To Dear Sybil

From Mum & Dad 1946

ODHAMS DICTIONARY
OF THE
ENGLISH LANGUAGE
ILLUSTRATED

ODHAMS DICTIONARY

OF THE

ENGLISH LANGUAGE

ILLUSTRATED

A Modern Guide to the Meaning, Pronunciation and Derivation of Words in literary and current use with a Supplement of Appendices giving much useful information commonly required

Edited by

A. H. SMITH, Ph.D., D.Lit.

Reader in English, University College, London

and

J. L. N. O'LOUGHLIN, M.A. (Oxon.)

Lecturer in the English Faculty and Librarian of the English Library, University of Oxford

ODHAMS PRESS LIMITED, LONG ACRE, LONDON, W.C.2

Published 1946

Printed in Great Britain by Odhams (Watford) Ltd., Watford

PREFACE

English is a living language, growing, changing, ever adapting itself to the resilient and enterprising civilization it serves; and for each generation of English-speaking people the publication of a new authoritative dictionary of the language they have inherited is an important event. To produce a dictionary that should be worthy of taking a place amongst the standard works of reference in the English language has, over a period of eight years, been the constant purpose of the present Editors and their corps of assistants. Dr. A. H. Smith shouldered the burden of the work on the *Dictionary* in its earlier stages, and, in spite of the urgent call of wider responsibilities, has continued to collaborate in the work throughout its progress to completion.

The main criteria that have guided both compilers and publishers were first, that the *Dictionary* should be easy to consult; second, that it should include all words in current use, even if this use be a colloquial or slang one, and words which, though obsolete, are found in some of the best-known works in English literature; third, that the definitions given should be adequate, accurate, and objective; and fourth, since this, as will be seen, is a pronouncing dictionary, that the system employed for this purpose should be sufficiently simple to be readily comprehensible even to the inexpert, and yet exact enough to convey the accepted pronunciation without ambiguity.

To ensure ease of consultation all words regarded as important enough to be defined have been included as separate entries, whether they are "root" words, derivatives, or cognates. Furthermore, the printing of the headword in bold capitals will be found to be a valuable aid to ease of reference. Words with the same spelling but different functions or derivation have been differentiated by a bold, bracketed numeral following the headword. Spelling follows accepted conservative practice, but permissible variants have been admitted.

It is rightly expected of a new dictionary that it should be up-to-date, and here will be found several hundred new words, senses, or usages that have not hitherto been recorded.

Since the definitions are at once the justification and the substance of a dictionary, no effort has been spared to make those given here both accurate and objective; complete almost to the point of obviousness where the distinction between different senses or usages is so fine as to warrant particularization. Although considerations of space in a work that is designed as a handy volume necessarily prohibit the reiteration of the substance of definitions each time a derived form of word is defined, it will be found that such forms are defined by reference to the "parent" word rather than in terms which might involve the reader in a chase from pillar to post throughout the whole work. The alternative, in face of such considerations, was to have employed a form of contracted or telegraphic language, but this was rejected as likely to prove a barrier to clarity and speedy reference.

After careful research, a method of indicating pronunciation was adopted which took more adequate account of the needs of the average reader than is, perhaps, usual in the observances of the specialist. It is simple, easily comprehended and memorized, and fulfils its essential purpose of conveying clearly the accepted pronunciation of all the words included in the *Dictionary*.

The derivations have been the subject of fresh research, and many of them have been identified more closely than in the past. Conjecture has been steadfastly avoided, and where speculation and guesswork, however entertaining, would have been untrustworthy, the simple avowal "Uncertain" has been preferred. The nearest relationship of the word has been given, and where the derivation, though incontestable, is indirect, the tilde (~) is prefixed to it.

Much information of a useful and often-wanted sort has been gathered into the Appendices in a form which gives a minimum of trouble to the inquirer. In short, it is hoped and believed that the work in its entirety will be found to be as indispensable in the office and the library as in the home and the school.

A.H.S.
J.L.N.O'L.

CONTENTS

KEY TO THE USE OF THE DICTIONARY

Odhams Dictionary of the English Language has been planned expressly to make reference to it as easy as possible. The following hints and reminders may be found useful:

(a) All words regarded as important enough to be defined will be found in the bold capitals in which all headwords are printed, thus: **SHANTUNG.**

(b) Some compound words are not included as headwords. They will be found in small black type under one element of the compound or the other; thus, under **NURSERY** will be found **n. school**; under **SCHOOL, high s.**

(c) Well-known phrases which employ a headword in a special idiomatic sense are also to be found in small black type following the definition of the headword; e.g. following **GOAT** we find **to act the g.**

(d) Permissible spelling variants are entered as headwords but are referred to the headword with the preferable spelling; e.g. if the reader looks for **ALINEMENT** he will find it as a headword but will be referred to **ALIGNMENT** for its definition.

(e) The same word may often be used in various senses and in such cases each sense is treated as a separate word, the differentiation being made by means of a bold bracketed numeral following the headword; for example **CARD (1)** and **CARD (2).** Words with the same spelling but different etymology are similarly differentiated; e.g. **PORT (1), PORT (2),** etc. In every such case the reader should make sure that he has found the correct word or sense.

(f) The whole entry against a headword should be read through. The definition or the information which best clarifies the usage in the reader's context may be in the last line of the entry.

(g) An abbreviation in italic type within brackets, e.g. (*chem.*), preceding part of the definition indicates a special sense of a word in general use. Where such an abbreviation precedes the whole definition it indicates that the word is used only in relation to the subject, etc., for which the abbreviation stands. A list of such abbreviations is given on p. x.

(h) If a word is not to be found in the main body of the *Dictionary* it may be in the Appendix of *Familiar Words and Phrases Adopted from Foreign Languages.*

(i) The *Key to Pronunciation* on page ix should be studied carefully. It is self-explanatory and should present no difficulties. For speedy checking the phonetic and other symbols most frequently required are printed at the foot of each page-opening of the *Dictionary* proper. When the reader has become familiar with the *Dictionary* and its pronunciation scheme this should normally be all the reference he will require, but in every case of uncertainty the full *Key to Pronunciation* should be consulted.

KEY TO PRONUNCIATION

Symbol	Example	As in:	Symbol	Example	As in:
a (unstressed)	a-bet′	abet	**m**	man, lam	man, lamb
a	bat	bat	**n**	nit	nit, knot
ā	ād	aid	**ng***	sing′-er	singer
āer	bāer	bear, bare	**ng-ǵ**	ling′-ger	linger
ah	pahst	past	**ngk**	thingk	think
ah(r)	kah(r)	car	**o** (unstressed)	pī′-lon	pylon
aw	aw′-ther	author	**o**	a-tom′-ik	atomic
aw(r)	waw(r)	war	**ō**	bōn	bone
b	bad, kab	bad, cab	**oi**	boi	boy, buoy
ch	chās	chase	**o͝o**	sto͝od	stood
d	dad	dad	**o͞o**	ro͞od	rude
e (unstressed)	ā′-jent	agent	**ow**	now	now
e	bet	bet	**ow(r)**	flow(r)	flour
ē	dēd	deed	**p**	po͝ot, nip	put, nip
ēer	rēer	rear	**r**	rat, bēer	rat, beer
er	bet′-er	better	**s**	sit, sit′-i	sit, city
ew	bew′-ti	beauty	**sh**	shīn, wosh	shine, wash
f	fāer, lahf	fair, laugh	**t**	tīm, bet′-er	time, better
ǵ	gām, eg	game, egg	**th**	thin, bahth	thin, bath
h	hēer	hear	**TH**	THis, bāTH	this, bathe
i (unstressed)	as′-id	acid	**u** (unstressed)	up-hēv′-al	upheaval
i	film	film	**u**	blud	blood
ī	hī	high	**ur**	slur	slur
īer	fīer	fire	**v**	ve′-ri, luv	very, love
j	jak′-it, rāj	jacket, rage	**w**	wāv	wave
k	kat	cat	**y**	yung	young
kh	splo͞o′-khan	spleuchan	**yo͝o**	an′-yo͝o-al	annual
ks	eks-klām′	exclaim	**yo͞o**	yo͞o-nī′-tid	united
kw	kwēn	queen	**z**	ri-zent′	resent
l	batl, liv	battle, live	**zh**	vizh′-un	vision

The stress mark (′) follows the syllable on which the stress falls.
* This symbol in round brackets, thus (**ng**), is used to indicate the typical nasal vowels in French words or words of French origin which retain them.

LANGUAGES REFERRED TO IN DERIVATIONS

Afrik.	Afrikaans	FrCan.	French Canadian	N.	North
AmerInd.	American Indian	Fris.	Frisian	NFr.	Norman French
Arab.	Arabic	Gael.	Gaelic	Norw.	Norwegian
Ass.	Assyrian	Germ.	German	ON.	Old Norse
Boh.	Bohemian	Gk.	Greek	Pers.	Persian
Braz.	Brazilian	Heb.	Hebrew	Pol.	Polish
Bret.	Breton	HighGerm.	High German	Portug.	Portuguese
Brit.	British	Hind.	Hindustani	Provenc.	Provençal
Can.	Canadian	Icel.	Icelandic	Russ.	Russian
Celt.	Celtic	IE.	Indo-European	Scand.	Scandinavian
Chin.	Chinese	Ir.	Irish	Skr.	Sanskrit
Corn.	Cornish	It.	Italian	Slav.	Slavonic
Dan.	Danish	Jap.	Japanese	Span.	Spanish
Du.	Dutch	L.	Latin	Swed.	Swedish
E.	English	LL.	Late Latin	Turk.	Turkish
Flem.	Flemish	Lith.	Lithuanian	U.S.	United States
Fr.	French			Wel.	Welsh
				WGerm.	West Germanic

These abbreviations may be prefixed by the following :—A, Anglo- ; M, Middle ; Md, Modern ; Med, Medieval ; O, Old ; Pr, Primitive.

(~) indicates indirect relationship ; (*) indicates a reconstructed or hypothetical form ; (-) before an auxiliary etymon indicates that it is a suffix ; following an auxiliary etymon, that it is a prefix. *Next* signifies that the derivation will be found under the headword following, and *Prec.* that the derivation is given under the headword preceding.

ABBREVIATIONS USED IN THE DICTIONARY

abs.	absolute
acc.	accusative
adj.	adjective
adv.	adverb
aeron.	aeronautics
agric.	agriculture
alg.	algebra
anat.	anatomy
anthrop.	anthropology
antiq.	antiquities
arch.	architecture
archae.	archaeology
arith.	arithmetic
art.	article
astrol.	astrology
astron.	astronomy
auxil.	auxiliary
bacteriol.	bacteriology
bibl.	biblical
biol.	biology
bot.	botany
carp.	carpentry
cf.	compare
chem.	chemistry
chron.	chronology
class.	classical
coll.	colloquial
comm.	commerce
comp.	comparative
conj.	conjunction
crystal.	crystallography
dat.	dative
def.	definite
dial.	dialect
dim.	diminutive
dram.	dramatic
eccles.	ecclesiastical
econ.	economics
elect.	electricity
eng.	engineering
entom.	entomology
esp.	especially
eth.	ethics
ethn.	ethnology
fem.	feminine
fig.	figurative
fort.	fortification
fut.	future
gen.	genitive
geneal.	genealogy
geog.	geography
geol.	geology
geom.	geometry
ger.	gerund(ive)
gram.	grammar
her.	heraldry
hist.	history
hort.	horticulture
i.	intransitive
ichth.	ichthyology
imper.	imperative
impers.	impersonal
ind.	indicative
indef.	indefinite
inf.	infinitive
int.	interjection
interrog.	interrogative
lang.	language
leg.	legal
lit.	literary
magn.	magnetism
malac.	malacology
mas.	masonry
masc.	masculine
math.	mathematics
mech.	mechanics
med.	medicine
met.	metaphysics
metal.	metallurgy
meteor.	meteorology
milit.	military
min.	mineralogy
mus.	music
myth.	mythology
n.	noun
nat. hist.	natural history
naut.	nautical
nav.	naval
neut.	neuter
nom.	nominative
N.T.	New Testament
numis.	numismatics
obj.	objective
opt.	optics
orig.	originally
ornith.	ornithology
O.T.	Old Testament
p.	past
paint.	painting
Parl.	Parliamentary
pass.	passive
path.	pathology
persp.	perspective
philol.	philology
philos.	philosophy
phon.	phonetics
phot.	photography
phr.	phrase
phys.	physics
pl.	plural
poet.	poetry
pol.	politics
pop.	popular
pos.	positive
p.pt.	past participle
pref.	prefix
prep.	preposition
pres.	present
pret.	past (preterite) tense
print.	printing
pron.	pronoun
pros.	prosody
prot.	protected trade-name
prov.	provincial
proverb	proverb
psych.	psychology
pt.	participle
pyr.	pyrotechny
R.C.	Roman Catholic
reflex.	reflexive
rel.	relative
rhet.	rhetoric
Rom.	Roman
sci.	science
sculp.	sculpture
sg.	singular
specif.	specific
subj.	subjunctive
superl.	superlative
surg.	surgical
t.	transitive
teleg.	telegraphy
teleph.	telephony
theol.	theology
transl.	translation
typ.	typography
uncert.	uncertain
unkn.	unknown
v.	verb
var.	variant
vet.	veterinary
vulg.	vulgar
wirel.	wireless
zool.	zoology

The dagger sign (†) indicates an obsolete word, spelling, or meaning.

A (1), [ā], the first letter of the English alphabet; (*mus.*) the sixth note in the natural diatonic scale of C major; the note produced by the tuned second string of the violin when unstopped.

A (2), AN (before vowels and silent *h*), [a, an], *indef. art.* chiefly used to denote a noun in the singular and meaning "one," also precedes collective nouns; used to signify proportion, e.g., *three pounds a week*; to describe a type of person, e.g., *a Caesar, a Shelley*. [OE. *an* a, one].

A (3), [ā], *prep.* compounded with participles to mean "in the act of," e.g., *a-hunting*; prefixed to words to form adverbial compounds, e.g., *afoot*. [Weakened form of OE. *on* in, into, on].

A (4), *pref.* in Latin words, is equal to "away from," e.g., *avulsion*; in Greek words, is equal to "not," or "without," e.g., *acentric*. [Gk., L. *a*].

A1 (1), [ā'-wun'], *adj.* a sign used in Lloyd's marine insurance practice to place a ship in the first class as regards condition and seaworthiness; the A denotes that the ship's hull is in good condition, the 1 denotes that its equipment maintains a first-rate standard; (*fig.*) excellent, first-rate, first-class; descriptive of the highest type of recruit for H.M. Forces.

AAM, [ahm], *n.* a measure of liquid capacity, roughly 30 to 35 gallons, used in Holland and Germany. [Du. *aam*].

AARD-VARK, [ahd'-vahk], *n.* an African ant-bear, without front teeth, feeding on ants, *Orycteropus*. [Du. *aarde* earth and *vark* pig].

AARD-WOLF, [ahd'-wŏŏlf], *n.* a carnivorous animal found in Africa, resembling the hyæna. [Du. *aarde* earth and WOLF].

AARONIC, [āer-on'-ik], *adj.* Aaronical.

AARONICAL, [āer-on'-ikl], *adj.* connected with, pertaining to Aaron or his priesthood. [*Aaron*, Exodus iv, 14].

AARONITE, [āer'-on-īt], *n.* one of Aaron's descendants, male or female; a Hebrew priest. [*Aaron*, Exodus iv, 14].

AARON'S BEARD, [āer'-onz-bēerd'], *n.* popular name for the large-flowered St. John's wort, *Hypericum calycinum*.

AARON'S ROD, [āer'-onz-rod'], *n.* (*arch.*) a rod entwined by a serpent; (*bot.*) the golden rod, *Solidago*, and the common mullein, *Verbascum thapsus*.

AASVOGEL, [ahs'-fōgl], *n.* a name for a vulture used in South Africa. [Afrik. *aas* carrion and *vogel* bird].

AB-, *pref.* from, away from. [L. *ab* from].

ABA, ABAYA, [ab'-a, ab-ā'-ya], *n.* a garment, shapeless, like a sack, worn by Arabs over their clothes. [Arab. *aba, abaya*].

ABACA, [ab'-ak-a'], *n.* Manilla hemp, the fibre of *Musa textilis*. [Heb. *ābāq* dust].

ABACIST, [ab'-as-ist], *n.* a person who uses an abacus.

ABACK, [a-bak'], *adv.* to or towards the back; backwards; (*naut.*) blown backwards to the mast; **taken a.**, surprised. [OE. *on bæc* backwards].

ABACTOR, [a-bak'-tor], *n.* a person who steals cattle by the herd. [LL. *abactor*].

ABACUS, [ab'-ak-us], *n.* a square board or tray covered with a thin layer of sand in which figures were traced for accounting purposes in Ancient Greece; an apparatus of firm parallel wires strung with beads, originally used by accountants and cashiers, now retained chiefly for teaching arithmetic in kindergarten schools; (*arch.*) a rectangular tablet functioning usually as the crowning unit of a column and its capital, occasionally as the base; **a. harmonicus,** the order and construction of the keys of a musical instrument. [L. *abacus* a square tablet for tracing figures].

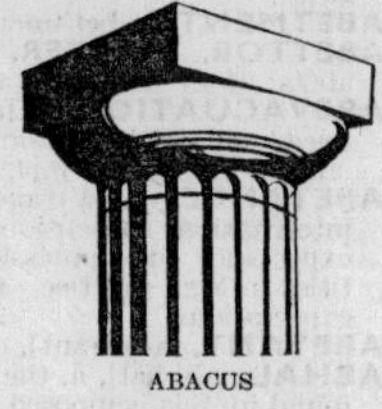
ABACUS

ABADDON, [ab-ad'-on], *n.* hell, the fathomless pit; the destroying angel. [Heb. *abaddon* destruction, from *abad* he perished].

ABAFT, [a-bahft'], *adv.* (*naut.*) at, on or towards the stern of a ship. [A (3) and OE. *be-æftan*, from *be* by, and *æftan* behind, back].

ABALIENATE, [ab-ā'-li-en-āt], *v.t.* (*leg.*) to transfer the title of a possession to another person. [L. *abalienatum*, *p.pt.* of *abalienare* to alienate].

ABALIENATION, [ab-ā'-li-en-ā'-shun], *n.* (*leg.*) the act of abalienating; (*med.*) amputation. [*Prec.*].

ABALONE, [ab'-al-ōn], *n.* a dark blue and green sea-shell, ear-shaped, a species of *Haliotis* which produces mother-of-pearl. [Unkn., possibly Span.].

ABANDON (1), [a-ban'-don], *n.* recklessness, impetuosity, unrestrained behaviour. [*Next*].

ABANDON (2), [a-ban'-don], *v.t.* to desert; to give up; to forsake; to neglect. [ME. *abandon* from OFr. *abandoner* from phrase *à bandon* at one's mercy or will].

ABANDONED, [a-ban'-dond], *adj.* deserted, left alone; wildly immoral, sexually unprincipled, continually yielding to vice.

ABANDONEDLY, [a-ban'-dond-li], *adv.* in an abandoned manner.

ABANDONEE, [a-ban'-don-ē'], *n.* one to whom the abandoned is assigned; (*leg.*) the underwriter who accepts the work of salvaging a sunken ship.

ABANDONMENT, [a-ban'-don-ment], *n.* the act of abandoning or the state of being abandoned.

ABASE, [a-bās'], *v.t.* to degrade, to humble, to lower in status. [OFr. *abaissier, abesier* to lower].

ABASEMENT, [a-bās'-ment], *n.* the condition of being abased.

ABASH, [a-bash'], *v.t.* to put to shame by revealing guilt, to discomfit, to confound. [~OFr. *esbaissier* to astonish, to shout "bah" at].

ABASHMENT, [a-bash'-ment], *n.* the state of being abashed.

ABASK, [a-bahsk'], *adv.* basking. [A (3) and BASK].

ABATABLE, [a-bāt'-abl], *adj.* capable of being abated.

ABATE, [a-bāt'], *v.t.* to diminish, lessen; to deduct; *v.i.* to become less, to decrease; to fail. [OFr. *abattre* from L. *batere, batuere* to bring down].

ABATEMENT, [a-bāt'-ment], *n.* the act of abating; sum subtracted from an account; (*her.*) a mark of dishonour in a coat of arms; (*leg.*) defeat of a writ.

ABATER, [a-bāt'-er], *n.* the person or thing that abates.

ABAT-JOUR, [ab'-ah-zhōōr'], *n.* a skylight. [MFr. (*ce qui*) *abat* (*le*) *jour* that which lets down the daylight].

ABATTIS, [ab-at'-is], *n.* (*fort.*) a defensive structure, a barricade, round a fort or across an avenue of approach, consisting of felled trees with the entangled branches facing the enemy. [Fr. *abatis* mass of fallen material].

ABATTOIR, [ab'-at-wah(r)], *n.* a slaughterhouse; place in which cattle are killed. [Fr. *abattoir*].

ABATURE, [ab'-a-chōō'-er], *n.* trail, track, spoor. [Fr. *abatture, abature* throwing down].

ABAT-VOIX, [ab-ah'-vwah], *n.* the sounding-board or canopy over a pulpit. [Fr. *abat-voix*].

ABAT-VOIX

ABAYA, *see* ABA.

ABB, [ab], *n.* the yarn for the wool or warp in a weaver's web; **a. wool,** the wool of which it is made. [OE. *ab, awebb*, from *awefan* to weave].

ABBA, [ab'-a], *n.* a father; a superior official in an ecclesiastical order. [Aramaic. *abba* father].

ABBACY, [ab'-as-i], *n.* the tenure, rank, and jurisdiction of an abbot. [L. *abbatia*].

ABBATIAL, [ab-ā'-shal], *adj.* pertaining to an abbey or an abbot. [L. *abbatialis*].

ABBATICAL, [ab-at'-ikl], *adj.* abbatial.

ABBE, abbé, [ab'-ā], *n.* an abbot; title of respect given to a French priest; one of a class of ecclesiastics in minor orders before the French Revolution expecting advancement in the Church. [Fr. *abbé*, from L. *abbas* abbot].

ABBESS, [ab'-es], *n.* the mother superior of a nunnery. [OFr. *abesse*].

ABBEY, [ab'-i], *n.* a society of people of either sex,

foregoing marriage, living in seclusion, and devoting their lives to religion; the edifice in which such a group resides; the church belonging, or formerly attached, to such a society; a private residence, or mansion, once an abbey. [OFr. *abbaie*].

ABBOT, [ab'-ot], *n.* the male superior or head of an abbey or monastery; **abbot's commendatory**, one of the abbey guardians receiving an allowance of the revenues. [OE. *abbod* from L. *abbas abbatis* abbot].

ABBOTSHIP, [ab'-ot-ship], *n.* the office and responsibilities of an abbot.

ABBREVIATE (1), [a-brē'-vi-at], *adj.* (*nat. hist.*) short. [*Next*].

ABBREVIATE (2), [a-brē'-vi-āt], *v.t.* to shorten; to curtail; to abridge. [L. *abbreviatum*, *p.pt.* of *abbreviare* to shorten].

ABBREVIATION, [a-brē'-vi-ā'-shun], *n.* the act of shortening; one letter or a few used to denote a word or phrase, e.g., *n.* for noun, *PrGerm.* for Primitive Germanic; (*math.*) the process of reducing fractions to their lowest terms; (*mus.*) one or more short strokes on the tail of a note to mark it as a quaver, etc.

ABBREVIATOR, [a-brē'-vi-āt'-or], *n.* a person who abridges.

ABBREVIATORY, [a-brē'-vi-āt'-or-i], *n.* whatever abbreviates or shortens.

ABBREVIATURE, [a-brē'-vi-ā'-cher], *n.* a letter, character or sign signifying abbreviation; a summary, epitome, abridgment, compound.

ABC, [ā'-bē'-sē'], *n.* a popular abbreviation for the alphabet, more particularly a book for children illustrating the alphabet; the basic principles or essentials of a subject; a railway time-table with the place-name entries in alphabetical order.

ABDALAVI, [ab-dal-ah'-vi], *n.* the Egyptian musk melon, *Cucurbita moschata*. [Egypt. *abdalavi*].

ABDALS, [ab'-dalz], *n.*(*pl.*) Persian fanatics. [Arab. *abd* servant, *allah* God].

ABDERIAN, [ab-dēer'-i-an], *adj.* inclined to laugh. [*Abdera*, a Thracian town].

ABDERITE, [ab'-der-īt], *n.* a person living in Abdera, a Thracian town; a dullard. Democritus, who laughed excessively, was an inhabitant of this town. [ABDERIAN].

ABDEST, [ab'-dest], *n.* a Mohammedan ceremony of purification by washing, participated in before prayers. [Pers. *abdast* from *ab* water and *dast* hand].

ABDICANT† [ab'-dik-ant], *adj.* abdicating; relinquishing; renouncing. [L. *abdicatem*, *pres.pt.* of *abdicare*].

ABDICATE [ab'-dik-āt], *v.t.* to resign from a position; to renounce power; to withdraw a claim or a right; to give up the right of exercising regal power; (*leg.*) to disown and disinherit. [L. *abdicatum*, *p.pt.* of *abdicare*].

ABDICATION, [ab'-dik-ā'-shun], *n.* the act of abdicating.

ABDICATIVE, [ab'-dik-at-iv, ab-dik'-at-iv], *adj.* signifying or causing abdication.

ABDIEL, [ab'-di-el], *n.* a servant of God; (*bibl.*) a descendant of God; in Milton's *Paradise Lost* the angel who opposed Satan's revolt. [Heb. *abdiel* servant of God].

ABDITORY, [ab'-dit-or-i], *n.* a hiding-place for secretly storing relics or riches. [L. *abditum*, *p.pt.* of *abdere* to hide].

ABDOMEN, [ab'-dom-en], *n.* (*anat.*) the belly; the lower part of a body, animal or human, with the thorax above and pelvis below, including the intestines and stomach, liver and gall-bladder, pancreas and spleen; (*entom.*) the posterior part of an insect. [L. *abdomen*].

ABDOMINAL, [ab-dom'-inl], *adj.* pertaining to, belonging to, or placed in, the belly; **a. ring**, a ring of sinew in each groin.

ABDOMINALLY, [ab-dom'-in-al-i], *adv.* with reference to the abdomen.

ABDOMINOSCOPY, [ab-dom'-in-os'-kop-i], *n.* the science of abdominal inspection and diagnosis. [ABDOMEN and Gk. *skopos* looking at].

ABDOMINOUS, [ab-dom'-in-us], *adj.* big in the belly.

ABDUCE, [ab-dews'], *v.t.* to separate one section from another; (*med.*) to open partially. [L. *abducere* to lead away].

ABDUCENT, [ab-dews'-ent], *adj.* (*anat.*) having the power of retracting; applied to those muscles, having the opposite function of the adducent muscles, which draw away or back the parts of the body to which they are applied. [L. *abducentem*, *pres.pt.* of *abducere* to lead away].

ABDUCT, [ab-dukt'], *v.t.* to lead away; to kidnap; to carry off by force or trickery. [L. *abductum*, *p.pt.* of *abducere* to lead away].

ABDUCTION, [ab-duk'-shun], *n.* the act of drawing or leading away; (*leg.*) the forcible or fraudulent carrying off of a person, particularly of a child or ward or wife; (*log.*) an argument or reasoning, whose minor premise being only probable, leads only to a probable conclusion. [~L. *abductio*].

ABDUCTOR, [ab-dukt'-or], *n.* a person who abducts another; (*anat.*) any muscle which retracts a part of the body.

ABEAM, [a-bēm'], *adv.* (*naut.*) at right angles to the ship's keel; facing the centre of the ship's hull; abreast of. [A (3) and OE. *beam* tree, beam].

ABECEDARIAN (1), [ā-bē-sē-dāer'-i-an], *n.* a person learning or teaching the alphabet. [ABC].

ABECEDARIAN (2), [ā-bē-sē-dāer'-i-an], *adj.* alphabetical; elementary.

ABECEDARY, [ā-bē-sē'-dar-i], *n.* an abecedarian.

ABED, [a-bed'], *adv.* in one's bed. [OE. *on bedde* in bed].

ABELE, [a-bēl'], *n.* the hoary or white poplar, *Populus alba*. [LL. *albellus*, *dim.* of *albus* white].

ABELIANS, [ā-bēl'-i-anz], *n.*(*pl.*) Abelites. [*Abel*, Genesis iv, 8].

ABELITES, [ā'-bel-īts], *n.*(*pl.*) an early religious order who believed in sexually chaste marriage following the accepted example of Abel. [*Abel*].

ABELMOSK, [ā'-bel-mosk], *n.* a variety of the Syrian mallow, with seeds of a musky scent, *Abelmoschus moschatus*. [Arab. *abul-misk* father or source of musk].

ABELONIANS, [ā-bel-ō'-ni-anz], *n.*(*pl.*) an earlier name for Abelites. [*Abel*].

ABERDEEN, [ab'-er-dēn'], *n.* the name of a city in Scotland; an Aberdeen terrier; **A. Angus**, a breed of cattle.

ABERDEEN TERRIER, [ab'-er-dēn'-te'-ri-er], *n.* a long- or rough-haired variety of terrier, known also as the Scotch terrier.

ABERDEVINE, [ab-er'-dev-in], *n.* a bird similar to the goldfinch, of the siskin species, *Carduelis spinus*. [Unkn.].

ABERDONIAN (1), [ab-er-dō'-ni-an], *n.* a native or inhabitant of Aberdeen. [MdL. *Aberdonia* Aberdeen].

ABERDONIAN (2), [ab'-er-dō'-ni-an], *adj.* belonging to, or appertaining to, Aberdeen.

ABERRANCE, [ab-e'-rans], *n.* a deviation; a mistake; a moral lapse; (*geom.*) the deviation of a line outside or inside its circular progression. [L. *aberrantia* a wandering away].

ABERRANCY, [ab-e'-ran-si], *n.* aberrance.

ABERRANT, [ab-e'-rant], *adj.* straying from the right path, lapsing morally; (*biol.* and *bot.*) abnormal, materially deviating from type. [L. *aberrantem*, *pres.pt.* of *aberrare* to go astray].

ABERRATION, [ab'-er-ā'-shun], *n.* the act of departing from the normal or correct line or course; a mental, emotional or moral lapse; an intellectual deviation; (*astron.*) to an observer, a slight apparent movement of the fixed stars, caused by the motion of light running counter to the earth's annual or diurnal movement in its orbit; (*opt.*) the deviation of light rays not converging in one focus by refraction or reflection; (*biol.*) material deviation from type; **crown of a.**, a circle of light round the sun's orb caused by aberration of the sun's rays. [~L. *aberratio* wandering].

ABERRING, [ab-ur'-ing], *adj.* wandering; going astray; deviating. [L. *aberrare* to go astray].

ABET, [a-bet'], *v.t.* to help, encourage, incite illegal or immoral action; to instigate. [ME. *abetten* to instigate].

ABETMENT, [a-bet'-ment], *n.* the act of abetting.

ABETTOR, ABETTER, [a-bet'-er], *n.* a person who abets; (*leg.*) a confederate, an accessory to a crime.

ABEVACUATION, [ab'-iv-ak'-yōō-ā'-shun], *n.* (*med.*) a partial expulsion of morbid affections. [AB- and L. *evacuatum*, *p.pt.* of *evacuare* to empty out].

ABEYANCE, [a-bā'-yans], *n.* remission, desistance, interruption, suspension; a condition of temporary expectancy or suppression, *esp.* used of hereditary titles in legal practice. [OFr. *a.* and *béer* to gape in expectation].

ABEYANT, [a-bā'-ant], *adj.* in abeyance.

ABHAL, [ab'-hal], *n.* the fruit of a variety of cypress found in Asia, supposed to be a strong stimulant for menstruation.

ABHOR, [ab-haw(r)'], *v.t.* to feel intense loathing and hatred for; to take an extreme aversion to; to recoil or turn aside in revulsion and horror from. [L. *abhorrere* to shrink back in horror].

ABHORRENCE, [ab-hor'-ens], *n.* abhorrency.

ABHORRENCY, [ab-hor′-en-si], *n.* detestation; abomination.
ABHORRENT, [ab-hor′-ent], *adj.* repellent, loathsome, hateful.
ABHORRENTLY, [ab-hor′-ent-li], *adv.* with abhorrence; in a detestable manner.
ABHORRER, [ab-haw′-rer], *n.* one who loathes a person or object; (*pl.*) the Tories who requested Charles II not to recall Parliament in 1680.
ABHORRING, [ab-hawr′-ing], *n.* the state of hatred or loathing.
ABIB, [ā′-bib], *n.* more generally known as Nisan, the first month of the Jewish religious year, March to April. [Heb. *abib* ear of corn].
ABIDE, (abiding, abode), [a-bīd′], *v.t.* to endure; to permit; to await; to be prepared for; *v.i.* to remain, stay; †to live in a place for a time; **to a. by,** to accept; to adhere to. [OE. *onbidan* to expect, wait for].
ABIDER, [a-bīd′-er], *n.* a resident; a tenant; a person living in a place, or one who remains in a place.
ABIDING, [a-bīd′-ing], *adj.* permanent; enduring.
ABIDINGLY, [a-bīd′-ing-li], *adv.* in an abiding way.
ABIES, [ab′-i-ēz], *n.* a genus of cone-bearing trees. [L. *abies*].
ABIETIC, [ab′-i-et′-ik], *adj.* belonging to the genus *Abies.*
ABIETIN, [ab′-i-et-in], *n.* resinous matter; the substance exuded by a fir tree.

ABIES
(Silver Fir Foliage)

ABIGAIL, [ab′-ig-āl], *n.* a woman's name in the Bible; (*coll.*) a lady's maid or lady-in-waiting. [Heb. *Abigayil,* 1 Samuel xxv].
ABIGEAT, [ab-ij′-i-at], *n.* (*leg.*) the crime of stealing herds of cattle; (*med.*) abortion induced by artificial methods. [L. *abigeat*].
ABILITY, [ab-il′-iti], *n.* power, physical or mental; capability and capacity; ableness; faculty of understanding; skill or competence in performance; efficiency; cleverness; means, wealth; **to the best of one's a.,** to the limit of one's capacity, as well as possible. [~OFr. *ableté* aptitude, cleverness].
ABINTESTATE, [ab′-in-tes′-tāt], *adj.* (*leg.*) inheriting the property and possessions of a person who has died intestate. [AB- and L. *intestatus* leaving no will].
ABIOGENESIS, [a-bī′-ō-jen′-is-is], *n.* the theory of spontaneous generation. [A (4) and Gk. *bios* life, and *genesis* origin, birth].
ABIOGENETIC, [a-bī′-ō-jen-et′-ik], *adj.* relating to spontaneous generation.
ABIOGENIST, [a-bī-oj′-en-ist], *n.* one believing in the doctrine of abiogenesis.
ABIOGENY, [a-bī-oj′-en-i], *n.* abiogenesis. [Gk. *abios* without life and *genes* born of].
ABJECT (1), [ab′-jekt], *n.* an outcast; a person accepting the most wretched and miserable conditions of life. [*Next*].
ABJECT (2), [ab′-jekt], *adj.* miserably reduced in means and condition; worthless; servile; vile; contemptible; fawning. [L. *abjectum, p.pt.* of *abjicere* to throw down].
ABJECTEDNESS, [ab-jekt′-ed-nes], *n.* a low or despicable condition; servility; vileness.
ABJECTION, [ab-jek′-shun], *n.* a state of moral and emotional depression; degradation; a low condition. [~L. *abjectio*].
ABJECTLY, [ab-jekt′-li], *adv.* in an abject way.
ABJECTNESS, [ab-jekt′-nes], *n.* the condition of being abject.
ABJOINT, [ab-joint′], *v.t.* (*biol.*) to divide or separate by formation of a joint. [AB- and JOINT].
ABJUDICATE†, [ab-jōō′-dik-āt], *v.t.* to transmit after judgment from one to another. [L. *abjudicatum, p.pt.* of *abjudicare* to take away by judgment].
ABJURATION, [ab-jōōer-ā′-shun], *n.* the act of abjuring; denial on oath; **a. of the realm,** the taking of a solemn oath to leave one's country. [~L. *abjuratio*].
ABJURE, [ab-jōōer′], *v.t.* to renounce upon oath; to relinquish one's sworn allegiance; to disclaim, abandon, retract; to recant an opinion, statement or belief. [L. *abjurare* to deny on oath].
ABJUREMENT, [ab-jōōer′-ment], *n.* renunciation; repudiation.
ABJURER, [ab-jōōer′-er], *n.* one who abjures.
ABKARI, ABKARY, [ab′-kar-i], *n.* the manufacture and sale of alcoholic drink in India; distilling; the tax levied on these activities. [Pers. *abkari* distilling].
ABLACTATE, [ab-lakt′-āt], *v.t.* to wean from the breast. [~L. *ablactare* to wean].
ABLACTATION, [ab′-lak-tā′-shun], *n.* the act of weaning a child from the breast; †(*hort.*) inarching, process of grafting by approach. [~L. *ablactatio*].
ABLAQUEATION, [ab-lak′-wi-ā′-shun], *n.* uncovering the roots of trees. [~L. *ablaqueare*].
ABLATION, [ab-lā′-shun], *n.* the act of taking away or removing; (*geol.*) the melting away of the surface of a glacier, or wearing away of rock through the action of water; (*surg.*) removal of part of the body by a surgical operation. [~L. *ablatio*].
ABLATIVE, [ab′-lat-iv], *n.* name given to the grammatical case in certain languages denoting *time* or *direction from.* [L. *ablativus*].
ABLAUT, [ab′-lowt], *n.* (*philol.*) vowel change, other than that caused by the influence of neighbouring sounds, occurring in certain words having the same base, e.g., *ring, rang, rung.* [Germ. *ablaut*].
ABLAZE, [a-blāz′], *adj.* on fire, in a blaze; (*fig.*) shining with dazzling brilliance; in a state of extreme excitement, thoroughly aroused. [A (3) and BLAZE].
ABLE, [ābl], *adj.* having physical or mental power to do a thing, equipped with the means or ability, or in a position to do something (which is usually specified); competent, adept at, talented, possessing some degree of skill; skilful, clever, good, highly satisfactory; (*leg.*) qualified by law for a position or office, legally entitled to. [OFr. *hable* from L. *habilis*].
ABLE-BODIED, [ābl′-bod′-id], *adj.* physically fit and robust, well fitted for physical or manual labour, strong and vigorous.
ABLEGATE, [ab′-lig-āt], *n.* a papal envoy, messenger or ambassador, *esp.* the bearer of the Red Hat, the traditional symbol of office, to a newly appointed cardinal. [L. *ablegatus* one sent on a mission].
ABLENESS†, [ābl′-nes], *n.* the state or quality of being able, ability.
ABLEPSY†, [ab-lep′-si], *n.* loss or absence of sight, blindness. [Gk. *ablepsia*].
ABLET, [ab′-let], *n.* a small freshwater fish, the bleak. [Fr. *ablette* from LL. *albula, dim.* of *alba* white].
ABLOCATE, [ab′-lō-kāt], *v.t.* to let out on hire, to lease. [L. *ablocatum, p.pt.* of *ablocare* to lease].
ABLOCATION, [ab′-lōk-ā′-shun], *n.* the act of ablocating.
ABLOOM, [a-blōōm′], *adj. and adv.* in bloom, flowering. [ME. *on blome* in bud].
ABLUENT (1), [ab′-lōō-ent], *n.* a blood purifier, a detergent. [*Next*].
ABLUENT (2), [ab′-lōō-ent], *adj.* able to cleanse; purifying. [~L. *abluens*].
ABLUSH, [a-blush′], *adv.* having the face suffused with blood. [A (3) and BLUSH].
ABLUTION, [ab-lōō′-shun], *n.* the act of cleansing; particularly a washing of the fingers before participating in a religious ceremony such as the celebration of the Eucharist; the water used for such a cleansing of the fingers; the water and wine which the priest, after communion, pours over the chalice and his fingers. [L. *ablutio* washing].
ABLUTIONARY, [ab-lōō′-shun-er-i], *adj.* related to ablution.
ABLUVION, [ab-lōō′-vi-on], *n.* whatever is washed away. [~L. *abluvio*].
ABLY, [āb′-li], *adv.* in able fashion.
ABNEGATE, [ab′-nig-āt], *v.t.* to renounce; to deny; to relinquish; to forbear. [L. *abnegare* to deny].
ABNEGATION, [ab′-nig-ā′-shun], *n.* renunciation; denial, disavowal. [L. *abnegatio*].
ABNEURAL, [ab-new′-ral], *adj.* belonging or appertaining to the part of the system opposite to the main nerve ganglion. [AB- and NEURAL].
ABNODATE, [ab′-nō-dāt], *v.t.* to prune away the knots, particularly of trees. [L. *abnodatum, p.pt.* of *abnodare* to clear of knots].
ABNORMAL, [ab-nawm′-al], *adj.* not conforming to type, rule or form; exceptional, peculiar; freakish. [L. *abnormis* deviating from rule].
ABNORMALISM, [ab-nawm′-al-izm], *n.* something abnormal; the state of being abnormal; deliberate cultivation of the abnormalities of life.
ABNORMALITY, [ab′-nawm-al′-i-ti], *n.* the condition of being abnormal.
ABNORMALLY, [ab-nawm′-a-li], *adv.* in an abnormal way.
ABNORMITY, [ab-nawm′-i-ti], *n.* abnormality, monstrosity. [L. *abnormitas*].
ABOARD (1), [a-bawd′], *adv.* (*naut.*) into or inside a ship; **hard a., close a.,** alongside. [A (3) and BOARD (1)].

ABOARD (2), [a-bawd'], *prep.* (*naut.*) on board of; **to step a. a boat, to go a.,** to embark; **to fall a.,** to collide with the side of a vessel; **all a.,** command giving warning of immediate departure of a ship or other vehicle.

ABODE, [a-bōd'], *n.* permanent or temporary dwelling, residence; a house; **to take up an a.,** to go to stay in. [*pret.* of ABIDE].

ABOIDEAU, [ah-bwah'-dō], *n.* a dam or sluice-gate, particularly for controlling drainage canals in marshland. [FrCan. *aboideau*].

ABOIL, [a-boil'], *adv.* boiling; in a raging emotion. [A (3) and BOIL (3)].

ABOLISH, [ab-ol'-ish], *v.t.* to destroy; to annul; to cancel; to dissolve; to repudiate; to declare null and void; to wipe out completely. [~Fr. *abolir*].

ABOLISHABLE, [ab-ol'-ish-abl], *adj.* fit to be abolished.

ABOLISHMENT, [ab-ol'-ish-ment], *n.* the act of abolishing; the condition or fact of being abolished.

ABOLITION, [ab'-ol-ish'-un], *n.* the act of abolishing; the fact of being abolished; complete elimination; cancellation of the existence of objects, persons, laws, practices, etc. [~L. *abolitio*].

ABOLITIONAL, [ab'-ol-ish'-unl], *adj.* concerned with the abolition of slavery.

ABOLITIONISM, [ab'-ol-ish'-un-izm], *n.* the doctrine held by an abolitionist.

ABOLITIONIST, [ab'-ol-ish'-un-ist], *n.* (*hist.*) a person who wished to abolish slavery.

ABOMA, [ab-ō'-ma], *n.* the thick-necked tree-boa found in Guiana, *Epicrates cenchris.* [Native].

ABOMASUS, [ab'-ō-mā'-sus], *n.* the fourth stomach of animals that chew the cud. [AB- and L. *omasum* bullock's tripe].

ABOMINABLE, [ab-om'-in-abl], *adj.* foul, hateful, detestable. [L. *abominabilis*].

ABOMINABLENESS, [ab-om'-in-abl-nes], *n.* the quality or state of being abominable.

ABOMINABLY, [ab-om'-in-ab-li], *adv.* in an abominable way; excessively.

ABOMINATE, [ab-om'-in-āt], *v.t.* to detest, abhor, to hate; to dislike. [L. *abominatum*, *p.pt.* of *abominari* to detest].

ABOMINATION, [ab-om'-in-ā'-shun], *n.* the act of abominating, repugnance, antipathy; the thing loathed; a disgusting action. [L. *abominationem*].

ABORAL, [ab-aw'-ral], *adj.* far away from the mouth. [AB- and ORAL].

ABORIGINAL (1), (*pl.* **aborigines**), [ab'-or-ij'-inl], *n.* an original and primitive native of a territory; applied to the flora and fauna native to the soil of a particular country. [AB- and ORIGINAL].

ABORIGINAL (2), [ab'-or-ij'-inl], *adj.* of the beginning; original; indigenous, applied to the native and natural plants, animals and inhabitants of a territory.

ABORIGINES, [ab'-or-ij'-in-ēz], *n.*(*pl.*) the original and primitive natives of a territory; applied also to the flora and fauna native to the soil of a particular country.

ABORT, [ab-awt'], *v.i.* to miscarry, to give birth to a child before the natural time; (*fig.*) of plans and processes and intentions, to fail to come to the intended conclusion. [L. *abortum*, *p.pt.* of *aboriri* to miscarry].

ABORTIFACIENT (1), [ab-awt'-if-āsh'-i-ent], *n.* a drug or medicine causing abortion. [*Next*].

ABORTIFACIENT (2), [ab-awt'-if-āsh'-i-ent], *adj.* causing, or cause of, abortion. [ABORT and L. *facientem*, *pres.pt.* of *facere* to make].

ABORTION, [ab-aw'-shun], *n.* a miscarriage, premature birth of a child; the foetus delivered ill-formed, and, perhaps, dead; whatever fails to mature, or is stunted in growth; a monstrosity; (*leg.*) procuration of a deliberate miscarriage. [L. *abortio*].

ABORTIONIST, [ab-aw'-shun-ist], *n.* a person procuring abortion.

ABORTIVE (1), [ab-awt'-iv], *n.* (*med.*) a physic bringing on abortion. [*Next*].

ABORTIVE (2), [ab-awt'-iv], *adj.* unsuccessful, premature; (*biol.*) imperfectly developed. [L. *abortivus*, from *abortus*, *p.pt.* of *aboriri* to be prematurely born].

ABORTIVELY, [ab-awt'-iv-li], *adv.* immaturely; prematurely, untimely.

ABORTIVENESS, [ab-awt'-iv-nes], *n.* condition of being abortive.

ABOULIA, [ab-ow'-li-a], *n.* (*path.*) loss of mental control, of the power of purposive thought or action, due to a brainstorm or psychological condition of chronic lethargy. [A (4) and Gk. *boule* will].

ABOUND, [a-bownd'], *v.i.* to have plenty, to be plentiful, to teem, to possess a large quantity, used both of natural things and inherent qualities. [OFr. *abonder* to overflow].

ABOUNDING, [a-bownd'-ing], *adj.* in abundance, plentiful.

ABOUT (1), [a-bowt'], *adv.* nearly, approximately, almost, thereabouts; here, there; around, in a circle; **a. ship,** command to place a ship on a different tack; **a. turn,** (*milit.*) turn and face the opposite direction. [OE. *abutan* around].

ABOUT (2), [a-bowt'], *prep.* around; close to, on the verge of; with regard to, relating to, appertaining to, concerning. [*Prec.*].

ABOVE (1), [a-buv'], *n.* heaven; the aforesaid, the aforementioned. [ABOVE (3)].

ABOVE (2), [a-buv'], *adj.* preceding; previous.

ABOVE (3), [a-buv'], *adv.* in a higher place, overhead, on high; higher in thought, power, motion or rank; before, in a previous position, in heaven. [OE. *abufan*].

ABOVE (4), [a-buv'], *prep.* superior or higher in any way, surpassing in number, quality or quantity; beyond, over; **a. all,** before everything else; **to be a. oneself,** to be over-confident, conceited; **a. par,** larger or finer than normal; **keep your head a. water,** keep out of danger.

ABOVE-BOARD, [a-buv'-bawd'], *adj.* fair, honest, frank, artless.

ABOVE-CITED, [a-buv'-sī'-tid], *adj.* cited before, quoted above.

ABOVE-GROUND, [a-buv'-grownd'], *adv.* on top of the ground, not buried; alive.

ABRACADABRA, [ab'-ra-kad-ab'-ra], *n.* a spell, a charm; a meaningless incantation, mumbo-jumbo, used to charm away evil and disease, the word being written down in lines in the form of a triangle by subtracting one end letter from each line, and the magic paper placed in a locket. [Unkn.]

ABRACALAN, [ab-rak'-al-an], *n.* a word used in Hebrew occult science, believed by the priests to have a power equivalent to that of the abracadabra. [Unkn.].

ABRADANT, [a-brād'-ant], *n.* a substance that will effect abrasion, e.g., emery paper, pumice stone, iron-filings, etc.

ABRADE, [a-brād'], *v.t.* to wear away, to rub off, by continual grazing, by friction; to scrape away, to file. [L. *abradere* to scrape off].

ABRADING, [a-brād'-ing], *n.* (*agr.*) the wearing away of mounds, dykes, or banks of soil by a succession of frosts or droughts and rains, or the pressure of running water on dry soil. [*Prec.*].

ABRAHAMIC, [ā'-bra-ham'-ik], *adj.* pertaining to Abraham.

ABRAHAM-MEN†, [ā'-bra-ham-men'], *n.*(*pl.*) lunatics of the sixteenth and seventeenth centuries.

ABRANCHIANS, [a-brangk'-i-anz], *n.*(*pl.*) (*zool.*) a species of *Annelida*, without gills, e.g., leeches and earthworms. [A (4) and Gk. *brankhia* gills].

ABRANCHIATE, [a-brangk'-i-at], *adj.* having no gills.

ABRASION, [a-brā'-zhun], *n.* friction, the act of wearing or rubbing away; substance worn off by attrition. [L. *abrasio*].

ABRASIVE (1), [a-brā'-ziv], *n.* an abradant. [*Next*].

ABRASIVE (2), [a-brā'-siv], *adj.* tending to cause abrasion. [L. *abrasivus*, from *abrasum*, *p.pt.* of *abradere* to rub away].

ABRASTOL, [ab'-ras-tol'], *n.* a preservative substance compounded from beta-naphthol, also used medicinally.

ABRAXAS, [ab-raks'-as], *n.* the Supreme Being recognized by the Egyptian Gnostics as the ruler of 365 separate and subordinate deities; an amulet of gems engraved with the word abraxas; (*entom.*) the magpie moth. [Gk. *abraxas* used numerically; the letters of the word *abraxas* add up to 365].

ABRAZITIC, [ab'-raz-it'-ik], *adj.* (*min.*) not effervescing. [A (4) and Gk. *brazo* I boil].

ABREAST, [a-brest'], *adv.* alongside, side by side, in a line; (*fig.*) up to date. [A (3) and BREAST (1)].

ABREPTION, [ab-rep'-shun], *n.* carrying away; the state of being carried away. [L. *abreptum*, *p. pt.* of *abripere* to drag away].

ABREUVOIR

ABREUVOIR, [ab-rur'-vwah(r)', ab-rōō'-vwah(r)'], *n.*

[ak-sep'-tid], *adj.* received, admitted.
ACCEPTOR, [ak-sept'-er, ak-sept'-or], cepts; (*comm.*) the person who accepts ange.
es], *n.* the approach to a person or place; approach, the opportunity of admission urrence of a fit or neurotic paroxysm. a approach].
Y, [ak-ses'-ar-il-i], *adv.* accessorily.
ESS, [ak-ses'-ar-in-es], *n.* accessoriness.
[ak-ses'-ar-i], *adj.* accessory.
Y, [ak-ses'-ib-il'-i-ti], *n.* the quality of e, of affording approach. [L. *accessi-*
[ak-ses'-ibl], *adj.* able to be approached; ch. [L. *accessibilis*].
ak-ses'-ib-li], *adv.* so as to be accessible.
ak-sesh'-un], *n.* the act of coming, a approach, the reaching or attaining to y, strength or state; whatever is added, gmentation, a joining to; an acquisi- or important acquisition; (*leg.*) incre- ty in value on account of attendant rowth or labour; (*med.*) the beginning ccles.) the transference of votes at a [L. *accessio* approach].
, [ak-sesh'-un-al], *adj.* additional.
, [ak'-ses-aw'-ri-al], *adj.* belonging to
, [ak-ses'-or-i-li], *adv.* in the fashion of
SS, [ak-ses'-or-in-es], *n.* the state of
), [ak-ses'-or-i], *n.* accomplice; a nt contributing to a general effect; bordinate, but useful device or detail ain body or design; (*leg.*) a person and abetting or protecting a criminal ; (*paint. and sculp.*) the decorative main theme or compositions. [L. *accessum, p.pt.* of *accedere* to ap-
), [ak-ses'-or-i], *adj.* contributing, onal, extra; subordinate to the main helpful to the chief person as object. k'-sid-ents], *n.* (*gram.*) that part of s concerned with the various termin- ension or conjugation of words. [OF. ent].
sid-ent], *n.* anything happening; an or unintended action, an unpre- apparently illogical occurrence, a une, a casualty, a calamity; (*log.*) ality, property, power, or attribute; ected symptom, usually of a dis- eol.) irregularity or variety in sur- ity; (*her.*) an unessential mark in a se inclusion is optional. [L. *acci-* happening].
, [ak'-sid-entl'], *n.* a non-essential ute; (*mus.*) an incidental semitone tonic key; the sign used in musical e note to be raised or lowered a
), [ak'-sid-entl'], *adj.* happening y chance, fortuitous; not essential, ous, extrinsic.
1, [ak'-sid-ent'-al-izm], *n.* effect ental rays of light.
, [ak'-sid-ent'-al-i], *adv.* in an acci-
SS, [ak'-sid-ent'-al-nes], *n.* the cidental.
k'-sid-ent'-id], *adj.* (*geol.*) varie- n surface.
'-it-er], *n.* (*zool.*) a member of a prey, including goshawks, eagles, *Accipitres*; (*surg.*) a dressing for pe of a claw. [L. *accipiter* hawk].
ip'-it-ral], *adj.* of accipitrine type.
k-sip'-it-ra-ri], *n.* a person who
-sip'-it-rīn], *adj.* seizing; rapaci- irds of prey.
-lām'], *n.* applause, a cheer of on. [*Next*].
lām'], *v.t.* to applaud loudly, to ure by cheering, show approval; hands. [L. *acclamare* to cry out].
[ak'-lam-ā'-shun], *n.* applause, a cheer of approval; (*archæ.*) a sculptural or numismatic image of the massed onlookers expressing joy; (*mus.*) the response phrases sung by the audience or congregation. [L. *acclamatio* a shouting out].
ACCLAMATORY, [ak-lam'-at-or-i], *adj.* expressing approval or applause by cheering, shouts or clapping.
ACCLIMATATION, [ak-lī'-mat-ā'-shun], *n.* the act or process of getting used to an unaccustomed climate.
ACCLIMATE, [ak-lī'-mat], *v.t.* to accustom any growing thing, plant, or animal, to a climate foreign to its nature. [Fr. *acclimater* to become used to a climate].
ACCLIMATION, [ak-lim-ā'-shun], *n.* acclimatation.
ACCLIMATIZATION, [ak-lī'-mat-iz-ā'-shun], *n.* acclimatation.
ACCLIMATIZE, [ak-lī'-mat-iz], *v.t. and i.* to acclimate.
ACCLIVITOUS, [ak-liv'-it-us], *adj.* acclivous.
ACCLIVITY, [ak-liv'-i-ti], *n.* an ascending slope of ground; (*fort.*) the slope of a rampart. [L. *acclivitas* an ascent].
ACCLIVOUS, [ak-lī'-vus], *adj.* ascending, uphill, sloping upwards. [L. *acclivus* rising with a slope].
ACCOLADE, [ak'-ol-ād'], *n.* in the ceremony of conferring knighthood, the laying on the shoulder of a sword, deriving from the earlier custom of embracing the recipient round the neck; (*mus.*) a perpendicular line across the staves connecting them. [It. *accollata* embrace round the neck].
ACCOLATED, [ak'-ol-ā'-tid], *adj.* accollé. [It. *accollata* embrace round the neck].
ACCOLENT† **(1),** [ak'-ol-ent], *n.* a person who lives near-by, a neighbour, a borderer. [*Next*].
ACCOLENT† **(2),** [ak'-ol-ent], *adj.* living close by. [L. *accolentem*].
ACCOLLE, accollé, [ak'-ol-ā], *adj.* (*her.*) of an animal, having a collar round the neck; (*numis.*) joined at the neck, as the profiles of two heads on a coin. [A (4) and L. *collum* neck].

ACCOLLÉ

ACCOMMODATE, [ak-om'-od-āt], *v.t.* to adjust, adapt, modify to suit; to reconcile, settle differences, to set right; to supply requisites, to equip, to furnish; to lend; to lodge. [L. *accommodatum, p.pt.* of *accommodare* to adapt].
ACCOMMODATING, [ak-om'-od-āt'-ing], *adj.* fitting in with, obliging, amiable, indulgent.
ACCOMMODATINGLY, [ak-om'-od-āt-ing-li], *adv.* in accommodating fashion.
ACCOMMODATION, [ak-om'-od-ā'-shun], *n.* adaptation, adjustment, modification to make correspond; reconciliation, settlement of differences; provision of requisites, equipment; a loan; a lodging; **a. bill, a. note,** (*comm.*) a bill exchanged authorizing a cash loan, and not for payment of goods received; **a. ladder,** a light ladder let down at the side of a vessel; **a. train,** a train that hauls both passenger and goods carriages. [~L. *accommodatio* an adjusting].
ACCOMMODATIVE, [ak-om'-od-ā'-tiv], *adj.* supplying accommodation.
ACCOMPANIER, [ak-um'-pan-i-er], *n.* a person who accompanies. [Fr. *accompagner* to accompany].
ACCOMPANIMENT, [ak-um'-pan-im-ent], *n.* whatever is found alongside or together with something, an adjunct, a complement; a symmetrical adornment; (*mus.*) the vocal or instrumental part or parts complementary to the melodic line. [Fr. *accompagnement* accompaniment].
ACCOMPANIST, [ak-um'-pan-ist], *n.* a person who plays the accompaniment.
ACCOMPANY, [ak-um'-pa-ni], *v.t.* to attend, to go with as a friend, to escort; to be connected with; (*mus.*) to play a supporting part subordinate to the main theme or leading singers or instruments. [Fr. *accompagner* from *à* to and *compagne* companion].
ACCOMPLICE, [ak-um'-plis], *n.* an associate in a crime. [A (2) and Fr. *complice*].
ACCOMPLICESHIP, [ak-um'-plis-ship], *n.* state of being an accomplice.
ACCOMPLISH, [ak-um'-plish], *v.t.* to complete, carry out, execute, to succeed in finishing, to realize in practice. [OFr. *accompliss* from *accomplir*, from L. *ad* to and *complere* to complete].
ACCOMPLISHABLE, [ak-um'-plish-abl], *adj.* capable of accomplishment.

watering-place for cattle; (*mas.*) the joint between two stones to be stopped up with cement or mortar. [~Fr. *abreuver* to water].
ABRIDGE, [a-brij'], *v.t.* to lessen, reduce, shorten, curtail, contract, compress, abbreviate, epitomize; to retrench; to deprive. [ME. *abregge* from OFr. *abregier* to shorten].
ABRIDGMENT, ABRIDGEMENT, [a-brij'-ment], *n.* an epitome, a précis, a synopsis, an abbreviation.
ABROACH, [a-brōch'], *adv.* opened up, broached, as of a cask; set at an angle to tap the cask of its liquor. [A (3) and BROACH (2)].
ABROAD, [a-brawd'], *adv.* widely, at large over a wide area; distant, far away; beyond the bounds of, overseas, in foreign lands; current; (*fig.*) uncertain, confused, far astray. [ME. *abrood*].
ABROGABLE, [ab'-rog-abl], *adj.* capable of being abrogated. [L. *abrogabilis*].
ABROGATE, [ab'-rog-āt], *v.t.* to repeal by authority; to annul, cancel. [L. *abrogatum, p.pt.* of *abrogare* to repeal].
ABROGATION, [ab'-rog-ā'-shun], *n.* the act of abrogating. [L. *abrogatio*].
ABROTANOID, [ab-rot'-an-oid], *n.* a variety of reef-coral with a form and pattern similar to the foliage of southernwood. [Gk. *abrotanon* southernwood, and *-oeides* like].
ABROTANUM, [ab-rot'-an-um], *n.* southernwood, *Artemisia Abrotanum.* [Gk. *abrotanon* southernwood].
ABRUPT, [ab-rupt'], *adj.* steep, craggy, broken, precipitous; sudden, unexpected, startling; uncivil, brusque, short; (*bot.*) terminated abruptly, as if the end were broken off; (*geol.*) of strata, that have suddenly broken out. [L. *abruptum, p.pt.* of *abrumpere* to break off].
ABRUPTED, [ab-rupt'-id], *adj.* broken off sharply, snapped off; torn apart.
ABRUPTION, [ab-rup'-shun], *n.* a sharp, sudden or violent separation.
ABRUPTLY, [ab-rupt'-li], *adv.* in an abrupt way.
ABRUPTNESS, [ab-rupt'-nes], *n.* a state of being abrupt.
ABSCESS, [ab'-sis], *n.* an inflamed gathering of pus in a part or organ of the body. [L. *abscessus* a going away, from *abscedere* to depart].
ABSCIND, [ab-sind'], *v.t.* to cut off; to rend apart. [L. *abscindere* to cut off].
ABSCISSA, [ab-sis'-a], *n.* (*geom.*) a line cut off, more particularly, a part of the diameter or transverse axis of a conic section intercepted between some fixed point and a semi-ordinate. [L. *abscissa* (*linea*), from *abscissum, p.pt.* of *abscindere* to cut off].
ABSCISSION, [ab-sizh'-un], *n.* a cutting off; the state of being cut off, separation, severance; (*surg.*) amputation, a separation of a limb or part of the body from the organism; (*rhet.*) a sudden stop in the middle of a sentence. [~L. *abscissum, p.pt.* of *abscindere* to cut off.
ABSCOND, [ab-skond'], *v.i.* to leave a place secretly, to depart abruptly and secretly, to flee in order to evade the law. [L. *abscondere* to conceal].
ABSCONDENCE, [ab-skond'-ens], *n.* the act of hiding; concealment.
ABSCONDER, [ab-skond'-er], *n.* one who absconds.
ABSENCE, [ab'-sents], *n.* state of being absent, not present, the state of being away; non-existence; the period when some person or thing is away; distraction, inattention; (*leg.*) failure to attend court. [L. *absentia*, from *absens, pres.pt.* of *abesse* to be absent].
ABSENT (1), [ab'-sent], *adj.* not present, away from a place, missing; non-existent; mentally distracted, inattentive to events as they occur, preoccupied, absent-minded. [L. *absens*].
ABSENT (2), [ab-sent'], *v. reflex.* to keep (oneself) deliberately in another place. [L. *absentare*].
ABSENTEE, [ab'-sent-ē'], *n.* one who is not present, particularly on an occasion when it is a duty to be present; a person who does not live at home; a person who resides apart from the position or district which is his source of income.
ABSENTEEISM, [ab'-sent-ē'-izm], *n.* residence apart from one's estate; the practice of absenting oneself from work.
ABSENTLY, [ab'-sent-li], *adv.* absent-mindedly, forgetfully.
ABSENTMENT, [ab'-sent-ment], *n.* state of being absent.
ABSENT-MINDED, [ab'-sent-mīnd'-id], *adj.* forgetful, preoccupied, not paying direct attention.
ABSENT-MINDEDLY, [ab'-sent-mīnd'-id-li], *adv.* in an absent-minded way, without paying attention.
ABSENT-MINDEDNESS, [ab'-sent-mīnd'-id-nes], *n.* the state of being absent-minded.
ABSINTH, [ab'-sinth], *n.* wormwood, a plant of bitter flavour with tonic properties, *Artemisia absinthium;* a French liqueur having among its ingredients wormwood oils, anise, and some aromatics. [L. *absinthium* wormwood].
ABSINTHE, [ab'-sa(ng)], *n.* the liqueur, absinth. [Fr. *absinthe*].
ABSINTHIAN, [ab-sinth'-i-an], *adj.* similar to, or consisting of, absinth.
ABSINTHIATED, [ab-sinth'-i-ā'-tid], *adj.* impregnated with absinth.
ABSINTHIC, [ab-sinth'-ik], *adj.* obtained from, or containing, absinth.
ABSINTHIN, [ab-sinth'-in], *n.* the bitter essence or principle in absinth.
ABSOLESCENCE, see OBSOLESCENCE.
ABSOLUTE (1), [ab'-sol-ewt, ab'-sol-ōōt], *n.* that which is complete in itself; the self-dependent and self-existent being, force or cause of things; the infinite. [ABSOLUTE (2)].
ABSOLUTE (2), [ab'-sol-ewt, ab'-sol-ōōt], *adj.* unconditional, complete, unqualified, not governed, unlimited; complete in itself, unequivocal, not relative, self-dependent, self-existent; perfect, pure, unmixed, untouched by imperfection; unlimited in power, supreme, authoritative, arbitrary, despotic; positive, real, definite, certain. [L. *absolutum, p.pt.* of *absolvere* to set free].
ABSOLUTELY, [ab'-sol-ewt-li, ab'-sol-ōōt'-li], *adv.* in an absolute way; (*coll.*) very, entirely.
ABSOLUTENESS, [ab'-sol-ewt-nes, ab'-sol-ōōt-nes], *n.* the quality or state of being absolute.
ABSOLUTION, [ab-sol-ew'-shun, ab-sol-ōō'-shun], *n.* a remission of sin after confession and penitence by a Catholic; the act of declaring such a remission after repentance by a Protestant; (*leg.*) a judge's declaration of acquittal. [L. *absolutio*].
ABSOLUTISM, [ab'-sol-ewt-izm, ab'-sol-ōōt-izm], *n.* the condition of being absolute; the political doctrine the central principle of which is the necessity for an absolute ruler; (*theol.*) the theory of predestination.
ABSOLUTIST (1), [ab'-sol-ewt'-ist, ab'-sol-ōōt'-ist], *n.* a person supporting or agreeing with the first principle of absolutism; (*philos.*) a thinker who equates object with subject.
ABSOLUTIST (2), [ab'-sol-ewt'-ist, ab'-sol-ōōt'-ist], *adj.* despotic, dictatorial or arbitrary.
ABSOLUTORY, [ab-sol'-ew-to-ri], *adj.* absolving.
ABSOLVATORY, [ab-solv'-at-or-i], *adj.* conferring absolution.
ABSOLVE, [ab-zolv'], *v.t.* to grant freedom from duty, oath, sin, guilt, obligation; to acquit; (*eccles.*) to grant absolution to. [L. *absolvere* to set free].
ABSONANT, [ab'-son-ant], *adj.* ridiculous, contrary to reason; unmusical, discordant. [L. *absonus* out of tune].
ABSONOUS, [ab'-son-us], *adj.* absonant. [L. *absonus* out of tune].
ABSORB, [ab-sawb'], *v.t.* to take in, eat or drink; to suck up; to swallow; (*fig.*) to assimilate ideas, to understand; to occupy completely, to take possession of the mind. [L. *absorbere* to swallow up].
ABSORBABILITY, [ab-sawb'-ab-il'-i-ti], *n.* the quality of being absorbable.
ABSORBABLE, [ab-sawb'-abl], *adj.* able to be absorbed.
ABSORBED, [ab-sawbd'], *adj.* deeply engaged in; engrossed.
ABSORBEDLY, [ab-saw'-bid-li], *adv.* in absorbed fashion.
ABSORBEFACIENT (1), [ab-sawb'-if-as'-i-ent], *n.* (*med.*) physic or whatever promotes absorption. [ABSORB and L. *facientem, pres.pt.* of *facere* to make].
ABSORBEFACIENT (2), [ab-sawb'-if-as'-i-ent], *adj.* inclined to cause absorption.
ABSORBENT (1), [ab-sawb'-ent], *n.* that which absorbs liquid; (*chem.*) any substance which can take in moisture from the atmosphere; (*med.*) any substance capable of absorbing abdominal acids. [ABSORBENT (2)].
ABSORBENT (2), [ab-sawb'-ent], *adj.* imbibing, sucking in; ready to absorb; spongy. [~L. *absorbens*].
ABSORBING, [ab-sawb'-ing], *adj.* anything engrossing; fully occupying the attention, interesting.
ABSORPTIOMETER, [ab-sawp'-shi-om'-it-er], *n.* an instrument for testing the absorption of gases in liquids. [ABSORPTION and Gk. *metron* measure].

ABSORPTION, [ab-sawp'-shun], *n.* the act of absorbing; the condition of being absorbed; the process of sucking in liquid; (*fig.*) mental preoccupation; (*physiol.*) assimilation through the blood, tissues or lymphatic matter of the body; (*chem.*) transformation, by fusion with another substance, of a gaseous liquid into a fluid or solid. [L. *absorptio*].

ABSORPTIVE, [ab-sawp'-tiv], *adj.* able to absorb. [L. *absorptivus*].

ABSORPTIVENESS, [ab-sawp'-tiv-nes], *n.* the tendency or power to absorb; (*fig.*) receptiveness.

ABSQUATULATE, [ab-skwot'-ew-lāt], *v.i.* (*U.S. slang*) depart, go away, decamp. [Unkn.].

ABSTAIN, [ab-stān'], *v.i.* to forbear, avoid, to hold back from, to refrain, particularly from food or drink or strong desires. [Fr. *abstenir* to keep away from].

ABSTAINER, [ab-stān'-er], *n.* a person who abstains, particularly from intoxicants.

ABSTAINING (1), [ab-stān'-ing], *n.* abstention, *esp.* from alcohol.

ABSTAINING (2), [ab-stān'-ing], *adj.* abstemious; teetotal.

ABSTEMIOUS, [ab-stēm'-i-us], *adj.* temperate, strictly controlled in satisfying the desire for food, drink or pleasure, not self-indulgent, practising self-denial. [L. *abstemius* sober].

ABSTEMIOUSLY, [ab-stēm'-i-us-li], *adv.* in an abstemious way.

ABSTEMIOUSNESS, [ab-stēm'-i-us-nes], *n.* the quality of being abstemious.

ABSTENTION, [ab-sten'-shun], *n.* the act of refraining; not exercising one's right to vote at an election; abstinence, self-restraint. [Fr. *abstention* holding back].

ABSTERGE, [ab-sturj'], *v.t.* to wipe clean; to purge, cleanse. [L. *abstergere* to wipe off].

ABSTERGENT (1), [ab-sturj'-ent], *n.* that which cleanses, a detergent. [*Next*].

ABSTERGENT (2), [ab-sturj'-ent], *adj.* possessing a cleansing quality. [~L. *abstergens*].

ABSTERSION, [ab-stur'-shun], *n.* the act of cleansing. [~L. *abstersum*, *p.pt.* of *abstergere* to wipe off].

ABSTERSIVE, [ab-stur'-siv], *adj.* cleansing.

ABSTINENCE, [ab'-stin-ents], *n.* temperance; a deliberate refraining from, voluntary self-denial; a strict allowance, or complete refusal to partake, of food or strong drink, or pleasure. [L. *abstinentia*, from *abstinentem*, *pres.pt.* of *abstinere* to refrain from].

ABSTINENCY, [ab'-stin-en-si], *n.* abstinence.

ABSTINENT, [ab'-stin-ent], *adj.* temperate, devoted to abstinence, refraining from indulgence, *esp.* in food and strong drinks. [L. *abstinens*].

ABSTINENTLY, [ab'-stin-ent-li], *adv.* with abstinence, in an abstinent manner.

ABSTRACT (1), [ab'-strakt], *n.* whatever is taken out; an extract, summary, epitome, essentially the same as the original. [*Next*].

ABSTRACT (2), [ab'-strakt], *adj.* separated in thought from material associations and connexions, abstruse, intellectual, mental in quality; thought apart from substance; **a. idea,** (*met.*) an idea considered as such, apart from material influences and relations; (*gram.*) the titles of various classes, varieties or orders of things. [L. *abstractum*, *p.pt.* of *abstrahere* to draw away].

ABSTRACT (3), [ab-strakt'], *v.t.* to remove, draw away, to separate, to detach either by intellect or by bulk; to take away illegally, to steal; to summarize; (*chem.*) to extract the volatile ingredients of a compound by means of heat. [ABSTRACT (2)].

ABSTRACTED, [ab-strakt'-id], *adj.* removed, separated; (*fig.*) mentally detached, absent-minded.

ABSTRACTEDLY, [ab-strakt'-id-li], *adv.* in an abstract way, forgetfully, absently.

ABSTRACTEDNESS, [ab-strakt'-id-nes], *n.* the state of being abstracted.

ABSTRACTER, [ab-strakt'-er], *n.* a person who abstracts; a maker of abstracts.

ABSTRACTION, [ab-strak'-shun], *n.* the state of being abstracted, the act of abstracting; withdrawal, separation or removal; illegal removal, pilfering; the act or process of thinking of a thing divorced from its substance, associations, or environment, of a substance apart from its attributes, or the converse; a condition of withdrawal from the physical distractions of life; a state of mental seclusion; an object or vision existing only in the mind; absent-mindedness; (*chem.*) the drawing away of the volatile ingredients of a compound by means of heat. [L. *abstractio*].

ABSTRACTIVE, [ab-strak'-tiv], *adj.* possessing the power or quality of abstracting.

ABSTRACTLY, [ab'-strakt-li], *adv.* in an abstract way.

ABSTRACTNESS, [ab-strakt'-nes], *n.* the state of being abstract.

ABSTRICTION†, [ab-strik'-shun], *n.* undoing, a loosening, a disjunction, an unbinding. [AB- and L. *strictio* binding].

ABSTRUSE, [ab-strōōs'], *adj.* hidden, obscure, unintelligible, undiscernible, difficult to understand. [L. *abstrusum*, *p.pt.* of *abstrudere* to hide].

ABSTRUSELY, [ab-strōōs'-li], *adv.* in an abstruse fashion.

ABSTRUSENESS, [ab-strōōs'-nes], *n.* the state or quality of being abstruse.

ABSURD, [ab-surd'], *adj.* nonsensical, senseless, irrational; eccentric, abnormal; ridiculous, laughable, comic, droll. [L. *absurdus* senseless].

ABSURDITY, [ab-surd'-i-ti], *n.* absurdness.

ABSURDLY, [ab-surd'-li], *adv.* in an absurd fashion.

ABSURDNESS, [ab-surd'-nes], *n.* the quality of being absurd.

ABUNDANCE, [a-bund'-ans], *n.* a great quantity, a great plenty; a sufficiency, plenitude, profusion, full measure; affluence; (*solo whist*) a player's bid to take nine tricks from the three opponents, naming his own trump suit. [L. *abundantia* an overflowing].

ABUNDANT, [a-bund'-ant], *adj.* plentiful; fully sufficient, ample, profuse. [L. *abundans*].

ABUNDANTLY, [a-bund'-ant-li], *adv.* in plenty.

ABUSABLE, [ab-ewz'-abl], *adj.* able to be abused.

ABUSE (1), [ab-ews'], *n.* misuse, a wrong or bad use; misapplication, perversion; ill-treatment; violation; an evil, unjust or tyrannical action or practice; a succession of insults. [L. *abusus*].

ABUSE (2), [ab-ewz'], *v.t.* to misuse, to use wrongly or badly; to pervert, misapply; to maltreat, mishandle; to insult, revile, to treat rudely or coarsely; to violate; to threaten, upbraid. [L. *abusus*, *p.pt.* of *abuti* to misuse].

ABUSER, [ab-ewz'-er], *n.* a person who abuses another.

ABUSIVE, [ab-ews'-iv], *adj.* characterized by or practising abuse; perverted, improper.

ABUSIVELY, [ab-ews'-iv-li], *adv.* in an abusive way.

ABUSIVENESS, [ab-ews'-iv-nes], *n.* the quality of being abusive; perversity; foulness of speech.

ABUT, [a-but'], *v.i.* to border upon, to lean on; to end at, to terminate; to put two planks end to end. [OFr. *abouter* to place end to end].

ABUTILON, [ab-ew'-til-on], *n.* (*bot.*) a genus of plant of shrub size having bell-shaped flowers of bright colours. [Arab. *aubutilon*].

ABUTMENT, [a-but'-ment], *n.* anything which abuts; (*arch.*) the fixture which supports the end of an arch.

ABUTMENT

ABUTTER, [a-but'-er], *n.* the landowner whose territory adjoins public or private land.

ABUZZ, [a-buz'], *adj.* and *adv.* full of buzzing noises. [A (3) and BUZZ].

ABYSM, [ab-izm'], *n.* any deep space, a gulf; the bottomless pit of ancient cosmogony. [OFr. *abisme* a gulf].

ABYSMAL, [ab-iz'-mal], *adj.* bottomless or fathomless.

ABYSMALLY, [ab-is'-mal-i], *adv.* in the manner of an abysm; (*fig.*) profoundly.

ABYSS, [ab-is'], *n.* a bottomless gulf, depth or chasm; whatever is fathomless or immeasurable; the earth in its primeval state of chaos; the formless centre of the earth; hell; (*her.*) the fesse point or centre of an escutcheon. [L. *abyssus*, Gk. *abussos* bottomless].

ABYSSAL, [ab-isl'], *adj.* unfathomable, bottomless; (*biol.*) pertaining to the lowest depths of the ocean; **a. rocks,** (*geol.*) rocks formed by intense heat at a very deep level below the surface.

ABYSSINIAN (1), [ab'-is-in'-yan], *n.* a native of Abyssinia.

ABYSSINIAN (2), [ab'-is-in'-yan], *adj.* belonging to, or appertaining to, Abyssinia.

A.C., [ā-sē], (*elect.*) abbreviation for ALTERNATING-CURRENT.

ACACIA, [ak-ā'-sha], *n.* a genus of mimosa trees, consisting of some four hundred shrubs and trees with feather-shaped leaves. [Gk. *akakia*].

ACACIO, [ak-ā'-shi-ō], *n.* acajou. [Perhaps from Fr. *acajou* mahogany].

ACADEME, [ak'-ad-ēm], *n.* an academy.

ACADEMIAN, [ak'-ad-ē'-mi-an], *n.* an associate of an academy; a person studying in a university or college.

ACADEMIC (1), [ak'-ad-em'-ik], *n.* academian; a follower of Plato's philosophy.

ACADEMIC (2), [ak-ad-em'-ik], *adj.* academical; theoretical.

ACADEMICAL, [ak-ad-em'-ikl], *adj.* belonging to an academy; related to the philosophy of Plato.

ACADEMICALLY, [ak-ad-em'-ik-a-li], *adv.* in an academical way.

ACADEMICIAN, [ak-ad'-em-ish'-un], *n.* a member of an academy or university or of a society for promoting the arts or sciences.

ACADEMISM, [ak-ad'-em-izm], *n.* the doctrine of the academic philosophy.

ACADEMIST, [ak-ad'-em-ist], *n.* an academician.

ACADEMY, [ak-a'-dem-i], *n.* an association of scholars and specialists formed to promote the teaching and learning, and to protect the interests, of the arts or sciences; the building in which such a society meets; an institution for the higher branches of education above university standard; originally, the grove near Athens in which Plato instructed his pupils; followers of Plato's philosophy; (*Scots*) a secondary school. [Gk. *akademeia* Plato's garden in which he taught, from the hero *Akademos* who owned it].

ACADIAN (1), [ak-ā'-di-an], *n.* a native of Nova Scotia.

ACADIAN (2), [ak-ā'-di-an], *adj.* pertaining to, belonging to, Nova Scotia.

ACAJOU, [ak'-aj-ōō], *n.* the cashew nut, *Anacardium occidentale.* [Fr. *acajou*].

ACANTHA, [ak-an'-tha], *n.* (*bot.*) the prickle of a plant; (*zool.*) a fish's fin or spine shaped like a prickle; one of the sharp protuberances of the vertebrae. [Gk. *akantha* a prickle].

ACANTHACEOUS, [ak'-an-thā'-shus], *adj.* having sharp prickles.

ACANTHINE, [ak-an'-thīn], *adj.* resembling the acanthus; from a prickly plant.

ACANTHOID, [ak-an'-thoid], *adj.* spiny. [ACANTHA and Gk. *-oeides* like].

ACANTHOPOD, [ak-an'-tho-pod'], *adj.* possessing spiny feet. [ACANTHA and Gk. *pous*, *podos* foot].

ACANTHOPTERYGII, [ak-an'-thop-ter-ij'-i-ī], *n.* (*pl.*) (*ichth.*) fishes having dorsal fins prickly at the ends, as the perch. [ACANTHA and Gk. *pterugion* a fin].

ACANTHOUS, [ak-an'-thus], *adj.* spinous.

ACANTHUS, [ak-an'-thus], *n.* the brank-ursine or bear's-breech plant, a group of prickly plants; (*arch.*) a formal leaf pattern copied from the foliage of the *Acanthus spinosus.* [Gk. *akanthos* a thorn].

ACANTHUS

ACARDIA, [ak-ahd'-i-a], *n.* lack of a heart. [Gk. *akardios* having no heart].

ACARDIAC, [ak-ahd'-i-ak], *adj.* without a heart.

ACARINA, [ak-a-rī'-na], *n.* (*entom.*) an order of arachnida which includes the ticks and mites. [~Gk. *akari* mite].

ACARPELOUS, [ak-ahp'-el-us], *adj.* without carpels. [A (4) and L. *carpellus*].

ACARPOUS, [ak-ahp'-us], *adj.* barren, unfruitful, sterile. [Gk. *akarpos* unfruitful].

ACARUS, [ak'-a-rus], *n.* a tick or mite. [Gk. *akari* mite].

ACATALECTIC (1), [ak-at'-al-ek'-tik], *n.* a form of verse numerically complete in syllables or feet. [*Next*].

ACATALECTIC (2), [ak-at'-al-ek'-tik], *adj.* complete in the required number of syllables or feet. [Gk. *akatalektikos*].

ACATALEPSY, [ak-at'-al-ep'-si], *n.* (*med.*) doubt in the prognosis or diagnosis of a disease; (*philos.*) form of scepticism based on the principle that no knowledge can be regarded as certain for what is known is only probable. [Gk. *akatalepsis* not understanding].

ACATALEPTIC (1), [ak-at'-al-ep'-tik], *n.* a sceptic, one who tends to doubt the truth of all knowledge.

ACATALEPTIC (2), [ak-at'-al-ep'-tik], *adj.* incomprehensible, improbable. [Gk. *akataleptikos*].

ACATHARSIA, [ak'-ath-ah'-si-a], *n.* impurity, suppuration; (*surg.*) pus forming in a cut or injury. [Gk. *akatharsia* foulness].

ACAULESCENT, [ak'-awl-es'-ent], *adj.* almost stemless. [~L. *acaulis* stemless].

ACAULINE, [ak-awl'-īn], *adj.* acaulose.

ACAUL[…] seeming[…] leaves […] a stem] ACAUL[…] *akaulos* ACCED[…] to succ[…] ACCELE[…] gradua[…] ACCELE[…] quicker[…] becom[…] *acceler*[…] ACCEL[…] speed, a mov[…] **force,** increa[…] ACCEL[…] accele[…] ated; body[…] ACCE[…] increa[…] ACCE[…] accel[…] which a cy[…] deve[…] ACCE[…] tive. ACCE[…] an […] resu[…] [L. […] ACCI[…] inst[…] sect[…] spe[…]

ACCEPTED, […] uncontested ACCEPTER, […] *n.* one who […] a bill of exc[…] ACCESS, [ak'[…] the means o[…] to; (*med.*) re[…] [L. *accessus* […] ACCESSARI[…] ACCESSARI[…] ACCESSARY ACCESSIBIL[…] being accessi[…] *bilitas*]. ACCESSIBLE […] easy of appro[…] ACCESSIBLY ACCESSION, […] coming to, ar[…] an office, dign[…] an addition, […] tion, a valuab[…] ment of prop[…] development, of a disease; pope's election ACCESSIONA[…] ACCESSORIA[…] an accessory. ACCESSORIL[…] an accessory. ACCESSORIN[…] being accessory ACCESSORY […] secondary elen[…] an inessential, added to the […] guilty of aiding from the polic[…] additions to th[…] *accessorius*, fro[…] proach]. ACCESSORY […] secondary, addi[…] purpose or plan ACCIDENCE, […] grammar which ations in the dec[…] *accidens* an acci[…] ACCIDENT, [ak[…] unexpected eve[…] meditated act, […] mishap, a misfo[…] a non-essential […] (*med.*) an unex[…] couraging kind; face, kind or qu[…] coat of arms wh[…] *dens accidentem* ACCIDENTAL […] property or attri[…] not proper to th[…] notation before semitone. ACCIDENTAL […] unexpectedly or incidental, extra[…] ACCIDENTALIS[…] produced by acc[…] ACCIDENTALLY […] dental way. ACCIDENTALN[…] quality of being […] ACCIDENTED, […] gated or irregular ACCIPITER, [ak-[…] group of birds of falcons, *Raptores* the nose, in the s[…] ACCIPITRAL, [ak[…] ACCIPITRARY […] snares birds of pr[…] ACCIPITRINE, [a[…] ous; belonging to ACCLAIM (1), [a[…] approval, acclama[…] ACCLAIM (2), [ak[…] signify joy or plea[…] to shout, to clap th[…] ACCLAMATION, […]

ACCOMPLISHED, [ak-um'-plisht], *adj.* finished, completed; talented, cultured, skilled.
ACCOMPLISHMENT, [ak-um'-plish-ment], *n.* the act of accomplishing; fulfilment, completion; a quality belonging to a cultured or talented person.
ACCOMPT, [ak-ompt'], *n.* account. [Fr. *accompter* account].
ACCOMPTANT, [ak-ompt'-ant], *n.* an accountant.
ACCORD (1), [ak-awd'], *n.* agreement, assent, concord, harmony of thoughts or sounds or actions; adjustment of differences; concurrence of factors. [OFr. *acord* agreement].
ACCORD (2), [ak-awd'], *v.t.* to grant, confer, concede; *v.i.* to be in agreement, to be in harmony, to correspond with. [ME. *accorden* to agree from LL. *accordare* to harmonize].
ACCORDANCE, [ak-awd'-ans], *n.* agreement with a person; conformity with a thing; harmony.
ACCORDANCY, [ak-awd'-an-si], *n.* agreement, harmony, conformity.
ACCORDANT, [ak-awd'-ant], *adj.* corresponding; consonant. [OFr. *accordant*].
ACCORDANTLY, [ak-awd'-ant-li], *adv.* in an accordant way.
ACCORDING, [ak-awd'-ing], *adv.* normally used in adverbial phrases; **a. to,** in a manner agreeing with, consistent with, conforming to; on the authority of; **a. as,** to the extent that, in proportion as.
ACCORDINGLY, [ak-awd'-ing-li], *adv.* logically; agreeably to something said; consequently.
ACCORDION, ACCORDEON, [ak-awd'-i-on], *n.* (*mus.*) a portable wind-instrument similar to a concertina operated on the metallic reed principle by the wind from bellows opened and closed by the hands. [Invented word, from ACCORD (1)].
ACCORDIONIST, [ak-awd'-i-on-ist], *n.* a person who plays on the accordion.
ACCOST, [ak-ost'], *v.t.* to approach and speak to a stranger familiarly, or with immoral intent, to speak before spoken to; to salute. [L. *accostare*].
ACCOSTABLE, [ak-ost'-abl], *adj.* easy of access; familiar.
ACCOSTED, [ak-ost'-id], *adj.* (*her.*) back to back or side by side, common position for two beasts on an escutcheon.
ACCOUCHEMENT, [ak-ōōsh'-mong], *n.* childbirth, delivery; the period just previous to the act of delivery, confinement, a lying-in. [Fr. *accouchement*].
ACCOUCHEUR, [ak-ōō-shur'], *n.* a male who practises midwifery; an obstetrician. [Fr. *accoucheur*].
ACCOUCHEUSE, [ak-ōō-shurz'], *n.* a midwife. [Fr. *accoucheuse*].
ACCOUNT (1), [ak-ownt'], *n.* a list, computation, reckoning, register, statement, calculation or record of money matters, services or goods; a recital, narrative or description, explanation or statement; the grounds, the conditions, the circumstances; sake, behalf, interest; estimation, evaluation, opinion, judgment; **current a.,** an account with a bank from which money may be withdrawn on demand. [OFr. *aconte*].
ACCOUNT (2), [ak-ownt'], *v.t.* to judge, estimate, value, assess; *v.i.* to explain, to give an adequate explanation, to make a satisfactory statement.
ACCOUNTABILITY, [ak-ownt'-ab-il'-i-ti], n. the power to give account; responsibility.
ACCOUNTABLE, [ak-ownt'-abl], *adj.* liable to be called to account; responsible.
ACCOUNTABLENESS, [ak-ownt'-abl-nes], *n.* the state of being accountable.
ACCOUNTABLY, [ak-ownt'-ab-li], *adv.* in an accountable way.
ACCOUNTANCY, [ak-ownt'-an-si], *n.* the profession or power of an accountant.
ACCOUNTANT (1), [ak-ownt'-ant], *n.* a person professionally engaged to keep accounts, or to examine and audit them; a person trained in keeping accounts, a book-keeper. [OFr. *acontant*].
ACCOUNTANT (2), [ak-ownt'-ant], *adj.* responsible for, accountable. [*Prec.*].
ACCOUNTANTSHIP, [ak-ownt'-ant-ship], *n.* the position or duties of an accountant.
ACCOUNT-BOOK, [ak-ownt'-bŏŏk'], *n.* a book in which accounts are recorded.
ACCOUTRE, [ak-ōō'-ter], *v.t.* to equip with costume or uniform, to dress for military service. [Fr. *accoutrer* to dress, deck out].
ACCOUTREMENTS, [ak-ōō'-tri-ments], *n.(pl.)* military equipment, all the articles and details except clothes and arms; (*fig.*) trappings. [*Prec.*].
ACCREDIT, [a-kred'-it], *v.t.* to invest with authority, sanction, authorize; to procure credit for; to dispatch as an official ambassador or envoy, to provide a messenger with credentials. [L. *ad* to and *creditum*, *p.pt.* of *credere* to trust].
ACCREDITED, [a-kred'-it-id], *adj.* having credentials, *esp.* to negotiate; **a. agent,** an authorized agent; **a milk,** milk guaranteed to satisfy a minimum government standard.
ACCREMENTITION, [ak'-rim-ent-ish'-un], *n.* gradual increase. [L. *accrementum* an increase].
ACCRESCENCE, [ak-res'-ents], *n.* gradual growth; accretion. [L. *accrescentia* continuous growth].
ACCRESCENT, [ak-res'-ent], *adj.* increasing; enlarged. [L. *accrescens*].
ACCRETE (1), [ak-rēt'], *adj.* (*bot.*) fastened to another body and growing with it. [L. *accretum*, *p.pt.* of *accrescere* to increase].
ACCRETE (2), [ak-rēt'], *v.t. and i.* to increase by growing; to join to. [*Prec.*].
ACCRETION, [ak-rē'-shun], *n.* an increase in size by additions from outside sources; that which is added in this way; (*bot.*) arboreal growth in girth or height; (*leg.*) process by which possessions and property left to a legatee pass on to co-legatee after the first claimant dies; (*med.*) the growing together of parts normally growing apart, as fingers or toes. [L. *accretio* an increasing].
ACCRUE, [ak-rōō], *v.t. and i.* to become added to, to be accumulated, to be increased, as of possessions, profit or damages; (*leg.*) to endow with a right. [Fr. *accrue* increase].
ACCRUEMENT, [ak-rōō'-ment], *n.* addition; the act of increasing.
ACCUBATION, [ak'-ew-bā'-shun], *n.* the act of lying or reclining, a custom of the Greeks at meal-times. [L. *accubatio* a lying near].
ACCUMBENCY, [ak-um'-ben-si], *n.* state of being accumbent.
ACCUMBENT, [ak-um'-bent], *adj.* leaning or reclining. [L. *accumbens*].
ACCUMULATE, [ak-ewm'-yōō-lāt], *v.t. and i.* to increase in bulk, quantity or number; to amass, store up, collect, heap up. [L. *accumulatum*, *p.pt.* of *accumulare* to heap up].
ACCUMULATION, [ak-ewm'-yōō-lā'-shun], *n.* the state of being accumulated; the act of accumulating; a mass; a heap.
ACCUMULATIVE, [ak-ewm'-yōō-lat-iv], *adj.* tending towards accumulation, acquisitive; effected by increase.
ACCUMULATIVELY, [ak-ewm'-yōō-lat-iv-li], *adv.* in an accumulative way.
ACCUMULATOR, [ak-ewm'-yōō-lā'-tor], *n.* a person who piles up or stores up, who accumulates anything, specifically wealth; battery storing electricity; an apparatus for transmitting water pumped up by pressure to another machine.
ACCURACY, [ak'-yōō-ras-i], *n.* correctness, precision, exactness.
ACCURATE, [ak'-yōō-rat], *adj.* correct, exact, precise; careful, strict, free from errors, without mistakes. [L. *accuratum*, *p.pt.* of *accurare* to prepare carefully].
ACCURATELY, [ak'-yōō-rat-li], *adv.* in an accurate fashion.
ACCURATENESS, [ak'-yōō-rat-nes], *n.* accuracy; exactness.
ACCURSED, [ak-urst', ak-ur'-sid], *adj.* under a curse, ill-fated, doomed to disaster; execrable, abominable; deserving of disaster. [A (3) and CURSE (1)].
ACCURST, [ak-urst'], *adj.* accursed, under a curse, detestable.
ACCUSABLE, [ak-ewz'-abl], *adj.* able to be accused, chargeable with a crime; blamable. [L. *accusabilis*].
ACCUSAL, [ak-ewzl'], *n.* an accusation.
ACCUSANT (1), [ak-ewz'-ant], *n.* a person who accuses another. [*Next*].
ACCUSANT (2), [ak-ewz'-ant], *adj.* accusing. [L. *accusans*, *pres.pt.* of *accusare* to blame].
ACCUSATION, [ak'-ewz-ā'-shun], *n.* the act of accusing; the charge of a crime or offence brought against a person; (*leg.*) an indictment. [L. *accusatio*].
ACCUSATIVE, [ak-ewz'-at-iv], *adj.* accusing; (*gram.*) denoting the objective case. [L. *accusativus* accusing].
ACCUSATIVELY, [ak-ewz'-at-iv-li], *adv.* in an accusative way, or the accusative case.
ACCUSATORIAL, [ak-ewz'-at-aw'-ri-al], *adj.* accusatory.
ACCUSATORY, [ak-ewz'-at-or-i], *adj.* making an accusation. [L. *accusatorius* of an accuser].
ACCUSE, [ak-ewz'], *v.t.* to bring a charge against a

person of a crime, fault or offence, to indict, arraign, to bring action against, to blame. [L. *accusare* to blame, accuse].

ACCUSER, [ak-ewz'-er], *n.* one who accuses.

ACCUSINGLY, [ak-ewz'-ing-li], *adv.* in accusing fashion.

ACCUSTOM, [ak-us'-tom], *v.t.* to familiarize by habit or use, to habituate, to make familiar, to inure, to naturalize. [OFr. *accostumer* to grow used to].

ACCUSTOMABLE†, [ak-ust'-om-abl], *adj.* usual, habitual, normal.

ACCUSTOMABLY, [ak-ust'-om-ab-li], *adv.* according to custom, in an habitual fashion.

ACCUSTOMED†, [ak-ust'-omd], *adj.* habitual, usual, normal, frequently practised; characteristic.

ACCUSTOMEDNESS, [ak-ust'-omd-nes], *n.* state of being accustomed.

ACE (1), [ās], *n.* a unit; the card or side of a die with one spot; the single spot or unit itself on a card or die side; (*fig.*) the best, the highest, the most expert, the winner; (*slang*) an expert airman; (*tennis*) an unreturnable service. [L. *as* a unit].

ACE (2), [ās], *v.t.* (*tennis*) to serve an ace to.

ACELDAMA, [ak-eld'-a-ma], *n.* (*eccles.*) a field near Jerusalem, bought with the money which bribed Judas to betray Jesus (Acts i, 19); (*fig.*) an arena or field of murder, slaughter, or bloodshed. [Aramaic *okeldama* field of blood].

ACENTRIC (1), [a-sen'-trik], *n.* (*aeron.*) descriptive of that type of aeroplane whose propeller thrust is not aligned with the centre of gravity. [*Next*].

ACENTRIC (2), [a-sen'-trik], *adj.* not centred, intentionally not centralized. [Gk. *akentros* without a centre].

ACEPHALAN, [as-ef'-al-an], *n.* (*zool.*) a specimen of a group of molluscs which is characterized by having no head, e.g., an oyster. [Gk. *akephalos* lacking a head].

ACEPHALISM, [as-ef'-al-izm], *n.* the condition of being without a head.

ACEPHALIST, [as-ef'-al-ist], *n.* a person who acknowledges no head.

ACEPHALITES, [as-ef'-al-īts], *n.(pl.)* sects and societies admitting no leader, or believing in going leaderless, e.g., Anarchists; (*eccles.*) clergymen who are not responsible to a bishop; (*myth.*) race of people supposed to be headless.

ACEPHALOUS, [as-ef'-al-us], *adj.* headless; (*bot.*) having no style to the seed vessel. [~Gk. *akephalos*].

ACER, [ā'-ser], *n.* (*bot.*) a genus of trees including the maple and the sycamore. [L. *acer* maple tree].

ACERA, [as'-er-a], *n.(pl.)* (*entom.*) a group of insects without wings or antennae; (*zool.*) a group of molluscs without tentacles and moving by muscular attachment of the stomach, e.g., snails, slugs. [Gk. *akeras* hornless].

ACERACEOUS, [as'-er-ā'-shus], *adj.* (*bot.*) belonging to the maple order.

ACERATE, [as'-er-āt], *n.* (*chem.*) a salt of aceric acid. [L. *acer* maple].

ACERB, [as-urb'], *adj.* sour, bitter, astringent. [L. *acerbus* bitter].

ACERBATE (1), [as'-urb-āt], *adj.* embittered, soured; irritated. [L. *acerbatus*].

ACERBATE (2), [as'-urb-āt], *v.t.* to make sour, embitter; to exasperate, irritate. [L. *acerbatum*, *p.pt.* of *acerbare*].

ACERBIC, [as-urb'-ik], *adj.* severe, sour, harsh, sharp.

ACERBITUDE, [as-urb'-it-ewd], *n.* acerbity.

ACERBITY, [as-urb'-it-i], *n.* astringency, sourness, unripeness, harshness to the taste; (*fig.*) severity, sharpness, harshness of nature, manner, bearing, speech. [L. *acerbitas* sourness].

ACERIC, [as-er'-ik], *adj.* belonging to the maple; **a. acid,** an acid yielded by maple juice. [L. *acericus*].

ACEROSE, [as'-er-ōs], *adj.* (*bot.*) chaffy, full of chaff; similar to the pine needle. [L. *acerosus* chaffy].

ACEROUS, [as'-er-us], *adj.* acerose.

ACERVATE, [as-ur'-vāt], *adj.* (*bot.*) growing in clusters, compact, compressed. [L. *acervatum*, *p.pt.* of *acervare* to heap up].

ACESCENCE, [as-es'-ents], *n.* souring by fermentation; the attribute of sourness. [L. *acescens* turning sour].

ACESCENT, [as-es'-ent], *adj.* turning sour; partly sour or acid. [L. *acescens*].

ACETABULUM, [as'-it-ab'-yōō-lum], *n.* (*anat.*) the socket of a bone which fits the end of another bone; a glandular secretion in the placenta of certain animals. [L. *acetabulum* a small cup for vinegar].

ACETARIOUS, [as'-it-āer'-i-us], *adj.* suitable for salads, as lettuce. [L. *acetaria* vegetables mixed with vinegar].

ACETARY, [as'-it-a-ri], *n.* the acidulous pulp formed round the cores of fruits, as in the pear. [L. *acetum* vinegar, and *-arium* receptacle].

ACETATE, [as'-it-āt], *n.* a salt of acetic acid.

ACETATED, [as'-it-āt'-id], *adj.* mixed with acetic acid.

ACETIC, [as-ē'-tik], *adj.* pertaining to vinegar; sour; **a. acid,** the pure acid of vinegar. [L. *acetum*].

ACETIFICATION, [as-et'-if-ik-ā'-shun], *n.* the process of acetifying.

ACETIFIER, [as-et'-if-ī'-er], *n.* an apparatus that effects acetification.

ACETIFY, [as-et'-if-ī], *v.t. and i.* to change into acid or vinegar.

ACETIMETER, [as'-et-im'-it-er], *n.* an instrument for testing the strength of acids. [ACETIC and METER].

ACETIMETRY, [as'-et-im'-it-ri], *n.* the process of testing the strength of acids. [ACETIC and Gk. *metria* measuring].

ACETONE, [as'-it-ōn], *n.* (*chem.*) a light inflammable liquid, dimethyl ketone, used as a solvent. [ACETIC and Gk. *one* descendant].

ACETOPATHY, [as'-et-op'-athi], *n.* the acetic acid cure. [ACETIC and Gk. *patheia* suffering].

ACETOSE, [as'-et-ōs], *adj.* resembling vinegar or acetic acid; sour.

ACETOUS, [as-ē'-tus], *adj.* acetose.

ACETYLENE, [as-et'-il-ēn], *n.* (*chem.*) a colourless, but strong-smelling gas, C_2H_2, evolved from calcium carbide and water.

ACHAEAN, [ak-ē'-yan], *adj.* relating to Achaia, a state of Ancient Greece.

ACHARNEMENT, [ash-ahn'-mong], *n.* bloodthirsty fury or ferocity. [Fr. *acharner* to give a taste of flesh].

ACHE (1), [āk], *n.* a strongly persistent pain, physical, mental or emotional. [ME. *ache*].

ACHE (2), [āk], *v.i.* to feel a dull persistent pain, to be persistently painful; (*fig.*) to feel a strong and persistent desire for something. [*Prec.*].

ACHENE, [a-kēn'], *n.* (*bot.*) a dry fruit consisting of a single seed-cell and case. [A (4) and Gk. *khaino* I gape].

ACHERON, [ak'-er-on], *n.* (*class. myth.*) one of the rivers of Hades, hence Hell, the infernal regions. [Gk. *akheron*, from *akhos* grief].

ACHEULIAN, [ash-ur'-li-an], *adj.* (*archæ.*) belonging to the palaeolithic period characterized by the remains found in France at St. Acheul.

ACHEWEED, [āk'-wēd], *n.* gout weed, *Aegopodium podagraria*.

ACHIEVABLE, [ach-ē'-vabl], *adj.* that may be achieved.

ACHIEVANCE, [ach-ē'-vants], *n.* performance, accomplishment. [OFr. *achevance*].

ACHIEVE, [ach-ēv'], *v.t.* to finish, effect an end to, perform, bring to a desired conclusion. [Fr. *achever* to complete].

ACHIEVEMENT, [ach-ēv'-ment], *n.* the act or fact of achieving, that which is successfully completed, brought to a desired conclusion; exploit, heroic deed, skilful act or performance.

ACHIEVER, [ach-ēv'-er], *n.* a person who achieves.

ACHILOUS, [ak-ī'-lus], *adj.* without lips, or having but undeveloped lips. [A (4) and Gk. *kheilos* lip].

ACHIRITE, [ak'-ir-īt], *n.* (*min.*) dioptase. [*Achir* Mahmet, a merchant who called attention to the dioptase].

ACHLAMYDEATE, [ak'-lam-id'-i-āt], *adj.* (*bot.*) having no calyx or corolla. [A (4) and Gk. *khlamus* a cloak].

ACHLAMYDEOUS, [ak'-lam-id'-i-us], *adj.* achlamydeate.

ACHOLIA, [ak-ō'-li-a], *n.* (*med.*) lack of bile. [Gk. *akholos* gall-less].

ACHOR, [ā'-kor], *n.* the scald-head disease, a scurvy eruption in the scalp, generally of a child. [L. *achor* scurf].

ACHROMATIC, [ak'-rō-mat'-ik], *adj.* colourless; (*opt.*) transmitting light without splitting it up into its prismatic colour components. [A (4) and Gk. *khroma khromatos* colour].

ACHROMATICALLY, [ak'-rō-mat'-ik-a-li], *adv.* in an achromatic way.

ACHROMATISM, [ak-rō'-mat-izm], *n.* the condition of being achromatic.

ACHROMATIZE, [ak-rō'-mat-īz], *v.t.* to make achromatic.

ACHROMATOPSY, [ak-rō'-mat-op'-si], *n.* colour-blindness. [ACHROMATIC and Gk. *opsis* sight].

ACICULAE, [as-ik'-yōō-lē], *n.(pl.)* (*nat. hist.*) prickly spikes. [L. *acicula*, *dim.* of *acus* needle].
ACICULAR, [as-ik'-yōō-ler], *adj.* having the form or sharpness of a needle.
ACICULARLY, [as-ik'-yōō-ler-li], *adv.* in the fashion of needles.
ACICULATE, [as-ik'-yōō-lāt], *adj.* in the shape of a needle.
ACICULIFORM, [as-ik'-yōō-li-fawm], *adj.* aciculate. [ACICULAE and FORM (1)].
ACID (1), [as'-id], *n.* sharp or sour matter or liquid; (*chem.*) a substance containing hydrogen and combining with salifiable bases to form salts, recognized by its action of turning blue litmus-paper red. [ACID (2)].
ACID (2), [as'-id], *adj.* sour, bitter, sharp to the taste; (*fig.*) testy, severe, curt, sarcastic; (*chem.*) possessing the qualities of acid; **a. drop,** an acidulated boiled sweet; **a. test,** final criterion of value. [L. *acidus* sour].
ACIDIC, [as-id'-ik], *adj.* pertaining to acid, having a fair percentage of acid.
ACIDIFEROUS, [as'-id-if'-er-us], *adj.* including or causing acid. [ACID (1) and L. *fero* I bring].
ACIDIFIABLE, [as-id'-if-ī'-abl], *adj.* capable of being acidified.
ACIDIFIC, [as'-id-if'-ik], *adj.* producing acid or acidity.
ACIDIFICATION, [as-id'-if-ik-ā'-shun], *n.* the act of acidifying. [ACID (1) and L. *ficatio*].
ACIDIFIER, [as-id'-if-ī-er], *n.* that which can acidify.
ACIDIFY, [as-id'-if-ī], *v.t.* to make acid; to change into acid.
ACIDIMETER, [as'-id-im'-it-er], *n.* an acetimeter. [ACID (1) and METER].
ACIDITY, [as-id'-it-i], *n.* acidness. [L. *aciditas*].
ACIDNESS, [as'-id-nes], *n.* the quality of being acid.
ACIDOSIS, [as'-id-ō'-sis], *n.* (*path.*) poisoning of the blood due to a superfluity of fatty acids in the system. [ACID (2) and Gk. *-osis* implying condition].
ACIDULATE, [as-id'-yōō-lāt], *v.t.* to make slightly acidulous. [L. *acidulus* slightly sour].
ACIDULENT, [as-id'-yōō-lent], *adj.* acidulous.
ACIDULOUS, [as-id'-yōō-lus], *adj.* slightly sour; caustic, sarcastic, petulant. [L. *acidulus* slightly sour].
ACIERAGE, [ā'-si-er-ij], *n.* the process of electrically plating a metal with a layer of steel to harden it. [Fr. *aciérage*].
ACIFORM, [as'-i-fawm], *adj.* sharp, thin, fine or shaped like a needle. [L. *acus* needle and FORM (1)].
ACINACEOUS, [as'-in-ā'-shus], *adj.* having clusters of berries, like the blackberry; full of kernels.
ACINACIFORM, [as'-in-as'-i-fawm], *adj.* (*bot.*) shaped like a scimitar. [L. *acinaces* Persian sabre and FORM (1)].
ACINARIOUS, [as'-in-āer'-i-us], *adj.* (*bot.*) covered with small round vesicles like grape seeds.
ACINI, [as'-i-nī], *n.(pl.)* (*anat.*) granulations; (*bot.*) berries in clusters. [L. *acinus* berry].
ACINIFORM, [as-in'-i-fawm], *adj.* (*bot.*) formed like the acini; (*anat.*) formed in grape-like clusters, particularly descriptive of glands. [*Prec.* and FORM (1)].
ACINOSE, [as'-in-ōs], *adj.* acinous.
ACINOUS, [as'-in-us], *adj.* (*min.*) having concretions of very small particles. [L. *acinus* berry].
ACIPENSER, [as'-ip-ens'-er], *n.* the sturgeon group of fishes including over twenty species. [L. *acipenser* sturgeon].

ACIPENSER

ACK-ACK, [ak'-ak'], *adj.* anti-aircraft. [Semaphore symbols for initial letters].
ACK EMMA, [ak'-em'-a], *adv.* (*slang*) abbreviation for *ante meridiem*, before twelve o'clock midday, popularized by army signallers during the war of 1914-1918.
ACKNOWLEDGE, [ak-nol'-ij], *v.t.* to admit, own, avow, recognize; to agree, assent, consent to; to confess; to reward, pay for. [~AD- and KNOWLEDGE].
ACKNOWLEDGEABLE, ACKNOWLEDGABLE, [ak-nol'-ij-abl], *adj.* capable of being acknowledged.
ACKNOWLEDGEABLY, ACKNOWLEDGABLY, [ak-nol'-ij-ab-li], *adv.* in an acknowledgable way.
ACKNOWLEDGEMENT, ACKNOWLEDGMENT, [ak-nol'-ij-ment], *n.* the act of acknowledging, a confession, admission of a fault; an expression of appreciation in recognition of a service or duty.
ACKNOWLEDGER, [ak-nol'-ij-er], *n.* a person who acknowledges.
ACLINIC, [ak-lin'-ik], *adj.* (*magn.*) not dipping, descriptive of a magnetic needle; placed where a magnetic needle will not dip; **a. line,** the magnetic equator where the needle does not respond and dip. [A (4) and CLINIC].
ACLIS, [ak'-lis], *n.* a spiked club with which the barbarians fought the Romans. [L. *aclis* small javelin].
ACME, [ak'-mi], *n.* the culminating point, the highest stage, the prime; (*med.*) the crisis. [Gk. *akme* a point].
ACNE, [ak'-ni], *n.* a skin disease, an eruption of inflamed pimples due to defective functioning of the skin and sweat glands. [Uncert.].
ACNESTIS, [ak-nest'-is], *n.* the part of an animal's back which the animal cannot scratch. [Gk. *aknestis* the spine of an animal].
ACOCK (1), [a-kok'], *adj.* awake, alert, listening intently. [A (3) and OE. *cocc* cock].
ACOCK (2), [a-kok'], *adv.* in a cocked position.
A-COCKBILL, [a-kok'-bil], *adv.* (*naut.*) an anchor in position at the cathead prepared for dropping; the yards, when dipped to denote mourning.
ACOEMETI, [a-sē'-me-tī], *n.(pl.)* an order of monks and nuns founded in the East in the fifth century that maintained a divine service day and night. [Gk. *akoimetos* sleepless].
ACOLOGY, [ak-ol'-o-ji], *n.* the science dealing with therapeutic agents or remedies. [Gk. *akos* cure and *logos* speech].
ACOLOTHIST, [ak-ol'-oth-ist], *n.* an acolyte, an attendant. [~MdL. *acolythus* acolyte].
ACOLYTE, [ak'-ol-īt], *n.* (*eccles.*) a layman or person in minor orders belonging to the Roman Catholic Church who attends to the lamps and prepares the accessories during Mass; (*fig.*) an attendant, a follower, subordinate. [~Gk. *akolouthos* follower].
ACONDYLOSE, [ak-ond'-il-ōs], *adj.* acondylous.
ACONDYLOUS, [ak-ond'-il-us], *adj.* (*bot.*) possessing jointless stalks. [Gk. *akondulos* jointless].
ACONITE, [ak'-on-īt], *n.* (*bot.*) the plant wolf's-bane, *Aconitum Napellus*, monk's-hood; the poison obtained from this plant. [L. *aconitum*].
ACONITIC, [ak'-on-it'-ik], *adj.* belonging to monk's-hood, *Aconitum Napellus*.
ACONITINE, [ak-on'-it-ēn], *n.* an extract of aconite which is poisonous.
ACOPIC, [ak-op'-ik], *adj.* (*med.*) able to cure or prevent tiredness. [~Gk. *akopos* unwearied].
ACORN, [ā'-kawn], *n.* the oak tree fruit or nut; (*naut.*) the piece of wood in the shape of an acorn fastened to the top of the vane's spindle to clamp the vane down. [OE. *æcern* acorn].

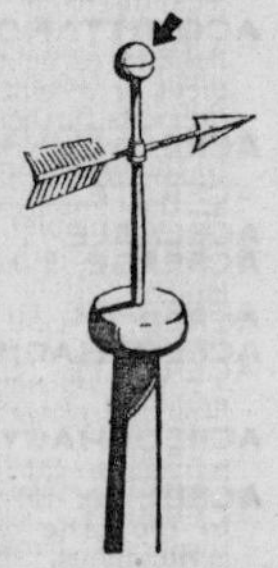
ACORN

ACORN-CUP, [ā'-kawn-kup'], *n.* the capsule containing the acorn.
ACORNED, [ā'-kawnd], *adj.* loaded, provided or fed with acorns; (*her.*) an oak tree pictured as bearing acorns.
ACORN-SHELL, [ā'-kawn-shel'], *n.* a kind of barnacle resembling an acorn.
ACORUS, [ā'-kaw-rus], *n.* the plant, sweet-flag, which gives off a sweet scent when bruised. [Gk. *akoros*.]
ACOSMISM, [ak-oz'-mizm], *n.* disbelief in the existence of a universal order or an external world. [Gk. *akosmos* without a world].
ACOTYLEDON, [ak-ot'-il-ē'-don], *n.* a cryptogam, a plant bearing no seedleaves, including those plants which have no flowers; ferns and mosses. [A (4) and COTYLEDON].
ACOTYLEDONOUS, [ak-ot'-il-ē'-don-us], *adj.* without seedleaves.
ACOUCHY, [ak-ōō'-shi], *n.* the common agouti. [Fr. *acouchi*].
ACOUMETER, [ak-ow'-mit-er], *n.* an apparatus for testing and measuring aural strength. [Gk. *akouo* I hear and METER].
ACOUSTIC, [ak-ows'-tik], *adj.* belonging to the science of sound, or connected with the sense of hearing; **a. duct,** (*anat.*) the passage of the ear leading to the aperture; **a. mine,** a sea mine detonated by sound waves; **a. nerve,** (*anat.*) the nerve responding to sound vibrations. [Gk. *akoustikos* from *akouo* I hear].

ACOUSTICAL, [ak-ow'-stikl], *adj.* acoustic.
ACOUSTICIAN, [ak'-ow-stish'-un], *n.* a person expert in acoustics.
ACOUSTICS, [ak-ow'-stiks], *n.* the science concerned with hearing and sound.
ACQUAINT, [ak-wānt'], *v.t.* to let know, inform, communicate, familiarize; to introduce; **a. oneself with,** to make oneself familiar with. [OFr. *acointer* to get to know].
ACQUAINTANCE, [ak-wānt'-ants], *n.* slight but direct knowledge of a person or fact; a person known socially but not intimately.
ACQUAINTANCESHIP, [ak-wānt'-ans-ship], *n.* the condition or state of being acquainted.
ACQUEST, [ak-west'], *n.* acquisition; (*leg.*) a possession not inherited. [~L. *acquisitio* act of acquiring].
ACQUIESCE, [ak'-wi-es'], *v.i.* to agree to, accept, tolerate; to continue satisfied with; to consent uneasily to. [L. *acquiescere* to remain satisfied].
ACQUIESCENCE, [ak'-wi-es'-ens], *n.* unwilling acceptance, submissive assent, tacit compliance.
ACQUIESCENT, [ak'-wi-es'-ent], *adj.* remaining satisfied; acquiescing.
ACQUIESCENTLY, [ak'-wi-es'-ent-li], *adv.* in an acquiescent way.
ACQUIRABILITY, [ak-wier'-ab-il'-it-i], *n.* the quality of being acquirable.
ACQUIRABLE, [ak-wier'-abl], *adj.* capable of being acquired.
ACQUIRE, [ak-wier'], *v.t.* to gain or obtain something which is to be owned more or less permanently, to take possession of; to put oneself in the way of possession of. [L. *acquirere*].
ACQUIRED, [ak-wierd'], *adj.* attained by artificial development, by practice, or by environmental influence, not innately possessed or inherited.
ACQUIREMENT, [ak-wier'-ment], *n.* the act of acquiring, the thing which is acquired; attainment.
ACQUISITION, [ak'-wiz-ish'-un], *n.* the act of acquiring; that which is acquired. [L. *acquisitio*].
ACQUISITIVE, [ak-wiz'-it-iv], *adj.* greedy, grasping, excessively desiring to acquire.
ACQUISITIVELY, [ak-wiz'-it-iv-li], *adv.* in an acquisitive way; by way of gain.
ACQUISITIVENESS, [ak-wiz'-it-iv-nes], *n.* the excessive desire to acquire and possess.
ACQUIT, [ak-wit'], *v.t.* to judge not guilty of a fault, offence, charge or suspicion; (*leg.*) to declare free from guilt. [OF. *aquiter*, from L. *ad* to and *quietare* to settle].
ACQUITTAL, [ak-witl'], *n.* (*leg.*) the act of acquitting; the verdict which frees a person from a charge; legal discharge.
ACQUITTANCE, [ak-wit'-ans], *n.* discharge from liability or debt, release from obligation; the document or receipt which is evidence of discharge and prevents further debt demands. [OFr. *aquitance*].
ACRE, [ā'-ker], *n.* a measure of land containing 160 square rods or perches, or 4,840 square yards; **God's a.,** the churchyard. [OE. *æcer* field].
ACREABLE, [ā'-ker-abl], *adj.* per acre.
ACREAGE, [ā'-ker-ij], *n.* number of acres in a piece of land.
ACRED, [ā'-kerd], *adj.* owning acres of land.
ACREOPHAGIST, [ak'-ri-of'-aj-ist], *n.* a vegetarian, a person refusing to eat meat. [A (4) and Gk. *kreas* flesh and *phago* I eat].
ACREOPHAGY, [ak-ri-of'-a-ji], *n.* the practice of refusing to eat meat, vegetarianism. [*Prec.*].
ACRID, [ak'-rid], *adj.* sharp, bitter, stinging, biting to the taste or smell; pungent; irritating; (*fig.*) acrimonious, sharp in speech, caustic, sarcastic, unpleasant in manner. [L. *acridus*].
ACRIDIAN, [ak-rid'-i-an], *n.* an insect of the locust family. [~Gk. *akridion*].
ACRIDITY, [ak-rid'-it-i], *n.* acridness.
ACRIDNESS, [ak'-rid-nes], *n.* an acrid quality.
ACRIMONIOUS, [ak'-ri-mō'-ni-us], *adj.* bitter, sharp, short in speech, nature or temper; discourteous, malevolent.
ACRIMONIOUSLY, [ak'-ri-mō'-ni-us-li], *adv.* in an acrimonious way.
ACRIMONIOUSNESS, [ak'-ri-mō'-ni-us-nes], *n.* the state or quality of being acrimonious.
ACRIMONY, [ak'-rim-on-i], *n.* sharpness, harshness, bitterness, severity of temper, speech, manner or nature. [L. *acrimonia* sharpness].
ACRISIA, [ak-ri'-si-a], *n.* (*med.*) a condition of illness or disease whose symptoms are difficult to identify, or in which a crisis does not occur. [Gk. *akrisia* want of judgment].
ACRISY, [ak'-ris-i], *n.* injudiciousness; acrisia.
ACRITA, [ak'-ri-ta], *n.*(*pl.*) plant-like animals, including polyps, sponges, which are without a definite nervous system. [Gk. *akritos* confused].
ACRITICAL, [ak-rit'-ikl], *adj.* (*med.*) having none of the symptoms or signs of a crisis. [A (4) and CRITICAL].
ACRITUDE, [ak'-rit-ewd], *n.* a corrosive quality, the power of acid. [L. *acritudo* bitterness].
ACRO-, *pref.* topmost, used in compound words, to denote growth to the highest stage or extreme. [Gk. *akros* topmost].
ACROAMATIC, [ak'-rō-am-at'-ik], *adj.* acroamatical. [Gk. *akroamatikos*].
ACROAMATICAL, [ak'-rō-am-at'-ikl], *adj.* belonging to the hearing; esoteric; confined to oral communication for the initiated only, such as the philosophy of Aristotle, not set down in writing, but communicated orally to his disciples. [*Prec.*].
ACROATIC, [ak'-rō-at'-ik], *adj.* acroamatic. [Gk. *akroatikos* of hearing].
ACROBAT, [ak'-rō-bat], *n.* a gifted gymnast performing skilful tricks, a tumbler, tight-rope walker, contortionist. [Gk. *akrobato* I walk on tiptoe].
ACROBATIC, [ak'-rō-bat'-ik], *adj.* agile, like an acrobat.
ACROBATICALLY, [ak'-rō-bat'-ik-a-li], *adv.* in the manner of an acrobat, with gymnastic skill.
ACROBATICS, [ak'-rō-bat'-iks], *n.* the art or practice of balancing, tumbling, tight-rope walking, etc.
ACROCARPOUS, [ak'-ro-kahp'-us], *adj.* (*bot.*) bearing the inflorescence at the apex of the stem. [ACRO- and Gk. *karpos* fruit].
ACROCEPHALIC, [ak'-rō-sef-al'-ik], *adj.* having a skull shaped like a pyramid, tending to grow to a point. [ACRO- and Gk. *kephalos* head].
ACROCERAUNIAN, [ak'-rō-ser-awn'-i-an], *adj.* thunderstruck (from the Grecian range of mountains of this name, often visited by heavy thunderstorms). [ACRO- and Gk. *keraunos* thunder].
ACROGEN, [ak'-rō-jen], *n.* (*bot.*) a cryptogam which increases by additions to the stem, as ferns and mosses. [ACRO- and Gk. *-genes* sprung from].
ACROGENOUS, [ak-roj'-en-us], *adj.* like an acrogen.
ACROGRAPHY, [ak-rog'-raf-i], *n.* the art of composing relief engravings on metal for the purpose of printing. [ACRO- and Gk. *graphia* writing].
ACROLITH, [ak'-rol-ith], *n.* a type of statue combining two materials, one being stone, which is used exclusively for the head and extremities of the body. [ACRO- and Gk. *lithos* stone].
ACROLITHAN, [ak-rol'-ith-an], *adj.* in the form of an acrolith.
ACROMANIA, [ak'-rō-mā'-ni-a], *n.* (*path.*) incurable insanity. [ACRO- and Gk. *mania* madness].
ACROMEGALY, [ak'-rō-meg'-a-li], *n.* (*path.*) abnormal and excessive development of the extremities of the body. [ACRO- and Gk. *megale* large].
ACROMONOGRAMMATIC, [ak'-rō-mon'-ō-gram-at'-ik], *n.* a form of poem, each line or verse beginning with the same letter as that which ends the preceding one. [ACRO-, Gk. *monos* alone and *gramma* a letter].
ACRONIC, [ak-ron'-ik], *adj.* (*astron.*) descriptive of the movements of a star rising at sunset and setting at dawn; the opposite of cosmical. [Gk. *akronukhos* at nightfall].
ACRONICALLY, [ak-ron'-ik-al-i], *adv.* in an acronic way.
ACROPETAL, [ak-rop'-etl], *adj.* directed towards the apex, growing upwards. [ACRO- and L. *petere* to seek].
ACROPOLIS, [ak-rop'-ol-is], *n.* a citadel, *esp.* the one in Athens. [Gk. *akropolis* higher city].
ACROSPIRE, [ak'-ros-pier], *n.* (*bot.*) a developed plumule, the first leaf sprouting, *esp.* of barley, developed by germination. [ACRO- and Gk. *speiro* I sow].
ACROSPIRED, [ak'-ros-spierd], *adj.* sprouting at both ends during the process of malting.
ACROSS (1), [a-kros'], *adv.* from side to side, crosswise, in a counter direction, in a position crossing at an angle. [*Next*].
ACROSS (2), [a-kros'], *prep.* from side to side of, from one side to another, not lengthwise, at an angle with; making a cross with; in opposition to; **to put it a.,** (*slang*) to get one's own back on (someone); to impose on, cheat, act a part. [A (3) and CROSS (2)].
ACROSTIC (1), [ak-ros'-tik], *n.* a poem, etc., with the first letters of each line spelling a word which is the subject of the poem; a puzzle, of which the solution

is a number of words written one above another. [Gk. *akrostikhion* from ACRO- and *stikhos* a row].

ACROSTIC (2), [ak-ros'-tik], *adj.* consisting of, or pertaining to, an acrostic. [*Prec.*].

ACROSTICALLY, [ak-ros'-tik-a-li], *adv.* in the same way as an acrostic.

ACROTELEUTIC, [ak-rot'-el-ewt'-ik], *n.* that which is added to the end of a psalm or hymn, such as the amen; a doxology. [Gk. *akroteleution* fag-end].

ACROTER, (*pl.* **acroteria**), [ak'-rot-er], *n.* a pedestal designed to take a statue or ornament placed on a pediment at either end or at the apex; the statue, pinnacle or other ornament placed in such a position. [Gk. *akroterion* apex].

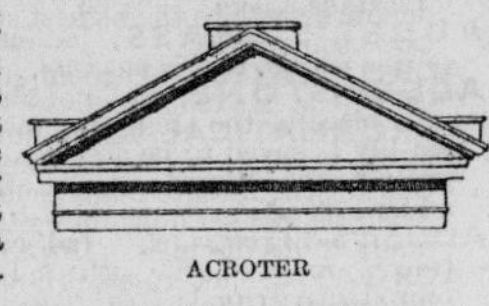

ACROTER

ACROTERIAL, [ak'-rot-ēer'-i-al], *adj.* belonging to acroteria.

ACROTHYMION, [ak'-rō-thim'-i-on], *n.* a species of wart. [ACRO- and Gk. *thumion*].

ACROTIC, [ak-rot'-ik], *adj.* (*med.*) having effect on the surface. [~Gk. *akrotes* top].

ACROTISM, [ak'-rot-izm], *n.* absence or weakening of pulse beats. [A (4) and Gk. *krotos* beat].

ACROTOMOUS, [ak-rot'-om-us], *adj.* (*min.*) characterized by a cleavage parallel with the top of a crystal. [Gk. *akrotomos* sharply cut off].

ACT (1), [akt], *n.* action, something done, the doing of something, a specific movement, deed, exploit, performance; a main division of a stage play consisting of a certain section in the development of the dramatic material; an administrative principle, a law, edict, decree; the document recording the principle; a thesis maintained in public by a candidate for a degree; **A. of God,** (*leg.*) the workings of the forces of Nature causing unavoidable and disastrous effects, such as earthquakes, tempests, floods and storms; **a. of grace,** king's pardon for an offender; a generous and voluntary action; **A. of Parliament,** a bill framed, passed and authorized by Parliament, which has received the royal assent. [L. *actum*].

ACT (2), [akt], *v.t.* to perform (a play); to play (a part); to simulate, imitate, mimic, personate, feign; *v.i.* to be in motion, to do things, to function, operate; to set in motion, bring power to bear upon, influence, cause effects; perform, deputize for; behave, comport, acquit oneself. [*Prec.*].

ACTA, [ak'-ta], *n.*(*pl.*) acts; (*leg.*) accounts of acts; **A. Sanctorum,** the biographies of the Christian saints and martyrs begun in 1643 by the Bollandists. [L. *acta*, *pl.* of *actum* deed, act].

ACTING (1), [akt'-ing], *n.* action, the practice of the dramatic art, the representation of a character in a play.

ACTING (2), [akt'-ing], *adj.* functioning, deputizing for, holding temporary office.

ACTINIA, [ak-tin'-i-a], *n.* a genus of sea-anemones. [Gk. *aktinos* radiant].

ACTINIC, [ak-tin'-ik], *adj.* (*phys.*) changing chemically by action of light.

ACTINIFORM, [ak-tin'-i-fawm], *adj.* radiated, having a radiated form. [ACTINO- and FORM (1)].

ACTINISM, [ak'-tin-izm], *n.* (*phys.*) the action of ultra-violet rays effecting chemical change, as distinct from heat or light changes; the power inherent in such rays.

ACTINIUM, [ak-tin'-i-um], *n.* a radio-active element in pitchblende.

ACTINO-, *pref.* (*phys.*) relating to actinic rays; (*nat. hist.*) having a radiated form. [Gk. *aktinos* radiance].

ACTINOGRAPH, [ak-tin'-ō-graf], *n.* an instrument for testing, measuring and registering actinic effects. [ACTINO- and GRAPH].

ACTINOLITE, [ak-tin'-ō-līt], *n.* a green stone, of the hornblende variety, having crystals formed in bunches or bundles. [ACTINO- and Gk. *lithos* stone].

ACTINOLITIC, [ak-tin'-ō-lit'-ik], *adj.* belonging to actinolite.

ACTINOLOGY, [ak'-tin-ol'-o-ji], *n.* the science of actinism. [ACTINO- and Gk. *logos* speech].

ACTINOMETER, [ak'-tin-om'-it-er], *n.* an instrument for measuring ultra-violet rays. [ACTINO- and METER].

ACTINOMYCES, [ak-tin'-ō-mī'-sēz], *n.* a ray-fungus; **a. bovis,** the ray-fungus infecting the ox. [ACTINO- and Gk. *mukes* fungus].

ACTINOMYCOSIS, [ak'-tin-ō-mī-kō'-sis], *n.* (*path.*) an infective disease, produced by ray-fungus of which suppurating boils in the jaw are symptomatic, affecting cattle and, very rarely, human beings. [*Prec.* and Gk. *osis* denoting condition].

ACTINOZOA, [ak'-tin-ō-zō'-a], *n.*(*pl.*) (*zool.*) a class of polyps including sea-anemones and coral animals, anthozoa. [ACTINO- and Gk. *zoa*, *pl.* of *zoon* animal].

ACTION, [ak'-shun], *n.* the state of acting, the condition of being in motion, the process of operating, the production of energy; operation, function; deed, exploit; conduct, behaviour, gesture; organic function; the series of events and incidents which are embodied in a stage play, the thematic progress of a play or film; (*leg.*) a lawsuit attempting to establish a claim; (*milit.*) a battle. [L. *actio* motion].

ACTIONABLE, [ak'-shun-abl], *adj.* (*leg.*) liable to an action, offering opportunity for action.

ACTIONABLY, [ak'-shun-ab-li], *adv.* in a way that calls for legal procedure.

ACTIVATE, [ak'-tiv-āt], *v.t.* to give cause for action, to stir into action, make active; (*phys.*) to convert so as to be capable of producing electrical effects.

ACTIVE, [ak'-tiv], *adj.* possessing the power to act, disposed to action, quick of movement; constantly busy, vigorous, energetic; agile, alert, assiduous; practical, as contrasted with meditative; involved in, engaged in, occupied in; (*gram.*) implying action done to a person or thing; **a. service,** service in the armed forces in the field of war. [L. *activus*].

ACTIVELY, [ak'-tiv-li], *adv.* in an active manner.

ACTIVENESS, [ak'-tiv-nes], *n.* the condition of being active.

ACTIVITY, [ak-tiv'-i-ti], *n.* activeness; alertness, agility; movement, busyness, rate of working.

ACTON, [ak'-ton], *n.* a medieval jerkin or jacket, padded with hair or wool, worn under a coat of mail for comfort and protection; later, a steel-plated waistcoat. [OFr. *auqueton* padded jacket].

ACTOR, [ak'-tor], *n.* a person who acts; one who takes a part in stage drama, a professional stage player; (*fig.*) a person participating in an event; (*leg.*) an advocate or proctor in civil cases. [L. *actor* doer].

ACTRESS, [ak'-tres], *n.* a female stage player.

ACTUAL, [ak'-tew-al, ak'-chōō-al], *adj.* real, having existence at present, existing as an act, object, idea, statement, in contrast to what is potential, probable or possible. [LL. *actualis*].

ACTUALIST, [ak'-tew-al-ist, ak'-chōō-al-ist], *n.* a realist, a practical person, a person who limits himself to what he believes to be real and lives unconcerned with the ideal.

ACTUALITY, [ak'-tew-al'-i-ti, ak'-chōō-al'-i-ti], *n.* the condition of being actual; reality, realism; **a. programme,** a broadcast programme or feature of a documentary nature aiming at realism in the reproduction of actual events.

ACTUALIZATION, [ak'-tew-al-īz-ā'-shun, ak'-chōō-al-īz-ā'-shun], *n.* making actual or real.

ACTUALIZE, [ak'-tew-al-īz, ak'-chōō-al-īz], *v.t.* to make actual, to present in real form.

ACTUALLY, [ak'-tew-al-i, ak'-chōō-a-li], *adv.* in truth, really; as a fact; at present, now.

ACTUARIAL, [ak'-tew-āer'-i-al], *adj.* belonging to an actuary or his profession.

ACTUARY, [ak'-tew-ar-i], *n.* the clerk of a court; a registrar; a statistician and calculator of premiums working for an insurance company. [L. *actuarius* a clerk].

ACTUATE, [ak'-tew-āt], *v.t.* to cause to act, influence, incite to action, motivate. [MdL. *actuatum*, *p.pt.* of *actuare*].

ACTUATION, [ak'-tew-ā'shun], *n.* the condition of being actuated or influenced. [~MdL. *actuatio*].

ACUITION, [ak'-ew-ish'-un], *n.* (*med.*) intensification of medicinal action. [~MdL. *acuitionem* sharpening].

ACUITY, [ak-ew'-i-ti], *n.* (of intelligence) keenness; (of a point) sharpness; (of illness) intensity. [LL. *acuitas*, from *acuere* to sharpen].

ACULEATE, [ak-ew'-li-āt], *adj.* (*bot.*) possessing prickles or a sting. [L. *aculeatus*].

ACULEATED, [ak-ew'-li-āt-id], *adj.* aculeate.

ACULEUS, [ak-ew'-li-us], *n.* (*bot.*) a prickle; (*zool.*) a sting. (L. *aculeus*, *dim.* of *acus* a needle].

ACUMEN, [ak-ew'-men], *n.* mental acuteness, keenness and quickness of perception. [L. *acumen* sharpened point].

ACUMINATE, [ak-ew'-min-āt], *adj.* (*bot.*) tapering to a point.

ACUMINATED, [ak-ew'-min-āt-id], *adj.* acuminate.

ACUMINATION, [ak-ew′-min-ā′-shun], *n.* an object culminating in a sharp point.
ACUMINOUS, [ak-ew′-min-us], *adj.* having acumen; quick in perception.
ACUPRESSURE, [ak′-ew-presh′-ur], *n.* (*surg.*) the stopping up of vents during a haemorrhage by pressure of a needle on the veins. [L. *acus* a needle and PRESSURE].
ACUPUNCTURATION, [ak′-ew-pungkt′-ewr-ā′-shun], *n.* (*surg.*) the pricking of an inflamed part of the body by a needle to relieve pain. [L. *acus* needle, and *punctura* puncture].
ACUPUNCTURE, [ak′-ew-pungk′-chur], *n.* acupuncturation.
ACUSHLA, [ak-ŏŏsh′-la], *n.* sweetheart, darling. [Ir. *a cuisle* O pulse].
ACUTE, [ak-ewt′], *adj.* sharp, pointed, keen, needle-like; perspicuous, shrewd, sharp-witted, penetrating, sensitive; (*math.*) less than ninety degrees; (*med.*) severely or violently symptomatic, as contrasted with chronic; (*mus.*) high, shrill, sharp; **a. accent,** a short line (′) marked over a letter. [L. *acutus* sharp-pointed].
ACUTELY, [ak-ewt′-li], *adv.* in an acute way.
ACUTENESS, [ak-ewt′-nes], *n.* the quality of being acute; the state of being intense.
ACUTIFOLIATE, [ak-ewt′-if-ō′-li-āt], *adj.* (*bot.*) possessing sharp-pointed leaves. [ACUTE and FOLIATE (1)].
ACYANOBLEPSY, [a-sī′-an-ō-blep′-si], *n.* inability to see the colour blue. [A (4) and Gk. *kuanos* blue, and *blepsia* sight].
AD, [ad], *n.* (*slang*) abbreviation for ADVERTISEMENT.
AD-, *pref.* to. [L. *ad*].
ADACTYL, [ad-ak′-til], *adj.* possessing no fingers or toes. [A (4) and Gk. *daktulos* finger].
ADAGE, [ad′-ij], *n.* a proverb, an old saying. [L. *adagium* proverb].
ADAGIAL, [ad-ā′-ji-al], *adj.* concerned with or full of adages; proverbial.
ADAGIO (1), [ad-ah′-ji-ō], *n.* a slow movement or piece of music. [*Next*].
ADAGIO (2), [ad-ah′-ji-ō], *adv.* (*mus.*) slowly, leisurely, gracefully. [It. *adagio* leisurely].
ADAMANT, [ad′-am-ant], *n.* an extremely hard substance; the diamond. [Gk. *adamas adamantos* unyielding].
ADAMANTEAN, [ad′-am-ant′-i-an], *adj.* unyielding and hard as adamant.
ADAMANTINE, [ad′-am-ant′-īn], *adj.* composed of adamant; (*fig.*) unbreakable, unyielding, impenetrable.
ADAMITES, [ad′-am-īts], *n.(pl.)* people who formed a sect and wore no clothes, assuming the innocence of Adam.
ADAM'S ALE, [ad′-amz-āl], *n.* (*coll.*) water.
ADAPT, [ad-apt′], *v.t.* to make to fit, to modify, to alter to suit, accommodate, to eliminate differences. [L. *adaptare* to fit to].
ADAPTABILITY, [ad-apt′-a-bil′-i-ti], *n.* adaptableness, the possession of the power of adapting.
ADAPTABLE, [ad-apt′-abl], *adj.* able to be adapted.
ADAPTABLENESS, [ad-apt′-abl-nes], *n.* adaptability, capability of adaptation.
ADAPTATION, [ad′-apt-ā′-shun], *n.* the act of adapting, the thing which is adapted.
ADAPTEDNESS, [ad-apt′-id-nes], *n.* the condition of being adapted.
ADAPTER, ADAPTOR, [ad-apt′-er], *n.* the person who adapts something, a modifier; (*chem.*) a double-necked vessel; any means or instrument enabling two or more other different instruments to work together; (*phot.*) a device fitted to a camera enabling it to take different-sized plates or films; (*elect.*) a fitting to a lamp-holder which carries an extension lead.
ADAPTIVE, [ad-apt′-iv], *adj.* capable of, or tending to, adaptation.
ADAR, [ā′-dah(r)], *n.* the twelfth month in the Hebrew sacred year. [Heb. *adar*].
ADD, [ad], *v.t.* to join one thing to another, to combine one number or thing with another, to augment, to increase, enlarge. [L. *addere* to give in addition].
ADDABLE, see ADDIBLE.
ADDAX, [ad′-aks], *n.* an antelope, *Addax nasomaculatus*, characterized by a mane and spiral horns, commonly found in Arabia and in the north of Africa. [Native].

ADDAX

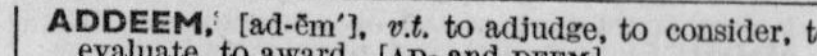

ADDEEM, [ad-ēm′], *v.t.* to adjudge, to consider, to evaluate, to award. [AD- and DEEM].
ADDENDUM, (*pl.* **addenda**), [ad-end′-um], *n.* appendix, that which is added or is to be added. [L. *addendum*, *gerund.* of *addere* give in addition].
ADDER (1), [ad′-er], *n.* a person who adds.
ADDER (2), [ad′-er], *n.* a poisonous snake of the viper species. [OE. *nædre*, *a nadder* becoming *an adder*].
ADDER-FLY, [ad′-er-flī], *n.* the dragon-fly.
ADDER-PIKE, [ad′-er-pīk], *n.* the viper weever fish, *Trachinus vipera*.
ADDER'S-GRASS, [ad′-erz-grahs], *n.* the early purple orchis, *Orchis mascula*.
ADDER-STONE, [ad′-er-stōn], *n.* a piece of the stem of a fossil sea-lily believed to be a charm to protect the bearer against the adder's sting.
ADDER'S-TONGUE, [ad′-erz-tung], *n.* a fern with spiky reproductive fronds, *Ophioglossum vulgatum*.
ADDIBILITY, [ad′-ib-il′-i-ti], *n.* the capacity of being addible.
ADDIBLE, ADDABLE, [ad′-ibl], *adj.* able to be added.
ADDICT (1), [ad′-ikt], *n.* a person who is addicted to a habit almost beyond cure. [*Next*].

ADDER'S-GRASS

ADDICT (2), [ad-ikt′], *v.t.* (with abnormality) to devote oneself to, to give oneself to, to accustom, to practise a habit of. [L. *addictum*, *p.pt.* of *addicere* to devote to].
ADDICTEDNESS, [ad-ikt′-id-nes], *n.* the condition or quality of being addicted.
ADDICTION, [ad-ik′-shun], *n.* addictedness.
ADDITION, [ad-ish′-un], *n.* the process or act of adding, the act of combining two or more numbers into one total; the final sum; (*her.*) that which is added to the escutcheon to indicate honour; (*leg.*) the title attached to a man's name signifying rank, position, profession, etc.; (*mus.*) the dot placed at the right side of a note which increases its duration by half. [L. *additio* a gift in addition].
ADDITIONAL, [ad-ish′-unl], *adj.* supplementary, extra.
ADDITIONALLY, [ad-ish′-un-a-li], *adv.* in addition to.
ADDITIVE, [ad′-it-iv], *adj.* that may be added, tending to addition.
ADDLE, [adl], *v.t.* to putrify, to make corrupt, to confuse, muddle. [~OE. *adel* filth, mud].
ADDLED, [adld], *adj.* rotten, putrid; barren, descriptive of eggs that can produce no chicks; (*fig.*) confused, muddled.
ADDLE-HEADED, [adl′-hed′-id], *adj.* muddle-minded.
ADDLEMENT, [adl′-ment], *n.* the condition of being addled.
ADDLE-PATED, [adl′-pā′-tid], *adj.* empty-headed, lacking brains.
ADDLEPLOT, [adl′-plot′], *n.* a person who upsets or betrays a plot by accident.
ADDOGRAPH, [ad′-ō-grahf], *n.* a machine that adds up numbers. [ADD and GRAPH (1)].
ADDORSED, [ad-awst′], *adj.* (*her.*) having the backs facing each other. [AD- and L. *dorsum* back].
ADDRESS (1), [ad-res′], *n.* the description of a direction; the residence of a person; a public speech or lecture; the bearing or behaviour of a person in public; a message of respect, a formal communication; (*pl.*) attentions of a lover. [*Next*].
ADDRESS (2), [ad-res′], *v.t.* to direct; to square up to, to take aim at, as in golf; to direct speech to; to direct a letter to; to inscribe with an address; to deliver a speech in public; to concentrate one's energies or interests; to direct one's attentions as a lover, to woo; to consign to an agent. [F. *adresser* to speak or send direct to].
ADDRESSEE, [ad-res-ē′], *n.* the person to whom a letter is addressed.
ADDRESSER, [ad-res′-er], *n.* a person who, or machine which, addresses.
ADDRESSOGRAPH, [ad-res′-ō-grahf], *n.* (*prot.*) a machine for stamping addresses rapidly on envelopes or papers. [ADDRESS (1) and GRAPH (1)].
ADDUCE, [ad-ews′], *v.t.* to bring forward as evidence, to allege as proof; to cite. [L. *adducere* to lead to].
ADDUCEABLE, see ADDUCIBLE.
ADDUCENT, [ad-ew′-sent], *adj.* (*anat.*) descriptive of muscles whose organic function is to draw close

together the parts of the body which they control.

ADDUCER, [ad-ew'-ser], *n.* a person who adduces.

ADDUCIBLE, ADDUCEABLE, [ad-ew'-sibl, ad-ew'-sabl], *adj.* able to be adduced.

ADDUCTION, [ad-uk'-shun], *n.* the act of bringing forward. [~L. *adductio*].

ADDUCTIVE, [ad-uk'-tiv], *adj.* tending to bring forward.

ADDUCTOR, [ad-uk'-tor], *n.* an adducent muscle.

ADELPHOUS, [ad-elf'-us], *adj.* (*bot.*) possessing stamens collected into a bundle. [~Gk. *adelphos* brother].

ADEMPTION, [ad-emp'-shun], *n.* (*leg.*) the revocation of a bequest or grant. [~L. *ademptio*].

ADEN-, *pref.* gland. [Gk. *aden* acorn, gland].

ADENALGIA, [ad'-en-al'-ji-a], *n.* (*med.*) a pain manifesting itself in a gland. [ADEN- and Gk. *algos* pain].

ADENIFORM, [ad-en'-i-fawm], *adj.* shaped like a gland. [ADEN- and FORM (1)].

ADENITIS, [ad'-en-ī'-tis], *n.* inflammation of a gland. [ADEN- and Gk. *itis* denoting inflammation].

ADENOGRAPHY, [ad'-en-og'-raf-i], *n.* the part of anatomy which deals with the glands. [ADEN- and Gk. *graphia* writing].

ADENOIDAL, [ad'-en-oidl], *adj.* glandiform.

ADENOIDS, [ad'-en-oidz], *n.(pl.)* (*med.*) enlarged growths of adenoidal tissue near the back of the throat which affect nasal breathing. [ADEN- and Gk. *-oeides* like].

ADENOLOGICAL, [ad'-en-ol-oj'-ikl], *adj.* belonging to the study of glands. [*Next*].

ADENOLOGY, [ad'-en-ol'-o-ji], *n.* the science and study of the glands, their nature and their uses. [ADEN- and Gk. *logos* speech].

ADENOSE, [ad'-en-ōs], *adj.* similar to, or appertaining to, a gland.

ADENOTOMY, [ad'-en-ot'-o-mi], *n.* incision or dissection of a gland. [ADEN- and Gk. *tome* cutting].

ADENOUS, [ad'-en-us], *adj.* adenose.

ADEPS, [ad'-eps], *n.* the fat on an animal or human being. [L. *adeps* fat of animals].

ADEPT (1), [ad'-ept], *n.* a person expert in any art or work. [*Next*].

ADEPT (2), [ad'-ept], *adj.* highly skilled, expert. [L. *adeptus*].

ADEQUACY, [ad'-ik-wa-si], *n.* the state of being adequate; adequateness, a sufficiency for a specific purpose.

ADEQUATE [ad'-ik-wat], *adj.* enough, sufficient, equal to, proportionate to, commensurate with, satisfactory. [L. *adaequatum*, *p.pt.* of *adaequare* to make equal to].

ADEQUATELY, [ad'-ik-wat-li], *adv.* in an adequate way.

ADEQUATENESS, [ad'-ik-wat-nes], *n.* the state of being adequate.

ADESPOTA, [ad-es'-pot-a], *n.(pl.)* literary works unclaimed by, or unattributed to, an author. [Gk. *adespota* without masters].

ADFECTED, [ad-fek'-tid], *adj.* (*alg.*) including different powers of an unknown quantity. [Variant of AFFECTED].

ADFILIATED†, [ad-fil'-i-āt-id], *adj.* affiliated. [Variant of AFFILIATED].

ADFILIATION†, [ad'-fil-i-ā'-shun], *n.* affiliation. [Variant of AFFILIATION].

ADHERE, [ad-hēer'], *v.i.* to stick fast to, to hold to, to rest firmly attached to; to persevere in. [L. *adhaerere* to cling to].

ADHERENCE, [ad-hēer'-ens], *n.* adherency.

ADHERENCY, [ad-hēer'-en-si], *n.* the quality or state of adhering; steady attachment.

ADHERENT (1), [ad-hēer'-ent], *n.* a supporter, a follower, a disciple. [*Next*].

ADHERENT (2), [ad-hēer'-ent], *adj.* sticking to; sticky, clinging; united with. [L. *adhaerens*, *pres. pt.* of *adhaerere* to cling].

ADHERENTLY, [ad-hēer'-ent-li], *adv.* in an adherent way.

ADHERER, [ad-hēer'-er], *n.* a person who adheres, adherent.

ADHESION, [ad-hē'-zhun], *n.* the action of adhering, the condition of sticking to, adherence, the fastening of two things together by a sticky substance; persistent attachment; (*path.*) the organic union of injured parts of the body by newly formed tissue; the joining up of adjacent parts of the body by inflammation; (*phys.*) the tendency of surfaces to form a contact. [L. *adhaesio*].

ADHESIVE (1), [ad-hē'-siv], *n.* an adhesive substance.

ADHESIVE (2), [ad-hē-siv], *adj.* sticking, tenacious.

ADHESIVELY, [ad-hē'-siv-li], *adv.* in an adhesive fashion.

ADHESIVENESS, [ad-hē'-siv-nes], *n.* the state of being adhesive; tenacity; the power to form attachments.

ADHIBIT, [ad-hib'-it], *v.t.* to apply; to affix, to attach. [L. *adhibitum*, *p.pt.* of *adhibere* to hold to].

ADHIBITION, [ad'-hib-ish'-un], *n.* act of applying; use. [L. *adhibitio*].

ADIABATIC, [ad'-i-ab-at'-ik], *adj.* (*phys.*) admitting no heat; referring to alterations in volume on account of pressure or volatility without loss or gain of heat. [Gk. *adiabatos* impassable].

ADIACTINIC, [ad'-i-ak-tin'-ik], *adj.* (*opt.*) not admitting actinic rays. [A (4) and Gk. *dia* through and ACTINIC].

ADIANTUM, [ad'-i-ant'-um], *n.* a maidenhair fern. [Gk. *adianton* maidenhair].

ADIAPHORISM, [ad'-i-af'-or-izm], *n.* the doctrine that specific theological controversies are essentially unimportant; religious indifferentism. [~Gk. *adiaphoros* indifferent].

ADIAPHOROUS, [ad'-i-af'-or-us], *adj.* indifferent, inessential; (*med.*) maintaining the same state, effecting neither good nor harm. [*Prec.*].

ADIATHERMIC, [ad-ī'-a-thurm'-ik], *adj.* (*phys.*) impervious to heat. [A (4) and Gk. *dia* through and THERMIC].

ADIEU, [a-dew'], *n. and int.* farewell, good-bye. [Fr. *adieu* from *à* to and *Dieu* God].

ADIPESCENT, [ad'-ip-es'-ent], *adj.* becoming fatty.

ADIPIC, [ad-ip'-ik], *adj.* of the nature of fat. [L. *adeps adipis* soft fat of animals].

ADIPOCERATE, [ad'-ip-ō'-ser-āt], *v.t.* to change into adipocere.

ADIPOCERATION, [ad'-ip-ō'-ser-ā'-shun], *n.* the act or process of changing into adipocere.

ADIPOCERE, [ad'-ip-ō'-sēer], *n.* the waxy substance which dead animal tissue changes into when surrounded by dampness; (*min.*) waxy mineral substance discovered in iron ore that is mixed with clay. [L. *adeps adipis* fat and *cera* wax].

ADIPOCEROUS, [ad'-ip-ō'-ser-us], *adj.* containing adipocere.

ADIPOMA, [ad'-ip-ō'-ma], *n.* a fatty growth. [L. *adeps* fat and Gk. *oma* tumour].

ADIPOSE, [ad'-ip-ōs], *adj.* fat; fatty; consisting of or including fat. [L. *adeps adipis* fat].

ADIPOSITY, [ad-ip-os'-it-i], *n.* fat, fatness; superfluous fatness.

ADIPOUS, [ad'-ip-us], *adj.* adipose.

ADIPSIA, [ad-ip'-si-a], *n.* (*med.*) a complete absence of thirst. [Gk. *adipsos* without thirst].

ADIT, [ad'-it], *n.* an entrance; (*mining*) a horizontal opening or tunnel leading into a mine. [L. *aditus* an approach].

ADJACENCE, [aj-ā'-sens], *n.* adjacency.

ADJACENCY, [aj-ā'-sen-si], *n.* the state of being adjacent.

ADJACENT, [aj-ā'-sent], *adj.* contiguous, neighbouring, lying near to. [L. *adjacens*].

ADJACENTLY, [aj-ā'-sent-li], *adv.* so as to be adjacent, in a nearby place.

ADJECT, [aj-ekt'], *v.t.* to add or put to, annex. [L. *adjectum*, *p.pt.* of *adjicere* to lay to].

ADJECTIVAL, [aj'-ek-tī'-val], *adj.* similar to or pertaining to an adjective.

ADJECTIVALLY, [aj'-ek-tī'-va-li], *adv.* adjectively, by means of an adjective.

ADJECTIVE (1), [aj'-ek-tiv], *n.* (*gram.*) a part of speech, a word, which qualifies a noun, describing, defining, limiting the attributes of the noun.

ADJECTIVE (2), [aj'-ek-tiv], *adj.* belonging to an adjective; (*dyeing*) descriptive of colours that are impermanent unless they have a base. [L. *adjectivus* added].

ADJECTIVELY, [aj'-ek-tiv-li], *adv.* as an adjective, adjectivally.

ADJOIN, [a-join'], *v.t.* to be next to, to border upon, to join on to, to be contiguous to, to abut on. [AD- and JOIN (2)].

ADJOINING, [a-join'-ing], *adj.* adjacent, neighbouring.

ADJOINT, [aj'-oint], *adj.* joined together, connected. [OFr. *ajoint* united].

ADJOURN, [a-jurn'], *v.t.* to postpone, to put off till another day or time, defer, to suspend proceedings. [LL. *adjurnare* to postpone].

ADJOURNMENT, [a-jurn'-ment], *n.* the act of adjourning; the duration of the postponement; postponement or suspension of proceedings.

ADJUDGE, [a-juj'], *v.t.* to consider, decide and pronounce a judgment; to make an award of judicial deliberation. [AD- and JUDGE (2)].
ADJUDGEMENT, ADJUDGMENT, [a-juj'-ment], *n.* the act of adjudging; a decision; an award.
ADJUDICATE, [a-jōō'-dik-āt], *v.t. and i.* to adjudge, to make a judicial decision; to act as a judge. [L. *adjudicatum*, *p.pt.* of *adjudicare* to decide].
ADJUDICATION, [a-jōō'-dik-ā'-shun], *n.* the act of adjudging; judgment or decision of a court, an award or sentence. [L. *adjudicatio* a decision].
ADJUDICATOR, [a-jōō'-dik-ā'-tor], *n.* a person who adjudicates.
ADJUNCT (1), [aj'-ungkt], *n.* a thing added or joined to another, an associate; (*met.*) a mental or physical quality, natural or acquired; (*gram.*) a word added to qualify or extend the meaning of another. [L. *adjunctus*, *p.pt.* of *adjungere* to join].
ADJUNCT (2), [aj'-ungkt], *adj.* joined or added to; united; associated with. [*Prec.*].
ADJUNCTION, [aj-ungk'-shun], *n.* the act of joining; the thing joined. [L. *adjunctio*].
ADJUNCTIVE (1), [aj-ungk'-tiv], *n.* the person or object joined.
ADJUNCTIVE (2), [aj-ungk'-tiv], *adj.* joining; possessing the qualities of an adjunct.
ADJUNCTIVELY, [aj-ungk'-tiv-li], *adv.* in the manner of an adjunctive.
ADJUNCTLY, [aj-ungkt'-li], *adv.* by way of adjunct; connected with.
ADJURATION, [aj'-ew-er-ā'-shun], *n.* the act of adjuring; a solemn appeal, an earnest affirmation; the form of a solemn oath to be taken. [L. *adjuratio* an adjuring].
ADJURATORY, [aj-ew'-er-at-o-ri], *adj.* solemnly urging; including an adjuration.
ADJURE, [aj-ew'-er], *v.t.* to urge with solemn emphasis; to charge on solemn oath. [L. *adjurare* to swear].
ADJUST, [aj-ust'], *v.t.* to settle differences, put in order, restore to harmony, set straight; to adapt, fit, make suit, regulate, make correspond. [MedL. *adjustare* to bring together].
ADJUSTABLE, [aj-ust'-abl], *adj.* able to be adjusted.
ADJUSTER, [aj-ust'-er], *n.* a person who adjusts.
ADJUSTIVE, [aj-ust'-iv], *adj.* serving to adjust.
ADJUSTMENT, [aj-ust'-ment], *n.* the act of adjusting; arrangement; settlement.
ADJUTAGE, [aj'-ut-ij], *n.* a tube connected with the mouth of a container to control the stream of water. [Fr. *ajoutage* tube].
ADJUTANCY, [aj'-ut-an-si], *n.* the office and duties of an adjutant; assistance.
ADJUTANT, [aj'-ut-ant], *n.* an officer beneath the rank of major who aids the commanding officer of a battalion in details of duty and discipline; **a. bird,** an Indian bird, a species of stork, which is protected as a scavenger. [L. *adjutans*, *pres. pt.* of *adjutare* to help].

ADJUTANT BIRD

ADJUTOR, [aj'-ut-or], *n.* a colleague; an ally. [~L. *adjutare* to help].
ADJUTRIX, [aj'-ut-riks], *n.* a woman adjutor. [*Prec.*].
ADJUVANT (1), [aj'-uv-ant], *n.* an assistant, aid; (*med.*) the substance in a compound of medicinals which facilitates the action of the principal ingredient. [*Next*].
ADJUVANT (2), [aj'-uv-ant], *adj.* assisting, helpful. [L. *adjuvans*, *pres.pt.* of *adjuvare* to assist].
ADLEGATION, [ad'-lig-ā'-shun], *n.* the right claimed by the former states of the German Empire to send their own delegates to confer with the Emperor on imperial matters of public concern. [AD- and LEGATION].
ADLOCUTION, [ad'-lok-ew'-shun], *n.* allocution.
ADMEASURE, [ad-mezh'-ur], *v.t.* to measure; to test or measure out proportional parts; (*leg.*) to give each claimant his proportionate right. [AD- and MEASURE (2)].
ADMEASUREMENT, [ad-mezh'-ur-ment], *n.* the act of admeasuring, the proportionate measurement itself; (*leg.*) the apportioned shares acquired by each claimant as his right. [AD- and MEASUREMENT].
ADMENSURATION, [ad-men'-sur-ā'-shun], *n.* the act or practice of measuring. [L. *admensuratio*].
ADMINICLE, [ad-min'-ikl], *n.* help, aid; (*leg.*) auxiliary, corroborative evidence helping to prove a point, but not in itself conclusive. [L. *adminiculum* a prop].
ADMINICULAR, [ad'-min-ik'-yōō-ler], *adj.* helping; helpful.
ADMINICULARLY, [ad'-min-ik'-yōō-ler-li], *adv.* in a helpful fashion.
ADMINICULATE, [ad'-min-ik'-yōō-lāt], *v.t. and i.* to add corroborative evidence.
ADMINICULATOR, [ad'-min-ik'-yōō-lā-tor], *n.* a person who gives help to the weak or the poor.
ADMINISTER, [ad-min'-ist-er], *v.t.* to act as agent for, to perform the duties of a deputy, to manage and look after affairs as an executor; to dispense, to direct or apply administratively rites, principles or laws; to tender or offer, as an oath; to give and/or bring supplies. [L. *administrare* to manage].
ADMINISTERIAL, [ad'-min-is-tēer'-i-al], *adj.* connected with administration, or the executive.
ADMINISTRABLE, [ad-min'-is-trabl], *adj.* capable of administration.
ADMINISTRANT, [ad-min'-is-trant], *n.* a person who administers.
ADMINISTRATE, [ad-min'-is-trāt], *v.t.* to administer. [L. *administratum*, *p.pt.* of *administrare* to manage].
ADMINISTRATION, [ad-min'-is-trā'-shun], *n.* the act of administering, the organizing and conducting of public affairs; the management of a business; the ministry, government or board of directors, any executive body; the office, duties or commission of an administrator; dispensation; execution; application of principles. [L. *administratio*].
ADMINISTRATIVE (1), [ad-min'-is-trat-iv], *n.* the department of a government, etc., which is concerned with administration. [*Next*].
ADMINISTRATIVE (2), [ad-min'-is-trat-iv], *adj.* concerned with administration, executive, that by which one administers. [L. *administrativus*].
ADMINISTRATIVELY, [ad-min'-is-trat-iv-li], *adv.* as a matter of, or by, administration.
ADMINISTRATOR, [ad-min'-is-trā'-tor], *n.* a person who is in charge of the estate of one dying without leaving a will; one who directs, manages, or organizes as a deputy. [L. *administrator* agent].
ADMINISTRATORSHIP, [ad-min'-is-trā-tor-ship], *n.* the duties and office of an administrator.
ADMINISTRATRIX, [ad-min'-is-trat-riks], *n.* a woman who administers.
ADMIRABILITY, [ad'-mir-ab-il'-i-ti], *n.* admirableness.
ADMIRABLE, [ad'-mir-abl], *adj.* possessing qualities to excite admiration; excellent, worth admiring. [L. *admirabilis*].
ADMIRABLENESS, [ad'-mir-abl-nes], *n.* the quality of being admirable.
ADMIRABLY, [ad'-mir-ab-li], *adv.* in an admirable way.
ADMIRAL, [ad'-mir-al], *n.* the naval officer in command of a fleet; the admiral's ship; **Lord High A.,** formerly an officer superintending all British naval affairs, now the Board of Admiralty; **A. of the Fleet,** the highest rank in the navy, senior to **Vice-A.,** who is senior to **Rear-A.**; the title customarily allowed to the senior captain of a fishing fleet; (*entom.*) a species of butterfly; (*zool.*) a single-valved shell-fish of the genus *Conus*. [Arab. *amir al* commander of the].

ADMIRAL BUTTERFLY

ADMIRALTY, [ad'-mir-al-ti], *n.* the Lords of the Admiralty, a board of commissioners granted power to conduct naval affairs; the building in which this board transacts its business; **Court of A.,** (*leg.*) the supreme court sitting in judgment of maritime cases.
ADMIRATION, [ad'-mir-ā'-shun], *n.* the act of admiring; that which excites wonder. [L. *admiratio*].
ADMIRATIVE, [ad'-mir-ā'-tiv], *adj.* expressing admiration.
ADMIRE, [ad-mier'], *v.t.* to look at a person or object and react with wonder and delight; to have mixed feelings of pleasure, awe and sympathy for something or someone; to have a high opinion of. [L. *admirari* to wonder at].
ADMIRER, [ad-mier'-er], *n.* one who admires; a lover.

ADMIRING, [ad-mier'-ing], *adj.* thinking highly of, wondering at.
ADMIRINGLY, [ad-mier'-ing-li], *adv.* with admiration.
ADMISSIBILITY, [ad-mis'-ib-il'-i-ti], *n.* the quality of being admissible.
ADMISSIBLE, [ad-mis'-ibl], *adj.* that may be admitted, entitled to be accepted and considered. [LL. *admissibilis* from *admissum*, *p.pt.* of *admittere* to let in].
ADMISSIBLY, [ad-mis'-ib-li], *adv.* so as to be admitted.
ADMISSION, [ad-mish'-un], *n.* the act of admitting; permission to enter; the right of entry; a confession, an agreement as to truth or fact, an acknowledgment; the price of entry.
ADMISSIVE, [ad-mis'-iv], *adj.* of the character of an admission. [L. *admissivus*].
ADMISSORY, [ad-mis'-or-i], *adj.* admitting.
ADMIT, [ad-mit'], *v.t.* to permit to enter, to give access to, to grant entrance into, to allow; to confess, acknowledge as true or false. [L. *admittere* to allow to enter].
ADMITTABILITY, [ad-mit'-ab-il'-i-ti], *n.* the quality of being admittable.
ADMITTABLE, [ad-mit'-abl], *adj.* capable of being admitted.
ADMITTABLY, [ad-mit'-ab-li], *adv.* admittedly.
ADMITTANCE, [ad-mit'-ans], *n.* the act of admitting; admission, permission to enter.
ADMITTEDLY, [ad-mit'-id-li], *adv.* accepted as correct, in agreement.
ADMIX, [ad-miks'], *v.t.* to mix with something else.
ADMIXTURE, [ad-miks'-chur], *n.* the act of mixing; the addition of another ingredient to a mixture; the mixture or compound itself formed by such an addition. [AD- and MIXTURE].
ADMONISH, [ad-mon'-ish], *v.t.* to exhort; warn, advise; reprove mildly. [L. *admonere* to warn].
ADMONISHMENT, [ad-mon'-ish-ment], *n.* admonition, the act of admonishing, reproof.
ADMONITION, [ad'-mon-ish'-un], *n.* mild reproof; friendly counsel; caution.
ADMONITIVE†, [ad-mon'-it-iv], *adj.* of the character of admonition. [L. **admonitivus*].
ADMONITIVELY, [ad-mon'-it-iv-li], *adv.* by admonition.
ADMONITOR†, [ad-mon'-it-or], *n.* a person who admonishes. [L. *admonitor*].
ADMONITORIAL, [ad-mon'-it-aw'-ri-al], *adj.* admonishing.
ADMONITORY, [ad-mon'-it-or-i], *adj.* serving as admonishment.
ADMORTIZATION, [ad-mawt'-iz-ā'-shun], *n.* amortization.
ADNASCENT, [ad-nā'-sent], *adj.* growing on to or upon. [L. *adnascens*, *pres.pt.* of *adnasci* to grow upon].
ADNATE, [ad'-nāt], *adj.* (*anat. and bot.*) organically attached by the whole surface. [L. *adnatum*, *p.pt.* of *adnasci* to grow upon].
ADNOMINAL, [ad-nom'-inl], *adj.* adjectival; connected with a noun. [AD- and NOMINAL].
ADNOUN, [ad'-nown], *n.* adjective; an attribute of a noun. [AD- and NOUN].
ADNUBILATED, [ad-new'-bil-ā'-tid], *adj.* clouded; obscured. [L. *adnubilatum*, *p.pt.* of *adnubilare* to involve in clouds].
ADO, [ad-ōō], *n.* to-do, fuss, stir, bustle; difficulty; trouble. [ME. *at do* to do].
ADOBE (1), [ad-ōb'-i], *n.* a brick baked by the sun; a house or building made of these bricks. [Span. *adobar* to plaster].
ADOBE (2), [ad-ōb'-i], *adj.* built of sun-baked bricks. [ADOBE (1)].
ADOLESCENCE, [ad'-ol-es'-ents], *n.* the state of growing up; the period of youth between puberty and maturity, the time of life between childhood and manhood or womanhood. [Fr. from L. *adolescentia* from *adolescere* to grow up].
ADOLESCENCY, [ad'-ol-es'-en-si], *n.* adolescence.
ADOLESCENT (1), [ad-ol-es'-ent], *n.* a boy or girl, becoming adult, a youth. [*Next*].
ADOLESCENT (2), [ad'-ol-es'-ent], *adj.* in the process of growing from puberty to maturity.
ADOLODE, [ad'-ol-ōd], *n.* an instrument for measuring the purity of distillation. [A (4) and Gk. *dolos* guile and *hodos* way].
ADONEAN, [ad-ō'-ni-an], *adj.* adonic.
ADONIC, [ad-on'-ik], *adj.* denoting a kind of short verse, first used in lamenting the death of Adonis.
ADONIS, [ad-ō'-nis], *n.* (*myth.*) name of a handsome young man whom Venus loved and followed when he was hunting—his favourite pastime—and whose life-blood she transformed into the wild anemone when she found him dying from a wound inflicted by a wild boar; a handsome man.
ADOPT, [ad-opt'], *v.t.* to treat as one's own, to appropriate; to choose; to take another's child, and treat and consider it as one's own. [L. *adoptare* to choose, select].
ADOPTABLE, [ad-opt'-abl], *adj.* able to be adopted.
ADOPTEDLY, [ad-opt'-id-li], *adv.* by adoption.
ADOPTION, [ad-op'-shun], *n.* the act of adopting; the acceptance of an unrelated child or person into one's family according it full privileges and rights; the acceptance of another's plan, belief, resolution, etc.
ADOPTIVE, [ad-opt'-iv], *adj.* that adopts, or that is adopted. [L. *adoptivus* acquired by adoption].
ADOPTIVELY, [ad-opt'-iv-li], *adv.* by adoption.
ADORABLE, [ad-aw'-er-abl], *adj.* worthy of being adored; calling for devoted love.
ADORABLENESS, [ad-aw'-er-abl-nes], *n.* the quality of being adorable.
ADORABLY, [ad-aw'-rab-li], *adv.* in a manner worthy of adoration.
ADORATION, [ad'-aw-rā'-shun], *n.* the act of worshipping; homage to that which is held sacred; devoted and intense affection. [L. *adoratio*].
ADORE, [ad-aw'-er], *v.t.* to worship with deep and intense reverence, to venerate; to pay ardent homage, to love beyond everything else, to idolize. [L. *adorare* to worship].
ADORER, [ad-aw'-rer], *n.* a person who adores, a lover; an admirer; a worshipper.
ADORN, [ad-awn'], *v.t.* to decorate, embellish, to add things of beauty to; to show the beauty of; to dress. [L. *adornare* to deck, embellish].
ADORNING, [ad-awn'-ing], *adj.* decorating, embellishing.
ADORNMENT, [ad-awn'-ment], *n.* decoration, ornament; embellishment.
ADOSCULATION, [ad-os'-kew-lā'-shun], *n.* (*bot.*) the process of impregnating plants by mere external contact of pollen meeting pistil; the insertion of one part of a plant into another. [L. *adosculatio* giving a kiss to].
ADOSSED, [ad-ost'], *adj.* (*her.*) placed back to back. [Fr. *adossé* back to back].
ADOWN, [a-down'], *prep. and adv.* down; towards the ground. [OE. *ofdune* from the hill, down].
ADPRESSED, [ad-prest'], *adj.* (*bot.*) pressed close to, parallel with the stem. [L. *adpressum*, *p.pt.* of *adprimere* to press].
ADRENAL, [ad-rē'-nal], *adj.* close to the kidneys; **a. glands**, the two small glands embedded in the face of the kidneys, the suprarenal capsules. [AD- and RENAL].
ADRENALIN, [ad-ren'-al-in], *n.* a hormone secreted by the suprarenal glands. [*Prec.*].
ADRIFT, [a-drift'], *adv. and adj.* without moorings, floating haphazardly; having no guiding or stabilizing moral power. [A (3) and DRIFT].
ADROIT, [ad-roit'], *adj.* skilful with the hands, dexterous; having expert resource and ability. [Fr. *à* to and *droit* right].
ADROITLY, [ad-roit'-li], *adv.* in an adroit way.
ADROITNESS, [ad-roit'-nes], *n.* the quality of being adroit, skilfulness.
ADRY, [a-dri'], *adv. and adj.* thirsty. [A (3) and DRY (1)].
ADSCITITIOUS, [ad-sit-ish'-us], *adj.* adopted by way of supplement, supplemental, additional. [~L. *adscitum*, *p.pt.* of *adsciscere* to accept].
ADSCRIPT, [ad'-skript], *n.* a person enrolled in service, as attached to a place; a serf. [L. *adscriptum*, *p.pt.* of *adscribere* to enrol].
ADSCRIPTIVE, [ad-skrip'-tiv], *adj.* attached as an adscript.
ADSTRICTION, [ad-strik'-shun], *n.* the act of binding together; costiveness. [L. *adstrictio*].
ADULARIA, [ad'-ew-lāer'-i-a], *n.* moonstone, a semi-transparent variety of felspar, found in granite. [*Adula*, the name of a Swiss mountain].
ADULATE, [ad'-ew-lāt], *v.t.* to give extreme praise; to flatter for a purpose. [L. *adulatum*, *p.pt.* of *adulari* to fawn like a dog].
ADULATION, [ad'-ew-lā'-shun], *n.* servile over-praise, excessive flattery, fawning. [L. *adulatio*].
ADULATOR, [ad'-ew-lā'-tor], *n.* one who adulates, a flatterer.
ADULATORY, [ad'-ew-lā'-to-ri], *adj.* overcharged with praise, servilely praising, flattering.

ADULLAMITE, [ad-ul'-am-it], *n.* the nickname given to the seceding section of the Liberal party in 1866, by John Bright. [*Adullam*, 1 Sam. xxii].

ADULT (1), [ad-ult'], *n.* any living thing or creature which is full grown. [*Next*].

ADULT (2), [ad'-ult], *adj.* grown up, mature as a person. [L. *adultus*, *p.pt.* of *adolescere* to grow up].

ADULTERANT, [ad-ult'-er-ant], *n.* a person or substance that adulterates.

ADULTERATE (1), [ad-ult'-er-āt], *adj.* bogus, not genuine, debased, contaminated.

ADULTERATE (2), [ad-ult'-er-āt], *v.t.* to debase the quality of a substance or mixture by adding inferior ingredients. [L. *adulteratum*, *p.pt.* of *adulterare* to defile].

ADULTERATELY, [ad-ult'-er-at-li], *adv.* in an adulterate fashion.

ADULTERATENESS, [ad-ult'-er-at-nes], *n.* the quality or state of being adulterated.

ADULTERATION, [ad-ult'-er-ā'-shun], *n.* the act of adulterating; the state of being adulterated, debasement.

ADULTERER, [ad-ult'-er-er], *n.* a man guilty of adultery. [L. *adulter* adulterer].

ADULTERESS, [ad-ult'-er-es], *n.* a woman guilty of adultery.

ADULTERINE (1), [ad-ult'-er-in], *n.* (*leg.*) a child of adultery. [L. *adulterinus* bastard, counterfeit].

ADULTERINE (2), [ad-ult'-er-in], *adj.* proceeding from adulterous intercourse, counterfeit, spurious.

ADULTEROUS, [ad-ult'-er-us], *adj.* guilty of adultery; illicit.

ADULTEROUSLY, [ad-ult'-er-us-li], *adv.* in an adulterous way.

ADULTERY, [ad-ult'-er-i], *n.* sexual intercourse breaking the marriage vow of faithfulness.

ADULTNESS, [ad-ult'-nes], *n.* the state of being adult.

ADUMBRANT, [ad-um'-brant], *adj.* giving a faint or sketchy idea or likeness of. [L. *adumbrans*, *pres.pt.* of *adumbrare* to outline].

ADUMBRATE, [ad-um'-brāt], *v.t.* to make a sketch of, to outline, indicate briefly, to forecast. [L. *adumbratum*, *p.pt.* of *adumbrare* to cast a shadow, outline].

ADUMBRATION, [ad'-um-brā'-shun], *n.* the act of adumbrating; a faint or imperfect representation, a brief indication, an incomplete forecast. [*Prec.*].

ADUMBRATIVE, [ad-um'-brat-iv], *adj.* faintly representing, characterized by adumbration.

ADUNCOUS, [ad-ungk'-us], *adj.* bent in the shape of a hook. [L. *aduncus* hooked].

ADUST, [ad-ust'], *adj.* scorched, parched, sunburnt. [L. *adustus*, *p.pt.* of *adurere* to burn up].

ADUSTED, [ad-ust'-id], *adj.* adust.

ADUSTION, [ad-ust'-yon], *n.* the act of burning up, parching, scorching; the state of being dried up; (*surg.*) cauterization. [L. *adustio* a burning up].

ADVANCE (1), [ad-vahns'], *n.* the act of moving forward, progression; (*fig.*) promotion; progress; rise in wages or offer of money; loan of money; a move towards someone with friendliness; **in a.**, beforehand, in front, before. [ADVANCE (3)].

ADVANCE (2), [ad-vahns'], *adj.* before; **a. note**, a draft, usually for one month's pay, on a shipowner issued to the crew being engaged by the captain when signing their articles of agreement. [ADVANCE (3)].

ADVANCE (3), [ad-vahns'], *v.t.* to move, lead or propel forward; to promote; to propose; improve, enhance; to arrange an earlier time for; to lend or pay money on security; *v.i.* to move forward; to be promoted; to make progress; (*milit.*) to attack; (*comm.*) to rise in price, to become dearer. [OFr. *avancer*].

ADVANCED, [ad-vahnst'], *adj.* in the van of progress, modern in ideas, beliefs and behaviour; old, well on in years, aged.

ADVANCEMENT, [ad-vahns'-ment], *n.* the act of advancing; the state of being advanced; progress, promotion; the payment of money on security; the money paid in advance; (*leg.*) a parent's provision for a child naming the child as heir after the parent's death.

ADVANCER, [ad-vahns'-er], *n.* one who advances, a promoter; the second branch (from the base upwards) of a buck's horn.

ADVANCIVE†, [ad-vahns'-iv], *adj.* able to advance or promote.

ADVANTAGE (1), [ad-vahn'-tij], *n.* any condition, event, circumstance or source of benefit and favourable effect, any means of gaining an elected end, conducive to happiness, success, favour or beneficial effects; gain, favour, profit, benefit; a superior position; (*tennis*) the point scored after both sides have drawn level at "40 all"; **to take a.**, to deceive, betray. [Fr. *avantage*].

ADVANTAGE (2), [ad-vahn'-tij], *v.t.* to promote the interest of; to be beneficial to; to create an advantage for; to profit, to benefit. [Fr. *avantager*].

ADVANTAGEOUS, [ad'-van-tā'-jus], *adj.* useful, being of advantage; profitable; serviceable; beneficial. [Fr. *avantageux*].

ADVANTAGEOUSLY, [ad'-van-tā'-jus-li], *adv.* in an advantageous way.

ADVANTAGEOUSNESS, [ad'-van-tā'-jus-nes], *n.* the quality or state of being advantageous.

ADVENE, [ad-vēn'], *v.i.* to accede. [L. *advenire* to come to].

ADVENT, [ad'-vent], *n.* an arrival, approach, a coming; the coming of Christ into the world; (*eccles.*) the period of four weeks previous to Christmas, preparatory to the Nativity. [OFr. from L. *adventum*, *p.pt.* of *advenire* to come to].

ADVENTITIOUS, [ad'-ven-tish'-us], *adj.* accidental; casual; not essentially inherent; out of the ordinary. [L. *adventicius* foreign].

ADVENTITIOUSLY, [ad'-ven-tish'-us-li], *adv.* in an adventitious way.

ADVENTITIOUSNESS, [ad'-ven-tish'-us-nes], *n.* the state of being adventitious.

ADVENTUAL†, [ad-ven'-chōō-al], *adj.* pertaining to the Advent.

ADVENTURE (1), [ad-ven'-cher], *n.* an enterprise full of risk and danger to person and property; an experience of unforeseen events endangering the participants' lives or persons; an unexpected and remarkable incident; an action involving an unforeseen gamble. [L. *adventurus*, *fut.pt.* of *advenire* to come to].

ADVENTURE (2), [ad-ven'-cher], *v.t.* to risk, to take a chance, to gamble on failure or success. [*Prec.*].

ADVENTUREFUL, [ad-ven'-cher-fōōl], *adj.* filled with a liking for adventure.

ADVENTURER, [ad-ven'-cher-er], *n.* a person who risks his life in difficult and extraordinary enterprises; a person who lives by his wits, an impostor; a speculator.

ADVENTURESOME, [ad-ven'-cher-sum], *adj.* adventurous, fond of adventure.

ADVENTURESOMENESS, [ad-ven'-cher-sum-nes], *n.* the quality of being adventurous.

ADVENTURESS, [ad-ven'-cher-es], *n.* a female adventurer.

ADVENTUROUS, [ad-ven'-cher-us], *adj.* venturesome, inclined to adventures: enterprising; risky full of danger.

ADVENTUROUSLY, [ad-ven'-cher-us-li], *adv.* in an adventurous way.

ADVENTUROUSNESS, [ad-ven'-cher-us-nes], *n.* the act or quality of being adventurous.

ADVERB, [ad'-vurb], *n.* a word qualifying the meaning of a verb, adjective, participle or other adverb in terms of place, time, manner, etc. [L. *ad* to and *verbum* a word].

ADVERBIAL, [ad-vurb'-i-al], *adj.* relating to an adverb.

ADVERBIALLY, [ad'-vurb'-i-a-li], *adv.* with an adverb's function, in the manner of an adverb.

ADVERSARIA, [ad'-ver-sāer'-i-a], *n.* a notebook, a collection of extracts, quotations, observations, remarks, etc. [L. *adversaria*, *pl.* of *adversarium* thing turned towards].

ADVERSARY (1), [ad'-ver-sa-ri], *n.* a person or organized group hostile to one, an opponent; an enemy. [L. *adversarius* one turned towards].

ADVERSARY (2), [ad'-ver-sa-ri], *adj.* (*leg.*) having an opposite party. [*Prec.*].

ADVERSATIVE (1), [ad-vur'-sat-iv], *n.* a word denoting antithesis or contrast. [L. *adversativus*].

ADVERSATIVE (2), [ad-vur'-sat-iv], *adj.* (*gram.*) denoting antithesis or contrast.

ADVERSE, [ad'-vers], *adj.* acting in a contrary direction; hostile; opposing; thwarting, unprosperous, injurious; situated opposite. [L. *adversum*, *p.pt.* of *advertere* to turn to].

ADVERSELY, [ad'-vurs-li], *adv.* in an adverse way.

ADVERSENESS, [ad-vurs'-nes], *n.* state of being adverse.

ADVERSITY, [ad-vur'-sit-i], *n.* an adverse state of affairs, distress, calamity; misfortune. [L. *adversitas*].

ADVERT, [ad-vurt'], *v.i.* to turn attention to; to allude

to; to regard or notice. [L. *advertere* to turn to].
ADVERTENCE, [ad-vurt'-ens], *n.* attention; regard.
ADVERTENCY, [ad-vurt'-en-si], *n.* advertence.
ADVERTENT, [ad-vurt'-ent], *adj.* attentive, heedful, interested. [L. *advertens, pres.pt.* of *advertere* to turn to].
ADVERTENTLY, [ad-vurt'-ent-li], *adv.* in an advertent way.
ADVERTISE, [ad'-ver-tīz], *v.t. and i.* to announce to the public; to display a public notice; to communicate merits and claims to the public by any means, by newspaper notice, placard, poster, radio, etc.; to boast, to push forward one's virtues with an almost vicious emphasis. [Fr. *avertir* to give notice to].
ADVERTISEMENT, [ad-vur'-tis-ment], *n.* an announcement, brought to the notice of the public, of products and prices; legal notification; notice of arrangements for public events.
ADVERTISER, [ad'-ver-tīz'-er], *n.* a person who advertises, a publicist.
ADVICE, [ad-vīs'], *n.* counsel, considered judgment, recommended opinion, professional information; report, notification; (*pl.*) diplomatic report; (*comm.*) detailed information concerning bills, drafts, advances or ledger balance passed between business firms. [ME. *avis* from OFr. *avis* opinion].
ADVICE-BOAT, [ad-vīs'-bōt], *n.* a fast vessel employed to carry dispatches.
ADVISABILITY, [ad-vīz'-ab-il'-i-ti], *n.* advisableness.
ADVISABLE, [ad-vīz'-abl], *adj.* prudent, proper to be advised; expedient.
ADVISABLENESS, [ad-vīz'-abl-nes], *n.* the quality of being advisable.
ADVISABLY, [ad-vīz'-ab-li], *adv.* with advice, wisely, prudently, advisedly.
ADVISE, [ad-vīz'], *v.t. and i.* to counsel, to give advice to; to inform, to give notice to, to communicate to; to consult with. [~Fr. *aviser* from LL. *advisare*].
ADVISED, [ad-vīzd'], *adj.* performed on advice or with deliberation; intended.
ADVISEDLY, [ad-vīz'-id-li], *adv.* in an advised way.
ADVISEDNESS, [ad-vīz'-id-nes], *n.* caution, deliberate consideration; prudent procedure.
ADVISER, [ad-vīz'-er], *n.* person who gives advice; in a bad sense, person who instigates.
ADVISORY, [ad-vīz'-or-i], *adj.* possessing power to advise; constituted to advise, containing advice.
ADVOCACY, [ad'-vok-a-si], *n.* a pleading for; intercessional or judicial pleading. [MedL. *advocatia*].
ADVOCATE (1), [ad'-vok-at], *n.* a person who pleads for another's cause, a professional representative in a legal case, a barrister; a person who recommends or vindicates a cause; a supporter of a proposal or plan; **Faculty of Advocates,** association of barristers allowed to plead in Scottish Supreme Court; **judge a.,** an officer in a court-martial who is appointed to conduct the prosecution; **Devil's a.,** in the Roman Catholic Church, the elected opposer obliged to argue against canonization of the person it is proposed to canonize. [OFr. *avocat* and L. *advocatus* one called in for legal aid].
ADVOCATE (2), [ad'-vok-āt], *v.t.* to plead on behalf of, to argue in favour of, to defend, recommend. [L. *advocatum, p.pt.* of *advocare* to call to help].
ADVOCATESHIP, [ad'-vok-at-ship], *n.* the office, rank or duty of an advocate; church patronage.
ADVOWEE, [ad-vow-ē'], *n.* one who owns the right of advowson. [OFr. *avouée*].
ADVOWSON, [ad-vow'-son], *n.* the right of presenting a cleric with or nominating him for a vacant benefice in the Church of England. [ME. *avoweisoun* and L. *advocatio* right of a patron].
ADYNAMIA, [ad'-in-ā'-mi-a], *n.* (*med.*) weakness brought on by disease; diminution of the vital powers. [Gk. *adunamia* want of strength].
ADYNAMIC, [ad'-ī-nam'-ik], *adj.* weak, without strength. [A (4) and DYNAMIC].
ADYTUM, [ad'-it-um], *n.* the innermost and most sacred part of the shrine of a temple; (*fig.*) an inner, private room. [Gk. *aduton* a place not to be entered].
ADZE, [adz], *n.* a tool with a curved steel blade whose cutting edge is set at right-angles to the wooden handle. Used for chipping the surface of wood. [OE. *adesa*].

ADZE

AEDILE, [ē'-dīl], *n.* a Roman magistrate whose duty it was to supervise public and private buildings, cleaning, draining and repair of highways, national games, etc. [L. *aedilis* from *aedes* a building, temple].
AEDOEOLOGY, [ē'-dē-ol'-o-ji], *n.* the branch of science that deals with the organs of generation. [Gk. *aidoia* the sexual organs and *logos* speech].
AEGER (1), [ē'-jer], *n.* sick leave in English schools and universities, excusing attendance. [*Next*].
AEGER (2), [ē'-jer], *adj.* sick, ill. [L. *aeger* sick].
AEGIS, [ē'-jis], *n.* a protecting shield; *esp.* the legendary shield of Minerva; hence, any protecting influence. [Gk. *aigis* shield].
AEGROTAT, [ē'-grō-tat], *n.* a certificate of exemption or absence from a part or the whole of an examination on account of illness; **a. degree,** a degree awarded to a candidate who has been absent for part or the whole of the final degree examination, and in which no classification is made. [L. *aegrotat* he is sick].
AENEID, ENEID, [ē'-nē-id], *n.* a famous classical epic poem by Virgil dealing with the wanderings and adventures of Aeneas and the origin of the city of Rome. [L. *Aeneida* pertaining to Aeneas].
AEOLIAN, [ē-ō'-li-an], *adj.* pertaining to or caused by the wind; **A. harp,** a musical instrument consisting of a bore of thin wood, furnished with low bridges at each end of its upper surface, over which are stretched strings or wires, placed in an exposed position and operated by the action of the wind blowing across the strings. [L. *Aeolius* from Gk. *Aiolos* the god of winds].
AEOLIC, [ē-ō'-lik], *adj.* pertaining to Aeolis a former Greek colony in Asia Minor; **A. dialect,** one of the five dialects of the Greek tongue; **A. verse,** consisting of an iambus or spondee followed by two anapæsts separated by a long syllable. [Gk. *Aiolikos*].
AEOLIPILE, [ē-ol'-ip-il], *n.* an instrument which measures the force of steam issuing through a small opening. [Gk. *Aiolou pulai* the gates of Aeolus, the god of winds].
AEOLIST, [ē'-ol-ist], *n.* a pretender to divine inspiration.
AEOLOTROPY, [ē'-ol-ot'-rop-i], *n.* a change in physical qualities or properties brought about by altering the position of a thing. [Gk. *aiolos* changeful and *tropia* turning].
AEON, [ē'-on], *n.* an immeasurably long indefinite period of time, eternity; (*philos.*) a spirit or power issuing from the Supreme Being from eternity and helping to create and influence the universe. [Gk. *aiōn* age, eternity].
AEPYORNIS, [ē'-pi-awn'-is], *n.* a large extinct flightless bird of Madagascar whose eggs have a circumference of thirty-six inches and a girth of thirty inches. [Gk. *aipus* tall and *ornis* bird].
AERARIAN (1), [ē-rāer'-i-an], *n.* a freeman in Rome who did not possess a vote and who paid only poll-tax. [L. *aerarius* fiscal].
AERARIAN (2), [ē-rāer'-i-an], *adj.* belonging to the treasury. [*Prec.*].
AERATE, [ā'-er-āt'], *v.t.* to allow air to act upon a substance, to charge with carbonic acid gas; (*med.*) to impregnate the blood with oxygen by respiration; **aerated waters,** a sparkling beverage of water charged with carbonic acid gas and at times flavoured.
AERATION, [ā'-er-ā'-shun], *n.* the process of aerating, or exposing to the action of air, or carbonic acid gas.
AERATOR, [ā'-er-ā'-tor], *n.* an apparatus used for aerating.
AERIAL (1), [āer'-i-al], *n.* a wire or wires supported in the air and used with wireless receiving sets to collect the electrical waves, or with transmitting sets or stations to send out the electrical waves. [Gk. *aerios* airy].
AERIAL (2), [ā-ēer'-i-al], *adj.* belonging to or resembling the air, consisting of or produced by air, existing or moving in the air; (*fig.*) light and delicate, at a great height, unsubstantial, ethereal; **a. plants** (*bot.*) plants which obtain nourishment from the air; **a. perspective,** expression of space or distance in a work of art; **a. ropeways,** method of transport by carriers suspended from ropes elevated on fixed supports. [*Prec.*].
AERIALLY, [ā-ēer'-i-a-li], *adv.* in an aerial fashion.

AERIE, [ãer'-i], *n.* the nest or brood of a bird of prey; (*fig.*) a dwelling place situated at a great height. [MedL. *aeria* from OFr. *aire* of uncertain origin].

AERIFEROUS, [ãer-if'-er-us], *adj.* conveying air. [L. *aer* air and *ferre* to bear].

AERIFICATION, [ãer'-if-ik-ā'-shun], *n.* the act of aerifying; the condition of being aerified; the act of becoming air, gas, or vapour; the state of being aeriform. [L. *aer* air and *ficatio*].

AERIFORM, [ãer'-i-fawm], *adj.* having the form or nature of air or gas; (*fig.*) ethereal, insubstantial, intangible. [L. *aer* air and FORM (1)].

AERIFY, (**aerifies, aerified, aerifying**), [ãer'-if-ī], *v.t.* to infuse air into; to fill with air. [L. *aer* and *-ficere* to make].

AERO-, *pref.* air, pertaining to the air. [Gk. *aer* air].

AEROBATICS, [ãer'-ō-bat'-iks], *n.* stunting in aeroplanes, a performance of spectacular, daring evolutions and manoeuvres by aircraft. [AERO- and ACROBATICS].

AEROBIA, [ãer-ō'-bi-a], *n.* bacteria that can live only in the presence of oxygen. [AERO- and Gk. *bios* life].

AEROBIC, [ãer-ō'-bik], *adj.* relating to aerobia.

AEROBIOSCOPE, [ãer'-ō-bī'-ō-skōp], *n.* an apparatus which calculates the number and shape of micro-organisms present in a specified volume of air. [AERO- and Gk. *bios* life and *skopos* watcher].

AEROCYST, [ãer'-o-sist], *n.* (*bot.*) the air cell of a plant of the seaweed family. [AERO- and Gk. *kustis* a bag, bladder].

AERODART, [ãer'-ō-daht], *n.* a steel weapon or missile that can be released from aircraft. [AERO- and DART (1)].

AERODENSIMETER, [ãer'-ō-den'-sim-ē'-ter], *n.* a gauge for measuring the pressure exerted by gases. [AERO- and DENSE and METER].

AERODONETICS, [ãer'-ō-dō-net'-iks], *n.* (*aeron.*) the science of gliding.

AERODROME, [ãer'-ō-drōm], *n.* an aircraft-station consisting usually of a large open flat area of land, at which aircraft may land or from which they may depart, and the buildings associated therewith, such as hangars, workshops, storerooms, etc. [AERO- and Gk. *dromos* a course].

AERODYNAMICALLY, [ãer'-ō-dīn-am'-ik-al-i], *adv.* as regards aerodynamics.

AERODYNAMICS, [ãer'-ō-dī-nam'-iks], *n.* the science dealing with the mechanical effects of air in motion, air resistance and pressure upon moving bodies in air, etc. [AERO- and Gk. *dunamis* power].

AEROFOIL, [ãer'-ō-foil], *n.* (*aeron.*) the wing of an aeroplane. [AERO- and FOIL (1)].

AEROGNOSY, [ãer-og'-nos-i], *n.* the science concerned with the properties of air. [AERO- and Gk. *gnosis* knowledge].

AEROGRAPHY, [ãer-og'-raf-i], *n.* description of the properties, limits, dimensions, etc., of the atmosphere. [AERO- and Gk. *graphia* writing].

AEROLITE, [ãer'-ol-īt], *n.* a meteoric stone, a meteorite. [AERO- and Gk. *lithos* stone].

AEROLITH, [ãer'-ol-ith], *n.* an aerolite. [*Prec.*].

AEROLITHOLOGY, [ãer'-ol-ith-ol'-o-ji], *n.* the study of meteorites. [AEROLITH and Gk. *logos* speech].

AEROLITIC, [ãer'-ol-it'-ik], *adj.* pertaining to aerolites.

AEROLOGIC, [ãer'-ol-oj'-ik], *adj.* aerological.

AEROLOGICAL, [ãer'-ol-oj'-ikl], *adj.* relating to aerology.

AEROLOGIST, [ãer-ol'-oj-ist], *n.* one who studies aerology.

AEROLOGY, [ãer-ol'-o-ji], *n.* the science which deals with the air, its constituent parts, properties, and phenomena. [AERO- and Gk. *logos* speech].

AEROMANCY, [ãer'-ō-man'-si], *n.* divination by means of the state of the air and winds; forecasting the weather. [AERO- and Gk. *manteia* prophesying].

AEROMETER, [ãer-om'-it-er], *n.* an instrument used to measure the weight or the density of air and gases. [AERO- and METER].

AEROMETRIC, [ãer'-ō-met'-rik], *adj.* relating to the measurement of the air.

AEROMETRY, [ãer-om'-et-ri], *n.* the science of measuring and weighing the air. [AERO- and Gk. *metria* measuring].

AERONAUT, [ãer'-ōn-awt], *n.* one who pilots or navigates any lighter-than-air flying-machine, one who makes ascents in a balloon, an air navigator. [AERO- and Gk. *nautes* a sailor].

AERONAUTIC, [ãer-ōn-awt'-ik], *adj.* pertaining to the science of navigating the air.

AERONAUTICAL, [ãer-ōn-awt'-ikl], *adj.* aeronautic.

AERONAUTICS, [ãer-ōn-awt'-iks], *n.* the science of navigating the air in aircraft of any description.

AERONAUTISM, [ãer-ōn-awt'-izm], *n.* aeronautics.

AEROPHOBIA, [ãer'-ō-fō-bi-a], *n.* fear of fresh air. [AERO- and Gk. *phobia* fear].

AEROPHONE, [ãer'-ō-fōn], *n.* an instrument invented by Edison and used for amplifying sound-waves, used in detecting the approach of or ascertaining the positions of aeroplanes in flight. [AERO- and Gk. *phone* sound].

AEROPHORE, [ãer'-ōf-aw(r)], *n.* an apparatus containing a supply of compressed air, oxygen, etc., which may be breathed by the wearer when working under water, in the case of a mine explosion, a gas attack, etc. [AERO- and Gk. *phoros* carrying].

AEROPHYTE, [ãer'-ō-fīt], *n.* a plant growing on trees or other plants but obtaining its nourishment from the air. [AERO- and Gk. *phuton* plant].

AEROPLANE, [ãer'-ō-plān], *n.* a mechanically propelled heavier than air flying-machine which keeps up in the air from the reaction of the air driven downwards by the rapid passage of the fixed wings through the air. [AERO- and PLANE].

AEROPLANE

AEROSCEPSY, [ãer'-ō-sep'-si], *n.* observation of changes in the state of the atmosphere. [AERO and Gk. *skepsis* an inquiry].

AEROSCOPY, [ãer-os'-kop-i], *n.* the observation of changes in the air. [AERO- and Gk. *skopos* watcher].

AEROSE, [ēer'-ōs], *adj.* coppery or brassy, containing copper or brass. [L. *aerosus* of copper or brass].

AEROSTAT, [ãer'-ō-stat], *n.* aircraft lighter than air, such as balloons, airships, etc. [AERO- and Gk. *statos* standing].

AEROSTATIC, [ãer'-ō-stat'-ik], *adj.* belonging to, concerning, weight, pressure and equilibrium of air and gases.

AEROSTATICAL, [ãer'-ō-stat'-ikl], *adj.* aerostatic.

AEROSTATICS, [ãer'-ō-stat'-iks], *n.* the science of the pressure, weight and equilibrium of the air and gases, or the equilibrium of bodies which move or are sustained in them; aeronautics.

AEROSTATION, [ãer'-ō-stā'-shun], *n.* the navigation of the air.

AEROTHERAPEUTICS, [ãer'-ō-ther'-ap-ewt'-iks], *n.* treatment of disease by air, sunshine or artificially produced ultra-violet rays. [AERO- and THERAPEUTICS].

AERTEX, [ãer'-teks], *n.* (*prot.*) a loosely woven fabric designed to act as a kind of insulating material against cold or heat, and used in making blankets and underclothing.

AERUGINOUS, [ēer-ōō'-jin-us], *adj.* like or having the nature of verdigris. [L. *aeruginosus* like copper-rust].

AERY, [ãer'-i], *adj.* ethereal; visionary, imaginary. [Gk. *aer* air].

AESTHESIOMETER, [ēs-thē'-zi-om'-it-er], *n.* an instrument for measuring the sensitiveness to, or of, the touch. [Gk. *aisthesis* perception and METER].

AESTHETE, [ēs'-thēt], *n.* one professing an extravagant sense of the beautiful. [Gk. *aisthetes* one who perceives].

AESTHETIC, [ēs-thet'-ik], *adj.* pertaining to the science and perception of the beautiful in art, able to appreciate beauty. [Gk. *aisthetikos* capable of perception].

AESTHETICALLY, [ēs-thet'-ik-a-li], *adv.* in an aesthetic fashion.

AESTHETICISM, [ēs-thet'-is-izm], *n.* zeal or devotion, real or affected, to the study of the beautiful.

AESTHETICS, [ēs-thet'-iks], *n.* the philosophy or science of the beautiful, being concerned with emotions or qualities which connote beauty.

AESTHO-PHYSIOLOGY, [ēs'-thō-fiz-i-ol'-o-ji], *n.* the physiology of the sensitory organs.

AESTIVAL, [ēs-tī'-val], *adj.* relating to summer. [L. *aestivālis*].

AESTIVATE, [ēs'-tiv-āt], *v.i.* to spend the summer; (*zool.*) to spend the summer in a state of rest and sleep. [L. *p.pt.* of *aestivare* to spend the summer].

AESTIVATION, [ēst'-iv-ā'-shun], *n.* (*zool.*) estivation; state of dormancy or extreme inactivity during the summer; (*bot.*) the arrangement of the petals within the bud.

AETHER, see ETHER.

AETIOLOGY, [ē'-ti-ol'-o-ji], *n.* the philosophy or science of causes; (*med.*) the study of origins or causes of disease or of pathological conditions. [Gk. *aitia* cause and *logos* speech].

AFAR, [a-fah(r)'], *adv.* (*poet.*) a long distance away. [OE. *on feor* afar].

AFEARD, [a-fēerd'], *adj.* (*poet.*) frightened; afraid, terrified.

AFFABILITY, [af'-ab-il-i-ti], *n.* cheerful good-naturedness, pleasant friendliness.

AFFABLE, [af'-abl], *adj.* friendly, pleasant, courteous, easily approachable, cheerful and polite. [L. *affabilis* able to be spoken to].

AFFABLENESS, [af'-abl-nes], *n.* the state of being affable.

AFFABLY, [af'-ab-li], *adv.* in an affable way.

AFFAIR, [af-āer'], *n.* concern, business, matter; a vague reference to a happening or adventure; a romantic intrigue; (*pl.*) public or private transactions or business, business accounts; (*coll.*) a thing, object or spectacle. [Fr. *affaire*].

AFFECT (1), [af-ekt'], *v.t.* to pretend, to lay claim to; to show a fondness for, to like, to adopt, to assume, to imitate in an unnatural manner, to assume a pose or artificial manner. [L. *affectare* to assume falsely].

AFFECT (2), [af-ekt'], *v.t.* to concern, to produce a change in, to influence, to move the emotions, to stir the feelings of, to produce an effect upon; to infect, to attack (of a disease). [L. *affectum*, *p.pt.* of *afficere* to do something to].

AFFECTATION, [af'-ekt-ā'-shun], *n.* a pretence, an artificially adopted mannerism; an assumed air or character, an artificial pose. [L. *affectatio*].

AFFECTED, [af-ekt'-id], *adj.* unnatural, artificially assumed, full of affectation, fond of adopting an artificial pose; influenced, emotionally stirred, exhibiting the effects of, inclined or disposed.

AFFECTEDLY, [af-ekt'-id-li], *adv.* in an affected way.

AFFECTEDNESS, [af-ekt'-id-nes], *n.* the condition of being affected; affectation.

AFFECTIBILITY, [af-ekt'-ib-il'-i-ti], *n.* the condition of being affectible.

AFFECTIBLE, [af-ekt'-ibl], *adj.* liable to be affected.

AFFECTING, [af-ekt'-ing], *adj.* capable of stirring the emotions, touching, moving, pathetic.

AFFECTINGLY, [af-ekt'-ing-li], *adv.* in an affecting way.

AFFECTION, [af-ek'-shun], *n.* feeling, warm attachment, fondness, love, kindly disposition; (*pl.*) emotions, feelings of love for, inclinations; (*med.*) disease, disorder; †attribute. [L. *affectio* fondness].

AFFECTIONAL, [af-ek'-shunl], *adj.* inferring affection.

AFFECTIONATE, [af-ek'-shun-at], *adj.* full of, or displaying affection, fond, loving, possessing an emotional attachment for, full of warmth.

AFFECTIONATELY, [af-ek'-shun-at-li], *adv.* in an affectionate manner.

AFFECTIONATENESS, [af-ek'-shun-at-nes], *n.* fondness, the quality of being affectionate.

AFFECTIONED†, [af-ek'-shund], *adj.* disposed, inclined.

AFFECTIVE, [af-ek'-tiv], *adj.* pertaining to the emotions, relating or belonging to the affections.

AFFECTIVELY, [af-ek'-tiv-li], *adv.* in an affective or impressive way.

AFFEER, [af-ēer'], *v.t.* (*leg.*) to determine the amount of an arbitrary fine, to make an assessment, to settle a fine. [L. *afforare* to fix a price].

AFFERENT, [af'-er-ent], *adj.* (*physiol.*) of nerves carrying impulses towards the central nervous system. [L. *afferens*, *pres.pt.* of *afferre* to carry to].

AFFETTUOSO, [af-et'-ew-ō'-sō], *adv.* (*mus.*) with feeling. [It. *affettuoso* with feeling].

AFFIANCE (1), [af-ī'-ans], *n.* a pledge of faith, a mutual agreement or promise of marriage between man and woman, faith, trust, reliance in a man. [LL. *affidantia* from *affidare* to trust].

AFFIANCE (2), [af-ī'-ans], *v.t.* to become engaged to be married, to betroth or promise in marriage.

AFFICHE, [af-ēsh'], *n.* a placard, a poster. [Fr. *affiche*].

AFFIDAVIT, [af'-i-dā'-vit], *n.* (*leg.*) a written statement of facts signed upon oath before a person qualified to witness oaths, and generally used in presenting evidence before a judge or court. [LL. *affidavit* he/she has pledged faith].

AFFILIABLE, [af-il'-i-abl], *adj.* able to be affiliated.

AFFILIATE, [af-il'-i-āt], *v.t.* to receive into a family or relationship as a child; to merge with a larger similar organization, or to become a branch of, attach oneself to, be connected with a larger similar organization; to establish the paternity of an illegitimate child in order that the putative father may contribute towards maintenance costs; (*fig.*) to be connected with on grounds of common origin (*esp.* of languages). [LL. *adfiliare* to adopt as a son].

AFFILIATION, [a-fil'-i-ā'-shun], *n.* the act of affiliating; the determining of the paternity of a bastard child; connexion with. [*Prec.*].

AFFINAGE†, [af-ī'-nij], *n.* (*metal.*) the process or act of refining metals.

AFFINE†, [af-īn'], *v.t.* (*chem.*) to refine. [Fr. *affiner*].

AFFINED, [af-īnd'], *adj.* (*zool.*) joined together by marriage or any other bond; leagued or allied; with natural affinities.

AFFINITY, [af-in'-i-ti], *n.* close relation or points of similarity between two objects; resemblance in structure between plants, animals, languages inferring an ultimate common origin; similarity of character, natural inclination or attraction, likeness serving as a connecting link; (*leg.*) relationship between one of two persons married to each other and the blood relations of the other; (*chem.*) the tendency of certain bodies to combine with each other. [L. *affinitas* neighbourhood].

AFFIRM, [af-urm'], *v.t.* to declare positively or formally, to state a thing to be true; (*leg.*) to confirm or ratify; *v.i.* (*leg.*) to confirm testimony by solemn declaration instead of taking an oath. [L. *affirmare* to make firm].

AFFIRMABLE, [af-urm'-abl], *adj.* able to be affirmed.

AFFIRMABLY, [af-urm'-ab-li], *adv.* so as to be capable of affirmation.

AFFIRMANCE, [af-urm'-ans], *n.* solemn statement, formal declaration, confirmation; (*leg.*) ratification. [OFr. *afermance*].

AFFIRMANT, [af-urm'-ant], *n.* one who affirms.

AFFIRMATION, [af'-urm-ā'-shun], *n.* a positive assertion, a declaration that something is so or is true, a statement, a confirmation; (*logic*) a positive assertion, inferring the mutual concernment of the terms of a proposition; (*leg.*) a solemn declaration made in a court of law as an alternative to the taking of an oath, and equally binding from a legal point of view. [L. *affirmatio*].

AFFIRMATIVE (1), [af-urm'-at-iv], *n.* a statement or expression which affirms the correctness or truth of something, or states a thing to be so.

AFFIRMATIVE (2), [af-urm'-at-iv], *adj.* stating that something is correct or true, or is a fact, confirmative, opposed to negative. [L. *affirmativus*].

AFFIRMATIVELY, [af-urm'-at-iv-li], *adv.* in an affirmative way.

AFFIRMATORY, [af-urm'-at-or-i], *adj.* confirmatory, that which affirms.

AFFIRMER, [af-urm'-er], *n.* a person who affirms.

AFFIX (1), [af'-iks], *n.* that which is added, attached, or fastened to; (*gram.*) a prefix or suffix added to a stem or base of a word. [*Next*].

AFFIX (2), [af-iks'], *v.t.* to attach, to fasten to, to fix upon, to append, to put at the end of a document. [L. *affixum*, *p.pt.* of *affigere* to fasten to].

AFFLATION, [af-lā'-shun], *n.* the act of breathing upon. [L. *afflatio* from *afflatum*, *p.pt.* of *afflare* to blow upon].

AFFLATUS, [af-lā'-tus], *n.* breathing or blowing upon; divine inspiration. [L. *afflatus* a blowing on].

AFFLICT, [af-likt'], *v.t.* to attack, to harass sorely, to distress, to oppress, to cause pain or grief, to bring trouble upon. [L. *afflictum*, *p.pt.* of *affligere* to dash down].

AFFLICTED, [af-likt'-id], *adj.* harassed, tormented, stricken with, oppressed or grieved with a calamity; (*med.*) diseased, injured.

AFFLICTEDNESS, [af-likt'-id-nes], *n.* the condition of being afflicted.

AFFLICTING, [af-likt'-ing], *adj.* causing sorrow or pain, distressing.

AFFLICTINGLY, [af-likt'-ing-li], *adv.* in an afflicting way.

AFFLICTION, [af-lik'-shun], *n.* the condition of being afflicted, distress, adversity, calamity, burden of suffering; (*pl.*) troubles, woes; (*med.*) a disorder, disease, or injury. [L. *afflictio*].

AFFLICTIVE, [af-likt'-iv], *adj.* producing affliction.

AFFLICTIVELY, [af-likt'-iv-li], *adv.* in an afflictive way.
AFFLUENCE, [af'-lōō-ens], *n.* profusion, abundance; prosperity, opulence, possession of riches, state of wealthiness. [L. *affluentia* riches].
AFFLUENCY†, [af'-lōō-en-si], *n.* affluence, riches, wealthiness. [*Prec.*].
AFFLUENT (1), [af'-lōō-ent], *n.* a tributary stream or river flowing into a larger river. [*Next*].
AFFLUENT (2), [af'-lōō-ent], *adj.* luxurious, rich, wealthy, prosperous; freely flowing, profuse, ample. [L. *affluens, pres.pt.* of *affluere* to flow to].
AFFLUENTLY, [af'-lōō-ent-li], *adv.* in an affluent way.
AFFLUX, [af'-luks], *n.* a flowing to, a gathering; (*med.*) a rush of blood. [L. *affluxum, p.pt.* of *affluere* to flow to].
AFFLUXION, [af-luk'-shun], *n.* afflux.
AFFORCE, [af-aws'], *v.t.* to exert force upon a person or thing; (*leg.*) to add technical experts or numbers of men to a judicial bench or jury in order to give it additional power or weight; †to ravish. [OFr. *aforcier* to force].
AFFORCEMENT, [af-aws'-ment], *n.* an addition of weight to, or strengthening. [OFr. *afforcement*].
AFFORD, [af-awd'], *v.t.* to give, to be able to supply, to be able to concede; to have the necessary means, to be able to spare the money for, to be able to allow a person to do something or a thing to happen; **can't a. to,** daren't. [OE. *geforthian* to further, advance].
AFFOREST, [af-or'-est], *v.t.* to turn into forest, to plant with trees. [MedL. *afforestare*].
AFFORESTATION, [af-or'-es-tā'-shun], *n.* the process of converting ground into forest.
AFFORMATIVE, [af-awm'-at-iv], *n.* a suffix or affix.
AFFRANCHISE, [af-ran'-chīz], *v.t.* to make free, to set free from an obligation. [OFr. *affranchir*].
AFFRANCHISEMENT, [af-ran'-chiz-ment], *n.* the process of affranchising, the state of being affranchised.
AFFRAY, [af-rā'], *n.* a fight, a brawl, a struggle or clash between two groups of disputants, a minor encounter between opposing sides in a war, a riot; (*fig.*) a struggle, dispute. [OFr. *effrei*].
AFFRIGHT (1), [a-frīt'], *n.* (*poet.*) sudden fear, terror. [*Next*].
AFFRIGHT (2), [a-frīt'], *v.t.* (*poet.*) to terrify, to alarm, to frighten exceedingly. [A (3) and FRIGHT].
AFFRIGHTEDLY, [a-frīt'-id-li], *adv.* in an affrighted manner, with fright.
AFFRONT (1), [a-frunt'], *n.* an insult, contemptuous or offensive treatment, act or speech. [*Next*].
AFFRONT (2), [a-frunt'], *v.t.* to insult openly, to offend, to speak insolently of a person to his face; to face boldly and impudently, to confront. [LL. *affrontare* to strike against].
AFFRONTEE, affrontée, [af-rawn'-tā], *adj.* (*her.*) facing each other, facing the front. [Fr. *affronté, p.pt.* of *affronter*].
AFFUSE, [af-ewz'], *v.t.* to pour upon; to sprinkle with a liquid. [L. *affusum, p.pt.* of *affundere* to pour upon].
AFFUSION, [af-ew'-zhun], *n.* sprinkling with water in baptism; (*med.*) pouring of tepid water upon patients suffering from fever. [L. *affusio*].
AFFY†, [af-ī'], *v.t.* to put one's trust in, to have faith in, to betroth, to bind with a pledge. [OFr. *affier*].
AFIELD, [a-fēld'], *adj. and adv.* in the field, out-of-doors; at some distance away from home, abroad; **to go too far a.**, to wander away from one's path, to stray. [OE. *on felda* in the field].
AFIRE, [a-fīer'], *adj. and adv.* (*lit. and fig.*) on fire. [OE. *on fyr* on fire].
AFLAME, [a-flām'], *adj. and adv.* ablaze, lit up; (*fig.*) eagerly excited, burning, glowing.
AFLAT, [a-flat'], *adv.* on a level with the ground.
AFLAUNT, [a-flawnt'], *adj. and adv.* flaunting.
AFLOAT, [a-flōt'], *adj. and adv.* at sea, floating, on board ship, awash, under water; (*fig.*) solvent, out of debt; abroad, being circulated, current; adrift. [OE. *on flote* on the sea].
AFOAM, [a-fōm'], *adj. and adv.* foaming.
AFOOT, [a-fŏŏt'], *adj. and adv.* on foot; on the move, in prospect, being prepared. [ME. *a fote* on foot].
AFORE, [a-faw(r)'], *adv. and prep.* in front; before; in or towards the front part of a ship. [OE. *on foran* before].
AFOREGOING (1), [a-faw'-gō'-ing], *adj.* going before, preceding.
AFOREGOING (2), [a-faw'-gō'-ing], *n.* that which has preceded, just been stated. [AFORE and *pr.pt.* of GO].
AFOREHAND, [a-faw(r)'-hand], *adv.* in time previous, in former time.
AFOREMENTIONED, [a-faw'-men'-shund], *adj.* mentioned before.
AFORENAMED, [a-faw'-nāmd], *adj.* cited before, already mentioned.
AFORESAID, [a-faw(r)'-sed], *adj.* said or mentioned before.
AFORETHOUGHT, [a-faw'-thawt], *adj.* premeditated, thought out previously or in advance.
AFORETIME, [a-faw'-tīm], *adv.* in time past; in a previous time.
AFOUL, [a-fowl'], *adj. and adv.* entangled; in collision, fouling.
AFRAID, [af-rād'], *adj.* frightened, scared, fear-stricken; (*coll.*) **I am a.**, phrase preceding some unpleasant news, or as a form of apology or excuse, or implying unwillingness. [~AFFRAY].
AFREET, AFRIT, [ā'-frēt], *n.* an evil spirit in Moslem folk-lore. [Arab. *ifrit*].
AFRESH, [a-fresh'], *adv.* anew, again.
AFRIKAANS (1), [af-rik-ahns'], *n.* the form of Dutch spoken in South Africa, the language of the Boers. [Du. *Afrikaansch* African].
AFRIKAANS (2), [af-rik-ahns'], *adj.* in, of, or pertaining to Afrikaans.
AFRIKANDER, [af'-rik-and'-er], *n.* a white person born in South Africa usually of Dutch stock; a coloured native of South Africa of mixed descent; **A. Bond**, organization devoted to South African interests and desiring the ultimate formation of a United States of South Africa. [Afrik. *Afrikaander* from *Afrikaans* African].
AFRIT, see AFREET.
AFT, [ahft], *adv.* (*naut.*) towards the stern or hinder part of a ship; **fore and a.**, (*naut.*) along the length of a ship, rigged with sails set lengthwise, from prow to stern; **right a.**, in a direct line with the stern. [OE. *æftan* from behind].
AFTER (1), [ahft'-er], *adj. and adv.* later, following; (*naut.*) near to or pertaining to the stern; in the rear, behind, later, subsequently. [OE. *æfter* behind].

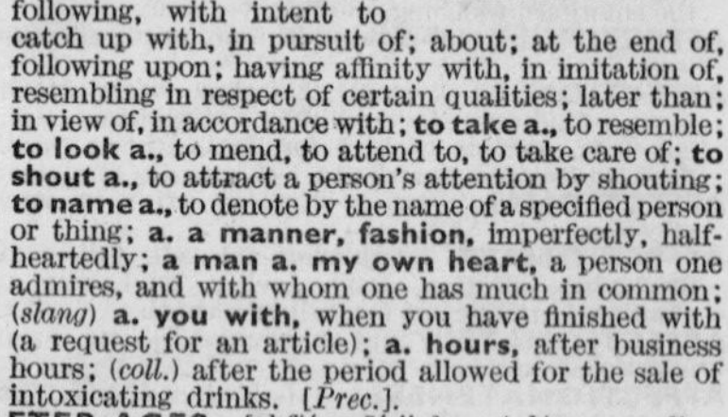
FORE-AND-AFT RIG

AFTER (2), [ahft'-er], *prep., adv. and conj.* immediately following, with intent to catch up with, in pursuit of; about; at the end of, following upon; having affinity with, in imitation of, resembling in respect of certain qualities; later than; in view of, in accordance with; **to take a.**, to resemble; **to look a.**, to mend, to attend to, to take care of; **to shout a.**, to attract a person's attention by shouting; **to name a.**, to denote by the name of a specified person or thing; **a. a manner, fashion**, imperfectly, half-heartedly; **a man a. my own heart**, a person one admires, and with whom one has much in common; (*slang*) **a. you with**, when you have finished with (a request for an article); **a. hours**, after business hours; (*coll.*) after the period allowed for the sale of intoxicating drinks. [*Prec.*].
AFTER-AGES, [ahft'-er-ā'-jiz], *n.(pl.)* succeeding ages, posterity.
AFTER ALL, [ahft'-er-awl'], *adv.* when all has been considered, in spite of everything said or done.
AFTERBIRTH, [ahft'-er-burth'], *n.* (*obstet.*) the placenta and membranes of the foetus expelled after parturition.
AFTER-BODY, [ahft'-er-bod'-i], *n.* (*naut.*) the part of a vessel to the rear of the midship section.
AFTERCLAP, [ahft'-er-klap'], *n.* an unexpected subsequent happening.
AFTERCOST, [ahft'-er-kost'], *n.* the expense incurred after the execution of the original plan.
AFTERCROP, [ahft'-er-krop'], *n.* the second crop in the same year from the same land.
AFTERDAMP, [ahft'-er-damp'], *n.* poisonous gases, suffocating fumes remaining after an explosion of fire-damp in mines.
AFTERGAME, [ahft'-er-gām'], *n.* an expedient after a failure; a later game to alter the results of a previous game.
AFTERGLOW, [ahft'-er-glō'], *n.* a glow remaining in the sky after sunset; also (*fig.*) in a metal becoming cool from white-heat.
AFTER-GRASS, [ahft'-er-grahs'], *n.* the new crop of grass growing after the mowing of the first crop.

AFTERGROWTH, [ahft'-er-grōth'], *n.* second and succeeding growth.
AFTERGUARD, [ahft'-er-gahd'], *n.* (*naut.*) seamen stationed aft whose duty it was to attend to the after-sails and upon whom most of the drudgery of the ship's routine fell.
AFTERHELP, [ahft'-er-help'], *n.* secondary or additional help.
AFTER-HOLD, [ahft'-er-hōld'], *n.* (*naut.*) that part of a vessel's hold to the rear of the mainmast.
AFTER-IMAGE, [ahft'-er-im'-ij], *n.* impression of an object or sensation remaining and perceptible to the senses after the external object or cause has been removed.
AFTERINGS, [ahft'-er-ingz], *n.(pl.)* the last drops of milk drawn from a cow.
AFTERLIFE, [ahft'-er-līf'], *n.* future life here on earth or hereafter.
AFTERLOVE, [ahft'-er-luv'], *n.* second or later love.
AFTERMATH, [ahft'-er-mahth'], *n.* a second crop of grass in a season; (*fig.*) consequences or results of some calamity. [AFTER and OE. *mæth* mowing].
AFTER-MENTIONED, [ahft'-er-men'-shund], *adj.* subsequently mentioned or said.
AFTERMOST, [ahft'-er-mōst], *adj.* (*naut.*) furthest aft, nearest the stern. [OE. *æftermest*].
AFTERNOON, [ahft'-er-nōōn'], *n.* time between noon and evening.
AFTERPAINS, [ahft'-er-pānz'], *n.(pl.)* pains following upon childbirth.
AFTERPART, [ahft'-er-paht'], *n.* the latter part; (*naut.*) the part of a ship towards the stern.
AFTERPIECE, [ahft'-er-pēs'], *n.* a short dramatic piece performed after an important play.
AFTERPROOF, [ahft'-er-prōōf'], *n.* proof known later.
AFTER-RAKE, [ahft'-er-rāk], *n.* (*naut.*) part of the hull projecting at the stern.

AFTER-RAKE

AFTERSAILS, [ahft'-er-sālz'], *n.(pl.)* the sails on the mizenmast and stays, between the main and mizenmasts.
AFTERSWARM, [ahft'-er-swawm'], *n.* a swarm of bees which leaves the hive after the first swarm, a cast.
AFTERTASTE, [ahft'-er-tāst'], *n.* the taste which remains in the mouth after eating or drinking.
AFTERTHOUGHT, [ahft'-er-thawt'], *n.* reflection upon a past act or happening, something thought of by way of an explanation or amplification.
AFTERTOSSING, [ahft'-er-tos'-ing], *n.* the swell occurring on the sea after a storm.
AFTERWARD(S), [ahft'-er-werd(z)], *adv.* in a later or subsequent time. [OE. *æftanweard*].
AFTERWISE, [ahft'-er-wīz], *adj.* wise after an event or too late.
AFTERWIT, [ahft'-er-wit'], *n.* wit that occurs too late.
AFTWARD, [ahft'-werd], *adj.* towards the stern.
AGA, [ah'-ga], *n.* formerly a military title of rank given to certain officers in the Turkish army, now used also as a civil title and applied to men holding high positions and men of great wealth and influence; **A. Khan,** hereditary spiritual and temporal chief of the Ismailite sect of Moslems, claiming direct lineal descent from Mohammed. [Turk. *agha* master].
AGAIN, [a-gān'], *adv.* back to the original or former place; anew, repeatedly, once more, in return, a second time; expressing a quantity equal to a stated quantity; moreover, besides, on the other hand; **now and a.,** occasionally; **time and a.,** repeatedly; **as much a.,** twice as much. [OE. *ongean* opposite, again].
AGAINST, [a-gānst'], *prep. and adv.* opposite, close to, in contrast with, in contact with, contrary to, in an opposite direction, in opposition to, in competition with, alongside, facing, in preparation for, in collision with; **to run up a.,** to encounter unexpectedly. [OE. *ongēanes*].
AGALACTIA, AGALAXY, [ag'-al-ak'-ti-a, ag'-al-ak'-si], *n.* (*med.*) absence of milk for suckling in mothers after childbirth. [Gk. *agalaktia* want of milk].
AGALACTOUS, [ag'-al-ak'-tus], *adj.* (*med.*) destitute of milk for suckling purposes. [Gk. *agalaktos* without milk].
AGALAXY, see AGALACTIA.
AGALLOCH†, [ag-al'-ok], *n.* a resinous wood with fragrant properties, of bluish-purple colour, of which aloes-wood is an example. [Gk. *agalokhon*].
AGALMA†, [ag-al'-ma], *n.* (*leg.*) impression of a figure on a seal. [Gk. *agalma* an ornament, statue, picture].
AGALMATOLITE, [ag'-al-mat'-ol-īt], *n.* a kind of clayey stone, easily cut and extensively used in China to model figures, for carving images, hence called figure-stone. [Gk. *agalma* statue, image and *lithos* stone].
AGAL-WOOD, [ah'-gal-wŏŏd'], *n.* wood of the aloes.
AGAMA, [ag'-a-ma], *n.* (*zool.*) a brightly coloured kind of lizard with a broad short tongue, able to change colour at will and allied to the iguana family. [Caribbean].
AGAMI, [ag'-a-mi], *n.* the trumpeter bird found in tropical America, *Psophia crepitans.* [Fr. *agamy* a native name in Guiana].
AGAMIC†, [ag'-am-ik], *adj.* asexual, reproduction without union of the sexes.
AGAMIST, [ag'-am-ist], *n.* one who is against matrimony.
AGAMOGENESIS, [ag'-am-oj-en'-es-is], *n.* reproduction asexually. [Gk. *agamos* unmarried and GENESIS].
AGAMOUS†, [ag'-am-us], *adj.* asexual, with the sexual organs not apparent. [Gk. *agamos* unmarried].

AGAMI

AGAPE, [a-gāp'], *adj. and adv.* staring with wide-open mouth in astonishment, surprise, bewilderment, expectation, etc.
AGAPE, [ag'-a-pi], *n.* (*eccles. hist.*) a primitive Christian love-feast of charity held in connexion with Communion, at which the rich contributed liberally towards the cost of food for their poorer co-religionists. [Gk. *agape* love].
AGAR-AGAR, [ā'-gahr-ā'-gah(r)], *n.* a gelatinous substance obtained from dried seaweed of the Asiatic archipelago and used for cultivating bacteria, in the manufacture of certain kinds of paper and silk, and soups and jellies in the East. [Malayan *agar-agar*].
AGARIC, [ag'-a-rik], *n.* (*bot.*) a large genus of fungi having a fleshy cap, and classified into five groups according to the colour of the spores; **a. mineral,** (*min.*) a deposit of carbonate of lime, formed in the fissures of limestone rocks and at the bottom of some lakes, so named from its resemblance to a fungus; a Tuscan stone, from which bricks can be made so light that they float in water, consisting of a hydrated silicate of magnesium containing also lime, aluminium and a slight amount of iron. [Gk. *agarikon* a kind of tree-fungus].
AGAST, see AGHAST.
AGASTRIC, [ag-as'-trik], *adj.* (*zool.*) lacking a distinct gullet, stomach or intestines. [A (4) and Gk. *gaster* stomach].
AGATE, [ag'-at], *n.* a very hard stone being a semi-transparent variegated compound variety of chalcedony, in which the bands or spots of colour are blended together or form stripes or layers, of which different varieties are distinguished in accordance with their appearance; an instrument used by gold-wire drawers containing an agate used for burnishing; (*print.*) ruby type. [Gk. *akhates* agate].
AGATIFEROUS, [ag-at-if'-er-us], *adj.* (*min.*) producing or containing agates. [AGATE and L. *ferre* to bear].
AGATINE, [ag'-at-īn], *adj.* resembling agate.
AGATIZE, [ag'-at-īz], *v.t.* to form into agate.
AGATIZED, [ag'-at-īzd], *adj.* (*min.*) with coloured lines like agate.
AGATY, [ag'-at-i], *adj.* like, of the nature of, or containing, agate.
AGAVE, [ag-ā'-vi], *n.* (*bot.*) a genus of plant popularly and erroneously known as American aloes or the century plant. [Gk. *Agave* the mother of Pentheus].
AGAZE, [a-gāz'], *adv.* gazing, staring.
AGAZED, [a-gāzd'], *adj.* struck with amazement, profoundly astonished.
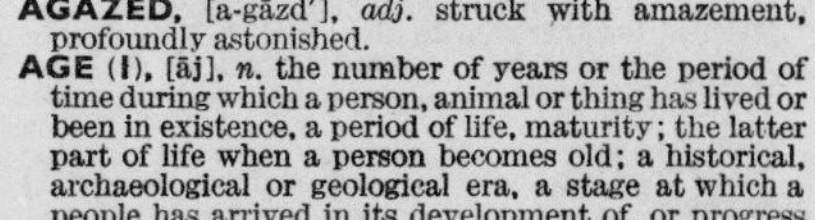
AGE (1), [āj], *n.* the number of years or the period of time during which a person, animal or thing has lived or been in existence, a period of life, maturity; the latter part of life when a person becomes old; a historical, archaeological or geological era, a stage at which a people has arrived in its development of, or progress towards, civilization; the people living at a certain

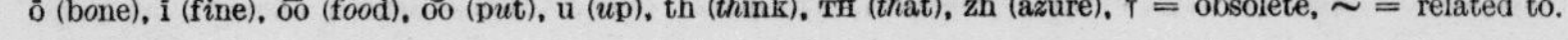

ō (bone), ī (fine), ōō (food), ŏŏ (put), u (up), th (think), TH (that), zh (azure), † = obsolete, ~ = related to.

period; a long, indefinite period of time; (*leg.*) the period of life at which certain legal rights and responsibilities are obtained; (*cards*) the player sitting to the left of the dealer at poker; (*pl.*) (*slang*) an unreasonably long time; **over/under a.,** too old/young; **to come of a.,** to be twenty-one years old; **to be of a.,** to be over twenty-one years old. [LL. *aetaticum* age].

AGE (2), [āj], *v.t. and i.* to grow old, to seem to have grown old, to cause to grow old; to make someone seem as if he is old. [AGE (1)].

AGED, [ājd', āj'-id], *adj.* of a certain age; advanced in years, old; *n.*(*pl.*) old persons.

AGELESS, [āj'-les], *adj.* never appearing to become old.

AGENCY, [ā'-jen-si], *n.* the occupation of an agent; the business or office of an agent; influence, power, instrumentality, acting force, means of action. [MedL. *agentia*].

AGENDA, [aj-en'-da], *n.* a statement of the business to be dealt with at a meeting, things to be done, or considered. [L. *agenda* things to be done, *neut.pl. ger.* of L. *agere* to do].

AGENDUM, [aj-en'-dum], *n.* an item of business to be considered at a meeting. [L. *agendum* that which must be done].

AGENESIS, [aj-en'-is-is], *n.* (*physiol.*) imperfect physical development. [A (4) and GENESIS].

AGENT, [ā'-jent], *n.* one who performs an action or causes something to occur, a business representative or substitute, one appointed to act on behalf of or to look after the interests or business of another; the cause of certain effects or phenomena; (*science*) a force acting on matter and bringing about certain results; an officer in India endowed with political power to deal with native states; **army a.,** a kind of authorized military banker who conducts the financial affairs of a regiment; **crown a.,** commercial or financial representative in Britain of a Dominion or Colony appointed by the Secretary of State for the Colonies; **A. General,** a crown agent appointed by certain self-governing colonies: **a. provocateur,** one employed in inciting suspected offenders to commit some crime or offence in order that the offenders may be caught in the act. [~L. *agens, pres.pt.* of *agere* to do].

AGENTIAL, [ā-jen'-shal], *adj.* pertaining to agency.

AGEUSIA, AGEUSTIA, [aj-ews'-(t)i-a], *n.* (*med.*) impairment or loss of taste. [Gk. *ageustos* not tasting].

AGGLOMERATE (1), [ag-lom'-er-at], *n.* an agglomeration of articles; (*min.*) masses of angular fragments of rock fused together, and erupted as ash and lava from a volcano. [AGGLOMERATE (3)].

AGGLOMERATE (2), [ag-lom'-er-at], *adj.* gathered into a heap, ball or mass. [AGGLOMERATE (3)].

AGGLOMERATE (3), [ag-lom'-er-āt], *v.t.* to gather together haphazardly into a confused pile, mass or heap. [L. *agglomeratum, p.pt.* of *agglomerare* to gather into a ball, to join].

AGGLOMERATION, [ag-lom-er-ā'-shun], *n.* the act of gathering into a mass; a confused heap of articles loosely and unmethodically thrown together in a mass; the state of being agglomerated, a piling up into a large quantity. [L. *agglomeratio*].

AGGLOMERATIVE, [ag-lom'-er-at-iv], *adj.* apt to collect together into a mass.

AGGLUTINANT (1), [ag-lōō'-tin-ant], *n.* any viscous substance which produces or strengthens adhesion; (*med.*) an adhesive application. [AGGLUTINANT (2)].

AGGLUTINANT (2), [ag-lōō'-tin-ant], *adj.* uniting as glue. [L. *agglutinans, pres.pt.* of *agglutinare* to fasten with glue].

AGGLUTINATE (1), [ag-lōō'-tin-āt], *adj.* fastened together as with glue. [AGGLUTINATE (2)].

AGGLUTINATE (2), [ag-lōō'-tin-āt], *v.t. and i.* to glue together, to fasten together by adhesion; to form into a glue-like substance; to combine words into compounds; to become glued together; to be made into a glue. [L. *agglutinatum, p.pt.* of *agglutinare*].

AGGLUTINATION, [ag-lōō'-tin-ā'-shun], *n.* the act of sticking together as with glue, the state of being fastened together as with glue; (*philol.*) a method of joining together two or more distinct elements so that the union does not appear to be so perfect or close as with inflexion, but with the same purpose; often applied to compounds formed by distinct words being joined together and each word retaining its original meaning.

AGGLUTINATIVE, [ag-lōō'-tin-at-iv], *adj.* tending to cause adhesion or agglutination; (*philol.*) formed by or exhibiting agglutination.

AGGLUTININ, [ag-lōō'-tin-in], *n.* (*biol.*) a substance, apparently proteid, found in animal organisms and bringing about agglutination.

AGGRANDIZABLE, [ag-rand-īz'-abl], *adj.* capable of being aggrandized.

AGGRANDIZATION, [ag-rand'-īz-ā'-shun], *n.* the act of making greater or more powerful.

AGGRANDIZE, [ag'-rand-iz], *v.t.* to make a person or state great or greater in power, rank or honour, to enlarge, to make more important. [Fr. *agrandir*].

AGGRANDIZEMENT, [aggrand'-iz-ment], *n.* increase in power, importance or wealth of a person or state, enlargement of the size of a state, increase in rank or honour of a person, advancement. [Fr. *agrandissement*].

AGGRAVATE, [ag'-rav-āt], *v.t.* to make worse, to increase or intensify the gravity or seriousness of anything; (*coll.*) to annoy, irritate, to exasperate. [L. *aggravatum, p.pt.* of *aggravare* to make heavy].

AGGRAVATING, [ag'-rav-ā'-ting], *adj.* making worse, increasing the gravity or seriousness of anything; provoking, exasperating, arousing irritation.

AGGRAVATINGLY, [ag'-rav-ā'-ting-li], *adv.* in an aggravating way.

AGGRAVATION, [ag'-rav-ā'-shun], *n.* an act or circumstance which increases the gravity or seriousness of anything; anything which aggravates; the act of aggravating; exasperation; annoyance.

AGGRAVATOR, [ag'-rav-ā'-tor], *n.* a person arousing aggravation.

AGGREGATE (1), [ag'-rig-at], *n.* the sum total; a collected mass, an amount; (*geol.*) a rock consisting of a compound of minerals; (*building*) material mixed with lime in order to make concrete; (*phys.*) a whole formed by the union of homogeneous particles.

AGGREGATE (2), [ag'-rig-at], *adj.* united into one body, and capable of being regarded as a whole, total, collective; (*geol.*) of rocks composed of a compound of different minerals, and able to be split up by machinery into the component minerals; (*bot.*) applied to flowers composed of small florets united at the base in a common undivided receptacle; (*leg.*) consisting of two or more persons in association, and maintained by a continued succession of new members.

AGGREGATE (3), [ag'-rig-āt], *v.t.* to collect together into a sum or mass, to add up to, to amount to. [L. *aggregatum, p.pt.* of *aggregare* to bring to the flock].

AGGREGATELY, [ag'-rig-at-li], *adv.* collectively, as a whole.

AGGREGATION, [ag'-rig-ā'-shun], *n.* an aggregate, a crowd, a collective body of persons or things, the act of aggregating, the state of being aggregated; †joining, affiliation.

AGGREGATIVE, [ag'-rig-at-iv], *adj.* considered together.

AGGRESS, [ag-res'], *v.i.* to be the first to attack; to start the quarrel. [LL. *aggressare* to attack].

AGGRESSION, [ag-resh'-un], *n.* an unprovoked attack upon a person or state. [L. *aggressio*].

AGGRESSIVE, [ag-res'-iv], *adj.* hostile, threatening, fiercely pugnacious, eager for violence, quarrelsome, always ready or disposed to attack.

AGGRESSIVELY, [ag-res'-iv-li], *adv.* in an aggressive way.

AGGRESSIVENESS, [ag-res'-iv-nes], *n.* state of being aggressive.

AGGRESSOR, [ag-res'-or], *n.* a state or individual that makes an unprovoked attack upon another, or first commences hostilities or a quarrel against another. [L. *aggressor*].

AGGRIEVE, [a-grēv'], *v.t.* to give pain or sorrow; to oppress; to injure the feelings of. [Fr. *agrever* to make more heavy].

AGGRIEVED, [a-grēvd'], *adj.* suffering from injustice, having one's feelings hurt, having a grievance.

AGGROUP, [a-grōōp'], *v.t.* to group together; to combine. [Fr. *agrouper* to group].

AGGROUPMENT, [a-grōōp'-ment], *n.* combination; grouping.

AGHAST, [a-gahst'], *adj.* terrified, horror-stricken, awe-struck, dumbfounded. [~OE. *gæstan*].

AGILE, [aj'-īl], *adj.* nimble, active, quick in movement, quick-witted. [Fr. from L. *agilis* nimble].

AGILELY, [aj'-īl-li], *adv.* in an agile way.

AGILENESS, [aj'-īl-nes], *n.* the quality of agility.

AGILITY, [a-jil'-i-ti], *n.* nimbleness, activity, quickness of movement (used also of the mind).

AGIO, [a'-jō, ā'-jō], *n.* the difference in value between paper money and actual coin, the difference between

two currencies in the same country or in different countries, the premium or discount to be paid in exchanging a currency of one country for that of another, the amount paid for money-changing. [It. *agio* discount].
AGIOTAGE, [aj'-ot-ij], *n.* business of money exchange.
AGIST, [a-jist'], *v.t.* (*leg.*) to take in cattle to pasture on one's land for a certain sum. [OFr. *agister*].
AGISTAGE, [a-jis'-tij], *n.* agistment.
AGISTER, see AGISTOR.
AGISTMENT, [a-jist'-ment], *n.* the pasturing of other men's cattle in the king's forest, or on one's own land; the price paid for such feeding; a tax. [OFr. *agistement*].
AGISTOR, AGISTER, [a-jist'-er], *n.* (*leg.*) a person pasturing cattle in return for a rent; (*hist.*) an official in charge of cattle so pastured in royal forests and domains. [AFr. *agistour*].
AGITABLE, [aj'-it-abl], *adj.* that may be agitated, disturbed, shaken, or discussed. [L. *agitabilis*].
AGITATE, [aj'-it-āt], *v.t.* to shake, to stir violently; (*fig.*) to disturb, to upset, to trouble, to disquiet, to excite (used of the mind and feelings); *v.i.* to cause public unrest, to arouse public attention in order to bring about something, to make efforts to cause something, to demand, often in a demonstrative fashion. [L. *agitatum*, *p.pt.* of *agitāre* to put into constant motion].
AGITATED, [aj'-it-ā'-tid], *adj.* aroused, upset, excited, emotionally aroused, in a state of mental disturbance or excitement due to fear.
AGITATION, [aj'-it-ā'-shun], *n.* disturbance, mental and emotional disquietude or excitement, perturbation, commotion, public excitement or unrest, a movement arousing public attention to gain some end, a demonstrative demand in favour of something.
AGITATIVE, [aj'-it-ā'-tiv], *adj.* displaying a tendency to agitate.
AGITATO, [aj'-it-ah'-tō], *adv.* (*mus.*) in a quick, excited, restless, disturbed manner. [It. *agitato*].
AGITATOR, [aj'-it-ā'-tor], *n.* one who produces an agitation, one who excites or causes a disturbance for party or private interests, one who is persistently stirring up public unrest by his actions and speeches; (*mech.*) a machine with a rotary beater or stirrer for breaking up wood-pulp, etc., in the preliminary stages of the manufacture of paper; †(*hist.*) a name by which the representatives of the different regiments in the English parliamentary army in 1647 were known.
AGLET, [ag'-let], *n.* the metal tag at the end of a lace; a metallic ornament worn on the dress; gold braid, cord, or pendant hanging down from the shoulder in certain military uniforms, a pendant, a flower in the shape of a pendant. [Fr. *aiguillette* point].

AGLET

AGLIMMER, [a-glim'-er], *adv.* in a glimmering way.
AGLOW, [a-glō'], *adj. and adv.* glowing; (*fig.*) aflame, eagerly excited.
AGLUTITION, [ag'-lōō-tish'-un], *n.* complete inability to swallow. [A (4) and L. *glutire* to swallow].
AGMATOLOGY, [ag'-mat-ol'-o-ji], *n.* the part of science that deals with fractures. [Gk. *agma* fracture and *logos* speech].
AGNAIL†, [ag'-nāl], *n.* a whitlow, bruised or torn skin below the finger-nail. [OE. *angnægl* corn on foot].
AGNAME, [ag'-nām], *n.* a nickname; a cognomen added to the name and surname, a third name. [L. *agnomen* in addition to the name].
AGNATE (1), [ag'-nāt], *n.* a male relation on the father's side. [L. *agnatus* a relation on the father's side].
AGNATE (2), [ag'-nāt], *adj.* related on the father's side by virtue of descent from a male ancestor.
AGNATIC, [ag-nat'-ik], *adj.* relating to descent by the male line.
AGNATICAL, [ag-nat'-ikl], *adj.* agnatic.
AGNATION, [ag-nā'-shun], *n.* (*leg.*) descent in a direct male line. [L. *agnatio*].
AGNEL, [an'-yel], *n.* an old French gold coin having a figure of the paschal lamb. [L. *agnus* a lamb].
AGNOMEN, [ag-nō'-men], *n.* a nickname, a name in addition to the surname; (*hist.*) formerly a fourth name occasionally adopted by certain Romans. [L. *agnomen*].
AGNOSTIC (1), [ag-nos'-tik], *n.* a person who recognizes knowledge only of material phenomena, and who consequently believes that there is nothing known about the absolute, the infinite, God, life hereafter, etc., and that therefore one cannot prove or disprove the existence of such phenomena. [Gk. *agnostos* not knowing].
AGNOSTIC (2), [ag-nos'-tik], *adj.* holding the belief of an agnostic, sceptical of non-material phenomena.
AGNOSTICISM, [ag-nos'-tis-izm], *n.* the doctrine and teaching of the agnostics.
AGNUS, [ag'-nus], *n.* a lamb; **A. castus**, a Mediterranean shrub of the order *Verbenaceæ* with white flowers, anciently thought to safeguard chastity; **A. Dei**, (*R.C.*) a prayer beginning with these words and sung before Communion, a consecrated medal or waxen disk stamped with the figure of a lamb supporting the cross and reputed to contain great virtues. [L. *agnus* a lamb].
AGO, [a-gō'], *adv.* past, previously, gone, in the past. [OE. *agan* gone away, past].
AGOG, [a-gog'], *adj. and adv.* in a state of eager excitement, expectancy or readiness. [Fr. *en gogues* mirthful].
AGOING, [a-gō'-ing], *adv.* in motion, moving.
AGONE (1), [ag-ōn'], *n.* a line which forms no angles; an agonic line. [A (4) and Gk. *gonia* angle].
AGONE† **(2)**, [a-gon'], *adv.* ago; past; since; previously. [OE. *agan*].
AGONIC, [ag-ō'-nik], *adj.* angle-less; pertaining to an agone; **a. line**, a line on the surface of the earth on which a magnetic needle points due north and south; hence, a line without magnetic declination.
AGONISM†, [ag'-on-izm], *n.* striving or contention for a prize. [Gk. *agonisma* a prize].
AGONIST†, [ag'-on-ist], *n.* a contender or competitor for a prize in a contest (usually athletic). [Gk. *agonistes* a contender in the games].
AGONISTIC, [ag'-on-is'-tik], *adj.* pertaining to athletic contests or to intellectual argument or discussion. [Gk. *agonistikos* relating to a combatant].
AGONISTICAL, [ag'-on-is'-tikl], *adj.* agonistic.
AGONISTICALLY, [ag'-on-is'-tik-a-li], *adv.* in an agonistic way.
AGONISTICS†, [ag'-on-is'-tiks], *n.* branch of gymnastics relating to the scientific study of athletics.
AGONIZE, [ag'-on-īz], *v.t. and i.* to be in extreme pain, to suffer great anguish, to be tortured; †to struggle, to strive, to put forth strenuous efforts; to torture, to afflict with extreme pain. [LL. *agonizare* from Gk. *agonizomai* I am in the death-agony].
AGONIZING, [ag'-on-iz-ing], *adj.* causing great suffering to the mind or body.
AGONIZINGLY, [ag'-on-iz'-ing-li], *adv.* in an agonizing way.
AGONOTHETE, [a-gō'-no-thēt], *n.* an official who presided over the Greek games. [Gk. *agon* contest and **thetes* a judge].
AGONOTHETIC, [a-gō'-no-thet'-ik], *adj.* relating to the duties of an agonothete.
AGONY, [ag'-on-i], *n.* intense physical pain or suffering, extreme anguish or mental suffering; the death pangs or last convulsive death struggles; the last sufferings in mind and body of Christ before His Crucifixion; †a severe struggle; **a. column**, column in a newspaper devoted to appeals for missing relatives and friends, personal messages (often in code), charitable appeals, etc. [Gk. *agonia* a struggle, anguish].
AGORA, [ag'-or-a], *n.* the market-place or assembly place of a Greek town. [Gk. *agora* an assembly].
AGORAPHOBIA, [ag'-or-a-fō'-bi-a], *n.* (*path.*) morbid fear of open places or of great crowds. [Gk. *agora* place of assembly and *phobia* fear].
AGOUTI, [a-gōō'-ti], *n.* a rodent found in South America and the West Indies, genus *Dasyprocta*, about the size of a rabbit, living on vegetables, particularly the sugar-cane, and having white edible flesh. [Span. *aguti* from native name].
AGRAFFE, [a-graf'], *n.* a kind of ornamental buckle or clasp often set with precious stones; (*med.*) an instrument for keeping together the edges of a wound in certain minor operations; (*milit.*) the coupling pin in artillery. [Fr. *agraffe*].
AGRAIL, [ag'-rāl], *n.* a rural railway with a narrow gauge. [Unkn.].
AGRAPHIA, [a-graf'-i-a], *n.* (*path.*) lack of ability to express oneself in writing, due to mental illness. [A (4) and Gk. *graphia* writing].
AGRARIAN (1), [a-grāer'-i-an], *n.* an agrarian law; a person who is in favour of equal division of landed

property amongst all the inhabitants of a country.

AGRARIAN (2), [a-grāer'-i-an], *adj.* pertaining to cultivated land, or landed property, or the apportioning of land; (*bot.*) growing in a state of wildness in the fields; **a. laws,** laws passed in former times in Rome relating to the division of public and conquered lands. [L. *agrārius* pertaining to land].

AGRARIANISM, [a-grāer'-i-an-izm], *n.* the principle of an equal division of lands, unrest or disorder caused by discontent with the existing system of land tenure.

AGRARIANIZE, [a-grāer'-i-an-īz], *v.t.* to share out or divide land equally; to infect with ideas of agrarianism.

AGREE, [a-grē'], *v.i.* to consent to, to accept, to be content with a proposition; to hold the same views as, to be of the same opinion as, (usually with *with*); to correspond with, to tally with, to conform with, to be the same as; to harmonize, to live in concord; to decide to, to resolve to; to come to terms; to have a healthy effect upon, to be suitable for one's constitution; to live in friendly relationship with; (*gram.*) to correspond in number, gender, case or person. [Fr. *agréer* to receive with favour].

AGREEABILITY, [a-grē'-ab-il'-i-ti], *n.* agreeableness; conformity; accordance; a quality that gives pleasure. [OFr. *agréableté*].

AGREEABLE, [a-grē'-abl], *adj.* pleasant, delightful, charming, ready to agree, favourable to, willing, conformable to; **I am a.,** I don't mind, I am ready to do what has been suggested. [Fr. *agréable*].

AGREEABLENESS, [a-grē'-abl-nes], *n.* condition or quality of being agreeable.

AGREEABLY, [a-grē'-ab-li], *adv.* pleasantly, charmingly, delightfully, in an agreeable manner; †in a manner conforming with, in accordance with.

AGREEMENT, [a-grē'-ment], *n.* correspondence of sympathies, sentiments, feelings, tastes, etc., state of having the same opinions as, holding the same views as, being of one mind with; a bargain, contract, understanding; (*leg.*) a written undertaking to perform a certain thing, between two or more persons, which though not a contract is subject to the law of contract; (*gram.*) correspondence of number, gender, case or person. [OFr. *agrément*].

AGRESTIC, [a-gres'-tik], *adj.* uncultured, rustic, uncouth., [L. *agrestis* a countryman].

AGRESTICAL, [a-gres'-tikl], *adj.* agrestic.

AGRICULTURAL, [ag'-ri-kul'-cher-al], *adj.* pertaining to agriculture; **a. show,** exhibition of farm produce, live-stock, implements, vehicles, etc.

AGRICULTURALIST, [ag'-ri-kul'-cher-al-ist], *n.* a farmer, one who obtains his living by, or who has made a special study of, agriculture.

AGRICULTURE, [ag'-ri-kul-cher], *n.* the art or practice of cultivating the ground, generally with a plough and over certain wide areas, for the purpose of raising crops, and including the preparation of the soil, the sowing of seed, the gathering of crops and the raising of live-stock; the theory and practice of farming. [L. *agricultura* field cultivation].

AGRICULTURIST, [ag'-ri-kul'-cher-ist], *n.* an agriculturalist.

AGRIMONY, [ag'-ri-mun'-i], *n.* (*bot.*) a genus of plants of the order *Rosaceae* found in temperate countries, one species of which, the *Agrimonia eupatoria*, possesses medicinal properties and provides a yellow dye. [L. *agrimonia* from Gk. *argemone*].

AGRIMOTOR, [ag'-ri-mō'-ter], *n.* a motor tractor used for certain agricultural processes formerly requiring a number of men, animals and implements. [L. *ager* land and MOTOR].

AGRIN, [a-grin'], *adv.* grinning, smiling broadly.

AGRIOLOGIST, [ag'-ri-ol'-oj-ist], *n.* one who studies agriology.

AGRIOLOGY, [ag'-ri-ol'-o-ji], *n.* the comparative study of man in his primitive condition or state. [Gk. *agrios* savage and *logos* speech].

AGROM, [ag'-rom], *n.* a disease frequently occurring in Bengal and other parts of the East Indies, in which the tongue chaps and cleaves, becomes rough, and is sometimes covered with white spots. [Gujerati *agrun* ulceration of the tongue].

AGRONOMIC, [ag'-ron-om'-ik], *adj.* pertaining to agronomics or agronomy.

AGRONOMICAL, [ag'-ron-om'-ikl], *adj.* agronomic.

AGRONOMICS, [ag'-ron-om'-iks], *n.* the science of the management and allotment of the land together with the theory and practice of production of crops.

AGRONOMIST, [ag-ron'-om-ist], *n.* one who studies agronomics, or a person practising agronomy.

AGRONOMY, [ag-ron'-o-mi], *n.* the study of the management of the land and the scientific cultivation of crops. [Gk. *agronomos* rural].

AGROSTOGRAPHY, [ag'-ros-tog'-raf-i], *n.* the science of the description of the species of grasses. [Gk. *agrostis* grass and *graphia* writing].

AGROSTOLOGY, [ag'-ros-tol'-o-ji], *n.* that branch of botany which treats of the grasses. [Gk. *agrostis* grass and *logos* speech].

AGROUND, [a-grownd'], *adv.* on the ground; (*naut.*) resting on the bottom in shallow water or a sand-bank, or wedged between rocks so that the ship is no longer floating in water and can no longer proceed, stranded.

AGUA, [ah'-gwa], *n.* the South American toad, *Bufo agua*, imported into Jamaica to kill off the rats.

AGUARDIENTE, [ah'-gwah-di-en'-ti], *n.* Spanish brandy of inferior quality. [Span. *agua* water and *ardiente* fiery].

AGUE, [ā'-gew], *n.* a kind of recurring malarial fever, characterized by fits of shivering; †a shivering fit or violent fever. [OFr. *ague* from L. (*febris*) *acuta* acute fever].

AGUE-CAKE, [ā'-gew-kāk'], *n.* a tumour brought on by a hardening of the spleen, frequently a concomitant of ague.

AGUED, [ā'-gewd], *adj.* having a fit of ague; shivering, suffering from ague.

AGUE-SPELL, [ā'-gew-spel'], *n.* a charm used to cure or prevent ague.

AGUE-TREE†, [ā'-gew-trē'], *n.* old name for the sassafras tree on account of its use as a remedy for fever.

AGUISH, [ā'-gew-ish], *adj.* characterized by shivering like an ague, causing an ague, prone to shivering fits and ague.

AGUISHNESS, [ā'-gew-ish-nes], *n.* the condition of being aguish.

AGYNOUS, [aj'-in-us], *adj.* (*bot.*) lacking female organs; male. [A (4) and Gk. *gune* a woman].

AH, [ah], *int.* an exclamation used to convey almost any emotion according to the manner of utterance. [OFr. *a*].

AHA, [a-hah, ah-hah'], *int.* an exclamation expressing triumph, surprise, contempt, mockery, etc., according to the way in which it is uttered.

AHEAD, [a-hed'], *adv.* further in advance, in front; forward; before (often with *of*); **to go a.,** (*coll.*) to start, begin; to keep on, continue.

AHEAP, [a-hēp'], *adv.* massed together in a heap, piled up.

AHEM, [a-hem'], *int.* an exclamation or interjection used to call attention, indicate embarrassment at an unpleasant subject, gain time in speaking, etc.

AHOY, [a-hoi'], *int.* (*naut.*) a sea term, used in hailing or attracting the attention.

AHRIMAN, [ah'-rim-an], *n.* the personification or source of all evil, the lord of darkness, death and the evil spirits according to the teaching of Zoroaster. [Pers. *Ahriman*].

AHULL, [a-hul'], *adv.* (*naut.*) applied to a ship with all sails furled, her helm lashed on the lee side on account of a storm, and lying with her side to wind and sea and somewhat inclined in the direction of the wind.

AI, [ah'-ē], *n.* the three-toed sloth native to South America, an animal destitute of front teeth. [Echoic].

AICH'S-METAL, [ā'-chiz-metl'], *n.* an alloy of copper, zinc and iron. [Johann *Aich*, the inventor of it].

AID (1), [ād], *n.* assistance, help, succour; a person who gives assistance, a means of help; (*hist.*) a grant or subsidy made to the king for a special purpose, an exchequer loan; a monetary tribute payable to a lord by a vassal; (*leg.*) legal help in the defence of an action claimed by a defendant; (*Fr. hist.*) customs dues; **first a.,** medical assistance rendered on the spot to a sick or injured person, often before the arrival of a doctor. [AID (2)].

AID (2), [ād], *v.t.* to help, to succour, to relieve, to give assistance to. [L. *adjutare* to help].

AIDE-DE-CAMP, (*pl.* **aides-de-camp**), [ād'-de-kah(ng)'], *n.* (*milit.*) an officer acting as secretary or agent to a king or general, and assisting him in the carrying out of his duties; formerly an officer attached to a general to convey his orders to the various divisions on the field of battle. [Fr. *aide-de-camp* assistant in the field].

AIDE-MEMOIRE, [ād'-mem'-wahr], *n.* an official intimation or declaration of policy or attitude upon a point in question sent by one government or state to another. [Fr. *aide memoire*].

AIDLESS, [ād'-les], *adv.* deprived of aid; unsupported.

AIGLET†, [āg'-let], *n.* (*her.*) a young eagle. [Fr. *aigle* an eagle].

AIGRE†, see EAGRE.

AIGREMORE, [āgr'-maw(r)], *n.* charcoal in a state of preparation for mixing with the other constituents of gunpowder. [Fr. *aigremore*].

AIGRET, AIGRETTE, [ā-gret'], *n.* the egret, the plume of an egret, the feathery plume attached to the seeds of several plants such as the thistle, etc., a head-dress in the form of a plume of feathers, or a spray of flowers or jewels, rays of light visible from the edge of the moon during a solar eclipse. [Fr. *aigrette*].

AIGRET

AIGUILLE, [ā-gwē'], *n.* one of the needle-like points of certain rocks and mountain peaks, or of sharp-pointed jagged ends of masses of ice. [Fr. *aiguille* needle].

AIGUILLETTE, AIGULET, [ā'-gwē-yet', ā'-gew-let], *n.* an aglet. [Fr. *aiguillette*, *dim.* of *aiguille* needle].

AIL, [āl], *v.t.* to trouble with pain or discomfort either physically or mentally, to be the matter with, to afflict; *v.i.* to be ill, to be in trouble, to be in a state of continued ill-health. [OE. *eglan* to molest, to trouble].

AILANTHUS, [ā-lan'-thus], *n.* (*bot.*) a tree of the order *Simarubaceae*, originally a native of China, on whose leaves a species of silkworm feeds and which produces a hard yellowy wood able to be polished well. [Native *aylanto* tree of the gods].

AILE, see AISLE.

AILERON, [āl'-er-on], *n.* (*arch.*) a side wall used to conceal a church aisle or a half-gable; (*aeron.*) a hinged flap on the outer extremities of the wings of an aeroplane by which lateral balance may be maintained, and which when depressed increases wind resistance of the wing and so causes it to rise. [Fr. *aileron* little wing].

AILERON

AILETTE, [āl-et'], *n.* a wing-shaped steel shoulder-plate affording protection to the shoulders in chain armour; an epaulet. [Fr. *ailette* little wing].

AILMENT, [āl'-ment], *n.* disease, indisposition, illness, slight affliction.

AIM (1), [ām], *n.* the pointing or levelling of a weapon, or the directing of a missile or blow towards an object to be hit; the estimation of direction, elevation, etc., necessary in order to hit an object; purpose, object, design, goal, end to be sought after. [AIM (2)].

AIM (2), [ām], *v.t.* *and i.* to train a weapon upon, to direct a blow or missile towards an object; to establish a goal or end to be striven after, to try to achieve some purpose or object; (*fig.*) to make a remark intended to affect some particular person; to direct, to point, to level at; to take aim; **to a. high**, to be ambitious. [ME. *aimen* to estimate, from OFr. *esmer*].

AIMLESS, [ām'-les], *adj.* without aim, fixed direction, intention, object of attainment, or plan of action.

AIMLESSLY, [ām'-les-li], *adv.* in an aimless fashion, haphazardly, without any fixed object, plan or purpose.

AIMLESSNESS, [ām'-les-nes], *n.* the state or quality of being aimless.

AIN'T, [ānt], (*coll.*) corruption of "are not" and "am not."

AIR (1), [āer], *n.* the gaseous substance forming the atmosphere which envelops the earth, consisting largely of oxygen and nitrogen, the state of the atmosphere at a particular time or place; (*fig.*) the space immediately above the earth, the sky, a light breeze or current of air; outward appearance, manner, look, mien, demeanour, a particular expression on a person's countenance, an affected manner, an assumed bearing or look implying superiority (generally in the *pl.*); a continuous musical melody, a composition for a solo voice or instrument with other voices or instruments providing an accompaniment, the tune, the principal melody part in a work for a number of instruments or voices, the principal vocal part providing the tune, usually the soprano part in a harmonious composition; **open-a.**, held outside a building, out of doors; **in the a.**, current, afloat (of rumours); shadowy, vague, unreal, unsettled or undecided upon (of projects); **castles in the a.**, fanciful dreams, unpractical, imaginary schemes or projects; **fresh a.**, non-vitiated air containing its full complement of oxygen; **on the a.**, broadcast by wireless; **over the a.**, by means of wireless; **hot a.**, boasting, tending to exaggeration; **to tread upon a.**, to be in a state of continued delight and exhilaration; **to beat the a.**, expend one's energy needlessly in futile endeavour; **to take a.**, to become known or current; **to give a person the a.** (*U.S. slang*) to shun, avoid the company of, to dismiss. [Fr. from Gk. *aer* air].

AIR (2), [āer], *v.t.* *and i.* to ventilate, to warm and dry before a fire, radiator, etc., to expose to the air in order to freshen, purify, etc.; (*fig.*) to express publicly, to display in a manner calculated to impress; to become ventilated, warmed and dried, or freshened.

AIR-BALLOON, [āer'-ba-lōōn'], *n.* a balloon; an inflated toy-balloon filled with air or gas.

AIR-BASE, [āer'-bās'], *n.* (*milit.*) an aerodrome or place used as a base of operations by military or naval aircraft.

AIR-BATH, [āer'-bahth'], *n.* a contrivance for drying chemical substances, exposure of the body to the air as a form of treatment.

AIR-BED, [āer'-bed'], *n.* an air-tight mattress inflated by air and used by the sick and invalids.

AIR-BLADDER, [āer'-blad'-er], *n.* a small membraneous cavity or sac containing air, the swimming-bladder of a fish, enabling the fish to rise or sink at will in the water.

AIR-BONE, [āer'-bōn], *n.* (*ornith.*) a hollow bone which contains air.

AIRBORNE, [āer'-baw(r)n], *adj.* carried by aircraft; (of troops) carried by air to the battle zone and dropped by parachute.

AIR-BRAKE, [āer'-brāk'], *n.* a brake worked by compression of air or by the action of air on a vacuum.

AIR-BRICK, [āer'-brik'], *n.* a brick containing holes used for ventilating purposes.

AIR-BUMP, [āer'-bump'], *n.* (*aeron.*) a sudden, uncontrolled movement of an aircraft caused by a change in the density of the air.

AIR-CASING, [āer'-kās'-ing], *n.* iron casing filled with air, enclosing a heated pipe and preventing conduction of heat from the pipe.

AIRCELLS, [āer'-selz'], *n.*(*pl.*) (*bot. and anat.*) air cavities or cells filled with air in plants, a cavity in the body containing air.

AIR-CHAMBER, [āer'-chām'-ber] *n.* a chamber enclosing air, as in a cushion or rubber tyre, for buoyancy and shock-absorption; a cavity in a hydraulic machine the air from which on the entrance of water acts as an equalizing force upon the flow of the water.

AIR-CHIEF-MARSHAL, [āer'-chēf'-mah'-shal], *n.* the second highest rank in the Royal Air Force, corresponding to an admiral in the Navy, or a general in the Army.

AIR-COCK, [āer'-kok'], *n.* a kind of valve or tap which allows air to escape from a pipe or engine.

AIR-COMMODORE, [āer'-kom'-od-aw(r)], *n.* a rank in the Royal Air Force corresponding to commodore in the Navy.

AIR-CONDENSER, [āer'-kon-dens'-er], *n.* an apparatus used to condense air; (*elect.*) a condenser in which the air acts as an insulator between the plates.

AIR-CONDITIONER, [āer'-kon-dish'-un-er], *n.* a plant used to maintain a constant supply of clean, warm fresh air in a building.

AIR-COOLING, [āer'-kōōl'-ing], *n.* a system of cooling or lessening heat in a motor engine by radiators through which currents of air pass.

AIRCOURSE, [āer'-kaws'], *n.* an airway.

AIRCRAFT, [āer'-krahft'], *n.* a flying machine or flying machines in general.

AIRCRAFT-CARRIER, [āer'-krahft-ka'-ri-er], *n.* a warship used for carrying aircraft, and having specially constructed decks where aircraft may land or take off.

AIRCRAFTMAN, [āer'-krahft-man], *n.* the lowest rank in the Royal Air Force. [AIRCRAFT and MAN].

AIR-CUSHION, [āer'-kōōsh'-un], *n.* a cushion that is blown up with air.

AIR-DRAIN, [āer'-drān'], *n.* a cavity round the external walls of a building for the purpose of keeping off the earth and preventing dampness.

AIR-DRAWN, [āer'-drawn'], *adj.* drawn in air; imaginary, ethereal.

AIRE, [āer], *n.* a freeman in ancient Ireland whose status was reckoned by his material possessions. [Unkn.].

AIREDALE, [āer'-dāl], *n.* the largest kind of terrier, originally bred for otter-hunting in the river Aire. [A district in the West Riding of Yorkshire].

AIR-ENGINE, [āer'-en'-jin], *n.* an engine worked by heated air which is either expanded or compressed.

AIRER, [āer'-er], *n.* one who airs, a framework on which clothes are hung in order to be aired.

AIR-EXHAUSTER, [āer'-egz-aws'-ter], *n.* an apparatus for draining off air.

AIRFIELD, [āer'-fēld], *n.* a flat open space where aircraft can land and take off.

AIR-FILTER, [āer'-fil'-ter], *n.* an apparatus for purifying air, an instrument for measuring impurities in air; (*motoring*) a device for removing grit and dust from air before it enters the carburettor of a motor-engine.

AIR-FLUE, [āer'-flōō'], *n.* a flue which distributes heated air in a building.

AIR-FORCE, [āer'-faws'], *n.* branch of the armed forces which is concerned with attack or defence from the air.

AIR-FOUNTAIN, [āer'-fownt'-en], *n.* an apparatus by which compressed air produces a jet of water.

AIR-FUNNEL, [āer'-funl], *n.* device for ventilating the hold of a ship.

AIR-FURNACE, [āer'-fur'-nas], *n.* a furnace in which the air is heated; a furnace other than a blast-furnace.

AIR-GAP, [āer'-gap'], *n.* (*elect.*) an air-filled gap left in an iron magnetic circuit or in an electric circuit.

AIR-GAS, [āer'-gas'], *n.* a gas used for heating and lighting purposes and consisting of dry air impregnated with vapour from hydrocarbons so that it becomes combustible.

AIRGRAPH, [āer'-graf'], *n.* (*prot.*) a letter photographed on a small scale for transmission by air.

AIR-GUN, [āer'-gun], *n.* a gun which fires bullets, etc., by means of compressed air.

AIR-HOLE, [āer'-hōl], *n.* an opening for the passage of air, a hole in the ice of a frozen sea, river, lake, etc., artificially made or formed by the rapid current, a hole in cast metal caused by bubbles of air escaping from the metal in its molten state.

AIRILY, [āer'-i-li], *adv.* in an airy manner, lightly, joyously, flippantly.

AIRINESS, [āer'-in-es], *n.* the state of being airy, lightness, frivolity, jollity.

AIRING, [āer'-ing], *n.* exposure to the air, or a fire, to warm or dry or ventilate; exercise in the open air.

AIR-INTAKE, [āer'-in'-tāk], *n.* a passage admitting air in a coal-mine; an aperture which allows air to enter an internal-combustion engine.

AIR-JACKET, [āer'-jak'-et], *n.* a swimming jacket or costume inflated with air to keep a person afloat in water; a covering for pipes or boilers filled with air to diminish or prevent loss of heat by radiation.

AIRLESS, [āer'-les], *n.* not well ventilated, not freely communicating with the open air, not open to a free current of air.

AIR-LINE, [āer'-līn'], *n.* (*aeron.*) a service of aeroplanes plying for hire; (*teleph.*) a line above the ground level, a straight line in the air between two points.

AIR-LINER, [āer'-līn'-er], *n.* a large passenger-aeroplane.

AIR-LOCK, [āer'-lok'], *n.* the intervening air-tight chamber between the outer air and the compressed air-chamber in a pneumatic or submarine caisson; an impediment or obstruction in the flow of air or liquid in a pipe caused by the presence of a bubble of air in the pipe.

AIR-MACHINE, [āer'-ma-shēn'], *n.* (*mining*) machine used for ventilation purposes.

AIR-MAIL, [āer'-māl'], *n.* mails carried by aircraft in conjunction with other forms of transport.

AIRMAN, [āer'-man], *n.* an aviator; one who navigates aircraft.

AIR-MARSHAL, [āer'-mah'-shal], *n.* the third highest rank in the Royal Air Force, corresponding to lieutenant-general in the Army and vice-admiral in the Navy.

AIR-PASSAGE, [āer'-pas'-ij], *n.* (*bot.*) extended air space between cells of certain plants.

AIRPLANE, [āer'-plān'], *n.* an aeroplane (originally U.S., now also a common form used in English journalism).

AIR-PLANT, [āer'-plahnt'], *n.* a non-parasitic plant which grows on another plant but obtains its nourishment and moisture from the air.

AIRPOCKET, [āer'-pok'-it], *n.* a localized atmospheric condition caused by irregular air currents and affecting an aeroplane so that it drops suddenly as into a cavity while flying.

AIRPOISE, [āer'-poiz'], *n.* an instrument used to measure the weight of air.

AIRPORT, [āer'-pawt'], *n.* an aerodrome provided with accommodation for customs and immigration officials, and used as a landing-place for aeroplanes coming from abroad.

AIRPUMP, [āer'-pump'], *n.* an apparatus for pumping air or gas into or out of a vessel; (*motoring*) a pressure pump which forces petrol to the carburettor.

AIR-RAID (1), [āer'-rād'], *n.* an attack by aircraft dropping bombs.

AIR-RAID (2), [āer'-rād], *adj.* of, or concerned with, air-raids or defence against them of a passive nature.

AIR-SACS, [āer'-saks'], *n.*(*pl.*) (*ornith.*) air receptacles, or vesicles, in the hollow bones and other cavities of birds.

AIR-SCOOP, [āer'-skōōp'], *n.* (*aeron.*) a projecting cowl which helps to keep up air pressure in the envelope of an airship.

AIRSCREW, [āer'-skrōō'], *n.* the propeller on an aircraft.

AIRSHAFT, [āer'-shahft], *n.* a shaft for ventilation purposes.

AIRSHED, [āer'-shed], *n.* a building for storing aircraft; a hangar.

AIRSHIP, [āer'-ship], *n.* an aircraft of the lighter-than-air type sustained in the air by gas, able to be steered, and propelled by means of an engine.

AIR-SICKNESS, [āer'-sik'-nes], *n.* sickness caused by the motion of aircraft in flight.

AIR-SILENCER, [āer'-sī'-lens-er], *n.* a device which reduces the noise made by air as it passes through the carburettor intake of a motor-vehicle.

AIRSPACE, [āer'-spās], *n.* the amount of space containing air in a room or building, intervening space between two parallel walls, a cavity in a bird's body containing air.

AIR-STOVE, [āer'-stōv], *n.* a stove from which heated air escapes into a room.

AIRSTREAM, [āer'-strēm], *n.* (*aeron.*) a current of air cooling an aero-engine.

AIRT†, [āert], *n.* a compass direction; a point of the compass. [Gael. *aird*, a quarter of the compass].

AIR-THERMOMETER, [āer'-thur-mom'-it-er], *n.* an instrument for measuring temperature by the expansion or contraction of air.

AIR-THREADS, [āer'-thredz], *n.*(*pl.*) light gauze-like material, fine threads of cobweb floating in the air or attached to bushes, etc., gossamer.

AIRTIGHT, [āer'-tīt'], *adj.* not admitting air.

AIRTRAP, [āer'-trap], *n.* a contrivance for preventing the escape of foul air from drains.

AIR-TRUCK, [āer'-truk], *n.* (*aeron.*) an aeroplane specially constructed for carrying freights.

AIRTRUNK, [āer'-trungk], *n.* an apparatus used for ventilation.

AIR-VESSEL, [āer'-ves'-el], *n.* (*zool.*) a vessel which contains air, a breathing tube in insects, a spiral vessel on the leaves of plants; (*hydraulics*) an air-chamber.

AIR-VICE-MARSHAL, [āer'-vīs'-mah'-shal], *n.* a rank in the Royal Air Force corresponding to major-general in the Army and rear-admiral in the Navy.

AIRWAY, [āer'-wā], *n.* ventilation shaft or passage in a mine; air route.

AIR WHEEL, [āer'-wēl], *n.* a kind of automobile wheel without spokes or rim, fastened directly on the hub.

AIRWORTHY, [āer'-wur'-THi], *adj.* in a fit state for flying, applied to machines.

AIRY (1), [āer'-i], *adj.* resembling or belonging to the air, open to a current of air, well-ventilated, unsubstantial, unreal, vague, unpractical, light, sprightly, gay, light of heart, vain, flippant, jaunty.

AIRY (2), see AERIE.

AISLE, AILE, [īl], *n.* (*arch.*) one of the lateral divisions of a church, running lengthwise, and separated from the central portion or nave by pillars or piers, a passage between two blocks of pews in a church. [L. *ala* wing].

AISLED, [īld], *adj.* provided with aisles.

AIT, [āt], *n.* a small island situated in a river or lake; an eyot. [OE. *igeoth* a little island].

AITCH-BONE, [āch'-bōn'], *n.* the buttock bone, the beef cut from over this bone. [OFr. *nache* buttock and BONE].

AJAR, [a-jah(r)'], *adv.* slightly open, as of a door or lid. [OE. *on cierre* on the turn].

AJOG, [a-jog'], *adv.* proceeding in a leisurely and steady manner.

AJUTAGE, see ADJUTAGE.

AKEE, [a-kē'], *n.* the tropical fruit-tree of Africa, *Blighea sapida.* [Native].

AKER-STAFF, ACRE-STAFF, [ā'-ker-stahf'], *n.* (*agr.*) an instrument for cleaning earth, soil, etc., from the blade of a plough.

AKIMBO, [a-kim'-bō], *adv.* only in the phrase **arms a.**, with hands on hips and elbows bent outwards. [ME. *in kene bowe* in a sharp curve].

AKIN, [a-kin'], *adj.* related, of similar kin, allied to, resembling in nature, connected with.

AL, [al], the article in the Arabic language. [Arab. *al* the].

ALA, [ā'-la], *n.* (*bot.*) the wing or side petal of a papilionaceous blossom, or membrane attached to a seed or stalk; (*anat.*) the upper outer parts of the external ear, the lateral cartilages of the nose; (*arch.*) a wing or side apartment of a Roman house. [L. *ala* wing].

ALABANDITES, [al'-ab-an'-dīt'-ēz], *n.* (*min.*) a black mineral being a sulphate of manganese, and found in Mexico, Transylvania, etc. [*Alabanda*, a town in Mexico].

ALABASTER (1), [al'-a-bas'-ter], *n.* a granular variety of gypsum, usually of a pure white colour and very soft, anciently used to manufacture ointment boxes, etc., now used for vases, statuettes and other ornamental articles. [Gk. *alabastros* from *Alabastron*, an Egyptian town].

ALABASTER (2), [al'-a-bas'-ter], *adj.* made of alabaster, resembling alabaster. [ALABASTER (1)].

ALABASTRIAN, [al'-a-bas'-tri-an], *adj.* relating to, or like, alabaster.

ALABASTRINE, [al'-a-bas'-trīn], *adj.* alabastrian.

ALABASTRITE, [al'-a-bas'-trīt], *n.* (*archæ.*) a vase, or other vessel, for containing perfumes, usually made of alabaster.

ALABASTRUM, [al'-a-bas'-trum], *n.* a flower-bud. [ALABASTER].

ALACK, [a-lak'], *int.* expression of sorrow, dismay, regret, remorse, etc. [Unkn.].

ALACK-A-DAY, [a-lak'-a-dā'], *int.* alas the day! an expression of sorrow.

ALACRIOUS, [al-ak'-ri-us], *adj.* active, brisk, eager, ready, lively. [L. *alacris* brisk].

ALACRITY, [al-ak'-rit-i], *n.* willing and eager quickness and readiness, brisk promptitude. [L. *alacritas* ardour].

ALADDINISTS, [al-ad'-in-ists], *n.*(*pl.*) Moslem freethinkers. [*Ala Eddin*, pinnacle of religion, a famous religious thinker in the days of Bajazet II].

ALALIA, [al-ā'-li-a], *n.* (*path.*) loss of speech. [Gk. *alalia* from *alalos* speechless].

ALAMEDA, [a'-lam-ā'-da], *n.* a wide promenade lined with trees, so called because in the south-western states of America these promenades are usually planted with *alamos* or cottonwood trees. [Span. *alameda*].

ALAMODE (1), [a'-la-mōd'], *n.* a thin glossy black silk used for hoods and scarves. [ALAMODE (2)].

ALAMODE (2), [a'-la-mōd'], *adj.* in accordance with the fashion, fashionable; **a. beef**, scraps of meat stewed with vegetables, particularly haricot beans. [Fr. *à la mode* in the fashion].

ALAN(T)†, [al-an(t)'], *n.* (*her.*) a mastiff dog having short ears. [OFr. *alan alant* a large hound for hunting].

ALANTIN, [al-ant'-in], *n.* a starch manufactured from the elecampane. [Germ. *alant* the elecampane].

ALAR, [ā'-ler], *adj.* pertaining to or having wings, shaped like wings, resembling wings; (*anat.*) connected with the armpit. [L. *alares* from *ala* a wing].

ALARM (1), [al-ahm'], *n.* a signal of a surprise attack or of impending danger, a call to arms, a warning of danger usually sounded on a bell; a bell or apparatus used to give the signal of sudden danger; (*fig.*) a warning; a state of sudden terror, excitement or apprehension aroused by a threat of unexpected danger, catastrophe, etc.; (*fencing*) a stamp on the ground with the advanced foot. [It. *all'arme* to arms].

ALARM (2), [al-ahm'], *v.t.* to arouse to a feeling of danger, to disturb with terror, to excite with sudden fear, to perturb, to frighten, to make a person uneasy and apprehensive; (*milit.*) to call to arms, to give a signal of danger. [ALARM (1)].

ALARM-BELL, [al-ahm'-bel'], *n.* a bell rung to sound an alarm.

ALARM-CLOCK, [al-ahm'-klok'], *n.* a clock provided with an alarm-bell which can be set to be rung by clockwork mechanism at a given time and used to rouse sleepers.

ALARM-GAUGE, [al-ahm'-gāj'], *n.* an appliance fastened to a steam engine to indicate a state of excessive steam pressure or dangerous deficiency of water in a boiler.

ALARM-GUN, [al-ahm'-gun'], *n.* gun fired to signal an enemy's approach.

ALARMING, [al-ahm'-ing], *adj.* perturbing, exciting alarm or apprehension, disturbing, frightening.

ALARMINGLY, [al-ahm'-ing-li], *adv.* in an alarming way.

ALARMIST (1), [al-ahm'-ist], *n.* one who is always arousing alarm, one who is always starting scares or attempting to cause panic, one who is always apprehensive of real or imaginary danger.

ALARMIST (2), [al-ahm'-ist], *adj.* of a nature to cause alarm.

ALARM-POST, [al-ahm'-pōst'], *n.* (*milit.*) a station appointed as a meeting place in case of alarm given of the unexpected approach of an enemy.

ALARM-WATCH, [al-ahm'-woch'], *n.* a watch having an alarm like an alarm-clock.

ALARUM, [al-ah'-rum], *n.* (*poet.*) alarm; the ringing mechanism on an alarm-clock, the ringing sound made by the bell on an alarm-clock. [*Var.* of ALARM].

ALARY, [ā'-lar-i], *adj.* (*bot. and anat.*) wing-shaped.

ALAS, [a-lahs', a-las'], *int.* an exclamation expressing sorrow, grief, pity, concern, or apprehension of evil. [OFr. *a las* Oh wretched one].

ALATE, [ā'-lāt], *adj.* provided with wings or wing-like appendages. [L. *alatus* furnished with wings].

ALATED, [ā-lā'-tid], *adj.* alate, wing-shaped.

ALB, [alb], *n.* a long robe of white linen reaching to the ground and bound round the waist with a girdle, worn by priests officiating at the celebration of Mass. [L. *alba* white].

ALB

ALBACORE, ALBICORE, [al'-bak-aw(r)'], *n.* a kind of tunny-fish; a species of *Thynnus.* [Arab. *al* the and *bukr* heifer, pig].

ALBATA, [al-bah'-ta], *n.* a mixture of nickel, tin, zinc, and copper, used as a substitute for silver. [L. *albata* fem. of *albatus* clothed in white].

ALBATROSS, [al'-bat-ros'], *n.* the largest known sea-bird, greyish-brown in its upper part and having a white belly, found in the southern seas and the Behring Straits, having a harsh cry and feeding voraciously on fish and other marine animals; a type of German aeroplane employed for scouting purposes in the War of 1914-18. [~Port. *alcatraz* cormorant].

ALBEIT, [awl-bē'-it], *conj.* (*poet.*) although, notwithstanding. [*Al*(though) *it be* (that)].

ALBERIA, [al-bēer'-i-a], *n.* (*her.*) a shield bearing no arms. [L. *albus* white].

ALBERT, [al'-bert], *n.* a kind of watch-chain fastened through a waistcoat buttonhole and held there by a small cross-piece. [*Albert*, Prince Consort].

ALBESCENCE, [al-bes'-ents], *n.* the process of growing white. [L. *albescens*, *pres.pt.* of *albescere* to become white].

ALBESCENT, [al-bes'-ent], *adj.* becoming white, or white-coloured.

ALBICORE, see ALBACORE.

ALBIGENSES, [al'-bi-jen'-sēz], *n.* a sect of religious reformers flourishing in the twelfth century who believed that all flesh or material substance is evil, and who consequently were in favour of extinction of bodily life particularly by suicide through starvation, and who were persecuted by the Roman Catholics. [*Albe* on the banks of a tributary of the Garonne where they chiefly flourished].

ALBINISM, [al'-bin-izm], *n.* the state or condition of being an albino; leucopathy.

ALBINO, [al-bē'-nō], *n.* a person or animal suffering from a hereditary disease whereby the dark colouring matter or pigment is absent from the skin, hair and eyes, having thus a pale skin, white hair and pink eyes with red pupils, unable to bear strong light; sometimes applied also to plants whose leaves suffer from lack of green colouring-matter. [Span. *albino* whitish from L. *albus* white].

ALBINOTIC, [al'-bin-ot'-ik], *adj.* pertaining to albinism; affected with leucopathy.

ALBION, [al'-bi-on], *n.* ancient and now poetic name for Great Britain; **a. metal**, a compound of tin and lead formed by combining the two metals under great pressure, and distinct from the alloy formed by fusion and known as pewter, used in the manufacture of toys, cheap jewellery, ornamental articles, etc. [Celt. *albainn*].

ALBITE, [al'-bīt], *n.* (*min.*) a kind of felspar usually white or whitish in colour, also known as soda-felspar, and consisting of a silicate of aluminium and sodium. [~L. *albus* white].

ALBUGINEA, [al'-bew-jin'-ē-a], *n.* (*anat.*) fibrous white substance covering the eye, testicle, and certain other organs.

ALBUGINEOUS, [al'-bew-jin'-ē-us], *adj.* relating to, or resembling the white of the eye or of an egg. [L. *albugineus*].

ALBUGO, [al-bew'-gō], *n.* an eye-disease in which a white opaque spot forms in the cornea and affects vision. [L. *albugo* a disease of the eye, whiteness].

ALBUM, [al'-bum], *n.* a book with blank leaves on which may be affixed autographs, literary extracts, photographs, stamps, cigarette-cards, newspaper cuttings, etc., a scrap-book; (*Rom. antiq.*) a white board or tablet on which were inscribed edicts, public notices, lists of public officials and transactions, etc.; (*leg.*) rent paid in silver. [L. *album* a white tablet for inscriptions].

ALBUMEN, ALBUMIN, [al'-bew-min], *n.* a type of protein compound, a complicated substance forming a chemical constituent of most organic matter including the white of an egg, the serum of blood, the juice of flesh, lymph, vegetable juice, etc., coagulable by various salts and used as a clarifier for syrupy liquors, in photography, cookery, etc., and also as an antidote to certain corrosive poisons; (*bot.*) farinaceous matter enclosing the embryo such as the hard white edible part of the coconut, the flour of cereals, etc. [L. *albumen* from *albus* white].

ALBUMENIZE, [al-bew'-min-īz], *v.t.* to impregnate with albumen, to treat or coat with a solution of albumen.

ALBUMIN, see ALBUMEN.

ALBUMINATE, [al-bew'-min-āt], *n.* a compound of albumen with certain bases.

ALBUMINOID (1), [al-bew'-min-oid], *n.* one of the proteids forming the chief part of organic matter. [ALBUMEN and Gk. *oeides* like].

ALBUMINOID (2), [al-bew'-min-oid], *adj.* resembling albumen. [ALBUMINOID (1)].

ALBUMINOSE (1), [al-bew'-min-ōs], *n.* a substance obtained from albumen by the action of dilute acid upon pepsin. [ALBUMINOSE (2)].

ALBUMINOSE (2), [al-bew'-min-ōs], *adj.* albuminous. [MdL. *albuminosus*].

ALBUMINOSIS, [al-bew'-min-ō'-sis], *n.* (*path.*) a morbid condition in which too much albumen is in the blood. [ALBUMEN and Gk. *osis* state, condition].

ALBUMINOUS, [al-bew'-min-us], *adj.* possessing the properties of albumen. [L. *albuminosus*].

ALBUMINURIA, [al-bew'-min-yōō'-ri-a], *n.* a condition in which albumen is present in the urine, usually a sign of a disease or disorder in the kidneys. [ALBUMEN and Gk. *ouria* urine].

ALBURNOUS, [al-burn'-us], *adj.* relating to or consisting of alburnum.

ALBURNUM, [al-burn'-um], *n.* (*bot.*) the soft white part of trees found between the inner bark and the wood, sap-wood which eventually hardens and becomes like wood. [L. *alburnum* from *albus* white].

ALCA, [al'-ka], *n.* a group of sea-birds which includes the razorbill. [OIcel. *alka* an auk].

ALCAIC, [al-kā'-ik], *adj.* belonging to the Greek poet Alcaeus of Mitylene, pertaining to or written in the metre invented by Alcaeus. [The Gk. poet *Alcaeus* circa 600 B.C.].

ALCAICS, [al-kā'-iks], *n.(pl.)* verses written in a metre invented by Alcaeus.

ALCAYDE, ALCAIDE, [al-kād'], *n.* the governor of a fortress, a Spanish or Portuguese magistrate responsible for the administration of justice and control of the police. [Sp. from Arab. *al qaid* the leader].

ALCAZAR, [al'-kath-ah(r)'], *n.* a Moorish or Spanish royal palace, a fortress. [Arab. *al-qacr* the castle].

ALCEDO†, [al-sē'-dō], *n.* a genus of birds including the kingfishers. [L. *alcedo* kingfisher].

ALCHEMIC, [al-kem'-ik], *adj.* pertaining to alchemy. [MedL. *alchimicus*].

ALCHEMICALLY, [al-kem'-ik-a-li], *adv.* by alchemy.

ALCHEMIST [al'-kem-ist], *n.* one versed in alchemy, a student of alchemy, one who practises alchemy. [MedL. *alchymista*].

ALCHEMISTIC, [al'-kem-ist'-ik], *adj.* alchemistical.

ALCHEMISTICAL, [al'-kem-ist'-ikl], *adj.* practising or pertaining to alchemy.

ALCHEMIZE, (**alchemizes, alchemized, alchemizing**), [al'-kem-īz], *v.t.* to change, as by alchemy.

ALCHEMY, ALCHYMY, [al'-kem-i], *n.* the study which aimed to prolong human life indefinitely, to find the philosopher's stone which would change all base metals into gold, and to find a universal solvent or *menstruum universale*. [OFr. *alchemie*].

ALCLAD, [al'-klad], *n.* an alloy of aluminium used in building aeroplanes. [*Al* chemical symbol for ALUMINIUM and (IRON)CLAD].

ALCOHOL, [al'-kō-hol'], *n.* an intoxicating product of fermentation from the juice of the grape and other substances, found in wine, beer, spirits and other fermented liquors; intoxicating liquors containing a certain amount of alcohol; (*chem.*) a large group of compounds containing carbon, hydrogen and oxygen, and having chemical properties analogous to ethyl alcohol; **absolute a.**, an alcohol with the water removed and containing more than 96 per cent pure alcohol. [Arab. *al kohl* a fine powder of antimony].

ALCOHOLATE, [al'-kō-hol'-āt], *n.* (*chem.*) a compound formed by a mixture of a metal and an alcohol, a compound in which alcohol takes the place of the water of crystallization.

ALCOHOLIC (1), [al'-kō-hol'-ik], *n.* a person who is strongly addicted to intoxicating beverages, and whose health is impaired by excessive consumption of these.

ALCOHOLIC (2), [al'-kō-hol'-ik], *adj.* pertaining to, caused by, containing a certain amount of, alcohol.

ALCOHOLIMETER, ALCOHOLOMETER, [al'-kō-hol-im'-it-er, al'-kō-hol-om'-it-er], *n.* an apparatus, similar in function to a hydrometer, used to calculate the percentage of alcohol in spirits by means of their specific gravity. [ALCOHOL and METER].

ALCOHOLISM, [al'-kō-hol-izm], *n.* an impaired condition of the body caused by immoderate consumption of alcoholic beverages; the habitual taking of alcoholic drinks and its effect upon the system.

ALCOHOLIZATION, [al'-kō-hol-īz-ā'-shun], *n.* process of subjection to the influence of alcohol.

ALCOHOLIZE, [al'-kō-hol-īz], *v.t.* to soak in alcohol, to cause someone or something to come under the influence of alcohol.

ALCOHOLOMETER, see ALCOHOLIMETER.

ALCOHOLOMETRY, [al'-kō-hol-om'-et-ri], *n.* the process of determining the amount of alcohol in spirituous liquids. [ALCOHOL and Gk. *metria* measuring].

ALCORAN†, ALKORAN†, [al'-kor-ahn'], *n.* the Koran. [Arab. *al koran* the Koran].

ALCOVE, [al'-kōv], *n.* a vaulted recess in a room often separated off by curtains, columns, etc., and sometimes containing a bed, a summer-house, a sheltered retreat. [Arab. *al gobbah* the vault].

ALDEHYDE, [al'-di-hīd], *n.* (*chem.*) the generic name of compounds of alcohol intermediate between the alcohols and the acids, a colourless volatile inflammable liquid, with a strong, suffocating smell, formed by oxidation of alcohol. [Shortened form of *alcohol dehydrogenatum*, i.e., deprived of hydrogen].

ALDEHYDIC, [al'-di-hīd'-ik], *adj.* containing aldehyde, characterized by aldehyde.

ALDER, [awl'-der], *n.* a plant of the order *Betulaceae*, growing in damp places and found in Europe, Asia and the United States, yielding a light soft reddish-coloured wood, the bark of the tree being used in tanning and leather dressing. [OE. *alor* the alder].

ALDER-FLY, [awl'-der-flī'], *n.* a small, large-winged insect, *Sialis superior*, usually found in marshy places, in the neighbourhood of alder trees.

ALDER-FLY

ALDERMAN, [awl'-der-man], *n.* a senior member of a county or municipal council who is concerned with the administration of local government and who holds office for a longer term than ordinary members or councillors. [OE. *aldorman* a chief, governor].

ALDERMANCY, [awl'-der-man-si], *n.* the position of an alderman.
ALDERMANIC, [awl'-der-man'-ik], *adj.* relating to an alderman.
ALDERMANLIKE, [awl'-der-man-līk], *adj.* like an alderman.
ALDERMANLY, [awl'-der-man-li], *adj.* aldermanlike.
ALDERMANRY, [awl'-der-man-ri], *n.* the office or rank of an alderman; a district or ward, whose representative on the municipal council is an alderman.
ALDERN, [awl'-dern], *adj.* made of alder [OE. *ælren*].
ALDERNEY, [awl'-der-ni], *n.* a breed of cattle originating in Alderney. [*Alderney*, the most northerly of the Channel Islands].
ALDINE, [awl'-dīn], *adj.* produced by the press of Aldus Manutius and family between 1494 and 1570 at Venice, Rome and Bologna, and of great importance in the history of printing; one of the nine kinds of Greek type, or fourteen kinds of Latin type used by Aldus in printing his editions. [*Aldus* Manutius].
ALE, [āl], *n.* a popular intoxicating beverage, consisting of fermented malt liquor generally flavoured with hops or other bitters, beer; **mild a.,** a sweeter form of ale, of lower gravity, and containing a higher proportion of malt. [OE. *alu* ale].
ALEATORY, [ā'-lē-at-or-i], *adj.* (*leg.*) depending on dice or chance; dependent on a contingency. [L. *aleātorius* from *aleātor* dice-player].
ALEBENCH, [āl'-bench], *n.* a bench placed in or before an alehouse.
ALEBERRY, [āl'-be'-ri], *n.* a mixture of ale, spice and sugar, boiled with soaked pieces of bread.
ALECONNER, [āl'-kon'-er], *n.* formerly an officer who had to inspect the strength, quality, and price of ale and beer, and also test the accuracy of the measures used in the sale of ale and beer in public-houses.
ALECOST, [āl'-kost], *n.* costmary, *Pyrethrum tanacetum*, used to give flavour to ale. [ALE and L. *costum* costmary].
ALECTOROMACHY, [al'-ek-tor-om'-ak-i], *n.* the practice of cock-fighting. [Gk. *alektruon* a cock and *mache* fighting].
ALECTOROMANCY, [al'-ek-tor-om-an'-si], *n.* an ancient custom of divination by means of a cock and a number of grains of corn. [Gk. *alektruon* a cock and *manteia* divination].
ALEE, [a-lē'], *adv.* (*naut.*) on or to the lee side. [OIcel. *á hlé* on the sheltered side].
ALEFOUNDER, [āl'-fownd'-er], *n.* an aleconner.
ALEGAR, [ā'-lig-er], *n.* sour ale, malt vinegar made from this. [ALE and Fr. *aigre* sour].
ALEGILL, [āl'-jil], *n.* malt liquor flavoured with ground-ivy.
ALE-HOOF, [āl'-hōōf'], *n.* ground-ivy, a species of *Nepeta*, formerly used instead of hops. [ALE and OE. *hofe*].
ALEHOUSE, [āl'-hows'], *n.* a public-house or shop where ale is sold. [OE.**alu-hūs*].
ALEMBIC, [al-em'-bik], *n.* an apparatus formerly used in distillation, made of glass or metal, or earthenware, having three main parts: the body, head and receiver, and slightly resembling the modern retort in shape; (*fig.*) refining and distilling influence. [ME. *alembykes* a still, from Arab. *al-ambiq*].
ALEMBROTH, [al-em'-broth], *n.* the salt of wisdom or philosopher's salt, believed to be the universal solvent sought after by the alchemists, †double chloride of mercury and ammonium. [Unkn.].
ALENGTH, [a-length'], *adv.* full-length or lengthwise.
ALEPIDOTE, [al-ep'-id-ōt], *adj.* (*ichth.*) having no scales. (A (4) and Gk. *lepis* a scale].
ALERT (1), [a-lurt'], *n.* the state of being alert; a signal to be alert, *esp.* an air-raid warning. [*Next*].
ALERT (2), [a-lurt'], *adj.* watchful, brisk, alive to all possibilities, ready to act immediately, lively, quick-witted, smart. [Fr. *alerte* from *à l'airte* on the look out].
ALERTLY, [a-lurt'-li], *adv.* in an alert manner, smartly, briskly, vigilantly.
ALERTNESS, [a-lurt'-nes], *n.* the condition of being alert.
ALESILVER, [āl'-sil'-ver], *n.* an ale-tax once imposed in London.
ALE-STAKE, [āl'-stāk'], *n.* a stake set in front of an alehouse as a sign itself, or to which a sign is affixed.
ALE-TASTER, [āl'-tāst'-er], *n.* an aleconner, an officer appointed to inspect the quality, strength, price and measures of ale sold in a public-house.
ALETHIOLOGY, [al-ē'-thi-ol'-o-ji], *n.* a division of logic, dealing with the nature of truth and falsehood. [Gk. *aletheia* truth and *logos* speech].
ALETTE, [al-et'], *n.* (*arch.*) a small wing, a buttress. [Fr. *alete*, *dim.* of *aile* wing].
ALETUDE†, [al'-it-ewd], *n.* bulkiness, fatness, corpulency. [L. *aletudo* fatness].
ALEUROMETER, [al'-yōō-rom'-it-er], *n.* an instrument for determining the bread-making qualities of wheaten flour. [Gk. *aleuron* wheat-flour and METER].

ALETTE

ALEURONE, [al-yōōer'-ōn], *n.* an albuminoid substance occurring in small shapeless particles found in the ripening seeds of cereals and other plants. [*Prec.*].
ALE-VAT, [āl'-vat], *n.* a vat in which ale is fermented.
ALEVIN, [al'-ev-in], *n.* a young salmon. [Fr. *alevin*].
ALEWIFE, [āl'-wīf'], *n.* a woman who keeps an alehouse; a fish related to the shad, ranging up to a foot in size and caught in the mouths of rivers in North America.
ALEXANDERS, [al'-eks-ahn'-derz], *n.* an umbelliferous biennial plant, *Smyrnium Olusatrum*, formerly raised for its aromatic leaf-stalks which were eaten as a vegetable. [Fr. *alexandre*].
ALEXANDRINE, [al'-eks-ahn'-drīn], *n.* (*pros.*) a line of six stresses or twelve syllables, usually having a pause after the sixth syllable. [Fr. poems in this metre on *Alexander* the Great].
ALEXANDRITE, [al'-eks-ahn'-drīt], *n.* a variety of chrysoberyl, occurring in mica schist. [*Alexander* I, Czar of Russia].
ALEXIN, [al-eks'-in], *n.* a defensive proteid; a substance in the body which kills germs. [Gk. *alexo* I ward off].
ALEXIPHARMIC (1), [al-eks'-i-fahm'-ik], *n.* an antidote to counteract the effects of poison. [ALEXIPHARMIC (2)].
ALEXIPHARMIC (2), [al-eks'-i-fahm'-ik], *adj.* acting as an antidote. [Gk. *alexi-* from *alexo* I ward off and *pharmakon* drug, poison].
ALEXIPYRETIC, [al-eks'-i-pīer-et'-ik], *n.* a remedy for fever. [Gk. *alexo* I ward off and *puretos* fever].
ALEXITERIC (1), [al'-eks-i-ter'-ik], *n.* a medicine which counteracts poison. [MedL. *alexiterium*].
ALEXITERIC (2), [al'-eks-i-ter'-ik], *adj.* counteracting poison.
ALFA, [al'-fa], *n.* esparto grass, a species of *Stipa*. [Unkn.].
ALFALFA, [al-fal'-fa], *n.* the plant, *Medicago sativa*, with leaves like clover, yellow or purple flowers, sometimes cultivated to provide green fodder and grown chiefly in Argentina and the U.S.A. [Span. *alfalfa* three-leaved plant].
ALFRESCO, [al-fres'-kō], *adj. and adv.* in the fresh air, under the open sky; **a. meal**, a picnic meal. [It. *al fresco* in the fresh (air)].
ALGAE, (*sg.* **alga**), [al'-jē], *n.*(*pl.*) (*bot.*) an order of plants, forming one of the divisions of cryptogamic plants, including the seaweeds, found in the sea and in fresh water or in damp places, often attached to rocks, and taking in nourishment through the whole of their surface. [L. *alga* seaweed].
ALGAL, [algl], *adj.* of, or pertaining to, alga or the algae.
ALGAROT, [al'-gar-ot], *n.* an emetic powder obtained from antimony. [*Algarotti*, its inventor, a Veronese doctor].
ALGEBRA, [al'-jib-ra], *n.* a kind of generalized arithmetic in which numbers, quantities, operations and often the results of operations are represented by symbols. [Arab. *al jebr* putting together of fragments].
ALGEBRAIC, [al'-jib-rā'-ik], *adj* algebraical.
ALGEBRAICAL, [al'-jib-rā'-ikl], *adj.* relating to algebra.
ALGEBRAICALLY, [al'-jib-rā'-ik-a-li], *adv.* by algebraic process, in accordance with algebra.
ALGEBRAIST, [al'-jeb-rā'-ist], *n.* one who studies algebra, an expert in algebra.
ALGEBRAIZE, [al'-jeb-rā'-iz], *v.t.* to reduce to algebraic form, to solve by means of algebra.
ALGERINE, [al'-jer-īn'], *n.* an inhabitant, usually a native, of Algiers; also a pirate because Algiers was formerly a great piratical stronghold. [Fr. *Alger*].

ALGID, [al'-jid], *adj.* (*med.*) cold. [L. *algidus* cold].
ALGIDITY, [al-jid'-i-ti], *n.* chiliness.
ALGIFIC, [al-jif'-ik], *adj.* causing cold. [L. *algificus* causing cold].
ALGIN, [al'-jin], *n.* a gummy substance obtained from certain seaweeds used in cookery to make jellies, soups, etc., soluble in water and resembling gelatine.
ALGOID, [al'-goid], *adj.* like algae. [ALGA and Gk. *oeides* like].
ALGOLOGY, [al-gol'-o-ji], *n.* (*bot.*) the study of algae, that branch of botany concerned with the algae. [ALGA and Gk. *logos* speech].
ALGOR, [al'-gor], *n.* (*med.*) a chilliness or coldness at the onset of fever. [L. *algor* cold].
ALGORISM, [al'-gor-izm], *n.* the Arabic system of notation of numerals, an arrangement or method of numeration. [Arab. *al-Khwarazmi* an Arab mathematician of the ninth century].
ALGOUS, [al'-gus], *adj.* relating to seaweed.
ALGUAZIL, [al'-gwaz-il'], *n.* a Spanish officer appointed to carry out the decrees of a judge, a kind of policeman. [Arab. *al-wazir* the minister].
ALGUM, [al'-gum], *n.* a tree mentioned in the Bible in the Books of Kings and Chronicles, and thought to be red sandal-wood of India. [Heb. *algūm*].
ALHENNA, see HENNA.
ALIAS (1), [ā'-li-as], *n.* an assumed name, a false name.
ALIAS (2), [ā'-li-as], *adv.* otherwise known as. [L. *alias* at another place/time].
ALIBI, [al'-ib-i], *n.* (*leg.*) a plea by the defence by which the accused endeavours to establish the fact that he was at a different place when the crime alleged was committed; (*slang*) excuse. [L. *alibi* elsewhere].
ALICANTE, [al'-i-kan'-ti], *n.* a red, sweet Spanish wine obtained from Alicante. [*Alicante* in Spain].
ALIDADE, [al'-id-ād], *n.* the movable arm of an instrument for measuring altitudes and distances, and carrying the sights and indicator. [Arab. *al hidada* a rule].

ALIDADE

ALIEN (1), [ā'-li-en], *n.* a person living in a different country from that of his birth, and who has not obtained the full rights of citizenship of that country, a stranger, a foreigner. [ALIEN (2)].
ALIEN (2), [ā'-li-en], *adj.* strange, foreign, belonging to a different country, pertaining to aliens; of a different character from, not native to, adverse, not in sympathy with. [L. *alienus* belonging to another].
ALIENABILITY, [ā'-li-en-ab-il'-i-ti], *n.* the quality of being alienated.
ALIENABLE, [ā'-li-en-abl], *adj.* able to be alienated.
ALIENAGE, [ā'-li-en-ij], *n.* the condition of being an alien, or alienated. [Fr. *aliénage*].
ALIENATE, [ā'-li-en-āt'], *v.t.* to make a person out of sympathy with, to turn against, to estrange, to make unfriendly or hostile to, to lose the sympathy or support of, to transfer property or rights to the ownership of another. [L. *alienatum*, *p.pt.* of *alienare* to estrange, to give up].
ALIENATION, [ā'-li-en-ā'-shun], *n.* the act of alienating, the condition of being alienated, estrangement, loss of friendship or affection; insanity, mental derangement, madness; (*leg.*) transference of rights or property to the ownership of another. [L. *alienatio*].
ALIENATOR, [ā'-li-en-ā'-tor], *n.* a person who alienates anything. [L. *alienator*].
ALIENEE, [ā'-li-en-ē'], *n.* (*leg.*) one to whom rights or property are conveyed or transferred.
ALIENER, [ā'-li-en-er], *n.* an alienator.
ALIENISM, [ā'-li-en-izm], *n.* state or condition of being an alien; (*med.*) the study and treatment of mental diseases.
ALIENIST, [ā'-li-en-ist], *n.* (*med.*) a physician who specializes in the study and treatment of insanity and mental diseases.
ALIFEROUS, [al-if'-er-us], *adj.* winged. [LL. *alifer* winged].
ALIFORM, [al'-i-fawm], *adj.* with the shape of a wing. [L. *ala* wing and FORM].
ALIGEROUS, [al-ij'-er-us], *adj.* having wings. [L. *aliger* wing-bearing].
ALIGHT (1), [a-līt'], *adj.* lighted, illumined.
ALIGHT (2), [a-līt'], *v.i.* to dismount, to get down from, to end one's journey (by vehicle) at, to get out at, to descend and come to rest upon or settle upon, to land upon; to fall on, to come upon unexpectedly. [OE. *alihtan*].
ALIGN, ALINE, [a-līn'], *v.t. and i.* to bring, form or draw up into a line, to bring the sights of a gun into line with the target; to form up, draw up into line, to fall into line with. [Fr. *aligner* to line].
ALIGNMENT, ALINEMENT, [a-līn'-ment], *n.* arrangement or formation into a line; (*milit.*) the act of adjusting or being adjusted to a straight line or lines (of soldiers); the ground-plan of a railway or road.
ALIKE (1), [a-līk'], *adj.* similar, possessing mutual resemblances, having the same characteristics, appearance, or effects. [OE. *gelic*].
ALIKE (2), [a-līk'], *adv.* equally, similarly, without determination, in the same manner, form or degree.
ALIMENT (1), [al'-im-ent], *n.* food, nourishment, sustenance; method of support, prop; (*Scots leg.*) alimony, financial provision for the support of a person. [L. *alimentum* nourishment].
ALIMENT (2), [al'-im-ent], *v.t. and i.* to keep up, to maintain; (*Scots leg.*) to provide for the support of a person. [ALIMENT (1)].
ALIMENTAL, [al'-im-entl'], *adj.* providing food; nourishing.
ALIMENTALLY, [al'-im-ent'-a-li], *adv.* so as to provide nourishment.
ALIMENTARINESS, [al'-im-en-ta'-rin-es], *n.* the state of being alimentary.
ALIMENTARY, [al'-im-ent'-a-ri], *adj.* nourishing, possessing nutritive value, providing support, furnishing a means of sustenance, connected with the process of nutrition or the organs of nutrition; **a. canal**, the passage through the body along which food travels, extending from the mouth to the anus, and including the gullet, stomach, and intestines. [L. *alimentarius* relating to nourishment].
ALIMENTATION, [al'-im-en-tā'-shun], *n.* nourishment, the act of affording nutriment, condition of being nourished. [MedL. *alimentatio*].
ALIMENTATIVENESS†, [al'-im-ent'-at-iv-nes], *n.* alimentiveness.
ALIMENTIVENESS†, [al'-im-ent'-iv-nes], *n.* the food-seeking instinct.
ALIMONY, [al'-i-mun-i], *n.* sustenance, provision for maintenance; (*leg.*) an allowance paid by a husband to his wife during or pending a matrimonial suit, or after a legal separation not brought about by adultery or elopement of the wife. [L. *alimōnia* sustenance].
ALINE, see ALIGN.
ALINEMENT, see ALIGNMENT.
ALIPED (1), [al'-ip-ed], *n.* an animal, like the bat, that has the toes joined by a membrane which serves as a wing. [L. *ala* wing and *pes pedis* foot].
ALIPED (2), [al'-ip-ed], *adj.* wing-footed. [ALIPED (1)].
ALIPHATIC, [al'-i-fat'-ik], *adj.* relating to fat; (*chem.*) a name applied to certain organic compounds known as the methane derivatives. [Gk. *aleiphar* fat].
ALIQUANT, [al'-i-kwont'], *adj.* (of a number) not dividing exactly into another number. [L. *aliquantum* somewhat].
ALIQUOT, [al'-i-kwot'], *adj.* (of a number) dividing without remainder into another number. [L. *aliquot* some].
ALISH, [āl'-ish], *adj.* resembling ale; having the qualities of ale.
ALITRUNK, [al'-i-trungk], *n.* the segment of the body of an insect to which the wings are joined. [L. *ala* wing and *truncus* trunk].
ALIVE, [a-līv'], *adj. and adv.* living, in a live state, in existence, thriving, in force, action or operation, active, vigorous; wideawake, alert, aware of, ready for, mindful of; crowded with, swarming with, full of; **look a.**, hurry up! be quick!; **sakes a.**, (*coll.*) an expletive. [OE. *on life* living].
ALIZARIN, [al-iz'-ar-in], *n.* a substance found in the root of the madder and used in dyeing to obtain shades of red, now synthetically prepared from anthracene, a constituent of coal-tar, in the form of yellowish-red crystals. [Fr. *alizarin* probably from Arab. *al-caçarah* juice of a plant].
ALKAHEST, [al'-ka-hest], *n.* the universal solvent sought by the alchemist. [A pseudo-Arab. word probably coined by Paracelsus].
ALKAHESTIC, [al'-ka-hes'-tik], *adj.* relating to the alkahest.
ALKALESCENCE, [al'-kal-es'-ens], *n.* alkalescency.
ALKALESCENCY, [al'-kal-es'-en-si], *n.* tendency or capacity to become alkaline.

ALKALESCENT, [al'-kal-es'-ent], *adj.* having to a certain degree the properties of an alkali. [Fr. *alcalescent*].
ALKALI, (*pl.* **alkalis**), [al'-kal-ī], *n.* the soluble product obtained from the ashes of certain plants, notably seaweed; (*chem.*) a base or compound which is soluble in water, neutralizes acids and combines with them to form salts, corrodes animal and vegetable matter and changes the colour of many vegetable colouring matters, as turning reds to blue, yellows to brown, and purples to green. [Arab. *al-qali* charred ashes].
ALKALIFIABLE, [al'-kal-if-ī'-abl], *adj.* able to be made alkaline.
ALKALIFY, [al'-kal-if-ī], *v.t.* to change into an alkali; *v.i.* to become an alkali. [ALKALI and L. *-ficere* to make].
ALKALIGENOUS, [al'-kal-ij'-en-us], *adj.* producing alkali. [ALKALI and Gk. *genes* producing].
ALKALIMETER, [al'-kal-im'-it-er], *n.* an instrument for determining the amount of pure alkali in an alkaline substance, by calculating the amount of acid of known strength required to neutralize an alkaline solution, from which the strength of the solution may be ascertained. [ALKALI and METER].
ALKALIMETRIC, [al'-kal-im-et'-rik], *adj.* pertaining to alkalimetry.
ALKALIMETRY, [al'-kal-im'-et-ri], *n.* the calculation of the strength of alkaline solutions or the amount of free alkali in an alkaline substance. [ALKALI and Gk. *metria* measuring].
ALKALINE, [al'-kal-īn], *adj.* having the properties or characteristics of an alkali.
ALKALINITY, [al'-kal-in'-i-ti], *n.* condition or quality of being alkaline, the characteristics of an alkaline substance or solution.
ALKALIZATION, [al'-kal-īz-ā'-shun], *n.* the act of making alkaline by impregnating with an alkali.
ALKALIZE, [al'-kal-īz], *v.t.* to make alkaline; *v.i.* to become an alkali. [MdL. *alcalizare*].
ALKALOID, [al'-kal-oid], *n.* (*chem.*) one of a class of nitrogenous compounds having the properties of a base or alkali, found in living plants, which are usually poisonous, and used as medicinal drugs. [ALKALI and Gk. *oeides* like].
ALKALOIDAL, [al'-kal-oidl], *adj.* like an alkaloid.
ALKANET, [al'-kan-et], *n.* the plant *Alkanna tinctoria* of the natural order *Boraginaceae* with spear-shaped leaves and clusters of dark-reddish flowers, the bark of whose root provides a deep red dye much used for colouring oils, plasters, artificial port-wine, etc.; the deep red dye obtained from this plant. [Arab. *al-henna* the henna plant].
ALKEKENGI, [al'-kik-en'-ji], *n.* (*bot.*) the winter cherry, a species of *Physalus* with bright red berries. [Arab. *al-kākany*].
ALKENNA, [al-ken'-a], *n.* henna. [Arab. *al-henna* the henna plant].
ALKERMES, [al-kurm'-ēz], *n.* the scarlet-grain insect anciently thought to be a berry; a cordial formerly popular, of which the kermes was an ingredient. [Arab. *al-qirmis* the kermes].
ALKORAN, see ALCORAN.
ALKORANIST, [al'-kor-ahn'-ist], *n.* one who closely follows the letter of the Koran, rejecting all Islamic traditions.
ALL (1), [awl], *n.* the whole, everything, everybody, the whole quantity, amount, quality, number, all people; (*fig.*) the whole of one's property, anything; **after a.**, considering everything; **a. in a.**, most precious thing; **all's one**, it is just the same; **in a.**, altogether, all told; **at a.**, in any way; **a. in**, inclusive; **a. my eye**, (*slang*) totally wrong, untrue, absurd, nonsense. [OE. *all*].
ALL (2), [awl], *adj.* the entire extent, amount or quantity of, every, any, the greatest possible; **for good and a.**, for ever; **once for a.**, for the last time, finally; **at a. events**, in any case; **a.-in wrestling**, wrestling in which any trick is permitted save biting or gouging. [OE. *all*].
ALL (3), [awl], *adv.* entirely, wholly, completely, totally, full of, so much; **a. one**, immaterial; **a. at once**, suddenly; **a. but**, almost; **a. the same**, immaterial, yet, notwithstanding, nevertheless; **a. over**, (*coll.*) just like; **a. there**, (*coll.*) perfectly sane, very shrewd; **a. along**, throughout; **a. out**, (*coll.*) with the throttle wide open, straining every nerve; **a. on**, (*cards*) set to make the remaining tricks; **a. for**, (*coll.*) enthusiastically supporting; **a. in**, completely exhausted, dead-beat; **to be a. over, or up, with**, (*coll.*) to be finished, beaten, done for, ruined. [OE. *all*].
ALLA, [al'-a], *prep.* (*mus.*) in the manner of. [It. *alla*].
ALLA-BREVE, [al'-a-brāv'-i], *n.* a musical direction indicating that the time values of the notes are to be reduced by one-half; originally indicating four minims to the measure, now indicating two minims to the measure and virtually amounting to a quick common time.
ALLA-CAPELLA, [al'-a-kap-el'-a], *n.* alla-breve.
ALLAH, [al'-a], *n.* the name for God in Arabic, the Moslem word for the Supreme Deity. [Arab. *allah* the true God].
ALLANITE, [al'-an-īt], *n.* (*min.*) a brownish-black mineral being a siliceous oxide of cerium. [T. *Allan*, mineralogist].
ALLANTOIC, [al'-an-tō'-ik], *adj.* contained in the allantois.
ALLANTOID, [al'-an-toid], *adj.* relating to the allantois; sausage-shaped. [Gk. *allas allantos* sausage and *oeides* like].
ALLANTOIDAL, [al'-an-toidl'], *adj.* allantoid.
ALLANTOIN, [al-an'-tō'-in], *n.* a substance found in allantoic fluid and synthetically produced by boiling uric acid and lead dioxide.
ALLANTOIS, [al-an'-tō-is], *n.* (*anat.*) a thin membranous sac in the foetus of reptiles, birds and mammals, largely made up of blood-vessels, and forming a kind of lining to the shell in birds. [Gk. *allas allantos* a sausage].
ALLANTOTOXICUM, [al-an'-tō-toks'-ik-um], *n.* a poison found in decayed liver-sausage. [Gk. *allas allantos* sausage and L. *toxicum* poison].
ALLAY, [al-ā'], *v.t.* to soothe, calm, appease, quieten, to put down, to repress; to calm, relieve, mitigate, assuage, abate, temper, diminish. [OE. *alecgan* to put down].
ALLAYMENT, [al-ā'-ment], *n.* the act of allaying, the process of being allayed, relief, alleviation, assuagement, abatement.
ALL-BEARING, [awl'-bāer'-ing], *adj.* producing everything.
ALL-CHANGING, [awl'-chānj'-ing], *adj.* changing everything.
ALL-DIVINE, [awl'-div-īn'], *adj.* divine in everything.
ALLECTATION, [al'-ek-tā'-shun], *n.* allurement. [L. *allectatio*].
ALLEGATION, [al'-ig-ā'-shun], *n.* a statement, an assertion (often unsupported by proof); (*leg.*) a statement believed to be true, but which has not been proved in a court of law, an assertion intended to be proved by evidence.
ALLEGE, [al-ej'], *v.t.* to state as a fact, to assert, to claim as true, to advance as an excuse, plea, argument, or evidence. [ME. *alleggen* to bring forward as evidence].
ALLEGEABLE, [al-ej'-abl], *adj.* able to be alleged.
ALLEGED, [al-ejd'], *adj.* stated to be true, averred, asserted, brought forward, levelled (of charges), ascribed.
ALLEGIANCE, [al-ē'-jans], *n.* obedience or loyalty which every subject owes to the state or to the king, fidelity, duty, loyalty or devotion to a cause or group. [ME. *allegiance* from OFr. *ligeance*].
ALLEGIANT (1), [al-ē'-jant], *n.* a person owing allegiance, as a subject to a ruler.
ALLEGIANT (2), [al-ē'-jant], *adj.* loyal.
ALLEGORIC, [al'-ig-or'-ik], *adj.* allegorical. [Gk. *allegorikos*].
ALLEGORICAL, [al'-ig-or'-ikl], *adj.* relating to allegory, symbolical, figurative.
ALLEGORICALLY, [al'-ig-or'-ik-a-li], *adv.* in a figurative or symbolical way.
ALLEGORICALNESS†, [al'-ig-or'-ik-al-nes], *n.* the condition of being allegorical.
ALLEGORIST, [al'-ig-or-ist], *n.* one who writes in allegory, one who treats a subject in an allegorical way.
ALLEGORIZATION, [al'-ig-or-īz-ā'-shun], *n.* the process of making an allegory.
ALLEGORIZE, [al'-ig-or-īz], *v.t.* to treat or interpret by means of allegory; *v.i.* to use allegory. [L. *allegorizare*].
ALLEGORY, [al'-ig-er-i], *n.* a figurative or symbolical description or story commenting upon or suggesting some real situation, yet placed in the realm of the imaginary, and in which the words and characters have often another significance in addition to their literal meaning, a figurative story in the form of a fable or parable generally having a moral import. [Gk. *allegoria* speech made in public assembly].
ALLEGRETTO, [al'-ig-ret'-ō], *adj. and adv.* (*mus.*) fairly fast, brisk and lively, not quite so quick as allegro. [It. *allegretto*, *dim.* of *allegro* gay].

ALLEGRISSIMO, [al'-ig-ris'-im-ō], *adj.* (*mus.*) very lively. [It. *allegrissimo*, *superl.* of *allegro*].

ALLEGRO (1), [al-eg'-rō], *n.* a piece of music or a movement to be played in a quick, lively way [ALLEGRO (2)].

ALLEGRO (2), [al-eg'-rō], *adj. and adv.* quick, lively, brisk; (*mus.*) with a quick lively rate of movement or time; at a quick lively rate. [It. *allegro* cheerful from L. *alacer* lively].

ALLELOMORPH, [al-ē'-lō-mawf], *n.* (*biol.*) the reproduction in an unmixed form in the offspring of one of a pair of mutually exclusive characteristics, existing separately in each of the parental forms crossed for the purposes of reproduction. [Gk. *allelon* of each other and *morphe* shape].

ALLELUIA, see HALLELUJAH.

ALLEMANDE, [al'-mahnd], *n.* a slow, stately graceful dance invented in France during the reign of Louis XVI; the music for this. [Fr. (*danse*) *allemande* German (dance)].

ALLERGY, [al'-er-ji], *n.* a pathological condition peculiar to certain individuals of extreme sensitivity to particular substances. [Gk. *allos* other and (EN)ERGY].

ALLERION, [al-ēer'-i-on], *n.* (*her.*) an eagle without beak or feet. [Fr. *alérion*].

ALLEVIATE, [al-ē'-vi-āt], *v.t.* to lessen, lighten, mitigate, to afford relief, to temper, to assuage. [L. *alleviatum*, *p.pt.* of *alleviare* to lighten].

ALLEVIATION, [al'-ē-vi-ā'-shun], *n.* the act or process of alleviating, that which provides relief, mitigation, assuagement.

ALLEVIATIVE, [al-ē'-vi-at-iv], *n. and adj.* (a substance) providing relief, or mitigation.

ALLEY, [al'-i], *n.* a narrow passage or corridor often between two buildings, and generally leading to a courtyard excluded from general view by intervening buildings, a narrow squalid slum street; avenue or walk bordered by trees or bushes, a bordered path in a garden; a long, narrow enclosed room or space in which bowls, skittles, etc., are played; a passage separating rows of pews; **blind a.**, one that is open at one end only; (*fig.*) a situation or project that leads nowhere; **The A.**, Change Alley, London, where gambling in South Sea and other stocks was carried on. [OFr. *alee* a passage].

ALL-FOOLS' DAY, [awl'-fōōlz'-dā'], *n.* the first of April.

ALL-FOURS, [awl'-fawz'], *n.* the legs of a quadruped animal, the arms and legs of a human being; a card game so called from its four points (high, low, jack and game) also known as *seven up*; **on a.-f.**, (of a person) on legs and arms; (*fig.*) on terms of equality, exactly similar.

ALL-GOOD, [awl'-good'], *n.* the plant Good King Henry, a species of *Chenopodium*.

ALL-HAIL, [awl'-hāl], *int.* a form of greeting, a wish of health.

ALL-HALLOWE'EN, [awl'-hal'-ō-ēn], *n.* the thirty-first of October.

ALL-HALLOWMASS, [awl'-hal'-ō-mas], *n.* All Saints' Day, the first of November; the festival of All Saints.

ALL-HALLOWS, [awl'-hal'-ōz], *n.* all the saints; All Saints' Day.

ALL-HALLOWTIDE†, [awl'-hal'-ō-tīd], *n.* the first of November.

ALL-HEAL†, [awl'-hēl'], *n.* a popular name given to several plants, such as valerian, mistletoe and self-heal, *Prunella vulgaris*.

ALLIACEOUS, [al'-i-ā'-shus], *adj.* (*bot.*) pertaining to plants of the genus *Allium*, including onion, leek, garlic, etc.; having the peculiar pungent smell and taste of the plants of the genus *Allium*. [L. *allium* garlic and *-aceus* resembling].

ALLIANCE, [al-ī'-ans], *n.* a relationship or union by marriage; a league or treaty between two or more powers for mutual offence and defence against a possible enemy, a union between parties (usually political) or sections, to help to bring about a common aim or object. [ME. *aliaunce* from OFr. *aliance*].

ALLICE, ALLIS, [al'-is], *n.* the Severn shad, *Clupea alosa*, an edible fish of the herring family. [L. *alausa* shad].

ALLICE

ALLIGATE†, [al'-ig-āt], *v.t.* (*arith.*) to endeavour to solve questions concerning the mixing of articles of different qualities or values. [L. *alligatum*, *p.pt.* of *alligare* to bind together].

ALLIGATOR, [al'-ig-ā'-tor], *n.* a genus of reptiles of the crocodile family, but with a shorter and flatter head, less webbed feet, and with teeth in the lower jaw fitting into cavities in the upper jaw, growing to a length of twenty feet and found in swamps and marshes in America and China. [Span. *el lagarto* the lizard].

ALLIGATOR-PEAR, [al'-ig-ā'-tor-pāer'], *n.* (*bot.*) a tree of the order *Lauraceae* bearing a fruit similar to a large pear, being a native of tropical America and the West Indies, and also known as avocado pear. [Corruption of AVOCADO].

ALLIGATURE†, [al-ig'-a-chōōer], *n.* ligature. [L. *alligatura* from *alligare* to bind].

ALL-IN, [awl'-in'], *adj.* all-embracing, comprehensive; **a. wrestling**, a form of wrestling in which no tactics except biting and gouging are barred.

ALLIS, see ALLICE.

ALLISION, [al-izh'-un], *n.* a striking against. [L. *allisio* from *allidere* to dash against].

ALLITERAL, [al-it'-er-al], *adj.* alliterative, a term applied to the Kaffir languages.

ALLITERATE, [al-it'-er-āt], *v.i.* (used of words in a phrase, sentence or verse), to have the same initial consonant or the same or different vowel sound; to write or make phrases, sentences or verses in which the words begin with a vowel or have the same initial consonant sound. [L. *ad* to and *littera* letter].

ALLITERATION, [al-it'-er-ā'-shun], *n.* repetition of the same initial consonantal sound or of initial vowel sounds in a group of words forming a phrase, sentence or line of verse. [*Prec.*].

ALLITERATIVE, [al-it'-er-at-iv], *adj.* characterized by alliteration; **a. verse**, verse in which alliteration marks the stress, and together with it forms the essential part of the structure.

ALLITERATIVELY, [al-it'-er-at-iv-li], *adv.* by means of alliteration, so as to alliterate.

ALLITERATIVENESS, [al-it'-er-at-iv-nes], *n.* the characteristic of being alliterative.

ALLO-, *pref.* other. [Gk. *allos* other].

ALLOCATE, [al'-o-kāt], *v.t.* to assign, to allot, to determine, to fix. [L. *allocatum*, *p.pt.* of *allocare* to place].

ALLOCATION, [al'-o-kā'-shun], *n.* allotment, distribution, apportionment, an allowance on account, arrangement. [MedL. *allocatio*].

ALLOCATUR, [al'-o-kā'-ter], *n.* (*leg.*) a certificate of allowance of costs. [MedL. *allocātur* it is allowed].

ALLOCHROITE, [al'-ok-rō'-īt], *n.* a species of garnet, so named from its changing colour under the blow-pipe. [Gk. *allokhroos* changed in colour].

ALLOCHROUS, [al'-ok-rus], *adj.* changing colour (as a symptom of illness). [*Prec.*].

ALLOCUTION, [al'-ok-ew'-shun], *n.* an address, anciently an exhortation to his troops made by a Roman general; (*R.C.*) a formal address made by the Pope to his cardinals on some important occasion. [L. *allocutio* from *alloqui* to speak to].

ALLODIAL, [al-ō'-di-al], *adj.* (of land) held without obligation to a superior, i.e., in absolute ownership, freehold. [MedL. *allodialis*].

ALLODIUM, [al-ō'-di-um], *n.* an ancient system of land-tenure, whereby land was the absolute property of the owner who held it, without any obligation or dues to an overlord or superior, as opposed to feudal tenure. [MedL. *allodium* entire property].

ALLOGAMOUS, [al-og'-am-us], *adj.* relating to cross-fertilization. [*Next*].

ALLOGAMY, [al-og'-a-mi], *n.* cross-fertilization by the transfer of the pollen of one flower to another. [ALLO and Gk. *gamia* marrying].

ALLOGRAPH, [al'-ō-grahf], *n.* writing or signature made by a person on behalf of the interested party. [ALLO and GRAPH].

ALLOMEROUS, [al-om'-er-us], *adj.* (*min. and chem.*) retaining the same form, yet varying in chemical composition. [ALLO and Gk. *meros* part].

ALLOMORPHISM, [al'-ō-mawf'-izm], *n.* the ability in substances to change their shape while they remain in other respects the same. [Gk. *allomorphos* of another shape].

ALLONGE†, [al-onzh'], *n.* (*fencing*) a thrust made by stepping forward and extending the arm, a lunge; (*leg. and comm.*) an appendage to a bill of exchange, or other commercial paper, to receive extra endorsements. [Fr. *allonge* lengthening].

ALLOPATHIC, [al'-ō-path'-ik], *adj.* relating to allopathy.

ALLOPATHICALLY, [al'-ō-path'-ik-a-li], *adv.* in an allopathic way.

ALLOPATHIST, [al-op′-ath-ist], *n.* one who practises allopathy.

ALLOPATHY, [al-op′-ath-i], *n.* (*med.*) the usual method of treatment of disease, whereby remedies are applied which produce results opposite to those produced by the disease to be cured, a term used in contrast to homoeopathy. [ALLO and Gk. *patheia* suffering].

ALLOPHANE, [al′-ō-fān], *n.* a hydrous aluminium silicate of varying colours, and found in the form of crust-like deposits in cavities of various rocks, losing its tint when subject to the influence of a blow-pipe. [Gk. *allophanos* appearing otherwise].

ALLOPHYLIAN (1), [al′-ō-fil′-i-an], *n.* a member of another race; (*specif.*) a member of a non-Aryan or Semitic race dwelling in Europe or Asia.

ALLOPHYLIAN (2), [al′-ō-fil′-i-an], *adj.* pertaining to the non-Aryan or Semitic peoples or languages of Europe and Asia. [Gk. *allophulos* of another tribe].

ALLOT, [al-ot′], *v.t.* to apportion, to assign, to distribute, to share out; to appoint, to determine, to fix; to set apart for a special purpose. [OFr. *aloter*].

ALLOTHEISM, [al′-ō-thē′-izm], *n.* worship of strange or foreign gods. [ALLO and Gk. *theos* god].

ALLOTMENT, [al-ot′-ment], *n.* the act of allotting; a share, portion or distribution, a small plot of land assigned or let out for cultivation; apportionment of shares; †destiny, fate, lot; **a. system,** the system of allotting small portions of land at a low rent for cultivation.

ALLOTROPIC, [al′-ō-trop′-ik], *adj.* (*chem.*) relating to allotropy.

ALLOTROPISM, [al-ot′-rop-izm], *n.* allotropy.

ALLOTROPY, [al-ot′-rop-i], *n.* (*chem.*) the existence of the same element in different forms, often with dissimilar external physical properties or characteristics. [Gk. *allotropia* variation].

ALLOTTABLE, [al-ot′-abl], *adj.* able to be allotted.

ALLOTTEE, [al′-ot-ē′], *n.* one to whom a share is allotted.

ALLOW, [al-ow′], *v.t. and i.* to permit, to agree to, to give consent to; to acknowledge, to admit, to grant, to concede; to render possible, to bring about; to grant, to give a certain periodical amount of money; to deduct; †to approve of; to concede, to provide for. [ME. *alouen* to allow from OFr. *alouer* to assign, and OFr. *aloer* to approve].

ALLOWABLE, [al-ow′-abl], *adj.* permissible, able to be allowed, lawful.

ALLOWABLENESS, [al-ow′-abl-nes], *n.* the characteristic of being allowable.

ALLOWABLY, [al-ow′-ab-li], *adv.* in an allowable way.

ALLOWANCE, [al-ow′-ans], *n.* a certain fixed sum of money or quantity of a substance periodically granted; a share, portion; deduction, discount; something taken into consideration of, permission. [OFr. *alouance*].

ALLOWEDLY, [al-ow′-ed-li], *adv.* admittedly.

ALLOXAN, [al-ok′-san], *n.* a product of the action of nitric acid on uric acid. [ALLANTOIN and OXALIC].

ALLOXANIC, [al′-ok-san′-ik], *adj.* relating to alloxan.

ALLOY (1), [al′-oi], *n.* a substance produced by melting together two or more metals; the relative purity of gold and silver, a mixture of a base metal with a precious one; (*fig.*) a mixture of good and bad, an impairing or detracting element. [ALLOY (2)].

ALLOY (2), [al′-oi], *v.t.* to mix metals, to lower the standard of purity in a metal by mixing with a base metal; (*fig.*) to debase, to impair, to detract from. [Fr. *aloier* to combine].

ALLOYAGE, [al-oi′-ij], *n.* the alloying of metals; an alloy.

ALL SAINTS' DAY, [awl′-sāntz′-dā], *n.* the first of November, on which day is held a festival in honour of all the saints.

ALLSEED, [awl′-sēd], *n.* a name often applied to plants which produce a large amount of seed, a term also given to the flax-seed, *Polycarpon* and *Radiola millegrana.*

ALL SOULS' DAY, [awl′-sōlz′-dā′], *n.* a day of prayer held on the second of November for the souls of the faithful dead.

ALLSPICE, [awl′-spīs], *n.* the dried, ground berry of a West Indian species of myrtle, having a flavour resembling a mixture of cinnamon, nutmegs and cloves, and employed in cooking and medicine.

ALLUDE, [al-ewd′], *v.i.* to refer to, often in a vague, indirect manner, to hint at, to make a casual, passing reference to. [L. *allūdere* to joke, to refer to].

ALLUMINATE†, [al-ew′-min-āt], *v.t.* to adorn with ornament; to illuminate.

ALLUMINOR†, [al-ew′-min-or], *n.* one who makes illuminated manuscripts; a limner. [AFr. *alluminour*].

ALLURE (1), [al-yōōer′], *n.* charm, fascination; (*coll.*) sex-appeal, attractiveness. [Fr. *allure*].

ALLURE (2), [al-yōōer′], *v.t.* to entice, to tempt, to attract, to charm, often implying a bad motive, to fascinate. [OFr. *aleurer* to tempt].

ALLUREMENT, [al-yōōer′-ment], *n.* enticement, fascination, charm, attraction (often implying a bad sense), attractive temptation.

ALLURING, (al-yōōer′-ing], *adj.* enticing, attractive and fascinating, tempting, possessing great charm.

ALLURINGLY, [al-yōōer′-ing-li], *adv.* in an alluring way.

ALLURINGNESS, [al-yōōer′-ing-nes], *n.* the quality of alluring, charm, allure.

ALLUSION, [al-ew′-zhun], *n.* a reference either direct or vague, a hint. [L. *allusio*].

ALLUSIVE, [al-ew′-ziv], *adj.* full of allusions, containing an allusion; **a. arms,** (*her.*) a device or motto on arms, that suggests a pun on the bearer's name.

ALLUSIVELY, [al-ew′-ziv-li], *adv.* in an allusive manner.

ALLUSIVENESS, [al-ew′-ziv-nes], *n.* the condition of being allusive.

ALLUSORY†, [al-ew′-zor-i], *adj.* making or containing allusions to. [L. **allusorius*].

ALLUVIAL, [al-ōō′-vi-al], *adj.* relating to soil which has been washed away by running water, and later deposited.

ALLUVION, [al-ōō′-vi-on], *n.* (*leg.*) the gradual increase of land on a shore, or the bank of a river, by the action of water; the land thus deposited; the mass of substances so collected. [Fr. from L. *alluvio*].

ALLUVIUM, [al-ōō′-vi-um], *n.* (*geol.*) deposits of soil collected and washed down by flowing water from rocks, etc., and usually found in valleys and plains, deltas, river-banks, consisting of loam, clay, gravel, etc. [L. *alluvium*].

ALL-WISE, [awl′-wiz′], *adj.* of infinite wisdom.

ALL-WORTHY, [awl′-wur′-THi], *adj.* having infinite worth.

ALLY (1), [al′-i], *n.* a large prize marble used in the game of marbles. [Shortened form of ALABASTER].

ALLY (2), (*pl.* **allies**), [al′-ī], *n.* a friend, confederate, a person who co-operates with or helps another in an attempt to achieve some common aim; a state leagued to another by treaty, agreement or mutual affinities for political, defensive or offensive purposes. [ALLY (3)].

ALLY (3), (**allies, allied**), [a-lī′], *v.t.* to unite or combine with, to league together by marriage, treaty or agreement; (*fig.*) to be connected by virtue of similar characteristics or affinities. [OFr. *alier* from L. *alligare* to join].

ALLYL, [al′-il], *n.* (*chem.*) the isolated radical of a series of organic compounds. [L. *allium* onion and Gk. *hule* substance].

ALMA (1), [al′-ma], *n.* an Egyptian dancing girl of the better class, who earns her living by singing and dancing for the wealthy. [Arab. *ςalmah* the learned].

ALMA (2), [al′-ma], *adj.* nourishing, fostering; **A. Mater,** the university, college or school at which a person received his education. [L. *alma* a foster-mother].

ALMACANTAR, ALMUCANTAR, [al′-mak-an′-tah(r)], *n.* a circle of the sphere parallel to the horizon; a circle of altitude; **almacantar's staff,** an instrument having an arc of 15 degrees formerly used in taking observations of the sun. [Arab. *al-muqantarat* from *qantarah* a bridge].

ALMADIE, [al′-mad-ē′], *n.* a raft, an Indian canoe or small native boat. [Arab. *al-maçdiya*].

ALMAGEST, [al′-maj-est], *n.* the name applied by the Arabs to a celebrated astronomical treatise written by Ptolemy of Alexandria, later applied to other treatises on astronomy or astrology. [Arab. *al* the and *majisti* greatest work].

ALMAGRA, [al-ma′-gra], *n.* a fine deep-red ochre. [Span. *almagra*].

ALMANAC, [awl′-man-ak], *n.* a document containing a list of days, months of the year, data about the movements of the sun and moon, indication of feasts, fasts, holidays, etc., prophecies and other miscellaneous information; **nautical a.,** a work published by the Government containing astronomical information, and used by sailors in determining their longitude at sea. [MedL. *almanac*].

ALMANDINE, [al'-man-dīn], *n.* a precious garnet of violet colour. [L. *alabandina* the name of a precious stone found at Alaband, in Asia Minor].

ALMANOGRAPHER, [awl'-man-og'-raf-er], *n.* a person who makes almanacs. [ALMANAC and GRAPH].

ALMIGHTILY, [awl'-mīt'-i-li], *adv.* omnipotently, in an all-powerful manner.

ALMIGHTINESS, [awl'-mīt'-in-es], *n.* omnipotence.

ALMIGHTY, [awl'-mīt'-i], *adj.* all-powerful, omnipotent; (*coll.*) great, disproportionate; **the A.** God. [OE. *ealmihtig*].

ALMOND, [ah'-mund], *n.* a tree related to the peach, with beautiful pinkish flowers; the seed or nut-kernel enclosed in the stone of the fruit of this tree, eaten as a palatable nut; (*fig.*) ornaments resembling an almond in shape; (*pl.*) †the tonsils. [L. *amygdala* an almond].

ALMOND-CAKE, [ah'-mund-kāk'], *n.* the solid residue which is left behind after the oil has been pressed out of almonds.

ALMOND-FURNACE, [ah'-mund-fur'-nas], *n.* a furnace used in the process of refining to separate out the metals from the impurities and ashes, a furnace in which the slag of litharge left in refining silver is reduced to lead.

ALMOND-ICING, [ah'-mund-is'-ing], *n.* a layer of paste made with ground almonds spread under a coating of icing on a cake.

ALMOND-OIL, [ah'-mund-oil'], *n.* an oil expressed from the kernels of bitter and sweet almonds, used by perfumers and also for medicinal purposes.

ALMOND-PASTE, [ah'-mund-pāst'], *n.* a cosmetic manufactured largely from almonds, and used to soften and protect the skin; a kind of hard thick paste made of icing sugar and almond meal mixed with water, which is placed on the top of certain cakes as an added delicacy.

ALMOND-WILLOW, [ah'-mund-wil'-ō], *n.* a species of willow, *Salix amygdalina*.

ALMONER, [ah'-mun-er], *n.* an official distributor of alms in a religious establishment; one who arranges the payments by patients at a hospital; **Lord High A.**, a person whose duty it is to distribute sums of money given by the king to certain of the poor on Maundy Thursday. [OFr. *aumoner*].

ALMONRY, [ah'-mun-ri], *n.* the place where the almoner lives, or where the alms are distributed; a cupboard. [Fr. *aumonerie*].

ALMOST, [awl'-mōst], *adv.* nearly; all but. [OE. *allmæst*].

ALMS, [ahmz], *n.(pl.)* money or other charitable gifts given for the relief of the poor, a donation for a religious or charitable purpose. [OE. *ælmesse* from L. *eleemosyna* mercy, alms].

ALMSBOX, [ahmz'-boks], *n.* a collecting box for the receipt of alms.

ALMSDEED, [ahmz'-dēd], *n.* almsgiving, a charitable act or gift to the poor, *esp.* as a religious duty.

ALMS-FEE, [ahmz'-fē], *n.* a tax formerly collected in Great Britain and Ireland for the Pope's use, and abolished by Henry VIII, now represented by the voluntary offerings of Roman Catholics to the Pope and known as Peter's Pence.

ALMSGATE, [ahmz'-gāt], *n.* the gate where alms were given out.

ALMSGIVING, [ahmz'-giv'-ing], *n.* charitable gift of money or alms.

ALMSHOUSE, [ahmz'-hows], *n.* a home maintained by private endowment or public support where certain aged poor people are housed and provided for.

ALMSMAN, [ahmz'-man], *n.* a person maintained by alms.

ALMUCANTAR, see ALMACANTAR.

ALNAGE, [al'-nij], *n.* (*hist.*) the measurement of cloth by the ell, the inspection, measurement and certification of wool. [OFr. *aulnage* from *aulne* ell].

ALNAGER, [al'-nij-er], *n.* an officer formerly appointed to inspect and certify the correct measurement of woollen cloth.

ALOE, [al'-ō], *n.* (*bot.*) a genus of plants of the order *Liliaceae* found largely in South Africa, having thick fleshy leaves and pointed red or yellow flowers, the juice of certain varieties of which possesses medicinal value; (*pl.*) (*med.*) the bitter juice of aloe leaves thickened by boiling and used as a purgative medicine. [Gk. *aloe* the aloe].

ALOED, [al'-ōd], *adj.* flavoured with aloes; bitter.

ALOES-WOOD, [al'-ōz-wood'], *n.* (*bot.*) the inner portion of the trunk of certain trees of the order *Aquilariaceae* found in Asia, and providing a resinous substance burned for its perfume, the eaglewood.

ALOETIC (1), [al'-ō-et'-ik], *n.* a medicine composed chiefly of aloes.

ALOETIC (2), [al'-ō-et'-ik], *adj.* containing aloes; **a. acid**, an acid obtained by the action of nitric acid upon aloes.

ALOETICAL, [al'-ō-et'-ikl], *adj.* aloetic.

ALOFT, [a-loft'], *adv.* high up, on high, up above; (*naut.*) to a more elevated part of the ship, as on deck from below, at the top of the mast, up the rigging. [OIcel. *a lopti*].

ALOGOTROPHY, [al'-og-ot'-raf-i], *n.* (*med.*) unequal nutrition of different parts of the body. [Gk. *alogos* unreasonable and *trophia* nourishment].

ALOIN, [al'-ō-in], *n.* the bitter element in aloes which acts as a purgative and forms pale yellow crystals.

ALOMANCY, [al'-ō-man-si], *n.* divination by salt. [Gk. *hals halos* salt and *manteia* divination].

ALONE, [a-lōn'], *adj. and adv.* unaccompanied, on one's own, by oneself; unaided, by one's own efforts, single, solitary, solely, exclusively; **to leave a.**, not to interfere with; **to let a.**, (*coll.*) not to interfere with. [ME. *al one* quite alone].

ALONG (1), [a-long'], *adv.* lengthwise, extending in a lengthwise direction; onward, forward, advancing from one's present position; **all a.**, repeatedly, from the commencement, all the time, the whole length of; **a. with**, together with; **lying a.**, (*naut.*) pressed down by weight of sail. [OE. *andlang* continuous].

ALONG (2), [a-long'], *prep.* in a line with or parallel to the length, in a lengthwise direction advancing towards one end; **a. shore**, (*naut.*) by the shore. [ALONG (1)].

ALONGSIDE, [a-long'-sīd], *adv. and prep.* by the side of, close to the side of, side by side with.

ALOOF, [a-lōōf'], *adv. and pred., adj.* at a distance away, away from, apart from (often implying absence of sympathy or approval); **to stand a.**, to take no part in voluntarily; **to hold oneself a.**, not to mix with, implying an attitude of reserve or disapproval. [A (3) and Du. *loef* on the luff].

ALOOFNESS, [a-lōōf'-nes], *n.* the condition or state of holding aloof.

ALOPECIA, [al'-ō-pē'-si-a], *n.* (*med.*) baldness, falling out of the hair. [Gk. *alopekia* bald patch on the head].

ALOUD, [a-lowd'], *adv.* in an audible manner, with a loud voice, loudly, in a manner so as to be heard. [ME. *aloude*].

ALOW, [a-lō'], *adv.* (*naut.*) in a lower part of a vessel, below the deck.

ALP, [alp], *n.* a high mountain, mountain pasture found below the level of the snow-line in summer; **the Alps**, the mountain ranges in Switzerland, northern Italy and south-eastern France. [L. *alpes*, ~Gael. *alp* a high mountain].

ALPACA, [al-pak'-a], *n.* an animal of the camel tribe found in the Andes, about the size of a sheep and with long soft woolly hair; the wool of this animal; cloth made from alpaca wool and generally mixed with cotton or silk. [Arab. *al* the and Peruvian *paco*, the native name of the animal].

ALPACA

ALPENHORN, [al'-pen-hawn'], *n.* a curved horn about three feet long used by the Swiss herdsmen to signal from one alp to another. [Germ. *alpenhorn*].

ALPENSTOCK, [al'-pen-stok'], *n.* a long, pointed iron-shod stick used in mountaineering. [Germ. *alpenstock* Alpine stick].

ALPHA, [al'-fa], *n.* the first letter in the Greek alphabet; (*fig.*) the first or beginning, the first of a series (in scientific terminology); †formerly the symbol of Christianity; **the a. and omega**, the beginning and end; **a. particles**, positively charged particles given off by radio-active substances; **a. rays**, streams of alpha particles. [Gk. *alpha*, ~Heb. *aleph* an ox, leader].

ALPHABET, [al'-fab-et], *n.* the whole series of characters used in writing a language, and arranged in a certain fixed order; (*fig.*) the first principles or elements of a study. [Gk. *alpha* and *beta*, the first two letters of the Gk. alphabet].

ALPHABETARIAN, [al'-fab-et-āer'-i-an], *n.* one who is just learning his alphabet, one who studies alphabets; (*fig.*) a beginner.

ALPHABETIC, [al'-fab-et'-ik], *adj.* alphabetical.

ALPHABETICAL, [al'-fab-et'-ikl], *adj.* pertaining to an alphabet, arranged according to the alphabet.

ALPHABETICALLY, [al'-fab-et'-ik-a-li], *adv.* in an alphabetical order or fashion.

ALPHABETIZE, [al'-fab-et-īz], *v.t.* to provide with an alphabet, to place in alphabetical order.

ALPHENIC, [al-fen'-ik], *n.* white barley-sugar. [Fr. *alphenic* sugar candy].

ALPHITOMANCY, [al-fit'-om-an-si], *n.* divination by barley-meal. [Gk. *alphiton* barley-meal and *manteia* divination].

ALPHONSIN, [al-fon'-sin], *n.* (*surg.*) an instrument fitted with three branches closed by a ring and used to extract bullets from wounds. [*Alphonsus* Ferrier, a physician of Naples].

ALPHONSINE, [al-fon'-sīn], *adj.* applied to astronomical data compiled under Alphonso X, king of Castile and Leon. [*Alphonso* X].

ALPHOS, [al'-fus], *n.* a cutaneous disease, also called vitiligo, in which the skin is rough and full of white spots. [Gk. *alphos* a dull white leprosy].

ALPINE, [al'-pīn], *adj.* pertaining to the Alps or other high mountainous range; (*fig.*) lofty, very high, belonging to or produced in high regions; **A. plants**, plants which grow in the region of the snow-line in mountainous districts. [L. *alpinus* belonging to the Alps].

ALPINIST, [al'-pin-ist], *n.* a climber in the Alps or other high mountains, a mountaineer.

ALPIST, [al'-pist], *n.* the seed of canary-grass used as bird food. [Span. *alpiste*].

ALQUIFOU, [al'-kif-ōō], *n.* a lead ore called potters' ore, found in Cornwall, and producing a green varnish. [Span. *alquifol* from Catalonian *alcofol*].

ALREADY, [awl-red'-i], *adv.* by or before a specified time, by this time, previously. [ME. *alredi* already].

ALSATIA, [al-sā'-shi-a], *n.* a frontier region between France and Germany, formerly often used as a place of shelter by fugitives from either country; a name given to Whitefriars, a London district between the Thames and Fleet Street, formerly possessing rights of sanctuary and thus a recognized retreat for criminals and debtors. [LL. *Alsatia* Alsace].

ALSATIAN (1), [al-sā'-shan], *n.* a large kind of wolf-hound, originally used as a sheep-dog in Alsace, now popular as a watchdog, police-dog, companion, etc.; a native of Alsace.

ALSATIAN (2), [al-sā'-shan], *adj.* pertaining to Alsace or the people of Alsace.

ALSIKE, [al'-sik], *n.* Swedish clover, *Trifolium hybridum*. [*Alsike* in Sweden where it flourished].

ALSIRAT, [al'-sēer-aht'], *n.* the bridge, according to Mohammedan belief, finer than a hair, as sharp as the edge of a sword-blade, and lined with thorns, built over hell and leading to paradise; (*fig.*) the narrow way of righteousness according to the Koran. [Arab. *al* the and *serat* road].

ALSO, [awl'-sō], *adv.* and *conj.* in addition, besides, as well, furthermore, likewise. [OE. *alswa* likewise].

ALT, [alt], *n.* (*mus.*) the high notes in the scale, the octave above the treble stave commencing on the top note of the treble stave G. [Provenc. from L. *altus* lofty, shrill].

ALTAR, [awl'-ter], *n.* a flat-topped raised structure of wood or stone at which religious sacrifices were received or performed; the communion table, the table on which the Mass is celebrated; **to lead to the a.**, to marry. [OE. *altare* from L. *altarium*].

ALTARAGE, [awlt'-er-ij], *n.* revenue derived from sacrificial offerings; revenue used to support an altar and priest.

ALTAR-BREAD, [awl'-ter-bred'], *n.* the bread used in the sacrament of Communion.

ALTAR-CLOTH, [awl'-ter-kloth'], *n.* a richly embroidered, ornamental cloth hanging down from the top of an altar and draping its front.

ALTAR-PIECE, [awl'-ter-pēs'], *n.* a painting or sculpture in a frame over the altar; the reredos.

ALTAR-RAILS, [awl'-ter-rālz'], *n.* the railing separating the raised platform on which stands an altar from the body of a church.

ALTAR-SCREEN, [awl'-ter-skrēn'], *n.* a screen between the altar and the choir.

ALTAR-TABLE, awl'-ter-tābl'], *n.* the Communion-table.

ALTAR-TOMB, [awl'-ter-tōōm'], *n.* a monument in the shape of an altar over a tomb.

ALTAR-WISE, [awl'-ter-wīz'], *adv.* like an altar, facing the same direction as an altar.

ALTAZIMUTH, [alt'-az'-im-uth], *n.* (*astron.*) a telescope so mounted as to register both altitude and azimuth. [ALT(ITUDE) and AZIMUTH].

ALTER, [awl'-ter], *v.t.* and *i.* to change, to make different, to modify; to become different, to change (in appearance or character). [LL. *alterare* to change].

ALTERABILITY, [awl'-ter-ab-il'-i-ti], *n.* degree to which a thing is capable of being altered or altering.

ALTERABLE, [awl'-ter-abl], *adj.* capable of being altered. [Fr. *altérable*].

ALTERABLENESS, [awl'-ter-abl-nes], *n.* susceptibility of alteration, power of being altered.

ALTERABLY, [awl'-ter-ab-li], *adv.* so as to be capable of alteration.

ALTERANT (1), [awl'-ter-ant], *n.* anything that changes or causes a change. [Fr. *altérant*].

ALTERANT (2), [awl'-ter-ant], *adj.* bringing about a change. [ALTERANT (1)].

ALTERATION, [awl'-ter-ā'-shun], *n.* change, a state of being changed, the act of altering, a correction, a modification. [MedL. *alterātio*].

ALTERATIVE (1), [awl'-ter-at-iv], *n.* (*med.*) a medicine which, when taken repeatedly, slowly brings about a change in the constitution, and gradually restores the healthy functions.

ALTERATIVE (2), [awl'-ter-at-iv], *adj.* bringing about alteration, susceptible to alteration.

ALTERCATE, [awl'-ter-kāt], *v.i.* to engage in violent argument with, to dispute hotly, to wrangle. [L. *altercāre* to wrangle with].

ALTERCATION, [awl'-ter-kā'-shun], *n.* a violent dispute, a heated argument, a wrangle.

ALTERCATIVE†, [awl'-ter-kā'-tiv], *adj.* scolding, quarrelling.

ALTER EGO, [al'-ter-eg'-ō], *n.* a second self, an intimate, a bosom friend; the administrative ambassador of the Sicilian kings.

ALTERNANT, [awl-tern'-ant], *adj.* (*geol.*) consisting of alternating layers.

ALTERNATE (1), [awl'-ter-nat], *n.* a person who shares alternatively with someone else in the execution of certain duties, offices, functions, etc.; (*leg.*) right to precedence in succession; precedence by rotation amongst persons of equal rank (as applied to diplomats, etc.); (*U.S.*) a substitute for a delegate. [ALTERNATE (2)].

ALTERNATE (2), [awl-tur'-nat], *adj.* of two things occurring in regular succession one behind the other as regards time or position; every other, every second; (*bot.*) occurring on opposite sides of an axis in regular succession at different levels; (*math.*) occurring on opposite sides of a line in regular succession; **a. generation**, (*biol.*) of young, reproduced after the manner in which their grandparents were reproduced, but in a different way from that in which their parents were reproduced. [L. *alternatum*, *p.pt.* of *alternare*].

ALTERNATE (3), [awl'-ter-nāt'], *v.t.* to perform, arrange or interchange two things in succession one after the other; (of two things) to cause to succeed in turn; *v.i.* to succeed or occur one after the other, to vary between two things occurring in alternate succession; (*elect.*) of a current which reverses direction regularly at certain periods. [*Prec.*].

ALTERNATELY, [awl-tur'-nat-li], *adv.* in alternate succession, first one then another in turn.

ALTERNATENESS, [awl-tur'-nat-nes], *n.* the characteristic of being alternate.

ALTERNATING-CURRENT, [awl'-ter-nāt'-ing-ku'-rent], *n.* (*elect.*) an electric current reversing its direction regularly at certain intervals.

ALTERNATION, [awl'-ter-nā'-shun], *n.* the act of alternating, the state of being alternate, the regular succession of one thing after another; (*eccles.*) response in the church service. [L. *alternatio*].

ALTERNATIVE (1), [awl-turn'-at-iv], *n.* a choice of one of two things, courses of action, solutions, etc.; a choice of several methods of approach, courses of action, solutions, etc.; (*pl.*) several courses of action, possibilities, etc., differing from the one suggested.

ALTERNATIVE (2), [awl-turn'-at-iv], *adj.* offering a choice of two, differing from the one suggested. [MedL. *alternativus*].

ALTERNATIVELY, [awl-turn'-at-iv-li], *adv.* in an alternative way, as an alternative, with a choice of.

ALTERNATIVENESS†, [awl-turn'-at-iv-nes], *n.* the

quality, state, or condition of being alternative.

ALTERNATOR, [awl'-ter-nāt'-or], *n.* a dynamo, or generator, that produces alternating electric current.

ALTHAEA, [al-thē'-a], *n.* a genus of plants including the marsh-mallow and hollyhock. [Gk. *althaia* marsh-mallow].

ALTHEINE, [al-thē'-ēn], *n.* an extract of marsh-mallow; asparagine.

ALTHORN, [alt'-hawn'], *n.* (*mus.*) a brass instrument, the tenor saxhorn.

ALTHORN

ALTHOUGH, [awl-THŌ'], *conj.* though, in spite of the fact that, even though. [ME. *al thogh* although].

ALTIMETER, [al-ti-mēt'-er], *n.* (*aeron.*) a kind of aneroid barometer, used in aircraft, to show the height above ground at which one is flying. [ALTI(TUDE) and METER].

ALTIMETRY, [al-tim'-et-ri], *n.* the art or science of measuring altitudes. [ALTI(TUDE) and Gk. *metria* measurement].

ALTINCAR, [al-tin'-kah(r)], *n.* a salt of unrefined borax employed in the fusion of metals. [Arab. *al-tinkar* crude borax].

ALTISCOPE, [al'-ti-skōp], *n.* a periscope, a telescope used in submarines. [L. *altus* high and SCOPE].

ALTISONANT, [al-tis'-on-ant], *adj.* high-sounding; lofty in language. [L. *altus* high and SONANT].

ALTISONOUS, [al-tis'-on-us], *adj.* high-sounding, altisonant.

ALTITUDE, [al'-ti-tewd], *n.* height of very tall objects measuring from bottom to top; height above horizon or sea-level; (*esp.* in *pl.*) high places or regions; (*astron.*) the height of a heavenly body measured by its angular distance above the horizon; (*geom.*) the perpendicular distance from the base of a triangle to its apex; **a. control**, (*aeron.*) a device fitted to the carburettor or other part of the induction system to obtain a weaker mixture of fuel gas at high altitudes, to compensate for reduced atmospheric pressure. [L. *altitudo*].

ALTITUDINAL, [al'-ti-tewd'-inl], *adj.* pertaining to altitude.

ALTITUDINARIAN, [al'-ti-tewd-in-āer'-i-an], *adj.* doctrinarian, lofty or idealistic.

ALTIVOLANT, [al-tiv'-ol-ant], *adj.* high-flying. [L. *altus* high and *volans* flying].

ALTO, [al'-tō], *n.* (*mus.*) originally the highest male voice or counter-tenor, now the lowest female or boy's voice, the contralto; the part taken by this voice in a score; a person who sings the alto part; the viola or tenor-violin. [It. *alto* from L. *altus* high].

ALTO-CLEF, [al'-tō-klef'], *n.* (*mus.*) the C clef placed on the third line of the stave.

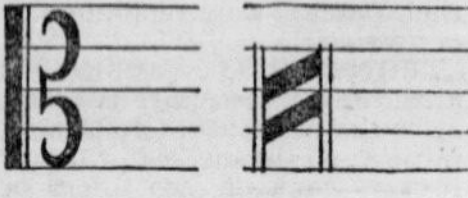

ALTO-CLEF

ALTOGETHER, [awl'-to-geTH'-er], *adv.* in all respects, wholly, entirely, totally. [ALL and TOGETHER].

ALTOMETER, [alt-om'-it-er], *n.* barometer for recording altitudes. [ALT(ITUDE) and (BAR)OMETER].

ALTO-RELIEVO, ALTO-RILIEVO, [al'-tō-ril-ē'-vō], *n.* (*sculp.*) high relief; figures that project half or more of their thickness from a flat surface. [It. *altorilievo*].

ALTO-RIPIENO, [al'-tō-rip-yā'-nō], *n.* a tenor part, instrumental or vocal, used only occasionally to fill out a grand chorus. [ALTO and It. *ripieno* that which fills up].

ALTRUISM, [al'-trōō-izm], *n.* the doctrine or principle which inculcates sacrifice of self for the interests of others. [Fr. *altruisme* from OFr. *altrui* others].

ALTRUIST, [al'-trōō-ist], *n.* one who practises altruism.

ALTRUISTIC, [al'-trōō-ist'-ik], *adj.* unselfish, in accordance with altruism.

ALTRUISTICALLY, [al'-trōō-ist'-ik-a-li], *adv.* in an altruistic way.

ALUDEL, [al'-ewd-el'], *n.* (*chem.*) a pear-shaped bottle with an opening at each end so that it can form one in a series of like objects used to make a condenser for sublimation. [Fr. *aludel* from Arab. *al-uthal*].

ALULA, [al'-yōō-la], *n.* (*ornith.*) the bastard wing, or winglet of a bird; (*entom.*) a small appendage at the base of the wing. [L. *alula* from *ala* wing].

ALUM (1), [al'-um], *n.* double sulphate of aluminium and potassium, a salt much used in medicine and the arts. [OFr. *alum*].

ALUM (2), [al'-um], *v.t.* to impregnate with alum.

ALUMINA, [al-ew'-min-a], *n.* the oxide of aluminium, the most abundant of the mineral earths, and the characteristic ingredient of common clay. [L. *alumen* alum].

ALUMINATE, [al-ew'-min-āt], *v.t.* to treat or impregnate with alum.

ALUMINIC, [al'-ew-min'-ik], *adj.* containing or resembling aluminium.

ALUMINIFEROUS, [al-ew'-min-if'-er-us], *adj.* containing quantities of alum or alumina. [L. *alumen* alum and *fero* I bear].

ALUMINIFORM, [al'-ew-min'-i-fawm], *adj.* having the form or appearance of alumina. [ALUMINA and FORM].

ALUMINITE, [al-ew'-min-īt], *n.* sulphate of alumina, also called Websterite.

ALUMINIUM, [al'-ew-min'-i-um], *n.* a soft light white metal much used for ornaments, instruments, household utensils and as an alloy, also used in the manufacture of aeroplanes on account of its lightness combined with strength, the chemical element Al; **a. gold**, an alloy of aluminium and copper, resembling gold, and hence much used for cheap jewellery. [Modification of ALUMINUM, the name given to it by its discoverer, Sir H. Davy].

ALUMINOUS, [al-ew'-min-us], *adj.* relating to or containing alum.

ALUMINUM, [al-ew'-min-um], *n.* (*U.S.*) aluminium. [ALUMINIUM].

ALUMISH, [al'-um-ish], *adj.* somewhat like alum.

ALUMNA, [al-um'-na], *n.* a woman graduate or a former pupil or student. [L. *alumna*, *fem.* of *alumnus* disciple, foster-child].

ALUMNUS, [al-um'-nus], *n.* a graduate, or a former pupil or student of a given school or university. [L. *alumnus* foster-son, disciple].

ALUMSTONE, [al'-um-stōn'], *n.* another name for alunite.

ALUNITE, [al'-ew-nīt], *n.* (*min.*) a hydrated sulphate of potassium and aluminium. [Fr. *alun* alum].

ALUNOGEN, [al-ew'-noj-en], *n.* (*min.*) a fibrous aluminium sulphate, also called keramohalite. [Fr. *alum* alum and Gk. *genes* born of, produced by].

ALUTA, [al-ew'-ta], *n.* a kind of soft leather treated with alum. [L. *aluta* soft leather].

ALUTACEOUS, [al'-ew-tā'-shus], *adj.* having the colour of tanned leather.

ALVEARY, [al'-vē'-a-ri], *n.* a beehive; (*anat.*) the hollow of the external ear where the wax is found. [L. *alvearium* a row of beehives].

ALVEATE, [al'-vē-āt], *v.t.* to make hollow, dome-shaped. [L. *alveus* a hollow or cavity].

ALVEOLAR, [al-vē'-ol-er], *adj.* containing or relating to sockets, and *esp.* to the ridge just behind the upper teeth. [ALVEOLUS].

ALVEOLARY, [al-vē'-ol-a-ri], *adj.* pertaining to the alveoli.

ALVEOLATE, [al-vē'-ol-āt], *adj.* pitted, so as to resemble a honeycomb.

ALVEOLE, [al'-vē-ōl], *n.* a cell or cavity in a honeycomb, or in a fossil; the socket in which a tooth is fixed. [L. *alveolus*].

ALVEOLUS, (*pl.* **alveoli**), [al-vē'-ōl-us, al-vē'-ōl-ī], *n.* an alveole; a cell in honeycomb or shell; the socket of a tooth. [L. *alveolus* a cavity].

ALVINE, [al'-vīn], *adj.* pertaining to the intestines. [L. *alvinus* from *alvus* belly].

ALWAY†, [awl'-wā], *adv.* (*poet.*) always. [OE. *alne weg*].

ALWAYS, [awl'-wāz], *adv.* on every occasion, at all times; continually, perpetually; in any circumstances, anyhow, whatever happens. [*Prec.*].

AM, [am, 'm], the *1st pers. sing.* of the verb *to be.* [OE. *eom eam*].

AMACRATIC, [am'-ak-rat'-ik], *adj.* applied to a lens so photographically perfect as to unite all the actinic rays into one focus. [Gk. *hama* together and *kratos* power].

AMADAVAT, [am'-ad-av-at'], *n.* a weaver-bird whose plumage is crimson spotted with white, *Sporoeginthus amandava.* [Indian].

AMADOU, [am'-ad-ōō], *n.* spongy substance used as tinder, prepared from a dried fungus, *Polyporus* *fomentarius*, steeped in saltpetre. [Fr. *amadou*].

AMAIN, [a-mān'], *adv.* with full force, with all one's might, violently, in full force of numbers, at full speed, without delay, at once, exceedingly, greatly. [OE. *on* and *mægn* strength].

AMALGAM, [am-al'-gam], *n.* an alloy of mercury; a mixture or compound of different substances. [Fr. *amalgame*].

AMALGAMATE (1), [am-al'-gam-āt], *adj.* alloyed (of mercury and another metal); combined, coalesced.

AMALGAMATE (2), [am-al'-gam-āt], *v.t.* to combine mercury with another metal; (*fig.*) to unite together, to combine (used of business houses, firms, societies, etc.); *v.i.* to combine in an amalgam; (*fig.*) to mix; unite, blend; agree (of classes, races, ideas, etc.).

AMALGAMATION, [am-al'-gam-ā'-shun], *n.* the act or process of amalgamating; the blending of different things; (*met.*) the process of separating gold and silver from ores by means of mercury; (*comm.*) a merger; the union of two or more companies of the same nature into one concern.

AMALGAMATIVE, [am-al'-gam-at-iv], *adj.* with a tendency to amalgamation.

AMALGAMATOR, [am-al'-gam-ā'-tor], *n.* one who amalgamates; a machine used in mining to mix mercury with the ore in order to extract free metal.

AMANDIN (1), [am-an'-din], *n.* the proteid represented in peach-kernels and sweet almonds. [Fr. *amandine*].

AMANDIN (2), **AMANDINE**, [am-an'-din], *n.* albuminous matter contained in, or an ointment made from, sweet almonds. [Fr. *amandine* from *amande* almond].

AMANDOLA, [am-an'-dol-a], *n.* a greenish marble with white spots resembling a honeycomb. [It. *amandola*].

AMANITIN, [am-an'-it-in], *n.* the poisonous principle contained in certain mushrooms; neurin. [Gk. *amanitai* a kind of fungi].

AMANUENSIS, [am-an'-ew-en'-sis], *n.* one who writes to another's dictation, or copies what has been written; a secretary. [L. *amanuensis*].

AMARACUS, [am-ar'-ak-us], *n.* the plant marjoram, *Origanum vulgare*. [L. *amaracus* from Gk. *amarakos*].

AMARANTH, [am'-ar-anth], *n.* another name for the plant called love-lies-bleeding; an imaginary flower that never fades; a colour inclining to purple. [Gk. *amarantos* never-fading].

AMARANTHINE, [am'-ar-anth'-in], *adj.* pertaining to amaranth; unfading; of a purple colour.

AMARYLLIS, [am'-ar-il'-is], *n.* a group of bulbous plants; (*poet.*) a country sweetheart or rustic maiden. [Gk. *Amarullis*, the name of a country maiden in Theocritus and Virgil].

AMASS, [a-mas'], *v.t.* to heap together, to accumulate, to collect in large quantities. [Fr. *amasser*].

AMASSABLE, [a-mas'-abl], *adj.* that can be amassed.

AMASSETTE, [am'-as-et'], *n.* a horn scraper used to collect and sort painters' colours on the stone in grinding. [Fr. *amassette*].

AMASSMENT, [a-mas'-ment], *n.* a heap or pile, an accumulation.

AMASTHENIC, [am'-as-then'-ik], *adj.* term applied to photographic lens, amacratic. [Gk. *hama* together and *sthenos* strength].

AMATEUR (1), [am'-at-ur', am'-ach-er], *n.* one who pursues any art, sport or study from a love of it for its own sake, not to make money; a non-professional (artist, sportsman, etc.); one who has incomplete knowledge of or is unskilful and clumsy in a subject through lack of training and practice. [Fr. *amateur* one who is fond of something].

AMATEUR (2), [am'-at-ur', am'-ach-er], *adj.* performed or done by an amateur.

AMATEURISH, [am'-at-ur'-ish], *adj.* like an amateur, betraying lack of training and skill; clumsily executed, not well done.

AMATEURISHLY, [am'-at-ur'-ish-li], *adv.*, in unskilful fashion.

AMATEURISHNESS, [am'-at-ur'-ish-nes], *n.* lack of practice and skill, clumsiness of execution.

AMATEURISM, [am'-at-ur'-izm], *n.* amateurishness, unskilfulness.

AMATIVE, [am'-at-iv], *adj.* pertaining to love, *esp.* sexual love; amorous. [L. *amatus* loved].

AMATIVENESS, [am'-at-iv-nes], *n.* a propensity to sexual love; the faculty supposed by phrenologists to govern this propensity.

AMATOL, [am'-at-ol], *n.* high explosive consisting of trinitrotoluene and ammonium nitrate. [AM(MONIUM) and TOL(UENE)].

AMATORIAL, [am'-at-aw'-ri-al], *adj.* lover-like, amatory. [L. *amator* lover].

AMATORIALLY, [am'-at-aw'-ri-a-li], *adv.* in an amatorial way.

AMATORY, [am'-at-or-i], *adj.* relating to love for the opposite sex; (*anat.*) applied to the muscles of the eye used in ogling. [L. *amatorius*].

AMAUROSIS, [am'-aw-rō'-sis], *n.* (*path.*) a decay or loss of sight due to disease of the optic nerve. [Gk. *amaurosis* darkening].

AMAUROTIC, [am'-aw-rot'-ik], *adj.* afflicted with amaurosis.

AMAZE (1), [a-māz'], *n.* (*poet.*) amazement, astonishment. [AMAZE (2)].

AMAZE (2), [a-māz'], *v.t.* to fill with awe, surprise or wonder, to astonish, to astound. [OE. *amasian*].

AMAZEDLY, [a-māz'-id-li], *adv.* in amazement, in an amazed manner.

AMAZEDNESS, [a-māz'-id-nes], *n.* surprise, amazement.

AMAZEMENT, [a-māz'-ment], *n.* the state or condition of being amazed, astonishment; perplexity.

AMAZING, [a-māz'-ing], *adj.* causing amazement, astonishment or surprise.

AMAZINGLY, [a-māz'-ing-li], *adv.* in an amazing way.

AMAZON, [am'-az-on], *n.* one of a fabled race of female warriors in Scythia who dispensed with men and were formidable to their neighbours; a masculine woman; a virago. [Gk. *amazon*].

AMAZONIAN, [am'-az-ō'-ni-an], *adj.* pertaining to or like an amazon.

AMAZON-STONE, [am'-az-on-stōn'], *n.* a variety of microline found in the valley of the river Amazon, amazonite.

AMB-, *pref.* about, around. [L. *ambi* about].

AMBAGES, [am-bā'-jēz], *n.* a winding; a roundabout way of speaking or acting; circumlocution; quibble; subterfuge. [L. *ambages* roundabout way].

AMBAGIOUS, [am-bā'-jus], *adj.* roundabout, circumlocutory.

AMBAGIOUSLY, [am-bā'-jus-li], *adv.* in a roundabout manner.

AMBAGIOUSNESS, [am-bā'-jus-nes], *n.* circuitous circumlocution.

AMBASSADOR, [am-bas'-ad-or], *n.* messenger, bringer of news; agent; a minister of highest rank who represents the supreme power of his state abroad, *esp.* at a foreign court, and whose duty it is to transact the diplomatic business between his own and the foreign country. [Fr. *ambassadeur*].

AMBASSADORIAL, [am-bas'-ad-aw'-ri-al], *adj.* relating to an ambassador.

AMBASSADRESS, [am-bas'-ad-res], *n.* the wife of an ambassador; a woman ambassador.

AMBER (1), [am'-ber], *n.* a yellow semi-transparent fossil resin, which when rubbed becomes electrified. [Fr. *ambre* from Arab. *çanbar* ambergris].

AMBER (2), [am'-ber], *adj.* consisting of or like amber.

AMBERGRIS, [am'-ber-grēs], *n.* an ash-coloured odorous wax-like substance, volatilized and used in perfumery, procured from the alimentary canal of the spermaceti whale and found floating in the seas it frequents. [Fr. *ambre gris* grey amber].

AMBERITE, [am'-ber-īt], *n.* name of a smokeless explosive.

AMBER-SEED, [am'-ber-sēd], *n.* musk-seed; a seed similar to millet.

AMBER-TREE, [am'-ber-trē], *n.* a shrub whose leaves, when crushed, yield a fragrant odour.

AMBIDEXTER, [am'-bi-deks'-ter], *n.* a person who uses both hands with equal facility; a double-dealer; (*leg.*) a juror who takes money from both parties. [L. *ambo* both and *dexter* right hand].

AMBIDEXTERITY, [am'-bi-deks-ter'-it-i], *n.* faculty or quality of being ambidextrous.

AMBIDEXTROUS, [am'-bi-deks'-ter-us], *adj.* capable of using both hands equally; double-dealing.

AMBIDEXTROUSLY, [am'-bi-deks'-ter-us-li], *adv.* in an ambidextrous way.

AMBIDEXTROUSNESS, [am'-bi-deks'-ter-us-nes], *n.* faculty of being ambidextrous.

AMBIENT, [am'-bi-ent], *adj.* encompassing; surrounding, going round about. [L. *ambiens* going round].

AMBIGUITY, [am'-big-ew'-i-ti], *n.* the state or quality of being ambiguous, double significance, lack of clarity. [L. *ambiguitas*].

AMBIGUOUS, [am-big'-ew-us], *adj.* liable to be interpreted in more than one way; doubtful; obscure; equivocal. [L. *ambiguus* uncertain, shifting].

AMBIGUOUSLY, [am-big'-ew-us-li], *adv.* in an ambiguous way.
AMBIGUOUSNESS, [am-big'-ew-us-nes], *n.* quality of being ambiguous.
AMBIT, [am'-bit], *n.* extent, scope, compass; precinct, circuit. [L. *ambitus* a moving round, circuit].
AMBITION, [am-bish'-un], *n.* strong desire of success and superiority, of prosperity, admiration, advancement, etc.; wish to achieve aspirations and ideals; the object of such aspirations and wishes. [L. *ambitio* a going round canvassing for votes].
AMBITIONLESS, [am-bish'-un-les], *adj.* lacking ambition.
AMBITIOUS, [am-bish'-us], *adj.* having ambition, desirous of attaining fame, power, wealth, etc.; (often) excessively desirous of attaining these; showing ambition, aspiring on a grand scale.
AMBITIOUSLY, [am-bish'-us-li], *adv.* in an ambitious way.
AMBITIOUSNESS, [am-bish'-us-nes], *n.* ambition, the quality of being ambitious.
AMBITUS, [am'-bit-us], *n.* the circumference or outer edge of an object, as a leaf or shell; (*arch.*) an open space surrounding a building or tomb. [L. *ambitus*].
AMBIVALENCE, [am-biv'-al-ens], *n.* (*psych.*) simultaneous operation in the mind of two irreconcilable wishes.
AMBIVALENCY, [am-biv'-al-en-si], *n.* ambivalence. [L. *ambo* both and VALENCY].
AMBIVALENT, [am-biv'-al-ent], *adj.* (*psych.*) operating simultaneously (of two irreconcilable wishes).
AMBLE (1), [ambl] *n.* an easy unhurried pace.
AMBLE (2), [ambl], *v.i.* to move at an amble, to move easily without hurry or jolts. [L. *ambulare*].
AMBLING, [am'-bling], *adj.* with an easy, rolling pace.
AMBLINGLY, [am'-bling-li], *adv.* with an ambling pace or gait.
AMBLOSIS, [am-blō'-sis], *n.* (*med.*) abortion. [Gk. *amblosis*].
AMBLOTIC, [am-blot'-ik], *adj.* tending to cause abortion.
AMBLYGONITE, [am-blig'-on-it], *n.* (*min.*) a pale greenish mineral found as obtuse-angled rhombic crystals. [Gk. *amblugonios* obtuse-angled].
AMBLYOPIA, [am'-bli-ō'-pi-a], *n.* incipient stage of amaurosis; defective vision. [Gk. *ambluopia* darkening of the sight].
AMBLYOPIC, [am'-bli-op'-ik], *adj.* weak-sighted.
AMBLYOPSIS, [am'-bli-op'-sis], *n.* a species of blind fish found in the Mammoth Cave of Kentucky.
AMBLYSTOMA, [am'-blis-tō'-ma], *n.* the adult form of the axolotl, a salamandroid amphibian found in Mexico. [Gk. *amblus* blunt and *stoma* mouth].
AMBON, [am'-bon], *n.* a raised reading-desk; a pulpit. [Gk. *ambon* hill-crest].
AMBOYNA, [am-boin'-a], *n.* a finely grained wood from the island of *Amboyna*.
AMBREADA, [ahm'-brā-ah'-da], *n.* a variety of factitious amber. [Span. *ambreada*].
AMBREATE, [am'-bri-āt], *n.* (*chem.*) a salt of ambreic acid.
AMBREIC, [am'-brē-ik], *adj.* pertaining to ambrein.
AMBREIN, [am'-brē-in], *n.* a fatty substance obtained from ambergris. [Fr. *ambréine*].
AMBRINE, [am'-brēn], *n.* remedy for burns and scalds, consisting of melted paraffin and amber resin, first extensively used during the War of 1914-1918.
AMBROSIA, [am-brō'-zi-a], *n.* (*myth.*) the food of the gods which rendered immortal anyone who tasted it; (*fig.*) anything having a very pleasing taste. [Gk. *ambrosia*].
AMBROSIAL, [am-brō'-zi-al], *adj.* having the qualities of ambrosia; fragrant; delicious.
AMBROSIALLY, [am-brō'-zi-a-li], *adv.* with ambrosial fragrance.
AMBROSIAN, [am-brō'-zi-an], *adj.* ambrosial; pertaining to St. Ambrose, who lived in the fourth century and was Bishop of Milan; **A. ritual, A. liturgy,** formula of worship still used in the church of Milan, instituted by St. Ambrose; **A. chant,** one composed by St. Ambrose.
AMBROSIN, [am'-brōz-in], *n.* an old Milanese coin with a picture of St. Ambrose on horseback. [*Ambrose*].
AMBRY, AUMBRY, [am'-bri, awm'-bri], *n.* a place where alms are left for distribution; a niche with a door near the altar for the sacred vessels; a cupboard. [OFr. **aumarie*].
AMBS-ACE, [āmz'-ās], *n.* a double ace; the worst throw at dice; hence ill luck. [OFr. *ambes as*].

AMBULACRAL, [am'-bew-la'-kral], *adj.* relating to an ambulacrum.
AMBULACRUM, [am'-bew-la'-krum], *n.* a row of pores on the outside of an echinoderm. [L. *ambulacrum* avenue, walk].
AMBULANCE, [am'-bew-lans], *n.* movable hospital for the wounded attached to the army in the field; the vehicle which carries the wounded, sick and injured to hospital. [Fr. *ambulance*].
AMBULANT, [am'-bew-lant], *adj.* that moves from place to place.
AMBULATE, [am'-bew-lāt], *v.t.* to move about from place to place, to walk backwards and forwards. [L. *ambulatum*, *p.pt.* of *ambulare* to walk].
AMBULATION, [am-bew-lā'-shun], *n.* the process of ambulating. [L. *ambulatio*].
AMBULATOR, [am'-bew-lā'-tor], *n.* a surveyor's wheel used for measuring distances traversed: an odometer; a walker. [L. *ambulator*].
AMBULATORY (1), [am'-bew-lat-er-i], *n.* a space in which to walk, generally within a religious building. [MedL. *ambulatorium*].
AMBULATORY (2), [am'-bew-lat-ri], *adj.* having the power of walking, moving from place to place (*ornith.*) formed for walking, applied to feet of birds with three toes before and one behind. [L. *ambulatorius* movable].
AMBURY, [am'-ber-i], *n.* see ANBURY.
AMBUSCADE (1), [am'-bus-kād'], *n.* ambush. [Fr. *embuscade* from Span. *emboscada*].

AMBULATOR

AMBUSCADE (2), [am'-bus-kād'], *v.t.* to set an ambush for, ambush. [AMBUSCADE (1)].
AMBUSH (1), [am'-bo͝osh], *n.* a lying in wait in a concealed position in order to attack an enemy by surprise; the place of concealment; the attack itself; the troops lying in wait. [AMBUSH (2)].
AMBUSH (2), [a'm-bo͝osh], *v.t. and i.* to arrange troops in hiding for a surprise attack, to lie in wait for an enemy, to attack suddenly from a hidden position. [ME. *embush* from L. *emboscare* to set in a bush].
AMBUSTION, [am-bus'-ti-on], *n.* a burn. [L. *ambustio*].
AMEER, [am-ēer'], *n.* a prince, commander or ruler, an emir, the title long borne by the Afghan kings. [Arab. *amir*].
AMELIORABLE, [am-ēl'-yer-abl], *adj.* which may be ameliorated.
AMELIORATE, [am-ēl'-yer-āt], *v.t.* to render better; to improve; *v.i.* to grow better. [OFr. *ameillorer*].
AMELIORATION, [am-ēl'-yer-ā'-shun], *n.* act or process of making or becoming better; improvement.
AMELIORATIVE, [am-ēl'-yer-at-iv], *adj.* conducing to make better.
AMEN (1), [ā'-men', ah'-men'], *n.* the word itself sung or said at the end of a prayer, hymn, etc.; *int.* so be it; a word used to ratify prayers or expressions of faith; **a. corner, a. seat,** (*U.S.*) part of a meeting-house occupied by people who make occasional and irregular responses, thereby assisting the preacher; **to say a. to,** to agree with. [Gk. *amen* verily from Heb. *amen*].
AMEN (2), [ā'-men', ah'-men'], *v.t.* to sanction, ratify.
AMENABILITY, [a-mēn'-ab-il'-i-ti], *n.* quality of being amenable.
AMENABLE, [a-mēn'-abl], *adj.* answerable, liable to be called to account; submissive, tractable, capable of being won over, capable of being influenced. [Fr. *amener* to lead, bring to].
AMENABLENESS, [a-mēn'-abl-nes], *n.* state or quality of being amenable.
AMENABLY, [a-mēn'-ab-li], *adv.* in an amenable way.
AMEND, [a-mend'], *v.t.* to change for the better; to improve; *v.i.* to grow or become better. [OFr. *amender*].
AMENDABLE, [a-mend'-abl], *adj.* that can be amended.
AMENDATORY, [a-mend'-at-o-ri], *adj.* tending to amend, conducing to amendment; corrective.
AMENDE, [am-ahnd'], *n.* compensation by way of a fine, reparation; **a. honorable,** a public apology for an insult offered or an injury done. [Fr. *amende*].
AMENDMENT, [a-mend'-ment], *n.* a change for the better; reformation; recovery of health; a word, clause or paragraph added, or proposed to be added, to a bill or a motion; (*leg.*) the correction of an error in a writ or process.

AMENDS, [a-mendz'], *n.(pl.)* compensation, reparation for an injury, (used chiefly in phrase **to make a.**).
AMENITY, [a-mĕn'-it-i, a-men-i-ti], *n.* delightfulness, pleasantness; (of places) due to agreeable climate, convenient situation, pleasant design, etc.; (of persons) to polished manners, gentle disposition, etc. [Fr. *aménité*].
AMENORRHOEA, [ā'-men'-o-rē'-a], *n.* absence or suppression of the menses from causes other than natural cessation or pregnancy. [A (4) and Gk. *men* month and *rhoia* flowing].
AMENT, [am'-ent], *n.* (*bot.*) a catkin, drooping inflorescence found on willows, hazels, etc. [L. *amentum* a thong].
AMENTACEOUS, [am'-en-tā'-shus], *adj.* growing in an ament, with flowers in catkins.
AMENTIA, [am-en'-shi-a], *n.* mental deficiency, imbecility. [L. *amentia* lack of mind].
AMERCE, [am-urs'], *v.t.* to punish with a fine the amount of which is left to the court to decide; to punish. [ME. *amercen* fine from AFr. *amercier*].
AMERCEABLE, [am-urs'-abl], *adj.* liable to be amerced.

AMENT

AMERCEMENT, AMERCIAMENT, [am-urs'-ment, am-urs'-i-am-ent], *n.* a fine or penalty inflicted at the discretion of the court.
AMERICAN (1), [am-e'-rik-an], *n.* an inhabitant of America, *esp.* of the United States of America. [AMERICAN (2)].
AMERICAN (2), [am-e'-rik-an], *adj.* pertaining to the continent of America, *esp.* to the United States; **A. Beauty,** a variety of rose; **A. blight,** a woolly aphis infesting apple trees; **A. cloth,** a kind of enamelled oilcloth; **A. ivy,** the Virginia creeper; **A. leather,** early name for a variety of American cloth with a surface imitating leather; **A. plan,** (in hotels) scheme by which board is paid for by time, instead of by separate items, as commonly in Europe; **A. sale of work,** a sale of work in which everyone is expected to bring one article to sell, and to buy one; **A. tea,** a function in which each guest brings an item of food; **A. tournament,** one in which each entrant plays each other entrant. [*Amerigo* Vespucci, an Italian who landed on the continent in 1499].
AMERICANI, [am-e'-rik-ah'-ni], *n.* a kind of cotton cloth. [Swahili *americani*].
AMERICANISM, [am-e'-rik-an-izm], *n.* an American peculiarity or idiom; the peculiar meaning given to an English word or phrase in the U.S.A.
AMERICANIZATION, [am-e'-rik-an-iz-ā'-shun], *n.* the making or becoming American in character.
AMERICANIZE, [am-e'-rik-an-iz], *v.t. and i.* to make American in character; to naturalize in America.
AMETABOLIAN, [a-met'-ab-ō'-li-an], *n.* a division of insects which are not subject to metamorphosis.
AMETABOLIC, [a-met'-ab-ol'-ik], *adj.* (*entom.*) not subject to metamorphosis. [Gk. *ametabolos* not changeable].
AMETHYST, [am'-ith-ist], *n.* a precious stone, usually violet, and of a crystalline nature, which was formerly supposed to prevent intoxication when worn about the person; a purple colour. [Gk. *amethustos* not drunken].
AMETHYSTINE, [am'-ith-ist'-in], *adj.* pertaining to, like, or composed of amethyst.
AMHARIC, [am-har'-ik], *n.* language of the Abyssinian nobility, official language of the country. [*Amhara* Abyssinian province].
AMIA, [am'-i-a], *n.* a genus of fishes found in North America, including the bow-fin or mud-fish. [Gk. *amia*].
AMIABILITY, [ām'-i-ab-il'-i-ti], *n.* the state or quality of being amiable.
AMIABLE, [ām'-i-abl], *adj.* possessing kindly qualities; lovable, worthy of affection. [OFr. *amiable* from L. *amicabilis* friendly].
AMIABLENESS, [ām'-i-abl-nes], *n.* quality of being amiable.
AMIABLY, [ām'-i-ab-li], *adv.* in an amiable way.
AMIANTHIFORM, [am'-i-an'-thi-fawm], *adj.* in the form of amianthus. [AMIANTHUS and FORM].
AMIANTHOID (1), [am'-i-an'-thoid], *n.* a kind of asbestos. [AMIANTHOID (2)].
AMIANTHOID (2), [am'-i-an'-thoid], *adj.* like amianthus in form. [AMIANTHUS and Gk. *oeides* like].
AMIANTHUS, [am'-i-an'-thus], *n.* a fine fibrous variety of asbestos. [Gk. *amiantos* undefiled].
AMIC, [am'-ik], *adj.* relating to or obtained from ammonia. [AM(MONIA)].
AMICABLE, [am'-ik-abl], *adj.* friendly, peaceable. [L. *amīcābilis*].
AMICABLENESS, [am'-ik-abl-nes], *n.* the state or quality of being amicable.
AMICABLY, [am'-ik-ab-li], *adv.* in an amicable way.
AMICE (1), AMICT, [am'-is, am'-ikt], *n.* a square piece of white linen, sometimes embroidered, worn round the shoulders by a priest when officiating at Mass. [OFr. *amis amit* from L. *amictus* cloak].
AMICE (2), [am'-is], *n.* a flowing hooded cloak, formerly worn by the clergy and pilgrims, a fur-lined hood with long ends first used as a cap. [OFr. *aumuce* from L. *almucia*].
AMICT, see AMICE (1).

AMICE (1)

AMID (1), AMIDE, [am'-id], *n.* a substance derived from ammonia by substituting univalent acid radicals for hydrogen atoms. [AM(MONIA)].
AMID (2), [a-mid'], *prep.* in the midst or middle of; among, surrounded by. [OE. *on middan* in the middle].
AMIDE, see AMID (1).
AMIDIN, AMIDINE, [am'-id-in], *n.* a substance obtained from wheat and potato starch. [Fr. *amidon* starch].
AMIDOL, [am'-id-ol], *n.* a compound of phenol used in photography for developing bromide plates. [Trade name from *(Di)amid(ophen)ol* of which it is a salt].
AMIDSHIPS, [a-mid'-ships], *adv.* (*naut.*) in the middle of a ship, on a line between stem and stern.
AMIDST, [a-midst'], *prep.* amid (2). [ME. *amiddes*].
AMINE, [am'-in], *n.* a substance derived from ammonia by substituting hydrocarbon radicals for the hydrogen atoms. [AM(MONIA)].
AMIR, [am-ēer'], *n.* an emir, an ameer, title given to some Mohammedan rulers. [Arab. *amir* prince].
AMISS (1), [a-mis'], *adj.* (only as predicate in negative constructions) wrong, inopportune, undesirable.
AMISS (2), [a-mis'], *adv.* badly, ill, wrongly; (in negative constructions only) inopportunely, undesirably; **to take something a.,** to take offence at something; **it will not come a. to him,** it will not be useless, unwelcome, distasteful to him. [ME. *a* from OE. *an* and MISS (2)].
AMISSING, [a-mis'-ing], *adj.* (*chiefly Scots*) wanting, missing, lacking. [From phrase *a-missing* wrongly taken as a single word].
AMITY, [am'-it-i], *n.* harmonious relationship, friendship. [Fr. *amitié*].
AMMA (1), [am'-a], *n.* the mother superior in a Greek or Syrian convent. [Gk. *amma*].
AMMA (2), [am'-a], *n.* (*med.*) a truss. [Gk. *amma* a tie].
AMMETER, [am'-it-er], *n.* an instrument for measuring the flow in amperes of an electric current. [AM(PERE) and METER].
AMMODYTE, [am'-od-it], *n.* (*ichth.*) name for the sand-eel. [Gk. *ammodutes*].
AMMONAL, [am'-onl], *n.* a class of high-explosive made by combining nitrate of ammonia with powdered aluminium. [AMMON(IA) and AL(UMINIUM)].
AMMONIA, [a-mō'-ni-a], *n.* a compound of nitrogen with three parts of hydrogen; the pungent volatile alkaline gas obtained from hartshorn. [*Next*].
AMMONIAC, [a-mō'-ni-ak], *adj.* like or containing ammonia; **sal a.,** hard salt used for medicinal purposes; **gum a.,** a bitter resin, used in medicine, and obtained from the tree *Dorema ammoniacum.* [L. *ammoniacum* pertaining or relating to *Ammon*, an Egyptian god identified with Jupiter. Ammonia was first obtained from trees growing round the temple of Jupiter Ammon].
AMMONIACAL, [a-mō'-ni-akl], *adj.* containing ammonia, or possessing its properties.
AMMONIAPHONE, [a-mō'-ni-af-ōn], *n.* an instrument through which ammonia may be inhaled to stimulate the voice. [AMMONIA and Gk. *phone* voice].
AMMONIATED, [a-mō'-ni-ā'-tid], *adj.* united or impregnated with ammonia.

AMMONITE (1), [am'-on-īt], *n.* an extinct mollusc. with flat, spiral shell resembling a ram's horn. [(Jupiter) *Ammon* who was always represented with ram's horns].

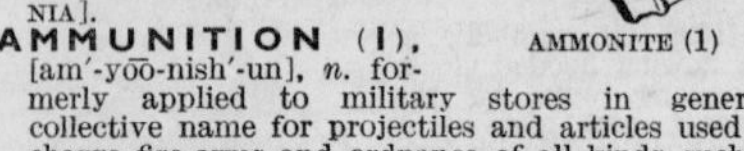

AMMONITE (1)

AMMONITE (2), [am-on'-īt], *n.* an explosive used in coal-mines, composed of ammonium nitrate and nitro-naphthalene. [AMMONIUM].

AMMONIUM, [a-mō'-ni-um], *n.* an alkaline radicle ammonia with one more atom of hydrogen. [AMMONIA].

AMMUNITION (1), [am'-yōō-nish'-un], *n.* formerly applied to military stores in general; collective name for projectiles and articles used to charge fire-arms and ordnance of all kinds, such as shells, explosives, cartridges, etc. [Fr. *amunition* from L. *munitio* defence].

AMMUNITION (2), [am'-yōō-nish'-un], *adj.* applied to articles made or issued *esp.* for use by soldiers, as boots; **a. wagon,** one used to carry ammunition. [AMMUNITION (1)].

AMNESIA, [am-nē'-zi-a], *n.* (*med.*) inability to remember, loss of memory. [Gk. *amnesia* lack of memory].

AMNESTY, [am'-nes-ti], *n.* pardon granted to political offenders. [Fr. *amnestie*].

AMNION, [am'-ni-on], *n.* (*anat.*) the innermost membrane enclosing the foetus in the womb; a gelatinous substance, in which the embryo of a seed is suspended and nourished at first. [Gk. *amnion*].

AMNIOTIC, [am'-ni-ot'-ik], *adj.* relating to or contained in the amnion.

AMOEBA, [am-ē'-ba], *n.* (*zool.*) a protozoon which, as a consequence of its habit of absorbing its food at every point all over its body, is constantly changing its shape. [Gk. *amoibe* change].

AMOEBAEAN, [am'-ē-bē'-an], *adj.* alternately answering, interchanging. [Gk. *amoibaios* alternate].

AMOEBAEUM, [am'-ē-bē'-um], *n.* a poem or verses in which persons are represented as speaking alternately. [L. *amoebeum* from Gk. *amoibaios* alternate].

AMOEBIFORM, [am-ē'-bi-fawm], *adj.* shaped like an amoeba. [AMOEBA and FORM].

AMOEBOID, [am-ē'-boid], *adj.* like the amoeba. [AMOEBA and Gk. *oeides* like].

AMOEBOUS, [am-ē'-bus], *adj.* relating to the amoeba.

AMOK, AMUCK, [a-muk'], *adv.* (only in phrase **to run a.**) to rush about in a frenzied manner with the intent to kill every person encountered, until finally killed oneself; (*fig.*) to get out of control, become violent. [Malay *amuq*].

AMOMUM, [am-ō'-mum], *n.* a group of tropical plants, including the cardamom and grains of paradise, whose seeds are remarkable for their pungency and aromatic properties. [L. *amomum* from Gk. *amomon*].

AMONG, [a-mung'], *prep.* mingled with, surrounded by, in the midst of, between. [OE. *on gemang* later *on mang* into a crowd, into the midst of].

AMONGST, [a-mungst'], *prep.* among, in the midst of. [ME. *amonges*].

AMONTILLADO, [am-on'-til-yah'-dō], *n.* a kind of pale sherry. [Span. *amontillado* from *Montilla* a town in Spain].

AMORAL, [am-or'-al], *adj.* non-moral, neither moral nor immoral. [A (4) and MORAL].

AMORCE, [am-aws'], *n.* priming-charge of finely-grained powder; cap for toy-pistol. [Fr. *amorce* from OFr. *amordre* to bite].

AMORIST, [am'-or-ist], *n.* one who practises and cultivates love; a gallant; a philanderer; one who writes amatory literature. [L. *amor* love].

AMOROSA, [am'-or-ō'-sa], *n.* a loose-living woman. [It. *amorosa*].

AMOROSO (1), [am'-or-ō'-sō], *n.* a lover, a man in love. [It. *amoroso*].

AMOROSO (2), [am'-or-ō'-sō], *adj. and adv.* tenderly, lovingly; (*mus.*) to be played with feeling. [*Prec.*].

AMOROUS, [am'-or-us], *adj.* easily inclined to love; fondly in love; inspired by love; pertaining to love.

AMOROUSLY, [am'-or-us-li], *adv.* in an amorous way.

AMOROUSNESS, [am'-or-us-nes], *n.* the state or quality of being amorous.

AMORPHISM, [a-maw'-fizm], *n.* shapelessness, state of being amorphous.

AMORPHOTAE, [am'-aw-fō'-tē], *n.(pl.)* (*astron.*) stars which do not fit into a constellation. [MdL. *amorphotae*].

AMORPHOUS, [am-aw'-fus], *adj.* having no determinate shape; uncrystallized. [Gk. *amorphos* shapeless].

AMORPHOUSNESS, [am-aw'-fus-nes], *n.* lack of form, the state of being shapeless.

AMORPHOZOA, [am-aw'-fō-zō'-a], *n.(pl.)* group of shapeless animals like sponges. [Gk. *amorphos* shapeless and *zoon* animal].

AMORT, [am-awt'], *adv.* in the state of death, lifeless; (*fig.*) dejected, spiritless. [Fr. *à mort* at or to death].

AMORTIZATION, [am-aw'-tīz-ā'-shun], the provision for the paying off of a debt by a sinking fund; the act or right of amortizing. [MdL. *admortizatio*].

AMORTIZE, [am-aw'-tīz], *v.t.* (*leg.*) to alienate property in mortmain, that is, to transfer in perpetuity to a corporation or fraternity; (*comm.*) to redeem by a sinking fund. [L. *admortizare*].

AMORTIZEMENT, [am-aw'-tiz-ment], *n.* amortization, act of amortizing.

AMOTION, [am-ō'-shun], *n.* (*leg.*) deprivation of property or office. [L. *amotio* a removing].

AMOUNT (1), [am-ownt'], *n.* sum total, quantity, substance, result. [AMOUNT (2)].

AMOUNT (2), [am-ownt'], *v.t.* to rise (to), or reach a certain sum; to come (to), to be equivalent (to). [OFr. *amonter* amount to].

AMOUR, [am-ōōr], *n.* a love-intrigue, usually of an illicit or discreditable nature. [L. *amor* love].

AMOURETTE, [am-ōōer-et'], *n.* a trifling love affair, a little romance; a cupid; (*bot.*) the quaking grass, *Briza media.* [Fr. *amourette, dim.* of AMOUR].

AMP, [amp], *n.* shortened colloquial form of AMPERE.

AMPELITE, [am'-pil-īt], *n.* a mineral anciently sprinkled on vines to protect them from pests. [Gk. *ampelitis* from *ampelos* a vine].

AMPELOPSIS, [am'-pel-op'-sis], *n.* an old family of climbing plants including the Virginia creeper, now united with *Vitis.* [Gk. *ampelos* a vine and *-opsis* resemblance.

AMPERAGE, [am'-per-ij], *n.* electric current, in a circuit, or given out by a generator or accumulator, measured in amperes.

AMPERE, ampère, [am'-pāer], *n.* unit of force in an electric current, the current sent by one volt through one ohm; **a.-turn,** product of number of turns in a coil of an electromagnet, and number of amperes flowing through; used as a practical unit of magnetizing force. [M. *Ampère,* a French physicist].

AMPERSAND, [am'-per-sand], *n.* name given to the symbol & which is a monogram of *et* and. [AND *per se and* "and by itself = and"].

AMPHI-, *pref.* both, about, around, on both sides. [Gk. *amphi* on both sides, of both kinds].

AMPHIARTHROSIS, [am'-fi-ah-thrō'-sis], *n.* (*anat.*) an articulation, which being, like that of the vertebrae, of the nature of both diarthrosis and synarthrosis, allows only a small degree of motion. [AMPHI and Gk. *arthron* joint and *-osis* expressing condition].

AMPHIBIA, [am-fib'-i-a], *n.(pl.)* (*zool.*) creatures capable of living both in water and on land, the class of vertebrates, intermediate between fishes and reptiles, which breathe by gills during their infancy in the water and by lungs when they attain their adult stage on land. [Gk. *amphibios* living a double life].

AMPHIBIAN, [am-fib'-i-an], *n. and adj.* member of the Amphibia, the class of vertebrates able to breathe in water and on land; (*aeron.*) aeroplane that can rise from and descend to either land or water.

AMPHIBIOLOGICAL, [am'-fib-i-ol-oj'-ikl], *adj.* relating to amphibiology. [AMPHI and BIOLOGICAL].

AMPHIBIOLOGY, [am'-fib-i-ol'-o-ji], *n.* the study of the Amphibia. [AMPHIBIA and Gk. *logos* speech].

AMPHIBIOUS, [am-fib'-i-us], *adj.* capable of living in air and water.

AMPHIBIOUSLY, [am-fib'-i-us-li], *adv.* in the manner of an amphibian.

AMPHIBIOUSNESS, [am-fib'-i-us-nes], *n.* the state or quality of being amphibious.

AMPHIBOLE, [am'-fib-ōl], *n.* a group of minerals, including hornblende. [Gk. *amphibolos* doubtful].

AMPHIBOLIC, [am'-fib-ol'-ik], *adj.* pertaining to or like amphibole.

AMPHIBOLITE, [am-fib'-ol-īt], *n.* a metamorphic

rock, the foundation of which is amphibole.

AMPHIBOLOGICAL, [am'-fib-ol-oj'-ikl], *adj.* capable of being interpreted in more than one way, ambiguous, amphibolous.

AMPHIBOLOGICALLY, [am'-fib-ol-oj'-ik-a-li], *adv.* in an amphibological manner.

AMPHIBOLOGY, [am'-fib-ol'-o-ji], *n.* (*logic.*) a phrase or sentence which may be interpreted in more than one way, ambiguous statement, obscure expression. [Gk. *amphibolos* doubtful and *logos* speech].

AMPHIBOLOID, [am-fib'-ol-oid], *n.* a rock consisting of amphibole and felspar. [AMPHIBOLE and Gk. *-oeides* like].

AMPHIBOLOUS, [am-fib'-ol-us], *adj.* capable of being interpreted in more than one way, uncertain, ambiguous. [Gk. *amphibolos*].

AMPHIBRACH, [am'-fib-rak], *n.* (*pros.*) metrical foot of three syllables, the middle long, the first and last short. [Gk. *amphibrakhus* short at both ends].

AMPHICARPIC, [am'-fi-kah'-pik], *adj.* (*bot.*) having two kinds of fruit, amphicarpous. [AMPHI and Gk. *karpos* fruit].

AMPHICARPOUS, [am'-fi-kah'-pus], *adj.* (*bot.*) having two kinds of fruit or seasons of ripening.

AMPHICOELOUS, [am'-fi-sē'-lus], *adj.* doubly concave; hollow at both ends, as the vertebrae of the fishes. [AMPHI and Gk. *koilos* hollow].

AMPHICTYONIC, [am-fik'-ti-on'-ik], *adj.* relating to the Amphictyons; **a. council,** a body of delegates, particularly the council at Delphi.

AMPHICTYONS, [am-fik'-ti-onz], *n.*(*pl.*) the delegates from twelve states of Greece, who sat alternately at Thermopylae and Delphi. [Gk. *amphiktuones* those who dwell around a place].

AMPHICTYONY, [am-fik'-ti-o-ni], *n.* (*hist.*) a federation of states in Ancient Greece for protection of common concerns. [Gk. *amphiktuonia*].

AMPHIMACER, [am-fim'-as-er], *n.* (*pros.*) a metrical foot of three syllables, the middle short, and the others long. [L. *amphimacrus*].

AMPHIMIXIS, [am'-fim-iks'-is], *n.* (*biol.*) the union of germ cells from the male and female in sexual reproduction. [AMPHI and Gk. *mixis* mingling].

AMPHIOXUS, [am'-fi-oks'-us], *n.* the lancelet, one of the primitive vertebrates of the sub-phylum Protochordata. [AMPHI and Gk. *oxus* sharp].

AMPHIPODA, [am-fip'-od-a], *n.*(*pl.*) a sub-order of Crustaceans, including sand-hoppers, freshwater shrimps, etc., with sessile eyes and two kinds of feet. [AMPHI and Gk. *pous podos* foot].

AMPHIPODOUS, [am-fip'-od-us], *adj.* relating to the Amphipoda.

AMPHIPROSTYLE, [am-fip'-ros-til], *n.* (*arch.*) a building having an equal-columned portico at each end, but without columns at the flanks. [Gr. *amphiprostulos* with a double prostyle].

AMPHISBAENA, [am'-fis-bē'-na], *n.* a species of lizards, supposed by the ancients, from the uniform thickness of their bodies, to have two heads, and to move forward with either end. [Gk. *amphisbaina*].

AMPHISCIANS, [am-fish'-i-anz], *n.*(*pl.*) the inhabitants of the torrid zone, whose shadows, at one season of the year, are cast to the north, and at the other, to the south. [Gk. *amphiskios* casting a shadow both ways].

AMPHISTOMOUS, [am-fis'-tom-us], *adj.* having a mouth at both ends. [AMPHI and Gk. *stoma* mouth].

AMPHITHEATRE, [am'-fi-thē'-at-er], *n.* an oval or circular arena with seats round it, raised in tiers so that an unobstructed view may be obtained from any part of the building; the lower gallery of a modern theatre. [Gk. *amphitheatron*].

AMPHITHEATRICAL, [am'-fi-thi-at'-rikl], *adj.* pertaining to, or performed in, an amphitheatre.

AMPHITRITE, [am'-fi-trī'-ti], *n.* (*astron.*) a minor planet between Mars and Jupiter. [*Amphitrite* the wife of Poseidon or Neptune in Greek and Roman mythology].

AMPHITROPAL, [am-fit'-ropl], *adj.* (*bot.*) applied to an embryo so curved upon itself that both ends point in the same direction.

AMPHITROPOUS, [am-fit'-rop-us], *adj.* (*bot.*) having the funicle attached to the middle of the ovule. [AMPHI and Gk. *tropos* turning].

AMPHITRYON, [am-fit'-ri-on], *n.* (*myth.*) a king of Thebes whom Jupiter impersonated in order to make love to his wife Alcmena, the mother of Hercules, and in whose person the god gave a great feast; (*fig.*) a host, entertainer. [Gk. *Amphitruon*].

AMPHORA, [am'-for-a], *n.* an ancient two-handled vessel, with a narrow neck, usually of earthenware, for wine or oil. [Gk. *amphoreus* two-handled urn].

AMPHORAL, [am'-for-al], *adj.* pertaining to or like an amphora.

AMPHORIC, [am-for'-ik], *adj.* (*med.*) emitting a sound similar to that yielded by blowing into an empty decanter; produced by an empty lung cavity.

AMPHOTERIC, [am'-fo'-ter-ik], *adj.* having both characters, neither acid nor alkaline, neutral. [Gk. *amphoteros* both].

AMPLE, [ampl], *adj.* large, of great size, spacious, abundant; sufficient; liberal; full. [Fr. *ample* from L. *amplus* large].

AMPLENESS, [ampl'-nes], *n.* the state of being ample, abundance.

AMPLEXICAUL, [am-pleks'-i-kawl], *adj.* (*bot.*) clasping the stem, used of sessile leaves the hollow base of which embraces the stem. [L. *amplexus* embracing and *caulis* stem].

AMPLIATIVE, [am'-pli-at-iv], *adj.* (*logic*) adding something to the primary idea or attributes of a subject. [~L. *amplicare* to enlarge].

AMPLIFICATION, [am'-plif-ik-ā'-shun], *n.* extension, enlargement; the act of amplifying; (*rhet.*) diffusiveness of description or argument; (*wirel.*) increasing of electrical signals (oscillations); **a. factor,** maximum voltage amplification, also called u (mu). [L. *amplificatio*].

AMPLIFICATIVE, [am'-plif-ik'-at-iv], *adj.* tending or serving to amplify.

AMPLIFIER, [am'-pli-fī-er], *n.* something that enlarges; (*opt.*) a magnifying lens; (*wirel.*) device for increasing power of radio waves, thereby magnifying the loudness of the sound.

AMPLIFY, [am'-pli-fī], *v.t. and i.* to increase, to enlarge (upon), to magnify, to describe or discuss in greater detail, to state more fully. [L. *amplificare*].

AMPLITUDE, [am'-pli-tewd], *n.* largeness, spaciousness, sufficiency, extent; (*astron.*) the arc of the horizon intercepted between the east or west point and the centre of the sun, or a star at its rising or setting during an alternation; (*elect.*) maximum value attained by an alternating quantity; **magnetical a.,** the arc of the horizon between the sun or a star at rising or setting, and the east or west point of the horizon by the compass; **a. of the range,** the line measuring the horizontal distance moved by a projectile. [L. *amplitudo*].

AMPLY, [am'-pli], *adv.* sufficiently, in an ample way.

AMPOULE, [am'-pōōl], *n.* a small container for a hypodermic dose. [Fr. *ampoule*].

AMPULLA, [am-pōōl'-a], *n.* a narrow-necked vessel used by the Romans for anointing the body after bathing, a cruet for the wine and water of the eucharist; (*anat.*) the dilated part of the semicircular canals of the ear; (*bot.*) a small membranaceous float attached to the leaves of some aquatic plants. [L. *ampulla*].

AMPULLA

AMPULLACEOUS, [am'-pōōl-ā'-shus], *adj.* resembling a bottle or inflated bladder; swelling. [L. *ampullaceus*].

AMPUTATE, [am'-pew-tāt], *v.t.* to cut off a limb or a portion of a limb, or larger bough of a tree. [L. *amputatum*, *p.pt.* of *amputare*].

AMPUTATION, [am'-pew-tā'-shun], *n.* the act or operation of amputating. [L. *amputatio*].

AMPUTATOR, [am'-pew-tā'-tor], *n.* a person who amputates.

AMUCK, [a-muk'], see AMOK.

AMULET, [am'-yōō-let], *n.* an ornament worn about the person as a charm against evil or disease; a charm; a talisman. [Fr. *amulette*].

AMULETIC, [am-yōō-let'-ik], *adj.* of the nature of or resembling an amulet.

AMURCA, [am-ur'-ka], *n.* a by-product in the preparation of olive oil, used in soap manufacture. [L. *amurca* lees of oil].

AMURCOUS, [am-ur'-kus], *adj.* full of dregs.

AMUSABLE, [am-ewz'-abl], *adj.* capable of being amused, that can be amused.

AMUSE, [am-ewz'], *v.t.* to occupy the attention agreeably, keep the mind pleasantly diverted, arouse laughter or interest, afford recreation or entertainment. [Fr. *amuser*].

AMUSEMENT, [am-ewz'-ment], *n.* the state of being amused, mirth; that which causes one to be amused, recreation, entertainment, diversion, pastime; **a.**

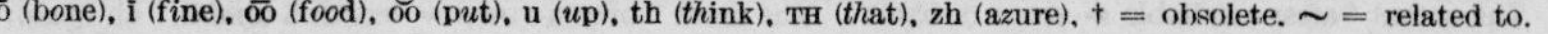

ō (bone), ī (fine), ōō (food), ŏŏ (put), u (up), th (think), TH (that), zh (azure), † = obsolete. ~ = related to.

park, a fair-ground in which are set up booths, stalls, swings, roundabouts and other forms of popular entertainment; **indoor amusements,** games and entertainments which can be played or given indoors, *esp.* in the home. [Fr. *amusement*].

AMUSING, [am-ewz'-ing], *adj.* capable of causing amusement, provoking mirth.

AMUSINGLY, [am-ewz'-ing-li], *adv.* in an amusing way.

AMUSIVELY, [am-ewz'-iv-li], *adv.* in an amusing manner.

AMYGDALATE (1), [am-ig'-dal-āt], *n.* (*med.*) an emulsion of almonds; (*chem.*) a salt of amygdalic acid.

AMYGDALATE (2), [am-ig'-dal-āt], *adj.* relating to or made of almonds. [L. *amygdalum* almond].

AMYGDALIC, [am-ig-dal'-ik], *adj.* obtained from or belonging to bitter almonds; **a. acid,** one obtained from amygdalin.

AMYGDALIN, [am-ig'-dal-in], *n.* a glucoside prepared from the kernel of the bitter almond and other stone fruit. [L. *amygdalum* almond].

AMYGDALINE, [am-ig'-dal-īn], *adj.* relating to or like the almond.

AMYGDALOID (1), [am-ig'-dal-oid], *n.* a rock embedding nodules of various minerals, looking like almonds in a cake. [AMYGDALOID (2)].

AMYGDALOID (2), [am-ig'-dal-oid], *adj.* like or shaped like an almond. [L. *amygdalum* almond and Gk. *oeides* like].

AMYGDALOIDAL, [am-ig'-dal-oidl'], *adj.* (*min.*) relating to, or consisting of, almond-shaped cavities in igneous rocks filled up with minerals. [*Prec.*].

AMYL, [am'-il], *n.* starch; (*chem.*) the supposed radical of such compounds as **a. alcohol,** and **a. nitrite.** [L. *amylum* from Gk. *amulon* starch].

AMYLACEOUS, [am'-il-ā'-shus], *adj.* relating to starch, or the farinaceous part of grain.

AMYLIC, [am-il'-ik], *adj.* of, or from starch.

AMYLOID (1), [am'-il-oid], *n.* a starchy substance found in some seeds. [AMYLOID (2)].

AMYLOID (2), [am'-il-oid], *adj.* starchy, like starch. [AMYL and Gk. *oeides* like].

AMYLOPSIN, [am'-il-op'-sin], *n.* the fermenting substance of the pancreatic juice in converting starch into sugar. [Gk. *amulon* starch and PEPSIN].

AN (1), [an], form of the indefinite article before a word beginning with a vowel. [OE. *ān* one, an].

AN (2), [an], *conj.* †if, and if. [OE. *and*].

AN- (3), *pref.* not, showing negation. [Gk. *a, an,* not, expressing negation].

ANA- (1), *pref.* up, towards, up to, again, back. [Gk. *ana*].

ANA (2), [ā'-na, ah'-na], *n.* collection of personal reminiscences, literary anecdotes, odd pieces of information, etc., usually associated with the name of some celebrity. [L. *-ana, neut. pl.* of L. *-anus adjectival suffix*].

ANA (3), [an'-a], *adv.* an equal quantity of each in a medical prescription, sometimes shortened thus, *āā* or *ā.* [ANA (1)].

ANABAPTISM, [an'-a-bap'-tizm], *n.* the religious doctrine of the Anabaptists. [ANA (1) and BAPTISM].

ANABAPTIST, [an'-a-bap'-tist], *n.* member of a sect founded at Zwickau in 1521, which believed that baptism should be by total immersion, and that those baptized in infancy should be baptized again when adults; one who believes that baptism should be administered to adults, and by total immersion.

ANABAPTISTIC, [an'-a-bap-tist'-ik], *adj.* pertaining to the Anabaptists, or Anabaptism.

ANABAS, [an'-ab-as], *n.* the Indian or climbing perch, *A. scandens,* a freshwater fish able to travel some distance on land, and supposed to climb trees. [Gk. *anabas, p.pt.* of *anabaino* I climb].

ANABASIS, [an-ab'-as-is], *n.* a military advance; so called from the famous march of Cyrus the Younger, recounted by Xenophon in his *Anabasis.* [Gk. *anabasis* a going up].

ANABATIC, [an'-a-bat'-ik], *adj.* (*meteor.*) term applied to winds caused by air flowing upwards.

ANABIOSIS, [an'-a-bī-ō'-sis], *n.* reanimation, resuscitation, a revival of life, the power of reviving in water. [Gk. *anabiosis*].

ANABOLISM, [an-ab'-ol-izm], *n.* (*biol.*) building up nutritive substances into living protoplasm, constructive metabolism. [Gk. *anabole* what is thrown up].

ANABRANCH, [an'-a-brahnch], *n.* a stream that turns out of a river, only to rejoin it lower down. [ANA (1) and BRANCH].

ANACAMPTIC, [an'-a-kamp'-tik], *adj.* reflected or reflecting, usually of sound. [Gk. *anakampto* I bend back].

ANACATHARTIC (1), [an'-a-kath-ah'-tik], *n.* that which cleanses, by exciting, vomiting or expectoration. [ANA (1) and CATHARTIC].

ANACATHARTIC (2), [an'-a-kath-ah'-tik], *adj.* cleansing, purging by causing vomiting or expectoration. [*Prec.*].

ANACEPHALAEOSIS, [an'-a-sef'-al-i-ō'-sis], *n.* (*rhet.*) recapitulation, summary. [Gk. *anakephalaiosis*].

ANACHRONISM, [an-ak'-ron-izm], *n.* a mistake in dating a historical event; (the representation of) an event or thing which is too early or too late for the period in which it is supposed to have happened or existed, or which appears out of keeping with the time at which it happens or exists. [Fr. *anachronisme* from Gk. *anakhronismos*].

ANACHRONISTIC, [an-ak'-ron-ist'-ik], *adj.* wrongly dated, out of its correct period, relating to an anachronism.

ANACHRONOUS, [an-ak'-ron-us], *adj.* wrongly dated, anachronistic.

ANACLASTIC, [an'-a-klas'-tik], *adj.* due to or connected with refraction. [Gk. *anaklastos* bent back].

ANACLISIS, [an-ak'-lis-is], *n.* (*med.*) a sore occasioned by prolonged lying back in bed. [Gk. *anaklisis* reclining].

ANACOENOSIS, [an'-a-sē-nō'-sis], *n.* (*rhet.*) appeal to an opponent for his views on the point in debate. [Gk. *anakoinosis* communication].

ANACOLUTHIC, [an'-a-kol-ew'-thik], *adj.* pertaining or relating to anacoluthon.

ANACOLUTHICALLY, [an'-a-kol-ew'-thik-a-li], *adv.* in a disjointed way.

ANACOLUTHON, (*pl.* **anacolutha**), [an'-a-kol-ew'-thon], *n.* a break in the structure or grammatical sequence of a sentence. [Gk. *anacoluthon* inconsequent].

ANACONDA, [an'-a-kon'-da], *n.* the large tropical South American snake *Eunectes murinus.* [Unkn.].

ANACREONTIC (1), [an-ak'-rē-on'-tik], *n.* a poem in the manner of the Greek poet *Anacreon,* praising love and wine.

ANACREONTIC (2), [an-ak'-rē-on'-tik], *adj.* in the style of the Greek poet *Anacreon*; in praise of love and wine; jovial; amatory.

ANACRUSIS, [an'-a-kroo'-sis], *n.* (*pros.*) an unstressed syllable or syllables preceding the first stressed syllable in a verse normally beginning with a stress; (*mus.*) introductory passage in a score. [Gk. *anakrousis* a thrusting back].

ANACRUSTIC, [an'-a-kroos'-tik], *adj.* relating to or connected with anacrusis.

ANACRUSTICALLY, [an'-a-kroos'-tik-a-li], *adv.* in an anacrustic way.

ANADEM, [an'-ad-em], *n.* a wreath, garland or chaplet. [Gk. *anadema* a headband].

ANADIPLOSIS, [an'-a-di-plō'-sis], *n.* (*rhet.*) the reiteration of the last word in a line or clause at the beginning of the next. [Gk. *anadiplosis* a doubling back].

ANADROMOUS, [an-ad'-rom-us], *adj.* (*ichth.*) passing from the sea into rivers to spawn. [Gk. *anadromos* running up].

ANAEMIA, [an-ē'-mi-a], *n.* a deficiency of blood involving a lack of red corpuscles. [Gk. *anhaimia* lack of blood].

ANAEMIC, [an-ē'-mik], *adj.* pertaining to, or suffering from anaemia.

ANAEMOTROPHY, [an'-ē-mot'-rof-i], *n.* (*med.*) deficiency in nourishment of the blood. [ANAEMIA and Gk. *trophe* nourishment].

ANAEROBIA, [an'-āer-ō'-bi-a], *n.*(*pl.*) (*biol.*) bacteria able to exist without oxygen. [AN (3) and Gk. *aer* air, and *bios* life].

ANAEROBIC, [an'-āer-ō'-bik], *adj.* able to live without free oxygen.

ANAESTHESIA, [an'-is-thē'-zi-a], *n.* (*med.*) loss, due to disease, drugs or anaesthetics, of the sense of touch or feeling. [Gk. *anaisthesia* insensibility].

ANAESTHETIC (1), [an'-is-thet'-ik], *n.* an agent to deaden sensibility, commonly used during surgical operations, etc. [*Next*].

ANAESTHETIC (2), [an'-is-thet'-ik], *adj.* deadening the sensibility, producing insensibility. [Gk. *anaisthetos* without feeling].

ANAESTHETIST, [an-ēs'-thet-ist], *n.* an expert in the administration of anaesthetics.

ANAESTHETIZATION, [an-ēs'-thet-īz-ā'-shun], *n.*

the process of administering anaesthetics; the state of being anaesthetized.
ANAESTHETIZE, [an-ēs'-thet-īz], *v.t.* to render insensible by administering an anaesthetic.
ANAGALLIS, [an'-ag-al'-is], *n.* a genus of plants of which the best known is *A. arvensis*, the scarlet pimpernel. [L. *anagallis*].
ANAGLYPH, [an'-ag-lif], *n.* an ornament embossed or sculptured in relief; a form of stereoscopic picture. [Gk. *anagluphon* carved in relief].

ANAGLYPH

ANAGLYPHIC, [an'-ag-lif'-ik], *adj.* connected with anaglyphy.
ANAGLYPHY, [an'-ag-lif-i], *n.* the art of sculpturing and embossing in relief.
ANAGLYPTIC, [an'-ag-lip'-tik], *adj.* anaglyphic. [Gk. *anagluptos* embossed].
ANAGNORISIS, [an'-ag-nor'-is-is], *n.* recognition, the denouement in a play. [Gk. *anagnorisis*].
ANAGOGE, see ANAGOGY.
ANAGOGICAL, [an'-ag-oj'-ikl], *adj.* allegorical, spiritual, mystical.
ANAGOGICALLY, [an'-ag-oj'-ik-a-li], *adv.* in an anagogic sense or manner.
ANAGOGY, ANAGOGE, [an'-ag-ō-ji], *n.* an allegorical or mystical interpretation of the Bible, particularly the Old Testament; (*path.*) the vomiting of blood from the lungs. [Gk. *anagoge* a leading up].
ANAGRAM, [an'-a-gram'], *n.* a word or phrase formed by transposing the letters it contains. [ANA (1) and Gk. *gramma* a letter].
ANAGRAMMATIC, [an'-a-gram-at'-ik], *adj.* containing an anagram.
ANAGRAMMATICAL, [an'-a-gram-at'-ikl], *adj.* containing an anagram.
ANAGRAMMATICALLY, [an'-a-gram-at'-ik-a-li], *adv.* after the manner of an anagram.
ANAGRAMMATISM, [an'-a-gram'-at-izm], *n.* the practice of making anagrams. [Gk. *anagrammatismos*].
ANAGRAMMATIST, [an'-a-gram'-at-ist], *n.* a composer of anagrams.
ANAGRAMMATIZE, [an'-a-gram'-at-īz], *v.i.* to compose anagrams.
ANAL, [ānl], *adj.* relating to or near the anus; (*ichth.*) under the tail. [MedL. *analis*].
ANALECT, (*pl.* **analecta**), [an'-al-ekt, an'-al-ek'-ta], *n.* a selection of extracts from different authors. [Gk. *analektos* choice].
ANALECTIC, [an'-al-ek'-tik], *adj.* consisting of selected parts or things. [Gk. *analektos* choice].
ANALEMMA, [an'-al-em'-a], *n.* a projection of the sphere made on the plane of the meridian, used for dialling, etc.; an astrolabe with the projection of the sphere on to wood or brass, fitted with a horizon, and formerly used to solve astronomical problems; a scale of the daily declination of the sun indicated on an artificial globe. [L. *analemma* pedestal of a sundial, from Gk. *analemma* support].
ANALEPSIS, [an'-al-ep'-sis], see ANALEPSY.
ANALEPSY, ANALEPSIS, [an'-al-ep-si], *n.* (*med.*) formerly applied to a form of epilepsy; support given during treatment of a fractured limb. [MdL. *analepsia*].
ANALEPTIC, [an'-al-ep'-tik], *n. and adj.* a restorative medicine, or tonic. [Gk. *analeptikos*].
ANALGESIA, [an'-al-jē'-zi-a], *n.* absence of, or local insensibility to, pain. [Gk. *analgesia* loss of feeling].
ANALGESIC (1), [an'-al-jēz'-ik], *n.* (*med.*) a substance tending to produce analgesia.
ANALGESIC (2), [an'-al-jēz'-ik], *adj.* tending to produce analgesia.
ANALOGIC, [an'-al-oj'-ik], *adj.* analogical; relating to analogy. [Gk. *analogikos*].
ANALOGICAL, [an'-al-oj'-ikl], *adj.* pertaining to or implying analogy.
ANALOGICALLY, [an'-al-oj'-ik-a-li], *adv.* in an analogical way.
ANALOGICALNESS, [an'-al-oj'-ikl-nes], *n.* the quality or state of being analogical.
ANALOGISM†, [an-al'-oj-izm], *n.* an argument from the cause to the effect; examination of things by their analogies. [Gk. *analogismos* proportionate calculation].
ANALOGIST, [an-al'-oj-ist], *n.* one who reasons by analogy.
ANALOGIZE, [an-al'-oj-īz], *v.t.* to explain or reason by analogy; to treat analogically.
ANALOGOUS, [an-al'-og-us], *adj.* having analogy, corresponding to, similar. [Gk. *analogos*].
ANALOGOUSLY, [an-al'-og-us-li], *adv.* in an analogous way.
ANALOGOUSNESS, [an-al'-og-us-nes], *n.* the quality or state of being analogous.
ANALOGUE, [an'-al-og], *n.* a word or object of any kind which bears resemblance or analogy to another; something that acts similarly, or has the same function; a corresponding part. [Gk. *analogon* in due proportion].
ANALOGY, [an-al'-o-ji], *n.* partial similitude or agreement between things; (*philol.*) process by which words and grammatical forms are constructed on the model of others with which they have some points of resemblance, or by which some forms are rebuilt in order to make them conform to the general rules and structure of a language; (*log.*) process of reasoning which concludes that if things are similar in certain respects they are probably similar in others as well; (*math.*) similitude of ratio, proportion; (*zool.*) resemblance in different species between organs that are essentially different, as that between the wings of bats and birds. [Fr. *analogie* from Gk. *analogia*].
ANALYSABLE, [an'-al-īz'-abl], *adj.* capable of being analysed.
ANALYSABLENESS, [an'-al-īz'-abl-nes], *n.* the quality of being analysable.
ANALYSE, [an'-al-īz], *v.t.* to resolve into its component elements; (*fig.*) to examine minutely and critically; (*chem.*) to split up a compound into its constituent parts; (*gram.*) to examine closely the structure of a phrase or sentence, observing the exact function of every word, and (often) indicating this by means of a system of tabulation. [Fr. *analyser*].
ANALYSER, [an'-al-īz-er], *n.* one who analyses.
ANALYSIS, (*pl.* **analyses**), [an-al'-is-is], *n.* the resolution or splitting up of a compound into its constituent elements; (*fig.*) a critical and detailed examination (of a discourse, statement, etc.), a classification (of the items of an account, chief points of a discussion, etc.); (*gram.*) arrangement or description of a sentence indicating the grammatical function of each word and its relation to the rest of the sentence; (*math.*) resolving of problems by reduction to equations; (*mus.*) a detailed study of a piece of music to discover primary and secondary subjects, their development and working-out, etc. [Gk. *analusis* an unloosing].
ANALYST, [an'-al-ist], *n.* one who performs analysis, *esp.* chemical or pathological analysis.
ANALYTIC, [an'-al-it'-ik], *adj.* analytical. [Gk. *analutikos*].
ANALYTICAL, [an'-al-it'-ikl], *adj.* relating to analysis; resolving a compound into its constituents; obtained by analysis; reasoning from particulars to principles, inductive.
ANALYTICALLY, [an'-al-it'-ik-a-li], *adv.* after the manner of analysis.
ANALYTICS, [an'-al-it'-iks], *n.(pl.)* the science or study of analysis.
ANAMNESIS, [an'-am-nē'-sis], *n.* remembrance, recollection, recalling to mind (*esp.* of events in a previous existence); (*med.*) the patient's account of his symptoms, from which diagnosis may sometimes be made. [Gk. *anamnesis* remembrance].
ANAMORPHOSIS, [an'-am-aw'-fō-sis], *n.* a distorted representation of an object which appears normal and in correct proportion when looked at from a certain angle or when reflected from a convex or concave mirror; (*biol.*) an evolutionary change in form, not such as may be classed as metamorphosis; (*bot.*) an abnormal development in the form of a plant often resulting in a resemblance to another species. [Gk. *anamorphosis* transformation].
ANAMORPHOUS, [an'-am-aw'-fus], *adj.* having an irregular or anomalous development.
ANANAS, [an-ahn'-as], *n.* the pineapple. [~Peruvian *nanas*].
ANANDROUS, [an-an'-drus], *adj.* (*bot.*) having no stamen. [Gk. *anandros* without a husband].
ANANIAS, [an-an-ī'-as], *n.* (*slang*) a liar. [*Ananias* one of the early Christians, who lied to St. Peter].
ANANTHEROUS, [an-an'-ther-us], *adj.* (*bot.*) having no anthers. [AN (3) and ANTHER].
ANANTHOUS, [an-an'-thus], *adj.* (*bot.*) having no flower. [Gk. *ananthes* flowerless].
ANAPAEST, [an'-a-pēst], *n.* (*pros.*) metrical foot

consisting of two short syllables followed by one long, or two unstressed syllables and a stressed one, a dactyl reversed. [L. *anapaestus*].

ANAPAESTIC (1), [an'-a-pēst'-ik], *n.* poetic measure composed of anapaests. [ANAPAESTIC (2)].

ANAPAESTIC (2), [an'-a-pēst'-ik], *adj.* pertaining to an anapaest, consisting of anapaests. [Gk. *anapaistikos*].

ANAPHORA, [an-af'-or-a], *n.* (*rhet.*) reiteration of the same word or words at the beginning of succeeding clauses of a sentence; the chief part of the eucharistic service of the Orthodox Church. [Gk. *anaphora* a carrying back].

ANAPHRODISIA, [an-af'-rod-iz'-i-a], *n.* want of sexual appetite. [Gk. *anaphrodisia*].

ANAPHRODISIAC, [an'-af-rod-iz'-i-ak], *n.* an agent to reduce sexual desire. [*Prec.*].

ANAPHYLACTIC, [an'-a-fil-ak'-tik], *adj.* relating to anaphylaxis.

ANAPHYLAXIS, ANAPHYLAXY, [an'-a-fil-aks'-is], *n.* (*med.*) an increasing responsiveness to small doses of a serum. [ANA (1) and Gk. *phulaxis* a guarding].

ANAPLASTY, [an'-a-plas'-ti], *n.* (*surg.*) the operation of restoring a part of the body by the transfer of tissue. [Gk. *anaplastos* that can be moulded].

ANAPLEROSIS, [an'-a-plēer-ō'-sis], *n.* (*med.*) renewal of destroyed or lost tissue, as in healing of wounds. [Gk. *anaplerosis* a means of filling up].

ANAPLEROTIC (1), [an'-a-plēer-ot'-ik], *n.* (*med.*) a remedy to renew flesh.

ANAPLEROTIC (2), [an'-a-plēer-ot'-ik], *adj.* (*med.*) capable of renewing flesh.

ANAPTOTIC, [an'-ap-tot'-ik], *adj.* uninflected (again), term applied to languages whose inflexion systems have broken down and for the most part disappeared. [ANA (1) and APTOTIC].

ANARCH, [an'-ahk'], *n.* an anarchist, a revolutionary. [Gk. *anarkhos* a revolutionary].

ANARCHIC, [an-ahk'-ik], *adj.* pertaining to anarchy.

ANARCHICAL, [an-ahk'-ikl], *adj.* having no civic rule; in a state of lawless confusion.

ANARCHICALLY, [an-ahk'-ik-al-i], *adv.* in a fashion tending to anarchy.

ANARCHISM, [an'-ahk-izm], *n.* political theory which regards any organized system of government as undesirable.

ANARCHIST, [an'-ahk-ist], *n.* one who follows the tenets of or promotes anarchy.

ANARCHY, [an'-ahk-i], *n.* condition of society in which there is no governing body; (*fig.*) political and social chaos, lack of order, lawlessness and confusion (in anything). [Gk. *anarkhia* condition of being without government].

ANARTHROUS, [an-ah'-thrus], *adj.* (*gram.*) without the article; (*zool.*) having no limbs. [Gk. *anarthros* jointless].

ANASARCA, [an'-a-sah'-ka], *n.* (*med.*) dropsy of the connective cellular tissue; subcutaneous dropsy. [ANA (1) and Gk. *sarx sarkos* flesh].

ANASARCOUS, [an'-a-sah'-kus], *adj.* relating to anasarca, or dropsy; dropsical.

ANASTATIC, [an'-as-tat'-ik], *adj.* (*print.*) a term defining a process of photographic reproduction, *esp.* of books. [Gk. *anastatos* made to stand up].

ANASTOMOSE, [an-as'-tom-ōs], *v.i.* to unite by anastomosis, join, communicate.

ANASTOMOSIS, [an-as'-tom-ō'-sis], *n.* intercommunication of a network of lines or streams; (*anat.* and *bot.*) inosculation, or the opening of one artery or vein into another. [Gk. *anastomosis* the furnishing of an opening].

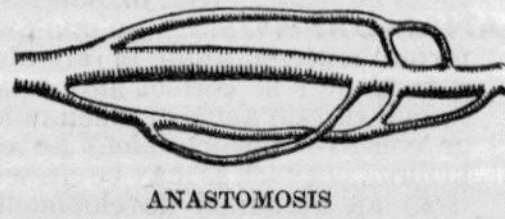

ANASTOMOSIS

ANASTOMOTIC, [an-as'-tom-ot'-ik], *adj.* relating to anastomosis; tending to open or remove obstructions. [Gk. *anastomotikos*].

ANASTROPHE, ANASTROPHY, [an-as'-trof-i], *n.* (*rhet.*) an inversion of the normal order of words. [Gk. *anastrophe* a turning upside down].

ANATASE, [an'-at-ās], *n.* (*min.*) one of the oxides of titanium. [Gk. *anatasis* extension].

ANATHEMA, [an-ath'-im-a], *n.* a curse solemnly pronounced by ecclesiastical authority, and accompanied by excommunication; the person or thing accursed; a curse or ban generally, a person or thing thoroughly disliked. [L. *anathema*].

ANATHEMATIC, [an-ath'-im-at'-ik], *adj.* pertaining to anathema. [Gk. *anathematikos*].

ANATHEMATICAL, [an-ath'-im-at'-ikl], *adj.* relating to or of the nature of anathema.

ANATHEMATICALLY, [an-ath'-im-at'-ik-al-i], *adv.* in an anathematical way.

ANATHEMATISM, [an-ath'-im-at-izm], *n.* excommunication, curse.

ANATHEMATIZATION, [an-ath'-im-at-īz-ā'-shun], *n.* the process of anathematizing. [MedL. *anathematizatio*].

ANATHEMATIZE, [an-ath'-im-at-īz], *v.t.* to utter an anathema against. [Gk. *anathematizo* I curse].

ANATOMICAL, [an'-at-om'-ikl], *adj.* pertaining to anatomy.

ANATOMICALLY, [an'-at-om'-ik-a-li], *adv.* in an anatomical way.

ANATOMISM, [an-at'-om-izm], *n.* a theory explaining vitality by anatomical structure, and thus opposed to animism; (in works of art) the application of anatomical principles. [Fr. *anatomisme*].

ANATOMIST, [an-at'-om-ist], *n.* one versed in anatomy.

ANATOMIZATION, [an-at'-om-īz-ā'-shun], *n.* the process of anatomizing.

ANATOMIZE, [an-at'-om-īz], *v.t.* to dissect, *esp.* animal bodies in order to see their structure; to analyse; to discriminate. [MedL. *anatomizare*].

ANATOMY, [an-at'-o-mi], *n.* (*orig.*) the dissection of bodies, human and animal, in order to study the structure and distribution of their parts; the art of dissecting; the science learnt from dissection; the parts and details with which the science deals; a treatise upon the science, or upon the structure of animals; †a skeleton; (*fig.*) the art of minutely examining anything, physical or intellectual; the examination or analysis itself, or a treatise thereupon. [Fr. *anatomie* from L. *anatomia*].

ANATREPTIC, [an'-a-trep'-tik], *adj.* overthrowing, overturning. [Gk. *anatreptikos*].

ANATRIPSIS, [an'-a-trip'-sis], *n.* (*med.*) friction applied to the body as a cure or aid, massage. [Gk. *anatripsis* chafing].

ANATRIPTIC, [an'-a-trip'-tik], *n.* connected with anatripsis. [Gk. *anatriptos* rubbed up].

ANATRON, [an'-at-ron], *n.* scum of melted glass; the salt which accumulates on the walls of vaults; glassgall. [Sp. *anatron* from Arab. *an natrun*].

ANATROPOUS, [an-at'-rop-us], *adj.* (*bot.*) having an inverted ovule. [L. *anatropus* from Gk. **anatropos* turned upside down].

ANBURY, [an'-ber-i, an'-bew-ri], *n.* a soft tumour found on necks of horses and oxen; disease affecting roots of cabbages, turnips and other plants. [Unkn.].

ANCESTOR, [an'-ses-tor], *n.* one from whom a person is descended; a forebear; (*leg.*) any lineal or collateral relative from whom property has been derived by descent. [OFr. *ancestre*].

ANCESTORIAL, [an'-ses-taw'-ri-al], *adj.* connected with ancestors, ancestral.

ANCESTRAL, [an-ses'-tral], *adj.* pertaining to ancestors; descending from ancestors.

ANCESTRESS, [an'-ses-tres], *n.* a woman ancestor.

ANCESTRY, [an'-ses-tri], *n.* ancestral lineage, persons composing the line of natural descent. [OFr. *ancestrie*].

ANCHILOPS, [angk'-il-ops], *n.* (*med.*) an abscess occurring in the inner angle of the eye. [Gk. *agkhilops* ulcer at the corner of the eye].

ANCHITHERE, [angk'-ith-ēer], *n.* the anchitherium, one of the ancestors of the modern horse, which had three toes on each foot. [MdL. *anchitherium* from Gk. *agkhi* near and *therion* wild beast].

ANCHOR (1), [angk'-er], *n.* a heavy iron or steel bar having at one end curved arms with hooks at each extremity so that when attached to a cable and thrown over the side of a ship it becomes firmly embedded in the sea or river-bottom, and moors the ship securely; (*fig.*) anything fixed and steady, giving a sense of security; **to cast a.,** to drop the anchor overboard; **to weigh a.,** to draw up the anchor from the sea; (*fig.*) to begin a voyage; **to come to a.,** to let down the anchor, stop sailing; **sheet a.,** the largest type of anchor; (*fig.*) chief support or security. [OE. *ancor* from L. *ancora*].

ANCHOR (2), [angk'-er], *v.t.* to make fast by casting anchor, to fix securely; *v.i.* to cast or come to anchor to come to a stop, rest. [*Prec.*].

ANCHORABLE, [angk'-er-abl], *adj.* that may be anchored.

ANCHORAGE, [angk'-er-ij], *n.* place suitable for anchoring; duty imposed on ships for anchoring in a harbour; (*motoring*) the point at which a component is secured to the chassis-frame.
ANCHORED, [angk'-erd], *adj.* with a shape like an anchor; (*her.*) having the extremities barbed like the flukes of an anchor.

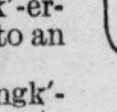
ANCHORED

ANCHORESS, [angk'-er-es], *n.* a female recluse or anchorite.
ANCHORET, [angk'-er-et], *n.* hermit, anchorite. [L. *anachoreta*].
ANCHORETIC, [angk'-er-et'-ik], *adj.* pertaining to an anchorite.
ANCHORETICAL, [angk'-er-et'-ikl], *adj.* pertaining to a hermit, or his way of life.
ANCHOR-GAP, [angk'-er-gap'], *n.* (*wirel.*) small safety spark-gap, between lead-in of receiving aerial and earth, to protect receiver from over-powerful oscillations.
ANCHOR-GROUND, [angk'-er-grownd'], *n.* ground where ships may anchor.
ANCHOR-HOLD, [angk'-er-hōld'], *n.* the hold taken by the anchor; (*fig.*) security, stability.
ANCHOR-ICE, [angk'-er-īs'], *n.* ice that forms at the bottom of streams; ground ice.
ANCHORITE, [angk'-er-īt], *n.* a hermit or anchoret; a religious recluse; a monk living in solitude with an allowance from his monastery. [L. *anachoreta*].
ANCHORSMITH, [angk'-er-smith'], *n.* one who forges anchors.
ANCHOVY, [an'-chov-i], *n.* a small rich-flavoured herring-like fish of the genus *Engraulis*, eaten salted or in sauces. [Span. *anchova*].
ANCHOVY-PEAR, [an'-chov-i-pāer'], *n.* the fruit of a West Indian tree of the genus *Grias*.
ANCHUSA, [an-chōō'-za, angk-ew'-za], *n.* varieties of hairy-stemmed plants, as bugloss. [L. *anchusa*].
ANCHYLOSE, [angk'-il-ōs], *v.t.* to become stiff by anchylosis.
ANCHYLOSIS, [angk-il-ō'-sis], *n.* (*med.*) stiffening of the joints. [Gk. *ankhulosis*].
ANCHYLOTIC, [angk'-il-ot'-ik], *adj.* (*med.*) pertaining to or afflicted with anchylosis.
ANCIENT (1), [ān'-shent], *n.* †old man; (*pl. only*) those who lived in the times of the Greek and Roman empires, the classical writers of antiquity (as opposed to modern), the elders of a people; (*leg.*) senior barristers, forming governing body of Inns of Court; **A. of Days**, God. [Fr. *ancien*].
ANCIENT† (2), [ān'-shent], *n.* flag, standard, ensign; the bearer of a standard, ensign. [OFr. *enseigne*].
ANCIENT (3), [ān'-shent], *adj.* old, former, that happened or existed in the past, or in antiquity, that has existed from past times to the present day; (*leg.*) enjoyed continuously for at least twenty years; **a. lights**, window which is protected by law whereby no one may erect a building that will keep the light from it. [Fr. *ancien*].
ANCIENTLY, [ān'-shent-li], *adv.* in days of old, in times gone by.
ANCIENTNESS, [ān'-shent-nes], *n.* extreme age, the state of being ancient; existence from old times.
ANCIENTRY, [ān'-shent-ri], *n.* ancient lineage; ancientness, seniority, antiquity.
ANCILLARY, [an-sil'-a-ri], *adj.* subordinate, auxiliary. [L. *ancillāris* pertaining to women-servants].
ANCIPITAL, [an-sip'-itl], *adj.* (*bot.*) having two edges, flattened, ancipitous. [L. *anceps ancipitis* having two heads].
ANCIPITOUS, [an-sip'-it-us], *adj.* double-faced or double-formed; (*bot.*) of stems, double-edged. [L. *anceps ancipitis* two-headed].
ANCON, [angk'-on], *n.* the upper end of the elbow; (*arch.*) a console bracket. [Gk. *agkon* a bend, elbow].
ANCONEAL, [an-kō'-nē-al], *adj.* pertaining to the elbow.
AND, [and], *conj.* having the sense of adding something to what has gone before, used as a link between words or sentences; (*coll.*) in order to (after TRY, COME, and GO). [OE. *and*].
ANDANTE (1), [an-dan'-ti], *n.* (*mus.*) a movement in slow time. [It. *andante*, *pres.pt.* of *andare* to go].
ANDANTE (2), [an-dan'-ti], *adv.* (*mus.*) slowly. [*Prec.*].
ANDANTINO, [an'-dan-tē'-nō], *adv.* (*mus.*) moderately slowly but quicker than andante. [It. *andantino*].
ANDERSON SHELTER, [an'-der-sun-shel'-ter], *n.* a small edifice made of corrugated steel intended for 4-8 people and used as a protection against bomb blast and splinters. [Sir John *Anderson*, Home Secretary 1939-40].
ANDESINE, [an'-dez-īn], *n.* (*geol.*) a constituent element of andesite; a felspar found in the Andes.
ANDESITE, [an'-dez-īt], *n.* a crystalline igneous rock found in lava flows, dykes and veins, in the *Andes*, etc.
ANDIRON, ENDIRON, [and'-iern'], *n.* a horizontal iron bar inserted at each end of a hearth, to hold the logs in a wood fire; a firedog; an iron fixed at either end of a grate, in which the spit turns; movable fire-irons. [OFr. *andier* andiron].

ANDIRON

ANDREOLITE, [an-drē'-ol-īt], *n.* harmotome, from its having been first found at *Andreas* in the Harz Mountains.
ANDRO-, *pref.* man. [Gk. *aner andros* man].
ANDROCEPHALOUS, [an'-drō-sef'-al-us], *adj.* having a human head with a non-human body, as the sphinx or Assyrian bull. [ANDRO and Gk. *kephale* head].
ANDROECIUM, [an-drē'-si-um], *n.* (*bot.*) the stamens of a flower. [ANDRO and Gk. *oikion* house].
ANDROGYNAL, [an-droj'-inl], *adj.* androgynous.
ANDROGYNALLY, [an-droj'-in-a-li], *adv.* (*bot.*) in the manner of a hermaphrodite.
ANDROGYNOUS, [an-droj'-in-us], *adj.* having the characteristics of both sexes, at once male and female, hermaphrodite; (*bot.*) having male and female organs on the same flower or plant. [Gk. *androgunos*].
ANDROID, (*pl.* **androides**), [an'-droid], *n.* an automaton, so made as to resemble a man in form and actions. [ANDRO and Gk. *oeides* like].
ANDROMEDA, [an-drom'-ed-a], *n.* (*astron.*) the name of a northern constellation; (*bot.*) a genus of shrubs of the heath family. [*Andromeda*, in Greek mythology, a young girl bound to a rock by the sea and exposed to a monster but delivered by the young hero Perseus].
ANDROPETALOUS, [an'-drō-pet'-al-us], *adj.* (*bot.*) having, as in double flowers, the stamens converted into petals. [ANDRO and PETALOUS].
ANDROPHAGI, [an-drof'-ag-ī], *n.(pl.)* man-eaters, cannibals. [ANDRO and Gk. *phago* I eat].
ANDROPHAGOUS, [an-drof'-ag-us], *adj.* man-eating. [Gk. *androphagos*].
ANDROTOMY, [an-drot'-o-mi], *n.* the dissection of the human body, as distinguished from zootomy. [Gk. *androtome*].
ANEAR, [a-nēer'], *prep. and adv.* near.
ANECDOTAGE, [an'-ik-dō'-tij], *n.* the telling of anecdotes; a state of garrulous senility. [ANEC(DOTE) and DOTAGE].
ANECDOTAL, [an'-ik-dōtl'], *adj.* relating to, or full of anecdotes.
ANECDOTE, [an'-ik-dōt], *n.* a short, vivid narrative concerning a single striking event or witty phrase, usually conversational and personal in tone; a story. [Gk. *anekdotos*].
ANECDOTIC, [an'-ik-dōt'-ik], *adj.* anecdotical.
ANECDOTICAL, [an'-ik-dōt'-ikl], *adj.* addicted to or pertaining to anecdotes.
ANECDOTIST, [an'-ik-dōt'-ist], *n.* one who collects or tells anecdotes.
ANELACE, [an'-las], *n.* (*arch.*) anlace; a short two-edged dagger or knife. [ANLACE].
ANELE, [an-ēl'], *v.t.* to put oil upon ; to give extreme unction to. [OE. *an* and *ele* oil].
ANELECTRODE, [an'-il-ek'-trōd], *n.* the positive pole of a galvanic battery. [Gk. *ana* up and ELECTRODE].
ANEMO-, *pref.* wind. [Gk. *anemos*].
ANEMOGRAM, [an-em'-ō-gram], *n.* the register made by an anemograph. [ANEMO and Gk. *gramma* what is written].
ANEMOGRAPH, [an-em'-ō-graf], *n.* an apparatus which registers the amount and variation of the force of the wind. [ANEMO and GRAPH].
ANEMOGRAPHY, [an'-im-og'-ra-fi], *n.* the study of the winds. [ANEMO and Gk. *graphia* writing].
ANEMOLOGY, [an'-im-ol'-o-ji], *n.* the science of the winds. [ANEMO and Gk. *logos* speech].
ANEMOMETER, [an'-im-om'-it-er], *n.* an instrument

which measures the direction, force and velocity of the wind. [ANEMO and METER].

ANEMOMETRY, [an'-im-om'-et-ri], *n.* the determination of the force, velocity and direction of the winds. [ANEMO and Gk. *metria* measuring].

ANEMONE, [an-em'-o-ni], *n.* the wind-flower, a genus of plant of the natural order *Ranunculaceae* growing widely in the temperate zone. [Gk. *anemone*].

ANEMOPHILOUS, [an'-im-of'-il-us], *adj.* (*bot.*) fertilized by the wind. [ANEMO and Gk. *philos* loving].

ANEMOSCOPE, [an-em'-ō-skōp], *n.* a machine which shows the direction of the wind. [ANEMO and Gk. *skopos* watcher].

ANENT, [an-ent'], *prep.* (of position) fronting, over against; in reference to, concerning, about. [OE. *on efen* near to, close by].

ANEROID, [an'-er-oid], *adj.* describing that type of barometer which employs no fluid, but measures the pressure of the atmosphere on the lid of a metal box exhausted of air. [A (4), Gk. *neros* wet and *oeides* like.]

ANETHOL, [an'-eth-ol], *n.* (*chem.*) an essential oil of anise and fennel. [L. *anethum*].

ANEURISM, ANEURYSM, [an'-yŏoer-izm], *n.* (*med.*) a hollow swelling that is filled with blood, in the diseased coat of an artery. [Gk. *aneurusma*].

ANEURISMAL, [an'-yŏoer-iz'-mal], *adj.* of or pertaining to an aneurism.

ANEURYSM, see ANEURISM.

ANEW, [a-new'], *adv.* over again, once more, in a new form.

ANFRACTUOSE, [an-frak'-tew-ōs], *adj.* anfractuous. [L. *anfractuosus*].

ANFRACTUOSITY, [an'-frak-tew-os'-i-ti], *n.* anfractuousness.

ANFRACTUOUS, [an-frak'-tew-us], *adj.* full of windings; (*fig.*) circumlocutory in speech. [L. *anfractus* winding].

ANFRACTUOUSNESS, [an-frak'-tew-us-nes], *n.* the condition of being anfractuous.

ANGARIA, [an-gāer-ī'-a], *n.* a term used in international law denoting the seizure or destruction by a belligerent state of property belonging to neutral states within its frontiers for which it pays an indemnity. [Gk. *aggareia* customs or port service].

ANGARIATE†, [an-gāer'-i-āt], *v.t.* to exact forced labour from. [L. *angaria* forced service].

ANGARY, [an-gar'-i], *n.* angaria. [ANGARIA].

ANGEKOK, [ang'-gi-kok'], *n.* Esquimo medicine man. [Esquimo *angekok*].

ANGEL, [ān'-jl], *n.* a spiritual being of powers greater than human and endowed with immortality who, according to Jewish, Christian and other theologies, is the attendant and messenger of God acting as an intermediary between Heaven and Earth; (*fig.*) a human being of great goodness and beauty; one who ministers unselfishly to the needs of others; (*hist.*) an old English gold coin, an angel noble, worth about ten shillings, bearing the figure of the archangel Michael; **guardian a.,** spiritual protector; **his good or evil a.,** a person who has a marked influence for good or evil on another; **to entertain an a. unawares,** to be unappreciative of the merits of one's company; **to rush in where angels fear to tread,** to interfere rashly where even those of great judgment would hesitate to intervene. [L. *angelus* from Gk. *angelos* a messenger].

ANGEL-BED, [ān'-jl-bed'], *n.* an open bed which has no posts.

ANGEL-FISH, [ān'-jl-fish'], *n.* a kind of shark, the monk fish, *Rhina squatina*, so named from its wing-like pectoral fins; also applied to certain small tropical fishes, which are brilliantly coloured and laterally compressed.

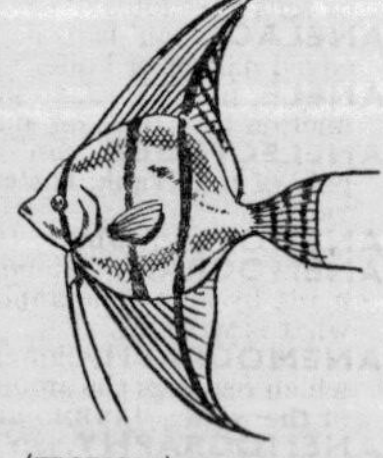

(TROPICAL) ANGEL-FISH

ANGELIC, [an-jel'-ik], *adj.* like an angel; having the physical and spiritual qualities of an angel; an angelic expression of face, looking either by art or nature supremely good or beautiful; **a. creature,** (*slang*), kind or very handsome person. [L. *angelicus*].

ANGELICA, [an-jel'-ik-a], *n.* an umbelliferous plant of the genus *Archangelica*, the preserved leaf-stalks of which are employed as a confection; a sweet wine of California. [MedL. (*herba*) *angelica*].

ANGELICAL, [an-jel'-ikl], *adj.* like or of the nature of, an angel.

ANGELICALLY, [an-jel'-ik-al-i], *adv.* in the manner of an angel.

ANGELICALNESS, [an-jel'-ikl-nes], *n.* the state of being angelic or more than human.

ANGELOLOGY, [ān'-jel-ol'-o-ji], *n.* the doctrine of angelic beings; a treatise on angels. [ANGEL and Gk. *logos* speech].

ANGELOPHANY, [ān'-jel-of'-an-i], *n.* the appearance of an angel to man. [ANGEL and Gk. *phaino* I appear].

ANGELUS, [an'-jel-us], *n.* a short form of prayer in the Roman Catholic Church in commemoration of the Incarnation, said in the morning, at noon, and in the evening, when the Angelus bell rings. [From the first words of the prayer *Angelus Domini nuntiavit Mariae*].

ANGEL-WATER†, [ān'-jel-waw'-ter], *n.* a strongly-scented liquid perfume and cosmetic.

ANGER (1), [ang'-ger], *n.* a passion of the mind prompted by a sense of wrong; resentment, ire, wrath, indignation, resentful sorrow, hot displeasure. [ME. *anger* from OIcel. *angr* sorrow].

ANGER (2), [ang'-ger], *v.t.* to excite to anger, to rouse resentment and indignation in a person, to provoke, to incense; (*fig.*) to make sore or inflammatory any part of the body. [*Prec.*].

ANGEVIN, [an'-jev-in], *adj.* (*hist.*) of or pertaining to Anjou, relating to the Plantagenet House that reigned in England from 1154 to 1485. [Fr. *angevin*].

ANGINA, [an-jī'-na], *n.* (*med.*) an inflammatory, and as if constricted, affection of the throat; tonsillitis, or quinsy, accompanied by spasmodic fits of suffocation; **a. pectoris,** an acutely painful constriction in the lower and left side of the chest, usually associated with the heart or great blood-vessels. [L. *angina* quinsy].

ANGIO-, [an'-ji-ō], *pref.* vessel, receptacle, hence contained in a seed-pod or blood-vessel. [Gk. *aggeion* vessel].

ANGIOCARPOUS, [an'-ji-ō-kahp'-us], *adj.* (*bot.*) having the fruit in an envelope distinct from the calyx. [ANGIO and Gk. *karpos* fruit].

ANGIOGRAPHY, [an'-ji-og'-raf-i], *n.* (*anat.*) an account of the blood-vessels and lymphatics of the human body. [ANGIO and Gk. *graphia* writing].

ANGIOLOGY, [an'-ji-ol'-o-ji], *n.* (*anat.*) the science of the blood-vessels and lymphatics of the human body. [ANGIO and Gk. *logos* speech].

ANGIONEUROSIS, [an'-ji-ō-new-rō'-sis], *n.* (*med.*) neurosis of the blood-vessels. [ANGIO and NEUROSIS].

ANGIOPATHY, [an'-ji-op'-ath-i], *n.* (*med.*) disease of the blood-vessels. [ANGIO and Gk. *pathos* an affection].

ANGIOSCOPE, [an'-ji-ō-skōp], *n.* an instrument for examining the capillary vessels of plants and animals. [ANGIO and Gk. *skopos* watcher].

ANGIOSPERM, [an'-ji-ō-spurm], *n.* (*bot.*) a plant that has the seeds enclosed in a pericarp. [ANGIO and SPERM].

ANGIOTOMY, [an'-ji-ot'-o-mi], *n.* (*med.*) the dissection of the blood-vessels and lymphatics of the body. [ANGIO and Gk. *tome* cutting].

ANGLE (1), [ang'-gl], *n.* (*geom.*) the inclination of one line to another which it meets; the space included between two meeting lines or surfaces; a narrowing space (as a corner or nook in a room); a projecting corner resembling an angle in shape (as of a building, etc.); (*astrol.*) the name given to the four astrological "houses" at the cardinal points of the compass; (*fig.*) position, point of view; (*U.S.*) a new approach to or light on a subject. (1. Acute angle. 2. Obtuse angle. 3. Curvilinear angle. 4. Mixed angle. 5. Right angle.) [Fr. *angle* from L. *angulus*].

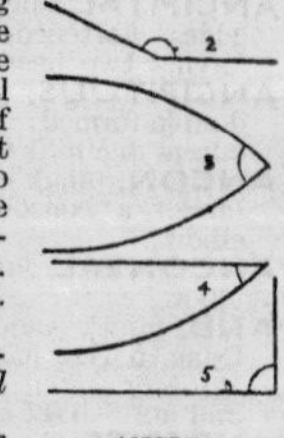

ANGLE

ANGLE (2), [ang'-gl], *n.* a fishing-hook, fishing-tackle. [OE. *angel* fish-hook].

ANGLE (3), [ang'-gl], *n.* a member of a Low German tribe who settled in Northern, Eastern, and Central England, and ultimately gave their name to the people of the whole country. [L. *Anglus*].

ANGLE (4), [ang'-gl], *v.i.* to use an angle for fishing, to fish; (*fig.*) to seek to obtain something by indirect means. [ANGLE (2)].
ANGLE (5), [ang'-gl], *v.t.* to direct at an angle (chiefly in sport). [ANGLE (1)].
ANGLE-BAR, [ang'-gl-bah(r)], *n.* the upright support at the angle of a polygonal window.
ANGLED, [ang'-gld], *adj.* having angles.
ANGLE-IRON, [ang'-gl-iern'], *n.* an L-shaped piece of iron used to fasten or strengthen the framework of various structures such as windows, etc.
ANGLEMETER, [ang'-gl-mē'-ter], *n.* an instrument used for measuring angles *esp.* in geology. [ANGLE and METER].
ANGLER (1), [ang'-gler], *n.* one who fishes with an angle.
ANGLER (2), [ang'-gler], *n.* (*ichth.*) a sea-fish, *Lophius piscatorius*, of which the front spines of the dorsal fin are modified into tentacles.
ANGLESITE, [ang'-gl-sīt], *n.* (*min.*) a sulphate of lead derived from the decomposition of galena (first recorded from *Anglesea*).
ANGLICAN (1), [ang'-glik-an], *n.* a member of the Church of England, *esp.* of the High Church party. [MedL. *anglicanus* English].
ANGLICAN (2), [ang'-glik-an], *adj.* English, connected with the Church of England.
ANGLICANISM, [ang'-glik-an-izm], *n.* attachment to English institutions; the principles of the English Church.
ANGLICE, [ang'-glis-ē], *adv.* in the English language or in an English style. [MedL. *anglicus* (*adj.*) English].
ANGLICISM, [ang'-glis-izm], *n.* English idiom.
ANGLICIZE, [ang'-glis-īz], *v.t.* to give an English form to, to make English.
ANGLIFY, [ang'-gli-fī], *v.t.* to make English, put into English idiom.
ANGLING, [ang'-gling], *n.* fishing with a rod and line; the art of the fisherman.
ANGLO-, [ang'-glō], *pref.* pertaining to the English. [L. *Anglo-* from ANGLE (3)].
ANGLO-AMERICAN (1), [ang'-glō-am-e'-rik-an], *n.* an American who is of English descent; an Englishman whose home is in the U.S.
ANGLO-AMERICAN (2), [ang'-glō-am-e'-rik-an], *adj.* of or pertaining to Anglo-Americans.
ANGLO-CATHOLIC (1), [ang'-glō-kath'-ol-ik], *n.* an English churchman of High Church principles.
ANGLO-CATHOLIC (2), [ang'-glō-kath'-ol-ik], *adj.* of or belonging to the Church of England and embracing High Church principles and ritual.
ANGLO-CATHOLICISM, [ang'-glō-kath-ol'-is-izm], *n.* the beliefs of the High Church party in the Church of England.
ANGLO-EIRE, [ang'-glō-āer'-a], *adj.* Anglo-Irish. [Ir. *Eire*].
ANGLO-FRENCH (1), [ang'-glō-frensh'], *n.* the French language used in England after the Norman Conquest.
ANGLO-FRENCH (2), [ang'-glō-frensh'], *adj.* of or pertaining to England and France.
ANGLO-INDIAN (1), [ang'-glō-ind'-i-an], *n.* an Englishman born or living in India; a Eurasian.
ANGLO-INDIAN (2), [ang'-glō-ind'-i-an], *adj.* of or pertaining to England and India or to Anglo-Indians.
ANGLO-IRISH (1), [ang'-glō-īer'-ish], *n.(pl.)* the descendants of the original settlers within the Pale; the offspring of marriages between the Irish and the English; English persons born or long resident in Ireland.
ANGLO-IRISH (2), [ang'-glō-īer'-ish], *adj.* of or pertaining to England and Ireland.
ANGLOMANIA, [ang'-glō-mā'-ni-a], *n.* an excessive admiration, *esp.* by foreigners, of everything English. [ANGLO and MANIA].
ANGLO-NORMAN (1), [ang'-glō-naw'-man], *n.* a Norman living in England after the Conquest; Norman-French as spoken in England after the Conquest.
ANGLO-NORMAN (2), [ang'-glō-naw'-man], *adj.* pertaining to Anglo-Norman.
ANGLOPHOBE (1), [ang'-glō-fōb], *n.* a hater of England and things English. [Fr. from ANGLO and Gk. *phobos* fear].
ANGLOPHOBE (2), [ang'-glō-fōb], *adj.* hating England and things English. [*Prec.*].
ANGLOPHOBIA, [ang'-glō-fō'-bi-a], *n.* hatred of everything English. [ANGLO and Gk. *phobos* fear].
ANGLO-SAXON (1), [ang'-glō-saks'-on], *n.* a native of England before the Norman Conquest; the language of England before the 12th century; (*pop.*) a person of British or American nationality descended from English stock.
ANGLO-SAXON (2), [ang'-glō-saks'-on], *adj.* pertaining to Anglo-Saxon.
ANGLO-SAXONISM, [ang'-glō-saks'-on-izm], *n.* anything peculiarly Anglo-Saxon; a belief in the superiority of the English-speaking races.
ANGOLA, [ang-gō'-la], *n.* cloth of angora wool; **A. cat,** a silky-haired cat, an Angora cat. [Corruption of ANGORA].
ANGOR, [ang'-gor], *n.* (*med.*) acute pain accompanied by great anxiety; intense anxiety. [L. *angor*].
ANGORA, [ang-gaw'-ra], *n.* an Anatolian city, also called Ankara; **a. wool,** the hair of the Angora goat, mohair; **a. rabbit,** a rabbit with fine white hair.
ANGOSTURA, [ang'-gos-tew'-ra], *n.* a place in Venezuela; **A. bark,** pungent bark of *Cusparia*; **A. bitters,** a drink made from angostura bark.
ANGRILY, [ang'-gri-li], *adv.* in angry manner.
ANGRINESS, [ang'-gri-nes], *n.* state of being angry.
ANGRY, [ang'-gri], *adj.* full of anger, enraged; (*fig.*) inflamed (of a sore).
ANGSTROM UNIT, ångström unit, [ang'-strōm, ong'-strurm ew'-nit], *n.* (*phys.*) a minute unit of measurement, the thousandth part of a millimetre. [*Ångström* a Swedish physicist].
ANGUIFORM, [ang'-gwi-fawm], *adj.* snake-shaped. [L. *anguis* snake and FORM].
ANGUILLIFORM, [ang-gwil'-i-fawm], *adj.* anguilloid. [L. *anguilla* eel and FORM].
ANGUILLOID, [ang'-gwil-oid], *adj.* like an eel. [L. *anguilla* and Gk. *oeides* like].
ANGUINE, [ang'-gwīn], *adj.* snake-like. [L. *anguineus*].
ANGUINEAL, [ang-gwin'-i-al], *adj.* snake-like, winding.
ANGUISH (1), [ang'-gwish], *n.* keen pain of body or mind, any intensely painful feeling. [OFr. *anguisse* from L. *angustia* difficulties].
ANGUISH (2), [ang'-gwish], *v.t.* to distress with acute pain or grief. [ANGUISH (1)].
ANGULAR, [ang'-gyŏŏ-ler], *adj.* having angles or corners; (*fig.*) (of people) thin and bony; stiff, over-formal in manner; difficult to get on with, crochety. [L. *angularis*].
ANGULARITY, [ang'-gyŏŏ-la'-rit-i], *n.* angularness.
ANGULARLY, [ang'-gyŏŏ-ler-li], *adv.* with angles or corners, in an angular manner.
ANGULARNESS, [ang'-gyŏŏ-ler-nes], *n.* the state of being angular.
ANGULATE (1), [ang'-gyŏŏ-lāt], *adj.* angulated.
ANGULATE (2), [ang'-gyŏŏ-lāt'], *v.t.* to make angular.
ANGULATED, [ang'-gyŏŏ-lāt'-id], *adj.* with angles, angled.
ANGUSTIFOLIATE, [ang-gust'-i-fōl'-i-at], *adj.* angustifolious.
ANGUSTIFOLIOUS, [ang-gust'-i-fōl'-i-us], *adj.* (*bot.*) with narrow leaves. [L. *angustus* narrow and *folium* leaf].
ANHARMONIC, [an'-hah-mon'-ik], *adj.* (*math.*) not harmonic. [AN (3) and HARMONIC].
ANHELATION, [an'-hel-ā'-shun], *n.* shortness of breath, a panting; (*fig.*) eager desire or aspiration. [~L. *anhelitus*].
ANHIMA, [an'-him-a], *n.* (*zool.*) the horned screamer, *Palamedea cornuta*, a South American bird with a horny structure on its head and two spurs on each wing. [Brazilian *anhima*].
ANHYDRITE, [an-hī'-drīt], *n.* (*min.*) anhydrous calcium sulphate.
ANHYDROUS, [an-hī'-drus], *adj.* (*chem.*) (of substances) without water of crystallization. [Gk. *an(h)udros* waterless].
ANICONIC, [an-ī-kon'-ik], *adj.* (of idols and symbols) not shaped in human or animal form. [AN (3) and ICONIC].
ANICUT, [an'-ik-ut], *n.* a dam for irrigation purposes in India. [Tamil *anai-kattu*].
ANIGH, [a-nī'], *adv.* (*poet.*) near. [A (3) and NIGH].
ANIL, [an'-il], *n.* (*bot.*) a kind of indigo plant, *esp. Indigofera Anil.* [Arab. *an-nil* from Skr. *nila* dark blue].
ANILE, [an'-īl], *adj.* old-womanish. [L. *anilis*].
ANILINE (1), [an'-il-ēn], *n.* a chemical obtained by the distillation of coal-tar, and used in the manufacture of numerous dyes. [ANIL].
ANILINE (2), [an'-il-ēn], *adj.* pertaining to anil or aniline. [*Prec.*].
ANILITY, [an-il'-i-ti], *n.* the state of being anile, dotage, senility. [~L. *anilitas*].

ANIMADVERSION, [an′-im-ad-vur′-shun], *n.* criticism of a hostile nature, censure; (*leg.*) judicial criticism of an offence or of evidence given. [~L. *animadversio*].

ANIMADVERSIVE†, [an′-im-ad-vur′-siv], *adj.* having the power of adversion, perceptive. [~L. *animadversus*].

ANIMADVERSIVENESS, [an′-im-ad-vur′-siv-nes], *n.* the power of animadverting.

ANIMADVERT, [an′-im-ad-vurt′], *v.i.* to observe, refer to, to direct attention to; to remark upon, in criticism or censure. [L. *animadvertere* to notice]

ANIMAL (1), [an′-im-al], *n.* an animate creature; a living being characterized by sensation and voluntary motion, as distinct from the other series of organized beings such as the vegetable; the lower animals as distinct from man; used contemptuously of a man little better than a beast, a brutish, sensual creature. [L. *animal* a living being, from *anima* breath, life].

ANIMAL (2), [an′-im-al], *adj.* pertaining to living beings; physical, belonging to the animal or sensual part as opposed to the spiritual; **a. heat**, the even temperature maintained within the bodies of living creatures; **a. magnetism**, mesmerism, the hypnotizing of one person by another; **a. spirits**, natural exuberance and vitality. [ANIMAL (1)].

ANIMALCULA, [an′-im-al′-kyōō-la], *n.(pl.)* (*zool.*) minute animals generally discernible only through a microscope. [L. *animalcula* small animals].

ANIMALCULAR, [an′-im-al′-kyōō-ler], *adj.* (*zool.*) pertaining to animalcula.

ANIMALCULE, [an′-im-al′-kewl], *n.* (*zool.*) a minute animal almost or quite invisible to the naked eye, one of the animalcula. [ANIMALCULA].

ANIMALCULINE, [an′-im-al′-kyōō-lin], *adj.* (*zool.*) animalcular.

ANIMALCULISM, [an′-im-al′-kyōō-lizm], *n.* (*path.*) a theory, now abandoned, by which some physiological and pathological phenomena were accounted for by the presence of animalcula.

ANIMALCULIST, [an′-im-al′-kyōō-list], *n.* a student of animalcula.

ANIMAL-FLOWER, [an′-im-al-flow′er], *n.* a zoophyte which resembles a flower, *esp.* the sea-anemone.

ANIMALISH, [an′-im-al-ish], *adj.* of or pertaining to an animal, brutish.

ANIMALISM, [an′-im-al-izm], *n.* conduct motivated by animal instincts; the doctrine that man is an animal.

ANIMALITY, [an′-im-al′-it-i], *n.* the qualities characteristic of an animal.

ANIMALIZATION, [an′-im-al-īz-ā′-shun], *n.* the act of animalizing.

ANIMAL-FLOWER

ANIMALIZE, [an′-im-al-īz], *v.t.* to give animal life or qualities to; to turn into an animal; to lower, abase; to brutalize.

ANIMALNESS, [an′-im-al-nes], *n.* animality, the condition of being animal.

ANIMATE (1), [an′-im-at], *adj.* living. [L. *animatus*].

ANIMATE (2), [an′-im-āt], *v.t.* to give life to, give spirit to; inspire. [~L. *animare*].

ANIMATED, [an′-im-āt′-id], *adj.* having life or spirit; vivacious, brisk; †**a. pictures**, cinema show.

ANIMATEDLY, [an′-im-āt′-id-li], *adv.* in a lively manner.

ANIMATING, [an′-im-āt′-ing], *adj.* enlivening, inspiring.

ANIMATINGLY, [an′-im-āt′-ing-li], *adv.* in an animating manner.

ANIMATION, [an′-im-ā′-shun], *n.* the act of animating, imparting vitality; the state of being animated; vivacity. [~L. *animatio*].

ANIMATISM, [an′-im-at-izm], *n.* belief that inanimate things possess reason.

ANIMATIVE, [an′-im-at-iv], *adj.* having the power of animating.

ANIMATOR, [an′-im-ā′-tor], *n.* a person or thing that animates.

ANIME, animé, [an′-im-ā], *n.* a transparent amber-coloured resin; any resin; Indian copal, white dammar, a species of *Vateria*. [Fr. *animé* living, from the number of insects embedded in it].

ANIMETTA, [an′-im-et′-a], *n.* a cloth to cover the chalice. [It. *animetta*].

ANIMISM, [an′-im-izm], *n.* the doctrine which regards the soul as the source of all forms of life; the attribution to inanimate objects of a soul; the belief in the existence of soul or spirit apart from matter. [L. *animus* soul].

ANIMIST, [an′-im-ist], *n.* one who believes in animism.

ANIMISTIC, [an′-im-ist′-ik], *adj.* pertaining to animism.

ANIMOSITY, [an′-im-os′-i-ti], *n.* active hostility of mind, bitter hatred, enmity, violent prejudice. [~L. *animositas*].

ANIMUS, [an′-im-us], *n.* soul, mind, purpose, spirit; hostile spirit. [L. *animus*].

ANISE, [an′-is], *n.* a Levantine umbelliferous plant, *Pimpinella Anisum*, cultivated for its aromatic and medicinal seeds. [Fr. *anis* from Gk. *anison*].

ANISEED, [an′-i-sēd], *n.* the seed of anise. [*Prec.* and SEED].

ANISETTE, [an′-i-set′], *n.* a liqueur flavoured with aniseed. [Fr. *anisette*].

ANISO-, [an′-is-ō], *pref.* unequal, unsymmetrical. [Gk. *anisos*].

ANISODACTYL, [an′-is-ō-dak′-til], *n.* (*ornith.*) a bird with toes of unequal length. [ANISO and Gk. *dactulos* toe].

ANISODYNAMOUS, [an′-is-ō-dī′-nam-us], *adj.* (*bot.*) growing more on one side of the axis than on the other. [ANISO and Gk. *dunamis* power].

ANISOMERIC, [an′-is-ō-me′-rik], *adj.* unsymmetrical. [ANISO and Gk. *meros* part].

ANISOPETALOUS, [an′-is-ō-pet′-al-us], *adj.* (*bot.*) with unequal petals. [ANISO and Gk. *petalon* a leaf].

ANISOPTEROUS, [an′-is-op′-ter-us], *adj.* having unequal wings. [ANISO and Gk. *pteron* wing].

ANISOSTEMONOUS, [an′-is-ō-stem′-on-us], *adj.* (*bot.*) having the number of stamens unequal to that of the petals or sepals. [ANISO and Gk. *stemon* stamen].

ANITROGENOUS, [an′-ī-troj′-en-us], *adj.* (*chem.*) non-nitrogenous. [AN (3) and NITROGENOUS].

ANKER, [angk-er], *n.* an old North European liquid measure of about 8½ gallons. [Du. *anker*].

ANKLE, [angkl], *n.* the joint in human beings which connects the foot and the leg; the slender part of the leg between the ankle joint and the calf. [ME. *ancle*].

ANKLET, [angk′-let], *n.* a ring-shaped ornament or fetter for the ankle.

ANKYLOSIS, *see* ANCHYLOSIS.

ANKYLOSTOMIASIS, [angk′-il-ō-stom-ī′-as-is], *n.* (*med.*) a disease caused by the parasitic hook-worm. [Gk. *agkulos* crooked and *stoma* mouth].

ANLACE†, [an′-las], *n.* a short, broad, tapering dagger. [OFr. *alenas*].

ANNA, [an′-a], *n.* a small copper coin, value one-sixteenth of a rupee. [Hind. *ana*].

ANNAL, [an′-al], *n.* a narrative of the events of a year; a Roman Catholic anniversary mass; *sg.* of annals. [L. *annalis*].

ANNALIST, [an′-al-ist], *n.* one who writes annals.

ANNALS, [an′-alz], *n.(pl.)* a historical narrative that records events year by year; a chronicle, year-book. [L. *annales*].

ANNATE, [an′-āt], *n.* †a year's revenue paid to the Pope by new bishops; (*Scots leg.*) an additional half-year's stipend due to the executors of a deceased minister. [LL. *annata*].

ANLACE

ANNATTO, ANNOTTO, [a-nat′-ō], *n.* the reddish pulp surrounding the seed of the Central American *Bixa orellana*, making a bright orange dye used in colouring butter and cheese. [Central Amer. *annatto*].

ANNEAL, [an-ēl′], *v.t.* to temper glass or metals by subjecting them to intense heat and then letting them cool slowly; to heat glass and earthenware so as to fix colours; to temper by heat; to bake, as of tiles. [OE. *on-ælan* to set on fire, bake (tiles, etc.)].

ANNEALING, [an-ēl′-ing], *n.* the process of tempering metal, etc.

ANNECTANT, [a-nekt′-ant], *adj.* joining on, connecting. [~L. *annectens*].

ANNELIDA, [an-el′-id-a], *n.(pl.)* (*zool.*) animals like the earth-worms, whose bodies are formed by a succession of rings. [~L. *annellus* a little ring].

ANNEX (1), ANNEXE, [an′-eks], *n.* something annexed, an addition; an additional, subsidiary building designed to supply extra accommodation. [Fr. *annexe*].

ANNEX (2), [a-neks'], *v.t.* to unite, add, attach; (of a state) to take over additional territory. [L. *annexum, p.pt.* of *annectere*].
ANNEXATION, [an'-eks-ā'-shun], *n.* the act of annexing.
ANNEXATIONIST, [an'-eks-ā'-shun-ist], *n.* one in favour of annexation.
ANNEXE, see ANNEX (1).
ANNIHILABLE, [an-ī'-hil-abl], *adj.* able to be annihilated.
ANNIHILATE, [an-ī'-il-āt], *v.t.* to reduce to nothing, completely destroy; (*fig.*) to reduce to defeated silence. [~L. *annihilare*].
ANNIHILATION, [a-nī'-il-ā'-shun], *n.* the act of annihilating; the condition of being annihilated. [Fr. *annihilation*].
ANNIHILATIONISM, [an-ī'-il-ā'-shun-izm], *n.* the doctrine that the wicked are punished after this life by annihilation.
ANNIHILATIONIST, [a-nī'-il'-ā'-shun-ist], *n.* a believer in annihilationism.
ANNIHILATOR, [a-nī'-il-āt'-er], *n.* one who or that which annihilates.
ANNIVERSARY (1), [an'-iv-urs'-er-i], *n.* the return in subsequent years of the date on which a certain event took place; a celebration taking place on an annually recurring date. [L. *anniversarius*].
ANNIVERSARY (2), [an'-iv-urs'-er-i], *adj.* pertaining to an anniversary. [ANNIVERSARY (1)].
ANNO DOMINI, [an'-ō-dom'-in-ī], *adv.* in the year since the birth of Christ, usually written A.D.; the dominical year. [L. *anno Domini*].
ANNOMINATION, [an-om'-in-ā'-shun], *n.* the use of words alike in sound but different in meaning, a pun, paronomasia. [L. *ad* to and *nomen* a name].
ANNONA, [an-ō'-na], *n.* a year's provisions. [L. *annona*].
ANNOTATE, [an'-ō-tāt], *v.t. and i.* to comment upon by means of notes, to write explanatory notes to any text or document. [~L. *annotare*].
ANNOTATED, [an'-ō-tāt-id], *adj.* with explanatory notes.
ANNOTATION, [an'-ō-tā'-shun], *n.* the act of annotating; an explanatory note. [~L. *annotatio*].
ANNOTATOR, [an'-ō-tāt'-er], *n.* one who annotates.
ANNOTATORY, [an'-ō-tāt'-er-i], *adj.* pertaining to an annotator or annotation.
ANNOTINOUS, [an-ot'-in-us], *adj.* (*bot.*) one year old. [L. *annotinus*].
ANNOTTO, [a-not'-ō], see ANNATTO.
ANNOUNCE, [a-nowns'], *v.t.* to make known, declare; to pronounce or declare judicially; to make known the approach or presence of. [Fr. *annoncer* from L. *annunciare*].
ANNOUNCEMENT, [a-nowns'-ment], *n.* the act of announcing.
ANNOUNCER, [a-nowns'-er], *n.* one who announces, used *esp.* of the officials who introduce programmes and broadcast news by wireless.
ANNOY, (annoys), [an-oi'], *v.t.* to irritate, discomfort, harass, plague, worry. [OFr. *anoier*].
ANNOYANCE, [an-oi'-ans], *n.* the action of annoying; vexation, trouble.
ANNOYER, [an-oi'-er], *n.* one who annoys.
ANNOYING, [an-oi'-ing], *adj.* causing annoyance.
ANNOYINGLY, [an-oi'-ing-li], *adv.* in an annoying manner.
ANNOYINGNESS, [an-oi'-ing-nes], *n.* the quality of being annoying; vexation.
ANNUAL (1), [an'-yōō-al], *n.* that which appears yearly; a plant that lives only one year or season; **hardy a.,** a hardy annual plant, (*fig.*) an event which recurs with tiresome monotony each year. [ANNUAL (2)].
ANNUAL (2), [an'-yōō-al], *adj.* returning every year, lasting only one year or season. [LL. *annualis*].
ANNUALLY, [an'-yōō-al-i], *adv.* every year.
ANNUENT, [an'-yōō-ent], *adj.* nodding, *esp.* of the muscles used in nodding the head. [~L. *annuens*].
ANNUITANT, [a-new'-it-ant], *n.* a person in receipt of an annuity.
ANNUITY, [a-new'-it-i], *n.* a sum of money paid every year for the lifetime of the recipient. [Fr. *annuité*].
ANNUL, (annulling, annulled), [a-nul'], *v.t.* to render void or null, reduce to nothing, cancel, declare invalid. [Fr. *annuler* from L. *ad nullum* to nothing].
ANNULAR, [an'-yōō-ler], *adj.* in the form of a ring, round; **a. eclipse of the sun,** (*astron.*) an eclipse in which the moon so covers the disk of the sun that only a bright ring is seen round the border; **a. space,** (*math.*) the space between an inner and outer cylinder; **a. ligament,** (*med.*) the strong muscular band ringing the wrist and ankle. [L. *annularis*].
ANNULARLY, [an'-yōō-ler-li], *adv.* in an annular manner.
ANNULARY, [an'-yōō-ler-i], *adj.* having a ring-like form.
ANNULATE, [an'-yōō-lāt], *adj.* annulated. [L. *annulatus*].
ANNULATED, [an'-yōō-lāt-id], *adj.* ringed, marked with ring-like grooves; **a. column,** (*arch.*) shafts clustered together or joined by bands of stone supported by a central pier.
ANNULATION, [an'-yōō-lā'-shun], *n.* a ring-like or annulate formation.
ANNULET, [an'-yōō-let], *n.* a little ring; (*her.*) a small ring or circle borne as a charge; (*arch.*) a small fillet round a column. [~L. *annulus*].

ANNULET

ANNULLER, [a-nul'-er], *n.* one who annuls. [ANNUL].
ANNULMENT, [a-nul'-ment], *n.* the act of annulling, of rendering null and void.
ANNULOSE, [an'-yōō-lōs], *adj.* (*zool.*) furnished with rings, formed of ring-like segments. [L. *annulosus*].
ANNUNCIATE, [a-nun'-si-āt], *v.t.* to announce officially, proclaim, to proclaim as about to come, to bring tidings of. [~L. *annunciare*].
ANNUNCIATION, [a-nun'-si-ā'-shun], *n.* the act of announcing; (*eccles.*) the announcing of the incarnation by the Angel Gabriel to the Virgin Mary; **A. Day,** a church festival on the 25th March in commemoration of the Annunciation. [~L. *annunciatio*].
ANNUNCIATOR, [a-nun'-si-ā'-tor], *n.* one who announces; a mechanism connected with a bell to indicate the room in which attendance is required; (*eccles.*) an officer of the Greek Church who proclaims holy days.
ANNUNCIATORY, [a-nun'-si-ā'-tor-i], *adj.* pertaining to announcing.
ANOA, [an-ō'-a], *n.* the smallest species of ox, *Bos depressicornis*.
ANODE, [an'-ōd], *n.* (*elect.*) the point at which an electric current passes from a source of electrical energy into an external circuit; a positive electrode; (*wirel.*) a metal plate or cylinder in a thermionic valve which attracts some of the electrons emitted by the filament. [Gk. *anodos* way up].
ANODYNE (1), [an'-ō-dīn], *n.* a medicine to alleviate pain; (*fig.*) anything which soothes wounded feelings or softens the sense of misfortune. [ANODYNE (2)].
ANODYNE (2), [an'-ō-dīn], *adj.* soothing, assuaging bodily or mental pain. [Gk. *anodunos*].
ANOESIS, [an-ō'-is-is], *n.* (*psych.*) consciousness with sensation but without thought. [~Gk. *anoetos*].
ANOINT, [an-oint'], *v.t.* to pour oil upon, to smear with oil or unctuous substance; (*eccles.*) to consecrate with oil; (*fig.*) **to a. the palm,** to bribe. [OFr. *enoint*, ~L. *inungere*].
ANOINTED (1), [an-oint'-id], *n.* a consecrated being; **the Lord's A.,** Christ; the king after his anointing.
ANOINTED (2), [an-oint'-id], *adj.* smeared with oil; **an a. king,** a king by divine right.
ANOINTING, [an-oint'-ing], *n.* the act of applying oil or ointment, consecration with oil.
ANOINTMENT, [an-oint'-ment], *n.* the act of anointing or condition of being anointed.
ANOMALIPED (1), [an-om'-al-i-ped'], *n.* (*ornith.*) a bird whose middle toe is joined to the outer and to the inner toes by dissimilar numbers of bones. [ANOMALOUS and L. *pes pedem* foot].
ANOMALIPED (2), [an-om'-al-i-ped], *adj.* pertaining to an anomaliped.
ANOMALISM, [an-om'-al-izm], *n.* anomaly, irregularity.
ANOMALISTIC, [an-om'-al-ist'-ik], *adj.* irregular, departing from established rule; **a. month,** the time taken by the moon to pass from perigee to perigee; **a. year,** the time taken by a planet to pass from perihelion to perihelion.
ANOMALOUS, [an-om'-al-us], *adj.* incongruous; deviating from rule, irregular. [Gk. *anomalos*].
ANOMALOUSLY, [an-om'-al-us-li], *adv.* in an irregular manner.

ANOMALOUSNESS, [an-om'-al-us-nes], *n.* the quality of being anomalous, irregularity.

ANOMALURE, [an-om'-al-ew-er], *n.* (*zool.*) the African scale-tailed squirrel. [~ANOMALOUS and Gk. *oura* tail].

ANOMALY, [an-om'-al-i], *n.* irregularity, deviation from rule, inconsistency (in human action); (*astron.*) the angular distance of a planet from its perihelion, an irregularity in a planet's motion. [L., Gk. *anomalia*].

ANON (1), [an-on'], *adv.* soon, in a short time, directly; **ever and a.**, every now and then. [OE. *on an*].

ANON (2), [an-on'], *n.* anonymous. [Abbrev. of ANONYMOUS].

ANONA, [an-ō'-na], *n.* a genus of plants including the pineapple. [L. *anona*].

ANONACEOUS, [an-ō-nā'-shus], *adj.* pertaining to the anona.

ANONYM, [an'-on-im], *n.* a nameless person; an assumed name. [Fr. *anonyme*].

ANONYMITY, [an'-on-im'-it-i], *n.* the state of being anonymous.

ANONYMOUS, [an-on'-im-us], *adj.* lacking a name, without any name acknowledged; of unknown or undeclared authorship. [Gk. *anonumos*].

ANONYMOUSLY, [an-on'-im-us-li], *adv.* without a name, in an anonymous manner.

ANONYMOUSNESS, [an-on'-im-us-nes], *n.* anonymity.

ANOPHELES, [an-of'-el-ēz], *n.* a genus of malarial mosquito. [Gk. *anopheles* harmful].

ANOPLOTHERIUM, [an'-ō-plō-thēer'-i-um], *n.* (*geol.*) a genus of extinct pachydermatous quadrupeds of the Eocene Age. [Gk. *anoplos* unarmed and *therion* wild beast].

ANOPSIA, [an-op'-si-a], *n.* deprivation of sight. [AN (3) and Gk. *opsis* sight].

ANOREXIA, ANOREXY, [an'-ō-rek'-si-(a)], *n.* (*med.*) lack of appetite. [Gk. *anorexia*].

ANORTHIC, [an-aw'-thik], *adj.* without right angles; (*geol.*) irregular in crystallization. [AN (3) and Gk. *orthos* straight].

ANORTHITE, [a-naw'-thīt], *n.* felspathic mineral found in translucent anorthic crystals. [ANORTHIC].

ANOSMIA, [an-oz'-mi-a], *n.* (*med.*) loss of the sense of smell. [AN (3) and Gk. *osme* a smell].

ANOTHER, [an-uTH'-er], *adj.* and *pron.* not the same, a second, further, additional, any other; a second similar; different in attributes though the same person or thing. [OE. *an* and OTHER].

ANOUROUS, [an-ower'-rus], *adj.* (*zool.*) tailless. [AN (3) and Gk. *oura*].

ANSA, [an'-sa], *n.* (*archæ.*) decorated vase handle; (*astron.*) the apparent end of the rings which surround the planet Saturn, projecting like handles from the planet. [L. *ansa* handle].

ANSERINE, [an'-ser-īn], *adj.* pertaining to the goose; stupid. [L. *anserinus*].

ANSWER (1), [ahn'-ser], *n.* a reply, response, statement made in reply to a question; an argument, a defence, a resulting action; (*math.*) solution of a problem; (*leg.*) a reply made to a charge, a counter-statement of facts in a course of pleadings. [OE. *andswaru*].

ANSWER (2), [ahn'-ser], *v.t.* to speak, write or act in consequence of another's words or actions; to reply to, to speak or write in return to, to say or do in reply, to refute, to be adequate for, to serve, to suit; *v.i.* to reply, to speak or reply by way of return, to rebut a charge, to defend oneself; (of a plan) to succeed; **to a. for**, to be responsible for; **to a. to**, (such a description, name), to be known by, to correspond to. [OE. *andswerian*].

ANSWERABLE, [ahn'-ser-abl], *adj.* capable of being answered; liable; **a. for**, responsible for; **a. to**, obliged to give an account to.

ANSWERABLENESS, [ahn'-ser-abl-nes], *n.* the quality of being answerable.

ANSWERABLY, [ahn'-ser-ab-li], *adv.* correspondingly, in due proportion.

ANSWERLESS, [ahn'-ser-les], *adj.* having no answer, incapable of being answered.

ANT (1), [ant], *n.* an emmet, a pismire, a small gregarious insect of the genus *Formica*. [OE. *æmete*].

ANT- (2), see ANTE-.

ANT- (3), see ANTI-.

ANTA, [an'-ta], *n.* (*arch.*) a pilaster or rectangular projection on the sides of the door or corners of a building. [L. *antae* (*pl.*)].

ANTACID (1), ANTIACID, [ant'-as'-id], *n.* a substance which counteracts or neutralizes an acid; an alkali; medicine for correcting stomach acidity. [ANT (3) and ACID].

ANTACID (2), [ant'-as'-id], *adj.* counteracting an acid.

ANTACRID, [ant'-ak'-rid], *n.* medicine for correcting acrid secretions. [ANT (3) and ACRID].

ANTAGONISM, [an-tag'-on-izm], *n.* the condition of being opposed; mutual resistance of two forces, physical or spiritual, an opposing force. [Gk. *antagonisma*].

ANTAGONIST, [an-tag'-on-ist], *n.* one who is opposed to, or contends with another; an adversary, an opponent. [Gk. *antagonistes*].

ANTAGONISTIC (1), [an-tag'-on-ist'-ik], *n.* (*anat.*) a muscle counteracting the action of another.

ANTAGONISTIC (2), [an-tag'-on-ist'-ik], *adj.* opposed to, unsympathetic, hostile.

ANTAGONISTICAL, [an-tag'-on-ist'-ikl], *adj.* antagonistic.

ANTAGONISTICALLY, [an-tag'-on-ist'-ik-al-i], *adv.* in an antagonistic manner.

ANTAGONIZE, [an-tag'-on-īz], *v.t.* to contend with, dispute the mastery with; to make antagonistic, to render hostile. [Gk. *antagonizomai*].

ANTALGIC, [ant-al'-jik], *n.* a medicine that relieves pain, an anodyne. [ANT (3) and Gk. *algos* pain].

ANTALKALI, [ant-al'-kal-ī], *n.* (*chem.*) a substance which neutralizes the effect of alkalis. [ANT (3) and ALKALI].

ANTALKALINE, [ant-al'-kal-īn], *adj.* pertaining to an antalkali.

ANTANACLASIS, [ant'-an-ak'-las-is], *n.* (*rhet.*) a figure of speech in which the same word is repeated in a different sense; the repetition, after a long parenthesis, of the preliminary words of the main sentence. [Gk. *antanaklasis*].

ANTAPHRODISIAC, [ant'-a-frō-diz'-i-ak], *adj.* and *n.* a drug or medicine counteracting sexual desire. [ANT (3) and APHRODISIAC].

ANTAPOPLECTIC, [ant-ap'-ō-plek'-tik], *adj.* and *n.* (*med.*) a drug or medicine efficacious against apoplexy. [ANT (3) and APOPLECTIC].

ANTARCTIC, [ant-ahk'-tik], *adj.* and *n.* pertaining to the zone round the South Pole. [ANT (3) and ARCTIC].

ANTARTHRITIC, ANTIARTHRITIC, [ant'-ah-thrit'-ik], *adj.* and *n.* (*med.*) a drug used for alleviating or remedying gout or arthritis. [ANT (3) and ARTHRITIS].

ANTASTHMATIC, ANTIASTHMATIC, [ant'-as-mat'-ik], *adj.* (*med.*) tending to alleviate asthma. [ANT (3) and ASTHMATIC].

ANTATROPHIC, [ant'-a-trof'-ik], *adj.* (*med.*) efficacious against atrophy. [ANT (3) and ATROPHIC].

ANT-BEAR, [ant'-bāer], *n.* the bear-like great ant-eater or tamanoa. [ANT (1) and BEAR (1)].

ANTE-, ANT-, *pref.* before, in front of, earlier than. [L. *ante*].

ANT-EATER, [ant'-ē'-ter], *n.* a South-American quadruped of the order *Myrmecophaga* which feeds on ants; a similar Australian quadruped of the *Monotremata*; (*ornith.*) the ant-thrush. [ANT (1) and EATER].

ANTEBRACHIAL, [an'-ti-brak'-i-al], *adj.* (*anat.*) pertaining to the forearm. [ANTE and L. *bracchium* arm].

ANTECEDANEOUS, [an'-ti-sid-ā'-ni-us], *adj.* preceding, going before.

ANTECEDE, [an'-ti-sēd'], *v.t.* to go before, to precede in place, time or rank. [L. *antecedere*].

ANTECEDENCE, [an'-ti-sē'-dens], *n.* the act or state of going before in place, time or rank; precedence; (*astron.*) an apparent motion of a planet towards the west, or contrary to the order of the signs. [L. *antecedentia*].

ANTECEDENCY, [an'-ti-sē'-den-si], *n.* the condition of being antecedent.

ANTECEDENT (1), [an'-ti-sē'-dent], *n.* that which goes before in time, place, or rank; (*gram.*) the noun or pronoun to which a relative pronoun refers; (*leg.*) the conditional clause of a hypothetical proposition; (*math.*) the former of two terms of a ratio; (*pl.*) prior conduct; one's previous record, circumstances of ancestry, birth, education, past experience. [ANTECEDENT (2)].

ANTECEDENT (2), [an'-ti-sē'-dent], *adj.* going before in time, place or rank; prior, previous. [~L. *antecedens*].

ANTECEDENTLY, [an'-ti-sē'-dent-li], *adv.* previously, before.

ANTECESSOR, [an'-ti-ses'-or], *n.* one who goes before, a predecessor; (*leg.*) previous possessor. [L. *antecessor*].

ANTECHAMBER, [an'-ti-chām'-ber], *n.* an entrance room, room leading to the chief apartment and often used as a waiting-room. [ANTE and CHAMBER].

ANTE-CHAPEL, [an'-ti-chapl'], *n.* (*arch.*) the ante-room to a chapel. [ANTE and CHAPEL].

ANTE-CHOIR, [an'-ti-kwīer'], *n.* (*arch.*) a space kept for clergy and choristers at the entrance to the choir. [ANTE and CHOIR].

ANTECIANS, [an-tē'-shanz], *n.(pl.)* (*geog.*) people living on the same meridian and at the same distance from, but on opposite sides of, the equator. [Gk. *antoikos*].

ANTEDATE, (antedating), [an'-ti-dāt'], *v.t.* to date before the actual time, to anticipate, to precede in time. [ANTE and DATE (2)].

ANTEDILUVIAN (1), [an'-ti-di-lōō'-vi-an], *n.* one who lived before the Deluge, a very old-fashioned thing or person. [ANTE and L. *diluvium* flood].

ANTEDILUVIAN (2), [an'-ti-di-lōō'-vi-an], *adj.* existing before the Deluge, antiquated.

ANT-EGGS, [ant'-egz'], *n.(pl.)* the ant's pupae, formerly thought to be eggs.

ANTEFIX, (pl. antefixa), [an'-ti-fiks'], *n.* (usually *pl.*) (*arch.*) ornamental tiles concealing the ends of the roofing tiles on ancient buildings. [L. *antefixum*].

ANTEFIX

ANTELOPE, [an'-til-ōp], *n.* a ruminant akin to the deer and goat, with cylindrical annulate horns. [OFr. *antelop*].

ANTELUCA†, [an'-ti-lōō'-ka], *n.* the time just before dawn. [ANTE and L. *lux lucem*, light].

ANTELUCAN, [an'-ti-lŏŏk'-an], *adj.* pertaining to the anteluca.

ANTEMERIDIAN, [an'-ti-mer-id'-i-an], *adj.* before noon. [ANTE and MERIDIAN].

ANTEMETIC (1), ANTIEMETIC, [ant'-im-et'-ik], *n.* a remedy to allay vomiting.

ANTEMETIC (2), [ant'-im-et'-ik], *adj.* allaying or checking vomiting. [ANT (3) and EMETIC].

ANTEMOSAIC, [an'-ti-mō-zā'-ik], *adj.* pertaining to the time before Moses. [ANTE and MOSES].

ANTEMUNDANE, [an'-ti-mun'-dān], *adj.* existing before the world was created. [ANTE and MUNDANE].

ANTENATAL, [an'-ti-nātl'], *adj.* existing or taking place before birth; **a. clinic,** a clinic where medical attention is given to pregnant women. [ANTE and NATAL].

ANTENNA, (pl. antennae), [an-ten'-a], *n.* a sensory organ or feeler on an insect's head (usually in pairs); (*wirel.*) an aerial. [L. *antenna* sail-yard].

ANTENNAL, [an-tenl'], *adj.* pertaining to an antenna.

ANTENNIFEROUS, [an'-ten-if'-er-us], *adj.* bearing or having antennae. [ANTENNA and L. *ferre* to bear].

ANTENNIFORM, [an-ten'-i-fawm], *adj.* having the form or shape of antennae. [ANTENNA and FORM].

ANTENUPTIAL, [an'-ti-nup'-shal], *adj.* pertaining to the time before marriage, pre-nuptial. [ANTE and NUPTIAL].

ANTEPASCHAL, [an'-ti-pas'-kal], *adj.* coming before Easter or the Jewish Passover. [ANTE and PASCHAL].

ANTEPAST, [an'-ti-pahst'], *n.* a foretaste, something taken before a meal as an appetizer, hors d'oeuvres. [ANTE and L. *pastus* food].

ANTEPENDIUM, [an'-ti-pend'-i-um], *n.* (*eccles.*) an ornamental cloth hanging in front of the altar. [ANTE and L. *pendere* to hang].

ANTEPENULT, [an'-ti-pen-ult'], *n.* the last but two. [ANTE and L. *penultimus* last but one].

ANTEPENULTIMATE, [an'-ti-pen-ult'-im-at], *adj.* pertaining to the antepenult.

ANTEPILEPTIC (1), [ant'-ep'-il-ep'-tik], *n.* a cure or remedy for epilepsy.

ANTEPILEPTIC (2), ANTIEPILEPTIC, [ant'-ep'-il-ep'-tik], *adj.* remedying epilepsy. [ANT (3) and EPILEPTIC].

ANTEPORT, ANTIPORT, [an'-ti-pawt'], *n.* an outer gate, door or harbour. [ANTE and L. *porta* gate].

ANTEPOSITION, [an'-ti-poz-ish'-un], *n.* (*gram.*) the placing of a word before another, which by ordinary rules of construction ought to follow it. [ANTE and POSITION].

ANTEPRANDIAL, [an'-ti-pran'-di-al], *adj.* pertaining to the time before dinner. [ANTE and PRANDIAL].

ANTERIOR, [an-tēer'-i-or], *adj.* before in time or place; preceding, earlier, prior. [L. *anterior*].

ANTERIORITY, [an-tēer'-i-or'-i-ti], *n.* the state of being anterior in time or position.

ANTERIORLY, [an-tēer'-i-or-li], *adv.* before, previously.

ANTEROOM, [an'-ti-rōōm'], *n.* an antechamber. [ANTE and ROOM].

ANTESTOMACH, [an'-ti-stum'-ak], *n.* (*anat.*) a cavity which leads into the stomach. [ANTE and STOMACH].

ANTETEMPLE, [an'-ti-templ'], *n.* (*arch.*) the western part of a divided nave of a church. [ANTE and TEMPLE].

ANTHAEMORRHAGIC, [ant-hem'-er-aj'-ik], *adj.* curing or preventing haemorrhage. [ANT (3) and HAEMORRHAGE].

ANTHELION, (pl. anthelia), [ant-hē'-li-on], *n.* a halo surrounding the shadow of an observer's head on a bank of fog or cloud opposite the sun. [Gk. *anthelios* opposite the sun].

ANTHELIX, see ANTIHELIX.

ANTHELMINTIC, [ant'-hel-min'-tik], *adj.* destroying intestinal worms. [ANTE and Gk. *helminthos* worm].

ANTHEM, [an'-them], *n.* a musical composition, usually from the Scriptures or Liturgy, sung antiphonally or by two voices or choirs responsively; any triumphant song of praise or gladness. [OE. *antefn*].

ANTHEMIS, [an'-thim-is], *n.* (*bot.*) a genus of many species of composite plants allied to camomile. [L. *anthemis* camomile].

ANTHER, [an'-ther], *n.* (*bot.*) the part of the stamen of a flowering plant containing the pollen. [Gk. *antheros* flowery].

ANTHERAL, [an'-ther-al], *adj.* pertaining to an anther.

ANTHER-DUST, [an'-ther-dust'], *n.* pollen.

ANTHERIDIUM, [an'-ther-id'-i-um], *n.* the male organ of cryptogams. [~Gk. *antheros* flowery].

ANTHERIFEROUS, [an'-ther-if'-er-us], *adj.* bearing anthers. [ANTHER and L. *fero* I bear].

ANTHEROGENOUS, [an'-ther-oj'-in-us], *adj.* (*bot.*) developing petals from anthers. [ANTHER and Gk. *genes* born].

ANTHEROID, [an'-ther-oid], *adj.* resembling an anther in appearance or function. [ANTHER and Gk. *oeides* like].

ANTHESIS, [an-thē'-sis], *n.* (*bot.*) the period of full bloom. [Gk. *anthesis*].

ANT-HILL, [ant'-hil], *n.* a small mound thrown up by ants in making their nest.

ANTHO-, *pref.* flower. [Gk. *anthos*].

ANTHOBIAN, [an-thō'-bi-an], *n.* a beetle which lives on flowers. [ANTHO and Gk. *bios* life].

ANTHOCARPOUS, [an'-thō-kah'-pus], *adj.* (*bot.*) bearing fruit formed by masses of flowers adhering together, as in the pineapple. [ANTHO and Gk. *karpos* fruit].

ANTHODIUM, [an-thō'-di-um], *n.* (*bot.*) the head of flowers of composite plants as of the thistle or daisy. [Gk. *anthodes* flower-like].

ANTHOID, [an'-thoid], *adj.* resembling a flower, flower-like. [ANTHO and Gk. *oeides* like].

ANTHOLITE, [an'-thō-līt], *n.* (*geol.*) an anthoid fossil plant. [ANTHO and Gk. *lithos* stone].

ANTHOLOGICAL, [an'-thō-loj'-ikl], *adj.* pertaining to an anthology.

ANTHOLOGY, [an-thol'-o-ji], *n.* a collection of flowers or choice specimens of verse, *esp.* applied to Greek verse; any collection of choice passages from the works of an author or different authors. [Gk. *anthologia* a nosegay].

ANTHOMANIA, [an'-thō-mā'-ni-a], *n.* passion for certain flowers. [ANTHOS and MANIA].

ANTHOPHORE, [an'-thō-faw(r)], *n.* (*bot.*) the receptacle extended into a stalk and bearing at its apex the petals, stamens and pistil. [ANTHO and Gk. *phoros* bearing].

ANTHOPHORE

ANTHOPHYLLITE, [an-thof'-il-īt], *n.* (*min.*) a Norwegian variety of hornblende, of a clove-brown colour. [MdL. *anthophyllum* clove].

ANTHORISM, [an'-thor-izm], *n.* (*rhet.*) a description or definition contrary to that given by the adverse party; a counter-definition. [Gk. *anthorismos*].

ANTHOZOA, [an'-thō-zō'-a], *n.(pl.)* (*zool.*) an order of marine polyps, the corals. [ANTHO and Gk. *zoon* animal].

ANTHRACENE, [an'-thras-ēn'], *n.* a hydro-carbon dyestuff, a crystalline hydro-carbon derived principally from anthracene oil; **a. oil**, a thick green oil distilled from coal tar; **a. red**, artificial alizarin. [~Gk. *anthrakos* coal].

ANTHRACIFEROUS, [an'-thras-if'-er-us], *adj.* bearing anthracite. [Gk. *anthrakos* coal and L. *ferre* to bear].

ANTHRACITE, [an'-thras-īt'], *n.* (*min.*) a hard, slow-burning, hot and smokeless non-bituminous coal. [Gk. *anthrakites* coal-like].

ANTHRACITIC, [an'-thras-it'-ik], *adj.* pertaining to, or resembling, anthracite.

ANTHRACOID, [an'-thrak-oid], *adj.* (*med.*) resembling anthrax. [ANTHRAX and Gk. *oeides* like].

ANTHRACOLITE, [an-thrak'-ol-īt'], *n.* anthraconite. [Gk. *anthrakos* coal and *lithos* stone].

ANTHRACONITE, [an-thrak'-on-īt], *n.* (*geol.*) a black Kilkenny marble, coal-black bituminous limestone; (*pop.*) swinestones or stinkstones. [Gk. *anthrakos* coal and *one* female descendant].

ANTHRACOSAURUS, [an'-thrak-ō-saw'-rus], *n.* (*geol.*) the large fossil lizard of the coal measures. [Gk. *anthrakos* coal and *sauros* lizard].

ANTHRACOTHERIUM, [an'-thrak-ō-thēer'-i-um], *n.* (*geol.*) an extinct genus of swine. [Gk. *anthrakos* coal and *therion* wild beast].

ANTHRAX, [an'-thraks], *n.* a carbuncle; a malignant disease common to sheep and cattle, occurring also in man; wool-sorter's disease. [L. *anthrax* a carbuncle].

ANTHRAXYLON, [an'-thraks-ī'-lon], *n.* a certain coal of homogeneous botanical origin from stems and roots. [Gk. *anthrax* coal and *xulon* wood].

ANTHROPIC, [an-throp'-ik], *adj.* pertaining to man. [~Gk. *anthropos* man].

ANTHROPO-, *pref.* man. [Gk. *anthropos*].

ANTHROPOCENTRIC, [an'-throp-ō-sen'-trik], *adj.* with man as the pivot of the universe. [ANTHROPO and CENTRIC].

ANTHROPOGENY, [an'-throp-oj'-en-i], *n.* the science which investigates the evolution of man. [ANTHROPO and Gk. *genes* born].

ANTHROPOGLOT, [an-throp'-ō-glot'], *n.* (*zool.*) a creature that has a tongue like man, as the parrot. [Gk. *anthropoglottos*].

ANTHROPOGRAPHY, [an'-thrō-pog'-raf-i], *n.* an account of the characteristics of the different races or peoples of mankind; ethnography. [ANTHROPO and Gk. *graphia* writing].

ANTHROPOID (1), [an'-throp-oid], *n.* a species of the *Anthropoidea*, the highest order of the primates which are nearest to man in structure, as the gorilla and other apes. [ANTHROPOID (2)].

ANTHROPOID (2), [an'-throp-oid], *adj.* (*zool.*) of human form, resembling man. [Gk. *anthropoeides*].

ANTHROPOLATRY, [an'-throp-ol'-at-ri], *n.* worship of man. [ANTHROPO and Gk. *latreia* worship].

ANTHROPOLITE, [an-throp'-ol-īt], *n.* a petrifaction of the human body; a petrified fossil man. [ANTHROPO and Gk. *lithos* stone].

ANTHROPOLOGICAL, [an'-throp-ō-loj'-ikl], *adj.* pertaining to anthropology.

ANTHROPOLOGIST, [an'-thrŏp-o'-loj-ist], *n.* one who studies anthropology.

ANTHROPOLOGY, [an'-thrŏp-o'-loj-i], *n.* the science of mankind, that branch of science which investigates the position of mankind zoologically, studying its evolution, history, physiology and psychology and their mutual bearing; the study of primitive customs, myths, and religions of mankind. [ANTHROPO and Gk. *logos* speech].

ANTHROPOMANCY, [an'-throp-om'-an-si], *n.* pretended divination by inspecting the entrails of a dead man. [ANTHROPO and Gk. *manteia* divination].

ANTHROPOMETRY, [an'-throp-om'-et-ri], *n.* measurement of the human body for scientific purposes. [ANTHROPO and Gk. *metron* measure].

ANTHROPOMORPHIC, [an'-throp-ō-maw'-fik], *adj.* relating to or characterized by anthropomorphism; resembling man. [ANTHROPO and Gk. *morphe* form].

ANTHROPOMORPHISM, [an'-throp-om-aw'-fizm], *n.* the attribution of the human form or human qualities and affections to the Deity, or of human faculties to the lower animals or inanimate things.

ANTHROPOMORPHIST, [an'-throp-ō-maw'-fist], *n.* one who attributes a human personality to God or to animals.

ANTHROPOMORPHITE, [an'-throp-ō-maw'-fīt], *n.* anthropomorphist.

ANTHROPOMORPHITIC, [an'-throp-ō-maw-fit'-ik], *adj.* pertaining to anthropomorphism.

ANTHROPOMORPHITISM, [an'-throp-ō-maw'-fit-izm], *n.* the beliefs of the anthropomorphites.

ANTHROPOMORPHIZE, [an'-throp-ō-maw'-fīz], *v.t.* to attribute to the Deity human form and qualities.

ANTHROPOMORPHOSIS, [an'-throp-ō-maw-fō'-sis], *n.* changing into human form. [Gk. *anthropomorphos* of human form and *osis* condition].

ANTHROPOMORPHOUS, [an'-throp-ō-maw'-fus], *adj.* of human form, having a form resembling that of man. [Gk. *anthropomorphos*].

ANTHROPOPATHICAL, [an'-throp-ō-path'-ikl], *adj.* pertaining to anthropopathy.

ANTHROPOPATHICALLY, [an'-throp-ō-path'-ik-a-li], *adv.* in an anthropopathical manner.

ANTHROPOPATHY, [an'-thrŏp-o'-path-i], *n.* the ascription of human passions and emotions to the Deity. [MedL. *anthropopathia*].

ANTHROPOPHAGI, [an'-throp-of'-aj-i], *n.(pl.)* man-eaters, cannibals, men that eat human flesh.

ANTHROPOPHAGITE, [an'-throp-of'-aj-īt], *n.* a man who eats human flesh. [ANTHROPO and Gk. *phago I* eat].

ANTHROPOPHAGOUS, [an'-throp-of'-ag-us], *adj.* man-eating, feeding on human flesh. [Gk. *anthropophagos* cannibal].

ANTHROPOPHAGY, [an'-throp-of'-aj-i], *n.* the eating of men, cannibalism. [Gk. *anthropophagia*].

ANTHROPOPHUISM, [an'-throp-ō-few'-izm], *n.* the ascription of a human nature to the gods. [ANTHROPO and Gk. *phue* nature].

ANTHROPOSCOPY, [an'-throp-os'-kop-i], *n.* the art of judging of character from bodily lineaments. [ANTHROPO and Gk. *skopos* watcher].

ANTHROPOSOPHIST, [an'-throp-os'-of-ist], *n.* one furnished with the knowledge or the wisdom of men. [ANTHROPO and Gk. *sophia* wisdom].

ANTHROPOSOPHY, [an'-throp-os'-o-fi], *n.* human wisdom; the knowledge of men. [ANTHROPO and Gk. *sophia* wisdom].

ANTHROPOTOMY, [an'-throp-ot'-o-mi], *n.* the anatomy or dissection of the human body. [ANTHROPO and Gk. *tome* cutting].

ANTHYPNOTIC, see ANTIHYPNOTIC.

ANTHYPOCHONDRIAC, see ANTIHYPOCHONDRIAC.

ANTHYPOPHORA, see ANTIHYPOPHORA.

ANTHYSTERIC, see ANTIHYSTERIC.

ANTI-, ANT-, *pref.* against, opposite, in hostility to; sometimes, in compound words directly from the Latin, it stands for ANTE-. [Gk. *anti* against].

ANTIABOLITIONIST, [an'-ti-ab'-ol-ish'-un-ist], *n.* a person who is opposed to the abolition of slavery. [ANTI and ABOLITIONIST].

ANTIACID, see ANTACID.

ANTIADES, [an-tī'-a-dēz], *n.(pl.)* (*anat.*) the tonsils. [Gk. *antiades*].

ANTIADITIS, [an'-tī-ad-ī'-tis], *n.* (*med.*) inflammation of the tonsils. [*Prec.* and Gk. *-itis* now denoting disease].

ANTI-AIRCRAFT, [an'-ti-āer'-krahft], *adj.* opposed to aircraft, used in defence against an attack by hostile aircraft.

ANTIAR, [an'-chah(r)], *n.* the upas tree of Java; the poison obtained from it. [Javanese *antjar*].

ANTIARINE, [an'-cha-rin], *n.* the virulent principle in antiar.

ANTIARISTOCRAT, [an'-ti-a'-ris-tō-krat'], *n.* one who is opposed to aristocrats.

ANTIARTHRITIC, see ANTARTHRITIC.

ANTIASTHMATIC, see ANTASTHMATIC.

ANTIATTRITION, [an'-ti-a-trish'-un], *n.* a counteractive of friction; (*mech.*) a substance applied to moving parts of machinery to eliminate friction. [ANTI and ATTRITION].

ANTIBACCHIUS, [an'-ti-bak'-i-us], *n.* (*pros.*) a foot of three syllables, the first two long, and the last short. [ANTI and BACCHIUS].

ANTIBASILICAN, [an'-ti-bas-il'-ik-an], *adj.* opposed to regal state and magnificence. [ANTI and Gk. *basilikos* regal].

ANTIBILIOUS, [an'-ti-bil'-i-us], *adj.* preventing or curative of bilious complaints. [ANTI and BILIOUS].

ANTIBODY [an'-ti-bod'-i], *n.* (*path.*) a substance in the blood which is a natural antidote to infection, a counteractive in the blood. [ANTI and BODY].

ANTIC (1), [an'-tik], *n.* an act of buffoonery; †a performer who plays a grotesque part, a clown; a mountebank; (*arch.*) †a grotesquely carved figure or face. [ANTIC (2)].

ANTIC (2), [an'-tik], *adj.* grotesque, ludicrous, whimsical, fantastic. [It. *antico* a grotesque antique from L. *antiquus* old].

ANTICACHECTIC, [an'-ti-kak-ek'-tik], *n.* (*med.*) a corrective to general malnutrition. [ANTI and CACHEXIA].

ANTICARDIUM, [an'-ti-kah'-di-um], *n.* (*anat.*) the pit of the stomach. [Gk. *antikardion*].

ANTICATARRHAL (1), [an'-ti-kat-ah'-ral], *n.* a remedy for or preventive of catarrh.

ANTICATARRHAL (2), [an'-ti-kat-ah'-ral], *adj.* remedying catarrh. [ANTI and CATARRHAL].

ANTICAUSOTIC (1), [an'-ti-kaw-sot'-ik], *n.* (*med.*) a remedy for a burning fever. [ANTI and Gk. *kausis* fever].

ANTICAUSOTIC (2), [an'-ti-kaw-sot'-ik], *adj.* (*med.*) remedying a burning fever.

ANTICHLOR, [an'-ti-klaw(r)], *n.* a substance used to free materials bleached by chloride of lime from the injurious effects of chlorine. [ANTI and CHLOR (IDE)].

ANTICHRIST, [an'-ti-krist], *n.* the opponent of Christ, name given to great opponent of Christ and His Kingdom expected by the early church to appear before the second coming of Christ, who would finally overthrow him; sometimes applied to the Pope or Papal power; a false prophet. [ANTI and CHRIST].

ANTICHRISTIAN, [an'-ti-kris'-ti-an], *adj.* opposed to Christ and Christianity.

ANTICHRISTIANISM, [an'-ti-kris'-ti-an-izm], *n.* opposition to the Christian religion.

ANTICHRISTIANIZE, [an'-ti-kris'-ti-an-iz], *v.t.* to render antichristian.

ANTICHTHON, (*pl.* **antichthones**), [an-tik'-thōn-(ēz)], *n.* †a supposed second earth on the opposite side of the sun; (*pl.*) †inhabitants of the antipodes. [Gk. *antichthon*].

ANTICIPANT (1), [an-tis'-ip-ant], *n.* one who anticipates. [ANTICIPANT (2)].

ANTICIPANT (2), [an-tis'-ip-ant], *adj.* expectant, looking forward, anticipating.

ANTICIPATE, [an-tis'-ip-āt], *v.t.* to be beforehand in acting or seeing, to forestall, to foresee, to look forward to, to be prepared for. [~L. *anticipare*].

ANTICIPATION, [an'-tis-ip-ā'-shun], *n.* the act of anticipating, forestalling, foreseeing or being prepared for; a foretaste; (*leg.*) assignment of income derived from a trust estate before it is actually due; (*mus.*) beginning one chord before the preceding one has ceased to sound. [~L. *anticipatio*].

ANTICIPATIVE, [an-tis'-ip-ā'-tiv], *adj.* anticipatory.

ANTICIPATOR, [an-tis'-ip-ā'-tor], *n.* one who anticipates.

ANTICIPATORY, [an-tis'-ip-ā'-tor-i], *adj.* being in anticipation of, in advance of.

ANTICIVIC, [an'-ti-siv'-ik], *adj.* opposed to citizenship. [ANTI and CIVIC].

ANTICLERICAL, [an'-ti-kle'-rikl], *adj.* opposed to the clergy, pertaining to anticlericalism. [ANTI and CLERICAL].

ANTICLERICALISM, [an'-ti-kle'-rik-al-izm], *n.* a movement opposed to the sacerdotal claims of the clergy or directed against the influence of the clergy; a movement against the intrusion of the clergy into politics. [*Prec.*].

ANTICLIMAX, [an'-ti-kli'-maks], *n.* the opposite of climax; (*rhet.*) sudden change from dignity to triviality of expression; an additional less moving scene at the end of a play after the scene of the climax. [ANTI and CLIMAX].

ANTICLINAL, [an'-ti-klīn'-al], *adj.* dipping or sloping down in opposite directions; **a. axis**, (*geol.*) a line from which strata dip on either side. [ANTI and Gk. *klino* I bend].

ANTICLINE, [an'-ti-klīn], *n.* (*geol.*) a line or ridge from which strata slope down on both sides. [*Prec.*].

ANTICLINE

ANTICLINIC, [an'-ti-klin'-ik], *adj.* anticlinal.

ANTICLY†, [an'-tik-li], *adv.* in antic manner, grotesquely.

ANTICONSTITUTIONAL, [an'-ti-kon'-sti-tew'-shun-al], *adj.* opposing the constitution.

ANTICONTAGIOUS, [an'-ti-kon-tā'-jus], *adj.* destructive or preventive of contagion.

ANTICONVULSIVE, [an'-ti-kon-vul'-siv], *adj.* remedying convulsions.

ANTICOR, [an'-ti-kaw(r)], *n.* a swelling in the chest of domestic animals. [ANTI and L. *cor* heart].

ANTICORROSIVE, [an'-ti-ker-ō'-siv], *n.* a substance for preventing corrosion. [ANTI and CORROSIVE].

ANTICOURT, [an'-ti-kawt], *adj.* opposed to the court.

ANTICOURTIER, [an'-ti-kawt'-i-er], *n.* an anti-court person.

ANTICOUS, [an'-tik-us], *adj.* (*bot.*) with the line of dehiscence in an anther pointing towards the pistil. [L. *anticus* front].

ANTICUM, [an'-tik-um], *n.* (*arch.*), a porch attached to the front of a building. [L. *anticus anticum* front].

ANTICYCLONE, [an'-ti-sī'-klōn], *n.* an atmospheric condition, with regard to wind and pressure, opposite to that of a cyclone; the central area of this condition, where winds blow spirally outwards, tending to produce improved and settled weather conditions. [ANTI and CYCLONE].

ANTI-DAZZLE, [an'-ti-dazl'], *adj.* designed to prevent visual glare (*esp.* from motor-car headlights). [ANTI and DAZZLE].

ANTIDEMOCRATIC, [an'-ti-dem'-ō-krat'-ik], *adj.* opposing democracy.

ANTIDEMOCRATICAL, [an'-ti-dem'-ō-krat'-ikl], *adj.* antidemocratic.

ANTIDISESTABLISHMENTARIANISM, [an'-ti-dis'-es-tab'-lish-ment-āer'-i-an-izm], *n.* opposition or hostility to the disestablishment of the Church.

ANTIDOTAL, [an'-ti-dōtl'], *adj.* pertaining to an antidote.

ANTIDOTALLY, [an'-ti-dōt'-al-i], *adv.* as an antidote.

ANTIDOTE, [an'-ti-dōt'], *n.* a medicine to counteract a poison or diseased condition; (*fig.*) a remedy. [Gk. *antidoton*].

ANTIDOTICAL, [an'-ti-dōt'-ikl], *adj.* serving as, or in the nature of, an antidote.

ANTIDOTICALLY, [an'-ti-dō'-tik-al-i], *adv.* in the manner of an antidote.

ANTIDYSENTERIC, [an'-ti-dis-en'-te'-rik], *adj.* curative of dysentery. [ANTI and DYSENTERY].

ANTIEMETIC, see ANTEMETIC.

ANTIENTHUSIASTIC, [an'-ti-en-thew'-zi-as'-tik], *adj.* counteracting or opposing enthusiasm.

ANTIEPILEPTIC, see ANTEPILEPTIC.

ANTIEPISCOPAL, [an'-ti-ip-is'-kō-pal], *adj.* opposed to episcopacy. [ANTI and EPISCOPAL].

ANTIEVANGELICAL, [an'-ti-ē'-van-jel'-ikl], *adj.* antagonistic to evangelicalism. [ANTI and EVANGELICAL].

ANTIFANATIC, [an'-ti-fan-at'-ik], *n.* an opponent of fanaticism.

ANTIFEBRILE, [an'-ti-fē'-bril], *n.* a medicine to counteract fever, a febrifuge. [ANTI and FEBRILE].

ANTIFEBRIN, [an'-ti-feb'-rin], *n.* a febrifuge obtained from aniline.

ANTIFEDERAL, [an'-ti-fed'-er-al], *adj.* opposed to federalism. [ANTI and FEDERAL].

ANTIFEDERALISM, [an'-ti-fed'-er-al-izm], *n.* opposition to federalism.

ANTIFOULING, [an'-ti-fowl'-ing], *n.* a substance for preventing the growth of barnacles and weeds on ships' hulls [ANTI and FOUL].

ANTIFRICTION (1), [an'-ti-frik'-shun], *n.* anti-attrition. [ANTI and FRICTION].

ANTIFRICTION (2), [an'-ti-frik'-shun], *adj.* decreasing or eliminating friction.

ANTIGALACTIC, [an'-ti-gal-ak'-tik], *adj.* (*med.*) diminishing the secretion of milk. [ANTI and Gk. *gala galaktos* milk].

ANTI-GAS, [an'-ti-gas'], *adj.* giving protection against poison gas.

ANTIGEN, [an'-ti-jen], *n.* (*med.*) a substance which forms antibodies in the blood. [ANTI and Gk. *genes* born].

ANTI-GURGLER, [an'-ti-gurg'-ler], *n.* a small siphon inserted into the mouths of carboys to admit air so that the liquor is drawn out without gurgling. [ANTI and GURGLE].

ANTIHECTIC, [an'-ti-hek'-tik], *n.* (*med.*) a medicine for remedying hectic disorders.

ANTIHELIX, ANTHELIX, [an'-t(i)-hē'-liks], *n.* (*anat.*) the semicircular prominence of the ear in front of and within the helix.

ANTIHYPNOTIC (1), **ANTHYPNOTIC**, [an'-t(i)-hip-not'-ik], *n.* (*med.*) a medicine used to prevent sleep. [ANTI and HYPNOTIC].

ō (bone), ī (fine), ōō (food), ŏŏ (put), u (up), th (*th*ink), TH (*th*at), zh (azure), † = obsolete, ~ = related to.

O.N.D.—E

ANTIHYPNOTIC (2), [an'-ti-hip-not'-ik], *adj.* tending to prevent sleep. [*Prec.*].

ANTIHYPOCHONDRIAC, ANTHYPOCHONDRIAC, [an'-t(i)-hip'-ō-kon'-dri-ak], *n.* a remedy for hypochondria.

ANTIHYPOPHORA, ANTHYPOPHORA, [an'-t(i)-hi-pof'-or-a] *n.*, (*rhet.*) the refutation of an objection by a sentence of contrary meaning. [ANTI and Gk. *hypophora* objection].

ANTIHYSTERIC, ANTHYSTERIC, [an'-t(i)-his-te'-rik], *n.* a medicine which counteracts hysteria.

ANTI-JACOBIN (1), [an'-ti-jak'-ō-bin], *n.* one opposed to the Jacobins; a member of a French political party opposed to the French Revolution of 1789. [ANTI and JACOBIN].

ANTI-JACOBIN (2), [an'-ti-jak'-ō-bin], *adj.* pertaining to the anti-Jacobins.

ANTILEGOMENA, [an'-ti-leg-om'-in-a], *n.*(*pl.*) the seven books of the New Testament whose inspiration was doubtful. [Gk. *antilegomena* things contradicted].

ANTILIBRATION, [an'-ti-lib-rā'-shun], *n.* the weighing of one thing against another, counterpoising, balancing. [ANTI and L. *libratio* balancing].

ANTILITHIC, [an'-ti-lith'-ik], *adj.* (*med.*) counteracting stone in the bladder. [ANTI and Gk. *lithos* stone].

ANTILOCAPRA, [an'-til-ō-kap'-ra], *n.* the prong-buck or North American antelope. [ANTELOPE and L. *capra* goat].

ANTILOG, [an'-ti-log'], *n.* antilogarithm.

ANTILOGARITHM, [an'-ti-log'-a-riTHm], *n.* (*math.*) the number represented by a logarithm; the complement of the logarithm of a sine, tangent or secant required to make up the logarithm of 90 degrees.

ANTILOGOUS (1), [an-til'-ō-gus], *n.* (*elect.*) that pole of a crystal which, when heating, is negative, and when cooling, positive. [Gk. *antilogia* contradiction].

ANTILOGOUS (2), [an-til'-ō-gus], *adj.* contradictory. [*Prec.*].

ANTILOGY, [an-til'-ō-ji], *n.* a contradiction in terms. [Gk. *antilogia* contradiction].

ANTILOIMIC, [an'-ti-loi'-mik], *adj.* efficacious against the plague. [ANTI and Gk. *loimos* plague].

ANTILOPE, [an'-ti-lōp], *n.* (*zool.*), the original genus of the antelopes. [ANTELOPE].

ANTILOQUY†, [an-til'-ō-kwi], *n.* a contradiction or overthrowing of an argument. [LL. *antiloquium*].

ANTIMACASSAR, [an'-ti-mak-as'-er], *n.* a loose covering on the backs of chairs and sofas to keep them from being soiled by oil on the hair. [ANTI and MACASSAR (OIL)].

ANTIMANIAC, [an'-ti-mā'-ni-ak], *adj.* antimaniacal.

ANTIMANIACAL, [an'-ti-mā'-ni-akl], *adj.* efficacious against madness. [ANTI and MANIACAL].

ANTIMASONIC, [an'-ti-ma-son'-ik], *adj.* opposed to freemasonry. [ANTI and MASONIC].

ANTIMASQUE, [an'-ti-mahsk'], *n.* a grotesque or comic interlude introduced into a masque. [ANTIC (1) and MASQUE].

ANTIMETABOLE, [an'-ti-met-ab'-ol-i], *n.* (*rhet.*) a figure of speech in which words are repeated in reverse order. [ANTI and Gk. *metabole*].

ANTIMETER, [an-tim'-it-er], *n.* an optical instrument for measuring angles under 10 degrees. [ANTI and Gk. *metron* measure].

ANTIMETRICAL, [an'-ti-met'-rikl], *adj.* contrary to the rules of metre.

ANTIMINISTERIAL, [an'-ti-min'-is-tēer'-i-al], *adj.* in opposition to the ministry.

ANTIMNEMONIC, [an'-ti-nim-on'-ik], *adj.* prejudicial or weakening to the memory. [ANTI and MNEMONIC].

ANTIMONARCHIC, [an'-ti-mon-ahk'-ik], *adj.* antimonarchical.

ANTIMONARCHICAL, [an'-ti-mon-ahk'-ikl], *adj.* opposed to monarchy.

ANTIMONARCHIST, [an'-ti-mon'-a-kist], *n.* a person opposed to monarchy. [ANTI and MONARCHIST].

ANTIMONIAL, [an'-ti-mō'-ni-al], *adj.* pertaining to, or composed of, antimony; **a. wine,** wine mixed with a solution of antimony tartrate. [ANTIMONY].

ANTIMONIATE, [an'-ti-mō'-ni-āt], *n.* a salt of antimonic acid.

ANTIMONIATED, [an'-ti-mō'-ni-ā-tid], *adj.* prepared with or containing antimony.

ANTIMONIC, [an'-ti-mō'-nik], *adj.* pertaining to antimony; (*chem.*) pertaining to compounds of antimony in which it combines as a pentad, as **a. acid,** a substance composed of two atoms of antimony and five of oxygen.

ANTIMONIOUS, [an'-ti-mō'-ni-us], *adj.* containing antimony; (*chem.*) pertaining to compounds of antimony, where it combines as a triad, as **a. acid,** a compound of two atoms of antimony and three of oxygen.

ANTIMONITE, [an'-tim'-ō-nīt], *n.* (*chem.*) a salt of antimonious acid; (*min.*) †stibnite.

ANTIMONY, [an'-ti-mun-i], *n.* a chemical element designated Sb (from L. *stibium*); a brittle, bluish-white metal of, flake-like crystals; **a. tartrate,** tartar emetic. [LL. *antimonium* from Arab. *uthmad*].

ANTINATIONAL, [an'-ti-nash'-un-al], *adj.* against or hostile to one's nation, opposed to a national party or policy. [ANTI and NATIONAL].

ANTINATURAL, [an'-ti-nach'-er-al], *adj.* opposed to that which is natural.

ANTINEPHRITIC (1), [an'-ti-nef-rit'-ik], *n.* a medicine for diseases of the kidneys. [ANTI and NEPHRITIC].

ANTINEPHRITIC (2), [an'-ti-nef-rit'-ik], *adj.* counteracting nephritis. [*Prec.*]

ANTINOMIAN, [an'-ti-nō'-mi-an], *n.* one of a sect who maintained that moral law is superseded and set aside by the Gospel. [ANTI and Gk. *nomos* law].

ANTINOMIANISM, [an'-ti-nō'-mi-an-izm], *n.* the doctrine of the Antinomians.

ANTINOMY, [an-tin'-om-i], *n.* a contradiction between two laws or two parts of a law; (*met.*) a contradiction between apparently equally logical conclusions. [Gk. *antinomia*].

ANTIPAPAL, [an'-ti-pā'-pal], *adj.* opposed to the pope or popery. [ANTI and PAPAL].

ANTIPAPISTIC, [an'-ti-pap-ist'-ik], *adj.* antipapal. [ANTI and PAPISTIC].

ANTIPAPISTICAL, [an'-ti-pap-ist'-ikl], *adj.* antipapal. [*Prec.*].

ANTIPARALYTIC (1), [an'-ti-pa'-ra-lit'-ik], *n.* a medicine efficacious for paralysis. [ANTI and PARALYTIC].

ANTIPARALYTIC (2), [an'-ti-pa'-ra-lit'-ik], *adj.* preventing or counteracting paralysis. [*Prec.*].

ANTIPATHETIC, [an'-ti-pa-thet'-ik], *adj.* having an antipathy to.

ANTIPATHETICAL, [an'-ti-pa-thet'-ikl], *adj.* antipathetic.

ANTIPATHIC, [an'-ti-path'-ik], *adj.* opposed to, of contrary nature or character; (*med.*) producing contrary symptoms.

ANTIPATHIST, [an-tip'-ath-ist], *n.* a person subject to antipathy; an opposite.

ANTIPATHY, [an-tip'-a-thi], *n.* hostile feeling, natural aversion or dislike; essential difference between substances (as oil and water) which prevents them uniting. [Gk. *antipatheia*].

ANTIPATRIOTIC, [an'-ti-pat'-ri-ot'-ik], *adj.* opposed or indifferent to the welfare of one's country; opposed to the narrow view of the welfare of one's country as being independent of that of other countries. [ANTI and PATRIOTIC].

ANTIPEDOBAPTIST, [an'-ti-ped'-ō-bap'-tist], *n.* one opposed to the baptism of infants. [ANTI and PEDOBAPTIST].

ANTIPERIODIC, [an'-ti-pēer'-i-od'-ik], *adj.* destroying the periodic return of diseases. [ANTI and PERIODIC].

ANTIPERISTALTIC, [an'-ti-pe'-ris-talt'-ik], *adj.* (*physiol.*) contrary to peristaltic motion. [ANTI and PERISTALTIC].

ANTIPERISTASIS, [an'-ti-pe-ris'-tas-is], *n.* the opposition of a contrary quality, resistance to an action; (*rhet.*) conceding a point, but drawing a different conclusion. [ANTI and Gk. *peristasis* standing round].

ANTIPERISTATIC, [an'-ti-pe-ris-tat'-ik], *adj.* pertaining to antiperistasis. [*Prec.*].

ANTI-PERSONNEL, [an'-ti-per-sun-el'], *adj.* of a bomb, intended to injure or destroy persons rather than material.

ANTIPESTILENTIAL, [an'-ti-pest'-il-en'-shal], *adj.* efficacious against pestilence, contagion or infection.

ANTIPHLOGISTIC, [an'-ti-flō-jis'-tik], *adj.* (*med.*) counteracting inflammation; opposed to the doctrine of phlogiston or the principle of inflammability. [ANTI and PHLOGISTIC].

ANTIPHLOGISTINE, [an'-ti-flō-jist'-ēn], *n.* (*prot.*) a registered trade-name for a plaster. [*Prec.*].

ANTIPHON, [an'-ti-fon], *n.* a composition in prose or verse consisting of passages or verses sung alternately by two church choirs; an anthem. [LL. *antiphona*].

ANTIPHONAL (1), [an-tif'-on-al], *n.* a book of antiphons. [*Prec.*].

ANTIPHONAL (2), [an-tif'-on-al], *adj.* (*mus.*) pertaining to an antiphon; sung alternately.

ANTIPHONALLY, [an-tif'-on-al-i], *adv.* (*mus.*) in antiphonal fashion.

ANTIPHONARY, [an-tif'-on-er-i], *n.* (*R.C., eccles.*) a service book which contains antiphons.

ANTIPHONIC, [an-tif'-on-ik], *adj.* antiphonal.

ANTIPHONY, [an-tif'-on-i], *n.* antiphon. [ANTIPHON].

ANTIPHRASIS, [an-tif'-ras-is], *n.* (*rhet.*) the use of a word in a sense opposite to its usual meaning. [Gk. *antiphrasis*].

ANTIPHRASTIC, [an'-tif-ras'-tik], *adj.* antiphrastical. [*Prec.*].

ANTIPHRASTICAL, [an'-tif-ras'-tikl], *adj.* of the nature of antiphrasis; ironical.

ANTIPHRASTICALLY, [an'-tif-ras'-tik-al-i], *adv.* in an antiphrastic manner.

ANTIPODAL, [an-tip'-ō-dal], *adj.* pertaining to the antipodes; (*fig.*) diametrically opposed to. [ANTIPODES].

ANTIPODE†, [an-tip'-ō-dē], *n.* one of the antipodes; a direct opposite. [ANTIPODES].

ANTIPODEAN, [an-tip'-od-ē'-an], *adj.* pertaining to the opposite side of the world.

ANTIPODES, [an-tip'-od-ēz], *n.(pl.)* those regions lying on the exact opposite side of the globe from any given point; (*fig.*) anything diametrically opposed to something else. [Gk. *antipous, -podos*, with the feet opposite].

ANTIPOISON, [an'-ti-poizn'], *n.* an antidote to poison. [ANTI and POISON].

ANTIPOLE, [an'-ti-pōl'], *n.* the opposite pole; (*fig.*) the direct opposite.

ANTIPOPE, [an'-ti-pōp'], *n.* a pope elected as rival to a properly elected pope. [ANTI and POPE].

ANTIPOPULAR, [an'-ti-pop'-yōō-ler], *adj.* opposing a popular cause or the people's cause.

ANTIPORT, see ANTEPORT.

ANTIPRELATICAL, [an'-ti-prel-at'-ikl], *adj.* opposed to the prelacy.

ANTIPSORIC, [an'-tip-saw'-rik], *adj.* remedying the itch. [ANTI and Gk. *psora* itch].

ANTIPTOSIS†, [an'-tip'-tō-sis], *n.* (*gram.*) the substitution of one case for another. [Gk. *antiptosis*].

ANTIPUTREFACTIVE, [an'-ti-pew'-tri-fak'-tiv], *adj.* antiseptic. [ANTI and PUTREFACTIVE].

ANTIPYRETIC, [an'-ti-pī-ret'-ik], *adj.* (*med.*) preventing or curing fever. [ANTI and PYRETIC].

ANTIPYRIN, [an'-ti-pīer'-in], *n.* (*prot.*) an antipyretic drug. [*Prec.*].

ANTIQUARIAN (1), [an'-ti-kwāer'-i-an], *n.* an antiquary.

ANTIQUARIAN (2), [an'-ti-kwāer'-i-an], *adj.* pertaining to an antiquary or to antiquity; **a. bookseller**, a seller of second-hand books. [L. *antiquarius*].

ANTIQUARIANISM, [an'-ti-kwāer'-i-an-izm], *n.* the work of an antiquarian; interest in or devotion to antiquities.

ANTIQUARY, [an'-ti-kwer-i], *n.* one devoted to the study of antiquity or antiquities; †a custodian of antiquities. [~L. *antiquarius*].

ANTIQUATE, [an'-ti-kwāt], *v.t.* to render obsolete, to put out of date. [~L. *antiquare*].

ANTIQUATED, [an'-ti-kwā-tid], *adj.* old, out of date, old-fashioned; (of persons) advanced in age. [*Prec.*].

ANTIQUATEDNESS, [an'-ti-kwā'-tid-nes], *n.* the state of being antiquated.

ANTIQUE (1), [an-tēk'], *n.* a relic, an artistic object of great antiquity; (*typ.*) a bold type-face in which all the strokes are of equal thickness.

ANTIQUE (2), [an-tēk'], *adj.* pertaining to olden times, ancient, old-fashioned, antiquated; pertaining to or in the style of an antique. [L. *antiquus*].

ANTIQUELY, [an-tēk'-li], *adv.* in an antique manner.

ANTIQUENESS, [an-tēk'-nes], *n.* the state of being antique.

ANTIQUITY, [an-tik'-wit-i], *n.* great age, the remote past, ancient times. [~L. *antiquitas*].

ANTIRABIC, [an'-ti-rā'-bik], *adj.* counteracting the rabies virus, relating to the cure of rabies. [ANTI and RABIES].

ANTIREVOLUTIONARY, [an'-ti-rev-ol-ōō'-shun-er-i], *adj.* opposed to revolutions in government.

ANTIREVOLUTIONIST, [an'-ti-rev-ol-ōō'-shun-ist], *n.* one opposed to revolution.

ANTIRHEUMATIC, [an'-ti-rōō-mat'-ik], *adj.* efficacious for curing rheumatism. [ANTI and RHEUMATISM].

ANTIRRHINUM, [an'-ti-rī'-num], *n.* (*bot.*) the genus of the snapdragon, the snout-like mouth of the flower being closed. [L. from Gk. *antirrhinon* from ANTI and Gk. *rhis* (*rhinos*) nose].

ANTIRRHINUM

ANTISABBATARIAN, [an'-ti-sab'-at-āer'-i-an], *n.* an opponent of the strict observance of the Sabbath.

ANTISACERDOTAL, [an'-ti-sas'-er-dō'-tal], *adj.* opposed to priests or priestcraft. [ANTI and SACERDOTAL].

ANTISCIANS, [an-tish'-anz], *n.(pl.)* people living on opposite sides of the equator whose shadows at noon fall in opposite directions. [ANTI and Gk. *skia* shadow].

ANTISCORBUTIC, [an'-ti-skaw-bew'-tik], *adj.* efficacious for scurvy. [ANTI and SCORBUTIC].

ANTISCRIPTURAL, [an'-ti-skrip'-chōō-ral], *adj.* opposed to the Holy Scriptures.

ANTI-SEMITE, [an'-ti-sem'-īt], *n.* one opposed to the Jews, racially, politically and economically. [ANTI and SEMITE].

ANTI-SEMITIC, [an'-ti-sem-it'-ik], *adj.* opposed to the Jews.

ANTISEPTIC (1), [an'-ti-sep'-tik], *n.* any substance used to destroy putrefaction and its causes. [ANTISEPTIC (2)].

ANTISEPTIC (2), [an'-ti-sep'-tik], *adj.* resisting the growth of septic bacteria which cause putrefaction. [ANTI and SEPTIC].

ANTISLAVERY, [an'-ti-slā'-ver-i], *adj.* opposed to slavery.

ANTISOCIAL, [an'-ti-sō'-shal], *adj.* averse to society and social intercourse, opposed to the principles underlying society.

ANTISOCIALIST, [an'-ti-sō'-shal-ist], *n.* an opponent of socialism.

ANTISPASIS, [an-tis'-pas-is], *n.* (*med.*) a revulsion or drawing back of any fluid from one part of the body to another. [Gk. *antispasis*].

ANTISPASMODIC, [an'-ti-spaz-mod'-ik], *adj.* efficacious in counteracting spasms. [ANTI and SPASMODIC].

ANTISPAST, [an'-ti-spast], *n.* (*pros.*) a foot of four syllables where the first and last are short, and the two middle ones long. [Gk. *antispastos*].

ANTISPASTIC, [an'-ti-spas'-tik], *adj.* (*med.*) turning into other parts, counteracting; (*pros.*) pertaining to antispasts. [Gk. *antispastikos*].

ANTISPLENETIC, [an'-ti-splen-et'-ik], *adj.* efficacious for splenetic diseases.

ANTISTASIS, [an-tis'-tas-is], *n.* (*rhet.*) the defence of an action by pointing out the evil which would have arisen if the action had not taken place. [Gk. *antistasis*].

ANTISTROPHE, [an-tis'-trof-i], *n.* (*dram.*) the return to the right of the chorus in Greek drama in answer to a previous move to the left; the stanza or lines sung during this movement; (*gram.*) the repetition of the words of a phrase in inverse order. [Gk. *antistrophe* turning about].

ANTISTROPHIC, [an'-ti-strof'-ik], *adj.* pertaining to an antistrophe.

ANTISTRUMATIC, [an'-ti-strōō-mat'-ik], *adj.* (*med.*) antistrumous.

ANTISTRUMOUS, [an'-ti-strōō'-mus], *adj.* (*med.*) efficacious for scrofula. [ANTI and L. *struma* scrofula].

ANTISYPHILITIC, [an'-ti-sif'-il-it'-ik], *adj.* efficacious for syphilis.

ANTITHEISM, [an'-ti-thē'-izm], *n.* opposition to theism.

ANTITHEIST, [an'-ti-thē'-ist], *n.* an opponent of theism.

ANTITHEISTIC, [an'-ti-thē-is'-tik], *adj.* pertaining to antitheism.

ANTITHENAR, [an-tith'-en-er], *n.* (*anat.*) the muscle that moves the thumb. [ANTI and Gk. *thenar* palm].

ANTITHESIS, [an-tith'-is-is], *n.* (*rhet.*) an emphatic contrast of ideas, usually attained by using two contrasting words with equivalent grammatical function in two adjacent clauses; a strong contrast. [ANTI and THESIS].

ANTITHETIC, [an′-ti-thet′-ik], *adj.* pertaining to antithesis; opposing, contrasting, directly opposite. [*Prec.*].

ANTITHETICAL, [an′-ti-thet′-ikl], *adj.* pertaining to the use of antithesis.

ANTITHETICALLY, [an′-ti-thet′-ik-al-i] *adv.* by antithesis.

ANTITOXIC, [an′-ti-tok′-sik], *adj.* pertaining to an antitoxin.

ANTITOXIN, [an′-ti-tok′-sin], *n.* (*physiol.*) one of several soluble chemical compounds in the blood, neutralizing specific poisons or toxins, *esp.* of disease. [ANTI and TOXIN].

ANTITRADE, [an′-ti-trād′], *n.* an upper tropical wind which blows in a direction contrary to and above the trade wind. [ANTI and TRADE (-WIND)].

ANTITRAGUS, [an-tit′-rag-us], *n.* (*anat.*) the conical prominence on the lower part of the outer ear, opposite the tragus. [Gk. *antitragos*].

ANTITRINITARIAN (1), [an′-ti-trin′-i-tāer′-i-an], *n.* one who rejects the doctrine of the Trinity.

ANTITRINITARIAN (2), [an′-ti-trin′-i-tāer′-i-an], *adj.* rejecting the doctrine of the Trinity.

ANTITRINITARIANISM, [an′-ti-trin′-i-tāer′-i-an-izm], *n.* (*theol.*) the doctrine which denies the Trinity.

ANTITYPE, [an′-ti-tīp′], *n.* that which is represented by a type or symbol. [ANTI and TYPE].

ANTITYPICAL, [an′-ti-tip′-ikl], *adj.* pertaining to an antitype, explaining the type. [*Prec.*].

ANTITYPICALLY, [an′-ti-tip′-ik-al-i], *adv.* in the manner of an antitype.

ANTIVARIOLOUS, [an′-ti-va-rī′-ō-lus], *adj.* (*med.*) efficacious for smallpox. [ANTI and VARIOLOUS].

ANTIVENENE, [an′-ti-ven-ēn′], *n.* an antidote against snake-bites. [ANTI and L. *venenum* poison].

ANTIVENEREAL, [an′-ti-ven-ēer′-i-al], *adj.* (*med.*) efficacious for venereal disease.

ANTIZYMIC, [an′-ti-zī′-mik], *adj.* preventing fermentation. [ANTI and Gk. *zume* leaven].

ANTIZYMOTIC, [an′-ti-zī-mot′-ik], *adj.* preventing decomposition or fermentation. [*Prec.*].

ANTLER, [ant′-ler], *n.* the lowest branch of a stag's horn; the whole or any part of this. [OFr. *antoillier*].

ANTLERED, [ant′-lerd], *adj.* bearing antlers. [*Prec.*].

ANTLIA, [ant′-li-a], *n.* (*zool.*) the suction tongue of lepidopterous insects. [L. *antlia* pump].

ANTLIKE, [ant′-līk], *adj.* resembling ants. [ANT (1) and LIKE].

ANT-LION, [ant′-lī′on], *n.* (*zool.*) a neuropterous insect of the genus *Myrmeleon.* [ANT (1) and LION].

ANTONOMASIA, [ant′-on-om-ā′-zi-a], *n.* (*rhet.*) a figure of speech in which a common noun is used for a proper noun or a proper noun for a common noun. [Gk. *antonomasia*].

ANTONYM, [ant′-on-im], *n.* the opposite of a synonym, a word which is opposite in meaning to another. [ANTI and Gk. *onoma* name].

ANTONYMOUS, [ant-on′-im-us], *adj.* of or pertaining to an antonym.

ANTRORSE, [ant-raws′], *adj.* (*bot.*) bent upwards or forwards. [MdL. *antrorsus*].

ANTRUM, [an′-trum], *n.* †a cave, den; (*anat.*) a large cavity in the upper maxillary bone connected with the nose; the maxillary sinus. [L. *antrum* cave].

ANT-THRUSH, [ant′-thrush], *n.* (*ornith.*) a bird belonging to the thrush family which feeds on ants. [ANT (1) and THRUSH].

ANURA, [an′-yōōer′-a], *n.* the order of tailless amphibia, such as frogs and toads. [MdL. *anura*].

ANUS, [ā′-nus], *n.* (*anat.*) the lower orifice of the alimentary canal, the fundament. [L. *anus*].

ANVIL, [an′-vil], *n.* a heavy iron block on which a smith hammers and shapes his work; anything on which blows are struck. [OE. *anfilte*].

ANVILLED, [an′-vild], *adj.* hammered, wrought on an anvil.

ANXIETY, [ang-zī′-et-i], *n.* the state of being anxious; intense solicitude, concern, uneasiness about some uncertain event; keen desire (to effect some end). [~L. *anxietas*].

ANXIOUS, [ang′-shus, angk′-shus], *adj.* greatly concerned about something, *esp.* in the future or the unknown; a state of being intensely solicitous, full of concern, earnestly desirous (to effect some purpose). [L. *anxius*].

ANXIOUSLY, [angk′-shus-li], *adv.* in an anxious manner, with painful uncertainty, solicitously.

ANXIOUSNESS, [angk′-shus-nes], *n.* the quality of being anxious.

ANY, [en′-i], *adj., pron. and adv.* one, one out of many, some; an indefinite number or quantity; one or more unspecified in a group; a small quantity. [OE. *ænig*].

ANYBODY, [en′-i-bod′-i], *n.* one person out of many, any person, someone; (*fig.*) a person of importance. [ANY and BODY].

ANYHOW, [en′-i-how], *adv.* by any means, in any possible way, in any case; (*fig.*) carelessly, in an easy, carefree manner, in disorder. [ANY and HOW].

ANYTHING, [en′-i-thing], *n.* something of any kind, a single thing; an unspecified object or notion. [ANY and THING].

ANYWHERE, [en′-i-wāer], *adv. and pron.* in any place. [ANY and WHERE].

ANYWISE†, [en′-i-wīz], *adv.* in any way. [ANY and WISE].

ANZAC, [an′-zak], *n.* the Australian-New Zealand Army Corps which fought in Gallipoli in 1915; a member of that corps. [The initial letters of the corps].

AONIAN, [a-ō′-ni-an], *adj.* belonging to Aonia, a district of ancient Bœotia in Greece.

AORIST, [āer′-ist], *n.* (*gram.*) an indefinite past tense in a verb. [Gk. *aoristos* indefinite].

AORISTIC, [āer′-ist′-ik], *adj.* pertaining to the aorist; indefinite. [*Prec.*].

AORTA, [ā-aw′-ta], *n.* (*anat.*) the great artery, proceeding from the left ventricle of the heart to the two iliac arteries. [Gk. *aorta*].

AORTAL, [ā-aw′-tal], *adj.* (*anat.*) of or pertaining to the aorta. [*Prec.*].

AORTIC, [ā-aw′-tik], *adj.* aortal.

AORTITIS, [ā′-aw-tī′-tis], *n.* (*med.*) disease of the aorta. [AORTA and Gk. *itis* now denoting disease].

APACE, [a-pās′], *adv.* at a pace, quickly, speedily; step by step, with steady speed. [A (3) and PACE].

APACHE, [ap-ahsh′], *n.* a tribe of North American Indians; a Parisian thief or cut-throat. [Amer. Ind. *apache* enemy].

APAGOGE, [ap′-a-gō′-ji], *n.* (*logic*) an argument in which the major is evident, but the minor requires further proof; the proof of a proposition by exposing the absurdity that would follow from denying it. [Gk. *apagoge* taking away].

APAGOGICAL, [ap′-a-gō′-jikl], *adj.* pertaining to apagoge; proving by showing the opposite to be absurd.

APAGYNOUS, [ap-aj′-in-us], *adj.* (*bot.*) fructifying once and then dying. [Gk. *hapax* once and *gune* female].

APANAGE, see APPANAGE.

APANTHROPY, [ap-an′-throp-i], *n.* an aversion to the society of human beings. [Gk. *apanthropia* dislike of men].

APART, [a-paht′], *adv.* (of space) on one side, separately, at a distance from; (of purpose, thought) separately, independently, individually; **to set a.,** to set aside for a special purpose, to separate, devote, consecrate. [Fr. *à part* to the side].

APARTMENT, [ap-aht′-ment], *n.* a set of rooms in a house set aside for the use of an individual or family; a single room in a house; (*pl.*) lodgings, a set of rooms set aside for the use of one person or family. [Fr. *appartement*].

APATHETIC, [ap′-ath-et′-ik], *adj.* of or pertaining to apathy; insensible, indifferent.

APATHETICALLY, [ap′-ath-et′-ik-al-i], *adv.* in apathetic fashion, listlessly.

APATHY, [ap′-ath-i], *n.* want of feeling, insensibility to passion or emotion, indifference, indolence of mind. [Gk. *apatheia*].

APATITE, [ap′-at-īt], *n.* (*min.*) a native crystallized phosphate of lime, varying in colour and transparency. [Gk. *apate* deceit].

APAUMEE, [ap-ō′-mi], *adj.* (*her.*) having the hand open and extended so as to show the palm. [Fr. *apaumé*].

APE (1), [āp], *n.* a monkey, *esp.* of the tailless species more closely related to man; (*fig.*) a servile or silly imitator. [OE. *apa*].

APE (2), [āp], *v.t.* to imitate servilely another's manners, speech, etc.; to mimic; to pretend to have, to assume. [APE (1)].

APEAK, [a-pēk′], *adv.* on the point; (*naut.*) perpendicularly, in a vertical line. [Fr. *à pic* perpendicularly].

APELLOUS, [ap-el′-us], *adj.* without a skin. [A (4) and L. *pellis* skin].

APEPSY, [ap-ep′-si], *n.* (*med.*) an imperfect digestion. [Gk. *apepsia* indigestion].

APER, [āp′-er], *n.* one who apes another. [APE (2)].

APERIENT (1), [ap-ēer′-i-ent], *n.* (*med.*) a laxative medicine; a medicine that opens rather than purges

APERIENT (2), [ap-ēer'-i-ent], *adj.* (*med.*) laxative. [~L. *aperiens*].
APERITIF, [ap-e'-rit-ēf], *n.* an alcoholic drink taken as an appetizer before meals. [Fr. *apéritif*].
APERITIVE, [ap-e'-rit-iv], *n.* an aperient; an aperitif. [Fr. *apéritif*].
APERT†, [a-purt'], *adj.* open, public, unconcealed. [OFr. *apert*].
APERTOR, [ap-urt'-or], *n.* (*anat.*) the muscle which raises the upper eyelid.
APERTURE, [ap'-er-cher], *n.* an opening, a gap, passage; the opening in a telescope or other optical instrument through which light passes; (*phot.*) the circular hole in a plate fitted to a lens to control the amount of light admitted to a camera. [L. *apertura*].
APERY, [āp'-eri], *n.* mimicry, aping. [APE (1)].
APETALOUS, [a-pet'-al-us], *adj.* (*bot.*) without petals. [A (4) and PETALOUS].
APETALOUSNESS, [a-pet'-al-us-nes], *n.* the state of having no petals. [*Prec.*].
APEX, (*pl.* **apices**), [ā'-peks], *n.* the tip, point, summit, peak, pointed end; (*geom.*) the top point of a triangle or cone. [L. *apex*].
APHAERESIS, APHERESIS, [a-fēer'-es-is], *n.* the taking away or loss of a letter or syllable from the beginning of a word; (*med.*) †the removal of anything noxious. [Gk. *aphairesis* taking away].
APHANIPTERA, [af'-an-ip'-ter-a], *n.*(*pl.*) (*zool.*) insects with rudimentary scales instead of wings. [Gk. *aphanes* invisible and *pteron* wing].
APHANISTIC, [af'-an-is'-tik], *adj.* indistinct, obscure. [Gk. *aphanes* invisible].
APHANITE, [af'-an-īt], *n.* (*min.*) a dark hornblende of uniform, grainless texture. [Gk. *aphanes* invisible].
APHASIA, [af-ā'-zi-a], *n.* (*med.*) loss of the power of speech through a lesion of the brain. [Gk. *aphasia*].
APHELION, (*pl.* **aphelia**), [af-ē'-li-on], *n.* (*astron.*) the point of a planet's or comet's orbit most distant from the sun. [APO and Gk. *helios* sun].

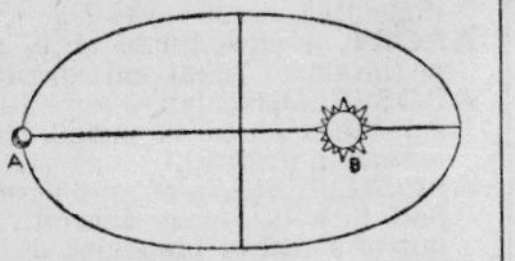

A B

APHELION

APHELIOTROPIC, [af-ē'-li-ō-trop'-ik], *adj.* pertaining to apheliotropism.
APHELIOTROPISM, [af-ē'-li-ō'-trop-izm], *n.* (*bot.*) the power of plants to turn away from the sun. [APO, Gk. *helios* sun and *tropos* turning].
APHEMIA, [a-fē'-mi-a], *n.* (*med.*) a form of aphasia marked by difficulty in articulation. [A (4) and Gk. *pheme* speech].
APHERESIS, see APHAERESIS.
APHESIS, [af'-is-is], *n.* (*philol.*) the occasional loss of an unstressed vowel at the beginning of a word. [Gk. *aphesis* dismissal].
APHID, (*pl.* **aphides**), [ā'-fid], *n.* (*zool.*) a minute plant-louse of the genus *Aphis*. [MdL. *aphis*].
APHIDIAN, [af-id'-i-an], *adj.* of or pertaining to the aphides. [*Prec.*].
APHIDIDES, [af-id'-id-ēz], *n.*(*pl.*) parasites on the aphides.
APHIDIVOROUS, [af-id-iv'-or-us], *adj.* devouring the aphides. [APHID and L. *voro* I devour].
APHILANTHROPY, [af'-il-an'-throp-i], *n.* lack of love to mankind; (*med.*) the first stage of melancholy, when solitude is preferred. [A (4) and PHILANTHROPY].
APHIS, (*pl.* **aphides**), [af'-is], *n.* (*zool.*) plant louse, green-fly. [MdL. *aphis*].
APHLOGISTIC, [af'-lō-jis'-tik], *adj.* burning without a flame. [Gk. *aphlogistos*].
APHONIA, APHONY, [af-ō'-ni-a], *n.* complete loss of the voice. [Gk. *aphonia*].
APHONOUS, [af'-on-us], *adj.* voiceless. [*Prec.*].
APHONY, see APHONIA.
APHORISM, [af'-or-izm], *n.* the concise statement of a principle; a maxim, precept. [Gk. *aphorismos* definition].
APHORIST, [af'-or-ist], *n.* one who makes aphorisms.
APHORISTIC, [af'-or-is'-tik], *adj.* pertaining to an aphorism, full of aphorisms.
APHORISTICALLY, [af'-or-is'-tik-al-i], *adv.* in an aphoristic manner, pithily.
APHORIZE, [af'-or-īz], *v.t. and i.* to make or use aphorisms or pithy sayings.
APHRISITE, [af'-riz-īt], *n.* (*min.*) black Norwegian tourmaline.
APHRITE, [af'-rīt], *n.* (*min.*) an earthy variety of calcite or carbonate of lime with a silvery lustre. [Gk. *aphros* foam].
APHRODISIAC (1), [af'-rō-diz'-i-ak], *n.* a drug which tends to produce sexual desire. [Gk. *aphrodisiakos* from *Aphrodite* the Greek goddess of love].
APHRODISIAC (2), [af'-rō-diz'-i-ak], *adj.* tending to excite sexual desires, venereal. [*Prec.*].
APHRODISIAN, [af'-rō-diz'-i-an], *adj.* pertaining to sexual love. [*Prec.*].
APHTHA, [af'-tha], *n.* (*path.*) a disease of the mouth, the thrush. [Gk. *aphtha*].
APHTHAE, [af'-thē], *n.*(*pl.*) (*path.*) small white specks or ulcers on the inside of the mouth symptomatic of the thrush. [Gk. *aphthai*].
APHTHITALITE, [af-thit'-al-īt], *n.* (*geol.*) glaserite, sulphate of potash occurring on lava and unchanged by exposure. [Gk. *aphthitos* imperishable, and *lithos* stone].
APHTHOUS, [af'-thus], *adj.* (*path.*) pertaining to the disease, aphtha.
APHYLLOUS, [af'-il-us], *adj.* (*bot.*) without leaves. [Gk. *aphullos*].
APIAN, [ā'-pi-an], *adj.* of or pertaining to bees. [L. *apianus*].
APIARIAN, [ā-pi-āer'-i-an], *adj.* relating to bee-keeping. [L. *apiarius* bee-keeper].
APIARIST, [ā'-pi-a-rist], *n.* one who keeps bees.
APIARY, [ā'-pi-ari], *n.* a place where bees or beehives are kept. [L. *apiarium*].
APICAL, [ap'-ikl], *adj.* pertaining to an apex. [L. *apex* (*apicem*)].
APICES, [ā'-pis-ēz'], *n.*(*pl.*) of APEX.
APICILLARY, [ā-pis-il'-ari], *adj.* at or near the apex.
APICULATED, [ā-pik'-yōō-lā'-tid], *adj.* (*bot.*) minutely pointed. [~L. *apex*].
APICULTURE, [ā'-pi-kul'-cher], *n.* bee-keeping. [L. *apis* bee and CULTURE].
APIECE, [a-pēs'], *adv.* for each piece, article or person; each severally or by itself. [A (2) and PIECE].
APIOCRINITE, [ap'-i-o-krin'-īt], *n.* (*geol.*) a pear-shaped oolitic encrinite. [Gk. *apion* pear and *krinon* lily].
APISH, [āp'-ish], *adj.* like an ape; foolishly imitative, affected, silly. [APE (1)].
APISHLY, [āp'-ish-li], *adv.* in apish fashion; in a foolishly imitative way.
APISHNESS, [āp'-ish-nes], *n.* the state of being apish.
APITPAT, [a-pit'-pat'], *adv.* in quick palpitations. [A (3) and PITPAT].
APLACENTAL, [a'-plas-ent'-al], *adj.* (*bot.*) without a placenta. [A (4) and PLACENTAL].
APLANATIC, [ap'-lan-at'-ik], *adj.* (*opt.*) totally free from aberration of the rays of light. [A (4) and Gk. *planao* I wander].
APLASTIC, [a-plas'-tik], *adj.* not plastic or easily moulded, tending to irregularity of organic structure. [Gk. *aplastos*].
APLOMB, [a-plom'], *n.* self-possession, poise, assurance of manner. [Fr. *aplomb* perpendicularity].
APLOME, [ap'-lōm], *n.* (*min.*) a brownish-coloured garnet. [Gk. *haplos* simple].
APLUSTRE, [ap-lust'-er], *n.* the ornament or flag carried by ancient ships at the stern. [Unkn.].
APNEUSIS, [ap-new'-sis], *n.* (*med.*) condition of suspended breathing. [A (4) and Gk. *pneusis* breathing].
APNOEA, [ap-nē'-a], *n.* (*med.*) temporary cessation of breathing. [Gk. *apnoia*].
APO-, *pref.* from, derived from, asunder, away, back again; (*chem.*) origin, derivation from. [Gk. *apo*].
APOCALYPSE, [ap-ok'-a-lips], *n.* a revelation; the revelation of the future to St. John; the New Testament book recording this; a revelation of an unusual kind. [Gk. *apokalupsis*].
APOCALYPTIC, [ap-ok'-al-ip'-tik], *adj.* pertaining to the Apocalypse; revealing. [*Prec.*].
APOCALYPTICAL, [ap-ok'-al-ip'-tikl], *adj.* of or pertaining to revelation or the Apocalypse.
APOCALYPTICALLY, [ap-ok'-al-ip'-tik-al-i], *adv.* in the manner of the Apocalypse.
APOCARPOUS, [ap'-ō-kah'-pus], *adj.* (*bot.*) with carpels entirely or partially distinct. [APO and Gk. *karpos* fruit].
APOCATASTASIS, [ap-ok'-at-as'-tas-is], *n.* (*astron.*) the time that a planet takes to return to the same point in the zodiac; the eventual re-establishment of lost souls in divine forgiveness. [Gk. *apokatastasis*].
APOCHROMATIC, [ap'-ō-krō-mat'-ik], *adj.* (*opt.*) highly achromatic. [APO and CHROMATIC].
APOCOPATE, [ap-ok'-ō-pāt], *v.t.* (*gram.*) to cut off or omit the last letter or syllable of a word. [*Next.*]

APOCOPE, [a-pok'-ō-pi], *n.* the cutting off or loss of the last letter or syllable of a word. [Gk. *apokope*].

APOCRUSTIC, [ap'-ō-krust'-ik], *adj.* (*med.*) astringent, repelling. [Gk. *apokroustikos*].

APOCRYPHA, [a-pok'-rif-a], *n.* those books appended to the Old Testament which are regarded as canonical by the Roman Catholic Church, but uncanonical by the Greek and Protestant Churches. [Gk. *apokruphos* hidden].

APOCRYPHAL, [ap-ok'-rifl], *adj.* of or pertaining to the Apocrypha, not canonical; of uncertain authorship or intent; fictitious.

APOCRYPHALLY, [ap-ok'-rif-al-i], *adv.* in apocryphal fashion; falsely.

APOD, (*pl.* **apodes**), [ap'-od], *n.* (*ichth.*) a fish which has no ventral fins. [Gk. *apous* without foot].

APODAL, [ap'-ōdl], *adj.* footless, without ventral fins. [*Prec.*].

APODEICTIC, APODICTIC, [ap'-ō-dīk'-tik], *adj.* apodeictical.

APODEICTICAL, [ap-ō-dīk'-tikl], *adj.* clearly demonstrative of absolute certainty. [Gk. *apodeiktikos*].

APODEICTICALLY, [ap-ō-dīk'-tik-al-i], *adv.* in apodeictic fashion.

APODEIXIS†, APODIXIS†, [ap-ō-dīk'-sis], *n.* complete demonstration or proof. [Gk. *apodeixis*].

APODICTIC, see APODEICTIC.

APODIXIS, see APODEIXIS.

APODOSIS, [ap-od'-os-is], *n.* (*gram.*) the consequent clause in conditional and other propositions; the concluding clause of a sentence. [Gk. *apodosis* giving back].

APODYTERIUM, [ap-ō'-dit-ēer'-i-um], *n.* the apartment in a Roman bath where the clothes were put; robing room. [Gk. *apoduterion*].

APOGEAN, [ap'-ō-jē'-an], *adj.* (*astron.*) of or belonging to the apogee.

APOGEE, [ap'-ō-jē], *n.* (*astron.*) the point in the moon's or a planet's orbit most distant from the earth; (*fig.*) topmost point. [Fr. *apogée* from Gk. *apogaion*].

APOGRAPH, [ap'-ō-grahf], *n.* a faithful transcript. [Gk. *apographon*].

APOLAUSTIC, [ap'-ō-laws'-tik], *adj.* entirely devoted to enjoyment or self-indulgence. [Gk. *apolaustikos*].

APOLLYON, [a-pol'-i-on], *n.* the destroying angel, the devil. [Gk. *apolluon* destroying].

APOLOGETIC, [a-pol'-ō-jet'-ik], *adj.* excusing with regret; (of manner) deferential, conciliatory; (of an opinion, essay, etc.) defending without admitting wrong. [Gk. *apologetikos*].

APOLOGETICAL, [a-pol'-ō-jet'-ikl], *adj.* apologetic.

APOLOGETICALLY, [a-pol'-ō-jet'-i-kal-i], *adv.* in an apologetic manner.

APOLOGETICS, [a-pol'-ō-jet'-iks], *n.*(*pl.*) (*theol.*) a branch of theology which sets out to defend the Christian religion.

APOLOGIA, [a-pol-ō'-ja], *n.* a defence in word or writing. [L. *apologia*].

APOLOGIST, [a-pol'-ō-jist], *n.* one who pleads in authority or defence; one who defends a cause or opinion.

APOLOGIZE, [a-pol'-ō-jīz'], *v.i.* to speak in excuse or defence; to make an excuse; to own to and express regret for an indefensible action. [APOLOGY].

APOLOGIZER, [a-pol'-ō-jīz'-er], *n.* a person who apologizes.

APOLOGUE, [ap'-ol-ōg], *n.* an allegorical story, a moral tale; a story in which the characters are birds, animals, trees, etc. [Fr. *apologue* from Gk. *apologos*].

APOLOGY, [a-pol'-ō-ji], *n.* an expression of regret for injury inflicted, explanation that no injury or offence was intended; (*fig.*) a bad attempt, a makeshift, a poor substitute for something else. [Gk. *apologia* defence].

APONEUROSIS, (*pl.* **aponeuroses**), [ap'-ō-new-rō'-sis], *n.* (*anat.*) a white, shining membrane of interlaced fibre in the form of an extension of a tendon or the envelope of a muscle. [Gk. *aponeurosis*].

APONEUROTIC, [ap'-ō-new-rot'-ik], *adj.* pertaining to aponeurosis.

APOPHASIS, [a-pof'-a-sis], *n.* (*rhet.*) the apparent denial by a speaker of that which he really desires to assert. [Gk. *apophasis* denial].

APOPHLEGMATIC† (1), [ap'-ō-fleg-mat'-ik], *n.* a medicine designed to cause discharges of phlegm or mucus.

APOPHLEGMATIC† (2), [ap'-ō-fleg-mat'-ik], *adj.* causing discharges of phlegm or mucus. [APO and PHLEGMATIC].

APOPHLEGMATISM, [ap'-ō-fleg'-mat-izm], *n.* the clearing of phlegm from the head; an apophlegmatic.

APOPHTHEGM, [ap'-ō-them], *n.* a terse, pithy saying, a brief sententious maxim. [Gk. *apophthegma*].

APOPHTHEGMATIC, [ap'-ō-the-mat'-ik], *adj.* of the character of an apophthegm; in the habit of using apophthegms; sententious.

APOPHTHEGMATICAL, [ap'-ō-the-mat'-ikl], *adj.* apophthegmatic.

APOPHTHEGMATIST, [ap'-ō-the'-mat-ist], *n.* a collector or inventor of apophthegms.

APOPHTHEGMATIZE, [ap'-ō-the'-mat-īz], *v.i.* to use or make apophthegms.

APOPHYGE, [a-pof'-i-ji], *n.* (*arch.*) that part of a column where it springs out of the base. [Gk. *apophuge* escape].

APOPHYGE

APOPHYSIS, (*pl.* **apophyses**), [a-pof'-i-sis], *n.* (*anat.*) a protuberance or offshoot of a bone; (*bot.*) a swelling beneath the spore-case in mosses. [Gk. *apophusis* offshoot].

APOPLECTIC (1), [ap'-ō-plek'-tik], *n.* one predisposed to apoplexy.

APOPLECTIC (2), [ap'-ō-plek'-tik], *adj.* having the character of, predisposed to apoplexy. [Gk. *apoplektikos*].

APOPLECTICAL, [ap'-ō-plek'-tik-al], *adj.* apoplectic.

APOPLEXY, [ap'-ō-plek'-si], *n.* a sudden deprivation of sense and movement usually caused by some effusion of blood in the brain. [Fr. *apoplexie*, Gk. *apoplexia*].

APORIA, [a-paw'-ri-a], *n.* (*rhet.*) pretence of not knowing where to begin or what to say; doubt; (*med.*) febrile uneasiness due to obstructions. [Gk. *aporia* difficulty].

APORT, [a-pawt'], *adv.* on or towards the port side of the ship. [A (3) and PORT (5)].

APOSEPEDIN, [ap'-ō-sep'-id-in], *n.* a crystallized substance found in putrid cheese. [APO and Gk. *sepedon* putridity].

APOSIOPESIS, [a-pō'-si-ō-pē-sis], *n.* (*rhet.*) an abrupt halt in a discourse, generally for rhetorical effect, out of a real or pretended disinclination to proceed further. [Gk. *aposiopesis*].

APOSTASY, [a-pos'-ta-si], *n.* the abandonment or renunciation of beliefs or of principles once professed; desertion from a religious sect or political party. [Gk. *apostasia*].

APOSTATE, [ap-os'-tāt], *n.* a person who has apostatized, a deserter, renegade. [Gk. *apostates*].

APOSTATICAL, [ap'-os-tat'-ikl], *adj.* in the manner of an apostate.

APOSTATIZE, [a-pos'-ta-tīz], *v.i.* to forsake religious or political principles. [APOSTATE].

APOSTEMATE†, [a-pos'-ti-māt], *v.i.* to form into an abscess; to suffer from an abscess. [APOSTEME].

APOSTEMATION†, [a-pos'-tim-ā'-shun], *n.* the formation of an abscess. [*Prec.*].

APOSTEMATOUS, [ap'-ost-em'-at-us], *adj.* of or pertaining to an aposteme. [*Next.*].

APOSTEME, [ap'-os-tēm], *n.* an abscess, a gathering or swelling filled with purulent matter. [Gk. *apostema*].

APOSTIL, [a-pos'-til], *n.* a marginal note. [Fr. *apostille*].

APOSTLE, [a-posl'], *n.* one chosen by Christ to preach the Gospel, one sent on or dedicated to some high mission; an early missionary; a messenger; **Apostles' Creed,** the earliest form of confession of Christian faith; **a. spoon,** an antique silver spoon whose handle is fashioned in the form of one of the Apostles. [OE. *apostol* from Gk. *apostolos*].

APOSTLESHIP, [a-posl'-ship], *n.* the status or condition of an apostle; protagonism of a lofty ideal.

APOSTOLATE, [a-pos'-tō-lāt'], *n.* the office or rank of an apostle; a mission.

APOSTOLIC, [ap'-os-tol'-ik], *adj.* of or pertaining to the Apostles; **A. Fathers,** Christian teachers contemporary with Christ's Apostles; **A. See,** the see of Rome; **A. succession,** the doctrine of the lineal transmission from the Apostles of spiritual power and authority. [Fr. *apostolique*].

APOSTOLICAL [ap'-os-tol'-ikl], *adj.* apostolic.

APOSTOLICALLY, [ap'-os-tol'-ik-al-i], *adv.* in the manner of the Apostles, according to the Apostles; through the Apostles.

APOSTOLICALNESS†, [ap'-os-tol'-ikl-nes], *n.* the quality of being apostolic.

APOSTROPHE, [a-pos'-trō-fi], *n.* (*rhet.*) a digression or interruption of an exclamatory or hortatory nature in the course of a speech or literary work, often one where an appeal is made to someone absent or dead as if he were present; (*gram.*) the contraction of a word by the omission of a letter or letters, and the insertion of a punctuation sign; (*gram.*) the sign (') denoting the possessive case. [Gk. *apostrophe* a turning away].

APOSTROPHIC, [ap'-os-trof'-ik], *adj.* pertaining to an apostrophe.

APOSTROPHIZE, [a-pos'-trō-fīz], *v.t.* to address an apostrophe to; to omit a letter of a word and insert an apostrophe.

APOTHECARY, [ap-oth'-ik-a-ri], *n.* one who prepares medicines and sells drugs, a chemist; †a partially-trained medical practitioner who prescribed as well as dispensed medicines. [LL. *apothecarius*].

APOTHECIUM, [ap'-ō-thē'-si-um], *n.* the peltate disks which contain the spores on the surface of lichens. [~Gk. *apotheke* storehouse].

APOTHEM, [ap'-ō-them], *n.* (*math.*) a perpendicular from the centre of a regular polygon to one of its sides. [APO and THEME].

APOTHEOSIS, [a-poth'-i-ō'-sis], *n.* deification, raising of a mortal to rank among the gods, supreme deification of a person or thing. [Gk. *apotheosis*].

APOTHEOSIZE, [a-poth'-i-ō-sīz'], *v.t.* to deify, make a god of.

APOTOMY, [a-pot'-o-mi], *n.* (*math.*) the difference between two quantities that are commensurate, or commensurable only in power; (*mus.*) a major semitone. [Gk. *apotome* cutting off].

APOTREPSIS, [ap'-ō-trep'-sis], *n.* (*med.*) the resolution of a suppurating tumour. [Gk. *apotrepsis* aversion].

APOZEM, [ap'-ō-zem], *n.* a decoction or infusion from plants. [APO and Gk. *zeo* I boil].

APPAL, (**appalling, appalled**), [a-pawl'], *v.t.* to depress with fear, to dismay, discomfort exceedingly, terrify. [OFr. *apalir* grow pale].

APPALLING, [a-pawl'-ing], *adj.* in a manner to dismay or shock. [*Prec.*].

APPALLINGLY, [a-pawl'-ing-li], *adv.* to a shocking extent, in an appalling way.

APPALMENT, [a-pawl'-ment], *n.* state or condition of being appalled.

APPANAGE, APANAGE, [ap'-a-nij], *n.* lands and revenue assigned to a younger son of a royal house; perquisite; a dependency; natural attribute or endowment. [OFr. *apanage* endowment].

APPANAGIST, [a-pan'-a-jist], *n.* a prince or younger son of a noble house to whom an appanage is granted.

APPARATUS, [ap'-a-rā'-tus], *n.* a collection of instruments or utensils for performing any operation or experiment, or for practising any art; the literary materials needed for the close study of a document. [L. *apparatus*].

APPAREL (1), [a-pa'-rel], *n.* clothes, dress; ecclesiastical vestments; an ornament embroidered on an alb or amice; (*naut.*) the equipment of a ship such as rigging, sails and anchors. [OFr. *apareille*].

APPAREL (2), (**apparelling, apparelled**), [ap-a'-rel], *v.t.* to clothe, dress, to adorn, to furnish. [OFr. *apareiller*].

APPARENT, [a-pa'-rent, a-pāer'-ent], *adj.* visible, easily seen, obvious, conspicuous; clear to the understanding, evident, palpable; appearing to be a fact, seeming; **heir a.**, the next rightful heir to a throne or estate.

APPARENTLY, [a-pa'-rent-li, a-pāer'-ent-li], *adv.* in an apparent manner; evidently, seemingly.

APPARENTNESS, [a-pa'-rent-nes, a-pāer'-ent-nes], *n.* the state of being apparent.

APPARITION, [ap'-a-rish'-un], *n.* the act of appearing, appearance, a visible object; the appearance of supernatural things, a ghost, spectre; (*astron.*) the first appearance of a star after having been obscured. [~L. *apparitio*].

APPARITIONAL, [ap'-a-rish'-un-al], *adj.* of or pertaining to an apparition.

APPARITOR, [ap-ar'-it-or], *n.* (*leg.*) an officer of ancient Rome who attended magistrates; (*eccles.*) an officer who serves the process of a spiritual court; the beadle in a university who carries the mace. [L. *apparitor*].

APPEACH†, [a-pēch'], *v.t.* to impede; to accuse, impeach. [OFr. *empechier*].

APPEAL (1), [ap-ēl'], *n.* urgent demand for aid, an entreaty; a challenge; a call to an authority for a decision in one's favour; (*leg.*) the action by which a case is brought from a lower to a higher court in the hope of obtaining a favourable judgment; **court of a.**, a court of law which investigates and confirms or reverses the decisions of lower courts. [OFr. *apel*].

APPEAL (2), [ap-ēl'], *v.i.* to call upon another to decide an issue; to refer to another as witness, to invoke aid, pity or mercy, to have recourse to; (*leg.*) to demand the judgment of a higher tribunal; (*fig.*) to move the feelings, attract, appear pleasing; *v.t.* to remove a case from an inferior to a superior court. [OFr. *apeler*].

APPEALABLE, [a-pēl'-abl], *adj.* which can be appealed to or against.

APPEALER, [a-pēl'-er], *n.* one who appeals, an appellant.

APPEALING, [a-pēl'-ing], *adj.* which appeals; (*leg.*) pertaining to a higher court; (*fig.*) imploring, affecting, moving.

APPEALINGLY, [a-pēl'-ing-li], *adv.* in an appealing manner.

APPEALINGNESS, [a-pēl'-ing-nes], *n.* the condition of being appealing.

APPEAR, [a-pēer'], *v.i.* to come into view, become visible, to be manifest; to come into public notice, to go into society; to be obvious to the mind, manifest; to seem, to convey the impression of; (*leg.*) to go before a court. [OFr. *aparoir*].

APPEARANCE, [a-pēer'-ans], *n.* the act of appearing, the act of coming before the public in some prominent role or of coming into society; the thing seen, a phenomenon; outward semblance, look; a particular impression; a strange phenomenon as a ghost, phantom; (*leg.*) the act of appearing in court; **to enter an a.**, appear in court; **to put in an a.** to come, appear; **to all appearances**, as far as may be seen; **to keep up appearances**, to maintain a good outward show. [OFr. *aparence*].

APPEASABLE, [ap-ēz'-abl], *adj.* able to be appeased. [OFr. *apaisable*].

APPEASABLENESS, [ap-ēz'-abl-nes], *n.* the quality of being appeasable.

APPEASE, [ap-ēz'], *v.t.* to pacify, allay; to soothe the feelings of; to satisfy the physical needs of. [OFr. *apaisier*].

APPEASEMENT, [ap-ēz'-ment], *n.* the action of appeasing; a peaceful condition; the policy of making concessions to win over potential enemies.

APPEASER, [ap-ēz'-er], *n.* one who appeases; a pacifier, peace-maker.

APPELLANT, [ap-el'-ant], *n.* one who asks for aid or justification; (*leg.*) one who appeals to a higher court. [OFr. *appellant*].

APPELLATE†, [ap-el'-āt], *adj.* (*leg.*) pertaining to an appeal; having power to deal with appeals. [L. *appellatus* called].

APPELLATION, [ap'-el-ā'-shun], *n.* the name, title or designation of a person or thing; a specific name. [~L. *appellatio*].

APPELLATIVE (1), [ap-el'-at-iv], *n.* a distinctive name, an appellation; a general name; (*gram.*) a name for a class of things or any specimen in that class; a common noun.

APPELLATIVE (2), [ap-el'-at-iv], *adj.* having the character of an appellation, serving to name or mark out; (*gram.*) pertaining to a common noun. [L. *appellativus*].

APPELLATIVELY, [ap-el'-at-iv-li], *adv.* in an appellative manner.

APPELLATORY†, [ap-el'-at-er-i], *adj.* pertaining to an appeal.

APPELLEE, [ap'-el-ē'], *n.* (*leg.*) †one who is appealed against, defendant in an appeal, a respondent. [Fr. *appelé* appealed].

APPELLOR, [ap-el'-or], *n.* (*leg.*) a prosecutor, accuser, informer. [AFr. *apelour*].

APPEND, [a-pend'], *v.t.* to hang something on, attach as a pendant, to subjoin; to add something in writing, to furnish additional matter as a supplement for a book. [L. *appendere*].

APPENDAGE, [a-pend'-ij], *n.* something hung on, attached to, hanging on; (*fig.*) a person closely attached to another, often as a dependant.

APPENDANT (1), [a-pend'-ant], *n.* something which is appended or attached as an adjunct.

APPENDANT (2), [a-pend'-ant], *adj.* hanging attached; (*leg.*) attached by right to a landed estate or property. [Fr. *appendant*].

APPENDICITIS, [a-pen'-dis-ī'-tis], *n.* (*med.*) acute inflammation of the vermiform appendix. [APPENDIX and Gk. *itis* denoting inflammation].

APPENDICLE, [a-pen'-dikl], *n.* a little appendage. [L. *appendicula*].

APPENDICULAR, [a'-pen-dik'-yoo-ler], *adj.* pertaining to or of the nature of an appendix.

APPENDICULATE, [a'-pen-dik'-yoo-lāt], *adj.* (*bot.*) having small appendages.

APPENDIX, (*pl.* **appendices**), [a-pen'-diks, a-pen'-di-sēz], *n.* something hung on or appended; matter added at the end of a book but not essential to its main argument; a very short, thin tube with closed end leading off the large intestine. [L. *appendix* something hung on].

APPENDIX

APPERCEIVE, [ap'-er-sēv'], *v.t.* to perceive, observe, recognize in the mind. [OFr. *aperceveir*].

APPERCEPTION, [ap'-er-sep'-shun], *n.* perception in the mind; the recognition by the mind of its own quality and power. [Fr. *aperception*].

APPERTAIN, [ap'-er-tān'], *v.i.* to belong to as parts to the whole; to be related; to pertain; to be appropriate or suitable. [OFr. *apertenir*].

APPERTINENT, [ap-ur'-tin-ent], *adj.* appertaining or belonging to; suitable for. [APPURTENANT].

APPETENCE, [ap'-it-ens], *n.* longing, desire or craving, *esp.* bodily craving; passion; inclination. [Fr. *appétence* instinctive desire].

APPETENCY, [ap'-it-en-si], *n.* the state of appetence, desire or craving.

APPETENT, [ap'-it-ent], *adj.* desiring, keenly desirous, longing. [~L. *appetens* seeking].

APPETITE, [ap'-it-īt], *n.* desire or inclination to obtain gratification, *esp.* for the natural activities and functions of the body; hunger, thirst, craving. [OFr. *apetit*].

APPETITIVE, [a-pet'-i-tiv], *adj.* having the quality of desiring, desiring gratification.

APPETIZE, [ap'-it-īz], *v.t.* to give an appetite to.

APPETIZER, [ap'-it-īz-er], *n.* something which creates an appetite for food; an aperitif.

APPETIZING, [ap'-it-īz-ing], *adj.* creating a desire or appetite, stimulating the appetite.

APPETIZINGLY, [ap'-it-iz-ing-li], *adv.* in a manner likely to stimulate the appetite.

APPLAUD, [a-plawd'], *v.t. and i.* to express approval by clapping the hands or in any other noisy way; to approve of, praise. [Fr. *applaudir*].

APPLAUSE, [a-plawz'], *n.* the action of applauding; loud praise; clapping. [L. *applausus*].

APPLAUSIVE, [a-plaw'-ziv], *adj.* applauding.

APPLE, [apl], *n.* the round, firm, red and yellow fleshy fruit of *Pyrus malus*, found wild as the crab-apple in Europe, and cultivated in many varieties; a fruit of similar structure or appearance, as the pineapple; **a. of the eye**, the pupil; (*fig.*) a very precious object; **a. of discord**, one contended for by the three goddesses, Juno, Minerva and Venus, any subject or matter of dispute; **Adam's a.**, the prominent part of the throat formed by the thyroid cartilage. [OE. *æppel*].

APPLE-BRANDY, [apl'-bran'-di], *n.* a liquor which is distilled from cider.

APPLE-BUTTER, [apl'-but'-er], *n.* a sauce made from apples stewed in cider.

APPLE-FACED, [apl'-fāst'], *adj.* with a round bright-complexioned face, chubby-faced.

APPLE-GRAFT, [apl'-grahft'], *n.* a graft of an apple-tree.

APPLE-JACK, [apl'-jak'], *n.* a spirit distilled from apple juice, apple-brandy.

APPLE-JOHN, [apl'-jon'], *n.* an apple which is considered best when it becomes shrivelled.

APPLE-MINT, [apl'-mint'], *n.* an aromatic herb, *Mentha rotundifolia*.

APPLE-PIE, [apl'-pī], *n.* a comestible of apples baked in a dish and covered with pastry; **a. order**, perfect order; **a. bed**, a bed with the sheets folded so as to prevent a person from lying down in it.

APPLE-PIP, [apl'-pip], *n.* apple seed.

APPLE-POMACE, [apl'-pom'-as], *n.* the pulp of the apples after the juice has been extracted from them in making cider.

APPLE-SAUCE, [apl'-saws'], *n.* sauce made of stewed apples.

APPLE-SCOOP, [apl'-skōōp'], *n.* an old-fashioned scooped fruit-knife.

APPLE-TREE, [apl'-trē], *n.* a tree which bears apples.

APPLIANCE, [ap-lī'-ans], *n.* the act of applying, putting into practice; a thing applied to achieve any purpose; a piece of apparatus, a utensil. [APPLY].

APPLICABILITY, [ap'-lik-ab-il'-i-ti], *n.* the quality of being applicable; suitability.

APPLICABLE, [ap'-lik-abl], *adj.* able to be applied, appropriate, fitting. [~L. *applicare*].

APPLICABLENESS, [ap'-lik-abl-nes], *n.* the quality of being applicable, appropriateness.

APPLICABLY, [ap'-lik-ab-li], *adv.* in such a manner that it can readily be applied.

APPLICANT, [ap'-lik-ant], *n.* one who applies, one who asks for something; a candidate for a post. [~L. *applicans*].

APPLICATE, [ap'-lik-āt], *n.* (*math.*) the chord bisected by the diameter. [L. *applicatus* applied].

APPLICATION, [ap'-lik-ā'-shun], *n.* the act of applying, of placing a thing in juxtaposition to another; the thing applied; the act of making a request or petition; a letter of request; the putting on of a remedy; the remedy so applied; close attention to study; the testing of something theoretical by applying it in practice. [~L. *applicatio*].

APPLICATIVE, [ap'-lik-at-iv], *adj.* which may be applied; practical.

APPLICATORY, [ap'-lik-at-er-i], *adj.* having the power or character of applying.

APPLIQUE, **appliqué**, [ap-lē'-kā], *n.* needlework of a material laid over and secured to another material. [Fr. *appliqué*].

APPLY, [a-plī'], *v.t.* to lay or put on; to put a thing into contact with another; to put into practice; to use or mention a word in reference to some person or thing; to direct the mind or attention to; to bring to bear on; *v.i.* to fit, be relevant; to make an application in order to obtain something. [OFr. *aplier* from ~L. *applicare*].

APPOGGIATURA, [a-poj'-at-ōō'-ra], *n.* (*mus.*) a grace-note which precedes as a support a full note in a melody. [It. *appoggiatura*].

APPOGGIATURA

APPOINT, [a-point'], *v.t.* to fix, designate, set apart; to decree, settle, determine authoritatively; to ordain or nominate a person to a certain office or to perform certain duties; (*leg.*) to determine the disposition of an estate. [OFr. *apointer*].

APPOINTED, [a-point'-id], *adj.* fixed, previously arranged or agreed upon; equipped, furnished. [*Prec.*].

APPOINTEE, [a-point'-ē'], *n.* one who is appointed; (*leg.*) one who is granted the power of appointment.

APPOINTER, [a-point'-er], *n.* one who appoints; one who arranges an agreement.

APPOINTMENT, [a-point'-ment], *n.* the act of appointing to an office; a situation, or office; fixing by mutual agreement; that which is decreed or appointed; command or order; (*leg.*) the grant to a person of the power to dispose of a property, whether he owns it or not; (*pl.*) equipment, furnishings, fittings. [OFr. *apointement*].

APPORTION, [a-paw'-shun], *v.t.* to divide and assign in due portions, to distribute. [OFr. *apportioner*].

APPORTIONMENT, [a-paw'-shun-ment], *n.* the act of apportioning, a division into fair shares.

APPOSITE, [ap'-oz-it], *adj.* suitable, entirely applicable. [L. *appositus* put to].

APPOSITELY, [ap'-oz-it-li], *adv.* in an apposite manner, appropriately, to the point.

APPOSITENESS, [ap'-oz-it-nes], *n.* the quality of being apposite.

APPOSITION, [ap'-oz-ish'-un], *n.* the action of adding to, application, addition; (*gram.*) the placing of a word in a parallel with another of the same function to explain and illustrate or modify it. [~L. *appositio*].

APPOSITIONAL, [ap'-oz-ish'-unl], *adj.* of or relating to apposition.

APPOSITIVE, [a-poz'-it-iv], *adj.* (*gram.*) pertaining to apposition.

APPRAISAL, [a-prāzl'], *n.* a valuation by authority, the fixing of a price; (*fig.*) estimate of worth.

APPRAISE, [a-prāz'], *v.t.* to set a price on, fix, evaluate;

to value as a professional valuer or appraiser; (*fig.*) to estimate the spiritual worth of. [OFr. *apreiser*].

APPRAISEMENT, [a-prāz'-ment], *n.* the action of appraising.

APPRAISER, [a-prāz'-er], *n.* one who values property, one licensed and sworn to estimate and fix the value of property.

APPRAISING, [a-prāz'-ing], *n.* the action of valuing or setting a price on.

APPRECIABLE, [a-prē'-shabl], *adj.* able to be estimated or recognized; perceptible; large enough to be perceived, of some size.

APPRECIABLY, [ap-rēsh'-ab-li], *adv.* to an appreciable extent.

APPRECIATE, [a-prē'-shi-āt'], *v.t.* to judge correctly, set a just value on, estimate duly; to perceive slight differences; set a high value on, be grateful for; to be alive to the merits of, to enjoy discriminatingly; *v.i.* to rise in value. [~L. *appretiare*].

APPRECIATION, [a-prē'-shi-ā'-shun], *n.* the act of appreciating or estimating; perception or recognition of merit, worth and excellence; the power of distinguishing slight variations; a rise in value.

APPRECIATIVE, [a-prē'-shi-at-iv], *adj.* having appreciation; recognizing merit; grateful.

APPRECIATIVELY, [ap-rēsh'-at-iv-li], *adv.* with appreciation.

APPRECIATOR, [a-prē'-shi-ā'-tor], *n.* one who appreciates; an instrument by which the amount of gluten present in flour can be determined.

APPRECIATORY, [a-prē'-shi-at-er-i], *adj.* capable of justly appreciating.

APPREHEND, [ap'-ri-hend'], *v.t.* to take hold of, to seize, to arrest, to grasp with the mind, to understand; to think with fear; *v.i.* to form a conception, to think. [L. *apprehendere*].

APPREHENSIBLE, [ap'-ri-hen'-sibl], *adj.* capable of being apprehended.

APPREHENSION, [ap'-ri-hen'-shun], *n.* the act of apprehending or seizing, the act of arresting; the faculty of conception, opinion; fear or dread of future evil, gloomy foreboding. [L. *apprehensio*].

APPREHENSIVE, [ap'-ri-hen'-siv], *adj.* capable of apprehending, understanding; fearful, suspicious, distrustful.

APPREHENSIVELY, [ap'-ri-hen'-siv-li], *adv.* in an apprehensive fashion.

APPREHENSIVENESS, [ap'-ri-hen'-siv-nes], *n.* the condition of being apprehensive.

APPRENTICE (1), [a-pren'-tis], *n.* a young person bound for a term of years to serve some craft or trade under a master who in turn binds himself to instruct him. [OFr. *aprentis*].

APPRENTICE (2), [a-pren'-tis], *v.t.* to bind under a master to learn a craft or trade.

APPRENTICESHIP, [a-pren'-tis-ship], *n.* the state of being an apprentice; the term during which the service must last.

APPRISE, [a-prīz'], *v.t.* to give notice to, to inform, acquaint. [Fr. *appris* instructed].

APPRIZE, [a-prīz'], *v.t.* to estimate the worth of, appreciate. [OFr. *aprisier*].

APPRIZING, [a-prīz'-ing], *n.* appraising, valuing.

APPRO, [ap'-rō], *n.* approval; **on a.,** on approval. [APPRO(VAL)].

APPROACH (1), [a-prōch'], *n.* the act of coming near or nearer; the means or way of coming near, a passage; an attempt to establish personal relationships; (*golf*) the stroke to place the ball on the green. [APPROACH (2)].

APPROACH (2), [a-prōch'], *v.t.* to advance to, come near or nearer; (*fig.*) to come near to so as to be compared with, to approximate to; to make advances or overtures to a person; *v.i.* to come nearer, (of time) to draw nearer. [Fr. *approcher*].

APPROACHABILITY, [ap-rōch'-ab-il'-it-i], *n.* the state or condition of being approachable.

APPROACHABLE, [a-prōch'-abl], *adj.* able to be approached, accessible.

APPROACHABLENESS, [a-prōch'-abl-nes], *n.* the condition of being approachable.

APPROACHING (1), [a-prōch'-ing], *n.* (*golf*) that stage in the game where the ball is played on to the putting-green; (*hort.*) the ingrafting of a shoot of one tree on to another without severing it from the parent stock.

APPROACHING (2), [a-prōch'-ing], *adj.* advancing towards, drawing nearer.

APPROACHLESS, [a-prōch'-les], *adj.* inaccessible.

APPROBATE†, [ap'-rō-bāt], *v.t.* to approve authoritatively, to license. [~L. *approbare* to assent].

APPROBATION, [ap'-rō-bā'-shun], *n.* the act of approving, approval, commendation, probation, formal sanction. [~L. *approbatio*].

APPROBATIVE, [ap-rō'-bat-iv], *adj.* approbatory.

APPROBATORY, [ap'-rō-bā-to-ri, a-prob'-a-to-ri], *adj.* tending to approve.

APPROPINQUITY, [ap'-rō-ping'-kwit-i], *n.* proximity, nearness to. [L. *appropinquitas*].

APPROPRIABLE, [a-prō'-pri-abl], *adj.* which can be appropriated.

APPROPRIATE (1), [a-prō'-pri-at], *adj.* set apart for a particular person or purpose, belonging to some person or thing; suitable, fitting. [L. *appropriatus*].

APPROPRIATE (2), [a-prō'-pri-āt], *v.t.* to make over to a person; to grant, take over; to set apart for a particular purpose; (*leg.*) to alienate a benefice.

APPROPRIATELY, [a-prō'-pri-at-li], *adv.* in an appropriate fashion, fittingly.

APPROPRIATENESS, [a-prō'-pri-at-nes], *n.* the quality of being appropriate, or essentially suitable.

APPROPRIATION, [a-prō'-pri-ā'-shun], *n.* the action of appropriating to one's own use or to some special purpose; (*leg.*) the sequestering of a benefice to the perpetual use of a spiritual corporation; **a. clause,** a clause in a money bill by which Parliament assigns revenue for a special purpose. [~L. *appropriatio*].

APPROPRIATIVE, [a-prō-pri-at-iv], *adj.* which appropriates, having a tendency to appropriation.

APPROPRIATOR, [a-prō'-pri-ā-tor], *n.* a person who appropriates; (*leg.*) the owner of an appropriated benefice.

APPROVABLE, [a-proov'-abl], *adj.* meriting approbation, deserving approval.

APPROVAL, [a-proov'-al], *n.* approbation, sanction, critical examination.

APPROVE, [a-proov'], *v.t.* to be pleased with, to think favourably of, to sanction formally, to ratify, to commend; (*reflex.*) to prove, give evidence of one's qualities; (*leg.*) to improve. [OFr. *aprover*].

APPROVED, [a-proovd'], *adj.* proved, tried, worthy of approbation; **a. course,** a course of action or study prescribed by regulations as suitable and adequate for a specified purpose; **a. school,** a State school to which convicted juvenile delinquents may be sent; **a. society,** a Trade Union or insurance company operating National Health Insurance with State approval.

APPROVEMENT, [a-proov'-ment], *n.* approbation; (*leg.*) the act of proving accomplices guilty by a confession of a crime; the improvement of common land by enclosure for cultivation.

APPROVER, [a-proov'-er], *n.* one who approves; one who makes approvement; (*leg.*) one who, originally an accomplice, turns King's evidence.

APPROVINGLY, [a-proov'-ing-li], *adv.* in an approving manner.

APPROXIMATE (1), [a-proks'-im-at], *adj.* approaching, nearly correct, nearly resembling or corresponding with. [L. *approximatus*].

APPROXIMATE (2), [a-proks'-im-āt], *v.t.* to bring near, to cause to be near; *v.i.* to come near, to approach, to agree nearly in quantity, character, etc. [~L. *approximare*].

APPROXIMATELY, [a-proks'-im-at-li], *adv.* in an approximate manner, nearly, almost.

APPROXIMATION, [a-proks'-im-ā'-shun], *n.* the act of approximating, approach; (*math.*) a continual approach nearer and nearer to a quantity which is sought, when no process is known for arriving at it exactly, an almost correct solution of a problem.

APPROXIMATIVE, [a-proks'-im-at-iv], *adj.* of an approximate nature.

APPUI, [ap-wē'], *n.* a prop or stay; (*milit.*) defensive support; **point d'appui** (*milit.*) the pre-determined position on which troops form into line. [Fr. *appui*].

APPULSE, [a-puls'], *n.* the driving motion at or against, the act of striking energetically against; (*astron.*) the approach of a planet to conjunction with the sun or a star. [~L. *appulsus* driven].

APPULSIVE, [a-pul'-siv], *adj.* characterized by striking or driving against.

APPULSIVELY, [a-pul'-siv-li], *adv.* in an appulsive manner.

APPURTENANCE, [ap-ur'-tin-ans], *n.* that which appertains to something else larger or of more consequence; an adjunct; an appendage. [AFr. *apurtenaunce*].

APPURTENANT, [ap-ur'-tin-ant], *adj.* belonging or pertaining to as of legal right; proper, suited, appropriate to. [*Prec.*].

APRICOT, [ā'-prik-ot], *n.* an orange-coloured, oval, soft stone-fruit allied to the plum, *Prunus armeniaca*. [Fr. *abricot*].

APRIL, [ā'-pril], *n.* the fourth month of the Christian year; **A. fool**, one who has a trick played on him on 1st April. [L. *aprilis*].

APRON, [ā'-pron], *n.* a piece of cloth, leather or baize worn over the front of the body to keep the clothes clean or protect them from injury; a piece of curved timber above the foremost end of the keel of a ship; (*mech.*) the guard on the slide-rest of a lathe to protect the lead-screw from shavings; **to be tied to the a-strings**, to be greatly influenced by a female. [ME. from OFr. *naperon*].

APRONED, [ā'-prund], *adj.* wearing an apron.

APROPOS (1), [ap'-rop-ō'], *adj.* to the point or purpose; pertinent to the place, time or subject; opportune. [Fr. *à propos*].

APROPOS (2), [ap'-rop-ō'], *prep.* in regard to or with reference to.

APSE, [apse], *n.* (*arch.*) an arched semi-circular or polygonal recess at the end of a church. [L. *apsis*].

APSE

APSIDAL, [ap'-sidl], *adj.* (*arch.*) in the shape of an apse.

APSIDIOLE, [ap'-sid'-i-ōl], *n.* (*arch.*) a small or subsidiary apse.

APSIS, (*pl.* **apsides**), [ap'-sis, ap'-si-dēz], *n.* an apse; (*astron.*) one of the two points in the orbit of a satellite, one nearest to, the other farthest from, its primary body. [L. *apsis*].

APT, [apt], *adj.* fit, suitable, appropriate, pertinent; skilled, promising, quick; liable to, having a tendency to. [L. *aptus*].

APTERA, [ap'-ter-a], *n.*(*pl.*) (*entom.*) wingless insects. [Gk. *apteros* wingless].

APTERAL, [ap'-ter-al], *adj.* (*entom.*) wingless; (*arch.*) with columns along the front and rear but none along the sides.

APTEROUS, [ap'-ter-us], *adj.* wingless.

APTERYX, [ap'-ter-iks], *n.* the kiwi, a rare reddish-brown New Zealand bird with rudiments of wings and tailless. [A (4) and Gk. *pterux* wing].

APTITUDE, [ap'-ti-tewd], *n.* fitness, natural capacity, readiness in learning, propensity. [Fr. *aptitude*].

APTLY, [apt'-li], *adv.* in an apt manner, suitably, fittingly. [APT].

APTNESS, [apt'-nes], *n.* the quality of being apt; fitness for a purpose.

APTOTE, [ap'-tōt], *n.* (*gram.*) a noun that has no distinction of cases, an indeclinable noun. [Gk. *aptoton*].

APTOTIC, [ap-tō'-tik], *adj.* uninflected.

APYRETIC, [ap'-īr-et'-ik], *adj.* (*med.*) without fever. [A (4) and Gk. *puretos* fever].

APYREXY, [ap'-īr-ek'-si], *n.* (*med.*) a temporary intermission of fever. [Gk. *apurexia*].

APYROUS, [a-pīer'-us], *adj.* unchanged by heat. [Gk. *apuros* fireless].

AQUA- (1), *pref.* water. [L. *aqua* water].

AQUA (2), [ak'-wa], *n.* water. [L. *aqua* water].

AQUAFORTIS, [ak'-wa-fawt'-is], *n.* (*pop.*) nitric acid. [L. *aqua fortis* strong fluid].

AQUAMARINE (1), [ak'-wa-ma-rēn'], *n.* bluish-green, sea-blue; (*min.*) blue-green beryl. [L. *aqua marina* sea-water].

AQUAMARINE (2), [ak'-wa-ma-rēn'], *adj.* bluish-green.

AQUA REGIA, [ak'-wa-rēj'-a], *n.* (*chem.*) a mixture of hydrochloric and nitric acids capable of dissolving the "royal" metals such as gold. [L. *aqua regia* royal fluid].

AQUARIUM, [ak-wāer'-i-um], *n.* a tank or a building containing tanks for aquatic plants and creatures. [L. *aquarium*].

AQUARIUS, [ak-wāer'-i-us], *n.* the water-bearer, the eleventh sign of the Zodiac. [L. *aquarius*].

AQUATIC (1), [ak-wat'-ik], *n.* a plant which grows in water; (*pl.*) exercises or games in or on the water.

AQUATIC (2), [ak-wat'-ik], *adj.* pertaining to water. [L. *aquaticus*].

AQUATINT, [ak'-wa-tint], *n.* a form of engraving and etching produced by aquafortis on copper. [AQUA (1) and TINT].

AQUEDUCT, [ak'-wi-dukt], *n.* an artificial conduit or structure for conveying water; (*anat.*) small passage connecting different organs of the body or separate parts of the same organ. [L. *aquæductus*].

AQUEOUS, [āk'-wi-us], *adj.* consisting of, containing, or deposited in, water; **a. humour**, a transparent limpid fluid which fills the space between the cornea and the crystalline lens; **a. rocks**, rocks formed by deposition of sand in water. [AQUA].

AQUEOUSNESS, [āk'-wi-us-nes], *n.* the quality of being aqueous; wateriness.

AQUIFEROUS, [ak-wif'-er-us], *adj.* bearing or conducting water. [AQUA and L. *ferre* to bear].

AQUIFORM, [ak'-wi-fawm], *adj.* of watery form; liquid. [AQUA and FORM].

AQUILATED, [ak'-wil-āt'-id], *adj.* (*her.*) adorned with the heads of eagles. [~L. *aquila* eagle].

AQUILEGE†, **AQUILEGIA**, [ak'-wil-ē'-ji-a], *n.* (*bot.*) the columbine. [LL. *aquilegia*].

AQUILINE, [ak'-wil-īn], *adj.* pertaining to an eagle; hooked, curved like an eagle's beak. [L. *aquilinus*].

AQUOSITY, [ak-wos'-i-ti], *n.* wateriness, moisture.

ARAB, [a'-rab], *n.* a native of Arabia; an Arab horse; **street a.**, a homeless urchin who wanders about the streets. [Fr. *arabe*].

ARABA, [ah-rah'-ba], *n.* a heavy springless Eastern cart drawn by oxen. [Arab. *arabah*].

ARABESQUE (1), [a'-rab-esk'], *n.* a style of decoration derived from the Moors and Arabs, exhibiting fantastic patterns of formalized foliage and flowers and of geometrical forms.

ARABESQUE (2), [a'-rab-esk'], *adj.* in the style of ornament in favour among the Moors and Arabs, exhibiting arabesque. [Fr. *arabesque*].

ARABIAN (1), [a-rā'-bi-an], *n.* a native of Arabia; an Arabian horse; the language of Arabia. [~L. *Arabia*].

ARABIAN (2), [a-rā'-bi-an], *adj.* pertaining to Arabia; **A. Nights**, a famous collection of Oriental tales, fabulous stories.

ARABIC (1), [a'-rab-ik], *n.* a Semitic language spoken by Arabs.

ARABIC (2), [a'-rab-ik], *adj.* of or pertaining to Arabia and its language; **A. numerals**, the numbers 1, 2, 3, etc.; **gum a.**, a gum derived from the *Acacia*.

ARABIN, [a'-rab-in], *n.* the chief soluble substance in gum arabic.

ARABIST, [a'-rab-ist], *n.* a student of Arabic language, literature or medicine.

ARABLE, [a'-rabl], *adj.* suitable for ploughing. [L. *arabilis*].

ARACHIS, [a'-rak-is], *n.* (*bot.*) a genus of leguminous plants including the ground-nut and the peanut. [Gk. *arakhis* weed].

ARACHNID, (*pl.* **arachnida**), [a-rak'-nid], *n.* a spider, mite or scorpion. [Gk. *arachnes* spider].

ARACHNOID, [a'-rak'-noid], *adj.* resembling a spider's web, appertaining to arachnida; **a. tunic**, (*anat.*) a thin membrane spread over the brain and spinal cord; a fine slender covering of the crystalline humour of the eye. [*Prec.* and Gk. *oeides* like].

ARACHNOLOGIST, [a'-rak-nol'-oj-ist], *n.* a person versed in arachnology.

ARACHNOLOGY, [a'-rak-nol'-o-ji], *n.* the science which deals with the arachnida. [Gk. *arachnes* spider and *logos* speech.]

ARAEOSTYLE, [a'-rē-ō-stil], *n.* (*arch.*) an arrangement of widely separated columns. [Gk. *araios* rare and *stulos* column].

ARAEOSTYLE

ARAF, [a'-rahf], *n.* the Moslem purgatory, the wall dividing heaven and hell. [Arab. *arafi*].

ARAGONITE, ARRAGONITE, [a'-rag-on-īt], *n.* (*geol.*) a type of calcium carbonate containing strontia, crystallizing in hexagonal prisms. [*Aragon* where first found].

ARAIGNEE, araignée, [a-rān'-yā], *n.* (*milit.*) a branch gallery in a military mine, constructed to avoid an obstacle. [Fr. *araignée* spider's web].

ARAMAIC (1), [a'-ram-ā'-ik], *n.* a northern Semitic language anciently spoken in Palestine and Syria.

ARAMAIC (2), [a'-ram-ā'-ik], *adj.* pertaining to Syria and Chaldaea. [Gk. *aramaios*].

ARAMEAN, [a'-ram-ē'-an], *adj.* Aramaic. [Gk. *aramaios*].

ARAMEANISM, [a'-ram-ē'-an-izm], *n.* an Aramaic idiom.

ARANEIDAE, [a'-ran-ē-id-ē], *n.(pl.)* (*zool.*) the spiders. [L. *aranea* spider and Gk. *eidos* form].

ARANEIDAN, [a'-ran-ē'-id-an], *adj.* pertaining to araneidae.

ARANEIFORM, [a'-ran-ē'-i-fawm], *adj.* shaped like a spider. [L. *aranea* spider and FORM].

ARANEOSE, [a-rā'-ni-ōs], *adj.* covered with crossed hairs in the same way as the rays of a spider's web. [L. *araneosus*].

ARANEOUS, [a-rā'-ni-us], *adj.* covered in cobwebs, like a cobweb. [*Prec.*].

ARAPAIMA, [a'-rap-ī'-ma], *n.* a large South American freshwater food-fish. [Brazilian *arapaima*].

ARAR, [ah'-rah(r)], *n.* the wood of a North African kind of *Callitris.* [Berber *arar*].

ARAUCARIA, [ar'-awk-āer'-i-a], *n.* a genus of trees including the monkey-puzzle, *A. imbricata.* [*Arauco* in South Chile].

ARBALEST, [ah'-bal-est], *n.* a powerful ancient military engine, working on the principle of the crossbow and discharging bolts and stones; a crossbow bent by a winch. [L. *arcuballista* a catapult fitted with a bow].

ARBALEST

ARBALESTER, [ah'-bal-est'-er], *n.* one who fires an arbalest; a crossbow man.

ARBITER, [ah'-bit-er], *n.* an impartial judge of a dispute, one given power by contending parties to decide their dispute; an umpire. [L. *arbiter*].

ARBITRAGE, [ah'-bit-rij], *n.* (*comm.*) the simultaneous buying and selling in different markets so as to profit by the difference in price; traffic in bills of exchange, stocks and shares, etc. [OFr. *arbitrage*].

ARBITRAL, [ah'-bit-ral], *adj.* pertaining to arbitration.

ARBITRAMENT, [ah-bit'-ram-ent], *n.* control; a decision, award by an arbiter. [OFr. *arbitrement*].

ARBITRARILY, [ah'-bit-rar-i-li], *adv.* in arbitrary fashion.

ARBITRARINESS, [ah'-bit-rar-in-es], *n.* the state of being arbitrary or capricious.

ARBITRARY, [ah'-bit-rar-i], *adj.* determined solely by personal judgment, dependent upon a person's caprice and discretion, capricious, uncertain, determined by individual chance; hastily decisive, tyrannical, beyond external control, unchecked by considerations outside oneself. [L. *arbitrarius*].

ARBITRATE, [ah'-bit-rāt], *v.t.* to hear and decide as an arbitrator; *v.i.* to decide, to judge between parties, to settle disputes by discussion. [~L. *arbitrari*].

ARBITRATION, [ah'-bit-rā'-shun], *n.* the hearing and decision of a dispute by a person or persons chosen by the disputants jointly; **Permanent Court of A.,** the Hague Tribunal. [~L. *arbitratio*].

ARBITRATOR, [ah'-bi-trā'-tor], *n.* an arbiter, one who arbitrates. [L. *arbitrator*].

ARBITRATRIX, [ah'-bi-trā'-triks], *n.* an arbitress. [L. *arbitratrix*].

ARBITRESS, [ah'-bi-tres], *n.* a female arbitrator. [OFr. *arbitresse*].

ARBOR, [ah'-ber], *n.* (*bot.*) a tree, as distinct from a shrub; an arbour; the axis of a wheel; **A. Day,** a public holiday in the Dominion of Canada and U.S.A., for tree-planting; **a. vitæ,** a tree of the genus *Thuja.* [L. *arbor* tree].

ARBORACEOUS, [ah'-ber-ā'-shus], *adj.* wooded, tree-like. [ARBOR].

ARBORATOR, [ah'-ber-ā'-tor], *n.* one who plants or prunes trees.

ARBOREAL, [ah-baw'-ri-al], *adj.* pertaining to trees; (*fig.*) rustic, leafy. [~L. *arboreus*].

ARBORESCENCE, [ah'-ber-es'-ens], *n.* the condition of being arborescent.

ARBORESCENT, [ah'-ber-es'-ent], *adj.* resembling or growing like a tree. [~L. *arborescens*].

ARBORET, [ah'-ber-et], *n.* a small tree, a shrub.

ARBORETUM, [ah'-ber-ē'-tum], *n.* a place for cultivating and displaying trees. [L. *arboretum*].

ARBORICULTURAL, [ah'-ber-i-kul'-cher-al], *adj.* of, or pertaining to, arboriculture.

ARBORICULTURE, [ah'-bor-i-kul'-cher], *n.* the cultivation of trees. [ARBOR and CULTURE].

ARBORICULTURIST, [ah'-bor-i-kul'-cher-ist], *n.* a cultivator of trees.

ARBORIFORM, [ah-bor'-i-fawm], *adj.* shaped like a tree. [ARBOR and FORM].

ARBORIST, [ah'-ber-ist], *n.* a student or grower of trees.

ARBORIZATION, [ah'-ber-īz-ā'-shun], *n.* tree-like figures in certain minerals; (*med.*) a similar phenomenon caused by distension of the blood-vessels in inflammation.

ARBORIZE, [ah'-ber-īz], *v.t.* to make arborescent.

ARBOROUS, [ah'-ber-us], *adj.* pertaining to trees.

ARBOUR, [ah'-ber], *n.* a seat shaded by trees; a bower. [~OFr. *herbier* from L. *herbarium* a collection of plants].

ARBOURED, [ah'-berd], *adj.* having an arbour; shady.

ARBUSCLE, [ah'-buskl], *n.* a tree-like shrub. [L. *arbuscula*].

ARBUSCULAR, [ah-bus'-kew-ler], *adj.* pertaining to a shrub.

ARBUSTUM, [ah'-bust'-um], *n.* a copse, plantation. [L. *arbustum*].

ARBUTEAN, [ah-bew'-ti-an], *adj.* of or pertaining to the *Arbutus.*

ARBUTUS, [ah-bew'-tus], *n.* a genus of evergreen trees and shrubs, including the strawberry-tree, *Arbutus unedo.* [L. *arbutus*].

ARC, [ahk], *n.* a segment of a circle, the apparent path of a heavenly body; **a. light,** a very bright lamp in which the current passes as a flame between two electrodes. [L. *arcus* bow].

ARCA, [ahk'-a], *n.* an ark, coffer. [L. *arca*].

ARCADE, [ah-kād'], *n.* a row of arches supported on columns; an arched walk; a long arched building or gallery lined with shops. [Fr. *arcade*].

ARCADIA, [ah-kā'-di-a], *n.* a mountainous region in the Peloponnesus whose inhabitants, being cut off from the rest of Greece and remaining largely uncultured, were supposed to be simple, rustic, and contented; hence a rural paradise, the restful innocence believed to exist in such circumstances. [Gk. *arkadia*].

ARCADIAN, [ah-kā'-di-an], *adj.* pastoral, ideally simple, rustic.

ARCANUM, (*pl.* **arcana**), [ah-kā'-num], *n.* a secret. [L. *arcanum*].

ARC-BOUTANT, [ahk'-bōōt'-ant], *n.* (*arch.*) a flying buttress. [Fr. *arc-boutant*].

ARCH (1), [ahch], *n.* an arc, curve, bow; a curved overhead structure of stone or brick; any place covered with an arch; **Court of Arches,** the supreme court of appeal in ecclesiastical causes lying within the province of Canterbury, so called from the church of St. Mary-le-Bow, where it was anciently held. [Fr. *arche* from ~L. *arcus* bow].

ARCH (2), [ahch], *adj.* coy, waggish, roguishly affecting a nice hypocrisy, shrewd. [ARCH (4)].

ARCH (3), [ahch], *v.t.* to cover with an arch; to form into a curve; *v.i.* to make an arch or arches. [ARCH (1)].

ARCH- (4), *pref.* chief, principal, pre-eminent, excelling in a class. [Gk. *arkhos* chief, leader].

ARCHAEAN, [ah-kē'-an], *adj.* belonging to the oldest geological period. [Gk. *arkhaios* ancient].

ARCHAEO-, *pref.* old, primitive. [Gk. *arkhaios*].

ARCHAEOLOGICAL, [ah'-ki-ol-oj'-ikl], *adj.* pertaining to archaeology.

ARCHAEOLOGICALLY, [ah'-ki-ol-oj'-ik-a-li'], *adv.* in archaeological fashion.

ARCHAEOLOGIST, [ah'-ki-ol'-oj-ist], *n.* one expert in archaeology.

ARCHAEOLOGY, [ah'-ki-ol'-o-ji], *n.* the study of ancient history and culture by means of material remains. [Gk. *arkhaiologia*].

ARCHAEOPTERYX, [ah'-kē-op'-ter-iks], *n.* a flying creature of the Jurassic period with teeth in its beak, vertebrae in its tail, and claws on its wings. [ARCHAEO and Gk. *pterux* wing].

ARCHAIC, [ah-kā'-ik], *adj.* ancient, very obsolete, primitive; (*philol.*) displaying an older form. [Gk. *arkhaikos*].

ARCHAICALLY, [ah-kā'-ik-al-i], *adv.* primitively.

ARCHAISM, [ah'-kā-izm], *n.* an archaic word or expression; literary affectation of an obsolete form or idiom.

ARCHAIST, [ah'-kā-ist], *n.* one given to archaism.

ARCHAISTIC, [ah'-kā-ist'-ik], *adj.* pertaining to, characterized by archaism.

ARCHAIZE, [ah'-kā-īz], *v.t. and i.* to use archaisms, to make archaic.

ARCHANGEL, [ahk'-ān'-jel], *n.* an angel of a superior order. [ARCH (4) and ANGEL].

ARCHANGELIC, [ahk'-an-jel'-ik], *adj.* in the manner of, pertaining to, an archangel.

ARCHBISHOP, [ahch'-bish'-op], *n.* a chief bishop, the chief bishop of a province, a metropolitan. [ARCH (4) and BISHOP].

ARCHBISHOPRIC, [ahch'-bish'-op-rik], *n.* an archbishop's jurisdiction or see. [ARCH (4) and BISHOPRIC].

ARCH-BRICK, [ahch'-brik'], *n.* a brick shaped for building arches. [ARCH (1) and BRICK].

ARCHBUTLER, [ahch'-but'-ler], *n.* the chief butler; the office held by the Kings of Bohemia in the Holy Roman Empire. [ARCH (4) and BUTLER].

ARCHBUTTRESS, [ahch'-but'-res], *n.* a flying buttress. [ARCH (4) and BUTTRESS].

ARCH-CHAMBERLAIN, [ahch'-chām'-ber-lin], *n.* the chief chamberlain in the Holy Roman Empire, an office held by the Elector of Brandenburg. [ARCH (4) and CHAMBERLAIN].

ARCH-CHANCELLOR, [ahch'-chahn'-sel-or], *n.* the chief chancellor of the Holy Roman Empire, an office held by the Elector-Archbishop of Mainz. [ARCH (4) and CHANCELLOR].

ARCHDEACON, [ahch'-dē'-kun], *n.* (*eccles.*) a dignitary, in rank below a bishop, with temporal jurisdiction over part of a diocese, with control of rural deans. [ARCH (4) and DEACON].

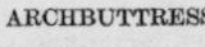
ARCHBUTTRESS

ARCHDEACONATE, [ahch'-dē'-kun-āt], *n.* (*eccles.*) the office of an archdeacon.

ARCHDEACONRY, [ahch'-dē'-kun-ri], *n.* (*eccles.*) the position, jurisdiction or residence of an archdeacon. [ARCH (4) and DEACONRY].

ARCHDIOCESE, [ahch'-dī'-os-is], *n.* the jurisdiction or see of an archbishop. [ARCH (4) and DIOCESE].

ARCHDRUID, [ahch'-drōō'-id], *n.* chief druid. [ARCH (4) and DRUID].

ARCHDUCAL, [ahch'-dewk'-al], *adj.* pertaining to an archduke.

ARCHDUCHESS, [ahch'-duch'-es], *n.* the consort of an archduke. [ARCH (4) and DUCHESS].

ARCHDUCHY, [ahch'-duch'-i], *n.* land ruled by an archduke. [ARCH (4) and DUCHY].

ARCHDUKE, [ahch'-dewk'], *n.* a chief duke; a prince of the former Austrian Royal Family. [ARCH (4) and DUKE].

ARCHDUKEDOM, [ahch'-dewk'-dom], *n.* archduchy.

ARCHEAL, [ah-kē'-al], *adj.* pertaining to the archeus.

ARCHEBIOSIS, [ah'-ki-bī-ō'-sis], *n.* the derivation of life from lifeless matter. [Gk. *arkhe* beginning and *bios* life].

ARCHEGONIUM, [ah'-ki-gō'-ni-um], *n.* the ovary of cryptogams. [~Gk. *arkhegonos* founder of a race].

ARCHEGONY, [ah-keg'-on-i], *n.* the doctrine of abiogenesis. [*Prec.*].

ARCHELOGY, [ahk-el'-o-ji], *n.* the scientific study of first principles. [Gk. *arkhe* beginning and *logos* speech].

ARCH-ENEMY, [ahch'-en'-i-mi], *n.* the greatest enemy; Satan.

ARCHER, [ah'-cher], *n.* one who shoots arrows with the bow; the ninth sign of the zodiac; **a. fish,** a species of fish that drown insects with drops of water, *Toxotes jaculator*. [L. *arcarium*].

ARCHERESS, [ahch'-er-es], *n.* a female archer.

ARCHERY, [ah'-cher-i], *n.* the art of shooting with bow and arrow. [OFr. *archerie*].

ARCHETYPAL, [ahk'-i-tīpl'], *adj.* pertaining to an archetype; original, primitive.

ARCHETYPE, [ahk'-i-tīp'], *n.* original model from which things are made, prototype; (*numis.*) the standard coin on which others are modelled; (*anat.*) an assumed original pattern for each great division of living creatures. [ARCH (4) and TYPE].

ARCHEUS, [ah-kē'-us], *n.* the life force that the Paracelsians believed to produce and animate all living organisms. [Gk. *arkhaios* original].

ARCH-FIEND, [ahch'-fēnd'], *n.* a chief fiend; Satan.

ARCH-FLAMEN, [ahch'-flā'-men], *n.* a chief priest, archbishop. [ARCH (4) and FLAMEN].

ARCH-FOE, [ahch'-fō'], *n.* the chief foe; Satan.

ARCH-HERESY, [ahch'-he'-res-i], *n.* a principal basic heresy.

ARCH-HYPOCRITE, [ahch'-hip'-ō-krit], *n.* a great hypocrite.

ARCHIATER, [ah-kī'-at-er], *n.* a chief physician; †the Imperial Russian physician. [Gk. *arkhiatros*].

ARCHIDIACONAL, [ah'-ki-dī-ak'-onl], *adj.* of or pertaining to an archdeacon. [ARCH (4) and DIACONAL].

ARCHIE, [ah'-chi], *n.* (*coll.*) an anti-aircraft gun. [Proper name *Archibald*].

ARCHIEPISCOPACY, [ah'-ki-ip-is'-kop-a-si], *n.* a method of ecclesiastical government by archbishops. [ARCH (4) and EPISCOPACY].

ARCHIEPISCOPAL, [ah'-ki-ip-is'-kō-pal], *adj.* pertaining to an archbishop.

ARCHIEPISCOPATE, [ah'-ki-ip-is'-kop-āt], *n.* an archbishop's office or tenure of office.

ARCHIL, ORCHIL, [ahch'-il], *n.* a species of lichen, *Roccella tinctoria*, producing a violet dye, litmus, etc. [OFr. *orchil*].

ARCHIMAGE, ARCHIMAGUS, [ahk'-im'-ij, ahk'-i-mā-gus], *n.* a chief wizard; high-priest of Persian fire-worshippers. [ARCH (4) and Gk. *magos* magician].

ARCHIMANDRITE, [ahk'-i-man'-drīt], *n.* the head or abbot of a Greek Orthodox monastery or monastic order. [Late Gk. *arkhimandrites*].

ARCHIMEDEAN, [ah'-ki-mē'-di-an], *adj.* relating to Archimedes; **A. principle,** his discovery that a body immersed in fluid displaces its own weight of liquid; **A. drill,** a drill in which a threaded bobbin, when pushed along the screwed shaft, causes rotation of the drill-point attached to the shaft, the rotary motion being sustained by a pair of balanced weights. [Gk. *Arkimedes*].

ARCHIMEDEAN DRILL

ARCHING (1), [ah'-ching], *n.* an arch, system of arches. [ARCH (1)].

ARCHING (2), [ah'-ching], *adj.* curving like an arch. [ARCH (3)].

ARCHIPELAGIC, [ahk'-i-pel-a'-jik], *adj.* pertaining to an archipelago.

ARCHIPELAGO, [ahk'-i-pel'-ag-ō], *n.* the Aegean Sea, between Greece and Asia Minor; a sea containing many islands; a group of islands. [ARCH (4) and Gk. *pelagos* sea].

ARCHITECT, [ahk'-i-tekt], *n.* one who draws plans for, and superintends the erection of a building; (*fig.*) one who frames a complex plan; one making a broad and detailed plan for a desired end, a constructor; **the Great A.,** God. [Gk. *arkhitekton* master-builder].

ARCHITECTONIC, [ahk'-it-ek-ton'-ik], *adj.* pertaining to, suited for architecture; having a controlling function; (*met.*) relating to the co-ordination of knowledge. [Gk. *arkhitektonikos*].

ARCHITECTONICS, [ahk'-it-ek-ton'-iks], *n.* (*pl.*) the science of architecture; (*met.*) the systematic arrangement of observed knowledge.

ARCHITECTURAL, [ah'-ki-tek'-cher-al], *adj.* relating to, or concerning the rules and science of architecture; an harmonious and impressive structure or conception.

ARCHITECTURALLY, [ah'-ki-tek'-cher-al-i], *adv.* in architectural manner.

ARCHITECTURE, [ah'-ki-tek-cher], *n.* the art and skill of building an edifice; the style in which a thing is built; construction, framework; the study of building methods and fashions; **naval a.,** the art of building warships. [~ARCHITECT].

ARCHITRAVE, [ahk'-i-trāv'], *n.* the part of an entablature resting immediately on the column; the ornamental mouldings round a door or window. [It. *architrave*].

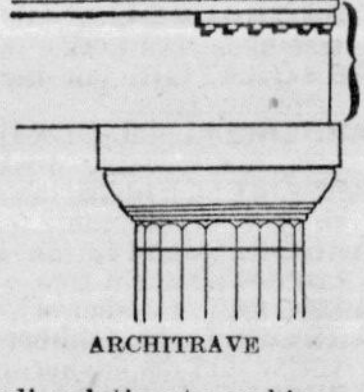
ARCHITRAVE

ARCHIVAL, [ah-kī'-val], *adj.* relating to archives.

ARCHIVAULT, see ARCHIVOLT.

ARCHIVE, (*pl.* **archives**), [ah'-kiv, ah'-kivz], *n.* a place of security for ancient documents; an historical document or record. [LL. *archivum* public office or building].

ARCHIVIST, [ahk'-iv-ist], *n.* a keeper of archives; one expert in the methods of preserving archives.

ARCHIVOLT, ARCHIVAULT, [ahk'-i-volt], *n.* (*arch.*) the inside curve of an arch; a band with mouldings on the faces of the arch. [It. *archivolto*].

ARCHLIKE, [ahch'-līk], *adj.* formed like an arch. [ARCH (1) and LIKE (3)].

ARCHLUTE, [ahch'-lōōt], *n.* a large, double-stringed lute having its bass strings lengthened. [ARCH (4) and LUTE].

ARCHLY, [ahch'-li], *adv.* in an arch manner. [ARCH (2)].

ARCH-MARSHAL, [ahch'-mah'-shal], *n.* the grand marshal of the Holy Roman Empire. [ARCH (4) and MARSHAL].

ARCHNESS, [ahch'-nes], *n.* arch behaviour, coyness. [ARCH (2)].

ARCHON, [ahk'-on], *n.* one of the nine chief magistrates of Athens; a ruler or chief magistrate; a creator of the world, held by the Gnostics to be inferior to God. [Gk. *arkhon*].

ARCHONSHIP, [ahk'-on-ship], *n.* an archon's office and tenure of office.

ARCH-PILLAR, [ahch'-pil'-er], *n.* a chief pillar.

ARCH-POLITICIAN, [ahch'-pol'-it-ish'-un], *n.* a principal politician.

ARCHPRESBYTER, [ahch'-prez'-bit-er], *n.* a chief presbyter. [ARCH (4) and PRESBYTER].

ARCHPRIEST, [ahch'-prēst'], *n.* †a priest acting as assistant under a bishop; a Lutheran rural dean. [ARCH (4) and PRIEST].

ARCHSTONE, [ahch'-stōn], *n.* a stone shaped for building arches; a keystone. [ARCH (1) and STONE].

ARCH-TREASURER, [ahch'-trezh'-er-er], *n.* the great treasurer of the Holy Roman Empire.

ARCHWAY, [ahch'-wā], *n.* a passage going under an arch. [ARCH (1) and WAY].

ARCHWAYED, [ahch'-wād], *adj.* with an archway.

ARCHWISE, [ahch'-wīz], *adv.* in the shape of an arch. [ARCH (1) and WISE].

ARCOGRAPH, [ahk'-ō-grahf], *n.* an instrument for describing a circular arc without using a central point. [L. *arcus* and GRAPH].

ARCTATION, [ahk-tā'-shun], *n.* arctitude. [~L. *arctatio*].

ARCTIC (1), [ahk'-tik], *n.* the North Polar region.

ARCTIC (2), [ahk'-tik], *adj.* pertaining to the Polar regions; (*fig.*) very cold; **A. Circle,** a lesser circle parallel to the equator 23 degrees 28 minutes from the North Pole. [L. *arcticus* from Gk. *arktos* (the Great Bear) the North].

ARCTITUDE, [ahk'-ti-tewd], *n.* (*med.*) constriction, compression as of an artery, or of the intestinal canal in constipation. [MedL. *arctitudo* constriction].

ARCTURUS, [ahk-tew'-rus], *n.* a star of the first magnitude in the constellation Boötes; (*pop.*) constellation, the Great Bear. [Gk. *arktouros* from *arktos* the Bear].

ARCUATE, [ahk'-yōō-āt], *adj.* arched, shaped like an arch. [L. *arcuatus*].

ARCUATION, [ahk'-yōō-ā'-shun], *n.* the act or state of curving; a series of arches; (*arch.*) use of arches in building; a method of raising trees by bending the branches to the ground and covering the shoots with earth. [~*Prec.*].

ARCUBALIST, [ah-kyōō'-bal-ist], *n.* an arbalest. [L. *arcuballista*].

ARCUBALISTER, [ah'-kyōō'-bal-ist'-er], *n.* an arbalester. [*Prec.*].

ARDASS†, [ah'-das], *n.* fine Persian silk. [Fr. *ardasse*, Pers. *ardan*].

ARDASSINE†, [ah-das'-ēn], *n.* a fabric made in France from ardass. [Pers. *ardan* raw silk].

ARDEB, [ah-deb], *n.* a measure of capacity of about 5 bushels, used in Egypt and the East. [Arab. *urdab*].

ARDENCY, [ah'-den-si], *n.* intense heat; (*fig.*) passion, lust, burning enthusiasm. [L. *ardentia*].

ARDENT, [ah'-dent], *adj.* (*fig.*) fiercely hot, glowing, intense, passionate, fervent, eager, hotly loyal, zealous. [~L. *ardens* burning].

ARDENTLY, [ah'-dent-li], *adv.* in ardent fashion.

ARDOUR, [ah'-der], *n.* heat; (*fig.*) warmth, violence of emotions, zeal, earnestness. [L. *ardor* heat].

ARDUOUS, [ahd'-yōō-us], *adj.* steep, difficult to climb; (*fig.*) difficult to accomplish, laborious. [L. *arduus* steep, difficult].

ARDUOUSLY, [ahd'-yōō-us-li], *adv.* in arduous fashion, laboriously.

ARDUOUSNESS, [ahd'-yōō-us-nes], *n.* the condition of being arduous.

ARE (1), [ah(r)], *n.* the metric unit of surface-area equal to 100 square metres. [Fr. *are* from L. *area*].

ARE (2), [ah(r)], *pres. ind., pl.* of the verb BE. [OE. *aron*].

AREA, [āer'-i-a], *n.* a piece of open or vacant land; a measure of the extent of a plane surface; a region, particular district; sunken courtyard before the basement of a town house; (*fig.*) range, scope; (*geom.*) the superficial content of a figure; (*comm.*) district allotted to travelling salesman. [L. *area* vacant piece of ground].

AREAL, [āer'-i-al], *adj.* relating to an area.

ARECA, [a-rē'-ka], *n.* a species of Asiatic palm, its fruit being chewed with the betel leaf. [Canarese *areca*].

AREFACTION, [a'-ri-fak'-shun], *n.* the act of drying, making arid. [~*Next*].

AREFY, [a'-ri-fī], *v.t.* to dry, parch, make dry. [L. *arefacere*].

ARENA, [a-rē'-na], *n.* the open space in the middle of an amphitheatre where combats and contests were held; a place where public contests are held; (*fig.*) the scene of any active conflict. [L. *arena* sanded place].

ARENACEOUS, [a'-ren-ā'-shus], *adj.* sandy. [L. *arenaceus*].

ARENG, [a-reng'], *n.* the palm tree which yields palm sugar, wine and fibre. [West Ind. *arenga*].

ARENICOLITES, [a'-ren-ik'-ol-īts], *n.(pl.)* (*geol.*) markings in sandstone like worm-burrows.

ARENILITIC, [a-ren'-il-it'-ik], *adj.* pertaining to sandstone. [L. *arena* sand and Gk. *lithos* stone].

ARENOSE, [a'-ren-ōs], *adj.* very sandy, consisting of sand. [L. *arenosus*].

AREOGRAPHY, [a'-ri-og'-raf-i], *n.* the study of the physical characteristics of the planet Mars. [Gk. *Ares* Mars and Gk. *graphia* writing].

AREOLA, (*pl.* **areolæ**), [a-rē'-ol-a], *n.* (*anat.*) the red circle round the nipple; the inflamed ring round a pustule; (*bot.* and *anat.*) an interstitial space in tissues. [L. *areola* small space].

AREOLAR, [a-rē'-ol-er], *adj.* pertaining to an areola; **a. tissue,** cellular tissue.

AREOLATE, [a-rē'-ol-āt], *adj.* separated into areolations.

AREOLATION, [a-rē'-ol-ā'-shun], *n.* separation into small areas by different colours, textures, etc.

AREOLE, [ar'-i-ōl], *n.* an areola. [Fr. *aréole*].

AREOMETER, [ar'-i-om'-it-er], *n.* an hydrometer. [Gk. *araios* diffuse and METER].

AREOMETRICAL, [ar'-i-ō-met'-rikl], *adj.* relating to areometry.

AREOMETRY, [ar'-i-om'-et-ri], *n.* the science of measuring the specific gravity of fluids.

AREOPAGITE, [ar'-i-op'-a-gīt], *n.* a member of the Areopagus.

AREOPAGITIC, [ar'-i-op'-a-git'-ik], *adj.* pertaining to the Areopagus.

AREOPAGUS, [a-ri-op'-ag-us], *n.* a hill near the Acropolis in Athens, where the ancient council was held; the highest judicial court of Athens. [Gk. *Areiopagos* Hill of Mars].

AREOSTYLE, see ARAEOSTYLE.

ARETE, arête, [a-rāt'], *n.* a sharp rising ridge on a mountain, a knife-edge. [Swiss Fr. *arête*].

ARGAL (1), [ah'-gal], *conj.* therefore. [~L. *ergo* therefore].

ARGAL (2), ARGOL, ORGAL, [ah'-gal], *n.* a hard tartar crust found on the sides of wine-casks, used in dyeing. [Uncert.].

ARGALA, [ah'-gal-a], *n.* (*ornith.*) a species of Indian stork, *Ciconia argala*, the adjutant-bird. [Hind *hargila*].

ARGALI, [ah'-gal-i], *n.* (*zool.*) an Asiatic horned wild sheep, *Ovis ammon*. [Tartar *argali*].

ARGAND, [ah'-gand], *n.* a hollow cylindrical burner in which the admission of air from inside and out increases the luminosity. [Aimé *Argand*, a Swiss physicist].

ARGEMA, [ah'-jem-a], *n.* (*med.*) a white spot on the edge of the cornea produced by ulceration. [Gk. *argema*].

ARGENT (1), [ah'-jent], *n.* silver, silvery white money; (*her.*) silver. [L. *argentum* silver].

ARGENT (2), [ah'-jent], *adj.* silvery, bright. [ARGENT (1)].

ARGENTAL, [ah-jentl'], *adj.* resembling or pertaining to silver.

ARGENTAN, [ah-jen'-tan], *n.* an alloy of nickel, zinc and copper, German silver. [L. *argentum* silver].

ARGENTIC, [ah-jen'-tik], *adj.* (*chem.*) containing silver as a monad.

ARGENTIFEROUS, [ah'-jen-tif'-er-us], *adj.* bearing or producing silver. [ARGENT (1) and L. *ferre* to bear].

ARGENTINE (1), [ah'-jen-tīn], *n.* a small fish of the salmon family having brilliant silver scales; a variety of porcelain coated with metal; (*bot.*) silverweed, *Potentilla anserina.* [L. *argentinus* silver].

ARGENTINE (2), [ah'-jen-tīn], *adj.* silvery, like silver. [L. *argentinus*].

ARGENTITE, [ah'-jent-īt], *n.* (*min.*) a greyish-black silver sulphide, a precious ore of silver. [~L. *argentum*].

ARGENTOUS, [ah-jent'-us], *adj.* (*chem.*) containing silver as a dyad. [~*Prec.*].

ARGENTUM, [ah-jen'-tum], *n.* silver; (*chem.*) a white metallic element (denoted by Ag). [L. *argentum*].

ARGHAN, [ah'-gan], *n.* a South American fibre-plant from which yarn is spun. [Uncert.].

ARGHOOL, [ah'-gōōl], *n.* an Egyptian musical reed having two tubes and a mouthpiece. [Arab. *arghool*].

ARGIL, [ah'-jil], *n.* potter's clay; †alumina. [Fr. *argile*, L. *argilla*, Gk. *argillos*].

ARGILLACEOUS, [ah'-jil-ā'-shus], *adj.* pertaining to clay, clayey. [~*Prec.*].

ARGILLIFEROUS, [ah'-jil-if'-er-us], *adj.* containing clay. [ARGIL and L. *ferre* to bear].

ARGILLITE, [ah'-jil-īt], *n.* clay-slate. [ARGIL].

ARGILLITIC, [ah'-jil-it'-ik], *adj.* pertaining to argillite.

ARGILLO-ARENACEOUS, [ah-jil'-ō-a-ren-ā'-shus], *adj.* containing or made of clay and sand.

ARGILLO-CALCAREOUS, [ah-jil'-ō-kal-kāer'-i-us], *adj.* containing or made of clay and lime.

ARGILLOUS, [ah'-jil-us], *adj.* clayey, containing or consisting of clay. [L. *argillosus*].

ARGIVE (1), [ah'-jīv], *n.* an inhabitant of Argos in Greece; a Greek, generally a noble and heroic one. [L. *Argivus*].

ARGIVE (2), [ah'-jīv], *adj.* pertaining to Argos; Greek; (*fig.*) rudely and hardily virtuous and noble. [*Prec.*].

ARGOL, see ARGAL (2).

ARGON, [ah'-gon], *n.* a chemical element (denoted by Ar), an inert gas, found in the atmosphere in very small quantities. [Gk. *argos* idle].

ARGONAUT, [ah'-gon-awt], *n.* one who sailed in Jason's ship *Argo*, in search of the golden fleece; (*fig.*) a daring sailor and adventurer; (*zool.*) a genus of molluscs, which includes the paper-nautilus. [L. *argonauta* from Gk. *Argo* and *nautes* sailor].

ARGONAUTIC, [ah'-go-nawt'-ik], *adj.* relating to the Argonauts.

ARGOSY, [ah'-gos-i], *n.* originally a ship from the wealthy Dalmatian port of Ragusa; a richly-laden merchant-ship, a rich sailing-ship. [It. *Ragusea*].

ARGOT, [ah'-gō], *n.* low Parisian slang; thieves' slang, low jargon. [Fr. *argot*].

ARGUABLE, [ah'-gew-abl], *adj.* able to be argued; possibly justifiable, reasonable.

ARGUE, [ah'-gew], *v.t. and i.* to maintain one opinion against another by stating reasons, to give reasons in a dispute, to oppose an opinion by reason, to dispute; to discuss in the light of reason, to debate keenly, to persuade by discussion, to indicate strongly. [L. *arguere* to prove].

ARGUER, [ah'-gew-er], *n.* one who argues.

ARGUFY, [ah'-gew-fī], *v.i.* (*coll.*) to argue in an irritating manner, to reiterate maddeningly small points in the form of argument, to wrangle.

ARGUING, [ah'-gew-ing], *n.* reasoning in argument.

ARGUMENT, [ah'-gew-ment], *n.* a disputation, discussion; a line of reasoning put forward in support of conclusions; a synopsis of the plot or subject of a play, book, or poem. [L. *argumentum*].

ARGUMENTAL, [ah'-gew-mentl'], *adj.* pertaining to argument.

ARGUMENTATION, [ah'-gew-men-tā'-shun], *n.* process of reasoning; debate. [~L. *argumentatio*].

ARGUMENTATIVE, [ah'-gew-ment'-at-iv], *adj.* given to argument or dispute; disputatious; controversial.

ARGUMENTATIVELY, [ah'-gew-ment'-at-iv-li], *adv.* in argumentative fashion.

ARGUMENTATIVENESS, [ah'-gew-ment'-at-iv-nes], *n.* disputatious behaviour or habit of mind.

ARGUS, [ah'-gus], *n.* a wakeful mythological creature with a hundred eyes, employed to guard the golden fleece; **a. eyed,** keen-sighted, vigilant; **a. pheasant,** an East-Indian bird allied to the peacock; **a. shell,** a porcelain-shell, variegated with spots. [Gk. *Argos*].

ARGUTE, [ah'-gewt], *adj.* subtle, acutely ingenious, quick, keen. [L. *argutus*].

ARGYRIA, [ah-jir'-i-a], *n.* (*med.*) a darkening of the skin caused by persistent application of silver nitrate. [Gk. *arguros* silver].

ARGYRODITE, [ah-jier'-ō-dīt], *n.* (*min.*) a rare mineral containing silver and germanium. [Gk. *argurodes* rich in silver].

ARIA, [ah'-ri-a], *n.* (*mus.*) air, melody; elaborate air sung solo in an oratorio or opera. [It. *aria*].

ARIAN (1), [āer'-i-an], *n.* a follower of the fourth century heresy of Arius, who denied that Christ was of one substance with God. [*Arius* the founder of this heresy].

ARIAN (2), [āer'-i-an], *adj.* pertaining to Arius or his heresy. [*Prec.*].

ARIANISM, [āer'-i-an-izm], *n.* the tenets of the Arians.

ARICINE, [ar'-is-ēn], *n.* an alkaloid extracted from cinchona bark. [*Arica* a place in Peru].

ARID, [a'-rid], *adj.* dry, parched with heat; infertile; (*fig.*) barren, incapable of feeling or imparting interest. [L. *aridus*].

ARIDAS, [a'-rid-as], *n.* an East Indian taffeta. [Native].

ARIDITY, [a-rid'-i-ti], *n.* the condition of being arid. [L. *ariditas*].

ARIDNESS, [a'-rid-nes], *n.* aridity.

ARIEL (1), [āer'-i-el], *n.* (*zool.*) the Arabian gazelle; the flying phalanger of Australia. [Arab. *aryil* stag].

ARIEL (2), [āer'-i-el], *n.* a spirit of the air; the inmost satellite of Uranus. [Heb. *Ariel*].

ARIES, [āer'-i-ēz], *n.* (*astron.*) the Ram, the first sign of the zodiac; the constellation. [L. *aries* ram].

ARIETTA, [a'-ri-et'-a], *n.* (*mus.*) a short air or song. [It. *arietta*].

ARIGHT, [a-rīt'], *adv.* rightly, correctly. [OE. *on riht*].

ARIL, [a'-ril], *n.* (*bot.*) an exterior seed-covering formed after fertilization. [MedL. *arillus* raisin].

ARILLATED, [ar'-il-ā-tid], *adj.* having an aril.

ARILLED, [a'-rild], *adj.* arillated.

ARILLUS, [a'-ril-us], *n.* (*bot.*) an aril. [ARIL].

ARIOLATION, [a'-ri-ō-lā'-shun], *n.* soothsaying. [~L. *hariolatio*].

ARIOSO, [a'-ri-ō'-sō], *adv.* (*mus.*) in a melodious fashion. [It. *arioso*].

A-RIOT, [a-rī'-ot], *adv.* in riotous fashion. [A (3) and RIOT].

ARISE, (**arose, arisen**), [a-rīz'], *v i.* to rise up, appear; (*fig.*) to develop, come about. [OE. *arisan*].

ARISTA, (*pl.* **aristæ**), [a-ris'-ta], *n.* (*bot.*) the beard or awn of grain, etc.; (*zool.*) the fibril on the edge of fishes' gills. [L. *arista*].

ARISTARCH, [a'-ris-tahk], *n.* a stern critic. [*Aristarkhos* a Gk. critic of Homer].

ARISTARCHIAN, [a'-ris-tahk'-i-an], *adj.* very critical.

ARISTATE, [a-ris'-tāt], *adj.* having awns; bearded. [ARISTA].

ARISTOCRACY, [a'-ris-tok'-ras-i], *n.* the government of a state by its best citizens, a state governed by such citizens; the nobles, those distinguished in lineage and inheritance, those succeeding to title or great estate; (*fig.*) the best people in any sphere. [Gk. *aristokrateia* rule by the best].

ARISTOCRAT, [a'-ris-tō-krat], *n.* a member of the aristocracy, a noble. [Fr. *aristocrate* a French Revolution formation].

ARISTOCRATIC, [a'-ris-tō-krat'-ik], *adj.* being or behaving like an aristocrat, showing well-bred haughtiness to inferiors. [Gk. *aristokratikos*].

ARISTOCRATICAL, [a'-ris-tō-krat'-ik-al], *adj.* aristocratic. [*Prec.*].

ARISTOCRATICALLY, [a'-ris-tō-krat'-ik-al-i], *adv.* in the manner of an aristocrat or aristocracy.

ARISTOCRATISM, [a'-ris-tok'-rat-izm], *n.* the principles and fashions of aristocracy.

ARISTOTELIAN, [a'-ris-tō-tē'-li-an], *adj.* relating to the teachings of Aristotle. [*Aristoteles* a Greek philosopher].

ARISTOTELIANISM, [a'-ris-tō-tē'-li-an-izm], *n.* the theories and doctrines of Aristotle.

ARISTOTELIC, [a'-ris-tō-tel'-ik], *adj.* Aristotelian.

ARITHMANCY, [a-rith'-man-si], *n.* divination by numbers. [ARITHMOMANCY].

ARITHMETIC (1), [a-rith'-met-ik], *n.* the science of numbers; the art of counting, computing or calculating. [Gk. *arithmetike*].

ARITHMETIC (2), [a'-rith-met'-ik], *adj.* arithmetical. [Gk. *arithmetikos*].

ARITHMETICAL, [a'-rith-met'-ikl], *adj.* pertaining to arithmetic; **a. progression,** a series of numbers increasing or decreasing by equal quantities, as 4, 7, 10, 13, 16 and 15, 10, 5, etc.

ARITHMETICALLY, [a'-rith-met'-ik-al-i], *adv.* in arithmetical fashion.

ARITHMETICIAN, [a'-rith-met-ish'-an], *n.* one learned in arithmetic. [Fr. *arithméticien*].

ARITHMOMANCY, [a-rith'-mō-man'-si], *n.* divination by numbers. [Gk. *arithmos* number and *manteia* divination].

ARITHMOMETER, [a'-rith-mom'-it-er], *n.* a calculating machine. [Gk. *arithmos* number and METER].

ARK, [ahk], *n.* a chest, box, coffer; the vessel in which Noah and his family rode safe from the Flood; **A. of the Covenant,** the sacred chest containing the tablets of Moses' Law; **Noah's A.,** a child's toy in the shape of an ark and containing toy animals. [L. *arca* chest].

ARM (1), [ahm], *n.* each of the human limbs attached to the body at the shoulder; part of a garment covering this limb, a sleeve; the part of a chair or seat supporting the arm; a branching-out of the sea, trees, etc.; the part of a lever from the fulcrum to the point where the force is applied; **to keep at arm's length,** to spurn; **to make a long a.,** to reach; **children in arms,** infants who, unable to walk, are carried. [OE. *earm*].

ARM (2), [ahm], *n.* an instrument for fighting, a weapon; power, authority; branch of the fighting services; (*pl.*) military equipment; (*her.*) (*pl.*) heraldic devices; **small arms,** pistols, revolvers; **to be up in arms,** to be roused to activity in indignation; **coat of arms,** an heraldic device; **Sergeant-at-arms,** a mace-bearer who carries out disciplinary measures in the British Houses of Parliament.

ARM (3), [ahm], *v.t.* to furnish with arms; to provide with equipment suitable for a task or situation; to be possessed of some mental, moral, or psychological advantage; *v.i.* to take up arms for oneself, to prepare oneself with the means of war. [L. *armare*].

ARMADA, [ah-mah'-da], *n.* a great fleet, *esp.* that of Philip II of Spain; a great fleet of aircraft. [Span. *armada*].

ARMADILLO, [ahm'-a-dil'-ō], *n.* (*zool.*) a South American edentate protected by hard bony plates. [Span. *armadillo*].

ARMADILLO

ARMAMENT, [ahm'-a'-ment], *n.* a force equipped for war, the equipment and materials of war; (*pl.*) weapons of war owned by the state. [Fr. *armement*, ~ARM (3)].

ARMATURE, [ahm'-a-cher], *n.* armour; a piece of iron connecting the two poles of a magnet; the rotating part of a dynamo or electric motor. [Fr. *armature* from L. *armatura* armour].

ARM-CHAIR, [ahm'-chāer'], *n.* a chair with side supports for the arms; an easy-chair.

ARMED, [ahmd], *adj.* provided with weapons, armoured; (*her.*) having the talons coloured differently from the rest of the body, having claws, talons, etc. [ARM (3)].

ARMENIAN, [ah-mē'-ni-an], *n.* a native of Armenia; *adj.* relating to that country; **A. stone,** lapis lazuli; **A. bole,** a red argillaceous earth used for colouring.

ARMET, [ahm'-et], *n.* a round fifteenth-century helmet with vizor and a large jointed neck-piece. [OFr. *armette*].

ARMFUL, [ahm'-fŏŏl], *n.* the quantity the arms can hold; (*fig.*) a difficult or unwieldy burden, a large quantity.

ARM-HOLE, [ahm'-hōl], *n.* a hole in a garment for the arm to pass through.

ARMIGER, [ahm'-ij-er], *n.* an esquire, a person entitled to bear heraldic arms, an armour-bearer. [L. *armiger*].

ARMET

ARMILLA, (*pl.* **armillae**), [ah-mil'-a], *n.* a bracelet for the arm. [L. *armilla* hoop].

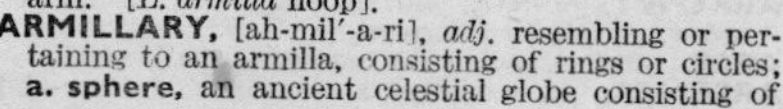

ARMILLARY, [ah-mil'-a-ri], *adj.* resembling or pertaining to an armilla, consisting of rings or circles; **a. sphere,** an ancient celestial globe consisting of a hollow sphere made up of the astronomical circles, and revolving upon its polar axis. [~*Prec.*].

ARMILLATED, [ah'-mil-ā'-tid], *adj.* having bracelets. [ARMILLA].

ARMINIAN (1), [ah-min'i-an], *n.* a follower of the sixteenth-century Dutch theologian Arminius, a believer in free will. [*Arminius*].

ARMINIAN (2), [ah-min'-i-an], *adj.* pertaining to Arminius or his doctrines.

ARMINIANISM, [ah-min'-i-an-izm], *n.* the theology and teachings of Arminius.

ARMIPOTENCE, [ahm-ip'-ot-ens], *n.* power in arms, military strength, valour in arms. [L. *armipotentia*].

ARMIPOTENT, [ahm-i'-pot-ent], *adj.* victorious, strong in battle, fierce in arms. [~L. *armipotens*].

ARMISTICE, [ahm'-is-tis], *n.* a temporary suspension of hostilities by agreement; a truce between armies. [ARM (2) and ~L. *sistere* to stop].

ARMLESS, [ahm'-les], *adj.* without an arm. [ARM (1) and LESS].

ARMLET, [ahm'-let], *n.* an ornament for the arm; a brassard; (*fig.*) a small branch of the sea or a river.

ARMORIAL (1), [ahm-aw'-ri-al], *n.* a book of armorial bearings.

ARMORIAL (2), [ahm-aw'-ri-al], *adj.* (*her.*) pertaining to arms or to the bearing of arms; **a. bearings,** a heraldic device or insignia.

ARMORICAN, [ah-mor'-ik-an], *n.* an ancient Breton; the Breton language. [*Armorica* the old name for Brittany].

ARMORIST, [ahm'-or-ist], *n.* one expert in heraldry.

ARMORY, [ahm'-er-i], *n.* the science of heraldry. [OFr. *armoirie*].

ARMOUR, [ahm'-er], *n.* a covering for the body, of iron or other material, to protect it in fighting; steel plates for the protection of warships and other war machines against hostile ammunition; any protective covering; **a.-piercing,** of bombs, shells, etc., designed to pierce armour-plate before exploding. [OFr. *armeure*, L. *armatara*].

ARMOUR-BEARER, [ahm'-er-bāer'-er], *n.* one who carried his lord's arms.

ARMOUR-CLAD, [ahm'-er-klad'], *adj.* clad in or protected with armour.

ARMOURED, [ahm'-erd], *adj.* provided with armour; **a. cruiser,** a heavily protected cruiser; **a. cable,** an electric wire with an outer protective covering of spirally wound metal tape; **a. car,** a motor vehicle employed in warfare and protected by armour-plate; **a. division,** a division provided with tanks and armoured cars.

ARMOURER, [ahm'-er-er], *n.* a person who makes or looks after armour or arms; (*milit., nav.*) one who has charge of a store of small arms.

ARMOUR-PLATE, [ahm'-er-plāt'], *n.* steel plates protecting warships, forts, or military machines.

ARMOURY, [ahm'-er-i], *n.* a place where arms are stored or repaired. [OFr. *armoirie*].

ARMOZINE, [ahm'-oz-īn], *n.* a strong silk, used in making ecclesiastical vestments. [OFr. *armesin*].

ARMPIT, [ahm'-pit], *n.* the axilla; the hollow underneath the arm at the junction with the trunk. [ARM (1) and PIT].

ARMS, see ARM (2).

ARMY, [ahm'-i], *n.* a body of armed men organized under one commander for warlike purposes on land; an armed force; any large body of people organized for a particular purpose; a crowd of people, a multitude; **a. corps,** (*milit.*, Brit.) a section of an army consisting of several divisions complete with auxiliary services; **a. list,** the official list of commissioned officers in the army; **standing a.,** a military force in service in time of peace. [Fr. *armée*].

ARMY-WORM, [ahm'-i-wurm'], *n.* larva of the fungus-midge, *Sciara militaris.*

ARNAUT, [ah-nowt], *n.* an inhabitant of the Albanian mountains. [Turk. *arnaut*].

ARNICA, [ah'-nik-a], *n.* a genus of plants including mountain tobacco, *Arnica montana*; a drug or liniment for bruises made from this plant. [Unkn.].

ARNOTTO, [ah-not'-ō], *n.* annatto.

AROID, [āer'-oid], *n.* (*bot.*) a plant akin to the arum. [ARUM and Gk. *oeides* like].

AROINT†, [a-roint'], *int.* Be off! Away with you! [OE. *geryme the* make yourself scarce].

AROMA, [a-rō'-ma], *n.* fragrance, perfume, a pleasant odour; the fragrance of plants; (*fig.*) characteristic atmosphere of something. [Gk. *aroma* spice].

AROMATIC (1), [a'-rō-mat'-ik], *n.* a drug having aromatic qualities.

AROMATIC (2), [a'-rō-mat'-ik], *adj.* spicy, fragrant, having a warm, pungent taste or smell. [Fr. *aromatique* from Gk. *aromatikos*].

AROMATITE, [a-rō'-mat-īt], *n.* (*min.*) a mineral resembling myrrh; a wine containing aromatics. [AROMA].

AROMATIZATION, [a-rō'-mat-iz-ā'-shun], *n.* the act or state of aromatizing.

AROMATIZE, [a-rō'-mat-īz], *v.t.* to make aromatic, impregnate with an aroma. [Gk. *aromatizo* I spice].

AROMATIZER, [a-rō'-mat-īz-er], *n.* a person or thing that aromatizes.

AROSE, [a-rōz'], *pret.* of ARISE. [OE. *aras*].

AROUND (1), [a-rownd'], *adv.* round about, in circles, in the neighbourhood.

AROUND (2), [a-rownd'], *prep.* about, surrounding, in the neighbourhood of.

AROUSE, [a-rowz'], *v.t.* to rouse up, stir, excite; to awaken from sleep or lethargy, incite to activity. [A (3) and ROUSE].

AROW, [a-rō'], *adv.* in a row; in order. [A (3) and ROW (1)].

ARPEGGIO, [ah-pej'-i-ō], *n.* (*mus.*) the sounding of the notes in a chord in quick succession from below upwards as if on a harp, instead of simultaneously; the distinct sound of the notes in an instrumental chord. [It. *arpeggio* from *arpeggiare* to play the harp].

ARQUEBUS, [ah'-kwi-bus], *n.* a primitive type of hand-gun, having a large bore and being fired from a rest to which it was attached by a hook. [It. *archibuso* from MHGerm. *hakenbusche* hook gun].

ARQUEBUSADE, [ah'-kwib-us-ād'], *n.* fire from arquebuses; (*med.*) a distilled curative water.

ARQUEBUSIER, [ah'-kwi-bew'-si-er], *n.* a man armed with an arquebus.

ARQUERITE, [ah'-ker-īt], *n.* (*min.*) a natural amalgam of silver found in Chile. [*Arqueros* a place in Chile].

ARQUIFOUX, [ah'-ki-fōō], *n.* a lead-ore used by potters. [Fr. *arquifoux*].

ARRACACHA, [a'-ra-kah'-cha], *n.* (*bot.*) a tropical American umbelliferous plant with edible roots, *Arracacha esculenta*. [Native].

ARRACH†, see ORACH.

ARRACK, [a'-rak], *n.* an Eastern spirit distilled from rice or molasses. [Arab. *arak* sweat].

ARRAGONITE, see ARAGONITE.

ARRAIGN, [a-rān'], *v.t.* (*leg.*) to accuse or indict on a criminal charge; to call to account, to charge, to call in question. [ME. *areinen* from AFr. *arainer*].

ARRAIGNER, [a-rān'-er], *n.* one who arraigns.

ARRAIGNMENT, [a-rān'-ment], *n.* the action of indicting, process of being arraigned; charge, accusation.

ARRANGE, [a-rānj'], *v.t.* to set in order for a purpose, to sort, adjust, settle, classify; to make preparations and prepare means for a thing; to fix the course of some event in advance; (*mus.*) to adapt; *v.i.* to come to agreement, adjust matters in advance. [OFr. *arangier*].

ARRANGEMENT, [a-rānj'-ment], *n.* the act of arranging, order, the state of things put in order; preparations for carrying out a thing, agreement or settlement, compromise, or understanding; (*mus.*) the adaptation of a musical score.

ARRANT, [a'-rant], *adj.* erring, notorious; complete, thorough. [ERRANT].

ARRANTLY, [a'-rant-li], *adv.* in an arrant manner.

ARRAS, [a'-ras], *n.* tapestry, wall-hangings of tapestry or similar material. [*Arras* a French town].

ARRAY (1), [a-rā'], *n.* a line of battle, a mass of troops, a large body set in order, an organized splendour for show or pageantry; a rich and splendid dress, ornaments of a splendid kind; (*leg.*) an impanelled jury.

ARRAY (2), [a-rā'], *v.t.* to set out in order, to draw up a body of troops in formation; to deck out, dress splendidly; (*leg.*) to impanel a jury. [ME. *arraien* from OFr. *araier*].

ARREAR, [a-rēer'], *n.* (of obligations) that which remains to be done; an overdue payment of a regular series; **in arrears**, in debt. [OFr. *arere* from LL. *ad retro* backwards].

ARREARAGE, [a-rēer'-ij], *n.* money overdue, a payment in arrears.

ARRECT, [a-rekt'], *adj.* attentive. [L. *arrectus* erected].

ARRENTATION, [a'-ren-tā'-shun], *n.* leave to enclose forest land in return for an annual rent. [MedL. *arrentatio*].

ARREST (1), [a-rest'], *n.* retardation or stoppage of motion, check; (*leg.*) seizure and detention of a person on a criminal or other charge, apprehension; **under a.**, detained by a legal authority; **a. of judgment**, a stopping of legal proceedings. [OFr. *areste*].

ARREST (2), [a-rest'], *v.t.* to stop check, hinder; (*leg.*) to seize and detain on legal grounds, to apprehend; (*fig.*) to seize, attract. [OFr. *arester* to stop].

ARRESTATION, [a'-res-tā'-shun], *n.* a stopping; an arrest.

ARRESTING, [a-rest'-ing], *adj.* striking, drawing the attention.

ARRESTIVE, [a-rest'-iv], *adj.* tending to draw the attention, arresting.

ARRESTMENT, [a-rest'-ment], *n.* a stopping, check, delay; (*Scots leg.*) apprehension, seizing of a person.

ARRET, arrêt, [a-rā', a-ret'], *n.* the decision of a court or council; the edict of a sovereign prince. [Fr. *arrêt*].

ARRIDE†, [a-rīd'], *v.t.* to laugh scornfully at a person; to gratify. [L. *arridere* to smile on].

ARRIERE, arrière, [a-ri-āer'], *n.* (*her.*) the back; **a.-ban**, a general proclamation of the French kings by which both their vassals and their tenants were called to arms. [OFr. *ariere-ban* from OG. *hari-ban* army edict].

ARRIS, [a'-ris], *n.* the line at which two planes meet to form an exterior angle; a sharp edge. [OFr. *areste* from L. *arista* ear of corn].

ARRISWISE, [a'-ris-wīz], *adv.* in a sharp edge, like a ridge.

ARRIVAL, [a-rīv'-al], *n.* the act of arriving, of coming to a place; the coming to its destination of a ship, train, or other means of conveyance; a person who arrives. [AFr. *arrivaille*].

ARRIVE, [a-rīv'], *v.i.* to come to a destination, to come to a place, to come to a conclusion; (*coll.*) to achieve success. [OFr. *ariver* from LL. *arripare* to come to shore].

ARROBA, [a-rō'-ba], *n.* an Iberian and South American weight equal to about 25 pounds; a Spanish wine-measure of about 3 gallons. [Span. *arroba*].

ARROGANCE, [a'-rog-ans], *n.* insolent pride or conceit, haughty bearing of authority, overbearing display of superiority. [L. *arrogantia*].

ARROGANT, [a'-rog-ant], *adj.* insolently superior, fiercely proud, overbearing, haughtily self-assertive. [~L. *arrogans* claiming for oneself].

ARROGANTLY, [a'-rog-ant-li], *adv.* in an arrogant manner.

ARROGATE, [a'-rog-āt], *v.t.* to make undue or excessive claims to power, place or importance, to usurp an undeserved superiority; to attribute. [~L. *arrogare*].

ARROGATION, [a'-rog-ā'-shun], *n.* the act of arrogating. [L. *arrogatio*].

ARROGATIVE, [a-rog'-at-iv], *adj.* tending to, pertaining to arrogance or arrogation.

ARRONDI, [a'-ron-dē], *adj.* (*her.*) rounded. [~Fr. *arrondir* to make round].

ARRONDI

ARRONDISSEMENT, [a'-ron-dēs'-mong], *n.* an administrative district of a department in France. [*Prec.*].

ARROSION, [a-rō'-zhun], *n.* corroding, or eating away. [~L. *arrodere* to gnaw at].

ARROW, [a'-rō], *n.* a straight, sharp-pointed stick (barbed at the point, feathered at the tail) made to be shot from a bow; an object resembling this; a sign indicating direction; **broad a.**, a mark shaped like the head of an arrow and used to signify ownership by the British Government. [~OE. *earh*].

ARROW-HEAD, [a'-rō-hed'], *n.* the metal, bone, or flint head of an arrow; anything resembling this in shape; (*bot.*) an aquatic plant with arrow-shaped leaves, *Sagittaria*.

ARROW-HEADED, [a'-rō-hed'-id], *adj.* shaped like an arrow-head; like any ancient characters resembling cuneiform.

ARROWROOT, [a'-rō-rōōt], *n.* an edible farinaceous substance, made from the roots of various species of *Maranta*, used by Indians to cure poisoned arrow wounds. [ARROW and ROOT].

ARROW-SHAPED, [a'-rō-shāpt'], *adj.* in the shape of an arrow.

ARROWY, [a'-rō-i], *adj.* moving, shaped like an arrow, pertaining to arrows.

ARSE, [ahs], *n.* (*vulg.*) the buttocks. [OE. *ears*].

ARSENAL, [ah'-sen-al], *n.* a government factory and

store for arms; **the A.,** a famous London football club. [It. *arsenale* from Arab.].

ARSENATE, [ah'-sen-āt], *n.* the salt formed by arsenic acid combined with a chemical base.

ARSENIC, [ah'-sen-ik], *n.* (*chem.*) a greyish brittle metal, the chemical element denoted by As ; (*pop.*) arsenious anhydrite, also called white arsenic [L. *arsenicum* from Gk. *arsenikon* yellow pigment].

ARSENICAL, [ah-sen'-ikl], *adj.* containing arsenic.

ARSENICATE, [ah-sen'-ik-āt], *v.t.* to compound with arsenic.

ARSENIOUS, [ah-sē'-ni-us], *adj.* (*chem.*) containing arsenic as a triad in chemical compounds; **a. acid,** white arsenic.

ARSENITE, [ah'-sen-īt], *n.* a salt produced by the combination of arsenious acid with a base.

ARSENIURET, [ah-sen'-yōō-ret], *n.* (*chem.*) a compound of arsenic with a metallic or other base.

ARSHIN, [ah-shēn'], *n.* an East European measure of about 2⅓ feet. [Turk. *arshin*].

ARSINE, [ah'-sēn], *n.* (*chem.*) hydride of arsenic. [ARS(ENIC) and (AM)INE].

ARSIS, (*pl.* **arses**), [ah'-sis], *n.* (*pros.*) the (un)accented part of the foot in classical verse; the stressed syllable in English verse; (*mus.*) the raising of the hand in beating time. [Gk. *arsis* lift].

ARSON, [ah'-son], *n.* the wilful and malicious burning of property. [OFr. *arson* from LL. *arsio*].

ART (1), [aht], *n.* craft or skill employed by man to do or make a thing, or to produce or improve a quality; skill or aptitude in aesthetics or in certain crafts; a branch of aesthetics itself; the organized general principles of many crafts, sciences and activities; cunning, skill in deception, a person's skill and subtlety generally; (*pl.*) occupations requiring sensibility, ingenuity, or intellect, primarily the fine arts such as poetry, painting, sculpture, music, architecture; secondarily the useful arts as of manufacture or the household, etc., third the purely intellectual arts such as mathematics, dialectics, pure chemistry, etc.; (*fig.*) wiles, tricks; academic term for all courses of study except the sciences and economics; **black arts,** black magic, alchemy; **Bachelor of Arts, Master of Arts,** graduates of British Universities qualified in humanistic branches of learning. [~L. *ars artes*].

ART (2), [aht], (*archaic*) *2nd pers. sg. pres. ind.* of BE.

ARTEL, [aht'-el], *n.* a guild of workers, undertaking work and sharing the profits. (Russ. *artel*].

ARTEMISIA, [ah'-ti-mi'-si-a], *n.* (*bot.*) a genus of plants including southernwood and wormwood. [Gk. *artemisia*].

ARTERIAL, [ah-tēer'-i-al], *adj.* pertaining to the arteries; **a. road,** a main-road between important centres. [ARTERY].

ARTERIALIZATION, [ah-tēer'-i-al-īz-ā'-shun], *n.* the making of arterial roads; (*med.*) the process of arterializing.

ARTERIALIZE, [ah-tēer'-i-al-īz], *v.t.* to change venous blood into arterial blood by its contact with oxygen.

ARTERIOGRAPH, [ah-tēer'-i-ō-graf'], *n.* a chart of the arteries. [ARTERY and GRAPH].

ARTERIOLE, [ah-tēer'-i-ōl], *n.* a lesser artery. [ARTERY].

ARTERIOLOGY, [ah'-tēer-i-ol'-o-ji], *n.* the study of the arteries. [ARTERY and Gk. *logos* speech].

ARTERIO-SCLEROSIS, [ah-teer'-i-ō-skler-ō'-sis], *n.* a disease of the arteries in which the walls are hardened and thickened. [Gk. *arteria* windpipe and *sklerosis* hardening].

ARTERIOTOMY, [ah'-tēer-i-ot'-o-mi], *n.* (*med.*) the cutting open or dissection of an artery. [Gk. *arteriotomia*].

ARTERY, [ah'-ter-i], *n.* one of the vascular tubes carrying blood from the heart to all parts of the body; (*fig.*) an important channel of communication. [Gk. *arteria* windpipe].

ARTESIAN, [ah-tē'-zi-an], *adj.* pertaining to Artois; **a. well,** a well bored to a lower stratum than the water's source, so as to obtain a continual upward flow. [OFr. *Arteis* the former French province].

ARTFUL, [aht'-fōōl], *adj.* cunning, crafty in a petty fashion, full of tricks, ingenious.

ARTFULLY, [aht'-fōōl-i], *adv.* in an artful fashion.

ARTFULNESS, [aht'-fōōl-nes], *n.* the quality of being artful.

ARTHRITIC, [ah-thrit'-ik] *adj.* pertaining to, or suffering from arthritis. [Gk. *arthritikos*].

ARTHRITIS, [ah-thrī'-tis], *n.* inflammation of the joints. [Gk. *arthritis* from *arthron* a joint].

ARTHRODIA, [ah-thrō'-di-a], *n.* articulation in which the head of one bone is received in the socket of another. [Gk. *arthrodia* good articulation].

ARTHRODIC, [ah-thrō'-dik], *adj.* pertaining to arthrodia.

ARTHRODYNIC, [ah'-thrō-dīn'-ik], *adj.* pertaining to a painful disease of the joints. [Gk. *arthron* and *odune* pain].

ARTHROLOGY, [ah-throl'-o-ji], *n.* (*anat.*) the science and study of the joints. [Gk. *arthron* joint and *logos* speech].

ARTHROPODA, [ah-throp'-o-da], *n.*(*pl.*) animals having jointed limbs, including insects, spiders and crustaceans. [Gk. *arthron* joint and *pous podos* foot].

ARTICHOKE, [ah'-ti-chōk], *n.* a species of vegetable, *Cynara*, akin to the thistle; **Jerusalem a.,** a species of sunflower with edible roots, *Helianthus tuberosus*. [It. *articiocco* from Arab. *alkharshuf*].

ARTICHOKE

ARTICLE (1), [ah'-tikl], *n.* an object distinct from others of a class, an item; a commodity of merchandise; a prose contribution on a subject published in a periodical; a tenet of belief; (*leg.*) an item in a legal document or contract; (*bot.*) part of a stem between two joints; (*gram.*) a definite or indefinite demonstrative adjective; **articles of association,** (*leg.*) a statement of the conditions under which a legally constituted association operates; **leading a.,** principal article in a newspaper, expressing editorial policy; **thirty-nine articles,** tenets of the Church of England set out as an appendix to the Book of Common Prayer. [L. *articulus* from *artus* joint].

ARTICLE (2), [ah'-tikl], *v.t.* to draw up in separate details; to bind by article of agreement, to enumerate charges in articles.

ARTICLED, [ah'-tikld], *adj.* (of apprentices, solicitors' clerks, etc.) bound by a legal agreement or articles to learn a trade or profession.

ARTICULAR, [ah-tik'-yōō-ler], *adj.* pertaining to the joints; jointed. [L. *articularis*].

ARTICULARLY, [ah-tik'-yōō-ler-li], *adv.* in an articular or articulate fashion.

ARTICULATE (1), [ah-tik'-yōō-lat], *adj.* having joints; composed of distinguishable syllables and words; (*fig.*) having the power of speech, expressed in articles. [L. *articulatus*].

ARTICULATE (2), [ah-tik'-yōō-lāt], *v.t. and i.* to unite by a joint; to utter a sound clearly and distinctly; to form into separate and distinct sounds; to speak clearly and with good enunciation. [*Prec.*].

ARTICULATELY, [ah-tik'-yōō-lat-li], *adv.* in articulate fashion.

ARTICULATENESS, [ah-tik'-yōō-lat-nes], *n.* the state of being articulate.

ARTICULATION, [ah-tik'-yōō-lā'-shun], *n.* the act or method of jointing; manner of speaking, speech; clear enunciation, distinct utterance; (*anat.*) a joint between two bones; (*bot.*) junction of separable parts of plants. [~L. *articulatio*].

ARTICULATOR, [ah-tik'-yōō-lāt'-or], *n.* one who articulates, a prosector; a dental instrument for ensuring proper connexion between artificial teeth.

ARTIFACT, [ah'-ti-fakt], *n.* a primitive object shaped by intelligent direction, as opposed to an object of use formed naturally. [ART (1) and L. *factus* made].

ARTIFICE, [ah'-ti-fis], *n.* an ingenious device, a trick; a cunning or deceptive contrivance. [L. *artificium* skill].

ARTIFICER, [ah'-ti-fis-er, ah-tif'-i-ser], *n.* a skilled workman, a mechanic; an inventor; (*nav.*) an engineer with petty officer's rank. [*Prec.*].

ARTIFICIAL, [ah'-ti-fish'-al], *adj.* made by art, not natural; contrived as a substitute for something real or genuine, imitation; (of persons) unnatural, constrained, shallow; false; **a. respiration,** inducement by force of breathing in suffocated persons. [L. *artificialis*].

ARTIFICIALITY, [ah'-ti-fish-i-al'-i-ti], *n.* the condition of being artificial; artificial behaviour or appearance; (*fig.*) unnaturalness; insincerity.

ARTIFICIALIZE, [ah'-ti-fish'-al-īz], *v.t.* to render artificial.

ō (bone), ī (fine), ōō (food), ŏŏ (put), u (up), th (*th*ink), TH (*th*at), zh (azure), † = obsolete, ~ = related to.

ARTIFICIALLY, [ah'-ti-fish'-al-i], *adv.* in artificial fashion.
ARTIFICIALNESS, [ah'-ti-fish'-al-nes], *n.* the condition of being artificial.
ARTILLERIST, [ah-til'-er-ist], *n.* one skilled in artillery.
ARTILLERY, [ah-til'-er-i], *n.* missile-throwing weapons larger than can be carried and fired by a single soldier; ordnance, the equipment required for its transport and discharge; troops by whom the weapons are worked; the science of gunnery; (*fig.*) arguments of an overwhelming sort; **field a.,** light guns attached to the forward troops; **a. train,** artillery grouped and ordered for transport. [OFr. *artillerie* weapons of war].
ARTILLERYMAN, [ah-til'-er-i-man], *n.* a soldier serving in the artillery.
ARTINESS, [ah'-ti-nes], *n.* the quality of being arty.
ARTIODACTYL, (*pl.* **artiodactyla**), [ah'-ti-ō-dak'-til], *n.* an even-toed ungulate, e.g., the hippopotamus. [Gk. *artios* even-numbered and *daktulos* toe].
ARTISAN, [ah'-tiz-an'], *n.* one skilled in a trade or mechanical art; a handicraftsman, manual worker. [Fr. *artisan*].
ARTIST, [ah'-tist], *n.* one skilled in a fine art, such as painting or drawing; a performer in an entertainment; one following an aesthetic pursuit; one taking intense and precise care over a thing for its own sake; one having aesthetic sensibility. [Fr. *artiste*].
ARTISTE, [ah-tēst'], *n.* (*coll.*) a music-hall or radio performer, etc. [Fr. *artiste*].
ARTISTIC, [ah-tis'-tik], *a.* having aesthetic sensibility; skilful in one of the fine arts; (*coll.*) (of an object) pleasing or tasteful in appearance; **a. temperament,** the temperament responsible for the alleged irrational behaviour of artists. [Fr. *artistique*].
ARTISTICALLY, [ah-tis'-tik-a-li], *adv.* in artistic fashion.
ARTISTRY, [ah'-tis-tri], *n.* artistic skill; (of conduct or action) attention to the smallest details so as to make an artistic whole.
ARTLESS, [aht'-les], *adj.* lacking art, guileless; natural, sincere; simple, innocent, unsophisticated.
ARTLESSLY, [aht'-les-li], *adv.* in artless fashion.
ARTLESSNESS, [aht'-les-nes], *n.* the state of being artless.
ARTOCARPAD, [ah'-tō-kahp'-ad], *n.* (*bot.*) the bread-fruit tree, *Artocarpus incisa.* [Gk. *artos* bread and *karpos* fruit].
ARTY, [ah'-ti], *adj.* (*coll.*) affecting singularities in dress or behaviour such as are popularly attributed to artists; **a. crafty,** showing artiness *esp.* in handicrafts.
ARUM, [āer'-um], *n.* the genus of plants including the wake-robin; **a. lily,** the white lily, a kind of *Richardia.* [Gk. *aron* reed].
ARUNDELIAN, [ar'-run-dē'-li-an], *adj.* pertaining to Arundel or the Earl thereof; pertaining to the Grecian marbles at Oxford collected by a former Earl. [*Arundel* in Sussex].
ARUNDINACEOUS, [a-rund'-i-nā'-shus], *adj.* relating to reeds, reedy. [L. *aharundo* reed].
ARUSPEX, [a'-roo-speks'], *n.* a soothsayer. [L. *haruspex*].
ARUSPICY, see HARUSPICY.
ARYAN (1), [āer'-i-an], *n.* an Indo-European; (*pop.*) a non-Jewish north European; a virile, fair-haired person; the hypothetical prototype of the Indo-European languages.
ARYAN (2), [āer'-i-an], *adj.* belonging to the Indo-European family of languages; (*pop.*) nobly Germanic; Nordic. [Skr. *arya* noble].
ARYTENOID, [ar'-i-tē'-noid], *adj.* cup-shaped, of the cartilages regulating the vocal chords in the larynx. [Gk. *arutainoeides* funnel-shaped].
AS (1), [as], *n.* the Roman pound of twelve ounces; a large coin of Republican Rome. [L. *as*].

AS

AS (2), [az], *adv., conj., and rel. pron.* like to, equal to; in the capacity of; in the aspect or having the appearance of; in the circumstances, since; because of; for instance; resembling; in relation to; though, when, while. [OE. *alswa*].
ASAFŒTIDA, ASSAFETIDA, [as'-a-fē-tid-a], *n.* a gum derived from the plant *Ferula asa-fœtida* and used as a cathartic. [Pers. *aza* resin and L. *foetidus* stinking].
ASARABACCA, [as'-ah-rab-ak'-a], *n.* a plant with bitter nauseous leaves used emetically and for snuff. [L. *asarum* hazelwort and *bacca* berry].
ASARIN, [as'-ar-in], *n.* a crystalline substance resembling camphor extracted from asarabacca. [~L. *asarum*].
ASBESTIC, [as-bes'-tik], *adj.* pertaining to asbestos.
ASBESTIFORM, [as-bes'-ti-fawm], *adj.* resembling asbestos in structure. [ASBESTOS and FORM].
ASBESTINE, [as-bes'-tīn], *adj.* like asbestos, non-inflammable.
ASBESTINITE, [as-bes'-tin-īt], *n.* actinolite or strahlstein; **calciferous a.,** a kind of actinolite.
ASBESTINIZED, [as-bes'-tin-īzd], *adj.* made incombustible.
ASBESTOID, [as-bes'-toid], *adj.* resembling asbestos. [ASBESTOS and Gk. *oeides* like].
ASBESTOS, [as-bes'-tos], *n.* an incombustible greyish-white fibrous mineral capable of being woven into fabric, and used in making fire-proof material or articles. [Gk. *asbestos* unquenchable].
ASBESTOUS, [as-bes'-tus], *adj.* asbestic.
ASBOLIN, [as'-bol-in], *n.* a bitter, yellow oil extracted from soot. [Gk. *asbole* soot].
ASCARIDES, [as-ka'-rid-ēz], *n.(pl.)* intestinal thread-worms. [Gk. *askaris*].
ASCEND, [a-send'], *v.t.* to climb, to get up or up to something; *v.i.* to move upwards, to go up, rise, come to a higher level; to rise in rank; (*mus.*) to rise in pitch. [L. *ascendere*].
ASCENDABLE, [a-send'-abl], *adj.* able to be ascended.
ASCENDANCY, ASCENDENCY, [a-send'-en-si], *n.* power, controlling influence, superiority, domination.
ASCENDANT (1), ASCENDENT†, [a-send'-ant], *n.* (*astrol.*) the sign of the zodiac that is just above the horizon at any particular time; †commanding influence, superiority; **in the a.,** becoming more important or influential.
ASCENDANT (2), ASCENDENT†, [a-send'-ant], *adj.* ascending, rising; dominating, having superiority; rising; (*astrol.*) having influence; (*astron.*) above the horizon. [~L. *ascendens*].
ASCENSION, [a-sen'-shun], *n.* the action of moving upwards, an ascending; Christ's ascent to Heaven; **A.-day,** a festival commemorating this on the sixth Thursday after Easter. [~L. *ascensio*].
ASCENSIONTIDE, [a-sen'-shun-tīd], *n.* the ten days between Ascension-day and Whitsun.
ASCENSIVE, [a-sen'-siv], *adj.* rising, likely to ascend.
ASCENT, [a-sent'], *n.* the act of ascending; slope of a hill; an upward way or path. [ASCEND].
ASCERTAIN, [as'-er-tān'], *v.t.* to find out, determine discover accurately. [OFr. *acertener*].
ASCERTAINABLE, [as'-er-tān'-abl], *adj.* able to be ascertained.
ASCERTAINMENT, [as'-er-tān'-ment], *n.* the act of ascertaining. [OFr. *acertenement*].
ASCESSENT, see ACESCENT.
ASCETIC (1), [a-set'-ik], *n.* one who pursues a life of asceticism.
ASCETIC (2), [a-set'-ik], *adj.* pertaining to asceticism or an ascetic, self-denying as to the more carnal pleasures. [Gk. *asketikos*].
ASCETICAL, [a-set'-ikl], *adj.* relating to asceticism.
ASCETICALLY, [a-set'-ik-al-i], *adv.* in ascetical fashion.
ASCETICISM, [a-set'-is-izm], *n.* the denial or suppression of bodily pleasures and appetites, the voluntary pursuit of an austere, frugal life; mortification of the flesh.
ASCI, [as'-sī], *n.(pl.)* see ASCUS.
ASCIANS, [ash'-i-anz], *n.* inhabitants of the torrid zone, whose bodies cast no shadow at noon twice a year, when the sun is in its zenith. [Gk. *askios* shadowless].
ASCIDIANS, [a-sid'-i-anz], *n.(pl.)* (*zool.*) a group of partially vertebrate molluscs, including the sea-squirt, whose outer covering is leathery. [Gk. *askidion* little bag].
ASCIDIFORM, [a-sid'-i-fawm], *adj.* (*bot.*) bottle-shaped. [ASCIDIUM and FORM].
ASCIDIUM, (*pl.* **ascidia**), [a-sid'-i-um], *n.* (*zool.*) one of the group of Ascidians; (*bot.*) a bag-shaped appendage on the leaves of certain plants. [ASCIDIANS].
ASCITES, [a-sī'-tēz], *n.* (*med.*) morbid fluid accumulation in the peritoneum. [Gk. *askites*].
ASCITIC, [a-sit'-ik], *adj.* pertaining to or having ascites.
ASCLEPIAD (1), [as-klē'-pi-ad], *n.* (*pros.*) a verse

having a spondee, a choriambus, and two dactyls. [*Asklepiades* a Greek poet].
ASCLEPIAD (2), [as-klē′-pi-ad], *n.* (*bot.*) a plant of the order *Asclepiadaceae*.
ASCLEPIADACEOUS, [as-klē′-pi-a-dā′-shus], *adj.* (*bot.*) pertaining to the order of Asclepiads. [ASCLEPIAD (2)].
ASCLEPIADAEAN, [as-klē′-pi-ad-ē′-an], *adj.* (*pros.*) asclepiadic.
ASCLEPIADIC, [as-klē′-pi-ad-ik], *adj.* (*pros.*) relating to, or resembling, an asclepiad. [ASCLEPIAD (1)].
ASCRIBABLE, [a-skrī′-ba-bl], *adj.* capable of being attributed, due.
ASCRIBE, [a-skrīb′], *v.t.* to impute, attribute, assign. [L. *ascribere*].
ASCRIPTION, [a-skrip′-shun], *n.* the act of ascribing; a statement or declaration that ascribes. [~L. *ascriptio*].
ASCUS, (*pl.* **asci**), [as′-kus], *n.* (*bot.*) the spore cell. [Gk. *askos* bag].
ASEITY, [a-sē′-it-i], *n.* (*met.*) independent origin and existence; God's quality of being His own First Cause. [L. *a* from and *se* oneself].
ASEPSIS, [ā′-sep′-sis, a-sep′-sis], *n.* state of wounds in which there is no pus. [A (4) and Gk. *sepsis* decay].
ASEPTIC, [a-sep′-tik], *adj.* free from pus. [*Prec.*].
ASEXUAL, [ā-sek′-shōō-al], *adj.* without sex or sexual organs; (*fig.*) frigid. [A (4) and SEXUAL].
ASEXUALITY, [a-sek-shōō-al′-it-i], *n.* the state or quality of having no sex. [A (4) and SEXUALITY].
ASEXUALLY, [a-sek′-shōō-al-i], *adv.* in an asexual manner.
ASH (1), [ash], *n.* the tree, *Fraxinus excelsior*; the wood of the ash-tree; **mountain a.**, the rowan tree, *Pyrus aucuparia*. [OE. *æsc*].
ASH (2), [ash], *n.* (usually in *pl.*), the greyish powdery material left after combustion; **A. Wednesday**, the first day of Lent when in the Roman Catholic Church ashes are sprinkled on the head. [OE. *æsce*].
ASH (3), [ash], *adj.* made from ash wood. [ASH (1)].
ASHAME†, [a-shām′], *v.t.* to put to shame. [OE. *ascamian*].
ASHAMED, [a-shāmd′], *adj.* moved by shame, abashed, feeling moral embarrassment, disconcerted by some guilty emotion. [*Prec.*].
ASHAMEDLY, [a-shām′-ed-li], *adv.* in an ashamed manner.
ASHEN (1), [ash′-en], *adj.* pertaining to or made of ash. [ASH (1)].
ASHEN (2), [ash′-en], *adj.* pertaining to ash; having the colour of ashes; pale, grey. [ASH (2)].
ASHES, [ash′-iz], *n.*(*pl.*) the residue of something burnt; the remains of a cremated corpse; (*pop.*) the result of a series of cricket matches between England and Australia, originally from a mock obituary in the *Sporting Times* of 1882 after Australia's victory; **in sackcloth and a.**, in repentant abasement; **to turn to dust and a.**, to destroy, thwart. [ASH (2)].
ASH-FLY, [ash′-flī′], *n.* the oak-fly.
ASH-HOLE, [ash′-hōl], *n.* a place for receiving ashes, the bottom of a furnace.
ASHIVER, [a-shiv′-er], *adv.* in a shiver, cold. [A (3) and SHIVER].
ASHLAR, [ash′-ler], *n.* hewn stones used for facing walls; (*arch.*) a facing of wrought and squared stones. [OFr. *aisseler*, ~L. *axis* plank].
ASHLARING, [ash′-ler-ing], *n.* a low wall of timbering in a roof to close off the angle between the floor and the rafters; ashlar stonework.
ASHLING, [ash′-ling], *n.* a young ash. [ASH (1)].
ASHORE, [a-shaw(r)′], *adv.* on shore, towards the shore. [A (3) and SHORE].
ASH-PAN, [ash′-pan′], *n.* a pan beneath a fire-grate to receive ashes.
ASH-PIT, [ash′-pit′], *n.* an ash-hole.
ASH-TRAY, [ash′-trā′], *n.* a small dish for tobacco-ash.
ASHY, [ash′-i], *adj.* pertaining to ashes. [ASH (2)].
ASIAN†, [ā′-shun], *adj.* Asiatic. [Gk. *asianos*].
ASIATIC (1), [ā′-shi-at′-ik], *n.* a native of Asia.
ASIATIC (2), [ā′-shi-at′-ik], *adj.* pertaining to Asia. [Gk. *asiatikos* from Gk. *Asia* a region in Lydia].
ASIATICISM, [ā-shi-at′-is-izm], *n.* imitation or affectation of Asiatic customs; effeminacy, cowardice.
ASIDE (1), [a-sīd′], *n.* a confidential remark slipped in between open statements, particularly a personal remark exchanged by actors or public speakers during the performance.
ASIDE (2), [a-sīd′], *adv.* on or to one side, out of mind, apart, away from the direct course, away from immediate use.
ASINEGO†, [as′-in-ē′-gō], *n.* small ass. [Span. *asnico*].
ASININE, [as′-in-īn], *n.* pertaining to the ass; (*fig.*) stupid, silly. [L. *asininus* from *asinus* ass].
ASININITY, [as′-in-in′-it-i], *n.* the state or quality of being asinine.
ASIPHONATE, [a-sī′-fon-at], *adj.* without a siphon. [A (4) and SIPHON].
ASK, [ahsk], *v.t. and i.* to beg or entreat for; to request, inquire; to seek information from; to claim, demand; to invite; to demand as a price; to publish banns. [OE. *ascian*].
ASKANCE, [a-skahns′], *adj.* sideways, obliquely, from the corner of the eye; **to look a. at**, to regard dubiously or with suspicion. [Unkn.].
ASKANT, [a-skant′], *adv.* askance. [*Prec.*].
ASKARI, [as-kah′-ri], *n.* a native African mercenary in the service of his European overlords, *esp.* a Somali in the British or Italian forces. [Arab. *askari* soldier].
ASKER (1), [ask′-er], *n.* a newt.
ASKER (2), [ahsk′-er], *n.* a person who asks.
ASKEW, [as-kew′], *adj.* awry, disordered, unbalanced; out of a straight line, crooked. [Uncert.].
ASLANT, [a-slahnt′], *adv.* askew, obliquely. [A (3) and SLANT (2)].
ASLEEP, [a-slēp′], *adj. and adv.* sleeping, unawakened; dull, unaroused. [OE. *on slæpe*].
ASLOPE, [a-slōp′], *adj. and adv.* sloping, leaning, tilted. [A (3) and SLOPE].
ASMOULDER, [a-smōl′-der], *adv.* smouldering.
ASOAK, [a-sōk′], *adj.* in a soaking condition. [A (3) and SOAK].
ASOMATOUS, [a-sō′-mat-us], *adj.* incorporeal, unsubstantial. [Gk. *asomatos*].
ASP (1), [asp], *n.* a small venomous Egyptian viper, the horned adder; any small poisonous snake. [Gk. *aspis*].
ASP (2), see ASPEN (1).
ASPARAGIN, [a-spa′-ra-jin], *n.* a crystallizable substance contained in asparagus.
ASPARAGINOUS, [as′-pa-raj′-in-us], *adj.* resembling asparagus, pertaining to asparagus.
ASPARAGUS, [a-spa′-ra-gus], *n.* a liliaceous plant, *Asparagus officinalis*, the young shoots of which are edible. [Gk. *asparagos*].
ASPARTATE, [as-pah′-tāt], *n.* salt of aspartic acid.
ASPARTIC, [as-pah′-tik], *adj.* pertaining to asparagin.
ASPECT, [as′-pekt], *n.* a look; outward appearance; view, direction faced, outlook; side of an opinion, a partial view of a subject or idea; (*astron.*) the situation of a planet in respect of another; **a. ratio**, (*aeron.*) the ratio of the chord to the span of an aeroplane. [L. *aspectus*].
ASPECTANT, [as-pek′-tant], *adj.* (*her.*) facing each other.
ASPEN (1), **ASP**, [as′-pen], *n.* a variety of poplar tree, *Populus tremula*. [OE. *æspe*].
ASPEN (2), [as′-pen], *adj.* pertaining to the aspen, made of aspen wood.
ASPERATE, [as′-per-āt], *v.t.* to roughen, make harsh or uneven. [~L. *asperare*].
ASPERGES, [a-spur′-jēz], *n.* the Roman Catholic ceremony of sprinkling altar, clergy and congregation with holy water. [L. *Asperges me hyssopo* thou shalt sprinkle, etc., (the opening words of the chant sung during the ceremony)].
ASPERGILLIFORM, [as′-per-jil′-i-fawm], *adj.* (*bot.*) in the shape of an aspergillum. [ASPERGILLUM and FORM].
ASPERGILLUM, [as′-per-jil′-um], *n.* a small brush used in Roman Catholic churches to scatter holy water over the congregation.
ASPERGILLUS, [as′-per-jil′-us], *n.* (*bot.*) a genus of fungi, resembling an aspergillum. [*Prec.*].
ASPERIFOLIATE, [as′-per-i-fō′-li-at], *adj.* possessing rough leaves. [L. *asper* rough and *folium* leaf].
ASPERIFOLIOUS, [as′-per-i-fō′-li-us], *adj.* rough-leaved.
ASPERITY, [as-per′-i-ti], *n.* roughness, sharpness, harshness, acerbity, severity. [L. *asperitas*].

ASPERGILLUS

ASPERMOUS, [as-purm′-us], *adj.* (*bot.*) having no seed. [Gk. *aspermos*].
ASPERSE, [as-purs′], *v.t.* to besprinkle; to cast

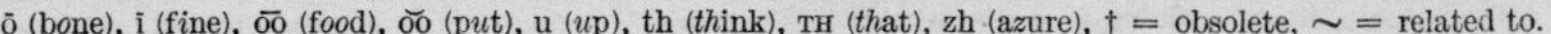

ō (bone), ī (fine), ōō (food), ŏŏ (put), u (up), th (think), TH (that), zh (azure), † = obsolete, ~ = related to.

aspersions upon, disparage. [L. *aspersum, p.pt.* of *aspergere* to sprinkle].

ASPERSION, [a-spur'-shun], *n.* spray; (*eccles.*) sprinkling; (*fig.*) slanderous remark or charge, disparagement, calumny. [L. *aspersio*].

ASPERSIVE, [a-spur'-siv], *adj.* slanderous, disparaging.

ASPERSORIUM, [as'-per-saw'-ri-um], *n.* a receptacle for holy water. [MedL. *aspersorium*].

ASPHALT (1), [as'-falt], *n.* mineral pitch, a hard, brittle, bituminous substance; bituminous pitch mixed with sand, gravel, etc., and used for surfacing roads and pavements. [Gk. *asphaltos* bitumen].

ASPHALT (2), [as'-falt], *v.t.* to surface with asphalt.

ASPHALTIC, [as-falt'-ik], *adj.* pertaining to asphalt.

ASPHODEL, [as'-fōd-el'], *n.* a flower similar to the lily; (*myth.*) a flower said to cover the Elysian fields. [Gk. *asphodelos*].

ASPHYXIA, [as-fik'-si-a], *n.* suffocation caused by lack of oxygen in the blood; suspended animation, insensibility. [Gk. *asphyxia* without pulsation].

ASPHYXIAL, [as'-fik'-si-al], *adj.* indicating, relating to asphyxia.

ASPHYXIANT, [as-fik'-si-ant], *n.* a gas or substance producing asphyxia.

ASPHYXIATE, [as-fik'-si-āt], *v.t.* to kill by asphyxia, to suffocate.

ASPIC, [as'-pik], *n.* a meat jelly in which certain foods such as fowl, etc., are suspended. [Fr. *aspic*].

ASPIDISTRA, [as'-pi-dis'-tra] *n.* a flowering plant of the lily family, originally from China; the popular parlour palm. [Modern word from Gk. *aspis* shield and *astron* star].

ASPIDISTRA

ASPIRANT, [as'-pir-ant], *n.* one who aspires, a candidate, an ambitious novice. [~L. *aspirans*].

ASPIRATE (1), [asp'-i-rat], *n.* a voiceless sound formed by friction of expired breath on the lining of the throat and mouth, represented by H. [L. *aspiratum, p.pt.* of *aspirare* to breathe].

ASPIRATE (2), [asp'-i-rāt'], *v.t.* to pronounce with an audible breathing; (*sci.*) to draw away gas or fluid by means of an aspirator. [~L. *aspirare* breathe].

ASPIRATION, [asp'-i-rā'-shun], *n.* an aspiring ambition, desire for some high attainment, an eager and noble seeking; the act of aspirating.

ASPIRATOR, [asp'-i-rā'-tor], *n.* (*med.*) an apparatus for removing gases or liquids by suction.

ASPIRE, [a-spier'], *v.t.* to desire highly, to have ambitions towards, to rise up, or strive to rise up, to attempt some high purpose. [L. *aspirare* breathe].

ASPIRIN, [asp'-i-rin], *n.* a compound of salicylic acid used for the relief of neuralgic and rheumatic pains. [Germ. *aspirin*].

ASPIRING, [a-spier'-ing], *adj.* ambitious, having aspirations.

ASPIRINGLY, [a-spier'-ing-li], *adv.* in an aspiring manner.

ASPORT, [as-pawt'], *v.t.* to remove by force or illegal means. [L. *absportare*].

ASPORTATION, [as'-pawt-ā'-shun], *n.* (*leg.*) the felonious removal of goods. [~L. *asportatio*].

ASPRAWL, [a-sprawl'], *adv.* sprawling.

ASPROUT, [a-sprowt'], *adv.* sprouting.

ASQUINT, [a-skwint'], *adv.* squinting, askew.

ASS, [as, ahs], *n.* a quadruped related to the horse, having large ears, a brownish-grey shaggy coat, and a tufted tail; (*fig.*) a stupid person, an utter fool. [OE. *assa* from L. *asinus*].

ASSAFETIDA, see ASAFOETIDA.

ASSAGAI, ASSEGAI, [as'-a-gī], *n.* a Kaffir stabbing spear. [OFr., Portug. *asagaye* from Berber *zaghayah*].

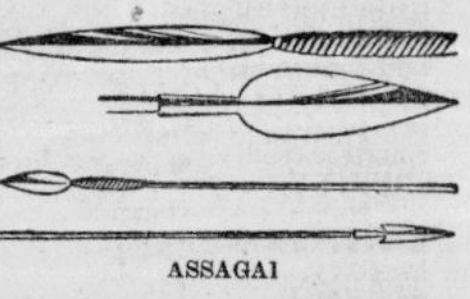

ASSAGAI

ASSAI, [a-sī'], *adv.* (*mus.*) fairly, sufficiently. [It. *assai*].

ASSAIL, [a-sāl'], *v.t.* to attack violently, to assault; to attack with criticism; to overwhelm or beset with questions, doubts, etc. [ME. *assailen* from OFr. *asalir*, L. *adsalire* to jump on].

ASSAILABLE, [a-sāl'-abl], *adj.* able to be assailed.

ASSAILANT, [a-sāl'-ant], *n.* one who assails, an attacker.

ASSAILER, [a-sāl'-er], *n.* an assailant.

ASSAPAN, [as'-a-pan], *n.* (*zool.*) the North American flying squirrel, *Sciuropterus volucella.* [Amer.Ind. *assapan*].

ASSART (1), [a-saht'], *n.* (*leg.*) an ancient offence of clearing away trees to make forest into arable land; a clearing. [AFr. *assart*].

ASSART (2), [as'-aht], *v.t.* to clear land of trees.

ASSASSIN, [a-sas'-in], *n.* a political murderer, a secret killer. [It. *assassino* from Arab. *hashishiyy* hashish-eaters, a Persian sect who murdered Crusaders].

ASSASSINATE, [a-sas'-i-nāt], *v.t.* to kill for political motives, to murder a person of political importance. [*Prec.*].

ASSASSINATION, [a-sas'-in-ā-shun], *n.* the act of assassinating, a political murder.

ASSASSINATOR, [a-sas'-in-ā-tor], *n.* one who assassinates, a killer.

ASSAULT (1), [a-sawlt'], *n.* a violent and sudden attack, an attack made on a fortress or town, a violent physical onslaught; (*leg.*) an attempt or threat to injure another bodily. [OFr. *asaut*].

ASSAULT (2), [a-sawlt'], *v.t. and i.* to make an assault upon, attack.

ASSAULTABLE, [a-sawlt'-abl], *adj.* exposed to attack.

ASSAULTER, [a-sawlt'-er], *n.* one who assaults.

ASSAY (1), [a-sā'], *n.* test, examination; estimation by test of the amount and value of precious metals in alloys. [OFr. *assai*].

ASSAY (2), [a-sā'], *v.t. and i.* to test, to determine the quality of precious metals in an alloy; to try, attempt. [OFr. *assayer* from L. *exigere* to examine, weigh].

ASSAYABLE, [a-sā-abl], *adj.* able to be assayed.

ASSAYER, [a-sā'-er], *n.* a metallurgist or mint official who assays bullion and coin.

ASSAYING, [a-sā'-ing], *n.* the act of making an assay.

ASSAY-MASTER, [a-sā'-mahst'-er], *n.* the official in charge of the assaying of precious metals.

ASSEGAI, see ASSAGAI.

ASSEMBLAGE, [a-sem'-blij], *n.* a gathering of persons or things; a concourse, meeting; the act of making an assembly; the putting together of the components of a machine; a machine put together. [Fr. *assemblage*].

ASSEMBLE, [a-sembl'], *v.t. and i.* to bring together (a number of persons or things) in one place; to come together, meet, congregate; to fit together the component parts of a machine. [Fr. *assembler*, L. *assimulare*].

ASSEMBLY, [a-sem'-bli], *n.* the act or state of being assembled; a concourse, a meeting for a specific purpose; (*milit.*) the signal and act of coming to general parade; **a. room,** a room for social functions. [OFr. *assemblee*].

ASSENT (1), [a-sent'], *n.* the act of agreeing, agreement, approval, consent; the agreement of the sovereign to the bills presented to him by Parliament. [OFr. *assente*].

ASSENT (2), [a-sent'], *v.i.* to agree, consent. [OFr. *assenter*, L. *assentire*].

ASSENTER, [a-sent'-er], *n.* a person who assents; one who agrees.

ASSENTIENT (1), [a-sent'-i-ent], *n.* an assenter.

ASSENTIENT (2), [a-sent'-i-ent], *adj.* assenting, expressing agreement. [~L. *assentiens*].

ASSENTINGLY, [a-sent'-ing-li], *adv.* in an assenting manner.

ASSENTOR, [a-sent'-er], *n.* (*leg.*) one who, not being proposer or seconder, adds his name in support at the nomination of a candidate in an election.

ASSERT, [a-surt'], *v.t.* to affirm, declare, state; to maintain and uphold (a right or claim); **to a. oneself,** to put oneself forward in an aggressive manner. [~L. *assertum, p.pt.* of *asserere* to claim].

ASSERTABLE, [as-urt'-abl], *adj.* that may be asserted.

ASSERTER, [a-surt'-er], *n.* a person who asserts.

ASSERTION, [a-sur'-shun], *n.* the act of asserting; a positive declaration, a statement or claim not yet tested. [~L. *assertio*].

ASSERTIVE, [a-surt'-iv], *adj.* positive, asserting strongly, insolently forward. [ASSERT].

ASSERTIVELY, [a-surt'-iv-li], *adv.* in assertive fashion.

ASSERTIVENESS, [a-surt'-iv-nes], *n.* the quality of being insistently assertive.

ASSERTOR, [a-surt'-or], *n.* one who asserts, a defender of a cause. [L. *assertor*].
ASSERTORY, [a-surt'-or-i], *adj.* asserting.
ASSESS, [a-ses'], *v.t. and i.* to determine the value of; to set an official value on property, income, etc., for the purpose of levying state taxes and rates; to determine the value of property damaged; (*leg.*) to estimate the liability of a person for damage or injury done to another. [OFr. *assesser*].
ASSESSABLE, [a-ses'-abl], *adj.* able to be assessed.
ASSESSMENT, [a-ses'-ment], *n.* the act of assessing; a valuation of property for taxation; the amount at which anything is assessed; a judicial determination of the extent of a loss or damage. [AFr. *assessement*].
ASSESSOR, [a-ses'-or], *n.* one who assesses property for taxation; an adviser assisting a judge or chairman upon technical matters. [OFr. *assessour*].
ASSET, [as'-et], *n.* a possession, an advantageous quality, factor or position, a gain; (*pl.*) possessions, property; (*leg.*) property as security against debts. [OFr. *asetz* enough].
ASSEVERATE, [as-ev'-er-āt], *v.t.* to affirm positively or solemnly. [~L. *asseverare* act seriously].
ASSEVERATION, [as-ev'-er-ā'-shun], *n.* a solemn and considered statement. [~L. *asseveratio*].
ASSIBILATE, [a-sib'-i-lāt], *v.t.* to pronounce with a hissing sound. [~L. *assibilare*].
ASSIBILATION, [a-sib'-i-lā'-shun], *n.* the action of assibilating. [*Prec.*].
ASSIDUITY, [as'-i-jōō'-i-ti], *n.* constant, close, and careful application to an enterprise, diligence, industry. [L. *assiduitas*].
ASSIDUOUS, [a-sij'-ōō-us], *adj.* attentive, persistent, diligent. [L. *assiduus*].
ASSIDUOUSLY, [a-sij'-ōō-us-li], *adv.* in assiduous fashion.
ASSIDUOUSNESS, [a-sij'-ōō-us-nes], *n.* assiduity.
ASSIETTE, [as-yet'], *n.* a preparation applied to the cut edges of books before gilding; an oblong, flat dish. [Fr. *assiette* seal].
ASSIGN (1), [a-sīn'], *n.* (*leg.*) one to whom property or rights are transferred. [*Next*].
ASSIGN (2), [a-sīn'], *v.t.* to apportion, to allot to someone; to determine, to fix or order (a military duty, etc.); to place, to ascribe to a cause, to attribute to a period (work of art, etc.), to ascribe a particular reason for a thing; (*leg.*) to transfer property to another. [L. *assignare*].
ASSIGNABLE, [a-sīn'-abl], *adj.* capable of being assigned.
ASSIGNAT, [as'-in-yah', as'-ig-nat], *n.* a bill issued by the French revolutionary government on the security of confiscated lands. [L. *assignatum*].
ASSIGNATION, [as'-ig-nā'-shun], *n.* an engagement to meet at a specified place and time, usually for a furtive, erotic, or dishonest purpose; assignment. [~L. *assignatio*].
ASSIGNEE, [as'-ī-nē'], *n.* (*leg.*) a person authorized to act for another, person to whom some right or charge is assigned. [OFr. *assigné*].
ASSIGNMENT, [a-sīn'-ment], *n.* the act of assigning; an allotment of work, duties, etc.; (*leg.*) transference of a right or property, the document in which such a transfer is made, the right or property transferred.
ASSIGNOR, [a-sīn'-or], *n.* (*leg.*) one who assigns. [AFr. *assignour*].
ASSIMILABILITY, [as-im'-il-ab-il'-it-i], *n.* the state or quality of being assimilable.
ASSIMILABLE, [a-sim'-il-abl], *adj.* capable of being assimilated.
ASSIMILATE, [a-sim'-i-lāt], *v.t.* to make similar; to convert into a substance similar to that of another organism; to absorb mentally with understanding; *v.i.* to become absorbed, to become amalgamated. [L. *assimilare*].
ASSIMILATION, [a-sim'-i-lā'-shun], *n.* the action of assimilating, the state of being assimilated. [~L. *assimilatio*].
ASSIMILATIVE, [a-sim'-i-lat-iv], *adj.* tending to assimilate.
ASSIMILATORY, [a-sim'-i-lā'-tor-i], *adj.* assimilative.
ASSIST, [a-sist'], *v.t.* to aid, help; (*coll.*) to lend money to; *v.i.* to help; to take part in, have a secondary position in; to be present at an event. [L. *assistere* to stand by].
ASSISTANCE, [a-sis'-tans], *n.* help, aid.
ASSISTANT (1), [a-sis'-tant], *n.* one who assists, an auxiliary, a junior co-worker.
ASSISTANT (2), [a-sis'-tant], *adj.* aiding, helping; subordinate.
ASSISTER, [a-sist'-er], *n.* a helper.
ASSIZE, [a-sīz'], *n.* a trial by a judge and jury; (*pl.*) a periodical sitting of judges of the High Court in each English county to deal with criminal and civil actions; (*hist.*) **A. of Bread and Ale,** edict of Henry III to control the price of articles of food, etc. [OFr. *assise* from L. *assidere* to sit by].
ASSIZER, [as-īz'-er], *n.* †an officer determining and inspecting measures and prices; (*Scots leg.*) a juryman.
ASSOCIABILITY, [a-sō'-shi-a-bil'-it-i], *n.* the condition of being associable.
ASSOCIABLE, [a-sō'-shi-abl], *adj.* capable of being associated in thought; (*med.*) liable to be affected sympathetically. [Fr. *associable*].
ASSOCIATE (1), [a-sō'-shi-at], *n.* a person connected with another by common activities, a companion, a colleague, partner; an inferior or subordinate partner in a work; one who has passed certain examinations below degree standard at certain universities; a junior member of certain academies; (*leg.*) a member of a body of officials of the High Court of Justice, deciding the court's business.
ASSOCIATE (2), [a-sō'-shi-at], *adj.* in close connexion; co-operating in an office without full power. [L. *associatus*].
ASSOCIATE (3), [a-sō'-shi-āt'], *v.t. and v.i.* to join, unite with; keep company with, frequent the society of; to join as a partner or co-worker; to express agreement with a policy, etc.; intellectually to connect ideas by thought; to give free play to irrational connexions, *esp.* in psychological treatment. [~L. *associare*].
ASSOCIATED, [a-sō'-shi-āt-id], *adj.* allied, united, connected.
ASSOCIATESHIP, [a-sō'-shi-at-ship], *n.* the office or position of an associate.
ASSOCIATION, [a-sō'-shi-ā'-shun], *n.* act of associating, state of being associated; group of people acting in co-operation for a common purpose; intellectual or psychological connexion; **a. football,** football played under the rules of the Football Association. [~L. *associatio*].
ASSOCIATIONAL, [a-sō'-shi-ā'-shun-al], *adj.* pertaining to an association.
ASSOCIATIONISM, [a-sō'-shi-ā'-shun-izm], *n.* the theory that association of ideas is the basic mental principle, and the fundamental explanation of intellectual processes.
ASSOCIATIONIST, [a-sō'-shi-ā'-shun-ist], *n.* one who believes in associationism.
ASSOCIATIVE, [as-ō'-shi-at-iv], *adj.* pertaining to association.
ASSOIL, [a-soil'], *v.t.* to free from guilt, to forgive or pardon, to absolve, to cleanse from sin. [OFr. *assoiler* from L. *absolvere* to loosen].
ASSONANCE, [as'-on-ans], *n.* similarity in sound between words or stressed syllables; the use of this for rhymes. [Fr. *assonance*].
ASSONANT, [as'-on-ant], *adj.* having the quality of assonance. [~L. *assonans*].
ASSORT, [a-sawt'], *v.t. and i.* to arrange or distribute into groups, to classify roughly on grounds of similarity; to sort out. [OFr. *assorter*].
ASSORTED, [a-sawt'-id], *adj.* of various sorts, mixed.
ASSORTMENT, [a-sawt'-ment], *n.* the act of assorting; a group or collection of assorted objects.
ASSUAGE, [a-swāj'], *v.t.* to soften, soothe, relieve. [OFr. *asouager*].
ASSUAGEMENT, [a-swāj'-ment], *n.* the act of assuaging, that which assuages. [OFr. *asouagement*].
ASSUAGER, [a-swāj'-er], *n.* a person or thing that assuages.
ASSUASIVE, [a-swā'-siv], *adj.* tending to assuage. L. *ad* and ~*suavis* sweet].
ASSUEFACTION†, [as'-wi-fak'-shun], *n.* the act of making accustomed, the state of being accustomed. [~L. *assuefacere*].
ASSUETUDE, [as'-wi-tewd], *n.* customs, wont, habit. [L. *assuetudo*].
ASSUME, [a-sewm'], *v.t.* to take, arrogate to oneself, to seize, to appropriate; to become like, to take on a quality or character; to pretend, to counterfeit something; to take for granted, to suppose without proof; to take for granted in an argument; *v.i.* to be arrogant; (*leg.*) to take on oneself an obligation. [L. *assumere* take to].
ASSUMED, [a-sewmd'], *adj.* pretended, feigned; supposed.
ASSUMER, [a-sewm'-er], *n.* one who assumes.
ASSUMING, [a-sewm'-ing], *adj.* presumptious, overbearing.
ASSUMPSIT, [a-sump'-sit], *n.* (*leg.*) an action to

obtain damages for breach of contract. [L. *assumpsit* he has undertaken].

ASSUMPTION, [a-sump'-shun], *n.* the act of assuming, the thing assumed; an arbitrary taking over; a pretence of possession of a quality; the act of taking something as true or correct, supposition; the thing so assumed; the Church feast commemorating the admission of the Virgin Mary into heaven (15th August). [~L. *assumptio*].

ASSUMPTIVE, [a-sump'-tiv], *adj.* capable of being assumed, overbearing; (*her.*) (of arms) assumed to mark a particular achievement.

ASSUMPTIVELY, [a-sump'-tiv-li], *adv.* in assumptive fashion.

ASSURABLE, [a-shōōer'-abl], *adj.* capable of being assured or insured.

ASSURANCE, [a-shōōer'-ans], *n.* a positive declaration, a firm statement to allay anxiety; a definite undertaking, a guarantee; certainty, confidence, self-possession, firmness of mind; self-conceit, presumption; insurance. [OFr. *asseurance*].

ASSURANT, [a-shōōer'-ant], *n.* one taking out an assurance policy.

ASSURE, [a-shōōer', a-shaw(r)'], *v.t.* to make certain, safe, to ensure; to assert confidently; allay the anxiety of; to convince; to undertake, to promise confidently; to insure. [OFr. *aseurer*].

ASSURED, [a-shōōerd'], *adj.* made safe, certain; insured; confident, self-possessed.

ASSUREDLY, [a-shōōer'-id-li], *adv.* certainly, beyond all doubt.

ASSUREDNESS, [a-shōōer'-id-nes], *n.* condition of being assured.

ASSURER, [a-shōōer'-er], *n.* one who assures.

ASSURGENT, [a-surj'-ent], *adj.* ascending; (*bot.*) rising in a curve. [~L. *assurgens* rising up].

ASSURINGLY, [a-shōōer'-ing-li], *adv.* in an assuring manner.

ASSYRIAN (1), [a-si'-ri-an], *n.* a native of Assyria.

ASSYRIAN (2), [a-si'-ri-an], *adj.* pertaining to Assyria.

ASSYRIOLOGIST, [a-si'-ri-ol'-o-jist], *n.* an expert in Assyriology.

ASSYRIOLOGY, [a-si'-ri-ol'-o-ji], *n.* the study of Assyrian history and culture. [*Assyria* and Gk. *logos* speech].

ASTARE, [a-stāer'], *adv.* staring.

ASTART, [a-staht], *adv.* suddenly. [A (3) and START].

ASTATIC, [a-stat'-ik], *adj.* (*elect.*) producing no external magnetic field; (*magn.*) without polarity, unaffected by terrestrial magnetism. [A (4) and STATIC].

ASTAY, [a-stā'], *adv.* held in line with the stays of a ship.

ASTEISM, [a'-stē-izm], *n.* delicate irony, subtle derision. [Gk. *asteismos* witty talk].

ASTER, [as'-ter], *n.* a genus of herbaceous plants with bright flowers, including the Michaelmas daisy; the Chinese aster. [Gk. *aster* star].

ASTERIA, [as-tēer'-i-a], *n.* a sapphire which, cut in a certain way, resembles a star of six rays. [L. *asteria*].

ASTERIALITE, [as-tēer'-i-al-it'], *n.* a fossil star fish. [Gk. *aster* and *lithos* stone].

ASTERIAS, (*pl.* **asteriæ**), [a-stēer'-i-as], *n.* the five-rayed and other star-fish. [Gk. *asterias* starry].

ASTERIAS

ASTERIATED, [a-stēer'-i-ā'-tid], *adj.* radiated like a star.

ASTERISK, [as'-ter-isk], *n.* the typographical sign (*). [Gk. *asteriskos* little star].

ASTERISM, [as'-ter-izm], *n.* (*astron.*) a cluster of stars; three asterisks ⁂; the use of asterisks instead of a proper name. [Gk. *asterismos*].

ASTERN, [a-sturn'], *adv.* in, at, or towards the back of a ship. [A (3) and STERN].

ASTEROID, [as'-ter-oid], *n* one of the numerous minor planets between the orbits of Mars and Jupiter. [Gk. *asteroeides* starlike].

ASTEROIDAL, [as'-ter-oidl'], *adj.* pertaining to the asteroids.

ASTEROIDEA, [as'-ter-oid'-i-a], *n.(pl.)* a group of polyps with radiate tentacles, star-fish.

ASTHENIA, [as-thē'-ni-a, as'-thin-ī'-a], *n.* (*med.*) debility, loss of strength, emaciation. [Gk. *astheneia*].

ASTHENIC, [as-thē'-nik], *adj.* feeble, weak.

ASTHMA, [as'-ma], *n.* (*med.*) chronic or acute spasm of the bronchial tubes. [Gk. *asthma* panting].

ASTHMATIC, [as-mat'-ik], *adj.* pertaining to, liable to asthma.

ASTHMATICAL, [as-mat'-ik-al], *adj.* asthmatic.

ASTHMATICALLY, [as-mat'-ik-al-i], *adv.* in an asthmatic manner.

ASTIGMATIC, [as'-tig-mat'-ik], *adj.* suffering from, pertaining to astigmatism; correcting astigmatism.

ASTIGMATISM, [a-stig'-mat-izm], *n.* (*med.*) a defect in the curvature of the eye which interferes with the focusing of images at a common point; blurred vision. [A (4) and Gk. *stigma* mark].

ASTIR, [a-stur'], *adv.* on the move, stirring.

ASTOMATOUS, [a-stom'-at-us], *adj.* (*zool.*) without a mouth.

ASTOMOUS, [as'-tom-us], *adj.* (*bot.*) having no mouth. [Gk. *astomos* without a mouth].

ASTONISH, [a-ston'-ish], *v.t.* to excite with sudden surprise, to surprise violently, to arouse feelings of shock and wonder. [~OFr. *astoner*].

ASTONISHING, [a-ston'-ish-ing], *adj.* very surprising, amazing, arousing astonishment.

ASTONISHINGLY, [a-ston'-ish-ing-li], *adv.* in astonishing fashion.

ASTONISHMENT, [a-ston'-ish-ment], *n.* the condition of being astonished, amazement, violent surprise, wonder.

ASTOUND, [a-stownd'], *v.t.* to overcome with amazement, to overwhelm with surprise and shock. [OFr. *astoner*].

ASTOUNDED, [a-stownd'-id], *adj.* surprised, shocked with surprise. [*Prec.*].

ASTOUNDING, [a-stownd'-ing], *adj.* extremely astonishing, amazing.

ASTRADDLE, [a-stradl'], *adv.* astride, in a straddling position.

ASTRAGAL, [as'-trag-al], *n.* (*arch.*) a rounded moulding at the top or bottom of a column; a ring moulding. [Gk. *astragalos*].

ASTRAGAL

ASTRAGALOID, [as-trag'-al-oid], *adj.* similar to, pertaining to the astragalus. [ASTRAGAL and Gk. *oeides* like].

ASTRAGALUS, [as-trag'-al-us], *n.* (*anat.*) the ball of the ankle-joint; (*bot.*) a genus of plants including the milk-vetches. [L. from Gk. *astragalos*].

ASTRAKHAN, [as'-tra-kan'], *n.* the skin of very young lambs from Astrakhan ; (*pop.*) any lambskin with curled fleece. [*Astrakhan* a place in Russia].

ASTRAL, [as'-tral], *adj.* pertaining to the stars; **a. lamp,** a lamp whose light is placed under a concave glass, so as to concentrate the light on the table leaving no shadow. [Fr. *astral*].

ASTRAY, [a-strā'], *adv.* wanderingly, in the wrong direction, from the true or proper course.

ASTRICT, [a-strikt'], *v.t.* to bind, confine; to restrict. [~L. *astrictum*, *p.pt.* of *astringere*].

ASTRICTION, [a-strik'-shun], *n.* the act of binding or constricting; (*med.*) constipation. [L. *astrictio*].

ASTRICTIVE, [a-strik'-tiv], *adj.* astringent.

ASTRICTORY, [a-strik'-tor-i], *adj.* astrictive.

ASTRIDE, [a-strīd'], *adv. and prep.* with legs apart, with a leg on either side of, astraddle.

ASTRINGE, [a-strinj'], *v.t.* to bind, constrict, to press together, to constipate. [L. *astringere* to bind tightly].

ASTRINGENCY, [a-strin'-jen-si], *n.* the quality of being astringent.

ASTRINGENT (1), [a-strin'-jent], *n.* an astringent medicine or drug.

ASTRINGENT (2), [a-strin'-jent], *adj.* having the property of binding or of drawing the tissues together; styptic; (*fig.*) severe, harsh. [ASTRINGE].

ASTRINGENTLY, [a-strin'-jent-li], *adv.* in astringent fashion.

ASTRO-, [as'-trō], *pref.* relating to the stars. [Gk. *astron* star].

ASTROGENY, [as-troj'-en-i], *n.* the study of the origins of the stars. [ASTRO and Gk. *geneia* birth].

ASTROGNOSY, [as-trog'-nos-i], *n.* the study of the fixed stars. [ASTRO and Gk. *gnosis* knowledge].

ASTRO-HATCH, [as'-trō-hach'], *n.* (*aeron.*) the transparent cover of the cockpit in an aeroplane. [ASTRO and HATCH (1)].

ASTROLABE, [as'-trō-lāb'], *n.* an instrument formerly used to ascertain the positions of the heavenly bodies. [ME. *astrelabe*, Gk. *astrolabon*].

ASTROLATRY, [as-trol'-at-ri], *n.* star-worship. [ASTRO and Gk. *latreia* worship].
ASTROLOGER, [as-trol'-ō-jer], *n.* a student of astrology, one foretelling the future by this means.
ASTROLOGICAL, [as'-trō-loj'-ikl], *adj.* pertaining to astrology.
ASTROLOGICALLY, [as'-trō-loj'-ik-al-i], *adv.* in astrological fashion.
ASTROLOGIZE, [as-trol'-ō-jīz], *v.i.* to practise astrology.
ASTROLOGY, [as-trol'-o-ji], *n.* practical primitive astronomy; (*astrol.*) the practical study of the stars and planets with the object of determining the future course of events by the position and relation of the heavenly bodies at a given moment. [ASTRO and Gk. *logos* speech].
ASTROMETER, [as-trom'-it-er], *n.* an instrument for measuring the comparative magnitude and brilliance of stars. [ASTRO and METER].
ASTROMETRY, [as-trom'-et-ri], *n.* determination of the comparative magnitude of the stars.
ASTRONOMER, [as-tron'-ō-mer], *n.* one skilled in astronomy. [~Gk. *astronomos*].
ASTRONOMIC, [as'-tro-nom'-ik], *adj.* pertaining to astronomy.
ASTRONOMICAL, [as'-tro-nom'-ikl], *adj.* astronomic.
ASTRONOMICALLY, [as'-tro-nom'-ik-a-li], *adv.* in an astronomical manner, in accordance with astronomy.
ASTRONOMY, [as-tron'-o-mi], *n.* the scientific study of the heavenly bodies. [OFr. *astronomie* from Gk. *astronomia*].
ASTRO-PHOTOGRAPHY, [as'-trō-fō-tog'-raf-i], *n.* photography of the stars.
ASTRO-PHOTOMETRY, [as'-trō-fō-tom'-et-ri], *n.* science of measuring the brightness of stars.
ASTRO-PHYSICS, [as'-trō-fiz'-iks], *n.*(*pl.*) that part of astronomy dealing with the physical characteristics of the stars.
ASTROSCOPE, [as'-trō-skōp], *n.* an ancient astronomical instrument showing the constellations delineated on two cones. [ASTRO and Gk. *skopos* watcher].
ASTROTHEOLOGY, [as'-trō-thē-ol'-o-ji], *n.* religion based on observation of the stars.
ASTRUT, [a-strut'], *adv.* in strutting fashion.
ASTUTE, [a-stewt'], *adj.* shrewd, mentally quick, cunning, sharp. [L. *astutus*].
ASTUTELY, [a-stewt'-li], *adv.* in astute fashion.
ASTUTENESS, [a-stewt'-nes], *n.* the quality of being astute.
ASTYLAR, [a-stil'-ar], *adj.* having no columns or pilasters. [A (4) and STYLAR].
ASUNDER, [a-sund'-er], *adv.* in, into two or more separate parts or places; apart. [OE. *on sundran*].
ASWARM, [a-swawm'], *adv.* swarming.
ASWAY, [a-swā'], *adv.* in swaying fashion.
ASYLUM, [a-si'-lum], *n.* a place of safety, sanctuary, refuge, a quiet retreat; an institution for the unfit, *esp.* the insane. [Gk. *asulon* sanctuary].
ASYMMETRICAL, [ā'-si-met'-rikl], *adj.* not symmetrical.
ASYMMETRY, [ā'-sim'-et-ri], *n.* lack of symmetry. [A (4) and SYMMETRY].
ASYMPTOTE, [a'-simp-tōt], *n.* (*math.*) a line approaching a curve, but never meeting it. [Gk. *asumptotos*].
ASYMPTOTICAL, [a'-sim-tōt'-ikl], *adj.* pertaining to an asymptote.
ASYNARTETE, [a-sin'-ah-tēt], *adj.* disconnected; (*pros.*) consisting of two parts having different rhythms. [Gk. *asunartetos*].
ASYNCHRONISM, [a-sin'-kron-izm], *n.* non-coincidence in time. [A (4) and SYNCHRONISM].
ASYNDETIC, [as'-in-det'-ik], *adj.* pertaining to an asyndeton.
ASYNDETON, [a-sin'-di-ton], *n.* (*gram.*) a construction in which the connectives are left out. [Gk. *asundetos* unconnected].
ASYNTACTIC, [a-sin-tak'-tik], *adj.* (*gram.*) irregular, ungrammatical. [Gk. *asuntaktos*].
ASYSTOLE, [a-sis'-tō-li], *n.* (*med.*) a stopping of the normal contractions of the heart. [A (4) and SYSTOLE].
AT, [at], *prep. expressing presence or proximity*, by, near; *or motion towards*, to, near to, towards; *expressing state or condition*, in, with; *expressing the hour or season of occurrence*, during, in, on; *expressing and governing number, quantity, etc.*, for, to be. [OE. *æt*].
ATABAL, [at'-ah-al], *n.* a Moorish kettledrum. [Arab. *at tabl*].
ATACAMITE, [a-tak'-a-mīt'], *n.* a native hydrous oxychloride of copper. [*Atacama*, a place in Chile].
ATAGHAN, see YATAGHAN.
ATARAXY, ATARAXIA, [at'-a-rak'-si], *n.* calmness of mind, impassivity. [Gk. *ataraxia* impassiveness].
ATAUNTO, [a-tawnt'-ō], *adv.* (*naut.*) with all sails set, shipshape. [Fr. *autant* as much].
ATAVISM, [at'-a-vizm], *n.* tendency in offspring to revert to an ancestral type, the appearance of physical and mental features more characteristic of earlier ancestors than of parents. [Fr. *atavisme* from L. *atavus* ancestor].
ATAVISTIC, [at'-a-vis'-tik], *adj.* tending to, due to, pertaining to atavism.
ATAXIA, see ATAXY.
ATAXIC, [a-tak'-sik], *adj.* pertaining to ataxy.
ATAXY, ATAXIA, [a-tak'-si, a-tak'-si-a], *n.* (*med.*) disease of the nerves and muscles resulting in faulty bodily co-ordination; **locomotor a.**, a disease in which the sufferer is unable to control the voluntary movements. [Gk. *ataxia* disorder].
ATE, [et, āt], *pret.* of EAT.
ATELIER, [at'-el-yā], *n.* an artist's studio. [Fr. *atelier*].
ATHALAMOUS, [ath-al'-a-mus], *adj.* (*bot.*) relating to lichens whose thallus lacks shields or beds for the spores. [A (4) and Gk. *thalamos* bed].
ATHANASIA, [ath'-an-ā'-zi-a], *n.* immortality. [Gk. *athanasia*].
ATHANASIAN (1), [ath'-a-nā'-zi-an], *n.* a follower of Athanasius, one believing in the Trinity. [*Athanasius* archbishop of Alexandria].
ATHANASIAN (2), [ath'-a-nā'-zi-an], *adj.* pertaining to Athanasius and his doctrines; **A. creed**, a formula of the Christian faith formerly attributed to Athanasius.
ATHANOR, [ath'-an-or], *n.* a furnace used in alchemy to keep up constant heat. [Arab. *at tannur* the furnace].
ATHEISM, [ā'-thi-izm], *n.* disbelief in a supreme personal god; denial of the existence of God. [Gk. *atheos* without god].
ATHEIST, [ā'-thi-ist], *n.* one who denies the existence of a God; (*fig.*) one who wilfully rejects and scoffs at any accepted belief.
ATHEISTIC, [ā'-thi-is'-tik], *adj.* pertaining to atheism.
ATHEISTICAL, [ā'-thi-is'-tikl], *adj.* atheistic.
ATHEISTICALLY, [ā'-thi-is'-tik-al-i], *adv.* in an atheistical manner.
ATHEIZE, [ā'-thi-iz], *v.t.* to convert to atheism.
ATHELING, [ath'-ling], *n.* (*hist.*) an Anglo-Saxon prince or noble. [OE. *ætheling*].
ATHENAEUM, [ath'-en-ē'-um], *n.* a temple of Athene; a club or institution for the encouragement of science and the arts, and the assembly of their devotees. [Gk. *Athenaion*].
ATHENIAN (1), [ath'-ē'-ni-an], *n.* a citizen of the Greek city of Athens.
ATHENIAN (2), [ath-ē'-ni-an], *adj.* pertaining to Athens; (*fig.*) noble.
ATHEOLOGY, [a'-thi-ol'-o-ji], *n.* hostility to theology. [A (4) and THEOLOGY].
ATHEOUS, [ā'-thi-us], *adj.* atheistic. [Gk. *atheos* godless].
ATHERMANCY, [a-thurm'-an-si], *n.* non-conductivity to radiant heat. [Gk. *athermantos* unheated].
ATHERMANOUS, [a-thurm'-an-us], *adj.* non-conductive of radiant heat.
ATHEROMA, [ath'-er-ō'-ma], *n.* (*med.*) an encysted tumour with curd-like matter. [Gk. *atheroma* from *athere* porridge].
ATHEROMATOUS, [ath'-er-ōm'-at-us], *adj.* pertaining to an atheroma.
ATHIRST, [a-thurst'], *adj.* thirsty; (*fig.*) desperately eager.
ATHLETE, [ath'-lēt], *n.* an expert in athletics; (*fig.*) one possessing bodily vigour and strength. [Gk. *athletes* contester].
ATHLETIC, [ath-let'-ik], *adj.* pertaining to athletics; strong and active, fit in body. [Gk. *athletikos*].
ATHLETICALLY, [ath-let'-ik-al-i], *adv.* in athletic fashion.
ATHLETICISM, [ath-let'-is-izm], *n.* devotion to athletics; the doctrine that athletics are all-important; over-insistence on athletics.
ATHLETICS, [ath-let'-iks], *n.*(*pl.*) physical sports; the practice of skilful games and sports (running, jumping, etc.) to develop the physical fitness of the body. [ATHLETE].
ATHLETISM, [ath'-let-izm], *n.* the qualities of an athlete, the physical poise of an athlete.

AT-HOME, [at-hōm'], *n.* a social function devoted to the general reception of visitors and guests at a stated time.

A-THROB, [a-throb'], *adv.* throbbing palpitatingly.

ATHWART, [a-thwawt'], *adv. and prep.* across, from side to side, against; (*naut.*) across the course or direction. [A (3) and THWART].

A-TILT, [a-tilt'], *adv.* tilted, tilting.

ATLANTEAN, [at'-lan-tē'-an], *adj.* pertaining to Atlas; strong. [ATLAS].

ATLANTES, [at-lan'-tēz], *n.(pl.)* supporting pillars shaped like men bearing burdens. [ATLAS]. [Gk. *Atlantes*].

ATLANTIC (1), [at-lan'-tik], *n.* the ocean dividing Europe and Africa from America. [Gk. *atlantikos* from ATLAS].

ATLANTIC (2), [at-lan'-tik], *adj.* relating to the ocean separating Europe from America.

ATLANTIDES, [at'-lan-tīd'-ēz], *n.(pl.)* the Pleiades. [Gk. *Atlanteides*].

ATLANTOSAURUS, [at-lan'-tō-saw'-rus], *n.* (*zool.*) a type of great extinct reptiles. [ATLAS and Gk. *sauros* lizard].

ATLANTES

ATLAS, [at'-las], *n.* (*myth.*) one of the older Greek gods who supports the sky on his shoulders; (*geog.*) a bound collection of maps of the world; (*anat.*) the first vertebra of the spine, supporting the head; **a. beetle,** a large olive-green beetle, *Chalcosoma atlas*; **a. moth,** a species of moth, *Saturnia atlas*, having a short body and very large wings. [Gk. *Atlas*].

ATLAS MOTH

ATMIDOMETER, [at'-mid-om'-it-er], *n.* an atmometer. [Gk. *atmis* vapour and METER].

ATMOLOGICAL, [at'-mol-oj'-ikl], *adj.* relating to atmology.

ATMOLOGIST, [at-mol'-o-jist], *n.* one learned in atmology.

ATMOLOGY, [at-mol'-o-ji], *n.* the study of aqueous vapours and vaporization. [Gk. *atmos* vapour and *logos* speech].

ATMOLYSIS, [at-mol'-is-is], *n.* (*phys.*) the separation of gases into their constituents, by passing them through porous substances. [Gk. *atmos* vapour and *lusis* loosing].

ATMOMETER, [at-mom'-it-er], *n.* an instrument for measuring the rate of evaporation from a humid surface. [Gk. *atmos* and METER].

ATMOSPHERE, [at'-mos-fēer], *n.* a gaseous substance surrounding some of the planets, *esp.* the earth; the air; (*fig.*) mental or moral environment, a psychological impression produced by a place; (*phys.*) a pressure of 15 lb. to the square inch. [Gk. *atmos* vapour and *sphaira* ball].

ATMOSPHERIC, [at'-mos-fe'-rik], *adj.* pertaining to the atmosphere, relating to air.

ATMOSPHERICAL, [at'-mos-fe'-rikl], *adj.* atmospheric.

ATMOSPHERICALLY, [at'-mos-fe'-rik-al-i], *adv.* by means of, through the air.

ATMOSPHERICS, [at'-mos-fe'-riks], *n.(pl.)* interference with wireless reception due to electrical disturbances in the ether.

ATOLL, [a-tol'], *n.* a coral reef or island. [Malay *atoll*].

ATOM, [at'-um], *n.* (*chem.*) the minutest portion of a chemical element which can exist by itself or in combination with other elements (formerly thought to be indivisible); (*fig.*) a very minute particle. [Gk. *atomos* indivisible].

ATOMIC, [a-tom'-ik], *adj.* pertaining to, consisting of atoms; **a. number,** (*chem.*) number given to an element to mark its place in the series of elements arranged in order of their atomic weights; **a. philosophy,** belief of the Epicureans that atoms are endowed with motion, and formed the universe without supernatural agency; **a. theory,** Dalton's theory of the formation of matter, to the effect that ultimate matter consists of uniform, indivisible particles in varying combinations; **a. weight,** relative weight of an atom to that of hydrogen.

ATOMICAL, [a-tom'-ikl], *adj.* atomic.

ATOMICITY, [at'-om-is'-i-ti], *n.* valency.

ATOMISM, [at'-um-izm], *n.* the theory that matter is made up of indivisible atoms.

ATOMIST, [at'-um-ist], *n.* one upholding the atomic theory.

ATOMIZATION, [at'-um-īz-ā'-shun], *n.* the breaking up of liquid into a fine spray.

ATOMIZE, [at'-um-īz], *v.t.* to reduce to atoms; to break a liquid up into a fine spray.

ATOMIZER, [at'-um-īz-er], *n.* an apparatus for breaking liquid up into a fine spray; a hand spray.

ATOMOLOGY, [at'-um-ol'-o-ji], *n.* atomism. [ATOM and Gk. *logos* speech].

ATOMY (1), [at'-um-i], *n.* (*coll.*) a skeleton. [ANATOMY].

ATOMY (2), [at'-um-i], *n.* atom, tiny being. [F. *atomi*].

ATONABLE, [a-tōn'-abl], *adj.* able to be atoned for.

ATONE, [a-tōn'], *v.i.* to make recompense for, expiate, make amends for an offence, to repair a wrong, suffer very heavily for a crime. [AT and ONE].

ATONEMENT, [a-tōn'-ment], *n.* the act or state of atoning.

ATONIC (1), [a-ton'-ik], *n.* (*phon.*) an unaccented syllable; (*med.*) a medicine for calming nervous excitement.

ATONIC (2), [a-ton'-ik], *adj.* (*phon.*) unaccented; (*med.*) in indifferent health, weak. [Gk. *atonos* toneless].

ATONY, [at'-on-i], *n.* (*med.*) debility, enervation, weakness. [Gk. *atonia* tonelessness].

ATOP, [a-top'], *adv.* on top of, at the top of.

ATRABILIAR, [at'-ra-bil'-yer], *adj.* having a melancholic humour, splenetic, hypochondriac. [L. *ater* black and BILE].

ATRABILIARY, [at'-ra-bil'-ya-ri], *adj.* atrabiliar.

ATRABILIOUS, [at'-ra-bil'-yus], *adj.* melancholic. [L. *ater* black and BILIOUS].

ATRABILIOUSNESS, [at'-ra-bil'-i-us-nes], *n.* the condition of being atrabiliar.

ATRAMENT, [at'-ra-ment'], *n.* blacking, ink. [L. *atramentum*].

ATRAMENTAL, [at'-ra-ment'-al], *adj.* very black, inky.

ATRAMENTOUS, [at'-ra-ment'-us], *adj.* atramental.

ATREMBLE, [a-trembl'], *adv.* tremblingly.

ATRIP, [a-trip'], *adv.* (*naut.*) (of sails) hoisted to the masthead for trimming; (of an anchor) raised slightly above the sea-bottom. [A (3) and TRIP].

ATRIUM, (*pl.* **atria**), [at'-ri-um], *n.* the entrance hall and principal room in a Roman house; a forecourt; (*anat.*) a cavity of the heart receiving blood from the veins. [L. *atrium*].

ATROCIOUS, [a-trō'-shus], *adj.* (of behaviour) extraordinarily cruel, wicked or infamous; (*coll.*) in very bad taste, terrible, abominable, horrible. [L. *atrox*].

ATROCIOUSLY, [a-trō'-shus-li], *adv.* in atrocious fashion.

ATROCIOUSNESS, [a-trō'-shus-nes], *n.* the quality of being atrocious.

ATROCITY, [a-tros'-i-ti], *n.* an act of cruelty and wickedness; violence done to non-combatants and prisoners by the enemy; a very bad work of art. [L. *atrocitas*].

ATROPHIC, [at-rof'-ik], *adj.* pertaining to atrophy.

ATROPHIED, [at'-ro-fid], *adj.* suffering or resulting from atrophy; wasted, shrunk, starved.

ATROPHY (1), [at'-rof-i], *n.* wasting away due to lack of nourishment; (*biol.*) wasting or cessation of development of parts of plants or animals for which there is no longer biological necessity; (*fig.*) the slow disappearance of some moral quality through lack of use. [Gk. *atrophos* unnourished].

ATROPHY (2), [at'-rof-i], *v.t. and i.* to waste away through atrophy; to cause atrophy in.

ATROPINE, [at'-ro-pin], *n.* a poisonous vegetable alkaloid obtained from deadly nightshade, *Atropa Belladonna*. [Gk. *atropa* deadly nightshade].

ATROPISM, [at'-rop-izm], *n.* a morbid state of the system caused by misuse of atropine.

ATROPOUS, [at'-rop-us], *adj.* (*bot.*) (of an ovule) unturned, with the foramen on top. [Gk. *atropos* unturned].

ATTABOY, [at'-a-boi'], *int.* an exclamation of enthusiastic congratulation on some feat and encouragement to further efforts. [*prob.* U.S. corruption of *That's the boy*].

ATTACH, [a-tach'], *v.t.* to fasten to, join to, connect with; to cause to adhere to, win over (support, etc.); to appoint to by authority; (*reflex.*) to unite with, accompany; (*fig.*) to attribute to, assign to; (*pass.*) to be fond of, interested in; (*leg.*) to arrest or seize (a person or property) under legal authority. [OFr. *attachier*].

ATTACHABLE, [a-tach'-abl], *adj.* able to be attached.

ATTACHE, attaché, [a-tash'-ā], *n.* a military or other expert attached to an embassy; **a. case,** a small hand-case for carrying documents or other papers. [Fr. *attaché, p.pt.* of *attacher*].

ATTACHMENT, [a-tach'-ment], *n.* state or condition of attaching or being attached; that by which a thing is attached; bond of affection, strong liking; (*leg.*) arrest of a person or legally authorized seizure of his property; writ authorizing this. [Fr. *attachement*].

ATTACK (1), [a-tak'], *n.* the state or condition of attacking or being attacked, a violent assault or hostile onslaught; (*fig.*) method of approach to, or starting upon. [Fr. *attaque*].

ATTACK (2), [a-tak'], *v.t. and i.* to make an assault upon, to make an onslaught on; (*milit.*) to make an offensive against an enemy; to advance and initiate (a conflict), to strike the first blow; (*fig.*) to open opposition with argument, to blame or reproach bitterly; to set to work on a task with furious energy; (of disease, etc.) to act violently or injuriously upon. [Fr. *attaquer*].

ATTACKABLE, [a-tak'-abl], *adj.* able to be attacked.

ATTAGHAN, see YATAGHAN.

ATTAIN, [a-tān'], *v.t. and i.* to gain, accomplish, reach, get, achieve (a place, position, or object); to come to, arrive at. [OFr. *attaindre* from L. *attingere*].

ATTAINABILITY, [a-tān'-a-bil'-i-ti], *n.* attainableness.

ATTAINABLE, [a-tān'-abl], *adj.* able to be attained.

ATTAINABLENESS, [a-tān'-abl-nes], *n.* the possibility of attainment.

ATTAINDER, [a-tān'-der], *n.* the act or state of attainting or being attainted, the deprivation of civil and legal rights on a sentence of death or outlawry; **Bill of A.,** legislation imposing the penalties of attainder without legal trial. [ATTAINT (2)].

ATTAINMENT, [a-tān'-ment], *n.* the act or state of attaining, the thing attained; an acquirement, skill, knowledge, or talent gained by effort and application.

ATTAINT (1), [a-tānt'], *n.* attainder; disgrace, stain; a wound on a horse's leg caused by an over-reaching. [OFr. *atteint*].

ATTAINT (2), [a-tānt'], *v.t.* to subject or sentence to attainder; to dishonour; to corrupt, taint, affect. [OFr. *atteindre*, L. *attingere*].

ATTAINTMENT, [a-tānt'-ment], *n.* the act or state of being attainted, attainder.

ATTAINTURE, [a-tān'-cher], *n.* attaintment.

ATTAR, OTTAR, OTTO, [at'-er], *n.* a perfume obtained from rose-petals. [Pers. *atar* scent].

ATTEMPER, [a-tem'-per], *v.t.* to mix in proportion, to modify by mixing, to temper; to adapt, to soothe. [L. *attemperare* to qualify].

ATTEMPERATE†, [a-tem'-per-at], *adj.* proportionate, tempered, qualified, suited, moderate.

ATTEMPERATOR, [a-tem'-per-āt'-or], *n.* an arrangement of hot-water pipes to regulate temperature in brewing.

ATTEMPT (1), [a-tempt'], *n.* an endeavour to do or obtain something (usually with difficulty and uncertainty); a violent attack against someone or something.

ATTEMPT (2), [a-tempt'], *v.t.* to strive after, to try, endeavour, seek to obtain, try to achieve or get something by sudden force, to attack. [L. *attemptare*].

ATTEMPTABILITY, [a-temp'-ta-bil'-i-ti], *n.* possibility of being attempted.

ATTEMPTABLE, [a-tempt'-abl], *adj.* able to be attempted.

ATTEMPTER, [a-tempt'-er], *n.* one who attempts.

ATTEND, [a-tend'], *v.i.* to wait upon in order to serve, to follow in attendance upon, to wait upon for orders and duties; to listen carefully to, give good heed to, fix the mind firmly upon; *v.t.* to be present at; wait upon; to visit to perform some service (*esp.* of a doctor); to accompany inseparably. [L. *attendere*].

ATTENDANCE, [a-tend'-ans], *n.* the act of attending; those who attend something; a waiting upon, attention. [OFr. *atendance*].

ATTENDANT (1), [a-tend'-ant], *n.* one who attends; a member of a retinue; a personal servant of a superior sort. [OFr. *attendant*].

ATTENDANT (2), [a-tend'-ant], *adj.* attending; accompanying, consequential, connected.

ATTENDER, [a-tend'-er], *n.* one who attends.

ATTENDINGLY, [a-tend'-ing-li], *adv.* with attention.

ATTENTION, [a-ten'-shun], *n.* the act or state of attending; state or act of mental application to the subject in hand, watchful notice; solicitous care; assiduous civility; (*pl.*) courtesies offered by a man to a woman; (*milit.*) a basic position in drill, in which a person stands rigidly upright with feet together and arms to the side. [~L. *attentio*].

ATTENTIVE, [a-tent'-iv], *adj.* paying attention; heedful. [Fr. *attentif*].

ATTENTIVELY, [a-tent'-iv-li], *adv.* in attentive fashion.

ATTENTIVENESS, [a-tent'-iv-nes], *n.* the condition of being attentive.

ATTENUANT (1), [a-ten'-yŏŏ-ant], *n.* a medicine for thinning the blood.

ATTENUANT (2), [a-ten'-yŏŏ-ant], *adj.* tending to dilution, thinning down. [~L. *attenuans*, ~ATTENUATE (2)].

ATTENUATE (1), [a-ten'-yŏŏ-at], *adj.* attenuated.

ATTENUATE (2), [a-ten'-yŏŏ-āt'], *v.t. and i.* to thin, to make slender, to dilute, to reduce the power of; to become thin, wasted. [~L. *attenuare*].

ATTENUATED, [a-ten'-yŏŏ-āt'-id], *adj.* made thin, slender or slim; diluted; tapering.

ATTENUATION, [a-ten'-yŏŏ-ā'-shun], *n.* the act of attenuating or state of being attenuated. [~L. *attenuatio*].

ATTEST, [a-test'], *v.t. and i.* to bear witness to, to certify; (*leg.*) to witness (a signature, etc.); to offer proof of; (*fig.*) to make manifest, show evidently; to put (a person) on oath; to testify to. [L. *attestari* to bear witness to].

ATTESTABLE, [a-test'-abl], *adj.* able to be attested.

ATTESTATION, [at'-es-tā'-shun], *n.* the act of attesting, the thing attested. [~L. *attestatio*].

ATTESTOR, ATTESTER, [a-test'-er], *n.* one who attests, a witness.

ATTIC (1), [at'-ik], *n.* the top room of a house immediately below the roof, with a ceiling following its angle; (*fig.*) any small and often sordid room at the top of a house, a garret. [Fr. *attique*].

ATTIC (2), [at'-ik], *adj.* pertaining to Attica, and hence to Greece generally; (*fig.*) artistic, noble, simple, austere; **A. base,** (*arch.*) the characteristic base of Ionic and Corinthian columns. [Gk. *Attikos*].

ATTICISM, [at'-is-izm], *n.* the style of or idioms peculiar to Athenian Greek; an elegant expression; partiality towards Athens.

ATTICIZE, [at'-i-siz], *v.i.* to affect the manners of Athens, or Greece.

ATTIC BASE

ATTINGE†, [a-tinj'] *v.t.* to touch lightly, to flavour or affect slightly. [L. *attingere*].

ATTIRE (1), [a-tier'], *n.* clothes, dress; ceremonial or elaborate dress; (*her.*) antlers.

ATTIRE (2), [a-tier'], *v.t.* to dress, clothe, adorn. [OFr. *atirer* equip].

ATTIRED, [a-tierd'], *adj.* dressed, adorned; (*her.*) having antlers.

ATTITUDE, [at'-i-tewd], *n.* posture of body, bearing of head and limbs; general mien; disposition of mind or opinion; position of a nation or class personified in relation to some circumstances. [Fr. *attitude*].

ATTITUDINAL, [at'-i-tewd'-in-al], *adj.* relating to attitude.

ATTITUDINARIAN, [at'-i-tewd'-in-āer'-i-an], *n.* a person who affects attitudes.

ATTITUDINIZE, [at'-i-tewd'-in-iz], *v.i.* to strike an attitude, to affect a pose, ape a deportment or mental disposition.

ATTIRED

ATTOLLENT (1), [a-tol'-ent], *n.* an attollent muscle.

ATTOLLENT (2), [a-tol'-ent], *adj.* (of functions of muscles) lifting up, raising up. [~L. *attollens*].

ATTORN, [a-turn'], *v.t.* (*leg.*) to transfer feudal

homage from one overlord to another, to agree to become tenant of a new landlord on the transfer of a property. [OFr. *atorner* turn to].

ATTORNEY, [a-turn′-i], *n.* (*leg.*) one legally empowered to act for another, a solicitor, a legal practitioner; **by a.,** by legal deputy; **A. General,** officer appointed to act for the sovereign in all state cases; **power of a.,** legal warrant to act for another. [OFr. *atorné*].

ATTORNEYSHIP, [a-turn′-i-ship], *n.* (*leg.*) the office of attorney.

ATTORNMENT, [a-turn′-ment], *n.* the act of attorning. [OFr. *atournement*].

ATTRACT, [a-trakt′], *v.t. and i.* to cause to approach, to draw towards; (*fig.*) to rouse feelings of interest and admiration in a person, to charm, allure, entice by moral and non-material means; to draw attention, to provoke observation on oneself; (*phys.*) to draw towards itself. [~L. *attractum*, *p.pt.* of *attrahere* to draw towards].

ATTRACTABILITY, [a-trakt′-a-bil′-i-ti], *n.* the condition of being attractable.

ATTRACTABLE, [a-trakt′-abl], *adj.* capable of being attracted.

ATTRACTILE, [a-trakt′-il], *adj.* having the power of attraction.

ATTRACTINGLY, [a-trakt′-ing-li], *adv.* in attracting fashion.

ATTRACTION, [a-trak′-shun], *n.* the act or condition of attracting; the influence of that which attracts; that which attracts. [~L. *attractio*].

ATTRACTIVE, [a-trakt′-iv], *adj.* having the power of attracting; (*fig.*) seductive, alluring. [Fr. *attractif*].

ATTRACTIVELY, [a-trakt′-iv-li], *adv.* in attractive fashion.

ATTRACTIVENESS, [a-trakt′-iv-nes], *n.* the quality of being attractive.

ATTRACTOR, [a-trakt′-or], *n.* person or thing that attracts.

ATTRAHENT (1), [a-trā′-ent], *n.* (*med.*) a liniment which attracts or draws by causing external irritation.

ATTRAHENT (2), [a-trā′-ent], *adj.* attracting, drawing towards. [~L. *attrahens*].

ATTRIBUTABLE, [a-trib′-yōōt-abl], *adj.* able to be attributed.

ATTRIBUTE (1), [at′-rib-yōōt], *n.* that which is attributed, a characteristic, a property, an inherent quality; an object or symbol, *esp.* associated with an office or position; (*gram.*) a word denoting quality, an adjective. [L. *attributum*].

ATTRIBUTE (2), [a-trib′-yōōt], *v.t.* to ascribe to, impute to, to take as belonging to; to assume as a property of, presume as a cause for; (*lit.*) to assign to a particular time, place, or authorship. [~L. *attribuere*].

ATTRIBUTION, [at′-rib-yōō′-shun], *n.* the act of attributing; the quality attributed; the statement or thing imputed. [~L. *attributio*].

ATTRIBUTIVE (1), [a-trib′-yōōt-iv], *n.* a thing attributed; (*gram.*) a word denoting an attribute.

ATTRIBUTIVE (2), [a-trib′-yōōt-iv], *adj.* pertaining to an attribute or attribution; (*gram.*) denoting an attribute.

ATTRIBUTIVELY, [a-trib′-yōōt-iv-li], *adv.* in an attributive manner.

ATTRITE†, [a-trīt′], *adj.* worn away by abrasion; (*theol.*) penitent only through fear of punishment. [L. *attritus*].

ATTRITED, [a-trīt′-id], *adj.* attrite.

ATTRITION, [a-trish′-un], *n.* the act, state or process of wearing away by abrasion; (*theol.*) penitence arising only through fear of punishment; (*milit.*) a tactic to exhaust the enemy in men and material before attempting a decisive onslaught. [L. *attritio*].

ATTRITUS, [at-rīt′-us], *n.* material produced by abrasion. [L. *attritus* worn away].

ATTUNE, [a-tewn′], *v.t.* to tune, to adjust one sound to another; (*fig.*) to bring into physical, spiritual, or psychological harmony. [TUNE].

ATWEEN, [a-twēn′], *adv. and prep.* between.

ATWIXT, [a-twikst′], *adv.* between, betwixt.

ATYPIC, [a-tip′-ik], *adj.* (*med.*) belonging to no special type. [A (4) and TYPE (1)].

ATYPICAL, [a-tip′-ikl], *adj.* not conforming to type.

AUBADE, [ō-bahd′], *n.* a song at dawn, a musical composition for morning performance, a morning concert. [Fr. *aubade* from Span. *albada* from *alba* dawn].

AUBAINE, [ō-bān′], *n.* former inheritance by the French crown of the property of an alien dying unnaturalized. [Fr. *aubaine*].

AUBERGINE, [ō-bāer-zhēn′], *n.* (*bot.*) the fruit of the egg plant, *Solanum Melongena*. [Fr. *aubergine*].

AUBURN, [aw′-bern], *adj.* brownish red. [OFr. *auborne* from L. *albus* white].

AUCTION (1), [awk′-shun], *n.* a public sale in which the goods go to the highest of competing bids, each bid having to be an increase on the last; **Dutch a.,** the offering of goods at high value, reducing the price until a purchaser is found; **a. bridge,** a variety of bridge in which overtricks count towards game. [~L. *auctio*].

AUCTION (2), [awk′-shun], *v.t.* to put up for sale by auction.

AUCTIONARY, [awk′-shun-a-ri], *adj.* relating to an auction.

AUCTIONEER, [awk′-shun-ēer′], *n.* one who officiates at an auction, one licensed to auction property for sale.

AUDACIOUS, [aw-dā′-shus], *adj.* bold, daring, recklessly brave, impudent, insolently presuming, contemptuously shameless. [~L. *audax*].

AUDACIOUSLY, [aw-dā′-shus-li], *adv.* in audacious fashion.

AUDACITY, [aw-das′-i-ti], *n.* the quality of being audacious. [AUDACIOUS].

AUDIBILITY, [aw′-di-bil′-i-ti], *n.* the state of being audible.

AUDIBLE, [awd′-ibl], *adj.* able to be heard, loud enough to be heard. [MedL. *audibilis*].

AUDIBLENESS, [awd′-ibl-nes], *n.* audibility.

AUDIBLY, [awd′-ib-li], *adv.* in audible fashion.

AUDIENCE, [aw′-di-ens], *n.* the act of hearing; a formal interview given by a potentate to an inferior person; a judicial session to hear cases; an assemblage of persons to witness some spectacle, *esp.* a dramatic entertainment. [L. *audientia*].

AUDILE, [awd′-il], *adj.* perceived through the auditory nerves; (of persons) specially sensitive to auditory impressions, tending to remember and recollect aurally instead of visually or tactually. [L. *audire* to hear].

AUDIOMETER, [awd-i-om′-it-er], *n.* a device for testing the hearing. [L. *audio* I hear and METER].

AUDIT (1), [awd′-it], *n.* an official examination of accounts of a business or institution; a settlement of accounts; **a. ale,** a strong ale, originally brewed at universities to enliven audit days; **commissioner of a.,** a commissioner to overlook public accounts. [L. *auditus*].

AUDIT (2), [awd′-it], *v.t.* to examine accounts, make an audit.

AUDIT-HOUSE, [awd′-it-hows′], *n.* an annex to a cathedral, for the transaction of its worldly business.

AUDITION, [aw-dish′-un], *n.* the act of hearing or listening, the sense and capacity of hearing; a preliminary test for wireless, film, and stage aspirants. [~L. *auditio*].

AUDITIVE, [awd′-it-iv], *adj.* pertaining to hearing.

AUDITOR, [awd′-it-or], *n.* a person appointed to carry out an audit; a listener. [L. *auditor*].

AUDITORIAL, [awd′-i-taw′-ri-al], *adj.* pertaining to an audit or an auditor.

AUDITORIUM, [awd′-i-taw′-ri-um], *n.* the part of a building in which the audience assembles. [L. *auditorium*].

AUDITORSHIP, [awd′-it-or-ship], *n.* the office or duty of an auditor.

AUDITORY (1), [awd′-it-er-i], *n.* an audience; an auditorium. [L. *auditorium*].

AUDITORY (2), [awd′-it-er-i], *adj.* pertaining to the sense of hearing. [L. *auditorius*].

AUF, [awf], *n.* oaf; a fool; a simple fellow. [OIcel. *alfr* elf, fairy].

AUGEAN, [aw-jē′-an], *adj.* filthy, unclean, filled with the accumulated dirt of years; **A. stable,** (*myth.*) the stable of Augeas, King of Elis, which contained three thousand oxen and remained uncleansed for thirty years. [Gk. *Augeias*].

AUGER, [aw′-ger], *n.* a tool used by carpenters for boring large holes; a tool for boring soil or rocks. [OE. *nafugar*].

AUGER

AUGET, AUGETTE, [ō-zhā′, aw′-jet], *n.* a tube filled with powder used for blasting. [Fr *auget*].

AUGHT (1), [awt], *n.* anything. [OE. *awiht*].

AUGHT (2), [awt], *adv.* at all, in any way. [*Prec.*].

AUGITE, [aw′-jīt], *n.* a dark or greenish coloured variety of pyroxene found in volcanic rocks. [Gk. *augites*].

AUGITIC, [aw-jit′-ik], *adj.* belonging to, or containing augite.

AUGMENT (1), [awg′-ment], *n.* a vowel prefixed to the verb in certain languages to denote the past tense. [L. *augmentum* increase].

AUGMENT (2), [awg-ment′], *v.t.* to make larger, increase; (*gram.*) to prefix an augment to; *v.i.* to grow bigger, increase. [*Prec.*, Fr. *augmenter*].

AUGMENTABLE, [awg-ment′-abl], *adj.* able to be augmented.

AUGMENTATION, [awg′-ment-ā′-shun], *n.* process or act of augmenting; state of being increased; that which is added; (*her.*) an addition to a coat-of-arms as a mark of honour; (*mus.*) repetition of a subject in notes of greater value. [~L. *augmentatio*].

AUGMENTATIVE (1), [awg-ment′-at-iv], *n.* (*gram.*) an affix used to enlarge or intensify the meaning of a root word.

AUGMENTATIVE (2), [awg-ment′-at-iv], *adj.* with the quality or power of augmenting; (*gram.*) enlarging the meaning. [Fr. *augmentatif*].

AUGMENTED, [awg-ment′-id], *adj.* added to; (*mus.*) larger by a semitone than the normal or major interval.

AUGMENTER, [awg-ment′-er], *n.* person or thing that augments.

AUGUR (1), [awg′-er], *n* an ancient Roman who foretold future events by observing birds and other omens; a soothsayer. [L. *augur*].

AUGUR (2), [awg′-er], *v.t.* to forebode, betoken, infer, be a sign of; *v.i.* to conjecture from signs or happenings; promise.

AUGURAL, [awg′-yōō-ral], *adj.* relating to augury. [L. *auguralis*].

AUGURIAL, [awg-yōōer′-i-al], *adj.* pertaining to augurs or augury. [L. *augurialis*].

AUGURY, [awg′-yōō-ri], *n.* the practice of divination by an augur; omen, prediction, auguring. [L. *augurium*].

AUGUST (1), [awg′-ust], *n.* the eighth month of the year, named after the Emperor Augustus. [L. *Augustus*].

AUGUST (2), [aw-gust′], *adj.* grand, majestic, inspiring awe or reverence. [L. *augustus*].

AUGUSTAN, [aw-gust′-an], *adj.* pertaining to Augustus Caesar or his time, *esp.* to the highly developed Latin literature of that time; **A. Age,** term applied to that period of a nation's history when its literary activity is marked by superlative refinement and finish; the age of the Emperor Augustus; the age of Queen Anne. [*Prec.*].

AUGUSTINIANS, [aw′-gust-in′-i-anz], *n.*(*pl.*) an order of friars, so called because they followed the tenets and rules of St. Augustine of Hippo. [St. *Augustine*].

AUGUSTLY, [aw-gust′-li], *adv.* in majestic manner.

AUGUSTNESS, [aw-gust′-nes], *n.* the state of being august.

AUK, [awk], *n.* a web-footed sea-bird of the genus *Alca* or *Mergulus*. [OIcel. *aukr*].

AULA, (*pl.* **aulae**), [aw′-la, aw′-lē], *n.* large hall or court of a Roman villa; (*anat.*) the front part of the third ventricle in the brain. [L. *aula*].

AULARIAN (1), [aw-lāer′-i-an], *n.* a member of a hall at a university as distinct from a college.

AULARIAN (2), [aw-lāer′-i-an], *adj.* pertaining to a hall. [L. *aularius*].

AULIC, [aw′-lik], *adj.* pertaining to or connected with a royal court; **A. Council,** formerly the privy council of the Holy Roman emperor; the imperial council of the Austro-Hungarian Empire. [L. *aulicus*].

AUMBRY, see AMBRY.

AUNCEL, [awn′-sel], *n.* an ancient form of balance. [AFr. *auncelle* for *launcelle*].

AUNT, [ahnt], *n.* the sister of one's father or mother, or the wife of an uncle; **A. Sally,** a dummy figure in the form of a woman at which missiles are thrown as a pastime. [OFr. *aunte* from L. *amita*].

AURA, [aw′-ra], *n.* aroma, effluvium as of blood or flowers; (*fig.*) atmosphere created by associations of words; (*elect.*) a current of air caused by an electrical discharge; (*med.*) a sensation of a current of air accompanied by oppression, palpitation, etc., which precedes an attack of epilepsy. [Gk. *aura* breeze].

AURAL (1), [aw′-ral], *adj.* pertaining to an aura.

AURAL (2), [aw′-ral], *adj.* belonging to or connected with the ear. [~L. *auris* ear].

AURATE, [aw′-rāt], *n.* (*chem.*) a compound produced by the action of auric acid on a base. [L. *aurum* gold].

AURATED, [aw′-rāt-id], *adj.* possessing ears, as in the scallop-shell. [L. *auris* ear].

AUREATE, [aw′-ri-at], *adj.* golden; gilded, splendid. [~L. *aureus* golden].

AURELIA, [aw-rēl′-i-a], *n.* the pupa of an insect; genus of large jelly-fish. [It. *aurelia* silkworm].

AURELIAN, [aw-rēl′-i-an], *adj.* pertaining to an aurelia.

AUREOLA, AUREOLE, [aw-rē′-ol-a], *n.* a halo or gold ring or disk with which painters surround the head of Christ, the Virgin, and the saints. [L. *aureola* (*corona*) golden crown].

AUREOLE, [aw′-ri-ōl], *v.t.* to place an aureole round or behind an object.

AUREUS, [aw′-rē-us], *n.* a Roman gold coin. [L. *aureus* golden].

AURIC, [aw′-rik], *adj.* pertaining to or like gold. [~L. *aurum* gold].

AURICLE, [aw′-rikl], *n.* (*anat.*) the outer ear; (*pl.*) two muscular cavities in the heart above the ventricles. [L. *auricula*].

AURICLES

AURICLED, [aw′-rikld], *adj.* with ear-like appendages.

AURICULA, [aw-rik′-yōō-la], *n.* a species of *Primula*, sometimes called, from the shape of its leaves, bear's ear. [L. *auricula*].

AURICULAR, [aw-rik′-yōō-ler], *adj.* relating to the ear, or to the sense of hearing; confided to the ear, *esp.* of a priest in the confessional; known by hearsay; pertaining to the auricles of the heart.

AURICULARLY, [aw-rik′-yōō-ler-li], *adv.* in auricular fashion.

AURICULATE, [aw-rik′-yōō-lāt], *adj.* ear-shaped; having ear-like protuberances.

AURICULATED, [aw-rik′-yōō-lāt-id], *adj.* auriculate.

AURIFEROUS, [aw-rif′-er-us], *adj* gold-bearing, containing gold. [L. *aurifer*].

AURIFORM, [aw′-ri-fawm], *adj.* in the shape of ears. [L. *auris* ear and FORM (1)].

AURIGNACIAN, [aw′-rig-nā′-shun], *adj.* represented by remains discovered in the Aurignac cave. [*Aurignac* in the Pyrenees].

AURILAVE, [aw′-ri-lāv], *n.* an ear-cleaner. [L. *auris* ear and LAVE].

AURIPIGMENTUM†, [aw′-ri-pig-ment′-um], *n.* orpiment. [L. *auripigmentum*].

AURISCALP†, [aw′-ri-skalp], *n.* an ear-probe. [L. *auriscalpium*].

AURISCOPE, [aw′-ri-skōp], *n.* a device used to examine the ear, an otoscope. [L. *auris* ear and Gk. *skopos* watcher].

AURIST, [aw′-rist], *n.* an ear specialist.

AURITED, [aw′-ri-tid], *adj.* (*zool., bot.*) having lobes or appendages like ears. [L. *auritus* eared].

AUROCHS, [ower-′oks], *n.* a primitive, almost extinct, European species of wild ox or bison. [Germ. *aurochse*].

AURORA, [aw-raw′-ra], *n.* dawn, goddess of the dawn, sunrise; **a. borealis,** luminous electrical phenomenon seen in the sky of the northern hemisphere at night, northern lights; **a. australis,** similar phenomenon occurring in the southern hemisphere. [L. *aurora* dawn].

AURORAL, [aw-raw′-ral], *adj.* pertaining to the dawn, or the northern lights.

AUROUS, [aw′-rus], *adj.* pertaining to or containing gold. [L. *aurum* gold].

AURULENT, [aw′-ryōō-lent], *adj.* of a golden hue. [L. *aurulentus*].

AURUM, [aw′-rum], *n.* Latin name for gold; the chemical element (denoted by Au). [L. *aurum*].

AUSCULTATE, [aws′-kult-āt], *v.t. and i.* to sound a person's lungs and heart with a stethoscope [L. *auscultare* listen].

AUSCULTATION, [aws′-kult-ā′-shun], *n.* listening; (*med.*) the art of diagnosis by sounding the lungs, heart, etc., with a stethoscope or by the ear alone. [~L. *auscultatio*].

AUSCULTATOR, [aws′-kult-āt′-er], *n.* one who auscultates. [L. *auscultator* listener].

AUSCULTATORY, [aws-kult′-at-or-i], *adj.* relating to auscultation.

AUSPEX†, (*pl.* **auspices**), [aws′-peks], *n.* one who makes auspices, divines. [L. *auspex*].

AUSPICATE†, [aw′-spik-āt], *v.t.* to give a good start to; to signalize one's entrance (by); to begin, inaugurate; *v.i.* to augur, predict. [~L. *auspicare*].

AUSPICE, (*pl.* **auspices**), [aw'-spis, aw'-spi-siz], *n.* an omen, generally favourable, derived from observation of the flight of birds; augury, prediction; (*pl.*) protection, patronage. [L. *auspicium* observing of birds].

AUSPICIOUS, [aw-spish'-us], *adj* auguring well, giving high promise, fortunate, favourable, gracious. [*Prec.*].

AUSPICIOUSLY, [aw-spish'-us-li], *adv.* in auspicious fashion.

AUSPICIOUSNESS, [aw-spish'-us-nes], *n.* condition of being auspicious.

AUSSIE, [aw'-si, os'-i], *n.* (*coll.*) Australia; an Australian. [AUSTRALIA].

AUSTER, [aws'-ter], *n.* the south or south-west wind; the south. [L. *auster*].

AUSTERE, [aws-tēer'], *adj.* severe, stern, strict; bare of decoration, severe in appearance. [L. *austerus* harsh, dry].

AUSTERELY, [aws-tēer'-li], *adv.* in austere fashion.

AUSTERENESS, [aws-tēer'-nes], *n.* austerity.

AUSTERITY, [aws-te'-ri-ti], *n.* severity in mode of life, manner or style. [OFr. *austerité*].

AUSTRAL, [aws'-tral], *adj.* southern. [L. *australis*].

AUSTRALASIAN, [aws'-tral-ā'-shan] *adj.* pertaining to or native to Australasia.

AUSTRALIA, [aws-trāl'-i-a], *n.* a continent in the southern hemisphere. [MdL. *terra australis* southern land].

AUSTRALIAN (1), [aws-trāl'-i-an] *n.* an inhabitant of Australia.

AUSTRALIAN (2), [aws-trāl'-i-an], *adj.* belonging to, connected with Australia.

AUTARCH, [aw'-tahk], *n.* a tyrant, despot, autocrat. [Gk. *autarkhos* independent ruler].

AUTARCHY, [aw'-tahk-i], *n.* despotism, absolute rule, self-government. [Gk. *autarkhia*].

AUTARKY, [aw'-tahk-i], *n.* self-sufficiency. [Germ. *autarkie* from Gk. *autarkeia*].

AUTHENTIC, [aw-then'-tik], *adj.* having a known origin or authority, being what it claims to be, genuine; (*leg.*) properly attested with all due formalities. [OFr. *autentique* from Gk. *authentikos* original].

AUTHENTICALLY, [aw-then'-tik-al-i], *adv.* in authentic fashion.

AUTHENTICALNESS, [aw-then'-tikl-nes], *n.* authenticity.

AUTHENTICATE, [aw-then'-tik-āt], *v.t.* to make authentic; to attest formally; to determine the origin or genuineness of; (*leg.*) to make valid. [*Prec.*].

AUTHENTICATION, [aw'-then-tik-ā'-shun], *n.* the act or process of authenticating.

AUTHENTICITY, [aw'-then-tis'-i-ti], *n.* condition of being authentic, genuineness.

AUTHENTICLY†, [aw-then'-tik-li], *adv.* authentically.

AUTHOR, [aw'-ther], *n.* one who creates or originates anything; one who creates or compiles a literary work; (*fig.*) the books or works of an author. [OFr. *autor*, L. *auctor*].

AUTHORESS, [aw'-ther-es], *n.* a woman author.

AUTHORITARIAN, [aw-thor'-i-tāer'-i-an], *adj.* undemocratic, dictatorial, repressive.

AUTHORITATIVE, [aw-thor'-it-at-iv], *adj.* accustomed to command, peremptory, dictatorial; having the approval of authority, having authority.

AUTHORITATIVELY, [aw-thor'-it-at-iv-li], *adv.* in authoritative fashion.

AUTHORITATIVENESS, [aw-thor'-it-at-iv-nes], *n.* the condition of being authoritative.

AUTHORITY, [aw-thor'-i-ti], *n.* the power or legal right to command and be obeyed; a person or group of persons having such right or power; influence, power or weight derived from rank, knowledge, experience, etc.; books giving accurate information and reliable judgments; a person expert in a particular subject. [Fr. *autorité*, L. *auctoritas*].

AUTHORIZABLE, [aw'-ther-iz-abl], *adj.* able to be authorized.

AUTHORIZATION, [aw'-ther-īz-ā'-shun], *n.* the act of authorizing; permission, sanction.

AUTHORIZE, [aw'-ther-īz], *v.t.* to give authority to; to sanction, allow; to approve or establish by authority. [Fr. *autoriser*].

AUTHORIZED, [aw'-ther-īzd], *adj.* having authority or permission; **A. Version,** an English translation of the Bible officially approved and issued in 1611.

AUTHORLESS, [aw'-ther-les], *adj.* having no known author.

AUTHORSHIP, [aw'-ther-ship], *n.* the state of being an author; the identity of the author of a work: the status of an author.

AUTO-, [aw'-tō], *pref.* done by or for oneself; spontaneous; without interference from others. [Gk *auto-*, *autos* self].

AUTO-ANALYSIS, [aw'-tō-an-al'-is-is], *n.* psychoanalysis self-applied. [AUTO and ANALYSIS].

AUTOBIOGRAPHER, [aw'-tō-bī-og'-raf-er], *n.* one who compiles autobiography.

AUTOBIOGRAPHICAL, [aw'-tō-bī-o-graf'-ikl], *adj.* relating to or containing autobiography.

AUTOBIOGRAPHICALLY, [aw'-tō-bī-og-raf'-i-kali], *adv.* in an autobiographical manner.

AUTOBIOGRAPHY, [aw'-tō-bī-og'-raf-i], *n.* an account of a man's life by himself. [AUTO and BIOGRAPHY].

AUTOBUS, [aw'-tō-bus'], *n.* a motor omnibus. [AUTOMOBILE and OMNIBUS].

AUTOCAR, [aw'-tō-kah(r)'], *n.* an automobile. [AUTOMOBILE and CAR].

AUTOCARPOUS, [aw'-tō-kahp'-us], *adj.* (*bot.*) consisting of pericarp only. [AUTO and Gk. *karpos* fruit].

AUTOCEPHALOUS, [aw'-tō-sef'-al-us], *adj.* (*eccles.*) self-governing or independent. [AUTO and Gk. *kephale* head].

AUTOCHTHON, (*pl.* **autochthones**), [aw-tok'-thon, aw-tok'-thon-ēz], *n.* one of the original primitive inhabitants of a country, an aboriginal. [Gk. *autokhthon* a native].

AUTOCHTHONAL, [aw-tok'-thon-al], *adj.* aboriginal.

AUTOCHTHONIC, [aw-tok-thon'-ik], *adj.* autochthonal.

AUTOCHTHONOUS, [aw-tok'-thon-us], *adj.* aboriginal, pertaining to the earliest known inhabitants of a place.

AUTOCLAVE, [aw'-tō-klāv], *n.* a cooking vessel with a cover that is steam-tight. [AUTO and L. *clavis* key].

AUTOCRACY, [aw-tok'-ra-si], *n.* government by a single all-powerful ruler; supreme and independent power in government. [Gk. *autokrateia* government by oneself].

AUTOCRAT, [aw'-tō-krat], *n.* an absolute monarch or ruler; a person who habitually behaves in a dictatorial and peremptory fashion. [Fr. *autocrate* from Gk. *autokrates*].

AUTOCRATIC, [aw'-to-krat'-ik], *adj.* pertaining to or behaving like an autocrat; dictatorial and overbearing in manner.

AUTOCRATICAL, [aw'-to-krat'-ikl], *adj.* autocratic.

AUTOCRATICALLY, [aw'-to-krat'-ik-al-i], *adv.* in autocratic fashion.

AUTO-CYCLE, [aw'-tō-sīkl'], *n.* a motor-cycle. [AUTOMOBILE and CYCLE].

AUTO-DA-FE, (*pl.* **autos-da-fé**), [aw'-tō-dah-fā'], *n.* a solemn trial and sentence of a heretic by a Court of the Inquisition; the execution of the sentence. [Portug. *auto-da-fé* act of faith].

AUTO-EROTISM, [aw'-tō-e'-rot-izm], *n.* (*psych.*) self-love or its manifestations. [AUTO and Gk. *eros* love].

AUTOGAMY, [aw-tog'-a-mi], *n.* (*bot.*) (of flowers) fertilization by their own pollen. [AUTO and Gk. *gamos* marriage].

AUTOGENIC, [aw'-tō-jen'-ik], *adj.* self-begotten. [AUTO and Gk. *genes* born].

AUTOGENOUS, [aw-toj'-en-us], *adj.* generated by, or generating, itself. [AUTO and Gk. *genes* born].

AUTOGRAPH (1), [aw'-tō-grahf], *n.* a person's own handwriting, *esp.* his signature, a writer's own manuscript; **a. album,** an album containing specimens of the handwriting of various people, etc. [Gk. *autographon*].

AUTOGRAPH (2), [aw'-tō-grahf], *v.t.* to write one's name as a mark of favour in a book, etc. [AUTOGRAPH (1)].

AUTOGRAPHIC, [aw'-to-graf'-ik], *adj.* autographical.

AUTOGRAPHICAL, [aw'-to-graf'-ikl], *adj.* pertaining to an autograph.

AUTOGRAPHY, [aw-tog'-raf-i], *n.* the study of autographs; the transference of a subject to a lithographing stone.

AUTOGRAVURE, [aw'-tō-grav-yŏŏer'], *n.* a type of photographic engraving. [AUTO and GRAVURE].

AUTOGYRO, [aw'-tō-jī'-rō], *n.* flying machine with a horizontal wind-driven screw which enables it to rise and descend vertically. [AUTO and GYRO].

AUTOGYRO

AUTOHARP, [aw'-tō-hahp'], *n.* musical instrument of the zither type, with dampers. [AUTO and HARP].

AUTO-INTOXICATION, [aw'-tō-in-toks'-i-kā'-shun], *n.* poisoning due to toxic matter produced by internal changes in the tissues of the body.

AUTOLATRY, [aw-tol'-at-ri], *n.* self-adoration. [AUTO and Gk. *latreia* worship].

AUTOLOGY, [aw-tol'-o-ji], *n.* the study of one's self. [AUTO and Gk. *logos* speech].

AUTOLYSIS, [aw-tol'-is-is], *n.* (*anat.*) destruction by its serum of cells in the body. [AUTO and Gk. *lusis* loosening].

AUTOMACY, [aw-tom'-a-si], *n.* the condition of being an automaton. [AUTOMATON].

AUTOMATA, see AUTOMATON.

AUTOMATH, [aw'-tō-math'], *n.* a person who is self-taught. [AUTO and Gk. *mathes* learned].

AUTOMATIC (1), [aw'-tō-mat'-ik], *n.* a quick-firing self-loading pistol or revolver.

AUTOMATIC (2), [aw'-tō-mat'-ik], *adj.* working by itself, self-acting, mechanically operated; involuntary. [Gk. *automatos* self-moving].

AUTOMATICAL, [aw'-tō-mat'-ikl], *adj.* automatic.

AUTOMATICALLY, [aw'-tō-mat'-ik-al-i], *adv.* in automatic fashion.

AUTOMATISM, [aw-tom'-at-izm], *n.* mechanical or automatic action; the theory that the behaviour of animals is automatic.

AUTOMATON, (*pl.* **automata, automatons**), [aw-tom'-at-on], *n.* anything which moves of itself; a machine or mechanical device which acts of itself; a mechanical figure constructed so as to imitate the movements of a human being; a human being who merely follows mechanically prescribed routine. [Gk. *automaton* self-acting].

AUTOMATOUS, [aw-tom'-at-us], *adj.* self-acting; acting without conscious stimulation.

AUTOMETRY, [aw-tom'-et-ri] *n.* measurement of parts of a figure in relation to the whole; self-measurement. [AUTO and Gk. *metria* measurement].

AUTOMOBILE (1), [aw'-to-mo-bēl'], *n.* a motor-car.

AUTOMOBILE (2), [aw'-tō-mō'-bil], *adj.* moving, or movable, of itself. [Fr. *automobile*, AUTO and MOBILE].

AUTOMORPHIC, [aw'-tō-maw'-fik], *adj.* pertaining to automorphism.

AUTOMORPHISM, [aw'-tō-maw'-fizm], *n.* the act or habit of ascribing to another one's own personal qualities; projection. [AUTO and Gk. *morphe* shape].

AUTONOMIAN, [aw'-tō-nō'-mi-an], *adj.* relating to autonomy.

AUTONOMIC, [aw'-tō-nom'-ik], *adj.* autonomous.

AUTONOMIST, [aw-ton'-om-ist], *n.* a supporter of autonomy.

AUTONOMOUS, [aw-ton'-om-us], *adj.* self-governing; independent.

AUTONOMY, [aw-ton'-o-mi], *n.* the power or right of self-government; independence in conducting one's own affairs; a self-governing community. [Gk. *autonomia*].

AUTONYM, [aw'-tō-nim], *n.* a literary work appearing under the author's own name. [AUTO and Gk. *onoma* name].

AUTOPHAGI, [aw-tof'-a-jī], *n.(pl.)* birds able to feed themselves as soon as hatched. [*Next*].

AUTOPHAGOUS, [aw-tof'-a-gus], *adj.* feeding on or by oneself. [Gk. *autophagos* self-feeding].

AUTOPHOBY, [aw-tof'-o-bi], *n.* inverted conceit, fear of mention of oneself. [AUTO and Gk. *phobia* fear].

AUTOPHONY, [aw-tof'-o-ni], *n.* (*med.*) a doctor's observation of the resonance of his own voice, when speaking loudly with his head close to his patient's chest. [AUTO and Gk. *phone* voice].

AUTOPLASTIC, [aw'-tō-plast'-ik], *adj.* pertaining to autoplasty.

AUTOPLASTY, [aw'-tō-plast'-i], *n.* (*surg.*) the grafting of skin or other tissue from another part of a person's body. [AUTO and Gk. *plastos* formed].

AUTOPLATE, [aw'-tō-plāt], *n.* machine for producing curved stereo-plates quickly for newspaper printing. [AUTO and PLATE].

AUTOPSY, [aw'-top'-si], *n.* (*med.*) personal observation; examination of a corpse by dissection. [Gk. *autopsia*].

AUTOPTICAL, [aw-top'-tikl], *adj.* observed or seen by oneself. [*Prec.*].

AUTOPTICALLY, [aw-top'-tik-al-i], *adv.* from personal observation.

AUTO-RADIOGRAM, [aw'-tō-rā'-di-ō-gram'], *n.* a radio-gramophone fitted with an automatic record-changing device. [AUTO and RADIOGRAM].

AUTOSCHEDIASM, [aw'-tō-skē'-di-azm], *n.* an extemporization, an impromptu. [Gk. *autoskhediasma*].

AUTOSOMES, [aw'-tō-sōmz], *n.(pl.)* chromosomes which are alike in male and female. [AUTO and Gk. *soma* body].

AUTO-SUGGESTION, [aw'-tō-su-jes'-chun], *n.* suggestion by oneself to oneself. [AUTO and SUGGESTION].

AUTOTHEISM, [aw'-tō-thē-izm], *n.* (*theol.*) the doctrine of the self-existence of God. [AUTO and THEISM].

AUTOTHERAPY, [aw'-tō-the'-rap-i], *n.* treatment of disease by use of pathological secretions of the patient. [AUTO and THERAPHY].

AUTOTOXAEMIA, [aw'-tō-toks-ē'-mi-a], *n.* auto-intoxication. [AUTO and TOXAEMIA].

AUTOTOXICATION, [aw'-tō-toks-ik-ā'-shun], *n.* auto-intoxication. [AUTO and TOXICATION].

AUTOTOXICOSIS, [aw'-tō-toks-ik-ō'-sis], *n.* auto-intoxication. [AUTO and TOXICOSIS].

AUTO-TOXIN, [aw'-tō-toks'-in], *n.* toxic matter produced by internal changes in the tissues in the body. [AUTO and TOXIN].

AUTO-TRANSFORMER, [aw'-tō-trans-fawm'-er], *n.* (*wirel.*) a transformer for a small change in voltage in which primary and secondary form a single winding [AUTO and TRANSFORMER].

AUTOTYPE, [aw'-tō-tīp'], *n.* a facsimile; (*phot.*) a reproduction by a process of photographic printing [*Prot.*; AUTO and TYPE].

AUTOTYPOGRAPHY, [aw'-tō-tī-pog'-raf-i], *n.* (*print.*) a process by which reproductions on a gelatine base are transferred to metal plates and printed therefrom. [*Prec.*].

AUTOVAC, [aw'-tō-vak'], *n.* (*eng.*) a vacuum device to raise petrol from a low tank to one from which it will run by gravity to the carburetter. [*Prot.*; AUTO and VACUUM].

AUTUMN, [aw'-tum], *n.* the third season of the year (September 21 to December 20), the fall; (*fig.*) maturity, late middle-age, the beginning of decline. [L. *autumnus*].

AUTUMNAL (1), [aw-tum'-nal], *n.* a plant that blooms in autumn.

AUTUMNAL (2), [aw-tum'-nal], *adj.* pertaining to autumn; produced or gathered in autumn; pertaining to the decline of life. [L. *autumnalis*].

AUXANOMETER, [awks'-an-om'-it-er], *n.* an apparatus to register the rate of growth of plants. [Gk. *auxano* I grow and METER].

AUXESIS, [awks-ē'-sis], *n.* (*rhet.*) hyperbole. [Gk. *auxesis* increase].

AUXETIC, [awks-ē'-tik], *adj.* (*rhet.*) pertaining to auxesis, magnifying, expanding.

AUXILIARY (1), [awg'-zil'-yer-i], *n.* a helper, assistant; (*gram.*) an auxiliary verb; (*pl.*) foreign troops, usually hired.

AUXILIARY (2), [awg-zil'-yer-i], *adj.* helping, assisting; **a. verb,** a verb which helps to form the moods and tenses of other verbs. [L. *auxiliaris*].

AVA, [ah'-va], *n.* the inebriating Hawaiian beverage yielded by a species of *Cordyline*. [Native].

AVAIL (1), [a-vāl'], *n.* profit, advantage, use, benefit.

AVAIL (2), [a-vāl'], *v.t.* to benefit, profit, be of use; *v.i.* to be of use, value, service; (*reflex.*) to take advantage of, make use of, profit by. [A (3) and Fr. *valoir* be worth].

AVAILABILITY, [a-vāl'-a-bil'-i-ti], *n.* condition of being available.

AVAILABLE, [a-vāl'-abl], *adj.* able to be made use of; close at hand, easy to get at; legally usable or valid. [AVAIL (2)].

AVAILABLENESS, [a-vāl'-abl-nes], *n.* availability.

AVAILABLY, [a-vāl'-a-bli], *adv.* in available fashion.

AVALANCHE, [av'-al-ahnch], *n.* a mass of loosened ice and snow hurtling down a mountain-side, a snow slip; (*fig.*) that which comes suddenly and with overwhelming force or in huge quantities. [Fr. dialect *avalanche*].

AVANT-COURIER, [av'-ahn-ko͝or'-i-er], *n.* a herald. [Fr. *avant-courier* forerunner].

AVANT-GARDE, [av'-ahn-gahd'], *n.* the vanguard of an army. [Fr. *avantgarde* advance guard].

AVANTURINE, AVENTURINE, [av-an'-tew-rin], *n.* a brownish variety of Venetian glass discovered by chance; a kind of micaceous quartz. [It. *avventurino* chance].

AVARICE, [av'-er-is] *n.* an immoderate greed for wealth; miserliness, covetousness. [L. *avaritia*].

AVARICIOUS, [av'-er-ish'-us], *adj.* afflicted with avarice; covetous, miserly, grasping. [Fr. *avaricieux*].

AVARICIOUSLY, [av'-er-ish'-us-li], *adv.* in avaricious fashion.

AVARICIOUSNESS, [av'-er-ish'-us-nes], *n.* the state or quality of being avaricious.

AVAST, [a-vahst'], *int.* (*naut.*) hold! stop! [Du. *houd vast* hold fast].

AVATAR, [av'-a-tah(r)], *n.* (*myth.*) descent to earth of a Hindu deity, and his incarnation as man or beast. [Skr. *avatara* descent].

AVAUNT, [a-vawnt'], *int.* †begone! depart! [Fr. *avant* forward!].

AVE (1), [ā'-vē, ah'-vā], *n.* a prayer to the Virgin Mary, so called from the opening words, *Ave Maria*, Hail Mary!

AVE (2), [ā'-vē, ah'-vā], *int.* hail! farewell! [L. *ave* hail].

AVELLAN, [av'-el-an, a-vel'-an], *n.* a filbert; **a. cross**, (*her.*) a rectangular cross formed by four filberts meeting. [L. *Avellanus*, now Avella, famed for nuts and fruit].

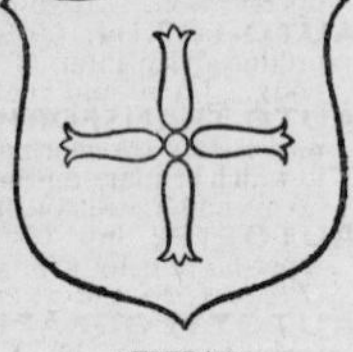

AVELLAN

AVENACEOUS, [av'-en-ā'-shus], *adj.* pertaining to oats. [L. *avena* oat].

AVENGE, [a-venj'], *v.t.* to exact satisfaction or retribution from, to obtain vengeance for, to inflict just punishment. [OFr. *avengier*].

AVENGEANCE†, [a-ven'-jens], *n.* punishment, revenge.

AVENGEMENT, [a-venj'-ment], *n.* the act of avenging, vengeance.

AVENGER, [a-ven'-jer], *n.* a person who avenges.

AVENS, [av'-enz], *n.* the herb bennet, a variety of *Geum*. [OFr. *avence*].

AVENTAIL, [av'-en-tāl], *n.* the movable mouthpiece of a helmet. [AFr. **aventail* an opening to let in air].

AVENTINE (1), [av'-en-tīn], *n.* a secure position; name of a political party in opposition to Fascism in Italy.

AVENTINE (2), [av'-en-tīn], *adj.* relating to Mount Aventinus, one of the seven hills of Rome. [L. *Aventinus*].

AVENTURE†, [a-ven'-cho͝oer], *n.* an accident resulting in a person's death. [OFr. *aventure*].

AVENTURINE, see AVANTURINE.

AVENUE, [av'-en-ew], *n.* a broad and usually tree-lined roadway, *esp.* one forming the drive to a mansion; a double line of trees or other objects between which one may walk; a street or road; (*fig.*) a way of approach. [Fr. *avenue*].

AVER, (averring, averred), [a-vur'], *v.t.* (*leg.*) to declare to be true; to affirm positively; to establish as just and right. [Fr. *avérer*].

AVERAGE (1), [av'-er-ij], *n.* a mean quantity or value of any number of unequal quantities, obtained by adding these together and dividing the resultant amount by the number of quantities concerned; a generalized estimate arrived at by this means; usual standard, common quantity or rate. [L. *averagium* cattle, property].

AVERAGE (2), [av'-er-ij], *adj.* constituting a mean proportion, obtained by average; ordinary, of the usual standard.

AVERAGE (3), [av'-er-ij], *v.t. and i.* to find the average of, to reduce to a mean, to distribute according to an average; **a. out, at**, to give an average of.

AVERAGELY, [av'-er-ij-li], *adv.* according to average.

AVERAGER, [av'-er-ij-er], *n.* one who estimates averages.

AVERMENT, [a-vur'-ment], *n.* the act of averring; a positive affirmation; something averred; (*leg.*) an offer to vindicate a plea advanced in a suit.

AVERNAL, [a-vurn'-al], *adj.* pertaining to Lake Avernus, anciently supposed to be the entrance to hell; pertaining to hell, hellish. [L. *Avernalis*].

AVERPENNY†, [av'-er-pen'-i], *n.* (*leg.*) a monetary contribution formerly paid towards conveying the king's carriages. [AVERAGE and PENNY].

AVERROISM, [av'-er-ō'-izm], *n.* the doctrines and tenets of *Averrhoes*, an Arabian philosopher.

AVERRUNCATE, [av'-er-ung'-kāt], *v.t.* to turn aside, ward off. [L. *averruncare*].

AVERRUNCATION, [av'-er-ung-kā'-shun], *n.* the action of averruncating.

AVERRUNCATOR, [av'-er-ung-kāt'-er], *n.* shears for pruning trees.

AVERSANT, [a-vurs'-ant], *adj.* (*her.*) displaying the back of the right hand.

AVERSE, [a-vurs'], *adj.* viewing with repugnance or disfavour; unwilling, disinclined. [L. *aversus* turned away].

AVERSELY, [a-vurs'-li], *adv.* in averse fashion.

AVERSENESS, [a-vurs'-nes], *n.* the state or quality of being averse.

AVERSION, [a-vur'-shun], *n.* a strong feeling of repugnance, dislike, loathing; disinclination; an object of dislike. [L. *aversio*].

AVERT, [a-vurt'], *v.t.* to turn away from, turn aside; ward off; (*fig.*) to ward off, prevent (a catastrophe, etc.). [L. *avertere*].

AVERTABLE, [a-vurt'-abl], *adj.* preventable, avoidable.

AVERTED, [a-vurt'-id], *adj.* turned aside (*esp.* of the eyes) as though in shame or horror.

AVERTEDLY, [a-vurt'-id-li], *adv.* in averted fashion.

AVERTER, [a-vurt'-er], *n.* one who averts.

AVIAN, [ā'-vi-an], *adj.* relating to birds. [L. *avis* bird].

AVIARY, [ā'-vi-er-i], *n.* a place for keeping or rearing birds. [L. *aviarium*].

AVIATE, [ā'-vi-āt], *v.i.* to fly (in aircraft). [AVIATOR].

AVIATION, [ā'-vi-ā'-shun], *n.* the art or science of flying aircraft. [Fr. *aviation*; L. *avis* bird].

AVIATOR, [ā'-vi-āt-or], *n.* one qualified to pilot aircraft. [Fr. *aviateur*].

AVIATRESS, [ā'-vi-āt-res], *n.* a woman flier.

AVICULTURE, [ā'-vi-kul'-cher], *n.* the breeding and keeping of birds. [L. *avis* bird and CULTURE].

AVID, [av'-id] *adj.* eager for, keenly desirous of, greedy. [L. *avidus*].

AVIDITY, [a-vid'-i-ti], *n.* vehement desire, eagerness, greed, hunger. [L. *aviditas*].

AVIDLY, [av'-id-li], *adv.* greedily.

AVIETTE, [ā-vi-et'], *n.* an engineless flying-machine, a glider. [Fr. *avion* aeroplane].

AVIFAUNA, [ā'-vi-fawn'-a], *n.* the birds of a given region. [L. *avis* bird and FAUNA].

AVIFORM, [ā'-vi-fawm], *adj.* shaped like a bird. [L. *avis* bird and FORM].

AVIGATO, see AVOCADO.

AVISO, [a-vē'-zō], *n.* a packet-boat. [Span. *aviso*].

AVITAL†, [av'-itl], *adj.* ancestral. [L. *avitus*].

AVIZANDUM, [av'-iz-and'-um], *n.* (*Scots leg.*) private consideration of a case. [MedL. *advisandum* from *advisare* to consider].

AVOCADO, AVIGATO, [av'-ō-kah'-dō], *n.* the alligator-pear, the fruit of a West Indian species of *Persea*. [Span. *avocado* from Mexican *ahuacatl*].

AVOCAT, [av'-ō-kah], *n.* a lawyer. [Fr. *avocat*].

AVOCATION, [av'-ō-kā'-shun], *n.* a person's proper calling, business or occupation. [L. *avocatio* calling away].

AVOCATIVE, [a-vok'-at-iv], *adj.* diverting, calling aside.

AVOCET, AVOSET, [av'-ō-set], *n.* a bird of the snipe group, having a bill curving upwards, *Recurvirostra avocetta*. [Fr. *avocette*].

AVOID, [a-void'], *v.t.* to keep away from, shun the company of; to abstain from; to evade, escape; (*leg.*) to make void, annul. [AFr. *avoider*].

AVOIDABLE, [a-void'-abl], *adj.* able to be avoided.

AVOIDANCE, [a-void'-ans], *n.* the act of avoiding, shunning a person's company.

AVOIDER, [a-void'-er], *n.* one who avoids.

AVOIDLESS, [a-void'-les], *adj.* (*poet.*) inevitable.

AVOIRDUPOIS (1), [av'-er-dew-poiz'], *n.* system of weights used for common commodities. [Corruption of *avoir de pois* from OFr. *aveir de pois* things of weight].

AVOIRDUPOIS (2), [av'-er-dew-poiz'], *adj.* pertaining to avoirdupois.

AVOSET, see AVOCET.

AVOUCH† **(1)**, [a-vowch'], *n.* evidence, assurance.
AVOUCH (2), [a-vowch'], *v.t. and i.* to affirm, attest; to admit openly; to vouch for, certify to. [OFr. *avochier*].
AVOUCHABLE, [a-vowch'-abl], *adj.* able to be avouched.
AVOUCHMENT, [a-vowch'-ment], *n.* the act of avouching.
AVOW, [a-vow'], *v.t.* to confess openly, to own up to, admit freely; (*leg.*) to admit and be prepared to justify, vindicate. [Fr. *avouer*].
AVOWABLE, [a-vow'-abl], *adj.* able to be avowed.
AVOWABLY, [a-vow'-ab-li], *adv.* in an avowable way.
AVOWAL, [a-vow'-al], *n.* a frank admission, confession, open acknowledgment.
AVOWANCE, [a-vow'-ans], *n.* avowal.
AVOWANT, [a-vow'-ant], *n.* (*leg.*) one who asserts his right to retain goods taken from another. [Fr. *avouant*].
AVOWED, [a-vowd'], *adj.* openly admitted, self-confessed.
AVOWEDLY, [a-vow'-id-li], *adv.* in openly acknowledged fashion.
AVOWEE, [a-vow'-ē'], *n.* (*leg.*) one who holds an advowson.
AVOWRY, [a-vow'-ri], *n.* (*leg.*) action of avowing. [OFr. *avouerie*].
AVULSION, [a-vul'-shun], *n.* a pulling or rending from or asunder; a forcible separation or removal. [L. *avulsio* tearing off].
AVUNCULAR, [a-vung'-kyōō-ler], *adj.* pertaining to an uncle. [L. *avunculus* maternal uncle].
AWAIT, [a-wāt'], *v.t.* to wait for, to look for, expect; to attend. [AFr. *awaitier*].
AWAKE (1), [a-wāk'], *adj.* not sleeping; aroused from sleep; (*fig.*) mentally alive, alert.
AWAKE (2), **(awoke, awaked)**, [a-wāk'], *v.t.* to cause to resume the power of mental and bodily activity after sleep or any state of inertia, to come out of sleep; to make aware of; to stir up, revive; *v.i.* to cease sleeping, rouse oneself; to become aware of. [OE. *awacan, awacian*].
AWAKEN, [a-wāk'-en], *v.t.* to awake, to stir up; *v.i.* to become awake. [OE. *awæcnian*].
AWAKENER, [a-wāk'-ner], *n.* one who awakens.
AWAKENING, [a-wāk'-ning], *n.* act of awaking or being awaked.
AWANTING, [a-wont'-ing], *adj.* lacking, absent. [A (3) and WANTING].
AWARD (1), [a-wawd'], *n.* a judgment, a decision or grant by judges; a payment granted by arbitrators; a prize, scholarship or distinction given.
AWARD (2), [a-wawd'], *v.t.* to make an award; to give as a prize or special distinction for outstanding merit; to grant, bestow. [AFr. *awarder*].
AWARDABLE, [a-wawd'-abl], *adj.* able to be awarded.
AWARDER, [a-wawd'-er], *n.* one who awards.
AWARDMENT†, [a-wawd'-ment], *n.* the giving of an award.
AWARE, [a-wāer']. *adj.* knowing, informed, conscious. [OE. *gewær*].
AWARENESS, [a-wāer'-nes], *n.* the condition of being aware.
AWASH, [a-wosh'], *adj.* washed about by the waves. [A (3) and WASH].
AWATCH, [a-woch'], *adv.* alert, on the look-out. [A (3) and WATCH].
AWAVE, [a-wāv'], *adv.* waving. [A (3) and WAVE].
AWAY, [a-wā'], *adv.* at or to some distance; not near; in the direction from; absent; **a. with you!** go away! begone!; **a. with it!** take it away!; **to explain (something) a.**, to excuse; **to pass a.**, to die. [OE. *onweg*].
AWE (1), [aw], *n.* fear and wonder at, mingled with reverence for, dread, feeling of respect tinged with terror at something sublimely impressive. [OScand. *agi*].
AWE (2), [aw], *v.t.* to strike with fear or dread, to inspire with awe.
AWEARY, [a-wēer'-i]. *adj.* (*poet.*) fatigued, tired out. [A (3) and WEARY].
AWEATHER, [a-weTH'-er], *adv.* to the windward side, facing the wind. [A (3) and WEATHER (1)].
AWE-BAND†, [aw'-band], *n.* a curb, check.
AWE-COMMANDING, [aw'-ko-mahnd'-ing], *adj.* inspiring awe.
AWEIGH, [a-wā'], *adv.* (*naut.*) with the anchor raised clear of the ground. [A (3) and WEIGH].
AWELESS, [aw'-les], *adj.* unabashed, having no awe; failing to arouse awe.
AWESOME, [aw'-sum], *adj.* fearsome, terrible; awe-inspiring.
AWE-STRUCK, [aw'-struk], *adj.* struck with fear.
AWFUL, [aw'-fŏŏl], *adj.* inspiring with awe or dread; solemn, worthy of reverence; terrible, dreadful, shocking.
AWFUL-EYED, [aw'-fŏŏl-īd'], *adj.* having eyes inspiring awe.
AWFULLY, [aw'-fŏŏl-i], *adv.* in an awful way; (*coll.*) very, exceedingly.
AWFULNESS, [aw'-fŏŏl-nes], *n.* the quality or condition of being awful.
AWHILE, [a-wīl'], *adv.* for a short time. [A (2) and WHILE (1)].
AWKWARD, [awk'-werd], *adj.* difficult to use; clumsy, unskilful; inconvenient; inelegant; disconcerting, difficult to deal with. [OScand. *afugr* backward].
AWKWARDLY, [awk'-werd-li], *adv.* in awkward fashion.
AWKWARDNESS, [awk'-werd-nes], *n.* the condition of being awkward.
AWL, [awl], *n.* a small sharp tool for piercing small holes. [OE. *æl*].
AWLWORT, [awl'-wurt], *n.* the plant, *Subularia aquatica*, with leaves shaped like awls.
AWN, [awn], *n.* the beard or slender sharp hair at the end of the seed-cluster in grasses, etc. [OScand. *agn*].
AWNED, [awnd], *adj.* bearded; (*bot.*) with awns.
AWNER, [awn'-er], *n.* a device by which the awns are separated from grain.
AWNING, [awn'-ing], *n.* a cover, usually of canvas fastened to a framework, to protect from the sun; (*naut.*) the part of the poop deck extending beyond the bulkhead of the cabin. [Uncert.]
AWNLESS, [awn'-les], *adj.* having no awns; beardless.
AWNY, [awn'-i], *adj.* having awns.
AWOKE, [a-wōk'], *p.t.* of AWAKE. [OE. *awoc*].

AWNS

AWRONG, [a-rong'], *adv.* wrongly. [A (3) and WRONG].
AWRY, [a-rī'], *adv.* unevenly, crookedly; wrongly, in the wrong way. [A (3) and WRY].
AXE (1), AX, [aks], *n.* a sharp-edged tool with a heavy head set at right-angles to a long handle, for cutting down trees, etc.; (*fig.*) execution by decapitation; drastic cutting down of public expenses; **to have an a. to grind**, to have an ulterior motive in adopting a line of action. [OE. *æxe*].
AXE (2), [aks], *v.t.* to abolish, *esp.* for the sake of economy.
AXED, [akst], *adj.* (*fig.*) discharged, usually from some civil service or government employment, as a result of a drastic reduction of expenditure.
AXE-HELVE, [aks'-helv'], *n.* the wooden handle of an axe. [AXE and OE. *helfe* handle].
AXE-STONE, [aks'-stōn'], *n.* jade.
AXIAL, [aks'-i-al], *adj.* relating to an axis.
AXIALLY, [aks'-i-al-i], *adv.* along an axis.
AXICLE†, [aks'-ikl], *n.* a small board, or shingle. [L. *axiculus* a little axis].
AXIFEROUS, [ak-sif'-er-us], *adj.* (*bot.*) having an axis. [AXIS and L. *ferre* to bear].
AXIFORM, [aks'-i-fawm], *adj.* in the shape of an axis. [AXIS and FORM].
AXIL, [aks'-il], *n.* (*bot.*) the angle made on the upper side by a leaf with the stem, or by a branch with the trunk. [AXILLA].
AXILE, [aks'-īl], *adj.* (*bot.*) resting in the axis of anything.
AXILLA, [ak-zil'-a], *n.* armpit; axil. [L. *axilla*].
AXILLARY, [ak-zil'-er-i], *adj.* relating to the armpit; developing from the axil of plants. [AXILLA].
AXINOMANCY, [ak-sin'-ō-man-si], *n.* divination with the aid of an axe. [Gk. *axinomanteia*].
AXIOM, [ak'-si-um], *n.* a generally accepted principle taken as the starting point of a science, or process of reasoning, a self-evident truth; (*math.*) a proposition so obvious that it requires no proof or demonstration. [Gk. *axioma*].
AXIOMATIC, [aks'-i-o-mat'-ik], *adj.* self-evident. [Gk. *axiomatikos*].
AXIOMATICAL, [aks'-i-o-mat'-ikl], *adj.* axiomatic.
AXIOMATICALLY, [aks'-i-o-mat'-ik-al-i], *adv.* in a self-evident manner.

AXIS (1), (*pl.* **axes**), [aks'-is, aks'-ēz], *n.* the straight line round which a figure or body revolves or appears to revolve; an axle; (*math.*) a straight line in a plane figure which may revolve round it to produce a solid figure of circular section; the line which divides a regular figure into two symmetrical parts; (*anat.*) the second vertebra on which the head turns; (*bot.*) the central line of a plant about which the organs are arranged; (*opt.*) the central line of a ray of light which meets a lens at right-angles; (*fig.*) a line about which the world is supposed to revolve; **the A.,** the international anti-Communist bloc headed by Hitlerite Germany. [L. *axis*].
AXIS (2), [ak'-sis], *n.* (*zool.*) the chital or spotted Indian deer, *Cervus axis*.
AXLE, [aksl], *n.* the spindle on which a wheel revolves. [OE. *axl* shoulder].
AXLE-BOX, [aksl'-boks'], *n.* a box accommodating the end of a revolving axle and containing lubricant.
AXLED, [aksld], *adj.* having an axle.
AXLE-PIN, [aksl'-pin], *n.* a pin or bolt securing the body of a cart to the axle-tree.
AXLE-TREE, [aksl'-trē'], *n.* a bar of wood or metal the ends of which form or hold the spindles or axles of a pair of wheels. [ME *axel-tre*].
AXMINSTER, [aks'-min-ster], *n.* a kind of carpet formerly made at *Axminster* in Devon.
AXOID, [aks'-oid], *n.* a cycloid. [AXIS and Gk. *oeides* like].
AXOIDEAN, [ak-soid'-i-an], *adj.* (*anat.*) axial.
AXOLOTL, [aks'-ol-otl], *n.* a Mexican larval salamander of the genus *Amblystoma*. [Mexican *axolotl*].
AXOTOMOUS, [aks-ot'-om-us], *adj.* (*min.*) with a cleavage perpendicular to the axis. [Gk. *axon* axis and *tome* cutting].
AXUNGE, [aks'-unj], *n.* goose-grease, pig's lard. [L. *axungia* from AXIS and *unguere* to grease].
AY (1), see AYE (3).
AY (2), [ā], *adv.* always, ever. [OScand. *ei*].
AYAH, [ī'-ya], *n.* a native Hindu waiting woman, a children's nurse. [Indian *aya* from Portug. *aia* nurse].
AYE (1), [ī], *n.* an affirmative answer; (*pl.*) those who vote in favour of a motion in Parliament. [Unkn.].
AYE (2) see AY (2).
AYE (3), AY, [ī], *int.* yes, indeed. [Unkn.].
AYE-AYE, [ī'-ī], *n.* a Madagascar lemur of the *Chiromys* family. [From the animal's cry].
AYELP, [a-yelp'], *adv.* yelping, whimpering. [A (3) and YELP].
AYRY†, see EYRIE.
AZALEA, [a-zā'-li-a], *n.* a genus of plants or shrubs with brightly coloured fragrant flowers. [Gk. *azaleos* dry].
AZAROLE, [az'-ar-ōl], *n.* the fruit from the Neapolitan medlar. [Fr. *azarole* from Arab. *azzucrur*].
AZEDARACH, [a-zed'-ar-ak], *n.* (*bot.*) a tall tree, a species of *Melia*, producing scented flowers. [Fr. *azédarac* from Pers. *azad dirakht* noble tree].
AZIMUTH, [az'-i-muth], *n.* angular horizontal direction point of the compass; the quadrant of a great circle which passes through the nadir and zenith cutting the horizon at right-angles; the horizontal angular distance from an observer between a fixed point on the horizon (such as the north) and a point where the horizon is cut at right-angles by a great circle which passes through a heavenly body; **a. compass,** a mariner's compass with vertical sights for determining the azimuth of a star. [Fr. *azimut*, Arab. *as-sumut* the directions].

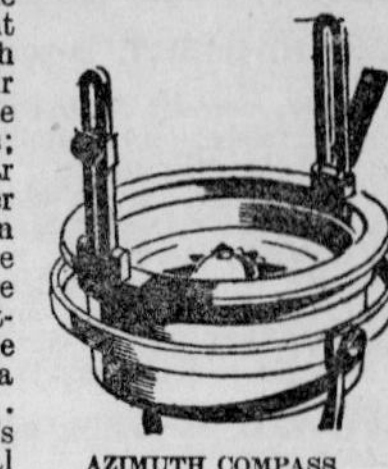
AZIMUTH COMPASS

AZIMUTHAL, [az'-i-mewth'-al], *adj.* pertaining to the azimuth.
AZOIC, [a-zō'-ik], *adj.* without sign of life. [Gr. *azōos* lifeless].
AZONIC, [a-zon'-ik], *adj.* not belonging to a particular region or zone. [A (4) and ZONE].
AZOTE†, [az'-ōt], *n.* (*chem.*) nitrogen. [A (4) and Gk. *zoo* I live].
AZOTH, [az'-oth], *n.* (*alchemy*) mercury; Paracelsus' universal cure containing mercury. [Fr. *azoth* from *Arab. az-zauq* the quicksilver].
AZTEC, [az'-tek], *n.* a member of an extinct Mexican race. [Native].
AZURE (1), [azh'-er, ā'-zher], *n.* the blue colour of the sky; (*poet.*) the sky itself, when unclouded; (*her.*) blue. [OFr. *azur*, Arab. *al-lazward*].
AZURE (2), [azh'-er, ā'-zher], *adj.* sky-blue; (*her.*) blue.
AZURED, [ā'-zherd], *adj.* blue-coloured.
AZURIN, [azh'-yōō-rin], *n.* a bluish coal-tar dye.
AZURINE, [azh'-yōō-rīn], *n.* the blue roach, a species of *Leuciscus*.
AZURITE, [azh'-yōō-rīt], *n.* the blue variety of malachite.
AZYGOUS, [az'-ig-us], *adj.* (*anat.*) occurring singly. [Gk. *azugos* unyoked].
AZYME, [az'-im], *n.* the unleavened bread eaten by the Jews at the Feast of the Passover. [Gk. *azumos* unleavened].
AZYMITE, [az'-im-īt], *n.* one who advocates the use of unleavened bread in the celebration of the eucharist. [*Prec.*].
AZYMOUS, [az'-im-us], *adj.* unleavened; not fermented.

B

B, [bē], the second letter of the English and related alphabets; (*mus.*) the seventh note of the major scale beginning on C.
BAA (1), [bah], *n.* the cry or bleat of a sheep. [Imitative].
BAA (2), [bah], *v.i.* to cry or bleat.
BAAL, (*pl.* **Baalim**), [bāl], *n.* the principal Phoenician god; (*fig.*) a false deity, idol. [Heb. *ba'al* a lord].
BABA (1), [bah'-ba], *n.* a church official in western Asia. [Turk. *baba*].
BABA (2), [bah'-ba], *n.* a small finger-shaped sponge-cake, soaked in wine, rum or brandy. [Fr. *baba*].
BABACOOTE, [bab'-a-kōōt'], *n.* the largest species of lemur, *Indris brevicaudata*. [Malagasy *babakoto*].
BABBIT-METAL, [bab'-it-met'-al], *n.* an alloy of copper, tin and antimony, used in bearings. [*Babbit* the inventor].
BABBLE (1), [babl], *n.* idle talk; incoherent speech; childish prattle; sound made by shallow water flowing over stones.
BABBLE (2), [babl], *v.t. and i.* to utter words indistinctly, as an infant; to talk incoherently and rapidly; to reveal secrets indiscreetly; to make a gentle and incessant murmuring sound as of a flowing stream. [Fr. *babiller*].
BABBLEMENT, [babl'-ment], *n.* idle talk or chatter.
BABBLER, [bab-ler], *n.* a person or thing that babbles; a tropical species of long-legged thrush.
BABBLING, [bab'-ling], *n.* empty or foolish talk.
BABE, [bāb], *n.* young child, baby; (*fig.*) an unsophisticated tyro. [ME. *baban*].
BABEL, [bābl], *n.* (*bibl.*) tower in Shinar where human speech first became confused; (*fig.*) uproar, din caused by several people all talking loudly at once; scene of disorder or tumult. [Heb. *Babel*, the capital of Babylonia].
BABIISM, [bah'-bi-izm], *n.* a religion started in Persia in 1844 by Mirza Ali, whose disciples called him the Bab. [Pers. *bab* gate].
BABIRUSA, BABYROUSSA, [bab'-i-rōōs'-a], *n.* an East Asiatic hog with curved, tusk-like upper canine teeth. [Malay *babi* hog and *rusa* stag].
BABISH, [bā'-bish], *adj.* like a babe, childish.

BABISHLY, [bā'-bish-li], *adv.* in childish fashion.
BABISHNESS, [bāb'-ish-nes], *n.* childishness, foolishness.
BABLAH, [bab'-lah], *n.* the rind of certain acacias found in the East and used in dyeing; certain kinds of thick, grey woollen cloth. [Unkn.].
BABOO, see BABU.
BABOON, [bab-ōōn'], *n.* a large monkey with short tail, long face and snout like that of a dog. [Fr. *babouin*].
BABOUCHE, [ba-bōōsh'], *n.* an Eastern slipper without heels. [Pers. *paposh*].
BABU, BABOO, [bah'-bōō], *n.* a Hindu clerk; a title of respect to a Hindu gentleman; a title of contempt for a Hindu of imperfect education, cultivating English speech and manners. [Hind. *babu*].
BABUL, [ba-bōōl'], *n.* a thorny tree of the mimosa genus; the gum-arabic tree, *Acacia arabica.* [Hind. *babul*].
BABY, [bā'-bi], *n.* a very young child; a doll; a person who behaves like a child; a thing which is a small example of its kind; (*slang*) sweetheart, girl-friend; **to hold the b.,** (*slang*) to be left to handle a difficult problem, to be the dupe. [ME. *babi*].
BABY-FARMING, [bā'-bi-fahm'-ing], *n.* the boarding-out of unwanted or illegitimate newly born infants to nurses for payment.
BABY-GRAND, [bā'-bi-grand'], *n.* a small grand-piano.
BABYHOOD, [bā'-bi-hŏŏd], *n.* infancy.
BABY-HOUSE, [bā'-bi-hows], *n.* a doll's house.
BABYISH, [bā'-bi-ish], *adj.* like a baby; childish, foolish.
BABYISHNESS, [bāb'-i-ish-nes], *n.* the quality of being babyish. [BABYISH].
BABYISM, [bā'-bi-izm], *n.* the qualities of a baby.
BABY-JUMPER, [bā'-bi-jump'-er], *n.* a suspended frame by which a very small child is supported to exercise its legs.
BABYLON, [bab'-il-on], *n.* capital of Babylonia, notorious for the vice and luxury of its citizens, later used as a derogatory term for Rome or the papal power; (*fig.*) a sinful city. [Heb. *Babel*].
BABYLONIAN (1), [bab'-il-ōn'-i-an], *n.* an inhabitant of Babylon; (*fig.*) a papist.
BABYLONIAN (2), [bab'-il-ōn'-i-an], *adj.* pertaining to Babylon; (*fig.*) luxurious, dissolute.
BABYLONIC, [bab'-il-ōn'-ik], *adj.* Babylonian.
BABYLONISH, [bab'-il-ōn'-ish], *adj.* pertaining to or resembling Babylon; popish.
BABYLONITE, [bab'-il-ōn'-īt], *n.* a Babylonian cuneiform character.
BABYROUSSA, see BABIRUSA.
BAC, [bak], *n.* a flat-bottomed French ferry-boat. [Fr. *bac*].
BACCALAUREATE, [bak'-a-lor-i-at], *n.* the lowest University degree, that of Bachelor. [MdL. *baccalaureatus*].
BACCARAT, BACCARA, [bak'-er-ah], *n.* a French gambling card game. [Fr. *baccarat*].
BACCATE, [bak'-āt], *adj.* berried, producing berries; like a berry. [L. *baccatus*].
BACCHANAL (1), [bak'-an-al], *n.* one who indulges in noisy, drunken revels ; a priest or follower of Bacchus, god of wine; a drunken orgy ; (*pl.*) dances or songs performed in honour of Bacchus.
BACCHANAL (2), [bak'-an-al], *adj.* belonging to Bacchus; noisily intoxicated. [L. *bacchanalis*].
BACCHANALIA, [bak'-an-ā'-li-a], *n.*(*pl.*) drunken and riotous feasts; feasts in honour of Bacchus. [L. *Bacchanalia*].
BACCHANALIAN (1), [bak'-an-āl'-i-an], *n.* an intoxicated reveller.
BACCHANALIAN (2), [bak'-an-āl'-i-an], *adj.* riotous, rowdily drunken.
BACCHANT (1), [bak'-ant], *n.* a priest or follower of Bacchus; (*fig.*) a Bacchanalian.
BACCHANT (2), [bak'-ant], *adj.* fond of drunken orgy and revelry. [L. *bacchans, pres.pt.* of *bacchare* celebrate the festival of Bacchus].
BACCHANTE, [bak'-ant, ba-kant'-i], *n.* a priestess of Bacchus; (*fig.*) a woman fond of wine and noisy revelry.
BACCHANTIC, [bak-ant'-ik], *adj.* pertaining to the priests of Bacchus.
BACCHIC, [bak'-ik], *adj.* belonging to Bacchus; (*fig.*) rowdily drunken in a frenzy of intoxication. [Gk. *Bakkhikos* of Bacchus].
BACCHIUS, [bak-ī'-us], *n.* (*pros.*) a foot of three syllables, the first short and the last two long. [Gk. *bakkheios*].
BACCHUS, [bak'-us], *n.* the god of wine in Greek and Roman religion. [Gk. *Bakkhos*].
BACCIFEROUS, [bak-sif'-er-us], *adj.* producing berries. [L. *baccifer*].
BACCIFORM, bak'-si-fawm], *adj.* shaped like a berry.
BACCIVOROUS, [bak-siv'-or-us], *adj.* living on berries. [BACCA and L. *vorus* eating].
BACCY, [bak'-i], *n.* (*coll.*) tobacco. [TOBACCO].
BACHELOR, [bach'-il-er], *n.* an unmarried man; one who has taken his first degree at a University; a member of the lowest stage of knighthood. [OFr. *bacheler*].
BACHELORDOM, [bach'-il-er-dom], *n.* the condition of being a bachelor.
BACHELORHOOD, [bach'-il-er-hŏŏd], *n.* bachelordom.
BACHELOR'S-BUTTON, [bach'-il-erz-but'-on], *n.* a button which can be attached without sewing; (*bot.*) one of several species of button-shaped flowers.
BACHELORSHIP, [bach'-il-er-ship], *n.* bachelorhood.
BACILLARY, [bas-il'-er-i], *adj.* composed of small rods, shaped like rods, relating to bacilli. [L. *bacillus* little rod].
BACILLIFORM, [bas-il'-i-fawm], *adj.* like bacilli in shape. [L. *bacillus* a little rod and FORM (1)].
BACILLUS, (*pl.* **bacilli**), [bas-il'-us, bas-il'-ī], *n.* rod-shaped, minute vegetable organisms causing decay in organic matter. [LL. *bacillus* a little rod].

BACILLI

BACK (1), [bak] *n.* the hinder part of the human or the upper rear part of an animal's body from the lower end of the spine to the base of the neck: the spine; the hinder part of anything, the part of an object most distant from an observer; a vertical support for the spine; the part of the hand opposite the palm; the non-cutting edge of a tool; that part of a brush to which the bristles are attached; (*football, hockey, etc.*) the rear line(s) of players; the upper surface of a wave; the rear part of a house, not containing the principal entrance; a ship's keel; a thick well-tanned hide; the covers of a book; the upper edge of a non-vertical beam; (*fig.*) the body; **behind one's b.,** in an underhand, deceitful way; **to put one's b. into anything,** to work zealously at; **to put someone's b. up,** to offend or anger someone; **to make a b. for,** to bend down at leap-frog; **to turn one's b. upon,** to desert, ignore; **to break one's b.,** to overburden, to make extremely strenuous efforts; **with one's b. to the wall,** hard-pressed, in difficult straits; **at the b. of one's mind,** dimly, half-remembered. [OE. *bæc*].
BACK (2), [bak], *n.* a shallow tray used in brewing, distilling and dyeing. [Fr. *bac*].
BACK (3), [bak], *adj.* situated in the rear, remote, inferior; overdue; no longer current, out of date; **to take a b. seat,** to occupy an inconspicuous position.
BACK (4), [bak], *adv.* to the rear; to the place from which one has come; again, in return; away from, at a distance; towards the past, to a former condition or time; behind; **to go b. upon,** to withdraw one's support or promise; **to answer b.** to reply with a rude retort; **to take b.,** to withdraw; **to pay someone b.,** to have one's revenge on someone.
BACK (5), [bak], *v.t.* to provide with a back; to give moral, legal or material support to; to mount or get upon the back; to bet or gamble in favour of a competitor in a contest; to cause to go backwards, to reverse; to sign one's name on the back of (a financial or legal document), thus assuming responsibility; *v.i.* to move or go backward or away from; to move in an opposite direction; **to b. up,** to support; **to b. down, b. out of,** to withdraw from, abandon; **to b. a sail,** to lay the sail so that it faces the wind.
BACK-BAND, [bak'-band], *n.* a strap fastened over the saddle of a horse to support the shafts of a cart.
BACK-BENCH, [bak'-bench'], *n.* (*pol.*) a seat or bench in the House of Commons where the less prominent members of a parliamentary party sit.
BACK-BENCHER, [bak'-bench'-er], *n.* a member who sits on the back-benches in the House of Commons.

ō (bone), ī (fine), ōō (food), ŏŏ (put), u (up), th (*th*ink), TH (*th*at), zh (azure), † = obsolete, ~ = related to.

BACKBITE, (backbit, backbitten), [bak'-bīt], *v.i.* to speak evil of persons absent. [ME. *bakbiten*].

BACKBITING, [bak'-bīt'-ing], *n.* maligning of absent persons, slander.

BACK-BLOCKS, [bak'-bloks], *n.(pl.)* sparsely populated and isolated regions in the interior of a country or continent.

BACKBOARD, [bak'-bawd], *n.* a board placed at the back, or forming the back of a cart, boat or picture-frame; a board fastened across the back of a person to correct a stoop.

BACK-BOILER, [bak'-boil'-er], *n.* a small boiler, in which water is heated, built immediately behind a domestic fire-range.

BACKBONE, [bak'-bōn], *n.* the spinal column; (*fig.*) steadiness of purpose, firmness of character, strength of will-power, determination; the chief support, prop, foundation or main constituent of anything. [ME. *bakbon*].

BACKBOXES, [bak'-bok-sez], *n.(pl.)* (*print.*) boxes on the top of the upper case for small capitals or peculiars.

BACK-BREAKER, [bak'-brāk'-er], *n.* (*coll.*) an extremely arduous task; a hard master, a slave-driver.

BACK-CASING, [bak'-kās'-ing], *n.* (*mining*) a temporary lining in a shaft, inside which the permanent lining is constructed.

BACK-CHAT, [bak'-chat], *n.* humorous cross-talk or repartee, exchange of facetious observations (often personal); impudent retort.

BACK-CLOTH, [bak'-kloth], *n.* painted cloth hung across the back of a stage in a theatre as part of the scenery and to provide a background.

BACKED, [bakt], *adj.* furnished with a back; having a back; on which bets have been placed.

BACK-END, [bak'-end'], *n.* (*coll.*) late autumn.

BACKER, [bak'-er], *n.* one who gives material or moral help, a supporter; one who bets in favour of a competitor in a sporting event

BACK-FALL, [bak'-fawl], *n.* a fall in wrestling in which one is thrown on the back; part of the coupling mechanism of an organ.

BACKFILLING, [bak'-fil'-ing], *n.* earth which has been dug up and then replaced.

BACK-FIRE (1), [bak'-fīer'], *n.* a premature explosion in the cylinder of an internal combustion engine, tending to reverse the motion; (*coll.*) an explosion in the silencer of a motor-vehicle; an ignited discharge from the breech of a gun.

BACK-FIRE (2), [bak'-fīer'], *v.i.* to experience a back-fire; (*fig.*) to undergo a sudden violent paroxysm of suppressed emotion.

BACK-FORMATION, [bak'-fawm-ā'-shun], *n.* (*philol.*) a grammatical form which, though derived analogically from a second form, would appear to be its base.

BACKGAMMON, [bak'-gam'-un], *n.* a game played by two persons on a board, on which the movements of the pieces are decided by the throwing of dice.

BACK-GEAR, [bak'-gēer'], *n.* a series of gear-wheels introduced to reduce the speed of the mandril in a lathe.

BACK-GREY, [bak'-grā'], *n.* (*calico printing*) a cloth inserted between the cloth being printed, and the woollen cloth covering the platen.

BACKGROUND, [bak'-grownd], *n.* (*paint.*) the pictorial representation of more distant or obscurely defined objects less significant, against which the principal figures stand out; back part of a stage or scene; an obscure position from which one is not easily noticed; (*fig.*) cultural environment, wide general knowledge of a subject.

BACKHAND, [bak'-hand'], *n.* writing that slopes upwards to the left; (*tennis, etc.*) a stroke made with the arm across the front of the body and the back of the hand facing forward.

BACKHANDED, [bak'-hand'-id], *adj.* with the back of the hand; (*of writing*) in which the letters slope upwards to the left; (*fig.*) unfair; ambiguous, doubtful.

BACKHANDER, [bak'-hand'-er], *n.* stroke delivered with the back of the hand; (*fig.*) unexpected news generally of an unpleasant nature; an extra glass of wine out of one's turn.

BACK-HEAD, [bak'-hed'], *n.* false hair formerly worn by ladies at the back of the head.

BACK-HEART, [bak'-haht], *n.* (*zool.*) the large blood-vessel of insects or other arthropods.

BACK-HEEL, [bak'-hēl'], *n.* a movement with the foot in wrestling to bring about a throw; a kick or flick at football made with the heel.

BACKING, [bak'-ing], *n.* the action of supporting; the act of putting or going back; the process of providing with a back; the mounting of a horse; material for making a back; assets to support an issue of paper-money; moral or material support.

BACKING-UP, [bak'-ing-up], *n.* support, help, readiness to help.

BACKLASH, [bak'-lash'], *n.* the irregular jerky rotary movement of gear-wheels not in perfect mesh, play; (*wirel.*) a defect in a system which causes it to go into oscillation at a different setting from that at which oscillation ceases.

BACKLESS, [bak'-les], *adj.* (of a woman's frock) having the upper portion of the back cut away.

BACK-LOCK, [bak'-lok'], *n.* a wrestling hold.

BACK-MARKER, [bak'-mahk'-er], *n.* the competitor with the largest handicap in a handicap sporting event.

BACK-NAILS, [bak'-nālz], *n.(pl.)* flat nails which remain secure and do not split wood along the grain.

BACK-NUMBER, [bak'-num'-ber], *n.* an out-of-date copy of a periodical; (*fig.*) a person who is old-fashioned, past his prime, and no longer of any account; (*coll.*) a nonentity.

BACK-PAGE, [bak'-pāj], *n.* the left-hand page of an open book; the last page of a newspaper.

BACKPAINTING, [bak'-pān'-ting], *n.* the method of staining mezzotint prints pasted on glass, so as to resemble stained glass.

BACK-PAY, [bak'-pā'], *n.* arrears of pay, wages due for work previously done.

BACK-PEDAL, [bak'-ped'-al], *v.i.* to reverse the normal direction of rotation of the pedals on a bicycle by which a braking mechanism may be made to operate; (*coll.*) to retreat.

BACKPIECE, [bak'-pēs'], *n.* the armour which protects the back.

BACKPLATE, [bak'-plāt'], *n.* (*aeron.*) the steel plate in front of the fuselage to which the engine is fastened.

BACK-PRESSURE, [bak'-presh'-er], *n.* the resistance of the exhaust steam or the atmosphere to the stroke of a piston in a steam-engine; resistance of burnt gas which has not escaped from the cylinder in an internal-combustion engine.

BACKRENT, [bak'-rent], *n.* (*leg.*) rent paid with money obtained after selling the first year's crop.

BACKREST, [bak'-rest], *n.* a support or rest at the back or rear of anything; a light frame attached to the back of certain typewriters to support the sheet of paper; a contrivance fastened to the slide-rest of a lathe to support the work; a contrivance to steady or ease the back of a person when seated or performing certain types of manual labour; (*weaving*) a bar used to support the warp passing from the warp-beam.

BACKSAW, [bak'-saw], *n.* a saw which is stiffened by having the non-cutting edge secured in a strip of stout metal.

BACK-SCENE, [bak'-sēn'], *n.* (*stage*) the background or rear part of a scene.

BACK-SCRATCHING, [bak'-skrach'-ing], *n.* (*vulg.*) mutual praise, reciprocal flattery.

BACKSET, [bak'-set'], *n.* a check, a temporary reverse; a counter-current.

BACK-SETTLEMENT, [bak'-setl'-ment], *n.* remote, outlying land that is being cultivated and settled.

BACKSHEESH, BAKSHEESH, BAKSHISH, [bak'-shēsh'], *n.* a tip, an Oriental begging cry. [Pers., Hind. *bakhshish*].

BACKSIDE, [bak'-sīd], *n.* the back or rear portion of anything; (*vulg.*) the buttocks.

BACKSIGHT, [bak'-sīt'], *n.* the sight facing the bench-mark with which the surveyor begins levelling; the gun-sight nearest the eye of the marksman.

BACK-SKIN, [bak'-skin'], *n.* a protective leather covering worn by coal-miners hewing in wet seams.

BACK-SLANG, [bak'-slang'], *n.* form of slang in which words are spelt backwards and pronounced in accordance with the changed spelling.

BACKSLIDE, [bak'-slīd'], *v.i.* to relapse into sin; to fall away from a previous high standard of moral virtue.

BACKSLIDER, [bak'-slīd'-er], *n.* one who backslides.

BACKSLIDING, [bak'-slīd'-ing], *n.* a relapsing into sin or evil ways; a forsaking of one's principles.

BACK-SPACER, [bak'-spās'-er], *n.* a device on a typewriter, operated by a key which, when depressed, causes the carriage to move backwards.

BACK-SPEED, [bak'-spēd'], *n.* the slowest gear of a lathe.

BACKSTAFF, [bak'-stahf], *n.* an old-fashioned quadrant in using which the back of the observer was turned towards the sun.

BACK-STAGE, [bak'-stāj'], *adv.* behind the scenes in a theatre.

BACKSTAIRS (1), [bak'-stāerz'], *n.(pl.)* private stairs or steps at the back of a house, a staircase for the use of servants.

BACKSTAIRS (2), [bak'-stāerz], *adj.* (*fig.*) secret, underhand.

BACKSTAYS, [bak'-stāz'], *n.(pl.)* (*naut.*) long ropes extending from the masthead to the sides of a ship, and helping the shrouds to support the mast when strained by the pull of sail.

BACK-STEP, [bak'-step'], *n.* a projecting step on the rear-hub of a bicycle.

BACKSTER, [bak'-ster], *n.* a flat piece of wood or cork resembling a snowshoe, and fastened to the feet to facilitate walking over a very loose, pebbly beach. [Unkn.].

BACK-STICKS, [bak'-stiks'], *n.* (*hockey*) a foul stroke with the wrong side of the stick.

BACKSTITCH, [bak'-stich'], *n.* a stitch which is looped through the front of the preceding one.

BACKSTONE, [bak'-stōn']. *n.* a piece of cast-iron placed at the rear of an ore-hearth.

BACK-STOP, [bak'-stop], *n.* † (*cricket*) a fieldsman placed well behind the striker's wicket in order to field such balls as the wicket-keeper fails to stop; (*baseball*) a fence placed behind the home base to stop balls missed by the catcher.

BACK-STRIKING, [bak'-strīk'-ing], *n.* (*agr.*) a method of ploughing in which the earth is turned and thrown back again.

BACK-STROKE, [bak'-strōk'], *n.* a stroke in swimming performed upon the back.

BACK-SWIMMER, [bak'-swim'-er], *n.* an insect belonging to the *Hemiptera*, which swims about on the surface of pools.

BACKSWORD, [bak'-sawd'], *n.* a sword having one sharp edge; a fencing-stick with a basket handle, a single-stick.

BACKWARD (1), [bak'-werd], *adj.* turned towards the back, or in a reverse or contrary direction; reluctant, unwilling, not eager for action; of subnormal intelligence, mentally retarded; not properly developed; behind in time or progress. [ME. *bakward*].

BACKWARD (2), [bak'-werd], *adv.* backwards, in backward fashion.

BACKWARDATION, [bak'-werd-ā'-shun], *n.* (*comm.*) allowance paid by sellers of stocks and shares to buyers in return for an extension of time for delivery.

BACKWARDLY, [bak'-werd-li], *adv.* in backward fashion.

BACKWARDNESS, [bak'-werd-nes], *n.* the condition of being backward.

BACK-SWORD

BACKWARDS, [bak'-werdz], *adv.* towards the back, in a reverse or contrary direction or manner to normal, with the back foremost, on the back; from a better to a worse condition; from the end to the beginning; towards the past.

BACKWASH, [bak'-wosh'], *n.* disturbance of waves behind a vessel as it moves through the water, water disturbed by oars at the end of the stroke; (*fig.*) disturbance.

BACKWATER (1), *n.* a pool or creek of still water, fed by or leading into a stream or river but cut off from the direct flow or course; water accumulated by an artificial obstruction; (*fig.*) the condition of being isolated from new ideas and progress.

BACK-WATER (2), [bak'-waw'-ter], *v.i.* to reverse the normal direction of motion of the oars in a rowing boat, in order to check its progress, or reverse its direction.

BACK-WIND, [bak'-wind'], *v.i.* (*naut.*) to have the sails forced back.

BACKWOODS, [bak'-wŏŏdz], *n.(pl.)* uncultivated forest-land far from towns or settlements.

BACKWOODSMAN, [bak'-wŏŏdz'-man], *n.* a settler in the backwoods; (*slang*) an uncultured, uncouth person; a peer who seldom visits the House of Lords.

BACK-WORD, [bak'-wurd], *n.* an announcement of the withdrawal from a promise or invitation previously given.

BACKWORM, [bak'-wurm'], *n.* a disease which attacks hawks.

BACON, [bā'-kun], *n.* the back and sides of a pig, cured for eating; **to save one's b.,** (*coll.*) to have a narrow escape. [OFr. *bacon*].

BACONER, [bā'-kun-er], *n.* a pig suitable for making into bacon.

BACONIAN (1), [bā-kō'-ni-an], *n.* a follower or disciple of Bacon; a person who thinks that Bacon wrote the plays usually ascribed to Shakespeare. [Sir Francis *Bacon*].

BACONIAN (2), [bā-kō'-ni-an], *adj.* belonging to the philosophy of Bacon.

BACTERIA, [bak-tēer'-i-a], *n.(pl.)* microscopic living things found on all organic matter and frequently acting deleteriously to their hosts. [Gk. *bakterion*, *dim.* of *baktron* staff].

BACTERIAL, [bak-tēer'-i-al], *adj.* of, or arising from, bacteria. [BACTERIUM].

BACTERICIDAL, [bak-tēer'-is-īd'-al], *adj.* causing bacteria to die. [Gk. *bakterion* little rod and L. *cidere* to kill].

BACTERIOLOGY, [bak-tēer'-i-ol'-o-ji], *n.* the study of bacteria. [*Prec.* and Gk. *logos* speech].

BACTERIOLYSIS, [bak'-tēer-i-ol'-is-is], *n.* the destruction of bacteria by dissolution in an anti-bacterial serum. [BACTERIA and *lusis* loosing].

BACTERIOLYTIC, [bak'-tēer-i-ol-it'-ik], *adj.* having the power to destroy bacteria.

BACTRIS, [bak'-tris], *n.* the peach-palm of Brazil, *Bactris minor*. [Gr. *baktron* staff].

BACULITE, [bak'-yŏŏ-līt], *n.* (*geol.*) a fossil cephalopod with straight cylindrical shell. [L. *baculum* rod and Gk. *lithos* stone].

BACULOMETRY, [bak'-yŏŏ-lom'-et-ri], *n.* the art of measuring distance or altitude by means of rods. [L. *baculum* a rod and Gk. *metria* measurement].

BAD (1), [bad], *n.* ill-fortune; evil ways; loss, deficit.

BAD (2), [bad], *adj.* lacking good or goodness; evil, wicked, immoral, ill; worthless, inferior, corrupt, debased, not reaching the required standard; offensive; decayed, unsound; painful, diseased; severe; harmful; unfortunate; not liked; incorrect; profane; (*leg.*) not valid; **b. debt,** a debt which cannot be collected; **b. lot,** worthless creature; **b. egg,** disreputable character; **b. blood,** unpleasant or angry feeling. [ME. *badde*].

BADDISH, [bad'-ish], *adj.* slightly bad.

BADE, [bad], *pret.* of BID. [OE. *bæd*].

BADGE, [baj], *n.* a distinguishing mark or token of a particular rank or office or party. [ME. *bage*].

BADGER (1), [baj'-er], *n.* a grey, short-legged carnivorous animal of the genus *Meles*, thick-bodied with long coarse hair; a paint-brush with its bristles made of badger's hair. [Unkn.].

BADGER (2), [baj'-er], *n.* a corn-chandler; †a licensed pedlar. [Unkn.].

BADGER (3), [baj'-er], *v.t.* to annoy, tease, pester; to worry by questioning.

BADGER-LEGGED, [baj'-er-legd'], *adj.* having short thick legs resembling those of a badger.

BADIAGA, [bad'-i-ah'-ga], *n.* a small river-sponge of northern Europe. [Russ. *bady-a-ga*].

BADIANE, BANDIAN, [bah'-di-an, ban'-di-an], *n.* the seed of the Chinese anise-tree, from which a seasoning oil is extracted. [Fr. *badiane* from Pers. *badyan* fennel].

BADIGEON, [bad-ij'-on], *n.* a mixture of plaster and freestone used by sculptors to fill up small holes in statues and repair other defects; a mixture of sawdust and glue used by joiners to hide faults in wood. [Fr. *badigeon*].

BADINAGE, [bad'-in-ahzh'], *n.* light, playful talk, or gentle banter. [Fr. *badinage*].

BADLY, [bad'-li], *adv.* in bad fashion; in an unsatisfactory, imperfect or bad manner; unwell; hopelessly; strongly, very much. [ME. *baddeliche*].

BADMINTON, [bad'-min-tun], *n.* game in which a shuttlecock is hit to and fro across a net with light rackets; a summer drink made with claret, soda-water and sugar. [*Badminton* the Duke of Beaufort's country seat].

BADNESS, [bad'-nes], *n.* the condition of being bad.

BAEDEKER, [bād'-ek-er], *n.* one of a series of guide-books for travellers. [K. *Baedeker* the original publisher].

BAEL, [bāl], *n.* (*bot.*) an Indian plant related to the orange, the fruit of which is used as a cure for dysentery. [Hind. *bel*].

BAFFETAS, see BAFTAS.

BAFFING-SPOON, see BAFFY.

BAFFLE (1), [bafl], *n.* a plate in a furnace to deflect the course of the air or burning gases; (*wirel.*) a screen of non-resonant material placed in loudspeakers in order that low frequencies may be reproduced, a large board on which a loudspeaker is mounted.

BAFFLE (2), [bafl], *v.t.* to puzzle, frustrate, disconcert, delude; to check, perplex. [OFr. *beffler* to ridicule].

BAFFLING, [baf′-ling], *adj*. puzzling, incomprehensible, perplexing.

BAFFLINGLY, [baf′-ling-li], *adv*. in a baffling fashion.

BAFFLINGNESS, [baf′-ling-nes], *n*. tendency or quality of baffling.

BAFFY, BAFFING-SPOON, [baf′-i], *n*. (*Scots*) a short wooden golf club with a sharply lofted face. [Scots *baff* a blow].

BAFTAS, BAFFETAS, [baf′-tas], *n*. a cotton cloth or plain muslin, woven in India. [Pers. *bafta* woven].

BAG (1), [bag], *n*. a receptacle for the conveyance of small or light articles, made of paper, cloth or leather, etc., and having an opening which can be closed; a sac or pouch in an animal's body containing some secretion; the number of game animals shot on a single outing; (*comm.*) a determinate quantity of a commodity; (*pl.*) a pair of trousers; (*slang*) a prostitute; (*pl.*) (*slang*) heaps, a great amount, a large number; **blue b.,** a small cloth bag filled with blue powder, used in laundry work; **the whole b. of tricks,** every possible device or feature, the whole issue, all the lot; **b. and baggage,** with everything belonging to one; **to let the cat out of the b.,** to reveal a secret carelessly. [ME. *bagge*].

BAG (2), [bag], *v.t. and i.* to put into a bag, to collect; (*sport*) to kill after a day's shooting; to acquire, obtain; to cut wheat or rough grass with a hook; (*slang*) to take without permission, to steal; to take on the grounds of priority of claim; to swell, to bulge out; (*naut.*) to drop away from the course.

BAGASSE, [ba-gas′], *n*. the refuse stalks of the sugar-cane after crushing. [Fr. *bagasse* from Span. *bagazo* husks of olives].

BAGATELLE, [bag′-a-tel′], *n*. a game resembling billiards, played with nine balls and a cue on a nine-holed board having a semicircular upper end; a thing of no importance, a trifle; a piece of music of light character. [It. *bagatella* worthless thing, trifle].

BAGFUL, [bag′-fŏŏl], *n*. the amount contained in a bag.

BAGGAGE, [bag′-ij], *n*. tents, utensils and other portable equipment of an army; a traveller's luggage; (*coll.*) a prostitute; an impudent, lively young girl. [OFr. *bagage*].

BAGGAGE-CHECK, [bag′-ij-chek′], *n*. a label attached to the luggage of passengers travelling on American railways.

BAGGINESS, [bag′-i-nes], *n*. baggy nature or appearance. [BAGGY].

BAGGING (1), [bag′-ing], *n*. material from which bags are made.

BAGGING (2), [bag′-ing], *adj*. bulging, distended, swelling out.

BAGGY, [bag′-i], *adj*. bulging out like a bag; shapeless.

BAGMAN, [bag′-man], *n*. a commercial traveller.

BAGNIO, [bahn′-yō], *n*. a public bath; a brothel; a Turkish gaol. [It. *bagno* bath from L. *balneum*].

BAGPIPE, [bag′-pip], *n*. a musical wind instrument, consisting of a leather bag, which is kept inflated, fitted with pipes containing reeds, into which a constant stream of air is pressed from the bag by the performer. [ME. *baggepipe*].

BAGPIPER, [bag′-pīp-er], *n*. one who performs upon the bagpipes.

BAGUETTE, [bag-et′], *n*. a small round moulding. [Fr. *baguette* from It. *bacchetta* little rod].

BAGUETTE

BAH, [bah], *int*. an exclamation indicating contempt.

BAHADUR, [ba-hah′-der], *n*. a word added as a title of honour in India; title of respect used by Orientals in speaking ceremoniously of European officers; (*slang*) a pompous person filled with a sense of his own importance. [Hind. *bahadur* hero, champion].

BAHAR, [bah-hah(r)′], *n*. a weight of approximately 3½ cwt. used in the East Indies. [Skr. *bhara* load].

BAIKALITE, [bāk′-al-it], *n*. (*min.*) a kind of augite. [Lake *Baikal*].

BAIL (1), [bāl], *n*. a sum of money paid to secure the release of a prisoner awaiting trial on condition that he will present himself for trial when required; the surety of a prisoner on bail; **to surrender one's b.,** to appear for trial at the prescribed time; **to forfeit one's b.,** to fail to appear for trial.

BAIL (2), [bāl], *n*. a bar which separates two horses in an open stable; the handle of a kettle; (*cricket*) one of the two small rods laid across the tops of the stumps to complete the wicket; (*milit.*) outer line of fortifications made of stakes, the wall of a castle court; (*Australian*) a frame which holds up a cow's head during milking; a half-hoop used to secure the covering canvas over a wagon; **swinging b.,** a bar slung from the manger to the ceiling. [L. *baculum* small stick].

BAIL (3), [bāl], *n*. a shallow vessel used in bailing, a ladle. [Fr. *baille* bucket].

BAIL (4), [bāl], *v.t.* to secure the release of a prisoner awaiting trial by paying the sum demanded as a guarantee of his appearance at the appointed time; to release upon bail or security; (*comm.*) to deliver goods in trust upon a contract; to confine. [BAIL (1)].

BAIL (5), [bāl], *v.t.* to throw water out of a boat by means of small hand-vessels or cupped hands. [BAIL (3)].

BAIL (6), [bāl], *v.t.* (*cricket*) to bowl out a batsman with a ball which removes the bails but does not disturb the stumps; **to b. up,** to fasten a cow's head during milking; (*Australian*) to make a person hold up his arms above his head, preparatory to robbing him.

BAILABLE, [bāl′-abl], *adj*. able to be bailed.

BAILAGE, see BALLIAGE.

BAILBOND, [bāl′-bond′], *n*. the bond deposited by a prisoner and his surety as bail.

BAILEE, [bāl-ē′], *n*. (*leg.*) a person with whom goods are deposited in trust.

BAILER, [bāl′-er], *n*. one who bails or stands bail.

BAILEY, [bāl-i], *n*. the outer walls round a castle, space enclosed by such walls and forming a court, **the Old B.,** the Central Criminal Court in London [BALLIUM].

BAILIE, BAILLIE, [bāl′-i], *n*. a municipal official in Scotland corresponding to an English alderman; †a bailiff.

BAILIFF, [bal′-if], *n*. the officer of a sheriff who serves writs, makes arrests and distrains goods; a land steward; **water b.,** an officer who protects rivers from poachers. [OFr. *baillif* custodian, magistrate].

BAILIWICK, [bāl′-i-wik], *n*. the jurisdiction of, or territory under, a bailiff. [*Prec.* and OE. *wic* farm, village].

BAILLIE, see BAILIE.

BAILMENT, [bāl′-ment], *n*. (*leg.*) a delivery of goods in trust under an agreement for their return after they have fulfilled their purpose; bailing out of a prisoner.

BAILPIECE, [bāl′-pēs], *n*. (*leg.*) the document which contains a recognizance of bail.

BAILSMAN, [bāls′-man], *n*. one who stands as bail; a surety or bailer.

BAIRAM, [bī′-ram], *n*. a Mohammedan festival lasting three days, which follows the month of fasting. [Turk. *bairam*].

BAIRN, [bāern], *n*. an infant. [OE. *bearn*].

BAIT (1), [bāt], *n*. real or imitation food used to entice animals into traps or fish on to the hook; food for horses; (*fig.*) a trap, enticement, snare.

BAIT (2), [bāt], *v.t. and i.* to provide with bait in order to catch fish or animals; to give food and refreshment to on a journey; to worry or harass (bulls, bears, etc.) with dogs; (*fig.*) to entice, to allure; to provoke, tease. [OScand. *beita* cause to bite].

BAITING, [bāt′-ing], *n*. that which is used as bait; the act of using bait.

BAIZE, BAYZE, [bāz], *n*. a coarse, woollen cloth chiefly used for linings, and usually green or red. [OFr. *baies*, *pl.* of *baie* bay-coloured].

BAJADERE, see BAYADERE.

BAJREE, [baj′-rē], *n*. the Indian grass, *Holcus spicatus*, grown as a grain plant. [Hind. *bajri*].

BAKE, [bāk], *v.t. and i.* to dry and harden by cooking in a closed chamber or on a hot surface; to harden and dry by the heat of the sun's rays; to become dry or hardened in heat; (*slang*) to become tanned or excessively hot by exposure to the sun's rays; **half-baked**, (*coll.*) undeveloped; dull, stupid. [OE. *bacan*].

BAKEHOUSE, [bāk′-hows], *n*. the building in which bread, cake, etc., is baked. [ME. *bakehouse*].

BAKELITE, [bāk-el-it], *n*. (*prot.*) an insulating material readily moulded and hardened by heating, used extensively in electrical fittings. [H. *Baekeland*, the inventor].

BAKEMEATS, [bāk′-mētz], *n.*(*pl.*) pastry baked in an oven.

BAKER, [bāk′-er], *n*. one who bakes or sells bread, cakes, etc.; a small oven; **baker's dozen,** thirteen. [OE *bæcere*].

BAKER-FOOT, [bāk'-er-fo͝ot'], *n.* a twisted foot.
BAKER-LEGGED, [bāk'-er-legd'], *adj.* having legs that bend in at the knees.
BAKERY [bāk-er-i], *n.* an establishment where baking is carried on, the business or premises of a baker.
BAKESTONE, [bāk'-stōn], *n.* a stone or iron plate in an oven on which cakes are baked. [ME. *bakeston*].
BAKING (1), [bāk'-ing], *n.* the cooking of bread, cakes, etc., *esp.* by a baker; the quantity baked at one time.
BAKING (2), [bāk'-ing], *adj.* extremely hot, straight from the oven.
BAKING-POWDER, [bāk'-ing-pow'-der], *n.* a mixture of bicarbonate of soda and tartaric acid used to leaven bread, cakes, etc.
BAKSHEESH, see BACKSHEESH.
BAKSHISH, see BACKSHEESH.
BALAAM, [bā'-lam'], *n.* old newspaper matter kept for filling up gaps in a newspaper. [*Balaam*, the prophet].
BALACLAVA-HELMET, [bal'-a-klah'-va-hel'-met], *n.* (*milit.*) woollen headgear protecting the head and neck, worn by certain soldiers on field service. [*Balaclava* in the Crimea].
BALALAIKA, [bal'-a-lī'-ka], *n.* a Russian musical instrument having a triangular body and resembling a guitar; a concert of popular Russian music and traditional songs. [Russ. *balalaika*].

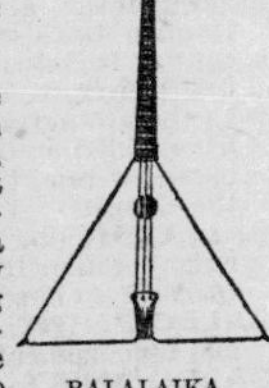
BALALAIKA

BALANCE (1), [bal'-ans], *n.* the condition of equilibrium between two opposing forces, weights, quantities, etc.; equality of weight or quantity; the method of determining this state of equality; a weighing apparatus actuated by levers or springs for determining the weight of an object by comparison with known weights; the amount required to make two different weights or quantities equal to each other; the sum of money required to equalize a credit and debit account; the amount of money required to complete a payment; (*fig.*) poise, a position of steadiness, equality and harmony of proportion; (*gymnastics*) an exercise performed on the parallel or horizontal bar; (*astron.*) the seventh sign of the zodiac; **b. of trade,** the difference in value between exports and imports; **to hold the b.,** to have power to determine anything; **to lose one's b.,** to fall, to lose one's grip mentally; **to strike a b.,** to make out a balance-sheet; **b. in hand,** sum of money left over after equalizing profit and loss, income and expenditure. [Fr. *balance* from L. *bi* two and *lanx* plate].
BALANCE (2), [bal'-ans], *v.t.* to bring to, or keep in, a state of equilibrium; to compare in one's mind in order to decide the relative worth; to adjust (accounts) in order to equalize the debit and credit side of the accounts; to have equal weight with; to pay the outstanding deficit on an account; *v.i.* to be in a state of equilibrium or equality; to be adjusted so as to be equal; to hesitate, waver.
BALANCE-FISH, [bal'-ans-fish'], *n.* the hammerhead shark, *Zygaena malleus*.
BALANCE KNIFE, [bal'-ans-nīf'], *n.* a table-knife balanced in such a way that the blade does not come into contact with the flat surface on which the knife rests.
BALANCER, [bal'-ans-er], *n.* an organ, shaped like a drumstick, which serves as a second pair of wings in flies and other two-winged insects.
BALANCE-REEF, [bal'-ans-rēf'], *n.* (*naut.*) a reef-band fastened diagonally across a sail, and used to contract the sail in a storm.
BALANCE-SHEET, [bal'-ans-shēt'], *n.* (*comm.*) a document which gives a summary of assets and liabilities of a person or company.
BALANCE-WHEEL, [bal'-ans-wēl'], *n.* a small wheel which regulates the beat in a watch.
BALANCING (1), [bal'-ans-ing], *n.* a state of balance or equilibrium, poise; the act of bringing to a state of balance.
BALANCING (2), [bal'-ans-ing], *adj.* having balance, equalizing.
BALANITE, [bal'-an-īt], *n.* (*geol.*) a fossil shell belonging to the barnacle family. [Gk. *balanitos* acorn-shaped].
BALAS, [bal'-as], *n.* a kind of rose-coloured ruby. [Arab. *balakhshi*].
BALATA, [bal-ah'-ta], *n.* a gum obtained from the tree, *Mimusops Balata*, used for purposes similar to rubber. [SAmer. *balata*].
BALAUSTINE, [bal-aws'-tin], *n.* the wild pomegranate tree, *Gunica Tranatum*. [*Next*].
BALAUSTION, [bal-aws'-tion], *n.* the flower of the pomegranate. [Gk. *balaustion*].
BALBRIGGAN, [bal-brig'-an], *n.* a kind of knitted cotton fabric used for underwear, etc. [*Balbriggan* a place in Ireland].
BALCONET, [bal'-kon-et'], *n.* a projecting railing round window-sills.
BALCONY, [bal'-kon-i], *n.* platform-like structure provided with a railing or parapet, and projecting from the external wall of a house, usually in front of windows; the rows of seats immediately below the gallery in a theatre. [It. *balcone*].
BALD, [bawld], *adj.* without hair on the head, *esp.* the top or back; bare, without vegetation; simple, unadorned; dull, graceless, monotonous; unconcealed; (*zool.*) (of certain animals or birds) having a white spot on their heads; **to go b.-headed,** to act without restraint or thought for the consequences. [ME. *balled*].
BALDACHIN, BALDAQUIN, [bawld'-ak-in], *n.* a silken canopy held over the pope's head and in processions, also over the Blessed Sacrament; a canopy of stone, supported by columns, placed over bishops' thrones and over altars. [It. *baldacchino* from *Baldacco* the It. name for *Bagdad*].
BALDERDASH, [bawl'-der-dash'], *n.* words jumbled together without meaning or sense; nonsense, rubbish. [Uncert.].
BALDHEAD, [bawld'-hed'], *n.* a bald person.
BALDICOOT, [bawld'-i-ko͞ot], *n.* a coot; (*slang*) a person with a bald head.
BALDLY, [bawld'-li], *adv.* in bald fashion.
BALDMONEY, [bawld'-mun-i], *n.* (*bot.*) †the purple gentian, *Gentiana campestris*; the spignel, *Meum athamanticum*. [Unkn.].
BALDNESS, [bawld'-nes], *n.* the state of being bald.
BALDPATE, [bawld'-pāt], *n.* a bald head.
BALDPATED, [bawld'-pāt'-id], *adj.* without hair on the head.
BALDRICK, [bawld'-rik], *n.* a richly ornamented belt hanging from the shoulder across the body and from which was slung a sword or bugle. [OFr. *baulderic*].
BALE (1), [bāl], *n.* a large bundle or package of goods, wrapped usually in canvas and corded or fastened with a metal band; (*pl.*) goods, merchandise. [OFr. *bale*].
BALE (2), [bāl], *n.* calamity, destruction, dire misfortune. [OE. *bealu* evil].
BALE† (3), [bāl], *n.* a beacon-fire, a funeral pyre. [OE. *bæl*].
BALE (4), [bāl], *v.t.* to make into a bale. [BALE (1)].
BALE (5), [bāl], *v.i.* to ladle with buckets; **b. out,** (*aeron.*) to descend from an aeroplane by parachute. [BAIL (5)].
BALEEN, [bal-ēn'], *n. and adj.* whalebone. [L. *balæna* whale].
BALE-FIRE, [bāl'-fīer], *n.* a large fire, bonfire; a signal fire; a pyre. [OE. *bæl-fyr*].
BALEFUL, [bāl'-fo͝ol], *adj.* harmful, bringing evil and misery, malicious, dire. [OE. *bealu-full*].
BALEFULLY, [bāl'-fo͝ol-i], *adv.* in baleful fashion.
BALEFULNESS, [bāl'-fo͝ol-nes], *n.* the condition of being baleful.
BALER, [bāl'-er], *n.* the bucket or bowl used in baling water out of a boat.
BALILLA, [ba-lē'-la], *n.* a militarist organization for children in Fascist Italy.
BALING-PAPER, [bāl'-ing-pāp'-er], paper used for packing.
BALING-PRESS, [bāl'-ing-pres'], *n.* a press for compressing goods to be made into bales.
BALISTER, [bal'-ist-er], *n.* a cross-bow; a ballista. [OFr. *balestre* and L. *ballistra*].
BALISTIC, see BALLISTIC.
BALISTRARIA, [bal'-ist-räer'-ia], *n.* a loophole in the wall of a fort or castle through which the cross-bowmen shot their arrows; a projecting turret from which to shoot. [MedL. *ballistraria*].
BALIZE, [bal-ēz'], *n.* a pole fixed on a bank as a sea-mark. [Fr. *balise*, Span. *valise*].
BALK, BAULK (1), [bawlk], *n.* an unploughed ridge of land between furrows, used formerly to separate the different strips into which a field was divided; a large rough beam of timber; house; (*fig.*) frustration, hindrance, check; (*billiards*) area at the bottom of a billiard-table, marked out by a line drawn parallel to the bottom cushion, the middle portion of the line

forming the base of a semicircle from which play begins. [OE. *balca*].

BALK, BAULK (2), [bawlk], *v.t. and i.* to impede the progress of, obstruct; to thwart, check, frustrate; to omit; to stop suddenly, to jib.

BALKER, [bawk'-er], *n.* (*fishing*) a man on shore who signals by shouting the movements of shoals of herrings.

BALKINGLY, [bawlk'-ing-li], *adv.* in a balking manner.

BALKY, [bawlk'-i], *adj.* liable to come to a sudden stop.

BALL (1), [bawl], *n.* a spherical or roundish object, solid or hollow, of any substance or size; a solid missile fired by a cannon, rifle, pistol, etc.; a round or oval-shaped object used in playing games; (*fig.*) the earth; any celestial body; material formed or wound into a round mass; a large pill used in veterinary practice; (*cricket*) a delivery of the ball by the bowler; golden sphere accompanying the sceptre as a sign of sovereignty; **b. of foot,** the rounded part of the foot below the joint of the big toe; **b. of eye,** the eye within the lids; **b. and socket,** a form of joint, usually of metal, in which a ball can turn in any direction within the close-fitting socket enclosing it; **b.-bearings,** a series of small steel balls placed in a groove between revolving parts and axles to reduce friction; **to keep the b. rolling,** to take one's share in conversation, keep anything going; **no b.,** (*cricket*) a ball which is unfairly delivered. [Fr. *balle* ball].

BALL (2), [bawl], *n.* an assembly or social gathering for dancing, a dance; **to open the b.,** to start the first dance; (*fig.*) to commence operations. [L. *ballare* to dance].

BALL (3), [bawl], *v.t. and i.* to form into a ball or spherical mass.

BALLAD, [bal'-ad], *n.* a popular, traditional story of adventure told in a simple metre, originally sung to a harp; (*mus.*) a short song of simple construction, generally of a sentimental character. [OFr. *ballade*].

BALLADE, [bal-ahd'], *n.* a poem consisting of three stanzas of eight lines each together with a stanza of four lines called an *envoy*, each verse and the *envoy* ending with the same line or refrain; a musical composition of a romantic nature. [OFr. *ballade*].

BALLADER, [bal'-ad-er], *n.* a composer or singer of ballads.

BALLADMAKER, [bal'-ad-māk'-er], *n.* one who composes ballads.

BALLADMONGER, [bal'-ad-mung'-ger], *n.* a maker or seller of ballads; (*coll.*) an inferior poet.

BALLADRY, [bal'-ad-ri], *n.* the subject or manner of writing ballads.

BALLADSINGER, [bal'-ad-sing'-er], *n.* one who sings ballads.

BALLAST (1), [bal'-ast], *n.* heavy material placed in the hold of a ship or in a balloon to keep it stable; that which is used to make anything steady; earth or gravel laid between the rails and sleepers on a railway line; (*fig.*) elements making for steadiness and stability of character. [Swed. *ballast*].

BALLAST (2), [bal'-ast], *v.t.* to provide with ballast; to keep steady by means of ballast.

BALLASTAGE, [bal'-ast-ij], *n.* a duty paid for permission to take ballast.

BALLASTING, [bal'-ast-ing], *n.* anything used as ballast.

BALL-CARTRIDGE, [bawl'-caht'-rij], *n.* a cartridge that is charged with a bullet.

BALL-COCK, [bawl'-kok'], *n.* a valve or cock controlling the supply of water to a cistern and actuated by a floating ball attached to it by a lever.

BALLERINA, [bal'-er-ēn'-a], *n.* a ballet girl, a female ballet dancer. [It. *ballerina* a dancer].

BALLET, [bal'-ā], *n.* a scenic representation of actions, characters, feelings, etc., by means of an elaborate series of dances performed to music. [Fr. *ballet* from *bal* dance].

BALLETOMANE, [bal'-et-ō-mān'], *n.* one who has an extravagant enthusiasm for attending ballet performances. [*Next*].

BALLETOMANIA, [bal'-et-o-mān'-ia], *n.* inordinate enthusiasm for attending ballet performances. [BALLET and MANIA].

BALL-FLOWER

BALL-FLOWER, [bawl'-flow'-er], *n.* a form of architectural ornament resembling a ball placed in a circular flower.

BALLIAGE, BAILAGE, [bal'-i-ahj], *n.* a small duty formerly paid to the City of London on certain goods exported. [Uncert.].

BALLING-GUN, [bawl'-ing-gun'], *n.* an instrument for introducing medicine in balls into a horse's throat.

BALLISTA, [bal-ist'-a], *n.* a military engine anciently used for hurling darts and stones. [L. *ballista*].

BALLISTIC, BALISTIC, [bal-ist'-ik], *adj.* concerning the throwing of missiles or shooting projectiles; **b. curve,** the path of a projectile.

BALLISTICS, [bal-ist'-iks], *n.(pl.)* the science of projectiles.

BALLISTITE, [bal-ist'-īt], *n.* a smokeless explosive compounded of nitro-glycerine and soluble nitro-cellulose.

BALLIUM, [bal'-i-um], *n.* the court inside a fortified castle; an outer bulwark; a bailey. [MedL. *ballium*].

BALLONET, [bal'-on-et'], *n.* small balloon, an air-bag inside an airship.

BALLOON (1), [ba-lōōn'], *n.* an inflated ball of air-tight material; a large spherical bag which rises and floats when filled with gas lighter than air; a small inflated sphere of thin rubber; the inflated bag which keeps an airship up in the air; (*chem.*) a large hollow glass receiver used in distilling; (*arch.*) a ball or globe surmounting a pillar or cupola; (*hort.*) a frame for training trees or plants; **b. barrage,** a system of captive balloons employed as a defence against low-flying aircraft; **observation b.,** a balloon anchored to the ground, and rising to a considerable height, from which an observer can watch the progress of a battle or report on the position and movements of the enemy. [It. *ballone*].

BALLOON (2), [bal-ōōn'], *v.t. and i.* (*of sails, etc.*) to bulge out like a balloon; to make an ascent in a balloon; (*football*) to kick the ball aimlessly high into the air.

BALLOONING, [bal-ōōn'-ing], *n.* the construction and management of balloons.

BALLOONIST, [bal-ōōn'-ist], *n.* one who builds or makes ascents in a balloon.

BALLOON-JUMPING, [bal-ōōn'-jump'-ing], *n.* the practice of leaping from great heights with a balloon to retard the rate of descent.

BALLOON-TYRE, [bal-ōōn'-tīer'], *n.* a large inflated pneumatic tyre used on motor vehicles.

BALLOT (1), [bal'-ot], *n.* a ball, ticket or paper used to record a secret vote; the act or practice of voting secretly, any voting by paper or ticket; the total number of votes cast. [It. *ballotta* little ball].

BALLOT (2), [bal'-ot], *v.i.* to vote by ballot, to vote secretly; to make a choice by ballot; **to b. for,** to elect by secret vote.

BALLOTADE, [bal'-ot-ād], *n.* the leap of a horse in which the horse bends his legs without kicking the rear legs backwards.

BALLOTAGE, [bal'-ot-ahzh'], *n.* a French system of a second ballot between the two highest candidates when a legal majority has not been obtained.

BALLOT-BOX, [bal'-ot-boks'], *n.* the box in which the voting papers are deposited at an election.

BALLOTING, [bal'-ot-ing], *n.* the action of voting by ballot.

BALLROOM, [bawl'-rōōm], *n.* a room or hall for dancing.

BALLY, [bal'-i], *adj.* (*coll.*) annoying, objectionable; very; (*often a mere vague expletive*). [Euphemistic form of BLOODY].

BALLYHOO, [bal'-i-hōō'], *n.* advance publicity of an exaggerated nature; (*fig.*) empty bombast, grossly deceitful talk. [U.S. slang].

BALM (1), [bahm], *n.* sap, juice or gum resin obtained from various aromatic or fragrant shrubs and trees; a fragrant or valuable healing ointment; (*fig.*) anything soothing mental or physical pain; (*bot.*) aromatic plants or garden herbs of the genus *Melissa*; **B. of Gilead,** the resin of the tree, *Commiphora Opobalsamum*, formerly used as an antiseptic ointment; the resin of a North American coniferous tree, *Abies balsamea*, also known as Canada balsam. [OFr. *baume*, L. *balsamum*].

BALM (2), [bahm], *v.t.* to anoint with balm.

BALM-CRICKET, [bahm'-krik'-it], *n.* the field-cricket.

BALMILY, [bahm'-il-i], *adv.* in balmy fashion.

BALMY, [bahm'-i], *adj.* like balm; fragrant, soothing.

BALNEAL, [bal'-ni-al], *adj.* pertaining to baths. [~L. *balneum* bath].

BALNEARY (1), [bal'-ni-er-i], *n.* a bathroom.

BALNEARY (2), [bal'-ni-er-i], *adj.* relating to bathing. [L. *balnearius*].

BALNEOLOGY, [bal'-ni-ol'-oj-i], *n.* the study or science of the use of natural and medicinal baths and waters in healing. [L. *balneum* bath and Gk. *logos* speech].

BALNEUM, [bal'-ni-um], *n.* (*chem.*) a bath. [L. *balneum*].

BALSA, [bal'-sa], *n.* a double-boat raft of great buoyancy used in Peru. [Span. *balsa* boat].

BALSAM (1), [bawl'-sam], *n.* an aromatic resinous substance obtained from certain plants or trees; artificial, oily or resinous ointment made by dissolving various substances in oil or turpentine; (*fig.*) a substance which heals or soothes; (*chem.*) compounds made from resins and volatile oils and insoluble in water; **Canada b.,** a type of balsam used in mounting microscopic objects. [L. *balsamum*].

BALSAM (2), see BALSAMINE.

BALSAMIC (1), [bawl'-sam-ik], *n.* a soothing oily medicine.

BALSAMIC (2), [bawl'-sam-ik], *adj.* having the qualities of balsam; soothing.

BALSAMICAL, [bawl-sam'-ikl], *adj.* balsamic.

BALSAMICALLY, [bawl-sam'-ik-a-li], *adv.* soothingly.

BALSAMIFEROUS, [bawl'-sam-if'-er-us], *adj.* yielding balsam. [BALSAM and L. *ferre* to bear].

BALSAMINE†, BALSAMIN, [bawl'-sam-in], *n.* the plant balsam, touch-me-not, *Impatiens noli-me-tangere*. [Gk. *balsamine* balsam plant].

BALTIMORE-BIRD, [bol'-ti-mawer-burd'], *n.* a small American migratory singing-bird with black head and upper-parts, and under-parts of brilliant orange. [*Baltimore*, Maryland, in the U.S.A.].

BALUSTER, [bal'-us-ter], *n.* a small pillar usually slender at its top and base but swelling out in the middle, used to support a hand-rail. [It. *balaustro*].

BALUSTERED, [bal'-ust-erd], *adj.* provided with balusters.

BALUSTRADE, [bal'-us-trād'], *n.* a row of balusters together with a coping supported by them, the whole serving as an ornamental parapet to a balcony, etc. [Fr. *balustrade*].

BALUSTRADE

BAM (1), [bam], *n.* a hoax, a falsehood. [Abbreviation of BAMBOOZLE].

BAM (2), (bammed, bamming), [bam], *v.t.* to cheat, to hoax. [*Prec.*].

BAMBINO, [bam-bēn'-ō], *n.* an Italian baby; a representation of the infant Christ. [It. *bambino* baby].

BAMBOCCIATA, [bam'-boch'-i-ah'-ta], *n.* a picture of rustic homely life, as seen in fairs and festivities. [Van Laar, a Dutch painter, nicknamed *bamboccio* cripple].

BAMBOO, [bam-bōō'], *n.* a genus of tropical and sub-tropical giant grasses with round jointed stalks and oval leaves, and ranging in height from a few feet to a hundred feet or over; the stalk of this plant used for innumerable purposes. [Malayan *bamba*].

BAMBOO

BAMBOOZLE, [bam'-boozl'], *v.t.* to hoax, deceive, mystify. [Fr. *bambocher* play the fool].

BAN (1), [ban], *n.* a prohibition, proscription; a sentence of excommunication passed by ecclesiastical authority; method of public disapproval; (*hist.*) proclamation summoning the king's vassals for military service; †a curse. [OE. *gebann* summons].

BAN (2), [ban], *n.* muslin made from banana fibre. [BANANA].

BAN (3), [ban], *v.t. and i.* to curse, to forbid, to prohibit. [OE. *gebannan* summon].

BANAL, [bān'-al, ban-al'], *adj.* commonplace, obvious; vulgar. [Fr. *banal*].

BANALITY, [ban-al'-i-ti], *n.* the condition of being banal; a commonplace, vulgarity, something which is obvious.

BANANA, [ban-ah'-na], *n.* a tropical or sub-tropical fruit-tree; the long curved edible fruit of this tree, hanging in clusters, and covered with a hard greenish-yellow rind. [Span. *banana*].

BANBURY CAKE, [ban'-ber-i-kāk'], *n.* a kind of pastry turnover originating in *Banbury*, Oxfordshire.

BANCO, [bang'-kō], *n.* a bench or bank; bank money in contrast with other currency; (*leg.*) **sittings in b.,** when several judges are present together on the bench. [LL. *bancus* a bench].

BAND (1), [band], *n.* a thin strip of material fastened round a number of objects or a mass of loose material to make a compact package or to fasten the objects together; a narrow flat strip of cloth forming part of a garment; a belt or stripe of material on an object, distinguishable in colour or appearance from the remainder of the object; (*pl.*) a pair of white strips of cloth hanging down from the collar in front and worn by barristers, certain clergymen, and with certain academic robes; (*arch.*) flat, square, shallow moulding, a succession of ornaments encircling a building or arranged along the whole length of a wall; (*mech.*) a belt for the transmission of power in a machine; (*bookbinding*) straps at the ends of the spine of a book which hold the sheets together; **b. stone,** a stone passing through a dry-stone wall and used to bind it together. [OE. *band*].

BAND (2), [band], *n.* a gathering of people; a company of persons brought together for a common purpose; (*mus.*) a company of instrumentalists gathered together to perform a musical composition; **B. of Hope,** an association of persons who have pledged themselves to total abstinence from intoxicating liquors. [*Prec.*].

BAND (3), [band], *v.t.and i.* to make a band, to secure or adorn with a band; to join together in a company, to associate; (*her.*) to bind with a band of different colour from the charge. [BAND (1)].

BANDAGE (1), [band'-ij], *n.* a strip of woven fabric used to dress and bind up wounds and injuries; that which is bound over something else. [Fr. *bandage*].

BANDAGE (2), [band'-ij], *v.t.* to bind with a bandage.

BANDAGING, [ban'-dij-ing], *n.* bandages; material for bandages.

BANDANNA, [band-an'-a], *n.* a brightly coloured Indian silk handkerchief spotted with white or yellow; a method of calico-printing or dyeing in which the above effect is obtained. [Hind. *bandhnu*].

BANDBOX, [band'-boks], *n.* a light box of cardboard or thin paper-covered bent-wood for hats and other light articles; a clergyman's case for holding his linen bands; **to have come out of a b.,** to be spruce and neat in appearance.

BANDBRAKE, [band'-brāk'], *n.* a brake on a bicycle or motor vehicle worked by the friction of a steel band on the axle of the wheel.

BANDEAU, [band-ō'], *n.* a ribbon tied round a woman's head to bind her hair; a flat ring inside a woman's hat. [Fr. *bandeau*].

BANDED, [band'-id], *adj.* united, joined together in a band; furnished or decorated with coloured bands.

BANDELET, [band'-let], *n.* a small band or flat moulding. [Fr. *bandelette*].

BANDERILLA, [ban'-de-rēl'-ya], *n.* the barbed dart used to excite the bull in bull-fighting. [Span. *banderilla*].

BANDEROL(E), [band'-er-ol], *n.* a long, narrow streamer flown at the masthead; an ornamental pennant fastened to the end of a knight's lance; (*arch.*) a flat ribbon-like band with an inscription; (*her.*) a narrow streamer under the crook of a crosier, and folding over the staff. [Fr. *banderole*].

BANDIAN, see BADIANE.

BANDICOOT, [band'-i-kōōt], *n.* a huge edible Indian rat, *Nesocia bandicota*; an Australian marsupial insect-eater of the genus *Perameles*. [Telugu *pandikokku* a pig-like rat].

BANDINESS, [band'-i-nes], *n.* the state or quality of having bandy legs.

BANDIT, (*pl.* **bandits, banditti**), [band'-it, band'-its, band-it'-i], *n.* an outlaw, an armed robber, a highwayman, a lawless or desperate person; **motor b.,** (*coll.*) a thief who uses a motor-car to make a swift raid and escape. [It. *bandito*].

BANDLE, [bandl], *n.* an Irish measure equal to two feet. [Ir. *bannlamh*].

BANDMASTER, [band'-mah'-ster], *n.* the conductor of a musical band.

BANDOG, [ban'-dog'], *n.* a large dog which is kept securely chained-up on account of its ferocious nature; a bloodhound or a mastiff. [BAND (1) and DOG].

BANDOLEER, BANDOLIER, [band'-ō-lēer'], *n.* a leather belt formerly worn by musketeers over the right shoulder to secure their firearms; a shoulder belt to which are attached small pockets of wood or leather for holding cartridges. [Fr. *bandoulière* from It. *bandoliera*].

BANDOLERO, [band'-o-lāer'-ō], *n.* a bandit, robber. [Span. *bandolero*].

BANDOLIER, see BANDOLEER.

BANDOLINE, [band'-ō-lēn], *n.* a substance rubbed in the hair to keep it flat. [BANDEAU].

BANDORE, [band-aw(r)'], *n.* an ancient kind of musical instrument resembling a guitar. [Portug. *bandurra*].

BAND-PASS, [band'-pahs'], *adj.* (*wirel.*) constructed so as to pass only a particular band of frequencies.

BANDROL, [band'-rōl], *n.* a small flag or streamer, a banderole. [It. *banduerola*].

BANDSAW, [band'-saw], *n.* a thin saw stretched on a frame; an endless saw running over two pulleys.

BANDSMAN, [bandz'-man], *n.* a performer in or member of a musical band.

BANDSTAND, [band'-stand'], *n.* a raised roofed outdoor platform in which a musical band gives performances.

BANDY (1), [band'-i], *n.* a kind of hockey played on the ice. [Unkn.].

BANDY (2), [band'-i], *n.* an Indian bullock cart. [Telugu *bandi*].

BANDY (3), [band'-i], *adj.* of legs having an outward curve at the knee; bow-legged.

BANDY (4), [band'-i], *v.t. and i.* to beat to and fro, to toss about; to exchange, to give and take, to circulate a rumour or story, to strive as at bandy; **to b. words,** to engage in violent and rapid discussion with someone. [BANDY (1)].

BANDY-LEGGED, [band'-i-legd'], *adj.* having curved or bowed legs.

BANE, [bān], *n.* a source of death or injury; a cause of vexation, worry or ruin; poison; destruction, death, woe; sheep-rot. [OE. *bana* slayer].

BANEBERRY, [bān'-be'-ri], *n.* the herb-christopher, a plant with poisonous berries, *Actæa spicata.*

BANEFUL, [bān'-fōōl], *adj.* destructive, deadly; evil.

BANEFULLY, [bān'-fōōl-i], *adv.* in a baneful way.

BANEFULNESS, [bān'-fōōl-nes], *n.* the condition of being baneful.

BANEWORT, [bān-wurt], *n.* the deadly-nightshade *Atropa Belladonna*; the lesser spearwort, *Ranunculus Flammula.* [OE. *bana* murderer and WORT].

BANEWORT
(*Ranunculus*)

BANG (1), [bang], *n.* a sudden, loud noise, the loud report of a firearm; a sudden noise caused by the slamming of anything; a hard violent blow. [BANG (4)].

BANG (2), [bang], *n.* (*U.S.*) hair cut straight across in a fringe, as a woman's hair across the forehead, or a horse's tail. [Uncert.].

BANG (3), [bang], *adv.* in the manner of a bang; (*coll.*) precisely and abruptly, exactly; completely. [BANG (4)].

BANG (4), [bang], *v.t. and i.* to make a sudden loud noise, to cause something to make a bang; to beat in a noisy manner, to thump, to thrash; to bring or come into violent contact with; to strike forcibly; to handle in a rough manner. [OScand. *banga* strike].

BANG (5), [bang], *v.t.* (*U.S.*) to cut hair in the form of a bang. [BANG (2)].

BANG (6), see BHANG.

BANGLE, [bang'-gl], *n.* an ornament in the form of a ring or bracelet encircling the arm. [Hind. *bangrī*].

BANGLE-EARS, [bang'-gl-ēerz], *n.(pl.)* loose hanging ears.

BANGUE, BANG, see BHANG.

BANIAN, BANYAN, [ban'-yan], *n.* a Hindu trader, *esp.* one who comes from the province of Gujerat; a name given by early travellers in Western India to persons of the Hindu religion; a native broker employed by business houses in Calcutta; a kind of dressing-gown resembling the loose garment worn by the Banyans; a kind of jacket of wool, silk or flannel; the Indian fig tree, *Ficus benghalensis.* [Portug. *banian* from Skr. *vanij* merchant].

BANISH, [ban'-ish], *v.t.* to condemn to exile; to drive or force away; to remove forcibly from one's thoughts or mind. [OFr. *banir*].

BANISHMENT, [ban'-ish-ment], *n.* the act of banishing; the condition of being banished; exile.

BANISTER, [ban'-is-ter], *n.* the handrail together with the supporting railings of a staircase. [A form of BALUSTER].

BANJO, [ban'-jō], *n.* a stringed instrument having a body like a tambourine and neck like a guitar, played with the fingers; the casing of the differential gear of a motor-car. [Negro corruption of BANDORE].

BANJOIST, [ban'-jō-ist], *n.* one who plays the banjo.

BANK (1), [bangk], *n.* a heaped-up mound of earth, snow or sand; a raised shelf of ground on the bed of a river or sea; the sloping ground forming the edge of a river, lake or cutting; an artificial slope or gradient built round a curve of a road or motor-racing track to allow a vehicle to maintain speed round the curve; a piled-up mass of clouds; (*naut.*) the rowing bench in a galley; (*min.*) the face of the coal in a mine, the top of a mine shaft. [ODan. *banke*, OIcel. *bakki*].

BANK (2), [bangk], *n.* an establishment which trades in, receives, lends or exchanges money; a building occupied by such an establishment; a company engaged in this business; a fund; the pool in a gambling game; **B. of England,** a London bank which manages the public debt, receives revenue, issues notes which are legal tender, etc.; **b. holiday,** a public holiday declared by Act of Parliament; **b. rate,** the rate at which the Bank of England discounts bills of exchange. [LL. *bancus* a bench, originally a table for moneylenders and changers].

BANK (3), [bangk], *v.t. and i.* to form a bank, to make into a bank, to heap, to become heaped; to raise a heap of earth or stones about, to fortify or strengthen with a bank, to confine with banks; (*aeron.*) to tilt an aeroplane at an angle in turning in order to avoid side-slip, to travel with one side higher than the other; **to b. a fire,** to heap a fire with fuel and reduce the draught so that it may burn slowly for a long time; **to b. on,** (*coll.*) to rely upon, to count on. [BANK (4)].

BANK (4), [bangk], *v.t. and i.* to deposit money in a bank, to change into money; to carry on the business of banking, to trade in money; (*gaming*) to hold the sum of money from which losses are paid. [BANK (2)].

BANKABLE, [bangk'-abl], *adj.* able to be accepted at a bank.

BANK-AGENT, [bangk'-āj'-ent], *n.* the manager of a branch-bank.

BANK-BILL, [bangk'-bil], *n.* a bill of exchange drawn by one bank upon another.

BANK-BOOK, [bangk'-bōōk], *n.* a pass-book which contains a statement of a customer's account at a bank.

BANK-CREDIT, [bangk'-kred'-it], *n.* permission, on security being given, for a customer to overdraw his account to a certain extent.

BANKER (1), [bangk'-er], *n.* one who keeps a bank or carries on the business of banking; a group of persons engaged in banking; a gambling card-game; (*gaming*) a person who holds the pool in a gambling game and who pays losses from the common fund.

BANKER (2), [bangk'-er], *n.* a vessel in the cod-fishery on the banks of Newfoundland; a stone or wooden bench on which masons cut and square their work; a horse trained to jump banks.

BANKET, [bangk'-et], *n.* the conglomerate rock forming the gold reef of the Transvaal; a cake having raisins in it. [Du. *banket* hard cake].

BANKING (1), [bangk'-ing], *n.* the act of erecting a bank; an artificially constructed sloping bank of a motor-racing track; fishing on a sea-bank; (*aeron.*) the tilting of an aeroplane at an acute angle when turning sharply.

BANKING (2), [bangk'-ing], *n.* the business of a banker, the act of carrying on the business of a banker; the depositing of money in a bank.

BANKING (3), [bangk'-ing], *adj.* pertaining to or conducted by a bank; **b. house,** a commercial firm transacting banking.

BANK-NOTE, [bangk'-nōt], *n.* a promissory note payable on demand, issued by a bank.

BANKOCRACY, [bangk'-ok'-ras-i], *n.* the virtual government of a state by banks; bank directors controlling the policy of a government. [BANK and Gk. *krateia* rule].

BANKRUPT (1), [bang'-krupt], *n.* a person who on becoming insolvent has, on his own or his creditors' petition, come under the jurisdiction of a court which administers and distributes his assets for the benefit of his creditors; a person legally declared to be unable to pay his debts; an insolvent person, one unable to pay his debts. [It. *bancarotta*].

BANKRUPT (2), [bang'-krupt], *adj.* unable to pay one's debts, insolvent; (*fig.*) without, destitute of.

BANKRUPT (3), [bang'-krupt], *v.t.* to make or declare bankrupt.

BANKRUPTCY, [bang'-krupt-si], *n.* the state of being legally declared bankrupt; the act of becoming a bankrupt; (*fig.*) absolute loss, the state of being morally or intellectually destitute; **Act of B.,** act by which a debtor renders himself liable to be declared a bankrupt; **B. Court,** the court of law which deals with this.

BANKSIA, [bangk'-si-a], *n.* (*bot.*) a genus of evergreen Australian shrubs of the order *Proteaceae* with dark-green velvety leaves and small yellow flowers. [Sir J. *Banks*, botanist].

BANKSMAN, [bangks'-man], *n.* an overseer who works at the pit-head in a coal-mine.

BANK-STOCK, [bangk'-stok], *n.* shares held in the capital stock of a bank.

BANLIEUE, [ban'-lew], *n.* the territory lying outside the walls, but within the legal limits of a town. [Fr. *banlieue*].

BANNER, [ban'-er], *n.* a flag or ensign supported on a pole and usually adorned with an emblem or device; a rectangular piece of cloth, suitably inscribed, fastened to and carried on one or two poles in a procession or demonstration; (*fig.*) the flag or cause of a country; anything used as a symbol of opinions or a cause; **to unfurl one's b.,** announce one's cause or principles; **b. headline,** a newspaper headline put prominently across the page; **b. screen,** a fire-screen suspended from a pole or mantelpiece. [OFr. *banere*].

BANNERED, [ban'-erd], *adj.* provided with banners.

BANNERET, [ban'-er-et'], *n.* a knight having his own vassals accompanying his banner in war; a Swiss officer in charge of the banner of his canton. [OFr. *baneret*].

BANNERETTE, [ban'-er-et'], *n.* a small banner. [OFr. *banerette*].

BANNEROLE, [ban'-er-ōl], *n.* a banner carried at the funerals of great men and placed over their tombs. [BANDEROLE].

BANNOCK, [ban'-ok], *n.* a cake of oatmeal baked on an iron plate over the fire. [OE. *bannuc* from Gael. *bannach*].

BANNS, [banz], *n.*(*pl.*) notice of intention of marriage given in church on three successive Sundays, to afford opportunity for possible objection to the marriage. [BAN (1)].

BANNY, [ban'-i], *n.* the minnow, *Leuciscus phoxinus*. [Unkn.].

BANQUET (1), [bang'-kwit], *n.* a sumptuous feast generally of a formal or official nature; a dinner with speeches in celebration of some occasion; (*pop.*) a very good meal. [It. *banchetto*].

BANQUET (2), [bang'-kwit], *v.t. and i.* to treat with a feast or rich entertainment; to feast sumptuously, to regale oneself with rich fare.

BANQUETER, [bang'-kwit-er], *n.* one who gives rich feasts; one who attends a banquet.

BANQUETING, [bang'-kwit-ing], *n.* the act of feasting sumptuously, luxurious living; **b. hall,** a large luxurious dining-room.

BANQUETTE, [bang-ket'], *n.* (*mil.*) a raised step behind a parapet from which to fire; the footpath of a bridge raised above the roadway. [Fr. *banquette*].

BANSHEE, [ban'-shē'], *n.* an Irish female spirit whose wail is said to give warning of death in the family to which she is attached; (*coll.*) an air-raid siren. [OIr. *ben sidhe* woman of the fairies].

BANSTICKLE, [ban'-stikl], *n.* a fish of the genus *Gasterosteus*, the stickleback. [Unkn.].

BANTAM, [ban'-tam], *n.* a small spirited breed of domestic fowl brought from Java; a kind of gaudy painted or carved work; a small highly spirited person; a boxer of bantam weight; **b. weight,** a boxer whose fighting weight lies between eight stone six pounds and nine stone; **b. battalions,** special battalions formed during the War of 1914-1918 of small but strong men. [*Bantam* a place in Java].

BANTER (1), [ban'-ter], *n.* joking or jesting; pleasant chaffing or ridicule. [Unkn.].

BANTER (2), [ban'-ter], *v.i.* to rail humorously. [Unkn.].

BANTERING, [ban'-ter-ing], *n.* the act of chaffing humorously.

BANTING, [ban-ting], *n.* a diet for reducing weight by avoiding sugar, starch and fat; the act of reducing corpulence. [William *Banting* (1797-1878), the originator].

BANTLING, [bant'-ling], *n.* an infant. [Germ. *bänkling* bastard].

BANTU (1), [ban'-tōō'], *n.* a group of South and Central African native languages; an African native belonging to a race whose native language is Bantu. [Native *Ba-ntu* the people].

BANTU (2), [ban'-tōō'], *adj.* pertaining to Bantu.

BANXRING, [bangks'-ring], *n.* a quadruped with a long pointed snout, somewhat like a squirrel in appearance, which is found in the Indian Archipelago and feeds on insects. [Javanese *bangsring*].

BANYAN, see BANIAN.

BANZAI, [bahn-zah'-ē], *n.* the Japanese shout of joy. [Jap. *banzai* live for ever].

BAOBAB, [bā'-ob-ab], *n.* the monkey-bread or sour gourd, an African tree, *Adansonia digitata*. [Unkn.].

BAP, [bap], *n.* (*Scots*) a small variously shaped loaf of bread with a thin soft crust. [Unkn.].

BAPHOMETIC, [baf'-o-met'-ik], *adj.* consecrated as a Templar and under the curse of Baphomet or Mahomet if found to be unfaithful. [*Baphomet* (Mahomet), the prophet].

BAPTISM, [bap'-tizm], *n.* initiation into membership of the Christian Church by sprinkling with or immersion in water as a sign of purification, usually accompanied by name-giving; **b. of fire,** a soldier's first battle; (*fig.*) a severe initiatory test or ordeal. [OFr. *baptesme*; Gk. *baptismos*].

BAPTISMAL, [bap-tiz'-mal], *adj.* pertaining to baptism.

BAPTIST, [bap'-tist], *n.* one who administers baptism, *esp.* John the Baptist; a member of a religious sect who believe in baptism of adults only and total immersion at the ceremony of baptism. [Gk. *baptistes*].

BAPTISTRY, [bap'-tis-tri], *n.* the place where baptism is administered; the receptacle in which the immersion takes place. [Gk. *baptisterion* bathing place].

BAPTIZABLE, [bap-tiz'-abl], *adj.* able to be baptized.

BAPTIZE, [bap-tīz'], *v.t. and i.* to administer baptism; to initiate into membership of the Christian Church by baptism; (*fig.*) to give a name to. [Gk. *baptizo* I immerse].

BAR (1), [bah(r)], *n.* a long narrow piece of wood, metal, or other rigid material, often used for the purposes of support or of obstruction or restriction; anything resembling this; a beam or ray of light; a barrier closing a road (for toll purposes); a gatehouse in a fortified town; a bank of sand or gravel heaped up at the mouth of a river or harbour partially blocking up the entrance; the place in a court of justice at which criminals stand when on trial, the part of the court where the judges sit (separated from the rest of the court by a railing); a railing enclosing the space occupied by barristers in a court of law; an enclosed space in a public-house, hotel, or place of refreshment from which drinks are served; a room in a public-house or hotel containing a bar; (*leg.*) barriers in the Inns of Court separating the unqualified students from the barristers and other members of the governing body; the whole body of qualified barristers; a plea which completely destroys a plaintiff's action or claim; a railing in the House of Commons to which persons are brought for the purpose of examination or censure by members of Parliament; (*fig.*) a moral or intellectual restriction, barrier or obstacle to progress; a tribunal of public opinion; (*mus.*) a vertical line drawn across the stave in a musical score; (*pop.*) a measure; (*her.*) a space enclosed by two straight lines drawn horizontally across the escutcheon, not wider than one-fifth the length of the shield; (*eng.*) an ingot, a moulded but unwrought piece of metal; (*meteor.*) the unit of atmospheric pressure; **b. sinister,** (*pop.*) bend sinister, an implication or sign of illegitimacy; **trial at b.,** (*leg.*) trial in the King's Bench division; **to practise at the B.,** to follow the profession of a barrister; **to be called to the B., to be at the B., to go to the B.,** to become a barrister; **to be called within the B.,** to be appointed King's Counsel. [ME. *barre*].

BAR (2), [bah(r)], *n.* a large sea-fish. [Fr. *barre*].

BAR (3), [bah(r)], *v.t.* to fasten by means of a bar, to obstruct, to hinder, to impede; to except or exclude; to prevent, to forbid; to take exception to; to mark with stripes of a different colour; (*leg.*) to stay by legal objection. [BAR (1)].

BAR (4), [bah(r)], *prep.* with the exception of; **b. none,** unreservedly, without exception. [*Prec.*].

BARATHEA, [ba'-ra-thē'-a], *n.* a finely woven cloth

made either of wool and silk or pure wool. [Unkn.].

BARB (1), [bahb], *n.* tuft of hair resembling a beard; the beard-like feelers growing from the mouth of a barbel; the curved points projecting outwards below the point of an arrow or fish-hook to prevent its withdrawal; the lateral filament of a feather springing from the quill. [L. *barba* beard].

BARB (2), [bahb], *n.* a Barbary horse; a pigeon. [Fr. *barbe*].

BARB (3), [bahb], *v.t.* to provide with a barb. [BARB (1)].

BARBACON, see BARBICAN.

BARBADOS-CHERRY, [bah-bād'-ōz-che'-ri], *n.* a Barbados tree producing a tart fruit. *Malpighia urens.* [*Barbados*, in the West Indies, and CHERRY].

BARBADOS-LEG, [bah-bād'-ōz-leg'], *n.* elephantiasis occurring in the tropics.

BARBARIAN (1), [bah-bāer'-ian], *n.* a member of a rough uncivilized community; an uncouth, wild, savage-like person, deficient in humanity and uncivilized; an uneducated uncultured person. [BARBARIAN (2)].

BARBARIAN (2), [bah-bāer'-ian], *adj.* rude, uncivilized, cruel, pitiless, inhuman. [Gk. *barbaros* foreign].

BARBARIC, [bah-ba'-rik], *adj.* pertaining to a barbarian; uncultured wild savage. [Gk. *barbarikos*].

BARBARISM, [bah'-ber-izm], *n.* the state of being barbaric or uncivilized; brutality, cruelty; a form of speech in which foreign or vulgar idioms are used. [Gk. *barbarismos* foreign speech].

BARBARITY, [bah-ba'-ri-ti], *n.* the state of being barbarous; cruelty; fierceness.

BARBARIZATION, [bah'-ber-ī-zā'-shun], *n.* the action of making or becoming barbarous.

BARBARIZE, [bah'-ber-īz], *v.t.* to make barbarous. [Gk. *barbarizo* I behave like a foreigner].

BARBAROUS, [bah'-ber-us], *adj.* barbaric, uncivilized, uncultured, cruel, unidiomatic. [Gk. *barbaros*].

BARBAROUSLY, [bah'-ber-us-li], *adv.* in barbarous fashion.

BARBAROUSNESS, [bah'-ber-us-nes], *n.* the condition of being barbarous.

BARBASTELLE, [bah'-ba-stel'], *n.* (*zool.*) a brown bat with bearded lips, *Plecotus barbastellus.* [Fr. *barbastelle*].

BARBATE, [bah'-bāt], *adj.* (*bot.*) bearded; awned. [L. *barbatus*].

BARBE, [bahb], *n.* part of the defensive armour of a knight's war-horse; a piece of linen worn by nuns and widows about the chin. [Fr. *barbe* beard].

BARBECUE (1), [bah'-bi-kew], *n.* a wooden framework on which meat is smoked or dried; a hog, ox, or any large animal broiled or roasted whole; hence, a function in the open air, at which animals are cooked whole; a terrace, a platform on which coffee beans are spread to dry in the sun. [Span. *barbacoa*].

BARBECUE (2), [bah'-bi-kew], *v.i.* to smoke or cure meat.

BARBED, [bahbd], *adj.* bearded; furnished with barbs; furnished with armour; **b. wire**, galvanized wire spun from short lengths of wire the ends of which are left projecting like barbs.

BARBE-FEATHERS, [bahb'-feᴛʜ'-erz], *n.* (*pl.*) the feathers growing under a hawk's beak.

BARBEL, [bah'-bel], *n.* a freshwater fish of the carp family having beard-like filaments hanging down from its mouth and nose; the beard-like filaments of such fishes. [OFr. *barbel*].

BARBELLATE, [bah'-bel-āt], *adj.* (*bot.*) bearded with short stiff bristles. [*Prec.*].

BARBER (1), [bah'-ber], *n.* one who shaves or trims beards and cuts hair, a man's hairdresser; **barber's itch**, sycosis thought to be contracted from a barber's brush; **barber's pole**, a pole spirally striped in red, white and blue, and used as a sign outside a barber's shop; **b. surgeon**, one who practised both shaving and bleeding. [OFr. *barbeour* from L. *barba* beard].

BARBER (2), [bah'-ber], *v.t.* to trim a beard, to shave, to cut the hair of.

BARBER(R)Y, BERBER(R)Y, [bah'-be-ri], *n.* (*bot.*) a kind of shrub of the family *Berberidaceæ*, with spiny shoots, hanging clusters of yellow flowers and small orange-red berries. [MdL. *berberis*].

BARBET, [bah'-bit], *n.* a species of tropical climbing birds having tufts of bristles at the base of the bill; a dog with long curly hair, resembling a French poodle. [Fr. *barbet*].

BARBETTE, [bah-bet'], *n.* (*fort.*) a terrace inside a parapet so raised as to allow a cannon to be fired over the top; the armoured turret of a warship. [Fr. *barbette*].

BARBICAN, BARBACON, [bah'-bi-kan], *n.* (*fort.*) a fortification erected to guard the entrance to a town or castle; an opening in a fortified wall through which guns are fired. [OFr. *barbacan*].

BARBICAN

BARBITON, [bahb'-i-ton], *n.* an ancient musical stringed instrument resembling a guitar. [Gk. *barbiton*].

BARBITONE, [bahb'-i-tōn], *n.* a hypnotic drug, veronal. [Fr. *barbitone*].

BARBOLA, [bah-bō'-la], *n.* the decoration of small articles with modelled plastic work painted. [Unkn.].

BARBULE, [bah'-bewl], *n.* a minute lateral filament projecting from the barb of a feather. [L. *barbula*].

BARCAROLLE, BARCAROLE, [bah'-ka-rōl'], *n.* a melody sung by Venetian gondoliers; a boating song. [It. *barcaruola* boatman].

BARD† (1), [bahd], *n.* the armoured breastplate of a war-horse. [Fr. *barde*].

BARD (2), [bahd], *n.* a wandering minstrel, an ancient Celtic minstrel-poet who glorified in verse the deeds of chieftains and warriors; a Welsh poet who has been recognized at the Eisteddfod; a poet or singer. [Ir. *bardh*].

BARD (3), [bahd], *n.* a thin slice of bacon used for larding. [BARD (1)].

BARDIC, [bahd'-ik], *adj.* pertaining to a bard or his poetry. [BARD (2)].

BARDISH, [bahd'-ish], *adj.* bardic.

BARDISM, [bahd'-izm], *n.* the learning and usage of bards.

BARDOLATRY, [bah-dol'-at-ri], *n.* undue reverence for (the works of) William Shakespeare, "*Bard* of Avon."

BARE (1), [bāer], *adj.* naked, without its normal covering; uncovered, stripped, without ornament, empty; poor, meagre; mere, slight, without further proof, plain, without concealment or disguise; **to lay b.**, to disclose, expose. [OE. *bær*].

BARE (2), [bāer], *v.t.* to strip, to make bare; to uncover, to reveal, to bring to light, to make known, to make a confession. [*Prec.*].

BARE (3)†, [bāer], *pret.*, *p.pt.* of BEAR. [OE. *bæron*].

BAREBACK, [bāer'-bak'], *adj.* and *adv.* without a saddle.

BAREBONED, [bāer'-bōnd], *adj.* so lean that the bones stand out.

BAREFACED, [bāer'-fāst], *adj.* with the face uncovered; (*fig.*) without attempt at concealment; brazen, shameless.

BAREFACEDLY, [bāer'-fās'-id-li], *adv.* in shameless fashion.

BAREFACEDNESS, [bāer'-fās'-id-nes], *n.* the state of being barefaced.

BAREFOOT, [bāer'-foot], *adj.* and *adv.* having the feet bare. [OE. *baerfot*].

BAREFOOTED, [bāer'-foot'-id], *adj.* with the feet bare.

BAREGE, [ba-rāzh'], *n.* a thin fabric-like gauze of worsted and silk or cotton. [*Barèges* a place in Southern France].

BAREGNAWN, [bāer'-nawn], *adj.* eaten bare.

BAREHEADED, [bāer'-hed'-id], *adj.* with the head uncovered.

BARELEGGED, [bāer'-leg'-id], *adj.* having the legs bare; with the knees and upper part of the calf uncovered.

BARELY, [bāer'-li], *adv.* in a bare or naked fashion; openly; scarcely, hardly, merely, only just. [OE. *bærlice*].

BARENECKED, [bāer-nekt], *adj.* with the neck uncovered.

BARENESS, [bāer'-nes], *n.* the condition of being bare.

BAREPICKED, [bāer'-pikt], *adj.* picked clean to the bone.

BARERIBBED, [bāer'-ribd], *adj.* extremely lean.

BARET, see BARRET.

BARETTER, see BARRETTER.

BARGAIN (1), [bah'-gen], *n.* an agreement between two persons usually concerning the selling and buying of a thing on terms mutually advantageous or acceptable; a thing obtained by this means; an article offered on advantageous terms to the purchaser;

something offered at a reduced price, an offer; **to make or strike a b.**, to come to terms with; **to make the best of a bad b.**, to face misfortune or trouble cheerfully and optimistically; **into the b.**, over and above, in addition to; **a Dutch, wet b.**, a bargain sealed with a drink; **a b. sale**, a seasonal sale at which the price of articles is reduced. [OFr. *bargaine*].

BARGAIN (2), [bah'-gen], *v.t. and i.* to argue about the purchase or sale of an article with a view to obtaining the most favourable terms; **to b. for**, to expect, to allow for, to be prepared for. [OFr. *bargaigner*].

BARGAIN-BASEMENT, [bah'-gen-bās'-ment], *n.* the lowest storey, below the street level, of a large store, where goods are sold cheaply.

BARGAINEE, [bah'-gen-ē'], *n.* one who accepts a bargain.

BARGAINER, [bah'-gen-er], *n.* one who makes a bargain.

BARGE (1), [bahj], *n.* a large flat-bottomed boat for transporting heavy burdens on canals or rivers, sometimes towed by horses; a large flat-bottomed boat used in loading and unloading ships; a boat for the use of the chief officers of a man-of-war; a large richly decorated boat of state propelled by oars and used on ceremonial occasions; a college house-boat. [*Var.* of BARQUE].

BARGE (2), [bahj], *v.i.* to transport by barge; to collide heavily with, to run into; (*slang*) to make an abrupt and unannounced entry, to meet with a person unexpectedly; **b. about**, to plunge about in a rough, clumsy manner. [*Prec.*].

BARGE-BOARD, [bahj'-bawd], *n.* (*arch.*) a board, often elaborately ornamented, hanging down from the outer edge of a gable. [MedL. *bargus* gallows and BOARD].

BARGE-BOARD

BARGE-COUPLE, [bahj'-kupl'], *n.* (*arch.*) a pair of gable-beams mortised one into the other to strengthen a building. [*Prec.* and COUPLE].

BARGE-COURSE, [bahj'-kaws'], *n.* that part of the tiling of a roof which juts out beyond the gable; the coping of a wall formed by a course of bricks placed edgeways.

BARGEE, [bah'-jē'], *n.* a person in charge of a barge; (*fig.*) a tough, pugnacious individual; **to swear like a b.**, to swear fluently and forcefully.

BARGEMAN, [bahj'-man], *n.* a bargee.

BARGEMASTER, [bahj'-mahs'-ter], *n.* a person who owns a barge.

BARGE-POLE, [bahj'-pōl'], *n.* a pole for propelling a barge.

BARIA, see BARYTA.

BARIC (1), [ba'-rik], *adj.* barometric. [Gk. *baros* weight].

BARIC (2), [bā'-rik], *adj.* pertaining to or containing barium. [BARIUM].

BARILLA, [ba-ril'-a], *n.* raw sodium carbonate obtained by burning to ashes certain Spanish seaweeds. [Sp. *barilla*].

BARILLET, [ba-ril'-et], *n.* the cylindrical case or barrel enclosing the mainspring of a watch. [Fr. *barillet*].

BAR-IRON, [bahr'-īern], *n.* iron cast into malleable bars.

BARITONE (1), BARYTONE, [ba'-ri-tōn], *n.* a male voice whose compass lies between the bass and tenor; a singer possessing such a voice; (Gk. *gram.*) a word whose final syllable does not bear the acute accent. [Ital. *baritono* from Gk. *barutonos*].

BARITONE (2), [ba'-ri-tōn], *adj.* (*mus.*) lying between bass and tenor; suitable for a baritone voice. [Gk. *barutonos* heavy-toned].

BARIUM, [bāer'-ium], *n.* a silver-white or pale yellow malleable metal found in baryta, the chemical element symbolized by Ba. [BARYTA].

BARK (1), see BARQUE.

BARK (2), [bahk], *n.* the outer protective covering of the trunk and branches of a tree; a particular kind of bark used medicinally, *esp.* that from the Peruvian tree of the family *Rubiaceae*; bark used in tanning leather. [OScand. *barkr*].

BARK (3), [bahk], *n.* the cry of certain animals such as the dog, fox or wolf; (*slang*) the sound made by a person coughing; the report of a fire-arm; **his b. is worse than his bite**, he is not so severe in his actions as in his words. [BARK (5)].

BARK (4), [bahk], *v.t.* to peel the bark from; (*slang*) to graze the skin. [BARK (2)].

BARK (5), [bahk], *v.i.* to utter a bark; (*slang*) to cough loudly; to speak sharply and loudly; to make a loud report; **to b. up the wrong tree**, to be on a false scent, to be mistaken. [OE. *beorcan* to bark].

BARK-BARED, [bahk'-bāerd], *adj.* deprived of the bark.

BARK-BED, [bahk'-bed'], *n.* (*hort.*) a hotbed made from tanner's bark.

BARK-BOUND, [bahk'-bownd'], *adj.* (*hort.*) not growing at a normal rate on account of its bark being too close and firm.

BARKER, [bah'-ker], *n.* one who barks; one who barks trees; †a tanner; (*coll.*) one who touts for customers at a shop-door, auction, etc.; (*slang*) a revolver.

BARKERY, [bahk'-er-i], *n.* a tannery.

BARKING-IRON, [bahk'-ing-īern], *n.* a tool for removing the bark of trees.

BARK-MILL, [bahk'-mil], *n.* a mill for grinding bark.

BARK-PIT, [bahk'-pit], *n.* a vat of bark and water for tanning.

BARKY, [bahk'-i], *adj.* made of or like bark.

BARLEY, [bah'-li], *n.* a cereal plant of the genus *Hordeum* whose grain is used for making malt in brewing and distilling, and also as a food; **Scotch b.**, barley grain which has had the husk stripped off in a mill; **pearl b.**, barley which has been polished, rounded and dressed; **patent b.**, flour obtained by grinding pearl barley. [OE. *bærlic*].

BARLEY-BREAK, [bah'-li-brāk'], *n.* a rustic game in which one person chases others round stacks of grain.

BARLEY-BREE, [bah'-li-brē], *n.* strong beer. [BARLEY and BREW].

BARLEY-BROTH, [bah'-li-broth'], *n.* broth made by boiling barley and flesh with certain vegetables; strong ale.

BARLEYCORN, [bah'-li-kawn], *n.* a grain of barley; an old measure of a third of an inch; the top of a rifle's fore-sight; **John B.**, malt liquor.

BARLEYMEAL, [bah'-li-mēl'], *n.* flour ground from barley.

BARLEYMILL, [bah'-li-mil'], *n.* a mill in which pearl-barley is made.

BARLEYMOW, [bah'-li-mō'], *n.* a store for reaped barley; a stack of barley.

BARLEY-SUGAR, [bah'-li-shŏŏg'-er], *n.* a translucent stick of sweetmeat made from sugar boiled and twisted into a spiral.

BARLEY-WATER, [bah'-li-waw'-ter], *n.* a refreshing drink made by boiling pearl barley in water.

BARLOW, [bah'-lō], *n.* (*Amer.*) a pocket knife with only one blade. [*Barlow*, the maker].

BARM, [bahm], *n.* yeast; the froth which forms upon malt liquor when fermenting, used as leaven. [OE. *beorma*].

BARMAID, [bah'-mād], *n.* a female attendant serving drinks in the bar of a public-house or hotel.

BARMAN, [bah'-man], *n.* a man who serves drinks in an hotel or public-house.

BARMASTER, [bah'-mah'-ster], *n.* an arbitrator for miners. [Germ. *bergmeister*].

BARMECIDE, [bahm'-i-sīd], *adj.* (*fig.*) unreal, disappointing. [The *Barmecide*, who, in *Arabian Nights*, gave a feast with rich but empty dishes].

BARMKIN, see BARNEKIN.

BARMY (1), [bahm'-i], *n.* a small fish of the genus *Gasterosteus*. [Unkn.].

BARMY (2), [bahm'-i], *adj.* containing barm, frothy; (*slang*) mad, insane, foolish. [BARM].

BARN (1), [bahn], *n.* a building in which hay, straw, grain, etc., is stored; (*fig.*) a large, bare, unadorned room or building. [OE. *bern*].

BARN (2), [bahn], *v.t.* to store in a barn. [*Prec.*].

BARNABAS, [bahn'-a-bus], *n.* the cornflower or corn bluebottle, *Centaurea cyanus*, which flowers about St. Barnabas' Day (June 11th).

BARNACLE, [bahn'-akl], *n.* a genus of marine crustaceous animals, family *Cirripedia*, which cling by long stalks to ship hulls, rocks, etc., covered by the sea; (*fig.*) a person who clings to an office or duty, one who cannot be shaken off; a kind of wild goose fabulously thought to have originated from the shell-fish of that name; pincers used for torture; (*her.*) heraldic pincers; (*pl.*) an instrument placed over a horse's nose to hold and restrain him while being shod, bled or clipped; (*slang*) spectacles. [OFr. *bernicle*].

BARNAGH, [bah'-nah], *n.* the large whelk, *Fusus antiquus.* [Unkn.].
BARN-DANCE, [bahn'-dahns], *n.* a rustic dance in which the members of each couple alternately move sideways to and from each other, and then dance together.
BARNDOOR (1), [bahn'-daw(r)], *n.* a large door of a barn; a very large target.
BARNDOOR (2), [bahn'-daw(r)], *adj.* reared in the farmyard; **b. fowls**, cross-bred domestic fowls.
BARNEKIN, BARMKIN, [bahn'-kin], *n.* (*fort.*) the outer ward of a castle. [Unkn.].
BARN-OWL, [bahn'-owl], *n.* the screech owl, *Strix flammea.*
BARNSTORMER, [bahn'-stawm'-er], *n.* an itinerant actor playing in barns and similar places; (*fig.*) a crude, boisterous player.
BARO-, *pref.* pertaining to atmospheric pressure. [Gk. *baros* weight].
BAROGRAPH, [ba'-rō-grahf'], *n.* a kind of aneroid barometer which records on paper successive variations of atmospheric pressure; a record of atmospheric changes drawn on a graph in this way. [BARO and GRAPH].
BAROLOGY, [ba-rol'-ō-ji], *n.* the science of weight. [BARO and Gk. *logos* speech].
BAROMETER, [ba-rom'-i-ter], *n.* an instrument which indicates variations in atmospheric pressure and relates them to variable weather conditions; (*fig.*) anything which indicates changes in public opinion. [BARO and METER].
BAROMETRIC, [ba'-rō-met'-rik], *adj.* pertaining to a barometer or atmospheric pressure.
BAROMETRICAL, [ba'-rō-met'-rik-al], *adj.* barometric.
BAROMETRICALLY, [ba'-rō-met'-rik-al-i], *adv.* by means of a barometer.
BAROMETZ, [ba'-ro-mets], *n.* (*bot.*) a fern, *Cibotium Barometz*, which looks like a crouching animal. [Russ. *baranets* little ram].
BARON, [ba'-ron], *n.* the lowest title or rank in the British peerage; a foreign title of nobility; (*hist.*) a tenant of the king whose lands were obtained in return for military service; **b. of beef**, two undivided sirloins of beef. [OFr. *baron*].
BARONAGE, [ba'-ron-ij], *n.* the collective body of barons; the peerage; a book containing a list of, and information about, barons and their families. [OFr. *baronage*].
BARONESS, [ba'-ron-es], *n.* a baron's wife or widow; a woman holding a barony in her own right. [OFr. *baronnesse*].
BARONET, [ba'-ron-et], *n.* the lowest British hereditary title or rank, in order of precedence between a knight and a baron. [Dim. of BARON].
BARONETAGE, [ba'-ron-et'-ij], *n.* the collective body of baronets; a book containing a list of, and information about, baronets and their families.
BARONETCY, [ba'-ron-et-si], *n.* the dignity and title of a baronet.
BARONIAL, [bar-ōn'-i-al], *adj.* pertaining to or belonging to a baron; sumptuous, suitable for a baron; (*arch.*) resembling a castle in style.
BARONY, [ba'-ron-i], *n.* the lands or estate of a baron; the rank or title of a baron; a division of an Irish county. [OFr. *baronie*].
BAROQUE (1), [ba-rok'], *n.* the baroque style in architecture, art, literature, etc.
BAROQUE (2), [ba-rok'], *adj.* elaborately grotesque, floridly irregular, fancifully ornamental, highly ornate and bizarre. [Fr. *baroque*, Portug. *barroco*].
BAROSELENITE†, [ba'-rō-sel'-en-it], *n.* barytes. [BARYTES and SELENITE].
BAROUCHE,]ba-rōōsh'], *n.* an old-fashioned, four-wheeled horse-drawn carriage having two double inside seats. [Germ. *barutsche* from It. *baroccio*, L. *bi-rotus* two-wheeled].
BAR-POST, [bah'-pōst], *n.* an upright post fixed in the ground, to which are fastened movable bars to form a gate.

BARQUE

BARQUE, BARK, [bahk], *n.* a sailing ship with three masts and having the fore and main masts square rigged and the mizzen mast fore-and-aft rigged. [Fr. *barque*].
BARQUENTINE, [bah'-ken-tēn], *n.* a three-masted vessel, square rigged on the foremast and fore-and-aft rigged on the main and mizzen masts. [*Prec.*].
BARRACAN, [ba'-ra-kan], *n.* a thick stout waterproof material. [Arab. *barrakan* camel-hair blanket].
BARRACK (1), [ba'-rak], *n.* (usually *pl.*) a large building in which military troops are quartered; a temporary hut or shelter; (*fig.*) a large bare gaunt building. [Fr. *baraque*, It. *baracca* wooden hut].
BARRACK (2), [ba'-rak], *v.t.and i.* to accommodate in barracks; (*sport*) to shout derisive remarks at, to cheer or applaud ironically.
BARRACKING, [ba'-rak-ing], *n.* (*sport*) ironical cheering or applause, cries of derision directed towards a player.
BARRACK-MASTER, [ba'-rak-mah'-ster], *n.* the officer who has charge of barracks.
BARRACOON, [ba'-ra-kōōn'], *n.* an African fortified place of temporary detention for slaves, convicts, etc. [Span. *barracon*].
BARRACOUTA, BARRACUDA, [ba'-ra-kōō'-ta], *n.* a large fish of the genus *Sphyræna.* [Unkn.].
BARRAGE, [ba'-rij, ba'-rahzh], *n.* the act of barring; an artificial embankment across the bed of a river to raise the water-level; (*milit.*) a violent concentration of artillery fire over a given area; **b. balloon**, a balloon forming part of a balloon barrage. [Fr. *barrage*].
BARRANCA, [ba-rang'-ka], *n.* a steep narrow valley. [Span.Amer. *barranca*].
BARRAS, [ba'-ras], *n.* a resinous secretion from *Pinus maritima.* [Fr. *barras*].
BARRATOR, [ba'-ra-ter], *n.* one who commits barratry. [OFr. *barateor* swindler].
BARRATROUS, [ba'-ra-trus], *adj.* guilty of or given to barratry.
BARRATRY [ba'-ra-tri], *n.* the practice of exciting or encouraging lawsuits; a dishonest or careless action by the captain or crew of a ship whereby loss is suffered by the owners and others. [OFr. *barraterie* deceit].
BARREL (1), [ba'-rel], *n.* a long cylindrical vessel, usually made of curved staves or bars of wood secured by hoops at the ends and in the middle, and having its maximum girth in the middle; the quantity contained in a barrel; hollow metal tube in a firearm through which the shot is fired; revolving cylinder on which a chain, rope or spring is wound; cylindrical object forming the trunk or body of an object; the belly and loins of a horse, etc.; the reservoir of a fountain pen; **b. of the ear**, hollow space in the ear situated behind the tympanum. [OFr. *bareil*].
BARREL (2), [ba'-rel], *v.t.* to put or pack in a barrel.
BARREL-BELLIED, [ba'-rel-bel'-id], *adj.* having a large rounded belly.
BARREL-BULK, [ba'-rel-bulk], *n.* (*naut.*) five cubic feet.
BARREL-ORGAN, [ba'-rel-awg'-un], *n.* a large musical instrument played by street musicians and automatically producing a series of tunes when a driving handle is turned.
BARREL-VAULTED, [ba'-rel-vawlt'-id], *adj.* with a semi-cylindrical roof.
BARREN (1), [ba'-ren], *n.* a barren region; (*pl.*) prairie land in Western America.
BARREN (2), [ba'-ren], *adj.* sterile, incapable of producing offspring; not producing fruit or seed; with little or no vegetation; (*fig.*) unfruitful, unprofitable; uninventive, lacking ideas; **b. of**, totally deficient in. [OFr. *baraigne*].
BARRENNESS, [ba'-ren-nes], *n.* the state of being barren, sterility.
BARRENWORT, [ba'-ren-wurt'], *n.* (*bot.*) a woodland plant of the genus *Epimedium* having purple and yellow flowers. [BARREN and WORT].
BARRET, BARET, [ba'-ret], *n.* a kind of flat clerical or military cap. [Fr. *barrette*].
BARRETTER, [ba-ret'-er], *n.* (*elect.*) a device for maintaining a constant flow of current in a circuit in spite of a possible change of voltage.
BARRICADE (1), BARRICADO+, [ba'-ri-kād'(-ō)], *n.* a hastily and roughly improvised barrier for obstruction, protection or shelter. [Fr. *barricade*].
BARRICADE (2), [ba'-ri-kād'], *v.t.* to make or use a barricade.
BARRICADO, see BARRICADE (1).
BARRICO, [ba-rē'-kō], *n.* a small keg; a large beaker. [Span. *barrica*].
BARRIER, [ba'-ri-er], *n.* an obstacle or obstruction, generally to bar an approach; a limit or boundary;

an erection designed to keep people from a particular place; (*fig.*) a hindrance, an obstacle preventing progress, restriction; **b. reef,** a coral barrier encircling islands or running parallel to a shore and enclosing a lagoon. [OFr. *barrière*].

BARRING, [bah'-ring], *prep.* excepting, excluding. [BAR (3)].

BARRING-OUT, [bah'-ring-owt'], *n.* exclusion of a schoolmaster by his pupils in sport at Christmas.

BARRISTER, [ba'-ris-ter], *n.* a person who has been called to the Bar by one of the Inns of Court, and who is entitled to plead as counsel in the higher courts. [BAR (1) and OE. suffix *-estre*].

BARROW (1), [ba'-rō], *n.* a small hand-cart with one or two wheels and legs usually having handles by which it is raised and pushed; the amount contained in a barrow; a conical basket used for draining wet sand; a bier. [ME. *barwe*].

BARROW (2), [ba'-rō], *n.* a heap of earth or stone anciently built over a grave, a mound. [OE. *beorg* hill].

BARROW (3), [ba'-rō], *n.* a castrated boar. [OE. *bearg* boar].

BARROW (4), *n.* a long sleeveless flannel coat worn by infants. [OE. *beorgan* to protect].

BARRULET, [ba'-rōō-let], *n.* (*her.*) a horizontal stripe, one quarter the width of a bar. [BAR (1)].

BARRULY, [ba'-rew-li], *adj.* (*her.*) divided horizontally by barrulets. [AFr. *barrulée*].

BARRY, [bah'-ri], *adj.* (*her.*) divided across by an equal number of horizontal bars of two alternately recurring colours; **b. bendy,** (*her.*) split up into bars and bends with two colours alternately arranged; **b. nebuly,** (*her.*) barry, but with the edges of the bar wavy instead of straight. [Fr. *barré* barred].

BAR-SHEARS, [bah'-sheerz'], *n.*(*pl.*) an instrument for cutting metal bars.

BAR-SHOE, [bah'-shōō'], *n.* a horseshoe crossed by a bar to protect the frog of a horse's foot.

BAR-SHOT, [bah'-shot'], *n.* (*milit.*) a projectile consisting of a bar with a shot at each end.

BAR-TENDER, [bah'-tend'-er], *n.* a waiter who serves drinks in a bar.

BARTER (1), [bah'-ter], *n.* trade carried on by exchange of goods instead of by money; that which is bartered.

BARTER (2), [bah'-ter], *v.t.* to exchange goods of approximately equal value; (*fig.*) to exchange; to give away for an unworthy reward; to bargain; *v.i.* to trade by exchanging goods; **to b. down,** to effect a reduction in price by bargaining. [OFr. *barrater* to cheat].

BARTIZAN, [bah-tiz-an'], *n.* a small turret overhanging the corner of an ancient fortification. [Scots *bertisene*, a misspelling of BRATTICING.]

BARTIZAN

BARTON, [bah'-tun], *n.* a barn used for storing grain from the farm of the lord of the manor; a farmyard. [OE. *bærtun*].

BARTRAM†, [bah'-tram], *n.* the plant pellitory, a variety of *Parietaria*. [Germ. *bertram*, L. *pyrethrum*].

BARU, [bah'-rōō], *n.* the fibre of an Indian sago-palm used to stuff pillows and caulk boats. [Native].

BARUKHZY, [ba-ruk'-zi], *n.* the Afghan hound. [*Barakzi*, the name of an Afghan tribe].

BARWOOD, [bah'-wŏŏd], *n.* a red African dye-wood used for dyeing cotton yarn. [BAR (1) and WOOD].

BARY-, *pref.* heavy. [Gk. *barus* heavy].

BARYCENTRIC, [ba'-ri-sen'-trik], *adj.* pertaining to the centre of gravity. [BARY and CENTRIC].

BARYPHONIA, [ba'-ri-fōn'-i-a], *n.* hoarseness. [BARY and Gk. *phone* voice].

BARYSPHERE, [ba'-ris-fēer'], *n.* (*geol.*) material forming the interior of the earth. [BARY and SPHERE].

BARYTA, BARIA, [ba-rī'-ta, bāer'-i-a], *n.* (*chem.*) barium monoxide. [*Next* and BARIUM].

BARYTES, [ba-rī'-tēz], *n.* (*min.*) barium sulphate occurring as a mineral deposit. [BARIUM and Gk. *-ites* connected with].

BARYTIC, [ba-rit'-ik], *adj.* relating to or containing baryta.

BARYTOCALCITE, [ba-rīt'-ō-kal'-sīt], *n.* (*min.*) a mineral containing barium carbonate and calcium carbonate. [BARYTES and CALCITE].

BARYTONE, see BARITONE.

BASAL, [bās'-al], *adj.* belonging to or forming the base; fundamental.

BASALT, [ba'-sawlt], *n.* (*geol.*) a dark, compact, crystalline, igneous rock, consisting of augite, felspar, etc., generally found in natural columns; a black porcelain first made by Wedgwood. [L. *basaltes*].

BASALTIC, [ba-sawl'-tik], *adj.* relating to or containing basalt.

BASALTIFORM, [ba-sawl'-ti-fawm], *adj.* possessing the columnar structure of basalt. [BASALT and FORM].

BASALTINE, [ba-sawl'-tin], *n.* a hornblende occurring in basalt and lava; a column of basalt.

BASANITE, [bas'-an-it], *n.* (*min.*) a black, compact, flinty slate. [Gk. *basanos* touchstone and *ites* connected with].

BASCINET, see BASINET.

BASCULE, [bas'-kewl], *n.* a balanced lever centrally pivoted, one end rising when the other is lowered; **b. bridge,** a bridge with a counterpoise operating in this way. [Fr. *bascule*].

BASE (1), [bās], *n.* the foundation on which an object rests, the bottom or lowest part of anything; the pedestal upon which a statue stands; (*fig.*) the chief element or constituent; the groundwork, starting point; (*arch.*) part of a column at the bottom of the shaft; (*milit.*) headquarters where equipment is stored, and from which military operations proceed; (*bot.*) the point of junction of an organ to a trunk; (*geom.*) the lowest line or side of a plane or solid figure on which it is regarded as standing; (*her.*) a space equal to the width of a bar at the bottom of a shield marked off by a horizontal line; (*chem.*) a substance combining with an acid to form a salt; (*surveying*) a line of which the length and position are accurately known, and which is used as starting point for trigonometrical calculations; (*math.*) the number used as a starting point for logarithms; (*philol.*) a root-form of a word from which cognate forms in different languages are derived; (*baseball*) the stations at the four points of the diamond over which the batsmen must cross to score a run; **b. on balls,** (*baseball*) a base allowed to the batsman after receiving four legitimate balls; **b. hit,** a hit by which a batsman is able to reach a base; **b. hospital,** a military hospital behind the field of battle. [Fr. *base* from Gk. *basis*].

BASE (2), [bās], *adj.* low-lying; low in rank or condition, of humble origin; cowardly; of poor spirit; impure, worthless, debased; (*leg.*) not free, obligatory upon the fulfilment of certain conditions; **b. metals,** metals of low worth. [Fr. *bas*].

BASE (3), [bās], *v.t.* to use as a starting point for one's ideas, thoughts, assumptions; to lay the foundation of; to rely upon; (*archaic*) to humble or debase. [BASE (1) and (2)].

BASEBALL, [bās-bawl], *n.* a ball game resembling rounders, in which a hard ball is struck with a truncheon-shaped bat, played by two teams of nine players on a field which is marked out as a diamond.

BASEBORN, [bās'-bawn], *adj.* of humble parentage, illegitimate.

BASEBRED, [bās'-bred], *adj.* of base upbringing.

BASECOURT, [bās'-kawt], *n.* (*fort.*) the outer court of a castle; the yard at the back of a house; farmyard. [OFr. *basse-cort*].

BASEL, [bazl], *n.* a tanned sheepskin. [Corruption of OFr. *basane* from Arab. *bizanah* lining].

BASELARD, BASLARD†, [baz'-lahd], *n.* a small dagger hung from the girdle. [AFr. *baselarde*].

BASELESS, [bās'-les], *adj.* without foundation, unwarranted.

BASELESSNESS, [bās'-les-nes], *n.* the state or quality of being baseless, *esp.* of an accusation or charge. [BASELESS].

BASELINE, [bās'-līn'], *n.* the line from which surveying and military operations begin; (*tennis*) one of the parallel lines marking the ends of a tennis court; (*baseball*) the space a yard wide reaching from base to base.

BASELY, [bās-li], *adv.* in base fashion.

BASEMENT, [bās'-ment], *n.* the lowest inhabited room of a house, usually below ground level.

BASENESS, [bās-nes], *n.* the quality of being base.

BASENET, see BASINET.

BASH (1), [bash], *n.* (*coll.*) a blow.

BASH (2), [bash], *v.t.* (*coll.*) to strike violently; to beat, thrash. [~Dan. *baske* beat].

BASHAW, [ba-shaw'], *n.* a pasha; a tyrannical person. [PASHA].

BASHFUL, [bash'-fŏŏl], *adj.* shy, timid, modest, retiring, shamefaced. [ABASH and FULL].

BASHFULLY, [bash'-fōōl-i], *adv.* in a bashful fashion.
BASHFULNESS, [bash'-fōōl-nes] *n.* the state of being bashful.
BASHI-BAZOUKS, [bash'-i-ba-zooks'], *n.(pl.)* irregular, unpaid volunteers in the Turkish army infamous for committing atrocities. [Turk. *bashi bazuq* one whose head is turned].
BASIAL, [bāz-i-al], *adj.* relating to kissing. [L. *basium* a kiss].
BASIC, [bās'-ik], *adj.* fundamental; forming the base; (*chem.*) having the base in excess of the acid; **B. English,** a variety of English, devised by C. K. Ogden, with a vocabulary of about eight hundred fundamental words, apart from technical and scientific words. [BASE (1)].
BASICITY, [ba-sis'-i-ti], *n.* (*chem.*) the capacity of an acid to combine with a base.
BASIC-SLAG, [bas'-ik-slag'], *n.* a fertilizer obtained as a by-product of steel-smelting.
BASIL (1), [baz'-il], *n.* an aromatic herb, *Ocymum basilicum,* used for culinary purposes. [OFr. *basile,* Gk. *basilikon*].
BASIL (2), [baz'-il], *n.* sheepskin tanned with bark. [~Fr. *basane*].
BASILAR, [baz'-i-ler], *adj.* (*anat.*) pertaining to the base. [L. *basilaris*].
BASILIAN, [baz-il'-i-an], *n.* a monk belonging to the order of St. Basil. [St. *Basil* (329-379), the patriarch].
BASILIC, [bas'-il-ik], *adj.* (*arch.*) pertaining to a basilica; (*anat.*) †pertaining to one of the principal veins in the upper arm. [Fr. *basilique* from Gk. *basilikos* royal].
BASILICA, [ba-sil'-i-ka], *n.* (*hist.*) a royal palace; a Roman public hall, oblong, with an apse at one end and an entrance at the other; a Christian church resembling this. [L. from Gk. *basilike* royal (dwelling)].
BASILICAL, [ba-sil'-ik-al], *adj.* basilic.
BASILICAN, [ba-sil'-ik-an], *adj.* basilic.
BASILICON, [ba-sil'-ik-on], *n.* a resinous ointment acting as a sovereign remedy. [Gk. *basilikon*].
BASILISK (1), [baz'-i-lisk], *n.* a fabulous African creature said to be hatched by a snake from a cock's egg whose look or breath was fatal; a species of lizard of the family *Iguanidae,* having a crest which can be erected at will on its head like a crown; †a brass cannon adorned with figures of serpents. [Gk. *basiliskos* little king, a serpent].
BASILISK (2), [baz'-i-lisk], *adj.* cold, relentless, deadly, full of venom.
BASIL-WEED, [baz'-el-wēd'], *n.* (*bot.*) wild basil, *Calamintha Clinopodium.*
BASIN, [bās'-in], *n.* a broad, shallow, hollow vessel with curved smooth sides sloping inwards towards a small flat circular base; the amount contained in such a vessel; a large hollow opening or depression in land containing water; a harbour or bay enclosed by land; that area of a country drained by a river; a hollow; (*geol.*) a trough or hollow formation in which the strata dip everywhere towards a common centre; a shallow valley or hollow depression circular or oval in shape; (*opt.*) concave tool used in making convex glasses. [OFr. *basin*].
BASINED, [bās'-end], *adj.* contained in a basin.
BASINET, BASENET, BASCINET, [bas'-i-net'], *n.* a light rounded helmet, originally without vizor, and often worn under the large heavy fighting-helmet. [OFr. *bacinet* from *bacin* basin].
BASIS, (*pl.* **bases**), [bās'-is], *n.* the foundation, base, the essential principle on which a thing is built up, the chief constituent; (*milit.*) a region from which military operations are originated. [Gk. *basis*].
BASK, [bahsk], *v.i.* to enjoy oneself; to expose oneself pleasurably to the sun's rays; to revel in. [OIcel. *bathask* to bathe oneself].
BASKET, [bahs'-kit], *n.* a hollow open receptacle made of cane, rushes, etc., usually provided with a handle across the top by which it is carried; a receptacle resembling this; the contents of a basket; a guard for the hand on a single-stick; **b. stitch,** one in which the stitches are taken into openings made by previous stitches; **pick of the b.,** the best, the choicest. [ME. *baskete*].
BASKET-BALL, [bahs'-kit-bawl'], *n.* game played with a large ball, in which a goal is scored by dropping the ball into a basket-like receptacle suspended from the top of a pole.
BASKET-CHAIR, [bahs'-kit-chāer'], *n.* a chair made of wickerwork.
BASKET-FISH, [bahs'-kit-fish'], *n.* a species of star-fish, *Astrophyton linckii.*
BASKETFUL, [bahs'-kit-fōōl'], *n.* that which will fill a basket.
BASKET-HILT, [bahs'-kit-hilt'], *n.* a hilt of basket-work used as a hand-guard on a fencing-stick or sword.
BASKET-HILTED, [bahs'-kit-hilt'-id], *adj.* provided with a basket-hilt.
BASKETRY, [bahs'-kit-ri], *n.* wickerwork.
BASKETWORK, [bahs'-kit-wurk'], *n.* wickerwork.
BASKING-SHARK, [bahsk'-ing-shahk'], *n.* a species of shark, *Selache maxima*; the sail-fish or sun-fish.
BASLARD†, see BASELARD.
BASQUE (1), [bahsk], *n.* a race of people dwelling in the Western Pyrenees, having their own unrelated language; the language spoken by the Basques; a bodice extending below the waist in a short skirt. [Fr. *Basque,* L *Vasco* an inhabitant of Vasconia in the Western Pyrenees].
BASQUE (2), [bahsk], *adj.* pertaining to the Basques or to their language.
BAS-RELIEF, BASS-RELIEF, [bas'-ri-lēf'], *n.* a method of sculpture or carving in which the figures stand out slightly above the surface upon which they are carved; a carving in this style. [It. *basso-rilievo*].
BASS (1), [bas], *n.* (*zool.*) the sea perch, *Labrax lupus*; (*bot.*) the American linden-tree, *Tilia americana*; the inner bark of this tree; matting made from its bark. [OE. *bærs* perch].
BASS (2), [bas], *n.* a proprietary brand of bitter ale. [*Bass,* the brewers].
BASS (3), [bās], *n.* (*mus.*) the lowest range of notes in a vocal or instrumental composition; the deepest male voice; one who sings the lowest part in the harmony; a singer with a deep voice; the lowest sounding string of certain musical instruments. [BASS (4)].
BASS (4), [bās], *adj.* very low and sonorous, deep sounding; indicating an instrument whose compass lies in the lowest register; suitable for a bass-singer; **b. clef,** the F clef in the bottom stave. [Fr. *bas,* It. *basso*].
BASS (5), [bās], *v.t. and i.* to sound in a deep tone, to take the bass part. [*Prec.*].
BASS-BAR, [bās'-bah(r)'], *n.* a strengthening strip of wood inserted lengthwise in the body of string instruments, to resist the pressure of the bridge.
BASS-BROOM, [bas'-brōōm'], *n.* a course fibre broom suitable for performing work of a rough nature. [BASS (1) and BROOM].
BASSELISSE, [bas'-lēs], *adj.* (of tapestry) with the warp running horizontally. [Fr. *basselisse*].
BASSET (1), [bas'-it], *n.* a long smooth-haired dog with short legs used in hunting. [Fr. *basset* a terrier, from *bas(se)* low].
BASSET (2), [bas'-it], *n.* (*geol.*) a portion of rock or stratum appearing at or showing above the level of the ground. [Uncert.].
BASSET (3), [bas'-it], *adj.* (*geol.*) inclined upwards. [*Prec.*].
BASSET (4), [bas'-it], *v.i.* to incline upwards (as of strata). [BASSET (3)].
BASSET-HORN, [bas'-it-hawn'], *n.* †a musical instrument with a curved mouthpiece and bell-shaped end; a tenor clarinet.
BASSETING, [bas'-it-ing], *n.* (*mining*) outcrop.
BASSETTE, [ba-set'], *n.* a tenor or small bass viol. [It. *bassetto*].
BASS-HORN, [bas'-hawn'], *n.* a bassoon with a deep tone.
BASSINETTE, BASSINET, [bas'-i-net'], *n.* a wicker-work cradle furnished with a hood; a perambulator (shaped like this). [Fr. *bassinet* a small basin].
BASSO, [bas'-ō], *n.* a singer with a bass voice. [It. *basso* low].
BASSOON, [ba-sōōn'], *n.* a musical instrument of the wood-wind class, having a double reed, and a deep bass tone. [Fr. *basson*].
BASSOONIST, [ba-sōōn'-ist], *n.* a player on the bassoon.
BASSORINE, [bas'-o-rin], *n.* a substance obtained by mixing Bassora gum with water, alcohol and ether. [*Bassora,* a city in Asia Minor].
BASS-RELIEF, see BAS-RELIEF.
BASS-VIOL, [bās'-vī'-ol], *n.* the violoncello.
BAST, [bast], *n.* (*hort.*) the inner bark of the lime and other trees cut up into strips and manufactured into cords, mats, etc., used by gardeners for tying. [OE. *bæst* bundle].
BASTA, [bas'-ta], *int.* stop! cease! [It. *basta* enough].

BASTARD (1), [bast'-erd, bahst'-erd], *n.* an illegitimate offspring. [OFr. *bastard*].
BASTARD (2), [bahst'-erd], *adj.* illegitimate; spurious, counterfeit; deviating from the normal in shape or size; **b. slip**, (*bot.*) a sucker springing in an unexpected place from a tree; **b. bar**, (*her.*) heraldic sign of illegitimate descent. [*Prec.*].
BASTARDIZATION, [bahst'-erd-ĭz-ā'-shun,] *n.* the act of bastardizing.
BASTARDIZE, [bahst'-erd-īz], *v.t.* to pronounce or make illegitimate.
BASTARDLY†, [bahst'-erd-li,] *adv.* in the manner of a bastard.
BASTARD-WING, [bahst'-erd-wing'], *n.* a set of small feathers like a quill fastened to a joint, which corresponds to a thumb, in a bird's wing.
BASTARDY, [bahst'-erd-i], *n.* the state of being a bastard; **b. order**, (*leg.*) an order demanding the support of an illegitimate child by its father. [OFr. *bastardie*].
BASTE (1), [bāst], *v.t.* to thrash or beat violently; to put butter or fat upon meat while roasting in order to keep it juicy; to pour melted wax over wicks in candle-making. [Unkn.].
BASTE (2), [bāst], *v.t.* to tack, to sew with long loose stitches. [OFr. *bastir*].
BASTERNA, [ba-sturn'-a], *n.* a closed litter for women, carried between two mules. [L. *basterna*].
BASTILLE, BASTILE, [bas-tēl'], *n.* (*milit.*) a wheeled wooden tower used at sieges; huts fortified by an entrenchment and used as dwelling-places for besieging soldiers; an old castle in Paris, long used as a state prison and demolished by the Revolutionary mob in 1789; (*coll.*) a workhouse. [Fr. *bastille*].
BASTINADO (1), **BASTINADE**, [bast'-in-ăd'-ō, bast'-in-ăd'], *n.* an Eastern form of corporal punishment or torture, in which the soles of the victim's feet were beaten with a bamboo cane; a beating with a stick. [Span. *bastonada*].
BASTINADO (2), **BASTINADE**, [bast-in-ăd'-ō, bast-in-ăd'], *v.t.* to punish or torture by the bastinado.
BASTING, [bāst'-ing], *n.* sewing long stitches, tacking.
BASTION, [bast'-i-on], *n.* (*fort.*) an advanced work with two flanks and two faces projecting from the angles of a rampart, as a salient angle. [Fr. *bastion*, It. *bastione*].

BASTION

BASTIONED, [bast'-i-ond], *adj.* furnished with bastions.
BASTO, [bast'-ō], *n.* the ace of clubs in quadrille. [Sp. *basto*].
BASTON, [bast'-on], *n.* a small cudgel; (*arch.*) a round convex moulding used in the bases of columns; (*her.*) a baton. [OFr. *baston*].
BAT (1), [bat], *n.* a flying mammal with a body shaped like a mouse and a pair of large membranes attached to the forelegs and body to form wings. [ME. *backe*, OScand. *bakka*].
BAT (2), [bat], *n.* one of various kinds of clubs or implements used in striking the ball in various ball-games; (*min.*) a shale occurring in strata between seams of coal, iron-ore, etc.; a sheet of cotton prepared for quilting; a layer of fur or hair and wool used in making hats; a quick violent blow; (*coll.*, *cricket*) a batsman; **to carry one's b.**, (*cricket*) to remain undefeated at the close of an innings; **off one's own b.**, (*coll.*) entirely unaided, without instruction. [OE. *batt* club].
BAT (3), [bat], *v.t. and i.* to beat, to wield a bat at cricket or baseball; (*cricket*) to have an innings; to beat with a stick or beater; to move the eyelid quickly, to wink. [BAT (2)].
BATATA, [ba-tah'-ta], *n.* the sweet potato, *Batatas edulis*. [Haiti *batata*].
BATAVIAN (1), [ba-tā'-vi-an], *n.* a native of Batavia; a Dutchman. [L. *Batavia*, now Betawe].
BATAVIAN (2), [ba-tā'-vi-an], *adj.* Dutch. [*Prec.*].
BATCH, [bach], *n.* the quantity of bread made at a single baking; a quantity of similar things, a group of things made at one time or arriving together. [ME. *bache*, ~BAKE].
BATE (1), [bāt], *n.* a strong alkaline solution used in tanning to soften hides. [Uncert.].
BATE (2), [bāt], *n.* (*slang*) rage, temper, fury. [Unkn.].
BATE (3), [bāt], *v.t.* to steep hides in bate. [BATE (1)].
BATE (4), [bāt], *v.t. and i.* to lessen, reduce, diminish. [Fr. *abattre* beat down].
BATEAU, [bat'-ō], *n.* a long narrow shallow boat; a pontoon. [Fr. *bateau* boat].
BATED, [bāt'-id], *adj.* held back by conscious effort; **with b. breath**, in a state of awe or tense apprehension.
BATEFUL, [bāt'-fŏŏl], *adj.* contentious, eager for strife.
BAT-FOWLING, [bat'-fowl'-ing], *n.* a method of catching birds at night by holding a light in front of a net, and, as they fly to the light, striking them down.
BATH (1), [bahth], *n.* a large elongated vessel containing sufficient water for a person to be immersed in so as to wash the whole body; the act of washing or soaking the body completely; a quantity of liquid in which the whole or part of the body of persons may be soaked for remedial or medicinal purposes; a swimming-pool; (usually *pl.*) a building in which baths of various kinds may be taken or swimming indulged in; (*dyeing*) a solution of colouring liquid used for soaking cloths; (*phot.*) a solution in which prints or plates are steeped; **Order of the B.**, a British order of chivalry; **B. Oliver**, a biscuit first made by Dr. W. Oliver of Bath. [OE. *bæth*].
BATH (2), [bahth], *v.t. and i.* to give a bath to; to take a bath. [*Prec.*].
BATHABLE, [bahth'-abl], *adj.* capable of being bathed.
BATH-BRICK, [bahth'-brik], *n.* a siliceous earth (from Bridgwater, near Bath) in the form of a brick for cleaning stone and metal.
BATH BUN, [bahth'-bun'], *n.* a spiced and sugared fruit bun originating from *Bath*.
BATH-CHAIR, [bahth'-chāer], *n.* a chair in which invalids may be wheeled, first used at Bath. [*Bath*, an English spa, and CHAIR].
BATHE (1), [bāᴛʜ], *n.* the act of bathing and swimming; immersion of the body in the sea, pools, etc., for pleasure. [BATH (2)].
BATHE (2), (**bathing**), [bāᴛʜ], *v.i.* to immerse the body in water either in a bath, the sea, river, pond, pool, etc., to cleanse it or for enjoyment and recreation; to expose the body to the sun's rays; *v.t.* to pour liquid over (part of the body), to soak in liquid; to flow by, to wash (of a river or sea); to suffuse, saturate; (*fig.*) to steep in or soak; **to b. in blood**, to cause bloodshed to. [OE. *bathian* to bathe].
BATHER, [bāᴛʜ'-er], *n.* one who bathes.
BATHETIC, [ba-thet'-ik], *adj.* relating to bathos. [BATHOS].
BATHING, [bāᴛʜ'-ing], *n.* the act of immersion of the body in water for recreation and enjoyment or for remedial purposes; **b. machine**, a small hut on wheels where bathers may undress. [BATHE (2)].
BATH-METAL, [bahth'-met'-al], *n.* an alloy of zinc and copper.
BATHOMETER, [bath-om'-it-er], *n.* an instrument used to measure the depth of water by the use of a spring-balance. [Gk. *bathos* depth and METER].
BAT-HORSE, [bat'-haws], *n.* a horse allowed to a batman to transport the equipment in his charge. [Fr. *bât* packsaddle and HORSE].
BATHOS, [bāth'-os], *n.* (*rhet.*) anti-climax, a sudden passing from the sublime to the ridiculous, unexpected descent from the elevated and dignified to the commonplace and mean. [Gk. *bathos* depth].
BATHROOM, [bahth'-rŏŏm], *n.* a room which contains a bath.
BATHYBIUS, [bath-ib'-i-us], *n.* (*zool.*) gelatinous matter found at great depths on the bottom of the Atlantic. [Gk. *bathus* deep and *bios* life].
BATHYMETRICAL, [bath'-i-met'-rik-al], *adj.* pertaining to bathymetry.
BATHYMETRY, [bath-im'-et-ri], *n.* the art of measuring the depth of water. [Gk. *bathus* deep and *metria* measurement].
BATHYSPHERE, [bath'-is-fēer], *n.* a hollow metal sphere which can be lowered to a great depth in the sea. [Gk. *bathus* deep and SPHERE].
BATIK, [bat-ēk'], *n.* (*print.*) a method used in printing coloured designs upon textiles, by which the parts to be left undyed are covered over with wax. [Javanese *batik* drawing].
BATING (1), [bāt'-ing], *n.* lessening, abating.
BATING (2), [bāt'-ing], *prep.* barring, excepting. [BATE (4)].
BATISTE, [bat-ēst'], *n.* a kind of cambric, a light fabric of cotton and linen. [*Baptiste* of Cambrai, the maker].
BATLET, [bat'-let], *n.* a small bat used for beating linen.
BATMAN, [bat'-man], *n.* (*milit.*) an officer's servant. [Fr. *bât* packsaddle and MAN].

BATON (1), [bat'-on], *n.* a short staff or truncheon carried as a badge of office; a slender tapering wand used by conductors of orchestras; a police officer's truncheon; (*her.*) a truncheon in a shield; **b. sinister,** (*her.*) a sign of illegitimacy. [Fr. *bâton* stick].

BATON (2), [bat'-on], *v.t.* to strike or beat with a baton. [*Prec.*].

BATRACHIA, [ba-trăk'-ia], *n.(pl.)* (*zool.*) the order of amphibians, comprising frogs, toads, and newts. [Gk. *batrakhos* frog].

BATRACHIAN (1), [ba-trăk'-i-an], *n.* (*zool.*) one of the batrachia; a water-buttercup.

BATRACHIAN (2), [ba-trăk'-i-an], *adj.* pertaining to a batrachian.

BATRACHITE, [bat'-ra-kīt], *n.* (*geol.*) a fossilized batrachian; a frog-hued gem; a kind of chrysolite. [Gk. *batrakhites*].

BATRACHOID, [bat'-ra-koid], *adj.* frog-like. [Gk. *batrakhos* a frog and *oeides* like].

BATRACHOMYOMACHY, [bat'-ra-kom'-i-om'-a-ki], *n.* the battle of the frogs and mice, a burlesque poem attributed to Homer. [Gk. *batrakhos* frog, *mus* mouse, and *makhia* fight].

BATRACOPHAGOUS, [bat'-ra-kof'-a-gus], *adj.* feeding on frogs. [Gk. *batrakhos* frog and *phago* I eat].

BATS, [bats], *adj.* crazy, having "bats in the belfry." [BAT (1)].

BATSMAN, [bats'-man], *n.* one who bats at cricket or baseball; one notable for his batting ability.

BATSWING, [bats'-wing], *n.* a gas-burner producing a flat flame.

BATTA (1), [bat'-a], *n.* an allowance, in addition to their pay, made to soldiers in India when in the field, or to public servants in special circumstances. [Hind. *bhat*, *bhanta* ploughman's wages].

BATTA (2), [bat'-a], *n.* an Indian discount on coins no longer current or below the normal weight. [Urdu *batta*].

BATTALIA†, [ba-tah'-ly-a], *n.* an army arrayed for battle. [It. *battaglia*].

BATTALION, [ba-tal'-i-on], *n.* (*milit.*) a body of troops, generally consisting of five companies; (*fig.*) a legion or great number. [It. *battaglione*].

BATTALIONED, [ba-tal'-i-ond], *adj.* divided into battalions.

BATTEL, [batl], *v.i.* to obtain one's food as battels. [Uncert.].

BATTELER, [batl'-er], *n.* one supplied with battels in an Oxford college.

BATTELS, [batlz], *n.(pl.)* provisions obtained from the buttery in an Oxford college; the charge made for these. [Uncert.].

BATTEN (1), BATTON, [batn], *n.* a long narrow board used for making floors, for strengthening laths, etc.; a long, narrow wooden bar nailed across a door as a clamp or support, or used to fasten down hatches on hatchways; a strip of wood nailed to masts and spars to act as a protection against rubbing. [BATON (1)].

BATTEN (2), [batn], *v.t.* to fasten or strengthen with battens.

BATTEN (3), [batn], *v.t. and i.* to become fat, to thrive or become prosperous, to feed luxuriously and parasitically. [OScand. *batna* improve].

BATTENING, [bat'-ning], *n.* the act of fastening battens; the battens thus secured.

BATTER (1), [bat'-er], *n.* a mallet used for flattening out potter's clay; (*cricket*) a batsman.

BATTER (2), [bat'-er], *n.* a mixture of flour, milk and eggs whipped together to a thick consistency, used in frying and in making certain puddings; (*print.*) defective type or stereotype-plate. [BATTER (4)].

BATTER (3), [bat'-er], *n.* deviation of a wall, bank, etc., from the vertical position.

BATTER (4), [bat'-er], *v.t.* to strike with a succession of violent blows; to disfigure by beating; (*milit.*) to attack heavily with artillery or bombs; to beat down or demolish. [OFr. *batre*].

BATTERED, [bat'-erd], *adj.* beaten; disfigured, dilapidated.

BATTERING-CHARGE, [bat'-er-ing-chahj'], *n.* †the amount of powder required to charge a cannon.

BATTERING-GUN, [bat'-er-ing-gun'], *n.* (*milit.*) a heavy gun used to attack defensive works.

BATTERING-RAM, [bat'-er-ing-ram'], *n.* (*milit.*) an ancient military engine consisting of a swinging beam or spar with a massive hardened cap of metal, used for demolishing walls.

BATTERING-TRAIN, [bat'-er-ing-trān], *n.* (*milit.*) a siege-train.

BATTERY, [bat'-er-i], *n.* an attack with blows; (*leg.*) an unlawful attack on the body of another; (*milit.*) a number of guns grouped for action, a unit of artillery with men and equipment; (*elect.*) a cell made of two electrodes in contact with certain chemicals to produce electricity on completing the external circuit; a storage cell for electricity; (*opt.*) a series of lenses in combination; (*fig.*) the full resources at one's command. [Fr. *batterie*].

BATTING, [bat'-ing], *n.* the wielding of a bat in cricket or baseball; cotton or wool in sheets, ready to be used to make quilts.

BATTISH, [bat'-ish], *adj.* like a bat. [BAT (1)].

BATTLE (1), [batl], *n.* a fight or combat between large opposing bodies of armed men; a contest, struggle, strife; the name of a type of fighter-aeroplane; **b. royal,** a fight of the greatest vigour; a cockfight in which several birds take part; **pitched b.,** one fought on a specified or limited ground; **line of b.,** troops or ships drawn up in readiness for fighting. [OFr. *bataille*].

BATTLE (2), [batl], *v.t. and i.* to fight, to contend, strive against.

BATTLE-AXE, [batl'-aks'], *n.* an axe anciently used as a fighting weapon.

BATTLE-CRUISER, [batl'-kroo'-zer], *n.* a speedy well-armed cruiser.

BATTLE-CRY, [batl'-crī'], *n.* a war-cry, a martial slogan, a rallying cry.

BATTLED†, [batld], *adj.* provided with battlements.

BATTLEDORE, [batl'-daw(r)], *n.* a light bat with a circular blade and short handle as used in the game of battledore and shuttlecock; a wooden instrument with a circular blade and a long handle used in laundry work; a similar object used to put loaves, etc., in a baker's oven. [Uncert.].

BATTLE-DRESS, [batl'-dress], *n.* the modern uniform of the British Army, as opposed to parade or ceremonial wear.

BATTLEFIELD, [batl'-fēld], *n.* the place where a battle is fought.

BATTLEGROUND, [batl'-grownd], *n.* a place of conflict; (*fig.*) a subject of dispute.

BATTLEMENT, [batl'-ment], *n.* (*arch.*) an indented parapet, the openings formerly being devised for military purposes. [OFr. *batillement*].

BATTLEMENT

BATTLEMENTED, [batl'-ment-id], *adj.* provided with battlements.

BATTLE-PIECE, [batl'-pēs], *n.* a painting depicting a battle, a verbal description of a battle.

BATTLE-PLANE, [batl'-plān], *n.* (*aeron.*) an aeroplane equipped with guns and bomb-dropping apparatus.

BATTLER, [bat'-ler], *n.* one who battles, a fighter; (*boxing*) a boxer with more vigour than skill.

BATTLESHIP, [batl'-ship], *n.* the largest and most heavily armed type of warship; **pocket b.,** a small warship of extreme power, yet of relatively light tonnage and armament.

BATTLING, [bat'-ling], *n.* fighting vigorously against great opposition.

BATTOLOGIST, [bat-ol'-o-jist], *n.* one addicted to battology.

BATTOLOGY, [bat-ol'-o-ji], *n.* an unnecessary repetition of words. [Gk. *battologia* from *Battos*, a personal name, and *logos* speech].

BATTON, see BATTEN.

BATTUE, [bat'-ew], *n.* a method of killing game by surrounding a game-preserve with beaters who drive the animals towards the place where the sportsmen lie in wait for them with guns; game beaten up from cover in this way; wanton massacre. [Fr. *battue*].

BATTY, [bat'-i], *adj.* (*slang*) crazy, mad, idiotic. [BATS].

BAUBEE, see BAWBEE.

BAUBLE, BAWBLE†, [bawbl], *n.* a thing of little intrinsic value with an attractive exterior, a trifle; (*fig.*) a symbol of the transitoriness of human greatness; †a jester's sign of office, consisting of a stick mounted with a carved head furnished with asses' ears. [OFr. *baubel* toy].

BAUDEKIN†, BAUDKIN†, [bawd'-i-kin], *n.* a richly embroidered medieval silk. [AFr. *baudekin*].

BAUGE, [bōzh], *n.* a variety of coarse cloth or drugget. [*Bauge*, in France, the place of manufacture].

BAULK, see BALK.

BAUSON†, [baw'-son], *n.* a badger. [OFr. *bausen*].

BAUXITE, [bawk'-sīt], *n.* a rock similar to clay from which aluminium is obtained. [Les *Baux*, in the south of France, where mined].

BAVIN, [bav'-in], *n.* a brushwood faggot. [Unkn.].

BAWBEE, BAUBEE, [baw'-bē'], *n.* a Scots halfpenny. [Unkn.].

BAWBLE†, see BAUBLE.

BAWD, [bawd], *n.* a procurer or procuress; a prostitute; the keeper of a brothel. [OFr. *baude* gay].

BAWDILY, [bawd'-i-li], *adv.* in bawdy fashion.

BAWDINESS, [bawd'-i-nes], *n.* obscenity, lewdness.

BAWDRY, [bawd'-ri], *n.* the practice of prostituting women; bawdiness. [ME. *bauderie*].

BAWDY (1), [bawd'-i], *n.* bawdy conversation or writing. [*Next*].

BAWDY (2), [bawd'-i], *adj.* unchaste, obscene. [ME. *baudi*].

BAWDY-HOUSE, [bawd'-i-hows'], *n.* a brothel.

BAWL (1), [bawl], *n.* a loud shout or cry. [Uncert.].

BAWL (2), [bawl], *v.t. and i.* to shout loudly in a rough, rude manner; to speak or sing in an unusually loud voice. [Uncert.].

BAWLEY, [baw'-li], *n.* a borley.

BAWLING, [bawl'-ing], *n.* the act of shouting in a loud rough voice.

BAWN, [bawn], *n.* a castle court; a cattle enclosure. [Ir. *babhun*].

BAY (1), [bā], *n.* an opening or recess in a wall, often between columns or buttresses; the space provided in a room by the outward projection of a window beyond the wall-line; a horse's stall; the forepart of a ship between decks, used as a dressing station or sick-room; a subordinate terminus line in a railway station surrounded by a platform; an embankment or barrier to dam up water to be used in driving a mill-wheel. [OFr. *baie* opening].

BAY (2), [bā], *n.* a large opening or indentation into the land, of a sea or lake; an opening in a mountain range. [Fr. *baie*].

BAY (3), [bā], *n.* a bay-tree; (*pl.*) a wreath of laurels or bay leaves awarded in recognition of a noteworthy achievement; (*fig.*) honour, fame, distinction. [OFr. *baie* from L. *baca* berry].

BAY (4), [bā], *n.* a bay horse. [BAY (6)].

BAY (5), [bā], *n.* the bark of a hound or a pack of hounds; noise made by a pack of hounds as they come upon the hunted animal; **at b.**, (of a hunted animal) forced to halt and face its pursuers; (*fig.*) cornered, in dire straits; **to keep at b.**, to ward off. [BAY (7)].

BAY (6), [bā], *adj.* of a chestnut or reddish brown colour. [Fr. *bai* from L. *badius*].

BAY (7), [bā], *v.t. and i.* to bark continuously (as hounds in pursuit of their quarry); to bark at, to pursue with barking. [OFr. *baier*].

BAYADERE, bayadère, [bā'-ya-dāer], *n.* an Indian dancing girl. [Fr. *bayadere*, Portug. *bailadeira*].

BAYARD (1), [bā'-ahd], *n.* a bay horse. [OFr. *bayard* bay-coloured].

BAYARD (2), [bā'-ahd], *n.* one who stares in a rude way. [OFr. *bayer* gape].

BAYARD (3), [bā'-ahd], *n.* a chivalrous person.

BAYARDLY, [bā'-ahd-li], *adj.* blind; stupid, ignorant.

BAYBERRY, [bā'-be'-ri], *n.* the wax-myrtle, *Myrica cerifera*, the berry of which is used in making bay-rum.

BAYED, [bād], *adj.* provided with bays.

BAYONET (1), [bā'-on-et], *n.* a short sword-shaped blade which can be rapidly attached by a clip to the muzzle of a rifle; **b. cap, b. catch, b. fitting, b. joint**, a cap, etc., in which one member with small projections is secured to another with corresponding grooves by sliding it in inside and twisting it. [Fr. *baïonette* from *Bayonne* where first made].

BAYONET (2), [bā'-on-et], *v.t.* to transfix with a bayonet.

BAYOU, [bī'-ōō], *n.* (*Amer.*) a marshy creek or outlet of a river or lake in the southern states of the U.S.A. [Uncert.].

BAY-RUM, [bā'-rum'], *n.* a fragrant spirit obtained by distillation from the West Indian bayberry.

BAYSALT, [bā'-solt], *n.* salt formed in pits by evaporating sea-water. [BAY (2) and SALT].

BAY-STONE, [bā'-stōn'], *n.* a foundation stone laid on the surface of the ground.

BAY-TREE, [bā'-trē], *n.* the laurel, *Laurus nobilis*.

BAY-WINDOW, [bā'-wind'-ō], *n.* a large window built as a projection from a room.

BAY-WOOD, [bā'-wŏŏd], *n.* mahogany obtained from Campeachy Bay.

BAY-YARN, [bā'-yahn], *n.* woollen yarn.

BAZAAR, [ba-zah(r)'], *n.* an Eastern market-place; a large store fitted up with stalls containing fancy goods; a social function in a hall fitted up with stalls at which goods are sold, often for charity, a sale-of-work. [Pers. *bazar*].

BDELLIUM, [del'-i-um], *n.* an aromatic gum-resin from certain African and East Indies trees. [Gk. *bdellion* fragrant gum].

BE (1), (am, is, are, was, were, been, being), *an auxiliary verb* (a) used with the past participle of verbs to denote the passive voice, (b) with the past participles of certain intransitive verbs to form the perfect tense, (c) to express continuous action (with the present participle); used also as a link joining subject and predicate; *v.* to exist, to have an existence, to live, to occur; to stay, to remain; to have visited; to be worth, to cost; to be made to be; to be established; to become; to be the cause of; to belong to; to amount to; to have to; to be the same as; to occupy the position or status of; **for the time being**, temporarily; **maybe**, perhaps; **to-be**, future, intended; **b.-all**, the essential thing; **would-be**, desirous of being; **to b. off**, to depart; **to b. for**, to intend to go; to support; **to b. in on**, (*coll.*) to take part in, to know about. [OE. *bean*].

BE- (2), *pref. used to intensify, to form transitive verbs, to form verbs from nouns and adjectives; also with sense* round, alongside. [OE. *bi, be*].

BEACH (1), [bēch], *n.* the edge of a sea, lake or other large tract of water, usually a narrow strip of land covered with sand or pebbles; a shore; the strip of land at the edge of the sea exposed at low tide and inundated at high tide. [Unkn.].

BEACH (2), [bēch], *v.t.* to drag up on to the beach, to run aground on a beach.

BEACHCOMBER, [bēch'-kō'-mer], *n.* a long rolling wave; an idle longshoreman, one who searches the beach for goods washed up by the sea.

BEACHED, [bēcht], *adj.* run aground on a beach.

BEACHMASTER, [bēch'-mah'-ster], *n.* an officer responsible for the disembarkation of attacking troops.

BEACHY, [bēch-i], *adj.* provided with a beach.

BEACON (1), [bē'-kon], *n.* a fire lighted on a prominent hill or slope as a signal of danger or of national rejoicing; a lighthouse or prominent object used as a signal of warning of danger; a hill forming a land-mark; a traffic-sign marking a place at which pedestrians may presume to cross the road in safety. [OE. *beacn*].

BEACON (2), [bē'-kon], *v.t. and i.* to act as a beacon; to guide, warn or give a signal.

BEACONAGE, [bē'-kon-ij], *n.* money paid for the upkeep of beacons, buoys, and lighthouses.

BEACONED, [bē-kond], *adj.* provided with a beacon.

BEAD (1), [bēd], *n.* a small perforated piece of precious stone, glass, etc., threaded with many others on to a string, generally to form a necklace; a small globular drop of liquid or moisture; (*arch.*) small rounded moulding or ornament; (*pl.*) a collection of beads on a string forming a necklace or rosary; a prayer; a small metal rounded protuberance forming the front-sight of a gun; the flange of a pneumatic tyre; **to tell one's beads**, to say one's prayers; **to draw a b. on**, to take aim at with a firearm. [OE. *gebed* prayer].

BEAD (2), [bēd], *v.t. and i.* to furnish with beads, to make into a string of beads, to form into beads.

BEADED, [bēd'-id], *adj.* covered or decorated with beads; shaped like a bead.

BEAD-FRAME, [bēd'-frām'], *n.* a frame containing a series of horizontal wires with beads, used in teaching the elements of counting to children.

BEADHOUSE†, [bēd'-hows], *n.* an almshouse. [OE. *gebed-hus* house of prayer].

BEADING, [bēd'-ing], *n.* a narrow wooden moulding.

BEADLE, BEDEL(L), [bēdl], *n.* †a parish officer appointed by the vestry to supervise poor-relief, act as constable, etc.; a court official or judicial servant of a trade guild or company; a mace-bearer at certain universities, a senior porter or attendant at a

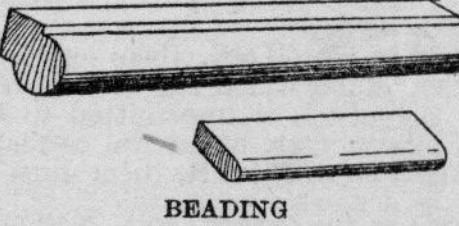

BEADING

university; a doorkeeper at a synagogue. [OE. *bydel, bedel* messenger].

BEADLEDOM, [bēdl'-dum], *n.* stupid officiousness. [BEADLE].

BEADLERY, [bēd'-ler-i], *n.* legal authority of a beadle.

BEADLESHIP, [bēdl'-ship], *n.* the position or rank of a beadle.

BEAD-PROOF, [bēd'-prōōf], *n.* a rough method of determining the strength of spirituous liquors by observing the time the bubbles remain on the surface after shaking.

BEADSMAN, BEDESMAN, [bēdz'-man], *n.* one who prays for another; a person receiving charitable gifts in return for which he has to pray for the souls of his benefactors; one residing in an almshouse; (*Scots*) a licensed beggar. [ME. *bedeman*].

BEADSWOMAN, BEDESWOMAN, [bēdz'-wōōm'-an], *n.* a woman employed in praying for the souls of others.

BEAD-TREE, [bēd'-trē], *n.* a species of *Melia*, the nuts of which are perforated and made into rosaries.

BEADWORK, [bēd'-wurk], *n.* ornamental work made with beads.

BEADY, [bē'-di], *adj.* of the shape or appearance of beads; covered with beads; protruding and shining.

BEAGLE (1), [bēgl], *n.* a small smooth-haired, long-eared hound for hunting rabbits or hares, and followed on foot by the field. [ME. *begle*].

BEAGLE (2), [bēgl], *v.i.* to hunt with the beagles, to follow on foot after the beagles.

BEAK, [bēk], *n.* the strong, hooked, sharp-pointed termination of the jaws of birds; pointed, horny, mandible ends of certain other animals such as the turtle; a curved sharp-pointed peak or projection; a curved piece of wood fastened to the prow of ancient warships as a kind of battering ram; (*chem.*) the spout of a retort; (*slang*) a prominent, curved nose; a magistrate or judge in a court; a headmaster. [Fr. *bec*].

BEAKER, [bēk'-er], *n.* a drinking cup; a cylindrical glass vessel, generally with a lip, for laboratory use. [OScand. *bikarr*].

BEAKIRON, [bēk'-ī'-ern], *n.* an anvil with two projecting pointed ends; one of these ends. [BICKERN].

BEAM (1), [bēm], *n.* a long straight heavy piece of timber or metal, often forming one of the main supports in a building or ship; a wooden roller in a loom, on which the warp is wound; the chief timber or bar in a plough to which the parts of the back are fastened; the bar forming the top pivoted member of a balance and from the extremities of which the scales are suspended; the shaft or shank of an anchor; the greatest width of a ship; a pivoted bar transmitting the reciprocating motion of the piston rod of a steam engine to the crank rod; the crank of the wheel-shaft; a ray or column of light emitted by the sun, moon, or other luminous body; (*fig.*) a cheerful happy smile; the expression of good-natured pleasure in a person's countenance; **on the b.,** (*naut.*) at right angles to the keel of a ship; **on her b. ends,** (*naut.*) (of a ship) keeled over and lying on her side; **broad in the b.,** stout, thick-set; **to be on one's b. ends,** (*coll.*) to be sorely pressed for money, to be out of work; to be at one's wit's end; **to turn the b.,** to weigh; **b. sea,** a sea broadside on to the ship. [OE. *beam* tree].

BEAM (2), [bēm], *v.i.* to shine, to emit rays of light; (*fig.*) to smile in kindly fashion, to radiate good-natured cheerfulness.

BEAM-BIRD, [bēm'-burd], *n.* the spotted flycatcher, a species of *Muscicapa*.

BEAM-COMPASS, [bēm'-kum'-pas], *n.* an instrument for drawing large circles, consisting of a wooden or metal beam with sliding sockets to accommodate steel and pencil points.

BEAM COMPASSES

BEAMED, [bēmd], *adj.* possessing all its antlers.

BEAM-ENGINE, [bēm'-en'-jin], *n.* (*eng.*) a steam-engine in which the vertical reciprocating motion of the piston is transmitted to the crank through an intermediate horizontal oscillating beam.

BEAM-FEATHER, [bēm'-feTH'-er], *n.* a long feather in a hawk's wing.

BEAM-FILLING, [bēm'-fil'-ing], *n.* masonry or plaster to fill the space between beams or joists; (*naut.*) cargo stowed between the beams.

BEAMING (1), [bēm'-ing], *n.* emission of rays of light.

BEAMING (2), [bēm'-ing], *adj.* radiant with happiness, smiling broadly.

BEAMLESS, [bēm'-les]' *adj.* having no beams.

BEAM-TRAWL, [bēm-trawl'], *n.* a net, used for trawling, in which the ends are kept open by a beam.

BEAM-TREE, [bēm'-trē], *n.* a tree related to the apple and pear, with white undersides to the leaves and red berries. [WHITEBEAM and TREE].

BEAM-WIRELESS, [bēm'-wī'-er-les], *n.* (*wirel.*) a system for emitting short-waves in a beam which does not disperse in all directions.

BEAMY, [bēm'-i], *adj.* like a beam; emitting rays of light; radiant; having antlers; broad.

BEAN, [bēn], *n.* one of several kinds of comestible leguminous seeds grown in pods; a plant of the order *Fabaceae*, which produces these seeds; **old b.,** (*slang*) old fellow; **full of beans,** in high spirits; **to give a person beans,** to punish severely; **not to have a b.,** to be penniless. [OE. *bean*].

BEAN-CAPER, [bēn'-kā'-per], *n.* a plant of the genus *Zygophyllum*, its buds being used as capers.

BEANFEAST, [bēn-fēst] *n.* a dinner or excursion of celebration; (*slang*) a good meal, jolly outing. [Gael. *beanfeis* a spree].

BEAN-GOOSE, [bēn'-gōōs], *n.* the migratory wild goose, *Anser segetum*.

BEANO, [bē'-nō], *n.* (*slang*) a beanfeast. [BEANFEAST].

BEAN-STALK, [bēn'-stawk], *n.* the stalk of the bean plant.

BEAN-TREFOIL, [bēn'-trē'-foil], *n.* the laburnum tree, *Laburnum vulgare*.

BEAR (1), [bāer], *n.* a powerfully built, large mammal of the genus *Ursus*, with a thick long-haired, shaggy coat, strong claws, a prominent nose and a short tail; (*fig.*) a clumsy ill-mannered person; (*Stock Exchange*) one who sells stock to be delivered at a certain price on a specified future date, in the hope that by that time the price will have fallen, and he will be able to purchase at a lower rate than that at which he has sold; **Great B. and Little B.,** name of two constellations in the northern hemisphere. [OE. *bera*].

BEAR (2), [bāer], *n.* a six-rowed ear of barley. [OE. *bere*].

BEAR (3), (bare, bore, borne), [bāer], *v.t.* to support, to carry; to push; to suffer, to endure; to wear, exhibit, be displayed on; to admit of, to be suitable for, to stand the test of; to possess and use, to wield; to behave; to have relation to, to concern; to pretend; to claim; to have written on, to be inscribed on; to have one's name on the books of; to cherish; to tolerate, to submit to; to bring forth, to give birth to, to yield; *v.i.* to suffer; to have or take effect; to be situated in a certain direction with respect to something else; to make one's way in a certain direction, to turn; to rest; **to b. away,** (*naut.*) to change the course of a ship so that it runs before the wind; **to b. down,** to overthrow, to force to the ground; (*naut.*) to drive towards; **to b. down upon,** to approach; (*naut.*) to crowd on all sail in order to come near; **to b. in,** (*naut.*) to run or sail towards; **to b. out,** to support, to confirm, to justify; **to b. up,** to take away; to keep up one's courage, to cheer up; **to b. with,** to endure anything (unpleasant), to tolerate, to allow for; to be patient with; **to b. a hand,** to help; **to b. in mind,** to remember, to take into consideration; **to b. witness,** to testify to, to give proof of; †**to b. a burden,** to sing the accompaniment. [OE. *beran*].

BEAR (4), [bāer], *v.i.* (*comm.*) to cause the depreciation of stocks and shares.

BEARABLE, [bāer'-abl], *adj.* able to be endured.

BEARABLENESS, [bāer-abl-nes], *n.* the condition of being bearable.

BEARABLY, [bāer'-ab-li], *adv.* in bearable fashion.

BEAR-BAITING, [bāer'-bā'-ting], *n.* the ancient amusement of baiting bears with dogs.

BEARBERRY, [bāer'-be'-ri], *n.* the plant *Arctostaphylos Uva-ursi*, whose leaves have tonic and astringent qualities.

BEARBIND, [bāer'-bīnd], *n.* a variety of bindweed, *Convolvulus sepium*.

BEARD (1), [bēerd], *n.* hair growing on a man's face, *esp.* on the cheeks, chin and adjacent parts; (*zool.*) the gills of the oyster and other bivalves; filaments growing round the mouths of certain fish, birds and insects; (*bot.*) the slender sharp bristles on the ears of grasses; the web of a feather; the barb of an arrow, fish-hook, etc.; the part of a horse's head, under the lower jaw and above the chin, which bears the curb of the bridle; the forepart of a rudder forming an angle; (*carp.*) the edge of a board; (*print.*) front part of type extending beyond the face, allowing for proper spacing between the lines; the horizontal additions to the letters. [OE. *beard*].

BEARD (2), [bēerd], *v.t.* to pull the beard of; to tackle boldly, to interview someone and discuss frankly some delicate question.

BEARDED, [bēerd'-id], *adj.* possessing a beard.

BEARDGRASS, [bēerd'-grahs], *n.* a grass of the genus *Polypogon*.

BEARDIE, [bēerd-i], *n.* the loach.

BEARDLESS, [bēerd-les], *adj.* lacking a beard; (*fig.*) youthful. [ME. *berdles*].

BEARDLESSNESS, [bēerd'-les-nes], *n.* condition of being beardless.

BEARD-MOSS, [bēerd-mos], *n.* the grey lichen, *Usnea barbata*.

BEARD-TONGUE, [bēerd-tung], *n.* the plant, *Pentstemon digitalis*.

BEARER, [bāer'-er], *n.* one who bears anything; a porter; one on whose shoulders the coffin is borne at a funeral; one who holds or walks beside the pall spread over the coffin at a funeral; (*bot.*) a fruit-yielding tree or plant; one who presents a cheque or bank-note payable on demand. [ME. *berere*].

BEAR-GARDEN, [bāer'-gahd'-en], *n.* a place where bears were baited for sport; a noisy assembly; a scene of great disorder.

BEARING, [bāer'-ing], *n.* connexion, relation, purport; aspect, mien, behaviour, conduct; suffering, endurance; direction, direction with respect to a meridian, the direction in which a point lies, or the situation of a point with regard to a fixed point with reference to the compass points; the action of producing or giving birth to; (*her.*) a charge or device on a shield; (*naut.*) part of the vessel greatest in width below the plank-shear; (*mech.*) surface upon which a machine shaft rotates, or which takes the end thrust of a shaft; (*carp.*) the unsupported length of a beam or rafter; **to take one's bearings,** to find out one's position and establish one's course (mentally or physically); **to lose one's bearings,** to lose one's sense of location, direction or proportion.

BEARING-REIN, [bāer'-ing-rān'], *n.* a rein fixed from the bit to the saddle to keep a horse's head lifted; (*fig.*) a restraining influence.

BEARISH, [bāer'-ish], *adj.* having the characteristics of a bear; (of a stock-market) showing a tendency for prices to fall.

BEARLEADER, [bāer'-lēd'-er], *n.* the keeper of a bear; (*coll.*) a tutor who travels around with his pupil.

BEARLIKE, [bāer'-līk], *adj.* like a bear.

BEAR-PIT, [bāer'-pit], *n.* a shallow pit where bears are kept.

BEAR'S-BREECH, [bāerz'-brēch], *n.* (*bot.*) the brank-ursine, *Acanthus mollis*.

BEAR'S-EAR, [bāerz'-ēer], *n.* the plant, *Primula auricula*; **B. sanicle,** the plant *Cortusa Matthioli*.

BEAR'S-FOOT, [bāerz'-fŏŏt], *n.* a plant of the species *Helleborus foetidus*, stinking hellebore.

BEAR'S-GREASE, [bāerz'-grēs], *n.* fat of bears made into a pomatum; an ointment made of a mixture of hog or veal fat perfumed and slightly tinted.

BEARSKIN, [bāer'-skin], *n.* the skin of a bear; a cap made of it; a shaggy woollen cloth for making overcoats; the tall fur cap worn by the Brigade of Guards.

BEARWARD, [bāer'-wawd], *n.* the keeper of a bear. [ME. *bereward*].

BEAST, [bēst], *n.* an animal, an animal of lower order than man, a mammal as distinct from birds, insects, fishes, etc.; a domestic bovine animal, an animal used for carrying burdens; (*fig.*) a human being with the unpleasant characteristics or behaviour of an animal; the coarser or lower nature in man; (*coll.*) an exceptionally difficult thing or person; **the B.,** Antichrist. [OFr. *beste*, L. *bestia* a beast].

BEASTINGS, see BIESTINGS.

BEASTISH, [bēst'-ish], *adj.* like a beast, brutal. [ME. *bestyssh*].

BEASTLINESS, [bēst'-li-nes], *n.* quality of being beastly.

BEASTLY (1), [bēst'-li], *adj.* like a beast in behaviour; brutal, filthy, coarse, rude; unpleasant, very bad; obscene, disgusting. [ME. *bestelich*].

BEASTLY (2), [bēst-li], *adv.* in the manner of a beast; (*coll.*) used in an intensifying sense.

BEAT (1), [bēt], *n.* a stroke or blow; a regularly recurring stroke, a pulsation or throb; a path or course habitually patrolled; (*mus.*) movement of the hand used to indicate rhythm and time in music; main stresses in a measure of music or of poetry, a grace-note; (*acoustics* and *mus.*) the pulsation arising from the joint vibrations of two sounds of slightly different pitch sounding simultaneously; (*wirel.*) pulsations caused by two wave-motions of slightly different frequency being superimposed. [BEAT (4)].

BEAT (2), [bēt], *n.* flax or hemp bundled up in readiness for soaking. [Unkn.].

BEAT (3), [bēt], *adj.* in a state of extreme fatigue. [BEAT (4)].

BEAT (4), [bēt], *v.t.* to strike or hit repeatedly or continuously, to chastise by repeated blows, to thrash; to conquer, to defeat, to surpass, to prove better than; to shape by hammering; to prove too difficult for, to baffle; to reduce to a powder by pounding; to stir up rapidly; to dash or strike against, to knock; to tread down; to force out of; *v.i.* to throb, to pulsate; to strike down with force; **to b. about,** to run in all directions in an endeavour to escape; (*naut.*) to sail against the wind by tacking; **to b. about the bush,** to evade the point at issue; **to b. down,** to force a person to reduce his price by bargaining; **to b. the bounds,** to traverse the boundaries of a district or parish and strike the principal boundary marks with rods as a method of indicating them; **to b. time,** to indicate the accents and time of a piece of music by regular motions of the hand or foot; **to b. up,** to thrash soundly; (*naut.*) to sail against the wind by tacking; **to b. up and down,** (*hunting*) to double on one's tracks; **to b. the tattoo,** to call to quarters; **to b. a retreat,** to run away; **to b. it,** (*slang*) to run away with all speed. [OE. *beatan*].

BEATEN, [bētn], *adj.* vanquished; fatigued; wrought or hammered out; thrashed; trodden down.

BEATER, [bēt'-er], *n.* one who strikes or beats; an instrument for pounding, hammering or whisking substances; one employed in beating up game.

BEATIFIC, [bē'-a-tif'-ik], *adj.* making happy; blessed, radiant. [L. *beatificus*].

BEATIFICAL, [bē'-a-tif'-ikl], *adj.* beatific.

BEATIFICALLY, [bē'-a-tif'-ik-a-li], *adv.* in beatific fashion.

BEATIFICATION, [bi-at'-if-i-kā'-shun], *n.* (*R.C.*) the act of beatifying.

BEATIFY, [bi-at'-i-fī], *v.t.* to make happy; to bless with heavenly enjoyment; (*R.C.*) to declare publicly and officially that a person is received into heaven, and is to be reverenced as blessed. [LL. *bĕatificāre*].

BEATING, [bēt-ing], *n.* the act of a person or thing that beats; punishment by infliction of repeated blows; defeat. [ME. *beatung*].

BEATITUDE, [bi-at'-it-ewd], *n.* happiness of the highest order, extreme felicity; a saying ascribing particular blessedness; (*pl.*) the heavenly joys enunciated in the Sermon on the Mount. [L. *beatitudo* happiness].

BEAU, (*pl.* **beaux**), [bō, bōz], *n.* a foppish, dandified, faultlessly attired, affected man; a lady's man; (*slang*) a young woman's boy friend. [Fr. *beau*].

BEAUFIGHTER, [bō'-fī-ter], *n.* a type of British fighting plane.

BEAUFREY, [bō'-frā], *n.* a beam or joist. [Fr. *beaufrey*].

BEAU-GESTE, [bō-zhest'], *n.* an act of kindness or graciousness, a good deed. [Fr. *beau geste*].

BEAU-IDEAL, [bō'-id-ē'-al], *n.* the ideal, the conception of perfection. [Fr. *beau idéal*].

BEAUISH, [bō-ish], *adj.* resembling a beau.

BEAUJOLAIS, [bō'-zhol-ā], *n.* a red Burgundy wine. [*Beaujolais*, a place in France, where made].

BEAU-MONDE, [bō'-mond'], *n.* the fashionable world, society. [Fr. *beau monde* fine world].

BEAUNE, [bōn], *n.* a red Burgundy wine. [*Beaune*, a French town, where made].

BEAUTEOUS, [bew'-ti-us], *adj.* beautiful.

BEAUTEOUSLY, [bew'-ti-us-li], *adv.* in a beauteous way.

BEAUTEOUSNESS, [bew'-ti-us-nes], *n.* the condition or quality of being beauteous.

BEAUTIFIER, [bew'-ti-fī'-er], *n.* a person or thing that beautifies, decorator.

BEAUTIFUL (1), [bew'-ti-fŏŏl], *n.* that which constitutes or has beauty.

BEAUTIFUL (2), [bew'-ti-fŏŏl], *adj.* endowed with beauty, pleasing and delighting the senses (*esp.* the ear and eye); approaching perfection of its kind, excellent, admirable, lovely.

BEAUTIFULLY, [bew'-ti-fŏŏl-i], *adv.* in a beautiful fashion; perfectly, admirably.

BEAUTIFULNESS, [bew'-ti-fŏŏl-nes], *n.* the quality or state of being beautiful.

BEAUTIFY, [bew'-ti-fī], *v.t.* to make beautiful; to ornament, adorn. [BEAUTY].

BEAUTILESS, [bew'-ti-les], *adj.* lacking beauty.

BEAUTY, [bew'-ti], *n.* a combination of qualities or attributes arousing a sense of aesthetic satisfaction or affording keen pleasure and delight to the senses; material and spiritual feature giving charm or satisfaction; a beautiful lady; an excellent example of its kind; used ironically as the reverse of its true meaning; a term of affection. [Fr. *beauté*].

BEAUTY-CULTURE, [bew'-ti-kul'-cher], *n.* the art of acquiring or maintaining personal beauty by artificial methods.

BEAUTY-PARLOUR, [bew'-ti-pah'-ler], *n.* an establishment where personal beauty may be attained by artificial methods.

BEAUTY-SLEEP, [bew'-ti-slēp'], *n.* sleep obtained before midnight.

BEAUTY-SPOT, [bew'-ti-spot'], *n.* a small patch or spot placed on the face to heighten beauty; a beautiful place amid pleasant surroundings.

BEAVER (1), [bēv'-er], *n.* a large rodent, living by rivers and lakes; the fur of the beaver; a hat made of beaver-fur; (*slang*) a person with a beard. [OE. *beofor*].

BEAVER

BEAVER (2), **BEVER**, [bēv'-er], *n.* a quick meal or snack, a quick drink. [OFr. *bievre*, L. *bibere* to drink].

BEAVER (3), [bēv'-er], *n.* the front lower guard of a helmet. [OFr. *bavière* a bib].

BEAVER

BEAVERED, [bēv'-erd], *adj.* wearing a beaver.

BEAVERTEEN, [bēv'-er-tēn], *n.* twilled cotton-cloth with the lengthwise threads making a pile of uncut loops. [BEAVER (1) on analogy with VELVETEEN].

BEAVER-TREE, [bēv'-er-trē], *n.* the white laurel, *Magnolia glauca*.

BEBEERINE, [bi-bēer'-in] *n.* an alkaloid, having properties of quinine, obtained from the British Guiana bibiru-tree, *Nectandra leucantha*. [Guiana *bibiru*].

BECALL, [bi-kawl'], *v.t.* to call a person names.

BECALM, [bi-kahm'], *v.t.* *and i.* to calm, appease; (*naut.*) to come to rest through the absence of wind (of a sailing ship).

BECALMED, [bi-kahmd'], *adj.* (*naut.*) unable to proceed through lack of wind.

BECAUSE, [bik-oz'], *conj.* *and adv.* for this reason; on account of this; since, seeing that; inasmuch as. [ME. *bicause*].

BECCAFICO, [bek'-a-fēk'-ō], *n.* (*ornith.*) the fig-pecker or garden-warbler, or other similar migratory birds eaten as delicacies, when fattened on figs and grapes. [It. from *beccare* to peck and *fico* a fig].

BECHAMEL, **béchamel**, [besh'-a-mel'], *n.* a white sauce of savoury herbs. [Marquis de *Béchamel*, the inventor].

BECHANCE (1), [bi-chahns'], *adv.* by chance.

BECHANCE (2), [bi-chahns'], *v.t.* to befall, to happen.

BECHARM, [bi-chahm'], *v.t.* to charm, to captivate. [ME. *becharmen*].

BECHE-DE-MER, **bêche-de-mer**, [bāsh'-de-māer'], *n.* a sea-slug, which is eaten by the Chinese; the South Sea trading dialect of Melanesia. [Fr. from *bêche* spade and *mer* sea].

BECK (1), [bek], *n.* a stream. [OScand. *bekkr*].

BECK (2), [bek], *n.* a silent signal or gesture made by a slight movement of the hand, finger or head; a nod; **at one's b. and call**, in continual and subservient attendance. [BECK (3)].

BECK (3), [bek], *v.t.* *and i.* to make a beck; to beckon. [Short form of BECKON].

BECKET, [bek'-it], *n.* a device in ships to secure loose ropes, tackles etc. [Unkn.].

BECKON, [bekn], *v.t.* *and i.* to call someone by means of a slight movement of the hand, finger or head; to greet by a gesture of acknowledgment. [OE. *becnan*].

BECLOUD, [bi-klowd'], *v.t.* to cloud, obscure.

BECOME, (**became**), [bi-kum'], *v.t.* to suit, to be in agreement with; to enhance one's personal appearance; to be suitable for; **to b. of**, to happen to; *v.i.* to come to be; to develop into, to acquire the characteristics, rank or position of. [OE. *becuman* arrive].

BECOMING, [bi-kum'-ing], *adj.* suitable, fit; charming.

BECOMINGLY, [bi-kum'-ing-li], *adv.* in a becoming fashion.

BECOMINGNESS, [bi-kum'-ing-nes], *n.* the condition of being becoming.

BECURLED, [bi-kurld'], *adj.* covered with curls.

BED (1), [bed], *n.* that on which something rests; something on which a person or animal may rest or sleep; a large rectangular framework, supported on four legs, on which is placed a mattress and coverings, and designed for purposes of resting or sleeping; (*fig.*) sexual relations; a plot of ground in which plants are cultivated; the bottom of a river, sea, stream, lake, etc.; a stratum of rock or other mineral; a solid, level surface forming a foundation upon which a structure, machine, etc., lies; the slate foundation of a billiard table; foundation of broken stones, gravel, etc., of a railroad; **b. and board**, lodging and food; **bring to b.**, to be delivered of a child; **to die in one's b.**, to die from natural causes; **to keep one's b.**, **to take to one's b.**, to become ill; **to make a b.**, to straighten and re-arrange the coverings, mattress and pillow; **to get out of b. on the wrong side**, to be cross-tempered and irritable. [OE. *bedd*].

BED (2), (**bedding**, **bedded**), *v.t.* *and i.* to place in a bed; to plant (flowers) in a bed; to lay flat on a bed or solid foundation. [*Prec.*].

BEDABBLE, [bi-dabl'], *v.t.* to sprinkle, moisten; to splash, to stain.

BEDAGGLE, [bi-dagl'], *v.t.* to soil by trailing and dangling in dirt.

BEDARKENED, [bi-dahk'-end], *adj.* in total darkness.

BEDASH, [bi-dash'], *v.t.* to hurl against; to ornament with splashes of colour.

BEDAUB, [bi-dawb'], *v.t.* to daub over; to besmear.

BEDAZZLE, [bi-dazl'], *v.t.* to confuse or cloud the sight by its brilliance, to dazzle completely.

BEDAZZLINGLY, [bi-daz'-ling-li], *adv.* in bedazzling fashion.

BED-BUG, [bed'-bug], *n.* the parasitic insect, *Cimex lectularius*.

BED-CARD, [bed'-kahd], *n.* a chart on which is recorded by means of a graph, or in a tabulated form, the daily progress of a sick or injured person.

BED-CHAIR, [bed'-chāer'], *n.* a frame provided with a movable back, to support a sick person while sitting up.

BEDCHAMBER, [bed'-chām-ber], *n* a room to sleep in; **Ladies of the B.**, certain ladies appointed to wait upon the queen; **Gentlemen and Grooms of the B.**, certain officers of the royal household, whose duty is to wait upon the sovereign.

BED-CLOTHES, [bed'-klōthz], *n.*(*pl.*) sheets, blankets, coverlets, etc., for a bed.

BEDCOVER, [bed'-kuv'-er], *n.* a bedspread.

BEDDER, [bed'-er], *n.* one who attends to the repose of animals; a plant suitable for cultivation in a flower-bed; (*slang*) a woman who makes the beds in the apartments of students in some universities; a bedroom.

BEDDING, [bed'-ing], *n.* blankets, covers, sheets, mattress, etc., which form a bed when placed on the framework; straw, hay, bracken, etc., used to make a bed for animals; the foundation layer; formation of rocks in strata; process of setting plants in flower-beds. [BED (1)].

BEDECK, [bi-dek'], *v.t.* to deck out, to adorn, embellish, to festoon.

BEDEGUAR, [bed'-i-gah(r)], *n.* a reddish mossy gall found on rose-bushes. [Pers. *badawar* brought by the wind].

BEDE-HOUSE, [bēd'-hows], *n.* a hospital or almshouse, where the poor prayed for their benefactors. [OE. *gebed-hus* prayer house].

BEDE-ROLL, [bēd'-rōl], *n.* (*R.C.*) a list of persons for whom prayers are to be said; a list of people. [OE. *gebed* and ROLL (2)].

BEDEL(L), see BEADLE.

BEDESMAN, see BEADSMAN.

BEDESWOMAN, see BEADSWOMAN.

BEDEVIL, (**bedevilling, bedevilled**), [bi-dev'-il], *v.t.* to throw into confusion and disorder, to upset thoroughly; to exasperate, bewitch.
BEDEVILMENT, [bi-dev'-il-ment], *n.* the state of being bedevilled, exasperation.
BEDEW, [bi-dew']; *v.t.* to moisten with dew; to suffuse or sprinkle with.
BEDEWER, [bi-dew'-er], *n.* that which bedews.
BEDFAST, [bed'-fahst], *adj.* confined to bed through sickness, injury, or old age.
BEDFELLOW, [bed'-fel'-ō], *n.* one who occupies a bed with another; (*fig.*) an associate, partner, companion.
BEDGOWN, [bed'-gown], *n.* a night-gown.
BED-HANGINGS, [bed'-hang'-ings], *n.*(*pl.*) drapery hung about a bed.
BEDIGHT†, [bi-dit'], *v.t.* to array, to adorn. [ME. *bedight*].
BEDIM, (**bedimming, bedimmed**), [bi-dim'], *v.t.* to make dim, to obscure.
BEDIZEN, [bi-dizn'], *v.t.* to deck out in garish fashion. [DIZEN].
BED-JOINT, [bed'-joynt'], *n.* (*geol.*) a crack or split parallel to the surface of the ground.
BED-KEY, [bed'-kē'], *n.* a key for moving the screws in the framework of a bedstead.
BEDLAM (**1**), [bed'-lam], *n.* originally a priory in London, St. Mary of Bethlehem, later turned into a hospital for lunatics; a mad-house, an asylum; (*fig.*) an uproarious assembly, pandemonium. [Late ME. *bedlam* from *Bethlehem*].
BEDLAM (**2**), [bed'-lam], *adj.* fit for a madhouse, resembling a madhouse.
BEDLAMISM, [bed'-lam-izm], *n.* a sign of lunacy.
BEDLAMITE, [bed'-lam-it], *n.* a patient of Bethlehem Hospital; a lunatic.
BED-LIFT, [bed'-lift], *n.* a contrivance to raise invalids to a sitting position.
BEDLINEN, [bed'-lin'-in], *n.* linen for beds.
BEDLINGTON, [bed'-ling-ton], *n.* a short-haired terrier, with a short body, long legs and a long, narrow head. [*Bedlington*, a place in Northumberland].
BEDMAKER [bed'-māk-er], *n.* one who makes beds; a bedder.
BEDMATE, [bed'-māt], *n.* a bed-fellow.
BED-MOULDING, [bed'-mōld-ing], *n.* (*arch.*) those members of a cornice which are found below the cornice.

BED-MOULDING

BEDOUIN (**1**), **BEDUIN**, [bed'-ōō-in], *n.* a nomadic race of Arabs; a member of such a tribe. [Arab. *badawin* dwellers in the desert].
BEDOUIN, (**2**), **BEDUIN**, [bed'-ōō-in], *adj.* pertaining to Bedouins.
BED-PAN, [bed'-pan], *n.* a chamber-pot for the use of the bedfast.
BEDPLATE, [bed'-plāt], *n.* a plate forming the bed of a machine.
BEDPOST, [bed'-pōst], *n.* one of the four posts at the corner of a bed to which the frame is fastened.
BED-PRESSER, [bed'-pres'-er], *n.* a lazy person.
BED-QUILT, [bed'-kwilt'], *n.* the top covering of a bed, placed over the blankets.
BEDRABBLED, [bi-drabld'], *adj.* besmeared with mud.
BEDRAGGLE, [bi-dragl'], *v.t.* to soil by trailing through mud and dirt in walking; to cause to hang down limply and untidily through being wet.
BEDRENCH, [bi-drench'], *v.t.* to drench completely; to saturate.
BED-REST, [bed'-rest], *n.* a piece of furniture for supporting the back when sitting up in bed.
BEDRIDDEN, BEDRID, [bed'-ridn, bed'-rid], *adj.* confined to bed by age or infirmity. [OE. *bedrida* a bed-rider].
BED-ROCK (**1**), [bed'-rok'], *n.* solid rock existing beneath alluvial or other loose formations; (*fig.*) the essential facts or foundations.
BED-ROCK (**2**), [bed'-rok], *adj.* lowest, fundamental.
BEDROOM, [bed'-rōōm], *n.* a chamber with a bed, a room for sleeping in.
BEDROP, (**bedropping, bedropped**), [bi-drop'], *v.t.* to besprinkle, to speckle.
BEDSIDE (**1**), [bed'-sīd], *n.* the side or immediate vicinity of a bed.
BEDSIDE (**2**), [bed'-sīd], *adj.* for use beside the bed; **b. manner**, (*fig.*) (of a doctor) a manner calculated to win confidence or inspire cheerfulness.
BED-SOCKS, [bed'-soks'], *n.*(*pl.*) knitted woollen socks worn in bed.
BEDSORE, [bed'-saw(r)], *n.* a sore on the skin caused through continued lying in bed in one position.
BEDSPREAD, [bed'-spred'], *n.* a linen or other cover spread upon the top of a bed in the daytime to keep out dust, etc.
BEDSTEAD, [bed'-sted], *n.* the frame supporting a mattress and other bedding.
BED-STONE, [bed'-stōn], *n.* a large heavy stone used as a foundation stone in building.
BEDSTRAW, [bed'-straw], *n.* a plant of the genus *Galium*; †a straw mattress. [ME. *bedstraw*].
BED-TABLE, [bed'-tābl'], *n.* a small short-legged table, which can be put on a bed, for the use of an invalid, etc.
BEDTICK, [bed'-tik'], *n.* a linen or cotton covering for a mattress, etc.
BEDTIME, [bed'-tīm'], *n.* the usual time for going to bed. [ME. *bed-time*].
BEDUCK, [bi-duk'], *v.t.* to immerse.
BEDUIN, see BEDOUIN.
BEDUST, [bi-dust'], *v.t.* to sprinkle or cover over with dust.
BEDWARD, [bed'-werd], *adv.* to bed.
BEDWARF, [bi-dwawf'], *v.t.* to make little, stunt.
BEDWORK, [bed'-wurk], *n.* (*coll.*) work easily accomplished.
BEE, [bē], *n.* a genus of hymenopterous insects with a brown and black body, *esp.* the honey-bee, *Apis mellifica*; a number of persons gathered together for some charitable purpose, competition, etc.; (*fig.*) a busy worker; **spelling b.**, a spelling game or contest; **to have a b. in one's bonnet**, to be obsessed with an idea to the point of madness. [OE. *beo*].
BEE-BIRD, [bē'-burd'], *n.* the spotted flycatcher.
BEE-BREAD, [bē'-bred'], *n.* flower-pollen gathered by bees as food for their young; the common clover, *Trifolium pratense*. [OE *beo-bread*].
BEECH, [bēch], *n.* a tree of the genus *Fagus*, with a hard, smooth bark slightly silvery in colour, and oval-shaped leaves. [OE. *bece*].
BEECHCOAL, [bēch'-kōl'], *n.* charcoal made from beechwood.
BEECHEN, [bēch'-en], *adj.* consisting of beechwood or beech bark. [OE. *becen*].
BEECH-GALL, [bēch'-gawl'], *n.* a hard excrescence on the leaf of a beech, caused by a fly maggot.
BEECH-MARTEN, [bēch'-mah'-tin], *n.* a species of marten distinguished by its white breast, the stone-marten.
BEECHMAST, [bēch'-mast'], *n.* the fruit or nut of the beech.
BEECH-NUT, [bēch'-nut'], *n.* the nut of the beech-tree.
BEECH-OIL, [bēch'-oil'], *n.* oil obtained from beech-nuts.
BEE-EATER, [bē'-ēt'-er], *n.* a genus of birds with brightly coloured plumage.
BEEF, (*pl.* **beeves**†), [bēf, bēvz], *n.* the name formerly given to an ox; now the flesh of an ox, bull or cow when killed; (*fig.*) flesh and muscle; power, vigour, force. [Fr. *boeuf*].
BEEFEATER, [bēf'-ēt'-er], *n.* a Yeoman of the Guard, a warder of the Tower of London; an African bird feeding on grubs in the hides of certain bovine animals.
BEEFINESS, [bēf'-in-es], *n.* the condition of being beefy.
BEE-FLOWER, [bē'-flow'-er], *n.* the bee orchis, *Ophrys apifera*.
BEEFSTEAK, [bēf'-stāk'], *n.* a thick slice of beef suitable for braising or grilling.
BEEF-TEA, [bēf-tē'], *n.* a broth made from stewed beef often given to invalids.
BEEF-WITTED, [bēf'-wit'-id], *adj.* stupid, slow-witted.
BEEF-WOOD, [bēf'-wōōd], *n.* hard, close-grained, reddish timber obtained from certain Australian trees of the genus *Casuarina*.
BEEFY, [bēf'-i], *adj.* resembling beef; resembling an ox in physical or mental characteristics. [BEEF].
BEE-GARDEN, [bē'-gah'-den], *n.* an enclosure where beehives are kept; a garden where plants favoured by bees are cultivated.
BEE-GLUE, [bē'-glōō'], *n.* propolis, the soft, waxy substance with which bees cement the combs to the hives and seal the cells.

BEE-HAWK, [bē'-hawk'], *n.* (*zool.*) the honey-buzzard, *Pernis apivora*, which feeds on hymenopterous insects.
BEEHIVE, [bē'-hīv'], *n.* a wooden or straw structure, often domed, in which bees are kept and in which they store up honey. [ME. *bee-hyve*].
BEEHIVE OVEN, [bē'-hīv-ovn'], *n.* the simplest form of coke-oven, resembling a domed beehive.
BEELINE, [bē'-līn], *n.* an undeviating direct line; **to make a b. for**, to rush straight towards, along the shortest possible path of approach.
BEELZEBUB, [bē-el'-zib-ub'], *n.* the prince of devils, Satan. [Heb. *Baal-zebub* Lord of flies].
BEEMASTER, [bē'-mah'-ster], *n.* a bee-keeper.
BEE-MOTH, [bē'-moth'], *n.* a moth of the genus *Macroglossa*, harmful to bees.
BEEN (1), [bēn, bin], *p.pt.* of the verb BE.
BEEN (2), [bēn], *n.* the vina, an Indian guitar with nineteen frets. [Unkn.].
BEE-ORCHIS, [bē'-awk-is], *n.* the bee-flower, *Ophrys apifera*.
BEER (1), [bēer], *n.* an alcoholic beverage usually made from fermented malted barley flavoured with hops; **small b.**, weak inferior beer; (*fig.*) of little account or value. [OE. *bēor*].
BEER (2), [bēer], *n.* one of the ends forming a division of the warp, and containing a certain number of threads. [BIER].
BEER-BARREL, [bēer'-ba'-rel], *n.* a barrel in which beer is kept.
BEER-ENGINE, [bēer'-en'-jin], *n.* a beer-pump.
BEER-MONEY, [bēer'-mun'-i], *n.* an allowance of money made to hired labourers instead of an allowance of beer.
BEER-PULL, [bēer'-pōōl], *n.* the handle of a beer-pump.
BEER-PUMP, [bēer'-pump], *n.* a hand-pump for drawing beer from barrels in a cellar or vault to the bar.
BEERSHOP, [bēer'-shop'], *n.* a licensed house at which beer may be sold.
BEERY, [bēer'-i], *adj.* having the taste or smell of beer; slightly intoxicated; showing signs of having consumed beer, or of fondness for beer.
BEESWAX (1), [bēz'-waks], *n.* a solid substance secreted by bees, with which they construct their combs, often used for polishing, etc.
BEESWAX (2), [bēz-waks], *v.t.* to polish with beeswax.
BEESWING, [bēz'-wing], *n.* a film of tartar which forms on old port-wine.
BEET, [bēt], *n.* a plant of the genus *Beta*, the crimson roots of which are eaten as a vegetable. [OE. *bete*].
BEET-BEETLE, [bēt'-bētl], *n.* (*zool.*) a beetle whose larvae are very harmful to the beet and mangel-wurzel plants.
BEETLE (1), [bētl], *n.* an insect of the order *Coleoptera*, having its wings covered and protected by hard outer wing-cases; (*pop.*) the large black variety, the cockroach. [OE. *bitel*].
BEETLE (2), [bētl], *n.* an industrial implement, consisting of a heavy, solid piece of wood furnished with a small projecting handle, and used for hammering in paving-blocks, etc. [OE. *bietel* mallet].
BEETLE (3), [bētl], *adj.* overhanging; (of eyebrows) bushy. [BEETLE (5)].
BEETLE (4), [bētl], *v.t.* to hammer or crush with a beetle. [BEETLE (2)].
BEETLE (5), [bētl], *v.i.* to project, hang over, jut out over. [Unkn.].
BEETLE-BROW, [bētl'-brow'], *n.* a prominent, over-hanging brow.
BEETLE-BROWED, [betl'-browd'], *adj.* having a beetle-brow.
BEETLE-HEAD, [bētl'-hed'], *n.* a dull, stupid person.
BEETLE-HEADED, [bētl'-hed'-id], *adj.* dull, stupid.
BEETLE-STOCK, [bētl'-stok'], *n.* the handle of a wooden beetle.

BEETLE

BEETLING, [bēt'-ling], *adj.* overhanging, projecting, prominent.
BEET-RADISH, [bēt'-rad'-ish], *n.* beet-rave.
BEET-RAVE†, [bēt'-rāv'], *n.* a small red beet used in salad. [Fr. *bette-rave*].
BEEVES†, *n. pl.* of BEEF.
BEFALL, (**befell, befallen**), [bi-fawl'], *v.t. and i.* to happen, occur, to take place; to happen to. [OE. *befallen*].
BEFIT, (**befitting, befitted**), [bi-fit'], *v.t.* to suit, to be fitting for, to become.
BEFLATTER, [bi-flat'-er], *v.t.* to flatter, cajole, to praise unduly.
BEFLOWER, [bi-flow'-er], *v.t.* to adorn it with flowers.
BEFOG, (**befogging, befogged**), [bi-fog'], *v.t.* to envelop completely in fog, to cloud over with fog; (*fig.*) to obscure, perplex.
BEFOOL, [bi-fōōl'], *v.t.* to delude, fool completely, deceive. [ME. *befolen*].
BEFORE (1), [bi-faw(r)'], *adv.* in front, farther on ahead; preceding, earlier; previously, ago; already.
BEFORE (2), [bi-faw(r)'], *prep. and conj.* in front of; in the presence or sight of; ahead of; under the influence of; in preference to, sooner than; earlier than, in less time than; confronting; rather than, previous to; **be b. the mast**, (*naut.*) to be a common sailor; (*naut.*) in the same direction as, and driven by, the wind. [OE. *beforan*].
BEFORE-CITED, [bi-faw'-sīt-id], *adj.* quoted above, mentioned in a previous place.
BEFORE-GOING, [bi-faw'-gō'-ing], *adj.* preceding, previous.
BEFOREHAND, [bi-faw'-hand'], *adv.* in advance, in anticipation of; in front, ahead of schedule; **to be b. with**, to foresee, be prepared in advance for. [ME. *beforen-hand*].
BEFORE-MENTIONED, [bi-faw'-men'-shund], *adj.* mentioned previously.
BEFOUL, [bi-fowl'], *v.t.* to soil, make dirty, pollute, to besmirch.
BEFRECKLE, [bi-frekl'], *v.t.* to freckle, spot.
BEFRIEND, [bi-frend'], *v.t.* to make friends with; to act kindly towards.
BEFRINGE, [bi-frinj'], *v.t.* to provide or ornament with a fringe.
BEFUR, (**befurred, befurring**), [bi-fur'], *v.t.* to cover or line with fur.
BEG (1), [beg], *n.* the governor of a town, district or sanjak in Turkey and other parts of the East. [Osmanli *beg* prince].
BEG (2), (**begging, begged**), [beg], *v.t. and i.* to make known to another a desire so that it may be effected; to ask for charity, to request as a gift; to ask a favour, to implore, to entreat earnestly, to beseech; (of animals) to sit up with the fore-paws outstretched; to ask humbly, politely or formally; **to b. to**, to take the liberty of, to presume; **to b. the question**, to avoid the point at issue; **to go a-begging**, to be not taken advantage of. [Uncert.].
BEGAD, [bi-gad'], *int.* an exclamation or polite oath. [BY-GOD].
BEGAN, [bi-gan'], *pret.* of BEGIN
BEGET, (**begetting, begot, begotten**), [bi-get'], *v.t.* to get, to procreate; (*fig.*) to cause, bring about. [OE. *begietan* influenced by GET].
BEGETTER, [bi-get'-er], *n.* a person who begets.
BEGGABLE, [beg'-abl], *adj.* capable of being begged.
BEGGAR (1), [beg'-er], *n.* one who begs, one who obtains his living by soliciting alms; a person living in a state of extreme poverty; (*coll.*) a rogue, a fellow. [ME. *beggere* from BEGHARD].
BEGGAR (2), [beg'-er], *v.t.* to reduce to poverty, to ruin; (*fig.*) to upset, to make useless, to spoil; **b. my neighbour**, a simple card-game in which the aim is to try to acquire the whole of an opponent's cards. [*Prec.*].
BEGGARLINESS, [beg'-er-li-nes], *n.* the condition of being beggarly.
BEGGARLY (1), [beg'-er-li], *adj.* poor, mean, trifling, meagre, squalid.
BEGGARLY (2), [beg'-er-li], *adv.* in a poor manner.
BEGGARY, [beg'-er-i], *n.* extreme poverty, destitution. [ME. *beggarie*].
BEGGING (1), [beg'-ing], *n.* the practice of asking for alms or gifts.
BEGGING (2), [beg'-ing], *adj.* asking for something; mendicant.
BEGHARD, BEGUARD, [beg'-ahd], *n.* an indepedent religious organization originating in Belgium in the thirteenth century, whose members led lives of extreme holiness without giving up their secular occupations. [OFr. *begard* from BEGUINE].
BEGILT, [bi-gilt'], *adj.* gilded.
BEGIN, (**beginning, began, begun**), [bi-gin'], *v.t. and i.* to start, commence, perform the initial act of; to enter upon; to originate; to have an original existence; **to b. with**, first of all. [OE. *beginnan*].
BEGINNER, [bi-gin'-er], *n.* one who begins; (*fig.*) a learner, a novice.
BEGINNING, [bi-gin'-ing], *n.* the start, origin, sources; (*pl.*) the rudiments, the elements.

BEGIRD, (**begirt**), [bi-gurd′], *v.t.* to fasten with a girdle; to surround, enclose, bind. [OE. *begyrdan*].
BEGIRDLE, [bi-gurdl′], *v.t.* to begird.
BEGLERBEG, [beg′-ler-beg], *n.* the governing official of a Turkish province. [Turk. *beglerbeg*].
BEGLOOM, [bi-glōōm′], *v.t.* to make gloomy; to depress.
BEGNAW, [bi-naw′], *v.t.* to eat away, to corrode, to nibble at, to gnaw through. [OE. *begnagan*].
BEGONE, [bi-gon′], *int.* go away ! depart ! flee ! [ME. *begone*].
BEGONIA, [bi-gō′-ni-a], *n.* a genus of tropical plants of the order *Begoniaceae* with gaily-coloured flowers. [Michel *Begon* (1638-1710), a French botanist].
BEGORED, [bi-gawd′], *adj.* smeared with blood.
BEGREASE, [bi-grēs′], *v.t.* to daub with grease.
BEGRIME, [bi-grīm′], *v.t.* to blacken with dirt, oil, soot, etc., to soil, make dirty.
BEGROAN, [bi-grōn], *v.t.* to hail with a groan.
BEGRUDGE, [bi-gruj′], *v.t.* to allow reluctantly, to envy for having something, to give unwillingly, to grudge. [ME. *bigrucchen*].
BEGUARD, see BEGHARD.
BEGUILE, [bi-gīl′], *v.t.* to deceive, cheat; to deprive of under false pretences; to pass (the time, etc.), in pleasant manner; (*reflex.*) to amuse oneself. [ME. *bigilen*].
BEGUILEMENT, [bi-gīl′-ment], *n.* act of beguiling; that which beguiles; the state of being beguiled.
BEGUILER, [bi-gīl′-er], *n.* the person or thing that beguiles.
BEGUILINGLY, [bi-gīl′-ing-li], *adv.* in a beguiling fashion.
BEGUINE, [beg′-ēn], *n.* a member of a twelfth century Netherlands order of women, who, without taking a monastic vow, spent their time in devotion and charity. [Lambert le *Bègue*, founder of the order].
BEGUM, [bē′-gum], *n.* Indian title for a Moslem princess or lady of rank. [Turk. *bigim*, *fem.* of BEG (1)].
BEGUN, [bi-gun′], *p.pt.* of BEGIN.
BEHALF, [bi-hahf′], **on b. (of)**, *adv.* instead of, in place of, as representative of. [BY and HALF].
BEHAVE, [bi-hāv′], *v.i. and reflex.* to act, to conduct oneself, to acquit oneself (in a particular way); to conduct oneself properly, to exhibit good manners; (*fig.*) (of a machine) to function; **well-, ill-behaved**, having good (bad) manners. [OE. *behabban* restrain].
BEHAVIOUR, [bi-hāv′-yer], *n.* the way in which a thing or person acts; conduct, manners, mode of behaving; reaction under a set of imposed conditions.
BEHAVIOURISM, [bi-hāv′-yer-izm], *n.* a psychological method of observing conduct in response to externally applied mental or physical stimuli; the theory that reactions to particular external stimuli will always be the same.
BEHEAD, [bi-hed′], *v.t.* to decapitate, cut off the head of. [OE. *beheafdian*].
BEHEADING, [bi-hed′-ing], *n.* the act of cutting off the head.
BEHELD, [bi-held′], *pret.* of BEHOLD.
BEHEST, [bi-hest′], *n.* command, request, order. [OE. *behæs*].
BEHIND (1), [bi-hīnd′], *n.* (*coll.*) the buttocks.
BEHIND (2), [bi-hīnd′], *adv.* in the rear, backwards; remaining after a departure; past; in arrears; on the further side and invisible to an observer; not apparent, held in reserve; **to fall b.**, to be in arrears; **to put b. oneself**, to dismiss from one's consideration. [OE. *behindan*].
BEHIND (3), [bi-hīnd′], *prep.* at the back of, to the rear of, on the remote side of; after; inferior to; in support of; **b. one's back**, without one's knowledge, in an underhand, deceitful way; **b. the scenes**, (*fig.*) not disclosed or known to the public, secret; **b. time**, late. [*Prec.*].
BEHINDHAND, [bi-hīnd′-hand], *adj. and adv.* late, slow, backward; in arrears, slightly antiquated.
BEHOLD, [bi-hōld′], *v.t. and i.* to see, to witness, to look carefully at, to fix one's eyes upon, to gaze upon; (*pass.*) to be regarded as; (*imper.*) look ! consider ! [OE. *behaldan* keep, consider, look at].
BEHOLDEN†, [bi-hōld′-en], *adj.* grateful, deeply obliged. [*P.pt.* of BEHOLD].
BEHOLDER, [bi-hōld′-er], *n.* one who beholds.
BEHONEY, [bi-hun′-i], *v.t.* to make sweet with honey.
BEHOOF, [bi-hōōf′], *n.* advantage, profit, benefit. [ME. *bihof*].
BEHOVE, [bi-hōv′], *v. impers.* to need, to be necessary, to be highly desirable. [OE. *behofian*].
BEHOVEFUL, [bi-hōv′-fōōl], *adj.* profitable, highly desirable, necessary.
BEIGE, [bāzh], *n.* an undyed, unbleached woollen fabric; a pinkish shade of buff. [Fr. from LL. *bisus* grey].
BEING, [bē′-ing], *n.* existence, life; a person who is alive; essential nature; the **Supreme B.**, God.
BEINKED, [bi-ingkt′], *adj.* smudged with ink.
BEJAN, [bēj′-an], *n.* a freshman at Scottish universities. [Fr. *béjaune* novice].
BEJEWELLED, [bi-jōō′-eld], *adj.* adorned with jewels.
BEJUCO, [bi-hōōk′-ō], *n.* a tropical American twisting cane-tree. [Span. *bejuco*].
BEKAH, [bē′-ka], *n.* half a shekel. [Heb. *bekah* half].
BEKISS, [bi-kis′], *v.t.* to give countless kisses to.
BEKNAVE, [bi-nāv], *v.t.* to brand as a knave.
BEKNOWN, [bi-nōn], *adj.* known.
BELABOUR, [bi-lāb′-er], *v.t.* to thrash soundly; (*fig.*) to exert strenuous efforts upon.
BELACE, [bi-lās′], *v.t.* to ornament with lace.
BELATE, [bi-lāt′], *v.t.* to cause to be late, to delay.
BELATED, [bi-lāt′-id], *adj.* arriving late, coming too late, overdue.
BELATEDNESS, [bi-lāt′-id-nes], *n.* the condition of being belated.
BELAUD, [bi-lawd′], *v.t.* to praise excessively.
BELAY, [bi-lā], *v.t.* (*naut.*) to secure (a running rope) by winding it round a fixed pin or cleat. [~OE. *belecgan* to lay round].
BELAYING-CLEAT, [bi-lā′-ing-klēt′], *n.* (*naut.*) a horizontal piece of wood or iron with projecting ends, to which a rope may be temporarily fastened.
BELAYING-PIN, [bi-lā′-ing-pin′], *n.* a belaying-cleat.
BEL CANTO, [bel′-cant′-ō], *n.* (*mus.*) a style of singing which pays special attention to a smooth, musical (as distinct from a dramatic) interpretation of a piece. [It. *bel canto* fine song].
BELCH (1), [belch, belsh], *n.* a noisy expulsion of wind upwards from the stomach, eructation; (*fig.*) a sudden eruption of smoke, flames, etc.
BELCH (2), [belch, belsh], *v.t. and i.* to make a belch; (*fig.*) spurt forth, emit suddenly in large quantities. [OE. *bealcian*].
BELCHER, [belch′-er], *n.* a coloured neckerchief. [J. *Belcher*, a famous English pugilist].
BELCHING, [belch′-ing], *n.* the emission of a belch.
BELDAM(E), [bel′-dam′], *n.* an old woman; a violent, dirty, obscene hag. [OFr. *beldame* grandmother].
BELEAGUER, [bi-lēg′-er], *v.t.* to besiege, blockade. [Du. *belegeren*].
BELEAGUERMENT [bi-lēg′-er-ment], *n.* the act of beleaguering, the state of being beleaguered.
BELEMNITE, [bel′-em-nīt], *n.* (*geol.*) a cylindrical fossil shell-fish, tapering to a point. [Gk. *belemnon* dart].
BELFRY, [bel′-fri], *n.* that part of a church tower or steeple in which the bells are hung; (*naut.*) an ornamented covered framework under which a ship's bell is hung; **to have bats in the b.**, to be crazy, mad, or eccentric. [OFr. *berfroi*].
BELGA, [bel′-ga], *n.* a Belgian unit of money equivalent to five francs. [L. *Belga* a Belgian].
BELGIAN (1), [bel′-jan], *n.* a native of Belgium. [*Belgium*].
BELGIAN (2), [bel′-jan], *adj.* pertaining to or belonging to Belgium.
BELGIC, [bel′-jik], *adj.* pertaining to the Belgae; Belgian. [L. *Belgae*, a Germanic and Celtic tribe once settled in the Netherlands].

BELEMNITE

BELGRAVIAN (1), [bel-grā′-vi-an], *n.* one of the upper classes. [*Belgravia*, a fashionable London district].
BELGRAVIAN (2), [bel-grā′-vi-an], *adj.* belonging to Belgravia or to fashionable society.
BELIAL (1), [bē′-li-al], *n.* Satan; the spirit of wickedness; **sons of B.**, worthless wicked persons.
BELIAL (2), [bē′-li-al], *adj.* worthless, wicked. [Heb. *b'li-yacal* worthless].
BELIBEL, (**belibelling, belibelled**), [bi-lī′-bel], *v.t.* to libel.
BELIE, [bi-lī′], *v.t.* to contradict by implication, to misrepresent, give the lie to, to fail to conform with. [OE. *beleogan* deceive].
BELIEF, [bi-lēf′], *n.* something regarded by a person as true; firm conviction, considered opinion; faith in the truth of a body of religious doctrines, a creed; confidence, trust; a formula or exposition of doctrine; **The B.**, the Apostles' Creed. [OE. *geleafa*].

BELIEVABILITY, [bi-lēv'-a-bil'-i-ti], *n.* believableness.

BELIEVABLE, [bi-lēv'-abl], *adj.* capable of being believed.

BELIEVABLENESS, [bi-lēv'-abl-nes], *n.* the quality of being believable.

BELIEVE, [bi-lēv'], *v.t.* to regard personally as true, to have faith in, to feel convinced of the truth of the remarks of (a person); to conceive, to imagine; to be under the impression that, to think; *v.i.* (with *in*) to hold a conviction or opinion; to place one's trust in; to set store by, to regard as advantageous; to profess faith in Christianity; **make-b.,** to imagine, to pretend. [ME. *bileven* from OE. *gelefan*].

BELIEVER, [bi-lēv'-er], *n.* one who believes, one who adheres to the Christian religion.

BELIEVING, [bi-lēv'-ing], *adj.* having complete faith in, accepting as true.

BELIEVINGLY, [bi-lēv'-ing-li], *adv.* in a believing way.

BELIKE, [bi-līk'], *adv.* probably, perhaps.

BELISHA-BEACON, [bel-ēsh'-a-bē'-kon], *n.* a traffic sign marking a place at which pedestrians may cross a busy road in perfect safety. [L. Hore-*Belisha*, who introduced it when Minister of Transport].

BELITTLE, [bi-litl'], *v.t.* to make light of, to minimize the importance of, disparage.

BELITTLEMENT, [bi-litl'-ment], *n.* the act of belittling, the state of being belittled.

BELL (1), [bel], *n.* a hollow bowl-shaped metal vessel which emits a clear musical sound when struck with a clapper; anything resembling a bell in shape; a hollow metal case in which divers may work under water; (*pl.*) (*naut.*) strokes of a ship's bell indicating half-hours of a watch, even numbers of strokes always denoting the hours; **to bear the b.,** to be the leader. [OE. *belle*].

BELL (2), [bel], *v.t. and i.* to provide with, or to adorn with bells; to open and grow like a bell in shape; **to b. the cat,** to undertake a hazardous adventure. [OE. *bellan*].

BELL (3), [bel], *v.i.* to bellow as a deer at rutting time. [OE. *bellan*].

BELLADONNA, [bel'-a-don'-a], *n.* (*bot.*) a poisonous British plant *Atropa Belladonna*, deadly nightshade, bearing shining, blackish-brown berries and lurid flowers; (*med.*) a medicine or drug prepared from this plant. [It. *bella donna* beautiful lady].

BELLBIND, [bel'-bīnd'], *n.* the bindweed, *Convolvulus sepium*.

BELL-BIRD, [bel'-burd'], *n.* (*zool.*) a South American perching bird with a sonorous bell-like note, *Arapunga alba*; an Australian bird, the *Myzanthra melanophrys*.

BELL-BUOY, [bel'-boi'], *n.* a buoy with a bell which gives audible warning of danger.

BELLCOTE, [bel'-kot], *n.* a protection for a bell.

BELL-CRANK, [bel'-krangk'], *n.* (*mech.*) an **L**-shaped lever pivoted at its centre with its two arms set at an angle to change the direction of the motion transmitted in a machine; formerly, a lever changing the vertical motion of a bell-pull to a horizontal motion of the bell-wire.

BELLE, [bel], *n.* a fashionable and beautiful lady; (*fig.*) the most beautiful or most admired lady in a group. [Fr. *belle* beautiful woman].

BELLED, [beld], *adj.* adorned with bells.

BELLEISLE, [bel'-īl'], *n.* the American cress, *Barbarea praecox*. [*Belle Isle* in Newfoundland].

BELLES-LETTRES, [bel'-letr'], *n.* artistic and literary writings; light literature; the aesthetic study of literature. [Fr. *belles-lettres* fine letters].

BELLETRIST, [bel'-let'-rist], *n.* one who writes belles-lettres.

BELL-FASHIONED, [bel'-fash'-und], *adj.* shaped like a bell.

BELL-FLOWER, [bel'-flow'-er], *n.* a plant of the genus *Campanula*, so called from the shape of its flowers.

BELLFOUNDER, [bel'-fownd'-er] *n.* one who casts large bells.

BELL-FOUNDRY, [bel'-fownd'-ri], *n.* a place in which bells are cast.

BELL-GABLE, [bel'-gābl'], *n.* a gable in which bells are hung.

BELL-GLASS, [bel'-glahs'], *n.* a bell-shaped protection for plants, or delicate ornaments and instruments.

BELL-HANGER, [bel'-hang'-er], *n.* one who is employed in fixing or hanging large bells.

BELLHANGING, [bel'-hang'-ing], *n.* the trade of hanging bells.

BELL-HOP, [bel'-hop'], *n.* (*U.S.*) (*coll.*) a page-boy.

BELLICOSE, [bel'-i-kōs], *adj.* warlike, aggressively hostile. [L. *bellicosus*].

BELLICOSITY, [bel-ik-os'-it-i], *n.* bellicoseness. [BELLICOSE].

BELLIED, [bel'-id], *adj.* (*bot.*) swollen out like a belly; bulging in the middle.

BELLIGERENCE, [bel-ij'-er-ents], *n.* the state of being a belligerent.

BELLIGERENCY, [bel-ij'-er-en-si], *n.* a state of war.

BELLIGERENT (1), [bel-ij'-er-ent], *n.* a nation, state, or party engaged in war.

BELLIGERENT (2), [bel-ij'-er-ent], *adj.* engaged in war; pugnacious; **b. rights,** the rights of a nation, state, or party at war.

BELLING (1), [bel'-ing], *n.* the cry of a roe at rutting-time; a loud cry or roar. [BELL (3)].

BELLING (2), [bel'-ing], *adj.* growing full and ripe (of hops). [Uncert.].

BELLIPOTENT, [bel-i'-pō-tent], *adj.* mighty in war. [L. *bellipotens*].

BELLMAN, [bel'-man], *n.* a town-crier who rings a bell to attract attention. [ME. *belman*].

BELL-METAL, [bel'-met'-al], *n.* an alloy of copper and tin from which bells are founded.

BELLON, [bel'-on], *n.* lead colic. [Unkn.].

BELLONA, [bel-ōn'-a], *n.* the Roman goddess of war; (*fig.*) a tall majestic woman. [L. *Bellona* goddess of war].

BELLOW (1), [bel'-ō], *n.* a deep, loud roar.

BELLOW (2), [bel'-ō], *v.i.* to roar as a bull or ox, to utter a loud resonant cry; to shout continuously, to speak or sing in an unnecessarily loud manner; to make a deep, loud roaring sound. [OE. *belgian*].

BELLOWING, [bel'-ō-ing], *n.* a loud hollow sound, a loud roar or clamour.

BELLOWS, [bel'-ōz], *n.*(*pl.*) a bag or other receptacle which when compressed produces a strong current of air; (*phot.*) the extending portion of a camera for varying the distance between lens and film or plate; **pair of b.,** a two-handled, portable bellows. [OE. *belg*].

BELLOWSFISH, [bel'-ōz-fish'], *n.* the trumpet-fish, or sea-snipe, *Centriscus scolopax*.

BELLOWS-MAKER, [bel'-ōz-māk'-er], *n.* one who makes bellows.

BELLOWS-SOUND, [bel'-ōz-sownd'], (*med.*) a puffing wheezy sound.

BELL-PEPPER, [bel'-pep'-er], *n.* Guinea pepper made from the bell-shaped fruit of the plant *Capsicum*.

BELLOWS

BELL-PULL, [bel'-pōōl], *n.* the cord or handle, which when pulled causes the bell to ring.

BELL-PUNCH, [bel'-punch'], *n.* a metal case containing a ticket-perforator and bell.

BELL-RINGER, [bel'-ring'-er], *n.* one who rings church or other bells, a campanologist.

BELL-ROPE, [bel'-rōp], *n.* the rope or cord by which a bell is rung.

BELL-SHAPED, [bel'-shāpt], *adj.* in the shape of a bell.

BELL-TENT, [bel'-tent'], *n.* a large conical tent.

BELL-TURRET, [bel'-tu'-ret], *n.* a turret which contains a bell.

BELLUM, [bel'-um], *n.* a small Persian boat. [Pers. *balam*].

BELLWETHER, [bel'-weTH'-er], *n.* the sheep which leads the flock and has a bell on its neck.

BELLWORT, [bel'-wurt], *n.* the bell-flower, *Campanula Trachelium*. [BELL (1) and WORT].

BELLY (1), [bel'-i], *n.* the lower part of the trunk extending from the diaphragm to the thighs in mammals; the stomach; that part of anything which swells out or forms a bulge-like protuberance, the thick part of a muscle, the front curved part of a violin; (*fig.*) greed, gluttony, the inside or interior; a hollow, enclosed space; **pot-b.,** a protruding abdomen. [OE. *belg* bag].

BELLY (2), [bel'-i], *v.i.* to swell out, to bulge, to become protuberant.

BELLY-ACHE, [bel'-i-āk], *n.* pain in the stomach or abdomen. [BELLY (1) and ACHE (1).

BELLY-BAND, [bel'-i-band'], *n.* a band passing under a horse's belly in harness, a girth; (*naut.*) a strengthening band of canvas on a sail.

BELLY-BOARD, [bel'-i-bawd'], *n.* (*mus.*) the wood from which sounding-boards are made.

BELLY-FRETTING, [bel'-i-fret'-ing], *n.* the chafing

of a horse's belly by a bellyband; a violent pain in a horse's belly, caused by internal worms.

BELLYFUL, [bel'-i-fōōl], *n.* as much as satisfies the appetite, a sufficiency; (*fig.*) as much as one can tolerate, more than enough.

BELLY-GOD, [bel'-i-god'], *n.* a glutton, a greedy person.

BELLYING, [bel'-i-ing], *adj.* protuberant, swelling out, distended.

BELLY-PINCHED, [bel'-i-pincht'], *adj.* very hungry, starving.

BELLY-ROLL, [bel'-i-rōl'], *n.* (*agr.*) a roller whose surface bulges out in the middle.

BELLY-SLAVE†, [bel'-i-slāv'], *n.* a slave to one's appetite.

BELOCK, [bi-lok'], *v.t.* to lock or secure with a lock.

BELOMANCY, [bel'-ō-man-si], *n.* divination by marked arrows. [Gk. *belos* arrow and *manteia* divination].

BELONE, [bel'-on-i], *n.* the garfish, or mackerel guide, *Belone vulgaris.* [Gk. *belone* needle].

BELONG, [bi-long'], *v.i.* to be the attribute of, to pertain to, to relate to; to be the business, duty or concern of, to be connected with; to be a resident or native of; to be the property of; to have its right place, to go with. [ME. *belongen*].

BELONGINGS, [bi-long'-ings], *n.(pl.)* goods, possessions, luggage.

BELOVE†, [bi-luv'], *v.t.* to love. [ME. *biluven*].

BELOVED (1), [bi-luv'-id], *n.* a person loved by someone, a betrothed person, a spouse.

BELOVED (2), [bi-luv'-id, bi-luvd'], *adj.* dearly loved.

BELOW (1), [bi-lō'], *adv.* beneath, in a lower place from a specified position, further or lower down; (*naut.*) underneath the deck, in the cabins or holds; **place b.,** hell; **here b.,** on earth. [ME. *bi-lowe*].

BELOW (2), [bi-lō'], *prep.* lower down than, lower in position than, not up to, beneath; inferior to (in merit, morals, rank, quality, etc.); too low to be affected by; unworthy of; **b. the ground,** dead and buried; **b. the mark,** not up to the usual standard; **b. par,** (*comm.*) not having their nominal value (of shares); (*fig.*) indisposed, unwell; **b. the surface,** not apparent, unrevealed. [ME. *bi-lowe*].

BELT (1), [belt], *n.* a strap or girdle encircling the waist, to confine or support garments, or from which weapons may be hung; a girdle indicating the rank of earl or knight; a leather strap or indiarubber band connecting wheels or shafts, and transmitting rotary motion, to drive machinery; a broad strip of approximately uniform width; a long, narrow region, a zone, an extended regular patch; a band of distinguishable colour or material laid upon another; a broad strip of armour-plating built along the water-line of a battle-ship; a strap containing cartridges, which feeds a machine-gun; **cartridge b.,** a belt containing cartridges, and worn over one shoulder and under the other arm; **Sam Browne b.,** (*milit.*) a belt supported by a strap crossing one shoulder, worn by an officer; **to hit below the b.,** (*boxing*) to hit unfairly; (*fig.*) to take an unfair advantage. [OE. *belt*].

BELT (2), [belt], *v.t.* to encircle or enclose with a belt; to secure by means of a belt; to distinguish with a belt of colour; (*coll.*) to thrash soundly.

BELTANE, [bel'-tān'], *n.* an ancient Gaelic and Irish spring festival. [Ir. *bealteine,* Gael. *bealltuinn* blaze-fire].

BELTED, [belt'-id], *adj.* wearing a belt, provided with a belt; marked by a belt; bearing the distinctive belt of an earl or knight.

BELTING, [belt'-ing], *n.* a system of belts driving machinery; the material of which belts are made; (*coll.*) a thrashing with a belt.

BELUGA, [bel-ewg'-a], *n.* a species of dolphin, the white whale, *Delphinapterus leucas.* [Russ. *byeluga*].

BELVEDERE, [bel'-ved-ēer], *n.* a small pavilion or turret on the top of a house; a summer-house built on raised land and so having a wide prospect. [It. *belvedere* fine view].

BEMA, [bēm'-a], *n.* (*eccles.*) the chancel; the raised platform in the apse of a basilica; the platform from which a Grecian orator spoke. [Gk. *bema* a step].

BEMASK, [bi-mahsk'], *v.t.* to mask, to conceal, to hide.

BEMIRE, [bi-mīer'], *v.t.* to soil or drag in the mud.

BEMOAN, [bi-mōn'], *v.t.* to lament, to bewail. [~OE. *bemænan*].

BEMOCK, [bi-mok'], *v.t.* to deride, to laugh at in mockery.

BEMOISTEN, [bi-mois'-ten], *v.t.* to moisten, to damp.

BEMOUTH, [bi-mowth'], *v.t.* to mouth, to express in an extravagant way.

BEMUDDLE, [bi-mudl'], *v.t.* to confuse, to stupefy, to muddle.

BEMUSED, [bi-mewzd'], *adj.* absorbed in musing; stupefied, dazed; as if in a trance.

BEN, [ben], *n.* (*bot.*) a British plant, *Silene inflata* or *Senecio jacobea*; the seed of the horse-radish tree, *Moringa.* [Arab. *ban*].

BENCH (1), [bench], *n.* a long wooden seat or form, often backless; a stone seat; a cross-seat in a boat; the work-table used by persons engaged in various forms of handicrafts; a seat where judges or magistrates sit in a court of justice; (*fig.*) the judge or magistrates in a court of law; a court of law or of enquiry; the dignity and rank of a judge or magistrate; a ledge left on the edge of a cutting in an earth-work for strengthening purposes; **b. of bishops,** the bishops of the Anglican Church who sit in the House of Lords; **King's B.** a court anciently presided over by the king in person, and accompanying the sovereign in his travels, now a division of the High Court of Justice. [OE. *benc*].

BENCH (2), [bench], *v.t. and i.* to provide with benches; to sit on a bench or seat of justice.

BENCHER, [ben'-cher], *n.* a senior member of an inn of court.

BENCH-MARK, [bench'-mahk'], *n.* (*surveying*) a surveyor's mark, in the form of an arrow with a horizontal bar across the top, used as a reference mark in determining altitudes.

BENCH-WARRANT, [bench'-wo'-rant], *n.* (*leg.*) a warrant issued by the judge.

BEND (1), [bend], *n.* a curve, anything not forming a straight line; a slight change of direction in a road; half a hide of the leather used for soles; (*naut.*) a kind of knot used by sailors; (*her.*) a diagonal band across a shield; (*pl.*) a kind of apoplexy affecting divers, and caused by too rapid changes of atmospheric pressure; (*naut.*) the curved sides of a ship; **b. sinister,** (*her.*) a diagonal band across a shield from upper left to right base to denote illegitimacy. [OE. *bend* a band].

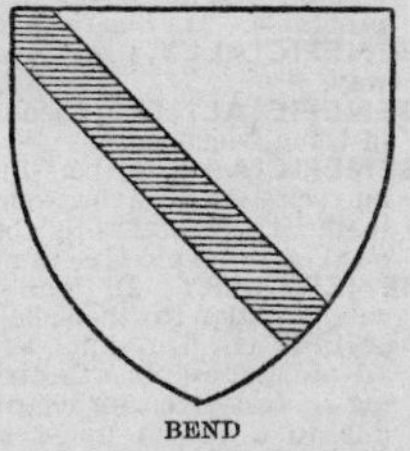

BEND

BEND (2), [bend], *v.t.* to alter the existing curve or direction of, to curve, to make crooked (of rather rigid material); to straighten something curved or crooked; to stoop, to arch (the eyebrows); to lower, to incline, to abase; (*fig.*) to direct one's thoughts to, to apply oneself closely to; (*naut.*) to fasten or bind a rope; *v.i.* to depart from an upright position; to be curved, to sag; (*pass. fig.*) to be determined upon, to have set one's mind upon; to be submissive to, to defer to. [OE. *bendan*].

BENDABLE, [bend'-abl], *adj.* able to be bent.

BENDER, [bend'-er], *n.* something that is used for bending; (*slang*) a sixpenny piece.

BENDIX-GEAR, [bend'-iks-gēer'], *n.(prot.)* (*motoring*) an automatic pinion on an electric starter.

BEND-LEATHER, [bend'-leTH'-er], *n.* the thickest kind of leather used for making soles.

BENDLET, [bend'-let], *n.* (*her.*) a narrow bend. [OE. *bendelette*].

BENDY, [bend'-i], *adj.* (*her.*) having the field divided into an equal number of bends, alternately coloured. [OFr. *bendé*].

BENE (1), [ben'-i], *pref.* well. [L. *bene* well].

BENE (2), [ben'-i], *n.* the species of oil-plant, *Sesamum orientale.* [Unkn.].

BENEAPED, [bi-nēpt'], *adj.* (*naut.*) left high and dry by the ebb of a neap tide.

BENEATH (1), [bi-nēth'], *adv.* below, at a lower place, lower down; (*bibl.*) on earth. [OE. *beneothan*].

BENEATH (2), [bi-nēth'], *prep.* under, below, underneath; inferior to, lower than (in social position or merit); unworthy of, at the foot of. [*Prec.*].

BENEDICK, [ben'-i-dik], *n.* a confirmed bachelor who suddenly marries, a newly married man. [*Benedick,* a character in Shakespeare's *Much Ado About Nothing*].

BENEDICTINE (1), [ben'-i-dik'-tēn], *n.* a monk of an

order founded by St. Benedict; a liqueur prepared by the Benedictine monks. [St. *Benedict* (480-543)].

BENEDICTINE (2), [ben'-i-dik'-tēn], *adj.* relating to the order of monks founded by St. Benedict.

BENEDICTION, [ben-i-dik'-shun], *n.* a blessing, the act of blessing or giving thanks, the pronouncement of a blessing at the close of a church service; (*R.C.*) a service for the blessing of the people by the priest with the Blessed Sacrament; (*fig.*) the advantages or benefits of blessing. [L. *benedictio*].

BENEDICTIVE, [ben'-i-dik'-tiv], *adj.* expressing benediction.

BENEDICTORY, [ben'-i-dik'-ter-i], *adj.* benedictive. [MedL. *benedictorius*].

BENEFACTION, [ben'-i-fak'-shun], *n.* a good action, a generous deed, a benefit rendered; a gift to charity. [L. *benefactio*].

BENEFACTOR, [ben'-i-fak'-tor], *n.* one who performs a beneficial act, one who gives help, money or service. [L. *benefactor*].

BENEFACTORY, [ben'-i-fak'-ter-i], *adj.* conferring benefits upon. [MdL. *benefactorius*].

BENEFACTRESS, [ben'-i-fak'-tres], *n.* a female benefactor.

BENEFICE, [ben'-i-fis], *n.* an ecclesiastical living, a church endowed with a revenue for the purpose of maintaining divine service. [L. *beneficium* good deed].

BENEFICED, [ben'-i-fist], *adj.* appointed to a benefice.

BENEFICENCE, [ben-e'-fis-ents], *n.* the practice of doing good, practical kindness, good and generous deeds. [L. *beneficentia* active goodness].

BENEFICENT, [ben-e'-fis-ent], *adj.* charitable, doing good, kindly, munificent. [L. *beneficens*].

BENEFICENTLY, [ben-e'-fis-ent-li], *adv.* in beneficent fashion.

BENEFICIAL, [ben'-i-fish'-al], *adj.* doing good, helpful, useful, advantageous, providing benefits, profitable. [L. *beneficialis*].

BENEFICIALLY, [ben'-i-fish'-al-i], *adv.* in a beneficial way.

BENEFICIALNESS, [ben'-i-fish'-al-nes], *n.* the state of being beneficial.

BENEFICIARY (1), [ben'-i-fish'-er-i], *n.* one who holds an ecclesiastical living, one who acquires benefits or material advantages by the terms of a will or trust; (*leg.*) one who receives as a gift. [L. *beneficiarius*].

BENEFICIARY (2), [ben'-i-fish'-er-i], *adj.* held in subordination to others, held as a gift or benefice.

BENEFIT (1), [ben'-i-fit], *n.* a favour, generous action; advantage; a public theatrical performance or sporting contest given for charity; a pension or allowance due to a person under an insurance scheme; **b. society,** a Friendly Society whose funds are used for the alleviation of sick, aged or poor members; **b. of clergy,** the right to be tried by the ecclesiastical courts of justice, claimed by clerical delinquents, and later extended to all who could read a particular verse of Psalm 51; **sick b.,** monetary allowance paid to an indisposed member by a Friendly Society; **unemployment b.,** money paid weekly under certain conditions by the State to a person who is out of work. [AFr. *benfet* from L. *benefactum*].

BENEFIT (2), [ben'-i-fit], *v.t. and i.* to do good to, to improve, to be advantageous to; to profit from, to be improved (by), to derive advantage (from). [*Prec.*].

BENEVOLENCE, [ben-ev'-ol-ents], *n.* disposition to do good, goodwill, kind-heartedness; an act of kindness; (*hist.*) a tax, formerly levied by the kings of England, regarded as a forced gratuity. [L. *benevolentia* goodwill].

BENEVOLENT, [ben-ev'-ol-ent], *adj.* kind-hearted, doing good to others, charitable; **b. society,** a society whose funds are used for the relief of distressed members. [L. *bene volens* well-wishing].

BENEVOLENTLY, [ben-ev'-ol-ent-li], *adv.* in benevolent fashion.

BENGAL, [ben'-gawl'], *n.* thin silk-like material of various kinds, formerly exported from Bengal. [*Bengal*, a province in India].

BENGALESE, [ben'-gal-ēz], *n.*(*pl.*) natives of Bengal.

BENGALI (1), [ben-gawl'-i], *n.* a language spoken in Bengal; a native of Bengal.

BENGALI (2), [ben-gawl'-i], *adj.* pertaining to the people or language of Bengal.

BENGAL LIGHT, [ben'-gawl-līt'], *n.* a firework giving a steady continuous brightly-coloured flame.

BENGAL STRIPES, [ben'-gawl-strīps'], *n.* a cotton fabric with coloured stripes.

BENIGHT, [bi-nīt'], *v.i.* to overtake by night, to envelop in darkness, to obscure.

BENIGHTED, [bi-nīt'-id], *adj.* overtaken by night; ignorant, backward, uninformed.

BENIGN, [bi-nīn'], *adj.* gracious, gentle, good-natured, pleasant; (*med.*) non-virulent not malignant. [L. *benignus*].

BENIGNANT, [bi-nig'-nant], *adj.* gracious, favourable, good-natured.

BENIGNANTLY, [bi-nig'-nant-li], *adv.* in a benignant way.

BENIGNITY, [bi-nig'-ni-ti], *n.* the quality of being benignant. [OFr. *benignité* from L. *benignitas*].

BENIGNLY, [bi-nīn'-li], *adv.* in benign fashion.

BENIGNNESS, [bi-nīn'-nes], *n.* benignity.

BENISON, [ben'-i-son], *n.* blessing, benediction. [OFr. *beniçon* from L. *benedictio*].

BENITIER, [be-nēt'-i-ā], *n.* a stone vessel containing holy water, placed near the entrance of a Roman Catholic church. [Fr. from (*eau*) *bénite* blessed (water)].

BENITIER

BENJAMIN, [ben'-ja-min], *n.* benzoin; a kind of overcoat. [A corrupted form of BENZOIN].

BENJY, [ben'-ji], *n.* (*coll.*) a shallow broad-brimmed hard straw hat. [Unkn.].

BENNET, [ben'-et], *n.* (*bot.*) a yellow-flowered wild herb, *Geum urbanum*. [OFr. *herbe beneit* blessed grass].

BEN-NUT, [ben'-nut'], *n.* the nut of the horse-radish tree, which yields a cosmetic oil.

BENOTE, [bi-nōt'], *v.t.* to provide with full notes, to annotate.

BENT (1), [bent], *n.* a stiff, wiry, creeping grass; the withered stalks of this grass; a place covered with stiff, wiry grass, a heath. [OE. *beonet*].

BENT (2), [bent], *n.* inclination, aptitude, skill for, inherent ability at and interest for; **to the top of one's b.,** to the utmost extent. [BEND].

BENT (3), [bent], *adj.* curved, crooked, not straight.

BENT-GRASS, [bent'-grahs'], *n.* (*bot.*) bent, a grass of the genus *Agrostis*. [BENT (1)].

BENTHAMISM, [ben'-tha-mizm], *n.* the utilitarian philosophy expounded by Jeremy Bentham which stressed mass satisfaction in preference to individual happiness. [Jeremy *Bentham* (1748-1832)].

BENTHAMITE, [ben'-tha-mīt], *n.* a follower of Bentham.

BENTHOS, [ben'-thos], *n.* minute aquatic organisms at the bottom of the sea. [Gk. *benthos* sea-bottom].

BENTY, [bent'-i], *adj.* overgrown with bent.

BENUMB, [bi-num'], *v.t.* to make numb, to deprive of feeling; to render (the mind) incapable of feeling or acting.

BENUMBEDNESS, [bi-numd'-nes], *n.* state of being benumbed.

BENUMBMENT, [bi-num'-ment], *n.* the act or process of benumbing.

BENZENE, [ben'-zēn], *n.* (*chem.*) a colourless, vaporizable liquid hydrocarbon, C_6H_6, made by distillation from coal-tar. [BENZOIN].

BENZINE, [ben'-zēn], *n.* a colourless volatile liquid obtained from crude petroleum and used with petrol as fuel for internal combustion engines. [*Prec.*].

BENZOATE, [ben'-zō-āt], *n.* a salt of benzoic acid.

BENZOIC, [ben-zō'-ik], *adj.* relating to benzoin; **b. acid,** an acid obtained from gum-benzoin and also prepared from the hydrocarbon, toluene.

BENZOIN, [ben'-zō-in], *n.* a solid brittle resin obtained from the tree *Styrax Benzoin*, used as incense, as a cosmetic, and in pharmacy, gum-benjamin. [It. *benzoi*, Fr. *benjoin*, Arab. *lubanjawi* incense of Jawa].

BENZOL, [ben'-zol'], *n.* benzene.

BENZOLINE, [ben'-zo-lēn], *n.* benzine.

BENZOYL, [ben'-zoil], *n.* the radical of benzoic acid, obtained from the volatile oil of bitter-almonds.

BEPAINT, [bi-pānt'], *v.t.* to paint over.

BEPATCH, [bi-pach'], *v.t.* to cover, adorn or mend with patches.

BEPEARL, [bi-purl'], *v.t.* to cover or adorn with pearls.

BEPEPPER, [bi-pep'-er], *v.t.* to rain blows upon, to direct a shower of missiles at.

BEPESTER, [bi-pest'-er], *v.t.* to annoy or trouble persistently.

BEPINCH, [bi-pinch'], *v.t.* to cover or mark with pinches or bruises.

BEPITY, [bi-pit'-i], *v.t.* to pity greatly, to be sorry for.

BEPLASTER, [bi-plahst'-er], *v.t.* to cover heavily with plaster.
BEPLUME, [bi-ploōm'], *v.t.* to cover or adorn with plumes.
BEPOMMEL, [bi-pum'-el], *v.t.* to belabour soundly.
BEPOWDER, [bi-powd'-er], *v.t.* to cover extravagantly with powder.
BEPRAISE, [bi-prāz'], *v.t.* to praise excessively.
BEPUDDLED, [bi-pudld'], *adj.* made muddy by being frequently trodden on.
BEPUFF, [bi-puf'], *v.t.* (*lit. and fig.*) to swell out; to praise excessively.
BEQUEATH, [bi-kwēTH], *v.t.* to leave (property or money) to a person by will, to transmit or hand down to posterity. [OE. *becwethan* declare].
BEQUEATHABLE, [bi-kwēTH'-abl], *adj.* able to be bequeathed.
BEQUEATHAL, [bi-kwēTH'-al], *n.* bequeathment.
BEQUEATHER, [bi-kwēTH'-er], *n.* a person who bequeaths.
BEQUEATHMENT, [bi-kwēTH'-ment], *n.* the act of bequeathing, that which is bequeathed.
BEQUEST, [bi-kwest'], *n.* something bequeathed, the act of bequeathing. [ME. *biqueste*].
BEQUOTE, [bi-kwōt'], *v.t.* to quote often.
BERATE, [bi-rāt], *v.t.* to chide vehemently, to scold, to rate soundly.
BERBER (1), [bur'-ber], *n.* a member of a tribe inhabiting North Africa; the language of this people. [Arab. *barbar* people of Barbary].
BERBER (2), [bur'-ber], *adj.* relating to the Berbers or their language.
BERBERIN, [bur'-ber-in], *n.* a bitter yellow substance obtained from the root of the barberry plant.
BERBERRY, see BARBERRY.
BERE†, [bēer], *n.* barley having six- or four-rowed ears. [OE. *bere* barley].
BEREAVE, [bi-rēv'], *v.t.* to deprive of, to make destitute of, to remove from; to suffer the loss by death of a friend or relative. [OE. *bereafian* to plunder].
BEREAVED, [bi-rēvd'], *adj.* deprived by death of a relative or friend.
BEREAVEMENT, [bi-rēv'-ment], *n.* the state of being bereaved.
BEREFT, [bi-reft'], *adj.* deprived of, suffering the loss of, destitute, devoid of. [*p.pt.* of BEREAVE].
BERET, [be'-rā], *n.* flat, round, peakless cap. [Fr. *béret*].
BERG, [burg], *n.* an iceberg. [(ICE)BERG].
BERGAMASK, see BERGOMASK.
BERGAMOT (1), BURGAMOT, [bur'-ga-mot], *n.* a kind of orange, *Citrus aurantium bergama*, producing an aromatic oil; the perfume or essence from this plant; a species of mint plant from which is prepared an oil of similar odour to the above; a coarse tapestry consisting of a mixture of flock and hair, and woven at Bergamo. [*Bergamo*, a place in North Italy].
BERGAMOT (2), [bur'-ga-mot], *n.* a kind of pear with a strong flavour. [Turk. *beg-armudi* prince's pear].
BERGANDER†, [bur'-gand-er], *n.* a bird allied to duck and goose, the sheldrake, *Tadorna cornuta*. [Uncert.].
BERGMANNITE, [burg'-man-īt], *n.* a mineral found in Norway, a species of natrolite. [J. *Bergmann*, a mineralogist].
BERGMEHL, [burg'-māl], *n.* (*geol.*) a fine, powdery freshwater deposit formed from the cell-walls of diatoms. [Germ. *berg* rock and *mehl* flour].
BERGOMASK, BERGAMASK, [burg'-ō-mahsk], *n.* a rustic dance; a citizen of Bergamo in North Italy. [It. *bergamasco* pertaining to Bergamo].
BERGYLT, [bur'-gilt], *n.* a northern fish related to the gurnards, of a bright orange-red colour, the Norway haddock. [Unkn.].
BERHYME, [bi-rīm], *v.t.* to write rhymes about, to celebrate in rhymed verse.
BERI-BERI, [be'-ri-be'-ri], *n.* (*med.*) a disease due to the lack of vitamin B. [Singhalese *beri* weakness].
BERLIN†, [bur-lin'], *n.* a four-wheeled carriage with an enclosed front part for two persons and a covered back seat for servants; **b. wool,** variegated wool. [*Berlin*, capital of Germany].
BERLIN BLACK, [bur'-lin-blak'], *n.* a dull black carbon paint.
BERLIN IRON, [bur'-lin-īern'], *n.* an easily moulded fusible iron containing phosphorus.
BERM, [burm], *n.* (*fort.*) a ledge, a level space a few feet wide between the outside slope of a rampart and the interior slope of the ditch. [Fr. *berme* ledge].
BERNACLE, see BARNACLE.
BERNARDINE (1), [bur'-nah-dēn], *n.* a monk of the Cistercian order, founded by St. Bernard of Clairvaux; a Trappist.
BERNARDINE (2), [bur'-nah-dēn], *adj.* relating to the order of monks founded by St. Bernard. [St. *Bernard* of Clairvaux (1090-1153)].
BERNICLE, [burn'-ikl], *n.* the barnacle-goose. [BARNACLE].
BERNOUSE, [burn-oōs'], *n.* a loose mantle worn by Arabs. [BURNOUSE].
BEROE, [be'-rō-i], *n.* (*zool.*) a genus of small globular, transparent, phosphorescent, marine animals. [Gk. *Beroe* daughter of Oceanus].
BERRIED, [be'-rid], *adj.* having berries.
BERRY (1), [be'-ri], *n.* the small spherical pulpy fruit of certain trees; (*bot.*) a fleshy fruit containing no hard parts except the seed; the eggs in the roe of certain fish. [OE. *berig*].
BERRY (2), [be'-ri], *v.i.* to bear or produce berries.
BERRY-BEARING, [be'-ri-bāer'-ing], *adj.* yielding berries.
BERSAGLIERI, [bāer'-sahl-yāer'-i], *n.(pl.)* a troop of Italian light-infantry or sharp-shooters. [It. *bersaglieri*].
BERSERK (1), BERSERKER, [bāer'-sahk(er)], *n.* an ancient Scandinavian warrior who in sudden fits of fury fought with terrific energy, often discarding his armour. [OIcel. *berserkr* bear-shirt].
BERSERK (2), [bāer'-sahk], *adj. and adv.* not wearing armour. [*Prec.*].
BERTH (1), [burth], *n.* a place in which a ship may be moored or swing at anchor; sufficient sea-room in which to manoeuvre; a sleeping-place in a ship or in other vehicles of transport, any lodging or sleeping place; employment on board ship; any post or situation of employment; **to give a wide b. to,** to avoid. [Unkn.].
BERTH (2), [burth], *v.t. and i.* to anchor, to bring a ship into a berth; to distribute berths or accommodate persons in berths; to settle a person in employment. [Unkn.].
BERTHA, [bur'-tha], *n.* a wide lace collar on a low-necked dress. [*Bertha*, a woman's name].
BERTHAGE, [burth'-ij], *n.* fees paid for berthing a ship, the berth provided.
BERTHING, [burth'-ing], *n.* (*naut.*) the raised projecting portion of a ship's sides, the bulwark.
BERTHOLLETIA, [burt'-ol-ēsh'-a], *n.* (*bot.*) a South American tree, a species of *Myrtaceae*, which yields the Brazil nut. [*Berthollet* (1748-1822), a famous French chemist].
BERTRAM†, [bur'-tram], *n.* (*bot.*) the bastard pellitory, a plant of the genus *Anacyclus*. [Germ. *berchtram* from Gk. *purethon*].
BERYL, [be'-ril], *n.* a pale green precious stone. [Gk. *berullos*].
BERYLLINE, [be'-ril-īn], *adj.* like beryl.
BERYLLIUM, [be-ril'-i-um], *n.* a metal found in beryl and certain other minerals, the element whose symbol is Be. [BERYL].
BESAINT, [bi-sānt'], *v.t.* to make into a saint.
BESANT, see BEZANT.
BESAYLE, [be-sāl'], *n.* (*leg.*) a great-grandfather. [OFr. *besayel*].
BESBOZHNIK, [bez-bozh'-nik], *n.* a member of the League of the Godless in Soviet Russia. [Russ. *bez* without and *bog* god].
BESCRAWL, [bi-skrawl'], *v.t.* to scribble all over.
BESCREEN, [bi-skrēn'], *v.t.* to screen, to shelter, to hide.
BESCRIBBLE, [bi-skribl'], *v.t.* to scribble all over.
BESEECH, [bi-sēch'], *v.t.* to beg, to pray to, to implore. [ME. *besechen*].
BESEECHER, [bi-sēch'-er], *n.* one who beseeches.
BESEECHING, [bi-sēch'-ing], *adj.* that beseeches or implores.
BESEECHINGLY, [bi-sēch'-ing-li], *adv.* in beseeching fashion.
BESEEM, [bi-sēm'], *v.t.* to become, to suit, to befit, to be worthy of, to be appropriate. [ME. *besemen*].
BESEEMING, [bi-sēm'-ing], *adj.* becoming.
BESEEMINGLY, [bi-sēm'-ing-li], *adv.* in a beseeming way.
BESEEMINGNESS, [bi-sēm'-ing-nes], *n.* the quality of being beseeming.
BESEEMLY, [bi-sēm'-li], *adj.* beseeming.
BESET, (besetting, beset), [bi-set'], *v.t.* to surround, to encompass, to press from all sides, to harass, perplex; (*pass.*) to be set round with, to be adorned with; to be fraught with, to be assailed with. [OE. *besettan*].

BESETMENT, [bi-set'-ment], *n.* the condition of being beset; a personal failing.

BESETTING, [bi-set'-ing], *adj.* that which besets, continually present and pressing.

BESHADOW, [bi-shad'-ō], *v.t.* to throw a shadow on, to overshadow.

BESHAME, [bi-shām'], *v.t.* to cause to be ashamed.

BESHMET, [besh'-met], *n.* grapes boiled down into a pulpy mass resembling honey. [Turk. *beshmet*].

BESHREW†, [bi-shroo'], *v.t.* to abuse; **b. thee,** may evil befall you! [ME. *beschrewen* to deprave].

BESHROUDED, [bi-shrowd'-id], *adj.* covered over as with a shroud.

BESIDE, [bi-sīd'], *prep.* near by, close by; alongside, by the side of; equal with, on a level with; in addition to; apart from, irrelevant to distinct from; **to be b. oneself,** to allow one's feelings to get out of hand. [OE. *be sidan*].

BESIDERY, [bi-sīd'-er-i], *n.* a kind of pear. [Unkn.].

BESIDES (1), [bi-sīdz'], *adv.* over and above, in addition; moreover, furthermore. [ME. *bisides*].

BESIDES (2), [bi-sīdz'], *prep.* in addition to, except, other than. [*Prec.*].

BESIEGE, [bi-sēj'], *v.t.* (*milit.*) to lay siege to; (*fig.*) to press upon, to crowd round, to hem in. [ME. *besegen*].

BESIEGEMENT, [bi-sēj'-ment], *n.* act of besieging, the state of being besieged.

BESIEGER, [bi-sēj'-er], *n.* one who besieges.

BESIEGING, [bi-sēj'-ing], *adj.* laying siege to.

BESIEGINGLY, [bi-sēj'-ing-li], *adv.* in a besieging fashion.

BESIGH, [be-sī'], *v.t.* to sigh over.

BESILVER, [bi-sil'-ver], *v.t.* to cover over with silver.

BESIT†, **(besat, besitting),** [bi-sit'], *v.t.* to besiege; to fit, suit. [OE. *besittan*].

BESLAVE, [bi-slāv'], *v.t.* to enslave, to call a person a slave.

BESLAVER, [bi-slav'-er], *v.t.* to slaver all over; (*fig.*) to praise and flatter fulsomely.

BESLIME, [bi-slīm'], *v.t.* to daub with slime; to befoul.

BESLOBBER, [bi-slob'-er], *v.t.* to slaver over; (*fig.*) to praise excessively, to embrace effusively.

BESMEAR, [bi-smēer'], *v.t.* to daub, to smear over, to soil; (*fig.*) to defile. [OE. *besmerwan*].

BESMIRCH, [bi-smurch'], *v.t.* to discolour, to soil, to darken; (*fig.*) to cast a stain upon, to blot.

BESMOKE, [bi-smōk'], *v.t.* to make dirty with smoke.

BESMUT, **(besmutting, besmutted),** [bi-smut'], *v.t.* to cover with smuts.

BESNOWED, [bi-snōd'], *adj.* snowed under. [OE. *besniwian* to snow].

BESNUFF, [bi-snuf'], *v.t.* to soil with snuff.

BESOIL, [bi-soil'], *v.t.* to soil, to make dirty, to defile. [ME. *besoilen*].

BESOM, [bez'-um, bēz'-um], *n.* a gardener's broom made of slender twigs bound to a long handle; (*coll.*) a hag, a worthless woman. [OE. *besma*].

BESOT, **(besotting, besotted),** [bi-sot'], *v.t.* to infatuate, to make a fool or sot of.

BESOTTED, [bi-sot'-id], *adj.* infatuated, stupid; stupefied as with drink, in a state of continual intoxication.

BESOTTEDLY, [bi-sot'-id-li], *adv.* in a besotted fashion.

BESOTTEDNESS, [bi-sot'-id-nes], *n.* the condition of being besotted.

BESOTTINGLY, [bi-sot'-ing-li], *adv.* so as to besot.

BESOUGHT, [bi-sawt'], *pret. and p.pt.* of BESEECH. [OE. *besohte*].

BESOULED, [bi-sōld'], *adj.* having a soul.

BESPANGLE, [bi-spangl'], *v.t.* to adorn with spangles.

BESPATTER, [bi-spat'-er], *v.t.* to cover or soil with splashes of mud, dirt, etc.; (*fig.*) to besmirch, abuse.

BESOM

BESPEAK, **(bespoke, bespoken),** [bi-spēk'], *v.t.* to speak for or engage beforehand, to order or reserve in advance, to claim; to betoken. [OE. *besprecan*].

BESPEAKER, [bi-spēk-er], *n.* a person who bespeaks.

BESPECKLE, [bi-spekl'], *v.t.* to cover with speckles or spots.

BESPECTACLED, [bi-spek'-takld], *adj.* having spectacles on.

BESPEED, [bi-spēd'], *v.t.* to hurry on with all speed.

BESPEW, [bi-spew'], *v.t.* to cover or soil with vomit.

BESPICE, [bi-spīs'], *v.t.* to flavour with spices or drugs.

BESPIT, **(bespitting, bespat),** [bi-spit'], *v.t.* to spit upon, to pollute with spittle.

BESPOKE, [bi-spōk'], *adj.* made to order. [BESPEAK].

BESPOT, **(bespotting, bespotted),** [bi-spot'], *v.t.* to mark or cover with spots. [ME. *bespotten*].

BESPREAD, [bi-spred'], *v.t.* to spread over. [ME. *bespreden*].

BESPRENT, [bi-sprent'], *adj.* (*poet.*) sprinkled over, scattered with. [ME. *bespreynt, p.pt.* of *besprengen* besprinkle].

BESPRINKLE, [bi-sprinkl'], *v.t.* to sprinkle on, to strew with, to scatter over. [ME. *besprengen*].

BESSEMER, [bés'-i-mer], *n. and adj.* a process of making steel by passing air through molten iron. [Sir H. *Bessemer* (1813-1898), the inventor].

BEST (1), [best], *n.* that which is in quality superior to all others; (*coll.*) the experts, the acknowledged superiors; **all for the b.,** to one's ultimate advantage; **for the b.,** with the best intentions; **to have the b. of it,** to win, to prove superior; **to make the b. of,** to derive as much benefit as possible from; **to the b. of,** to the utmost extent of; **to be at one's b.,** to excel oneself; **to come off second b.,** to lose; **to give someone b.,** to admit someone's superiority.

BEST (2), [best], *adj.* (*superl. of* GOOD *and* WELL), good or excellent in the highest degree, unsurpassed in quality, most advantageous, suitable or appropriate, greatest, of most value or merit, unequalled; largest; **b. man,** the chief groomsman at a wedding. [OE. *betst*].

BEST (3), [best], *adv.* to the highest degree, in the most excellent way or manner; to an unsurpassed extent, above all others; **we had b.,** it would be most advantageous for us to, we ought to.

BEST (4), [best], *v.t.* to get the better of, to overcome. [BEST (2)].

BESTAIN, [bi-stān'], *v.t* to mark or cover with stains.

BESTEAD, [bi-sted'], *adj.* beset, treated, placed. [ME. *bestad, p.pt.* of *besteden* to place].

BESTIAL (1), [best'-i-al], *n.* (*Scots leg.*) cattle. [L. *bestialia*].

BESTIAL (2), [best'-i-al], *adj.* like a beast; brutal, beastly, depraved; obscene, sexually unnatural. [L. *bestialis*].

BESTIALITY, [best'-i-al'-it-i], *n.* the quality of being bestial; (*leg.*) unnatural sexual intercourse between a human being and an animal.

BESTIALIZE, [best'-i-al-īz'], *v.t.* to make bestial.

BESTIALLY, [best'-i-al-i], *adv.* in a bestial manner.

BESTIARIAN, [best'-i-āer'-i-an], *n.* one who is opposed to vivisection.

BESTIARY, [best'-i-er-i], *n.* a medieval collection of animal stories with allegorical and religious explanations. [MedL. *bestiarium*].

BESTICK, **(bestuck),** [bi-stik'], *v.t.* to stick over or on.

BESTIR, **(bestirring, bestirred),** [bi-stur'], *v. reflex.* to rouse oneself to vigorous activity. [OE. *bestyrian* to pile up].

BESTOW, [bi-stō'], *v.t.* to put in a certain place, to deposit; to give, to confer ceremoniously, to award. [ME. *bestowen* to place].

BESTOWAL, [bi-stō'-al], *n.* the act or ceremony of bestowing.

BESTOWER, [bi-stō'-er], *n.* a person who bestows.

BESTOWMENT, [bi-stō'-ment], *n.* the act of bestowing; that which is bestowed.

BESTRADDLE, [bi-stradl'], *v.t.* to bestride.

BESTREAK, [bi-strēk'], *v.t.* to mark or cover with streaks.

BESTREW, [bi-strōō'], *v.t.* to scatter, to scatter over with, to litter up with. [OE. *bestreowian*].

BESTRIDE, **(bestrode, bestrid, bestridden),** [bi-strīd'], *v.t.* to stand or sit with the legs on either side of anything; to mount (a horse); to extend or stretch across, to span; to stride over. [OE. *bestridan*].

BEST-SELLER, [best'-sel'-er], *n.* a book which sells in abnormally large quantities.

BESTUCK, [bi-stuk'], *adj.* pierced through in many places.

BESTUD, **(bestudding, bestudded),** [bi-stud'], *v.t.* to ornament with studs or bosses.

BET (1), [bet], *n.* a wager, the supporting of one's opinion upon some past or future event against that of another, by depositing or staking a sum of money to be forfeited to the winner by the loser; the amount wagered.

BET (2), [bet], *v. t. and i.* to wager on an event, to indulge in betting, to make a bet; **I b., I'll b.,** (*coll.*) it is my opinion. [Unkn.].

BETAIL, [bi-tāl'], *v.t.* to furnish with or to deprive of a tail.

BETAINE, [bē'-tān], *n.* the alkaloid obtained from beet. [L. *beta* beet].

BETAKE, [bi-tāk'], *v.reflex.* to depart, to make one's way, to go. [ME. *betaken* to entrust].
BETA-RAYS, [bē'-ta-rāz], *n.(pl.)* a flow of electrons from radio-active substances such as radium. [Gk. *beta* (a letter of the alphabet) and RAY].
BETEARED, [bi-tēerd'], *adj.* wet with tears, full of tears.
BETEL, [bētl], *n.* (*bot.*) an East Indian variety of pepper, *Piper Betél*, the leaves of which are used to contain a piece of betel-nut and lime, chewed by natives; **b.-nut**, the nut of the fruit of the areca-palm found in the East Indies, so named from being chewed with betel leaf. [Port. *betle*, Malayan *vettila*].
BETE-NOIRE, bête noire, [bāt'-nwah(r)'], *n.* a bugbear, a pet aversion, a person or thing especially disliked. [Fr. *bête-noire*].
BETHANK, [bi-thangk'], *v.t.* to thank profusely.
BETHEL, [beth'-el'], *n.* a spot or place for divine worship; a Nonconformist chapel; a chapel for seamen. [Heb. *beth-el* house of God].
BETHINK, [bi-thingk'], *v. reflex.* to recall, to recollect, to remember; to consider, to reflect. [OE. *bithencan* consider].
BETHRAL, (**bethralling, bethralled**), [bi-thrawl'], *v.t.* to enslave, make captive.
BETHUMB, [bi-thum'], *v.t.* to mark or crease with the thumb.
BETHUMP, [bi-thump'], *v.t.* to beat soundly, to thrash.
BETHWACK, [bi-thwak'], *v.t.* to thrash soundly.
BETIDE, [bi-tīd'], *v.t. and i.* to happen to, to occur to, to take place, to come about. [ME. *bitiden* happen].
BETIMES, [bi-tīmz'], *adv.* in good time, early in the morning; soon, quickly. [ME. *betimes*].
BETISE, bêtise, [bet-ēz'], *n.* nonsense, foolishness. [Fr. *bêtise*].
BETITLE, [bi-tītl'], *v.t.* to bestow a title upon.
BETOKEN, [bi-tōkn'], *v.t.* to signify, to be a sign of, to foreshadow, to augur. [ME. *bitacnien*].
BETON, [bet'-on], *n.* a concrete made from sand, lime and gravel. [Fr. *béton* concrete].
BETONGUE, [bi-tung'], *v.t.* to chide, dispute with.
BETONY, [bet'-on-i], *n.* (*bot.*) a plant of the genus *Stachys*, with spiked purple flowers. [LL. *betonia*].
BETOOK, [bi-to͝ok'], *pret.* of BETAKE.
BETORN, [bi-tawn'], *adj.* torn in pieces, tattered.
BETOSS, [bi-tos'], *v.t.* to toss, throw about.
BETRAP, [bi-trap'], *v.t.* to ensnare, to trap. [OE. *betræppan*].
BETRAY, [bi-trā'], *v.t.* to deliver treacherously or by breach of trust into the hands of an enemy; to be unfaithful to, to deal falsely with, to reveal what has been entrusted as a secret; to seduce, to lead astray; to reveal unconsciously or inadvertently; to show signs of, to display. [ME. *betraien*].
BETRAYAL, [bi-trā-al], *n.* the act of betraying, a breach of trust or confidence, a deceitful act.
BETRAYER, [bi-trā'-er], *n.* a traitor; a person who betrays.
BETREAD, (**betrod, betrodden**), [bi-tred'], *v.t.* to tread on or over. [ME. *bitreden*].
BETRIM, (**betrimming, betrimmed**), [bi-trim'], *v.t.* to set out in order; to deck.
BETROTH, (**betroths**), [bi-trōTH'], *v.t.* to affiance; to promise to marry; (*pass.*) to become engaged to be married. [ME. *betrewthien*].
BETROTHAL, [bi-trōTH'-al], *n.* the act of being betrothed.
BETROTHED, [bi-trōTHd'], *n.* a person engaged to be married.
BETROTHMENT, [bi-trōTH'-ment], *n.* betrothal.
BETTER (1), [bet'-er], *n.* (usually *pl.*) one superior in quality, rank or merit; **to get the b. of**, to overcome, to prove superior, to defeat; **to think the b. of**, to have a higher opinion of.
BETTER (2), BETTOR, [bet'-er], *n.* a person who bets. [BET (2)].
BETTER (3), [bet'-er], *adj.* (*comp. of* GOOD *and* WELL), good or excellent in a greater degree than another, superior to, more desirable, of higher merit, worth or rank; more efficient, useful, suitable, advantageous or appropriate; larger, chief, greater; improved in health, well again; **b. half**, (*coll.*) wife; **to have seen b. days**, to have become relatively poor, to be old and shabby; **to think b. of (it)**, to decide not to do (a thing). [OE. *betera*].
BETTER (4), [bet'-er], *adv.* (*comp. of* WELL), in a superior way, to a higher degree; again and again, frequently, repeatedly; **to know b. than to**, not to be so stupid as to; **to think b. of**, to change one's mind or intentions; **b. off**, in better circumstances, more favourably situated; **to go one b. than**, to surpass; **to feel b.**, to have recovered from an illness or indisposition; **I had b.**, I ought to. [OE. *bet* and *Prec.*].
BETTER (5), [bet'-er], *v.t. and i.* to make better, improve, ameliorate.
BETTERMENT, [bet'-er-ment], *n.* the act of bettering, improvement.
BETTERMOST, [bet'-er-mōst], *adj.* best.
BETTERNESS, [bet'-er-nes], *n.* the quality of being better, superiority.
BETTING, [bet'-ing], *n.* the making of bets; the allocation of money wagered as bets.
BETTONG, [bet'-ong], *n.* a species of kangaroo rat, *Hypsiprymnus setosus*. [Maori *bettong*].
BETTOR, see BETTER (2).
BETTY, [bet'-i], *n.* an instrument used for breaking open doors, a jemmy. [*Betty*, a woman's name].

BETTONG

BETULINE, [bet'-ew-lēn], *n.* the plant, birch camphor. [L. *betula* birch].
BETUMBLED, [bi-tumbld'], *adj.* rolled about; disordered, upset.
BETUTOR, [bi-tew'-tor], *v.t.* to instruct, to tutor, to teach.
BETWEEN (1), [bi-twēn'], *adv.* midway, at certain intervals.
BETWEEN (2), [bi-twēn'], *prep.* lying in an intermediary position in relation to, near to without the interposition of one of the objects specified; with something specified placed on either side of; *with a specified temporal or spatial unit or period occurring or situated on either side of a unit*; *implying a choice of two or more alternatives*; *implying a condition related to two stated extremes within which it lies*; *extending from one stated place to another, implying communication from one stated place to another*; *expressing a relationship of two things whether of difference, similarity, separation or connexion*; restricted to and shared by, amongst; by the combined efforts of; **b. two fires**, torn by two opposing forces or desires; **b. the devil and the deep blue sea**, faced with no favourable alternative, vulnerable spot; **b. you and me**, in confidence. [OE. *betweonan*].
BETWEEN-DECKS, [bi-twēn'-deks'], *adv.* between two decks; below deck.
BETWEEN-MAID, [bi-twēn'-mād'], *n.* a servant who helps other servants.
BETWEEN-WHILES, [bi-twēn'-whīlz'], *adv.* during the intervals.
BETWIXT, [bi-twikst'], *prep. and adv.* between. [OE. *be-tweox*].
BEUDANTITE, [bew'-dan-tīt], *n.* (*min.*) a crystalline mineral containing iron, lead and silica. [*Beudant*, a French mineralogist].
BEVEL (1), [bev'-el], *n.* an oblique or sloping-edge, an edge that does not form a right-angle to the surface; an instrument consisting of a fixed arm with a movable tongue or square which can be set to form any angle with the fixed arm, used for marking out angles. [OFr. *bevel*].
BEVEL (2), BEVILE, [bev'-el], *adj.* having a sloping edge which does not form a right-angle; (*her.*) a bevilled bar; **b. angle**, an angle other than a right-angle; **b. wheel**, a gear wheel whose teeth are set at an angle to the shaft; **b. edge**, the sloping edge of a chisel or other similar cutting tool; **b. joint**, an oblique joint formed by two bevelled edges of wood being fastened together.
BEVEL (3), (**bevelling, bevelled**), [bev'-el], *v.t. and i.* to cut to a bevel angle, to provide with a bevel edge; to have an edge which does not form a right-angle.
BEVEL-GEAR, [bev'-el-gēer'], *n.* a system of engaging bevel wheels to transmit motion from one shaft to another set at an angle to the first shaft; a bevel wheel.
BEVELLED, [bev'-eld], *adj.* having a bevel edge.
BEVELLING, [bev'-el-ing], *n.* the cutting of the edge of timber to an oblique or bevel angle; a bevelled edge.
BEVELMENT, [bev'-el-ment], *n.* (*min.*) the cutting away of the edge of a crystal, so that in place of the original edge there are two similar planes, each forming an equal angle with the adjacent faces.
BEVERAGE, [bev'-er-ij], *n.* a drink, a liquid that can be drunk. [OFr. *bevraige*].
BEVILE, see BEVEL.

BEVILLED, [bev'-eld], *adj.* (*her.*) having a bar in which one side running parallel to the other is continued at a greater distance from, but still parallel to the first by the introduction of two acute angles. [BEVEL].

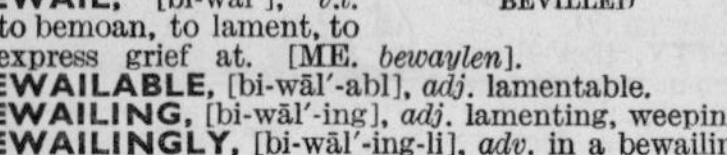

BEVILLED

BEVILWAYS, [bev'-il-wāz'], *adv.* (*her.*) shown as bevilled.
BEVY, [bev'-i], *n.* a group of roes, quails or larks; a company, assembly or gathering, *esp.* of girls; (*fig.*) a collection, a group of objects. [Fr. *bevée*].
BEWAIL, [bi-wāl'], *v.t.* to bemoan, to lament, to express grief at. [ME. *bewaylen*].
BEWAILABLE, [bi-wāl'-abl], *adj.* lamentable.
BEWAILING, [bi-wāl'-ing], *adj.* lamenting, weeping.
BEWAILINGLY, [bi-wāl'-ing-li], *adv.* in a bewailing way.
BEWAILMENT, [bi-wāl'-ment], *n.* the act of bewailing.
BEWARE, [bi-wāer'], *v.t. and i.* to guard against, to take care about, to regard with caution, to be wary of. [OE. *bewarian* to guard over].
BEWEEP, [bi-wēp], *v.t.* to weep over; to moisten with tears. [OE. *beweepan*].
BEWELTERED, [bi-welt'-erd], *adj.* gory, soaked in blood.
BEWET (1), BEWIT, [bew'-it], *n.* the leather strap fastening a bell to a hawk's leg. [OFr. *beuette*, *dim.* of *beue* collar].
BEWET (2), (**bewetting, bewetted**), [bi-wet'], *v.t.* to set, to moisten, to damp.
BEWILDER, [bi-wil'-der], *v.t.* to puzzle, to baffle, to perplex, to confuse utterly. [ME. *bewilden* to lead into the wilderness].
BEWILDERINGLY, [be-wil'-der-ing-li], *adv.* in bewildering fashion.
BEWILDERMENT, [bi-wil'-der-ment], *n.* the condition of being bewildered; act of bewildering.
BEWITCH, [bi-wich'], *v.t.* to lay under a spell of magic or witchcraft; (*fig.*) to charm, to allure. [ME. *biwicchen*].
BEWITCHEDNESS, [bi-wicht'-nes], *n.* the condition of being bewitched.
BEWITCHERY, [bi-wich'-er-i], *n.* the power to bewitch; resistless fascination, enchantment.
BEWITCHFUL, [bi-wich'-fool], *adj.* bewitching, enchanting.
BEWITCHING, [bi-wich'-ing], *adj.* fascinating, alluring.
BEWITCHINGLY, [bi-wich'-ing-li], *adv.* in bewitching fashion.
BEWITCHINGNESS, [bi-wich'-ing-nes], *n.* bewitchery.
BEWITCHMENT, [bi-wich'-ment], *n.* bewitchery.
BEWONDERED†, [bi-wund'-erd], *adj.* astonished, full of amazement and admiration.
BEWRAP†, (**bewrapping, bewrapped**), [bi-rap'], *v.t.* to wrap up, to enclose; (*fig.*) to envelop, to conceal. [ME. *bewrappen*].
BEWRAY, [bi-rā'], *v.t.* to disclose, to betray unintentionally. [ME. *biwreyen* reveal].
BEWRAYER, [bi-rā'-er], *n.* a revealer of secrets.
BEWRAYINGLY, [bi-rā'-ing-li], *adv.* in a bewraying manner.
BEWRAYMENT, [bi-rā'-ment], *n.* the act of bewraying.
BEWROUGHT, [bi-rawt'], *adj.* worked round, adorned with embroidery or fancy-work. [OE. *beworhte*, *p.pt.* of *bewyrcan* to work round].
BEY, [bā], *n.* a Turkish governor, a ruler over a sanjak; a major serving in Egypt; a person of high rank. [Turk. *beg* lord].
BEYLIK, [bā'-lik], *n.* a province or district governed by a bey. [Turk. *beglik*].
BEYOND (1), [bi-yond'], *n.* the future life; the unknown or unexplored.
BEYOND (2), [bi-yond'], *adv.* on the farther side, at a distance. [OE. *begeondan* beyond].
BEYOND (3), [bi-yond'], *prep.* farther on than, past, on the far side of; later than; out of reach of, exceeding the range or limit of, surpassing; in addition to, more or greater than; except (*with negative*); **to be b. someone**, (*coll.*) to be incomprehensible to someone; **b. one's depth**, (*fig.*) too difficult to grasp. [OE. *begeondan*].
BEZAN, [bez'-an], *n.* a variety of cotton cloth made in Bengal. [Unkn.].
BEZANT, BESANT, [bez'-ant], *n.* a gold coin formerly current in Europe, varying in value from ten to twenty shillings; (*her.*) such a coin used as an heraldic charge, a plain circular figure of gold. [OFr. *besan* from *Byzantium*, where first coined].
BEZ-ANTLER, [bā-ant-ler, bāz-ant'-ler], *n.* the tine of a deer's horn above the brow antler.
BEZEL, BEZIL, [bezl], *n.* the sloping cutting edge of a chisel or similar tool; the sloping facets of a cut gem, *esp.* the sloping facets adjacent to the large flat side on the upper surface of a gem; that part of a ring in which the stone is set; the groove into which the glass of a watch fits. [OFr. *bezel*].
BEZETTA, [bi-zet'-a], *n.* linen rags soaked in various colouring solutions and used as a dye or colouring agent. [It. *pezzetta*, *dim.* of *pezza* piece].
BEZIL, see BEZEL.
BEZIQUE, [be-zēk'], *n.* a game of cards for two or four persons, usually played with two packs of cards; a hand at this game containing the queen of spades and the knave of diamonds. [Fr. *bésique*].
BEZOAR, [be-zōer'], *n.* a hard concretion found in the stomach or intestines of certain animals, particularly ruminants, due to the formation of spherical layers of digested food around some foreign object; once considered to be an antitoxin. [Fr. *bezoar* from Pers. *padzhar* antidote].
BEZOARDIC (1), [be'-zō-ah'-dik], *n.* an antidote, a remedy.
BEZOARDIC (2), [be'-zō-ah'-dik], *adj.* pertaining to bezoar or to an antidote.
BEZONIAN, [bi-zōn-i-an], *n.* a beggar, a knave. [It. *bisogno* army recruit].
BHANG, BANG, BANGUE, [bang], *n.* Indian hemp, *Cannabis indica*; the leaves and small stalks of this, dried and used as an intoxicant or a sweetmeat; hashish. [Hind. *bhang*].
BHEESTIE, [bēst'-i], *n.* a Hindu servant who brings water for the family. [Urdu *bhisti* paradise].
BHEL, [bel], *n.* (*bot.*) the Bengal quince, *Aegle Marmelos*, the rind of which provides perfume and yellow dye. [Hind. *bhel*].
BHOOSA, [bōōs'-a], *n.* Indian fodder of broken husks, etc. [Hind. *bhusa*].
BI-, *pref.* two, twice, twofold; having two; lasting for or occurring every, two; (*chem.*) having twice the quantity of acid or base. [L. *bi(s)* twice].
BIACID, [bī-as'-id], *adj.* (*chem.*) combining in two different proportions with an acid. [BI and ACID].
BIANGULAR, [bī-ang'-gyōō-ler], *adj.* containing two angles. [BI and ANGULAR].
BIARTICULATE, [bī-ah-tik'-yōō-lāt], *adj.* possessing two joints. [BI and ARTICULATE].
BIAS (1), [bī'-as], *n.* a wedge-shaped piece of cloth, cut in a slanting direction across the texture; (*bowls*) the weighted or slightly elongated side of a bowl, which causes it to depart from a straight course when rolled; (*fig.*) a leaning in a particular direction, a partiality, a strong preference, a prejudice, an influence producing a marked inclination; **on the b.**, cut in a diagonal direction to the texture of the cloth or fabric. [Fr. *biais* oblique].
BIAS (2), [bī'-as], *v.t.* to provide with a bias, to cut with a bias; (*fig.*) to cause to incline or lean in a particular direction, to prejudice, to influence in a particular (often unfavourable) way.
BIASED, [bī'-ast], *adj.* partial, prejudiced, unfairly influenced, opinionated.
BIAURICULATE, [bī-aw-rik'-yōō-lat], *adj.* (*anat.*) possessing two auricles.
BIAXIAL, [bī-aks'-i-al], *adj.* possessing two axes.
BIB (1), [bib], *n.* a small piece of linen fastened under the chin of an infant when feeding, etc. [BIB (3)].
BIB (2), [bib], *n.* a fish of the cod family, the whiting pout. [Unkn.].
BIB (3), (**bibbing, bibbed**), [bib], *v.i.* to drink excessively, to tipple. [L. *bibere* to drink].
BIBACIOUS, [bi-bā'-shus], *adj.* fond of drinking. [L. *bibax*].
BIBASIC, [bī-bās'-ik], *adj.* (*chem.*) combining in two different proportions with a base. [BI and BASIC].
BIBBER, [bib'-er], *n.* a tippler, a person addicted to excessive drinking.
BIBBING, [bib'-ing], *n.* excessive drinking of intoxicating liquor tippling.
BIBBLE-BABBLE, [bibl-babl], *n.* prating, idle talk, foolish chatter.
BIBBS, [bibz], *n.(pl.)* (*naut.*) wooden brackets bolted

to the projections at the masthead to support the trestle-trees. [BIB (1)].

BIB-COCK, [bib'-kok'], *n.* a tap or valve with a bent nozzle.

BIBLE, [bībl], *n.* the collection of sacred and historical writings forming the body of belief of the Christian religion; (*fig.*) any sacred book; a book regarded as the ultimate authority on a subject; **B. oath,** a solemn oath sworn on the Bible; **B. societies,** societies formed for the distribution of the Bible in various languages. [Gk. *biblia* a collection of writings].

BIBLE-CLERK, [bībl'-klahk'], *n.* a scholarship-holder at All Souls' College, Oxford, who reads the lessons in chapel.

BIBLICAL, [bib'-lik-al], *adj.* pertaining to, contained in, or authorized by the Bible.

BIBLICALLY, [bib'-lik-al-i], *adv.* according to the Bible, in the manner of the Bible.

BIBLICIST, [bib'-li-sist], *n.* one who follows out literally the instruction of the Bible; a student of the Bible.

BIBLIO-, [bib'-li-ō], *pref.* pertaining to or referring to books. [Gk. *biblion* little book.]

BIBLIOGRAPHER, [bib'-li-og'-ra-fer], *n.* one skilled in bibliography.

BIBLIOGRAPHIC, [bib'-li-ō-graf'-ik], *adj.* pertaining to bibliography.

BIBLIOGRAPHICAL, [bib'-li-ō-graf'-ikl], *adj.* bibliographic.

BIBLIOGRAPHY, [bib'-li-og'-raf-i], *n.* the study of the history of books, their publication, printing, etc., as distinct from their subject matter; list of books or writings about a particular subject; the list of an author's works. [Gk. *bibliographia* writing of books].

BIBLIOLATER, [bib'-li-ol'-at-er], *n.* a biblicist.

BIBLIOLATRY, [bib'-li-ol'-at-ri], *n.* excessive respect for, or devotion to, the letter of the Holy Scriptures. [BIBLIO and Gk. *latreia* worship].

BIBLIOLOGICAL, [bib'-li-ō-loj'-ikl], *adj.* pertaining to bibliology.

BIBLIOLOGY, [bib'-li-ol'-oj-i], *n.* literature or doctrine relating to the Bible; bibliography. [BIBLIO and Gk. *logos* speech].

BIBLIOMANCY, [bib'-li-ō-man'-si], *n.* divination by interpretation of passages of Scripture opened at random. [BIBLIO and Gk. *manteia* divination].

BIBLIOMANIA, [bib'-li-ō-mān'-ia], *n.* extravagant zeal or love for book-collecting. [BIBLIO and MANIA].

BIBLIOMANIAC, [bib'-li-ō-mān'-i-ak], *n.* a rabid book-collector.

BIBLIOMANIACAL, [bib'-li-ō-mān'-i-akl], *adj.* obsessed by a passion for books.

BIBLIOMANIST, [bib'-li-ō'-man-ist], *n.* a bibliomaniac.

BIBLIOPEGY, [bib-li-op'-ej-i], *n.* the art of book-binding. [BIBLIO and Gk. *pegia* fixing].

BIBLIOPHIL(E), [bib'-li-ō-fil'], *n.* a lover or collector of books. [BIBLIO and Gk. *philos* lover].

BIBLIOPHILISM, [bib'-li-of'-il-izm], *n.* love of bibliography or of books.

BIBLIOPHILIST, [bib'-li-of'-il-ist], *n.* a bibliophile.

BIBLIOPHOBIA, [bib'-li-ō-fōb'-ia], *n.* a horror of books. [BIBLIO and Gk. *phobia* dread].

BIBLIOPOLE, [bib'-li-ō-pōl'], *n.* a dealer in books, a bookseller. [BIBLIO and Gk. *poles* merchant].

BIBLIOPOLIC, [bib'-li-ō-pol'-ik], *adj.* bibliopolical.

BIBLIOPOLICAL, [bib'-li-ō-pol'-ik-al], *adj.* pertaining to bookselling or booksellers.

BIBLIOPOLIST, [bib'-li-op'-ol-ist], *n.* a bookseller.

BIBLIOPOLY, [bib'-li-op'-ol-i], *n.* bookselling.

BIBLIOTHECA, [bib'-li-ō-thēk'-a], *n.* a library; a collection of books or writings. [L. *bibliotheca*].

BIBLIOTHECARY, [bib'-li-ō-thēk'-er-i], *n.* a librarian.

BIBLIST, [bib'-list, bī'-blist], *n.* one who knows or one who believes in the Bible.

BIBLUS, [bib'-lus], *n.* the papyrus or paper-reed, *Cyperus Papyrus*, used as writing material. [Gk. *biblos*].

BIBULOUS, [bib'-yōō-lus], *adj.* addicted to drink; slightly intoxicated; absorbent. [L. *bibulus*].

BIBULOUSLY, [bib'-yōō-lus-li], *adv.* in a bibulous way.

BICALCARATE, [bī'-kal'-ka-rāt], *adj.* provided with two spurs. [BI and L. *calcar* a spur].

BICAMERAL, [bī'-kam'-er-al], *adj.* (of legislative assemblies) composed of two chambers. [BI and L. *camera* chamber].

BICAPITATED, [bī'-kap'-i-tāt-id], *adj.* two-headed. [BI and L. *capitatus* having a head].

BICAPSULAR, [bī'-kap'-sew-lar], *adj.* (*bot.*) having two seed-capsules to a flower. [BI and L. *capsula* small box].

BICARBONATE, [bī'-kah'-bon-āt], *n.* (*chem.*) an acid salt of carbonic acid. [BI and CARBONATE].

BICARINATE, [bī'-ka'-rin-āt], *adj.* having two keels or ridges. [BI and L. *carinatus* having a keel].

BICARPELLARY, [bī'-kah-pel'-er-i], *adj.* possessing two carpels. [BI and L. *carpellum* fruit].

BICAUDAL, [bī'-kaw'-dal], *adj.* having two tails. [BI and L. *cauda* tail].

BICE, [bīs], *n.* a basic pigment used in painting. [Fr. *bis*].

BICENTENARY, [bī'-sen-tēn'-er-i], *n.* an anniversary at the end of two hundred years. [BI and CENTENARY].

BICENTENNIAL, [bī'-sen-ten'-i-al], *adj.* lasting two hundred years, happening every two hundred years.

BICEPHALOUS, [bī'-sef'-al-us], *adj.* having two heads. [BI and Gk. *kephale* head].

BICEPS, [bī'-seps], *n.* a muscle having two heads; the chief flexor muscle of the upper arm; the corresponding muscle in the leg. [L. *biceps* two-headed].

BICHLORIDE, [bī'-klaw'-rīd], *n.* (*chem.*) a compound having two equivalents of chlorine to one of a base. [BI and CHLORIDE].

BICHROMATE, [bī'-krōm'-āt], *n.* (*chem.*) a compound having two molecules of chromic acid to one of a base. [BI and CHROMATE].

BICIPITAL, [bī'-sip'-it-al], *adj.* (*anat.*) with two heads (as a muscle). [L. *bicipitus*].

BICIPITOUS, [bī-sip'-it-us], *adj.* bicipital.

BICKER (1), [bik'-er], *n.* a quarrel, skirmish.

BICKER (2), [bik'-er], *n.* a bowl for holding liquor, *esp.* of wood; a vessel made of wooden staves for holding porridge.

BICKER (3), [bik'-er], *v.i.* to quarrel, to dispute petulantly, to wrangle. [ME. *bikeren*].

BICKERING, [bik'-er-ing], *n.* quarrelling, squabbling, petty dispute, altercation.

BICKERN, [bik'-ern], *n.* an anvil with one, formerly two, beak-like ends. [L. *bicornus* two-horned].

BICKERN

BICONJUGATE, [bī-kon'-jōō-gat], *adj.* forking twice, paired twice. [BI and CONJUGATE].

BICORN, [bī'-kawn], *adj.* two-horned. [L. *bicornus*].

BICORNOUS, [bī'-kawn'-us], *adj.* (*bot.*) bicorn.

BICORPORAL, [bī'-kaw'-por-al], *adj.* with two bodies. [BI and CORPORAL].

BICRURAL, [bī'-krōō'-ral], *adj.* two-legged. [BI and L. *crus cruris* leg].

BICUSPID (1), [bī'-kus'-pid], *n.* a tooth with two fangs.

BICUSPID (2), [bī'-kus'-pid], *adj.* having two fangs. [BI and L. *cuspis cuspidis* point].

BICUSPIDATE, [bī'-kus'-pid-āt], *adj.* with two points or fangs.

BICYCLE, [bī'-sikl], *n.* a vehicle with two wheels in series propelled by rotating two pedals with the feet. [BI and Gk. *kuklos* wheel, circle].

BICYCLIST, [bī'-sik-list], *n.* a person who rides a bicycle.

BID (1), [bid], *n.* an offer of a sum of money for an article, as at an auction; (*cards*) an undertaking at certain card games to obtain a specified number of tricks.

BID (2), (bidding, bade, bidden), [bid], *v.t. and i.* to command, to order; to ask pressingly, to beg, to invite; to announce, to proclaim; to wish; to offer, to make an offer of a price at a sale or auction; (*cards*) to make a bid at certain card games; **to b. fair,** to appear likely. [OE. *biddan* to entreat, confused with *beodan* to offer, command].

BIDALE†, [bid'-āl], *n.* a feast at which an open invitation is given to persons to drink ale, and to contribute to the relief of a poor person for whom the feast is held.

BIDARKA, [bī-dah'-ka], *n.* a portable Eskimo canoe. [Eskimo *bidarka*].

BIDDABLE, [bid'-abl], *adj.* obedient, willing; (*cards*) that can be bid successfully.

BIDDER, [bid'-er], *n.* a person who bids.

BIDDERY, BIDRI, [bid'-ri], *n.* a rustless alloy composed of copper, lead, etc., used for Indian metalware. [*Bidar* a town in India].

BIDDING, [bid'-ing] *n.* command; request; offer; invitation; bids or offers of prices at an auction or at the opening of certain card games; **b. prayer,** an exhortation in which the congregation are directed to pray for a certain thing, and ending with the Lord's Prayer.

BIDDY, [bid'-i], *n.* †a fowl, a chicken; **red b.,** a harmful intoxicating drink containing methylated spirit. [Unkn.].

BIDE, [bīd], *v.i.* (*archaic*) to remain, to await, to endure. [OE. *bidan* await].

BIDENT, [bī'-dent], *n.* an implement having two prongs or forks. [BI and L. *dens dentis* tooth].

BIDENTAL, [bī'-dent'-al], *adj.* having two prongs or teeth.

BIDENTATE, [bī-dent'-at], *adj.* having two tooth-like projections.

BIDENTATED, [bī-dent'-āt-id], *adj.* bidentate.

BIDET, [bid-et', bi'-dā], *n.* a small horse formerly allowed to a trooper for carrying his baggage; a kind of sitz-bath. [Fr. *bidet*].

BIDIGITATE, [bī-dij'-it-āt], *adj.* having two fingers or two toes [BI and L. *digitus* finger].

BIDRI, see BIDDERY.

BIENNIAL (1), [bī-en'-i-al], *n.* a plant which does not flower until the second year. [L. *biennium* two years].

BIENNIAL (2), [bī-en'-i-al], *adj.* lasting for only two years; occurring once in two years. [*Prec.*].

BIENNIALLY, [bī'-en'-i-al-i], *adv.* once in two years; at two-yearly periods.

BIER, [bēer], *n.* a carriage or framework for conveying a corpse to its grave; (*fig.*) a grave, tomb. [OE. *bær* litter].

BIER-BALK, [bēer'-bawlk'], *n.* a strip of land in a field along which the dead may be borne to their graves.

BIESTINGS, BEASTINGS, [bēst'-ings], *n.* first milk yielded by a cow after calving. [OE. *bysting*].

BIFACIAL, [bī-fāsh'-al], *adj.* having two similar faces. [BI and FACIAL].

BIFARIOUS, [bī-fāer'-i-us], *adj.* double, twofold; (*bot.*) arranged or set out in double rows. [L. *bifarius*].

BIFARIOUSLY, [bī-fāer'-i-us-li], *adv.* in a bifarious manner.

BIFEROUS, [bi'-fer-us], *adj.* producing fruit or flowers twice a year. [BI and L. *ferre* to bear].

BIFF (1), [bif], *n.* (*slang*) a heavy blow, a violent smack. [Symbolic].

BIFF (2), [bif], *v.t.* (*slang*) to strike heavily, to administer a violent blow to.

BIFFIN, [bif'-in], *n.* a dried variety of cooking apple of the colour of beef; such an apple baked in the oven and made flat in the form of a cake. [BEEF].

BIFID, [bī'-fid], *adj.* separated into two parts by a cleft; (*bot.*) split up into two equal portions. [L. *bifidus*].

BIFIDATE, [bī'-fid-āt'], *adj.* bifid.

BIFIDLY, [bī'-fid-li], *adv.* in a bifid fashion.

BIFILAR, [bī-fīl'-er] *adj.* having two fine threads. [BI and L. *filum* thread].

BIFLEX, [bī'-fleks], *adj.* doubly curved. [BI and L. *flexum*, *p.pt.* of *flectere* to bend].

BIFLORATE, [bī-flaw'-rāt], *adj* biflorous. [BI and FLORATE].

BIFLOROUS, [bī'-flaw'-rus], *adj.* producing two flowers on a stem. [BI and L. *flos, floris* flower].

BIFOCAL, [bī-fō'-kal], *adj.* (of spectacles) having two segments of different focus. [BI and FOCAL].

BIFOLD, [bī'-fōld], *adj.* twofold, double, of two kinds.

BIFOLIATE, [bī-fōl'-i-at], *adj.* (*bot.*) two-leaved.

BIFOLIOLATE, [bī-fōl'-i-ō-lat], *adj.* with two leaflets.

BIFOLLICULAR, [bī-fol-ik'-yōō-ler], *adj.* (*bot.*) with two follicles. [BI and L. *folliculus* little bag].

BIFORATE, [bī-for'-at], *adj.* with two pores. [BI and L. *foratus* pierced].

BIFORM, [bī'-fawm'], *adj.* with two forms. [BI and FORM].

BIFORMITY, [bī-fawm'-it-i], *n.* the condition of being biform.

BIFRONTED, [bī'-frunt'-id], *adj.* with two fronts or faces. [BI and FRONT].

BIFURCATE (1), [bī'-fer-kat'], *v.t. and i.* to divide into two branches, to fork. [MedL. *bifurcatus*].

BIFURCATE (2), [bī-fer-kat'], *adj.* two-forked; having two prongs or branches.

BIFURCATED, [bī'-fer-kā-tid], *adj.* divided into two branches or forks.

BIFURCATION, [bī'-fer-kā'-shun], *n.* a forking into two branches; the point at which such forking takes place; the two branches produced by forking.

BIFURCOUS, [bī-furk'-us], *adj.* bifurcate. [L. *bifurcus*].

BIG, [big], *adj. and adv.* large in size, power or quality, great in bulk, ample; tall, broad, capacious; (*fig.*) noble, generous, magnanimous, proud, lofty; (*coll.*) important, influential; grown up; †pregnant; **b. words,** words intended to intimidate or impress; **to talk b.,** (*coll.*) to boast; **to be too b. for one's shoes,** to be conceited; *often used in compound words.* [ME. *big*].

BIGA, [bī'-ga], *n.* a kind of chariot drawn by two horses abreast. [L. *biga* from *bijugae* two-yoked].

BIGAMIST, [big'-a-mist], *n.* a person guilty of bigamy.

BIGAMOUS, [big'-a-mus], *adj.* having committed bigamy, involving bigamy.

BIGAMOUSLY, [big'-a-mus-li], *adv.* in a bigamous way.

BIGAMY, [big'-a-mi], *n.* the crime of marrying another whilst still legally married. [BI and Gk. *gamos* wedding].

BIGAROON, [big'-a-rōōn'], *n.* the large red and yellow white-heart cherry. [OFr. *bigarreau* variegated].

BIG-BELLIED, [big'-bel'-id], *adj.* corpulent; †pregnant.

BIG BERTHA, [big-bur'-tha], *n.* a German field gun of great range. [Frau *Berta* Krupp von Bohlen und Halbach].

BIG-BONED, [big'-bōnd'], *adj.* having large bones, strong, heavy.

BIGEMINATE, [bī'-jem'-in-at], *adj.* (*bot.*) set out or growing in double pairs. [BI and L. *geminatus* doubled].

BIG-END, [big'-end'], *n.* (*eng.*) that part of a connecting rod bearing a crank-shaft.

BIGENER, [bī'-jen-er], *n.* a cross between two different species. [BI and L. *genera* (*pl.*) kinds].

BIGENTIAL, [bī'-jen'-shal], *adj.* of two nations or races. [BI and L. *gens gentis* race].

BIGG, [big], *n.* the four-rowed barley. [OIcel. *bygg* barley].

BIGGIN (1), [big'-in], *n.* a child's cap; a night-cap. [Fr. *béguin*].

BIGGIN (2), [big'-in], *n.* a small wooden vessel; a percolator coffee-pot. [Mr. *Biggin*, the inventor].

BIGGISH, [big'-ish], *adj.* rather big.

BIGGONET, [big'-on-et], *n.* a large cap having ear-like flaps, worn by the Beguines. [Fr. *béguinet*].

BIGHORN, [big'-hawn], *n.* the wild sheep with large horns found in the Rocky Mountains. [BIG and HORN].

BIGHT, [bīt], *n.* a bend, curve; a loop or coil in a rope; a break in the straightness of a coast-line formed by a creek, a small, shallow bay. [OE. *byht*].

BIGLANDULAR, [bī'-gland'-yōō-ler], *adj.* (*bot.*) with two glands. [BI and GLANDULAR].

BIGLY, [big'-li], *adv.* in a haughty, blustering way, loudly.

BIGNESS, [big'-nes], *n.* the quality of being big.

BIGNONIA, [big-nōn'-i-a], *n.* (*bot.*) a genus of climbing shrubs of the order *Bignoniaceae.* [Abbé *Bignon*, a French scholar].

BIGOT, [big'-ot], *n.* a narrow-minded person holding stubbornly to a particular opinion or belief. [Uncert.].

BIGOTED, [big'-ot-id], *adj.* prejudiced, narrow-minded.

BIGOTEDLY, [big'-ot-id-li], *adv.* in a bigoted manner.

BIGOTRY, [big'-ot-ri], *n.* the quality of being bigoted.

BIG-SOUNDING, [big'-sownd'-ing], *adj.* having an impressive sound.

BIGWIG, [big'-wig], *n.* (*coll.*) a person of considerable importance or influence, formerly such a person who wore a large wig. [BIG and WIG].

BIJOU (1), (*pl.* **bijoux**), [bē'-zhōō], *n.* a jewel, trinket. [Fr. *bijou*].

BIJOU (2), [bē'-zhōō], *adj.* small, neat.

BIJOUTERIE, [bē-zhōō'-ter-ē'], *n.* jewellery, trinkets. [Fr. *bijouterie*].

BIJUGATE, [bī'-jōōg-āt'], *adj.* bijugous.

BIJUGOUS, [bī'-jōōg-us], *adj.* (*bot.*) having two pairs; yoked in pairs. [BI and L. *jugum* yoke].

BIKE, [bīk], *n.* (*coll.*) a bicycle. [Abbreviation of BICYCLE].

BILABIATE, [bī'-lāb'-i-at], *adj.* (*bot.*) with two lips. [BI and L. *labium* lip].

BILAMELLATE, [bī'-lam'-el-āt], *adj.* bilaminar. [BI and L. *lamella* small thin plate].

BILAMINAR, [bī'-lam'-in-ar], *adj.* with two thin plates. [BI and L. *laminas* thin plate].

BILANDER, [bil'-and-er], *n.* (*naut.*) a small two-masted Dutch trading vessel. [Du. *bijlander* a single-masted coastal vessel].

BILATERAL, [bī'-lat'-er-al], *adj.* two-sided; affecting two parties; arranged upon or forming two sides. [BI and LATERAL].

BILATERALLY, [bī-lat'-er-al-i], *adv.* in bilateral fashion; from both sides.

BILBERRY, [bil'-ber-i], *n.* (*bot.*) the common whortleberry, a hardy shrub-like plant, yielding a small purple berry with a sweet taste. [Uncert.].

BILBO†, (*pl.* **bilboes**†), [bil'-bō], *n.* a rapier; a kind of sword; (*pl.*) an apparatus for confining the feet of prisoners or offenders. [*Bilbao* in Spain].

BILBOQUET, [bil'-bok-et], *n.* the game of cup-and-ball, the object of which is to catch the ball in a cup fastened to the end of a stick. [Fr. *bilboquet*].

BILBOES

BILE, [bīl], *n.* a yellow, bitter secretion of the liver, retained in the gall-bladder and aiding in the digestion of fatty substances; unhealthy condition arising from disorders of the bile; (*fig.*) ill-humour, bitter feeling. [Fr. from L. *bilis* gall].

BILEDUCT, [bīl'-dukt], *n.* (*anat.*) a channel or duct for conveying bile.

BILESTONE, [bīl'-stōn], *n.* a gall-stone.

BILGE (1), [bilj], *n.* the broadest and flattest part of a ship's hull; filth, dirt and noisome material accumulating there; the bulging part of a cask; (*fig.*) (*coll.*) rubbish, stupid, nonsensical statements; **b. ways,** planks put under a vessel's bilge for support during launching. [Uncert.].

BILGE (2), [bilj], *v.t. and i.* to split the bottom of a ship; to spring a leak by a fracture of the bilge.

BILGED, [biljd], *adj.* provided with a large bilge; springing a leak by a fracture of the bilge.

BILGE-WATER, [bilj-wa'-ter], *n.* water which collects in the bilge of a ship having a strong offensive smell.

BILHARZIA, [bil-haht'-si-a], *n.* a liver-fluke found in the veins and in the bladder of human beings. [T. *Bilharz*, the discoverer of the worm as a disease-producing agent].

BILHARZIOSIS, [bil-haht'-si-ō'-sis], *n.* a chronic internal disorder set up by the bilharzia. [BILHARZIA and Gk. *-osis* denoting condition].

BILIARY, [bil'-i-ar-i], *adj.* pertaining to the bile.

BILIATION, [bil'-i-ā'-shun], *n.* the excretion of bile.

BILIN, [bīl'-in], *n.* (*chem.*) resinous matter obtained from bile.

BILINGUAL, [bī-ling'-gwal], *adj.* characterized by or formed from two languages; speaking two languages naturally; written in two languages. [L. *bilinguis*].

BILINGUAR, [bī-ling'-gwer], *adj.* bilingual.

BILINGUOUS, [bī-ling'-gwus], *adj.* bilingual.

BILIOUS, [bil'-yus], *adj.* caused by or relating to disorder of the bile; liable to be afflicted by disorder of the bile; (*fig.*) morose, peevish; (*coll.*) sick. [L. *biliosus*].

BILIOUSLY, [bil'-yus-li], *adv.* in bilious fashion, irritably.

BILIOUSNESS, [bil'-yus-nes], *n.* the state or condition of being bilious.

BILIRUBIN, [bil'-i-rōōb'-in], *n.* the red colouring matter present in bile. [BILE and L. *ruber* red].

BILITERAL, [bī-lit'-er-al], *adj.* composed of, or based on, two letters. [BI and LITERAL].

BILIVERDINE, [bil'-i-vur'-din], *n.* a green pigment occurring in bile. [BILE and ~L. *viridis* green].

BILK (1), [bilk], *n.* a person who cheats, a bilker.

BILK (2), [bilk], *v.t.* to defraud or swindle by non-payment, in a mean, underhand way; to escape from; to cheat, to deceive. [Unkn.].

BILKER, [bilk'-er], *n.* a person who bilks.

BILL (1), [bil], *n.* the beak of a bird; a small, narrow promontory; the point of the fluke of an anchor. [OE. *bile*].

BILL (2), [bil], *n.* an obsolete infantry axe, a halberd; a tool used for chopping hedges, etc., in the form of a long curved blade on the end of a wooden handle. [OE. *bill* sword].

BILL (3), [bil], *n.* a written list or statement of particulars; a legislative measure put before the Houses of Parliament for approval; an account of money due for services rendered or goods purchased; a printed proclamation or advertisement; (*leg.*) a statement of a case in writing put before a grand jury; **b. of exchange,** (*comm.*) a promissory note, a signed written order authorizing the person to whom it is addressed to pay to the bearer, on a specified date, a certain sum of money for value received; **b. of credit,** (*comm.*) a document authorizing a person to receive money from a third party; a note issued on the credit of the state and passed as money; **b. of entry,** a written account of goods entered at a customs house; **b. of fare,** a menu; **b. of health,** (*naut.*) a certificate issued by the port authorities to masters of ships certifying the state of health of the crew at the time of departure; **b. of lading,** a receipt given by a shipmaster for goods consigned to him; **b. of sale,** a formal document authorizing the conveyance or transfer of personal chattels, given as security to a creditor; **a true b.,** a declaration by a grand jury that evidence furnished by a plaintiff warrants a trial. [L. *bulla* document].

BILL (4), [bil], *v.i.* to rub or stroke beak against beak; (*fig.*) to caress; **to b. and coo,** to make love like doves. [BILL (1)].

BILL (5), [bil], *v.t. and i.* to advertise or announce by means of a placard; to appear upon a bill of entertainment as playing a certain role. [BILL (3)].

BILL-BOOK, [bil'-bōōk'], *n.* a book in which a trader formally enters all his bills.

BILL-BROKER, [bil'-brōk'-er], *n.* a person who trades in money bills.

BILL-DISCOUNTER, [bil'-dis-kown'-ter], *n.* a broker who discounts bills of exchange.

BILLED, [bild], *adj.* provided with a bill; advertised on a placard.

BILLET (1), [bil'-it], *n.* a log of firewood; (*metal.*) a gold ingot or bar of steel; (*arch.*) an ornamental moulding in Roman or Norman architecture, consisting of round pieces of wood placed in a hollow moulding at regular intervals; (*her.*) rectangular charges filling a coat of arms. [Fr. *billot* block of wood].

BILLET (2), [bil'-it], *n.* a young coal-fish, *Gadus virens.* [Uncert.].

BILLET (3), [bil'-it], *n.* a formal note; a document demanding the feeding and lodging of soldiers, etc., in a town by householders; accommodation of this type; soldier's lodgings; apartments in general. [AFr. *billette*].

BILLET (4), [bil'-it], *v.t.* to quarter in billets, to place in a billet. [*Prec.*].

BILLET-DOUX, [bil'-i-dōō'], *n.* a love-letter, a note. [Fr. *billet-doux* sweet note].

BILL-FISH, [bil'-fish'], *n.* the gar-pike or long-nosed gar.

BILL-FISH

BILLHEAD, [bil'-hed'], *n.* the printed heading of a bill, a bill form.

BILLHOOK, [bil'-hōōk], *n.* a knife with a hooked end, used for chopping hedges, etc.

BILLIARD, [bil'-i-erd], *adj.* relating to the game of billiards.

BILLIARDS, [bil'-i-erdz], *n.*(*pl.*) an indoor game played by striking three small balls with a leather-tipped cue, on an oblong flat table enclosed by a raised rubber cushion, and fitted with six pockets. [Fr. *billard* billiard table].

BILLING, [bil'-ing], *n.* the act of caressing or fondling in the manner of doves. [BILL].

BILLINGSGATE, [bil'-ingz-get], *n.* bad or abusive language of the type associated with the fish market at *Billingsgate.*

BILLION, [bil'-i-on], *n.* a million millions; in France and America a thousand millions. [Fr. *billion*].

BILLHOOK

BILLON, [bil'-on], *n.* an alloy of copper and silver containing an excess of copper. used in debased coinage. [Fr. *billon* lump].

BILLOT, [bil'-ot], *n.* gold or silver in bars or blocks. [Fr. *billot* wooden block].

BILLOW (1), [bil'-ō], *n.* a large rolling wave of the sea; (*fig.*) (*pl.*) the sea; (*poet.*) a sudden sweep, surge or roll of flame, cloud, smoke, etc. [OScand. *bylgja* a wave].

BILLOW (2), [bil'-ō], *v.i.* to form into billows, to surge or roll in sweeping waves.

BILLOWED, [bil'-ōd], *adj.* like a billow.

ō (bone), ī (fine), ōō (food), ŏŏ (put), u (up), th (*th*ink), TH (*th*at), zh (*az*ure), † = obsolete, ~ = related to.

BILLOWY, [bil'-ō-i], *adj.* like a billow, full of billows, sweeping, surging or rolling like billows.
BILL-POSTER, [bil'-pōst-er], *n.* one who posts up bills or employs others to do so. [BILL (3) and POST (3)].
BILLSTICKER, [bil'-stik'-er], *n.* one who pastes up bills on hoardings.
BILLY, [bil'-i], *n.* (*coll.*) a tin can used for cooking. [Uncert.].
BILLYBOY, [bil'-i-boi'], *n.* a flat-bottomed, bluff-bowed vessel, rigged as a sloop, and having a detachable mast.
BILLYCOCK, [bil'-i-kok'], *n.* (*coll.*) a bowler hat. [Originally *bully-cocked*, cocked at an angle, in the way bullies wore their hats].
BILLY-GOAT, [bil'-i-gōt], *n.* a male goat. [*Billy*, a male name].
BILOBATE, [bī'-lōb'-āt], *adj.* bilobed. [BI and Gk. *lobos* lobe].
BILOBED, [bī'-lōbd'], *adj.* having two lobes.
BILOBULAR, [bī'-lōb'-yŏŏ-lar], *adj.* bilobed.
BILOCATION, [bī-lōk-ā'-shun], *n.* the power of being in two places at the same time.
BILOCULAR, [bī'-lok'-yŏŏ-ler], *adj.* (*bot.*) possessing two cells. [BI and L. *loculus* small place].
BILTONG, [bil'-tong], *n.* strips of lean meat dried in the sun, and eaten as food in South Africa. [Du. *bil* buttock and *tong* tongue].
BIMACULATE, [bī'-mak'-yŏŏ-lat], *adj.* with two spots. [BI and L. *maculatus* spotted].
BIMANAL, [bī'-man-al], *adj.* (*zool.*) bimanous.
BIMANOUS, [bī'-man-us], *adj.* having two hands. [BI and L. *manus* hand].
BIMARGINATE, [bī-mah'-jin-at], *adj.* with a double margin. [BI and MARGIN].
BIMARINE, [bī'-ma-rēn'], *adj.* between two seas. [BI and MARINE].
BIMBASHI, [bim'-bash-ē] *n.* a captain or commander in the Turkish Army; a British officer in Egyptian service.
BIMENSAL, [bī'-men'-sal], *adj.* happening every two months. [BI and L. *mensis* month].
BIMESTRIAL, [bī'-mes'-tri-al], *adj.* bimensal; lasting for two months. [L. *bimestris* every two months].
BIMETALLIC, [bī'-met-al'-ik], *adj.* based on or consisting of two metals (of currency). [BI and METALLIC].
BIMETALLISM, [bī'-met'-al-izm], *n.* the use of coins of two metals as currency, at a fixed ratio of value to each other. [BI and METALLISM].
BIMETALLIST, [bī'-met'-al-ist], *n.* an advocate of bimetallism.
BIMONTHLY, [bī'-munth'-li], *adj.* every two months. [BI and MONTHLY].
BIMUSCULAR, [bī'-mus'-kyŏŏ-ler], *adj.* with two attaching muscles. [BI and MUSCULAR].
BIN (1), [bin], *n.* a large receptacle provided with a lid in which bread, grain or corn may be stored; a receptacle in which dust, ashes, etc., are temporarily kept; a division or partition in a wine-cellar for storing; a kind of basket used in hop-picking. [OE. *binn* manger].
BIN (2), (binning, binned), [bin], *v.t.* to store in a bin.
BINARY, [bīn'-er-i], *adj.* characterized by, or composed of, two; **b. form,** (*mus.*) music based on the interchange of two themes to a set pattern; **b. stars,** (*astron.*) two stars revolving round a common centre, or one which revolves round another. [L. *binarius* consisting of two].
BINATE, [bī'-nāt'], *adj.* (*bot.*) growing or set out in pairs. [BINAL].
BINAURAL, [bin-aw'-ral], *adj.* having two ears; adapted to the two ears. [L. *bini* two by two and AURAL].
BIND (1), [bīnd], *n.* a stalk of hops; (*min.*) hardened clay occurring between levels of coal; (*mus.*) a curved mark denoting a tied note; a measure of quantity of eels or salmon.
BIND (2), (bound), [bīnd], *v.t.* to fasten together or confine (a loose mass) by means of a band, to join objects together; to wrap round firmly with a band, to bandage up; to tie up or render incapable of movement with fetters, chains, ropes, etc.; to fasten a strip of material round an object or along the edge of an object for strengthening purposes; to cause to be constipated; to pledge oneself to, to lay under an obligation; to fasten together the leaves of a book in a cover; to conclude (an agreement); to subject to a legal obligation; to apprentice; *v.i.* to form into a hard mass under pressure; to contract; **bound up in,** completely absorbed in; **I'll be bound,** I am certain. [OE. *bindan*].
BINDER, [bīnd'-er], *n.* a person who binds; a piece of material used for binding purposes; a piece of material used to confine the body (*esp.* of a baby); a machine that binds.
BINDERY, [bīnd'-er-i], *n.* a place where books are bound.
BINDING (1), [bīnd'-ing], *n.* the act of binding; anything that binds; the strong material used to bind a book, the manner of binding it; strong protective material fastened to the edges of carpet, fabric, etc.; (*eng.*) excessive friction causing loss of power in machinery; a bandage.
BINDING (2), [bīnd-ing], *adj.* that which binds, obligatory; tending to cause constipation.
BINDINGLY, [bīnd'-ing-li], *adv.* in binding fashion.
BINDINGNESS, [bīnd'-ing-nes], *n.* the condition of being binding.
BINDWEED, [bīnd-wēd], *n.* (*bot.*) the common name for plants of the genus *Convolvulus* and certain other climbing plants.
BINE, [bīn], *n.* (*bot.*) the creeping, slender stem of various climbing plants, the long pliant stem of the hop. [BIND (1)].
BINERVATE, [bī'-nur'-vāt], *adj.* possessing two nerves; (*bot.*) having two longitudinal ribs. [BI and NERVE].
BING, [bing], *n.* (*archaic*) a heap of grain, potatoes, etc.; a fixed amount of ore; a charcoal kiln. [OScand. *bingr* a heap].
BINGE, [binj], *n.* (*slang*) a drinking-bout or outing, a hilarious jollification. [Uncert.].
BINGLE (1), [bing'-gl], *n.* a style of hairdressing between bobbing and shingling.
BINGLE (2), [bing'-gl], *v.t.* to dress the hair in a bingle.
BINNACLE, [bin'-akl], *n.* (*naut.*) the box which contains the compass on a ship. [Span. *bitacula*].
BINOCLE†, [bin'-okl], *n.* a pair of binoculars. [L. *bini* two and *oculus* eye].
BINOCULAR (1), [bin-ok'-yŏŏ-ler], *n.* a field-glass, opera-glass or microscope through which an object may be seen with both eyes simultaneously. [*Prec.*].
BINOCULAR (2), [bin-ok'-yŏŏ-ler], *adj.* suited for or employing both eyes simultaneously.
BINOCULATE, [bin-ok'-yŏŏ-lāt], *adj.* with two eyes.
BINOMIAL (1), [bī'-nōm'-i-al], *n.* (*alg.*) an expression containing two terms, connected by a plus or minus sign. [BI and ~L. *nomen* a name].

BINNACLE

BINOMIAL (2), [bī'-nōm'-ial], *adj.* pertaining to binomials; consisting of two terms; binominal; **b. theorem,** a formula for raising a binomial equation to any power, or for extracting any root of it without lengthy multiplication or division, by a converging infinite series. [*Prec.*].
BINOMINAL, [bī-nom'-in-al], *adj.* (*bot.* and *zool.*) possessing two names. [BI and L. *nomen* name].
BINOTONOUS, [bī'-not'-on-us], *adj.* containing two notes. [*L. bini* two together and TONE].
BINOUS, [bī'-nus], *adj.* (*bot.*) double, in pairs. [L. *bini* two together].
BINOXALATE, [bī'-noks'-al-āt], *n.* a combination of two equivalents of oxalic acid and a base [L. *bini* two together and OXALATE].
BINOXIDE, [bin'-oks'-īd], *n.* (*chem.*) a dioxide. [L. *bini* two together and OXIDE].
BINTURONG, [bin-chŏŏ'-rong], *n.* the bear-cat of Malaya, *Arctitis binturong*. [East Indian *binturong*].
BINUCLEAR, [bī-nŏŏk'-li-er], *adj.* having two nuclei. [BI and NUCLEAR].
BIO-, [bī'-o], *pref.* life. [Gk. *bios* life].
BIOBLAST, [bī'-ō-blast'], *n.* a minute mass of protoplasm, possessing formative power. [BIO and Gk. *blastos* germ, bud].
BIOCELLATE, [bī-os'-il-at], *adj.* with two eyelike markings. [BI and L. *ocellatus* having eyelets].
BIOCHEMISTRY, [bī'-ō-kem'-is-tri], *n.* the study of the chemical composition of animal and plant structure. [BIO and CHEMISTRY].
BIODYNAMICS, [bī'-ō-dī-nam'-iks], *n.(pl.)* the study of vital forces. [BIO and DYNAMICS].
BIOGENESIS, [bī'-ō-jen'-is-is], *n.* the science of the origin and development of life or of new species. [BIO and GENESIS].
BIOGENETIC, [bī'-ō-jen-et'-ik], *adj.* relating to biogenesis.

BIOGENETICALLY, [bī'-ō-jen-et'-ik-al-i], *adv.* according to biogenesis.

BIOGEOGRAPHY, [bī'-ō-ji-og'-raf-i], *n.* the study of the geographical distribution of animals and plants. [BIO and GEOGRAPHY].

BIOGRAPH, [bī'-ō-grahf], *n.* an earlier name for the cinematograph. [BIO and GRAPH].

BIOGRAPHER, [bī-og'-ra-fer], *n.* one who writes the life story of a person.

BIOGRAPHIC, [bī'-ō-graf'-ik], *adj.* biographical.

BIOGRAPHICAL, [bī'-ō-graf'-ik-al], *adj.* relating to, or containing, biography.

BIOGRAPHICALLY, [bī'-ō-graf'-ik-a-li], *adv.* in biographical fashion.

BIOGRAPHY, [bī-og'-raf-i], *n.* an account of the life of a particular person; that section of literature concerned with accounts of the lives of individuals. [BIO and Gk. *graphia* writing].

BIOLOGICAL, [bī-ō-loj'-ik-al], *adj.* pertaining to biology.

BIOLOGICALLY, [bī'-ō-loj'-ik-al-i], *adv.* from the biological standpoint, as a matter of biology.

BIOLOGIST, [bī-ol'-ō-jist], *n.* one expert in biology.

BIOLOGY, [bī-ol'-o-ji], *n.* the study of living plants and animals, their relationship, distribution, origin, structure, functions and manner of living. [BIO and Gk. *logos* speech].

BIOLYTIC, [bī'-ō-lit'-ik], *adj.* life-destroying. [BIO and Gk. *lutikos* loosing].

BIOMAGNETISM, [bī'-ō-mag'-net-izm], *n.* animal magnetism. [BIO and MAGNETISM].

BIOMETRICS, [bī'-o-met'-riks], *n.(pl.)* the study of the statistics and quantitative valuation of biological facts. [BIO and METRIC].

BIOMETRY, [bī-om'-et-ri], *n.* biometrics. [BIO and Gk. *metria* measuring].

BIONOMICS, [bī'-ō-nom'-iks], *n.(pl.)* that aspect of biology dealing with organisms in relation to their environment. [BIO and (ECO)NOMICS].

BIOPHAGOUS, [bī-of'-ag-us], *adj.* existing on living food. [BIO and Gk. *phagos* eating].

BIOPHYSICS, [bī-ō-fiz'-iks], *n.(pl.)* the study of biological phenomena according to the laws of physics.

BIOPLASM, [bī'-ō-plazm'], *n.* protoplasm. [BIO and PLASM].

BIOPLAST, [bī'-ō-plast'], *n.* a germ plasm. [BIO and Gk. *plastos* moulded].

BIOSCOPE, [bī'-os-kōp'], *n.* a kind of cinematograph. [BIO and SCOPE].

BIOSTATICS, [bī'-ō-stat'-iks], *n.(pl.)* the study and science of living structure. [BIO and STATIC].

BIOTAXY, [bī'-ō-taks'-i], *n.* the branch of biology dealing with the classification of organisms according to likenesses and differences. [BIO and Gk. *taxis* order].

BIOTIC, [bī-ot'-ik], *adj.* pertaining to life, vital. [Gk. *biotikos*].

BIOTINE, [bī'-ō-tēn], *n.* anorthite, aluminium silicate. [*Biot*, a French physicist].

BIOTITE, [bī'-ō-tīt'], *n.* the magnesia mica. [*Prec.*].

BIOTRON, [bī'-ō-tron], *n.* (*wirel.*) two thermionic valves coupled so as to give a very steep curve.

BIPAROUS, [bip'-er-us], *adj.* producing or yielding two at once. [BI and L. *parus* producing].

BIPARTIBLE, [bī-pah'-tibl], *adj.* divisible into two portions. [BI and L. *partibilis*].

BIPARTIENT (1), [bī-paht'-i-ent], *n.* a number which exactly divides another number into two equal parts.

BIPARTIENT (2), [bī'-pah'-ti-ent], *adj.* dividing into two parts. [L. *bipartiens*].

BIPARTITE, [bī-paht'-īt], *adj.* set out in or consisting of two corresponding parts; shared by the two parties concerned; (*bot.*) divided into two parts to the base. [L. *bipartitus*].

BIPARTITION, [bī'-pah-tish'-un], *n.* the act of making bipartite.

BIPED (1), [bī'-ped'], *n.* an animal having two feet. [BI and L. *pes pedis* foot].

BIPED (2), [bī'-ped'], *adj.* having two feet.

BIPEDAL, [bī'-ped'-al], *adj.* biped; caused or made by two feet.

BIPELTATE, [bī'-pelt'-āt], *adj.* (*zool.*) protected by a double shield. [BI and L. *peltatus* from Gk. *pelte* a shield].

BIPENNATE, [bī'-pen'-āt], *adj.* with two wings.

BIPENNATED, [bī'-pen-āt'-id], *adj.* bipennate.

BIPENNIS, [bī-pen'-is], *n.* a double-edged battle-axe. [L. *bipennis* with two wings].

BIPETALOUS, [bī-pet'-al-us], *adj.* with two petals.

BIPINNATE, [bī'-pin'-āt], *adj.* doubly pinnate; (*zool.*) having a feathery tail in which the feathers are arranged in opposed pairs.

BIPINNATED, [bī'-pin-āt'-id], *adj.* bipinnate.

BIPINNATIFID, [bī'-pin-at'-if-id], *adj.* (*bot.*) pinnatifid and having the pinnae similarly divided.

BIPLANE, [bī'-plān], *n.* an aeroplane having two planes. [BI and PLANE].

BIPLICATE, [bī'-plik-at], *adj.* doubly folded. [BI and L. *plicatus* folded].

BIPOLAR, [bī-pōl'-er], *adj.* with two poles.

BIPUNCTATE, [bī-pungk'-tat], *adj.* possessing two points. [BI and L. *punctatus* pointed].

BIQUADRATE, [bī'-kwod'-rāt], *n.* the fourth power in arithmetic or algebra, the square (root) of the square (root). [BI and QUADRATE].

BIQUADRATIC (1), [bī'-kwod-rat'-ik], *n.* (*math.*) the biquadrate.

BIQUADRATIC (2), [bī'-kwod-rat'-ik], *adj.* (*math.*) relating to the biquadrate.

BIRAMOUS, [bī'-rām'-us], *adj.* having two branches. [BI and L. *ramus* a branch].

BIRCH (1), [burch], *n.* (*bot.*) a genus of hardy trees of the order *Betulaceae*, having a smooth, shining, whitish bark; the wood of this tree; a bundle of twigs fastened together, and used to inflict corporal punishment (especially upon schoolboys). [OE. *bierce*].

BIRCH (2), [burch], *adj.* made of or consisting of birch.

BIRCH (3), [burch], *v.t.* to flog with a birch.

BIRCHEN, [burch'-en], *adj.* made of birch; consisting of birch trees.

BIRCH-WATER, [burch'-waw'-ter], *n.* the sugary sap yielded by the birch.

BIRCH-WINE, [burch'-wīn'], *n.* a medicinal drink obtained from birch-water.

BIRD, [burd], *n.* a two-legged feathered vertebrate animal which lays eggs; (*slang*) a physically attractive woman; a person, fellow; a bad reception; **birds of a feather**, persons with similar interests; **b. of passage**, a migratory bird, (*fig.*) a restless nomadic person; **b. of prey**, a bird which preys on living birds or animals. [OE. *bird* nestling].

BIRD-BOLT, [burd'-bōlt'], *n.* a short, thick, blunt arrow fired from a crossbow.

BIRDCAGE, [burd'-kāj'], *n.* a receptacle of wire or wicker, provided with a wooden or metal bottom, in which captive birds may be kept.

BIRDCAGE

BIRD-CALL, [burd'-kawl'], *n.* a pipe which can imitate the notes of birds and decoy them.

BIRDCATCHER, [burd'-kach'-er], *n.* a person who catches birds.

BIRDCATCHING, [burd'-kach'-ing], *n.* the art of catching birds.

BIRD-CHERRY, [burd'-che'-ri], *n.* (*bot.*) a species of cherry, *Prunus Padus*, with a purple bark, white flowers, and berries eagerly sought after by birds.

BIRD-EYE, see BIRD'S-EYE.

BIRDFANCIER, [burd'-fan'-si-er], *n.* one who rears and keeps birds for pleasure.

BIRDIE, [burd'-i], *n.* (*golf*) a holing-out in one stroke less than bogey.

BIRDLIKE, [burd'-līk], *adj.* resembling a bird.

BIRDLIME, [burd'-līm], *n.* a viscous substance prepared from holly-bark and mistletoe-berries, smeared on branches to entangle birds.

BIRDLIMED, [burd'-līmd'], *adj.* smeared over with birdlime.

BIRDMAN, [burd'-man], *n.* a fowler, birdcatcher.

BIRD-ORGAN, [burd'-awg'-an], *n.* a small kind of organ used in teaching birds to sing.

BIRD-PEPPER, [burd'-pep'-er], *n.* (*bot.*) the plant *Capsicum minimum*.

BIRDSEED, [burd'-sēd], *n.* grain suitable for small cage-birds. [BIRD and SEED (1)].

BIRD'S-EYE (1), BIRD-EYE, [burd(z)'-ī], *n.* (*bot.*) one of various species of flowers having central spots or eyes; the germander speedwell; a kind of cut-tobacco containing sections of stems like mottled stalks.

BIRD'S-EYE (2), [burdz'-ī], *adj.* seen from above; **b. view**, panoramic view seen from a height; (*fig.*) a general survey.

BIRD'S-FOOT, [burdz'-fŏot'], *n.* (*bot.*) one of several

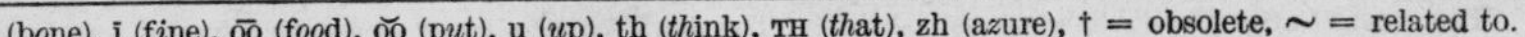

plants of the genus *Ornithopus* with cylindrical claw-like fruits.
BIRD'S-FOOT-TREFOIL, [burdz'-foot-tri-foil'], *n.* (*bot.*) a leguminous pasture-plant, *Lotus corniculatus*.
BIRD'S-MOUTH, [burdz'-mowth], *n.* (*carp.*) a groove cut at the end of a piece of timber to receive another piece.
BIRD'S-NEST, [burdz'-nest'], *n.* the nest of a bird; the nest of the salangane and other kinds of swifts eaten as a delicacy by the Chinese; name given to various plants from the shape of their roots.
BIRD'S-TONGUE, [burdz'-tung'], *n.* (*bot.*) the plant *Senecio paludosus*.
BIREME, [bī'-rēm], *n.* a galley having two tiers of oars. [BI and L. *remus* oar].
BIRETTA, [bi-ret'-a], *n.* a square-shaped, stiff-sided cap with a tassel on the top, worn by Roman Catholic priests. [It. *berretta*].
BIRHOMBOIDAL, [bī'-rom-boid'-al], *adj.* having a surface made up of twelve rhombic faces. [BI and RHOMBOIDAL].
BIROSTRATE, [bī'-ros'-trāt], *adj.* possessing a double beak. [BI and L. *rostrum* beak].
BIROSTRATED, [bī-ros-trāt'-id], *adj.* birostrate.
BIRR, [bur], *n.* a whirring, rattling noise; the rush or force of a rapidly moving object; a violent thrust; forceful, energetic pronunciation; a strongly trilled consonant *r*. [OScand. *byrr* a good wind].
BIRTH, [burth], *n.* the process of being born; that which is born; family, descent, lineage, environment into which a person is born; noble rank by birth; (*fig.*) origin, beginning. [OE. *gebyrd*].
BIRTH-CONTROL, [burth'-kon-trōl'], *n.* the regulation or prevention of conception by the use of chemical or mechanical contraceptives.
BIRTHDAY, [burth'-dā], *n.* the day of one's birth; the anniversary of that day; **in one's b. suit,** naked.
BIRTHLESS, [burth'-les], *adj.* abortive, unsuccessful; of very low birth.
BIRTHMARK, [burth'-mahk], *n.* a disfigurement in the form of a discoloured patch on the skin, a naevus.
BIRTHPLACE, [burth'-plās], *n.* the place where a person was born.
BIRTHRATE, [burth'-rāt], *n.* the ratio of births to the population of a country.
BIRTHRIGHT, [burth'-rīt], *n.* the rights and privileges acquired at birth as a member of a family, nation, etc.
BIRTHSONG, [burth'-song], *n.* a song sung at a birth.
BIRTH-STRANGLED, [burth'-strangld], *adj.* strangled at birth.
BIRTHWORT, [burth'-wurt'], *n.* the plant *Aristolochia Clematitis*, so called from its supposed medicinal value in parturition. [BIRTH and WORT].
BIS, [bis], *adv.* (*mus.*) again, to be repeated. [L. *bis* twice].
BISCOTIN, [bis'-kot-in], *n.* a variety of biscuit made of flour, sugar, marmalade and eggs. [It. *biscottino* little biscuit].
BISCUIT, [bis'-kit], *n.* a thin, hard, crisp, dry cake or bread made of flour, water, eggs, etc., often flavoured; porous, unglazed porcelain or earthenware after the first firing; **sea b.,** a coarse, unfermented biscuit much used at sea instead of bread; **to take the b.,** to surpass (in impudence) everything. [Fr. *biscuit* from L. *bis coctus* twice cooked].
BISE, [bēz], *n.* a keen north-easterly wind frequently occurring in Switzerland and north of the Mediterranean. [Fr. *bise*].
BISECT, [bī-sekt'], *v.t.* to divide into two portions; (*math.*) to cut or divide into two equal parts. [BI and L. *sectum*, *p.pt.* of *secare* to cut].
BISECTION, [bī'-sek'-shun], *n.* the act of bisecting. [BI and SECTION].
BISECTOR, [bī'-sek'-tor], *n.* that which bisects.
BISEGMENT, [bī-seg'-ment], *n.* one half of a bisected line. [BI and SEGMENT].
BISERIATE, [bī-sēer'-i-āt], *adj.* (*zool.*) set out in two series.
BISERRATE, [bī-se'-rāt], *adj.* doubly notched, with the notches themselves further notched. [BI and SERRATE].
BISETOSE, [bī-sēt'-ōs], *adj.* (*bot. and zool.*) with two bristle-like appendages. [BI and L. *setosus* bristly].
BISETOUS, [bī'-sēt'-us], *adj.* bisetose.
BISEXUAL, [bī-seks'-yōō-al], *adj.* of two sexes; containing both sexes in one body.
BISHOP (1), [bish'-op], *n.* a priest who is given charge over spiritual matters and the supervision of the clergy in his diocese; a piece in chess, which has a carved top in the form of a mitre; a drink made by pouring red wine upon oranges and adding spice and sugar. [OE. *biscop* from Gk. *episkopos* overseer].
BISHOP (2), [bish'-op], *v.t.* to improve the appearance of a horse, make it look younger, by doctoring its teeth. [*Bishop*, a man who did this].
BISHOP-BIRD, [bish'-op-burd'], *n.* a South African bird of the genus *Pyromelana* of beautiful plumage.
BISHOP-LIKE, [bish'-op-līk'], *adj.* resembling a bishop.
BISHOPRIC, [bish'-op-rik'], *n.* the office of bishop; the jurisdiction and diocese of a bishop. [OE. *biscoprice*].
BISHOP'S-CAP, [bish'-ops-kap'], *n.* mitre-wort, a plant of the genus *Cyclamen*.
BISHOP-SLEEVE, [bish'-op-slēv'], *n.* sleeves of a lady's dress when shaped like those worn by a bishop.
BISHOP'S-WEED, [bish'-ops-wēd'], *n.* the grub-weed, *Aegopodium Podagraria*, with creeping roots or underground stems.
BISK, [bisk], *n.* a rich soup made from birds or crayfish. [Fr. *bisque* crayfish soup].
BISMILLAH, [bis-mil'-a], *int.* (*Mohammedan*) in God's name. [Arab. *bismillah*].
BISMITE, [biz'-mīt], *n.* (*min.*) a yellowish, earthy mineral, bismuth oxide or bismuth ochre. [BISMUTH].
BISMUTH, [biz'-muth], *n.* a brittle pale reddish-white metal, the chemical element whose symbol is Bi. [Germ. *Wismuth*].
BISMUTHAL, [biz'-muth-al], *adj.* bismuthic.
BISMUTHIC, [biz'-muth-ik], *adj.* containing bismuth, pertaining to bismuth.
BISMUTHINE, [biz'-muth-ēn], *n.* a compound of bismuth.
BISMUTHITE, [bīz'-muth-īt], *n.* a natural bismuth carbonate.
BISON, (*pl.* **bison**), [bī'-sun], *n.* the European aurochs; the American buffalo. [L. *bison*].
BISQUE (1), [bisk], *n.* bisk.
BISQUE (2), [bisk], *n.* a handicap allowance given to a player in a tennis or a golf tournament, to be used once only at some stage of the match; an extra turn allowed to a player at croquet by his opponent. [Fr. *bisque*].
BISQUE (3), [bisk], *n.* a kind of unglazed white porcelain used for ornaments. [BISCUIT].
BISSEXTILE (1), [bis-seks'-tīl], *n.* a leap-year.
BISSEXTILE (2), [bis-seks'-tīl], *adj.* containing the extra day added in a leap-year. [L. *bis* twice and *sextus* sixth; in leap year the sixth day before the kalends of March, i.e., February 24 was reckoned twice].
BISTIPULED, [bī'-stip'-yōōld], *adj.* (*bot.*) with two stipules.
BISTORT, [bis'-tawt], *n.* (*bot.*) a perennial plant of the buckwheat family, snakeweed or *Polygonum Bistorta*, used occasionally in medicine as an astringent. [LL. *bis torta* twice-twisted].
BISTOURY, [bis-tōōer'-i], *n.* a scalpel. [Fr. *bistouri*].
BISTRE, [bis'-ter], *n. and adj.* a brown oily pigment obtained from the soot of wood. [Fr. *bistre*].
BISULCATE, [bī'-sul'-kāt], *adj.* having cloven feet. [BI and L. *sulcus* a furrow].
BIT (1), [bit], *n.* the cutting edge of a tool; a boring tool used with a drill, brace, etc.; that part of a key which moves or grips the levers of a lock; the part of a bridle which is put in a horse's mouth, and to which the reins are fastened. [OE. *bite* biting].
BIT (2), [bit], *n.* a morsel, a small portion or piece; a share; a small amount; a short interval of time; a small silver coin; (*slang*) a woman. [OE. *bita* piece bitten off].
BIT (3), (**bitting, bitted**), [bit], *v.t.* to place a bit in a horse's mouth; (*fig.*) to hold back, curb. [BIT (1)].
BITCH, [bich], *n.* the female of dog, wolf or fox; (*vulgar*) a term of reproach for a woman. [OE. *bicce*].
BITE (1), [bīt], *n.* a small portion of food, a mouthful; a wound made by the teeth or a sting; a piercing with the teeth; a smart, sharp pain; sting; sharp taste; sudden seizing or snap at bait made by a fish; (*coll.*) a fish; an attractive, enticing offer; the gripping action of an edge upon another surface; (*print.*) a part of the impression improperly printed, owing to the frisket not being sufficiently cut away. [OE. *bite*].
BITE (2), (**bit, bitten**), [bīt], *v.t. and i.* to pierce, sever or wound with the teeth; to cut into; to snap at; to grip, to hold by friction; to eat into so as to corrode; to wound the feelings of; to nip, damage; to be liable to attack persons with the teeth; (*fig.*) to cause sharp pain; to possess a sharp taste; to seize the bait with the teeth; to pinch with cold; (*pass.*) to be tempted by an attractive offer; (*coll.*) to swindle, deceive,

hoax; **to be bitten with,** (*coll.*) to be very enthusiastic about; **to b. the dust,** to be utterly defeated and humbled. [OE. *bitan*].

BITER, [bīt'-er], *n.* a person or thing that bites.

BITERNATE, [bī-turn'-at], *adj.* (*bot.*) doubly ternate.

BITING, [bīt'-ing], *adj.* sharp, severe, very cold, piercing; painfully sarcastic, bitter.

BITING-IN, [bīt'-ing-in'], *n.* corrosion by acids used in etching.

BITINGLY, [bīt'-ing-li], *adv.* in biting fashion.

BITLESS, [bit'-les], *adj.* without a bit. [BIT (1)].

BITMAKER, [bit'-māk'-er], *n.* a person who makes bits.

BITMOUTH, [bit'-mowth'], *n.* the bit of a bridle.

BITNOBEN, [bit-nōb'-en], *n.* a salt of bitumen, valued as remedial by the natives of India. [Unkn.].

BITT, [bit], *v.t.* (*naut.*) to put a cable, rope, etc., round the bitts. [BITTS].

BITTER (1), [bit'-er], *n.* anything bitter; bitter beer.

BITTER (2), [bit'-er], *adj.* having an acrid, sharp, pungent taste, sour; (*fig.*) keen, piercing, harsh, malignant, full of animosity; cruel, stinging; distressing, lamentable; **b. beer,** a light, clear ale; **to the b. end,** to the very end, however unpleasant. [OE. *biter*].

BITTERCRESS, [bit'-er-kres'], *n.* a plant of the genus *Cardamine*.

BITTERING, [bit'-er-ing], *n.* a mixture used to adulterate beer.

BITTERISH, [bit'-er-ish], *adj.* rather bitter.

BITTERISHNESS, [bit'-er-ish-nes], *n.* the condition of being bitterish.

BITTERLING, [bit'-er-ling], *n.* small freshwater carp with a bitter taste.

BITTERLY, [bit'-er-li], *adv.* in a bitter manner. [OE. *biterlice*].

BITTERN (1), [bit'-ern], *n.* a marsh-haunting bird of the genus *Botaurus*, related to the heron. [OFr. *butor*].

BITTERN (2), [bit'-ern], *n.* the product remaining from evaporated sea-water after the removal of the common salt; bittering. [BITTER (2)].

BITTERNESS, [bit'-er-nes], *n.* the quality of being bitter, a bitter taste.

BITTER-ROOT, [bit'-er-rōōt'], *n.* (*bot.*) a North American plant with bitter edible roots, *Lewisia rediviva*.

BITTERS, [bit'-erz], *n.* a liquor brewed from bitter herbs or roots, used for flavouring drinks, and taken as an appetizer.

BITTER-SALT, [bit'-er-sawlt'], *n.* Epsom salts.

BITTER-SPAR, [bit'-er-spah(r)'], *n.* (*min.*) rhomb-spar, the crystallized form of magnesian limestone.

BITTER-SWEET (1), [bit'-er-swēt'], *n.* woody nightshade, *Solanum Dulcamara*, whose root, when chewed, tastes first bitter then sweet; the meadow-sweet.

BITTER-SWEET (2), [bit'-er-swēt'], *adj.* that which is partly bitter and partly sweet; (*fig.*) pleasant with some feeling of mental pain.

BITTER-VETCH, [bit'-er-vech'], *n.* a plant of the genus *Orobus* with purple flowers and edible tubers.

BITTERWEED, [bit'-er-wēd'], *n.* (*bot.*) †the poplar; a variety of North American wormwood.

BITTERWOOD, [bit'-er-wŏŏd'], *n.* quassia, the plant *Picræna excelsa*.

BITTERWORT, [bit'-er-wurt'], *n.* the yellow gentian, *Gentiana lutea*.

BITTOCK, *n.* a little bit.

BITTOUR†, [bit'-ōō-er], *n.* the bittern. [BITTERN].

BITTS, [bitz], *n.*(*pl.* (*naut.*) pairs of strong vertical posts fastened to the deck of a ship to secure ropes, etc. [Uncert.].

BITUBERCULATE, [bī'-tyōō-bur'-kyōō-lat], *adj.* with two tubercles.

BITULITHIC, [bit-ew-lith'-ik], *adj.* (*prot.*) made up of a mixture of broken stone and bitumen or asphalt. [BITUMEN and Gk. *lithos* stone].

BITUMEN, [bit'-ew-men], *n.* (*min.*) mineral pitch, asphalt. [L. *bitumen* mineral-pitch].

BITUMINATE, [bit-ew'-min-āt], *v.t.* to bituminize, to impregnate with bitumen.

BITUMINIFEROUS, [bit'-ew-min-if'-er-us], *adj.* yielding bitumen. [BITUMEN and L. *ferre* to bear].

BITUMINIZATION, [bit'-ew'-min-ī-zā'-shun], *n.* the act of bituminizing.

BITUMINIZE, [bit-ewm'-in-īz], *v.t.* to turn into or impregnate with bitumen.

BITUMINOUS, [bit-ew'-min-us], *adj.* containing or like bitumen.

BIVALENT, [bī'-vāl'-ent], *adj.* (*chem.*) able to replace two atoms of hydrogen. [BI and L. *valens* being worth].

BIVALVE (1), [bī'-valv'], *n.* a mollusc having a hinged shell of two halves, as an oyster, etc.; (*bot.*) a seed-envelope whose seed-vessels open in two valves. [BI and VALVE].

BIVALVE(D) (2), [bī'-valv(d)'], *adj.* having a double, hinged shell; (*bot.*) having a seed-vessel of two halves.

BIVALVOUS, [bī'-val'-vus], *adj.* having bivalve shells.

BIVALVULAR, [bī-valv'-yōō-ler], *adj.* with two small valves.

BIVAULTED, [bī'-vawlt'-id], *adj.* with two vaults.

BIVALVE

BIVENTRAL, [bī'-ven'-tral], *adj.* with two belly-shaped parts. [BI and VENTRAL].

BIVIOUS, [biv'-i-us], *adj.* offering a choice of two paths. [L. *bivius*].

BIVOUAC (1), [biv'-ōō-ak'], *n.* an encampment of soldiers in the open for the night. [Fr. *bivouac* from Germ. *beiwacht* a guard].

BIVOUAC (2), [biv'-ōō-ak'], *v.i.* to camp out for the night.

BI-WEEKLY, [bī'-wēk'-li], *adj.* fortnightly; occurring twice in a week.

BIXIN, [biks'-in], *n.* a variety of anatta, a dye obtained from the Central American shrub, *Bixa orellana*. [*Bixa*, the native name of the shrub].

BIZARD, [biz'-ahd], *n.* a carnation having two stripes and a variety of colours. [Unkn.].

BIZARRE, [bi-zah(r)'], *adj.* eccentric, odd, peculiar, fantastic, grotesque. [Fr. *bizarre*].

BLAB (1), [blab], *n.* a blabber.

BLAB (2), (**blabbing, blabbed**), [blab], *v.i.* to reveal secrets unwisely, to betray confidences. [BLABBER (2)].

BLABBER (1), [blab'-er], *n.* a tell-tale. [*Prec.*].

BLABBER (2), [blab'-er], *v.i* to blab. [OScand. *blabbra* babble].

BLACK (1), [blak], *n.* the absence of light or visible colour; the colour, dye or pigment which absorbs all incident light; a smut of soot; black clothing; a negro; dirt; (*fig.*) mourning apparel; (*bot.*) a dark fungus which injures wheat.

BLACK (2), [blak], *adj.* having no colour or light, absorbing all visible colours; of the darkest colour; pertaining to negroes, having dark features, swarthy-skinned, dusky; dirty; (*fig.*) unpropitious, gloomy, dismal, mournful; wicked, foul, infamous; sullen, cross; **b. art,** magic, necromancy; **b. cap,** a cap worn by judges when passing sentence of death; **b. draught,** a black-coloured purgative; **b. eye,** dark-coloured bruise around the eye; **in b. and white,** written down; **b. guard,** a member of the German protective guards who wear a black uniform; **b. market,** illegal dealing in Government-controlled commodities; **B. Monks,** the Benedictines; **B. Rod,** the usher to the Lord Chamberlain and the House of Lords, so called from his black rod of office. [OE. *blæc*].

BLACK (3), [blak], *v.t.* to make black; to polish with blacking or black-lead; to soil; **to b. out,** to delete, to obliterate; to cause a black-out.

BLACKAMOOR, [blak'-a-maw(r)'], *n.* a negro; a black man. [BLACK and MOOR].

BLACKBALL (1), [black'-bawl], *n.* a small wooden or ivory black ball used to indicate an adverse vote in balloting.

BLACKBALL (2), [blak'-bawl], *v.t.* to vote against by putting a black ball into the voting box; to vote against, to reject, to expel.

BLACK-BAND, [blak'-band'], *n.* (*min.*) a mineral carbonate of iron found in the coal-measures.

BLACK-BEETLE, [blak'-bētl'], *n.* the cockroach, *Periplaneta orientalis*.

BLACKBERRY, [blak'-be'-ri], *n.* (*bot.*) the small, black berry of the bramble; (*pop.*) the bramble, *Rubus fruticosus*.

BLACKBIRD, [blak'burd], *n.* a dark-coloured species of thrush; a species of American birds related to the starling and crow.

BLACKBIRDING, [blak'-burd'-ing], *n.* the kidnapping of negroes into slavery.

BLACKBOARD, [blak'-bawd'], *n.* a large board painted black, which is written upon with chalk.

BLACK-BODING, [blak'-bōd'-ing], *adj.* promising evil.

BLACK-BONNET, [blak'-bon'-et], *n.* the reed-bunting, *Emberiza schœniclus*.

BLACKBROWED, [blak'-browd'], *adj.* frowning, sullen.
BLACKBUCK, [blak'-buk'], *n.* the Indian antelope.
BLACKCAP, [blak'-kap'], *n.* (*zool.*) a European warbler bird, *Sylvia atricapilla*, the upper part of the head of which is black; an American species of titmouse.
BLACK-CHALK, [blak'-chawk'], *n.* a soft bluish-black variety of clayish slate used for drawing.
BLACK-COAT, [blak'-kōt], *n.* (*coll.*) a clergyman; **a black-coated worker**, one engaged in non-manual labour, and who receives weekly wages as distinct from a salary.
BLACK-COCK, [blak'-kok'], *n.* the heath-cock, *Tetrao tetrix*.
BLACK-CURRANT, [blak'-ku'-rant], *n.* a small black fruit, *Ribes nigra*, made into jam, used as flavouring, etc.
BLACKDROP, [blak'-drop'], *n.* a drink made of opium mixed with vinegar and spices; (*astron.*) a dark band or spot visible during the passage of the planets Venus and Mercury across the sun's disk.
BLACK-EARTH, [blak'-urth], *n.* rich black soil.
BLACKEN, [blak'-en], *v.t. and i.* to make black, to darken; (*fig.*) to defame, to sully, disparage; to become black or gloomy.
BLACKEY, [blak'-i], *n.* (*coll.*) a black person; a negro.
BLACKFELLOW, [blak'-fel'-ō], *n.* an aboriginal of Australia.
BLACK-FISH, [blak'-fish'], *n.* an American edible sea-fish, *Tautoga americana* with black back and sides and white belly; a Mediterranean fish allied to the mackerel, *Zentrolophus morio*; a species of small pilot-whale of the genus *Globiocephalus*.
BLACK-FLAG, [blak'-flag'], *n.* a pirate flag; a flag symbolizing death.
BLACK-FLUX, [blak'-fluks], *n.* a mixture of carbonate of potash and charcoal used to help the fusion of metals or minerals.
BLACK-FLY, [blak'-flī], *n.* the turnip-flea beetle.
BLACKFRIAR, [blak'-frī'-er], *n.* a Dominican friar.
BLACK-GAME, [blak'-gām'], *n.* black grouse.
BLACKGUARD (1), [blag'-ahd], *n.* a base, unprincipled, dishonourable scoundrel. [Uncert.].
BLACKGUARD (2), [blag'-ahd], *v.t.* to revile in violent language, to call a blackguard.
BLACKGUARDISM, [blag'-ahd-izm], *n.* the behaviour or language of a blackguard.
BLACKGUARDLY (1), [blag'-ahd-li], *adj.* like a blackguard; vile, dishonourable.
BLACKGUARDLY (2), [blag'-ahd-li], *adv.* in the manner of a blackguard.
BLACK-GUM, [blak'-gum'], *n.* a North American tree, *Nyssa multiflora*, producing a close-grained wood.
BLACKHEAD, [blak'-hed], *n.* a small black pimple, due to the stopping-up of a pore.
BLACK-HEART, [blak'-haht], *n.* a dark-coloured variety of cherry.
BLACKHEARTED, [blak'-haht'-id], *adj.* having an evil, wicked character.
BLACKHOLE, [blak'-hōl'], *n.* a place of confinement for insubordinate prisoners.
BLACKING, [blak'-ing], *n.* a black liquid or paste used for cleaning and polishing footwear.
BLACKISH, [blak'-ish], *adj.* rather black.
BLACK-JACK, [blak'-jak], *n.* a black draught; †a leather jug made like a jack-boot.
BLACK-LEAD (1), [blak'-led'], *n.* plumbago, graphite, used in making pencils, cleaning and blackening fire-grates, etc.; a writing or drawing pencil.
BLACK-LEAD (2), [blak'-led'], *v.t.* to polish and blacken with black-lead.
BLACKLEG, [blak'-leg], *n.* a swindler, a fraud; one who continues to work during an official strike; a non-union member who will work for less than union rates of pay; a cattle disease.
BLACK-LETTER (1), [blak'-let'-er], *n.* (*print.*) an ornate form of type, Gothic, Old English type.
BLACK-LETTER (2), [blak'-let'-er], *adj.* printed in black-letter.
BLACK-LIST (1), [blak'-list'], *n.* an official or private list of fraudulent or insolvent people; a list of convicted, suspected or discredited persons.
BLACK-LIST (2), [blak'-list'], *v.t.* to put down (a person's name) on the black-list.
BLACKLY, [blak'-li], *adj.* in a black manner.
BLACKMAIL (1), [blak'-māl], *n.* (*hist.*) a levy or tax of money, produce, livestock, etc., formerly paid on the Scottish Border to robbers to secure immunity from pillage or molestation; (*leg.*) the obtaining or attempt to exact money from a person under threats of violence or exposure. [BLACK and OScand. *mal* agreement].
BLACKMAIL (2), [blak'-māl], *v.t.* to obtain money from a person by blackmail.
BLACKMAILER, [blak'-māl'-er], *n.* one who blackmails.
BLACK-MARK, [blak'-mahk], *n.* a mark set down against the name of a person who does wrong.
BLACK-MARTIN, [blak'-mah'-tin], *n.* the swift.
BLACK-MATCH, [blak'-mach'], *n.* a firework match or sponge.
BLACK-MONDAY, [blak'-mun'-dā], *n.* any unfavourable day; originally a fatal Easter Monday, in the reign of Edward III.
BLACK-MOUTHED, [blak'-mowTHd'], *adj.* foul-mouthed, slanderous.
BLACKNESS, [blak'-nes] *n.* the state of being black.
BLACK-OUT (1), [blak'-owt], *n.* a sudden cutting off of all stage-lights to end a scene with effect; a complete failure of a public supply of electricity at night; the extinction or screening of all lights in a particular area; a state of temporary unconsciousness due to a sudden turn or dive while navigating an aircraft.
BLACK-OUT (2), [blak'-owt'], *v.t. and i.* to screen or extinguish lights so that their effects are not seen from outside the building in which they are.
BLACK-PEOPLED, [blak'-pēpld'], *adj.* possessing a black population.
BLACK-PUDDING, [blak'-pŏŏd'-ing], *n.* a kind of black sausage made from meat, suet, pig's blood, etc.
BLACK-RENT, [blak'-rent'], *n.* rent paid in kind or base coin; money paid to the Irish chiefs by the English for allegiance.
BLACK-ROT, [blak'-rot'], *n.* a destructive blight or fungus afflicting certain vegetables.
BLACK-RUST, [blak'-rust'], *n.* a disease occurring in wheat.
BLACK-SHEEP, [blak'-shēp'], *n.* a person of bad character, a scapegoat.
BLACK-SHIRT, [blak'-shurt'], *n.* a member of the Fascist party in Italy or Great Britain.
BLACK-SILVER, [blak'-sil'-ver], *n.* a mineral composed of silver, antimony and sulphur.
BLACKSMITH, [blak'-smith], *n.* a smith who works in iron.
BLACKSNAKE, [blak'-snāk'], *n.* one of various snakes of dark colour, *Zamenis constrictor*, etc.
BLACK-START, [blak'-staht'], *n.* (*ornith.*) the black redstart, *Ruticilla titys*.
BLACKSTRAP, [blak'-strap], *n.* (*coll.*) a strong inferior kind of port wine; a mixture of rum and molasses often served to sailors.
BLACKTAIL, [blak'-tāl], *n.* a kind of perch.
BLACK-TANG, [blak'-tang'], *n.* the seaweed, *Fucus vesiculosus*.
BLACKTHORN, [blak'-thawn], *n.* the sloe, a kind of thorn-tree, *Prunus spinosa*, with white flowers and black round berries; a staff made of the wood of this tree.

BLACKTHORN

BLACK-WAD, [black'-wod'], *n.* an ore of manganese used as a drying agent in paints.
BLACK-WASH (1), [blak'-wosh'], *n.* a black solution used for blackening an object; (*med.*) a lotion of calomel and lime-water.
BLACK-WASH (2), [blak'-wosh'], *v.t.* to cover or treat with black-wash.
BLACKWATER FEVER, [blak'-waw-ter fēv'-er], *n.* (*med.*) a tropical West African fever.
BLACK-WORK, [blak'-wurk'], *n.* blacksmiths' work in iron.
BLACKWORT, [blak'-wurt], *n.* the comfrey, *Symphytum officinale*.
BLADDER, [blad'-er], *n.* (*anat.*) a thin muscular bag, lined with mucous membrane, in the bodies of animals, serving as a receptacle for secreted fluids such as urine; the thin membranous sac of an animal used as a windbag for bagpipes, etc.; a tough rubber or membranous bag inflated with air; (*bot.*) a hollow, small baglike protuberance in certain plants; (*fig.*) an excessively talkative person. [OE. *blædre* bladder].
BLADDER - ANGLING, [blad'-er-ang'-gling], *n.* angling by means of a hook fastened to an inflated bladder.

BLADDERED, [blad'-erd], *adj.* swollen out like a bladder.
BLADDER-KELP, [blad'-er-kelp'], *n.* (*bot.*) a seaweed with small bladder-like protuberances on its fronds.
BLADDER-WORT, [blad'-er-wurt'], *n.* (*bot.*) a water-plant of the genus *Utricularia*, with tiny bladders on the leaves.
BLADDER-WRACK, [blad'-er-rak'], *n.* bladder-kelp, black-tang.
BLADDERY, [blad'-er-i], *adj.* resembling a bladder; containing bladders
BLADE, [blād], *n.* a narrow leaf of grass or corn; the broad part of a leaf; anything similar in shape to this; the cutting part of a tool or weapon apart from its handle; the broad part of an oar, propeller, paddle, etc.; a flattened broad bone; the front part of the tongue; (*fig.*) a sword or similar weapon; a company of men armed with swords; (*coll.*) a dashing young man. [OE. *blæd* leaf].
BLADEBONE, [blād'-bōn'], *n.* the shoulder-blade.
BLADED, [blād'-id], *adj.* possessing a blade or blades; blade-like.
BLADEFISH, [blād'-fish'], *n.* the hairtail, *Trichiurus lepturus.*
BLADESMITH†, [blād'-smith], *n.* a sword forger.
BLAEBERRY, [blā'-ber-i], *n.* (*bot.*) the bilberry or whortleberry. [OScand. *bla* dark-blue and BERRY].
BLAGUE, [blahg], *n.* swagger, conceited bluster. [Fr. *blague*].
BLAH, [blah], *n.* (*slang*) foolish, empty, exaggerated talk or writing. [Uncert.].
BLAIN (1), [blān], *n.* the whiting pout, *Gradus luscus.* [Unkn.].
BLAIN (2), [blān], *n.* an inflamed swelling, a pustule, a blister; a growth on the root of the tongue in cattle. [OE. *blegen*].
BLAKELING, [blāk'-ling], *n.* (*ornith.*) the yellow bunting. [OE. *blāc* pale, yellow].
BLAMABLE, [blām'-abl], *adj.* deserving blame.
BLAMABLENESS, [blām'-abl-nes], *n.* the condition of being blamable.
BLAMABLY, [blām'-ab-li], *adv.* in a blamable way.
BLAME (1), [blām], *n.* censure, reproof, disapproval, imputation of a fault; responsibility for failure or wrong action, guilt.
BLAME (2), [blām], *v.t.* to censure, to find fault with; to hold responsible for an offence or fault, to accuse. [OFr. *blamer* from L. *blasphemare*].
BLAMEFUL, [blām'-fo͞ol], *adj.* blamable.
BLAMEFULLY, [blām'-fo͝ol-i], *adv.* in a blameful way.
BLAMEFULNESS, [blām'-fo͝ol-nes], *n.* the condition of being blameful.
BLAMELESS, [blām'-les], *adj.* free from guilt or blame, innocent.
BLAMELESSLY, [blām'-les-li], *adv.* in blameless fashion.
BLAMELESSNESS, [blām'-les-nes], *n.* the quality of being blameless.
BLAMEWORTHINESS, [blām'-wurTH-i-nes], *n.* the quality of being blameworthy.
BLAMEWORTHY, [blām'-wurTH'-i], *adj.* deserving reproof.
BLANCH, [blahnch], *v.t.* and *i.* to make white, to deprive of colour, bleach; to remove the skin of (almonds); (*fig.*) to gloss over, to palliate; to grow white; to turn pale, to be drained of colour. [Fr. *blanchir*].
BLANCHED, [blahncht], *adj.* whitened, bleached; skinned (of almonds).
BLANCHER, [blahnch'-er], *n.* one who blanches.
BLANCHIMETER, [blahnch-im'-it-er], *n.* an apparatus for determining the bleaching effects of chloride of lime. [BLANCH and METER].
BLANCHING, [blahnch'-ing], *adj.* whitening; **b. liquor,** a bleaching solution of chloride of lime.
BLANCMANGE, [bla-monzh'], *n.* an opaque jelly pudding, originally white but now often coloured, made from cornflour, etc. [Fr. *blanc-manger* white food].
BLAND, [bland], *adj.* gentle, affable, ingratiatingly polite; mild, balmy. [L. *blandus*].
BLANDILOQUENCE, [bland-il'-ō-kwens], *n.* flattering speech. [L. *blandiloquentia*].
BLANDISH, [bland'-ish], *v.t.* to flatter, to coax, to wheedle with soft, ingratiating words. [~Fr. *blandir* from L. *blandiri* to flatter].
BLANDISHING, [bland'-ish-ing], *n.* blandishment.
BLANDISHMENT, [bland'-ish-ment], *n.* flattering cajolery; an alluring manner or thing.
BLANDLY, [bland'-li], *adv.* in a bland manner.
BLANDNESS, [bland'-nes], *n.* the quality of being bland.
BLANK (1), [blangk], *n.* an unmarked whiteness; a piece of paper having nothing written or printed upon it; an unsuccessful ticket in a lottery; emptiness, a state of vacancy or emptiness; a piece of metal ready for stamping or finishing; a white point in the centre of a target; an empty space in a document to be filled up later; an unmarked half of a domino; **a double b.,** a domino with no spots; **to draw a b.,** to be unsuccessful, to fail.
BLANK (2), [blangk], *adj.* appearing as a blank; white without mark; devoid of all writing or marks; vacant; destitute of interest or incident; abortive, unrelieved, pure; expressionless, nonplussed; (*poet.*) not rhyming; **a b. cheque,** a signed cheque with the amount to be drawn left to be filled in by the possessor; (*fig.*) a free hand; **b. cartridge,** one without ball or bullet. [Fr. *blanc* white].
BLANK (3), [blangk], *v.t.* to make blank.
BLANK-DOOR, [blangk'-daw(r)'], *n.* a recess in a wall resembling a door.
BLANKET (1), [blang'-ket], *n.* a thick, soft, loosely-woven cloth used as a covering; (*print.*) a piece of such a fabric or of rubber inserted between paper and platen to absorb uneven pressure, etc.; (*fig.*) a thick bank of clouds, a belt of fog; **a wet b.,** (*fig.*) one who spoils enjoyment for others. [OFr. *blankette* white cloth].
BLANKET (2), [blang'-ket], *n.* (*bot.*) the mullein, *Verbascum Thapsus.* [*Prec.*].
BLANKET (3), [blang'-ket], *v.t.* to cover with a blanket; (*naut.*) to take the wind out of a vessel's sails by drawing up alongside to windward.
BLANKETING, [blang'-ket-ing], *n.* cloth or material for blankets; tossing in a blanket.
BLANKLY, [blangk'-li], *adv.* in a blank fashion; utterly, absolutely.
BLANKNESS, [blangk'-nes], *n.* quality of being blank.
BLANQUETTE, [blong-ket'], *n.* a highly-seasoned stew. [Fr. *blanquette*].
BLARE (1), [blāer], *n.* a loud sonorous noise or blast as of a trumpet, etc.
BLARE (2), [blāer], *v.t.* and *i.* to bellow, to make a deafening sound. [Du. *blaren*].
BLARNEY (1), [blah'-ni], *n.* coarse flattery; grossly deceitful speech; crude cajolery; nonsense. [*Blarney*, in Ireland, where a stone stands which if kissed is said to endow a person with a flattering persuasive tongue].
BLARNEY (2), [blah'-ni], *v.t.* and *i.* to flatter, to coax.
BLASE, blasé, [blah'-zā], *adj.* extremely sophisticated and bored. [Fr. *blaser* to pall].
BLASPHEME, [blas-fēm'], *v.t.* and *i.* to curse, swear, use bad language; to desecrate in speech, to utter impious, profane remarks about; to abuse, revile. [Gk. *blasphemi* I speak profanely].
BLASPHEMER, [blas-fēm'-er], *n.* one who blasphemes.
BLASPHEMING, [blas-fēm'-ing], *n.* the utterance of blasphemy.
BLASPHEMOUS, [blas'-fim-us], *adj.* speaking or containing blasphemy.
BLASPHEMOUSLY, [blas'-fim-us-li], *adv.* in a blasphemous way.
BLASPHEMY, [blas'-fem-i], *n.* impious, profane, contemptuous speech or behaviour with regard to things held sacred; foul abuse, bad language. [Gk. *blasphemia*].
BLAST, [blahst], *n.* a sudden strong current of air, natural as in a gust of wind or artificially produced as in a current of air driven through a furnace or by an explosive; the loud sound produced by blowing certain wind-instruments, chiefly brass; the explosion in splitting up rocks by dynamite, gunpowder, etc.; the amount of explosive used; a pernicious, blighting disease attacking plants and animals, a flatulent disease in sheep; (*fig.*) a withering destructive influence; **in full b.,** (*fig.*) in a state of great activity; **b.-proof,** impervious to, giving protection against, bomb blast. [OE. *blæst*].
BLAST (2), [blahst], *v.t.* to shrivel up, to wither, to blight; to break up or blow up by the use of explosives; (*fig.*) to discredit, to ruin, to curse; to indulge in profane abuse. [OE. *blæstan* to blow].
BLAST (3), [blahst], *int.* (*a profane exclamation*) confound.
BLASTED, [blahst'-id], *adj.* blighted, withered; (*coll.*) confounded, infernal.
BLASTEMA, [blahs-tēm'-a], *n.* the primary material out of which plants or animals are formed and developed. [Gk. *blastema* a germ].

BLASTEMAL, [blahs-tēm'-al], *adj.* pertaining to the blastema.
BLASTER, [blahst'-er], *n.* anything that blasts or produces a blast.
BLAST-FURNACE, [blahst'-furn'-is], *n.* a smelting furnace in which heated air is driven through the molten metal.
BLASTING, [blahst'-ing], *n.* the breaking up of rocks by explosion; a shrivelling or withering, a blighting; the blaring of certain wind-instruments; (*wirel.*) distortion, *esp.* on loud notes.
BLASTOCARPOUS, [blast'-ō-kahp'-us], *adj.* (*bot.*) germinating inside the pericarp. [Gk. *blastos* a germ and *karpos* fruit].
BLASTOCOLLA, [blast'-ō-kol'-a], *n.* (*bot.*) a sticky substance with which several kinds of buds are coated. [Gk. *blastos* a germ and *kolla* gum].
BLASTODERM, [blast'-ō-durm'], *n.* (*biol.*) the external layers of cells of an embryo in its earliest form. [Gk. *blastos* germ and *derma* skin].
BLASTOGENESIS, [blast'-ō-jen'-is-is], *n.* (*biol.*) the theory that life originates from the germ plasma. [Gk. *blastos* germ and GENESIS].
BLASTOSPHERE, [blast'-ō-sfēer], *n.* an embryo having a blastoderm and a cavity. [Gk. *blastos* germ and SPHERE].
BLAST-PIPE, [blast'-pīp], *n.* a pipe in locomotives to convey waste steam up the chimney, creating a draught through the fire.
BLATANCY, [blāt'-an-tsi], *n.* the condition of being blatant.
BLATANT, [blāt'-ant], *adj.* noisily vulgar, loud-voiced, clamorous. [The *blatant* beast in Spenser's *Faerie Queene*].
BLATANTLY, [blāt'-ant-li], *adv.* in blatant fashion.
BLATE, [blāt], *adj.* (*Scots*) bashful, dull. [OE. *blāt* pale].
BLATHER (**1**) and (**2**), see BLETHER (1) and (2).
BLATHERSKITE, [blaTH'-er-skīt], *n.* empty talk, nonsense; (*U.S.*) a noisy empty person. [*Prec.* and SKATE].
BLATTA, [blat'-a], *n.* the cockroach; purple-dyed silk. [L. *blatta*].
BLATTER, [blat'-er], *v.i.* to speak rapidly, volubly and foolishly. [L. *blaterare*].
BLATTERING, [blat'-er-ing], *n.* senseless chatter.
BLAY, [blā], *n.* a small river-fish, the bleak. [OE. *blæge* gudgeon].
BLAZE (**1**), [blāz], *n.* a burst or jet of flame, a stream of light from a fire; a fire; a dazzlingly brilliant glow; (*fig.*) sudden flaring up of emotion; a white spot or mark on the forehead of a horse; a white mark made by notching the bark of trees; **like blazes**, with great vigour. [OE. *blæse* fire].
BLAZE (**2**), [blāz], *v.t. and i.* to burst into flames, to burn with a bright, strong light; to shine brilliantly and powerfully; to fire off ammunition continuously and rapidly; (*fig.*) to shine with anger; to mark trees by cutting away part of the bark; **to b. up, out,** to give way to a sudden burst of anger; **to b. a trail**, to mark out a path by blazing the trees; (*fig.*) to engage in pioneer work. [*Prec.*].
BLAZE (**3**), [blāz], *v.t.* to proclaim far and wide, to spread or publish abroad. [OScand. *blaza* to blow].
BLAZER, [blāz'-er], *n.* a light, often brightly-coloured, flannel sports jacket. [BLAZE (2)].
BLAZING, [blāz'-ing], *adj.* that blazes; (*fig.*) furiously angry; (of a fox's scent) very strong; glaring, extreme, wanton.
BLAZON (**1**), [blāz'-on], *n.* a shield or coat of arms together with its heraldic devices; a description in heraldic terms, or drawing, of armorial bearings; (*fig.*) display of excellences, titles, etc. [OFr. *blason* a shield].
BLAZON (**2**), [blāz'-on], *v.t.* to depict or inscribe armorial bearings; to describe coats of arms in proper terms; to embellish; to make known far and wide.
BLAZONER, [blāz'-on-er], *n.* one who blazons, a herald.
BLAZONMENT, [blāz'-on-ment], *n.* the act of blazoning.
BLAZONRY, [blāz'-on-ri], *n.* a collection of coats of arms or armorial bearings; the art of describing coats of arms in proper heraldic terms.
BLEA, [blē], *n.* (*bot.*) the inner bark of a tree. [Uncert.].
BLEACH, [blēch], *v.t. and i.* to whiten, to pale, to deprive of colour by chemical action or exposure to sunlight; to become lighter in this way. [OE. *blæcan* make white].
BLEACH CREAM, [blēch'-krēm'], *n.* cream, ointment, containing bleaching powder, used as an antidote for mustard gas.
BLEACHER, [blēch-er], *n.* a person or thing that bleaches.
BLEACHERY, [blēch'-er-i], *n.* a place where bleaching is carried out.
BLEACHFIELD, [blēch'-fēld], *n.* a field in which cloth is bleached.
BLEACHING, [blēch'-ing], *n.* the process of whitening or making lighter by chemical agents or exposure to sunlight.
BLEAK (**1**), [blēk], *n.* a small silvery river fish, *Leuciscus albumus*, allied to the carp. [Uncert.].
BLEAK (**2**), [blēk], *adj.* cheerless; bare, unsheltered, exposed; dismal, uninviting. [OScand. *bleikr* pale, colourless].
BLEAKISH, [blēk'-ish], *adj.* somewhat bleak.
BLEAKLY, [blēk-li], *adv.* in a bleak way.
BLEAKNESS, [blēk'-nes], *n.* the condition of being bleak.
BLEAR (**1**), [blēer], *adj.* (of the eyes) dim, watery. [ME. *blere*].
BLEAR (**2**), [blēer], *v.t. and i.* (of the eyes) to dim, to make indistinct, to blur, to dull or cloud; **to b. the eyes**, to deceive, hoax. [ME. *bleren*].
BLEAREDNESS, [blēerd'-nes], *n.* the condition of being bleared.
BLEAR-EYED, [blēer'-īd'], *adj.* not able to see distinctly.
BLEARY, [blēer'-i], *adj.*, blear.
BLEAT (**1**), [blēt], *n.* the cry of a sheep; (*fig.*) a feeble wail.
BLEAT (**2**), [blēt], *v.t. and i.* to make the cry of a sheep; (*fig.*) to babble, to blurt out foolishly. [OE. *blætan* to bleat].
BLEATING, [blēt'-ing], *n.* the crying of a sheep.
BLEB, [bleb], *n.* a small blister or swelling. [Unkn.].
BLEBBY, [bleb'-i], *adj.* covered with blebs.
BLEED, [blēd], *v.t.* to take blood from a person surgically; (*fig.*) to exact large amounts of money from a person wrongfully; (*motoring*) to draw fluid from an hydraulic braking system; *v.i.* to lose blood, to emit blood; (*bot.*) to emit sap; (of a book illustration) to extend to the edge of a page so as to leave no margin. [OE. *bledan*].
BLEEDER, [blēd'-er], *n.* a person suffering from haemophilia.
BLEEDING (**1**), [blēd'-ing], *n.* flow of blood from a wound; haemorrhage; the operation of letting blood; (*bot.*) the flow of sap from cut stems.
BLEEDING (**2**), [blēd'-ing], *adj.* that bleeds; (*fig.*) full of anguish or pity.
BLEMISH (**1**), [blem'-ish], *n.* a fault or flaw marring anything, a disfigurement, a physical or moral defect.
BLEMISH (**2**), [blem'-ish], *v.t.* to mar, to impair; tarnish, sully; to deface, to spoil the perfection of. [OFr. *blesmir* to become pale].
BLEMISHLESS, [blem'-ish-les], *adj.* without blemish, perfect.
BLENCH, [blench], *v.i.* to flinch, quail, shrink back. [OE. *blencan* to deceive].
BLEND (**1**), [blend], *n.* a mixture of wholly or slightly different substances to form a harmonious or pleasing whole.
BLEND (**2**), [blend], *v.t. and i.* to make a blend, to mix together so as to form an agreeable compound or combination; to mingle easily, to mix well together; to unite imperceptibly. [ME. *blenden*].
BLENDE, [blend], *n.* (*min.*) a native sulphide of zinc; certain other minerals of a peculiar lustre. [Germ. *blende*].
BLENDER, [blend'-er], *n.* one who blends.
BLEND-WATER, [blend'-waw'-ter], *n.* distemper of the liver in cattle.
BLENHEIM, [blen'-em], *n.* a breed of spaniel. [Originally bred at *Blenheim*, near Oxford].
BLENHEIM-ORANGE, [blen'-em-o'-rinj], *n.* a large orange-red variety of eating apple. [*Prec.*].
BLENNOGENOUS, [blen-oj'-in-us], *adj.* (*path.*) yielding mucus. [Gk. *blenna* mucus and *genes* producing].
BLENNORRHOEA, [blen'-o-rē'-a], *n.* excessive discharge of mucus; gonorrhoea. [Gk. *blenna* mucus and *rheo* I flow].
BLENNY, [blen'-i], *n.* a small freshwater fish covered with mucus. [Gk. *blennos* blenny from *blenna* mucus, slime].
BLESBOK, [bles'-bok], *n.* a South African antelope, *Alcelaphus albifrons*, having a white face. [Du. *bles* blaze and *bok* goat].
BLESS, [bles], *v.t.* to pronounce holy, to consecrate; to worship, to adore, to praise; to thank, to remember

with gratitude; to invoke God's favour upon; to make happy or prosperous, to be favoured with; **to b. oneself,** to make the sign of the Cross; **to b. one's stars,** to count oneself fortunate. [OE. *bletsian* to bless].

BLESSED (1), BLEST, [bles'-id, blest], *n.* those who are beatified.

BLESSED (2), BLEST, [bles'-id, blest], *adj.* prosperous, fortunate; consecrated, venerated; beatified, possessing or enjoying certain joys; eternally happy.

BLESSEDLY, [bles'-id-li], *adv.* in a blessed way.

BLESSEDNESS, [bles'-id-nes], *n.* the state of being blessed.

BLESSED-THISTLE, [bles'-id-thisl'], *n.* a medicinal herb, *Carduus benedictus.*

BLESSING, [bles'-ing], *n.* a prayer, invocation for Divine favour or happiness; a benediction, grace; a divine gift, favour or benefit; a cause of happiness; something to be remembered with gratitude.

BLEST, see BLESSED.

BLETHER (1), [bleTH'-er], *n.* foolish empty talk.

BLETHER (2), [bleTH'-er], *v.i.* to talk nonsense. [OScand. *blathra* talk nonsense].

BLETONISM, [blet'-on-izm], *n.* the faculty of water divining. [M. *Bléton* a water-diviner].

BLETONIST, [blet'-on-ist], *n.* a water-diviner.

BLEWIT, [blo͞o'-it], *n.* the mushroom, *Agaricus personatus.* [Uncert.].

BLIGHT (1), [blīt], *n.* an effect produced by disease, attacks of insects or parasitic fungi which cause plants to wither or decay; (*fig.*) anything which destroys hope. [Uncert.].

BLIGHT (2), [blīt], *v.t.* to affect with blight; to wither, cause to decay. [Uncert.].

BLIGHTER, [blīt'-er], *n.* (*slang*) an utter cad; a fellow.

BLIGHTING, [blīt'-ing], *n.* the action of affecting or being affected with blight.

BLIGHTINGLY, [blīt'-ing-li], *adv.* in a blighting way.

BLIGHTY, [blīt'-i], *n.* (*coll.*) England; **a b. one,** a severe wound which led to the return of a soldier to England. [Hind. *Billait* Europe].

BLIMEY, [blīm'-i], *int. expressing amazement,* (*vulg.*) [(God) BLIND ME].

BLIMP, [blimp], *n.* a small non-rigid dirigible military airship; (*coll.*) a person, usually of official rank, with exaggeratedly nationalist and imperialist ideas. [Unkn.].

BLIMP

BLIND (1), [blīnd], *n.* a screen of cloth or other material, which can be lowered from a roller to cover a window; a deception, something intended to produce a misleading impression; (*coll.*) a drinking bout; **the b.,** blind people.

BLIND (2), [blīnd], *adj.* unable to see, deprived of sight; (*fig.*) without understanding, judgment or appreciation; dark, obscure, concealed, admitting no light; having no outlet; pertaining to the blind; **to turn a b. eye to,** to pretend not to notice. [OE. *blind*].

BLIND (3), [blīnd], *v.t. and i.* to make blind, to obscure the perception, vision or judgment of; (*fig.*) to deceive; (*coll.*) to drive a motor vehicle at a highly dangerous speed.

BLINDAGE, [blīnd'-ij], *n.* a screen used for military purposes.

BLIND-COAL, [blīnd'-kōl'], *n.* anthracite.

BLINDER, [blīnd'-er], *n.* a horse-blinker.

BLIND-FIRE, [blīnd'-fier'], *n.* a fire laid ready for igniting.

BLIND-FLYING, [blīnd'-flī'-ing], *n.* (*aeron.*) aerial navigation entirely by means of instruments.

BLINDFOLD (1), [blīnd'-fōld], *adj. and adv.* having the eyes covered over with a bandage; (*fig.*) lacking understanding or judgment; deceived.

BLINDFOLD (2), [blīnd-fōld], *v.t.* to make a person unable to see by covering his eyes with a bandage.

BLIND-GUT, [blīnd'-gut], *n.* (*anat.*) the caecum.

BLIND-HARRY, [blīnd'-ha'-ri], *n.* blind-man's-buff.

BLINDLY, [blīnd'-li], *adv.* as if blind; (*fig.*) recklessly, without judgment, ignorantly.

BLIND-MAN'S-BUFF, [blīnd'-manz'-buf'], *n.* a game in which one, who is blindfolded, tries to catch any other player and guess his identity.

BLINDNESS, [blīnd'-nes], *n.* the state of being blind.

BLINDS, [blīndz], *n.(pl.)* (*milit.*) a screen of branches to protect the men in trenches.

BLIND-SIDE, [blīnd'-sīd], *n.* the vulnerable side.

BLIND-SPOT, [blīnd'-spot'], *n.,* a part of the retina insensible to light.

BLIND-VESSEL, [blīnd'-ves'-el], *n.* (*chem.*) a vessel having an opening on one side only.

BLINDWORM, [blīnd'-wurm], *n.* the slow-worm, *Anguis fragilis,* a legless lizard with extremely small eyes.

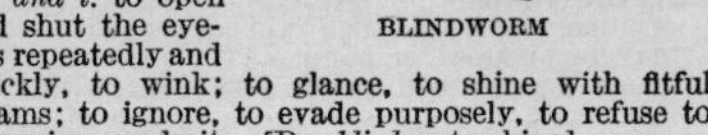

BLINDWORM

BLINK (1), [blingk], *n.* a sudden flash of light; a glimpse, a glance, a wink.

BLINK (2), [blingk], *v.t. and i.* to open and shut the eyelids repeatedly and quickly, to wink; to glance, to shine with fitful gleams; to ignore, to evade purposely, to refuse to recognize or admit. [Du. *blinken* to shine].

BLINKARD, [blingk'-erd], *n.* a person with weak eyes; (*fig.*) a person lacking in intellectual perception or understanding.

BLINK-BEER, [blingk'-bēer'], *n.* beer kept till it is slightly sour.

BLINKERS, [blingk'-erz], *n.(pl.)* broad rectangular pieces of leather fastened on each side of a horse's head over the eyes.

BLINKING, [blingk'-ing], *adj.* (*coll. as a mild expletive*) confounded.

BLINKS, [blingks], *n.* water chickweed, *Montia fontana.*

BLINKY, [blingk'-i], *adj.* with blinking eyes.

BLIRT, [blurt], *n.* (*naut.*) a gust of wind accompanied by a sudden, fierce shower of rain. [Unkn.].

BLISS, [blis], *n.* supreme happiness; perfect joy and blessedness of souls in paradise; the highest spiritual or physical delight. [OE. *bliths, bliss*].

BLISSFUL, [blis'-fo͝ol], *adj.* happy, enjoyable, full of bliss.

BLISSFULLY, [blis'-fo͝ol-i], *adv.* in a blissful manner.

BLISSFULNESS, [blis'-fo͝ol-nes], *n.* the condition of being blissful.

BLISSLESS, [blis'-les], *adj.* lacking bliss.

BLISTER (1), [blis'-ter], *n.* a pustule or bladder-like protuberance on the skin containing serum or watery matter, and caused by a burn, injury, etc.; a similar swelling on a heated or painted surface; (*med.*) that which causes a blister; (*naut.*) the outer covering of a ship having two hulls. [OFr. *blestre*].

BLISTER (2), [blis'-ter], *v.t. and i.* to raise a blister; to come out in blisters; (*fig.*) to shrivel with scorn or sarcasm.

BLISTER-FLY, [blis'-ter-flī'], *n.* the Spanish fly, *Lytta vesicatoria,* used medically to blister.

BLISTER GAS, [blis'-ter-gas'], *n.* a kind of poison gas which forms blisters on the human skin or membranes.

BLISTER-STEEL, [blis'-ter-stēl'], *n.* steel whose surface is covered with blisters during conversion from iron.

BLISTERY, [blis'-ter-i], *adj.* covered with blisters.

BLITE, [blīt, blit], *n.* (*bot.*) one of several plants of the order *Chenopodiaceae.* [Gk. *bliton*].

BLITHE, [blīTH], *adj.* merry, joyous, happy. [OE. *blithe*].

BLITHELY, [blīTH'-li], *adv.* in a blithe way. [OE. *blithelice*].

BLITHENESS, [blīTH'-nes], *n.* the condition of being blithe or blithesome.

BLITHERING, [bliTH-er-ing], *adj.* drivelling, utter. [BLETHER (2)].

BLITHESOME, [blīTH'-sum], *adj.* gay, cheerful, jolly.

BLITHESOMENESS, [blīTH'-sum-nes], *n.* blitheness.

BLITZ (1), [blits], *n.* a violent and sudden attack. [Shortened form of BLITZKRIEG].

BLITZ (2), [blits], *v.t.* to subject to a violent and sudden attack, *esp.* from the air. [*Next*].

BLITZKRIEG, [blits'-krēg], *n.* a form of warfare dependent on the very rapid movement of attacking forces, *esp.* of aeroplanes and tanks. [Germ. *Blitzkrieg* from *Blitz* lightning and *Krieg* war].

BLIZZARD, [bliz'-erd], *n.* a violent snowstorm, accompanied by a heavy gale. [Imitative].

BLOAT, BLOTE†, [blōt], *v.t. and i.* to cure herrings by salting and smoking them over an oak-fire; to cause to swell; to become swollen. [~OScand. *blautr* soaked].

BLOATED, [blōt'-id], *adj.* swollen with self-indulgence, turgid, flabby, fat by gluttony; (*fig.*) swollen with pride; (of fish, etc.), cured by salting and smoking.

BLOATEDNESS, [blōt'-id-nes], *n.* the condition of being bloated.
BLOATER, [blōt'-er], *n.* a herring that has been cured by salting and smoking.
BLOB, [blob], *n.* a blot, a globule of a liquid or semi-liquid; (*coll. cricket*) nought, a duck.
BLOBBER, [blob'-er], *n.* a bubble.
BLOBBER-LIP, [blob'-er-lip'], *n.* a thick protruding, loose lip.
BLOBBER-LIPPED, [blob'-er-lipt'], *adj.* having thick hanging lips.
BLOC, [blok], *n.* a group of parties supporting a government; a group of nations acting in concert. [Fr. *bloc*].
BLOCK (1), [blok], *n.* a regular or irregular solid mass of stone, wood, etc.; such a thing on which substances may be chopped or hammered, a piece of wood on which persons laid their necks when about to be beheaded; a continuous row or group of buildings without intervening spaces; a large quantity of shares; a frame casing which can be attached to an object and on which are mounted one or more grooved pulleys; an obstruction to the natural flow or free passage of anything, especially liquid or gas, traffic, etc.; a small piece of hard wood on which an engraving is made, an etched metal plate mounted on wood for printing illustrations; a dull, stupid person; (*cricket*) that part of the crease in which a batsman rests his bat in readiness for play; **b. system**, a traffic system whereby a section of a railway line has to be reported clear before a train is allowed to enter it; **b. tin**, impure tin run into ingots; (*coll.*) **a chip of the old b.**, a child who strongly resembles his father in person, interests, character or ability. [Fr. *bloc* from OHGerm. *bloh*].
BLOCK (2), [blok], *v.t.* to obstruct; to shut in, to enclose, to blockade; to shape on a block; to cut out in blocks; to support with blocks; to prevent or delay anything; (*cricket*) to stop a ball without attempting a scoring stroke; **to b. out**, to shape out roughly, to make a rough draft; to obstruct the line of vision, etc.
BLOCKADE (1), [blok-ād'], *n.* the surrounding of a port by enemy warships to prevent communication with, or receiving of supplies from, other nations; the besieging of a place by hostile forces, so as to cut it off from the outside world; **a paper b.**, an alleged but ineffective blockade; **to raise a b.**, to end a blockade; **b. runner**, a ship which tries to get through a blockade. [BLOCK].
BLOCKADE (2), [blok-ād'] *v.t.* to subject hostile territory to a blockade.
BLOCKHEAD, [blok'-hed], *n.* a stupid person.
BLOCKHEADISM, [blok'-hed-izm], *n.* the characteristics of a blockhead.
BLOCK-HOUSE, [blok'-hows], *n.* (*milit.*) a small temporary fortified hut.
BLOCKISH, [blok'-ish], *adj.* stupid, clumsy.
BLOCKISHLY, [blok'-ish-li], *adv.* in a blockish way.
BLOCKISHNESS, [blok'-ish-nes], *n.* the state of being blockish.
BLOCK-LETTERS, [blok'-let'-erz], *n.*(*pl.*) capital sans-serif letters.
BLOCK-LIKE, [blok'-līk'], *adj.* like a block: stupid, foolish.
BLOCK-PLANE, [blok'-plān'], *n.* a plane having the blade set so as to work across the grain of wood.

BLOCK-PLANE

BLOCK-PRINTING, [blok'-print'-ing], *n.* a method of printing from engraved blocks.
BLOKE, [blōk], *n.* (*slang*) a fellow. [Unkn.].
BLOMARY, BLOOMERY, [bloom'-er-i], *n.* the first forge through which iron passes after it is smelted from the ore.
BLOND (1), [blond], *n.* a person with light hair and fair complexion.
BLOND (2), [blond], *adj.* having light hair and fair complexion. [Fr. *blond*].
BLONDE, [blond], *n.* a woman with light hair and fair complexion; a kind of silk lace with hexagonal meshes.
BLOOD (1), [blud], *n.* an opaque red fluid circulating through the arteries, etc., of the human body and of other animals; (*fig.*) temper, passion, character; carnal nature as opposed to spiritual; bloodshed, murder, guilt of murder; sacrifice; life or essence, vital being; connexion by descent, lineage, relationship by birth; noble birth; good pedigree; a smart, dashing man-about-town; the juice of anything; (*slang*) a sensational thriller or mystery story; **flesh and b.**, human nature; **in cold b.**, deliberately; **blue b.**, noble birth or lineage; **base b.**, illegitimacy; **fresh b.**, (*fig.*) new influences, members, ideas, etc.; **to taste b.**, to kill and eat a hunted animal; (*fig.*) to be initiated into a new experience; **to spill b.**, to commit murder; **to have a person's b. on one's head**, to be guilty of his death; **to make one's b. run cold**, to terrify, horrify a person; **to make bad b.**, to arouse ill-feeling; **to make one's b. boil**, to make a person extremely angry or indignant; **one's b. is up**, used of a person whose anger is aroused; **b. sports**, the hunting and killing of animals for pleasure. [OE. *blod*].
BLOOD (2), [blud], *v.t.* to cause to let blood; to initiate a hound to the taste, scent, etc., of blood; to smear with blood; (*fig.*) to initiate.
BLOOD-BESPOTTED, [blud'-bi-spot'-id], *adj.* spotted or stained with blood.
BLOOD-BOUGHT, [blud'-bawt'], *adj.* obtained by the sacrifice of life.
BLOOD-BROTHER, [blud'-bruTH'-er], *n.* a male person born of the same parents as another.
BLOODED, [blud'-id], *adj.* smeared with blood, given the first taste of blood.
BLOOD-FEUD, [blud'-fewd'], *n.* a feud between two families arising out of the murder of a member of one by a member of the other.
BLOOD-FLOWER, [blud'-flow'-er], *n.* the red-flowered *Hæmanthus*.
BLOOD-GROUP, [blud'-grōōp'], *n.* (*med.*) a classification of the different types of blood; a classification of all persons who have the same type of blood.
BLOOD-GUILTINESS, [blud'-gilt'-i-nes], *n.* the guilt of murder.
BLOOD-GUILTY, [blud'-gilt'-i], *adj.* responsible for bloodshed or murder.
BLOOD-HEAT, [blud'-hēt'], *n.* the temperature of the human blood, about 98·4° Fahrenheit.
BLOOD-HORSE, [blud'-haws'], *n.* a thoroughbred horse.
BLOOD-HOT, [blud'-hot'], *adj.* of the same temperature as the blood.
BLOODHOUND, [blud'-hownd], *n.* a variety of dog with long pendulous ears and an acute sense of smell, used to pursue game or criminals.

BLOODHOUND

BLOODILY, [blud'-i-li], *adv.* in a bloody fashion.
BLOODINESS, [blud'-i-nes], *n.* condition of being bloody.
BLOODLESS, [blud'-les], *adj.* without bloodshed; lacking in blood; (*fig.*) devoid of energy or passion.
BLOODLESSLY, [blud'-les-li], *adv.* without loss of blood, without loss of life.
BLOODLETTING, [blud'-let'-ing], *n.* (*surg.*) the drawing of blood from a vein.
BLOOD-MONEY, [blud'-mun'-i], *n.* the reward paid to an informer for information leading to a conviction for murder.
BLOOD-ORANGE, [blud'-o'-rinj], *n.* a variety of orange yielding a fruit streaked with red and having red juice.
BLOOD-POISONING, [blud'-poiz'-on-ing], *n.* an infected condition of the blood, often characterized by the formation of abscesses on different parts of the body.
BLOOD-PUDDING, [blud'-pud'-ing], *n.* black-pudding.
BLOOD-RED, [blud'-red'], *adj.* red with blood, of the colour of blood.
BLOOD-RELATION, [blud'-ri-lā'-shun], *n.* one related by birth or descent.
BLOOD-ROOT, [blud'-rōōt'], *n.* (*bot.*) a plant related to the poppy family, *Sanguinaria canadensis*, whose root-stock produces a blood-red sap.
BLOODSHED, [blud'-shed'], *n.* the shedding of blood, slaughter, fierce fighting. [BLOOD and SHED].
BLOODSHEDDING, [blud'-shed'-ing], *n.* bloodshed.
BLOODSHOT, [blud'-shot'], *adj.* (of the eyeball)

streaked with blood, due to inflammation or breaking of small blood-vessels.

BLOOD-SPAVIN, [blud'-spav'-in], *n.* dilatation of the vein along the inside of a horse's hock.

BLOODSTAIN, [blud'-stān], *n.* a discoloration caused by smearing with blood.

BLOODSTAINED, [blud'-stānd], *adj.* coloured or smeared with blood.

BLOOD-STOCK, [blud'-stok'], *n.* thoroughbred or pedigree horses.

BLOODSTONE, [blud'-stōn], *n.* one of several precious stones streaked with red, and worn as amulets to stop or prevent bleeding; heliotrope; hæmatite.

BLOODSUCKER, [blud'-suk'-er], *n.* a creature that sucks blood; (*fig.*) one who extorts money from another.

BLOOD-SUCKING (1), [blud'-suk'-ing], *n.* the act of sucking blood by leeches.

BLOOD-SUCKING (2), [blud'-suk'-ing], *adj.* that sucks blood.

BLOOD-THIRST, [blud'-thurst], *n.* thirst for blood, lust for slaughter.

BLOODTHIRSTINESS, [blud'-thurst'-i-nes], *n.* the state of being bloodthirsty.

BLOODTHIRSTY, [blud'-thurst-i], *adj.* eager for slaughter, fierce, desirous of bloodshed.

BLOOD-TRANSFUSION, [blud'-trans-few'-zhun], *n.* transference of blood from one person to another who suffers from loss or lack of blood.

BLOOD-VESSEL, [blud'-ves'-el], *n.* an artery; a vein; a vessel through which blood circulates.

BLOODWARM, [blud'-wahm], *adj.* of the same temperature as human blood.

BLOOD-WON, [blud'-wun'], *adj.* gained by slaughter.

BLOODWOOD, [blud'-wŏŏd], *n.* one of various trees whose wood is red in colour.

BLOODWORM, [blud'-wurm'], *n.* the blood-red larva of a gnat found in water; a blood-red worm used as bait by anglers.

BLOODWORT, [blud'-wurt], *n.* the plant, *Rumex sanguineus.*

BLOODY (1), [blud'-i], *adj.* covered or stained with blood; (*fig.*) cruel, murderous; accompanied with bloodshed; of the same colour as blood; *used also as a common vulgar expletive.* [OE. *blodig*].

BLOODY (2), [blud'-i], *v.t.* to stain with blood.

BLOODY-EYED, [blud'-i-īd'], *adj.* having blood-shot or fierce eyes.

BLOODY-FACED, [blud'-i-fāst'], *adj.* having a bloody or fierce appearance.

BLOODY-FLUX, [blud'-i-fluks'], *n.* dysentery accompanied with blood.

BLOODY-MINDED, [blud'-i-mīnd'-id], *adj.* of a cruel, bloodthirsty disposition.

BLOODY-SCEPTRED, [blud'-i-sep'-terd], *adj.* having a sceptre won only after much bloodshed.

BLOODY-SWEAT, [blud'-i-swet'], *n.* a sweat accompanied by a discharge of blood, the sweating sickness.

BLOOM (1), [blōōm], *n.* the blossom or flower of a plant; the prime, time of life in which the nearest state to perfection is reached and enjoyed; rosy flush of health; the fine dust found on certain fruits, such as the plum, when newly gathered; name given to yellowish powdery deposit on leather, new coins. [OScand. *blomi*].

BLOOM (2), [blōōm], *n.* a lump of puddled iron forming a rough mass after smelting, and not yet rolled out into shapes; a lump of iron manufactured directly from the ore in a blomary. [OE. *bloma*].

BLOOM (3), [blōōm], *v.i.* to blossom, to flower; (*fig.*) to flourish, to prosper, to reach the prime of life, to enjoy the highest degree of perfection.

BLOOMER, [blōōm'-er], *n.* (*coll.*) a mistake. [Unkn.].

BLOOMERS, [blōōm'-erz], *n.(pl.)* women's knickers; a woman's garment (now obsolete) characterized by its jacket and its long knickers fastened round the ankles. [Mrs. *Bloomer* of New York, the inventor].

BLOOMERY, see BLOMARY.

BLOOMING (1), [blōōm'-ing], *n.* the state of being in bloom; the process of converting cast iron into a malleable form; a clouded appearance sometimes assumed by varnish on the surface of a picture.

BLOOMING (2), [blōōm'-ing], *adj.* in bloom, in a state of flower or blossom; in the full flush of health and beauty; (*coll.*) *as a mild expletive.*

BLOOMINGLY, [blōōm'-ing-li], *adv.* in a blooming fashion.

BLOOMINGNESS, [blōōm'-ing-nes], *n.* condition of being blooming.

BLOOMY, [blōōm'-i], *adj.* full of bloom, blooming, blossoming.

BLOSSOM (1), [blos'-um], *n.* the flower on a tree preceding the fruit; the mass of flowers on certain trees. [OE. *blostma*].

BLOSSOM (2), [blos'-um], *v.i.* to bloom, grow blossom; (*fig.*) to achieve success suddenly.

BLOSSOMY, [blos'-um-i], *adj.* full of blossoms, bloomy.

BLOT (1), [blot], *n.* a stain, a spot, a disfiguring mark, one caused by ink on paper; (*fig.*) a disgrace, fault. [ME. *blot*].

BLOT (2), (**blotting, blotted**), [blot], *v.t.* to make blots or disfiguring marks upon, to dry up (ink) with blotting paper; to obliterate; to render completely obscure to the sight; (*fig.*) to sully, blemish.

BLOTCH (1), [bloch], *n.* an eruption or pimple on the skin; spot or discoloured patch. [Unkn.].

BLOTCH (2), [bloch], *v.t.* to disfigure with blotches.

BLOTCHY, [bloch'-i], *adj.* disfigured with blotches.

BLOTE†, see BLOAT.

BLOTTER, [blot'-er], *n.* anything used to dry up ink, whether pad, book of blotting paper, or implement having a base covered with blotting paper.

BLOTTING, [blot'-ing], *n.* the drying up of ink by blotting paper; **b. paper**, unsized absorbent paper used for drying up ink quickly; **b. out**, total obliteration, complete effacement.

BLOTTO, [blot'-ō], *adj.* (*slang*) drunk. [BLOT (2)].

BLOUSE, BLOWSE, [blowz], *n.* a light, loose upper outer garment or bodice. [Fr. *blouse*].

BLOW (1), [blō], *n.* a sudden forceful expulsion of breath through the mouth; an outing in a strong breeze or gale, a walk in the fresh air; a stream of water emitted by a whale through its blow-hole; an egg deposited by a fly; **a b.-out**, (*slang*) a feast, a banquet, a beano. [BLOW (3)].

BLOW (2), [blō], *n.* a violent stroke, a hard knock, a sudden, violent impact; (*fig.*) an unpleasant shock, a sudden calamity, a strong disappointment or set-back. [Uncert.].

BLOW (3), (**blew, blown**), [blō], *v.t.* to drive or direct a current of air from a bellows, or from the lungs through the mouth, upon or through (an object); to drive or carry by a current of air; to clear or empty of matter by forcing a current of air through; to direct a stream of air from the lungs through the mouth into (a musical wind instrument), thus causing it to sound; (of a fly) to deposit (eggs); to cause to get out of breath by undue exertion; (*coll.*) to reveal, disclose; (*imper.*) a mild expletive equivalent to confound, or damn; *v.i.* to cause a current of air or gust; to expel air forcibly through the nose or mouth; to pant, to puff; (of a whale) to eject a stream of water from its blow-hole, to sound when blown, used of a wind-instrument; **to b. over**, to pass away without effect, to subside, to be forgotten; **to b. out**, to extinguish by blowing upon; **to b. out one's brains**, to kill oneself by firing a shot through the head; **to b. up**, to pump or force air into and cause to distend, to inflate; to explode; to destroy by means of explosives; (*coll.*) to fall into a sudden rage, to rate soundly, to scold; **to b. off steam**, (*coll.*) to give vent to one's feelings; **to b. in**, (*coll.*) to arrive, to visit; **to b. hot and cold**, to vacillate, to waver; **to b. one's own trumpet**, to boast, to speak well of oneself. [OE. *blawan*].

BLOW (4), [blō], *v.i.* (*poet.*) to blossom, to be in flower. [OE. *blowan* to flower].

BLOW-BALL, [blō'-bawl], *n.* (*bot.*) the fluffy head of a dandelion or similar plant when in seed.

BLOW-BALL

BLOWER, [blō'-er], *n.* one who blows; a whale; a contrivance for producing a forced current of air through a fire; an escape of fire-damp from fissures in the coal.

BLOW-FLY, [blō'-flī], *n.* (*zool.*) a fly which taints meat by laying eggs in it, usually applied to the *Musca vomitoria* and other species of two-winged flies of the genus *Calliphora.*

BLOW-GUN, [blō'-gun], *n.* a tube from which darts are propelled by the breath.

BLOW-HOLE, [blō'-hōl], *n.* the opening in a whale's head for ejecting a spout of water; a hole for the escape of foul air, steam, etc.

BLOWLAMP, [blō'-lamp'], *n.* a lamp with its fuel under pressure and vaporized by its own heat which produces an intensely hot beam of flame, used in brazing, etc.
BLOW-MILK, [blō'-milk], *n.* milk after the cream has been blown off.
BLOWPIPE, [blō'-pīp'], *n.* an instrument, usually in the form of a tube, through which air is blown on a flame to concentrate it at a particular place and increase its heat; a blow-gun.
BLOWSE, see BLOUSE.
BLOWY, [blō'-i], *adj.* windy, gusty.
BLOWZE, [blowz], *n.* a ruddy, fat-faced slattern. [Uncert.].
BLOWZED, [blowzd], *adj.* blowzy.
BLOWZY, [blow'-zi], *adj.* dishevelled, fat, tawdry.
BLUBBER (1), [blub'-er], *n.* the fat of whales and other large sea-animals; the sea-nettle, a kind of jelly-fish. [ME. *blober*].
BLUBBER (2), [blub'-er], *v.t. and i.* to weep or cry noisily; to make the cheeks red and swollen with weeping. [ME. *blubren*].
BLUBBERING, [blub'-er-ing], *n.* weeping noisily and persistently].
BLUCHER, [bloo'-cher], *n.* strong leather boot covering half the calf. [Marshal von *Blücher*, a Prussian soldier].
BLUDGEON (1), [bluj'-on], *n.* a short heavy stick, a stout cudgel. [Unkn.].
BLUDGEON (2), [bluj'-on], *v.t.* to injure by beating with a bludgeon.
BLUE (1), [bloo], *n.* the colour of a cloudless sky; a colour of an approximate wave-length of about .00045 of a millimetre; a colour of the visible spectrum between violet and green; a pigment or dye of this colour; a person who has taken part in an inter-university sporting or athletic contest between Oxford and Cambridge; a preparation used in laundering linen; (*fig.*) the sky; the sea; **a bolt from the b.,** an unexpected occurrence.
BLUE (2), [bloo], *adj.* having the colour blue, the livid colour of the skin when affected by intense cold, a bruise, etc.; (*fig.*) depressed, in low spirits; **true b.,** staunch, firm and loyal, genuine; **b. cat,** a species of Siberian cat; **b. gum,** a tree of the eucalyptus family; **B. John,** (*min.*) fluorspar; **once in a b. moon,** very rarely; **B. Peter,** (*naut.*) a blue flag with a white square in the centre used to indicate the departure of a ship; **b. ribbon,** the Order of the Garter; the ribbon worn by total abstainers; **the b. riband,** the distinction of holding the fastest sea-crossing of the Atlantic; (*fig.*) a coveted honour or prize in certain sports, racing, etc.; **b. rock,** the rock dove; **b. vitriol,** copper sulphate. [Fr. *bleu* from OHG. *blao*].
BLUE (3), [bloo], *v.t.* to make blue, to launder with blue; (*coll.*) to squander.
BLUEBACK, [bloo'-bak], *n.* the fieldfare, a migratory bird of the thrush family.
BLUEBEARD, [bloo'-bēerd], *n.* one who marries, and subsequently murders, more than one wife. [*Bluebeard*, a character in fiction].
BLUE-BELL, [bloo'-bel'], *n.* the wild hyacinth, *Hyacinthus non-scriptus*.
BLUEBERRY, [bloo'-be'-ri], *n.* (*bot.*) an American species of whortleberry, *Vaccinium pennsylvanicum*.
BLUEBIRD, [bloo'-burd], *n.* a small singing bird of the genus *Scalia*, blue in colour except for a red throat and breast.
BLUE-BLACK, [bloo'-blak'], *adj.* dark blue.
BLUE-BOOK, [bloo'-book], *n.* general name given to official reports or publications printed and published by order of Parliament, usually appearing as books or pamphlets with a blue cover.
BLUE-BONNET, [bloo'-bon'-it], *n.* the cornflower, *Centaurea Cyanus*; a Scottish trooper; the flat cap worn by a Scottish peasant.
BLUE-BOTTLE, [bloo'-botl'], *n.* a British plant with blue flowers, *Centaurea Cyanus*, growing in cornfields; a large blue species of blow-fly, *Musca vomitoria*.
BLUE-BREAST, [bloo'-brest], *n.* the bluethroat.
BLUE-CAP, [bloo'-kap], *n.* the blue titmouse, *Parus caeruleus*; the blue-bonnet; a salmon less than one year old.
BLUECOAT (1), [bloo'-kōt], *n.* a pupil at Christ's Hospital School, so called from the school uniform.
BLUE-COAT (2), [bloo'-kōt], *adj.* belonging to Christ's Hospital.
BLUE-FISH, [bloo'-fish], *n.* a fish, a species of *Chilodipterus*, related to the mackerel.
BLUEING, [bloo'-ing], *n.* the giving of a bluish tint to white clothes; heating of metals until blue; the discoloration of lenses by condensation; (*coll.*) extravagant spending of money.
BLUEJACKET, [bloo'-jak'-et], *n.* a seaman of the Royal Navy.
BLUENESS, [bloo'-nes], *n.* the quality of being blue, blue colour.
BLUENOSE, [bloo'-nōs], *n.* the popular name for an inhabitant of Nova Scotia.
BLUE-OINTMENT, [bloo'-oint'-ment], *n.* mercurial ointment.
BLUE-PILL, [bloo'-pil'], *n.* (*med.*) a preparation of mercury, used as a purgative.
BLUEPOLL, [bloo'-pōl], *n.* a fish related to the salmon, *Salmo albus*.
BLUE-PRINT, [bloo'-print'], *n.* a technical diagram or plan photographed on blue paper.
BLUES, [blooz], *n.* U.S. Negro folk songs *orig.* consisting of improvised three-line stanzas in jazz rhythm; (*coll.*) melancholy; **The B.,** name given to the Royal Horse Guards from the colour of their tunics.
BLUE-STOCKING, [bloo'-stok'-ing], *n.* a literary or pedantic woman belonging, originally, to an eighteenth century club which met to discuss literature, and at which men wore blue stockings to defy convention which insisted on black.
BLUE-STOCKINGISM, [bloo'-stok'-ing-izm], *n.* female pedantry.
BLUESTONE, [bloo'-stōn], *n.* a dark blue crystalline salt, copper sulphate.
BLUE-THROAT, [bloo'-thrōt], *n.* a migratory bird, *Sylvia suecica*, having sky-blue markings on its breast.
BLUFF (1), [bluf], *n.* a headland formed by the steep banks of a lake, stream, etc. [BLUFF (3)].
BLUFF (2), [bluf], *n.* deliberate deception as to true motives or state of affairs. [BLUFF (4)].
BLUFF (3), [bluf], *adj.* steep and almost perpendicular, rising sheer; (*fig.*) rough, hearty, outspokenly honest. [Unkn.].
BLUFF (4), [bluf], *v.i.* to disguise one's real intentions, to give a misleading impression of one's strength. [Unkn.].
BLUFF-BOWED, [bluf'-bowd], *adj.* (*naut.*) having broad, almost perpendicular bows.
BLUFFER, [bluf'-er], *n.* person given to bluffing.
BLUFF-HEADED, [bluf'-hed'-id], *adj.* (*naut.*) with an upright stem.
BLUFFNESS, [bluf'-nes], *n.* steepness; blunt heartiness.
BLUFFY, [bluf'-i], *adj.* abounding in prominent headlands.
BLUISH, [bloo'-ish], *adj.* tinged with blue.
BLUISHNESS, [bloo'-ish-nes], *n.* the condition of being bluish.
BLUISM, [bloo'-izm], *n.* female pedantry.
BLUNDER (1), [blun'-der], *n.* a stupid mistake, an error; an ill-advised or careless action.
BLUNDER (2), [blun'-der], *v.t. and i.* to flounder about, to proceed in a clumsy, stumbling manner; to make a careless mistake, commit a tactless, stupid action; to mismanage by clumsy inefficiency. [ME. *blondren*].
BLUNDERBUSS, [blun'-der-bus], *n.* an old-fashioned short gun having a bell-shaped muzzle and a wide bore, and fired by a flintlock. [Du. *donderbus* thunder-box].
BLUNDERER, [blun'-der-er], *n.* a stupid, clumsy person continually committing blunders.
BLUNDERHEAD, [blun'-der-hed], *n.* a stupid person.
BLUNDERING, [blun'-der-ing], *adj.* that blunders, clumsy, erratic.
BLUNDERINGLY, [blun'-der-ing-li], *adv.* in blundering fashion.
BLUNT (1), [blunt], *n.* a thick needle.
BLUNT (2), [blunt], *adj.* having an edge or point that is not sharp; (*fig.*) dull, thickheaded; abrupt, unpolished in manners. [Unkn.].
BLUNT (3), [blunt], *v.t.* to dull the edge or point of; (*fig.*) to make less sensitive (of feelings, sensibilities), to make less acute or refined.

BLUNDERBUSS

BLUNTISH, [blunt'-ish], *adj.* rather blunt.
BLUNTLY, [blunt'-li], *adv.* roughly, abruptly, unceremoniously.
BLUNTNESS, [blunt'-nes], *n.* the condition of being blunt.
BLUNT-WITTED, [blunt'-wit'-id], *adj.* stupid, thick-headed.

BLUR (1), [blur], *n.* a smear, a blot or stain; an indistinct outline or appearance.

BLUR (2), (blurring, blurred), [blur], *v.t. and i.* to smear, smudge; to make indistinct, to obscure the outlines of, to dim; to weaken or confuse the impression of. [Unkn.].

BLURB, [blurb], *n.* a publisher's eulogistic description of a book, often printed on the jacket of the book. [Invented word].

BLURT, [blurt], *v.t.* to reveal by means of a hasty and often inadvertent utterance. [Uncert.].

BLUSH (1), [blush], *n.* redness suffusing the cheeks of a person when moved by some strong feeling of modesty, shame, confusion, indignation; a rosy colour; **at the first b.,** at the first glance.

BLUSH (2), [blush], *v.i.* to grow red in the cheeks or face when moved by some strong emotion or feeling of modesty or embarrassment; (*fig.*) to feel ashamed. [OE. *blyscan* to blush].

BLUSHFUL, [blush'-fōōl], *adj.* prone to blush.

BLUSHFULLY, [blush'-fōōl-i], *adv.* in a blushful fashion.

BLUSHING (1), [blush'-ing], *n.* the act of becoming red in the face or cheeks under the stress of strong feeling, or through modesty.

BLUSHING (2), [blush'-ing], *adj.* covered or suffused with blushes; (*fig.*) modest, embarrassed, bashful.

BLUSHINGLY, [blush'-ing-li], *adv.* in a blushing fashion.

BLUSHLESS, [blush'-les], *adj.* without a blush; (*fig.*) shameless.

BLUSTER (1), [blus'-ter], *n.* a loud, roaring noise of stormy waves or gusts of wind; (*fig.*) boisterous, empty boasting; excited commotion, noisy display of temper.

BLUSTER (2), [blus'-ter], *v.i.* to rage in boisterous fashion (of winds, waves); (*fig.*) to threaten, scold, boast or rave in a noisy manner; to bully in an empty, swaggering way. [Unkn.].

BLUSTERER, [blus'-ter-er], *n.* one who blusters.

BLUSTERING, [blus'-ter-ing], *adj.* noisy, stormy, boisterous (of wind or waves); threatening, boasting or scolding in a loud manner.

BLUSTERINGLY, [blus'-ter-ing-li], *adv.* in a blustering fashion.

BLUSTEROUS, [blus'-ter-us], *adj.* boisterous, tempestuous; given to blustering.

BO, [bō], *int.* (*a word used to startle*); **to say b. to a goose,** to perform an action requiring the minimum of courage. [Imitative].

BOA, [baw'-a, bō'-a], *n.* a genus of non-venomous snakes of the family *Boidae*, found in South America, which crush their prey in their coils; (*pop.*) a python or any similar serpent; a boa-shaped fur worn by women round the neck; **b. constrictor,** a large snake of this genus. [SAmer. *boa*].

BOA

BOANERGES, [bō'-an-ur'-jēz], *n.* a loud-voiced, vehement orator or preacher. [Gk. *Boanerges* from Heb. *b'ney regesh*, Mark iii,17, "sons of thunder"].

BOAR, [baw(r)], *n.* the male uncastrated pig; the European wild boar, *Sus scrofa*. [OE. *bar*].

BOARD (1), BORD†, [bawd], *n.* a long, narrow, thin prepared piece of timber, usually rectangular, a plank; a table; a rectangular, vertical piece of wood on which notices are placed; food received at a table, meals taken regularly at a house in return for a specific charge; a thin piece of wood or cardboard on which certain games are played; an official body of persons, often a government department, having the management, control or superintendence of some public company, office or trust; strong pasteboard used as the outside cover of a book; (*naut.*) the deck or side of a ship; the line of a ship's course between two tacks; (*mining*) a cutting or hewing in a mine at right-angles to the face of the coal; (*pl.*) the stage; **above b.,** openly, honestly, fairly; **to sweep the b.,** to take all the prizes or rewards, to be extremely successful; **to go by the b.,** (*naut.*) to be swept away (of masts); (*fig.*) to be lost for good; **on b.,** aboard ship. [OE. *bord* plank, table].

BOARD (2), [bawd], *v.t.* to cover with boards; to supply with regular meals in return for a stipulated payment; to go on board a ship, to enter a vehicle of transport; (*fig.*) to accost; *v.i.* to receive meals at one's lodging in return for a specified payment; (*naut.*) to tack; **to b. out,** to take one's meals as a boarder; to put out in lodgings.

BOARDABLE, [bawd'-abl], *adj.* that can be boarded; (*fig.*) approachable.

BOARDER, [bawd'-er], *n.* one who receives board and lodgings at the house of another in return for a stipulated payment; a schoolboy who lives at school during term-time, as opposed to a day boy; one who boards a ship.

BOARDING-HOUSE, [bawd'-ing-hows'], *n.* a lodging-house, where persons board.

BOARDING-PIKE, [bawd'-ing-pīk'], *n.* a weapon used by sailors in boarding a ship.

BOARDING-SCHOOL, [bawd'-ing-skōōl'], *n.* a school where the pupils are housed and fed during term.

BOARD-RULE, [bawd'-rōōl], *n.* a figured scale for obtaining the area of a board without calculation.

BOARD-SCHOOL, [bawd'-skōōl], *n.* an elementary school under the management of one of the now obsolete school boards.

BOARD-WAGES, [bawd'-wāj'-iz], *n.* wages together with money allowed to domestic servants to keep themselves in food when living away from their employers.

BOARFISH, [baw'-fish], *n.* the red and silver fish, *Capros aper*.

BOARHOUND, [baw'-hownd], *n.* a hound used in the hunting of boars.

BOARISH, [baw'-rish], *adj.* cruel and depraved.

BOAR-SPEAR, [baw'-spēer], *n.* a spear used in hunting boars.

BOAST (1), [bōst], *n.* an arrogant expression of self-conceit; a proud assertion; a cause for boasting. [ME. *bost*].

BOAST (2), [bōst], *v.t. and i.* to make a statement of self-glorification, to brag, to glory in oneself or one's possessions; to assert in an arrogant, conceited manner; to be graced with, to possess as an attraction.

BOASTER (1), [bōst-er], *n.* one who boasts.

BOASTER (2), [bōst'-er], *n.* a broad chisel used by stone-masons. [Unkn.].

BOASTFUL, [bōst'-fōōl], *adj.* given to boasting; arrogant; containing boasts.

BOASTFULLY, [bōst'-fōōl-i], *adv.* in a boastful fashion.

BOASTFULNESS, [bōst'-fōōl-nes], *n.* the condition of being boastful.

BOASTING (1), [bōst'-ing], *n.* the making of boasts.

BOASTING (2), [bōst'-ing], *adj.* full of boasts.

BOASTINGLY, [bōst'-ing-li], *adv.* in a boasting fashion.

BOASTLESS, [bōst'-les], *adj.* without boasting.

BOAT (1), [bōt], *n.* a long symmetrically shaped hollow vessel or receptacle that floats upon water, is propelled either by oars, the action of wind on sails, or by mechanical means, and which is used as a means of transport; a small dish or utensil in the shape of a boat, used as a tureen; **to be in the same b.,** to be placed in like circumstances; **to burn one's boats,** to be irretrievably bound to a certain line of action. [OE. *bat*].

BOAT (2), [bōt], *v.t. and i.* to travel or sail in a boat, to place in a boat.

BOATABLE, [bōt'-abl], *adj.* navigable by small boats.

BOATBILL, [bōt'-bil], *n.* a South American bird of the heron family, *Cancroma cochlearia*, having a beak shaped like an upturned boat.

BOATBUILDER, [bōt'-bild'-er], *n.* one who builds boats.

BOAT-CAR, [bōt'-kah(r)], *n.* a trolley used for carrying canal boats on inclined planes.

BOATER, [bōt'-er], *n.* (*coll.*) a hard round straw hat with a flat top and rim, adorned with a band.

BOAT-FLY, [bōt'-flī'], *n.* the water-boatman, an aquatic insect, *Notonecta glauca*, which has oar-like hind legs and swims on its back.

BOATFUL, [bōt'-fōōl], *n.* that which one boat will hold.

BOATHOOK, [bōt'-hŏŏk], *n.* a hook on a long pole, used to control the movement of a boat near land, etc.

BOAT-HOUSE, [bōt'-hows], *n.* a shed for storing small boats.

BOATING, [bōt'-ing], *n.* the act of rowing or sailing in boats.

BOATMAN, [bōt'-man], *n.* a man who hires out or is in charge of a small boat.

BOAT-RACE, [bōt'-rās'], *n.* a race between crews of

two or more boats rowing in craft usually specially adapted for such racing.

BOAT-ROPE, [bōt'-rōp'], *n.* the painter.

BOAT-SHAPED, [bōt'-shāpt], *adj.* possessing the shape of a boat.

BOATSWAIN, BOSUN,† [bō'-sn], *n.* a warrant officer in the Royal Navy or a Mercantile Marine officer, who has charge of the boats, sails, rigging, etc., and summons the men to duty. [OE. *batswegen* a boatman].

BOAT-TRAIN, [bōt'-trān], *n.* a railway train whose arrival at or departure from a port is timed to approximate to the departure or arrival of a passenger-steamer.

BOB (1), [bob], *n.* a short, jerky ducking motion, a curtsey; the weighted ball on a pendulum, plumb-line or kite; a slight tap; a method of dressing women's hair by cutting it short behind and close to the neck, a horse's tail when docked; a bunch or knot of ribbon-like tassels; a bunch of worms used as eel-bait; (*pros.*) a short line ending a stanza; an implement for polishing metal surfaces; a pendant, an ear-ring; a wig of short hair; a peal of several sets of changes in bell-ringing; (*coll.*) a shilling. [Unkn.].

BOB (2), (**bobs, bobbed, bobbing**), [bob], *v.i.* to move about or up and down, with a short jerking motion; to make a rough curtsey; to angle for eels, using a bob as bait; to ride on a bob-sleigh; *v.t.* to move with a sudden, sharp, jerking motion; to cut short a horse's tail, to cut a woman's hair so that it lies close and thick round the back of the neck; to cheat; to snatch with the mouth at a suspended object; to tap lightly; **to b. up**, (*coll.*) to appear suddenly and unexpectedly. [Unkn.].

BOBBED, [bobd], *adj.* (of hair) cut short.

BOBBERY, [bob'-er-i], *n.* a disturbance, noisy squabble. [Hind. *bap-re* O father!].

BOBBIN, [bob'-in], *n.* a wooden cylinder with a flange at each end on which thread, wire, etc., is wound. [Fr. *bobine* a reel].

BOBBINET, [bob'-in-et], *n.* machine-made cotton net in imitation of lace.

BOBBIN-LACE, [bob'-in-lās'], *n.* lace made by hand with bobbins.

BOBBIN-WORK, [bob'-in-wurk'], *n.* work woven by means of bobbins.

BOBBISH, [bob'-ish], *adj.* (*slang*) lively, hearty.

BOBBLE, [bobl], *n.* the agitated movement of disturbed water; a small spherical ornament on a dress or hat. [Onomatopoeic word].

BOBBY, [bob'-i], *n.* (*coll.*) a policeman. [Sir *Robert* (*Bobby*) Peel, Home Secretary during the passing of the Metropolitan Police Act, 1828].

BOBBY-DAZZLER, [bob'-i-daz'-ler], *n.* a brilliant object.

BOB-CAT, [bob'-kat], *n.* (*U.S.*) a lynx.

BOBOLINK, [bob'-o-lingk], *n.* a migratory North American song bird, *Dolichonyx oryzivorus.* [Imitative.]

BOB-SLED, [bob'-sled], *n.* a bob-sleigh.

BOB-SLEIGH, [bob'-slā], *n.* a sleigh holding two or more persons.

BOBSTAY, [bob'-stā], *n.* (*naut.*) the rope which steadies the bowsprit.

BOBTAIL, [bob'-tāl], *n.* a horse or dog with a docked tail.

BOBTAILED, [bob'-tāld], *adj.* with the tail cut short; **b. wig**, a bobwig.

BOB-WHITE, [bob'-wīt], *n.* the American partridge, *Ortyx virginianus.* [So called from its note].

BOBWIG, [bob'-wig], *n.* a wig of short hair.

BOCAL, [bokl, bōkl], *n.* a cylindrical glass jar having a short, wide neck. [Gk. *baukalion*].

BOCHE, [bosh], *n.* (*slang*) a German. [Fr.].

BOCK-BEER, [bok'-bēer'], *n.* a German lager, containing a large proportion of malt. [Germ. *Bockbier*].

BOCKING, [bok'-ing], *n.* a coarse woollen cloth; a red herring. [*Bocking*, an English village].

BODE, [bōd], *v.t.* to portend, to be an omen of. [OE. *bodian* announce].

BODEFUL, [bōd'-fool], *adj.* ominous, threatening.

BOCAL

BODEGA, [bod-ē'-ga], *n.* a wine shop. [Span. *bodega* from Gk. *apotheke* store].

BODEMENT, [bōd'-ment], *n.* an omen, a presentiment.

BODGE, [boj], *n.* a coarse repair or patch. [BOTCH].

BODHI-TREE, [bod'-i-trē'], *n.* the bo-tree. [Skr. *buddhi* knowledge].

BODICE, [bod'-is], *n.* a close-fitting woman's garment covering the part of the body above the waist, the upper part of a woman's dress. [BODIES *pl.* of BODY].

BODIED, [bod'-id], *adj.* having a body, embodied.

BODILESS, [bod'-i-les], *adj.* having no body.

BODILY (1), [bod'-i-li], *adj.* pertaining to the body.

BODILY (2), [bod'-i-li], *adv.* in person, physically, in the flesh; (*fig.*) in a body, as a whole.

BODING (1), [bōd'-ing], *n.* an omen, a presentiment.

BODING (2), [bōd'-ing], *adj.* threatening, ominous.

BODKIN, [bod'-kin], *n.* a large blunt needle for threading tape through a hem or piercing holes. [ME. *bodekyn*].

BODY (1), [bod'-i], *n.* the material, physical structure or organism of living creatures; the trunk as distinct from the head and limbs; a corpse; a bodice; the main portion of a structure or work as distinct from appendages; a material object or substance; a group of persons united by a common purpose, the majority of the people, a number of individuals legally constituted or organized, and usually having some official function or position; strength, quality, consistency; (*coll.*) a person, a human being; (*theol.*) the bread in the sacrament of communion; **heavenly bodies**, the sun, moon and planets. [OE. *bodig*].

BODY (2), [bod'-i], *v.t.* to display in some external form, to give shape to; to be an example of.

BODY-CLOTHES, [bod'-i-klōTHz], *n.*(*pl.*) clothing for the body, coverings for a horse.

BODY-COLOUR, [bod'-i-kul'-er], *n.* a pigment possessing consistence, body and colouring power as distinct from a wash; an opaque colour containing a certain amount of white.

BODYGUARD, [bod'-i-gahd'], *n.* a group of soldiers connected with and guarding the person of a sovereign, ruler or high dignitary; a protective escort.

BODY-LINE, [bod'-i-līn], *n.* (*cricket*) short-pitched, fast bowling on the leg-side.

BODY-SERVANT, [bod'-i-sur'-vant], *n.* a valet or other personal servant.

BODY-SNATCHER, [bod'-i-snach'-er], *n.* one who disinterred and sold dead bodies for dissection.

BODY-SNATCHING, [bod'-i-snach'-ing], *n.* the illegal exhumation of corpses for dissection.

BODY-WHORL, [bod'-i-wurl'], *n.* (*biol.*) the last and largest turn of the spiral in the shell of molluscs.

BOEOTIAN, [bē-ō'-shun], *adj.* pertaining to Boeotia; dull, stupid. [*Boeotia* a district in ancient Greece noted for its stupid people].

BOER, [bōō'-er, baw(r)], *n.* an inhabitant of the Transvaal of Dutch descent, a Dutch colonist in South Africa. [Du. *boer* peasant, farmer].

BOG (1), [bog], *n.* marshy ground, a quagmire; (*vulg.*) a latrine, water-closet. [Ir. *bogach*].

BOG (2), (**bogging, bogged**), [bog], *v.t.* to sink or become entangled in a bog; (*pass.*) to become fast or trapped in a bog.

BOG-BEAN, [bog'-bēn], *n.* the marsh plant, *Menyanthes trifoliata.*

BOG-BERRY, [bog'-be'-ri], *n.* a popular name of the cranberry.

BOG-BUTTER, [bog'-but'-er], *n.* a fatty hydrocarbon found in peat-bogs.

BOG-EARTH, [bog'-urth], *n.* an earth or soil consisting of sand and decomposed vegetable fibre.

BOGEY (1), BOGY, [bō'-gi], *n.* a ghost, an evil spirit, the devil; a bugbear, a pet dislike; (*coll.*) a crust of mucus in the nose. [Uncert.].

BOGEY (2), [bō'-gi], *n.* (*golf*) the number of strokes in which a "scratch" golfer would hole out at each hole on a golf-course, the bogey for the course being the sum total of these strokes. [The mythical Colonel *Bogey*].

BOGEY-MAN, [bō'-gi-man'], *n.* a bogey.

BOGGARD, [bog'-erd], *n.* bogey; (*fig.*) imaginary terror, evil spirit, object of special dislike.

BOGGLE, [bogl], *v.i.* to falter, to shrink from, to raise scruples about; to bungle, to blunder; to dissemble. [BOGLE].

BOGGLER, [bog'-ler], *n.* an over-scrupulous, timorous person, a doubter.

BOGGY, [bog'-i], *adj.* full of bogs, marshy.

BOGIE, [bō'-gi], *n.* a frame provided with one or more pairs of wheels and pivoted below the frame of a railway carriage or locomotive to reduce the fixed wheel base and enable the vehicle to take curves of small radius. [Unkn.].

BOG-LAND, [bog'-land], *n.* marshy land.

BOGLE, [bōgl], *n.* a goblin, a bogey; a bugbear; a scarecrow. [Unkn.].

BOGMOSS, [bog'-mos], *n.* peat-moss of the genus *Sphagnum.*
BOG-OAK, [bog'-ōk], *n.* black oak found in bogs and used for ornamental purposes.
BOG-ORE, [bog'-aw(r)], *n.* a loose porous ore of iron hydroxide found in peat bogs and swamps.
BOG-RUSH, [bog'-rush], *n.* a sedgegrass of the genus *Schoenus.*
BOG-SPAVIN, [bog'-spav'-in], *n.* an encysted tumour on the inside of a horse's hock.
BOG-TROTTER, [bog'-trot'-er], *n.* an Irishman; one who shows agility in escaping over bogs.
BOGUS, [bō'-gus], *adj.* sham, counterfeit. [Unkn.].
BOG-WORT, [bog'-wurt], *n.* the bilberry.
BOGY, see BOGEY.
BOH, [bō], *n.* a chief of the Dacoits. [Burmese *bo*].
BOHEA, [bō-hē'], *n.* one of the varieties of black tea. [Chin. *Wu-i* hills in the north of Fukien].
BOHEMIAN (1), [bō-hē'-mi-an], *n.* a gipsy; one whose mode of living is free and unconventional. [Fr. *bohémien*].
BOHEMIAN (2), [bō-hē'-mi-an], *adj.* unconventional, gipsy-like.
BOHEMIANISM, [bō-hē'-mi-an-izm], *n.* the habits of a Bohemian.
BOIL (1), [boil], *n.* a small inflamed swelling on the skin, containing pus. [OE. *byle*].
BOIL (2), [boil], *n.* the state of boiling.
BOIL (3), [boil], *v.i.* to be heated to such a temperature as to cause a liquid to bubble and be agitated; to reach boiling point; to be cooked by boiling; (of a river or sea) to be violently stirred up by wind or strong currents; (*fig.*) to be wildly aroused by passion; (*coll.*) to be excessively hot and perspiring; *v.t.* to heat (a liquid) to such a temperature as to cause it to bubble; to heat (a liquid) to boiling point; to cook by immersing in boiling water; to subject to heat in a boiling liquid, for cleansing purposes, as a torture, etc.; **to b. away,** to evaporate by boiling; **to b. down,** to reduce by boiling. [OFr. *boillir* from L. *bullire*].
BOILER, [boil'-er], *n.* a person who boils; a vessel in which anything is boiled; a metallic vessel in which water is heated or converted into steam for various domestic and industrial purposes; **b. suit,** a trousered outer garment covering the body and limbs and used for dirty work.
BOILING (1), [boil'-ing], *n.* the process of bringing a liquid to the boil; the process of cooking by boiling; the amount of material boiled at a time.
BOILING (2), [boil'-ing], *adj.* in a state of boiling; (*fig.*) extremely hot and perspiring; violently agitated with emotion; **b. point,** the temperature at which a liquid turns to vapour.
BOISTEROUS, [bois'-ter-us], *adj.* rough, noisy, hearty. [ME. *boistous*].
BOISTEROUSLY, [bois'-ter-us-li], *adv.* in a boisterous fashion.
BOISTEROUSNESS, [bois'-ter-us-nes], *n.* the state of being boisterous.
BOK, [bok], *n.* an antelope. [Du. *bok*].
BOLAS, [bō'-las], *n.* a native missile used in South America consisting of a rope or thong to which are attached heavy metal or clay balls, which when hurled at an animal entangles its legs and causes it to trip up. [Span. *bolas, pl.* of *bola* ball].

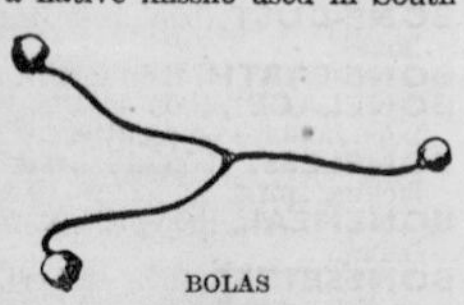
BOLAS

BOLD, [bōld], *adj.* daring, courageous; impudent; standing out, conspicuous; emphatic; steep. [OE. *bald*].
BOLD-FACE, [bōld'-fās], *n.* impudence; (*typ.*) letters made up of thick bold strokes.
BOLD-FACED, [bōld'-fāst], *adj.* impudent, brazen; (*typ.*) having heavy thick strokes.
BOLDLY, [bōld'-li], *adv.* in a bold fashion.
BOLDNESS, [bōld'-nes], *n.* courage, daring; impudence, lack of modesty.
BOLD-SPIRITED, [bōld'-spi'-rit-id], *adj.* courageous, adventurous.
BOLE (1), [bōl], *n.* the trunk of a tree. [OScand. *bolr*].
BOLE (2), [bōl], *n.* a compact, red or yellowish clayey earth. [Gk. *bolos* clod].
BOLECTION, [bol-ek'-shun], *n.* (*arch.*) a projecting moulding. [Unkn.].
BOLERO, [bol-āer'-ō], *n.* a popular Spanish dance distinguished by changes of time and rhythm; a short jacket or blouse barely reaching the waist. [Span. *bolero*].
BOLETIC†, [bol-et'-ik], *adj.* found in a fungus of the genus *Boletus.* [Gk. *bolites* mushroom].
BOLIDE, [bol'-id], *n.* a meteor that explodes in the air. [Gk. *bolis bolidos* a thing thrown].
BOLIVAR, [bol-ē'-vah(r)], *n.* the unit of currency in Venezuela. [Simon *Bolivar*].
BOLL (1), [bōl], *n.* a globular seed-vessel of flax or the cotton plant. [OE. *bolla* a bowl].
BOLL (2), [bōl], *n.* a measure of grain varying from two to six bushels. [OScand. *bolli*].
BOLL (3), [bōl], *v.i.* to form into round seed-vessels or bolls. [BOLL (1)].
BOLLARD, [bol'-ahd], *n.* strong post on the deck of a boat or quayside for securing ropes. [Uncert.].
BOLLING, [bol'-ing], *n.* a tree having its top and branches cut off.
BOLL-WEEVIL, [bōl'-wē'-vil], *n.* a weevil, *Anthonomus grandis,* which attacks the American cotton crops.
BOLL-WORM, [bōl'-wurm'], *n.* a caterpillar, the larva of the owl moth *Heliothis armigera,* which destroys the flowers, buds and pods of the cotton plant.
BOLO, [bō'-lō], *n.* the long knife used by the natives of the Philippine Islands. [Span. *bolo*].
BOLOGNA-FLASK, [bol-ōn'-ya-flahsk'], *n.* a flask of glass suddenly cooled, which flies into fragments if scratched. [*Bologna,* an Italian town, and FLASK].
BOLOGNA-SAUSAGE, [bol-ōn'-ya-sos'-ij], *n.* a large sausage containing bacon, veal and pork suet; a polony.
BOLOGNESE, [bol-ōn'-yēz], *adj.* relating to Bologna; **b. stone,** radiated sulphate of barium, first discovered near Bologna. [*Bologna,* an Italian town].
BOLOMETER, [bol-om'-it-er], *n.* an apparatus for measuring radiant heat. [Gk. *bole* ray of light and METER].
BOLSHEVIK (1), [bol'-shiv-ik], *n.* a member of that extremist, and majority, party at the split in the Russian Social Democratic Party in 1903, which later came into power after the Russian Revolution of 1917; (*pop.*) a Communist or extreme revolutionary. [Russ. *pl. Bolsheviki* members of a majority].
BOLSHEVIK (2), [bol'-shiv-ik], *adj.* pertaining to the Bolsheviks or Bolshevism.
BOLSHEVISM, [bol'-shiv-izm], *n.* the political principles and policy of the Bolsheviks.
BOLSHEVIST (1), [bol'-shiv-ist], *n.* a Bolshevik.
BOLSHEVIST (2), [bol'-shiv-ist], *adj.* pertaining to the Bolsheviks or their policy.
BOLSHY (1), [bol'-shi], *n.* a Bolshevik. [Shortened form of BOLSHEVIK].
BOLSHY (2), [bol'-shi], *adj.* Bolshevik. [*Prec.*].
BOLSTER (1), [bōl'-ster], *n.* a long, round underpillow of a bed; a pad; a base; a strengthening in various pieces of mechanism. [OE. *bolster*].
BOLSTER (2), [bōls'-ter], *v.t.* to support with a bolster or pad; **to b. up,** to give support to, to prop up.
BOLSTER-CASE, [bōl'-ster-kās·], *n.* a cover for a bolster.
BOLSTERER, [bōl'-ster-er], *n.* one who bolsters, a supporter.
BOLSTERING, [bōl'-ster-ing], *n.* propping up, support.
BOLT (1), [bōlt], *n.* a short thick arrow shot from a crossbow; a thick metal bar fastened to a door, and sliding out into a socket in the door-post to prevent the door opening; a window catch which prevents the window from being opened from the outside, a sliding pin which locks a rifle breech; a metal pin with a head and screwed shank; a thunderbolt, lightning; a rapid start or dart away, a sudden dash; a long roll of fabric; a rapid gulp of unchewed food; **to shoot one's b.,** (*coll.*) to make a final effort. [OE. *bolt* arrow].
BOLT (2), [bōlt], *v.t.* to secure or fasten with a bolt; to swallow hastily and without proper mastication; to fasten together by nut and bolt; *v.i.* to dart off, to run away quickly in an unexpected manner.
BOLT-AUGER, [bōlt'-awg'-er], *n.* a large boring tool.
BOLT-BOAT†, [bōlt'-bōt], *n.* a strong boat able to withstand a rough sea.
BOLT-HEAD, [bōlt'-hed], *n.* the head of a bolt; (*chem.*) a spherical distillation flask fitted with a long cylindrical neck.
BOLTING, [bōlt'-ing], *n.* the act of fastening with a bolt, a sudden dash or dart; the act of gulping down food.
BOLTONITE, [bōlt'-on-īt], *n.* a granular mineral, a kind of olivine. [*Bolton,* U.S.A., where found].
BOLT-ROPE, [bōlt'-rōp], *n.* (*naut.*) rope sewn to the edges of sails for strengthening purposes.
BOLT-SPRIT, see BOWSPRIT.

BOLT-UPRIGHT, [bōlt'-up'-rīt], *adj.* perfectly erect.
BOLUS, [bō'-lus], *n.* a large pill. [L. from Gk. *bolos* lump].
BOMB (1), [bom], *n.* a metal case filled with explosive, etc., which detonates or catches fire; an apparatus arranged to explode at a given time; a porous mass of igneous rock from a volcano; **b. rack,** the rack in which bombs are packed in an aeroplane ready for release. [Fr. *bombe*].
BOMB (2), [bom], *v.t.* to attack with bombs.
BOMBARD (1), [bom'-bahd], *n.* a primitive cannon; a ship carrying mortars for bombing purposes. [OFr. *bombarde*].

BOMBARD

BOMBARD (2), [bom-bahd'], *v.t.* to attack with artillery; (*fig.*) to fire or direct a continuous stream (of questions, etc.) at.
BOMBARDIER, [bom'-ber-dēer'], *n.* the lowest grade of non-commissioned artillery officer; **b. beetle,** a beetle of the general *Brachinus* or *Aptinus*, which when assailed expels an acrid fluid. [Fr. *bombardier*].
BOMBARDMENT, [bom-bahd'-ment], *n.* an attack with bombs, or artillery.
BOMBARDON, [bom-bahd'-on], *n.* (*mus.*) a brass wind instrument; an organ stop producing a similar sound.

BOMBARDON

BOMBAST, [bom'-bast], *n.* high-sounding, pompous language. [L. *bombyx* silk from Gk. *bombux* silkworm, hence padding].
BOMBASTIC, [bom-bast'-ik], *adj.* high-flown, pompous.
BOMBAX, [bom'-baks], *n.* a genus of large, soft-wooded tropical trees of the order *Sterculiaceae*, whose seeds are enclosed in a mass of silky hair from which silk-cotton is obtained. [Gk. *bombux* silkworm].
BOMBAY-DUCK, [bom'-bā-duk'], *n.* a small Indian transparent fish, *Saurus ophiodon*, which, salted and dried, is esteemed a great delicacy.
BOMBAZETTE, [bom'-ba-zet'], *n.* a kind of thin woollen cloth. [Fr. *bombasette*].
BOMBAZINE, [bom'-baz-ēn'], *n.* a twilled fabric of silk or cotton and worsted, generally used for mourning. [OFr. *bombasin* from L. *bombyx* silk].
BOMBE, [bawmb], *n.* a sweet or iced pudding made in a cone-shaped mould.
BOMBER, [bom'-er], *n.* a bomb-carrying aeroplane; a soldier who throws bombs.
BOMBERNICKEL, [bom'-ber-nikl'], *n.* a sort of coarse bran bread. [Uncert.].
BOMBIATE, [bom'-bi-at], *n.* (*chem.*) a salt of bombic acid. [*Gk. bombux* silkworm].
BOMBIC, [bom'-bik], *adj.* pertaining to the silkworm; **b. acid,** (*chem.*) an acid obtained from the silkworm.
BOMB-KETCH, [bom'-kech'], *n.* a small ship containing mortars for firing bombs.
BOMB-PROOF, [bom'-proof], *adj.* affording protection against bombs.
BOMBSHELL, [bom'-shel], *n.* a bomb; (*fig.*) a violent surprise.
BOMB-VESSEL, [bom'-ves'-el], *n.* a bomb-ketch.
BOMBYCINOUS, [bom-bis'-in-us], *adj.* silken, of the colour of the silkworm. [L. *bombycinus* silken from Gk. *bombux*].
BOMBYX, [bom'-biks], *n.* the silkworm, the genus of moths to which the silkworm moth belongs. [L. *bombyx* from Gk. *bombux*].
BONA FIDE (1), [bō'-na-fī'-di], *adj.* genuine.
BONA FIDE (2), [bō'-na-fī'-di], *adv.* without fraud or deception. [L. *bona fide* in good faith].
BONA FIDES, [bō'-na-fī'-diz], *n.* (*leg.*) good faith, sincerity.
BONANZA, [bon-an'-za], *n.* a vein of rich ore in a mine; (*fig.*) a windfall of good fortune, prosperity. [Span. *bonanza* good luck].
BONASUS, [bon-ā'-sus], *n.* a variety of bison or wild ox, *Bos bonasus*. [Gk. *bonasos* bison].
BONBON, [bon'-bon'], *n.* a sweetmeat or confection. [Fr. *bonbon* from *bon* good].
BONBONNIERE, bonbonnière, [bon'-bon-i-āer'], *n.* a small dish or box for sweetmeats. [*Prec.*].
BOND (1), [bond], *n.* that which binds; chain, fetter; (*fig.*) a connecting link, an element which serves to join together; (*leg.*) a written agreement or promise to perform a certain action or pay a certain sum of money; an acknowledgment of money lent; a method of arranging bricks in a wall, endwise and longitudinally, so that they overlap and hold together; government custody of goods until duty has been paid. [OE. *bond*].
BOND (2), [bond], *adj.* in a state of bondage.
BOND (3), [bond], *v.t.* to connect (bricks in building) by means of a bond; to change (a loan) into a bond; to hold (imported goods) until the duties are paid.
BONDAGE, [bond'-ij], *n.* lack of freedom, slavery, captivity; (*fig.*) the subjugating influence of anything. [ME. *bondage*].
BOND-CREDITOR, [bond'-kred'-it-er], *n.* a creditor secured by a bond.
BOND-DEBT, [bond'-det], *n.* a debt incurred under a bond.
BONDED, [bond'-id], *adj.* secured or held by a bond; **b. goods,** goods retained by the government until duty on them is paid; **b. warehouse,** a store for goods so retained.
BONDHOLDER, [bond'-hōld'-er], *n.* a bond-creditor.
BONDING, [bond'-ing], *n.* the joining of bricks by a bond; (*aeron.*) gauze used to make a good electrical earth.
BONDMAID, [bond'-mād], *n.* a female slave.
BONDMAN, [bond'-man], *n.* a slave. [OScand. *bondi* yeoman].
BONDSERVANT, [bond'-sur'-vant], *n.* a slave.
BONDSERVICE, [bond'-sur'-vis], *n.* a condition of slavery.
BONDSLAVE, [bond'-slāv], *n.* a person in slavery.
BONDSMAN, [bondz'-man], *n.* a surety; a slave.
BOND(S)WOMAN, [bond(z)'-woom'-an], *n.* a female slave.
BONE (1), [bōn], *n.* the hard substance forming the skeleton or framework of mammals, birds, fishes, and reptiles; each of the parts which are joined together to form the skeleton; other hard substances in the animal body resembling this; (*pl.*) corpse; pieces of bone held between the fingers and rattled together rhythmically; (*fig.*) system, nature; **a b. of contention,** a cause of dispute; **to have a b. to pick,** to intend a dispute about a certain matter; **to make no bones,** (*coll.*) to have no scruples. [OE. *ban*].
BONE (2), [bōn], *v.t.* to remove the bones from; to stiffen or manure with bones; (*slang*) to steal; (*surveying*) to test the level of with boning rods.
BONE-ACHE, [bōn'-āk], *n.* pain in the bones.
BONE-ASH, [bōn'-ash'], *n.* the residue of burnt bones.
BONE-BED, [bōn'-bed'], *n.* a stratum of rock containing fossil bones.
BONE-BLACK, [bōn'-blak'], *n.* charcoal obtained from burnt bones and used as an absorbent or filter.
BONE-BREAKER, [bōn'-brāk'-er], *n.* the osprey or fish-hawk.
BONED, [bōnd], *adj.* possessing bones; with the bones taken out.
BONE-DUST, [bōn'-dust], *n.* manure made of crushed bones.
BONE-EARTH, [bōn'-urth], *n.* bone-ash.
BONELACE†, [bōn'-lās], *n.* lace made by hand with bone bobbins on a pattern of pins.
BONELESS, [bōn'-les], *adj.* without bones; (*fig.*) lacking spirit.
BONEMEAL, [bōn-mēl], *n.* meal made from ground bones.
BONESETTER, [bōn'-set'-er], *n.* one who sets broken or dislocated bones.
BONESETTING, [bōn'-set'-ing], *n.* the art of setting broken or dislocated bones.
BONESHAKER, [bōn'-shāk'-er], *n.* an old-fashioned bicycle; any decrepit rattling vehicle.
BONE-SPAVIN, [bōn'-spav'-in], *n.* a bony growth on the inside of the hock of a horse's leg.
BONETTA, see BONITO.
BONFIRE, [bon'-fīer], *n.* a large fire in the open air lighted as a beacon at festivities or to destroy rubbish.

BONGO

BONGO, [bong'-gō], *n.* a large striped antelope native to East and West Africa. [Native].

BONHOMIE, [bon'-om-ē], *n.* good-nature, geniality. [Fr. *bonhomie*].

BONING, [bōn'-ing], *n.* (*surveying*) the act or method of judging a plane surface, or of setting objects on the level by looking along the top of a line of rods spaced out at intervals.

BONISM, [bōn'-izm], *n.* the doctrine that the world is good but not perfect. [L. *bonus* good].

BONITO, BONETTA, [bōn-ē'-tō], *n.* one of several fishes of the mackerel family, the stripe-bellied tunny. [Span. *bonito*].

BON MOT, (*pl.* **bons mots**), [bon'-mō'], *n.* a witty repartee. [Fr. *bon mot* good saying].

BONNET (1), [bon'-it], *n.* a soft, brimless head-covering fastened under the chin with strings and worn by women and babies, a flat cap worn by Scotsmen; the cowl on a chimney or locomotive, the protective covering of thin metal sheets encasing the engine of a motor-car, the safety or protective cap over the works of certain kinds of machinery; (*naut.*) a small sail attached to a larger one in order to attract more wind. [OFr. *bonet*].

BONNET (2), [bon'-it], *v.t.* to put on a bonnet, to pull down forcibly a person's hat over his eyes.

BONNETED, [bon'-it-id], *adj.* wearing a bonnet; having the hat crushed down over the eyes.

BONNET-PEPPER, [bon'-it-pep'-er], *n.* a variety of *Capsicum* with a bonnet-shaped fruit.

BONNET-ROUGE, [bon'-ā-rōōzh'], *n.* an extreme Republican, so called from the red caps worn by the Sansculottes in 1793. [Fr. *bonnet rouge*].

BONNILY, [bon'-i-li], *adv.* in a bonny fashion.

BONNINESS, [bon'-i-nes], *n.* quality of being bonny.

BONNY, [bon'-i], *adj.* handsome, pretty, comely, naturally good-looking. [ME. *boni*].

BONNY-CLABBER, [bon'-i-klab'-er], *n.* milk thickened and clotted when sour. [Ir. *bainne* milk and *claba* thick].

BONSPIEL, [bon'-spēl], *n.* (*Scots*) a curling match. [Uncert.].

BONTEBOK, [bon'-ti-bok'], *n.* the South African pied antelope, *Alcelaphus pygarga*. [Du. *bont* pied and *bok* goat].

BON TON, [baw(ng)'-taw(ng)'], *n.* good breeding, the height of fashion. [Fr. *bon ton*].

BONUS, [bō'-nus], *n.* extra remuneration, or money paid in excess of salary to workmen for services performed; an extra dividend to shareholders, insurance policy-holders, etc., paid out of profits made. [L. *bonus* good].

BON-VIVANT, [bon'-vē-vah(ng')], *n.* an epicure. [Fr. *bon vivant* good living].

BONXIE, [bongk'-si], *n.* the great skua, one of the pirate gulls of Shetland. [Unkn.].

BONY, [bōn'-i], *adj.* resembling or pertaining to a bone, hard; full of or characterized by bones; having large prominent bones; (*coll.*) emaciated.

BONZE, [bonz], *n.* a Buddhist monk in China or Japan. [Jap. *bonzi*].

BOO (1), [bōō], *int.* a verbal indication of disapproval.

BOO (2), (**booes, booed**), [bōō], *v.t. and i.* to express verbal disapproval by saying "boo", to drive away an animal by this cry; to greet with boos.

BOOB, [bōōb], *n.* (*slang*) a stupid clumsy fellow.

BOOBY, [bōōb'-i], *n.* a stupid blockhead, a dunce; a species of supposedly stupid swimming-bird, the *Sula*, related to the gannet. [Span. *bobo* fool].

BOOBY-HATCH, [bōōb'-i-hach'], *n.* (*naut.*) the covering over the hatchway to the forepeak.

BOOBY-HUT, [bōōb'-i-hut'], *n.* a kind of covered sleigh.

BOOBY-HUTCH, [bōōb'-i-huch'], *n.* a small, clumsy covered cart formerly used in England, a hand-barrow.

BOOBY-PRIZE, [bōōb'-i-priz'], *n.* a prize awarded as a jest to the least successful competitor.

BOOBY-TRAP, [bōōb'-i-trap'], *n.* a trap in the form of an object arranged so as to fall on the head of a passer-by or to cause him to trip up.

BOODHISM, see BUDDHISM.

BOODLE (1), [bōōdl], *n.* (*slang*) a crowd, the whole lot; money for political bribery; a card game. [Unkn.].

BOODLE (2), [bōōdl], *n.* the corn marigold, *Chrysanthemum segetum*. [Unkn.].

BOOHOO (1), [bōō'-hōō'], *n.* a noisy weeping. [Imitative].

BOOHOO (2), [bōō-hōō'], *v.i.* to weep loudly.

BOOK (1), [bŏŏk], *n.* a collection of blank, printed or written sheets bound together at the back, usually enclosed in protective covers and forming a compact whole, a written or printed treatise sufficiently large to constitute a book, a large section of a long literary work; the words of an opera, etc., as distinct from the music; the financial records of a business or other undertaking; a record of the bets made by a bookmaker on the result of a race or sporting contest, together with the variations in odds offered, as determined by the money wagered; the Bible; (*fig.*) medium providing instruction; (*pl.*) studies; list of patients, clients, customers; **b. matches,** matches packed in the form of a booklet; **bring to b.,** to call to reckoning; **in one's good** or **bad books,** in or out of favour; **to take a leaf out of a person's b.,** to copy or imitate a person; **to suit one's b.,** to please, to satisfy; **to make a b.,** to act as a bookmaker. [OE. *boc*].

BOOK (2), [bŏŏk], *v.t.* to enter or write down in a book; to order in advance, to reserve a place or seat; to buy a ticket; to engage a person in advance to perform a certain action on a future specified occasion.

BOOKBINDER, [bŏŏk'-bind'-er], *n.* one who binds books.

BOOKBINDERY, [bŏŏk'-bind'-er-i], *n.* a factory or workshop for binding books.

BOOKBINDING, [bŏŏk'-bind'-ing], *n.* the art or trade of binding books.

BOOKCASE, [bŏŏk'-kās], *n.* an upright case fitted with shelves for holding books.

BOOK-DEBT, [bŏŏk'-det'], *n.* a debt charged in an account book.

BOOKED, [bŏŏkt], *adj.* reserved, engaged, registered in a book, bound, engaged to perform a certain action, having an appointment fixed with; **b. up,** completely engaged or reserved.

BOOK-ENDS, [bŏŏk'-endz'], *n.*(*pl.*) a pair of heavy ornaments or plates to keep erect a row of unshelved books.

BOOKFUL, [bŏŏk'-fŏŏl], *n.* as much as can be contained in a book.

BOOK-HUNTER, [bŏŏk'-hunt'-er], *n.* a collector of old and rare books.

BOOKIE, [bŏŏk'-i], *n.* (*coll.*) a bookmaker or commission agent.

BOOKING, [bŏŏk'-ing], *n.* act of entering or registering in a book, anything so entered or registered; (*pl.*) reservations; seats at a public entertainment, on a vehicle, etc., engaged in advance; **b. clerk,** person who enters up or makes bookings, *esp.* a clerk who issues railway tickets, a person who reserves seats at a theatre, etc., or rooms at an hotel; **b. office,** office where tickets are obtained for a journey, a public entertainment, etc.

BOOKISH, [bŏŏk'-ish], *adj.* relating to books or studies; studious, fond of reading, based on or obtained from books.

BOOKISHLY, [bŏŏk'-ish-li], *adv.* in the fashion of one who is bookish.

BOOKISHNESS, [bŏŏk'-ish-nes], *n.* studiousness, fondness for reading, pedantry.

BOOK-KEEPER, [bŏŏk'-kēp'-er], *n.* a person who keeps the accounts of a business or other undertaking.

BOOK-KEEPING, [bŏŏk'-kēp'-ing], *n.* the art or method of recording financial transactions in an accurate and comprehensible manner.

BOOK-KNOWLEDGE, [bŏŏk'-nol'-ij], *n.* knowledge derived solely from books or reading.

BOOKLAND†, [bŏŏk'-land], *n.* (*leg.*) land held by a charter or simple deed; land taken from the common land and given to a private owner. [OE. *bocland* land granted by book or charter].

BOOK-LEARNED, [bŏŏk'-lurn'-ed], *adj.* well-read.

BOOK-LEARNING, [bŏŏk'-lurn'-ing], *n.* learning acquired by reading and study, as opposed to knowledge derived from personal experience or observation.

BOOKLESS, [bŏŏk'-les], *adj.* without books, unlearned.

BOOKLET, [bŏŏk'-let], *n.* a small tract, a pamphlet.

BOOK-MADNESS, [bŏŏk'-mad'-nes], *n.* a desire to own rare or curious books.

BOOK-MAKER (1), [bŏŏk'-māk'-er], *n.* one who makes or compiles books.

BOOKMAKER (2), [bŏŏk'-mā-ker], *n.* a person professionally engaged in making or taking bets on a race or other sporting event.

BOOKMAKING, [bŏŏk'-mak'-ing], *n.* the profession or business of a bookmaker.

BOOKMAN, [bŏŏk'-man], *n.* a scholar, a learned man; one interested in books.

BOOKMARK, [bŏŏk'-mahk'], *n.* a thin strip of material such as paper, leather, metal, etc., placed in a book so as to enable a person to find a particular page rapidly and easily.

BOOKMATE, [bŏŏk'-māt], *n.* a fellow student.
BOOK-MUSLIN, [bŏŏk'-muz'-lin], *n.* a kind of fine muslin.
BOOK-NAME, [bŏŏk'-nām'], *n.* the name of a plant or animal having little currency outside books.
BOOK-OATH, [bŏŏk'-ōth], *n.* an oath sworn on the Bible.
BOOKPLATE, [bŏŏk'-plāt], *n.* an ornamental label pasted on the inside of a book-cover to indicate the owner's name.
BOOK-POST, [bŏŏk'-pōst'], *n.* (the rates and regulations governing) the sending of books through the post.
BOOKSELLER, [bŏŏk'-sel'-er], *n.* a person who trades in books.
BOOKSELLING, [bŏŏk'-sel'-ing], *n.* the business of a bookseller.
BOOKSHELF, [bŏŏk'-shelf], *n.* a shelf on which books are kept.
BOOKSTALL, [bŏŏk'-stawl], *n.* an open stall where books are sold.
BOOKSTAND, [bŏŏk'-stand'], *n.* a stand or case for holding books.
BOOKSTORE, [bŏŏk'-staw(r)], *n.* a bookseller's shop; a section of a library where little-used books are stacked.
BOOKWORM, [bŏŏk'-wurm], *n.* the larva of several genera of beetle, such as *Arobium* and *Ptinus*, which eat into the bindings and leaves of books; (*fig.*) a person continually reading or poring over books.
BOOM (1), [bōōm], *n.* an obstruction in the form of beams fastened together, iron chains, etc., across the mouth of a harbour or river to prevent entry; (*naut.*) a long pole or spar used to extend the bottom of certain sails; (*Amer.*) a barrier of floating logs to enclose timber felled by the lumber-jack; (*cinema*) a movable arm from which a film-camera is suspended in photographing people or scenes from above. [Du. *boom* beam].
BOOM (2), [bōōm], *n.* a deep, resonant hollow sound (as of thunder, drums, the firing of cannon, or the cry of the bittern, etc.); sudden rapid activity in a particular trade, commercial enterprise, etc., resulting in increased prosperity for those concerned, sudden activity in financial speculation in a certain commodity or business concern, resulting in a rapid increase in the value of stocks and shares; a vigorous advertising or electioneering campaign. [BOOM (3)].
BOOM (3), [bōōm], *v.t.* *and i.* to make a deep, hollow, resonant or humming sound; to prosper, to increase rapidly in value or price, to advance in favour or popularity; to come with a sudden violent rush; to boost, to make known by vigorous publicity or an advertising campaign. [ME. *bommen*].
BOOMER, [bōōm'-er], *n.* the great grey kangaroo, *Macropus giganteus.* [*Prec.*].
BOOMERANG, [bōōm'-er-ang'], *n.* a curved flat missile of hard wood which returns to the thrower if it misses its objective, chiefly used by the aborigines of Australia; (*fig.*) an action recoiling on the performer or instigator. [Native].

BOOMERANG

BOOMKIN, see BUMPKIN.
BOON (1), [bōōn], *n.* (*archaic, poet.*) a favour, a request; a blessing, gift. [OScand. *bon* a petition].
BOON (2), [bōōn], *n.* refuse from dressed flax. [Unkn.].
BOON (3), [bōōn], *adj.* pleasant, delightful; genial, jovial. [ME. *bon* from L. *bonus* good].
BOOPIC, [bō-op'-ik], *adj.* having prominent bulging eyes like an ox. [Gk. *bo-opis* ox-eyed].
BOOPS, [bō'-ops], *n.* the pike-headed whale, *Megaptera boops.* [*Prec.*].
BOOR, [bōō'-er], *n.* a peasant, a rustic; (*fig.*) a coarse, ill-mannered, uneducated person. [Du. *boer*].
BOORISH, [bōoer'-ish], *adj.* ill-bred, rude in manner, uneducated.
BOORISHLY, [bōoer'-ish-li], *adv.* in boorish fashion.
BOORISHNESS, [bōoer'-ish-nes], *n.* the condition of being boorish.
BOORT, [bōoert], *n.* a variety of diamond used for polishing. [BORT.].
BOOSE†, see BOOZE.
BOOST (1), [bōōst], *n.* a lift, a help-up, an advance or increase in popularity, favour or value; helpful publicity. [Unkn.].
BOOST (2), [bōōst], *v.t.* to lift or raise by pushing; to increase the popularity, value, or sale of an article, or the fame or popularity of a person by a campaign of vigorous publicity or advertising.
BOOSTER, [bōōst'-er], *n.* one who boosts; (*eng.*) a small additional steam-engine fitted to one of the bogies of large locomotives.
BOOT (1), [bōōt], *n.* a covering for the foot, generally of leather, and extending over the ankle, and laced in front; a box or compartment for luggage on a coach, situated under the coachman's seat; a luggage compartment at the back of a motor-car; a protective leather covering worn over the hoof or round the fetlock of a horse; a leather case in which to hold a bottle while it is being corked; **riding b.,** a long boot covering the foot and calf of the leg. [OFr. *bote*].
BOOT (2), [bōōt], *n.* advantage, profit; **to b.,** in addition. [OE. *bot*].
BOOT (3), [bōōt], *v.t.* *and i.* to put on boots; to kick; **to b. out,** (*coll.*) to dismiss.
BOOT (4), [bōōt], *v.i.* (*impers.*) to profit, to do good, to be of use or advantage.
BOOTBLACK, [bōōt'-blak], *n.* a person who earns his living by cleaning boots, usually in the street.
BOOTCRIMP, [bōōt'-krimp], *n.* a machine or tool for shaping the pieces of leather used in making the uppers of boots.
BOOTEE, [bōōt-ē'], *n.* a knitted woollen boot worn by babies; a kind of half-boot for ladies.
BOOTH, [bōōTH], *n.* a covered stall at a market, a temporary wooden shed or shelter, a tent at a fair-ground; **polling b.,** a building or temporary structure where voters register their votes at an election. [ODan. *both*].
BOOT-HOOK, [bōōt'-hŏŏk], *n.* a hook to draw on long boots.
BOOT-HOSE, [bōōt'-hōz], *n.* knitted coverings for the leg, worn over boots.
BOOTIED, [bōōt'-id], *adj.* laden with booty.
BOOTJACK, [bōōt'-jak], *n.* an appliance for pulling off long boots.
BOOTLACE, [bōōt'-lās], *n.* a thong or lace used for fastening boots.
BOOT-LAST, [bōōt'-lahst], *n.* a mould or model of the foot upon which a shoemaker makes or repairs boots, a boot-tree inserted into boots to keep them in shape.
BOOTLEG†, [bōōt'-leg], *v.i.* (*U.S. slang*) to carry prohibited alcoholic liquor, etc., hidden on one's person, to indulge in wholesale smuggling of alcoholic liquor, etc. [So called because the smuggled liquor was originally hidden in the leg of a tall boot].
BOOTLEGGER, [bōōt'-leg'-er], *n.* a person engaged in the wholesale smuggling of prohibited alcoholic liquor, etc.
BOOTLESS, [bōōt'-les], *adj.* unavailing, useless, unprofitable. [BOOT (2) and LESS].
BOOTLESSLY, [bōōt'-les-li], *adv.* in a bootless manner.
BOOTLESSNESS, [bōōt'-les-nes], *n.* condition of being bootless.
BOOTLICK, [bōōt'-lik], (*U.S. slang*) a despicable flatterer.
BOOTMAKER, [bōōt'-māk-er], *n.* one who makes boots.
BOOTS, [bōōts], *n.* a hotel servant who cleans the boots and performs other odd jobs.
BOOT-TOPPING, [bōōt'-top'-ing], *n.* the cleansing and greasing of a ship's hull near the surface of the water.
BOOT-TREE, [bōōt'-trē'], *n.* a shaped block inserted into boots or shoes to stretch them or preserve their shape.
BOOTY, [bōōt'-i], *n.* plunder, spoils of war captured from an enemy, goods or loot seized and distributed amongst the captors. [Uncert.].
BOOZE (1), BOOSE†, [bōōz], *n.* (*coll.*) alcoholic drink, a drinking party.
BOOZE (2), [bōōz], *v.i.* (*coll.*) to drink large quantities of alcoholic liquor. [MDu. *buzen* to drink].
BOOZY, BOOSY†, [bōōz'-i], *adj.* fond of excessive quantities of alcoholic liquor; partially intoxicated.
BORA, [baw'-ra], *n.* a cold north wind of the Upper Adriatic. [It. *bora* from L. *boreas* north wind].
BORACHIO, [bor-ach'-i-ō], *n.* a bottle or flask to contain liquid for drinking purposes; a drunkard. [Span. *borracha* a leather wine bag].
BORACIC, [bor-as'-ik], *adj.* containing, derived from, or pertaining to, borax; **b. acid,** a compound of boron with hydrogen and oxygen forming white crystals, used as an antiseptic and food preservative.

BORACITE, [bo'-ras-it], *n.* native borate and chloride of magnesium.
BORAGE, [bu'-rij], *n.* a genus of plants of the order *Boraginaceae*, used in making cordials. [OFr. *bourage*].
BORATE, [baw'-rāt], *n.* a salt of boracic acid.
BORAX, [baw'-raks], *n.* (*chem.*) a white crystalline salt, sodium tetraborate, or the sodium salt of pyroboric acid. [L. *borax* from Arab. *bauraq*].
BORCER, [baw'-ser], *n.* an instrument to bore holes in rocks in preparation for blasting. [Unkn.].
BORD†, see BOARD.
BORDAR, [bawd'-er], *n.* †a villein or cottar holding his cottage from the lord of the manor in return for service. [LL. *bordarius*].
BORDEAUX, [baw-dō'], *n.* white or red wine produced in the wine-growing district of Bordeaux; claret. [*Bordeaux* in France].
BORDEAUX-MIXTURE, [baw-dō'-miks'-cher], *n.* a preparation of copper sulphate and lime for spraying plants.
BORDEL†, [baw'-del], *n.* a brothel. [OFr. *bordel*].
BORDER (1), [bawd'-er], *n.* edge, margin, extremity, boundary, frontier; a narrow strip running along the edge of anything, and distinguished in appearance, material, etc., from the thing to which it is attached; a strip of ground in a garden, often in the form of a flower-bed, forming a fringe or margin to a portion of the garden; **The B.**, the frontier of England and Scotland. [OFr. *bordure*].
BORDER (2), [bawd'-er], *v.t.* *and i.* to furnish with a border, to mark the limits of, to be adjacent to; to be situated on the border of; (*fig.*) to approach, to verge on.
BORDEREAU, [bawd'-er-ō], *n.* a memorandum, an abstract or summary. [Fr. *bordereau*].
BORDERER, [bawd'-er-er], *n.* one who lives on the frontiers of a country.
BORDERLAND, [bawd'-er-land'], *n.* land adjoining the boundaries of two adjacent countries; (*fig.*) intervening region.
BORDLAND†, [bawd'-land], *n.* (*hist.*) land held by a bordar.
BORDURE, [bawd'-yōō-er], *n.* (*her.*) the border running round a shield. [OFr. *bordure*].
BORE (1), [baw(r)], *n.* an instrument used for drilling holes; a hole made by boring; the hollow inside of a tube or barrel of a gun, the diameter of the cavity of a tube or gun-barrel; (*fig.*) dull, uninteresting, monotonous work or method of passing one's time; a person whose conversation or remarks are wearisome and tedious. [BORE (3)].
BORE (2), [baw(r)], *n.* a high tidal wave on a river caused by the sudden, rapid influx of an unusually high tide in a narrow or funnel-shaped estuary. [OScand. *bara* wave].
BORE (3), [baw(r)], *v.t.* to drill a hole into by means of a revolving sharp-pointed tool, to furnish with a bore or hollow inside; (*racing*) to impede by moving too closely to another horse to force it out of its course; (*fig.*) to bring about a complete lack of interest in a thing, to weary with repetition of what is dull and tedious; *v.i.* to make a hole, to burrow through; (*fig.*) to push one's way through a crowd of people. [OE. *borian*].
BORE (4), [baw(r)], *pret.* of BEAR.
BOREAL, [baw'-ri-al], *adj.* northerly, relating to the north or north wind. [L. *borealis*].
BOREAS, [baw'-re-as], *n.* the north wind.
BORECOLE, [baw'-kōl'], *n.* a winter cabbage with wrinkled leaves, *Brassica oleracea* var. *acephala*. [BOOR and KALE].
BOREDOM, [baw'-dom], *n.* state of being bored, tedium.
BORER, [baw'-rer], *n.* an instrument for boring, a drill; the sea-worm *Teredo*, the larvæ of certain insects which bore holes in wood.
BOREWORM, [baw'-wurm'], *n.* the shipworm, a variety of *Teredo*.
BORIC, [bor'-ik], *adj.* pertaining to or containing boron or borax, boracic.
BORING (1), [baw'-ring], *n.* the process of piercing by means of drills or bores; the hole made by boring.

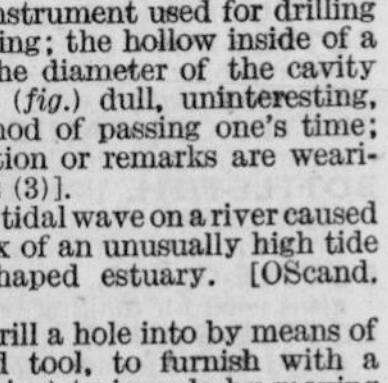

BORLEY

BORING (2), [baw'-ring], *adj.* dull, tedious, causing boredom; used for boring.
BORLEY, [baw'-li], *n.* a Thames fishing boat.
BORN, [bawn], *adj.* natural, perfect; destined or inheriting by birth. [OE. *boren*, *p.pt.* of *beran* to bear].
BORNE, [bawn], *p.pt.* of BEAR. [*Prec.*].
BORNITE, [bawn'-it], *n.* a tellurite of bismuth. [*Born*, an Austrian scientist].
BORON, [baw'-ron], *n.* (*chem.*) a non-metallic substance found in borax and other compounds; the chemical element denoted by B. [BORAX].
BOROUGH, [bu'-ro], *n.* a corporate town; **municipal b.**, a town possessing an organized municipal government with a mayor and corporation, and certain privileges granted by royal charter; **parliamentary b.**, a town sending at least one representative to Parliament; **rotten** or **pocket b.**, (*hist.*) a borough in which a wealthy or influential person controlled the election of a parliamentary representative. [OE. *burg* a fortified place, town].
BOROUGH-ENGLISH, [bu'-ro-ing'-glish], *n.* †(*leg.*) a custom, found in certain English boroughs, by which lands descended to the youngest son, instead of the eldest.
BOROUGH-MASTER†, [bu'-ro-mahst'-er], *n.* the mayor, governor, or bailiff of a borough; a burgomaster.
BOROUGHMONGER†, [bu'-ro-mung'-ger], *n.* one who bought or sold the parliamentary representation of boroughs.
BORROW, [bor'-ō], *v.t.* *and i.* to accept something to be repaid or returned later, often with other conditions of security; (*fig.*) to make use of, to obtain or copy from; to obtain the loan of money or articles. [OE. *borgian*].
BORROWER, [bor'-ō-er], *n.* one who borrows.
BORROWING, [bor'-ō-ing], *n.* act of one who borrows; the thing borrowed.
BORSCH, [bawsh], *n.* a highly seasoned Russian beetroot soup. [Russ. *borshch*].
BORSTAL, [baws'-tal], *n.* a system whereby young offenders between the ages of sixteen and twenty-one are sent to an institution to acquire a trade or occupation instead of going to prison; an institution for such a purpose. [*Borstal*, village in Kent, the site of the original institution].
BORT, [bawt], *n.* waste pieces left over after the cutting of diamonds, made into dust, and used for grinding and polishing; a massive coarse form of diamond used in making drills for rock-boring. [OFr. *bort* bastard].
BORZOI, [baw'-zoi], *n.* a Russian wolfhound, a long-haired variety of greyhound with silky, white coat. [Russ. *borzii* swift].
BOSA, [bō'-za], *n.* a fermented liquor made from hemp and other seed. [Turk. *boza*].
BOSCAGE, BOSKAGE, [bos'-kij], *n.* dense woody undergrowth. [OFr. *boscage*].
BOSH (1), [bosh], *n.* *and int.* (*coll.*) rubbish, nonsense, empty talk. [Turk. *bosh* nonsense].
BOSH (2), [bosh], *n.* the lower sloping portion of the shaft of a blast furnace. [Unkn.].
BOSHBOK, see BUSHBUCK.
BOSH-BUTTER, [bosh'-but'-er], *n.* a mixture of butter and margarine.
BOSJESMANS, [bŏŏsh'-manz], *n.* an aboriginal tribe dwelling to the north of the Cape of Good Hope in the western part of South Africa. [Du. *boschjesman* bushman].
BOSK, [bosk], *n.* a thicket, woody grove. [ME. *boske* from L. *boscus* wood].
BOSKAGE, see BOSCAGE.
BOSKET, [bos'-kit], *n.* a woody grove or plantation, a bosk. [Fr. *bosquet*, BOSK].
BOSKY, [bos'-ki], *adj.* with much undergrowth, full of dense thickets, bushy; (*coll.*) drunk. [BOSK].
BOSOM (1), [bŏŏz'-um], *n.* the breast; the portion of a garment covering the breast; (*fig.*) the surface of the sea or earth, the innermost part, the interior, the depths; emotions, the feelings, affections or passions; an embrace. [OE. *bosm*].
BOSOM (2), [bŏŏz'-um], *adj.* dear, intimate.
BOSOM (3), [bŏŏz'-um], *v.t.* to enclose or conceal in the bosom, to cherish.
BOSPHORIAN, [bos-faw'-ri-an], *adj.* pertaining to the Bosphorus straits. [*Bosphorus*, the strait between the Black Sea and the Sea of Marmora].
BOSS (1), [bos], *n.* a protuberant part, a knob, stud, the central stud on a shield; (*arch.*) a sculptured or carved raised ornament or moulding placed at the intersection of arches or ribs in a roof. [Fr. *bosse* protuberance].
BOSS (2), [bos], *n.* (*coll.*) a master, supervisor, manager. [Du. *baas* master].

BOSS (3), [bos], *v.t.* to emboss, to furnish with bosses.
BOSS (4), [bos], *v.t.* to supervise; (*coll.*) to bully, to attempt to domineer.
BOSSAGE, [bos'-ij], *n.* (*arch.*) a rough stone left projecting from the surface of a wall ready to be carved; rustic work formed of stones which project beyond the end of the building.
BOSS-EYED, [bos'-īd], *adj.* (*coll.*) squinting, cross-eyed; (*fig.*) crooked, out of shape.
BOSSINESS, [bos'-i-nes], *n.* a tendency to domineer; masterfulness.
BOSSY (1), [bos'-i], *adj.* containing a boss; ornamented with bosses.
BOSSY (2), [bos'-i], *adj.* (*coll.*) masterful.
BOSTANGI, [bos-tan'-ji], *n.*(*pl.*) the guards attached to the Sultan's seraglio. [Turk. *bostangi* palace guard].
BOSTON, [bos'-ton], *n. and adj.* a kind of whist; a kind of two-step; a method of cutting the hair. [*Boston*, U.S.A.].
BOSTRYCHITE, [bos'-trik-īt], *n.* a gem in the shape of a lock of hair. [Gk. *bostruchos* a curl].
BOSUN†, see BOATSWAIN.
BOSWELLIAN, [boz-wel'-i-an], *adj.* after the manner of Boswell. [James *Boswell* (1740-1794), biographer of Dr. Samuel Johnson].
BOT, BOTT, [bot], (*pl.* **botts**,) *n.* the larva of the bot-fly, a species of *Gastrophilus*, attacking the skin and intestines of horses, sheep and cattle; (*pl.*) disease or swelling set up by this fly. [Unkn.].
BOTANIC, [bot-an'-ik], *adj.* botanical. [Gk. *botanikos*].
BOTANICAL, [bot-an'-ik-al], *adj.* pertaining to botany or to plant life.
BOTANICALLY, [bot-an'-ik-a-i], *adv.* according to botany.
BOTANIST, [bot'-an-ist], *n.* a student of botany.
BOTANIZE, [bot'-an-īz], *v.i.* to make a botanical investigation; to gather plants.
BOTANIZER, [bot'-an-ī-zer], *n.* one who collects plants for purposes of botanical study.
BOTANOMANCY, [bot'-an-o-man'-si], *n.* divination by plants. [BOTANY and Gk. *manteia* divination].
BOTANY (1), [bot'-an-i], *n.* the science of the structure, growth, and function of plants. [Gk. *botanikos* pertaining to plants].
BOTANY (2), [bot'-an-i], *n.* fine Australian wool. [*Botany* Bay, New South Wales].
BOTARGO, [bot-ah'-gō], *n.* a relish made of the salted roe of the mullet or tunny. [Arab. *butarkhah*].
BOTCH (1), [boch], *n.* a plague or disease of eruptive discoloured swellings on the skin; clumsy, makeshift work; unskilful, ill-finished work. [OFr. *boche* a swelling].
BOTCH (2), [boch], *v.t. and i.* to mend or patch clumsily, to bungle, to put together or make in an unskilful, rough way.
BOTCHER (1), [boch'-er], *n.* a person who does clumsy, rough, ill-finished work.
BOTCHER (2), [boch'-er], *n.* a grilse, a young salmon.
BOTCHERY, [boch'-er-i], *n.* clumsy, rough workmanship.
BOTCHILY, [boch'-i-li], *adj.* in a botchy manner.
BOTCHY, [boch'-i], *adj.* marked with botches; full of botches.
BOT-FLY, [bot'-flī], *n.* a fly of the genus *Gastrophilus* or bot. [BOT and FLY].
BOTH, [bōth], *adj.* the two together; *pron.* the one and the other; *adv.* as well as, not only . . . but also. [OScand. *bathir*].
BOTHER (1), [boTH'-er], *n.* disturbance, fuss; trouble, worry, annoyance; difficulty. [Unkn.].
BOTHER (2), [boTH'-er], *v.t. and i.* to worry, to annoy, to trouble, to present difficulty to, to make anxious, to worry about, to be anxious or troubled; to trouble oneself, to take care; to pay too much attention to; to take the trouble to. [Unkn.].
BOTHERATION, [boTH'-er-ā'-shun], *n.* bother, trouble, worry.
BOTHERSOME, [boTH'-er-sum], *adj.* tiresome, troublesome, annoying.
BOTHRODENDRON, [boTH'-rō-den'-dron], *n.* (*geol.*) a genus of *Lycopodiales* or fossil plants occurring in coal measures. [Gk. *bothros* pit and *dendron* tree].
BOTHY, BOTHIE, [both'-ē], *n.* a hut or cottage; a one-roomed building for housing workmen.
BOTOCUDOS, [bot'-ok-ew'-doz], *n.*(*pl.*) the aboriginal race inhabiting the forests of Eastern Brazil, so named from the pieces of wood, shaped like the bung of a barrel, which they insert in their lips and ears. [Portug. *botoque* barrel stopper].

BOTONY, [bot'-on-i], *adj.* (*her.*) having an ornament at each extremity in the form of three buds, knots or buttons (of a cross). [OFr. *botoné* furnished with buttons].

BOTONY

BO-TREE, [bō'-trē], *n.* the pipal or sacred fig-tree of India and Ceylon, *Ficus religiosa*, regarded as holy by the Buddhists, as being the tree under which Buddha was sitting when he received enlightenment. [Singhalese *bo* enlightenment].
BOTRYOID, [bot'-ri-oid], *adj.* botryoidal.
BOTRYOIDAL, [bot'-ri-oidl'], *adj.* having the appearance or shape of a bunch of grapes. [Gk. *botrus* bunch of grapes and *oeides* like].
BOTRYOLITE, [bot'-ri-ō-līt'], *n.* (*min.*) a variety of datolite, found in botryoidal form. [Gk. *botrus* bunch of grapes and *lithos* stone].
BOTTINE, [bot'-ēn], *n.* a large, light boot covering part of the leg, formerly worn by ladies and children. [Fr. *bottine*].

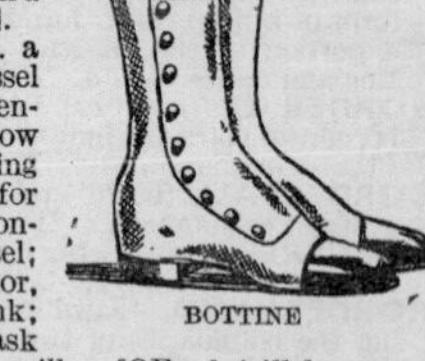
BOTTINE

BOTTLE (1), [botl], *n.* a symmetrical hollow vessel usually of glass or earthenware, having a narrow neck with a small opening at the top, and used for holding liquid; the contents of such a vessel; (*fig.*) intoxicating liquor, alcoholic beverage, drink; a baby's feeding flask from which it sucks milk. [OFr. *boteille*].
BOTTLE (2), [botl], *n.* a bundle or truss of hay. [OFr. *botel*].
BOTTLE (3), [botl], *v.t.* to put into bottles; (*fig.*) to restrain, to repress, to keep in check. [BOTTLE (1)].
BOTTLE-BELLIED, [botl'-bel'-id], *adj.* pot-bellied.
BOTTLE-BRUSH, [botl'-brush'], *n.* a brush adapted for cleaning bottles; (*bot.*) an Australian plant of the genus *Callistemon*.
BOTTLE-COMPANION, [botl'-kom-pan'-yon], *n.* a companion in drinking.
BOTTLE-FISH, [botl'-fish], *n.* a sea-fish found at great depths, *Saccopharynx ampullaceus*, so named from the shape of its body when distended.
BOTTLE-GLASS, [botl'-glahs], *n.* a coarse green glass used for making bottles.
BOTTLE-GOURD, [botl'-gōōerd], *n.* a variety of gourd of the genus *Lagenaria*, whose dried fruits are often used as a receptacle for liquids.
BOTTLE-GREEN, [botl'-grēn], *n.* a dark green colour.
BOTTLE-HEAD, [botl'-hed], *n.* the bottlenose whale.
BOTTLE-HOLDER, [botl'-hōld'-er], *n.* a second at a prize-fight; (*fig.*) a supporter, a backer.
BOTTLENECK, [botl'-nek], *n.* short strip of road narrowing suddenly so that it becomes congested or unsafe; a stage in manufacture which holds up production.
BOTTLENOSE, [botl'-nōs], *n.* a variety of whale of the dolphin family of the genus *Hyperoodon*, having a bleached snout.
BOTTLE-NOSED, [botl'-nōzd], *adj.* having a swollen, red, bulbous nose.
BOTTLE-PARTY, [botl'-pah'-ti], *n.* a social gathering or party to which each guest brings a bottle of some alcoholic drink; a night club.
BOTTLER, [bot'-ler], *n.* one who bottles liquors.
BOTTLE-RACK, [botl'-rak], *n.* a rack on which bottles are placed in an inverted position in order to drain.
BOTTLE-TIT, [botl'-tit], *n.* the long-tailed tit, *Parus longicaudatus*, so called from the shape of its nest.
BOTTLE-WASHER, [botl'-wosh'-er], *n.* one who washes bottles; a general drudge, servant, hack; (*coll.*) **head cook and b.**, one in charge.
BOTTOM (1), [bot'-um], *n.* the lowest or deepest part, the part most remote from the top, the foot, the base; the end or surface on which an object rests; the ground or bed underneath a mass of water; the keel of a ship; the seat of a chair; the lowest part of a

valley; (*coll.*) the buttocks; (*fig.*) a ship; foundation, basis, the depths of one's thoughts, feelings; strength, endurance, stamina; (*motoring*) the lowest gear of a motor engine; **to touch b.,** to run aground, (*fig.*) to reach the worst; **to be at the b. of,** to be the cause of; **to get to the b. of,** to sift or probe thoroughly; to get a complete understanding of. [OE. *botm*].

BOTTOM (2), [bot'-um], *adj.* lowest, last, at the bottom; **b. heat,** heat supplied to certain plants by fermenting and decomposing substances placed below their soil.

BOTTOM (3), [bot'-um], *v.t. and i.* to provide with a bottom; to reach or get to the bottom of, to understand thoroughly, to sift fully; to found, to base, to start from, to build upon, to rest upon.

BOTTOMLESS, [bot'-um-les], *adj.* having no bottom; (*fig.*) unfathomable, of immeasurable depth; groundless, without foundation or base, unjustifiable.

BOTTOMMOST, [bot'-um-mōst], *adj.* lowest down, at the extreme bottom.

BOTTOMRY, [bot'-um-ri], *n.* (*leg.*) a form of contract in which the ship is pledged by the owner or master in order to raise money to enable her to complete her voyage. [Du. *bodmerij*].

BOTULIFORM, [bot'-yōō-li-fawm'], *adj.* sausage-shaped. [L. *botulus* sausage and FORM].

BOTULISM, [bot'-yōō-lizm], *n.* a form of food-poisoning caused by eating preserved meat, etc., infected with the *Bacillus botulinus.* [L. *botulus* sausage].

BOUCHE (1), [bōōsh], *n.* †provision granted by the king or lord to his household or knights on military service; mouth. [Fr. *bouche* a mouth].

BOUCHE (2), [bōōsh], *v.t.* (*milit.*) to fix a vent into a cannon. [Fr. *boucher* to plug, to stop].

BOUDOIR, [bōōd'-wah(r)], *n.* a lady's private sitting-room. [Fr. from *bouder* to sulk, originally a room for sulking in].

BOUGAINVILLEA, [bōō'-găn-vil'-i-a], *n.* a genus of tropical South American spinous climbing shrubs of the order *Nyctaginaceae.* [*Bougainville*, a French explorer].

BOUGE†, [bōōzh], *n.* the part of a cask or barrel having the greatest girth. [OFr. *bouge* leather tag].

BOUGH, [bow], *n.* a large branch of a tree. [OE. *boh*].

BOUGHT, [bawt], *pret., p.pt.* of BUY.

BOUGIE, [bōō'-zhi], *n.* a smooth cylindrical rod introduced into the rectum, urethra or oesophagus in order to distend these canals to remove obstructions. [Fr. *bougie* wax candle].

BOUILLABAISSE, [bōō-ya-bes'], *n.* a French dish of fish-stew.

BOUILLI, [bōō'-yē'], *n.* boiled or stewed meat; bully-beef. [Fr. *bouilli, p.pt.* of *bouillir* to boil].

BOUILLON, [bōō'-yaw(ng)], *n.* broth; soup. [Fr. *bouillon*].

BOULDER, [bōld'-er], *n.* a large detached rock with its edges smoothed and rounded by the effect of water; (*geol.*) a large, weather-worn mass of stone, detached from its original position, and transported elsewhere by glacial action; **b. period,** the Ice Age. [ME. *bulder-ston*].

BOULDER-CLAY, [bōld'-er-klā'], *n.* a clay containing boulders deposited by glaciers.

BOULE (1), see BUHL.

BOULE (2), [bow'-lē], *n.* a legislative assembly of Greece. [Gk. *boule*].

BOULET, [bōōl'-ā], *n.* a horse whose fetlock is bent forward and displaced. [Fr. *boulet* fetlock].

BOULEVARD, [bōōl'-vahd], *n.* †the rampart or bulwark of a fortified city; a street or promenade, a promenade planted with trees. [Fr. *boulevard* bulwark].

BOULEVERSEMENT, [bōōl-vāers'-mah(ng)], *n.* overthrow; turning upside down. [Fr. *bouleversement*].

BOULTER, [bōlt'-er], *n.* a long fishing-line with many hooks. [Unkn.].

BOULTINE, [bōlt'-in], *n.* (*arch.*) a plain concave moulding. [Unkn.].

BOUNCE (1), [bowns], *n.* the power of rebounding, elasticity, resilience; the rebound; (*fig.*) impudence. [ME. *bounse*].

BOUNCE (2), [bowns], *v.t. and i.* to strike against and rebound; to rush about or move in a boisterous, violent manner; to cause to bounce; to cause a person to perform a hurried, unconsidered action. [ME. *bouncen*].

BOUNCER, [bowns'-er], *n.* a blusterer, a boaster; a brazen lie; (*fig.*) anything large or well-developed.

BOUNCING, [bowns'-ing], *adj.* that which bounces; (*fig.*) large, healthy, well-developed, bustling, boisterous; **b. bet,** (*bot.*) the soap-wort, *Saponaria officinalis.*

BOUNCINGLY, [bowns'-ing-li] *adv.* in a bouncing manner.

BOUND (1), [bownd], *n.* the edge, limit, boundary; (*pl.*) a prescribed area; (*fig.*) limit, restraints; **out of bounds,** beyond the lawful or prescribed boundary, and therefore forbidden to a person. [OFr. *bonne*].

BOUND (2), [bownd], *n.* a vigorous upward spring or leap, a sudden, violent throb (of the heart). [BOUND (5)].

BOUND (3), [bownd], *adj.* prepared, destined, intending to go, journeying. [OScand. *buinn* ready].

BOUND (4), [bownd], *v.t.* to mark the boundary of, to confine, to set limits to; (*fig.*) to restrain, to restrict. [BOUND (1)].

BOUND (5), [bownd], *v.i.* to leap, to move forward with a series of rapid springs or leaps; to rebound. [OFr. *bonder*].

BOUND (6), [bownd], *pret., p.pt.* of BIND.

BOUNDARY, [bownd'-er-i], *n.* that which marks the limits or extreme edge of anything; the bounds; (*cricket*) that which marks the limits of the field of play; a stroke which causes the ball to cross the boundary line, and which counts a certain number of runs to the batsman. [BOUND (1)].

BOUNDEN, [bownd'-en], *adj.* morally binding, under compulsion or obligation. [OE. *bunden, p.pt.* of *bindan* to bind].

BOUNDER, [bownd'-er], *n.* (*coll.*) a vulgar ill-mannered cad, a rank outsider. [BOUND (5)].

BOUNDLESS, [bownd'-les], *adj.* without bound or limit. [BOUND (1)].

BOUNDLESSLY, [bownd'-les-li], *adv.* in a boundless fashion.

BOUNDLESSNESS, [bownd'-les-nes], *n.* the quality or state of being boundless.

BOUNTEOUS, [bown'-ti-us], *adj.* liberal, generous, full of goodness; freely given, munificent, plentiful. [BOUNTY].

BOUNTEOUSLY, [bown'-ti-us-li], *adv.* in bounteous fashion.

BOUNTEOUSNESS, [bown'-ti-us-nes], *n.* the quality or condition of being bounteous.

BOUNTIFUL, [bown'-ti-fōōl], *adj.* generous, liberal; freely given, abundant.

BOUNTIFULLY, [bown'-ti-fōōl-i], *adv.* in bountiful fashion.

BOUNTIFULNESS, [bown'-ti-fōōl-nes], *n.* the quality or state of being bountiful.

BOUNTY, [bown'-ti], *n.* generosity, open-handedness, liberality, munificence; a gratuity, reward; a premium given to encourage enlistment in the Services, or a branch of industry; **Queen Anne's b.,** provision formerly made for supplementing poor church livings; **King's b.,** a gift or grant made to the parents of triplets. [OFr. *bontet* from L. *bonitas*].

BOUQUET, [bōō-kā'], *n.* a bunch of flowers; the aromatic perfume of wine. [Fr. *bouquet*].

BOUQUETIN, [buk'-et-in], *n.* the ibex or wild Alpine goat. [Fr. *bouc-estain*].

BOURBON, [bōōer'-bon], *n.* a crude whisky manufactured from Indian corn and rye. [*Bourbon*, U.S.A., where first made].

BOURBONISM, [bōōer'-bon-izm], *n.* loyalty to the French legitimate royal line of the *Bourbon* family.

BOURBONIST, [bōōer'-bon-ist], *n.* a supporter of the Bourbons.

BOURDON, [bōōer'-don], *n.* the bass stop in an organ or harmonium; the drone of a bagpipe. [Fr. *bourdon*].

BOURGEOIS (1), [bur-jois'], *n.* a printing type which provides 8½ lines to an inch. [*Bourgeois*, a French typographer].

BOURGEOIS (2), [bōōer'-zhwah], *n.* a member of the (upper) middle classes. [Fr. *bourgeois*].

BOURGEOIS (3), [bōōer'-zhwah], *adj* pertaining to the (upper) middle classes.

BOURGEOISIE, [bōōer'-zhwah-zē'], *n.* the middle classes; **petit b.,** the lower middle classes.

BOURGEON, see BURGEON.

BOURN (1), [bawn], *n.* a stream. [OE. *burna*].

BOURN(E) (2), [bawn], *n.* a boundary, limit; destination. [Fr. *borne*].

BOURNONITE, [bōōern'-on-it], *n.* (*min.*) an antimonial sulphide of lead and copper. [Count *Bournon*, its discoverer].

BOURREE, bourrée, [bōōer'-ā], *n.* a lively Spanish or

French dance, music written for this. [Fr. *bourrée*].

BOURSE, [bōō'-ers], *n.* a continental exchange where financial business is transacted. [Fr. *bourse*, Gk. *bursa* leather bag].

BOUR-TREE, [bōōer'-trē'], *n.* the elder, *Sambucus nigra* [ME. *biwer-tre*].

BOUSE, see BOWSE.

BOUSTROPHEDON, [bows'-trof-ē'-don], *n.* an ancient mode of writing from right to left and left to right alternately, as in ploughing. [Gk. *boustrophedon* ox-turning].

BOUT, [bowt], *n.* a spell of more or less continuous activity, a round, the amount done at one time; a contest, fight, encounter; an attack or turn of illness or indisposition [Uncert.].

BOUTS-RIMES, bouts-rimés, [bōō'-rē'-mā], *n.* a list of rhyming words, a form of verse-making in which verses are written to fit given rhymes. [Fr. *bouts-rimés* rhymed endings].

BOVEY-COAL, [bōv'-i-kōl'], *n.* a kind of lignite. [*Bovey* Tracy, in Devon, where found].

BOVIFORM, [bō'-vi-fawm], *adj.* having the form of an ox. [L. *bos bovem* ox and FORM].

BOVINE, [bō'-vīn], *adj.* pertaining to the ox; (*fig.*) dull, sluggish, heavy-witted. [LL. *bovinus*].

BOVRIL, [bov'-ril], *n.* an extract of beef. [(*Prot.*) *Prec.* and *vril* an electric fluid in Lytton's *Comino Lace*].

BOW (1), [bow], *n.* a respectful inclination of the head or bending of the body as a sign of greeting or departure; **to make one's b.**, to arrive; to retire. [BOW (4)].

BOW (2), [bow], *n.* the fore-end of a ship or boat, consisting of the curving sides meeting at the prow; (*coll.*) the oarsman nearest the bow. [OE. *bog* shoulder, bough].

BOW (3), [bō], *n.* weapon from which arrows are shot, consisting of a piece of flexible wood, steel, horn, etc., slightly curved so that its ends are joined by a taut string, which when drawn back and released, propels the arrow; anything in the form of a bow, a rainbow; (*mus.*) slender staff of slightly curved wood strung with horsehair, which produces the tone in stringed instruments; a metal ring or hoop used as a handle or means of attachment; double-looped slip-knot, a necktie or piece of ribbon tied in such a way; **to have more than one string to one's b.**, (*fig.*) to have several resources or courses of action, etc.; **to draw the long b.**, (*coll.*) to exaggerate. [OE. *boga*].

BOW (4), [bow], *v.i.* to incline the head or bend the body as a respectful gesture of greeting, departure, polite acknowledgment, etc.; to express by a bow; to incline the person or stoop in sign of reverence or submission; (*fig.*) to submit to, to acknowledge as superior, to yield to; *v.t.* to bend, to crush, to subdue, to incline, to oppress, to depress; (*lit. and fig.*) to usher in or out with bows; **to b. the knee to**, to worship, to revere; **a bowing acquaintance**, a slight acquaintance. [OE. *bugan* to bend, incline].

BOW (5), [bō], *v.t. and i.* to use a bow in playing stringed musical instruments. [BOW (3)].

BOW-BACK, [bō'-bak], *n.* a crooked back.

BOW-BENT, [bō'-bent], *adj.* bent like a bow.

BOW-BRACE, [bō'-brās], *n.* a guard on the left arm for protection against friction of the bow-string.

BOW-COMPASSES, [bō'-kum'-pas-iz], *n.*(*pl.*) a pair of compasses having jointed legs which turn inwards.

BOWDLERISM, [bowd'-ler-izm], *n.* expurgation of what is thought obscene.

BOWDLERIZE, [bowd'-ler-īz], *v.t.* to expurgate a book, to remove from a book all things considered indelicate or profane. [Dr. T. *Bowdler*, who published in 1818 an expurgated edition of Shakespeare].

BOW-DRILL, [bō'-dril'], *n.* a drill operated by a bow.

BOW-DYE, [bō'-dī'], *n.* a scarlet dye. [*Bow*, in London].

BOWED, [bōd], *adj.* played or furnished with a bow.

BOWEL (1), [bow'-el], *n.*(*pl.*) the intestines of man or animals; (*fig.*) the interior, the depths; feelings, emotions. [OFr. *bueille* bowel].

BOWEL (2), [bow'-el], *v.t.* to remove the bowels from.

BOWER (1), [bow'-er], *n.* a lady's chamber, a private apartment; an arbour, a shady retreat, a sheltered recess covered in with shrubs, branches of trees; a rustic dwelling. [OE. *bur*].

BOWER (2), [bow'-er], *n.* either of the two anchors together with their cables carried at the bow of a ship.

BOWER (3), [bō'-er], *n.* one who bows. [BOW (5)].

BOWER-BIRD, [bow'-er-burd'], *n.* one of several species of Australian birds of the starling family, which build bowers.

BOWERY (1), [bow'-er-i], *n.* the name of a district of a New York popularly supposed to be insalubrious. [Du. *bouwerij* a farm].

BOWERY (2), [bow'-er-i], *adj.* like a bower, characterized by bowers.

BOWESS, [bow'-es], *n.* a young hawk.

BOWFIN, [bō'-fin], *n.* the mudfish, the North American ganoid fish, *Amia calva*.

BOWFIN

BOW-GRACE, [bō'-grās], *n.* (*naut.*) a protective fender placed round the bows of a ship to guard against injury from floating ice, timber, etc.

BOW-HAND, [bō'-hand], *n.* the hand that holds a bow.

BOWIE-KNIFE, [bō'-i-nīf'], *n.* a sheath knife or hunting dagger having a long blade double-edged at the point. [Colonel James *Bowie* (1790-1835), an American].

BOWING, [bō'-ing], *n.* (*mus.*) the art of using a bow.

BOWINGLY, [bow'-ing-li], *adv.* in a bowing manner.

BOWL (1), [bōl], *n.* a wide hollow vessel or rimless basin of various sizes and materials, a drinking vessel, the rounded hollow part of a tobacco-pipe in which the tobacco is put, the hollow bowl-shaped part of a utensil or implement. [OE. *bolla*].

BOWL (2), [bōl], *n.* a heavy wooden ball provided with a bias, and rolled along a bowling green in the game of bowls. [Fr. *boule* a ball].

BOWL (3), [bōl], *v.t. and i.* to trundle or roll a hoop; to deliver the ball at cricket; to deliver a ball which hits the striker's wicket and dislodges a bail; to roll a bowl; to play the game of bowls; **to b. over**, to nonplus, to upset thoroughly; **to b. out**, to defeat, to disconcert. [*Prec.*].

BOW-LEG, [bō'-leg], *n.* a leg which bends outwards in the shape of a bow from the hip downwards; malformation arising from this condition.

BOW-LEGGED, [bō'-leg'-id], *adj.* having bow-legs.

BOWLER (1), [bōl'-er], *n.* a person who plays bowls; the person who delivers the ball to the batsman at cricket.

BOWLER (2), [bōl'-er], *n.* a hard round felt hat with a curved brim. [BOWL (1)].

BOWLESS, [bō'-les], *adj.* without a bow.

BOWLINE, [bō'-lin], *n.* (*naut.*) a rope fastened by bridles to loops on the perpendicular edge of a square sail, and used to steady the weather edge of the sail forward when the ship is sailing close to the wind; **b. knot**, a knot used for fastening the bowline bridles to the cringles.

BOWLING, [bōl'-ing], *n.* the act or recreation of playing bowls; the act of delivering the ball to the batsman at cricket, the method or skill with which this is done; the sport of playing skittles in a bowling alley; **b. alley**, a long, narrow, enclosed alley provided with raised edges in which the game of skittles is played; **b. crease**, the line from behind which the bowler delivers the ball; **b. green**, a smooth prepared lawn, either level or having a crown, upon which the game of bowls is played.

BOWLS, [bōlz], *n.* a game played on a bowling green with bowls.

BOWMAN, [bō'-man], *n.* one who uses a bow; an archer.

BOW-NET, [bō'-net], *n.* a kind of wicker basket with a narrow, funnel-shaped opening, used for catching lobsters, crayfish, etc.

BOW-OAR, [bow'-aw(r)], *n.* the oarsman nearest the bow.

BOW-PEN, [bō'-pen], *n.* a metallic ruling-pen, having the part which holds the ink bowed out towards the middle.

BOW-PIECE, [bow'-pēs], *n.* a gun placed in the bow of a ship.

BOW-SAW, [bō'-saw], *n.* a saw consisting of a narrow blade stretched across the ends of a strong frame in the manner of a bow-string, and used in cutting curves.

BOW-SAW

BOWSE, BOUSE, [bowz], *v.i.* (*naut.*) to haul with tackle. [Unkn.].

BOW-SHOT, [bō'-shot], *n.* the distance an arrow will travel when shot from a bow.

BOWSPRIT, BOLT-SPRIT, [bō'-sprit], *n.* (*naut.*) the large spar projecting over the stern of a ship to which are fastened the foremast and fore-topmast stays and stay-sails. [BOW (3) and OE. *spreot*].

BOWSPRIT

BOW-STRING (1), [bō'-string], *n.* the string of a bow; cord formerly used by the Turks in strangling people.
BOW-STRING (2), (bō'-string), *v.t.*, to strangle with a bow-string.
BOW-WINDOW, [bō'-win'-dō], *n.* a curved window frame projecting from a wall.
BOWYER, [bō'-yer], *n.* a person who makes bows. [ME. *bowyere*].
BOX (1), [boks], *n.* a case, receptacle, or chest, usually provided with a lid, of various shapes and sizes, and made of various hard materials; the contents of a box; the driver's seat on a coach; a compartment in the auditorium of a theatre, with seats for several persons; a square pew; a small wooden hut or shelter; a small country lodge; a protective case over various kinds of machinery or mechanism; the piston of a pump, closed with a valve; an axle-box; (*print.*) one of the cells of a type case; an enclosed portion of a court of law for the jury, or for witnesses; **Christmas-b.**, a Christmas gift. [OE. *box* box-tree].
BOX (2), [boks], *n.* an evergreen tree or shrub of the order *Euphorbiaceae*, having dark green leaves and a hard, yellow, close-grained wood; the wood of this tree. [OE. *box* from L. *buxus*].
BOX (3), [boks], *n.* a blow with the open hand, usually on the side of the head; a cuff. [ME. *box*].
BOX (4), [boks], *v.t.* to put into a box; to furnish with a box; to enclose or confine in an uncomfortably narrow space; to make a cut in the trunk of a tree to obtain the sap; (*cards*) to disarrange the cards in shuffling so that the backs of the cards do not all face the same way; **to b. the compass,** (*naut.*) to repeat all the points of the compass in their proper order; (*fig.*) to make a complete turn; **to b. off,** (*naut.*) to turn the head of a vessel by altering the sails. [BOX (1)].
BOX (5), [boks], *v.t. and i.* to strike the side of a person's head; to fight with the closed fists protected by padded gloves. [BOX (3)].
BOX-CALF, [boks'-kahf], *n.* a kind of leather treated with chromic oxide and having a double grain. [I. *Box* a bootmaker].
BOX-COAT, [boks'-kōt], *n.* a heavy overcoat worn for driving or riding on the outside of coaches or carriages.
BOX-DAY, [boks'-dā], *n.* (*leg.*) a day when the law-courts are closed in Scotland and papers may be lodged by lawyers and litigants.
BOX-DRAIN, [boks'-drān], *n.* a rectangular, closed, underground drain.
BOX-ELDER, [boks'-eld'-er], *n.* the United States ash-leaved maple, *Negundo aceroides*.
BOXEN, [boks'-en], *adj.* relating to the box-tree, made of box-wood.
BOXER (1), [boks'-er], *n.* a person trained in the art of fighting with the fists; a professional pugilist.
BOXER (2), [boks'-er], *n.* a member of a Chinese secret society of an extremely nationalist and anti-foreign nature.
BOXHAUL, [boks'-hawl], *v.t.* to veer a ship suddenly round on her keel.
BOXING, [boks'-ing], *n.* the art of fighting with the fists.
BOXING-DAY, [boks'-ing-dā'], *n.* the first week-day after Christmas-day, when Christmas-boxes are given.
BOX-IRON, [boks'-īern'], *n.* a hollow smoothing iron containing a heater.
BOX-KEEPER, [boks'-kēp'-er], *n.* an attendant in charge of the boxes in a theatre.
BOX-KITE, [boks'-kīt], *n.* a kite resembling a rectangular oblong box without ends.
BOX-OFFICE, [boks'-of'-is], *n.* an office at a theatre, etc., where seats may be booked.
BOX-PLEAT, [boks'-plēt], *n.* a double pleat or fold in a cloth.
BOX-THORN, [boks'-thawn], *n.* a plant of the genus *Lycium*.
BOX-TREE, [boks'-trē], *n.* a shrubby evergreen tree, the box.
BOX-WOOD, [boks'-wŏŏd], *n.* the wood of the box-tree.
BOY, [boi], *n.* a male child, often applied also to a young man; a native personal servant. [ME. *boi* from AFr. **embuié* serf].
BOYAR, [boi'-ah(r)], *n.* †a former order of the old Russian aristocracy ranking next to the ruling princes; a class in Rumania possessing special privileges. [Russ. *boyarin* lord].
BOYAU, (*pl.* **boyaux**), [boi'-ō], *n.* (*fort.*) a connecting trench serving as a means of communication. [Fr. *boyau* intestine].
BOYCOTT (1), [boi'-kot], *n.* an organized system of social or commercial ostracism. [Captain *Boycott*, an Irish land-agent, against whom it was first employed].
BOYCOTT (2), [boi'-kot], *v.t.* to combine together to have no dealings or intercourse with (a person); to refrain deliberately from buying, using or dealing in an article or merchandise as a means of reprisal or injury; (*fig.*) to ostracize, to shun the company of.
BOYER, [boi'-er], *n.* a Flemish sloop, with a castle at each end. [Du. *boeijer* a smack].
BOYHOOD, [boi'-hŏŏd], *n.* the period of life of a male child from birth to puberty.
BOYISH, [boi'-ish], *adj.* like a boy; fresh, lively; inexperienced, puerile.
BOYISHLY, [boi'-ish-li], *adv.* in a boyish fashion.
BOYISHNESS, [boi'-ish-nes], *n.* the quality of being boyish.
BOY'S-PLAY, [boiz'-plā], *n.* an amusement worthy of a boy, child's-play.
BRABBLE (1), [brabl], *n.* a quarrel, altercation.
BRABBLE (2), [brabl], *v.i.* to quarrel, to dispute noisily and obstinately, to wrangle. [Uncert.].
BRACCATE, [brak'-āt], *adj.* (*ornith.*) having the feet hidden by long feathers. [L. *braccatus* breeched].
BRACE (1), [brās], *n.* anything used as a support, stay, steadying or stiffening influence; a rope to adjust the sails of a ship; cords used to keep a drum taut; a carpenter's drilling tool consisting of a handle in the form of a crank to rotate; a socket into which a bit fits; (*print.*) a bracket in the form { } connecting two or more words or lines of type; a pair; (*pl.*) two adjustable straps passing over the shoulders, and uniting on the back, fastened to buttons on the trousers, both back and front, in order to support them; †an arm guard. [OFr. *brasse* clamp].
BRACE (2), [brās], *v.t.* to fasten together, to bind or tie, to strengthen, support or steady; to tighten, to stretch tightly, to make taut; to fasten and support with braces; (*fig.*) to prepare oneself for a special effort; to freshen, to stimulate, to strengthen, to invigorate. [*Prec.*].
BRACELET, [brās'-let], *n.* a circular ornament worn by women round the wrist or arm; a bracer; (*coll., pl.*) handcuffs. [Fr. *bracelet*].
BRACER, [brās'-er], *n.* anything that braces; a leather or metal protective covering for the arm or wrist. [OFr. *brasseure*].

BRACER

BRACH, [brach], *n.* a female hound. [OFr. *brache*].
BRACHELYTROUS, [brak-el'-it-rus], *n.* (*entom.*) relating to beetles characterized by short wing-cases. [BRACHY and Gk. *elytron* wing-case].
BRACHIAL, [brā'-ki-al], *adj.* pertaining to the arm; resembling an arm. [L. *brachialis* from Gk. *brachion* an arm].
BRACHIATE, [brā'-ki-āt], *adj.* (*bot.*) with branches arranged in pairs. [L. *brachiatus* provided with arms].
BRACHIOCEPHALIC, [brak'-i-ō-si-fal'-ik], *adj.* (*anat.*) pertaining to the arm and head, *esp.* to the blood-vessels in these parts. [Gk. *brakhion* arm and *kephale* head].
BRACHIOPOD, [brak'-i-ō-pod'], *n.* (*zool.*) a group of shell-bearing animals having a long spirally-coiled appendage on either side of the mouth which acts as a respiratory organ. [Gk. *brachion* arm and *pous podos* foot].
BRACHIOPODOUS, [brak'-i-op'-od-us], *adj.* pertaining to the brachiopods.
BRACHISTOCEPHALIC, [brak-is'-tō-si-fal'-ik], *adj.* having a short, broad head. [Gk. *brakhistos* shortest, and *kephale* head].

BRACHISTOCHRONE, [brak-is'-tō-krōn], *n.* the curve of quickest descent under the influence of gravity. [Gk. *brakhistos* shortest, and *khronos* time].
BRACHY-, *pref.* short. [Gk. *brakhus* short].
BRACHYCATALECTIC, [brak'-i-kat-a-lek'-tik], *n.* a verse lacking two syllables at the end. [BRACHY and Gk. *katalektos* deficient].
BRACHYCEPHALIC, [brak'-i-sef-al'-ik], *adj.* short-headed, having a head whose lateral diameter is at least four-fifths of its longitudinal diameter. [BRACHY and Gk. *kephale* head].
BRACHYDIAGONAL, [brak'-i-dī-ag'-on-al], *n.* the shorter diagonal of a rectangular prism. [BRACHY and DIAGONAL].
BRACHYGRAPHY, [brak-ig'-raf-i], *n.* shorthand writing. [BRACHY and Gk. *graphia* writing].
BRACHYLOGY, [brak-il'-o-ji], *n.* (*rhet.*) conciseness in speech, abbreviated form of expression. [BRACHY and Gk. *logos* speech].
BRACHYPTEROUS, [brak-ip'-ter-us], *adj.* (*ornith.*) short-winged. [BRACHY and Gk. *pteron* wing].
BRACHYTYPOUS, [brak-it'-ip-us], *adj.* (*min.*) of a short form. [BRACHY and Gk. *tupos* a mark].
BRACHYURAL, [brak'-i-yōōer'-al], *adj.* pertaining to the *Brachyura*, a genus of crab having a short jointed tail. [BRACHY and Gk. *oura* tail].
BRACHYUROUS, [brak'-i-yōōer'-us], *adj.* brachyural.
BRACING, [brās'-ing], *adj.* invigorating, freshening, stimulating. [BRACE (2)].
BRACKEN, [brakn], *n.* a species of coarse fern, *Pteris aquilina*. [OE. *bracen*].
BRACKET (1), [brak'-it], *n.* an angular piece of metal or wood projecting as a support from a wall; (*arch.*) a flat-topped projecting support for an arch, statue, shelf, etc.; a short shelf fastened to a wall; a gas pipe with burner, usually attached to an ornamental hinged fixture, and projecting from a wall; (*print.*) one of the marks [ ] used in printing to enclose or separate words, or a portion of a mathematical formula. [Unkn.].

BRACKET

BRACKET (2), [brak'-it], *v.t.* to enclose in brackets, to join by means of a bracket; to associate or mention two persons together; to provide with brackets.
BRACKISH, [brak'-ish], *adj.* salty. [Du. *brak* salt].
BRACKISHNESS, [brak'-ish-nes], *n.* the quality of being brackish.
BRACT, [brakt], *n.* (*bot.*) a leaf growing out beneath the calyx from the peduncle of a flower. [L. *bractea* a thin leaf of metal].
BRACTEATE (1), [brak'-ti-āt], *n.* (*archæ.*) a thin gold or silver plaque ornamented on one face.
BRACTEATE (2), [brak'-ti-āt], *adj.* (*bot.*) having bracts. [L. *bracteatus* covered with thin plates].
BRACTEATED, [brak'-ti-āt-id], *adj.* (*numis.*) plated over with a richer metal.
BRACTEOLATE, [brak'-ti-ō-lāt], *adj.* (*bot.*) having bracteoles.
BRACTEOLE, [brak'-ti-ōl], *n.* (*bot.*) a little bract. [L. *bracteola* thin gold leaf].
BRACTLESS, [brakt'-les], *adj.* (*bot.*) without bracts.
BRAD, [brad], *n.* a thin wire nail with a small head. [ME. *brod* spike].
BRADAWL, [brad'-awl], *n.* a small hand boring tool for making holes for nails or screws.
BRADSHAW, [brad'-shaw], *n.* a British railway guide. [*Bradshaw*, the original compiler].
BRADYPOD, [brad'-i-pod'], *n.* a sloth of the genus *Bradypus*. [Gk. *bradus* slow and *pous podos* foot].
BRAE, [brā], *n.* (*Scots*) the side of a hill, a slope. [OScand. *bra* eyebrow].
BRAG (1), [brag], *n.* a boast, boastful language; a gambling game at cards at which the players bet on the value of their cards.
BRAG (2), (**bragging, bragged**), [brag], *v.i.* to boast, to indulge in self-praise. [ME. *braggen*].
BRAGGADOCIO, [brag'-a-dō'-chi-ō], *n.* one who brags; bragging. [Coined by Spenser, *Faerie Queene*].
BRAGGART (1), [brag'-ert], *n.* a boaster. [OFr. *bragard*].
BRAGGART (2), [brag'-ert], *adj.* boastful.
BRAGGING, [brag'-ing], *n.* boastful language.
BRAGGINGLY, [brag'-ing-li], *adv.* in a boasting manner.
BRAHMA, [brah'-ma], *n.* the Divine Reality or Universal Power; the creator God of Hinduism. [Skr. *brahma* prayer].
BRAHMANAS, [brah-man'-as], *n.*(*pl.*) writings on Brahminism.
BRAHMIN, BRAHMAN, [brah'-min] *n.* a member of the highest caste or hereditary priests of Hinduism claiming direct descent from Brahma. [Skr. *brahmana* from *brahma* prayer].
BRAHMINEE, [brah'-min-ē], *n.* a female Brahmin. [Skr. *brahmani*].
BRAHMINEE-BULL, [brah'-min-i-bōōl'], *n.* one of the sacred humped cattle of India.
BRAHMINICAL, [brah-min'-ikl], *adj.* pertaining to the Brahmins.
BRAHMINISM, [brah'-min-izm], *n.* the beliefs and customs of Brahmins.
BRAHMOISM, [brah'-mō-izm], *n.* rational, enlightened theistic Hinduism.
BRAHMO-SOMAJ, [brah'-mō-so-mahj'], *n.* a revival of Hinduism on deistic and rationalistic principals. [Bengali *brahmo-somaj* Society of Brahman].
BRAID (1), [brād], *n.* a plait of hair; a narrow band of woven fabric used for trimming or binding the edges of cloth, a woven band of gold or silver thread used as ornamentation on uniforms.
BRAID (2), [brād], *v.t.* to weave by intertwining strands, to plait (hair), to trim or bind with braid. [OE *bregdan* to twist, plait].
BRAIDING, [brād'-ing], *n.* a trimming of braid.
BRAIL (1), **BRAYLE,** [brāl], *n.* (*naut.*) a rope at the corner of a sail passing through a block and used to truss up the bottoms, corners and skirts of a sail before furling. [OFr. *brail* girdle].
BRAIL (2), [brāl], *v.t.* (*naut.*) to haul in a fore-and-aft sail by means of a brail.
BRAILLE, [brāl], *n.* a system of printing in relief for the blind by an alphabet of raised dots read by touch. [Louis *Braille* (1809-1852), the inventor].
BRAIN (1), [brān], *n.* a convoluted mass of soft substance enclosed in the skull, the centre of the nervous system and of mental processes; the cephalic ganglion in invertebrates; (*fig.*) the mind, intelligence, understanding, thought, imagination; (*pl.*) the most intellectual person, the cleverest person of a group or organization; **to have something on the b.,** to be obsessed by an idea; **to pick a person's brains,** to make use of the fruits of another's mental effort; **to turn one's b.,** to cause to become mad. [OE. *brægen*].
BRAIN (2), [brān], *v.t.* to dash out the brains of.
BRAINED, [brānd], *adj.* having a brain (*usually with a preceding qualifying word*); having the brains beaten out.
BRAIN-FAG, [brān'-fag], *n.* nervous exhaustion due to continued mental strain.
BRAIN-FEVER, [brān'-fē'-ver], *n.* inflammation of the brain; meningitis.
BRAINLESS, [brān'-les], *adj.* without brains, stupid, silly.
BRAINPAN, [brān'-pan], *n.* the skull containing the brain.
BRAINSICK, [brān'-sik], *adj.* mentally deranged.
BRAINSICKNESS, [brān'-sik'-nes], *n.* the condition of being brainsick.
BRAINSTORM, [brān'-stawm], *n.* sudden mental derangement.
BRAINS TRUST, [brānz'-trust], *n.* a committee of experts appointed by a government or other body to aid in planning; (*coll.*) a group of persons appointed to answer without previous preparation questions asked by an audience or the general public on subjects of current interest.
BRAINWAVE, [brān'-wāv], *n.* (*coll.*) sudden, brilliant idea or inspiration.
BRAINY, [brān'-i], *n.* (*coll.*), clever, highly intelligent.
BRAISE (1), [brāz], *n.* the fish generally known as the roach. [Unkn.].
BRAISE (2), [brāz], *v.t.* to cook by stewing in a covered pan. [Fr. *braiser* to stew].
BRAISING-PAN, [brāz'-ing-pan'], *n.* a covered pan for braising meat in.
BRAIZE, [brāz], *n.* a red fish, the pandora, *Pagellus erythrinus*. [Unkn.].
BRAKE (1), [brāk], *n.* bracken, the fern, *Pteris aquilina*; a place overgrown with bracken, etc.; a thicket. [ME. *brake* fern, bracken].
BRAKE (2), [brāk], *n.* an instrument used for pounding flax or hemp; a baker's kneading board; a heavy wooden machine for breaking up clods of earth; a machine for crushing hops in brewing. [ODu. *braeke*].

BRAKE (3), [brāk], *n.* an apparatus for slowing down or arresting the motion of a wheel by friction applied to the axle or wheel.
BRAKE (4), BREAK, [brāk], *n.* a large open wagonette, a heavy four-wheeled carriage used for breaking-in horses; (*fig.*) a restraining influence. [Unkn.].
BRAKE (5), [brāk], *v.t.* to crush or beat hemp; to break up clods of earth; to knead dough. [BRAKE (2)].
BRAKE (6), [brāk], *v.i.* to apply the brake(s) to a revolving wheel. [BRAKE (3)].
BRAKELESS, [brāk'-les], *adj.* having no brakes; (*fig.*) unchecked.
BRAKE-MAN, [brāk'-man'], *n.* a brakesman.
BRAKESMAN, [brāks'-man], *n.* a man in charge of a brake.
BRAKE-VAN, [brāk'-van'], *n.* the compartment in a train from which the brakes are controlled.
BRAKY, [brāk'-i], *adj.* overgrown with bracken, thorns.
BRAMBLE, [brambl], *n.* a coarse, wild shrub; the wild blackberry. [OE. *bremel*].
BRAMBLED, [brambld], *adj.* covered with brambles.
BRAMBLE-NET, [brambl'-net], *n.* a net for catching birds.
BRAMBLING, [bramb'-ling], *n.* the mountain finch, *Fringilla montifringilla.*
BRAMBLY, [bramb'-li], *n.* thorny, covered with brambles.
BRAN, [bran], *n.* the husk of ground oats, wheat, etc., separated from the flour after grinding and used as meal, the coarsest part of the grain. [OFr. *bran*].

BRAMBLE

BRANCARD, [brangk'-ahd], *n.* a horse-borne litter. [Fr. *brancard*].
BRANCH (1), [brahnch], *n.* the limb or arm of a tree, an off-shoot or out-growth from anything; a subdivision or extension of anything; a division or group of some subject of knowledge, etc. [Fr. *branche*].
BRANCH (2), [brahnch], *v.i.* to grow branches, to separate into divisions, to extend at various angles; **to b. out,** to extend, expand, turn in new directions; to display unexpected potentialities.
BRANCHER, [brahnch'-er], *n.* that which branches out; a young hawk when it begins to take to the trees away from its nest.
BRANCHERY, [branch'-er-i], *n.* a mass of branches; ramification of vessels through the pulp of the fruit.
BRANCHIAE, [brangk'-i-ē], *n.*(*pl.*) fish gills. [Gk. *brankhia*].
BRANCHIAL, [brangk'-i-al], *adj.* relating to gills.
BRANCHIATE, [brangk'-i-at], *adj.* possessing gills.
BRANCHIFEROUS, [brank-if'-er-us], *adj.* branchiate. [BRANCHIAE and L. *fero* I bear].
BRANCHINESS, [brahnch'-i-nes], *n.* possession of branches.
BRANCHIOPOD, [brangk'-i-ō-pod'], *n.* a crustacean having gills on the feet. [BRANCHIAE and Gk. *pous podos* foot].
BRANCHIOPODOUS, [brangk'-i-op'-od-us], *adj.* pertaining to branchiopods, having gills on the feet.
BRANCHIOSTEGOUS, [brangk'-i-os'-teg-us], *adj.* with the gills covered with membranes. [BRANCHIAE and Gk. *stego* I cover].
BRANCHIOSTOMA, [brangk'-i-os'-tom-a], *n.* a genus of semi-vertebrates comprising the lancelets. [BRANCHIAE and Gk. *-stomos* mouthed].
BRANCHIREME, [brangk'-i-rēm], *n.* an animal having setiform legs. [BRANCHIAE and L. *remus* oar].
BRANCHLESS, [brahnch'-les], *adj.* without branches.
BRANCHLET, [brahnch'-let], *n.* a little branch.
BRANCH-PILOT, [brahnch'-pil'-ot], *n.* a pilot possessing a Trinity House certificate.
BRANCHY, [brahnch'-i], *adj.* having branches, covered with branches.
BRAND (1), [brand], *n.* a burning piece of wood; a mark made by burning, such a mark made on criminals as a punishment or on cattle or other property for identification; (*fig.*) a mark of infamy; a trade mark, used as an evidence of quality, the vintage date and shipper's name stamped on wine corks; a disease in vegetables; (*poet.*) †a sword. [OE. *brand*].
BRAND (2), [brand], *v.t.* to mark with a brand; to attach a stigma to; to designate.
BRANDED, [brand'-id], *adj.* marked with a brand.
BRAND-GOOSE, see BRANT-GOOSE.
BRANDIED, [brand'-id], *adj.* strengthened, mixed with brandy.
BRANDING-IRON, [brand'-ing-īern'], *n.* an iron for branding; a trivet for holding a pot.
BRANDISH, [brand'-ish], *v.t.* to wave or flourish in threatening fashion. [OFr. *brandisser*].
BRANDLING, [brand'-ling], *n.* a dunghill worm striped with red and yellow; a young salmon.
BRAND-NEW, [brand'-new'], *adj.* absolutely new.
BRANDRITH, [brand'-rith], *n.* a gridiron. [OScand. *brandreith*].
BRANDY, [brand'-i], *n.* a strong alcoholic spirit distilled from wine; **b. ball,** a round brown sweet. [Du. *brandewijn* burned wine].
BRANDY-PAWNEE, [brand'-i-paw'-nē], *n.* brandy and water. [BRANDY and Hind. *pani* water].
BRANDY-SNAP, [brand'-i-snap'], *n.* a thin, brown, sticky cylindrical biscuit.
BRANDY-WINE, [brand'-i-wīn], *n.* (*archaic*) brandy.
BRANKS†, [brangks], *n.* an iron halter for gagging nagging women. [Uncert.].
BRANK-URSINE, [brangk'-ur'-sin], *n.* the plant bear's-breech, a species of *Acanthus.* [Fr. *branche-ursine* bear's paw].
BRANLIN, [bran'-lin], *n.* brandling.
BRANNY, [bran'-i], *adj.* containing bran.
BRANTAIL, [bran'-tāl], *n.* the redstart [Uncert.].
BRANT-FOX, [brant'-foks'], *n.* a small, blackish fox.
BRANT-GOOSE, [brant'-gōōs], *n.* the small wild goose, *Branta bernicla,* the brent-goose. [~Germ. *brandgans, cf.* ME. *brant* burnt].
BRASEN†, see BRAZEN.
BRASH (1), [brash], *n.* small fragments of broken rock, rubble. [Fr. *brèche*].
BRASH (2), [brash], *n.* a belch of acidulous fluid from the stomach. [Uncert.].
BRASH (3), [brash], *adj.* impetuous, hasty; brittle. [Uncert.].
BRASIER, see BRAZIER.
BRASIL, [braz-il'], *n.* Brazil-wood. [*Brazil*].
BRASS (1), [brahs], *n.* an alloy of copper and zinc; a plate of this substance engraved with effigies, etc., and set on a church wall or floor as a memorial; (*numis.*) Roman bronze coinage; (*coll.*) coined money; (*coll.*) impudence, effrontery; (*mus.*) the metal wind instruments of an orchestra. [OE. *bræs*].
BRASS (2), [brahs], *adj.* made of brass.
BRASS (3), [brahs], *v.t. and i.* to cover with brass; to brazen, put a bold face on.
BRASSAGE, [brahs'-ij], *n.* a tax levied to cover the expense of minting money. [Fr. *brassage*].
BRASSARD, BRASSART, [bras'-ahd], *n.* †armour protecting the upper arm; an armlet worn as a badge. [Fr. *brassard*].
BRASS-BAND, [brahs'-band'], *n.* a band, consisting only of brass instruments; (*coll.*) a military band.
BRASSE, [bras], *n.* the pale-spotted perch. [LGerm. *brassen*].
BRASSERIE, [bras'-er-i], *n.* a beer hall and eating place. [Fr. *brasser* brew].
BRASSET, [bras'-et], *n.* a brassard. [BRASSARD].
BRASS-FOIL, [brahs'-foil'], *n.* brass beaten into foil.
BRASSFOUNDER, [brahs'-fownd'-er], *n.* a worker in a brass foundry, one who casts brass.
BRASS HAT, [brahs'-hat'], *n.* (*coll.*) a military staff-officer. [From the strip of brass formerly round his cap].
BRASSIE (1), BRASSY, [bras'-i], *n.* a golf-club having a brass sole. [BRASS].
BRASSIE (2), [bras'-i], *n.* the whiting pout, *Gadus luscus.* [BRASS (1)].
BRASSIERE, brassière, [bras'-i-āer], *n.* an under-garment worn by women to shape and support the breasts. [Fr. *brassière*].
BRASSINESS, [brahs'-i-nes], *n.* the condition of being brassy, or resembling brass; insolence, unrelenting hardness.
BRASS-VISAGED, [brahs'-viz'-ijd], *adj.* impudent, brazen.
BRASSY (1), [brahs'-i], *adj.* made of brass; (of sound) harsh, loudly metallic; glaringly hot; impudent.
BRASSY (2), see BRASSIE (1).
BRAT, [brat], *n.* a small, nasty, troublesome child; (*coll.*) a child. [OE. *bratt* rough cloak].
BRATLING, [brat'-ling], *n.* a little brat.
BRATTICE, BRETTICE, [brat'-is], *n.* an air-tight section for ventilating mines. [OFr. *bretesche*].
BRATTICING†, [brat'-is-ing], *n.* (*fort.*) a removable wooden tower, parapet, or defence for a fortress. [*Prec.*].
BRAUNITE, [brown'-īt], *n.* a natural oxide of manganese. [W. *Braun,* its discoverer].
BRAVADO, [brav-ah'-dō], *n.* an arrogant challenging

boast, an ostentatious show of courage; a braggart, a valiant boaster. [Span. *bravada*].

BRAVE (1), [brāv], *n.* a brave man; a Red Indian warrior; a hired thug. [Fr. *brave*].

BRAVE (2), [brāv], *adj.* courageous, valiant, gallantly bearing suffering or misfortune, unflinching in the face of danger; fine, attractive, gay. [BRAVE (1)].

BRAVE (3), [brāv], *v.t.* to face boldly, brazen out, venture; to vaunt, swagger. [BRAVE (1)].

BRAVELY, [brāv-li], *adv.* in brave fashion.

BRAVERY, [brāv'-er-i], *n.* courage, intrepidity; splendour of apparel. [Fr. *braverie*].

BRAVISSIMO, [brav-is'-im-ō], *int.* well done! [It. *bravissimo*].

BRAVO (1), brah'-vō'], *n.* a hired bully. [It. *bravo*].

BRAVO (2), [brah'-vō'], *int.* well done! [*Prec.*].

BRAVURA, [brav-o͞o'-ra], *n.* a dashing display, a show of spirit, something executed with a flourish; (*mus.*) a spirited passage. [It. *bravura*].

BRAWL (1), [brawl], *n.* a noisy fight; a vulgar, loud quarrel; an uproar. [ME. *braule*].

BRAWL (2), [brawl], *v.i.* to create or take part in a brawl. [*Prec.*].

BRAWLING, [brawl'-ing], *adj.* noisy, quarrelsome.

BRAWLINGLY, [brawl'-ing-li], *adv.* in brawling fashion.

BRAWN, [brawn], *n.* a compressed mould of pieces of spiced meat; muscle, muscular power. [OFr. *braon* meat].

BRAWNER, [brawn'-er], *n.* a boar slaughtered for food.

BRAWNINESS, [brawn'-i-nes], *n.* the condition of being brawny.

BRAWNY, [brawn'-i], *adv.* muscular.

BRAY (1), [brā], *n.* the cry of the ass; any loud noisy cry. [OFr. *braire*].

BRAY (2), [brā], *v.i.* to make a bray. [*Prec.*].

BRAY (3), [brā], *v.t.* to crush, pound; (*coll.*) to beat. [OFr. *breyer*, from OHG. *brehhan* to break].

BRAYER†, [brā'-er], *n.* (*print.*) a pestle for smoothing printer's ink.

BRAYING, [brā'-ing], *n.* senseless noise.

BRAYLE, see BRAIL (1).

BRAZE, [brāz], *v.t.* to join metals together by heating or fusing the joint with silver, brass or spelter. [OScand. *brasa* to heat].

BRAZED, [brāzd], *adj.* (*her.*) having three chevrons clasping one another.

BRAZEN (1), BRASEN†, [brāz'-en], *adj.* made from brass, relating to or resembling brass; (*fig.*) impudently bold; (of a sound) resembling that given out by a brass instrument. [OE. *bræsen*].

BRAZEN (2), [brāzn], *v.t.* **to b. a thing out,** to avoid criticism of something by acting brazenly.

BRAZEN-BROWED, [brāz'-en-browd'], *adj.* shameless; insolent.

BRAZEN-FACE, [brāz'-en-fās'], *n.* a shameless person.

BRAZEN-FACED, [brāz'-en-fāsd'], *adj.* shameless; insolent.

BRAZENLY, [brāz'-en-li], *adv.* in brazen fashion.

BRAZENNESS, [brāz'-en-nes], *n.* impudence.

BRAZIER (1), [brāz'-i-er], *n.* an open pan containing burning coals or charcoal. [Fr. *brasier*].

BRAZIER (2), BRASIER, [brāz'-i-er], *n.* one who works in brass. [BRASS].

BRAZILETTO, [braz'-il-et'-ō], *n.* a Jamaican dye-wood. [Span. *brasilete*].

BRAZILIN, [braz'-il-in], *n.* the red colouring in Brazil-wood. [*Brazil*].

BRAZIL-NUT, [braz-il'-nut'], *n.* a three-sided edible nut, the fruit of *Bertholletia excelsa*, a great myrtaceous tree, native to Brazil.

BRAZIL-WOOD, [bra-zil'-wo͝od], *n.* a red dye-wood from Brazil.

BRAZING-LAMP, [brāz'-ing-lamp'], *n.* a blow-lamp.

BREACH (1), [brēch], *n.* a breaking, an infringement, a violation, the dishonouring of an obligation; the thing broken; a material gap, a hole made in something; (*milit.*) a gap in fortifications made by bombardment or assault; (*naut.*) the breaking of waves; a whale's leap from the water; **b. of the peace,** (*leg.*) a riot, public disorder. [~BREAK].

BREACH (2), [brēch], *v.t.* to make a breach; (*milit.*) to break a way through walls or defences. [*Prec.*].

BREACHFUL, [brēch'-fo͝ol], *adj.* with many breaches.

BREAD, [bred], *n.* man's staple food, made of flour baked usually with yeast, etc.; (*fig.*) food generally; means of livelihood. [OE. *bread*].

BREAD-BASKET, [bred'-bahs'-kit], *n.* a basket for bread; (*pop.*) the belly; a type of bomb consisting of a number of small bombs which are scattered by impact and burst separately.

BREAD-BERRY, [bred'-be'-ri], *n.* bread soaked in sweetened water.

BREAD-CORN, [bred'-kawn], *n.* corn from which bread is made.

BREADCRUMB, [bred'-crum'], *n.* a crumb of bread.

BREAD-FRUIT, [bred'-fro͞ot], *n.* the fruit of *Artocarpus incisa*, a native of the Pacific Islands, resembling bread.

BREADLESS, [bred'-les], *adj.* without bread; starving.

BREAD-NUT, [bred'-nut], *n.* the fruit of *Brosimum alicastrum*.

BREAD-ROOM, [bred'-ro͞om], *n.* that part of a ship's hold in which the biscuit is stored.

BREADSTUFFS, [bred'-stufs], *n.*(*pl.*) flour, meal, etc.; cereals used for making bread.

BREADTH, [bretth], *n.* the shorter lineal dimension of surface, the distance across from edge to edge at right angles to the length and depth; the quality of being broad; (*fig.*) broad tolerance, wideness of interest or understanding. [OE. *braedu*].

BREADTHWAYS, [bretth'-wāz], *adv.* from side to side, across.

BREADTHWISE, [bretth'-wiz], *adv.* breadthways.

BREAD-WINNER, [bred'-win'-er], *n.* one who maintains a family by his or her earnings.

BREAK (1), see BRAKE (4).

BREAK (2), [brāk], *n.* the forcible division of anything into (often irregular) parts; fracture, the thing broken; an interruption in time, an interference with continuity; a period for rest between the classes in a school; an escape from prison; (*slang*) a piece of good (or bad) fortune; (*billiards*) a continuous score at one period of play; a change in direction of the ball in cricket after pitching. [BREAK (3)].

BREAK (3), (broke, broken), [brāk], *v.t. and i.* to divide forcibly into pieces; to make or cause a break; to ruin, make bankrupt; to interrupt or disturb continuity; to open ground for planting; to come apart, to be fractured; to give way, to collapse; to disregard, ignore (the laws); to deviate from the original direction (of a ball); to become harsh and deep (of the male voice at puberty); **to b. down,** to crush down, remove, destroy; **to b. in,** to tame (of horses); **to b. into,** to enter by force; to begin to use (one's resources, etc.); **to b. off,** to discontinue; **to b. out,** to become violent; to become infected as to the skin; **to b. up,** to disperse; **to b. the ice,** (*fig.*) to make first social advances; **to b. a record,** to surpass the previous best performance. [OE. *brecan*].

BREAKABLE, [brāk'-abl], *adj.* easily broken, fragile.

BREAKAGE, [brāk'-ij], *n.* act of breaking, things broken; amount of damage by breaking.

BREAKDOWN (1), [brāk'-down], *n.* a complete break; the unforeseen cessation of action or work; the accidental stoppage of a machine; nervous collapse; a statistical analysis.

BREAKDOWN (2), [brāk'-down], *n.* an American negro jig.

BREAKER (1), [brāk'-er], *n.* a small water-barrel carried in boats. [Span. *barrica*].

BREAKER (2), [brāk'-er], *n.* one who breaks; a wave breaking in foam.

BREAKFAST (1), [brek'-fast], *n.* the earliest meal of the day (which breaks a person's fast). [BREAK (3) and FAST].

BREAKFAST (2), [brek'-fast], *v.i.* to eat breakfast.

BREAKFASTING, [brek'-fast-ing], *n.* the act of taking breakfast.

BREAK-JOINT, [brāk'-joint], *n.* the laying of stones or bricks so that the joints in an upper layer do not coincide with those of the layer immediately below.

BREAKNECK, [brāk'-nek', brek'-nek'], *adj.* dangerously fast. [BREAK (3) and NECK].

BREAKWATER, [brāk'-waw-ter], *n.* a barrier or wall run at an angle into the sea to break the force of the waves.

BREAM, [brēm], *n.* a broad, thin freshwater carp of the genus *Abramis*; one of the sea fishes of the genus *Pagellus* or *Labrus*. [Fr. *brême*, from OHGerm. *brahsino*].

BREAM

BREAM, [brēm], *v.t.* (*naut.*) to burn off the seaweed, barnacles, etc., from a ship's bottom. [Uncert.].

BREAST (1), [brest], *n.* that part of the body between the throat and the navel; the soft protuberance on

the chest terminating in the nipple; the mammary glands in women; (*fig.*) the heart, the seat of the emotions and passions; (*arch.*) the torus of a column; **to make a clean b. of it,** confess fully to some fault. [OE. *breost*].
BREAST (2), [brest], *v.t.* to face resolutely, oppose face to face; rise over the top of. [*Prec.*].
BREASTBAND, [brest'-band'], *n.* a band across a horse's breast, used in place of a collar.
BREASTBONE, [brest'-bōn], *n.* the flat bone supporting the breast, the sternum.
BREAST-DEEP, [brest'-dēp'], *adv.* as deep as breast-height; coming up to the breast.
BREAST-DRILL, [brest'-dril'], *n.* a drill held against the breast for pressure on the work.
BREASTED, [brest'-id], *adj.* having breasts.
BREASTFAST, [brest'-fahst], *n.* (*naut.*) a strong rope to hold a ship sidewise to a wharf or quay, or to another ship.
BREAST-HIGH, [brest'-hī'], *adj. and adv.* as high as the breast.
BREAST-HOOKS, [brest'-hŏŏks], *n.(pl.)* horizontal timbers strengthening the forepart of a ship.
BREAST-KNOT, [brest'-not'], *n.* a knot of ribbons, worn as a decoration on the breast.
BREAST-PIN, [brest'-pin], *n.* a brooch, a pin worn to keep a blouse together at the breasts.
BREASTPLATE, [brest'-plāt], *n.* a plate of armour worn to protect the breast; the name-plate on a coffin; a piece of a harness.
BREAST-PLOUGH, [brest'-plow], *n.* a small plough driven by hand and used for cutting turf.
BREASTROPE, [brest'-rōp], *n.* (*naut.*) the rope fastening the yards to the parrels.
BREASTSUMMER, see BRESSUMMER.
BREAST-WALL, [brest'-wawl], *n.* a low wall across the top of a slope.
BREAST-WHEEL, [brest'-wēl], *n.* a water-wheel receiving the water at the level of the axle.

BREAST-PLOUGH

BREASTWORK, [brest'-wurk], *n.* (*milit.*) a rough parapet, a low earthen rampart.
BREATH, [breth], *n.* the air drawn into and exhaled from the lungs at a single respiration; (*poet.*) life; (*fig.*) a light breeze; **to take one's b. away,** utterly to astound one. [OE. *braeth*].
BREATHABLE, [brēTH'-abl], *adj.* able to be breathed.
BREATHABLENESS, [brēTH'-abl-nes], *n.* the state of being breathable.
BREATHE, [brēTH], *v.t. and i.* to inhale and exhale air, to give vent to breath, to blow gently and pleasantly; to blow gently on, to utter softly; (*fig.*) to express a quality. [OE. *braethan*].
BREATHED, [brēTHd], *adj.* (*phon.*) uttered without voice; voiceless; (*philol.*) having a breathing.
BREATHER, [brēTH'er], *n.* (*coll.*) mild open-air exercise as relief from a task, a relaxation from violent effort.
BREATHFUL, [breth'-fŏŏl], *adj.* full of breath.
BREATHING, [brēTH'-ing], *n.* respiration, the action of inhaling and exhaling the breath continuously; a gentle sound or movement; (*philol.*) aspiration, a stressed breath, a mark indicating aspiration; **rough b.,** the strong aspiration of an initial vowel or *r* in Greek.
BREATHING-PORE, [brēTH'-ing-paw(r)'], *n.* a microscopic opening in the cuticle of plants.
BREATHING-SPACE, [brēTH'-ing-spās'], *n.* an opportunity to get one's breath, a short respite.
BREATHING-TIME, [brēTH'-ing-tīm'], *n.* a short interval of rest, a brief relaxation.
BREATHLESS, [breth'-les], *adj.* out of breath, breathing heavily and rapidly; scarcely able, or unable, to breathe, gasping; (*fig.*) tensely expectant, fearfully eager.
BREATHLESSLY, [breth'-les-li], *adv.* in breathless fashion.
BREATHLESSNESS, [breth'-les-nes], *n.* the state or quality of being breathless.
BRECCIA, [brech'-a], *n.* a mass of rough grit or stones held together by a natural bonding. [It. *breccia*].
BRECCIATED, [brech'-āt-id], *adj.* having the quality or appearance of breccia.
BRED, [bred], *adj.* possessing inherited qualities. [BREED (2)].
BREDSORE, [bred'-saw(r)], *n.* a whitlow. [Uncert.].
BREECH (1), (*pl.* **breeches**), [brēch'], *n.* the lower rear part of the body, the buttocks; the part of the trousers covering the buttocks; the hinder part of a gun, the part of a gun that opens for loading. [OE. *brec*].
BREECH (2), [brich], *v.t.* to dress (*esp.* for the first time) in breeches.
BREECH-BAND, [brēch'-band'], *n.* the breeching.
BREECH-BLOCK, [brēch'-blok'], *n.* the part of a gun closing the breech after loading.
BREECHES, [brich'-iz], *n.(pl.)* garments worn on the legs and lower part of the body, trousers; garment fitting tightly round the knees as worn for riding; **b. buoy,** canvas breeches slung along a rope to carry people from a sinking ship. [*pl.* of BREECH].
BREECHING, [brich'-ing], *n.* the harness-strap passing round a horse's haunches; the ropes lashing a gun to the sides of a ship.
BREECH-LOADER, [brēch'-lōd'-er], *n.* a cannon or gun loaded at the breech.
BREED (1), [brēd], *n.* race or stock, racial variety, kind, a group possessing common qualities; good breeding. [BREED (2)].
BREED (2), [brēd], *v.t. and i.* to beget, to bear; to cause to arise; to educate, develop, bring up; to propagate desired types by ordered pairing of selected mates; to reproduce, to give birth; (*fig.*) to grow and increase of itself. [OE. *bredan*].
BREEDER, [brēd'-er], *n.* one who breeds, one who supervises the breeding of animals.
BREEDING, [brēd'-ing], *n.* the act or process of reproducing; descent, ancestry; aristocratic manners; education.
BREEKS, [brēks], *n.(pl.)* (*Scots*) trousers. [BREECH].
BREEZE (1), [brēz], *n.* the gad-fly. [OE. *breosa*].
BREEZE (2), [brēz], *n.* a light wind; (*fig.*) a brief, sharp disturbance; a sudden quarrel. [Fr. *brise*].
BREEZE (3), [brēz], *n.* coal refuse, small cinders; building blocks made of such material. [OFr. *brese*].
BREEZELESS, [brēz'-les], *adj.* without breezes.
BREEZILY, [brēz'i-li], *adv.* in breezy fashion.
BREEZY, [brēz'-i], *adj.* subject to breezes; (*fig.*) lively and jovial in manner.
BREN GUN, [bren'-gun'], *n.* a type of machine gun, *orig.* made at Brno (Brunn) in Czechoslavakia.
BRENNAGE, [bren'-ij], *n.* a feudal due paid in lieu of bran for the lord's hounds. [MedL. *brennagium*].
BRENT-GOOSE, [brent'-gōōs], *n.* the brant-goose, *Branta bernicla.* [Uncert.].
BRESSOMER, see BRESSUMER.
BRESSUMMER, BRESSOMER, BREAST-SUMMER, [bres'-um-er], *n.* (*arch.*) a horizontal beam placed above a door or window to bear the weight of the wall above. [BREAST and Fr. *sommier* beast of burden].
BRET, [bret], *n.* a fish related to the turbot. [Uncert.].
BRETHREN, [breTH'-ren], *n.* †brothers, members of the same group. [*pl.* of BROTHER].
BRETON (1), [bret'-on], *n.* a native of Brittany; the Celtic language spoken in Brittany. [OFr. *breton*].
BRETON (2), [bret'-on], *adj.* pertaining to Brittany or the language of Brittany. [*Prec.*].
BRETTICE, see BRATTICE.
BRETWALDA, [bret'-wawld-a], *n.* a title given to certain Anglo-Saxon kings. [OE. *bretwalda* ruler of the Britons].
BREVE, [brēv], *n.* (*mus.*) a note equal to two semi-breves; a mark (˘) denoting a short syllable. [L. *brevis* short].
BREVET (1), [brev'-it], *n.* (*milit.*) a document recording the appointment of an officer to a higher rank without extra pay. [Fr. *brevet* diploma].
BREVET (2), [brev'-it], *adj.* holding rank by brevet. [*Prec.*].
BREVETCY, [brev'-it-si], *n.* rank held by brevet.
BREVIARY, [brēv'-i-a-ri], *n.* a Roman Catholic book containing the daily services for the year. [L. *breviarium* summary].
BREVIER, [bri-vēer'], *n.* (*print.*) type of a size which prints 9½ lines to an inch, formerly used in printing breviaries. [*Prec.*].
BREVIPED, [brev'-i-ped], *adj.* having short legs. [L. *brevis* short, and *pes pedem* foot].
BREVIPEN, [brev'-i-pen], *n.* (*ornith.*) a bird having short wings, such as the ostrich. [L. *brevis* short and *pennis* wing].
BREVIPENNATE, [brev-ip'-en-āt], *adj.* having short wings. [*Prec.*].
BREVIROSTRATE, [brev'-i-ros'-trāt], *adj.* (*zool.*) short-beaked. [L. *brevis* and *rostrum* beak].

BREVITY, [brev'-i-ti], *n.* the quality of briefness, concision. [L. *brevitas*].
BREW (1), [broo], *n.* something brewed, a particular brewing of beer. [BREW (2)].
BREW (2), [broo], *v.t. and i.* to make beer and similar liquor by boiling and fermenting from malt or hops; to prepare any liquid by mingling and boiling; (*fig.*) cunningly to plot and contrive mischief; to undergo the process of brewing. [OE. *breowan*].
BREWAGE, [broo'-ij], *n.* a brewing, something brewed; (*pop.*) a conglomeration.
BREWER, [broo'-er], *n.* one who brews.
BREWERY, [broo'-er-i], *n.* a factory where brewing is carried out.
BREWHOUSE, [broo'-hous], *n.* a brewery.
BREWING, [broo'-ing], *n.* the act of making ale or beer, the liquor so brewed at any one time.
BREWIS, [broo-is], *n.* broth. [~BROSE].
BREWSTER, [broo'-ster], *n.* a brewer; **b. sessions,** a sitting of magistrates to grant licences to sell alcoholic liquor.
BREWSTERITE, [broo-ster-it], *n.* a white siliceous mineral. [Sir D. *Brewster*].
BRIABOT, [brī'-a-bot], *n.* the angler-fish. [Uncert.].
BRIAR (1), BRIER, [brī'-er], *n.* the wood of *Erica arborea*; a pipe made from this. [Fr. *bruyere* heather].
BRIAR (2), BRIER, [brī'-er], *n.* the wild rose; any prickly bush or shrub; a thorn or prickle; (*fig.*) (*pl.*) difficulties, troubles. [OE. *brere*].
BRIAR (3), BRIER, [brī'-er], *adj.* made from briar.
BRIAREAN, BRIERIAN, [bri-āer'-i-an], *adj.* many-handed. [*Briareus*, the hundred-handed giant of Greek legend].
BRIAR-ROOT, BRIER-ROOT, [brī'-er-root'], *n.* root of the tree heath, *Erica arborea*.
BRIBABLE, [brīb'-abl], *adj.* open to bribery.
BRIBE (1), [brīb], *n.* a reward promised or given for an act contrary to right or duty. [OFr. *bribe* piece of bread].
BRIBE (2), [brīb], *v.t.* to seduce, influence by a bribe. [*Prec.*].
BRIBELESS, [brīb'-les], *adj.* without a bribe.
BRIBERY, [brīb'-eri], *n.* the practice of giving and taking bribes.
BRIC-A-BRAC, bric-à-brac, [brik'-a-brak'], *n.* a collection of miscellaneous, ornamental oddments or knick-knacks; curiosities of little value and less use. [Fr. *bric-à-brac*].
BRICK (1), [brik], *n.* a rectangular block of clay baked hard and used as a building stone; (*pl.*) blocks of wood used as children's toys; (*coll.*) a person of sterling qualities; **to drop a b.,** to make a tactless and indiscreet blunder. [OFr. *brique* piece].
BRICK (2), [brik], *adj.* made of brick.
BRICK (3), [brik], *v.t.* (usually **b. in** or **b. up**) to fill up, build up with bricks.
BRICK-BAT, [brik'-bat'], *n.* a broken piece of brick; such a piece used as a missile. [BRICK and BAT].
BRICK-BUILT, [brik'-bilt], *adj.* built of bricks.
BRICK-CLAY, [brik'-klā], *n.* clay used for making bricks.
BRICK-DUST, [brik'-dust], *n.* powdered brick.
BRICK-EARTH, [brik'-urth], *n.* earth used in brick-making.
BRICK-FIELD, [brik'-fēld], *n.* a field where brick-clay is obtained and baked into bricks.
BRICK-KILN, [brik'-kiln], *n.* a kiln for baking bricks.
BRICKLAYER, [brik'-lā'-er], *n.* a workman skilled in building with bricks.
BRICKLAYING, [brik'-lā'-ing], *n.* the craft of building with bricks.
BRICK-MAKER, [brik'-māk'-er], *n.* a man who makes bricks.
BRICK-NOGGING, [brik'-nog'-ing], *n.* (*arch.*) brick-work fitted in between timber framing.
BRICK-RED, [brik'-red'], *adj.* the reddish colour of bricks.
BRICK-TEA, [brik'-tē], *n.* China tea packed in blocks.
BRICKWORK, [brik'-wurk], *n.* building in brick, those parts of an edifice made with brick.
BRICKYARD, [brik'-yahd'], *n.* a place in which bricks are made.

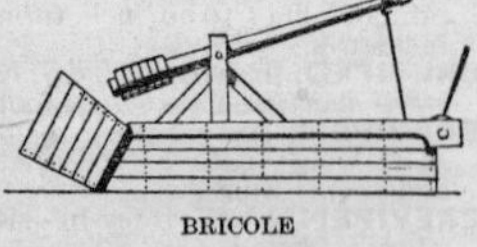
BRICOLE

BRICOLE, [brik'-ōl], *n.* a medieval siege-catapult; (*billiards*) a shot off the cushion. [Fr. *bricole*].
BRIDAL, [brīd'-al], *adj.* pertaining to a bride or wedding. [OE. *brydealu* wedding feast].
BRIDE, [brīd], *n.* a woman about to be or just married, a newly married woman. [OE. *bryd*].
BRIDE-CAKE, [brīd'-kāk], *n.* a very rich cake decorated with white icing, eaten at a wedding feast.
BRIDE-CHAMBER, [brīd'-chām'-ber], *n.* the bedroom shared by a couple on their wedding night.
BRIDEGROOM, [brīd'-groom], *n.* a man about to be or just married. [OE. *brydguma*].
BRIDESMAID, [brīds'-mād], *n.* an unmarried woman attending the bride at a wedding.
BRIDESMAN, [brīds'-man], *n.* a male attendant at a wedding.
BRIDEWELL, [brīd'wel], *n.* a gaol; house of correction. [St. *Bride's Well*, London].
BRIDE-WORT, [brīd'-wurt], *n.* the meadowsweet, *Spiraea Ulmaria*.
BRIDGE (1), [brij], *n.* a structure carrying a road, railway, etc., across a gap, river, etc., linking the two sides; anything resembling this in shape or purpose; a way between two points passing above some intervening obstacle; the raised deck from which a ship is navigated; a rest for a billiard cue; a wooden support for the taut strings of a violin or similar instrument; the hard upper structure of the nose; metal bar for keeping false teeth in place. [OE. *brycg*].
BRIDGE (2), [brij], *n.* a card game for four people, similar to whist, in which one of the two sets of partners undertakes to win so many tricks; **auction b.,** a variety of the game in which the declarers undertake to score a certain minimum number of tricks; **contract b.,** a variety in which the players contract to win a stated number of tricks, with trifling gain for over-tricks and heavy penalties for failure. [Unkn.].
BRIDGE (3), [brij], *v.t.* to build or erect a bridge; (*fig.*) to surmount, overcome. [BRIDGE (1)].
BRIDGEBOARD, [brij'-bawd], *n.* a board to support stair-ends.
BRIDGE-HEAD, [brij'-hed], *n.* the land at the end of a bridge, leading to it and dominating it; the defences guarding the approach to a bridge.
BRIDGELESS, [brij'-les], *adj.* lacking a bridge.
BRIDGE-TRAIN, [brij'-trān], *n.* (*milit.*) the engineers and equipment for building a military bridge.
BRIDLE (1), [brīdl], *n.* the head-gear of a horse's harness to which the controlling reins are attached; (*fig.*) a galling constraint. [OE. *brigdel*].
BRIDLE (2), [brīdl], *v.t. and i.* to control a horse with a bridle, to put on a bridle; (*fig.*) to restrain; to draw oneself up in haughty anger. [*Prec.*].
BRIDLE-HAND, [brīdl'-hand'], *n.* the hand holding the reins; the left hand.
BRIDLE-MAKER, [brīdl'-māk'-er], *n.* one who makes bridles, a loriner.
BRIDLE-PATH, [brīdl'-pahth] *n.* a horse-track, a path wide enough for a single mounted horse.
BRIDLE-REIN, [brīdl'-rān'], *n.* the thong of a bridle, attached to the bit.
BRIDLE-ROAD, [brīdl'-rōd], *n.* a bridle-path.
BRIDLE-WAY, [brīdl'-wā], *n.* a bridle-path.
BRIDOON, [brid-oon'], *n.* the snaffle and rein of a cavalry bridle. [Fr. *bridon*].
BRIEF (1), [brēf], *n.* a statement of a client's case given to the barrister who is to conduct it; the engagement of a barrister to argue a case; a papal letter; an authorization to collect money in churches; a size of note-paper. [OFr. *bref* letter].
BRIEF (2), [brēf], *adj.* short, concise; abrupt (of conversation). [OFr. *bref* from L. *brevis*].
BRIEF (3), [brēf], *v.t.* to instruct a barrister to conduct a case. [BRIEF (1)].
BRIEFLESS, [brēf'-les], *adj.* lacking a brief; (*fig.*) (of a barrister) unsuccessful.
BRIEFLY, [brēf'-li], *adv.* shortly, in brief.
BRIEFNESS, [brēf'-nes], *n.* the quality of being brief, brevity.
BRIER, see BRIAR (2).
BRIERED, [brī'-erd], *adj.* covered with briers.
BRIERY, [brī'-er-i], *adj.* abounding in briers, rough, prickly. [OE **braerig*].
BRIG, [brig], *n.* a vessel having two square-rigged masts. [BRIGANTINE].
BRIGADE (1), [brig-ād'], *n.* a military unit subsidiary to a division, and under the command of a brigadier; an organized semi-military body, usually uniformed, with some common purpose. [Fr. *brigade*].

BRIGADE (2), [brig-ād], *v.t.* to join together into brigades; (*fig.*) to press into service.
BRIGADE-MAJOR, [brig-ād'-māj'-er], *n.* the adjutant or staff officer of a brigade.
BRIGADIER, [brig'-a-dēer'], *n.* the commander of a brigade. [Fr. *brigadier*].
BRIGAND, [brig'-and], *n.* a bandit, a member of a band of robbers who waylay travellers in country districts. [OFr. *brigand*].
BRIGANDAGE, [brig'-an-dij], *n.* the occupation of a brigand, lawless robbery by companies of bandits. [Fr. *brigandage*].
BRIGANTINE, [brig'-an-tēn], *n.* a two-masted vessel, square-rigged on the fore-mast and fore-and-aft rigged on the mainmast. [Fr. *brigantin*].

BRIGANTINE

BRIGHT, [brīt], *adj.* reflecting light, giving out light, glittering; vivid, vividly coloured; cheerful; encouraging; quick in mind, lively; honourable, illustrious. [OE. *beorht*].
BRIGHTEN, [brītn], *v.t. and i.* to make bright, become bright.
BRIGHTLY, [brīt'-li], *adv.* in bright fashion, brilliantly, gaily.
BRIGHTNESS, [brīt'-nes], *n.* the quality of being bright.
BRIGHT'S DISEASE, [brīts'-di-zēz'], *n.* (*med.*) a disease of the kidneys. [Dr. *Bright*, a physician].
BRIGHTSOME, [brīt'-sum], *adj.* bright, cheery, jolly.
BRIGUE†, [brēg], *n.* a cabal, faction; strife. [Fr. *brigue*].
BRILL, [bril], *n.* a smooth flat fish of the genus *Rhombus*, akin to the turbot. [Cornish *brilli* mackerel].
BRILLANTE, [bril-ant'-i], *adj.* (*mus.*) in gay and lively fashion.
BRILLIANCE, [bril'-yans], *n.* the quality of being extremely bright; exceptional talent.
BRILLIANCY, [bril'-yan-si], *n.* brilliance.
BRILLIANT (1), [bril'-yant], *n.* a brightly sparkling jewel, a fine diamond.
BRILLIANT (2), [bril'-yant], *adj.* shining, sparkling, blazingly bright; exceptionally talented; splendid, fashionable. [Fr. *brillant*].
BRILLIANTINE, [bril'-yan-tēn'], *n.* a liquid or solid preparation of alcohol and oil for brightening, scenting, and fixing the hair. [Fr. *brillantine*].
BRILLIANTLY, [bril'-yant-li], *adv.* in brilliant fashion.
BRILLIANTNESS, [bril'-yant-nes], *n.* the condition of being brilliant.
BRIM (1), [brim], *n.* the edge of the rim around the opening of a vessel; the flattish rim round the crown of a hat; the edge of the sea or a river, the extreme edge of a chasm. [ME. *brymme* seashore].
BRIM (2), [brim], *v.i.* to be filled up to the brim. [*Prec.*].
BRIMFUL, [brim'-fōōl], *adj.* full to the top.
BRIMLESS, [brim'-les], *adj.* without a brim.
BRIMMED, [brimd], *adj.* having a brim; brimming over.
BRIMMER, [brim'-er], *n.* a vessel filled to the brim.
BRIMMING, [brim'-ing], *adj.* filled to the very top, overflowing.
BRIMSTONE (1), [brim'-stōn], *n.* sulphur; (*fig.*) hell-fire. [ME. *brinston*, ~BURN, STONE].
BRIMSTONE (2), [brim'-stōn], *adj.* made of or like brimstone.
BRIN, [brin], *n.* the inner radiating bar of a fan. [Fr. *brin*].
BRINDLE, BRINDLED, [brindl], *adj.* having tawny streaks on black. [BRAND].
BRINE, [brīn], *n.* water saturated with salt; sea-water; salt water used in pickling. [OE. *bryne*].
BRINEPAN, [brīn'-pan'], *n.* a pit in which brine is evaporated in order to extract the salt.
BRINEPIT, [brīn'-pit], *n.* a brinepan.
BRINESHRIMP, [brīn'-shrimp], *n.* a small crustacean of the genus *Artemia*.
BRINE-SPRING, [brīn'-spring], *n.* a salt water spring.
BRING, (**brings, brought**), *v.t.* to cause to come; to carry along (to a place where the speaker is or will be), to produce, cause to arise; (*leg.*) to initiate an action; **to b. about,** to cause to arise; **to b. back,** to call to mind; **to b. down,** to shoot down; **to b. forth,** give birth to; **to b. forward,** to carry on a total, etc., to the following page in book-keeping; **to b. off,** to accomplish, usually by luck or exceptional skill or in face of difficulty; **to b. on,** to induce; **to b. over,** to convert; **to b. round,** to restore to consciousness, convert; **to b. up,** to educate, rear; to vomit; to raise a matter. [OE. *bringan*].
BRINISH, [brīn'-ish], *adj.* salty, resembling brine.
BRINISHNESS, [brīn'-ish-nes], *n.* the state of being brinish.
BRINJAL, [brin'-jawl], *n.* the fruit of the egg-plant, *Solanum Melongena*. [Portug. *bringella*, Arab. *bādiyān*].
BRINK, [bringk], *n.* the extreme edge of a hill top or precipice; (*fig.*) the immediate neighbourhood of anything alarming. [ODan. *brinke*].
BRINY (1), [brīn-i], *n.* (*coll.*) the sea.
BRINY (2), [brīn-i], *adj.* brinish, like brine.
BRIO, [brē'-ō], *n.* (*mus.*) vivacity. [It. *brio*].
BRIOCHE, [bri'-osh], *n.* a kind of horseshoe-shaped bread or pastry. [Fr. *brioche*].
BRIONY, see BRYONY.
BRIQUETTE, [brik-et'], *n.* a brick-shaped cake of compressed material used in household fires; a similarly shaped piece of ice-cream. [Fr. *briquette*].
BRISE-BISE, [brēz'-bēz], *n.* a short curtain in front of a window. [Fr. *brise-bise*].
BRISK (1), [brisk], *adj.* active, spirited, quick and efficient in movement; (of fires) burning brightly; (of wind) sharp and fresh. [Uncert.].
BRISK (2), [brisk], *v.t. and i.* to make or become brisk.
BRISKET, [bris'-kit], *n.* the breast of an animal; the part of the breast nearest the ribs. [OFr. *breschet*].
BRISKLY, [brisk'-li], *adv.* in brisk fashion.
BRISKNESS, [brisk'-nes], *n.* the quality of being brisk.
BRISLING, [briz'-ling], *n.* the sprat, *Clupea sprattus*. [Norw. *brisling*].
BRISTLE (1), [brisl], *n.* the quills of a hedgehog, the stiff hair of swine, any short, stiff, rough hair; the stiff hairs in a brush. [ME. *bristel*].
BRISTLE (2), [brisl], *v.i.* to raise the bristles from rage or fear; (*fig.*) to bridle with anger; to show or make a group of projecting points, to display many weapons ominously; (*fig.*) to be beset with. [*Prec.*].
BRISTLINESS, [bris'-li-nes], *n.* the condition of being bristly.
BRISTLING, [bris'-ling], *adj.* displaying, having bristles; rising in anger. [BRISTLE (2)].
BRISTLY, [bris'-li], *adj.* with bristles; rough, unshaven.
BRISTOL BOARD, [brist'-ol-bawd'], *n.* a fine smooth cardboard used by artists. [*Bristol*, Gloucestershire].
BRISTOL BRICK, [brist'-ol-brik'], *n.* a brick for cleaning cutlery.
BRISTOL CREAM, [brist'-ol-krēm'], *n.* a fine rich brand of sherry.
BRISTOL DIAMOND, [brist'-ol-dī'-a-mond], *n.* rock-crystal found near Bristol.
BRISTOL STONE, [brist'-ol-stōn'], *n.* Bristol diamond.
BRIT, [brit], *n.* young mackerel; young sea-fish of various kinds. [Unkn.].
BRITANNIA METAL, [brit-an'-ya-met'-al], *n.* a white metal alloy, somewhat resembling and used as a cheap substitute for silver.
BRITANNIC, [brit-an'-nik], *adj.* pertaining to Britain or the inhabitants of Britain. [L. *britannicus*].
BRITHOLITE, [brith'-ō-līt], *n.* (*min.*) a rare form of phosphate and silicate of calcium and cerium. [Gk. *brithos* weight and *lithos* stone].
BRITISH, [brit'-ish], *adj.* pertaining to Britain or to the inhabitants of Britain, or to the British Empire; **B. warm,** a short overcoat worn by British Army officers. [OE. *Brittisc*].
BRITISHER, [brit'-ish-er], *n.* (*U.S.*) a Briton.
BRITISHNESS, [brit'-ish-nes], *n.* the quality and character peculiar to the British race.
BRITON, [brit'-on], *n.* a native of Great Britain; an ancient Brythonic inhabitant of England. [OFr. *breton*].
BRITTLE, [britl], *adj.* fragile, liable to break easily. [ME. *brutel, britel*].
BRITTLENESS, [britl'-nes], *n.* the condition of being brittle.
BRITTLESTAR, [britl'-stah(r)], *n.* a species of star-fish, having long arms.
BRITZSKA†, [brit'-ska], *n.* a carriage with a folding hood. [Pol. *britzka* wagon].
BRIZA, [brī'-za], *n.* (*bot.*) quaking grass. [MdL.].

BROACH (1), [brōch], *n.* a pointed hand tool for making small holes, a bodkin, awl, any boring-bit tapered to an end; a roasting-spit. [Fr. *broche* from L. *broccus* having prominent teeth].

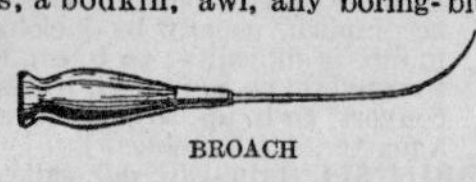
BROACH

BROACH (2), [brōch], *v.t.* to bore a hole in a cask of liquor, to tap; to enter upon, begin, approach a subject, mention a matter for discussion. [*Prec.*].

BROACHER, [brōch'-er], *n.* one who starts a new subject for discussion.

BROACH-SPIRE, [brōch'-spī-er], *n* a spire rising directly from a church-tower wall without resting on a parapet.

BROAD (1), [brawd], *n.* a wide stretch of a river, etc. [Uncert.].

BROAD (2), [brawd], *adj.* wide, extended, extensive, not narrow, of long measurement from side to side; general, comprehensive, widespread; liberal, unprejudiced; bold, distinct, decided; indelicate, immodest, coarse gross; **as b. as it is long**, the same either way; **b. church**, Protestants who tend to regard dogma with indifference. [OE. *brad*].

BROAD ARROW, [brawd'-a'-rō], *n.* the mark in the shape of an arrow-head set up on government property, and also upon the uniforms of convicts.

BROAD AWAKE, [brawd'-a-wāk'], *adj.* wide awake.

BROAD-AXE, [brawd'-aks'], *n.* an ancient military weapon in the form of an axe; an axe for hewing timber.

BROAD-BEAN, [brawd'-bēn], *n.* a large edible bean, the fruit of *Vicia Jaba.*

BROAD-BILL, [brawd'-bil], *n.* a variety of duck having a broad beak shaped like a shovel, the spoon-bill.

BROAD-BRIM†, [brawd'-brim], *n.* a hat with a broad brim, formerly worn by Quakers; a Quaker.

BROADCAST (1), [brawd'-kahst], *n.* (*agr.*) a scattering of seed when sowing; (*wirel.*) an entertainment transmitted by wireless telephony.

BROADCAST (2), [brawd'-kahst], *adj.* sown by scattering, scattered by hand; (*fig.*) widely disseminated; transmitted by wireless telephony.

BROADCAST (3), (*pret., p.pt.* **broadcast**), [brawd'-kahst], *v.t.* to transmit by wireless telephony; to speak or perform before a transmitting microphone.

BROADCLOTH, [brawd'-cloth], *n.* a fine woollen cloth, woven to a broad width.

BROADEN, [brawd'-en], *v.t. and i.* to grow broad; to make broad.

BROAD-EYED, [brawd'-īd], *adj.* taking a wide survey.

BROAD-GAUGE, [brawd'-gāj], *n.* a railway track with the rails set wider apart than the standard width of four feet eight and a half inches.

BROAD-HORNED, [brawd'-hawnd], *adj.* having a pair of horns, with the two tips spread wide apart.

BROADISH, [brawd'-ish], *adj.* tending to broadness.

BROADLY, [brawd'-li], *adv.* in a broad manner; on the whole; approximately.

BROAD-MINDED, [brawd'-mīnd'-id], *adj.* tolerant.

BROADMINDEDNESS, [brawd'-mīnd'-id-nes], *n.* a tolerant and liberal attitude of mind.

BROADNESS, [brawd'-nes], *n.* the state or quality of being broad.

BROADSHEET, [brawd'-shēt], *n.* a sheet of paper printed only on the face; a tract or ballad printed on one side of a sheet of paper and sold to the public, a broadside.

BROADSIDE, [brawd'-sīd], *n.* a broadsheet; the whole length of one side of a ship; the simultaneous firing of all guns on one side of a ship aiming at the same objective; (*fig.*) a concentrated attack against an individual.

BROADSIDE, [brawd'-sīd], *adv.* on or facing the broadside.

BROAD-SIGHTED, [brawd'-sīt'-id], *adj.* having an extended view.

BROAD-SPOKEN, [brawd'-spōkn'], *adj.* speaking frankly or rudely, outspoken.

BROADSWORD, [brawd'-sawd], *n.* a sword with a broad blade.

BROADWAYS, [brawd'-wāz], *adv.* broadwise.

BROADWISE, [brawd'-wīz], *adv.* towards the side, laterally, along the breadth.

BROBDINGNAGIAN, [brob'-ding-nag'-i-an], *adj.* gigantic. [*Brobdingnag*, a country of giants in Swift's *Gulliver's Travels*].

BROCADE (1), [brōk-ād'], *n.* a fabric usually of silk embossed or decorated with silver and gold threads. [Span. *brocado*].

BROCADE (2), [brōk-ād'], *v.t. and i.* to make brocade; to stitch designs on cloth.

BROCADED, [brōk-ād'-id], *adj.* woven or worked with brocade; dressed in brocade.

BROCADE-SHELL, [brōk-ād'-shel], *n.* a species of cone-shell.

BROCAGE, see BROKAGE.

BROCATEL, [brok'-a-tel'], *n.* a coarse kind of brocade, or a cheap substitute for it. [Fr. *brocatelle*].

BROCATELLO, [brok'-a-tel'-ō], *n.* a variegated brocade-coloured marble; Sienna marble. [*Prec.*].

BROCCOLI, [brok'-ol-i], *n.* a hardy species of cauliflower bearing a number of small sproutings. [It. *broccolo* sprout].

BROCH, [brok], *n.* a prehistoric North-Scottish circular tower, open in the centre, built of stone and left uncemented. [OScand. *borg* stronghold].

BROCHANTITE, [brok'-an-tīt'], *n.* (*min.*) a sulphate of copper, having green crystals. [*Brochant* de Villiers, a French mineralogist].

BROCHE, broché (1), [brosh'-ā], *n.* a fabric, particularly of silk, on the surface of which an embossed pattern is woven. [Fr. *broché*, *p.pt.* of *brocher* to stitch].

BROCHE, broché (2), [brosh'-ā], *adj.* woven like broché.

BROCHURE, [brosh'-yŏoer], *n.* a small descriptive pamphlet. [Fr. *brochure*].

BROCK, [brok], *n.* a badger. [OE. *broc*, Wel. *broch*].

BROCKET, [brok'-it], *n.* a two-year-old stag. [Fr *broquart*].

BROG, [brog], *n.* (*dial.*) an awl. [Uncert.].

BROGAN, [brōg'-an], *n.* a brogue. [Ir. *brogan*].

BROGUE (1), [brōg], *n.* a coarse leather shoe; a heavy leather shoe with hand-tooled reinforcements for hard wear. [Ir. *brog* shoe].

BROGUE (2), [brōg], *n.* the accent of an Irishman speaking English; English as spoken in Ireland. [Unkn.].

BROGUISH, [brōg'-ish], *adj.* speaking with a trace of brogue. [BROGUE (1)].

BROIDER, [broid'-er], *v.t.* to embroider. [EMBROIDER].

BROIL (1), [broil], *n.* a turmoil; a row, a brawl, a noisy quarrel. [Fr. *brouille*].

BROIL (2), [broil], *v.t. and i.* to grill, to cook in the flames of a fire, generally upon a gridiron; to be heated; to sweat with heat. [OFr. *broiller*].

BROIL (3), [broil], *n.* broiled meat.

BROILER, [broil'-er], *n.* a person who enjoys or excites broils; a person who cooks meat by broiling; a gridiron; (*coll.*) an extremely hot day.

BROILING, [broil'-ing], *adj.* being cooked by fire; extremely hot.

BROKAGE, BROCAGE, [brōk'-ij], *n.* brokerage. [Short form of BROKERAGE].

BROKE (1), [brōk], *pret.* of BREAK (3)].

BROKE (2), [brōk], *adj.* (*coll.*) penniless, ruined, bankrupt. [BREAK (3)].

BROKEN, [brōk'-en], *adj.* (*p.pt.* of BREAK), being in fragments, crushed, dispirited, weak; interrupted; (*bot.*) variegated. [BREAK (2)].

BROKEN-BACKED, [brōk'-en-bakt'], *adj.* having the spine broken.

BROKEN-DOWN, [brōk'-en-down'], *adj.* worn out by illness or work, stopped through a breakdown; decrepit; useless.

BROKEN-HEARTED, [brōk'-en-haht'-id] *adj.* overcome by sorrow, inconsolable.

BROKENLY, [brōk'-en-li], *adv.* in a broken fashion with breaks, intermittently.

BROKEN MEAT, [brōk'-en-mēt'], *n.* the remains of a meal.

BROKENNESS, [brōk'-en-nes], *n.* the state of being broken.

BROKEN WIND, [brōk'-en-wind'], *n.* an affection of the lungs of horses causing laboured and spasmodic breathing.

BROKEN-WINDED, [brōk'-en-wind'-id], *adj* affected by broken wind.

BROKER, [brōk'-er], *n.* an agent working on a commission basis who buys and sells stocks and shares or goods in bulk for clients; a dealer in second-hand goods. [OFr. *brocour* seller of wine].

BROKERAGE, [brōk'-er-ij], *n.* the business of a broker; the commission charged by a broker for handling a transaction.

BROKING, [brōk'-ing], *n.* the business of a broker.

BROLLY, [brol'-i], *n.* (*slang*) an umbrella.

BROMA†, [brōm-a], *n.* (*med.*) solid food. [Gk. *broma* food].
BROMAL, [brōm'-al], *n.* an oily liquid obtained by adding bromine to alcohol.
BROMATE, [brōm'-āt] *n.* (*chem.*) a salt of bromic acid.
BROMATOLOGY, [brom'-a-tol'-o-ji], *n.* the study of food, dietetics. [BROMA and Gk. *logos* speech].
BROMELIA, [brom-ēl'-ya], *n.* a plant of the order *Bromeliaceae*, the pine-apple. [*Bromel*, a botanist].
BROMELIN, [brōm'-el-in], *n.* a ferment derived from pine-apple juice. [*Prec.*].
BROMIC, [brōm'-ik], *adj.* (*chem.*) containing bromine; **b. acid**, an acid containing hydrogen, bromine and oxygen, $HBrO_3$.
BROMIDE, [brōm'-īd], *n.* a compound of bromine with a base, used medically as a sedative.
BROMIDIC, [brōm-id'-ik], *adj.* containing bromide.
BROMINE, [brōm'-ēn], *n.* non-metallic poisonous brownish-red liquid giving off a bad stench, the chemical element denoted by Br. [Gk. *bromos* stink].
BROMIZE, [brōm'-īz], *v.t.* (*phot.*) to treat with a bromide.
BROMOIL, [brōm'-oil], *n.* (*phot.*) a bleached bromide print treated with a pigment.
BRONCHIA, (*pl.* **bronchiae**), [brong'-ki-a], *n.* (*anat.*) extension of the windpipe which carries air into the lung. [Gk. *brogkhos* throat].
BRONCHIAL, [brong'-ki-al], *adj.* pertaining to, affected in, the bronchiae.
BRONCHIC, [brong'-kik], *adj.* bronchial.
BRONCHITIS, [brong-kīt'-is], *n.* inflammation of the bronchial tubes, with rawness of the chest, characterized by spasmodic coughing bouts. [BRONCHO and Gk. *-itis* denoting inflammation].
BRONCHO-, *pref.* appertaining to the windpipe. [Gk. *bronkhos*].
BRONCHOCELE, [brong'-ko-sēl'], *n.* (*med.*) goitre. [BRONCHO and Gk. *kele* swelling].
BRONCHOPHONY, [brong-kof'-on-i], *n.* the sound peculiar to the human voice; (*med.*) sound in the chest heard by auscultation. [BRONCHO and Gk. *phone* sound].
BRONCHOSCOPE, [brong'-kō-skōp'], *n.* (*med.*) an instrument fitted with a reflector and electric bulb for inspecting the interior of the bronchiae. [BRONCHO and Gk. *skopos* watcher].
BRONCHOTOMY, [brong-kot'-om-i], *n.* (*surg.*) the operation of cutting into the windpipe. [BRONCHO and Gk. *tome* cutting].
BRONCO, [brong'-kō], *n.* (*U.S.*) an untamed horse. [Span. *bronco* rough].
BRONTOSAURUS, [bron'-tō-sawr'-us], *n.* (*geol.*) an extinct herbivorous giant lizard of the prehistoric age, about seventy feet in length. [Gk. *bronte* thunder, and *sauros* lizard].

BRONTOSAURUS

BRONX, [brongks], *n.* (*U.S.*) the district in New York City, lying north of Manhattan, bounded by the Bronx river; a kind of cocktail.
BRONZE (1), [bronz], *n.* an alloy of copper and tin with lead or zinc; an ornament or cast statue of this metal; the reddish colour of the alloy; **B. age**, (*archae.*) historical period between 1800 and 1000 B.C. when most implements were made of bronze. [It. *bronzo* from L. *aes Brundisinum* brass from Brindisi].
BRONZE (2), [bronz], *adj.* made of bronze; of the colour of bronze.
BRONZE (3), [bronz], *v.t.* *and i.* to give or acquire the colour or appearance of bronze.
BRONZE-POWDER, [bronz'-pow'-der], *n.* a metallic powder used to produce the effect of bronze.
BRONZE-WING, [bronz'-wing], *n.* the Australian bronze-winged pigeon, a species of *Phaps*.
BRONZING-LIQUOR, [bronz'-ing-lik'-er], *n.* chloride of antimony and sulphate of copper, used in the process of bronzing.
BRONZITE, [bronz'-īt], *n.* (*min.*) a bronze-like variety of diallage.
BROOCH, [brōch], *n.* a clasp, usually ornamented with precious or semi-precious stones, fastened by a clip and catch to the clothes at the breast or throat. [Variant of BROACH].
BROOD (1), [brōōd], *n.* the number of young birds hatched at one sitting; all the offspring of one parent; (*fig.*) offspring, progeny, children. [OE. *brod*].
BROOD (2), [brōōd]. *v.i.* to sit on eggs to hatch them; to cover and guard with the wings and feathers; (*fig.*) to sit quietly, to be at rest; meditate, to ponder for a long time. [*Prec.*].
BROODING, [brōōd'-ing], *adj.* meditating deeply and for long.
BROODINGLY, [brōōd'-ing-li], *adv.* meditatively.
BROOD-MARE, [brōōd'-māer], *n.* a mare kept for breeding purposes.
BROODY, [brōōd'-i], *adj.* having a natural urge to brood.
BROOK (1), [brŏŏk], *n.* a small stream. [OE. *broc*].
BROOK (2), [brŏŏk], *v.t.* to bear; to endure; to tolerate. [OE. *brucan* enjoy].
BROOKLET, [brŏŏk'-let], *n.* a small brook. [*Dim.* of BROOK].
BROOKLIME, [brŏŏk'-līm], *n.* (*bot.*) the water-speedwell, a species of *Veronica*.
BROOKMINT, [brŏŏk'-mint], *n.* (*bot.*) the water-mint.
BROOKWEED, [brŏŏk'-wēd], *n.* (*bot.*) the cosmopolitan plant, *Samolus Valerandi*.
BROOKY, [brŏŏk'-i], *adj.* having many brooks.
BROOM, [brōōm], *n.* a shrub bearing clusters of small yellow flowers and having short spiky leaves, of the genus *Cytisus* or *Genista*; a besom, a long handle with a short board bearing a bush of bristles attached to one end, used for sweeping. [OE. *brom*].
BROOMCORN, [brōōm'-kawn], *n.* the common millet, a species of *Sorghum*, whose panicles provide bristles for brooms and brushes.
BROOMLAND, [brōōm'-land'], *n.* land overgrown with broom.
BROOMRAPE, [brōōm'-rāp'], *n.* (*bot.*) the strangleweed, a parasitic plant of the genus *Orobanche*. [BROOM and L. *rapum* knot, lump].

BROOM

BROOMSTICK, [brōōm'-stik], *n.* the handle of a broom.
BROOMY, [brōōm'-i], *adj.* overgrown with, or looking like broom.
BROSE, [brōz], *n.* porridge; **Athole b.**, a drink of honey, cream and whisky. [OFr. *broues*].
BROTH, [broth], *n.* stock water in which meat has been cooked or vegetables boiled; a kind of soup with meat and vegetables. [OE. *broth*].
BROTHEL, [broth'-el], *n.* an establishment kept for prostitution. [ME. *brothel* a prostitute].
BROTHELLER, [broth'-el-er], *n.* a person who frequents brothels.
BROTHER, (*pl.* **brothers**, **†brethren**), [bruTH'-er], *n.* a male having the same father and mother as another person; a person closely connected with another; a member of the same society as another person, an associate; a member of a religious order; a person resembling another in any characteristic; a fellow-man; **half b.**, a son having one parent in common with another person. [OE. *brothor*].
BROTHER-GERMAN, [bruTH'-er-jur'-man], *n.* a man having the same two parents as another person, a full brother.
BROTHERHOOD, [bruTH'-er-hŏŏd], *n.* the state of being a brother; a society, fraternity, association, any group of persons working towards a common end.
BROTHER-IN-LAW, [bruTH'-er-in-law'], *n.* the brother of a husband or wife, or a sister's husband.
BROTHERLESS, [bruTH'-er-les], *adj.* having no brother.
BROTHERLIKE, [bruTH'-er-līk'], *adj.* resembling or acting like a brother.
BROTHERLINESS, [bruTH'-er-li-nes], *n.* state of being brotherly, friendliness.
BROTHERLY, [bruTH'-er-li], *adj.* like a brother, affectionate.
BROTHER-UTERINE, [bruTH'-er-yŏŏ'-ter-īn], *n.* a son related to another by having the same mother.
BROUGHAM†, [brō'-um, brōōm], *n.* a closed carriage with a light chassis and body on four wheels, drawn by one horse. [Lord *Brougham* (1778-1868), the designer].
BROUGHT, [brawt], *p.pt.* of BRING.
BROW, [brow], *n.* the forehead, the part of the forehead above the eyes, the ridge above each eye, supported by the top bone of each eye-socket; the slight crescent of hair that covers this ridge; the top edge of a steep hill; a movable gangway from the ship to a quayside. [OE. *bru*].

BROW-ANTLER, [brow'-ant'-ler], *n.* the first antler appearing in growth on a deer's head.
BROWBEAT, [brow'-bēt], *v.t.* to act overbearingly towards, threaten arrogantly, intimidate, bully.
BROWN (1), [brown], *n.* a colour which is a mixture of yellow, red and black in various shades; a large flock of game-birds on the wing having the effect of a brown mass.
BROWN (2), [brown], *adj.* having the colour of brown; **b. study,** deep thought; **b.-shirt,** a Nazi (from the colour of his uniform). [OE. *brun*].
BROWN (3), [brown], *v.t.* and *i.* to make brown; to cause to become brown in colour by applying heat, to roast or grill; to become brown; **b. off,** (*slang*) to disappoint.
BROWNBILL†, [brown'-bil], *n.* a brown halberd.
BROWN COAL, [brown'-kōl'], *n.* wood coal, lignite.
BROWNIAN, [brown'-i-an], *adj.* (*phys.*); **B. movement,** the motion of finely divided particles suspended in a fluid, caused by the impact of molecules on one another. [Dr. R. *Brown* who first described the phenomenon].
BROWNIE, [brown'-i], *n.* an elf or fairy helpful to human beings; a member of the Girl Guides of the youngest age.
BROWNING (1), [brown'-ing], *n.* the process of imparting a brown colour to the surfaces of articles made of iron; a liquid used in cookery as a colouring.
BROWNING (2), [brown'-ing], *n.* an automatic pistol. [*Browning*, the inventor].
BROWNISH, [brown'-ish], *adj.* slightly brown.
BROWNIST, [brown'-ist], *n.* a follower of the religious principles of Robert *Brown* who seceded from the Established Church of England about 1580.
BROWNNESS, [brown'-nes], *n.* the quality or state of being brown in colour.
BROWN-POST, [brown'-pōst], *n.* a beam which runs horizontally across a building.
BROWN-RUST, [brown'-rust], *n.* a disease in wheat caused by the fungus *Puccinia graminis*.
BROWN-SPAR, [brown'-spah(r)], *n.* (*min.*) a variety of dolomite.
BROWSE (1), [browz], *n.* the tender shoots of herbage eaten by cattle.
BROWSE (2), [browz], *v.i.* to feed on grass and young shoots while moving aimlessly from place to place; to graze; (*fig.*) to study or read fitfully. [OFr. *brouster* to shoot, sprout].
BROWSING, [browz'-ing], *n.* ground for browsing.
BRUCINE, [brōōs'-in], *n.* a poisonous vegetable alkaloid found in *Nux vomica*. [James *Bruce*, the African explorer].
BRUCITE, [brōōs'-īt], *n.* (*min.*) a hydrate of magnesia. [*Bruce*, an American mineralogist].
BRUIN, [brōō'-in], *n.* a bear. [Du. *bruin* brown].
BRUISE (1), [brōōz], *n.* an injury to the flesh accompanied by discoloration due to a blow, a contusion.
BRUISE (2), [brōōz], *v.t.* and *i.* to injure the flesh without drawing blood, to cause the flesh to discolour by a heavy blow, to contuse; to crush by squeezing or pounding; to display the effects of a blow. [OE. *brysan*].
BRUISER, [brōōz'-er], *n.* a person who bruises; a concave tool for grinding the specula of telescopes; (*slang*) a professional boxer.
BRUIT (1), [brōōt], *n.* report; rumour. [Fr. *bruit*].
BRUIT (2), [brōōt], *v.t.* to rumour.
BRUMAL, [brōōm'-al], *adj.* pertaining to winter. [L. *bruma* shortest day of the year].
BRUME, [brōōm], *n.* fog. [Fr. *brume* fog from L. *bruma* the shortest day].
BRUNCH, [brunch], *n.* (*slang*) a meal heavier than breakfast, lighter than lunch, at which dishes from both meals are eaten. [BR(EAKFAST) and (L)UNCH].
BRUNETTE (1), [brōōn-et'], *n.* a woman or girl with a brown complexion and colouring, with dark eyes and hair. [Fr. *brunette*].
BRUNETTE (2), [brōōn'-et'], *adj.* dark-haired; of dark complexion.
BRUNION, [brun'-yon], *n.* a smooth-skinned peach, a nectarine, a cross between a plum and a peach. [Fr. *brugnon* peach].
BRUNSWICK-BLACK, [brunz'-wik-blak'], *n.* a dull black paint. [*Brunswick*, a German state].
BRUNSWICK-GREEN, [brunz'-wik-grēn'], *n.* a pigment composed of copper carbonate and chalk.
BRUNT, [brunt], *n.* the fiercest attack; the heaviest shock; the first blow. [Unkn.].
BRUSH (1), [brush], *n.* a hand utensil made of a bunch of bristles, feathers or twigs set in a piece of wood or other material with a handle, used for sweeping, removing dirt, brushing hair or wearing apparel, etc.; a stick with a small bunch of fine hair used to apply paint; the bushy tail of a fox; rough, wild shrubs growing close together, undergrowth; skirmish, an insignificant encounter with opponents; (*elect.*) a discharge of electricity with the sparks resembling the bristles of a brush; a piece of copper gauze or carbon for conducting an electric current to or from the commutator of a dynamo or electric motor; **b. work,** painting. [OFr. *brosse* bush].
BRUSH (2), [brush], *v.t.* and *i.* to use a brush; to graze against, to rub lightly in passing; **to b. away, to b. off,** to remove with a quick movement; **to b. aside,** to ignore, summarily reject; **to b. up,** (*fig.*) to learn again. [*Prec.*].
BRUSH-BURN, [brush'-burn], *n.* a burn produced by friction.
BRUSHINESS, [brush'-i-nes], *n.* the quality of being brushy.
BRUSHING (1), [brush'-ing], *n.* (*mining*) the work of demolishing by blasting or cutting walls and roof of a blocked section of a gallery.
BRUSHING (2), [brush'-ing], *adj.* sweeping; cutting brushwood; (*fig.*) brisk.
BRUSH-TURKEY, [brush'-turk'-i], *n.* a game-bird of the megapode family.
BRUSHWOOD, [brush'-wŏŏd], *n.* undergrowth, scrub, a thicket.
BRUSHY, [brush'-i], *adj.* rough or bushy, like a brush.
BRUSQUE, [brusk], *adj.* curt, abrupt in manner. [Fr. *brusque*].
BRUSQUELY, [brusk'-li], *adv.* in brusque fashion.
BRUSQUENESS, [brōōsk'-nes], *n.* the quality of being brusque
BRUSSELS, [brus'-elz], *n.* (*coll.*) carpet. [*Next*].
BRUSSELS CARPET, [brus'-elz-kahp'-it], *n.* a type of carpet originally imported from *Brussels*.
BRUSSELS-SPROUTS, [brus'-el-sprowts'], *n.*(*pl.*) vegetables resembling small cabbages, which sprout from an upright stem or stalk.
BRUT, [brōōt], *adj.* (of wines) unsweetened. [Fr. *brut*].
BRUTAL, [brōōt'-al], *adj.* characteristic of a brute; cruel, coarse, rough. [Fr. *brutal*].
BRUTALISM, [brōōt'-al-izm], *n.* brutality.
BRUTALITARIAN, [brōōt-al'-i-tāer'-i-an], *n.* a person who advocates consistent practice of brutality.
BRUTALITY, [brōōt-al'-i-ti], *n.* the state of being brutal; a brutal act.
BRUTALIZE, [brōōt'-al-īz], *v.t.* to make brutal, to treat brutally.
BRUTALLY, [brōōt'-al-i], *adv.* in brutal fashion.
BRUTE (1), [brōōt], *n.* a beast, a mammal, as distinct from a man; a brutal person, a savage, an uncivilized human being, a crude and cruel person. [Fr. *brut*. from L. *brutus* heavy, stupid].
BRUTE (2), [brōōt], *adj.* brutal, inhuman, irrational.
BRUTIFY, [brōōt'-i-fī], *v.t.* to make brutal, to brutalize.
BRUTISH, [brōōt'-ish], *adj.* like a brute, stupid unfeeling; savage.
BRUTISHLY, [brōōt'-ish-li], *adv.* in a brutish fashion.
BRUTISHNESS, [brōōt'-ish-nes], *n.* the state of being brutal.
BRUTISM, [brōōt'-izm], *n.* brutishness.
BRYOLOGIST, [brī-ol'-o-jist], *n.* one who studies bryology.
BRYOLOGY, [brī-ol'-o-ji], *n.* the study of mosses. [Gk. *bruon* moss and *logos* speech].
BRYONINE, [brī'-on-in], *n.* a bitter principle from the root of the white bryony.
BRYONY, BRIONY, [brī'-on-i], *n.* (*bot.*) a wild climbing plant of the genus *Bryonia*. [Gk. *bruonia*].
BRYOZOA, [brī'-oz-ō'-a], *n.*(*pl.*) the polyzoa. [Gk. *bruon* moss and *zoon* animal].
BRYTHONIC, [brith-on'-ik], *adj.* pertaining to the Celtic races of southern Britain, British. [Wel. *Brython* Briton].
BUBAL, [bōō'-bal], *n.* a kind of North African antelope. [Gk. *boubalos*].
BUBBLE (1), [bubl], *n.* a thin globular or hemispherical skin of liquid inflated with air or gas; a small round air- or gas-filled pocket in a liquid or solid; (*fig.*) anything lacking a solid or sound basis, any scheme in danger of being destroyed by the intrusion of the facts of reality; a fraudulent plan. [~Du. *bobbel*, Swed. *bubla*].
BUBBLE (2), [bubl], *v.i.* to make or cause bubbles, to effervesce, to be in a state of activity due to the formation of bubbles, to contain bubbles; to flow with the noise of innumerable bubbles bursting.

BUBBLE-AND-SQUEAK, [bubl'-and-skwēk'], *n.* a dish composed of potato and cabbage mashed, sometimes mixed with balls of mincemeat, and fried.
BUBBLEMENT, [bubl'-ment], *n.* effervescence.
BUBBLER, [bub'-ler], *n.* a person who cheats.
BUBBLING, [bub'-ling], *n.* the process of forming bubbles, the sound of boiling or flowing water.
BUBBLY, [bub'-li], *adj.* full of bubbles; *n.* (*slang*) champagne.
BUBO (1), [bew'-bō], *n.* the eagle owl. [Uncert.].
BUBO (2), [bew'-bō], *n.* (*med.*) a pus-emitting swelling in the groin or armpit, due to an inflamed gland, often of a venereal origin. [L. *bubo* groin].
BUBONIC, [bew-bon'-ik], *n.* (*med.*) affected with, characterized by, buboes; **b. plague,** plague, the Black Death.
BUBONOCELE, [bew-bon'-o-sēl'], *n.* (*med.*) a rupture in the groin. [Gk. *boubon* groin and *kele* tumour].
BUCCAL, [buk'-al], *adj.* pertaining to the cheek. [L. *bucca* cheek].
BUCCAN (1), [bo͞ok'-an], *n.* (*S.Amer.*) a hurdle of sticks bound together. [Fr. *boucan*].
BUCCAN (2), [bo͞ok'-an], *v.i.* to smoke meat over a fire on a buccan.
BUCCANEER, [buk'-an-ēer'], *n.* a seventeenth-century pirate; originally a French settler in Haiti who cooked meat on a buccan. [BUCCAN].
BUCCHERO, [(buk-āer'-ō], *n.* (*archae.*) a type of ancient black Tuscan pottery decorated in low relief.
BUCCINAL, [buk'-sin-al], *adj.* shaped, resembling or sounding like a trumpet. [L. *buccina* trumpet].
BUCCINATOR, [buk'-sin-āt'-or], *n.* (*anat.*) a muscle which forms the side of the cheek, used in blowing. [*Prec.*].
BUCCINITE, [buk'-sin-īt'], *n.* (*geol.*) a fossil shell like a buccinum.
BUCCINUM, [buk'-sin-um], *n.* a whelk or trumpet-shaped shell. [BUCCINAL].
BUCENTAUR, [bew-sen'-taw(r)], *n.* a fabulous monster supposed to be part man, part ox; the state barge of a Venetian doge. [Gk. *bous* ox and *kentauros* centaur].
BUCEPHALUS, [bew-sef'-al-us], *n.* the name of a horse celebrated as the favourite charger of Alexander the Great; a charger. [Gk. *boukephalos* ox-headed].
BUCEROS, [bew'-ser-os], *n.* a rhinoceros hornbill found in Malaya.
BUCHMANITE, [buk'-man-īt], *n.* a member of the Oxford Groups. [Frank *Buchman*, the founder].
BUCK (1), [buk], *n.* the male of the deer family, of rabbits and hares, antelope; (*fig.*) a fop, a dandy, a beau; a lye in which clothes are washed or bleached; (*U.S.*) a dollar; (*poker*) any article of value put in the pool in place of chips; **to pass the b. to,** (*slang*) to transfer responsibility to. [OE. *bucc* male deer, *bucca* he-goat].
BUCK (2), [buk], *v.t. and i.* to swagger, strut; (of horses) to jump up and down with all four feet leaving the ground; to jump, to kick the legs out; to wash or bleach in lye; **to b. up,** (*fig.*) to cheer up, to take confidence; to increase efforts. [*Prec.*].

BUCEROS

BUCKBEAN, [buk'-bēn], *n.* (*bot.*) a water plant belonging to the genus *Menyanthes*, the bog-bean.
BUCKBOARD†, [buk'-bawd], *n.* a light carriage with four wheels between which is slung a spring-board supporting the seats.
BUCKET (1), [buk'-it], *n.* a cylindrical tapering vessel for holding water or waste matter; **to kick the b.,** (*slang*) to die. [OFr. *buket*].
BUCKET (2), [buk'-it], *v.t.* to take it out of a horse by hard riding; (in rowing) to splash water with the blade of the oar. [*Prec.*].
BUCKETFUL, [buk'-et-fo͝ol], *n.* the amount a bucket will hold.
BUCKET-SHOP, [buk'-et-shop], *n.* the office of stockbrokers, not members of the Stock Exchange, dealing chiefly in trashy shares.
BUCKEYE, [buk'-ī], *n.* (*U.S.*) a horse-chestnut, *Aesculus ohioensis*.
BUCKHOUND, [buk'-hownd], *n.* a breed of dog for tracking down stags.
BUCKING, [buk'-ing], *n.* the act of bleaching cloth or clothes; the lye or liquid in which the clothes are bleached; a washing. [BUCK (2)].
BUCKING-STOOL, [buk'-ing-sto͞ol], *n.* a washing block.
BUCKISH, [buk'-ish], *adj.* pertaining to a buck; foppish.
BUCKISM, [buk'-izm], *n.* the quality of a buck; the behaviour of a fop.
BUCK-JUMP, [buk'-jump], *n.* (of an unbroken horse) a leap with all four feet clear of the ground.
BUCK-JUMPER, [buk'-jump-er], *n.* a vicious or unbroken horse.
BUCKLE (1), [bukl], *n.* a metal or bone frame with a crossbar on which a hinged prong is often placed, usually attached to one end of a strap or strip of material to fasten it temporarily to the other end; a clasp for adorning a shoe or handbag; a well-set coiffure of curls; a curl of hair. [Fr. *boucle*].
BUCKLE (2), [bukl], *v.t. and i.* to fasten with a buckle; to gird oneself with armour; to curl up, bend under pressure, crumple; **to b. to,** to devote one's energy to. [*Prec.*].
BUCKLER, [buk'-ler], *n.* round shield with a boss in the centre; (*zool.*) the thick-skinned, shell or bone parts covering some animals, such as the armadillo.
BUCKLER-THORN, [buk'-ler-thawn'], *n.* (*bot.*) a species of *Rhamnus*.
BUCK-NIGGER, [buk'-nig-er], *n.* (*U.S. slang*) a male negro.
BUCKO (1), [buk'-ō], *n.* (*naut. slang*) a swaggerer, boaster, a bragging fellow.
BUCKO (2), [buk'-ō], *adj.* (*naut. slang*) boastful, swaggering.
BUCKRAM, [buk'-ram], *n.* a coarse linen cloth stiffened with gum and used in book-binding and tailoring. [OFr. *boqueran*].
BUCK-RAREBIT, [buk'-rāer'-bit], *n.* a Welsh rarebit with an egg added.
BUCKSAW, [buk'-saw], *n.* a frame-saw.
BUCKSHEE (1), [buk'-shē'], *n.* (*slang*) extra army rations; anything given away or obtained free. [Variant of BACKSHEESH].
BUCKSHEE (2), [buk'-shē], *adj.* (*slang*) free, gratis.
BUCK'S-HORN, [buks'-hawn], *n.* (*bot.*) one of several species of plants with leaves like the horns of a buck; a plantain.

BUCKSAW

BUCKSHOT, [buk'-shot'], *n.* a large-sized shot used with sporting guns.
BUCKSKIN (1), [buk'-skin], *n.* the skin of a buck; the soft yellow leather made from this skin; (*pl.*) breeches made from this leather.
BUCKSKIN (2), [buk'-skin], *adj.* made of buckskin.
BUCKSTALL†, [buk'-stawl], *n.* a large net for trapping deer.
BUCKTHORN, [buk'-thawn], *n.* (*bot.*) a thorny shrub of the genus *Rhamnus* bearing berries which yield a powerful cathartic; **sea b.,** a plant of the genus *Hippophae*.
BUCK-TOOTH, [buk'-to͞oth], *n.* a prominent tooth.
BUCK-WASHING, [buk'-wosh'-ing], *n.* a process of rough washing in lye.
BUCKWHEAT, [buk'-wēt'], *n.* (*bot.*) a species of *Polygonum*, bearing seeds like beech-nuts. [OE. *boc* beech, and WHEAT].
BUCOLIC (1), [bew-kol'-ik], *n.* a poem having a pastoral subject-matter. [Gk. *boukolikos* pastoral].
BUCOLIC (2), [bew-kol'-ik], *adj.* pertaining to the countryside or to pastoral poetry.
BUCOLICAL, [bew-kol'-ik-al], *adj.* bucolic.
BUCRANIA, [bew-krān'-i-a], *n.*(*pl.*) ornamental ox-skulls depicted on Greek friezes. [Gk. *bous* ox and *kranion* skull].
BUD (1), [bud], *n.* (*bot.*) an embryonic growth of compact leaves or flower breaking out of the main stem; a half-opened flower; **to nip in the b.,** (*fig.*) to kill or put an end to an action or idea by stopping it in its initial stages. [ME. *budde*].
BUD (2), [bud], *v.t. and i.* to graft (a bud) into another plant; to put out buds, to grow buds.
BUDDHISM, BOODHISM, [bo͝od'-izm], *n.* a great Asiatic religious system perfected by Siddhartha, or Buddha. [Skr. *buddha* awakened].
BUDDHIST, [bo͝od'-ist], *n.* one who believes in Buddhism.
BUDDHISTIC, [bo͝od-ist'-ik], *adj.* pertaining to Buddhism.
BUDDING (1), [bud'-ing], *n.* the growth of buds; (*hort.*) the act of grafting a bud to another plant or tree.
BUDDING (2), [bud'-ing], *adj.* opening out as a bud; (*fig.*) promising, likely to do well.

BUDDLE (1), [budl], *n.* a large square frame of boards used in washing ore. [Uncert.].

BUDDLE (2), [budl], *v.i.* to wash ore.

BUDDLEIA, [bud'-lē-a], *n.* a variety of shrub with purple or yellow flowers of many forms. [A. *Buddle*, the botanist].

BUDDY, [bud'-i] *n.* (*U.S. coll.*) a brother, comrade. [Uncert.].

BUDE-LIGHT, [bewd'-līt], *n.* a very brilliant light produced by burning oxyhydrogen gas in the centre of an Argand burner. [*Bude*, in Cornwall, where the inventor Gurney lived].

BUDGE (1), [buj], *n.* the skin of lambs prepared for trimming clothes. [Uncert.].

BUDGE (2), [buj], *v.t. and i.* to cause to move slightly with difficulty, shift; to make a slight movement under pressure, to shift. [Fr. *bouger*].

BUDGERIGAR, [buj'-er-i-gah(r)], *n.* the Australian green parakeet, *Melopsittacus undulatus*, a love-bird. [Native].

BUDGERO, [buj'-er-ō], *n.* a passenger-boat used in Bengal. [Hind. *bajra*].

BUDGET (1), [buj'-it], *n.* †a small bag, the contents of such a bag; the annual statement made in the House of Commons by the Chancellor of the Exchequer summarizing the country's financial position; a financial statement presented by official organizations; a record of financial expenditure. [OFr. *bouget*].

BUDGET (2), [buj'-it], *v.i.* to estimate financial expenditure.

BUDGETARY, [buj'-it-er-i], *adj.* of, or pertaining to, a budget.

BUDLET, [bud'-let], *n.* a little bud.

BUFF (1), [buf], *n.* leather prepared from the skin of the buffalo or ox; a polisher made of leather; the colour of buff leather, a pale muddy yellow; (*med.*) a substance having the colour of buff discharged by blood in an infected condition. [Fr. *buffle* buffalo].

BUFF† (2), [buf], *n.* a blow, bang. [OFr. *buffe*].

BUFF (3), [buf], *adj.* having the colour of buff.

BUFF (4), [buf], *v.t.* to polish with a buff.

BUFFALO, [buf'-al-ō], *n.* a wild ox; **b. bird,** an African bird of the genus *Buphago* that lives on parasitic insects attached to buffaloes; **b. grass,** prairie grass. [Portug. *bufalo*].

BUFFEL, [buf'-el], *n.* a North American duck with a large, well-feathered head, *Charitonetta albeola*. [BUFFALO].

BUFFER, [buf'-er], *n.* a shock-absorbing contrivance consisting of spring-loaded flat metal plates so placed on a vehicle as to make contact with similar plates on other vehicles; such a contrivance fitted to the platform of a terminus functioning by hydraulic pressure; **b. state,** a small state situated between two larger, acting as an absorber of hostile differences. [BUFF (2)].

BUFFER, [buf'-er], *n.* (*slang*) a fool; a blockhead. [BUFFOON].

BUFFET (1), [bo͝of'-ā], *n.* a sideboard; a place for light refreshments. [Fr. *buffet*].

BUFFET (2), [buf'-it], *n.* a blow struck with the hand, a cuff; (*fig.*) a misfortune, calamity. [~OFr. *buffe* a blow].

BUFFET (3), [buf'-it], *v.t. and i.* to strike with the hand or fist, to cuff; to struggle, to contend.

BUFFETING, [buf'-it-ing], *n.* a beating with the hands or fists, any series of slaps; the action of waves beating against a ship.

BUFFING, [buf'-ing], *n.* the process of polishing on a buff.

BUFFING-SPRING, [buf'-ing-spring'], *n.* a spring fitted to a buffer.

BUFFLE-HEADED, [bufl'-hed'-id], *adj.* possessing a large head; stupid.

BUFFO, [bo͝of'-ō], *n.* a comedian, a comic actor; a clown. [It. *buffo*, comic].

BUFFOON, [bu-fo͞on'], *n.* a person who amuses others with simple knockabout humour; a clown, a jester. [Fr. *bouffon*, It. *buffone*].

BUFFOONERY, [bu-fo͞on'-er-i], *n.* the behaviour of a buffoon; practical joking.

BUFFOONISH, [bu-fo͞on'-ish], *adj.* like a buffoon.

BUFFOONISM, [bu-fo͞on'-izm], *n.* buffoonery.

BUFFOONLIKE, [bu-fo͞on'-līk], *adj.* resembling a buffoon.

BUFFS, [bufs], *n.(pl.)* (*milit.*) the East Kent Regiment, whose uniform was faced with buff material.

BUFFY, [buf'-i], *adj.* having the colour of buff; (*med.*) pertaining to buff.

BUFONITE, [bew'-fōn-īt], *n.* toadstone; the teeth of certain fossil fishes. [L. *bufo* toad.]

BUG, [bug], *n.* a verminous insect of the genus *Cimex*, often blood-sucking and often infesting old or dirty houses; **big b.,** (*coll.*) a person considering himself important. [OScand. *buggi*].

BUGABOO, [bug'-a-bo͞o'], *n.* a bugbear. [Uncert.].

BUGBEAR (1), [bug'-bāer], *n.* an object of dread, often spectral. [Uncert.].

BUGGER, [bug'-er], *n.* †a heretic (originally from Bulgaria); (*leg.*) one guilty of buggery; (*vulg.*) term of abuse for a fellow. [Fr. *bougre* from L. *bulgarus* Bulgarian].

BUGGERY, [bug'-er-i], *n.* (*leg.*) unnatural intercourse with another male; sodomy. [*Prec.*].

BUGGINESS, [bug'-i-nes], *n.* the condition of being buggy.

BUGGY (1), [bug'-i], *n.* a light two- or four-wheeled carriage drawn by one horse; a gig. [Uncert.].

BUGGY

BUGGY (2), [bug'-i], *adj.* infested with bugs.

BUGLE (1), [bewgl], *n.* a small trumpet for sounding calls to troops; **key b.,** a bugle fitted with keys. [OFr. *bugle* from L. *buculus* young ox].

BUGLE (2), [bewgl], *n.* a long glass bead, usually black, sewn on to a woman's dress as an ornament. [Uncert.].

BUGLE (3), [bewgl], *n.* (*bot.*) a creeping plant of the genus *Ajuga*. [Fr. *bugle*].

BUGLE (4), [bewgl], *v.i.* (*milit.*, *mus.*) to play or blow a bugle.

BUGLER, [bewg'-ler], *n.* one who sounds a bugle.

BUGLET, [bewg'-let], *n.* a small bugle.

BUGLOSS, [bew'-glos], *n.* (*bot.*) one of two plants, *Echium vulgare* and *Lycopsis arvensis*. [Fr. *buglosse*].

BUGWORT, [bug'-wurt], *n.* (*bot.*) the plant, *Cimicifuga foetida*.

BUHL, BOULE, [bo͞ol], *n.* style of inlaying wood with gold or brass and mother-of-pearl. [A. *Boulle*, a French cabinet-maker].

BUHR-STONE, [bur'-stōn], *n.* burr-stone.

BUILD (1), [bild], *n.* shape, form, construction; the proportions of the human body.

BUILD (2), (built), [bild], *v.t. and i.* to construct by fixing securely together various component parts according to a plan, to raise, to rear; to develop gradually, to strengthen, improve; to practise building; **to b. on,** to rely upon. [OE. *byldan*].

BUILDER, [bild'-er], *n.* a person who builds.

BUILDING, [bild'-ing], *n.* the occupation of a builder; an edifice; **b. society,** a co-operative loan society lending capital at interest to subscribers building or buying their own houses.

BUILT, [bilt], *adj.* formed, composed of parts.

BULB (1), [bulb], *n.* an enlarged, ovoid base of the stem of certain plants such as the daffodil; an expanded section of a stem or tube of a similar shape; an electric lamp. [Gk. *bolbos* bulb].

BULB (2), [bulb], *v.i.* to be protuberant; to form a bulb.

BULBACEOUS, [bul-bāsh'-us], *adj.* bulbous; round-headed.

BULBED, [bulbd], *adj.* having a bulb; round-headed.

BULBIFEROUS, [bulb-if'-er-us], *adj.* (*bot.*) bearing bulbs. [BULB and L. *fero* I bear].

BULBIFORM, [bulb'-i-fawm], *adj.* possessing the form of a bulb. [BULB and FORM].

BULBOSITY, [bul-bos'-i-ti], *n.* the quality or state of being bulbous.

BULBOUS, [bulb-us], *adj.* possessing a bulb; bulb-shaped; round, swollen.

BULB-TUBER, [bulb'-tew'-ber], *n.* a corm.

BULBUL, [bo͞ol'-bo͞ol'], *n.* a genus of Asiatic singing birds; the Persian nightingale. [Arab. *bulbul*].

BULBULE, [bulb'-yo͞ol], *n.* a little bulb.

BULGARIAN (1), [bo͞ol-gāer'-i-an], *n.* a native of Bulgaria.

BULGARIAN (2), [bo͞ol-gāer'-ian], *adj.* of, or relating to, Bulgaria.

BULGE (1), [bulj], *n.* a protuberant part, a swelling; an irregular protuberance. [L. *bulga* swelling].

BULGE (2), [bulj], *v.t. and i.* to swell out, to expand in an ungainly way.

BULGER, [bul'-jer], *n.* a golf club with a wooden convex face. [*Prec.*].

BULGILY, [bulj'-i-li], *adv.* in a bulgy manner.

BULGING, [bulj'-ing], *adj.* protuberant, swelling.
BULIMIA, [bew-lim'-i-a], *n.* (*med.*) an excessive morbid appetite. [Gk. *boulimia*].
BULK, [bulk], *n.* magnitude of mass, large volume; a large quantity; (*naut.*) the cargo in a ship's hold; **laden in b.,** left unbattened in the hold; **to sell in b.,** to sell in large unpacked amounts. [OIcel. *bulki*].
BULKHEAD, [bulk'-hed], *n.* a main partition in a ship's hull.
BULKINESS [bulk'-i-nes], *n.* the condition of being bulky.
BULKY, [bulk'-i], *adj.* large and clumsy in size.
BULL (1), [bŏŏl], *n.* the male of any species of the bovine group still able to propagate; (*fig.*) a person as powerful and crude as a bull; a stock-exchange speculator who has gambled on a rise of share prices; a bull's-eye; the constellation *Taurus*; *Taurus*, one of the twelve Zodiac signs; **to take the b. by the horns,** to take courage and grapple with danger without flinching; **a b. in a china shop,** an excessively clumsy or tactless person. [OE. *bula*].
BULL (2), [bŏŏl], *n.* an edict issued by the Pope. [L. *bulla* a seal].
BULL (3), [bŏŏl], *n.* a ludicrous mistake in speech. [Fr. *boule* a lie from L. *bulla* bubble].
BULL (4), [bŏŏl], *adj.* of large size, gross. [BULL (1)].
BULL (5), [bŏŏl], *v.t. and i.* to deal as a bull with stock-exchange shares. [BULL (1)].
BULLA, [bŏŏl'-a], *n.* a genus of thin-shelled mollusc. [L. *bulla* bubble].
BULLACE, [bŏŏl'-is], *n.* the wild plum. [ME. *bolace*].
BULLATE, [bŏŏl'-āt], *adj.* (*bot.*) forming blisters. [L. *bullatus*].
BULL-BAITING, [bŏŏl'-bāt'-ing], *n.* a sport of baiting bulls with dogs.
BULL-BEE, [bŏŏl'-bē], *n.* the stag beetle.
BULL-BEEF, [bŏŏl'-bēf'], *n.* a coarse beef; bully beef.
BULL-CALF, [bŏŏl'-kahf'], *n.* a male calf.
BULLDOG, [bŏŏl'-dog], *n.* a squat, flat-faced English breed of dog, remarkable for its tenacity, formerly used in baiting bulls.
BULLDOZER, [bŏŏl'-dō-zer], *n.* a powerful excavating and lifting machine used in road-making; (*fig.*) a person who gains his point by overbearing argument. [Unkn.].
BULLET, [bŏŏl'-it], *n.* a lead pellet or short, solid, pointed rod of metal, fired from a rifle or revolver. [Fr. *boulette*].
BULLETIN (1), [bŏŏl'-it-in], *n.* an official report or public announcement, often concerning the health of a distinguished invalid. [Fr. *bulletin*].
BULLETIN (2), [bŏŏl'-it-in], *v.t.* to announce by bulletin.
BULLET-PROOF, [bŏŏl'-it-prōōf'], *adj.* able to resist a bullet.
BULL-FACED, [bŏŏl'-fāst'], *adj.* having a large coarse face.
BULL-FIGHT, [bŏŏl'-fīt'], *n.* a Spanish sport in which a bull is goaded, attacked, and finally slain.
BULL-FIGHTER, [bŏŏl'-fīt'-er], *n.* a matador.
BULLFINCH (1), [bŏŏl'-finch'], *n.* a high hedge with a ditch alongside. [Earlier *bull-fence*].
BULLFINCH (2), [bŏŏl'-finch'], *n.* a British singing bird of the genus *Pyrrhula*, with short beak, large head, and thick neck.

BULLFINCH

BULL-FLY, [bool'-flī'], *n.* the gad-fly.
BULL-FROG, [bŏŏl'-frog], *n.* a species of large frog.
BULL-HEAD, [bŏŏl'-hed'], *n.* a small freshwater fish with a large head; (*fig.*) a stupid man.
BULLION, [bŏŏl'-yon], *n.* uncoined gold and silver; gold and silver money assessed for its raw material value. [Fr. *bouillon*].
BULLIONIST, [bŏŏl'-yon-ist], *n.* one who opposes the use of a paper currency.
BULLIRAG, BULLYRAG, [bŏŏl'-i-rag], *v.t.* to bully, to badger. [BULLY and RAG (2)].
BULLISH, [bŏŏl'-ish], *adj.* pertaining to or like a bull.
BULLOCK, [bŏŏl'-ok], *n.* a young bull; a gelded bull. [OE. *bulluc*].
BULLRING, [bŏŏl'-ring], *n.* the arena for a bull-fight.
BULL-ROARER, [bŏŏl'-rawr'-er], *n.* an oblong piece of wood attached to a string and whirled rapidly round until it booms.
BULL'S-EYE, [bŏŏlz'-ī'], *n.* a small round window or opening; the centre of a target; a small sweetmeat ball.
BULL'S-NOSE, [bŏŏlz'-nōz], *n.* (*archae.*) the external angle of a polygon or of two lines meeting at an obtuse angle.
BULL-TERRIER, [bŏŏl'-te'-ri-er], *n.* a breed of dog, a cross between a terrier and a bulldog.
BULL-TROUT, [bŏŏl'-trowt'], *n.* a large-headed trout resembling a small salmon.
BULLY (1), [bŏŏl-i], *n.* a blustering, overbearing person; the putting of the ball in play by two opposing players in hockey; a miner's hammer. [Unkn.].
BULLY (2), [bŏŏl'-i], *adj.* (*slang*) excellent.
BULLY (3), (**bullies, bullied**), [bŏŏl-i], *v.t.* to attack with blustering menaces, to tyrannize over, treat cruelly, *esp.* the young or weak.
BULLY BEEF, [bŏŏl'-i-bēf'], *n.* tinned boiled beef.
BULLYRAG, see BULLIRAG.
BULRUSH, [bŏŏl'-rush'], *n.* a rush with a large thick velvety head, of the genus *Scirpus*. [BULL and RUSH].
BULRUSHY, [bŏŏl'-rush'-i], *adj.* overgrown with bulrushes.
BULSE†, [bŏŏls], *n.* a parcel of diamonds or gold-dust. [Span. *bolsa* from L. *bursa* pause].
BULWARK (1), [bŏŏl'-wak], *n.* (*fort.*) a rampart; (*naut.*) a ship's side above the deck; (*fig.*) any form of defence which gives security. [Du. *bolverk*].
BULWARK (2), [bŏŏl'-wak], *v.t.* to protect with a bulwark.
BUM (1), [bum], *n.* (*slang*) the buttocks. [Unkn.].
BUM (2), [bum], *n.* (*U.S. slang*) an habitual loafer. [~BUMMEL].
BUM (3), [bum], *v.i.* to hum loudly, to boom. [Unkn.].
BUMBAILIFF, [bum'-bā'-liff], *n.* (*coll.*) a sheriff's officer; a bailiff who apprehends debtors, etc. [BUM (1) and BAILIFF].
BUMBLE-BEE, [bumbl'-bē'], *n.* a hairy wild bee with a loud hum.
BUMBLEDOM, [bumbl'-dom], *n.* the fussy pomposity of petty officialdom. [Mr. *Bumble*, the beadle in Dickens's *Oliver Twist*].
BUMBLEPUPPY, [bumbl'-pup'-i], *n.* a game played with racquets and a tennis ball slung to a tall post, the players hitting the ball so as to wind it spirally round the post and prevent each other doing so. [Unkn.].
BUMBOAT, [bum'-bōt], *n.* a boat used for carrying provisions to, and refuse from, ships at some distance from shore. [Dan. *bun* a boat's fish box]
BUMKIN, see BUMPKIN.
BUMMALO, [bum'-al-ō], *n.* a small fish, known also as the Bombay duck. [Hind. *bombil*].
BUMMAREE, [bum'-er-ē], *n.* a dealer in the fish trade; (*slang*) a money-lender. [Unkn.].
BUMMEL, [bum'-el], *v.i.* to stroll aimlessly. [Germ. *bummeln* to dawdle].
BUMP (1), [bump], *n.* a heavy blow, a dull thud caused by a collision; the action whereby a boat-race is won when the boat immediately ahead is caught up and touched; a swelling or lump caused by a collision; a protuberance like this; (*aeron.*) irregularity in an aeroplane's motion. [Echoic].
BUMP (2), [bump], *v.i.* to strike dully against anything hard or solid; to jolt along an uneven road in a vehicle; *v.t.* to cause a protuberance to rise on the skin by violent collision; (in a boat-race) to come up with and touch the boat immediately in front; **to b. off,** (*slang*) to kill, murder.
BUMPER (1), [bump'-er], *n.* a horizontal metal bar attached before or behind a motor car to protect it in collisions.
BUMPER (2), [bump'-er], *n.* a glass or cup brimful.
BUMPER (3), [bump'-er], *adj.* large, plentiful.
BUMPINESS, [bump'-i-nes], *n.* irregularity of surface, unevenness.
BUMPKIN (1), BUMKIN†, [bump'-kin], *n.* (*naut.*) a short boom standing out from the bows; a small outrigger over the stern of a boat. [BOOM].
BUMPKIN (2), [bump'-kin], *n.* a rough, loutish countryman. [Du. *boomken* little tree].
BUMPTIOUS, [bump'-shus], *adj.* conceited, arrogant. [Invented].
BUMPY, [bump'-i], *adj.* uneven, abounding in bumps; jolting.
BUN, [bun], *n.* a small, round sweet cake; a small round bunch (as of hair); (*slang*) **to take the b.,** to be first or worst in anything, to behave startlingly. [ME. *bunne*].
BUNA, [bōōn'-a], *n.* synthetic rubber. [Germ. *buna*].
BUNCE, [buns], *n.* (*slang*) extra profit, something gained.

BUNCH (1), [bunch], *n.* a bundle, cluster or group of objects of a similar kind; a knot, a tuft, a portion of any garment or material gathered closely together; (*coll.*) a group of people; **the best of the b.**, the pick of anything. [Unkn.].

BUNCH (2), [bunch], *v.t. and i.* to gather up into a bunch.

BUNCH-BACKED, [bunch'-bakt'], *adj.* with a bunch on the back.

BUNCHINESS, [bunch'-i-nes], *n.* the state of being bunchy.

BUNCHY, [bunch-i], *adj.* forming a bunch; growing in bunches.

BUNCO, [bung'-kō], *v.t.* (*U.S. slang*) to swindle (as at cards). [Span. *banca* a card game].

BUNCOMBE, see BUNKUM.

BUND, [bund], *n.* (*Indian*) an embankment, dyke, causeway. [Hind. *band*].

BUNDLE (1), [bundl], *n.* a number of things gathered together loosely; anything wrapped in a form convenient for carrying; a package. [ME. *bundel*].

BUNDLE (2), [bundl], *v.t.* to tie in, or make up into, a bundle; to collect, gather into a mass; *v.i.* to depart hurriedly with all one's incumbrances; to sleep in one's clothes on the same bed with a person of the opposite sex.

BUNDOOK, [bun'-dōōk], *n.* a musket. [Hind. *banduq*].

BUNG (1), [bung], *n.* a stopper for the hole in a cask. [ODu. *bongh* hole].

BUNG (2), [bung], *v.t.* to stop the hole of a cask with a bung; (*fig.*) to stop; to shut up; to close by the swelling of surrounding parts; (*slang*) to throw missiles at.

BUNGALOID, [bung'-gal-oid], *adj.* consisting of, covered with, bungalows; **b. growth**, a large area covered with bungalows and made hideous by them.

BUNGALOW, [bun'-gal-ō], *n.* a detached, one-storied house. [Hind. *bangala*].

BUNGHOLE, [bung'-hōl], *n.* the hole in a cask through which it is filled. [BUNG and HOLE].

BUNGLE (1), [bungl], *n.* a clumsy performance, a blunder. [Unkn.].

BUNGLE (2), [bungl], *v.t.* to perform clumsily; to botch, to spoil by inexpert handling.

BUNGLER, [bung'-gler], *n.* one who bungles; an unskilful workman; a tactless negotiator.

BUNGLING, [bung'-gling], *adj.* clumsy, awkward, unskilful.

BUNGLINGLY, [bung'-gling-li], *adv.* in a bungling manner, unskilfully, awkwardly.

BUNGY, [bung'-gi], *n.* (*Bombay*) a sweeper, low caste servant, scavenger. [Hind. *bhangi*].

BUNION, [bun'-yon], *n.* a large inflamed swelling on the foot, *esp.* at the base of the big toe. [OFr. *buigne* a bump].

BUNK (1), [bungk], *n.* a recessed shelf fitted with bedding in a ship's cabin, railway carriage, etc., for sleeping in; a sleeping berth; **to do a b.**, (*slang*) to disappear, run away hastily. [Unkn.].

BUNK (2), [bungk], *n.* (*slang*) humbug, bunkum. [BUNKUM].

BUNK (3), [bungk], *v.i.* to lie down on one's bunk; (*slang*) to run away.

BUNKAGE, [bung'-kij], *n.* (*naut.*) the charge for coaling.

BUNKER, [bung'-ker], *n.* a large receptacle or storage for coal in a steamship; a seat or bench; a sandy hollow or other obstruction on a golf-course; (*fig.*) any obstruction. [Uncert.].

BUNKERED, [bung'-kerd], *adj.* (*golf*) stopped by a bunker or other obstruction; (*fig.*) in a difficult place, obstructed.

BUNKUM, BUNCOMBE, [bung'-kum], *n.* nonsense; empty, futile talk spoken to impress. [*Buncombe*, constituency in Carolina whose member in Congress spoke in this way].

BUNNIA, [bun'-ya], *n.* (*Indian*) an Indian trader, merchant. [Hind. *banya*].

BUNNY, [bun'-i], *n.* a rabbit. [Unkn.].

BUNODONT, [byōō'-nō-dont], *adj.* with tuberculated molar teeth. [Gk. *bounos* a hill, and *odous odontos* a tooth].

BUNSEN BURNER

BUNSEN BATTERY, [bun'-sen -bat'-er-i], *n.* (*elect.*) a voltaic battery. [*Bunsen*, a German chemist].

BUNSEN BURNER, [bun'-sen-burn'-er], *n.* a jet which burns gas and air to produce great heat. [*Prec.*].

BUNT (1), [bunt], *n.* a parasitic fungoid which attacks wheat and turns the grain black. [Unkn.].

BUNT (2), [bunt], *n.* the pouched part of a fishing net; (*naut.*) the middle part of a sail gathered to form a cavity. [Unkn.].

BUNT (3), [bunt], *n.* (*aeron.*) a manoeuvre consisting of half an outside loop followed by a half roll to regain normal equilibrium. [BUNT (4)].

BUNT (4), [bunt], *v.t.* to strike, knock, push; (*baseball*) to stop the ball with the bat without swinging the latter; (*aeron.*) to execute a bunt. [Unkn.].

BUNTING (1), [bunt'-ing], *n.* a group of birds of the genus *Emberiza*, including the yellow-hammer. [Unkn.].

BUNTING (2), [bunt'-ing], *n.* open-mesh, coarse, bright-coloured cloth used for flags and streamers, employed on ships and in the streets for decorative purposes. [Uncert.].

BUOY (1), [boi], *n.* (*naut.*) a floating sphere or drum moored to indicate the presence of a shoal, rock, etc., dangerous to shipping. [OFr. *boye*].

BUOY (2), [boi], *v.t.* to keep afloat, bear up; (*fig.*) to hold up, to sustain.

BUOYAGE, [boi'-ij], *n.* the placing of buoys.

BUOYANCY, [boi'-an-si], *n.* the power of floating lightly; (*fig.*) lightness, gaiety.

BUOYANT, [boi'-ant], *adj.* floating, capable of rising to the surface if submerged; (*fig.*) light-hearted, not easily crushed.

BUOYANTLY, [boi'-ant-li], *adv.* in buoyant fashion.

BUPHAGA, [bew'-fag-a], *n.* the beef-eater bird which lives on the larvae beneath the hides of cattle. [Gk. *bous* ox and *phago* I eat].

BUR (1), BURR, [bur], *n.* a prickly fruit or flower head, the husk of the chestnut; (*fig.*) anything which clings like a bur; a person hard to get rid of. [ME. *borre*].

BUR (2), BURR, [bur], *n.* in etching or engraving, the rough edge or ridge left by the tool on the copper-plate; a rough coarse stone of which millstones or whetstones are made. [Unkn.].

BUR (3), BURR, [bur], *n.* (*anat.*) the outer cavity of the ear, leading to the tympanum. [Unkn.].

BUR (4), BURR, [bur], *n.* the dialectal pronunciation of *r* with a uvular trill. [Echoic].

BUR (5), BURR, [bur], *v.i.* to articulate with a bur.

BURBOT, [bur'-bot], *n.* a freshwater fish of the genus *Lota*. [AFr. *bourbotte*].

BURBOT

BURDEN (1), BURTHEN†, [bur'-den], *n.* something borne or carried, a load, weight; (*fig.*) anything that is wearisome or oppressive to bear; (*naut.*) the freightage capacity of a ship; **beast of b.**, an animal used for carrying loads; **b. of proof**, responsibility of proving. [OE. *byrthen* load].

BURDEN (2), BURTHEN†, [bur'-den], *n.* the chorus of a song; the main topic. [Fr. *bourdon*].

BURDEN (3), BURTHEN†, [bur'-den], *v.t.* to load, encumber, impose a burden on, oppress.

BURDENSOME, [bur'-den-sum], *adj.* heavy to bear; oppressive.

BURDENSOMELY, [bur'-den-sum-li], *adv.* in burdensome fashion.

BURDENSOMENESS, [bur'-den-sum-nes], *n.* the condition of being burdensome.

BURDOCK, [bur'-dok], *n.* a plant of the genus *Arctium*, with prickly flowers and dock-like leaves. [BUR and DOCK].

BUREAU, [bew-rō'], *n.* a desk with drawers and a movable flap for writing on; a public office; a government department. [Fr. *bureau*].

BUREAUCRACY, [bew-rok'-ras-i], *n.* the system of government administration in departments each under the control of a chief; government by officials; officials as a body. [BUREAU and Gk. *krateia* rule].

BUREAUCRAT, [bew'-rō-krat], *n.* an advocate of bureaucracy; a state official with an undue reverence for the letter rather than the spirit of the law.

BUREAUCRATIC, [bew'-rō-krat'-ik], *adj.* having the nature of a bureaucrat, relating to a bureaucracy.

BUREAUCRATIST, [bew-rok'-rat-ist], *n.* a bureaucrat.

BURETTE, [bew-ret′], *n.* a graduated glass tube with stopcock at the bottom, for measuring fluids. [Fr. *burette*].

BURG, [burg], *n.* a stronghold; a borough. [OE. *burg*].

BURGAGE, [burg′-ij], *n.* (*leg.*) the holding of lands or tenements in a town or city from an overlord for a certain yearly rent. [BURG, OFr. *bourgage*].

BURGAMOT, see BERGAMOT (1).

BURGEE (1), [bur-jē′], *n.* a small swallow-tailed pennant or flag used by yachts as a distinguishing flag of their club. [Unkn.].

BURGEON, [bur′-jon], *v.i.* to sprout, come into bud. [Fr. *bourgeonner*].

BURGESS, [bur′-jes], *n.* a citizen, a borough freeman, one who has the full rights of citizenship. [OFr. *burgeis*].

BURGESS-SHIP, [bur′-jes-ship], *n.* citizenship, freedom of a borough.

BURETTE

BURGH, [bu′-ra], *n.* (*Scots*) a borough; **royal b.**, a corporate body erected by a charter from the crown. [BOROUGH].

BURGHAL, [bur′-gel], *adj.* pertaining to a borough.

BURGHER, [bur′-ger], *n.* an inhabitant or freeman of a borough, a citizen, *esp.* of Dutch and German towns. [Du. *burger*].

BURGH-MOTE, [burg′-mōt], *n.* (*hist.*) a borough court. [BURG and OE. *mot* assembly].

BURGLAR, [burg′-ler], *n.* one who commits burglary. [Uncert.].

BURGLARIOUS, [burg-lāer′-i-us], *adj.* pertaining to burglary.

BURGLARIOUSLY, [burg-lāer′-i-us-li], *adv.* in the manner of a burglar.

BURGLARY, [burg′-ler-i], *n.* the act or crime of breaking into a house after sunset with intent to steal.

BURGLE, [burgl], *v.t.* to commit burglary. [BURGLAR].

BURGOMASTER (1), [burg′-ō-mah′-ster], *n.* the mayor of a Dutch or Flemish town. [Du. *burgemeester*].

BURGOMASTER (2), [burg′-ō-mah′-ster], *n.* (*ornith.*) the glaucous gull, *Larus glaucus*.

BURGUNDIAN, [bur-gund′-i-an], *adj.* belonging to Burgundy.

BURGUNDY, [bur-gund-i], *n.* (red) wine made in Burgundy.

BURHEL, [bu′-rel], *n.* Himalayan wild sheep. [Hind. *bharal*].

BURIAL, [be′-ri-al], *n.* the act of burying or placing in the ground, *esp.* a dead person; a funeral; **b. board**, public authority controlling a cemetery. [OE. *byrgels* a grave].

BURIAL-GROUND, [be′-ri-al-grownd′], *n.* a cemetery.

BURIN, [bew′-rin], *n.* a graver, a tool for engraving. [Fr. *burin*].

BURKE, [burk], *v.t.* to murder, particularly by suffocation; to smother quietly and get rid of; (*fig.*) to hush up, avoid any discussion of. [*Burke*, who committed such murders in Edinburgh in 1828].

BURL (1), [burl], *n.* a matted lump in wool or cloth. [OFr. *bourle* tuft of wool].

BURL (2), [burl], *v.t.* to dress cloth by removing knots and matted lumps.

BURLACE†, [bur′-lās], *n.* a variety of grape from the Bordeaux district. [Fr. *bourdelais*].

BURLAP, [bur′-lap], *n.* a coarse cloth of hemp or jute for packing. [Unkn.].

BURLER, [bur′-ler], *n.* one who burls or dresses cloth.

BURLESQUE (1), [ber-lesk′], *n.* a ludicrous representation; a parody of a serious work. [Fr. *burlesque*].

BURLESQUE (2), [ber-lesk′], *adj.* tending to excite laughter by burlesque.

BURLESQUE (3), [ber-lesk′], *v.t.* to turn into ridicule by parody; to caricature.

BURLETTA, [ber-let′-a], *n.* a comic opera. [It. *burletta*].

BURLINESS, [bur′-li-nes], *n.* the condition of being burly.

BURLY, [bur′-li], *adj.* stout, massively built, corpulent, robust. [ME. *burlich*].

BURMESE (1), [burm′-ēz′], *n.* a native of Burma; the native language of Burma.

BURMESE (2), [burm′-ēz], *adj.* of, or pertaining to, Burma or its language.

BURN (1), [burn], *n.* a brook, small stream. [BOURN].

BURN (2), [burn], *n.* an injury or bodily hurt caused by fire or heat.

BURN (3), [burn], *v.t.* destroy or injure by subjecting to fire or great heat; to put to death by burning; to scorch; to harden by treatment with fire; to parch, crack by heat, to dry up, shrivel up; **to b. down**, to destroy utterly by fire; **to b. one's fingers**, to suffer from interfering in dangerous enterprises. [OE. *byrnan*].

BURN (4), [burn], *v.i.* to be on fire, in a state of conflagration, to glow; (*fig.*) feel excess of heat; to be inflamed with passion or desire; to suffer from the heat of a fever.

BURNER, [burn′-er], *n.* a device which permits gas, etc., to burn for heat or illumination.

BURNET, [burn′-et], *n.* (*bot.*) a brown-leaved plant of the genus *Poterium*; (*zool.*) a moth of the genus *Zygaena*. [BRUNETTE].

BURNING, [burn′-ing], *adj.* on fire, much heated; (*fig.*) vehement, excited, intense; **b. bush**, name of several shrubs which give off highly volatile oil; **b. glass**, a lens which concentrates the sun's rays to produce intense heat.

BURNISH (1), [burn′-ish], *n.* polish, brightness, lustre.

BURNISH (2), [burn′-ish], *v.t.* to polish by friction, to make bright, to give a lustre to by polishing; *v.i.* to take a polish. [OFr. *burnisser*].

BURNISHER, [burn′-ish-er], *n.* one who burnishes; an implement used in polishing.

BURNOOSE, [bern-ōōs′], *n.* a hooded cloak worn by desert dwellers in Arabia. [Fr. *burnous* from Arab. *burnus*].

BURNT, BURNED, [burnt], *adj.* acted on by fire; (*fig.*) hurt, injured by some intensity of suffering.

BURNT-EAR, [burnt′-ēer], *n.* a disease in corn caused by a fungus in which the ear seems black as if burnt.

BURNT-OFFERING, [burnt′-of′-er-ing], *n.* an offering sacrificed by fire to a deity.

BURNT-SACRIFICE, [burnt′-sak′-rif-is], *n.* a burnt-offering.

BURNT-SIENNA, [burnt′-si-en′-a], *n.* an orange-red pigment produced by burning sienna; the pigment sienna.

BUR-REED, [bur′-rēd′], *n.* a plant of the genus *Sparganium*; the reed-mace.

BURREL-FLY, [bu′-rel-flī′], *n.* the gad-fly. [Unkn.].

BURRO, [bŏŏ′-rō], *n.* (*U.S.*) a donkey. [Span. *burro*].

BURROW (1), [bu′-rō], *n.* a hole made in the ground by rabbits, foxes, etc., as a lair. [Uncert.].

BURROW (2), [bu′-rō], *v.t.* to make a burrow, dig a way underground; (*fig.*) to penetrate below the surface of a subject.

BURROW-DUCK, [bu′-rō-duk′], *n.* the sheldrake.

BURROWER, [bu′-rō-er], *n.* one that burrows.

BURROWING-OWL, [bu′-rō-ing-owl′], *n.* an American owl, *Athene cunicularia*, which lives in burrows scooped out either by itself or by other animals.

BURR-PUMP, [bur′-pump], *n.* (*naut.*) a large bilge-pump in which the piston is devised so as to eliminate check-valves.

BURRY, [bur′-i], *adj.* prickly, covered with spines.

BURSAR, [bur′-ser], *n.* a treasurer, particularly in a college; a student who holds a scholarship at a university. [MedL. *bursarius* from *bursa* a purse].

BURSARSHIP, [bur′-ser-ship], *n.* the office of a bursar.

BURSARY, [bur′-ser-i], *n.* the treasury of a college or monastery; a grant to assist a scholar to continue his studies; a scholarship.

BURSE, [burs], *n.* a purse; †a place where merchants meet for the transacting of business, an exchange. [MedL. *bursa* purse].

BURSIFORM, [bur′-si-fawm], *adj.* shaped like a purse.

BURST (1), [burst], *n.* the act of bursting; sudden explosion or tearing asunder; sudden activity; a brief vigorous effort, a spurt. [OE. *byrst*].

BURST (2), [burst], *v.t.* to break or tear open with violence; to cause to break open, come apart; *v.i.* to break or fly open suddenly and with violence; to disrupt violently; to explode; to break; (*fig.*) to be plentifully endowed with, to overflow with; to appear suddenly and unexpectedly; **to b. with laughing**, to be helpless with excess of laughter; **to b. out**, begin to speak violently. [OE. *berstan*].

BURTHEN†, see BURDEN (2).

BURTON (1), [bur′-ton], *n.* (*naut.*) tackle formed by two blocks or pulleys used to tighten rigging. [BARTON].

BURTON (2), [burt′-on], *n.* a kind of beer brewed at *Burton*-on-Trent.

BURY, [be′-ri], *v.t.* to put a dead body into the earth; to inter with funeral rites in the earth or at sea; to put anything into the earth; to hide, immerse; (*fig.*) to forget and forgive; **to b. the hatchet**, to settle a quarrel. [OE. *byrgan*].

BURYING, [be'-ri-ing], *n.* a burial, interment; the action of putting anything into the earth to cover it over.

BURYING-GROUND, [be'-ri-ing-grownd'], *n.* a cemetery.

BURYING-PLACE, [be'-ri-ing-plās'], *n.* a place of burial, a tomb, a sepulchre.

BUS, [bus], *n.* an omnibus; **to miss the b.**, to miss a good opportunity. [Short form of OMNIBUS].

BUSBY, [buz'-bi], *n.* the tall fur cap, usually bearskin, worn by certain regiments of the British army. [Unkn.].

BUSH (1), [bo͞osh], *n.* a shrub with densely growing branches, a wild uncultivated forest region with a thick undergrowth; †a bush hung outside a tavern as its sign; (*fig.*) anything thick or bushy, *esp.* the tail of a fox; **to beat about the b.**, to go indirectly to work; **good wine needs no b.**, a good article requires no advertisement. [ME. *bush*].

BUSH (2), [bo͞osh], *v.i.* to grow thick and bushy.

BUSH (3), [bo͞osh], *n.* a short length of tube forming the bearing of a rotating shaft. [MDu. *busse* box].

BUSHBUCK, BOSHBOK, [bo͞osh'-buk], *n.* an antelope of the genus *Tragelaphus*.

BUSH-CAT, [bo͞osh'-kat'], *n.* the serval, *Felis serval*.

BUSHEL, [bo͞osh'-el], *n.* a dry measure of eight gallons; **to hide one's light under a b.**, to conceal one's merits unnecessarily. [OFr. *boissel*].

BUSHELAGE, [bo͞osh'-el-ij], *n.* a duty levied by the bushel.

BUSH-HARROW, [bo͞osh'-ha'-rō], *n.* a harrow in which bushes or bushy branches are interwoven to scour the land.

BUSHINESS, [bo͞osh'-i-nes], *n.* the quality of being bushy.

BUSHMAN, [bo͞osh'-man], *n.* a woodsman, settler in the bush.

BUSHRANGER, [bo͞osh'-rān'-jer], *n.* an Australian outlaw, a man who has taken to the bush and lives by robbery.

BUSHY, [bo͞osh'-i], *adj.* overgrown with bushes, full of branches; thick and spreading.

BUSILY, [biz'-i-li], *adv.* in a busy manner, actively; officiously.

BUSINESS, [biz'-nis], *n.* a trade or profession followed for a livelihood; commercial enterprise, trading; that which has to be done, a special and necessary duty; an affair, subject, concern; **to send a man about his b.**, to dismiss a man, snub him. [BUSY].

BUSINESS-LIKE, [biz'-nis-līk], *adj.* suitable for business; orderly, efficient.

BUSK (1), [busk], *n.* a piece of steel or whalebone used to strengthen corsets. [~Fr. *busc*].

BUSK (2), [busk], *v.t.* to get ready, prepare oneself; to improvise. [OScand. *buask*].

BUSKER, [busk'-er], *n.* an itinerant musician or actor. [*Prec.*].

BUSKIN, [bus'-kin], *n.* a kind of leather boot reaching halfway up the calf and with a thick sole worn by Greek and Roman tragic actors; (*fig.*) tragedy. [OFr. *broissequin*].

BUSKINED, [bus'-kind], *adj.* wearing buskins; of, or pertaining to, tragedy.

BUSKY, [busk'-i], *adj.* bosky, wooded. [BOSKY].

BUSMAN, [bus'-man], *n.* the driver or conductor of a bus; **busman's holiday**, a holiday in name only.

BUSS (1), [bus], *n.* a kiss, *esp.* a loud, hearty one. [Wel. *bus*].

BUSS (2), [bus], *n.* (*naut.*) a three-masted or two-masted herring lugger, having the mizen smaller than the mainsail. [Du. *buis*].

BUSS

BUST (1), [bust], *n.* the head, neck, shoulders and chest of the human figure; a representation of these in sculpture; the bosom. [Fr. *buste*].

BUST (2), [bust], *v.i.* (*slang*) burst. [BURST].

BUSTARD, [bust'-erd], *n.* a European bird of the genus *Otis*, related to cranes and plovers. [OFr. *bistarde*].

BUSTLE (1), [busl], *n.* hurry; noisy, fussy activity; a great stir.

BUSTLE (2), [busl], *v.t.* to move, stir up to activity; *v.i.* to stir about fussily, to be actively busy, bestir oneself. [ME. *bustlen*].

BUSTLE (3), [busl], *n.* a stuffed pad or framework to cause a skirt to project behind from the waist. [Unkn.].

BUSTLER, [bus'ler], *n.* an active bustling person.

BUSY (1), [biz'-i], *n.* (*slang*) a detective. [BUSY (2)].

BUSY (2), [biz'-i], *adj.* working hard, actively employed; diligent; full of activity or occupation; meddlesome, officious. [OE. *bysig*].

BUSY (3), [biz'-i], *v.t.* to cause to be busy; to occupy. [OE. *bysgian*].

BUSYBODY, [biz'-i-bod'-i], *n.* one who meddles in others' business.

BUSYNESS, [biz'-i-nes], *n.* the state of being busy.

BUT (1), [but], *prep.* without, with the exception of, except, save. [OE. *butan*].

BUT (2), [but], *adv.* only, not more than, without, outside; **all b.**, very nearly.

BUT (3), [but], *conj.* except that, unless, than, only.

BUTCHER (1), [bo͝och'-er], *n.* one who slaughters animals for meat; one who sells meat; one who kills others violently and unnecessarily; a murderer. [OFr. *bouchier*].

BUTCHER (2), [bo͝och'-er], *v.t.* to kill animals for food; to murder with cruelty; to slaughter human beings ruthlessly; to massacre.

BUTCHER-BIRD, [bo͝och'-er-burd'], *n.* one of various kinds of shrike, of the genus *Lanius*.

BUTCHER'S-BROOM, [bo͝och'-erz-bro͞om'], *n.* (*bot.*) the knee holly, *Ruscus aculeatus*.

BUTCHERY, [bo͝och'-er-i], *n.* the occupation of a butcher; the place where animals are killed; massacre. [Fr. *boucherie*].

BUTLER, [but'-ler], *n.* the principal man-servant in an establishment and one who has charge of the plate and wines. [OFr. *bouteiller* from L. *buticula* bottle].

BUTLERAGE†, [but'-ler-ij], *n.* a duty payable on imported wine, so called as being originally payable to the king's butler.

BUTLERSHIP, [but'-ler-ship'], *n.* the office of a butler.

BUTLERY, [but'-ler-i], *n.* a butler's pantry.

BUTT (1), [but], *n.* large cask for beer or wine; a barrel. [OFr. *bout*].

BUTT (2), [but], *n.* an object to aim at in shooting; the mound behind a target; a thrust given by the head of an animal; (*fig.*) a person or object of ridicule. [Fr. *but*].

BUTT (3), [but], *n.* the end of a thing, *esp.* the thick or handle end of a weapon or tool. [OScand. *buttr*].

BUTT (4), [but], *n.* a flat fish. [~Swed. *butta* turbot].

BUTT (5), [but], *v.t.* and *i.* to strike, thrust, push violently with the head or the horns; to jut out, project. [OFr. *boter*].

BUTT-END, [but'-end'], *n.* a butt [BUTT (3)].

BUTTER (1), [but'-er], *n.* a firm fatty substance obtained from cream by churning; a similar foodstuff obtained from other materials; (*fig.*) flattery. [OE. *butere*].

BUTTER (2), [but'-er], *v.t.* to cover or spread with butter; **to b. up**, to flatter; **to know which side one's bread is buttered**, to be aware of one's own best interests.

BUTTER-AND-EGGS, [but'-er-and-egz'], *n.*(*pl.*) certain daffodils whose petals are two shades of yellow.

BUTTER-BEAN, [but'-er-bēn], *n.* a large dried haricot bean.

BUTTER-BIRD, [but'-er-burd'], *n.* the rice-bunting, the bobolink.

BUTTER-BOAT, [but'-er-bōt'], *n.* a small tureen for sauce.

BUTTERBUMP, [but'-er-bump'], *n.* the bittern. [BITTER(N) and BUMP].

BUTTERBUR, [but'-er-bur'], *n.* (*bot.*) the plant, *Petasites vulgaris*, with large soft leaves formerly used for wrapping butter. [BUTTER and BUR].

BUTTER-COOLER, [but'-er-ko͞ol'-er], *n.* a water vessel with an inner container to keep butter cool.

BUTTERCUP, [but'-er-kup], *n.* a variety of *Ranunculus* with bright yellow cup-shaped flowers.

BUTTER-DISH, [but'-er-dish'], *n.* a small dish in which butter is served at table.

BUTTER-DOCK, [but'-er-dok], *n.* the dock, *Rumex obtusifolius*.

BUTTER-FINGERED, [but'-er-fing'-gerd], *adj.* having weak or nerveless fingers; not able to grasp firmly; clumsy.

BUTTER-FINGERS, [but'-er-fing'-gerz], *n.* one who is butter-fingered.

BUTTER-FISH, [but'-er-fish'], *n.* one of the blennies, *Centronotus gunnellus*.

BUTTERFLOWER, [but'-er-flow'-er], *n.* a flower that reflects a yellow colour on the skin; the buttercup.

BUTTERFLY, [but'-er-flī], *n.* an insect of the order *Lepidoptera*, having four wings and knobbed antennae, and usually brightly coloured; (*fig.*) any gay, rather trivial person. [Uncert.].
BUTTERINE, [but'-er-ēn], *n.* a butter substitute, a product of oleomargarine churned up with milk.
BUTTERINESS, [but'-er-i-nes], *n.* buttery quality.
BUTTERIS, BUTTRICE, [but'-ris], *n.* a knife for paring horse's hoofs when shoeing. [Unkn.].
BUTTER-KNIFE, [but'-er-nīf'], *n.* a blunt knife, usually of silver, for cutting butter at table.
BUTTER-MAN, [but'-er-man'], *n.* a retailer of butter.
BUTTERMILK, [but'-er-milk'], *n.* the liquid which remains when butter has been churned.
BUTTER-MOULD, [but'-er-mōld'], *n.* a mould in which butter is shaped.
BUTTER-MUSLIN, [but'-er-muz'-lin], *n.* thin, loosely woven cloth with fine mesh, used primarily as a wrapping for butter.
BUTTER-NUT, [but'-er-nut'], *n.* the nut of the genus *Caryocar*; an oily edible nut of the American white walnut tree.
BUTTER-PRINT, [but'-er-print'], *n.* a carved or ridged piece of wood with handles for rolling pats of butter.
BUTTER-SCOTCH, [but'-er-skotch'], *n.* a hard toffee made of sugar and butter. [BUTTER and SCORCH].
BUTTER-STAMP, [but'-er-stamp'], *n.* a carved piece of wood for stamping patterns on butter.
BUTTER-TOOTH, [but'-er-tōōth'], *n.* a broad front tooth; a buck-tooth.
BUTTER-TREE, [but'-er-trē'], *n.* an African plant of the genus *Butyrospermum*, the nuts of which yield a substance of the consistency of butter called shea-butter.
BUTTER-WIFE, [but'-er-wīf'], *n.* a butter-woman, a maker or seller of butter.
BUTTER-WOMAN, [but'-er-wōōm'-an], *n.* a woman who hawks butter for sale.
BUTTERWORT, [but'-er-wurt'], *n.* (*bot.*) a marsh plant, *Pinguicula*, with oil-secreting prickles that catch small insects.
BUTTERY (1), [but'-er-i], *n.* the room where provisions are stored, *esp.* in colleges. [OFr. *boterie* wine store].
BUTTERY (2), [but'-er-i], *adj.* of the nature of or containing butter; (*fig.*) oily, nauseatingly flattering.
BUTTOCK (1), [but'-ok], *n.* one of the fleshy protuberances of the rump; (*pl.*) rump, posterior; (*naut.*) the convexity of a ship behind, under the stern. [ME. *buttok*].
BUTTOCK (2), [but'-ok], *v.t.* to throw a wrestler by using the buttock.
BUTTON (1), [butn], *n.* a knob or disk of metal or other material used for the purpose of fastening one part of the dress to another by being passed through a slit or loop in a corresponding place on the opposite side of a garment; a similar small disk worn for ornament or as a badge; any small round object resembling this. [Fr. *bouton*].
BUTTON (2), [butn], *v.t. and i.* to fasten with buttons.
BUTTON-BUSH, [butn'-bōōsh'], *n.* (*bot.*) the North American shrub, *Cephalanthus occidentalis*.
BUTTONHOLE (1), [butn'-hōl'], *n.* hole, slit or loop through which a button slips and is fastened; a flower or small nosegay worn in a buttonhole on the breast.
BUTTONHOLE (2), [butn'-hōl'], *v.t. and i.* to make buttonholes; (*fig.*) to detain a reluctant victim in conversation.
BUTTONHOLER, [butn'-hōl'-er], *n.* one who makes buttonholes.
BUTTONHOOK, [butn'-hōōk'], *n.* a small metal or bone hook fitted to a handle for drawing a button through a buttonhole.
BUTTON-MOULD, [butn'-mōld], *n.* a metal or wooden shape over which material is stretched to make a button.
BUTTONS (1), [butnz], *n.* a uniformed boy attendant, a page.
BUTTONS (2), [butnz], *n.* (*bot.*) the popular name for the tansy because of its button-shaped flowers.
BUTTON-STICK, [butn-stik], *n.* soldier's instrument for polishing buttons.
BUTTONWEED, [butn'-wēd'], *n.* (*bot.*) the knapweed, *Centaurea nigra*.
BUTTONWOOD, [butn'-wōōd'], *n.* (*bot.*) the western plane-tree of North America, *Platanus occidentalis*.
BUTTONY, [but'-o-ni], *adj.* resembling a button; having many buttons.
BUTTRESS (1), [but'-res], *n.* (*arch.*) a construction of wood, stone or brick against the outside of a wall to strengthen it by receiving part of the thrust; (*fig.*) a prop or support. [OFr. *bouterez*].

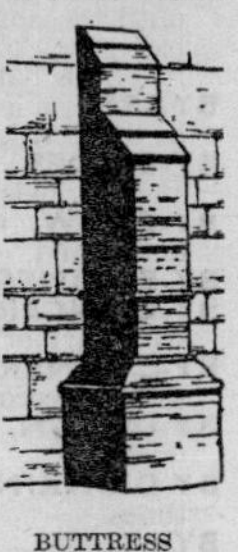
BUTTRESS

BUTTRESS (2), [but'-res], *v.t.* to support by a buttress, to prop; (*fig.*) to support, give strength to. [BUTTRESS (1)].
BUTTRICE, see BUTTERIS.
BUTTS, [buts], *n.(pl.)* a place for archery; a rifle range. [BUTT].
BUTTY, [but'-i], *n.* a foreman; (*min.*) a middleman who contracts to raise a certain amount of coal and pays workmen to do it. [Unkn.].
BUTYRACEOUS, [bew'-ti-rā'-shus], *adj.* with the qualities of butter, buttery. [Gk. *bouturon* butter].
BUTYRIC, [bew'-ti-rik], *adj.* pertaining to, made of, butter; **b. acid,** a colourless acid, having a rancid smell, found in butter.
BUTYRINE, [bew'-ti-rēn], *n.* an oily substance found in butter.
BUTYROUS, [bew'-ti-rus], *adj.* butyraceous.
BUXEOUS, [buks'-ē-us], *adj.* of or pertaining to the box or box-tree. [L. *buxus* box-tree].
BUXINE, [buks'-ēn], *n.* a bitter alkaloid extracted from the box-tree.
BUXOM, [buks-um], *adj.* plump and good-looking. [ME. *boghsom* pliable, obedient, ~BOW].
BUXOMLY, [buks'-um-li], *adv.* in a buxom manner.
BUXOMNESS, [buks'-um-nes], *n.* plump comeliness.
BUY (1), [bī], *n.* (*orig. U.S.*) a purchase. [*Next*].
BUY (2), (**buys, bought**), [bī], *v.t.* to acquire in exchange for payment in money, or goods or services; to purchase; to obtain by bribery; **to b. in,** to buy for oneself what one has already set up for sale, to purchase a stock of commodities; **to b. off,** to pay a price for release from some obligation; **to b. out,** to purchase the share of another person in any concern; to obtain release from the army by a money payment; **to b. up,** to purchase the entire available amount of anything, *esp.* goods or stock. [OE. *bycgan, bohte*].
BUYABLE, [bī'-abl], *adj.* able to be bought.
BUYER, [bī'-er], *n.* one who buys, purchaser; person in large stores who is responsible for the choosing and buying of goods from wholesalers.
BUZZ (1), [buz], *n.* the hum of a bee or a fly; a confused murmuring, hum made by a number of people talking together; **b. saw,** a circular saw. [Echoic].
BUZZ (2), [buz], *v.t. and i.* to make the humming sound of a bee, etc.; to whisper, to spread abroad secretly; **b. off,** (*coll.*) to go away, depart.
BUZZARD, [buz'-erd], *n.* one of the various birds of the falcon family and the genus *Buteo*. [OFr. *busart*].
BUZZARD-CLOCK, [buz'-erd-klok'], *n.* the dor beetle.
BUZZARDET, [buz'-erd-et], *n.* a species of hawk with long legs.
BUZZER, [buz'-er], *n.* a tattler, gossip; a steam whistle or hooter to summon people to work as in a factory; a fog-horn; (*electr.*) a vibrating armature which produces a buzzing sound.
BUZZING, [buz'-ing], *adj.* making or characterized by a buzz; whispering, chattering.
BUZZINGLY, [buz'-ing-li], *adv.* in a buzzing manner.

BUZZARD

BY (1), [bī], *prep.* close to; near; through, with (*denoting the author, means, etc.*); according to; by direction, authority or example of; to the amount or number of; during the course of, within the compass or period of; **b. all means,** certainly, without doubt; **b. no means,** not at all. [OE. *bi*].
BY (2), [bī], *adv.* near; in the same place; at hand; aside; so as to pass; **b. and b.,** in the near future, soon, presently; **to stand b.,** to support; (*naut.*) be in readiness; **b. the by,** by the way, in passing; **b. and large,** in general.
BY- (3), BYE-, [bī], *pref.* secondary, minor, subsidiary; indirect, secret, private. [OE. *bi*].
BY (4), BYE, [bī], *n.* something not the immediate object

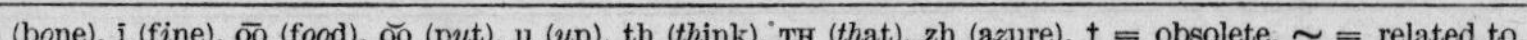

of regard; (*cricket*) run scored when ball passes batsman without touching him and is neither a wide nor a no-ball; in games, the odd man or team that waits until the next round to compete; **leg b.**, (*cricket*) a ball which touches the striker's person but does not touch his bat or hand. [BY (1)].

BYARD, [bī'-erd], *n.* a miner's breast-strap with which he drags trucks. [Unkn.].

BY-BIDDER, [bī'-bid'-er], *n.* a person who, at an auction, bids in order to tempt others to bid higher.

BY-BLOW, [bī'-blō], *n.* a side blow; (*dial.*) an illegitimate child. [BY and BLOW].

BY-BUSINESS, [bī'-biz'-nes], *n.* a subsidiary business.

BY-CONCERNMENT, [bī'-kon-surn'-ment], *n.* a secondary or subsidiary business or interest.

BY-CORNER, [bī'-kawn'-er], *n.* a private or out-of-the-way corner.

BY-DESIGN, [bī'-di-zīn'], *n.* a subsidiary design or purpose.

BY-DRINKING, [bī'-dringk'-ing], *n.* drinking between times.

BYE, see BY.

BYE-BYE, [bī'-bī'], *n.* (*slang*) good night, good-bye. [(GOOD)BYE].

BYE-ELECTION, [bī'-i-lek'-shun], *n.* an election held owing to a special vacancy and not at a General Election.

BYE-LAW, [bī'-law], *n.* a special law made by a corporation, town council, or society. [ODan. *by* town and LAW].

BY-END, [bī'-end'], *n.* a secondary objective; a private, selfish end.

BYGONE (1), [bī'-gon'], *n.* the past; a past incident; **let bygones be bygones**, forget past grievances.

BYGONE (2), [bī'-gon'], *adj.* over and past, belonging to the past.

BY-INTEREST, [bī'-int'-er-est], *n.* a private, selfish interest.

BY-LANE, [bī'-lān], *n.* a small side lane.

BY-NAME, [bī'-nām], *n.* a nickname, name of reproach or contempt.

BY-PASS (1), [bī'-pahs], *n.* a pipe or outlet used when the main supply or current is cut off; an arterial road which passes by, without going through, a town.

BY-PASS (2), [bī'-pahs'], *v.t.* to divert traffic, etc., by means of a by-pass.

BY-PASSAGE, [bī'-pas'-ij], *n.* a secluded passage; a private passage.

BYPATH, [bī'-pahth'], *n.* a side path, a little used way; (*fig.*) an unimportant or little known part of a subject. [BY and PATH].

BY-PLAY, [bī'-plā], *n.* (*drama*) significant action taking place as an aside while the main action goes forward.

BY-PLOT, [bī'-plot'], *n.* a subsidiary or secondary plot taking place within the main plot of a drama or story.

BY-PRODUCT, [bī'-prod'-ukt], *n.* an incidental product; (in manufactures) a subsidiary article produced incidentally in the manufacture of some other article.

BY-PURPOSE, [bī'-pur'-pus], *n.* an incidental or concealed purpose.

BYRE, [bīer], *n.* a cow-house. [OE. *byre*].

BY-ROAD, [bī'-rōd], *n.* a side or subsidiary road.

BYRONIC, [bī-ron'-ik], *adj.* applied to poetry or conduct supposedly in the manner of Lord *Byron*; cynical, daring and picturesque.

BY-SPEECH, [bī'-spēch], *n.* an incidental or casual speech. [BY and SPEECH].

BYSSINE, [bis'-īn], *adj.* made of fine linen. [Gk. *bussos*].

BYSSOID, [bis'-oid], *adj.* like a byssus; fringed with threads of unequal length.

BYSSOLITE, [bis'-ō-līt], *n.* a fine fibrous tremolite; a kind of asbestos. [*Next*, and Gk. *lithos* stone].

BYSSUS, [bis'-us], *n.* a fine linen fabric, formerly used for wrapping Egyptian mummies. [Gk. *bussos* linen]

BYSTANDER, [bī'-stand'-er], *n.* one who stands by, an onlooker.

BY-STREET, [bī'-strēt'], *n.* a side street, one leading out of a main thoroughfare; a poor street.

BY-STROKE, [bī'-strōk'], *n.* an incidental or sly stroke.

BY-VIEW, [bī'-vew], *n.* a glimpse; a private end or purpose.

BY-WALK, [bī'-wawk], *n.* a secluded or private walk.

BY-WAY, [bī'-wā], *n.* a side road; (*fig.*) **b. of learning**, line of study off the main track.

BY-WIPE, [bī'-wīp], *n.* (*slang*) a secret stroke of sarcasm or raillery; a side stroke.

BY-WORD, [bī'-wurd], *n.* †a common saying, proverb; an object of contempt or derision.

BYZANT, see BEZANT.

BYZANTIAN, [biz-ant'-i-an], *n.* Byzantine.

BYZANTINE, [biz-ant'-īn, bī-zant'-ēn], *adj.* pertaining to Byzantium (Constantinople), the former capital of the Eastern Roman Empire.

C

C, [sē], the third letter of the English alphabet; (*mus.*) the dominant or fifth note of the scale of F major; the key of C major.

CAAING-WHALE, [kah'-ing-wāl', kaw'-ing-wāl], *n.* the pilot whale; porpoise.

CAB (1), [kab], *n.* a Hebrew measure, equivalent to nearly three pints. [Heb. *qab* vessel].

CAB (2), [kab], *n.* a small horse-drawn or motor-driven carriage plying for public hire; the covered part of a locomotive engine sheltering the driver and fireman. [Fr. *cab(riolet)*].

CABAL (1), [ka-bal'], *n.* a small party of persons engaged in a secret state intrigue, the intrigue itself; (*hist.*) a small committee of the Privy Council of 1671, the initials of the surnames of five members chancing to spell *cabal* (*C*lifford, *A*rlington, *B*uckingham, *A*shley, *L*auderdale). [Fr. *cabale*, ~CABALA].

CABAL (2), **(caballing, caballed)**, [ka-bal'], *v.i.* to engage in intrigue, to plot.

CABALA, CABBALA, KABBALA, [kab'-al-a], *n.* the mystical interpretation of the Scriptures handed down orally through generations of Jewish Rabbis; any occult science. [Heb. *qabbalah* mysterious teaching].

CABALISM, [kab'-al-izm], *n.* the mystical interpretation of the Jewish Scriptures; occultism.

CABALIST, [kab'-al-ist], *n.* one skilled in the cabala.

CABALISTIC, [kab'-al-ist'-ik], *adj.* connected with the cabala; having an occult meaning.

CABALISTICAL, [kab'-al-is'-tik-al], *adj.* pertaining to the cabala.

CABALISTICALLY, [kab'-al-ist'-ik-al-i], *adv.* in a cabalistic way.

CABALLER, [kab-al'-er], *n.* one who cabals, a schemer.

CABALLINE, [kab'-al-īn], *adj.* of or pertaining to a horse. [L. *caballinus*].

CABANA, [kab-ahn'-ya], *n.* a brand of cigars. [*Cabaña*, a Spanish surname].

CABANE, [kab-ahn'], *n.* (*aeron.*) the mast-like structure projecting above the body of a monoplane, and to which the upper strengthening wires of the wings are attached. [Fr. *cabane*].

CABARET, [kab'-er-ā], *n.* a licensed restaurant where smart singing and dancing shows are given at night; a small tavern. [Fr. *cabaret*].

CABBAGE (1), [kab'-ij], *n.* the plant *Brassica oleracea*, eaten as a green vegetable; a white butterfly which, in the caterpillar stage, feeds on cabbages; **sea c.**, sea-kale; **c. rose**, a large coarse double red rose. [Fr. *caboche* big head].

CABBAGE (2), [kab'-ij], *n.* clippings of cloth pilfered by tailors. [Variant of GARBAGE].

CABBAGE (3), [kab'-ij], *v.i.* to filch. [*Prec.*].

CABBAGE-TREE, [kab'-ij-trē'], *n.* (*bot.*) a palm of the genus *Oreodoxa*.

CABBALA, see CABALA.

CABBLE, [kab'-al], *v.t.* to smash up partly finished iron into small pieces for smelting. [Unkn.].

CABBY, [kab'-i], *n.* (*coll.*) the driver of a cab. [CAB (2)].

CABECA, cabeça, [kab-ās'-a], *n.* see CABESSE.

CABER, [kā'-ber], *n.* a roughly trimmed tree-trunk used in Highland games for hurling as a trial of strength. [Gael. *cabar* pole].

CABESSE, [ka-bes'], *n.* the finest variety of Indian silk. [Fr. *cabesse*, ~Port. *cabeça*].

CABIN (1), [kab'-in], *n.* a hut; a poor man's house; room in a ship; a building on a railway from which points and signals are worked; **c. boy,** a junior servant on a ship, who waits on the officers. [Fr. *cabane*].

CABIN (2), [kab'-in], *v.i.* to confine in a small space.

CABINET, [kab'-in-et], *n.* a small room, a closet; a piece of furniture for preserving or displaying valuable objects, china, glass, etc., the objects contained in this; (*pol.*) the group of ministers who hold the principal offices in the government; **c. pudding,** a pudding made of bread, eggs, milk, raisins, and covered with a sauce; **shadow c.,** a council formed from the Opposition with a view to taking office on coming into power. [*Dim.* of CABIN].

CABINETED, [kab'-in-et-id], *adj.* conferring closely.

CABINET-MAKER, [kab'-in-et-māk'-er], *n.* a skilled wood-worker who designs and makes cabinets and other high-class furniture.

CABINET MINISTER, [kab'-i-net min'-is-ter], *n.* the parliamentary head of a government department who is also a member of the cabinet.

CABLE (1), [kābl], *n.* a thick rope of twisted strands of hemp or wire; insulated wires for transmitting electricity; such a wire on the sea-bottom or underground to transmit telegraphic messages, etc.; a message transmitted in this way; (*arch. and goldsmith's work*) a moulding shaped like a rope; (*naut.*) a rope carrying the anchor; a measure of depth equal to 100 fathoms. [OFr. *cable*].

CABLE (2), [kābl], *v.t. and i.* to secure or provide with a cable; to transmit a message by submarine telegraphy; (*arch.*) to ornament with cable moulding.

CABLEGRAM, [kābl'-gram], *n.* a message sent by cable. [CABLE (1) and Gk. *gramma* writing].

CABLE-LAID, [kābl'-lād], *adj.* twisted like a cable with three strands.

CABLET, [kā'-blet], *n.* a cable-laid rope less than ten inches in circumference. [*Dim.* of CABLE (1)].

CABLE-TIER, [kābl'-tēer], *n.* a place where cables are stored; (*naut.*) a heap of coiled cable.

CABMAN, [kab'-man], *n.* one who drives a cab.

CABOB (1), [kā'-bob, ka-bob'], *n.* oriental dish of beef or mutton roasted in small pieces and spiced with ginger, garlic, etc. [Arab. *kabab*].

CABOB (2), [kā'-bob, ka-bob'], *v.t.* to prepare cabobs.

CABOCHED, CABOSHED, [kab-osht'], *adj.* (*her.*) having an animal's head drawn from the front, without any of the neck or body showing. [OFr. *caboché* from *caboche* large head].

CABOCHON, [kab'-osh-on(g)'], *n.* a jewel, polished but not cut. [Fr. *cabochon*].

CABOODLE, [ka-bōōdl'], *n.* (*slang*) lot, crowd. [Unkn.].

CABOOSE, [ka-bōōs'], *n.* (*naut.*) a room on deck where food is cooked. [Du. *kabuys*].

CABOCHED

CABOSHED, see CABOCHED.

CABOTAGE, [kab'-ot-ahzh], *n.* coasting, carrying along the coast from port to port; the carriage of persons and goods for hire within the territory of a Sovereign State, such territory including colonies, protectorates, and mandated territories and the territorial waters adjacent thereto. [Fr. *cabotage*].

CAB-RANK, [kab'-rangk'], *n.* an approved parking place for taxi-cabs in a street.

CABRIOLE (1), [kab'-ri-ōl], *n.* curved leg typical of Queen Anne and Chippendale furniture. [Fr. *cabriole* goat's leap].

CABRIOLE (2), [kab'-ri-ōl], *adj.* (of furniture) having a cabriole.

CABRIOLET, [kab'-ri-ō-lā], *n.* a small covered carriage on two wheels drawn by a single horse. [Fr. *cabriolet* from *cabriole* goat's leap].

CABRIT, [kab'-rit], *n.* the pronghorn antelope. [Span. *cabrito* kid, young goat].

CAB-STAND, [kab'-stand'], *n.* a cab-rank.

CABURN, [kab'-ern], *n.* (*naut.*) a thin thread of spun yarn. [Uncert.].

CACAO, [ka-kah'-ō], *n.* a tropical American plant the seeds of which provide cocoa. [Span. *cacao* from Mexican *kaka-uatl*].

CACHAEMIA, [ka-kē'-mi-a], *n.* (*med.*) a condition of the blood. [Gk. *kakos* bad and *haima* blood].

CACHALOT, [kach'-a-lot], *n.* the sperm whale which is distinguished by having teeth growing in its lower jaw. [Fr. *cachalot*].

CACHE (1), [kash], *n.* a store or storehouse where things are hidden; an illegal hoard of arms and ammunition; (*zool.*) the hoard of food which some animals make ready for the winter. [Fr. *cache*].

CACHE (2), [kash], *v.t.* to place in a cache.

CACHECTIC, [ka-kekt'-ik], *adj.* (*med.*) afflicted with or pertaining to cachexy.

CACHECTICAL, [ka-kekt'-ik-al], *adj.* cachectic.

CACHET, [kash'-ā], *n.* a seal, stamp; (*fig.*) any mark or sign of excellence or authenticity; (*med.*) a capsule. [Fr. *cachet* seal].

CACHEXY, [ka-kek'-si], *n.* (*med.*) a low physical condition. [Gk. *kakhexia*].

CACHINNATE, [kak'-in-āt], *v.i.* to laugh boisterously. [L. *cachinnare*].

CACHINNATION, [kak'-in-ā'-shun], *n.* loud, uproarious laughter. [L. *cachinnatio*].

CACHOU, [ka'-shōō], *n.* a small lozenge taken by smokers to sweeten the breath; any small scented sweet. [Fr. *cachou*].

CACHUCHA, [ka-chōō'-cha], *n.* a vigorous Spanish dance. [Span. *cachucha*].

CACIQUE, [ka-sēk'], *n.* a West Indian, an American Indian native chieftain; a Spanish political boss. [Span. *cacique*].

CACIQUISM, [ka-sēk'-izm], *n.* a form of local government in Spanish politics.

CACKLE (1), [kakl], *n.* the cry of a hen or goose; (*fig.*) loud silly talk or laughter.

CACKLE (2), [kakl], *v.i.* to make a cackle; (*fig.*) to chatter and laugh in a loud silly fashion. [ME. *kakelen*].

CACO-, [kak'-ō-], *pref.* badly, ill-, mis-. [Gk. *kakos* bad].

CACODEMON, CACODAEMON, [kak'-ō-dēm'-on], *n.* an evil spirit, malignant person; (*fig.*) a bad dream. [CACO and Gk. *daimon* spirit].

CACODOXY, [kak'-ō-dok'-si], *n.* a mistaken opinion. [Gk. *kakodoxia* heterodoxy].

CACODYL, KAKODYL, [kak'-ō-dil], *n.* a highly inflammable and evil-smelling compound of arsenic and methyl. [CACO and Gk. *odme* smell].

CACOEPY, [ka-kō'-ep-i], *n.* bad enunciation. [CACO and Gk. *epos* speech].

CACOETHES, [kak'-ō-ēth'-ēz], *n.* an evil propensity of mind or body; a constant desire to be doing something which it is not wise to do; recurrent bad health. [Gk. *kakoethes* bad habit].

CACOGASTRIC, [kak'-ō-gas'-trik], *adj.* suffering from indigestion. [Gk. *kakos* bad and GASTRIC].

CACOGRAPHY, [ka-kog'-raf-i], *n.* bad handwriting or spelling. [CACO and Gk. *graphia* writing].

CACOLET, [kak'-ō-let], *n.* a mule-chair; a litter for the wounded borne by mules. [Fr. dialect *cacolet*].

CACOLOGY, [ka-kol'-ō-ji], *n.* bad pronunciation or choice of words. [Gk. *kakologia* slander].

CACOPHONIC, [kak'-o-fon'-ik], *adj.* discordant.

CACOPHONOUS, [kak-of'-on-us], *adj.* cacophonic.

CACOPHONY, [kak-of'-on-i], *n.* a discordant sound, unpleasantly-sounding speech. [Gk. *kakophonia*].

CACOTROPHY, [kak-ot'-rof-i], *n.* malnutrition. [Gk. *kakotrophia*].

CACTACEOUS, [kak-tā'-shus], *adj.* (*bot.*) pertaining to the cactus family, *Cactaceae*.

CACTUS, (*pl.* **cactuses, cacti**), [kak'-tus, kak'-tus-iz, kak'-tī], *n.* (*bot.*) family of cactaceous plants distinguished by their fleshy and prickly leaves and stems. [Gk. *kaktos*].

CACUMINAL, [ka-kewm'-in-al], *adj.* (*phon.*) with the tip of the tongue turned upwards and pointing backwards to the hard palate. [L. *cacumen* top, peak].

CAD, [kad], *n.* an ill-bred person who is always ready to take a mean advantage. [Fr. *cad(et)* a junior].

CADASTRAL, [kad-ast'-ral], *adj.* pertaining to a survey of landed property and its taxable value. [Fr. *cadastre*].

CADAVER, [kad-av'-er], *n.* a corpse. [L. *cadaver*].

CADAVERIC, [kad-av'-er-ik], *adj.* relating to corpses; resembling one.

CADAVEROUS, [kad-av'-er-us], *adj.* corpse-like, pale and emaciated like a corpse.

CADAVEROUSLY, [kad-av'-er-us-li], *adv.* in a cadaverous fashion.
CADAVEROUSNESS, [kad-av'-er-us-nes], *n.* the quality of being cadaverous.
CADDICE, see CADDIS.
CADDIE, see CADDY (1).
CADDIS, CADDICE, [kad'-is], *n.* the larva of a caddis-fly; a ribbon lint for dressing wounds. [Unkn.].
CADDIS-FLY, [kad'-is-flī'], *n.* a species of the Trichoptera, whose larvae live in fresh water and are used as bait for fish.
CADDISH, [kad'-ish], *adj.* in the manner of a cad.
CADDY (1), CADDIE, [kad'-i], *n.* a young lad or other servant who accompanies a golfer round the course, chiefly to carry the clubs. [Fr. *cadet* junior].
CADDY (2), [kad'-i], *n.* a container for tea. [Malay *kati* a measure].
CADE (1), [kād], *n.* a young animal, abandoned by its mother, and brought up as a pet; a pet lamb. [Unkn.].
CADE (2), [kād], *n.* a cask. [L. *cadus* wine-jar].
CADENCE, [kād'-ens], *n.* rhythm; the rhythm and tonal quality of speech, a falling intonation of voice; (*mus.*) a closing phrase or concluding chords. [Fr. *cadence* from L. *cadens* falling].
CADENCY, [kād'-en-si], *n.* cadence; descent from a younger member of a family as distinct from the main branch. [*Prec.*].
CADENE, [kad-ēn'], *n.* an inferior kind of Turkey carpet, with a chain-like warp. [Fr. *cadène* chain].
CADENT, [kād'-ent], *adj.* falling, modulating. [L. *cadens*].
CADENZA, [kad-enz'-a], *n.* (*mus.*) an elaborate ornamental passage outside the general structure, but bringing it to a conclusion. [It. *cadenza*].
CADET, [ka-det'], *n.* a younger son; a member of a school which prepares men to hold commissions in the forces; a member of a Cadet Corps; **C. Corps**, a military body where boys are trained for the Officers' Training Corps. [Fr. *cadet* junior].
CADETSHIP, [kad-et'-ship], *n.* the state of being a cadet; the post of a cadet.
CADGE (1), [kaj], *n.* the act of cadging.
CADGE (2), [kaj], *v.t. and i.* to get by begging, to beg. [Uncert.].
CADGER, [kaj'-er], *n.* a person who cadges.
CADI, KADI, [kād'-i, kah'-di], *n.* a minor Arab or Turkish judge. [Arab. *qadi*].
CADMEAN, [kad-mē'-an], *adj.* (*class. myth.*) pertaining to Cadmus, who is supposed to have introduced the sixteen simple letters of the alphabet into Greece; **C. victory**, a victory fatal in its consequences for the victor; doubtful praise or compliment. [Gk. *Kadmos*, legendary founder of Thebes].
CADMIUM, [kad'-mi-um], *n.* (*chem.*) a soft bluish-white metal, the chemical element denoted by Cd; **c. yellow**, a brilliant yellow pigment containing cadmium. [L. *cadmia* calamine].
CADRANS, [kad'-ranz], *n.* an implement used by jewellers when cutting facets.
CADRE, [kahdr], *n.* (*milit.*) the men and officers forming the permanent nucleus of a battalion; the officers of a battalion. [Fr. *cadre* frame].
CADUCEUS, (*pl.* **caducei**), [kad-ew'-si-us], *n.* (*antiq.*) a herald's wand. [L. *caduceus*].
CADUCIBRANCHIATE, [kad-ews'-i-brang'-ki-at], *adj.* (*zool.*) having gills which fall off before maturity is reached, as in frogs and other amphibians. [L. *caducus* inclined to fall, and BRANCHIATE].
CADUCITY, [kad-ews'-it-i], *n.* fleetingness, perishableness; (*bot.*) the tendency to fall very early. [Fr. *caducité*].
CADUCOUS, [kad-ewk'-us], *adj.* (*bot.*) tending to fall at an early date. [L. *caducus*].
CAECAL, [sēk'-al], *adj.* (*anat.*) of, or pertaining to, the caecum.
CAECUM, [sēk'-um], *n.* (*anat.*) the blind gut, a sac in the large intestine with only one opening. [L. *caecus* blind].

CADUCEUS

CAESAR, [sē'-zer], *n.* the title taken by Augustus, the first Roman emperor, and held by his successors; an emperor. [The family name of Caius Julius *Caesar*].
CAESARIAN, [sēz-āer'-ian], *adj.* pertaining to Caesar; **c. operation, c. section**, a surgical operation to effect the birth of a child through the abdomen, as at the birth of Julius *Caesar*.
CAESARISM, [sēz'-er-izm], *n.* a system of autocratic government like that of the Roman emperors.
CAESIOUS, [sē'-zhi-us], *adj.* greyish-blue. [L. *caesius*].
CAESIUM, [sēz'-i-um], *n.* a silvery-coloured metal; the chemical element denoted by Cs. [L. *caesius* bluish-grey].
CAESPITOSE, [ses'-pit-ōs], *adj.* (*bot.*) occurring in tufts. [~L. *caespes caespitem* turf].
CAESURA, [si-zhŏŏer'-a], *n.* (*pros.*) a pause in the rhythm of a line of verse. [L. *caesura*].
CAESURAL, [si-zhŏŏer'-al], *adj.* (*pros.*) relating to caesura.
CAFE, café, [kaf'-ā], *n.* a coffee-house, restaurant where (non-alcoholic) drinks and other refreshments are served; **c. au lait**, coffee with milk. [Fr. *café* coffee].
CAFELITE, [kaf'-i-līt], *n.* a plastic material made from coffee beans. [Fr. *café* coffee and (BAKE)LITE].
CAFETERIA, [kaf'-i-tēer'-i-a], *n.* a restaurant without waiters, where customers serve themselves. [Span. *cafeteria* café].
CAFFEIC, [kaf-ē'-ik], *adj.* pertaining to coffee or caffeine.
CAFFEINE, [kaf'-ēn], *n.* an alkaloid present in coffee, etc., sometimes used as a drug. [Fr. *caféine*].
CAFFRE, see KAFFIR.
CAFTAN, KAFTAN, [kaf'-tan, kaft-ahn'], *n.* a long-sleeved garment worn with a girdle in the Near East. [Turk. *qaftan*].
CAGE (1), [kāj], *n.* a room or edifice with bars, trellis, or other open work on at least one side, in which an animal may be kept; a small, often portable, metal box with sides of wire trellis work where birds and other small pets may be kept; anything resembling this; the lift in a mine. [Fr. *cage*].
CAGE (2), [kāj], *v.t.* to shut up in, or as if in, a cage.
CAGELING, [kāj'-ling], *n.* a bird kept in a cage.
CAGMAG, [kag'-mag], *n.* a tough goose; any meat unfit to eat. [Unkn.].
CAGOT, [kag-ō'], *n.* a member of a nearly extinct outcast race in the Pyrenees. [Fr. *cagot*].
CAGOULARD, [ka-gŏŏ-lah(r)'], *n.* a member of a former secret French organization run by pro-Nazi industrialists and financiers. [Fr. *cagoule* hooded cloak].
CAHOOT (1), [ka-hŏŏt'], *n.* (*U.S.*) a partnership or league. [Fr. *cahute* cabin].
CAHOOT (2), [ka-hŏŏt'], *v.i.* to act conjointly or in partnership.
CAIMACAM, see KAIMAKAM.
CAIMAN, see CAYMAN.
CAIN, [kān], *n.* a fratricide; **to raise C.**, to create a violent disturbance. [Gen. iv].
CAINOZOIC, KAINOZOIC, [kān'-ō-zō'-ik], *adj.* (*geol.*) pertaining to the age which followed the mesozoic and lasted up to the present era, including the tertiary and quaternary periods. [Gk. *kainos* new and *zoe* life].
CAIQUE, [kah-ēk'], *n.* a small boat common in the Bosphorus. [Fr. *caïque*, from Turk. *kaik*].
CAIRN, [kāern], *n.* a heap of stones, *esp.* when erected as a memorial; a cairn-terrier. [Gael. *carn* a heap].
CAIRNGORM, [kāern'-gawm'], *n.* a mountain in Inverness which produces a yellowish-brown crystal; the crystal itself. [CAIRN and Gael. *gorm* blue].

CAIQUE

CAIRN-TERRIER, [kāern'-te'-ri-er], *n.* a breed of small Scots terriers, with a shaggy coat usually grey or brindled.
CAISSON, [kāsn], *n.* a wooden framework or casing; a chest containing bombs to be buried under the road of an enemy, so as to explode beneath him; (*milit.*) a movable chest for holding ammunition; (*eng.*) a water-tight chamber which can be lowered into water and supplied with air from pumps above, so that men can work in it; an iron container filled with cement in which the supports of a bridge are sunk. [Fr. *caisson*].
CAITIFF (1), [kā'-tif], *n.* (*poet.*) a low-spirited, despicable wretch, a coward. [OFr. *caitif* from L. *captivus* prisoner].
CAITIFF (2), [kā'-tif], *adj.* mean, cowardly, contemptible.
CAJEPUT, CAJUPUT, [kaj'-i-pŏŏt], *n.* (*bot.*) a tree

of the genus *Melaleuca* which yields an aromatic oil. [Malay *kaya-putih* white wood].

CAJOLE, [ka-jōl'], *v.t.* to flatter (someone) so as to influence his actions, opinions, feelings as one wishes; to seduce or persuade by blandishment. [Fr. *cajoler*].

CAJOLEMENT, [ka-jōl'-ment], *n.* the act of cajoling.

CAJOLER, [ka-jōl'-er], *n.* a person who cajoles.

CAJOLERY, [ka-jōl'-er-i], *n.* the process of cajoling, the arts of flattery and blandishment.

CAJOLINGLY, [ka-jōl'-ing-li], *adv.* in a cajoling fashion.

CAJUPUT, see CAJEPUT.

CAKE (1), [kāk], *n.* a small lump of dough sweetened, flavoured and baked in a symmetrical form; the material itself or a piece of it; any other piece of food similar in appearance; any substance resembling this; **cakes and ale,** jollity and rejoicing; **to take the c.,** to be very excellent or remarkable; **c.-walk,** a grotesque dance among American negroes, the prize for which was a cake; an Edwardian dance called after this. [Uncert.].

CAKE (2), [kāk], *v.t. and i.* to form into a cake; to dry hard.

CALABAR BEAN, [kal'-a-bah'-bēn'], *n.* the seed of an African plant, from which a poisonous drug is extracted. [*Calabar* in West Africa].

CALABASH, [kal'-a-bash'], *n.* a South American tree bearing gourds; a gourd from this tree; any kind of gourd, *esp.* one that has been dried. [Fr. *calebasse* from Arab. *qar aibas* dry gourd].

CALABER, [kal'-a-ber], *n.* the skin or fur of the grey squirrel. [*Calabria*, a province in Italy].

CALABOOSE, [kal'-a-bōōs'], *n.* (*U.S. slang*) a prison. [Span. *calabozo* cell].

CALADE, [ka-lād'], *n.* a piece of sloping ground down which horses are ridden quickly to train them to stop suddenly. [Fr. *calade*].

CALAMANCO, [kal'-a-mang'-kō], *n.* woollen material of fine gloss and checkered in the warp. [Uncert.].

CALAMARY, [kal'-a-ma-ri], *n.* a kind of cuttle-fish, with inner shell shaped like a pen. [L. *calamus* reed, pen].

CALAMBAC, [kal'-am-bak'], *n.* a calambour. [Uncert.].

CALAMBOUR, [kal'-am-bōō-er], *n.* the *Aquilaria Agallocha*, a variety of aloes-wood used in making furniture. [Fr. *calambour*].

CALAMIFEROUS, [kal'-am-if'-er-us], *adj.* reedy, producing reeds. [L. *calamus* reed and *ferre* to bear].

CALAMINE, [kal'-a-mēn], *n.* an ore of zinc used medicinally for soothing inflammation of the skin, etc. [MdL. *calamina* from L. *cadmia*].

CALAMINT, [kal'-a-mint], *n.* (*bot.*) an aromatic plant of the genus *Calamintha*. [Gk. *kalaminthe*].

CALAMITE, [kal'-a-mīt], *n.* (*geol.*) a kind of lustrous tremolite, frequently reed-shaped; a fossil plant resembling a horsetail. [L. *calamus* reed].

CALAMITOUS, [kal-am'-it-us], *adj.* disastrous, arising out of or producing calamity.

CALAMITOUSLY, [kal-am'-it-us-li], *adv.* in a calamitous way.

CALAMITOUSNESS, [kal-am'-it-us-nes], *n.* the state or condition of being calamitous.

CALAMITY, [kal-am'-it-i], *n.* a disaster, an event causing terrible and often widespread misery; misfortune, very often more acute on account of its suddenness. [Fr. *calamité* from L. *calamitas*].

CALAMUS, [kal'-a-mus], *n.* (*bot.*) a reed; a genus of palms whose stems provide rattan-canes and sometimes the resin called dragon's-blood; a wind instrument made of a reed. [L. *calamus*].

CALANDER†, [kal-an'-der], *n.* (*ornith.*) a large Mediterranean lark. [Fr. *calandre*].

CALANDO, [kal-and'-ō], *adv.* (*mus.*) gradually dying away. [It. *calando*].

CALANDRA, [kal-and'-ra], *n.* the grain-weevil. [Uncert.].

CALANGAY, [kal-ang'-gā], *n.* a kind of white cockatoo. [Unkn.].

CALASH†, [ka-lash'], *n.* a light low-wheeled carriage, generally with a folding hood and a box for the coachman. [Fr. *calèche*].

CALAVANCES, [kal'-av-an-siz], *n.(pl.)* haricot-beans. [Span. *garbanzo* pea].

CALC-, *pref.* lime, chalk. [L. *calx calcis* lime].

CALCANEAL, [kal-kān'-i-al], *adj.* (*anat.*) pertaining to the calcaneum.

CALCANEUM, [kal-kān'-i-um], *n.* (*anat.*) a bone that forms part of the ankle-bone; the hypotarsus in birds. [L. *calcaneum*].

CALCAR (1), [kal'-kah(r)], *n.* a furnace used in making glass. [It. *calcara* calcining furnace].

CALCAR (2), [kal'-kah(r)], *n.* (*bot.*) a spur-like formation in flowers. [L. *calcar* spur].

CALCARATE, [kal'-ker-at], *adj.* (*bot.*) having a spur.

CALCAREO-ARGILLACEOUS, [kal-kāer'-i-ō-ah'-jil-ā-shus], *adj.* containing lime and sulphur. [CALCAREOUS and ARGILLACEOUS].

CALCAREO-BITUMINOUS, [kal-kāer'-i-ō-bi-tew'-min-us], *adj.* consisting of lime and bitumen.

CALCAREO-SILICEOUS, [kal-kāer'-i-ō-sil-ish'-us], *adj.* containing lime and flint or silica. [CALCAREOUS and SILICEOUS].

CALCAREO-SULPHUROUS, [kal-kāer'-i-ō-sul'-fer-us], *adj.* containing lime and sulphur. [CALCAREOUS and SULPHUROUS].

CALCAREOUS, [kal-kāer'-i-us], *adj.* relating to or containing lime. [L. *calcarius*].

CALCAVELLA, [kal'-kav-el'-a], *n.* a Portuguese sweet wine. [*Carcavelhos*, a place in Portugal].

CALCED, [kalst], *adj.* wearing shoes. [L. *calceus* boot].

CALCEDON, [kal'-sid-on], *n.* a foul vein, like chalcedony, found in some precious stones. [*Chalcedon*, town in Asia Minor].

CALCEDONIC, see CHALCEDONIC.

CALCEDONY, see CHALCEDONY.

CALCEOLARIA, [kal'-si-ō-lāer'-i-a], *n.* (*bot.*) a numerous genus of plants comprising the slipperworts. [L. *calceolarius* shoemaker].

CALCEOLATE, [kal'-si-ō-lāt'], *adj.* (*bot.*) resembling a slipper in shape. [L. *calceolus* little shoe].

CALCIC, [kal'-sik], *adj.* (*chem.*) resembling or containing calcium.

CALCIFEROL, [kal-sif'-er-ol], *n.* vitamin D in pure crystalline form.

CALCIFEROUS, [kal-sif'-er-us], *adj.* containing or producing lime or carbonate of lime. [L. *calx* lime and *ferre* to bear].

CALCIFICATION, [kal'-sif-ik-ā'-shun], *n.* conversion into chalk with salts of lime, as in petrifaction by impregnating. [L. *calcificatio*].

CALCIFY, [kal'-sif-i], *v.t. and i.* to make or become stony by deposit of lime. [Fr. *calcifier*].

CALCIMINE (1), KALSOMINE, [kal'-sim-īn], *n.* a white or slightly coloured wash for distempering walls and ceilings. [L. *calx* lime].

CALCIMINE (2), KALSOMINE, [kal'-sim-īn], *v.t.* to whitewash with calcimine.

CALCINABLE, [kal-sīn'-abl], *adj.* able to be calcined.

CALCINATION, [kal'-sin-ā'-shun], *n.* reduction to ashes by burning.

CALCINATORY, [kal-sin'-at-or-i], *n.* a vessel employed in calcination.

CALCINE, [kal'-sīn], *v.t. and i.* to reduce to lime by burning, to reduce to ashes by burning. [Fr. *calciner* from L. *calcinare*].

CALCITE, [kal'-sīt], *n.* calc-spar, a native carbonate of lime. [L. *calx* lime].

CALCITRATE, [kal'-sit-rāt], *v.t. and i.* to kick, strike a blow with the foot. [L. *calcitrare* strike with the heels].

CALCIUM, [kal'-si-um], *n.* the metallic element in lime, found naturally in compounds only, the chemical element denoted by Ca. [~L. *calx* (*calceum*) lime].

CALCOGRAPHY, [kal-kog'-ra-fi], *n.* engraving in the style of chalk drawing. [CALC and Gk. *graphia* writing].

CALCOURANITE, [kal'-kō-yōōer'-a-nīt], *n.* hydrated phosphate of calcium and uranium.

CALC-SINTER, [kalk'-sin'-ter], *n.* stalactitic calcium carbonate, calcareous tufa. [CALC and Germ. *sinter* dross].

CALC-SPAR, [kalk'-spah(r)'], *n.* calcareous spar; calcite. [CALC and SPAR].

CALC-TUFF, [kalk'-tuf'], *n.* carbonate of lime in alluvial deposit, calcareous tufa. [CALC and TUFF].

CALCULABLE, [kal'-kyōōl-abl], *adj.* able to be calculated.

CALCULATE, [kal'-kyōō-lāt], *v.t. and i.* to reckon by mathematics; to compute or estimate. [L. *calculare*].

CALCULATING, [kal'-kyōō-lāt-ing], *adj.* that calculates; careful; designing, cunning.

CALCULATION, [kal'-kyōō-lā'-shun], *n.* the act or process of calculating; the result of a mathematical computation; estimation, forecast of likely results. [L. *calculatio*].

CALCULATIVE, [kal'-kyōō-lāt-iv], *adj.* relating to calculation.

CALCULATOR, [kal'-kyōō-lāt-or], *n.* one who calculates; a calculating machine.

CALCULATORY, [kal'-kyōō-lāt-or-i], *adj.* pertaining to calculation.
CALCULOUS, [kal'-kyōō-lus], *adj.* (*med.*) pertaining to calculus.
CALCULUS (1), (*pl.* **calculi**), [kal'-kyōō-lus, kal-kyōō-lī], *n.* (*med.*) a morbid hard or stony concretion formed in organs of the body. [L. *calculus* small stone].
CALCULUS (2), [kal'-kyōō-lus], *n.* a mathematical process, a method of calculating. [*Prec.*].
CALDARIUM, [kal-dāer'-i-um], *n.* (*antiq.*) a room for hot baths in a Roman villa. [L. *caldarium*].
CALDRON, see CAULDRON.
CALECANNON, [kāl-kan'-on], *n.* an Irish dish consisting of green vegetables, etc. [KALE].
CALECHE†, [kal-āsh'], *n.* a calash. [Fr. *calèche*].
CALEDONIAN (1), [kal'-i-dōn'-i-an], *n.* a native of Caledonia, a Scotsman.
CALEDONIAN (2), [kal-i-dōn'-i-an], *adj.* pertaining to or of Caledonia or Scotland.
CALEFACIENT (1), [kal'-i-fāsh'-ent], *n.* (*med.*) a substance exciting or producing heat.
CALEFACIENT (2), [kal'-i-fāsh'-ent], *n.* (*med.*) generating heat. [L. *calefaciens*].
CALEFACTION, [kal'-i-fak'-shun], *n.* the act or process of producing heat, the state of being heated. [L. *calefacere* to make hot].
CALEFACTOR, [kal'-i-fak'-tor], *n.* a variety of small cooking-stove.
CALEFACTORY, [kal'-i-fak'-tor-i], *adj.* producing or imparting heat.
CALEMBOUR, [kal'-om-bōōer'], *n.* a play upon words, pun. [Fr. *calembour*].
CALENDAR (1), [kal'-in-der], *n.* a system by which the beginning and end and subdivisions of the year are fixed; a list of days and months in a given year; an almanac; a list of days in the year of special interest to a particular class or group of persons; a list of documents in a collection giving the date and a summary of each; the register of cases up for trial before a criminal court; **c. or date line,** that imaginary line through the Pacific Ocean, to be east or west of which signifies a day's difference in time. [OFr. *calendier* from L. *calendarium* account-book].
CALENDAR (2), [kal'-in-der], *v.t.* to enter on a calendar.
CALENDER (1), [kal'-in-der], *n.* a machine consisting of two hot rollers for pressing cloth, smoothing paper, etc.; a person who calenders. [Fr. *calandre* from Gk. *kulindros* cylinder].
CALENDER (2), [kal'-in-der], *v.t.* to press, smooth or polish in a calender.
CALENDER (3), [kal'-end-er], *n.* a wandering dervish, begging for his livelihood. [Pers. *qalender*].
CALENDS, KALENDS, [kal'-endz], *n.*(*pl.*) the first day of every month, in the Roman year; **Greek c.,** a date or occasion which never arrives. [L. *calendae*].
CALENDULA, [kal-end'-ew-la], *n.* (*bot.*) a variety of marigold. [CALENDS, because it flowers the whole year round].
CALENDULIN, [kal-end'-ew-lin], *n.* a gum obtained from the marigold.
CALENTURE, [kal'-en-chōōer], *n.* a delirious fever due to exposure in a hot climate, sunstroke. [Fr. *calenture* from L. *calens* growing hot].
CALESCENCE, [kal-es'-ens], *n.* increasing warmth.
CALF (1), (*pl.* **calves**), [kahf, kahvz], *n.* a young bull or cow; also applied to other animals when young, such as the elephant, seal, etc.; leather from the skin of a calf; stupid, clumsy youth; **c.-love,** an immature fondness in a girl or boy for one of the other sex; **to kill the fatted c.,** to prepare a hearty welcome for a prodigal. [OE. *calf*].
CALF (2), (*pl.* **calves**), [kahf, kahvz], *n.* the muscles of the leg between ankle and knee. [OScand. *kalfi*].
CALFSKIN, [kahf'-skin], *n.* the hide of a calf of which leather is made.
CALIBAN, [kal'-i-ban'], *n.* a subhuman monster; an ugly, brutal person. [*Caliban*, a character in Shakespeare's *Tempest*].
CALIBRATE, [kal'-i-brāt], *v.t.* to determine the calibre of; to make marks of measurement on a gauge or measure. [CALIBRE].
CALIBRATION, [kal'-i-brā'-shun], *n.* the measuring of the calibre of a gun; the marking of standard measurements on a gauge or other measure; the marks so made.
CALIBRE, [kal'-i-ber], *n.* the diameter of the bore of a gun; the size of a bomb, bullet or shell; (*fig.*) mental or moral capacity or quality. [Fr. *calibre*].
CALIBRED, [kal'-i-berd], *adj.* possessing a calibre.
CALICLE, [kal'-ikl], *n.* a small cup or hollow, as in coral; (*biol.*) small body or organ like a cup. [L. *caliculus* little cup].
CALICO, [kal'-i-kō], *n.* fine cotton cloth; **c. printing,** the process of printing figured patterns on calico. [*Calicut*, the town from which it originally came].
CALICO-BALL, [kal'-i-kō-bawl'], *n.* a dance at which fancy dresses made of cotton are worn.
CALICO-PRINTER, [kal'-i-kō-print'-er], *n.* one who prints patterns on calico.
CALICULAR, [kal-ik'-yōō-ler], *adj.* (*biol.*) relating to or resembling a calicle.
CALID, [kal'-id], *adj.* hot. [L. *calidus*].
CALIDUCT, [kal'-i-dukt], *n.* a pipe to convey hot air or water through a house. [L. *calere* to heat and *ducere* to lead].
CALIGINOUS†, [kal-ij'-in-us], *adj.* misty, obscure, dark. [L. *caliginosus*].
CALIGO, [kal-īg'-ō], *n.* feebleness of vision. [L. *caligo*].
CALIN, [kāl'-In], *n.* an alloy of tin and lead used by the Chinese for making tea-canisters and the like. [Fr. *calin* from Arab. *qalai*].
CALIPASH, [kal'-i-pash], *n.* the dull green fat on a turtle's upper shell. [Uncert.].
CALIPEE, [kal'-i-pē], *n.* the pale yellow fat on a turtle's lower shell. [Uncert.].
CALIPERS, see CALLIPERS.
CALIPH, KALIF, [kā'-if], *n.* a title assumed by the descendants of Mohammed as leaders. [Arab. *Khalifah* successor].
CALIPHATE, [kal'-i-fāt], *n.* the office or rule of a caliph or caliphs.
CALISAYA, [kal'-is-ā'-ya], *n.* a bark found in Peru. [Peruvian *calisaya*].
CALISAYINE, [kal-is-ā'-in], *n.* an extract of calisaya used for making bitters.
CALISTHENIC, see CALLISTHENIC.
CALIVER, [kal'-i-ver], *n.* a sixteenth century musket. [CALIBRE].
CALIX, [kā-liks], (*pl.* **calices**), *n.* (*biol., bot.*) an organ or part of the body shaped like a cup. [L. *calix*].
CALK (1), [kawlk], *n.* a piece of sharp-pointed iron fixed to shoe heels in America to prevent slipping in cold weather; a calker or calkin. [L. *calx* heel].
CALK (2), [kawlk], *v.t.* to provide with a calk or calkin.
CALK (3), see CAULK.
CALK (4), [kalk], *v.t.* to take a copy of a drawing by chalking its back and tracing the design on other paper placed under the chalked back, by running a blunt point or pencil over the lines of the original drawing. [Fr. *calquer* from L. *calcare* tread].
CALKER, [kaw'-ker], *n.* a man who calks; a calkin.
CALKIN, [kawk'-in, kal'-kin], *n.* a projection at the ends of a horseshoe to make a grip. [OFr. *calcain* from L. *calcaneum* heel].
CALKING (1), see CAULKING.
CALKING (2), [kawlk'-ing], *n.* the act of one who calks a drawing; a drawing so prepared. [CALK (4)].
CALL (1), [kawl], *n.* a shout or loud interjection to attract attention; a cry of one bird or animal to another; a note on a bugle or huntsman's horn; a message over the telephone; a reading over of names to discover those present and those absent; a summons of any sort; a vocation; a feeling that one is fitted to take up certain work; the attraction of a person, thing or idea; a claim on one's generosity; a short visit; a message to one's partner at cards by playing one's hand in a particular way, a bid; **a port of c.,** a port at which a ship calls regularly; **a house of c.,** a public-house; **within c.,** nearby, within ear-shot; **a c. box,** a telephone booth; **c. sign,** the identification sign used by a wireless-station when transmitting; **to have no c. to,** to have no need to.
CALL (2), [kawl], *v.t. and i.* to cry out, utter a call, shout for attention or help; to summon, attract, draw; to give a name to; to waken, rouse from sleep; to summon someone to take up a particular position or duty; to consider to be, reckon; to pay a visit; **to c. for,** to demand, to deserve; **to c. forth,** to occasion; **to c. in,** to order the return of or payment of; to send for request services and opinion of; **to c. on,** to pay a short visit to; to invoke (usually the Deity); to request (a person, *esp.* for a speech); **to c. out,** to utter cries in a loud voice; to summon to action; to challenge to a duel; **to c. over,** to read out a list of names to find out if any one is missing; **to c. up,** to summon for military service; (*fig.*) to evoke (a mental image); **to c. the banns,** to publish banns of a marriage in Church; **to c. attention to,** to bring to notice; **to c. into being,** to create, produce, give life to; **to c. to mind,** to

remember, recollect; **to c. in question,** to cast doubt upon; **to c. to order,** to make a request for orderly conduct at a public meeting; **to c. (a person) names,** abuse and insult (a person). [OE. *ceallian* from OScand. *kalla*].

CALLA, [kal'-a], *n.* (*bot.*) a genus of floating water-plants, including the bog arum. [Invented name].

CALL-BIRD, [kawl'-burd], *n.* a bird trained to entice others.

CALL-BOY, [kawl'-boi], *n.* a boy who calls actors to be ready to appear on the stage; a messenger boy at an hotel; a captain's boy.

CALLER (1), [kaw'-ler], *n.* a visitor; the card player who calls.

CALLER (2), [kal'-er], *adj.* fresh, brisk, cool; **c. herring,** fresh herrings. [Scots].

CALLID, [kal'-id], *adj.* skilful, expert. [L. *callidus* shrewd].

CALLIGRAPHIC, [kal'-i-graf'-ik], *adj.* calligraphical.

CALLIGRAPHICAL, [kal'-i-graf'-ik-al], *adj.* pertaining to calligraphy.

CALLIGRAPHIST, [kal-ig'-raf-ist], *n.* one who practises calligraphy, a skilled penman.

CALLIGRAPHY, [kal-ig'-ra-fi], *n.* the art of beautiful writing, skilful penmanship; handwriting. [Gk. *kallos* beauty and *graphia* writing].

CALLING, [kaw'-ling], *n.* trade, profession, vocation.

CALLIONYMUS, [kal'-i-on'-im-us], *n.* the dragonet fish. [Gk. *kallionymos*].

CALLIOPE, [kal-ī'-ōp-i], *n.* a mechanical organ. [*Calliope* the Muse of Song].

CALLIPERS, CALIPERS, [kal'-i-perz], *n.*(*pl.*) an instrument resembling compasses made with curved legs for measuring the internal or external diameters of round bodies. [CALIBRE].

CALLISTHENIC, CALISTHENIC, [kal'-is-then'-ik], *adj.* pertaining to callisthenics.

CALLISTHENICS, [kal'-is-then'-iks], *n.*(*pl.*) exercises developing graceful carriage and physical strength. [Gk. *kallos* beauty and *sthenos* strength].

CALL-NOTE, [kawl'-nōt], *n.* the cry of a bird to its mate.

CALLOSITY, [kal-os'-it-i], *n.* a part of the skin hardened by friction. [Fr. *callosité* from L. *callus* hardened skin].

CALLIPERS

CALLOUS, [kal'-us], *adj.* (of skin) hardened; (*fig.*) unfeeling, indifferent to other people's pain and sorrow. [L. *callosus* hard-skinned].

CALLOUSLY, [kal'-us-li], *adv.* in a callous way.

CALLOUSNESS, [kal'-us-nes], *n.* the condition of being callous.

CALLOW, [kal'-ō], *adj.* (of birds) unfledged, bare of feathers; (*fig.*) (of boys and youths) immature, clumsy. [OE. *calu* bald, bare].

CALLOWNESS, [kal'-ō-nes], *n.* the condition of being callow.

CALLUS, [kal'-us], *n.* (*med.*) a callosity, a lump forming round a bone during healing after fracture. [L. *callus*].

CALM (1), [kahm], *n.* the condition of the atmosphere or weather when there is no wind at all; (*fig.*) (of the mind or of a state of affairs) quiet, tranquillity. [Fr. *calme*].

CALM (2), [kahm], *adj.* windless; tranquil, not agitated, leisurely.

CALM (3), [kahm] *v.t. and i.* to make or become calm; to smooth, pacify, settle down; **to c. down,** to soothe, appease.

CALMATIVE (1), [kahm'-a-tiv], *n.* (*med.*) sedative, a drug which induces calmness and quiet in the patient.

CALMATIVE (2), [kahm'-a-tiv], *adj.* having a calming or sedative effect.

CALMLY, [kahm'-li], *adv.* in a calm way.

CALMNESS, [kahm'-nes], *n.* the condition of being calm.

CALOMEL, [kal'-ō-mel], *n.* (*med.*) a chloride of mercury, useful as a purgative. [Gk. *kalos* fair and *melas* black].

CALORESCENCE, [kal'-or-es'-ents], *n.* (*phys.*) the changing of light rays into heat rays. [L. *calescens* growing hot, influenced by CALORIE].

CALORIC (1), [kal-or'-ik], *n.* warmth, heat.

CALORIC (2), [kal-or'-ik], *adj.* relating to heat.

CALORICITY, [kal'-or-is'-i-ti], *n.* the power of producing heat.

CALORIE, [kal'-or-i], *n.* a standard unit of heat, a heat unit in the determination of nutrition values; **large c.,** a unit of a thousand calories. [Fr. *calorie* from L. *calor* heat].

CALORIFACIENT (1), [kal'-or-i-fā'-shent], *n.* a substance supplying animal heat.

CALORIFACIENT (2), [kal'-or-i-fā'-shent], *adj.* heat-producing, supplying animal heat. [CALORIE and L. *faciens* making].

CALORIFERE, [kal-or'-i-fēer], *n.* a device for distributing heat, *esp.* in conservatories. [CALORIE and L. *ferre* to bear].

CALORIFIC, [kal'-or-if'-ik], *adj.* producing heat; relating to heat; **c. rays,** the invisible heat-giving rays of the sun. [Fr. *calorifique*].

CALORIFICATION, [kal-or'-i-fi-kā'-shun], *n.* the production of heat.

CALORIFIER, [kal-or'-i-fī-er], *n.* an apparatus by which water for domestic and other purposes is heated by contact with steam pipes or hot-water pipes.

CALORIMETER, [kal'-or-im'-it-er], *n.* an apparatus for measuring heat. [CALORIE and METER].

CALOTTE, [kal-ot'], *n.* a skull-cap worn by Roman Catholic ecclesiastics and by English serjeants-at-law; (*arch.*) a small round cavity resembling a cap. [Fr. *calotte*].

CALOTYPE†, [kal'-ō-tīp], *n.* (*phot.*) a process of photography. [Gk. *kalos* beautiful and *typos* form].

CALOYER, [kal'-oi-er], *n.* a monk of the Greek Orthodox Church. [Fr. *caloyer*].

CALPAC, [kal'-pak], *n.* a tall, black, sheepskin hat, worn in the Near East. [Turk. *qal paq*].

CALTHA, [kal'-tha], *n.* (*bot.*) the kingcup, or marsh-marigold.

CALTROP, [kal'-trop, kawl'-trop], *n.* a small instrument with four iron spikes arranged so that when thrown on the ground one always projects upwards, used in medieval warfare to lame enemy horses; (*bot.*) variety of spiny plant or thistle. [OE. *colte-træppe* thistle].

CALUMBA, [kal-um'-ba], *n.* the East African climbing plant *Jateorhiza Calumba,* the root of which is used as a bitter tonic. [*Colombo,* capital of Ceylon].

CALTROP

CALUMET, [kal'-ew-met], *n.* a ceremonial pipe used among the North American Indians. [Fr. *calumet,* L. *calamus* reed].

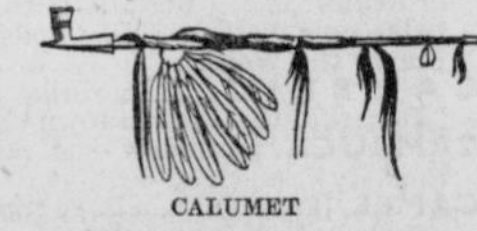

CALUMET

CALUMNIATE, [kal-um'-ni-āt], *v.t.* to spread evil reports concerning, to slander, to speak ill of. [CALUMNY].

CALUMNIATION, [kal-um'-ni-ā'-shun], *n.* the act of calumniating.

CALUMNIATOR, [kal-um'-ni-āt-or], *n.* a person who calumniates.

CALUMNIATORY, [kal-um'-ni-āt-er-i], *adj.* slanderous, calumnious.

CALUMNIOUS, [kal-um'-ni-us], *adj.* pertaining to calumny, slanderous.

CALUMNIOUSLY, [kal-um'-ni-us-li], *adv.* in a calumnious way.

CALUMNIOUSNESS, [kal-um'-ni-us-nes], *n.* the condition of being calumnious.

CALUMNY, [kal'-um-ni], *n.* a false charge, slander, an injurious report about a person. [Fr. *calomnie* from L. *calumnia* intrigue].

CALVARY, [kal'-va-ri], *n.* the place where the Crucifixion took place; a model of the Crucifixion in the open air, consisting of the figures of Christ and the two thieves crucified, and erected for devotional purposes; (*her.*) a cross erected upon steps. [L. *calvaria* skull, a translation of Heb. *gulgoleth* skull].

CALVE, [kahv], *v.i.* to give birth to a calf. [OE. *calfian*].

CALVES-FOOT, [kahvz'-fŏŏt], *adj.* denoting a jelly for invalids made from the boiled foot of a calf.

CALVES-SNOUT, [kahvz'-snowt], *n.* the flowering plant snapdragon.

CALVINISM, [kal'-vin-izm], *n.* an austere religious system evolved by Jean *Calvin* (1509-1564), a French Protestant reformer.

CALVINIST, [kal'-vin-ist], *n.* a follower of Calvin and his doctrines.
CALVINISTIC, [kal'-vin-ist'-ik], *adj.* relating to Calvinism; (*fig.*) stern, morally strict.
CALVINISTICAL, [kal'-vin-ist'-ik-al], *adj.* Calvinistic.
CALX, [kalks], *n.* lime, chalk; the residue of a substance after calcination. [L. *calx*].
CALYCINAL, [kal-is'-in-al], *adj.* relating to a calyx.
CALYCINE, [kal'-ī-sīn], *adj.* calycinal.
CALYCLE, [kal'-ikl], *n.* (*bot.*) a row of small leaves on the outside of the base of a calyx. [L. *calyculus*].
CALYPTRA, [kal-ip'-tra], *n.* (*bot.*) the hood of mosses. [Gk. *kaluptra* covering].
CALYPTRATE, [kal-ip'-trāt], *adj.* (*bot.*) possessing a calyptra.
CALYPTRIFORM, [kal-ip'-tri-fawm], *adj.* having the form of a calyptra.
CALYX, [kāl'-iks], *n.* (*bot.*) the cup-shaped whorl of sepals of a flower. [Gk. *kalux* cup].
CAM (1), [kam], *n.* (*mech.*) a projection on the edge of a wheel, for converting a rotary motion to a sudden reciprocal motion. [Du. *kam* comb].
CAM (2), KAM, [kam], *adj.* awry, crooked. [Wel. *cam*].
CAMAIEU, [kam'-ī-yur'], *n.* a cameo; the technique of painting in monochrome. [Fr. *camaieu*].
CAMARADERIE, [kam'-er-ahd'-er-ē'], *n* loyalty and good fellowship. [Fr. *camaraderie*].
CAMARILLA, [kam'-ar-ēl'-ya], *n.* a little room, an audience chamber in a palace; (*fig.*) a cabal. [Span. *camarilla*].
CAMATINA, [kam'-a-tēn'-a], *n.* immature acorns used in tanning. [It. *camatina*].
CAMBER (1), [kam'-ber], *n.* a slight convex curving of a road section or ship's deck; the gradual raising of the level of a curved road towards its outer radius; the curvature of the wing sections of an aeroplane.
CAMBER (2), [kam'-ber], *v.t. and i.* to curve or arch; to make a camber. [Fr. *cambrer* to curve, bend].
CAMBERING, [kam'-ber-ing], *adj.* having a camber.
CAMBIST, [kam'-bist], *n.* a banker; one expert in cambistry. [Fr. *cambiste*].
CAMBISTRY, [kam'-bis-tri], *n.* (*comm.*) a knowledge of foreign exchange.
CAMBIUM, [kam'-bi-um], *n.* (*bot.*) the pith or soft tissue lying beneath the bark from which both new wood and bark is developed. [L. *cambium* change].
CAMBLET, see CAMLET.
CAMBREL, [kam'-brel], *n.* a wooden hook for hanging up meat. [Unkn.].
CAMBRIAN, [kam'-bri-an], *adj.* relating to Cambria, or Wales; (*geol.*) pertaining to the first stage of the palaeozoic period. [L. *Cambria* Wales from Wel. *Cymry* the Welsh].
CAMBRIC, [kām'-brik], *n.* fine white linen. [*Kamerijk*, the French town Cambrai].
CAMBUCA, [kam-bew'-ka], *n.* a bishop's staff. [L. *cambuca*].
CAMEL, [kam'-el], *n.* a large ruminant ungulate quadruped of genus *Camelus*, with a thick coarse coat, large flat feet and one (**Arabian c.** or dromedary) or two humps (**Bactrian c.**), used in desert regions for transport; a large floating device used to carry ships over bars into a port. [OE. *camel*, L. *camelus*].

CAMBUCA

CAMEL-BACKED, [kam'-el-bakt'], *adj.* having a hump on the back like a camel.
CAMEL-CORPS, [kam'-el-kaw'], *n.* a troop of soldiers mounted on camels.
CAMELEAN, see CHAMELEON (1).
CAMEL-HAIR, [kam'-el-hāer'], *n.* the rough hair of the camel; fine hair from a squirrel's tail for making paint brushes.
CAMELLIA, [kam-ēl'-ia], *n.* a species of Asiatic evergreen shrub. [Joseph *Kamel*, a Jesuit who brought it to Europe from China in the eighteenth century].
CAMELOPARD, [kam-el'-o-pahd'], *n.* †a giraffe; (*fig.*) a tall, ungainly woman. [L. *camelopardus*].
CAMELOT†, see CAMLET.
CAMELRY, [kam'-el-ri], *n.* a troop of soldiers mounted on camels. [CAMEL and (CAVAL)RY].
CAMEMBERT, [kam'-om-bāer], *n.* a rich cheese with a powerful odour. [*Camembert*, a village in Normandy, where first made].
CAMEO, [kam'-i-ō], *n.* a piece of jewellery cut from a stone that has layers of different colours, e.g. agate, so that the design cut in one layer contrasts with the background formed by the next; **c. ware,** a pottery such as that produced by Wedgwood in which the raised design is contrasted with a background in a different colour. [It. *cameo*].
CAMERA, [kam'-er-a], *n.* (*phot.*) a light-tight box or other structure with a lens at one end throwing an inverted image of what stands before it upon a sensitized photographic plate or film placed at the other end; (*arch.*) a vaulted roof; **c. lucida,** (*opt.*) prismatic apparatus which projects an image from a microscope eyepiece upon a piece of paper so that the image can be easily drawn; **c. obscura,** (*opt.*) a dark room fitted with a lens to throw an image of things outside upon a screen; **in c.,** (*leg.*) in private, with the public excluded. [L. *camera* vault].

CAMERA

CAMERA-CRAFT, [kam'-er-a-krahft'], *n.* the art of photography.
CAMERALISTICS, [kam'-er-al-ist'-iks], *n.* the specialized study of public finance. [Germ. *kameral* pertaining to chamber, bureau in which state business is performed].
CAMERA-REPORTER, [kam'-er-a-ri-pawt'-er], *n.* a press photographer.
CAMERATE (1), [kam'-er-āt], *adj.* (*zool.*) separated into compartments. [L. *cameratus*].
CAMERATE†, (2), [kam'-er-āt], *v.t.* (*arch.*) to construct in the form of an arch or vault.
CAMERATED, [kam'-er-āt-id], *adj.* (*zool.*) camerate; (*arch.*) †arched or vaulted.
CAMERLENGO, CAMERLINGO, [kam'-er-leng'-gō], *n.* the papal chamberlain, invariably a cardinal, in charge of the papal treasury. [It. *camerlingo* chamberlain].
CAMERON, [kam'-er-on], *n.* a large freshwater prawn, like a crayfish. [Span. *cameron* shrimp].
CAM-GEAR, [kam'-gēer], *n.* (*motoring*) a train of wheels actuating the camshaft.
CAMI-KNICKS, CAMI-KNICKERS, [kam'-i-niks], *n.*(*pl.*) a woman's undergarment, a bodice and knickers in one piece. [CAMI(SOLE) and KNICK(ER)S].
CAMION, [kam'-i-on], *n.* a flat low four-wheeled motor or horse truck.
CAMISADE, CAMISADO, [kam'-i-sād'(-ō)], *n.* a nocturnal attack by soldiers wearing shirts over their armour, so as to recognize each other. [Span. *camisada* from *camisa* shirt].
CAMISOLE, [kam'-i-sōl], *n.* a woman's garment, consisting of a short bodice worn under the dress. [Fr. *camisole*].
CAMLET, CAMBLET, CAMELOT, [kam'-let, kam'-i-lot], *n.* a thin material originally made of camel's hair, but now usually of wool and silk. [Fr. *camelot*].
CAMOMILE, CHAMOMILE, [kam'-om-il], *n.* a strong-scented bitter plant used medicinally and for toilet purposes. [Fr. *camomille*].
CAMOUFLAGE (1), [kam'-ōō-flahzh'], *n.* (*milit.*) the disguising or hiding of objects from the enemy; the practice of making an object or idea appear different from what it is. [Fr. *camouflage*].
CAMOUFLAGE (2), [kam'-ōō-flahzh], *v.t.* to conceal or disguise by camouflage.
CAMOUFLET, [kam'-ōō-flā], *n.* (*milit.*) a small mine placed so as to kill or cut off the line of escape of counterminers; a similar kind of bomb. [Fr. *camouflet*].
CAMP (1), [kamp], *n.* a tract of ground where tents and other temporary shelters are erected for soldiers or others; persons inhabiting such a place; any structure erected for temporary shelter in open country; (*fig.*) the soldier's life; a faction, party. [Fr. *camp* from L. *campus* field].
CAMP (2), [kamp], *v.i.* to pitch a camp; to encamp; to take up temporary quarters; **to c. out,** to live, sleep in a tent or the open-air.
CAMPAGNOL, [kam'-pan-yol'], *n.* the short-tailed field-mouse, or field-vole. [Fr. *campagnol*].
CAMPAIGN (1), [kam-pān'], *n.* (*milit.*) a series of concerted military operations towards a single objective; the length of time that an army is in the field at a stretch; a series of actions planned with a definite purpose. [Fr. *campagne* tract of open country].
CAMPAIGN (2), [kam-pān'], *v.i.* to direct or work in a campaign.
CAMPAIGNER, [kam-pān'-er], *n.* one who campaigns; one who has served in many campaigns, a veteran soldier.

CAMPANERO, [kam'-pan-āer-ō], *n.* the white-plumaged South American bell-bird. [Span. *campanero* bell-ringer].
CAMPANIFORM, [kam-pan'-i-fawm], *adj.* (*bot.*) shaped like a bell.
CAMPANILE, [kam'-pan-īl, kam-pan-ēl'-i], *n.* a high detached bell-tower. [It. *campanile*].
CAMPANOLOGIST, [kam'-pan-ol'-oj-ist] *n.* an exponent of campanology.
CAMPANOLOGY, [kam'-pan-ol'-o-ji], *n.* the art of bell-ringing. [L. *campana* bell and Gk. *logos* speech].
CAMPANULA, [kam-pan'-ew-la], *n.* (*bot.*) a genus of plants, including the bell-flowers. [~L. *campana* bell].
CAMPANULATE, [kam-pan'-ew-lāt], *adj.* (*bot.*) shaped like a bell.
CAMP-BED, [kamp'-bed'], *n.* a camp-bedstead.
CAMP-BEDSTEAD, [kamp'-bed'-sted], *n.* a narrow bedstead made to fold up so that it can be readily carried or packed away.
CAMPEACHY-WOOD, [kam-pēch'-i-wŏŏd], *n.* logwood. [*Campeche*, a town in Mexico].
CAMPER, [kam'-per], *n.* one who camps in the open.
CAMPESTRAL, [kam-pes'-tral], *adj.* pertaining to or growing in fields. [L. *campester*].
CAMP-FIGHT, [kamp'-fīt'], *n.* (*leg.*) †a legal trial by duel.
CAMP-FOLLOWER, [kamp'-fol'-ō-er], *n.* a non-combatant, male or female, who follows an army on the march or hangs about a military camp.
CAMPHINE, CAMPHENE, [kam'-fēn], *n.* a hydrocarbon which crystallizes in white prisms.
CAMPHOR, [kam'-fer], *n.* a volatile, strong-smelling, semi-transparent solid substance, whitish in colour, useful in medicine, procured by distillation chiefly from the Japanese camphor-laurel; **c. balls,** small pellets or balls of naphthalene placed amongst clothes to keep away moths. [MdL. *camphora*, Arab *kafur*].
CAMPHORACEOUS, [kam'-for-ā'-shus], *adj.* resembling camphor.
CAMPHORATE (1), [kam'-for-āt], *n.* a salt formed from camphoric acid and a base.
CAMPHORATE (2), [kam'-for-āt], *v.t.* to permeate or impregnate with camphor.
CAMPHORIC, [kam-for'-ik], *adj.* containing or pertaining to camphor; **c. acid,** an acid produced by successive distillations of camphor.
CAMPHOR-OIL, [kam'-for-oil'], *n.* a fragrant essence distilled from the *Dryobalanops Camphora* of Borneo.
CAMPHOR-TREE, [kam'-for-trē], *n.* the tree which bears the common camphor, a species of *Cinnamomum*.
CAMPING, [kamp'-ing], *n.* the act of living in camp.
CAMPION, [kam'-pi-on], *n.* (*bot.*) one of the plants included in the genera *Lychnis* or *Silene*. [Uncert.].
CAMP-MEETING, [kamp'-mēt'-ing], *n.* an open-air religious meeting.
CAMP-STOOL, [kamp'-stōōl'], *n.* a folding stool.
CAMPUS, [kamp'-us], *n.* (*U.S.*) the grounds of a school or university. [L. *campus* a field].
CAMPYLOSPERMOUS, [kamp'-il-ō-spur'-mus], *adj.* (*bot.*) having the seed curved at the margin. [Gk. *kampulos* bent and SPERM].
CAMPYLOTROPAL, [kam'-pil-ot'-rop-al], *adj.* (*bot.*) campylotropous.
CAMPYLOTROPOUS, [kam'-pil-ot'-rop-us], *adj.* (*bot.*) curved so that the apex of the ovule is close to the base. [Gk. *kampulos* bent and *tropos* turned].
CAMSHAFT, [kam'-shahft'], *n.* (*motoring*) a rotating shaft to which cams are attached to lift the valves.

CAMSHAFT

CAM-WHEEL, [kam'-wēl'], *n.* a wheel with a cam on its periphery.
CAMWOOD, [kam'-wŏŏd], *n.* a red dye-wood, a variety of *Baphia*. [Unkn.].
CAN (1), [kan], *n.* a small metal container. [OE. *canne* cup].
CAN (2), [kan], *v.t.* to put into, preserve in, an air-tight can; **c. it,** (*slang*) stop such talk.

CAM-WHEEL

CAN (3), (**could**), [kan], *pres.t. of v.* to be able to; to know how to, to have the power to. [OE. *cann*, *pres.t.* of *cunnan*].
CANADIAN (1), [kan-ā'-di-an], *n.* a native of Canada.
CANADIAN (2), [kan-ā'-di-an], *adj.* pertaining to Canada.
CANAILLE, [kan-ī'], *n.* the rabble. [Fr. *canaille* from L. *canis* dog].
CANAL, [kan-al'], *n.* an artificial watercourse made for navigation or irrigation; (*anat.*) a duct in a living body; (*zool.*) flute or groove in structure of a shell to allow for the passage of the breathing-tube; **c. rays,** (*phys.*) positive rays. [L. *canalis* water-pipe].
CANALICULATE, [kan'-al-ik'-yōō-lāt], *adj.* (*biol.*) finely channelled, furrowed, ridged.
CANALICULATED, [kan'-al-ik'-yōō-lāt-id], *adj.* (*biol.*) canaliculate.
CANALIZATION, [kan'-al-īz-ā'-shun] *n.* the making of canals; the canal system of a district.
CANALIZE, [kan'-al-īz], *v.t.* to make into a canal; provide with canals.
CANARD, [kan-ahr'], *n.* a hoax; an invented story palmed off as a fact; (*aeron.*) an aeroplane with the elevator in front of the main planes. [Fr. *canard* duck, breach of etiquette].
CANARY (1), [kan-āer'-i], *n.* a yellow or greenish-yellow song-bird; †a wine very popular in England in the sixteenth and seventeenth centuries. [*Canary* Islands, where found].
CANARY (2), [kan-āer'-i], *adj.* like a canary; bright yellow.
CANARY-COLOURED, [kan-āer'-i-kul'-erd], *adj.* bright yellow.
CANARY-CREEPER, [kan-āer'-i-krēp'-er], *n.* a climbing plant with yellow flowers, a species of *Tropaeolum*.
CANARY-GRASS, [kan-āer'-i-grahs], *n.* the canary-seed plant, a species of *Phalaris*.
CANASTER, [kan-ast'-er], *n.* a rush basket used for packing tobacco, a kind of coarse tobacco. [Span. *canastro*].
CAN-BUOY, [kan'-boi], *n.* (*naut.*) a large buoy in the shape of a cone.
CAN-CAN, [kan'-kan'], *n.* a wild dance, in which there is much high kicking. [Fr. *cancan*].
CANCEL (1), [kan'-sel], *n.* something deleted; a punch for tickets; a leaf in a book substituted for that originally printed; the leaf so deleted.
CANCEL (2), [kan'-sel], *v.t. and i.* to cross out, delete; to wipe out; to countermand, to annul; to neutralize, balance; (*math.*) to take out the same factor on both sides of an equation or fraction; **c. out,** to balance, neutralize. [L. *cancellare* to enclose with a lattice, to strike out with crosswise strokes].
CANCELLATED, [kan'-sel-āt-id], *adj.* (*bot.*) reticulated. [L. *cancellatus* latticed].
CANCELLATION, [kan'-sel-ā-shun], *n.* the act of cancelling, the fact of being cancelled.
CANCER, [kan'-ser], *n.* the constellation of the Crab, the fourth sign of the Zodiac; (*med.*) malignant tumour having the appearance of a crab with claws outstretched, which gradually consumes the tissues of the body; (*fig.*) any similar corruptive or destructive evil; **tropic of C.,** parallel of latitude 23° 27′ north of the equator. [L. *cancer* crab].
CANCERATE, [kan'-ser-āt], *v.i.* to grow cancerous.
CANCERATION, [kan'-ser-ā-shun], *n.* the process of becoming cancerous.
CANCEROUS, [kan'-ser-us], *adj.* pertaining to, or like, a cancer.
CANCEROUSLY, [kan'-ser-us-li], *adv.* after the manner of a cancer.
CANCEROUSNESS, [kan'-ser-us-nes], *n.* the condition of being cancerous.
CANCRIFORM, [kang'-kri-fawm], *adj.* shaped like a crab; (*path.*) like a cancer tumour.
CANCRINE, [kang'-krīn], *adj.* possessing the qualities of a crab.
CANCRINITE, [kang'-krin-īt], *n.* (*min.*) a silicate of aluminium and sodium found in Russia. [*Cancrin*, a Russian statesman].
CANCROID, [kang'-kroid], *adj.* resembling cancer; resembling a crab.
CANDELABRA, (*pl.* **candelabras**), [kan'-dil-ab'-ra], *n.* a branched candlestick holding several candles. [L. *candelabra*, *pl.* of *candelabrum* candlestick].
CANDENT, [kand'-ent], *adj.* white-hot, glowing with heat. [L. *candens* shining, glowing].
CANDID, [kand'-id], *adj.* frank, outspoken, sincere; (*phot.*) of, or pertaining to, informal photographs. [Fr. *candide* from L. *candidus* white, pure].
CANDIDACY, [kand'-id-as-i], *n.* the state of being a candidate for any office, examination or prize.
CANDIDATE, [kand'-i-dāt], *n.* one offering himself

for appointment, election or examination. [L. *candidatus* dressed in white (as customary for candidates for office in Rome)].

CANDIDATESHIP, [kand'-i-dat-ship']. *n.* candidacy.

CANDIDATURE, [kand'-i-da-chooer], *n.* the condition of being a candidate.

CANDIDLY, [kand'-id-li], *adv.* in a candid fashion.

CANDIDNESS, [kand'-id-nes], *n.* the state or quality of being candid.

CANDIED, [kand'-id], *adj.* sweet, covered with sugar; (*fig.*) suave, flattering. [CANDY (2)].

CANDLE, [kandl], *n.* a simple device for illumination consisting of a narrow cylinder of wax, tallow, etc., surrounding a wick which is ignited; **c.-power**, unit of measurement of light, being the amount of light given by a standard weight candle (2½ oz.), burning at a rate of 120 grains per hour; **Roman c.**, a firework discharging coloured stars; **not fit to hold a c. to**, not to be compared with, vastly inferior to; **with bell, book and c.**, with the observance of due form and ceremony (the objects named being used in excommunication); **to burn the c. at both ends**, to dissipate one's energy by doing too many things at once, or for too long at a stretch. [OE. *candel* from L. *candela*].

CANDLEBERRY, [kandl'-be'-ri], *n.* the wax-myrtle or its berry.

CANDLE-BOMB, [kandl'-bom'], *n.* a small glass bubble, filled with water, placed in the wick of a candle so that it explodes.

CANDLE-COAL, see CANNEL-COAL.

CANDLE-LIGHT, [kandl'-lit'], *n.* the light of a candle.

CANDLEMAS, [kandl'-mas], *n.* the Feast of the Purification of the Blessed Virgin (February 2). [OE. *Candelmæsse*].

CANDLESTICK, [kandl'-stik], *n.* a stand for a candle. [OE. *candelsticca*].

CANDLE-TREE, [kandl'-trē], *n.* the Central American tree, wax-myrtle, *Parmentiera cerifera*.

CANDLE-WICK, [kandl'-wik], *n.* the wick in a candle.

CANDOCK, [kand'-ok], *n.* the yellow or the white water-lily. [CAN (1) and DOCK].

CANDOUR, [kand'-er], *n.* impartiality, frankness and justice of speech and thought. [L. *candor* whiteness].

CANDY (1), [kand'-i], *n.* a form of sugar obtained after repeated boiling and evaporation; (*U.S.*) a sweetmeat, sweets. [Fr. (*sucre*) *candi* from Arab. *qand* sugar].

CANDY (2), [kand'-i], *v.t. and i.* to encrust (fruit, etc.) with candy.

CANDYTUFT, [kand'-i-tuft'], *n.* a plant of the genus *Iberis*. [*Candia*, a place in Crete, and TUFT].

CANE (1), [kān], *n.* the hollow jointed hard stem of large reeds, bamboo, etc.; a walking-stick, a stick for punishing schoolboys; canes prepared for use in making chairs, etc.; stem of fruit-bushes such as the raspberry and loganberry; a slender stick of sealing-wax, sulphur, etc. [Gk. *kanna* reed].

CANE (2), [kān], *v.t.* to punish by beating with a cane; to make or repair the back or seat of a chair with strips of split cane.

CANE-BRAKE, [kān'-brāk], *n.* a cane thicket.

CANE CHAIR, [kān chāer'], *n.* a chair made of, or with a seat of, woven cane.

CANE-HOLE, [kān'-hōl], *n.* a ditch for planting sugar-cane cuttings.

CANE-MILL, [kān'-mil'], *n.* a mill for grinding down sugar-canes.

CANEPHOR, [kan-ĕ'-fawr], *n.* a sculptured figure of a Greek youth or maiden carrying a basket on the head. [Gk. *kanephoros* bearing a basket].

CANESCENT, [kan-es'-ent], *adj.* dull white or hoary. [L. *canescens* growing hoary].

CANE-SUGAR, [kān'-shoog'-er], *n.* sugar extracted from sugar-cane.

CANE-TRASH, [kān'-trash'], *n.* the refuse of sugar-cane.

CANGUE, [kang], *n.* a form of Chinese pillory consisting of a large, square, wooden board which is placed round the victim's neck. [Fr. *cangue* from Portug. *canga* yoke].

CANGUE

CANHOOK, [kan'-hook], *n.* an instrument for slinging a cask.

CANICULAR, [kan-ik'-yool-er], *adj.* relating to the dog-star; excessively hot, as in the dog-days.

CANINE, [kan'-īn], *adj.* pertaining to a dog; **c. teeth**, two pairs of sharp, pointed teeth between the incisors and the premolars. [L. *caninus*].

CANING, [kān'-ing], *n.* corporal punishment with a cane.

CANISTER, [kan'-ist-er], *n.* a small box or can generally of metal, in which tea, sugar, tobacco, etc., are stored; **c. shot**, old-fashioned ammunition in the form of a case containing shot, which, when discharged, exploded and sprayed out the shot. [L. *canistrum* wicker-basket].

CANKER (1), [kang'-ker], *n.* an ulcerous sore, a small sore found in the mouth of children; a disease in a horse's foot; an ulcer affecting the ears of dogs and cats; a disease which attacks and rots the bark and wood of trees; the dog-rose; (*fig.*) anything which corrupts and destroys. [L. *cancer*].

CANKER (2), [kang'-ker], *v.t.* to corrupt or destroy by canker; *v.i.* to be afflicted with canker.

CANKERED, [kang'-kerd], *adj.* disgruntled; ill-natured.

CANKER-FLY, [kang'-ker-flī'], *n.* a fly that eats and damages fruit.

CANKEROUS, [kang'-ker-us], *adj.* affected by, corroding like, a canker.

CANKER-WORM, [kang'-ker-wurm'], *n.* an insect very destructive to plants and fruit-trees.

CANKERY, [kang'-ker-i], *adj.* cankered.

CANNA, [kan'-a], *n.* a numerous genus of tropical plants. [L. *canna* cane].

CANNABIN, [kan'-a-bin], *n.* a resin obtained from hemp. [~L. *cannabis* hemp].

CANNED, [kand], *adj.* packed and sold in cans; (*coll.*) (of music) recorded; (*coll.*) intoxicated.

CANNEL-COAL, CANDLE-COAL, [kan'-el-kōl'], *n.* a variety of hard bituminous smokeless coal. [CANDLE and COAL].

CANNELON, [kan'-el-on], *n.* a narrow roll of paste filled with minced meat or jam, baked or fried. [Fr. *cannelon*].

CANNELURE, [kan'-el-ewer], *n.* (*arch.*) a groove or fluting. [Fr. *cannelure*].

CANNEQUIN, [kan'-ek-in], *n.* an East Indies white cotton cloth. [Fr. *cannequin* from Portug. *canequim*].

CANNERY, [kan'-er-i], *n.* a factory where foodstuffs are canned.

CANNIBAL (1), [kan'-i-bal], *n.* a human being who eats the flesh of other human beings; an animal which eats others of its own kind. [Span. *Caribal* a native of the Carib Islands].

CANNIBAL (2), [kan'-i-bal], *adj.* pertaining to cannibals or cannibalism.

CANNIBALISM, [kan'-ib-al-izm], *n.* the act of being a cannibal; (*fig.*) monstrous, inhuman cruelty.

CANNIBALLY, [kan'-ib-al-i], *adv.* in cannibal fashion.

CANNIKIN, [kan'-i-kin], *n.* a small can. [*Dim.* of CAN (1)].

CANNILY, [kan'-i-li], *adv.* in canny fashion.

CANNINESS, [kan'-i-nes], *n.* the quality of being canny.

CANNING, [kan'-ing], *n.* the trade or process of preserving foodstuffs in sealed cans.

CANNON (1), [kan'-on], *n.* a large mounted gun for heavy ammunition. [It. *cannone* large tube or pipe].

CANNON (2), [kan'-on], *n.* a stroke in billiards in which the cue-ball is made to strike the other two balls in succession. [Uncert.].

CANNON (3), [kan'-on], *v.i.* to make a cannon in billiards; **to c. into**, to bump heavily into.

CANNONADE, [kan'-un-ād'], *n.* a rapid and sustained discharge of artillery, a bombardment; the noise of this.

CANNON-BALL, [kan'-on-bawl'], *n.* a ball of iron or stone discharged from a cannon.

CANNON-BIT, CANON-BIT, [kan'-on-bit'], *n.* a round smooth bit for a horse.

CANNON-BONE, [kan'-on-bōn'], *n.* the bone in a horse's leg between the hock and the fetlock.

CANNONEER, CANNONIER, [kan'-on-ēer'], *n.* a soldier who fires a cannon.

CANNON-PROOF, [kan'-on-proof'], *adj.* safe from damage by cannon-shot.

CANNON-SHELL, [kan'-on-shel'], *n.* a shell for use in a cannon, *esp.* one of small calibre.

CANNON-SHOT, [kan'-on-shot'], *n.* ammunition for cannon, cannon-balls; the firing range of a cannon.
CANNOT, [kan'-ot], *pres.t.* (*negative*) of CAN.
CANNULA, [kan'-yŏŏl-a], *n.* a surgical metal tube. [L. *cannula*].
CANNULAR, [kan'-yŏŏl-er], *adj.* tubular.
CANNY, [kan'-i], *adj. and adv.* (*coll.*) shrewd; cautious; knowing; **to ca' c.** (=**to call c.**), to be cautious, go carefully; to slack off work during working hours, to limit output. [OScand. *kaenn* skilful].
CANOE (1), [kan-ōō'], *n.* a light boat propelled by paddles. [Span. *canoa*].
CANOE (2), [kan-ōō'], *v.i.* to go in a canoe.
CANOEIST, [kan-ōō'-ist], *n.* one skilled in propelling a canoe.
CANON, cañon (1), see CANYON.
CANON (2), [kan'-on], *n.* (*eccles.*) a body of laws or rules set up by the Church to which doctrine and conduct, etc., must conform; the collection of books of Holy Scripture recognized by the Christian Church as divinely inspired models of faith and conduct; general standard, rule or criterion for conduct, taste, or for sorting the genuine and spurious works of an author; those writings of an author which are accepted as authentic; (*mus.*) a continued fugue; (*typ.*) name of a large kind of type; (*surg.*) implement used in sewing up wounds; **c. law,** ecclesiastical law. [OFr. *canun* from Gk. *kanon* carpenter's rule, standard].
CANON (3), [kan'-on], *n.* a dignitary of the Church, a member of a cathedral chapter; **minor c.,** a canon who conducts services in a cathedral, but who is not a member of the chapter. [OFr. *canoine* from L. *canonicus* man subject to rule].
CANON-BIT, see CANNON-BIT.
CANONESS, [kan'-on-es], *n.* a woman who holds an ecclesiastical benefice; a nun following a rule similar to that of canons.
CANONIC, [kan-on'-ik], *adj.* canonical.
CANONICAL, [kan-on'-ikl], *adj.* prescribed by, according to or pertaining to the canon; orthodox; regular; **c. hours,** official times for prayer. [*Prec.*].
CANONICALLY, [kan-on'-ik-al-i], *adv.* in a canonical manner.
CANONICALNESS, [kan-on'-ik-al-nes], *n.* the state or quality of being canonical.
CANONICALS, [kan-on'-ik-alz], *n.*(*pl.*) the robes and vestments prescribed for any particular ecclesiastical or academic rank or office.
CANONICATE, [kan-on'-ik-āt], *n.* the rank or office of a canon.
CANONICITY, [kan'-on-is'-i-ti], *n.* canonicalness.
CANONIST, [kan'-on-ist], *n.* one expert in canon law.
CANONISTIC, [kan'-on-ist'-ik], *adj.* relating to a canonist.
CANONIZATION, [kan'-on-iz-ā'-shun], *n.* the act or process of canonizing.
CANONIZE, [kan'-on-īz], *v.t.* (*R.C.*) to declare officially to be a saint.
CANONRY, [kan'-on-ri], *n.* the office of a canon.
CANOODLE, [ka-nōōdl'], *v.t. and i.* (*coll.*) to caress, fondle, cuddle. [Unkn.].
CAN-OPENER, [kan'-ōp'-ner], *n.* an instrument for opening sealed cans of preserved food.
CANOPIED, [kan'-ōp-id] *adj.* provided with a canopy.
CANOPUS, [kan-ōp'-us], *n.* a star in the constellation *Argo.* [Gk. *kanopos*].
CANOPY (1), [kan'-o-pi], *n.* a covering, often richly embroidered, forming a roof over a bed, throne, etc.; a covering supported by poles and held over the head of a distinguished person at state functions; (*arch.*) a wood or stone roof over a pulpit, a statue, etc. [Gk. *konopeion* a bed with mosquito net].
CANOPY (2), [kan'-op-i], *v.t. and i.* to provide or cover with a canopy.
CANOROUS, [kan-awr'-us], *adj.* tuneful, sonorous. [L. *canorus*].
CANT (1), [kant], *n.* the plaintive whining of beggars; the peculiar slang of beggars and thieves; the clichés or catchphrases of any sect or group of people; insincere platitudes; hypocritical religious or political jargon. [CANT (3)].
CANT (2), [kant], *n.* an inclining of anything, a slope, slant. [ODan. *kant*].
CANT (3), [kant], *v.i.* to utter platitudes or clichés, the truth of which is not doubtful. [L. *cantare* sing, talk in sing-song fashion].
CANT (4), [kant], *v.t.* to cause to slope; *v.i.* to slope, incline to one side. [CANT (2)].
CANTAB, [kant'-ab], *n.* member, past or present, of the university of Cambridge. [Abbreviation of L. *Cantabrigiensis* of Cambridge].
CANTABILE, [can-tah'-bil-i], *adj.* (*mus.*) in a tuneful singing style. [It. *cantabile*].
CANTALOUPE, CANTALOUP, [kan'-ta-lōōp'], *n.* a small round species of musk-melon. [*Cantalupo,* a castle in Italy, where first grown in Europe].
CANTANKEROUS, [kan-tang'-ker-us], *adj.* quarrelsome, surly, cross-grained. [Uncert.].
CANTATA, [kan-tah'-ta], *n.* (*mus.*) a dramatic choral work; a musical setting of a narrative or dramatic poem, containing choruses, recitatives and arias. [It. *cantata*].
CANTATRICE, [kant'-at-rēs], *n.* a female singer. [Fr. *cantatrice*].
CANTEEN, [kant-ēn'], *n.* a refreshment bar and store, *esp.* in a camp, barracks, factory, etc.; soldier's drinking-bottle; a complete outfit of table cutlery. [Fr. *cantine* from It. *cantina* wine-cellar].
CANTER (1), [kant'-er], *n.* a light gentle gallop; **preliminary c.,** (*fig.*) a trial outing. [Abbreviation of *Canter*(*bury pace*), the slow and easy pace of Canterbury pilgrims].
CANTER (2), [kant'-er], *v.t.* to make to canter; *v.i.* to ride or move at a canter.
CANTERBURY, [kant'-er-be-ri], *n.* a stand with rows of partitions for holding music, papers, etc. [*Canterbury* in Kent].
CANTERBURY-BELL, [kant'-er-be-ri-bel'], *n.* the flower *Campanula medium.*
CANTHARIDES, [kanth-a'-rid-ēz], *n.*(*pl.*) blister-beetles, the so-called Spanish flies, used for medicinal purposes when dried. [Gk. *kantharis*].
CANTHARIDIN, [kan-tha'-rid-in], *n.* the principle of cantharides, which causes blistering.
CANTHARUS, [kanth'-a-rus], *n.* a deep drinking-cup with a long stem and loop-shaped handles. [L. *cantharus*].
CANTHOOK, [kant'-hŏŏk], *n.* (*U.S.*) instrument for levering logs.
CANTHUS, [kanth'-us], *n.* the angle or corner of the eye. [Gk. *kanthos*].
CANTICLE, [kant'-ikl], *n.* a short chant or hymn; one of the songs in the Prayer Book; (*pl.*) the Song of Solomon. [L. *canticulum* little song].
CANTILEVER, [kant'-i-lēv-er], *n.* (*arch. eng.*) a long beam projecting from a single support, usually arranged in pairs projecting from adjacent piers and joined by a centre support; a long projecting piece of wood, iron or stone giving support to a balcony, cornice, etc. [CANT (2) and LEVER].

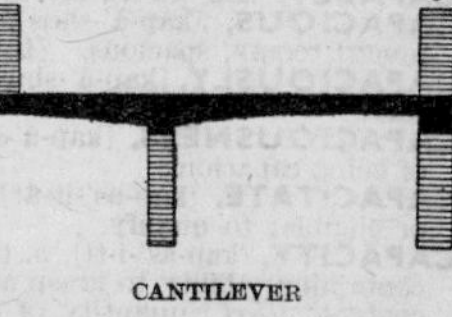
CANTILEVER

CANTILLATE, [kant'-i-lāt], *v.i.* to chant, intone, as in Jewish synagogues. [L. *cantillare* to sing softly].
CANTING, [kant'-ing], *adj.* whining, hypocritical, insincere; (*her.*) allusive. [CANT (3)].
CANTINGLY, [kant'-ing-li], *adv.* in a canting fashion.
CANTLE, [kantl], *n.* the rear, upward, sloping part of a saddle; a segment cut out of anything; a thick slice. [OFr. *cantel*].
CANTLET, [kant'-let], *n.* a small piece or slice, a fragment. [*Prec.*].
CANTO, [kant'-ō], *n.* one of the main divisions of a long poem; (*mus.*) the upper melody of a composition in several parts; **c. fermo,** (*mus.*) the melody on which the counterpoint is based; plainsong. [It. *canto*].
CANTON (1), [kan'-ton', kan'-ton], *n.* a small division of territory; one of the separate states of which Switzerland is composed; (*her.*) a small square division in the upper corner of a shield or flag. [OFr. *canton* corner].
CANTON (2), [kan'-ton], *v.t.* (*her.*) to place in the upper corner of a shield or standard; to quarter troops.
CANTONAL, [kant'-on-al], *adj.* relating to a canton.
CANTONIZE, [kant'-on-īz], *v.t.* to divide into cantons; to parcel out.
CANTONMENT, [kant-ōōn'-ment], *n.* (usually *pl.*) quarters for soldiers.
CANTOR, [kant'-or], *n.* (*eccles.*) a precentor, *esp.* in a synagogue. [L. *cantor* singer].

ō (bone), ī (fine), ōō (food), ŏŏ (put), u (up), th (*th*ink), TH (*th*at), zh (a*z*ure), † = obsolete, ~ = related to.

CANTORIAL, [kant-awr'-i-al], *adj.* belonging to the precentor's or northern side of a choir.
CANVAS (1), [kan'-vas], *n.* a strong coarse cloth made of hemp, etc., used for sacks, tents, sails, etc., and for painting on; **under c.,** (*milit.*) in tents; (*naut.*) under sail. [Fr. *canevas* from L. *cannabis* hemp].
CANVAS (2), [kan'-vas], *adj.* made of canvas.
CANVAS-BACK, [kan'-vas-bak'], *n.* a species of mottled American duck, *Fuligula vallisneriana*.
CANVASS, [kan'-vas], *v.t. and i.* to discuss, examine closely; to solicit votes or orders systematically. [CANVAS, with the idea of 'throwing about in canvas, to discuss,' etc.].
CANVASSER, [kan'-vas-er], *n.* one who canvasses.
CANY, [kān'-i], *adj.* made of cane, full of canes.
CANYON, cañon, [kan'-yon], *n.* a deep and precipitous ravine. [Span. *cañon*].
CANZONE, [kan-tzōn'-ā], *n.* (*mus.*) a two- or three-part song. [It. *canzone*].
CANZONET, [kan'-zon-et'], *n.* (*mus.*) a short air. [*Prec.*].
CAOUTCHINE, [kow-chēn'], *n.* a hydrocarbon found in oil of caoutchouc.
CAOUTCHOUC (1), [kow'-chŏŏk], *n.* rubber in its raw state; india-rubber. [Fr. *caoutchouc*].
CAOUTCHOUC (2), [kow'-chŏŏk], *adj.* made of rubber.
CAP (1), [kap], *n.* a covering for the head usually of cloth or similar material, without a brim and often having a stiffened peak; a round covering over various objects; **c. in hand,** humbly, as a petitioner; **if the c. fits,** if the allusion is applicable; **to set one's c. at,** to try to attract the admiration and attention of. [OE. *cæppe*].
CAP (2), (capping, capped), [kap], *v.t.* to put a cap on (a person's head); to cover or provide with a cap; (*fig.*) to surpass, go one better than, top; to reply to and complete (a quotation); to raise one's cap by way of greeting.
CAPA, [kah'-pa], *n.* the tobacco leaf used to make the outer covering of Havana cigars. [Span. *capa*].
CAPABILITY, [kā'-pa-bil'-i-ti], *n.* the quality of being capable.
CAPABLE, [kāp'-abl], *adj.* possessing ability, competent, clever, skilful, qualified; susceptible of, liable to. [LL. *capabilis* able to seize].
CAPABLENESS, [kāp'-abl-nes], *n.* capability.
CAPABLY, [kāp'-ab-li], *adv.* in a capable fashion.
CAPACIOUS, [kap-ā'-shus], *adj.* able to contain much; roomy, spacious. [L. *capax capacem*].
CAPACIOUSLY, [kap-ā'-shus-li], *adv.* in a capacious way.
CAPACIOUSNESS, [kap-ā'-shus-nes], *n.* the state of being capacious.
CAPACITATE, [kap-as'-it-āt], *v.t.* to make capable or eligible; to qualify.
CAPACITY, [kap-as'-i-ti], *n.* the power of holding or containing; ability to grasp and retain; room; cubic content; (*elect.*) quantity of electricity that a condenser can store; the number of ampère-hours a battery is capable of when charged. [Fr. *capacité* from L. *capacitas*].
CAP-A-PIE, cap-à-pie, [kap'-a-pē'], *adv.* from head to foot; all over; completely. [OFr. *cap a pie*].
CAPARISON (1), [kap-a'-ris-on], *n.* harness, trappings (of a horse); equipment of an armed man. [OFr. *caparasson* preparation].
CAPARISON (2), [kap-a'-ris-on], *v.t.* to furnish with equipment or trappings.
CAPE (1), [kāp], *n.* a loose-fitting sleeveless cloak, usually short; a loose covering for the neck and shoulders, worn chiefly by women or as part of military or police uniforms. [Fr. *cape* from Span. *capa* head-covering].
CAPE (2), [kāp], *n.* a headland, a piece of coast projecting into the sea, a promontory. [Fr. *cap* from L. *caput* head].
CAPE GOOSEBERRY, [kāp-gŏŏz'-ber-i], *n.* the plant, *Physalis capensis*, or its bright orange fruit. [*Cape* of Good Hope].
CAPELIN, CAPLIN, [kap'-el-in], *n.* a small Canadian smelt, *Mallotus villosus*, used as bait. [Fr. *capelin*].
CAPELINE, [kap'-el-ēn], *n.* a lady's evening hood; (*surg.*) hood-shaped bandage.
CAPER (1), [kāp-er], *n.* the flower-bud of a species of shrub, *Capparis*, used in making sauces; the plant itself. [Gk. *kapparis*].
CAPER (2), [kāp'-er], *n.* a playful leap; lively frisking about; (*fig.*) (*pl.*) pranks, giddy and irresponsible behaviour; **to cut capers,** to frisk about in a lively way; (*fig.*) to play foolish tricks. [Uncert.].
CAPER (3), [kāp' er], *v.i.* to jump about, frolic in sprightly fashion.
CAPERCAILZIE, [kā'-per-kāl'-zi], *n.* wood grouse. [~Gael. *capul coille* horse of the wood].
CAPIAS, [kāp'-i-as], *n.* (*leg.*) a writ to authorize seizure of person or goods. [L. *capias* thou mayest take].
CAPIBARA, see CAPYBARA.
CAPILLACEOUS, [kap'-il-ā'-shus], *adj.* hair-like, thin, fine.
CAPILLAIRE, [kap'-il-āer'], *n.* the maidenhair fern; a syrup flavoured with this. [Fr. *capillaire*].
CAPILLAMENT†, [kap-il'-a-ment], *n.* a hair-like filament.
CAPILLARITY, [kap'-il-a'-rit-i], *n.* the quality of being capillary, power of capillary attraction.
CAPILLARY (1), [kap-il'-er-i], *n.* one of the minute hair-like blood vessels.
CAPILLARY (2), [kap-il'-er-i], *adj.* pertaining to hair; resembling a hair; **c. attraction,** physical attraction between a solid and a liquid, which determines the rise and fall of fluid in capillary vessels. [L. *capillaris* from *capillus* hair].
CAPILLIFORM, [kap-il'-i-fawm], *adj.* in the form of hair.
CAPILLITIUM, [kap'-il-ish'-i-um], *n.* (*bot.*) a hair-like structure enclosing the spores of some fungi.
CAPILLOSE, [kap'-il-ōs], *adj.* hairy, covered with hair.
CAPITAL (1), [kap'-itl], *n.* the principal city of a state or country; the wealth amassed by an individual or company and set apart to produce further wealth; money or stock used in starting and carrying on a business; the class of people who possess such wealth; (*print.*) a capital letter; (*fig.*) that which is turned to one's account, personal advantage. [CAPITAL (3)].
CAPITAL (2), [kap'-itl], *n.* (*arch.*) the head of a column. [L. *capitellum*].
CAPITAL (3), [kap'-itl], *adj.* relating to life; punishable by the loss of life; of first importance; chief, principal; excellent; pertaining to or employed as capital. [L. *capitalis*].

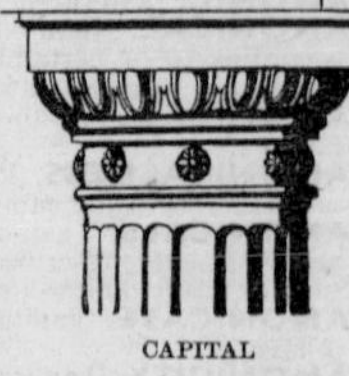
CAPITAL

CAPITALISM, [kap'-it-al-izm], *n.* an economic system under which capital or wealth is owned by individuals.
CAPITALIST, [kap'-it-al-ist], *n.* one who possesses capital, by which he may live; one who believes in and conforms to capitalism.
CAPITALIZATION, [kap'-it-al-iz-ā'-shun], *n.* the act of capitalizing.
CAPITALIZE, [kap'-it-al-iz], *v.t.* to convert into capital; to invest with capital; to convert a periodical payment into a sum equivalent to the amount of capital that would produce it.
CAPITALLY, [kap'-it-al-i], *adv.* in a first-rate or capital way.
CAPITATE, [kap'-it-āt], *adj.* (*bot.*) having a head (of flowers); growing in a head. [L. *capitatus*].
CAPITATION, [kap'-it-ā'-shun], *n.* a tax upon each person; a levy on each individual in a group. [L. *capitatio* poll tax].
CAPITOL, [kap'-it-ol], *n.* a large Roman temple; an important public building, as the seat of the U.S. government at Washington. [L. *Capitolium*, the temple of Jupiter on the Capitol in Rome].
CAPITOLIAN, [kap'-it-ōl'-i-an], *adj.* Capitoline.
CAPITOLINE, [kap'-it-ōl-in], *adj.* belonging or relating to the Capitol in Rome.
CAPITULAR, [ka-pich'-ŏŏ-ler], *adj.* pertaining to a chapter. [L. *capitularis*].
CAPITULARY, [ka-pich'-ŏŏ-ler-i], *n.* a collection of ordinances or decrees of a chapter.
CAPITULATE, [ka-pich'-ŏŏ-lāt], *v.i.* to yield, give in, surrender; (*milit.*) to surrender on terms. [L. *capitulare* to draw up a treaty].
CAPITULATION, [ka-pich'-ŏŏ-lā'-shun], *n.* the act of capitulating; the terms of surrender.
CAPITULATOR, [ka-pich'-ŏŏ-lāt'-or], *n.* a person who capitulates.
CAPITULUM, [ka-pich'-ŏŏ-lum], *n.* (*bot.*) a little head; small compact cluster of flowers in a composite plant; (*anat.*) a piece of bone protruding so as to fit into a hollow of another bone. [L. *capitulum*].
CAPIVI, see COPAIBA.
CAPLIN, see CAPELIN.

CAPNOMANCY, [kap'-nō-man-si], *n.* divination from smoke. [Gk. *kapnos* smoke and *manteia* divination].

CAPNOMOR, [kap'-nom-or], *n.* an oily fluid obtained from the smoke of wood-tar and other organic matter. [Gk. *kapnos* smoke].

CAPOC, KAPOK, [kā'-pok, kap-ok'], *n.* a soft light fibre obtained from cotton-seeds. [Malay *kapoq* cotton-tree].

CAPON, [kāp'-on], *n.* a castrated male fowl, *esp.* one fattened for eating; (*fig.*) a coward, faint-hearted fellow. [Fr. *capon*].

CAPONIER, [kap'-on-ēer'], *n.* (*fort.*) a covered structure across a ditch. [Fr. *caponnier* capon cage].

CAPORAL, [kap'-or-ahl'], *n.* a kind of French tobacco. [Fr. *caporal* corporal].

CAPOT (1), [ka-pot'], *n.* the winning of all tricks at piquet. [Fr. *capot*].

CAPOT (2), [ka-pot'], *v.t.* to make a capot against.

CAPOTE, [ka-pōt'], *n.* a long cloak. [Fr. *capote*].

CAPPAGH-BROWN, [kap'-a-brown'], *n.* a colouring matter obtained from manganese and iron earth-deposits. [*Cappagh*, a place in Ireland, where found].

CAPRATE, [kap'-rāt], *n.* (*chem.*) a salt of capric acid. [~L. *caper* goat].

CAPREOLATE, [kap'-ri-ō-lāt'], *adj.* (*bot.*) having tendrils. [L. *capreolus* tendril].

CAPRIC, [kap'-rik], *adj.* (*chem.*) related to capric acid; **c. acid,** an acid found in butter, etc., having a slight goat-like smell. [~L. *caper* goat].

CAPRICCIO, [kap-rich'-ō], *n.* (*mus.*) a free and often fanciful composition. [It. *capriccio*].

CAPRICCIOSO, [kap-rich'(-i)'ōs'-ō], *adv.* (*mus.*) in a free and fanciful style. [It. *capriccioso*].

CAPRICE, [kap-rēs'], *n.* an irrational change of opinion or humour, a whim. [Fr. *caprice*].

CAPRICIOUS, [kap-rish'-us], *adj.* acting by caprice, whimsical, irrational.

CAPRICIOUSLY, [kap-rish'-us-li], *adv.* in a capricious fashion.

CAPRICIOUSNESS, [kap-rish'-us-nes], *n.* the state or quality of being capricious.

CAPRICORN, [kap'-ri-kawn], *n.* a constellation, the Goat; the tenth sign of the Zodiac. [L. *capricornus* goat-horn].

CAPRID, [kap'-rid], *adj.* (*zool.*) pertaining to goats.

CAPRIFICATION, [kap'-rif-ik-ā'-shun], *n.* a method by which figs are unnaturally matured by fertilizing with the stings of a gall-insect. [L. *caprificatio*].

CAPRIFOIL, [kap'-ri-foil'], *n.* the honeysuckle, *Lonicera Periclymenum.* [MdL. *caprifolium*].

CAPRIFORM, [kap'-ri-fawm], *adj.* in the form of a goat. [L. *caper* goat and FORM].

CAPRIGENOUS, [kap-rij'-en-us], *adj.* springing from or produced by a goat. [L. *caper* goat and Gk. *genes* born].

CAPRIN, [kap'-rin], *n.* a flavouring principle in butter. [CAPRIC].

CAPRINE, [kāp'-rīn], *adj.* goat-like.

CAPRIOLE (1), [kap'-ri-ōl], *n.* a leap, prance. [It. *capriola*, *dim.* of L. *capra* goat].

CAPRIOLE (2), [kap'-ri-ōl], *v.i.* to leap about, caper, skip, prance.

CAPRIPED, [kap'-ri-ped'], *n.* an animal with feet resembling those of a goat. [L. *caper* goat and *pes pedem* foot].

CAPROATE, [kap'-rō-āt], *n.* (*chem.*) a salt obtained from caproic acid.

CAPROIC, [kap-rō'-ik], *adj.* like a goat; **c. acid,** an acid with a goat-like odour obtained from butter and other oils. [CAPRIC].

CAPRONE, [kap'-rōn], *n.* a flavouring oil found in butter.

CAPSICINE, [kap'-sis-ēn], *n.* an alkaloid present in capsicums.

CAPSICUM, [kap'-sik-um], *n.* a genus of American tropical plants whose fruits, chillies or red peppers are ground to produce cayenne. [L. *capsa* a box].

CAPSIZE, [kap-sīz'], *v.t. and i.* to turn upside down, upset (*esp.* of boats). [Uncert.].

CAPSTAN

CAPSTAN, [kap'-stan], *n.* an upright revolving drum turned by detachable projecting bars and round which a cable is wound in hoisting up an anchor or similar operations. [Fr. *cabestan*].

CAPSTONE, [kap'-stōn], *n.* (*arch.*) a stone forming a crown or top; a coping-stone; a fossil encrinite.

CAPSULAR, [kaps'-yŏŏl-er], *adj.* relating to a capsule.

CAPSULATE, [kaps'-yŏŏ-lāt], *adj.* like or contained in a capsule.

CAPSULE, [kaps'-yŏŏl], *n.* a small case or vessel; a metal or rubber cap to enclose the neck of a bottle, etc.; (*anat.*) a membranous sac, or protective covering; (*bot.*) a seed-vessel; (*med.*) a gelatinous sheath containing an unpleasant medicine. [L. *capsula*].

CAPTAIN (1), [kap'-tin], *n.* a naval officer immediately below a rear-admiral in rank; a military officer immediately below a major; the commanding officer of a merchant ship or of certain trained bodies of men; the leader of a sports team; (*fig.*) a gifted commander and leader. [OFr. *capitain*].

CAPTAIN (2), [kap'-tin], *v.t.* to lead, command as captain.

CAPTAINCY, [kap'-tin-si], *n.* the rank and status of a captain.

CAPTAIN-GENERAL, [kap'-tin-jen'-er-al], *n.* a supreme commander.

CAPTAINSHIP, [kap'-tin-ship], *n.* captaincy; military skill.

CAPTATION, [kap-tā'-shun], *n.* an appeal for applause or approval. [L. *captatio* a reaching out after].

CAPTION, [kap'-shun], *n.* a heading, a short title of a film scene, a section of a book, etc.; a title under a picture; (*leg.*) a seizure, lawful arrest; a certificate appended to a legal document to show its authority. [L. *captio* a seizing].

CAPTIOUS, [kap'-shus], *adj.* inclined to catch at faults; fault-finding, apt to cavil; ensnaring. [L. *captiosus* deceiving].

CAPTIOUSLY, [kap'-shus-li], *adv.* in a captious way.

CAPTIOUSNESS, [kap'-shus-nes], *n.* inclination to be captious.

CAPTIVATE, [kap'-tiv-āt], *v.t.* to enthral, charm, fascinate; capture the fancy of. [L. *captivare* to take captive].

CAPTIVATING, [kap'-tiv-āt'-ing], *adj.* enchanting, charming; fascinating.

CAPTIVATION, [kap'-tiv-ā'-shun], *n.* the act of captivating.

CAPTIVE (1), [kap'-tiv], *n.* a prisoner, one who has been captured.

CAPTIVE (2), [kap'-tiv], *adj.* taken prisoner, captured; **c. balloon,** a balloon secured to the ground. [L. *captivus*].

CAPTIVITY, [kap-tiv'-it-i], *n.* the condition of being captive. [Fr. *captivité* from L. *captivitas*].

CAPTOR, [kap'-tor], *n.* one who captures a prisoner or prize. [L. *captor*].

CAPTURE (1), [kap'-cher], *n.* the act of seizing, taking prisoner; that which is seized or caught. [L. *captura*].

CAPTURE (2), [kap'-cher], *v.t.* to catch, seize as prisoner, take as prize.

CAPUCHIN, [kap'-yŏŏ-chin], *n.* an order of Franciscan friars wearing pointed cowls; **c. monkey,** a South American hooded monkey; **c. pigeon,** a pigeon with a crest of feathers like a cowl. [Fr. *capucin* from It. *cappuccino* little cowl].

CAPUCINE†, [kap'-ew-sēn], *n.* a hooded cloak worn by women. [Fr. *capucine*].

CAPULIN, [kap'-yŏŏ-lin], *n.* the Mexican cherry.

CAPYBARA, CAPIBARA, [kap'-i-bah'-ra], *n.* (*zool.*) the largest extant rodent, *Hydrochaerus capibara.* [Brazil. *capybara*].

CAR, [kah(r)], *n.* a wheeled vehicle; a mechanically propelled passenger vehicle; a railway carriage; a motor-car; the passenger section of an aeroplane. [OFr. *carre* from L. *carrus*].

CARABINEER, [ka'-ra-bin-ēer], *n.* a mounted soldier armed with a carbine. [Fr. *carabinier*].

CARACAL, [ka'-rak-al], *n.* the Persian lynx, or its fur. [Fr. *caracal* from Pers. *qarah qulaq* black ear].

CARACARA, CARCARA, [ka'-ra-kah'-ra], *n.* the South American carrion-hawk, a species of *Polyborus.* [Brazilian *carcara*].

CARACK, CARRACK, [ka'-rak], *n.* a large armed trading vessel. [Fr. *caraque*].

CARACOLE (1), [ka'-ra-kōl], *n.* a half-turn or a series of these by a horse; (*arch.*) a spiral staircase. [Fr. *caracole* a spiral].

CARACOLE (2), [ka'-ra-kōl], *v.i.* to make a caracole.

CARAFE, [ka-rahf′], *n.* a glass bottle, usually for wine, water, or perfume. [Fr. *carafe*].

CARAMBOLA, [ka′-ram-bōl′-a], *n.* the tree or fruit of the Coromandel gooseberry, a species of *Averrhoa*. [Portug. *carambola*].

CARAMBOLE, [ka′-ram-bōl′], *n.* a cannon at billiards. [Fr. *carambole*].

CARAMEL, [ka′-ra-mel], *n.* burnt sugar, used for colouring and flavouring; a kind of toffee. [Fr. *caramel* from L. *canna mellis* sugar-cane].

CARANX, [ka′-rangks], *n.* a genus of fishes including the horse-mackerel. [Fr. *carangue*].

CARAPACE, [ka′-ra-pās′], *n.* the hard upper shell of certain reptiles and crustaceans. [Span. *carapacho*].

CARAP-OIL, [ka′-rap-oil′], *n.* oil obtained from the seeds of the crab-wood tree, *Carapa guianensis*.

CARAT, [ka′-rat], *n.* a measure of weight for diamonds and other gems; a standard of purity of gold, reckoned in twenty-fourths. [Fr. *carat*].

CARAUNA, [ka-rawn′-a], *n.* a resinous matter obtained from certain South American trees.

CARAVAN, [ka′-ra-van′], *n.* a company of travellers journeying together, *esp.* in the desert; a covered wagon used as a domicile by gipsies and holiday-makers; a kind of small house on wheels; vehicles transporting a travelling circus. [Fr. *caravane* from Pers. *karwan*].

CARAVANEER, [ka′-ra-van-ēer′], *n.* a man in charge of the camels of a caravan.

CARAVANSERAI, [ka′-ra-van′-ser-ī′], *n.* a large bare Eastern inn with a central courtyard, affording accommodation for the night to caravans. [CARAVAN and Pers. *sara* large house].

CARAVEL, [ka′-ra-vel], *n.* a lateen-rigged four-masted sailing vessel. [Fr. *caravelle*].

CARAWAY, CARRAWAY, [ka′-ra-wā], *n.* a plant with aromatic seeds, *Carum Carui*. [Fr. *carvi* from Arab. *karwia*].

CARBIDE, [kah′-bīd], *n.* a combination of carbon with another element, usually a metal; calcium carbide used in the preparation of acetylene. [CARBON].

CARBINE, [kah′-bīn], *n.* †a short rifle used by mounted soldiers. [Fr. *carabine*].

CARBOHYDRATE, [kah′-bō-hīd′-rāt], *n.* an organic compound of carbon, oxygen and hydrogen. [CARBON and HYDRATE].

CARBOLIC (1), [kah-bol′-ik], *n.* carbolic acid.

CARBOLIC (2), [kah-bol′-ik], *adj.* derived from carbon; **c. acid,** an antiseptic prepared from coal-tar, phenol. [CARBON and L. *oleum* oil].

CARBON, [kah′-bon], *n.* a non-metallic substance existing, other than in compounds, as charcoal, graphite and diamond; a chemical element denoted by C; a thin rod of this used in an electric arc-light; a copy reproduced by carbon-paper; **c. paper,** a sheet of thin paper covered with a pigment on one side, used for producing duplicate copies of written work. [L. *carbo carbonem* charcoal].

CARBONACEOUS, [kah′-bon-ā′-shus], *adj.* belonging to, containing or composed of coal.

CARBONADO†, [kah′-bon-ah′-dō], *n.* meat cut across with a knife and grilled on an open fire. [Span. *carbonada*].

CARBONATE, [kah′-bon-āt], *n.* (*chem.*) a salt obtained from carbonic acid.

CARBONATED, [kah′-bon-āt-id], *adj.* combined or impregnated with carbonic acid gas.

CARBONIC, [kah-bon′-ik], *adj.* pertaining to, coming from carbon; **c. acid gas,** carbon dioxide, a gas produced in respiration, etc.

CARBONIFEROUS, [kah′-bon-if′-er-us], *adj.* yielding coal. [CARBON and L. *ferre* to bear].

CARBONIZATION, [kah′-bon-īz-ā′-shun], *n.* the process of carbonizing.

CARBONIZE, [kah′-bon-īz], *v.t.* to turn into carbon.

CARBORUNDUM, [kah′-bo-rund′-um], *n.* a compound of silicon and carbon formed under great heat, used as an abrasive for grinding. [CARBON and CORUNDUM].

CARBOY

CARBOY, [kah′-boi], *n.* a large globular glass-bottle usually encased in basket-work. [Arab. *qarabah*].

CARBUNCLE, [kah′-bungkl], *n.* an inflamed boil or tumour; a brilliant deep red gem, *esp.* a garnet; (*her.*) a bearing with four radii forming a cross and another four making a saltire. [L. *carbunculus*].

CARBUNCLED, [kah′-bungkld], *adj.* adorned with carbuncles; afflicted with carbuncles.

CARBUNCULAR, [kah-bungk′-yŏŏl-er], *adj.* pertaining to a carbuncle; like a carbuncle.

CARBURET, (carburetting, carburetted), [kahb′-yŏŏ-ret], *v.t.* to impregnate or cause to combine with carbon. [CARB(ON) and (SULPH)UR].

CARBURETTED, [kahb′-yŏŏ-ret′-id], *adj.* combined with carbon.

CARBURETTOR, CARBURETTER, [kahb′-yŏŏ-ret′-er], *n.* a device in an internal-combustion engine in which petrol is vaporized and mixed with air to form an explosive mixture.

CARBURIZE, [kahb′-yŏŏ-rīz], *v.t.* to carburet.

CARCAJOU, [kah′-ka-zhŏŏ′], *n.* the wolverine. [Fr. *carcajou*].

CARCANET, [kah′-kan-et], *n.* a necklet or collar of jewels. [~Fr. *carcan* iron collar].

CARCASE, CARCASS, [kah′-kas], *n.* a dead body of an animal, *esp.* when dressed by a butcher; the framework of a ship, building, etc.; a kind of bomb. [OFr. *carceis*].

CARCINOLOGY, [kah′-sin-ol′-oj-i], *n.* the scientific study of crustaceans. [Gk. *karkinos* crab and *logos* speech].

CARCINOMA, [kah′-sin-ōm′-a], *n.* (*med.*) a kind of cancer affecting the organs or connective tissue. [Gk. *karkinoma*].

CARCINOMATOUS, [kah′-sin-ōm′-at-us], *adj.* (*med.*) affected by cancer, cancerous.

CARD (1), [kahd], *n.* a piece of thin pasteboard bearing a person's name and address, an invitation, an expression of good wishes for a special occasion, a postcard, a programme of events or score sheet, or an advertisement; one of fifty-two pieces of thin pasteboard marked with red hearts or diamonds, black spades or clubs, or with the traditional representations of King, Queen and Knave and used in many games; (*coll.*) a queer, peculiar person; **on the cards,** likely to occur, possible; **to put one's cards on the table,** to act openly and reveal one's intentions, plans, etc.; **a house of cards,** an impracticable scheme doomed to early failure. [Fr. *carte* from L. *charta* paper].

CARD (2), [kahd], *n.* a machine for combing flax, hemp, wool, etc. [Fr. *carde* from L. *carduus* thistle].

CARD (3), [kahd], *v.t.* to comb flax, hemp and wool with a card. [*Prec.*].

CARDAMOM, [kahd′-a-mom], *n.* an aromatic, pungent spice made from the seeds of *Elettaria Cardamomum*. [Gk. *kardamon* cress].

CARDAN, [kah′-dan], *adj.* (*eng.*) **c. joint,** a universal join; **c. shaft,** a shaft with a cardan joint at both ends. [*Cardano*, an Italian mathematician].

CARDBOARD, [kahd′-bawd], *n.* stiff pasteboard.

CARD-CASE, [kahd′-kās], *n.* a case for visiting-cards.

CARDIA, [kahd′-i-a], *n.* (*anat.*) the opening where the gullet enters the stomach. [Gk. *kardia* heart].

CARDIAC, [kah′-di-ak], *adj.* relating to, concerned with the heart, and heart-disease. [Gk. *kardiakos*].

CARDIACE, [kahd′-i-ās], *n.* a precious stone in the shape of a heart.

CARDIALGY, [kahd′-i-al′-ji], *n.* heartburn. [Gk. *kardia* heart and *algos* pain].

CARDIGAN, [kah′-dig-an], *n.* a short knitted jacket. [Earl of *Cardigan*].

CARDINAL (1), [kah′-din-al], *n.* (*R.C.*) one of the seventy members of the Pope's Council, next in rank to the Pope himself; a woman's cloak; a kind of mulled wine, red like the robes of a cardinal; the cardinal-bird.

CARDINAL (2), [kah′-din-al], *adj.* pertaining to a cardinal; of primary importance; principal; chief; **c. numbers,** the numbers one, two, three, etc.; **c. church,** one of the seventy chief churches of Rome. [L. *cardinalis* pertaining to a pivot or that on which everything depends].

CARDINALATE, [kah′-din-al-āt], *n.* the office, rank, or status of a cardinal.

CARDINAL-BIRD, [kah′-din-al-burd′], *n.* a North American song-bird with red plumage, *Cardinalis virginianus*.

CARDINAL-FLOWER, [kah′-din-al-flow′-er], *n.* a plant, *Lobelia cardinalis*, with brilliant red flowers.

CARDINALLY, [kahd′-in-al-i], *adv.* fundamentally.

CARDINALSHIP, [kah′-din-al-ship], *n.* cardinalate.

CARD-INDEX (1), [kahd′-in′-deks], *n.* an index in which each item is entered on a separate card for easy reference.

CARD-INDEX (2), [kahd′-in′-deks], *v.t.* to make a card-index of.

CARDING-MACHINE, [kahd′-ing-mash-ēn′], *n.* a machine for carding and cleansing flax or hemp.

CARDIOGRAPH, [kahd′-i-ō-grahf′], *n.* a device for recording the beats of the heart. [Gk. *kardia* heart and *graphia* writing].

CARDIOID, [kah′-di-oid], *n.* a curve shaped like a heart. [Gk. *kardia* heart and *oeides* like].

CARDIOID

CARDIOLOGY, [kah′-di-ol′-oj-i], *n.* the specialized study of the heart. [Gk. *kardia* heart and *logos* speech].

CARDIOMETRY, [kah′-di-om′-et-ri], *n.* the measurement of the beats of the heart. [Gk. *kardia* heart and *metria* measurement].

CARDITIS, [kah-dīt′-is], *n.* (*med.*) inflammation of the muscles of the heart. [Gk. *kardia* heart and *itis* denoting inflammation].

CARDOL, [kah′-dol], *n.* an oil of a vesicant nature extracted from the cashew-nut.

CARDOON, [kah′-dōōn′], *n.* the globe artichoke, *Cynara Cardunculus.* [OFr. *cardon* from L. *cardus* thistle].

CARD-PLAYER, [kahd′-plā′-er], *n.* one who plays card games.

CARDSHARPER, [kahd′-shah′-per], *n.* a cheat at cards.

CARD-TABLE, [kahd′-tābl], *n.* a small collapsible table with a green baize top for playing cards on.

CARE (1), [kāer], *n.* attention, solicitude; worry, anxiety; heed, regard; responsibility; (*poet.*) sorrow, grief. [OE. *caru*].

CARE (2), [kāer], *v.i.* to feel anxious, sorrowful, to display a strong interest, to mind; to be concerned; **to c. for,** to be fond of, to like; to look after. [OE. *carian* be anxious].

CARE-CRAZED, [kāer′-krāzd], *adj.* driven crazy by care.

CAREEN, [ka-rēn′], *v.t.* to lay a ship on her side for caulking or repairing; *v.i.* to heel over. [~L. *carina* keel].

CAREENAGE, [ka-rēn′-ij], *n.* a place suitable for, or the cost of, careening.

CAREER (1), [ka-rēer′], *n.* a rapid motion, a rushing onwards; the gradual improvement of status through life, advance through life; profession or business providing means of personal advancement. [Fr. *carrière* from LL. *carraria* carriage, carriage-way, course].

CAREER (2), [ka-rēer′], *v.i.* to rush madly, to race; gallop.

CAREERIST, [ka-rēer′-ist], *n.* a person whose whole aim in life is personal advancement and success.

CAREFUL, [kāer′-fŏŏl], *adj.* full of care; anxious, solicitous; provident; heedful, cautious.

CAREFULLY, [kāer′-fŏŏl-i], *adv.* in a careful way.

CAREFULNESS, [kāer′-fŏŏl-nes], *n.* the condition of being careful.

CARELESS, [kāer′-les], *adj.* without care, care-free; indifferent, unconcerned; heedless; negligent, thoughtless, slovenly, inconsiderate.

CARELESSLY, [kāer′-les-li], *adv.* in a careless fashion.

CARELESSNESS, [kāer′-les-nes], *n.* the condition of being careless.

CARESS (1), [ka-res′], *n.* a movement or act of endearment or affection; an embrace. [Fr. *caresse*].

CARESS (2), [ka-res′], *v.t.* to fondle, embrace, touch with affection; flatter; soothe.

CARESSING, [ka-res′-ing], *adj.* loving, affectionate, soothing.

CARESSINGLY, [ka-res′-ing-li], *adv.* in a caressing fashion.

CARET, [ka′-ret], *n.* a mark ∧ placed below the line in writing or in proof correcting to indicate that something has been omitted and must be added at that place. [L. *caret* it lacks].

CARGO, [kah′-gō], *n.* freight, the goods carried by a ship. [Span. *cargo* from L. *carricum* cart-load].

CAR-GOOSE, [kah′-gōōs], *n.* the crested grebe.

CARIACOU, [ka′-ri-a-kōō], *n.* the Virginian deer

CARIATIDES, see CARYATIDES.

CARIBOU, CARIBOO, [ka′-ri-bōō], *n.* the North American reindeer. [American Indian *caribou*].

CARICA, [ka′-ri-ka], *n.* (*bot.*) the papaw-tree. [L. *carica* fig].

CARICATURE (1), [ka-rik′-a-chŏŏer], *n.* a ludicrous, exaggerated imitation of someone's mannerisms, style, or appearance; a grotesque drawing of a person exaggerating his peculiarities; an ill-formed or ugly person or thing. [It. *caricatura*].

CARICATURE (2), [ka-rik′-a-chŏŏer], *v.t.* to make a caricature of.

CARICATURIST, [ka-rik′-a-chŏŏer-ist], *n.* a person who caricatures.

CARICOUS, [ka′-rik-us], *adj.* like a fig. [CARICA].

CARIES, [kāer′-i-ēz], *n.* decay of a bone or tooth. [L. *caries*].

CARILLON, [ka′-ril-yon], *n.* a chime of bells, usually operated by one person; the tune played on a peal of bells. [Fr. *carillon*].

CARINA, [ka-rīn′-a], *n.* (*bot.*) the keel of papilionaceous plants. [L. *carina*].

CARINATE, [ka′-rin-āt], *adj.* (*bot. and zool.*) with a keel-shaped ridge.

CARINATED, [ka′-rin-āt-id], *adj.* carinate.

CARIOSITY, [ka′-ri-os′-i-ti], *n.* (*path.*) a condition of decay. [CARIES].

CARIOUS, [kāer′-i-us], *adj.* rotten or decayed.

CARK†, [kahk], *v.i.* to worry, be anxious. [OFr. *carkier*].

CARKING, [kahk′-ing], *adj.* harassing; worrying.

CARL(E), [kahl], *n.* a chap; rough fellow; bumpkin. [OScand. *karl*].

CARLINE (1), [kahl′-in], *n.* old woman. [OScand. *kerling*].

CARLINE (2), [kah′-līn], *n.* (*bot.*) a genus of plants related to the thistle. [L. *Carolinus* or Charlemagne, after whom it is called].

CARLINE (3), [kah′-lin], *n.* (*naut.*) a light joist placed from beam to beam. [Uncert.].

CARLINGUE, [kah′-ling], *n.* (*aeron.*) the foundation of a nacelle.

CARLISM, [kahl′-izm], *n.* the movement supporting the claims of Don Carlos and his heirs to the Spanish throne.

CARLOCK, [kah′-lok], *n.* a kind of isinglass obtained from sturgeon's bladder. [Russ. *karluk*].

CARLOVINGIAN, [kahl′-ō-vin′-ji-an], *adj.* relating to Charlemagne or the dynasty he founded.

CARMAGNOLE, [kah′-man-yōl′], *n.* a noisy, boisterous dance, popular with the revolutionaries in France; a Jacobin soldier in the French Revolution. [Fr. *carmagnole* short jacket worn by Jacobins].

CARMAN, [kah′-man], *n.* a carter, a man who drives a cart or horse-driven vehicle carrying goods.

CARMELITE (1), [kah′-mel-īt], *n.* a member of the religious order of White Friars; a variety of pear.

CARMELITE (2), [kah′-mel-īt], *adj.* pertaining to the order of White Friars and its members. [Mount *Carmel*, where the order was founded in the twelfth century].

CARMINATIVE (1), [kah′-min-at-iv], *n.* an agent to relieve flatulence.

CARMINATIVE (2), [kah′-min-at-iv], *adj.* relieving or curing flatulence. [L. *carminare* cleanse].

CARMINE (1), [kah′-mīn], *n.* a crimson-red pigment obtained from cochineal. [Fr. *carmin*].

CARMINE (2), [kah′-mīn], *adj.* crimson, carmine-coloured.

CARNAGE, [kah′-nij], *n.* heavy wanton slaughter of human beings; bloodshed. [Fr. *carnage*].

CARNAL, [kahnl], *adj.* of the flesh; sexual, sensual; worldly; **c. knowledge,** sexual intercourse. [L. *carnalis* fleshly].

CARNALIST, [kah′-nal-ist], *n.* a sensualist; a materialist.

CARNALITY, [kah-nal′-i-ti], *n.* worldliness; sensuality; lust.

CARNALLY, [kah′-nal-i], *adv.* in a carnal way.

CARNAL-MINDEDNESS, [kah′-nal-mīnd′-id-nes], *n.* carnality.

CARNASSIAL, [kah-nas′-i-al], *adj.* (*anat.*) suited for the eating of flesh; (*pl.*) the flesh teeth of carnivorous animals.

CARNATION, [kah-nā′-shun], *n.* a pink colour, like that of flesh; a kind of pink, *Dianthus Caryophyllus.* [L. *carnatio*].

CARNAUBA, [kah-now′-ba], *n.* the Brazilian palm. *Corypha cerifera.* [Brazilian *carnauba*].

CARNELIAN, see CORNELIAN.

CARNEOUS†, [kah′-ni-us], *adj.* fleshy. [L. *carneus*]

CARNEY, CARNY, [kah′-ni], *v.t. and i.* to coax, wheedle, cajole. [Unkn.].

CARNIFEX, [kah′-ni-feks], *n.* an executioner. [L. *carnifex*].

CARNIFICATION, [kah′-ni-fik-ā′-shun], *n.* the process or act of carnifying.

CARNIFY, [kah'-ni-fī], *v.t.* to turn into flesh or a fleshy substance. [L. *carnificare*].
CARNIVAL, [kah'-ni-val], *n.* a week of revelry and festivity just before Lent *esp.* in Roman Catholic countries; revelry, an organized jollification. [It. *carnevale* farewell to flesh].
CARNIVORA, [kah-niv'-or-a], *n.(pl.)* (*zool.*) flesh-eating mammals. [L. *carnivora*].
CARNIVOROUS, [kah-niv'-or-us], *adj.* living on flesh.
CARNOSE, [kah'-nōs], *adj.* fleshy. [L. *carnosus*].
CARNOSITY, [kahn-os'-it-i], *n.* a fleshy growth.
CAROB, [ka'-rob], *n.* the locust or algaroba tree, *Ceratonia Siliqua*, or its fruit. [Fr. *carobe* from Arab. *kharrubah* bean-pods].
CAROL (1), [ka'-rol], *n.* a song of gladness and rejoicing, *esp.* to celebrate Christmas; a happy song. [OFr. *carole* a round dance].
CAROL (2), (carolling, carolled), [ka'-rol], *v.i.* to sing carols; to sing joyfully.
CAROLINGIAN, [ka'-rō-lin'-jan], *adj.* Carlovingian.
CAROLUS, [ka'-rō-lus], *n.* a gold coin of Charles I. [L. *Carolus* Charles].
CAROM, [ka'-rom], *n.* a cannon in French billiards; an American variation of croquet. [Fr. *carambole*].
CAROSS, see KAROSS.
CAROTEEL, [ka'-rot-ēl], *n.* an Oriental weight equal to about seven pounds. [Arab. *qirtal*].
CAROTID (1), [ka-rot'-id], *n.* one of the two main arteries in the neck which carry blood from the aorta to the head. [Gk. *karotides*].
CAROTID (2), [ka-rot'-id], *adj.* pertaining to or connected with either of the carotids.
CAROTIN, [ka'-rot-in], *n.* the vitamin present in carrots. [L. *carota* carrot and (VITAM)IN].
CAROUSAL, [ka-rowz'-al], *n.* a feast; a merry, rowdy drinking bout.
CAROUSE (1), [ka-rows'], *n.* a carousal.
CAROUSE (2), [ka-rows'], *v.i.* to drink and make merry; to feast; to revel. [Fr. *carousse* from Germ. *gar aus* to the very bottom (of a cup)].
CAROUSER, [ka-rowz'-er], *n.* a person who carouses.
CAROUSINGLY, [ka-rowz'-ing-li] *adv.* in a carousing fashion.
CARP (1), [kahp], *n.* the common freshwater fish *Cyprinus carpio*. [OFr. *carpe*, L. *carpa*].
CARP (2), [kahp], *v.i.* to cavil; criticize sharply and persistently. [OScand. *karpa* to boast].
CARPAL, [kahp'-al], *adj.* pertaining to the carpus or wrist.
CARPEL, [kahp'-el'], *n.* (*bot.*) a single cell into which a compound fruit may be divided; a simple fruit having only a single cell. [L. *carpellum* from Gk. *karpos* fruit].
CARPELLARY, [kah-pel'-er-i], *adj.* pertaining to a carpel.
CARPELLUM, [kah-pel'-um], *n.* a carpel. [MdL. *carpellum*].
CARPENTER (1), [kah'-pint-er], *n.* one who works in wood, a wood-worker. [OFr. *carpentier*].
CARPENTER (2), [kah'-pint-er], *v.i.* to work in wood, as a carpenter.
CARPENTERING, [kah'-pint-er-ing], *n.* carpentry.
CARPENTRY, [kah'-pint-ri], *n.* the art or work of a carpenter.
CARPER, [kah'-per], *n.* a person who speaks or acts in a carping way.
CARPET (1), [kah -pit], *n.* a covering for floors and stairs usually of some heavy woven fabric; a quantity or piece of this fabric; an even natural covering for the ground; **on the c.,** being reproved, reprimanded; under discussion; **c. bagger,** a candidate for parliament who does not live in his constituency and who is a stranger to it; **c. knight,** a knight or soldier who has never seen service in the field. [OFr. *carpite*].
CARPET (2), [kah'-pit], *v.t.* to cover with or as with a carpet; (*coll.*) reprimand.
CARPET-BAG, [kahp'-it-bag], *n.* a bag made of carpeting, often used to carry tools.
CARPETING, [kah'-pit-ing], *n.* material for carpets; carpets.
CARPETMONGER, [kah'-pit-mung'-ger], *n.* an idler.
CARPHOLITE, [kah'-fol-it], *n.* a yellow fibrous mineral composed of silica, alumina and manganese. [Gk. *karphos* straw and *lithos* stone].
CARPHOLOGY, [kah-fol'-oj-i], *n.* floccilation. [Gk. *karphologia*].
CARPHOSIDERITE, [kah'-fōs-id'-er-it], *n.* a straw-coloured hydrated sulphate of iron with sand and gypsum. [Gk. *karphos* straw and *sideros* iron].
CARPING, [kah'-ping], *adj.* critical in a petty and disagreeable way, cavilling, captious. [CARP (2)].
CARPINGLY, [kah'-ping-li], *adv.* in a carping way.
CARPOLITE, [kah'-pol-it], *n.* (*geol.*) a fossilized fruit. [Gk. *karpos* fruit and *lithos* stone].
CARPOLOGY, [kah-pol'-o-ji], *n.* the scientific study of fruits. [Gk. *karpos* fruit and *logos* speech].
CARPOPHAGOUS, [kah-pof'-ag-us], *adj.* feeding on fruits. [Gk. *karpos* fruit and *phago* I eat].
CARPOPHORE, [kah'-pō-faw(r)'], *n.* the continuation of the stem between the carpels. [Gk. *karpos* fruit and *phero* I bear].
CARPUS, [kah'-pus], *n.* (*anat.*) wrist. [L. *carpus*].
CARR, [kah(r)], *n.* boggy land, marshland reclaimed or being reclaimed by draining. [OScand. *kjarr*].
CARRACK, see CARACK.
CARRAGEEN, [ka'-ra-gēn], *n.* an edible Irish sea-weed or moss, *Chondrus crispus*. [*Carragheen*, on the Irish coast, where found].
CARRAWAY, see CARAWAY.
CARREL†, [ka'-rel], *n.* an arrow for the crossbow; a little oratory. [Fr. *carrel*].
CARRIABLE, [ka'-ri-abl], *adj.* portable.
CARRIAGE, [ka'-rij], *n.* the act of carrying or transporting; charge made for transport and delivery of goods; a wheeled passenger-vehicle, *esp.* one with four wheels and drawn by a horse; a passenger-compartment on a railway train; device used to support and move heavy objects, as guns; the movable part of a typewriter that holds the paper; way of holding one's self, deportment, bearing; (*print.*) part of a press in which type formes are placed for printing; **c. forward,** an indication that the fee for conveyance is to be paid by addressee. [OFr. *cariage*].
CARRICK BEND, [ka'-rik-bend'], *n.* (*naut.*) a kind of knot. [Uncert.].
CARRICK BITTS, [ka'-rik-bits'], *n.* (*pl.*)(*naut.*) a pair of bitts supporting the windlass.

CARRICK BEND

CARRIER, [ka'-ri-er], *n.* one who conveys goods from one place to another, an out-porter; a contrivance for carrying luggage, attached to the back of a car or bicycle; any person or thing that transmits infection; (*mech.*) the part of a machine which carries something from one position to another; **c. pigeon,** a pigeon trained to carry messages.
CARRIOLE, [ka'-ri-ōl], *n.* a light single-seater carriage, a Canadian sledge. [Fr. *carriole* from L. *carrus* wagon].
CARRION (1), [ka'-ri-on], *n.* dead and rotting flesh; bad meat. [OFr. *caroigne*].
CARRION (2), [ka'-ri-on], *adj.* like, pertaining to, or feeding on, carrion.
CARRONADE†, [ka'-ron-ād'], *n.* a ship's cannon. [*Carron* in Scotland, where they were made].
CARRON-OIL, [ka'-ron-oil'], *n.* oil for treating scalds as used at *Carron* ironworks.
CARROT, [ka'-rot], *n.* the yellowish-red edible root of *Daucus Carota*; (*pl.*) (*coll.*) (a person with) red hair. [Fr. *carotte*].
CARROTINESS, [ka'-rot-i-nes], *n.* the state or quality of being carroty.
CARROTY, [ka'-rot-i], *adj.* resembling a carrot in colour; reddish yellow.
CARRY (1), [ka'-ri], *n.* the position of gun or sword held ready for a salute; range, length of flight, distance anything carries.
CARRY (2), (carrying, carried), [ka'-ri], *v.t.* to bear; to transport, convey, lift and move from one place to another; to support; to extend; to storm, take by force; to retain (in the memory); to succeed in passing; to gain approval for; to involve, imply; (*math.*) to bring over from one column to another; (*naut.*) to have (sail); *v.i.* to transport, to lift and bear things from one place to another; to reach to a certain distance; to be audible; (of a hare) to run over ground that sticks to the feet; (of a horse) to hold the head in a particular way; **to c. one's bat,** (*cricket*) to be still "in" at the close of an innings; **to c. weight,** (*horse-racing*) to be handicapped by extra weight; to be reasonable and convincing, to tend to influence; **to c. the day,** to win, gain one's point; **to be carried away,** to be wildly stirred; **to c. forward,** to proceed with; (*book-keeping*) to transfer an entry to the next page; **to c. off,** to remove by force; to kill; **to c. off well,** to handle with ease and equanimity, make the best of; **to c. on,** to continue;

to persevere; (*coll.*) to complain in a foolish, excited, and angry manner; **to c. out,** to complete, accomplish, fulfil; **to c. over,** (*Stock Exchange*) to keep till next day for selling; **to c. through,** to complete, achieve; to maintain, sustain. [Northern OFr. *carier*].

CARRYING, [ka'-ri-ing], *adj.* bearing, conveying, removing, or transporting; **c. trade,** transport of goods, particularly by water.

CARRY-TALE, [ka'-ri-tāl], *n.* gossip; telltale.

CART (1), [kaht], *n.* a wheeled vehicle drawn by horses or oxen for transporting goods; **dog c.,** light two-wheeled passenger-vehicle; **in the c.,** (*coll.*) in trouble, in a difficult situation. [OE. *craet*].

CART (2), [kaht], *v.t. and i.* to transport in a cart; to undertake the carrying of loads in a cart.

CARTAGE, [kaht'-ij], *n.* the act or cost of carting.

CARTE (1), [kaht], *n.* bill of fare, menu card; **à la c.,** selected from items on the bill of fare. [Fr. *carte* card].

CARTE (2), QUARTE, [kaht], *n.* a particular movement or pass at fencing. [Fr. *quarte* fourth].

CARTE-BLANCHE, [kaht'-blahnch'], *n.* a blank piece of paper to be filled in as the possessor pleases; **to give a person c.,** to give him a free hand, *esp.* with regard to expenditure. [Fr. *carte-blanche* blank card].

CARTE-DE-VISITE, [kaht'-de-viz'-ēt], *n.* a particular size of small photograph. [Fr. *carte-de-visite* visiting card].

CARTEL, [kaht'-el], *n.* a written agreement between opposing parties in a war as to exchanging prisoners; an unarmed vessel used for such an exchange; a written challenge to a duel; a trust; a working agreement between rival commercial concerns. [Fr. *cartel*].

CARTER, [kaht'-er], *n.* one who drives a cart or is employed in carting.

CARTESIAN (1), [kaht-ēzh'-un], *n.* a disciple of the French philosopher, Descartes, or his doctrines. [(*Des*)*cartes*, a French philosopher].

CARTESIAN (2), [kaht-ēz'-i-an], *adj.* relating to Descartes and his philosophy.

CARTHAMINE, [kah'-tham-in], *n.* a red substance extracted from the bastard saffron. [*Next*].

CARTHAMUS, [kah'-tham-us], *n.* a genus of saffrons including *Carthamus tinctorius*, the safflower or bastard saffron. [Arab. *qartum*].

CART-HORSE, [kaht'-haws], *n.* a heavy horse.

CARTHUSIAN (1), [kah-thew'-zi-an], *n.* a member of a religious order founded by St. Bruno at Chartreuse in the eleventh century; a pupil of Charterhouse School.

CARTHUSIAN (2), [kah-thew'-zi-an], *adj.* pertaining to a Carthusian or to Charterhouse School. [L. *Cartusianus*, *adj.* from *Chartreuse*].

CARTILAGE, [kaht'-il-ij], *n.* gristle, the elastic tissue from which bone is formed. [L. *cartilago*].

CARTILAGINOUS, [kaht'-il-aj'-in-us], *adj.* connected with, or consisting of, cartilage.

CART-JADE, [kaht'-jād], *n.* a horse suitable only for a cart.

CART-LOAD, [kaht'-lōd'], *n.* as much as a cart will hold; a rough measure for hay, straw, gravel, etc.

CARTOGRAPHER, [kaht-og'-raf-er], *n.* a map-maker.

CARTOGRAPHIC, [kaht'-ō-graf'-ik], *adj.* pertaining to cartography.

CARTOGRAPHICAL, [kaht'-ō-graf'-ik-al], *adj.* cartographic.

CARTOGRAPHY, [kaht-og'-ra-fi], *n.* the art or science of map-making. [Fr. *cartographie*].

CARTOMANCY, [kaht'-ō-man'-si], *n.* fortune-telling by means of playing-cards. [Fr. *carte* card and Gk. *manteia* divination].

CARTON, [kaht'-on], *n.* a small cardboard box or container; the white disk in the centre of a target. [Fr. *carton* pasteboard].

CARTON-PIERRE, [kaht'-on-pyāer'], *n.* papier-mâché designed to give the appearance of stonework. [CARTON and Fr. *pierre* stone].

CARTOON (1), [kah-toon'], *n.* a design or sketch on strong paper, as for tapestry, etc.; a picture, usually of the nature of a caricature, illustrating and usually satirizing topical events; a cartoon-film. [Fr. *carton* pasteboard].

CARTOON (2), [kah-tōōn'], *v.t. and i.* to draw, represent in a cartoon; to draw a cartoon.

CARTOON-FILM, [kah-tōōn'-film'], *n.* a film, usually humorous, photographed from black-and-white or coloured drawings, with appropriate music and sound effects.

CARTOONIST, [kaht-ōōn'-ist], *n.* one who draws cartoons.

CARTOPHILE, [kaht'-ō-fīl], *n.* one who collects cigarette-cards or coupons. [Fr. *carte* card and Gk. *philos* love].

CARTOPHILIST, [kaht-of'-il-ist], *n.* a cartophile.

CARTOUCHE (1), [kah-tōōsh'], *n.* an oval-shaped device, containing titles and names, on ancient Egyptian monuments; (*arch.*) a scroll forming the top of a column; an ornamental device with an inscription inside. [Fr. *cartouche* from It. *cartoccio*].

CARTOUCHE

CARTOUCHE (2), [kah'-tōōsh'], *n.* a cartridge; a case for cartridges or cannon-balls; a soldier's pass. [Fr. *cartouche* cartridge].

CARTRIDGE, [kah'-trij], *n.* a container in which a charge of explosive for a firearm, etc., is packed; **ball c.,** a cartridge which contains both shot and explosive; **blank c.,** a cartridge containing explosive, but no shot. [Corruption of CARTOUCHE (2)].

CARTRIDGE-BOX, [kah'-trij-boks'], *n.* a box holding cartridges.

CARTRIDGE-PAPER, [kah'-trij-pāp'-er], *n.* a strong paper used for making cartridge-cases and for artists' drawings.

CARTULARY, CHARTULARY, [kah'-chōō-la-ri], *n.* a collection of deeds and charters transcribed in a book. [MdL. *cartularium*].

CART-WHEEL, [kaht'-wēl], *n.* the wheel of a cart; (*coll.*) a sideways somersault.

CARTWRIGHT, [kaht'-rīt], *n.* a man who makes carts.

CARUCAGE, [ka'-rōō-kij], *n.* †a medieval tax on ploughs. [MdL. *carrucagium*].

CARUCATE, [ka'-rōō-kāt], *n.* (*hist.*) a measure of land, that which can be ploughed by one plough in a year. [L. *caruca* plough].

CARUNCLE, [ka'-rungkl], *n.* a soft excrescence of flesh, as in a cock's comb; (*bot.*) swelling in a seed-vessel where the seed is joined to its covering. [L. *caruncula*].

CARUNCULAR, [ka-rungk'-yōō-ler], *adj.* in the shape of a caruncle.

CARUNCULATED, [ka-rungk'-yōō-lāt-id], *adj.* furnished with a caruncle.

CARUS, [kāer'-us], *n.* (*med.*) complete loss of consciousness. [L. *caros* deep sleep].

CARVE, [kahv], *v.t. and i.* to cut, chisel, or engrave a design or figure upon wood, stone, etc.; to cut or serve up meat or fowl prepared for the table into slices; (*fig.*) to shape, make, mould. [OE. *ceorfan*].

CARVEL, [kah'-vel], *n.* a kind of jelly-fish. [CARAVEL].

CARVEL-BUILT, [kah'-vel-bilt'], *adj.* (*naut.*) with the edges of the planks flush instead of over-lapping as in clinker-built.

CARVER, [kah'-ver], *n.* one who carves; a knife used to carve meat at table.

CARVING, [kah'-ving], *n.* the act of one who carves; a figure carved in stone or wood.

CARYATIC, [ka'-ri-at'-ik], *adj.* relating to caryatides; **c. order,** (*arch.*) one in which the entablature is supported by draped female figures in stone.

CARYATIDES, CARIATIDES, [ka'-ri-at'-id-ēz], *n.* (*pl.*) (*arch.*) carved stone figures of women, serving to support entablatures. [Gk. *karuatides* priestesses at Karuai].

CARYOKAR, [ka'-ri-ō'-ker], *n.* the butternut tree. [Gk. *karuon* nut].

CARYOPHYLLIC, [ka'-ri-of'-il-ik], *adj.* obtained from oil of cloves. [Gk. *karuophullon*].

CARYOPHYLLINE, [ka'-ri-of'-il-ēn], *n.* a crystalline substance obtained from cloves.

CARYOPSIS, (*pl.* **caryopsides**), [ka'-ri-op'-sis], *n.* (*bot.*) a fruit in which seed and pericarp are one, as in grasses. [Gk. *karuon* nut and *opsis* appearance].

CARYOTA, [ka'-ri-ōt'-a], *n.* the fish-tail palm.

CASAL, [kās'-al], *adj.* (*gram.*) pertaining to case.

CASCABEL, [kask'-a-bel], *n.* the pommel at the end of a cannon; the rear end of a cannon. [Span. *cascabel* little round bell].

CASCADE (1), [kas-kād'], *n.* a waterfall; (*fig.*) something falling freely like a waterfall; **in c.,** (*elect.*) so connected that the output of the first constitutes the input for the second. [Fr. *cascade*].

CASCADE (2), [kas-kād'], *v.i.* to fall in a cascade.

CASCALHO, [kas-kal'-yō], *n.* the alluvial deposit in which diamonds are found. [Brazil.].

CASCARA, [kas-kah'-ra], *n.* a mild laxative extracted from the bark of the Californian buckthorn. [Span. *cascara (sagrada)* (sacred) bark].
CASCARILLA, [kask'-a-ril'-a], *n.* the acrid aromatic bark of *Croton Cascarilla*. [MdL. *cascarilla*].
CASE (1), [kās], *n.* that which falls, or happens; circumstances; special or actual state of affairs; event; predicament; instance, example; fact; (*leg.*) a question to be settled, a cause to be tried or which has been tried and decided; facts or evidence supporting one side; (*med.*) an example of a particular disease in someone; a person afflicted with a particular disease; (*gram.*) a change in the form of a noun, pronoun or adjective, to show its relation to other words in the sentence; grammatical relationship of a noun, pronoun or adjective; **in c.**, lest, in the event that; **leading c.**, (*leg.*) one often quoted in subsequent actions. [OFr. *cas* from L. *casum* that which has befallen].
CASE (2), [kās], *n.* a box or chest of various kinds in which things may be kept; a leather bag for toilet articles, writing materials, travelling, etc.; a box and glass covering to exhibit and protect the contents; (*zool.*) a sheath for insect's wings; linen or cotton bag to hold pillow or bolster, etc.; (*print.*) box divided up into compartments for holding type; **lower c.**, box for small letters; small letters themselves; **upper c.**, box for capital letters; capital letters themselves. (OFr. *casse*].
CASE (3), [kās], *v.t.* to encase. [*Prec.*].
CASEATE, [kās'-i-āt], *n.* a salt obtained from caseic acid. [L. *caseus* cheese].
CASEHARDEN, [kās'-hahd'-en], *v.t.* to give a hard skin to steel or iron; to render insensitive, hard and unfeeling.
CASEIC, [kās'-i-ik], *adj.* pertaining to, obtained from cheese. [L. *caseus* cheese].
CASEIN, [kās'-i-in], *n.* the coagulated cheesy substance in milk, present also in certain leguminous plants.
CASE-KNIFE, [kās'-nīf], *n.* a large knife carried in a sheath.
CASE-LAW, [kās'-law'], *n.* (*leg.*) the administration of justice on the basis of decisions made in previous cases.
CASEMATE, [kās'-māt], *n.* (*fort.*) a strong shell-proof vault in fortification, with openings for guns; the armoured covering surrounding guns on a warship. [Fr. *casemate*].
CASEMATED, [kās'-māt'-id], *adj.* provided with a casemate.
CASEMENT, [kās'-ment], *n.* a window opening outwards on side hinges. [Fr. *casement*].
CASEMENT-CLOTH, [kās'-ment-kloth'], *n.* a strong cotton cloth, used chiefly for curtains.
CASEOUS, [kās'-i-us], *adj.* like cheese. [L. *caseus*].
CASERN, CASERNE, [ka-zurn'], *n.* barracks. [Fr. *caserne*].
CASE-SHOT, [kās'-shot'], *n.* shrapnel.
CASE-WORM, [kās'-wurm], *n.* an aquatic larva, the caddis, which envelops its body in a protective case.
CASH (1), [kash], *n.* money in coin or notes, ready money; (*coll.*) money in any form; **c. down**, payment immediately on receiving goods; **c.-on-delivery (C.O.D.)**, payment by the addressee on delivery of goods by a postman. [Fr. *casse* box, treasury].
CASH (2), [kash], *n.* small Eastern coin, usually perforated so that it can be carried on a string. [Tamil *casu*].
CASH (3), [kash], *v.t.* to give or receive coins or notes in exchange for a cheque; to convert into ready money; **to c. in on**, to take advantage of (an event or state of affairs).
CASH-ACCOUNT, [kash'-a-kownt'], *n.* an account of sales and purchases for cash.
CASH-BOX, [kash'-boks'], *n.* a small steel box in which coins are kept.
CASHEW, [ka-shōō'], *n.* a tropical American tree, *Anacardium occidentale*, with kidney-shaped nuts. [Fr. *acajou* from Brazil. *acajoba*].
CASHIER (1), [ka-shēer'], *n.* one who pays out and receives cash, and who keeps an account of monetary transactions in a bank or other commercial institution. [Fr. *caissier*].
CASHIER (2), [kash-ēer], *v.t.* to dismiss or discharge with ignominy from the fighting services, to deprive of rank. [Du. *kasseren* from Fr. *casser* break].
CASHMERE, [kash'-mēer], *n.* the soft, silky hair of the Cashmere goat; a material woven from this or resembling it. [*Kashmir* in India].
CASHOO, see CATECHU.
CASH-REGISTER, [kash'-rej'-ist-er], *n.* a machine which records the amount of money placed in it.
CASING, [kās'-ing], *n.* that which envelops or encases the framework of windows and doors.
CASINO, [ka-sē'-no], *n.* a place of public amusement at a pleasure resort, with facilities for gambling. [It. *casino* little house].
CASK, [kahsk], *n.* a kind of barrel; the amount contained in a cask; a measure of capacity. [Span. *casco* skull, shell].
CASKET, [kahs'-kit], *n.* a small case for jewels, trinkets, etc. [Uncert.].
CASLON, [kaz'-lon], *n.* a type-face popularized by W. *Caslon*.
CASQUE, [kahsk], *n.* (*archaic*) a helmet. [Fr. *casque*].
CASQUE-SHAPED, [kahsk'-shāpt], *adj.* like a helmet in shape.
CASSAMUNAR, [kas'-a-mewn'-er], *n.* the aromatic root of an East Indies plant related to ginger.
CASSAREEP, [kas'-a-rēp], *n.* a sauce used in Guiana, made from the juice of the cassava.
CASSATION (1), [ka-sā'-shun], *n.* (*leg.*) the reversal or annulment of a judgment. [Fr. *cassation*].
CASSATION (2), [kas-ā'-shun], *n.* an informal suite of music for chamber orchestra. [G. *kassation*].
CASSAVA, [kas-ah'-va], *n.* a plant with tuberous roots; the starch or flour made from the roots. [Haiti *casabi*].
CASSEROLE, [kas'-er-ōl], *n.* an earthenware or glass cooking dish with a lid; food cooked in such a utensil. [Fr. *casserole* saucepan].
CASSIA, [kas'-i-a], *n.* a large genus of plants including the senna. [L. *cassia* tree with fragrant bark].
CASSIDEOUS, [ka-sid'-i-us], *adj.* (*bot.*) shaped like a helmet. [L. *cassis* helmet].
CASSIMERE, [kas'-i-mēer], *n.* a twilled woollen material. [Fr. *casimere*, CASHMERE].
CASSINETTE, [kas'-i-net'], *n.* a material with cotton warp with a fine wool woof. [Uncert.].
CASSINO, [ka-sēn'-ō], *n.* a card game. [CASINO].
CASSIOPEIA, [kas'-i-ō-pē'-a] *n.* (*astron.*) a northern constellation shaped like a W.
CASSITERITE, [ka-sit'-er-īt], *n.* tinstone, the principal ore of tin. [Gk. *kassiteros* tin].
CASSIUS, [kas'-i-us], *n.* a purple pigment obtained by mixing chlorides of gold and tin. [A. *Cassius*, a German chemist].
CASSOCK, [kas'-ok], *n.* a long, sleeved (black) garment, worn, usually over ordinary secular attire, by clergymen, choristers, etc. [Fr. *casaque* from It. *casacca* great-coat].
CASSOLETTE, [kas'-ō-let'], *n.* a small box for perfume. [Fr. *cassolette*].
CASSOWARY, [kas'-ō-wer-i], *n.* a large bird of the genus *Casuarius*, resembling a small ostrich. [Malay *casuari*].
CAST (1), [kahst], *n.* the act of casting; a throw; something thrown or shed; the distance thrown; the skin of a snake; a little pile of earth left by earthworms; a piece of gut to which a fish-hook and bait are fixed; plaster or other material moulded into a particular shape; a mould; the actors of a play; characteristic feature, expression or mien.
CAST (2), [kahst], *v.t.* to throw, hurl, fling; to direct towards; to shed, throw off; to let fall, throw overboard; to produce, cause to appear; to reject; to assign parts in a play to actors; to record, give (votes); to mould; to work out, reckon up; *v.i.* to throw a fishing-line; to mould iron or other metals; **to c. the lead** (*naut.*) to measure the depth of water, by letting down a plumb-line; **the die is c.**, there is no going back; **to c. about for**, to seek a way, devise a plan; **to c. down** (*fig.*) to depress, fill with gloom; **to c. off**, to leave destitute, abandon; (in knitting) to finish off a piece of work by slipping stitches off the needles, and securing them; (*print.*) to find how many printed pages a manuscript will make; **to c. on**, to knit the first row of stitches on to a needle. [OScand. *kasta*].
CASTALIAN, [ka-stāl'-yan], *adj.* belonging to Castalia, a spring on Mount Parnassus, sacred to the Muses; (*fig.*) poetic.
CASTANETS, [kas'-tan-ets'], *n.*(*pl.*) a pair of small concave clappers of hard wood or ivory, attached to the thumb, and struck against each other to music. [Span. *castanetas* from L. *castanea* chestnut].
CASTAWAY, [kahst'-a-wā], *n.* one wrecked on a desolate shore; (*fig.*) an outcast.
CASTE, [kahst], *n.* an hereditary social division among the Hindus; any exclusive social class; **to lose c.**, to lose respect and social prestige. [Portug. *casta* pure strain].

CASTELLAN, [kast'-el-an], *n.* the governor or warden of a castle. [OFr. *castelain*].
CASTELLANY, [kast'-el-an-i], *n.* the lordship of a castle.
CASTELLATED, [kast'-el-āt-id], *adj.* having turrets, parapets, or battlements like a castle; **c. shaft** (*eng.*) a spliced shaft; **c. nut** (*eng.*) a nut with grooves in its top surface to accommodate a securing pin. [L. *castellatus*].

CASTELLATED

CASTER (1), CASTOR, [kahst'-er], *n.* a bottle or other receptacle with a perforated lid, for pepper, sugar, etc.; small wheel on a swivel fixed to the legs of chairs, etc.; **c. action,** (*motoring*) a trailing action in steering which tends to keep the wheels on a straight course.
CASTER (2), [kahst'-er], *n.* one who casts, a computer.
CASTER-SUGAR, CASTOR-SUGAR, [kahst'-er-shoog'-er], *n.* finely powdered sugar.
CASTIGATE, [kast'-i-gāt], *v.t.* to chastise; administer punishment to; to scold; to criticize severely; to emend, correct. [L. *castigare*].
CASTIGATION, [kast'-i-gā'-shun], *n.* the act of castigating. [L. *castigatio*].
CASTIGATOR, [kast'-i-gā'-tor], *n.* one who castigates.
CASTIGATORY, [kast'-i-gāt-or-i], *adj.* corrective; punishing.
CASTILE-SOAP, [ka-stēl'-sōp'], *n.* a fine white, hard soap. [*Castile* in Spain, where first made].
CASTILIAN, [kast-il'-yan], *n.* a native of Castile; the dialect spoken there. [*Castile* in Spain].
CASTING, [kahst'-ing], *n.* the act of throwing; act of shaping metal in moulds; a piece of metal shaped in this way.
CASTING-NET, [kahst'-ing-net'], *n.* a net thrown into the water, and drawn up again immediately.
CASTING-VOTE, [kahst'-ing-vōt'], *n.* the vote of a president or chairman at a meeting, to decide the issue when the votes of each party are otherwise equal; a decisive vote.
CAST-IRON, [kahst'-iern'], *n.* iron melted in a furnace and poured into moulds.
CASTLE (1), [kahsl], *n.* a large building elaborately fortified, with battlements and often a moat, a fortress; a large house resembling this in architectural style, a mansion; a chess piece shaped like a tower, the rook; **c. in Spain,** an impracticable ideal or plan. [OE. *castel* from L. *castellum* citadel].
CASTLE (2), [kahsl], *v.i.* in the game of chess, to move simultaneously the king and rook, subject to certain conditions, so as to bring them side by side. [*Prec.*].
CASTLE-BUILDER, [kahsl'-bild'-er], *n.* (*fig.*) a dreamer, an idealist.
CASTLED, [kahsld], *adj.* possessing castles.
CASTLET, [kahs'-let], *n.* a small type of castle.
CAST-OFF, [kahst'-of], *n.* something put aside as useless; a calculation of the number of printed pages a manuscript will make.
CASTOR (1), [kahst'-or], *n.* a genus of rodents, including the beaver. [Gk. *kastor* beaver].
CASTOR (2), [kahst'-or], *n.* a knob-like hard growth on the inside of a horse's leg; a chestnut. [Uncert.].
CASTOR (3), [kast'-or], *n.* the twin brother of Pollux, commemorated with him in the sign of the Zodiac *Gemini*; (*meteor.*) a fiery halo, shaped like twin balls, seen round a ship's rigging at sea. [Gk. *Castor*].
CASTOR (4), see CASTER (1).
CASTOREUM, [cast-awr'-i-um], *n.* an oily secretion of the beaver. [L. *castoreum*].
CASTORINE, [kast'-or-ēn], *n.* (*chem.*) the active principle of castoreum.
CASTOR-OIL, [kahst'-er-oil'], *n.* a natural oil, with purgative action, obtained from the Indian plant *Ricinus communis*. [CASTOREUM].
CASTOR-SUGAR, see CASTER-SUGAR.
CASTRAL, [kast'-ral], *adj.* relating to a camp. [L. *castra* camp].
CASTRAMETATION, [kast'-ra-met-ā'-shun], *n.* the art or act of pitching a camp. [L. *castra* camp and *metatio* measuring].
CASTRATE, [kast'-rāt], *v.t.* to make sexually impotent by excising the testicles, to emasculate, geld; (*fig.*) to expurgate, censor. [L. *castrare*].
CASTRATION, [kast-rā'-shun], *n.* the process of castrating.
CASTRATO, [kast-rah'-tō], *n.* a person who was castrated in boyhood so that his singing voice should remain unbroken. [It. *castrato* eunuch].
CAST-STEEL, [kahst'-stēl'], *n.* steel fused and poured into moulds.
CASUAL, [kaz'-yoo-al], *adj.* accidental, occasional, resulting from chance, haphazard; unsettled, uncertain; incidental; unmethodical, slack; **c. labourer,** a worker who lives by taking odd jobs; **c. ward,** a ward for vagrants. [L. *casualis*].
CASUALISM, [kaz'-yoo-al-izm], *n.* the doctrine that events, realities, etc., are merely the outcome of accident.
CASUALLY, [kaz'-yoo-al-i], *adv.* in a casual fashion.
CASUALNESS, [kaz'-yoo-al-nes], *n.* the condition of being casual.
CASUALTY, [kaz'-yoo-al-ti], *n.* an accident involving physical injury; (*pl.*) those wounded or dead in a battle; **c. ward,** hospital ward for those hurt in accidents.
CASUARINA, [kaz'-yoo-a-rīn'-a], *n.* a large genus of Australian and Polynesian trees, with branches thought to resemble a cassowary's feathers. [CASSOWARY].
CASUIST, [kaz'-yoo-ist], *n.* one skilled in casuistry. [Fr. *casuiste* from L. *casus* case].
CASUISTIC, [kaz'-yoo-ist'-ik], *adj.* pertaining to casuistry.
CASUISTICAL, [kaz-yoo-ist'-ik-al], *adj.* casuistic.
CASUISTRY, [kaz'-yoo-ist-ri], *n.* the doctrine which professes to arrive at conclusive judgments on particular problems of conduct, by arguing from general principles of ethics; a quibbling line of argument, sophistry.
CASULA, [kaz'-yoo-la], *n.* a chasuble. [L. *casula* vestment].
CASUS BELLI, [kāz'-us-bel'-i], *n.* an act considered a sufficient cause of war; (*fig.*) ground for a quarrel. [L. *casus belli*].
CAT (1), [kat], *n.* a small carnivorous animal of the genus *Felis*, with short jaws, sharp teeth, and soft fur, of which there are both wild and domesticated varieties; (*zool.*) any species of the genus *Felis*; (*fig.*) a spiteful woman; (*naut.*) a type of single-masted sailing boat, with narrow stern and deep waist; (*naut.*) strong tackle or gear for drawing up the anchor to the cathead; a double tripod designed to stand upright on three of its six feet; the cat-o'-nine-tails; **to let the c. out of the bag,** to divulge a secret. [OE. *catt*].

CAT

CAT (2), (catting, catted), [kat], *v.t.* (*naut.*) to hoist to the cathead.
CAT (3), [kat], *v.* (*slang*) to vomit. [CAT (1)].
CATA-, *pref.* back, against, down to, along, over, thoroughly. [Gk. *kata*].
CATABAPTIST, [kat'-a-bap'-tist], *n.* an opponent of baptism. [CATA and BAPTIST].
CATABOLISM, [kat-ab'-ol-izm], *n.* (*biol.*) the breaking down of complex organic matter to a simpler form. [CATA and Gk. *bole* cast].
CATACAUSTIC (1), [kat-a-kaw'-stik], *n.* a curve produced by reflection. [CATA and CAUSTIC].
CATACAUSTIC (2), [kat'-a-kaw'-stik], *adj.* (*opt.*) formed by reflection into curves.
CATACHRESIS, [kat'-a-krē'-sis], *n.* (*rhet.*) misapplication of a metaphor or other figure of speech; alteration of a word by folk etymology. [CATA and Gk. *khresis* use].
CATACHRESTIC, [kat-a-krēs'-tik], *adj.* (*rhet.*) misused, wrongly applied.
CATACLYSM, [kat'-a-klizm], *n.* a deluge, an all-enveloping flood; (*geol.*) a violent alteration in the face of the earth; (*fig.*) violent and radical shift of mental and emotional balance, a revolutionary upheaval. [Gk. *kataklusmos* flood].
CATACLYSMAL, [kat'-a-klizm'-al], *adj.* pertaining to or like a cataclysm.
CATACLYSMICALLY, [kat'-a-klizm'-ik-al-i], *adv.* by means of a cataclysm.
CATACLYSMIST, [kat'-a-kliz'-mist], *n.* a person who ascribes change of any kind, and particularly geological change, to cataclysms.
CATACOMB, [kat'-a-koom], *n.* an underground vault or gallery, or series of these, in which the dead are buried. [Fr. *catacombe*].
CATACOUSTICS, [kat'-a-kowst'-iks], *n.* the study

of echoes or reflected sounds. [CATA and ACOUSTICS].

CATADIOPTRIC, [kat'-a-dī-op'-trik], *adj.* (*opt.*) having the power of refracting and reflecting light. [CATA and DIOPTRIC].

CATADROMOUS, [kat-ad'-rom-us], *adj.* (*zool.*) leaving a river to spawn in the sea, as salmon. [CATA and Gk. *dromos* course].

CATAFALQUE, [kat'-a-falk'], *n.* a temporary structure upon which the coffin is placed during a lying-in-state. [Fr. *catafalque*].

CATAGENESIS, [kat'-a-jen'-is-is], *n.* retrogressive evolution. [CATA and GENESIS].

CATAGMATIC, [kat'-ag-mat'-ik], *adj.* (*med.*) pertaining to fractures and their cure. [Gk. *katagma* fracture].

CATALAN (1), [kat'-al-an], *n.* a native or the language of Catalonia. [*Catalonia* in Spain].

CATALAN (2), [kat'-al-an], *adj.* pertaining to Catalonia or its language.

CATALANIST, [kat-al-an'-ist], *n.* an advocate of the independence of Catalonia.

CATALECTIC, [kat'-a-lek'-tik], *adj.* (*pros.*) lacking a syllable. [Gk. *katalektikos*].

CATALEPSY, [kat'-a-lep'-si], *n.* (*med.*) a state of insensibility, suspension of sensation brought on suddenly as in a fit. [CATA and Gk. *lepsis* grasping].

CATALEPTIC, [kat-a-lep'-tik], *adj.* of, or pertaining to, catalepsy.

CATALLACTICS, [kat'-a-lak'-tiks], *n.* political economy. [Gk. *katallaktikos* exchange].

CATALOGUABLE, [kat'-a-log'-abl], *adj.* able to be catalogued.

CATALOGUE (1), [kat'-a-log'], *n.* a list or register systematically compiled and set out; a list, often illustrated, of goods offered for sale; **c. raisonné,** a catalogue arranged in order of subjects with explanatory matter under each entry. [Gk. *katalogos* enrolment].

CATALOGUE (2), [kat'-a-log], *v.t.* to make a catalogue of.

CATALPA, [ka-tal'-pa], *n.* an American genus of trees including the catawba and shawnie-wood. [Amer. Indian *catalpa*].

CATALYSIS, [kat-al'-is-is], *n.* (*chem.*) a change effected in a chemical substance by something which does not undergo any change itself. [Gk. *katalusis* dissolving].

CATALYST, [kat'-a-list], *n.* (*chem.*) a substance producing catalysis.

CATALYTIC (1), [kat'-a-lit'-ik], *n.* (*chem.*) a catalyst; (*med.*) a medicine which destroys toxins in the blood.

CATALYTIC (2), [kat'-a-lit'-ik], *adj.* effecting or pertaining to catalysis.

CATALYTICAL, [kat'-a-lit'-ik-al], *adj.* catalytic.

CATAMARAN, [kat'-a-ma-ran'], *n.* a log raft; a flat-bottomed boat formed by lashing together two shallow hulls. [Tamil *cattamaram*].

CATAMENIA, [kat'-a-mēn'-ya], *n.*(*pl.*) the menses. [Gk. *katamenia*].

CATAMENIAL, [kat'-a-mēn'-yal], *adj.* relating to catamenia.

CATAMOUNT, [kat'-a-mownt], *n.* the puma. [CAT of the MOUNT(AIN)].

CATANADROMOUS, [kat'-an-ad'-rom-us], *adj.* catandromous.

CATANDROMOUS, [kat'-an-drom'-us], *adj.* catadromous.

CATAPAN, [kat'-ap-an'], *n.* an administrative governor of a Byzantine province. [MdL. *catapanus*].

CATAPETALOUS, [kat'-a-pet'-al-us], *adj.* (*bot.*) having the petals fastened together by stamens at their bases. [CATA and Gk. *petalon* leaf].

CATAPHONICS, [kat'-a-fon'-iks], *n.* the theory of the nature and action of reflected sounds. [CATA and PHONICS].

CATAPHORESIS, [kat'-a-faw-rēs'-is], *n.* (*med.*) the passing of medicine through the pores of the skin by electricity.

CATAPHRACT, [kat'-a-frakt'], *n.* a suit of armour, consisting largely of overlapping scales; a soldier clad in such armour. [Gk. *kataphraktos* covered up].

CATAPHRACTED, [kat'-a-frakt'-id], *adj.* (*zool.*) covered with horny plates as a defensive device.

CATAPHYLLARY, [kat'-a-fil'-a-ri], *adj.* belonging to a rudimentary leaf. [CATA and Gk. *phullon* leaf].

CATAPLASM, [kat'-a-plazm'], *n.* (*med.*) a poultice.

CATAPLEXY, [kat'-a-pleks'-i], *n.* actual or feigned hypnotic sleep brought on in an animal by extreme fear. [CATA and Gk. *plexis* striking].

CATAPULT (1), [kat'-a-pult'], *n.* a small forked stick with a length of rubber fastened to both ends of the fork for shooting pebbles; an ancient military device for hurling boulders, rocks, etc. [Gk. *katapeltes*].

CATAPULT (2), [kat'-a-pult'], *v.t. and i.* to shoot with a catapult; to hurl, throw or propel as from a catapult.

CATARACT, [kat'-a-rakt'], *n.* a great waterfall or series of waterfalls; (*med.*) a disease of the eye affecting the crystalline lens. [Gk. *kataraktes*].

CATARACTOUS, [kat'-a-rakt'-us], *adj.* pertaining to cataract.

CATARRH, [ka-tah(r)'], *n.* (*med.*) inflammation of the mucuous membrane; a cold. [Gk. *katarrhous* running down].

CATARRHAL, [ka-tahr'-al], *adj.* of, or infected with, catarrh.

CATARRHINE (1), [kat'-a-rīn], *n.* (*zool.*) one of the narrow-nosed group of the family of primates.

CATARRHINE (2), [kat'-a-rīn], *adj.* (*zool.*) having a narrow nose. [CATA and Gk. *rhis rhinos* nose].

CATARRHOUS, [ka-tahr'-us], *adj.* catarrhal.

CATASTA, [ka-tast'-a], *n.* the platform upon which slaves were placed to be sold. [L. *catasta* scaffold].

CATASTASIS, [ka-tast'-a-sis], *n.* the climax of a play; (*rhet.*) a narrative setting forth the subject under discussion; (*med.*) the constitution or condition of the body. [Gk. *katastasis* settling].

CATASTROPHE, [ka-tast'-ro-fi], *n.* a disaster, a calamity with irremediable effects, an overwhelming upheaval in the accepted order of things; the decisive action in a play which produces the climax; (*fig.*) the final issue; (*geol.*) a cataclysm. [Gk. *katastrophe* overthrowing].

CATASTROPHIC, [kat'-a-strof'-ik], *adj.* having the characteristics of a catastrophe.

CATASTROPHISM, [ka-tast'-rof-izm], *n.* (*geol.*) the theory that violent and sudden disturbances are the main causes of changes in nature.

CATASTROPHIST, [ka-tast'-rof-ist], *n.* one who believes in catastrophism.

CATAWBA, [kat-awb'-a], *n.* an Ohio grape; the wine obtained from it. [*Catawba*, an American river].

CAT-BIRD, [kat'-burd], *n.* an American thrush, a species of *Galeoscoptes*.

CAT-BLOCK, [kat'-blok'], *n.* a block to hoist up an anchor to the cathead.

CATBOAT, [kat'-bōt], *n.* a boat with a mast erected in the bow.

CAT-BURGLAR, [kat'-burg'ler], *n.*, a thief who enters a house by climbing drain-pipes, etc.

CATCALL, [kat'-kawl], *n.* a squealing instrument used to express disapproval in public places, theatres, etc.; a noise of disapproval intended to interrupt.

CATCH (1), [kach], *n.* the act of seizing or grasping; a sudden halt or break; the thing which catches or holds; (*fig.*) a trick to deceive or trap; the thing caught, a haul of fish; (*coll.*) a thing worth catching; (*mus.*) a round.

CATCH (2), (**caught**), [kach], *v.t. and i.* to seize, get hold of, to seize after pursuit, capture; to ensnare, trap; to draw level with; to receive in communication; to hear with difficulty; to entangle; to hold (one's breath); to grasp; to attract, engage; to receive by contagion or infection; to be in time for; to detect, discover, find out; to intercept; to lay hold of, fasten on to; to become entangled, to become fastened to; **to c. on,** (*slang*) to become popular, take the public fancy; to understand; **to c. a crab,** to get the oar jammed under water while rowing; **to c. it.,** (*coll.*) to be severely reprimanded. [OFr. *cachier* to seize].

CATCHABLE, [kach'-abl], *adj.* able or liable to be caught.

CATCH CROP, [kach'-krop'], *n.* a subsidiary crop sown after the main crop has been harvested.

CATCH-DRAIN, [kach'-drān'], *n.* a drain dug across a slope to catch the water from the surface; a drain cut parallel to a canal to contain the overflow.

CATCHFLY, [kach'-flī], one of the several genera of plants which catch flying insects by sticky secretions.

CATCHINESS, [kach'-i-nes], *n.* (of a tune) the quality of being catchy.

CATCHING, [kach'-ing], *adj.* taking; contagious, infectious; charming.

CATCHLAND, [kach'-land], *n.* public land having no definite owner.

CATCH-MEADOW, [kach'-med'-ō], *n.* a meadow irrigated by water drained from a hillside.

CATCHMENT, [kach'-ment], *n.* a stretch of land which may be drained of its water; drainage.

CATCHPENNY, [kach'-pen'-i], *adj.* worthless yet superficially attractive, showy.

CATCHPOLL, [kach'-pōl], *n.* †a constable. [OE. *kæcepol* from MedL. *chassipullus* chicken-chaser].

CATCHWEED, [kach'-wēd], *n.* (*bot.*) the madwort, *Asperugo procumbens*; the goosegrass, *Galium Aparine*.

CATCHWEIGHT, [kach'-wāt], *n.* a boxer or wrestler engaged in a competition without restriction as to weight.

CATCHWORD, [kach'-wurd], *n.* a word placed at the bottom of a page which is the same as the first on the succeeding page; the word at the head of a page or column in reference books; the word an encyclopaedia or dictionary explains or defines; an actor's cue; a popular cliché or slogan.

CATCHY, [kach'-i], *adj.* appealing, attractive to the eye; deceptive, tricky; easy to remember (of a tune).

CATECHETIC(AL), [kat'-i-ket'-ik(-al)], *adj.* having the form of a catechism.

CATECHETICALLY, [kat-i-ket'-ik-al-i], *adv.* in a catechetical form.

CATECHISM, [kat'-i-kizm'], *n.* instruction in the form of question and answer, *esp.* in religious doctrine; **the C.**, the formulae expressing the religious principles of the Church of England. [L. *catechismus*].

CATECHIST, [kat'-i-kist], *n.* one who teaches by means of a catechism; a church official who instructs in the principles and doctrines of religion.

CATECHISTIC, [kat'-i-kist'-ik], *adj.* having the form of a catechism.

CATECHISTICAL, [kat'-i-kist'-ik-al], *adj.* catechistic.

CATECHISTICALLY, [kat'-i-kist'-ik-al-i], *adv.* in a catechistical way.

CATECHIZATION, [kat'-i-kiz-ā'-shun], *n.* the procedure or act of catechizing.

CATECHIZE, [kat'-i-kīz], *v.t.* to instruct by asking set questions in a definite order with the answers already formulated and supposed to have been learned by heart; to question thoroughly. [Gk. *katekhizo* I instruct orally].

CATECHU, CASHOO, [kat'-ech-ōō, kash'-ōō], *n.* a brown astringent substance obtained from the *Acacia Catechu*. [Malay *kachu*].

CATECHUIC, [kat'-ech-ōō'-ik], *adj.* consisting of, or pertaining to, catechu.

CATECHUMEN, [kat'-i-kyŏŏ'-men], *n.* a convert obtaining religious education before being baptized; a novice, a beginner; a person taught orally. [Gk. *katekhoumenos* instructed].

CATEGOREMATIC, [kat'-i-go'-ri-mat'-ik], *adj.* (*log.*) (of a word) usable by itself as a term. [Gk. *kategorema* asserting].

CATEGORICAL, [kat'-i-go'-rik-al], *adj.* belonging or pertaining to a category; absolute, positive, unqualified, not conditional.

CATEGORICALLY, [kat'-i-go'-rik-al-i], *adv.* in a categorical way.

CATEGORY, [kat'-i-ger-i], *n.* a class or group of which the individual members or elements share certain common characteristics; one of the ten basic forms of thought existing in the understanding independent of experience. [Gk. *kategoria* statement].

CATELECTRODE, [kat'-i-lekt'-rōd], *n.* the negative electrode of a battery. [CATA and ELECTRODE].

CATENA, [kat-ēn'-a], *n.* a chain; a series of arguments. [L. *catena*].

CATENARIAN, [kat'-in-āer'-i-an], *adj.* catenary.

CATENARY (1), [kat-ēn'-er-i], *n.* (*geom.*) the curve formed by a chain of uniform weight and strength hanging freely between two points of suspension placed at the same height. [L. *catenarius*].

CATENARY (2), [kat-ēn'-er-i], *adj.* having the form of a chain, like a chain.

CATENULATE, [ka-tēn'-yŏŏ-lat], *adj.* composed of links or chains; resembling a small chain; having a series of tubercles hanging together to form a chain. [L. *catenula* little chain].

CATER, [kāt'-er], *v.i.* to provide food or amusement. [OFr. (*a*)*catour* buyer].

CATERAN, [kat'-er-an], *n.* an irregular Scots or Irish soldier living by plunder. [Gael. *ceathairne* common people].

CATERER, [kāt'-er-er], *n.* a person who caters.

CATERPILLAR, [kat'-er-pil'-er], *n.* the larva of a moth or butterfly, having many pairs of legs; **c. wheel**, an endless jointed band of strong material, running over two or more wheels, and used in place of ordinary wheels on a vehicle. [OFr. *chate pelouse* hairy cat].

CATERPILLAR WHEEL

CATERPILLAR-TRACTOR, [kat'-er-pil'-er-trak'-tor], *n.* a motor-vehicle driven by caterpillar wheels for drawing very heavy loads over rough ground.

CATERWAUL, [kat'-er-wawl], *v.i.* to make a noise like a howling cat. [ME. *caterwawen*].

CATES, [kāts], *n.*(*pl.*) viands; dainties. [OFr. *acate* purchase].

CAT-EYED, [kat'-īd], *adj.* able to see in the dark (like a cat).

CAT-FALL, [kat'-fawl], *n.* (*naut.*) a rope to draw up the anchor.

CAT-FISH, [kat'-fish], *n.* a fish with cat-like whiskers, the wolf-fish, *Anarrhicas lupus*; the nurse-hound, *Scyllium catulus*.

CATGUT, [kat'-gut], *n.* a strong resilient cord made from the twisted intestines of animals, used as strings for musical instruments, tennis rackets, and for stitching wounds. [Uncert.].

CATHARISM, [kath'-er-izm], *n.* the beliefs held by a catharist. [Gk. *katharizo* I purify].

CATHARIST, [kath'-er-ist], *n.* a person who pretends to greater purity than others.

CATHARMA†, [kath-ah'-ma], *n.* a purge. [Gk. *katharmos* purification].

CAT-HARPINGS, [kat'-hah'-pingz], *n.*(*pl.*) (*naut.*) ropes used to tighten the shrouds.

CATHARSIS, [kath-ah'-sis], *n.* (*med.*) cleansing of the body by purging; (*fig.*) an emotional and moral purgation. [Gk. *katharsis* cleansing].

CATHARTIC (1), [kath-ah'-tik], *n.* a purgative.

CATHARTIC (2), [kath-ah'-tik], *adj.* purgative. [Gk. *kathartikos* cleansing].

CATHARTICAL, [kath-ah'-tik-al], *adj.* cathartic.

CATHARTINE, [kath-ah'-tēn], *n.* the bitter principle of senna.

CATHEAD (1), [kat'-hed'], *n.* (*naut.*) a pair of bars projecting (like a cat's whiskers) from the sides of a ship's bows and bearing pulley blocks at their outer extremities for weighing anchor. [CAT and HEAD].

CATHEAD (2), [kat'-hed'], *v.t.* (*naut.*) to secure to the cathead.

CATHEDRA, [kath-ēd'-ra], *n.* a bishop's throne; **ex c.**, with authority. [Gk. *kathedra* chair].

CATHEDRAL (1), [kath-ēd'-ral], *n.* the principal church in a diocese, in which the bishop's throne is set. [*Prec.*].

CATHEDRAL (2), [kath-ēd'-ral], *adj.* pertaining to, possessing, regarded as, a cathedral.

CATHERETIC, [kath'-er-et'-ik], *n.* (*med.*) a caustic substance used for burning away warts, etc. [Gk. *kathairetikos* destructive].

CATHERINE-PEAR, [kath'-er-in-pāer'], *n.* a variety of small pear. [*Catherine*, a woman's name, and PEAR].

CATHERINE-WHEEL, [kath'-er-in-wēl'], *n.* (*arch.*) an ornamental circular window with divisions radiating outwards from a common centre; (*pyr.*) a firework which rotates like a wheel when set alight; a cart-wheel.

CATHERINE-WHEEL

CATHETER, [kath-ēt'-er], *n.* (*surg.*) a slender tubular instrument used to draw off urine or other fluid from the body. [Gk. *katheter*].

CATHETOMETER, [kath'-it-om'-et-er], *n.* an apparatus for measuring the levels of liquids in tubes or retorts. [*Prec.* and Gk. *metron* measure].

CATHISMA, [kath-iz'-ma], *n.* a part of the psalter. [Gk. *kathisma* a seat].

CATHODE, [kath'-ōd], *n.* (*elect.*) the negative electrode; (*wirel.*) the filament of a thermionic valve which emits a stream of electrons to the anode. [Gk. *kathados* descent].

CATHODE-RAY, [kath'-ōd-rā'], *n.* (*elect.*) a negative emission at the cathode of a vacuum tube; **c. tube**, a tube in which a minute beam of electrons is controlled by plates of various potentials and directed to a fluorescent screen at the end.

CATHOLIC (1), [kath'-ol-ik] *n.* a member of the Catholic Church; a Roman Catholic; **C. Church**,

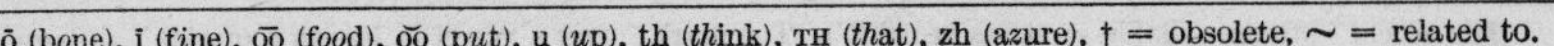

the Christian Church in all its sects; the Roman Catholic Church.

CATHOLIC (2), [kath'-ol-ik], *adj.* universal, applicable to all, embracing all people and all things, liberal, comprehensive, impartial, broad-minded; pertaining to the Catholic Church or to Roman Catholics. [Gk. *katholikos* universal].

CATHOLICISM, [kath-ol'-is-izm], *n.* the religious doctrine, liturgy and observances of Catholics; the state of being a Catholic.

CATHOLICITY, [kath'-ol-is'-i-ti], *n.* the quality of being catholic.

CATHOLICON, [kath-ol'-ik-on], *n.* a universal cure; a bishop's church in the Greek Church. [Gk. *katholikon*].

CATHOLICOS, [kath-ol'-ik-os], *n.* the head of the Armenian Church; a treasurer in the early Christian Church. [Gk. *katholikos*].

CATILINARIAN, [kat'-il-in-āer -i-an], *n.* a person whose behaviour resembles that of Catiline, a conspirator. [*Catiline*, a Roman conspirator].

CATILINISM, [kat'-il-in-izm], *n.* conduct like that of Catiline, conspiracy. [*Prec.*].

CATKIN, [kat'-kin], *n.* the long, fluffy hanging flower of the willow or hazel, etc.; catgut. [*Dim.* of CAT].

CATLING, [kat'-ling], *n.* (*surg.*) a small knife for delicate work in amputation; the down or bloom on walnut trees; catgut.

CATMINT, [kat'-mint], *n.* a scented plant like mint, a species of *Nepeta*.

CATODONT, [kat'-o-dont], *adj.* having teeth only on the lower jaw. [CATA and Gk. *odous odontos* tooth].

CATONIAN, [kāt-ōn'-i-an], *adj.* like Cato, severe. [*Cato* the Censor, a Roman of famed severity].

CAT-O'-NINE-TAILS, [kat'-ō-nīn'-tālz], *n.* a whip with nine thongs or knotted cords used for scourging prisoners.

CATOPSIS, [kat-op'-sis], *n.* morbid sharp-sightedness. [CATA and Gk. *opsis* sight].

CATOPTRIC, [kat-op'-trik], *adj.* pertaining to catoptrics.

CATOPTRICS, [kat-op'-triks], *n.* (*opt.*) the study of reflected light. [Gk. *katoptrikos* from *katoptron* mirror].

CATOPTROMANCY, [kat-op'-trō-man'-si], *n.* foretelling events by looking into a mirror under water. [Gk. *katoptron* mirror and *manteia* divination].

CAT-SALT, [kat'-sawlt], *n.* salt composed of bittern.

CAT'S-CRADLE, [kats'-krādl'], *n.* a game played with a length of string, with its two ends tied together, alternately lifted by each of two players from the fingers of the other on to his own, to form fresh and more intricate symmetrical designs.

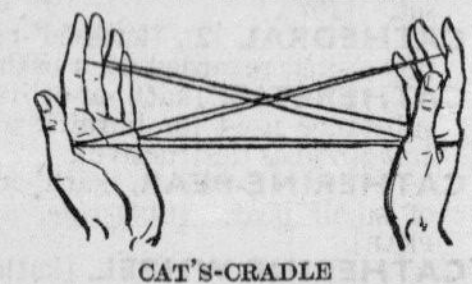
CAT'S-CRADLE

CAT'S-EYE, [kats'-ī], *n.* a chrysoberyl, a semi-precious opalescent stone, resembling the eye of a cat, a variety of chalcedonic quartz.

CAT-SILVER, [kat'-sil'-ver], *n.* a variety of mica.

CATSMEAT, [kats'-mēt], *n.* meat, usually horseflesh, sold for feeding cats.

CAT'S-PAW, [kats'-paw], *n.* a dupe, a person tricked into acting on behalf of another in a dangerous or illegal undertaking (as in the fable of the monkey which induced the cat to remove hot chestnuts from the fire with its paw); (*naut.*) a slight breeze; a hitch twisted in the bight of a rope for hooking on tackle.

CAT'S-TAIL, [kats'-tāl], *n.* (*bot.*) one of several plants and grasses resembling the catkin, the horse-tail, etc.

CATTISH, [kat'-ish], *adj.* feline; (*fig.*) spiteful, vindictive.

CATTLE, [katl], *n.*(*pl.*) domesticated farm beasts such as cows, bulls, oxen. [OFr. *catel* cattle, property].

CATTY (1), [kat'-i], *n.* the Chinese pound. [Malay-Javanese *kati*].

CATTY (2), [kat'-i], *adj.* cat-like; cattish; spiteful.

CATWHIN, [kat'-win], *n.* (*bot.*) the plant *Genista anglica*, the needle-gorse.

CAUCASIAN (1), [kaw-kā'-zhun], *n.* one living in the Caucasus; a member of the white races of man. [*Caucasus*, a mountain range near the Black Sea].

CAUCASIAN (2), [kaw-kā'-zhun], *adj.* of or pertaining to the Caucasus or to the white races of man.

CAUCUS, [kaw'-kus], *n.* a small committee of people privately formed to decide policy and tactics for electoral purposes or for arranging administrative details. [Unkn.].

CAUDAL, [kawdl], *adj.* relating to a tail; having a tail. [L. *caudalis* from *cauda* tail].

CAUDATE, [kaw'-dāt], *adj.* (*bot.*) having a tail or tail-like appendage.

CAUDEX, (*pl.* **caudices**), [kaw'-deks], *n.* (*bot.*) the stalk of a palm or fern. [L. *caudex* tree-trunk].

CAUDILLO, [kow-dēl'-yō], *n.* the head of the Spanish government after the Civil War of 1936-1939. [Span. *caudillo*].

CAUDLE, [kawdl], *n.* a hot spiced drink, a warm gruel mixed with wine for invalids. [L. *calidus* hot].

CAUGHT, [kawt], *pret., p.pt.,* of CATCH.

CAUL, [kawl], *n.* a membrane covering the foetus; a kind of net or cap for the hair. [OFr. *cale* cap].

CAULDRON, CALDRON, [kawl'-dron], *n.* a large bowl-shaped kettle or boiler of copper or iron for cooking purposes. [OFr. *c(h)alderon* from L. *calidus* hot].

CAULESCENT, [kawl-es'-ent], *adj.* (*bot.*) having a true stem. [~L. *caulis* stalk].

CAULICLE, [kawl'-ikl], *n.* (*bot.*) a short stalk. [L. *cauliculus*].

CAULICULE, [kawl'-i-kewl], *n.* (*bot.*) a small stalk, particularly one rising from the top of the root.

CAULIFEROUS, [kawl-if'-er-us], *adj.* (*bot.*) possessing a stalk. [L. *caulis* stem and *ferre* to bear].

CAULIFLOWER, [kol'-i-flow-er], *n.* a variety of cabbage, with a large white edible flower *Brassica oleracea* var. *cauliflora*. [L. *caulis* stalk and FLOWER].

CAULIFORM, [kawl'-i-fawm], *adj.* stalk-like. [L. *caulis* stalk and FORM].

CAULINE, [kawl'-īn], *adj.* (*bot.*) of or pertaining to the stem. [L. *caulis* stalk].

CAULK, CALK, [kawlk], *v.t.* to make water-tight by filling in the seams of a ship's hull or deck with oakum, tow, and pitch; to stop a crack. [OFr. *cauquer*, L. *calcare* tread].

CAULKING, CALKING, [kawlk'-ing], *n.* the process of making a ship's seams water-tight; a mixture of oakum, tow, and pitch.

CAUSAL (1), [kawzl], *n.* (*gram.*) a word introducing a phrase or clause expressing a reason or cause.

CAUSAL (2), [kawzl], *adj.* expressing or pertaining to a cause.

CAUSALITY, [kawz-al'-it-i], *n.* the state of being a cause; the operation of cause and effect.

CAUSALLY, [kawz'-al-i], *adv.* in a causal sequence or manner.

CAUSATION, [kawz-ā'-shun], *n.* the act of causing, the progress from cause to effect.

CAUSATIONAL, [kawz-ā'-shun-al], *adj.* pertaining to causation.

CAUSATIONIST, [kawz-ā'-shun-ist], *n.* a person who believes that every event occurs in causal sequence.

CAUSATIVE, [kawz'-a-tiv], *adj.* able to cause an effect, causing; (*gram.*) expressing cause.

CAUSATIVELY, [kawz'-a-tiv-li], *adv.* in a causative fashion.

CAUSE (1), [kawz], *n.* the motivating force or inspiration of any act; the person or thing which produces, or contributes to, an effect; that which moves a person to action, a reason, motive; the principle, ideal or interest to which are devoted all the energies, beliefs, and fervour of a person or group; the object of thought and action held as an end in itself; lawsuit, case, the grounds for litigation; **c. célèbre,** a famous lawsuit. [OFr. *cause* from L. *causa* reason].

CAUSE (2), [kawz], *v.t.* to effect, to bring about, produce, induce, to actuate, motivate. [*Prec.*].

CAUSELESS, [kawz'-les], *adj.* without apparent cause.

CAUSELESSLY, [kawz'-les-li], *adv.* without cause or justification.

CAUSELESSNESS, [kawz'-les-nes], *n.* the condition of being causeless.

CAUSERIE, [kōz-er-ē'], *n.* gossip, light discussion, particularly in a newspaper; any short and informal essay or article. [Fr. *causerie* talk].

CAUSEUSE, [kōz-urz'], *n.* a settee for two people. [Fr. *causeuse* a talkative female].

CAUSEWAY, [kawz'-wā, kawz'-i], *n.* a stone-paved roadway; a highway; a raised pavement at the side of a thoroughfare. [OFr. *causie* a path from L. (*via*) *calciata* trodden (way)].

CAUSIDICAL, [kawz-id'-ik-al], *adj.* (*leg.*) belonging to an advocate. [L. *causidicus* pleader].

CAUSTIC (1), [kaws'-tik], *n.* a substance which burns or corrodes. [Gk. *kaustikos* corrosive].

CAUSTIC (**2**), [kaws'-tik], *adj.* corrosive, burning or eating away or into; (*fig.*) sharp, severe, sarcastic, cutting; **c. curve**, (*phys.*) a curve of light-rays which are reflections from a curved surface; **c. soda**, sodium hydroxide.
CAUSTICITY, [kaws-tis'-it-i], *n.* the property of being caustic.
CAUTER, [kaw'-ter], *n.* hot iron used as a cauterizing instrument. [Gk. *kauterion* branding iron].
CAUTERANT, [kawt'-er-ant], *n.* a cauterizing substance.
CAUTERISM, [kawt'-er-izm], *n.* (*med.*) the use of cautery.
CAUTERIZATION, [kawt'-er-īz-ā'-shun], *n.* (*med.*) the process of cauterizing.
CAUTERIZE, [kawt'-er-īz], *v.t.* to apply heat with a caustic or a hot iron, *esp.* to diseased tissue; to sear.
CAUTERY, [kawt'-er-i], *n.* the process of cauterizing; an iron caustic for cauterizing.
CAUTION (**1**), [kaw'-shun], *n.* prudence, carefulness; deliberate care when expecting danger; a warning; reproof, admonition; (*coll.*) a mischievous child or person. [L. *cautio*].
CAUTION (**2**), [kaw'-shun], *v.t.* to give a warning or caution to. [*Prec.*].
CAUTIONARY, [kaw'-shun-a-ri], *adj.* acting or designed as a warning, cautioning.
CAUTIONER, [kaw'-shun-er], *n.* one who cautions.
CAUTIOUS, [kaw'-shus], *adj.* exercising caution, careful, wary. [L. *cautus* careful].
CAUTIOUSLY, [kaw'-shus-li], *adv.* in a cautious fashion.
CAUTIOUSNESS, [kaw'-shus-nes], *n.* the quality of being cautious.
CAVALCADE, [kav'-al-kād'], *n.* an official procession, a procession on horseback; an historical sequence. [Fr. *cavalcade* from It. *cavalcado*].
CAVALIER (**1**), [kav'-a-lēer'], *n.* a horseman; a knight; a gentleman escort, a lady's man, a dashing gallant; (*hist.*) a follower of Charles I in the Civil War; (*fort.*) a raised place for cannon in a fort or rampart. [Fr. *cavalier*].

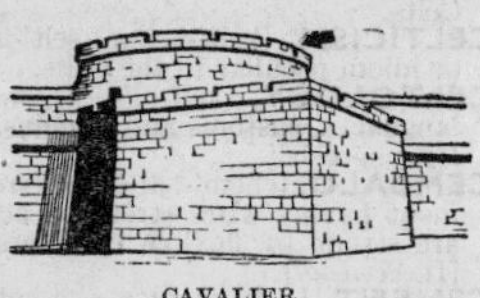
CAVALIER

CAVALIER (**2**), [kav'-a-lēer'], *adj.* gay, free and easy; having the qualities of a gentleman; disdainful, haughty, offhand.
CAVALIERLY, [kav-a-lēer'-li], *adv.* in a cavalier fashion.
CAVALRY, [kav'-al-ri], *n.* (*milit.*) troops mounted on horseback. [Fr. *cavallerie* from L. *caballus* a nag].
CAVATINA, [kav'-a-tēn'-a], *n.* (*mus.*) a short simple melody. [It. *cavatina*].
CAVATION, [kav-ā'-shun], *n.* (*arch.*) the hollowing out and levelling of earth for the foundation of a building. [L. *cavatio* excavation].
CAVE (**1**), [kāv], *n.* a space hollowed out of the earth, a subterranean den or chamber, naturally or artificially produced in a rock or cliff; anything resembling this; a group of seceders from a political party. [Fr. from L. *cava* hollows].
CAVE (**2**), [kā'-vi], *int.* (*school slang*) have care; beware. [*Imper. sg.* of L. *cavere* to beware].
CAVE (**3**), [kāv], *v.i.* †to hollow out; **to c. in**, to fall in and leave a hollow; (*fig.*) to give in. [CAVE (1)].
CAVEAT, [kāv'-i-at], *n.* a warning; (*leg.*) a notice to bring about a temporary cessation of proceedings. [L. *caveat, 3rd sg. pres.subj.* of *cavere* to beware].
CAVEATING, [kāv'-i-āt-ing] *n.* (*fencing*) a disengaging of one's sword.
CAVEATOR, [kāv'-i-āt-or], *n.* a person who enters a caveat.
CAVE-DWELLERS, [kāv'-dwel-erz], *n.*(*pl.*) dwellers in caves.
CAVE-MAN, [kāv'-man], *n.* one dwelling in a cave; (*slang*) a boisterous, virilemale.
CAVENDISH, [kav'-en-dish], *n.* a cake of tobacco mixed with molasses. [Uncert.].
CAVERN, [kav'-ern], *n.* a deep hollow in the earth, an underground cave. [L. *caverna*].
CAVERNED, [kav'-ernd], *adj.* with caverns; cavernous.
CAVERNOUS, [kav'-ern-us], *adj.* resembling a cavern, full of caverns, hollow.
CAVERNULOUS, [ka-vurn'-yŏŏ-lus], *adj.* riddled with tiny cavities.
CAVESSON, [kav'-es-on], *n.* a nose-band with a ring used instead of a bit for breaking in horses. [Fr. *caveçon*].
CAVIAR, CAVIARE, [kav'-i-ah(r)'], *n.* the roe of the sturgeon salted and prepared for eating; (*fig.*) that which is relished only by a highly developed taste. [Turk. *khavyar*].
CAVICORN, [kav'-i-kawn], *adj.* having hollow horns. [L. *cavus* hollow and *cornu* horn].
CAVIL (**1**), [kav'-il], *n.* a trivial objection, quibble, sophism.
CAVIL (**2**), [kav'-il], *v.i.* to quibble, carp, to raise unnecessary objections. [L. *cavillari*].
CAVILLER, [kav'-il-er], *n.* a person who cavils.
CAVILLING, [kav'-il-ing], *adj.* quibbling, raising captious objections.
CAVILLINGLY, [kav'-il-ing-li], *adv.* in a cavilling fashion.
CAVITY, [kav'-i-ti], *n.* a hollow place or part. [Fr. *cavité* from L. *cavus* hollow].
CAVORT, [ka-vawt'], *v.i.* (*coll.*) to frisk about like a horse.
CAVY, [kāv'-i], *n.* a small rodent, any species of *Cavia*, as the guinea-pig. [Fr. *cavié* from Braz. *cabiai*].
CAW (**1**), [kaw], *n.* the hoarse cry of a rook. [Echoic].
CAW (**2**), [kaw], *v.i.* to utter the cry of a rook.
CAXON, [kaks'-on], *n.* a type of wig. [Uncert.].
CAXTON, [kaks'-ton], *n.* a book printed by Caxton; (*typ.*) type similar to that used by Caxton. [W. *Caxton*, the first English printer (1422-1491)].
CAY, [kā], *n.* a reef or shoal. [Span. *cayo* shoal].
CAYENNE-PEPPER, [kā-yen'-pep'-er], *n.* a red and very pungent pepper.
CAYMAN, CAIMAN, [kā'-man], *n.* a variety of South American tropical alligator. [Carib. *caiman*].
CEASE, [sēs], *v.t. and i.* to stop, discontinue, to leave off; to cut short, pull up; to desist; to come to an end, finish. [L. *cessare*].
CEASELESS, [sēs'-les], *adj.* continuous, unending.
CEASELESSLY, [sēs'-les-li], *adv.* in a ceaseless manner.
CEASING, [sēs'-ing], *n.* a pause or cessation.
CECILS, [ses'-ilz], *n.*(*pl.*) balls of seasoned mincemeat fried in breadcrumbs. [Unkn.].
CECITY, [sēs'-it-i], *n.* loss of sight; (*fig.*) moral blindness. [Fr. *cécité* from L. *caecus* blind].
CEDAR (**1**), [sēd'-er], *n.* a coniferous evergreen tree having a fragrant wood. [Gk. *kedros*].
CEDAR (**2**), [sēd'-er], *adj.* made of cedar; **c. bird**, the American waxwing; **c. oil**, oil extracted from a species of juniper.
CEDARED, [sēd'-erd], *adj.* covered or planted with cedars.
CEDARN, [sēd-ern], *adj.* belonging to, or made of, cedar.
CEDE, [sēd], *v.t. and i.* to yield, surrender, submit; allow. [L. *cedere*].
CEDILLA, [sid-il'-a], *n.* a sign in the form of a comma sometimes placed under the letter *c* in French or Portuguese. [Span. *cedilla* a little z].
CEDRAT, [sēd'-rat], *n.* a species of citron-tree; its fruit, the lemon. [Fr. *cédrat* citron].
CEDRINE, [sed'-rēn], *adj.* cedarn.
CEE-SPRING, [sē'-spring], *n.* a spring resembling in form the letter C, used in supporting carriage bodies.
CEIL, [sēl], *v.t.* to cover over with a ceiling, to plaster a ceiling. [~L. *cælum* heaven].
CEILING, [sēl'-ing], *n.* the inside surface of a house roof, the upper side of a room, the layer of plaster spread under the timber which supports an overhead floor; (*naut.*) the lining or interior framework of a ship's hull; (*aeron.*) the altitude above which an aeroplane cannot fly; the highest price which may be charged for an article. [*Prec.*].
CELADON, [sel'-ad-on], *n.* porcelain which has had colour laid on it when the clay is wet and baked into it at the first baking. [Uncert.].
CELANDINE, [sel'-an-dīn], *n.* **greater c.**, the swallowwort, with a yellow flower, flowering in the season of the swallow's return to England, a species of *Chelidonium*; **lesser c.**, the pilewort, a variety of ranunculus.

GREATER CELANDINE

[Gk. *khelidonion* from *khelidon* swallow].
CELANESE, [sel'-an-ēz'], *n.* (*prot.*) a proprietary brand of artificial silk fabrics.
CELEBRANT, [sel'-i-brant], *n.* a person who celebrates; an officiating priest. [L. *celebrans*].
CELEBRATE, [sel'-i-brāt], *v.t.* to praise, to honour publicly, to commemorate by an official ceremony, to commend; to remember the past with joy and ritual; (*slang*) to have a good time. [L. *celebrare* solemnize, praise].
CELEBRATED, [sel'-i-brāt'-id], *adj.* widely praised, well-known, renowned.
CELEBRATION, [sel'-i-brā'-shun], *n.* the act of celebrating; a festivity. [L. *celebratio*].
CELEBRITY, [sel-eb'-rit-i], *n.* the status of being widely known for important achievements, fame, renown; a celebrated or greatly distinguished person. [Fr. *celebrité* from L. *celebritas*].
CELERIAC, [sel-e'-ri-ak], *n.* a turnip-rooted variety of celery which sprouts biennially.
CELERITY, [sel-e'-ri-ti], *n.* speed, rapidity, swiftness. [L. *celeritas*].
CELERY, [sel'-er-i], *n.* a vegetable, *Apium graveolens*, having edible stalks. [Gk. *selinon* wild parsley].
CELESTE, [sē-lest'], *n.* (*mus.*) a musical instrument resembling a glockenspiel; an organ-stop having a similar tone to this. [Fr. *céleste* heavenly].
CELESTIAL (1), [si-lest'-i-al], *n.* a Chinaman.
CELESTIAL (2), [si-lest'-i-al], *adj.* belonging to the heavens or sky, heavenly, divine; (*fig.*) excellent; having the colour of the sky; **C. Empire**, the former Chinese empire. [OFr. *celestial*].
CELESTIALLY, [si-lest'-i-al-i], *adv.* in a celestial fashion.
CELESTIALNESS, [si-lest'-i-al-nes], *n.* the condition or the quality of being celestial.
CELESTINE, [sel'-es-tēn], *n.* (*min.*) sulphate of strontium having a sky-blue colour. [It. *celestino* blue (of the sky)].
CELESTINES, [sel'-es-tēnz], *n.*(*pl.*) an order of Benedictine monks founded by Pietro da Morrone and so called when he became Pope Celestine V in 1294.
CELIAC, [sē'-li-ak], *adj.* belonging or referring to the lower abdomen. [COELIAC].
CELIBACY, [sel'-i-ba-si], *n.* the condition of being unmarried. [~L. *cælebs* unmarried].
CELIBATARIAN (1), [sel'-ib-a-tāer'-i-an], *n.* a person who favours celibacy.
CELIBATARIAN (2), [sel'-ib-a-tāer'-i-an], *adj.* favouring celibacy.
CELIBATE (1), [sel'-i-bat], *n.* one who is unmarried.
CELIBATE (2), [sel'-i-bat], *adj.* unmarried.
CELIDOGRAPHY, [sel'-id-og'-raf-i], *n.* an account of spots on the sun or on planets. [Gk. *kelis* spot and *graphia* writing].
CELL, [sel], *n.* a small room in a prison; a monk's or nun's small room; the hut or small refuge of a hermit; a single unit of a whole composed of similar units, particularly a unit of a honeycomb; a subsidiary unit of a political organization, of particular value for illegal propaganda work; (*biol.*) the smallest unit of living tissue; (*elect.*) one complete unit in a battery. [L. *cella* storeroom].
CELLAR, [sel'-er], *n.* a storeroom beneath ground-level, a basement used for storage purposes, a vault. [L. *cellarium*].
CELLARAGE, [sel'-er-ij], *n.* cellars; space for cellars, the storage capacity of a cellar, or cellars; charge for storage in a cellar.
CELLARER, [sel'-er-er], *n.* a monk looking after the monastery cellars; any person detailed to look after a cellar; a wine-merchant.
CELLARET, [sel'-er-et'], *n.* a case, or a cupboard in a sideboard fitted for storing wine, etc.
CELLARING, [sel'-er-ing], *n.* cellarage; storing in cellars, a place in a cellar.
CELLARIST, [sel'-er-ist], *n.* a person in charge of a cellar, a cellarer.
CELLARMAN, [sel'-er-man], *n.* a person employed in a cellar where liquor is stored.
CELLED, [seld], *adj.* having cells, being in the form of cells.
CELLIFEROUS, [sel-if'-er-us], *adj.* producing or growing in the form of cells. [L. *cella* and *ferre* to bear].
CELLIST, [chel'-ist], *n.* a violoncellist.
CELLO, [chel'-ō], *n.* a violoncello. [Short form of VIOLONCELLO].
CELLOPHANE, [sel'-ō-fān], *n.* (*prot.*) a transparent material made of wood pulp and used as a wrapping paper.
CELLULAR, [sel'-yōō-ler], *adj.* containing or consisting of cells; porous; **c. tissue**, an organic mass of minute living cells.
CELLULATED, [sel'-yōō-lāt-id], *adj.* formed with or composed of cells.
CELLULE, [sel'-yōōl], *n.* a small cell. [L. *cellula*].
CELLULIFEROUS, [sel'-yōō-lif'-er-us], *adj.* producing or bearing little cells. [*Prec.* and L. *ferre* to bear].
CELLULOID (1), [sel'-yōō-loid], *adj.* consisting of or pertaining to celluloid; **c. base**, (*phot.*) the negative film before being treated with sensitized emulsion.
CELLULOID (2), [sel'-yōō-loid], *n.* a synthetic substance, consisting of cellulose treated with camphor, highly inflammable, used as a substitute for bone, ivory, tortoise-shell, etc., and as a base for photographic film. [CELLULE and Gk. *oeides* like].
CELLULOSE (1), [sel'-yōō-lōs], *n.* a chemical substance obtained from the cell walls of vegetables or plants, chiefly composed of carbohydrate, and extensively used in the manufacture of artificial silk, paints, paper, etc.
CELLULOSE (2), [sel'-yōō-lōs], *adj.* consisting of cells, cellular; pertaining to or containing cellulose.
CELO, [sē'-lō], *n.* a unit of acceleration measured as one velo a second. [~L. *celer* swift].
CELSIUS (1), [sel'-si-us], *n.* the scale of the Centigrade thermometer. [A. *Celsius* (1701-1744), the inventor].
CELSIUS (2), [sel'-si-us], *adj.* Centigrade.
CELT (1), KELT, [kelt, selt], *n.* a member of those peoples whose languages include Welsh, Breton, Gaelic and Erse. [L. *Celta*, Gk. *Keltoi*].
CELT (2), [selt], *n.* (*archæ.*) a prehistoric flint cutting-implement. [L. *celtis* a cutting instrument].
CELTIC (1), [kelt'-ik, selt'-ik], *n.* one of the languages of the Celts.
CELTIC (2), [kelt'-ik, selt'-ik], *adj.* pertaining to the Celts.
CELTICISM, [kelt'-is-izm, selt'-is-izm], *n.* a custom or idiom peculiar to the Celts.
CELTOLOGY, [kelt-ol'-o-ji], *n.* the study of Celtic languages, customs and remains. [CELT (1) and Gk. *logos* speech].
CEMBALO, [chem'-bal-ō], *n.* (*mus.*) a musical instrument having wires stretched across a frame, which are struck by flexible hammers held in the hands. [It. *cembalo*].
CEMENT (1), [si-ment'], *n.* a substance compounded of ground limestone and water which, when placed in thin layers between stones or bricks, hardens rapidly and binds them firmly together; any adhesive substance used for securing joints; (*fig.*) that which has the power of uniting people, groups or units. [L. *cæmentum*].
CEMENT (2), [si-ment'], *v.t.* to join together, or cause to cohere, with cement; (*fig.*) to unite firmly; to effect a firmer, closer, alliance, to consolidate.
CEMENTATION, [sēm'-en-tā'-shun], *n.* the process of cementing or of being cemented; (*chem.*) the process of surrounding a solid body with another powdered substance or substances, and fusing them together by heat to produce a chemical change; the conversion of iron into steel by covering the iron with powdered charcoal and heating.
CEMENTATORY, [sim-ent'-at-er-i], *adj.* cementing.
CEMETERY, [sem'-it-er-i], *n.* a burying-place, a piece of ground having no parish church on it, consecrated for the burial of the dead. [Gk. *koimeterion* resting-place].
CENACLE, [sĕn'-akl], *n.* a supper-room, particularly that which was the scene of the Last Supper. [L. *coenaculum*].
CENOBITE, [sen'-ō-bīt], *n.* a member of a religious order living communally in a convent. [~Gk. *koinobion* communal life].
CENOBITIC, [sen'-ō-bit'-ik], *adj.* living in community, participating in a communal life.
CENOBITICAL, [sen'-ō-bit'-ikl], *adj.* cenobitic.
CENOTAPH, [sen'-ō-taf], *n.* a monument or tomb not containing the body of the person whose life and death it commemorates; the monument raised in Whitehall, London, commemorating British soldiers killed in the War of 1914-18. [Gk. *kenotaphion* empty tomb].
CENSE, [sens], *v.t.* to burn incense. [CENSER].
CENSER, [sen'-ser], *n.* a vessel designed for burning incense in. [OFr. *encensier* from L. *incendere* to burn].
CENSOR (1), [sen'-ser], *n.* an official authorized by a public body to ban books, plays or films, before or

after publication or performance, on the grounds of their containing material injurious to public morals, to religious beliefs, to individual reputations or subversive of the established social order; an officer appointed by the University of Oxford to supervise men students not attached to a college; (*hist.*) an officer in ancient Rome with duties of tax-collecting, census-taking and protecting public morals. [L. *censor* from *censere* to assess].

CENSOR (2), [sen'-ser], *v.t. and i.* to do the work of a censor, to examine material for the purpose of censorship; to delete or suppress by authority.

CENSORIAL, [sen-saw'-ri-al], *adj.* belonging to a censor; censorious.

CENSORIOUS, [sen-saw'-ri-us], *adj.* given to censure; severe in criticism; expressing censure.

CENSORIOUSLY, [sen-saw'-ri-us-li], *adv.* in a censorious fashion.

CENSORIOUSNESS, [sen-saw'-ri-us-nes], *n.* the condition of being censorious.

CENSORSHIP, [sen'-ser-ship], *n.* the act of censoring; the office, duties or tenure of a censor.

CENSUAL, [sen'-shōō-al], *adj.* belonging to a census. [L. *censualis*].

CENSURABLE, [sen'-sher-abl], *adj.* deserving or liable to censure.

CENSURABLENESS, [sen'-sher-abl-nes], *n.* the quality of being censurable.

CENSURABLY, [sen'-sher-ab-li], *adv.* in a censurable way.

CENSURE (1), [sen'-sher], *n.* blame, condemnation, stricture, criticism, admonition, imputation of wrong. [L. *censura* criticism].

CENSURE (2), [sen'-sher], *v.t.* to blame, reproach; to admonish, chide, reprimand; to stigmatize; to find fault with; to condemn after judgment. [*Prec.*].

CENSUS, [sen'-sus], *n.* an official count of a country's population, hence, any official collection of statistics. [L. *census* assessment].

CENT, [sent], *n.* abbreviation of L. *centum* one hundred; a hundredth part of any unit, as of a U.S. dollar; the name of an American coin of this value; **per c.**, a rate by the hundred, rate of interest in units of a hundred; **hundred per c.**, (*slang*) wholly, completely. [L. *centum* hundred].

CENTAGE, [sent'-ij], *n.* rate of measurement counted by the hundred.

CENTAL, [sent'-al], *n.* a hundred pounds weight, particularly of corn.

CENTAUR, [sent'-aw(r)], *n.* a creature of mythological origin, half man and half horse. [Gk. *kentauros*].

CENTAUR

CENTAURY, [sent'-aw-ri], *n.* (*bot.*) the plant *Erythræa Centaurium*, having medicinal properties. [*Prec.*].

CENTAVO, [sen-tā'-vō], *n.* a small Spanish coin. [Span. *centavo*, L. *centum* hundred].

CENTENARIAN, [sent'-en-āer'-i-an], *n.* a person a hundred years of age or more.

CENTENARY (1), [sen-tēn'-a-ri], *n.* a period of a hundred years; a commemoration after a hundred years. [L. *centenarius* from *centum* hundred].

CENTENARY (2), [sen-tēn'-a-ri], *adj.* relating to a hundred or a centenary.

CENTENNIAL (1), [sen-ten'-i-al], *n.* a centenary.

CENTENNIAL (2), [sen-ten'-i-al], *adj.* lasting or having lived a hundred years; happening once every hundred years. [L. *centum* hundred and *annus* year].

CENTERING, [sen'-ter-ing], *n.* a moving towards the centre; (*arch.*) a temporary frame supporting an arch or vault whilst under construction.

CENTESIMAL (1), [sen-tes'-im-al], *n.* a hundredth part. [L. *centesimum*].

CENTESIMAL (2), [sen-tes'-im-al], *adj.* hundredth.

CENTESIMATION, [sen'-tes-im-ā'-shun], *n.* an arbitrary mode of punishment in the army, one in each hundred being executed. [L. *centesimatio* selection of one in a hundred].

CENTI-, *pref.* one hundred. [L. *centum*].

CENTIARE, [sahn'-ti-āer'], *n.* an area of one square meter. [Fr. *centiare* square meter].

CENTICIPITOUS, [sen'-ti-sip'-it-us], *adj.* hundred-headed, having innumerable heads. [CENTI and L. *caput* head].

CENTIFOLIOUS, [sen'-ti-fō'-li-us], *adj.* possessing a hundred leaves. [CENTI and L. *folium* leaf].

CENTIGRADE, [sen'-ti-grād], *adj.* graded into a hundred degrees; **C. thermometer**, a thermometer having the interval between the freezing and the boiling points of water divided into 100 degrees. [CENTI and L. *gradus* step].

CENTIGRAMME, [sen'-ti-gram], *n.* one-hundredth part of a gramme. [CENTI and GRAMME].

CENTILITRE, [sen'-ti-lē'-ter], *n.* one-hundredth part of a litre. [CENTI and LITRE].

CENTILLION, [sen-til'-yon], *n.* the one-hundredth power of one million. [CENTI and (MI)LLION].

CENTIME, [sahn'-tēm], *n.* a coin of the value of one-hundredth part of a franc. [Fr. *centime* from L. *centesimus* hundredth part].

CENTIMETRE, [sen'-ti-mē-ter], *n.* one-hundredth part of a metre. [CENTI and METRE].

CENTIPEDE, [sen'-ti-pēd], *n.* a many-legged wingless arthropod. [L. *centipeda*].

CENTNER, [sent'-ner], *n.* a German measure of weight of 110·2 pounds avoirdupois. [L. *centenarius*].

CENTO, [sen'-tō], *n.* a form of composition in literature or music made up of selections from the works of various writers or musicians; an anthology. [L. *cento* patchwork].

CENTRAL, [sent'-rall, *adj.* pertaining to or situated in or near the centre of anything; accessible, important, chief; **c. heating**, a system of heating a building by a series of pipes heated from a single boiler.

CENTRALISM, [sen'-tral-izm], *n.* the quality of being concentrated in a centre; centralization of government or control.

CENTRALIST, [sen'-tral-ist], *n.* a person who advocates centralization in government.

CENTIPEDE

CENTRALITY, [sen-tral'-i-ti], *n.* the quality or the state of being central.

CENTRALIZATION, [sen'-tral-iz-ā'-shun], *n.* the act of centralizing, the act of concentrating at one centre the government of a country or the administration and directorate of a large business firm.

CENTRALIZE, [sen'-tral-iz], *v.t.* to draw to a centre, to concentrate in one place or at one point.

CENTRALLY, [sen'-tral-i], *adv.* in a central position, in the centre, accessibly.

CENTRE (1), [sen'-ter], *n.* (*geom.*) the point round which a circle is described, the point in a circle or sphere which is equidistant from all points on the circumference, a point equally distant from two extremities; (*fig.*) the point or position round which persons or objects are grouped, the person or object in the middle; an important position in the middle of an environment in which a particular activity is carried on, the environment itself; (*phys.*) that point in a body acting as a pivot for some particular activity or phenomenon; (*pol.*) the party standing for a moderate programme holding principles which are neither entirely reactionary nor entirely revolutionary; **c. forward**, the player occupying the middle position of five forwards in association football; **c. of gravity**, (*phys.*) the point about which all the parts of a body exactly balance each other, whether in motion or at rest. [Gk. *kentron* point].

CENTRE (2), [sen'-ter], *v.t.* to place on or in the centre, to determine the central point of, to draw towards the middle, to concentrate in the middle; (*fig.*) to concentrate; *v.i.* to be concentrated at a point, to be moved towards the middle, to be placed on or in the middle, to converge. [*Prec.*].

CENTRE (3), [sen'-ter], *adj.* central.

CENTREBIT, [sen'-ter-bit], *n.* a boring tool worked with a brace, and rotating on a projecting central point.

CENTREBOARD, [sen'-ter-bawd], *n.* an adaptable keel fitted to a boat which can be raised or lowered as desired.

CENTRE-PIECE, [sen'-ter-pēs], *n.* an ornament in the centre of a table.

CENTRIC, [sen'-trik], *adj.* central.

CENTRICALLY, [sen'-trik-a-li], *adv.* in a central position, centrally.

CENTRICITY, [sen-tris'-i-ti], *n.* the quality or the state of being centric.

CENTRIFUGAL, [sen-tri'-fewgl], *adj.* tending to move away from the centre of a revolving body; (*bot.*) of the flowers of a plant, opening at the centre before those at the outside; **c. force,** (*phys.*) the force which impels a revolving body to fly outwards from the centre. [CENTRE and L. *fugere* fly from].

CENTRIPETAL, [sen-trip'-it-al], *adj.* tending to move towards the centre; (*bot.*) (of a plant's flowers) opening first at the outside; (*biol.*) proceeding from the periphery to the nerve centre. [CENTRE and L. *petere* to seek].

CENTROBARIC, [sen'-trō-ba'-rik], *adj.* belonging to the centre of gravity. [L. *centrum* centre and Gk. *baros* weight].

CENTROID, [sen'-troid], *n.* centre of gravity. [CENTRE and Gk. *oeides* like].

CENTROLINEAD, [sen'-trō-lin'-i-ad], *n.* an instrument for drawing lines converging on a centre that is external to the drawing. [CENTRE and L. *linea* line].

CENTROLINEAL (1), [sen'-trō-lin'-i-al], *n.* a centrolinead.

CENTROLINEAL (2), [sen'-trō-lin'-i-al], *adj.* pertaining to lines converging towards a centre.

CENTUMVIR, [sen-tum'-ver], *n.* a Roman judge appointed by the prætor to deal with civil suits; a body of such judges. [L. *centum* hundred and *vir* man].

CENTUPLE (1), [sen'-tewpl], *adj.* hundredfold. [L. *centuplex*].

CENTUPLE (2), [sen'-tewpl], *v.t.* to multiply a hundredfold.

CENTUPLICATE, [sen-tew'-pli-kāt], *v.t.* to increase a hundredfold. [CENTI and L. *plicare* fold].

CENTURION, [sen-chōoer'-i-on], *n.* (*hist.*) an officer in the Roman army having command of a hundred men. [L. *centurio*].

CENTURY, [sen'-cher-i], *n.* a period of a hundred consecutive years; any period of a hundred years following on the conventionally accepted year of Christ's birth, e.g., twentieth century; a hundred things of the same kind, a collective hundred, particularly a hundred runs made by a batsman at cricket; (*hist.*) a Roman division of infantry numbering a hundred men; **c. plant,** the American aloe or agave. [L. *centuria*].

CEPHAL(O)-, *pref.* head. [Gk. *kephale*].

CEPHALALGIC (1), [sef'-al-al'-jik], *n.* a medicine for headache.

CEPHALALGIC (2), [sef'-al-al'-jik], *adj.* (*med.*) having or relating to headache. [CEPHAL(O) and Gk. *algos* pain].

CEPHALASPIS, [sef'-al-as'-pis], *n.* (*geol.*) a fossil fish, a ganoid. [CEPHAL(O) and Gk. *aspis* shield].

CEPHALIC, [sef-al'-ik], *adj.* of, or relating to, the head; **c. index,** (*anthrop.*) the ratio of length to breadth in a skull. [Gk. *kephale* head].

CEPHALITIS, [sef'-al-i'-tis], *n.* (*med.*) inflammation of the nerve centres in the brain. [CEPHAL(O) and Gk. *itis* denoting inflammation].

CEPHALOGRAPHY, [sef'-al-og'-raf-i], *n.* a descriptive analysis of the head. [CEPHALO and Gk. *graphia* writing].

CEPHALOID, [sef'-al-oid], *adj.* (*bot.*) head-shaped. [CEPHALO and Gk. *oeides* like].

CEPHALOMETRY, [sef'-al-om'-it-ri], *n.* the art of taking measurements of the skull. [CEPHALO and Gk. *metria* measuring].

CEPHALOPOD, [sef'-al-ō-pod'], *n.* a class of molluscs, including the cuttlefish and octopus, having tentacles growing from the head. [CEPHALO and Gk. *pous podos* foot].

CEPHALOPODIC, [sef'-al-ō-pod'-ik], *adj.* of, or relating to, the cephalopods.

CEPHALOPODOUS, [sef'-al-op'-od-us], *adj.* cephalopodic.

CEPHALOTHORAX, [sef'-al-ō-thaw'-raks], *n.* (*anat.*) the head and chest together. [CEPHALO and THORAX].

CEPHALOTOMY, [sef'-al-ot'-om-i], *n.* (*anat.*) dissection of the head. [CEPHALO and Gk. *tome* cutting].

CEPOLA, [sep'-ol-a], *n.* the bandfish or snakefish. [L. *cepola* small onion].

CEPOLA

CERACEOUS, [se-rā'-shus], *adj.* waxy, or resembling wax. [L. *cera* wax]

CERAMIC, KERAMIC, [ser-am'-ik], *adj.* relating to pottery. [Gk. *keramikos* made of clay].

CERAMICS, [ser-am'-iks], *n.* the art of making objects with clay, pottery.

CERARGYRITE, KERARGYRITE, [ser-ah'-jer-īt], *n.* (*min.*) horn silver; a natural chloride of silver. [Gk. *keras* horn and *arguros* silver].

CERASIN, [se'-ras-in], *n.* a gum formed by the cherry and the plum. [L. *cerasus* cherry-tree].

CERASTES, [se-ras'-tēz], *n.* a horned venomous snake, a species of viper. [Gk. *kerastes* horned; horned snake].

CERATE, [sēer'-āt], *n.* an ointment composed of wax, oil, etc. [L. *cerare* to smear with wax].

CERATED, [sēer'-āt-id], *adj.* smeared or covered with wax.

CERATITE, [se'-ra-tīt], *n.* a species of ammonite with oviculated lobes.

CERATOID, [se'-rat-oid], *adj.* horny. [Gk. *keras* horn and *oeides* like].

CERBEREAN, [ser-bēer'-i-an], *adj.* (*myth.*) pertaining to Cerberus, the three-headed dog guarding the entrance to Hell. [Gk. *Kerberos*].

CERE (1), [sēer], *n.* (*ornith.*) the waxy film which envelops the base of some birds' beaks, as of the hawk. [L. *cera* wax].

CERE (2), [sēer], *v.t.* to smear or cover with wax.

CEREAL (1), [sēer'-i-al], *n.* a plant which bears edible grain; the grain itself; a breakfast food made from this. [L. *cerealis* relating to *Ceres* goddess of corn].

CEREAL (2), [sēer'-i-al], *adj.* pertaining to or made of edible grain.

CEREALIA, [sēer'-i-ā'-li-a], *n.*(*pl.*) the species of edible grasses that include the cereals.

CEREALIN, [sēer'-i-al-in], *n.* (*chem.*) a substance containing nitrogen found in bran.

CEREBELLAR, [se'-rib-el'-er], *adj.* pertaining to the cerebellum.

CEREBELLUM, [se'-rib-el'-um], *n.* (*anat.*) the tissue of nerves forming the hinder and lower part of the brain. [L. *cerebellum* the smaller brain, from CEREBRUM].

CEREBRAL, [se'-rib-ral], *adj.* relating to the brain; **c. hemispheres,** the two main sections of the brain.

CEREBRALISM, [se'-rib-ral-izm], *n.* the theory that the mind works according to the actions of the brain.

CEREBRATE, [se'-rib-rāt], *v.i.* to be exercising the brain. [L. *cerebrum* brain].

CEREBRATION, [se'-rib-rā'-shun], *n.* action of the brain. [L. *cerebratio*].

CEREBRIC, [ser-ēb'-rik], *adj.* (*chem.*) extracted from the brain.

CEREBRIFORM, [ser-eb'-ri-fawm], *adj.* brain-shaped.

CEREBRINE, [se'-rib-rin], *n.* (*chem.*) a substance obtained from the brain.

CEREBROPATHY, [se'-rib-rop'-ath-i], *n.* the scientific study of treating morbid affections of the brain. [CEREBRUM and Gk. *pathos* suffering].

CEREBRO-SPINAL, [ser'-ib-rō-spīn-al], *adj.* (*anat.*) relating to or connected with both brain and spine; **c. meningitis,** an epidemic affection of the membranes surrounding the cerebrum and spine, spotted fever.

CEREBRUM, [se'-rib-rum], *n.* the higher nerve centre of the brain. [L. *cerebrum* brain].

CERECLOTH, [sēer'-kloth], *n.* a cloth smeared with wax used for shrouding a corpse. [L. *cera* wax and CLOTH].

CEREMENT, [sēer'-ment], *n.* a winding-sheet smeared with wax. [Fr. *cirement*].

CEREMONIAL (1), [se'-ri-mō'-ni-al], *n.* a sequence of customs and rites in formal order, observed on a solemn occasion, and expressing reverence; ritual.

CEREMONIAL (2), [se'-ri-mō'-ni-al], *adj.* pertaining to ceremony.

CEREMONIALISM, [se'-ri-mō'-ni-al-izm], *n.* ritualism.

CEREMONIALLY, [se'-ri-mō'-ni-al-i], *adv.* in a ceremonial fashion.

CEREMONIALNESS, [se'-ri-mō'-ni-al-nes], *n.* the state or quality of being ceremonial.

CEREMONIOUS, [se'-ri-mō'-ni-us], *adj.* characterized by ceremony, ritualistic, deferential, formal, courteous.

CEREMONIOUSLY, [se'-ri-mō'-ni-us-li], *adv.* in a ceremonious fashion.

CEREMONIOUSNESS, [se'-ri-mō'-ni-us-nes], *n.* the condition of being ceremonious.

CEREMONY, [se'-rim-un-i], *n.* an act, or series of acts or rites in a formal order, observed in public for the expression of reverence in honour of a solemn event; formality of manners, courteousness; **master of ceremonies,** the person who superintends the order of events at a public function. [L. *cærimonia* religious ceremony].

CEREOPSIS, [se'-ri-op'-sis], *n.* the Cape Barren goose. [CERE and Gk. *opsis* appearance].

CEREOUS, [sēer'-i-us], *adj.* waxen; resembling wax.

CERES, [sēer'-ēz], *n.* the Roman goddess of nature; mother of the earth. [L. *Ceres*].

CERGE, see CIERGE.

CERIFEROUS, [se-rif'-er-us], *adj.* wax-producing. [CERE and L. *ferre* to bear].

CERIN, [sēer'-in], *n.* a component of common wax.

CERINE, [sēer'-ēn], *n.* (*min.*) a cerium ore.

CERIPH, see SERIF.

CERISE (1), [se-rēs'], *n.* a tint of red with a tone of purple in it, the colour of a ripe cherry. [Fr. *cerise* cherry].

CERISE (2), [se-rēs'], *adj.* having the colour of cerise.

CERITE, [sēer'-īt], *n.* (*min.*) the red-coloured silicate of cerium.

CERIUM, [sēer'-i-um], *n.* (*chem.*) a greyish malleable metal, the chemical element denoted by Ce. [*Ceres* a star discovered at the same time].

CERNUOUS, [surn'-yōō-us], *adj.* (*bot.*) drooping. [L. *cernuus* turned earthwards].

CERO-, *pref.* wax. [Gk. *keros*].

CEROGRAPHICAL, [se-rō-graf'-ik-al], *adj.* relating to cerography.

CEROGRAPHIST, [se-rog'-raf-ist], *n.* an expert in cerography.

CEROGRAPHY, [se-rog'-raf-i], *n.* the art of engraving on wax; painting in coloured wax. [CERO and Gk. *graphia* writing].

CEROMANCY, [se'-rō-man'-si], *n.* divination by dropping melted wax into water and studying the patterns produced. [CERO and Gk. *manteia* divination].

CEROON, see SEROON.

CEROPLASTIC, [se'-rō-plas'-tik], *n.* the art of modelling in wax. [Gk. *keroplastikos*].

CEROTIC, [ser-ot'-ik], *adj.* of the nature of, or obtained from, beeswax.

CEROXYLON, [ser-oks'-il-on], *n.* the wax-palm of the Andes. [CERO and Gk. *xulon* tree].

CERRIS, [se'-ris], *n.* the Turkey oak, a species of *Quercus*. [L. *cerrus* oak].

CERT, [surt], *n.* (*slang*) a certainty, particularly a race-horse regarded as certain to win. [CERT(AINTY)].

CERTAIN, [sur'-ten], *adj.* sure, positive, unequivocal, definite, beyond doubt, undisputed; inevitable; accurate; fixed, accepted; unspecified, some, more than one. [OFr. *certein* from L. *certus* sure, resolved].

CERTAINLY, [sur'-ten-li], *adv.* for sure, without doubt, without fail.

CERTAINTY, [sur'-ten-ti], *n.* that which is certain; assurance, conviction; security.

CERTIFIABLE, [sur'-ti-fī'-abl], *adj.* able or liable to be certified; insane.

CERTIFIABLY, [sur'-ti-fī'-ab-li], *adv.* in a certifiable manner.

CERTIFICATE, [ser-tif'-ik-at], *n.* a document which certifies a fact; a written testimony bearing official recognition of achievement or fact; an authorized statement. [CERTIFY].

CERTIFICATION, [ser-tif'-ik-ā'-shun], *n.* the act of certifying.

CERTIFIER, [sur'-ti-fī'-er], *n.* one who certifies.

CERTIFY, [sur'-ti-fī], *v.t.* *and i.* to make certain; to give assurance, to give a certificate; to testify officially in writing; to judge insane. [Fr. *certifier* from LL. *certificare*].

CERTIORARI, [sur'-ti-ō-rāer'-ī], *n.* (*leg.*) a writ issued from a superior court to take a case out of the jurisdiction of a lower court together with all relevant records. [LL. *certiorari*, *pass.inf.* of *certiorare* to certify].

CERTITUDE, [sur'-ti-tewd], *n.* certainty; assurance. [LL. *certitudo*].

CERULEAN, [si-rōō'-li-an], *adj.* a deep blue having a transparent quality, sky-blue. [L. *caeruleus*].

CERULIFIC, [se'-rōō-lif'-ik], *adj.* producing a blue colour.

CERULIN, [se'-ryōō-lin], *n.* a substance of intense blueness obtained from indigo.

CERUMEN, [se'-rōō-men], *n.* the yellow wax secreted by the ear. [L. *cerumen* from *cera* wax].

CERUSE, [sē'-rōōs], *n.* white-lead, a carbonate of lead used as white paint. [L. *cerussa*].

CERUSED, [sē'-rōōst'], *adj.* painted with white lead.

CERUSSITE, [se'-rus-īt], *n.* (*min.*) carbonate of lead, white lead ore.

CERVICAL, [sur-vīk'-al, sur'-vik-al], *adj.* of, or relating to, the neck. [L. *cervix* neck].

CERVINE, [sur'-vīn], *adj.* relating to a stag or deer. [L. *cervus* stag].

CESAREWITCH, [sez-ah'-re-vich, sēz'-er-wich], *n.* the eldest son or successor of the Russian Tsar; a horse-race at Newmarket, England, run in late autumn. [~TSAR].

CESPITOSE, [ses'-pit-ōs], *adj.* (*bot.*) growing in tufts. [~L. *caespes* turf].

CESPITOUS, [ses'-pit-us], *adj.* consisting of or similar to turf; turfy.

CESSATION, [ses-ā'-shun], *n.* stoppage, a ceasing; pause; rest. [L. *cessatio*].

CESSION, [sesh'-un], *n.* (*leg.*) the act of formal surrender. [L. *cessio* giving up].

CESSPIT, [ses'-pit], *n.* a cesspool.

CESSPOOL, [ses'-pōōl], *n.* a pit for the sewage from a house. [Uncert.].

CEST, [sest], *n.* a lady's girdle. [Gk. *kestos*].

CESTOID, [ses'-toid], *n.* a tapeworm. [Gk. *kestos* girdle and *oeides* like].

CESTRACION, [ses-trā'-shun], *n.* the Port Jackson shark, *Heterodontus philippi*. [Gk. *kestra* hammer].

CETACEAN, [sit-ā'-shan], *n.* a whale, dolphin. [Gk. *ketos* whale].

CETACEOUS, [sit-ā'-shus], *adj.* relating to the cetaceans.

CETATE, [sē'-tāt], *n.* a salt of cetic acid.

CETIC, [sēt'-ik], *adj.* relating to the whale; obtained from spermaceti. [CETACEAN].

CETINE, [sē'-tin], *n.* a crystalline mass of spermaceti.

CETOLOGY, [sit-ol'-o-ji], *n.* (*zool.*) the scientific study of the natural history of the cetaceans. [Gk. *ketos* large fish and *logos* speech].

CETOTOLITES, [sēt-ot'-ol-its], *n.*(*pl.*) (*geol.*) fossil whale ear-bones. [Gk. *ketos* large fish, *ota* ears and *lithos* stone].

CETRARIA, [sit-rāer'-i-a], *n.* (*bot.*) a genus of lichens which includes the Iceland moss. [L. *cetra* small shield].

CETRARINE, [sē'-trar-in], *n.* (*chem.*) a principle extracted in white crystals from cetraria.

CETYL, [sē'-til], *n.* a radical principle in spermaceti. [Gk. *ketos* large fish and *hule* wood].

CEYLONITE, [sil-on'-īt], *n.* (*min.*) a variety of spinel found in Ceylon.

CHABAZITE, [kab'-a-zit], *n.* (*min.*) the colourless silicate of aluminium and lime. [Uncert.].

CHABLIS, [sha-blē'], *n.* a white Burgundy wine. [*Chablis* a French town].

CHABOUK, CHABUK, [chah'-bōōk], *n.* a scourge used in the East. [Pers. *chabuk*].

CHABUK, see CHABOUK.

CHACMA, [chak'-ma], *n.* a large pig-tailed baboon.

CHACONNE, [shak-on'], *n.* a stately Spanish dance; slow music for this dance. [Span. *chacona*].

CHAD, [chad], *n.* (*dial.*) the young of the sea-bream, a species of *Pagellus*; the *Pagrus auratus*. [SHAD].

CHAFE, [chāf], *v.i.* to rub against, to fret, to be made sore by rubbing; (*fig.*) to fret, to be goaded or fretted into impatience; *v.t.* to rub so as to make warm, to abrade, to rub till sore; (*fig.*) to cause anger, goad. [OFr. *chaufer* from L. *calefacere* make warm].

CHAFER, [chāf'-er], *n.* a winged beetle that feeds on leaves. [OE. *ceafor*].

CHAFERY, [chāf'-er-i], *n.* (*metal.*) a furnace in which metal is reheated. [Fr. *chaufferie* heating place].

CHAFF (1), [chahf], *n.* the husk of grain; fodder of finely-chopped straw; (*fig.*) worthless matter; spurious imitation; banter. [OE. *ceaf* gnawings].

CHAFF (2), [chahf], *v.t.* to banter.

CHAFF-CUTTER, [chahf'-kut'-er], *n.* a machine for cutting chaff.

CHAFFER (1), [chaf'-er], *n.* bargaining, haggling over prices. [OE. *ceap-faru*, ME. *chapfare*].

CHAFFER (2), [chaf'-er], *v.t.* *and i.* to buy, purchase as a bargain; to bargain, haggle.

CHAFFINCH, [chaf'-inch], *n.* a small British bird, *Fringilla cœlebs*, frequenting shrubberies and gardens. [OE. *ceaf-finc*].

CHAFFLESS, [chahf'-les], *adj.* having no chaff.

CHAFFY, [chahf'-i], *adj.* similar to or full of chaff; light; spurious, worthless; full of jokes and banter.

CHAFING-BOARD, [chāf'-ing-bawd'], *n.* (*naut.*) a batten to protect the ropes from chafing.

CHAFING-DISH, [chāf'-ing-dish'], *n.* a portable stove; a dish heated at table.

ō (bone), ī (fine), ōō (food), ŏŏ (put), u (up), th (*th*ink), TH (*th*at), zh (azure), † = obsolete, ~ = related to.

CHAGRIN (1), [shag-rēn′], *n.* annoyance, vexation; ill-humour. [Fr. *chagrin* grief].
CHAGRIN (2), [shag-rēn′], *v.t.* to fret, to vex.
CHAIN (1), [chān], *n.* a number of circular or oval metal links, each link passing through the next; a fetter; a device for measuring land, consisting of 100 links, equal to 66 ft.; (*pl.*) bondage, imprisonment; (*fig.*) sequence of similar things or ideas connected in series. [OFr. *chaeine* from L. *catena* chain].
CHAIN (2), [chān], *v.t.* to secure or fasten with a chain; to confine by chains, to fetter; (*fig.*) to bind, restrain, to restrict the freedom of.
CHAIN-BELT, [chān′-belt′], *n.* a chain in the form of a driving belt running on sprockets in a machine.
CHAIN-BRIDGE, [chān′-brij], *n.* suspension-bridge supported by chains from points higher than road level.
CHAIN-GANG, [chān′-gang′], *n.* a number of prisoners, each secured to the next by chains.
CHAINLESS, [chān′-les], *adj.* having no chains; out of bondage, free.
CHAIN-LIGHTNING, [chān′-līt′-ning], *n.* forked lightning flashing continuously.
CHAINLET, [chān′-let], *n.* a small chain.
CHAIN-LETTER, [chān′-let′-er], *n.* a letter intended to be forwarded by each recipient in turn.
CHAIN-MAIL, [chān′-māl], *n.* armour of interwoven iron rings.
CHAIN-PUMP, [chān′-pump′], *n.* a pump in which the liquid is elevated by a series of small buckets secured at intervals on a rotating endless belt let down into the well.
CHAIN-SHOT†, [chān′-shot′], *n.* (*milit.*) two cannon-balls joined together by a length of chain for wrecking the rigging of an enemy ship.
CHAIN-SMOKER, [chān′-smōk′-er], *n.* a person who smokes cigarettes in unbroken succession, lighting each new cigarette with the end of the previous one.
CHAIN-STITCH, [chān′-stich], *n.* (*sewing*) an arrangement of stitches to form a chain; a stitch made with two threads.

CHAIN-STITCH

CHAIN-STORE, [chān′-staw(r)′], *n.* one of a large series of shops owned and operated by a single firm.
CHAIR (1), [chāer], *n.* a movable seat made of various materials with a seat, four legs and a back-rest; the block of steel which secures a railway line to a sleeper; (*fig.*) a seat of authority, the post of university professor, the chairmanship of a meeting. [OFr. *chaiere* from Gk. *kathedra* seat].
CHAIR (2), [chāer], *v.t.* to carry a person on high through a public throng as a token of enthusiasm for an achievement.
CHAIRMAN, [chāer′-man], *n.* the person presiding over a meeting; the principal director of a commercial company; a sedan-chair or bath-chair attendant.
CHAIRMANSHIP, [chāer′-man-ship], *n.* the status of a chairman.
CHAIROPLANE, [chāer′-ō-plān], *n.* a roundabout with chairs hung on long chains. [CHAIR and PLANE].
CHAISE, [shāz], *n.* a light one-horsed four-wheeled carriage; **c. longue,** a sofa or couch. [Fr. *chaise* seat].
CHALAZA, [kal-ā′-za], *n.* (*bot.*) the spot on a seed where the nucleus and integuments meet. [Gk. *khalaza* hailstone].
CHALCEDONIC, CALCEDONIC, [kal′-sid-on′-ik], *adj.* relating to chalcedony.
CHALCEDONY, CALCEDONY, [kal-sed′-on-i], *n.* one of various forms of translucent quartz valued as semi-precious. [*Chalcedon* a town in Asia Minor].
CHALCEDONYX, [kal-sed′-on-iks], *n.* (*min.*) a variety of agate composed of white and grey layers.
CHALCOGRAPHY, [kal-kog′-raf-i], *n.* the art of engraving on copper. [Gk. *khalkos* copper and *graphia* writing].
CHALDAIC (1), [kal-dā′-ik], *n.* the language of the Chaldeans or Babylonians.
CHALDAIC (2), [kal-dā′-ik], *adj.* pertaining to Chaldea or its inhabitants.
CHALDER, [chold′-er], *n.* the oyster-catcher; (*naut.*) a gudgeon. [Unkn.].
CHALDRON, [chawl′-dron], *n.* a measure of coal of one ton and a quarter. [OFr. *chauldron* kettle].
CHALET, [shal′-ā], *n.* a Swiss cottage, a hut built on a mountain-side; a summer bungalow. [Swiss Fr. *chalet*].
CHALICE, [chal′-is], *n.* (*eccles.*) a sacramental cup. [L. *calix*].

CHALICE

CHALICED, [chal′-ist], *adj.* (*bot.*) possessing a cell or cup. [*Prec.*].
CHALK (1), [chawk], *n.* an opaque, soft, earthy, white limestone; the geological rock strata in which this is found; material consisting of or similar to chalk for drawing or sketching purposes; a mark made with chalk; **french c.,** soapstone; **not to know c. from cheese,** not to recognize things obviously different; **better by a long c.,** being more likely to win or score, thus finer by a considerable degree. [OE. *cealc* from L. *calx* lime].
CHALK (2), [chawk], *v.t.* to make a mark with chalk; (*fig.*) to score, to record the score in a game.
CHALK-CUTTER, [chawk′-kut′-er], *n.* one who digs for chalk.
CHALKINESS, [chawk′-i-nes], *n.* the quality or the state of being chalky.
CHALKPIT, [chawk′-pit], *n.* a pit from which chalk is obtained.
CHALKSTONE, [chawk′-stōn], *n.* (*med.*) a chalky accretion of urate of sodium in the feet and hands, a symptom of gout.
CHALKY, [chawk′-i], *adj.* containing, or resembling, chalk.
CHALLENGE (1), [chal′-enj], *n.* a provocation or deliberate defiance; a call to account; an invitation to a contest or athletic competition, an incitement to prove one's skill or strength; a sentry's call; an objection to a person as a member of a jury. [OFr. *chalonge* from L. *calumnia* accusation].
CHALLENGE (2), [chal′-enj], *v.t.* to make a challenge to. [*Prec.*].
CHALLENGEABLE, [chal′-enj-abl], *adj.* liable or able to be challenged.
CHALLENGER, [chal′-enj-er], *n.* one who challenges.
CHALLIS, [shal′-i], *n.* a fine soft silk and woollen fabric. [Unkn.].
CHALONE, [chal′-ōn], *n.* a secretion restricting growth.
CHALUMEAU, [shal-ew-mō′], *n.* a shepherd's pipe cut from a reed. [OFr. *chalemel* from L. *calamellus* reed].
CHALYBEATE (1), [kal-ib′-i-āt], *n.* water or a liquor into which iron has entered.
CHALYBEATE (2), [kal-ib′-i-āt], *adj.* containing iron. [Gk. *khalups* steel].
CHALYBITE, [kal′-ib-īt], *n.* (*min.*) spathic iron ore, a native carbonate of iron; siderite.
CHAM, [kam], *n.* an Oriental despot; a literary dictator. [KHAN].
CHAMADE, [sham-ahd′], *n.* (*milit.*) signal given by trumpet or drum to retreat or call a truce with the enemy. [Portug. *chamada* from L. *clamare* to shout].
CHAMBER (1), [chām′-ber], *n.* an apartment, a room in a house or public building, the room of a high official such as lawyer or judge; the large room in which legislative bodies assemble; the assembly of such bodies itself; an apartment rented for lodging in; a cavity, a hollow space; a chamber-pot; (*milit.*) the part of a gun's breech made to hold the projectile or charge. [OFr. *chambre* from L. *camera* vault].
CHAMBER (2), [chām′-ber], *v.t. and i.* to make a hollow, to hollow out; to be residing in a chamber.
CHAMBER-CONCERT, [chām′-ber-kon′-sert], *n.* a concert of chamber-music.
CHAMBER-COUNCIL, [chām′-ber-kown′-sil], *n.* a council held in private.
CHAMBER-COUNSEL, [chām′-ber-kown′-sel], *n.* (*leg.*) a barrister giving his opinion in chambers, but not pleading in court.
CHAMBERED, [chām′-berd], *adj.* divided into compartments.
CHAMBERER, [chām′-ber-er], *n.* a frequenter of ladies' rooms, a wanton; a gallant.
CHAMBER-FELLOW, [chām′-ber-fel′-ō], *n.* a person who sleeps in the same bedroom.
CHAMBER-HANGING, [chām′-ber-hang′-ing], *n.* a curtain or tapestry for a chamber.

CHAMBERING, [chām′-ber-ing], *n.* habitual frequenting of ladies' rooms; licentious indulgence.

CHAMBERLAIN, [chām′-ber-lin], *n.* the officer in charge of the private apartments of a king or noble; the treasurer of a corporation or city; **Lord C.,** the head of the Royal Household. [OFr. *chambrelain*].

CHAMBERLAINSHIP, [chām′-ber-lin-ship′], *n.* the rank and office of a chamberlain.

CHAMBERMAID, [chām′-ber-mād], *n.* a female servant whose task is to keep the bedrooms clean and tidy.

CHAMBER-MUSIC, [chām′-ber-mew′-zik], *n.* music to be played in a room by a few performers as distinct from music to be played by a full orchestra in a public hall.

CHAMBER-POT, [chām′-ber-pot′], *n.* a bedroom utensil to receive urine.

CHAMBER-PRACTICE, [chām′-ber-prak′-tis], *n.* the practice of a chamber-counsel.

CHAMBERS, [chām′-berz], *n.(pl.)* apartments situated in the Inns of Court; private rooms in the law courts for settling cases or details of routine.

CHAMBERTIN, [shahm′-bāer-tan(g)′], *n.* a rich red Burgundy wine. [*Chambertin*, in France, where grown].

CHAMBREL, [kam′-brel], *n.* a joint above the hoof in a horse's hind leg; a gambrel. [GAMBREL].

CHAMELEON (1), CAMELEON, [kam-ē′-li-on], *n.* one of a genus of lizard with a long extensile tongue and a prehensile tail, and the power of changing its colour to match its surroundings. [Gk. *khamaileon* ground-lion].

CHAMELEON (2), [kam-ē′-li-on], *adj.* pertaining to the chameleon; (*fig.*) changeable, fickle, inconstant.

CHAMFER (1), [sham′-fer], *n.* a bevel cut at the line of union of two planes. [Fr. *chanfrein*].

CHAMFER (2), [sham′-fer], *v.t.* to cut a bevel in. [OFr. *chanfraindre*].

CHAMFRON, [sham′-fron], *n.* armour to protect a horse's head. [OFr. *chanfrein*].

CHAMOIS (1), [sham′-wah], *n.* an agile horned animal of ruminant habits of the antelope kind found in Europe, *Rupicapra tragus*. [Fr. *chamois*].

CHAMOIS (2), [sham′-i], *n.* a soft leather made from the skin of the chamois, used for washing and cleaning.

CHAMFRON

CHAMOMILE, see CAMOMILE.

CHAMP, [champ], *v.t.* and *i.* (of a horse) to keep biting with the teeth; (*fig.*) to chew; to crunch, munch. [Uncert.].

CHAMPAGNE, [sham-pān′], *n.* a light and effervescent French wine. [*Champagne*, a district in France, where made].

CHAMPAIGN, [cham′-pān], *n.* a stretch of level open country. [OFr. *champaigne* from L. *campania*].

CHAMPAK, [cham′-pak], *n.* an Indian magnolia cultivated for its perfumed yellow flowers, *Michelia Champaca*. [Hind. *champak*].

CHAMPERTOR, [cham′-per-ter], *n.* (*leg.*) one who makes a champerty.

CHAMPERTY, [cham′-per-ti], *n.* (*leg.*) a bargain with one of the parties in a lawsuit to share what may be recovered in the suit in return for sharing the cost. [Fr. *champart* from L. *campi partio* sharing of land].

CHAMPIGNON, [sham-pēn′-yon(g)], *n.* a small mushroom. [Fr. *champignon*].

CHAMPION (1), [cham′-pi-on], *n.* defender, usually publicly acknowledged, of a cause, faith, title or another person; the person proved as superior to all others in skill or strength; an expert in skill or strength; an expert in a form of athletics; the animal winning the first prize in a show. [OFr. *champiun* from LL. *campio* fighter].

CHAMPION (2), [cham′-pi-on], *adj.* (*dial.*) finest, best.

CHAMPIONSHIP, [cham′-pi-on-ship], *n.* the rank or status of champion, the position of a winner of a series of eliminating contests.

CHAMPLEVE, champlevé, [shahm-lev′-ā], *adj.* enamelled by a process in which the lines of the design are left raised. [Fr. *champlevé* raised field].

CHANCE (1), [chahns], *n.* the result of untraced causes; the course of events, occurrence; unforeseen circumstance; luck, fortune; opportunity, possibility, probability. [OFr. *cheance*].

CHANCE (2), [chahns], *adj.* fortuitous, happening by chance, accidental, unforeseen.

CHANCE (3), [chahns], *v.t.* and *i.* to happen; to occur, to experience by accident; (*coll.*) to risk, to dare, to take a gamble on; **to c. upon,** to meet or find unexpectedly.

CHANCECOMER, [chahns′-kum′-er], *n.* a person who comes by chance.

CHANCEFUL, [chahns′-fo͞ol], *adj.* hazardous.

CHANCEL, [chahn′-sel], *n.* the eastern part of a church in which the clergy and choir sit during service; that part of a church where the altar is, and usually railed off. [OFr. *chancel*, L. *cancelli* lattice].

CHANCELLOR, [chahn′-sel-er], *n.* the title of certain high officials; **c. of a diocese,** the legal adviser to a bishop; **C. of the Duchy of Lancaster,** a minister of the crown who exercises certain special duties in relation to crown lands in the Duchy of Lancaster; **C. of the Exchequer,** the minister of finance; **Lord High C.,** the keeper of the Great Seal, the principal judge presiding over the House of Lords. [OFr. *chanceler* from LL. *cancellarius*].

CHANCELLORSHIP, [chahn′-sel-er-ship], *n.* the office and tenure of a chancellor.

CHANCEL-SCREEN, [chahn′-sel-skrēn′], *n.* the screen, usually of open woodwork, partitioning the chancel from the main body of a church.

CHANCE-MEDLEY, [chahns′-med′-li], *n.* (*leg.*) manslaughter upon a chance encounter. [AFr. *chance medlee*].

CHANCERY, [chahn′-ser-i], *n.* a division of the High Court of Justice dealing with equity cases, presided over by the Master of the Rolls. [*Var.* of *chancellery*].

CHANCRE, [shangk′-er], *n.* a venereal ulcer. [Fr. *chancre*, CANKER].

CHANCROUS, [shangk′-rus], *adj.* (*med.*) ulcerous.

CHANCY, [chahn′-si], *adj.* (*slang*) risky; uncertain.

CHANDELIER, [shan′-del-ēer′], *n.* a fitting usually in the form of symmetrical brackets or arms, hanging from the ceiling for holding a number of lights, formerly candles; **c. flame,** a kind of flare. [CANDLE].

CHANDLER, [chahnd′-ler], *n.* a candle-maker; a dealer in soap, candles, etc.; **ship's c.,** a seller of ship's provisions. [CANDLE].

CHANDLERY, [chahnd′-ler-i], *n.* articles sold by a chandler.

CHANFRIN, [shan′-frin], *n.* the fore-part of a horse's head; the chamfron. [OF. *chanfrein*].

CHANGE (1), [chānj], *n.* an alteration, variation or replacement of one thing for another; variety; a passing from one condition or state to another, transition; coins of low denomination given as equivalent in value for coins of higher denomination; money in excess of the purchase price returned by the seller to the buyer of a commodity; (*coll.*) the Exchange; the order in which a chime of bells is rung; (*fig.*) **to ring the changes on,** to repeat in different forms; to swindle. [Fr. *change* from LL. *cambium* exchange].

CHANGE (2), [chānj], *v.t.* to make a change or modification; to cause to become different; to substitute or adopt one thing for another; to alter the order or nature of a thing or person; to exchange coins of lower denomination equivalent in value to higher; *v.i.* to undergo a change, to become different, to be in a state of transition, to pass into a new phase; to undress and put on different clothes; **to c. with,** to exchange. [OFr. *changier*].

CHANGEABILITY, [chānj′-ab-il′-i-ti], *n.* the quality or condition of being changeable, changeableness.

CHANGEABLE, [chānj′-abl], *adj.* liable to change; capable of being changed, variable, fickle, inconstant.

CHANGEABLENESS, [chānj′-abl-nes], *n.* changeability.

CHANGEABLY, [chānj′-ab-li], *adv.* in a changeable fashion.

CHANGEFUL, [chānj′-fo͞ol], *adj.* constantly changing, full of change; inconstant, fickle.

CHANGEFULLY, [chānj′-fo͞ol-i], *adv.* in a changeful fashion.

CHANGEFULNESS, [chānj′-fo͞ol-nes], *n.* the condition or the quality of being changeful.

CHANGELESS, [chānj′-les], *adj.* unchanging, immutable.

CHANGELING, [chānj′-ling], *n.* a child substituted for another; any substitute; a fickle person.

CHANGER, [chānj′-er], *n.* a person who changes; a money-changer.

CHANGING, [chānj'-ing], *adj.* that changes, changeful.

CHANK, [changk], *n.* a species of conch-shell, *Turbinella pyrum.* [Skr. *chanka* conch-shell].

CHANNEL, [chan'-el], *n.* a watercourse, the bed of a river; a deep in a harbour or bay taking the main current; a narrow sea between two land-masses and joining two seas; a groove, passage or duct naturally or artificially formed to carry water; (*fig.*) a path, means of communication. [OFr. *chanel*].

CHANK

CHANNEL-IRON, [chan'-el-iern'], *n.* a rolled iron bar with a groove or channel formed on one side.

CHANNELLED, [chan'-eld], *adj.* grooved lengthwise, connected by means of channels.

CHANSON, [shahn'-son(g)], *n.* a song; **c. de geste,** a medieval French narrative heroic poem. [Fr. *chanson* song].

CHANSONETTE, [shahn'-son-et'], *n.* a short song, a ditty. [Fr. *chansonette*].

CHANT (1), [chahnt], *n.* a song, melody, one which accompanies church canticles; the words in a church service, half-sung, half-recited. [Fr. *chante* from L. *cantus* song].

CHANT (2), [chahnt], *v.t. and i.* to sing a song; to recite poetry; to repeat monotonously; to intone. [Fr. *chanter* from L. *cantare*].

CHANTER, [chahnt'-er], *n.* a person who chants; a solo singer; the tenor or treble pipe in a bagpipe.

CHANTERELLE, [shan'-ter-el'], *n.* a species of yellow mushroom, *Cantharellus cibarius.* [Fr. *chanterelle*].

CHANTICLEER, [chahn'-tik-lēer'], *n.* a cock, particularly one that crows lustily and clearly. [OFr. *chantecler*].

CHANTRESS†, [chahn'-tres], *n.* a woman singer.

CHANTRY, [chahn'-tri], *n.* an endowment of a chapel in which a priest is to chant mass daily for the soul of the founder or other deceased person; the chapel or part of the chapel so endowed. [OFr. *chanterie* singing].

CHANTY, [shan'-ti], *n.* a shanty.

CHAOS, [kā'-os], *n.* the formless confusion, the abyss, supposed to exist before the creation of the universe; the state of anything before it is put in order; disorder, muddle. [Gk. *khaos*].

CHAOTIC, [kā-ot'-ik], *adj.* having or resembling the nature of chaos; confused.

CHAOTICALLY, [kā-ot'-ik-a-li], *adv.* in chaotic fashion.

CHAP (1), [chap], *n.* a crack, a slit, particularly on the skin. [CHAP (4)].

CHAP (2), [chap], *n.* (*coll.*) a boy, man, fellow. [CHAPMAN].

CHAP (3), [chap], *n.* the jaw; **Bath c.,** dressed pig's cheek. [Uncert.].

CHAP (4), (**chapping, chapped**), [chap], *v.t. and i.* to cause a crack or cracks or soreness, particularly in the skin. [~CHOP].

CHAPBOOK, [chap'-bŏŏk], *n.* a small book, pamphlet or tract of popular tales and verses sold by chapmen or hawkers.

CHAPE, [chāp], *n.* a catch, as of a buckle; a thin metal plate at the end of a scabbard protecting the point of the sword. [*Var.* of CAPE].

CHAPEAU, [shap-ō'], *n.* a hat; (*her.*) a cap of maintenance. [Fr. *chapeau*].

CHAPEL, [chap'-el], *n.* a small building for worship, generally belonging to or part of a church; part of a church with an altar; a hall used for worship in a remote part of a parish; a private place of worship; a place of worship for Nonconformists; a union organization for printers to safeguard their interests, a meeting held by these workers. [OFr. *chapel*, L. *capella*].

CHAPELESS, [chāp'-les], *adj.* having no chape.

CHAPELET†, [chap'-let], *n.* a pair of stirrup leathers fitted with stirrups. [CHAPLET].

CHAPELLARY, [chap-el'-er-i], *n.* a chapel within a church; an ecclesiastical foundation subordinate to another.

CHAPELLING, [chap'-el-ing], *n.* (*naut.*) the act of reversing a ship in a light breeze.

CHAPELRY, [chap'-el-ri], *n.* a part of a parish served by a chapel. [Fr. *chapelerie*].

CHAPERON (1), [shap'-er-ōn], *n.* a responsible person, usually an elderly lady, in charge of a young unmarried girl in assemblies where men are present. [Fr. *chaperon* hood].

CHAPERON (2), [shap'-er-ōn'], *v.t.* to act as a chaperon.

CHAPERONAGE, [shap'-er-ōn'-ij], *n.* the duty of a chaperon.

CHAPFALLEN, CHOPFALLEN, [chap'-fawl'-en], *adj.* having the lower jaw drooping; dejected.

CHAPITER, [chap'-it-er], *n.* (*arch.*) a capital. [Fr. *chapitre*].

CHAPLAIN, [chap'-lin], *n.* a clergyman appointed to serve official bodies such as the army. [OFr. *chaplain*].

CHAPLAINCY, [chap'-lin-si], *n.* the office or rank of a chaplain.

CHAPLAINSHIP, [chap'-lin-ship], *n.* chaplaincy.

CHAPLESS, [chap'-les], *adj.* having little flesh round the mouth.

CHAPITER

CHAPLET (1), [chap'-let], *n.* a wreath, garland or band worn round the crown of the head; a rosary; (*arch.*) a small moulding of semicircular section carved with beading. [OFr. *chaplet*].

CHAPLET

CHAPLET (2), [chap'-let], *v.t.* to adorn or provide with a chaplet.

CHAPMAN, [chap'-man], *n.* a hawker, pedlar. [OE. *ceapman*].

CHAPPED, [chapt], *adj.* with chaps, sore-skinned. [CHAP (4)].

CHAPPY, [chap'-i], *adj.* chapped.

CHAPTER, [chap'-ter], *n.* one of the main sections of a book; a heading, a principal topic or aspect, episode; an Act of Parliament; a decretal epistle; the governing body of a cathedral church presided over by the dean; a meeting held by such a body; **a c. of accidents,** a series of misfortunes; **c. and verse,** exact authority. [OFr. *chapitre* from L. *caput* head].

CHAPTER-HOUSE, [chap'-ter-hows'], *n.* a building attached to a cathedral in which the chapter meets.

CHAPTREL, [chap'-trel], *n.* (*arch.*) a capital supporting an arch. [CHAPTER].

CHAR (1), [chah(r)], *n.* a species of trout living in cold-water lakes. [Gael. *ceara* blood-red].

CHAR (2), [chah(r)], *n.* a charwoman.

CHAR (3), (**charring, charred**), [chah(r)], *v.i.* to do house-work for payment by the hour. [OE. *cerran* to turn].

CHAR (4), (**charring, charred**), [chah(r)], *v.t.* to reduce to charcoal by burning; to burn partially. [Uncert.].

CHAR-A-BANC, CHARABANC, [sha'-ra-bang'], *n.* a long open brake or motor-car with seats for many people; a motor coach. [Fr. *char-à-banc*].

CHARACTER (1), [ka'-rak-ter], *n.* an inscribed mark, a letter or alphabetical symbol, a symbol; a style of letter forms; a mark that distinguishes, a peculiarity; the qualities which give individuality to a person, the expressive habits of a person in action and emotional reaction; a good reputation; (*biol.*) the characteristics and peculiarities, organic or conditioned, typical of the species; a written estimate of mental and physical abilities, a testimonial; a person well known for certain individual traits or achievements; an odd individual, an eccentric; a person taking part in the action of a play or novel; the representation on the stage by an actor of a person. [Gk. *kharakter*].

CHARACTER (2), [ka'-rak-ter], *v.t.* to characterize, to describe a character; to inscribe.

CHARACTERFUL, [ka'-rak-ter-fŏŏl], *adj.* intensely expressive of character.

CHARACTERISTIC (1), [kar'-ak-ter-ist'-ik], *n.* that which constitutes or exposes the character, an individual feature or peculiarity, mental or physical.

CHARACTERISTIC (2), [kar'-ak-ter-ist'-ik], *adj.* pertaining to or revealing character. [Gk. *kharakteristikos*].

CHARACTERISTICALLY, [ka'-rak-ter-ist'-ik-a-li], *adv.* in a characteristic fashion.

CHARACTERIZATION, [kar'-ak-ter-iz-ā'-shun], *n.* the act of characterizing, a descriptive or dramatic portrayal of character.
CHARACTERIZE, [kar'-ak-ter-iz], *v.t.* to expose the character of, to give character to; to distinguish; to describe the peculiar qualities of. [Gk. *kharakterizo* I engrave].
CHARACTERLESS, [kar'-ak-ter-les], *adj.* possessing little distinctive character.
CHARADE, [sha-rahd'], *n.* a riddle game, usually in the form of extempore dramatizations of the syllables of a word. [Fr. *charade*].
CHARCOAL, [chah'-kōl], *n.* the residue of partially burnt wood, etc., being an impure form of carbon. [CHAR (4) and COAL].
CHARD, [chahd], *n.* an American artichoke. [Fr. *chardon* from ~L. *carduus* thistle].
CHARFRON, [chah'-fron], *n.* chamfron.
CHARGE (1), [chahj], *n.* a full loading, *esp.* of something meant to be emptied out, such as muskets or glasses; the thing loaded; the electricity contained in a battery; a liability, a tax, claim, or debt; the price demanded or extracted for a thing; a debit entry; an injunction, exhortation, obligation; responsibility for something, control, jurisdiction over; a judicial instruction and command; a formal accusation of some crime; a furious approach to attack; (*her.*) a bearing on an escutcheon. [OFr. *charge*].
CHARGE (2), [chahj], *v.t. and i.* to load, fill with; to fill with electricity; to ask payment for something, to make a claim, to exhort, to enjoin; to entrust someone with something; (*leg.*) to accuse, make a charge against, to instruct the jury; to run violently against, to make a violent rush. [OFr. *chargier*].
CHARGEABLE, [chahj'-abl], *adj.* able to be charged for.
CHARGEABLENESS, [chahj'-abl-nes], *n.* the condition of being chargeable.
CHARGE D'AFFAIRES, chargé d'affaires, [shah-zhā-daf-āer'], *n.* an ambassador's representative. [Fr. *chargé d'affaires* one charged with business].
CHARGELESS, [chahj'-les], *adj.* free from charge.
CHARGER (1), [chahj'-er], *n.* a battle horse.
CHARGER (2), [chahj'-er], *n.* a large dish for carrying joints. [OFr. *chargeoir*].
CHARGE-SHEET, [chahj'-shēt], *n.* a list of offenders taken into custody by the police, with the charges against them.
CHARILY, [chāer'-i-li], *adv.* warily.
CHARINESS, [chāer'-i-nes], *n.* the quality of being chary, prudence.
CHARIOT, [cha'-ri-ot], *n.* a two-wheeled, horse-drawn vehicle. [OFr. *charette*].
CHARIOTEER, [cha'-ri-ot-ēer'], *n.* one who drives a chariot.
CHARIOTEERING, [cha'-ri-ot-ēer'-ing], *n.* the act of driving a chariot.
CHARISM, [ka'-rizm], *n.* the grace of God; a talent. [Gk. *kharisma*].
CHARITABLE, [cha'-rit-abl], *adj.* generous to the needy, benevolent; giving help of various kinds to the necessitous without asking payment. [OFr. *charitable*].
CHARITABLENESS, [cha'-rit-abl-nes], *n.* the condition of being charitable.
CHARITABLY, [cha'-rit-ab-li], *adv.* in charitable fashion.
CHARITY, [cha'-ri-ti], *n.* the fact, act or quality of being charitable; liberality, generosity without expectation or call for repayment of any kind; an institution or trust with a charitable object. [L. *caritas*].
CHARIVARI, [sha'-ri-vah'-ri], *n.* a mock serenade of discordant music; a satirical journal. [Fr. *charivari*].
CHARKA, [chahk'-a], *n.* an Indian spinning-wheel. [Hind. *charka*].
CHARLADY, [chah'-lā-di], *n.* a charwoman.
CHARLATAN, [shah'-lat-an], *n.* a quack, an impostor, a flaunter of sham learning and skill. [It. *ciarlatano*].
CHARLATANIC, [shah'-la-tan'-ik], *adj.* pertaining to a charlatan.
CHARLATANICAL, [shah'-la-tan'-ik-al], *adj.* charlatanic.
CHARLATANICALLY, [shah'-lat-an'-ik-al-i], *adv.* in charlatanical fashion.
CHARLATANISM, [shah'-lat-an-izm], *n.* the quality of being a charlatan, quackery.
CHARLATANRY, [shah'-lat-an-ri], *n.* charlatanism.
CHARLES'S-WAIN, [chahlz'-iz-wān], *n.* (*astron.*) the Plough, seven stars in the constellation of the Great Bear. [OE. *Carles-wægn* Charlemagne's wagon].
CHARLESTON, [chahls'-ton], *n.* an energetic ball-room dance popular in the nineteen-twenties. [*Charleston*, U.S.A.].
CHARLOCK, [chah'-lok], *n.* the wild mustard, *Sinapis arvensis*. [OE. *cerlic*].
CHARLOTTE, [shah'-lot], *n* a sweet, usually made with apples, consisting of the fruit, sugar, and bread-crumbs baked together; **c. russe**, a sweet having sponge cake and cream as its basis. [Queen *Charlotte*].
CHARM (1), [chahm], *n.* an incantation with supposed magical effect, a magical or occult effect or influence; a trinket or ornament believed to possess magical powers for aiding the wearer; (*fig.*) a quality of attractiveness, indefinable fascination. [Fr. *charme* from L. *carmen* song].
CHARM (2), [chahm], *v.t.* to bewitch, influence by magic, to reduce to service and affection by magic or apparent magic; (*fig.*) to enchant, fascinate.
CHARMER, [chahm'-er], *n.* one who charms, fascinates; an attractive young woman; one who tames snakes.
CHARMEUSE, [shah-murz'], *n.* a kind of rich dress-material. [Fr. *charmeuse*].
CHARMING, [chahm'-ing], *adj* delightful, attractive.
CHARMINGLY, [chahm'-ing-li], *adv.* in charming fashion.
CHARMINGNESS, [chahm'-ing-nes], *n.* the quality of being charming.
CHARNEL-HOUSE, [chah'-nel-hows'], *n.* a place where corpses are kept; any place reeking of death, or dismally morbid. [OFr. *charnel* from L. *carnale* graveyard].
CHARPIE, [shah'-pi], *n.* lint used for dressing wounds. [Fr. *charpie*].
CHARPOY, [chah'-poi], *n.* a light Indian bedstead with a bamboo frame. [Hind. *charpoi*].
CHARQUI, [chahk'-i], *n.* beef strips dried in the sun. [Span. *charqui*].
CHARRY, [chah'-ri], *adj.* pertaining to or like charcoal.
CHART (1), [chaht], *n.* a navigation map, recording features and dangers of the sea or coast; any detailed map or plan; a graph. [Fr. from L. *carta*].
CHART (2), [chaht], *v.t.* to make a chart of.
CHARTACEOUS, [kah-tā'-shus], *adj.* (*bot.*) resembling paper. [L. *charta* paper].
CHARTER (1), [chah'-ter], *n.* a document granting or confirming rights, properties, etc.; a manifesto of rights and liberties claimed by the people for themselves. [OFr. *chartre*].
CHARTER (2), [chah'-ter], *v.t.* to hire a vessel, to hire any vehicle.
CHARTERED, [chah'-terd], *adj.* holding some right or position by virtue of a charter; (*fig.*) acting as though under charter.
CHARTER-LAND, [chah'-ter-land'], *n.* land granted by charter.
CHARTER-PARTY, [chah'-ter-pah'-ti], *n.* an agreement concerning the hire of a vessel and the freight. [Fr. *chartre partie* a shared charter].
CHARTISM, [chaht'-izm] *n.* early nineteenth-century radicalism whose supporters demanded, and were penalized for demanding, such things as universal suffrage, payment of Members of Parliament, annual parliaments and other democratic reforms. [The People's *Charter*, the programme of the movement].
CHARTIST, [chaht'-ist], *n.* a follower of chartism.
CHARTLESS, [chaht'-les], *adj.* without a chart.
CHARTOGRAPHER, [kah-tog'-raf-er], *n.* cartographer.
CHARTOGRAPHIC, [kah'-tog-raf'-ik], *adj.* cartographic.
CHARTOGRAPHY, [kah-tog'-raf-i], *n.* cartography.
CHARTREUSE, [shah-trurz'], *n.* a Carthusian monastery; a very fine liqueur (green or yellow) made by the Carthusians. [Fr. *la grande Chartreuse* the chief Carthusian house].
CHARTREUX, [shah-trur'], *n.* a Carthusian.
CHARTULARY, see CARTULARY.
CHARWOMAN, [chah'-wŏŏm'-an], *n.* a woman who chars. [CHAR (3)].
CHARY, [chāer'-i], *adj.* doubtful, cautious, hesitating [OE. *cearig* sad].
CHASE (1), [chās], *n.* the act of chasing; the quarry pursued; land in which game is bred and hunted; the liberty to hunt over certain land. [CHASE (3)].
CHASE (2), [chās], *n.* the part of a cannon taking the charge; (*print.*) a metal frame for holding type when it has been set up. [Fr. *châsse*].
CHASE (3), [chās], *v.t. and i.* to pursue (an animal)

in order to catch and kill; to hunt; to drive away by pursuing in threatening fashion, to drive out; to rush about for some purpose. [OFr. *chacier*].
CHASE (4), [chās], *v.t.* to engrave on metal. [OFr. *(en)chasser* to enshrine].
CHASEABLE, [chās'-abl], *adj.* able to be chased.
CHASER (1), [chās'-er], *n.* one who chases; (*eng.*) a flat tool with a serrated edge for cutting screw-threads in a lathe. [CHASE (4)].
CHASING, [chās'-ing], *n.* chased work on metal; the patterns so engraved on the metal.
CHASM, [kazm], *n.* a deep cleft in the earth, a deep and alarming gap; (*fig.*) an irreconcilable division of outlook. [Gk. *khasma.*]
CHASSE, chassé, [shas'-ā], *n.* a rapid movement in ballroom dancing. [Fr. *chassé*].
CHASSEUR, [shas-ur'], *n.* a light cavalryman; a French pageboy. [Fr. *chasseur* huntsman].
CHASSIS, [shas'-i], *n.* the frame supporting the engine and body of a motor-car, aeroplane or gun. [Fr. *chassis* framework].
CHASTE, [chāst], *adj.* continent, sexually pure, undefiled, pure; (*fig.*) clean and simple in design. [Fr. from L. *castus*].
CHASTE-EYED, [chāst'-īd'], *adj.* not given to ogling.
CHASTELY, [chāst'-li], *adv.* in chaste fashion.
CHASTEN, [chāsn], *v.t.* to punish for a just cause, particularly to humble pride and insolence, to restrain. [OFr. *chastier* from L. *castigare* punish].
CHASTENED, [chāsnd], *adj.* subdued in spirit as though punished.
CHASTENESS, [chāst'-nes] *n.* the condition of being chaste.
CHASTENING, [chās'-ning], *adj.* humbling, punishing, restraining.
CHASTE-TREE, [chāst'-trē'], *n.* a shrub related to the verbena, *Vitex Agnus-castus.*
CHASTISABLE, [chas-tīz'-abl], *adj.* able or fit to be chastised.
CHASTISE, [chas-tīz'], *v.t.* to punish with justice, to chasten and restrain erring or unruly inferiors as by beating; to beat. [CHASTEN].
CHASTISEMENT, [chast-īz'-ment], *n.* the process of chastising, corporal punishment.
CHASTITY, [chas'-tit-i], *n.* the quality or condition of being chaste, virgin purity; (*fig.*) restraint. [OFr. *chasteté*].
CHASUBLE, [chaz'-yōōbl], *n.* an outer vestment usually highly ornamented and made of silk, worn over the alb by the priest officiating at Mass. [MedL. *casubula* little house].

CHASUBLE

CHAT (1), [chat], *n.* casual talk of a light, informal kind, idle and familiar conversation; chatter; **back-c.**, brightly offensive questions and answers. [CHATTER].
CHAT (2), [chat], *n.* a bird of the thrush family. [CHATTER].
CHAT (3), (**chatting, chatted**), [chat], *v.i.* to converse lightly and informally on casual subjects.
CHATEAU, [shat'-ō], *n.* a castle. [Fr. *château*].
CHATELAINE, [shat'-el-ān], *n.* the lady of a house, hostess; a lady's chain to hold keys, etc. [Fr. *châtelaine*].
CHATELET, [shat'-el-ā], *n.* a small castle, a country house. [Fr. *châtelet*].
CHATELLANY, [shat'-el-an-i], *n.* a castle lordship.
CHATOYANT (1), [shat-oi'-ant], *n.* a stone with a changing lustre.
CHATOYANT (2), [shat-oi'-ant], *adj.* glowing with varying colour and lustre. [Fr. *chatoyant* shining like a cat's eyes].
CHAT-POTATOES, [chat'-pot-ā'-tōz], *n.(pl.)* potatoes cut up for pigs' food.
CHATTEL, [chat'-el], *n.* a possession; (*leg.*) a movable article of property. [OFr. *chattel* cattle].
CHATTER (1), [chat'-er], *n.* rapid, casual talk; noise made by monkeys, magpies, etc.
CHATTER (2), [chat'-er], *v.i.* to talk rapidly and pointlessly, to talk with careless indiscretion; to click together rapidly and continuously, from fear or cold; to jabber rapidly, to utter shrill inarticulate cries. [ME. *chateren*].
CHATTERBOX, [chat'-er-boks'], *n.* a chatterer.
CHATTERER, [chat'-er-er], *n.* one who chatters, a talkative person; (*ornith.*) a bird related to the waxwing.
CHATTY (1), [chat'-i], *n.* an Indian earthen pot. [Hind. *chati*].
CHATTY (2), [chat'-i], *adj.* talkative.
CHATWOOD, [chat'-wood], *n.* little sticks, tinder.
CHAUCERIAN, [chaw-sēer'-i-an], *adj.* pertaining to or resembling Chaucer, and his works. [G. *Chaucer*, a fourteenth century English poet].
CHAUD-FROID, [shō-frwa'], *n.* a cold poultry dish. [Fr. *chaud-froid* warm-cold].
CHAUFFER, [shō'-fer], *n.* a small stove. [Fr. *chauffoir*].
CHAUFFEUR, [shō'-fer], *n.* a servant employed to drive a private automobile. [Fr. *chauffeur* a stoker].
CHAUMONTELLE, [shō'-mon-tel'], *n.* a variety of pear. [Fr. *chaumontelle*].
CHAUNTER, [chahn'-ter], *n.* a chanter.
CHAUSSES, [shōs], *n.* armour for the legs. [Fr. *chausses*].
CHAUSSURE, [shō-sōō'-er], *n.* hose; shoes. [OFr. *chauceure*].
CHAUVINISM, [shō'-vin-izm], *n.* nationalist militarism, belief in the patriotic mailed fist, jingoism. [N. *Chauvin* a supporter of Napoleon].
CHAUVINIST, [shō'-vin-ist], *n.* a devotee of chauvinism.
CHAYA-ROOT, CHAY-ROOT, CHOY-ROOT, [chā'-ya-rōōt'], *n.* the root of a species of *Oldenlandia*, from which a red dye may be extracted. [Tamil *chaya*].
CHEAP, [chēp], *adj.* low in price, inexpensive; second-rate, in bad taste, vulgar, facile. [OE. *ceap* a bargain].

CHAUSSES

CHEAPEN, [chēp'-en], *v.t. and i.* to make cheap; to degrade; to become cheap, lessen in value.
CHEAP-JACK, [chēp'-jak], *n.* a hawker of cheap articles. [CHEAP and JACK].
CHEAPLY, [chēp'-li], *adv.* at a low price.
CHEAPNESS, [chēp'-nes], *n.* the quality of being cheap.
CHEAT (1), [chēt], *n.* one who cheats, a fraud, trickster; a deception, sham. [ESCHEAT].
CHEAT (2), [chēt], *v.t. and i.* to trick, deceive, swindle; to escape from; to break some rule in order to gain advantage.
CHEATABLE, [chēt'-abl], *adj.* able to be cheated.
CHEATABLENESS, [chēt'-abl-nes], *n.* the state of being cheatable.
CHEATERY, [chēt'-er-i], *n.* cheating, trickery.
CHEATING, [chēt'-ing], *n.* being a cheat at cards, unfair play.
CHEATINGLY, [chēt'-ing-li], *adv.* in cheating fashion.
CHECK (1), [chek], *n.* a notification in chess when a piece threatens the king, the situation when a king is so threatened; an obstruction, a rebuff, an interference with progression, a sudden slowing down or hesitation; control or supervision or the means of supervising; a record of some event or action kept for purposes of comparison; token or pledge of identification, cloakroom ticket; bill, invoice; cheque; chessboard pattern, pattern of alternate dark and light coloured squares; (*pl.*) a suit of such a pattern. [OFr. *(e)schec* from Pers. *shah* king].
CHECK (2), [chek], *adj.* with squares alternately light and dark.
CHECK (3), [chek], *v.t. and i.* to threaten the king in chess; to obstruct, cause to slow down, interrupt, hinder, restrain; to verify, test; (*naut.*) to ease off a rope; to come to a stop, pause in motion, hesitate.
CHECK-BOOK, see CHEQUE-BOOK.
CHECKER (1), [chek'-er], *n.* one who checks.
CHECKER (2), see CHEQUER.
CHECKER-TREE, [chek'-er-trē'], *n.* the service tree, *Pyrus torminalis.*
CHECKER-WORK, see CHEQUER-WORK.
CHECKLESS, [chek'-les], *adj.* unchecked.
CHECKMATE (1), [chek'-māt], *n.* the winning position in chess, when a king is in such a situation that he must inevitably be taken at the next move; (*fig.*) a move or situation by which someone's plans are brought to an impotent standstill. [Arab. *shah mata* the king is dead].
CHECKMATE (2), [chek'-māt'], *v.t.* (*chess*) to bring one's opponent to checkmate; (*fig.*) to frustrate.
CHECK-REIN, [chek'-rān], *n.* a coupling strap between harness and bridle preventing the horse from lowering its head.
CHECK-ROLL, [chek'-rōl], *n.* a list of employees in an

office or works used to check attendance, pay, etc.
CHECKWEIGHER, [chek'-wā'-er], *n.* a colliery worker who represents the miners, and checks the amount of coal mined.
CHECKY, [chek'-i], *adj.* (*her.*) a field divided into squares of alternate colours.
CHEDDAR, [ched'-er], *n.* a variety of cheese. [*Cheddar*, in Somerset, where made].
CHEDDAR-PINK, [ched'-er-pingk'], *n.* the wild flower *Dianthus cæsius*.
CHEDDITE, [shed'-īt], *n.* an explosive. [*Chedde*, in Savoy].
CHEEK (1), [chēk], *n.* one of the two fleshy sides of the face, one of two corresponding sides; (*fig. and coll.*) insolence, smart rudeness. [OE. *ceoce*].
CHEEK (2), [chēk], *v.t.* (*coll.*) to insult impertinently.
CHEEK-BONE, [chēk'-bōn], *n.* the bone supporting the cheek.
CHEEK-TOOTH, [chēk'-tōōth], *n.* a molar tooth.
CHEEKY, [chēk'-i], *adj.* (*slang*) impertinent.
CHEEP (1), [chēp], *n.* the shrill chirrup of a young bird. [Imitative].
CHEEP (2), [chēp], *v.i.* to utter a cheep.
CHEEPER, [chēp'-er], *n.* a young bird.
CHEER (1), [chēer], *n.* mood, state of mind; encouragement; a shout of triumph and delight, a roar of applause; entertainment, rich food. [OFr. *chere* from LL. *cara* face].
CHEER (2), [chēer], *v.t. and i.* to encourage, to make or be made cheerful; to enliven; to applaud.
CHEERER, [chēer'-er], *n.* one who cheers.
CHEERFUL, [chēer'-fōōl], *adj.* full of cheer, brightly happy, inspiriting, bright, tending to gladden.
CHEERFULLY, [chēer'-fōōl-i], *adv.* in cheerful fashion.
CHEERFULNESS, [chēer'-fōōl-nes], *n.* the condition of being cheerful.
CHEERILY, [chēer'-i-li], *adv.* in cheery fashion.
CHEERINESS, [chēer'-i-nes], *n.* the state of being cheery.
CHEERING (1), [chēer'-ing], *n.* the sound of cheers, continuous cheers.
CHEERING (2), [chēer'-ing], *adj.* gladdening, encouraging, tending to make cheerful.
CHEERINGLY, [chēer'-ing-li], *adv.* in cheering fashion.
CHEERIO, [chēer-i-ō'], *int.* goodbye. [CHEERY and HO].
CHEER-LEADER, [chēer'-lēd'-er], *n.* a person whose duty it is to lead the cheers at a sports meeting, etc.
CHEERLESS, [chēer'-les], *adj.* joyless, dreary, gloomy.
CHEERLESSNESS, [chēer'-les-nes], *n.* the condition of being cheerless.
CHEERY, [chēer'-i], *adj.* heartily cheerful, bright.
CHEESE (1), [chēz], n. a milk-curd compressed into a solid mass; various substances resembling cheese; **the c.,** (*coll.*) the right thing. [OE. *cese*].
CHEESE (2), [chēz'], *v.t.* (*slang*) **to c. it,** to stop, desist.
CHEESECAKE, [chēz'-kāk], *n.* a cake made from curds, sugar, and butter.
CHEESE-FLY, [chēz'-flī], *n.* a small black fly breeding in cheese.
CHEESE-HOPPER, [chēz'-hop'-er], *n.* the maggot of the cheese-fly, *Piophila casei*.
CHEESE-MITE, [chēz'-mīt], *n.* an arachnid occurring in cheese.
CHEESEMONGER, [chēz'-mung'-ger], *n.* a dealer in cheese and other farm produce.
CHEESEPARING (1), [chēz'-pāer'-ing], *n.* a thin piece of rind cut from a cheese; (*fig.*) stinginess.
CHEESEPARING (2), [chēz'-pāer'-ing], *adj.* pettily mean, stingy.
CHEESEPRESS, [chēz'-pres], *n.* a press for forming curd into cheese.
CHEESE-RENNET, [chēz'-ren'-et], *n.* the yellow lady's bedstraw, *Galium verum*, used in coagulating milk for cheese.
CHEESEVAT, [chēz'-vat], *n.* a vat for pressing curds.
CHEESY, [chēz'-i], *adj.* tasting, smelling, or looking like cheese.
CHEETAH, [chē'-ta], *n.* the Indian hunting leopard. [Skr. *chitta* spotted].
CHEF, [shef], *n.* a head male cook, the chief cook in a restaurant. [Fr. *chef* head].
CHEF-D'ŒUVRE, [shā'-durvr'], *n.* a masterpiece. [Fr. *chef-d'œuvre*].
CHEIRANTHUS, [kīer-an'-thus], *n.* the genus including the wallflower. [Gk. *kheir* hand and *anthos* flower].
CHEIROLEPIS, [kīer'-ol-ēp'-is], *n.* a fossil scale. [Gk. *kheir* hand and *lepis* scale].
CHEIROPTERA, [kīer-op'-ter-a], *n.* the order of flying mammals. [Gk. *kheir* hand and *pteron* wing].
CHEKA, [chā'-ka], *n.* the Russian secret police. [The initials of Russ. *Chresvychainaya Kommissiya* Extraordinary Commission].
CHELA (1), [chā'-la], *n.* a Buddhist novice; an Anglo-Indian convict battalion. [Hind. *chela* servant].
CHELA (2), [kē'-la] *n.* the pincers of crabs and lobsters. [Gk. *khele* claw].
CHELIFEROUS, [kel-if'-er-us], *adj.* having claws. [Gk. *khele* claw and L. *ferre* to bear].
CHELIFORM, [kel'-i-fawm], *adj.* shaped like a claw. [Gk. *khele* claw and FORM].
CHELONE, [kel-ō'-ni], *n.* the tortoise flower. [Gk. *khelone* tortoise].
CHELONIA, [kel-ō'-ni-a], *n.*(*pl.*) a class of the reptiles including the tortoises and turtles. [Gk. *khelone*].
CHELONIAN, [kel-ō'-ni-an], *adj.* pertaining to the chelonia.
CHELSEA, [chel'-si], *n.* an artistic quarter of London; **C. bun,** a kind of rolled currant-bun.
CHEMICAL (1), [kem'-ik-al], *n.* a substance used or made in chemistry.
CHEMICAL (2), [kem'-ik-al], *adj.* pertaining to, used or made in chemistry.
CHEMICALLY, [kem'-ik-al-i], *adv.* in accordance with the principles of chemistry, by chemical process.
CHEMICO-ELECTRIC, [kem'-ik-ō-il-ek'-trik], *adj.* electrical and chemical action.
CHEMIN DE FER, [shem-an(g)'-de-fāer'], *n.* baccarat. [Fr. *chemin de fer* railway].
CHEMISE, [shem-ēz'], *n.* a woman's undergarment, supported by shoulder-straps and hanging down to the thigh; (*fort.*) a wall strengthening a bastion or earthwork. [Fr. *chemise*].
CHEMISETTE, [shem'-ēz-et'], *n.* a woman's undergarment for the shoulders and breast. [Fr. *chemisette*].
CHEMIST, CHYMIST†, [kem'-ist], *n.* one practising or skilled in chemistry; a trader in drugs. [ALCHEMIST].
CHEMISTRY, CHYMISTRY†, [kem'-ist-ri], *n.* the science of the properties of elements and their combinations and of the behaviour and reactions of substances to each other.
CHEMITYPE, [kem'-i-tīp], *n.* a process by which a stereotype is made by chemical means. [CHEM(ICAL) (2) and TYPE].
CHEMOSMOSIS, [kem'-oz-mō'-sis], *n.* chemical action through an intervening membrane. [CHEM(ICAL) (2) and OSMOSIS].
CHEMO-THERAPY, [kem'-ō-ther'-a-pi], *n.* (*med.*) treatment by synthetic drugs.
CHENG, [cheng], *n.* a Chinese reed instrument. [Chin. *cheng*].
CHENILLE, [shen-ēl'], *n.* tufted silk or cotton cord used in embroidery work. [Fr. *chenille* caterpillar].
CHENOPODIUM, [ken'-op-ō'-di-um], *n.* the goosefoot genus of plants. [Gk. *khenopous* goosefoot].
CHEQUE, [chek], *n.* a bill of exchange or a draft by which a bank is authorized by a client to make a payment to another person from funds held by the bank on his behalf; a printed form on which this instruction is given. [CHECK (1)].
CHEQUE-BOOK, CHECK-BOOK, [chek'-bŏŏk], *n.* blank cheques issued bound in convenient book-form.

CHENG

CHEQUER (1), CHECKER, [chek'-er], *n.* a check pattern, a pattern of alternate squares of different colour. [OFr. (*e*)*schekier* from L. *scaccarium* chessboard].
CHEQUER (2), CHECKER, [chek'-er], *v.t.* to mark in check pattern; to variegate, to cause to alternate between opposites; **chequered career,** a career marked by very varying fortune.
CHEQUER-WORK, CHECKER-WORK, [chek'-er-wurk'], *n.* cross-stripes of different coloured materials.
CHERIMOYER, [che'-rim-oi'-er], *n.* the fruit of *Anona Cherimolia*, a South American tree.
CHERISH, [che'-rish], *v.t.* to hold very dear, to protect, to show great solicitude for, nourish affectionately; to keep in mind. [OFr. *cheriser* from ~L. *carus* dear].
CHERISHING, [che'-rish-ing], *adj.* so as to cherish.
CHERISHINGLY, [che'-rish-ing-li], *adv.* in cherishing fashion.
CHERMES, see KERMES.

CHEROOT, [sher-ōōt'], *n.* a small strong cigar, open at both ends. [Tamil *cheroot* roll].
CHERRY (1), [che'-ri], *n.* a fruit of the genus *Cerasus*; the tree bearing this fruit. [OFr. *cherise* from Gk. *kerasos*].
CHERRY (2), [che'-ri], *adj.* relating to a cherry; red.
CHERRY-BAY, [che'-ri-bā'], *n.* the Portuguese laurel.
CHERRY-BRANDY, [che'-ri-bran'-di], *n.* a sweet liqueur made by steeping ripe cherries in brandy.
CHERRY-CHEEKED, [che'-ri-chēkt'], *adj.* rosy-cheeked.
CHERRY-PIE, [che'-ri-pī'], *n.* pie made with cherries; the purple heliotrope.
CHERRY-PIT, [che'-ri-pit'], *n.* a children's game of throwing cherry-stones into a hole.
CHERT, [churt], *n.* a flint-like quartz, hornstone. [Uncert.].
CHERTY, [churt'-i], *adj.* flinty.
CHERUB, (*pl.* **cherubim**), [che'-rub], *n.* an angel next in order to the seraphim; a beautiful, chubby childlike angel; (*coll.*) a pretty rosy-cheeked chubby child. [Heb. *kerub*].
CHERUBIC, [che-rōōb'-ik], *adj.* pertaining to or like a cherub, angelic; chubby and rosy-cheeked.
CHERUBICAL, [che-rōō'-bik-al], *adj.* cherubic.
CHERVIL, [chur'-vil], *n.* a plant of the genus *Chærophyllum*, used for flavouring. [OE. *cerfille* from Gk. *khairephullon*].
CHESHIRE, [chesh'-er], *n.* an English county; **C. cheese**, a reddish cheese made there.
CHESIBLE, [chez'-ibl], *n.* a chasuble.
CHESIL, [ches'-il], *n.* shingle. [OE. *ceosob*].
CHESS, [ches], *n.* a game of high intellectual skill played upon a board of sixty-four squares with thirty-two pieces. [OFr. *(e)schès*, *pl.* of *(e)schec*].
CHESS-APPLE, [ches'-apl'], *n.* the checker-berry, the fruit of the service tree.
CHESSBOARD, [ches'-bawd], *n.* the board of sixty-four squares, alternately black and white, on which chess is played.
CHESSEL, [ches'-el], *n.* a mould used in pressing cheese. [Uncert.].
CHESSMAN, [ches'-man], *n.* a piece used in chess.
CHESSPLAYER, [ches'-plā'-er], *n.* one who plays or is skilled in chess.
CHESS-TREE, [ches'-trē], *n.* (*naut.*) a piece of wood bolted vertically to a ship's side to hold the clews of the mainsail.
CHEST, [chest], *n.* a large heavy box with a lid for storage; the financial office of an institution, a treasury; (*anat.*) the front part of the body between throat and abdomen, thorax; (*coll.*) the lungs; **c. of drawers**, a series of drawers arranged above one another in a piece of furniture; **c. of tea**, 108 pounds of tea. [OE. *cest*].
CHESTED, [ches'-tid], *adj.* having a chest; kept in a chest.
CHESTERFIELD, [ches'-ter-fēld], *n.* a long sofa with upright ends; an overcoat. [The Earl of *Chesterfield*].
CHEST-FOUNDERING, [chest'-fownd'-er-ing], *n.* a rheumatic disease of the chest and forelegs of horses.
CHESTNUT (1), [ches'-nut], *n.* the edible nut of the *Castanea vulgaris*; the bitter, inedible *Æsculus Hippocastanum* or horse-chestnut; the trees bearing either of these; (*slang*) an old, worn-out joke; a reddish-brown horse. [OFr. *chastaigne* from Gk. *Kasthanaia* (a place in Greece) and NUT].
CHESTNUT (2), [ches'-nut], *adj.* reddish brown.
CHESTON, [ches'-ton], *n.* a kind of plum. [CHESTNUT].
CHEVAL, [shev-al'], *n.* a frame; **c. glass**, a tall narrow mirror. [Fr. *cheval* horse; support, frame].
CHEVALIER, [shev'-al-ēer'], *n.* cavalier; a foreign title of honour; a gallant young man. [Fr. *chevalier*].
CHEVELURE, [shev'-el-ew(r)'], *n.* a periwig. [Fr. *chevelure*].
CHEVERIL†, [chev'-er-il], *n.* soft leather, kid. [OFr. *chevril*].
CHEVILLE, [shev-ēl'], *n.* the bridge of a violin. [Fr. *cheville* a (carpenter's) plug].
CHEVIN, [chev'-in], *n.* a fish, the chub, *Leuciscus cephalus*. [OFr. *chevesne*].
CHEVIOT, [chev'-i-ot], *n.* a sheep bred on the Cheviots; cloth made from the wool of such sheep. [*Cheviot* Hills].
CHEVISANCE†, [chev'-is-ans], *n.* (*leg.*) an agreement; the raising of money. [OFr. *chevisance*].
CHEVRETTE, [shev-ret'], *n.* a device for lifting guns or mortars into their carriages; a thin glove-leather. [Fr. *chevrette* from L. *capra* goat].
CHEVRON, [shev'-ron], *n.* (*her.*) an honourable ordinary representing two rafters of a house meeting at the top; (*arch.*) a **V**-shaped device, an ornament of zigzag work; (*milit.*) the mark on the coat-sleeves of a non-commissioned officer. [OFr. *chevron*].

CHEVRON

CHEVRONED, [shev'-rund], *adj.* having a chevron, decorated with chevrons.
CHEVRONEL, [shev'-ron-el'], *n.* (*her.*) half a chevron. [Fr. *chevronel*].
CHEVROTAIN, [shev'-rot-ān], *n.* a small ruminant of the genus *Tragulus*. [Fr. *chevrotain*, *dim.* of OFr. *chevrot* goat].
CHEVY, [chev'-i], *v.t.* to chivy.
CHEW, [chōō], *v.t.* and *i.* to bite and grind up with the teeth into small pieces, to masticate, to champ; (*fig.*) to meditate deeply on some problem. [OE. *ceowan*].
CHEWING-GUM, [chōō'-ing-gum'], *n.* a sweetened and variously flavoured preparation of chicle or similar gums, used for masticating.
CHIAN (1), [kī'-an], *n.* a wine from Chios. [*Chios* in the Aegean].
CHIAN (2), [kī'-an], *adj.* pertaining to the island of Chios.
CHIANTI, [kē-an'-ti], *n.* a light Italian red wine. [*Chianti*, a district in Italy].
CHIAROSCURO, [kē-ah'-rōs-kōōer'-ō], *n.* variation in light and shade. [It. *chiaroscuro* light-dark].
CHIASM, [kī'-azm], *n.* (*anat.*) a crossing of two portions of the optic nerve, resembling the Greek letter *x*. [Gk. *khiasmos* placing crosswise].
CHIASMUS, [kī'-az'-mus], *n.* (*rhet.*) the inversion of word order in a repeated phrase. [*Prec.*].
CHIASTOLITE, [kī-as'-tol-īt], *n.* a kind of andalusite, showing, when polished, a white cross on a black ground. [*Prec.*].
CHIBOUK, [chi-bōōk'], *n.* a Turkish tobacco-pipe. [Turk. *chibouk*].
CHIC (1), [shik, shēk], *n.* smartness.
CHIC (2), [shik, shēk], *adj.* smartly dressed, just right, in good taste. [Fr. *chic*].
CHICA, [chē'-ka], *n.* a fermented liquor made from Indian corn. [Native].
CHICANE (1), [shik-ān'], *n.* obstruction by quibble, deceit by verbal subterfuge; (*bridge*) a small score allowed to players holding no trumps. [Fr. *chicane*].
CHICANE (2), [shik-ān'], *v.t.* and *i.* to employ chicane, to cheat by chicane.
CHICANERY, [shik-ān'-er-i], *n.* quibbling, the method and employment of chicane, sophistry. [Fr. *chicanerie*].
CHICH, [chich], *n.* a chick-pea.
CHICK, [chik], *n.* a very young chicken. [CHICKEN].
CHICKADEE, [chik'-a-dē'], *n.* an American titmouse. [Imitative].
CHICKAREE, [chik'-a-rē], *n.* the American red squirrel. [Imitative].
CHICKEN (1), [chik'-en], *n.* a young bird, a young domestic fowl; a domestic fowl as a dish; a very young, helpless person. [OE. *cicen*].
CHICKEN (2), [chik'-en], *adj.* made of chicken flesh.
CHICKEN-HEARTED, [chik'-en-haht'-id], *adj.* cowardly, spiritless.
CHICKEN-POX, [chik'-en-poks'], *n.* a pustulous contagious disease, common in childhood, *Varicella*.
CHICKLING, [chik'-ling], *n.* a small chicken.
CHICK-PEA, [chik'-pē], *n.* an edible pea, *Cicer arietinum*. [L. *cicer* vetch].
CHICKWEED, [chik'-wēd], *n.* the creeping plant *Cerastium arvense*.
CHICLE, [chik'-li], *n.* the gum from which chewing-gum is prepared. [Mexican *tzictli*].
CHICORY, [chik'-er-i], *n.* a plant of the genus *Cichorium*, which has a root sometimes ground and mixed with coffee. [OFr. *cichoree* from Gk. *kikhoreia*].
CHIDE, [chīd], *v.t.* and *i.* to scold, rebuke; to complain, fret. [OE. *cidan*].
CHIDING, [chīd'-ing], *n.* a scolding, a rebuke, complaint.
CHIDINGLY, [chīd'-ing-li], *adv.* in a reproving fashion.

CHIEF (1), [chēf], *n.* the head of a body of people, leader of a tribe, head of a clan, a native tribal ruler; (*coll.*) a boss, the active head of a business; (*her.*) the upper third of an escutcheon. [OFr. *chef* from L. *caput* head].

CHIEF (2), [chēf], *adj.* principal, supreme, the highest of its kind, primary, most important.

CHIEFLESS, [chēf'-les], *adj.* without a chief.

CHIEFLY, [chēf'-li], *adv.* principally.

CHIEFTAIN, [chēf'-tan], *n.* the leader and senior man of a clan or tribe, a chief. [OFr. *chevetain* captain].

CHIEFTAINCY, [chēf'-tan-si], *n.* the rank and rule of a chieftain.

CHIEFTAINSHIP, [chēf'-tan-ship], *n.* chieftaincy.

CHIFF-CHAFF, [chif'-chaf'], *n.* the British warbler, *Phylloscopus collybita.* [Imitative].

CHIFFON, [shif'-on], *n.* a light gauzy material used for dresses. [Fr. *chiffon*].

CHIFFONIER, [shif'-on-ēer'], *n.* a low sideboard with shelves for ornaments. [Fr. *chiffonier*].

CHIGNON, [shēn'-yon(g)], *n.* a coil of hair, natural or artificial, worn by women at the back of the head. [Fr. *chignon* nape].

CHIGOE, [chig'-ō], *n.* an insect, the female of which burrows under the skin of the feet and causes great irritation; the harvest-mite. [West Indian].

CHILBLAIN, [chil'-blān], *n.* a painful inflamed swelling on hands or feet, caused by cold and bad circulation of the blood.

CHILD, (*pl.* **children**), [chīld], *n.* a very young infant, an unborn infant, a young person before the age of puberty, a minor; a simple, undeveloped person, a very innocent and harmless person; a descendant, offspring, progeny; a disciple, follower; one produced by certain circumstances, one apparently having origin in some class; something produced by something, the result of some process. [OE. *cild*].

CHILDBEARING, [chīld'-bāer'-ing], *n.* childbirth.

CHILDBED, [chīld'-bed'], *n.* parturition, the state of labour.

CHILDBIRTH, [chīld'-burth], *n.* parturition, the act of bringing forth a child.

CHILDE†, [chīld], *n.* a young man of noble birth. [CHILD].

CHILDERMAS, [chil'-der-mas], *n.* the Feast of the Innocents (28th December). [OE. *cildra-mæsse*].

CHILDHOOD, [chīld'-hŏŏd], *n.* the state of being a child, the period before adolescence; **second c.**, extreme senility inducing childishness of mind.

CHILDING†, [chīld'-ing], *n.* parturition.

CHILDISH, [chīld'-ish], *adj.* like a child, innocent, simple; pertaining to, fit for, a child; silly, foolish, ridiculous.

CHILDISHLY, [chīld'-ish-li], *adv.* in childish fashion.

CHILDISH-MINDED, [chīld'-ish-mīnd'-id], *adj.* very simple, mentally undeveloped, senile.

CHILDISHNESS, [chīld'-ish-nes], *n.* the condition of being childish.

CHILDLESS, [chīld'-les], *adj.* without children or descendants.

CHILDLESSNESS, [chīld'-les-nes], *n.* the condition of being childless.

CHILDLIKE, [chīld'-līk], *adj.* like a child in appearance or outlook; innocent, simple, gullible, unspoilt.

CHILDLY, [chīld'-li], *adj.* like a child. [OE. *cildlic*].

CHILDRENITE, [chil'-dren-īt], *n.* a native hydrated phosphate of aluminium, iron and manganese. [M. *Children*, a geologist].

CHILDSPLAY, [chīldz'-plā], *n.* the play of children; an absurdly easy task.

CHILI, see CHILLI.

CHILIAD, [kil'-i-ad], *n.* a thousand, a span of a thousand years. [Gk. *khilias* thousand].

CHILIAGON, [kil'-i-a-gon], *n.* a plane geometrical figure having a thousand equal angles. [Gk. *khilias* thousand and *gonia* angle].

CHILIAHEDRON, [kil'-i-a-hē'-dron], *n.* a figure having a thousand equal sides. [Gk. *khilias* thousand and *hedra* seat].

CHILIARCH, [kil'-i-ahk], *n.* the commander of a thousand men. [Gk. *khilias* thousand and *arkhos* leader].

CHILIARCHY, [kil'-i-ahk-i], *n.* a regiment of a thousand men.

CHILIASM, [kil'-i-azm], *n.* belief in the millennium.

CHILIAST, [kil'-i-ast], *n.* a believer in millennia. [Gk. *khiliastes*].

CHILIASTIC, [kil'-i-ast'-ik], *adj.* relating to millennia or belief in them.

CHILL (1), [chil], *n.* a sudden sensation of cold; internal inflammation or illness caused by cold, damp, etc.; (*fig.*) depressing atmosphere. [OE. *ciele*].

CHILL (2), [chil], *adj.* cold, chilly; dismal, unenthusiastic.

CHILL (3), [chil], *v.t. and i.* to make or become chill, to strike with a chill, to make cold internally; to depress make dismal; to keep meat cold, to preserve it; to strengthen steel by suddenly cooling it.

CHILLER, [chil'-er], *n.* a machine for chilling; one who chills.

CHILLI, CHILI, [chil'-i], *n.* the dried pod of the capsicum. [Mexican *chili*].

CHILLINESS, [chil'-i-nes], *n.* coolness, cold; coldness, unfriendliness.

CHILLINGLY, [chil'-ing-li], *adv.* in chilling fashion.

CHILLNESS, [chil'-nes], *n.* the state of being, making or feeling chill.

CHILLUM, [chil'-um], *n.* the bowl of a hookah. [Hind. *chillum*].

CHILLY, [chil'-i], *adj.* rather cold, suddenly cold.

CHILOMA, [kīl-ō'-ma], *n.* the upper lip of an ungulate, such as the camel. [Gk. *kheiloma*].

CHILONEAN, [kī-lō'-ni-an], *adj.* concise. [*Khilon*, one of the seven wise men of Greece].

CHILTERN, [chil'-tern], *adj.* relating to the Chilterns; **C. Hundreds**, nominal stewardship in Buckinghamshire and Oxfordshire under the Crown, an office which a Member of Parliament may accept to obtain his resignation from the House.

CHIMB, CHIME, [chīm], *n.* the projecting rim formed by the staves at the ends of a barrel. [OE. *cimb*].

CHIME (1), [chīm], *n.* a resonant musical sound of pure timbre, such as is produced by a bell; a bell itself, a group of tuned bells set in a church tower, the sound made by such bells, the sound made by a clock striking the hours; harmony. [L. *cymbalum*].

CHIME (2), [chīm], *v.t. and i.* to make, strike or sound chimes; to harmonize; **to c. in**, to intervene suddenly in conversation.

CHIMERA, CHIMAERA, [ki-mēer'-a], *n.* a creature with a lion's head, goat's body, and serpent's tail, a very furious and terrifying beast; an imagined but non-existent thing. [Gk. *khimaira* she-goat].

CHIMERA

CHIMERE, [chi-mēer'], *n.* the black outer robe of a bishop, with side openings for the sleeves of the rochet. [OFr. *chamarre*].

CHIMERICAL, [ki-me'-rik-al], *adj.* unfounded, unreasoned and imaginary.

CHIMERICALLY, [ki-me'-rik-al-i], *adv.* in chimerical fashion.

CHIMNEY, [chim'-ni], *n.* a hollow shaft or tube above a fire to carry away the fumes and gaseous products of combustion, as that built in a house wall or above a factory, a steamship or locomotive; a vertical glass cylinder surrounding the flame of an oil-lamp; the opening of a volcano; a narrow cleft in a rock by which a climber can ascend. [OFr. *cheminée*].

CHIMNEY-BOARD, [chim'-ni-bawd'], *n.* a fire-board.

CHIMNEY-BREAST, [chim'-ni-brest'], *n.* the projecting part built out of a wall to contain the fireplace in a house.

CHIMNEY-CAP, [chim'-ni-kap'], *n.* the cowl of a chimney-pot.

CHIMNEY-CORNER, [chim'-ni-kawn'-er], *n.* an inglenook.

CHIMNEY-HOOK, [chim'-ni-hŏŏk'], *n.* a hook for hanging pots above a fire.

CHIMNEY-PIECE, [chim'-ni-pēs'], *n.* an ornamental border set into the wall round a fireplace.

CHIMNEY-POT, [chim'-ni-pot'], *n.* an earthenware tube set at the top end of a house chimney.

CHIMNEY-SHAFT, [chim'-ni-shahft'], *n.* that part of a chimney rising from the roof of a building.

CHIMNEY-STACK, [chim'-ni-stak], *n.* a tall factory chimney; the masonry from which the chimney-pots of a house project.

CHIMNEY-SWEEP, [chim'-ni-swēp'], *n.* one who clears soot from the insides of chimneys.

CHIMPANZEE, [chim'-pan-zē'], *n.* an African anthropoid ape of the genus *Anthropopithecus.* [Native].

CHIN, [chin], *n.* the front extremity of the lower jaw. [OE. *cin*].

CHINA (1), [chī'-na], *n.* glazed porcelain ware; household crockery. [*China*, the country where originally made].

CHINA (2), [chī'-na], *adj.* made of china; (*fig.*) fragile, delicate.

CHINA-ASTER, [chī'-na-as'-ter], *n.* (*bot.*) a species of *Callistephus*.

CHINA-CLAY, [chī'-na-klā'], *n.* kaolin, fine potter's clay.

CHINA-GRASS, [chī'-na-grahs'], *n.* a small shrubby Chinese plant, *Boehmeria rivea*.

CHINAMAN, [chī'-na-man], *n.* a native of China.

CHINAMPA, [chin-am'-pa], *n.* a wooden raft covered with earth and used as a floating garden on the lakes of Mexico. [Mexican *chinampa*].

CHINA-ORANGE, [chī'-na-or'-inj], *n.* the sweet orange, originally imported from China.

CHINA-ROOT, [chī'-na-rōōt'], *n.* the root of a variety of *Smilax*, used as sarsaparilla.

CHINA-ROSE, [chī'-na-rōz'], *n.* one of several varieties of garden roses, *esp. Rosa indica*; the mallow or *Hibiscus rosa, var. sinensis*, a Chinese plant.

CHINA-SHOP, [chī'-na-shop'], *n.* a shop where chinaware is sold.

CHINATOWN, [chī'-na-town'], *n.* the Chinese quarter of a city.

CHINAWARE, [chī'-na-wāer'], *n.* articles made of china.

CHINCAPIN, see CHINKAPIN.

CHINCH, [chinch], *n.* the bed-bug, a species of *Cimex*. [Span. *chinche*].

CHINCHILLA, [chin-chil'-a], *n.* the small South American rodent, *Chinchilla lanigera*, etc., prized for its fur. [Span. *chinchilla*].

CHIN-CHIN, [chin'-chin'], *n.* (*coll.*) a polite greeting before drinking. [Chin. *ts'ing ts'ing* please, please].

CHIN-COUGH, [chin'-kof'], *n.* whooping-cough. [~Du. *kinkhoest*].

CHINE (1), [chīn], *n.* the back of an animal; a rock ridge. [OFr. (*e*)*schine*].

CHINE (2), [chīn], *n.* a small, deep, narrow ravine. [OE. *cine*].

CHINE (3), [chīn], *n.* the protruding rim at the top of a cask, etc. [CHIME].

CHINE (4), [chīn], *v.t.* to cut along or through the backbone, to remove the backbone of a fish. [CHINE (1)].

CHINED, [chīnd], *adj.* relating to the back or having a back.

CHINEE, [chī-nē'], *n.* (*coll.*) a Chinese. [A supposed singular form of CHINESE].

CHINESE (1), [chī-nēz'], *n.* a native of China, the language of China; (*pl.*) the race native to China.

CHINESE (2), [chī'-nēz], *adj.* pertaining to China or the Chinese; **C. lantern,** a collapsible lantern made of coloured paper, and used as a decoration; **C. white,** white oxide of zinc, used as a pigment.

CHINGLE†, see SHINGLE (1).

CHINK (1), [chingk], *n.* a long narrow opening, a slit. [Unkn.].

CHINK (2), [chingk], *n.* a sound as of two coins or pieces of glass striking together; (*coll.*) money. [Imitative].

CHINK (3), [chingk], *n.* (*coll.*) a Chinaman.

CHINK (4), [chingk], *n.* a convulsive, spasmodic gasp for breath. [CHINK (5)].

CHINK (5), [chingk], *v.i.* to gasp in a violent spasm of coughing or laughter. [~Du. *kinken*].

CHINK (6), [chingk], *v.i.* to make a light metallic sound. [CHINK (2)].

CHINKAPIN, CHINCAPIN, [chingk'-a-pin], *n.* the dwarf chestnut tree of North America, *Castanea pumila*. [Amer.Indian *chechinquamins*].

CHINKY, [chingk'-i], *adj.* full of chinks.

CHINNED, [chind], *adj.* possessing a chin.

CHINOOK, [chin-ōōk'], *n.* a North West American Indian tribe; the dialect used between the North American traders and the Indian tribes; the warm dry wind along the western slope of the Rocky Mountains. [Amer.Indian *Chinook*, the name of the tribe].

CHINSCAB, [chin'-skab'], *n.* a disease attacking sheep, the dartars.

CHINSE, [chins], *v.t.* (*naut.*) to repair seams by temporary caulking. [CHINK].

CHINTZ, [chints], *n.* cotton cloth or calico, printed with flowers, etc., in different colours. [Hind. *chint* spotted cotton stuff].

CHIOPPINE, see CHOPINE.

CHIP (1), [chip], *n.* a small thin strip or splinter of wood, a small fragment of brittle substance broken away from a vessel or implement, the rough crack or cut left by the breaking away of such a fragment, (*pl.*) thin slices of fried potato; (*cards*) counters used in a gambling game; (*naut.*) the small block of wood at the end of a log-line; **a c. of the old block,** one who inherits certain paternal characteristics; **c. shot,** (*golf*) a short lofted approach shot on to a green. [Uncert.].

CHIP (2), (chipping, chipped), [chip], *v.t. and i.* to cut into chips; to break off a chip from; to fry slices of potato; (*slang*) to tease, to banter; to break off in chips; **to c. in,** to intervene in a conversation.

CHIP-AXE, [chip'-aks'], *n.* a small light axe used for chipping timber.

CHIP-BASKET, [chip'-bahsk'-it], *n.* a light basket of thin plaited strips of wood for flowers or fruit.

CHIP-HAT, [chip'-hat'], *n.* a hat manufactured from thin strips of woody fibre or thick straw.

CHIPMUNK, [chip'-mungk], *n.* a small American ground-squirrel of the genus *Tamias*. [Amer. Indian].

CHIPPENDALE, [chip'-en-dāl], *n.* a fine style of furniture made in the eighteenth century. [Thos. *Chippendale* (1718-1779), a cabinet-maker].

CHIPPER (1), [chip'-er], *n.* light chatter.

CHIPPER (2), [chip'-er], *adj.* (*U.S. slang*) lively, cheerful, nimble.

CHIPPER (3), [chip'-er], *v.i.* to twitter, to chirp [CHIRRUP].

CHIPPING, [chip'-ing], *n.* the act of cutting off in chips; a chip; the breaking off in chips or pieces from the edges of earthenware; banter.

CHIPPY, [chip'-i], *adj.* full of chips; (*coll.*) indisposed through alcoholic excess.

CHIRAGRA, [kī-rag'-ra], *n.* gout in the hands. [Gk. *kheiragra*].

CHIRM (1), [churm], *n.* noise, the subdued sound of voices.

CHIRM (2), [churm], *v.i.* to cry out, to chirp, to chatter. [OE. *cirman*].

CHIRO-, *pref.* hand. [Gk. *kheir* hand].

CHIROGNOMY, [kī-rog'-nom-i], *n.* judgment of character from the hand. [CHIRO and Gk. *gnome* knowing].

CHIROGRAPH, [kī'-rō-grahf], *n.* (*leg.*) a formal document, engrossed and duly signed, an indenture, a charter. [Gk. *kheirographos* written by hand].

CHIROGRAPHER, [kī-rog'-raf-er], *n.* a copying clerk.

CHIROGRAPHIC, [kī'-rō-graf'-ik], *adj.* belonging to chirography.

CHIROGRAPHICAL, [kī'-rō-graf'-ik-al], *adj.* chirographic.

CHIROGRAPHIST, [kī-rog'-raf-ist], *n.* a chirographer; one who tells fortunes by the hand, a palmist.

CHIROGRAPHY, [kī-rog'-raf-i], *n.* handwriting, penmanship. [CHIRO and Gk. *graphia* writing].

CHIROGYMNAST, [kī'-rō-jim'-nast], *n.* (*mus.*) an instrument used to strengthen the fingers in piano-playing. [CHIRO and GYMNAST].

CHIROLOGICAL, [kī'-rō-loj'-ik-al], *adj.* relating to chirology.

CHIROLOGIST, [kī-rol'-oj-ist], *n.* one skilled in chirology.

CHIROLOGY, [kī-rol'-oj-i], *n.* the science or study of the hand. [CHIRO and Gk. *logos* speech].

CHIROMANCER, [kī'-rō-man-ser], *n.* one versed in chiromancy.

CHIROMANCY, [kī'-ro-man-si], *n.* palmistry. [Gk. *kheiromanteia* divination by the hand].

CHIROMANTIC, [kī-rō-man'-tik], *adj.* relating to chiromancy.

CHIRONOMY, [kī-ron'-om-i], *n.* expression by the use of gesture. [Gk. *kheironomia* management of the the hands and feet.

CHIROPEDIST†, see CHIROPODIST.

CHIROPLAST, [kī'-rō-plast], *n.* (*mus.*) an instrument used to train the hand to a particular position when playing on the piano. [CHIRO and Gk. *plastos* moulded].

CHIROPODIST, CHIROPEDIST†, [kī-rop'-od-ist], *n.* one skilled in treatment of diseases or disorders of the hands and feet. [Gk. *kheiropous, -podus* chapped feet].

CHIROPRACTIC, [kī'-rō-prak'-tik], *n.* a method of healing by manipulative massage-treatment joints displaced in the spine. [CHIRO and Gk. *praktikos* fit for use].

CHIROPRACTOR, [kī'-rō-prak'-tor], *n.* an exponent of chiropractic.
CHIRP (1), [churp], *n.* the shrill cry of a bird.
CHIRP (2), [churp], *v.t. and i.* to utter a series of short, shrill cheerful notes as a bird; to speak in a thin, shrill, cheerful, ineffective voice. [Imitative].
CHIRPER, [churp'-er], *n.* a chirping bird or insect
CHIRPINGLY, [churp'-ing-li], *adv.* in a chirping fashion.
CHIRPY, [churp'-i], *adj.* cheerful, lively.
CHIRR (1), [chur], *n.* the monotonous chirp of the grasshopper or cricket. [Imitative].
CHIRR (2), [chur], *v.i.* to utter a chirr.
CHIRRUP (1), [chi'-rup], *n.* a cheerful, lively chirp.
CHIRRUP (2), [chi'-rup], *v.i.* to chirp, to twitter. [CHIRP].
CHIRURGEON†, [kī-rur'-jun], *n.* a surgeon. [OFr. *cirurgien* from Gk. *kheirourgos*].
CHISEL (1), [chizl], *n.* a cutting tool having a long steel or iron blade with a bevelled cutting edge at the end, sometimes fitted with a wooden handle. [OFr. *chisel*].
CHISEL (2), (chiselling, chiselled), [chizl], *v.t.* to cut, pare or shape with a chisel; (*slang*) to cheat, to defraud.
CHISELLED, [chizld], *adj.* cut, as with a chisel, clear cut, having a bold outline.
CHISELLY, [chiz'-li], *adj.* sandy and clayey, (of land) containing a large mixture of small pebbles. [OE. *cisel* gravel].
CHISLEV, [kis'-lev], *n.* the ninth month of the Jewish ecclesiastical year, and the third of the civil year. [Heb. *Kislev*].
CHIT (1), [chit], *n.* a first shoot, a sprout. [OE. *cith*].
CHIT (2), [chit], *n.* a child, an inexperienced, immature young woman or girl. [*Prec.*].
CHIT (3), [chit], *n.* a short letter, a memorandum, a certificate. [Hind. *chitthi*].
CHIT (4), [chit], *v.i.* to sprout, to shoot forth roots. [CHIT (1)].
CHITAL, [chit'-al], *n.* the spotted deer of India, *Cervus axis*; a poisonous sea-snake of the genus *Hydrophis*. [Hind. *chital*].
CHIT-CHAT, [chit'-chat], *n.* gossip. [CHAT].
CHITIN, [kī'-tin], *n.* a hard horny substance forming the protective shell of certain crustaceans and the wing-cases of certain insects. [Fr. *chitine* from Gr. *khiton* tunic].
CHITINOUS, [kī'-tin-us], *adj.* made of chitin.
CHITON, [kī'-ton], *n.* the ancient tunic formerly worn by the Greeks; (*zool.*) a genus of molluscs.
CHITTACK, [chit'-ak], *n.* an Indian measure of weight equal to about an ounce. [Bengali *chhatak*].
CHITTAGONG-WOOD, [chit'-a-gong'-wood'], *n.* the wood of several Indian trees valued for cabinet-making, the chief being *Chickrassia tabularis*. [*Chittagong*, a place in Bengal].
CHITTER, [chit'-er], *v.i.* to twitter, to chirp; to shiver with cold. [CHATTER].
CHITTERLINGS, [chit'-er-lingz], *n.(pl.)* part of the smaller intestines, particularly of swine, used as food. [Uncert.].
CHITTY, [chit'-i], *adj.* childish. [CHIT (2)].
CHIVALERESQUE, [shiv-al'-er-esk'], *adj.* filled with the spirit of chivalry. [Fr. *chevaleresque*].
CHIVALRIC, [shiv'-al-rik], *adj.* pertaining to chivalry, chivalrous.
CHIVALROUS, [shiv'-al-rus], *adj.* pertaining to chivalry; endowed with the qualities possessed by the ideal knight, courageous, courteous, noble, gallant, protective of the weak.
CHIVALROUSLY, [shiv'-al-rus-li], *adv.* in a chivalrous fashion.
CHIVALRY, [shiv'-al-ri], *n.* the organization, institution, aims and spirit of knighthood in the Middle Ages; the body or order of knights; military prowess, knightly skill, display of qualities of an ideal knight, courtesy, daring, nobility, respect for weaker persons. [OFr. *chevalerie* knighthood].
CHIVE, [chīv], *n.* the small onion, *Allium Schoenoprasum*, related to the garlic. [Fr. *cive* from L. *cepa* onion].
CHIVY (1), [chiv'-i], *n.* a playground game resembling prisoner's base. [CHIVY (2)].
CHIVY (2), [chiv'-i], *v.t.* to chase, to cause to run away; (*fig.*) to harass, to worry continually, to tease persistently. [*Chevy* Chase, a ballad].
CHLAMYDOPHORUS, [klam'-i-dof'-or-us], *n.* a genus of South American armadillos. [Gk. *khlamus* cloak and *phero* I bear].

CHLAMYS, [klam'-is], *n.* an ancient Greek scarf or loose outdoor cloak fastened at the shoulder. [Gk. *khlamus*].
CHLOANTHITE, [klō'-an-thīt], *n.* an ore of nickel in which is found arsenic. [Gk. *khloanthes* budding].
CHLOASMA, [klō'-az-ma], *n.* a skin disease characterized by yellowish-brown or dark patches, caused by internal irritation. [Gk. *khloazo* I become green].
CHLOR-, CHLORO-, *pref.* green, containing chlorine. [Gk. *khloros*].
CHLORACETIC, [klawr'-a-sē'-tik], *adj.* (*chem.*) formed by the action of chlorine on acetic acid. [CHLOR and ACETIC].
CHLORAL, [klaw'-ral], *n.* (*chem.*) a liquid prepared by passing dry chlorine gas through absolute alcohol; (*pop.*) a white crystalline chloral hydrate used as a hypnotic and anaesthetic. [CHLOR and AL(COHOL)].

CHLAMYS

CHLORALISM, [klaw'-ral-izm], *n.* a diseased condition of the body induced by excessive use of chloral.
CHLORATE, [klaw'-rāt], *n.* a salt of chloric acid.
CHLORIC, [klo'-rik], *adj.* of or from chlorine; **c. acid,** an acid of chlorine and oxygen, $HClO_3$.
CHLORID, see CHLORIDE.
CHLORIDATE, [klaw'-ri-dāt], *v.t.* (*chem.*) to treat with a chloride.
CHLORIDE, CHLORID, [klaw'-rīd], *n.* a compound of chlorine with another element.
CHLORINATE, [klo'-ri-nāt], *v.t.* (*chem.*) to treat with chlorine.
CHLORINATION, [klaw'-rin-ā'-shun], *n.* (*chem.*) the act of chlorinating.
CHLORINE, [klaw'-rēn], *n.* a heavy greenish gas with a suffocating odour, used as a powerful disinfectant and bleaching agent, and as a poison gas in warfare; the chemical element denoted by Cl. [CHLOR].
CHLORIODATE, [klaw'-rī-ō-dāt], *n.* a salt of chloriodic acid.
CHLORIODIC, [klaw'-rī-od'-ik], *adj.* consisting of or derived from chlorine and iodine.
CHLORIODINE, [klawr-ī'-od-ēn], *n.* a compound of chlorine and iodine. [CHLOR and IODINE].
CHLORITE, [klaw'-rīt], n. (*geol.*) a group of soft green minerals consisting of magnesium, iron and aluminium silicates; (*chem.*) a salt of chlorous acid.
CHLORITIC, [klaw-rit'-ik], *adj.* containing chlorite.
CHLOROCARBONIC, [klaw'-rō-kah-bon'-ik], *adj.* made of, or containing chlorine and carbonic oxide.
CHLOROCARBONOUS, [klaw'-rō-kah'-bon-us], *adj.* chlorocarbonic.
CHLOROCYANIC, [klaw'-rō-sī-an'-ik], *adj.* consisting of chlorine and cyanogen.
CHLOROFORM (1), [klor'-ō-fawm], *n.* a volatile, colourless, sweet-smelling liquid used as an anaesthetic. [CHLORO and FORMIC].
CHLOROFORM (2), [klor'-o-fawm], *v.t.* to administer chloroform to in order to render insensible.
CHLOROMETER, [klaw-rom'-it-er], *n.* an instrument for testing the bleaching powers of chloride of lime, etc. [CHLORO and METER].
CHLOROMETRY, [klaw-rom'-et-ri], *n.* the process of testing the bleaching power of any compound of chlorine. [CHLORO and Gk. *metria* measurement].
CHLOROPAL, [klo-rōp'-al], *n.* a greenish earthy mineral consisting of silica and oxide of iron. [CHLOR and OPAL].
CHLOROPHAEITE, [klo'-rō-fē'-īt], *n.* a green mineral which becomes black or brown when broken or exposed. [CHLORO and Gk. *phaios* brown].
CHLOROPHANE, [klo'-rō-fān], *n.* a kind of fluorspar which shines with a bright green phosphorescence when heated. [CHLORO and Gk. *phainomai* I appear].
CHLOROPHYLL, [klo'-rō-fil], *n.* (*bot.*) the green colouring matter of plants. [CHLORO and Gk. *phullon* leaf].
CHLOROSIS, [klaw-rō'-sis], *n.* (*med.*) a form of anaemia affecting young girls in which the skin assumes a yellowish-green colour, green-sickness; (*bot.*) a disease in plants in which the leaves turn yellow on account of insufficient production of chlorophyll. [CHLORO and Gk. *osis* denoting condition].
CHLOROTIC, [klaw-rot'-ik], *adj.* relating to, or affected by, chlorosis.
CHLOROUS, [klaw'-rus], *adj.* (*chem.*) similar to,

pertaining to, or containing chlorine; **c. acid,** the acid $HClO_2$.

CHOANITE, [kō'-an-īt], *n.* (*geol.*) a fossil funnel-shaped zoophyte found in chalk formations. [Gk. *khoane* funnel].

CHOBDAR, [chob'-dah], *n.* a state attendant upon an Indian noble. [Pers. *chobdar* stick-bearer].

CHOCK (1), [chok], *n.* a small block of wood; (*naut.*) a wooden block or wedge to support articles or prevent them rolling about on board ship. [OFr. *choque* log].

CHOCK (2), [chok], *v.t.* to support or secure with chocks.

CHOCK-A-BLOCK, [chok'-a-blok'], *adj.* (*naut.*) hoisted up so as to touch the blocks of the hoisting tackle; (*fig.*) crammed full, packed tightly.

CHOCK-FULL, CHOKE-FULL, [chok'-fōōl'], *adj.* quite full, full to capacity.

CHOCOLATE (1), [chok'-(ō)-lat], *n.* a sweetmeat in the form of a hard, dark-brown paste composed of the kernels of the cacao-tree, ground down, sweetened and combined with some flavouring substance; a drink made by mixing this in boiling milk or water. [Span. *chocolate* from Mexican *chocolatl*].

CHOCOLATE (2), [chok'-(ō)-lat], *adj.* of the colour of chocolate, dark brown.

CHOCOLATE-NUT, [chok'-lat-nut'], *n.* the seed of the cacao-tree.

CHOCTAW, [chok'-taw], *n.* a tribe of civilized North American Indians; a step in figure-skating. [*Choctaw*, the name of the Indian tribe].

CHOICE (1), [chois], *n.* the act or process of selecting or discriminating; the thing selected; opportunity for selection or preference; the best or most preferable; a number of things from which a selection may be made; **Hobson's c.,** a choice with no alternative. [OFr. *chois*].

CHOICE (2), [chois], *adj.* selected with care, select, of special value; careful, fastidious, scrupulous.

CHOICELESS, [chois'-les], *adj.* offering no alternative, unable to discriminate.

CHOICELY, [chois'-li], *adv.* with care in choosing; carefully, in a choice manner.

CHOICENESS, [chois'-nes], *n.* the condition of being choice, superiority.

CHOIR (1), [kwīer], *n.* an organized body of singers (*esp.* those taking part in church services) trained to sing together under the guidance of a conductor; that part of the church extending eastward from the nave to the altar, and set apart for the singers. [OFr. *cuer* from Gk. *khoros* chorus].

CHOIR (2), [kwīer], *v.t. and i.* to sing together as a choir or in chorus.

CHOIRMAN, [kwīer'-man], *n.* a male singer in a choir.

CHOIR-ORGAN, [kwīer'-awg'-an], *n.* the softest of the three organs of which a large, multiple three-manual organ is built up.

CHOIR-SCREEN, [kwīer'-skrēn'], *n.* a partition of carved lattice work dividing off the choir from the nave of the church.

CHOIR-SERVICE, [kwīer'-sur'-vis], *n.* the part of a church service performed by the choir.

CHOKE (1), [chōk], *n.* a device for closing the air-inlet of a petrol engine; (*wirel.*) a choking coil, a coil offering, by self-induction, a high impedance to the flow of an alternating current; the narrow part of a gun; (*slang*) prison, gaol.

CHOKE (2), [chōk], *v.t.* to block or compress the wind-pipe or introduce fumes into the lungs, so as to stop the passage of breath; to impede a free passage partially or completely; to stifle, to smother through lack of air or light; (*fig.*) to suppress forcibly (one's feelings); *v.i.* to suffer a stoppage of breath; **to c. off,** to kill by choking, to discourage, cause to abandon; **to c. down,** to swallow or repress with great difficulty. [ME. *choken*].

CHOKE-BORE, [chōk'-baw(r)'], *n.* a sporting gun having a bore narrowed or tapering towards the extremity.

CHOKE-BORE

CHOKE-CHERRY, [chōk'-che'-ri], *n.* the fruit of *Prunus virginiana*.

CHOKE-DAMP, [chōk'-damp'], *n.* poisonous gas found in disused wells, pits, and in coal mines after the explosion of fire-damp.

CHOKE-FULL†, see CHOCK-FULL.

CHOKE-PEAR, [chōk'-pāer], *n.* a pear with a bitter taste.

CHOKER, [chōk'-er], *n.* anything that chokes or is very difficult to answer; (*slang*) a large, high collar or scarf worn round the neck.

CHOKRA, [chok'-ra], *n.* a young male servant. [Hind. *chhokra*].

CHOKY (1), [chōk'-i], *n.* (*slang*) gaol. [Hind. *chauki* police-station].

CHOKY (2), [chōk'-i], *adj.* causing, or producing a feeling of, choking.

CHOL-, *pref.* bile. [Gk. *khole*].

CHOLAGOGUE, [kol'-a-gog'], *n.* a medicine to get rid of bile. [CHOL and Gk. *agogos* leading out].

CHOLEDOGRAPHY, [kol'-id-og'-raf-i], *n.* an account of the organs connected with biliary secretion. [CHOL and Gk. *graphia* writing].

CHOLEDOLOGY, [kol'-id-ol'-o-ji], *n.* a treatise on the bile. [CHOL and Gk. *logos* speech].

CHOLEIC, [kol-ē'-ik], *adj.* derived from bile.

CHOLER, [kol'-er], *n.* bile; anger, hot-temper; †one of the four humours of medieval physiology, thought to produce quickness or heat of temper. [Gk. *kholera* bile].

CHOLERA, [kol'-er-a], *n.* a malignant disease, characterized by violent vomiting, diarrhoea, severe cramps, and intense thirst, and generally fatal. [Gk. *kholera* bile].

CHOLERAIC, [kol'-er-ā'-ik], *adj.* relating to cholera.

CHOLERIC, [kol'-er-ik], *adj.* hot-tempered, angry, quickly enraged.

CHOLERINE, [kol'-er-ēn], *n.* a mild form of cholera, the early stages of cholera.

CHOLESTERIC, [kol-es'-ter-ik], *adj.* obtained from cholesterin.

CHOLESTERIN, [kol-es'-ter-in], *n.* a form of alcohol present in protoplasm, occurring in excess in bile. [CHOL and Gk. *stereos* stiff].

CHOLIAMB, [kōl'-i-amb], *n.* (*pros.*) an iambic verse having a spondee or trochee in the last foot instead of an iamb. [Gk. *kholiambos*].

CHOLIAMBIC (1), [kōl'-i-amb-ik], *n.* a choliamb.

CHOLIAMBIC (2), [kōl'-i-amb-ik], *adj.* pertaining to a choliamb.

CHOLIC, [kol'-ik], *adj.* pertaining to bile.

CHOLOCHROME, [kol'-o-krōm], *n.* colouring matter in the bile. [CHOL and CHROME].

CHOLTRY, see CHOULTRY.

CHONDRAL, [kon'-dral], *adj.* cartilaginous.

CHONDRINE, [kon'-drin], *n.* a gelatinous liquid obtained from cartilage.

CHONDRITIS, [kon-drī'-tis], *n.* inflammation of the cartilage. [CHONDRO and Gk. *itis* denoting inflammation].

CHONDRO- *pref.* cartilage, grain. [Gk. *khondros*].

CHONDRODITE, [kon'-drō-dīt], *n.* (*min.*) a form of silicate of magnesium, humite. [Gk. *khondrodes* granular].

CHONDROGRAPHY, [kon-drog'-raf-i], *n.* the description of cartilages. [CHONDRO and Gk. *graphia* writing].

CHONDROLOGY, [kon-drol'-oj-i], *n.* the scientific study of cartilages. [CHONDRO and Gk. *logos* speech].

CHONDROMETER, [kon-drom'-it-er], *n.* a steel-yard for weighing corn. [CHONDRO and METER].

CHONDROPTERYGIAN, [kon'-drōp-ter-ij'-i-an], *n.* one of the two great divisions of fishes, the bones and fin-spines of which are formed of gristle, as in the sturgeons and sharks. [CHONDRO and Gk. *pterugion* fin].

CHONDROTOMY, [kon-drot'-om-i], *n.* the dissection of cartilage. [CHONDRO and Gk. *tome* cutting].

CHONIKRITE, [kon'-i-krīt], *n.* a massive white mineral, hydrosilicate of aluminium, magnesium and lime. [Gk. *khoneia* melting and *kritos* separated].

CHOOSE, (chose, chosen), [chōōz], *v.t. and i.* to select, to make a choice (of), to discriminate in favour (of), to pick out; to elect; to decide to, to feel inclined to, to prefer. [OE. *ceosan*].

CHOOSER, [chōōz'-er], *n.* a person who chooses.

CHOOSINGLY, [chōōz'-ing-li], *adv.* by choosing.

CHOOSY, [chōōz'-i], *adj.* fussy, over-particular. [CHOOSE].

CHOP (1), [chop], *n.* the act of cutting by striking with an axe or knife; something chopped off, a chopped-off piece of meat, usually with a rib; (*cricket*) a stroke in which the bat cuts down heavily on the ball; (*tennis*) a similar stroke in tennis, which causes the ball to rebound to a lesser height than usual. [CHOP (5)].

CHOP (2), [chop], *n.* jaw; (*pl.*) the side of the face, the jaws and mouth. [CHAP (3)].

CHOP (3), [chop], *n.* a stamp, seal, an official permit; **first c.,** of first rate quality. [Hind. *chhap* seal].

CHOP (4), [chop], *n.* an exchange, a change. [Unkn.].

CHOP (5), [chop], *v.t. and i.* to cut off by a quick downward blow from a sharp instrument such as an axe, etc.; to hew, to hack, to direct a chopping blow at; (*fig.*) to exchange arguments with, to exchange, to barter; (*naut.*) to veer round (of the wind); **to c. up,** to cut up into pieces, to mince; **to c. down,** to fell; **to c. off,** to sever by means of a chopping blow; **to c. and change,** to alter, to be variable; **to c. logic,** to wrangle. [Uncert.].

CHOP-CHOP, [chop'-chop'], *adv. and int.* (*Pidgin English*) quickly. [Chin. *k'wai-k'wai*].

CHOPFALLEN, see CHAPFALLEN.

CHOP-HOUSE, [chop'-hows], *n.* an eating house.

CHOPIN, [chop'-in], *n.* a French liquid measure of approximately half a pint, a Scots liquid measure equal to an English quart. [Fr. *chopine*].

CHOPINE, CHIOPPINE, [chop-ēn'], *n.* a seventeenth-century woman's thick-soled high shoe, made of wood, covered with leather. [OFr. *chapine*].

CHOPPER (1), [chop'-er], *n.* an axe.

CHOPPER (2), [chop'-er], *n.* a roof of grass thatch. [Hind. *chappar*].

CHOPPING (1), [chop'-ing], *n.* the rough motion of waves caused by a sudden freshening of the wind; **c. and changing,** altering, substituting.

CHOPPING (2), [chop'-ing], *adj.* abrupt, jerky, interrupted, having a rough, jerky, agitated movement.

CHOPPING-BLOCK, [chop'-ing-blok'], *n.* a wooden block on which anything is placed to be chopped.

CHOPPING-KNIFE, [chop'-ing-nīf'], *n.* a chopper, a double-handled knife used for mincing.

CHOPPY, [chop'-i], *adj.* (of wind) constantly veering; (of the sea) rough, agitated by a sudden freshening of the breeze.

CHOPSTICKS, [chop'-stiks], *n.(pl.)* two smooth pieces of wood, ivory or bamboo, used by the Chinese to convey food to the mouth. [CHOP-CHOP and STICK].

CHOP-SUEY, [chop'-sōō'-i], *n.* a Chinese dish of fried meat, onions, etc., accompanied with rice. [Chin. *chap sui*].

CHORAGIC, [kor-aj'-ik], *adj.* relating to a choragus; **c. monument,** (*antiq.*) a monument in honour of the choragus who produced the best musical or theatrical entertainment at the festival of Bacchus. [Gk. *khoregikos*].

CHORAGUS, CHOREGUS, [kor-ā'-gus], *n.* (*antiq.*) the leader of a chorus amongst the ancient Greeks; an official in the University of Oxford who organizes the practice of music; a choir-master. [Gk. *khoregos* chorus-leader].

CHORAL, [kaw'-ral], *adj.* pertaining to a choir, written or arranged for a choir, sung by a choir; **c. service,** a service in the Church of England with intoned responses. [CHORUS].

CHORALE, [kaw-rahl'], *n.* a sacred hymn or psalm tune of the German Protestant churches sung in harmony or unison. [*Prec.*].

CHORALLY, [kaw'-ral-i], *adv.* in a choral manner.

CHORD (1), [kawd], *n.* the string of a musical instrument; anything resembling this in structure or function; (*mus.*) a combination of musical notes sounding simultaneously and arranged according to the rules of harmony; an harmonious and unbroken feeling or emotion considered as a musical chord; harmonious combination of colours; (*geom.*) a straight line connecting two points on the circumference of a circle; (*aeron.*) the distance from the leading edge to the trailing edge of the wings of an aeroplane. [Gk. *khorde* string of gut].

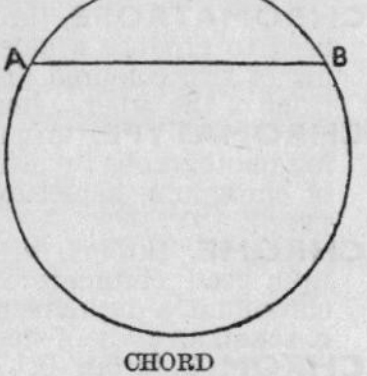

CHORD

CHORD (2), [kawd], *v.t. and i.* to form a musical chord; to furnish with chords.

CHORDATA, [kaw-dā'-ta], *n.(pl.)* (*zool.*) a division or class of animals characterized by a well-developed cartilaginous structure corresponding to the spinal column.

CHORE, [chaw(r)], *n.* (*U.S.*) a small task or job of work. [CHAR].

CHOREA, [ko-rē'-a], *n.* a nervous disease characterized by convulsive muscular twitches; St. Vitus's dance. [Gk. *khoreia* choral dance].

CHOREE, [ko-rē'], *n.* a trochee. [Gk. *khoreios* relating to a dance].

CHOREGRAPHY, see CHOREOGRAPHY.

CHOREGUS, see CHORAGUS.

CHOREOGRAPHER, [ko'-ri-og'-raf-er], *n.* an arranger of ballets.

CHOREOGRAPHY, CHOREGRAPHY, [ko'-ri-og'-raf-i], *n.* the art of representing a dance by signs, as a tune is represented by notes; ballet-dancing. [Gk. *khoreia* dance and *graphia* writing].

CHOREPISCOPAL, [ko'-ri-pis'-kō-pal], *adj.* relating to a chorepiscopus.

CHOREPISCOPUS†, [ko'-ri-pis'-kō-pus], *n.* a local or suffragan bishop. [Gk. *khorepiskopos*].

CHORIAMB, [ko'-ri-amb'], *n.* (*pros.*) a foot of four syllables, the first and last being long, and the rest short. [Gk. *khoriambos*].

CHORIAMBIC (1), [ko'-ri-amb'-ik], *n.* a choriamb.

CHORIAMBIC (2), [ko'-ri-amb'-ik], *adj.* containing a choriamb.

CHORIC, [ko'-rik], *adj.* relating to a chorus. [Gk. *khorikos*].

CHORION, [kō'-ri-on], *n.* (*anat.*) the exterior membrane enclosing the foetus in the womb; (*bot.*) the pulpy matter forming the nucleus of the seed. [Gk. *khorion*].

CHORIPETALOUS, [kaw'-ri-pet'-al-us], *adj.* (*bot.*) with separate petals. [Gk. *khoris* separate and PETALOUS].

CHORISIS, [kaw-rī'-sis], *n.* (*bot.*) the separation of an organ into parts which are each perfect facsimiles of the original. [Gk. *khorisis*].

CHORISTER, [ko'-ris-ter], *n.* a singer in a choir, a choir boy.

CHOROGRAPHER, [ko-rog'-raf-er], *n.* a person describing the features of a particular district or country.

CHOROGRAPHY, [ko-rog'-raf-i], *n.* the art of describing or a description of the physical features of a particular district or country, regional physical geography. [Gk. *khorographia*].

CHOROID (1), [kō'-roid], *n.* (*anat.*) the vascular membrane forming a lining to the ball of the eye. [CHORION and Gk. *oeides* like].

CHOROID (2), [kō'-roid], *adj.* resembling the chorion, forming an enclosing membrane.

CHOROLOGY, [kor-ol'-o-ji], *n.* the science and study of the distribution of plants and animals over the surface of the earth. [Gk. *khora* place and *logos* speech].

CHORTLE (1), [chawtl], *n.* a chuckle.

CHORTLE (2), [chawtl], *v.i.* to chuckle loudly. [Invented].

CHORUS (1), [kaw'-rus], *n.* a group of actors or singers helping to interpret and pass comment upon the action in a Greek drama, the words uttered by the chorus; an organized group of singers who, whilst not playing an individually important part, sing together the choral parts of a musical drama, parts of a musical drama sung by such a group; a group of female performers, distinguished rather by their physical charms and dancing ability than by their histrionic talent; the recurring part of a song sung together by a number of persons as a refrain; a musical composition for a number of voices singing in harmony; (*fig.*) remarks, cries or shouts uttered simultaneously by a group of persons or animals. [Gk. *khoros* a ring dance].

CHORUS (2), [kaw'-rus], *v.t. and i.* to sing or speak in chorus.

CHORUS-GIRL, [kaw'-rus-gurl'], *n.* a girl who sings and dances in the chorus of a variety show or a musical comedy.

CHOSE, [shōz], *n.* (*leg.*) property; **c. in action,** money due for a bond or as a debt and recoverable in law. [Fr. *chose* thing].

CHOSEN, [chōz'-en], *adj.* specially selected, elect, distinguished by preference. [ME. *chosen*, *p.pt.* of CHOOSE].

CHOU, [shōō], *n.* an ornamental ribbon or lace worn on a woman's dress or hat; small pastry cake containing cream or jelly. [Fr. *chou* cabbage].

CHOUGH, [chuf], *n.* a bird of the crow family, *Pyrrhocorax graculus*; (*pop.*) the jackdaw; (*fig.*) a chatterer, babbler. [ME. *chogh*].

CHOULTRY, CHOLTRY, [chōl'-tri], *n.* (*Anglo-Indian*) an inn; a building where public business is transacted; a temple hall adorned with pillars. [Telugu *chawadi*].

CHOUSE (1), [chows], *n.* a swindle, a hoax; †a rogue, a cheat. [Turk. *chaush* a herald].
CHOUSE (2), [chowz], *v.t.* to dupe, to swindle.
CHOUSINGHA, [chow'-sing-ha], *n.* the Indian four-horned antelope, *Tetraceros quadricornis.* [Native].
CHOW, [chow], *n.* a Chinese dog having a black tongue and a thick furry coat usually red or brown in colour; (*Austral.*) a Chinaman. [CHOW-CHOW].
CHOW-CHOW, [chow-chow], *n.* a Chinese mixture of pickles or preserves; any mixture. [Uncert.].
CHOWDER (1), [chow'-der], *n.* an American dish of fish or clams cooked with biscuit, salt pork, etc.; **c. beer,** a kind of spruce beer. [Fr. *chaudière* pot, kettle].
CHOWDER (2), [chow'-der], *v.t.* to make a chowder of.
CHOWRY, [chow'-ri], *n.* a flapper to keep away flies. [Hind. *chaunri*].
CHOY-ROOT, see CHAYA-ROOT.
CHREMATISTIC, [krē'-mat-is'-tik], *adj.* pertaining to the acquiring or pursuit of wealth. [Gk. *khrematistikos*].
CHREMATISTICS, [krē'-mat-is'-tiks], *n.* the science of wealth, political economy. [*Prec.*].
CHRESTOMATHY, [kres-tom'-ath-i], *n.* a book of specimen passages from literature with notes; an anthology. [Gk. *khrestos* useful and *matho* I learn].
CHRISM, [krizm], *n.* consecrated oil used in the Roman Catholic and Greek Churches in the sacraments. [Gk. *khrisma*].
CHRISMAL, [kriz'-mal], *adj.* relating to the chrism.
CHRISMATORY, [kriz'-mat-or-i], *n.* a vessel in which the chrism is contained. [MedL. *chrismatorium*].
CHRISOM, [kris'-um], *n.* a white robe, laid on a child at baptism to cover the chrism; a christening robe; one used as the shroud of a child dying before a month old; **c. child,** a child in its first month, a child dead within a month of baptism. [CHRISM].
CHRIST, [krist], *n.* the Jewish Messiah or Lord's Anointed One, name given to Jesus as the Messiah. [Gk. *khristos* the anointed one].
CHRISTADELPHIAN, [kris'-ta-del'-fi-an], *n.* a member of a religious sect, established in 1848, which believe in Jesus, but not the Trinity; a Thomasite. [Gk. *khristadelphia* brotherhood with Christ].

CHRISMATORY

CHRIST-CROSS-ROW, [krist'-kros'-rō'], *n.* a cross, the sign of the cross; †the alphabet, so called from the figure of the cross which usually preceded the row of letters.
CHRISTEN, [krisn], *v.t.* to baptize, to admit into the Christian faith by the ceremony of baptism; to give a name to. [OE. *cristnian*].
CHRISTENDOM, [krisn'-dum], *n.* the whole body of Christians, Christian countries.
CHRISTENING, [krisn'-ing], *n.* the act or ceremony of baptism.
CHRISTIAN (1), [kris'-chan], *n.* one who professes to follow Christ or his teaching, one whose life and conduct conform to the example and precepts given by Christ; (*coll.*) a decent human being.
CHRISTIAN (2), [kris'-chan], *adj.* pertaining to Christ or to his teaching, pertaining to a Christian; **C. era,** the period regarded as beginning with the year of the birth of Christ; **C. name,** a name given to a person at baptism as distinct from the surname; **C. Science,** an American religious organization which maintains that sin and disease are due solely to wrong thinking. [L. *christianus*].
CHRISTIANISM, [kris'-ti-an-izm], *n.* Christianity.
CHRISTIANITY, [kris'-ti-an'-i-ti], *n.* the religion and teaching of Christ, the Christian faith; the beliefs and conduct characteristic of a Christian. [L. *christianitas*].
CHRISTIANIZATION, [kris'-ti-an-iz-ā'-shun], *n.* the process of conversion to Christianity.
CHRISTIANIZE, [kris'-ti-an-īz], *v.t.* to make Christian, to convert to Christianity.
CHRISTIANLIKE, [kris'-ti-an-līk'], *adj.* as befits a Christian.
CHRISTIANLY, [kris'-ti-an-li], *adj. and adv.* befitting a Christian; in a Christian fashion.
CHRISTLESS, [krīst'-les], *adj.* heathen, without the spirit of Christ.
CHRISTMAS, [kris'-mas], *n.* the church festival in memory of the birth of Christ, observed annually on December 25; **C. card,** a decorated card sent out as a greeting at Christmas; **C. daisy,** the plant *Aster grandiflorus*; **C. Day,** December 25; **C. Eve,** December 24; **C. number,** a special Christmas issue of a periodical, usually in an enlarged form; **C. pride,** the plant *Ruellia paniculata*; **C. rose,** the black hellebore, *Helleborus niger*, so called from its flower which resembles a large white rose. [OE. *Cristes-mæsse*].
CHRISTMAS-BOX, [kris'-mas-boks'], *n.* a present or gift of money given at Christmas-time.
CHRISTMASTIDE, [kris'-mas-tīd'], *n.* the days about Christmas.
CHRISTMAS-TIME, [kris'-mas-tīm'], *n.* the season of Christmas which officially lasts from December 24 to January 6 (Epiphany).
CHRISTMAS-TREE, [kris'-mas-trē'], *n.* a Christmas decoration consisting of a small tree, usually a fir, decorated with tinsel, ornaments, and presents.
CHRISTOLOGY, [kris-tol'-oj-i], *n.* that branch of theology which deals with Christ. [CHRIST and Gk. *logos* speech].
CHRISTOPHANY, [kris-tof'-an-i], *n.* the appearance of Christ after his resurrection. [CHRIST and Gk. *phainomai* I appear].
CHRIST'S-THORN, [krīsts'-thawn], *n.* the prickly shrub, *Paliurus aculeata*, supposed to be the plant from which Christ's crown of thorns was made.
CHROMA-, CHROMAT-, CHROMO-, *pref.* colour. [Gk. *khromatos*, *gen.* of *khroma* colour].
CHROMAT-, see CHROMA.
CHROMATE, [krōm'-āt], *n.* (*chem.*) a salt of chromic acid.
CHROMATIC, [krōm-at-'-ik], *adj.* of or pertaining to colour, highly coloured; (*mus.*) including or referring to notes not included in a major or minor diatonic scale, foreign to the key in which a passage of music is written; (*biol.*) capable of taking a stain. [Gk. *khromatikos* relating to colour].
CHROMATICALLY, [krōm-at'-ik-al-i], *adv.* in a chromatic fashion.
CHROMATICS, [krōm-at'-iks], *n.* (*opt.*) the branch of optics dealing with the science of colour; (*mus.*) chromatic notes.
CHROMATIN, [krōm'-at-in], *n.* that part of the nucleus of cells which can be stained by dyes.
CHROMATISM, [krōm'-at-izm], *n.* (*opt.*) chromatic aberration; (*bot.*) abnormal coloration.
CHROMATO-, see CHROMA.
CHROMATOGRAPHY, [krōm'-at-og'-raf-i], *n.* a treatise on colours. [CHROMATO and Gk. *graphia* writing].
CHROMATOMETER, [krōm'-at-om'-it-er], *n.* a chart, measure or scale of colours. [CHROMATO and METER].
CHROMATOPHORE, [krōm'-at-ō-faw(r)'], *n.* a pigment-carrying cell which produces change of colour in certain animals. [CHROMATO and Gk. *phero* I bear].
CHROMATOPSIA, [krō'-ma-top'-si-a], *n.* (*med.*) chromatic sight. [CHROMATO and Gk. *opsia* seeing].
CHROMATOSCOPE, [krōm'-at-os-kōp'], *n.* an apparatus for mingling different-coloured rays of light to produce new colours or shades. [CHROMATO and SCOPE].
CHROMATROPE, [krōm'-a-trōp], *n.* an instrument used to produce a kaleidoscopic effect, and consisting of two coloured disks, one of which revolves in front of the other. [CHROMA and TROPE].
CHROMATYPE, [krōm'-a-tīp], *n.* a method of obtaining photographs by using a paper sensitized by a salt of chromium, a picture so obtained. [CHROMA and TYPE].
CHROME, [krōm], *n.* a yellow pigment obtained from lead chromate; yellow; **c. green,** oxide of chromium, a dark green pigment used in enamelling; **c. steel,** an alloy of steel and chromium. [CHROMA].
CHROMIC, [krōm'-ik], *adj.* pertaining to, containing, or obtained from chromium.
CHROMIDIUM, [krōm-id'-i-um], *n.* an alloy of chromium used in making brake-drums, etc.
CHROMITE, [krōm'-īt], *n.* (*min.*) a brownish-black metal, the chief ore of chromium.
CHROMIUM, [krōm'-i-um], *n.* (*chem.*) a greyish white metal used in giving hardness to alloys, the chemical element denoted by Cr. [CHROME].
CHROMIUM-PLATE, [krōm'-i-um-plāt'], *n.* a coating of chromium electrically deposited on metal giving it a hard, lustrous, and untarnishable surface.
CHROMOGENE, [krōm'-o-jēn'], *n.* a vegetable colouring matter or compound which, when acted

upon by an acid or alkali, is converted into a dyestuff. [CHROMO and Gk. *genes* producing].

CHROMOGRAPH, [krōm'-ō-grahf'], *n.* an apparatus for duplicating copies of matter written in aniline dye, and transferred to a gelatinous surface from which a number of copies can be taken. [CHROMO and GRAPH].

CHROMO-LITHOGRAPH, [krō'-mō-lith'-o-grahf], *n.* a coloured lithograph.

CHROMO-LITHOGRAPHY, [krō'-mō-lith-og'-raf-i], *n.* the art of printing lithographs in colours.

CHROMOPLASM, [krōm'-o-plazm], *n.* the part of a cell having a tendency to absorb colouring matter. [CHROMO and PLASM].

CHROMOSOME, [krōm'-o-sōm], *n.* a minute body formed from chromatin and occurring in the germ-cells of animals. [CHROMO and Gk. *soma* body].

CHROMOSPHERE, [krōm'-os-fēer'], *n.* the incandescent gaseous sphere surrounding the sun. [CHROMO and SPHERE].

CHROMOTYPOGRAPHY, [krō'-mō-tī-pog'-raf-i], *n.* colour-printing.

CHROMULE, [krōm'-ewl], *n.* (*bot.*) the colouring matter (other than chlorophyll) in plants. [CHROMO and Gk. *hule* matter].

CHRONIC, [kron'-ik], *adj.* continuous, lingering, (of a disease) long-lasting, slowly-developing and of a rather mild nature; (*coll.*) bad, boring. [Gk. *khronikos* relating to time].

CHRONICALLY, [kron'-ik-al-i], *adv.* in a chronic manner.

CHRONICITY, [kron-is'-it-i], *n.* (*med.*) the condition of being chronic.

CHRONICLE (1), [kron'-ikl], *n.* a record of events, systematically arranged in order of time; a narrative, a history; **The Chronicles,** name given to two historical books of the kingdom of Judah in the Old Testament. [ME. *cronicle* from Gk. *khronika* annals].

CHRONICLE (2), [kron'-ikl], *v.t.* to record in a chronicle, to record in order of occurrence.

CHRONICLER, [kron'-ik-ler], *n.* the compiler of a chronicle, an historian.

CHRONO-, *pref.* time. [Gk. *khronos* time].

CHRONOGRAM, [kron'-ō-gram], *n.* an inscription recording an event in which certain letters, marked out in some way, give (when taken as Roman numerals) the date of the event recorded. [CHRONO and Gk. *gramma* something written].

CHRONOGRAMMATIC, [kron'-ō-gram-at'-ik], *adj.* pertaining to a chronogram.

CHRONOGRAMMATICAL, [kron'-ō-gram-at'-ik-al], *adj.* chronogrammatic.

CHRONOGRAMMATIST, [kron'-ō-gram'-at-ist], *n.* a composer of chronograms.

CHRONOGRAPH, [kron'-ō-grahf], *n.* an instrument used for measuring and registering minute portions of time with great precision, and for recording the time of an event with extreme exactness and accuracy. [CHRONO and GRAPH].

CHRONOGRAPHER, [kron-og'-raf-er], *n.* a chronologer.

CHRONOGRAPHY, [kron-og'-raf-i], *n.* a chronological description of past events. [CHRONO and Gk. *graphia* writing].

CHRONOLOGER, [kron-ol'-oj-er], *n.* one expert in chronology.

CHRONOLOGICAL, [kron'-ō-loj'-ik-al], *adj.* pertaining to chronology; arranged in order of time.

CHRONOLOGICALLY, [kron'-ō-loj'-ik-al-i], *adv.* in a chronological fashion.

CHRONOLOGIST, [kron-ol'-o-jist], *n.* a chronologer.

CHRONOLOGY, [kron-ol'-o-ji], *n.* the art of reckoning time or periods of time and arranging events in the correct sequence of time; the correct dating of events; a register or table of dates. [CHRONO and Gk. *logos* speech].

CHRONOMETER, [kron-om'-it-er], *n.* a very accurate watch or clock, usually with a compensation adjustment for temperature, used in determining longitude at sea. [CHRONO and METER].

CHRONOMETRIC, [kron'-ō-met'-rik], *adj.* relating to, or measured by, a chronometer.

CHRONOMETRICAL, [kron'-ō-met'-rik-al], *adj.* chronometric.

CHRONOMETRY, [kron-om'-et-ri], *n.* the science of measuring time with great precision and accuracy. [CHRONO and Gk. *metria* measuring].

CHRONOPHER, [kron'-ō-fer], *n.* an electrical apparatus for transmitting time signals by wireless. [CHRONO and Gk. *phero* I carry].

CHRONOSCOPE, [kron'-ō-skōp], *n.* an instrument for measuring accurately extremely small intervals of time, such as the duration of an electric spark. [CHRONO and SCOPE].

CHRYSALID (1), [kris'-al-id], *n.* a chrysalis.

CHRYSALID (2), [kris'-al-id], *adj.* pertaining to a chrysalis.

CHRYSALIS, (*pl.* **chrysalides,** or **chrysalises**), [kris'-al-is], *n.* the membranous sheath in which the larva of a moth, etc., is enclosed when developing into its final winged state; the torpid state of a larva when so enclosed. [Gk. *khrusallis* gold-coloured butterfly sheath].

CHRYSANTHEMUM, [kris-an'-thim-um], *n.* a large genus of composite plants consisting of herbs with single flowers and with many small petals thickly set, of which the oxeye daisy and corn-marigold are common British representatives. [Gk. *khrusanthemon* gold-flower].

CHRYSELEPHANTINE, [kris'-el-if-an'-tīn], *adj.* partly made of, or overlaid with, gold and ivory. [CHRYS(O) and Gk. *elephantinos* made of ivory].

CHRYSO-, *pref.* gold. [Gk. *khrusos* gold].

CHRYSOBERYL, [kris'-ō-be'-ril], *n.* (*min.*) a precious stone yellowish-green in colour. [CHRYSO and BERYL].

CHRYSOCHLORIS, [kris'-ō-klaw'-ris], *n.* a South African genus of insectivorous mammals related to the mole, whose fur shines with green and gold; a golden mole. [CHRYSO and Gk. *khloros* green].

CHRYSOCOLLA, [kris'-ō-kol'-a], *n.* (*min.*) a green lustrous hydrous silicate of copper. [Gk. *khrusokolla* gold solder].

CHRYSOCRACY, [kris-ok'-ras-i], *n.* plutocracy. [CHRYSO and Gk. *krateia* power].

CHRYSOGRAPHY, [kris-og'-raf-i], *n.* the art and practice of writing in gold. [Gk. *khrusographia*].

CHRYSOLITE, [kris'-ol-īt], *n.* the most transparent form of olivine, a hard yellowish-green semi-precious stone. [Gk. *khrusolithos* yellow stone].

CHRYSOLOGY, [kris-ol'-o-ji], *n.* that branch of political economy which deals with the production of wealth. [CHRYSO and Gk. *logos* speech].

CHRYSOPHAN, [kris'-ō-fan], *n.* a bitter substance obtained by alcoholic extraction from rhubarb. [CHRYSO and Gk. *phainomai* I appear].

CHRYSOPHANIC, [kris'-ō-fan'-ik], *adj.* pertaining to chrysophan.

CHRYSOPRASE, [kris'-ō-prāz], *n.* a golden green variety of chalcedony. [Gk. *khrusoprasos*].

CHRYSOTYPE, [kris'-ō-tīp], *n.* a photographic process in which gold chloride is used as a developer. [CHRYSO and TYPE].

CHTHONIAN, [kthō'-ni-an], *adj.* pertaining to the gods of the earth. [Gk. *khthonios* earthy].

CHTHONIC, [kthō'-nik], *adj.* chthonian.

CHUB, [chub], *n.* a thick, rounded fresh-water fish, *Leuciscus cephalus,* of the carp family. [ME. *chubbe*].

CHUBBINESS, [chub'-i-nes], *n.* the condition of being chubby.

CHUBBY, [chub'-i], *adj.* fat, plump. [Uncert.].

CHUB-FACED, [chub'-fāst], *adj.* having a plump face.

CHUCK (1), [chuk], *n.* a cluck, a clicking sound made with the tongue against the hard palate. [Echoic].

CHUCK (2), [chuk], *n.* a word of endearment, a childish name for a chicken or fowl. [Corruption of CHICKEN].

CHUCK (3), [chuk], *n.* a light, playful or amorous tap under the chin; **to give a person the c.,** (*slang*) to dismiss, to sack; to finish with. [Uncert.].

CHUCK (4), [chuk], *n.* a small block or lump; a device for holding a piece of wood or metal on the revolving mandril of a lathe. [CHOCK].

CHUCK (5), [chuk], *n.* (*slang*) food, provisions; **hard c.,** (*naut.*) ship's biscuit. [Unkn.].

CHUCK (6), [chuk], *v.i.* to make a click, to cluck. [CHUCK (1)].

CHUCK (7), [chuk], *v.t.* to give a light, playful or amorous pat under the chin; to throw, to hurl, to toss; (*coll.*) to stop, to break off relations with, to give up; **to c. away,** to squander; **to c. out,** to throw out forcibly, to cause to be withdrawn (of a bill, motion, proposal); **to c. up,** to give up, to abandon. [Uncert.].

CHUCK (8), [chuk], *v.t.* to secure in position in a chuck. [CHUCK (4)].

CHUCKER-OUT, [chuk'-er-owt'], *n.* an attendant whose duty is to remove by force disorderly persons from a public assembly.

CHUCK-FARTHING, [chuk'-fah'-THing], *n.* a game in which farthings are thrown at a mark.
CHUCK-HOLE, [chuk'-hōl], *n.* a deep hole in a rut.
CHUCKLE (1), [chukl], *n.* a quiet half-suppressed laugh. [CHUCKLE (2)].
CHUCKLE (2), [chukl], *v.t. and i.* to cluck; to make a chuckle; (*fig.*) to have a feeling of inward triumph or exultation. [Imitative].
CHUCKLE-HEAD, [chukl'-hed'], *n.* a thick-headed stupid person.
CHUCKLE-HEADED, [chukl'-hed'-id], *adj* thick-headed.
CHUCKLING, [chuk'-ling], *n.* a series of chuckles, half-suppressed laughter.
CHUCK-WAGON, [chuk'-wag'-on], *n.* (*U.S.*) a provision cart.
CHUDDAR, [chud'-er], *n.* a shawl or head-covering worn by Indian women. [Hind. *chadar*].
CHUET†, [chōō'-it], *n.* a dish of minced meat flavoured with spice and fruit. [Unkn.].
CHUFFILY, [chuf'-i-li], *adv.* in a chuffy fashion.
CHUFFINESS, [chuf'-i-nes], *n.* the condition of being chuffy.
CHUFFY, [chuf'-i], *adj.* rude, boorish; plump, chubby. [Unkn.].
CHUG, [chug], *v.i.* to emit steady low explosive sounds. [Echoic].
CHUKKER, [chuk'-er], *n.* one of the periods of play in the game of polo. [Hind. *chukkur* a bout].
CHUM (1), [chum], *n.* a familiar friend, a partner; pal, chap. [Unkn.].
CHUM (2), (**chumming, chummed**), [chum], *v.i.* to live with another person, to share a room or dwelling with another; to strike up an intimate friendship.
CHUMMY, [chum'-i]. *adj.* friendly, intimate.
CHUMP, [chump], *n.* a short, thick piece of wood, a solid lump of meat; (*fig.*) the head; a stupid person; **off one's c.**, (*coll.*) out of one's mind, crazy. [Uncert.].
CHUMP-END, [chump'-end'], *n.* the thick end of a loin of meat nearest the rump.
CHUNAM, [chōō-am'], *n.* a fine quicklime made from calcined shells or limestone, a kind of cement from sand and calcined shells. [Tamil *chunnam* lime].
CHUNK, [chungk], *n.* a thick roughly-cut piece, a rough, unhewn lump or block. [Uncert.].
CHUPATTY, [chōō-pat'-i], *n.* unleavened bread of coarse meal, the native bread of Upper India. [Hind. *chapati*].
CHUPRASSIE, [chōō-pras'-i], *n.* an office-messenger bearing a badge which gives the name of the office to which he belongs. [Hind. *chaprasi*].
CHURCH (1), [church], *n.* a building specially devoted to religion, one consecrated to the (Christian) worship of God; a religious sect; the Christian religion; a branch of this; the collective body of Christians; a building in which Church of England services only are held (as distinct from a chapel); the clergy; **C. Army**, an organization in the Church of England for mission and relief work amongst the poor; **Established C.**, the form of religion, doctrine and ritual, recognized and supported by the State; **C. Militant**, the body of Christians, considered as warring against all spiritual evil; **to enter the C.**, to become a clergyman. [OE. *cirice* from Gk. *kuriakon* (house) of the Lord].
CHURCH (2), [church], *v.t.* to bring into membership of the Church; to bring a woman to church for thank-offering for safe delivery after childbirth.
CHURCH-ALE†, [church'-āl], *n.* a periodical church festival at which there was ale-drinking, dancing, and merrymaking.
CHURCH-BENCH, [church'-bench'], *n.* a seat placed in a church porch.
CHURCH-BROOM, [church'-brōōm], *n.* the teasel, *Dipsacus sylvestris*.
CHURCH-BURIAL, [church'-be'-ri-al], *n.* burial according to the rites of a church.
CHURCH-COURT, [church'-kawt], *n.* a court which tries ecclesiastical cases.
CHURCH-GOER, [church'-gō'-er], *n.* one who regularly attends church.
CHURCH-GOING (1), [church'-gō'-ing], *n.* habitual attendance at church.
CHURCH-GOING (2), [church'-gō'-ing], *adj.* regularly attending church.
CHURCHING, [church'-ing], *n.* (*eccles.*) the ceremony of thank-offering of a woman safely delivered of a child.
CHURCHISM, [church'-izm], *n.* a strong belief in the doctrines and ritual of a particular church.
CHURCHITE, [church'-īt], *n.* a native Cornish hydrous phosphate of cerium and didymium. [Prof. A. H. *Church*].
CHURCH-LAND, [church'-land'], *n.* land belonging to the church.
CHURCHLIKE, [church'-līk], *adj.* befitting a church or churchman.
CHURCHMAN, [church'-man], *n.* an ecclesiastic, a clergyman; a member of the church.
CHURCHMANLY, [church'-man-li], *adj.* like a churchman.
CHURCHMANSHIP, [church'-man-ship], *n.* the condition of being a churchman.
CHURCH-MEMBER, [church'-mem'-ber], *n.* a recognized member of a church, one entitled to receive communion.
CHURCH-MEMBERSHIP, [church'-mem'-ber-ship], *n.* the condition of being a church-member.
CHURCH-MUSIC, [church'-mew'-zik], *n.* music written for or suitable for performance in church.
CHURCH-OUTED†, [church'-owt'-id], *adj.* excommunicated.
CHURCH-OWL, [church'-owl'], *n.* the common barn-owl, *Strix flammea*.
CHURCH-RATE, [church'-rāt'], *n.* a ground-rent or house-rate which is collected for the upkeep of the parish church.
CHURCH-SCOT, [church'-skot'], *n.* (*archaic*) a payment formerly made in aid of the parish clergy.
CHURCH-SERVICE, [church'-sur'-vis], *n.* a religious service held in a church.
CHURCH-TEXT, [church'-tekst'], *n.* (*print.*) Old English or black-letter type.
CHURCHWARDEN, [church'-waw'-den], *n.* one of two honorary officials elected in every Anglican parish to look after the church fabric, enforce decorum in church, and distribute gifts to the church (other than collections); (*coll.*) a long-stemmed clay pipe.
CHURCH-WAY, [church'-wā], *n.* a road that leads to a church.
CHURCH-WORK, [church'-wurk], *n.* work on behalf of a church.
CHURCHY, [church'-i], *adj.* (*coll.*) excessively devoted to the Church, and displaying this in an obtrusive manner; displaying an excessive preference for the Established Church as against the Nonconformist churches.
CHURCHYARD, [church'-yahd], *n.* a piece of consecrated ground surrounding a church and used for interments.
CHURINGA, [chu-ring'-ga], *n.* a charm used by Australian aborigines. [Native].

CHURINGA

CHURL, [churl], *n.*† a peasant; a rude, ill-bred person, a niggard. [OE. *ceorl*].
CHURLISH, [churl'-ish], *adj.* boorish, rude, uncivil; niggardly; mean. [OE. *ceorlisc* rustic].
CHURLISHLY, [churl'-ish-li], *adv.* in a churlish fashion.
CHURLISHNESS, [churl'-ish-nes], *n.* the state of being churlish.
CHURLY, [churl'-i], *adj.* churlish.
CHURN (1), [churn], *n.* a rotating drum or other vessel in which cream is agitated for the production of butter; a large milk can. [OE. *cyren*].
CHURN (2), [churn], *v.t. and i.* to agitate or beat up in a churn in order to produce butter; (*fig.*) to stir, agitate with continued violence (of liquids) so that a froth appears; to make butter in a churn.
CHURNING, [churn'-ing], *n.* the process of making butter in a churn, a quantity of butter so produced at one time; (*fig.*) violent agitation or disturbance (of liquids).
CHURN-STAFF, [churn'-stahf], *n.* a staff used in churning.
CHURRUS, [chu'-rus], *n.* a resinous substance obtained from the dried hemp-plant, and used as an intoxicating narcotic in India. [Hind. *charas*].
CHURR-WORM, [chur'-wurm], *n.* the mole-cricket, *Gryllotalpa vulgaris*.
CHUT, [chut], *int.* an exclamation of impatience.
CHUTE, [shōōt], *n.* a steeply sloping channel or enclosed passage down which heavy objects are quickly slid to a lower level; a steep channel which causes an abrupt descent to a lower level and along which water flows; a steep cutting; **water c.**, a steep framework leading into water, down which specially

constructed boats are shot so that they bump about after hitting the water; (*coll.*) a parachute. [Fr. *chute* a fall].

CHUTNEY, [chut'-ni], *n.* an East Indies spiced sauce made of fruit, vinegar, etc. [Hind. *chatni*].

CHYLACEOUS, [kī-lā'-shus], *adj.* chylous; consisting of chyle.

CHYLE, [kīl], *n.* (*physiol.*) a milky fluid into which food is converted in the intestines by the process of digestion, before absorption into the blood-stream. [Gk. *khulos* juice].

CHYLE-DUCT, [kīl'-dukt'], *n.* a part of the thoracic duct which acts as reservoir for the chyle.

CHYLIFACTIVE, [kīl'-i-fak'-tiv], *adj.* forming or turning into chyle; having the power to make chyle. [CHYLE and L. *facere* to make].

CHYLIFEROUS, [kīl-if'-er-us], *adj.* containing or transmitting chyle. [CHYLE and L. *ferre* to bear].

CHYLIFICATION, [kīl'-if-ik-ā'-shun], *n.* the process of making chyle.

CHYLIFICATORY, [kīl'-if-i-kā'-tor-i], *adj.* chylifactive.

CHYLIFIC, [kīl-if'-ik], *adj.* producing chyle.

CHYLIFY, [kīl'-i-fī] *v.t.* to turn into chyle.

CHYLOPOIETIC, [kīl'-ō-poi-et'-ik], *adj.* pertaining to the production of chyle. [CHYLE and Gk. *poietikos* making].

CHYLOUS, [kīl'-us], *adj.* relating to, or consisting of, chyle.

CHYLURIA, [kīl-ew'-ri-a], *n.* the disorder of chyle in the urine. [CHYLE and Gk. *ouron* urine].

CHYME, [kīm], *n.* a pulpy mass into which food is converted in the stomach by the action of the gastric juices. [Gk. *khumos* juice].

CHYMIC†, [kim'-ik], *adj.* chemical.

CHYMIFICATION, [kīm'-if-ik-ā'-shun], *n.* the process of becoming, or being made into, chyme.

CHYMIFY, (**chymified, chymifies, chymifying**), [kīm'-i-fī], *v.t. and i.* to form, or be formed into, chyme.

CHYMIST†, see CHEMIST.

CHYMISTRY†, see CHEMISTRY.

CHYMOUS, [kīm'-us], *adj.* pertaining to, or consisting of, chyme.

CIBARIOUS, [sib-āer'-i-us], *adj.* pertaining to food, edible. [L. *cibarius*].

CIBOL, [sib'-ol], *n.* a Welsh onion; a shallot. [Fr. *ciboule*].

CIBORIUM, [sib-aw'-ri-um], *n.* an ornamental cup of precious metal in which the bread of the sacrament is kept; (*arch.*) a canopy or arch above the high altar. [Gk. *kiborion* a drinking cup].

CIBORIUM

CICADA, [sik-ah'-da], *n.* one of a group of insects belonging to the order *Homoptera*. [L. *cicada* cricket].

CICALA, [sik-ah'-la], *n.* a cicada. [It. *cicala*].

CICATRICE, CICATRIX, [sik-ā'-tris, sik-ā'-triks], *n.* a scar remaining on the skin after a wound has healed; (*bot.*) a scar left on the bark of a tree. [L. *cicitrix*].

CICATRICLE, [sik'-a-trikl], *n.* a scar-like germinating point in the embryo of a seed or the yolk of an egg; (*bot.*) scar formed when the leaf separates from its stem. [L. *cicatricula* small scar].

CICATRICULA, [sik'-a-trik'-yōō-la], *n.* a cicatricle.

CICATRISANT, [sik'-a-trīz'-ant], *n.* a medicinal healing application which causes a scar to form. [CICATRICE].

CICATRISIVE, [sik'-a-trīz'-iv], *adj.* having the power to form a cicatrice.

CICATRIX, see CICATRICE.

CICATRIZATION, [sik'-a-trīz-ā'-shun], *n.* the formation of a scar in the healing of a wound.

CICATRIZE, [sik'-a-trīz], *v.t. and i.* to heal a wound or to heal by the formation of new skin or a cicatrice.

CICATROSE, [sik'-a-trōs], *adj.* full of, or covered with, scars. [L. *cicatricosus*].

CICELY, [sis'-i-li], *n.* the plant *Myrrhis odorata* and similar umbelliferous plants. [Gk. *seselis*].

CICER†, [sis'-er], *n.* a genus of Mediterranean plants including the chick-pea. [L. *cicer*].

CICERONE, (*pl.* **ciceroni**), [chich'-er-ō'-ni], *n.* a guide, a person who shows sightseers the historical curiosities or objects of interest of a place. [It. *cicerone* from L. *Cicero*, the name of a great Roman orator].

CICERONIAN (1), [sis'-er-ō'-ni-an], *n.* an admirer or follower of the style of Cicero.

CICERONIAN (2), [sis'-er-ō'-ni-an], *adj.* resembling Cicero in style, classical and eloquent. [*Cicero*, a great Roman orator].

CICERONIANISM, [sis'-er-ō'-ni-an-izm], *n.* a Ciceronian style of expression.

CICHLID, [sik'-lid], *n.* a member of the genus of fishes, the *Cichlidae*, found mainly in Lake Tanganyika.

CICHORACEOUS, [sik'-or-ā'-shus], *adj.* pertaining to the order of plants *Cichoraceae*, including chicory, dandelion, etc. [CHICORY].

CICINDELA, [sis'-in-dē'-la], *n.* a genus of beetles, tiger-beetles, or sparklers, so called on account of their rich colours. [L. *cicindela* glow-worm].

CICISBEISM, [chich'-iz-bā'-izm], *n.* the practice of a cicisbeo.

CICISBEO, [chich-iz-bā'-o], *n.* the recognized lover of a married woman. [It. *cicisbeo*].

CICONIA, [sik-ō'-ni-a], *n.* (*ornith.*) a genus of birds comprising the storks. [L. *ciconia*].

CICURATE†, [sik'-yōō-rāt], *v.t.* to tame. [L. *cicurare*].

CID, [sid], *n.* a chief, a commander, *esp.* the eleventh century Spanish national hero, Rodrigo Diaz, who fought the Moors; the epic of his life and deeds. [Arab. *sayyid* lord].

CIDER, CYDER, [sī'-der], *n.* a liquor made from the fermented juice of apples. [OFr. *cisdre*, Heb. *shekar* strong liquor].

CIDERIST, [sī'-der-ist], *n.* a maker of cider.

CIDER-KIN, [sī'-der-kin], *n.* an inferior drink made from the crushed apples after the juice has been extracted for cider.

CIDER-PRESS, [sī'-der-pres'], *n.* a machine which extracts the juice for cider from apples.

CI-DEVANT, [sē'-de-vahn(g)'], *adj.* late, former. [Fr. *ci-devant* formerly].

CIERGE, [sēerj], *n.* a wax candle used in religious ceremonies. [OFr. *cerge*].

CIGAR, [si-gah(r)'], *n.* a small roll of tobacco-leaf for smoking. [Span. *cigarro*].

CIGARETTE, [sig'-a-ret'], *n.* a small roll of finely cut tobacco-leaf enclosed in a small thin paper cylinder for smoking. [*Dim.* of CIGAR].

CIGARETTE-CARD, [sig'-a-ret'-kahd'], *n.* a small illustrated card, enclosed in a packet of cigarettes.

CIGARETTE-COUPON, [sig'-a-ret'-kōō'-pon], *n.* a voucher enclosed in a packet of cigarettes, and exchangeable for goods, when a sufficient number have been collected.

CIGARETTE-HOLDER, [sig'-a-ret'-hōld'-er], *n.* a small tube shaped so as to hold a cigarette at one end, the other end tapering to a small slit-like aperture which is held in the mouth.

CIGAR-SHAPED, [sig-ah'-shāpt'], *adj.* cylindrical but tapering towards the ends.

CILERY, [sil'-er-i], *n.* (*arch.*) the ornamental drapery or foliage carved on the heads of columns. [L. *caelatura*].

CILIA, [sil'-i-a], *n.(pl.)* the eye-lashes; (*bot.*) fine hairy appendages on plants; (*zool.*) microscopic filaments found on the surface of animal tissue. [L. *cilia*, *pl.* of *cilium* an eyelash].

CILIARY, [sil'-i-a-ri], *adj.* relating to the eyelids or to cilia.

CILIATE, [sil'-i-āt], *adj.* provided with cilia.

CILIATED, [sil'-i-āt'-id], *adj.* ciliate.

CILICE, [sil'-is], *n.* a cloth woven from goat's-hair, a garment made from this cloth. [L. *cilicium*, Gk. *kilikion* cloth of Cilician goats' hair, from *Kilikia* Cilicia].

CILICIOUS, [sil-ish'-us], *adj.* of coarse hair-cloth. [*Prec.*].

CILIFORM, [sil'-i-fawm], *adj.* resembling cilia. [CILIA and FORM].

CILIOGRADE, [sil'-i-ō-grād'], *adj.* moving by means of cilia. [CILIA and L. *gradus* step].

CIMA, see CYMA.

CIMBIA, [sim'-bi-a], *n.* (*arch.*) a strengthening fillet round a column. [It. *cimbia*].

CIMBRIC (1), [sim'-brik], *n.* the language of the Cimbri.

CIMBRIC (2), [sim'-brik], *adj.* pertaining to the Cimbri, an ancient North Germanic tribe. [L. *Cimbri*, the name of the tribe].

CIMELIARCH†, [sim-ē'-li-ahk'], *n.* the keeper of the church plate; the room where plate was kept. [Gk. *keimeliarkhos* store-keeper].

CIMETER†, see SCIMITAR.

CIMEX, (*pl.* **cimices**), [sī'-meks, sī'-mi-sēz], *n.* the genus of bed-bugs, including *Cimex lectularius*. [L. *cimex*].

CIMMERIAN (1), [si-mēer'-i-an], *n.* a member of an ancient nomadic tribe of the Crimea and the Volga basin; a mythical race described by Homer living in the far west in perpetual gloom. [Gk. *Kimmerioi*].

CIMMERIAN (2), [si-mēer'-i-an], *adj.* pertaining to the Cimmerians; **C. darkness,** perpetual and profound darkness.

CIMOLITE, [sim'-ō-līt], *n.* (*min.*) a soft hydrated silicate of aluminium used as a cleansing agent. [Gk. *kimolia* a soft earth found in the island of Cimolus].

CINCH (1), [sinch], *n.* a saddle-girth; (*slang*) a certainty, a sure thing. [Span. *cincha*].

CINCH (2), [sinch], *v.t. and i.* to fix by means of a girth, to tighten the saddle-girth; (*slang*) to have a hold upon.

CINCHONA, [sing-kō'-na], *n.* a South American evergreen tree of the order *Rubiaceæ* which yields quinine; the bark of this species of tree; a drug extracted from the bark. [Countess of *Chinchon*, vicereine of Peru in 1638, who was cured of a fever by taking this bark].

CINCHONACEOUS, [sing'-kon-ā'-shus], *adj.* relating to cinchona.

CINCHONATE, [sing'-kon-āt], *n.* a salt of cinchonic acid.

CINCHONIC, [sing-kon'-ik], *adj.* obtained from cinchona bark.

CINCHONINE, [sing'-kon-ēn], *n.* an alkaloid obtained from several species of cinchona, used medically to alleviate fever.

CINCHONISM, [sing'-kon-izm], *n.* a disordered condition due to excessive use of cinchona.

CINCINNATUS, [sin'-sin-ā'-tus], *n.* a retired statesman capable of aiding his nation in a crisis. [*Cincinnatus*, an early Roman statesman].

CINCTURE (1), [singk'-cher], *n.* a belt, a girdle, a ring; (*arch.*) a ring or band at the top and bottom of the shaft of a column; an encircling band. [L. *cinctura* girdle].

CINCTURE

CINCTURE (2), [singk'-cher], *v.t.* to encircle, to encompass.

CINCTURED, [singk'-cherd], *adj.* provided with a cincture or girdle.

CINDER, [sin'-der], *n.* the hard friable residue of coal after it has ceased to burn or flame, but before it has been reduced to ashes, refuse from smelting processes. [OE. *sinder*].

CINDERELLA, [sin'-der-el'-a], *n.* any person (usually in humble surroundings) whose beauty or goodness of character escapes general notice; (*fig.*) that which is continually neglected or overlooked. [*Cinderella*, in the fairy-tale].

CINDERELLA-DANCE, [sin'-der-el'-a-dahns'], *n.* an informal dance ending at midnight. [*Prec.*].

CINDERPATH, [sin'-der-pahth'], *n.* a path or running track made of, or covered with, an even layer of cinders.

CINDERSIFTER, [sin'-der-sif'-ter], *n.* a sieve for sifting cinders from ashes.

CINDER-WENCH, [sin'-der-wench'], *n.* a cinder-woman.

CINDER-WOMAN, [sin'-der-wŏŏm'-an], *n.* a woman who gains her living by raking cinders from amongst ashes.

CINDERY, [sin'-der-i], *adj.* resembling or composed of cinders.

CINDROUS, [sin'-drus], *adj.* like or composed of cinders.

CINE-CAMERA, [sin'-i-kam'-er-a], *n.* a camera which takes a continuous series of photographs at momentary intervals on a cinematograph film.

CINEFACTION†, [sin'-i-fak'-shun], *n.* reduction to ashes. [MedL. *cinefactio*].

CINE-FILM, [sin'-i-film'], *n.* a film wound on a spool, and used with a cine-camera or a cinematograph.

CINEMA, KINEMA, [sin'-i-mah] *n.* a theatre in which moving pictures are projected upon a screen; (*fig.*) the showing of moving pictures as a medium of entertainment and instruction. [Abbreviation of CINEMATOGRAPH].

CINEMA-ORGAN, [sin'-i-mah-awg'-an], *n.* a large organ fitted with many mechanical devices, and containing many unusual stops from which an almost endless variety of effects may be obtained, played in certain large cinemas, as a break between, or to introduce, the films shown.

CINEMATOGRAPH, KINEMATOGRAPH, [sin-i-mat'-ō-grahf], *n.* an apparatus by which a continuous succession of photographs, taken at very brief intervals of time, are magnified and projected on to a screen in rapid sequence, so that an impression of steady movement is produced. [Gk. *kinema* motion and GRAPH].

CINEMATOGRAPHY, KINEMATOGRAPHY, [sin'-im-at-og'-raf-i], *n.* the art of making and exhibiting pictures by a cinematograph. [Gk. *kinema* motion and *graphia* writing].

CINENCHYMA, [sin'-eng-kī'-ma], *n.* (*bot.*) tissue forming the vessels of latex or milky juice. [Gk. *kino* I move and *khuma* infusion].

CINE-PROJECTOR, [sin'-i-prō-jek'-tor], *n.* a projector used in the showing of cinematograph films.

CINERARIA, [sin'-er-āer'-i-a], *n.* (*bot.*) a South African genus of composite plants with small brightly coloured flowers. [L. *cinerarius* of ashes].

CINERARIUM, [sin'-er-āer'-i-um], *n.* a place where a cinerary urn is deposited. [L. *cinerarius* of ashes].

CINERARY, [sin'-er-a-ri], *adj.* pertaining to or containing ashes; **c. urn,** a vase or urn in which the ashes of cremated persons are kept. [L. *cinerarius*].

CINERATION, [sin'-er-ā'-shun], *n.* reduction to ashes. [Fr. *cinération*].

CINEREAL†, [sin-ēer'-i-al], *adj.* cinereous. [L. *cinis, cineris* ashes].

CINEREOUS, [sin-ēer'-i-us], *adj.* like ashes, having the colour of ashes, ashen-grey. [L. *cinereus* ash-coloured].

CINERITIOUS, [sin'-er-ish'-us], *adj.* ashen-grey, like ashes. [L. *cinericius*].

CINE-VARIETY, [sin'-i-va-rī'-et-i], *n.* an entertainment in which the showing of cinematograph films is varied with stage turns of a vaudeville type.

CINGALESE, see SINGHALESE.

CINGLE, [sing'-gl], *n.* a girdle or horse-girth. [L. *cingulum*].

CINGULUM, [sing'-gew-lum], *n.* a band encircling the waist, worn over the alb by priests, and adorned with coloured tassels; a surgical belt encircling the waist; the bony structures surrounding the body of certain animals. [L. *cingulum* girdle].

CINNABAR, [sin'-a-bah(r)], *n.* (*min.*) a red mineral substance, the crystalline form of mercuric sulphide; a red or vermilion pigment obtained from this. [OFr. *cinabre* from Pers. *zinjarf* red lead].

CINNABARINE, [sin'-a-ba'-rēn], *adj.* relating to or containing cinnabar.

CINNAMIC, [sin-am'-ik], *adj.* pertaining to cinnamon.

CINNAMON, [sin'-am-on], *n.* the bark found on the under branches of a species of laurel, *Cinnamomum zeylanicum*, chiefly flourishing in Ceylon, used as a spice and for medicinal purposes; the tree from which the bark is obtained; the yellowish-brown colour of dried cinnamon. [Gk. *kinamomon*].

CINNAMONIC, [sin'-a-mon'-ik], *adj.* obtained from cinnamon.

CINNAMON-STONE, [sin'-a-mon-stōn'], *n.* essonite, a yellowish-red garnet.

CINQUE, [singk], *n.* five, a five at cards or dice; **C. Ports,** the five English ports of Dover, Sandwich, Hastings, Romney and Hythe, which had special privileges in return for providing a navy. [Fr. *cinq* from L. *quinque* five].

CINQUECENTIST, [chingk'-wi-chen'-tist], *n.* an artist or writer of the Italian sixteenth-century school characterized by a reversion to classical models, one who models his style upon that school. [It. *cinquecentista*].

CINQUEFOIL

CINQUEFOIL, [singk'-foil], *n.* (*bot.*) one of several plants of the genus *Potentilla*, having leaves made up of five leaflets; (*arch.*) a form of ornament used in circular windows, etc., and consisting of five foliated divisions. [L. *quinque-folium* five-leaf].

CINQUEPACE†, [singk'-pās], *n.* a lively dance performed to music written in quintuple time. [Fr. *cinq pas* five steps].

CINQUE-SPOTTED, [singk'-spot'-id], *adj.* having five spots.

CINTRE, [sin'-ter], *n.* (*arch.*) the centering of a bridge or arch. [Fr. *cintre*].

CIPHER, CYPHER (1), [sī'-fer], *n.* the arithmetical character 0 or zero, the Arabic numerals, any arithmetical number; a disguised or secret method of writing which can only be understood by those holding the key to it, the key by which such writing is made intelligible; a monogram having several initials or letters interwoven to form a whole; an organ note that continues to sound (after the key is released) through an imperfect valve; (*fig.*) a person of no importance, a nonentity. [OFr. *ciphre* from Arab. *sifr* zero].

CIPHER, CYPHER (2), [sī'-fer], *v.t. and i.* to calculate by arithmetic; to write in cipher or secret writing; to work out arithmetical problems; to sound continuously (of an organ note) owing to a faulty valve.

CIPHERING, [sī'-fer-ing], *n.* calculating with numerals; arithmetic; writing in cipher; sounding continuously (of an organ note).

CIPHER-KEY, [sī'-fer-kē'], *n.* a key by which writing in cipher is made intelligible.

CIPOLIN, [sip'-ol-in], *n.* an Italian marble streaked with green and white. [It. *cipollino*, *dim.* of *cipolla* onion].

CIPPUS, [sip'-us], *n.* a small monumental column with an inscription. [L. *cippus* a post].

CIRC, see CIRQUE.

CIRCA, [surk'-a], *adv. and prep.* about, approximately. [L. *circa*].

CIRCAR, [surk'-ah(r)], *n.* a district under Mogul rule. [Pers. *sarkar* administrator].

CIRCASSIAN, [ser-ka'-shan], *n.* a kind of thin worsted cloth; a native of Circassia. [*Circassia*].

CIRCE, [sur'-si], *n.* the name of the sorceress who changed men into swine by her magic potions; (*fig.*) an enchantress, a vamp. [Gk. *Kirke*].

CIRCEAN, [ser-sē'-an], *adj.* dangerously infatuating, fascinating but harmful.

CIRCENSIAL, [ser-sen'-shal], *adj.* circensian.

CIRCENSIAN, [ser-sen'-si-an], *adj.* (*Rom. antiq.*) pertaining to, or taking place in, the circus in ancient Rome. [L. *circensis*].

CIRCINATE (1), [sur'-sin-āt], *adj.* (*bot.*) rolled up inwardly in a coil with the tip occupying the centre (of a leaf). [L. *circinatum*, *p.pt.* of *circinare* to make round].

CIRCINATE† (2), [sur'-sin-āt'], *v.t.* to construct a circle; to compass. [L. *circinare*].

CIRCLE (1), [surkl], *n.* (*geom.*) a plane figure enclosed by a curved line, every point of which is equidistant from a point within called the centre; anything of this form, such as a ring, a planet's orbit, a group of prehistoric upright stones, a halo; the lowest gallery of a theatre, usually semicircular in shape; a system or series making a complete revolution and returning to the starting point; a recurring succession of events, a cycle; (*logic*) a fallacious method of argument by which the thing to be proved is stated as a major premise, a conclusion inferred from it, and the conclusion used to prove the major premise; a number of persons drawn or associated together by affinity of interests; social class; (*fig.*) compass, limits; area of influence or action; **vicious c.,** an argument in a circle, in which the thing to be proved is assumed; **to square the c.,** (*fig.*) to attempt the impossible; **great c.,** a circle on the surface of a sphere whose plane cuts through the centre of the sphere; **small c.,** a similar circle whose plane does not cut through the centre of the sphere. [L. *circulus* a round figure].

CIRCLE (2), [surkl], *v.t. and i.* to surround as with a circle, to make a complete circle round, to move in a circle.

CIRCLET, [sur'-klet], *n.* a small circle, a ring, a small circular band. [*Dim.* of CIRCLE (1)].

CIRCLEWISE, [surkl'-wīz], *adv.* in a circle.

CIRCLING, [sur'-kling], *adj.* encircling, proceeding in a circle.

CIRCUIT (1), [sur'-kit], *n.* a round, a path or journey round an area, the act of moving or going round in a circle, the distance round, the space enclosed in moving round an area; (*fig.*) the periodical visitation of judges to different towns in a district to hold assizes; the district so served; (*elect.*) the closed path traversed by an electric current; (*fig.*) a roundabout method, detour; a chain of cinemas owned by one distributing company and generally showing the same films at the same time. [L. *circuitus*].

CIRCUIT (2), [sur'-kit], *v.t. and i.* to pass round, to encircle; to move round in a circuit.

CIRCUITEER, [sur'-kit-ēer'], *n.* one who travels on a circuit.

CIRCUITOUS, [ser-kew'-it-us], *adj.* indirect, roundabout.

CIRCUITOUSLY, [ser-kew'-it-us-li], *adv.* in a circuitous fashion.

CIRCUITY, [ser-kew'-it-i], *n.* indirect proceeding.

CIRCULABLE, [sur'-kyōōl-abl], *adj.* capable of being circulated.

CIRCULAR (1), [sur'-kyŏŏ-ler], *n.* a letter, notice, advertisement, etc., printed and sent to large numbers of people. [L. *circulus* circle].

CIRCULAR (2), [sur'-kyŏŏ-ler], *adj.* pertaining to, or in the shape of, a circle, forming part of a circle; moving in a circle, making a circle; sent to a number of persons; **c. ticket,** a ticket for a tour which returns to the point of departure by a different route; **c. note,** a letter of credit furnished by a banker to travellers, and exchangeable for cash at different places; **c. number,** (*math.*) a number whose power terminates in the same digits as the root. [*Prec.*]

CIRCULARITY, [sur-kyŏŏ-la'-rit-i], *n.* the condition of being circular.

CIRCULARIZE, [sur'-kyŏŏ-ler-īz], *v.t.* to send circulars to.

CIRCULARLY, [sur'-kyŏŏ-ler-li], *adv.* in a circular fashion.

CIRCULATE, [sur'-kyŏŏ-lāt'], *v.i.* to move round and return to the point of departure; to move around freely, to pass through many hands or channels, to be handed round; (*math.*) to recur; *v.t.* to pass round, to cause to move from person to person or from place to place, to spread. [L. *circulare* form a circle].

CIRCULATING, [sur'-kyŏŏ-lāt'-ing], *adj.* that which circulates or causes circulation; **c. decimal,** a recurring decimal; **c. library,** an institution which lends or hires out books to members or subscribers for a definite period of time; **c. medium,** currency, medium of exchange.

CIRCULATION, [sur'-kyŏŏ-lā'-shun], *n.* the process or act of circulating; state of being circulated; (*anat.*) the flow of blood from the heart through the arteries and back by way of the veins; (*bot.*) the flow of sap through the veins of a plant; the extent to which a thing is circulated, the number of copies sold or otherwise reaching the public; continual passage of water through pipes, so that it returns to its starting point. [L. *circulatio*].

CIRCULATIVE, [sur'-kyŏŏ-lat-iv], *adj.* tending to circulate or to cause to circulate.

CIRCULATOR, [sur'-kyŏŏ-lā'-ter], *n.* one who circulates.

CIRCULATORY, [sur'-kyŏŏ-lāt-er-i], *adj.* pertaining to circulation. [L. *circulatorius*].

CIRCUM, *pref.* round. [L. *circum* round].

CIRCUMAMBAGES, [sur'-kum-am'-baj-ēz], *n.(pl.)* indirect, roundabout methods of speaking. [CIRCUM and AMBAGES].

CIRCUMAMBIENCY, [sur'-kum-am'-bi-en-si], *n.* the action of encompassing or surrounding.

CIRCUMAMBIENT, [sur'-kum-am'-bi-ent], *adj.* going round about, surrounding. [CIRCUM and AMBIENT].

CIRCUMAMBULATE, [sur'-kum-am'-byŏŏ-lāt], *v.t. and i.* to walk or go round; (*fig.*) to approach in an indirect fashion, to avoid coming straight to the point. [L. *circumambulare*].

CIRCUMAMBULATION, [sur'-kum-am-byŏŏ-lā'-shun], *n.* the act of circumambulating.

CIRCUMAMBULATORY, [sur'-kum-am-byŏŏ-lā'-tor-i], *adj.* indirect, round about.

CIRCUMBENDIBUS, [sur'-kum-ben'-dib-us], *n.* circumlocution. [Humorous formation from CIRCUM and BEND (1)].

CIRCUMCISE, [sur'-kum-sīz], *v.t.* to cut off the foreskin; (*fig.*) to purify, to cleanse from sin. [L. *circumcidere* to cut round].

CIRCUMCISER, [sur'-kum-sīz-er], *n.* a person who circumcises.

CIRCUMCISION, [sur'-kum-sizh'-un], *n.* the act of circumcising; (*fig.*) purification, cleansing of the spirit; (*eccles.*) the festival in celebration of the circumcision of Christ (January 1). [L. *circumcisio*].

CIRCUMCLUSION, [sur'-kum-klōō'-zhun], *n.* the act of surrounding on all sides. [L. *circumclusum*, *p.pt.* of *circumcludere*].

CIRCUMDUCT, [sur'-kum-dukt'], *v.t.* (*leg.*) to annul, to nullify. [L. *circumductum*, *p.pt.* of *circumducere* to lead round].

CIRCUMDUCTILE, [sur'-kum-duk'-tīl], *adj.* that can be led about.

CIRCUMDUCTION, [sur'-kum-duk'-shun], *n.* the act of circumducting.

CIRCUMFERENCE, [ser-kum'-fer-ens], *n.* the curved line that marks or encloses a circle, the length of this line. [L. *circumferentia*].

CIRCUMFERENTIAL, [ser-kum'-fer-en'-shal], *adj.* relating to the circumference.

CIRCUMFERENTOR, [ser-kum'-fer-en'-tor], *n.* (*surveying*) an instrument used for measuring angles in a horizontal plane, a kind of theodolite.

CIRCUMFERENTOR

CIRCUMFLECT, [sur'-kum-flekt], *v.t.* to bend round, to mark with a circumflex accent. [L. *circumflectere* to bend round].

CIRCUMFLECTION, see CIRCUMFLEXION.

CIRCUMFLEX (1), [sur'-kum-fleks], *n.* (*gram.*) a mark or accent used in Greek ͂ and in French ^. [L. *circumflexus, p.pt.* of *circumflectere* to bend round].

CIRCUMFLEX (2), [sur'-kum-fleks'], *v.t. and i.* to mark with a circumflex accent; to bend round.

CIRCUMFLEXION, CIRCUMFLECTION, [sur'-kum-flek'-shun], *n.* a bending or curving round; the addition of a circumflex. [L. *circumflexio*].

CIRCUMFLEXUS, [sur'-kum-flek'-sus], *n.* (*anat.*) a muscle of the palate; the axillary nerve. [L. *circumflexus* bent about].

CIRCUMFLUENCE, [ser-kum'-flōō-ents], *n.* a flowing round on all sides. [L. *circumfluentia*].

CIRCUMFLUENT, [ser-kum'-flōō-ent], *adj.* flowing around. [*Prec.*].

CIRCUMFLUOUS, [ser-kum'-flōō-us], *adj.* circumfluent. [L. *circumfluus*].

CIRCUMFORANEOUS, [sur'-kum-for-ān'-i-us], *adj.* strolling from market to market, vagabond, wandering. [CIRCUM and L. *forum* market-place].

CIRCUMFULGENT, [sur'-kum-ful'-jent], *adj.* glowing all around. [CIRCUM and L. *fulgens* shining].

CIRCUMFUSE, [sur'-kum-fewz'], *v.t.* to pour round, to spread round. [L. *circumfusus, p.pt.* of *circumfundere*].

CIRCUMFUSILE, [sur'-kum-few'-zīl], *adj.* poured round, able to be circumfused.

CIRCUMFUSION, [sur'-kum-few'-zhun], *n.* the act of pouring round. [L. *circumfusio*].

CIRCUMGYRATE, [sur'-kum-jī'-rāt], *v.i.* to revolve, to rotate, to whirl round on an axis. [CIRCUM and GYRATE].

CIRCUMGYRATION, [sur'-kum-jī-rā'-shun], *n.* the act of circumgyrating, rotation, revolution.

CIRCUMINCESSION, [sur'-kum-in-sesh'-un], *n.* (*theol.*) the existence of the Three in One or of each person of the Trinity in the others. [MedL. *circumincessio* going round].

CIRCUMJACENT, [sur'-kum-jā'-sent], *adj.* lying round anything, lying on every side. [L. *circumjacens*].

CIRCUMLITTORAL, [sur'-kum-lit'-or-al], *adj.* lying along the edge of the shore. [CIRCUM and LITTORAL].

CIRCUMLOCUTION, [sur'-kum-lok-ew'-shun], *n.* a talking round, an indirect verbose mode of speech or writing, an example of this. [L. *circumlocutio*].

CIRCUMLOCUTIONIST, [sur'-kum-lok-ew'-shun-ist], *n.* one given to circumlocution.

CIRCUMLOCUTORY, [sur'-kum-lok'-ew-ter-i], *adj.* given to, characterized by, circumlocution, indirect, verbose.

CIRCUM-MERIDIAN, [sur'-kum-mer-id'-i-an], *adj.* near the meridian. [CIRCUM and MERIDIAN].

CIRCUMMURED, [sur'-kum-mew'-erd], *adj.* walled round on all sides. [CIRCUM and L. *murare* to wall].

CIRCUMNAVIGABLE, [sur'-kum-nav'-ig-abl], *adj.* capable of being sailed round.

CIRCUMNAVIGATE, [sur'-kum-nav'-ig-āt], *v.t.* to sail round. [L. *circumnavigare*].

CIRCUMNAVIGATION, [sur'-kum-nav'-ig-ā'-shun], *n.* the act of sailing round, *esp.* round the world. [CIRCUM and NAVIGATION].

CIRCUMNAVIGATOR, [sur'-kum-nav'-ig-ā'-ter], *n.* one who sails round, *esp.* the world. [L. *circumnavigator*].

CIRCUMNUTATION, [sur'-kum-new-tā'-shun], *n.* (*bot.*) the tendency of plant stems to rotate as they grow. [CIRCUM and NUTATION].

CIRCUMORAL, [sur'-kum-aw'-ral], *adj.* placed round the mouth. [CIRCUM and ORAL].

CIRCUMPLEXION†, [sur'-kum-plek'-shun], *n.* a folding round. [CIRCUM and L. *plexus* folding].

CIRCUMPOLAR, [sur'-kum-pōl'-er], *adj.* about the Poles; (*astron.*) (of stars) never disappearing below the horizon. [CIRCUM and POLAR].

CIRCUMPOSE, [sur'-kum-pōz], *v.t.* to place round. [CIRCUM and POSE].

CIRCUMPOSITION, [sur'-kum-poz-ish'-un], *n.* the act of circumposing or the state of being placed around. [*Prec.*].

CIRCUMROTARY, [sur'-kum-rō'-ter-i], *adj.* spinning or rotating round an axis. [CIRCUM and ROTARY].

CIRCUMROTATION, [sur'-kum-rō-tā'-shun], *n.* the act of rotating; the state of being rotated. [*Prec.*].

CIRCUMROTATORY, [sur'-kum-rō-tāt'-er-i], *adj.* circumrotary.

CIRCUMSCISSILE, [sur'-kum-sis'-il], *adj.* (*bot.*) opening by a circular section across the sides of the ovary. [CIRCUM and L. *scissum, p.pt.* of *scindere* to cut].

CIRCUMSCRIBABLE, [sur'-kum-skrīb'-abl], *adj.* able to be circumscribed.

CIRCUMSCRIBE, [sur'-kum-skrīb'], *v.t.* to draw a line round, to hem in on all sides; (*fig.*) to limit, restrict. [L. *circumscribere*].

CIRCUMSCRIBER, [sur'-kum-skrīb'-er], *n.* a person who circumscribes.

CIRCUMSCRIPTIBLE, [sur'-kum-skript'-ibl], *adj.* circumscribable. [*Prec.*].

CIRCUMSCRIPTION, [sur'-kum-skrip'-shun], *n.* the act of circumscribing; the state of being circumscribed; that which circumscribes, a circular inscription. [L. *circumscriptio*].

CIRCUMSCRIPTIVE, [sur'-kum-skrip'-tiv], *adj.* pertaining to circumscription.

CIRCUMSCRIPTIVELY, [sur'-kum-skrip'-tiv-li], *adv.* in a circumscribed manner.

CIRCUMSOLAR, [sur'-kum-sōl'-er], *adj.* surrounding or round the sun. [CIRCUM and SOLAR].

CIRCUMSPECT, [sur'-kum-spekt'], *adj.* careful, warily cautious, prudent; decorous, proper. [L. *circumspectum, p.pt.* of *circumspicere* to look round].

CIRCUMSPECTION, [sur'-kum-spek'-shun], *n.* the quality of being circumspect, circumspect behaviour. [L. *circumspectio*].

CIRCUMSPECTIVE, [sur'-kum-spek'-tiv], *adj.* circumspect.

CIRCUMSPECTLY, [sur'-kum-spekt'-li], *adv.* in a circumspect fashion.

CIRCUMSPECTNESS, [sur'-kum-spekt'-nes], *n.* circumspection.

CIRCUMSTANCE, [sur'-kum-stans], *n.* the accidental accompaniments or unrelated factors of an event, the independent conditions in which something happens, a single event, a detail, a factor; (*pl.*) economic conditions, monetary situation; **pomp and c.,** gorgeous formalities, worldly glory. [L. *circumstantia*].

CIRCUMSTANCED, [sur'-kum-stanst], *adj.* in a specific situation, situated.

CIRCUMSTANTIAL, [sur'-kum-stan'-shal], *adj.* very detailed, minutely describing the circumstances; incidental, indirect, unrelated to the essential events; **c. evidence**, presumptive evidence inferred from numerous circumstances attendant on an event but not directly linked to the event itself.

CIRCUMSTANTIALITY, [sur'-kum-stan-shi-al'-i-ti], *n.* the quality or condition of being circumstantial.

CIRCUMSTANTIALLY, [sur'-kum-stan'-shal-i], *adj.* inferentially, by virtue of the circumstantial details; in minute detail.

CIRCUMSTANTIATE, [sur'-kum-stan'-shi-āt], *v.t.* to confirm, support circumstantially.

CIRCUMUNDULATION, [sur'-kum-un'-jōō-lā'-shun], *n.* a flowing round in waves. [CIRCUM and UNDULATION].

CIRCUMVALLATE, [sur'-kum-val'-āt], *v.t.* to throw up ramparts or trenches around. [L. *circumvallare*].

CIRCUMVALLATION, [sur'-kum-val-ā'-shun], *n.* the act of circumvallating; the fortifications so thrown up. [L. *circumvallatio*].

CIRCUMVENT, [sur'-kum-vent'], *v.t.* to outwit, overreach, to prevent, to outmanoeuvre. [L. *circumventum, p.pt.* of *circumvenire* to come round].

CIRCUMVENTION, [sur'-kum-ven'-shun], *n.* act of circumventing.

CIRCUMVENTIVE, [sur'-kum-ven'-tiv], *adj.* circumventing, scheming to circumvent.

CIRCUMVOLATION, [sur'-kum-vol-ā'-shun], *n.* a flying round. [CIRCUM and L. *volare* to fly].

CIRCUMVOLUTION, [sur'-kum-vol-ōō'-shun], *n.* the act of rolling or winding round; something coiled up, a winding. [L. *circumvolvere*].
CIRCUMVOLVE, [sur'-kum-volv'], *v.t. and i.* to revolve round, to cause to revolve round. [L. *circumvolvere*].
CIRCUS, [sur'-kus], *n.* (*Rom. antiq.*) a circular sports arena built round with tiers of seats; a show derived from this consisting of exhibitions of horsemanship and tricks with wild beasts, interspersed with clowning and acrobatic feats; an open, circular space at the junction of several roads. [L. *circus* a ring].
CIRL, [surl], *n.* the cirl bunting, *Emberiza cirlus.* [It. *zirlare* to twitter].
CIRQUE, CIRC, [sēerk], *n.* a natural arena at the head of a valley. [Fr. *cirque*].
CIRRHOSIS, [si-rō'-sis], *n.* a morbid state of the liver. [Gk. *kirrhos* tawny and *osis* denoting condition].
CIRRHOTIC, [si-rot'-ik], *adj.* suffering from or relating to cirrhosis.
CIRRHOUS, see CIRROUS.
CIRRI-, CIRRO-, *pref.* curl, tuft, tendril. [L. *cirrus* curl].
CIRRIFEROUS, [si-rif'-er-us], *adj.* with twisting tendrils. [CIRRI and L. *ferre* to bear].
CIRRIFORM, [si'-ri-fawm], *adj.* in the shape of a tendril. [CIRRI and FORM].
CIRRIGEROUS, [si-rij'-er-us], *adj.* having curls or coils. [CIRRI and L. *gerere* to bear].
CIRRIGRADE, [si'-ri-grād], *adj.* moving by means of tendrils. [CIRRI and GRADE].
CIRRIPEDE, [si'-ri-pēd], *n.* a crustacean moving by means of curling legs. [CIRRI and L. *pes pedem* foot].
CIRRO-, see CIRRI-.
CIRRO-CUMULUS, [si'-rō-kewm'-yŏŏ-lus], *n.* a type of cloud characterized by small, fleecy masses. [CIRRO and L. *cumulus* heap].
CIRROSE, [si'-rōs], *adj.* resembling a lock of hair; (*bot.*) ending in a tendril. [L. *cirrus*].
CIRRO-STRATUS, [si'-rō-strā'-tus], *n.* a type of cloud consisting of layers of fleecy cloud. [CIRRI and STRATA].
CIRROUS, CIRRHOUS, [si'-rus], *adj.* cirrose.
CIRRUS, [si'-rus], *n.* a series of tufted fleecy clouds, faintly resembling hair; (*bot.*) a curling tendril; (*zool.*) a tendril-like filament. [L. *cirrus* curl].
CIRSOCELE, [surs'-ō-sēl'], *n.* a morbid enlargement of the spermatic vein, a varicocele. [Gk. *kirsokele*].
CIS-, *pref.* on this side, on the near side of. [L. *cis*].
CISALPINE, [sis-al'-pīn], *adj.* on the south or Italian side of the Alps. [L. *cisalpinus*].
CISATLANTIC, [sis'-at-lan'-tik], *adj.* on the eastern side of the Atlantic. [CIS and ATLANTIC].
CISCO, [sis'-kō], *n.* a species of *Coregonus,* an American herring. [U.S. *cisco*].
CISELURE, [sēzl'-yŏŏer], *n.* chased metal work. [Fr. *ciselure*].
CISMONTANE, [sis-mon'-tān], *adj.* on this (the near) side of the Alps. [CIS and L. *montanus* relating to a mountain].
CISPADANE, [sis'-pad'-ān], *adj.* south of the Po. [CIS and L. *Padanus* the river Po].
CISSOID, [sis'-oid], *n.* (*geom.*) a curve to trisect a plane angle and to construct two means between two given straight lines. [Gk. *kissoeides* resembling ivy].
CISSUS, [sis'-us], *n.* wild ivy. [Gk. *kissos* ivy].
CIST, [sist], *n.* a rough sepulchral chamber or tomb; (*Gk. antiq.*) the casket containing the sacred utensils carried in procession during the mysteries. [L. *cista*].
CISTED, [sis'-tid], *adj.* contained in a cist.
CISTELLA, [sis-tel'-a], *n.* a capsular shield in some lichens. [L. *cistella*].
CISTERCIAN (1), [sis-tur'-shan], *n.* a member of the monastic order founded by St. Bernard at Cîteaux in the eleventh century. [L. *Cistercium* Cîteaux in France].
CISTERCIAN (2), [sis-tur'-shan], *adj.* relating to the Cistercian Order and its members.
CISTERN, [sis'-tern], *n.* a tank for storing water. [L. *cisterna*].
CISTUS, [sis'-tus], *n.* a genus of shrubs related to the rock-rose. [L. from Gk. *kisthos*].
CITABLE, [sīt'-abl], *adj.* able to be cited.
CITADEL, [sit'-a-del], *n.* a fortress commanding or protecting a city. [It. *cittadella*].
CITAL, [sī'-tal], *n.* summons, quotation, reference.
CITATION, [sī-tā'-shun], *n.* a reference, a quotation; the act of referring to or quoting; (*leg.*) an order to appear before a court; (*milit.*) a special mention of an individual or unit in despatches. [Fr. *citation*].
CITATOR, [sī-tā'-ter], *n.* one citing or having a citation made against another. [L. *citator*].
CITATORY, [sī-tā'-tor-i], *adj.* citing, in the manner of citation.
CITE, [sīt], *v.t.* to quote from an authority, to instance as an example or precedent; (*leg.*) to summon to appear before a court; to name as a participant in a legal cause. [L. *citare* to put in motion].
CITHARA, [sith'-er-a], *n.* an ancient triangular musical instrument. [Gk. *kithara*].
CITHARISTIC, [sith'-a-ris'-tik], *adj.* pertaining to a cithara or its music.
CITHERN, CITTERN, [sith'-ern, sit'-ern], *n.* a medieval lute, a sort of zither. [OE. *cytere*].
CITIED, [sit'-id], *adj.* having many cities.
CITIGRADE, [sit'-i-grād], *adj.* nimble in movement. [L. *citus* quick and GRADE].
CITIZEN, [sit'-iz-en], *n.* an inhabitant of a city, one having rights and duties by virtue of belonging to a city; a townsman; a civilian, a national. [ME. *citezein* from OFr. *citezin*].
CITIZENIZE, [sit'-iz-en-iz], *v.t.* to give citizenship to; (*fig.*) to sophisticate.
CITIZENSHIP, [sit'-iz-en-ship], *n.* the status, rights and duties of a citizen.

CITHERN

CITOLE, [sit'-ōl], *n.* a medieval lute. [OFr. *citole*].
CITRATE, [si'-trāt], *n.* (*chem.*) a salt of citric acid.
CITRENE, [sit'-rēn], *n.* a hydrocarbon obtained from oil of lemons.
CITRIC, [sit'-rik], *n.* pertaining to citron; **c. acid,** the acid to which oranges, lemons, limes, etc., owe their peculiar flavour.
CITRIL, [sit'-ril], *n.* an Italian and South European song finch. [It. *citrinella*].
CITRINATION†, [sit'-rin-ā'-shun], *n.* the condition of turning yellow. [MdL. *citrinatio*].
CITRINE (1), [sit'-rēn], *n.* a variety of yellowish quartz.
CITRINE (2), [sit'-rēn], *adj.* yellowish green, lemon coloured. [Fr. *citrin*].
CITRON, [sit'-ron], *n.* a large fruit of the lemon and lime family; the tree producing this fruit; a pale yellow-green colour. [Gk. *kitron*].
CITRONELLA, [sit'-ron-el'-a], *n.* an oil used to ward off mosquitoes. [*Prec.*].
CITRUL, [sit'-rul], *n.* the yellow pumpkin. [~CITRON].
CITRUS, [sit'-rus], *n.* the genus of trees bearing such fruits as the lemon, lime, citron, etc. [L. *citrus*].
CITTERN, see CITHERN.
CITY, [sit'-i], *n.* a great town, a town having a Royal Charter, a cathedral town; (*fig.*) the seat or headquarters of some force; the centre of finance in a state; **in the c.,** in business; **c. company,** a guild of merchants in a particular trade. [OFr. *cité* from L. *civitas*].
CITYWARDS, [sit'-i-werdz], *adv.* towards the city.
CIVET, [siv'-it], *n.* a small African and Asian carnivore of the genus *Viverra*; a musk-like substance used in perfumery, extracted from glands in the anus of this creature. [Arab. *zabad*].

CIVET

CIVET-CAT, [siv'-it-kat'], *n.* a civet.
CIVIC, [siv'-ik], *adj.* pertaining to a city, a citizen or citizenship; **c. crown,** a garland of oak leaves, the highest Roman award for valour; **c. virtues,** the qualities that make the state possible. [L. *civicus*].
CIVIC CENTRE, [siv'-ik-sen'-ter], *n.* a building or group of buildings housing the offices of a local authority, and some or all of the amenities run by it.
CIVICS, [siv'-iks], *n.* the study of civil administration.
CIVIL, [siv'-il], *adj.* pertaining to, based on the social life of organized groups; pertaining to citizens, citizenship, and the state; pertaining to the non-military members or organization of a community; courteous, polite, urbane, obediently respectful; **c. engineer,** one concerned with non-mechanical construction; **c. case,** (*leg.*) a case concerned with the personal and private relations of the citizens and not with criminal charges; **c. law,** a legal system

regulating the obligations of society; **c. list,** an annual parliamentary grant for Royal maintenance, etc.; **C. Service,** the state departments of administration, etc., as distinct from the armed forces; **c. war,** war between parties who are members of the same state; **c. defence,** defence of the civilian population by non-combatants; **c. disobedience,** mass refusal to pay taxes, etc., for political reasons. [L. *civilis*].

CIVILIAN (1), [siv-il'-yan], *n.* one who is not a member of the armed forces; a member of the Indian Civil Service.

CIVILIAN (2), [siv-il'-yan], *adj.* pertaining to civil life, non-military. [L. *civilianus*].

CIVILIST, [siv'-il-ist], *n.* a practitioner in Civil Law.

CIVILITY, [siv-il'-i-ti], *n.* politeness, courtesy, the quality of being civil; (*pl.*) conventional attentions. [OFr. *civilité*].

CIVILIZABLE, [siv'-il-īz'-abl], *adj.* capable of being civilized.

CIVILIZATION, [siv'-il-īz-ā'-shun], *n.* the process of civilizing and the achievement of this process; the structure of organized society; a highly developed culture of mankind.

CIVILIZE, [siv'-il-īz], *v.t.* to instruct in the culture and organization of a more developed form of society, to raise from barbarism; (*fig.*) to educate out of ignorance and lack of breeding.

CIVILLY, [siv'-il-i], *adv.* in relation to civil life; in civil fashion.

CIVISM, [siv'-izm], *n.* the principles of civic virtue.

CIVVIES, [siv'-iz], *n.*(*pl.*) (*coll.*) mufti; plain clothes. [*Dim.* of CIVILIAN].

CLABBER (1), [klab'-er], *n.* thick, sour milk. [Gael. *clabar* mud].

CLABBER (2), [klab'-er], *v.i.* to become thickened.

CLACHAN, [kla'-khan], *n.* a Scottish hamlet. [Gael. *clach* stone].

CLACK (1), [klak], *n.* a loud click; a sharp abrupt sound, frequently repeated; that which clacks; a continual talking; the tongue; a hinged flap forming a valve in a pump. [ME. *clacke*].

CLACK (2), [klak], *v.t.* and *i.* to make a clack; to keep up a continual nagging talk. [ME. *clacken*].

CLACK-DISH†, [klak'-dish], *n.* a dish carried by medieval mendicants, who clacked its cover to attract attention.

CLACKER, [klak'-er], *n.* that which clacks, a valve hinged at one edge.

CLAD, [klad], *adj.* clothed. [OE. *clathod, p.pt.* of *clathian* to clothe].

CLADODE, [klad'-ōd], *n.* a phylloclade; a leaf-like branch. [Gk. *klados* young shoot].

CLAIK, [klāk], *n.* the barnacle goose; the cry of this bird. [OScand. *klaka* to chatter].

CLAIM (1), [klām], *n.* the demanding of a right; the right demanded; the mode in which the demand is made; a legitimate right; a piece of land acquired by a settler; **to stake one's c.,** to mark out a plot of new land with stakes; (*fig.*) to establish oneself in a position. [OFr. *claime*].

CLAIM (2), [klām], *v.t.* to make a claim for; to seek to establish as fact; to state that lost property is one's own; to require, need; to ask for damages in a court of law in respect of an injury. [L. *clamare* declare].

CLAIMABLE, [klām'-abl], *adv.* able to be claimed.

CLAIMANT, [klām'-ant], *n.* one who claims. [OFr. *clamant*].

CLAIR-AUDIENCE, [klāer'-aw'-di-ens], *n.* an alleged psychic faculty of hearing sounds normally inaudible. [Fr. *clair* and L. *audiens, pres.pt.* of *audire* to hear].

CLAIRSCHACH, [klāer'-shakh], *n.* an ancient Celtic wire harp. [Gael. *clairseach*].

CLAIRVOYANCE, [klāer-voi'-ans], *n.* the alleged psychic faculty of perceiving objects and events not normally perceptible to the senses. [Fr. *clairvoyance*].

CLAIRVOYANT (1), [klāer-voi'-ant], *n.* one having the power of clairvoyance.

CLAIRVOYANT (2), [klāer'-voi'-ant], *adj.* pertaining to clairvoyance. [Fr. *clair* clear and *voyant, pres.pt.* of *voir* to see].

CLAM (1), [klam], *n.* an edible mollusc; (*U.S. slang*) a very reserved, often puritanical person; **as close as a c.,** secretive. [Uncert.].

CLAM (2), [klam], *n.* clamminess. [OE. *clam* mud].

CLAMANT, [klam'-ant], *adj.* clamorous, beseeching urgently, crying out for immediate attention. [L. *clamans, pres.pt.* of *clamare* to shout].

CLAMBER (1), [klam'-ber], *n.* a rough climb.

CLAMBER (2), [klam'-ber], *v.t.* to climb awkwardly, scramble up. [ME. *clambren*].

CLAMMINESS, [klam'-i-nes], *n.* the quality of being clammy. [CLAM (2)].

CLAMMY, [klam'-i], *adj.* damp and cold. [OE. *clam* mud].

CLAMOROUS, [klam'-er-us], *adj.* vociferous, noisily insistent.

CLAMOROUSLY, [klam'-er-us-li], *adv.* in clamorous fashion.

CLAMOROUSNESS, [klam'-er-us-nes], *n.* the condition of being clamorous.

CLAMOUR (1), [klam'-er], *n.* a noisy, confused outbreak of voices, a loud threatening and demanding outcry; insistent noisy complainings. [L. *clamor*].

CLAMOUR (2), [klam'-er], *v.t.* and *i.* to raise a clamour, to overpower with noise, to shout at [*Prec.*].

CLAMP (1), [klamp], *n.* a device, usually of wood or iron, for holding things together, *esp.* when being assembled; a thick plank on the inner side of a ship strengthening the end beams. [Du. *klamp*].

CLAMP (2), [klamp], *n.* a pile of bricks; a heap of potatoes covered with straw and earth for storage; a dung heap. [MDu. *klamp*].

CLAMP (3), [klamp], *n.* a heavy stamping tread, a lumbering tramping. [Onomatopoeic].

CLAMP (4), [klamp], *v.t.* to hold together or fasten with a clamp; (*fig.*) to hold very firmly.

CLAMP (5), [klamp], *v.t.* to store potatoes in a clamp.

CLAMP (6), [klamp], *v.i.* to tramp heavily with a clamp.

CLAMP

CLAMPER, [klamp'-er], *n.* an iron plate studded with points fitted to the shoe for walking on ice. [CLAMP (1)].

CLAMS, [klamz], *n.*(*pl.*) a pair of pincers for extracting nails; a kind of vice or clamp; the movable jaws of a vice used for holding delicate work. [OE. *clamm* cramp].

CLAN (1), [klan], *n.* a tribal group, *esp.* in Scotland, Ireland, etc., under the leadership of a hereditary chief, united by supposed descent from the same individual; (*fig.*) an exclusive group of people having common interests, a jealously self-sufficient set. [Gael. *clann* family].

CLAN (2), [klan], *v.i.* to join together in a clan, to unite in a clique.

CLANCULAR†, [klang'-kyŏŏ-ler], *adj.* secret, underhand. [L. *clancularius* from *clam* secretly].

CLANDESTINE, [klan'-des-tin], *adj.* secret, surreptitious, furtively hidden. [L. *clandestinus*].

CLANDESTINELY, [klan'-des-tin-li], *adv.* in clandestine fashion.

CLANDESTINENESS, [klan'-des-tin-nes], *n.* the quality of being clandestine.

CLANG (1), [klang], *n.* the resonant ringing sound made by the striking together of metal objects, as bells, etc. [~OHG. *klank*].

CLANG (2), [klang], *v.t.* and *i.* to make or cause to make a clang.

CLANGOROUS, [klang'-er-us], *adj.* loudly clanging.

CLANGOUR, [klang'-er], *n.* a continual loud clanging sound. [L. *clangor* noise].

CLANGOUS, [klang'-us], *adj.* clangorous.

CLANK (1), [klangk], *n.* a dull, heavy, metallic sound, such as that made by iron chains. [Onomatopoeic].

CLANK (2), [klangk], *v.t.* and *i.* to make or cause to make a clank.

CLANNISH, [klan'-ish], *adj.* pertaining to a clan; cliquish; regarding outsiders with suspicion and hostility, concerned solely with the welfare of one's own small social group.

CLANNISHLY, [klan'-ish-li], *adv.* in clannish fashion.

CLANNISHNESS, [klan'-ish-nes], *n.* the quality of being clannish.

CLANSHIP, [klan'-ship], *n.* the state of belonging to a clan.

CLANSMAN, [klanz'-man], *n.* a member of a clan; a male member of a clan old enough to bear arms.

CLAP (1), [klap], *n.* the sound made by the sudden forcible impact of two hard flat surfaces; a sudden burst of thunder; the noise made by striking together the palms of the hands; a friendly slap; the tongue of a bell; the lower, mandible of a hawk. [ME. *clap*].

CLAP (2), [klap], *n.* (*vulg.*) gonorrhoea. [~OFr. *clapoir*].
CLAP (3), (**clapping, clapped**), [klap], *v.t.* to make or cause to make a clap; to applaud by claps; to strike in friendly fashion with the palm of the hand; to bring into contact in a rapid and forcible manner; **to c. into,** to confine forcibly and expeditiously. [OE. *clæppan*].
CLAP (4), [klap], *v.t.* to infect with gonorrhoea. [CLAP (2)].
CLAP-BOARD, [klap'-bawd], *n.* a stave used in making barrels; a plank thicker at one edge than the other, used for the outside walls of wooden buildings. [Uncert.].
CLAP-DISH†, [klap'-dish], *n.* a clack-dish.
CLAP-NET, [klap'-net'], *n.* a fowler's net which can be suddenly closed by bringing the two halves of the rim together.
CLAPPER, [klap'-er], *n.* a person or thing that claps; the tongue of a bell; the striker of a mill-hopper which causes the corn to run on to the mill-stones; (*slang*) the tongue.
CLAPPER-CLAW†, [klap'-er-klaw'], *v.t.* to scratch with the nails; (*fig.*) to abuse loudly and vulgarly.
CLAPPING, [klap'-ing], *n.* applause shown by claps.
CLAP-SILL, [klap'-sil], *n.* the bottom part of the frame, into which lock-gates shut.
CLAP-TRAP, [klap'-trap], *n.* pretentious, plausible nonsense.
CLAQUE, [klak], *n.* an organized group of bribed applauders, or noisy vehement supporters. [Fr. *claque*].
CLAQUEUR, [klak'-er], *n.* one bribed to applaud.
CLARABELLA, [kla'-ra-bel'-a], *n.* an organ-stop with a flute-like note. [L. *clarus* clear and *bellus* lovely].
CLARAIN, [klāer'-ān], *n.* a sort of laminated coal.
CLARENCE, [kla'-rens], *n.* a closed, four-wheeled carriage carrying four persons inside and two out. [Named after the Duke of *Clarence*, afterwards William IV].
CLARENCEUX, [kla'-ren-sew], *n.* the King-of-Arms of the district south of the Trent. [Lionel, Duke of *Clarence*, third son of Edward III].
CLARENDON, [kla'-ren-don], *n.* (*typ.*) a bold-faced type. [The *Clarendon* Press, Oxford].
CLARE-OBSCURE, [klāer'-obs-kew'-er], *n.* chiaroscuro.
CLARET (1), [kla'-ret], *n.* a red Bordeaux wine; a dark red colour. [ME. *claret* from L. *claratum* clarified].
CLARET (2), [kla'-ret], *adj.* dark red in colour.
CLARET-CUP, [kla'-ret-kup'], *n.* a refreshing drink made of claret, lemon, spices, etc.
CLARICORD, [kla'-ri-kawd], *n.* a clavicord. [CLAVICORD confused with L. *clarus* clear].
CLARIFICATION, [kla'-ri-fik-ā'-shun], *n.* the process of clarifying, the state of being clarified. [L. *clarificatio*].
CLARIFIER, [kla'-ri-fī'-er], *n.* that which clarifies; a vessel for clarifying liquor.
CLARIFY, [kla'-ri-fī], *v.t.* and *i.* to make clear, to purify, to render intelligible, to clear up obscurities. [L. *clarificare* make famous].
CLARINET, [kla'-ri-net'], *n.* a wood-wind instrument having a single reed in the mouthpiece; an organ stop with a note similar to that of this instrument. [Fr. *clarinette* from L. *clarus* clear].
CLARION (1), [kla'-ri-on], *n.* a shrill slender trumpet; an organ-stop resembling the note produced by this; a shrill ringing call. [OFr. *clarion* from L. *clarus*].
CLARION (2), [kla'-ri-on], *adj.* shrill; (*fig.*) nobly inspiring.
CLARIONET, [kla'-ri-on-et'], *n.* a clarinet. [*Dim.* of CLARION].
CLARISONOUS, [kla-ri'-son-us], *adj.* clear sounding. [L. *clarus* clear and *sonus* sounding].
CLARITY, [kla'-ri-ti], *n.* the quality of being clear. [L. *claritas*].
CLARKIA, [klahk'-i-a], *n.* (*bot.*) a brightly coloured flowering plant allied to the willow-herb. [J. *Clark*, an American explorer].
CLARY, [klāer'-i], *n.* the sweet herb *Salvia Sclarea* used as a seasoning. [ME. *clarie*].
CLARY-WATER, [klāer'-i-waw'-ter], *n.* a cordial made from brandy, sugar, clary flowers, etc.
CLASH (1), [klash], *n.* a harsh metallic sound produced by the violent impact of metals; (*fig.*) a sudden violent conflict of opinions, hostile armed forces, etc.
CLASH (2), [klash], *v.t.* and *i.* to make or cause to make a clash; to come into violent contact (with); (of events) to take place at the same or approximately the same time and so interfere with each other; (of colours) to be violently inharmonious. [Onomatopoeic].
CLASHING, [klash'-ing], *adj.* making a clash, conflicting, opposing.
CLASHINGLY, [klash'-ing-li], *adv.* in clashing fashion.
CLASP (1), [klahsp], *n.* a secure grasp, a hearty grip, a strong encompassing embrace; a catch or hook for fastening two ends together; a metal bar attached to the ribbon of a medal to mark the stages of a campaign. [ME. *claspe*].
CLASP (2), [klahsp], *v.t.* to embrace firmly, to fold in the arms, hug; to grip hands; to secure with a clasp. [ME. *claspen*].
CLASPER, [klahsp'-er], *n.* a person or thing that clasps; a tendril; (*pl.*) rudimentary limbs possessed by the males of certain insects and fishes and used to hold the female.
CLASPERED, [klahsp'-erd], *adj.* having claspers.
CLASP-KNIFE, [klahsp'-nīf], *n.* a knife in which the blade folds up into the handle.
CLASP-LOCK, [klahsp'-lok], *n.* a spring-lock.
CLASP-NAIL, [klahsp'-nāl], *n.* a nail with a flat, broad head.
CLASS (1), [klahs], *n.* a category, a type, kind, sort, a division of things according to some common characteristic; a group of organisms, subordinate to a kingdom, but embracing orders and genera; an economic and social division of society; a group of students studying the same subject at the same place and time, a form; a division of candidates according to their success in an examination; a distinction according to quality; a distinction in the style and comfort of accommodation on a train or ship according to the price paid; a standard of approximation to a fixed ideal of excellence; **no c.,** vulgar; **working c.,** industrial proletariat. [L. *classis* fleet].
CLASS (2), [klahs], *adj.* relating to a class or to class in general.
CLASS (3), [klahs], *v.t.* to assign to a class, place in a group or category by some standard.
CLASSABLE, [klahs'-abl], *adv.* able to be classed.
CLASSIC (1), [klas'-ik], *n.* a Greek or Latin work of art or literature; a work of art of established excellence and value; an author, artist, composer or poet of the highest rank of merit; an example of his work; a student of Greek and Latin.
CLASSIC (2), [klas'-ik], *adj.* relating to Greece and Rome and their culture; alleged to be in accordance with the spirit of ancient Greece and Rome; (of art and literature) of accepted importance and merit; in the best taste; austerely balanced and restrained; uniquely perfect, constituting the best example of its kind; pertaining to one of the five great horse-races. [L. *classicus* pertaining to the classes of the Roman people].
CLASSICAL, [klas'-ikl], *adj.* relating to the classics or to Greek and Roman culture; pertaining to or expert in the study of the classics; (of literature, music, etc.) the best and most balanced in taste.
CLASSICALISM, [klas'-ik-al-izm], *n.* devotion to the classics; an aesthetic mode following the classics; a classical turn of phrase.
CLASSICALIST, [klas'-ik-al-ist], *n.* one learned in or following the classics.
CLASSICALITY, [klas'-ik-al'-it-i], *n.* the quality of being classical or classic.
CLASSICALLY, [klas'-ik-al-i], *adv.* in classical fashion.
CLASSICALNESS, [klas'-ik-al-nes], *n.* classicality.
CLASSICISM, [klas'-is-izm], *n.* a classical turn of phrase; classic proportion of form; an affectation of the classics.
CLASSICIZE, [klas'-is-īz], *v.t.* and *i.* to imitate the classic style; to cause to conform to the classic.
CLASSIFIABLE, [klas'-if-ī'-abl], *adv.* able to be classified.
CLASSIFICATION, [klas'-if-ik-ā'-shun], *n.* the act, method, or result of classifying.
CLASSIFICATORY, [klas'-if-ik-ā'-ter-i], *adj.* relating to classification.
CLASSIFIER, [klas'-i-fī-er], *n.* one who classifies.
CLASSIFY, [klas'-i-fī], *v.t.* to arrange, sort or allot into classes. [Fr. *classifier*].
CLASSY, [klah'-si], *adj.* (*coll.*) of high class, superior.
CLASTIC, [klas'-tik], *adj.* (*geol.*) consisting of broken pieces. [Gk. *klastos* broken].
CLATHRATE, [klath'-rāt], *adj.* (*bot.*) latticed. [~L. *clathri* bars].

CLATHROID, [klath'-roid], *adj.* clathrate. [*Prec.* and Gk. *oeides* like].

CLATTER (1), [klat'-er], *n.* a confused, repeated sharp rattling din, a noisy babble of voices. [Du. *klater*].

CLATTER (2), [klat'-er], *v.t. and i.* to make or cause to make a clatter; to walk about in a noisy manner. [OE. *clatrian*].

CLATTERER, [klat'-er-er], *n.* one who clatters.

CLATTERINGLY, [klat'-er-ing-li], *adv.* in clattering fashion.

CLAUSE, [klawz], *n.* (*leg.*) a distinct and particular section or part of a contract, agreement, etc.; (*gram.*) a division of a main sentence, grammatically complete in itself, but subordinate to a sentence; **a saving c.**, the solitary but decisive element of good in a person or situation. [~L. *clausum*, *p.pt.* of *claudere* to shut].

CLAUSTHALITE, [klaws'-tal-īt], *n.* a selenide of lead. [*Klausthal*, a place in Germany].

CLAUSTRAL, [klaws'-tral], *adj.* pertaining to or restrained by cloisters; living a monastic life. [L. *claustrum* cloister].

CLAUSTRATION, [klaws-trā'-shun], *n.* the act of confining in a monastery.

CLAUSTROPHOBIA, [klaws'-tro-fō'-bi-a], *n.* a neurotic fear of small or confined spaces. [L. *claustrum* and Gk. *phobia* fear].

CLAUSTRUM, [klaws'-trum], *n.* grey matter in the cerebellum. [L. *claustrum*].

CLAUSULAR, [klawz'-yōō-ler], *adj.* pertaining to clauses.

CLAUSURE†, [klawz'-yer], *n.* the act, state, means of confinement or constriction; (*anat.*) a stopped-up canal.

CLAVATE, [klā'-vāt], *adj.* †studded with nails, knobbed; (*bot.*) like a club in shape. [L. *clava* club].

CLAVATED, [klā'-vāt-ed], *adj.* clavate.

CLAVATION, [kla-vā'-shun], *n.* the quality of being clavate; (*anat.*) gomphosis.

CLAVIARY, [klāv'-i-a-ri], *n.* (*mus.*) an index of keys, a scale. [L. *clavis* key].

CLAVICHORD, [klav'-i-kawd], *n.* (*mus.*) an early type of piano in which the strings were struck by small brass hammers. [MdL. *clavichordium*].

CLAVICLE, [klav'-ikl], *n.* the collar-bone. [L. *clavicula*, *dim.* of *clavis* key].

CLAVICORN, [klav'-i-kawn], *n.* a family of beetles with club-shaped antennae. [L. *clava* club and *cornu* a horn].

CLAVICULAR, [klav-ik'-yōō-ler], *adj.* pertaining to the collar-bone.

CLAVIER, [klav-ēer'], *n.* the keyboard of an organ or piano. [Germ. from L. *claviarius* key-bearer].

CLAVIFORM, [klav'-i-fawm], *adj.* clavate. [L. *clava* club and FORM].

CLAVIGEROUS, [klav-ij'-er-us], *adj.* bearing a key. [~L. *claviger* key-bearer].

CLAVIS, [klāv'-is], *n.* a key; (*fig.*) a literal translation, *esp.* from the classics, a key to a cipher. [L. *clavis*].

CLAW (1), [klaw], *n.* the sharp nails on the feet of birds and some animals; the limbs or pincers of certain crustaceans; anything resembling these; a tool for extracting nails from wood; a grappling hook. [OE. *clawu*].

CLAW (2), [klaw], *v.t.* to scratch or pluck with a claw; (*fig.*) to grab at ravenously; **to c. away**, (*naut.*) to turn to windward from a lee shore.

CLAWED, [klawd], *adj.* having claws; scratched.

CLAWHAMMER, [klaw'-ham'-er], *n.* a hammer with one end of the head curved into two claws.

CLAWHAMMER

CLAWLESS, [klaw'-les], *adj.* having no claws.

CLAY (1), [klā], *n.* a plastic and sticky earth, which, when mixed with water, can be moulded and baked hard; (*fig.*) a corpse, human flesh. [OE. *clæg*].

CLAY (2), (**clays, clayed**), [klā], *v.t.* to daub, cover with clay.

CLAY-BRAINED, [klā'-brānd], *adj.* stupid.

CLAY-COLD, [klā'-kōld], *adj.* (*poet.*) dead.

CLAYES, [klāz], *n.(pl.)* (*fort.*) hurdles of stakes interwoven with osiers. [Fr. *claie*].

CLAYEY, [klā'-i], *adj.* like clay, sticky, clammily tenacious.

CLAYISH, [klā'-ish], *adj.* like clay.

CLAY-MARL, [klā'-mahl], *n.* a whitish chalky kind of clay.

CLAYMORE, [klā'-maw(r)], *n.* the double-edged ancient Highland broadsword. [Gael. *claidheamh* sword and *mor* great].

CLAY-PIGEON, [klā'-pij'-un], *n.* a small clay disk sent spinning into the air to be fired at.

CLAY-PIT, [klā'-pit], *n.* a pit from which clay is dug.

CLAY-SLATE, [klā'-slāt], *n.* argillaceous schist; roofing-slate.

CLAY-STONE, [klā'-stōn], *n.* a felspathic igneous rock, resembling marl.

CLAYWEED, [klā'-wēd], *n.* the coltsfoot, *Tussilago Farfara*.

CLEAN (1), [klēn], *adj.* free from dirt, infection or impurity; freshly washed; honest, free from guilt or vice; undefiled; smooth, sharp-edged, without jagged edges; new, unblemished; clear-cut; blank; **to make a c. breast of**, to confess completely. [OE. *claene*].

CLEAN (2), [klēn], *adv.* (*coll.*) completely, in every respect; exactly.

CLEAN (3), [klēn], *v.t.* to make clean, to free from dirt or impurity of any kind, to polish, brighten and smarten; **to c. out**, (*slang*) to drain completely of money; **to c. up**, to finish up arrears of work or remnants of difficulties; to purge of vice or dishonesty.

CLEANER, [klēn'-er], *n.* one who, or that which, cleans; one who cleans a public building.

CLEAN-HANDED, [klēn'-hand'-id], *adj.* guiltless, free from blame.

CLEANING, [klēn'-ing], *n.* the act of making clean.

CLEANISH, [klēn'-ish], *adj.* fairly clean.

CLEANLILY, [klēn'-li-li], *adv.* in cleanly fashion.

CLEANLIMBED, [klēn'-limd], *adj.* well proportioned and strong.

CLEANLINESS, [klen'-li-nes], *n.* the quality of being and keeping clean.

CLEANLY (1), [klen'-li], *adj.* clean in habits and in person.

CLEANLY (2), [klēn'-li], *adv.* in a clean manner.

CLEANNESS, [klēn'-nes], *n.* the state of being clean.

CLEANSABLE, [klenz'-abl], *adj.* able to be cleaned.

CLEANSE, [klenz], *v.t.* to make clean, to purify. [OE. *claesensian*].

CLEANSER, [klenz'-er], *n.* one who, or that which, cleanses.

CLEAN-SHAPED, [klēn'-shāpt], *adj.* well-proportioned.

CLEANSIBLE, [klenz'-ibl], *adj.* able to be cleansed.

CLEANSING (1), [klenz'-ing], *n.* the act of making clean.

CLEANSING (2), [klenz'-ing], *adj.* making clean, tending to cleanse or purify.

CLEANSING STATION, [klenz'-ing sta'-shun], *n.* a post or depôt where persons who have been in contact with poison-gas may be cleansed.

CLEAN-TIMBERED, [klēn'-tim'-berd], *adj.* (*naut.*) well-proportioned, having graceful lines; (*vulg.*) clean-limbed.

CLEAR (1), [klēer], *adj.* free from obscurity, plain lucid; obvious, open; bright, free from cloud, etc.; translucent, transparent; unobstructed; free; distinct; with a pure ringing sound; whole, entire; **a c. head**, sound judgment. [OFr. *cler* from L. *clarus*].

CLEAR (2), [klēer], *adv.* completely; unhindered.

CLEAR (3), [klēer], *v.t.* to make clear; to make a space; to make tidy; to get rid of, to disentangle; to free from suspicion of guilt; to surmount, to pass an obstacle; to get payment on (a cheque or bill); *v.i.* to become clear; (*naut.*) to pay harbour dues, etc.; to become free of encumbrances; **to c. away**, to tidy up, remove debris of a meal; to go away; **to c. out**, to go away; **to c. up**, to put into order, make tidy; to solve; to improve (*esp.* the weather).

CLEARAGE, [klēer'-ij], *n.* clearing, a clearance.

CLEARANCE, [klēer'-ans], *n.* the act or result of clearing; a certificate that a ship has been cleared; room to pass clear; the amount of space required to enable one thing to move past or in another without touching it; **c. sale**, a sale at a shop, intended to get rid of stock at any price.

CLEARCOLE, [klēer'-kōl], *n.* the first coat of paint applied to woodwork. [Fr. *claire colle*].

CLEAR-CUT, [klēer'-kut], *adj.* distinct, clear in outline, obvious.

CLEARER, [klēer'-er], *n.* that which clears.

CLEAR-EYED, [klēer'-īd], *adj.* clear-sighted, honest.

CLEAR-HEADED, [klēer'-hed'-id], *adj.* acute, intelligent, sound in judgment.

CLEARING, [klēer'-ing], *n.* the act of making clear; justification; a tract of land cleared for cultivation; (*comm.*) the exchanging of the drafts on banking houses, and settling of the differences.

CLEARING-HOUSE, [klēer'-ing-hows'], *n.* a central organization at which the cheques and bills payable to various banks are credited and exchanged; a similar organization for settling the apportionment of combined receipts to different railway companies.
CLEARING-NUT, [klēer'-ing-nut'], *n.* the kernel of the nut of *Strychnos potatorum*, used in India for purifying dirty water.
CLEARING-STATION, [klēer'-ing-stā'-shun], *n.* a temporary front-line hospital for receiving casualties for immediate treatment before they are passed to the base.
CLEARLY, [klēer'-li], *adv.* in clear fashion, obviously
CLEARNESS, [klēer'-nes], *n.* the quality of being clear.
CLEAR-SEEING, [klēer'-sē'-ing], *adj.* clear-sighted.
CLEAR-SHINING, [klēer'-shīn'-ing], *adj.* shining brightly.
CLEAR-SIGHTED, [klēer'-sīt'-id], *adj.* able to see distinctly, discerning.
CLEAR-SIGHTEDNESS, [klēer'-sīt'-id-nes], *n.* the quality of being clear-sighted.
CLEARSTARCH, [klēer'-stahch], *v.t.* to stiffen and launder with clear starch.
CLEARSTARCHER, [klēer'-stahch'-er], *n.* one who clearstarches.
CLEARSTORY, see CLERESTORY.
CLEARWING, [klēer'-wing], *n.* one of a family of moths, *Sesiadae*, with translucent wings.
CLEAT (1), [klēt], *n.* (*naut.*) small tapering piece of wood fastened sideways to a spar, etc.; a device for belaying ropes, either with two projecting ends, or having a pair of parallel holes, and fastened to the ship; narrow lateral strengthening strip of wood or metal in joinery; a wedge-like projection. [ME. *clete* wedge].
CLEAT (2), [klēt], *v.t.* to belay, fasten by a cleat.
CLEAVABLE, [klēv'-abl], *adj.* able to be cleaved.
CLEAVAGE, [klēv'-ij], *n.* a division, particularly by cutting or splitting; a place where anything is split; condition of being split; (*min.*) a natural line of division in a mineral or rock; (*fig.*) a sharp division of opinion leading to a split.
CLEAVE (1), **(cleft)**, [klēv], *v.t. and i.* to divide forcibly by cutting, to split, make a fissure; to fall apart; **in a cleft stick**, in a hopeless position between several choices, mutually incompatible and individually inadequate. [OE. *cleofan*].
CLEAVE (2), [klēv], *v.i.* to adhere, stick; (*fig.*) to join oneself with, to stand by closely and loyally. [OE. *cleofian*].
CLEAVER, [klēv'-er], *n.* a person or thing that cleaves; a butcher's chopper.
CLEAVERS, [klēv'-ers], *n.* goose-grass, a plant of the genus *Galium*, with clinging bristly leaves. [OE. *clife*].
CLECHÉ, [klesh-ā'], *n.* (*her.*) a cross voided. [Fr. *cleché* from L. *clavis* a key].
CLEDGE, [klej], *n.* clay; the upper of the two strata of fuller's earth. [Uncert.].
CLEDGY, [klej'-i], *adj.* clayey.
CLEEK, [klēk], *n.* an iron-faced golf club, with a narrow head; a large grappling-hook. [A northern form of CLUTCH].
CLEF, [klef], *n.* (*mus.*) a sign denoting the pitch of a stave. [Fr. *clef* from L. *clavis* key].
CLEFT, [kleft], *n.* a split made by cleaving, a natural fissure in rock, a chasm. [ME. *clift*].
CLEFT-FOOTED, [kleft'-fŏŏt'-id], *adj.* cloven-footed.
CLEFT-GRAFT, [kleft'-grahft], *v.t.* (*hort.*) to engraft by cleaving the stock and grafting on a scion.
CLEFT-PALATE, [kleft'-pal'-at], *n.* deformity of the roof of the mouth, in which the two halves are imperfectly joined.
CLEG, [kleg], *n.* the horse-fly, gadfly, *Tabanus bovinus*. [OScand. *cleggi*].
CLEISTOGAMOUS, [klīst'-og'-am-us], *adj.* having a flower that does not open and is self-pollinated. [Gk. *kleistos* shut and *gamos* marriage].
CLEM, [klem], *v.t. and i.* to starve, or discomfort severely with hunger or adversity; to be pinched with cold or hunger, to be in dire want. [CLAM].

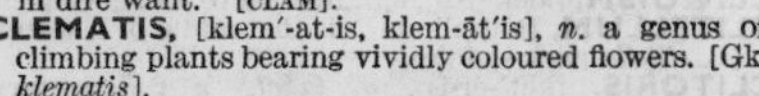

CLEMATIS

CLEMATIS, [klem'-at-is, klem-āt'is], *n.* a genus of climbing plants bearing vividly coloured flowers. [Gk. *klematis*].
CLEMENCY, [klem'-en-tsi], *n.* the quality of being clement. [L. *clementia*].
CLEMENT, [klem'-ent], *adj.* merciful, lenient, mild. [L. *clemens*].
CLEMENTLY, [klem'-ent-li], *adv.* in clement fashion.
CLENCH, [klench], *v.t. and i.* to grip tightly, hold firmly with the hand; to secure (a rivet, etc.) by hammering down the ends; to double the hand; (*fig*). to conclude definitely. [ME. *clenchen*].
CLEPE†, [klēp], *v.t.* to name, call. [OE. *cleopian*].
CLEPSAMMIA, [klep-sam'-i-a], *n.* a sand clock, an hour glass. [Gk. *klepto* I steal and *ammos* sand].
CLEPSYDRA, [klep-sid'-ra], *n.* a water-clock. [Gk. *klepto* I steal and *hudor* water].
CLERESTORY, **CLEARSTORY**, [klēer'-staw-ri], *n.* the upper row of windows above the nave in Gothic and other churches. [CLEAR and STORY].

CLERESTORY

CLERGY, [klur'-ji], *n.* people consecrated and professionally engaged in religion in any Christian denomination; **benefit of c.**, the former right of clergy, and others able to read, to be tried before the ecclesiastical courts. [OFr. *clergie*].
CLERGYABLE, [klur'-ji-abl], *adj.* entitled to benefit of clergy.
CLERGYMAN, [klur'-ji-man], *n.* a minister of religion.
CLERIC, [kle'-rik], *n.* a clergyman. [OE. *cleric* from Gk. *klerikos* picked by lot].
CLERICAL, [kle'-rikl], *adj.* relating to the clergy; pertaining to a clerk. [*Prec.*].
CLERICALISM, [kle'-rik-al-izm], *n.* the belief in the domination and importance of the clergy.
CLERISY†, [kle'-ris-i], *n.* the clergy.
CLERK, [klahk], *n.* a religious, legal or political officer, whose duties formerly involved writing, copying and recording; a minor parish official; a person employed to do simple and monotonous tasks in the offices of a business; one in holy orders; †a scholar, one who can read and write. [CLERIC].
CLERK-LIKE, [klahk'-līk], *adj.* like a clerk; learned.
CLERKLY, [klahk'-li], *adj.* pertaining to a clerk.
CLERKSHIP, [klahk'-ship], *n.* the position and duty of a clerk.
CLEROMANCY, [kle'-ro-man'-si], *n.* divination by casting lots. [Gk. *kleros* lot and *manteia* divination].
CLERONOMY, [kle-ron'-om-i], *n.* heritage. [Gk. *kleros* lot and *nomos* share].
CLEVE, [klēv], *n.* a cliff. [OE. *clife*].
CLEVER, [klev'-er], *adj.* intelligent, quick-witted; apt with the hands, skilful in devising, adroit; displaying powers of foresight, resource and good management. [Uncert.].
CLEVERISH, [klev'-er-ish], *adj.* fairly clever.
CLEVERLY, [klev'-er-li], *adv.* in clever fashion.
CLEVERNESS, [klev'-er-nes], *n.* the quality of being clever.
CLEVIS, [klev'-is], *n.* a curved iron at the end of a beam of a plough, cart, etc., to which harness or tackle is attached. [CLEAVE (2)].
CLEVY, [klev'-i], *n.* a clevis.
CLEW (1), [klōō], *n.* thread or yarn wound into a ball; (*naut.*) the lower corner of a square sail; the cords supporting a hammock. [OE. *cliwen* a ball (of thread)].
CLEW (2), [klōō], *v.t.* to wind into a ball; (*naut.*) to pull up to the yard-arm (a sail); *v.i.* (*naut.*) to complete some task.
CLICHE, **cliché**, [klē'-shā], *n.* a much used, hackneyed phrase, trite and cheap in form. [Fr. *cliché*, *p.pt.* of *clicher* to stereotype].
CLICK (1), **KLICK**†, [klik], *n.* a short, sharp snapping sound.
CLICK (2), [klik], *v.t. and i.* to make a click; to fasten or bring together with a clicking sound; (*slang*) to succeed in attracting the amorous attention of a member of the opposite sex. [Fris. *klikken*].
CLICK-BEETLE, [klik'-bētl], *n.* a coleopterous insect of the family *Elateridae*, the fire-fly.
CLICK-CLACK, [klik'-klak'], *n.* a repeated clicking noise.
CLICKER, [klik'-er], *n.* one employed to stand at the door of a shop to inveigle customers inside; (*print.*)

a head compositor; a foreman who cuts out and distributes leather to shoemakers; a tape machine.

CLICKET, [klik'-it], *n.* a light knocker, a door-latch.

CLIENT, [klī'-ent], *n.* a customer; one who employs members of a profession as his agents, as in legal affairs, etc. [~L. *cliens* follower].

CLIENTAGE, [klī'-ent-ij], *n.* a clientèle; the state of being a client.

CLIENTELE, clientèle, [klēon'-tel'], *n.* the clients or customers of a business collectively; customers or clients as a class. [Fr. *clientèle*].

CLIENTSHIP, [klī'-ent-ship], *n.* the state of being a client.

CLIFF, [klif], *n.* a steep declivity, lofty wall of rock, high edge of land bordering the sea. [OE. *clif*].

CLIFFY, [klif'-i], *adj.* having cliffs.

CLIFT, [klift], *n.* a cleft, a break in a cliff.

CLIMACTERIC (1), [klī-mak'-ter-ik], *n.* a period of supposed great physical and mystical importance in human life associated with the failing of physical powers or the menopause; a period of great importance; an event of great importance; **grand c.,** 63rd year. [Gk. *klimakterikos* from *klimakter* rung of a ladder].

CLIMACTERIC (2), [klī-mak'-ter-ik], *adj.* pertaining to the climacteric; crucially important.

CLIMACTERICAL, [klī'-mak-ter'-ik-al], *adj.* climacteric.

CLIMACTIC, [klī-mak'-tik], *adj.* pertaining to a climax.

CLIMATARCHIC, [klī'-mat-ahk'-ik], *adj.* determining climates. [CLIMATE and Gk. *arkho* I rule].

CLIMATE, [klī'-mat], *n.* the general weather conditions as affecting the atmosphere of a region. [Gk. *klima klimatos* region of the earth].

CLIMATIC, [klī-mat'-ik], *adj.* pertaining to climate.

CLIMATICAL, [klī-mat'-ik-al], *adj.* climatic.

CLIMATION, [klī-mā'-shun], *n.* acclimatization.

CLIMATIZE, [klī'-mat-īz], *v.t. and i.* to acclimatize.

CLIMATOGRAPHICAL, [klī'-mat-o-graf'-ik-al], *adj.* pertaining to climatography.

CLIMATOGRAPHY, [klī'-mat-og'-raf-i], *n.* the study of climate. [CLIMATE and Gk. *graphia* writing].

CLIMATOLOGICAL, [klī'-mat-ō-loj'-ik-al], *adj.* relating to climatology.

CLIMATOLOGY, [klī'-mat-ol'-ō-ji], *n.* the science of climate and the factors governing it. [CLIMATE and Gk. *logos* speech].

CLIMATURE, [klī'-ma-chooer], *n.* climate.

CLIMAX, [klī'-maks], *n.* the culminating event of a series, the final stage of a happening; the highest point; (*rhet.*) a figure by which the phrases rise in dignity and importance to the end of a series; the culminating point of a drama. [Gk. *klimax* ladder].

CLIMB (1), [klīm], *n.* the act or way of ascending; the thing ascended; an ascent, a rise in status.

CLIMB (2), [klīm], *v.t. and i.* to ascend, to reach a higher position, to mount; (*fig.*) to rise socially; (*bot.*) to creep upwards clinging by tendrils; **to c. down,** to abandon a claim or position rather ignominiously in face of pressure. [OE. *climban*].

CLIMBABLE, [klīm'-abl], *adj.* able to be climbed.

CLIMBER, [klīm'-er], *n.* one who climbs; (*bot.*) a climbing plant.

CLIMBING, [klīm'-ing], *adj.* ascending, that climbs, relating to a climber.

CLIME, [klīm], *n.* (*poet.*) a region of the earth with a characteristic climate. [L. *clima*].

CLINCH (1), [klinch], *n.* a firm grip, a hold; a position in boxing in which one of the boxers closes and holds his opponent with his arms, thus avoiding punishment; a rivet. [CLENCH].

CLINCH (2), [klinch], *v.t. and i.* to hold fast, make fast; hold with a rivet, fall into a clinch in boxing; (*fig.*) to conclude an agreement finally and definitely.

CLINCHER, [klinch'-er], *n.* that which clinches, a riveter, a tool for clinching.

CLINCHER-BUILT†, see CLINKER (2).

CLING, (clung), [kling], *v.i.* to adhere, hold on to by clasping with the arms; (*fig.*) to pervade, remain present by or associated with; to keep close to; to remain constant to; to hold to for support. [OE. *clingan*].

CLINGSTONE, [kling'-stōn], *n.* a sort of peach, in which the pulp adheres closely to the stone.

CLINGY, [kling'-i], *adj.* tending to cling.

CLINIC, [klin'-ik], *n.* an institution for medical, hygienic, or psychological treatment or instruction, usually specializing in a single method of treatment; the teaching of surgery and medicine by practical demonstration on actual cases or patients in hospitals; a class of students receiving such instruction. [Fr. *clinique*].

CLINICAL, [klin'-ikl], *adj.* relating to a clinic or its methods; pertaining to practical instruction or demonstrations on patients in a hospital; taking place on the sick-bed; **c. thermometer,** an instrument for taking the bodily temperature. [Gk. *klinikos* pertaining to a bed].

CLINICALLY, [klin'-ik-a-li], *adv.* in clinical fashion.

CLINK (1), [klingk], *n.* a light resonant sound caused by the gentle impact of metals; (*slang*) prison, gaol.

CLINK (2), [klingk], *v.t. and i.* to make or cause to make a clink. [Du. *klinken*].

CLINKANT, see CLINQUANT.

CLINKER (1), [klingk'-er], *n.* hard, fused cinders from a furnace. [LGerm. *klinker*].

CLINKER (2), [klingk'-er], *adj.* having overlapping strakes; **clinker-built, clincher-built†,** (*naut.*) built of planks each overlapping the next and fastened together with clinched nails.

CLINKER BUILT

CLINKSTONE, [klingk'-stōn], *n.* a greyish-blue resonant felspathic rock.

CLINO-, *pref.* sloping.[Gk. *kline* a (sloping) couch].

CLINOID, [klin'-oid], *adj.* like a bed; of the knobs of the sphenoid bone. [Gk. *kline* bed and *oeides* like].

CLINOMETER, [klī-nom'-it-er], *n.* an instrument for measuring angles of inclination. [CLINO and METER].

CLINOMETRIC, [klī'-no-met'-rik], *adj.* pertaining to, ascertained by, clinometry.

CLINOMETRICAL, [klī'-no-met'-rik-al], *a.* clinometric.

CLINOMETRY, [klī-nom'-et-ri], *n.* the art of measuring angles of inclination. [CLINO and Gk. *metria* measurement].

CLINQUANT, CLINKANT, [klingk'-ant], *adj.* glittering, spangled; (*rhet.*) having a cheap polish. [CLINK].

CLINT, [klint], *n.* a hard rock, a rock projecting from a hillside; the stone first thrown in curling. [ODan *klint*].

CLIONE, [klī'-ō-ni], *n.* a genus of pteropods on which the whalebone whales chiefly feed. [Gk. *Kleio*, the sea-nymph].

CLIP (1), [klip], *n.* a device for holding two things together, usually two bars drawn together on each side of the object. [OE. *clypp* an embrace].

CLIP (2), [klip], *n.* a snip, the act of clipping off; the thing clipped off; the wool of a season's sheep-shearing; the sharp, clicking sound made by snipping or clipping; a neat, sharp blow with the open hand on the face or side of the head. [Uncert.].

CLIP (3), (clipping, clipped), [klip], *v.t. and i.* to hold or be held with a clip; to hold fast by squeezing. [OE. *clyppan* to embrace].

CLIP (4), (clipping, clipped), [klip], *v.t.* to snip off, to cut off by nipping between two blades; to cut short and trim; to shear (a sheep); to cut pieces from the rims of (coins); to cut off sharp (words); to strike with a sharp blow with the open hand; (*slang*) to move fast; **to c. the wings of,** (*fig.*) to restrain from free activity. [Uncert.].

CLIPPER, [klip'-er], *n.* one who clips, that which clips; (*naut.*) a speedy sailing-vessel with a forward raking bow; a transatlantic flying-boat.

CLIPPER

CLIPPERS, [klip'-erz], *n.* (*pl.*) small shears.

CLIPP-FISH, [klip'-fish], *n.* split and salted fish. [Dan. *klip-fisk*].

CLIPPING, [klip'-ing], *n.* a piece cut off by clipping; a cutting from a newspaper.

CLIQUE, [klēk], *n.* a group of persons united by the consciousness of a common superiority; a self-conscious coterie. [Fr. *clique*].

CLIQUISH, [klēk'-ish], *adj.* tending to join in cliques.

CLITELLUM, [klit-el'-um], *n.* the saddle of a worm. [L. *clitella* pack-saddle].

CLITORIS, [klit'-er-is], *n.* (*anat.*) a rudimentary

organ in females corresponding to the penis. [Gk. *kleitoris*].
CLITTER, [klit'-er], *v.t. and i.* to make a gentle clatter. [CLATTER].
CLITTER-CLATTER, [klit'-er-klat'-er], *n.* continual clattering.
CLIVERS, [kliv'-erz], *n.* goose-grass.
CLIVITY, [kliv'-i-ti], *n.* declivity. [DECLIVITY].
CLOACA, [klō-ā'-ka], *n.* a sewer; (*anat.*) a cavity in birds, fishes, etc., into which the alimentary canal and urinary ducts open. [L. *cloaca* a sewer in Rome]
CLOACAL, [klō-ākl'], *adj.* pertaining to a cloaca; dirty, revolting.
CLOAK (1), [klōk], *n.* a long loose outer garment wrapped round the body, and without arms or arm-holes; (*fig.*) a disguise, concealment, pretext. [OFr. *cloke* from LL. *clocca* bell].
CLOAK (2), [klōk], *v.t.* to wrap, conceal with a cloak; (*fig.*) to hide, cover up.
CLOAK-BAG, [klōk'-bag'], *n.* a portmanteau.
CLOAKEDLY, [klōk'-ed-li], *adv.* in concealed fashion.
CLOAKING, [klōk'-ing], *n.* wrapping in a cloak; material for making cloaks; (*fig.*) concealment, disguise.
CLOAK-ROOM, [klōk'-ro͞om], *n.* a place in stations, restaurants, and hotels, where coats and luggage may be left till called for; a toilet.
CLOBBER, [klob'-er], *n.* a paste used for cobbling up old shoes to conceal cracks in the leather; (*coll.*) kit, clothes. [Uncert.].
CLOCHE, [klosh], *n.* bell-shaped glass covering for forcing outdoor plants; a woman's close-fitting hat. [Fr. *cloche* a bell].
CLOCK (1), [klok], *n.* a device for telling the time of the day employing water, sand, swinging weights or metal springs, etc. [LL. *clocca* bell].
CLOCK (2), [klok], *v.t.* **to c. in, on, out, off,** to register the time of arrival at and departure from work by means of some timing device; to start or finish any work.
CLOCK-GOLF, [klok'-golf'], *n.* a form of putting played clockwise into holes set out as the numbers on a clock-face.
CLOCKMAKER, [klok'-māk'-er], *n.* a person employed in making clocks.
CLOCK-SETTER, [klok'-set'-er], *n.* a person who regulates clocks.
CLOCKWISE, [klok'-wīz], *adv.* moving in the same direction as the hands of a clock.
CLOCKWORK, [klok'-wurk], *n.* the machinery operating a clock; a prime mover driven by a coiled spring unwinding and transmitting its rotary motion through gear-wheels; **like c.,** without hitch or interruption.
CLOD (1), [klod], *n.* a lump of earth or clay, a mass of turf; the ground; (*fig.*) that which is earthy or base; (*fig.*) a gross, stupid fellow, a dolt. [ME. *clodde*].
CLOD (2), (**clodding, clodded**), [klod], *v.t. and i.* to clot; to pelt with clods.
CLOD-BREAKER, [klod'-brāk'-er], *n.* (*slang*) a stupid peasant.
CLODDINESS, [klod'-i-nes], *n.* the state of being cloddy.
CLODDISH, [klod'-ish], *adj.* stupid, grossly vulgar, doltish.
CLODDY, [klod'-i], *adj.* earthy; (*fig.*) stupid.
CLODHOPPER, [klod'-hop'-er], *n.* a stupid rustic a heavy-witted farm labourer; a heavy clumsy shoe or boot.
CLODPATE, [klod'-pāt], *n.* a clodhopper.
CLODPATED, [klod'-pāt-id], *adj.* stupid, dull, oafish.
CLODPOLL, CLOTPOLL, [klod'-pōl], *n.* a clodpate.
CLOFF, [klof], *n.* overweight given to wholesale purchasers of certain goods so that they have full weight when selling retail. [Uncert.].
CLOG (1), [klog], *n.* a heavy shoe with a wooden sole shod with a protective iron; a block of wood tied to the legs of animals to restrain them; an impediment, *esp.* dirt in machinery; (*fig.*) anything that hinders. [ME. *klogge* block of wood].
CLOG (2), (**clogging, clogged**), [klog], *v.t. and i.* to hamper, hinder, to slow up by encumbrances; to choke up, block up; to hamper free activity; to become coagulated.
CLOG-ALMANAC, [klog'-awl'-man-ak'], *n.* an almanac in the form of a notched square block of wood or bone.
CLOG-DANCE, [klog'-dahns], *n.* a kind of tap dance in clogs.
CLOGGINESS, [klog'-i-nes], *n.* the state of being cloggy.
CLOGGING, [klog'-ing], *n.* a clog; the process of becoming clogged.
CLOGGY, [klog'-i], *a.* that clogs, adhesively encumbering.
CLOISONNE, cloisonné (1), [kloiz-on'-ā], *n.* cloisonné work.
CLOISONNE, cloisonné (2), [kloiz-on'-ā], *adj.* (of enamelled work) having the design in metal raised above the level of the enamelled surfaces. [Fr. *cloisonné*].
CLOISTER (1), [klois'-ter], *n.* a covered way, open on the inside, running round an open court or quadrangle in a monastic or similar building, and often vaulted and supported on the open side by pillared arches; a monastery, convent; a retreat. [OFr. *cloistre* from L. *claustrum* locked place].
CLOISTER (2), [klois'-ter], *v. reflex. and t.* to confine in a cloister; to withdraw from the world.
CLOISTERAL, [klois'-ter-al], *adj.* cloistral.
CLOISTERED, [klois'-terd], *adj.* having a cloister; living in a cloister; retired, secluded, sheltered.
CLOISTERER, [klois'-ter-er], *n.* one inhabiting a cloister.
CLOISTER-GARTH, [klois'-ter-gahth'], *n.* a court surrounded by cloisters.
CLOISTRAL, [klois'-tral], *adj.* relating to, or resembling, a cloister; retired.
CLOISTRESS, [klois'-tres], *n.* a nun.
CLONIC, [klon'-ik], *adj.* (*med.*) relating to, or resembling, clonus. [Gk. *klonikos*].
CLONUS, [klō'-nus], *n.* (*med.*) violent spasmodic muscular contractions and relaxations in rapid succession. [Gk. *klonos* violent motion].
CLOSE (1), [klōs], *n.* a piece of open ground, partly enclosed by walls or buildings, and usually having only one entrance; a blind passage leading only to an inner courtyard. [OFr. *clos*].
CLOSE (2), [klōz], *n.* a conclusion, end; a coming to grips in fighting; (*mus.*) a cadence. [CLOSE (5)].
CLOSE (3), [klōs], *adj.* near, next to; firm, intimate; restricted; solid, compact, not porous; imprisoned; secluded; (*fig.*) reserved; reticent; stingy; nearly equal, almost exact or identical; thorough, careful, detailed; keen; sultry, stuffy, promising storms; (*philol.*) protected by or ending in a consonant; **c. vowel,** a vowel uttered with the tongue near the roof of the mouth; **c.-up,** a photograph taken near to the subject. [OFr. *clos* from L. *claus(um)*, *p.pt.* of *claudere* to shut].
CLOSE (4), [klōs], *adv.* closely; at hand. [*Prec.*].
CLOSE (5), [klōz], *v.t.* to bring to an end, finish; to shut, to shut up, enclose completely; to make access impossible to anything; (*milit.*) to arrange in close formation; *v.i.* to come to an end, finish; to cease speaking; become closed, to shut; to come to grips; **to c. in,** to approach on several sides, usually with hostile intention; (of days) to become shorter; **to c. with,** to come to blows or grips; to come to an agreement, accept an offer. [L. *clausum*, *p.pt.* of *claudere*].
CLOSE-BANDED, [klōs'-band'-id], *adj.* in close order.
CLOSE-BARRED, [klōs'-bahd], *adj.* with small spaces between the bars; closely confined.
CLOSE-COUCHED, [klōs'-kowcht], *adj.* completely concealed.
CLOSE-FISTED, [klōs-fist'-id], *adj.* mean, stingy.
CLOSE-GRAINED, [klōs'-grānd], *adj.* compact.
CLOSE-HANDED, [klōs'-hand'-id], *adj.* close-fisted.
CLOSE-HANDEDNESS, [klōs-hand'-id-nes], *n.* the property of being close-handed.
CLOSE-HAULED, [klōs'-hawld], *adj.* (*naut.*) with the corners of the sails drawn in tightly for sailing close to the wind.
CLOSELY, [klōs'-li], *adv.* in close fashion.
CLOSENESS, [klōs'-nes], *n.* condition of being close.
CLOSE-PENT, [klōs'-pent'], *adj.* rigorously confined.
CLOSE-QUARTERS, [klōs'-kwawt'-erz], *n.(pl.)* strong wooden barriers used for defence when a ship is boarded; **to come to c.,** to come to grips with an enemy.
CLOSER, [klōz'-er], *n.* the speaker who sums up in a debate; (*arch.*) the brick ending the horizontal course of a wall.
CLOSE-REEFED, [klōs'-rēft'], *adj.* (*naut.*) with all reefs taken in.
CLOSE-SEASON, [klōs'-sēz'-on], *n.* the breeding season when it is illegal to catch certain fish and shoot

certain game; any annual period when some sport does not take place.
CLOSE-STOOL, [klōs'-stōōl], *n.* a chamber-pot with a wooden seat.
CLOSET (1), [kloz'-it], *n.* a small retiring room entered from a large room, a private chamber for undisturbed rest; a lavatory, a privy; a large cupboard. [OFr. *closet*].
CLOSET (2), [kloz'-it], *v.t.* to take into a private apartment for secret conclave, to shut away; **to be closeted with**, to talk secretly with.
CLOSE-TIME, [klōs'-tīm], *n.* close-season.
CLOSE-TONGUED, [klōs'-tungd'], *adj.* reticent, uncommunicative.
CLOSET-SIN, [kloz'-it-sin'], *n.* sin committed secretly.
CLOSING, [klōz'-ing], *n.* conclusion, end.
CLOSING-TIME, [klōz'-ing-tīm'], *n.* the hour at which shops or public-houses close.
CLOSURE, [klō'-zher], *n.* an application for a vote to be taken in order to bring a debate to a close; (*elect.*) the completion of a circuit; a declaration at cricket; a bringing to an end. [OFr. *closure*].
CLOT (1), [klot], *n.* a coagulation of fluid, a small coagulated lump. [OE. *clott* lump].
CLOT (2), (**clotting, clotted**), [klot], *v.t. and i.* to make or become clotted.
CLOTH (1), [kloth], *n.* a pliable stuff woven from various fibrous materials, principally used for garments; a piece of this material, *esp.* as used for dusting, or as a covering for anything; a breadth of canvas in a sail; (*fig.*) the clergy; **C. of Estate**, a canopy held above the King. [OE. *clath*].
CLOTH (2), [kloth], *adj.* made of cloth.
CLOTHE, [klōTH], *v.t.* to put garments on, dress, supply with clothes; (*fig.*) to adorn as if with clothes; to deck out in; to conceal; to surround, endue with. [OE *clathian*].
CLOTHES, [klōTHz], *n.* garments, articles of dress; bodily coverings; bed-coverings; **plain c.** civilian dress. [OE. *clathas*].
CLOTHES-BASKET, [klōz'-bahsk'-it], *n.* a basket in which soiled clothes are taken to be washed.
CLOTHES-BRUSH, [klōz'-brush], *n.* a brush for coats and other heavy garments.
CLOTHES-HORSE, [klōz'-haws], *n.* a frame to dry clothes on.
CLOTHES-LINE, [klōz'-līn], *n.* a line on which clothes are hung out to dry.
CLOTHES-MAN, [klōz'-man], *n.* a dealer in second-hand clothes.
CLOTHES-MOTH, [klōz'-moth'], *n.* a moth of the genus *Tinea*, whose larvae feed on woollen fabric.

CLOTHES-HORSE

CLOTHES-PEG, [klōz'-peg'], *n.* a forked peg for fastening clothes to a clothes-line.
CLOTHES-PRESS, [klōz'-pres'], *n.* a device for pressing clothes; a chest for storing clothes.
CLOTH-HALL, [kloth'-hawl], *n.* a medieval cloth exchange, a building formerly used for this purpose.
CLOTHIER, [klōTH'-i-er], *n.* a dealer in cloth or clothes; an outfitter, tailor.
CLOTHING, [klōTH'-ing], *n.* clothes or garments in general, attire, dress.
CLOTH-SHEARER, [kloth'-shēer'-er], *n.* one who removes unnecessary nap on woollen cloth.
CLOTHWORKER, [kloth'-wurk'-er], *n.* a maker of cloth.
CLOTHYARD, [kloth'-yahd], *n.* a former unit of measurement for cloth; the rod used to determine such measurement; the arrow fired from the long-bow.
CLOTPOLL, see CLODPOLL.
CLOTTED, [klot'-id], *adj.* coagulated, formed into clots.
CLOTTER, [klot'-er], *v.t.* to clot, to coagulate.
CLOTTING, [klot'-ing], *n.* the process or result of forming into clots, the substance clotted.
CLOTTY, [klot'-i], *adj.* full of clots.
CLOU, [klōō], *n.* a central point, focus, the finishing touch. [Fr. *clou* a peg].
CLOUD (1), [klowd], *n.* a mass of thick vapour, a mass of water-vapour suspended in the atmosphere; a mass of suspended dust; (*fig.*) anything resembling this; a vast mass of rapidly-moving particles or objects; a vast multitude; that which shadows, darkens or disgraces; that which threatens; a dark or blurred colour in a stone or translucent body; (*pl.*) the sky, heaven, a great height; **under a c.**, in disgrace; **up in the clouds**, abstracted, not noticing ordinary happenings; very happy. [OE. *clud* rock].
CLOUD (2), [klowd], *v.t. and i.* to cast a cloud on, become dark, blurred; to mark or cover with a cloud; to spoil, disparage; to lour.
CLOUDAGE, [klowd'-ij], *n.* cloudiness; a mass of clouds.
CLOUDBERRY, [klowd'-be'-ri], *n.* the mountain bramble, *Rubus Chamaemorus*.
CLOUD-BORN, [klowd'-bawn], *adj.* ethereal.
CLOUD-BUILT, [klowd'-bilt], *adj.* unsubstantial.
CLOUDBURST, [klowd'-burst], *n.* a torrential rainstorm, a deluge.
CLOUD-CAPT, [klowd'-kapt'], *adj.* lost in the clouds, lofty.
CLOUD-CASTLE, [klowd'-kahsl'], *n.* a day-dreamed ambition.
CLOUDED, [klowd'-id], *adj.* covered with clouds, cloudy; blurred; spoilt; with the colours blended unevenly, with the colours confusedly merging.
CLOUDILY, [klowd'-i-li], *adv.* in cloudy fashion.
CLOUDINESS, [klowd'-i-nes], *n.* the condition of being cloudy.
CLOUDLESS, [klowd'-les], *adj.* lacking clouds, clear, untroubled.
CLOUDLET, [klowd'-let], *n.* a little cloud.
CLOUDLINE, [klowd'-līn], *n.* the level below which cloud rarely descends.
CLOUDWARDS, [klowd'-werdz], *adj.* in the direction of the clouds, skyward.
CLOUD-WRACK, [klowd'-rak'], *n.* ragged and scattered clouds remaining after a storm.
CLOUD-WRAPT, [klowd'-rapt'], *adj.* wrapped in mist or clouds; surrounded by obscurity; abstracted.
CLOUDY, [klowd'-i], *adj.* covered in, surrounded by clouds; (of the weather) dull, overcast; dim, indistinct, obscure; not clarified, thick, opaque; blurred.
CLOUGH, [kluf], *n.* a small deep valley or depression in a hillside. [OE. *cloh*].
CLOUT (1), [klowt], *n.* a heavy swinging blow with the hand; a rough cloth, a rag for cleaning; the centre of the target in archery; an iron plate fixed on the heel of a shoe or on an axletree to prevent wear. [OE. *clut*].
CLOUT (2), [klowt], *v.t. and i.* to mend with a patch; to make fast with clout-nails; to strike with a clout. [OE. *clutian* to patch].
CLOUT-NAIL, [klowt'-nāl], *n.* a short large-headed nail for securing the soles of shoes; the copper nail formerly used in coating ships.

CLOUT

CLOVE (1), [klōv], *n.* the aromatic Moluccan spice from the dried flower-bud of *Caryophyllus aromaticus*. [OFr. *clou* from L. *clavus* nail].
CLOVE (2), [klōv], *n.* a small bulb growing separate from another. [OE. *clofe*].
CLOVE (3), [klōv], *n.* a former unit of weight of about 8 lb. used for cheese and wool. [OFr. *clou*].
CLOVE (4), [klōv], *n.* a cleft, ravine. [Du. *klove*].
CLOVE-GILLYFLOWER, [klōv'-jil'-i-flow-er], *n.* a species of *Dianthus*, the flower of which has a clove-like fragrance.
CLOVE-HITCH, [klōv'-hich], *n.* a knot in the form of two half-hitches round a spar or rope.
CLOVEN, [klōv'-en], *adj.* split up into two parts; **to show the c. hoof**, to reveal evil characteristics. [OE. *clofen*].
CLOVEN-FOOTED, [klōv'-en-fōōt'-id], *adj.* cloven-hoofed.
CLOVEN-HOOFED, [klōv'-en-hōōft'], *adj.* having the hoof split up into two parts, as the ox.
CLOVE-PINK, [klōv'-pingk], *n.* the clove-gillyflower.
CLOVER, [klōv'-er], *n.* a plant of the genus *Trifolium*, with fragrant pink or white flowers; **to be in c.**, to be in easy circumstances. [OE. *claefre*].
CLOVERED, [klōv'-erd], *adj.* filled with clover.
CLOVER-GRASS, [klōv'-er-grahs'], *n.* clover.
CLOWN (1), [klown], *n.* a buffoon, *esp.* an intentional one; the buffoon in pantomime or a circus who amuses by tumbling, somersaulting, etc.; (*archaic*) a rustic; a bad-mannered oaf. [OScand. *klunni* a boor].
CLOWN (2), [klown], *v.i.* to act the fool.

CLOWNERY, [klown'-er-i], *n.* behaviour like that of a clown, buffoonery.
CLOWNISH, [klown'-ish], *adj.* like a clown; ill-mannered, clumsy.
CLOWNISHLY, [klown'-ish-li], *adv.* in clownish fashion.
CLOWNISHNESS, [klown'-ish-nes], *n.* the condition of being clownish.
CLOY, [kloi], *v.t. and i.* to satiate, glut, sicken with sweetness or plenty, to dull with richness or abundance. [Fr. *enclouer*].
CLOYLESS, [kloi'-les], *adj.* uncloying.
CLOYMENT, [kloi'-ment], *n.* surfeit, excess.
CLUB (1), [klub], *n.* a heavy, thick-ended piece of wood used for striking blows; a stick with a knobbed or heavy end for striking the ball in several games, as golf, etc.; the lowest valued suit in playing cards, bearing a trefoil emblem; a number of persons meeting together for some common, generally social, purpose, usually bound by self-devised regulations; the building in which such an assembly is held; an organization for the pursuit of a common interest. [OScand. *klubba*].
CLUB (2), (**clubbing, clubbed**), [klub], *v.t. and i.* to strike with a club, to use as a club (some other weapon); to join in a club; **to c. together**, to pool resources to achieve some common object.
CLUBBABLE, [klub'-abl], *adj.* sociable, disposed to club life.
CLUBBED, [klubd], *adj.* used, held like a club; thickened at the end.
CLUBBER, [klub'-er], *n.* a clubbist.
CLUBBISH, [klub'-ish], *adj.* clubbable.
CLUBBIST, [klub'-ist], *n.* a club-member.
CLUB-FIST, [klub'-fist], *n.* a large heavy fist, a deformity of the hand.
CLUB-FISTED, [klub'-fist'-id], *adj.* suffering from a club-fist.
CLUB-FOOT, [klub'-foot], *n.* a congenital deformity of the foot in which it is short, distorted, and thickened.
CLUB-FOOTED, [klub'-foot'-id], *adj.* having a club-foot.
CLUB-GRASS, [klub'-grahs], *n.* (*bot.*) the grey hair-grass, *Aira canescens*.
CLUB-HAUL, [klub'-hawl], *n.* a desperate method of tacking a ship about, by dropping the lee anchor, thus bringing her head to the wind, and then casting off the cable as soon as she pays off.
CLUB-HEADED, [klub'-hed'-id], *adj.* having a heavy thick head.
CLUB-HOUSE, [klub'-hows], *n.* the building occupied by a club; a sports pavilion for rest and refreshment.
CLUB-LAND, [klub'-land], *n.* the district round St. James's and Pall Mall in London, where the leading clubs are found.
CLUB-LAW, [klub'-law], *n.* rule by brute force.
CLUB-MAN, [klub'-man], *n.* one frequenting clubs.
CLUB-MOSS, [klub'-mos'], *n.* (*bot.*) a plant of the genus *Lycopodium*.
CLUB-ROOM, [klub'-room], *n.* a room reserved for social relaxation in some building.
CLUB-ROOT, [klub'-root], *n.* (*bot.*) a plant disease due to a fungus, *Plasmodiophora brassicae*.
CLUB-RUSH, [klub'-rush], *n.* (*bot.*) a plant of the genus *Scirpus*.
CLUB-SHAPED, [klub'-shāpt], *adj.* in the form of a club.
CLUCK (1), [kluk], *n.* a thick clicking sound made by the tongue against the back of the palate; the call of the hen. [Imitative].
CLUCK (2), [kluk], *v.i.* to utter a series of clucks.
CLUE, [kloo], *n.* a fact helping to solve or throw light on, some puzzle or mystery. [CLEW].
CLUMBER, [klum'-ber], *n.* a species of spaniel bred at Clumber, formerly the Duke of Newcastle's seat. [*Clumber*, a place in Nottinghamshire].
CLUMP (1), [klump], *n.* a small, solid group of people or objects (*esp.* trees) in an open place; a shapeless lump, a clod; clay in coal strata; a thick slab of leather on the sole of a boot; (*coll.*) a heavy blow, clout. [Swed. *klump* lump].
CLUMP (2), [klump], *v.t. and i.* to gather, come together in a clump; to fasten a clump; to tread heavily; (*coll.*) to clout heavily.
CLUMPER, [klump'-er], *v.t.* to form into clumps.
CLUMPS, [klumps], *n.* a dolt, a heavy oaf.
CLUMPY, [klump'-i], *adj.* consisting of clumps, in heavy clods.
CLUMSILY, [klum'-zi-li], *adv.* in clumsy fashion.
CLUMSINESS, [klum'-zi-nes], *n.* the state of being clumsy.
CLUMSY, [klum'-zi], *adj.* awkward, apt to stumble and fumble; with the muscles and movements imperfectly co-ordinated; ungainly, heavy-handed, lacking in grace; slow, unskilful; inelegant, gauche. [Swed. *klumsen* numbed].
CLUNG, [klung], *pret. and p.pt.* of CLING.
CLUNIAC (1), [kloon'-yak], *n.* a member of a reformed Benedictine order of monks. [*Cluny*, in Burgundy, the home of the order].
CLUNIAC (2), [kloon'-yak], *adj.* relating to the Cluniacs or their order.
CLUPEA, [kloo'-pi-a], *n.* the genus of fishes of which the herring, sprat and pilchard are members. [L. *clupea*].
CLUPEOID, [kloo'-pi-oid], *adj.* pertaining to the genus *Clupea*, like a herring. [CLUPEA and Gk. *oeides* like].
CLUSTER (1), [klus'-ter], *n.* a small group of people or objects collected together in fairly close formation; a bunch of flowers, fruit, etc., growing together or from the same stem; a mass of bees lumped together during swarming; a mass of septic matter. [OE. *clustor* confinement].
CLUSTER (2), [klus'-ter], *v.i.* to grow in a cluster, to crowd round in a cluster or clusters.
CLUSTERED, [klus'-terd], *adj.* grouped in a cluster; **c. column**, a Gothic pillar resembling a mass of slender columns arranged in a single group.
CLUSTER-GRAPE, [klus'-ter-grāp'], *n.* a small black grape; a currant.
CLUSTERINGLY, [klus'-ter-ing-li], *adv.* in clusters.
CLUSTERY, [klus'-ter-i], *adj.* growing in, or forming, clusters.
CLUTCH (1), [kluch], *n.* a gripping with the hands, a sudden snatch, a desperate grab at; a firm, sudden grasp; a mechanical device for connecting or disconnecting at will one rotating shaft with another in the same axis by means of a projecting tooth or a friction plate between the two.
CLUTCH (2), [kluch], *n.* the eggs laid by a bird at one sitting; the chickens hatched from these. [OScand. *klekja*].
CLUTCH (3), [kluch], *v.t. and i.* to grab at desperately, to contract the fingers spasmodically, to snatch, to seize with the hand. [OE. *clyccan* to clench].
CLUTTER (1), [klut'-er], *n.* a mess of litter, a confused, disorderly bustle. [Uncert.].
CLUTTER (2), [klut'-er], *v.t.* to make untidy, choke up, clog up.
CLYPEATE, [klip'-i-āt], *adj.* shaped like a buckler, shield-like. [L. *clypeatus* bearing a shield].
CLYPEIFORM, [klip'-ē-i-fawm], *adj.* clypeate. [L. *clypeus* shield and FORM(1)].
CLYPEUS, [klip'-i-us], *n.* (*hist.*) a round curved shield with a central boss; (*zool.*) the forepart of an insect's head. [L. *clypeus* shield].
CLYSMIC, [kliz'-mik], *adj.* purging, cleansing. [Gk. *klusmos* washing].
CLYSTER, [klis'-ter], *n.* an enema. [Gk. *kluster*].
CLYSTERIZE, [klis'-ter-iz], *v.t.* to apply a clyster to.
CLYSTER-WISE, [klis'-ter-wīz], *adv.* in the fashion of a clyster.
CO-, *pref.* together, together with, joint action, coincidence of some kind. [L. from *cum*].
COACERVATE (1), [kō-as'-er-vāt], *adj.* piled together.
COACERVATE (2), [kō-as'-er-vāt], *v.t.* to pile up together. [L. *coacervare* to keep together].
COACH (1), [kōch], *n.* a large closed horse-drawn carriage, with a box outside for the driver, and two seats within, one of several four-wheeled varieties of horse-drawn passenger conveyances; a motor char-a-banc carrying passengers for long distances; a passenger carriage of a railway train; a number of compartments; a teacher, instructor, *esp.* one employed to train and prepare for a particular contest or examination; the trainer to a team of athletes. [Hungarian *kocsi*].
COACH (2), [kōch], *v.t. and i.* to travel by coach; to give special instruction or training for an examination or athletic contest.
COACHBOX, [kōch'-boks'], *n.* the driver's seat on a coach.
COACHBUILDER, [kōch'-bild'-er], *n.* one who makes coaches; one who makes the bodies of motor vehicles.
COACH-BUILT, [kōch'-bilt], *adj.* of a car, having the bodywork made by a coachbuilder.
COACH-DOG, [kōch'-dog'], *n.* a carriage-dog; a Dalmatian hound.

COACHFUL, [kōch'-fŏŏl], *n.* as many as a coach will hold.
COACH-HIRE, [kōch'-hier], *n.* the act or process of hiring a coach; the fee paid for so doing.
COACH-HORSE, [kōch'-haws], *n.* a horse trained to draw a coach.
COACH-HOUSE, [kōch'-hows], *n.* a shed to keep a coach in.
COACHING, [kōch'-ing], *n.* the driving of a coach; the tutoring or training of a person for an examination or athletic contest.
COACHMAKER, [kōch'-māk'-er], *n.* a coachbuilder.
COACHMAN, [kōch'-man], *n.* the driver of a coach; an artificial fly used as a bait for trout.
COACHMANSHIP, [kōch'-man-ship], *n.* skill in driving a coach.
COACHMASTER, [kōch'-mahst'-er], *n.* the proprietor of a coach or stable.
COACH-OFFICE, [kōch'-of'-is], *n.* the booking-office for a stage coach or motor coach.
COACHSTAND, [kōch'-stand'], *n.* a place where coaches stood for hire.
COACT, [kō-akt'], *v.t.* to compel. [L. *coactum*, *p.pt.* of *coagere*].
COACTION, [kō-ak'-shun], *n.* a compulsion; conjoint action. [L. *coactio*].
COACTIVE, [kō-ak'-tiv], *adj.* compulsive, concurrent.
COACTIVELY, [kō-ak'-tiv-li], *adv.* in coactive fashion.
COADAPTED, [kō'-ad-apt'-id], *adj.* mutually adapted. [co and ADAPT].
COADJUSTMENT, [kō'-a-just'-ment], *n.* mutual adjustment.
COADJUTANT (1), [kō-aj'-ŏŏt-ant], *n.* an assistant.
COADJUTANT (2), [kō-aj'-ŏŏt-ant], *adj.* assisting.
COADJUTOR, [kō-aj'-ŏŏt-or], *n.* an assistant, a bishop who assists another bishop. [L. *coadjutor*].
COADJUTORSHIP, [kō-aj'-ŏŏt-or-ship], *n.* the office or duty of a coadjutor.
COADJUTRIX, [kō-aj'-ŏŏt-riks], *n.* a female coadjutor.
COADJUVANT, [kō-aj'-ŏŏv-ant], *n.* (*med.*) an ingredient in a prescription designed to make the medicine more effective. [co and L. *adjuvans*, *pres.pt.* of *adjuvare* to help].
COADUNATE, [kō-aj'-ŏŏn-āt], *adj.* (*bot.*) united at the base. [LL. *coadunatus*].
COADVENTURE, [kō'-ad-ven'-cher], *n.* a common adventure.
COAGENCY, [kō-ā'-jen-si], *n.* a joint agency.
COAGENT, [kō-ā'-jent], *n.* a joint agent.
COAGULABILITY, [kō-ag'-yŏŏ-lab-il'-i-ti], *n.* the quality of being coagulable.
COAGULABLE, [kō-ag'-yŏŏl-abl], *adj.* capable of coagulation.
COAGULANT, [kō-ag'-yŏŏ-lant], *n.* a substance producing coagulation. [L. *coagulans*].
COAGULATE, [kō-ag'-yŏŏ-lāt], *v.t.* and *i.* to make partly solid, to clot, to curdle and semi-solidify; to become clotted or curdled, to congeal. [L. *coagulare*].
COAGULATING-PAN, [kō-ag'-yŏŏ-lāt'-ing-pan'], *n.* an apparatus used in various coagulating processes.
COAGULATION, [kō'-ag-yŏŏ-lā'-shun], *n.* the process or state of coagulating; the substance coagulated. [L. *coagulatio*].
COAGULATIVE, [kō-ag'-yŏŏ-lat-iv], *adj.* producing, liable to, coagulation.
COAGULATOR, [kō-ag'-yŏŏ-lāt-or], *n.* that which produces coagulation.
COAGULATORY, [kō'-ag-yŏŏ-lā'-tor-i], *adj.* coagulative.
COAGULUM, [kō-ag'-yŏŏ-lum], *n.* a blood clot; a coagulating substance. [L. *coagulum*].
CO-AID, [kō'-ād'], *n.* an assistant.
COAK (1), [kōk], *n.* a dowel let into the end of one of two pieces of wood to be joined, and fitting into sockets in the other, to strengthen the joint; (*naut.*) the metal pin-hole in a sheave. [It. *cocca* notch].

COAK

COAK (2), [kōk], *v.t.* to join by coaks.
COAL (1), [kōl], *n.* a solid black combustible mineral, chiefly carbon, burnt as fuel; a piece of this material; a piece of burning matter; **to haul over the coals**, to rate, rebuke, reprimand; **to heap coals of fire on**, to give good for evil; **to carry coals to Newcastle**, to take something where there is already plenty of it. [OE. *col*].
COAL (2), [kōl], *v.t.* and *i.* to load with, take on board, coal.
COALBACKER, [kōl'-bak'-er], *n.* a coal-porter at the docks.
COALBED, [kōl'-bed'], *n.* a coal-stratum.
COAL-BLACK, [kōl'-blak'], *adj.* very black.
COALBOX, [kōl'-boks'], *n.* a domestic box for holding coal.
COALBRAND, [kōl'-brand'], *n.* a disease affecting wheat in which the ear becomes filled with a coal-black powder.
COAL-BRASS, [kōl'-brahs], *n.* iron pyrites.
COAL-BUNKER, [kōl'-bungk'-er], *n.* that part of a ship in which the coal is stored.
COAL-CELLAR, [kōl'-sel'-er], *n.* a cellar or shed in which coal is stored.
COALESCE, [kō'-a-les'], *v.i.* to grow together, fuse, unite completely and inseparably, intermingle, to combine so as to merge individual characteristics into a single fresh whole; (*fig.*) to unite, join together as one. [L. *coalescere* to grow together].
COALESCENCE, [kō'-a-les'-ens], *n.* the process of coalescing, state of having coalesced.
COALESCENT, [kō'-a-les'-ent], *adj.* coalescing; tending to coalesce.
COAL-FACTOR, [kōl'-fak'-tor], *n.* the middleman between the coal-owner and retailer.
COALFIELD, [kōl'-fēld], *n.* a seam of coal; a region in which coal is mined.
COALFISH, [kōl'-fish], *n.* a species of codfish having a greenish-black back, *Gadus virens*.
COALFITTER, [kōl'-fit'-er], *n.* a middleman in the coal trade.
COAL-FORMATION, [kōl'-fawm-ā'-shun], *n.* geological strata in which coal is found.
COAL-GAS, [kōl'-gas'], *n.* an inflammable gas obtained from coal and extensively used for purposes of illumination and heating.
COALHEAVER, [kōl'-hēv'-er], *n.* one employed in carrying or loading coals.
COAL-HOLE, [kōl'-hōl], *n.* a small circular opening in the pavement through which coal may be tipped into the cellar of a house, etc.; a place in which coal is stored.
COAL-HOUSE, [kōl'-hows], *n.* a small building by a house for keeping coals.
COALING, [kōl'-ing], *n.* the act of filling a ship's bunkers with coal.
COALITION, [kō-al-ish'-un], *n.* the act of coalescing; an alliance between two or more persons or organizations by which they temporarily co-operate while maintaining their individuality entire; a temporary union between several fundamentally incompatible political parties to form a government. [COALESCE].
COALITIONIST, [kō'-al-ish'-un-ist], *n.* one supporting some political coalition.
COALMASTER, [kōl'-mahst'-er], *n.* a mineowner or lessee of a coalmine.
COAL-METER, [kōl'-mēt'-er], *n.* one in charge of the measuring of coals.
COAL-MINE, [kōl'-mīn'], *n.* underground workings from which coal is dug.
COAL-MINER, [kōl'-mīn'-er], *n.* a worker in a coal-mine.
COALPIT, [kōl-pit], *n.* a unit of a coal mine, a group of workings sharing and grouped round a common entrance and pithead.
COALPLATE, [kōl'-plāt], *n.* the circular lid over a coal-hole.
COAL-SCREEN, [kōl'-skrēn], *n.* a mechanical sieve for sorting coal.
COAL-SCUTTLE, [kōl'-skutl'], *n.* a container in which coals are stored for a domestic fire.
COAL-SHIP, [kōl'-ship], *n.* a ship transporting coal; a collier.
COAL-TAR, [kōl'-tah(r)'], *n.* tar obtained by the destructive distillation of coal.
COAL-TIT, [kōl'-tit], *n.* a small passerine bird, *Parus britannicus*, having black markings on head and throat.
COAL-TRIMMER, [kōl'-trim'-er], *n.* one employed in coaling ships.
COAL-WHIPPER, [kōl'-wip'-er], *n.* one who unloads coal from ships.
COALWORK, [kōl'-wurk'], *n.* a colliery; a mine and pithead as a whole.
COALY, [kōl'-i], *adj.* resembling coal, very black.

COAMING, [kōm′-ing], *n.* the raised ledge round a trapdoor or a ship's hatch to prevent water from entering. [Uncert.].
CO-ANNEX, [kō′-an-eks′], *v.t.* to annex jointly.
COAPTATION, [kō′-apt-ā′-shun], *n.* mutual adjustment; the fitting of parts into each other; (*med.*) the setting of a fractured bone. [L. *coaptatio*].
COARB, COMARB, [kō′-ahb], *n.* the head of a Celtic clan; a bishop, abbot. [Ir. *comharba*].
COARCTATE, [kō-ahk′-tāt], *adj.* compressed, pressed together; (*entom.*) (of a pupa) enclosed in a hard, opaque case; (*bot.*) compact. [L. *coarctare* to compress].
COARCTATION, [kō′-ahk-tā′-shun], *n.* compression, restriction.
COARSE, [kaws], *adj.* rough, harsh, not smooth; unpolished; unrefined; not finely finished; (of screws) having the threads widely spaced; made of, or having, large particles; (*fig.*) ill-mannered; lacking in sensibility, rude, vulgar. [Uncert.].
COARSE-GRAINED, [kaws′-grānd], *adj.* having a rough widely spaced grain (of wood); (*fig.*) crude, lacking in sensibility.
COARSELY, [kaws′-li], *adv.* in coarse fashion.
COARSEN, [kaws′-en], *v.t.* and *i.* to make coarse, become coarse.
COARSENESS, [kaws′-nes], *n.* the state of being coarse.
COARSISH, [kaws′-ish], *adj.* fairly coarse.
CO-ARTICULATION, [kō′-ah-tik′-yōō-lā′-shun], *n.* the articulation of two jointed parts; the articulation of bones.
CO-ASSESSOR, [kō′-as-es′-or], *n.* a joint assessor.
CO-ASSUME, [kō′-as-ewm′], *v.t.* to take (some rank or dignity) jointly with another.
COAST (1), [kōst], *n.* the part of the land bordering on the sea or on any large tract of water; (*fig.*) land bordering any utterly different territory; a (silver) decanter-tray; **the c. is clear**, the immediate danger is past. [OFr. *coste* from L. *costa* rib].
COAST (2), [kōst], *v.t.* and *i.* to skirt the coast; to skirt the edge of anything; to travel in a mechanical vehicle without help of engine or restraint of brakes, to free wheel.
COASTAL, [kōst′-al], *adj.* relating to, or near, the coast.
COASTER, [kōst′-er], *n.* a vessel employed in trading between ports in the same country; a (silver) decanter-tray; a bicycle with a free wheel.
COASTGUARD, [kōst′-gahd], *n.* a guard stationed on the coast to prevent and detect smuggling or illicit entry, and keep a sharp look-out in general.
COASTING, [kōst′-ing], *adj.* that coasts; **a c. vessel**, a coaster.
COASTLINE, [kōst′-līn′], *n.* the coastal outline of a country; a stretch of coast, *esp.* when viewed from the sea.
COAST-WAITER, [kōst′-wāt′-er], *n.* a customs official in charge of the examination of the cargoes of coasters.
COASTWARDS, [kōst′-werdz], *adv.* in the direction of the coast.
COASTWISE, [kōst′-wīz], *adv.* along the coast.
COAT (1), [kōt], *n.* a (sleeved) outer garment buttoning down the front; the outer furry or hairy skin of an animal; (*anat.*) the membranous layer enclosing an organ of the body; a layer of some substance spread over the surface of a body; (*her.*) the background on which armorial bearings are portrayed; (*bot.*) the outer layer of a bulb. [OFr. *cote* from L. *cota* tunic].
COAT (2), [kōt], *v.t.* to cover with a coat.
COAT-ARMOUR, [kōt′-ahm′-er], *n.* armorial bearings of a person or family.
COAT-CARD, [kōt′-kahd], *n.* a court card.
COATEE, [kōt-ē′], *n.* a short close-fitting tunic worn by women.
COAT-FROCK, [kōt′-frok′], *n.* a dress resembling a coat and skirt but made as a single garment.
COATI, [kō-ah′-ti], *n.* one of two species of *Nasua*, a long-nosed South American genus of mammals related to the racoons. [Native].
COATING, [kōt′-ing], *n.* a coat, a layer of something covering something else; material for making coats.
COAT-LINK, [kōt′-lingk], *n.* two buttons held loosely together by a link.
COAX, [kōks], *v.t.* to persuade by flattery or fondling; to humour into doing something, cajole. [Uncert.].
COAXER, [kōk′-ser], *n.* one who coaxes.
CO-AXIAL, [kō-ak′-si-al], *adj.* (*maths.* and *phys.*) having a common axis.
COAXINGLY, [kōks′-ing-li], *adv.* in a coaxing way.
COB (1), [kob], *n.* the spike of maize; a pellet of mixed bran and seed for feeding chickens; a compound of clay and straw, used as a cheap substitute by cottagers for stone and brick; a small lump of coal; a small wicker basket to contain seeds for sowing; a greedy or avaricious person; a stocky, sturdy horse, in size between a horse and a pony; the male swan. [Unkn.].
COB (2), [kob], *n.* the greater black-backed gull. [~Fris. *kobbe*].
COB (3), (**cobbing, cobbed**), *v.t.* to beat a child on the buttocks; to hit over the head; to fight. [Unkn.].
COBALT, [kō′-bawlt], *n.* a brittle, greyish or reddish grey metal, the chemical element denoted by Co; the pigment obtained from a compound of this metal; **c. blue**, a deep blue pigment obtained from this compound. [Germ. *kobalt*].
COBALTIC, [kō-bawlt′-ik], *adj.* pertaining to, mixed with, cobalt.
COBALTINE, [kō′-bawlt-īn], *n.* cobaltite.
COBALTITE, [kō′-bawlt-īt], *n.* cobalt glance.
COBBLE (1), [kobl], *n.* a small round stone, formerly used for paving streets; a lump of coal of similar size. [Unkn.].
COBBLE (2), see COBLE.
COBBLE (3), [kobl], *v.t.* to mend or make boots or shoes; sew or patch rudely; *v.i.* to work clumsily. [Unkn.].
COBBLE (4), [kobl], *v.t.* to pave with cobbles.
COBBLER, [kob′-ler], *n.* a boot and shoe repairer; a clumsy mender, a botcher; (U S.) an iced drink flavoured with lemon and sweetened; **cobbler's punch**, hot spiced beer.
COBBLESTONE, COPPLESTONE†, [kobl′-stōn], *n.* a large rounded pebble.
COBBLY, [kob′-li], *adj.* paved with cobblestones; uneven.
COBBY, [kob′-i], *adj.* stocky, stumpy.
COBCAL, [kob′-kal], *n.* a kind of sandal worn by Eastern women. [Arab. *cobcal*].
COBCOALS, [kob′-kōlz], *n.*(*pl.*) large round coals the size of cobbles.
CO-BELLIGERENT (1), [kō′-bel-ij′-er-ent], *n.* an active ally in war.
CO-BELLIGERENT (2), [kō′-bel-ij′-er-ent], *adj.* allied in war.
COBIRON, [kob′-īern], *n.* an andiron with a knob at the top for supporting a roasting-spit.
CO-BISHOP, [kō′-bish′-op], *n.* a joint or associate bishop.
COBLE, COBBLE, KOBIL†, [kōbl], *n.* a flat-bottomed fishing boat with a deep rudder, driven by one lug sail; a flat-bottomed rowing boat. [Wel. *ceubal*, Bret. *caubal* flat-bottomed boat].
COBLOAF, [kob′-lōf], *n.* a round, flat-bottomed crusty loaf baked in the oven without a tin.
COBNUT, [kob′-nut], *n.* a variety of large hazel-nut, *Corylus tubulosa*.
COB-PIPE, [kob′-pīp], *n.* a pipe made of a corn-cob.
COBRA, [kō′-bra, kob′-ra], *n.* a venomous Asiatic snake with erectile hood-like folds of skin round its neck, *Naja tripudians*; a similar African species, *Naja haje*; **King C.**, the ring cobra or hamadryad, *Naja bungarus*. [Port. *cobra* from L. *colubra* female adder].
COBRES, [kō′-bres], *n.* a South American indigo. [Uncert.].
COBSTONE, [kob′-stōn], *n.* a cob. [COB (1)].
COBURG, [kō′-burg], *n.* a thin fabric of mixed cotton or silk and worsted, with one side twilled; a kind of loaf. [The Prince Consort, Albert of Saxe-*Coburg*].
COB-WALL, [kob′-wawl], *n.* a wall of mud or clay, mixed with straw.
COBWEB, [kob′-web′], *n.* a spider's network of gossamer threads, usually of circular and symmetrical shape, for catching insects; (*fig.*) any thin transparent fabric; that which is fluffy or obscure. [ME. *copweb*].
COBWEBBED, [kob′-webd′], *adj.* thick with cobwebs; (*bot.*) covered with a thick interwoven pubescence.
COBWEBBERY, [kob′-web′-er-i], *n.* a mass of cobweb.
COBWEBBY, [kob′-web′-i], *adj.* covered with cobwebs, resembling cobwebs.
COCA, [kōk′-a], *n.* a South American plant, the leaves of which have strong tonic properties, *Erythroxylon Coca*. [Peruvian *koka*].
COCA-COLA, [kōk′-a-kōl′-a], a mildly stimulating beverage. [*Prot.*].
COCAINE, [kō-kān′], *n.* an alkaloid substance

obtained from the coca plant, taken as a drug, and employed as a local anaesthetic. [*Prec.*].

COCAINISM, [kok-ān′-izm], *n.* cocaine poisoning; a morbid craving for cocaine.

COCAINIST, [kok-ān′-ist], *n.* an habitual taker of cocaine.

COCAINIZATION, [kok-ān′-īz-ā′-shun], *n.* the state of being drugged with cocaine.

COCAINIZE, [kok-ān′-iz], *v.t.* to give cocaine to; to drug with cocaine.

COCALON, [kok′-al-on], *n.* a large cocoon of a weak texture. [Gk. *kokkalon* kernel].

COCCAGEE, [kok′-a-jē′], *n.* a cider apple, the cider made from it. [Ir. *cac a gheidh* goose dung (from its similar colour)].

COCCIDIA, [kok-sid′-i-a], *n.(pl.)* parasitic organisms formed in the cell-tissues of animals. [Gk. *kokkidia*, *dim.* of *kokkos* berry].

COCCIFEROUS, [kok-sif′-er-us], *adj.* bearing berries. [L. *coccum* berry and *ferre* to bear].

COCCINELLA, [kok′-sin-el′-a], *n.* a genus of beetles including the ladybirds. [Span. *cochinella*, *dim.* from L. *coccinus* scarlet].

COCCOLITE, [kok′-ō-līt], *n.* a variety of pyroxene. [coccus and Gk. *lithos* stone].

COCCOLITH, [kok′-ō-lith], *n.* a minute algoid organism found in silted mud.

COCCOMILIA, [kok′-o-mē′-li-a], *n.* a plum-tree whose bark has medicinal properties. [COCCUS and It. *milia* plum].

COCCOSPHERE, [kok′-os-fēer′], *n.* a globular mass of coccoliths found in the depths of the North Atlantic. [COCCUS and SPHERE].

COCCUS, [kok′-us], *n.* a spherical kind of bacteria producing disease; a genus of four-winged insects harmful to plants; (*bot.*) a capsule, a single cell. [Gk. *kokkos* berry].

COCCYGEAL, [kok-sij′-i-al], *adj.* of, or relating to, the coccyx.

COCCYX, [kok′-siks], *n.* (*anat.*) the bone at the base of the spine. [L. *coccyx* from Gk. *kokkux* cuckoo, the bone being similar in shape to a cuckoo's beak].

COCHIN, [koch′-in], *n.* a breed of domestic fowls originally imported from China. [Abbreviation for *Cochin-China*].

COCHINEAL, [koch′-in-ēl′], *n.* a base for scarlet dye formed from compounded bodies of a South American insect, *Coccus cacti.* [Span. *cochinella* from L. *coccinus* scarlet].

COCHINEAL-FIG, [koch′-in-ēl′-fig], *n.* the cactaceous plant, *Nopalea coccinellifera*, which harbours the cochineal insect.

COCHLEA, [kok′-li-a], *n.* (*anat.*) a part of the internal ear, shaped like a snail-shell. [L. *cochlea* from Gk. *kokhlias* snail].

COCHLEAN, [kok′-li-an], *adj.* cochleate.

COCHLEARE, [kok′-li-āer′-i], *n.* a spoon; (*med.*) a spoonful. [L. *cochlear* spoon].

COCHLEARIFORM, [kok′-li-āer′-i-fawm], *adj.* cochleate.

COCHLEARY, [kok′-li-āer′-i], *adj.* cochleate.

COCHLEATE, [kok′-li-āt], *adj.* twisted in the form of a snail-shell, spiral.

COCHLEATED, [kok′-li-āt-id], *adj.* cochleate.

COCINATE, [kō′-sin-āt], *n.* (*med.*) a salt of cocinic acid.

COCINIC, [kō-sin′-ik], *adj.* (*chem.*) obtained from cocoa.

COCK (1), [kok], *n.* the male of the domestic fowl or other birds; a weathervane in the form of a cock; a device for regulating the flow of water through a pipe; the gnomon of a sundial; the needle or pointer of a balance; the small bracket in a clock which supports the pivot of the pendulum; (*fig.*) a swaggering, ostentatious man; an alert, quick, movement; a smart curl or angle, particularly of a hat; part of a gun operated by the trigger to fire the cartridge; the notch in an arrow for taking the bowstring; (*slang*) fellow, chap, pal; the penis. [OE. *cocc*].

COCK (2), [kok], *n.* a heap of farm-produce, hay, or or manure, piled in a cone. [OE. *cocc*]

COCK (3), [kok], *v.i.* to lift up alertly; to strut, swagger; to look smart; *v.t.* to set erect, to place at an angle, as a hat; to draw back the hammer of (a gun) ready for firing. [COCK (1)].

COCK (4), [kok], *v.t.* to heap up into a cock. [COCK (2)].

COCKABONDY, [kok′-a-bon′-di], *n.* the artificial fly coch-a-bonddu, used by anglers. [Wel. *coch a bon ddu* red with black body].

COCKADE, [kok-ād′], *n.* an ornamental rosette or badge of office fastened to the side of a hat. [Fr. *cocarde* from *coq* cock].

COCKADED, [kok-ād′-id], *adj.* wearing a cockade.

COCKADE

COCKAHOOP, [kok′-a-hōōp′], *adj.* exultant. [Uncert.].

COCKAL, [kok′-al], *n.* a game played with knuckle-bones.

COCKALORUM, [kok′-a-law′-rum], *n.* (*coll.*) a strutting conceited man of small stature.

COCKATEEL, [kok′-a-tēl′], *n.* a crested parrot of the cockatoo group, found in Australia, *Callopsittacus.* [Du. *kaketielje* from Portug. *cacatu*].

COCKATOO, [kok′-a-tōō′], *n.* one of several highly coloured birds of the parrot family, characterized by a crest of feathers on the head. [Malay *kakatua*].

COCKATRICE, [kok′-a-tris], *n.* a mythical reptile supposed to be hatched from a cock's egg and to have a deadly poisonous glance, a basilisk; (*her.*) a fabulous creature with the head, wings, and legs of a cock and a snake's body and tail. [OFr. *cocatrice*].

COCKAYNE, COCKAIGNE, [kok-ān′], *n.* a country of the imagination offering idleness and luxury; London and its suburbs. [OFr. *cocaigne* abundance].

COCK-BILL, [kok′-bil], *n.* (*naut.*) the anchor when hung perpendicularly from the cathead ready to be dropped.

COCKBOAT, [kok′-bōt], *n.* a small boat towed behind a ship.

COCK-BRAINED, [kok′-brānd], *adj.* giddy, light-headed, silly.

COCK-BROTH, [kok′-broth′], *n.* broth made from a boiled cock.

COCKCHAFER, [kok′-chāf-er], *n.* a beetle of the genus *Melolontha*, which makes a loud whirring noise when flying.

COCK-CROW, [kok′-krō], *n.* dawn.

COCK-CROWING, [kok′-krō′-ing], *n.* dawn.

COCKED, [kokt], *adj.* erect; set at a rakish angle; ready for firing.

COCKER (1), [kok′-er], *n.* cock-fighter; a kind of spaniel.

COCKER (2), [kok′-er], *v.t.* to fondle, indulge. [~Dan. *kokre* to call often].

COCKEREL, [kok′-er-il], *n.* a young cock not more than a year old. [*Dim.* of COCK].

COCKET (1), [kok′-it], *n.* the official seal of the custom-house; a certificate for goods which have passed through the custom-house. [Uncert.].

COCKET† (2), [kok′-it], *n.* a fine quality wheaten bread. [Unkn.].

COCKEYE, [kok′-ī], *n.* a squinting eye.

COCKEYED, [kok′-īd], *adj.* having squinting eyes; (*slang*) slanted, crooked, clumsy, topsy-turvy.

COCKFIGHT, [kok′-fīt], *n.* a fight between trained gamecocks.

COCKFIGHTING, [kok′-fīt′-ing], *n.* the sport of matching two fighting gamecocks.

COCKHEADED, [kok′-hed′-id], *adj.* having a head like a cock's.

COCKHORSE, [kok′-haws], *n.* a hobby-horse; **a c.,** on horseback, astride.

COCKILY, [kok′-i-li], *adv.* boastfully, impudently.

COCKINESS, [kok′-i-nes], *n.* the quality of being cocky.

COCKING, [kok′-ing], *n.* the action of drawing back the hammer of a gun ready to fire.

COCKLE (1), [kokl], *n.* a plant growing amongst corn. [OE. *coccel* tares].

COCKLE (2), [kokl], *n.* an edible bivalve mollusc of the genus *Cardium*; **to warm the cockles of one's heart,** to cheer up, comfort and please. [Fr. *coquille* from L. *concha* shell].

COCKLE (3), [kokl], *v.t. and i.* to contract into wrinkles, to pucker. [*Prec.*].

COCKLE-OAST, [kokl′-ōst′], *n.* the furnace of a hop-kiln.

COCKLER, [kok′-ler], *n.* a person who catches and sells cockles.

COCKLE-STAIR, [kokl′-stāer], *n.* a spiral stairway.

COCKLOFT, [kok′-loft′], *n.* the top loft immediately under the roof.

COCK-MASTER, [kok'-mahst'-er], *n.* a person who breeds gamecocks.
COCKNEY (1), [kok'-ni]. *n.* a Londoner, a person born within sound of Bow Bells; the vulgar London dialect. [ME. *cokeney* cock's egg].
COCKNEY (2), [kok'-ni], *adj.* belonging to, or connected with, a cockney, belonging to London.
COCKNEYDOM, [kok'-ni-dum], *n.* the city of London.
COCKNEYFIED, [kok'-ni-fīd], *adj.* having acquired the characteristics of a cockney.
COCKNEYISH, [kok'-ni-ish], *adj.* pertaining to, or like, a cockney.
COCKNEYISM, [kok'-ni-izm], *n.* the dialect of a cockney; a cockney idiom.
COCK-PADDLE, [kok'-padl'], *n.* the lump-fish, *Cyclopterus lumpus.*
COCKPIT, [kok'-pit], *n.* the enclosed space or pit in which fighting gamecocks are matched against each other; (*fig.*) a battlefield; (*naut.*) a temporary ward on the lower deck of a warship for the wounded; the confined space in an aeroplane where the pilot or passenger sits.
COCKROACH, [kok'-rōch], *n.* a large black creeping insect frequenting kitchens and larders, *Blatta orientalis.*
COCKSCOMB, [koks'-kōm], *n.* the comb of a cock; (*bot.*) a plant of the genus *Celosia*; (*fig.*) a fop, a dandy.
COCK'S-FOOT, [koks'-fŏŏt], *n.* the pasture grass, *Dactylis glomerata.*
COCK'S-HEAD, [koks'-hed'], *n.* (*bot.*) the common red clover, so called from the shape of the pod.
COCK-SHOT, [kok'-shot'], *n.* (*coll.*) a shot or shy at an object for amusement; the object itself aimed at.
COCK-SHY, [kok'-shī], *n.* a cock-shot.
COCK-SPARROW, [kok'-spa'-rō], *n.* the male of the sparrow; (*fig.*) a pert, self-important dapper little man.
COCKSPUR, [kok'-spur], *n.* the spur of a cock; the white hawthorn.
COCKSURE, [kok'-shŏŏer], *adj.* conceitedly sure of success, confidently certain.
COCKSWAIN, see COXSWAIN.
COCKSY, [kok'-si], *adj.* cocky.
COCKTAIL, [kok'-tāl], *n.* a short iced drink of mixed ingredients, usually gin, bitters and a flavouring of some kind, well shaken up; a beetle, the Devil's Coach-horse, which erects the hind section of its body.
COCK-UP, [kok'-up], *n.* (*typ.*) a superior letter used in abbreviations.
COCKY, [kok'-i] *adj.* vain, conceited, confidently and aggressively certain of ability and importance.
COCKY-LEEKIE, [kok'-i-lē'-ki], *n.* a vegetable soup. [COCK and LEEK].
COCOA, [kō'-kō], *n.* a brown powder from the seeds of the cacao plant; the drink of chocolate flavour made from this. [CACAO].
COCOA-BEAN, [kō'-kō-bēn], *n.* the seed of the cacao plant.
COCOA-NIBS, [kō'-kō-nibz'], *n.*(*pl.*) uncrushed cocoa-beans after husking.
COCOA-NUT, [kō'-kō-nut'], *n.* the coconut.
COCOA-PLUM, [kō'-kō-plum'], *n.* the fruit of *Chrysobalanus Icaco*; the tree itself.
COCO-DE-MER, [kō'-kō-de-māer'], *n.* the double coconut, *Lodoicea sechellarum.*
COCONUT, [kō'-kō-nut'], *n.* the fruit of the tropical palm, *Cocos nucifera*, in the form of a white hollow kernel containing milk, and covered with a hard brown shell; **c. butter**, a buttery substance obtained from the coconut.
COCOON, [kok-ōōn'], *n.* the small silken case spun by certain insects. [Fr. *cocon* from *coque* egg-shell].

COCOON

COCOONERY, [kok-ōōn'-er-i], *n.* a building or apartment in which silkworms are kept to spin their cocoons.
COCTIBLE, [kok'-tibl], *adj.* able to be cooked.
COCTILE, [kok'-tīl], *adj.* baked (as a brick), formed of baked bricks. [L. *coctilis*].
COCTION, [kok'-shun], *n.* the act of boiling. [L. *coctio* cooking].
COCUS, [kō'-kus], *n.* green ebony. [Uncert.].
COD (1), [kod], *n.* the scrotum; a pod, husk; a small bag, pillow; **pease c.** a pod of peas. [OE. *codd*].
COD (2), [kod], *n.* a large sea-fish, *Gadus morrhua.* [Unkn.].
COD (3), (**codding, codded**), [kod], *v.t.* (*slang*) to play tricks on a person, to hoax, fool. [Unkn.].
CODA, [kō'-da], *n.* (*mus.*) a short separate concluding section. [It. from L. *cauda* tail].
CODBER, [kod'-ber], *n.* a pillowslip.
CODDED, [kod'-id], *adj.* encased; hoaxed; in a pod.
CODDER, [kod'-er], *n.* a gatherer of cods or peas; (*coll.*) a hoaxer.
CODDLE (1), CODLE†, [kodl], *v.t.* to nurse excessively, spoil. [Uncert.].
CODDLE (2), CODLE†, [kodl], *v.t.* to boil, seethe, simmer. [Unkn.].
CODE (1), [kōd], *n.* accepted social customs; a system of principles or laws, tacit or authorized; a system of special symbols for conveying messages rapidly or secretly. [Fr. *code* from CODEX].
CODE (2), [kōd], *v.t.* to put in code form (a message).
CO-DECLINATION, [kō'-dek'-lin-ā'-shun], *n.* (*astron.*) the complement of declination, the north polar distance.
CODEINE, [kō'-dēn], *n.* an alkaloid produced from opium. [Gk. *kodeia* head of a poppy].
CODEX, (*pl.* **codices**), [kō'-deks, kō'-di-sēz], *n.* an ancient manuscript, particularly of the scriptures or of a system of laws; (*med.*) a collection of prescriptions. [L. *codex* writing tablet].
CODFISH, [kod'-fish], *n.* the cod.
CODGER, [koj'-er], *n.* (*coll.*) an old man with eccentric ways; a miser. [CADGER].
CODICIL, [kod'-is-il], *n.* a supplement to a will, altering or explaining it further. [Fr. *codicille* from L. *codicillus*, *dim.* of CODEX].
CODICILLARY, [kod'-i-sil'-er-i], *adj.* connected with, of the nature of, a codicil.
CODIFICATION, [kōd'-if-ik-ā'-shun], *n.* the process of codifying.
CODIFIER, [kōd'-i-fī'-er], *n.* one who codifies.
CODIFY, [kōd'-i-fī], *v.t.* to make into a code or system.
CODILLA, [kod'-il'-a], *n.* the coarsest part of flax or hemp. [Uncert.].
CODILLE, [kod-ēl'], *n.* a win at ombre. [Fr. *codille*].
CO-DIRECTOR, [kō'-di-rek'-tor], *n.* a joint director.
CODIST, [kōd'-ist], *n.* a person who codifies.
CODLE, see CODDLE.
CODLING (1), [kod'-ling], *n.* a cooking-apple. [Ir. *cueirt* apple-tree].
CODLING (2), [kod'-ling], *n.* a young cod.
CODLIVER-OIL, [kod'-liv-er-oil'], *n.* oil extracted from cod's liver, and employed medicinally.
CO-ED, [kō'-ed], *n.* (*U.S. coll.*) a female student at a co-educational high-school or university. [Abbreviation of CO-EDUCATIONAL].
CO-EDUCATION, [kō'-ej'-ōō-kā'-shun], *n.* the education of boys and girls together.
CO-EDUCATIONAL, [kō'-ej'-ōō-kā-shun-al], *adj.* pertaining to, characterized by, co-education.
COEFFICACY, [kō-ef'-i-ka-si], *n.* joint efficacy.
COEFFICIENCY, [kō'-i-fish'-en-si], *n.* co-operation.
COEFFICIENT (1), [kō'-i-fish'-ent], *n.* that which is united with a unit to bring about a specific result; (*alg.*) a number preceding other numbers or symbols which it multiplies; (*phys.*) the number expressing the deviation of various substances from a standard unit.
COEFFICIENT (2), [kō'-i-fish'-ent], *adj.* co-operating, combining, uniting.
COEFFICIENTLY, [kō'-i-fish'-ent-li], *adv.* in a coefficient manner.
COEHORN, [kō'-hawn], *n.* a small mortar for throwing grenades. [Baron *Coehorn*, its Dutch inventor].
COELEBS, [sē'-lebs], *n.* a bachelor. [L. *coelebs*].
CO-ELECTION, [kō'-i-lek'-shun], *n.* joint election.
COELENTERATA, [sē-len'-ter-ah'-ta], *n.*(*pl.*) the group of invertebrates comprising sea-anemones, corals, jelly-fish, etc. [Gk. *koilos* hollow and *enteron* intestine].
COELIAC, [sē'-li-ak], *adj.* relating to the lower abdomen; **c. artery**, the artery connected with the aorta just below the diaphragm; **c. passion**, a discharge or diarrhoea of undigested food. [Gk. *koiliakos*].
COELOM, [sē'-lum], *n.* the body cavity. [Gk. *koilos* hollow].
COEMPTION, [kō-emp'-shun], *n.* the act of cornering the market in any commodity. [L. *coemptio* buying up].

ō (bone), ī (fine), ōō (food), ŏŏ (put), u (up), th (*th*ink), TH (*th*at), zh (azure), † = obsolete, ~ = related to.

COENAESTHESIS, [sēn-as-thē'-sis], *n.* (*psych.*) the amalgam of sensations constituting the consciousness of the whole body. [COENO and Gk. *aisthesis* sensation].

COENO-, [sē-nō], *pref.* common, together. [Gk. *koinos* common].

COENOBITE, [sēn'-o-bīt], *n.* a member of a religious order living in a convent or monastery, in community with others. [L. *coenobita* associated member from COENO and Gk. *bios* life].

COENOECIUM, [sēn-ē'-si-um], *n.* the dermal system of a polyzoon. [COENO and Gk. *oikos* house].

COENOGAMY, [sēn-og'-a-mi], *n.* community of wives or of husbands. [COENO and Gk. *gamos* marriage].

COENOSARC, [sēn'-ō-sahk], *n.* the common tissue uniting separate polypites of a compound hydrozoon. [COENO and Gk. *sarx* flesh].

COENURE, [sēn'-yōōer], *n.* the larva of the tapeworm. [COENO and Gk. *oura* tail].

COEQUAL (1), [kō'-ē'-kwal], *n.* a person equal to another.

COEQUAL (2), [kō'-ē'-kwal], *adj.* having complete equality with another person or thing.

COEQUALITY, [kō'-i-kwol'-i-ti], *n.* the condition of being coequal.

COEQUALLY, [kō-ē'-kwal-i], *adv.* in coequal fashion.

COERCE, [kō-urs'], *v.t.* to force, constrain, compel, restrain or keep in submission or subjection by force. [L. *coercere*].

COERCIBLE, [kō-urs'-ibl], *adj.* able to be coerced.

COERCIBLENESS, [kō-urs'-ibl-nes], *n.* the quality of being coercible.

COERCION, [kō-ur'-shun], *n.* the act of coercing; the state of being coerced.

COERCIVE, [kō-urs'-iv], *adj.* tending or intended to coerce.

COERCIVELY, [kō-urs'-iv-li], *adv.* in coercive fashion.

CO-ESSENTIAL, [kō'-i-sen'-shal], *adj.* possessing the same essence, being equally essential.

CO-ESSENTIALITY, [kō'-i-sen'-shi-al'-i-ti], *n.* the quality of being co-essential.

CO-ESSENTIALLY, [kō'-i-sen'-shal-i], *adv.* in a co-essential way.

CO-ESTABLISHMENT, [kō-es-tab'-lish-ment], *n.* a joint establishment.

CO-ESTATE, [kō'-es-tāt'], *n.* an association of estates.

COETANEAN, [kō'-i-tā'-ni-an], *adj.* coetaneous.

COETANEOUS, [kō'-i-tā'-ni-us], *adj.* coeval, contemporary. [L. *coaetaneus*].

CO-ETERNAL, [kō'-i-tur'-nal], *adj.* equally eternal.

CO-ETERNALLY, [kō'-i-turn'-al-i], *adv.* in a co-eternal way.

CO-ETERNITY, [kō'-i-turn'-i-it-i], *n.* joint eternity.

COEVAL (1), [kō-ē'-val], *n.* one of the same age, a contemporary object or person. [CO and L. *aevum* age].

COEVAL (2), [kō-ē'-val], *adj.* equally old, of contemporaneous origin.

CO-EXECUTOR, [kō'-egz-ek'-yōō-ter], *n.* an executor acting with another.

COEXIST, [kō'-egz-ist'], *v.i.* to exist at the same time or together.

COEXISTENCE, [kō'-egz-is'-tents], *n.* existence at the same time.

COEXISTENT, [kō'-egz-is'-tent], *adj.* existing at the same time.

CO-EXPAND, [kō'-eks-pand'], *v.t. and i.* to expand equally.

CO-EXTEND, [kō'-eks-tend'], *v.t. and i.* to extend equally through the same space.

CO-EXTENSION, [kō'-eks-ten'-shun], *n.* the act or state of co-extending.

CO-EXTENSIVE, [kō'-eks-ten'-siv], *adj.* equally extensive, extending simultaneously.

CO-EXTENSIVELY, [kō'-eks-ten'-siv-li], *adv.* in co-extensive fashion.

CO-EXTENSIVENESS, [kō'-eks-ten'-siv-nes], *n.* equal extensiveness, simultaneous extension.

COFFEE, [kof'-i], *n.* an evergreen shrub bearing small berries possessing highly-flavoured seeds; these berries ground and roasted; a drink made from this. [Arab. *qahveh*].

COFFEE-BEAN, [kof'-i-bēn'], *n.* the seed of a coffee berry.

COFFEE-BUG, [kof'-i-bug'], *n.* one of the gall insects, *Lecania coffeae*.

COFFEE-CUP, [kof'-i-kup'], *n.* a small cup used for drinking coffee.

COFFEE-HOUSE, [kof'-i-hows'], *n.* a house where coffee and other refreshments can be taken.

COFFEE-MILL, [kof'-i-mil'], *n.* a mill for grinding coffee-beans.

COFFEE-POT, [kof'-i-pot'], *n.* a pot in which coffee is brewed or contained.

COFFEE-ROASTER, [kof'-i-rōs'-ter], *n.* an apparatus for roasting coffee-beans before grinding.

COFFEE-ROOM, [kof'-i-rōōm'], *n.* a public refreshment room in an hotel.

COFFEE-TAVERN, [kof'-i-tav'-ern], *n.* a coffee-house.

COFFER, [kof'-er], *n.* a box or chest for storing money, jewellery, etc., a large cash-box; (*arch.*) an ornamental panel sunk in the ceiling, vault or dome; (*hydraulics*) a watertight box; a lock in a canal. [OFr. *coffre* box from Gk. *kophinos* basket].

COFFER-DAM, [kof'-er-dam'], *n.* a watertight enclosure on a sea or river bed, emptied of water and filled with concrete to form a foundation for erections above the surface.

COFFERED, [kof'-erd], *adj.* provided with coffers.

COFFERER, [kof'-er-er], *n.* a treasurer; †officer of the Royal Household, immediately under the Comptroller.

COFFER-FISH, [kof'-er-fish'], *n.* a fish with a protective layer of overlapping plates, a trunk-fish.

COFFIN (1), [kof'-in], *n.* a wooden chest or case in which the dead are interred; anything resembling this in form or use; the hollow hoof of a horse below the coronet; the wooden frame on the bed of a hand printing press which holds the stone; **c. block**, a wooden or metal block fitted with a brass frame to take electrotype or stereotype plates; **c. bone**, a small pulpy bone inside a horse's hoof. [OFr. *cofin* from Gk. *kophinos* basket].

COFFIN (2), [kof'-in], *v.t.* to place in a coffin; (*fig.*) to enclose, shut in, entomb.

COFFIN-MAKER, [kof'-in-māk'-er], *n.* a person who makes coffins.

COFFIN-NAIL, [kof'-in-nāl'], *n.* (*slang*) a cigarette.

COFFIN-SHIP, [kof'-in-ship'], *n.* an unseaworthy vessel.

COFFLE, [kofl], *n.* a caravan; a train of beasts of burden or slaves. [Arab. *qafilah*].

COG (1), [kog], *n.* a toothlike projection repeated at regular intervals round the rim of a wheel as a means of communicating power and motion to a similar wheel; (*slang*) a crib book, a literal translation. [~Dan. *kogge*].

COG

COG (2), [kog], *n.* a small boat for fishing. [OIcel. *koggi*].

COG (3), (**cogging, cogged**), [kog], *v.t.* to provide with cogs.

COG (4), (**cogging, cogged**), [kog], *v.t.* to cheat by using loaded dice; (*fig.*) to swindle, cheat. [Unkn.].

COGENCY, [kō'-jen-si], *n.* the quality of being cogent.

COGENT, [kō'-jent], *adj.* compelling, forcible; convincing. [L. *cogens*, *pres.pt.* of *cogere* to force].

COGENTLY, [kō'-jent-li], *adv.* in cogent fashion.

COGGERY, [kog'-er-i], *n.* swindling, trickery.

COGGING, [kog'-ing], *n.* cheating; cribbing.

COGGLESTONE, [kogl'-stōn'], *n.* a pebble; a cobble-stone. [Variant of COBBLE and STONE].

COGITABLE, [koj'-it-abl], *adj.* conceivable. [L. *cogitabilis*].

COGITATE, [koj'-i-tāt], *v.t. and i.* to reflect, to think, to meditate, weigh over in the mind; to think out. [L. *cogitare*].

COGITATION, [koj'-i-tā'-shun], *n.* the act of cogitating.

COGITATIVE, [koj'-it-āt'-iv], *adj.* meditative, reflective; capable of thinking; relating to reasoning.

COGITATIVITY, [koj'-i-tāt-iv'-i-ti], *n.* the capacity to think.

COGNAC, [kōn'-yak], *n.* a brandy of the highest quality distilled in France; brandy. [*Cognac*, a French town].

COGNATE (1), [kog'-nāt], *n.* (*philol.*) a word in one language corresponding in form to, and derived from the same etymon as, a word in another language; (*Scots law*) a male related to the mother's side of the family.

COGNATE (2), [kog'-nāt], *adj.* having blood relationship, akin; related in origin; resembling, similar in kind; (*philol.*) (of a word) mutually corresponding and derived from the same etymon; (of languages) having a common prototype; (*leg.*) descending from the same ancestor. [L. *cognatus*].

COGNATENESS, [kog'-nāt-nes], *n.* quality of being cognate.

COGNATION, [kog-nā'-shun], *n.* kinship, affinity of origin or of nature.

COGNITION, [kog-nish'-un], *n.* the fundamental faculty of the mind to know, recognize and conceive; knowledge acquired personally and empirically by the senses and retained by the mind in an abstract form. [L. *cognitio*].

COGNITIVE, [kog'-ni-tiv], *adj.* of, or relating to, cognition, having the power to cognize. [L. *cognitum*, *p.pt.* of *cognoscere* to understand].

COGNIZABLE, [kog'-niz-abl], *adj.* able to be known or apprehended; liable to come under judicial notice.

COGNIZABLY, [kog'-niz-ab-li], *adv.* in a cognizable fashion.

COGNIZANCE, [kog'-niz-ans], *n.* knowledge, recognition, conscious awareness; (*her.*) a badge or mark of distinction; (*leg.*) the official notice and trial of a case in court; the judicial right of conducting a trial; acknowledgment of an alleged fact in evidence; a defendant's plea substantiating the right of taking another's goods as his bailiff; **to take c. of,** to take notice of.

COGNIZANT, [kog'-niz-ant], *adj.* knowing, having cognizance of; competent to judge.

COGNIZE, [kog-nīz'], *v.t.* to perceive, to become aware of, to know consciously. [~L. *cognoscere* to understand].

COGNIZEE, [kog'-niz-ē], *n.* (*leg.*) a person in whose favour a fine in land or tenements is acknowledged.

COGNIZOR, [kog'-niz-or], *n.* (*leg.*) a person who acknowledges the right of the plaintiff or cognizee in a fine.

COGNOMEN, [kog-nō'-men], *n.* a surname, a family name. [L. *cognomen* family name].

COGNOMINAL, [kog-nom'-in-al], *adj.* pertaining to a cognomen.

COGNOMINATE, [kog-nom'-in-āt], *v.t.* to give a surname to.

COGNOMINATION, [kog-nom'-in-ā'-shun], *n.* the act of naming; a surname.

COGNOSCE, [kog-nos'], *v.t.* (*leg.*) to investigate officially, to inquire into judicially. [L. *cognoscere* to understand].

COGNOSCENTE, (*pl.* **cognoscenti**), [kon'-yō-shen'-ti], *n.* a connoisseur, a knowing person. [It. *cognoscente*].

COGNOSCIBLE, [kog-nos'-ibl], *adj.* cognizable.

COGNOVIT, [kog-nō'-vit], *n.* (*leg.*) a signed acknowledgment by a defendant of the plaintiff's claim, and agreement to judgment being entered against him. [L. *cognovit* he has acknowledged, *3rd pers. sg. pret.* of *cognoscere*].

COG-WHEEL, [kog'-wēl], *n.* a wheel fitted with cogs.

COGWOOD, [kog'-wŏŏd], *n.* wood from the Jamaican tree, *Laurus chloroxylon*, used to make cogs for the wheels of sugar-mills.

COHABIT, [kō-hab'-it], *v.i.* to live together, particularly as husband and wife without being married. [L. *cohabitare*].

COHABITANT, [kō-hab'-it-ant], *n.* one who cohabits with another.

COHABITATION, [kō'-hab-it-ā'-shun], *n.* the act or state of cohabiting.

CO-HEIR, [kō'-āer'], *n.* a joint heir.

CO-HEIRESS, [kō'-āer'-es], *n.* a joint heiress.

COHERE, [kō-hēer'], *v.t.* to stick together, to adhere, to unite; (*fig.*) to agree, to be logically connected or consistent. [L. *cohaerere*].

COHERENCE, [kō-hēer'-ens], *n.* the quality of being coherent.

COHERENCY, [kō-hēer'-en-si], *n.* coherence.

COHERENT, [kō-hēer'-ent], *adj.* sticking together; (*fig.*) connected, consistent; clear and rational; logical.

COHERENTLY, [kō-hēer'-ent-li], *adv.* in coherent fashion.

COHERER, [kō-hēer'-er], *n.* a person or thing that coheres; (*wirel.*) a device in early forms of receivers in which the cohering of metal filings indicated the presence of electro-magnetic waves.

COHERITOR, [kō-he'-rit-er], *n.* a co-heir.

COHESIBILITY, [kō-hēz'-i-bil'-i-ti], *n.* the capacity for cohesion.

COHESIBLE, [kō-hēz'-ibl], *adj.* capable of cohering. [L. *cohaesum*, *p.pt.* of *cohaerere* to stick].

COHESION, [kō-hē'-zhun], *n.* the act or power of cohering; the state of cohering; (*fig.*) emotional or purposive unity, agreement. [L. *cohaesio*].

COHESIVE, [kō-hē'-siv], *adj.* characterized by or producing cohesion.

COHESIVELY, [kō-hē'-siv-li], *adv.* in cohesive fashion.

COHESIVENESS, [kō-hē'-siv-nes], *n.* the quality of being cohesive.

COHIBIT, [kō-hib'-it], *v.t.* to restrain. [L. *cohibitum*, *p.pt.* of *cohibere* to restrain].

COHIBITION, [kō'-hib-ish'-un], *n.* hindrance; restraint.

COHOBATE, [kō-hō'-bāt], *v.t.* to distil repeatedly (the same liquid) from the same matter. [L. *cohobare* to distil].

COHORT, [kō'-hawt], *n.* a company of the Roman army comprising one tenth of a legion; a detachment or body of soldiers; (*bot.*) an allied group superior to a natural order. [L. *cohors*].

COHORTATIVE, [kō-hawt'-at-iv], *adj.* emboldening, encouraging. [~L. *cohortari* exhort].

COHUNE-OIL, [kō-hōōn'-oil'], *n.* oil derived from the fruit of the Central American palm, *Attalea Cohune*.

COIF (1), [koif], *n.* a head-dress or cap fitting close to the scalp; the white cap, later becoming a black-centred white patch on the wig, distinguishing serjeants-at-law. [OFr. *coife* from OHGerm. *chuppha* cap worn under a knight's helmet].

COIF (2), [koif], *v.t.* to cover the head with a coif.

COIFFEUR, [kwah-fur'], *n.* a hairdresser. [Fr. *coiffeur*].

COIFFURE, [kwah-few'-er], *n.* a style of woman's hairdressing. [Fr. *coiffure*].

COIGN, [koin], *n.* a corner, a corner-stone; (*arch.*) the external angle of a wall; a wedge; **a c. of vantage,** a splendid view-point. [OFr. *coign* corner from L. *cuneus* wedge].

COIL (1), [koil], *n.* a series of spiral rings or loops placed next to, or on top of, one another; a single ring or fold of this nature; (*elect.*) a device consisting of insulated wire wound round a former, creating a magnetic field when electricity is passed through it.

COIL (2), [koil], *v.t. and i.* to gather, form or loop into a coil or coils. [OFr. *coillir* from L. *colligere* to gather].

COIN (1), [koin], *n.* a piece of metal, usually of circular shape, embossed, stamped and authorized as money; a unit of money made of metal; cash; a die used in minting pieces of money. [L. *cuneus* wedge].

COIN (2), [koin], *v.t.* to stamp (money) out of metal, to mint; (*fig.*) to invent, create; **to c. money,** (*coll.*) to be extremely prosperous. [OFr. *coignier* to strike].

COINAGE, CUINAGE†, [koin'-ij], *n.* the practice or art of coining money; coins of a particular period or country; the expense of coining; invention, fabrication of phrases or words; words or phrases so coined.

COINCIDE, [kō'-in-sīd'], *v.i.* to occupy the same position, to correspond, or come together, in time or space; to concur, to be in agreement; to be equivalent to. [co and L. *incidere* to happen].

COINCIDENCE, [kō-in'-sid-ens], *n.* the act or fact of coinciding; a combination of events which happens purely by chance. [Fr. *coincidence*].

COINCIDENCY, [kō-in'-sid-en-si], *n.* coincidence.

COINCIDENT, [kō-in'-sid-ent], *adj.* coinciding.

COINCIDENTAL, [kō'-in-sid-ent'-al], *adj.* coincident.

COINCIDENTLY, [kō-in'-sid-ent-li], *adv.* by coincidence.

COINCIDER, [kō'-in-sīd'-er], *n.* the person who, or object which, coincides.

COINDICATION, [kō-in'-dik-ā'-shun], *n.* (*med.*) a concurrent symptom.

COINER, [koin'-er], *n.* a person who coins, one who makes counterfeit money.

COINHABITANT, [kō'-in-hab'-it-ant], *n.* a person who inhabits the same town or country as another.

CO-INHERE, [kō'-in-hēer'], *v.i.* to exist together.

CO-INHERITANCE, [kō'-in-he'-rit-ans], *n.* joint inheritance.

CO-INHERITOR, [kō'-in-he'-rit-or], *n.* a joint heir.

COINSTANTANEOUS, [kō'-in-stan-tān'-i-us], *adj.* occurring at precisely the same moment, exactly simultaneous.

COINTENSE, [kō'-in-tens'], *adj.* equally intense.

COINTENSITY, [kō'-in-tens'-i-ti], *n.* the state of being equally intense.

CO-INTEREST, [kō'-in'-ter-est], *n.* joint or mutual interest.
COIR, [koi'-er], *n.* a coarse fibre made from coconut husks; cordage manufactured from this. [Malay *kayar* cord].
COITION, [kō-ish'-un], *n.* sexual intercourse. [L. *coitio*].
COIX, [kō'-iks], *n.* a tropical grass, Job's tears. [L. *coix*].
COJUROR, [kō-jew'-rer], *n.* a witness to another's oath or word.
COKE (1), [kōk], *n.* a dark-grey brittle fuel, which is the residue of coal from which most of the gas has been extracted by heating in a furnace. [Unkn.].
COKE (2), [kōk], *v.t.* to transform into coke.
COKERNUT, [kōk'-er-nut'], *n.* coconut.
COL (1, [kol], *n.* a high pass through a mountain-range. [Fr. *col*, neck].
COL- (2), *pref.* standing for CON or CUM before *l.*
COLA, [kō'-la], *n.* a West African tree. [West African *kola*].
COLANDER, CULLENDER, [kul'-in-der], *n.* a vessel with a perforated bottom used as a strainer in cookery. [L. *colare* to strain].
COLA-NUT, [kō'-la-nut'], *n.* the nut from the cola tree, having tonic properties.
COLATION, [kol-ā'-shun], *n.* purifying by filtration, the action of passing through a strainer. [L. *colare* to strain].
COLATITUDE, [kō-lat'-it-yōōd], *n.* the complement of the latitude, 90° minus the latitude.
COLATURE, [kol'-a-tew-er], *n.* the act of straining; the substance strained. [L. *colatura*].
COLCANNON, [kōl-kan'-on], *n.* a dish of mashed cabbage and potatoes. [Uncert.].
COLCHICINE, [kol'-kis-ēn], *n.* an alkaloid of colchicum. [Gk. *Kolkhikos* pertaining to Colchis, a region east of the Black Sea].
COLCHICUM, [kol'-chik-um], *n.* the meadow saffron or autumn crocus, *Colchicum autumnale*; a narcotic preparation from the seeds of this. [*Prec.*].
COLCOTHAR, [kol'-koth-ah(r)'], *n.* a brown-red iron oxide, jeweller's rouge. [Arab. *qolqotar*].
COLD (1), [kōld], *n.* a sensation or state of being cold; the cause of this sensation, a low temperature, the absence of heat; (*med.*) a chill, acute nasal catarrh.
COLD (2), [kōld], *adj.* lacking in heat, having relatively little warmth, low in temperature, frigid; (*fig.*) having no passion, spiritless; indifferent, apathetic; unfriendly; chaste, virginal, modest; lacking in brilliance of colour; **c. as charity,** extremely indifferent; **c. comfort,** poor consolation, small compensation; **c. feet,** fear; **c. steel,** hand-to-hand fighting without firearms or other long-range weapons; **to pour c. water on,** to discourage. [OE. *cald*].
COLD-BLAST, [kōld'-blahst], *n.* a blast of cold air, *esp.* one forced into a furnace.
COLD-BLOODED, [kōld'-blud'-id], *adj.* having cold blood; readily feeling the cold; (*fig.*) unsympathetic, hard-hearted, pitiless.
COLD-CHISEL, [kōld'-chiz'-el], *n.* a chisel for working on cold metal.
COLD-CREAM, [kōld'-krēm'], *n.* a cooling scented ointment for the skin.
COLD-HAMMER, [kōld'-ham'-er], *v.t.* to work cold metal.
COLD-HEARTED, [kōld'-haht'-id], *adj.* lacking feeling, unfriendly, unsympathetic.
COLD-HEARTEDLY, [kōld'-haht'-id-li], *adv.* in cold-hearted fashion.
COLD-HEARTEDNESS, [kōld'-haht'-id-nes], *n.* the quality of being cold-hearted.
COLDIAL, [kōld-i'-al], *n* a refrigerator control. [COLD and DIAL].
COLDISH, [kōld'-ish], *adj.* rather cold, cool, chilly.
COLDLY, [kōld'-li], *adv.* in a cold fashion.
COLDNESS, [kōld'-nes], *n.* the condition of being cold.
COLD-SERVED, [kōld'-survd], *adj.* served up cold; dull, boring, stale.
COLDSHORT, [kōld'-shawt], *adj.* brittle when cold.
COLD-SHOULDER (1), [kōld'-shōld'-er], *n.* studied neglect, a snub.
COLD-SHOULDER (2), [kōld'-shōld'-er], *v.t.* to shun deliberately, snub.
COLE, [kōl], *n.* a cabbage. [OE. *cal* cawl].
COLECTOMY, [kol-ek'-tom-i], *n.* (*surg.*) the removal of part of the colon. [COLON and Gk. *ektomia* cutting out].
COLE-GARTH, [kōl'-gahth], *n.* a cabbage plot.
COLEOPTERA, [kol'-i-op'-ter-a], *n.* (*zool.*) the beetle order of insects, having external protective wing-cases. [Gk. *koleos* sheath and *pteron* wing].
COLEOPTERAL, [kol'-i-op'-ter-al], *adj.* coleopterous.
COLEOPTERIST, [kol'-i-op'-ter-ist], *n.* a student of beetles.
COLEOPTEROUS, [kol'-i-op'-ter-us], *adj.* relating to the coleoptera.
COLEORHIZA, [kol'-i-ō-rī'-za], *n.* (*bot.*) the sheath of the root in a grass embryo. [Gk. *koleos* sheath and *rhiza* root].
COLE-PERCH, [kōl'-purch], *n.* a small fish resembling the perch.
COLE-RAPE, [kōl'-rāp], *n.* the common turnip.
COLESEED, [kōl'-sēd], *n.* the seed of *Brassica campestris* from which is obtained rape or sweet oil; the plant itself.
COLEWORT, [kōl'-wurt], *n.* cabbage cut young.
COLIC (1), [kol'-ik], *n.* an abdominal gripe, a severe pain in the bowels. [COLON].
COLIC (2), [kol'-ik], *adj.* pertaining to the colic.
COLICKY, [kol'-i-ki], *adj.* having or resembling colic.
COLIN, [kol'-in], *n.* a quail of the genus *Ortyx.* [Mexican *kolin*].
COLISEUM, see COLOSSEUM.
COLITIS, [kol-ī'-tis], *n.* (*med.*) inflammation of the colon. [COLON and *itis* denoting inflammation].
COLL (1), [kol], *n.* the line across a curling rink, across which the stones have to pass to score.
COLL (2), [kol], *v.t.* to hug, to clasp heartily with both arms. [L. *collum* neck].
COLLABORATE, [kol-ab'-or-āt] *v.i.* to work together with someone for some object; to produce work jointly with another. [L. *collaborare* to work with].
COLLABORATEUR, [kol-ab'-or-āt'-ur], *n.* collaborator.
COLLABORATION, [kol-ab'-or-ā'-shun], *n.* the act or process of collaborating.
COLLABORATOR, [kol-ab'-or-āt'-or], *n.* one who collaborates.
COLLAGE, [kol'-ahj], *n.* pictorial art in which objects, photographs, etc., are pasted on a canvas or otherwise fixed in juxtaposition. [Fr. *collage*].
COLLAGEN, [kol'-a-jen], *n.* a chief constituent in cartilage and bone which turns into gelatine when boiled. [Gk. *kolla* glue].
COLLAPSABLE, [kol-aps'-abl], *adj.* collapsible.
COLLAPSE (1), [ko-laps'], *n.* a sudden falling down, falling to pieces or breaking up, a falling in, a crumbling into a heap; (*fig.*) cessation of resistance; complete physical or nervous prostration, a breakdown.
COLLAPSE (2), [ko-laps'], *v.i.* to fall to pieces, break up, break down, crumble to ruin, fall in, disintegrate suddenly; (*fig.*) to be suddenly prostrated, to go to pieces, give way suddenly and completely under strain or opposition; to fail completely. [L *collapsus*, *p.pt.* of *collabi* to fall in pieces].
COLLAPSIBLE, [ko-laps'-ibl], *adj.* made to collapse, able to fold up into a small space.
COLLAPSION, [ko-lap'-shun], *n.* the act or state of collapsing.
COLLAR (1), [kol'-er], *n.* something worn round the neck, an article of masculine dress worn around the neck and attached to the shirt permanently or by studs; a leather or metal harness put round the neck of a dog for control and identification, the neck harness of a horse or similar animal; a jewelled band worn round the throat by women; that part of the coat or upper garment fitting round the neck; a part of the insignia of numerous orders worn round the neck; anything resembling these things in form or function; (*mech.*) a band joining two rods of a machine, encircling band strengthening the joints of a pipe; (*naut.*) the upper part of a stay; (*zool.*) any marking about the neck of an animal; (*bot.*) the part of a plant next to, and above the ground; (*arch.*) an astragal. [L. *collare* from *collum* neck].

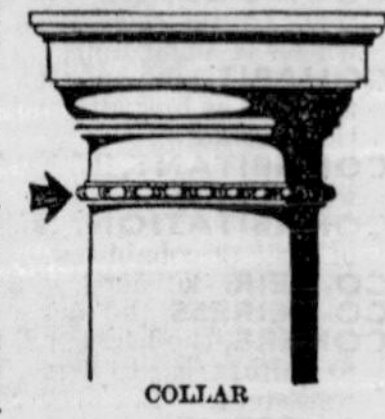
COLLAR

COLLAR (2), [kol'-er], *v.t.* to encircle, restrain with a collar; to tackle successfully in rugby football; (*coll.*) to seize, to grab, catch; to get hold of.
COLLARAGE, [kol'-er-ij], *n.* a tax formerly levied on the collars of draught horses.

COLLAR-BONE, [kol'-er-bōn'], *n.* the clavicle.
COLLARED, [kol'-erd], *adj.* (*coll.*) wearing a collar; seized, caught and held fast.
COLLARET, COLLARETTE, [kol'-er-et'], *n.* a piece of lace or fur worn by women round the neck. [Fr. *collerette*].
COLLAR-MAKER, [kol'-er-māk'-er], *n.* one who makes collars for horses.
COLLATABLE, [kol-āt'-abl], *adj.* capable of being collated.
COLLATE, [kol-āt'], *v.t.* to bring together for comparison, to compare and contrast in detail one manuscript, etc., with another; to put together the sheets of a book in preparation for binding; to present to a benefice. [L. *collatum*, *p.pt.* of *conferre* to bring together].
COLLATERAL (1), [kol-at'-er-al], *n.* a collateral relation; collateral security.
COLLATERAL (2), [kol-at'-er-al], *adj.* running parallel or side by side; coexistent but subsidiary; derived from a common ancestor but through a different line; **c. security**, an additional security given with the principal security. [co and LATERAL].
COLLATERALLY, [kol-at'-er-al-i], *adv.* in a collateral manner.
COLLATERALNESS, [kol-at'-er-al-nes], *n.* the state of being collateral.
COLLATION, [kol-ā'-shun], *n.* the act, process, or result of collating; a light meal quickly brought together. [L. *collatio*].
COLLATIVE, [kol-āt'-iv], *adj.* (*eccles.*) in the patronage of the bishop of the diocese.
COLLATOR, [kol-āt'-or], *n.* one who collates.
COLLAUD, [ko-lawd'], *v.t.* to unite in praise. [L. *collaudare*].
COLLEAGUE (1), [kol'-ēg], *n.* a professional associate, a co-worker, a fellow worker appointed by the same authority. [L. *collega* associate].
COLLEAGUE (2), [kol-ēg'], *v.t.* and *i.* to join in league.
COLLEAGUESHIP, [kol'-ēg-ship], *n.* the status of a colleague.
COLLECT (1), [kol'-ikt], *n.* a short prayer used in church on appointed days or occasions. [L. *collectum*, *p.pt* of *colligere* to gather].
COLLECT (2), [kol-ekt'], *v.t.* and *i.* to gather together scattered things or persons; to accumulate specimens of some kind as a hobby; to beg money for some cause from scattered sources by an appeal to charity; (*reflex.*) to put the mind in order, to pull oneself together; to infer something; to come together, to accumulate. [L. *collectum*, *p.pt.* of *colligere* to gather].
COLLECTABLE, COLLECTIBLE, [kol-ekt'-abl], *adj.* able to be collected.
COLLECTANEA, [kol'-ek-tā'-ni-a], *n.(pl.)* a miscellany of selected literary work. [L. *collectanea*, *neut. pl.* of *collectaneus* collected].
COLLECTED, [kol-ekt'-id], *adj.* cool, self-possessed, sensible; works of an author gathered together into one book or series of books.
COLLECTEDLY, [kol-ekt'-id-li], *adv.* in collected fashion.
COLLECTEDNESS, [kol-ekt'-id-nes], *n.* a collected state of mind.
COLLECTIBLE, see COLLECTABLE.
COLLECTION, [kol-ek'-shun], *n.* the act or process of collecting, a sum of money obtained for charity or religion by collecting from individuals; the assemblage of objects collected; the gathering of matter in an abscess; a terminal examination in Oxford colleges. [L. *collectio* gathering together].
COLLECTIVE, [kol-ekt'-iv], *adj.* regarded as a whole; belonging, or related, to the whole body, or to the sum of all the constituents of a group; **c. noun**, (*gram.*) a noun, singular in form but plural in meaning; **c. security**, security to be obtained by uniting rival states to protect peace, justice, and their own interests.
COLLECTIVELY, [kol-ekt'-iv-li], *adv.* as a whole, in collective fashion.
COLLECTIVENESS, [kol-ekt'-iv-nes], *n.* the state of being collective.
COLLECTIVISM, [kol-ekt'-iv-izm], *n.* the doctrine of centralized state control of all the means of production and distribution; state capitalism.
COLLECTIVIST, [kol-ekt'-iv-ist], *n.* a believer in collectivism.
COLLECTIVIZATION, [kol-ekt'-iv-iz-ā'-shun], *n.* the substitution of collective for private ownership.
COLLECTIVIZE, [kol-ekt'-iv-iz], *v.t.* to transfer ownership of property from private persons to public or co-operative bodies.
COLLECTOR, [kol-ekt'-or], *n.* one who, or that which, collects; one who assembles specimens, objets d'art, etc., as a hobby; one who gathers payments or taxes, or who collects tickets, passes, etc.; chief administrator in a district of an Indian province; an Oxford Bachelor of Arts superintending certain proceedings in Lent; (*bot.*) (*pl.*) hairs covering the styles of certain plants, clearing the pollen out of the anthers. [L. *collector*].
COLLECTORATE, [kol-ekt'-or-āt], *n.* a collector's district.
COLLECTORSHIP, [kol-ekt'-or-ship], *n.* the position or office of a collector.
COLLEEN, [kol'-ēn], *n.* a girl. [Ir. *cailin*].
COLLEGATARY, [kol-eg'-at-er-i], *n.* (*leg.*) a joint legatee. [L. *collegatarius*].
COLLEGE, [kol'-ij], *n.* a self-governing group acting or living by common rules for a common purpose; a semi-independent unit of a university; any school or educational establishment of a senior or superior sort; the buildings in which a college is housed; **c. pudding**, a pudding made with flour, suet and dried fruit. [L. *collegium* association of persons under rules].
COLLEGER, [kol'-ij-er], *n.* a foundation scholar at Eton College.
COLLEGIAL, [kol-ē'-ji-al], *adj.* constituted as a college.
COLLEGIAN, [kol-ē'-ji-an], *n.* a member of a college.
COLLEGIATE, [kol-ē'-ji-at], *adj.* constituted as or pertaining to a college; **c. church**, a non-cathedral church governed by a dean and chapter. [L. *collegiatus*].
COLLENCHYMA, [kol-en'-ki-ma], *n.* elastic cell tissue. [Gk. *kolla* glue and *egkhuma* an infusion].
COLLET, [kol'-it], *n.* a collar, neckband; anything resembling this; that part of a finger ring in which a jewel is set; (*bot.*) the part of a plant between the root and the stalk. [Fr. *collet*, L. *collum* neck].

COLLET

COLLETIC (1), [kol-et'-ik], *n.* an agglutinant.
COLLETIC (2), [kol-et'-ik], *adj.* agglutinant. [Gk. *kolletikos*].
COLLIDE, [kol-id'], *v.i.* to run into violent impact with; to bump forcibly into something; (*fig.*) to come into direct conflict, to clash violently. [L. *collidere* dash together].
COLLIE, [kol'-i], *n.* a long-haired Scottish sheep-dog. [Gael. *cuilean*].
COLLIER, [kol'-i-er], *n.* a coal-miner; a dealer in coals; a ship employed in the transportation of coal. [ME. *colyere*].
COLLIERY, [kol'-i-er-i], *n.* a coal-mine.
COLLIGATE, [kol'-i-gāt], *v.t.* to link together, to sort out and bring together under one head. [L. *colligare* bind together].
COLLIGATION, [kol'-ig-ā'-shun], *n.* the act of colligating. [L. *colligatio*].
COLLIMATE, [kol'-i-māt], *v.t.* (*opt.*) to bring into line, or render parallel, to bring to the line of sight. [L. *collimare* bring into line].
COLLIMATING, [kol'-i-māt-ing], *adj.* (*opt.*) correcting, or adjusting to the line of sight.
COLLIMATION, [kol'-i-mā'-shun], *n.* adjustment to the line of sight; **line of c.**, the line of sight of a telescope. [L. *collimatio*].
COLLIMATOR, [kol'-i-mā'-ter], *n.* a small auxiliary telescope fastened to a larger one to correct deviation from the line of sight.
COLLINEAR, [kol-in'-i-er], *adj.* in the same straight line.
COLLINEATION, [kol-in'-i-ā'-shun], *n.* the act or process of aligning.
COLLINGUAL, [ko-ling'-gwal], *adj.* speaking the same language.
COLLIQUABLE†, [kol-ik'-wabl], *adj.* liquefiable. [L. *colliquare* to liquefy].
COLLIQUAMENT†, [ko-lik'-wa-ment], *n.* something melted; the earliest stage of an embryo.
COLLIQUANT†, [ko'-lik-want], *adj.* capable of melting or dissolving.
COLLIQUATION†, [kol'-i-kwā'-shun], *n.* (*med.*) a bodily wasting, attended by excessive and foul excretions. [L. *colliquatio*].

COLLIQUATIVE, [ko-lik'-wat-iv], *adj*. causing, resulting from, resembling colliquation.
COLLIQUEFACTION, [ko-lik'-wi-fak'-shun], *n*. melting together. [L. *colliquefacere*].
COLLISION, [kol-izh'-un], *n*. the act or process of colliding, a violent impact between objects, *esp*. between moving vehicles. [L. *collisio*].
COLLISIVE, [kol-iz'-iv], *adj*. tending to, relating to collision.
COLLITIGANT, [kol-it'-ig-ant], *n*. one who litigates with another.
COLLOCATE, [kol'-ō-kāt], *v.t.* to arrange, to station, to put in order. [L. *collocare* place together].
COLLOCATION, [kol'-ō-kā'-shun], *n*. the act of collocating; disposition, arrangement; things arranged or grouped in association. [L. *collocatio*].
COLLOCUTION, [kol'-ō-kew'-shun], *n*. a conversation, conference. [L. *collocutio*].
COLLOCUTOR, [kō-lok'-yōō-ter], *n*. a speaker. [L. *colloqui* speak].
COLLODION, [kol-ōd'-i-on], *n*. a gummy solution of gun-cotton in ether and alcohol, used to produce thin films in surgery and photography. [Gk. *kollodes* glue-like].
COLLODIONIZE, [kol-ōd'-i-on-īz], *v.t.* to treat with collodion.
COLLOGUE, [kol-ōg'], *v.i.* to discuss together confidentially; to plot, scheme together. [L. *colloqui* speak together].
COLLOID (1), [kol'-oid], *n*. (*chem*.) any non-crystalloid inert substance, such as gelatine, which, suspended in a liquid, does not pass through a membrane. [Gk. *kolla* glue and *oeides* like].
COLLOID (2), [kol'-oid], *adj*. glue-like; pertaining to colloid.
COLLOIDAL, [kol-oid'-al], *adj*. like a colloid.
COLLOIDALITY, [kol'-oid-al'-i-ti], *n*. the condition of being colloid.
COLLOP, [kol'-op], *n*. (*Scots*) coarse minced meat; a thick slice of meat. [Unkn.].
COLLOQUIAL, [kol-ō'-kwi-al], *adj*. pertaining to, found in, everyday speech; characteristic of ordinary conversation; unaffected, unliterary in phrase.
COLLOQUIALISM, [kol-ō'-kwi-al-izm], *n*. a colloquial usage or expression.
COLLOQUIALITY, [kol-ō'-kwi-al'-i-ti], *n*. the use of colloquialisms.
COLLOQUIALLY, [kol-ō'-kwi-a-li], *adv*. in colloquial fashion.
COLLOQUIST, [kol'-o-kwist], *n*. one taking part in a colloquy.
COLLOQUIZE, [kol'-o-kwīz], *v.i.* to hold colloquy.
COLLOQUY, [kol'-ok-wi], *n*. a conference, conversation, discussion, debate, discourse. [L. *colloquium*].
COLLOTYPE, [kol'-o-tīp'], *n*. (*print*.) a process of reproducing photographs from a sensitized gelatine plate suitably developed and inked. [Gk. *kolla* glue and TYPE].
COLLUCTATION, [kol'-uk-tā'-shun], *n*. a conflict. [L. *colluctari* to contend].
COLLUDE, [kol-ewd'], *v.i.* to work in collusion. [L. *colludere* play together].
COLLUM, [kol'-um], *n*. (*bot*.) a collet. [L. *collum* neck].
COLLUSION, [kol-ew'-zhun], *n*. a working together in secret for a dishonest purpose. [L. *collusio*].
COLLUSIVE, [kol-ew'-siv], *adj*. in collusion.
COLLUSIVELY, [kol-ew'-siv-li], *adv*. in collusive fashion.
COLLUSIVENESS, [kol-ew'-siv-nes], *n*. the quality of being collusive.
COLLUSORY, [kol-ew'-ser-i], *adj*. collusive.
COLLUVIES, [kol-ōō'-vi-ēz], *n*. a collection of filthy refuse; (*med*.) a discharge of foul matter. [L. *colluvies* swillings].
COLLYRITE, KOLLYRITE, [kol'-i-rīt], *n*. white clay. [Gk. *kollurion* Samian earth].
COLLYRIUM, [kol-i'-ri-um], *n*. an eye ointment. [*Prec*.].
COLLY-WOBBLES, [kol'-i-wob-elz], *n*.(*pl*.) internal digestive disturbances. [Echoic].
COLMEY, [kōl'-mi], *n*. the coal-fish, *Gadus virens*. [Uncert.].
COLOBUS, [kol'-ob-us], *n*. a genus of African monkeys with tufted tails. [Gk. *kolobos*].
COLOCASIA, [kol'-ok-ā'-si-a], *n*. (*bot*.) taro, the edible root of *Colocasia antiquorum*. [Gk. *kolokasia* water-lily root].
COLOCOLLO, [kol'-ō-kol'-ō], *n*. a black and white South American cat with grey legs, *Felis colocollo*. [Native].
COLOCYNTH, [kol'-o-sinth], *n*. (*bot*.) the Asiatic or North African plant *Citrullus Colocynthis*, the fruit having purgative properties; a violent purgative. [Gk. *kolokunthis*].
COLOCYNTHIN, [kol'-o-sin'-thin], *n*. the purgative essence of colocynth.
COLOGNE-EARTH, [kol-ōn'-urth'], *n*. lignite earth. [*Cologne*, a German city].
COLOGNE-WATER, [kol-ōn'-waw'-ter], *n*. eau-de-Cologne.
COLOMBIER, see COLUMBIER.
COLON, [kō'-lon], *n*. (*anat*.) the large intestine; (*gram*.) the punctuation mark (:) used to denote the completion of the grammatical structure rather than of the sense of a sentence. [Gk. *kolon*].
COLONEL, [kur'-nel], *n*. the officer commanding a battalion in the British Army. [It. *colonello* from *colonna* column].
COLONELCY, [kur'-nel-si], *n*. the office or rank of a colonel.
COLONELSHIP, [kur'-nel-ship], *n*. colonelcy.
COLONIAL (1), [kol-ō'-ni-al], *n*. an inhabitant of a colony.
COLONIAL (2), [kol-ō'-ni-al], *adj*. pertaining to a colony; **C. Office**, the State department responsible for the colonies.
COLONIALISM, [kol-ō'-ni-al-izm], *n*. a colonial characteristic.
COLONIST, [kol'-on-ist], *n*. one who colonizes, a pioneer settler in a colony.
COLONIZATION, [kol'-on-īz-ā'-shun], *n*. the act of colonizing.
COLONIZATIONIST, [kol'-on-īz-ā'-shun-ist], *n*. an advocate of colonization.
COLONIZE, [kol'-on-īz], *v.t. and i.* to people with one's own nation or race, to provide with a settlement or colony; to settle in a colony.
COLONNADE, [kol'-on-ād'], *n*. a row of columns ranged at regular intervals; a double row of columns forming a passage. [It. *colonnata*].

COLONNADE

COLONY, [kol'-on-i], *n*. a settlement established in a distant, and usually uncivilized and sparsely inhabited, country by people of another race, living together and preserving their national characteristics; the people taking part in such a settlement; (*biol*.) a body of organisms grouped closely together. [L. *colonia*].
COLOPHON, [kol'-o-fon], *n*. an inscription or device, often ornamental, at the beginning or end of a book. [Gk. *kolophon* finishing stroke].
COLOPHONIC, [kol'-o-fon'-ik], *adj*. obtained from colophony.
COLOPHONITE, [kol-of'-on-īt], *n*. a kind of garnet.
COLOPHONY, [kol-of'-on-i], *n*. a dark resin obtained from coniferous trees. [L. *Colophonia*, a place in Lydia, where first obtained].
COLOQUINTIDA, [kol'-o-kwin'-tid-a], *n*. the bitter apple. [Gk. *kolokunthis*].
COLORADO-BEETLE, [kol-er-ahd'-ō-bētl], *n*. a destructive beetle of the genus *Doryphora*. [*Colorado* in the U.S.A.].
COLORATE, [kul'-er-āt], *adj*. tinged with colour.
COLORATION, COLOURATION, [kul'-er-ā'-shun], *n*. the process or effect of colouring, the disposition and blending of colours. [L. *coloratio*].
COLORATURA, [kol'-er-a-tew'-ra], *n*. (*mus*.) highly ornate variations for embellishment. [It. *coloratura* coloration].
COLORIFIC, [kul'-er-if'-ik], *adj*. able to colour; brightly coloured. [Fr. *colorifique*].
COLORIMETER, [kul'-er-im'-it-er], *n*. an instrument for calculating the strength of dyes or colours. [COLOUR and METER].
COLORINE, [kol'-or-in], *n*. an extract of madder.
COLOSSAL, [kol-os'-al], *adj*. gigantic, stupendous. [COLOSSUS].
COLOSSEAN, [kol'-os-ē'-an], *a*. colossal.
COLOSSEUM, COLISEUM, [kol'-os-ē'-um], *n*. Vespasian's great amphitheatre at Rome; any large amphitheatre or place of public entertainment. [L. *colosseum*].
COLOSSUS, [kol-os'-us], *n*. a gigantic statue; the immense statue of Apollo that stood in the harbour

at Rhodes; (*fig.*) a man of great power or stature. [Gk. *kolossos*].

COLOSSUS-WISE, [kol-os'-us-wīz'], *adv.* like a Colossus.

COLOSTRUM, [kol-os'-trum], *n.* the first milk after parturition. [L. *colostrum*].

COLOTOMY, [kol-ot'-om-i], *n.* an incision in the colon. [COLON and Gk. *tomia* cutting].

COLOUR (1), [kul'-er], *n.* hue, tint; the different sensations of this produced on the retina by light waves of varying frequencies; variously tinted pigments and their use in painting; human complexion; (*fig.*) appearance, show; false show, pretence; kind, quality; (*fig.*) life, vividness, zest; (*mus.*) variety of tone; (*pl.*) a military standard; the distinguishing badges of jockeys, athletic teams, etc.; **to see the c. of,** to test the reality of; **a man of c.,** an Indian, a negro; **local c.,** vivid detail used as a literary background; **to come off with flying colours,** to emerge triumphantly from some test or ordeal; **off c.,** unwell, slightly indisposed. [L. *color* colour, complexion].

COLOUR (2), [kul'-er], *v.t. and i.* to stain, paint, dye or tint with colour; (*fig.*) to distort, exaggerate, to tinge strongly with one's own feelings or ideas; to become coloured, to flush.

COLOURABLE, [kul'-er-abl], *adj.* specious, plausible.

COLOURABLENESS, [kul'-er-abl-nes], *n.* speciousness.

COLOURABLY, [kul'-er-ab-li], *adv.* in colourable fashion.

COLOURATION, see COLORATION.

COLOUR-BLIND, [kul'-er-blīnd'], *adj.* unable to distinguish colours.

COLOUR-BLINDNESS, [kul'-er-blīnd'-nes], *n.* the condition of being colour-blind.

COLOUR-BOX, [kul'-er-boks'], *n.* a box of artist's paints.

COLOUR-COMPANY, [kul'-er-kum'-pan-i], *n.* the company which carries the colours of a battalion.

COLOURED, [kul'-erd], *adj.* having a colour; not white-skinned.

COLOURING, [kul'-er-ing], *n.* the process, effect, manner or skill of laying on colour; the colour so laid on; complexion.

COLOURIST, [kul'-er-ist], *n.* one who colours, one skilled in commercial colouring.

COLOURLESS, [kul'-er-les], *adj.* having no colour; dull, drab; (*fig.*) lifeless, uninteresting.

COLOURLESSLY, [kul'-er-les-li], *adv.* in a colourless manner; uninterestingly.

COLOURMAN, [kul'-er-man], *n.* a dealer in paints, oils, artists' materials, etc.

COLOUR-SERGEANT, [kul'-er-sah'-jant], *n.* the senior sergeant of the colour company.

COLOURY, [kul'-er-i], *adj.* (*comm.*) possessing a colour denoting good quality, as coffee.

COLPORTAGE, [kol'-pawt-ij], *n.* the distribution of tracts by hawkers.

COLPORTEUR, [kol'-pawt-ur'], *n.* one who hawks bibles or distributes religious tracts. [F. *colporteur* hawker].

COLSTAFF, [kol'-stahf], *n.* a staff for carrying a load on the shoulders of two persons. [L. *collum* neck].

COLT (1), [kōlt], *n.* a young horse; a young, frolicsome, inexperienced person. [Uncert.].

COLT (2), [kōlt], *n.* an early American revolver. [Samuel *Colt*, the inventor].

COLTER, see COULTER.

COLTISH, [kōlt'-ish], *adj.* like a colt, frolicsome.

COLTSFOOT, [kōlts'-fo͝ot], *n.* a species of *Tussilago*, with yellow flowers, and leaves used medically.

COLUBER, [kol'-yo͞o-ber], *n.* a genus of harmless Mediterranean snakes. [L. *coluber* snake].

COLUBRINE, [kol'-yo͞o-brīn], *adj.* relating to the snake; (*fig.*) cunning, subtle. [L. *colubrinus*].

COLUMBA (1), see CALUMBA.

COLUMBA (2), [kol-um'-ba], *n.* a dove-shaped vessel used to reserve the elements of the Eucharist. [L. *columba* dove].

COLUMBARIUM, [kol'-um-bāer'-i-um], *n.* a dove-cote; a chamber with wall-niches for receiving the ashes or bodies of the dead. [L. *columbarium* from *columba* dove].

COLUMBA

COLUMBARY, [kol'-um-ber-i], *n.* a dove-cote. [*Prec.*].

COLUMBATE, [kol-um'-bāt], *n.* (*chem.*) a salt of columbic acid. [*Columbia* in America].

COLUMBIAN, [kol-um'-bi-an], *adj.* American. [*Columbus*, the discoverer of America].

COLUMBIC, [kol-um'-bik], *adj.* pertaining to columbium.

COLUMBIER, COLOMBIER, [kol-um'-bēer], *n.* a size of drawing paper generally 34½ inches by 23. [Fr. *colombier* dove-cote].

COLUMBINE (1), [kol'-um-bīn] *n.* perennial plant of the genus *Aquilegia*. [LL. *columbinus* dove-like].

COLUMBINE (2), [kol'-um-bīn], *n.* Harlequin's partner in pantomime. [*Prec.*].

COLUMBINE (3), [kol'-um-bīn], *adj.* dovelike, dove-coloured.

COLUMBITE, [kol-um'-bīt], *n.* niobite, a mineral composed of niobium, iron, and manganese.

COLUMBIUM, [kol-um'-bi-um], *n.* niobium. [*Columbia*, in America].

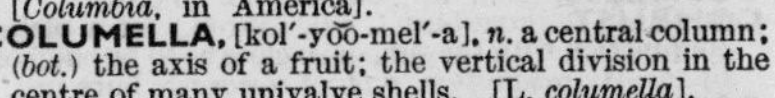

COLUMBINE

COLUMELLA, [kol'-yo͞o-mel'-a], *n.* a central column; (*bot.*) the axis of a fruit; the vertical division in the centre of many univalve shells. [L. *columella*].

COLUMN, [kol'-um], *n.* a pillar, an upright shaft, a lofty support to the arch or roof of a building; anything resembling this; any tall, slender, upright body; a vertical division of a page of type; a set of figures arranged vertically; a body of troops arranged so that there are fewer abreast than there are deep. [L. *columna* pillar].

COLUMNAR, [kol-um'-ner], *adj.* in the form of, pertaining to, a column. [L. *columnaris*].

COLUMNATED, [kol'-um-nāt'-id], *adj.* embellished with columns. [L. *columnatus*].

COLUMNED, [kol'-umd], *adj.* having columns.

COLUMNIATION, [kol-um'-ni-ā'-shun], *n.* (*arch.*) the use of columns.

COLURE, [kol-ew'-er], *n.* one of two theoretical circles in the heavens, intersecting at right angles at the poles. [Gk. *kolouros* cut off].

COLZA, [kol'-za], *n.* rape oil extracted from *Brassica Rapa*. [Du. *koolzaad* cabbage-seed].

COMA (1), [kō'-ma], *n.* a trance-like stupor produced by disease or injury; (*fig.*) deep abstraction. [Gk. *koma*].

COMA (2), [kō'-ma], *n.* (*astron.*) the nebulous covering round the nucleus of a comet; (*bot.*) the tufted ends of certain seeds; the leafy head of a tree. [Gk. *kome* hair]

COMARB, see COARB.

COMATE, [kōm'-āt], *adj.* (*bot.*) hairy.

CO-MATE, [kō'-māt], *n.* a companion.

COMATOSE, [kōm'-at-ōs], *adj.* suffering from coma, lethargic.

COMATOUS, [kōm'-at-us], *adj.* comatose.

COMB (1), [kōm], *n.* an instrument having many tooth-like projections in a row for cleaning, adjusting or holding the hair, a similar article for separating and cleansing wool, flax, etc.; the crest of a cock; the cellular store-place built by bees for their honey. [OE. *comb*].

COMB (2), [kōm], *v.t. and i.* to adjust and smooth with a comb; to separate and cleanse with a comb; (*fig.*) to search a place minutely.

COMBAT (1), [kom'-bat], *n.* a physical contest, a fight, battle.

COMBAT (2), (combating, combated), [kom'-bat], *v.t. and i.* to fight, strive against; to struggle, be opposed to. [Fr. *combattre*].

COMBATABLE, [kom'-bat-abl], *adj.* that may be combated.

COMBATANT (1), [kom'-bat-ant], *n.* one who fights or struggles; a soldier, etc. [Fr. *combattant, pres.pt.* of *combattre* to fight].

COMBATANT (2), [kom'-bat-ant], *adj.* taking part in combat; **c. officer,** (*milit.*) a leader of a unit actively engaged in fighting.

COMBATIVE, [kom'-bat-iv], *adj.* pugnacious.

COMBATIVENESS, [kom'-bat-iv-nes], *n.* the quality of being combative.

COMB-BRUSH, [kōm'-brush], *n.* a brush for cleaning combs.

COMBE, [ko͞om], *n.* a small valley. [COOMBE].

COMBER (1), [kōm'-er], *n.* one who or that which combs, a machine for combing flax.

COMBER (2), [kum'-ber], *n.* the sea-perch, *Serranus cabrilla*.

COMBINABLE, [kom-bīn'-abl], *adj.* that may be combined.
COMBINABLENESS, [kom-bīn'-abl-nes], *n.* the quality of being combinable.
COMBINATION, [kom'-bin-ā'-shun], *n.* the act or process of combining; the state of being combined; a union, league, amalgamation, alliance; (of persons) a league, partnership; (*math.*) various arrangements of common factors; (*pl.*) a long undergarment reaching from neck to knee. [L. *combinatio*].
COMBINATIVE, [kom'-bin-āt-iv], *adj.* tending to combine.
COMBINE (1), [kom'-bīn], *n.* a combination; a union of companies or trading organizations for business purposes.
COMBINE (2), [kom-bīn'], *v.t. and i.* to make to unite, amalgamate, fuse, join together, unite closely; to mix, come together, coalesce; **combined operations**, military operations carried out by air, sea and land forces under a single command. [LL. *combinare*].
COMBINER, [kom-bīn'-er], *n.* one who or that which combines.
COMBING, [kōm'-ing], *n.* treating with a comb; dead hair, etc., removed by combing.
COMBLESS, [kōm'-les], *adj.* having no crest.
COMBUST, [kom-bust'], *adj.* (*astron.*) (of a planet) conjunction with the sun, or so close as to be outshone by it. [L. *combustum*, *p.pt.* of *comburere* burn up].
COMBUSTIBILITY, [kom-bus'-tib-il'-i-ti], *n.* liability to combustion.
COMBUSTIBLE (1), [kom-bus'-tibl], *n.* an inflammable material.
COMBUSTIBLE (2), [kom-bus'-tibl], *adj.* inflammable; (*fig.*) easily excited. [LL. *combustibilis*].
COMBUSTIBLENESS, [kom-bus'-tibl-nes], *n.* combustibility.
COMBUSTION, [kom-bus'-chun], *n.* the process or state of burning, a sudden bursting into flame. [LL. *combustio*].
COME, (**came**), [kum], *v.i.* to approach, be in motion towards, to move towards something; to arrive, to reach; (*fig.*) to appear; to occur, take place, happen; to originate in; **to c. about**, to happen; **to c. across**, (*slang*) to hand over under pressure; to find by chance; **to c. at**, to attack furiously; **to c. back**, to return; **to c. down**, to decline economically, socially, etc.; **to c. down on**, to blame; **to c. in**, to prove useful; to be the fashion; **to c. in for**, to meet with, to inherit; **to c. into**, to inherit; **to c. off**, to succeed by luck; to take place; **to c. on**, to improve; **to c. over**, to become (faint, etc.); **to c. out**, to become apparent; to go on strike; (of a girl) to appear in society as a débutante; **to c. out with**, to blurt out; **to c. round**, to recover, become placated; **to c. through**, to survive; **to c. to**, to recover consciousness; **to c. under**, to be classed as. [OE. *cuman*].
COME-BACK, [kum'-bak'], *n.* a return to one's former state after a decline or retirement.
COMEDIAN, [kom-ē'-di-an], *n.* an actor of comedy; a buffoon. [Fr. *comédien*].
COMEDIENNE, [kom-ē'-di-en'], *n.* a female comedian. [Fr. *comédienne*].
COMEDIETTA, [kom-ē'-di-et'-a], *n.* a light comedy with music. [It. *comedietta*].
COMEDIST, [kom'-id-ist], *n.* a comedy-writer.
COMEDO, [kom-ē'-dō], *n.* a blackhead. [L. *comedo* glutton].
COME-DOWN, [kum'-down], *n.* a fall in position, humiliation.
COMEDY, [kom'-id-i], *n.* drama intended to arouse laughter rather than pity or terror, or in which the humour is obtained from normal behaviour in every-day life; a play of this kind; an amusing incident in real life arising from the combination of character and situation rather than farcical event. [Gk. *komoidia*].
COMELILY, [kum'-li-li], *adv.* in comely fashion.
COMELINESS, [kum'-li-nes], *n.* the condition of being comely.
COMELY, [kum'-li], *adj.* becoming, pleasing to the eye. [OE. *cymlic* splendid].
COMER, [kum'-er], *n.* one who comes.
COMESTIBLE (1), [kom-es'-tibl], *n.* food.
COMESTIBLE (2), [kom-es'-tibl], *adj.* edible, relating to food. [L. *comestibilis*].
COMET, [kom'-it], *n.* a heavenly body consisting of a solid nucleus and a gaseous, luminous tail. [Gk. *kometes* long-haired].
COMETARIUM, [kom'-it-āer'-i-um], *n.* an instrument for representing the eccentric orbit of a comet.
COMETARY (1), [kom'-it-er-i], *n.* a cometarium.
COMETARY (2), [kom'-it-er-i], *adj.* pertaining to a comet.
COMETIC, [kom-et'-ik], *adj.* cometary.
COMETOGRAPHY, [kom'-it-og'-raf-i], *n.* the study and description of comets. [COMET and Gk. *graphia* writing].
COMETOLOGY, [kom'-it-ol'-o-ji], *n.* the study of comets. [COMET and Gk. *logos* speech].
COMFIT, [kum'-fit], *n.* a fruit, nut, etc., preserved in a thick covering of sugar; a sweetmeat. [Fr. *confit*].
COMFORT (1), [kum'-fert], *n.* consolation; solace; encouragement in fear, trouble or anxiety; the person or thing that comforts; well-being, feeling of physical satisfaction and ease, freedom from, or release from pain; freedom from physical want or unease.
COMFORT (2), [kum'-fert], *v.t.* to provide comfort for. [LL. *confortare* to strengthen].
COMFORTABLE, [kum'-fert-abl], *adj.* providing or enjoying comfort; enough to satisfy one's needs or wants. [OFr. *confortable*].
COMFORTABLENESS, [kum'-fert-abl-nes], *n.* the condition of being comfortable.
COMFORTABLY, [kum'-fert-ab-li], *adv.* in comfortable fashion.
COMFORTER, [kum'-fert-er], *n.* one who or that which comforts; the Holy Ghost; a thick woollen muffler; a dummy teat for infants.
COMFORTFUL, [kum'-fert-fōōl], *adj.* that comforts.
COMFORTLESS, [kum'-fert-les], *adj.* lacking all comfort; unable to be comforted.
COMFORTLESSLY, [kum'-fert-les-li], *adv.* in comfortless fashion.
COMFORTLESSNESS, [kum'-fert-les-nes], *n.* the quality of being comfortless.
COMFREY, [kum'-fri], *n.* (*bot.*) the plant *Symphytum officinale*, formerly used as a remedy for wounds. [OFr. *comfirie*].
COMFY, [kum'-fi], *adj.* (*coll.*) comfortable. [~COMFORTABLE].
COMIC (1), [kom'-ik], *n.* (*coll.*) a comedian; a comic paper.
COMIC (2), [kom'-ik], *adj.* relating to comedy; funny, laughter-provoking. [Gk. *komikos*].
COMICAL, [kom'-ik-al], *adj.* comic, extremely funny, amusing by ludicrous antics.
COMICALITY, [kom'-ik-al'-i-ti], *n.* the quality or condition of being comical.
COMICALLY, [kom'-ik-a-li], *adv.* in comical fashion.
COMICALNESS, [kom'-ik-al-nes], *n.* comicality.
COMIC-STRIP, [kom'-ik-strip'], *n.* a humorous newspaper cartoon continued from day to day in which the amusing adventures of a group of stock characters are told in a series of drawings.
COMING (1), [kum'-ing], *n.* approach, movement towards; **second c.**, Christ's return to judge the world.
COMING (2), [kum'-ing], *adj.* about to come, approaching, future, inevitable.
COMINTERN, [kom'-in-turn], *n.* the *Com*munist *International*.
COMITIAL, [kom-ish'-al], *adj.* pertaining to assemblies. [L. *comitialis*].
COMITY, [kom'-i-ti], *n.* mutual courtesy, common civility, respect of manners; **c. of nations**, mutual respect and tolerance amongst nations. [L. *comitas*].
COMMA, [kom'-a], *n.* the mark of punctuation (,) used to mark off the phrases and clauses of a sentence; (*mus.*) an enharmonic interval; **c. butterfly**, the butterfly *Polygonia comma-album*, so named from the mark on its wing; **inverted commas** (" "), commas placed above the line to enclose a quotation. [Gk. *komma* something cut, a clause].
COMMAND (1), [kom-ahnd'], *n.* complete power, rule or authority, control; an order that must be obeyed; the position of one holding such authority; the body of troops under such control; the words in which such orders are given. [Fr. *commande*].
COMMAND (2), [kom-ahnd'], *v.t. and i.* to have command or authority over; to compel, to order, demand without questioning; (*milit.*) to dominate a position; to bring, be sold for; to possess. [L. *commandare*].
COMMANDABLE, [kom-ahnd'-abl], *adj.* capable of being commanded.
COMMANDANT, [kom'-and-ant'], *n.* a military officer commanding a post, fort, or town. [Fr. *commandant*].
COMMANDANTSHIP, [kom'-and-ant'-ship], *n.* the position of a commandant.
COMMANDEER, [kom'-and-ēer'], *v.t.* to seize for military purposes; to convert arbitrarily to one's

own use; to take by virtue of command; to conscript. [Du. *kommandeeren*].

COMMANDER, [kom-ahnd'-er], *n.* one who commands; (*milit.*) an officer in command of any military division; (*nav.*) the officer immediately below the rank of captain; a member of one of the higher ranks of certain Orders of Knighthood; a heavy wooden mallet. [OFr. *commandere*].

COMMANDERSHIP, [kom-ahnd'-er-ship], *n.* the rank of officer or commander.

COMMANDERY, COMMANDRY, [kom-ahnd'-er-i], *n.* (*hist.*) an estate belonging to an Order of Knights and governed by one of them; the commandership in an Order of Knights. [MedL. *commendaria*].

COMMANDING, [kom-ahnd'-ing], *adj.* having command over, chief; having a broad view; overlooking; dignified, nobly striking.

COMMANDINGLY, [kom-ahnd'-ing-li], *adv.* in commanding fashion.

COMMANDMENT, [kom-ahnd'-ment], *n.* a solemn command; a holy law, one of the clauses in the Decalogue formulated by Moses. [OFr. *commandement*].

COMMANDO, [kom-ahnd'-ō], *n.* a body of irregular troops, *esp.* a body of armed Boers in the South African War; a small, mobile, independent body of special service troops; a member of such a body. [Portug. *commando*].

COMMANDRY, see COMMANDERY.

COMMARK, [kom'-ahk], *n.* a frontier. [Sp. *comarca*].

COMMATERIAL, [kom'-at-ēer'-i-al], *adj.* of the same substance.

COMMATIC, [kom-at'-ik], *adj.* having short clauses or sentences. [Gk. *kommatikos*].

COMMATISM, [kom'-at-izm], *n.* literary concision or abruptness. [Fr. *commatisme*].

COMMEASURABLE, [kom-ezh'-er-abl], *adj.* commensurable.

COMMEMORABLE, [kom-em'-or-abl], *adj.* fitting for commemoration. [L. *commemorabilis*].

COMMEMORATE, [kom-em'-or-āt], *v.t.* to call to remembrance some act or person by a memorial or a celebration; to perpetuate, honour the memory of, something. [L. *commemorare*].

COMMEMORATION, [kom-em'-or-ā'-shun], *n.* the act of commemorating, a ceremony in honour and memory of something or someone. [L. *commemoratio*].

COMMEMORATIVE, [kom-em'-or-at-iv], *adj.* serving to commemorate.

COMMEMORATORY, [kom-em'-or-a-ter-i], *adj.* commemorative.

COMMENCE, [kom-ens'], *v.t. and i.* begin, initiate; start. [Fr. *commencer*].

COMMENCEMENT, [kom-ens'-ment], *n.* the beginning, start, origin; the time of a beginning. [OFr. *comencement*].

COMMEND, [kom-end'], *v.t.* to entrust, commit; to recommend; to praise, express appreciation of; to send one's good wishes to. [L. *commendare* recommend].

COMMENDABLE, [kom'-end-abl], *adj.* able to be commended.

COMMENDABLENESS, [kom-end'-abl-nes], *n.* the quality of being commendable.

COMMENDABLY, [kom'-end-ab-li], *adv.* in commendable fashion.

COMMENDATION, [kom'-end-ā'-shun], *n.* the act of commending; recommendation, praise. [L. *commendatio*].

COMMENDATORY, [kom'-end-ā'-ter-i], *adj.* commending. [LL. *commendatorius*].

COMMENSAL (1), [kom-en'-sal], *n.* (*biol.*) an organism living on the food of another without being a parasite; a fellow diner.

COMMENSAL (2), [kom-en'-sal], *adj.* living on the food of another; dining at the same table. [MedL. *commensalis*].

COMMENSALISM, [kom-en'-sal-izm], *n.* the habit or condition of being commensal.

COMMENSURABILITY, [kom-en'-sher-ab-il'-i-ti], *n.* the quality of being commensurable.

COMMENSURABLE, [kom-en'-sher-abl], *adj.* in proportion, able to be measured by the same standard. [L. *commensurabilis*].

COMMENSURABLENESS, [kom-en'-sher-abl-nes], *n.* commensurability.

COMMENSURABLY, [kom-en'-sher-ab-li], *adv.* in commensurable fashion.

COMMENSURATE, [kom-en'-sher-at], *adj.* commensurable, in just accordance with, corresponding. [L. *commensuratus*].

COMMENSURATELY, [kom-en'-sher-at-li], *adv.* in commensurate fashion.

COMMENSURATENESS, [kom-en'-sher-at-nes], *n.* the quality of being commensurate.

COMMENSURATION, [kom-ens'-yōō-rā'-shun], *n.* commensurateness; the measuring of things against each other. [L. *commensuratio*].

COMMENT (1), [kom'-ent], *n.* a critical remark, an observation on something; an editorial note explaining some difficulty or obscurity in a text. [L. *commentum*].

COMMENT (2), [kom'-ent], *v.i.* to make a comment on something; to utter an observation, notice something.

COMMENTARY, [kom'-en-tri], *n.* critical comments on a text, often published as an independent work; a continuous series of observations on some happening. [L. *commentarium*].

COMMENTATE, [kom'-en-tāt], *v.t. and i.* to make comments on, annotate; to give a running commentary on.

COMMENTATION, [kom'-ent-ā'-shun], *n.* the making of a commentary. [L. *commentatio*].

COMMENTATIVE, [kom-ent'-at-iv], *adj.* relating to commentation.

COMMENTATOR, [kom'-ent-ā'-ter], *n.* one who commentates.

COMMENTATORIAL, [kom'-ent-at-aw'-ri-al], *adj.* relating to the function of a commentator.

COMMENTITIOUS, [kom'-en-tish'-us], *adj.* fictitious, imaginary. [L. *commenticius*].

COMMERCE, [kom'-urs], *n.* trade (on a large scale), the exchange of goods and the organization of such exchange; **Chamber of C.,** a body set up to foster and organize trade in a district. [L. *commercium*].

COMMERCIAL (1), [kom-ur'-shal], *n.* (*coll.*) a commercial traveller.

COMMERCIAL (2), [kom-ur'-shal], *adj.* relating to, characteristic of, commerce or business, run on business lines; **c. traveller,** one employed in arranging the sale of a manufacturer's products to tradesmen.

COMMERCIALISM, [kom-ur'-shal-izm], *n.* an outlook based purely upon motives of commerce.

COMMERCIALIST, [kom-ur'-shal-ist], *n.* one who is actuated by commercialism.

COMMERCIALIZE, [kom-ur'-shal-iz], *v.t.* to make into a matter of business; to make some uneconomic scheme or product a commercial possibility.

COMMERCIALLY, [kom-ur'-shal-i], *adv.* in commerce, from a commercial standpoint.

COMMERGE, [kom-urj'], *v.i.* to merge, coincide.

COMMIGRATE, [kom'-mi-grāt], *v.i.* to migrate in a group.

COMMINATION, [kom'-in-ā'-shun], *n.* a threatening of punishment, *esp.* of God's vengeance on the wicked; **c. service,** a service held by the Church of England on Ash Wednesday, threatening divine punishment of sinners. [L. *comminatio*].

COMMINATORY, [kom-in'-at-er-i], *adj.* threatening, denouncing.

COMMINGLE, [kom-in'-gl], *v.t. and i.* to mix, mingle together; to merge.

COMMINUIBLE, [kom-in'-ew'-ibl], *adj.* able to be comminuted.

COMMINUTE, [kom'-in-ewt], *v.t.* to reduce to powder, break into parts; **a comminuted fracture,** a fracture in which the bone is broken into fragments. [L. *comminuere*].

COMMINUTION, [kom'-in-ew'-shun], *n.* the act of comminuting. [L. *comminutio*].

COMMISERABLE, [kom-iz'-er-abl], *adj.* deserving pity.

COMMISERATE, [kom-iz'-er-āt], *v.t. and i.* to sympathize, to express or feel pity or sorrow at, deplore. [L. *commiserari*].

COMMISERATION, [kom-iz'-er-ā'-shun], *n.* the act of commiserating; pity, sympathy. [L. *commiseratio*].

COMMISERATIVE, [kom-iz'-er-at-iv], *adj.* relating to commiseration.

COMMISERATIVELY, [kom-iz'-er-at-iv-li], *adv.* in commiserative fashion.

COMMISERATOR, [kom-iz'-er-ā'-tor], *n.* one who commiserates.

COMMISSAR, [kom'-is-ah(r)'], *n.* a commissioner; a Soviet state official. [COMMISSARY].

COMMISSARIAL, [kom'-is-āer'-i-al], *adj.* relating to a commissar or commissary.

COMMISSARIAT, [kom'-is-āer'-i-at], *n.* (*milit.*) that section of an army in charge of the rations and food supplies; the supplies themselves. [Fr. *commissariat*].

COMMISSARY, [kom'-is-er-i], *n.* a commissioner, one to whom an office, duty or special responsibility has been delegated; (*eccles.*) a bishop's delegate, having authority in his absence; †(*milit.*) an officer in charge of food supplies. [LL. *commissarius*].

COMMISSARYSHIP, [kom'-is-er-i-ship'], *n.* the office of a commissary.

COMMISSION (1), [kom-ish'-un], *n.* the act of committing; a warrant, a written authority permitting and enjoining the execution of some office, *esp.* that of an officer in the armed forces; the rank of officers generally; a body set up to conduct an enquiry and issue a report; authority to act on behalf of another, *esp.* to make purchases or conclude deals, etc.; an agreed percentage paid as recompense for such action; **to put into c.**, to make a naval vessel ready for sea; **c. agent**, a bookmaker. [L. *commissio*].

COMMISSION (2), [kom-ish'-un], *v.t.* to grant a commission to, instruct someone to act on one's behalf; to authorize the fitting out of a warship.

COMMISSIONAIRE, [kom-ish'-un-āer], *n.* a uniformed door-keeper; a member of the corps of ex-soldiers organized for such duties. [Fr. *commissionaire*].

COMMISSIONAL, [kom-ish'-un-al], *adj.* appointing or appointed by commission.

COMMISSIONARY, [kom-ish'-un-er-i], *adj.* commissional.

COMMISSION-DAY, [kom-ish'-un-dā'], *n.* the opening day of assizes, on which the judge's commission is read aloud.

COMMISSIONED, [kom-ish'-und], *adj.* holding, appointed by, a commission.

COMMISSIONER, [kom-ish'-un-er], *n.* a person acting under a commission; a local governor in certain colonies; a high administrative official of the Indian Civil Service; a member of a commission. **High C.**, the London representative of a Dominion. [MedL. *commissionarius*].

COMMISSION-MERCHANT, [kom-ish'-un-mur'-chant], *n.* a merchant who transacts business on commission.

COMMISSIVE, [kom-is'-iv], *adj.* committing.

COMMISSURAL, [kom-ish'-ōōer-al], *adj.* of, or pertaining to, a commissure. [L. *commissuralis*].

COMMISSURE, [kom'-ish-ew'-er], *n.* (*anat.*) the junction of two parts of the body, a suture; the line formed by the closing of the lips or eyelids, the corner of the lips or eyelids when closed; (*bot.*) the junction of the carpels in umbelliferous plants. [L. *commissura* joint].

COMMISSURE

COMMIT, (**committing, committed**), [kom-it'], *v.t.* to entrust, give to someone's charge, to commend to keeping; to pledge, to engage (oneself) irretrievably; to do; to perform (a wicked action); to send to prison; (*leg.*) to send for trial before a superior court. [L. *committere* to join].

COMMITMENT, [kom-it'-ment], *n.* the act of committing; an undertaking, pledge or monetary obligation to which one is committed.

COMMITTABLE, [kom-it'-abl], *adj.* liable to be committed (to prison); (of an offence) rendering the one who commits it liable to trial.

COMMITTAL, [kom-it'-al], *n.* the act of committing.

COMMITTEE, [kom-it'-i], *n.* a body of persons set up to examine and report on some problem and present their conclusions to the person or group that appointed them; the governing body of a club or society. [Fr. *comité*].

COMMITTEE-MAN, [kom-it'-i-man'], *n.* a member of a committee, one addicted to committees.

COMMITTEE-ROOM, [kom-it'-i-rōōm'], *n.* a room where a committee meets.

COMMITTEESHIP, [kom-it'-i-ship], *n.* the office of a committee.

COMMITTER, [kom-it'-er], *n.* one who commits.

COMMITTOR, [kom-it'-er], *n.* a magistrate who commits a minor or insane person to the care of others.

COMMIX, [kom-iks'], *v.t.* (*archaic*) to mix together, to mingle.

COMMIXTURE, [kom-iks'-cher], *n.* the act of mixing; the state of being mixed; the substance or solution formed by mixing. [L. *commixtura*].

COMMODATE, [kom'-od-āt], *n.* (*leg.*) a free loan to be returned intact by the borrower. [L. *commodatum*].

COMMODE, [kom-ōd'], *n.* a chamber-pot; a chest of drawers. [Fr. from L. *commodus* suitable].

COMMODIOUS, [kom-ōd'-i-us], *adj.* roomy, ample in space. [L. *commodiosus*].

COMMODIOUSLY, [kom-ōd'-i-us-li], *adv.* in commodious fashion.

COMMODIOUSNESS, [kom-ōd'-i-us-nes], *n.* the condition of being commodious.

COMMODITY, [kom-od'-i-ti], *n.* merchandise, something for sale; (*pl.*) (*econ.*) goods in which direct dealings can be made. [L. *commoditas*].

COMMODORE, [kom'-od-aw(r)], *n.* a naval courtesy title given to a captain performing special duties, or acting in seniority to others of the same rank; the captain of a yacht squadron or a merchant fleet. [LL. *commandator*].

COMMON (1), [kom'-un], *n.* a piece of land open to all, and on which certain tenants have grazing rights; (*pl.*) the common people; the lower elective House in the British Parliament; **on short commons**, on a restricted diet.

COMMON (2), [kom'-un], *adj.* shared by two or more, not private; open to or related to all; undertaken by, affecting the whole of a group; plentiful, widespread, regularly happening, familiar; ordinary, nondescript; of low birth; vulgar, ill-bred, coarse; cheap, shoddy; in bad taste; **a c. noun**, (*gram.*) a name applicable to any single one of a group ; **a c. room**, a living-room shared at a school or university; **c. sense**, good sense, normal understanding, sensible self-interest; **c. serjeant**, a judge in the City of London. [L. *communis*].

COMMONABLE, [kom'-un-abl], *adj.* held in common; permitted to be pastured on common land.

COMMONAGE, [kom'-un-ij], *n.* the right of pasturing on a common; the use of something in common; the common people.

COMMONALTY, COMMONALITY, [kom'-un-al-ti, kom'-un-al'-i-ti], *n.* the common people. [MedL. *communalitas*].

COMMONER, [kom'-un-er], *n.* one of the common people, one without hereditary rank; one with a right in a common.

COMMONEY, [kom'-un-i], *n.* a clay playing-marble.

COMMONITION, [kom'-un-ish'-un], *n.* a formal admonition. [L. *commonitio*].

COMMONITIVE, [kom-on'-it-iv], *adj.* warning, monitory.

COMMONITORY (1), [kom-on'-it-er-i], *n.* a warning.

COMMONITORY (2), [kom-on'-it-er-i], *adj.* warning. [L. *commonitorius*].

COMMONLY, [kom'-un-li], *adv.* usually.

COMMONNESS, [kom'-un-nes], *n.* the quality of being common.

COMMONPLACE (1), [kom'-un-plās], *n.* a trite and platitudinous remark.

COMMONPLACE (2), [kom'-un-plās], *adj.* ordinary, common, unremarkable, happening frequently, trite.

COMMONPLACE-BOOK, [kom'-un-plās-bōōk'], *n.* a note-book for recording other people's thoughts and observations.

COMMONPLACENESS, [kom'-un-plās-nes], *n.* the property of being commonplace.

COMMON PLEAS, [kom'-un-plēz'], *n.* civil legal actions; **Court of C.**, a former court for trying civil cases.

COMMONTY, [kom'-un-ti], *n.* land shared in common; a common. [OFr. *comuneté*].

COMMONWEAL, [kom'-un-wēl], *n.* the public good, the common profit.

COMMONWEALTH, [kom'-un-welth], *n.* the state, a political community or union; the protectorate under Cromwell; the Federated States of Australia.

COMMONWEALTHSMAN, [kom'-un-welths-man], *n.* a supporter of the commonwealth.

COMMORANCE, [kom'-er-ans], *n.* (*leg.*) residence, domicile. [~L. *commorari* to stay].

COMMORANCY, [kom'-er-an-si], *n.* commorance.

COMMORANT, [kom'-er-ant], *adj.* (*leg.*) ordinarily residing (at), domiciled.

COMMORATION, [kom'-or-ā'-shun], *n.* a tarrying. [L. *commoratio*].

COMMORIENT, [kom-aw'-ri-ent], *adj.* (*astrol.*) dying at exactly the same time as another. [L. *commoriens*].

COMMOTION, [kom-ō'-shun], *n.* agitation, disturbance, uproar, violent stir. [L. *commotio* violent movement].

COMMOVE, [kom-ōōv'], *v.t.* to stir up, excite, incite, rouse to passion. [Fr. *commouvoir*].

COMMUNAL, [kom'-yōōn-al], *adj.* relating to common ownership; shared by others; relating to a commune; public. [LL. *communalis*].

COMMUNALISM, [kom'-yo͞on-al-izm], *n.* government by local communes.

COMMUNALIST, [kom'-yo͞on-al-ist], *n.* a supporter of communalism.

COMMUNALISTIC, [kom'-yo͞on-al-is'-tik], *adj.* pertaining to communalism.

COMMUNARD, [kom'-yo͞on-ahd], *n.* a supporter of the Paris Commune of 1871. [Fr. *communard*].

COMMUNE (1), [kom'-yo͞on], *n.* a local French administrative division under the direction of a mayor and council; the democratic movement that controlled Paris for part of 1871. [L. *communis*].

COMMUNE (2), [kom-ewn'], *v.i.* to talk quietly and intimately with a person, to be in close spiritual contact (with). [L. *communicare*].

COMMUNICABILITY, [kom-ewn'-ik-ab-il'-i-ti], *n.* the quality of being communicable.

COMMUNICABLE, [kom-ewn'-ik-abl], *adj.* able to be communicated. [L. *communicabilis*].

COMMUNICABLENESS, [kom-ewn'-ik-abl-nes], *n.* communicability.

COMMUNICABLY, [kom-ewn'-ik-ab-li], *adv.* in communicable fashion.

COMMUNICANT (1), [kom-ewn'-ik-ant], *n.* (*eccles.*) one who receives Holy Communion; one who communicates.

COMMUNICANT (2), [kom-ewn'-ik-ant], *adj.* communicating, linking. [L. *communicans*].

COMMUNICATE, [kom-ewn'-ik-āt], *v.t. and i.* to impart, pass on or transmit a message, information, etc.; to exchange ideas or information with, be in touch with; to have access to, be connected (with); to take Holy Communion. [L. *communicare*].

COMMUNICATION, [kom-ewn'-ik-ā'-shun], *n.* the act of communicating; the thing communicated; the means of communicating; (*pl.*) (*milit.*) the means of connexion between an army and its base for the replenishment of supplies; **c. cord**, chain passing through all compartments of a railway train which, when pulled, operates the brake in an emergency. [L. *communicatio*].

COMMUNICATIVE, [kom-ewn'-ik-at-iv], *adj.* ready or eager to communicate.

COMMUNICATIVENESS, [kom-ewn'-ik-at-iv-nes], *n.* the quality of being communicative.

COMMUNICATOR, [kom-ewn'-ik-ā'-ter], *n.* one who, or that which, communicates.

COMMUNICATORY, [kom-ewn'-ik-ā'-ter-i], *adj.* useful for the communication of information.

COMMUNION, [kom-ewn'-i-on], *n.* mutual intercourse between two or more persons, fellowship, communication, mutual intercourse or spiritual contact in religious worship or doctrine; a body of Christians who have one common belief and are members of a particular church; the celebration of the Lord's Supper. [L. *communio* fellowship].

COMMUNIONIST, [kom-ewn'-i-on-ist], *n.* one of the same communion; one holding strong views about Holy Communion.

COMMUNIQUE, **communiqué**, [kom-ewn'-ik-ā], *n.* an official bulletin, or official statement on military operations. [Fr. *communiqué*].

COMMUNISM, [kom'-yo͞on-izm], *n.* the political theory of those Socialists who maintain that their objective can be obtained only by violent overthrow of capitalism and the establishment of proletarian dictatorship. [Fr. *communisme*].

COMMUNIST (1), [kom'-yo͞on-ist], *n.* a believer in communism, a militant socialist.

COMMUNIST (2), [kom'-yo͞on-ist], *adj.* pertaining to communism.

COMMUNISTIC, [kom'-yo͞on-is'-tik], *adj.* inclined, appertaining, to communism.

COMMUNITARIAN, [kom'-yo͞on-it-āer'-i-an], *n.* a member of a communist community.

COMMUNITY (1), [kom-ewn'-i-ti], *n.* a society; a group living together and linked by national, economic or social relationships or under a common religious authority; the people of a state generally, the public; that which is held or shared in common. [L. *communitas*].

COMMUNITY (2), [kom-ewn'-i-ti], *adj.* pertaining to a community, common to a group.

COMMUNIZATION, [kom'-ewn-iz-ā'-shun], *n.* the liquidation of private ownership.

COMMUNIZE, [kom'-yo͞on-iz], *v.t.* to transfer to public ownership, to convert to communism.

COMMUTABILITY, [kom-ewt'-ab-il'-i-ti], *n.* the quality of being commutable. [L. *commutabilitas*].

COMMUTABLE, [kom-ewt'-abl], *adj.* able to be commuted. [L. *commutabilis*].

COMMUTATION, [kom'-yo͞o-tā'-shun], *n.* the act of commuting. [L. *commutatio*].

COMMUTATIVE, [kom-ew'-tat-iv], *adj.* relating to commutation.

COMMUTATIVELY, [kom-ewt'-at-iv-li], *adv.* by way of exchange or substitution.

COMMUTATOR, [kom'-yo͞o-tā'-ter], *n.* a device for changing the direction of a current in an electric circuit.

COMMUTE, [kom-ewt'], *v.t.* to substitute; to change a mode of payment; (*leg.*) to reduce a legal sentence. [L. *commutare*].

COMMUTUAL, [kom-mewt'-yo͞o-al], *adj.* mutual, reciprocal.

COMOSE, [kō'-mōs], *adj.* (*bot.*) hairy, downy. [L. *comosus* from *coma* hair].

COMPACT (1), [kom'-pakt], *n.* an agreement, an unwritten but binding understanding. [L. *compactum*].

COMPACT (2), [kom'-pakt], *n.* face-powder, etc., enclosed in a small case, a pocket vanity case.

COMPACT (3), [kom-pakt'], *adj.* packed together, dense, firmly and neatly compressed; convenient to handle; concise, briefly comprehensive. [L. *compactum*, *p.pt.* of *compingere*].

COMPACTED, [kom-pakt'-id], *adj.* closely united, compressed together.

COMPACTEDLY, [kom-pakt'-id-li], *adv.* in compact fashion.

COMPACTEDNESS, [kom-pakt'-id-nes], *n.* the condition of being compact.

COMPACTIBLE, [kom-pakt'-ibl], *adj.* able to be joined.

COMPACTION, [kom-pak'-shun], *n.* the act of making a compact; the state or quality of being compact.

COMPACTLY, [kom-pakt'-li], *adv.* in compact fashion.

COMPACTNESS, [kom-pakt'-nes], *n.* the quality of being compact.

COMPACTURE, [kom-pak'-cher], *n.* the manner of joining; compagination. [L. *compactura* joint].

COMPAGES, [kom-pā'-jēz], *n.* a complex framework or structure. [L. *compages*].

COMPAGINATE, [kom-paj'-in-āt], *v.t.* to unite firmly. [L. *compaginare*].

COMPAGINATION, [kom-paj'-in-ā'-shun], *n.* structure, joining of parts; complex connection. [L. *compaginatio*].

COMPANION (1), [kum-pan'-yun], *n.* one who accompanies, a comrade, a familiar friend, associate; a person hired to attend, accompany and amuse an old, invalid, lonely, or bored person; a low rank in an Order of Knighthood; an exact match, the complement of one of a pair; a handbook, a guide. [OFr. *compainon*].

COMPANION (2), [kum-pan'-yun], *n.* the shelter over a stairway on a ship; **c. hatch**, an opening leading from the deck to cabins below; **c. ladder**, the ladder by which officers reach the quarter-deck; **c. way**, the staircase descending to the cabins. [It. *compagna* store-room].

COMPANION (3), [kum-pan'-yun], *adj.* matching, completing a pair or set of objects.

COMPANION (4), [kum-pan'-yun], *v.t.* to be companion to.

COMPANIONABLE, [kum-pan'-yun-abl], *adj.* sociable, friendly, making a good companion.

COMPANIONABLY, [kum-pan'-yun-ab-li], *adv.* in companionable fashion.

COMPANIONLESS, [kum-pan'-yun-les], *adj.* without a companion.

COMPANIONSHIP, [kum-pan'-yun-ship], *n.* fellowship, the state of being companions, association; the status of companion in an order of knighthood; (*print.*) a group of compositors working together.

COMPANY, [kum'-pan-i], *n.* a group of people gathered together in companionship, a gathering of persons with a common bond; the qualities that make a person a (pleasant) companion; the quality of being entertaining socially or to oneself personally; an association of persons for business purposes; a ship's crew; a group of actors working together under common management; (*milit.*) a sub-division of a battalion; **to keep c. with**, to associate habitually with. [LL. *compania*].

COMPARABLE, [kom'-per-abl], *adj.* able to be compared, having some affinity with, within measurable similarity. [L. *comparabilis*].

COMPARABLY, [kom'-per-ab-li], *adj.* in a comparable manner.

COMPARATES, [kom'-per-ats], *n.*(*pl.*) (*log.*) two things or ideas that may be compared.

COMPARATIVE, [kum-pa'-rat-iv], *adj.* based on, related to, judged by, comparison; qualified from the point of comparisons, relative; that compares; **c. degree**, (*gram.*) the form of an adjective or adverb denoting a higher degree than the positive. [L. *comparativus*].

COMPARATIVELY, [kum-pa'-rat-iv-li], *adv.* in a comparative manner.

COMPARE (1), [kum-pāer'], *n.* comparison.

COMPARE (2), [kum-pāer'], *v.t. and i.* to examine things in relation to each other, to examine things in respect of their similarities; to note the resemblance between things; to be similar, resemble; to be worthy of comparison. [L. *comparare*].

COMPARISON, [kum-pa'-ris-un], *n.* the act of comparing; state of being compared; relative resemblance, closeness of degree between persons or objects; the degree of similarity, possibility of comparing two objects; an expression which compares two or more things. [L. *comparatio*].

COMPART, [kom-paht'], *v.t.* to lay out according to a plan. [L. *compartiri* to divide and share].

COMPARTITION, [kom'-pah-tish'-un], *n.* the act of dividing into parts; the part divided, a single part. [L. *compartitio*].

COMPARTMENT, [kum-paht'-ment], *n.* a division or separate part partitioned off; one of the separate units which make up a railway coach; the part of a parliamentary bill for which a limit of time is allowed. [LL. *compartimentum*].

COMPASS (1), [kum'-pas], *n.* circumference, encircling boundary; extent, span, range, reasonable or inevitable limit; an instrument containing a needle sensitive to the magnetic pole and used to find direction; (*pl.*) an instrument, pivoting on a fixed leg, used for describing arcs and circles. [LL. *compassus* from L. *passus* step].

COMPASS (2), [kum'-pas], *v.t.* to extend round, enclose, surround; to plot, plan, devise (some wicked act). [Fr. *compasser* to measure].

COMPASSABLE, [kum'-pas-abl], *adj.* that may be compassed.

COMPASS-BOX, [kum'-pas-boks'], *n.* the container of a mariner's compass; a case for a compass.

COMPASS-CARD, [kum'-pas-kahd'], *n.* the card on which the points of the compass are marked.

COMPASS-DIAL, [kum'-pas-dī'-al], *n.* a pocket sundial fitted with a compass needle.

COMPASSING, [kum'-pas-ing], *adj.* surrounding, hemming in, encompassing; arched; bringing about, causing to happen.

COMPASSION, [kom-pash'-un], *n.* pity mingled with kindness, sympathy and wish to alleviate suffering or distress. [L. *compassio*].

COMPASSIONATE (1), [kom-pash'-un-at], *adj.* inclined to compassion, showing pity and mercy; granted without legal obligation, on grounds of compassion.

COMPASSIONATE (2), [kom-pash'-un-āt], *v.t.* to take compassion on.

COMPASSIONATELY, [kom-pash'-un-at-li], *adv.* in compassionate fashion.

COMPASSIONATENESS, [kom-pash'-un-at-nes], *n.* the quality of being compassionate.

COMPASS-NEEDLE, [kum'-pas-nēdl'], *n.* the magnetized needle of a compass.

COMPASS-PLANE, [kum'-pas-plān'], *n.* a plane with a rounded bottom for planing concave surfaces.

COMPASS-PLANT, [kum'-pas-plahnt'], *n.* (*bot.*) the prickly lettuce, *Lactuca Scariola*, which turns its leaves to north and south.

COMPASS-SAW, [kum'-pas-saw'], *n.* a narrow saw designed for cutting curves.

COMPASS-SIGNAL, [kum'-pas-sig'-nal], *n.* a flag signal indicating the points of the compass.

COMPASS-TIMBER, [kum'-pas-tim'-ber], *n.* curved beams.

COMPASS-WINDOW, [kum'-pas-win'-dō], *n.* a bow-window.

COMPATERNITY, [kom'-pat-urn'-i-ti], *adj.* godfathership. [L. *compater* godfather].

COMPATIBILITY, [kun-pat'-ib-il'-i-ti], *n.* the quality of being compatible.

COMPATIBLE, [kum-pat'-ibl], *adj.* congruous, suitable; agreeing with, circumstantially feasible or natural; able to live or get on with someone. [MedL. *compatibilis*].

COMPATIBLENESS, [kum-pat'-ibl-nes], *n.* compatibility.

COMPATIBLY, [kum-pat'-ib-li], *adv.* in compatible fashion.

COMPATRIOT (1), [kum-pat'-ri-ot], *n.* a fellow-countryman. [Fr. *compatriote*].

COMPATRIOT (2), [kum-pat'-ri-ot], *adj.* of the same country.

COMPEER, [kom-pēer'], *n.* an equal, an associate, a companion. [L. *compar* equal to another].

COMPEL, (**compelling**, **compelled**), [kom-pel'], *v.t.* to force, to make someone do something, to bring about by force. [L. *compellere* to drive together].

COMPELLABLE, [kom-pel'-abl], *adj.* able to be compelled.

COMPELLABLY, [kom-pel'-ab-li], *adv.* by compulsion.

COMPELLATION, [kom'-pel-ā'-shun], *n.* the addressing of a person by some style or title; the title or form of address itself. [L. *compellare* to accost].

COMPELLATIVE, [kom-pel'-at-iv], *n. and adj.* (pertaining to) compellation.

COMPELLINGLY, [kom-pel'-ing-li], *adv.* in compelling fashion.

COMPEND, [kom-pend'], *n.* a compendium.

COMPENDIOUS, [kom-pend'-i-us], *adj.* concisely comprehensive, containing a great volume of necessary information in extremely compact form. [L. *compendiosus* abridged].

COMPENDIOUSLY, [kom-pend'-i-us-li], *adv.* in compendious fashion.

COMPENDIOUSNESS, [kom-pend'-i-us-nes], *n.* the state of being compendious.

COMPENDIUM, (*pl.* **compendiums** or **compendia**), [kom-pend'-i-um], *n.* a comprehensive but compact summary of all relevant information. [L. *compendium* a weighing together].

COMPENSABLE, [kom-pens'-abl], *adj.* able to be compensated.

COMPENSATE, [kom'-pen-sāt], *v.t. and i.* to recompense for a loss or injury, *esp.* by monetary payment, to give something of equal value to make amends for some loss for which one is to blame; (*mech.*) to counterbalance a variation. [L. *compensare* to weigh together].

COMPENSATION, [kom'-pen-sā'-shun], *n.* the act of compensating; the thing given to make amends for some loss or injury; (*psych.*) the development of a physical or mental condition to compensate for some psychological disability. [L. *compensatio*].

COMPENSATIVE, [kom'-pen-sā'-tiv], *adj.* compensatory.

COMPENSATOR, [kom'-pen-sā-ter], *n.* one who, or that which, compensates.

COMPENSATORY, [kom'-pen-sā'-ter-i], *adj.* making compensation, in compensation.

COMPERE, **compère**, [kom'-pāer], *n.* a person introducing the turns in a cabaret or revue. [Fr. *compère* gossip].

COMPESCE, [kom-pes'], *v.t.* to check, curb. [L. *compescere*].

COMPETE, [kom-pēt'], *v.i.* to strive against others for a common object, to rival something in quality; to take part in a test or contest of ability. [L. *competere* to strive together].

COMPETENCE, [kom'-pit-ens], *n.* the quality of being competent; ability; means or money sufficient for life. [LL. *competentia*].

COMPETENT, [com'-pit-ent], *adj.* capable, efficient; satisfactory; fitted; of sound mind; (*leg.*) having legal authority, legally capable. [L. *competens*].

COMPETENTLY, [kom'-pit-ent-li], *adv.* in competent fashion.

COMPETITION, [kom'-pit-ish'-un], *n.* the act of competing; a struggle of two or more persons for a prize; an organized contest, a public test of skill for some prize or distinction; international struggles for trade and raw materials. [L. *competitio* rivalry].

COMPETITIVE, [kom-pet'-it-iv], *adj.* relating to, by means of, competition.

COMPETITIVELY, [kom-pet'-it-iv-li], *adv.* in competitive fashion.

COMPETITOR, [kom-pet'-it-er], *n.* one engaging in competition, a rival. [L. *competitor*].

COMPETITORY, [kom-pet'-it-er-i], *adj.* engaging in competition.

COMPETITRESS, [kom-pet'-it-res], *n.* a female competitor.

COMPETITRIX, [kom-pet'-it-riks], *n.* a competitress.

COMPILATION, [kom'-pil-ā'-shun], *n.* the act or result of compiling; a book made up from other works or sources. [L. *compilatio*].

COMPILATOR, [kom'-pil-ā'-tor], *n.* a compiler.
COMPILE, [kom-pil'], *v.t.* to amass together material, *esp.* literary material, so as to produce a new work; to make out, draw up, compose, write, from various data or sources of information. [L. *compilare*].
COMPILEMENT, [kom-pil'-ment], *n.* compilation.
COMPILER, [kom-pil'-er], *n.* one who compiles.
COMPLACENCE, [kom-plās'-ens], *n.* self-satisfied serenity, contented tranquillity. [MedL. *complacentia*].
COMPLACENCY, [kom-plās'-en-si], *n.* complacence.
COMPLACENT, [kom-plās'-ent], *adj.* unruffled, feeling or showing complacence. [L. *complacens*].
COMPLACENTIAL, [kom'-plā-sen'-shal], *adj.* distinguished by complacence.
COMPLACENTLY, [kom-plā'-sent-li], *adv.* in complacent fashion.
COMPLAIN, [kom-plān'], *v.i.* to express discontent at a circumstance; to show this discontent by sounds of grief, to grumble at, find fault with; to bewail, to state that one is suffering; to make a formal accusation. [LL. *complangere*].
COMPLAINANT, [kom-plān'-ant], *n.* a complainer; (*leg.*) one who commences a legal action against an offender, a plaintiff.
COMPLAINING, [kom-plān'-ing], *n.* complaint.
COMPLAININGLY, [kom-plān'-ing-li], *adv.* in complaining fashion.
COMPLAINT, [kom-plānt'], *n.* the expression of complaining; an expression or cause of dissatisfaction; a statement of injury or grievance; ailment, illness; formal accusation. [Fr. *complainte*].
COMPLAISANCE, [kom-plās'-ans], *n.* civility, conscious courtesy, desire to oblige or appear agreeable, over-readiness to defer or comply. [Fr. *complaisance*].
COMPLAISANT, [kom-plās'-ant], *adj.* showing complaisance. [Fr. *complaisant*].
COMPLAISANTLY, [kom-plās'-ant-li], *adv.* in complaisant fashion.
COMPLAISANTNESS [kom-plās'-ant-nes], *n.* complaisance.
COMPLECT, [kom-plekt'], *v.t.* to interweave; †to embrace. [L. *complectere*].
COMPLEMENT (1), [kom'-plim-ent], *n.* that which completes or is needed to complete; (*milit. and nav.*) the full number of men to a unit or ship; (*math.*) the number of degrees by which an acute angle is less than a right angle; (*gram.*) that part which completes the meaning; (*mus.*) the interval needed to make an octave with a given interval. [L. *complementum*].
COMPLEMENT (2), [kom'-plim-ent], *v.t.* to make complete.
COMPLEMENTAL, [kom'-plim-en'-tal], *adj.* pertaining to or standing as a complement.
COMPLEMENTARY, [kom'-pli-ment'-er-i], *adj.* completing; supplying a deficiency; **c. angles**, angles whose sum equals a right angle; **c. colours**, colours which, together with a specified colour, make up white.
COMPLETE (1), [kom-plēt'], *adj.* entire, whole, lacking nothing, finished; (*coll.*) absolute, utter. [L. *completum*, *p.pt.* of *complere* fill up].
COMPLETE (2), [kom-plēt'], *v.t.* to finish, bring to an end; to make complete.
COMPLETELY, [kom-plēt'-li], *adv.* entirely, wholly, in complete fashion.
COMPLETENESS, [kom-plēt'-nes], *n.* the condition of being complete.
COMPLETION, [kom-plē'-shun], *n.* the act of completing; state of being complete. [L. *completio*].
COMPLETIVE, [kom-plē'-tiv], *adj.* completing.
COMPLETORY, [kom-plē'-ter-i], *adj.* completive.
COMPLEX (1), [kom'-pleks], *n.* a complexity, a complex confusion; (*psych.*) a confusion of repressed emotions producing a neurotic state. [L. *complexus* an embrace].
COMPLEX (2), [kom'-pleks], *adj.* complicated, intricate, composed of many interlocking parts; (*fig.*) difficult, involved; (*gram.*) **c. sentence**, a sentence containing subordinate clauses.
COMPLEXED, [kom'-plekst], *adj.* complex.
COMPLEXEDNESS, [kom-plek'-sid-nes], *n.* complexity.
COMPLEXION, [kom-plek'-shun], *n.* the colour of the face; (*fig.*) the outlook, the external prospect; a complexity; †the combination of the bodily humours determining one's nature. [L. *complexio* close connection].
COMPLEXIONAL, [kom-plek'-shun-al], *adj.* depending on or relating to the complexion.
COMPLEXIONARY, [kom-plek'-shun-er-i], *adj.* complexional.
COMPLEXITY, [kom-plek'-si-ti], *n.* the state of being complex.
COMPLEXLY, [kom-pleks'-li], *adv.* in complex fashion.
COMPLEXNESS, [kom-pleks'-nes], *n.* complexity.
COMPLEXURE, [kom-plek'-sher], *n.* the complication of something with others.
COMPLEXUS, [kom-pleks'-us], *n.* a large neck-muscle. [L. *complexus*].
COMPLIABLE, [kom-plī'-abl], *adj.* compliant.
COMPLIANCE, [kom-plī'-ans], *n.* the state of being compliant; the act of complying with.
COMPLIANT, [kom-plī'-ant], *adj.* complying, yielding, giving way, obliging, readily agreeing to. [COMPLY].
COMPLIANTLY, [kom-plī'-ant-li], *adv.* in compliant fashion.
COMPLICACY, [kom'-plik-a-si], *n.* the state of being complicated.
COMPLICATE (1), [kom'-plik-āt], *adj.* complicated; (*bot.*) conduplicate. [L. *complicatus*, *p.pt.* of *complicare* to fold].
COMPLICATE (2), [kom'-plik-āt], *v.t.* to involve, to make more complex, difficult or awkward. [*Prec.*].
COMPLICATED, [kom'-plik-ā-tid], *adj.* complex, involved, difficult, intricate; **c. fracture**, a fracture accompanied by adjacent injuries.
COMPLICATELY, [kom'-plik-āt-li], *adv.* in complicated fashion.
COMPLICATENESS, [kom'-plik-āt-nes], *n.* the condition of being complicated.
COMPLICATION, [kom'-plik-ā'-shun], *n.* act of complicating, state of being complicated; that which complicates; (*med.*) a fresh trouble arising during an illness, increasing the danger. [L. *complicatio*].
COMPLICATIVE, [kom'-plik-ā-tiv], *adj.* tending to complicate.
COMPLICITY, [kom-plis'-i-ti], *n.* the state of being an accomplice in some wrong. [Fr. *complicité*].
COMPLIER, [kom-plī'-er], *n.* one who complies readily.
COMPLIMENT (1), [kom'-pli-ment], *n.* an expression of praise or regard uttered with intention to please irrespective of its truth; a formal courtesy; (*pl.*) a polite greeting, an expression of good wishes. [Fr. *compliment*].
COMPLIMENT (2), [kom'-pli-ment], *v.t.* to utter a compliment; to praise, congratulate.
COMPLIMENTAL, [kom'-pli-ment-al'], *adj.* complimentary.
COMPLIMENTARY, [kom'-pli-ment'-er-i], *adj.* pertaining to a compliment; containing compliments; flattering, full of praise; given with the compliments of the donor.
COMPLIMENTER, [kom'-plim-ent'-er], *n.* one who pays compliments.
COMPLIN, COMPLINE, [kom'-plin], *n.* the last prayer or service of the day in the Roman Catholic Church. [OFr. *complie* from L. *completus* complete].
COMPLOT (1), [kom'-plot'], *n.* a joint plot, a conspiracy. [COM and PLOT (1)].
COMPLOT (2), (**complotting, complotted**), [kom-plot'], *v.i.* to plot together, to conspire.
COMPLOTTINGLY, [kom-plot'-ing-li], *adv.* in conspiracy.
COMPLUVIUM, [kom-ploo'-vi-um], *n.* (*antiq.*) an opening in the roof of a Roman villa to admit light and air. [L. *compluvium*].

COMPLUVIUM

COMPLY, [kom-plī'], *v.i.* to give way, yield (to a request), consent, oblige; **to c. with**, to observe, agree to. [L. *complere* to fill up].
COMPO, [kom'-pō], *n.* stucco, a kind of concrete used by plasterers. [COMPO(SITION)].
COMPONED, [kom-pōnd'], *adj.* (*her.*) formed of a row of chequered squares generally of a colour and a metal alternately. [Fr. *componé*].
COMPONENT (1), [kom-pō'-nent], *n.* a constituent, one of the elements of which a thing is composed.
COMPONENT (2), [kom-pō'-nent], *adj.* constituting, forming part of a whole, forming a component. [L. *componens*].

COMPORT, [kom-pawt'], *v.t., refl., and i.* to bear, conduct oneself; to be appropriate or suitable; to be consistent with. [L. *comportare* to bear together].

COMPORTABLE, [kom-pawt'-abl], *adj.* suitable, appropriate, consistent.

COMPORTMENT, [kom-pawt'-ment], *n.* deportment, bearing.

COMPOSE, [kom-pōz'], *v.t.* to make up, form from constituents, put together, to constitute by combining parts; (*mus.*) to create a work of music; to create any work of art or literature; to make calm; to restore the bearing or features to calmness or repose; to put in order, adjust, so as to suit the occasion; to arrange properly; (*print.*) to set up type or in type. [L. *compositum*, *p.pt.* of *componere* to put together].

COMPOSED, [kom-pōzd'], *adj.* formed by composing; calm, undisturbed.

COMPOSEDLY, [kom-pōz'-id-li], *adv.* in composed fashion.

COMPOSEDNESS, [kom-pōz'-id-nes], *n.* the condition of being composed.

COMPOSER, [kom-pōz'-er], *n.* one who composes, *esp.* music.

COMPOSING, [kom-pōz'-ing], *adj.* putting together; fitted for composing; restoring to reposeful calm; **c. frame**, (*print.*) a frame holding a printer's typecases; **c. stick**, (*print.*) a receptacle of adjustable width in which type is set up in lines by the compositor.

COMPOSITAE, [kom-poz'-it-ē], *n.*(*pl.*) (*bot.*) the largest natural order of plants, in which many small flowers are closely grouped to form a single flowerhead as in the dandelion, etc. [L. (*plantae*) *compositae*].

COMPOSITE (1), [kom'-poz-it], *n.* that which is composite; (*bot.*) a composite flower; a composite candle.

COMPOSITE (2), [kom'-poz-it], *adj.* made up of distinct parts; mixed; (*bot.*) of the order *Compositae*; (*math.*) capable of being divided into whole numbers other than one. [L. *compositum*, *p.pt.* of *componere* to put together].

COMPOSITION, [kom'-poz-ish'-un], *n.* the act of composing or of putting together; the thing composed; the writing of music; the music composed; an essay or other short piece of writing; the arrangement and proportion of a work of art; a compound of various substances; a settlement, an agreement to settle a debt by the payment of a proportion of the amount due, a legal compromise; (*print.*) the setting up of type. [L. *compositio* putting together].

COMPOSITIVE, [kom-poz'-it-iv], *adj.* able to compound, suitable for compounding; pertaining to composition.

COMPOSITOR, [kom-poz'-it-er], *n.* (*print.*) a typesetter. [L. *compositor* one who arranges].

COMPOSSESSOR, [kom'-poz-es'-or], *n.* a joint possessor.

COMPOSSIBILITY, [kom'-pos-i-bil'-i-ti], *n.* the possibility of co-existence.

COMPOSSIBLE, [kom-pos'-ibl], *adj.* capable of co-existence, compatible.

COMPOST (1), [kom'-post], *n.* a mixture of soil and various manures as a fertilizer; a mixture for plastering the exterior of houses; compo. [OFr. *composite*].

COMPOST (2), [kom'-post'], *v.t.* to apply compost to.

COMPOSTO, [kom-pos'-tō], *adj.* (*mus.*) compounded or doubled. [It. *composto*].

COMPOSURE, [kom-pō'-zher], *n.* calmness, severity, unruffled frame of mind.

COMPOT, see COMPOTE.

COMPOTATION, [kom'-pō-tā'-shun], *n.* the act of drinking together.

COMPOTE, COMPOT, [kom'-pōt], *n.* fruit stewed or preserved in syrup; a fruit or cake dish. [Fr. *compôte*].

COMPOUND (1), [kom'-pound], *n.* a compound substance, something compounded; (*chem.*) a substance containing chemically united elements.

COMPOUND (2), [kom'-pownd], *n.* the fenced-in ground round a dwelling-place or factory in India, China, etc. [Malay *kampung* village quarter].

COMPOUND (3), [kom'-pownd], *adj.* made up of several elements, not simple; **c. interest**, interest accumulating on to interest; **c. householder**, a householder whose rent includes his rates; **c. quantity**, a quantity composed of several simple quantities connected by a mathematical sign, as (*a-b*); **c. word**, a word made up of two or more separate words.

COMPOUND (4), [kom-pound'], *v.t. and i.* to bring together different elements to form a compound substance; to make a mixture; to settle by mutual agreement or composition; (*leg.*) to overlook an offence for gain; to come to a composition. [L. *componere*].

COMPOUNDABLE, [kom-pownd'-abl], *adj.* able to be compounded.

COMPOUNDER, [kom-pound'-er], *n.* one who compounds, *esp.* crime or debt.

COMPRADOR, [kom'-prahd-or'], *n.* native middleman or agent employed in the Far East by a European firm. [Portug. *comprador* from L. *comparator*].

COMPRECATION, [kom'-prik-ā'-shun], *n.* a joint prayer. [MedL. *comprecatio*].

COMPREHEND, [kom'-pri-hend'], *v.t.* to include, to contain within a bound or scope; to understand. [L. *comprehendere* to seize].

COMPREHENSIBLE, [kom'-pri-hen'-sibl], *adj.* able to be comprehended.

COMPREHENSIBLENESS, [kom'-pri-hen'-siblnes], *n.* the quality of being comprehensible.

COMPREHENSIBLY, [kom'-pri-hen'-sib-li], *adv.* in comprehensible fashion.

COMPREHENSION, [kom'-pri-hen'-shun], *n.* the act or power of comprehending, intellectual capacity. [L. *comprehensio* perception].

COMPREHENSIVE, [kom'-pri-hen'-siv], *adj.* covering a wide range, inclusive, extensive, encyclopedic.

COMPREHENSIVELY, [kom'-pri-hen'-siv-li], *adv.* in comprehensive fashion.

COMPREHENSIVENESS, [kom'-pri-hen'-siv-nes], *n.* the quality of being comprehensive.

COMPRESS (1), [kom'-pres], *n.* (*surg.*) a pad of wet material held down by a bandage.

COMPRESS (2), [kom-pres'], *v.t.* to press together, bring pressure on to, constrict, crush into a small space, condense. [L. *compressum*, *p.pt.* of *comprimere* squeeze together].

COMPRESSED, [kom-prest'], *adj.* pressed together; (*fig.*) made concise, condensed.

COMPRESSIBILITY, [kom'-pres-ib-il'-i-ti], *n.* the quality of being compressible.

COMPRESSIBLE, [kom-pres'-ibl], *adj.* able to be compressed.

COMPRESSIBLENESS, [kom-pres'-ibl-nes], *n.* compressibility.

COMPRESSION, [kom-presh'-un], *n.* the act of compressing, the state of being compressed; (*motoring*) the condition of a petrol engine in regard to its efficiency in holding the explosive gas when compressed in the cylinder by the piston; (*fig.*) conciseness. [L. *compressio*].

COMPRESSIONAL, [kom-presh'-un-al], *adj.* relating to compression.

COMPRESSION-TAP, [kom-presh'-un-tap'], *n.* a tap in a motor-engine by which the compressed gas can escape from the cylinder-head to reduce compression.

COMPRESSIVE, [kom-pres'-iv], *adj.* tending to, able to compress.

COMPRESSOR, [kom-pres'-or], *n.* an apparatus for compressing air; anything used to compress.

COMPRESSURE, [kom-presh'-er], *n.* compression.

COMPRISAL, [kom-priz'-al], *n.* the act of comprising, the sum of things comprised.

COMPRISE, [kom-priz'], *v.t.* to contain, to be made up of, consist of. [Fr. *compris*, *p.pt.* of *comprendre* from L. *comprehendere*].

COMPROBATION, [kom'-prob-ā'-shun], *n.* joint attestation or approbation. [MedL. *comprobatio*].

COMPROMISE (1), [kom'-prom-iz], *n.* an agreement in which the parties make mutual concessions for the sake of settlement, a decision endeavouring to make the best of incompatibles. [L. *compromissum*].

COMPROMISE (2), [kom'-prom-iz], *v.t. and i.* to come to agreement by compromise; to throw into danger by careless folly; to bring under suspicion, *esp.* of illicit sexual intercourse. [*Prec.*].

COMPROVINCIAL, [kom'-prov-in'-shal], *n.* (*eccles.*) one belonging to the same province or archiepiscopal jurisdiction.

COMPTOIR, [kompt'-wahr], *n.* a cash-desk; a counting house. [Fr. *comptoir*].

COMPTOMETER, [komp-tom'-it-er], *n.* a calculating machine. [Fr. *compter* to count and METER].

COMPTROLLER, see CONTROLLER.

COMPULSATIVE, [kom-pul'-sat-iv], *adj.* compulsory.

COMPULSATIVELY, [kom-pul'-sat-iv-li], *adv.* by compulsion.

COMPULSATORY†, [kom-pul'-sat-er-i], *adj.* compulsative.

COMPULSION, [kom-pul'-shun], *n.* the act of compelling; force, constraint. [L. *compulsio*].

COMPULSIVE, [kom-pul'-siv], *adj.* compelling.

COMPULSIVELY, [kom-pul'-siv-li], *adv.* in compulsive fashion.

COMPULSIVENESS, [kom-pul'-siv-nes], *n.* the quality of being compulsive.

COMPULSORILY, [kom-pul'-ser-i-li], *adv.* in compulsory fashion.

COMPULSORY, [kom-pul'-ser-i], *adj.* coercive, compelling; that must be made or performed, enforced by compulsion.

COMPUNCTION, [kom-pungk'-shun], *n.* scruple; impulse to show mercy; moral qualm or hesitation in regard to a wrong; prick of conscience. [L. *compunctio*].

COMPUNCTIONLESS, [kom-pungk'-shun-les], *adj.* without compunction.

COMPUNCTIOUS, [kom-pungk'-shus], *adj.* feeling, inducing compunction.

COMPUNCTIOUSLY, [kom-pungk'-shus-li], *adv.* with compunction.

COMPUNCTIVE†, [kom-pungk'-tiv], *adj.* compunctious.

COMPURGATION†, [kom'-pur-gā'-shun], *n.* (*leg.*) the exculpation of someone charged with an offence, by the solemn oath of others as to his innocence. [MedL. *compurgatio* purification].

COMPURGATORS†, [kom'-pur-gā-terz], *n.*(*pl.*) (*leg.*) the men who testified on oath to a man's innocence. [MedL. *compurgator*].

COMPUTABLE, [kom-pewt'-abl], *adj.* able to be computed.

COMPUTATE, [kom'-pew-tāt], *v.t.* to compute. [L. *computatum*, *p.pt.* of *computare*].

COMPUTATION, [kom'-pew-tā'-shun], *n.* the process or result of computing, a reckoning. [L. *computatio*].

COMPUTATOR, [kom'-pew-tā'-tor], *n.* a computer. [L. *computator*].

COMPUTE, [kom-pewt'], *v.t.* *and* *i.* to count, to calculate, estimate. [L. *computare*].

COMPUTER, [kom-pewt'-er], *n.* one who computes.

COMPUTIST, [kom'-pewt-ist], *n.* a computer.

COMRADE, [kom'-rād], *n.* a companion, an associate. [OFr. *camerade*].

COMRADERY, [kom'-rad-ri], *n.* jolly comradeship, hearty good-fellowship [Fr. *camaraderie*].

COMRADESHIP, [kom'-rad-ship], *n.* fellowship, friendly feeling.

COMS, [kōōmz], *n.*(*pl.*) malt-dust.

COMTISM, [kom'-tizm], *n.* (*philos.*) positivism. [A. *Comte*, a French philosopher].

COMTIST, [kom'-tist], *n.* (*philos.*) a positivist. [*Prec.*].

CON- (1), *pref.* with, together. [L. *con-* ~ *cum*].

CON (2), **(conning, conned)**, [kon], *v.t.* to study carefully, scrutinize, learn by heart. [OE. *conn* I know how to].

CON (3), **(conning, conned)**, [kon], *v.t.* to direct a ship. [L. *conducere* to guide].

CONARIUM, [kon-āer'-i-um], *n.* (*anat.*) the pineal gland. [L. from Gk. *konarion*].

CONATION, [kō-nā'-shun], *n.* the faculty of will, the volitional impulse. [L. *conatio* endeavour].

CONATIVE, [kō'-nat-iv], *adj.* pertaining to the exercise of conation.

CONATUS, [kō-nā'-tus], *n.* a natural impulse, the desire to live. [L. *conatus* endeavour].

CONCAMERATE, [kon-kam'-er-āt], *v.t.* to arch over, to vault. [L. *concameratus* arched].

CONCAMERATION, [kon'-kam-er-ā'-shun], *n.* a vaulting. [L. *concameratio*].

CONCATENATE, [kon-kat'-in-āt], *v.t.* to link together in a series, to join as in a chain. [L. *concatenare* from *catena* a chain].

CONCATENATION, [kon-kat'-in-ā'-shun], *n.* a series of links united, a series of interdependents; the act of concatenating. [L. *concatenatio*].

CONCAVE

CONCAUSE, [kon-kawz'], *n.* a co-assistant cause. [MedL. *concausa*].

CONCAVATION, [kon'-ka-vā'-shun], *n.* a making concave. [L. *concavatio*].

CONCAVE (1), [kon'-kāv], *n.* a concavity, a curving inwards.

CONCAVE (2), [kon'-kāv], *adj.* hollow, curving inwards, forming a curved hollow; (*opt.*) with the surface of a lens ground to a hollow curved profile. [L. *concavus*].

CONCAVELY, [kon-kāv'-li], *adv.* in concave fashion.

CONCAVENESS, [kon-kāv'-nes], *n.* the condition of being concave.

CONCAVITY, [kon-kav'-i-ti], *n.* hollowness; the inside surface of a hollow spherical or vaulted body. [L. *concavitas*].

CONCAVO-CONCAVE, [kon-kā'-vō-kon'-kāv], *adj.* (*opt.*) concave on both surfaces.

CONCAVO-CONVEX, [kon-kā'-vō-kon'-veks], *adj.* concave on one side and convex on the other.

CONCAVO-PLANE, [kon-kā'-vō-plān'], *adj.* (*opt.*) plane on one side and concave on the other.

CONCAVOUS, [kon-kā'-vus], *adj.* concave.

CONCEAL, [kon-sēl'], *v.t.* to hide, keep from sight or knowledge; to keep secret. [L. *concelare*].

CONCEALABLE, [kon-sēl'-abl], *adj.* able to be concealed.

CONCEALED, [kon-sēld'], *adj.* hidden, secret.

CONCEALMENT, [kon-sēl'-ment], *n.* the act of concealing; the state of being concealed; a hiding place, a disguise. [OFr. *concelement*].

CONCEDE, [kon-sēd'], *v.t.* *and* *i.* to yield, give way, admit, to grant something previously denied; to let go without resistance, to surrender without contesting. [L. *concedere*].

CONCEDENCE, [kon-sēd'-ens], *n.* the state or act of conceding. [L. *concedens*].

CONCEIT, [kon-sēt'], *n.* the state of being conceited; exaggerated self-admiration; a quaint intellectual fancy; a witty and ingenious notion. [CONCEIVE].

CONCEITED, [kon-sēt'-id], *adj.* full of self-esteem, displaying petty personal pride.

CONCEITEDLY, [kon-sēt'-id-li], *adv.* in conceited fashion.

CONCEITEDNESS, [kon-sēt'-id-nes], *n.* the state or quality of being conceited.

CONCEIVABILITY, [kon-sēv'-a-bil'-i-ti], *n.* conceivableness.

CONCEIVABLE, [kon-sēv'-abl], *adj.* imaginable, possible.

CONCEIVABLENESS, [kon-sēv'-abl-nes], *n.* the quality of being conceivable.

CONCEIVABLY, [kon-sēv'-ab-li], *adv.* in conceivable or intelligible fashion, possibly.

CONCEIVE, [kon-sēv'], *v.t.* *and* *i.* to become pregnant; to generate, to form mentally; to devise, plan, formulate; to imagine, to consider possible. [OFr. *concevre* from L. *concipere*].

CONCELEBRATE, [kon-sel'-ib-rāt], *v.t.* *and* *i.* to celebrate together, *esp.* mass.

CONCENT†, [kon-sent'], *n.* harmony, concord, singing together. [L. *concentus*].

CONCENTRATE (1), [kon'-sen-trāt], *n.* a substance in a state of concentration, *esp.* cattle food.

CONCENTRATE (2), [kon'-sen-trāt], *adj.* produced by concentration, in a state of concentration.

CONCENTRATE (3), [kon'-sen-trāt], *v.t.* to bring together in a single place and body, *esp.* to mass troops in a place; to fix one's attention, energy on a single object; (*chem.*) to intensify the strength of a substance or liquid by evaporation or purification; *v.i.* to come together round a single centre, to mass in a single place; to exercise intense mental effort, to focus all the intellect on one point; to devote oneself entirely. [CON (1) and L. *centrum* centre].

CONCENTRATION, [kon'-sen-trā'-shun], *n.* the act of concentrating; the condition of being concentrated; that which is concentrated; **c. camp**, a prison camp in which political prisoners are confined.

CONCENTRATIVE, [kon-sen'-trat-iv], *adj.* relating to concentration, that concentrates.

CONCENTRATIVENESS, [kon-sen'-trat-iv-nes], *n.* the faculty of concentration.

CONCENTRATOR, [kon'-sen-trā'-tor], *n.* a pneumatic machine used in mining to concentrate particles of ore; an apparatus for producing a concentrated substance or solution.

CONCENTRE, [kon-sen'-ter], *v.t.* *and* *i.* to gather together in a common centre; to come together for a common object. [Fr. *concentrer*].

CONCENTRIC, [kon-sen'-trik], *adj.* having a common centre. [MedL. *concentricus*].

CONCENTRICAL, [kon-sen'-trik-al], *adj.* concentric.

CONCENTRICALLY, [kon-sen'-trik-a-li], *adv.* in concentric fashion.

CONCENTRICITY, [kon'-sen-tris'-i-ti], *n.* condition of being concentric.

CONCENTUAL, [kon-sen'-chōō-al], *adj.* accordant. [L. *concentus*].

CONCEPT, [kon'-sept], *n.* an idea, an abstract or general notion. [L. *conceptum, p.pt.* of *concipere* to conceive].

CONCEPTACLE, [kon-sept'-akl], *n.* a container, a receptacle, a cavity containing the reproductive parts in certain primitive organisms. [L. *conceptaculum*].

CONCEPTIBILITY, [kon-sept'-ib-il'-i-ti], *n.* the quality of being conceivable.

CONCEPTIBLE, [kon-sept'-ibl], *adj.* conceivable.

CONCEPTION, [kon-sep'-shun], *n.* the act of conceiving; the thing conceived; (*physiol.*) the first forming of the embryo in the womb; the imaginative or creative intellectual faculty; an idea, plan, notion. [L. *conceptio*].

CONCEPTIONAL, [kon-sep'-shun-al], *adj.* conceptive.

CONCEPTIONALIST, [kon-sep'-shun-al-ist], *n.* a conceptualist.

CONCEPTIVE, [kon-sept'-iv], *adj.* pertaining to conception.

CONCEPTUAL, [kon-sep'-chōō-al], *adj.* pertaining to conception or to concepts.

CONCEPTUALISM, [kon-sep'-chōō-al-izm], *n.* (*philos.*) the medieval philosophical doctrine that universals have only subjective reality; the epistemological doctrine that the mind is capable of creating an idea corresponding to the general term.

CONCEPTUALIST, [kon-sep'-chōō-al-ist], *n.* a believer in conceptualism.

CONCERN (1), [kon-surn'], *n.* that which concerns, that which affects or is related to; anxiety; responsibility; business.

CONCERN (2), [kon-surn'], *v.t.* to relate to, to have to do with, to affect, be connected with the interests of; to disturb, cause anxiety in; to be a responsibility to; (*reflex.*) to take trouble over, show a strong interest in. [L. *concernere* to mix].

CONCERNED, [kon-surnd'], *adj.* having concern with or for, interested, anxious.

CONCERNEDLY, [kon-surn'-ed-li], *adv.* in concerned fashion.

CONCERNING, [kon-surn'-ing], *prep.* relating to.

CONCERNMENT, [kon-surn'-ment], *n.* that with which one is concerned, the state of being concerned.

CONCERT (1), [kon'-sert], *n.* concord, harmony, unison; agreement; (*specif.*) a musical entertainment in which singers or instrumentalists take part. [It. *concerto*].

CONCERT (2), [kon-surt'], *v.t.* to join together in an operation, to agree to undertake in common. [Fr. *concerter*].

CONCERTANTE, [kon'-cher-tan'-ti], *n.* (*mus.*) a musical composition for solo instruments or voices with accompaniments. [It. *concertante*].

CONCERTATION, [kon'-sert-ā'-shun], *n.* contention. [L. *concertatio*].

CONCERTED, [kon-surt'-id], *adj.* in harmony, by mutual effort, joint; (*mus.*) arranged in parts.

CONCERT-GRAND, [kon'-sert-grand'] *n.* a large grand-piano for use at concerts.

CONCERTINA, [kon'-sert-ē'-na], *n.* (*mus.*) a manual wind-instrument, the air stream being provided by bellows and controlled by the note keys on the ends. [Invented].

CONCERTINA

CONCERTO, [kon-chāer'-to], *n.* (*mus.*) a composition usually for a single instrument with orchestral accompaniment. [It. *concerto*].

CONCERT-PITCH, [kon'-sert-pich'], *n.* a musical tuning to a pitch slightly higher than normal; (*fig.*) at the top of condition.

CONCESSION, [kon-sesh'-un], *n.* the act of conceding, the thing conceded; land or privilege granted by a government, *esp.* to a foreign commercial undertaking; a grant of specially favourable terms to a customer. [L. *concessio*].

CONCESSIONAIRE, [kon-sesh'-un-āer'], *n.* the person to whom a concession has been made. [Fr. *concessionaire*].

CONCESSIONARY (1), [kon-sesh'-un-er-i], *n.* a concessionaire.

CONCESSIONARY (2), [kon-sesh'-un-er-i], *adj.* pertaining to concessions.

CONCESSIONIST, [kon-sesh'-un-ist], *n.* one advocating concession.

CONCESSIVE, [kon-ses'-iv], *adj.* relating to concession; (*gram.*) expressing concession. [L. *concessivus*].

CONCESSIVELY, [kon-ses'-iv-li], *adv.* by concession.

CONCESSORY, [kon-ses'-er-i], *adj.* concessive.

CONCETTO, [kon-chet'-ō], *n.* affected wit or conceit. [It. *concetto*].

CONCH, [kongk], *n.* a large spiral shell of the marine mollusc, *Strombus gigas*, such a shell used as a trumpet in Hindu temples, or sounded by the Tritons; (*arch.*) the vault of a semicircular apse; the apse itself. [*Next*].

CONCH

CONCHA, [kongk'-a], *n.* a conch; (*anat.*) the larger cavity of the external ear. [L. *concha* shell].

CONCHIFER, [kongk'-i-fer], *n.* a shell-bearing mollusc. [CONCH and L. *ferre* to bear].

CONCHIFEROUS, [kongk-if'-er-us], *adj.* having a shell; (*geol.*) containing shells.

CONCHITE, [kongk'-īt], *n.* a petrified shell.

CONCHITIC, [kongk-it'-ik], *adj.* (*geol.*) conchiferous.

CONCHOID, [kongk'-oid], *n.* (*math.*) a curve for finding two mean proportionals. [Gk. *kogkhoeides* shell-like].

CONCHOIDAL, [kongk'-oid-al], *adj.* (*min.*) breaking with shell-like surfaces.

CONCHOLOGICAL, [kongk'-ō-loj'-ik-al], *adj.* relating to conchology.

CONCHOLOGIST, [kongk-ol'-oj-ist], *n.* one expert in conchology.

CONCHOLOGY, [kongk-ol'-o-ji], *n.* the scientific study of shells and molluscs. [CONCH and Gk. *logos* speech].

CONCHOMETER, [kongk-om'-it-er], *n.* an instrument for measuring the spiral angle of shells. [CONCH and METER].

CONCHOMETRY, [kongk-om'-it-ri], *n.* the art of measuring shells. [CONCH and Gk. *metria* measurement].

CONCHO-SPIRAL, [kongk'-ō-spier'-al], *n.* the curve of a shell.

CONCHYLACEOUS, [kongk'-i-lā'-shus], *adj.* relating to or resembling a shell. [Gk. *konkhulion* small shell].

CONCHYLIACEOUS, [kongk'-il-i-ā'-shus'], *adj.* conchylaceous.

CONCHYLIOLOGY, [kongk'-il-i-ol'-o-ji], *n.* conchology. [*Prec.* and Gk. *logos* speech].

CONCHYLIOUS, [kongk-il'-i-us], *adj.* relating to shells.

CONCIERGE, [kon'-si-āerzh'], *n.* a hall porter, a janitor. [Fr. *concierge*].

CONCILIABLE, [kon-sil'-i-abl], *adj.* able to be conciliated.

CONCILIAR, [kon-sil'-i-er], *adj.* relating to a council *esp.* to an ecclesiastical council.

CONCILIATE, [kon-sil'-i-āt], *v.t.* to modify the hostility of, to mollify, placate, make peace between. [L. *conciliare*].

CONCILIATION, [kon-sil'-i-ā'-shun], *n.* the act or result of conciliating. [L. *conciliatio*].

CONCILIATIVE, [kon-sil'-i-at-iv], *adj.* conciliatory.

CONCILIATOR, [kon-sil'-i-ā-ter], *n.* a person who conciliates. [L. *conciliator*].

CONCILIATORINESS, [kon-si'-li-at-er-i-nes], *n.* the state or quality of being conciliatory.

CONCILIATORY, [kon-sil'-i-at-er-i], *adj.* tending to conciliate.

CONCINNITY, [kon-sin'-i-ti], *n.* polished elegance of style in literature or rhetoric. [L. *concinnitas* elegance].

CONCINNOUS, [kon-sin'-us], *adj.* (*rhet.*) elegant, fitting, harmonious. [L. *concinnus*].

CONCIPIENT, [kon-sip'-i-ent], *adj.* conceiving. [L. *concipiens*].

CONCISE, [kon-sīs'], *adj.* briefly clear and comprehensive, terse, short and to the point. [L. *concisus*].

CONCISELY, [kon-sīs'-li], *adv.* in concise fashion.

CONCISENESS, [kon-sis'-nes], *n.* the quality of being concise.
CONCISION, [kon-sizh'-un], *n.* conciseness; a division, mutilation. [L. *concisio* cutting up].
CONCITATION†, [kon'-sit-ā'-shun], *n.* mental agitation. [L. *concitatio*].
CONCLAMATION, [kon'-klam-ā'-shun], *n.* a concerted outcry. [L. *conclamatio*].
CONCLAVE, [kon'-klāv], *n.* (*R.C.*) the assembly of cardinals for a papal election; the place in which this assembly meets; any secret meeting or discussion. [L. *conclave*].
CONCLAVIST, [kon'-klav-ist], *n.* an ecclesiastic attending upon a cardinal in conclave.
CONCLUDE, [kon-klo͝od'], *v.t.* and *i.* to bring or come to an end or a decision; to finish, end; to infer, form an opinion. [L. *concludere*].
CONCLUDING, [kon-klo͝od'-ing], *adj.* finishing, completing, final.
CONCLUDINGLY, [kon-klo͝od'-ing-li], *adv.* in conclusion.
CONCLUSION, [kon-kloo'-zhun], *n.* the act of concluding; the state of being concluded, an end, finish; that which is concluded, deduction. [L. *conclusio*].
CONCLUSIONAL, [kon-kloo'-zhun-al], *adj.* relating to conclusion.
CONCLUSIVE, [kon-kloo'-siv], *adj.* bringing to a conclusion; decisive, convincing. [Fr. *conclusif*].
CONCLUSIVELY, [kon-kloo'-siv-li], *adj.* in conclusive fashion.
CONCLUSIVENESS, [kon-kloo'-siv-nes], *n.* the condition of being conclusive.
CONCLUSORY, [kon-kloo'-zer-i], *adj.* concluding.
CONCOCT, [kon-kokt'], *v.t.* to form or devise, by the mixture of various ingredients; (*fig.*) to plan, scheme. [L. *concoctum*, *p.pt.* of *concoquere* to cook together].
CONCOCTER, [kon-kokt'-er], *n.* a person who concocts.
CONCOCTION, [kon-kok'-shun], *n.* the act of concocting; that which is concocted, a mixture.
CONCOLOROUS, [kon-kul'-er-us], *adj.* of uniform colour.
CONCOMITANCE, [kon-kom'-it-ans], *n.* the state of being concomitant; (*theol.*) the complete presence of the body and blood of Christ in each of the Eucharistic elements. [MedL. *concomitantia*].
CONCOMITANCY, [kon-kom'-it-an-si], *n.* concomitance.
CONCOMITANT (1), [kon-kom'-it-ant], *n.* an attendant circumstance, an accompaniment.
CONCOMITANT (2), [kon-kom'-it-ant], *adj.* accompanying. [L. *concomitans*].
CONCOMITANTLY, [kon-kom'-it-ant-li], *adv.* as a concomitant.
CONCORD, [kon'-kawd], *n.* agreement, personal harmony, *esp.* in opinions or ideas; (*gram.*) grammatical agreement in number, person and case; (*mus.*) an harmonious combination of intervals. [L. *concordia*].
CONCORDANCE, [kon-kawd'-ans], *n.* the state of being concordant; an index of the words in a book or author's works. [L. *concordantia*].
CONCORDANCY, [kon-kawd'-an-si], *n.* agreement.
CONCORDANT, [kon-kawd'-ant], *adj.* harmonious, agreeing, in accord.
CONCORDANTLY, [kon-kawd'-ant-li], *adv.* in concordant fashion.
CONCORDAT, [kon-kawd'-at], *n.* an agreement between a temporal sovereign or government and the Pope; a compact, agreement.
CONCORDIAL, [kon-kawd'-i-al], *adj.* agreeing.
CONCORDIST, [kon-kawd'-ist], *n.* one who compiles a concordance.
CONCORPORAL, [kon-kaw'-por-al], *adj.* of the same body.
CONCORPORATE, [kon-kaw'-por-āt], *v.t.* to unite different elements into the same body.
CONCORPORATION, [kon'-kaw-por-ā'-shun], *n.* the uniting of things in one body.
CONCOURSE, [kon'-kaws], *n.* a great assembly, a vast throng; a gathering or flowing together. [L. *concursus*].
CONCREATE, [kon'-kri-āt'], *v.t.* to create together with someone else.
CONCREMATION, [kon'-kri-mā'-shun], *n.* the burning of different things together at the same time.
CONCREMENT, [kon'-kri-ment'], *n.* a mass formed by concretion.
CONCRESCENCE, [kon-kres'-ents], *n.* a coalescence of organisms. [L. *concrescentia*].
CONCRESCIBLE, [kon-kres'-ibl], *adj.* capable of growing together.
CONCRESCIVE, [kon-kres'-iv], *adj.* concrescible.
CONCRETE (1), [kon'-krēt], *n.* a mixture of sand, gravel and cement used in building; a concrete thing, a real object; **reinforced c.**, concrete strengthened with steel.
CONCRETE (2), [kon'-krēt], *adj.* formed into a solid mass, possessing mass or matter; tangible, real; particular; made of concrete; (*gram.*) denoting a material object. [L. *concretus* grown together].
CONCRETE (3), [kon-krēt'], *v.t.* and *i.* to form into a solid mass, to cause to become concrete; to surface with concrete.
CONCRETELY, [kon-krēt'-li], *adv.* in concrete fashion.
CONCRETENESS, [kon-krēt'-nes], *n.* the quality of being concrete.
CONCRETION, [kon-krē'-shun], *n.* the act of becoming concrete; the state of being concrete; a concreted mass; (*med.*) an internal stone or calculus.
CONCRETIONAL, [kon-krē'-shun-al], *adj.* concretionary.
CONCRETIONARY, [kon-krē'-shun-er-i], *adj.* pertaining to a concretion.
CONCRETIONISM, [kon-krē'-shun-izm], *n.* the belief that soul and body originate and grow together.
CONCRETIVE, [kon-krē'-tiv], *adj.* tending to concretion.
CONCUBINAGE, [kon-kew'-bin-ij], *n.* the state of being a concubine.
CONCUBINAL, [kon-kew'-bin-al], *adj.* relating to, born in, concubinage.
CONCUBINARY, [kon-kew'-bin-er-i], *adj.* concubinal.
CONCUBINE, [kon'-kew-bīn'], *n.* a woman cohabiting with a man without marriage. [L. *concubina*].
CONCULCATE, [kon'-kul-kāt], *v.t.* to tread underfoot. [L. *conculcare*].
CONCUPISCENCE, [kon-kew'-pis-ens], *n.* lust, continuous sexual desire. [L. *concupiscentia*].
CONCUPISCENT, [kon-kew'-pis-ent], *adj.* lustful. [L. *concupiscens*, *pres.pt.* of *concupiscere* to desire].
CONCUPISCIBLE, [kon-kew'-pis-ibl], *adj.* libidinous.
CONCUR, (**concurring, concurred**), [kon-kur'], *v.i.* to agree, *esp.* to assent to another's opinion or decision; to coincide, meet at a point. [L. *concurrere* to run together].
CONCURRENCE, [kon-ku'-rens], *n.* the act or state of concurring; agreement.
CONCURRENT (1), [kon-ku'-rent], *n.* something concurring, a cause acting with another.
CONCURRENT (2), [kon-ku'-rent], *adj.* agreeing, coinciding, taking place at the same time, contributory, converging. [L. *concurrens*].
CONCURRENTLY, [kon-ku'-rent-li], *adv.* in concurrent fashion.
CONCURRENTNESS, [kon-ku'-rent-nes], *n.* the condition of being concurrent.
CONCUSS, [kon-kus'], *v.t.* to shake, strike heavily; to cause concussion in. [L. *concussum*, *p.pt.* of *concutere*].
CONCUSSATION, [kon'-kus-ā'-shun], *n.* a violent shock.
CONCUSSION, [kon-kush'-un], *n.* shock, violent impact; (*med.*) an injury resulting from a heavy blow, collision, etc., *esp.* to the brain. [L. *concussio* a shaking].
CONCUSSIVE, [kon-kus'-iv], *adj.* tending to cause concussion.
CONCUTIENT, [kon-kew'-shyent], *adj.* colliding violently.
CONCYCLIC, [kon-sīk'-lik], *adj.* lying in the circumference of a circle.
CONDEMN, [kon-dem'], *v.t.* to pronounce guilty; to declare to be unfit for use; to sentence to destruction; to censure, deprecate, express disapproval of; (*leg.*) to pass sentence on. [L. *condemnare*].
CONDEMNABLE, [kon-dem'-nabl], *adj.* fit to be condemned.
CONDEMNATION, [kon'-dem-nā'-shun], *n.* the act of condemning; state of being condemned; censure. [L. *condemnatio*].
CONDEMNATORY, [kon-dem'-na-ter-i], *adj.* that condemns.
CONDEMNED, [kon-demd'], *adj.* having suffered condemnation; **c. cell**, the cell where a prisoner under sentence of death is kept.
CONDEMNEDLY, [kon-dem'-nid-li], *adv.* in condemnable fashion.

ō (bone), ī (fine), o͞o (food), o͝o (put), u (up), th (*th*ink), TH (*th*at), zh (azure), † = obsolete, ~ = related to.

CONDENSABILITY, [kon-dens'-a-bil'-i-ti], *n.* the capacity for being condensed.

CONDENSABLE, [kon-dens'-abl], *adj.* able to be condensed.

CONDENSATION, [kon'-den-sā'-shun], *n.* the act of condensing; the state of being condensed.

CONDENSATIVE, [kon-dens'-at-iv], *adj.* tending to condense.

CONDENSE, [kon-dens'], *v.t. and i.* to make dense, compact, to compress; (*phys.*) to make more dense, to change from vapour to liquid; (*fig.*) to make concise, to reduce to a few words; (*opt.*) to focus, concentrate; to become denser or more compact. [L. *condensare* to press together].

CONDENSED, [kon-denst'], *adj.* compressed, compact, terse, liquefied; **c. milk**, tinned evaporated milk.

CONDENSER, [kon-dens'-er], *n.* that which condenses; a vessel in which vapour is reduced to liquid form; (*elect.*) a device for storing an electric charge.

CONDESCEND, [kon'-di-send], *v.i.* to lower one's actions or behaviour consciously and voluntarily below one's position of superiority; to perform actions unworthy of, or beneath, one; to descend socially and deliberately to the level of an inferior. [L. *condescendere*].

CONDESCENDENCE, [kon'-dis-end'-ens], *n.* condescension.

CONDESCENDING, [kon'-dis-end'-ing], *adj.* characterized by condescension.

CONDESCENDINGLY, [kon'-dis-end'-ing-li], *adv.* in condescending fashion.

CONDESCENSION, [kon'-dis-en'-shun], *n.* the act of condescending; the display of familiarity to inferiors. [L. *condescensio*].

CONDIGN, [kon-dīn'], *adj.* appropriate, just, merited. [L. *condignus*].

CONDIGNITY, [kon-dig'-ni-ti], *n.* (*theol.*) merit, desert. [MedL. *condignitas*].

CONDIGNLY, [kon-dīn'-li], *adv.* in condign fashion.

CONDIGNNESS, [kon-dīn'-nes], *n.* the quality of being condign.

CONDIMENT, [kon'-di-ment], *n.* seasoning, highly-flavoured spices. [L. *condimentum*].

CONDIMENTAL, [kon'-di-ment'-al], *adj.* pertaining to a condiment.

CONDISCIPLE, [kon'-dis-ipl'], *n.* a fellow student. [L. *condiscipulus*].

CONDITION (1), [kon-dish'-un], *n.* the state of being, existence; the state of repair; health, physique; rank, social status; a qualification, stipulation, a limitation; a determining cause; (*pl.*) environment; (*psych.*) a factor determining behaviour, the cause producing a reflex. [L. *conditio*].

CONDITION (2), [kon-dish'-un], *v.t.* to make conditions; to bring to good health; to produce a condition; (*psych.*) to treat so that certain stimuli will produce determined reflexes.

CONDITIONAL, [kon-dish'-un-al], *adj.* depending upon conditions, qualified; (*gram.*) expressing a condition.

CONDITIONALISM, [kon-dish'-un-al-izm], *n.* the belief that survival after death depends upon the holding of the right faith.

CONDITIONALITY, [kon-dish'-un-al'-i-ti], *n.* the quality of being conditional.

CONDITIONALLY, [kon-dish'-un-a-li], *adv.* upon conditions.

CONDITIONARY, [kon-dish'-un-er-i], *adj.* conditional.

CONDITIONATE (1), [kon-dish'-un-āt], *adj.* conditional.

CONDITIONATE (2), [kon-dish'-un-āt], *v.t.* to put under conditions.

CONDITIONED, [kon-dish'-und], *adj.* limited by conditions; (*psych.*) done as an acquired reflex to certain causes; **well c.**, in good condition.

CONDITORY, [kon'-dit-er-i], *n.* a repository, container. [L. *condere* to hide].

CONDOLATORY, [kon'-dol-ā'-ter-i], *adj.* expressing condolence.

CONDOLE, [kon-dōl'], *v.t. and i.* to express sympathy with; to share the grief of another in sympathy. [L. *condolere* to suffer pain with].

CONDOLEMENT, [kon-dōl'-ment], *n.* condolence.

CONDOLENCE, [kon-dōl'-ens], *n.* an expression of sympathy and commiseration upon a cause of grief.

CONDOMINIUM, [kon'-dō-min'-yum], *n.* joint sovereignty. [CON (1) and L. *dominium* rule].

CONDONATION, [kon'-dō-nā'-shun], *n.* the act of condoning. [L. *condonatio*].

CONDONE, [kon-dōn'], *v.t.* to overlook or forgive an offence, *esp.* adultery. [L. *condonare* to pardon].

CONDOR, [kon'-daw(r)], *n.* the large South American vulture, *Sarcorhamphus gryphus*; a Chilean gold coin. [Span. *condor*].

CONDOR

CONDOTTIERE, (*pl.* **condottieri**), [kon-dot-yāer'-i], *n.* an Italian leader of mercenaries of the Renaissance period. [It. *condottiere*].

CONDUCE, [kon-dews'], *v.i.* to tend to produce, promote, bring on. [L. *conducere* bring together].

CONDUCEMENT†, [kon-dews'-ment], *n.* tendency; that which conduces.

CONDUCENT†, [kon-dews'-ent], *adj.* conducive.

CONDUCIBILITY, [kon-dews'-i-bil'-i-ti], *n.* the condition of being conducible.

CONDUCIBLE†, [kon-dews'-ibl], *adj.* conductive.

CONDUCIVE, [kon-dews'-iv], *adj.* tending to bring about, inducing.

CONDUCIVENESS, [kon-dews'-iv-nes], *n.* the quality of being conducive.

CONDUCT (1), [kon'-dukt], *n.* management, carrying out; behaviour, comportment; **a safe-c.**, a warrant granting safe passage through hostile territory. [LL. *conductus* escort].

CONDUCT (2), [kon-dukt'], *v.t.* to direct, manage, look after; to lead, guide, escort; (*mus.*) to direct and control the performance of an orchestra or choir; (*reflex.*) to behave; (*phys.*) to transmit, to allow to pass through. [L. *conductum*, *p.pt.* of *conducere* to bring together].

CONDUCTIBILITY, [kon-dukt'-ib-il'-i-ti], *n.* (*phys.*) the power of conducting electricity, heat, etc.

CONDUCTIBLE, [kon-dukt'-ibl], *adj.* able to conduct or to be conducted.

CONDUCTION, [kon-duk'-shun], *n.* conductivity; the act of conducting; (*phys.*) the transmission of heat through adjacent bodies. [L. *conductio*].

CONDUCTIVE, [kon-duk'-tiv], *adj.* able to conduct (heat, etc.).

CONDUCTIVITY, [kon'-duk-tiv'-i-ti], *n.* ability to conduct heat, electricity, etc.

CONDUCT-MONEY, [kon'-dukt-mun'-i], *n.* travelling expenses refunded to a witness in a legal case.

CONDUCTOR, [kon-duk'-tor], *n.* a guide, one who conducts, *esp.* a choir or orchestra; the attendant who collects fares and issues tickets on a bus, tram, etc.; a substance or instrument able to conduct heat, electricity, etc.; (*milit.*) a warrant officer. [LL. *conductor* carrier].

CONDUCTORSHIP, [kun-duk'-ter-ship], *n.* the position of conductor.

CONDUCTORY, [kon-duk'-ter-i], *adj.* relating to conduction.

CONDUCTRESS, [kon-duk'-tres], *n.* a female conductor.

CONDUIT, [kon'-dit], *n.* a pipe or channel to convey water or other fluid; a narrow connecting passage or channel. [Fr. *conduit*, from LL. *conductus*].

CONDUPLICATE, [kon-dew'-plik-āt], *adj.* (*bot.*) doubled over together lengthwise.

CONDUPLICATION, [kon-dew'-plik-ā'-shun], *n.* the state of being conduplicate.

CONDURRITE, [kon-dur'-rit], *n.* a black ore of copper. [*Condurrow*, a place in Cornwall].

CONDYLE, [kon'-dīl], *n.* (*anat.*) the protuberance at the end of a bone fitting into the socket of another. [Gk. *kondulos* knuckle].

CONDYLOID, [kon'-dil-oid], *adj.* (*anat.*) resembling a condyle. [CONDYLE and Gk. *oeides* like].

CONE, [kōn], *n.* a solid body tapering regularly to a point from a circular base; anything having a similar shape; (*bot.*) the fruit of conifers; (*geom.*) a straight line always fixed at one point, any other point of which describes a fixed closed curve; (*zool.*) any species of *Conus*, a genus of univalve molluscs having inversely conical shells. [Gk. *konos* pine-cone].

CONE-PULLEY

CONE-PULLEY, [kōn'-pōōl'-i], *n.* a kind of pulley which resembles or is shaped like a cone.

CONES, [kōnz], *n.* very fine flour with which a baker's troughs and loaves are sprinkled.
CONE-SHAPED, [kōn'-shāpt], *adj.* shaped like a cone.
CONEY, see CONY.
CONFAB [kon'-fab'], *n.* (*coll.*) a confabulation. [CONFAB(ULATION)].
CONFABULATE, [kon-fab'-yōō-lāt], *v.i.* to chat confidentially. [L. *confabulari* to talk together].
CONFABULATION, [kon-fab'-yōō-lā'-shun], *n.* a confidential chat.
CONFABULATORY, [kon-fab'-yōō-lā-ter-i], *adj.* relating to confabulation.
CONFALON, [kon'-fal-on], *n.* (*R.C.*) one of a fraternity of seculars. [Fr. *gonfalon* banner].
CONFAMILIAR, [kon'-fam-il'-yer], *adj.* of the same family.
CONFECT, [kon'-fekt], *n.* a sweetmeat. [L. *confectus* made up].
CONFECTION, [kon-fek'-shun], *n.* a mixing into a compound preparation; a sweetmeat. [L. *confectio*].
CONFECTIONARY (1), [kon-fek'-shun-er-i], *n.* the place where sweetmeats are made; a sweetmeat.
CONFECTIONARY (2), [kon-fek'-shun-er-i], *adj.* pertaining to confections.
CONFECTIONER, [kon-fek'-shun-er], *n.* a maker of, or dealer in, confectionery.
CONFECTIONERY, [kon-fek'-shun-er-i], *n.* sweetmeats, pastries, cakes and other confections; the business or shop making and selling these.
CONFECTORY, [kon-fek'-ter-i], *adj.* pertaining to the making of confectionery.
CONFEDERACY, [kon-fed'-er-a-si], *n.* a uniting in alliance; a league, a number of independent states united in close alliance for a common purpose; a criminal conspiracy.
CONFEDERATE (1), [kon-fed'-er-at], *n.* a member of a confederacy; an accomplice.
CONFEDERATE (2), [kon-fed'-er-at], *adj.* allied, in confederacy, leagued together. [L. *confoederatus* leagued together].
CONFEDERATE (3), [kon-fed'-er-āt], *v.t.* and *i.* to form into a confederacy.
CONFEDERATION, [kon-fed'-er-ā'-shun], *n.* the formation of a confederacy, a close alliance between states. [LL. *confederatio*].
CONFEDERATIVE, [kon-fed'-er-at-iv], *adj.* pertaining to a confederacy.
CONFER, (**conferring**, **conferred**), [kon-fur'], *v.t.* and *i.* to bestow upon, to award; to consult with, to discuss. [L. *conferre*].
CONFEREE, [kon'-fer-ē'], *n.* a person with whom one confers; one on whom something is conferred.
CONFERENCE, [kon'-fer-ens], *n.* a consultation; a formal gathering to discuss or examine a problem or situation and exchange views. [Fr. *conférence*].
CONFERENTIAL, [kon'-fer-en'-shal], *adj.* pertaining to a conference.
CONFERMENT, [kon-fur'-ment], *n.* the act of conferring.
CONFERRABLE, [kon-fur'-abl], *adj.* able to be conferred.
CONFERRER, [kon-fur'-er], *n.* one who confers.
CONFERRING, [kon-fur'-ing], *n.* deliberation, conference; bestowal.
CONFERVA, (*pl.* **confervae**), [kon-fur'-va], *n.* (*bot.*) green fresh-water algae. [L. *conferva*].
CONFERVACEOUS, [kon'-fer-vā'-shus], *adj.* relating to, or resembling, a conferva.
CONFERVITE, [kon-fur'-vīt], *n.* (*geol.*) a fossil plant allied to the confervae.
CONFERVOID, [kon-fur'-void], *adj.* articulated like the confervae. [CONFERVA and Gk. *oeides* like].
CONFESS, [kon-fes'], *v.t.* and *i.* to admit, to disclose, own up to, acknowledge (error or misdeed); (*eccles.*) to hear a confession; to declare one's sins to a priest. [L. *confessum*, *p.pt.* of *confiteri* confess].
CONFESSANT, [kon-fes'-ant], *n.* one who confesses to a priest.
CONFESSARY, [kon-fes'-er-i], *n.* a confessor; a confessant.
CONFESSEDLY, [kon-fes'-id-li], *adv.* admittedly.
CONFESSION, [kon-fesh'-un], *n.* the act of confessing; the thing confessed; a declaration or avowal of faith or belief. [L. *confessio*].
CONFESSIONAL (1), [kon-fesh'-un-al], *n.* the curtained box in which the priest hears confessions.
CONFESSIONAL (2), [kon-fesh'-un-al], *adj.* relating to, or based upon, a confession.
CONFESSIONALISM, [kon-fesh'-un-al-izm], *n.* the theory upon which religious confession is based.
CONFESSIONARY (1), [kon-fesh'-un-er-i], *n.* a confessional.
CONFESSIONARY (2), [kon-fesh'-un-er-i], *adj.* relating to confession.
CONFESSIONIST, [kon-fesh'-un-ist], *n.* one who makes a profession of faith.
CONFESSOR, [kon-fes'-or], *n.* †one who makes a declaration of his religious faith, a martyr; a priest who hears confession. [MedL. *confessor*].
CONFETTI, [kon-fet'-i], *n.*(*pl.*) small pieces of thin coloured paper thrown at a bridal pair. [It. *confetti*, *pl.* of *confetto* sweetmeat].
CONFICIENT, [kon-fish'-ent], *adj.* efficient.
CONFIDANT, [kon'-fid-ant'], *n.* one to whom something is confided, an intimate friend.
CONFIDANTE, [kon'-fid-ahnt'], *n.* a female confidant.
CONFIDE, [kon-fīd'], *v.t.* and *i.* to entrust to, to tell a secret to; to have trust or reliance in. [L. *confidere* entrust].
CONFIDENCE, [kon'-fid-ens], *n.* trust; steadfast reliance, assurance, self-assurance; that which is confided as a secret; **c. trick**, a deception in which the victim's confidence is gained with a view to cheating him; **in c.**, in secrecy. [L. *confidentia*].
CONFIDENT, [kon'-fid-ent], *adj.* trusting; sure of oneself and one's powers, self-reliant; certain, convinced (of success). [L. *confidens*].
CONFIDENTIAL, [kon'-fid-en'-shal], *adj.* told in confidence, secret; intimate, familiar.
CONFIDENTIALLY, [kon'-fid-en'-shal-i], *adv.* in confidence; privately.
CONFIDENTLY, [kon'-fid-ent-li], *adv.* in confident fashion.
CONFIDENTNESS, [kon'-fid-ent-nes], *n.* confidence.
CONFIDER, [kon-fīd'-er], *n.* one who confides.
CONFIDING, [kon-fīd'-ing], *adj.* tending to confide, trusting.
CONFIGURATION, [kon-fig'-yōō-rā'-shun], *n.* the figure or appearance formed by the arrangement and relation of parts; (*geog.*) variation in the surface elevation of a region; (*astron.*) the relative position of the planets at a given time. [L. *configuratio*].
CONFIGURE, [kon-fig'-er], *v.t.* to arrange in a certain form, figure, or shape. [L. *configurare*].
CONFINABLE, [kon-fīn'-abl], *adj.* able to be confined.
CONFINE (1), [kon'-fīn], *n.* the boundary, frontier; (*pl.*) area. [Fr. *confins* (*pl.*)].
CONFINE (2), [kon-fīn'], *v.t.* to keep or restrict within limits; to imprison, shut up. [Fr. *confiner*].
CONFINED, [kon-fīnd'], *adj.* restricted, imprisoned, limited; giving, or having just given, birth to a child.
CONFINELESS, [kon-fīn'-les], *adj.* without confines.
CONFINEMENT, [kon-fīn'-ment], *n.* imprisonment, detention, restriction; childbearing, labour.
CONFINER, [kon-fīn'-er], *n.* that which confines.
CONFINITY, [kon-fin'-i-ti], *n.* adjacency.
CONFIRM, [kon-furm'], *v.t.* to make firm, strengthen, fortify; to ratify; to corroborate; (*eccles.*) to admit to full membership of the church. [L. *confirmare*].
CONFIRMABLE, [kon-furm'-abl], *adj.* able to be confirmed.
CONFIRMATION, [kon'-fer-mā'-shun], *n.* the act of confirming, the state of being confirmed; supporting evidence, that which confirms; (*eccles.*) the ceremony of admission to full membership of the church. [L. *confirmatio*].
CONFIRMATIVE, [kon-furm'-at-iv], *adj.* confirmatory.
CONFIRMATIVELY, [kon-furm'-at-iv-li], *adv.* in confirmative fashion.
CONFIRMATORY, [kon'-ferm-ā'-ter-i], *adj.* that confirms; relating to confirmation.
CONFIRMED, [kon-furmd'], *adj.* established, settled; inveterate.
CONFIRMEDLY, [kon-furm'-id-li] *adv.* in confirmed fashion.
CONFIRMEDNESS, [kon-furm'-id-nes], *n.* the state of being confirmed.
CONFIRMEE, [kon'-furm-ē'], *n.* (*eccles.*) one about to be confirmed.
CONFIRMER, [kon-furm'-er], *n.* one who, or that which, confirms.
CONFIRMINGLY, [kon-furm'-ing-li], *adv.* so as to confirm.
CONFISCABLE, [kon'-fisk-abl], *adj.* liable to confiscation.
CONFISCATE (1), [kon'-fis-kāt], *adj.* confiscated; deemed to be forfeited.

CONFISCATE (2), [kon'-fis-kāt'], *v.t.* to seize by legal authority, to appropriate legally without compensation, to deem to be forfeited. [L. *confiscare*].
CONFISCATION, [kon'-fis-kā'-shun], *n.* the act of confiscating, legal appropriation as a forfeit. [L. *confiscatio*].
CONFISCATOR, [kon'-fis-kā'-tor], *n.* one who confiscates. [L. *confiscator*].
CONFISCATORY, [kon'-fis-kā'-ter-i], *adj.* pertaining to confiscation.
CONFITENT, [kon'-fit-ent], *n.* one who confesses to a priest. [L. *confitens*].
CONFITEOR, [kon-fit'-i-aw(r)], *n.* (*R.C.*) the general form of confession of faith used at the beginning of mass. [L. *confiteor* I confess].
CONFIX, [kon-fiks'], *v.t.* to fix firmly, to fasten. [L. *confixum*, *p.pt.* of *configere*].
CONFLAGRANT, [kon-flā'-grant], *adj.* burning. [L. *conflagrans*].
CONFLAGRATION, [kon'-flag-rā'-shun], *n.* a huge fire or blaze. [L. *conflagratio*].
CONFLATE, [kon-flāt'], *v.t.* to blow together; to assemble; to make a composite text from different versions. [L. *conflare*].
CONFLATION, [kon-flā'-shun], *n.* the act of conflating. [L. *conflatio*].
CONFLICT (1), [kon'-flikt], *n.* a fight, struggle; a quarrel, strong difference of opinion; a marked disagreement, incompatibility. [L. *conflictus*].
CONFLICT (2), [kon-flikt'], *v.i.* to strive, fight, contend; to be in opposition, to be contradictory or mutually incompatible, to clash. [L. *conflictum*, *p.pt.* of *confligere* strike against].
CONFLICTIVE, [kon-flikt'-iv], *adj.* tending to conflict.
CONFLUENCE, [kon'-flōō-ens], *n.* a flowing together; place where streams join; (*fig.*) a concourse, gathering. [L. *confluentia*].
CONFLUENT (1), [kon'-flōō-ent], *n.* a stream which joins another; a tributary.
CONFLUENT (2), [kon'-flōō-ent], *adj.* flowing together, joining; (*bot.*) joined at some part; (*med.*) merging together, as of pustules. [L. *confluens*, *pres.pt.* of *confluere* to flow together].
CONFLUX, [kon'-fluks], *n.* a confluence of people or things. [L. *confluxus*].
CONFLUXIBILITY, [kon-fluks'-ib-il'-i-ti], *n.* a tendency to unite.
CONFLUXIBLE, [kon-fluks'-ibl], *adj.* tending to unite.
CONFORM, [kon-fawm'], *v.t.* to make similar to, cause to agree with; *v.i.* to correspond, be similar to in form; (*fig.*) to agree or comply with, obey, observe; to observe the practices of the Established Church. [Fr. *conformer* from L. *conformare*].
CONFORMABILITY, [kon-fawm'-ab-il'-i-ti], *n.* the condition of being conformable.
CONFORMABLE, [kon-fawm'-abl], *adj.* alike in form, resembling; agreeable, compliant; (*geol.*) in parallel formation.

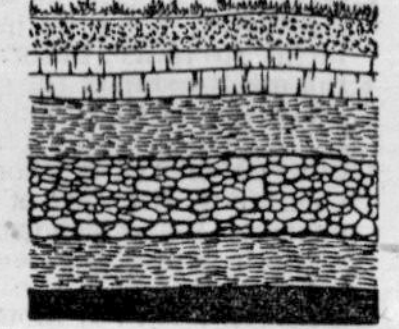
CONFORMABLE (STRATA)

CONFORMABLY, [kon-fawm'-ab-li], *adv.* in conformable fashion.
CONFORMANCE, [kon-fawm'-ans], *n.* conformity.
CONFORMATION, [kon'-fawm-ā'-shun], *n.* the manner of formation; agreement, shape, structure. [L. *conformatio*].
CONFORMER, [kon-fawm'-er], *n.* one who conforms, or agrees.
CONFORMIST, [kon-fawm'-ist], *n.* one who conforms to the observances of the Established Church.
CONFORMITY, [kon-fawm'-i-ti], *n.* likeness in structure, shape, manner, etc.; consistency; agreement; (*eccles.*) observance of the forms of worship of the Established Church.
CONFOUND (1), [kon-fownd'], *v.t.* to confuse, perplex; to mix up, to put to shame; to destroy. [L. *confundere* to pour together].
CONFOUND (2), [kon-fownd'], *int.* (*coll.*) bother.
CONFOUNDED, [kon-fownd'-id], *adj.* confused, abashed; (*coll.*) infernal, abominable.
CONFOUNDEDLY, [kon-fownd'-id-li], *adv.* (*coll.*) extremely, infernally, abominably.
CONFOUNDEDNESS, [kon-fownd'-id-nes], *n.* the condition of being confounded.
CONFRATERNITY, [kon'-frat-urn'-i-ti], *n.* a brotherhood; brotherly friendship.
CONFRERE, confrère, [kon'-frāer], *n.* fellow-member, associate, colleague. [Fr. *confrère*].
CONFRONT, [kon-frunt'], *v.t.* to face, stand facing and staring at; to stand up boldly to; to bring face to face with, set before. [Fr. *confronter*].
CONFRONTATION, [kon'-frunt-ā'-shun], *n.* the act of confronting.
CONFUCIAN, [kon-few'-shun], *adj.* pertaining to Confucius or his philosophy. [*Confucius* or *Kung Fu-tsze*, an ancient Chinese philosopher].
CONFUCIANISM, [kon-few'-shun-izm], *n.* the religion or philosophy established by Confucius.
CONFUSABILITY, [kon-fewz'-a-bil'-i-ti], *n.* liability to be confused.
CONFUSABLE, [kon-fewz'-abl], *adj.* able to be confused.
CONFUSE, [kon-fewz'], *v.t.* to mix up; to muddle; to mistake for; to be unable to discriminate between; to bewilder, perplex; to embarrass. [L. *confusum*, *p.pt.* of *confundere* pour together].
CONFUSED, [kon-fewzd'], *adj.* mixed together; muddled; perplexed; embarrassed.
CONFUSEDLY, [kon-fewz'-id-li], *adv.* in a confused fashion.
CONFUSEDNESS, [kon-fewz'-id-nes], *n.* the condition of being confused.
CONFUSION, [kon-few'-zhun], *n.* the state of being confused, the act of confusing. [L. *confusio*].
CONFUTABLE, [kon-fewt'-abl], *adj.* able to be confuted.
CONFUTANT, [kon-fewt'-ant], *n.* a person who confutes. [L. *confutans*].
CONFUTATION, [kon'-few-tā'-shun], *n.* the act of confuting. [L. *confutatio*].
CONFUTE, [kon-fewt'], *v.t.* to disprove; to prove to be false or wrong. [L. *confutare* repress, check].
CONFUTEMENT, [kon-fewt'-ment], *n.* confutation.
CONGA, [cong'-ga], *n.* a modern ballroom dance based on West Indian rhythms.
CONGE, congé, [kon'-zhā], *n.* dismissal, *esp.* from service or employment; leave; **c. d'élire,** [kon'-zhā-dā-lēer'], the authority to elect a bishop granted by the sovereign to the dean and chapter. [Fr. *congé*].
CONGEAL, [kon-jēl'], *v.t. and i.* to freeze; to become solid through cold; to coagulate. [Fr. *congeler* from L. *congelare*].
CONGEALABLE, [kon-jēl'-abl], *adj.* able to be congealed.
CONGEALMENT, [kon-jēl'-ment], *n.* the process of congealing.
CONGELATION, [kon'-jel-ā'-shun], *n.* congealment. [L. *congelatio*].
CONGENER, [kon'-jen-er], *n.* a person or thing of the same genus or nature. [L. *congener*].
CONGENERIC, [kon'-jen-e'-rik], *adj.* of the same genus or nature; akin.
CONGENIAL, [kon-jē'-ni-al], *adj.* having similar tastes or views; agreeable, suitable.
CONGENIALITY, [kon-jē'-ni-al'-i-ti], *n.* the condition of being congenial.
CONGENIALIZE, [kon-jē'-ni-al-īz], *v.t.* to render congenial.
CONGENIALLY, [kon-jē'-ni-a-li], *adv.* in congenial fashion.
CONGENIALNESS, [kon-jē'-ni-al-nes], *n.* congeniality.
CONGENITAL, [kon-jen'-it-al], *adj.* inherited, present from birth; since birth. [L. *congenitus*].
CONGER, [kong'-ger], *n.* a large variety of sea-eel, *Conger vulgaris*. [L. *conger*].
CONGERIES, [kon-jēer'-i-ēz], *n.* a collection of several particles or small bodies in one mass. [L. *congeries*].

CONGER

CONGEST, [kon-jest'], *v.t.* to crowd together in a dense mass; to overcrowd, to pack so tightly as to impede normal movement; (*med.*) to accumulate abnormally in an organ (of blood). [L. *congestum*, *p.pt.* of *congerere* collect together].
CONGESTED, [kon-jest'-id], *adj.* overcrowded, blocked; (*med.*) having too much blood accumulated in one place.

CONGESTIBLE, [kon-jest'-ibl], *adj.* that may be congested.

CONGESTION, [kon-jes'-chun], *n.* the act of congesting; the state of being congested; (*med.*) an excess of blood in any organ. [L. *congestio*].

CONGESTIVE, [kon-jes'-tiv], *adj.* inducing or indicating congestion.

CONGLOBATE (1), [kon'-glōb-āt], *adj.* formed or gathered into a ball or round mass. [L. *conglobatus*].

CONGLOBATE (2), [kon'-glōb-āt], *v.t.* to collect into a ball. [*Prec.*].

CONGLOBATELY, [kon'-glōb-āt-li], *adv.* in the form of a ball.

CONGLOBATION, [kon'-glōb-ā'-shun], *n.* formation into a globe; something conglobate. [L. *conglobatio*].

CONGLOBE, [kon-glōb'], *v.t.* and *i.* to conglobate. [L. *conglobare*].

CONGLOBULATE, [kon-glob'-yŏŏ-lāt], *v.i.* to form into a little round mass.

CONGLOMERATE (1), [kon-glom'-er-āt], *n.* a quantity of objects piled up together; (*geol.*) a rock composed of pebbles embedded in some finer substance.

CONGLOMERATE (2), [kon-glom'-er-āt], *adj.* formed from a number of separate parts gathered securely together in one mass.

CONGLOMERATE (3), [kon-glom'-er-āt], *v.t.* and *i.* to collect together in one rounded mass. [L. *conglomerare* to roll together].

CONGLOMERATION, [kon-glom'-er-ā'-shun], *n.* the act of conglomerating; the state of being conglomerated; a mixture.

CONGLUTINANT (1), [kon-glōōt'-in-ant], *n.* (*med.*) an agent that heals wounds by uniting.

CONGLUTINANT (2), [kon-glōōt'-in-ant], *adj.* uniting; sticking together.

CONGLUTINATE, [kon-glōōt'-in-āt], *v.t.* to stick together; to join the parts of a wound by an adhesive substance; *v.i.* to unite; join together. [L. *conglutinare*].

CONGLUTINATION, [kon-glōō'-tin-ā'-shun], *n.* the act of sticking together. [L. *conglutinatio*].

CONGLUTINATIVE, [kon-glōōt'-in-at-iv], *adj.* able to conglutinate.

CONGLUTINATOR, [kon-glōōt'-in-āt-er], *n.* a substance which conglutinates wounds.

CONGOU, [kong'-gōō], *n.* a kind of black China tea. [Chin. *kung fu* labour].

CONGRATULABLE, [kon-gra'-chŏŏl-abl], *adj.* suitable for congratulation.

CONGRATULANT, [kon-grach'-ŏŏ-lant], *adj.* expressing congratulation.

CONGRATULATE, [kon-grach'-ŏŏ-lāt], *v.t.* to express one's appreciation of the success of another, to compliment; to wish joy to. [L. *congratulari*].

CONGRATULATION, [kon-grach'-ŏŏ-lā'-shun], *n.* the act of congratulating; words used in congratulating anyone.

CONGRATULATORY, [kon-grach'-ŏŏ-lat-er-i], *adj.* expressing congratulations.

CONGREGATE, [kong'-grig-āt], *v.t.* and *i.* to collect; to bring or come together; to assemble, gather. [L. *congregare*].

CONGREGATION, [kong'-gri-gā'-shun], *n.* an assembly of people, *esp.* in church; those attending worship at a church or chapel. [L. *congregatio*].

CONGREGATIONAL, [kong'-grig-ā'-shun-al], *adj.* relating to a congregation or to congregationalism.

CONGREGATIONALISM, [kong'-grig-ā'-shun-al-izm], *n.* a system of church government amongst nonconformists whereby each church and congregation is autonomous.

CONGREGATIONALIST, [kong'-grig-ā'-shun-al-ist], *n.* one who believes in congregationalism.

CONGRESS, [kong'-gres], *n.* a gathering, assembly, conference; the federal governing body of the United States of America. [L. *congressus*].

CONGRESSIONAL, [kong-gresh'-un-al], *adj.* relating to a congress, *esp.* the United States Congress.

CONGRESS-MAN, [kong'-gres-man'], *n.* a member of the U.S. Congress.

CONGREVE, [kong'-grēv], *n.* a kind of phosphorized match; **c.-rocket**, a powerful, destructive rocket. [Sir William *Congreve*, the inventor].

CONGRUENCE, [kong'-grōō-ens], *n.* the quality of being congruent, agreement. [L. *congruentia*].

CONGRUENCY, [kong'-grōō-en-si], *n.* congruence.

CONGRUENT, [kong'-grōō-ent], *adj.* agreeing, according; corresponding exactly; (*math.*) (of two numbers) leaving the same remainder when divided by a third number. [L. *congruens*, *pres.pt.* of *congruere* to agree].

CONGRUITY, [kong-grōō'-i-ti], *n.* the condition of being congruous.

CONGRUOUS, [kong'-grōō-us], *adj.* suitable; consistent, in keeping. [L. *congruus*].

CONGRUOUSLY, [kong'-grōō-us-li], *adv.* in congruous fashion.

CONGRUOUSNESS, [kong'-grōō-us-nes], *n.* the condition of being congruous.

CONIA, [kō'-ni-a], *n.* (*chem.*) conine. [L. *conium* hemlock].

CONIC, [kon'-ik], *adj.* relating to cones and their properties; in the shape of a cone; **c. sections**, curves formed by the intersection of the surface of a cone with planes that cut the cone in various directions.

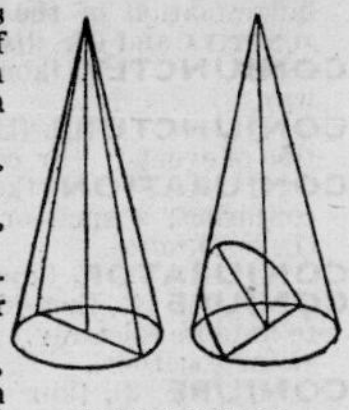

CONIC SECTIONS

CONICAL, [kon'-ik-al], *adj.* conic.

CONICALLY, [kon'-ik-a-li], *adv.* in the shape of a cone.

CONICALNESS, [kon'-ikl-nes], *n.* the condition or quality of being conical.

CONICO-CYLINDRICAL, [kon'-ik-ō-sil-in'-drikl], *adj.* in the form of a cylinder, but tapering to a point like a cone.

CONICS, [kon'-iks], *n.*(*pl.*) (*math.*) the theory of cones.

CONIFER, [kōn'-i-fer], *n.* (*bot.*) a cone-bearing shrub or tree. [CONE and L. *fero* I bear].

CONIFERAE, [kōn-if'-er-ē], *n.*(*pl.*) an order of plants with cone-shaped seed vessels.

CONIFEROUS, [kōn-if'-er-us], *adj.* cone-bearing.

CONIFORM, [kōn'-i-fawm], *adj.* having the form of a cone. [CONE and FORM].

CONIMA, [kon'-i-ma], *n.* a fragrant gum-resin, obtained from a British Guiana species of *Icica*, and used for making pastilles. [Native].

CONIN, CONINE (1), [kōn'-ēn], *n.* a poisonous yellow alkaloid found in hemlock. [Gk. *koneion* hemlock].

CONINE (2), [kōn'-ēn], *adj.* pertaining to, derived from, hemlock.

CONIROSTRAL, [kōn-i-ros'-tral], *adj.* (*ornith.*) with a cone-shaped beak. [CONE and L. *rostrum* beak].

CONJECTURABLE, [kon-jek'-cher-abl], *adj.* able to be conjectured.

CONJECTURAL, [kon-jek'-cher-al], *adj.* based on conjecture. [L. *conjecturalis*].

CONJECTURALLY, [kon-jek'-cher-a-li], *adv.* in conjectural fashion.

CONJECTURE (1), [kon-jek'-cher], *n.* a guess, supposition, an inference with little proof. [L. *conjectura*].

CONJECTURE (2), [kon-jek'-cher], *v.t.* to guess, surmise, suppose, to judge as likely; *v.i.* to make a conjecture.

CONJECTURER, [kon-jek'-cher-er], *n.* a person who conjectures.

CONJOIN, [kon-join'], *v.t.* and *i.* to unite, join, blend. [Fr. *conjoindre* from L. *conjungere*].

CONJOINT (1), [kon'-joint], *n.* (*coll.*) the final examination of the Conjoint Board of the Royal College of Physicians and that of Surgeons.

CONJOINT (2), [kon-joint'], *adj.* united, joined, associated; in conjunction with. [Fr. *conjoint*, *p.pt.* of *conjoindre*].

CONJOINTLY, [kon-joint'-li], *adv.* in conjoint fashion.

CONJUGAL, [kon'-jŏŏg-al], *adj.* pertaining to marriage. [L. *conjugalis*].

CONJUGALLY, [kon'-jŏŏg-a-li], *adv.* in a conjugal manner.

CONJUGATE (1), [kon'-jŏŏg-āt], *adj.* joined; united in pairs. [L. *conjugatus*].

CONJUGATE (2), [kon'-jŏŏg-āt'], *v.t.* and *i.* (*gram.*) to inflect, recite the parts of (a verb); to have inflexions. [L. *conjugare*].

CONJUGATION, [kon'-jŏŏg-ā'-shun], *n.* (*gram.*) the act of conjugating; one of the classes into which verbs may be divided according to their terminations.

CONJUGATIONAL, [kon'-jŏŏg-ā'-shun-al], *adj.* pertaining to conjugation.

CONJUNCT, [kon-jungkt'], *adj.* conjoined, united. [L. *conjunctus*].

CONJUNCTION, [kon-jungk'-shun], *n.* the act of conjoining; the state of being conjoined; combination; (*astron.*) nearness to each other of two heavenly bodies; (*gram.*) an indeclinable particle joining sentences or parts of them. [L. *conjunctio*].

CONJUNCTIONAL, [kon-jungk'-shun-al], *adj.* pertaining to a conjunction.

CONJUNCTIVA, [kon'-jungk-tī'-va], *n.* (*anat.*) the membrane in contact with the eyeball.

CONJUNCTIVE, [kon-jungk'-tiv], *adj.* that connects or joins; (*gram.*) used as a conjunction. [L. *conjunctivus*].

CONJUNCTIVELY, [kon-jungk'-tiv-li], *adv.* in a conjunctive way.

CONJUNCTIVENESS, [kon-jungk'-tiv-nes], *n.* the state of being conjunctive.

CONJUNCTIVITIS, [kon-jungk'-tiv-ī'-tis], *n.* inflammation of the conjunctiva, pink-eye. [CONJUNCTIVA and Gk. *itis* denoting inflammation].

CONJUNCTLY, [kon-jungkt'-li], *adv.* in a conjunct way.

CONJUNCTURE, [kon-jungk'-cher], *n.* a combination of events. [Fr. *conjoncture* from L. *conjunctura*].

CONJURATION, [kon'-jōō-rā'-shun], *n.* the act of conjuring; a spell or charm; an earnest entreaty. [L. *conjuratio*].

CONJURATOR, [kon'-jōō-rāt-or], *n.* a conspirator.

CONJURE (1), [kon-jōō'-er], *v.t.* to entreat earnestly, to implore solemnly. [Fr. *conjurer* from L. *conjurare* swear together].

CONJURE (2), [kun'-jer], *v.i.* to practise magic; to perform tricks of sleight-of-hand or mystifying illusions; **a name to c. with**, an influential name; **to c. up**, to invoke, bring forth by magic and sorcery; (*fig.*) to invoke an image in the mind. [*Prec.*].

CONJUREMENT, [kun'-jer-ment], *n.* adjuration, solemn demand or entreaty.

CONJURER, [kun'-jer-er], *n.* one skilled in conjuring.

CONJURING (1), [kun'-jer-ing], *n.* the art of performing tricks of legerdemain or creating baffling illusions.

CONJURING (2), [kun'-jer-ing], *adj.* executed by legerdemain.

CONJUROR, [kon-jōōer'-or], *n.* one bound by oath with others.

CONJURY, [kun'-jer-i], *n.* the art of performing conjuring tricks.

CONK (1), [kongk], *n.* (*slang*) a nose, a large nose. [Fr. *conque* shell].

CONK (2), [kongk], *v.i.* (*coll.*) to fire badly or fail to fire; **to c. out**, (*coll.*) to cease to fire; to break down. [Echoic].

CONKER, [kongk'-er], *n.* (*slang*) a horse-chestnut. [CONK (1)].

CON MAN, [kon'-man'], *n.* (*coll.*) a confidence trickster. [CON(FIDENCE) and MAN].

CONNASCENCE, [kon-ās'-ens], *n.* the condition of being connascent.

CONNASCENT, [kon-ās'-ent], *adj.* born at the same time as; produced together. [L. *connascens*, *pres.pt.* of *connasci* to be born].

CONNATE, [kon'-āt], *adj.* congenital; (*bot.*) of the same origin. [CON (1) and L. *natus* born].

CONNATURAL, [kon-ach'-er-al], *adj.* inborn; of similar nature. [Fr. *connaturel*].

CONNATURALITY, [kon-ach'-er-al'-i-ti], *n.* the state of being connatural.

CONNATURALIZE, [kon-ach'-er-al-īz], *v.t.* to render connatural.

CONNATURALLY, [kon-ach'-er-a-li], *adv.* in a connatural manner.

CONNATURALNESS, [kon-ach'-er-al-nes], *n.* connaturality.

CONNECT, [kon-ekt'], *v.t.* to join, fasten together; to show the relationship between events; to associate; *v.i.* to unite, join on to, fix together; to follow logically. [L. *connectere* bind together].

CONNECTED, [kon-ekt'-id], *adj.* joined, linked; associated with; related by family.

CONNECTEDLY, [kon-ekt'-id-li], *adv.* in a connected fashion.

CONNECTEDNESS, [kon-ek'-tid-nes], *n.* the state or quality of being connected.

CONNECTING-ROD, [kon-ekt'-ing-rod'], *n.* a rod or bar that connects a piston to a crank.

CONNECTION, see CONNEXION.

CONNECTIVE, CONNEXIVE†, [kon-ekt'-iv, kon-eks'-iv], *adj.* connecting, able to connect; **c. tissue**, the tissue which binds together the organs of the body.

CONNECTIVELY, [kon-ekt'-iv-li], *adv.* in connective fashion.

CONNECTOR, [kon-ekt'-or], *n.* one who, or that which, connects.

CONNER (1), [kon'-er], *n.* a salt-water fish, the bass *Labrax lupus*. [Variant of CUNNER].

CONNER (2), [kon'-er], *n.* one who cons.

CONNEXION, CONNECTION, [kon-ek'-shun], *n.* the act of connecting; the state of being connected; anything that connects; relation, close union; sexual intimacy; clientele; the fitting in of hour of arrival of one train and the departure of another; a train or boat timed to meet the arrival or departure of another; (*pl.*) influential friends; relatives; a group of persons bound together in the pursuit of some common object. [L. *connexio*].

CONNEXIONAL, [kon-ek'-shun-al], *adj.* having connexion; relating to a connexion.

CONNEXIVE†, see CONNECTIVE.

CONNING, [kon'-ing], *n.* (*naut.*) the directions of the helmsman; the reading of a book or lesson.

CONNING-TOWER, [kon'-ing-tow'-er], *n.* (*nav.*) the armoured compartment in a warship or submarine, from which it is steered. [CON (3)].

CONNING-TOWER

CONNIVANCE, [kon-īv'-ans], *n.* act of conniving; intentional oversight, implying consent or help.

CONNIVE, [kon-īv'], *v.i.* to overlook and deliberately encourage wrongdoing, to be a secret accessory to. [L. *connivere* to turn a blind eye to].

CONNIVENT, [kon-īv'-ent], *adj.* deliberately inattentive; (*bot.*) convergent.

CONNOISSEUR, [kon'-e-sur'], *n.* a critical expert in matters of art.

CONNOISSEURSHIP, [kon'-e-sur'-ship], *n.* the skill or taste of a connoisseur.

CONNOTATE, [kon'-ō-tāt], *v.t.* to connote, suggest, imply. [CONNOTE].

CONNOTATION, [kon'-ō-tā'-shun], *n.* the act of connoting; that which is connoted; (*logic*) all that is comprehended by a term.

CONNOTATIVE, [kon-ōt'-at-iv], *adj.* having connotation; implying in addition.

CONNOTE, [kon-ōt'], *v.t.* to imply, infer, indicate; to suggest beyond its original meaning; to signify. [L. *connotare* to work together].

CONNUBIAL, [kon-ew'-bi-al], *adj.* relating to the married state or to marriage. [L. *connubialis*].

CONNUMERATION, [kon-ew'-mer-ā'-shun], *n.* a joint reckoning.

CONNUSANCE, [kon-ews'-ans], *n.* (*leg.*) cognizance. [OFr. *connusance*].

CONOID (1), [kōn'-oid], *n.* a cone-shaped object; (*geom.*) a solid figure formed by the revolution of a conic section about its axis; (*anat.*) the pineal gland.

CONOID (2), [kōn'-oid], *adj.* almost conical, like a cone in shape. [Gk. *konoeides*].

CONOIDAL, [kōn-oid'-al], *adj.* conoid.

CONOIDIC, [kōn-oid'-ik], *adj.* conoid.

CO-NOMINEE, [kō'-nom'-in-ē'], *n.* a person nominated with another.

CONQUER, [kongk'-er], *v.t.* to overcome by force, defeat, to overpower, subjugate; (*fig.*) to put down, vanquish; *v.i.* to overcome, to win. [L.'*conquaerere*].

CONQUERABLE, [kongk'-er-abl], *adj.* able to be conquered.

CONQUERABLENESS, [kongk'-er-abl-nes], *n.* the state of being conquerable, vulnerability.

CONQUERESS, [kongk'-er-es], *n.* a female conqueror.

CONQUERINGLY, [kongk'-er-ing-li], *adv.* in the manner of a conqueror.

CONQUEROR, [kongk'-er-er], *n.* one who conquers; **The C.**, (*hist.*) William I, King of England.

CONQUEST, [kongk'-west], *n.* the act of conquering; that which is conquered; **The C.**, (*hist.*) the conquest of England by William I, in 1066. [OFr. *conqueste*].

CONQUISTADOR, [kon-kist'-a-dor], *n.* one of the Spanish conquerors of Peru and Mexico. [Span. *conquistador*].

CON-ROD, [kon'-rod], *n.* (*motoring*) connecting rod. [CON(NECTING)-ROD].

CONSANGUINEOUS, [kon'-sang-gwin'-i-us], *adj.* of the same blood; connected by birth.

CONSANGUINITY, [kon'-sang-gwin'-i-ti], *n.* blood-relationship.

CONSCIENCE, [kon'-shens], *n.* the power of distinguishing right and wrong; a moral feeling for this; **c. clause**, a clause in law making allowance for possible conscientious scruples in religious matters; **c. money,** money paid to salve one's conscience; **in all c.,** certainly, by all means. [Fr. *conscience* from L. *conscientia* knowledge].

CONSCIENCELESS, [kon'-shens-les], *adj.* lacking a conscience.

CONSCIENCE-PROOF, [kon'-shens-pro͞of'], *adj.* proof against the prickings of conscience.

CONSCIENCE-SMITTEN, [kon'-shens-smit'-en], *adj.* struck with compunction or remorse.

CONSCIENTIOUS, [kon'-shi-en'-shus], *adj.* governed by conscience; scrupulous, taking one's duties and responsibilities seriously; **c. objector,** one who refuses to fight in wartime on grounds of conscience.

CONSCIENTIOUSLY, [kon'-shi-en'-shus-li], *adv.* in a conscientious fashion.

CONSCIENTIOUSNESS, [kon'-shi-en'-shus-nes], *n.* the quality of being conscientious.

CONSCIONABLE, [kon'-shun-abl], *adj.* governed by conscience; reasonable.

CONSCIONABLENESS, [kon'-shun-abl-nes], *n.* the state or quality of being conscionable.

CONSCIONABLY, [kon'-shun-ab-li], *adv.* in a conscionable fashion.

CONSCIOUS, [kon'-shus], *adj.* having the faculty of thought; able to think, perceive and feel; aware, possessing knowledge (of); in control of one's mental powers; able to know and recognize what is happening; awake and sensible. [L. *conscius*].

CONSCIOUSLY, [kon'-shus-li], *adv.* wittingly; in conscious fashion.

CONSCIOUSNESS, [kon'-shus-nes], *n.* the quality or state of being conscious.

CONSCRIBE, [kon-skrīb'], *v.t.* to enrol as a soldier, etc., under compulsion. [L. *conscribere*].

CONSCRIPT (1), [kon'-skript], *n.* a conscript soldier.

CONSCRIPT (2), [kon'-skript], *adj.* enlisted, enrolled under compulsion. [L. *conscriptus*].

CONSCRIPT (3), [kon-skript'], *v.t.* to enrol by conscription, conscribe.

CONSCRIPTION, [kon-skrip'-shun], *n.* compulsory enrolment for national service.

CONSECRATE (1), [kon'-sik-rāt], *adj.* consecrated; sanctified. [L. *consecratus*].

CONSECRATE (2), [kon'-sik-rāt], *v.t.* to make holy, to hallow; to set aside for, or dedicate to, the service of the church. [*Prec.*].

CONSECRATEDNESS, [kon'-sik-rāt'-id-nes], *n.* the quality or state of being consecrated.

CONSECRATION, [kon'-sik-rā'-shun], *n.* the act or ceremony of consecrating. [L. *consecratio*].

CONSECRATOR, [kon'-sik-rāt'-or], *n.* a person who consecrates.

CONSECRATORY, [kon'-sik-rāt'-er-i], *adj.* that consecrates.

CONSECTANEOUS†, [kon'-sek-tā'-ni-us], *adj.* following as a matter of course. [L. *consectaneus*].

CONSECTARY (1), [kon-sek'-ter-i], *n.* consequence, deduction. [L. *consectarium*].

CONSECTARY (2), [kon-sek'-ter-i], *adj.* consequent.

CONSECUTION, [kon'-sik-ew'-shun], *n.* a train of reasoning, natural sequence; (*gram.*) logical sequence of related tenses or words. [L. *consecutum*, *p.pt.* of *consequi* to follow].

CONSECUTIVE, [kon-sek'-ew-tiv], *adj.* following in correct, suitable or regular order; coming in uninterrupted succession; (*gram.*) expressing consequence; **c. chords,** (*mus.*) a succession of similar intervals. [*Prec.*].

CONSECUTIVELY, [kon-sek'-ew-tiv-li], *adv.* in consecutive fashion.

CONSECUTIVENESS, [kon-sek'-ew-tiv-nes], *n.* the state of being consecutive.

CONSENESCENCE, [kon'-sen-es'-ens], *n.* the process of growing old; senility.

CONSENSUAL, [kon-sen'-sho͝o-al], *adj.* (*leg.*) arranged by consent of all parties; (*physiol.*) reacting in sympathy.

CONSENSUS, [kon-sen'-sus], *n.* agreement or unanimity in opinion or response. [L. *consensus*].

CONSENT (1), [kon-sent'], *n.* mutual agreement, concurrence; permission, assent. [OFr. *consente*].

CONSENT (2), [kon-sent'], *v.i.* to agree to accept, to acquiesce in another's propositions; to yield to another's demands. [L. *consentire*].

CONSENTANEITY, [kon-sent'-an-ē'-i-ti], *n.* the quality of being consentaneous.

CONSENTANEOUS, [kon'-sent-ā'-ni-us], *adj.* suited, consistent with; unanimous. [L. *consentaneus*].

CONSENTANEOUSLY, [kon'-sent-ā'-ni-us-li], *adv.* in consentaneous fashion.

CONSENTANEOUSNESS, [kon'-sent-ā'-ni-us-nes], *n.* consentaneity.

CONSENTER, [kon-sent'-er], *n.* a person who consents.

CONSENTIENT, [kon-sen'-shent], *adj.* agreeing, unanimous, giving mutual consent. [L. *consentiens*].

CONSENTINGLY, [kon-sent'-ing-li], *adv.* with consent.

CONSEQUENCE, [kon'-sik-wens], *n.* the fact or event dependent on an immediate cause, effect, result; a logical conclusion or inference; importance, value. [L. *consequentia*].

CONSEQUENT (1), [kon'-sik-went], *n.* that which is given existence by a cause, an effect; that which follows on something else.

CONSEQUENT (2), [kon'-sik-went], *adj.* existing as a result of what has previously occurred; following on logically as an effect or by inference. [L. *consequens*].

CONSEQUENTIAL, [kon'-sik-wen'-shal], *adj.* arising or resulting as a consequence; pretentiously claiming importance, pompous.

CONSEQUENTIALLY, [kon'-sik-wen'-shal-i], *adv.* in consequential fashion.

CONSEQUENTIALNESS, [kon'-sik-wen'-shal-nes], *n.* the condition of being consequential.

CONSEQUENTLY, [kon'-sik-went-li], *adv.* in consequence of something.

CONSERVABLE, [kon-surv'-abl], *adv.* able to be preserved.

CONSERVANCY, [kon-surv'-an-si], *n.* a body of officials appointed to safeguard rivers or forests; conservation of rivers or forests in this way.

CONSERVATION, [kon'-surv-ā'-shun], *n.* the act of conserving, preservation. [L. *conservatio*].

CONSERVATIONAL, [kon'-surv-ā'-shun-al], *adj.* relating to conservation, conserving.

CONSERVATISM, [kon-surv'-at-izm], *n.* a permanent desire to conserve what is established; (*pol.*) the principles of the Conservative Party.

CONSERVATIVE (1), [kon-surv'-at-iv], *n.* a person of conservative temperament or conviction; a preservative; (*pol.*) a person who believes in the necessity for keeping unchanged the traditional system of law and government, a member of the Conservative Party.

CONSERVATIVE (2), [kon-surv'-at-iv], *adj.* inclined or tending to conserve; disliking innovation, moderate, cautious; (*pol.*) advocating the maintenance of traditional social conditions and governing system.

CONSERVATOIRE, [kon-surv'-at-wah(r)], *n.* an institution devoted to the study of music. [Fr. *conservatoire*].

CONSERVATOR, [kon'-surv-āt'-or], *n.* a person who preserves from harm, a protector; an official keeper or custodian of a museum or similar public building. [L. *conservator*].

CONSERVATORY, [kon-surv'-at-er-i], *n.* a shed built of framed glass in which young or delicate plants are grown or kept, a green-house. [CONSERVATOIRE].

CONSERVATORY

CONSERVATRIX, [kon-surv'-at-riks], *n.* a woman who preserves.

CONSERVE (1), [kon-surv'], *n.* a sweetmeat made of preserved fruits; preserved fruit, jam.

CONSERVE (2), [kon-surv'], *v.t.* to keep unchanged or in a sound state, to preserve, safeguard. [L. *conservare* to preserve].

CONSERVER, [kon-surv'-er], *n.* one who conserves.

CONSIDER, [kon-sid'-er], *v.t.* and *i.* to think, to examine closely in the mind, to meditate on, to pay attention to; to take into account; to judge, hold; to have regard for, to respect; to come to a conclusion. [L. *considerare*].

CONSIDERABLE, [kon-sid'-er-abl], *adj.* worthy of note, worth considering, important; relatively large, much, great.

CONSIDERABLENESS, [kon-sid'-er-abl-nes], *n.* the quality of being considerable.

CONSIDERABLY, [kon-sid'-er-ab-li], *adv.* to a considerable degree.

CONSIDERATE, [kon-sid'-er-at], *adj.* thoughtful, mindful of others.
CONSIDERATELY, [kon-sid'-er-at-li], *adv.* in considerate fashion.
CONSIDERATENESS, [kon-sid'-er-at-nes], *n.* the quality of being considerate.
CONSIDERATION, [kon-sid'-er-ā'-shun], *n.* the act of considering, thought; a determining cause or reason; payment for a particular action or service, compensation; careful regard for the feelings of others; (*leg.*) a stipulation governing a contract. [L. *consideratio* contemplation].
CONSIDERER, [kon-sid'-er-er], *n.* one who considers carefully.
CONSIDERING, [kon-sid'-er-ing], *prep.* in view of, taking into account.
CONSIDERINGLY, [kon-sid'-er-ing-li], *adv.* in a considering manner.
CONSIGN, [kon-sīn'], *v.t. and i.* to deliver or give up into another's charge; (*comm.*) to dispatch goods for delivery. [L. *consignare* stamp with a seal].
CONSIGNABLE, [kon-sīn'-abl], *adj.* able to be consigned.
CONSIGNATION, [kon'-sig-nā'-shun], *n.* the act of consigning.
CONSIGNATORY, [kon-sig'-nat-er-i], *n.* the person to whom any trust or transaction is consigned.
CONSIGNATURE†, [kon-sig'-nach-er], *n.* the act of signing conjointly.
CONSIGNEE, [kon'-sīn-ē'], *n.* the person to whom goods are consigned.
CONSIGNER, CONSIGNOR, [kon-sīn'-er], *n.* the person who consigns goods.
CONSIGNMENT, [kon-sīn'-ment], *n.* the act of consigning; the thing consigned, goods dispatched to a customer.
CONSIGNOR, see CONSIGNER.
CONSILIENCE, [kon-sil'-i-ens], *n.* the act of concurring or coinciding, a coincidence.
CONSIMILITUDE†, [kon'-sim-il'-i-tewd], *n.* resemblance, similarity.
CONSIST, [kon-sist'], *v.i.* to be made up; **c. in**, to comprise, to be derived from; **c. of**, to be composed of, to have as constituent parts. [L. *consistere* to remain firm].
CONSISTENCE, [kon-sist'-ens], *n.* the state or quality of being consistent, the degree of solidity, firmness, density.
CONSISTENCY, [kon-sist'-en-si], *n.* consistence.
CONSISTENT, [kon-sist'-ent], *adj.* having a nature which is fixed; in keeping with, not contradictory, uniform; regular.
CONSISTENTLY, [kon-sist'-ent-li], *adv.* in a consistent fashion.
CONSISTORIAL, [kon'-sist-aw'-ri-al], *adj.* pertaining to a consistory.
CONSISTORIAN, [kon'-sist-aw'-ri-an], *n.* a Presbyterian.
CONSISTORY (**1**), [kon-sist'-er-i], *n.* a council, assembly; (*eccles.*) the court under the jurisdiction of a bishop; the College of Cardinals at Rome; an assembly of Presbyterian elders. [LL. *consistorium* assembly chamber].
CONSISTORY (**2**), [kon-sist'-er-i], *adj.* consistorial.
CONSOCIATE† (**1**), [kon-sō'-shi-āt], *n.* an associate.
CONSOCIATE (**2**), [kon-sō'-shi-āt], *v.t. and i.* to take into an alliance, to meet or group together as associates. [L. *consociare* to associate with].
CONSOCIATED, [kon-sō'-shi-āt'-id], *adj.* united; associated in a body.
CONSOCIATION, [kon-sō'-shi-ā'-shun], *n.* the act of consociating; (*eccles.*) an association of Christian churches. [L. *consociatio*].
CONSOLABLE, [kon-sōl'-abl], *adj.* able to be comforted.
CONSOLATION, [kon'-sol-ā'-shun], *n.* the act of consoling; that which consoles or is intended to console; **c. prize**, a prize given to a runner up. [L. *consolatio*].
CONSOLATORY† (**1**), [kon-sol'-at-er-i], *n.* a speech or writing intended to console.
CONSOLATORY (**2**), [kon-sol'-at-er-i], *adj.* tending to console or comfort.
CONSOLE (**1**), [kon'-sōl], *n.* a table with legs in the form of carved scrolls; the key-board of an organ; (*arch.*) an ornamental bracket resembling a scroll, which supports a mantelpiece, shelf or cornice. [Fr. *console* a bracket].

CONSOLE

CONSOLE (**2**), [kon-sōl'], *v.t.* to comfort a person suffering grief or disappointment; to compensate, afford solace. [L. *consolari*].
CONSOLER, [kon-sōl'-er], *n.* a person who consoles.
CONSOLIDANT† (**1**), [kon-sol'-id-ant], *n.* a medicine that heals or binds wounds or fractures.
CONSOLIDANT (**2**), [kon-sol'-id-ant], *adj.* tending to consolidate or to heal. [L. *consolidans*].
CONSOLIDATE, [kon-sol'-id-āt], *v.t. and i.* to strengthen or make more secure, to give greater solidarity to; to combine or unite into a single strong unit; to solidify, grow firm and hard. [L. *consolidare*].
CONSOLIDATED, [kon-sol'-id-āt-id], *adj.* brought into a compact state, united; **c. fund**, a fund for the payment of interest on the national debt controlled by the government.
CONSOLIDATION, [kon-sol'-id-ā'-shun], *n.* the act of consolidating. [L. *consolidatio*].
CONSOLIDATIVE, [kon-sol'-id-at-iv], *adj.* having the power to consolidate. [Fr. *consolidatif*].
CONSOLIDATOR, [kon-sol'-id-āt'-er], *n.* one who, or that which, consolidates.
CONSOLS, [kon-solz'], *n.(pl.)* (*comm.*) British Government stock. [CONSOL(IDATED)].
CONSOMME, consommé, [kon-som'-ā], *n.* a clear soup. [Fr. *consommé*].
CONSONANCE, [kon'-son-ans], *n.* the quality of being consonant. [L. *consonantia*].
CONSONANCY, [kon'-son-an'-si], *n.* consonance.
CONSONANT (**1**), [kon'-son-ant], *n.* (*phon.*) a speech sound in which the flow of air from the lungs is partially or completely impeded in its passage through the mouth; an alphabetical letter or symbol denoting such a sound.
CONSONANT (**2**), [kon'-son-ant], *adj.* consistent, agreeing in accordance. [L. *consonans*].
CONSONANTAL, [kon'-son-ant-al], *adj.* consisting of, resembling, relating to a consonant.
CONSONANTLY, [kon'-son-ant-li], *adv.* in a consonant fashion.
CONSONANTNESS, [kon'-son-ant-nes], *n.* the condition of being consonant.
CONSONOUS†, [kon'-son-us], *adj.* agreeing in sound, harmonious. [L. *consonus*].
CONSORT (**1**), [kon'-sawt], *n.* an intimate associate, a spouse, *esp.* a royal spouse; a ship accompanying another as an escort; **Prince C.**, the husband of a reigning queen; **Queen C.**, the wife of a king. [L. *consors* comrade].
CONSORT (**2**), [kon-sawt'], *v.t. and i.* to associate with, to be habitually in the company of; to mix with, agree with.
CONSORTABLE, [kon-sawt'-abl], *adj.* capable of consorting, suitable.
CONSORTIUM, [kon-sawt'-i-um], *n.* a union of several powers for the purpose of joint action. [L. *consortium* from *consors* comrade].
CONSORTSHIP, [kon'-sawt-ship], *n.* the status of a consort; the period of consorting with; fellowship.
CONSPECIFIC, [kon'-spes-if'-ik], *adj.* belonging to the same species.
CONSPECTUS, [kon-spekt'-us], *n.* a general view; a brief survey. [L. *conspectus*].
CONSPICUITY, [kon'-spik-ew'-i-ti], *n.* conspicuousness.
CONSPICUOUS, [kon-spik'-yōō-us], *adj.* readily seen or noticed; commanding the attention, standing out well from a background; attracting notice because of unusual qualities. [L. *conspicuus*].
CONSPICUOUSLY, [kon-spik'-yōō-us-li], *adv.* in conspicuous fashion.
CONSPICUOUSNESS, [kon-spik'-yōō-us-nes], *n.* the quality of being conspicuous.
CONSPIRACY, [kon-spi'-ra-si], *n.* the act of conspiring; a secret association of people planning to commit some illegal act, a plot; a prearranged and secret determination or agreement. [L. *conspiratio*].
CONSPIRATOR, [kon-spi'-ra-ter], *n.* a person who conspires.
CONSPIRE, [kon-spier'], *v.i.* to plot, combine secretly for some unlawful purpose. [L. *conspirare* to breathe together].
CONSPIRER, [kon-spier'-er], *n.* a conspirator.
CONSPIRING, [kon-spier'-ing], *adj.* plotting together.
CONSPIRINGLY, [kon-spier'-ing-li], *adv.* in a conspiring manner.
CONSPUE, [kon-spew'], *v.t.* to raise an outcry against.

to express hatred or strong dislike of. [Fr. *conspuer* from L. *conspuere*].

CONSPURCATION†, [kon'-sper-kā'-shun], *n.* pollution, defilement. [L. *conspurcare* to defile].

CONSTABLE, [kun'-stabl], *n.* a policeman; **chief c.**, the head of a city or county constabulary; **special c.**, a civilian called upon to act as constable upon special occasions; **to outrun the c.**, to get into debt. [OFr. *conestable*].

CONSTABLESHIP, [kun'-stabl-ship], *n.* the office or rank of a constable.

CONSTABLEWICK, [kun'-stabl-wik], *n.* the jurisdiction of a constable.

CONSTABULARY (1), [kun-stab'-yōō-ler-i], *n.* the police force of a city or district.

CONSTABULARY (2), [kun-stab'-yōō-ler-i], *adj.* pertaining to, or consisting of, constables. [L. *constabularius*].

CONSTANCY, [kon'-stans-i], *n.* the quality of being constant. [L. *constantia*].

CONSTANT (1), [kon'-stant], *n.* (*math.*) an unvarying quantity.

CONSTANT (2), [kon'-stant], *adj.* steadfast; faithful; unchanging; continual. [L. *constans*, *pres.pt.* of *constare* to be steadfast].

CONSTANTIA, [kon-stan'-shi-a], *n.* a sweet wine from South Africa. [*Constantia*, near Cape Town].

CONSTANTLY, [kon'-stant-li], *adv.* in constant fashion.

CONSTAT, [kon'-stat], *n.* (*leg.*) an exemplification of letters patent under the Great Seal. [L. *constat* it is established].

CONSTELLATE, [kon'-stel-āt], *v.t.* and *i.* to group or form into a constellation. [L. *constellatus* in groups of stars].

CONSTELLATED, [kon'-stel-āt'-id], *adj.* abounding in, adorned with stars.

CONSTELLATION, [kon'-stel-ā'-shun], *n.* a cluster or group of stars, often named after some mythological figure; (*fig.*) a gathering or collection of notabilities; (*astrol.*) disposition of the stars at one's birth. [L. *constellatio*].

CONSTERNATION, [kon'-ster-nā'-shun], *n.* alarm, dismay. [L. *consternatio*].

CONSTIPATE, [kon'-stip-āt], *v.t.* to bind, render the bowels inactive or irregular in functioning. [CON and L. *stipatum*, *p.pt.* of *stipare* pack].

CONSTIPATION, [kon'-stip-ā'-shun], *n.* the state of being constipated. [L. *constipatio*].

CONSTITUENCY, [kon-stit'-yōō-en-si], *n.* the electorate of a parliamentary division; a parliamentary division.

CONSTITUENT (1), [kon-stit'-yōō-ent], *n.* a component part; a voter in a parliamentary constituency.

CONSTITUENT (2), [kon-stit'-yōō-ent], *adj.* forming part of, making up a whole; having the right to elect. [L. *constituens*, *pres.pt.* of *constituere* to construct].

CONSTITUTE, [kon'-stit-ewt], *v.t.* to set up, establish by authority; to compose, make what it is; to appoint or elect, to create officially; to be legally or officially regarded as. [L. *constituere* to construct].

CONSTITUTED, [kon'-stit-ewt-id], *adj.* established; appointed; made up.

CONSTITUTION, [kon'-stit-ew'-shun], *n.* the act or manner of constituting; a person's physical condition, qualities or capacities; the principles according to which a state, society, institution, etc., is organized and governed; (*hist.*) an official decree. [L. *constitutio*].

CONSTITUTIONAL (1), [kon'-stit-ew'-shun-al], *n.* a walk habitually taken for the sake of health.

CONSTITUTIONAL (2), [kon'-stit-ew'-shun-al], *adj.* connected with the bodily constitution; pertaining to the constitution of a state or society, restricted or limited by the constitution.

CONSTITUTIONALISM, [kon'-stit-ew'-shun-al-izm], *n.* the principles of the constitution, or of constitutional government; constitutional government.

CONSTITUTIONALIST, [kon'-stit-ew'-shun-al-ist], *n.* a supporter of constitutional government or of a constitution.

CONSTITUTIONALITY, [kon'-stit-ew'-shun-al'-i-ti], *n.* the state of being constitutional.

CONSTITUTIONALIZE, [kon'-stit-ew'-shun-al-īz], *v.t.* to make constitutional.

CONSTITUTIONALLY, [kon'-stit-ew'-shun-a-li], *adv.* according to the constitution.

CONSTITUTIONIST, [kon'-stit-ew'-shun-ist], *n.* a constitutionalist.

CONSTITUTIVE, [kon'-stit-ewt-iv], *adj.* that constitutes; determinative.

CONSTITUTIVELY, [kon'-stit-ewt'-iv-li], *adv.* in a constitutive way.

CONSTRAIN, [kon-strān'], *v.t.* to compel, force; to effect by compulsion; to bring pressure to bear upon. [OFr. *constreindre* to fetter, restrain].

CONSTRAINABLE, [kon-strān'-abl], *adj.* able to be constrained.

CONSTRAINED, [kon-strānd'], *adj.* compelled; embarrassed.

CONSTRAINEDLY, [kon-strān'-id-li], *adv.* in a constrained manner.

CONSTRAINT, [kon-strānt'], *n.* compulsion, force; self-consciousness, embarrassment; control. [OFr. *constreinte*].

CONSTRICT, [kon-strikt'], *v.t.* to draw together, contract, bind close. [L. *constrictum*, *p.pt.* of *constringere* to restrain].

CONSTRICTION, [kon-strik'-shun], *n.* the act of constricting; (in the chest, etc.) a feeling of tightness. [L. *constrictio*].

CONSTRICTIVE, [kon-strikt'-iv], *adj.* that constricts or tends to constrict.

CONSTRICTOR, [kon-strikt'-er], *n.* (*anat.*) a muscle that contracts or constricts a part; (*zool.*) a large kind of South American snake which kills its victims by crushing them in its coils.

BOA CONSTRICTOR

CONSTRINGE, [kon-strinj'], *v.t.* to draw together; to contract; to constrict; to cramp. [L. *constringere*].

CONSTRINGENCY, [kon-strinj'-en-si], *n.* the act of constringing.

CONSTRINGENT, [kon-strinj'-ent], *adj.* constricting; contracting.

CONSTRUCT, [kon-strukt'], *v.t.* to build, fit together, form; to compose, make up; (*geom.*) to draw. [L. *constructum*, *p.pt.* of *construere* build].

CONSTRUCTION, [kon-struk'-shun], *n.* the act of constructing; that which is constructed; an interpretation, meaning; (*gram.*) the arrangement and connexion of words in a sentence. [L. *constructio*].

CONSTRUCTIONAL, [kon-struk'-shun-al], *adj.* pertaining to construction.

CONSTRUCTIVE, [kon-strukt'-iv], *adj.* possessing ability to construct; creative, formative; pertaining to construction; inferred from interpretation and not directly expressed.

CONSTRUCTIVELY, [kon-strukt'-iv-li], *adv.* in a constructive fashion.

CONSTRUCTIVENESS, [kon-strukt'-iv-nes], *n.* ability to construct.

CONSTRUCTOR, [kon-strukt'-er], *n.* a person who constructs; a builder.

CONSTRUCTURE, [kon-struk'-cher], *n.* an edifice, structure.

CONSTRUE, [kon-strōō'], *v.t.* to discover the meaning or syntactical construction of a sentence by analysis; to translate; (*fig.*) to interpret, ascribe a particular meaning to; *v.i.* to analyse syntactically; to be capable of syntactic analysis. [L. *construere* to set in order].

CONSUBSIST, [kon'-sub-sist'], *v.i.* to subsist together.

CONSUBSTANTIAL, [kon'-sub-stan'-shal], *adj.* of the same substance, essence, or nature.

CONSUBSTANTIALIST, [kon'-sub-stan'-shal-ist], *n.* a person who believes in consubstantiation.

CONSUBSTANTIALITY, [kon'-sub-stan-shi-al'-i-ti], *n.* the quality of being consubstantial.

CONSUBSTANTIATE, [kon'-sub-stan'-shi-āt], *v.t.* and *i.* to unite; to join together in one common substance.

CONSUBSTANTIATION, [kon'-sub-stan'-shi-ā'-shun], *n.* the theological doctrine that the sacramental elements in the Eucharist are united with Christ's body and blood after consecration.

CONSUETUDE, [kon'-swi-tewd], *n.* usage, habit, custom, *esp.* when enforceable by law. [L. *consuetudo*].

CONSUETUDINARY (1), [kon'-swi-tewd'-in-er-i], *n.* a handbook of customary religious observances, etc.

CONSUETUDINARY (2), [kon'-swi-tewd'-in-er-i], *adj.* customary.

CONSUL, [kon'-sul], *n.* an official agent of a state in a foreign country, who looks after its nationals and commercial affairs there; (*hist.*) one of two chief magistrates of the Roman Republic holding office for one year; (*hist.*) one of the three chief magistrates of the French Republic from 1799 till 1804. [L. *consul*].

CONSULAGE, [kon'-sul-ij], *n.* a duty levied on imports and exports by the consul, in exchange for protecting them.

CONSULAR, [kon'-sew-ler], *adj.* pertaining to a consul or his office.

CONSULATE, [kon'-sew-lat], *n.* the rank or office of a consul; the term of office of a consul; the official residence of a consul. [L. *consulatus*].

CONSULSHIP, [kon'-sul-ship], *n.* the post of a consul; the duration of his office.

CONSULT, [kon-sult'], *v.t.* to ask or seek advice from or the opinion of, to refer to for information; to consider, have regard to; *v.i.* to take counsel with another. [L. *consultare*].

CONSULTANT, [kon-sult'-ant], *n.* a person who consults another; an expert who may be consulted for professional advice for a fee. [L. *consultans*].

CONSULTATION, [kon'-sŏolt-ā'-shun], *n.* the act of consulting; a conference. [L. *consultatio*].

CONSULTATIVE, [kon-sult'-at-iv], *adj.* pertaining to consultation.

CONSULTEE, [kon'-sul-tē'], *n.* one who is consulted.

CONSULTER, [kon-sult'-er], *n.* one who consults.

CONSULTING, [kon-sult'-ing], *adj.* giving (expert) advice; **c. room**, the room in which a doctor or lawyer sees his patients or clients professionally.

CONSULTIVE†, [kon-sult'-iv], *adv.* consultative.

CONSUMABLE, [kon-sewm'-abl], *adj.* capable of being consumed.

CONSUME, [kon-sewm'], *v.t.* to destroy; to waste; to eat, devour; to obsess. [L. *consumere* to use up].

CONSUMER, [kon-sewm'-er], *n.* a person or thing that consumes; one who buys for use or consumption.

CONSUMMATE (1), [kon-sum'-at], *adj.* brought to perfection, complete, supreme. [L. *consummatus*].

CONSUMMATE (2), [kon'-sum-āt], *v.t.* to complete, perfect, finish; to make a marriage legally complete by sexual intercourse. [*Prec.*].

CONSUMMATELY, [kon-sum'-at-li], *adv.* to perfection; completely; perfectly.

CONSUMMATION, [kon'-sum-ā'-shun], *n.* the act of consummating; sexual intercourse at marriage. [L. *consummatio*].

CONSUMMATIVE, [kon-sum'-at-iv], *adj.* that consummates.

CONSUMPT, [kon-sumpt'], *n.* consumption.

CONSUMPTION, [kon-sump'-shun], *n.* the act of consuming; the quantity consumed; (*econ.*) the use or amount used of commercial or industrial products; (*med.*) tuberculosis of the lungs, phthisis. [L. *consumptio*].

CONSUMPTIONARY, [kon-sump'-shun-er-i], *adj.* pertaining to consumption.

CONSUMPTIVE (1), [kon-sump'-tiv], *n.* a person suffering from consumption.

CONSUMPTIVE (2), [kon-sump'-tiv], *adj.* tending to consume; suffering from tuberculosis.

CONSUMPTIVENESS, [kon-sump'-tiv-nes], *n.* the condition of being consumptive.

CONSUTE, [kon'-sewt], *adj.* (*entom.*) marked as if with stitches.

CONTABESCENCE, [kon'-tab-es'-ens], *n.* (*bot.*) absence of pollen through diseased stamens; (*med.*) consumption. [~L. *contabescens* wasting away].

CONTABULATE, [kon-tab'-yŏo-lāt], *v.t.* to cover (a floor) with boards. [L. *contabulare*].

CONTABULATION, [kon-tab'-yŏo-lā'-shun], *n.* the act of contabulating. [L. *contabulatio*].

CONTACT (1), [kon'-takt], *n.* a state of touching; close sympathetic communication; clash, collision; (*elect.*) proximity to each other of two conductors so that the electric current can pass from one to the other; (*med.*) one who has been in contact with an infectious case; (*math.*) meeting of two curves, surfaces or straight line and curve; (*milit.*) communication. [L. *contactus*].

CONTACT (2), [kon-takt'], *v.t. and i.* to have personal dealings with, to get in touch with. [CONTACT (1)].

CONTACT-BREAKER, [kon'-takt-brāk'-er], *n.* a device for interrupting an electric circuit.

CONTACTUAL, [kon-tak'-chŏo-al], *adj.* relating to, or implying, contact.

CONTADINO, [kon'-ta-dē'-nō], *n.* an Italian peasant. [It. *contadino*].

CONTAGION, [kon-tā'-jon], *n.* the communication of a disease by contact; a disease communicated by contact; (*fig.*) evil influence communicated from one to another. [L. *contagio*].

CONTAGIONIST, [kon-tā'-jun-ist], *n.* one who believes in the contagious nature of certain diseases.

CONTAGIOUS, [kon-tā'-jus], *adj.* (*med.*) communicated by contact, liable to spread disease by contact with others; (*fig.*) catching, affecting others by contact. [L. *contagiosus*].

CONTAGIOUSLY, [kon-tāj'-us-li], *adv.* in contagious fashion.

CONTAGIOUSNESS, [kon-tā'-jus-nes], *n.* the condition of being contagious.

CONTAGIUM, [kon-tā'-ji-um], *n.* an agent which transmits a disease from one person to another.

CONTAIN, [kon-tān'], *v.t.* to hold, to have as a component part, comprise, include; to have space for; (*arith.*) to be divisible by; (*geom.*) to enclose, bound; (*reflex.*) to maintain self-control. [OFr. *contenir* from L. *continere*].

CONTAINABLE, [kon-tān'-abl], *adj.* able to be contained.

CONTAINANT, [kon-tān'-ant], *n.* container.

CONTAINER, [kon-tān'-er], *n.* one who, or that which, contains; a vessel, receptacle.

CONTAMINATE, [kon-tam'-in-āt], *v.t.* to render impure or noxious, pollute, taint; (*fig.*) to exert a bad influence upon. [L. *contaminare*].

CONTAMINATION, [kon-tam'-in-ā'-shun], *n.* the act of contaminating; the state or quality of being contaminated, *esp.* with poison-gas; corruption of a text. [L. *contaminatio*].

CONTAMINATIVE, [kon-tam'-in-āt-iv], *adj.* that contaminates.

CONTANGO, [kon-tang'-go], *n.* (*Stock Exchange*) the percentage paid by the buyer to the seller of stock for the privilege of carrying over completion of purchase to a following account day. [MedL. *contango* I postpone].

CONTE, [kawnt], *n.* a short story. [Fr. *conte*].

CONTEMN, [kon-tem'], *v.t.* to scorn, despise. [L. *contemnere*].

CONTEMNER, [kon-tem'-er], *n.* one who contemns.

CONTEMPER, [kon-tem'-per], *v.t.* to blend, mix together. [L. *contemperare*].

CONTEMPERATE†, [kon-tem'-per-āt], *adj.* tempered by blending. [L. *contemperatus*].

CONTEMPLATE, [kon'-tem-plāt], *v.t.* to observe, look at fixedly, gaze upon; to meditate on, think closely about; to intend; to anticipate; *v.i.* to meditate, reflect. [L. *contemplari*].

CONTEMPLATED, [kon'-tem-plāt-id], *adj.* deliberate, intended.

CONTEMPLATION, [kon'-tem-plā'-shun], *n.* the act of contemplating. [L. *contemplatio*].

CONTEMPLATIVE, [kon-tem'-plat-iv], *adj.* given to contemplation or meditation; studious, thoughtful.

CONTEMPLATIVELY, [kon-tem'-plat-iv-li], *adv.* in contemplative fashion.

CONTEMPLATIVENESS, [kon-tem'-plat-iv-nes], *n.* the quality of being contemplative.

CONTEMPLATOR, [kon'-tem-plāt-er], *n.* one who contemplates.

CONTEMPORANEITY, [kon-tem'-per-an-ē'-i-ti], *n.* contemporariness.

CONTEMPORANEOUS, [kon-tem'-per-ā'-ni-us], *adj.* existing or happening at the same time. [L. *contemporaneus*].

CONTEMPORANEOUSLY, [kon-tem'-per-ā'-ni-us-li], *adv.* at the same time.

CONTEMPORANEOUSNESS, [kon-tem'-per-ā'-ni-us-nes], *n.* the state of being contemporaneous.

CONTEMPORARINESS, [kon-tem'-per-er-i-nes], *n.* contemporaneousness.

CONTEMPORARY (1), [kon-tem'-per-er-i], *n.* one who, or that which, is contemporary.

CONTEMPORARY (2), [kon-tem'-per-er-i], *adj.* living, existing at the time (of speaking or writing); contemporaneous; belonging to the same period of time.

CONTEMPORIZE, [kon-tem'-per-īz], *v.t.* to make contemporary; *v.i.* to be contemporary.

CONTEMPT, [kon-tempt'], *n.* scorn, disdain; disgrace, the state of being despicable; **c. of court**, disrespect for, or disobedience to, a court of law. [L. *contemptus*].

CONTEMPTIBILITY, [kon-tempt'-ib-il'-i-ti], *n.* the state of being contemptible.

CONTEMPTIBLE (1), [kon-temp'-tibl], *n.* that which is contemptible; **Old C.**, a member of the "contemptibly small" British Expeditionary Force of 1914. [*Next*].

CONTEMPTIBLE (2), [kon-tempt'-ibl], *adj.* despicable, provoking contempt. [L. *contemptibilis*].
CONTEMPTIBLENESS, [kon-tempt'-ibl-nes], *n.* contemptibility.
CONTEMPTIBLY, [kon-tempt'-ib-li], *adv.* in a contemptible fashion.
CONTEMPTUOUS, [kon-temp'-choo-us], *adj.* expressing contempt, scornful; disdainful.
CONTEMPTUOUSLY, [kon-temp'-choo-us-li], *adv.* in contemptuous fashion.
CONTEMPTUOUSNESS, [kon-temp'-choo-us-nes], *n.* quality of being contemptuous.
CONTEND, [kon-tend'], *v.i.* to strive, to compete; to dispute; to maintain; to face in opposition. [L. *contendere*].
CONTENDENT, [kon-tend'-ent], *n.* a contender.
CONTENDER, [kon-tend'-er], *n.* one who contends.
CONTENDING, [kon-tend'-ing], *adj.* striving, opposing.
CONTENT (1), [kon'-tent], *n.* that which is contained, essential part, true significance, material contained; the capacity of a receptacle; (*philos.*) the substance of an idea; (*geom.*) area or volume contained within a certain space; (*pl.*) that which is contained in anything; that which makes up or comprises a book, treatise, etc. [L. *contentum*, *p.pt.* of *continere* to contain].
CONTENT (2), [kon-tent'], *n.* contentedness; (*pl.*) (*parl.*) those members of the House of Lords who vote in favour of a motion.
CONTENT (3), [kon-tent'], *adj.* satisfied, easy in mind, happy. [L. *contentus*].
CONTENT (4), [kon-tent'], *v.t.* to make contented; (*reflex.*) to satisfy oneself with, to accept without demur, limit oneself to. [Fr. *contenter* from L. *contentare*].
CONTENTED, [kon-tent'-id], *adj.* content, satisfied, easy in mind.
CONTENTEDLY, [kon-tent'-id-li], *adv.* in a contented fashion.
CONTENTEDNESS, [kon-tent'-id-nes], *n.* satisfaction, pleasure, happiness.
CONTENTION, [kon-ten'-shun], *n.* conflict; a contest of words, controversy; the point contended in argument; **bone of c.,** a disputed point. [L. *contentio*].
CONTENTIOUS, [kon-ten'-shus], *adj.* argumentative, quarrelsome; controversial. [L. *contentiosus*].
CONTENTIOUSLY, [kon-ten'-shus-li], *adv.* in contentious fashion.
CONTENTIOUSNESS, [kon-ten'-shus-nes], *n.* the condition of being contentious.
CONTENTLESS, [kon'-tent-les], *adj.* discontented.
CONTENTMENT, [kon-tent'-ment], *n.* contentedness.
CONTERMINABLE, [kon-tur'-min-abl], *adj.* terminated by the same limits.
CONTERMINAL, [kon-tur'-min-al], *adj.* conterminous.
CONTERMINANT, [kon-tur'-min-ant], *adj.* conterminous.
CONTERMINATE, [kon-tur'-min-at], *adj.* equally extensive in time or space; with two ends meeting; within the same bounds; neighbouring, approaching.
CONTERMINOUS, [kon-tur'-min-us], *adj.* conterminate. [L. *conterminus* neighbouring].
CONTEST (1), [kon'-test], *n.* a fight, dispute; a competition, struggle for victory or pre-eminence.
CONTEST (2), [kon-test'], *v.t.* to fight or struggle for; (*pol.*) to offer oneself as a parliamentary candidate for (a constituency) in opposition to some other candidate; (*leg.*) to take legal action about, defend at law; *v.i.* to vie, contend. [Fr. *contester* from L. *contestari* to call to witness].
CONTESTABLE, [kon-test'-abl], *adj.* able to be disputed.
CONTESTANT, [kon-test'-ant], *n.* one who contests. [Fr. *contestant*].
CONTESTATION, [kon'-test-ā'-shun], *n.* the act of contesting. [L. *contestatio*].
CONTESTED, [kon-test'-id], *adj.* disputed; settled by contest; opposed.
CONTESTINGLY, [kon-test'-ing-li], *adv.* in a contesting manner.
CONTESTLESS, [kon'-test-les], *adj.* without contest.
CONTEX, [kon'-teks'], *n.* an attachment to a gas mask.
CONTEXT (1), [kon'-tekst], *n.* the adjacent parts of a passage in a specimen of literature or other writing. [L. *contextus*].
CONTEXT (2), [kon-tekst'], *adj.* woven together; close, firm, well-knit.
CONTEXT (3), [kon-tekst'], *v.t.* to knit together closely.
CONTEXTUAL, [kon-teks'-choo-al], *adj.* pertaining to the context.
CONTEXTUALLY, [kon-teks'-choo-al-i], *adv.* by, or arising from, the context.
CONTEXTURAL, [kon-teks'-cher-al], *adj.* relating to the contexture.
CONTEXTURE, [kon-teks'-cher], *n.* the interweaving of several parts into one; the disposition and proportion of the constituent parts of a thing with respect to each other; way in which anything is constructed; something woven.
CONTEXTURED, [kon-teks'-cherd], *adj.* woven or knitted together into a tissue.
CONTICENT, [kon'-tis-ent], *adj.* silenced, hushed. [L. *conticens*].
CONTIGNATION†, [kon'-tig-nā'-shun], *n.* a frame of beams; a storey, a floor; the act of framing together into a structure or fabric; the method by which this is done. [L. *contignatio*].
CONTIGUITY, [kon'-tig-ew'-i-ti], *n.* the state of being contiguous. [L. *contiguitas*].
CONTIGUOUS, [kon-tig'-yoo-us], *adj.* touching, adjoining, in contact. [L. *contiguus*].
CONTIGUOUSLY, [kon-tig'-yoo-us-li], *adv.* near.
CONTIGUOUSNESS, [kon-tig'-yoo-us-nes], *n.* contiguity.
CONTINENCE, [kon'-tin-ens], *n.* restraint, moderation in sexual indulgence, chastity. [L. *continentia*].
CONTINENCY, [kon'-tin-en-si], *n.* continence.
CONTINENT (1), [kon'-tin-ent], *n.* one of the five main territorial divisions of the earth's surface; any very large unbroken stretch of land; the mainland, *esp.* of Europe.
CONTINENT (2), [kon'-tin-ent], *adj.* chaste; abstaining from indulgence in sexual intercourse; moderate, temperate, showing self-restraint. [L. *continens* restraining].
CONTINENTAL (1), [kon'-tin-ent'-al], *n.* an inhabitant of the mainland of Europe.
CONTINENTAL (2), [kon'-tin-ent'-al], *adj.* pertaining to a continent, *esp.* to that of Europe.
CONTINENTALIZE, [kon-tin-ent'-al-iz], *v.t.* to make continental.
CONTINENTLY, [kon'-tin-ent-li] *adv.* in a continent fashion.
CONTINGENCE, [kon-tin'-jens], *n.* contingency. [Fr. *contingence*].
CONTINGENCY, [kon-tin'-jen-si], *n.* liability to happen; that which may happen, a possibility; a chance occurrence; a resultant event.
CONTINGENT (1), [kon-tin'-jent], *n.* contingency; a share, a due proportion; a predetermined number of soldiers, ships, etc.
CONTINGENT (2), [kon-tin'-jent], *adj.* that may or may not happen, liable to occur, possible, conditional; (*leg.*) dependent upon a possibility. [L. *contingens*, *pres.pt.* of *contingere*].
CONTINGENTLY, [kon-tin'-jent-li], *adv.* in contingent fashion.
CONTINUABLE, [kon-tin'-yoo-abl], *adj.* that can be continued.
CONTINUAL, [kon-tin'-yoo-al], *adj.* unceasing, unremitting; persistent, recurring, often repeated. [OFr. *continual*].
CONTINUALLY, [kon-tin'-yoo-a-li], *adv.* without ceasing; persistently.
CONTINUANCE, [kon-tin'-yoo-ans], *n.* persistence; duration; continuity.
CONTINUANT, [kon-tin'-yoo-ant], *n.* (*phon.*) a consonantal sound produced by allowing the breath to escape in a continuous stream.
CONTINUATE, [kon-tin'-yoo-āt], *adj.* knit closely together; holding together; continuous.
CONTINUATELY, [kon-tin'-yoo-at-li], *adv.* continuously.
CONTINUATION, [kon-tin'-yoo-ā'-shun], *n.* the act or process of continuing; the state of being continued; that which continues, an extension, prolongation, uninterrupted succession. [L. *continuatio*].
CONTINUATION-DAY, [kon-tin'-yoo-ā'-shun-dā'] *n.* (*Stock Exchange*) the day on which interest is paid.
CONTINUATIVE, [kon-tin'-yoo-at-iv], *adj.* that continues. [L. *continuativus*].
CONTINUATOR, [kon-tin'-yoo-āt-or], *n.* one who, or that which, continues.

CONTINUE, [kon-tin'-yōō], *v.t.* to extend, prolong; to unite without a break; to carry on after interruption; *v.i.* to go on, extend; to go on doing something; to remain. [L. *continuere*].
CONTINUED, [kon-tin'-yōōd], *adj.* sustained; extended in length; proceeding without stop; continuous.
CONTINUEDLY, [kon-tin'-yōōd-li], *adv.* in a continued fashion.
CONTINUER, [kon-tin'-yōō-er], *n.* one who, or that which, continues.
CONTINUING, [kon-tin'-yōō-ing], *adj.* lasting, enduring.
CONTINUITY, [kon'-tin-ew'-i-ti], *n.* the state or condition of being continuous. [L. *continuitas*].
CONTINUOUS, [kon-tin'-yōō-us], *adj.* joined in unbroken succession, uninterrupted; unceasing. [L. *continuus*].
CONTINUOUSLY, [kon-tin'-yōō-us-li], *adv.* in a continuous fashion.
CONTINUOUSNESS, [kon-tin'-yōō-us-nes], *n.* the state or quality of being continuous.
CONTINUUM, [kon-tin'-yōō-um], *n.* sequence; unbroken quantity, continuous entity. [L. *continuum*].
CONTLINE, [kont'-lin], *n.* the space between casks when stowed, or between the twisted strands of a rope. [Unkn.].
CONTO, [kon'-tō], *n.* a million Portuguese reis. [Portug. *conto*].
CONTORNIATI, [kon-tawn'-i-ah'-ti], *n.(pl.)* (*numis.*) ancient bronze medals, with a groove on both sides encircling the edge. [It. *contorniati*].
CONTORT, [kon-tawt'], *v.t.* to distort, to twist out of shape; (*fig.*) to twist the meaning of. [L. *contortum*, *p.pt.* of *contorquere* to twist].
CONTORTION, [kon-taw'-shun], *n.* the act of contorting; twisting, distorting; the state of being contorted. [L. *contortio*].
CONTORTIONIST, [kon-taw'-shun-ist], *n.* an acrobat or dancer who twists his body into contortions.
CONTOUR (1), [kon'-tōōer], *n.* an outline of a figure or object; a contour-line; **c.-line**, a line drawn on a map to show relative elevation; **c.-map**, a map with lines to show the surface of the country. **c. ploughing**, a method of ploughing in dry soils which follows land contours in order to collect moisture for the crops. [Fr. *contour*].

CONTOUR-LINES

CONTOUR (2), [kon'-tōōer], *v.t.* to show the contour of; to indicate contour-lines on.
CONTRA- (1), *pref.* against; (*mus.*) opposite to, indicating an octave lower than the usual form. [L. *contra*].
CONTRA (2), [kon'-tra], *n.* a contrary vote; **pros and contras**, votes or points for and against.
CONTRA (3), [kon'-tra], *prep. and adv.* against, opposing; to the contrary, in opposition. [L. *contra*].
CONTRABAND (1), [kon'-tra-band'], *n.* smuggling; goods smuggled and offered for sale illegally; **c. of war**, goods which may not be sold to a warring nation by neutrals. [Fr. *contrebande*].
CONTRABAND (2), [kon'-tra-band'], *adj.* prohibited by law, smuggled.
CONTRABANDIST, [kon'-tra-band'-ist], *n.* a smuggler.
CONTRABASS, [kon'-tra-bās'], *n.* the largest kind of bass-viol, the double-bass.
CONTRACEPTION, [kon'-tra-sep'-shun], *n.* the prevention of conception, by drugs or mechanical means. [CONTRA (1) and (CON)CEPTION].
CONTRACEPTIVE (1), [kon'-tra-sept'-iv], *n.* an appliance or drug preventing conception.
CONTRACEPTIVE (2), [kon'-tra-sept'-iv], *adj.* preventing conception.
CONTRACT (1), [kon'-trakt], *n.* a solemn agreement; bargain, compact; a bond; a betrothal; a solemn and binding promise; a document containing the terms of an agreement; the terms or conditions of a solemn agreement or compact; **c. bridge**, a form of bridge in which tricks won above those contracted for do not count towards game. [OFr. *contract*].
CONTRACT (2), [kon-trakt'], *v.t.* to draw together, tighten up; to knit together, causing to wrinkle; to shrink, narrow, shorten; to bring on, incur; to catch (a disease); *v.i.* to draw together; become tighter or shorter; to shrink. [L. *contractum*, *p.pt.* of *contrahere* to collect].
CONTRACT (3), [kon-trakt'], *v.t.* to draw up an agreement with another, to arrange by contract; *v.i.* to enter into a contract to do something. [CONTRACT (1)].
CONTRACTED, [kon-trakt'-id], *adj.* drawn up, knit together; shortened; wrinkled; (*fig.*) narrow, limited.
CONTRACTEDLY, [kon-trakt'-id-li], *adv.* in a contracted fashion.
CONTRACTEDNESS, [kon-trakt'-id-nes], *n.* the condition or quality of being contracted.
CONTRACTIBILITY, [kon-trakt'-ib-il'-i-ti], *n.* the condition of being contractible.
CONTRACTIBLE, [kon-trakt'-ibl], *adj.* liable to contract.
CONTRACTIBLENESS, [kon-trakt'-ibl-nes], *n.* contractibility.
CONTRACTILE, [kon-trakt'-il], *adj.* tending to contract; able to contract.
CONTRACTILITY, [kon'-trakt-il'-i-ti], *n.* the power or capacity of contracting. [Fr. *contractilité*].
CONTRACTING, [kon-trakt'-ing], *adj.* drawing together; shortening; able to contract; bound or engaged in contract.
CONTRACTION, [kon-trak'-shun], *n.* the act or process of contracting; that which is contracted; an abbreviated form of a word. [L. *contractio*].
CONTRACTIVE, [kon-trakt'-iv], *adj.* tending to contract.
CONTRACTOR, [kon-trakt'-or], *n.* a person who solemnly contracts to do work at an agreed price; a builder and house repairer; (*anat.*) a contracting muscle.
CONTRACTUAL, [kon-trak'-chōō-al], *adj.* pertaining to a contract.
CONTRA-DANCE, [kon'-tra-dahns'], *n.* a dance in which the partners are arranged in two rows or in a ring. [COUNTRY DANCE].
CONTRADICT, [kon'-tra-dikt'], *v.t.* to deny emphatically; to state the exact opposite of what someone says; to be at variance with. [L. *contradicere*].
CONTRADICTABLE, [kon'-tra-dikt'-abl], *adj.* that may be contradicted.
CONTRADICTION, [kon'-tra-dik'-shun], *n.* the act of contradicting; that which contradicts, a contrary statement. [L. *contradictio*].
CONTRADICTIOUS, [kon'-tra-dik'-shus], *adj.* contradictory.
CONTRADICTIVE, [kon'-tra-dikt'-iv], *adj.* contradictory.
CONTRADICTIVELY, [kon'-tra-dikt'-iv-li], *adv.* contradictorily.
CONTRADICTORILY, [kon'-tra-dikt'-or-i-li], *adv.* in contradictory fashion.
CONTRADICTORINESS, [kon'-tra-dikt'-or-i-nes], *n.* the state of being contradictory.
CONTRADICTORY (1), [kon'-tra-dikt'-or-i], *n.* an assertion to the contrary; anything that contradicts something else.
CONTRADICTORY (2), [kon'-tra-dikt'-or-i], *adj.* that contradicts.
CONTRADISTINCTION, [kon'-tra-dis-tingk'-shun], *n.* distinction by contrasting qualities.
CONTRADISTINCTIVE, [kon'-tra-dis-tingk'-tiv], *adj.* distinguished by contrast.
CONTRADISTINGUISH, [kon'-tra-dis-ting'-gwish], *v.t.* to distinguish by contrast.
CONTRAFISSURE, [kon'-tra-fish'-ōōer], *n.* (*surg.*) a fracture in the cranium on the opposite side to that which suffered the blow.
CONTRAHENT, [kon'-tra-hent], *adj.* contracting. [L. *contrahens*, *pres.pt.* of *contrahere* to draw together].
CONTRA-INDICANT, [kon'-tra-in'-dik-ant], *n.* (*path.*) a symptom discouraging the usual treatment.
CONTRA-INDICATE, [kon'-tra-in'-dik-āt], *v.t.* (*path.*) to indicate a different treatment from usual.
CONTRA-INDICATION, [kon'-tra-in'-dik-ā'-shun], *n.* (*path.*) an indication that discourages the usual treatment.
CONTRAJERVA, see CONTRAYERVA.
CONTRALATERAL, [kon'-tra-lat'-er-al], *adj.* on the opposite side.
CONTRALTO (1), [kon-tral'-tō], *n.* (*mus.*) the part sung by the lowest pitched female voice or, rarely, by the highest pitched male voice; a deep female voice; a woman with such a voice. [CONTRA and ALTO].
CONTRALTO (2), [kon-tral'-tō], *adj.* (*mus.*) resembling or suitable for a contralto.

CONTRAMURE, [kon'-tra-mew-er], *n.* a countermure. [Fr. *contremur*].

CONTRAPLEX, [kon'-tra-pleks'], *adj.* having two telegraphic messages passing each other simultaneously in opposite directions. [CONTRA and L. *plex* fold].

CONTRAPOSE, [kon'-tra-pōz'], *v.t.* to set against.

CONTRA-POSITION, [kon'-tra-poz-ish'-un], *n.* opposition, contrast; (*log.*) a form of conversion.

CONTRAPTION, [kon-trap'-shun], *n.* a makeshift, a contrivance, a strange device. [Invented word].

CONTRAPUNTAL, [kon'-tra-punt'-al], *adj.* relating to counterpoint. [It. *contrappunto*].

CONTRAPUNTIST, [kon'-tra-punt'-ist], *n.* (*mus.*) an expert in counterpoint. [It. *contrappuntista*].

CONTRARIANT, [kon-trāer'-i-ant], *adj.* inconsistent, contradictory. [OFr. *contrariant*].

CONTRARIETY, [kon'-tra-rī'-i-ti], *n.* the state or quality of being contrary; an inconsistency. [L. *contrarietas*].

CONTRARILY, [kon'-tra-ri-li], *adv.* in contrary fashion.

CONTRARINESS, [kon'-tra-ri-nes], *n.* the state of being contrary; perverseness.

CONTRARIOUS, [kon-trāer'-i-us], *adj.* perverse, deliberately awkward; harmful, disastrous. [OFr. *contrarios*].

CONTRARIWISE, [kon'-tra-ri-wiz], *adv.* in contrary fashion; on the contrary; in reverse directions.

CONTRA-ROTATION, [kon'-tra-rō-tā'-shun], *n.* reverse rotation.

CONTRARY (1), [kon'-tra-ri], *n.* the very opposite; (*log.*) a contrary proposition or term; **on the c.**, on the other hand; **to the c.**, in opposition. [L. *contrarius*].

CONTRARY (2), [kon'-tra-ri], *adj.* opposed to, contradicted by, against; opposite; unfavourable; **c. propositions**, (*log.*) propositions which contradict each other; **c. terms**, (*log.*) terms which express the exact opposites. [L. *contrarius*].

CONTRAST (1), [kon'-trahst], *n.* the act of contrasting; dissimilarity between things set in comparison; the things which show such unlikeness; unfavourable comparison; (*phot.*) the degree of variation between the lightest and darkest parts of a photograph. [Fr. *contraste*].

CONTRAST (2), [kon-trahst'], *v.t.* to compare objects so as to cause their differences to stand out clearly; to compare; *v.i.* to show dissimilarity when set in comparison, to stand out sharply. [Fr. *contraster*].

CONTRA-STIMULANT, [kon'-tra-stim'-yŏŏ-lant], *n.* (*med.*) a drug to counteract over-stimulation.

CONTRASTIVE, [kon-trahst'-iv], *adj.* that can be contrasted.

CONTRA-TENOR, [kon'-tra-ten'-or], *n.* the male alto voice or part.

CONTRATE-WHEEL, [kon'-trāt-wēl'], *n.* a gear-wheel whose teeth project at right angles to the plane of the wheel. [CONTRA].

CONTRATE-WHEEL

CONTRAVALLATION, COUNTERVALLATION, [kon'-tra-val-ā'-shun], *n.* (*milit.*) trenches or ramparts built by besiegers to protect themselves from the sorties of the besieged. [Fr. *contrevallation*].

CONTRAVENE, [kon'-tra-vēn'], *v.t.* to oppose, violate, be at variance with; to contradict; to oppose. [L. *contravenire*].

CONTRAVENTION, [kon'-tra-ven'-shun], *n.* the act of contravening.

CONTRAVERSION, [kon'-tra-vur'-shun], *n.* an antistrophe.

CONTRAYERVA, CONTRAJERVA, [kon'-tra-yur'-va], *n.* the root of several kinds of *Dorstenia*, used as an antidote. [Span. *contrayerva*].

CONTRETEMPS, [kon'-tra-taw(m)], *n.* an unexpected and unfortunate accident; a hitch, set-back. [Fr. *contretemps*].

CONTRIBUTABLE, [kon-trib'-yŏŏt-abl], *adj.* that may be contributed.

CONTRIBUTE, [kon-trib'-yŏŏt], *v.t. and i.* to give, subscribe along with others for a common end; to supply (help); to add (to knowledge); to write articles, stories, etc., (fairly regularly) for a publication. [L. *contribuere*].

CONTRIBUTION, [kon'-trib-ew'-shun], *n.* the act of contributing; the amount or thing contributed. [L. *contributio*].

CONTRIBUTIVE, [kon-trib'-yŏŏt-iv], *adj.* that contributes.

CONTRIBUTOR, [kon-trib'-yŏŏt-or], *n.* a person who contributes.

CONTRIBUTORY, [kon-trib'-yŏŏt-er-i], *adj.* pertaining to, maintained by, contributions; that contributes.

CONTRITE, [kon'-trit], *adj.* broken-hearted; deeply penitent or repentant, stricken with remorse. [L. *contritus* bruised].

CONTRITELY, [kon'-trit-li, kon-trit'-li], *adv.* in contrite fashion.

CONTRITENESS, [kon'-trit-nes], *n.* contrition.

CONTRITION, [kon-trish'-un], *n.* penitence; remorse. [L. *contritio* bruising, wearing down].

CONTRITURATE, [kon-trit'-yŏŏ-rāt], *v.t.* to pulverize, to grind to powder. [CON and TRITURATE].

CONTRIVABLE, [kon-trīv'-abl], *adj.* able to be contrived.

CONTRIVANCE, [kon-trīv'-ans], *n.* the act of contriving; that which is contrived; a device.

CONTRIVE, [kon-trīv'], *v.t.* to devise, to plan; to invent; *v.i.* to scheme or devise, to manage. [OFr. *controver*].

CONTRIVEMENT, [kon-trīv'-ment], *n.* the act of contriving.

CONTRIVER, [kon-trīv'-er], *n.* one who contrives.

CONTROL (1), [kon-trōl'], *n.* authority and guidance, restraint, supervision, the manual or mechanical management of machines, etc.; an accepted standard for comparison; the spirit alleged to direct the movements of a medium at spiritualistic séances; part of a road in which a racing car has to observe certain regulations; (*pl.*) instruments by which the movements of a machine are guided. [Fr. *controle*].

CONTROL (2), (**controlling, controlled**), [kon-trōl'], *v.t.* to curb, restrain; to regulate; to guide, superintend; to direct, supervise; to verify by the aid of an accepted standard. [Fr. *controler*].

CONTROLLABLE, [kon-trōl'-abl], *adj.* able to be controlled.

CONTROLLER, COMPTROLLER, [kon-trōl'-er], *n.* one who controls; an official who supervises the expenditure of the services, the King's household, etc.; a mechanical device for controlling machines.

CONTROLLERSHIP, [kon-trōl'-er-ship], *n.* the office or rank of a controller.

CONTROLMENT, [kon-trōl'-ment], *n.* the act of controlling.

CONTROL ROOM, [kon-trōl'-rōōm], *n.* the room from which (military) operations are directed.

CONTROVERSARY†, [kon'-trō-vurs'-er-i], *adj.* controversial.

CONTROVERSIAL, [kon'-tro-vur'-shal], *adj.* pertaining to, or inducing, controversy.

CONTROVERSIALIST, [kon'-tro-vur'-shal-ist], *n.* one skilled in, or fond of, controversy.

CONTROVERSIALLY, [kon-tro-vur'-shal-i], *adv.* in controversial fashion.

CONTROVERSION, [kon'-trō-vur'-shun], *n.* a turning to the opposite side. [MedL. *controversio*].

CONTROVERSY, [kon'-tro-vur-si], *n.* a dispute, argument, disputation, discussion. [L. *controversia*].

CONTROVERT, [kon'-tro-vurt'], *v.t.* to debate, argue, dispute about; to deny. [From CONTRA and L. *vertere* to turn].

CONTROVERTER, [kon'-tro-vurt'-er], *n.* one who controverts.

CONTROVERTIBLE, [kon'-tro-vurt'-ibl], *adj.* able to be controverted.

CONTROVERTIBLY, [kon'-tro-vurt'-ib-li], *adv.* in controvertible fashion.

CONTROVERTIST, [kon'-tro-vurt-ist], *n.* one who controverts.

CONTUMACIOUS, [kon'-tew-mā'-shus], *adj.* disobedient, refractory, insubordinate; (*fig.*) showing contempt of court. [L. *contumax*].

CONTUMACIOUSLY, [kon'-tew-mā'-shus-li], *adv.* in contumacious fashion.

CONTUMACIOUSNESS, [kon'-tew-mā'-shus-nes], *n.* the quality of being contumacious.

CONTUMACY, [kon'-tew-mas-i], *n.* wilful disobedience, insubordination. [L. *contumacia*].

CONTUMELIOUS, [kon'-tew-mēl'-i-us], *adj.* reproachful; insolent, contemptuously abusive.

CONTUMELIOUSLY, [kon'-tew-mēl'-i-us-li], *adv.* in contumelious fashion.

CONTUMELIOUSNESS, [kon'-tew-mēl'-i-us-nes], *n.* the quality of being contumelious.
CONTUMELY, [kon-tewm'-li], *n.* insolent language, behaviour or treatment; disgrace. [L. *contumelia*].
CONTUSE, [kon-tewz'], *v.t.* to cause injury without breaking the skin, to bruise. [L. *contusum*, *p.pt.* of *contundere* to bruise].
CONTUSION, [kon-tew'-zhun], *n.* (*med.*) a bruise; the act of contusing. [L. *contusio*].
CONTUSIVE, [kon-tew'-ziv], *adj.* causing a contusion.
CONUNDRUM, [kon-un'-drum], *n.* a riddle, a puzzling question. [Unkn.].
CONURBATION, [kon'-er-bā'-shun], *n.* a group of neighbouring towns which have grown by peripheral development into a single continuous built-up area. [CON (1) and L. *urbs urbis* town].
CONVALESCE, [kon'-val-es'], *v.i.* to recover one's strength and normal health after illness. [L. *convalescere*].
CONVALESCENCE, [kon'-val-es'-ens], *n.* the process of convalescing; the period necessary for this. [Fr. *convalescence*].
CONVALESCENCY, [kon'-val-es'-en-si], *n.* convalescence.
CONVALESCENT (1), [kon'-val-es'-ent], *n.* one who is convalescing.
CONVALESCENT (2), [kon'-val-es'-ent], *adj.* regaining health after illness; pertaining to convalescence.
CONVECTION, [kon-vek'-shun], *n.* the transmission of heat or electricity by the movement of a substance that is heated or electrified. [L. *convectio* carrying together].
CONVECTIVE, [kon-vek'-tiv], *adj.* that conveys; pertaining to convection.
CONVENABLE, [kon-vēn'-abl], *adj.* that may be convened.
CONVENANCES, [kaw(n)'-ven-ahnses], *n.(pl.)* an accepted standard of conduct or behaviour; conventional propriety. [Fr. *les convenances*].
CONVENE, [kon-vēn'], *v.t. and i.* to summon, to cause to gather together, to assemble, to meet. [L. *convenire*].
CONVENER, [kon-vēn'-er], *n.* one who convenes.
CONVENIENCE, [kon-vēn'-i-ens], *n.* the quality of being convenient, that which is convenient; material comfort; a useful contrivance or fitting, *esp.* in a house; a lavatory, water-closet; **to make a c. of someone,** to take advantage of a person's good nature. [L. *convenientia* fitness, suitability].
CONVENIENCY, [kon-vēn'-i-en-si], *n.* convenience.
CONVENIENT, [kon-vēn'-i-ent], *adj.* suitable, fitting, commodious; not causing trouble; suiting one's personal comforts; (*coll.*) comfortably accessible, near at hand. [L. *conveniens*, *pres.pt.* of *convenire* to be suitable].
CONVENIENTLY, [kon-vēn'-i-ent-li], *adv.* in a convenient manner.
CONVENING, [kon-vēn'-ing], *n.* the act of summoning or coming together.
CONVENT, [kon'-vent], *n.* a religious community, particularly of nuns, observing the rule of a religious order; the building in which such a community lives. [L. *conventus* an assembly].
CONVENTICLE, [kon-vent'-ikl], *n.* formerly a secret religious meeting of Dissenters; the building where such meetings were held; a small Nonconformist chapel. [L. *conventiculum* little assembly, meeting-place].
CONVENTION, [kon-ven'-shun], *n.* the act of convening; a formal assembly convened to conduct business; an agreement; an accepted mode of conduct or play. [L. *conventio*].
CONVENTIONAL, [kon-ven'-shun-al], *adj.* according to convention, or generally accepted practice; rigidly adhering to convention; traditional, stilted; unoriginal. [L. *conventionalis*].
CONVENTIONALISM, [kon-ven'-shun-al-izm], *n.* the state of being conventional; the rigid acceptance of convention.
CONVENTIONALITY, [kon-ven'-shun-al'-i-ti], *n.* the quality of being conventional; that which is conventional.
CONVENTIONALIZE, [kon-ven'-shun-al-iz], *v.t.* to make conventional.
CONVENTIONALLY, [kon-ven'-shun-a-li], *adv.* in a conventional fashion.
CONVENTIONARY (1), [kon-ven'-shun-er-i], *n.* a party to a convention; a tenant on agreed terms.
CONVENTIONARY (2), [kon-ven'-shun-er-i], *adj.* on terms settled by a convention or special contract or agreement.
CONVENTUAL (1), [kon-ven'-choo-al], *n.* an inmate of a convent; a member of the more lenient branch of the Franciscan order.
CONVENTUAL (2), [kon-ven'-choo-al], *adj.* pertaining to a convent; pertaining to the Conventuals. [L. *conventualis*].
CONVERGE, [kon-vurj'], *v.t.* to cause to converge; *v.i.* to approach and meet at a point; (*math.*) (of a series) to approximate towards a definite limit in certain of its terms; (*fig.*) to be focused on. [L. *convergere*].
CONVERGENCE, [kon-vurj'-ens], *n.* the act of converging; the tendency to converge.
CONVERGENCY, [kon-vurj'-en-si], *n.* convergence.
CONVERGENT, [kon-vurj'-ent], *adj.* converging, inclined to converge. [L. *convergens*, *pres.pt.* of *convergere*].
CONVERSABLE, [kon-vurs'-abl], *adj.* easy and ready in conversation, sociable, affable.
CONVERSABLENESS, [kon-vurs'-abl-nes], *n.* the quality of being conversable.
CONVERSABLY, [kon-vurs'-ab-li], *adv.* in a conversable manner.
CONVERSANCE, [kon-vurs'-ans], *n.* the quality of being conversant.
CONVERSANT, [kon-vurs'-ant], *adj.* familiar, acquainted; having intimate knowledge of, experienced in. [L. *conversans*].
CONVERSANTLY, [kon-vurs'-ant-li], *adv.* in a conversant manner.
CONVERSATION, [kon'-ver-sā'-shun], *n.* talk, as a form of social intercourse; (*leg.*) †sexual intercourse; **c. piece,** a painting of a group of figures; **to make c.,** to talk merely in order to avoid a silence, without having anything special to say. [L. *conversatio*].
CONVERSATIONAL, [kon'-ver-sā'-shun-al], *adj.* skilled in the art of conversation; relating or suited to conversation; chatty and informal.
CONVERSATIONALIST, [kon'-ver-sā'-shun-al-ist], *n.* a good talker.
CONVERSATIONISM, [kon'-ver-sā'-shun-izm], *n.* a colloquial expression.
CONVERSATIONIST, [kon-ver-sā'-shun-ist], *n.* a conversationalist.
CONVERSATIVE, [kon-vurs'-at-iv], *adj.* inclined to converse; conversable.
CONVERSAZIONE, [kon'-ver-sat-si-ō'-ni], *n.* a meeting for conversation, a soirée given by a learned, scientific, or literary body. [It. *conversazione*].
CONVERSE (1), [kon'-vurs], *n.* conversation, social intercourse or friendly dealings.
CONVERSE (2), [kon'-vurs], *n.* the exact opposite, antithesis.
CONVERSE (3), [kon'-vurs], *adj.* reverse, opposite, contrary. [L. *conversus*].
CONVERSE (4), [kon-vurs'], *v.i.* to talk, have conversation with. [L. *conversari* to associate with].
CONVERSELY, [kon-vurs'-li], *adv.* in converse fashion. [CONVERSE (3)].
CONVERSION, [kon-vur'-shun], *n.* the act of converting; the state of being converted, *esp.* to another form of religion; a spiritual awakening; (*log.*) interchanging of the terms of a proposition; **fraudulent c.,** the misappropriation to one's own use of funds entrusted to one by a body or a number of individuals. [L. *conversio*].
CONVERSIVE, [kon-vur'-siv], *adj.* able to convert.
CONVERT (1), [kon'-vurt], *n.* one who has been converted, *esp.* to a new religious creed.
CONVERT (2), [kon-vurt'], *v.t.* to transform, to change from one form or function to another; to persuade to adopt some particular religious creed; to awaken spiritually; (*comm.*) to change one kind of stock to another of like value; (*leg.*) to misappropriate to one's own use; (*Rugby football*) to complete a try by kicking a goal. [L. *convertere* to turn round].
CONVERTEND, [kon'-vurt-end'], *n.* (*log.*) the proposition for conversion.
CONVERTER, [kon-vurt'-er], *n.* one who converts; the receptacle in which molten iron is converted into steel; **rotary c.,** an electric motor and dynamo for converting the applied current into another form.
CONVERTIBILITY, [kon-vurt'-i-bil'-i-ti], *n.* the capacity for being converted.
CONVERTIBLE, [kon-vurt'-ibl], *adj.* able to be converted.
CONVERTIBLENESS, [kon-vurt'-ibl-nes], *n.* convertibility.
CONVERTIBLY, [kon-vurt'-ib-li], *adv.* interchangeably.
CONVERTITE, [kon'-vert-īt], *n.* a convert.

CONVEX, [kon'-veks'], *adj.* with the surface curving outwards; (*opt.*) (*a*) convexo-concave, (*b*) convexo-convex, (*c*) convexo-plane (see illustration). [L. *convexus* vaulted].

(*a*) (*b*) (*c*)
CONVEX

CONVEXED, [kon'-vekst], *adj.* made convex in form.
CONVEXEDLY, [kon-vek'-sid-li], *adv.* convexly.
CONVEXITY, [kon-vek'-sit-i], *n.* the quality or state of being convex.
CONVEXLY, [kon'-veks'-li], *adv.* in a convex shape.
CONVEXNESS, [kon-veks'-nes], *n.* convexity.
CONVEY, [kon-vā'], *v.t.* to transport, take, carry from one place to another; to lead, conduct; (*fig.*) to communicate, make known; (*leg.*) to transfer real property. [OFr. *conveier* to escort].
CONVEYABLE, [kon-vā'-abl], *adj.* able to be conveyed.
CONVEYANCE, [kon-vā'-ans], *n.* the act or process of conveying; the means by which something is conveyed; a vehicle, carriage; (*leg.*) the making over of real property to different ownership; the legal document embodying such a transfer.
CONVEYANCER, [kon-vā'-ans-er], *n.* (*leg.*) one employed in drawing up conveyances of property.
CONVEYANCING, [kon-vā'-ans-ing], *n.* (*leg.*) the drawing up of conveyances of property; the branch of law dealing with this.
CONVEYER, CONVEYOR, [kon-vā'-er], *n.* one who, or that which, conveys; a mechanical apparatus for conveying goods.
CONVICINITY, [kon'-vis-in'-i-ti], *n.* the immediate neighbourhood.
CONVICT (1), [kon'-vikt], *n.* a person convicted after trial in a court of law; a person serving a sentence of penal servitude. [L. *convictus*].
CONVICT (2), [kon-vikt'], *v.t.* to find guilty of a crime after trial in a judicial court; (*fig.*) to prove guilty of a fault. [L. *convictum*, *p.pt.* of *convincere* to prove guilty].
CONVICTED, [kon-vikt'-id], *adj.* declared guilty.
CONVICTION, [kon-vik'-shun], *n.* the act of convicting; the fact of being convicted; the state of being convinced; a firm belief, convinced opinion; **to carry c.,** to sound convincing. [L. *convictio*].
CONVICTIVE, [kon-vikt'-iv], *adj.* able to convince or convict.
CONVINCE, [kon-vins'], *v.t.* to satisfy the mind, or compel belief by evidence; to cause to feel certain that, to persuade to believe something. [L. *convincere* to overcome by argument].
CONVINCEMENT, [kon-vins'-ment], *n.* conviction.
CONVINCIBLE, [kon-vins'-ibl], *adj.* capable of being convinced.
CONVINCINGLY, [kon-vins'-ing-li], *adv.* in convincing fashion.
CONVINCINGNESS, [kon-vins'-ing-nes], *n.* the power of convincing.
CONVIVE, [kon'-vēv], *n.* a fellow guest at a banquet. [Fr. *convive*].
CONVIVIAL, [kon-viv'-i-al], *adj.* festive, jovial, social. [L. *convivialis*].
CONVIVIALIST, [kon-viv'-i-al-ist], *n.* one displaying conviviality.
CONVIVIALITY, [kon-viv'-i-al'-i-ti], *n.* festivity; good humour befitting a feast; good-fellowship.
CONVIVIALLY, [kon-viv'-i-al-i], *adv.* in convivial fashion.
CONVOCATE, [kon'-vō-kāt], *v.t.* to convoke. [L. *convocare*].
CONVOCATION, [kon'-vō-kā'-shun], *n.* the act of convoking; a formal assembly convoked for a particular purpose; (*eccles.*) a synod of provincial clergy; a legislative body in the Universities of Oxford and Durham; the collective body of registered graduates at certain universities. [L. *convocatio*].
CONVOCATIONAL, [kon'-vō-kā'-shun-al], *adj.* pertaining to a convocation.
CONVOKE, [kon-vōk'], *v.t.* to call together, to summon, to assemble; to convene. [L. *convocare*].
CONVOLUTE, [kon'-vol-ewt], *adj.* (*bot.*) rolled together or upon itself; coiled. [L. *convolutus*].
CONVOLUTED, [kon'-vol-ewt'-id], *adj.* (*zool.*) coiled, rolled up into a spiral.
CONVOLUTION, [kon'-vol-ew'-shun], *n.* the act of convolving; the state of being convolved; a winding, a fold, a coil.
CONVOLVE, [kon-volv'], *v.t. and i.* to roll together; to roll one part on another; to roll back upon itself. [L. *convolvere*].
CONVOLVULUS, [kon-volv'-vŏŏ-lus], *n.* (*bot.*) a large genus of plants, including the bindweed. [L. *convolvulus*].
CONVOY (1), [kon'-voi], *n.* ships of war which convoy merchant vessels; the merchant ships so convoyed.
CONVOY (2), [kon'-voi], *v.t.* to accompany for purposes of protection; to escort non-combatant vessels in time of war. [OFr. *convoier*].
CONVULSE, [kon-vuls'], *v.t.* to agitate violently; to unsettle, upset deeply; to set up a series of violent spasmodic muscular contractions; to overcome with a paroxysm of emotion. [L. *convulsum*, *p.pt.* of *convellere* to shake].
CONVULSION, [kon-vul'-shun], *n.* a sudden, violent shaking or disturbance; strong social or political upset or upheaval; (*pl.*) a fit characterized by a series of spasmodic, involuntary twitchings of the muscles; an overpowering paroxysm of strong emotion. [L. *convulsio*].
CONVULSIONARY, [kon-vul'-shun-er-i], *adj.* connected with, relating to, convulsion.
CONVULSIVE, [kon-vul'-siv], *adj.* producing or attended by convulsions. [Fr. *convulsif*].
CONVULSIVELY, [kon-vul'-siv-li], *adv.* in convulsive fashion.
CONY, CONEY, [kō'-ni], *n.* the rabbit, *Lepus cuniculus*. [OFr. *coniz* from L. *cuniculus*].
CONY-CATCHER†, [kō'-ni-kach'-er], *n.* (*slang*) a sharper, a cheat.
CONY-CATCHING†, [kō'-ni-kach'-ing], *n.* (*slang*) cheating, sharping.
CONY-SKIN, [kō'-ni-skin'], *n.* the skin of rabbits.
COO (1), [kōō], *n.* the soft cry of doves or pigeons; a soft, gentle sound resembling this.
COO (2), [kōō], *v.i.* to utter the soft cry of pigeons and doves; (of babies) to utter gentle inarticulate sounds of content; to speak gently and soothingly; **to bill and c.,** to make love by endearments and fondling. [Imitative].
COOEE, [kōō'-ē], *int.* a call of the Australian bushmen; a similar cry to attract attention.
COOING, [kōō'-ing], *n.* the act of one who coos.
COOK (1), [kŏŏk], *n.* one who cooks, *esp.* a domestic employed to prepare food for eating. [OE. *coc* from L. *coquus*].
COOK (2), [kŏŏk], *v.t.* to prepare food for eating by roasting, boiling, frying, etc ; (*fig.*) to subject to great heat; to prepare something falsely, fake; *v.i.* to be prepared for eating by subjection to heat; **to c. one's goose,** to spoil one's scheme.
COOKER, [kŏŏk'-er], *n.* a stove or other apparatus for cooking; a fruit particularly fitted for cooking.
COOKERY, [kŏŏk'-er-i], *n.* the art and practice of cooking.
COOK-HOUSE, [kŏŏk'-hows], *n.* a camp-kitchen; caboose.
COOKIE, [kŏŏk'-i], *n.* (*Scots*) a plain bun; (*U.S.*) a small cake.
COOK-ROOM, [kŏŏk'-rōōm], *n.* a cook-house; an outdoor kitchen.
COOK-SHOP, [kŏŏk'-shop'], *n.* an eating-house, a shop where cooked food is sold.
COOKY, [kŏŏk'-i], *n.* (*coll.*) a female cook.
COOL (1), [kōōl], *n.* coolness; that which is cool.
COOL (2), [kool], *adj.* pleasantly cold; chilly; fresh, not too warm; (*fig.*) clear-headed; deliberate, calm; lukewarm, apathetic; lacking in friendliness or warmth of feeling; offhand, impudent; (*hunting*) (of scent) faint. [OE. *col*].
COOL (3), [kōōl], *v.t.* to make cool; *v.i.* to become cool, to grow cool; **to c. one's heels,** to be kept waiting; **to keep one's breath to c. one's porridge,** not to waste one's words. [OE. *colian*].
COOLER, [kōōl'-er], *n.* anything that abates heat or excitement; a vessel in which things are cooled.
COOL-HEADED, [kōōl'-hed'-id], *adj* not easily excited or alarmed.
COOLIE, [kōōl'-i], *n.* a hired native servant or porter in India, China, and Malaya. [Native].
COOLISH, [kōōl'-ish], *adj.* rather cool.
COOLLY, [kōōl'-li], *adv.* in a cool manner.
COOLNESS, [kōōl'-nes], *n.* the state or quality of

being cool; a difference of opinion, disagreement.

COOM, [kōōm], *n.* soot accumulating in the mouth of an oven; black stuff that works out of the axles of wheels. [ME. *colm*].

COOMBE, COMBE, [kōōm], *n.* a deep, narrow valley often wooded; a hollow on the slope of a hill. [OE. *cumb*].

COON, [kōōn], *n.* a racoon; (*coll.*) a negro; a shrewd fellow. [(RA)COON].

COON-CAN, [kōōn'-kan'], *n.* an American and Mexican card game. [Span. *con quien?* with whom?].

COOP (1), [kōōp], *n.* a cask or barrel; a wooden cage for hens; a wicker basket for catching fish. [L. *cupa* cask].

COOP (2), [kōōp], *v.t.* to put in a coop; to confine; **to c. in, up,** to confine within a small space.

CO-OP, [kō-op'], *n.* a co-operative society or shop. [CO-OP(ERATIVE)].

COOPER (1), [kōōp'-er], *n.* one who makes barrels and casks. [ME. *couper*].

COOPER (2), see COPER (1).

COOPER (3), [kōōp'-er], *v.t.* to repair barrels; to ply the trade of a cooper.

COOPERAGE, [kōōp'-er-ij], *n.* the price paid for work done by the cooper; a cooper's work or workshop.

CO-OPERANT, [kō-op'-er-ant], *adj.* working together.

CO-OPERATE, [kō-op'-er-āt], *v.i.* to work or act together for a common end; to aid one another in producing an effect. [CO and OPERATE].

CO-OPERATION, [kō-op'-er-ā'-shun], *n.* the act of co-operating; a group of people working together in the production or provision of goods for the common profit.

CO-OPERATIVE, [kō-op'-er-at-iv], *adj.* working or acting together for the same end or a common purpose; (of a trading concern) owned or controlled by its customers.

CO-OPERATIVELY, [kō-op'-er-at-iv-li], *adv.* in co-operative fashion.

CO-OPERATOR, [kō-op'-er-āt'-or], *n.* a person who co-operates.

COOPERING, [kōōp'-er-ing], *n.* the trade of a cooper.

CO-OPT, [kō-opt'], *v.t.* to elect to membership of a body by the votes of the existing members. [L. *co-optare* to elect].

CO-OPTATION, [kō-op-tā'-shun], *n.* election to a body by the votes of its existing members.

CO-OPTATIVE, [kō-opt'-at-iv], *adj.* eligible for co-optation.

CO-ORDINATE (1), [kō-awd'-in-at], *n.* that which is co-ordinate; (*math.*) any one of a system of magnitudes used to fix the position of a line or point.

CO-ORDINATE (2), [kō-awd'-in-at], *adj.* in the same order; of equal rank or importance. [L. *co-ordinatus* set in order].

CO-ORDINATE (3), [kō-awd'-in-āt], *v.t.* to make co-ordinate; to bring into proper order or relation. [L. *co-ordinatum*, *p.pt.* of *co-ordinare* to set in order].

CO-ORDINATELY, [kō-awd'-in-at-li], *adv.* in the same order or in equal rank.

CO-ORDINATENESS, [kō-awd'-in-at-nes], *n.* the state or quality of being co-ordinate.

CO-ORDINATION, [kō-awd'-in-ā'-shun], *n.* the act of co-ordinating; the condition of being co-ordinate.

CO-ORDINATIVE, [kō-awd'-in-at-iv], *adj.* that co-ordinates.

COOT, [kōōt], *n.* the water-fowl, *Fulica atra.* [ME. *cote*].

COP (1), [kop], *n.* a small hill; a ball of thread or yarn on a spindle. [OE. *copp* summit, top].

COP (2), [kop], *n.* (*slang*) the act of catching or finding out; a policeman; **no great c.,** not much of a haul, not much use. [COP (3)].

COP (3), (**copping, copped**), [kop], *v.t.* (*slang*) to catch, to take in charge; to detect, to find in the act (of committing an offence). [Uncert.].

COPAIBA, [kop-ī'-ba], *n.* a balsam, made from a liquid resinous juice obtained from the copaiva tree, a species of *Copaifera.* [Span. *copaiba* from Brazilian *cupauba*].

COPAL, [kōpl], *n.* the juice of certain tropical trees, used for varnishing. [Mexican *copalli* resin].

COPANG, [kō'-pang], *n.* a Japanese coin. [Jap. *coping*].

COPARCENARY, [kō-pah'-sen-er-i], *n.* joint inheritance, or heirship. [CO and PARCENARY].

COPARCENER, [kō-pah'-sen-er], *n.* a co-heir, fellow parcener.

COPARTNER, [kō-paht'-ner], *n.* a joint partner, fellow partner.

COPARTNERSHIP, [kō-paht'-ner-ship], *n.* joint business concern; the persons who own or direct a joint concern; partnership between employers and employed.

COPARTNERY, [kō-paht'-ner-i], *n.* copartnership.

CO-PATRIOT, [kō-pā'-tri-ot], *n.* a fellow patriot; fellow loyalist.

COPE (1), [kōp], *n.* a vestment in the form of a long ornamented cloak, worn by the clergy on special occasions; (*fig.*) anything that covers, envelops, like a cope; (*arch.*) coping. [MedL. *capa* cape].

COPE (2), [kōp], *v.t.* to array in a cope; (*arch.*) to furnish with a coping.

COPE (3), [kōp], *v.i.* to handle, deal with a difficult person or situation successfully. [OFr. *couper* to strike].

COPECK, KOPECK, [kō'-pek], *n.* a Russian copper coin, the hundredth part of a rouble. [Russ. *kopeika*].

COPEPODA, [kō-pep'-od-a], *n.*(*pl.*) an order of crustaceans, including the water-fleas and fish-lice. [Gk. *kope* handle and *pous* foot].

COPER (1), COOPER, [kōp'-er], *n.* a ship surreptitiously supplying grog to deep-sea fishermen in the North Sea. [Du. *kooper*].

COPER (2), [kōp'-er], *n.* a horse-dealer, usually a dishonest one. [~Du. *koopen* to buy].

COPERNICAN, [kop-ur'-nik-an], *adj.* relating to the astronomical theories of Copernicus. [*Copernicus*, an astronomer (1473-1543)].

COPESTONE, [kōp'-stōn], *n.* a top-stone.

COPHOSIS, [kof-ō'-sis], *n.* (*med.*) total deafness. [Gk. *kophosis*].

COPIER, [kop'-i-er], *n.* a person who copies.

COPING, [kōp'-ing], *n.* (*arch.*) the top course of a wall; a projecting edge running along the top of a wall. [COPE (1)].

COPING-SAW, [kōp'-ing-saw'], *n.* a triangular-shaped frame with a handle and a detachable, narrow saw-blade, used for the purposes of fine metal work.

COPING-SAW

COPING-STONE, [kōp'-ing-stōn'], *n.* a stone that forms a coping.

COPIOUS, [kō'-pi-us], *adj.* abundant; plentiful; prolific; diffuse. [L. *copiosus*].

COPIOUSLY, [kō'-pi-us-li], *adv.* in a copious way; diffusely.

COPIOUSNESS, [kō'-pi-us-nes], *n.* plenteousness, abundance; diffusiveness of style in treating a subject.

COPOS†, [kō'-pos], *n.* weariness, lassitude. [Gk. *kopos* fatigue].

COPPER (1), [kop'-er], *n.* a malleable metal, reddish-brown in colour, and a good conductor; (*chem.*) the chemical element denoted by Cu ; a coin made of copper, a penny or halfpenny; a large vessel (formerly made of copper) for boiling clothes in when washing them. [OE. *coper* from LL. *cuper*].

COPPER (2), [kop'-er], *n.* (*slang*) policeman. [COP (3)].

COPPER (3), [kop'-er], *v.t.* to cover with copper.

COPPERAS, [kop'-er-as], *n.* sulphate of iron, also called green vitriol. [Fr. *couperose*].

COPPER-BEECH, [kop'-er-bēch'], *n.* a beech-tree with copper-coloured leaves.

COPPER-BOTTOMED, [kop'-er-bot'-omd], *adj.* (*naut.*) plated with copper below the waterline.

COPPER-CAPTAIN, [kop'-er-kap'-tin], *n.* a sham or false captain.

COPPER-FASTENED, [kop'-er-fahs'-end], *adj.* secured by copper bolts.

COPPER-GLANCE, [kop'-er-glahnts'], *n.* redruthite, an ore consisting of copper and sulphur.

COPPERHEAD, [kop'-er-hed'], *n.* a venomous North American snake; (*fig.*) a defeatist.

COPPERISH, [kop'-er-ish], *adj.* containing copper; resembling copper.

COPPER-NICKEL, [kop'-er-nik'-el], *n.* a native Westphalian copper-coloured ore of nickel and arsenic.

COPPER-NOSE, [kop'-er-nōz'], *n.* a red nose, *esp.* one caused by drink.

COPPERPLATE (1), [kop'-er-plāt'], *n.* (*print.*) a plate or sheet of polished copper with an engraving or etching upon it; the print taken from the plate.

COPPERPLATE (2), [kop'-er-plāt'], *adj.* like a print made from a copperplate; neat, beautifully and carefully formed with fine lines, *esp.* of hand-writing.
COPPER-PYRITES, [kop'-er-pi-ri'-tēz], *n.* a copper ore.
COPPERSMITH, [kop'-er-smith'], *n.* a craftsman who works in copper.
COPPER-TOP, [kop'-er-top'], *n.* (*slang*) a red-headed person.
COPPER-WORK, [kop'-er-wurk'], *n.* work carried out in copper.
COPPER-WORM, [kop'-er-wurm'], *n.* a little worm found in ships.
COPPERY, [kop'-er-i], *adj.* blended with copper, made of copper; like copper.
COPPICE, [kop'-is], *n.* a thicket of brushwood; a small wood, cut periodically for fuel. [OFr. *copeiz*].
COPPIN, [kop'-in], *n.* the cone of thread which is formed round the spindle of a wheel. [COP].
COPPLESTONE†, see COBBLESTONE.
COPRA, [ko'-pra], *n.* dried coconut kernels, from which coconut oil is extracted. [Malayalam *koppara* cocoa-nut].
COPROLITE, [kop'-rol-īt], *n.* fossilized dung, chiefly of extinct saurians. [Gk. *kopros* dung and *lithos* stone].
COPROLITIC, [kop'-rol-it'-ik], *adj.* containing, or like, coprolite.
COPROLOGY, [kop-rol'-o-ji], *n.* obscenity, indecency in art and literature. [Gk. *kopros* dung and *logos* speech].
COPROPHAGAN, [kop-rof'-ag-an], *n.* a beetle which lives on or in dung. [Gk. *kopros* dung and *phago* I eat].
COPROPHAGOUS, [kop-rof'-ag-us], *adj.* eating or feeding on dung.
COPSE, [kops], *n.* a small wood, a thicket of small trees and undergrowth; coppice. [OFr. *copeiz*].
COPSE-WOOD, [kops'-wŏŏd], *n.* a coppice.
COPSY, [kops'-i], *adj.* studded with copses, having copses.
COPT, [kopt], *n.* a Christian Egyptian. [Gk. (*ai*)*guptos* Egyptian].
COPTIC (1), [kop'-tik], *n.* the language of the Copts, or Christian descendants of the Ancient Egyptians.
COPTIC (2), [kop'-tik], *adj.* pertaining to the Copts.
COPULA, [kop'-ew-la], *n.* (*anat.*) a joining, a connecting bone or cartilage; (*gram.*) the word that links subject and predicate. [L. *copula* band, link].
COPULATE, [kop'-yōō-lāt], *v.i.* to join, unite in copulation. [L. *copulare*].
COPULATION, [kop'-yōō-lā'-shun], *n.* union, binding together; the sexual act, coition. [L. *copulatio*].
COPULATIVE (1), [kop'-yōō-lat-iv], *n.* a connecting word.
COPULATIVE (2), [kop'-yōō-lat-iv], *adj.* pertaining to copulation; (*gram.*) serving to connect as a copula. [L. *copulativus*].
COPULATORY, [kop'-yōō-lāt-er-i], *adj.* pertaining to copulation.
COPY (1), [kop'-i], *n.* an imitation; a transcript; a reproduction; one of a number of similar examples of a book or other document; literary or other matter in manuscript ready to be printed; (*leg.*) a record of the admissions of tenants to land under copyhold. [Fr. *copie* from L. *copia* ability, means].
COPY (2), [kop'-i], *v.t.* and *i.* to make a copy, an imitation or a transcript of; to imitate. [L. *copiare*].
COPY-BOOK, [kop'-i-bŏŏk'], *n.* a book in which specimens of handwriting are provided for the young to imitate in learning to write.
COPYHOLD, [kop'-i-hōld'], *n.* (*leg.*) the tenure of land at the will of the lord of the manor; land held under this system.
COPYHOLDER, [kop'-i-hōld'-er], *n.* one who holds land in copyhold.
COPYING-PRESS, [kop'-i-ing-pres'], *n.* a machine for taking an exact copy of handwritten documents.
COPYIST, [kop'-i-ist], *n.* one who copies; a transcriber; an imitator.
COPYRIGHT (1), [kop'-i-rīt'], *n.* the exclusive right of an author, artist, etc. to reproduce his works over a fixed period.
COPYRIGHT (2), [kop'-i-rīt'], *adj.* protected by copyright.
COPYRIGHT (3), [kop'-i-rīt'], *v.t.* to protect by copyright.
COQUE, [kok, kōk], *n.* a loop of ribbon. [Fr. *coque* shell].
COQUET, [kōk-et'], *v.i.* to flirt, try to attract the admiration of the male sex; (*fig.*) to play with an idea for a short time. [Fr. *coqueter* to strut like a cock].
COQUETRY, [ko'-ket-ri], *n.* flirtatious behaviour; superficial prettiness. [Fr. *coquetterie*].
COQUETTE, [kōk-et'], *n.* a woman who attempts to win the admiration of the other sex by coquetry; a kind of crested humming-bird. [Fr. *coquette*].
COQUETTISH, [kōk-et'-ish], *adj.* behaving like a coquette.
COQUETTISHLY, [kōk-et'-ish-li], *adv.* in a coquettish fashion.
COQUILLA-NUT, [ko-kil'-ya-nut'], *n.* the fruit of the Brazilian palm, *Attalea funifera*. [Span. *coquilla* little shell].
COQUIMBITE, [kok-im'-bīt], *n.* a kind of ferric sulphate from Coquimbo. [*Coquimbo*, a place in Chile].
COQUITO, [kok-ē'-tō], *n.* the Chilean honey-yielding palm, *Jubaea spectabilis*. [Span. *coquito* little palm].
COR, [kaw(r)], *n.* a homer, a Hebrew measure of capacity. [Heb. *cor*].
CORACITE, [kor'-as-īt], *n.* a kind of black uraninite. [Gk. *korax* crow].
CORACLE, [kor'-akl], *n.* a small row-boat used by the ancient Britons, and still used in Wales and Ireland, consisting of a wicker frame covered with skin, leather or canvas. [~Welsh *corwgl*].
CORACOID (1), [kor'-ak-oid], *n.* (*anat.*) a small bone helping to articulate the fore-limb.
CORACOID (2), [kor'-ak-oid], *adj.* like a crow's beak in shape. [Gk. *korax* crow and *oeides* like].
CO-RADICATE, [kō-rad'-ik-āt], *adj.* (*philol.*) pertaining to, derived from, the same root. [CO and L. *radix* root].
CORAL (1), [kor'-al], *n.* a sea-water zoophyte, akin to sea-anemones, found in the tropical oceans; the white or reddish hard substance left by coral organisms; a bead or ornament made of this. [OFr. *coral*].
CORAL (2), [kor'-al], *adj.* made of coral; resembling coral in colour.

CORAL

CORALLACEOUS, [kor'-al-ā'-shus], *adj.* containing or like coral.
CORALLIAN, [kor-al'-i-an], *n.* (*geol.*) Jurassic rocks formed between the Oxford and Kimmeridge clays, coral-rag.
CORALLIFEROUS, [kor'-al-if'-er-us], *adj.* containing, producing coral. [CORAL and L. *ferre* to bear].
CORALLIFORM, [kor-al'-i-fawm], *adj.* like coral.
CORALLIGENOUS, [kor'-al-ij'-en-us], *adj.* producing coral. [CORAL and Gk. *genes* born].
CORALLINE (1), [kor'-al-īn], *n.* a sea-weed or animal like coral in appearance.
CORALLINE (2), [kor'-al-īn], *adj.* made of, or like, coral.
CORALLITE, [kor'-al-īt], *n.* a petrified coral; (*zool.*) the skeleton of a single zoophyte. [CORAL and Gk. *lithos* stone].
CORALLOID, [kor'-al-oid'], *adj.* like coral; branching like coral. [CORAL and Gk. *oeides* like]
CORALLOIDAL, [kor'-al-oid'-al], *adj.* coralloid.
CORAL-RAG, [kor'-al-rag'], *n.* (*geol.*) a limestone containing petrified coral.
CORAL-REEF, [kor'-al-rēf'], *n.* a series of marine ridges formed by the deposit of coral.
CORAL-ROOT, [kor'-al-rōōt'], *n.* an orchid of the genus *Corallorhiza*.
CORAL-SNAKE, [kor'-al-snāk'], *n.* any species of the genus *Elaps*.
CORAL-TREE, [kor'-al-trē'], *n.* a tropical African or American flowering shrub of the genus *Erythrina*.
CORALWORT, [kor'-al-wurt'], *n.* (*bot.*) the tooth-violet, toothwort, *Dentaria bulbifera*.
CORANACH, see CORONACH.
COR ANGLAIS, [kaw(r)'-ong'-glā], *n.* a wood-wind instrument, the tenor oboe. [Fr. *cor anglais*].
CORANTO, [kor-an'-tō], *n.* a rapid sprightly dance, courante; a tune to which this could be danced. [Span. *coranto* running].
CORB, [kawb], *n.* an iron basket used in collieries, corf; an alms-basket. [L. *corbis* basket].
CORBAN, [kawb'-an], *n.* an offering dedicated exclusively to God. [Heb. *qorban* offering].
CORBEIL†, [kawb'-el], *n.* a basket filled with earth and used as a protection against the enemy's fire. [Fr. *corbeille* basket].

CORBEL (1), [kawb'-el], *n.* (*arch.*) a bracket or stone projection from the face of the wall used as a support; a short beam set lengthwise under a girder. [OFr. *corbel* raven].

CORBEL (2), (corbelling, corbelled), [kawb'-el], *v.t.* to support by a corbel.

CORBICULA, [kaw-bik'-yoo-la], *n.* the hairy surface of the hind-leg of a bee where the pollen is carried. [L. *corbicula* little basket].

CORBIE, [kaw'-bi], *n.* (*Scots*) a crow. [~OFr. *corbel* a crow].

CORBEL

CORCASS, [kaw'-kas], *n.* the salt-marshes along the banks of some Irish rivers. [Irish *corcach*].

CORCLE, CORCULE, [kaw'-kl], *n.* (*bot.*) the embryo in a seed. [L. *corculum* little heart].

CORD (1), [kawd], *n.* a thin rope; thick, stout string; (*anat.*) parts of the body resembling this; a ribbed cloth; (*pl.*) breeches made of ribbed cloth. [Gk. *khorde* gut].

CORD (2), [kawd], *v.t.* to make fast or tie with a cord.

CORDAGE, [kawd'-ij], *n.* ropes or cords in general; the series of cords forming the rigging of a ship; a store of ropes. [Fr. *cordage*].

CORDATE, [kawd'-āt], *adj.* (*bot.*) shaped like a heart. [~L. *cor* heart].

CORDATED, [kawd'-āt-id], *adj.* cordate.

CORDATELY, [kawd'-āt-li], *adv.* in a cordate fashion.

CORDED, [kawd'-id], *adj.* fastened with cords; made of cords; ribbed.

CORDELIER, [kawd'-el-i-ā], *n.* a Franciscan friar; a machine for making ropes. [Fr. *cordelier*].

CORDIAL (1), [kaw'-di-al], *n.* a medicinal drink to strengthen and encourage the action of the heart; a warming or refreshing drink.

CORDIAL (2), [kaw'-di-al], *adj.* connected with the heart; stimulating; hearty, sincere, cheerfully friendly; heart-felt. [L. *cordialis*].

CORDIALITY, [kaw'-di-al'-i-ti], *n.* the condition of being cordial.

CORDIALLY, [kaw'-di-a-li], *adv.* in cordial fashion.

CORDIALNESS, [kaw'-di-al-nes], *n.* cordiality.

CORDIERITE, [kaw'-dēer-it], *n.* (*min.*) a silicate of magnesium, iron, and aluminium; iolite. [*Cordier*, a French geologist].

CORDIFORM, [kawd'-i-fawm], *adj.* shaped or formed like a heart. [L. *cor cordis* heart and FORM].

CORDILLERA, [kaw'-dil-yāer'-a], *n.* a ridge in a group of parallel mountain ranges, *esp.* in South America. [Span. *cordillera*, *dim.* of *cordilla* a little rope].

CORDITE, [kawd'-īt], *n.* a smokeless explosive in the form of short lengths of cord.

CORDON, [kaw'-don], *n.* a ribbon worn as a badge of honour; (*fort.*) a row of stones jutting before a rampart in fortifications; (*milit.*) a line of military posts; a ring of people surrounding anything to cut it off from outside communication; **c. bleu,** blue ribbon on which hung the insignia of the order of the Holy Ghost in France; (*fig.*) a first-class distinction; an excellent cook. [Fr. *cordon*].

CORDOVAN, [kaw'-dō-van'], *n.* a leather from Cordova. [*Cordova*, in Spain].

CORDUROY (1), [kaw'-dyoo-roi'], *n.* a thick cotton material corded or ribbed with a velvety finish; (*pl.*) trousers made of this. [Fr. *corde du roi* the king's cord].

CORDUROY (2), [kaw'-dyoo-roi'], *adj.* made of corduroy.

CORDWAIN, [kawd'-wān], *n.* a kind of Spanish leather. [Corruption of CORDOVAN].

CORDWAINER, [kawd'-wān-er], *n.* †a worker in cordwain, shoemaker; a member of the Cordwainers' Company in London. [OFr. *cordouanier*].

CORE (1), [kaw(r)], *n.* the innermost part of anything, the heart; the central dry radical part of certain fruits that contains the pips; (*elect.*) the central soft iron bar in a magnetic coil; (*founding*) the inner part of a mould; (*fig.*) the inmost part, kernel, root, substance. [OFr. *cor* horn, corn].

CORE (2), [kaw(r)], *v.t.* to remove the core of.

CO-REGENT, [kō-rē'-jent], *n.* a joint regent.

CO-RELATION, see CORRELATION.

CO-RELATIVE, see CORRELATIVE (1) and (2).

CO-RELIGIONIST, CORRELIGIONIST, [kō'-ri-lij'-un-ist], *n.* a person of the same religious faith as another.

COREOPSIS, [ko'-ri-op'-sis], *n.* a yellow daisy-like garden-plant. [Gk. *koris* bug and *opsis* appearance].

CO-RESPONDENT, [kō'-res-pond'-ent], *n.* (*leg.*) a man charged with adultery with the plantiff's wife in a divorce suit; **c. shoes,** shoes of white canvas and brown leather.

CORF, [kawf], *n.* a basket for carrying minerals in mines; a floating basket in which fish are kept alive. [Du. *korf*].

CORGI, CORGY, [kaw'-gi], *n.* a breed of small dogs. [Wel. *corgi*].

CORIACEOUS, [kor'-i-ā'-shus], *adj.* made of or resembling leather; tough. [L. *coriaceus* leathern].

CORIANDER, [kor'-i-an'-der], *n.* the *Coriandrum sativum*, whose seeds have aromatic and carminative properties. [L. *coriandrum*].

CORINTHIAN (1), [kor-inth'-i-an], *n.* a native of Corinth; †a profligate, libertine.

CORINTHIAN (2), [kor-inth'-i-an], *adj.* pertaining to Corinth; **C. column,** the most ornate of the three types of column in Greek architecture, having a capital embellished with flowing acanthus leaves.

CORIUM, [kaw'-ri-um], *n.* the innermost layer of the skin. [L. *corium* hide, leather].

CO-RIVAL, [kō'-rī'-val], *n.* a fellow rival.

CO-RIVALRY, [kō'-rī'-val-ri], *n.* joint rivalry.

CO-RIVALSHIP, [kō'-rī'-val-ship], *n.* co-rivalry.

CORK (1), [kawk], *n.* the light, resilient bark of the cork oak, *Quercus suber*; a piece of this cut down and shaped to make a stopper for a bottle; (*bot.*) the bark, the external covering of woody plants. [Span. *corcho*].

CORK (2), [kawk], *adj.* made of cork.

CORK (3), [kawk], *v.t.* to stop up a bottle by fitting a cork in its neck; to give wine the taste of the cork.

CORKAGE, [kawk'-ij], *n.* a charge made at hotels for serving a guest's own wine; the corking or uncorking of bottles.

CORKED, [kawkt], *adj.* stopped up or filled with a cork; (of wine) tasting of cork.

CORKER, [kawk'-er], *n.* (*slang*) anything conclusive; an outrageous lie; a strikingly attractive person.

CORKING-PIN, [kawk'-ing-pin'], *n.* a large pin, such as that formerly used to fasten the hair to a cork.

CORK-JACKET, [kawk'-jak'-it], *n.* a jacket lined with cork, worn as a support in swimming.

CORKSCREW, [kawk'-skroo], *n.* a screw with a handle to extract corks from bottles.

CORK-TREE, [kawk'-trē], *n.* a western European species of oak, *Quercus suber*, the thick rough bark of which is manufactured into corks.

CORKWING, [kawk'-wing], *n.* a salt-water fish, the goldsinny, *Crenilabrus cornubicus*.

CORKWOOD, [kawk'-wood], *n.* the American tree, *Ochroma lagopus*, producing a very light wood.

CORKY, [kawk'-i], *adj.* consisting of cork; like a cork in taste or appearance; (*slang*) lively or skittish.

CORM, [kawm], *n.* (*bot.*) a short solid bulb-like underground stem. [Gk. *kormos* tree-trunk].

CORK-TREE

CORMOPHYTE, [kaw'-mof-it], *n.* (*bot.*) a plant in which the stem and leaves are distinct. [Gk. *kormos* trunk and *phuton* plant].

CORMORANT, [kaw'-mor-ant], *n.* a voracious sea-bird of the genus *Phalacrocorax*; (*fig.*) a glutton. [Fr. *cormoran* sea-raven].

CORMORANT

CORN (1), [kawn], *n.* grain, the seed of cereal plants; cereal plants which yield grain; wheat; (*U.S.*) maize. [OE. *corn*].

CORN (2), [kawn], *n.* a small painful excrescence of hardened, horny skin, usually on the foot; **to tread on a person's corns,** (*fig.*) to hurt his feelings. [OFr. *corn*].

CORN (3), [kawn], *v.i.* to form into grains; to

granulate, to preserve meat by salting; to feed with oats. [CORN (1)].
CORN-APHIS, [kawn'-ā'-fis], *n.* a plant-louse often destructive to grain crops.
CORNBRAKE, [kawn'-brāk'], *n.* a maize plantation.
CORNBRASH, [kawn'-brash'], *n.* a coarse shelly limestone of lower Jurassic age; a favourable soil for corn.
CORN-BREAD, [kawn'-bred'], *n.* bread made from maize.
CORN-CHANDLER, [kawn'-chahnd'-ler], *n.* a dealer in corn.
CORN-COB, [kawn'-kob], *n.* the woody centre part of the stalk, or spike, on which the ears of maize grow; a pipe having this for a bowl.
CORN-COCKLE, [kawn'-kok'-al], *n.* (*bot.*) a purple-flowered plant, *Lychnis Githago*, growing in corn-fields.
CORN-CRAKE, [kawn'-krāk], *n.* the bird, *Crex pratensis*, with a peculiarly harsh cry.
CORNEA, [kaw'-nē-a], *n.* the strong transparent membrane protecting the ball of the eye. [L. *cornea fem.* of *corneus* horny].
CORNED-BEEF, [kawnd'-bēf'], *n.* pickled and salted beef.
CORNEL, [kawn'-el], *n.* the cornelian-tree. [OFr. *cornille* cornel-tree].
CORNELIAN, CARNELIAN, [kaw-nē'-li-an], *n.* a precious stone, a kind of red chalcedony. [Fr. *corneline*].
CORNELIAN-TREE, [kaw-nēl'-i-an-trē'], *n.* (*bot.*) the dogwood, *Cornus mascula*, yielding a small edible fruit like a cherry. [L. *cornolium*].
CORNEL-TREE, [kaw'-nel-trē'], *n.* cornelian-tree.
CORNEOUS, [kawn'-i-us], *adj.* horny, hard, tough. [L. *corneus*].
CORNER (1), [kaw'-ner], *n.* the point or line where two lines or surfaces meet; an angle, *esp.* one formed by two plane sides of any object; a secluded place; a region of the earth; (*comm.*) a system by which the whole of the available supply of an article is bought up, so that the buyers can sell again at their own price; (*football*) a corner-kick; **to turn the c.,** (*fig.*) to start to improve; **to drive into a c.,** (*fig.*) to bring to bay; **a tight c.,** a difficult position. [OFr. *cornier*].
CORNER (2), [kawn'-er], *v.t.* to drive into a corner; to bring to bay, to trap; (*comm.*) to make a corner in some commodity.
CORNERED, [kawn'-erd], *adj.* with corners or angles; (*fig.*) caught, trapped.
CORNER-KICK, [kawn'-er-kik], *n.* (*Association football*) a free kick taken from one of the opponent's corners of the field.
CORNER-STONE, [kawn'-er-stōn'], *n.* (*arch.*) the stone which joins two walls of a building at the corner; the principal stone; (*fig.*) the foundation, prop.
CORNER-TEETH, [kawn'-er-tēth'], *n.*(*pl.*) the lateral incisors of a horse.
CORNER-WISE, [kawn'-er-wīz'], *adv.* diagonally; with the corner forward.
CORNET, [kawn'-et], *n.* a hollow cone-shaped wafer for holding ice-cream; (*mus.*) a brass instrument like a trumpet with pistons; a player of this instrument in an orchestra; †(*milit.*) officer in a cavalry troop who formerly carried the colours. [OFr. *cornet*, *dim.* of *corn* horn].

CORNET

CORNETCY†, [kawn'-et-si], *n.* the rank or office of a cornet.
CORNETIST, [kawn-et'-ist], *n.* a performer on the cornet.
CORNFLAG, [kawn'-flag'], *n.* (*bot.*) the wild gladiolus, *Gladiolus communis*.
CORNFLOUR, [kawn'-flow'-er], *n.* finely ground flour of Indian corn or other grain.
CORN-FLOWER, [kawn'-flow'-er], *n.* (*bot.*) *Centaurea Cyanus*, a plant growing in corn-fields, and having a deep blue flower.
CORN-GROWING, [kawn'-grō'-ing], *adj.* growing or producing corn.
CORNICE, [kawn'-is], *n.* (*arch.*) an ornate moulding capping a building; a part of the entablature, above the frieze; a plaster moulding running round the walls of a room, just below the ceiling. [Fr. *cornice*].
CORNICLE, [kawn'-ikl], *n.* a small horn. [L. *corniculum*].
CORNICULATE, [kawn-ik'-yŏŏ-lat], *adj.* having horns or small horn-like projections. [L. *corniculatus*].
CORNIFIC, [kawn-if'-ik], *adj.* growing, producing horns. [L. *cornu* horn and *facere* to make].
CORNIFORM, [kawn'-i-fawm'], *adj.* shaped like a horn.
CORNIGEROUS, [kawn-ij'-er-us], *adj.* having horns. [L. *corniger*].
CORNINE, [kawn'-in], *n.* a principle in the bark of *Cornus florida*, somewhat like quinine.
CORNING-HOUSE, [kawn'-ing-hows'], *n.* a place where gunpowder is granulated.
CORNISH (1), [kawn'-ish], *n.* the native language of Cornwall.
CORNISH (2), [kawn'-ish], *adj.* pertaining to Cornwall.
CORNLAND, [kawn'-land'], *n.* land used for or suitable for the production of corn.
CORNLOFT, [kawn'-loft'], *n.* a granary.
CORN-MARIGOLD, [kawn'-ma'-ri-gōld], *n.* (*bot.*) the composite plant, *Chrysanthemum segetum*, which grows in corn-fields.
CORN-METER, [kawn'-mē'-ter], *n.* a measure for corn.
CORN-MILL, [kawn'-mil], *n.* a mill where corn is ground.
CORN-MOTH, [kawn'-moth'], *n.* a moth, *Tinea granella*, whose larvae destroy corn.
CORNO, [kawn'-ō], *n.* (*mus.*) the French horn. [It. *corno*].
CORNOPEAN, [kawn-ō'-pi-an], *n.* a cornet.
CORN-PARSLEY, [kawn'-pahs'-li], *n.* (*bot.*) the umbelliferous plant, *Petroselinum segetum*, found in grain-fields.
CORN-POPPY, [kawn'-pop'-i], *n.* the common red poppy, *Papaver Rhoeas*.
CORN-RENT, [kawn'-rent'], *n.* a rent paid in corn instead of money.
CORN-RIG, [kawn'-rig], *n.* (*Scots*) a strip of land, growing corn. [CORN and RIDGE].
CORN-SALAD, [kawn'-sal'-ad], *n.* any kind of *Valerianella*, used as salad.
CORN-STONE, [kawn'-stōn'], *n.* (*geol.*) a kind of speckled limestone of Devonian age.
CORNUBIANITE, [kawn-ew'-bi-an-īt], *n.* (*geol.*) a slaty rock found in Cornwall in contact with granite. [*Cornubia*, the Latin name for Cornwall].
CORNUCOPIA, [kawn'-yŏŏ-kō'-pi-a], *n.* (*myth.*) the horn of the goat that suckled Zeus, the symbol of plenty; the representation of this in sculpture, painting, etc.; (*fig.*) plenty, abundance. [L. *cornucopia*].
CORNULITES, [kawn'-yŏŏ-lits], *n.*(*pl.*) (*geol.*) a genus of tube-worms present in the Silurian limestones and sandstones. [L. *cornu* horn and Gk. *lithos* stone].
CORNUTE (1), [kawn'-yŏŏt], *adj.* cornuted. [L. *cornutus* horned].
CORNUTE (2), [kawn'-yŏŏt], *v.t.* to bestow horns upon; to cuckold.
CORNUTED, [kawn-ŏŏt'-id], *adj.* having horns; horn-shaped.
CORN-VIOLET, [kawn'-vī'-ol-et], *n.* (*bot.*) a purple-coloured bell-flower, *Campanula hybrida*.
CORN-WAIN, [kawn'-wān], *n.* a wagon for carrying corn.
CORN-WEEVIL, [kawn'-wē'-vil], *n.* an insect *Calandra granaria*, harmful to corn.
CORNY, [kawn'-i], *adj.* horny; like horn; producing, containing, or extracted from, corn; (*U.S. slang*) old-fashioned.
COROCORE, [kor'-ō-kaw(r)], *n.* a large-sized Malayan boat. [Uncert.].
CORODY, CORRODY, [kor'-o-di], *n.* provision for maintenance; pension. [L. *corrodium*].
COROLLA, [kor-ol'-a], *n.* (*bot.*) the inner whorl of a flower, comprising the petals. [L. *corolla* little crown, garland].
COROLLACEOUS, [kor'-ol-ā'-shus], *adj.* relating to, or resembling, a corolla.
COROLLARY, [kor-ol'-er-i], *n.* a further inference from an established proposition; (*geom.*) a proposition following naturally upon one that has been proved; a natural result, logical consequence. [L. *corollarium* deduction].
COROLLATE, [kor'-ol-āt], *adj.* like a corolla; ornamented with corollas.
COROLLATED, [kor'-ol-āt'-id], *adj.* corollate.
COROLLET†, [kor'-ol-et], *n.* a floret of a composite flower.

COROLLINE, [kor'-ol-in], *adj.* relating to a corolla.

COROLLITIC, CAROLITIC, [kor-ol-it'-ik], *adj.* (*arch.*) having foliated shafts decorated with leaves and branches.

COROLLULE, [kor'-ol-ewl], *n.* a corollet. [L. *corollula*, *dim.* of *corolla* garland].

CORONA, [kor-ō'-na], *n.* (*astron.*) a halo round the sun or moon; a disk of light round the sun, seen beyond the moon's rim in a total eclipse of the sun; a crown-shaped chandelier for holding the tapers in a church; (*anat.*) the upper surface of a tooth; (*arch.*) a large flat projecting part of a cornice; (*bot.*) an appendage of the corolla in certain flowers; (*elect.*) a blue discharge of electricity from a transmitting aerial using a high voltage. [L. *corona* crown].

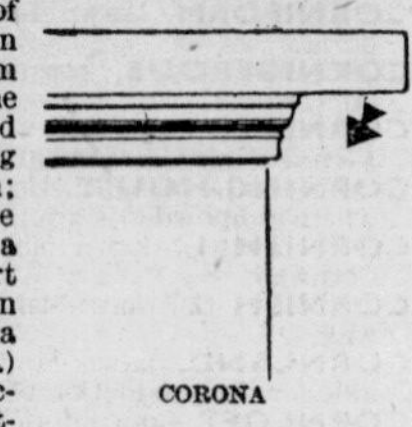

CORONA

CORONACH, CORANACH, [kor'-on-ak], *n.* a funeral dirge in the Scottish Highlands; public lamentation by hired mourners at an Irish burial. [Gael. *comh* together and *rainach* wailing].

CORONAL (1), [kor'-on-al], *n.* a circlet of precious gems for the head; a circular garland of flowers worn as a crown.

CORONAL (2), [kor'-on-al], *adj.* pertaining to the crown of the head; pertaining to or resembling a corona. [L. *coronalis*].

CORONAMEN, [kor'-on-ā'-men], *n.* the upper edge of a hoof. [~L. *corona* crown].

CORONARY, [kor'-on-er-i], *adj.* pertaining to a crown, resembling a crown; (*anat.*) placed like a crown (of vessels, ligaments, etc.); **c. gold**, gifts collected from the ancient Roman provinces to celebrate a Roman victory. [L. *coronarius*].

CORONATE, [kor'-on-āt], *v.t.* to crown. [L. *coronare* to crown].

CORONATED, [kor'-on-āt'-id], *adj.* (*bot. and zool.*) provided or adorned with a crown or crest. [*Prec.*].

CORONATION, [kor'-on-ā'-shun], *n.* the solemn ceremony of crowning a sovereign. [OFr. *coronacion*].

CORONER, [kor'-on-er], *n.* an officer appointed to hold an inquest or inquiry into the cause of death of persons killed or dying unexpectedly, or to determine the ownership of treasure-trove. [AFr. *corouner*].

CORONERSHIP, [kor'-on-er-ship'], *n.* the office or position of a coroner.

CORONET, CROWNET†, [kor'-on-et, †krown'-et], *n.* a small crown worn by princes and peers; an ornamental gold head-dress worn by ladies of rank or position; a wreath of flowers worn round the head; (*bot.*) the flowering head of certain plants; the upper part of a horse's hoof; **c. moth**, the moth *Acronycta ligustri*. [OFr. *coronette*].

CORONETED, [kor'-on-et-id], *adj.* wearing or entitled to wear a coronet.

CORONIFORM, [kor-on'-i-fawm], *adj.* in the shape of a crown.

CORONIS, [kor-ō'-nis], *n.* (*gram.*) the sign used to indicate vowel-contraction in Greek. [Gk. *koronis* curved stroke].

CORONOID, [kor'-on-oid], *adj.* (*anat.*) curved like the beak of a crow. [Gk. *korone* crow and *oeides* like].

CORONULE, [kor'-on-ewl], *n.* (*bot.*) a downy crown-like tuft above a seed; (*zool.*) a barnacle of the genus *Coronula*. [L. *coronula*].

COROZO-NUT, [kor-ō'-zō-nut'], *n.* the nut of a South American palm, *Phytelephas macrocarpa*, used as vegetable ivory. [Native].

CORPORAL (1), [kaw'-por-al], *n.* a non-commissioned officer ranking between a sergeant and a private; (*naut.*) a petty officer dealing with disciplinary matters. [It. *caporale*].

CORPORAL (2), CORPORALE, [kaw'-por-al], *n.* a fine white linen cloth placed over the altar during the celebration of mass and in which the elements are afterwards wrapped. [L. *corporalis* (*palla*) body cloth].

CORPORAL (3), [kaw'-por-al], *adj.* pertaining to the human body; bodily; **c. punishment**, whipping or flogging. [L. *corporalis*].

CORPORALE, see CORPORAL (2).

CORPORALITY, [kaw'-por-al'-i-ti], *n.* the state of existing in bodily form. [LL. *corporalitas*].

CORPORALLY, [kaw'-por-a-li], *adv.* bodily.

CORPORALSHIP, [kaw'-por-al-ship], *n.* the office or position of corporal.

CORPORAS, [kaw'-por-as], *n.* the corporale. [OFr. *corporaus*].

CORPORATE, [kaw'-por-at], *adj.* united into a corporation, pertaining to or belonging to a corporation. [L. *corporatus*, *p.pt.* of *corporare* to embody].

CORPORATELY, [kaw'-por-at-li], *adv.* in a corporate way.

CORPORATENESS, [kaw'-por-at-nes], *n.* the condition of being a corporate body.

CORPORATION, [kaw'-por-ā'-shun], *n.* a group or body of persons constituting a single legal entity; a body appointed by election to conduct civic business; (*U.S.*) a joint-stock company; (*slang*) a large belly. [L. *corporatio*].

CORPORATIVE, [kaw'-por-at-iv], *adj.* pertaining to a corporation.

CORPORATOR, [kaw'-por-āt'-er], *n.* a member of a corporation.

CORPOREAL, [kaw-paw'-ri-al], *adj.* bodily, physical, material; (*leg.*) tangible, consisting of physical objects or substances. [L. *corporeus* belonging to the body].

CORPOREALIST†, [kaw-paw'-ri-al-ist], *n.* a materialist.

CORPOREALITY, [kaw'-paw-ri-al'-i-ti], *n.* the condition of being corporeal.

CORPOREALIZE, [kaw-paw'-ri-al-īz], *v.i.* to assume bodily or tangible form, to materialize.

CORPOREALLY, [kaw-paw'-ri-al-i], *adv.* in bodily form.

CORPOREITY, [kaw'-paw-rē'-i-ti], *n.* material being, bodily substance or existence.

CORPOSANT, [kaw'-pōz-ant], *n.* luminous electric flashes occasionally seen about the rigging and mast-heads of a ship, St. Elmo's fire. [Port. *corpo santo* holy body].

CORPS, (*pl.* **corps**), [kaw(r)], *n.* one of the largest manoeuvrable subdivisions of an army; a particular section or department of the army; an organized group of trained persons; **c. de ballet**, the whole company of dancers in a ballet; **c. diplomatique**, the entire group of persons attached to the diplomatic service in a foreign country [Fr. *corps* body].

CORPSE, [kawps], *n.* the dead body, generally of a human being. [L. *corpus* body].

CORPSE-CANDLE, [kawps'-kandl'], *n.* a weird flame seen in a churchyard, etc., and due to marsh-gas; a tall candle placed by a bier.

CORPSE-GATE, [kawps'-gāt], *n.* a lichgate.

CORPULENCE, [kawp'-yōō-lents], *n.* the state of being corpulent. [L. *corpulentia*].

CORPULENCY, [kawp'-yōō-len-si], *n.* corpulence.

CORPULENT, [kawp'-yōō-lent], *adj.* stout, fat, excessively plump, obese. [L. *corpulentus*].

CORPULENTLY, [kawp'-yōō-lent-li], *adv.* in a corpulent fashion.

CORPUS, [kaw'-pus], *n.* a corpse; a body or collection of writings extant upon a subject; the principal of a fund; one of the special structures of the body; (*leg.*) a body of rules, precedents, examples, etc., which establish the law; **C. Christi**, a church festival in honour of the Eucharist. [L. *corpus*].

CORPUSCLE, [kaw'-pusl], *n.* a minute physical body; (*biol.*) a small fragment of protoplasm; (*physiol.*) a microscopic body forming part of the blood; [(*phys.*) an electron. [L. *corpusculum* little body].

CORPUSCULAR, [kaw-pus'-kyōō-ler], *adj.* pertaining to or consisting of corpuscles; **c. philosophy**, the philosophy holding that the universe is produced by adjustments of corpuscles into various forms of matter; **c. theory**, (*phys.*) a former theory that light consists of emanations of minute particles of matter from a luminous body.

CORPUSCULARIAN, [kaw-pus'-kyōō-lāer'-i-an], *n.* one who upholds the corpuscular philosophy or theory of light.

CORRADIATION, [ko-rā'-di-ā'-shun], *n.* divergence of rays from a radiating centre.

CORRAL (1), [kor-al'], *n.* an enclosure or pen for cattle, or for imprisoning wild animals; the space within an enclosed defence of wagons and equipment. [Span. *corro* circle].

CORRAL (2), (**corralling, corralled**), [kor-al'], *v.t.* to enclose in a corral.

CORRECT (1), [kor-ekt'], *adj.* free from error, right, accurate, true; conforming to a recognized conventional standard or code, proper, fitting, in good taste. [L. *correctum*, *p.pt.* of *corrigere* to make straight].

CORRECT (2), [kor-ekt'], *v.t.* to make correct; to put right; to reprove, to censure, to punish for misbehaviour; to modify or adjust in order to make a thing conform with a required standard; to nullify or cure malformity or disorder.

CORRECTION, [kor-ek'-shun], *n.* the act of correcting; the corrected or amended version; **house of c.**, a reformatory, prison. [L. *correctio*].

CORRECTIONAL, [kor-ek'-shun-al], *adj.* pertaining to correction, intended to correct.

CORRECTIVE (1), [kor-ekt'-iv], *n.* that which corrects or tends to correct.

CORRECTIVE (2), [kor-ekt'-iv], *adj.* able, intended or tending to correct. [Fr. *correctif*].

CORRECTLY, [kor-ekt'-li], *adv.* in correct fashion.

CORRECTNESS, [kor-ekt'-nes], *n.* the quality of being correct.

CORRECTOR, [kor-ekt'-or], *n.* one who, or that which, corrects; (*print.*) a proof-reader; (*hist.*) a governor or director. [L. *corrector*].

CORREGIDOR, [ko-rej'-id-aw(r)'], *n.* a Spanish chief magistrate. [Span. *corregidor*].

CORRELATABLE, [kor'-el-āt'-abl], *adj.* able to be correlated.

CORRELATE (1), [kor'-el-āt], *n.* either of two mutually connected things, so related that one forms the complement of the other.

CORRELATE (2), [kor'-el-āt], *v.t.* *and i.* to stand in mutual relationship; to bring into relation with, to show the proper connexion between. [CO and RELATE].

CORRELATION, CO-RELATION, [kor'-el-ā'-shun], *n.* reciprocal relation; the act of correlating.

CORRELATIVE (1), **CO-RELATIVE**, [ko-rel'-at-iv], *n.* that which stands in reciprocal relation to something else.

CORRELATIVE (2), **CO-RELATIVE**, [ko-rel'-at-iv], *adj.* so related that one implies or involves the other, mutually dependent; (*gram.*) corresponding or complementary to one another and regularly used together (as *either . . . or*).

CORRELATIVELY, [kor-el'-at-iv-li], *adv.* in a correlative relation or manner.

CORRELATIVENESS, [kor-el'-at-iv-nes], *n.* the quality of being correlative.

CORRELIGIONIST, see CO-RELIGIONIST.

CORREPTION, [kor-ep'-shun], *n.* shortening in pronunciation. [L. *correptio* from *corripere* to snatch].

CORRESPOND, [kor'-es-pond'], *v.i.* to agree, be in accordance with, suit, fit; to be similar, conform to; to be equivalent to; to write letters, to maintain connexion or communication with a person by the writing of letters. [MedL. *correspondere*].

CORRESPONDENCE, [kor'-es-pond'-ens], *n.* the act of corresponding, conformity, similarity; communication between persons by means of letters; the letters so exchanged; **c. course**, a course of study by postal tuition; **c. column**, the portion of a newspaper devoted to letters from readers.

CORRESPONDENCY, [kor'-es-pond'-en-si], *n.* correspondence.

CORRESPONDENT (1), [kor'-es-pon'-dent], *n.* one who corresponds with another; a special writer on a newspaper or magazine who contributes periodical articles, or who is sent abroad to report some special happening; a person who occasionally writes letters to a newspaper to air his views or grievances; (*comm.*) a firm having regular business dealings with another.

CORRESPONDENT (2), [kor'-es-pon'-dent], *adj.* corresponding, suitable, analogous to. [MedL. *correspondens*, *pres.pt.* of *correspondere*].

CORRESPONDENTLY, [kor'-es-pon'-dent-li], *adv.* in a corresponding fashion.

CORRESPONDING, [kor'-es-pond'-ing], *adj.* that corresponds.

CORRIDOR, [kor'-id-or], *n.* a long narrow passage in a building connecting several rooms or sections on the same floor; a narrow passage extending along the whole length of certain types of railway coach; (*pol. geog.*) a narrow strip of territory not under the control of the state through which it passes; **c. train**, a train made up of coaches with corridors. [It. *corridore* runner].

CORRIE, [ko'-ri], *n.* (*Scots*) a valley on a mountain-side. [Gael. *coire* a cauldron].

CORRIGENDUM, (*pl.* **corrigenda**), [kor'-ij-end'-um], *n.* something to be corrected; (*pl.*) list of corrections to be made in a book. [L. *corrigendum* which must be corrected, *ger.* of *corrigere* to correct].

CORRIGIBLE, [kor'-ij-ibl], *adj.* capable of being corrected. [L. *corrigibilis*].

CORRIVATION, [kor'-iv-ā'-shun], *n.* the merging of different streams into one. [L. *corrivatio*].

CORROBORANT (1), [kor-ob'-or-ant], *n.* a fact which corroborates; (*med.*) a tonic, a pick-me-up.

CORROBORANT (2), [kor-ob'-or-ant], *adj.* strengthening, tonic, invigorating; corroborating. [L. *corroborans*, *pres.pt.* of *corroborare*].

CORROBORATE, [kor-ob'-or-āt], *v.t.* to strengthen, confirm, support by additional information. [L. *corroborare* strengthen].

CORROBORATION, [kor-ob'-or-ā'-shun], *n.* the act of corroborating; that which corroborates.

CORROBORATIVE (1), [kor-ob'-or-at-iv], *n.* a corroborant.

CORROBORATIVE (2), [kor-ob'-or-at-iv], *adj.* tending to confirm or corroborate.

CORROBORATOR, [kor-ob'-or-āt'-or], *n.* one who corroborates.

CORROBORATORY, [kor-ob'-or-āt'-er-i], *adj.* corroborative.

CORROBOREE, [kor-ob'-or-ē], *n.* a traditional Australian aboriginal dance performed in the moonlight around a camp-fire. [Native].

CORRODE, [kor-ōd'], *v.t.* *and i.* to eat away or destroy by degrees, to wear away gradually, to rust; (*fig.*) to gnaw, to prey upon. [L. *corrodere*].

CORRODENT (1), [kor-ōd'-ent], *n.* a substance that corrodes.

CORRODENT (2), [kor-ōd'-ent], *adj.* causing corrosion. [L. *corrodens*].

CORRODIBILITY, [kor-ōd'-i-bil'-i-ti], *n.* corrosibility.

CORRODIBLE, [kor-ōd'-ibl], *adj.* corrosible.

CORRODY, see CORODY.

CORROSIBILITY, [kor-ōz'-ib-il'-i-ti], *n.* susceptibility to corrosion.

CORROSIBLE, [kor-ōz'-ibl], *adj.* capable of corrosion.

CORROSIBLENESS, [kor-ōz'-ibl-nes], *n.* corrosibility.

CORROSION, [kor-ō'-zhun], *n.* the act or process of corroding. [L. *corrosio*].

CORROSIVE (1), [kor-ō'-siv], *n.* a substance that corrodes.

CORROSIVE (2), [kor-ō'-siv], *adj.* tending to set up corrosion; **c. sublimate**, mercuric chloride, a white virulent poison. [OFr. *corosif*].

CORROSIVELY, [kor-ō'-siv-li], *adv.* in corrosive fashion.

CORROSIVENESS, [kor-ō'-siv-nes], *n.* the power of corroding.

CORRUGANT, [kor'-ŏŏg-ant], *adj.* readily contracting into wrinkles or folds. [L. *corrugans*, *pres.pt.* of *corrugare*].

CORRUGATE, [kor'-ŏŏg-āt], *v.t.* *and i.* to wrinkle, to contract into wrinkles and folds; to form into small rounded ridges and furrows. [L. *corrugare* to wrinkle].

CORRUGATED, [kor'-ŏŏg-āt-id], *adj.* wrinkled, contracted into folds and ridges, furrowed; **c. iron**, sheet iron formed into a series of rounded, parallel ridges and hollows.

CORRUGATED IRON

CORRUGATION, [kor'-ŏŏg-ā'-shun], *n.* the act of corrugating, the state of being corrugated; a wrinkle, fold.

CORRUGATOR, [kor'-ŏŏg-āt'-or], *n.* (*anat.*) a muscle that wrinkles or furrows the forehead in frowning.

CORRUPT (1), [kor-upt'], *adj.* putrid; tainted; impure, depraved, perverted, morally evil; open to bribery, dishonest; mixed (of languages); (of texts) not representing the original or correct version. [L. *corruptum*, *p.pt.* of *corrumpere* destroy].

CORRUPT (2), [kor-upt'], *v.t.* *and i.* to make corrupt; to consume, wear away; to become corrupt. [*Prec.*].

CORRUPTER, [kor-upt'-er], *n.* one who or that which corrupts.

CORRUPTIBILITY, [kor-upt'-ib-il'-i-ti], *n.* the quality of being corruptible.

CORRUPTIBLE (1), [kor-upt'-ibl], *n.* a corruptible substance, the body.

CORRUPTIBLE (2), [kor-upt'-ibl], *adj.* capable of being corrupted.

CORRUPTIBLENESS, [kor-upt'-ibl-nes], *n.* corruptibility.

CORRUPTIBLY, [kor-upt'-ib-li], *adv.* in a corruptible manner.
CORRUPTION, [kor-up'-shun], *n.* the act of corrupting; the state of being corrupt; that which corrupts. [L. *corruptio*].
CORRUPTIVE, [kor-upt'-iv], *adj.* causing corruption.
CORRUPTLESS†, [kor-upt'-les], *adj.* incorruptible.
CORRUPTLY, [kor-upt'-li], *adv.* in corrupt fashion.
CORRUPTNESS, [kor-upt'-nes], *n.* the condition of being corrupt.
CORSAC, CORSAK, [kaw'-sak], *n.* a yellowish Asiatic fox, *Canis corsac.* [Turk. *corsac*].
CORSAGE, [kaw'-sij], *n.* the bodice of a dress. [OFr. *corsage*].
CORSAIR, [kaw'-sāer], *n.* a pirate, a Barbary privateer; a pirate-ship. [Fr. from LL. *cursarius* runner].
CORSAK, see CORSAC.
CORSE, [kaws], *n.* (*archaic*) a corpse. [OFr. *cors*].
CORSET, [kaws'-et], *n.* a woman's close-fitting under-garment worn to give shape to the figure; stays. [Fr. *corset, dim.* of OFr. *cors* body].
CORSETRY, [kaws'-et-ri], *n.* the art of fitting or making corsets.
CORSITE, [kaw'-sīt], *n.* (*min.*) a mixture of anorthite, quartz, and hornblende, a variety of diorite. [Fr. *Corse,* Corsica, where found].
CORSLET, [kaws'-let], *n.* close-fitting sleeveless armour covering the body; a pliable form of corset; (*entom.*) the thorax of an insect. [Fr. *corselet, dim.* of OFr. *cors* body].
CORTEGE, cortège, [kaw-tāzh'], *n.* an accompanying train of attendants on official occasions; a procession, a funeral procession. [Fr. from It. *corteggio* court].
CORTES, [kaw'-tez], *n.(pl.)* the legislative assembly of the states of Spain and Portugal. [Span. *cortes, pl.* of *corte* court].
CORTEX, (*pl.* **cortices**), [kaw'-teks, kaw'-tis-ēz], *n.* (*bot.*) the bark of a tree; (*anat.*) the external layer or part of an organ; the outer mass of grey matter of the brain. [L. *cortex* tree bark].
CORTICAL, [kaw'-tik-al], *adj.* pertaining to, or resembling, the cortex.
CORTICATE, [kaw'-tik-āt], *adj.* corticated. [L. *corticatus*].
CORTICATED, [kaw'-tik-āt-id], *adj.* resembling or covered with bark.
CORTICIFEROUS, [kaw'-ti-sif'-er-us], *adj.* producing bark. [CORTEX and L. *ferre* to bear].
CORTICIFORM, [kaw-tis'-i-fawm], *adj.* resembling cortex.
CORTICOSE, [kaw'-tik-ōs], *adj.* containing bark. [L. *corticosus*].
CORTICOUS, [kaw'-tik-us], *adj.* corticose.
CORTILE, [kaw-tēl'-ā], *n.* the courtyard of a building. [It. *cortile*].
CORUNDUM, [kor-und'-um], *n.* (*min.*) a mineral aluminium oxide of great hardness, known as sapphire when blue, and ruby when red. [Tamil *kurundam* ruby].
CORUSCANT, [kor-us'-kant], *adj.* flashing, sparkling. [L. *corruscans, pres.pt.* of *corruscare* to flash].
CORUSCATE, [kor'-us-kāt], *v.i.* to sparkle, glitter, flash, gleam. [L. *corruscare*].
CORUSCATION, [kor'-us-kā'-shun], *n.* a sudden gleam of light, a sparkle. [L. *coruscatio*].
CORVEE, corvée, [kaw-vā'], *n.* a laborious uncongenial task; forced labour. [Fr. *corvée*].
CORVETTE, [kaw-vet'], *n. orig.* a full-rigged warship having one row of guns and no quarter-deck; a small anti-submarine escort vessel. [Fr. from L. *corbita* transport ship].
CORVINE, [kaw'-vīn], *adj.* relating to the crow family. [L. *corvinus*].
CORVUS, [kaw'-vus], *n.* the crow; a genus of birds, including the raven, jackdaw, and the rook; (*antiq.*) an ancient Roman military engine for grappling and boarding ships. [L. *corvus* crow].
CORYBANT, [kor'-ib-ant], *n.* one of the frenzied priests or attendants of Cybele. [Gk. *korubas*].
CORYBANTIC, [kor'-ib-ant'-ik], *adj.* resembling the Corybantes; wild, unrestrained. [*Prec.*].
CORYDALIN, [kor-id'-al-in], *n.* an alkaloid extracted from the root of the *Corydalis tuberosa.* [L. *corydalis*].
CORYDON, [kor'-id-on], *n.* the traditional shepherd of pastoral poetry; a young rustic. [Gk. *Korudon,* the classical name of a shepherd].
CORYMB, [kor'-imb], *n.* (*bot.*) a form of inflorescence in which the stalks of the lower flowers rise approximately to the same level as those of the upper, forming a broad, level cluster of flowers. [Gk. *korumbos* cluster].
CORYMBIATED†, [kor-imb'-i-āt-id], *adj.* adorned with clusters of berries. [L. *corymbiatus*].
CORYMBIFEROUS, [kor'-imb-if'-er-us], *adj.* (*bot.*) having flowers, fruit, or berries in corymbs. [L. *corymbifer*].
CORYMBOSE, [ko-rimb'-ōs], *adj.* like, or relating to, a corymb.
CORYMBULOSE, [ko-rimb'-yōō-lōs], *adj.* consisting of little corymbs.
CORYPHAEUS, [kor'-if-ē'-us], *n.* the leader of a chorus; (*fig.*) chief, leader. [Gk. *koruphaios*].
CORYPHEE, coryphée, [kor'-if-ā], *n.* the principal dancer in a ballet.
CORYPHENE, [kor'-if-ēn], *n.* a lustrous fish, with the dorsal fin extending along the whole back, *Coryphaena hippuris,* the dolphin. [Gk. *korus* helmet and *phainomai* I appear].

CORYPHENE

CORYSTES, [kor-is'-tēz], *n.* a long-armed or masked crab, *Corystes cassivelaunus.* [Gk. *korustes* helmeted soldier].
CORYZA, [kor-īz'-a], *n.* (*med.*) inflammation of the mucous membrane of the nose; catarrh in the head. [Gk. *koruza*].
COS, [kos], *n.* a lettuce grown originally in the island of Cos. [Gk. *Kos,* one of the Aegean Islands].
COSE, [kōz], *v.i.* to make oneself cosy. [COSY].
COSECANT, [kō-sē'-kant], *n.* (*geom.*) the secant of the complement of an arc or angle.
CO-SEISMAL (1), [kō-sīz'-mal], *n.* a line or curve connecting places where simultaneous shocks from an earthquake wave are felt.
CO-SEISMAL (2), [kō-sīz'-mal], *adj.* pertaining to a co-seismal.
CO-SEISMIC (1), [kō-sīz'-mik], *n.* a co-seismal.
CO-SEISMIC (2), [kō-sīz'-mik], *adj.* co-seismal.
CO-SENTIENT, [kō'-sen'-shent], *adj.* feeling or perceiving together with.
COSEY, see COSY (1).
COSH (1), [kosh], *n.* (*slang*) a heavy, thick truncheon, a life-preserver. [Unkn.].
COSH (2), [kosh], *v.t. and i.* (*slang*) to strike or fell with a cosh; to strike vigorously.
COSHER, [kosh'-er], *v.t. and i.* to pamper, to indulge, to feast, to be the guest of another. [Ir. *coisir* feasting].
CO-SIGNATORY, [kō'-sig'-nat-ori], *n.* one who takes part in the signing of an official document along with others.
CO-SIGNIFICATIVE, [kō'-sig-nif'-ik-at-iv], *adj.* possessing like signification.
COSILY, [kō'-zi-li], *adv.* snugly, comfortably.
COSINAGE, [kuz'-in-ij], *n.* cousinhood; (*leg.*) a writ to regain possession of an estate in lands. [Fr. *cousinage*].
COSINE, [kō'-sīn], *n.* (*geom.*) the sine of the complement of an arc or angle.
COSINESS, [kō'-zi-nes], *n.* the state of being cosy.
COSLETTIZE, [koz'-let-īz], *v.t.* to render steel rust-proof by a special process. [From the name of the inventor].
COSMETIC (1), [kos-met'-ik], *n.* a substance applied externally to the skin or hair to aid the complexion or appearance.
COSMETIC (2), [kos-met'-ik], *adj.* intended to heighten the beauty of the skin or hair. [Gk. *kosmetikos* well-arranged].
COSMIC, [koz'-mik], *adj.* pertaining to the universe as a systematized entity; harmonious, orderly; vast, enormous; **c. philosophy,** the doctrine of the evolution of the universe; **c. rays,** rays of extremely high penetrative power, thought to originate above the atmosphere. [Gk. *kosmikos* connected with the world].
COSMICAL, [koz'-mik-al], *adj.* cosmic.
COSMICALLY, [koz'-mik-a-li], *adv.* in relation to the universe, coinciding with the rising of the sun.
COSMISM, [koz'-mizm], *n.* the philosophy based on the doctrine of evolution.
COSMO-, *pref.* the universe. [Gk. *kosmos*].
COSMOGONIC, [koz'-mo-gon'-ik], *adj.* pertaining to cosmogony.
COSMOGONIST, [koz-mog'-on-ist], *n.* a student of cosmogony.
COSMOGONY, [koz-mog'-on-i], *n.* the evolution or origin of the universe, the study of this; a theory about this. [Gk. *kosmogonia* creation of the world].

COSMOGRAPHER, [koz-mog'-raf-er], *n.* one who studies cosmography.

COSMOGRAPHICAL, [koz'-mo-graf'-ik-al] *adj.* relating to cosmography.

COSMOGRAPHY, [koz-mog'-raf-i], *n.* a description of the universe; the science which deals with this. [Gk. *kosmographia*].

COSMOLABE, [koz'-mo-lāb], *n.* an ancient instrument for measuring distances, an astrolabe. [COSMO and (ASTRO)LABE].

COSMOLATRY, [koz-mol'-at-ri], *n.* worship of the universe. [COSMO and Gk. *latreia* worship].

COSMOLOGICAL, [koz'-mol-oj'-ik-al], *adj.* relating to cosmology.

COSMOLOGIST, [koz-mol'-oj-ist], *n.* one who studies cosmology.

COSMOLOGY, [koz-mol'-oj-i], *n.* the study of the universe as a system; the branch of metaphysics which deals with the ideas underlying the universe. [COSMO and Gk. *logos* speech].

COSMOMETRY†, [koz-mom'-et-ri], *n.* measurement of the world. [COSMO and Gk. *metria* measurement].

COSMOPLASTIC, [koz'-mo-plast'-ik], *adj.* forming or moulding the world. [Gk. *kosmoplastikos*].

COSMOPOLITAN (1), [koz'-mo-pol'-it-an], *n.* a citizen of the world, a much-travelled person who is at home anywhere and unprejudiced by national feelings.

COSMOPOLITAN (2), [koz'-mo-pol'-it-an], *adj.* without national prejudices or attachments; universal, belonging or common to the whole world; (*nat. hist.*) found all over the world. [COSMO and Gk. *polites* citizen].

COSMOPOLITANISM, [koz'-mo-pol'-it-an-izm], *n.* the quality or state of being a cosmopolitan.

COSMOPOLITE, [koz-mop'-ol-īt], *n.* a cosmopolitan. [Gk. *kosmopolites*].

COSMOPOLITICAL, [koz'-mo-pol-it'-ik-al], *adj.* pertaining to international politics.

COSMOPOLITISM, [koz'-mo-pol'-it-ism], *n.* cosmopolitanism, universal outlook.

COSMORAMA, [koz'-mo-rah'-ma], *n.* a series of views of different parts of the world, giving the illusion of actual vision. [COSMO and Gk. *horama* a view].

COSMORAMIC, [koz'-mo-ram'-ik], *adj.* relating to a cosmorama.

COSMOS (1), [koz'-mos], *n.* the universe as a well-planned system; a planned and regulated system; harmony, order. [Gk. *kosmos* order, the universe].

COSMOS (2), [koz'-mos], *n.* (*bot.*) a garden plant producing single flowers of various colours. [Gk. *kosmos* ornament].

COSMOSPHERE, [koz'-mo-sfēer], *n.* an apparatus for showing the relative position of the earth and fixed stars at any moment.

COSMOTHEISM, [koz'-mo-thē'-izm], *n.* worship of the world as God.

COSS, [kos], *n.* a Hindu measure of length of approximately two miles. [Hind. *kos*].

COSSACK, [kos'-ak], *n.* a member of a tribe inhabiting the south-eastern parts of Russia, and skilled in horsemanship. [Turk. *quzzaq* vagabond].

COSSAS, [kos'-as], *n.(pl.)* plain Indian muslins, of differing qualities and widths. [Native].

COSSET (1), [kos'-et], *n.* a pet lamb; (*fig.*) a pampered child. [Uncert.].

COSSET (2), (**cossetting, cossetted**), [kos'-et], *v.t.* to fondle, to pamper, to indulge.

COST (1), [kost], *n.* the price charged for an article, the expense of some undertaking; (*leg.*) (*pl.*) the expenses incurred in a lawsuit; (*fig.*) expenditure or sacrifice involved in the accomplishment of an object; pain, suffering, detriment; **c. price**, wholesale price; **at all costs**, whatever happens.

COST (2), [kost], *v.t.* to be purchasable or accomplishable at (a certain price), to require or involve (a stated expenditure of money, effort, etc.); to cause to forfeit or lose, to bring about some painful or detrimental experience; (*comm.*) to calculate or determine the cost of. [OFr. *coster*].

COSTAL, [kos'-tal], *adj.* pertaining to the ribs. [L. *costalis*].

CO-STAR, (**co-starring, co-starred**), [kō'-stah(r)'], *v.i.* to share the chief rôles or parts in a play or film.

COSTARD, [kos'-tahd], *n.* a large variety of apple; (*archaic*) the head. [Uncert.].

COSTATE, [kos'-tāt], *adj.* (*bot. and zool.*) ribbed. [L. *costatus*].

COSTATED, [kos'-tāt-id], *adj.* costate.

COSTEAN, [kos-tēn'], *v.i.* (*min.*) to bore small shafts to the level of the rock in order to expose or ascertain the course of a mineral vein. [Cornish *cothas stean* dropped tin].

COSTEANING, [kos-tēn'-ing], *n.* the boring of small pits to ascertain the presence or course of mineral veins.

COSTERMONGER, [kos'-ter-mung'-ger], *n.* a person hawking fruit and vegetables through the streets on a handcart or barrow. [COSTARD and MONGER].

COSTING, [kos'-ting], *n.* the scientific calculation of the cost of, or analysis of expenses to be incurred in, a business undertaking.

COSTIVE, [kos'-tiv], *adj.* constipated, bound; (*fig.*) sluggish, very reserved and shy. [OFr. *costivé* from L. *constipatus*].

COSTIVENESS, [kos'-tiv-nes], *n.* the condition of being costive.

COSTLESS, [kost'-les], *adj.* costing nothing.

COSTLINESS, [kost'-li-nes], *n.* the quality of being costly.

COSTLY, [kost'-li], *adj.* of a high price, expensive; sumptuous, precious.

COSTMARY, [kost'-māer-i], *n.* (*bot.*) a composite perennial aromatic plant formerly used for flavouring ale, *Chrysanthemum Balsamita*. [Gk. *kostos* aromatic plant and the Virgin *Mary*].

COSTREL, [kos'-trel], *n.* a large flask of wood, leather, or earthenware hung from the waist. [OFr. *costerel*].

COSTUME (1), [kos'-tewm], *n.* fashion or mode of dress, outer clothes, *esp.* when characteristic of a people, period, etc.; period dress worn by actors in an historical play; two-piece female attire consisting usually of a short coat and a skirt; **c. piece**, a play, etc., in which the actors wear clothes characteristic of an earlier period of history; **c. ball**, a fancy-dress ball. [OFr. *costume* from L. *consuetudo* custom].

COSTUME (2), [kos'-tewm], *v.t.* to dress, to clothe in a costume.

COSTUMER, [kos'-tewm-er], *n.* a dealer in or maker of period costumes or fancy dress.

COSTUMIER, [kos-tewm'-i-er], *n.* one who makes, sells, or deals in costumes; a dressmaker. [Fr. *costumier*].

CO-SUPREME†, [kō'-sōō-prēm'], *n.* one who is equally or jointly supreme.

CO-SURETY, [kō'-shōōer'-i-ti], *n.* a surety with another.

COSY (1), COSEY, [kō'-zi], *n.* a thick cover put over a tea-pot to keep it hot when the tea has been brewed. [COSY (2)].

COSY (2), [kō'-zi], *adj.* snug, comfortable. [~Norw. *koselig* snug].

COT (1), [kot], *n.* a shelter or protective covering; a small cottage. [OE. *cot*].

COT (2), [kot], *n.* a small, roughly-fashioned boat. [Ir. *cot* small boat].

COT (3), [kot], *n.* a small bed; a child's crib; a bed in a children's hospital; (*naut.*) a hammock-like bed suspended from beams for officers and sick persons. [Hind. *khat* bed].

COT (4), (**cotting, cotted**), [kot], *v.t.* to shelter or confine in a cot.

COTANGENT, [kō-tan'-jent], *n.* (*geom.*) the tangent of the complement of an arc or angle. [CO and TANGENT].

COTE (1), [kōt], *n.* a dwelling or shed for small farm animals or birds. [OE. *cote*].

COTE (2), [kōt], *v.t.* (of dogs) to outstrip. [Uncert.].

COTEAU, [kot-ō'], *n.* a ridge. [Fr. *coteau*].

COTELINE, [kōt'-el-ēn], *n.* ribbed muslin.

COTEMPORARY (1), [kō-tem'-per-er-i], *n.* a contemporary. [COTEMPORARY (2)].

COTEMPORARY (2), [kō-tem'-per-er-i], *adj.* contemporary.

CO-TENANT, [kō'-ten'-ant], *n.* a joint tenant.

COTERIE, [kō'-ter-ē], *n.* a group or circle of people bound together in association by similarity of interests, outlook, position, etc.; an exclusive social set, clique. [Fr. *coterie* a company of rustics].

COTERMINOUS, [kō-tur'-min-us], *adj.* having a common border or boundary. [L. *conterminus*].

COTHURNATE, [kō-thur'-nāt], *adj.* buskined; (*fig.*) pertaining to tragedy.

COTHURNATED, [kō-thur'-nāt-id], *adj.* cothurnate.

COTHURNUS, [kō-thur'-nus], *n.* the high buskin worn by actors in Greek and later Roman tragedies; (*fig.*) tragedy. [Gk. *kothornos*].

COTICULAR†, [kō-tik'-yōō-ler], *adj.* relating to, or suitable for, a whetstone. [L. *coticula* whetstone].

CO-TIDAL, [kō-tīd'-al], *adj.* pertaining to the simultaneous occurrence of a high tide at different places; **c. line**, a line on a map connecting all places at which high tide occurs at approximately the same time.

COTILLION, COTILLON, [kot-il'-yun], *n.* a brisk lively dance for eight persons; the music to which it is danced. [Fr. *cotillon* petticoat].

COTISE, [kot'-is], *n.* (*her.*) a bendlet, usually arranged in parallel pairs, one on either side of a bend or other charge. [Fr. *cotice*].

COTISE

COTLAND†, [kot'-land], *n.* (*hist.*) arable land held by a cottar.

COTONEASTER, [kot-ō'-ni-as'-ter], *n.* (*bot.*) a genus of small trees or shrubs of the family *Rosaceae*, bearing orange-red berries. [L. *cotonea* quince].

CO-TRUSTEE, [kō'-trus-tē'], *n.* a joint trustee.

COTSWOLD, [kots'-wōld], *n.* long-haired sheep occurring on the Cotswolds. [The *Cotswold* hills in Gloucestershire].

COTTA, [kot'-a], *n.* (*eccles.*) a short ecclesiastical vestment in the form of a surplice. [LL. *cotta* tunic].

COTTAGE, [kot'-ij], *n.* a small, humble dwelling house in a village or the country; **c. loaf**, a round loaf of bread with a small rounded lump of dough on top; **c. piano**, a small upright piano. [ME. *cottage*].

COTTAGED, [kot'-ijd], *adj.* containing cottages.

COTTAGER, [kot'-ij-er], *n.* a person who lives in a cottage.

COTTAR, COTTER, [kot'-er], *n.* (*hist.*) a villein who occupies a cot with the accompanying strip of arable land in return for services to his overlord; (*Scots*) a peasant or farm-labourer dwelling in a cottage attached to a farm in return for farm service. [MedL. *cottarius*].

COTTER (2), [kot'-er], *n.* a thin wedge, bolt or pin, driven through a slot or hole to fasten machinery. [Unkn.].

COTTERITE, [kot'-er-īt], *n.* an Irish quartz with a pearly lustre. [Miss *Cotter*, the discoverer].

COTTIER, [kot'-i-er], *n.* an Irish peasant holding his land by cottier tenure; **c. tenure**, a system of annual tenure in which the land is rented by public auction. [MedL. *cotarius*].

COTTON (1), [kotn], *n.* (*bot.*) a plant of the genus *Gossypium* of the family *Malvaceae*; the soft downy hairs on the seeds of this plant used in the manufacture of cloth and thread; thread made from these hairs; cloth woven from this thread. [Arab. *qutun*].

COTTON (2), [kotn], *adj.* made of cotton.

COTTON (3), [kotn], *v.i.* (*fig.*) to be attracted by; to be on terms of friendship with; **to c. on to**, to like; to gather (an idea); **to c. up to**, to make friends with.

COTTON-CAKE, [kotn'-kāk], *n.* compressed cotton-seed, with the oil expressed, used as food for cattle.

COTTON-GIN, [kotn'-jin'], *n.* a machine for separating the seeds from cotton.

COTTON-GRASS, [kotn'-grahs], *n.* (*bot.*) a sedge of the genus *Eriophorum*, having long cottony heads.

COTTON-LORD, [kotn'-lawd], *n.* one who controls the cotton industry.

COTTONOCRACY, [kotn'-ok'-ras-i], *n.* the heads of the cotton-trade. [COTTON and Gk. *krateia* rule].

COTTONOUS†, [kotn'-us], *adj.* like cotton.

COTTON-PLANT, [kotn'-plahnt], *n.* (*bot.*) a species of *Gossypium* with large yellow flowers and a cellular capsule.

COTTON-PRESS, [kotn'-pres'], *n.* a machine in which cotton is compressed into bales.

COTTON-SEED, [kotn'-sēd], *n.* the seed of the cotton-plant.

COTTON-TAIL, [kotn'-tāl], *n.* an American rabbit having a short distinctive white tail.

COTTON-WASTE, [kotn'-wāst], *n.* refuse from the manufacture of cotton, used for cleaning machinery.

COTTON-WEED, [kotn'-wēd], *n.* (*bot.*) the composite plant, *Diotis maritima.*

COTTON-WOOD, [kotn'-wŏŏd], *n.* a North American species of poplar tree, *Populus monilifera.*

COTTON-WOOL, [kotn'-wŏŏl'], *n.* the thick fluffy mass of the hairs of the cotton-plant after cleansing and extraction of seeds, used as packing and for surgical purposes.

COTTON-WORM, [kotn'-wurm'], *n.* the larva of the owlet moth, *Aletia xylina.*

COTTONY, [kot'-on-i], *adj.* soft, downy; resembling cotton.

COTYLE, [kot'-il-i], *n.* (*antiq.*) a Greek cup or vase with curved sides and a flat base; (*anat.*) the cup-like cavity of a bone made to receive the end of another bone; (*zool.*) a cup-shaped sucker on the heads or arms of cephalopods. [Gk. *kotule* small vessel].

COTYLEDON, [kot'-il-ē'-don], *n.* (*bot.*) the seed-leaves of the embryo plant; a genus of plants of the family *Crassulaceae*, with brightly-coloured flowers; (*physiol.*) a cup-shaped vascular body on the chorion of certain animals. [Gk. *kotuledon* a cup-like hollow].

COTYLEDONAL [kot'-il-ē'-don-al], *adj.* (*bot.*) in the form of a seed-leaf; (*physiol.*) possessing cotyledons.

COTYLEDONOUS, [kot'-il-ē'-don-us], *adj.* (*bot.*) relating to cotyledons; having a seed-leaf.

COTYLIFORM, [kot-il'-i-fawm], *adj.* cotyloid.

COTYLOID, [kot'-il-oid], *adj.* (*anat.*) (of the socket of the hip-bone) cup-shaped. [Gk. *kotule* cup and *oeides* like].

COUCAL, [kōō'-kal], *n.* a ground-cuckoo of the genus *Centropus.* [Unkn.].

COUCH (1), [kowch], *n.* a sofa, a long piece of furniture on which a person may recline and rest; (*poet.*) a bed; a place for rest and sleep, a lair; (*paint.*) a first coat of colour covering the surface to be painted; (*malting*) the framework on which a mass of grain germinates. [OFr. *couche*].

COUCH (2), [kowch], *v.t.* to lay down as in rest; to hold a spear or lance ready for immediate use; to bend, lower; to express in speech or writing; (*surg.*) to perform the operation for removal of a cataract from the eye; (*malting*) to heap grain on the floor to germinate; *v.i.* to lie down, as on a couch, to recline; to crouch down; to stoop; to lie hidden. [OFr. *couchier*].

COUCHANT, [kowch'-ant], *adj.* (*her.*) lying down with the head lifted up. [Fr. *couchant*].

COUCHEE, [kōō'-shā], *n.* an evening reception. [Fr. *couché*].

COUCHER, [kowch'-er], *n.* one who couches, a sluggard.

COUCH-FELLOW, [kowch'-fel'-ō], *n.* a companion in lodgings.

COUCH-GRASS, [kowch'-grahs], *n.* (*bot.*) a creeping weed, *Agropyrum repens.* [~QUITCH].

COUCHING, [kowch'-ing], *n.* the act of one who couches; (in needle-work) the laying down of one or more threads held by single transverse stitches at certain intervals.

COUCHING

COUCHLESS, [kowch'-les], *adj.* without couch.

COUCH-MATE, [kowch'-māt], *n.* a bedfellow.

COUGAR, [kōō'-gah(r)], *n.* a large South American cat-like quadruped, *Felix concolor*, the puma. [Native].

COUGH (1), [kof, kawf], *n.* a sudden and forcible expulsion of air from the lungs, accompanied by an abrupt harsh sound, and caused by temporary irritation of the wind-pipe; catarrh, etc.; diseased or inflamed condition of the larynx or wind-pipe causing frequent bouts of coughing.

COUGH (2), [kof, kawf], *v.i.* to utter a cough, or a series of coughs periodically; to clear the throat audibly; **to c. up**, to get rid of by coughing; (*coll.*) to reveal, disclose information, to pay up, under compulsion. [OE. *cohhetan*].

COUGH-DROP, [kof'-drop'], *n.* a medicinal lozenge sucked to alleviate a cough; (*slang*) a blow, an unpleasant surprise; a "character."

COULD, [kŏŏd], *pret.* of CAN. [OE. *cuthe*].

COULEE, [kōō-lā'], *n.* (*geol.*) a deep ravine or creek; a lava-stream. [Fr. *coulée* a flow].

COULEUR-DE-ROSE, [kōōl'-ur-de-rōz'], *adj.* rose colour; (*fig.*) pleasant. [Fr. *couleur-de-rose*].

COULISSE, [kōōl-ēs'], *n.* a slide along which the side-scenes of a stage run; the wings of a stage. [Fr. *coulisse* passage].

COULOIR, [kōōl'-wah(r)], *n.* deep cleft or gully in the side of a mountain. [Fr. *couloir* strainer].

COULOMB, [kōōl'-om], *n.* (*elect.*) the unit of quantity at the rate of one ampère in one second. [C. A. de *Coulomb*, the French physicist (1736-1806)].

COULTER, COLTER, [kōl'-ter], *n.* the front vertical blade of a plough immediately before the share.

which cuts the soil vertically in ploughing. [OE. *culter* from L. *culter*].

COUMARIN, [kōō'-mar-in], *n.* an aromatic substance obtained from the Tonka bean, *Dipteryx odorata*, found in Guiana, having the fragrance of new-mown hay. [Native].

COUNCIL, [kown'-sil], *n.* an assembly summoned together for deliberation and consultation or to perform some executive or legislative function; a group of men elected to carry on the local government of a borough, city, etc.; (*fig.*) a discussion of proposed action; **Privy C.**, a select group of persons appointed to advise the king in the administration of the government upon certain occasions. [L. *concilium*].

COUNCIL-BOARD, [kown'-sil-bawd'], *n.* the table round which a council meets.

COUNCIL-CHAMBER, [kown'-sil-chām'-ber], *n.* a room in which the members of a council officially and habitually meet.

COUNCILLOR, [kown'-sil-er], *n.* a member of a council.

COUNCILMAN, [kown'-sil-man], *n.* a member of a city or borough council.

COUNSEL (1), [kown'-sel], *n.* deliberation, consultation; advice, direction; a legal adviser, a barrister retained to plead his client's case in a court of law; the group of advocates or barristers who conduct the prosecution and defence in a law-suit; **King's C.**, an English barrister acting as Counsel to the Crown, and thus taking precedence. [L. *consilium*].

COUNSEL (2), (**counselling, counselled**), [kown'-sel], *v.t.* to advise, to recommend a certain course of action. [L. *consiliari* to take or give counsel].

COUNSELABLE, [kown'-sel-abl], *adj.* willing to receive, and act upon, counsel.

COUNSELLOR, [kown'-sel-er], *n.* an adviser; a barrister, advocate or counsel. [OFr. *counseilleur* from L. *consiliator*].

COUNSELLORSHIP, [kown'-sel-er-ship], *n.* the office of a counsellor.

COUNT (1), [kownt], *n.* the act of numbering or reckoning; the total counted; account, reckoning, consideration; (*leg.*) a charge in an indictment setting forth a cause for prosecution; (*cotton-spinning*) the number of hanks equal to a pound weight; (*boxing*) the process of counting out; **on all counts**, in every respect. [AFr. *counte* from L. *computum* reckoning].

COUNT (2), [kownt], *n.* a foreign title of nobility about equivalent to an English earl, but often merely honorary. [OFr. *counte* from L. *comes* (*comitem*)].

COUNT (3), [kownt], *v.t.* to name the numerals in a correct sequence up to a stated number; to reckon, to sum up the total number of things; to calculate; to take into account, to include; to consider, value, esteem; *v.i.* to repeat the numerals in their correct order; to enter into consideration in determining or reckoning something; to be of value, to be important, help; to be of some consequence; to keep the number or score of anything; **to c. for**, to be considered as; **to c. on**, to rely upon, to expect; **to c. out**, (*parl.*) to adjourn a meeting after counting those present, and finding that there are not enough present to constitute a quorum; (*boxing*) to declare a boxer defeated upon his failure to stand up within ten seconds of the referee beginning to count. [AFr. *counter* from L. *computare*].

COUNTABLE, [kownt'-abl], *adj.* capable of being counted.

COUNTENANCE (1), [kownt'-in-ans], *n.* the face, facial expression, the features; composure, demeanour; encouragement; patronage; **to keep one's c.**, to appear unruffled by any expression of emotion; **out of c.**, disconcerted, confounded; **to put out of c.**, to abash; **to lose c.**, to show disappointment or dejection. [L. *continentia* self-control].

COUNTENANCE (2), [kownt'-in-ans], *v.t.* to favour, view with approval; to stomach; to tolerate, allow, permit.

COUNTER (1), [kown'-ter], *n.* a small thin disk used as stakes or as a means of reckoning in card or other games; a long flat-topped table or desk behind which shopkeepers, bankers and others stand to carry on exchange of goods and money with the public; one who counts.

COUNTER (2), [kown'-ter], *n.* (*fencing*) a circular parry made without changing the position of the hand; (*boxing*) a blow dealt in answer to, and at the same time as, that of an opponent; (*coursing*) the opposite direction to that taken by the game; (*mus.*) an under part in contrast to the principal voice part. [COUNTER (4)].

COUNTER (3), [kown'-ter], *n.* (*naut.*) the curved part of a ship's stern; the part of a horse lying between the shoulders and under the neck; stiff leather round the heel of a boot or shoe. [Unkn.].

COUNTER (4), [kown'-ter], *adj.* opposite, contrary, in opposition. [L. *contra* against].

COUNTER (5), [kown'-ter], *adv.* in the opposite direction to, contrary to, against, in antagonism to. [*Prec.*].

COUNTER (6), [kown'-ter], *v.t. and i.* to give a return blow; to oppose, to reply in opposition to; (*boxing*) to reply with a counter. [COUNTER (4)].

COUNTERACT, [kown'-ter-akt'], *v.t.* to have a counter effect upon, to neutralize, to check, to mitigate, to hinder, defeat.

COUNTERACTION, [kown'-ter-ak'-shun], *n.* contrary action.

COUNTERACTIVE (1), [kown'-ter-akt'-iv], *n.* anything that counteracts.

COUNTERACTIVE (2), [kown'-ter-akt'-iv], *adj.* tending to counteract.

COUNTER-AGENT, [kown'-ter-ā'-jent], *n.* that which counteracts.

COUNTER-APPROACH, [kown'-ter-a-prōch'], *n.* (*fort.*) a series of defences in front of a besieged place to hinder or oppose the besiegers.

COUNTER-ATTRACTION, [kown'-ter-a-trak'-shun], *n.* a rival or competing attraction.

COUNTERBALANCE (1), [kown'-ter-bal'-ans], *n.* a weight used to balance another; (*fig.*) a force or power equal in effect to and neutralizing another.

COUNTERBALANCE (2), [kown'-ter-bal'-ans], *v.t.* to weigh against with an equal weight or power; to neutralize the effect of, to make up for.

COUNTERBLAST, [kown'-ter-blahst], *n.* a vigorous reply to an opponent.

COUNTER-BOND, [kown'-ter-bond'], *n.* a bond of security to one who has given bond for another.

COUNTER-BRACE (1), [kown'-ter-brās'], *n.* (*naut.*) the lee-brace of the foretopsail yard.

COUNTER-BRACE (2), [kown'-ter-brās'], *v.t.* (*naut.*) to brace the head-yards and after-yards in opposite directions.

COUNTERBUFF (1), [kown'-ter-buf'], *n.* a return blow.

COUNTERBUFF (2), [kown'-ter-buf'], *v.t.* to strike back in return.

COUNTERCAST†, [kown'-ter-kahst], *n.* a trick; a delusive contrivance.

COUNTERCASTER†, [kown'-ter-kahst'-er], *n.* a book-keeper, an accountant, an arithmetician.

COUNTERCHANGE (1), [kown'-ter-chānj], *n.* an exchange, an alternation; a design consisting of squares containing identical patterns, in which the arrangement of colouring is alternately reversed in successive squares.

COUNTERCHANGE (2), [kown'-ter-chānj], *v.t. and i.* to interchange, to transpose; (*her.*) to reverse the colouring, to chequer.

COUNTERCHARGE (1), [kown'-ter-chahj], *n.* (*milit.*) a charge made in retaliation; an attack or accusation in which the attacker or accuser is charged in reply.

COUNTERCHARGE (2), [kown'-ter-chahj], *v.t.* to make a countercharge.

COUNTERCHARM (1), [kown'-ter-chahm'], *n.* that which neutralizes or lessens the effect of a charm.

COUNTERCHARM (2), [kown'-ter-chahm], *v.t.* to destroy the effect of a charm.

COUNTERCHECK (1), [kown'-ter-chek'], *n.* a check in reply; a double check.

COUNTERCHECK (2), [kown'-ter-chek], *v.t.* to restrain with a countercheck; to check doubly.

COUNTERCLAIM (1), [kown'-ter-klām] *n.* (*leg.*) a claim made by a defendant against a plaintiff.

COUNTERCLAIM (2), [kown'-ter-klām], *v.t.* to make a counterclaim.

COUNTER-CLOCKWISE, [kown'-ter-klok'-wiz], *adj.* in a circular direction or motion opposite to that of the hands of a clock.

COUNTER-CURRENT, [kown'-ter-ku'-rent], *n.* a current running in an opposite direction to another.

COUNTERDEED, [kown'-ter-dēd], *n.* a deed which invalidates.

COUNTER-DIE, [kown'-ter-dī], *n.* the upper stamp of a die.

COUNTERDRAIN, [kown'-ter-drān], *n.* a drain parallel to a watercourse for collecting leakage water and running it off through a drain under the water-course.

COUNTERDRAW†, [kown'-ter-draw], *v.t.* (*paint.*) to copy a design by means of tracing material.

COUNTER-ERMINE, [kown'-ter-ur'-min], *n.* (*her.*) the reverse of ermine, black with white spots.

COUNTER-ESPIONAGE, [kown'-ter-es'-pi-on-ahzh], *n.* a system of spy-work designed to frustrate the activities of enemy spies.

COUNTER-EVIDENCE, [kown'-ter-ev'-id-ents], *n.* evidence offered to set off other evidence.

COUNTERFEIT (1), [kown'-ter-fēt], *n.* a forgery, anything made, usually dishonestly, in skilful imitation of another article; a cheat, an impostor, a fraud; (*archaic*) a copy.

COUNTERFEIT (2), [kown'-ter-fēt'], *adj.* forged, not genuine, made in skilful imitation in order to deceive; spurious, false, pretended. [OFr. *contrefet*].

COUNTERFEIT (3), [kown'-ter-fēt], *v.t.* to feign, simulate, pretend; to make in imitation of, with a view to passing it off as genuine.

COUNTERFEITED, [kown'-ter-fēt'-id], *adj.* forged, copied, imitated, assumed.

COUNTERFEITER, [kown'-ter-fēt-er], *n.* a forger.

COUNTERFLORY, [kown'-ter-flaw'-ri], *adj.* (*her.*) with flowers placed opposite each other in pairs.

COUNTERFOIL, [kown'-ter-foil], *n.* the counterpart of a document such as a cheque, postal order, etc., retained by the giver or issuer, and on which are detailed the essential particulars of the document.

COUNTERFORCE, [kown'-ter-faws], *n.* a counteracting force.

COUNTERFORT, [kown'-ter-fawt], *n.* (*arch.*) a buttress built to support a wall or terrace.

COUNTER-GAUGE, [kown'-ter-gāj], *n.* (*carp.*) the measuring of joints by transferring the breadth of a mortise to the proposed tenon.

COUNTERGUARD, [kown'-ter-gahd'], *n.* (*fort.*) a small narrow rampart in front of a work to strengthen it against breaching.

COUNTER-IRRITANT, [kown'-ter-i'-rit-ant], *n.* (*med.*) a substance used to produce counter-irritation.

COUNTER-IRRITATION, [kown'-ter-i'-rit-ā'-shun], *n.* (*med.*) the production of a slight secondary irritation in order to relieve the main irritation.

COUNTERJUMPER, [kown'-ter-jump'-er], *n.* a shop assistant.

COUNTERLATH, [kown'-ter-lahth], *n.* a lath placed between two gauged laths in roofing; (*plastering*) a lath nailed to a beam in order to leave space between the cross-laths and the surface of the timber, into which the plaster may penetrate.

COUNTERMAND (1), [kown'-ter-mahnd], *n.* an order cancelling a previous order; (*leg.*) an action which nullifies a previous act. [OFr. *contremander*].

COUNTERMAND (2), [kown'-ter-mahnd], *v.t.* to issue a countermand; to reverse a command; to prohibit, cancel or revoke by a countermand. [OFr. *contremander*].

COUNTERMARCH (1), [kown'-ter-mahch'], *n.* (*milit.*) a marching back again; a change of the wings or face of a battalion, so as to bring the right to the left, or the front into the rear.

COUNTERMARCH (2), [kown'-ter-mahch], *v.i.* to march back again, to perform a countermarch.

COUNTERMARK (1), [kown'-ter-mahk], *n.* an additional mark placed on goods for greater security; a hall-mark of the Goldsmiths' Company put on silver or gold articles in addition to that of the maker; a mark added to a coin, after it has been struck, to signify a change of value; an artificial cavity made in the teeth of horses to disguise their age.

COUNTERMARK (2), [kown'-ter-mahk'], *v.t.* to mark with a countermark.

COUNTERMINE (1), [kown'-ter-mīn], *n.* (*milit.*) a mine constructed by the besieged to intercept and destroy one made by the attackers; (*nav.*) a mine laid to blow up an enemy's mines; (*fig.*) a plot to defeat another plot.

COUNTERMINE (2), [kown'-ter-mīn], *v.t. and i.* to make or sink a countermine; (*fig.*) to frustrate by a counterplot.

COUNTERMOVE, [kown'-ter-mōōv'], *n.* a move in reply to, or to check, another.

COUNTER-MOVEMENT, [kown'-ter-mōōv'-ment], *n.* a movement in reply to another.

COUNTERMURE, [kown'-ter-mew'-er], *n.* (*milit.*) a wall raised behind another as an additional defence. [Fr. *contre-mur*].

COUNTER-OPENING, [kown'-ter-ōp'-ning], *n.* (*surg.*) an opening made on the side opposite to an existing one to assist in the discharge of matter.

COUNTERPACE†, [kown'-ter-pās], *n.* a countermove.

COUNTER-PALED, [kown'-ter-pāld'], *adj.* (*her.*) (of an escutcheon) divided into twelve pales, and charged fess-wise, the two colours of the upper and lower halves being counterchanged.

COUNTER-PALED

COUNTERPANE, [kown'-ter-pān], *n.* a coverlet for a bed; one half of an indenture. [OFr. *contrepointe* embroidered pillow].

COUNTER-PAROLE, [kown'-ter-pā-rōl'], *n.* (*milit.*) a word given as a signal of alarm.

COUNTERPART, [kown'-ter-paht'], *n.* a part corresponding to another part; (*leg.*) the opposite and subsidiary part of an indenture; a duplicate, a copy; a complementary part; (*mus.*) a part written as an accompaniment to another part; a person or thing resembling another.

COUNTER-PASSANT, [kown'-ter-pas'-ant], *adj.* (*her.*) (of two animals) facing opposite ways.

COUNTERPLEA, [kown'-ter-plē'], *n.* (*leg.*) a reply to a plea or request.

COUNTERPLEAD†, [kown'-ter-plēd'], *v.t.* to plead in opposition, to deny. [AFr. *contrepleder*].

COUNTERPLOT (1), [kown'-ter-plot], *n.* a plot to frustrate another, a subsidiary plot of a play.

COUNTERPLOT (2), (**counterplotting, counterplotted**), [kown'-ter-plot'], *v.i.* to defeat with a counterplot.

COUNTERPOINT†, **(1)**, [kown'-ter-point'], *n.* a counterpane. [OFr. *contrepointe*].

COUNTERPOINT (2), [kown'-ter-point], *n.* a style of musical composition in which a melody or melodies are written above or below a given melody so as to harmonize with it.

COUNTERPOISE (1), [kown'-ter-poiz], *n.* a weight or force sufficient to balance another; a condition of equilibrium; (*fig.*) a neutralizing or counterbalancing force; (*wirel.*) insulated wire(s) placed beneath an aerial. [OFr. *contrepois*].

COUNTERPOISE (2), [kown'-ter-poiz], *v.t. and i.* to balance by a counterpoise; to bring into a state of equilibrium; to act against with equal power or force.

COUNTERPOISON, [kown'-ter-poiz'-on], *n.* an antidote.

COUNTER-PROJECT, [kown'-ter-pro'-jekt], *n.* a plan in opposition to one already put forward.

COUNTER-PROOF, [kown'-ter-prōōf'], *n.* (*engraving*) an impression taken from one newly printed.

COUNTER-PROVE, [kown'-ter-prōōv'], *v.t.* to take a counter-proof from.

COUNTER-REVOLUTION, [kown'-ter-rev'-ol-ōō'-shun], *n.* a revolution, in opposition to one which has taken place, to restore a former state of affairs.

COUNTER-ROLL†, [kown'-ter-rōl], *n.* (*leg.*) the counterpart or copy of a legal document kept as a check.

COUNTER-SALIENT, [kown'-ter-sāl'-i-ent], *adj.* (*her.*) representing two beasts leaping in opposite directions.

COUNTERSCARP, [kown'-ter-skahp'], *n.* (*fort.*) the outer slope of a ditch. [Fr. *contrescarpe*].

COUNTERSEAL†, [kown'-ter-sēl], *n.* a small seal on the reverse side of a main seal as an additional seal; the reverse part of a seal.

COUNTER-SECURITY, [kown'-ter-sik-ew'-ri-ti], *n.* a security given to one who is security for another.

COUNTERSIGN (1), [kown'-ter-sīn], *n.* a soldier's password or watchword to be given when challenged by the guard; a secret signal in reply to another; a countermark.

COUNTERSIGN (2), [kown'-ter-sīn], *v.t.* to sign a document already signed by another person; (*fig.*) to confirm, attest.

COUNTER-SIGNAL, [kown'-ter-sig'-nal], *n.* a signal in reply to another.

COUNTER-SIGNATURE, [kown'-ter-sig'-nach-er], *n.* a signature added to a signed document for confirmation or ratification.

COUNTERSINK (1), [kown'-ter-singk], *n.* a drill or bit for countersinking.

COUNTERSINK (2), (**countersank, countersunk**), [kown'-ter-singk], *v.t.* to drill a shallow conical-shaped hole in wood or metal to receive the head of a bolt or screw.

COUNTERSINK

COUNTERSTAND, [kown'-ter-stand'], *n.* resistance.

COUNTER-STROKE, [kown'-ter-strōk'], *n.* a stroke in reply.

COUNTER-TALLY, [kown'-ter-tal'-i], *n.* a tally corresponding to another.

COUNTER-TENOR, [kown'-ter-ten'-or], *n.* (*mus.*) a high tenor part sung by a male alto voice; a male alto voice; a singer possessing such a voice.

COUNTER-TURN, [kown'-ter-turn'], *n.* a turn or swing in the reverse direction; an unexpected development in a plot at the climax.

COUNTERVAIL (1), [kown'-ter-vāl], *n.* an equivalent, a counterbalance.

COUNTERVAIL (2), [kown'-ter-vāl], *v.t. and i.* to act against with equal effect or power; to neutralize the effect of. [OFr. *contrevaloir*].

COUNTERVAILING, [kown'-ter-vāl'-ing], *adj.* equalizing, counterbalancing.

COUNTERVALLATION, see CONTRAVALLATION.

COUNTER-VIEW, [kown'-ter-vew'], *n.* an opposite view, reverse opinion.

COUNTER-VOTE, [kown'-ter-vōt'], *v.t.* to vote against.

COUNTER-WEIGH, [kown'-ter-wā'], *v.t.* to counterbalance.

COUNTERWEIGHT, [kown'-ter-wāt'], *n.* a counterpoise.

COUNTER-WHEEL, [kown'-ter-wēl'], *v.i.* to wheel in the reverse direction.

COUNTER-WORK (1), [kown'-ter-wurk], *n.* work in opposition to another work; (*milit.*) a raised mound or fortification in opposition to a similar enemy structure.

COUNTER-WORK (2), [kown'-ter-wurk'], *v.t.* to work in opposition to, to counteract.

COUNTER-WROUGHT, [kown'-ter-rawt'], *adj.* counteracted.

COUNTESS, [kown'-tes], *n.* the wife or widow of an earl or count; a roofing slate 20 inches by 10 inches. [AFr. *cuntesse*].

COUNTING-HOUSE, [kownt'-ing-hows'], *n.* a business office devoted to the keeping of accounts.

COUNTING-ROOM, [kownt'-ing-rōōm'], *n.* a counting-house.

COUNTLESS, [kownt'-les], *adj.* innumerable.

COUNT-OUT, [kownt'-owt'], *n.* the premature close of a debate, meeting, etc., when it is found that there are not enough members present to form a quorum.

COUNTRIFIED, [kun'-tri-fīd], *adj.* resembling or belonging to the country, rural, rustic.

COUNTRIFY, [kun'-tri-fī], *v.t.* to make rustic.

COUNTRY (1), [kun'-tri], *n.* a land or territory known by a particular name, possessing clearly established limits, and inhabited by a particular nation; the nation, the inhabitants of such a land; one's native land; the rural part of the land characterized by fields, woods, etc., and by the absence of industrial settlement; the physical characteristics of an area of land; (*naut.*) a particular region of the sea; (*fig.*) fields of learning; (*cricket*) the outfield; **to go to the c.,** to resort to a general election. [OFr. *contrée* from LL. *contrata* land lying against].

COUNTRY (2), [kun'-tri], *adj.* rural, rustic, pertaining to, or peculiar to, a country.

COUNTRY-DANCE, [kun'-tri-dahns'], *n.* a dance in which the partners are arranged opposite to each other in lines at the start.

COUNTRY-GENTLEMAN, [kun'-tri-jentl'-man], *n.* one of the leisured upper classes, possessing landed estates in the country.

COUNTRYMAN, [kun'-tri-man], *n.* a compatriot, a member of the same nation; one who lives in the country, a rustic.

COUNTRY-MEMBER, [kun'-tri-mem'-ber], *n.* a member of a social or sports club in town, who, being resident in the country, is admitted at a reduced subscription.

COUNTRYPARTY, [kun'-tri-paht'-i], *n.* a political party representing agricultural interests.

COUNTRY-SEAT, [kun'-tri-sēt'], *n.* a country mansion.

COUNTRYSIDE, [kun'-tri-sīd'], *n.* a rural district, an expanse of country.

COUNTRYWOMAN, [kun'-tri-wŏŏm'-an], *n.* a female compatriot, a woman who dwells in the country.

COUNT-WHEEL, [kownt'-wēl], *n.* the wheel in a clock which causes it to strike correctly.

COUNTY (1), [kown'-ti], *n.* an administrative division of a country, a shire; the inhabitants of a county, the landed gentry of a county; **c. borough,** a borough whose local administration is independent of the county in which it lies; **c. palatine,** a county whose lord formerly possessed royal privilege; **c. town,** the administrative centre of the county. [AFr. *counté* from L. *comitatus* court].

COUNTY (2), [kown'-ti], *adj.* pertaining to a county or the landed gentry.

COUNTY-COURT, [kown'-ti-kawt'], *n.* a local civil court used chiefly for the recovery of small debts, etc.

COUP, [kōō], *n.* a sudden and drastic action; a strikingly successful business deal or gamble; **c. d'état,** (*pol.*) sudden forcible change of government by illegal methods; **c. de grâce,** finishing blow; **c. d'œil,** a rapid general survey and appreciation of a situation or a scene; **c. de théâtre,** a surprise turn of events or sensational action; a theatrical success. [Fr. *coup* a blow].

COUPE, coupé, [kōō'-pā], *n.* a short four-wheeled closed carriage for two; a closed two-seater motor-car; an end-compartment of a railway carriage with seats on one side only. [Fr. *coupé, p.pt.* of *couper* to cut].

COUPED, [kōōpt], *adj.* obtained by a coup.

COUPEE, coupée, [kōō'-pā], *n.* a dance-step in which one leg is stationary whilst the other moves forward or backward. [Fr. *coupé*].

COUPER, [kowp'-er], *n.* a dealer. [OScand. *koupari*].

COUPHOLITE, [kow'-fol-īt], *n.* a zeolite. [Gk. *kouphos* light and *lithos* stone].

COUPLE (1), [kupl], *n.* two similar things connected or related to each other; two of a kind; a pair, brace; a husband and wife; a betrothed man and woman; two dance-partners; (*mech.*) two equal parallel forces acting in opposite directions upon a body; (*arch.*) a principal rafter in a roof. [OFr. *couple* from L. *copula* a band].

COUPLE (2), [kupl], *v.t. and i.* to fasten together, to connect; to associate, to join; to copulate; to unite in marriage, to mate. [OFr. *coupler*].

COUPLEMENT†, [kupl'-ment], *n.* union. [OFr. *couplement*].

COUPLER, [kup'-ler], *n.* anything that couples; a mechanical device for coupling two parts of machinery.

COUPLET, [kup'-let], *n.* two consecutive lines of verse of the same metre which rhyme and form a complete unit; (*music*) two notes introduced for cross-rhythm in a passage of triple rhythm and having the same time-value as a triplet. [Fr. *couplet*].

COUPLING, [kup'-ling], *n.* that which couples or connects; the act of fastening together; an apparatus for connecting together parts of systems of shafting of machinery; the contrivance which joins one railway carriage to another; (*elect.*) connexion of two circuits so that a change of current in one affects the other inductively.

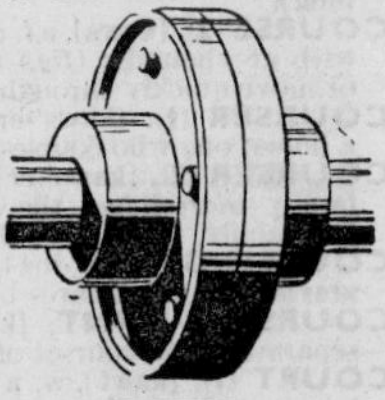

COUPLING

COUPLING-BOX, [kup'-ling-boks'], *n.* (*mech.*) a metal box connecting the ends of two shafts.

COUPLING-PIN, [kup'-ling-pin'], *n.* a bolt used to couple together railway carriages and other machinery.

COUPON, [kōō'-pon], *n.* a detachable piece of a ticket or document; a detachable certificate attached to bearer bonds to be presented for payment of interest due; a detachable ticket which may be exchanged for goods, etc.; a part of an advertisement in a periodical or newspaper, to be filled in and returned to the advertiser in exchange, or part exchange, for a sample of goods advertised, or to be used as an entry form for a competition; an entry

form for a football pool. [Fr. *coupon* piece cut off].
COUPURE, [kōō-pew'-er], *n.* (*milit.*) a ditch and parapet cut as an entrenchment for defensive purposes. [Fr. *coupure* a cutting].
COURAGE, [ku'-rij], *n.* strength of character to resist danger, hardship or suffering without flinching; bravery, pluck, stout-heartedness; **Dutch c.**, temporary courage acquired by drink. [OFr. *corage*].
COURAGEOUS, [ku-rāj'-us], *adj.* displaying or requiring courage. [OFr. *corageus*].
COURAGEOUSLY, [ku-rāj'-us-li], *adv.* in courageous fashion.
COURAGEOUSNESS, [ku-rāj'-us-nes], *n.* the quality of being courageous.
COURANT (1), [kōō-rant'], *n.* that which spreads news quickly, a newspaper. [Fr. *courant* runner].
COURANT (2), [kōō-rant'], *adj.* (*her.*) shown as running. [OFr. *courant* running].
COURANTE, [kōō-rahnt'], *n.* a quick French dance in triple time with a regular flowing rhythm; music to which this was performed. [Fr. *courante*].
COURAP, [kōō'-rap], *n.* (*med.*) a kind of herpes attacking the armpits, groin, breast, and face, common in the East Indies. [Ind. *khurap*].
COURBARIL, [kōōer'-ba-ril], *n.* a resinous substance obtained from the West Indian locust-tree, *Hymenaea Courbaril*; the tree itself. [Native].
COURIER, [kōō'-ri-er], *n.* an express messenger, a bearer of special dispatches; an attendant who makes all arrangements on a conducted foreign tour. [Fr. *courier*].
COURLAN, [kōōer'-lan], *n.* a tropical South American bird related to the cranes, *Aramus scolopaceus*. [Native].

COURLAN

COURSE (1), [kaws], *n.* continuous progress or trend; the route traversed (of a moving body), direction or path of motion; ground over which a race is run; a specially prepared and marked-out tract of land over which certain games (e.g. golf) are played; channel along which a moving body flows; the duration of a period of time; a method of procedure, line of action; a regular succession of related events, a sequence, progress; one of a succession of dishes comprising a meal; (*arch.*) a continuous layer of bricks at the same level throughout the whole length of a building; a race between two greyhounds, both of which are chasing a hare; (*pl. naut.*) the lower squaresails, the staysails on the lower masts, the main staysails of brigs and schooners; a point of the compass to which a ship sails; (*vulgar*) the menstrual discharge; **in due c.**, at the proper time, in a natural succession; **of c.**, naturally; **as a matter of c.**, automatically. [OFr. *cours* from L. *cursus* a running].
COURSE (2), [kaws], *v.t.* and *i.* to hunt; to hunt game with greyhounds; (*fig.*) to pursue, traverse; to race or move quickly through.
COURSER (1), [kaws'-er], *n.* a swift horse; (*poet.*) a horse; one who courses.
COURSER (2), [kaws'-er], *n.* a genus of birds of the family *Glareolidae*; the cream-coloured member of this family, *Cursorius gallicus*.
COURSING, [kaws'-ing], *n.* a form of sport in which greyhounds hunt hares by sight.
COURSING-JOINT, [kaws'-ing-joint'], *n.* a joint separating two courses of masonry.
COURT (1), [kawt], *n.* a paved yard surrounded by houses and usually entered by a narrow passage; an open space or quadrangle enclosed by buildings; a large mansion or manor; an enclosed area or building in which certain ball games may be played; a lawn or hard, level surface on which lawn tennis may be played; the residence of a sovereign, members of the personal retinue of a sovereign and royal family; an official function at which distinguished people formally meet the sovereign; a place where judicial inquiries are held or cases heard; the judges, magistrates, or officials assembled for administering justice; a session of such an assembly; solicitous attention to gain favour, amorous attentions; **to put oneself out of c.**, (*fig.*) to behave in a very unreasonable and objectionable way. [OFr. *curt* from L. *cohors cohortis* enclosure].
COURT (2), [kawt], *v.t.* and *i.* to endeavour to please or gain the favour of, by assiduous attention or deference; to pay amorous attentions to, to woo; (*fig.*) to act in such a way as to merit, run the risk of.
COURT-BARON, [kawt'-ba'-ron], *n.* (*leg. hist.*) a manorial court having jurisdiction over actions relating to freehold land within the manor.
COURT-CARD, [kawt'-kahd], *n.* the king, queen or knave in playing-cards. [COURT and CARD].
COURT-DAY, [kawt'-dā], *n.* a day on which a judicial court sits.
COURT-DRESS, [kawt'-dres'], *n.* formal dress prescribed for appearance at a royal court.
COURTEOUS, [kur'-ti-us], *adj.* courtly; displaying courtesy; polite, well-mannered. [OFr. *corteis*].
COURTEOUSLY, [kur'-ti-us-li], *adv.* in courteous fashion.
COURTEOUSNESS, [kur'-ti-us-nes], *n.* the quality of being courteous.
COURTER, [kawt'-er], *n.* one who courts; a wooer.
COURTESAN, [kurt'-iz-an'], *n.* a woman of easy virtue, a prostitute. [Span. *cortesana*].
COURTESY, [kurt'-is-i], *n.* politeness of manners and good breeding accompanied by kindness, dignity, and considerateness; favour; a respectful act; **c. title**, a title given by social custom to certain persons not strictly entitled to it; **tenure by c.**, (*leg.*) tenure by which a man holds property inherited by his wife after her death, if there are any living issue from the marriage. [OFr. *cortesie*].
COURT-FAVOUR, [kawt'-fā'-ver], *n.* royal favour.
COURT-FOOL, [kawt'-fōōl'], *n.* a buffoon or jester formerly kept at a royal court for amusement.
COURT-GUIDE, [kawt'-gīd'], *n.* a directory of persons presented at court, or of the upper classes.
COURT-HAND, [kawt'-hand'], *n.* a cursive style of handwriting formerly used in legal and official documents.
COURT-HOUSE, [kawt'-hows], *n.* a building in which courts of law are held.
COURTIER, [kawt'-i-er], *n.* a person attached to a royal court; an exceedingly deferential person, flatterer. [OFr. *courteur*].
COURTIERISM, [kawt'-i-er-izm], *n.* the manners of a courtier.
COURTING, [kawt'-ing], *n.* courtship.
COURT-LEET, [kawt'-lēt'], *n.* (*hist.*) a local court formerly presided over by the lord of the manor.
COURTLIKE, [kawt'-līk], *adj.* elegant, courtly.
COURTLINESS, [kawt'-li-nes], *n.* the quality of being courtly.
COURTLY, [kawt'-li], *adj.* pertaining to or characteristic of a court; dignified, well-bred, polite, nobly refined.
COURT-MARTIAL (1), (*pl.* **courts-martial**), [kawt'-mah'-shal], *n.* a tribunal of naval or military officers legally authorized to conduct an inquiry into and to punish offences against, naval or military law; a trial of a sailor, soldier or airman by this means.
COURT-MARTIAL (2), (**court-martialling, court-martialled**), [kawt'-mah'-shal], *v.t.* to try a person by court-martial.
COURT-PARTY, [kawt'-pah'-ti], *n.* a political party having only the interests of a royal court at heart.
COURT-PLASTER, [kawt'-plahst'-er], *n.* sticking plaster consisting of coloured or transparent silk applied to cuts, etc.
COURTSHIP, [kawt'-ship], *n.* the period of wooing with a view to marriage.
COURT-YARD, [kawt'-yahd], *n.* a large paved court wholly or partly enclosed by a building entered from it.
COUSCOUS, [kōōs'-kōōs], *n.* an African food of millet flour, flesh and the leaves of the baobab, *Adansonia digitata*. [Arab. *kuskus*].
COUSIN, [kuzn], *n.* the offspring of one's uncle or aunt; †a kinsman or distant relative; formal royal title of address to another sovereign or peer of the realm; **c. german**, the child of an uncle or aunt, (*fig.*) a closely related thing. [Fr. *cousin*].
COUSINSHIP, [kuzn'-ship], *n.* the relationship of cousins.
COUTEAU, [kōō'-tō], *n.* a knife-like sword. [Fr. *couteau* knife].
COUTILLE, [kōō-tēl'], *n.* close-woven material resembling canvas. [Fr. *coutil* quilt].
COUVADE, [kōō-vahd'], *n.* a custom among primitive peoples by which the male spouse pretends to be ill and retires to bed, when his wife is about to give birth. [Fr. *couvade*].
COVE (1), [kōv], *n.* a small creek or inlet; a cavern;

a narrow gap in the side of a mountain; (*arch.*) a concave moulding or vault. [OE. *cofa* chamber].

COVE (2), [kōv], *n.* (*slang*) a person a creature. [Uncert.].

COVE (3), [kōv], *v.t.* to arch over in concave form. [COVE (1)].

COVEN, [kuvn], *n.* a meeting of witches. [OFr. *covent* assembly].

COVENANT (1), [kuv'-en-ant], *n.* a mutual agreement, a solemn undertaking; (*leg.*) a signed agreement in writing between two parties with respect to a promise; a clause of a legal document containing such a promise; **Solemn League and C.,** (*hist.*) a contract between the Church of Scotland and the English Parliament in 1643 recognizing and establishing Presbyterianism in Scotland. [OFr. *covenant* from L. *convenire* to agree].

COVENANT (2), [kuv'-en-ant], *v.t. and i.* to grant by a covenant; to bind oneself by a covenant.

COVENANT-BREAKER, [kuv'-en-ant-brāk'-er], *n.* one who breaks a covenant.

COVENANTED, [kuv'-en-ant-id], *adj.* pledged or bound by covenant.

COVENANTER, [kuv'-en-ant-er], *n.* a person who covenants; a supporter of the National Covenant of Scotland or the Solemn League and Covenant.

COVENTRY, [kov'-en-tri], *n.* **to send to C.,** to ostracize, to ignore deliberately, refuse to talk to. [*Coventry*, a town in Warwickshire].

COVER (1), [kuv'-er], *n.* anything made to fit over and cover an object, a lid, wrapper, case, screen; anything affording reasonable protection or hiding; (*pl.*) dining utensils laid for each person at a meal; the outer boards of a book; (*comm.*) money deposited against loss that could be sustained by a fall in prices; (*fig.*) pretence, cloak; (*slang*) a press report of a public meeting or social function.

COVER (2), [kuv'-er], *v.t.* to place one thing over another so as to hide it wholly or in part; to spread, lie over; to clothe; to lay down a sum of money equal to one offered or wagered; to place something in front of or over an object to protect it, to shield; to protect against possibility of loss; to allow for, to be adequate for, to provide for; to stain or splash extensively, to bedaub, to envelop; to travel (a certain distance); (*fig.*) to treat of, to include, embrace; to overwhelm; to conceal, to refrain from disclosing; to level a firearm at ; (of animals) to mate with, to incubate; (*slang*) to report (a meeting, etc.); **to remain covered,** to keep one's hat on one's head; **to c. in,** to fill in (a hole); **to c. up,** (*boxing*) to adopt a defensive attitude, and protect one's vulnerable parts. [OFr. *covrir* from L. *cooperire* to cover].

COVERCHIEF†, [kuv'-er-chēf], *n.* a covering for the head. [OFr. *cuevre-chef*].

COVER-CLIP, [kuv'-er-klip'], *n.* a fish, the sole.

COVERED-WAY, COVERT-WAY, [kuv'-erd-wā'], *n.* a roofed passage or corridor having one or both of its sides open to the air.

COVERING, [kuv'-er-ing], *n.* that which covers; a case, a cover.

COVERING-LETTER, [kuv'-er-ing-let'-er], *n.* a letter accompanying a document in explanation or amplification of it.

COVERING-PARTY, [kuv'-er-ing-pah'-ti], *n.* (*milit.*) a body of soldiers sent out to cover the activities of trench-diggers, wire-repairers, etc.

COVERLET, [kuv'-er-let], *n.* the outer cover or quilt of a bed; any cover.

COVER-POINT, [kuv'-er-point'], *n.* (*cricket*) a position in the cricket-field behind and to the right of point; the player fielding in this position.

CO-VERSED SINE, [kō'-vurst-sīn'], *n.* the difference of the sine of an arc or angle from unity.

COVERT (1), [kuv'-er(t)], *n.* a shelter, a hiding-place (*esp.* for game); a small feather covering parts of larger feathers in birds; (*archaic*) a cover; **to draw a c.,** to search thickets, brushwood, etc., for game or a fox. [OFr. *covert*].

COVERT (2), [kuv'-ert], *adj.* disguised, surreptitious; **femme c.,** (*leg.*) a married woman as being under the protection of her husband.

COVERT-COAT, [kuv'-ert-kōt'], *n.* a short, light, waterproof overcoat.

COVERTLY, [kuv'-ert-li], *adv.* in covert fashion.

COVERTNESS, [kuv'-ert-nes], *n.* the condition of being covert.

COVERTURE, [kuv'-er-cher], *n.* covering, shelter; disguise, veil; (*leg.*) the state of a married woman. [OFr. *coverture*].

COVERT-WAY, see COVERED-WAY.

COVET, [kuv'-it], *v.t. and i.* to desire earnestly and unlawfully, to long for, hanker after. [OFr. *coveiter* from LL. *cupiditare* to desire].

COVETABLE, [kuv'-it-abl], *adj.* liable to be coveted.

COVETINGLY, [kuv'-it-ing-li], *adv.* so as to covet.

COVETIVENESS†, [kuv'-it-iv-nes], *n.* cupidity, avarice, greed.

COVETOUS, [kuv'-it-us], *adj.* inordinately desirous of possessing, excessively eager to acquire, avaricious, greedy, grasping.

COVETOUSLY, [kuv'-it-us-li], *adv.* in a covetous manner.

COVETOUSNESS, [kuv'-it-us-nes], *n.* the state of being covetous.

COVEY, [kuv'-i], *n.* a group or brood of partridges; (*fig.*) a company, party, family. [OFr. *covée* a brood].

COVIN, [kuv'-in], *n.* a fraudulent agreement made to the detriment of others. [OFr. *covin* a trick from MedL. *convenium* agreement].

COVING, [kōv'-ing], *n.* (*arch.*) an arched part of a roof; the curved part of a vault or ceiling; the curved sides of a fireplace.

COVING

COVINOUS†, [kuv'-in-us], *adj.* collusive, fraudulent.

COW (1), [kow], *n.* the female of the ox or other animals of the genus *Bos*, *esp.* when domesticated; the female of certain other animals; **sea-c.,** a marine mammal of the order *Sirenia*; **c. gun,** (*slang*) a large naval gun. [OE. *cu*].

COW (2), [kow], *v.t.* to intimidate with threats or bullying; to reduce to a state of perpetual fear or docility. [OIcel. *kuga* to tyrannize].

COWAGE, see COWHAGE.

COWARD (1), [kow'-erd], *n.* a person destitute of courage, a craven; one who is afraid to face danger or hardship. [OFr. *couard*].

COWARD (2), [kow'-erd], *adj.* lacking courage, faint-hearted, weak-spirited; (*her.*) with its tail between its legs.

COWARDICE, [kow'-erd-is], *n.* want of courage, faint-heartedness, ignoble fear. [OFr. *couardise*].

COWARD-LIKE, [kow'-erd-līk'], *adj.* cowardly.

COWARDLINESS, [kow'-erd-li-nes], *n.* the condition of being cowardly.

COWARDLY (1), [kow'-erd-li], *adj.* like a coward, faint-hearted, craven.

COWARDLY (2), [kow'-erd-li], *adv.* in the manner of a coward.

COW-BANE, [kow'-bān], *n.* (*bot.*) water-hemlock, *Cicuta virosa.*

COWBERRY, [kow'-be'-ri], *n.* (*bot.*) the whortleberry, *Vaccinium Vitis-Idaea.*

COW-BIRD, [kow'-burd], *n.* an American starling of the genus *Molothrus*, which deposits its eggs in the nests of other birds.

COWBOY, [kow'-boi], *n.* (*U.S.*) a man employed in looking after cattle grazing on a ranch.

COWCATCHER, [kow'-kach'-er], *n.* (*U.S.*) a strong framework or grating fitted to the front of a locomotive to clear obstructions from the rails, and as a safety-guard.

COWED, [kowd], *adj.* dispirited, subdued.

COWER, [kow'-er], *v.i.* to crouch or gather oneself into a squat posture through fear, cold, etc.; to shrink back or cringe in fear. [OIcel. *kura* to lie still].

COWHAGE, COWAGE, COWITCH, [kow'-ij], *n.* (*bot.*) a leguminous plant of the genus *Macuna*, with hairy pods that cause intolerable itching when touched. [Hind. *kawanch*].

COWHAND, [kow'-hand], *n.* (*U.S.*) a cowboy.

COW-HEEL, [kow'-hēl'], *n.* the stewed edible heel or foot of a cow.

COWHERD, [kow'-hurd'], *n.* one who looks after cows.

COWHIDE (1), [kow'-hīd], *n.* leather made of the hide of a cow; a coarse riding-whip of this.

COWHIDE (2), [kow'-hīd], *v.t.* to flog with a cowhide.

COW-HOUSE, [kow'-hows], *n.* a cow-shed.

COWITCH, see COWHAGE.

COWKEEPER, [kow'-kēp'-er], *n.* a cowherd.

COWL (1), [kowl], *n.* a hooded garment worn by monks; the hood itself; a movable hood-shaped metal contrivance attached to the top of a chimney pot; the wire-cap of a locomotive funnel; a hood-shaped ventilator on the deck of a large ship. [OE. *cugele* from L. *cucullus* a hood].

COWL (2), [kowl], *n.* a large water-vessel carried on a pole between two men. [OFr. *covelle*].
COWLED, [kowld], *adj.* provided with a cowl.
COW-LEECH, [kow'-lēch], *n.* a cow doctor.
COWLICK, [kow'-lik], *n.* a tuft of hair straying over the forehead.
COWLIKE, [kow'-līk], *adj.* resembling a cow.
COWLING, [kowl'-ing], *n.* (*aeron.*) the casing over radiators or air-cooled cylinders to direct the air-stream.
COWLSTAFF, [kowl'-stahf], *n.* the pole on which a cowl is supported.
COWMAN, [kow'-man], *n.* a cowherd.
CO-WORKER, [kō-wurk'-er], *n.* one who works along with another.
COW-PARSLEY, [kow'-pahs'-li], *n.* (*bot.*) an umbelliferous plant, *Anthriscus sylvestris*.
COW-PARSNIP, [kow'-pahs'-nip], *n.* (*bot.*) a plant of the genus *Heracleum*.
COW-POCK, [kow'-pok'], *n.* a pustule of cow-pox.
COW-POX, [kow'-poks'], *n.* a vaccine disease in which pustules appear on the teats of a cow, the pus from these pustules formerly used for vaccination.
COWRY, COWRIE, [kow'-ri], *n.* a small shell of the genus *Cypraea*, used as native money in parts of India and Africa. [Hind. *kauri*].
COWSHED, [kow'-shed'], *n.* a building in which cows are housed.
COWSLIP, [kow'-slip], *n.* a plant of the primrose family, *Primula veris*, with fragrant yellow flowers. [OE. *cu-slyppe* cow-dung].
COW-TREE, [kow'-trē], *n.* a Venezuelan tree, *Brosimum galactodendron*, which yields a milky fluid.
COW-WHEAT, [kow'-wēt], *n.* a plant of the genus *Melampyrum*, with wheat-like seeds.
COX (1), [koks], *n.* the steersman of an oar-propelled racing boat. [COXSWAIN].
COX (2), [koks], *v.t.* to act as cox to.
COXA, (*pl.* **coxae**), [kok'-sa, kok'-sī], *n.* (*anat.*) the hip-joint; (*entom.*) the joint next to the body on an insect's leg. [L. *coxa* hip].
COXAL, [koksl], *adj.* of, or pertaining to, the coxa.
COXALGIA, [kok-sal'-ji-a], *n.* disease of the hip-joint. [COXA and Gk. *algia* pain].
COXCOMB, [koks'-kōm], *n.* †a red cap resembling a cock's comb, formerly worn by professional jesters or fools; a conceited dandy, a vain, swaggering fop. [COCK and COMB].
COXCOMBRY, [koks'-kōm-ri], *n.* the manners or behaviour of a coxcomb, conceited affectation.
COXCOMICAL, [koks-kom'-ik-al], *adj.* foppish, vain, swaggering.
COXSWAIN, [koksn], *n.* the sailor in charge of the steering of a boat, the leader and helmsman of a lifeboat; a cox. [COCK and SWAIN].
COXSWAINLESS, [koksn'-les], *adj.* (*rowing*) having no cox.
COY, [koi], *adj.* modest, bashful, shy. [OFr. *coi* from L. *quietus*].
COYISH, [koi'-ish], *adj.* rather coy.
COYLY, [koi'-li], *adv.* in a coy fashion.
COYNESS, [koi'-nes], *n.* the condition of being coy.
COYOTE, [kī-ō'-ti, koi'-ōt], *n.* the prairie wolf *Canis latrans*. [Mexican *coyotl*].
COYPU, [koi'-pōō], *n.* a South American rodent of aquatic habits, *Myopotamus coypu*, valued for its fur. [Native].
COZ, [kuz], *n.* (*archaic*, as a term of address) cousin.
COZEN, [kuzn], *v.t. and i.* to cheat, defraud. [Uncert.].
COZENAGE, [kuzn'-ij], *n.* deceit, cheating.
COZENER, [kuzn'-er], *n.* one who cozens.
CRAB (1), [krab], *n.* a ten-footed crustacean of the suborder *Brachyura*, having a shallow, rounded body and strong claws like nippers; one of the signs of the Zodiac; (*pl.*) crab-lice; mechanical apparatus of various forms, with claws for hoisting or hauling heavy objects; a kind of capstan, the drum of a portable winch; (*pl. slang*) the lowest throw at dice; **to catch a c.**, to make a faulty rowing stroke so that the handle of the oar is forced against the rower, causing him to lose balance. [OE. *crabba*].
CRAB, (2), [krab], *n.* the small sour fruit of the wild apple tree; the tree itself; (*fig.*) a cross-tempered, embittered person. [ME. *crabbe*].
CRAB (3), [krab], *v.t.* (*falconry*) to scratch, claw; to find fault with unfairly, to disparage, carp at. [CRAB (1)].
CRABBED, [krabd], *adj.* sour, peevish, embittered; difficult to read, badly-formed; obtuse, difficult to understand.
CRABBEDLY, [krab'-id-li], *adv.* in crabbed fashion.
CRABBEDNESS, [krab'-id-nes], *n.* the condition of being crabbed.
CRABBY, [krab'-i], *adj.* perplexing; peevish.
CRABER†, [krab'-er], *n.* the water-rat, *Microtus amphibius*. [Fr. *crabier*].
CRAB-FACED, [krab'-fāst], *adj.* having a sour, embittered countenance.
CRAB-LOUSE, (*pl.* **crab-lice**), [krab'-lows], *n.* the body louse, *Phthirius inguinalis*.
CRAB-POT, [krab'-pot'], *n.* a wickerwork receptacle for catching crabs.
CRAB'S-EYES, [krabz'-īz], *n.*(*pl.*) round, hard masses of lime in the stomach of the crayfish, used medically.
CRABSIDLE, [krab'-sīdl], *v.i.* to move sideways with a crab-like motion.
CRABWOOD, [krab'-wood], *n.* a South American tree of the genus *Caraipa*. [Corruption of CARAP].
CRAB-YAWS, [krab'-yawz], *n.* a West Indian disease in which ulcers form on the soles of the feet or the palms of the hand.
CRACK (1), [krak], *n.* a sudden, loud report; a sharp blow; a chink, a long, narrow opening or slit; a slight fissure or break in a brittle substance, usually marked by a thin line of fracture; an instant, a very short interval of time; (*slang*) an expert performer; (*slang*) an attempt, a shot, an endeavour to accomplish something; (*slang*) a wise-crack; **c. of doom**, judgment-day.
CRACK (2), [krak], *adj.* expert; champion, first-rate.
CRACK (3), [krak], *v.t.* to fracture, break by pressure; to cause a crack in; to flick or let off with a crack; (*coll.*) to tell (a joke); to decompose (petroleum) by heat or pressure into lighter hydrocarbons; (*slang*) to hit with a crack; **to c. up**, (*coll.*) to boost, boast of; **to c. a crib**, (*slang*) to burgle a house; **to c. on**, (*naut.*) to crowd on all sail; *v.i.* to break into a crack; (of a male voice) to undergo a lowering in tone at puberty; (of a voice) to become hoarse and broken; to wilt, to snap; (*pass.*) (*coll.*) to be crazy. [OE. *cracian* to resound].
CRACK-BRAINED, [krak'-brānd], *adj.* crazy, senseless.
CRACKED, [krakt], *adj.* containing cracks, split, broken; harsh, dissonant, untuneful; (*coll.*) slightly crazy, weak in the head; damaged, containing flaws.
CRACKER, [krak'-er], *n.* a small explosive firework emitting a series of loud reports when lit; a firework enclosed in a cylinder of brightly coloured paper together with a motto and paper cap or cheap trinket, which explodes with a loud crack when the ends are pulled; a thin, dry, flaky biscuit; (*pl.*) a tool for cracking nuts.
CRACKERS, [krak'-erz], *adj.* (*slang*) mad, crazy.
CRACK-HEMP, [krak'-hemp], *n.* one destined to be or worthy of being hanged.
CRACKJAW, [krak'-jaw], *n.* (*coll.*) a tongue-twister; a hard sort of toffee.
CRACKLE (1), [krakl], *n.* a series of faint crisp reports rapidly sounding; china, porcelain or glassware whose surface is ornamented with a tracery of small cracks.
CRACKLE (2), [krakl], *v.i.* to make a crackling sound. [*Dim.* of CRACK (2)].
CRACKLING, [krak'-ling], *n.* the making of frequently repeated crackles; the crisp rind of roast pork.
CRACKNEL, [krak'-nel], *n.* a variety of light, dry flaky biscuit. [Fr. *craquelin*].
CRACKSMAN, [kraks'-man], *n.* (*slang*) a burglar.
CRACOVIENNE, [krak-ō'-vi-en'], *n.* a Polish peasant dance. [Fr. (*danse*) *cracovienne* a dance of Cracow, in Poland].
CRADLE (1), [krādl], *n.* a little cot or crib, usually on rockers, for babies; anything resembling this; (*fig.*) infancy; birthplace, place of origin; (*naut.*) a rigid bedstead for a wounded seaman; a basket suspended from a rope in which people are swung ashore from wrecks; a supporting frame placed under a ship during construction or repairs; a small movable framework slung from pulleys fastened to scaffolding, and used by steeplejacks, etc.; (*surg.*) a protective framework for a broken or injured limb; a chisel with one bevelled side, used in mezzotint engraving; **the c. of the deep**, the sea. [OE. *cradol*].
CRADLE (2), [krādl], *v.t. and i.* to lay or rock in a cradle; to soothe or lull as in a cradle; to rear, to nurse from birth; (*min.*) to wash gold in a cradle.
CRADLE-WALK, [krādl'-wawk], *n.* a walk under an avenue of trees.
CRADLING, [krādl'-ing], *n.* (*arch.*) a framework of wood; the timber to support the lathing and plastering of vaulted ceilings.

CRAFT, [krahft], *n.* art, skill, dexterity, workmanship; cunning, guile, cleverness; a skilled trade or occupation requiring special manual training; the members of such a trade, especially when banded into a collective body; a boat; **the c.**, the collective body of Freemasons. [OE. *cræft*].

CRAFTILY, [krahft'-i-li], *adv.* in a crafty fashion.

CRAFTINESS, [krahft'-i-nes], *n.* the quality of being crafty.

CRAFTSMAN, [krahfts'-man], *n.* a skilled artificer or other manual worker; (*fig.*) an artist; one skilled in the aesthetic arts.

CRAFTSMANSHIP, [krahfts'-man-ship], *n.* highly skilled workmanship.

CRAFTSMASTER, [krahfts'-mahst'-er], *n.* one skilled in a craft.

CRAFTY, [krahft'-i], *adj.* skilful, cunning, full of guile. [OE. *cræftig* powerful].

CRAG, [krag], *n.* a rough, steep, jutting, rugged rock or point of rock. [Ir. *carraig*].

CRAGGINESS, [krag'-i-nes], *n.* the condition of being craggy.

CRAGGY, [krag'-i], *adj.* full of crags, characterized by crags.

CRAGSMAN, [kragz'-man], *n.* a skilled rock-climber.

CRAKE (1), [krāk], *n.* a small bird of the genus *Crex*, the corn-crake; the grating cry of this bird. [Imitative].

CRAKE (2), [krāk], *v.i.* to utter the cry of the corn-crake. [Imitative].

CRAKEBERRY, [krāk'-be'-ri], *n.* (*bot.*) the crowberry, *Empetrum nigrum*.

CRAM (1), [kram], *n.* information obtained by cramming; a lie.

CRAM (2), [kram], *v.t.* to stuff, force or pack into a small space; to thrust in by force; to feed excessively in order to fatten; (*fig.*) to coach intensively for a particular examination; *v.i.* to eat greedily and to excess; (*coll.*) to tell an untruth; (*fig.*) to undergo a period of intensive concentrated study in order to pass an examination. [OE. *crammian* to stuff].

CRAMBO, [kram'-bō], *n.* a game in which one person gives a word, to which another finds a rhyme; a rhyming word; **dumb c.**, a kind of charade in which a rhyme to the word to be found is given. [L. *crambe* (*repetita*) (warmed-up) cabbage, a story often repeated].

CRAMMABLE, [kram'-abl], *adj.* capable of being crammed.

CRAMMER, [kram'-er], *n.* one who crams, a person who gives intensive coaching for examinations; a specially prepared book for cramming purposes.

CRAMOISY, [kram'-wa-zē], *n.* cloth of crimson; crimson. [Fr. *cramoisi*].

CRAMP (1), [kramp], *n.* sudden spasmodic and involuntary muscle contraction attended with great pain. [LGerm. *kramp*].

CRAMP (2), [kramp], *n.* a piece of iron bent at the ends, to bind objects together; a kind of screw-clamp; (*fig.*) a restraining or confining influence. [Du. *krampe*].

CRAMP (3), [kramp], *v.t.* to affect with cramp; to bind with a cramp, to clamp together; (*fig.*) to restrain, hinder, to restrict the freedom of, to hamper.

CRAMP-BARK, [kramp'-bahk], *n.* (*bot.*) a medicinal plant, *Viburnum Oxycoccus*, with an acid fruit.

CRAMP-BONE, [kramp'-bōn], *n.* a sheep's patella, formerly thought to be a remedy against cramp.

CRAMP-FISH, [kramp'-fish], *n.* the torpedo-fish, *Torpedo nobiliana*.

CRAMP-IRON, [kramp'-iern'], *n.* a piece of metal, bent at right angles at each end, for fastening stone-work together; a crampon.

CRAMPON, [kramp'-on], *n.* a grappling-iron, a hooked bar of iron; a tool in the form of two hooked bars of iron for raising stone or timber; spiked plate attached to the sole of the shoe in order to get a better foothold. [Fr. *crampon*].

CRAMPON

CRAN, [kran], *n.* a measure for herrings containing 37½ gallons, or about 800 herrings, a barrel-ful. [Gael. *crann* measure].

CRANAGE, [krān'-ij], *n.* the right of using a crane at a wharf; the price paid for this.

CRANBERRY, [kran'-be'-ri], *n.* (*bot.*) a small dark red berry, the fruit of *Oxycoccus palustris*. [CRANE and BERRY].

CRANE (1), [krān], *n.* a wading bird with long legs, slender neck and narrow bill, *Grus cineraria*; a machine for raising or moving heavy loads; a siphon for drawing liquid out of a vessel. [OE. *cran*].

CRANE

CRANE (2), [krān], *v.t.* to stretch forward the neck as far as possible; to hoist or lower with a crane.

CRANE-FLY, [krān'-flī], *n.* an insect of the genus *Tipula*, the daddy-longlegs.

CRANE'S-BILL, [krānz'-bil], *n.* (*bot.*) any species of *Geranium*; (*surg.*) a pair of long forceps.

CRANIAL, [krān'-i-al], *adj.* pertaining to the cranium.

CRANIO-, *pref.* the cranium. [Gk. *kranion*].

CRANIOFACIAL, [krān'-i-ō-fā'-shal], *adj.* belonging to the face and head.

CRANIOGNOMY, [krān-i-on'-o-mi], *n.* the science dealing with the physical characteristics of the skull. [CRANIO and Gk. *gnome* knowledge].

CRANIOLOGICAL, [krān'-i-o-loj'-ik-al], *adj.* relating to craniology.

CRANIOLOGIST, [krān'-i-ol'-oj-ist], *n.* one skilled in craniology.

CRANIOLOGY, [krān'-i-ol'-o-ji], *n.* the science of the structure of the skull as significant of race. [CRANIO and Gk. *logos* speech].

CRANIOMETER, [krān'-i-om'-it-er], *n.* an instrument for measuring skulls. [CRANIO and METER].

CRANIOMETRICAL, [krān'-i-ō-met'-rik-al], *adj.* belonging to craniometry.

CRANIOMETRY, [krān'-i-om'-et-ri], *n.* the measurement of the cranium. [CRANIO and Gk. *metria* measurement].

CRANIOSCOPY, [krān'-i-os'-kop-i], *n.* phrenology, examination of the shape, contours and size of the skull as a means of character-telling. [CRANIO and Gk. *skopia* viewing].

CRANIOTOMY, [krān'-i-ot'-o-mi], *n.* (*surg.*) the operation of opening the head of the foetus. [CRANIO and Gk. *tome* cutting].

CRANIUM, [krān'-i-um], *n.* the bones enclosing and forming a protective covering for the brain, the skull. [L. from Gk. *kranion* skull].

CRANK (1), [krangk], *n.* a bent axle or handle to convert lineal into rotary motion or vice-versa, or to impart motion to a wheel; the starting handle of a motor vehicle; an angular-shaped device used in bell-hanging to change the direction of motion; (*fig.*) a twist or strange turn of speech, a verbal conceit; a mental kink or caprice; a person with a mental twist or kink, an eccentric individual. [ME. *crank*, ~OE. *crincan* to bend].

CRANK

CRANK (2), [krangk], *adj.* cranky.

CRANK (3), [krangk], *v.t.* to bend in the form of a crank; to fasten with a crank, to impart motion to by means of a crank; to provide with a crank; **to c. up**, (*coll.*) to start up a motor-car engine by hand.

CRANKILY, [krangk-i-li], *adv.* in cranky fashion.

CRANKINESS, [krangk'-i-nes], *n.* the quality of being cranky.

CRANKLE (1), [krangkl], *n.* a twist, turn, bend, a curve. [*Dim.* of CRANK (1)].

CRANKLE (2), [krangkl] *v.i.* to twist, bend, wind in tortuous manner.

CRANK-PIN, [krangk'-pin], *n.* (*engin.*) a pin, eccentric to a shaft, which rotates in the big-end bearing of a connecting-rod.

CRANKY, [krangk'-i], *adj.* out of order; unstable, shaky; sickly, weak; ill-tempered; eccentric, faddish; full of twists, tortuous.

CRANNIED, [kran'-id], *adj.* full of chinks.

CRANNOG, [kran'-og], *n.* in Scotland and Ireland, a fortified dwelling and refuge on an island in a lake. [Gael. *crannag* timber-structure].

CRANNY (1), [kran'-i], *n.* a small aperture, a chink, a crack, a cleft; a secret hiding-place; (*glass-making*)

an iron instrument for forming the necks of glasses. [Fr. *cran*].
CRANNY (2), [kran'-i], *adj.* (*prov.*) pleasant, cheerful, jovial.
CRANTS†, [krahntz], *n.*(*pl.*) garlands carried before the bier of a maiden and hung over her grave. [Germ. *kranz*].
CRAPE, [krāp], *n.* a thin, light, transparent stuff made from gummed raw silk, usually dyed black, and used for mourning attire; a band of this as a sign of mourning. [Fr. *crêpe* curled from L. *crispus*].
CRAPS, [kraps], *n.* (*U.S.*) a gambling dice game. [Fr. *crabs*, *craps*].
CRAPULENCE, [krap'-yōō-lens], *n.* sickness or indisposition occasioned by excessive drinking; excessive drinking, debauchery. [L. *crapula* drunkenness].
CRAPULENT, [krap'-yōō-lent], *adj.* pertaining to, or suffering from, crapulence. [L. *crapulentus* extremely intoxicated].
CRAPULOUS, [krap'-yōō-lus], *adj.* crapulent.
CRAPY, [krāp'-i], *adj.* resembling crape.
CRASH (1), [krash], *n.* a sudden loud explosive sound; the violent impact of a heavy fall or collision; an aircraft accident involving a sudden fall to the ground; (*fig.*) ruin; failure, heavy financial loss. [CRASH (3)].
CRASH (2), [krash], *n.* a coarse linen cloth, chiefly used for towels. [Unkn.].
CRASH (3), [krash], *v.t. and i.* to fall and break with a crash; to collide with something with a crash; (*aeron.*) to fall suddenly to the ground with a heavy impact; (*fig.*) to collapse, fall in ruins, fail hopelessly; (*slang*) to gate-crash. [Imitative].
CRASH-HELMET, [krash'-hel'-mit], *n.* a stout padded helmet worn by aviators and racing motorists, to protect the head in case of accident.
CRASHING (1), [krash'-ing], *n.* the noise of a crash.
CRASHING (2), [krash'-ing], *adj.* that crashes; (*slang*) utter and unmistakable (of a fool, bore, etc.).
CRASIS, [krā'-sis], *n.* (*gram.*) the contraction of two vowels belonging to different syllables into one long vowel or diphthong. [Gk. *krasis* blending].
CRASS, [kras], *adj.* thick, coarse, gross; utter, unmistakable, complete. [L. *crassus* thick].
CRASSAMENTUM, [kras'-am-ent'-um], *n.* the thick red part of the blood, the clot. [L. *crassamentum* thickness].
CRASSITUDE, [kras'-i-tewd], *n.* coarseness, grossness; utter stupidity, unmistakable foolishness or dullness. [L. *crassitudo* thickness].
CRASSLY, [kras'-li], *adv.* in crass fashion, impenetrably.
CRASSNESS, [kras'-nes], *n.* the quality of being crass.
CRATAEGUS, [krā-tē'-gus], *n.* (*bot.*) a genus of large shrubs including the hawthorn, *Crataegus Oxyacantha*. [L. *crataegus* hawthorn].
CRATCH, [krach], *n.* a grated rack for fodder in a stable; a wooden framework or grating. [Fr. *crèche* a crib].
CRATE, [krāt], *n.* a framework packing-case, or wickerwork basket in which fragile goods are transported. [L. *cratis* wickerwork].
CRATER, [krāt'-er], *n.* the mouth of a volcano; (*milit.*) a rounded hole in the ground caused by an explosion. [Gk. *krater* bowl].
CRATERIFORM, [krā-ter'-i-fawm'], *adj.* in the shape of a crater.
CRAUNCH, [krahnch], *v.t.* to crunch. [CRUNCH].
CRAVAT, [krav-at'], *n.* an old-fashioned necktie. [Fr. *cravate*].
CRAVATTED, [krav-at'-id], *adj.* wearing a cravat.
CRAVE, [krāv], *v.t.* to beg earnestly, to entreat humbly, to implore or demand, to long for intensely. [OE. *crafian* from OScand. *krefja*].
CRAVEN (1), [krāvn], *n.* a coward. [Unkn.].
CRAVEN (2), [krāvn], *adj.* cowardly. [Unkn.].
CRAVER, [krāv'-er], *n.* one who craves.
CRAVING (1), [krāv'-ing], *n.* uncontrollable desire, persistent longing, intense yearning.
CRAVING (2), [krāv'-ing], *adj.* imploring, entreating, longing.
CRAVINGLY, [krāv'-ing-li], *adv.* in a craving fashion.
CRAVINGNESS, [krāv'-ing-nes], *n.* the condition of craving.
CRAW, [kraw], *n.* the crop of fowls. [ME. *crawe*].
CRAW-CRAW, [kraw'-kraw], *n.* a West African skin disease. [Native].
CRAWFISH, see CRAYFISH.
CRAWL (1), [krawl], *n.* the act of crawling; a slow, laborious rate of progress; a racing stroke in swimming, in which the arms are alternately brought past the head; (*slang*) a leisured tour of public-houses. [CRAWL (3)].
CRAWL (2), [krawl], *n.* a pen or enclosure of stakes and hurdles for sea-fish. [Du. *kraal* from Span. *corral*].
CRAWL (3), [krawl], *v.i.* to move slowly and laboriously on hands and knees; to advance at a slow laboured pace; (*fig.*) to humble oneself abjectly; to be full of, or covered with, crawling objects. [OScand. *krafla* to paw].
CRAWLER, [krawl'-er], *n.* one who, or that which, crawls; (*fig.*) a lazy or servile creature.
CRAWLING, [krawl'-ing], *adj.* moving at a crawl; insinuating, fawning; full of crawling things.
CRAWLINGLY, [krawl'-ing-li], *adv.* in crawling fashion.
CRAYFISH, CRAWFISH, [krā'-fish, kraw'-fish], *n.* the freshwater crustacean, *Astacus fluviatis* the langouste or rock lobster, an edible saltwater crustacean of the genus *Palinurus*. [OFr. *crevisse* crab].

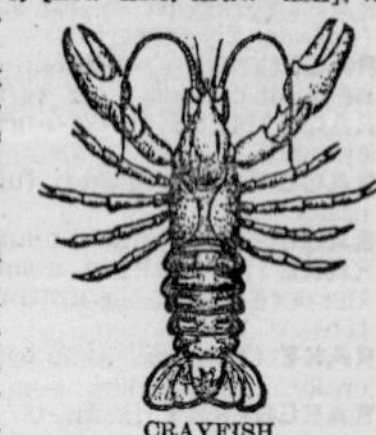
CRAYFISH

CRAYON (1), [krā'-on], *n.* a thin stick of coloured chalk, a wax-like pencil, charcoal used as a drawing implement; a drawing done by this means; the carbon point in an electric arc-lamp. [Fr. *crayon* pencil].
CRAYON (2), [krā'-on], *v.t.* to sketch or draw with crayons.
CRAYON-PAINTING, [krā'-on-pānt'-ing], *n.* the act or art of drawing with crayons.
CRAZE (1), [krāz], *n.* an inordinate passion, an exaggerated enthusiasm or fondness for; the attraction of the moment.
CRAZE (2), [krāz], *v.t.* to derange the mind, make insane, drive mad; to crack; to produce or obtain the effect of a network of small cracks on the glaze of pottery. [Swed. *krasa* to break].
CRAZED, [krāzd], *adj.* crazy; having the crackle effect.
CRAZEDNESS, [krāzd'-nes], *n.* the condition of being crazed.
CRAZILY, [krāz'-i-li], *adv.* in crazy fashion.
CRAZINESS, [krāz'-i-nes], *n.* crazy condition.
CRAZING-MILL, [krāz'-ing-mil'], *n.* a mill for grinding tin.
CRAZY, [krāz'-i], *adj.* mad, mentally deranged; wildly enthusiastic about; broken-down, decrepit; unreasonable, senseless, wild; **c. pavement, c. paving**, a pavement constructed of flat stones of varying unsymmetrical shapes. [Fr. *écrasé* crushed].
CREAK (1), [krēk], *n.* a sharp, harsh, grating sound.
CREAK (2), [krēk], *v.t. and i.* to make a creak. [Imitative].
CREAKY, [krēk'-i], *adj.* liable to creak.
CREAM (1), [krēm], *n.* a rich fatty substance forming on the surface of undisturbed milk; a sauce or dressing resembling this in thickness; a cosmetic ointment or hair fixative of the rich oily nature of this; a whitish-yellow colour; (*fig.*) the choicest part, the flower; **cold c.**, a cosmetic ointment applied to the face and neck; **c. of tartar**, potassium bitartrate used medicinally and in cookery. [Fr. *crême* from Gk. *khrisma*].
CREAM (2), [krēm], *v.t. and i.* to form into a cream; to foam, to form a frothy scum on its surface; to skim the cream from; to add cream to.
CREAM-CAKE, [krēm'-kāk], *n.* a light puffy sponge-cake containing cream.
CREAM-CHEESE, [krēm'-chēz'], *n.* a soft white cheese made from cream and curdled milk.
CREAM-COLOURED, [krēm'-kul'-erd], *adj.* of a very pale yellow.
CREAMER, [krēm'-er], *n.* an instrument which separates the cream from the milk.
CREAMERY, [krēm'-er-i], *n.* a place at which cream is skimmed from milk; a shop where cream, milk, and butter, etc., are sold.
CREAM-FACED, [krēm'-fāst], *adj.* having a pale, cowardly look.
CREAM-LAID, [krēm'-lād], *adj.* (of laid paper) of a smooth, glossy, cream colour.
CREAM-NUT, [krēm'-nut], *n.* the Brazil nut, one of the two species of *Bertholletia*.
CREAM-POT, [krēm'-pot'], *n.* a vessel for holding cream.

CREAM-WOVE, [krēm'-wōv'], *adj.* (of wove paper) of a cream colour.
CREAMY, [krēm'-i], *adj.* full of cream; like cream in colour or consistency.
CREASE (1), [krēs], *n.* the line at which the two surfaces of a fold meet; a fold or continuous mark made on the surface of soft pliable material by pressure; the continuous straight fold down the back and front of trousers; (*cricket*) two parallel straight lines marked in white at each wicket, marking the limits of the legitimate position of the batsman and bowler. [Unkn.].
CREASE (2), [krēs], *v.t. and i.* to make a crease, to wrinkle, furrow (the brow); to press trousers in order to produce a straight crease in them; to make irregular creases in cloth by careless folding or wear; to acquire creases. [Unkn.].
CREASOTE†, see CREOSOTE.
CREASY, [krēs'-i], *adj.* full of creases.
CREATABLE, [krē-āt'-abl], *adj.* able to be created.
CREATE, [krē-āt'], *v.t.* to bring into being, to cause the existence of, produce, give an independent existence to; to produce or make something new or original; to develop, to cause to arise. [L. *creatum*, *p.pt.* of *creare* to make].
CREATIN, [krē'-at-in], *n.* a crystalline substance present in blood and urine. [Gk. *kreas* flesh].
CREATION, [krē-ā'-shun], *n.* the act or process of creating, the bringing into existence of the world; that which is created, the universe; a strikingly original and fashionable garment; an original invention or production of the mind. [L. *creatio*].
CREATIONAL, [krē-ā'-shun-al], *adj.* belonging to creation.
CREATIONISM, [krē-ā'-shun-izm], *n.* the doctrine that the soul is specially created for each human being at birth, the doctrine that the universe was created by God out of nothing; the doctrine that all living species were simultaneously created by God.
CREATIVE, [krē-āt'-iv], *adj.* that creates, original; pertaining to creation.
CREATIVELY, [krē-āt'-iv-li], *adv.* in creative fashion.
CREATIVENESS, [krē-āt'-iv-nes], *n.* the quality of being creative.
CREATOR, [krē-āt'-or], *n.* a person who creates; God as the one who created the universe.
CREATRESS, [krē-āt'-res], *n.* a woman who creates.
CREATURE, [krē'-cher], *n.* anything created, a living being; a dupe, puppet, dependant; (*fig.*) the product or offspring of creation; (*coll.*) strong spirits, particularly whisky. [L. *creatura*].
CREATURELY, [krē'-cher-li], *adj.* pertaining to the creature; having the qualities of a creature.
CRECHE, crèche, [krāsh], *n.* a day nursery where babies and small children may be left while their mothers are at work. [Fr. *crèche* cradle].
CRECK, [krek], *n.* the corncrake. [CRAKE].
CREDENCE, [krēd'-ens], *n.* belief, credit; (*rel.*) a small side-table on which the bread and wine are placed before consecration in the Eucharist; **letter of c.,** a letter of introduction, a reference. [MedL. *credentia*].
CREDENDA, [krēd-en'-da], *n.* things to be believed, doctrine of faith. [L. *credenda*].
CREDENT, [krēd'-ent], *adj.* believing, ready to credit, trusting. [L. *credens*].
CREDENTIAL, [krēd-en'-shal], *n. and adj.* a document or attestation of confidence and trust in a person entitling to credence or credit.
CREDIBILITY, [kred'-ib-il'-i-ti], *n.* the state of being credible. [MedL. *credibilitas*].
CREDIBLE, [kred'-ibl], *adj.* trustworthy, capable of being believed or of being accepted as true. [L. *credibilis*].
CREDIBLENESS, [kred'-ibl-nes], *n.* credibility.
CREDIBLY, [kred'-ib-li], *adv.* in a credible manner.
CREDIT (1), [kred'-it], *n.* belief, faith; anything that adds to a person's honour or merit, a person or action of which one may be justly proud; personal honour, good name; reputation, prestige, personal power; just reward or recognition, acknowledgment of merit; (*comm.*) faith in a person's promise or ability to pay subsequently for goods received on trust; reputation for solvency, trustworthiness or honesty; (*banking*) sum standing to a person's account in a bank; (*book-keeping*) that part of an account in which are entered all sums received in payment; **letter of c.,** a banker's letter sanctioning a payment to the holder; **public c.,** confidence in the ability of a nation to fulfil its financial obligations. [L. *creditum*, *p.pt.* of *credere* to believe].
CREDIT (2), [kred'-it], *v.t.* to believe, accept as true; to allow a person credit for something, assign; (*book-keeping*) to set to the credit of.
CREDITABLE, [kred'-it-abl], *adj.* honourable, reputable; bringing credit to a person.
CREDITABLENESS, [kred'-it-abl-nes], *n.* the quality of being creditable.
CREDITABLY, [kred'-it-ab-li], *adv.* in creditable fashion.
CREDITOR, [kred'-it-or], *n.* a person to whom a debt is owed; (*book-keeping*) the credit side of an account. [OFr. *crediteur*].
CREDITRIX†, [kred'-it-riks], *n.* a female creditor. [L. *creditrix*].
CREDO, [krē'-dō], *n.* a creed, *esp.* the Apostles' creed. [L. *credo* I believe].
CREDULITY, [kred-ew'-lit-i], *n.* the quality of being credulous. [L. *credulitas*].
CREDULOUS, [kred'-yōō-lus], *adj.* readily believing or accepting as true all that one is told, without sufficient evidence or verification, gullible. [L. *credulus*].
CREDULOUSLY, [kred'-yōō-lus-li], *adv.* in credulous fashion.
CREDULOUSNESS, [kred'-yōō-lus-nes], *n.* credulity.
CREE, [krē], *v.t.* to soften (grain). [Fr. *crever* to burst].
CREED, [krēd], *n.* a form of belief or body of beliefs held by the members of a particular religious faith; a set of principles consistently followed; a summary of the main points of the Christian faith. [OE. *creda* from L. *credo* I believe].
CREEK, [krēk], *n.* a narrow opening in the coast; a small, narrow harbour; a small tributary river; a narrow, winding passage. [OScand. *kriki*].
CREEKY, [krēk'-i], *adj.* full of creeks; winding.
CREEL, [krēl], *n.* an angler's wicker fishing-basket. [OFr. *creil*].
CREEP (1), [krēp], *n.* the action of creeping; (*mining*) a forcing up of the floor of a gallery by the downward pressure of the props; (*geol.*) the gradual movement of loose rock or earth; (*mech.*) the small increase in length in a bar of rigid material when subjected to heavy pressure; (*pl.*) a nervous sensation of horror or fear.
CREEP (2), [krēp], *v.t.* to move stealthily and silently, *esp.* on hands and knees, in order to avoid attracting attention; (*bot.*) to grow with branches and stem close to the ground or to a wall; (*fig.*) to approach unobtrusively and imperceptibly; (*coll.*) to worm one's way into favour, to ingratiate oneself; to experience a sensation of living things moving over the surface of the skin; (*naut.*) to drag with a creeper; (*mech.*) to increase in length under great pressure; (*phys.*) to form crystals by evaporation along the sides of a receptacle. [OE. *creopan*].
CREEPER, [krēp'-er], *n.* a person or thing that creeps; a family of birds which run along the stems of trees; (*bot.*) a plant which grows along the ground or clings to the side of a wall by tendrils; an iron-hooked instrument resembling a grapnel, used for dragging; a spiked plate fitted to the sole of a shoe for climbing, etc.; a grain-conveyor; (*slang*), one who is unduly deferential to his superiors. [OE. *creopere*].
CREEPHOLE, [krēp'-hōl], *n.* a hole in which an animal may hide; (*fig.*) an excuse, subterfuge.
CREEPINGLY, [krēp'-ing-li], *adv.* in a creeping manner.
CREEPY, [krēp'-i], *adj.* producing a tingling sensation of horror.
CREMAILLERE, crémaillère, [krem'-i-yāer'], *n.* arrangement of the inside line of a parapet in zigzag formation to increase its length. [OFr. *cramaillère*].
CREMATE, [kri-māt'], *v.t.* to burn a corpse to ashes. [L. *cremare* to burn].
CREMATION, [kri-mā'-shun], *n.* the act of cremating. [L. *crematio*].
CREMATIONIST, [kri-mā'-shun-ist], *n.* a supporter of cremation.
CREMATOR, [kri-māt'-or], *n.* a person employed in cremating the dead; a furnace used in cremation.
CREMATORIUM, [krem'-a-taw'-ri-um], *n.* a place where bodies are cremated; a refuse-destructor.
CREMATORY (1), [kre'-mat-er-i], *n.* a crematorium.
CREMATORY (2), [kre'-mat-er-i], *adj.* relating to cremation.
CREME-DE-MENTHE, crême-de-menthe, [krām-der-mont'], *n.* a green liqueur with a strong peppermint flavour. [Fr. *crême-de-menthe*].
CREMONA, [kri-mō'-na], *n.* an old and valuable make of violin. [*Cremona*, an Italian town].

CREMOR, [krē′-mor], *n.* a kind of broth or thick juice; a foamy scum on liquids. [L. *cremor* thick juice].

CRENATE, [krē′-nāt], *adj.* (*bot.*) having the edge indented with rounded notches; (*physiol.*) (of a blood corpuscle) with toothed edges. [L. *crena* indentation].

CRENATED, [kri-nāt′-id], *adj.* crenate.

CRENATURE, [kren′-ach-er], *n.* a rounded indentation on the edge of a leaf.

CRENEL, CRENELLE, (*pl.* **crenaux, crenelles**), [kren′-el, kren′-ō], *n.* a small opening or gap at regular intervals in the parapet of a battlement; anything resembling this in form. [MedL. *crenellum*].

CRENELLATE, [kren′-el-āt], *v.t.* to provide with crenaux or battlements.

CRENELLATED, [kren′-el-āt-id] *adj.* (*arch.*) having crenelles or indented mouldings resembling these.

CRENELLATED

CRENULATE, [kren′-yōō-lāt], *adj.* (*bot.*) having the edges indented with small round notches.

CRENULATED, [kren′-yōō-lāt-id], *adj.* crenulate.

CREOLE (**1**), [krē′-ōl], *n.* a native of the West Indies, parts of South America, etc., of European ancestry; a person of mixed European and native descent born in these regions. [Span. *criollo*].

CREOLE (**2**), [krē′-ōl], *adj.* pertaining to a creole.

CREOPHAGOUS, [krē-of′-ag-us], *adj.* eating flesh. [Gk. *kreas* flesh and *phagos* eating].

CREOSOL, [krē′-os-ol], *n.* a colourless aromatic liquid found in creosote.

CREOSOTE, CREASOTE†, **KREASOTE**†, [krē′-os-ōt], *n.* a thick, pungent, dark-brown antiseptic liquid used medicinally and as a protective coating for wood. [Gk. *kreas* flesh and *sozo* I save].

CREOSOTE-PLANT, [krē′-os-ōt-plahnt′], *n.* a Mexican plant that binds drifting sand together, and has a similar smell to wood creosote, *Larrea mexicana*.

CREPE, crêpe, [krāp], *adj.* crape; **c. paper**, crinkled or pleated paper; **c. rubber**, rubber rolled into a corrugated surface. [Fr. *crêpe* from L. *crispus* curled].

CREPITANT, [krep′-it-ant], *adj.* (*med.*) crackling. [L. *crepitans*].

CREPITATE, [krep′-it-āt], *v.i.* to crackle, to rattle; (*entom.*) (of certain beetles) to emit a strong-smelling liquid with a sharp explosive sound when attacked. [L. *crepitare* to crackle].

CREPITATION, [krep′-it-ā′-shun], *n.* the act of crepitating; a crackling or rattling sound.

CREPON, [krep′-on], *n.* a crape-like material of worsted or silk. [Fr. *crépon*].

CREPT, [krept], *pret. and p.pt.* of CREEP.

CREPUSCULAR, [krep-us′-kyōō-ler], *adj.* pertaining to, or resembling, twilight; (*fig.*) dim, obscure; (*zool.*) seen only at twilight. [*Next*].

CREPUSCULE, [krep′-us-kewl], *n.* twilight. [L. *crepusculum*].

CREPUSCULOUS, [krep-us′-kyōō-lus], *adj.* crepuscular.

CRESCENDO (**1**), [krish-en′-dō], *n.* (*mus.*) a gradual increase in loudness, a direction signifying this, a passage of this character; (*fig.*) a progressive heightening towards a climax. [It. *crescendo*, *pres.pt.* of *crescere* to grow].

CRESCENDO (**2**), [krish-en′-dō], *adj. and adv.* (*mus.*) with, or characterized by, a crescendo.

CRESCENT (**1**), [krez′-ent], *n.* the moon as it waxes or wanes in the first or last quarter, when it appears as a convexo-concave area of light terminating in points; any figure resembling this in shape; (*her.*) a half-moon; the national emblem of Turkey; (*fig.*) the Turkish power; the Mohammedan religion; a row of buildings built in the form of an arc; a bone disease in a horse's foot. [CRESCENT (2)].

CRESCENT (**2**), [krez′-ent], *adj.* growing, increasing, waxing, developing; like the crescent of the moon; in the shape of a crescent. [L. *crescens*, *pres.pt.* of *crescere* to grow].

CRESCENTED, [krez′-ent-id], *adj.* adorned with, or shaped like, a crescent.

CRESCIVE, [kres′-iv], *adj.* increasing, waxing.

CRESS, [kres], *n.* any of several edible species of plants of the order *Cruciferae*, having a pungent taste. [OE *cærse*, *cresse*].

CRESSELLE, [kres′-el], *n.* a wooden rattle used in certain Roman Catholic countries to announce divine worship. [Fr. *crécelle*].

CRESSET, [kres′-it], *n.* an iron vessel containing fuel, suspended and lit as a torch, beacon or lamp. [Fr. *craisset*].

CREST (**1**), [krest], *n.* tuft of hair or feathers on the top of the head of certain animals, birds, fishes or reptiles; a distinguishing plume of feathers fastened to the top of a helmet as a badge; (*her.*) a distinctive personal device placed over the shield and helmet on a coat of arms; such a device stamped on personal articles as a badge of ownership, etc.; (*poet.*) a helmet; the top or highest point of anything; the line of the neck of a dog or horse; (*anat.*) a ridge along the surface of a bone; (*bot.*) an outgrowth on the surface of an organ; (*arch.*) the crown of a roof, the topmost layer of a wall. [L. *cresta*].

CREST (**2**), [krest], *v.t. and i.* to provide or ornament with a crest; to reach the topmost point of; to crown as a crest; to form into a crest.

CRESTFALLEN, [krest′-fawl-en], *adj.* having a drooping crest; (*fig.*) dejected, disheartened, chastened, downcast.

CRESTLESS, [krest′-les], *adj.* without crest; (*fig.*) of humble birth.

CRETACEOUS, [krit-ā′-shus], *adj.* chalky, composed of, or resembling, chalk; (*geol.*) belonging to the period of the highest system of the Mesozoic group of strata, between the Jurassic and Eocene. [L. *cretaceus* chalk-like].

CRETIC, [krēt′-ik], *n.* (*class. pros.*) a metrical foot of two long syllables separated by one short. [L. *creticus* (*pes*) a Cretan foot].

CRETIN, [kret′-in], *n.* a person suffering from cretinism. [Swiss Fr. from L. *christianus* a Christian].

CRETINISM, [kret′-in-izm], *n.* a disease producing a form of idiocy, with physical deformity or stunted growth, due to defective action or deficiency of the thyroid gland.

CRETONNE, [kret′-on], *n.* a strong, unglazed cotton cloth decorated with a printed, coloured pattern. [*Creton*, a village in Normandy].

CRETOSE†, [krit′-ōs], *adj.* chalky, cretaceous. [L. *cretosus*].

CREUX, [krur], *n.* anything hollowed out. [Fr. *creux*].

CREVASSE, [krev-as′], *n.* a breach, a deep crack in a glacier. [Fr. *crevasse*].

CREVET, [krev′-it], *n.* a melting-pot used by goldsmiths. [Fr. *crevet*].

CREVICE, [krev′-is], *n.* a crack, a cleft, a fissure. [OFr. *crevace*].

CREW, [krōō], *n.* the group of sailors belonging to, and employed in sailing a ship (often excluding the officers); a gang of workmen; (*coll.*) a body of people with similar interests. [OFr. *creue* increase].

CREWEL, [krōō′-el], *n.* a thin worsted yarn suitable for tapestry or embroidery. [Unkn.].

CRIB (**1**), [krib], *n.* a child's cot; a small room; a hut, a small dwelling place; a rack or manger in which fodder is contained; a wicker-work fishing trap; (*archaic*), an ox-stall; (*mining*) a wooden framework for lining and strengthening the sides of a shaft; (*cards*) cards discarded to the dealer at cribbage; (*coll.*) a literary theft, a plagiarism; a translation of a foreign or classical work; (*slang*) a dwelling or other building (to be burgled). [OE. *cribb*].

CRIB (**2**), (**cribbing, cribbed**), [krib], *v.t. and i.* to provide with a crib, to copy from the works of another author, and misrepresent as one's own work; to translate by copying from a crib; to cheat or defraud in a test or examination; to confine in a small space so as to cramp.

CRIBBAGE, [krib′-ij], *n.* a card game for two or more persons in which five or six cards are dealt to each person. [CRIB (1)].

CRIBBING, [krib′-ing], *n.* the act of one who cribs; the lining of a mine-shaft.

CRIB-BITING, [krib′-bīt′-ing], *n.* a bad habit amongst horses of biting the manger or other object and noisily breathing in.

CRIBBLE, [kribl], *n.* a sieve. [L. *cribellum*, *dim.* of *cribrum* a sieve].

CRIBRATION†, [krib-rā′-shun], *n.* the process of sifting or riddling.

CRIBRIFORM, [krib′-ri-fawm], *adj.* like a sieve [L. *cribrum* sieve and FORM].

CRIBROSE, [krib′-rōs], *adj.* cribriform.

CRICHTONITE, [krī′-ton-īt], *n.* (*min.*) a black titaniferous iron crystallizing in rhomboidal form. [Dr. *Crichton*, its discoverer].
CRICK (1), [krik], *n.* painful spasmodic stiffness chiefly affecting the muscles of the neck or back. [CREEK].
CRICK (2), [krik], *v.t.* to cause a crick in.
CRICKET (1), [krik′-it], *n.* a small brown insect of the genus *Gryllus*, characterized by the chirruping noise produced by the friction of its wing-covers. [OFr. *criquet*].

CRICKET

CRICKET (2), [krik′-it], *n.* an outdoor summer game played with bats, ball, and wickets, between two teams of eleven players; **not c.**, (*coll.*) not sporting, unfair. [~OFr. *criquet* a bat].
CRICKETER, [krik′-it-er], *n.* one who plays cricket.
CRICOID, [krik′-oid], *adj.* ring-shaped; (*anat.*) **c. cartilage**, the cartilage of the larynx. [Gk. *krikoeides* ring-shaped].
CRIER, [krī′-er], *n.* one who cries; an usher in a court of justice; a person whose duty it is to proclaim public announcements. [CRY].
CRIM-CON, [krim′-kon], *n.* abbreviation of CRIMINAL CONVERSATION.
CRIME, [krīm], *n.* an offence against public laws and social welfare, and punishable in a court of justice; (*fig.*) sin, wrongdoing, an extremely ill-advised or unjust action. [Fr. from L. *crimen* a charge].
CRIMEFUL, [krīm′-fōōl], *adj.* criminal, wicked.
CRIMELESS, [krīm′-les], *adj.* free from crime, innocent, guiltless.
CRIMINAL (1), [krim′-in-al], *n.* a person guilty of a crime; (*pop.*) a perpetual or grave offender against the law.
CRIMINAL (2), [krim′-in-al], *adj.* amounting to a crime; guilty of a crime; pertaining to crime and its punishment; **c. conversation**, unlawful sexual intercourse. [L. *criminalis*].
CRIMINALITY, [krim′-in-al′-i-ti], *n.* the state or quality of being criminal, crime. [L. *criminalitas*].
CRIMINALLY, [krim′-in-a-li], *adv.* in a criminal fashion.
CRIMINALNESS†, [krim′-in-al-nes], *n.* criminality.
CRIMINATE, [krim′-in-āt], *v.t.* to accuse of a crime; to find fault with, condemn. [L. *criminari* to charge].
CRIMINATION, [krim′-in-ā′-shun], *n.* the act of criminating, the state of being criminated. [L. *criminatio*].
CRIMINATORY, [krim′-in-āt′-er-i], *adj.* criminating. [L. *criminator* accuser].
CRIMINOLOGY, [krim′-in-ol′-o-ji], *n.* the study of crime. [L. *crimen* crime and Gk. *logos* speech].
CRIMINOUS, [krim′-in-us], *adj.* wicked, guilty of a grave crime. [L. *criminosus*].
CRIMP (1), [krimp], *n.* one who entraps or decoys persons to complete the crew of a short-handed ship. [Unkn.].
CRIMP (2), [krimp], *n.* a crease, wrinkle or fold. [CRIMP (4)].
CRIMP (3), [krimp], *adj.* crisp, friable, brittle. [CRIMP (4)].
CRIMP (4), [krimp], *v.t.* to wrinkle, to make crimps in; to curl (of hair); to gash the flesh of (a fish) when caught so as to make it more firm and hard; to cut. [OE. *crimpan* to curl].
CRIMP (5), [krimp], *v.t.* to decoy or engage illegally as seamen to make up a ship's crew. [CRIMP (1)].
CRIMPAGE, [krimp′-ij], *n.* the act of crimping.
CRIMPING-IRON, [krimp′-ing-īern′], *n.* an apparatus for curling hair, or for crimping material.
CRIMPING-MACHINE, [krimp′-ing-mash-ēn′], *n.* a machine used for crimping frills.
CRIMPLE, [krimpl], *v.t.* and *i.* to curl, wrinkle, frill. [ME. *crimplen*].
CRIMPY, [krimp-i], *adj.* full of, or characterized by, short fuzzy curls (of hair), wavy.
CRIMSON (1), [krim′-zon], *n.* a deep red colour with a purplish tinge.
CRIMSON (2), [krim′-zon], *adj.* of a deep, purplish-red colour; (*fig.*) bloody. [ME. *crimosine* from Arab. *qirmisi* an insect of this colour].
CRIMSON (3), [krim′-zon], *v.t.* and *i.* to turn crimson; (*fig.*) to blush.
CRIMSON-WARM, [krim′-zon-wahm′], *adj.* warm to redness.
CRINAL, [krīnl], *adj.* pertaining to hair. [L. *crinalis*].
CRINATED, [krin-āt′-id], *adj.* hairy. [CRINITE].
CRINCUM†, [krin′-kum], *n.* a cramp, a turn, a whim; (*slang*) venereal disease. [Unkn.].
CRINGE (1), [krinj], *n.* a fawning civility, the act of cringing.
CRINGE (2), [krinj], *v.i.* to shrink back from, to cower; to bow or stoop in a servile or frightened manner, to fawn in terror upon. [OE. *cringan*, *crincgan* to fall].
CRINGELING, [krinj′-ling], *n.* one who cringes abjectly.
CRINGING, [krinj′-ing], *adj.* shrinking back in cowardice or servility, fawning.
CRINGINGLY, [krinj′-ing-li], *adv.* in a cringing fashion.
CRINGLE, [kring′-gel], *n.* (*naut.*) a hole, lined with a metal ring or thimble, in the bolt-rope of a sail. [LGerm. *kringel* ring].
CRINICULTURAL, [krin′-i-kul′-cher-al], *adj.* pertaining to the growth of hair. [L. *crinis* hair and CULTURAL].
CRINIGEROUS, [krin-ij′-er-us], *adj.* hairy, furnished or covered with hair. [L. *criniger* bearing hair].
CRINITE, [krin′-īt], *adj.* hairy; (*bot.* and *zool.*) resembling tufts of hair. [L. *crinitus* hairy].
CRINKLE (1), [kringkl], *n.* a wrinkle, a winding or turn, a wave.
CRINKLE (2), [kringkl], *v.t.* and *i.* to twist or curl into crinkles; to cringe, bend; to rumple, crease, to crush into innumerable irregular folds (of paper, etc.). [OE. *crincan*].
CRINKLY, [krink′-li], *adj.* wavy, curly; wrinkled, rumpled.
CRINOID (1), [krin′-oid], *n.* (*zool.*) one of the encrinites or sea-lilies, a class of *Echinodermata* shaped like a lily. [Gk. *krinoeides* lily-like].
CRINOID (2), [krin′-oid], *adj.* lily-shaped, applied to the crinoids.
CRINOIDAL, [krin-oid′-al], *adj.* relating to the crinoids.
CRINOIDEA, [krin-oid′-i-a], *n.*(*pl.*) the sea-lilies, a class of echinoderms, growing on long jointed stalks at the bottom of the sea. [Gk. *krinoeides* lily-like].
CRINOIDEANS, [krin-oid′-i-anz], *n.*(*pl.*) the crinoidea.
CRINOLINE, [krin′-ol-in], *n.* a stout fabric made from horse-hair and coarse thread; a petticoat of this material stiffened with narrow steel hoops, and worn to distend or support the skirt of the dress; a torpedo-net fitted round the sides of a warship. [L. *crinis* hair and *linum* thread].
CRINOLINED, [krin′-ol-ind], *adj.* wearing a crinoline.
CRINOSE, [krin′-ōs], *adj.* hairy. [L. *crinis* hair].
CRIO-SPHINX, [krī′-ō-sfingks], *n.* a ram-headed sphinx. [Gk. *krios* a ram and SPHINX].

CRIO-SPHINX

CRIPPLE (1), [kripl], *n.* a lame person, one who has a maimed limb. [OE. *crypel*].
CRIPPLE (2), [kripl], *adj.* lame, having a maimed limb; (*fig.*) ruined, impaired.
CRIPPLE (3), [kripl], *v.t.* to lame, to disable, to maim in a limb; (*fig.*) to lessen, to handicap severely, to injure, weaken.
CRIPPLENESS, [kripl′-nes], *n.* lameness.
CRIPPLINGS, [krip′-lingz], *n.*(*pl.*) timbers placed as supports against the side of a building.
CRISIS, (*pl.* **crises**), [krī′-sis, krī′-sēz], *n.* the critical moment in any business or affair; (*med.*) the turning point; a period at which a dangerous climax is reached. [Gk. *krisis* decision].
CRISP (1), [krisp], *n.* a thin wafer of potato fried hard.
CRISP (2), [krisp], *adj.* (of hair) curly, frizzy, full of short curls; brittle, dry and firm; bracing, cold and dry; lively, clear-cut, brisk, sharp. [OE. *crisp* from L. *crispus* curled].
CRISP (3), [krisp], *v.t.* and *i.* to curl in short, firm curls; to make crisp; to become crisp.
CRISPATE, [krisp′-āt], *adj.* crisp; (*bot.*) curled over at the edge. [L. *crispatus*].
CRISPATED, [krisp′-āt-id], *adj.* crispate.
CRISPATION, [krisp-ā′-shun], *n.* the act of crisping or curling; the state of being crisped.
CRISPATURE, [krisp′-a-chōōer], *n.* the condition of being curled.
CRISPED, [krispt], *adj.* curled.

CRISPER, [krisp'-er], *n.* an apparatus for crisping cloth; that which crisps.
CRISPIN, [krisp'-in], *n.* a shoemaker. [St. *Crispin*, the patron saint of shoemakers].
CRISPING-IRON, [krisp'-ing-īern'], *n.* an iron for crisping.
CRISPING-PIN, [krisp'-ing-pin'], *n.* a simple type of crisping-iron.
CRISPISULCANT†, [krisp'-i-sulk'-ant], *adj.* waved or forked, as lightning. [L. *crispisulcans*].
CRISPLY, [krisp'-li], *adv.* in a crisp fashion.
CRISPNESS, [krisp'-nes], *n.* the condition of being crisp.
CRISPY, [krisp'-i], *adj.* frizzy, full of short curls (of hair); brittle, dry and hard.
CRISS-CROSS (1), [kris'-kros'], *n.* †a child's alphabet at the beginning of which was a cross; the force resulting from the union of two forces moving at an angle to each other; a child's game resembling noughts and crosses; a network of intersecting lines. [CHRIST CROSS].
CRISS-CROSS (2), [kris'-kros'], *adj.* arranged in, or marked with, intersecting lines.
CRISS-CROSS (3), [kris'-kros'], *adv.* in opposite directions, crosswise, at cross-purposes.
CRISS-CROSS (4), [kris'-kros'], *v.t.* to mark with intersecting lines; *v.i.* to form a network of crossing lines.
CRISS-CROSS-ROW, [kris'-kros'-rō'], *n.* the alphabet.
CRISTATE, [kris'-tāt], *adj* crested, tufted. [L. *cristatus* having a crest].
CRISTATED, [kris'-tāt-id], *adj.* cristate.
CRITERION, (*pl.* **criteria**), [krī-tēer'-i-on, krī-tēer'-i-a], *n.* a standard of quality by which a thing is judged, a guide. [Gk. *kriterion*].
CRITH, [krith], *n.* a unit of weight in measuring gases, the weight of a litre of hydrogen at a standard temperature and pressure. [Gk. *krithe* a barley-corn].
CRITHOMANCY, [krith'-o-man'-si], *n.* divination by scattering barley over sacrificed animals. [Gk. *krithe* barley-corn and *manteia* divination].
CRITIC, [krit'-ik], *n.* a person who criticizes, *esp.* literary or artistic works; a person employed in writing critical reviews of musical or dramatic performances, works of art, books, etc.; one skilled in textual criticism; (*pop.*) a fault-finder, a severe judge. [Gk. *kritikos* able to pass judgment].
CRITICAL, [krit'-ikl], *adj.* pertaining to a moment or point at which a great change may take place in the course of events; pertaining to a crisis; fateful, dangerous, involving risk; discriminating, expressing a reasoned judgment; (of an edition) containing textual criticism; fault-finding, judging harshly; (*phys., math.*) indicating or constituting a limit beyond which a change occurs; (*zool., bot.*) differing but slightly.
CRITICALLY, [krit'-ik-a-li], *adv.* in a critical fashion or condition.
CRITICALNESS, [krit'-ik-al-nes], *n.* the condition of being critical.
CRITICISM, [krit'-is-izm], *n.* the guiding principles of a critic; the art or act of estimating the quality of literary or artistic work by an analysis of its merits and defects; an analysis or review of anything; an expression of adverse opinion about; (*philos.*) the philosophy of Kant; **textual c.**, scientific examination or analysis of manuscripts in order to establish the transmission of the original text.
CRITICIZABLE, [krit'-is-īz'-abl], *adj.* capable of being criticized.
CRITICIZE, [krit'-is-īz], *v.t.* to give a critical estimate of, point out the merits and defects of; to discuss in a critical manner; to censure, find fault with, to point out defects in.
CRITICIZER, [krit'-is-īz-er], *n.* one who criticizes.
CRITICKIN, [krit'-ik-in], *n.* a petty critic.
CRITIQUE, [krit-ēk'], *n.* a critical review of a literary, artistic or musical work; the critical art. [Fr. *critique*].
CRIZZEL†, see CRIZZLE.
CRIZZELING†, see CRIZZLING.
CRIZZLE (1), **CRIZZEL**†, [krizl], *n.* a roughness on the surface of glass; a rough, scorched, sunburnt condition of the skin.
CRIZZLE (2), **CRIZZEL**†, [krizl], *v.i.* to become rough and harsh on the surface. [Unkn.].
CRIZZLING, **CRIZZELING**†, [kriz'-ling], *n.* a crizzle.
CROAK (1), [krōk], *n.* the low, harsh, dissonant cry of a frog or raven.
CROAK (2), [krōk], *v.t.* (*slang*) to kill; *v.i.* to utter a croak; (*fig.*) to grumble, to talk or think as a pessimist. [OE. *cracettan* to croak].
CROAKER, [krōk'-er], *n.* a fish or animal that croaks, a fish of the genus *Micropogon*; a person who croaks; a person with a deep voice or cough.
CROAKING, [krōk'-ing], *adj.* that croaks; grumbling; pessimistic; foreboding evil; **c. lizard**, a species of gecko, *Cadactylus laevis*, common in Jamaica, so called from its croak.
CROAKY, [krōk'-i], *adj.* croaking.
CROATIAN, [krō-āshn'], *adj.* of, or pertaining to, the Croats or their language. [Serbian *Hrvat* a Croat].
CROATS, [krō'-atz], *n.(pl.)* the inhabitants of Croatia; light irregular cavalry of the former Austro-Hungarian Empire in which many Croats served.
CROCEATE, [krō'-si-āt], *adj.* of the colour of saffron, yellow. [L. *croceus* saffron-coloured].
CROCEOUS†, [krō'-shi-us], *adj.* croceate; consisting of saffron. [*Prec.*].
CROCHET (1), [krō'-shā], *n.* a form of knitting-work done with a small hook. [Fr. *crochet* small hook].
CROCHET (2), [krō'-shā], *v.t. and i.* to work in crochet, to work with a crochet-needle.
CROCIDOLITE, [kros-id'-ol-īt], *n.* a fibrous silicate of iron and sodium occurring in Griqualand West. [Gk. *krokis* cloth and *lithos* stone].
CROCK (1), [krok], *n.* an earthenware or iron vessel; a broken piece of earthenware. [OE. *croc* earthenware pot].
CROCK (2), [krok], *n.* a smut of dirt or soot. [Unkn.].
CROCK (3), [krok], *n.* an old ewe; an old broken-down horse; (*fig.*) a cripple or injured person; a useless, inefficient person. [Unkn.].
CROCK (4), [krok], *v.t. and i.* to become a crock, to breakdown in health; (*coll.*) to be injured or lamed, to suffer a breakdown in health; to injure, to lame. [CROCK (3)].
CROCK (5), [krok], *v.t.* to blacken with soot. [CROCK (2)].
CROCKERY, [krok'-er-i], *n.* domestic earthenware or china vessels; (*coll.*) china and porcelain ornaments or vessels.
CROCKET, [krok'-it], *n.* (*arch.*) an ornamentation of curved and bent foliage along the edge of a gable or spire. [AFr. *croquet*].
CROCODILE, [krok'-ō-dīl], *n.* (*zool.*) a large long-tailed aquatic reptile, partly covered with hard, bony scales and having powerful jaws which can open to a great width; (*coll.*) a group of schoolgirls walking out in double file; (*rhet.*) a captious sophism; (*fig.*) a person shedding false tears; **c. tears**, sham grief, false sorrow. [Gk. *krokodilos* lizard].

CROCKET

CROCODILE-BIRD, [krok'-od-īl-burd'], *n.* a small bird of the plover family which eats the insect parasites of the crocodile.
CROCODILIAN, [krok'-od-il'-i-an], *adj.* of, or like, the crocodile.
CROCODILITY, [krok'-od-il'-i-ti], *n.* (*log.*) captious sophistry.
CROCOITE, [krōk'-ō-īt], *n.* a red translucent chromate of lead. [Gk. *krokoeis* saffron-coloured].
CROCUS, [krō'-kus], *n.* (*bot.*) a genus of plants of the family *Iridaceae*, bearing brightly-coloured flowers. [Gk. *krokos* saffron].
CROFT, [kroft], *n.* a small piece of land for pasture or tillage, usually adjoining a house; a small farm-holding. [OE. *croft*].
CROFTER, [kroft'-er], *n.* one who rents and farms a croft, *esp.* in the Scottish Highlands.
CROID, [kroid], *n.* (*prot.*) a high-quality glue, used in aeroplane manufacture, etc. [*Croydon* in Surrey where made].
CROISE, **croisé**, [kroiz'-ā], *n.* one of the crusaders, a soldier who took part in a crusade. [Fr. *croisés* crusaders].
CROIX DE FEU, [krwah'-d-fu(r)'], *n.* a French pro-Fascist party.
CROMA, [krō'-ma], *n.* (*mus.*) a quaver. [It. *croma* quaver].
CRO-MAGNON, [krō'-man'-yong], *n.* (*anthrop.*) a prehistoric European race dwelling in the late palaeolithic age. [*Cro-Magnon*, a series of caves in France].

CROMFORDITE, [krom'-fawd-īt], *n.* phosgenite, a compound of lead carbonate and chloride. [*Cromford*, in Derbyshire, where found].

CROMLECH, [krom'-lek], *n.* a prehistoric structure consisting of a large flat stone laid across two or more upright stones. [Wel. *crom* bent and *llech* flagstone].

CROMORNA, [krom-awn'-a], *n.* a reed stop on an organ. [Germ. *krummhorn* crooked horn].

CRONE, [krōn], *n.* a hideously decrepit old hag; an old ewe. [ME. *krone* from ODu. *karonie* an old ewe].

CRONET, [kron'-it], *n.* the head of a spear used for tilting; the tuft of hair over the top of a horse's hoof. [CORONET].

CRONY, [krō'-ni], *n.* an intimate companion, bosom friend. [Unkn.].

CROODLE, [kroōdl], *v.i.* to nestle close to, to snuggle; to collapse. [Unkn.].

CROOK (1), [kro͝ok], *n.* a stick bent at the top in the form of a hook; a shepherd's staff bent in this way; a crosier; anything bent or curved, a hook; (*slang*) a dishonest person, a swindler, sharper; (*pl.*) (*mus.*) curved metal tubes attached to brass wind instruments to change the pitch of the instrument to suit the key of the music; **by hook or by c.**, by fair means or foul. [OScand. *krókr*].

CROOK (2), [kro͝ok], *v.t. and i.* to bend or curve into a crook; to bend, to be turned from a direct line.

CROOKBACK, [kro͝ok'-bak'], *n.* one who has a crooked back.

CROOKBACKED, [kro͝ok'-bakt'], *adj.* hunch-backed.

CROOKED, [kro͝ok'-id], *adj.* bent, curved, twisted, winding; deformed; dishonest.

CROOKEDLY, [kro͝ok'-id-li], *adv.* in crooked fashion.

CROOKEDNESS, [kro͝ok-'id-nes], *n.* the condition of being crooked.

CROOKES, [kro͝oks], *adj.* denoting various inventions or discoveries made by Sir William *Crookes*.

CROOKESITE, [kro͝ok'-sīt], *n.* a selenide of copper and thallium containing about one-twentieth of silver. [Sir William *Crookes*, the scientist].

CROOM, [kroōm], *n.* a tool with crooked prongs; a pitchfork. [Gael. *crom* twisted].

CROON, [kroōn], *v.t. and i.* to sing in the soft, plaintive manner cultivated by vocalists in a dance band; to hum in a gentle undertone. [Du. *kreunen* to groan].

CROONER, [kroōn'-er], *n.* a person who croons, one engaged by a dance band to croon vocal numbers.

CROONING, [kroōn'-ing], *n.* a style of subdued singing into a microphone.

CROP (1), [krop], *n.* the stock or handle of a whip; a short hunting-whip with a leather loop at the end; a pouch-like swelling in the gullet of birds, the craw; produce yielded by cultivation of the earth; (*pl.*) grain, grass, fruit, vegetables, etc., growing in a particular district at certain seasons; (*fig.*) a group or mass of objects accumulated together; a whole tanned hide; (*mining*) an outcrop; a hair-cut; **neck and c.**, completely and bodily. [OE. *cropp*].

CROP (2), (**cropping, cropped**), [krop], *v.t. and i.* to cut, lop or break off the tops of plants; to cut short (the hair), to cut off; (*fig.*) to cut short, to put a sudden end to; to gather, mow, reap; to produce crops; **to c. out, up**, (*mining and geol.*) to be exposed (of a stratum); **to c. up**, (*fig.*) to arise in an unforeseen manner.

CROP-EAR, [krop'-ēer], *n.* a horse with ears cut short.

CROP-EARED, [krop'-ēerd], *adj.* with the ears cropped.

CROPFUL, [krop'-fo͝ol], *adj.* having a full crop; satiated.

CROPPER (1), [krop'-er], *n.* a person or thing that crops; a cloth-facing machine; a plant producing a crop; a pouter pigeon; (*coll.*) a heavy fall; **to come a c.**, to have a crashing fall; to meet with sudden disaster.

CROPPER (2), [krop'-er], *n.* a treadle printing machine. [H. S. *Cropper*, the inventor].

CROPPING, [krop'-ing], *n.* the act of cutting off; the raising of crops.

CROPPY, [krop'-i], *n.* a person with hair cut close to the head, as the Roundheads, and Irish rebels in 1798.

CROP-SICK, [krop'-sik], *adj.* having the stomach upset through over-indulgence.

CROQUET (1), [krō'-ki], *n.* a game played on a lawn, with balls struck by long-handled wooden mallets through iron hoops in succession. [ONFr. *croquet*, *dim.* of *croc* crook].

CROQUET (2), (**croqueted, croqueted**), [krō'-ki], *v.t. and i.* after having struck an opponent's ball with one's own and then having placed the two together, to strike one's own ball and so drive both away.

CROQUETTE, [krok-et'], *n.* a crisply-fried forcemeat ball of minced meat, potato or rice, and butter, seasoned; a rissole. [Fr. *croquer* to crunch].

CRORE, [kraw'-er], *n.* (generally) ten million rupees. [Hind. *krōr*].

CROSIER, CROZIER, [krō'-si-er], *n.* a bishop's staff; (*bot.*) the top of a young fern when curled. [OFr. *crossier* crossbearer, confused in meaning with OFr. *croce* crook].

CROSIER

CROSLET, see CROSSLET.

CROSS (1), [kros], *n.* a bar or line intersected with a transverse bar at right angles; the intersection of two bars; a kind of (wooden) instrument of this shape (+ † X) to which malefactors were nailed; a structure of this shape upon which Christ suffered; the symbol of Christianity; (*fig.*) Christ's sufferings or passion; an affliction; anything (a mark, ornament, monument, etc.) fashioned with the intersection of two lines or bars; that which crosses, thwarts or perplexes; a mixing of breeds in the production of plants or animals; a plant or animal so produced; (*her., art, etc.*) a figure consisting of two intersecting bars, represented by engraving or enamelling upon a medal or other insignia; **C. of Calvary**, a cross set up on three steps ; **fiery c.**, a wooden cross with its ends alight and extinguished in the blood of a goat, used as a call to arms by Scottish Highlanders; **George C.**, a cross awarded as a distinction for deeds of valour by British civilians; **Iron C.**, a medal of iron awarded for distinguished service in the German army; **C. of Jerusalem**, a cross with a small crossbar at the end of each arm; **Latin c.**, a vertical cross with the lower member longer than the three other members; **Maltese c.**, a cross in which the four members gradually widen from the point of intersection so as to form a nearly complete square; **St. Andrew's c.**, a cross shaped like X; **St. Anthony's c.**, shaped like T (also called a **Tau c.**); **Southern C.**, a constellation in the form of a cross, visible in the southern hemisphere; **Victoria C.**, a bronze cross awarded as the highest distinction in the British Services for personal valour in action; **to take up one's c.**, to suffer one's afflictions; **to cut on the c.**, to cut obliquely across the texture, grain, etc. [L. *crux* borrowed in OIr. as *cros* and thence introduced by Vikings into OE. as *cross*].

CROSS (2), [kros], *adj. and adv.* lying or falling athwart, transverse, moving at an angle to the main direction, or from side to side ; opposite ; perverse, peevish, contrary; crossbred.

CROSS (3), [kros], *v.t. and i.* to make the sign of a cross on, to draw a line or place a thing across or athwart another; to erase by lines passing from side to side; to move athwart or from side to side, to move over a line, river, sea, etc.; to pass; to thwart, to obstruct; to interbreed; **to c. a cheque**, to draw two parallel lines on a cheque and write *& Co.* between them; **to c. one's mind**, (*impers.*) to occur or appear suddenly to one's mind; **to c. a person's hand with silver**, to give a silver coin to a person; **to c. the suit**, (*cards*) to change trumps from a red suit to a black suit at euchre.

CROSSABLE, [kros'-abl], *adj.* which can be crossed.

CROSS-ACTION, [kros'-ak-shun], *n.* (*leg.*) a legal case in which one person brings an action against a second person and the second person brings an action arising out of the same transaction against the first.

CROSS-AISLE†, [kros'-īl], *n.* (*arch.*) a transept.

CROSS-ARMED, [kros'-ahmd], *adj.* with the arms crossed; (*bot.*) brachiate.

CROSS-ARROW†, [kros'-a'-rō], *n.* an arrow for a crossbow.

CROSSBANDED, [kros'-band'-id], *adj.* (*carp., arch.*) covered with a veneer of wood the grain of which runs in the direction of the shorter dimension.

CROSSBAR (1), [kros'-bah(r)], *n.* a transverse bar, a bar fixed between other bars; **c. shot**, a ball with an iron bar through it.

CROSSBAR (2), (**crossbarring, crossbarred**), [kros-bah(r)'], *v.t.* to put bars across.

CROSSBEAM, [kros'-bēm], *n.* a transverse beam; a beam running from side to side of a structure.

CROSSBEARER, [kros'-bāer'-er], *n.* one who bears

a cross in a procession; the priest who bears an archbishop's cross.

CROSS-BEARINGS, [kros'-bāer'-ingz], *n.(pl.)* the bearings of two known points or more from a fixed point, the position of the fixed point being determined from the angles so formed.

CROSS-BELT, [kros'-belt'], *n.* a belt worn over one shoulder and under the opposite arm.

CROSS-BENCH, [kros'-bensh'], *n.* a bench placed at right angles to the other benches in the House of Lords on which independent members sit.

CROSSBILL (1), [kros'-bil], *n.* a bird, the curved tips of whose beak cross when the bill is closed, *Loxia curvirostra*.

CROSS-BILL (2), [kros'-bil], *n.* (*leg.*) a bill filed by a defendant against the plaintiff, to pray relief against the plaintiff.

CROSSBILL

CROSS-BIRTH, [kros'-burth'], *n.* (*surg.*) a labour in which the child is placed transversely in the uterus.

CROSSBITE† **(1)**, [kros'-bit], *n.* a trick, swindle.

CROSSBITE† **(2)**, [kros'-bit], *v.t.* to cheat, to deceive.

CROSS-BLOW, [kros'-blō], *n.* a counter-blow, an indirect blow.

CROSSBONES, [kros'-bōnz], *n.(pl.)* a symbol of two human thigh-bones placed obliquely across each other, generally below a skull, as an emblem of piracy and death.

CROSSBOW, [kros'-bō], *n.* a medieval weapon for shooting arrows, consisting of a grooved stock for the arrow, a bow fixed across the end of the stock, and a catch for releasing the bow-string.

CROSSBOWER†, [kros'-bō'-er], *n.* one who uses a crossbow.

CROSSBOWMAN†, [kros'-bō'-man], *n.* a soldier who uses a crossbow.

CROSSBRED, [kros'-bred'], *adj. and n.* hybrid, mongrel.

CROSSBREED (1), [kros'-brēd], *n.* a mongrel breed.

CROSSBREED (2), (**crossbred**), [kros'-brēd], *v.t. and i.* to breed from plants or animals of different species or kinds.

CROSS-BUN, [kros'-bun], *n.* a bun marked with a cross; **hot c.**, such a bun eaten hot on Good Friday.

CROSS-BUTTOCK, [kros'-but'-ok], *n.* (*wrestling*) a throw in which an opponent is pulled round the hip and hurled head first to the ground across the buttocks.

CROSS-CHANNEL, [kros'-chan'-el], *adj.* that crosses the English Channel.

CROSS-COUNTRY, [kros'-kun'-tri], *adj. and adv.* across fields and open country between the roads.

CROSS-COURSE, [kros'-kaws], *n.* (*mining*) a mineral vein lying at an angle across a main vein.

CROSS-CROSSLET, [kros'-kros'-let], *n.* (*her.*) a cross with the end of each member in the form of a small cross.

CROSSCUT (1), [kros'-kut], *n.* a cut from side to side; a path connecting two roads.

CROSSCUT (2), [kros'-kut], *adj.* used for cross-cutting; having crosscuts; **c. chisel**, a chisel with a long narrow cutting edge for making grooves in metal; **c. file**, a file whose teeth are formed by two sets of diagonal crosscuts; **c. saw**, a large saw with a handle at each end for use by two men in sawing logs, etc.

CROSSCUT (3), (**cross-cutting**), [kros'-kut], *v.t.* to cut transversely, to cut from side to side.

CROSSED, [krost], *adj.* marked with a cross or the sign of a cross; with a line or lines drawn from side to side; (*fig.*) cancelled, thwarted.

CROSSER, [kros'-er], *n.* one who crosses.

CROSSETTE, [kros'-it, kros-et'], *n.* (*arch.*) a small shouldered projection on an architrave or voussoir, which rests in a corresponding recess in the surrounding wall or adjacent voussoir. [Fr. *crossette*].

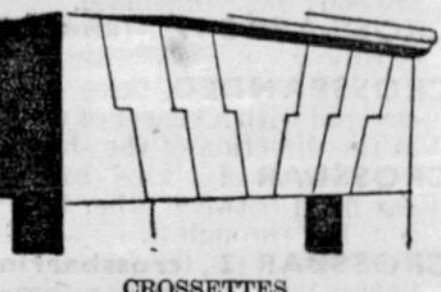

CROSSETTES

CROSS-EXAMINATION, [kros'-egz-am'-in-ā'-shun], *n.* the process of cross-examining.

CROSS-EXAMINE, [kros'-egz-am'-in], *v.t.* to examine carefully by questions to control the results of a previous examination; (*leg.*) to subject a witness who has given evidence for one side to questioning by the opposing side.

CROSS-EXAMINER, [kros'-egz-am'-in-er], *n.* one who cross-examines.

CROSS-EYED, [kros'-īd], *adj.* squinting, suffering from internal strabismus.

CROSS-FERTILIZATION, [kros'-furt'-il-iz-ā'-shun], *n.* the process of cross-fertilizing.

CROSS-FERTILIZE, [kros'-furt'-il-iz], *v.t.* to fertilize by pollen brought from another plant.

CROSS-FIRE, [kros'-fīer], *n.* (*milit.*) lines of fire from different directions that cross each other.

CROSS-FISH, [kros'-fish], *n.* a starfish, *Uraster*.

CROSS-FROG, [kros'-frog'], *n.* (*eng.*) the intersection of two rails grooved to allow the free passage of a flanged wheel on either rail.

CROSS-GARNET, [kros'-gah'-nit], *n.* a hinge formed of two metal plates, one broad and the other a long, narrow strap joined by a pin to the middle of the long edge of the broadplate, the long strap being generally attached to the movable door, partition, etc.; a T-hinge. [ME. *garnet* hinge from L. *cardo*].

CROSS-GRAINED (1), [kros'-grānd], *adj.* (of wood, etc.) with the grain running transversely from side to side or irregularly; (*fig.*) intractable, perverse, contrary.

CROSS-GRAINED (2), [kros'-grānd], *adv.* against or across the grain.

CROSS-GUARD, [kros'-gahd], *n.* a short transverse bar on a sword forming a guard.

CROSS-HATCH, [kros'-hach'], *v.i.* to hatch or engrave two sets of parallel lines at an angle to produce effects of shade (in an engraving).

CROSS-HATCHING, [kros'-hach'-ing], *n.* the process of engraving with two intersecting sets of parallel lines; the shadow effect so produced.

CROSSHEAD, [kros'-hed'], *n.* a bar or rod stretching across the top of something; (*antiq.*) the upper part of an ornamental stone cross; (*eng.*) the bar or block fixed to the end of the piston-rod of a reciprocating steam-engine and moving to and fro between parallel guide bars to transmit the motion to the connecting-rod; (*print.*) a heading across a page or column.

CROSSING, [kros'-ing], *n.* the act of making a cross, marking or drawing a cross; the process of cross-breeding; a moving across; the place of crossing; a pathway or track across a road or railway; **pedestrian c.**, a track across a road marked by two parallel lines where pedestrians have a preferential right of way over traffic.

CROSSISH, [kros'-ish], *adj.* (*coll.*) rather cross, slightly peevish.

CROSSJACK, [kros'-jak], *n.* (*naut.*) the lowest square sail on the mizen-mast.

CROSS-LEGGED, [kros'-legd'], *adj.* having one leg lying across the other when sitting.

CROSSLET, **CROSLET**†, [kros'-let], *n.* (*her.*) a small cross, usually at one of the extremities of a larger cross.

CROSSLY, [kros'-li], *adv.* in a cross manner.

CROSSNESS, [kros'-nes], *n.* the state of being cross.

CROSS-OVER, [kros'-ō'-ver], *n.* that which crosses from side to side; a bodice with its two ends drawn across the front of the body and tied behind; a short set of rails connecting two parallel sets of rails.

CROSSPATCH, [kros'-pach], *n.* a cross, bad-tempered person.

CROSSPIECE, [kros'-pēs], *n.* a piece of anything lying at an angle over anything else or extending from one thing to another.

CROSS-POLLINATION, [kros'-pol'-in-ā'-shun], *n.* (*bot.*) cross-fertilization.

CROSS-PURPOSE, [kros'-pur'-pos], *n.* a contrary, opposing purpose or intention; **to be at cross-purposes**, to deal with another person in a contrary manner through unintentional misunderstanding of each other's purposes.

CROSS-QUARTERS, [kros'-kwawt'-erz], *n.(pl.)* (*arch.*) an ornamental cruciform flower in tracery work.

CROSS-QUESTION (1), [kros'-kwes'-chun], *n.* a question asked in a cross-examination; a question asked in return by someone who has been questioned.

CROSS-QUESTION (2), [kros'-kwes'-chun], *v.t. and i.* to ask questions in cross-examination.

CROSS-REFERENCE, [kros'-ref'-er-ens], *n.* a reference from one place in a book to another place in the same book.

CROSSROAD, (*pl.* **crossroads**), [kros'-rōd(z)'], *n.* the place where two roads cross.

CROSS-ROW†, [kros'-rō], *n.* the alphabet. [So called because the row of letters was usually preceded by a cross ✠].

CROSS-RUFF (1), [kros'-ruf], *n.* alternate trumping of different suits by partners.

CROSS-RUFF (2), [kros-ruf'], *v.i.* to trump one's partner's lead, and then return with a suit that one's partner is trumping.

CROSS-SEA, [kros'-sē], *n.* the sea with two series of waves running across each other at an angle.

CROSS-SECTION, [kros'-sek'-shun], *n.* the cutting across of anything; a plane exposed or visualized by cutting transversely across anything; a drawing of such a plane; (*fig.*) a representative sample.

CROSS-SILL, [kros'-sil], *n.* a long block of wood or stone laid in a prepared bed to support wooden sleepers laid transversely across it.

CROSS-SPALL, [kros'-spawl], *n.* (*naut.*) a temporary wooden strut fixed across a boat's frame to keep the frame in shape until the deck-knees are fitted.

CROSS-SPIDER, [kros'-spī'-der], *n.* a common British spider with a cross-mark on its foreparts, *Epeira diadema.*

CROSS-SPRINGER, [kros'-spring'-er], *n.* (*arch.*) a rib which passes diagonally from one pier to another in groined vaulting.

CROSS-SPRINGER

CROSS-STAFF, [kros'-stahf], *n.* †an archbishop's cross; †an instrument used for finding the sun's altitude; a surveyor's staff for taking offsets.

CROSS-STITCH, [kros'-stich], *n.* a stitch made by two stitches crossing (X); needlework embroidered with such stitches.

CROSS-STONE, [kros'-stōn], *n.* (*min.*) chiastolite, harmotome, staurolite, minerals with cruciform crystals.

CROSS-TALK, [kros'-tawk], *n.* (*coll.*) talking back at someone, back-chat.

CROSSTIE, [kros'-tī], *n.* (*eng.*) a bar used to tie or secure two parallel rails; a sleeper; (*arch.*) a bar or beam to hold two things together.

CROSSTINING, [kros'-tīn'-ing], *n.* (*prov.*) a harrowing transversely to a previous harrowing.

CROSSTREES, [kros'-trēz], *n.*(*pl.*) (*naut.*) transverse horizontal timbers at the top ends of the upper and lower masts.

CROSS-VALVE, [kros'-valv'], *n.* a valve inserted at a four-way joint in a pipe.

CROSS-VAULT(ING), [kros'-vawlt'-(ing)], *n.* (*arch.*) a vault(ing) formed by the intersection of simple vaults.

CROSSWAY, [kros'-wā], *n.* a crossroad.

CROSSWAYS, [kros'-wāz'], *adv.* transversely, crosswise.

CROSS-WIND, [kros'-wind'], *n.* a wind blowing from the side.

CROSSWISE, [kroz'-wiz'], *adv.* in the form of a cross, across, athwart.

CROSS-WORD, [kros'-wurd'], *n.* a puzzle, consisting of a square marked off in smaller squares some of which are blacked to form stops, the remaining squares being filled with letters which form words horizontally and vertically from clues provided; **c. puzzle,** such a puzzle.

CROSSWORT, [kros'-wurt], *n.* (*bot.*) a plant with leaves in groups of four in the form of a cross, *Galium cruciatum.*

CROSSWORT

CROTALID, [krō'-tal-id], *n.* (*zool.*) a rattlesnake.

CROTALIN, [krō'-tal-in], *n.* (*chem.*) a substance in the venom of rattlesnakes.

CROTALINE, [krō'-tal-ēn], *adj.* belonging to the rattlesnake family.

CROTALO, [krō'-tal-ō], *n.* a Turkish musical percussion instrument. [It. *crotalo* from L. *crotalum* rattle].

CROTCH, [kroch], *n.* a stake with a forked top, used as a support; the fork of a tree or bough; (*naut.*) forked timbers placed under the keel fore and aft. [ONFr. *croc(h)e* a shepherd's crook, cf. CROSIER].

CROTCHED, [krocht], *adj.* having a crotch, forked, bifurcated.

CROTCHET (1), [kroch'-it], *n.* a hook, a hook-shaped figure or symbol; (*typ.*) a square bracket [ ]; (*mus.*) the representation of a note of half the time value of a minim, ♩; a note represented in this way; (*fig.*) a fancy, a whim, a perverse idea. [Fr. *crochet* hook].

CROTCHET (2), [kroch'-it], *v.t. and i.* †to ornament with crotchets; (*mus.*) to play in regular crotchets.

CROTCHETINESS, [kroch'-i-ti-nes], *n.* the state of being crotchety.

CROTCHETY, [kroch'-i-ti], *adj.* having crotchets; (*fig.*) of fanciful, whimsical or perverse ideas.

CROTON, [krō'-ton], *n.* (*bot.*) a euphorbiaceous plant, such as *Croton Cascarilla*, cascarilla bark, and *Croton Tiglium*; (*pop.*) a beautifully foliated plant, *Codiæum Pictum*; **c. oil,** a fatty purgative oil obtained from the seeds of *Croton Tiglium.* [Gk. *kroton* a tick or mite, from the appearance of the seeds].

CROTONATE, [krō'-ton-āt], *n.* the salt of crotonic acid.

CROTONIC, [krō-ton'-ik], *adj.* (*chem.*) of or from croton oil; **c. acid,** an acid derived from croton oil.

CROTTLE, [krotl], *n.* (*Scots*) a lichen used in dyeing. [Gael. *crotal*].

CROUCH (1), [krowch], *n.* the action of crouching. [OFr. *croche* crook].

CROUCH† **(2),** [krowch], *n.* a cross. [OE. *cruc* from L. *crux* cross].

CROUCH (3), [krowch], *v.i.* to stoop with the whole body, to bend down with the legs, with the trunk pressed against the thighs; (*fig.*) to cringe, to fawn. [CROUCH (1)].

CROUCHED-FRIARS, CRUTCHED-FRIARS, [krowcht'-frī'-erz], *n.* an order of friars who wore or carried a cross.

CROUCH-WARE, [krowch'-wāer], *n.* old, finely-glazed pottery formerly made in Staffordshire. [Unkn.].

CROUD, CROWD, see CRUTH.

CROUP (1), [kroop], *n.* an inflammation, usually of the larynx, resulting in a hoarse cough and difficult breathing. [CROUP (3)].

CROUP(E) (2), [kroop], *n.* the hind-quarters or buttocks of a horse, ass, etc. [Fr. *croupe*].

CROUP (3), [kroop], *v.i.* to cough or cry hoarsely, to croak. [OScand. *kropja* to shout].

CROUPADE, [kroop-ād], *n.* (*equitation*) a jump in which a horse kicks up its hind-legs towards its belly. [Fr. *croupade*].

CROUPIER, [kroop'-i-er], *n.* one who presides at a gambling-table; the vice-chairman at a banquet who sits at the lower end of the table. [Fr. *croupier* a man who rides behind on the croup of a horse].

CROUPINESS, [kroop'-i-nes], *n.* the condition of having croup or some affection like it; a tendency towards croup.

CROUPY, [kroop'-i], *adj.* having, or like, croup.

CROUT, see SAUERKRAUT.

CROUTON, croûton, [kroo'-ton], *n.* a small portion of fried bread eaten with soups. [Fr. *croûton*].

CROW (1), [krō], *n.* a large, black bird of the genus *Corvus*; the cry of such a bird or of a cock; the joyful cry of an infant. [OE. *crawe*].

CROW (2), [krō], *n.* a crowbar. [OE. *croh* crook].

CROW (3), [krō], *v.i.* to utter a crow or a succession of crows; (*fig.*) to boast, swagger. [OE. *crawan*].

CROWBAR, [krō'-bah(r)], *n.* an iron bar with one end slightly flattened and bent, and used as a lever.

CROWBERRY, [krō'-be-ri], *n.* a heath or moorland plant, *Empetrum nigrum*, producing a black berry; the fruit of this plant. [Dan. *kragebær*].

CROW-BILL, CROW'S-BILL, [krō(z)'-bil], *n.* (*surg.*) a kind of surgical forceps for extracting bullets, etc., from wounds.

CROWD (1), [krowd], *n.* a large number of people gathered into a closely packed mass; a large collection of things placed close together; a large number of people in a small room.

CROWD (2), [krowd], *v.t. and i.* to form a crowd, to throng, to swarm, to press round or on, to confine; to gather in crowds in or at (a place); to press into too small a space; **to c. sail,** (*naut.*) to run up an extraordinary number of sails, to carry a press of sail. [OE. *crudan* to press].

CROWD (3), see CRUTH.

CROWDED, [krowd'-id], *adj.* filled with a large number of people; closely packed.

CROWDING, [krowd'-ing], *n.* the action of crowding, overcrowding.

CROWFOOT, [krō'-foot], *n.* (*bot.*) a buttercup of the genus *Ranunculus*; (*naut.*) a number of small cords passing through a long block and spreading out to support an awning or the like.

CROW-GARLIC, [krō'-gah'-lik], *n.* (*bot.*) wild garlic, *Allium vineale.*
CROWGER, [krow'-jer], *n.* (*zool.*) a fish, the striped wrasse, *Labrus mixtus.* [Unkn.].
CROWKEEPER, [krō'-kēp'-er], *n.* a person employed to scare crows from newly sown land; a scarecrow.
CROWMILL, [krō'-mil], *n.* a snare or trap for catching crows.
CROWN (1), [krown], *n.* a fillet, wreath or garland placed on the head as a mark of honour; a headband or head-dress of precious metal ornamented with jewels, worn as an emblem of sovereignty; sovereignty, regal power, royalty, dignity; the wearer of a crown, the king's office, the king; the figure or shape of a crown; anything which bears such a mark; a coin of the value of five shillings, formerly stamped with a crown; a size of paper (20 ins. by 15 ins.); the top of the head, the top of other things, the head; the exposed part of a tooth; the rounded top of a bell; the crest of a bird; (*arch.*) the highest part of a cornice; (*naut.*) the end of an anchor shank; (*fig.*) the completion, perfection. [Scand. *kruna* from L. *corona*].
CROWN (2), [krown], *adj.* pertaining to or belonging to the crown, as a symbol of regal authority, belonging to the kingdom; **C. Agents**, a government department having charge of the financial and commercial affairs of the Crown Colonies; **C. Colony**, a colony governed direct by the Crown and not self-governing; **C. law**, the common law of England as applicable to criminal matters; **C. office**, a section of the High Court of Justice which deals with the administration of Crown law (criminal matters).
CROWN (3), [krown], *v.t. and i.* to place a crown upon the head; to invest with a crown as a symbol of royal power and dignity, to enthrone; to honour, to adorn in a dignified and splendid manner; to reward; to complete successfully, to finish; to cover the head or crown of something; (*draughts*) to put one draught upon another to make a king which can then move backwards. [L. *coronare*].
CROWN-AND-ANCHOR, [krown'-and-angk'-er], *n.* a gambling game played with dice marked with crowns or anchors.
CROWN-ANTLER, [krown'-ant'-ler], *n.* the highest tine of a stag's horns.
CROWN-COURT, [krown'-kawt], *n.* an assize court in which criminal affairs are dealt with.
CROWNED, [krownd], *adj.* adorned with, invested with a crown; crested; (*fig.*) perfect.
CROWNER, [krown'-er], *n.* one who crowns; †a coroner.
CROWNET†, see CORONET.
CROWN-GLASS, [krown'-glahs], *n.* a circular window glass, generally thick at the centre, made without lead.
CROWN-IMPERIAL, [krown'-im-pēer'-i-al], *n.* (*bot.*) a cultivated flowering plant, *Fritillaria Imperialis.*
CROWNING (1), [krown'-ing], *n.* the action of crowning, coronation; that which crowns; the top of an arch.
CROWNING (2), [krown'-ing], *adj.* finishing, perfecting, perfect.
CROWN-LANDS, [krown'-landz'], *n.*(*pl.*) lands belonging to the Crown or State.
CROWNLESS, [krown'-les], *adj.* without a crown.
CROWN-PIECE, [krown'-pēs], *n.* a silver coin worth five shillings, a crown.
CROWNPOST, [krown'-pōst], *n.* (*arch.*) the middle upright post supporting the crown of a roof.
CROWN-PRINCE, [krown'-prins'], *n.* a prince who is heir to the throne.
CROWN-SAW, [krown'-saw], *n.* (*eng.*) a circular saw with the teeth formed on the edge of a hollow cylinder.
CROWN-SCAB, [krown'-skab'], *n.* a cancerous and painful scab in the coronet of a horse's hoof.
CROWN-SHEET, [krown'-shēt], *n.* the top plate of the fire-box of a steam-locomotive.
CROWN-STAY, [krown'-stā], *n.* a stay or rod joining the crown-plate to the top boiler-plate to prevent distortion of the plates through steam-pressure.

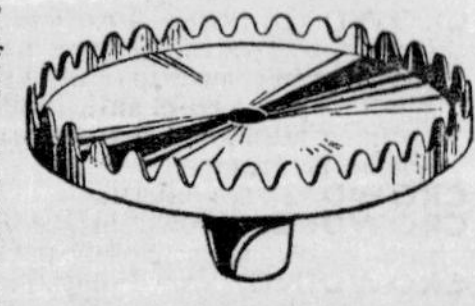
CROWN-WHEEL

CROWN-WHEEL, [krown'-wēl], *n.* a gear-wheel with its teeth set on the periphery at right angles to the plane of the wheel; the balance-wheel of a watch.
CROWN-WITNESS, [krown'-wit'-nes], *n.* a witness who gives evidence for the Crown in a criminal case.
CROWQUILL, [krō'-kwil], *n.* a fine steel pen for delicate penmanship.
CROW'S-BILL, see CROW-BILL.
CROW'S-FEET, [krōz'-fēt'], *n.*(*pl.*) (*coll.*) wrinkles at the outer corners of the eyes.
CROW-SILK, [krō'-silk], *n.* a freshwater alga, *Conferva rivularis.*
CROW'S-NEST, [krōz'-nest], *n.* a cylindrical look-out shelter fixed to the upper part of a ship's mast.
CROWSTEPS, [krō'-steps'], *n.*(*pl.*) (*arch.*) a set of steps ornamenting the top of a gable wall.
CROW-STONE, [krō'-stōn], *n.* (*geol.*) a hard light-coloured sandstone from Yorkshire; (*arch.*) the top stone of a gable wall.
CROY, [kroi], *n.* an embankment built into a river to check the current; an enclosure in a river for catching fish. [Scots].
CROYDON†, [kroi'-don], *n.* a gig, formerly made of basket-work. [*Croydon*, Surrey].
CROYLSTONE†, [kroil'-stōn], *n.* cawk. [Prov. *croyl* a kind of clay].
CROZE (1), [krōz], *n.* a groove cut in the ends of the timbers of a barrel to fit the cask-head; a tool for making this groove. [OFr. *croz* groove].
CROZE (2), [krōz], *v.t. and i.* to make a croze (in). [OFr. *crozer* to hollow].
CROZIER, see CROSIER.
CRUCIAL, [kroo'-shal], *adj.* (*anat.*, *surg.*) in the form of a cross; (*fig.*) decisive, conclusive, critical, severe. [Fr. *crucial*, ~L. *crux* cross].
CRUCIAN, [kroo'-shun], *n.* a yellow freshwater fish, allied to the carp, *Carassius.* [L. *coracinus* black perch].
CRUCIATE, [kroo'-shi-at], *adj.* (*bot.*) cross-shaped [MedL. *cruciatus*, from L. *crux* cross].
CRUCIBLE, [kroo'-sibl], *n.* a small earthenware pot used for melting metals; a hollow place at the bottom of a furnace where molten metal is received; (*fig.*) a severe test; **c. steel**, hard cast-steel used in tool-making. [MedL. *crucibulum* night-lamp].
CRUCIFERAE, [kroo-sif'-er-ē], *n.* (*bot.*) a family of plants whose flowers have four petals arranged in the form of a cross. [CRUX and L. *ferre* to bear].
CRUCIFEROUS, [kroo-sif'-er-us], *adj.* adorned with a cross; (*bot.*) having four petals arranged in a cross.
CRUCIFIED, [kroo'-sif-īd], *adj.* nailed on the cross.
CRUCIFIER, [kroo'-si-fī'-er], *n.* one who crucifies.
CRUCIFIX, [kroo'-sif-iks], *n.* a representation or image of Christ on the cross. [OFr. *crucifix*, L. *cruci fixus* fixed to a cross].
CRUCIFIXION, [kroo'-sif-ik'-shun], *n.* the act of crucifying; the punishment of being crucified; the death of Christ on a cross.
CRUCIFORM, [kroo'-si-fawm], *adj.* cross-shaped; (*bot.*) arranged in the form of a cross. [L. *crux* and FORM].
CRUCIFY, [kroo'-si-fī], *v.t. and i.* to nail a person to a cross by the hands and feet; to put to death in this way; (*fig.*) to mortify, to torment, to subject to severe pain. [OFr. *crucifier*, L. *crucifigere* to fix to a cross].
CRUCIFYING, [kroo'-si-fī-ing], *adj.* torturing, excruciating.
CRUCIGEROUS†, [kroo-sij'-er-us], *adj.* bearing a cross. [L. *crux* cross and *gerere* to bear].
CRUCITE, [kroo'-sīt], *n.* a red oxide of iron with crystals in cross form. [L. *crux*].
CRUDE, [krood], *adj.* raw, in the natural state, unripe; untreated by any artificial process; undigested; uncooked; (*fig.*) immature; ill-considered, rough, unpolished; (of colours, music) gaudy, unrefined. [L. *crudus*].
CRUDELY, [krood'-li], *adv.* in a crude fashion.
CRUDENESS, [krood'-nes], *n.* the quality of being crude.
CRUDITY, [krood'-i-ti], *n.* crudeness; that which is crude; (*med.*) the immature stage in a disease. [L. *cruditas*].
CRUEL, [kroo'-el], *adj.* inflicting pain or sorrow upon others, unkind, unreasonably harsh; intended to produce distress or suffering, painful; (*vulg.*) very hard, severe. [Fr. *cruel* from L. *crudelis* fierce].
CRUEL-HEARTED, [kroo'-el-haht'-id], *adj.* of a cruel disposition.
CRUELLY, [kroo'-el-i], *adv.* in a cruel fashion.

CRUELNESS, [krōō'-el-nes], *n.* the state of being cruel.
CRUELTY, [krōō'-el-ti], *n.* the state of being cruel; a cruel act; severity, harsh treatment causing pain and distress. [L. *crudelitas*].
CRUENTATE†, [krōō'-en-tāt], *adj.* covered with blood. [L. *cruentatum*, *p.pt.* of *cruentare* to stain with blood].
CRUET, [krōō'-it], *n.* a small glass bottle for condiments; a group of these placed in a stand; (*eccles.*) a small vessel in which wine or water for the Eucharist is contained. [AFr. *cruet*].
CRUET-STAND, [krōō'-it-stand'], *n.* a small stand fitted with several compartments for cruets.
CRUISE (1), [krōōz], *n.* a leisurely sea-voyage with calls at various places; a sea-voyage of a warship to patrol a wide area with no particular destination in view.
CRUISE (2), [krōōz], *v.i.* to sail about on a cruise; (of a taxi) to drive slowly looking for a fare. [Du. *kruizen* to cross].
CRUISER, [krōō'-zer], *n.* a ship, particularly a warship, that cruises; a lightly armoured and speedy type of warship specially designed for cruising; a boxer who fights at cruiser-weight; **c.-weight,** (*boxing*) light-heavy-weight, between middle- and heavy-weight.
CRUISKEEN†, [krōōz'-kin], *n.* a small bottle. [OFr. *creusequin*].
CRUIVE, [krōōv], *n.* a wicker-work enclosure or trap for catching fish. [Scots].
CRUMB (1), [krum], *n.* a small fragment of bread broken from a loaf; the soft inner part of bread; (*fig.*) a small portion or amount, a scrap. [OE. *cruma*].
CRUMB (2), [krum], *v.t.* to break or rub into crumbs; to spread over with crumbs.
CRUMB-BRUSH, [krum'-brush], *n.* a curved narrow brush for sweeping crumbs from a table-cloth.
CRUMB-CLOTH, [krum'-kloth'], *n.* a cloth laid under a table to catch crumbs.
CRUMBLE, [krumbl], *v.t.* and *i.* to break into small pieces or crumbs; to disintegrate, fall to bits.
CRUMBLY, [krum'-bli], *adj.* easily crumbled, friable.
CRUMBY, [krum'-i], *adj.* soft and spongy; full of crumbs.
CRUMMABLE, [krum'-abl], *adj.* capable of being crumbled.
CRUMMY, [krum'-i], *n.* a cow with a crumpled horn.
CRUMP (1), [krump], *n.* (*slang*) a heavy explosive shell; a dull heavy explosion. [Echoic].
CRUMP† (2), [krump], *adj.* crooked, deformed. [OE. *crump*].
CRUMPET, [krum'-pit], *n.* a soft thin sponge-like yeast-cake; (*slang*) the head. [Uncert.].
CRUMPLE, [krumpl], *v.t.* and *i.* to fold up or press into creases in careless fashion, to rumple, to ruffle; to squeeze (paper) into a compact ball; (*fig.*) to cause a person to collapse completely; to become ruffled or full of creases; to wilt and collapse completely, to fall to pieces. [CRUMP].
CRUMPLING†, [krump'-ling], *n.* a small shrivelled apple. [OHGerm. *krümmeling* a crooked man].
CRUNCH (1), [krunch], *n.* the act or noise of crunching.
CRUNCH (2), [krunch], *v.t.* and *i.* to crush or crumble noisily with the teeth, to grind or crush with a harsh grating noise. [Imitative].
CRUOR, [krōō'-or], *n.* coagulated blood. [L. *cruor* blood].
CRUORIN†, [krōō'-er-in], *n.* the red colouring matter in the blood, haemoglobin.
CRUP, [krup], *n.* the buttocks. [CROUP (1)].
CRUPPER, [krup'-er], *n.* the hind-quarters of a horse; a leather strap in harness extending from the back of a saddle under a horse's tail, to keep the saddle firmly fixed. [OFr. *cropiere*].
CRURAL, [krōōer'-al], *adj.* (*anat.*) pertaining to the leg. [L. *cruralis*].
CRUSADE (1), [krōō-sād'], *n.* one of the military expeditions undertaken in the Middle Ages, under the banner of the Cross, by Christian rulers, to win back Palestine and the Holy Sepulchre from the Saracens; a holy war against infidels, sanctioned by the Pope; (*fig.*) an enthusiastic campaign or drive against some social evil or abuse. [MedL. *cruciata* from *cruciare* mark with a cross].
CRUSADE (2), [krōō-sād'], *v.i.* to take part in a crusade.
CRUSADER, [krōō-sād'-er], *n.* one taking part in a crusade.
CRUSADO, [krōō-sād'-ō], *n.* a Portuguese coin stamped with a cross. [Portug. *cruzado* marked with a cross].
CRUSE, [krōōz], *n.* a small earthenware receptacle, a drinking vessel. [OScand. *krus* a pot].
CRUSH (1), [krush], *n.* a closely packed mass of people collected or moving in a restricted space; violent pressure, the act of crushing; a gang, set or group of people habitually associating together; **a c. on,** (*slang*) a strong and secret passion for.
CRUSH (2), [krush], *v.t.* and *i.* to press, to squeeze forcibly, to apply pressure to so as to break, injure or destroy; to press or squeeze tightly in order to express the contents, change the form or shape of; to crease, to rumple; to grind or pound to small particles; to squeeze into a confined or restricted space; (*fig.*) to subdue, to put down, to suppress; to overwhelm, to destroy completely; to abash; to force one's way into an already crowded space; to become creased or crumpled. [OFr. *croissir*].
CRUSHER, [krush'-er], *n.* one who, or that which, crushes.
CRUSH-HAT, [krush'-hat'], *n.* a collapsible opera-hat.
CRUST (1), [krust], *n.* the hard, crisp brown covering of a loaf or roll of bread; a hard stale piece of bread; the outer covering of pastry baked over a pie; any hard shell or protective covering; the solid exterior surface of the earth; a crystal-like film from wine collecting on the inside of the bottle. [L. *crusta*].
CRUST (2), [krust], *v.t.* and *i.* to cover with a crust; to form or gather into a crust.
CRUSTACEA, [krust-ā'-shi-a], *n.*(*pl.*) (*zool.*) one of the classes of *Arthropoda*, comprising a large number of aquatic animals with a hard protective shell as lobsters, shrimps, crabs, etc. [L. *crusta* crust].
CRUSTACEAN (1), [krust-ā'-shi-an], *n.* one of the crustacea.
CRUSTACEAN (2), [krust-ā'-shi-an], *adj.* belonging to the crustacea.
CRUSTACEOLOGICAL, [krust-ā'-si-o-loj'-ik-al], *adj.* belonging to crustaceology.
CRUSTACEOLOGIST, [krust-ā'-si-ol'-oj-ist], *n.* one expert in crustaceology.
CRUSTACEOLOGY, [krust-ā'-si-ol'-o-ji], *n.* the study or science of the crustacea. [CRUSTACEA and Gk. *logos* speech].
CRUSTACEOUS, [krust-ā'-shus], *adj.* relating to a crust; of the nature of crust or shell; hard and brittle; crustacean.
CRUSTACEOUSNESS, [krust-ā'-shus-nes], *n.* the condition of being crustaceous.
CRUSTATED, [krust-āt'-id], *adj.* covered with a crust. [L. *crustatus* crusted].
CRUSTATION, [krust-ā'-shun], *n.* an incrustation.
CRUSTILY, [krust'-i-li], *adv.* in a crusty fashion.
CRUSTINESS, [krust'-i-nes], *n.* the quality of being crusty.
CRUSTY, [krust'-i], *adj.* like crust; hard; surly; morose.
CRUT, [krut], *n.* the rough uneven part of oak-bark; a dwarf. [Uncert.].
CRUTCH (1), [kruch], *n.* a long staff with a padded top which rests under the armpit, used as a support in walking, by the crippled; (*fig.*) a support, a prop, a fork-shaped contrivance in certain machinery; a fork; a forked leg-rest in a side-saddle; the fork of the human body. [OE. *crycc*].
CRUTCH (2), [kruch], *v.t.* and *i.* to prop up with a crutch, to support on crutches; to walk on crutches.
CRUTCHED, [krucht], *adj.* supported on crutches; distinguished by a cross; **c. friars,** crouched friars.
CRUTCHET, [kruch'-it], *n.* a freshwater fish, the perch. [Unkn.].
CRUTH, CROUD, CROWD, [kruth], *n.* a Welsh violin. [Wel. *crwth* fiddle].
CRUX, [kruks], *n.* a difficult problem, a trouble-some point, a difficult passage; the real issue. [L. *crux* a cross, torture].
CRY (1), [krī], *n.* the distinguishing call of an animal; a loud vocal sound, expressive of strong emotion, uttered by human beings; a call for help; a shout or call of excitement; a shriek, a scream, a wail; the act of weeping; a popular rumour or report; a party slogan or political catchword; a prayer, an audible entreaty; a characteristic shout uttered by street hawkers, etc., to attract attention to their wares; a pack of hounds; **hue and c.,** pursuit, public agitation or clamour; **a far c.,** a long way removed; **within c.,** within earshot; **in full c.,** in hot pursuit. [Fr. *cri*].
CRY (2), [krī], *v.t.* and *i.* to utter a cry; to call loudly in order to attract notice; to weep, sob, shed tears; to proclaim loudly and publicly; **to c. up,** to praise; **to c. down,** to disparage; **to c. off,** to withdraw from, to ask to be excused; **to c. quits,** to declare matters

equal; **to c. shame,** to protest against; **to c. for the moon,** to want what is beyond one's means to acquire. [OFr. *crier* from L. *quiritare* to wail].

CRY-BABY, [krī′-bāb′-i], *n.* a child who cries when it meets with opposition or difficulty.

CRYING (1), [krī′-ing], *n.* outcry, clamour, the act of crying.

CRYING (2), [krī′-ing], *adj.* calling for immediate redress.

CRYOGEN, [krī′-oj-en], *n.* a freezing mixture. [Gk. *kruos* frost and *genes* produced].

CRYOLITE, [krī′-ol-īt], *n.* (*min.*) a mineral found in Greenland, a double fluoride of aluminium and sodium. [Gk. *kruos* frost and *lithos* stone].

CRYOMETER, [krī-om′-it-er], *n.* an instrument used for measuring low temperatures. [Gk. *kruos* frost and METER].

CRYOPHORUS, [krī-of′-er-us], *n.* an instrument for freezing water by its own evaporation, consisting of a tube with a spherical bulb at each end. [Gk. *kruos* frost and *phoros* bearing].

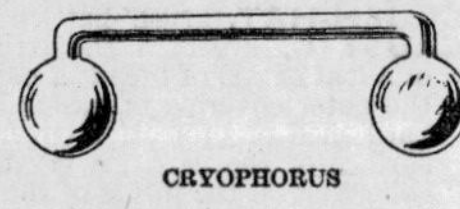

CRYOPHORUS

CRYPT, [kript], *n.* a subterranean vaulted cell or cave, *esp.* a burial-chamber under a church. [Gk. *krupte* a vault].

CRYPTAESTHESIA, [kript′-es-thēz′-ya], *n.* supernatural knowledge or perception. [CRYPTO and Gk. *aisthesis* perception].

CRYPTIC, [kript′-ik], *adj.* secret, mysterious, occult; (*zool.*) hiding, concealing. [Gk. *kruptikos* hidden].

CRYPTICAL, [kript′-ik-al], *adj.* cryptic.

CRYPTICALLY, [kript′-ik-a-li], *adv.* secretly, in a cryptic manner.

CRYPTO-, *pref.* hidden, secret. [Gk. *kruptos* hidden, secret].

CRYPTOBRANCHIATE, [kript′-ō-brangk′-i-āt], *adj.* (*zool.*) having partly-hidden gills.

CRYPTOGAM, [kript′-o-gam], *n.* (*bot.*) one of the cryptogamia. [CRYPTO and Gk. *gamos* marriage].

CRYPTOGAMIA, [kript′-ō-găm′-i-a], *n.*(*pl.*) (*bot.*) a class of plants having no apparent flowers or seeds, as mosses, ferns, etc. [*Prec.*].

CRYPTOGAMIC, [kript′-o-gam′-ik], *adj.* relating to the cryptogamia.

CRYPTOGAMIST, [kript-og′-am-ist], *n.* a botanist who makes a special study of the cryptogamia.

CRYPTOGAMOUS, [kript-og′-am-us], *adj.* cryptogamic.

CRYPTOGAMY, [kript-og′-a-mi], *n.* (*bot.*) concealed reproduction.

CRYPTOGRAM, [kript′-o-gram], *n.* anything written in cipher. [CRYPTO and Gk. *gramma* writing].

CRYPTOGRAPH, [kript′-o-grahf], *n.* a cryptogram.

CRYPTOGRAPHER, [kript′-og′-raf-er], *n.* one skilled in writing in cipher.

CRYPTOGRAPHICAL, [kript′-o-graf′-ik-al], *adj.* written in cipher.

CRYPTOGRAPHY, [kript-og′-ra-fi], *n.* the art of writing in secret characters. [CRYPTO and Gk. *graphia* writing].

CRYPTOLOGY, [kript-ol′-o-ji], *n.* a secret language. [CRYPTO and Gk. *logos* speech].

CRYPTOMERIA, [kript′-o-mēer′-i-a], *n.* the Japanese cedar, *Cryptomeria japonica.* [CRYPTO and Gk. *meros* part].

CRYPTONYM, [kript′-on-im], *n.* a secret name. [CRYPTO and Gk. *onoma* name].

CRYSTAL (1), [kris′-tal], *n.* (*min.*) a clear transparent variety of quartz; (*chem., min.*) a body having a more or less symmetrical form, any structure resembling a crystal in form, and bounded by plane surfaces; (*fig.*) anything clear and transparent; a spherical piece of rock-crystal used in fortune-telling; fine cut-glassware of high transparency; (*wirel.*) a natural mineral deposit that passes an electric current in one direction only; **rock c.,** transparent or colourless quartz. [Gk. *krustallos*].

CRYSTAL (2), [kris′-tal], *adj.* made of crystal, resembling crystal, clear, transparent, limpid.

CRYSTALFORM, [kris′-tal-fawm′], *adj.* in the form of crystal.

CRYSTAL-GAZING, [kris′-tal-gāz′-ing], *n.* fortune-telling by means of a crystal.

CRYSTALLINE, [krist′-a-līn′], *adj.* made of or like a crystal; clear, transparent; (*min., chem.*) having the structure of a crystal; **c. lens,** (*anat.*) the transparent body behind the iris of the eye, which focuses the rays of light on the retina. [Gk. *krustallinos*].

CRYSTALLITE, [kris′-tal-īt], *n.* masses of microscopic crystal-like particles in rock.

CRYSTALLIZABLE, [kris′-tal-īz′-abl], *adj.* able to be crystallized.

CRYSTALLIZATION, [kris′-tal-īz-ā′-shun], *n.* the process of crystallizing; **water of c.,** the water contained in certain crystalline substances.

CRYSTALLIZE, [kris′-tal-īz], *v.t.* and *i.* to form into crystals; to cover with sugar crystals; (*fig.*) to give a definite concrete form to; (*fig.*) to become clearly defined and settled.

CRYSTALLOGENIC, [kris′-tal-ō-jen′-ik], *adj.* producing a crystalline arrangement. [CRYSTAL and Gk. *genes* producing].

CRYSTALLOGRAPHER, [kris′-tal-og′-raf-er], *n.* one skilled in crystallography.

CRYSTALLOGRAPHIC, [kris′-tal-o-graf′-ik], *adj.* relating to crystallography.

CRYSTALLOGRAPHICAL, [kris′-tal-o-graf′-ik-al], *adj.* crystallographic.

CRYSTALLOGRAPHICALLY, [kris′-tal-o-graf′-ik-a-li], *adv.* in the manner of crystallography.

CRYSTALLOGRAPHY, [kris′-tal-og′-raf-i], *n.* the scientific study of crystals. [CRYSTAL and Gk. *graphia* writing].

CRYSTALLOID (1), [kris′-tal-oid], *n.* a substance resembling a crystalline substance. [CRYSTAL and Gk. *oeides* like].

CRYSTALLOID (2), [kris′-tal-oid], *adj.* resembling a crystal, crystalline.

CRYSTALLOMANCY, [kris′-tal-ō-man′-si], *n.* divination by crystals. [CRYSTAL and Gk. *manteia* divination].

CRYSTAL-SET, [kris′-tal-set′], *n.* (*wirel.*) a simple form of wireless receiving apparatus in which a crystal is used to rectify the incoming waves.

CRYSTOLEUM, [kris-tōl′-i-um], *n.* photographs painted in oil on glass. [CRYSTAL and L. *oleum* oil].

CTENOID (1), [ten′-oid], *n.* a ctenoid fish.

CTENOID (2), [ten′-oid], *adj.* (of certain fishes) having scales with comb-like edges. [Gk. *kteis ktenos* a comb and *oeides* like].

CTENOIDANS, [ten-oid′-anz], *n.*(*pl.*) an order of fishes with ctenoid scales.

CTENOPHORE, [ten′-o-faw(r)], *n.* an animal that swims by means of rows of ctenoid plates. [Gk. *kteis ktenos* comb and *phoros* bearing].

CUB (1), [kub], *n.* the young of the fox, bear, or other beast; (*fig.*) a rough-mannered inexperienced youth; (*coll.*) a young person. [Ir. *cuib* whelp].

CUB (2), [kub], *n.* a cattle-pen; a receptacle for fodder. [Unkn.].

CUB (3), (cubbing, cubbed), [kub], *v.i.* to give birth to cubs; to hunt cubs. [CUB (1)].

CUBAGE, [kewb′-ij], *n.* the cubic content of a solid; the calculation of this. [CUBE].

CUBAN (1), [kew′-ban], *n.* a native of Cuba.

CUBAN (2), [kew′-ban], *adj.* relating to Cuba.

CUBATURE, [kewb′-a-cher], *n.* the calculation of the cubage.

CUBBING, [kub′-ing], *n.* the hunting of fox-cubs.

CUBBISH, [kub′-ish], *adj.* ill-mannered, rough.

CUBBY, [kub′-i], *n.* a cosy retreat. [CUB (2)].

CUBE (1), [kewb], *n.* a regular six-sided solid body, with all its sides square and identical; anything resembling this; (*math.*) the third power, the product of the square of a number multiplied by the number itself. [Gk. *kubos*].

CUBE (2), [kewb], *v.t.* (*math.*) to raise to the third power, to calculate the cube of.

CUBEB, [kew′-beb′], *n.* the small aromatic spicy berry of the plant *Piper Cubeba,* used medicinally. [Arab. *kababah*].

CUBEBINE, [kew′-bib-in], *n.* a vegetable substance extracted from the seeds of the cubeb.

CUBIC, [kewb′-ik], *adj.* resembling a cube; involving three dimensions; (*math.*) pertaining to the cube or third power. [Gk. *kubikos*].

CUBICAL, [kewb′-ik-al], *adj.* cubic.

CUBICALLY, [kewb′-ik-a-li], *adv.* in the manner of a cube.

CUBICALNESS, [kewb′-ik-al-nes], *n.* the quality of being cubical.

CUBICLE, [kewb′-ik-al], *n.* one of the small, separate enclosed changing-rooms or sleeping-compartments in a building. [L. *cubiculum* rest room].

CUBICULAR, [kewb-ik′-yōō-ler], *adj.* pertaining to a cubicle. [L. *cubicularis*].

CUBIFORM, [kewb′-i-fawm], *adj.* having the form of a cube.

CUBISM, [kewb'-izm], *n.* a style of painting in which only geometrical figures in three dimensions are employed.
CUBIST (**1**), [kewb'-ist], *n.* an exponent of cubism.
CUBIST (**2**), [kewb'-ist], *adj.* of, or pertaining to, cubism or cubists.
CUBIT†, [kewb'-it], *n.* a measure of length, being the distance from the elbow to the tip of the middle finger; (*anat.*) the forearm. [L. *cubitum* elbow].
CUBITAL, [kewb'-it-al], *adj.* of the length of a cubit; (*anat.*) relating to the elbow.
CUBITED†, [kewb'-it-id], *adj.* of the measure of a cubit.
CUBITUS, [kewb'-it-us], *n.* the forearm, the ulna. [L. *cubitus*].
CUBO-DODECAHEDRAL, [kewb'-ō-dō'-dek-a-hē'-dral], *adj.* having a combination of the two forms, a cube and a dodecahedron.
CUBOID (**1**), [kewb'-oid], *n.* anything shaped like a cube, but not strictly cubical. [CUBE and Gk. *oeides* like].
CUBOID (**2**), [kewb'-oid], *adj.* resembling a cube.
CUBOIDAL, [kewb'-oid-al], *adj.* cuboid.
CUBO-OCTAHEDRAL, [kewb'-ō-ok'-ta-hē'-dral], *adj.* having a combination of two forms, a cube and an octahedron.
CUBSHA, [kub'-sha], *n.* an Indian drug. [Native].
CUCA, COCA, [kōō'-ka], *n.* (*bot.*) the Peruvian plant, *Erythroxylum Coca*, the leaves of which yield cocaine. [Peruvian *cuca*].
CUCKING-STOOL, [kuk'-ing-stōōl'], *n.* a chair or stool in which scolds, rogues, and disreputables were fastened and publicly exhibited or ducked. [OScand. *kuka* to excrete].
CUCKOLD (**1**), [kuk'-ōld], *n.* a man whose wife commits adultery. [ME. *cokewold*].
CUCKOLD (**2**), [kuk'-ōld], *v.t.* to make a husband a cuckold.
CUCKOLDLY†, [kuk'-ōld-li], *adj.* like a cuckold.
CUCKOLD-MAKER, [kuk'-ōld-māk'-er], *n.* one who has sexual intercourse with another man's wife.
CUCKOLDOM, [kuk'-ōld-om], *n.* the act of adultery; the state of being a cuckold.
CUCKOLDRY, [kuk'-ōld-ri], *n.* adultery.
CUCKOO, [kŏŏk'-ōō], *n.* the migratory bird *Cuculus canorus*; (*slang*) a fool, a stupid person; **c. ray**, the skate, *Raia circularis*; **cuckoo's mate**, the wryneck, *Iynx torquilla*; **cuckoo's meat**, the wood sorrel, a plant of the genus *Oxalis*. [Imitative].
CUCKOO-CLOCK, [kŏŏk'-ōō-klok'], *n.* a clock in which the hours are announced by the appearance and cry of an imitation cuckoo.
CUCKOO-FLOWER, [kŏŏk'-ōō-flow'-er], *n.* (*bot.*) one of several plants including the lady's smock, *Cardamine pratensis*, and the wild orchis.
CUCKOO-PINT, [kŏŏk'-ōō-pint'], *n.* the plant, *Arum maculatum*.
CUCKOO-SPIT, [kŏŏk'-ōō-spit'], *n.* the cuckoo-spittle.
CUCKOO-SPITTLE, [kŏŏk'-ōō-spitl'], *n.* a spittle-like secretion deposited on plants by certain parasitic insects such as the froghopper.
CUCULLATE, [kew'-kul-āt], *adj.* (*zool.*) hooded; (*bot.*) shaped like a hood. [L. *cucullatus* hooded].
CUCULLATED, [kew'-kul-āt-id], *adj.* cucullate.
CUCUMARIA, [kew'-kyŏŏ-māer'-i-a], *n.* the sea-cucumber.
CUCUMBER, [kew'-kumb-er], *n.* the edible fruit of a plant of the gourd family, *Cucumis sativus*; the plant itself. [L. *cucumis cucumeris*].
CUCUMIFORM, [kew-kewm'-i-fawm], *adj.* resembling a cucumber in appearance. [L. *cucumis* and FORM].
CUCURBITA, [kew-kurb'-it-a], *n.* a gourd; the genus of plants of which the gourd is a species. [L. *cucurbita* gourd].
CUCURBITACEOUS, [kew-kurb'-it-ā'-shus], *adj.* (*bot.*) belonging to the family *Cucurbitaceae* or gourds.
CUD, [kud], *n.* food which ruminating animals return to the mouth to chew at leisure; **to chew the c.**, to ponder. [OE. *cwidu*].
CUDBEAR, [kud'-bāer], *n.* (*bot.*) the lichen, *Lecanora tartarea*, used in dyeing purple. [Dr. *Cuthbert* Gordon].
CUDDLE (**1**), [kudl], *n.* a hug, an embrace.
CUDDLE (**2**), [kudl], *v.t.* *and i.* to hug, to embrace warmly, to fondle; **c. up**, to lie close together, to curl up in sleeping. [Unkn.].
CUDDY (**1**), [kud'-i], *n.* (*naut.*) a small cabin under the poop where the officers dine. [Unkn.].
CUDDY (**2**), [kud'-i], *n.* a donkey; the coal-fish; (*fig.*) a stupid fool. [Uncert.].
CUDGEL (**1**), [kuj'-el], *n.* a short heavy thick stick, a stout club; **to take up the cudgels**, to defend vigorously. [OE. *cycgel].
CUDGEL (**2**), (**cudgelling**, **cudgelled**), [kuj'-el], *v.t.* to beat with a cudgel; **to c. one's brains**, to rack one's brains, puzzle over.
CUDWEED, [kud'-wēd], *n.* a species of *Gnaphalium*; **c. moth**, *Cucullia gnaphalii*; **mountain c.**, *Antennaria dioica*.
CUE (**1**), [kew], *n.* the last words of a speech in a play, forming a guide or signal to an actor to enter or begin speaking; (*mus.*) a lead in, a signal to begin playing or singing after a rest; (*fig.*) a hint, a lead; a guide to the attitude to adopt. [Uncert.].
CUE (**2**), [kew], *n.* a pigtail, the plait of hair attached to the back of a wig; a long slender tapering rod with a leather tip used in billiards, etc. [Fr. *queue* from L. *coda* a tail].
CUFF (**1**), [kuf], *n.* a blow with the open palm. [CUFF (3)].
CUFF (**2**), [kuf], *n.* the lower portion of the sleeve, often starched or ornamental; the strengthened band at the end of a shirt-sleeve, by which it is fastened round the wrist; (*pl.*) (*coll.*) handcuffs. [ME. *coffe*].
CUFF (**3**), [kuf], *v.t.* to give a cuff or succession of cuffs to. [Swed. *kuffa* to beat].
CUFF-LINK, [kuf'-lingk], *n.* two small and often ornamental pieces of metal, joined by a short link, and used to fasten the cuff of a shirt-sleeve round the wrist.
CUFIC, KUFIC, [kew'-fik], *n.* the style of writing Arabic which originated at Cufa. [*Kufa*, an ancient city near Babylon].
CUINAGE†, see COINAGE.
CUIRASS, [kwi-ras'], *n.* a piece of body-armour of leather or metal. [Fr. *cuirasse*].
CUIRASSIER, [kwi-ras-ēer'], *n.* a cavalryman wearing a cuirass. [Fr. *cuirassier*].
CUIR-BOUILLY, [kwēer'-bōō-yē'], *n.* leather boiled and treated with certain gums to harden it. [Fr. *cuir-bouilli* boiled leather].
CUISH, see CUISSE.
CUISINE, [kwiz-ēn'], *n.* the cooking department; cookery; style of cooking. [Fr. *cuisine*].
CUISINERIE, [kwiz-ēn'-er-ē'], *n.* cookery.

CUIRASS

CUISSE, CUISH, [kwēs, kwish], *n.* armour protecting the thighs. [Fr. *cuisse*].
CULCH, CULTCH, [kulch], *n.* rubbish; a mass of shells or other hard substances forming an oyster-bed. [OFr. *culche* couch].
CULDEE, [kul'-dē], *n.* a member of an old order of monks settled in the west of Scotland, Ireland, and Wales. [OIr. *céle dé* servant of God].
CUL-DE-FOUR, [kul'-de-fōōer'], *n.* (*arch.*) a low spherical arched vault shaped like an oven. [Fr. *cul de four* furnace bottom].
CUL-DE-SAC, [kul'-de-sak'], *n.* a street or passage closed at one end; (*fig.*) a situation offering no way of escape. [Fr. *cul de sac* bottom of a bag].
CULET, [kew'-let], *n.* the flat plane forming the base of a diamond when cut; (*pl.*) overlapping plates of armour to protect the bottom of the back and buttocks. [OFr. *culet*].
CULEX, [kew'-leks], *n.* (*entom.*) a genus of insects including gnats and mosquitoes. [L. *culex*].
CULICIFORM, [kew-lis'-i-fawm], *adj.* in the form of a gnat.
CULINARY, [ku'-lin-er-i], *adj.* pertaining to a kitchen or cookery; that may be cooked and eaten. [L. *culinarius*].
CULL (**1**), [kul], *n.* anything selected, an animal weeded out from the flock.
CULL (**2**), [kul], *v.t.* to pick out, to gather; to select, collect. [OFr. *cuillir*].
CULLENDER, see COLANDER.
CULLET, [kul'-it], *n.* broken glass to be melted down again. [Fr. *collet* little neck].
CULLING, [kul'-ing], *n.* the act or process of selecting or gathering; the thing culled.
CULLION, [kul'-yun], *n.* a rascal. [OFr. *coillon* testicle].
CULLIONLY†, [kul'-yun-li], *adj.* mean, base, like a cullion.
CULLIS, [kul'-is], *n.* meat broth; strained jelly. [OFr. *coleis*].
CULLY (**1**), [kul'-i], *n.* a gullible fool, a dupe; (*slang*) a friend. [CULLION].

CULLY (2), [kul'-i], *v.t.* (*slang*) to impose on, cheat.
CULLYISM, [kul'-i-izm], *n.* the state of being a cully.
CULM (1), [kulm], *n.* (*bot.*) the jointed hollow stalk or stem of grasses. [L. *culmus* a stalk].
CULM (2), [kulm], *n.* slack, coal-dust; slack from anthracite, an inferior shaly coal; (*geol.*) deposits of shale. [Unkn.].
CULMIFEROUS, [kul-mif'-er-us], *adj.* full of culm coal. [CULM and L. *ferre* to bear].
CULMINANT, [kul'-min-ant], *adj.* having reached its topmost point; (*astron.*) at the zenith. [L. *culminans*].
CULMINATE, [kul'-min-āt], *v.i.* (*astron.*) to reach the zenith; (*fig.*) to reach the highest point, to attain the highest point of development; to come to a head. [L. *culminare*].
CULMINATION, [kul'-min-ā'-shun], *n.* the highest point attained; (*astron.*) the highest altitude reached by a heavenly body.
CULPABILITY, [kulp'-ab-il'-i-ti], *n.* culpableness. [L. *culpabilitas*].
CULPABLE, [kulp'-abl], *adj.* censurable, criminal, blameworthy. [L. *culpabilis*].
CULPABLENESS, [kulp'-abl-nes], *n.* the quality of being culpable.
CULPABLY, [kulp'-ab-li], *adv.* in culpable fashion.
CULPRIT, [kul'-prit], *n.* a guilty person, offender, one responsible for a crime; (*leg.*) a prisoner brought to trial. [AFr. *culp(able)* guilty and OFr. *prist* ready].
CULT, [kult], *n.* a system of religious worship with its particular ritual or observances; devotion or homage paid to anything or anyone; adoration, worship; (*coll.*) a popular fad or fashion. [L. *cultus* worship].
CULTCH, see CULCH.
CULTIVABLE, [kul'-tiv-abl], *adj.* cultivatable. [Fr. *cultivable*].
CULTIVATABLE, [kul'-tiv-āt-abl], *adj.* able to be cultivated.
CULTIVATE, [kul'-tiv-āt], *v.t.* to till, to prepare land for the raising of crops; to grow; (*fig.*) to improve, develop by labour or study, to foster. [L. *cultivare*].
CULTIVATED, [kul'-tiv-āt-id], *adj.* tilled; (*fig.*) possessing culture, refined.
CULTIVATION, [kul'-tiv-ā'-shun], *n.* the art or practice of cultivating, the state of being cultivated; culture.
CULTIVATOR, [kul'-tiv-āt'-er], *n.* one who cultivates; that which serves to cultivate, an agricultural machine for tilling the land.
CULTRATE, [kul'-trāt], *adj.* in the form of a pruning-knife; knife-edged. [L. *cultratus*].
CULTRATED, [kul'-trāt-id], *adj.* cultrate.
CULTRIFORM, [kul'-tri-fawm], *adj.* cultrate.
CULTURAL, [kul'-cher-al], *adj.* of, or pertaining to, culture.
CULTURE, [kul'-cher], *n.* cultivation; the artificial rearing of plants, animals, germs, etc.; the things so reared; (*fig.*) the education of the mind for improvement and refinement; the result of such education; possession of a correct, sensitive taste, rational judgment, refinement of manner, and highly developed intellectual outlook; a form of civilization or state of intellectual progress. [L. *cultura*].
CULTURELESS, [kul'-cher-les], *adj.* devoid of culture.
CULTURIST, [kul'-cher-ist], *n.* a cultivator.
CULTUS, [kul'-tus], *n.* cult. [L. *cultus*].
CULVER, [kul'-ver], *n.* a pigeon, wood-pigeon. [OE. *culfre* dove].
CULVER-HOUSE, [kul'-ver-hows'], *n.* a dovecote.
CULVERT, [kul'-vert], *n.* a large pipe or enclosed brick drain for conveying water beneath a road, canal, etc. [Uncert.].
CUMBENT, [kum'-bent], *adj.* lying down, reclining. [L. *cumbens*].
CUMBER (1), [kum'-ber], *n.* an encumbrance.
CUMBER (2), [kum'-ber], *v.t.* to burden, hinder, to restrict or obstruct freedom of movement by unwieldiness. [OFr. *combrer*].
CUMBERLESS, [kum'-ber-les], *adj.* unhampered, unburdened.
CUMBERSOME, [kum'-ber-sum], *adj.* burdensome, difficult to manage on account of its weight or size.
CUMBERSOMELY, [kum'-ber-sum-li], *adv.* in a cumbersome fashion.
CUMBERSOMENESS, [kum'-ber-sum-nes], *n.* the quality of being cumbersome.
CUMBER-WORLD†, [kum'-ber-wurld'], *n.* one who merely gets in the way.
CUMBRANCE†, [kum'-brants], *n.* trouble; an encumbrance.
CUMBRIAN, [kum'-bri-an], *adj.* pertaining to Cumberland. [L. *Cumbria*, an ancient British kingdom].
CUMBROUS, [kum'-brus], *adj.* cumbersome. [CUMBER].
CUMBROUSLY, [kum'-brus-li], *adv.* in a cumbrous fashion.
CUMBROUSNESS, [kum'-brus-nes], *n.* the condition of being cumbrous.
CUMIN, [kum'-in], *n.* (*bot.*) a plant, *Cuminum Cyminum*, with bitterish, pungent, carminative seeds. [Heb. *kammon*].
CUMMERBUND, KAMARBAND, [kum'-er-bund], *n.* a sash worn round the waist. [Pers. *kamarband* loin-cloth].
CUMQUAT, [kum'-kwot], *n.* a fruit like a small orange, with a sweet rind and sharp bitter pulp. [Chin. *kin ku* golden orange].
CUMULATE, [kewm'-yōō-lāt'], *v.t. and i.* to accumulate. [L. *cumulare*].
CUMULATION, [kewm'-yōō-lā'-shun], *n.* accumulation.
CUMULATIVE, [kewm'-yōō-lat-iv], *adj.* continually piling up or increasing; increasing in force by successive accumulations; **c. vote,** a system of voting by which each voter may keep all his votes for only one candidate; **c. preference shares,** (*comm.*) shares entitling the holder to a special dividend before other shareholders receive the current interest or dividend.
CUMULATIVELY, [kewm'-yōō-lat-iv-li], *adv.* by accumulation.
CUMULUS, [kewm-yōō-lus], *n.* a heap, an accumulation; a common cloud-formation in which the clouds appear as heaped-up convex masses; **cumulo-stratus,** a cloud formation combining the cumulus and the stratus and having a flattened top overhanging its base. [L. *cumulus* a heap].
CUNABULA, [kewn-ab'-yōō-la], *n.*(*pl.*) cradle; (*fig.*) a birthplace. [L. *cunabula* cradle].
CUNARDER, [kew-nahd'-er], *n.* a vessel belonging to the Cunard Line. [The *Cunard* White Star Company].
CUNCTATIVE, [kungk'-tat-iv], *adj.* delaying, dilatory. [L. *cunctatum*, *p.pt.* of *cunctari* to delay].
CUNCTATOR, [kungk-tāt'-er], *n.* one who delays. [L. *cunctator*].
CUNEAL, [kew'-ni-al], *adj.* wedge-shaped. [L. *cunealis*].
CUNEATE, [kew'-ni-āt], *adj.* (*bot.*) wedge-shaped. [L. *cuneatum*, *p.pt.* of *cuneare* to form a wedge].
CUNEATED, [kew'-ni-āt-id], *adj.* cuneate.
CUNEIFORM (1), [kew'-ni-i-fawm], *n.* cuneiform characters.
CUNEIFORM (2), [kew'-ni-i-fawm], *adj.* wedge-shaped; **c. characters,** wedge-shaped characters in which ancient Eastern inscriptions were written. [L. *cuneus* a wedge and FORM].
CUNETTE, [kew-net'], *n.* (*fort.*) a trench at the bottom of a dry ditch. [Fr. *cunette*].
CUNNER, CONNER, [kun'-er], *n.* a fish, the gilt-head, the blue perch. [Uncert.].
CUNNING (1), [kun'-ing], *n.* subtle craft, astuteness, cleverness, artfulness; (*archaic*) skill, power. [ME. *cunning* skill, knowledge].
CUNNING (2), [kun'-ing], *adj.* skilful, dexterous; wily, crafty, astute, subtle, clever, artful; ingenious. [OE. *cunnan* to know].
CUNNINGLY, [kun'-ing-li], *adv.* in cunning fashion.
CUNNINGNESS, [kun'-ing-nes], *n.* the quality of being cunning.
CUP (1), [kup], *n.* a small drinking-vessel with a handle; the contents of such a vessel; a large ornamental vessel of precious metal given as a prize in games, etc.; (*eccles.*) the vessel containing the wine used in the Communion Service; anything resembling these in shape; (*pl.*) indulgence in intoxicating liquor, drinking bout; any of the several drinks made from wine mixed with other ingredients; (*surg.*) a cupping glass; **in one's cups,** in a state of intoxication. [OE. *cuppe* from LL. *cuppa* cup].
CUP (2), (**cupping, cupped**), [kup], *v.t. and i.* (*surg.*) to apply a cupping glass to; to form into the shape of a cup.
CUP-BEARER, [kup'-bāer'-er], *n.* the official wine server in a prince's household, a person who performs a similar function at official banquets.
CUPBOARD, [kub'-erd], *n.* a large wooden cabinet fitted with shelves and doors, fastened to the wall, and used for storing domestic crockery, provisions, etc.; **c. love,** a display of affection from motives of self-interest.
CUPEL, [kew'-pel], *n.* a shallow vessel used in testing the purity of precious metals. [LL. *cupella* a cup].

CUPELLATION, [kew'-pel-ā'-shun], *n.* (*metal.*) refining or assaying by cupel.
CUPFUL, [kup'-fo͞ol], *n.* the measure of the contents of a cup when full.
CUP-GALL, [kup'-gawl], *n.* a gall found on oak-leaves.
CUPID, [kew'-pid], *n.* the Roman god of love, a representation in sculpture or painting of Cupid; (*fig.*) a beautiful young boy. [L. *Cupido*].
CUPIDITY, [kew-pid'-i-ti], *n.* an inordinate desire to possess; covetousness. [L. *cupiditas* desire].
CUPOLA, [kew'-pol-a], *n.* (*arch.*) a small dome projecting above a roof; (*metal.*) a furnace for melting; a rounded revolving gun-turret on a warship; (*anat.*) a dome-shaped organ or process. [L. *cupula*, *dim.* of *cupa* cup].

CUPOLA

CUPPED, [kupt], *adj.* bled by cupping, formed like a cup.
CUPPER, [kup'-er], *n.* one who cups.
CUPPING, [kup'-ing], *n.* (*surg.*) the application of a cupping glass to a part of the skin in order to draw an increased amount of blood to that part; **c. glass,** a cup-shaped glass vessel heated and applied to a portion of the skin in cupping.
CUPRENE, [kew'-prēn], *n.* a derivative of copper used in the manufacture of gas-masks. [L. *cuprum* copper].
CUPREOUS, [kew'-pri-us], *adj.* of or like copper. [L. *cupreus*].
CUPRIC, [kew'-prik], *adj.* (*chem.*) containing copper in its higher valency. [L. *cuprum* copper].
CUPRIFEROUS, [kew-prif'-er-us], *adj.* producing copper. [L. *cuprum* copper and *ferre* to bear].
CUPRITE, [kew'-prīt], *n.* (*min.*) ruby copper, the red oxide of copper. [L. *cuprum* copper].
CUPRO-URANITE, [kew'-prō-yo͞o'-ran-īt], *n.* hydrated phosphate of uranium and copper.
CUPROUS, [kew'-prus] *adj.* (*chem.*) containing copper in its lower valency.
CUP-TIE, [kup'-tī], *n.* a football match in a round of a knock-out competition.
CUPULA, CUPULE, [kew'-pyo͝o-la], *n.* (*bot.*) the small, hard, cup-like receptacle holding the acorn, the hazel-nut, etc.; (*zool.*) a cup-like organ; a small round cavity. [L. *cupula*, *dim.* of *cupa* cup].
CUPULIFEROUS, [kew'-pyo͝o-lif'-er-us], *adj.* bearing cupules. [L. *cupula* small cup and *ferre* to bear].
CUR, [kur], *n.* a low-bred or mongrel dog; (*fig.*) a cowardly wretch. [OIcel. *kurra* to grumble].
CURABILITY, [kew-ra-bil'-i-ti], *n.* ability to be cured.
CURABLE, [kew'-rabl], *adj.* able to be cured. [L. *curabilis*].
CURABLENESS, [kew'-rabl-nes], *n.* a curable state.
CURACOA, curaçoa, [kew'-ra-sō'-a], *n.* a liqueur flavoured with orange peel, cinnamon, and mace. [*Curaçao*, a Dutch island in the Caribbean Sea, where made].
CURACY, [kew'-ras-i], *n.* the office or post of a curate.
CURARI, CURARE, [ko͞o-rah'-ri], *n.* the poisonous extract from the bark of the tree *Strychnos toxifera*, used by South American natives for tipping arrows. [Native].
CURARINE, [kew-rah'-rēn], *n.* an alkaloid obtained from curari.
CURASSOW, [kew-ras'-ō], *n.* a bird of the genus *Crax*, resembling a turkey. [*Curaçao*, the island].
CURATE, [kew'-rat], *n.* a clergyman appointed to assist the incumbent of a parish; a priest who has the cure of souls. [LL. *curatus*].
CURATESHIP, [kew'-rat-ship], *n.* a curacy.
CURATIVE (1), [kew'-rat-iv], *n.* a remedy, a cure.
CURATIVE (2), [kew'-rat-iv], *adj.* remedial, intended to cure.
CURATOR, [kew-rāt'-er], *n.* one who is in charge of official property or possessions; an official in charge of a museum, art-gallery, library, etc.; (*Scots leg.*) a guardian appointed to manage the affairs of a minor or a lunatic. [L. *curator* custodian].
CURATORSHIP, [kew-rāt'-er-ship], *n.* the office or tenure of a curator.
CURB (1), [kurb], *n.* a chain or strap under the lower jaw of a horse and attached to the bit, used as a check; (*fig.*) a check, a framework or border round something (often spelt *kerb*), a rim round a fireplace or round the top of a well or copper; long stone setts placed lengthwise along the edge of a pavement; **c. roof,** a roof having two slopes of differing steepness on each side. [L. *curvus* bent, curved].
CURB (2), [kurb], *v.t.* to restrain, check, keep under control. [*Prec.*].
CURBLESS, [kurb'-les], *adj.* without curb or restraint.
CURCAS, [kur'-kas], *n.* the physic-nut of tropical America, *Jatropha Curcas*. [Native].
CURCULIO, [kur-kew'-li-ō], *n.* a fruit-weevil or corn-worm. [L. *curculio*].
CURCUMA, [kur'-kyo͝o-ma], *n.* a genus of plants of the ginger family, from which arrowroot and turmeric are obtained; **c. paper,** a paper stained with turmeric, used to detect the presence of an alkali. [MdL. from Arab. *kurkum*].
CURCUMIN, [kur'-kyo͝o-min], *n.* the colouring matter extracted from the roots of the turmeric plant. [*Prec.*].
CURD (1), [kurd], *n.* the thickened substance which separates and coagulates when milk is left, or treated with acid, and from which cheese is made; any substance similar to this. [ME. *curd*].
CURD (2), [kurd], *v.t. and i.* to curdle.
CURDLE, [kurdl], *v.t. and i.* to thicken into curd; to coagulate, to congeal (of blood).
CURDY, [kurd'-i], *adj.* like curd; full of curd.
CURE (1), [kew'-er], *n.* the act of curing; that which cures or is intended to cure, a remedy for disease; (*eccles.*) the spiritual care of souls, the office or parish of a priest; (*fig.*) an alleviation, remedy; vulcanization of rubber. [L. *cura*].
CURE (2), [kew'-er], *v.t.* to heal, to restore to normal health; to remedy, banish; (*fig.*) to put right, remedy, to cause a person to give up that which is harmful or evil; to preserve (foodstuffs) by salting, drying and pickling; to vulcanize (rubber). [L. *curare*].
CURE, curé, [kew'-rā], *n.* a French parish-priest. [Fr. *curé*].
CURELESS, [kew'-er-les], *adj.* incurable.
CURER, [kew'-rer], *n.* one who cures foodstuffs, etc.
CURETTE (1), [kew-ret'], *n.* (*surg.*) an instrument shaped like a small scoop. [Fr. *curette*].
CURETTE (2), [kew-ret'], *v.t. and i.* to scrape with a curette.
CURFEW, [kur'-fyo͞o], *n.* (*hist.*) the ringing of a bell at a fixed hour of the evening as a signal that all fires and lights were to be put out; the bell so rung; the time at which it was rung; a fixed time by which all persons must be within their houses. [AFr. *coever-feu* cover fire].
CURIA, [kew'-ri-a], *n.* one of the subdivisions into which the Roman tribes were divided; a senate house or public place of worship; (*hist.*) the medieval court of judicature of the king, being the supreme court; **The C.,** the Papal court. [L. *curia*].
CURIALISTIC, [kew'-ri-al-ist'-ik], *adj.* pertaining to the Papal court.
CURIE, [kew'-ri], *n.* amount of radio-activity produced by one gramme of radium. [M. and Mme. *Curie*, the discoverers of radium].
CURING-HOUSE, [kew'-er-ing-hows'], *n.* a building in which sugar is drained and dried.
CURIO, [kew'-ri-ō], *n.* an object having some unusual characteristics of value to collectors. [CURIO(SITY)].
CURIOLOGIC, see KYRIOLOGIC.
CURIOSITY, [kew'-ri-os'-i-ti], *n.* the quality of being curious; that which is curious; a curio. [L. *curiositas*].
CURIOSO, [kew'-ri-ō'-sō], *n.* (*archaic*) an admirer or collector of curios. [It. *curioso* curious person].
CURIOUS, [kew'-ri-us], *adj.* of a rare or unusual nature, surprising, strange, remarkable; odd, peculiar, singular; indecent; desirous of knowing or ascertaining, eager to obtain information about; inquisitive, displaying an unwarranted interest in what does not concern one. [L. *curiosus* careful, inquisitive].
CURIOUSLY, [kew'-ri-us-li], *adv.* in a curious manner.
CURIOUSNESS, [kew'-ri-us-nes], *n.* curiosity.
CURL (1), [kurl], *n.* a lock of hair twisted into a spiral roll or ringlet; anything resembling this in shape; (*pl.*) curly hair. [Dan. *kurle*].
CURL (2), [kurl], *v.t. and i.* to form into a curl or curls; to ripple (of water); to roll up at the edges; to play at curling; **to c. up,** (*fig.*) to collapse suddenly; to overwhelm.
CURLEW, [kur'-lew], *n.* a wading bird, *Numenius arquatus*. [OFr. *courlieue*].
CURLICUE, [kurl'-ik-ew], *n.* a quaintly-twisted curl. [CURLY and CUE (2)].

CURLINESS, [kurl'-i-nes], *n.* the quality of being curly.

CURLING (1), [kurl'-ing], *n.* a Scottish winter game resembling bowls, played on the ice with large, round flat-bottomed stones, thrust with a curling movement of the arm. [CURL (2)].

CURLING (2), [kurl'-ing], *adj.* curly, that curls.

CURLING-IRONS, [kurl'-ing-ïernz'], *n.(pl.)* curling-tongs.

CURLINGLY, [kurl'-ing-li], *adv.* in a curly fashion.

CURLING-PINS, [kurl'-ing-pinz'], *n.* clips round which locks of hair are twisted to form curls.

CURLING-TONGS, [kurl'-ing-tongz'], *n.(pl.)* a pair of tongs heated for curling the hair.

CURL-PAPER, [kurl'-pā'-per], *n.* a piece of paper into which a lock of hair is twisted and set to form a curl.

CURLY, [kurl'-i], *adj.* having curls; tending to curl; full of ripples or small waves.

CURMUDGEON, [kur-muj'-un], *n.* a bad-tempered, surly, miserable misanthrope. [Unkn.].

CURMUDGEONLY, [kur-muj'-un-li], *adj.* churlish, like a curmudgeon.

CURR, [kur], *v.i.* to coo like a dove, or purr like a cat, to snore like the barn owl. [Imitative].

CURRAGH (1), [ku'-rah], *n.* a coracle. [Ir. *curach*].

CURRAGH (2), [ku'-rah], *n.* boggy waste land, marshy swamp; **The C.**, a military camp and famous racecourse near Dublin. [Ir. *corrach* marsh].

CURRANT, [ku'-rant], *n.* a small sweet dried Levantine grape; the juicy fruit of several species of *Ribes*. [*Corinth*, in Greece, where grown].

CURRE, [kur], *n.* the golden-eye duck, *Clangula glaucion*. [Unkn.].

CURRENCY, [ku'-ren-si], *n.* the condition of being in current use; that which is current; the particular form or system of money in use in a state; value.

CURRENT (1), [ku'-rent], *n.* a continuous flow, generally in one direction, of air or water or of electricity; part of such a mass, moving at a more rapid rate than the main body; (*fig.*) course, trend, drift.

CURRENT (2), [ku'-rent], *adj.* running, flowing; in circulation; in general use at the present time; prevalent, generally accepted at the moment; present; of the latest issue. [*Prec.*].

CURRENTLY, [ku'-rent-li], *adv.* in current fashion; generally.

CURRENTNESS, [ku'-rent-nes], *n.* the state of being current.

CURRICLE (1), [ku'-rikl], *n.* a two-wheeled carriage drawn by two horses abreast. [L. *curriculum* a running].

CURRICLE (2), [ku'-rikl], *v.i.* to ride in a curricle.

CURRICULUM, [ku-rik'-yōō-lum], *n.* a course of study or training given or prescribed. [L. *curriculum* course].

CURRIER, [ku'-ri-er], *n.* one who curries and colours leather after tanning. [L. *coriarius*].

CURRISH, [kur'-ish], *adj.* like a cur; snarling, spiteful, snappish.

CURRISHLY, [kur'-ish-li], *adv.* in a currish fashion.

CURRISHNESS, [kur'-ish-nes], *n.* a currish disposition, the state of being currish.

CURRY (1), [ku'-ri], *n.* a highly-flavoured Indian dish made from stewed meat, fish, fruit, etc., seasoned with spices and turmeric; a hash or stew flavoured with this or curry-powder; **c.-powder**, a compound of strong spices and turmeric used as a sauce or relish. [Tamil *kari* sauce].

CURRY (2), [ku'-ri], *v.t.* to season with curry, to make a curry from.

CURRY (3), [ku'-ri], *v.t.* to dress leather after it is tanned; to rub down and clean (a horse's coat) with a comb; **to c. favour**, to try to win a person's favour by flattery and fawning. [OFr. *correier*].

CURRYCOMB, [ku'-ri-kōm'], *n.* a metal comb with a handle, used in currying horses' coats.

CURRYING, [ku'-ri-ing], *n.* the art of dressing tanned skins; the act of rubbing down a horse with a currycomb.

CURSE (1), [kurs], *n.* an utterance invoking evil or misfortune upon a person; a profane oath, a blasphemy; a cause or source of evil or misfortune; (*eccles.*) censure, excommunication; **c. of Scotland**, the nine of diamonds. [OE. *curs*].

CURSE (2), [kurs], *v.t. and i.* to lay under a curse; to swear (at); to regard with bitter regret; to pursue with misfortune or calamity; (*eccles.*) to excommunicate. [OE. *cursian*].

CURSED, CURST, [kurst], *adj.* blasted by a curse; deserving a curse; detestable, execrable; (*coll.*) confounded.

CURSEDLY, [kurs'-id-li], *adv.* in a cursed fashion miserably.

CURSEDNESS, [kurs'-id-nes], *n.* the state of being cursed.

CURSING, [kurs'-ing], *n.* the utterance of a curse blasphemy, swearing.

CURSITOR†, [kur'-sit-or], *n.* a clerk in the Court of Chancery, employed in drafting original writs [MedL. *cursitor* a runner].

CURSIVE, [kur'-siv], *adj.* (of handwriting) flowing in which the characters are formed and connected by curved strokes. [MedL. *cursivus*].

CURSOR, [kur'-sor], *n.* a transparent slide marked with a vertical hair-line, attached to a slide-rule to facilitate accurate readings. [L. *cursor* runner].

CURSORIAL, [kur-saw'-ri-al], *adj.* fitted for running. [L. *cursorius*].

CURSORILY, [kur'-ser-i-li], *adv.* in a cursory fashion.

CURSORINESS, [kur'-ser-i-nes], *n.* the condition of being cursory.

CURSORY, [kur'-ser-i], *adj.* hasty, hurried, superficial. [L. *cursorius* running].

CURST, see CURSED.

CURSUS, [kur'-sus], *n.* a racecourse; a ritual of prayer or celebration; a curriculum. [L. *cursus* course].

CURT, [kurt], *adj.* short, brief, terse, rudely abrupt. [L. *curtus* shortened].

CURTAIL, [ker-tāl'], *v.t.* to cut short, abridge, shorten, to cut down. [Uncert.].

CURTAILMENT, [ker-tāl'-ment], *n.* the act of curtailing; the state of being curtailed.

CURTAIL-STEP, [kur'-tāl-step'], *n.* the bottom step in a flight of stairs, ending at its outer edge in a scroll.

CURTAIN (1), [kur'-tan], *n.* a long piece of cloth hanging from a bed or window, and which can be drawn to screen it completely; a long piece of cloth drawn across a room to partition it; a sheet of heavy material which can be lowered, to conceal the stage in a theatre from the audience; the descent of this; a protective barrier; (*fig.*) anything serving as a cover or screen; (*fort.*) part of a rampart between the flanks of two bastions; **to draw a c. over**, (*fig.*) to say nothing about; **to lift the c.**, (*fig.*) to reveal, to disclose information. [LL. *cortina* a small court].

CURTAIN (2), [kur'-tan], *v.t.* to cover, screen, or partition off by a curtain.

CURTAIN-LECTURE, [kur'-tan-lek'-cher], *n.* a reproof delivered by a wife to her husband in bed.

CURTAINLESS, [kur'-tan-les], *adj.* without curtain.

CURTAIN-RAISER, [kur'-tan-rāz'-er], *n.* a short dramatic piece performed before the play of the evening.

CURTAL (1), [kur'-tal], *n.* a horse or other animal with its tail cut short. [OFr. *cortald*].

CURTAL (2), [kur'-tal], *adj.* having the tail cut short, docked, shortened, brief.

CURTAL-AXE, [kur'-tal-aks'], *n.* a short, broad, heavy sword. [*Var.* of CUTLASS].

CURTANA, [kur-tā'-na], *n.* the pointless sword carried before the kings of England at the coronation. [MedL. *curtana*].

CURTATE, [kur'-tāt], *adj.* cut short, reduced; **c. distance**, (*astron.*) the distance of a planet from the sun or earth reduced to the plane of the ecliptic. [L. *curtatus* shortened].

CURTATION, [ker-tā'-shun], *n.* (*astron.*) the difference between the actual and the curtate distance of a planet from the sun.

CURTESY, [kur'-tes-i], *n.* (*leg.*) the life interest in his wife's estate falling to a husband after her death, if there has been issue capable of inheriting. [COURTESY].

CURTILAGE, [kur'-til-ij], *n.* (*leg.*) a yard, garden, enclosure or field, around and belonging to a dwelling-house. [MedL. *curtilagium*].

CURTANA

CURTLY, [kurt'-li], *adv.* in curt fashion.

CURTNESS, [kurt'-nes], *n.* the quality of being curt.

CURTSEY (1), CURTSY, [kurt'-si], *n.* a bending of the knees as a sign of respect or acknowledgment by women. [COURTESY].

CURTSEY (2), CURTSY, [kurt'-si], *v.i.* to make a curtsey.

CURUKU-OIL, [kōō'-rōōk-ōō-oil'], *n.* a yellow oil obtained from the prickly poppy.

CURVATE, [kurv'-āt], *adj.* curvated. [L. *curvatus* curved].
CURVATED, [kurv'-āt-id], *adj.* curved.
CURVATION, [kurv-ā'-shun], *n.* bending, curving. [L. *curvatio*].
CURVATIVE, [kurv'-at-iv], *adj.* (*bot.*) having margins slightly curved.
CURVATURE, [kurv'-ach-er], *n.* the act of curving; the state of being curved; the amount of curve; a curve; (*geom.*) the rate of change of direction of the tangent per unit length of arc. [L. *curvatura* bending].
CURVE (1), [kurv], *n.* a line with a finite radius of curvature; a rounded bend, a bend not in the form of an angle; a curved part of anything. [L. *curvus* bent, curved].
CURVE (2), [kurv], *v.t. and i.* to bend in a curve, to have the form of a curve. [L. *curvare*].
CURVET (1), [kur-vet'], *n.* a leap of a horse in which the forelegs are raised together, and then, while these are still in mid-air, the hind legs are raised. [It. *corvetto* a small curve].
CURVET (2), (curvetting, curvetted), [kur-vet'], *v.i.* to perform a curvet.
CURVI-, *pref.* curved. [L. *curvus*].
CURVICAUDATE, [kurv'-i-kawd'-āt], *adj.* possessing a curved tail.
CURVICOSTATE, [kurv'-i-kos'-tāt], *adj.* marked with small curved ribs. [CURVI and L. *costa* a rib].
CURVIFOLIATE, [kurv'-i-fō'-li-āt], *adj.* having curved leaves.
CURVIFORM, [kurv'-i-fawm], *adj.* curved.
CURVILINEAL, [kurv'-i-lin'-i-al], *adj.* curvilinear.
CURVILINEAR, [kurv'-i-lin'-i-er], *adj.* bounded by, or formed of, curved lines.
CURVILINEARITY, [kurv'-i-lin'-i-a'-ri-ti], *n.* the state of being curvilinear.
CURVILINEARLY, [kurv'-i-lin'-i-er-li], *adv.* in a curvilinear way.
CURVING (1), [kurv'-ing], *n.* a curve, the state or process of forming a curve.
CURVING (2), [kurv'-ing], *adj.* in the form of a curve.
CURVIROSTRAL, [kurv'-i-ros'-tral], *adj.* having a curved beak. [CURVI and L. *rostrum* a beak].
CUSCO-BARK, [kus'-kō-bahk'], *n.* Arica bark, the bark of the South American tree, *Cinchona pubescens*. [*Cuzco*, in South America].
CUSCUS (1), [kus'-kus], *n.* a species of phalanger, found in the East Indian Archipelago, having greyish spotted fur. [Native].
CUSCUS (2), [kōōs'-kōōs], *n.* the fibrous aromatic root of the pearl-millet. [Pers. *khas-khas*].
CUSHAT, [kush'-at], *n.* the ringdove or wood-pigeon, the stockdove. [OE. *cuscote* wild pigeon].
CUSHION (1), [kŏŏsh'-un], *n.* a large pad or case of cloth, silk, etc., stuffed with soft, yielding material, and used for sitting or resting upon; anything resembling this and used to form a resilient support of anything; the hard elastic rubber lining round the raised inner sides of a billiard-table; steam left in a steam-engine, to resist the movement of the piston; the fleshy frog of a horse's hoof; **lady's c.,** (*bot.*) a species of saxifrage; **sea c.,** the sea pink, *Armeria maritima*. [AFr. *quissine* a rest for the thighs].
CUSHION (2), [kŏŏsh'-un], *v.t.* to provide with or bolster up with a cushion.
CUSHIONET, [kŏŏsh'-un-et], *n.* a small cushion.
CUSHY, [kŏŏsh'-i], *adj.* (*slang*) comfortable, pleasant, easy. [Hind. *khashi* pleasant].
CUSP, [kusp], *n.* (*geom.*) the point in a curve at which its two branches have a common tangent; (*arch.*) a projecting point from which two foils or curves spring in Gothic tracery; (*astron.*) either horn of the crescent moon; a pointed projection, a sharp pointed end of anything. [L. *cuspis* a point].

CUSP

CUSPID, [kusp'-id], *n.* a tooth with a fang or fangs. [L. *cuspis cuspidis* point].
CUSPIDAL, [kusp'-id-al], *adj.* pointed; terminating in a cusp.
CUSPIDATE, CUSPIDATED, [kusp'-id-āt(-id)], *adj.* having a cusp.
CUSPIDOR, [kusp'-id-aw(r)], *n.* a spittoon. [Portug. *cuspideira*].
CUSS, [kus], *n.* (*vulg.*) a curse; a fellow, person, customer. [CURSE, CUS(TOMER)].
CUSSEDNESS, [kus'-id-nes], *n.* obstinacy, perverseness. [CURSEDNESS].
CUSTARD, [kust'-erd], *n.* a mixture of milk and eggs, sweetened and baked or boiled to a thick consistency. [L. *crustatum* covered with a crust].
CUSTARD-APPLE, [kust'-erd-apl'], *n.* the fruit of *Anona reticulata*, a West Indian plant with a soft pulp.
CUSTODIAL (1), [kus-tō'-di-al], *n.* a vessel in which sacred objects are kept.
CUSTODIAL (2), [kus-tō'-di-al], *adj.* pertaining to custody.
CUSTODIAN, [kus-tō'-di-an], *n.* one who looks after, or is in charge of, some public building, etc.; a guardian, a keeper.
CUSTODY, [kus'-to-di], *n.* care, guardianship, responsibility for looking after; detention by imprisonment; the safe-keeping of the police; **to take into c.,** to arrest. [L. *custodia* a guard].
CUSTOM (1), [kus'-tum], *n.* habit, usual practice; established usage having the status of authority or law; continual patronage of a trader by a customer; (*pl.*) duties imposed by law upon exported or imported goods. [OFr. *custome* from L. *consuetudo*].
CUSTOM† (2), [kus'-tum], *v.t. and i.* to accustom, to give custom. [*Prec.*].
CUSTOMABLE, [kus'-tum-abl], *adj.* on which custom duties may be paid.
CUSTOMABLY, [kus'-tum-ab-li], *adv.* according to custom.
CUSTOMARILY, [kus'-tum-er-i-li], *adv.* habitually; commonly, usually.
CUSTOMARINESS, [kus'-tum-er-i-nes], *n.* the quality of being customary.
CUSTOMARY (1), [kus'-tum-er-i], *n.* a book of laws and usages established by custom.
CUSTOMARY (2), [kus'-tum-er-i], *adj.* according to custom, usual, habitual, in common practice; originating in or founded on custom. [MedL. *custumarius*].
CUSTOMER, [kus'-tum-er], *n* one who makes or intends to make a purchase from a trader, dealer, or seller; a regular purchaser or patron at a particular shop or trading establishment; (*coll.*) a person, a fellow. [MedL. *custumarius*].
CUSTOM-HOUSE, [kus'-tum-hows'], *n.* an establishment where customs revenue is collected; the place where customs duties are paid.
CUSTOS, [kus'-tos], *n.* keeper, guardian; **c. rotulorum,** the chief civil officer of a county who has charge of its rolls and records. [L. *custos* keeper].
CUT (1), [kut], *n.* the act of cutting; a smart stroke, slash; the result of cutting or being cut, a wound, mark made by cutting; that which is cut or cut off; the method or style in which anything is cut; (*print.*) an engraved block from which prints are impressed, a print obtained in this way; **a c. above,** a class superior to; **a short c.,** a more direct method of approach.
CUT (2), [kut], *adj.* divided, gashed, wounded; shaped, ornamented, or otherwise altered by cutting; detached, severed; shortened, reduced; shredded (of tobacco); **c. grass,** spear-grass; **c. and dried,** ready made, straightforward, stereotyped.
CUT (3), (cutting, cut), [kut], *v.t.* to gash, wound or make an incision by means of a sharp-edged instrument; to chisel, carve into shape; to engrave or incise marks or characters upon a hard substance; to grind, shape, and polish (gems, etc.) into facets; to detach, separate into small portions, carve; to mow, reap; to trim, crop in order to shorten (hair); to pare; to abridge, curtail; to omit, delete; to reduce in amount; (of teeth) to appear in the gums; to intersect; to deliver a smart, sharp stroke; to divide a pack of cards; to castrate, to construct (a road) by removing obstacles; to perform, execute, (*fig.*) to ignore; (*cricket*) to hit the ball with a chopping stroke; (*tennis*) to hit the under-side of the ball so as to produce back-spin; (*billiards*) to strike on its extreme edge with the cue-ball; (*slang*) to absent oneself unlawfully from; *v.i.* to gash, make an incision, sever; to be sharp enough to gash or sever easily; (*fig.*) to produce a painful smarting sensation; (*slang*) to run away, be off; **to c. no ice,** to fail to impress; **to c. to the quick,** to offend or distress deeply; **to c. a dash,** to make a show; **to c. a poor figure,** to show up in an unfavourable light; **to c. in,** (*motoring*) to speed past a car in a line of traffic, in face of oncoming traffic;

to interrupt; (*cards*) to take the place of someone else; **to c. loose,** to cease to be connected with; to behave in a frivolous, wild manner; **to c. off,** to discontinue supplies of, to exclude from, to deprive of; (of a telephone call) to disconnect; (*pass.*) to die suddenly; **to c. off with a shilling,** to disinherit; **to c. up,** to criticize severely, to censure, to review very unfavourably; to become rough and uneven; to distress sorely; **to c. up rough,** to become angry or insulting; **to c. both ways,** to have an opposite effect in addition to the one intended. [ME. *cutten*].

CUT-AND-COVER, [kut'-and-kuv'-er], *n.* (*eng.*) a method of constructing a tunnel by making a cutting for the brick-work lining, arching it over, and covering it in again.

CUTANEOUS, [kew-tā'-ni-us], *adj.* pertaining to the skin. [MedL. *cutaneus*].

CUT-AWAY, [kut'-a-wā'], *n.* (*archaic*) a coat cut so as to curve back from the waist.

CUT-BACK, [kut'-bak], *n.* (*cinema*) a repetition of shots previously shown to heighten the dramatic effect.

CUTCH, KUTCH, [kuch], *n.* catechu, tannin obtained from mangrove bark. [Malay *kachu*].

CUTCHA, [kuch'-a], *adj.* of inferior quality, poor. [Hind. *kacha* raw].

CUTCHERY, [kuch'-er-i], *n.* an Indian court-house or administrative office; a business office of a planter in India. [Hind. *kachari*].

CUTE, [kewt], *adj.* sharp, cunning, clever, keen-witted; (*U.S. slang*) attractive, pretty, charming; quaint. [Abbreviation of ACUTE].

CUTENESS, [kewt'-nes], *n.* the quality of being cute.

CUTICLE, [kewt'-ikl], *n.* the epidermis, the outer skin of animals, thin external covering of plants. [L. *cuticula* external skin].

CUTICULAR, [kewt-ik'-yōō-ler], *adj.* belonging to the cuticle.

CUTIS, [kewt'-is], *n.* the true skin beneath the cuticle. [L. *cutis*].

CUTLASS, [kut'-las], *n.* a short sword with a broad, slightly curving, single-edged blade. [Fr. *coutelas*].

CUTLER, [kut'-ler], *n.* one who makes, sells, or repairs knives or cutting instruments. [ME. *coteliere*].

CUTLERY, [kut'-ler-i], *n.* the business of a cutler; knives and other sharp-edged instruments. [OFr. *coutelerie*].

CUTLET, [kut'-let], *n.* a small chop or slice of meat cut off from the rib-bones. [Fr. *côtelette* little rib].

CUT-OFF, [kut'-of], *n.* a device in the valve-gear of a steam engine by which the steam can be cut off from the cylinder in the course of the piston-stroke; a device to prevent the flow of a liquid; a device to prevent cartridges moving from the magazine of a rifle into the breech-chamber.

CUT-OUT, [kut'-owt], *n.* (*elect.*) a device which automatically breaks the circuit of an electric current when it exceeds a fixed strength.

CUTPURSE, [kut'-purs], *n.* (*archaic*) a thief, robber, pickpocket.

CUTTER, [kut'-er], *n.* one who, or that which, cuts; one who cuts out cloth to measure; a small boat used by ships of war; a single-masted vessel with a running bowsprit, fore-and-aft rigged, with gaff mainsail, foresail, and jib; (*U.S.*) a light sledge; (*pl.*) variety of bricks, chiefly used for the arches of windows and doorways; **revenue c.,** a small fast motor vessel, used for customs purposes.

CUTTER-BAR, [kut'-er-bah(r)'], *n.* (*mech.*) the bar of a boring machine, in which the cutters are fixed.

CUT-THROAT (1), [kut'-thrōt], *n.* a murderer, an assassin, a fierce ruffian.

CUT-THROAT (2), [kut'-thrōt], *adj.* murderous, cruel; (*fig.*) merciless; **c. bridge, whist,** three-handed bridge, whist, etc.

CUTTING (1), [kut'-ing], *n.* the act of one who cuts; that which is cut out; an excavation, channel or passage cut through a hill for a railway, road, etc.; a printed extract cut out of a publication; a slip from a plant, cut off and replanted to form a new plant; a reduction in prices.

CUTTING (2), [kut'-ing], *adj.* that which cuts or is used to cut; (of wind, etc.) penetrating, biting; (*fig.*) sarcastic, intended to hurt the feelings, cruel.

CUTTINGLY, [kut'-ing-li], *adv.* in a cutting fashion.

CUTTLE-BONE, [kutl'-bōn], *n.* the internal shell of the cuttle-fish.

CUTTLE-FISH, [kutl'-fish], *n.* a marine cephalopod animal of the order *Sepiidae*, with long tentacles, and a sac from which it shoots out a black fluid when attacked. [OE. *cudele*].

CUTTY-STOOL, [kut'-i-stōōl'], *n.* a bench in old Scottish churches, where loose women were compelled to sit three Sundays for public rebuke.

CUT-WATER, [kut'-waw'-ter], *n.* (*naut.*) the forepart of a ship's prow; a wedge-shaped end of a pier of a bridge against which the current flows and is divided; an American water-fowl, *Rhynchops nigra*.

CUT-WORM, [kut'-wurm], *n.* a caterpillar, grub, or worm destructive to young cultivated plants.

CUVETTE, [kew-vet'], *n.* a shallow dish or basin; a large clay crucible to receive melted glass in making plate-glass; (*fort.*) a cunette. [Fr. *cuvette* small basin].

CYANATE, [sī'-an-āt], *n.* a salt of cyanic acid.

CYANIC, [sī-an'-ik], *adj.* blue; containing cyanogen. [Gk. *kuanos* blue].

CYANIDE, [sī'-an-īd], *n.* a salt of hydrocyanic acid, prussic acid.

CYANINE, [sī'-an-in], *n.* a blue colouring principle.

CYANITE, [sī'-an-īt], *n.* an anorthic silicate of aluminium, a hard, infusible mineral, occurring in long, thin bluish crystals. [Gk. *kuanos* blue].

CYANO-, *pref.* blue. [Gk. *kuanos* blue].

CYANOGEN, [sī-an'-ō-jen], *n.* (*chem.*) a compound radical of nitrogen and carbon, a colourless, poisonous gas. [CYANO and Gk. *genes* producing].

CYANOMETER, [sī'-an-om'-it-er], *n.* an instrument to measure the blueness of the sky.

CYANOSIS, [sī'-an-ō'-sis], *n.* a disease in which the skin becomes blue because of the lack of the normal amount of oxygen in the blood. [CYANO and Gk. *osis* state].

CYANOTYPE, [sī-an'-ō-tīp], *n.* a process of making photographs on paper treated with a cyanide.

CYANURIN, [sī'-an-yōō'-rin], *n.* a blue deposit found in urine.

CYAR, [sī'-ah(r)], *n.* the aperture of the internal ear. [Gk. *kuar*].

CYATHIFORM, [sī-ath'-i-fawm], *adj.* in the shape of a cup widening towards the top. [Gk. *kuathos* a cup and FORM].

CYCAD, [sī'-kad], *n.* a palm-like plant of the genus *Cycas*. [Gk. *koikas* Egyptian palm tree].

CYCADACEOUS, [sī-kad-ā'-shus], *adj.* belonging to, or resembling, the cycads. [*Prec.*].

CYCLAMEN, [sik'-lam-en], *n.* (*bot.*) a genus of plants related to the primrose with beautiful flowers and fleshy root-stocks; the colour of this flower. [Gk. *kuklaminos*].

CYCLAMEN

CYCLAMINE, [sik'-lam-in], *n.* a poisonous substance obtained from the roots of the cyclamen.

CYCLE (1), [sīkl], *n.* a succession of the same events regularly returning at uniform intervals of time; the period of time taken for this recurrence; a fixed period of time regularly recurring; (*astron.*) one of the heavenly circles; a long indefinite period of time, an age; a complete series, round or course; a group of poems, songs, or legends revolving round or associated with some theme; (*coll.*) a bicycle. [Gk. *kuklos* a ring].

CYCLE (2), [sīkl], *v.i.* to recur or revolve through a cycle; to ride a bicycle.

CYCLE-CAR, [sīkl'-kah(r)'], *n.* a cycle with a small car attached.

CYCLIC, [sī'-klik], *adj.* pertaining to, revolving or returning in, connected with, a cycle; **c. poets,** certain epic poets who wrote of one cycle of events, the Trojan War; **c. arrangement,** (*bot.*) growth in which leaves, etc., are attached at the same level.

CYCLICAL, [sī'-klik-al], *adj.* cyclic.

CYCLING, [sī'-kling], *n.* riding a bicycle.

CYCLIST, [sī'-klist], *n.* one who rides a cycle.

CYCLO-, *pref.* circle. [Gk. *kuklos* circle].

CYCLOGRAPH, [sī'-klō-grahf], *n.* an instrument for drawing arcs of large circles.

CYCLOID (1), [sī'-kloid], *n.* a geometrical curve described by a point in the circumference of a circle as it completes a single revolution in moving along a straight line. [CYCLO and Gk. *oeides* like].

CYCLOID

CYCLOID (2), [sī'-kloid], *adj.* circular, resembling a circle in form.

CYCLOIDAL, [sī-kloid'-al], *adj.* relating to a cycloid.

CYCLOIDEANS, [sī-kloid'-i-anz], *n.(pl.)* fishes belonging to the order *Cycloidei*, with smooth rounded scales.

CYCLOMETER, [sī-klom'-it-er], *n.* an instrument for measuring circles or circular arcs; an instrument attached to the wheel of a vehicle to record the distance travelled, by registering the number of revolutions of the wheel.

CYCLOMETRY, [sī-klom'-it-ri], *n.* the art of measuring circles. [CYCLO and Gk. *metria* measuring].

CYCLONE, [sī'-klōn], *n.* a system of winds blowing or rotating spirally inwards towards a centre of lower barometric pressure; a hurricane, a tornado, a sudden violent whirling wind, a storm. [Gk. *kuklon* moving in a circle].

CYCLONIC, [sī-klon'-ik], *adj.* pertaining to a cyclone.

CYCLONOLOGY, [sī'-klon-ol'-o-ji], *n.* the study of cyclones. [CYCLONE and Gk. *logos* speech].

CYCLONOSCOPE, [sī-klon'-o-skōp], *n.* an apparatus used to discover the centre of a cyclone. [CYCLONE and SCOPE].

CYCLOPEAN, [sī'-klō-pē'-an], *adj.* pertaining to, or resembling, the Cyclops; gigantic, vast; pertaining to an ancient style of architecture using huge blocks of unhewn or uncemented stone. [Gk. *Kuklopeios* of the Cyclops, a fabulous race of one-eyed giants].

CYCLOPEDIA, [sī'-klō-pē'-di-a], *n.* an encyclopedia. [CYCLO and Gk. *paideia* education].

CYCLOPIC, [sī-klop'-ik], *adj.* Cyclopean.

CYCLOPS, [sī'-klops], *n.* a fabulous race of one-eyed giants, in Greek mythology, dwelling in Sicily; (*zool.*) a small crustacean of the order *Copepoda*, having only one eye, which is placed in the middle of its head; a one-eyed person. [Gk. *kuklops* round-eye].

CYCLORAMA, [sī'-klō-rahm'-a], *n.* a series of pictures of a landscape or scene arranged to form a hollow cylinder round an observer. [CYCLO and Gk. *orama* spectacle].

CYCLOSIS, [sī-klō'-sis], *n.* (*bot.*) the rotation of latex or protoplasmic matter in the cells. [Gk. *kuklosis* encircling].

CYCLOSTOMATA, [sī'-klō-stom'-at-a], *n.(pl.)* the lowest class of vertebrate animals, comprising the lampreys, the hagfishes, and the extinct *Palaeosondylus*. [CYCLO and Gk. *stoma* mouth].

CYCLOSTOMOUS, [sī-klos'-tom-us], *adj.* with a circular mouth.

CYCLOSTYLE, [sī'-klos-tīl], *n.* an apparatus in the form of a pen fitted with a small toothed wheel which cuts a stencil in specially prepared paper, from which many copies of a written document may be printed. [CYCLO and STYLE].

CYDER, see CIDER.

CYESIOLOGY, [sī'-ēz-i-ol'-o-ji], *n.* that part of physiology dealing with pregnancy. [Gk. *kuesis* pregnancy and *logos* speech].

CYGNET, [sig'-net], *n.* a young swan. [L. *cygnus* swan].

CYLINDER, [sil'-in-der], *n.* the solid enclosed by a circle or other closed curve moving perpendicularly in one direction only; an object of similar form to this, a roller; (*eng.*) a cylindrical chamber in which the piston is driven; (*print.*) a hollow metal roller inking or bearing the type. [Gk. *kulindros* a roller].

CYLINDER-BLOCK, [sil'-in-der-blok'], *n.* the main casting containing the group of cylinders of an engine.

CYLINDER-HEAD, [sil'-in-der-hed'], *n.* the detachable end of an engine's cylinder.

CYLINDRACEOUS, [sil'-in-drā'-shus], *adj.* cylindrical.

CYLINDRIC, [sil-in'-drik], *adj.* cylindrical.

CYLINDRICAL, [sil-in'-drikl], *adj.* having the shape of a cylinder.

CYLINDRICALLY, [sil-in'-drik-a-li], *adv.* in a cylindrical manner.

CYLINDRICITY†, [sil'-in-dris'-i-ti], *n.* a cylindrical form.

CYLINDRIFORM, [sil-in'-dri-fawm], *adj.* cylindrical.

CYLINDROID, [sil'-in-droid], *n.* a solid body like a cylinder, the ends of which form an ellipse. [CYLINDER and Gk. *oeides* like].

CYLIX, [sī'-liks], *n.* a shallow bowl-shaped drinking-cup with two handles, used by the ancient Greeks. [Gk. *kulix*].

CYMA, CIMA, [sī'-ma], *n.* (*arch.*) the moulding of a cornice the profile of which is formed of a convex curve joined to a concave curve. [Gk. *kuma* a swelling, a wave].

CYMAR, [sē'-mah(r)], *n.* a loose light undergarment worn by women; an official vestment worn by a bishop. [OFr. *simarre*].

CYMBAL, [simbl], *n.* a musical percussion instrument in the form of a thin, hollow plate of brass. [Gk. *kumbalon* a hollow cup].

CYMBAL

CYMBIFORM, [sim'-bi-fawm], *adj.* shaped like a boat. [Gk. *kumbe* a boat and FORM].

CYMBOCEPHALIC, [sim'-bō-sef'-al-ik], *adj.* having a long boat-shaped head. [Gk. *kumbe* boat and *kephale* head].

CYME, [sīm], *n.* (*bot.*) a flowering process in which the principal single-flowered stem bears several single-flowered stems, which in turn bear similar stems, all the stems being of proportionate length so that a flat-topped or rounded mass of flowers is produced. [Gk. *kuma* swelling].

CYMOGRAPH, [sī'-mō-grahf], *n.* a revolving cylinder covered with graph paper on which anything is recorded. [Gk. *kuma* wave and GRAPH].

CYMOID, [sī'-moid], *adj.* like a cyme. [Gk. *kuma* wave and *oeides* like].

CYMOMETER, [sī-mom'-it-er], *n.* a device used in wireless telegraphy to measure the wavelengths. [Gk. *kuma* wave and METER].

CYMOPHANE, [sīm'-ō-fān], *n.* a variety of chrysoberyl. [Gk. *kuma* wave and *phanes* showing].

CYMOPHANOUS, [sīm-of'-an-us], *adj.* having a wavy light; opalescent.

CYMOSCOPE, [sī'-mo-skōp], *n.* a wave detector in wireless telegraphy or telephony. [Gk. *kuma* wave and SCOPE].

CYMOSE, [sī'-mōs], *adj.* containing a cyme; in the shape of a cyme. [L. *cymosus*].

CYMOUS, [sī'-mus], *adj.* cymose. [L. *cymosus*].

CYMRIC, [kim'-rik], *adj.* Welsh. [Wel. *Cymru* Wales].

CYMRY, [kim'-ri], *n.* the Welsh people. [*Prec.*].

CYNANCHE, [sin-angk'-i], *n.* (*med.*) disease of the throat and tonsils. [Gk. *kunagkhe* dog collar, sore throat].

CYNANTHROPY, [sin-an'-throp-i], *n.* a form of insanity in which a person believes he is a dog. [Gk. *kunanthropos* dog man].

CYNIC (1), [sin'-ik], *n.* a member of a group of ancient Greek philosophers who believed in rigid self-control, self-denial, and complete independence of external conditions; one incapable of seeing good in anything, a pessimistic realist. [Gk. *kunikos* like a dog].

CYNIC (2), [sin'-ik], *adj.* pertaining to the Cynics or their philosophy; cynical.

CYNICAL, [sin'-ik-al], *adj.* resembling the Cynics in philosophy or opinions; having the frame of mind of a cynic.

CYNICALLY, [sin'-ik-a-li], *adv.* in cynical fashion.

CYNICALNESS, [sin'-ik-al-nes], *n.* the quality of being cynical.

CYNICISM, [sin'-is-izm], *n.* the opinions, character, or frame of mind of a cynic; a particular example of this.

CYNOCEPHALOUS, [sī'-nō-sef'-al-us], *adj.* dog-headed. [Gk. *kunokephalos*].

CYNOSURE, [sin'-ō-shooer], *n.* (*astron.*) the northern constellation, the Little Bear; (*fig.*) a centre of attraction, an object of immediate attention or interest. [Gk. *kunosoura* dog's tail].

CYOPHORIA, [sī'-of-aw'-ri-a], *n.* the period of gestation. [Gk. *kuos* foetus and *phoros* bearing].

CYPERUS, [sī'-per-us], *n.* (*bot.*) a genus of plants of the sedge family, producing many flowered spikelets. [Gk. *kuperos* sedge].

CYPHEL, [sī'-fel], *n.* (*bot.*) the white-flowered caryophyllaceous plant, *Cherleria sedoides*. [Gk. *kuphella* ear cavity].

CYPHER, see CIPHER.

CYPHONISM, [sīf'-on-izm], *n.* (*Gk. antiq.*) a method of punishment by fastening a heavy wooden yoke or collar round the neck. [Gk. *kuphonismos* punishment by pillory].

CY-PRES, [sē'-prā'], *adj. and adv.* (*leg.*) near; to be applied to an object as near as possible to that specified by the benefactor. [AFr. *cy près* nearby].

CYPRESS (1), [sī'-pres], *n.* a genus of dark-coloured evergreen coniferous trees; the hard reddish wood of this tree; (*poet.*) the tree or its branches as the emblem of mourning. [Gk. *kuparissos*].

CYPRESS (2), CYPRUS, [sī'-pres], *n.* a light, thin, transparent, gauze-like material, often dyed black and used in mourning wear. [OFr. *Cypre* Cyprus].
CYPRIAN (1), [sip'-ri-an], *n.* an immoral woman.
CYPRIAN (2), [sip'-ri-an], *adj.* belonging to the island of Cyprus. [L. *Cyprius* of Cyprus].
CYPRINE (1), [sip'-rīn], *n.* (*min.*) a blue Norwegian variety of idocrase or vesuvianite. [L. *cyprius* of copper].
CYPRINE (2), [sip'-rīn], *adj.* pertaining to fish of the carp family. [Gk. *kuprinos* carp].
CYPRIOT, [sip'-ri-ot], *n.* an inhabitant of Cyprus. [L. *Cyprius* of Cyprus].
CYPRIPEDIUM, [sip'-ri-pē'-di-um], *n.* (*bot.*) a slipper-orchid. [Gk. *Kupris* Venus and L. *pes pedis* foot].
CYPRIS, (*pl.* **cyprides**), [sī'-pris], *n.* a genus of small freshwater bivalve crustaceans, swimming by means of cilia. [Gk. *Kupris* Venus].
CYPRUS, see CYPRESS (2).
CYRENAIC, [sī'-ren-ā'-ik], *adj.* pertaining to the Hedonistic school of philosophy originated by Aristippus of Cyrene. [Gk. *kurenaikos* of Cyrene].
CYRILLIC, [si-ril'-ik], *adj.* pertaining to the Slavonic alphabet. [St. *Cyril*, its supposed inventor].
CYRIOLOGIC, see KYRIOLOGIC.
CYST, [sist], *n.* a membranous cavity in the body containing fluid; a closed sac containing pus or other morbid matter. [Gk. *kustis* bladder].
CYSTI-, CYSTO-, *pref.* a cyst or bladder. [Gk. *kustis* bladder].
CYSTIC, [sist'-ik], *adj.* pertaining to, resembling or containing, cysts; pertaining to the gall-bladder or urinary bladder.
CYSTICLE, [sist'-ikl], *n.* a small cyst.
CYSTIFORM, [sist'-i-fawm], *adj.* in the form of a cyst.
CYSTINE, [sist'-in], *n.* a yellowish crystalline organic base occurring in a certain type of urinary calculus.
CYSTITIS, [sis-tī'-tis], *n.* inflammation of the bladder. [CYST and Gk. *itis* denoting inflammation].
CYSTOCELE, [sist'-ō-sēl], *n.* a rupture of the urinary bladder. [CYST and Gk. *kele* tumour].
CYSTOID, [sist'-oid], *adj.* like a cyst. [CYST and Gk. *oeides* like].
CYSTOMA, [sist-ō'-ma], *n.* a tumour full of cysts. [CYST and Gk. *oma* denoting disease].
CYSTOSCOPE, [sist'-os-kōp'], *n.* an instrument used to examine the inside of the bladder. [CYST and SCOPE].
CYSTOSE†, [sist'-ōs], *adj.* containing cysts.
CYSTOTOMY, [sist-ot'-omi], *n.* the operation of cutting into the bladder to remove a stone, etc. [CYST and Gk. *tome* cutting].
CYTHEREAN, [sith'-er-ē'-an], *adj.* belonging, or pertaining, to Venus. [Gk. *Kuthereia* Venus].
CYTISIN, [sit'-is-in], *n.* a poisonous alkaloid substance from the ripe seeds of the laburnum. [Gk. *kutisos* a shrubby plant].
CYTOBLAST, [sī'-tō-blahst], *n.* the nucleus of a cell [Gk. *kutis* hollow and *blastos* germ].
CYTOGENOUS, [sī-toj'-en-us], *adj.* cell-forming [Gk. *kutis* hollow and *genes* producing].
CYTOLOGICAL, [sīt'-ō-loj'-ikl], *adj.* of, or pertaining to, cytology.
CYTOLOGIST, [sīt-ol'-ō-jist], *n.* one who studies cytology.
CYTOLOGY, [sīt-ol'-ō-ji], *n.* the study of cell-division in its bearing on heredity. [Gk. *kutos* vessel and *logos* speech].
CYTOPLASM, [sī'-tō plazm], *n.* the protoplasm of a living cell. [Gk. *kutos* hollow and PLASM].
CZAR, [zah(r)], *n.* a king, a chief, the title of the former emperors of Russia. [Russ. *tsar* from L. *Caesar* emperor].
CZARDAS, [zah'-das, chah'-dash], *n.* a native Hungarian dance; music written for this. [Hung. *czardas*].
CZAREVITCH, [zah'-rev-ich], *n.* the title of the eldest son of the former emperors of Russia. [Russ. *tsarevitch* son of a czar].
CZAREVNA, [zah-rev'-na], *n.* a daughter of the former emperors of Russia. [Russ. *tsarevna*].
CZARINA, [zah-rē'-na], *n.* a title of the former empress of Russia. [Russ. *tsarina*].
CZARISM, [zah'-rism], *n.* autocratic government by a czar.
CZECH (1), [chek], *n.* a native of Bohemia or Moravia the language of this people. [Polish *Čech*].
CZECH (2), [chek], *adj.* pertaining to the Czechs or their language.
CZECHISH, [chek'-ish], *adj.* Czech.
CZECHO-SLOVAK, [chek'-ō-slō'-vak], *adj.* pertaining to Czecho-Slovakia.

D

D, [dē], the fourth letter in the English alphabet; (*mus.*) the second note of the scale of C major; (Roman numerals) 500.
DAB (1), [dab], *n.* a light tap, a gentle blow; that which is dabbed on; a dabber. [DAB (4)].
DAB (2), [dab], *n.* (*coll.*) an expert at anything. [Unkn.].
DAB (3), [dab], *n.* a sea flatfish frequenting sandy places. [Unkn.].
DAB (4), [dab], *v.t.* to apply by dabbing; *v.i.* to touch lightly, to repeat this action for a time. [ME. *dabben*].
DABBER, [dab'-er], *n.* that which dabs; (*print.*) a ball or pad for inking type.
DABBLE, [dabl], *v.t. and i.* to dip repeatedly in, to play with, or splash about in, water; to make wet with little splashes; (*fig.*) to take a superficial interest in anything, to meddle with. [DAB].
DABBLER, [dab'-ler], *n.* a person who dabbles.
DABBLINGLY, [dab'-ling-li], *adv.* in a dabbling fashion.
DABCHICK, [dab'-chik], *n.* a small species of grebe, *Podiceps fluviatilis*; the moorhen.
DABSTER, [dab'-ster], *n.* (*slang*) an expert.
DA CAPO, [dah'-kah'-pō], (*mus.*) repeat from the beginning. [It. *da capo* from the beginning].
DACE, [dās], *n.* a freshwater fish, *Leuciscus vulgaris*. [OFr. *dars*].
DACHSHUND, [daks'-hoond], *n.* a variety of long-nosed dog, long in the body, with short, bandy legs. [Germ. *dachshund* badgerhound].
DACOIT, DAKOIT, [dak-oit'], *n.* a member of a gang of Burmese thieves; a river pirate. [Hind. *dacait*].
DACOITY, DAKOITY, [dak-oit'-i], *n.* the practices of a dacoit.
DACRYOMA, [dak'-ri-ō'-ma], *n.* a tumour on the lachrymal duct. [Gk. *dakruon* tear].
DACTYL, [dak'-til], *n.* a finger, toe; (*pros.*) a foot of one long and two short syllables. [Gk. *daktulos*].
DACTYLAR, [dak'-til-er], *adj.* connected with the finger or toe; (*pros.*) dactylic.
DACTYLIC (1), [dak-til'-ik], *n.* a dactylic line of verse; a poem in this metre.
DACTYLIC (2), [dak-til'-ik], *adj.* relating to a dactyl [Gk. *daktulikos*].
DACTYLIOGLYPH, [dak-til'-i-ō-glif'], *n.* the engraved name of the artist on a finger-ring or gem a jewel engraver. [DACTYL and Gk. *gluphos* carving].
DACTYLIOGLYPHY, [dak-til'-i-og'-lif-i], *n.* the art of engraving gems.
DACTYLION, [dak-til'-i-on], *n.* (*surg.*) the organic adhesion of two fingers.
DACTYLIST, [dak'-til-ist], *n.* one expert in writing dactylics.
DACTYLOLOGY, [dak'-til-ol'-ō-ji], *n.* the study and use of the dumb alphabet; conversation by signs of the fingers. [DACTYL and Gk. *logos* word].
DACTYLOMANCY, [dak-til'-ō-man-si], *n.* divination by means of finger-rings. [DACTYL and Gk. *manteia* divination].
DACTYLOPTERUS, [dak'-til-op'-ter-us], *n.* (*zool.*) the flying gurnard. [DACTYL and Gk. *pteron* wing].
DACTYLORHIZA, [dak'-til-o-rīz'-a], *n.* finger-and-toe disease attacking turnips. [DACTYL and Gk. *rhiza* root].
DAD, [dad], *n.* a father. [Unkn.].
DADDA, [dad'-a], *n.* a father. [*Prec.*].

DADDLE, [dadl], *v.i.* to stagger like a child. [Unkn.].
DADDY, [dad'-i], *n.* father. [DAD].
DADDY-LONGLEGS, [dad'-i-long'-legz], *n.* a crane-fly of the genus *Tipula.*
DADE, [dād], *v.t. and i.* to hold up by leading-strings while walking; to toddle. [Uncert.].
DADO, [dā'-dō], *n.* (*arch.*) the square part between the cornice and base of a pedestal; the wainscoting of a wall; the decorated part of a wall close to the floor. [It. *dado*].
DAEDAL, [dēdl], *adj.* skilful, intricate. [Gk. *Daidalos,* a mythical builder].
DAEDALIAN, [dēd-ā'-li-an], *adj.* daedal.
DAEDALOUS, [dē'-dal-us], *adj.* (*bot.*) irregularly jagged.
DAFFODIL, [daf'-od-il], *n.* (*bot.*) a yellow spring flower of the genus *Narcissus*; a pale yellow colour. [Gk. *asphodelos*].
DAFT, [dahft], *adj.* foolish, idiotic. [OE. *gedæfte* meek].
DAG (1), [dag], *n.* a shred, a loose end; a slash in a garment; a leather latchet. [Uncert.].
DAG† (2), [dag], *n.* an old-fashioned pistol. [Unkn.].
DAGGER, [dag'-er], *n.* a short double-edged weapon for stabbing; (*fencing*) a blunt blade having a basket hilt; (*print.*) a mark of reference shaped like a dagger (†), or a double-dagger (‡); **at daggers drawn,** at enmity. [Fr. *dague*].
DAGGLE, [dagl], *v.t.* to drag in wet grass and mud. [Uncert.].
DAGGLE-TAIL (1), [dagl'-tāl], *n.* a woman with dirty torn skirts, a slut.
DAGGLE-TAIL (2), [dagl'-tāl], *adj.* dirty-skirted, having muddy clothes.
DAG-LOCK, [dag'-lok'], *n.* wool on a sheep that drags in the wet.
DAGO, [dā'-gō], *n.* (*slang*), a person of dark complexion; a half-breed. [Span. *Diego* James].
DAGOBA, [dag-ō'-ba], *n.* a Buddhist temple in Ceylon. [Singhalese *dagaba*].
DAGON, [dā'-gon], *n.* the Philistine god of farmers. [Heb. *dagon* little fish].
DAG-SWAIN, [dag'-swān], *n.* a coarse woollen fabric; a cover of such material. [Unkn.].
DAG-TAILED, [dag'-tāld], *adj.* daggle-tail.
DAGUERREOTYPE (1), [dag-āer'-ō-tīp], *n.* a photograph on a glass or metal plate which has an emulsion developed in mercury vapour. [L. *Daguerre,* the inventor].
DAGUERREOTYPE (2), [dag-āer'-ō-tīp], *v.t.* to photograph by the daguerreotypic process.
DAGUERREOTYPIC, [dag-āer-ō-tip'-ik], *adj.* relating to daguerreotype.
DAHABIAH, [dah'-hab-ē'-a], *n.* a passenger-boat plying on the Nile with a large triangular sail and accommodation for oarsmen. [Arab. *dahabiya*].

DAHABIAH

DAHLIA, [dā'-li-a], *n.* (*bot.*) a much-cultivated herbaceous plant with large bright flowers, originally from Mexico. [A. *Dahl,* a Swedish botanist].
DAHLIN, [dāl'-in], *n.* a starch-like substance extracted from the roots of the dahlia.
DAI, [dī], *n.* a wet-nurse. [Hind. *dai*].
DAIL-EIREANN, [dawl'-āer'-an], *n.* the lower chamber of the Irish parliament. [Ir. *dail eireann* council of Ireland].
DAILY (1), [dā'-li], *n.* a newspaper published every day; a maid-servant who does not live in.
DAILY (2), [dā'-li], *adj.* happening, issued every day; **d. bread,** one's means of livelihood.
DAILY (3), [dā'-li], *adv.* on every day. [OE. *dæglic*].
DAIMIO, [dīm'-i-ō], *n.* a member of the Japanese aristocracy. [Jap. *dai* great and *myo* name].
DAINTILY, [dān'-ti-li], *adv.* in a dainty manner.
DAINTINESS, [dān'-ti-nes], *n.* the condition of being dainty.
DAINTY (1), [dān'-ti], *n.* a delicacy, something very pleasant to the palate. [OFr. *deinté* from L. *dignitas*].
DAINTY (2), [dān'-ti], *adj.* fastidious, delicate, elegant; affectedly refined.
DAIRY (1), [dāer'-i], *n.* the building or room in a farm for making and storing butter and cheese; a shop where milk, eggs, etc., are sold. [ME. *deierie*].
DAIRY (2), [dāer'-i], *adj.* relating to, or made in, a dairy.
DAIRY-FARM, [dāer'-i-fahm'], *n.* a farm dealing only in dairy produce.
DAIRYING, [dāer'-i-ing], *n.* the business of running a dairy.
DAIRYMAID, [dāer'-i-mād], *n.* a woman employed in a dairy.
DAIRYMAN, [dāer'-i-man], *n.* a man who keeps or works for a dairy.
DAIS, [dā'-is], *n.* a raised platform placed usually at one end of a room. [OFr. *deis*].
DAISIED, [dāz'-id], *adj.* full of, decorated with, daisies.
DAISY, [dā'-zi], *n.* (*bot.*) a small, composite, wild plant of the genus *Bellis,* having white petals and a yellow centre. [OE. *dæges-eage* the day's eye].
DAISY-BUSH, [dā'-zi-bŏŏsh'], *n.* (*bot.*) a plant belonging to the genus *Olearia.*
DAISY-CHAIN, [dā'-zi-chān'], *n.* a string of daisies fastened together by their stems.
DAISYCUTTER, [dā'-zi-kut'-er], *n.* (*cricket*) a ball sent along very fast and close to the ground; a horse that barely lifts its hooves.
DAK, [dahk], *n.* a system of transmitting letters in the East. [Hind. *dak*].
DAKER, [dā'-ker], *n.* ten in number. [~DICKER].
DAKOIT, see DACOIT.
DAKOITY, see DACOITY.
DAL, see DHAL.
DALAI-LAMA, [dal-ī'-lah'-ma], *n.* the ruler of Tibet, believed, after death, to be reincarnated in his successor. [Native].
DALE, [dāl], *n.* a valley. [OE. *dæl,* OScand. *dalr*].
DALESMAN, [dālz'-man], *n.* a person who lives in the northern dales.
DALI, [dah'-li], *n.* a large South American tree. [Native].
DALLIANCE, [dal'-i-ans], *n.* dallying. [OFr. *daliance*].
DALLOP, [dal'-op], *n.* a tuft or clump, a lump of anything. [~DOLLOP].
DALLY, [dal'-i], *v.i.* to waste time, to trifle; to play or flirt with; (*fig.*) to contemplate (a scheme or idea). [AFr. *dalier* to chat].
DALLYING, [dal'-i-ing], *n.* the act of one who dallies.
DALMATIAN, [dal-mā'-shun], *n.* a breed of spotted dog, originally bred in Dalmatia.

DALMATIAN

DALMATIC, [dal-mat'-ik], *n.* a robe with wide sleeves, worn by kings at their coronation, and by deacons and bishops. [L. *dalmatica* (*tunica*) a robe of Dalmatian wool].
DALTONIAN, [dawl-tōn'-i-an], *n.* a colour-blind person. [J. *Dalton,* a famous chemist so affected].
DALTONISM, [dawl'-ton-izm], *n.* colour-blindness.
DAM (1), [dam], *n.* a female parent. [DAME].
DAM (2), [dam], *n.* an obstruction built across a river to control its flow. [ME. *dam*].
DAM (3), [dam], *n.* an Indian copper coin worth a fortieth of a rupee. [Hind. *dam*].
DAM (4), (damming, dammed), *v.t.* to obstruct with a dam. [DAM (2)].
DAMAGE (1), [dam'-ij], *n.* injury to an object, person or a reputation; (*coll.*) the estimated cost of repair; (*pl.*) (*leg.*) amount of money claimed or awarded as compensation; **d. feasant,** (*leg.*) compensation claimed for damage to property by cattle. [OFr. *damage*].
DAMAGE (2), [dam'-ij], *v.t.* to injure, reduce the value of.
DAMAGEABLE, [dam'-ij-abl], *adj.* liable to be damaged.
DAMAR, see DAMMAR.
DAMASCENE (1), [dam'-a-sēn'], *n.* a damson. [L. *Damascenus* of Damascus].
DAMASCENE (2), [dam'-a-sēn'], *adj.* relating to Damascus.
DAMASCENE (3), [dam'-a-sēn'], *v.t.* to decorate (steel) with gold and silver patterns.
DAMASK (1), [dam'-ask], *n.* a fabric of silk or linen with a raised pattern woven into it; the colour of the damask rose; steel made in Damascus. [*Damascus,* a place in Syria].
DAMASK (2), [dam'-ask], *adj.* of the colour of a damask rose.
DAMASK (3), [dam'-ask], *v.t.* to weave a pattern on

fabrics; to decorate steel in the Damascene fashion.
DAMASKIN, [dam'-ask-in], *n.* a Damascus or damascened sword.
DAMASK-ROSE, [dam'-ask-rōz'], *n.* a pink rose from Damascus.
DAMASK-STEEL, [dam'-ask-stēl'], *n.* a fine steel made in the Levant for sword blades.
DAMASSIN, [dam'-as-in], *n.* a type of damask cloth interwoven with flowers of gold and silver. [Fr. *damas* Damask].
DAME, [dām], *n.* a woman holding authority; the wife of a baronet or knight; a female knight of the Order of the British Empire; **dame's school**, a kindergarten school run by a woman. [OFr. *dame* from L. *domina*].
DAME'S-VIOLET, [dāmz'-vī'-o-let], *n.* (*bot.*) the plant *Hesperis matronalis*.
DAMMAR, DAMAR, [dam'-ah(r)], *n.* a pine resin extracted from *Agathis Dammara*. [Malay *damar*].
DAMN (1), [dam], *n.* (an oath); (*coll.*) a jot. [DAMN (2)].
DAMN (2), [dam], *v.t.* to pass a sentence of eternal punishment on, to condemn; to swear, curse; to ruin a reputation, to criticize heavily. [L. *damnare*].
DAMNABILITY, [dam'-na-bil'-it-i], *n.* the quality of being damnable.
DAMNABLE, [dam'-nabl], *adj.* worthy of damnation.
DAMNABLENESS, [dam'-nabl-nes], *n.* the condition of being damnable.
DAMNABLY, [dam'-nab-li], *adv.* in a damnable fashion.
DAMNATION, [dam-nā'-shun], *n.* the act of damning; the state of being damned. [L. *damnatio*].
DAMNATORY, [dam'-na-ter-i], *adj.* effecting condemnation, condemnatory. [L. *damnatorius*].
DAMNIFIC, [dam-nif'-ik], *adj.* causing damage or loss, pernicious. [L. *damnificus*].
DAMNIFICATION, [dam'-ni-fik-ā'-shun], *n.* the act of injuring.
DAMNIFY†, [dam'-ni-fī], *v.t.* to cause damage to. [L. *damnificare*].
DAMNING, [dam'-ing], *adj.* causing or exposing to damnation.
DAMNINGNESS†, [dam'-ing-nes], *n.* the quality of being damning.
DAMOCLEAN, [dam'-ōk-lē'-an], *adj.* constantly menacing. [Gk. *Damokles*, over whose head a sword was hung on a thread by Dionysius the tyrant].
DAMOSEL, [dam'-ō-zel], *n.* a maid, a virgin. [~DAMSEL].
DAMP (1), [damp], *n.* humidity, slight wetness; moist vapour, fog; gas accumulating in coal-mines; (*fig.*) dejection; **choke-d.**, carbonic acid gas; **fire-d.**, noxious explosive gas in coal-mines. [Du. *damp*].
DAMP (2), [damp], *adj.* moist, humid.
DAMP (3), [damp], *v.t.* to make damp, to slow the combustion of a boiler fire by checking the entry of air; (*fig.*) to depress, discourage; (*mus.*) to stop the vibration of a string.
DAMPEN, [damp'-en], *v.t.* to make damp.
DAMPER, [damp'-er], *n.* a person or thing which damps; an iron plate controlling the draught in a furnace; (*mus.*) a felt pad checking the vibration of a piano string.
DAMPING, [damp'-ing], *n.* the rate at which wireless oscillations lessen in intensity.
DAMPISH, [damp'-ish], *adj.* somewhat damp.
DAMPISHLY, [dam'-pish-li], *adv.* in a dampish fashion.
DAMPISHNESS, [dam'-pish-nes], *n.* the condition of being dampish.
DAMPNESS, [damp'-nes], *n.* the condition of being damp.
DAMP-PROOF, [damp'-proōf], *adj.* water-proof.
DAMPY, [damp'-i], *adj.* dampish; (*fig.*) dejected.
DAMSEL, [dam'-zel], *n.* a maiden. [OFr. *damoisel*].
DAMSON, [dam'-zon], *n.* a small sour plum. [OFr. *damascene* from L. *Prunus Damascenum* (plum of) Damascus].
DAN†, [dan], *n.* a former title of respect. [~DON].
DANCE (1), [dahnts], *n.* a series of rhythmic, bodily movements usually performed to music; any special form of dance; a party or gathering for dancing; music for a dance; **St. Vitus's d.**, the convulsive nervous movements of muscles, chorea; **to lead a person a d.**, to distract or obstruct a person deliberately.
DANCE (2), [dahnts], *v.t.* to perform (a dance); to make to dance; *v.i.* to execute a dance; to caper about; **to d. attendance upon**, to accompany constantly, to fawn round. [OFr. *danser*].
DANCER, [dahn'-ser], *n.* a person who dances; a ballet girl.
DANCETTE, dancetté, [dans-et'-i], *n.* (*her.*) the outline of an indented border; (*arch.*) the zigzag moulding of Norman architecture. [Fr. *dancetté*].

DANCETTÉ

DANCING, [dahns'-ing], *n.* the art of the dance; **d.-master**, a man who teaches dancing.
DANDELION, [dan'-di-li-on], *n.* (*bot.*) a plant of the genus *Taraxacum*, with a bright yellow flower and a deeply indented leaf. [Fr. *dent de lion* tooth of a lion].
DANDER (1), [dan'-der], *n.* dandruff; anger. [Unkn.].
DANDER (2), [dan'-der], *v.i.* to talk incoherently. [Unkn.].
DANDIE, [dand'-i], *n.* a breed of Scottish terriers. [*Dandie* Dinmont, a character in Sir Walter Scott's *Guy Mannering*].
DANDIFIED, [dand'-i-fīd], *adj.* having the dress or manners of a dandy.
DANDIFY, [dand'-i-fī], *v.t.* to give the appearance of a dandy to.
DANDLE, [dandl], *v.t.* to jiggle (a child) on the knee; to fondle. [It. *dandolare*].
DANDRUFF, DANDRIFF, [dand'-ruf, dand'-rif], *n.* a scurf of dry skin on the scalp. [Uncert.].
DANDY (1), [dan'-di], *n.* a fop, a man of fashion; a yawl's mizen; a yawl. [Uncert.].
DANDY (2), [dan'-di], *adj.* in the style of a dandy, foppish; (*coll.*) fine, excellent.
DANDY-BRUSH, [dand'-i-brush'], *n.* a hard brush used in grooming horses.
DANDY-COCK, [dand'-i-kok'], *n.* a bantam fowl.
DANDY-HORSE, [dand'-i-haws'], *n.* the earliest form of bicycle propelled by the legs.
DANDYISH, [dand'-i-ish], *adj.* resembling a dandy.
DANDYISM, [dand'-i-izm], *n.* foppishness, the manners and dress of a dandy.
DANDY-NOTE, [dan'-di-nōt'], *n.* (*coll.*) a custom-house form recording bonded goods. [Corruption of *Addenda note*].
DANE, [dān], *n.* a native of Denmark; **great d.**, a breed of large dogs trained in Denmark for hunting boars. [OScand. *Danir* Danes].
DANEGELD, [dān'-geld], *n.* (*hist.*) a tax levied in the tenth century to buy off the invading Danes. [*Prec.* and YIELD].
DANELAW, [dān'-law], *n.* (*hist.*) laws imposed by the invading Danes; the northern part of England assigned to the Danes by King Alfred. [DANE and LAW].
DANE-WORT, [dān'-wurt], *n.* (*bot.*) the plant *Sambucus Ebulus*, the dwarf elder.
DANGER, [dān'-jer], *n.* whatever produces risk of injury or death; the condition or cause of peril; exposure to risk of injury or death. [OFr. *danger* power].
DANGEROUS, [dān'-jer-us], *adj.* full of danger, unsafe, menacing.
DANGEROUSLY, [dān'-jer-us-li], *adv.* in a dangerous fashion.
DANGEROUSNESS, [dān'-jer-us-nes], *n.* the condition of being dangerous.
DANGER-SIGNAL, [dān'-jer-sig'-nal], *n.* a signal denoting the presence of danger.
DANGLE, [dang'-gl], *v.t. and i.* to swing loosely. [OSwed. *dangla*].
DANGLER, [dang'-gler], *n.* a person who dangles.
DANISH (1), [dā-nish], *n.* the language of the Danes, the people of Denmark.
DANISH (2), [dā'-nish], *adj.* of or relating to the Danes or Denmark or its language.
DANK (1), [dangk], *n.* humidity.
DANK (2), [dangk], *adj.* moist, rotting. [ME. *dank*].
DANKISH, [dangk'-ish], *adj.* slightly damp.
DANTEAN, [dant-ē'-an], *adj.* resembling the manner of Dante. [*Dante*, the Italian poet].
DANTESQUE, [dant-esk'], *adj.* resembling the work of Dante.
DANUBIAN, [dan-ew'-bi-an], *adj.* relating to the Danube. [The river *Danube*].

DAP, (dapped, dapping), [dap], *v.i.* to drop bait gently into the water. [Uncert.].

DAPHNAL, [daf'-nal], *adj.* relating to laurels.

DAPHNE, [daf'-ni], *n.* a genus of flowering shrubs. [Gk. *daphne* laurel].

DAPHNIA, [daf'-ni-a], *n.* (*zool.*) a genus of water-fleas.

DAPHNIN, [daf'-nin], *n.* the bitter principle found in certain species of daphne.

DAPIFER†, [dap'-i-fer], *n.* (*hist.*) a person who brings meat to the table; a royal steward. [MedL. *dapifer* from L. *daps* feast].

DAPPER, [dap'-er], *adj.* smart, neat, well-dressed; sprightly. [ME. *dapper*].

DAPPERLING, [dap'-er-ling], *n.* a pigmy, a dwarf.

DAPPLE (1), [dapl], *adj.* marked with spots of different colours or shades. [Unkn.].

DAPPLE (2), [dapl], *v.t.* to speckle, variegate with spots.

DARBIES, [dah'-biz], *n.(pl.)* (*slang*) handcuffs. [Unkn.].

DARBY, [dah'-bi], *n.* a tool for levelling plaster on a ceiling. [Unkn.].

DARBYITES, [dah'-bi-its], *n.(pl.)* the Plymouth Brethren. [J. *Darby*, a leader of the sect].

DARCALL, [dah'-kawl], *n.* the long-tailed duck, *Harelda glacialis*.

DARCOCK, [dah'-kok'], *n.* the water-rail, *Rallus aquaticus*.

DARE (1), [dāer], *n.* the dace. [DACE].

DARE (2), [dāer], *v.t.* and *i.* to challenge or defy a person to do something by an implication of cowardice; to venture upon, to have sufficient courage for; **I d. say,** I believe it possible (often with irony). [OE. *dear(r)*, *pres.* of *durran* to dare].

DAREDEVIL, [dāer'-dev'-il], *n.* a person who dares any danger.

DARG, [dahg], *n.* (*Scots*) a day's work; the batch of peat cut and stored in one day. [DAY-WORK].

DARGER, [dahg'-er], *n.* (*Scots*) a worker hired by the day.

DARI, [du'-rē], *n.* Indian millet, Guinea corn. [Hind. *dari*].

DARIC, [da'-rik], *n.* a Persian gold coin of Darius stamped with an archer; any coin so stamped. [Gk. *dareikos*].

DARING (1), [dāer'-ing], *n.* a method of capturing larks by means of a daring-net and a mirror.

DARING (2), [dāer'-ing], *n.* reckless courage.

DARING (3), [dāer'-ing], *adj.* brave, fearless, audacious.

DARINGLY, [dāer'-ing-li], *adv.* in a daring fashion.

DARINGNESS, [dāer'-ing-nes], *n.* the quality of being daring.

DARING-NET, [dāer'-ing-net'], *n.* a net for capturing birds. [DARING (1) and NET (1)].

DARK (1), [dahk], *n.* darkness, obscurity, gloom; (*fig.*) ignorance, secrecy.

DARK (2), [dahk], *adj.* completely without light, with very little light, black, almost black; gloomy, sombre; sallow complexioned; (*fig.*) without understanding or knowledge; hidden, obscure; secret; evil, sinister; **d. ages,** (*hist.*) the period from the fifth to the eleventh centuries in Europe; **d. blues,** athletes representing Oxford University; **d. horse,** a competitor whose form or potentialities are unknown; **d. room,** (*phot.*) a light-proof room in which negatives are developed. [OE. *deorc*].

DARK-BROWED, [dahk'-browd'], *adj.* severe in countenance.

DARKEN, [dah'-ken], *v.t.* and *i.* to make dark or darker, to shut out light from; (*fig.*) to render ignorant, immoral or foul; to cause confusion; to sadden; to give a darker tone to; to become dark or darker.

DARK-HOUSE†, [dahk'-hows], *n.* a lunatic asylum.

DARKISH, [dahk'-ish], *adj.* slightly dark.

DARKLING (1), [dahk'-ling], *adj.* gloomy, dim.

DARKLING (2), [dahk'-ling], *adv.* in the dark. [DARK (2) and *ling* an old adverbial suffix].

DARKLY, [dahk'-li], *adv.* in the dark; not clearly, mysteriously.

DARKNESS, [dahk'-nes], *n.* the condition or quality of being dark; (*fig.*) ignorance, wickedness.

DARKSOME, [dahk'-sum], *adj.* dark; dismal.

DARKY, [dahk'-i], *n.* (*coll.*) a negro.

DARLING (1), [dah'-ling], *n.* a person dearly beloved, a sweetheart. [OE. *deorling*].

DARLING (2), [dah'-ling], *adj.* much loved; pretty.

DARN (1), [dahn], *n.* a place mended by darning.

DARN (2), [dahn], *v.t.* to mend a hole or tear in a material by imitating the texture of the stuff with new threads. [OE. *dernan* to hide].

DARN (3), [dahn], *v.t.* (*coll.*) to confound. [~DAMN].

DARNEL, [dahn'-el], *n.* (*bot.*) a grass, *Lolium temulentum*, which grows among corn. [ME. *dernel*].

DARNER, [dahn'-er], *n.* a person or instrument that darns.

DARNING, [dahn'-ing], *n.* the action of making a darn.

DARNING-NEEDLE, [dahn'-ing-needl'], *n.* a large needle used in darning.

DARREIN, [da-rān'], *n.* (*leg.*) the final presentation to a vacant benefice. [OFr. *derrein*].

DART (1), [daht], *n.* a light, pointed weapon usually fitted with guide feathers, thrown by hand, formerly used in close fighting and now in the game of darts; a rapid movement forward; (*dressmaking*) a small fold made in the cloth so that it fits more closely. [OFr. *dart*].

DART (2), [daht], *n.* a dace.

DART (3), [daht], *v.t.* and *i.* to jerk rapidly forward, to shoot out; to play a game of darts; to move suddenly and rapidly forward; (*fig.*) to fly in the air like a swallow.

DARTARS†, [daht'-erz], *n.* an ulcer forming under the skin of lambs. [Fr. *dartre*].

DART-BOARD, [daht'-bawd], *n.* a marked board, usually circular in form, for throwing darts at.

DARTER, [daht'-er], *n.* a Brazilian bird with a long, supple neck, which darts into the water after prey; the kingfisher.

DART

DARTINGLY, [daht'-ing-li], *adv.* with darting movements.

DARTS, [dahts], *n.* a game in which two or more persons compete in throwing darts at a suitably marked board.

DARWINIAN (1), [dah-win'-i-an], *n.* a believer in the Darwinian theory.

DARWINIAN (2), [dah-win'-i-an], *adj.* pertaining to Charles Darwin and his theories.

DARWINISM, [dah'-win-izm], *n.* the scientific theories of Darwin. [C. *Darwin*, a scientist].

DASH (1), [dash], *n.* a sudden, short, rapid run, a rush; a flavouring of one liquid in another; (*fig.*) resolute energetic action; a swift stroke with pen, pencil or brush, *esp.* a horizontal line, as —, to signify a pause or parenthesis; a mild expletive; show, swagger, ostentation; **to cut a d.,** to make a show, give a false impression of wealth or ability.

DASH (2), [dash], *v.t.* and *i.* to throw violently; to smash, shatter; to bespatter; to rush with fury or violence; (*fig.*) to abash, lower the spirits of. [ME. *daschen*].

DASH-BOARD, [dash'-bawd], *n.* a wooden screen to protect the driver of a horse-drawn vehicle from mud, etc.; a board in front of the driver in a motor vehicle fitted with gauges, switches, etc.

DASHER, [dash'-er], *n.* the plunger in a churn; (*coll.*) a modish fellow.

DASHING, [dash'-ing], *adj.* bold, energetic; showy.

DASH-WHEEL, [dash'-wēl], *n.* a wheel in a washing machine.

DASTARD, [das'-terd], *n.* a contemptible coward; a person who takes mean advantages. [ME. *dastard* a fool].

DASTARDLINESS, [dast'-erd-li-nes], *n.* the condition of being dastardly.

DASTARDLY, [dast'-erd-li], *adj.* cowardly, taking a mean advantage, brutal.

DASTARDNESS†, [dast'-erd-nes], *n.* dastardliness.

DASTARDY†, [dast'-erd-i], *n.* cowardice.

DASTUR, [dust-ōō(r)'], *n.* convention; usual commission. [Pers. *dastur*].

DASYMETER, [das-im'-it-er], *n.* an instrument for determining the density of gases. [Gk. *dasus* dense and *metron* measure].

DASYURES, [das'-i-yŏŏerz], *n.(pl.)* the Australian marsupials called native cats. [Gk. *dasus* dense and *oura* tail].

DATA, [dāt'-a], *n.(pl.)* facts assumed to be fixed or true, from which inferences are drawn and opinions formed. [DATUM].

DATABLE, [dāt'-abl'], *adj.* able to be dated.

DATARIA, [dat-āer'-i-a], *n.* a chancery of the Popes from which papal bulls are issued.

DATARY, [dāt'-er-i], *n.* the official who affixes *datum Romae* (given at Rome) to papal bulls. [L. *datarius*].

DATE (1), [dāt], *n.* the day, month and year when something occurred; a specified moment in time; the numerical designation of a day; **to make a d.,**

to arrange an appointment; **out of d.**, old-fashioned, obsolete; **up to d.**, modern, fashionable. [L. *datum* given].

DATE (2), [dāt], *n.* the oval, sweet, firm-fleshed fruit of the date-palm. [Fr. *datte* from Gk. *daktulos* finger].

DATE (3), [dāt], *v.t. and i.* to assign a date to; to derive from a past period or point of time; to become obsolete or old-fashioned.

DATELESS, [dāt'-les], *adj.* having no particular date.

DATE-LINE, [dāt'-līn], *n.* a hypothetical line in the Pacific on the east of which time is a day ahead of time on the west side; the heading giving the origin of a press message.

DATE-PALM, [dāt'-pahm], *n.* the palm-tree, *Phoenix dactylifera*, yielding dates.

DATE-PLUM, [dāt'-plum'], *n.* a South European species of tree, *Diospyros Lotus*, having cherry-sized fruit; the persimmon.

DATISCA, [dat-isk'-a], *n.* bastard hemp, *Datisca cannabina*. [Unkn.].

DATIVAL, [dat-ī'-val], *adj.* relating to the dative.

DATIVE, [dā'-tiv], *n.* (*gram.*) the case of a noun which denotes the indirect object of a verb, and used after some prepositions in certain languages. [L. *dativus* relating to the act of giving].

DATOLITE, [dā'-tō-līt], *n.* (*min.*) a borosilicate of calcium forming in white compact masses. [Gk. *dateomai* I divide and *lithos* stone].

DATUM, (*pl.* **data**), [dā'-tum], *n.* something ascertained or assumed; a fact given or known and from which inferences are made. [L. *datum*, *p.pt.* of *dare* to give].

DATUM-LINE, [dā'-tum-līn'], *n.* (*surveying*) the line from which are reckoned all the heights along a section.

DATURA, [dat-ew'-rah], *n.* (*bot.*) a genus of poisonous plants including the thorn-apple. [Skr. *dhattura*]

DATURINE, [dat-ew'-rin], *n.* a poisonous alkaloid extracted from the thorn-apple.

DAUB (1), [dawb], *n.* paint of mixed colours applied widely; a poorly painted picture.

DAUB (2), [dawb], *v.t. and i.* to smear with any sticky matter; to paint badly. [OFr. *dauber* from L. *dealbare* to whitewash].

DAUBER, [dawb'-er], *n.* a person who daubs.

DAUBING, [dawb'-ing], *n.* crude painting; (*fig.*) gross flattery.

DAUBSTER, [dawb'-ster], *n.* a dauber.

DAUBY, [dawb'-i], *adj.* soft and sticky; clumsily painted.

DAUGHTER, [daw'-ter], *n.* a female child or descendant; (*fig.*) a woman deriving certain characteristics from a specified source. [OE. *dohtor*].

DAUGHTER-IN-LAW, [daw'-ter-in-law'], *n.* a son's wife.

DAUGHTERLIKE, [daw'-ter-līk'], *adj.* befitting a daughter.

DAUGHTERLINESS, [daw'-ter-li-nes], *n.* the state of being daughterly.

DAUGHTERLY (1), [daw'-ter-li], *adj.* like, or appertaining to, a daughter.

DAUGHTERLY (2), [daw'-ter-li], *adv.* in a daughterly way.

DAUK, [dauk], *n.* a dent or crack in wood. [Unkn.].

DAUNT, [dawnt], *v.t.* to quell; to intimidate. [OFr. *daunter*, L. *domitare* to tame].

DAUNTLESS, [dawnt'-les], *adj.* courageous, intrepid.

DAUNTLESSLY, [dawnt'-les-li], *adv.* in a dauntless fashion.

DAUNTLESSNESS, [dawnt'-les-nes], *n.* the quality of being dauntless, fearlessness.

DAUPHIN†, [daw'-fin], *n.* the title of the eldest son of the King of France. [Fr. *dauphin* dolphin].

DAUPHINE, [daw-fēn'], *n.* dauphiness. [Fr. *dauphine*].

DAUPHINESS, [daw'-fin-es], *n.* the wife of the dauphin.

DAVENPORT, [davn'-pawt], *n.* a small writing table. [Uncert.].

DAVINA, [dā'-vē'-na], *n.* (*min.*) a variety of volcanic mineral of a hexahedral form, found on Vesuvius. [Sir H. *Davy*, a scientist].

DAVINE, [dav-ēn'], *n.* davina. [*Prec.*].

DAVITS, [dav'-itz], *n.(pl.)* (*naut.*) the metal uprights in which a boat is slung on a ship's deck, ready to be lowered to the water; **fish d.**, a small crane over the bows for hoisting up the anchor. [OFr. *daviot*].

DAVY, [dā'-vi], *n.* (*slang*) an affidavit.

DAVY JONES, [dā'-vi-jōnz'], *n.* (*naut.*) the Devil; **Davy Jones's locker**, the sea as a grave. [Unkn.].

DAVY LAMP, [dā'-vi-lamp'], *n.* a safety-lamp lessening the risk of explosions for miners. [Sir Humphry *Davy*, the inventor].

DAVY LAMP

DAW, [daw], *n.* the jackdaw. [ME. *dawe* chough].

DAWDLE, [dawdl], *v.i.* to waste time, hang about, wander aimlessly. [Unkn.].

DAWDLER, [dawd'-ler], *n.* one who dawdles.

DAWISH, [daw'-ish], *adj.* resembling a daw.

DAWK (1), [dawk], *n.* a flaw or incision in timber.

DAWK (2), [dawk], *v.t.* to mark (timber) with an incision. [Uncert.].

DAWM, [dawm], *n.* an Indian coin, valued at one-fortieth of a rupee. [Native].

DAWN (1), [dawn], *n.* daybreak; (*fig.*) a beginning.

DAWN (2), [dawn], *v.i.* to begin to grow light; (*fig.*) to begin to open, or appear; **to d. upon**, (*coll.*) to enter the consciousness or mind of. [ME. *dawnen*].

DAWNING, [dawn'-ing], *n.* dawn; the action of that which dawns.

DAY, [dā], *n.* the time from sunrise to sunset; a period of twenty-four hours; daylight; an appointed time; **d. by d.**, daily, occurring on each successive day; **d. of doom**, the day of judgment; **d. of grace**, (*theol.*) the time mercy is granted to sinners; **d. of judgment**, the time of the Last Judgment; **d. rule**, (*leg.*) licence granted to a prisoner to go beyond the bounds of prison; **day's work**, labour completed in one day; **d. ticket**, a return ticket available for both journeys on one day only; **days of grace**, (*leg.*) a period of delay granted a defendant; a period of delay after the stipulated day of settlement of credit notes; **to-d.**, this day; **this d. week**, the corresponding day of next week; **to win the d.**, to gain the victory; **to call it a d.**, to agree to finish; **astronomical d.**, a period from noon to the next noon; **civil d.**, the period of twenty-four hours from midnight to midnight; **lunar d.**, the period taken by the earth in making one complete revolution on its axis. [OE. *dæg*].

DAY-BED, [dā'-bed'], *n.* a bed or long couch for resting on by day.

DAY-BLINDNESS, [dā'-blind'-nes], *n.* a form of partial blindness resulting in indistinct vision during the day.

DAY-BOOK, [dā'-book], *n.* (*comm.*) a record of day to day sales or business transactions.

DAY-BOY, [dā'-boi'], *n.* a non-resident boy attending a secondary or public school.

DAYBREAK, [dā'-brāk], *n.* dawn.

DAY-COAL, [dā'-kōl], *n.* the upper stratum of coal.

DAYDREAM (1), [dā'-drēm], *n.* a foolish fancy; a reverie; a visionary scheme offering little hope of materialization.

DAYDREAM (2), [dā'-drēm], *v.i.* to indulge in daydreams.

DAYDREAMER, [dā'-drē'-mer], *n.* one who daydreams.

DAY-FLY, [dā'-flī], *n.* a May-fly, any species of *Ephemera*.

DAY-LABOUR, [dā'-lā'-ber], *n.* work performed during the daytime.

DAY-LABOURER, [dā'-lā'-ber-er], *n.* a labourer engaged by the day.

DAYLIGHT, [dā'-līt], *n.* the light of the sun; natural light; **to see d.**, to see one's way out of a difficulty; **D. Saving Act**, an Act passed by Parliament in 1916 whereby the clock is set forward in the summer months.

DAY-LILY, [dā'-lil'-i], *n.* a lily which blooms only for a day, *Hemerocallis fulva*.

DAY-MAID, [dā'-mād], *n.* a dairy-maid; a maid engaged to work in the daytime.

DAY-SCHOOL, [dā'-skool], *n.* a school where the pupils come daily to be taught, but are not boarded.

DAY-SIGHT, [dā'-sīt], *n.* ability to see clearly only by day.

DAY'S-MAN†, [dāz'-man], *n.* an arbitrator; a day-labourer.

DAYSPRING, [dā'-spring], *n.* the dawn; (*fig.*) beginning.

DAY-STAR, [dā'-stah(r)], *n.* the morning star.

DAYTIME, [dā'-tīm], *n.* the period when there is day light, from dawn to sunset.

DAY-WOMAN, [dā'-woom'-an], *n.* a woman engaged to work by the day.

DAY-WORK, [dā′-wurk], *n.* work undertaken by the day; work during the daytime.
DAZE (1), [dāz], *n.* a state of stupefaction; (*min.*) a glittering stone.
DAZE (2), [dāz], *v.t.* to numb the brain, stupefy; to dazzle. [OScand. *dasa* to be sluggish].
DAZZLE (1), [dazl], *n.* that which dazzles.
DAZZLE (2), [dazl], *v.t. and i.* to confuse or cause to be temporarily blinded by a powerful glaring light; to camouflage by painting; (*fig.*) to be agreeably overwhelmed by some quality in a person or object so that the power of judgment is affected. [~DAZE].
DAZZLEMENT, [dazl′-ment], *n.* power of dazzling.
DAZZLING, [daz′-ling], *adj.* that dazzles.
DAZZLINGLY, [daz′-ling-li], *adv.* in a dazzling fashion.
DE-, *pref.* away, down; over; completely; also expressing negation, deprivation, deficiency. [L. *de* away from, from; OFr. *des* from L. *dis* apart].
DEACON, [dē′-kon], *n.* (*eccles.*) a church official helping the priest; one who has been ordained to the ecclesiastical order next below the priesthood; a person responsible for the secular management of a Presbyterian church; a church official helping the minister and taking part in the secular administration of a Congregational church. [OE. *diacon* from Gk. *diakonos* minister].
DEACONESS, [dē′-kon-es], *n.* a female deacon; a member of a Protestant religious and charitable organization for women.
DEACONRY, [dē′-kon-ri], *n.* deaconship.
DEACONSHIP, [dē′-kon-ship], *n.* the office or status of a deacon.
DEAD (1), [ded], *n.*(*pl.*) those who have died; **the d. of night,** the time of night characterized by the absence of all sound or activity.
DEAD (2), [ded], *adj.* deprived of life, no longer alive; deathlike, resembling death; inorganic, inanimate; numbed; no longer operative; not now spoken as a language; inert; heavy, (of a sound) dull; tasteless; useless, unprofitable; (*coll.*) absolute, certain; unresponsive; not glossy, having a matt surface; (*sport*) out of play; (*leg.*) without rights of citizenship; **d. ropes,** (*naut.*) ropes uncontrolled by blocks or grooves; **d. set,** a steady and unwavering concentration of activity upon; **d. shot,** an expert marksman; **d. water,** (*naut.*) eddying water closing in behind the stern of a moving ship. [OE. *dead*].
DEAD (3), [ded], *adv.* (*coll.*) thoroughly, completely, utterly.
DEAD-AND-ALIVE, [ded′-and-a-līv′], *adj.* lethargic, dreary; monotonous, boring, exasperatingly quiet.
DEAD-BEAT (1), [ded′-bēt′], *n.* an escapement in a watch by which the seconds hand halts at each second.
DEAD-BEAT (2), [ded′-bēt], *adj.* (*coll.*) utterly tired out, exhausted.
DEAD-CENTRE, [ded′-sen′-ter], *n.* (*eng.*) one of the two points in a revolution of a cranked shaft when the piston, connecting rod and crank are all in line.
DEAD-COLOURING, [ded′-kul′-er-ing], *n.* the first layer of colours in a picture, roughly sketching in its composition and emphasis of tone.
DEADEN, [dedn], *v.t.* to lessen, to diminish the force of; to numb; to blunt; to make spiritless; to dull the gloss or brilliancy of.
DEADEYE, [ded′-ī′], *n.* (*naut.*) a round, wooden block pierced with three holes to receive the lanyards.
DEAD-FREIGHT, [ded′-frāt], *n.* the cost of space booked for, but not occupied by freight.
DEAD-GROUND, [ded′-ground], *n.* (*milit.*) folds in the ground sheltered from direct enemy gun-fire.
DEAD-HEAD, [ded′-hed′], *n.* the tail stock of a lathe; (*U.S. slang*) a person using a free ticket for a theatrical performance; (*coll.*) a fool.
DEAD-HEAT, [ded′-hēt′], *n.* the result of a race in which two or more competitors arrive at the winning post simultaneously.
DEAD-HEDGE, [ded′-hej′], *n.* a hedge of close-trimmed branches.
DEAD-HOUSE, [ded′-hows], *n.* a mortuary.
DEADISH, [ded′-ish], *adj.* rather dead.
DEAD-LETTER, [ded′-let′-er], *n.* a letter that the Post Office has been unable to deliver; a defunct, inoperative law.
DEADLIGHTS, [ded′-lītz], *n.*(*pl.*) (*naut.*) strong wooden or metal coverings made exactly to fit over the cabin windows, and used during stormy weather.
DEADLIHOOD†, [ded′-li-hŏŏd], *n.* the state of the dead.
DEAD-LINE, [ded′-līn′], *n.* an arbitrary line barring further progress; (*sport*) a line which when crossed puts a ball out of play; (*print*) the time of going to press.
DEADLINESS, [ded′-li-nes], *n.* the quality of being deadly.
DEADLOCK, [ded′-lok′], *n.* a complete standstill of progress; an impasse.
DEADLY (1), [ded′-li], *adj.* having the power to cause death; fatal; relentless; like death; (*coll.*) unbearable.
DEADLY (2), [ded′-li], *adv.* in a manner like that of death; (*coll.*) excessively.
DEADLY NIGHTSHADE, [ded′-li-nīt′-shād], *n.* (*bot.*) the poisonous plant, *Atropa Belladonna.*

DEADLY NIGHTSHADE

DEADNESS, [ded′-nes], *n.* the condition of being dead.
DEAD-NETTLE, [ded′-netl′], *n.* (*bot.*) any species of the genus *Lamium.*
DEAD-POINT, [ded′-point], *n.* dead-centre.
DEAD-RECKONING, [ded′-rek′-ning], *n.* (*naut.*) a calculation of a ship's position without the aid of the stars.
DEAD-STRUCK, [ded′-struk′], *adj.* resolute.
DEAD-TOP, [ded′-top′], *n.* a disease attacking the shoots of young trees.
DEAD-WEIGHT, [ded′-wāt′], *n.* heavy weight of an inanimate thing; a loan by the Bank of England to the Government on account of the half-pay and pensions of retired officers of the army and navy; a useless encumbrance.
DEADWOOD, [ded′-wŏŏd′], *n.* (*naut.*) certain supporting blocks of timber on the keel of a ship, particularly at the extremities; the dead branches of trees; (*fig.*) useless material.
DEADWORT, [ded′-wurt], *n.* (*bot.*) a variety of elder, *Sambucus Ebulus.*
DEAF (1), [def], *n.*(*pl.*) those who are deaf.
DEAF (2), [def], *adj.* completely unable to hear; only able to hear imperfectly; (*fig.*) disregarding, wilfully ignoring. [OE. *deaf*].
DEAFEN, [defn], *v.t.* to make deaf; to prevent from being heard by the interposition of a loud noise; (*arch.*) to render sound-proof.
DEAFLY, [def′-li], *adv.* in a deaf fashion.
DEAF-MUTE, [def′-mewt′], *n.* one who is deaf and dumb.
DEAFNESS, [def′-nes], *n.* the condition of being deaf.
DEAF-NUT, [def′-nut′], *n.* a nut in which a kernel has not grown.
DEAL (1), [dēl], *n.* pinewood, firwood; a plank of firwood not more than 3 inches thick, 7 or more inches broad and 6 feet or more long. [LGerm. *dele*].
DEAL (2), [dēl], *n.* a considerable number or amount. [DEAL (5)].
DEAL (3), [dēl], *n.* a business transaction, a successfully concluded negotiation; the act or result of dealing out cards. [DEAL (5)].
DEAL (4), [dēl], *adj.* made of deal wood. [DEAL (1)].
DEAL (5), [dēl], *v.t. and i.* to give, share out, distribute; to strike; to distribute playing cards to the players; **to d. in,** to trade in; **to d. with,** to be concerned with; to contend, treat, behave; to handle, settle, manage; to trade or do business with. [OE. *dælan* to share].
DEALER, [dēl′-er], *n.* a trader, a merchant; one who deals the playing cards.
DEAL-FISH, [dēl′-fish], *n.* a thin fish, *Trachypterus arcticus,* having a tail which projects at an angle to the backbone.
DEALING, [dēl′-ing], *n.* conduct in relation to others; (*pl.*) transactions in buying and selling; traffic, trade.
DEAN, [dēn], *n.* (*eccles.*) the head of a cathedral chapter; the head of a university faculty; **rural d.,** a clergyman appointed to supervise a portion of a diocese. [OFr. *deien* from LL. *decanus* supervisor of ten].
DEANERY, [dē′-ner-i], *n.* the office, status or jurisdiction of a dean; the official residence of a dean.
DEANSHIP, [dēn′-ship], *n.* the office, status or tenure of a dean.
DEAR (1), [dēer], *n.* a darling, a loved one, sweetheart, a lovable person.
DEAR (2), [dēer], *adj.* beloved, lovable, charming; costly, expensive; in excess of the normal or reasonable price; used as the conventional mode of address in letter-writing. [OE. *deore*].
DEAR-BOUGHT, [dēer′-bawt], *adj.* expensive.
DEARIE, see DEARY.

DEARLY, [dēer'-li], *adv.* at a high price; with great lovingness.
DEARNESS, [dēer'-nes], *n.* the quality of being dear.
DEARTH, [durth], *n.* lack, deficiency. [ME. *derthe*].
DE-ARTICULATE, [dē'-ah-tik'-yōō-lāt], *v.t.* to disjoint.
DEARY, DEARIE, [dēer'-i], *n.* (*coll.*) a dear.
DEATH, [deth], *n.* the act of dying, the state or fact of being dead; the cause of death; the manner of dying; **black d.,** the bubonic plague that swept Europe in the fourteenth century; **civil d.,** the taking away of rights of citizenship; **at death's door,** apparently about to die; **d. duties,** taxes collected by the State on the estate owned by a person who has just died. [OE. *death*].
DEATH-ADDER, [deth'-ad'-er], *n.* the most venomous of Australian snakes, *Pseudechis porphyriaca.*
DEATHBED, [deth'-bed'], *n.* the bed on which a person dies.
DEATH-BELL, [deth'-bel'], *n.* the bell rung upon the death of someone.
DEATH-BLOW, [deth'-blō'], *n.* a blow destroying life or hope.
DEATHFUL, [deth'-fōōl], *adj.* deadly, bringing death.
DEATHFULNESS, [deth'-fōōl-nes], *n.* the quality of being deathful.
DEATHLESS, [deth'-les], *adj.* incapable of death, immortal, everlasting.
DEATHLESSLY, [deth'-les-li], *adv.* in deathless fashion.
DEATHLESSNESS, [deth'-les-nes], *n.* the quality of being deathless, immortality.
DEATHLIKE, [deth'-līk], *adj.* resembling death.
DEATHLY (1), [deth'-li], *adj.* like death.
DEATHLY (2), [deth'-li], *adv.* in a deathly fashion.
DEATH-MASK, [deth'-mahsk], *n.* a plaster cast of the face made shortly after death.
DEATH-RATE, [deth'-rāt], *n.* the percentage of deaths in a given district during a given period.
DEATH-RATTLE, [deth'-ratl'], *n.* the rattling sound in the throat, signifying approaching death.
DEATH-ROLL, [deth'-rōl], *n.* a record of the dead.
DEATH'S-HEAD, [deths'-hed'], *n.* a human skull; a representation of it; the pirate flag decorated with a skull and cross-bones; **d. moth,** a species of hawk-moth, *Acherontia atropos,* so called from the markings resembling a human skull on its thorax.

DEATH'S-HEAD

DEATH'S-MAN, [deths'-man], *n.* an executioner.
DEATH-STROKE, [deth'-strōk'], *n.* a fit resulting in death; death-blow.
DEATH-STRUGGLE, [deth'-strugl], *n.* the struggle ending in death.
DEATH-THROES, [deth'-thrōz'], *n.(pl.)* the pangs of death.
DEATH-TOKEN, [deth'-tōk'-en], *n.* a sign of approaching death.
DEATH-TRAP, [deth'-trap'], *n.* a source of potential death.
DEATHWARD, [deth'-werd], *adv.* towards death.
DEATH-WARRANT, [deth'-wo'-rant], *n.* an official order for the execution of a criminal.
DEATH-WATCH, [deth'-woch'], *n.* a small beetle which eats its way into woodwork, the male of which when mating makes a call like the tick of a clock, *Arobium tessellatum.*
DEB, [deb], *n.* (*slang*) a débutante.
DEBACLE, débâcle, [dā-bahkl'], *n.* (*geol.*) a torrential flow of water sweeping along with it rocks, trees, etc.; the breaking up of ice on a river; (*fig.*) a crushing and unexpected overthrow. [DE and Fr. *bacler* to hurry through].

DEATH-WATCH BEETLE

DEBAG, (debagging, debagged), [de-bag'], *v.t.* forcibly to remove the trousers from. [DE and BAG (1)].
DEBAR, (debarred, debarring), [di-bah(r)'], *v.t.* to forbid the privilege or enjoyment of, or the approach or entry to, to bar from.
DEBARK, [dē'-bahk'], *v.t. and i.* to land from a vessel; to disembark.
DEBARKATION, [dē'-bahk-ā'-shun], *n.* the act of debarking.
DEBASE, [di-bās'], *v.t.* to lower in purity or value, to adulterate, to degrade, depreciate. [DE and ABASE].
DEBASEMENT, [di-bās'-ment], *n.* the act of debasing; the state of being debased.
DEBASER, [di-bās'-er], *n.* one who, or that which, debases.
DEBASING, [di-bās'-ing], *adj.* tending to debase, degrading.
DEBASINGLY, [di-bās'-ing-li], *adv.* in a debasing manner.
DEBATABLE, [di-bāt'-abl], *adj.* able to be disputed, of a contentious character; **d. land,** borderland.
DEBATE (1), [di-bāt'], *n.* a formal discussion of a motion, usually in public and according to recognized procedure; argument, disputation, controversy.
DEBATE (2), [di-bāt'], *v.t. and i.* to take part in a debate; to discuss a subject from all angles, to argue, engage in controversy; (*fig.*) to endeavour to make up one's mind about, consider, reflect, to deliberate; **debating point,** an argument which is intended to silence the opponent by logic or wit rather than truth. [OFr. *debater*].
DEBATER, [di-bāt'-er], *n.* one who debates.
DEBATINGLY, [di-bāt'-ing-li], *adv.* in a debating manner.
DEBAUCH (1), [di-bawch'], *n.* an occasion of drunken and immoral conduct, a drinking bout.
DEBAUCH (2), [di-bawch'], *v.t. and i.* to corrupt or vitiate; to seduce from duty or from virtue; to plunge into an orgy of immorality. [OFr. *debaucher* to draw away from work].
DEBAUCHEDLY, [di-bawch'-id-li], *adv.* in a dissipated manner.
DEBAUCHEDNESS, [di-bawch'-id-nes], *n.* intemperance, dissipation.
DEBAUCHEE, [deb'-awch-ē'], *n.* dissipated person; a libertine, profligate.
DEBAUCHERY, [di-bawch'-er-i], *n.* indulgence in debauch.
DEBAUCHMENT, [di-bawch'-ment], *n.* the act of debauching.
DEBENTURE, [di-ben'-cher], *n.* (*comm.*) written acknowledgment issued by a public company in exchange for money subscribed, entitling the holder to a first claim on dividends as interest arising from profits; one bond of an issue of such bonds; a certificate granted by the custom-house, entitling an exporter to an allowance on import duties previously paid on commodities which he re-exports. [L *debentur*, 3rd *pers. pl.* of *deberi* to be owing].
DEBENTURED, [di-ben'-cherd], *adj.* entitled to an allowance as a drawback.
DEBILITATE, [di-bil'-i-tāt], *v.t.* to make feeble, to impair the strength of, to enervate. [L. *debilitare* weaken].
DEBILITATING, [di-bil'-i-tāt-ing], *adj.* that debilitates.
DEBILITATION, [di-bil'-i-tā'-shun], *n.* the act of debilitating; the state of being debilitated.
DEBILITY, [di-bil'-it-i], *n.* functional weakness, absence of normal power, feebleness. [L. *debilitas*].
DEBIT (1), [deb'-it], *n.* (*comm.*) an entry in an account-book of a debt; the left-hand side of a ledger devoted to such entries. [L. *debitum*, *p.pt.* of *debere* to owe].
DEBIT (2), [deb'-it], *v.t.* to record a debt in an account-book, to enter as a debit.
DEBITOR†, [deb'-it-er], *n.* a debtor.
DEBITUMINIZE, [di-bi-tew'-min-īz'], *v.t.* to extract the bitumen from.
DEBLAI, déblai, [dē-blā'], *n.* (*fort.*) a trench or cavity excavated in taking soil to form the parapet. [Fr. *débléer* to clear of corn].
DEBONAIR, [deb'-on-āer'], *adj.* well-mannered and spruce; genial and well-bred, bright and cheerful. [OFr. *de bonne aire* of pleasing manner].
DEBONAIRLY, [deb'-on-āer'-li], *adv.* in debonair fashion.
DEBONAIRNESS, [deb'-on-āer'-nes], *n.* the quality of being debonair.
DEBOUCH, [di-bowch'], *v.i.* (*milit.*) to march out of a confined place into the open; to flow out into a wider outlet. [Fr. *déboucher*].
DEBOUCHMENT, [di-bowch'-ment], *n.* the act of debouching; the embouchure of a river.
DEBOUCHURE, [di-bōōsh'-yōōer], *n.* debouchment.

DEBOUT†, [di-bōō(t)'], *v.t.* to expel, thrust out, oust; (*coll.*) to belch, eructate. [OFr. *deboter*].
DEBRIS, [deb'-rē, dā'-brē], *n.* confused and ruined remains left by a destructive force; an accumulation of broken fragments; (*geol.*) loose, worn and crumbled rock heaped up. [Fr. *débris*].
DEBT, [det], *n.* something owed or due to be paid to another; material or moral obligation or liability; **bad d.**, a debt which will not be paid; **national d.**, the money owed to investors in state securities. [OFr. *dette*, ~DEBIT].
DEBTEE, [det'-ē], *n.* a creditor.
DEBTLESS, [det'-les], *adj.* free from debt.
DEBTOR, [det'-er], *n.* a person in debt to another person; (*comm.*) a debit.
DEBUNK, [dē-bungk'], *v.t.* (*slang*) to remove the accumulated cant, hypocrisy, and sentimentality which surrounds anything, to expose. [DE and BUNK].
DEBUT, **début**, [dā-bew'], *n.* first public or social appearance of a player, performer, society girl, etc.; beginning, start. [Fr. *début*].
DEBUTANTE, débutante, [dā-bew-tahnt'], *n.* a lady making her début, a lady who has been, or is to be, presented to the King and Queen at a recent or specified formal court reception. [Fr. *débutante*].
DECA-, *pref.* ten, tenfold. [Gk. *deka* ten].
DECACHORD, [dek'-a-kawd], *n.* an ancient Greek ten-stringed harp.
DECACUMINATED†, [dē'-ka-kew'-min-āt-id], *adj.* decapitated. [L. *decacuminare*].
DECADAL, [dek'-ad-al], *adj.* relating to a decade; consisting of, counted in, a series of tens.
DECADE, [dek'-ād], *n.* a series or aggregate of ten, a period of ten years. [Gk. *dekas dekada* a group of ten].
DECADENCE, [dek'-ad-ents], *n.* decay, deterioration in moral quality. [LL. *decadentia* pulling down].
DECADENCY, [dek'-ad-en-si], *n.* decadence.
DECADENT (1), [dek'-ad-ent], *n.* a degenerate.
DECADENT (2), [dek'-ad-ent], *adj.* marked by decadence.
DECADENTLY, [dek'-ad-ent-li], *adv.* in decadent fashion.
DECAGON, [dek'-ag-on], *n.* (*geom.*) a plane figure of ten sides and angles. [DECA and Gk. *gonia* angle].
DECAGONAL, [dek-ag'-on-al], *adj.* pertaining to a decagon.
DECAGRAMME, [dek'-a-gram'], *n.* a metric weight of ten grammes.
DECAHEDRAL, [dek'-a-hēd'-ral], *adj.* possessing ten sides.
DECAHEDRON, [dek'-a-hēd'-ron], *n.* (*geom.*) a solid body possessing ten sides. [DECA and Gk. *hedra* base].
DECALCIFICATION, [dē-kal'-si-fik-ā'-shun], *n.* the act of decalcifying.
DECALCIFY, [dē-kal'-si-fī], *v.t.* to extract the lime from. [DE and CALCIFY].
DECALCOMANIA, [dē-kal'-kō-mān'-i-a], *n.* a process of transferring a coloured picture from paper to glass or china. [Fr. *décalcomanie*].
DECALITRE, [dek'-a-lē'-ter], *n.* a metric measure of capacity consisting of ten litres.
DECALOGUE, [dek'-a-log], *n.* the Ten Commandments. [DECA and Gk. *logos* speech].
DECAMERON, [di-kam'-er-on], *n.* a collection of a hundred short stories by Boccaccio, represented as related in ten days. [DECA and Gk. *hemera* day].
DECAMETRE, [dek'-a-mē'-ter], *n.* a metric measure of length containing ten metres.
DECAMP, [di-kamp'], *v.i.* to depart from a camp; to run away secretly, escape.
DECAMPMENT, [di-kamp'-ment], *n.* the act of decamping.
DECANAL, [dek'-an-al, di-kān'-al], *adj.* relating to a deanery or to a dean. [~L. *decanus* dean].
DECANDRIAN, [dek-and'-ri-an], *adj.* decandrous.
DECANDROUS, [dek-and'-rus], *adj.* possessing ten stamens.
DECANGULAR, [dek-ang'-gyōōl-er], *adj.* possessing ten angles.
DECANT, [di-kant'], *v.t.* to pour off gently; to pour wine or other liquid from one vessel into another without disturbing the sediment; to pour into a decanter from a bottle. [DE and L. *canthus* lip of a vessel].
DECANTATION, [dē'-kant-ā'-shun], *n.* the process of decanting.
DECANTER, [di-kant'-er], *n.* a glass bottle for holding decanted liquor.
DECAPHYLLOUS, [di-kaf'-il-us], *adj.* possessing ten leaves. [DECA and Gk. *phullon* leaf].
DECAPITATE, [di-kap'-it-āt], *v.t.* to cut off the head of, to behead. [L. *decapitare*].
DECAPITATION, [di-kap'-it-ā'-shun], *n.* the act of beheading. [L. *decapitatio*].
DECAPOD (1), [dek'-a-pod], *n.* a crustacean having ten feet. [DECA and Gk. *pous podos* foot].
DECAPOD (2), [dek'-a-pod], *adj.* possessing ten limbs, as a crustacean.
DECAPODAL, [dek-ap'-od-al], *adj.* possessing ten feet; belonging to the order of decapoda.
DECAPODOUS, [dek-ap'-od-us], *adj.* decapodal.
DECARBONATE, [dē-kah'-bon-āt], *v.t.* to remove carbonic acid from.
DECARBONIZATION, [dē-kah'-bon-īz-ā'-shun], *n.* the process of decarbonizing.
DECARBONIZE, [dē-kah'-bon-īz], *v.t.* to deprive of carbonic acid or carbon; to remove carbon accumulated on the pistons and cylinder head of an internal combustion engine.
DECARE, [dek'-āer], *n.* a metric unit of measurement consisting of a thousand square metres. [Fr. *décare*].
DECASTICH, [dek'-a-stik], *n.* a poem limited to ten lines. [DECA and Gk. *stikhos* line of poetry].
DECASTYLE, [dek'-a-stīl], *n.* (*arch.*) a portico having ten columns. [DECA and Gk. *stulos* column].
DECASYLLABIC (1), [dek'-a-sil-ab'-ik], *n.* (*pros.*) a line of verse containing ten syllables.
DECASYLLABIC (2), [dek'-a-sil-ab'-ik], *adj.* having ten syllables.
DECASYLLABLE, [dek'-a-sil'-abl], *n.* a word composed of ten syllables.
DECATHLON, [dek-ath'-lon], *n.* a contest in athletic skill consisting of ten events. [DECA and *athlon* competition].
DECAY (1), [di-kā'], *n.* a decline towards dissolution, decomposition, disintegration, rotting; gradual weakening.
DECAY (2), [di-kā'], *v.i.* to suffer or undergo decay. [L. *decadere*].
DECAYED, [di-kād'], *adj.* rotten, decomposed; deteriorated.
DECAYEDNESS, [di-kād'-nes], *n.* decayed state.
DECAYER, [di-kā'-er], *n.* that which induces decay.
DECEASE (1), [di-sēs'], *n.* death. [L. *decessum*, *p.pt.* of *decedere* depart].
DECEASE (2), [di-sēs], *v.i.* to die.
DECEASED (1), [di-sēst'], *n.* (*leg.*) a dead person.
DECEASED (2), [di-sēst'], *adj.* dead.
DECEIT, [di-sēt'], *n.* the act of deceiving; a deception, fraud; the quality of being deceitful, duplicity; (*leg.*) any fraudulent practice. [OFr. *deceite*].
DECEITFUL, [di-sēt'-fōōl], *adj.* tending or intended to deceive; given to deceiving; deceptive, misleading.
DECEITFULLY, [di-sēt'-fōōl-i], *adv.* in deceitful fashion.
DECEITFULNESS, [di-sēt'-fōōl-nes], *n.* the quality of being deceitful.
DECEITLESS, [di-sēt'-les], *adj.* free from deceit.
DECEIVABLE, [di-sēv'-abl], *adj.* able to be deceived.
DECEIVABLENESS, [di-sēv'-abl-nes], *n.* the quality of being deceivable.
DECEIVABLY, [di-sēv'-ab-li], *adv.* in deceivable fashion.
DECEIVE, [di-sēv'], *v.t.* to practise deceit on, to mislead deliberately, impose on, delude; to put under a delusion. [L. *decipere*].
DECEIVER, [di-sēv'-er], *n.* a person who deceives.
DECELERATE, [dē-sel'-er-āt], *v.t.* to slow down, to cause the rate of motion to diminish. [DE and L. *celer* swift].
DECEM-, *pref.* ten. [L. *decem* ten].
DECEMBER, [di-sem'-ber], *n.* the twelfth and last month of the year. [L. *december* the tenth month of the Roman year].
DECEMDENTATE, [des'-em-dent'-āt], *adj.* possessing ten points or teeth.
DECEMFID, [di-sem'-fid], *adj.* (*bot.*) separated into ten parts. [DECEM and L. *fidus* divided].
DECEMLOCULAR, [des'-em-lok'-yōōl-er], *adj.* (*bot.*) possessing ten small seed-cells. [DECEM and L. *loculus* cell].
DECEMPEDAL, [di-sem'-pid-al], *adj.* having ten feet. [DECEM and PEDAL].
DECEMVIR†, [*pl.* **decemviri**), [di-sem'-vur], *n.* (*hist.*) a member of a body of ten, one of a Roman commission appointed to codify the laws. [L. *decemviri* ten men].
DECEMVIRAL, [di-sem'-ver-al], *adj.* relating to the decemviri.

DECEMVIRATE, [di-sem'-vėr-āt], *n.* the office or tenure of office of the decemviri; any official body of ten men.

DECEMVIRI, see DECEMVIR.

DECENCY, [dē'-sen-si], *n.* the quality of being decent; modesty, decorum; (*coll.*) good manners. [L. *decentia*].

DECENNARY, [di-sen'-er-i], *n.* a period of ten years. [DECEM and L. *annus* year].

DECENNIAD, [di-sen'-i-ad], *n.* a decennium.

DECENNIAL, [di-sen'-i-al], *adj.* consisting of, lasting for ten years, or occurring every ten years.

DECENNIUM, [di-sen'-i-um], *n.* a decade. [L. *decennium*].

DECENNOVAL†, [di-sen'-o-val], *adj.* relating to, consisting of, nineteen years. [L. *decennovalis*].

DECENNOVARY†, [di-sen'-o-ver-i], *adj.* relating to the nineteenth year.

DECENT, [dēs'-ent], *adj.* becoming, fitting, seemly, chaste, proper, modest; (*coll.*) tolerable, satisfactory, likeable. [L. *decens*].

DECENTISH, [dē'-sent-ish], *adj.* (*coll.*) quite decent.

DECENTLY, [dē'-sent-li], *adv.* in a decent fashion.

DECENTNESS, [dē'-sent-nes], *n.* the quality of being decent.

DECENTRALIZATION, [dē-sent'-ral-īz-ā'-shun], *n.* the act of decentralizing.

DECENTRALIZE, [dē-sent'-ral-īz], *v.t.* to remove from the centre; to split up an administration amongst branches instead of concentrating in one central place or authority.

DECEPTIBILITY, [di-sep'-tib-il'-i-ti], *n.* the condition of being deceptible.

DECEPTIBLE, [di-sept'-ibl], *adj.* liable or able to be deceived.

DECEPTION, [di-sep'-shun], *n.* the act of deceiving; the state of being deceived; that which deceives or is intended to deceive. [L. *deceptio*].

DECEPTIVE, [di-sep'-tiv], *adj.* tending to deceive, misleading. [L. *deceptivus*].

DECEPTIVELY, [di-sep'-tiv-li], *adv.* in a deceptive fashion.

DECEPTIVENESS, [di-sep'-tiv-nes], *n.* the quality of being deceptive.

DECEPTIVITY, [dē'-sep-tiv'-i-ti], *n.* deceptiveness.

DECEPTORY†, [di-sep'-ter-i], *adj.* apt to mislead.

DECERN, [di-surn'] *v.t.* to decide, to judge; to discern; (*Scots leg.*) to decree. [L. *decernere* decide].

DECESSION†, [di-sesh'-un], *n.* departure. [L. *decessio*].

DECHARM†, [di-chahm'], *v.t.* to disenchant.

DECHRISTIANIZE, [di-kris'-chan-īz], *v.t.* to turn or pervert from Christianity.

DECI-, [des'-i], *pref.* tenth. [L. *deci(mus)* tenth].

DECIARE, [de'-si-ah(r)], *n.* a metric unit of measurement, the tenth of an are. [Fr. *déciare*].

DECIDABLE, [di-sīd'-abl], *adj.* capable of being decided.

DECIDE, [di-sīd'], *v.t. and i.* to judge, to select as best or right; to settle; to determine. [L. *decidere* to cut off, settle].

DECIDED, [di-sīd'-id], *adj.* firm, resolute, determined; definite, unmistakable.

DECIDEDLY, [di-sīd'-id-li], *adv.* in a decided way.

DECIDENCE†, [di-sīd'-ens], *n.* the act of falling off. [L. *decidentia*].

DECIDER, [di-sīd'-er], *n.* a further race or contest to decide a tie; a person or thing that decides.

DECIDUOUS, [di-sid'-yōō-us], *adj.* (*bot.*) shedding its leaves annually; (of leaves, etc.) falling off seasonally. [L. *deciduus* falling down].

DECIDUOUSNESS, [dis-id'-yōō-us-nes], *n.* (*bot.*) the condition of being deciduous.

DECIGRAMME, [des'-i-gram'], *n.* a metric measure of weight, one-tenth of a gramme.

DECILE, [des'-īl], *n.* (*astrol.*) the aspect of two planets when at a distance of thirty-six degrees from each other. [Fr. *décile*].

DECILITRE, [des'-i-lē'-ter], *n.* a metric measure of cubic capacity equal to one-tenth of a litre.

DECILLION, [di-sil'-yon], *n.* the tenth power of a million. [DECI and (MI)LLION].

DECIMA, [des'-im-a], *n.* (*mus.*) the interval of a tenth. [L. *decimus* tenth].

DECIMAL (1), [des'-i-mal], *n.* (*math.*) a fraction having some power of ten as its denominator; **recurring d.,** a fraction in which the final figure or group of figures repeats indefinitely.

DECIMAL (2), [des'-i-mal], *adj.* numbered by tens, expressed or reckoned in tens or powers of ten, arranged in multiples of ten; **d. fraction,** a fraction whose denominator is taken as ten or a power of ten; **d. system,** system of calculation of weights and measures based on powers of ten. [L. *decimus* tenth].

DECIMALISM, [des'-i-mal-izm], *n.* the principles and method of the decimal system.

DECIMALIST, [des'-im-al-ist], *n.* an advocate of the decimal or metric system.

DECIMALIZATION, [des'-i-mal-ī-zā'-shun], *n.* the act of decimalizing.

DECIMALIZE, [des'-i-mal-īz], *v.t.* to reduce to terms of the decimal system, to convert into decimals.

DECIMALLY, [des'-i-mal-i], *adv.* by tens; by means of decimals.

DECIMATE, [des'-im-āt], *v.t.* to eliminate every tenth part; to put to death every tenth man as reprisals; (*fig.*) to destroy in great numbers. [L. *decimare* to choose every tenth man for punishment or death].

DECIMATION, [des'-im-ā'-shun], *n.* the act of decimating; the condition of being decimated. [L. *decimatio*].

DECIMATOR, [des'-i-mā'-tor], *n.* a person or thing that decimates.

DECIMETRE, [des'-i-mē'-ter], *n.* a metric measure of length equal to the tenth of a metre.

DECIMO-SEXTO, [des'-im-ō-seks'-tō], *n.* a book with its pages one-sixteenth the size of a full sheet, usually written 16mo. [L. *sextus decimus* sixteenth].

DECIPHER, [di-sī'-fer], *v.t.* to interpret a cipher in terms of a recognized language, to decode; to make out, read and understand, discover the meaning of.

DECIPHERABLE, [di-sī'-fer-abl], *adj.* able to be deciphered.

DECIPHERMENT, [di-sī'-fer-ment], *n.* the act of deciphering.

DECISION, [di-sizh'-un], *n.* final judgment; settlement; firmness and stability of purpose, resolution; (*leg.*) the authoritative opinion or verdict of a judge. [L. *decisio*].

DECISIVE, [di-sī'-siv], *adj.* that decides, conclusive; exhibiting decision; decided.

DECISIVELY, [di-sī'-siv-li], *adv.* in a decisive way.

DECISIVENESS, [di-sī'-siv-nes], *n.* the quality of being decisive.

DECISTERE, [des'-ist-āer'], *n.* the tenth part of a stere.

DECIVILIZE, [di-civ'-il-īz], *v.t.* to cause to revert to barbarism.

DECK (1), [dek], *n.* a horizontal covering enclosing the top of a ship's hull; the floor of an omnibus or tramcar; a pack of cards; **to clear the decks,** to prepare for action. [MDu. *dek*].

DECK (2), [dek], *v.t.* to adorn, decorate; to provide with a deck. [MDu. *decken* to cover].

DECK-CHAIR, [dek'-chāer'], *n.* a portable, folding chair with a canvas support across a light wooden frame.

DECKER, [dek'-er], *n.* one who, or that which, decks or adorns; a ship or omnibus with a specified number of decks.

DECK-HAND, [dek'-hand'], *n.* a man employed in doing work on deck.

DECK-HOUSE, [dek'-hows'], *n.* a cabin or shelter on deck.

DECK-CHAIR

DECKING, [dek'-ing], *n.* ornament; embellishment.

DECKLE, DEKLE†, [dekl], *n.* the adjustable apparatus which determines the size of a sheet of paper in manufacture or cutting. [Germ. *deckel* cover].

DECKLED, [dekld], *adj.* (of paper) having untrimmed edges.

DECK-LOAD, [dek'-lōd'], *n.* a deck cargo.

DECK-PASSENGER, [dek'-pas'-in-jer], *n.* (*naut.*) a passenger travelling without cabin accommodation.

DECK-TENNIS, [dek'-ten'-is], *n.* a game adapted from lawn tennis played on board ship.

DECLAIM, [di-klām'], *v.t. and i.* to speak or recite to an audience vigorously with exaggerated gesture for effect; to deliver poetry or a set speech to an audience in a rhetorical and dramatic manner; **to d. against,** to raise an outcry against. [L. *declamare*].

DECLAIMANT, [di-klā'-mant], *n.* a declaimer.

DECLAIMER, [di-klā'-mer], *n.* a person who declaims.

DECLAIMING, [di-klā'-ming], *n.* a rhetorical harangue.

DECLAMATION, [dek'-lam-ā'-shun], *n.* the act of declaiming; a speech declaimed.
DECLAMATORY, [di-klam'-a-ter-i], *adj.* characterized by, or suited to, declamation.
DECLARABLE, [di-klāer'-abl], *adj.* able to be declared; dutiable.
DECLARANT, [di-klāer'-ant], *n.* (*leg.*) a person who makes a declaration.
DECLARATION, [dek'-ler-ā'-shun], *n.* the act of declaring; that which is declared; a document recording this; an affidavit; (*leg.*) a formal statement of a claim by the plaintiff. [L. *declaratio* a making known].
DECLARATIVE, [di-kla'-ra-tiv], *adj.* having the nature of a declaration, explanatory.
DECLARATIVELY, [di-kla'-ra-tiv-li], *adv.* in a declarative manner.
DECLARATORILY, [di-kla'-ra-ter-i-li], *adv.* by declaration.
DECLARATORY, [di-kla'-ra-ter-i], *adj* making a declaration.
DECLARE, [di-klāer'], *v.t. and i.* to make known, announce; to assert, affirm; to state directly and explicitly; (*cards*) to name a suit as trumps; (*leg.*) to enumerate the grounds of complaint against the defendant; to announce that one has certain dutiable goods in one's possession; (*cricket*) to announce one's innings to have finished. [L. *declarare*].
DECLAREDLY, [di-klāer'-id-li], *adv.* confessedly, admittedly.
DECLASSED, [di-klahst'], *adj.* having declined in social status.
DECLENSION, [di-klen'-shun], *n.* the act of declining; a tendency towards a lower level of quality, power, etc.; (*gram.*) the changes in the endings of nouns, pronouns and adjectives according to the different cases; a particular type of inflexion. [L. *declinatio*].
DECLINABLE, [di-klīn'-abl], *adj.* capable of declension.
DECLINATE, [dek'-lin-āt], *adj.* (*bot.*) leaning or bent downward in a curve; declining. [L. *declinatus* fallen down].
DECLINATION, [dek'-lin-ā'-shun], *n.* a downward slope; (*astron.*) the distance, measured at an angle north or south, that a heavenly body is situated from the celestial equator; (*elect.*) the angular difference between the true north and south and the magnetic north and south.
DECLINATOR, [di-klīn'-at-er], *n* (*astron.*) an instrument for recording and measuring the angle of sloping planes; a clinometer.

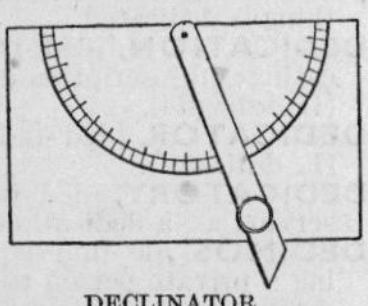
DECLINATOR

DECLINATORY, [di-klīn'-at-er-i], *adj.* relating to declination; indicating a refusal; **d. plea,** (*leg.*) a plea claiming exemption from jurisdiction.
DECLINATURE, [di-klin'-a-chooer], *n.* the act of declining; (*Scots leg.*) refusal of jurisdiction in a case.
DECLINE (1), [di-klīn'], *n.* a gradual falling off in quality or strength; a tendency towards a lower level of health; (*comm.*) a slow fall in price; (*med.*) tuberculosis.
DECLINE (2), [di-klīn'], *v.t. and i.* to slope downward; to droop; to degenerate, drop to a lower level of excellence, deteriorate; to diminish; to refuse, reject; (*gram.*) to inflect; to waste away; (*comm.*) to fall in price. [L. *declinare* to turn aside].
DECLINER, [di-klī'-ner], *n.* a dial which cuts the plane of the meridian or the plane of the horizon obliquely.
DECLINOMETER, [dek'-lin-om'-it-er], *n.* an instrument for measuring the declination of the magnetic needle. [DECLINE and Gk. *metron* measure].
DECLIVITOUS, [di-kliv'-it-us], *adj.* having a declivity, steeply sloping.
DECLIVITY, [di-kliv'-i-ti], *n.* the downward slope of the ground; a surface that slopes downward. [L. *declivitas*].
DECLIVOUS, [di-klī'-vus], *adj.* declivitous. [L. *declivus*].
DECLUTCH, [di-kluch'], *v.i.* to disconnect the engine shaft from the transmission shaft in a motor-car by depressing the clutch.
DECOCT, [dē-kokt'], *v.t.* to prepare by boiling; to extract substances by boiling. [L. *decoctum*, *p.pt.* of *decoquere*].
DECOCTIBLE, [dē-kokt'-ibl], *adj.* able to be decocted.
DECOCTION, [dē-kok'-shun], *n.* the act of decocting; the essence decocted. [L. *decoctio*].
DECOCTIVE, [dē-kok'-tiv], *adj.* relating to decoction, that may be readily decocted.
DECOCTURE†, [di-kok'-chooer], *n.* a decoction.
DECODE, [dē-kōd'], *v.t.* to decipher.
DE-COKE, [di-kōk'], *v.i.* (*coll.*) to decarbonize.
DECOLLATE, [di-kol'-āt], *v.t.* to behead. [L. *decollare*].
DECOLLATION, [dē'-kol-ā'-shun], *n.* the act of beheading, the beheading of John the Baptist.
DECOLLETAGE, décolletage, [dā-kolt'-ahzh], *n.* the practice of wearing low-backed dresses. [Fr.].
DECOLLETE, décolleté, [dā-kol'-tā], *adj.* low-necked; wearing a low-necked gown. [Fr. *décolleté* bare at the neck].
DECOLORATE, [dē-kul'-er-āt], *v.t.* to render colourless, to bleach. [L. *decolorare*].
DECOLORATION, [dē-kul'-er-ā'-shun], *n.* the act or result of decolorating.
DECOLOUR, [dē-kul'-er], *v.t.* to decolorate.
DECOLOURANT, [dē-kul'-er-ant], *n.* a substance which decolours.
DECOLOURIZE, [dē-kul'-er-īz], *v.t.* to decolour.
DECOMPLEX, [dē'-kom'-pleks], *adj.* consisting of complex component parts; formed of complex ideas.
DECOMPOSABLE, [dē'-kom-pō'-zabl], *adj.* able to be decomposed.
DECOMPOSE, [dē'-kom-pōz'], *v.t. and i.* to break up into component parts or elements; to disintegrate; to decay, go bad.
DECOMPOSITE (1), [dē-kom'-poz-it], *n.* a decomposite substance.
DECOMPOSITE (2), [dē-kom'-poz-it], *adj.* consisting of compounds; compounded further.
DECOMPOSITION, [dē'-kom'-poz-ish'-un], *n.* the act of decomposing; the state of becoming or being decomposed.
DECOMPOUND (1), [dē-kom'-pownd], *n.* a substance composed of compounded parts.
DECOMPOUND (2), [dē-kom'-pownd], *adj.* composed of compound parts.
DECOMPOUND (3), [dē'-kom-pownd'], *v.t.* to decompose; to combine into a fresh compound something already compounded.
DECOMPOUNDABLE, [dē'-kom-pownd'-abl], *adj.* able to be decompounded.
DECOMPRESS, [dē'-kom-pres'], *v.t.* to reduce a high pressure to a more normal one.
DECONCENTRATE, [dē-kon'-sen-trāt], *v.t.* to spread, to scatter, diffuse.
DECONSECRATE, [dē-kon'-sik-rāt], *v.t.* to deprive of sacred character, to secularize.
DECONTAMINATE, [dē-kon-tam'-in-āt], *v.t.* to free from contamination, *esp.* gas-contamination.
DECONTAMINATION, [dē'-kon-tam'-in-ā'-shun], *n.* the act or process of decontaminating, *esp.* from poison gas.
DECONTROL, (decontrolling, decontrolled), [de'-kon-trōl'], *v.t.* to release from control, *esp.* from state control and management; to abolish an official restriction of speed on a road.
DECONTROLLED, [dē'-kon-trōld'], *adj.* without control; (of a road) having no restriction of speed for vehicular traffic.
DECOR, décor, [dā'-kaw(r)], *n.* the stage-setting of a ballet, play, or opera. [Fr. *décor*].
DECORATE, [dek'-or-āt], *v.t.* to adorn, to deck with ornament; to ornament, to embellish; to confer an honour; to award a badge or medal of honour to; to paint and paper the interior of a room or house. [L. *decorare*].
DECORATION, [dek'-or-ā'-shun], *n.* the act or manner of decorating; the state of being decorated; that which decorates; a badge or medal of honour.
DECORATIVE, [dek'-or-at-iv], *adj.* that decorates; suitable as, or pertaining to, decoration, ornamental.
DECORATIVENESS, [dek'-or-at-iv-nes], *n.* the condition of being decorative.
DECORATOR, [dek'-or-āt-er], *n.* a person who decorates; a person employed in house painting and interior decoration.
DECOROUS, [de'-ker-us], *adj.* seemly, proper, suitable. [L. *decorus*].
DECOROUSLY, [de'-ker-us-li], *adj.* in decorous fashion.
DECOROUSNESS, [di-kawr'-us-nes], *n.* the quality of being decorous.

DECORTICATE, [di-kawt'-i-kāt], *v.t.* to strip off bark; to peel, to husk.
DECORTICATION, [dē-kawt'-ik-ā'-shun], *n.* the act of decorticating. [L. *decorticatio*].
DECORUM, [dik-awr'-um], *n.* propriety of speech or behaviour, decency, social convention. [L. *decorum*].
DECOY (1), [di-koi'], *n.* a tame bird or animal used to entice wild birds or animals into a snare; place in which wild birds may be easily ensnared; (*fig.*) a trap; a person used to lead someone into a trap. [DE and Du. *kooi* a snare].
DECOY (2), [di-koi'], *v.t.* to entice into a trap, ensnare by means of a decoy.
DECOY-DUCK, [di-koi'-duk'], *n.* a real or imitation duck used to decoy others into a snare; (*fig.*) a person who decoys others.
DECREASE (1), [dē'-krēs], *n.* the act of decreasing; the state of being decreased; a lessening, diminution.
DECREASE (2), [di-krēs'], *v.t. and i.* to cause to become less or smaller, to lessen, diminish; to become less or smaller. [L. *decrescere*].
DECREASINGLY, [di-krē'-sing-li], *adv.* in a decreasing fashion.
DECREE (1), [di-krē'], *n.* an order or law authorized by a legislative body; established law; a judgment; an arbitrary law enforced by undemocratic means; (*fig.*) an inevitable principle; (*leg.*) a decision of a judge, court of law, etc.; (*theol.*) the absolute principle of God; a law authorized by a church council; **d. nisi,** an order for divorce subject to ratification. [L. *decretum*].
DECREE (2), [di-krē'], *v.t. and i.* to order, command, to make or impose a decree; to settle, appoint or fix by decree.
DECREEABLE, [di-krē'-abl], *adj.* able to be decreed.
DECREMENT, [dek'-rim-ent], *n.* the process of decreasing; the amount by which anything is decreased. [L. *decrementum*].
DECREPIT, [di-krep'-it], *adj.* worn out, broken down and weakened by age, illness, etc.; tumbledown, rickety, in the last stages of decay. [L. *decrepitus*].
DECREPITATE (1), [di-krep'-it-āt], *v.t. and i.* to heat to the point of crackling, to roast; to crackle under extreme heat.
DECREPITATION, [di-krep'-it-ā'-shun], *n.* the act of decrepitating.
DECREPITNESS, [di-krep'-it-nes], *n.* decrepitude.
DECREPITUDE, [di-krep'-i-tewd], *n.* the state of being decrepit. [MedL. *decrepitudo*].
DECRESCENDO, [dē'-kresh-end'-ō], *n.* (*mus.*) a gradual lessening of sound. [It. *decrescendo*].
DECRESCENT, [di-kres'-ent], *adj.* decreasing, becoming smaller, waning.
DECRETAL (1), [di-krē'-tal], *n.* an authorized decree; (*eccles.*) a decree issued by the Pope, establishing an ecclesiastical precedent; (*pl.*) a collection of these constituting canon law. [L. *decretale*].
DECRETAL (2), [di-krē'-tal], *adj.* pertaining to a decree.
DECRETION, [di-krē'-shun], *n.* the process of decreasing.
DECRETIST, [di-krē'-tist], *n.* (*eccles.*) a person expert in the decretals; a student of canon law.
DECRETIVE, [di-krē'-tiv], *adj.* like a decree.
DECRETORILY, [di-krēt'-er-i-li], *adv.* in an authoritative or dictatorial manner.
DECRETORY, [di-krēt'-er-i], *adj.* authorized by a decree; decretal. [L. *decretorius*].
DECRIAL, [di-krī'-al], *n.* the act of decrying.
DECRIER, [di-krī'-er], *n.* one who decries.
DECROWN, [dē-krown'], *v.t.* to deprive of a crown.
DECRUSTATION, [dē'-krus-tāsh'-un], *n.* removal of a crust.
DECRY, [di-krī'], *v.t.* to cry down the value of, to disparage, depreciate.
DECUBATION†, [dek'-yōō-bā'-shun], *n.* the act of lying down. [L. *decubatio*].
DECUBITAL, [di-kewb'-it-al], *adj.* resulting from lying down.
DECUBITUS, [di-kewb'-it-us], *n.* (*med.*) the way in which a patient lies in bed. [L. *decubitus*].
DECUMAN, [dek'-yōō-man], *adj.* (*hist.*) pertaining to the main gate of a Roman camp next to which was stationed the tenth cohort; tenth; large, as every tenth wave. [L. *decumanus* relating to the tenth part].
DECUMBENCE, [di-kum'-bents], *n.* decumbency.
DECUMBENCY, [di-kum'-ben-si], *n.* the state or act of lying down.
DECUMBENT, [di-kum'-bent], *adj.* lying down, recumbent, prostrate; (*bot.*) lying close to the ground.
DECUMBENTLY, [di-kum'-bent-li], *adv.* in a decumbent position.
DECUMBITURE†, [di-kum'-bit-yōōer], *n.* the act of going to bed when ill, the state of lying in bed of an invalid; (*astrol.*) a figure in the heavens taken as foretelling the course of an illness. [~DECUBITUS].
DECUPLE (1), [dek'-yōōpl], *n.* a number ten times a specified number.
DECUPLE (2), [dek'-yōōpl], *adj.* tenfold. [L. *decuplus* tenfold].
DECUPLE (3), [dek'-yōōpl], *v.t.* to increase tenfold.
DECURION, [dē-kew'-ri-on], *n.* (*hist.*) a Roman officer in charge of ten soldiers. [L. *decurio*].
DECURRENCY, [di-ku'-ren-si], *n.* (*bot.*) the state of being decurrent.
DECURRENT, [di-ku'-rent], *adj.* (*bot.*) extending downwards along the stem. [L. *decurrens*].
DECURRENTLY, [di-ku'-rent-li], *adv.* in decurrent fashion.
DECURSIVE, [di-kurs'-iv], *adj.* running downwards, decurrent. [L. *decursus*].
DECURSIVELY, [dē-kurs'-iv-li], *adv.* in a decursive form.
DECURTATE, [di-kurt'-āt], *adj.* cut short. [L. *decurtatus*].
DECUSSATE (1), [dē-kus'-āt], *adj.* crossing or intersecting to form an X; (*bot.*) arranged in pairs successively set crosswise to each other.
DECUSSATE (2), [dē-kus'-āt], *v.t.* to grow, cross, or intersect at right angles or in the form of an X. [L. *decussare*].
DECUSSATED, [dē-kus'-at-id], *adj.* decussate.
DECUSSATELY, [dē-kus'-at-li], *adv.* in a decussate form.
DECUSSATION, [dē'-kus-ā'-shun], *n.* the act of decussating. [L. *decussatio*].
DECUSSATIVELY, [dē-kus'-at-iv-li], *adv.* crosswise.
DEDENTITION, [dē-dent-ish'-un], *n.* (*physiol.*) the shedding of teeth, particularly of the milk teeth.
DEDICANT, [ded'-i-kant], *n.* a dedicator. [L. *dedicans*].
DEDICATE (1), [ded'-ik-āt], *adj.* devoted, consecrated, dedicated.
DEDICATE (2), [ded'-ik-āt], *v.t.* to consecrate solemnly to a holy purpose; to assign to a special purpose by solemn ritual; to devote exclusively to some specific cause; to write an inscription in a book assigning it to a particular person. [L. *dedicare*].
DEDICATEE, [ded'-i-kat-ē'], *n.* one to whom something is dedicated.
DEDICATION, [ded'-ik-ā'-shun], *n.* the act of dedicating; an inscription dedicating a book to someone. [L. *dedicatio*].
DEDICATOR, [ded'-ik-ā'-tor], *n.* one who dedicates. [L. *dedicator*].
DEDICATORY, [ded'-ik-ā'-ter-i], *adj.* relating to, or serving as, a dedication.
DEDIMUS, [dē'-dim-us], *n.* (*leg.*) a writ commissioning a private person to act in place of a judge. [L. *dedimus(potestatem)* we have given the power].
DEDITION†, [dē-dish'-un], *n.* surrender. [L. *deditio*].
DEDOUBLEMENT, [dē-dubl'-ment], *n.* doubling down; (*bot.*) chorisis.
DEDUCE, [di-dews'], *v.t.* to trace the steps in; to reason from preceding facts or statements; to infer. [L. *deducere* to lead down, derive].
DEDUCEMENT†, [di-dews'-ment], *n.* deduction.
DEDUCIBILITY, [di-dews'-ib-il'-i-ti], *n.* deducibleness.
DEDUCIBLE, [di-dews'-ibl], *adj.* able to be deduced.
DEDUCIBLENESS, [di-dews'-ibl-nes], *n.* the quality of being deducible.
DEDUCT, [di-dukt'], *v.t.* to take away, to subtract. [L. *deductum*, *p.pt.* of *deducere* to lead away].
DEDUCTION, [di-duk'-shun], *n.* the act of deducting; that which is subtracted; the act of deducing; that which is deduced.
DEDUCTIVE, [di-duk'-tiv], *adj.* using or dependent upon deduction; **d. reasoning,** (*logic*) a process of reasoning proceeding from the general to the particular.
DEDUCTIVELY, [di-duk'-tiv-li], *adv.* by way of deduction.
DEED, [dēd], *n.* something done, an action, an act; an actual fact; (*leg.*) a sealed document embodying the terms of an agreement, settlement, etc.; a document setting out a title to real estate; **d.-poll,** a deed made by one party only, recorded on polled paper. [OE. *ded*].
DEEDFUL, [dēd'-fōōl], *adj.* marked by effective deeds.

DEEDLESS, [dēd'-les], *adj.* not performing any deeds, inactive.

DEEM, [dēm], *v.t.* to consider, to judge. [OE. *deman* to judge].

DEEMSTER, [dēm'-ster], *n.* a judge in the Isle of Man. [OE. *demestre*].

DEEP (1), [dēp], *n.* that which is deep; the sea; (*cricket*) the outfield; (*naut.*) the distance between two depths on a load-line.

DEEP (2), [dēp], *adj.* extending far down, situated a long distance beneath a certain level; extending a long distance across a surface; penetrating far into a mass; profound, having the power to deal with abstruse, difficult ideas, problems, etc.; thoroughly preoccupied by; difficult to comprehend; hidden; cunning, tricky, artful; having a powerful emotional effect; intense, dark, rich in tone; (*mus.*) low in pitch; (*milit.*) some distance behind the front-line; (*tennis*) placed near the opponent's base-line; **to go (in) off the d. end,** to become temporarily mad; to lose one's temper suddenly; to become suddenly reckless. [OE. *deop*].

DEEP (3), [dēp], *adv.* far down, thoroughly, deeply.

DEEPEN, [dēp'-en], *v.t.* and *i.* to make or become deeper.

DEEPLY, [dēp'-li], *adv.* to an extreme depth; profoundly; with considerable emotion; gravely; thoroughly; considerably.

DEEP-MOUTHED, [dēp'-mowтнd'], *adj.* having a loud, hollow voice; possessing a deep bark.

DEEPNESS, [dēp'-nes], *n.* the condition of being deep; depth.

DEEP-READ, [dēp'-red'], *adj.* well-informed.

DEEP-SEA, [dēp'-sē'], *adj.* belonging to the sea at its deeper levels.

DEEP-TONED, [dēp'-tōnd'], *adj.* possessing a very low tone.

DEER, [dēer], *n.* a family of ruminant horned ungulates with deciduous antlers. [OE. *deor* wild animal].

DEER-HOUND, [dēer'-hownd'], *n.* a large breed of dog employed originally for deer-hunting.

DEER-NECK, [dēer'-nek'], *n.* a horse having a thin neck.

DEERSKIN, [dēer'-skin], *n.* the skin of a deer; the soft supple leather made from it.

DEERSTALKER, [dēer'-stawk'-er], *n.* a person stalking deer to shoot them; (*slang*) a low-crowned soft felt hat.

DEER

DEERSTALKING, [dēer'-stawk'-ing], *n.* the act of stalking deer.

DEFACE, [di-fās'], *v.t.* to destroy or spoil the face of anything, to disfigure; (of writing) to obliterate or make indistinct.

DEFACEABLE, [di-fās'-abl], *adj.* able to be defaced.

DEFACEMENT, [di-fās'-ment], *n.* the act of defacing; that which defaces; the injury effected by defacing.

DEFACER, [di-fā'-ser], *n.* one who, or that which, defaces.

DEFACINGLY, [di-fā'-sing-li], *adv.* in a defacing way.

DE FACTO, [dē-fak'-tō], *adv.* in actual fact though not by legal right. [L. *de* from and *factum* fact, deed].

DEFALCATE, [dē'-fal-kāt'], *v.i.* to misappropriate or embezzle money. [L. *defalcare* to lop].

DEFALCATION, [dē'-fal-kā'-shun], *n.* the art of defalcating; an irregular deficit in funds left in the charge of a person.

DEFALCATOR, [dē'-fal-kā'-tor], *n.* one who defalcates.

DEFAMABLE, [di-fā'-mabl], *adj.* able to be defamed.

DEFAMATION, [de-fa-mā'-shun], *n.* the act of defaming; calumny; slander.

DEFAMATORY, [di-fam'-a-ter-i], *adj.* defaming, slanderous.

DEFAME, [di-fām'], *v.t.* to harm the reputation of by calumny, to make slanderous or libellous remarks about, to speak or write evilly and falsely about. [L. *diffamare*].

DEFAMER, [di-fām'-er], *n.* one who defames another.

DEFAMING, [di-fām'-ing], *n.* defamation.

DEFAMINGLY, [di-fām'-ing-li], *adv.* so as to defame.

DEFAULT (1), [di-fawlt'], *n.* failure to fulfil an obligation, a neglect of duty; a fault, deficiency; (*leg.*) failure to appear in court at the proper time. [OFr. *defaute*].

DEFAULT (2), [di-fawlt'], *v.t.* and *i.* to fail in fulfilling an obligation, to neglect to perform a duty; to fail to complete a contract; (*leg.*) to fail to appear in court at the proper time; to nominate a person as failing to appear in court when officially required. [*Prec.*].

DEFAULTER, [di-fawlt'-er], *n.* one, *esp.* a soldier, who defaults.

DEFEASANCE, [di-fē'-zants], *n.* a rendering null and void; (*leg.*) a conditional clause in a document which, if taking effect, renders the whole null and void; a document containing such a clause. [OFr. *defesance* undoing].

DEFEASANCED, [di-fē'-zanst], *adj.* forfeited.

DEFEASIBLE, [di-fē'-zibl], *adj.* able to be annulled.

DEFEASIBLENESS, [di-fēz'-ibl-nes], *n.* the quality of being defeasible.

DEFEAT (1), [di-fēt'], *n.* the act of defeating, overthrow, conquest; frustration, ruin, destruction.

DEFEAT (2), [di-fēt'], *v.t.* to conquer, overthrow, vanquish, to render an opponent ineffectual; to frustrate, nullify, destroy, ruin, cause to fail. [OFr. *defeit* from L. *deficere* to fail].

DEFEATISM, [di-fē'-tizm], *n.* advocacy of surrender, acceptance of defeat as inevitable.

DEFEATIST (1), [di-fēt'-ist], *n.* one who overrates the possibilities of defeat.

DEFEATIST (2), [di-fēt'-ist], *adj.* of, or pertaining to, a defeatist or his views.

DEFEATURE†, [di-fē'-cher], *n.* defacement, marring; a rendering difficult of identification. [OFr. *desfaiture*].

DEFECATE, [dēf'-e-kāt], *v.t.* and *i.* to purify, clarify; (*physiol.*) to empty the bowels. [L. *defaecare* to excrete].

DEFECATION, [dēf'-ek-ā'-shun], *n.* the act of defecating.

DEFECT, [di-fekt'], *n.* want; imperfection, flaw, fault, error, mistake. [L. *defectus*, *p.pt.* of *deficere* to fail].

DEFECTIBLE, [di-fekt'-ibl], *adj.* defective, tending to fail.

DEFECTION, [di-fek'-shun], *n.* desertion from allegiance or duty; revolt; apostasy. [L. *defectio*].

DEFECTIONIST, [di-fek'-shun-ist], *n.* an advocate of defection.

DEFECTIVE, [di-fekt'-iv], *adj.* having defects, lacking in something; imperfect, incomplete.

DEFECTIVELY, [di-fekt'-iv-li], *adv.* in defective fashion.

DEFECTIVENESS, [di-fekt'-iv-nes], *n.* the condition of being defective.

DEFENCE, [di-fents'], *n.* the act of defending; that which defends, a fortification; (*leg.*) the case of a defendant in reply to charges made by the prosecution; (*pl.*) (*milit.*) series of fortified positions one behind another; **d. area,** a district in which civilian movements are restricted by military authorities in wartime. [OFr. *defense*].

DEFENCED, [di-fenst'], *adj.* fortified, protected by defences.

DEFENCELESS, [di-fens'-les], *adj.* without defence, helpless.

DEFENCELESSLY, [di-fens'-les-li], *adv.* in defenceless fashion.

DEFENCELESSNESS, [di-fens'-les-nes], *n.* the state of being defenceless.

DEFEND, [di-fend'], *v.t.* to protect from, to shield against assault, resist, repulse an enemy; to assert a case in reply to an attack; to support by a speech; to vindicate, excuse; (*leg.*) to plead not guilty in a court and attempt to establish one's innocence; to seek to prove the innocence of (the accused). [L. *defendere*].

DEFENDABLE, [di-fend'-abl], *adj.* able to be defended.

DEFENDANT, [di-fend'-ant], *n.* one who defends; (*leg.*) a person accused or prosecuted. [Fr. *défendant*].

DEFENDER, [di-fend'-er], *n.* a person who defends.

DEFENSATIVE†, [di-fens'-at-iv], *n.* defence.

DEFENSIBLE, [di-fen'-sibl], *adj.* offering a means of defence, defendable; excusable. [L. *defensibilis*].

DEFENSIBLY, [di-fents'-ib-li], *adv.* in a defensible way.

DEFENSIVE (1), [di-fens'-iv], *n.* the condition of expecting, and being ready to meet attack; (*milit.*) the limitation of activities to those of defence.

DEFENSIVE (2), [di-fens'-iv], *adj.* prepared for defence; serving as a defence. [MedL. *defensivus*].

DEFENSIVELY, [di-fens'-iv-li], *adv.* in a defensive fashion.

DEFER (1), (deferring, deferred), [di-fur'], *v.t. and i.* to delay, postpone, to transfer from one date to a later one; to put off; to reserve for a subsequent occasion. [L. *differre* to put off].
DEFER (2), (deferring, deferred), [di-fur'], *v.i.* to submit, to yield to another's opinion. [L. *deferre* to bear away].
DEFERENCE, [def'-er-ents], *n.* the act of deferring; regard, respect, consideration.
DEFERENT (1), [def'-er-ent], *n.* (*anat.*) a duct in the human body to carry off fluids. [L. *deferens*].
DEFERENT (2), [def'-er-ent], *adj.* deferential; (*anat.*) conveying away fluids. [*Prec.*].
DEFERENTIAL, [def'-er-en'-shal], *adj.* showing deference.
DEFERENTIALLY, [def'-er-en'-shal-i], *adv.* in a deferential manner.
DEFERMENT, [di-fur'-ment], *n.* the act of deferring, the state of being deferred.
DEFERRABLE, [di-fur'-abl], *adj.* able to be deferred.
DEFERRED, [di-furd'], *adj.* delayed, postponed; having the right to a dividend after paying off prior charges; **d. annuity,** an annuity becoming payable only after the lapse of a certain period of time or at death.
DEFERRER, [di-fur'-er], *n.* one who continually defers.
DEFERVESCENCE, [dē-fur-ves'-ents], *n.* (*med.*) the process of cooling down, abatement of fever. [L. *defervescens*].
DEFEUDALIZE, [dē-fewd'-al-īz], *v.t.* to deprive of feudal characteristics and forms.
DEFIANCE, [di-fī'-ants], *n.* the act of defying; **in d. of,** contrary to, disobeying. [OFr. *deffiance*].
DEFIANT (1), [di-fī'-ant], *n.* a type of British fighter aeroplane.
DEFIANT (2), [di-fī'-ant], *adj.* expressive of defiance; insolent; aggressively disobedient.
DEFIANTLY, [di-fī'-ant-li], *adv.* in a defiant way.
DEFIANTNESS, [di-fī'-ant-nes], *n.* the condition of being defiant.
DEFIATORY†, [di-fī'-a-ter-i], *adj.* conveying defiance.
DEFICIENCE†, [di-fish'-ents], *n.* deficiency. [LL. *deficientia*].
DEFICIENCY, [di-fish'-en-si], *n.* the state of being deficient; the amount by which anything is deficient; **d. bills,** a Bank of England loan to government facilitating payment of dividends on government stock; **d. disease,** a disease caused by lack of protective foods.
DEFICIENT, [di-fish'-ent], *adj.* lacking, wanting; not sufficient, inadequate; not having enough, defective; incomplete; **mentally d.,** slightly or completely imbecile. [L. *deficiens* lacking].
DEFICIENTLY, [di-fish'-ent-li], *adv.* in a deficient manner.
DEFICIT, [def'-i-sit], *n.* deficiency, the amount short; shortage; excess of debts over credit. [L. *deficit* it is lacking].
DEFIER, [di-fī'-er], *n.* a person who defies.
DEFILADE, [def'-il-ād'], *v.t. and i.* (*fort.*) to shelter from enfilading fire.
DEFILADING, [def'-il-ād'-ing], *n* (*milit.*) the act of protecting against enfilading fire.
DEFILE (1), [dē'-fīl], *n.* a very narrow passageway or pass in the hills.
DEFILE (2), [di-fīl'], *v.i.* to march in single file. [Fr. *defiler* to unthread].
DEFILE (3), [di-fīl'], *v.t.* to make dirty, to soil, pollute; (*fig.*) to corrupt, to render morally unclean. [OE. *fylan* to make foul].
DEFILEMENT, [di-fīl'-ment], *n.* the act of defiling; the state of being defiled; that which defiles.
DEFILER, [di-fīl'-er], *n.* one who, or that which, defiles.
DEFINABLE, [di-fīn'-abl], *adj.* able to be defined.
DEFINABLY, [di-fīn'-ab-li], *adv.* in definable fashion.
DEFINE, [di-fīn'], *v.t.* to mark clearly and fix the boundaries or limits of something; to describe accurately and comprehensively; to state in exact terms the meaning of a word, idiom or phrase; to outline. [L. *definire* to limit].
DEFINER, [di-fīn'-er], *n.* a person who defines.
DEFINITE, [def'-in-it], *adj.* having exact and fixed limits; settled; precise, exact; (*gram.*) limiting the application. [*Prec.*].
DEFINITELY, [def'-in-it-li], *adv.* in a definite fashion.
DEFINITENESS, [def'-in-it-nes], *n.* the quality of being definite.
DEFINITION, [def'-in-ish'-un], *n.* the act of defining; the process of being defined; an exact description of the nature of a thing; a concise explanation of the exact meaning of a word or phrase; (*phot.*) sharpness of detail, clearness; (*opt.*) the power of a lens to form a sharp image.
DEFINITIVE, [di-fin'-it-iv], *adj.* conclusive, determinate, positive, final. [L. *definitivus*].
DEFINITIVELY, [di-fin'-it-iv-li], *adv.* in a definitive manner.
DEFINITIVENESS, [di-fin'-it-iv-nes], *n.* the quality of being definitive.
DEFINITUDE, [di-fin'-it-ewd], *n.* definiteness.
DEFLAGRABILITY, [di-flā'-gra-bil'-i-ti], *n.* the quality of being deflagrable.
DEFLAGRABLE†, [di-flā'-grabl], *adj.* burning with a sudden rapid combustion.
DEFLAGRATE, [dē'-flag-rāt], *v.t.* to burn with fierce rapid combustion; *v.i.* to blaze and burn away.
DEFLAGRATION, [dē'-flag-rā'-shun], *n.* (*chem.*) the act or process of deflagrating. [L. *deflagratio*].
DEFLAGRATOR, [dē'-flag-rāt'-er], *n.* an electric battery producing intense heat.
DEFLATABLE, [di-flāt'-abl], *adj.* able to be deflated.
DEFLATE, [di-flāt'], *v.t.* to release or let out air; to reduce the amount of paper money in circulation. [DE and L. *flatus*, *p.pt.* of *flare* to blow].
DEFLATION, [di-flā'-shun], *n.* the act or result of deflating.
DEFLECT, [di-flekt'], *v.t. and i.* to turn aside from a straight or direct line or course. [L. *deflectere* to bend aside].
DEFLECTED, [di-flekt'-id], *adj.* (*bot.*) bending down archwise.
DEFLECTION, DEFLEXION, [di-flek'-shun], *n.* the act of deflecting, the state of being deflected. [L. *deflectio*].
DEFLECTIVE, [di-flek'-tiv], *adj.* tending to deflect.
DEFLECTOR, [di-flek'-ter], *n.* an appliance for improving combustion, fitted to a lamp burning gas.
DEFLEX, [dē-fleks'], *v.t.* (*bot.*) to bend down.
DEFLEXED, [di-flekst'], *adj.* (*bot.*) bent sharply down.
DEFLEXION, see DEFLECTION.
DEFLEXURE†, [di-flek'-sher], *n.* deflection.
DEFLORATE, [di-flaw'-rāt], *adj.* (*bot.*) having shed its pollen; with the flowers fallen off. [L. *defloratus*].
DEFLORATION, [dē'-flaw-rā'-shun], *n.* the act of deflowering. [L. *defloratio* picking of flowers].
DEFLOWER, [di-flow'-er], *v.t.* to deprive a woman of her virginity; (*fig.*) to take from anything its original beauty and purity.
DEFLOWERER, [di-flow'-er-er], *n.* one who deflowers.
DEFLUENT, [dē'-flōō-ent], *adj.* flowing down.
DEFLUX, [di-fluks'], *n.* defluxion.
DEFLUXION, [di-fluk'-shun], *n.* (*med.*) a discharge of mucus due to catarrh. [L. *defluxio* a flowing down].
DEFOLIATE (1), [di-fō'-li-āt], *adj.* (*bot.*) deprived of leaves.
DEFOLIATE (2), [dē-fō'-li-āt], *v.t.* to deprive of leaves.
DEFOLIATION, [di-fōl'-i-ā'-shun], *n.* (*bot.*) the shedding of leaves; the time of shedding leaves.
DEFORCE, [di-faws'], *v.t.* (*leg.*) to retain wrongfully by force.
DEFORCEMENT, [di-faws'-ment], *n.* (*leg.*) the act of deforcing.
DEFORCIANT, [di-faws'-i-ant], *n.* (*leg.*) a person who deforces. [AFr. *deforceant*].
DEFORCIATION†, [di-faws'-i-ā'-shun], *n.* deforcement. [MedL. *deforciatio*].
DEFOREST, [dē-for'-ist], *v.t.* to clear of trees; to disafforest.
DEFORM, [di-fawm'], *v.t.* to mar the form of, to disfigure, to make ugly or misshapen.
DEFORMATION, [dē'-fawm-ā'-shun], *n.* the act of deforming; the state of being deformed.
DEFORMED, [di-fawmd'], *adj.* abnormally formed in limb or body, disfigured, misshapen.
DEFORMEDLY, [di-fawm'-id-li], *adv.* in a deformed manner.
DEFORMEDNESS, [di-fawm'-id-nes], *n.* the condition of being deformed.
DEFORMER, [di-fawm'-er], *n.* a person who deforms.
DEFORMITY, [di-fawm'-i-ti], *n.* the state of being deformed; malformation; a misshapen organ or limb; disfigurement, ugliness. [L. *deformitas*].
DEFRAUD, [di-frawd'], *v.t.* to deprive of, to withhold from wrongfully, by fraud; to cheat, swindle. [L. *defraudare*].
DEFRAUDER, [di-frawd'-er], *n.* a person who defrauds.

DEFRAY, [di-frā'], *v.t.* to pay the cost of. [Fr. *défrayer*].
DEFRAYAL, [di-frā'-al], *n.* the act of defraying.
DEFRAYER, [di-frā'-er], *n.* a person who defrays.
DEFRAYMENT, [di-frā'-ment], *n.* defrayal.
DEFROCK, [dē'-frok'], *v.t.* to remove from the office or status of priest. [DE and FROCK (2)].
DEFROST, [dē-frost'], *v.t.* to render unfrozen; to unfreeze meat frozen for storage purposes.
DEFT, [deft], *adj.* dexterous, manually skilful, handy. [OE. *gedæft*].
DEFTLY, [deft'-li], *adv.* in a deft fashion.
DEFTNESS, [deft'-nes], *n.* the quality of being deft.
DEFUNCT (1), [di-fungkt'], *n.* a dead person.
DEFUNCT (2), [di-fungkt'], *adj.* dead. [L. *defunctus*, *p.pt.* of *defungi* to die].
DEFUNCTIVE†, [di-fungkt'-iv], *adj.* relating to the dead.
DEFY, [di-fī'], *v.t.* to challenge; to resist; to disobey; to flout, go in the face of; to baffle, frustrate. [Fr. *défier*].
DEGARNISH†, [dē-gah'-nish], *v.t.* to unfurnish; to deprive of a garrison.
DEGAUSS, [dē-gows'], *v.t.* to make (iron, etc.) incapable of affecting a magnet. [DE and GAUSS].
DEGENERACY, [di-jen'-er-a-si], *n.* the state of being degenerate.
DEGENERATE (1), [di-jen'-er-at], *n.* one who is degenerate.
DEGENERATE (2), [di-jen'-er-at], *adj.* being in a condition of development lower than a norm previously attained; fallen from a physical, mental or moral standard, depraved, defective, subnormal; having deteriorated. [L *degeneratus*].
DEGENERATE (3), [di-jen'-er-āt], *v.i.* to become degenerate; to worsen, deteriorate, to develop into something inferior.
DEGENERATELY, [di-jen'-er-at-li], *adv.* in degenerate fashion.
DEGENERATENESS, [di-jen'-er-at-nes], *n.* the condition of being degenerate.
DEGENERATION, [di-jen'-er-ā'-shun], *n.* the act of degenerating; the state of being degenerate.
DEGENERATIONIST, [di-jen'-er-ā'-shun-ist], *n.* one who believes that man has not improved but has degenerated.
DEGENERATIVE, [di-jen'-er-at-iv], *adj.* tending to degeneracy.
DEGENEROUS†, [di-jen'-er-us], *adj.* degenerate.
DEGENEROUSLY†, [di-jen'-er-us-li], *adv.* in a degenerous fashion.
DEGLUTINATE, [di-glew'-tin-āt], *v.t.* to unglue, to unstick. [L. *deglutinare*].
DEGLUTITION, [dē'-glew-tish'-un], *n.* the act or power of swallowing. [L. *deglutire* to swallow].
DEGRADATION, [deg'-rad-ā'-shun], *n.* the act of degrading; the state of being degraded; a condition of sordid poverty and misery; (*geol.*) attraction of surfaces; (*biol.*) degenerate state; (*chem.*) reduction.
DEGRADE, [di-grād'], *v.t. and i.* to reduce or lower the moral or physical level; to degenerate; to reduce in rank as a form of punishment; to take away honours and official recognition; to lower the dignity and self-respect of, to dishonour; to reduce the value of; (*geol.*) to wear down by attrition. [LL. *degradare*].
DEGRADED (1), [di-grā'-did], *adj.* having suffered degradation, mean, debased.
DEGRADED (2), [di-grā'-did], *adj.* (*her.*) placed on steps.
DEGRADING, [di-grā'-ding], *adj.* that degrades.
DEGRADINGLY, [di-grā'-ding-li], *adv.* in a degrading manner.
DEGREE, [di-grē'], *n.* a position, rank or grade relative to a line of development; an extent, amount, measure in relation to a larger; rank, status; an award conferred by a university as a mark of a certain proficiency in a branch of learning; (*alg.*) the rank of an equation as denoted by the highest power of the unknown quantity; (*phys.*) a unit of measurement of heat; (*geom.*) one of the three hundred and sixty divisions of a circle, constituting a unit of measurement; (*geog.*) a measure of sixty miles; (*gram.*) a form of qualification of adjectives; **by degrees,** step by step, gradually; **to a d.,** exceedingly; **third d.,** (*coll.*) a severe examination often accompanied by direct or indirect physical and mental torture for the purpose of extracting or forcing a confession; **degrees of latitude,** hypothetical lines at equal distances from each other drawn round the globe parallel to the equator; **degrees of longitude,** hypothetical lines encircling the earth and passing through the poles. [Fr. *degré* from LL. *degradus*].
DEGRESSION, [di-gresh'-un], *n.* a lowering of the rate of taxation on sums below a certain level. [L. *degressio* descent].
DEGUST, [dē-gust'], *v.t.* to taste, relish. [L. *degustare*].
DEGUSTATION, [dē'-gust-ā'-shun], *n.* the act of degusting. [L. *degustatio*].
DEHISCE, [dē-his'], *v.i.* (*bot.*) to burst asunder, as the capsules of plants, to release the ripened seeds or pollen. [L. *dehiscere* to burst open].
DEHISCENCE, [dē-his'-ents], *n.* (*bot.*) the act of dehiscing.
DEHISCENT, [dē-his'-ent], *adj.* (*bot.*) characterized by dehiscence.
DEHORS, [de-hawr'], *adj.* (*leg.*) irrelevant, outside the limits of. [OFr. *dehors*].
DEHORT†, [di-hawt'], *v.t.* to advise to the contrary, dissuade. [L. *dehortari* to dissuade].
DEHORTATION, [dē'-hawt-ā'-shun], *n.* dissuasion.
DEHORTATIVE, [di-hawt'-at-iv], *adj.* dehortatory.
DEHORTATORY, [di-hawt'-at-ter-i], *adj.* characterized by dehortation, dissuading, designed to dissuade.
DEHUMANIZE, [dē-hew'-man-īz], *v.t.* to deprive of human qualities, to render brutal or savage.
DEHYDRATE, [dē-hī'-drāt], *v.t.* (*chem.*) to extract or remove water from.
DEHYDRATION, [dē'-hī-drā'-shun], *n.* (*chem.*) the act of dehydrat.ng.
DEHYDROGENIZE, [dē-hī'-dro-jen-īz], *v.t.* (*chem.*) to extract the hydrogen from a chemical compound.
DEHYPNOTIZE, [dē-hip'-not-īz], *v.t.* to awake from a hypnotic trance.
DE-ICE, [dē-īs'], *v.t.* to prevent ice from forming on the surface of (an aeroplane).
DEICIDE, [dē'-i-sīd], *n.* the putting of a god to death; a person who kills a god. [L. *deus* god and *cidere* to kill].
DEICTIC, [dīk'-tik], *adj.* (*log.*) proving directly. [Gk. *deiktikos* able to prove].
DEIFIC, [dē-if'-ik], *adj.* making divine, godlike.
DEIFICAL†, [dē-if'-ik-al], *adj.* deific.
DEIFICATION, [dē'-if-ik-ā'-shun], *n.* the act of deifying; the state of being deified.
DEIFIED, [dē'-if-īd], *adj.* ranked with the gods.
DEIFORM, [dē'-i-fawm'], *adj.* having a divine form, like a god. [L. *deus* god and FORM].
DEIFY, [dē'-i-fī], *v.t.* to exalt to the rank of a god, to worship as a god, to make a god of. [LL. *deificare*].
DEIGN, [dān], *v.t. and i.* to condescend, to lower one's dignity. [OFr. *deigner* from L. *dignari*].
DEINTEGRATE, [dē-in'-tig-rāt], *v.t. and i.* to disintegrate.
DEIPAROUS, [dē-ip'-ar-us], *adj.* giving birth to a god. [L. *deus* god and *parus* bearing].
DEIPNOSOPHIST, [dīp-nos'-o-fist], *n.* a member of a group of philosophers who carried on their discussions at meal-times. [Gk. *deipnosophistes* culinary expert].
DEISM, [dē'-izm], *n.* the philosophical doctrine accepting a Divine Being existing apart from the world, but rejecting the manifestation of God in Christ. [L. *deus* god].
DEIST, [dē'-ist], *n.* a person believing in deism; a freethinker.
DEISTIC, [dē-ist'-ik], *adj.* relating to deism or to deists.
DEISTICAL, [dē-ist'-ik-al], *adj.* deistic.
DEISTICALLY, [dē-ist'-ik-al-i], *adv.* in the manner of deists.
DEITY, [dē'-it-i], *n.* the condition of being a god, divinity, the Supreme Being; a god or goddess. [L. *deitas*].
DEJECT, [di-jekt'], *v.t.* to depress; to discourage, dishearten. [L. *dejectum*, *p.pt.* of *dejicere* to throw down].
DEJECTED, [di-jekt'-id], *adj.* depressed, disheartened.
DEJECTEDLY, [di-jekt'-id-li], *adv.* in a dejected fashion.
DEJECTEDNESS, [di-jekt'-id-nes], *n.* the condition of being dejected.
DEJECTION, [di-jek'-shun], *n.* the state of being dejected; lowness of spirit; (*med.*) the act of evacuating the bowels. [L. *dejectio*].
DEJECTLY, [di-jekt'-li], *adv.* in a disheartened manner.
DEJECTORY, [di-jekt'-er-i], *adj.* (*med.*) encouraging evacuation, laxative.
DEJECTURE, [di-jek'-cher], *n.* excrement.
DEJEUNER, [dā'-zhur-nā], *n.* breakfast; luncheon. [Fr. *déjeuner*].

DE JURE, [dē-jew'-ri], *adv.* by law, as lawful. [L. *de* from and *ius iuris* law].
DEKKO, [dek'-ō], *n.* (*slang*) a look, a sight of. [Hind. *dekho*].
DEKLE, see DECKLE.
DELACERATION, [dē'-las'-er-ā'-shun], *n.* the act of tearing to pieces; the state of being torn in pieces.
DELACRYMATION†, [dē'-lak'-rim-ā'-shun], *n.* (*med.*) wateriness of the eyes, epiphora. [L. *delacrimatio* weeping].
DELACTATION, [dē'-lak-tā'-shun], *n.* weaning.
DELAINE, [di-lān'], *n.* a light material, originally of wool, but now of cotton and wool mixed. [Fr. *de laine* of wool].
DELATE, [di-lāt'], *v.t.* to inform against. [L. *delatum*, *p.pt.* of *deferre* to bring down].
DELATION, [di-lā'-shun], *n.* the act of delating. [L. *delatio* accusation].
DELATOR, [di-lā'-tor], *n.* an accuser, informer. [L. *delator*].
DELAY (1), [di-lā'], *n.* the act of delaying, the condition of being delayed, interval of waiting, a pause or retarding.
DELAY (2), [di-lā'], *v.t. and i.* to defer, postpone; to retard, detain; to procrastinate, linger, waste time. [OFr. *delaier* from L. *dilatare* to prolong].
DELAYMENT†, [di-lā'-ment], *n.* the act of delaying.
DEL-CREDERE, [del'-krād'-er-i], *n.* (*comm.*) a guarantee of the solvency of a purchaser. [It. *del credere* of trust].
DELE, [dē'-li], *v.t. imper.* (*print.*) omit, delete. [DELETE].
DELECTABLE, [di-lekt'-abl], *adj.* delightful, pleasant, charming. [L. *delectabilis*].
DELECTABLENESS, [di-lekt'-abl-nes], *n.* the quality of being delectable.
DELECTABLY, [di-lekt'-ab-li], *adv.* in a delectable manner.
DELECTATION, [dē'-lekt-ā'-shun], *n.* the act of pleasing, delight. [L. *delectatio*].
DELECTUS, [di-lekt'-us], *n.* an anthology of selected passages from classical authors for construing. [L. *delectus*, *p.pt.* of *deligere* to choose].
DELEGACY, [del'-ig-a-si], *n.* the system of representing by delegates; a group of delegates.
DELEGATE (1), [del'-ig-at], *n.* a person sent as a representative of a group or class of people. [L. *delegatus*].
DELEGATE (2), [del'-ig-āt], *v.t.* to elect or send as a delegate; to entrust to another as representative or deputy. [L. *delegare* to transfer].
DELEGATION, [del'-ig-ā'-shun], *n.* the act of delegating; a group or body of delegates; a group of delegates appointed to represent a State in international negotiations. [L. *delegatio*].
DELENDA, [di-lend'-a], *n.*(*pl.*) things to be deleted. [L. *delenda*].
DELETE, [di-lēt'], *v.t.* to erase, expunge, take out. [L. *deletum*, *p.pt.* of *delere* to efface].
DELETERIOUS, [del'-i-tēer-i-us], *adj.* harmful to life, injurious, noxious. [Gk. *deleterios*].
DELETION, [di-lē'-shun], *n.* the act of deleting, the state of being deleted; that which is deleted. [L. *deletio*].
DELETIVE†, [di-lē'-tiv], *adj.* effacing, deletory.
DELETORY, [di-lē'-ter-i], *adj.* effacing, deleting, removing.
DELF, [delf], *n.* an excavation, a hollow or hole dug in the earth; (*her.*) a square representing a clod of earth. [OE. *delf* trench].
DELFT, [delft], *n.* a kind of earthenware glazed over. [*Delft*, in Holland, where originally made].
DELIAC, [dē'-li-ak], *n.* a Grecian sculptured vase. [*Delos*, a Grecian island].
DELIBATE†, [del'-i-bāt], *v.t.* to taste, to sip, to sample. [L. *delibare*].
DELIBERATE (1), [di-lib'-er-at], *adj.* intentional; done with deliberation, studied; slow and decided in speech and movement. [L. *deliberatus*].

DELF

DELIBERATE (2), [di-lib'-er-āt'], *v.t. and i.* to reflect upon, consider; to think over carefully, study closely; to confer about, debate. [L. *deliberare*].
DELIBERATELY, [di-lib'-er-at-li], *adv.* in a deliberate fashion.
DELIBERATENESS, [di-lib'-er-at-nes], *n.* the quality of being deliberate.
DELIBERATION, [di-lib'-er-ā'-shun], *n.* the act of deliberating; deliberateness.
DELIBERATIVE, [di-lib'-er-at-iv], *adj.* pertaining to, acting by, deliberation.
DELIBERATIVELY, [di-lib'-er-at-iv'-li], *adv.* by deliberation.
DELIBLE, [del'-ibl], *adj.* able to be deleted.
DELICACIES, [del'-ik-as-iz], *n.*(*pl.*) choice eatables, food delicate to the taste; luxuries.
DELICACY, [del'-ik-as-i], *n.* the condition of being delicate; anything delicate to the palate.
DELICATE, [del'-ik-at], *adj.* fine in texture, material, and form, of slight and shapely proportions; soft, slender, neat, refined; subtle in sensibility, precisely adjusted; chaste; nice in perception; susceptible to illness or injury, fragile, frail; (*of colours*) pale or subtly blended; difficult to deal with; complex and highly responsive in nature. [L. *delicatus* tender, charming].
DELICATELY, [del'-ik-at-li], *adv.* in a delicate manner.
DELICATENESS, [del'-ik-at-nes], *n.* the quality of being delicate.
DELICATES, [del'-ik-ats], *n.*(*pl.*) delicacies.
DELICATESSEN, [del'-ik-at-es'-en], *n.* a shop or store selling cooked savoury foodstuffs; the goods sold by such a shop. [Germ. *delikatessen*].
DELICIOUS, [di-lish'-us], *adj.* very agreeable to the palate, highly pleasing to the taste or the senses; giving exquisite pleasure. [L. *deliciosus*].
DELICIOUSLY, [di-lish'-us-li], *adv.* in delicious fashion.
DELICIOUSNESS, [di-lish'-us-nes], *n.* the quality of being delicious.
DELICT, [di-likt'], *n.* (*leg.*) a legal offence; a crime. [L. *delictum*].
DELIGATION, [del'-ig-ā'-shun], *n.* (*med.*) bandaging binding up; a ligature. [L. *deligare* to bind up].
DELIGHT (1), [di-līt'], *n.* intense pleasure or satisfaction; that which causes such pleasure or satisfaction.
DELIGHT (2), [di-līt'], *v.t. and i.* to please intensely, to gladden, give delight to; to be highly pleased, to enjoy greatly. [OFr. *deliter* from L. *delectare*].
DELIGHTED, [di-lī'-tid], *adj.* full of delight, very pleased, charmed.
DELIGHTEDLY [di-lī'-tid-li], *adv.* in delighted fashion.
DELIGHTFUL, [di-līt'-fŏŏl], *adj.* giving delight charming, pleasant.
DELIGHTFULLY, [di-līt'-fŏŏl-i], *adv.* in a delightful manner.
DELIGHTFULNESS, [di-līt'-fool-nes], *n.* the quality of being delightful.
DELIGHTLESS, [di-līt'-les], *adj.* producing no delight.
DELIGHTSOME, [di-līt'-sum], *adj.* delightful.
DELIGHTSOMELY, [di-līt'-sum-li] *adv.* delightfully.
DELIGHTSOMENESS, [di-līt'-sum-nes], *n.* the quality of being delightsome.
DELIMIT, [dē-lim'-it], *v.t.* to fix the boundaries of; to take off a specific restriction.
DELIMITATE, [dē-lim'-it-āt], *v.t.* to delimit.
DELIMITATION, [dē-lim'-it-ā'-shun], *n.* the act of delimiting; the state of being delimited.
DELINEABLE, [di-lin'-i-abl], *adj.* able to be delineated.
DELINEAMENT†, [di-lin'-i-a-ment], *n.* delineation.
DELINEATE, [di-lin'-i-āt], *v.t.* to mark or sketch in outline, to trace out, sketch; to describe. [L. *delineare*].
DELINEATION, [di-lin'-i-ā-shun], *n.* the act of delineating; that which is delineated, a sketch, outline.
DELINEATOR, [di-lin'-i-āt-er], *n.* one who, or that which, delineates.
DELINQUENCY, [di-ling'-kwen-si], *n.* failure or omission of duty; fault, offence, a crime. [L. *delinquentia*].
DELINQUENT (1), [di-ling'-kwent] *n.* a criminal type, an offender; one who fails in or neglects a duty.
DELINQUENT (2), [di-ling'-kwent], *adj.* guilty of delinquency.
DELIQUESCE, [del'-i-kwes'], *v.i.* (*chem.*) to melt or turn to liquid by absorption of moisture from the atmosphere. [L. *deliquescere* to dissolve].
DELIQUESCENCE, [del'-i-kwes'-ents], *n.* the process or characteristic of deliquescing.
DELIQUESCENT, [del'-i-kwes'-ent], *adj.* that deliquesces.
DELIQUIUM†, [di-lik'-wi-um], *n.* (*chem.*) deliquescence. [L. *deliquium*].

DELIRATION, [del'-i-rā'-shun], *n.* delirium, temporary madness. [L. *deliratio*].

DELIRIANT [di-li'-ri-ant], *n.* (*med.*) a poison inducing delirium.

DELIRIFACIENT (1) [di-li'-ri-fāsh'-ent], *n.* an agent causing delirium.

DELIRIFACIENT (2), [di-li'-ri-fāsh'-ent], *adj.* inducing delirium. [DELIRIUM and L. *faciens* making].

DELIRIOUS, [di-li'-ri-us], *adj.* suffering from delirium.

DELIRIOUSLY [di-li'-ri-us-li], *adv.* in a delirious fashion.

DELIRIOUSNESS, [di-li'-ri-us-nes], *n.* the state of being delirious.

DELIRIUM, [di-li'-ri-um], *n.* a mental disorder in which the patient is unconscious of his surroundings and suffers from hallucinations; **d. tremens**, a state of delirium induced by alcoholic excesses. [L. *delirium* madness].

DELITESCENCE, [del'-it-es'-ents], *n.* (*med.*) the condition of being delitescent; incubation; sudden subsidence of a tumour.

DELITESCENT, [del'-it-es'-ent], *adj.* (*med.*) (of diseases or symptoms) latent, unmanifested, present but not appearing. [L. *delitescens*, *pres.pt.* of *delitescere* to hide].

DELIVER, [di-liv'-er], *v.t.* to set free, to save from something objectionable or injurious; to send, to forward; to give up, to hand over, to transfer; to help at childbirth; to pronounce, utter, make (a speech); to aim a blow; (*cricket*) to bowl a ball; (*leg.*) to hand over formally or officially. [LL. *deliberare* to set free].

DELIVERABLE, [di-liv'-er-abl], *adj.* able or requiring to be delivered.

DELIVERANCE, [di-liv'-er-ants], *n.* the act of delivering; the state of being delivered.

DELIVERER, [di-liv'-er-er], *n.* a person who delivers.

DELIVERY, [di-liv'-er-i], *n.* the act of delivering; a giving out or taking of postal matter to the addressee; a style of speaking; a ball bowled at cricket; the style of a bowler at cricket; childbirth. [*Prec.*].

DELL, [del], *n.* a small wooded valley, a dale. [OE. *dell*].

DELLA-ROBBIA WARE, [del'-a-rob'-i-a-wāer'], *n.* earthenware founded on terra-cotta enamelled and moulded. [*Della Robbia*, the Italian originator].

DELOCALIZE, [dē-lō'-kal-īz], *v.t.* to centralize.

DELOUSE, [dē'-lows], *v.t.* (*coll.*) to remove lice from.

DELPHIAN, [del'-fi-an], *adj.* Delphic.

DELPHIC, [del'-fik], *adj.* relating to Delphi, or the oracle of Apollo there; resembling in ambiguity one of Apollo's oracular statements. [*Delphi*, the ancient Greek temple of Apollo].

DELPHIN, [del'-fin], *adj.* relating to the Dauphin.

DELPHINE, [del'-fēn], *adj.* relating to the dolphin.

DELPHINIC, [del-fin'-ik], *adj.* pertaining to dolphin oil.

DELPHININE, [del'-fin-ēn], *n.* the alkaloid of larkspur.

DELPHINIUM, [del-fin'-i-um], *n.* (*bot.*) the genus of plants to which the larkspur belongs. [L. from Gk. *delphinion* larkspur].

DELTA, [del'-ta], *n.* the fourth letter in the Greek alphabet; the flat triangular-shaped area of land at the mouth of the Nile; flat alluvial land through which a river finds several outlets to the sea; **d. metal**, an alloy of zinc, copper, and ferro-manganese. [Gk. *delta* the fourth letter in alphabet].

DELTAFICATION, [del'-ta-fik-ā'-shun] *n.* the forming of a delta. [DELTA and L. *ficatio* making].

DELTAIC, [del-tā'-ik], *adj.* relating to, or resembling, a delta.

DELPHINIUM

DELTA-LEAVED, [del'-ta-lēvd'], *adj.* (*bot.*) having leaves in the form of a delta.

DELTOHEDRON, [del'-tō-hēd'-ron], *n.* a solid having a surface of twenty-four deltoids. [DELTA and Gk. *hedra* base].

DELTOID (1), [del'-toid], *n.* (*anat.*) the large triangular muscle of the shoulder used to elevate or move the arm.

DELTOID (2), [del'-toid], *adj.* (*anat.*) (of a muscle) triangular in shape; (*bot.*) shaped like a delta. [DELTA and Gk. *oeides* like].

DELUDABLE, [di-lewd'-abl], *adj.* able to be deluded.

DELUDE, [di-lewd'], *v.t.* to impose on, deceive, to mislead deliberately; (*reflex.*) to convince oneself by false hopes. [L. *deludere*].

DELUGE (1), [del'-ewj], *n.* an overwhelming flood of water; (*fig.*) a spate of words; (*coll.*) a cloudburst; **the D.**, Noah's flood. [F. *déluge*].

DELUGE (2), [del'-ewj], *v.t.* to overwhelm with water; to inundate; (*fig.*) to overwhelm.

DELUSION, [di-lew'-zhun], *n.* the act of deluding; the state of being deluded; a mistaken belief, a fallacy, deception, an illusion; a firm and absurd belief of a pathological nature. [L. *delusio*].

DELUSIONAL, [di-lōōzh'-an-al], *adj.* exhibiting delusions.

DELUSIVE, [di-lews'-iv], *adj.* tending to delude.

DELUSIVELY, [di-lews'-iv-li], *adv.* in a delusive fashion.

DELUSIVENESS, [di-lews'-iv-nes] *n.* the condition of being delusive.

DELUSORY, [di-lews'-er-i], *adj.* delusive.

DELVE, [delv], *v.t. and i.* to dig with a spade; (*fig.*) to make an active and exhaustive study of. [OE. *delfan*].

DELVER, [delv'-er], *n.* a person who digs or delves.

DEMAGNETIZE, [dē'-mag'-net-īz], *v.t.* to eliminate magnetic qualities from; to deprive of polarity.

DEMAGOGIC, [dem'-a-gog'-ik], *adj.* relating to, or resembling, a demagogue or demagogy.

DEMAGOGICAL, [dem'-a-gog'-ik-al], *adj.* demagogic.

DEMAGOGISM, [dem'-a-gog'-izm], *n.* the methods and practices of a demagogue.

DEMAGOGUE, [dem'-a-gog'], *n.* a person speaking for the interests of the mass of the people, agitating on their behalf, and leading them against the ruling classes; a politician with principles of dubious sincerity playing on the emotions of the people. [Gk. *demagogos* leader of the people].

DEMAGOGY, [dem'-a-gog'-i], *n.* the principles and tactics of a demagogue.

DEMAIN, [di-mān'], *n.* demesne.

DEMAND (1), [di-mahnd'], *n.* a claim by right of agreement, an authorized request; an urgent request, a claim requiring immediate settlement; an aggressive request; (*econ.*) the necessities or requirements of consumers.

DEMAND (2), [di-mahnd'], *v.t.* to make a demand for; to require, need, ask for. [L. *demandare* to hand over to the charge of].

DEMANDABLE, [di-mahnd'-abl], *adj.* able to be demanded.

DEMANDANT, [di-mahnd'-ant], *n.* a person who demands; (*leg.*) a plaintiff.

DEMARCATE, [dē'-mah-kāt'], *v.t.* to mark out and fix a boundary.

DEMARCATION, [dē'-mahk-ā'-shun], *n.* the act of demarcating; the dividing line or boundary demarcated. [Fr. *démarcation*].

DEMARCHE, démarche, [dā'-mahsh], *n.* (in diplomacy) an announcement of a fresh plan of action, or a new departure in policy. [Fr. *démarche* step aside].

DEMATERIALIZE, [dē'-mat-ēer'-i-al-īz], *v.t.* to deprive of material aspect, to spiritualize; *v.i.* to become spiritualized.

DEMEAN (1), [di-mēn'], *v.t. and refl.* to lower, to degrade, to humiliate.

DEMEAN† (2), [di-mēn'], *v.t.* to behave; to conduct. [OFr. *demener* to manage].

DEMEANOUR, [di-mēn'-er], *n.* behaviour, bearing, deportment. [ME. *demenure*].

DEMENT, [di-ment'], *v.t.* to render insane, drive mad. [L. *dementare*].

DEMENTATE†, [di-ment'-āt], *v.t.* to dement. [*Prec.*].

DEMENTED, [di-ment'-id], *adj.* insane, crazy, infatuated. [L. *dementatus*].

DEMENTEDNESS, [di-ment'-id-nes], *n.* the state of being demented.

DEMENTI, démenti, [dem-on'-ti], *n.* a denial, an official contradiction. [Fr. *démenti*].

DEMENTIA, [di-men'-shi-a], *n.* insanity. [L. *demens dementis*].

DEMEPHITIZATION, [dē-mef'-i-tīz-ā'-shun], *n.* the act of demephitizing.

DEMEPHITIZE, [dē-mef'-i-tīz], *v.t.* to free from noxious air. [DE and Gk. *mephitis* bad air].

DEMERARA, [dem'-er-āer'-a], *n.* a kind of brown sugar from the island of this name.

ō (bone), ī (fine), ōō (food), ŏŏ (put), u (up), th (*th*ink), TH (*th*at), zh (a*z*ure), † = obsolete, ~ = related to.

DEMERIT, [dē-me'-rit], *n.* an undesirable trait, defect; a characteristic worthy of censure. [L. *demeritum*].
DEMERITORIOUS, [dē-me'-ri-taw'-ri-us], *adj.* blameworthy.
DEMERSED, [dē-murst'], *adj.* sub-aqueous; (*bot.*) growing under water. [L. *demersum*, *p.pt.* of *demergere* to submerge].
DEMESMERIZE, [dē-mez'-mer-iz], *v.t.* to free from a state of mesmerism.
DEMESNE, [di-mān', di-mēn'], *n.* land immediately surrounding a country house; land not worked by tenants but by the owner himself. [AFr. *demesne*].
DEMESNIAL, [di-mān'-i-al], *adj.* of, or belonging to, a demesne.
DEMI-, *pref.* half, partial. [Fr. *demi*].
DEMIBASTION, [dem-i-bas'-chun], *n.* (*arch.*) part of a crown work with one face and one flank cut off by a capital.
DEMICADENCE, [dem'-i-kā'-dents], *n.* (*mus.*) a cadence which falls on any other than the key note.
DEMICULVERIN, [dem-i-kul'-ver-in], *n.* a piece of ordnance, used in the sixteenth century, firing a ball of nine or ten pounds. [Fr. *demi-coulevrine*].
DEMIDEIFY, [dem'-i-dē'-i-fī], *v.t.* to make into a demigod.
DEMI-DISTANCE, [dem'-i-dis'-tants], *n.* (*fort.*) the space between the outward polygons and the flank.
DEMIDITONE, [dem'-i-dī'-tōn], *n.* (*mus.*) a minor third.
DEMIGOD, [dem'-i-god'], *n.* a half divine being sprung from the union of a god and a mortal; (*fig.*) one possessing god-like qualities, or regarded as a god.
DEMIGORGE, [dem'-i-gawj'], *n.* (*fort.*) that portion of the polygon remaining after the flank is raised, and running from the curtain to the angle of the polygon.
DEMIJOHN, [dem'-i-jon'], *n.* a glass or earthenware bottle with a large body and small neck, enclosed in wicker-work. [Fr. *dame-jeanne* Dame Jane].
DEMILANCE, [dem'-i-lahnts'], *n.* a light lance, a half-pike.
DEMILUNE, [dem'-i-lōōn], *n.* (*fort.*) a fortification shaped like a half-moon. [Fr. *demilune* half-moon].
DEMI-MONDAINE, [dem-i-mond'-ān], *n.* a member of the demi-monde.
DEMI-MONDE, [dem-i-mond'], *n.* a class of women of doubtful character and uncertain social position. [Fr. *demi-monde* half-world].
DEMI-OFFICIAL, [dem'-i-o-fish'-al], *adj.* semi-official, partially authorized.
DEMIREP, [dem'-i-rep'], *n.* a woman of doubtful character. [DEMI and REPUTE].
DEMISABLE, [di-mīz'-abl], *adj.* that may be transferred by lease or inheritance.
DEMISE (1), [di-mīz'], *n.* the action of conveying property; the transmission of an estate or hereditary privilege by death, especially on the death of the sovereign; death. [OFr. *demise* sent away, dismissed].
DEMISE (2), [di-mīz'], *v.t.* to grant by deed, lease, etc.; to transmit by inheritance. [DEMISE (1)].
DEMISEMIQUAVER, [dem'-i-sem'-i-kwā'-ver], *n.* (*mus.*) a note half the length of a semiquaver.
DEMISS†, [di-mis'], *adj.* submissive, downcast; (*bot.*) depressed, flattened. [L. *demissus*].
DEMISSION, [di-mish'-un], *n.* the act of resigning an office. [L. *demissio*].
DEMISSIVE†, [di-mis'-iv], *adj.* downcast, submissive.
DEMISSLY†, [di-mis'-li], *adv.* in a demissive or humble fashion.
DEMIT, **(demitting, demitted)**, [di-mit'], *v.t.* (*Scots leg.*) to lay down formally, to give up office, resign. [Fr. *démettre*].
DEMI-TINT, [dem'-i-tint], *n.* (*paint.*) a half-tint; a tint intermediate between strong light and shade.
DEMITONE, [dem'-i-tōn], *n.* (*mus.*) a semitone.
DEMIURGE, [dem'-i-urj], *n.* a magistrate in ancient Greece; the world builder and agent, the Creator. [Gk. *demiourgos* skilled workman, creator].
DEMIURGIC, [dem'-i-urj'-ik], *adj.* pertaining to the demiurge; creative.
DEMI-VOLT, [dem'-i-volt'], *n.* a partial turn by a horse, with forelegs in mid-air. [Fr. *demi-volte*].
DEMOB, [dē-mob'], *v.t.* (*coll.*) to demobilize. [DEMOB(ILIZE)].
DEMOBILIZATION, [dē'-mōb'-i-līz-ā'-shun], *n.* the act of demobilizing.
DEMOBILIZE, [dē-mōb'-i-līz], *v.t.* to disband military forces; to dismiss a person from the fighting forces after a war. [DE and MOBILIZE].
DEMOCRACY, [di-mok'-ra-si], *n.* government by all classes for the benefit of all classes; a state having this form of government; the people, especially the working classes, of such a state. [Gk. *demokratia*].
DEMOCRAT, [dem'-ō-krat], *n.* a person who believes in democracy; (U.S.) a member or supporter of the Democratic Party. [Fr. *démocrate*].
DEMOCRATIC, [dem'-ō-krat'-ik], *adj.* pertaining to in favour of, founded on democracy.
DEMOCRATICAL, [dem'-ō-krat'-ik-al] *adj.* democratic.
DEMOCRATICALLY, [dem'-ō-krat'-ik-al-i], *adv.* in a democratic fashion.
DEMOCRATIZE, [di-mok'-ra-tīz], *v.t.* to make democratic.
DEMOCRITEAN, [di-mok'-ri-tē'-an], *adj.* pertaining to Democritus.
DEMODE, démodé, [dā-mōd'-ā], *adj.* out of fashion, dated. [Fr. *démode*].
DEMOGORGON, [dē'-mō-gaw'-gon], *n.* a terrible deity of the lower regions. [Gk. *demos* people and *gorgos* terrible].
DEMOGRAPHER, [di-mog'-ra-fer], *n.* a student of demography.
DEMOGRAPHIC, [dem'-ō-graf'-ik], *adj.* pertaining to demography.
DEMOGRAPHY, [di-mog'-ra-fi], *n.* the social study of a community as revealed by statistics of its births, deaths or diseases. [Gk. *demos* people and *graphia* writing].
DEMOISELLE, [dem'-wah-zel'], *n.* a young unmarried woman. [Fr. *demoiselle*].
DEMOLISH, [di-mol'-ish], *v.t.* to pull down, destroy; (*coll.*) to eat up completely. [Fr. *démolir*].
DEMOLISHER, [di-mol'-ish-er], *n.* one who demolishes.
DEMOLISHMENT, [di-mol'-ish-ment], *n.* demolition.
DEMOLITION, [dē-mol-ish'-un], *n.* the act of demolishing. [L. *demolitio*].
DEMOLOGY, [di-mol'-o-ji], *n.* demography. [Gk *demos* people and *logos* speech].
DEMON, [dē'-mon], *n.* a spirit, supernatural being; one's guiding genius; an evil spirit or genius, a devil; (*coll.*) a naughty child; a wicked or supremely evil person. [Gk. *daimon*].
DEMONESS, [dē'-mon-es], *n.* a she-devil.
DEMONETIZE, [dē-mun'-i-tīz], *v.t.* to deprive of standard value, as money; to withdraw from use as currency. [Fr. *démonetiser*].
DEMONIAC (1), [di-mō'-ni-ak], *n.* a person possessed by a demon.
DEMONIAC (2), [di-mō'-ni-ak], *adj.* pertaining to demons; influenced or produced by demons or wicked spirits. [L. *daemoniacus*].
DEMONIACAL, [dē'-mon-ī'-ak-al], *adj.* demoniac, diabolical; possessed of a demon.
DEMONIACALLY, [dē'-mon-ī'-ak-al-i], *adv.* in a demoniacal fashion.
DEMONIACISM, [dē'-mon-ī'-a-sizm], *n.* a demoniacal condition, demoniacal practices.
DEMONIC, [di-mo'-nik], *adj.* relating to a demon; possessed or inspired by a demon.
DEMONISM, [dē'-mon-izm], *n.* belief in the existence and power over human beings of demons.
DEMONIST, [dē'-mon-ist], *n.* a believer in demons.
DEMONIZE, [dē'-mon-īz], *v.t.* to turn into a demon; to put under the power of a demon.
DEMONOCRACY, [dē-mon-ok'-ra-si], *n.* the rule or dominion of demons. [DEMON and Gk. *kratos* power].
DEMONOLATRY, [dē-mon-ol'-a-tri], *n.* demon-worship. [DEMON and Gk. *latreia* worship].
DEMONOLOGIC, [dē'-mon-ol-oj'-ik], *adj.* demonological.
DEMONOLOGICAL, [dē'-mon-ol-oj'-ik-al], *adj.* pertaining to demonology.
DEMONOLOGIST, [dē'-mon-ol'-oj-ist], *n.* a person skilled in demonology.
DEMONOLOGY, [dē'-mon-ol'-o-ji], *n.* the study concerned with the belief in demons or evil spirits. [DEMON and Gk. *logos* speech].
DEMONOMANIA, [dē'-mon-ō-mā'-ni-a], *n.* a mania in which the patient imagines himself to be possessed by devils. [DEMON and MANIA].
DEMONOMY†, [dē-mon'-om-i], *n.* belief in the dominion of demons. [DEMON and Gk. *nomos* a law].
DEMONRY, [dē'-mon-ri], *n.* demoniacal power.
DEMONSHIP, [dē'-mon-ship], *n.* the state of being a demon.
DEMONSTRABLE, [de'-mon-strabl], *adj.* able to be demonstrated. [L. *demonstrabilis*].

DEMONSTRABLENESS, [de'-mon-strabl-nes], *n.* the state of being demonstrable.

DEMONSTRABLY, [de'-mon-strab-li], *adv.* in demonstrable fashion.

DEMONSTRATE, [dem'-on-strāt], *v.t. and i.* to offer logical proof of, set forth the arguments supporting, to prove; to give practical examples of the working of, to use or make work for inspection; to organize a public meeting in support of one's opinions; (*milit.*) to show willingness for action. [L. *demonstrare* to point out].

DEMONSTRATION, [dem'-on-strā'-shun], *n.* the act of demonstrating; an exhibition, a practical illustration; a public exhibition of feeling; an active expression of public dissatisfaction; (*anat.*) the exhibiting of parts dissected; (*milit.*) a movement of troops with a view to deceive; (*log.*) a series of syllogisms all of whose premises are either definitions, self-evident truths, or propositions already established. [L. *demonstratio*].

DEMONSTRATIVE, [di-mon'-strat-iv], *adj.* logically conclusive; clearly demonstrating; forcibly frank, given to demonstration; (*gram.*) that points out emphatically a specific thing.

DEMONSTRATIVELY, [di-mon'-strat-iv-li], *adv.* in a demonstrative fashion.

DEMONSTRATIVENESS, [di-mon'-strat-iv-nes], *n.* the quality of being demonstrative.

DEMONSTRATOR, [dem'-on-strāt-er], *n.* one who demonstrates; one who assists a professor of science in his practical demonstrations and experiments; a practical teacher of science.

DEMONSTRATORY, [di-mon'-strat-er-i], *adj.* tending to demonstrate.

DEMORALIZATION, [di-mor'-al-īz-ā'-shun] *n.* the act of demoralizing; the condition of being demoralized.

DEMORALIZE, [di-mor'-al-īz], *v.t.* to undermine or corrupt the morals, courage or discipline of, to destroy the moral fibre of. [Fr. *démoraliser*].

DEMOS, [dē'-mos], *n.* the common people, *esp.* those of an ancient Greek state. [Gk. *demos* a district, the people of a district].

DEMOSTHENIC, [dē-mos-then'-ik], *adj.* pertaining to Demosthenes, the Greek orator; eloquent.

DEMOTIC, [di-mot'-ik], *adj.* in common use. [Gk. *demotikos* common].

DEMPSTER, [demp'-ster], *n.* a deemster. [DEEMSTER].

DEMULCENT (1), [di-mul'-sent], *n.* a soothing ointment or medicine. [DEMULCENT (2)].

DEMULCENT (2), [di-mul'-sent], *adj.* having a soothing quality; softening. [L. *demulcens*].

DEMUR (1), [di-mur'], *n.* objection, hesitation, questioning. [Fr. *demeure*].

DEMUR (2), (demurring, demurred), [di-mur'], *v.i.* to hesitate from uncertainty, disapprove, feel scruples concerning; (*leg.*) to raise an objection which stops proceedings until it is decided. [Fr. *demeurer*].

DEMURE, [di-myōō'-er], *adj.* serious, grave, quietly decorous, modest. [DE and OFr. *mure* ripe].

DEMURELY, [di-myōō'-er-li], *adv.* in demure fashion.

DEMURENESS, [di-myōō'-er-nes], *n.* the state or quality of being demure.

DEMURRABLE, [di-mu'-rabl], *adj.* (*leg.*) of such a nature as to call for a demurrer.

DEMURRER, [di-mur'-rer], *n.* a person who demurs; (*leg.*) a pleading which, while it admits the truth of the facts as set out by the opponent, declares that he is not legally entitled to redress, and brings the action to a halt pending a decision on this question by the court. [AFr. *demurrer*].

DEMY, [di-mī'], *n.* a regulation size of paper, measuring $22\frac{1}{2}$ by $17\frac{1}{2}$ inches for printing, and 20 by $15\frac{1}{2}$ inches for writing on; a foundation scholar at Magdalen College, Oxford. [DEMI].

DEMYSHIP, [di-mī'-ship], *n.* a foundation scholarship at Magdalen College, Oxford.

DEN, [den], *n.* the lair, home, or hiding-place of a wild animal; a cage for wild beasts in a menagerie, etc.; (*fig.*) a place of retreat or abode; a hiding place of thieves; a small, dark, sordid room or dwelling, a small private room for work or leisure. [OE. *denn*].

DENARIUS, [den-āer'-i-us], *n.* an ancient Roman silver coin worth 10 asses, or $7\frac{3}{4}$d.; (in books on law) an English penny. [L. *denarius*].

DENARY, [den'-er-i], *adj.* pertaining to the number ten; decimal. [L. *denarius*].

DENATIONALIZATION, [dē-nash'-un-al-īz-ā'-shun], *n.* the act of denationalizing; the condition of being denationalized.

DENATIONALIZE, [dē-nash'-un-al-īz], *v.t.* to divest of national rights; to deprive of the status of a nation; to divest of its national character. [DE and NATIONALIZE].

DENATURALIZATION, [dē'-nach-er-al-īz-ā'-shun], *n.* the act of denaturalizing; the state of being denaturalized.

DENATURALIZE, [dē-nach'-er-al-īz], *v.t.* to render unnatural; to deprive of the rights and standing of a citizen. [DE and NATURALIZE].

DENATURANT, [dē-nā'-cher-ant], *n.* that which changes the nature of a thing; an adulterative addition.

DENATURATION, [dē'-nā-cher-ā'-shun], *n.* the process of denaturing.

DENATURE, [dē-nā'-cher], *v.t.* to adulterate so as to change the essential quality of; to make unsuitable for consumption. [Fr. *dénaturer*].

DENDRACHATE, [den'-dra-kāt], *n.* (*min.*) an agate with markings resembling vegetable forms. [DENDRO and Gk. *akates* agate].

DENDRIFORM, [den'-dri-fawm], *adj.* of the form of a tree; branching. [Gk. *dendron* tree and FORM (1)].

DENDRITE, [den'-drīt], *n.* a mineral in which are embedded the figures of vegetable forms. [Gk. *dendrites* of a tree].

DENDRITIC, [den-drit'-ik], *adj.* resembling dendrite.

DENDRITICAL, [den-drit'-ik-al], *adj.* dendritic.

DENDRO-, *pref.* of a tree or trees. [Gk. *dendron* a tree].

DENDRODONT, [den'-drō-dont], *adj.* a fossil fish the teeth of which show a branch-like tissue. [DENDRO and Gk. *odous odontos* tooth].

DENDROID, [den'-droid], *adj.* resembling a tree tree-like. [DENDRO and Gk. *oeides* like].

DENDROLATRY, [den-drol'-a-tri], *n.* the worship of trees. [DENDRO and Gk. *latreia* worship].

DENDROLITE, [den'-drō-līt], *n.* a fossil plant or section of a plant. [DENDRO and Gk. *lithos* a stone].

DENDROLOGIST, [den-drol'-oj-ist], *n.* one learned in dendrology. [*Next*].

DENDROLOGY, [den-drol'-o-ji], *n.* the study of trees. [DENDRO and Gk. *logos* speech].

DENDROMETER, [den-drom'-i-ter], *n.* an instrument for measuring the height and diameter of trees. [DENDRO and Gk. *metron* a measure].

DENE (1), [dēn], *n.* a bare, sandy stretch by the sea; a low sand-hill. [OE. *dyne*, **dene*, a hill, mound].

DENE (2), [dēn], *n.* a little hollow on a hillside or on downland. [OE. *denu*].

DENEGATE†, [dē'-ni-gāt], *v.t.* to deny. [L. *denegare*].

DENEGATION, [dē-ni-gā'-shun], *n.* denial, contradiction.

DENEHOLE, [dēn'-hōl], *n.* an ancient, deep excavation, usually in chalk, widening into horizontal passages at the bottom.

DENGUE, [deng'-ā], *n.* (*med.*) break-bone fever, a tropical fever characterized by redness of the skin and severe rheumatic pains. [W. Indian Span. *dengue*].

DENIABLE, [di-nī'-abl], *adj.* which may be denied.

DENIAL, [di-nī'-al], *n.* the act of denying; a statement which denies something.

DENIER (1), [di-nī'-er], *n.* one who denies.

DENIER (2), [den'-i-er], *n.* a small French copper coin of low value. [Fr. *denier*].

DENIGRATE, [den'-i-grāt], *v.t.* to blacken; (*fig.*) to blacken the character of, to slander. [L. *denigrare*].

DENIM, [den'-im], *n.* coarse cotton drill used for making aprons and overalls, and manufactured first at Nîmes in France. [Fr. (*serge*) *de Nîmes* Nîmes (serge)].

DENITRATE, [dē-nī'-trāt], *v.t.* to rid of nitric acid or nitrate. [DE and NITRATE].

DENITRATION, [dē-nī-trā'-shun], *n.* the act of denitrating.

DENIZATION, [den'-iz-ā'-shun], *n.* the action of declaring a person a subject or citizen.

DENIZEN (1), [den'-iz-en], *n.* an inhabitant of a place, native or otherwise; a naturalized alien; an inhabitant, dweller. [OFr. *deinzein*].

DENIZEN (2), [den'-iz-en], *v.t.* to make a denizen or subject; to populate, settle a country.

DENIZENSHIP, [den'-iz-en-ship], *n.* the status of a denizen.

DENNET, [den'-et], *n.* an open, two-wheeled vehicle resembling a gig. [The surname *Dennet*].

DENOMINABLE, [di-nom'-i-nabl], *adj.* capable of being named.

DENOMINATE, [di-nom'-i-nāt], *v.t.* to give a name to; to call. [L. *denominare*].

DENOMINATION, [di-nom'-i-nā'-shun], *n.* the act of naming; a name, title; a group called by the same name; a religious sect; (*arith.*) a unit of measure. [L. *denominatio*].

DENOMINATIONAL, [di-nom'-i-nā'-shun-al], *adj.* pertaining or belonging to a religious denomination; sectarian.

DENOMINATIONALISM, [di-nom'-i-nā'-shun-al-izm], *n.* a spirit of exclusive devotion to the interests and tenets of a sect or party.

DENOMINATIONALIZE, [di-nom-i-nā'-shun-al-iz], *v.t.* to make denominational.

DENOMINATIONALLY, [di-nom'-i-nā'-shun-al-i], *adv.* by denomination.

DENOMINATIVE, [di-nom'-i-nat-iv], *adj.* that gives a name to; (*gram.*) derived from a noun. [L. *denominativus*].

DENOMINATIVELY, [di-nom'-i-nat-iv-li], *adv.* by way of denomination.

DENOMINATOR, [di-nom'-i-nā'-ter], *n.* a person or thing that names; (*arith.*) the number placed below the line in a vulgar fraction. [L. *denominator*].

DENOTABLE, [di-nōt'-abl], *adj.* that may be denoted.

DENOTATE†, [dē'-nōt-āt], *v.t.* to denote. [L. *denotare*].

DENOTATION, [dē'-nōt-ā'-shun], *n.* the act of denoting; the thing by which anything is denoted; (*log.*) the meaning of a word, the extent of a term's application. [L. *denotatio*].

DENOTATIVE, [di-nōt'-at-iv], *adj.* having power to denote.

DENOTE, [di-nōt'], *v.t.* to mark out; to show; to indicate; to stand as a symbol for. [L. *denotare*].

DENOTEMENT, [di-nōt'-ment], *n.* the fact of denoting; an indication.

DENOUEMENT, dénouement [dā-nōō'-mo(ng)], *n.* the last dramatic revelation in a plot, the unravelling of a plot or situation, the climax. [Fr. *dénouement* an unravelling].

DENOUNCE, [di-nownts'], *v.t.* to censure openly and threateningly; to accuse publicly; to bring to an end. [OFr. *denoncier*].

DENOUNCEMENT, [di-nowns'-ment], *n.* denunciation.

DENOUNCER, [di-nowns'-er], *n.* one who denounces.

DENSE, [dents], *adj.* tightly packed together; crowded, thick; opaque, impenetrable; (*fig.*) stupid, dull of comprehension. [L. *densus* thick].

DENSELY, [dens'-li], *adv.* in a dense fashion.

DENSENESS, [dens'-nes], *n.* the state or quality of being dense.

DENSIMETER, [dens-im'-i-ter], *n.* a scientific instrument for measuring density. [DENSE and METER].

DENSITY, [dens'-i-ti], *n.* the quality of being dense; (*phys.*) the relation of mass to bulk; specific gravity. [L. *densitas*].

DENT (1), [dent], *n.* a depression or slight hollow mark made by pressure or a blow; indentation; (*pl.*) the wires of the reed-frame of a weaver's loom. [OE. *dent*, a S.E. variant of W. Saxon *dynt*].

DENT (2), [dent], *v.t.* to make a dent in.

DENTAL, [dent'-al], *adj.* pertaining to the teeth or to dentistry; (of certain consonants) pronounced by putting the tip of the tongue to the upper teeth. [MedL. *dentalis*].

DENTARY, [dent'-er-i], *n.* (*anat.*) a bone in the lower jaw of certain vertebrates for supporting the teeth. [L. *dentarius*].

DENTATE, [dent'-āt], *adj.* edged with teeth or tooth-like projections. [L. *dentatus*].

DENTATED, [dent-āt'-id], *adj.* dentate.

DENTATELY, [dent'-āt-li], *adv.* in a dentate manner.

DENTATION, [dent-ā'-shun], *n.* the state of being dentate.

DENTATO-, *pref.* dentately, with teeth. [L. *dentatus*].

DENTATO-CRENATE, [dent-ā'-tō-krēn'-āt], *adj.* with triangular notches.

DENTATO-LACINIATE, [dent-ā'-tō-la-sin'-i-āt], *adj.* with teeth irregularly extended into long points.

DENTATO-SERRATE, [dent-ā'-tō-se'-rāt], *adj.* having regular tapering teeth pointed forwards.

DENTATE

DENTATO-SINUATE, [dent-ā'-tō-sin'-yōō-at], *adj.* (*bot.*) (of a leaf) intermediate in form between the dentate and the sinuate.

DENTED, [dent'-id], *adj.* with indentations; toothed.

DENTELS, [dent'-elz], *n.(pl.)* dentils. [Fr. *dentelle*].

DENTI-, *pref.* of, or relating to, teeth. [L. *dens dentis* tooth].

DENTICLE, [dent'-ikl], *n.* a little tooth; a small tooth-shaped projection. [L. *denticulus*].

DENTICULAR, [dent-ik'-yōō-ler], *adj.* like a small tooth; slightly notched.

DENTICULATE, [dent-ik'-yōō-lāt], *adj.* with small teeth or tooth-like projections. [L. *denticulatus*].

DENTICULATELY, [dent-ik'-yōō-lat-li], *adv.* in denticulate fashion.

DENTICULATION, [dent-ik'-yōō-lā'-shun], *n.* the state of being finely toothed.

DENTIFORM, [dent'-i-fawm], *adj.* in the form of a tooth, tooth-shaped. [DENTI and FORM (1)].

DENTIFRICE, [dent'-i-fris], *n.* a powder or paste for cleaning the teeth. [L. *dentifricium*].

DENTIGEROUS, [dent'-ij-er-us], *adj.* bearing teeth. [DENTI and L. *gerere* to bear].

DENTIL, [dent'-il], *n.* (*arch.*) one of the small projecting blocks in the moulding of certain cornices. [Fr. *dentille*].

DENTILATION, [dent-i-lā'-shun], *n.* dentition.

DENTILAVE, [dent'-i-lāv], *n.* a wash for the teeth. [DENTI and L. *lavare* to wash].

DENTILINGUAL, [dent'-i-ling'-gwal], *adj.* (*phon.*) (of certain consonants) pronounced by applying the tongue to the gum above the upper teeth. [DENTI and LINGUAL].

DENTIL

DENTINE, [dent'-in], *n.* the hard, bone-like ivory tissue forming the body of a tooth.

DENTIROSTER, [dent'-i-ros'-ter] *n.* (*ornith.*) a passerine bird having tooth-like processes on the bill. [DENTI and L. *rostrum* a beak].

DENTISCALP, [dent'-i-skalp'], *n.* an instrument used in scaling teeth. [L. *dentiscalpium*].

DENTIST, [dent'-ist], *n.* a person skilled in, and professionally engaged in, the care of the teeth. [Fr. *dentiste*].

DENTISTIC, [dent-ist'-ik], *adj.* of, or pertaining to, dentistry.

DENTISTRY, [dent'-is-tri], *n.* the profession or skill of a dentist.

DENTITION, [dent-ish'-un], *n.* the production of the teeth, teething; the character and arrangement of the teeth; the teeth themselves. [L. *dentitio*].

DENTIZE, [dent'-īz], *v.i.* to renew the teeth.

DENTOID, [dent'-oid], *adj.* resembling a tooth. [L. *dens dentis* and Gk. *oeides* like].

DENTURE, [den'-cher], *n.* a set of false teeth. [Fr. *denture*].

DENUDATE, [di-newd'-āt, den'-yōō-dāt], *v.t.* to denude. [L. *denudare*].

DENUDATION, [den'-yōō-dā'-shun], *n.* the act of denuding; (*geol.*) the uncovering of an underlying formation by the erosion of the outer layer of soil or soft rock. [L. *denudatio*].

DENUDE, [di-newd'], *v.t.* to make or lay bare; to strip, divest. [L. *denudare*].

DENUNCIATE, [di-nun'-si-āt], *v.t.* to denounce. [L. *denuntiare*].

DENUNCIATION, [di-nun'-si-ā'-shun], *n.* the act of denouncing. [L. *denuntiatio*].

DENUNCIATOR, [di-nun'-si-āt-er], *n.* one who denounces, an accuser. [L. *denuntiator*].

DENUNCIATORY, [di-nun'-si-āt'-er-i], *adj.* characterized by denouncing, that denounces.

DENY, [di-nī'], *v.t.* to say that a statement is untrue or untenable; to disown, repudiate, to refuse; to cause to abstain from. [Fr. *dénier*].

DEOBSTRUCT, [dē-ob-strukt'], *v.t.* to remove obstructions.

DEOBSTRUENT (1), [dē-ob'-strōō-ent], *n.* a deobstruent medicine.

DEOBSTRUENT (2), [dē-ob'-strōō-ent], *adj.* (*med.*) removing obstructions by opening the bowels or pores. [MdL. *deobstruens*].

DEODAND, [dē'-ō-dand], *n.* (*leg.*) any personal chattel which is the immediate occasion of the death of a human being, and, for that reason, is forfeited for pious or charitable use. [L. *deo dandum* that must be given to God].

DEODAR, [dē'-ō-dah(r)], *n.* a cedar of the Western

Himalayas, a Hindu sacred tree, *Cedrus Deodarus*. [Hind. *deodar*].
DEODATE†, [dē'-ō-dāt], *n.* a gift from God; a gift made to God. [L. *deo datum* given to God].
DEODORANT, [dē-ō'-der-ant], *n.* a deodorizer.
DEODORIZATION, [dē-ō'-der-īz-ā'-shun], *n.* the act of deodorizing.
DEODORIZE, [dē-ō'-der-īz'], *v.t.* to take away the smell of; to disguise or remove unpleasant or unhealthy smells from an object by the use of chemicals.
DEODORIZER, [dē-ō'-der-īz-er], *n.* a deodorizing agent.
DEONTOLOGICAL, [dē-on'-tō-loj'-ik-al] *adj.* relating to deontology.
DEONTOLOGY, [dē-on-tol'-o-ji], *n.* the science which deals with moral obligations. [Gk. *deon* that which is binding and *logos* speech].
DEOSCULATE [dē-os'-kyōō-lāt], *v.t.* to kiss warmly. [L. *deosculari*].
DEOXIDATE, [dē-oks'-i-dāt], *v.t.* to deoxidize.
DEOXIDATION, [dē-oks'-i-dā'-shun], *n.* deoxidization.
DEOXIDIZATION, [de-oks'-i-dīz-ā'-shun], *n.* the act of deoxidizing.
DEOXIDIZE, [dē-oks'-i-dīz], *v.t.* to remove oxygen from; to reduce from the state of an oxide.
DEOXYGENATE, [dē-oks'-i-jen-āt], *v.t.* to deoxidize.
DEOXYGENATION, [dē-oks'-i-jen-ā'-shun], *n.* deoxidization.
DEPAINT†, [di-pānt'], *v.t.* to picture; to depict in colours. [ME. *depeinten* from OFr. *depeindre*].
DEPART, [di-paht'], *v.i.* to go away, leave; to die; to start; **d. from**, to turn aside from an accustomed course; to change; to break. [OFr. *departir*].
DEPARTED, [di-paht'-id], *adj.* gone, vanished, dead.
DEPARTER, [di-paht'-er], *n.* one who departs.
DEPARTING, [di-paht'-ing], *n.* going away, separating; leaving; dying.
DEPARTMENT, [di-paht'-ment], *n.* a separate part, section, division or branch; an administrative division of territory in France; **d. store**, a large shop supplying a great variety of goods. [Fr. *département*].
DEPARTMENTAL, [dē'-paht-ment'-al], *adj.* pertaining to a department of business or of territory; concerned with, affecting, a particular department or departments.
DEPARTURE, [di-pah'-cher], *n.* the act of departing; (*naut.*) the distance travelled east or west of a meridian. [OFr. **desparteure*].
DEPASTURAGE, [di-pahs'-cher-ij], *n.* the act or right of grazing or pasturing.
DEPASTURE, [di-pahs'-cher], *v.t.* to turn cattle out to pasture, to graze upon; *v.i.* to graze.
DEPAUPERATE, [dē-paw'-per-āt], *v.t.* to impoverish, weaken, deprive of goods. [MedL. *depauperare*].
DEPAUPERIZE, [dē-paw'-per-īz], *v.t.* to free from paupers; to free from a state of pauperism.
DEPEND, [di-pend'], *v.i.* to be suspended; **to d. on**, to be waiting to be decided; to rely on; to look to for help, support, maintenance, sympathy; to be a question of; to follow as a result of; to trust. [L. *dependere*].
DEPENDABLE, [di-pend'-abl], *adj.* that may be depended upon; trustworthy.
DEPENDABLENESS, [di-pend'-abl-nes], *n.* the quality of being dependable.
DEPENDANT, DEPENDENT, [di-pend'-ant], *n.* one who is dependent on, or supported by, another; a servant, retainer. [Fr. *dépendant*].
DEPENDENCE, [di-pend'-ents], *n.* the condition of being dependent on another; reliance, trust, faith. [Fr. *dépendance*].
DEPENDENCY, [di-pend'-en-si], *n.* that which is attached but subordinate to something; a state or dominion governed by another.
DEPENDENT (1), see DEPENDANT.
DEPENDENT (2), [di-pend'-ent], *adj.* hanging down; subsisting or supported by; relying on for support, favour, benefit; that depends on something. [L. *dependens*].
DEPENDENTLY, [di-pend'-ent-li], *adv.* in a dependent manner.
DEPENDING, [di-pend'-ing], *adj.* pendent, hanging down; dependent; (*leg.*) awaiting settlement.
DEPERDITION, [dē-per-dish'-un], *n.* slow destruction by wasting away.
DEPERSONALIZE, [dē-pur'-son-al-īz], *v.t.* to divest of personality; to look upon as impersonal.
DEPHLEGMATE, [dē-fleg'-māt], *v.i.* to free spirits and acids from excess water; to rectify. [MedL. *dephlegmare*].
DEPHLEGMATION, [dē-fleg-mā'-shun], *n.* the act of dephlegmating.
DEPHOSPHORIZE, [dē-fos'-fer-īz], *v.t.* to remove phosphorus from.
DEPICT, [di-pikt'], *v.t.* to delineate, draw, paint, sculpture; to portray; to draw a word-picture. [L. *depict(um)*, *p.pt.* of *depingere*].
DEPICTION, [di-pik'-shun], *n.* the act of depicting.
DEPICTOR, [di-pikt'-er], *n.* an artist who depicts or describes.
DEPICTURE, [di-pik'-cher], *v.t.* to depict.
DEPILATE, [dē'-pi-lāt], *v.t.* to strip off, remove, pull out hair. [L. *depilare*].
DEPILATION, [dē-pi-lā'-shun], *n.* the removing of the hair.
DEPILATORY (1), [dē-pil'-at-er-i], *n.* a preparation which removes superfluous hair.
DEPILATORY (2), [dē-pil'-at-er-i], *adj.* able to remove unwanted hair. [L. *depilatorius*].
DEPILOUS, [dē'-pil-us], *adj.* deprived of, without, hair.
DEPLANATE, [dē'-plan-āt], *adj.* made flat, levelled down. [L. *deplanatus*].
DEPLENISH, [di-plen'-ish], *v.t.* to empty, take away the contents from. [DE and OFr. *plenir* to fill].
DEPLETE, [di-plēt'], *v.t.* to let out contents of; to empty out; to exhaust; to diminish considerably. [L. *depletum*, *p.pt.* of *deplere*].
DEPLETION, [di-plē'-shun], *n.* the act of depleting; the state of being depleted; (*med.*) bloodletting.
DEPLETIVE, [di-plē'-tiv], *adj.* inducing depletion.
DEPLETORY, [di-plē'-ter-i], *adj.* depletive.
DEPLICATION†, [dē'-plik-ā'-shun], *n.* an unfolding, display.
DEPLORABLE, [di-plaw'-rabl], *adj.* causing grief or pity; wretched; lamentable. [Fr. *déplorable*].
DEPLORABLENESS, [di-plaw'-rabl-nes], *n.* the condition of being deplorable.
DEPLORABLY, [di-plaw'-rab-li], *adv.* in deplorable fashion.
DEPLORATION, [dē'-plaw-rā'-shun], *n.* the act of deploring. [L. *deploratio*].
DEPLORE, [di-plaw(r)'], *v.t.* to lament; express regret about. [L. *deplorare*].
DEPLORINGLY, [di-plaw'-ring-li], *adv.* in a deploring manner.
DEPLOY, [di-ploi'], *v.t.* (*milit.*) to open out for action; *v.i.* to spread out into open formation. [Fr. *déployer*].
DEPLOYMENT, [di-ploi'-ment], *n.* the act of deploying.
DEPLUMATION, [dē'-plōōm-ā'-shun], *n.* the act of depluming; (*med.*) an affection of the eyelids causing loss of eyelashes.
DEPLUME, [di-plōōm'], *v.t.* to pull out or pluck the feathers of. [Fr. *déplumer*].
DEPOLARIZATION, [dē-pōl'-er-īz-ā'-shun], *n.* the act of depolarizing.
DEPOLARIZE, [dē-pōl'-er-īz], *v.t.* (*elect.*) to destroy the polarity of; (*fig.*) to unsettle; to de-orientate.
DEPONE, [di-pōn'], *v.t.* (*leg.*) to make a statement upon oath; to depose. [L. *deponere*].
DEPONENT (1), [di-pōn'-ent], *n.* one who depones, a sworn witness.
DEPONENT (2), [di-pōn'-ent], *adj.* laying down; **d. verb**, (in Latin and Greek grammar) a verb passive in form but otherwise active. [L. *deponens*].
DEPOPULATE, [dē-pop'-yōō-lāt], *v.t.* to lessen or destroy population of an area; *v.i.* to become sparsely populated. [L. *depopulare*].
DEPOPULATION, [dē'-pop-yōō-lā'-shun], *n.* the act of depopulating. [L. *depopulatio*].
DEPOPULATOR, [dē-pop'-yōō-lāt-er] *n.* one who depopulates.
DEPORT, [di-pawt'], *v.t.* to expel; to send back by force to one's own country; (*v. reflex.*) to behave. [Fr. *déporter* from L. *deportare*].
DEPORTATION, [dē'-pawt-ā'-shun], *n.* the act of deporting; the state of being deported. [L. *deportatio*].
DEPORTEE, [dē-pawt-ē'], *n.* one who is deported.
DEPORTMENT, [di-pawt'-ment], *n.* carriage, bearing, behaviour. [Fr. *déportement*].
DEPOSABLE, [di-pōz'-abl], *adj.* capable of being deposed.
DEPOSAL, [di-pōz'-al], *n.* the act of deposing. [AFr. *deposaille*].
DEPOSE, [di-pōz'], *v.t.* to remove from a throne or

other high office or rank; (*leg.*) to give evidence on oath. [Fr. *déposer*].

DEPOSIT (1), [di-poz'-it], *n.* that which is deposited; the sediment from a liquid; money paid into a banking account; money paid on account to render a contract binding.

DEPOSIT (2), [di-poz'-it], *v.t.* to lay or drop down; to leave as a sediment; to entrust for safe keeping; to pay money in advance to render a contract binding. [L. *depositum*, *p.pt.* of *deponere*].

DEPOSITARY, [di-poz'-it-er-i], *n.* one to whom a deposit is paid. [L. *depositarius*].

DEPOSITION, [dē'-poz-ish'-un], *n.* the act of deposing; sworn testimony; the state of being deposed. [L. *depositio*].

DEPOSITOR, [di-poz'-it-or], *n.* one who pays deposits into a bank; a person or machine for laying a deposit. [L. *depositor*].

DEPOSITORY, [di-poz'-it-er-i], *n* a storehouse or place of safe keeping. [MedL. *depositorium*].

DEPOT, [dep'-ō], *n.* a place of deposit for goods of any kind, *esp.* for military stores; (*milit.*) the headquarters of a regiment or recruiting centre when the main body is abroad; a railway terminus; a place where transport vehicles are housed. [Fr. *dépôt*].

DEPRAVATION, [dē'-prav-ā'-shun], *n.* the act of depraving; moral debasement. [L. *depravatio*].

DEPRAVE, [di-prāv'], *v.t.* to corrupt, morally debase, pervert. [L. *depravare*].

DEPRAVEDLY, [di-prāv'-id-li], *n.* in depraved fashion.

DEPRAVEDNESS, [di-prāvd'-nes], *n.* the state of being depraved.

DEPRAVEMENT, [di-prāv'-ment], *n.* a depraved state.

DEPRAVER, [di-prāv'-er], *n.* one who depraves.

DEPRAVINGLY, [di-prāv'-ing-li], *adv.* in a depraved manner.

DEPRAVITY, [di-prav'-it-i], *n.* moral corruption; (*theol.*) man's inherent sinfulness.

DEPRECABLE, [dep'-ri-kabl], *adj.* to be deprecated. [Eccles. L. *deprecabilis*].

DEPRECATE, [dep'-ri-kāt], *v.t.* to feel and express regret or reluctance about; to protest against, condemn. [L. *deprecare*].

DEPRECATINGLY, [dep-ri-kāt'-ing-li], *adv.* in a deprecating manner.

DEPRECATION, [dep-ri-kā'-shun], *n.* the act of deprecating. [L. *deprecatio*].

DEPRECATIVE, [dep'-ri-ka-tiv], *adj.* deprecatory. [L. *deprecativus*].

DEPRECATOR, [dep'-ri-kāt'-er], *n.* one who deprecates. [L. *deprecator*].

DEPRECATORY, [dep-ri-kāt'-er-i], *adj.* tending to deprecate. [L. *deprecatorius*].

DEPRECIATE, [di-prē'-shi-āt], *v.t.* to bring down the value of; (*fig.*) to disparage, belittle; *v.i.* to fall in value; to become less valuable through wear and tear. [L. *depretiare*].

DEPRECIATINGLY, [di-prēsh'-i-āt-ing-li], *adv.* in depreciating fashion; so as to depreciate.

DEPRECIATION, [di-prē-shi-ā'-shun], *n.* the act of depreciating; the condition of being depreciated; allowance for wear and tear in assessment; (*fig.*) disparagement.

DEPRECIATIVE, [di-prē'-shi-at-iv], *adj.* depreciatory.

DEPRECIATOR, [di-prē'-shi-āt-er], *n.* a person who depreciates. [L. *depretiator*].

DEPRECIATORY, [di-prē'-shi-at-er-i], *adj.* tending to depreciate or undervalue.

DEPREDATE, [dep'-ri-dāt], *v.t.* to plunder or pillage; *v.i.* to make depredations. [L. *depraedare*].

DEPREDATION, [dep-ri-dā'-shun], *n.* the act of plundering or ravaging; robbery. [L. *depraedatio*].

DEPREDATOR, [dep'-ri-dāt-er], *n.* a person or thing that makes depredations. [L. *depraedator*].

DEPREDATORY, [dep'-ri-dāt'-er-i], *adj.* plundering, laying waste.

DEPREHEND†, [dep'-ri-hend], *v.t.* to apprehend by surprise, to detect; to prove guilty of. [L. *deprehendere*].

DEPRESS, [di-pres'], *v.t.* to press down, lower; to make dispirited, dreary; to weaken in vigour or intensity; (*fig.*) to render lower in rank or fortune. [OFr. *depresser*].

DEPRESSANT, [di-pres'-ant], *n.* (*med.*) a sedative.

DEPRESSED, [di-prest'], *adj.* pressed down; flattened; (*fig.*) crippled in vitality and power for action; low, dejected; **the d. areas**, those parts of the country where poverty and unemployment are widespread.

DEPRESSIBLE, [di-pres'-ibl], *adj.* capable of being depressed.

DEPRESSING, [di-pres'-ing], *adj.* tending to depress.

DEPRESSINGLY, [di-pres'-ing-li], *adv.* in depressing fashion.

DEPRESSION, [di-presh'-un], *n.* the act of depressing, the state of being depressed; a little valley, a slight concavity on the surface of anything; (*fig.*) low spirits, lethargy, melancholy; (*comm.*) a period of timidity and slump; (*meteor.*) an area in which there is a low barometric pressure.

DEPRESSIVE, [di-pres'-iv], *adj.* apt to depress.

DEPRESSOR, [di-pres'-er], *n.* a person or thing that depresses; (*anat.*) a muscle that pulls down a part of the body. [L. *depressor*].

DEPRIVABLE, [di-prīv'-abl], *adj.* subject to deprivation.

DEPRIVATION, [dep'-ri-vā'-shun], *n.* the act of depriving; loss; (*leg.*) deposition from the clerical order or a church benefice. [MedL. *deprivatio*].

DEPRIVATIVE, [di-priv'-at-iv], *adj.* depriving, that deprives.

DEPRIVE, [di-prīv'], *v.t.* to take from, debar from use or enjoyment of; to dispossess; to strip of ecclesiastical rank or office. [Fr. *dépriver*].

DEPRIVEMENT, [di-prīv'-ment], *n.* deprivation.

DEPRIVER, [di-prīv'-er], *n.* a person or thing that deprives.

DEPTH, [depth], *n.* the state or quality of being deep; the measure of anything downward or inward; extent of penetration or of distance from front to back; the quality of being intellectually deep, learned, or difficult; profundity, intensity of feeling, warmth; strength of colour; (*mus.*) the quality of being rich and low in pitch; (*pl.*) that which is deep; (*fig.*) the heart; **out of one's d.**, too deep for the bottom to be touched with the feet; (*fig.*) confronted with something beyond one's power of comprehension; **defence in d.**, (*milit.*) a defence system involving interlinked strong points spread over a wide area rather than one solid front line. [ME. *depthe*].

DEPTH-CHARGE, [depth'-chahj'], *n.* an explosive weapon against submarines, which is designed to explode under water at a certain predetermined depth.

DEPTH-GAUGE, [depth'-gāj], *n.* an instrument for measuring depth.

DEPTHLESS, [depth'-les], *adj.* unfathomable.

DEPURATE, [dep'-yōōer-āt], *v.i.* to purify. [L. *depurare*].

DEPURATION, [dep'-yōō-er-ā'-shun], *n.* the act of purifying.

DEPURATIVE, [di-pyōōer-at-iv], *adj.* serving to cleanse of impurities. [MedL. *depurativus*].

DEPURATOR, [dep'-yōōer-āt'-er], *n.* the person or thing that purifies.

DEPURATORY, [dep'-yōōer-āt'-er-i], *adj.* purifying.

DEPURITION, [dep'-yōōer-ish'-un], *n.* depuration.

DEPUTATION, [dep'-yōō-tā'-shun], *n.* the act of deputing; a body of representatives or delegates.

DEPTH-GAUGE

DEPUTE, [di-pewt'], *v.t.* to appoint as proxy or proxies; to delegate (duties) to others. [L. *deputare*].

DEPUTIZE, [dep'-yōō-tīz], *v.i.* to act on behalf of someone else.

DEPUTY, [dep'-yōō-ti], *n.* one who deputizes; a member of a deputation; a coal-miner who is in charge of the working conditions and output of a group of other miners; the manager of a doss-house; (in France) a member of the lower house of the legislature. [Fr. *député*, *p.pt.* of *députer*].

DERACINATE, [dē-ras'-i-nāt], *v.t.* to uproot, destroy completely. [Fr. *déraciner*].

DERAIGN, [di-rān'], *v.t.* to vindicate, settle, or establish a claim by law or by battle. [OFr. *deraisnier*].

DERAIGNMENT, [di-rān'-ment], *n.* the act of deraigning.

DERAIL, [di-rāl'], *v.t.* and *i.* to run off the rails; to cause to run off the rails.

DERAILMENT, [di-rāl'-ment], *n.* the act of derailing; the condition of being derailed.

DERANGE, [di-rānj'], *v.t.* to put out of order, throw into confusion; to upset the normal function of; to cause an abnormal state of mind in. [Fr. *déranger*].

DERANGEMENT, [di-rānj'-ment], *n.* the act of deranging; the state of being deranged.

DERATE, [dē-rāt'], *v.t.* to free from or reduce liability to rating; to relieve industries from municipal taxation by Act of Parliament.

DERBIO, [dur'-bi-ō], *n.* a green sea-fish, *Lichia glauca*, having a black tail. [Uncert.].

DERBIO

DERBY, [dah'-bi], *n.* a horse race instituted by the twelfth Earl of Derby in 1780, and run at the Epsom Summer Meeting; a hard felt hat.

DERELICT (1), [de'-ri-likt], *n.* a wreck adrift on the open sea; anything thrown away, relinquished, or abandoned by the owner, *esp.* goods found at sea; a tract of land left dry by the sea, and unfit for cultivation or use. [DERELICT (2)].

DERELICT (2), [de'-ri-likt], *adj.* abandoned by its owner; (*fig.*) (of a person) old and considered of no further use. [L. *derelictum*, *p.pt.* of *derelinquere* to forsake].

DERELICTION, [de'-ri-lik'-shun], *n.* neglect of duty; permanent abandonment; the condition of being abandoned. [L. *derelictio*].

DERESERVE, [dē'-rē-zurv'], *v.t.* to remove from a reserved status.

DERIDE, [di-rīd'], *v.t.* to mock at with scorn; to hold in contempt or ridicule. [L. *deridere*].

DERIDER, [di-rīd'-er], *n.* one who derides.

DERIDINGLY, [di-rīd'-ing-li], *adv.* in a deriding fashion.

DERISION, [di-rizh'-un], *n.* the act of deriding; the state of being derided, mockery, ridicule. [L. *derisio*].

DERISIVE, [di-rī'-siv], *adj.* expressing derision; worthy of derision.

DERISIVELY, [di-rī'-siv-li], *adv.* in a derisive fashion.

DERISIVENESS, [di-rīs'-iv-nes], *n.* the quality or state of being derisive.

DERISORY, [di-rī'-ser-i], *adj.* characterized by derision, mocking. [L. *derisorius*].

DERIVABLE, [di-rīv'-abl], *adj.* that may be derived; deducible.

DERIVABLY, [di-rīv'-ab-li], *adv.* in a derivative fashion.

DERIVATE, [de'-ri-vāt], *n.* a derivative. [L. *derivare*].

DERIVATION, [de'-ri-vā'-shun], *n.* the act of deriving; the origin, source; the original form or word from which the present form of a word is derived, the etymology. [L. *derivatio*].

DERIVATIONAL, [de'-ri-vā'-shun-al], *adj.* of, or pertaining to, derivation.

DERIVATIVE (1), [di-riv'-a-tiv], *n.* that which is derived from another word. [DERIVATIVE (2)].

DERIVATIVE (2), [di-riv'-a-tiv], *adj.* derived; proceeding from another; secondary; **d. chord**, (*mus.*) a chord derived from a fundamental combination; **d. conveyances**, (*leg.*) secondary deeds, such as releases, surrenders, consignments, etc. [L. *derivativus*].

DERIVATIVELY, [di-riv'-a-tiv-li], *adv* in a derivative fashion.

DERIVATIVENESS, [di-riv'-a-tiv-nes], *n.* the condition or quality of being derivative.

DERIVE, [di-rīv'], *v.t.* to receive by regular transmission or conveyance; to obtain, get as from a source; to trace from; to give the etymology as being; *v.i.* to come or proceed from. [L. *derivare* to draw off or aside].

DERM, DERMA, [durm-a], *n.* the true skin or layer of skin underneath the epidermis; the corium. [Gk. *derma*].

DERMAL, [durm'-al], *adj.* pertaining to the derma.

DERMATIC, [der-mat'-ik], *adj.* pertaining to the skin.

DERMATITIS, [durm'-a-tī'-tis], *n.* (*path.*) eruption of, or inflammation on, the true skin. [DERMA and Gk. *itis* denoting inflammation].

DERMATO-, *pref.* pertaining to the skin. [Gk. *dermatos* of the skin].

DERMATOGRAPHY, [durm'-a-tog'-ra-fi], *n.* description of the skin. [DERMATO and Gk. *graphia* writing].

DERMATOID, [durm'-a-toid], *adj.* like or resembling skin. [DERMATO and Gk. *oeides* like].

DERMATOLOGIST, [durm'-a-tol'-oj-ist], *n.* a student of dermatology.

DERMATOLOGY, [durm'-a-tol'-o-ji], *n.* the study of the skin and its diseases. [DERMATO and Gk. *logos* speech].

DERMATOPHYTE, [durm'-at-ō-fīt], *n.* (*med.*) a certain fungoid growth under the cuticle which causes skin diseases. [DERMATO and Gk. *phuton* plant].

DERMATORRHOEA, [durm'-a-to-rē'-a], *n.* a morbid increase of secretion from the skin. [DERMATO and Gk. *rheo* I flow].

DERMATO-SKELETON, [durm'-a-tō-skel'-i-ton], *n.* the hard outer skin of crustaceans and of certain insects.

DERMIC, [durm'-ik], *adj.* dermal.

DERMOGRAPHY, [derm-og'-ra-fi], *n.* a scientific description of the skin; dermatography. [DERM and Gk. *graphia* writing].

DERMOHAEMIA, [durm'-o-hē'-mi-a], *n.* congestion of the skin. [DERM and Gk. *haima* blood].

DERMOID, [durm'-oid], *adj.* dermatoid. [DERM and Gk. *oeides* like].

DERNIER, [dāer'-ni-ā], *adj.* last, final; **d. cri**, latest fashion. [Fr. *dernier*].

DEROGATE, [de'-ro-gāt'], *v.t.* to take away some part; to detract from; to disparage; to invalidate some part of a law or established rule; *v.i.* to detract; to lessen. [L. *derogare*].

DEROGATION, [de'-ro-gā'-shun], *n.* the act of derogating; detraction. [L. *derogatio*].

DEROGATORILY, [di-rog'-at-er-il-i], *adv.* in derogatory fashion.

DEROGATORINESS, [di-rog'-at-er-i-nes], *n.* the quality of being derogatory.

DEROGATORY, [di-rog'-at-er-i], *adj.* detracting from authority, honour, prestige; disparaging, disrespectful. [L. *derogatorius*].

DERRICK, [de'-rik], *n.* a contrivance in various forms, for raising heavy weights, so called from its resemblance to a gallows; a kind of crane; a framework over an oil-well or similar boring. [*Derrick*, a former famous hangman in London].

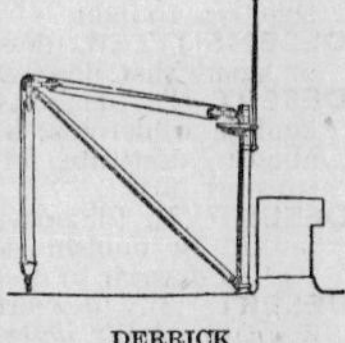
DERRICK

DERRING-DO, [de'-ring-dōō'], *n.* desperate courage, valiant action. [From *in derryng don* in daring to do, misunderstood by Spenser as a noun].

DERRINGER, [de'-rinj-er], *n.* (*U.S.*) a short, rifled pistol of large bore, so named from the inventor.

DERVISH, [dur'-vish], *n.* a member of a Mohammedan religious sect or order professing extreme poverty and leading an austere life; **dancing d.**, a member of one of the orders of dervishes who dance to attain religious ecstasy. [Pers. *darvish* poor, a religious mendicant].

DESCANT (1), [des'-kant], *n.* a melody played or sung above an air as a variation or accompaniment to it; a part song; the air or soprano in a part song; a lengthy conversation or discussion; a series of comments upon a theme. [OFr. *deschant*].

DESCANT (2), [des-kant'], *v.i.* (*mus.*) to sing or play a descant; to converse at length on one theme or topic. [OFr. *deschanter*].

DESCANTER, [des-kant'-er], *n.* a person who descants.

DESCEND, [di-send'], *v.t.* to walk, move, or pass downward upon or along; to pass from the top to the bottom of; (*astron.*) to move to the southward; (*mus.*) to pass from sharp to flat; **to d. to**, (*fig.*) to stoop, lower oneself to; **to d. upon**, to attack unexpectedly, (*fig.*) to visit without notice; *v.i.* to move in a downward course, proceed to a lower position; to sink; to proceed from a source or origin; to be derived; to pass from one heir to another; to lower or degrade oneself. [L. *descendere*].

DESCENDABLE, [di-send'-abl], *adj.* descendible. [OFr. *descendable*].

DESCENDANT, DESCENDENT†, [di-send'-ant], *n.* a person or animal descended from another; progeny. [Fr. *descendant*, from L. *descendens*].

DESCENDIBILITY, [di-send'-i-bil'-i-ti], *n.* the quality of being descendible.

DESCENDIBLE, [di-send'-ibl], *adj.* capable of being transmitted by inheritance.

DESCENSION, [di-sen'-shun], *n.* the act of descending; descent. [L. *descensio*].

DESCENSIONAL, [di-sen′-shun-al], *adj.* pertaining to descent.
DESCENSIVE, [di-sens′-iv], *adj.* tending to descend, characterized by downward motion.
DESCENT, [di-sent′], *n.* the act of descending; a declivity, downward slope; a fall; ancestry; hereditary transmission; a sudden unexpected invasion. [OFr. *descente*].
DESCRIBABLE, [di-skrīb′-abl], *adj.* capable of description.
DESCRIBE, [di-skrīb′], *v.t.* to give a detailed account of; to delineate by word or pictorial representation; (*geom.*) to mark out, draw. [L. *describere*].
DESCRIBENT, [di-skrīb′-ent], *n.* (*geom.*) a point, line or surface which describes by its motion a line, surface or solid. [L. *describens*].
DESCRIED, [di-skrīd′], *adj.* observed, noticed.
DESCRIPTION, [di-skrip′-shun], *n.* the act of describing; that which describes, the representation or account of anything by words and images; class, sort, kind, variety. [L. *descriptio*].
DESCRIPTIVE, [di-skrip′-tiv], *adj.* that describes, fond of or skilled in description; **d. geometry**, the application of geometrical rules to the representation of the figures and the various relations of the forms of bodies. [LL. *descriptivus*].
DESCRIPTIVELY, [di-skrip′-tiv-li], *adv.* in descriptive fashion.
DESCRIPTIVENESS, [di-skrip′-tiv-nes], *n.* the quality or state of being descriptive.
DESCRY, [di-skrī′], *v.t.* to espy, discover by sight; to see something in the distance. [OFr. *descrier* to cry out].
DESECRATE, [des′-i-krāt], *v.t.* to divert from a sacred purpose or character; to profane. [DE and L. *secratum*, *p.pt.* of *secrare* to hallow].
DESECRATION, [des′-i-krā′-shun], *n.* the act of desecrating; the condition of being desecrated.
DESENSITIZE, [dē-sents′-it-īz], *v.t.* to make insensitive, *esp.* to light.
DESENSITIZER, [dē-sents′-it-īz-er], *n.* an apparatus or agent that desensitizes.
DESERT (1), [dez′-ert], *n.* an uninhabited tract of land; a wilderness; a vast sandy or stony expanse almost destitute of moisture and vegetation. [DESERT (3)].
DESERT (2), [di-zurt′], *n.* what one deserves as a reward or punishment; due return. [OFr. *desert*, *p.pt.* of *deservir* to deserve].
DESERT (3), [dez′-ert], *adj.* barren, uninhabited, desolate. [OFr. *desert*, *p.pt.* of *deserter*].
DESERT (4), [di-zurt′], *v.t. and i.* to forsake, leave without warning given or permission granted; (*milit.*) to make an unauthorized departure from the fighting services, to run away. [OFr. *deserter*, LL. *desertare*].
DESERTER, [di-zurt′-er], *n.* one who deserts, *esp.* a soldier or sailor who leaves the service without permission.
DESERTION, [di-zur′-shun], *n.* the act of deserting; the condition of being deserted.
DESERTLESS (1), [di-zurt′-les], *adj.* undeserving.
DESERTLESS (2), [dez′-ert-les], *adj.* without desert lands.
DESERTLESSLY, [di-zurt′-les-li], *adv.* in desertless fashion.
DESERVE, [di-zurv′], *v.t. and i.* to merit, be worthy of, have a title to; to earn. [L. *deservire* to serve well].
DESERVEDLY, [di-zurv′-id-li], *adv.* according to desert.
DESERVER, [di-zurv′-er], *n.* a person who deserves.
DESERVING, [di-zurv′-ing], *adj.* worthy of reward, meritorious.
DESERVINGLY, [di-zurv′-ing-li], *adv.* in a deserving fashion.
DESHABILLE, see DISHABILLE.
DESICCANT (1), [des′-i-kant, di-sik′-ant], *n.* (*med.*) a medicine applied to a sore to dry up discharging matter. [DESICCANT (2)].
DESICCANT (2), [des′-i-kant, di-sik′-ant], *adj.* serving to dry. [L. *desiccans*].
DESICCATE, [de′-si-kāt], *v.t.* to dry up; to draw all moisture from; (*chem.*) to dry thoroughly so as to form a powder; *v.i.* to become dry. [L. *desiccare*].
DESICCATION, [des-i-kā′-shun], *n.* the act of desiccating; the condition of being desiccated. [L. *desiccatio*].
DESICCATIVE, [di-sik′-a-tiv], *adj.* that dries up. [MedL. *desiccativus*].
DESICCATOR, [des′-ik-āt-er], *n.* an agent or apparatus that desiccates.
DESIDERATE, [di-sid′-er-āt], *v.t.* to feel the want of, to miss; to wish to have. [L. *desiderare*].
DESIDERATION, [di-sid′-er-ā′-shun], *n.* the act of desiderating. [L. *desideratio*].
DESIDERATIVE, [di-sid′-er-a-tiv], *adj.* having or implying desire; (*gram.*) of or pertaining to a verb formed from another to denote desire to perform the action of the original verb [L. *desiderativus*].
DESIDERATUM, (*pl.* **desiderata**), [di-zid′-er-ā′-tum], *n.* a real or felt want; that which is greatly desired. [L. *desideratum* something desired].
DESIGHTMENT, [di-sīt′-ment], *n.* the act of making unsightly; disfiguration
DESIGN (1), [di-zīn′], *n.* a plan or representation of a thing by an outline; a draft or scheme to serve as a guide in subsequent practical work; a mental plan, intention, aim; the adapting of means to a preconceived end; a form of painting or drawing based on the harmony of line and colour rather than the representation of objects; the art of making such paintings or drawings. [DESIGN (2)].
DESIGN (2), [di-zīn′], *v.t.* to plan or delineate by drawing; to draft a scheme for the construction of some object; to project; to plan in the mind; to give, set apart for, in intention; to intend, purpose. [L. *designare* to mark out].
DESIGNABLE, [di-zīn′-abl], *adj.* capable of being designed or marked out.
DESIGNATE (1), [dez′-ig-nāt], *adj.* nominated to an office. [DESIGNATE (2)].
DESIGNATE (2), [dez′-ig-nāt], *v.t.* to indicate by visible lines, marks, descriptions; to name and settle the identity of; to assign for appointment. [L. *designare* to mark out].
DESIGNATION, [dez′-ig-nā′-shun], *n.* the act of designating; the state of being designated; that which designates, a distinctive appellation or title. [L. *designatio*].
DESIGNATIVE, [dez′-ig-nā′-tiv], *adj.* serving to designate. [MedL. *designativus*].
DESIGNATOR, [dez′-ig-nā′-tor], *n.* one who designates; (*Rom. antiq.*) the officer who allotted each person his place in public shows. [L. *designator*].
DESIGNATORY, [dez′-ig-nā′-ter-i], *adj.* serving to designate.
DESIGNED, [di-zīnd′], *adj.* delineated, planned, intended.
DESIGNEDLY, [di-zīn′-ed-li], *adv.* intentionally, on purpose.
DESIGNER, [di-zīn′-er], *n.* one who designs, *esp.* patterns, a draughtsman; a designing person.
DESIGNFUL, [di-zīn′-fŏŏl], *adj.* intentional.
DESIGNING (1), [di-zīn′-ing], *n.* the art of drawing designs or patterns; the act of planning.
DESIGNING (2), [di-zīn′-ing], *adj.* intriguing, given to crafty scheming.
DESIGNLESS, [di-zīn′-les], *adj.* purposeless, without design.
DESIGNLESSLY, [di-zīn′-les-li], *adv.* unintentionally.
DESIGNMENT†, [di-zīn′-ment], *n.* indication of or by design; delineation; a sketch; designation.
DESILVER, [dē′-sil′-ver], *v.t.* to clean the silver from.
DESILVERIZATION, [dē-sil′-ver-īz-ā′-shun], *n.* the process of desilverizing.
DESILVERIZE, [dē′-sil′-ver-īz], *v.t.* to extract silver from other metals.
DESINENCE, [des′-i-nens], *n.* conclusion, end; (*gram.*) a suffix. [Fr. *désinence*].
DESIPIENCE, [di-sip′-i-ens], *n.* weakening of intellect, silliness. [L. *desipientia*].
DESIPIENT, [di-sip′-i-ent], *adj.* silly. [L. *desipiens*].
DESIRABILITY, [di-zīer′-a-bil-i-ti], *n.* the condition of being desirable.
DESIRABLE, [di-zīer′-abl], *adj.* worthy of desire, exciting a wish to possess; agreeable, choice. [Fr. *désirable*].
DESIRABLENESS, [di-zīer′-abl-nes], *n.* desirability.
DESIRABLY, [di-zīer′-ab-li], *adv.* in a desirable fashion.
DESIRE (1), [di-zīer′], *n.* a strong wish to possess or enjoy some object; a prayer or request; the object desired; lust, sexual passion. [DESIRE (2)].
DESIRE (2), [di-zīer′], *v.t.* to wish to possess or enjoy; to long for, to covet; to utter a wish; to ask, beg; to request. [Fr. *désirer* from L. *desiderare*].
DESIRED, [di-zīerd′], *adj.* wished for, coveted.
DESIRELESS, [di-zīer′-les], *adj.* without desire.
DESIROUS, [di-zīer′-us], *adj.* having a wish or desire for; longing; covetous.
DESIROUSLY, [di-zīer′-us-li], *adv.* in desirous fashion.

DESIROUSNESS, [di-zier'-us-nes], *n.* the condition of being desirous.
DESIST, [di-zist'], *v.i.* to cease to act, to leave off, stop; to forbear, discontinue. [L. *desistere*].
DESISTANCE, [di-zist'-ans], *n.* the act of desisting.
DESK, [desk], *n.* a table, board, or box, usually with a sloping top, for writing on or reading from; a similar flat-topped piece of furniture fitted with drawers at each side; the place from which prayers are read. [ME. *deske* from LL. *desca* desk, table].
DESMAN, [des'-man], *n* a musk-rat, an aquatic insectivore related to the shrews and moles. [Swed. *desman (ratta)* musk-rat].

DESMAN

DESMID, [des'-mid], *n.* (*bot.*) a plant of the genus *Desmidium*, a single-celled freshwater alga. [MdL. *desmidium*].
DESMINE, [des'-min], *n.* (*min.*) stilbite. [Gk. *desme* bundle].
DESMO-, *pref.* bond, fastening, chain, ligature. [Gk. *desmos*].
DESMOGRAPHY, [des-mog'-ra-fi], *n.* an account of the ligaments of the body.
DESMOID, [des'-moid], *adj.* arranged in tufts or bundles; (*anat.*) ligamentous. [DESMO and Gk. *oeides* like].
DESMOLOGY, [des-mol'-o-ji], *n.* (*anat.*) the study of ligaments and sinews. [DESMO and Gk. *logos* speech].
DESMOTOMY, [des-mot'-o-mi], *n.* the practical anatomy or dissection of ligaments and sinews. [DESMO and Gk. *tome* cutting].
DESOLATE (1), [des'-ō-lat], *adj.* destitute or deprived of inhabitants, desert, dismal, barren and dreary; neglected, lonely, extremely unhappy [L. *desolatus*].
DESOLATE (2), [des'-ō-lāt], *v.t.* to strip of inhabitants, lay waste; to ruin; ravage; to make lonely; to bereave. [*Prec.*].
DESOLATELY, [des'-o-lat-li], *adv.* in a desolate manner.
DESOLATENESS, [des'-o-lat-nes], *n.* the condition of being desolate.
DESOLATING, [des'-o-lāt-ing], *adj.* wasting, ravaging.
DESOLATION, [des'-o-lā'-shun], *n.* the act of desolating; devastation; the condition of being desolate; extreme sadness.
DESOLATORY, [des-o-lāt'-er-i], *adj.* causing desolation.
DESPAIR (1), [di-spāer'], *n.* hopelessness, despondency, desperation. [ME. *despeir*].
DESPAIR (2), [di-spāer'], *v.i.* to have no hope; to abandon hope. [L. *desperare*].
DESPAIRING, [di-spāer'-ing], *adj.* that despairs, prone to despair; indicating despair.
DESPAIRINGLY, [di-spāer'-ing-li], *adv.* in a despairing manner.
DESPAIRINGNESS, [di-spāer'-ing-nes], *n.* despairing condition; hopelessness.
DESPATCH, see DISPATCH.
DESPERADO, [des'-per-ah'-dō], *n.* a violent ruffian; a desperate, lawless fellow. [OSpan. *desperado*].
DESPERATE, [des'-per-at], *adj.* reckless of danger; furious, sticking at nothing; without hope, hopeless; beyond hope of recovery; done in despair. [L. *desperare*].
DESPERATELY, [des'-per-at-li], *adv.* in a desperate fashion.
DESPERATENESS, [des'-per-at-nes], *n.* the condition of being desperate.
DESPERATION, [des-per-ā'-shun], *n.* a state of despair or of being desperate; a desperate disregard of safety or danger; **to drive to d.**, to make violently angry, to goad to extreme measures. [L. *desperatio*].
DESPICABLE, [des'-pik-abl, di-spik'-abl], *adj.* deserving of being despised; contemptible; vile; mean. [L. *despicabilis*].
DESPICABLENESS, [di-spik'-abl-nes], *n.* the quality or state of being despicable.
DESPICABLY, [di-spik'-ab-li], *adv.* in a despicable fashion.
DESPISABLE, [di-spīz'-abl], *adj.* capable of being despised; despicable.
DESPISAL, [di-spīz'-al], *n.* contempt, scorn.
DESPISE, [di-spīz'], *v.t.* to look down on; to feel contempt for. [ME. *despisen* from OFr. *despire*].
DESPISEDNESS, [di-spīz'-id-nes], *n.* the state or condition of being despised.
DESPISER, [di-spīz'-er], *n.* a person who despises.
DESPISINGLY, [di-spīz'-ing-li], *adv.* with contempt.
DESPITE (1), [di-spīt'], *n.* malice, spite; defiance with contempt; (*archaic*) injury. [OFr. *despit*].
DESPITE (2), [di-spīt'], *prep.* notwithstanding, in spite of. [DESPITE (1)].
DESPITEFUL, [di-spīt'-fŏŏl], *adj.* spiteful, malignant.
DESPITEFULLY, [di-spīt'-fŏŏl-i], *adv.* spitefully, maliciously.
DESPITEFULNESS, [di-spīt'-fŏŏl-nes], *n.* the condition of being despiteful.
DESPOIL, [di-spoil'], *v.t.* to rob; to strip by force. [L. *despoliare*].
DESPOILER, [di-spoil'-er], *n.* a person who despoils.
DESPOILMENT, [di-spoil'-ment], *n.* despoliation.
DESPOLIATION, [di-spō'-li-ā'-shun], *n.* the act of despoiling; the condition of being despoiled. [OFr. *despoliation*].
DESPOND, [di-spond'], *v.i.* to be in low spirits or dejected; to despair. [L. *despondere*].
DESPONDENCE, [di-spond'-ents], *n.* despondency
DESPONDENCY, [di-spond'-en-si], *n.* a desponding state of mind, dejection, low spirits.
DESPONDENT, [di-spond'-ent], *adj.* dejected in spirit, depressed, despairing. [L. *despondens*].
DESPONDENTLY, [di-spond'-ent-li], *adv.* in despondent fashion.
DESPONDING [di-spond'-ing], *adj.* yielding to despondency, depressed, dejected.
DESPONDINGLY, [di-spond'-ing-li], *adv.* in a desponding fashion.
DESPOT, [des'-pot], *n.* one who rules with absolute power or authority in a state irrespective of the wishes of the governed; a tyrant. [Gk. *despotes* lord of a household].
DESPOTIC, [des-pot'-ik], *adj.* pertaining to a despot or to despotism; having the power of a despot; arbitrary, tyrannical.
DESPOTICAL, [des-pot'-ik-al], *adj.* despotic.
DESPOTICALLY [des-pot'-ik-al-i], *adv.* in despotic fashion.
DESPOTICALNESS, [des-pot'-ik-al-nes], *n.* the quality or state of being despotic.
DESPOTISM, [des'-pot-izm], *n.* rule by a despot; a state governed by a despot; tyrannical government.
DESPUMATE, [di-spewm'-āt], *v.t. and i.* to skim; to rid of impurities, *esp.* of froth or scum. [L. *despumare*].
DESPUMATION, [des'-pyŏŏ-mā'-shun], *n.* the act of despumating. [L. *despumatio*].
DESQUAMATE, [des'-kwam-āt], *v.i.* to scale off, peel. [L. *desquamare*].
DESQUAMATION, [des'-kwam-ā'-shun], *n.* the process of desquamating.
DESQUAMATORY, [des-kwam'-at-er-i], *adj.* characterized by desquamation.
DESSERT, [di-zurt'], *n.* a course of fruit and confections when the substantial part of a meal is completed; (*U.S.*) pies, puddings, sweets, etc. [OFr. *desserte*].
DESSERT-SPOON, [di-zurt'-spōōn'], *n.* a spoon intermediate in size between a tablespoon and a teaspoon, used mainly for eating puddings or dessert; **d.-ful**, the quarter of a liquid ounce.
DESTEMPER†, see DISTEMPER (1).
DESTINABLE†, [des'-tin-abl], *adj.* fixed by destiny; fated. [OFr. *destinable*].
DESTINATE (1), [des'-tin-āt], *adj.* destined, fated, appointed. [DESTINATE (2)].
DESTINATE (2), [des'-tin-āt], *v.t.* to destine. [L. *destinare*].
DESTINATION, [des'-tin-ā'-shun], *n.* the place for which one has set out, the place to which anything is to be sent, goal.
DESTINE, [des'-tin], *v.t.* to ordain, appoint; to fix or predetermine unalterably; to devote or doom; to intend. [L. *destinare* to fasten, fix].
DESTINIST, [des'-tin-ist], *n.* one who believes in destiny; a fatalist.
DESTINY, [des'-tin-i], *n.* the fate to which a person or thing is preappointed; the inevitable power which governs and determines action; the personification of this power. [OFr. *destinée*].
DESTITUTE, [des'-ti-tewt], *adj.* not having or possessing, lacking; in a condition of great poverty; lacking means of support. [L. *destitut(um)*, *p.pt.* of *destituere* to abandon].
DESTITUTENESS, [des'-ti-tewt-nes], *n.* destitution.
DESTITUTION, [des'-ti-tew'-shun], *n.* the state of

being abandoned or left destitute; lack of the necessaries of life. [L. *destitutio*].

DESTRIER, [des'-trē-er], *n.* (*hist.*) a war-horse, charger. [OFr. *destrier* from LL. *equus dextrarius* a horse led by the right hand].

DESTROY, [di-stroi'], *v.t.* to reduce to nothing, to ruin; to pull down, demolish, to lay waste; to kill. [ME *destroien* from OFr. *destruire*].

DESTROYABLE, [di-stroi'-abl], *adj.* that may be destroyed.

DESTROYER, [di-stroi'-er], *n.* one who, or that which, destroys; (*nav.*) a small, lightly-armed, swift warship firing torpedoes.

DESTRUCTIBILITY, [di-struk'-ti-bil'-i-ti], *n.* the state of being destructible.

DESTRUCTIBLE, [di-struk'-tibl], *adj.* able to be destroyed. [L. *destructibilis*].

DESTRUCTIBLENESS, [di-struk'-tibl-nes], *n.* the state of being destructible.

DESTRUCTION, [di-struk'-shun], *n.* the act of destroying; the state of being destroyed; ruin; that which destroys. [L. *destructio*].

DESTRUCTIONIST, [di-struk'-shun-ist], *n.* a destructive; (*theol.*) a person who believes that the wicked will be finally and utterly destroyed.

DESTRUCTIVE (1), [di-struk'-tiv], *n.* that which is destructive; a radical reformer.

DESTRUCTIVE (2), [di-struk'-tiv], *adj.* causing destruction; ruinous, injurious, destroying. [L. *destructivus*].

DESTRUCTIVELY, [di-struk'-tiv-li], *adv.* in a destructive manner.

DESTRUCTIVENESS, [di-struk'-tiv-nes], *n.* the quality of being destructive.

DESTRUCTOR, [di-struk'-ter], *n.* a person or thing that destroys; a furnace where refuse is destroyed by burning.

DESUETUDE, [des'-wi-tewd], *n.* the state of being disused; discontinuance, disuse. [L. *desuetudo*].

DESULPHUR, [dē-sul'-fer], *v.t.* to remove sulphur from.

DESULPHURATE, [dē-sul'-fer-āt] *v.t.* to desulphurize.

DESULPHURATION, [dē-sul'-fer-ā-shun], *n.* desulphurization.

DESULPHURIZATION, [dē-sul'-fer-īz-ā'-shun], *n.* the operation of desulphurizing.

DESULPHURIZE, [dē-sul'-fer-īz], *v.t.* to remove the sulphur from.

DESULTORILY, [dez'-ul-ter-i-li], *adv.* in desultory fashion.

DESULTORINESS, [dez'-ul-ter-i-nes], *n.* the state of being desultory.

DESULTORY, [dez'-ul-ter-i], *adj.* rambling from one thing to another without order or connexion; occurring abruptly and suddenly; casual, spasmodic. [L. *desultorius* relating to a circus rider].

DESYNONYMIZE, [dē'-si-non'-i-mīz], *v.t.* to cause synonyms to acquire a different shade of meaning from each other.

DETACH, [di-tach'], *v.t.* to separate, unloosen; to unfasten; (*milit.*) to bring men from the main contingent for some special duty. [Fr. *détacher*].

DETACHABLE, [di-tach'-abl], *adj.* able to be detached.

DETACHED, [di-tacht'], *adj.* separated, standing apart or separately; (*fig.*) impartial, free from personal bias.

DETACHEDLY, [dē-tach'-id-li], *adv.* in detached fashion.

DETACHEDNESS, [di-tacht'-nes], *n.* the state of being detached.

DETACHMENT, [di-tach'-ment], *n.* the act of detaching; the condition of being detached; (*fig.*) freedom from personal concern; aloofness; (*milit.*) a unit separated from the main body of troops for some special service.

DETAIL (1), [de'-tāl], *n.* one item; an individual fact, circumstance or portion taken in conjunction with others; something of slight importance; **in d.**, item by item; thoroughly and exactly. [DETAIL (2)].

DETAIL (2), [dē'-tāl], *v.t.* to make a detailed report of, to recount item by item; (*milit.*) to appoint for certain work. [Fr. *détailler* to cut into pieces].

DETAILED, [dē'-tāld], *adj.* related item by item; exact, thorough and minute.

DETAILER, [dē-tāl'-er], *n.* a person who details.

DETAIN, [di-tān'], *v.t.* to hold or keep back; to cause to be delayed, to prevent from continuing, to keep possession of; (*leg.*) to retain in custody. [OFr. *détenir* from L. *detinere*].

DETAINER, [di-tān'-er], *n.* (*leg.*) one who unlawfully withholds or keeps property which belongs to another; **writ of d.**, a writ issued against prisoners in custody in order that they may be detained on further charges.

DETAINMENT, [di-tān'-ment], *n.* the act of detaining.

DETECT, [di-tekt'], *v.t.* to notice, perceive; to become aware of the existence of; see, discover, apprehend. [L. *detectum*, *p.pt.* of *detegere* to uncover].

DETECTABLE, [di-tekt'-abl], *adj.* able to be detected.

DETECTION, [di-tek'-shun], *n.* the act of detecting; criminal investigation. [L. *detectio*].

DETECTIVE (1), [di-tek'-tiv], *n.* a police officer who investigates cases of crime; a private person who is engaged professionally in investigating cases of crime or irregular conduct.

DETECTIVE (2), [di-tek'-tiv], *adj.* of or pertaining to detection; employed in detecting; **d. story**, a type of fiction dealing with crimes and the detection of those responsible for them.

DETECTOPHONE, [di-tek'-to-fōn], *n.* an instrument for tapping telephone wires. [DETECT and Gk. *phone* sound].

DETECTOR, [di-tek'-tor], *n.* a discoverer; one who, or that which, detects; (*wirel.*) a device for rectifying high-frequency oscillations. [L. *detector*].

DETENT, [di-tent'], *n.* a catch in a machine; a stop in a clock, which controls the striking mechanism. [Fr. *détente*].

DETENTE, détente, [dā'-tahnt'], *n.* a condition of tension in the diplomatic relations of two states. [Fr. *détente*].

DETENTION, [di-ten'-shun], *n.* the act of detaining; condition of being detained; custody; confinement; the punishment of being kept in school after hours; **d. barrack**, a military prison. [L. *detentio*].

DETENU, détenu, [dā'-ten-yōō], *n.* a man who is detained in custody. [Fr. *détenu*].

DETER, [di-tur'], *v.t.* to hold back or restrain; to prevent; to dissuade by describing the consequences of action [L. *deterrere* to frighten from].

DETERGE, [di-turj'], *v.t.* to wipe away; to cleanse a sore of pus or other harmful matter. [L. *detergere*].

DETERGENCY, [di-turj'-en-si], *n.* cleansing quality.

DETERGENT (1), [di-turj'-ent], *n.* (*med.*) a cleansing agent. [DETERGENT (2)].

DETERGENT (2), [di-turj'-ent], *adj.* cleansing. [L. *detergens*].

DETERIORATE, [di-tēer'-i-er-āt], *v.t.* to lower the value of, to make inferior or worse; *v.i.* to become worse; to degenerate. [L. *deteriorare*].

DETERIORATION, [di-tēer'-i-er-ā'-shun], *n.* the act of deteriorating; the condition of having deteriorated.

DETERIORATIVE, [di-tēer'-i-er-ā-tiv], *adj.* that deteriorates.

DETERIORITY, [di-tēer'-i-or'-i-ti], *n.* a worse state or quality, deterioration.

DETERMA, [di-tur'-ma], *n.* a species of wood grown in Guiana. [Uncert.].

DETERMENT, [di-tur'-ment], *n.* the act of deterring; that which deters.

DETERMINABILITY, [di-tur'-min-a-bil'-i-ti], *n.* the state or quality of being determinable.

DETERMINABLE, [di-tur'-min-abl], *adj.* that may be determined. [L. *determinabilis*].

DETERMINABLENESS, [di-tur'-min-abl-nes], *n.* determinability.

DETERMINANT (1), [di-tur'-min-ant], *n.* that which determines.

DETERMINANT (2), [di-tur'-min-ant], *adj.* having the power of determining; serving to determine or fix. [L. *determinans*].

DETERMINATE, [di-tur'-min-at], *adj.* limited, fixed, definite, settled, **d. problem**, (*math.*) a problem having a limited number of solutions.

DETERMINATELY, [di-tur'-min-at-li], *adv.* in a determinate fashion.

DETERMINATENESS, [di-tur'-min-at-nes], *n.* the state of being determinate.

DETERMINATION, [di-tur'-min-ā'-shun], *n.* the act of determining; the condition of being determined; firm resolution, decision of character; (*leg.*) judicial sentence; (*med.*) tendency of blood to flow to any part more copiously than is normal. [L. *determinatio*].

DETERMINATIVE (1), [di-tur'-min-a-tiv], *n.* that which determines.

DETERMINATIVE (2), [di-tur'-min-a-tiv], *adj.* that determines anything.

DETERMINATOR, [di-tur'-min-āt'-or], *n.* one who determines. [L. *determinator*].
DETERMINE, [di-tur'-min], *v.t. and i.* to fix the size or range of; to settle by mental or judicial decision; to give a direction to influence the choice; to resolve, settle (an issue); to find out, ascertain; to decide, make up one's mind; (*leg.*) to end. [L. *determinare*].
DETERMINED, [di-tur'-mind], *adj.* having a firm or fixed purpose; resolute.
DETERMINEDLY, [di-tur'-mind-li], *adv.* in a determined manner.
DETERMINEDNESS, [dē-turm'-ind-nes], *n.* the state or quality of being determined.
DETERMINISM, [di-tur'-min-izm], *n.* the doctrine that man is not free to act as he wills, but is governed entirely by forces outside himself.
DETERMINIST, [di-tur'-min-ist], *n.* a person who maintains the determinist doctrine.
DETERMINISTIC, [di-tur'-min-is'-tik], *adj.* pertaining to determinism.
DETERRATION†, [dē-ter-ā'-shun], *n.* (*geog.*) the carrying down of earth from higher to lower levels by action of certain physical processes as rain, etc. [DE and L. *terra* the earth].
DETERRENCE, [di-te'-rents], *n.* the act of deterring; something that deters.
DETERRENT (1), [di-te'-rent], *n.* something that deters.
DETERRENT (2), [di-te'-rent], *adj.* that deters or tends to deter. [L. *deterrens*].
DETERRING, [di-tur'-ing], *n.* the action of hindering or dissuading through fear.
DETERSION, [di-tur'-shun], *n.* the act of cleansing a sore. [L. *detersio*].
DETERSIVE (1), [di-tur'-siv], *n.* a cleansing agent.
DETERSIVE (2), [di-tur'-siv], *adj.* that cleanses; (*med.*) detergent. [L. *detersivus*].
DETERSIVENESS, [di-tur'-siv-nes], *n.* the quality of being detersive.
DETEST, [di-test'], *v.t.* to feel a loathing of; to hate deeply; to abominate. [L. *detestare* to denounce].
DETESTABILITY, [di-test'-a-bil'-i-ti], *n.* the quality of being detestable.
DETESTABLE, [di-test'-abl], *adj.* to be detested, loathsome, execrable. [L. *detestabilis*].
DETESTABLENESS, [di-test'-abl-nes], *n.* detestability.
DETESTABLY, [di-test'-ab-li], *adv.* in a detestable fashion.
DETESTATION, [dē'-test-ā'-shun], *n.* extreme hatred, intense dislike, abhorrence. [L. *detestatio*].
DETESTED, [di-test'-id], *adj.* intensely hated; abhorred.
DETESTER, [di-test'-er], *n.* one who detests.
DETHRONE, [di-thrōn'], *v.t.* to remove from the throne; to strip of royal power; to remove from a position of power or influence.
DETHRONEMENT, [di-thrōn'-ment], *n.* the act of dethroning.
DETHRONER, [di-thrōn'-er], *n.* a person who dethrones.
DETHRONIZATION, [di-thrōn'-iz-ā'-shun], *n.* the act of dethroning.
DETINUE, [det'-i-nyōō], *n.* (*leg.*) a writ against one who wrongfully seeks to keep goods or chattels belonging to another. [OFr. *détenue* detained].
DETONATE, [det'-on-āt], *v.t.* to cause to explode; *v.i.* to explode with a sudden bang. [L. *detonare*].
DETONATING, [det'-on-āt-ing], *adj.* that detonates; exploding; containing explosive.
DETONATION, [det-on-ā'-shun], *n.* the act of detonating; a sudden, loud explosion; the noise of this.
DETONATIVE, [det'-on-āt-iv], *adj.* causing detonation or explosion.
DETONATOR, [det'-on-āt-er], *n.* a contrivance that explodes an explosive; a percussion cap; a fog signal that explodes on a railway line.
DETONIZATION, [det'-on-iz-ā'-shun], *n.* the act of detonating.
DETONIZE, [det'-on-īz], *v.t.* to detonate.
DETORT†, [di-tawt'], *v.t.* to wrest from their purpose or meaning; to distort. [L. *detortum*, *p.pt.* of *detorquere*].
DETORTION, [dē-taw'-shun], *n.* twisting, distortion (of a meaning, etc.).
DETOUR, détour, [dē'-tōōr], *n.* a circuitous or indirect way; a deviation from the shortest way of approach. [Fr. *détour*].
DETRACT, [di-trakt'], *v.t.* to take away from the quality, excellence, or standing of; to derogate from; to diminish. [~L. *detrahere* to pull down].
DETRACTINGLY, [di-trakt'-ing-li], *adv.* in a detracting fashion.
DETRACTION, [di-trak'-shun], *n.* the act of detracting; calumny, depreciation. [L. *detractio*].
DETRACTIOUS, [di-trak'-shus], *adj.* fond of detracting, calumnious.
DETRACTIVE, [di-trakt'-iv], *adj.* that detracts from anything.
DETRACTIVENESS, [di-trakt'-iv-nes], *n.* the quality of being detractive.
DETRACTOR, [di-trakt'-er], *n.* one who disparages the merits or reputation of a person or thing. [L. *detractor*].
DETRACTORY, [di-trakt'-er-i], *adj.* detractive. [L. *detractorius*].
DETRACTRESS, [di-trak'-tres], *n.* a woman who detracts.
DETRAIN, [di-trān'], *v.t. and i.* to remove from a railway train, to alight from a railway train.
DETRIMENT, [det'-ri-ment], *n.* loss, damage, hurt, mischief, injury. [L. *detrimentum*].
DETRIMENTAL (1), [det-ri-ment'-al], *n.* an undesirable person.
DETRIMENTAL (2), [det-ri-ment'-al], *adj.* occasioning loss or damage, harmful.
DETRIMENTALLY, [det-ri-ment'-al-i], *adv.* in detrimental fashion; so as to occasion detriment.
DETRIMENTALNESS, [det-ri-ment'-al-nes], *n.* the quality of being detrimental.
DETRITAL, [di-trīt'-al], *adj.* of, or belonging to, detritus.
DETRITED, [di-trīt'-id], *adj.* worn down; produced through detrition.
DETRITION, [di-trish'-un], *n.* the act of wearing down by continual rubbing.
DETRITUS, [di-trīt'-us], *n.* waste or disintegrated material; (*geol.*) a mass of fragments produced by the wearing away of exposed surfaces of rocks, etc. [L. *detritus* a rubbing off].
DETRUDE, [di-trōōd'], *v.t.* to thrust or force down. [L. *detrudere*].
DETRUNCATE, [dē-trung'-kāt], *v.t.* to lop off a portion of; to shorten by lopping off. [L. *detruncare*].
DETRUNCATION, [de'-trung-kā'-shun], *n.* the act of detruncating. [L. *detruncatio*].
DETRUSION, [di-trōō'-zhun], *n.* the act of detruding. [L. *detrusio*].
DETRUSOR, [di-trōōs'-er], *n.* that which thrusts away; (*anat.*) the muscular covering of the bladder which when contracted causes the expulsion of the urine.
DETUMESCENCE, [dē'-tew-mes'-ents], *n.* the going down of swelling. [L. *detumescere*].
DEUCE, [dews], *n.* two, a card or die marked with two pips; the score of forty all at lawn tennis; (*slang*) the devil. [OFr. *deux* two].
DEUCE-ACE, [dews'-ās], *n.* a throw of two dice in which two and one are scored respectively.
DEUCED, [dewst], *adj.* (*slang*) confounded, devilish, extreme.
DEUCEDLY, [dews'-id-li], *adv.* (*slang*) confoundedly, extremely.
DEUT-, see DEUTO-.
DEUTERAGONIST, [dew'-ter-ag'-on-ist], *n.* the second actor in order of importance in a Greek drama. [Gk. *deuteragonistes*].
DEUTER(O)-, *pref.* second, secondary. [Gk. *deuteros*].
DEUTEROCANONICAL, [dew'-ter-ō-kan-on'-i-kal], *adj.* (of certain books of Scripture) accepted into the canon after the rest. [DEUTERO and CANONICAL].
DEUTEROGAMIST, [dew'-ter-og'-am-ist], *n.* a person who marries a second time or believes in second marriages.
DEUTEROGAMY, [dew'-ter-og'-a-mi], *n.* a second marriage after the death of a first husband or wife. [DEUTERO and Gk. *gamos* marriage].
DEUTERONOMIST, [dew'-ter-on'-om-ist], *n.* the writer of the book of Deuteronomy.
DEUTEROPATHIC, [dew'-ter-op'-ath-ik], *adj.* pertaining to deuteropathy.
DEUTEROPATHY, [dew'-ter-op'-ath-i], *n.* (*med.*) a sympathetic affection of one part of the body with another, as headache from indigestion. [DEUTERO and Gk. *pathos* disease].
DEUTEROSCOPY†, [dew'-ter-os'-kop-i], *n.* the second view, or meaning; second sight. [DEUTERO and Gk. *skopos* view].
DEUTO-, DEUT-, *pref.* (*chem.*) of the second in any series; (*biol.*) second. [Gk. *deuteros* (in abbreviated form)].

DEUTOGENIC, [dew'-tō-jen'-ik], *adj.* (*geol.*) of secondary formation. [DEUTO and Gk. *genes* producing].
DEUTOPLASM, [dew'-tō-plazm], *n.* (*biol.*) the substance in the yolk of an egg which is the food of the embryo. [DEUTO and PLASM].
DEUTOPLASTIC, [dew'-tō-plas'-tik], *adj.* pertaining to, resembling, deutoplasm.
DEUTOXIDE, [dew-tok'-sīd], *n.* (*chem.*) the second of the series of oxides of a metal containing the second smallest quantity of oxygen. [DEUT and OXIDE].
DEUTZIA, [doit'-si-a], *n.* (*bot.*) a Chinese and Japanese shrub with small white flowers. [*Deutz*, an eighteenth-century Dutch botanist].
DEVA, [de'-va], *n.* a god; a beneficent spirit in Hindu mythology. [Skr. *deva* a god].
DEVANAGARI, [dē-van-ah'-ger-i], *n.* the Sanskrit alphabet. [DEVA and Skr. *nagari* alphabet].
DEVAPORATION†, [di-vap'-er-ā'-shun], *n.* the change of vapour into water, condensation. [DE and L. *vapor* vapour].
DEVASTATE, [dev'-as-tāt], *v.t.* to lay waste, ravage; (*slang*) to captivate, charm, fascinate. [L. *devastare*].
DEVASTATION, [dev'-as-tā'-shun], *n.* the act of devastating; the condition of being devastated.
DEVASTAVIT, [dē-vast-ā'-vit], *n.* (*leg.*) a writ against an executor for bad management of property resulting in loss. [L. *devastavit* he has wasted].
DEVELOP, [di-vel'-op], *v.t.* to unfold, bring out all that is contained within; to expand, cause to be on a bigger scale; to enable to evolve what is latent or in embryo; to explain more fully, to enlarge upon; (*phot.*) to cause the images to show up on a photographic negative by the use of certain chemical agents; *v.i.* to grow, enlarge, to be more completely evolved; to become more mature in appearance or character. [Fr. *développer*].
DEVELOPABLE, [di-vel'-op-abl], *adj.* capable of being developed or of developing.
DEVELOPER, [di-vel'-op-er], *n.* a person or thing that develops; (*phot.*) the chemical compound or solution employed in developing photographic negatives.
DEVELOPMENT, [di-vel'-op-ment], *n.* the act of developing; the state of being developed; that which has developed from something; (*biol.*) evolution; (*mus.*) that part of a complex musical composition in which a certain theme is developed.
DEVELOPMENTAL, [di-vel'-op-ment'-al], *adj.* pertaining to development.
DEVELOPMENTALLY, [di-vel'-op-ment'-al-i], *adv.* in course of development.
DEVEST, [di-vest'], *v.i.* (*leg.*) to take away goods or privileges vested in anyone; to alienate. [OFr. *desvestir*].
DEVIATE, [dē'-vi-āt], *v.i.* to turn aside, diverge; (*fig.*) to stray or swerve from a certain moral course. [L. *deviare*].
DEVIATION, [dē-vi-ā'-shun], *n.* the act of deviating; deflection; **d. of the compass,** the deflection of the needle from the magnetic meridian due to external causes. [MedL. *deviatio*].
DEVICE, [di-vīs'], *n.* the act of devising; the result of contriving; something devised; a plan, scheme, trick; a gadget, contrivance; (*her.*) an emblematic figure or design adopted by some family or association of people, as a badge; **left to one's own devices,** left to do as one thinks fit. [OFr. *devis* division, device].

DEVICE

DEVICEFUL, [di-vīs'-fōōl], *adj.* ingenious, full of devices.
DEVICEFULLY, [di-vīs-fōōl-i], *adv.* ingeniously.
DEVIL (1), [dev'-il], *n.* the great leader of the spirits of evil, Satan; any evil spirit, a demon; a false god or idol; (*fig.*) a human being of fiendish wickedness; a poor wretched creature; a clever rogue, a mischievous or reckless person; one doing subordinate unpaid work as a legal junior counsel under a leader; a writer employed by another for hack work; (*coll.*) temper, spirit; (*cookery*) highly seasoned dish; **printer's d.,** (*print.*) an errand-boy to a printer; **between the d. and the deep sea,** on the horns of a dilemma; **devil's advocate,** the advocate who opposes a proposed canonization; one whose advocacy does more harm than good; **d. to pay,** trouble ahead; **to give the d. his due,** to be fair even to the undeserving; **to go to the d.,** to be on the road to ruin; **to play the d. with,** to ruin, injure; **the very d.,** a source of great trouble. [OE. *deofol*].
DEVIL (2), (devilling, devilled), [dev'-il], *v.t.* to cook by grilling with hot condiments, *esp.* mustard; *v.i.* to do hack work for another. [DEVIL (1)].
DEVILET, [dev'-il-et], *n.* a little devil.
DEVIL-FISH, [dev'-il-fish'], *n.* one of the several gigantic Atlantic rays of the genus *Myliobatis*.
DEVILISH (1), [dev'-il-ish], *adj.* like the devil, extremely wicked or mischievous.
DEVILISH (2), [dev'-il-ish], *adv.* (*coll.*) exceedingly.
DEVILISHLY, [dev'-il-ish-li], *adv.* in a devilish manner; excessively.
DEVILISHNESS, [dev'-il-ish-nes], *n.* the condition of being devilish.
DEVILISM, [dev'-il-izm], *n.* the attributes or behaviour of a devil; devil-worship.
DEVILKIN, [dev'-il-kin], *n.* a little devil, an imp.
DEVIL-MAY-CARE, [dev'-il-mā'-kāer'], *adj.* reckless, rollicking, happy-go-lucky.
DEVILMENT, [dev'-il-ment], *n.* action characteristic of a devil; mischief.
DEVILRY, [dev'-il-ri], *n.* devilment, devilish practices or conduct.
DEVIL'S-COACH-HORSE, [dev'-ilz-kōch'-haws], *n.* a species of large black beetle.
DEVIL-WORSHIP, [dev'-il-wur'-ship], *n.* the propitiation by primitive tribes of the devil or spirit of evil.
DEVIOUS, [dē'-vi-us], *adj.* off the common way, remote; departing from a straight course, circuitous; indirect; (*fig.*) erratic; crooked, deceitful. [L. *devius* off the high road].
DEVIOUSLY, [dē'-vi-us-li], *adv.* in devious fashion.
DEVIOUSNESS, [dē'-vi-us-nes], *n.* the state of being devious.
DEVISABLE, [di-vīz'-abl], *adj.* that may be devised; (*leg.*) that can be bequeathed. [OFr. *devisable*].
DEVISE (1), [di-vīz'], *n.* (*leg.*) the act of devising property; the statement in a will concerned with such assignment.
DEVISE (2), [di-vīz'], *v.t.* to arrange, contrive, think out; to plan out, invent, design; (*leg.*) to assign real estate by will. [OFr. *deviser*].
DEVISEE, [di-vīz'-ē], *n.* (*leg.*) the person to whom property is devised.
DEVISER, [di-vīz'-er], *n.* an inventor, a schemer.
DEVISOR, [di-vīz'-er], *n.* (*leg.*) one who devises property. [AFr. *devisour*].
DEVITALIZATION, [dē-vī'-tal-īz-ā'-shun], *n.* the act of devitalizing.
DEVITALIZE, [dē-vī'-tal-īz], *v.t.* to deprive of vitality; to drain of energy or vigour.
DEVITRIFICATION, [dē-vit'-ri-fi-kā'-shun], *n.* the act of devitrifying.
DEVITRIFY, [dē-vit'-ri-fī], *v.t.* to deprive glass of its transparency, to make opaque.
DEVOCALIZE, [dē-vō'-kal-īz], *v.t.* to make a speech-sound voiceless.
DEVOID, [di-void'], *adj.* empty, destitute of, lacking in, without. [ME. *devoiden* to rid of].
DEVOIR, [duv'-wahr], *n.* duty, appointed task; (*pl.*) courteous attention, conventional civilities. [Fr. *devoir*].
DEVOLUTE, [dē'-vol-ewt], *v.t.* to transfer, devolve. [L. *devolutum*, *p.pt.* of *devolvere*].
DEVOLUTION, [dē-vol-ew'-shun], *n.* the act of devolving; (*biol.*) degeneration, deterioration in course of descending. [L. *devolutio*].
DEVOLVE, [di-volv'], *v.t.* to roll down; to deliver over, pass on; to hand down, transfer; to delegate; *v.i.* to fall to the lot of; cause to be performed by; (*leg.*) to descend by inheritance. [L. *devolvere* to roll down].
DEVOLVEMENT, [di-volv'-ment] *n.* devolution.
DEVONIAN, [di-vōn'-i-an], *adj.* of or belonging to Devonshire; (*geol.*) pertaining to the geological formation which lies above the Silurian and below the Carboniferous systems as found in Devonshire.
DEVOTE, [di-vōt'], *v.t.* to set apart, dedicate; to give oneself to, direct the attention wholly or chiefly to. [L. *devotum*, *p.pt.* of *devovere*].
DEVOTED, [di-vōt'-id], *adj.* given up to, consecrated to; strongly attached to; zealous.
DEVOTEDLY, [dē-vōt'-id-li], *adv.* with devotion.

DEVOTEDNESS, [di-vōt'-id-nes], *n.* the state or quality of being devoted.
DEVOTEE, [dev'-ō-tē], *n.* one who is deeply devoted; an enthusiastic supporter.
DEVOTEMENT, [di-vōt'-ment], *n.* devotion, dedication.
DEVOTER, [di-vōt'-er], *n.* a votary, devotee.
DEVOTION, [di-vō'-shun], *n.* the state of being devoted to anything or anyone; a devout yielding of the heart and affections to God; religious worship, an act of respect; ardent love or affection; strong attachment. [L. *devotio*].
DEVOTIONAL, [di-vō'-shun-al], *adj.* relating or suited to devotion.
DEVOTIONALISM, [di-vō'-shun-al-izm], *n.* extreme devoutness of a formal character.
DEVOTIONALIST, [di-vō'-shun-al-ist], *n.* a person given to religious devotion.
DEVOTIONALLY, [di-vō'-shun-al-i], *adv.* in a devotional fashion.
DEVOTIONIST, [di-vō'-shun-ist], *n.* one who formally practises or professes devotion.
DEVOUR, [di-vow'-er], *v.t.* to eat up greedily; consume, ravage, destroy; (*fig.*) to look fiercely, intently at; to read avidly, with consuming interest. [L. *devorare*].
DEVOURABLE, [di-vow'-er-abl], *adj.* capable of being devoured.
DEVOURER, [di-vow'-er-er], *n.* one who, or that which, devours.
DEVOURING, [di-vow'-er-ing], *adj.* consuming, wasting, destroying; (*fig.*) overwhelming, intense.
DEVOURINGLY, [di-vow'-er-ing-li], *adv.* in a devouring manner.
DEVOUT, [di-vowt'], *adj.* reverential, pious, religious; expressing devotion; (*fig.*) earnest, deep, heartfelt. [L. *devotus*].
DEVOUTLESS, [di-vowt'-les], *adj.* without devoutness.
DEVOUTLESSNESS, [di-vowt'-les-nes], *n.* the state of being devoutless.
DEVOUTLY, [di-vowt'-li], *adv.* in a devout fashion.
DEVOUTNESS, [di-vowt'-nes], *n.* the state or quality of being devout.
DEW (1), [dew], *n.* aqueous vapour condensed on the cool surfaces of plants, etc., during the night; (*fig.*) anything soft, fresh and shining like this. [OE. *deaw*].
DEW (2), [dew], *v.t. and i.* to wet with dew, to bedew; to fall as dew.
DEWAN, [di-wahn'], *n.* a finance minister in the Mohammedan States of India. [Arab. *diwan*].
DEW-BEATER, [dew'-bēt-er], *n.* a person who shakes off the dew for others following; a pioneer.
DEW-BERRY, [dew'-be'-ri], *n.* a species of blackberry, *Rubus cæsius*; the fruit of this tree.
DEW-CLAW, [dew'-klaw], *n.* (*anat.*) a rudimentary claw occurring in dogs and deer.
DEW-DROP, [dew'-drop], *n.* one of the drops of moisture in which dew collects.
DEW-FALL, [dew'-fawl], *n.* the time when the dew begins to fall in the evening.
DEWINESS, [dew'-i-nes], *n.* the state of being dewy; (*fig.*) freshness.
DEWLAP [dew'-lap], *n.* the loose flesh that hangs from the throat of cattle and certain other animals.

DEWLAP

DEWLAPPED, [dew'-lapt], *adj.* having a dewlap.
DEWLESS, [dew'-les] *adj.* without dew.
DEW-POINT, [dew'-point], *n.* the temperature at which dew can be deposited.
DEW-POND [dew'-pond'], *n.* a shallow pool on chalk downs thought to be replenished by drainage of dew and condensed mist from neighbouring ground.
DEW-RETTING, [dew'-ret'-ing], *n.* the exposure of flax to the weather or dew to decompose by maceration the gum which coats the fibre.
DEWSTONE, [dew'-stōn], *n.* a species of limestone which collects dew readily.
DEW-WORM, [dew'-wurm], *n.* the common earthworm, *Lumbricus terrestris*.
DEWY, [dew'-i], *adj.* wet with dew; (*fig.*) like dew in its freshness and softness, glistening.
DEXTER, [deks'-ter], *adj.* on the right-hand side; (*her.*) on the right-hand side of a shield or coat of arms, i.e., the left-hand side of the drawing. [L. *dexter*].
DEXTERITY, [deks-te'-ri-ti], *n.* the quality of being dexterous, manipulative skill, adroitness. [L. *dexteritas*].
DEXTEROUS, DEXTROUS, [deks'-ter-us], *adj.* right-handed; quick and expert in bodily or mental activity; adroit, skilful, deft.
DEXTEROUSLY, DEXTROUSLY, [deks'-ter-us-li], *adv.* in dexterous fashion.
DEXTEROUSNESS, [deks'-ter-us-nes], *n.* dexterity, adroitness.
DEXTRAL, [deks'-tral], *adj.* situated on the right-hand side; running from left to right.
DEXTRALITY, [deks-tral'-i-ti], *n.* right-handedness.
DEXTRIN, [deks'-trin], *n.* starch gum, the soluble matter into which the interior substance of starch globules is convertible by acids, diastase, or heating. [Fr. *dextrine*].
DEXTRO-, *pref.* turning towards the right; (*chem.*) causing the plane of a ray of polarized light to turn to the right. [L. *dextro* to the right].
DEXTRO-GLUCOSE, [deks'-trō-glōō'-kōs], *n.* (*chem.*) granular sugar, so named as being dextrogyrate.
DEXTRO-GYRATE, [deks'-trō-jī'-rāt], *adj.* (*min.*) revolving the plane of polarization to the right. [DEXTRO and L. *gyratus* turned round].
DEXTRORSE, [deks-traws'], *adj.* turned to the right. [L. *dextrorsum*, *dextroversum* turned to the right].
DEXTROSE, [deks'-trōs], *n.* dextro-glucose; ordinary glucose or grape-sugar.
DEXTROUS, see DEXTEROUS.
DEXTROUSLY, see DEXTEROUSLY.
DEY, [dā], *n.* a title of dignity, at one time given to the governors of Algiers and Tripoli. [Fr. *dey* from Turk. *dai* maternal uncle].
DEZINC, [dē-zingk'], *v.t.* to remove the zinc from.
DEZYMOTIZE, [di-zī'-mot-īz], *v.t.* to rid of disease-germs.
DHAGOBA, [dag-ō'-ba], *n.* a mound with a dome-shaped top, which contains Buddhist relics. [Hind. *dhagoba*].
DHAK, [dawk], *n.* an East Indian tree, *Butea frondosa*, producing brilliant flowers. [Hind. *dhak*].
DHAL, DAL, [dahl], *n.* Indian split pulse. [Hind. *dhal*].
DHARMA, [dah'-ma], *n.* the law of Buddha; the moral system underlying that law. [Skr. *dharma*].
DHOBI(E), [dō'-bi], *n.* a native washerman in India. [Hind. *dhobi*].
DHOLE, [dōl], *n.* the wild dog of the Indian Deccan, *Canis deccanensis*. [Unkn.].
DHOOTIE, DHOTI, [dōō'-ti, dō'-ti], *n.* the Indian loin-cloth. [Hind. *dhoti*].
DHOW, [dow], *n.* an Arab vessel, *esp.* one which has a lateen sail on one or two masts. [Unkn.].

DHOW

DHURRA, [dōōer'-a], *n.* Indian millet, *Panicum miliaceum*. [Hind. *dhurra*].
DHURRIE, [du'-ri], *n.* a strong Indian cotton fabric resembling carpeting. [Hind. *dari*].
DI- (1), *pref.* expressing separation. [L. *dis*.]
DI- (2), *pref.* two, twice, double. [Gk. *di-* twice, double].
DIA-, DI- (3), *pref.* through the influence of, by means of; through, throughout. [Gk. *dia*].
DIABASE, [dī'-a-bās], *n.* trap or greenstone, crystalline granular rock, an altered form of basalt. [Gk. *diabasis* a crossing over].
DIABASIC, [dī'-a-bās'-ik], *adj.* pertaining to diabase.
DIABATERIAL, [dī-a-bat-ēer'-i-al], *adj.* relating to the passing over of a border or river. [Gk. *diabateria*].
DIABETES, [dī'-a-bē'-tēz], *n* (*med.*) a disease characterized by an abnormal amount of sugar in the urine, which is passed excessively. [Gk. *diabetes* a moving through].
DIABETIC (1), [dī'-a-bē'-tik], *n.* (*med.*) a person having diabetes.
DIABETIC (2), [dī'-a-bē'-tik], *adj.* (*med.*) of, or pertaining to, diabetes.
DIABLERIE, DIABLERY, [dē-ah'-bler-i], *n.* machinations of the devil, witchery, devilment. [Fr. *diablerie*].
DIABOLIC, [dī-a-bol'-ik], *adj.* diabolical.

DIABOLICAL, [dī'-a-bol'-ik-al], *adj.* devilish, fiendish, extremely wicked. [Gk. *diabolikos*].
DIABOLICALLY, [dī'-a-bol'-ik-al-i], *adv.* in diabolical fashion.
DIABOLICALNESS, [dī-a-bol'-ik-al-nes], *n.* the state of being diabolical.
DIABOLIFY, [dī'-a-bol'-i-fī], *v.t.* to make a devil of; to ascribe diabolical attributes to.
DIABOLISM, [dī-ab'-ol-izm], *n.* worship of the devil or demons; dealings with the devil, witchcraft; diabolical behaviour or nature.
DIABOLIZATION, [dī-ab'-o-līz-ā'-shun], *n.* the act of rendering diabolical.
DIABOLIZE, [dī-ab'-o-līz], *v.t.* to render diabolical.
DIABOLO, [dē-ab'-o-lō], *n.* a game played with a top shaped like an hour-glass spun on and thrown from a string tied between two sticks. [DIA and Gk. *bole* a throw].
DIACATHOLICON, [dī'-a-kath-ol'-i-kon], *n.* a purgative so named from its general usefulness. [DIA and CATHOLIC].
DIACAUSTIC, [dī-a-kaws'-tik], *adj.* (*med.*) cauterizing by refraction; **d. curve,** (*math.*) the curve made by the intersection of refracted rays of light. [DIA and CAUSTIC].
DIACHASTIC, [dī-a-kas'-tik], *adj.* coming asunder spontaneously. [Gk. *diakhasko* I yawn].
DIACHYLON, DIACHYLUM, [dī-ak'-i-lon], *n.* sticking-plaster compounded by boiling litharge with olive oil and water, originally prepared from expressed juices. [Gk. *diakhulos* very juicy].
DIACHYMA, [dī-ak'-i-ma], *n.* (*bot.*) parenchyma. [DIA and Gk. *khuma* juice].
DIACODIUM, [dī'-a-kō'-di-um], *n.* a preparation distilled from the syrup of poppies. [DIA and Gk. *kodis* a poppyhead].
DIACONAL, [dī-ak'-on-al], *adj.* of or belonging to a deacon. [L. *diaconalis*].
DIACONATE, [dī-ak'-on-āt], *n.* the rank or position of a deacon; period of tenure of a deacon's office; deacons generally. [L. *diaconatus*].
DIACOPE, [dī-ak'-o-pi], *n.* (*rhet.*) a tmesis; (*gram.*) the separation of two halves or syllables of a word by interpolating another between them. [DIA and Gk. *kope* cutting].
DIACOUSTIC, [dī-a-kows'-tik], *adj.* pertaining to diacoustics. [DIA and ACOUSTIC].
DIACOUSTICS, [dī-a-kows'-tiks], *n.(pl.)* branch of acoustics concerned with the science of refracted sounds.
DIACRITIC (1), [dī-a-krit'-ik], *n.* a distinguishing sign; a diacritic mark.
DIACRITIC (2), [dī-a-krit'-ik], *adj.* distinguishing, distinctive; (*gram.*) (of certain marks) used on letters to indicate a special sound or value. [Gk. *diakritikos*].
DIACRITICAL, [dī'-a-krit'-ik-al], *adj.* diacritic.
DIACTINIC, [dī-ak-tin'-ik], *adj.* capable of transmitting the actinic rays of light. [DI (3) and Gk. *aktis* a ray].
DIADEM, [dī'-a-dem], *n.* the arch on a crown; a headband or fillet worn on the head as a badge of royalty or eminence; a crown; sovereign power; **d. spider,** the garden spider, *Araneus diadema*. [L. *diadema*].

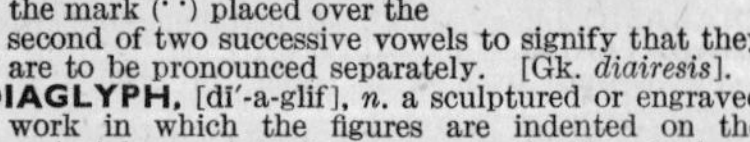

DIADEM

DIADEMED, [dī'-a-demd], *adj.* wearing a diadem, crowned.
DIADROM†, [dī'-a-drom], *n.* vibration of a pendulum. [Gk. *diadromos*].
DIAERESIS, [dī-ēer'-i-sis], *n.* the resolution of a diphthong or syllable into two parts; the mark (¨) placed over the second of two successive vowels to signify that they are to be pronounced separately. [Gk. *diairesis*].
DIAGLYPH, [dī'-a-glif], *n.* a sculptured or engraved work in which the figures are indented on the material; an intaglio. [DIA and Gk. *glypho* I carve].
DIAGNOSE, [dī'-ag-nōs], *v.t.* to find out the nature of an illness from an investigation of its symptoms.
DIAGNOSIS, [dī-ag-nōs'-is], *n.* the identification of an illness from an investigation of its symptoms; the statement embodying this; (*fig.*) conclusions reached about any unsatisfactory condition by accurate observation of its manifestations. [Gk. *diagnosis*].
DIAGNOSTIC (1), [dī-ag-nos'-tik], *n.* the sympto[m] of a disease; (*pl.*) the study of symptoms.
DIAGNOSTIC (2), [dī-ag-nos'-tik], *adj.* indicatin[g] the nature of a disease or unsatisfactory state [of] affairs.
DIAGNOSTICALLY [dī-ag-nos'-tik-al-i], *adv.* b[y] means of diagnosis.
DIAGNOSTICIAN, [dī'-ag-nos-tish'-an], *n.* a[n] expert in diagnosis.
DIAGOMETER, [dī-ag-om'-it-er], *n.* an instrumen[t] for measuring electro-conductive power. [F. *diagomètre*].
DIAGONAL (1), [dī-ag'-on-al], *n.* (*geom.*) a diagona[l] line.
DIAGONAL (2), [dī-ag'-on-al], *adj.* extending as [a] straight line between any two non-adjacent angl[es] of a rectilineal figure; stretching from corner [to] corner; oblique; forming or crossed with obliqu[e] lines. [L. *diagonalis*].
DIAGONALLY, [dī-ag'-on-al-i], *adv.* in a diagona[l] fashion.
DIAGRAM, [dī'-a-gram'], *n.* (*geom.*) a figure draw[n] to help in demonstrating the proof of a propositio[n]; an explanatory sketch or drawing; a pictorial sum[-]mary of statistics. [Gk. *diagramma*].
DIAGRAMMATIC, [dī'-a-gram-at'-ik], *adj.* involv[-]ing a diagram; resembling a diagram.
DIAGRAMMATICALLY, [dī'-a-gram-at'-ik-al-i], *adv.* by means of a diagram.
DIAGRAMMATIZE, [dī-a-gram'-at-īz], *v.t.* to pu[t] into the form of a diagram.
DIAGRAPH, [dī'-a-graf], *n.* an instrument for th[e] mechanical enlargement of diagrams, maps, etc., [or] for the drawing of projections. [DIA and GRAPH].
DIAGRAPHIC, [dī'-a-graf'-ik], *adj.* connected wit[h] drawings or figures.
DIAGRAPHICAL, [dī'-a-graf'-ik-al], *adj.* diagraphic.
DIAGRYDIATES, [dī'-ag-rid'-i-āts], *n.(pl.)* (*pharm.*) powerful purgatives made with diagrydium.
DIAGRYDIUM, [dī-a-grid'-i-um], *n.* (*med.*) a prepara[-]tion of scammony and quince-juice. [L. *diagrydium*].
DIAHELIOTROPIC, [dī'-a-hē'-li-o-trop'-ik], *ad[j.]* turning sideways to the light. [DIA and HELIO[-]TROPE].
DIAHELIOTROPISM, [dī'-a-hē'-li-o'-trop-izm], *n.* (*bot.*) a tendency to fall at right angles to the ligh[t].
DIAL (1), [dī'-al], *n.* the graduated face of any instru[-]ment for telling the time of day; any scale resemblin[g] a clock-face with a movable index; (*teleph.*) a mov[-]able disk marked with numbered and lettered finge[r-]holes for operating an automatic telephone system; (*slang*) the human face. [LL. *dialis*].
DIAL (2), (**dialling, dialled**), [dī'-al], *v.t.* to measu[re] by a dial; (*teleph.*) to use the dial of an automat[ic] telephone system to call a particular numbe[r]. [DIAL (1)].
DIALECT, [dī'-a-lekt], *n.* a recognized local [or] personal variation in the pronunciation, grammar, [or] vocabulary of a language. [Gk. *dialektos* way [of] speaking].
DIALECTAL, [dī-a-lek'-tal], *adj.* of, or belonging t[o] a dialect.
DIALECTALLY, [dī-a-lek'-tal-i], *adv.* in dialect.
DIALECTIC, [dī'-a-lek'-tik], *n.* the investigation [of] truth by argument or by the logical examinatio[n] of hypotheses and theories. [Gk. *dialektike*].
DIALECTICAL, [dī-a-lek'-tik-al], *adj.* belonging t[o] dialectic.
DIALECTICALLY, [dī-a-lek'-tik-al-i], *adv.* b[y] dialectic; in dialectic.
DIALECTICIAN, [dī-a-lek-tish'-an], *n.* one skille[d] in dialectic.
DIALECTICS, [dī-a-lek'-tiks], *n.(pl.)* the art of employ[-]ing dialectic.
DIALECTOLOGIST, [dī-a-lek-tol'-oj-ist], *n.* o[ne] who studies dialects.
DIALECTOLOGY, [dī-a-lek-tol'-o-ji], *n.* the stud[y] of dialects. [DIALECT and Gk. *logos* speech].
DIALECTOR, [dī-a-lek'-ter], *n.* a person skilled [in] dialects.
DIALIST, [dī'-al-ist], *n.* a manufacturer of dials; o[ne] accustomed to dialling.
DIALLAGE (1), [dī-al'-a-ji], *n.* (*rhet.*) a rhetorical figu[re] by which arguments are examined from differen[t] aspects and then turned to one conclusion. [Gk. *diallage*].
DIALLAGE (2), [dī'-al'-a-ji], *n.* (*min.*) an olive-gree[n] or bronze-coloured laminate mineral, a variety [of] augite. [DIALLAGE (1)].
DIALLAGIC, [dī-a-laj'-ik], *adj.* (*min.*) belonging t[o] or formed of diallage.

DIALLAGOID, [dī-al'-a-goid], *adj.* (*min.*) containing or resembling diallage. [DIALLAGE and Gk. *oeides* like].

DIALLING, [dī'-al-ing], *n.* the art of making or using dials.

DIALOGIC, [dī-a-loj'-ik], *adj.* dialogical. [MedL. *dialogicus*].

DIALOGICAL, [dī-a-loj'-ik-al], *adj.* of the nature of dialogue.

DIALOGISM, [dī-al'-o-jizm], *n.* (*rhet.*) a discussion in the form of a dialogue; a dialogue. [Gk. *dialogismos*].

DIALOGIST, [dī-al'-o-jist], *n.* one who speaks or writes dialogues.

DIALOGISTIC, [dī-al-o-jist'-ik], *adj.* dialogistical.

DIALOGISTICAL, [dī-al-o-jist'-ik-al], *adj.* in the form of a dialogue; argumentative.

DIALOGISTICALLY, [dī-al-o-jist'-ik-al-i], *adv.* as in a dialogue.

DIALOGITE, [dī-al'-o-jīt], *n.* (*chem.*) a rose-red carbonate of manganese. [Gk. *dialoge*].

DIALOGIZE, [dī-al'-o-jīz], *v.t.* to put in dialogue form; *v.i.* to carry on a dialogue.

DIALOGUE (1), [dī'-a-log], *n.* a conversation in speech or writing between two or more persons; the words spoken by the actors in a drama. [Gk. *dialogos*].

DIALOGUE (2), [dī'-a-log], *v.t.* and *i.* to put in the form of a dialogue; to hold a conversation.

DIAL-PLATE, [dī'-al-plāt'], *n.* the face-plate of a dial.

DIALURIC, [dī-al-yo͞oer'-ik], *adj.* pertaining to the urine. [DI (3) and AL(LOXAN) and URIC].

DIALYSIS, [dī-al'-i-sis], *n.* (*chem.*) the separation of substances by diffusion through a parchment membrane. [Gk. *dialusis* a setting free].

DIALYTIC, [dī-a-lit'-ik], *adj.* pertaining to dialysis; **d. telescope**, a telescope producing achromatism by the use of lenses of flint and crown glass.

DIALYZE, [dī'-a-līz], *v.t.* (*chem.*) to separate two substances by dialysis.

DIALYZER, [dī'-a-līz-er], *n.* (*chem.*) a membrane permeable to crystalloids, used in dialysis.

DIAMAGNETIC (1), [dī-a-mag-net'-ik], *n.* (*phys.*) a diamagnetic substance.

DIAMAGNETIC (2), [dī'-a-mag-net'-ik], *adj.* exhibiting diamagnetism. [DIA and MAGNETIC].

DIAMAGNETICALLY, [dī'-a-mag-net'-ik-al-i]. *adv.* in a diamagnetic manner.

DIAMAGNETISM, [dī'-a-mag'-net-izm], *n.* (*phys.*) the property possessed by some substances of adopting a position at right angles to a magnetic current. [DIA and MAGNETISM].

DIAMANTIFEROUS, [dī'-a-man-tif'-er-us], *adj.* bearing diamonds. [Fr. *diamantifère*].

DIAMETER, [dī-am'-it-er], *n.* (*geom.*) a straight line, bounded by the circumference, passing through the centre of a circle or sphere which it bisects; a chord passing through the centre of a conic; the measurement from side to side through the centre, the width or thickness of objects having a circular contour; (*opt.*) a unit of measurement of the magnifying power of lenses. [OFr. *diametre* from Gk. *diametros*].

DIAMETRAL, [dī-am'-it-ral], *adj.* diametrical.

DIAMETRICAL, [dī'-a-met'-rik-al], *adj.* pertaining to a diameter; exactly opposite.

DIAMETRICALLY, [dī-a-met'-rik-al-i], *adv.* exactly, directly.

DIAMOND (1), [dī'-a-mond], *n.* the hardest, and most precious of all the precious stones, being a crystal of pure carbon, a glazier's tool for cutting glass; (*typ.*) the second smallest type, intermediate between pearl and brilliant; (*geom.*) a rhomboidal figure stood on end; (*her.*) a lozenge; a playing-card marked with red lozenge-shaped figures; the suit at cards characterized in this way; **d. drill**, a boring tool in which the cutters are boort diamonds fixed in a groove round a cylinder; **d. jubilee**, the sixtieth anniversary; **d. wedding**, the sixtieth anniversary of the wedding day; **d. knot**, (*naut.*) an ornamental knot worked with the separated strands of a rope; **a rough d.**, (*fig.*) a good and intelligent but uncultured man; **d. cut d.**, cunning matched against equal cunning; **black d.**, coal. [OFr. *diamant* from L. *adamas adamantis*, the hardest substance].

DIAMOND (2), [dī'-a-mond], *adj.* made of, or ornamented with, diamonds; having many diamonds, like a diamond in shape.

DIAMOND (3), [dī'-a-mond], *v.t.* to set with diamonds.

DIAMONDIFEROUS, [dī'-a-mond-if'-er-us], *adj.* producing diamonds. [DIAMOND (1) and L. *ferre* to bear].

DIAMOND-POINT, [dī'-a-mond-point'], *n.* an engraving tool whose point is a diamond; (*pl.*) a diamond-shaped figure formed by the crossing of two sets of railway lines.

DIAMOND-SHAPED, [dī'-a-mond-shāpt'], *adj.* in the form of a diamond.

DIANA, [dī-an'-a], *n.* (*myth.*) a Roman virgin goddess of the moon and hunting; (*fig.*) a huntress, the moon. [L. *Diana*].

DIANDROUS, [dī-an'-drus], *adj.* (*bot.*) of the class Diandria, two-stamened; (*zool.*) mating with two males.

DIANOETIC, [dī-an'-ō-et'-ik], *adj.* of or relating to thought; thinking; intellectual. [Gk. *dianoetikos*].

DIANTHUS, [dī-an'-thus], *n.* (*bot.*) the genus of plants of which the pinks and carnations are members. [Gk. *Dios* of Zeus and *anthos* flower].

DIAPASM, [dī'-a-pazm], *n.* a perfumed powder for dusting over the body. [Gk. *diapasma*].

DIAPASON, [dī'-a-pā'-zon], *n.* (*mus.*) music written in harmony; a musical passage containing an harmonious arrangement of parts; the natural range of a voice or instrument; a scale by which instruments are tuned; (*fig.*) a rich, harmonious sound; **open d., closed d.**, two stops in an organ which open or close its whole compass. [Gk. *dia pason* through all the tones].

DIAPEDESIS, [dī'-a-ped-ē'-sis], *n.* (*path.*) the passing of blood corpuscles through the walls of the veins without causing rupture. [Gk. *diapedesis* a jumping through].

DIAPER (1), [dī'-a-per], *n.* a cloth woven in a diamond or some other regular pattern; a baby's napkin or towel; a design based on a diamond-shaped pattern; (*her.*) a pattern in diamonds forming the groundwork of a design. [OFr. *diapre*].

DIAPER (2), [dī'-a-per], *v.t.* to decorate in a diaper pattern.

DIAPERING, [dī'-a-per-ing], *n.* decoration in a diaper pattern.

DIAPERING

DIAPHANE, [dī'-a-fān], *n.* a diaphanous substance, *esp.* the transparent membrane of a cell. [Gk. *diaphanes* transparent].

DIAPHANED, [dī'-a-fānd], *adj.* rendered diaphanous; transparent.

DIAPHANEITY, [dī'-a-fan-ē'-i-ti], *n.* transparency.

DIAPHANIC, [dī-a-fan'-ik], *adj.* diaphanous.

DIAPHANIE, [dī-af'-a-ni], *n.* the art of affixing coloured transparencies on glass, creating an effect of staining.

DIAPHANOMETER, [dī'-a-fan-om'-it-er], *n.* an instrument for measuring the degree of transparency of the air. [DIAPHANE and METER].

DIAPHANOUS, [dī-af'-an-us], *adj.* transparent.

DIAPHORESIS, [dī'-a-for-ē'-sis], *n.* (*med.*) perspiration, *esp.* when artificially promoted. [Gk. *diaphoresis*].

DIAPHORETIC (1), [dī'-a-for-et'-ik], *n.* (*med.*) a diaphoretic medicine.

DIAPHORETIC (2), [dī'-a-for-et'-ik], *adj.* promoting perspiration. [Gk. *diaphoretikos*].

DIAPHRAGM, [dī'-a-fram], *n.* (*anat.*) the midriff or large circular movable muscle separating the chest or thorax from the abdomen or lower belly; a dividing membrane; a partition; (*opt.*) a plate with an opening through it for cutting off superfluous rays of light. [Gk. *diaphragma* a barrier].

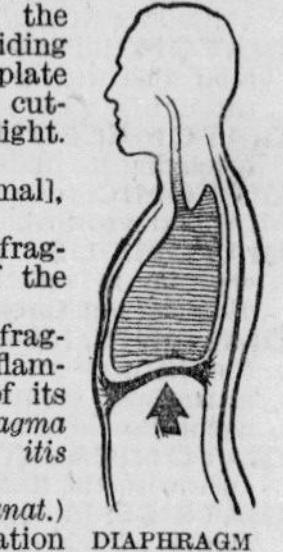
DIAPHRAGM

DIAPHRAGMAL, [dī-a-frag'-mal], *adj.* belonging to the diaphragm.

DIAPHRAGMATIC, [dī'-a-frag-mat'-ik], *adj.* pertaining to, of the nature of a diaphragm.

DIAPHRAGMATITIS, [dī'-a-frag-mat-ī'-tis], *n.* (*path.*) acute inflammation of the diaphragm, or of its peritoneal coats. [Gk. *diaphragma diaphragmatos* diaphragm and *itis* denoting inflammation].

DIAPHYSIS, [dī-af'-i-sis], *n.* (*anat.*) the place in a bone where ossification begins; (*bot.*) prolongation of an inflorescence. [Gk. *diaphusis* the bursting open of a bud].

DIAPNOIC, [dī-ap-nō'-ik], *adj.* (*med.*) causing a gentle sweat. [Gk. *diapnoe*].

DIAPYETIC, [dī'-a-pi-et'-ik], *adj.* (*med.*) causing suppuration. [Gk. *diapuein* to suppurate].
DIARCHY, [dī'-ah-ki], *n.* a system of government in which two powers have sovereignty. [DI (2) and Gk. *arkhia* rule].
DIARIAN, [dī-āer'-i-an], *adj.* belonging to a diary daily.
DIARIST, [dī'-er-ist], *n.* one who writes a diary.
DIARIZED, [dī'-er-īzd], *adj.* entered in a diary.
DIARRHOEA, [dī-er-ē'-a], *n.* a disorder causing fluid stools and frequent evacuations. [Gk. *diarrhoia*].
DIARRHOETIC, [dī-ar-ēt'-ik], *adj.* inducing diarrhoea.
DIARTHROSIS, [dī'-ah-thrō'-sis], *n.* (*anat.*) the articulation of a bone which is movable in every direction. [DIA and Gk. *arthron* a joint].
DIARY, [dī'-er-i], *n.* a record of daily events; the book in which this is recorded; a small engagement-book with dated pages. [L. *diarium*].
DIASPORA, [dī-as'-per-a], *n.* the Dispersion of the Jews after their captivity in Egypt. [Gk. *diaspora*].
DIASPORE, [dī'-a-spaw(r)], *n.* (*chem.*) native hydrate of aluminium which decrepitates and disperses when subjected to the heat of the blowpipe. [Gk. *diaspora* dispersive].
DIASTALTIC, [dī-a-stal'-tik], *adj.* (*mus.*) (of an interval) extended; (of a melody) exalting the mind; (*phys.*) (of reflex actions) operating through the spinal cord. [Gk. *diastaltikos*].
DIASTASE, [dī'-a-stās], *n.* (*chem.*) an enzyme found in malt which changes starch into sugar. [Gk. *diastasis*].
DIASTASIS, [dī-as'-ta-sis], *n.* (*anat.*) a forcible separation of bones without causing fracture. [Gk. *diastasis*].
DIASTATIC, [dī-a-stat'-ik], *adj.* pertaining to, or of the nature of, diastase.
DIASTEMA, [dī-a-stē'-ma], *n.* the space between two kinds of teeth or two successive teeth of the same kind, in certain mammals. [Gk. *diastema*].
DIASTOLE, [dī'-a-stol'], *n.* (*med.*) the rhythmic dilation of the heart. [Gk. *diastole*].
DIASTOLIC, [dī-a-stol'-ik], *adj.* connected with or resembling diastole.
DIASTYLE (1), [dī'-a-stīl], *n.* (*arch.*) a building with surrounding columns grouped in pairs with three diameters of one column between each pair.
DIASTYLE (2), [dī'-a-stīl], *adj.* with columns arranged as in a diastyle. [Gk. *diastulos* with a space between columns].
DIATESSARON, [dī-a-tes'-er-on], *n.* (*mus.*) a concord or harmonic interval consisting of a greater tone, a lesser tone, and one great semitone; (*theol.*) a harmony of the four gospels; the four gospels. [Gk. *dia tessaron* comprising four].
DIATHERMAL, [dī-a-thur'-mal], *adj.* diathermic.
DIATHERMANCY, [dī-a-thur'-man-si], *n.* the property of transmitting radiant heat. [DIA and Gk. *thermansis* heating].
DIATHERMIC, [dī-a-thur'-mik], *adj.* able to transmit radiant heat.
DIATHERMY, [dī-a-thur'-mi], *n.* (*med.*) the theory or practice of administering radiant heat to break down obstinate physical conditions such as arthritis. [DIA and Gk. *thermos* heat].
DIATHESIS, [dī-ath'-is-is], *n.* (*med.*) a physical condition making the body particularly susceptible to a disease. [Gk. *diathesis*].
DIATOM, [dī'-a-tom], *n.* (*zool.*) a microscopic unicellular alga with a flinty skeleton. [Gk. *diatomos* cut through].
DIATOMACEOUS, [dī'-a-tom-ā'-shus], *adj.* of, or belonging to, diatoms.
DIATOMIC, [dī-a-tom'-ik], *adj.* (*chem.*) of two atoms. [DI and ATOMIC].
DIATOMOUS, [dī-at'-om-us], *adj.* (*min.*) with crystals in one distinct diagonal cleavage. [Gk *diatomos* cut through].
DIATONIC, [dī'-a-ton'-ik], *adj.* (*mus.*) pertaining to the natural scale of any key without chromatic intrusions; composed of the notes proper to the natural scale of a certain key. [Gk. *diatonikos*].
DIATONICALLY, [dī-a-ton'-ik-al-i], *adv.* in accordance with the diatonic scale.
DIATRIBE, [dī'-a-trīb], *n.* a discourse; a spirited and wordy attack on some person or work, a piece of invective or abuse. [Gk. *diatribe*].
DIATRIBIST [dī-a-trīb'-ist], *n.* one who indulges in diatribe.
DIAZO-COMPOUNDS, [dī-at'-zō-kom'-powndz], *n.(pl.)* (*chem.*) compounds derived from aromatic hydrocarbons with characteristic grouping of two atoms of nitrogen with phenyl. [DI (2) and AZO].
DIB, [dib], *n.* a counter used in playing at cards; (*pl.*) a game played by children with pebbles or sheep knuckle-bones; the name of these pebbles or bones; (*pl.*) (*slang*) money. [DAB].
DIBASIC, [dī-bās'-ik], *adj.* (*chem.*) (of acids) with two atoms of hydrogen replaced by bases. [DI (2) and BASIC].
DIBBER, [dib'-er], *n.* an agricultural implement having teeth or prongs for making holes in the ground, a dibble.
DIBBLE (1), [dibl], *n.* a pointed tool used in gardening for making holes for planting. [DIB].
DIBBLE (2), [dibl], *v.t.* to use a dibble.
DIBBLER, [dib'-ler], *n.* a man using a dibble.
DIBOTHRIANS, [dī-both'-ri-anz], *n.(pl.)* (*zool.*) a division of the entozoa, which includes the tape-worms. [DI (2) and Gk. *bothros* a pit].
DIBRANCHIATA, [dī-brang'-ki-āt'-a], *n.(pl.)* (*ichth.*) the order of cephalopods with two gills. [DI (2) and Gk. *bragkhia* gills].
DIBSTONE, [dib'-stōn], *n.* a stone or knuckle-bone used in the game dib.
DICACITY, [dī-kas'-i-ti], *n.* pertness in speech; raillery. [L. *dicacitas*].
DICAST, [dik'-ast], *n.* an Athenian juryman. [Gk. *dikastes*].

DIBBLE

DICE (1), [dīs], *n.(pl.)* small cubes marked with a different number of pips on each surface and used for games of chance; dicing; (*cookery*) meat or vegetables cut into small cubes. [*Pl.* of DIE].
DICE (2), [dīs], *v.i.* to play with dice; to cut into the shape of dice.
DICE-BOX, [dīs'-boks], *n.* the small tubular box used for shaking dice in gaming.
DICED, [dīst], *adj.* cut into small cubes like dice; ornamented with figures shaped like dice.
DICEPHALOUS, [dī-sef'-al-us], *adj.* two-headed [Gk. *dikephalos*].
DICER, [dīs'-er], *n.* a person who plays with dice.
DICHLAMYDEOUS, [dī-klam-id'-i-us], *adj.* (*bot.*) with both calyx and corolla. [DI (2) and Gk. *khlamys* a short dress].
DICHOGAMOUS, [dī-kog'-am-us], *adj.* (*bot.*) of or pertaining to dichogamy.
DICHOGAMY, [dī-kog'-a-mi], *n.* (*bot.*) the system whereby stamens and pistils of an hermaphrodite plant mature at different times and so prevent self-fertilization. [Gk. *dicho* apart and *gamos* marriage].
DICHORD, [dī'-kawd], *n.* a two-stringed instrument, usually of the lyre type; an instrument with a pair of strings to each note. [DI (2) and CHORD].
DICHOTOMIC, [dī-kot'-om-ik], *adj.* dichotomous.
DICHOTOMIZE, [dī-kot'-om-īz] *v.t. and i.* to divide in two.
DICHOTOMOUS, [dī-kot'-om-us], *adj.* dividing in two; (*bot.*) dividing regularly in pairs. [Gk. *dichotomos*].
DICHOTOMOUSLY, [dī-kot'-om-us-li], *adv.* in dichotomous fashion.
DICHOTOMY [dī-kot'-o-mi], *n.* (*log.*) continuous division by pairs into groups distinguished by contradictory qualities, (*bot.*) a continuous forking into pairs. [Gk. *dicho* apart and *tome* cutting].

DICHORD

DICHROIC, [dī-krō'-ik], *adj.* exhibiting dichroism, *esp.* of a kind of fog on a photographic negative. [Gk. *dikhroos* two-coloured].
DICHROISM, [dī-krō'-izm], *n.* the property possessed by certain doubly-refracting crystals of showing different colours when viewed in different directions.
DICHROMATIC, [dī-krō-mat'-ik], *adj.* having two different colours. [DI (2) and CHROMATIC].
DICHROMIC, [dī-krōm'-ik], *adj.* recognizing only two of the primary colours; showing a different colour when looked at, from the one seen when looked through. [DI (2) and CHROMIC].
DICING, [dīs'-ing], *n.* the act of playing or gambling with dice.
DICING-HOUSE [dīs'-ing-hows'], *n.* a gaming-house.

DICK (1), [dik], *n.* a leather apron. [The Christian name *Dick*].
DICK (2), [dik], *n.* (*dial.*) the bank of a ditch. [DYKE].
DICKENS, [dik'-inz], *int.* (*slang*) the devil! the deuce! [Uncert.].
DICKENSIAN, [dik-en'-si-an], *adj.* relating to Charles Dickens, or anything written in his style.
DICKER (1), [dik'-er], *n.* (*comm.*) a group of ten. [ME. *dyker* from L. *decuria*].
DICKER (2), [dik'-er], *v.i.* to haggle, bargain. [DICKER (1)].
DICKEY, [dik'-i], *n.* the driving seat of a horse carriage; a small seat usually folding in behind a car, coach, or cab; (*slang*) a false shirt-front. [Unkn.].
DICKY (1), [dik'-i], *n.* a childish name for any bird. [Unkn.].
DICKY (2), [dik'-i], *adj.* (*slang*) shaky, unsteady; liable to ill-health; financially unstable. [Unkn.].
DICLINATE, [dī-klin'-āt], *adj.* diclinic.
DICLINIC, [dī-klin'-ik], *adj.* (of crystals) having two obliquely inclined axes. [DI (2) and Gk. *klino* I incline].
DICLINOUS, [dī'-klin-us], *adj.* (*bot.*) bearing the stamens and the pistils in different flowers, each flower being unisexual. [DI (2) and Gk. *kline* a bed].
DICOCCOUS, [dī-kok'-us], *adj.* (*bot.*) dividing into two cocci; consisting of two cohering grains. [DI (2) and Gk. *kokkos* a kernel].
DICOELOUS, [dī-sē'-lus], *adj.* (*anat.*) having two cavities. [DI (2) and Gk. *koile* a hollow].
DICONDYLIAN, [dī-kon-dil'-i-an], *adj.* (*zool.*) with two occipital condyles. [Gk. *dikondulos* double-jointed].
DICOTYLEDON, [dī'-kot-i-lē'-don], *n.* (*bot.*) a plant which bears two seed-leaves. [DI (2) and COTYLEDON].
DICOTYLEDONOUS, [dī'-kot-i-lē'-don-us], *adj.* (*bot.*) bearing two cotyledons.
DICOTYLES, [dī-kot'-i-lēz], *n.*(*pl.*) (*zool.*) the peccaries.
DICROTIC, [dī-krot'-ik], *adj.* (*path.*) having two beats of the pulse for each heart-beat. [Gk. *dikrotos* double-beating].
DICTA, [dik'-ta], *n.*(*pl.*) proverbial sayings; authoritatively sounding or brilliant phrases. [*Pl.* of DICTUM].
DICTAPHONE, [dik'-ta-fōn], *n.* (*prot.*) a machine for the recording of dictations to be subsequently reproduced audibly. [DICTA(TE) and Gk. *phone* sound].
DICTATE (1), [dik'-tāt], *n.* a command; a precept; that which is dictated. [DICTATE (2)].
DICTATE (2), [dik-tāt'], *v.t.* *and* *i.* to command, to give orders for; to tell another what to do, say, or write; to compose letters, speeches, etc., orally for someone to write down; to recite something to be copied down verbatim by others, to override, play the despot. [L. *dictare* to say frequently].
DICTATED, [dik-tāt'-id], *adj.* commanded; spoken so as to be taken down verbatim.
DICTATION, [dik-tā'-shun], *n.* the act or habit of dictating; material that is dictated; a passage spoken slowly to be written down verbatim as a spelling exercise. [LL. *dictatio*].
DICTATOR, [dik-tāt'-er], *n.* one who dictates; a despot, an absolute ruler; an occasional magistrate in ancient republican Rome. [L. *dictator*].
DICTATORIAL, [dik'-tat-aw'-ri-al], *adj.* after the manner of a dictator; absolute, authoritative, overbearing; having an assertive tone of voice or manner.
DICTATORIALLY, [dik-tat-aw'-ri-al-i], *adv.* in a dictatorial fashion.
DICTATORSHIP, [dik-tāt'-er-ship], *n.* the rule or status of a dictator in a state; the period of a dictator's office; any position of absolute authority; **d. of the proletariat**, a system in which all classes except the wage-earning class are deprived of political power.
DICTATORY, [dik-tāt'-er-i], *adj.* dictatorial. [L. *dictatorius*].
DICTATRESS, [dik-tā'-tres], *n.* a female dictator.
DICTATRIX, [dik-tā'-triks], *n.* a dictatress.
DICTATURE, [dik-tā'-cher], *n.* dictatorship; a body of dictators.
DICTION, [dik'-shun], *n.* the style of speech or writing so far as it concerns the choice of words and phrases; enunciation; **poetic d.**, a specialized poetical vocabulary. [L. *dictio*].
DICTIONARY, [dik'-shun-er-i], *n.* a lexicon, a book consisting of an alphabetical list of the words of a language or of an author, showing their forms, meanings, and sometimes their etymologies, etc.; a book of precise information on any subject, usually arranged under alphabetical readings. [MedL. *dictionarius*].
DICTOGRAPH, [dik'-to-graf], *n.* (*prot.*) an instrument for recording sounds, *esp.* speech sounds. [DICTUM and Gk. *graphia* writing].
DICTUM, [dik'-tum], *n.* a saying; an authoritative pronouncement; (*leg.*) a personal opinion given by a judge, not having the force of an official pronouncement or decision. [L. *dictum* something said].
DICTYOGENS, [dik'-ti-o-jenz], *n.*(*pl.*) (*bot.*) plants having net-veined leaves, intermediate between those of an endogenous and those of an exogenous structure. [Gk. *diktuon* a net and *genes* born].
DICYNODON, [dī-sin'-o-don], *n.* (*geol.*) a fossil reptile of South Africa, with a beak like a turtle and two large tusks in the upper jaw. [DI (2) and Gk. *kuon* dog and *odous odontos* a tusk, tooth].
DID, [did], *v.t.* *pret.* of DO.
DIDACTIC, [dī-dak'-tik], *adj.* designed to impart information and instruct, *esp.* morally; giving instruction out of season, unpleasantly superior. [Gk. *didaktikos*].
DIDACTICAL, [dī-dak'-tik-al], *adj.* didactic.
DIDACTICALLY, [dī-dak'-tik-al-i], *adv.* in didactic fashion.
DIDACTICISM, [dī-dak'-ti-sizm], *n.* the quality of being didactic.
DIDACTICS, [dī-dak'-tiks], *n.*(*pl.*) the method or art of teaching.
DIDACTYL, [dī-dak'-til], *adj.* (*zool.*) having two fingers, toes or claws. [DI (2) and Gk. *daktulos* a finger].
DIDACTYLOUS, [dī-dak'-til-us], *adj.* didactyl.
DIDAPPER, DIEDAPPER, [dī'-dap-er], *n.* the dabchick or little grebe. [ME. *dydoppar*].
DIDASCALIC, [dī-das-kal'-ik], *adj.* didactic. [Gk. *didaskalikos* instructive].
DIDDER, [did'-er], *v.i.* (*dial.*) to shiver, shake. [DITHER].
DIDDLE (1), [didl], *v.t.* (*coll.*) to cheat, trick, or dupe. [Unkn.].
DIDDLE (2), [didl], *v.i.* to totter, to walk unsteadily. [DIDDER].
DIDDLER, [did'-ler], *n.* (*coll.*) a person who diddles, a swindler, cheat.

DIDAPPER

DIDECAHEDRAL, [dī'-dek-a-hē'-dral], *adj.* (*min.*) in the form of a ten-sided prism, with five-sided summits. [DI and (2) DECAHEDRAL].
DIDELPHIA, [dī-del'-fi-a], *n.*(*pl.*) (*zool.*) the mammalian sub-class comprising the marsupials. [DI (2) and Gk. *delphus* womb].
DIDELPHOID, [dī-delf'-oid], *adj.* (*zool.*) double-wombed. [DIDELPHIA and Gk. *oeides* like].
DIDELPHYS, [dī-delf'-is], *n.* (*zool.*) a genus of marsupial mammals which includes the opossum.
DIDIDAE, [dī'-did-ē], *n.*(*pl.*) (*zool.*) the family of birds including the dodo and the solitaire, *Pezophaps solitaria*.
DIDODECAHEDRAL, [dī'-dō-dek-a-hē'-dral], *adj.* (*min.*) in the form of a twelve-sided prism, with six-sided summits, making twenty-four faces in all. [DI (2) and DODECAHEDRAL].
DIDRACHM, [dī'-dram], *n.* an ancient Greek silver coin worth two drachmae. [DI (2) and DRACHMA].
DIDUCTION†, [di-duk'-shun], *n.* a drawing or pulling apart. [L. *diductio*].
DIDUNCULUS, [di-dung'-kyōō-lus], *n.* (*zool.*) the tooth-billed pigeon native to Samoa.
DIDYMIUM, [did-im'-i-um], *n.* (*chem.*) a very rare metal occurring only with lanthanum and cerium, the chemical element denoted by Di. [Gk. *didumos* twin].
DIDYMOUS, [did'-im-us], *adj.* (*bot.*) twin; growing in pairs. [Gk. *didumos* twin].
DIDYNAMIA, [did'-in-ā'-mi-a], *n.*(*pl.*) didynamous plants. [DI and Gk. *dunamis* power].
DIDYNAMIAN, [did'-in-ā'-mi-an], *adj.* didynamous.
DIDYNAMOUS, [dī-din'-am-us], *adj.* (*bot.*) containing four stamens arranged in pairs, with one pair shorter than the other.
DIE (1), (*pl.* **dice, dies**), [dī], *n.* (*pl.* **dice**), a small solid cube having each of its faces marked with dots from one to six, and thrown from a box or the hand in games of chance (only used in the *pl.*); (*pl.* **dies**),

a piece of metal or stamp engraved with a design which can be impressed in reverse upon some softer material; a specially shaped piece of metal with a screwed hole for cutting the thread on a rod; the dado of a pedestal; **the d. is cast,** all is irretrievably settled and decided. [OFr. *dei*].

DIE (2), [dī], *v.i.* to depart from life, to cease to exist, pass away; to perish, to be eternally lost, to pass out of existence; to wither; to fade away; (*coll.*) **to be dying for,** to long for something; (*fig., poet.*) to languish; **to d. away,** to become fainter, to diminish in intensity; **to d. back,** (*bot.*) to wither from the branches down to the root; **to d. down,** to subside, lessen. [OE. **degan*].

DIE-AWAY, [dī'-a-wā'], *adj.* languishing away.

DIEB, [dēb], *n.* a North African jackal, *Canis anthus.* [Arab. *dib* wolf].

DIEDAPPER, see DIDAPPER.

DIEGESIS, [dī'-i-jē'-sis], *n.* an explanation or statement of anything; narrative. [Gk. *diegesis*].

DIEHARD (1), [dī'-hahd], *n.* one who resists to the end (particularly innovation or change).

DIE-HARD (2), [dī'-hahd], *adj.* extreme, out-and-out.

DIELECTRIC (1), [dī'-il-ek'-trik], *n.* an insulating substance, a non-conductor of electricity. [DI (1) and ELECTRIC].

DIELECTRIC (2), [dī'-il-ek'-trik], *adj.* insulating, non-conductive.

DIESEL-ENGINE, [dē'-zel-en'-jin], *n.* an internal-combustion engine burning heavy oil ignited by compression. [R. *Diesel*, the inventor (1858-1913)].

DIE-SINKER, [dī'-singk'-er], *n.* an engraver of dies.

DIE-SINKING, [dī'-singk'-ing], *n.* the process of engraving dies.

DIESIS, [dī'-es-is], *n.* (*print.*) the double dagger reference mark (‡); (*mus.*) one of various intervals less than a tone, the difference between three major thirds and an octave. [Gk. *diesis* a quarter-tone].

DIES NON, [dī'-ēz-non'], *n.* (*leg.*) day on which no legal business may be done. [L. *dies non* (*juridicus*) a day there is no court].

DIESOLIUM, [dē-sō'-li-um], *n.* (*prot.*) a heavy crude-oil fuel. [DIE(SEL) and L. *oleum* oil].

DIE-STOCK, [dī'-stok], *n.* a device for holding the dies used in screw-cutting.

DIET (1), [dī'-et], *n.* an international or national conference or congress; a regular national assembly of elected representatives in certain European countries, for purposes of government. [MedL. *dieta*].

DIET (2), [dī'-et], *n.* a specially prescribed course of food for medical purposes, as a punishment, etc.; the type of meals or food habitually eaten. [Gk. *diaita*].

DIET (3), [dī'-et], *v.t. and i.* to follow out or keep to a diet; to subject to, prescribe a diet for.

DIETARIAN, [dī'-et-āer'-i-an], *n.* one who strictly keeps to his diet.

DIETARY (1), [dī'-et-er-i], *n.* a diet; an allowance of food.

DIETARY (2), [dī'-et-er-i], *adj.* pertaining to a diet.

DIET-DRINK, [dī'-et-dringk'], *n.* a medicinal drink.

DIETED, [dī'-et-id], *adj.* fed according to a diet.

DIETER, [dī'-et-er], *n.* one who diets.

DIETETIC, [dī'-et-et'-ik], *adj.* pertaining to a diet. [Gk. *diaitetikos*].

DIETETICAL, [dī'-et-et'-ik-al], *adj.* dietetic.

DIETETICS, [dī'-et-et'-iks], *n.*(*pl.*) the scientific study of food and diets required for sound health.

DIETETIST, [dī'-et-et'-ist], *n.* one who seeks to cure disease by prescribing a diet.

DIETIST, [dī'-et-ist], *n.* one who studies, undergoes, or prescribes a system of dieting.

DIETITIAN, [dī'-et-ish'-un], *n.* a dietist.

DIF-, *pref.* a form of the prefix DIS used before *f*.

DIFFAREATION, [dif-āer'-i-ā'-shun], *n.* an ancient Roman method of divorce. [L. *diffareatio*].

DIFFER, [dif'-er], *v.i.* to be unlike, to be dissimilar; to disagree, to hold a contrary opinion; to be at variance; **to d. from,** to be distinguished from, to disagree with. [L. *differre*].

DIFFERENCE, [dif'-er-ents], *n.* dissimilarity; the act of differing; the state or quality of being different; that by which things differ, that which makes anything different; the amount by which anything differs; (*her.*) a figure or device added to a coat-of-arms to distinguish a younger member or branch; **to split the d.,** to compromise. [L. *differentia*].

DIFFERENT, [dif'-er-ent], *adj.* not the same, unlike; various, separate; changed, altered; distinct. [L. *differens*].

DIFFERENTIA, [dif'-er-en'-shi-a], *n.* a mark of difference; (*log.*) a distinguishing feature peculiar to a particular species. [L. *differentia*].

DIFFERENTIAL (1), [dif'-er-en'-shal], *n.* (*math.*) an infinitely small difference between two consecutive states of a variable quantity.

DIFFERENTIAL (2), [dif'-er-en'-shal], *adj.* pertaining to, causing or forming a difference, distinguishing; (*math.*) pertaining to infinitely small differences of quantity; (*econ.*) varying according to differing conditions; (*mech.*) pertaining to, showing, causing, or marked by, a difference of pressure, motion, etc., or other physical attributes; **d. calculus,** (*math.*) a method of calculation dealing with differentials and the determination of the relative rate of change in magnitude between the two interdependent variable quantities; **d. equation,** (*math.*) an equation involving differentials; **d. gear,** a combination of toothed gear wheels connecting two axles and allowing them to rotate at different speeds; **d. thermometer,** (*phys.*) a thermometer consisting of two bulbs joined by a bent tube containing liquid which registers differences in temperature between the two bulbs. [MedL. *differentialis*].

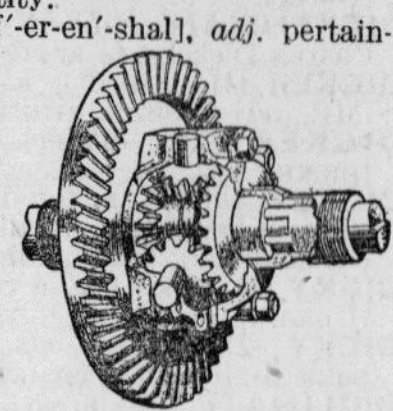

DIFFERENTIAL GEAR

DIFFERENTIALLY, [dif'-er-ensh'-al-i], *adv.* by means of a differentia or differential.

DIFFERENTIATE, [dif'-er-en'-shi-āt], *v.t. and i.* to discriminate between, to recognize, form, or establish a difference between, to distinguish; to make different; (*math.*) to find the differential of; to become different. [MedL. *differentiatum*, *p.pt.* of *differentiare*].

DIFFERENTIATION, [dif'-er-en'-shi-ā'-shun], *n.* the act of differentiating; the state of being differentiated.

DIFFERENTLY, [dif'-er-ent-li], *adv.* in a different way; variously.

DIFFERINGLY, [dif'-er-ing-li], *adv.* so as to differ.

DIFFICILE, [dif'-i-sēl], *adj.* difficult to deal with; hard to persuade. [Fr. *difficile* difficult].

DIFFICULT, [dif'-i-kult], *adj.* hard, not easy, causing trouble; involving strenuous mental or physical exertion; needing skill to perform; not easy to understand or appreciate; awkward, involving strain, worrying; hard to satisfy, troublesome to deal with, refractory, taking offence or bursting into fits of temper. [L. *difficilis*].

DIFFICULTLY, [dif'-ik-ult-li], *adv.* with difficulty.

DIFFICULTY, [dif'-ik-ul-ti], *n.* the quality of being difficult, trouble; that which is difficult, or which makes anything difficult, an obstacle; (*pl.*) financial trouble. [L. *difficultas*].

DIFFIDENCE, [dif'-id-ents], *n.* the state or quality of being diffident. [L. *diffidentia*].

DIFFIDENT, [dif'-id-ent], *adj.* shy, modest, retiring, bashful; wanting self-confidence; self-effacing. [L. *diffidens*].

DIFFIDENTLY, [dif'-id-ent-li], *adv.* in diffident fashion.

DIFFIDENTNESS, [dif'-id-ent-nes], *n.* the quality of being diffident.

DIFFLUENCE, [di-flōō'-ens], *n.* condition of being diffluent, the degree of fluidity.

DIFFLUENT, [di-flōō'-ent], *adj.* flowing away in all directions; fluid; deliquescent. [L. *diffluens*].

DIFFRACT, [di-frakt'], *v.t.* to break into pieces; (*opt.*) to break up rays of light into the coloured bands of the spectrum by passing close to the edge of, or through a slit in, an opaque substance; to break up or deflect sound-waves. [L. *diffractum*, *p.pt.* of *diffringere*].

DIFFRACTION, [di-frak'-shun], *n.* the act of diffracting.

DIFFRACTIVE, [di-frak'-tiv], *adj.* causing diffraction.

DIFFUSE (1), [di-fews'], *adj.* not concise, unnecessarily wordy or verbose, prolix; spread out, widely dispersed; (*path.*) attacking a large area of the body.

DIFFUSE (2), [di-fewz'], *v.t. and i.* to spread over a large area, to shed, to disperse widely; to send out, radiate; (*phys.*) to mingle by diffusion. [L. *diffusum*, *p.pt.* of *diffundere* pour forth].

DIFFUSEDLY, [di-fewzd'-li], *adv.* in a diffused fashion.

DIFFUSEDNESS, [di-fewzd'-nes], *n.* the condition of being diffused.
DIFFUSELY, [di-fews'-li], *adv.* in diffuse fashion.
DIFFUSENESS, [di-fews'-nes], *n.* the condition or quality of being diffuse.
DIFFUSER, [di-fewz'-er], *n.* one who, or that which, diffuses.
DIFFUSIBILITY, [di-fewz'-i-bil'-i-ti], *n.* diffusibleness.
DIFFUSIBLE, [di-fewz'-ibl], *adj.* able to be diffused.
DIFFUSIBLENESS, [di-fewz'-ibl-nes], *n.* the quality of being diffusible.
DIFFUSION, [di-few'-zhun], *n.* the act or process of diffusing; the state of being diffused; diffusiveness; (*phys.*) the gradual unaided mingling of gases, liquids, or solids when brought into contact with each other. [L. *diffusio*].
DIFFUSION-TUBE, [di-few'-zhun-tewb'], *n.* an instrument for finding the rate of diffusion for different gases.
DIFFUSIVE, [di-fews'-iv], *adj.* tending to diffuse or be diffused; diffuse.
DIFFUSIVELY, [di-fews'-iv-li], *adv.* in a diffusive fashion.
DIFFUSIVENESS, [di-fews'-iv-nes], *n.* the quality of being diffusive.
DIG (1), [dig], *n.* (*coll.*) a nudge, a poke, a light smart blow; (*fig.*) a sarcastic remark directed against anything or anyone; (*pl.*) (*slang*) lodgings.
DIG (2), (**dug**), [dig], *v.t.* and *i.* to break and turn up the earth with a spade or similar sharp-bladed instrument; to break up the ground with paws, claws; etc.; to hollow out or construct in the earth; (*coll.*) to poke, nudge sharply, prod; (*fig.*) to unearth or discover by careful and diligent research or investigation; (*slang*) to lodge; **to d. in**, to mix with and cover over with soil by digging; **to d. oneself in**, to establish oneself firmly in slow but sure fashion; **to d. out**, to unearth; (*coll.*) to find, to discover. [OFr. *diguer* to dike].
DIGAMIST, [dī'-gam-ist], *n.* one who lawfully marries a second time.
DIGAMMA, [dī-gam'-a], *n.* a double gamma (F) pronounced like *f*. [Gk. *digamma*].
DIGAMY, [dī'-ga-mi], *n.* second marriage. [Gk. *digamia*].
DIGASTRIC (1), [dī-gas'-trik], *n.* (*anat.*) the muscle working the lower jaw.
DIGASTRIC (2), [dī-gas'-trik], *adj.* (*anat.*) having two belly-like protuberances separated by a thin portion; (*anat.*) pertaining to the digastric muscle, which is of this shape. [DI (2) and Gk. *gaster* belly].
DIGEST (1), [dī'-jest], *n.* a systematic summary, a condensed compilation, an abstract; the code of Roman laws drawn up by order of the Emperor Justinian. [L. *digesta*, *neut.*(*pl.*) of *digestum*, *p.pt* of *digerere* to sort].
DIGEST (2), [di-jest', dī-jest'], *v.t.* and *i.* to convert food in the stomach and intestines into a liquid form which can be assimilated into the system; (*fig.*) to study and master the details of, to absorb into the mind as knowledge; to stomach, to endure; (*chem.*) to dissolve by boiling or heating with a solvent; to undergo the process of digestion; to dissolve gradually in a slow heat. [L. *digestum*, *p.pt.* of *digerere* to sort, to digest].
DIGESTEDLY, [dī-jest'-id-li], *adv.* in a methodical and regular manner.
DIGESTER, [dī-jest'-er], *n.* one who, or that which, digests; a strong metal vessel in which bony substances are digested; an apparatus in which carcases of animals are boiled down.
DIGESTIBILITY, [di-jest'-ib-il'-i-ti], *n.* digestibleness.
DIGESTIBLE, [dī-jest'-ibl], *adj.* able to be digested.
DIGESTIBLENESS, [dī-jest'-ibl-nes], *n.* the quality of being digestible.
DIGESTIBLY, [dī-jest'-ib-li], *adv.* in a form capable of digestion.
DIGESTION, [dī-jes'-chun], *n.* the process of digesting, or of being digested; ability to digest food thoroughly and completely. [L. *digestio*].
DIGESTIVE (1), [di-jest'-iv], *n.* a preparation which encourages or helps digestion; (*surg.*) an application which causes a wound or ulcer to generate, and so become rid of, pus.
DIGESTIVE (2), [di-jest'-iv], *adj.* pertaining to digestion; encouraging or helping digestion; easily digested. [L. *digestivus*].
DIGESTIVELY, [di-jest'-iv-li], *adv.* so as to digest.
DIGGABLE, [dig'-abl], *adj.* capable of being dug.
DIGGER, [dig'-er], *n.* one who, or that which, digs; a person who digs for gold; a burrowing wasp; (*pl.*) a tribe of North American Indians existing on roots and herbs; (*slang*) an Australian.
DIGGING, [dig'-ing], *n.* the act of one who digs; (*pl.*) a gold-field and mine where gold is dug; (*pl.*) (*coll.*) lodgings.
DIGHT†, [dīt], *adj.* arrayed, dressed, decked. [OE. *gediht*].
DIGIT, [dij'-it], *n.* a finger or toe; a finger's breadth, three-fourths of an inch; any integer less than ten, from 0 to 9; (*astron.*) the twelfth part of the diameter of the sun or moon. [L. *digitus* finger, inch].
DIGITAL (1), [dij'-it-al], *n.* a key of a musical instrument, such as a pianoforte, struck with the finger; (*coll.*) a finger.
DIGITAL (2), [dij'-it-al], *adj.* pertaining to the fingers, resembling a digit. [L. *digitalis*].
DIGITALIN, [dij'-it-ā'-lin], *n.* a poisonous vegetable alkaloid obtained from the leaves of the foxglove, used medicinally.
DIGITALIS, [dij'-it-ā'-lis], *n.* (*bot.*) a genus of plants of the order *Scrophulariaceae*, including the foxglove; a poisonous drug prepared from this used medicinally in cases of heart disease. [L. *digitalis*].
DIGITATE, [dij'-it-āt], *adj.* (*bot.*) branching into distinct leaflets or lobes like fingers; (*zool.*) having separate fingers or toes. [L. *digitatus*].
DIGITATED, [dij'-it-āt-id], *adj.* digitate.
DIGITATELY, [dij'-it-āt'-li], *adv.* in digitate fashion.
DIGITATION, [dij-it-ā'-shun], *n.* the state of being digitate; (*zool.*, *bot.*) one of a series of finger-like processes.
DIGITIFORM, [dij'-it-i-fawm'], *adj.* finger-shaped.
DIGITIGRADE (1), [dij'-it-i-grād'], *n.* (*zool.*) a digitigrade animal.
DIGITIGRADE (2), [dij'-it-i-grād'], *adj.* (*zool.*) walking on its toes.
DIGITORIUM, [dij'-it-aw'-ri-um], *n.* a small portable dumb keyboard with five keys, used to train the fingers for playing the pianoforte.
DIGITOXIN, [dij'-i-tok'-sin], *n.* a poisonous substance obtained from the foxglove. [DIGIT(ALIS) and TOXIN].
DIGLOT, [dī'-glot], *adj.* speaking two languages. [Gk. *diglottos*].
DIGLYPH, [dī'-glif], *n.* (*arch.*) a projecting face having two grooves in it. [Gk. *digluphos* doubly indented].
DIGNIFICATION, [dig'-ni-fik-ā'-shun], *n.* the act of dignifying. [MedL. *dignificatio*].
DIGNIFIED, [dig'-ni-fīd], *adj.* possessing and expressing dignity, stately, nobly austere, majestic, commanding respect.
DIGNIFY, [dig'-ni-fī], *v.t.* to invest with honour, to confer distinction on; to render exalted; to give dignity to, to represent as impressive. [LL. *dignificare*].
DIGNITARY, [dig'-nit-er-i], *n.* a person with a high rank or official position.
DIGNITY, [dig'-ni-ti], *n.* a sense of one's superior position; ability to command respect; unaffected stateliness of manner, natural air of distinction or nobility; a high office, rank, title, position or honour; high estimation or reputation in which a thing is held; majesty or deference naturally associated with an institution, a dignitary; (*astrol.*) increased influence of a planet on account of its particular position in the zodiac, or its position with respect to other planets. [L. *dignitas*].
DIGONOUS, [dig'-on-us], *adj.* (*bot.*) having two angles. [DI (2) and Gk. *gonos* angled].
DIGRAM, [dī'-gram], *n.* a digraph. [DI (2) and Gk. *gramma* writing].
DIGRAPH, [dī'-graf], *n.* two letters representing only a single sound. [DI (2) and GRAPH].
DIGRAPHIC, [dī-graf'-ik], *adj.* relating to a digraph.
DIGRESS, [dī-gres'], *v.i.* to turn aside, to wander from one's course; (*fig.*) to stray or depart temporarily from the main topic, to start to talk or write about something which, while not strictly relevant to the main topic, is suggested by it. [L. *digressum*, *p.pt.* of *digredi* to deviate].
DIGRESSION, [dī-gresh'-un], *n.* the act of digressing; that which digresses. [L. *digressio*].
DIGRESSIONAL, [dī-gresh'-un-al], *adj.* digressive.
DIGRESSIVE, [dī-gres'-iv], *adj.* that forms a digression; habitually digressing. [L. *digressivus*].
DIGRESSIVELY, [dī-gres'-iv-li], *adv.* by way of digression.
DIGYNIA, [dī-jin'-i-a], *n.*(*pl.*) (*bot.*) digynous plants. [DI (2) and Gk. *gune* female].
DIGYNIAN, [dī-jin'-i-an], *adj.* (*bot.*) digynous.

DIGYNOUS, [dij'-in-us], *adj.* (*bot.*) with two pistils.

DIHEDRAL, [dī-hē'-dral], *adj.* having two plane faces or sides; **d. angle**, the angle between two planes; (*aeron.*) the angle at which the wings of an aeroplane are inclined to each other from the horizontal to minimize rolling. [DI and Gk. *hedra* base].

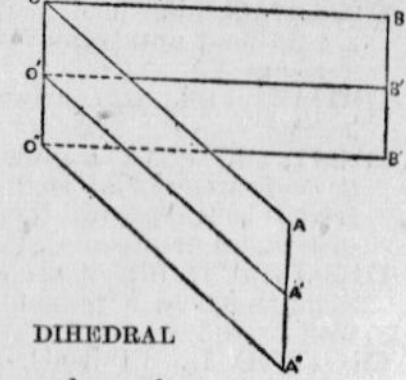

DIHEDRAL

DIHEDRON, [dī-hē'-dron], *n.* a figure with two sides or surfaces; (*geom.*) that part of two planes placed one on the other enclosed by a regular polygon.

DIHEXAGONAL, [dī'-heks-ag'-on-al], *adj.* having twelve angles of which either alternate six are not equal to the other, though equal among themselves. [DI and HEXAGONAL].

DIHEXAHEDRAL†, [dī'-heks-a-hē'-dral], *adj.* (*min.*) in the shape of a hexahedral prism with trihedral summits. [DI and HEXAHEDRAL].

DIJUDICATE, [dī-jew'-di-kāt], *v.t.* to judge or determine between two; to adjudicate. [L. *dijudicare*].

DIJUDICATION, [dī'-jew-di-kā'-shun], *n.* the act of judging or of passing judgment; a judge's decision, a legal judgment. [L. *dijudicatio*].

DIKA, [dē-kah], *n.* the West African mango, *Mangifera gabonensis*. [Native].

DIKAMALI, [dik'-a-mah'-li], *n.* the gum of *Gardenia lucida*, used for dressing wounds. [Marathi *dikamali*].

DIK-DIK, [dik'-dik'], *n.* a small antelope, the duikerbok, *Cephalophus grimmi*. [Unkn.].

DIKE (1), DYKE, [dīk], *n.* a ditch, a channel along which water flows; a high bank of earth, stones, clay, etc., constructed to safeguard low-lying country from the sea, rivers or streams; (*fig.*) a barrier; (*geol.*) a mass of igneous rock formed while molten in the fissures of stratified rocks. [OScand. *dikr*].

DIKE (2), [dīk], *v.t. and i.* to protect or provide with dikes; to make a dike.

DIK-DIK

DIKING, [dīk-ing], *n.* the act of ditching or protecting by a dike.

DILACERATE, [dī-las'-er-āt], *v.t.* to tear up in pieces. [L. *dilacerare*].

DILACERATION, [dī-las'-er-ā'-shun], *n.* the act of dilacerating; (*dental surg.*) a shifting of a growing tooth on its base, and its subsequent misplaced development. [L. *dilaceratio*].

DILANIATE†, [di-lā'-ni-āt], *v.t.* to rend in pieces, to tear to bits. [L. *dilaniare*].

DILAPIDATE, [di-lap'-i-dāt], *v.t. and i.* to allow to fall into a state of ruin or disrepair; (*fig.*) to waste, to squander; to decay through neglect. [L. *dilapidare* to demolish].

DILAPIDATED, [di-lap'-id-ā-tid], *adj.* in a state of ruin or decay, tumble-down; shabby, in great need of repair.

DILAPIDATION, [di-lap'-id-ā'-shun], *n.* the state of being dilapidated; the process of becoming or causing to be dilapidated; (*leg.*) the act of permitting church property to become dilapidated while in the possession of an incumbent; the crumbling or wearing away of masses of rock by natural forces. [L. *dilapidatio*].

DILAPIDATOR, [di-lap'-id-āt'-er], *n.* one who causes or allows a building to become dilapidated.

DILATABILITY, [dī-lā'-tab-il'-i-ti], *n.* the quality of being dilatable.

DILATABLE, [dī-lā'-tabl], *adj.* able to be dilated.

DILATANCY, [dī-lā'-tan-si], *n.* the power to dilate.

DILATATION, [dī-lat-ā'-shun], *n.* the state of being dilated, the act of dilating. [L. *dilatatio*].

DILATE, [dī-lāt'], *v.t. and i.* to become larger, to expand, to grow wider and bigger; (*fig.*) to speak or expound at great length; to make larger. [L. *dilatare*].

DILATION, [dī-lā'-shun], *n.* dilatation.

DILATOR, DILATER, [dī-lā'-ter], *n.* one who, or that which, dilates.

DILATORILY, [dil'-at-er-i-li], *adv.* in dilatory fashion.

DILATORINESS, [dil'-at-er-i-nes], *n.* the quality of being dilatory.

DILATORY, [dil'-at-er-i], *adj.* slow, tardy, causing delay, dallying. [L. *dilatorius*].

DILEMMA, [dil-em'-a, dī-lem'-a], *n.* a perplexing situation in which all the possible courses of action are equally unfavourable, a quandary; (*log.*) an argument offering only a choice of two equally difficult alternatives. [Gk. *dilemma* double proposition].

DILEMMATIC, [dil'-em-at'-ik], *adj.* belonging to dilemmas.

DILETTANTE, (*pl.* **dilettanti**), [dil'-it-ant'-i], *n.* one who trifles in the fine arts in a superficial or casual way; an amateur dabbler in anything. [It. *dilettante* from L. *delectare* to delight].

DILETTANTISH, [dil'-it-ant'-ish], *adj.* that becomes a dilettante, amateurish.

DILETTANTISM, [dil-it-ant'-izm], *n.* the casual and rather superficial cultivation of the fine arts, the method of a dilettante.

DILIGENCE (1), [dil'-ij-ents], *n.* careful steady application, constant industry, zealous and assiduous labour; (*leg.*) reasonable and careful attention demanded from persons under certain conditions. [L. *diligentia* carefulness].

DILIGENCE (2), [dil'-ij-ents], *n.* a heavy, lumbering, four-wheeled, horse-drawn stage-coach, with a hood, a deck and a dickey.

DILIGENT, [dil'-ij-ent], *adj.* exhibiting diligence, careful and industrious, assiduous; hard-working and steady, laboriously zealous. [L. *diligens*].

DILIGENTLY, [dil'-ij-ent-li], *adv.* in a diligent way.

DILL, [dil], *n.* (*bot.*) an umbelliferous Mediterranean medicinal plant, *Anethum graveolens*; **d. water**, a medicinal preparation obtained from the fruits or the oil of the dill. [OE. *dile*].

DILL-OIL, [dil'-oil'], *n.* a yellow oil obtained from the seeds of dill, used as a carminative.

DILLY (1), [dil'-i], *n.* a heavy cart, truck or wagon [DILIGENCE (2)].

DILLY (2), [dil'-i], *n.* a native Australian plaited rush or bark bag. [Native].

DILLY-DALLY, [dil'-i-dal'-i], *v.i.* to waste time in indecision, to delay continually in making up one's mind. [DALLY].

DILOGY, [dil'-o-ji], *n.* a phrase with a double meaning. [Gk. *dilogia* twice speaking].

DILUENT (1), [dil'-yōō-ent], *n.* that which dilutes; (*med.*) a remedy which dilutes the blood.

DILUENT (2), [dil'-yōō-ent], *adj.* used for, or causing, dilution. [L. *diluens* washing away].

DILUTE (1), [dī'-lewt, dī-lewt'], *adj.* reduced in strength, weakened, watered down.

DILUTE (2), [dī-lewt'], *v.t.* to weaken, thin down, or reduce in strength, by adding more fluid to; (*fig.*) to lessen the force or effect of, to tone down. [L. *dilutum*, *p.pt.* of *diluere* to wash away].

DILUTEDLY, [dī-lew'-tid-li], *adv.* in a diluted manner.

DILUTER, [dī-lew'-ter], *n.* that which dilutes.

DILUTION, [dī-lew'-shun], *n.* the act of diluting; the condition of being diluted; that which is diluted.

DILUVIAL, [dī-lōōv'-i-al], *adj.* pertaining to a flood, *esp.* that recorded in the Old Testament; caused by a flood; (*geol.*) pertaining to the theory that certain geological phenomena are the result of floods. [LL. *diluvialis*].

DILUVIALIST, [dī-lōōv'-i-al-ist], *n.* one who believes that certain geological phenomena are the result of a world-wide flood.

DILUVIAN, [dī-lōōv'-ian], *adj.* pertaining to a flood, or the Great Flood.

DILUVIUM, [dī-lōōv'-i-um], *n.* (*geol.*) comparatively recent and superficial deposits of loam, sand, gravel, etc., produced by a flood or a sudden strong rush of water. [L. *diluvium* flood].

DIM (1), [dim], *adj.* faint, not bright or clear; indistinct, with the outlines not clearly defined, shadowy; dull; scarcely heard; not seeing clearly; (*fig.*) vague. [OE. *dimm*].

DIM (2), (**dimming, dimmed**), [dim], *v.t. and i.* to make or become dim.

DIME (1), [dīm], *n.* (*U.S.*) a silver coin of the value of ten cents. [Fr. *dîme* tenth part].

DIME (2), [dīm], *adj.* cheap, inferior, costing a dime.

DIMENSION, [di-men'-shun], *n.* measurement or extent in space of length, breadth or depth or a combination of these; (*pl.*) size, magnitude, proportions; scope; (*math.*) spatial measurement in any direction or form; factors of a term of an algebraic expression. [L. *dimensio* a measuring].

DIMENSIONAL, [di-men'-shun-al], *adj.* pertaining to the number of dimensions involved, relating to dimension.

DIMENSIONED, [di-men'-shund], *adj.* having dimensions.

DIMEROUS, [dim'-er-us], *adj.* (*bot., entom.*) having two parts. [Gk. *dimeros*].

DIMETALLIC, [dī'-met-al'-ik], *adj.* having two equivalents of a metal. [DI and METALLIC].

DIMETER, [dim'-it-er], *n.* (*pros.*) a verse made up of two measures. [Gk. *dimetros*].

DIMETRIC, [dī-met'-rik], *adj.* tetragonal; (applied to crystals) of three axes, the vertical axis being unequal to the two equal, lateral axes.

DIM-EYED, [dim'-īd'], *adj.* possessing indistinct vision.

DIMICATORY, [dim'-ik-āt'-er-i], *adj.* pertaining to fighting or fencing. [L. *dimicatio* fighting].

DIMIDIATE (1), [dī-mid'-i-āt], *adj.* divided into halves; (*bot.*) split into two unequal parts; (*zool.*) split into two halves of different function. [L. *dimidiatus*, *p.pt.* of *dimidiare* to halve].

DIMIDIATE (2), [dī-mid'-i-āt], *v.t.* to divide into two equal parts. [*Prec.*].

DIMIDIATION, [dī-mid-i-ā'-shun], *n.* the act of dimidiating; the state of being dimidiated; (*her.*) the combination of the right half of one coat-of-arms with the left half of another. [L. *dimidiatio*].

DIMINISH, [di-min'-ish], *v.t. and i.* to lessen, to reduce, to decrease; (*mus.*) to reduce an interval by a semitone. [Fr. *diminuer* to reduce].

DIMINISHABLE, [di-min'-ish-abl], *adj.* able to be diminished.

DIMINISHED, [di-min'-isht], *adj.* lessened, reduced, made smaller; (*mus.*) (of intervals) decreased by a semitone.

DIMINISHER, [di-min'-ish-er], *n.* one who, or that which, diminishes.

DIMINISHINGLY, [di-min'-ish-ing-li], *adv.* in a diminishing manner.

DIMINUENDO, [di-min'-yōō-end'-ō], *n.* (*mus.*) a progressive lessening of the loudness of sound, a sign > denoting this; a passage in which the tone becomes gradually softer. [It. *diminuendo*].

DIMINUTION, [dim-in-ew'-shun], *n.* the act of diminishing, the state of being diminished; (*mus.*) the repetition of a contrapuntal theme in notes whose time value is half or a quarter that of the original; (*her.*) the disfiguring of an escutcheon; a difference; (*leg.*) the omission of part of the record of a case sent up to a Court of Appeal; (*arch.*) the tapering of a column shaft. [L. *diminutio*].

DIMINUTIVAL, [dim-in'-ew-tīv'-al], *adj.* relating to a diminutive.

DIMINUTIVE (1), [dim-in'-yōō-tiv], *n.* (*gram.*) a word formed from another word by the addition of an affix denoting diminution.

DIMINUTIVE (2), [dim-in'-yōō-tiv], *adj.* small; (*gram.*) conveying the idea of, or indicating, diminution. [L. *diminutivus*].

DIMINUTIVELY, [dim-in'-yōō-tiv-li], *adv.* in a diminutive fashion.

DIMINUTIVENESS, [dim-in'-yōō-tiv-nes], *n.* the state of being diminutive.

DIMISSORY, [dim-is'-er-i], *adj.* (*eccles.*) sending away, or granting leave to depart, to another jurisdiction. [LL. *dimissorius*].

DIMITY, [dim'-it-i], *n.* a stout cotton cloth, ornamented with raised stripes or decorative patterns. [Gk. *dimitos* of a double thread].

DIMLY, [dim'-li], *adv.* in a dim fashion.

DIMMER, [dim'-er], *n.* (*motoring*) a device to dim headlamps.

DIMMISH, [dim'-ish], *adj.* rather dim.

DIMNESS, [dim'-nes], *n.* the state of being dim.

DIMORPHIC, [dī-maw'-fik], *adj.* dimorphous.

DIMORPHISM, [dī-maw'-fizm], *n.* the property of crystallizing in two distinct forms; (*biol.*) the existence of two different forms in the same plant, or in different plants or animals of the same species. [DI and Gk. *morphe* shape].

DIMORPHOUS, [dī-maw'-fus], *adj.* exhibiting dimorphism.

DIMPLE (1), [dimpl], *n.* a small, natural rounded hollow in the cheek or other fleshy part of the body; a shallow hollow in the ground. [OE. *dympel* hollow].

DIMPLE (2), [dimpl], *v.t. and i.* to form into dimples; to cause dimples to appear.

DIMPLED, [dimpld], *adj.* having dimples.

DIMPLY, [dimp'-li], *adj.* full of dimples.

DIMYARIAN, [dī-mī-āer'-i-an], *n.* a bivalve mollusc, the shells of which are opened and closed by two muscles. [DI and Gk. *mus* muscle].

DIN (1), [din], *n.* a loud, continued noise, a persistent clamour or uproar. [OE. *dyne*].

DIN (2), **(dinning, dinned)**, [din], *v.t. and i.* to impress with noisy persistence; to create a din. [OE. *dynian*].

DINANDERIE, [din-ahnd'-er-ē], *n.* ornamental brass or copper ware. [*Dinant*, a Belgian town where formerly made].

DINAR, [dē-nah(r)'], *n.* an Eastern gold coin; a Yugo-Slavian coin worth about twopence. [Arab. and Serb. *dinar* from L. *denarius*].

DINARCHY†, [dī'-nahk-i], *n.* government by two persons. [DI and Gk. *arche* rule].

DINE, [dīn], *v.t. and i.* to have dinner; to give or provide dinner. [Fr. *dîner*].

DINER, [dī'-ner], *n.* one who dines; a railway restaurant car.

DINER-OUT, [dī'-ner-owt'], *n.* one who is fond of dining away from home.

DING, [ding], *v.t. and i.* (*archaic*) to dash with violence, to beat, to ring, to hurl. [OScand. *dengja* to hammer].

DING-DONG (1), [ding'-dong'], *n.* a loud continuous ringing noise, the sound produced by the striking of two differently toned bells. [Imitative].

DING-DONG (2), [ding'-dong'], *adj.* closely and fiercely contested.

DINGHY, DINGEY, [ding'-gi], *n.* a small ship's boat, a small pleasure skiff or rowing boat; a collapsible rubber boat used by airmen in case of forced landings on water. [Hind. *dengi* rowing boat].

DINGHY

DINGINESS, [din'-ji-nes], *n.* the state or quality of being dingy.

DINGLE, [ding'-gl], *n.* a wooded dell. [ME. *dingel*].

DINGLE-DANGLE, [ding'-gl-dang'-gl], *adj. and adv.* hanging loosely, dangling.

DINGO, [ding'-gō], *n.* the native wild dog of Australia, *Canis dingo*. [Native].

DINGO

DINGY, [din'-ji], *adj.* dark, dull, lacking lustre; disreputable; dirty, drab, shabby. [Unkn.].

DINING-CAR, [dī'-ning-kah(r)'], *n.* a railway carriage in which meals are provided during a journey.

DINING-HALL, [dī'-ning-hawl'], *n.* a hall or large room used for dining.

DINING-ROOM, [dī'-ning-rōōm'], *n.* a room in which meals are taken.

DINING-TABLE, [dī'-ning-tābl'], *n.* a table on which meals are taken.

DINKUM, [ding'-kum], *adj.* (*Austral. slang*) genuine, straightforward. [Unkn.].

DINKY, [dingk'-i], *adj.* (*coll.*) neat, attractive, dainty. [Scots *dink* neat].

DINNER, [din'-er], *n.* the principal meal of the day; a formal official banquet to mark some occasion; **d. jacket**, a black dress-coat without tails; **d. wagon**, a set of shelves on wheels on which articles used at dinner are placed. [Fr. *diner*].

DINNERLESS, [din'-er-les], *adj.* without dinner.

DINNER-TABLE, [din'-er-tābl'], *n.* a dining-table.

DINNER-TIME, [din'-er-tīm'], *n.* the usual time for dining.

DINOCERAS, [dīn-os'-er-as], *n.* (*geol.*) a great fossil horned mammal with two tusks in the upper jaw. [Gk. *deinos* fearsome and *keras* horn].

DINORNIS, [dī-naw'-nis], *n.* (*zool.*) an extinct New Zealand genus of gigantic birds, including the moa. [Gk. *deinos* fearsome and Gk. *ornis* bird].

DINOSAURIA, [dī'-no-saw'-ri-a], *n.(pl.)* (*geol.*) a group of large, prehistoric extinct reptiles. [Gk. *deinos* fearsome and *sauros* lizard].

DINOTHERE, [dī'-no-thēer], *n.* one of a genus of extinct gigantic mammals, the forerunner of the elephant. [Gk. *deinos* fearsome and *ther* wild beast].

DINT (1), [dint], *n.* a blow, a powerful stroke; effort, force, violence; a large crease or hollow in something hard, made by a violent blow; **by d. of**, as a result of, after. [OE. *dynt*].

DINT (2), [dint], *v.t.* to make a dint or dints in. [OE. *dyntan*].

DIOCESAN (1), [dī-os'-i-zan], *n.* a bishop; one of the members of a diocese.

DIOCESAN (2), [dī-os'-i-zan], *adj.* pertaining to a diocese.

DIOCESE, [dī'-os-is], *n.* the ecclesiastical district over which a bishop holds authority. [Gk. *dioikesis* control].

DIODE, [dī'-ōd], *n.* a thermionic valve having only two electrodes. [DI and Gk. *odos* way].

DIODON, [dī'-od-on'], *n.* a family of fishes to which the globe-fish and porcupine-fish belong, having two continuous bones, one in each jaw, for teeth. [DI and Gk. *odous odontos* tooth].

DIOECIA, [dī-ē'-shi-a], *n.(pl.)* (*bot.*) plants having flowers with stamens on one individual and flowers with pistils on another. [DI and Gk. *oikos* house].

DIOECIOUS, [dī-ē'-shi-us], *adj.* (*bot., zool.*) having the male generative organs in one individual and the female in another.

DIONAEA, [dī-on-ē'-a], *n.(pl.)* (*bot.*) a genus of plants comprising the Venus's fly-traps. [*Dione*, the mother of Venus].

DIOPHANTINE, [dī-o-fant'-in], *adj.* pertaining to the analysis of Diophantus, the Greek mathematician. [Gk. *Diophantos*].

DIOPSIDE, [dī-op'-sīd], *n.* (*min.*) a calcium magnesium silicate, a greyish-green foliated variety of augite. [DI and Gk. *opsis* appearance].

DIOPSIS, [dī-op'-sis], *n.* (*zool.*) an insect having stalk-like processes to support its eyes. [*Prec.*].

DIOPTASE, [dī-op'-tās], *n.* a silicate of copper found in emerald-green crystals. [Gk. *dioptos* one who looks through].

DIOPTER, [dī-op'-ter], *n.* (*opt.*) a dioptric; the index arm of a graduated circle. [Gk. *dioptra*].

DIOPTRIC (1), [dī-op'-trik], *n.* the unit of measurement used in determining the refractive power of a lens or curved mirror; (*pl.*) that branch of optics concerned with the refraction of light by lenses.

DIOPTRIC (2), [dī-op'-trik], *adj.* pertaining to the refraction of light; aiding vision by refracting light through lenses. [Gk. *dioptrikos*].

DIOPTRICAL, [dī-op'-trik-al], *adj.* dioptric.

DIORAMA, [dī'-o-rah'-ma], *n.* a pictorial representation of a natural scene, viewed through an aperture, cleverly distanced and illuminated by a strong hidden and varied lighting; the building in which such an exhibition takes place. [DI and Gk. *horama* view].

DIORAMIC, [dī'-o-ram'-ik], *adj.* belonging to a diorama.

DIORISM†, [dī'-o-rism], *n.* definition. [Gk. *diorismos* distinction].

DIORISTIC†, [dī-o-rist'-ik], *adj.* defining.

DIORITE, [dī'-o-rīt], *n.* (*min.*) a crystalline igneous rock consisting of hornblende and calcium sodium felspar. [DI and Gk. *horizo* I mark a boundary].

DIORITIC, [dī-o-rit'-ik], *adj.* relating to diorite.

DIORTHOSIS, [dī'-aw-thō'-sis], *n.* the act of setting right; (*surg.*) the setting of crooked or broken limbs; revision and correction of literary work. [Gk. *diorthosis*].

DIORTHOTIC, [dī'-aw-tho'-tik], *adj.* pertaining to literary diorthosis.

DIOSMOSIS, [dī'-os-mō'-sis], *n.* the passage of liquid through a membrane. [Gk. *dia* through and OSMOSIS].

DIOTA, [dī-ō'-ta], *n.* a full-bodied receptacle for liquids, having a narrow neck and two handles. [Gk. *diote* two-eared].

DIOXIDE, [dī-oks'-īd], *n.* (*chem.*) a compound having two equivalents of oxygen to one of metal. [DI (2) and OXIDE].

DIP (1), [dip], *n.* the act of dipping, a short rapid immersion; a brief bathe; the liquid in which anything is plunged for washing or dyeing; a tub of bran, sawdust, etc., in which prizes are hidden, to be obtained by dipping the hand into the tub; a candle, a wick soaked in hot tallow and used as a candle; a slope or depression; (*magn.*) inclination of a magnetic needle from a horizontal line; (*surveying*) apparent sloping of the horizon seen by an observer standing above sea-level; (*geol.*) downward slope of strata.

DIP (2), **(dipping, dipped)**, [dip], *v.t.* to immerse quickly in a liquid and take out again immediately; to dye by plunging in a liquid dye for a brief time; to wash (sheep) in an antiseptic solution; to soak (a wick) in hot tallow to make a candle; to move quickly down and up again; (*motoring*) to lower (headlights of a car); *v.i.* to submerge in liquid and quickly reappear; to plunge into a receptacle or liquid in order to remove something from it; to slope gently down; to sink down and disappear; (*geol.*) (of strata) to incline so as to form an angle with the horizontal; **to d. into**, to make a casual, incomplete examination of; to read here and there in (a book). [OE. *dyppan*].

DIPCHICK, [dip'-chik], *n.* the dabchick.

DIPETALOUS, [dī-pet'-al-us], *adj.* (*bot.*) with two petals. [DI and PETAL].

DIPHENYL-ARSINE, [dī-fen'-il-ah'-sēn] *n.* a deadly poison gas, pepper gas.

DIPHTHERIA, [dif-thēer'-i-a], *n.* a serious infectious disease attacking the throat and air-passages. [Gk. *diphthera* leather].

DIPHTHERIAL, [dif-thēer'-i-al], *adj.* relating to diphtheria.

DIPHTHERIC, [dif-ther'-ik], *adj.* diphtheritic.

DIPHTHERITIC, [dif'-ther-it'-ik], *adj.* pertaining to, or caused by, diphtheria.

DIPHTHERITIS, [dif'-ther-īt'-is], *n.* diphtheria. [Gk. *diphthera* leather and *itis* denoting inflammation].

DIPHTHEROID, [dif'-ther-oid], *adj.* pertaining to, resembling diphtheria. [DIPHTHERIA and Gk. *oeides* like].

DIPHTHONG, [dif'-thong], *n.* (*phon.*) a sound of two vowels together dominated by a single accent or stress. [Gk. *diphthongos*].

DIPHTHONGAL, [dif-thong'-gal], *adj.* pertaining to a diphthong.

DIPHTHONGALLY, [dif-thong'-al-i], *adv.* in a diphthongal way.

DIPHTHONGIZATION, [dif'-thong-ī-zā'-shun], *n.* the process of diphthongizing.

DIPHTHONGIZE, [dif'-thong-īz], *v.t. and i.* to form into a diphthong.

DIPHYCERCAL, [dif'-is-urk'-al], *adj.* having the tail split into two equal divisions by the caudal spine. [Gk. *diphues* double and *kerkos* a tail].

DIPHYLLOUS, [dī-fil'-us], *adj.* (*bot.*) two-leaved. [DI and Gk. *phullon* a leaf].

DIPHYODONT, [dif'-i-o-dont], *n.* (*zool.*) an animal that has two successive and distinct sets of teeth. [Gk. *diphues* double and *odous odontos* tooth].

DIPLEGIA, [dī-plē'-ji-a], *n.* (*med.*) paralysis of corresponding parts on each side of the body. [DI and Gk. *plege* stroke].

DIPLEIDOSCOPE, [dip-lī'-do-skōp], *n.* an instrument for determining the transit of the sun or other heavenly body over the meridian. [Gk. *diploos* double, *eidos* form and SCOPE].

DIPLOBLASTIC, [dip-lō-blast'-ik], *adj.* (*biol.*) having only two germinal layers. [Gk. *diploos* double and *blastos* bud].

DIPLOCARDIAC, [dip'-lō-kah'-di-ak], *adj.* (*biol.*) having the heart divided into two separate halves. [Gk. *diploos* double and CARDIAC].

DIPLODOCUS, [dip'-lō-dok'-us], *n.* (*geol.*) a huge extinct dinosaur. [Gk. *diploos* double and *dokos* bar].

DIPLOE, [dip'-lō-i], *n.* (*anat.*) the tissue between the inner and outer layers of the bones of the skull. [Gk. *diploe* doubling].

DIPLOGEN, [dip'-lo-jen], *n.* (*chem.*) a form of hydrogen about twice as heavy as ordinary hydrogen. [Gk. *diploos* double and *genes* producing].

DIPLOGENIC, [dip-lō-jen'-ik], *adj.* producing two substances; having the nature of two bodies. [*Prec.*].

DIPLOMA, [dip-lō'-ma], *n.* an official state document or charter; a certificate or document awarded by a recognized authority as an honour, distinction, licence, or privilege, *esp.* one granted by a university or other authority attesting the recipient's proficiency in some subject of study. [Gk. *diploma*].

DIPLOMACY, [dip-lō'-ma-si], *n.* the art of conducting business between nation and nation; the forms and formalities of such business and the skill with which it is carried out; dexterity and tact in social or business relationships. [Fr. *diplomatie*].

DIPLOMAT, [dip'-lom-at'], *n.* a person paid for his services in international diplomacy, a person of tact and social dexterity. [Fr. *diplomate*].

DIPLOMATE (1), [dip'-lom-āt], *n.* a person who holds a diploma.

DIPLOMATE (2), [dip'-lom-āt], *v.t.* to confer a diploma upon.

DIPLOMATIC, [dip'-lom-at'-ik], *adj.* pertaining to (international) diplomacy; skilled and adroit in managing people; tactful; pertaining to the study or text of original documents; (of printed texts) representing an exact transliteration of the original; **d. corps**, the body of diplomatic representatives accredited to a government. [Fr. *diplomatique*].

DIPLOMATICALLY, [dip'-lom-at'-ik-al-i], *adv.* in a diplomatic manner.

DIPLOMATICS, [dip'-lom-at'-iks], *n.* the science of deciphering and studying of old documents.

DIPLOMATIST, [dip-lō'-mat-ist], *n.* a diplomat.

DIPLOPIA, [dīp-lō'-pi-a], *n.* (*med.*) a disease of the eye in which objects are seen double. [Gk. *diploos* double and *opia* from *ops* eye].

DIPLOSTEMONOUS, [dip'-lo-stē'-mon-us], *adj.* (*bot.*) having twice as many stamens as petals. [Gk. *diploos* double and *stemon* a warp].

DIPNOAN, [dip'-nō-an], *adj.* (of a fish) having both gills and lungs. [Gk. *dipnoos* having two breathing holes].

DIPNOI, [dip'-nō-ī], *n.*(*pl.*) (*zool.*) a group of dipnoan fishes, able to live in or out of water.

DIPODY, [dip'-od-i], *n.* (*pros.*) a measure containing two feet. [Gk. *dipodia*].

DIPOLAR, [dī-pōl'-er], *adj.* having two magnetic poles.

DIPOLARIZE, [dī-pōl'-er-īz], *v.t.* to magnetize.

DIPPER, [dip'-er], *n.* one who, or that which, dips; a water-ouzel or other diving bird; a Baptist, *esp.* a member of an American group of Baptists; (*motoring*) a device which lowers and raises the headlights of a motor-car.

DIPPING-NEEDLE, [dip'-ing-nēdl'], *n.* (*magn.*) an instrument which shows the angle of dip of a magnetic needle.

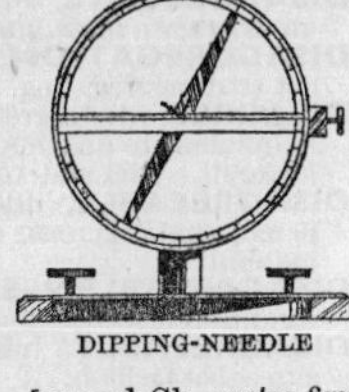
DIPPING-NEEDLE

DIPPY, [dip'-i], *n.* (*slang*) mad, crazy.

DIPRISMATIC†, [dī'-priz-mat'-ik], *adj.* (*min.*) doubly prismatic; having cleavages parallel to the sides of a four-sided vertical and horizontal prism.

DIPROTODON, [dī-prōt'-od-on], *n.* a genus of gigantic extinct marsupials characterized by two incisors in the bottom jaw. [DI and Gk. *protos* first and *odous odontos* tooth].

DIPSAS, [dip'-sas], *n.* a serpent whose bite was supposed to cause an unquenchable thirst; a genus of long, slender, tropical, non-venomous tree snakes; a genus of freshwater bivalves of the mussel family. [Gk. *dipsas*].

DIP-SECTOR, [dip'-sek'-tor], *n.* a reflector for measuring the angle of dip of the horizon.

DIPSOMANIA, [dip'-sō-mā'-ni-a], *n.* (*med.*) a nervous disease characterized by an uncontrollable desire for alcohol. [Gk. *dipsa* thirst and MANIA].

DIPSOMANIAC, [dip'-sō-mā'-ni-ak'], *n.* one suffering from dipsomania; a confirmed drunkard.

DIPSOSIS, [dip-sō'-sis], *n.* (*med.*) excessive unnatural thirst. [Gk. *dipsa* thirst and *osis* denoting condition].

DIPSTICK, [dip'-stik], *n.* (*motoring*) a measuring rod inserted in the sump of a car engine to ascertain the amount of oil present.

DIPTERA, [dip'-ter-a], *n.*(*pl.*) (*zool.*) the two-winged order of insects, including the house-fly. [Gk. *dipteros* two-winged].

DIPTERAL, [dip'-ter-al], *adj.* (*entom.*) dipterous; (*arch.*) having a double peristyle; **d. temple,** a temple flanked by two rows of columns.

DIPTERAN, [dip'-ter-an], *n.* one of the diptera.

DIPTEROUS, [dip'-ter-us], *adj.* (*bot.*) (of seeds) having two wings; (*entom.*) two-winged, belonging to the diptera.

DIPTERYGIANS, [dip'-ter-ij'-i-anz], *n.*(*pl.*) a genus of two-finned fishes. [DI and Gk. *pterugion* fin].

DIPTYCH, (*pl.* **diptycha**), [dip'-tich], *n.* a writing tablet, folded in two, of ivory, metal, or wood, covered on the inside with wax; a picture on two leaves opening like a screen and often beautifully carved. [Gk. *diptukha* a double tablet].

DIPUS, [dī'-pus], *n.* (*zool.*) a genus of rodents, the jerboas; a small Australian marsupial, *Chaeropus castanotis.* [Gk. *dipous* two-footed].

DIPUS

DIPYRE, [dī-pī'-er], *n.* (*min.*) aluminium calcium sodium silicate, which fuses with phosphorescence when heated. [Gk. *dipuros* double fired].

DIRADIATION, [dī'-rā'-di-ā'-shun], *n.* the emission of rays of light from a luminous body. [DI (3) and RADIATION].

DIRE, [dī-er'], *adj.* evil, dreadful, horrible. [L. *dirus*].

DIRECT (1), [di-rekt'], *adj.* straight; without interference; (*fig.*) immediate, unaffected, without intervening agent; straightforward, plain, frank, undisguised; complete; (*geneal.*) lineal, in uninterrupted succession from father to son; (*astron.*) onward, forward, advancing from east to west; (*mus.*) with both hands moving in the same direction along the keyboard; (*mus.*) not inverted; (*gram.*) in the actual words used by the speaker; **d. action,** strike or lock-out action in a labour dispute; **d. current,** (*elect.*) a current flowing continuously in one direction only; **d. hit,** the impact of a bomb dropped from the air on a building; **d. method,** a method of teaching foreign languages by continual conversation, reading, and use of the language, the native tongue being employed as little as possible; **d. tax,** tax levied upon a person's income or revenue. [L. *directus*].

DIRECT (2), [di-rekt'], *adv.* in an undeviating line, straight, in a direct manner.

DIRECT (3), [di-rekt'], *v.t. and i.* to conduct, control, manage, supervise, guide, to be in charge of, to superintend, to govern the actions or movements of; to give orders, to command; to turn, to cause to be focused upon; to draw to, to attract to; to address postal matter; to address to, to aim at, to intend for; to point out the right way or road to. [L. *directum*, *p.pt.* of *dirigere*].

DIRECTION, [di-rek'-shun], *n.* the act of directing, management, control, leadership, supervision, guidance; line or path along which a body moves; point to which, or from which, movement is made, way; a group of directors; (often *pl.*) instructions on how to proceed, information as to what to do; order, command; the address on a letter; **in the d. of,** towards. [L. *directio*].

DIRECTIONAL, [di-rek'-shun-al], *adj.* pertaining to direction; **d. aerial,** an aerial which will transmit or receive wireless waves better from one direction than from others.

DIRECTION-FINDER, [di-rek'-shun-fīnd'-er], *n.* (*wirel.*) an instrument for finding the direction from which wireless signals are coming.

DIRECTIVE, [di-rek'-tiv], *adj.* tending to direct, that directs.

DIRECTLY (1), [di-rekt'-li], *adv.* in a direct manner; immediately, at once; shortly, presently.

DIRECTLY (2), [di-rekt'-li], *conj.* as soon as.

DIRECTNESS, [di-rekt'-nes], *n.* the quality of being direct.

DIRECTOIRE, [di-rekt'-wah(r)], *adj.* in the style or fashion of the period of the Directory in France (1795-99). [Fr. *Directoire*].

DIRECTOR, [di-rekt'-er], *n.* one who directs, an instructor, supervisor; a person elected to assist in the management of the affairs of a commercial company; an instrument that directs the course of anything; (*hist.*) a member of the French Directory.

DIRECTORATE, [di-rekt'-er-at], *n.* a board of directors; directorship.

DIRECTORIAL, [dī'-rekt-aw'-ri-al], *adj.* relating to directors; containing directions.

DIRECTORSHIP, [di-rekt'-er-ship], *n.* the office of director.

DIRECTORY (1), [di-rekt'-er-i], *n.* that which directs or instructs; a book of directions; a book containing classified lists of the inhabitants of a district, of telephone numbers, or of trades or professions; a list of the streets in a place, with a system of cross-reference to enable anyone to find a particular street; the government or executive council of the French Republic, 1795-1799.

DIRECTORY (2), [di-rekt'-er-i], *adj.* containing instructions, that directs.

DIRECTRESS, [di-rekt'-res], *n.* a female director.

DIRECTRIX, [di-rekt'-riks], *n.* a directress; (*geom.*) a fixed line required in drawing a curve, the straight line perpendicular to the axis of a conic section in relation to which its nature may be defined. [MedL. *directrix*].

DIREFUL, [dī-er'-fŏŏl], *adj.* dire, horrible, terrible.

DIREFULLY, [dīer'-fŏŏl-i], *adv.* in direful fashion.

DIREFULNESS, [dīer'-fŏŏl-nes], *n.* the quality of being direful.

DIRELY, [dīer'-li], *adv.* in dire fashion; with dire results.

DIREMPTION, [dī-remp'-shun], *n.* separation by force. [L. *diremptio*].

DIRENESS, [dīer'-nes], *n.* the quality of being dire.

DIREPTION†, [dī-rep'-shun], *n.* plundering, ravaging; the act of snatching or tearing by force. [L. *direptio*].

DIRGE, [durj], *n.* a funeral hymn, a song of lament or mourning. [L. *dirige*, *imp.* of *dirigere* to direct].

DIRHEM, [dēer'-hem], *n.* a small Moslem silver coin, or unit of weight. [Arab. *dirhem*].

DIRIGENT† (1), [di'-rij-ent], *n.* anything that guides

or directs; (*geom.*) the line of motion along which the describing line or surface moves in the production of any plane or solid figure.

DIRIGENT† (2), [di'-rij-ent], *adj.* directing. [L. *dirigens*].

DIRIGIBLE (1), [di'-rij-ibl], *n.* a navigable airship

DIRIGIBLE (2), [di'-rij-ibl], *adj.* able to be steered.

DIRIMENT, [di'-ri-ment], *adj.* invalidating, annulling; **d. impediment**, an impediment that nullifies marriage. [L. *dirimens*].

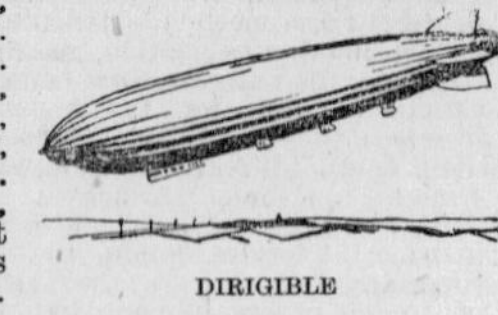

DIRIGIBLE

DIRK (1), [durk], *n.* a short Highland dagger. [Uncert.].

DIRK (2), [durk], *v.t.* to stab with a dirk.

DIRT, [durt], *n.* unclean matter, filth, mud, dust, soil; refuse or valueless matter; (*fig.*) sordidness, uncleanliness, foulness; a thing of no account or value; (*coll.*) land, earth; **yellow d.**, (*slang*) gold; **d. cheap**, (*coll.*) very cheap. [OScand. *dritr*].

DIRTILY, [durt'-i-li], *adv.* in a dirty fashion; meanly, dishonourably.

DIRTINESS, [durt'-i-nes], *n.* the condition of being dirty.

DIRT-TRACK, [durt'-trak'], *n.* a track of cinders or earth, evenly rolled, and used for motor-cycle racing.

DIRTY (1), [durt'-i], *adj.* covered with, or containing dirt, not clean, soiled, foul; (of weather) stormy, rainy; (*fig.*) dishonourable, mean, unfair; obscene, indecent; **to do the d. on**, (*coll.*) to treat in a mean fashion.

DIRTY (2) [durt'-i], *v.t.* to make dirty, soil.

DIRZI, DIRZEE, [dur'-zi], *n.* a native Indian tailor. [Pers. *darzi*].

DIS-, *pref.* indicating or expressing negation; deprivation, removal from; separation, parting from. [L. *dis-*].

DISA, [dē'-zah], *n.* (*bot.*) the South African orchid, *Disa grandiflora*. [Native].

DISABILITY, [dis'-ab-il'-i-ti], *n.* the state of being disabled; that which disables.

DISABLE, [dis-ābl'], *v.t.* to render unfit, incapacitate, maim, to make unable to perform competently; (*leg.*) to render or pronounce legally incapable. [DIS and ABLE].

DISABLEMENT, [dis-ābl'-ment], *n.* the act of disabling, the condition of being disabled.

DISABUSE, [dis'-ab-ewz'], *v.t.* to free from mistaken belief or error, to undeceive. [DIS and ABUSE].

DISACCOMMODATE, [dis'-ak-om'-od-āt], *v.t.* to inconvenience.

DISACCOMMODATION, [dis'-ak-om-od-ā'-shun], *n.* inconvenience.

DISACCORD (1), [dis'-ak-awd], *n.* lack of agreement, variance.

DISACCORD (2), [dis'-ak-awd], *v.i.* to disagree; to be out of accord with. [DIS and ACCORD (2)].

DISACCUSTOM, [dis'-ak-us'-tom], *v.t.* to destroy the force of a habit, to cause a person to break off a custom.

DISACKNOWLEDGE, [dis'-ak-nol'-ij] *v.t.* to disown, to refuse to acknowledge.

DISACQUAINTANCE, [dis'-a-kwānt'-ants], *n.* lack of familiarity or acquaintance with.

DISADVANTAGE (1), [dis'-ad-vahn'-tij], *n.* a drawback, an unfavourable circumstance, position or quality harmful to one's advantage or success; loss, detriment. [OFr. *desavauntage*].

DISADVANTAGE (2), [dis'-ad-vahn'-tij], *v.t.* to act to the prejudice of, to affect unfavourably.

DISADVANTAGEOUS, [dis'-ad-van-tāj'-us], *adj.* unfavourable to success or prosperity, causing disadvantage, detrimental.

DISADVANTAGEOUSLY, [dis'-ad-van-tāj'-us-li], *adv.* in a disadvantageous fashion.

DISADVANTAGEOUSNESS, [dis'-ad-van-tāj'-us-nes], *n.* the quality of being disadvantageous.

DISADVENTUROUS†, [dis'-ad-ven'-cher-us], *adj.* unprosperous, ill-fated.

DISAFFECT, [dis'-af-ekt'], *v.t.* to alienate the affection or loyalty of, to discontent, to estrange, to make dissatisfied.

DISAFFECTED, [dis'-af-ekt'-id], *adj.* disloyal; dissatisfied, unfriendly.

DISAFFECTEDLY, [dis'-af-ekt'-id-li], *adv* in a disaffected fashion.

DISAFFECTEDNESS, [dis'-af-ekt'-id-nes] *n.* the quality of being disaffected.

DISAFFECTION, [dis'-af-ek'-shun], *n.* the state of being disaffected; hostility, dislike; discontent.

DISAFFECTIONATE†, [dis'-af-ek'-shun-at], *adj* not well disposed; unfriendly.

DISAFFIRM, [dis'-a-furm'] *v.t.* to show to be false, to deny to contradict; (*leg.*) to reverse, to overthrow annul.

DISAFFIRMANCE, [dis'-a-furm'-ants], *n.* (*leg.*) the act of disaffirming.

DISAFFOREST, [dis'-a-fo'-rist], *v.t.* to clear of trees; to regard as ordinary land no longer subject to forest laws.

DISAFFORESTATION, [dis'-a-fo'-rist-ā'-shun], *n.* the act of disafforesting; the condition of being disafforested.

DISAGGREGATE, [dis-ag'-rig-āt], *v.t.* to split up an aggregate mass into its component parts.

DISAGGREGATION, [dis-ag'-rig-ā'-shun], *n.* the act of disaggregating.

DISAGREE, [dis'-a-grē'], *v.i.* to be different; to differ in opinion; to quarrel; to be unsuitable for; to upset, make ill. [DIS and AGREE].

DISAGREEABLE, [dis'-a-grē'-abl], *adj.* bad-tempered, cantankerous, cross-grained; unpleasant, distasteful.

DISAGREEABLENESS, [dis'-a-grē'-abl-nes], *n.* the condition of being disagreeable.

DISAGREEABLY, [dis'-a-grē'-ab-li], *adv.* in a disagreeable fashion.

DISAGREEMENT, [dis'-a-grē'-ment], *n.* want of agreement; difference of opinion; dissension, discord; a quarrel.

DISALLOW, [dis'-al-ow'], *v.t. and i.* not to permit, to refuse to sanction; not to allow or admit as just; not to grant.

DISALLOWABLE†, [dis'-al-ow'-abl], *adj.* not allowable.

DISALLOWANCE, [dis'-al-ow'-ants], *n.* the act of disallowing, rejection.

DISALLY, [dis'-al-ī'], *v.refl.* to break off an alliance with. [DIS and ALLY].

DISANCHOR, [dis-angk'-er], *v.t. and i.* to haul up the anchor, to release from anchorage.

DISANIMATE, [dis-an'-im-āt], *v.t.* to render inanimate; (*fig.*) to dishearten, to discourage. [DIS and ANIMATE].

DISANIMATION, [dis'-an'-im-ā'-shun], *n.* the act of disanimating, the state of being disanimated.

DISANNEX, [dis'-an-eks'] *v.t.* to disunite.

DISANNUL, [dis'-an-ul'], *v.t.* to annul, make void. [DIS and ANNUL].

DISANNULMENT, [dis'-an-ul'-ment], *n.* the act of disannulling.

DISANOINT, [dis'-an-oint'], *v.t.* to make void the anointment or consecration of.

DISAPPAREL, [dis'-a-pa'-rel], *v.t.* to disrobe; to strip of clothing.

DISAPPEAR, [dis'-a-pēer'], *v.i.* to vanish from sight, to be lost. [DIS and APPEAR].

DISAPPEARANCE, [dis'-a-pēer'-ans], *n.* the state of having disappeared; the act of disappearing.

DISAPPOINT, [dis'-a-point'], *v.t.* to fail to fulfil the expectations of, to dash the hopes of; to balk, to thwart, defeat. [Fr. *désappointer*].

DISAPPOINTED, [dis'-a-point'-id], *adj.* with one's hopes or expectations not realized, frustrated in one's wishes.

DISAPPOINTING, [dis'-a-point'-ing], *adj.* that disappoints, unsatisfactory.

DISAPPOINTINGLY, [dis-a-point'-ing-li], *adv.* in disappointing fashion.

DISAPPOINTMENT, [dis'-a-point'-ment], *n.* the state of being disappointed; that which disappoints; the feeling of regret or dejection upon the frustration of one's expectations, intentions, or wishes.

DISAPPRECIATE, [dis-ap-rē'-shi-āt], *v.t.* to undervalue, to fail to appreciate.

DISAPPROBATION, [dis-ap'-rōb-ā'-shun], *n.* disapproval; condemnation.

DISAPPROBATIVE, [dis'-ap-rō'-bat-iv], *adj.* disapprobatory.

DISAPPROBATORY, [dis'-ap-rō-bāt'-er-i], *adj.* showing or causing disapproval.

DISAPPROPRIATE (1), [dis'-ap-rō'-pri-at], *adj.* not appropriated, severed from connexion with or appropriation to. [MedL. *disappropriatus*].

DISAPPROPRIATE (2) [dis'-ap-rō'-pri-āt], *v.t.* to

withdraw or annul the appropriation of, to free from appropriation by. [L. *disappropriare*].

DISAPPROVAL, [dis'-a-prōōv'-al], *n.* censure, condemnation, adverse opinion.

DISAPPROVE, [dis'-a-prōōv'], *v.t.* to condemn, to have an adverse opinion of, not to approve. [DIS and APPROVE].

DISAPPROVINGLY, [dis'-a-prōōv'-ing-li], *adv.* in disapproving fashion.

DISARM, [dis-ahm'], *v.t.* and *i.* to deprive of arms or weapons; (*fig.*) to render harmless; to deprive of hostile force or intent, to allay; to reduce armaments. [DIS and ARM].

DISARMAMENT, [dis-ahm'-a-ment], *n.* the reduction and limitation of armaments; the state of being disarmed.

DISARRANGE, [dis'-a-rānj'], *v.t.* to cause to be out of place, to disturb the order or arrangement of, disorder, upset.

DISARRANGEMENT, [dis'-a-rānj'-ment], *n.* confusion, disorder.

DISARRAY (1), [dis'-a-rā'], *n.* disorder, confusion. [OFr. *desrei*].

DISARRAY (2), [dis'-a-rā'], *v.t.* to throw into disorder, to confuse, upset; to undress, to disrobe. [DIS and ARRAY].

DISARTICULATE, [dis'-ah-tik'-yōō-lāt], *v.t.* and *i.* to take to pieces at the joints.

DISASSIMILATION, [dis'-a-sim'-il-ā'-shun], *n.* the act of transforming assimilated substances into simpler forms.

DISASSOCIATE, [dis'-as-ō'-shi-āt], *v.t.* to sever or repudiate connexion or association with.

DISASTER, [diz-ahst'-er], *n.* a calamity, a sudden great misfortune, an event producing widespread distress, ruin, harm, loss of life, etc., a severe mishap. [Fr. *désastre* ill-omened star].

DISASTROUS, [diz-ahst'-rus], *adj.* calamitous, causing or resulting in disaster. [Fr. *désastreux*].

DISASTROUSLY, [diz-ahst'-rus-li], *adv.* in disastrous fashion.

DISASTROUSNESS, [diz-ahst'-rus-nes], *n.* the state of being disastrous.

DISATTACH, [dis'-a-tach'], *v.t.* to separate, detach.

DISAUTHORIZE†, [dis-aw'-ther-īz], *v.t.* to take away authority from.

DISAVOUCH†, [dis'-a-vowch'], *v.t.* to disavow, to disown. [DIS and AVOUCH].

DISAVOW, [dis'-a-vow'], *v.t.* to deny, to disclaim, to repudiate, to refuse to acknowledge. [Fr. *désavouer*].

DISAVOWAL, [dis'-a-vow'-al], *n.* the act of disavowing; that which disavows; repudiation.

DISAVOWMENT, [dis-a-vow'-ment], *n.* disavowal.

DISBAND, [dis-band'], *v.t.* and *i.* to break up or cause to cease as an organized body or band; to disperse, to cease to exist as an organized band; (of troops) to break ranks. [DIS and BAND].

DISBANDMENT, [dis-band'-ment], *n.* the act of disbanding.

DISBAR, (**disbarring, disbarred**), [dis-bah(r)'] *v.t.* (*leg.*) to expel (a barrister) from the bar, to strike off the list of barristers. [DIS and BAR].

DISBARK, [dis-bahk'], *v.t.* to remove the bark from; to disembark. [DIS and BARK].

DISBELIEF, [dis'-bi-lēf'], *n.* refusal or disinclination to believe; want of belief.

DISBELIEVE, [dis'-bi-lēv'], *v.t.* and *i.* to refuse, or be unable, to believe.

DISBELIEVER, [dis-bi-lēv'-er], *n.* one who disbelieves.

DISBENCH, [dis-bench'], *v.t.* (*leg.*) to deprive of membership of an Inn of Court. [DIS and BENCH].

DISBODIED, [dis-bod'-id], *adj.* spiritualized, etherealized.

DISBOWEL, [dis-bow'-el], *v.t.* to remove the bowels from.

DISBRANCH, [dis-brahnch'], *v.t.* to strip the branches from.

DISBUD, (**disbudding, disbudded**), [dis-bud'], *v.t.* to deprive of buds.

DISBURDEN, [dis-bur'-den], *v.t.* and *i.* to ease or relieve of a burden, to unload, to get rid of.

DISBURSE, [dis-burs'], *v.t.* and *i.* to pay out, to spend, to distribute, to give away money, to contribute sums of money. [OFr. *desbourser*].

DISBURSEMENT, [dis-burs'-ment], *n.* the act of disbursing money; the sum paid out.

DISBURSER, [dis-burs'-er], *n.* one who disburses money.

DISC, see DISK.

DISCAL, [disk'-al], *adj.* pertaining to a disk.

DISCALCEATE, [dis-kal'-si-āt], *adj.* unshod; (of members of religious orders) barefooted. [L. *discalceatus*].

DISCALCED, [dis-kalst'], *adj.* discalceate.

DISCANDY†, [dis-kand'-i], *v.i.* to melt; to dissolve. [DIS and CANDY].

DISCAPACITATE, [dis'-ka-pas'-it-āt], *v.t.* to incapacitate.

DISCARD (1), [dis-kahd'], *n.* the act of discarding, the card or cards discarded.

DISCARD (2), [dis-kahd'], *v.t.* and *i.* (*cards*) to throw away a card that is not a trump when unable to follow suit; to throw aside as valueless or useless; (of an article of clothing) to cease to wear, to remove or take off; to reject, dismiss, abandon as unworthy or of little account. [DIS and CARD].

DISCARNATE†, [dis-kah'-nāt], *adj.* deprived of flesh. [DIS and CARNATE].

DISCEPTATION, [dis'-ept-ā'-shun], *n.* (*archaic*) dispute, discussion. [L. *disceptatio*].

DISCERN, [dis-urn'], *v.t.* to perceive, to distinguish clearly by the sight, to see; to recognize, to perceive distinctly. [L. *discernere*].

DISCERNER, [dis-urn'-er], *n.* one who discerns.

DISCERNIBLE, [dis-urn'-ibl], *adj.* capable of being discerned.

DISCERNIBLENESS, [dis-urn'-ibl-nes], *n.* the condition of being discernible.

DISCERNIBLY, [dis-urn'-ib-li], *adv.* in a discernible manner.

DISCERNING (1), [dis-urn'-ing], *n.* discernment.

DISCERNING (2), [dis-urn'-ing], *adj.* able to discern, quick to perceive, that discerns.

DISCERNINGLY, [dis-urn'-ing-li], *adv.* in a discerning manner.

DISCERNMENT, [dis-urn'-ment], *n.* the act of discerning; ability to discern, insight, penetration.

DISCERP, [dis-urp'], *v.t.* to tear in pieces, to sever. [L. *discerpere*].

DISCERPTIBILITY, [dis-urp'-tib-il'-i-ti], *n.* the quality of being discerptible.

DISCERPTIBLE, [dis-urp'-tibl], *adj.* capable of being torn asunder; separable.

DISCERPTION, [dis-urp'-shun], *n.* the act of pulling to pieces; the state of being torn asunder. [L. *discerptio*].

DISCESSION†, [dis-esh'-un], *n.* departure. [L. *discessio*].

DISCHARGE (1), [dis-chahj'], *n.* the act of discharging; the state or process of being discharged; that which is discharged; a testimonial or order certifying freedom from liability; (*med.*) the emission of matter from a sore. [OFr. *descharge*].

DISCHARGE (2), [dis-chahj'], *v.t.* to remove or expel the contents of; to eject, to emit, to give off; (of a sore, wound) to emit matter; to fire (a gun); to unload; to take away electricity from a charged body; to release from service, care, or attention; to dismiss from employment; to acquit, to liberate from custody; to relieve from legal liability; to pay, to rid oneself of; to perform, to carry out (duties, etc.). [OFr. *descharger*].

DISCHARGER, [dis-chahj'-er], *n.* one who, or that which, discharges.

DISCHARGE-VALVE, [dis-chahj'-valv'], *n.* (*eng.*) a valve which covers the top of the barrel of the air-pump in marine engines.

DISCHARGING-ARCH, [dis-chahj'-ing-ahch'], *n.* (*arch.*) an arch over a door, window, etc., to distribute or take part of the pressure.

DISCHARGING-ARCH

DISCHARGING-ROD, [dis-chahj'-ing-rod'], *n.* a discharger of electricity.

DISCHURCH†, [dis-church'], *v.t.* to unchurch, to make no longer a church; to deprive of, or exclude from, a church.

DISCINCT, dis-ingkt'], *adj.* ungirded. [L. *discinctus*].

DISCIPLE, [dis-īpl'], *n.* one of the twelve Apostles, an early follower of Christ; (*fig.*) a follower, student, or adherent of any particular group holding common principles, or of the leader of such a group; an American sect of Baptists. [L. *discipulus*].

DISCIPLE-LIKE, [dis-īpl'-līk'], *adj.* befitting a disciple.

DISCIPLESHIP, [dis-īpl'-ship], *n.* the condition of being a disciple.

DISCIPLINABLE, [dis'-ip-lĭn'-abl], *adj.* capable of being disciplined.
DISCIPLINABLENESS, [dis'-ip-lĭn'-abl-nes], *n.* the quality of being disciplinable.
DISCIPLINAL, [dis'-ip-lĭn'-al], *adj.* relating to discipline.
DISCIPLINANT, [dis'-ip-lĭn'-ant], *n.* a member of a Spanish religious order, who publicly beat themselves with rods. [L. *disciplinans*].
DISCIPLINARIAN (1), [dis'-ip-lin-āer'-i-an], *n.* one who keeps strict discipline; an expert in the art of discipline.
DISCIPLINARIAN (2), [dis'-ip-lin-āer'-i-an], *adj.* pertaining to discipline.
DISCIPLINARY, [dis'-ip-lin'-er-i], *adj.* pertaining to, or involving, discipline.
DISCIPLINE (1), [dis'-ip-lin], *n.* systematic training intended to develop the mind along certain lines, to teach restraint, respect for, and willing obedience to, recognized authority; the result of such training, self-restraint, readiness with which commands, precepts, instructions, etc., are carried out, ability to act in orderly manner in unforeseen or abnormal circumstances; control over the behaviour of a group of persons; corrective punishment, chastisement; (*eccles.*) penance; moral precepts and their enforcement upon members of the Church. [L. *disciplina* instruction, teaching].
DISCIPLINE (2), [dis'-ip-lin], *v.t.* to subject to, or enforce discipline upon, to bring about discipline in. [MedL. *disciplinare*].
DISCIPLINER, [dis'-ip-lin-er], *n.* a disciplinarian.
DISCIPULAR, [dis-ip'-yōō-ler], *adj.* relating to a disciple.
DISCLAIM, [dis-klām'], *v.t. and i.* to renounce or repudiate a claim to, to deny connexion with; to disown, to refuse to admit; to repudiate a legal claim. [OFr. *desclamer*].
DISCLAIMANT, [dis-klām'-ant], *n.* one who disclaims.
DISCLAIMATION, [dis'-klam-ā'-shun], *n.* the act of disclaiming.
DISCLAIMER, [dis-klām'-er], *n.* (*leg.*) a refusal to admit; repudiation, renunciation, rejection of a legal claim, right, interest, etc.; one who disclaims.
DISCLOISTERED, [dis-klois'-terd], *adj.* freed from religious vows. [DIS and CLOISTER].
DISCLOSE, [dis-klōz'], *v.t.* to uncover, to reveal, to bring to light. [OFr. *descloser*].
DISCLOSER, [dis-klōz'-er], *n.* one who discloses.
DISCLOSURE, [dis-klō'-zher], *n.* the act of disclosing; that which is disclosed.
DISCOBOLIC, [dis'-kob-ol'-ik], *adj.* quoit-throwing. [Gk. *diskobolos*].
DISCOHERENT†, [dis'-kō-hēer'-ent], *adj.* incoherent.
DISCOID, [disk'-oid], *adj.* having the form of a disk; (*bot.*) consisting of a disk. [DISK and Gk. *oeides* like].
DISCOIDAL, [disk-oid'-al], *adj.* discoid.
DISCOLORATION, DISCOLOURATION, [dis'-kul-er-ā'-shun], *n.* the act of discolouring; the state of being discoloured. [OFr. *descoloracion*].
DISCOLOUR, [dis-kul'-er], *v.t. and i.* to alter or spoil the colour of, to stain; to become stained or tarnished. [OFr. *descolorer*].
DISCOLOURATION, see DISCOLORATION.
DISCOLOURED, [dis-kul'-erd], *adj.* stained, tarnished, having its natural colour changed or spoiled.
DISCOLOURMENT, [dis-kul'-er-ment], *n.* alteration in colour.
DISCOMFIT, [dis-kum'-fit], *v.t.* to defeat, overcome; to upset, to disconcert. [OFr. *desconfit*].
DISCOMFITURE, [dis-kum'-fich-er], *n.* the act of discomfiting, the state of being discomfited, confusion arising from defeat or frustration. [OFr. *desconfiture* defeat].
DISCOMFORT (1), [dis-kum'-fert], *n.* want of comfort, inconvenience, hardship, unpleasantness, uncomfortableness. [OFr. *desconfort*].
DISCOMFORT (2), [dis-kum'-fert], *v.t.* to cause discomfort to.
DISCOMFORTABLE, [dis-kum'-fert-abl], *adj.* uncomfortable.
DISCOMMEND, [dis'-kom-end'], *v.t.* to find fault with, to censure, to advise against. [OFr. *descommander*].
DISCOMMENDABLE, [dis'-kom-end'-abl], *adj.* censurable; deserving disapproval.
DISCOMMENDATION, [dis'-kom-end-ā'-shun], *n.* the act of discommending, disapprobation.
DISCOMMENDER, [dis'-kom-end'-er], *n.* one who discommends.
DISCOMMISSIONED†, [dis'-kom-ish'-und], *adj.* deprived of a commission; discharged.
DISCOMMODE, [dis'-kom-ōd'], *v.t.* to inconvenience, to annoy. [DIS and COMMODE].
DISCOMMODIOUS†, [dis'-kom-ōd'-i-us], *adj.* inconvenient; troublesome.
DISCOMMODIOUSLY†, [dis'-kom-ōd'-i-us-li], *adv.* in discommodious fashion.
DISCOMMODITY, [dis'-kom-od'-i-ti], *n.* inconvenience.
DISCOMMON, [dis-kom'-on], *v.t.* (*leg.*) to appropriate common land by enclosing it; (*fig.*) to deprive of a privilege.
DISCOMMUNITY, [dis'-kom-ewn'-i-ti], *n.* lack of community.
DISCOMPOSE, [dis'-kom-pōz'], *v.t.* to disquiet, to disturb, to upset the composure of.
DISCOMPOSEDNESS, [dis'-kom-pōz'-id-nes], *n.* the condition of being discomposed.
DISCOMPOSINGLY, [dis'-kom-pōz'-ing-li], *adv.* in a discomposing fashion.
DISCOMPOSURE, [dis'-kom-pōzh'-er], *n.* agitation, disturbed state of mind, lack of composure, perturbation.
DISCONCERT, [dis'-kon-surt'], *v.t.* to put out of countenance, to discompose, to abash, shake; to upset, frustrate.
DISCONCERTION, [dis'-kon-sur'-shun], *n.* the act of disconcerting.
DISCONCERTMENT, [dis'-kon-surt'-ment], *n.* the act of disconcerting; the state of being disconcerted.
DISCONFORMITY, [dis'-kon-fawm'-i-ti], *n.* lack of conformity; inconsistency.
DISCONGRUITY†, [dis'-kon-grōō'-i-ti], *n.* incongruity; inconsistency.
DISCONNECT, [dis'-kon-ekt'], *v.t.* to separate, to disunite, to break or remove the connexion between.
DISCONNECTED, [dis'-kon-ekt'-id], *adj.* separated, disjointed; not connected with, unrelated to; incoherent.
DISCONNECTEDLY, [dis'-kon-ekt'-id-li], *adv.* in a disconnected manner.
DISCONNECTEDNESS, [dis'-kon-ekt'-id-nes], *n.* the state of being disconnected.
DISCONNEXION, DISCONNECTION, [dis'-kon-ek'-shun], *n.* the act of disconnecting; the state or quality of being disconnected.
DISCONSENT†, [dis-kon-sent'], *v.i.* to differ; to disagree, to be at variance with. [OFr. *desconsentir*].
DISCONSOLATE, [dis-kon'-sol-at], *adj.* unable or unwilling to be consoled, extremely unhappy or dejected, utterly miserable; without comfort or consolation. [MedL. *disconsolatus*].
DISCONSOLATELY, [dis-kon'-sol-at-li], *adv.* in disconsolate fashion.
DISCONSOLATENESS, [dis-kon'-sol-at-nes], *n.* the condition of being disconsolate.
DISCONSOLATION, [dis-kon'-sol-ā'-shun], *n.* the state of being disconsolate, absence of comfort or consolation.
DISCONTENT (1), [dis'-kon-tent'], *n.* lack of contentment, dissatisfaction; one who is discontented.
DISCONTENT (2), [dis'-kon-tent'], *v.t.* to dissatisfy, to cause to be disquieted in the mind. [DIS and CONTENT].
DISCONTENTED, [dis'-kon-tent'-id], *adj.* dissatisfied, not contented.
DISCONTENTEDLY, [dis'-kon-tent'-id-li], *adv.* in discontented fashion.
DISCONTENTEDNESS, [dis'-kon-tent'-id-nes], *n.* the condition of being discontented.
DISCONTENTFUL, [dis'-kon-tent'-fōōl], *adj.* full of discontent, dissatisfied.
DISCONTENTMENT, [dis'-kon-tent'-ment], *n.* the condition of being discontented.
DISCONTIGUOUS, [dis'-kon-tig'-yōō-us], *adj.* not contiguous.
DISCONTINUABLE, [dis'-kon-tin'-yōō-abl], *adj* capable of being discontinued.
DISCONTINUANCE, [dis'-kon-tin'-yōō-ants], *n.* the act of discontinuing; the state of being discontinued; (*leg.*) interruption or dismissal of a suit owing to irregular continuance or breaking off of the proceedings by the plaintiff. [AFr. *discontinuance*].
DISCONTINUATION, [dis'-kon-tin'-yōō-ā'-shun], *n.* discontinuance.
DISCONTINUE, [dis'-kon-tin'-yōō], *v.t. and i.* to

interrupt, to cease, to stop, to leave off, to break off, to give up; to finish, to cease. [MedL. *discontinuare*].

DISCONTINUER, [dis'-kon-tin'-yōō-er], *n.* one who discontinues.

DISCONTINUITY, [dis'-kon'-tin-ew'-i-ti], *n.* lack of continuity, interrupted sequence.

DISCONTINUOUS, [dis'-kon-tin'-yōō-us], *adj.* not continuous, interrupted, broken off; separated by gaps or intervals.

DISCONTINUOUSLY, [dis'-kon-tin'-yōō-us-li], *adv.* in a discontinuous manner.

DISCONVENIENCE†, [dis'-kon-vēn'-i-ents], *n.* inconvenience, incongruity, unsuitableness. [L. *disconvenientia*].

DISCONVENIENT†, [dis'-kon-vēn'-i-ent], *adj.* incongruous, inconvenient. [L. *disconveniens*].

DISCOPHORA, [dis-kof'-er-a], *n.(pl.)* (*zool.*) a subdivision of hydrozoa, the jelly-fishes. [Gk. *diskophoros* bearing a discus].

DISCORD (1), [dis'-kawd], *n.* disagreement, variance, dissension, want of harmony; a confused, inharmonious jumble of sounds; (*mus.*) a dissonant chord, requiring resolution into a concord. [OFr. *descorde*].

DISCORD (2), [dis-kawd'], *v.t.* to disagree, to differ, to be at variance; (*mus.*) to be dissonant or inharmonious. [L. *discordare*].

DISCORDANCE, [dis-kawd'-ants], *n.* disagreement, lack of harmony, dissonance. [OFr. *descordance*].

DISCORDANCY, [dis-kawd'-an-si], *n.* the state of being discordant; discordance.

DISCORDANT, [dis-kawd'-ant], *adj.* not agreeing, at variance, quarrelling; harsh, unmusical, inharmonious, unpleasant to the ear. [OFr. *descordant*].

DISCORDANTLY, [dis-kawd'-ant-li], *adv.* in discordant fashion.

DISCORDANTNESS, [dis-kawd'-ant-nes], *n.* discordancy.

DISCORDFUL, [dis-kawd'-fōōl], *adj.* quarrelsome, contentious.

DISCORPORATE, [dis-kaw'-por-at], *adj.* deprived of corporate rights, not joined together in a corporation. [MedL. *discorporatus* dissolved].

DISCOUNT (1), [dis'-kownt], *n.* a sum of money deducted from the usual price for prompt payment, payment in cash, as a special concession to privileged persons, etc.; an allowance off the full amount normally due; charge made by a banker, as interest, on advancing a sum of money on a bill of exchange or other document not due; **at a d.**, of little account or value.

DISCOUNT (2), [dis-kownt'], *v.t.* to lend or receive money subject to discount on bills of exchange, etc.; to diminish in value, to depreciate, to offset; to disregard, to refuse to believe or accept. [OFr. *desconter* from MedL. *discomputare*].

DISCOUNTABLE, [dis-kownt'-abl], *adj.* capable of being discounted.

DISCOUNT-BROKER, [dis'-kownt-brōk'-er], *n.* one who cashes bills of exchange or advances money on securities at a discount.

DISCOUNT-DAY, [dis'-kownt-dā'], *n.* the day on which a bank discounts notes and bills.

DISCOUNTENANCE, [dis-kownt'-in-ants], *v.t.* to disapprove of, to view with disfavour, to discourage; to disconcert, to abash. [OFr. *descontenancer*].

DISCOUNTENANCER, [dis-kownt'-en-ans-er], *n.* a person who discountenances.

DISCOUNTER, [dis-kownt'-er], *n.* a person who discounts.

DISCOUNTING, [dis-kownt'-ing], *n.* (*comm.*) the act or practice of advancing money on discounts.

DISCOURAGE, [dis-ku'-rij], *v.t.* to dishearten, to deter, to take away one's enthusiasm, courage or confidence; to endeavour to deter from; to try to prevent or repress. [OFr. *descouragier*].

DISCOURAGEABLE, [dis-ku'-rij-abl], *adj.* capable of being discouraged.

DISCOURAGEMENT, [dis-ku'-rij-ment], *n.* the act of discouraging; that which discourages; the state of being discouraged. [OFr. *descouragement*].

DISCOURAGER, [dis-ku'-rij-er], *n.* one who, or that which, discourages.

DISCOURAGING, [dis-ku'-rij-ing], *adj.* tending to discourage.

DISCOURAGINGLY, [dis-ku'-rij-ing-li], *adv.* in a discouraging fashion.

DISCOURSE (1), [dis'-kaws], *n.* a formal speech, address, lecture, etc.; a written dissertation; conversation, talk. [L. *discursus* a running to and fro].

DISCOURSE (2), [dis-kaws'], *v.t. and i.* to converse, to talk; to speak or write at length in a learned or formal manner; to preach, to lecture.

DISCOURSER, [dis-kaws'-er], *n.* one who discourses.

DISCOURSIVE†, [dis-kaws'-iv], *adj.* reasoning; discursive; communicative, in the manner of a discourse.

DISCOURTEOUS, [dis-kur'-ti-us], *adj.* rude, ill-mannered, lacking in courtesy.

DISCOURTEOUSLY, [dis-kur'-ti-us-li], *adv.* in a discourteous fashion.

DISCOURTEOUSNESS, [dis-kur'-ti-us-nes], *n.* the quality of being discourteous.

DISCOURTESY, [dis-kur'-tes-i], *n.* lack of courtesy, discourteous behaviour, incivility, rudeness; a discourteous act.

DISCOVENANT†, [dis-kuv'-en-ant], *v.t.* to break a covenant with.

DISCOVER, [dis-kuv'-er], *v.t.* to find out; to establish the presence of; (*archaic*) to reveal, to disclose. [OFr. *descovrir*].

DISCOVERABILITY, [dis-kuv'-er-ab-il'-i-ti], *n.* the quality of being discoverable.

DISCOVERABLE, [dis-kuv'-er-abl], *adj.* capable of being discovered.

DISCOVERER, [dis-kuv'-er-er], *n.* one who discovers.

DISCOVERT, [dis-kuv'-ert], *n.* (*leg.*) (of a woman) unmarried or widowed. [OFr. *descouverte*].

DISCOVERTURE, [dis-kuv'-er-cher], *n.* (*leg.*) the condition of being discovert.

DISCOVERY, [dis-kuv'-er-i], *n.* the act of discovering; that which is discovered; (*leg.*) the disclosure of evidence or facts affecting the action at issue by one of the parties at the instigation of the other. [DISCOVER].

DISCRASITE, [dis'-kras-īt], *n.* antimonide of silver. [Gk. *duskrasia* bad mixture].

DISCREDIT (1), [dis-kred'-it], *n.* loss of credit, ill-repute; that which discredits; doubt, disbelief.

DISCREDIT (2), [dis-kred'-it], *v.t.* to bring into ill-repute, to shake one's confidence in, create an unfavourable opinion about; to doubt strongly, refuse to believe.

DISCREDITABLE, [dis-kred'-it-abl], *adj.* that discredits; mean, base, unworthy.

DISCREDITABLY, [dis-kred'-it-ab-li], *adv.* in a discreditable fashion.

DISCREDITOR†, [dis-kred'-it-er], *n.* one who discredits.

DISCREET, [dis-krēt'], *adj.* circumspect, wary, prudent, cautious, endeavouring to avoid ill-advised action or anything likely to produce trouble. [LL. *discretus* discerning].

DISCREETLY, [dis-krēt'-li], *adv.* in a discreet manner.

DISCREETNESS, [dis-krēt'-nes], *n.* the quality of being discreet.

DISCREPANCE, [dis-krep'-ants], *n.* discrepancy. [L. *discrepantia* dissimilarity].

DISCREPANCY, [dis-krep'-an-si], *n.* the quality of being discrepant; anything which is discrepant, an inconsistency.

DISCREPANT, [dis-krep'-ant], *adj.* inconsistent, different, disagreeing, contradictory, inconsequent, incompatible. [L. *discrepans*, *pres.pt.* of *discrepare* to differ].

DISCRETE, [dis-krēt'], *adj.* separate, discontinuous, disconnected; (*path.*) (of spots, etc.) scattered singly. [L. *discretum*, *p.pt.* of *discernere* divide].

DISCRETENESS, [dis-krēt'-nes], *n.* the quality of being discrete.

DISCRETION, [dis-kresh'-un], *n.* ability to realize and follow the most advantageous line of behaviour, carefulness, cautiousness, avoidance of unnecessary risks or hazards; ability or liberty to act or make free decisions as seems best; **to surrender at d.**, to surrender unconditionally; **years of d.**, age at which a person is considered capable of making his own decisions on how to act. [L. *discretio* separation, distinction].

DISCRETIONAL, [dis-kresh'-un-al], *adj.* discretionary.

DISCRETIONALLY, [dis-kresh'-un-al-i], *adv.* discretionarily.

DISCRETIONARILY, [dis-kresh'-un-er-i-li], *adv.* according to discretion.

DISCRETIONARY, [dis-kresh'-un-er-i] *adj.* controlled or determined by discretion.

DISCRETIVE, [dis-krēt'-iv], *adj.* disjunctive, expressing a difference or distinction. [L. *discretivus* distinguishing].

DISCRETIVELY, [dis-krēt'-iv-li], *adv.* in a discretive way.

DISCRIMINABLE, [dis-krim'-in-abl], *adj.* capable of being discriminated.
DISCRIMINATE (1), [dis-krim'-in-at], *adj.* exercising, showing or characterized by discrimination. [L. *discriminatus*].
DISCRIMINATE (2), [dis-krim'-in-āt], *v.t. and i.* to show, make, or note the difference between, to differentiate, to distinguish; to recognize a difference, to see or make a distinction between; to deal differently with, to show bias and unfair partiality in one's treatment of. [L. *discriminare* to separate, to distinguish].
DISCRIMINATELY, [dis-krim'-in-at-li], *adv.* in a discriminate manner.
DISCRIMINATENESS, [dis-krim'-in-at-nes], *n.* the quality of being discriminate.
DISCRIMINATING, [dis-krim'-in-āt-ing], *adj.* able to discriminate, able to distinguish slight differences; (of a duty, tariff) differential; showing discrimination.
DISCRIMINATINGLY, [dis-krim'-in-āt-ing-li], *adv.* in a discriminating manner.
DISCRIMINATION, [dis-krim'-in-ā'-shun], *n.* the act of discriminating; the ability to discriminate. [L. *discriminatio*].
DISCRIMINATIVE, [dis-krim'-in-at-iv], *adj.* able to discriminate; constituting a mark of difference, that discriminates.
DISCRIMINATIVELY, [dis-krim'-in-at-iv-li], *adv.* with discrimination.
DISCRIMINATOR, [dis-krim'-in-āt-er], *n.* one who discriminates. [L. *discriminator*].
DISCRIMINATORY, [dis-krim'-in-at-er-i], *adj.* discriminative.
DISCROWN, [dis-krown'], *v.t.* to deprive of a crown, dethrone.
DISCULPATE, [dis-kulp'-āt], *v.t.* to absolve from blame or guilt. [L. *disculpare*].
DISCUMBENCY†, [dis-kum'-ben-si], *n.* reclining posture adopted when dining. [L. *discumbens*].
DISCUMBER, [dis-kum'-ber], *v.t.* to disencumber. [DIS and CUMBER].
DISCURSION, [dis-kur'-shun], *n.* digression, reasoning. [L. *discursio* running to and fro].
DISCURSIVE, [dis-kurs'-iv], *adj.* rambling, wandering haphazardly from one topic to another, covering a variety of subjects; reasoning. [DISCOURSE].
DISCURSIVELY, [dis-kurs'-iv-li], *adv.* in discursive fashion.
DISCURSIVENESS, [dis-kurs'-iv-nes], *n.* the condition of being discursive.
DISCURSORY, [dis-kurs'-er-i], *adj.* discursive.
DISCURSUS, [dis-kurs'-us], *n.* reasoned discourse or discussion. [L. *discursus*].
DISCUS, [dis'-kus], *n.* a circular, slightly convex piece of metal, stone or heavy material thrown in athletic contests. [L. from Gk. *diskos* quoit].

DISCUS

DISCUSS, [dis-kus'], *v.t.* to debate, to argue about, to consider (a topic) in all its aspects and implications, to examine the various points of view about a subject upon which diversity of opinion is possible; (*civil leg.*) to exhaust the means of, or proceedings against, a principal debtor before taking action against the surety or person secondarily liable. [L. *discussum*, *p.pt.* of *discutere* to disperse].
DISCUSSIBLE, [dis-kus'-ibl], *adj.* capable of being discussed.
DISCUSSION, [dis-kush'-un], *n.* the act of discussing; the state of being discussed; an argument, debate, a mutual consideration of a problem. [L. *discussio*].
DISCUSSIVE, [dis-kus'-iv], *adj.* pertaining to, or characterized by, discussion.
DISCUTIENT (1), [dis-kew'-shent], *n.* a discutient medicine.
DISCUTIENT (2), [dis-kew'-shent], *adj.* (*med.*) able to disperse morbid matter. [L. *discutiens*].
DISDAIN (1), [dis-dān'], *n.* contempt, scorn, haughty disregard of what is considered inferior or derogatory, arrogant indifference. [OFr. *desdein*].
DISDAIN (2), [dis-dān'], *v.t.* to despise, to look down upon, to regard or treat with disdain; to scorn; to consider it as unworthy of one, to refuse to degrade oneself by. [L. *dedignare* to scorn].
DISDAINFUL, [dis-dān'-fo͝ol], *adj.* haughty, scornful, contemptuous, proudly indifferent or aloof.
DISDAINFULLY, [dis-dān'-fo͝ol-i], *adv.* in a disdainful fashion.
DISDAINFULNESS, [dis-dān'-fo͝ol-nes], *n.* the quality of being disdainful.
DISEASE, [diz-ēz'], *n.* an illness, a specific form of derangement or disorder of an organ, organism, mind, etc., characterized by distinct and recognizable symptoms; abnormal condition of the body, deviation from normal health; disorder of physical, mental, or social structure or function. [OFr. *desaise* lack of ease].
DISEASED, [diz-ēzd'], *adj.* affected by disease, not healthy, suffering from disease.
DISEASEDNESS, [diz-ēzd'-nes], *n.* the condition of being diseased.
DISEASEFUL, [diz-ēz'-fo͝ol], *adj.* bringing on disease.
DISEDIFICATION, [dis-ed'-i-fik-ā'-shun], *n.* moral retrogression.
DISEMBARK, [dis'-em-bahk'], *v.t. and i.* to land, to go ashore, to put ashore. [Fr. *désembarquer*].
DISEMBARKATION, [dis'-em'-bahk-ā'-shun], *n.* the act of disembarking.
DISEMBARKMENT, [dis'-em-bahk'-ment], *n.* disembarkation.
DISEMBARRASS, [dis'-em-ba'-ras], *v.t.* to free from embarrassment or trouble; to separate.
DISEMBARRASSMENT, [dis'-em-ba'-ras-ment], *n.* the act of disembarrassing; the state of being disembarrassed.
DISEMBELLISH, [dis'-em-bel'-ish], *v.t.* to strip of embellishment, to make bare.
DISEMBITTER, [dis'-em-bit'-er], *v.t.* to rid of bitterness or acrimony.
DISEMBODIMENT, [dis'-em-bod'-i-ment], *n.* the act of disembodying, the state of being disembodied.
DISEMBODY, [dis'-em-bod'-i], *v.t.* to free from bodily form; to disband, to discharge (a military body).
DISEMBOGUE, [dis-em-bōg'], *v.t. and i.* (of a river) to discharge or empty its waters at its mouth; (*fig.*) to pour or flow forth. [Span. *disembocar*].
DISEMBOGUEMENT, [dis'-em-bōg'-ment], *n.* the act of disemboguing; the place where a river disembogues.
DISEMBOSOM, [dis'-em-bo͝oz'-um], *v.t. and reflex.* to reveal, to disclose; to unburden one's troubles or secrets to.
DISEMBOUCHURE, [dis'-em-bo͞o'-sho͞oer], *n.* the mouth of a river, or the place where the waters of a river are discharged. [DIS and EMBOUCHURE].
DISEMBOWEL, [dis'-em-bow'-el], *v.t.* to remove the bowels of, to eviscerate; to wound so as to expose the entrails.
DISEMBOWELLED, [dis'-em-bow'-eld], *adj.* eviscerated; wounded so as to lay open the entrails.
DISEMBOWELMENT, [dis'-em-bow'-el-ment], *n.* the act of disembowelling; the state of being disembowelled.
DISEMBROIL, [dis'-em-broil'], *v.t.* to rid of trouble or confusion.
DISEMBURDENMENT, [dis'-em-burd'-en-ment], *n.* the action of disburdening, the state of being disburdened.
DISEMPLOYED, [dis'-em-ploid'], *adj.* unemployed.
DISENABLE, [dis'-en-ābl'], *v.t.* to deprive of the power to do, to cause to be unable, to disable.
DISENAMOURED, [dis'-en-am'-erd], *adj.* free from being enamoured of.
DISENCHAINED, [dis-en-chānd'], *adj.* set free, liberated from bondage.
DISENCHANT, [dis'-en-chahnt'], *v.t.* to disillusion, to destroy the power of a charm or spell; to remove the enchantment from. [OFr. *desenchanter*].
DISENCHANTER, [dis'-en-chahnt'-er], *n.* one who disenchants.
DISENCHANTMENT, [dis'-en-chahnt'-ment], *n.* the act of disenchanting; the condition of being disenchanted.
DISENCHANTRESS, [dis'-en-chahnt'-res], *n.* a female disenchanter.
DISENCLOSE†, **DISINCLOSE**†, [dis'-en-klōz], *v.t.* to throw open land that has been enclosed.
DISENCUMBER, [dis'-en-kum'-ber], *v.t.* to set free of an encumbrance, to relieve of a burden.
DISENCUMBRANCE†, [dis'-en-kum'-brants], *n.* freedom from encumbrance or burden.
DISENDOW, [dis'-en-dow'], *v.t.* to deprive of endowments.
DISENDOWMENT, [dis'-en-dow'-ment], *n.* the act of disendowing; the state of being disendowed.
DISENFRANCHISE, [dis'-en-franch'-īz], *v.t.* to disfranchise.

DISENFRANCHISEMENT, [dis'-en-franch'-iz-ment], *n.* disfranchisement.
DISENGAGE, [dis'-en-gāj'], *v.t.* to set free or unfasten from that which binds or joins, to detach, disconnect, release; (*fencing*) to transfer one's blade smartly to the other side of the opponent's foil.
DISENGAGED, [dis'-en-gājd'], *adj.* free, not occupied or engaged at the moment, at liberty.
DISENGAGEDNESS, [dis'-en-gājd'-nes], *n.* the quality or state of being disengaged.
DISENGAGEMENT, [dis'-en-gāj'-ment], *n.* the act of disengaging; the condition of being disengaged.
DISENNOBLE, [dis'-en-nōbl'], *v.t.* to make ignoble, to degrade.
DISENROL†, **(disenrolling, disenrolled)**, [dis'-en-rōl'], *v.t.* to remove from a roll or list.
DISENSLAVE, [dis'-en-slāv'], *v.t.* to free from slavery.
DISENTAIL, [dis'-en-tāl'], *v.t.* to break the entail of.
DISENTANGLE, [dis'-en-tang'-gl], *v.t.* and *i.* to unravel, untwist, free from entanglement; (*fig.*) to straighten out.
DISENTANGLEMENT, [dis'-en-tang'-gl-ment], *n.* the act of disentangling; the state of being disentangled.
DISENTHRAL, DISINTHRAL, **(disenthralling, disenthralled)**, [dis'-en-thrawl'], *v.t.* to release from bondage or oppression.
DISENTHRALMENT, DISINTHRALMENT, [dis'-en-thrawl'-ment], *n.* release from bondage.
DISENTHRONE, [dis'-en-thrōn'], *v.t.* to dethrone.
DISENTITLE, [dis'-en-tītl'], *v.t.* to deprive of title.
DISENTOMB, [dis'-en-tōōm'], *v.t.* to take out of a tomb; (*fig.*) to unearth.
DISENTRAIN, [dis'-en-trān'], *v.t.* (*milit.*) to disembark from a train; to detrain.
DISENTRANCE, [dis'-en-trahns'], *v.t.* to arouse from a trance, to free from a state of entrancement.
DISENTWINE, [dis'-en-twīn'], *v.t.* to untwist, to unravel.
DISENVELOP, [dis'-en-vel'-op], *v.t.* to unwrap.
DISENVIRON, [dis'-en-vīer'-on], *v.t.* to take out of its environment.
DISESPOUSE, [dis'-es-powz'], *v.t.* to separate after betrothal; (*fig.*) to dissociate oneself from.
DISESTABLISH, [dis'-es-tab'-lish], *v.t.* to depose or remove from an established position or state; to sever the connexion between church and state, to remove state control and support from an institution (*esp.* the church). [DIS and ESTABLISH].
DISESTABLISHMENT, [dis'-es-tab'-lish-ment], *n.* the act of disestablishing, the state of being disestablished.
DISESTEEM (1), [dis'-es-tēm'], *n.* lack of esteem, disrepute.
DISESTEEM (2), [dis'-es-tēm'], *v.t.* to hold in slight esteem, to think lightly of, to disrespect.
DISESTIMATION†, [dis-es'-tim-ā'-shun], *n.* disesteem.
DISEUSE, [dēz-urz'], *n.* an actress who entertains by means of spoken monologue. [Fr. *diseuse* fem. of *diseur* speaker].
DISFAME, [dis-fām'], *n.* disrepute, infamy.
DISFAVOUR (1), [dis-fā'-ver], *n.* dislike, disapproval; lack of favour, discredit.
DISFAVOUR (2), [dis-fā'-ver], *v.t.* to disapprove of, to dislike.
DISFEATURE, [dis-fē'-cher], *v.t.* to disfigure, to spoil the appearance of.
DISFIGURATION, [dis-fig'-er-ā'-shun], *n.* the act of disfiguring, the state of being disfigured; that which disfigures. [OFr. *desfiguration*].
DISFIGURE, [dis-fig'-er], *v.t.* to spoil or mar the appearance or beauty of, to deface; (*fig.*) to impair, to render ugly, to make defective. [OFr. *desfigurer*].
DISFIGUREMENT, [dis-fig'-er-ment], *n.* the act of disfiguring; the state of being disfigured; that which disfigures, a blemish, a deformity.
DISFOREST, [dis-fo'-rist], *v.t.* to disafforest.
DISFRANCHISE, [dis'-fran'-chīz], *v.t.* to deprive of civic rights and privileges, *esp.* of the right to vote, or of representation upon an elected body. [DIS AND FRANCHISE].
DISFRANCHISEMENT, [dis-fran'-chiz-ment], *n.* the act of disfranchising; the condition of being disfranchised.
DISFROCK, [dis-frok'], *v.t.* to unfrock.
DISFURNISH, [dis-fur'-nish], *v.t.* to strip of furniture; to make bare of apparatus, habiliments, or equipage.
DISGARNISH, [dis-gah'-nish], *v.t.* to strip of decoration or adornment, to lay bare of ornament.
DISGARRISON, [dis-ga'-ris-un], *v.t.* to take away a garrison from.
DISGAVEL†, [dis-gav'-el], *v.t.* (*leg.*) to deprive of tenure of gavelkind. [DIS and GAVEL].
DISGORGE, [dis-gawj'], *v.t.* and *i.* to eject from the throat, to vomit; to discharge violently, to pour forth, to empty; (*fig.*) to give up, hand over. [OFr. *desgorger*].
DISGORGEMENT, [dis-gawj'-ment], *n.* the act of disgorging.
DISGORGER, [dis-gawj'-er], *n.* an instrument for removing a hook from a fish's mouth.
DISGRACE (1), [dis-grās'], *n.* discredit, shame, loss of esteem or honour, ignominy; the state of being out of favour; a cause of shame, discredit, dishonour or reproach; a person who, or thing that, disgraces. [Fr. *disgrâce*].
DISGRACE (2), [dis-grās'], *v.t.* to bring disgrace upon, to bring into disrepute; to banish from favour or grace. [Fr. *disgracier*].
DISGRACEFUL, [dis-grās'-fōōl], *adj.* shameful, discreditable, bringing into disgrace.
DISGRACEFULLY, [dis-grās'-fōōl-i], *adv.* in disgraceful fashion.
DISGRACEFULNESS, [dis-grās'-fōōl-nes], *n.* the quality of being disgraceful.
DISGRACER, [dis-grās'-er], *n.* one who, or that which, disgraces.
DISGRADE, [dis-grād'], *v.t.* to degrade. [OFr. *desgrader*].
DISGREGATION, [dis'-greg-ā'-shun], *n.* splitting up into constituent parts, dispersal. [L. *disgregatum*, *p.pt.* of *disgregare* to separate].
DISGRUNTLED, [dis-gruntld'], *adj.* discontented, dissatisfied, continually grumbling, out of humour. [DIS and *gruntle* a form of GRUNT].
DISGUISE (1), [dis-gīz'], *n.* the act of disguising; the state of being disguised; that which disguises.
DISGUISE (2), [dis-gīz'], *v.t.* to alter the normal appearance of, to cause to resemble something else for the purposes of deception or concealment; to conceal under an assumed outward expression or air, to cloak, mask, hide. [OFr. *desguiser*].
DISGUISEDLY, [dis-gīz'-id-li], *adv.* in a disguised manner.
DISGUISEMENT, [dis-gīz'-ment], *n.* the act of disguising; the state of being disguised; a disguise.
DISGUISER, [dis-gīz'-er], *n.* one who, or that which, disguises.
DISGUISING, [dis-gīz'-ing], *n.* the act of one who disguises.
DISGUST (1), [dis-gust'], *n.* strong feeling of distaste and repugnance, loathing, abhorrence. [Fr. *desgoust* from DIS and L. *gustus* a taste].
DISGUST (2), [dis-gust'], *v.t.* to fill with disgust, to offend the moral feelings, to displease profoundly. [OFr. *desgouster*].
DISGUSTEDLY, [dis-gust'-id-li], *adv.* in disgusted fashion.
DISGUSTFUL, [dis-gust'-fōōl], *adj.* offensive to the taste; nauseous; arousing disgust.
DISGUSTFULNESS, [dis-gust'-fōōl-nes], *n.* the condition of being disgustful.
DISGUSTING, [dis-gust'-ing], *adj.* arousing disgust, loathsome, revolting, repulsive; (*coll.*) awful.
DISGUSTINGLY, [dis-gust'-ing-li], *adv.* in a disgusting fashion.
DISH (1), [dish], *n.* a rimmed, wide, shallow vessel with a flat bottom, used for holding food; anything resembling this; the food contained in this; a particular kind of food. [OE. *disc* from L. *discus*].
DISH (2), [dish], *v.t.* to put in a dish, to serve in a dish; (*coll.*) to spoil, upset, frustrate, defeat; to hollow out like a dish; **to d. up**, to present for notice or acceptance; to serve (a meal).
DISHABILITATE, [dis'-hab-il'-it-āt], *v.t.* to disqualify. [DIS and HABILITATE].
DISHABILITATION, [dis'-hab-il'-it-ā'-shun], *n.* disqualification.
DISHABILLE, DESHABILLE, dishabillé, déshabillé, [dis-ab-ēl'], *n.* undress, the state of being partly dressed or undressed, a loose informal garment. [Fr. *déshabillé* undressed].
DISHABIT†, [dis-hab'-it], *v.t.* to drive from a habitation, to dislodge from a settlement. [DIS and HABIT].
DISHABITUATE, [dis-hab-ich'-yōō-āt], *v.t.* to cause to be unaccustomed, to break off a habit, to disaccustom.
DISHALLOW, [dis-hal'-ō], *v.t.* to profane, to cause to be unhallowed, desecrate. [DIS and HALLOW].

DISHALLUCINATION, [dis'-hal-ōō-sin-ā'-shun], *n.* disillusionment.
DISHARMONIOUS, [dis'-hah-mō'-ni-us], *adj.* inharmonious, discordant.
DISHARMONIOUSLY, [dis'-hah-mō'-ni-us-li], *adv.* in disharmonious fashion.
DISHARMONIZE, [dis-hah'-mun-iz], *v.t.* to throw into discord, to upset, to cause to disagree. [DIS and HARMONIZE].
DISHARMONY, [dis-hah'-mun-i], *n.* discord, lack of harmony.
DISHCLOTH, [dish'-kloth'], *n.* a cloth used for washing dishes.
DISHCOVER, [dish'-kuv'-er], *n.* a metal or earthenware cover placed over a dish to retain the heat of its contents.
DISHEARTEN, [dis-haht'-en], *v.t.* to discourage, to dispirit, to cause to lack confidence or enthusiasm, to depress.
DISHEARTENING, [dis-haht'-ning], *adj.* discouraging, that disheartens.
DISHELM, [dis-helm'], *v.t. and i.* to remove the helmet from. [OFr. *desheaulmer*].
DISHERISON, [dis-he'-ris-on], *n.* the act of disinheriting. [OFr. *disheriteisun*].
DISHERIT†, [dis-he'-rit], *v.t.* to disinherit; (*fig.*) to deprive of. [OFr. *desheriter*].
DISHERITOR†, [dis-he'-rit-er], *n.* one who disinherits another.
DISHEVEL, (**dishevelling, dishevelled**), [dish-ev'-el], *v.t.* to let the hair hang down loosely and untidily. [OFr. *descheveler* from DIS and OFr. *chevel* hair].
DISHEVELMENT, [dish-ev'-el-ment], *n.* the condition of being dishevelled.
DISHFUL, [dish'-fōōl], *n.* as much as a dish will contain.
DISHMAT, [dish'-mat'], *n.* a table-mat.
DISHONEST, [dis-on'-ist], *adj.* not honest, given to cheating or defrauding; unfair, fraudulent, deceitful. [OFr. *deshoneste*].
DISHONESTLY, [dis-on'-ist-li], *adv.* in a dishonest fashion.
DISHONESTY, [dis-on'-is-ti], *n.* the quality of being dishonest; that which is dishonest. [OFr. *deshonesté*].
DISHONORARY, [dis-on'-er-er-i], *adj.* causing dishonour.
DISHONOUR (1), [dis-on'-er], *n.* disgrace, ignominy, loss of honour or reputation, shame, disrespect. [OFr. *deshonor*].
DISHONOUR (2), [dis-on'-er], *v.t.* to bring dishonour or shame upon; to treat with indignity, to act discreditably towards; to violate the chastity of; (*comm.*) to decline to pay or accept for payment, to refuse to meet (one's debts); to go back upon one's promise or word. [OFr. *deshonnorer*].
DISHONOURABLE, [dis-on'-er-abl], *adj.* without honour, dishonest, not honourable; discreditable, mean, base.
DISHONOURABLENESS, [dis-on'-er-abl-nes], *n.* the quality of being dishonourable.
DISHONOURABLY, [dis-on'-er-ab-li], *adv.* in a dishonourable fashion.
DISHONOURED, [dis-on'-erd], *adj.* disgraced, brought into disrepute; violated; (*comm.*) not accepted for payment; repudiated.
DISHONOURER, [dis-on'-er-er], *n.* one who brings dishonour upon anything.
DISHORN, [dis-hawn'], *v.t.* to rid of horns. [DIS and HORN].
DISHORSE, [dis-haws'], *v.t. and i.* to unhorse; to dismount.
DISHUMOUR†, [dis-hew'-mer], *n.* peevishness; ill-humour.
DISHWASHER, [dish'-wosh'-er], *n.* one who washes dishes; (*ornith.*) the pied wagtail, *Motacilla lugubris*.

DISHWASHER

DISHWATER, [dish'-wawt-er], *n.* water in which greasy plates, dishes, etc., have been washed.
DISH-WHEEL, [dish'-wēl], *n.* a wheel concave on one side and convex on the other.
DISILLUDE, [dis-i-lewd'], *v.t.* to disillusion. [DIS and ILLUDE].
DISILLUMINATE, [dis'-i-lew'-min-āt], *v.t.* to turn off the lights of; to make dark.

DISILLUSION (1), [dis'-i-lew'-zhun], *n.* the dispelling of an illusion, state of being disillusioned.
DISILLUSION (2), [dis'-i-lew'-zhun], *v.t.* to free from illusion, to undeceive, to acquaint with the tru[e] state of affairs.
DISILLUSIONMENT, [dis'-i-lew'-zhun-ment], *n.* the act of disillusioning; the state of being disillusioned.
DISIMMURE, [dis'-im-ew'-er], *v.t.* to free from imprisonment, to release from seclusion. [DIS and IMMURE].
DISIMPARK†, [dis'-im-pahk'], *v.t.* to free from the enclosure of a park.
DISIMPRISON, [dis'-im-priz'-on], *v.t.* to set free from imprisonment, to liberate.
DISIMPROVE, [dis'-im-prōōv'], *v.t. and i.* to make or grow worse.
DISIMPROVEMENT, [dis'-im-prōōv'-ment], *n.* deterioration, worsening.
DISINCARCERATE, [dis'-in-kah'-ser-āt], *v.t.* t[o] release from prison.
DISINCLINATION, [dis'-in-klin-ā'-shun], *n.* wan[t] of inclination, unwillingness, reluctance, mil[d] aversion.
DISINCLINE, [dis'-in-klīn'], *v.t.* to make unwilling or reluctant.
DISINCLOSE, see DISENCLOSE.
DISINCORPORATE, [dis'-in-kaw'-per-āt], *v.t.* t[o] deprive of corporate status or power.
DISINCORPORATION, [dis'-in-kaw'-per-ā'-shun], *n.* the act of disincorporating.
DISINDIVIDUALIZE, [dis'-in-div-id'-yōō-al-īz], *v.* to destroy the individuality of, to deprive of individual character.
DISINFECT, [dis'-in-fekt'], *v.t.* to render free from infection.
DISINFECTANT (1), [dis'-in-fekt'-ant], *n.* a substance used to disinfect.
DISINFECTANT (2), [dis'-in-fekt'-ant], *adj.* preventing infection, destroying the germs of infectious disease. [Fr. *désinfectant*].
DISINFECTION, [dis'-in-fek'-shun], *n.* the act of disinfecting.
DISINFECTOR, [dis'-in-fekt'-er], *n.* an apparatu[s] for spraying disinfectant.
DISINGENUITY, [dis'-in-jin-ew'-i-ti], *n.* insincerity, unfairness, dishonesty.
DISINGENUOUS, [dis'-in-jen'-yōō-us], *adj.* insincere, not frank, displaying a crafty meanness.
DISINGENUOUSLY, [dis'-in-jen'-yōō-us-li], *adv.* in a disingenuous fashion.
DISINGENUOUSNESS, [dis'-in-jen'-yōō-us-nes], *n.* the state or quality of being disingenuous.
DISINHABIT†, [dis'-in-hab'-it], *v.t.* to deprive of inhabitants, to cause to be uninhabited.
DISINHERISON†, [dis'-in-he'-ris-on], *n.* the act of disinheriting; the state of being disinherited.
DISINHERIT, [dis'-in-he'-rit], *v.t.* to deprive of inheritance, to refuse to allow to inherit.
DISINHERITANCE, [dis'-in-he'-rit-ants], *n.* the ac[t] of disinheriting; the state of being disinherited.
DISINHUME, [dis'-in-hewm'], *v.t.* to disinter, exhume. [DIS and INHUME].
DISINTEGRABLE, [dis-in'-tig-rabl], *adj.* able [to] be disintegrated.
DISINTEGRATE, [dis-in'-tig-rāt], *v.t. and i.* [to] separate into constituent parts; to break up in[to] fragments or parts, to fall to bits.
DISINTEGRATION, [dis-in'-tig-rā'-shun], *n.* th[e] process of disintegrating.
DISINTEGRATOR, [dis-in'-tig-rāt'-er], *n.* one wh[o] or that which, disintegrates; a machine for pulveri[z]ing or grinding to powder.
DISINTER, (**disinterring, disinterred**), [dis'-in-tur'], *v.t.* to take out of a grave, to dig up out of the earth, [to] unearth.
DISINTERESTED, [dis-in'-trest-id], *adj.* unmoved by considerations of personal interest, scrupulously fair and impartial.
DISINTERESTEDLY, [dis-in'-trest-id-li], *adv.* in disinterested fashion.
DISINTERESTEDNESS, [dis-in'-trest-id-nes], *n.* th[e] condition or quality of being disinterested.
DISINTERMENT, [dis'-in-tur'-ment], *n.* the act [of] disinterring.
DISINTHRAL, see DISENTHRAL.
DISINTHRALMENT, see DISENTHRALMENT.
DISINTRICATE, [dis-in'-trik-āt], *v.t.* to disentangle, to simplify.
DISINURE†, [dis-in-ew'-er]. *v.t.* to disaccustom, [to] make unaccustomed. [DIS and INURE].

DISINVEST, [dis'-in-vest'], *v.t.* to deprive of, divest.

DISINVESTITURE, [dis'-in-ves'-tich-er], *n.* the act of disinvesting.

DISINVOLVE, [dis'-in-volv'], *v.t.* to disentangle, to free from being involved in.

DISJECT, [dis-jekt'], *v.t.* to scatter, to hurl apart. [L. *disjectum*, *p.pt.* of *disjicere* to scatter].

DISJOIN, [dis-join'], *v.t.* to part, to disunite, to break the connexion with, to separate. [OFr. *desjoindre* from L. *disjungere* to separate].

DISJOINT, [dis-joint'], *v.t.* to put out of joint, to dislocate; to sever at the joints, to break the natural order or logical arrangement of.

DISJOINTED, [dis-joint'-id], *adj.* separated at the joints, not connected in compact fashion; out of joint; incoherent, disconnected, not progressing logically or in orderly sequence.

DISJOINTEDLY, [dis-joint'-id-li], *adv.* in disjointed fashion.

DISJOINTEDNESS, [dis-joint'-id-nes], *n.* the condition of being disjointed.

DISJOINTLY, [dis-joint'-li], *adv.* disjointedly; separately.

DISJUNCT, [dis-jungkt'], *adj.* separated, not connected with, discontinuous. [L. *disjunctum*, *p.pt.* of *disjungere* to separate].

DISJUNCTION, [dis-jungk'-shun], *n.* the act of disjoining, the state of being disjoined, absence or severance of connexion; (*logic*) a proposition offering a choice of alternatives. [L. *disjunctio*].

DISJUNCTIVE (1), [dis-jungk'-tiv], *n.* a disjunctive conjunction or proposition.

DISJUNCTIVE (2), [dis-jungk'-tiv], *adj.* separating, disjoining, severing connexion between; **d. conjunction,** (*gram.*) a conjunction linking two or more alternatives, or connecting words, phrases, or sentences suggesting opposing ideas (as *either . . . or*); **d. proposition,** (*logic*) a proposition offering a choice of alternatives, one of which must be true. [L. *disjunctivus*].

DISJUNCTIVELY, [dis-jungk'-tiv-li], *adv.* in disjunctive fashion.

DISK, DISC, [disk], *n.* a flat circular surface; a thin circular plate; (*astron.*) the visible face of the sun, moon or a planet; (*bot.*) the central rounded, flattened part of the flower-head of a radiate composite flower. [Gk. *diskos* quoit].

DISK-COUPLING, [disk'-kup'-ling], *n.* a method of coupling two rods by means of two disks keyed on the adjoining ends of the two shafts.

DISKIFEROUS, [disk-if'-er-us], *adj.* disk-bearing. [DISK and L. *ferre* to bear].

DISKIFORM, [disk'-i-fawm], *adj.* in the shape of a disk. [DISK and FORM].

DISKINDNESS, [dis-kīnd'-nes], *n.* lack of kindness.

DISKOUS†, [dis'-kus], *adj.* shaped like a disk, containing a disk. [DISK].

DISK-WHEEL, [disk'-wēl], *n.* (*motoring*) an automobile wheel having circular metal disks in place of spokes.

DISLIKE (1), [dis-līk'], *n.* distaste, aversion, repugnance.

DISLIKE (2), [dis-līk'], *v.t.* to regard with aversion, not to like.

DISLIKEN†, [dis-līk'-en], *v.t.* to make dissimilar.

DISLIKENESS†, [dis-līk'-nes], *n.* unlikeness, dissimilarity.

DISLIMB, [dis-lim'], *v.t.* to tear the limbs from, to dismember.

DISLIMN, [dis-lim'], *v.t.* to obliterate, to efface, to make the outlines indistinct. [DIS and LIMN].

DISLINK, [dis-lingk'], *v.t.* to uncouple, to disconnect.

DISLOCATE, [dis'-lok-āt'], *v.t.* to displace from its rightful position, to put out of joint; (*fig.*) to upset the normal course of, to disorganize, to interrupt the efficient functioning of. [MedL. *dislocare*].

DISLOCATION, [dis'-lok-ā'-shun], *n.* the act of dislocating; (*geol.*) displacement of portions of a stratified rock. [MedL. *dislocatio*].

DISLODGE, [dis-loj'], *v.t.* to remove from its previous established or normal position; to drive out from a position after a struggle. [OFr. *desloger*].

DISLODG(E)MENT, [dis-loj'-ment], *n.* the act of dislodging; the state of being dislodged.

DISLOYAL, [dis-loi'-al], *adj.* unfaithful, not loyal, traitorous. [OFr. *desloial*].

DISLOYALIST, [dis-loi'-al-ist], *n.* one who is disloyal to a king or government.

DISLOYALLY, [dis-loi'-al-li], *adv.* in disloyal fashion.

DISLOYALTY, [dis-loi'-al-ti], *n.* the quality or act of being disloyal.

DISMAL, [diz'-mal], *adj.* depressing, gloomy, dreary, melancholy, sorrowful. [OFr. *dismal* unlucky day from L. *dies mala*].

DISMALITY, [diz-mal'-i-ti], *n.* that which is dismal; dismal condition or quality.

DISMALLY, [diz'-mal-i], *adv.* in dismal fashion; (*coll.*) hopelessly, utterly.

DISMALNESS, [diz'-mal-nes], *n.* the condition of being dismal.

DISMAN, (**dismanning, dismanned**), [dis-man'], *v.t.* to unman; to deprive a country of its men.

DISMANTLE, [dis-mantl'], *v.t.* to strip of furnishings, essential parts, equipment, etc.; (*naut.*) to remove the sails and riggings (of a ship); (*fort.*) to pull down the defences and fortifications; to put out of action by removing the detachable parts, to take to pieces. [OFr. *desmanteller*].

DISMANTLEMENT, [dis-mantl'-ment], *n.* dismantling.

DISMARSHAL†, [dis-mah'-shal], *v.t.* to disarrange. [DIS and MARSHAL].

DISMASK†, [dis-mahsk'], *v.t.* to unmask.

DISMAST, [dis-mahst'], *v.t.* to deprive of masts, to carry away the masts of a ship.

DISMASTMENT, [dis-mahst'-ment], *n.* the act of dismasting; the state of being dismasted.

DISMAY (1), [dis-mā'], *n.* surprised alarm and dejection, apprehension and discouragement.

DISMAY (2), [dis-mā'], *v.t.* to fill with dismay, to alarm and dishearten. [OFr. *desmaier*].

DISMAYEDNESS, [dis-mād'-nes], *n.* the condition of being dismayed.

DISME, [dīm], *n.* a tenth part; a tithe. [DIME].

DISMEMBER, [dis-mem'-ber], *v.t.* to rend limb from limb, to tear to pieces, to cut off the limbs from; (*fig.*) to partition, to divide up. [OFr. *desmembrer*].

DISMEMBERMENT, [dis-mem'-ber-ment], *n.* the act of dismembering; the state of being dismembered.

DISMETTLED†, [dis-met'-ld], *adj.* deprived of mettle.

DISMISS, [dis-mis'], *v.t.* to send away, to allow to depart; (*milit.*) to allow to break ranks or organized formation upon the word of command; to release from further service or attention; to discharge from office or employment; to cease to have in one's mind; to regard lightly and take no further notice of; (*leg.*) to reject, to refuse to allow as valid. [L. *dismissum*, *p.pt.* of *dimittere* send away].

DISMISSAL, [dis-mis'-al], *n.* the act of dismissing; the state of being dismissed.

DISMISSIBLE, [dis-mis'-ibl], *adj.* liable to be dismissed.

DISMISSION, [dis-mish'-un], *n.* dismissal. [L *dimissio*].

DISMISSIVE, [dis-mis'-iv], *adj.* relating to dismissal.

DISMISSORY, [dis-mis'-er-i], *adj.* dismissive; parting.

DISMORTGAGE†, [dis-maw'-gij], *v.t.* to release from mortgage.

DISMOUNT, [dis-mount'], *v.t.* *and i.* to unhorse, to get down or cause to get down from a horse, to alight; to remove or take down from the support on which it is set.

DISNATURALIZE, [dis-nach'-er-al-īz], *v.t.* *and reflex.* to make an alien; to renounce one's native land.

DISNATURE, [dis-nā'-cher], *v.t.* to make unnatural, to cause to lose natural feelings or quality.

DISNEST, [dis-nest'], *v.t.* to dislodge from, to eject (as from a nest), to empty of.

DISOBEDIENCE, [dis'-ō-bē'-di-ents], *n.* the quality of being disobedient. [OFr. *desobedience*].

DISOBEDIENT, [dis'-ō-bē'-di-ent], *adj.* refusing to obey what is commanded, defying or wilfully disregarding orders. [OFr. *desobedient*].

DISOBEDIENTLY, [dis'-ō-bē'-di-ent-li], *adv.* in disobedient fashion.

DISOBEY, [dis-ō-bā'], *v.t.* *and i.* to refuse to obey, to disregard wilfully what is commanded or ordered. [Fr. *désobéir*].

DISOBLIGATION†, [dis-ob'-lig-ā'-shun], *n.* a disobliging act; freedom from obligation.

DISOBLIGATORY†, [dis'-ob-lig'-at-er-i], *adj.* not obligatory, freeing from obligation.

DISOBLIGE, [dis'-ob-līj'], *v.t.* to refuse to comply with or meet the wishes of, to fail to do that which would help or oblige another, to offend, hurt the feelings of. [Fr. *désobliger*].

DISOBLIGEMENT, [dis'-ob-līj'-ment], *n.* the act of disobliging.

DISOBLIGING, [dis'-ob-līj'-ing], *adj.* not obliging, unwilling or refusing to consult the wishes of others, unaccommodating.

DISOBLIGINGLY, [dis'-ob-lij'-ing-li], *adv.* in disobliging fashion.

DISOBLIGINGNESS, [dis'-ob-lij'-ing-nes], *n.* reluctance to oblige.

DISOMATOUS, [dī-sō'-mat-us], *adj.* having two bodies. [Gk. *disomatos*].

DISORB, [dis-awb'], *v.t.* to throw out from its proper orbit, to deprive of the orb.

DISORDER (1), [dis-awd'-er], *n.* lack of order, untidiness, confusion; political or social disturbance or unrest, a breach of the peace, conduct violating law and order; derangement in the bodily health or functions, disease, illness.

DISORDER (2), [dis-awd'-er], *v.t.* to throw into disorder; to disturb the normal healthy functioning of mind and body; to disarrange.

DISORDERED, [dis-awd'-erd], *adj.* out of order, upset; disarranged; thrown into disorder.

DISORDEREDNESS, [dis-awd'-erd-nes], *n.* a state of disorder.

DISORDERLINESS, [dis-awd'-er-li-nes], *n.* the condition of being disorderly.

DISORDERLY (1), [dis-awd'-er-li], *adj. and adv.* confused, untidy, without order; contrary to, or violating, law and order; unruly, creating a public disturbance; **d. house**, a brothel.

DISORDERLY (2), [dis-awd'-er-li], *adv.* in a disorderly manner.

DISORDINATE†, [dis-awd'-in-āt], *adj.* disorderly, inordinate. [OFr. *desordené*].

DISORDINATELY†, [dis-awd'-in-at-li], *adv.* in a disordinate manner.

DISORGANIZATION, [dis-awg'-an-iz-ā'-shun], *n.* the act of disorganizing, the state of being disorganized.

DISORGANIZE, [dis-awg'-an-īz], *v.t.* to throw into confusion, to upset the normal smooth functioning of. [Fr. *désorganiser*].

DISORGANIZER, [dis-awg'-an-īz-er], *n.* one who, or that which, disorganizes.

DISORIENTATE, [dis-aw'-ri-ent-āt], *v.t.* to turn away from the east; to cause to lose one's sense of direction; (*fig.*) to puzzle, to perplex.

DISOWN, [dis-ōn'], *v.t.* to renounce the ownership of, to disclaim, to refuse to acknowledge, to deny connexion with.

DISOWNMENT, [dis-ōn'-ment], *n.* the act of disowning.

DISPAIR†, [dis-pāer'], *v.t.* to break up as a pair.

DISPARADISE†, [dis-pa'-rad-īs], *v.t.* to remove from paradise.

DISPARAGE, [dis-pa'-rij], *v.t.* to pour scorn on, to depreciate, to attempt to discredit. [OFr. *desparagier* to marry into a different class].

DISPARAGEABLE, [dis-pa'-rij-abl], *adj.* liable to be disparaged.

DISPARAGEMENT, [dis-pa'-rij-ment], *n.* the act of disparaging; that which disparages; indignity, loss of credit.

DISPARAGINGLY, [dis-pa'-rij-ing-li], *adv.* in a disparaging manner.

DISPARATE, [dis'-pa-rāt], *adj.* unequal; dissimilar totally different, unable to be compared. [DIS and L. *paratum*, *p.pt.* of *parare* to prepare].

DISPARITION†, [dis-pa-rish'-un], *n.* disappearance. [OFr. *disparition*].

DISPARITY, [dis-pa'-ri-ti], *n.* inequality, dissimilarity, incongruity. [Fr. *disparité*].

DISPARK, [dis-pahk'], *v.t.* to deprive of its character or status as a park.

DISPART (1), [dis-paht'], *n.* (*gunnery*) the difference between the thickness of the metal of a gun at its mouth and at its breech, which must be allowed for in sighting; the sight placed at the mouth of a gun.

DISPART (2), [dis-paht'], *v.t. and i.* to separate, divide, cleave; to become separated, to part. [L. *dispartire*].

DISPASSION, [dis-pash'-un], *n.* freedom from passion; composure of mind.

DISPASSIONATE, [dis-pash'-un-at], *adj.* calm, not swayed by passion; impartial, uninfluenced by personal feeling, fair and unbiased.

DISPASSIONATELY, [dis-pash'-un-at-li], *adv.* in dispassionate fashion.

DISPASSIONED, [dis-pash'-und], *adj.* dispassionate, free from passion.

DISPATCH (1), DESPATCH, [dis-pach'], *n.* the act of dispatching, the state of being dispatched; alacrity, promptness, speedy performance; that which is dispatched, an official letter, report, document, or paper sent by means of a special messenger.

DISPATCH (2), DESPATCH, [dis-pach'], *v.t.* to send off; to perform, to finish; to carry out, transact with alacrity; to put to death. [It. *dispacciare* to hasten].

DISPAUPER, [dis-pawp'-er], *v.t.* to deprive of public assistance as a pauper.

DISPAUPERIZE, [dis-pawp'-er-īz], *v.t.* to release from pauperism, to free from paupers.

DISPEACE†, [dis-pēs'], *n.* lack of peace.

DISPEL, (**dispelling**, **dispelled**), [dis-pel'], *v.t.* to drive away, to banish, to scatter, to disperse, to cause to depart or vanish. [L. *dispellere*].

DISPELLER, [dis-pel'-er], *n.* one who, or that which, dispels.

DISPEND†, [dis-pend'], *v.t.* to expend; to squander; to dispense. [OFr. *despendre*].

DISPENSABLE, [dis-pens'-abl], *adj.* able to be dispensed with; (*eccles.*) conditional upon dispensation.

DISPENSABLENESS, [dis-pens'-abl-nes], *n.* the quality of being dispensable.

DISPENSARY, [dis-pens'-er-i], *n.* a place where medicines are dispensed.

DISPENSATION, [dis'-pens-ā'-shun], *n.* the act of dispensing; that which is dispensed; (*eccles.*) a system of religion, a set of divine laws; a divine decree, a judgment or purpose of fate; (*R.C.*) a licence from the Pope granting special exemption or privilege; permission granted by a bishop to a clergyman to enjoy certain privileges; (*leg.*) exception or mitigation of a law as a special concession to a particular person. [L. *dispensatio* distribution, management].

DISPENSATIVE, [dis-pens'-at-iv], *adj.* giving or issuing dispensation. [L. *dispensativus*].

DISPENSATIVELY, [dis-pens'-at-iv-li], *adv.* by dispensation.

DISPENSATOR, [dis'-pens-āt'-er], *n.* one who dispenses. [AFr. *dispensatour*].

DISPENSATORY (1), [dis-pens'-at-er-i], *n.* a book containing information about the dispensing of medicines.

DISPENSATORY (2), [dis-pens'-at-er-i], *adj.* having power to grant dispensations. [L. *dispensatorius*].

DISPENSE, [dis-pens'], *v.t and i.* to distribute, to deal out; to administer; to make up medicines from prescriptions; (*R.C.*) to issue dispensations; **to d. with**, to do without, to do away with. [L. *dispensare* to pay out].

DISPENSER, [dis-pens'-er], *n.* one who dispenses, one employed in making up medicines from prescriptions. [AFr. *dispenseor*].

DISPENSING, [dis-pens'-ing], *n.* the act of one who dispenses.

DISPEOPLE, [dis-pēpl'], *v.t.* to depopulate. [OFr. *despeupler* from L. *depopulare*].

DISPEOPLER, [dis-pēp'-ler], *n.* a depopulator.

DISPERMOUS, [dī-spurm'-us], *adj.* (*bot.*) with only two seeds. [DI and Gk. *sperma* a seed].

DISPERSAL, [dis-purs'-al], *n.* the act of dispersing; the state of being dispersed.

DISPERSE, [dis-purs'], *v.t. and i.* to scatter, to cause to depart or disappear, to banish; to spread or place with wide gaps between, so as to cover a large area; (*opt.*) to break up (rays of light); to depart, to disappear in several directions. [L. *dispersum*, *p.pt.* of *dispergere* scatter].

DISPERSEDLY, [dis-purs'-id-li], *adv.* in a dispersed fashion.

DISPERSEDNESS, [dis-purs'-id-nes], *n.* the condition of being dispersed.

DISPERSENESS†, [dis-purs'-nes], *n.* dispersedness.

DISPERSER, [dis-purs'-er], *n.* one who, or that which, disperses.

DISPERSION, [dis-pur'-shun], *n.* the act of dispersing; the state of being dispersed; diffusion; (*opt.*) the angular separation of light into its different coloured rays; **the D.**, the scattering of the Jewish tribes, *esp.* after the Babylonian Captivity. [L. *dispersio*].

DISPERSIVE, [dis-purs'-iv], *adj.* tending to disperse, or cause dispersion. [L. *dispersivus*].

DISPERSIVELY, [dis-purs'-iv-li], *adv.* in a dispersive fashion.

DISPERSONATE, [dis-purs'-on-āt], *v. reflex.* to put off one's personality.

DISPIRIT, [dis-pi'-rit], *v.t.* to deject, discourage, depress, dishearten.

DISPIRITED, [dis-pi'-rit-id], *adj.* depressed, dejected, disheartened.

DISPIRITEDLY, [dis-pi'-rit-id-li], *adv.* in a dispirited manner or mood.

DISPIRITEDNESS, [dis-pi'-rit-id-nes], *n.* the state of being dispirited.
DISPIRITMENT, [dis-pi'-rit-ment], *n.* that which dispirits.
DISPITEOUS, [dis-pit'-i-us], *adj.* without pity heartless.
DISPITEOUSLY, [dis-pit'-i-us-li], *adj.* pitilessly ruthlessly.
DISPITEOUSNESS, [dis-pit'-i-us-nes], *n.* the state of being dispiteous.
DISPLACE, [dis-plās'], *v.t.* to put out of the usual or proper place; to take the place of.
DISPLACEABLE, [dis-plās'-abl], *adj.* able to be displaced.
DISPLACEMENT, [dis-plās'-ment], *n.* the act of displacing; the state of being displaced; the amount displaced, the volume of liquid displaced by anything immersed or floating in it, the amount of water a ship can displace.
DISPLAIT, [dis-plat'], *v.t.* to untwist; to uncurl.
DISPLANT, [dis-plahnt'], *v.t.* to uproot. [OFr. *desplanter*].
DISPLAY (1), [dis-plā'], *n.* a show, an exhibition, anything spread out or shown prominently, or to attract attention; a parade, an exaggerated expression of feelings or talents in order to impress; (*print*) the arrangement of a printed page. [*Next*].
DISPLAY (2), [dis-plā'], *v.t.* to show, to exhibit, to spread out prominently to be seen; to parade; to reveal in a marked manner; (*print.*) to arrange and print in a conspicuous way. [OFr. *despleier* from L. *displicare* to unfold].
DISPLAYED, [dis-plād'], *adj.* (*her.*) having the wings expanded, and legs extended.

DISPLAYED

DISPLAYER, [dis-plā'-er], *n.* one who, or that which, displays.
DISPLEASE, [dis-plēz'], *v.t.* to offend, make angry, annoy, vex. [OFr. *desplaisir*].
DISPLEASEDNESS, [dis-plēzd'-nes], *n.* displeasure, dissatisfaction.
DISPLEASING, [dis-plēz'-ing], *adj.* disagreeable, unpleasant, arousing anger, annoying.
DISPLEASINGNESS, [dis-plēz'-ing-nes], *n.* the quality of being displeasing.
DISPLEASURE (1), [dis-plezh'-er], *n.* feeling of anger, mild indignation, annoyance, irritation. [OFr. *desplaisir*].
DISPLEASURE (2), [dis-plezh'-er], *v.t.* (*archaic*) to displease.
DISPLODE†, [dis-plōd'], *v.t. and i.* to discharge; to explode. [L. *displodere* to burst].
DISPLOSION†, [dis-plō'-zhun], *n.* the act of disploding.
DISPLUME, [dis-plo͞om'], *v.t.* to strip of plumes.
DISPONDEE, [dī-spond'-ē], *n.* (*pros.*) a double spondee containing four long syllables. [Gk. *dispondeios*].
DISPONE, [dis-pōn'], *v.t.* (*Scots leg.*) to convey, to make over. [L. *disponere* to dispose].
DISPONEE, [dis-pōn'-ē], *n.* (*Scots leg.*) the person to whom property is conveyed.
DISPONER, [dis-pōn'-er], *n.* (*Scots leg.*) one who dispones.
DISPONGE, see DISPUNGE.
DISPOPE, [dis-pōp'], *v.t.* to deprive of the position or status of pope. [MedL. *dispapare*].
DISPORT (1), [dis'-pawt], *n.* (*archaic*) play, sport recreation. [OFr. *desport*].
DISPORT (2), [dis-pawt'], *v.i. and reflex.* to play, sport, amuse oneself in pleasurable recreation, to frolic. [OFr. *desporter*].
DISPORTMENT, [dis-pawt'-ment], *n.* sport; diversion, amusement.
DISPOSABLE, [dis-pōz'-abl], *adj.* able to be disposed of, free for one's disposal.
DISPOSAL, [dis-pōz'-al], *n.* the act of disposing or disposing of; freedom or power to dispose of as one chooses.
DISPOSE, [dis-pōz'], *v.t. and i.* to arrange, set out in order, distribute; to bring about, manage, order, settle, decide; to turn, incline, to cause to adopt (a line of action, an attitude); (*archaic*) to prepare, to make ready for; **to d. of**, to get rid of, to deal effectively with; to settle; to bestow, give away; to sell; to part with. [Fr. *disposer*].
DISPOSED, [dis-pōzd'], *adj.* arranged; (*fig.*) inclined.
DISPOSEDNESS, [dis-pōzd'-nes], *n.* disposition; inclination.
DISPOSER, [dis-pōz'-er], *n.* one who, or that which, disposes.
DISPOSING, [dis-pōz'-ing], *n.* the act of one who disposes.
DISPOSITION, [dis'-poz-ish'-un], *n.* the act of disposing, the way in which anything is disposed, arrangement, order, disposal; tendency; temperament, sum of qualities constituting a person's nature; (*psych.*) an innate tendency to react in a specific way towards an object; (*Scots leg.*) a deed conveying property. [L. *dispositio*].
DISPOSITIONAL, [dis-poz-ish'-un-al], *adj.* relating to disposition.
DISPOSITIONED, [dis'-poz-ish'-und], *adj.* temperamentally inclined.
DISPOSITIVE, [dis-poz'-it-iv], *adj.* pertaining to the disposal of, directing, controlling, determining. [Fr. *dispositif*].
DISPOSITIVELY, [dis-poz'-it-iv-li], *adv.* in a dispositive fashion.
DISPOSITOR, [dis-poz'-it-or], *n.* (*astrol.*) a planet which because it is in its own house is more powerful than another in that house.
DISPOSSESS, [dis'-poz-es'], *v.t.* to cause to give up, to deprive or relieve of the possession of, to dislodge from occupation of land, etc. [OFr. *despossesser*].
DISPOSSESSION, [dis'-poz-esh'-un], *n.* the act of dispossessing; the state of being dispossessed.
DISPOSSESSOR, [dis'-poz-es'-er], *n.* one who dispossesses.
DISPOST, [dis-pōst'], *v.t.* to discharge or dismiss from a post.
DISPOSURE, [dis-pō'-zher], *n.* the disposition; disposal.
DISPRAISE (1), [dis-prāz'], *n.* censure, blame, disparagement; a dishonourable thing.
DISPRAISE (2), [dis-prāz'], *v.t.* to disparage, to censure, to speak ill of, belittle. [OFr. *despreisier* from L. *depretiare* to depreciate].
DISPRAISER, [dis-prāz'-er], *n.* one who dispraises.
DISPRAISINGLY, [dis-prāz'-ing-li], *adv.* so as to dispraise.
DISPREADER, [di-spred'-er], *n.* one who spreads about.
DISPREJUDICE, [dis-pre'-jo͝o-dis], *v.t.* to free from prejudice.
DISPRISON, [dis'-priz'-un], *v.t.* to set free, to release from prison.
DISPRIVILEGE, [dis-priv'-il-ij], *v.t.* to take away a privilege from.
DISPRIZE, [dis-prīz'], *v.t.* (*archaic*) to regard with scorn, consider of small worth. [OFr. *despriser*].
DISPROFIT, [dis-prof'-it], *v.t.* (*archaic*) to undervalue.
DISPROOF, [dis-pro͞of'], *n.* the act of disproving; the state of being disproved; that which disproves.
DISPROPORTION (1), [dis'-prop-aw'-shun], *n.* lack or absence of proportion, want of symmetry.
DISPROPORTION (2), [dis'-prop-aw'-shun], *v.t.* to make or cause to be out of proportion.
DISPROPORTIONABLE, [dis'-prop-aw'-shun-abl], *adj.* disproportionate.
DISPROPORTIONABLENESS, [dis'-prop-aw'-shun-abl-nes], *n.* the state of being disproportionate.
DISPROPORTIONABLY, [dis'-prop-aw'-shun-ab-li], *adv.* in a disproportionate manner.
DISPROPORTIONAL, [dis'-prop-aw'-shun-al], *adj.* disproportionate.
DISPROPORTIONALITY, [dis'-prop-aw'-shun-al'-i-ti], *n.* the condition of being disproportionate.
DISPROPORTIONALLY, [dis'-prop-aw'-shun-a-li], *adv.* in a disproportionate manner.
DISPROPORTIONALNESS, [dis'-prop-aw'-shun-al-nes], *n.* the condition of being disproportional.
DISPROPORTIONATE, [dis'-prop-aw'-shun-at], *adj.* not in the proper proportion, incommensurate.
DISPROPORTIONATELY, [dis'-prop-aw'-shun-at-li], *adj.* in a disproportionate manner; excessively.
DISPROPORTIONATENESS, [dis'-prop-aw'-shun-at-nes], *n.* the state or condition of disproportion.
DISPROPORTIONED, [dis'-prop-aw'-shund], *adj.* not proportioned; out of proportion.
DISPROPRIATE†, [dis-prō'-pri-āt], *v.t.* to disappropriate; to take away from.
DISPROVABLE, [dis-pro͞ov'-abl], *adj.* able to be disproved.
DISPROVAL, [dis-pro͞ov'-al], *n.* act of disproving.
DISPROVE, [dis-pro͞ov'], *v.t.* to show to be false or wrong, to refute. [OFr. *desprover*].

DISPROVER, [dis-pro͞ov'-er], *n.* one who disproves.

DISPROVIDE, [dis'-prov-īd'], *v.t.* (*archaic*) to neglect to provide for to leave unprovided.

DISPUNGE, DISPONGE, [dis-punj'], *v.t.* to express or squeeze as from a sponge.

DISPUTABLE, [dis-pewt'-abl], *adj.* open to question capable of being argued about, doubtful. [L. *disputabilis*].

DISPUTABLENESS, [dis-pewt'-abl-nes], *n.* the condition of being disputable.

DISPUTABLY, [dis-pewt'-ab-li], *adv.* in a disputable fashion.

DISPUTACITY†, [dis'-pewt-as'-i-ti], *n.* the state of being disputatious.

DISPUTANT (1), [dis'-pewt-ant], *n.* one engaged in dispute, a debater.

DISPUTANT (2), [dis'-pewt-ant], *adj.* engaged in dispute or argument, disputing.

DISPUTATION, [dis'-pewt-ā'-shun], *n.* the act of disputing, a debate, an argument, an exercise in controversy. [L. *disputatio*].

DISPUTATIOUS, [dis'-pewt-ā'-shus], *adj.* contentious, fond of disputing, argumentative.

DISPUTATIOUSLY, [dis'-pewt-ā'-shus-li], *adv.* in disputatious fashion.

DISPUTATIOUSNESS, [dis'-pewt-ā'-shus-nes], *n.* the quality of being disputatious.

DISPUTATIVE, [dis-pewt'-at-iv], *adj.* disputatious [LL. *disputativus*].

DISPUTE (1), [dis-pewt'], *n.* a verbal argument, a controversy, a discussion in which opposing points of view are debated; a quarrel, an altercation; **in d.**, under discussion.

DISPUTE (2), [dis-pewt'], *v.t. and i.* to debate, to discuss; to question, to contest, oppose, to argue about; to strive against; to engage in controversy. [L. *disputare* to investigate, to discuss].

DISPUTED, [dis-pewt'-id], *adj.* argued about, contested, controversial.

DISPUTELESS, [dis-pewt'-les], *adj.* indisputable.

DISPUTER, [dis-pewt'-er], *n.* one who disputes, a disputant.

DISQUALIFICATION, [dis-kwol'-i-fik-ā'-shun], *n.* the act of disqualifying, the state of being disqualified; that which disqualifies.

DISQUALIFY, [dis-kwol'-i-fī], *v.t.* to incapacitate, to render unfit or ineligible; to debar, to eliminate on account of failure to comply with rules or conditions.

DISQUIET (1), [dis-kwī'-et], *n.* restlessness, uneasiness, unrest, anxiety.

DISQUIET (2), [dis-kwī'-et], *adj.* restless, uneasy, disturbed, unsettled.

DISQUIET (3), [dis-kwī'-et], *v.t.* to make uneasy, to disturb, to cause to be anxious, to trouble, to upset.

DISQUIETER, [dis-kwī'-et-er], *n.* one who, or that which, disquiets.

DISQUIETFUL†, [dis-kwī'-et-fo͝ol], *adj.* full of, or causing, disquiet.

DISQUIETLY†, [dis-kwī'-et-li], *adv.* in a disquieting manner.

DISQUIETMENT†, [dis-kwī'-et-ment], *n.* act of disquieting; condition of disquiet.

DISQUIETNESS, [dis-kwī'-et-nes], *n.* the condition of disquiet.

DISQUIETOUS†, [dis-kwī'-et-us], *adj.* causing uneasiness or disquiet.

DISQUIETUDE, [dis-kwī'-it-yo͞od], *n.* want of quietude, uneasiness, anxiety, restlessness.

DISQUISITION, [dis'-kwiz-ish'-un], *n.* a systematic examination or formal investigation of a subject; a learned treatise or account, a lengthy discourse. [L. *disquisitio* enquiry].

DISQUISITIONAL, [dis'-kwiz-ish'-un-al], *adj.* pertaining to, or of the nature of, a disquisition.

DISQUISITIONARY, [dis'-kwiz-ish'-un-er-i], *adj.* disquisitional.

DISQUISITIVE, [dis-kwiz'-it-iv], *adj.* inquiring, curious, seeking information about. [L. *disquisitum*, *p.pt.* of *disquirere* to inquire].

DISRANK, [dis-rangk'], *v.t.* to reduce in rank.

DISRATE, [dis-rāt'], *v.t.* (*nav.*) to reduce in rating or rank.

DISREGARD (1), [dis'-ri-gahd'], *n.* indifference, lack of regard for, or attention to; wilful neglect.

DISREGARD (2), [dis'-ri-gahd'], *v.t.* to take no notice of, to refuse to heed, to ignore, to pay no attention to.

DISREGARDFUL, [dis'-ri-gahd'-fo͝ol], *adj.* unmindful of, ignoring, neglectful, heedless.

DISREGARDFULLY, [dis'-ri-gahd'-fo͝ol-i], *adv.* in disregardful fashion.

DISRELISH (1), [dis-rel'-ish], *n.* dislike, disfavour, distaste.

DISRELISH (2), [dis-rel'-ish], *v.t.* to dislike, to show distaste for, to view with aversion.

DISRELISHING, [dis-rel'-ish-ing], *adj.* distasteful unpleasant, repugnant.

DISREMEMBER, [dis'-ri-mem'-ber], *v.t.* to forget.

DISREPAIR, [dis'-ri-pāer'], *n.* a state of neglect, dilapidation, bad condition caused by lack of proper attention and repair.

DISREPUTABLE, [dis-rep'-yo͞ot-abl], *adj.* not reputable or respectable, degraded, discreditable, insalubrious.

DISREPUTABLY, [dis-rep'-yo͞ot-ab-li], *adv.* in disreputable fashion.

DISREPUTATION, [dis'-rep-yo͞ot-ā'-shun], *n.* (*archaic*) dishonour, disrepute.

DISREPUTE, [dis'-ri-pewt'], *n.* discredit, dishonour loss of good name, ill repute.

DISRESPECT (1), [dis'-ri-spekt'], *n.* lack of courtesy, impoliteness, absence of due deference or regard.

DISRESPECT (2), [dis'-ri-spekt'], *v.t.* to fail to respect, to treat with disrespect.

DISRESPECTABLE, [dis'-ri-spekt'-abl], *adj.* not respectable.

DISRESPECTFUL, [dis'-ri-spekt'-fo͝ol], *adj.* uncivil rude, impolite, showing want of respect or proper deference.

DISRESPECTFULLY, [dis'-ri-spekt'-fo͝ol-i], *adv.* in a disrespectful fashion.

DISRESPECTFULNESS, [dis'-ri-spekt'-fo͝ol-nes], *n.* lack of respect.

DISROBE, [dis-rōb'], *v.t. and i.* to take off the clothes or robes, undress, strip.

DISROOT, [dis-ro͞ot'], *v.t.* to tear up by the roots, to uproot.

DISRUDDERED, [dis-rud'-erd], *adj.* deprived of the rudder.

DISRUPT, [dis-rupt'], *v.t.* to break asunder, to split, to shatter, to break up. [L. *disruptum*, *p.pt.* of *disrumpere* to break into pieces].

DISRUPTION, [dis-rup'-shun], *n.* the act of disrupting; the condition of being disrupted. [L. *disruptio*].

DISRUPTIVE, [dis-rupt'-iv], *adj.* tending to disrupt.

DISRUPTURE, [dis-rup'-cher], *n.* disruption.

DISS, [dis], *n.* the fibre, *Arundo tenax*, used in making cordage. [Arab *dis*].

DISSATISFACTION, [dis-sat'-is-fak'-shun], *n.* the state of being dissatisfied, discontent; a cause of discontent; a feeling of annoyance mingled with disappointment.

DISSATISFACTORINESS, [dis-sat'-is-fakt'-er-i-nes], *n.* the quality of being dissatisfactory.

DISSATISFACTORY, [dis-sat'-is-fakt'-er-i], *adj.* unsatisfactory.

DISSATISFIED, [dis-sat'-is-fīd], *adj.* discontented; displeased and disappointed with, not satisfied.

DISSATISFY, [dis-sat'-is-fī], *v.t.* to fail to please, to make discontented, to displease by its unsatisfactoriness.

DISSEAT, [dis-sēt'], *v.t.* to remove from a seat, to unseat.

DISSECT, [di-sekt'], *v.t.* to cut in pieces; (*anat.*) to cut up systematically a dead body, plant, etc., in order to examine its structure; (*fig.*) to analyse minutely and critically, to probe. [L. *dissecare* to cut in pieces].

DISSECTIBLE, [di-sekt'-ibl], *adj.* capable of being dissected.

DISSECTING, [di-sekt'-ing], *adj.* used in dissection.

DISSECTION, [di-sek'-shun], *n.* the act of dissecting; that part which is dissected.

DISSECTIVE, [di-sekt'-iv], *adj.* relating to dissection.

DISSECTOR, [di-sekt'-er], *n.* one who dissects, one employed in making anatomical dissections.

DISSEIZE, [di-sēz'], *v.t.* (*leg.*) to deprive of possession of estates, property, etc., *esp.* wrongfully or illegally. [AFr. *disseisir*].

DISSEIZEE, [di-sēz'-ē], *n.* a person illegally dispossessed of an estate.

DISSEIZIN, [di-sēz'-in], *n.* (*leg.*) the act of disseizing; the state of being disseized. [AFr. *disseisine*].

DISSEIZOR, [di-sēz'-er], *n.* one who disseizes. [AFr. *disseizour*].

DISSELBOOM, [dis'-el-bo͞om'], *n.* the pole of an ox-wagon. [Du. *dissel* shaft and *boom* tree].

DISSEMBLANCE, [dis-em'-blants], *n.* (*archaic*) lack of resemblance; act of dissembling.

DISSEMBLE, [dis-embl'], *v.t. and i.* to conceal, to make anything seem other than it really is, to hide under a false exterior; to disguise or misrepresent one's real feelings, opinions, motives, plans, etc., in order to deceive. [L. *dissimulare*].

DISSEMBLER, [dis-emb'-ler], *n.* one who dissembles.

DISSEMBLING (1), [dis-em'-bling], *n.* dissimulation.

DISSEMBLING (2), [dis-em'-bling], *adj.* that dissembles, intended to deceive or mislead, hypocritical.

DISSEMBLINGLY, [dis-em'-bling-li], *adv.* in a dissembling manner.

DISSEMINATE, [dis-em'-in-āt], *v.t.* to scatter as seed; (*fig.*) to spread far and wide. [L. *disseminare*].

DISSEMINATION, [dis-em'-in-ā'-shun], *n.* the act of disseminating. [L. *disseminatio*].

DISSEMINATIVE, [dis-em'-in-at-iv], *adj.* liable or tending to disseminate, or become disseminated.

DISSEMINATOR, [dis-em'-in-āt-er], *n.* one who disseminates.

DISSENSION, [dis-en'-shun], *n.* disagreement, quarrel, discord, strife, lack of harmony or unanimity. [L. *dissensio*].

DISSENT (1), [dis-ent'], *n.* difference of opinion, disagreement; (*rel.*) nonconformity, refusal to accept the form of worship of the established church.

DISSENT (2), [dis-ent'], *v.i.* to disagree; (*rel.*) to observe a form of worship different from that of the established church. [L. *dissentire*].

DISSENTANEOUS, [dis'-en-tā'-ni-us], *adj.* (*archaic*) disagreeing; contrary. [L. *dissentaneus*].

DISSENTATION†, [dis-en-tā'-shun], *n.* dissension.

DISSENTER, [dis-ent'-er], *n.* one who dissents; one who practises a different form of worship from that of the established church.

DISSENTERAGE, [dis-ent'-er-ij], *n.* the condition of being a dissenter.

DISSENTERISM, [dis-ent'-er-izm], *n.* the beliefs of dissenters.

DISSENTIENT (1), [dis-en'-shent], *n.* one who holds and expresses a different opinion.

DISSENTIENT (2), [dis-en'-shent], *adj.* disagreeing, dissenting. [L. *dissentiens*].

DISSENTING, [dis-ent'-ing], *adj.* disagreeing, holding a different opinion; nonconformist, practising a different form of worship from that of the established church.

DISSENTINGLY, [dis-ent'-ing-li], *adv.* in dissenting fashion.

DISSENTIOUS, [dis-en'-shus], *adj.* quarrelsome, contentious.

DISSEPIMENT, [dis-ep'-im-ent], *n.* (*bot.*) a partition in an organ, a separating wall. [L. *dissaepimentum* partition].

DISSEPIMENTAL, [dis-ep'-im-ent-al'], *adj.* of the nature of, pertaining to, a dissepiment.

DISSERT, [dis-urt'], *v.i.* to write or deliver a dissertation upon. [L. *dissertum*, *p.pt.* of *disserere* to discuss].

DISSERTATION, [dis'-er-tā'-shun], *n.* a written or spoken discourse or systematic treatise upon some particular topic or subject, *esp.* a thesis written for a university degree. [L. *dissertatio* discourse].

DISSERTATIONAL, [dis'-er-tā'-shun-al], *adj.* pertaining to a dissertation.

DISSERTATIVE, [dis'-er-tā'-tiv], *adj.* resembling a dissertation.

DISSERTATOR, [dis'-er-tāt'-or], *n.* one who writes or delivers a dissertation. [L. *dissertator*].

DISSERVE, [di-surv'], *v.t.* to do a disservice to.

DISSERVICE, [di-surv'-is], *n.* an ill-turn; injury or harm.

DISSERVICEABLE, [di-surv'-is-abl], *adj.* injurious; hurtful, harmful.

DISSERVICEABLENESS, [di-surv'-is-abl-nes], *n.* the quality of being disserviceable.

DISSERVICEABLY, [di-surv'-is-ab-li], *adv.* in a disserviceable manner.

DISSETTLEMENT, [di-setl'-ment], *n.* (*archaic*) the act of unsettling or dislodging.

DISSEVER, [dis-ev'-er], *v.t.* to separate, divide, part, cut off. [AFr. *deseverer*].

DISSEVERANCE, [dis-ev'-er-ans], *n.* the act of dissevering; the state of being dissevered. [OFr. *desevrance*].

DISSEVERATION, [dis-ev'-er-ā'-shun], *n.* disseverance.

DISSEVERED, [dis-ev'-erd], *adj.* separated from, cut off from, divided.

DISSEVERING, [dis-ev'-er-ing], *adj.* dividing, separating.

DISSEVERMENT, [dis-ev'-er-ment], *n.* disseverance.

DISSIDENCE, [dis'-i-dens], *n.* disagreement, dissent. [L. *dissidentia*].

DISSIDENT (1), [dis'-i-dent], *n.* a dissentient, a dissenter.

DISSIDENT (2), [dis'-i-dent], *adj.* dissenting, disagreeing, differing. [L. *dissidens*].

DISSILIENCE†, [dis-il'-i-ens], *n.* the act of leaping, springing, or falling asunder.

DISSILIENT, [dis-il'-i-ent], *adj.* starting asunder; (*bot.*) bursting open sharply when ripe. [L. *dissiliens*].

DISSIMILAR, [di-sim'-il-er], *adj.* unlike, different.

DISSIMILARITY, [di-sim-il-a'-ri-ti], *n.* the quality of being dissimilar; that which is dissimilar.

DISSIMILARLY, [di-sim'-il-er-li], *adv.* in dissimilar fashion.

DISSIMILATE, [di-sim'-il-āt], *v.i.* (*philol.*) to undergo dissimilation. [L. *dissimilis* unlike].

DISSIMILATION, [di-sim'-il-ā'-shun], *n.* (*philol.*) the changing of one of two adjacent similar sounds in a word, so as to make them unlike. [*Prec.*].

DISSIMILE, [di-sim'-i-li], *n.* (*rhet.*) comparison or illustration by contraries or dissimilarities. [L. *dissimile*].

DISSIMILITUDE, [dis'-im-il'-i-tewd], *n.* unlikeness; lack of resemblance; (*rhet.*) a dissimile. [L. *dissimilitudo*].

DISSIMULATE, [di-sim'-yōō-lāt], *v.t.* and *i.* to conceal or disguise the true nature of anything in order to deceive, to dissemble; to feign, counterfeit. [L. *dissimulare*].

DISSIMULATION, [di-sim'-yōō-lā'-shun], *n.* the act of dissimulating. [L. *dissimulatio*].

DISSIMULATOR, [di-sim'-yōō-lāt'-er], *n.* a person who dissimulates.

DISSIPABLE†, [dis'-ip-abl], *adj.* capable of being dissipated. [L. *dissipabilis*].

DISSIPATE, [dis'-i-pāt], *v.t.* and *i.* to banish, to cause to disappear; to squander, to waste in wanton gaiety; to fritter away one's talents and energies in frivolous pursuits or dissolute pleasures. [L. *dissipare* to scatter].

DISSIPATED, [dis'-i-pāt'-id], *adj.* scattered; squandered; dissolute, debauched, debilitated by excessive self-indulgence.

DISSIPATION, [dis'-i-pā'-shun], *n.* the act of dissipating; debauchery, licentiousness, loose and frivolous pursuits. [L. *dissipatio*].

DISSIPATIVE, [dis'-i-pāt-iv], *adj.* inclined, tending to dissipate.

DISSIPATOR, [dis'-i-pāt'-er], *n.* one who dissipates.

DISSOCIABILITY, [di-sō'-shi-a-bil'-i-ti], *n.* the quality of being dissociable.

DISSOCIABLE, [di-sō'-shi-abl], *adj.* able to be dissociated; (*archaic*) unsociable. [L. *dissociabilis*].

DISSOCIAL, [di-sō'-shal], *adj.* anti-social, misanthropic. [L. *dissocialis*].

DISSOCIALIZE, [di-sō'-shal-īz], *v.t.* to make unsocial.

DISSOCIATE, [di-sō'-shi-āt], *v.t.* and *reflex.* to separate, to disunite; to disclaim connexion or association with; (*psych.*) to cause to develop additional centres of consciousness; **dissociated personality**, the simultaneous existence of more than one distinct personality in the same person. [L. *dissociare* to part].

DISSOCIATION, [di-sō'-shi-ā'-shun], *n.* the act of dissociating, the state of being dissociated; (*chem.*) the temporary reduction of a gas into its elements by heating; (*psych.*) the development or existence of a dissociated personality. [L. *dissociatio*].

DISSOCIATIVE, [di-sō'-shi-at-iv], *adj.* tending to dissociate.

DISSOLUBILITY, [di-sol'-yōō-bil'-i-ti], *n.* the quality of being dissoluble.

DISSOLUBLE, [di-sol'-yōōbl], *adj.* that may be dissolved. [L. *dissolubilis*].

DISSOLUBLENESS, [di-sol'-yōōbl-nes], *n.* dissolubility.

DISSOLUTE, [dis'-ol-ōōt], *adj.* loose in thought and behaviour, profligate, given to vice, debauched, licentious. [L. *dissolutum*, *p.pt.* of *dissolvere* to dissolve].

DISSOLUTELY, [dis'-ol-ōōt-li], *adv.* in a dissolute fashion.

DISSOLUTENESS, [dis'-ol-ōōt-nes], *n.* the state or quality of being dissolute.

DISSOLUTION, [dis-ol-ōō'-shun], *n.* the act of dissolving; the state of being dissolved; (*fig.*) death. [L. *dissolutio*].

DISSOLVABLE, [di-zolv'-abl], *adj.* capable of being dissolved.

DISSOLVABLENESS, [di-zolv'-abl-nes], *n.* the condition of being dissolvable.

DISSOLVE (1), [di-zolv'], *n.* (*cinema*) a method by which one sequence is made to fade into another.

DISSOLVE (2), [di-zolv'], *v.t. and i.* to cause to melt completely, to absorb in water or other liquid; to terminate, annul, rescind (an agreement or bond); to break up, to put an end to; to change into a liquid state; (*fig.*) to vanish, to melt away; to disperse, to come to an end. [L. *dissolvere* to loosen].

DISSOLVENT (1), [di-solv'-ent], *n.* a substance which has the power of dissolving.

DISSOLVENT (2), [di-solv'-ent], *adj.* able to dissolve. [L. *dissolvens*].

DISSOLVER, [di-zolv'-er], *n.* that which dissolves, a dissolvent.

DISSOLVIBLE, [di-zolv'-ibl], *adj.* dissolvable.

DISSOLVING, [di-zolv'-ing], *adj.* melting, disintegrating, fading away.

DISSONANCE, [dis'-on-ants], *n.* (*mus.*) a sound which by its introduction changes a concord into a discord; a discord; (*fig.*) disagreement. [L. *dissonantia*].

DISSONANCY†, [dis'-on-an-si], *n.* dissonance.

DISSONANT, [dis'-on-ant], *adj.* (*mus.*) inharmonious, harsh-sounding, discordant, unpleasant to the ear; (*fig.*) disagreeing, exhibiting a lack of unity, out of keeping with. [L. *dissonans*].

DISSONANTLY, [dis'-son-ant-li], *adv.* in dissonant fashion.

DISSUADE, [di-swād'], *v.t.* to advise against; to persuade to refrain, to discourage. [L. *dissuadere*].

DISSUASION, [di-swā'-zhun], *n.* the act of dissuading; advice against a thing.

DISSUASIVE, [di-swāz'-iv], *adj.* tending or endeavouring to dissuade.

DISSUASIVELY, [di-swāz'-iv-li], *adv.* in a dissuasive manner.

DISSUASORY†, [di-swāz'-er-i], *adj.* dissuasive.

DISSUNDER, [di-sund'-er], *v.t.* to separate, to rend, to tear in pieces.

DISSYLLABIC, DISYLLABIC, [dis'-il-ab'-ik], *adj.* containing two syllables. [DI (2) and SYLLABIC].

DISSYLLABIFICATION, [dis'-il-ab'-i-fi-kā'-shun], *n.* the act of forming into two syllables.

DISSYLLABIFY, [dis'-il-ab'-i-fī], *v.t.* to form into two syllables.

DISSYLLABISM, [di-sil'-ab-izm], *n.* the state of having two syllables.

DISSYLLABIZE, [di-sil'-ab-iz], *v.t.* to dissyllabify.

DISSYLLABLE, DISYLLABLE, [di-sil'-abl], *n.* a word made up of two syllables.

DISSYMMETRY, [di-sim'-et-ri], *n.* lack of symmetry, symmetry arranged contrariwise.

DISTAFF, [dis'-tahf], *n.* the staff on which the flax wool or tow was formerly wound in spinning; that part of a spinning-wheel to which the flax or wool was fastened; (*fig.*) the female line; women's occupation; **d. side**, the female ancestors or heirs in a pedigree; **d. thistle**, the thistle, *Carthamus alatus*, so called from its woolly flowers. [OE. *distæf*].

DISTAFF

DISTAIN†, [di-stān'], *v.t.* to stain; to sully, to tarnish. [OFr. *desteindre*].

DISTAL, [dis'-tal], *adj.* (*anat.*) away from, or farthest from, the point of growth or attachment, terminal. [DISTANT].

DISTANCE (1), [dis'-tants], *n.* the intervening space between two objects or separate points; the amount of such space, *esp.* when considerable; a remote point; remoteness; a considerable intervening period of time; difference, degree of remoteness; (*milit.*) the space between soldiers in rank, or the space between ranks; (*paint.*) the representation of different relative positions of various objects in a landscape; (*horse-racing*) an arbitrary point approximately one furlong from the winning-post; (*archaic*) coldness, reserve, aloofness; **in the d.**, far away; **to keep one's d.**, to keep away from; **to keep at a d.**, to treat with reserve. [Fr. from L. *distantia*].

DISTANCE (2), [dis'-tants], *v.t.* to separate by some distance; to outstrip.

DISTANT, [dis'-tant], *adj.* far off, separated or removed from by some considerable distance; remote; not closely related; cold, aloof, reserved; slight, faint; **d. signal**, a railway signal placed well in advance of a home signal, as an indication of the way in which the latter is set. [L. *distans*].

DISTANTLY, [dis'-tant-li], *adv.* remotely, at a distance; coldly.

DISTASTE (1), [dis-tāst'], *n.* dislike, disrelish feeling of repugnance or disgust.

DISTASTE (2), [dis-tāst'], *v.t.* (*archaic*) to have a distaste for; to displease, hurt.

DISTASTEFUL, [dis-tāst'-fōōl], *adj.* unpleasant, offensive, disagreeable.

DISTASTEFULLY, [dis-tāst'-fōōl-i], *adv.* in distasteful fashion.

DISTASTEFULNESS, [dis-tāst'-fōōl-nes], *n.* disagreeableness.

DISTASTIVE†, [dis-tāst'-iv], *adj.* distasteful.

DISTEMPER (1), **DESTEMPER**†, [dis-tem'-per], *n* a catarrhal disease affecting the mucous membrane of dogs; (*fig.*) disturbance, unrest, discontent; (*archaic*) a disordered condition of the mind or body, indisposition. [DISTEMPER (3)].

DISTEMPER (2), [dis-tem'-per], *n.* a special preparation of colour mixed with size or a gluey solution, applied to walls and ceilings in interior decoration; a method of painting using this. [DISTEMPER (4)].

DISTEMPER (3), [dis-tem'-per], *v.t.* to disorder, to indispose; (*archaic*) to upset, make bad-tempered. [DIS and L. *temperare* to mingle, proportion].

DISTEMPER (4), [dis-tem'-per], *v.t.* to coat or paint with distemper. [OFr. *destremper* to soak].

DISTEMPERANCE†, [dis-tem'-per-ants], *n.* distemper, intemperance. [OFr. *destemprance*].

DISTEMPERATE†, [dis-tem'-per-at], *n.* intemperate; disordered, diseased; immoderate. [MedL. *distemperatus*].

DISTEMPERATURE†, [dis-tem'-per-ach-er], *n.* bad weather; unhealthy state of the atmosphere; disorder of the mind or body; intemperance; (*fig.*) unrest.

DISTEMPERED, [dis-tem'-perd], *adj.* diseased in body or mind; (*fig.*) discontented, disaffected.

DISTEMPEREDNESS, [dis-tem'-perd-nes], *n.* the condition of being distempered.

DISTEND, [dis-tend'], *v.t. and i.* to cause to swell out, to stretch out, inflate, to expand in all directions; to swell out; to be greatly increased in size. [L. *distendere*].

DISTENSIBILITY, [dis-ten'-si-bil'-i-ti], *n.* the quality or state of being distensible.

DISTENSIBLE, [dis-tens'-ibl], *adj.* that may be distended. [L. *distensum*, *p.pt.* of *distendere*].

DISTENSION, DISTENTION, [dis-ten'-shun], *n.* the act of distending; the state of being distended. [L. *distensio*].

DISTENSIVE, [dis-tens'-iv], *adj.* distensible.

DISTENT†, [dis-tent'], *adj.* distended. [L. *distentus*].

DISTENTION, see DISTENSION.

DISTERITE, [dis'-ter-īt], *n.* a silicate of aluminium and magnesium; a species of clintonite. [Unkn.].

DISTHENE, [dis-thēn'], *n.* (*min.*) kyanite. [DI (2) and Gk. *sthenos* strength].

DISTICH, [dis'-tik], *n.* (*pros.*) a couplet, a pair of lines, often rhyming, and together forming a unit. [Gk. *distikhon*].

DISTICHOUS, [dis'-tik-us], *adj.* (*bot.*) arranged in two rows. [Gk. *distikhos* in two lines].

DISTIL, (**distilling, distilled**), [dis-til'], *v.t. and i.* to cause to fall in drops; to evaporate a liquid and cause it to condense again, to extract or refine in this way; to manufacture alcoholic spirits, etc., by this means; (*fig.*) to refine; to flow slowly and gently. [L. *distillare* to trickle].

DISTILLABLE, [dis-til'-abl], *adj.* capable of being distilled; fit for distillation.

DISTILLATE, [dis'-til-āt], *n.* the refined substance extracted by distillation. [L. *distillare*].

DISTILLATION, [dis'-til-ā'-shun] *n.* the act of distilling; the distillate; (*fig.*) the extracted or refined essence; **fractional d.**, distillation of a compound by heating gradually so that all the constituent liquids may be distilled and collected separately; **destructive d.**, the distillation of substances at high temperatures so that the compounds are broken down. [L. *distillatio*].

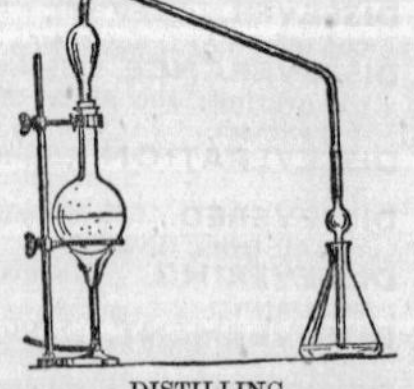
DISTILLING

DISTILLATORY, [dis-til'-at-er-i], *adj.* pertaining to distilling.

DISTILLER, [dis-til'-er], *n.* one who distils, *esp.* alcoholic spirits.

DISTILLERY, [dis-til'-er-i], *n.* the place where distilling is extensively carried on.

DISTILLING, [dis-til'-ing], *n.* the act or process of extracting or purifying a fluid by distillation.

DISTILMENT, [dis-til'-ment], *n.* distillation; the distillate.

DISTINCT, [dis-tingkt'], *adj.* separate, individual, different, distinguishable; clear, plain, well defined; marked, perceptible. [L. *distinctus* separate, adorned].

DISTINCTION, [dis-tingk'-shun], *n.* the act of distinguishing, that which distinguishes, a difference, distinctive traits of pre-eminence or merit; a special award or honour as a recognition of superior merit or outstanding conduct; the quality of being distinguished by something unusually good. [L. *distinctio*].

DISTINCTIVE, [dis-tingkt'-iv], *adj.* that distinguishes; peculiar, distinguishable.

DISTINCTIVELY, [dis-tingkt'-iv-li], *adv.* in a distinctive or distinct manner.

DISTINCTIVENESS, [dis-tingkt'-iv-nes], *n.* state or quality of being distinctive.

DISTINCTLY, [dis-tingkt'-li], *adv.* in a distinct manner, plainly.

DISTINCTNESS, [dis-tingkt'-nes], *n.* the quality or condition of being distinct.

DISTINCTURE†, [dis-tingk'-cher], *n.* distinction, distinctness.

DISTINGUISH, [dis-ting'-gwish], *v.t. and i.* to recognize a difference between; to separate or make distinct by some characteristic mark or feature; to mark out as different, to differentiate; to perceive; (*reflex.*) to become eminent, to achieve prominence. [L. *distinguere*].

DISTINGUISHABLE, [dis-ting'-gwish-abl], *adj.* able to be distinguished.

DISTINGUISHABLENESS, [dis-ting'-gwish-abl-nes], *n.* the state or quality of being distinguishable.

DISTINGUISHABLY, [dis-ting'-gwish-ab-li], *adv.* in a distinguishable manner.

DISTINGUISHED, [dis-ting'-gwisht], *adj.* marked out by some outstanding trait or feature; celebrated, famous, eminent, noteworthy.

DISTINGUISHEDLY, [dis-ting'-gwisht-li], *adv.* in a distinguished fashion.

DISTINGUISHER, [dis-ting'-gwish-er], *n.* a person who, or that which, distinguishes.

DISTINGUISHINGLY, [dis-ting'-gwish-ing-li], *adj.* with distinction; so as to distinguish.

DISTINGUISHMENT, [dis-ting'-gwish-ment], *n.* the act of distinguishing; the state of being distinguished; that which distinguishes.

DISTITLE†, [dis-tītl'], *v.t.* to deprive of right or title.

DISTOMUM, [dis'-tom-um], *n.* a genus of intestinal worms with two suckers at the extremity of their mouth. [Gk. *distomos* double-mouthed].

DISTORT, [dis-tawt'], *v.t.* to twist out of the habitual or regular shape or natural position; (*fig.*) to cause to seem other than it actually is, to misrepresent, to warp. [L. *distortum*, *p.pt.* of *distorquere* to twist].

DISTORTION, [dis-taw'-shun], *n.* the act of distorting; the state of being distorted; that which is distorted; the degree to which anything is distorted; (*wirel.*) the change of wave form of vibrations during transmission or reception, causing lack of clearness of reception. [L. *distortio*].

DISTORTIONIST, [dis-taw'-shun-ist], *n.* a contortionist.

DISTORTIVE, [dis-tawt'-iv], *adj.* producing distortion; distorted.

DISTORTOR, [dis-tawt'-er], *n.* (*anat.*) a muscle that distorts. [L. *distortor*].

DISTRACT, [dis-trakt'], *v.t.* to divert, to turn (the attention) away from an object; to prevent or hinder from concentrating upon; to bewilder or perplex by conflicting alternatives or too many problems and interests; to harass the mind to the state of derangement. [L. *distractum*, *p.pt.* of *distrahere* to pull apart].

DISTRACTED, [dis-trakt'-id], *adj.* perplexed, harassed, extremely worried or disturbed, driven to a state of madness.

DISTRACTEDLY, [dis-trakt'-id-li], *adv.* in distracted fashion.

DISTRACTEDNESS, [dis-trakt'-id-nes], *n.* condition of being distracted.

DISTRACTER, [dis-trakt'-er], *n.* one who, or that which, distracts.

DISTRACTIBLE, [dis-trakt'-ibl], *adj.* that may be drawn aside or distracted.

DISTRACTILE†, [dis-trakt'-īl], *adj.* (*bot.*) elastic, able to be drawn apart.

DISTRACTINGLY, [dis-trakt'-ing-li], *adv.* so as to distract.

DISTRACTION, [dis-trak'-shun], *n.* the act of distracting, the state of being distracted; that which distracts; diversion, relaxation from serious affairs; extreme agitation or disturbance of the mind; disorder, confusion; **to d.**, to the point of madness. [L. *distractio* a pulling apart].

DISTRACTIVE, [dis-trakt'-iv], *adj.* tending to distract.

DISTRAIN, [dis-trān'], *v.i.* to confiscate the goods and possessions of a debtor by way of, or to secure, payment of the debt. [OFr. *destraindre*].

DISTRAINABLE, [dis-trān'-abl], *adj.* liable to be distrained upon.

DISTRAINEE, [dis-trān-ē'], *n.* a person upon whom distraint is levied.

DISTRAINER, DISTRAINOR, [dis-trān'-er], *n.* (*leg.*) one who levies distraint. [AFr. *destreinor*].

DISTRAINT, [dis-trānt'], *n.* the act of distraining a debtor's goods and possessions. [OFr. *destraint*].

DISTRAIT, [dis-trā'], *adj.* absent-minded, thinking of something else. [Fr. *distrait*].

DISTRAUGHT, [dis-trawt'], *adj.* wildly agitated or upset, beside oneself with anxiety, fear or worry; mad. [ME. *distrauht* from L. *distractus*].

DISTRESS (1), [dis-tres'], *n.* sorrow, grief, extreme unhappiness; a state of danger, peril; a source of affliction or anxiety; want of necessaries of life, severe poverty and affliction; physical exhaustion; (*leg.*) the right of a creditor or landlord to distrain upon a debtor or tenant for non-payment of debt or rent; distraint. [OFr. *destresse*].

DISTRESS (2), [dis-tres'], *v.t.* to grieve, pain, to cause distress to; to harass; to cause misery and suffering to; (*leg.*) to distrain; (*reflex.*) to worry. [OFr. *destresser*].

DISTRESSED, [dis-trest'], *adj.* suffering distress; exhausted, harassed; lacking the bare necessaries of life; **d. area**, an industrial area in which there is mass unemployment and widespread poverty.

DISTRESSEDNESS, [dis-tres'-id-nes], *n.* a state or condition of being distressed.

DISTRESSFUL, [dis-tres'-fŏŏl], *adj.* causing distress; showing marked signs of distress.

DISTRESSFULLY, [dis-tres'-fŏŏl-i], *adv.* in a distressful manner.

DISTRESSING, [dis-tres'-ing], *adj.* causing distress, that distresses.

DISTRESSINGLY, [dis-tres'-ing-li], *adv.* in distressing fashion.

DISTRIBUTABLE, [dis-trib'-yōōt-abl], *adj.* able to be distributed.

DISTRIBUTARY (1), [dis-trib'-yōōt-er-i], *n.* a tributary or fork of a river that does not rejoin the main stream after leaving it.

DISTRIBUTARY (2), [dis-trib'-yōōt-er-i], *adj.* that distributes or is distributed.

DISTRIBUTE, [dis-trib'-yōōt], *v.t.* to divide amongst a number, to share out, apportion; to administer, deal out; to deliver, give out to a number of people, etc.; to divide into parts or classes; to spread out over a large surface; (*typ.*) to separate type used for printing, and replace the letters in their proper boxes; (*log.*) to employ a term in all the implications of its meaning. [L. *distributum*, *p.pt.* of *distribuere*].

DISTRIBUTER, see DISTRIBUTOR.

DISTRIBUTION, [dis'-trib-ew'-shun], *n.* the act of distributing; the state of being distributed; the way in which anything is distributed; (*political economy*) the distributing of commodities amongst consumers; the sharing-out of profits on products amongst those concerned in their production. [L. *distributio*].

DISTRIBUTIONAL, [dis'-trib-ew'-shun-al], *adj.* relating to distribution.

DISTRIBUTISM, [dis-trib'-yōōt-izm], *n.* the theory that the ownership of land and capital should be vested in the greatest possible number of individuals.

DISTRIBUTIST, [dis-trib'-yōōt-ist], *n.* a supporter of, or believer in, distributism.

DISTRIBUTIVE (1), [dis-trib'-yōōt-iv], *n.* (*gram.*) a distributive pronoun or adjective.

DISTRIBUTIVE (2), [dis-trib'-yōōt-iv], *adj.* pertaining to, or engaged in, distribution; (*log.*, *gram.*) pertaining or referring to each separate individual of a class or group. [L. *distributivus*].

DISTRIBUTIVELY, [dis-trib'-yōōt-iv-li], *adv.* in a distributive manner, singly, individually.

DISTRIBUTIVENESS, [dis-trib'-yōōt-iv-nes], *n.* the quality or state of being distributive.

DISTRIBUTOR, DISTRIBUTER, [dis-trib'-yōōt-er], *n.* one who, or that which, distributes; (*motoring*) that part of a magneto which distributes the current to the plugs.

DISTRICT (1), [dis'-trikt], *n.* a limited area of land

under the management and authority of an official person or administrative body; a region, a particular part of a country, city, town, etc., a locality; **D. Commissioner**, a magistrate or government official exercising semi-judicial authority in India or a British Crown Colony; **d. visitor**, a church-worker helping a clergyman in a particular area in his parish. [MedL. *districtus*].

DISTRICT (2), [dis'-trikt], *v.t.* to divide into districts.

DISTRICTION†, [dis-trik'-shun], *n.* severity, strictness. [L. *districtio*].

DISTRINGAS, [dis-tring'-gas], *n.* (*leg.*) a writ commanding the sheriff to distrain a person for debt, or to secure his appearance at court at a certain time; a notice served upon a company or public body and demanding notification to the server before transferring shares or stock or paying dividends. [L. *distringas, 2nd person pres.subj.* of *distringere* to distrain].

DISTRUST (1), [dis-trust'], *n.* doubt, want of confidence or trust in, suspicion.

DISTRUST (2), [dis-trust'], *v.t.* to be unable to trust to place no reliance or belief in, to doubt, suspect.

DISTRUSTER, [dis-trust'-er], *n.* one who distrusts.

DISTRUSTFUL, [dis-trust'-fōōl], *adj.* having no trust in, suspicious, doubtful, provoking or feeling distrust for.

DISTRUSTFULLY, [dis-trust'-fōōl-i], *adv.* in a distrustful fashion.

DISTRUSTFULNESS, [dis-trust'-fōōl-nes], *n.* the quality or state of being distrustful.

DISTRUSTINGLY, [dis-trust'-ing-li], *adv.* in a distrustful fashion.

DISTRUSTLESS†, [dis-trust'-les], *adj.* having no distrust.

DISTUNE, [dis-tewn'], *v.t.* to put out of tune.

DISTURB, [dis-turb'], *v.t.* to stir from a state of rest or tranquility, to ruffle the calmness of; to cause to alter its position or condition; to trouble, disquiet, make uneasy; to interrupt, upset, interfere with; to agitate, unsettle. [L. *disturbare*].

DISTURBANCE, [dis-turb'-ants], *n.* the act of disturbing; that which disturbs; anything disturbed; a row, disorder, uproar; a breach of the peace; (*leg.*) the hindering or disquieting of a person in the lawful and peaceable enjoyment of his rights.

DISTURBANT, [dis-turb'-ant], *adj.* disturbing. [L. *disturbans*].

DISTURBATIVE†, [dis-turb'-at-iv], *adj.* tending to disturb.

DISTURBED, [dis-turbd'], *adj.* agitated, upset; moved or altered from its position or normal condition; ruffled; made uneasy, disquieted.

DISTURBER, [dis-turb'-er], *n.* one who, or that which, disturbs.

DISTURBING, [dis-turb'-ing], *adj.* that disturbs, unsettling, upsetting.

DISTYLE, [dis'-tīl], *n.* a portico with two columns. [DI (2) and STYLE (1)].

DISTYLE

DISULPHATE, [dī-sulf'-āt], *n.* (*chem.*) a substance containing two equivalents of sulphuric acid with one of the base.

DISULPHIDE, [dī-sulf'-īd], *n.* (*chem.*) a compound in which two atoms of sulphur are combined with another element or radical.

DISUNIFORM, [dis-yōō'-ni-fawm], *adj.* not uniform.

DISUNIFORMITY, [dis'-yōō-ni-fawm'-i-ti], *n.* lack of uniformity.

DISUNION, [dis-yōō'-ni-on], *n.* severance, the breaking of a union, rupture; dissension, lack of concord.

DISUNIONIST, [dis-yōō'-ni-on-ist], *n.* (*U.S.*) a person opposed to union; a supporter of disunion.

DISUNITE, [dis'-yōō-nīt'], *v.t. and i.* to separate, part; to break the union or bond between; to become separate.

DISUNITER, [dis'-yōō-nīt'-er], *n.* one who, or that which, disunites.

DISUNITY, [dis-yōō'-nit-i], *n.* lack of unity.

DISUSAGE†, [dis-yōōz'-ij], *n.* disuse.

DISUSE (1), [dis-yōōs'], *n.* the state of being no longer in use, discontinuance of a custom or practice, lack of use.

DISUSE (2), [dis-yōōz'], *v.t.* to cease to use.

DISUSED, [dis-yōōzd'], *adj.* no longer used, obsolete.

DISVALUATION†, [dis'-val'-yōō-ā'-shun], *n.* depreciation, disparagement.

DISVALUE, [dis-val'-yōō], *v.t.* to undervalue, to treat as worthless, depreciate.

DISVELOP†, [dis-vel'-op], *v.t.* (*her.*) to unfurl, to spread, to display. [DEVELOP].

DISVOUCH†, [dis-vowch'], *v.t.* to contradict, disavow.

DISWARN†, [dis-wawn'], *v.t.* to warn not to.

DISWARREN, [dis-wo'-ren], *v.t.* to deprive of the status or condition of a warren.

DISWIT†, (**diswitting, diswitted**), [dis-wit'], *v.t.* to drive insane.

DISWORSHIP, [dis-wur'-ship], *n.* a disgrace, a discredit.

DISYLLABIC, see DISSYLLABIC.

DISYLLABLE, see DISSYLLABLE.

DISYOKE, [dis-yōk'], *v.t.* to unyoke, untrammel.

DITAL, [dit'-al], *n.* a thumb-key on stringed plucked instruments such as the guitar, to raise the pitch of a string by a semitone. [It. *dito* finger].

DITCH (1), [dich], *n.* a long, narrow trench round a fortified place for purposes of defence; a long, narrow channel dug as a watercourse or an open drain; any natural channel by the side of the road that drains water. [OE. *dic*].

DITCH (2), [dich], *v.t. and i.* to construct or repair ditches; (*coll.*) to drive into a ditch.

DITCHER, [dich'-er], *n.* one who constructs and repairs ditches.

DITCHING, [dich'-ing], *n.* the art of digging and repairing ditches.

DITCH-WATER, [dich'-wawt-er], *n.* stagnant water; **dull as d.**, (*coll.*) extremely dull and boring.

DITETRAHEDRAL†, [dī'-tet-ra-hē'-dral], *adj.* (*min.*) in the form of a tetrahedral prism with dihedral summits.

DITHECAL, [dī-thē'-kal], *adj.* dithecous.

DITHECOUS, [dī-thē'-kus], *adj.* (*bot.*) having two cells, bilocular. [DI (2) and Gk. *theke* case].

DITHEISM, [dī'-thē-izm], *n.* belief in the existence of two gods or supreme powers, *esp.* belief in good and evil as the two guiding forces.

DITHEIST, [dī-thē-ist], *n.* one who believes in ditheism.

DITHEISTIC, [dī'-thē-ist'-ik], *adj.* relating to ditheism.

DITHEISTICAL, [dī'-thē-ist'-ik-al], *adj.* ditheistic.

DITHER, [dITH'-er], *v.i.* (*coll.*) to shiver, shake or quiver continually, to tremble violently, to quake. [Unkn.].

DITHYRAMB, [dith'-i-ram], *n.* a hymn in honour of Bacchus, written in an extravagantly rhapsodical style; an ode or chant of a similar boisterous character. [Gk. *dithurambos*].

DITHYRAMBIC, [dith'-i-ram'-bik], *adj.* of the nature of a dithyramb; wild, impetuous, vehement.

DITHYRAMBUS, [dith'-i-ram'-bus], *n.* a dithyramb.

DITONE, [dī'-tōn], *n.* (*mus.*) a major third, an interval consisting of two tones. [Gk. *ditonos* two-toned].

DITRICHOTOMOUS, [dit'-ri-kot'-om-us], *adj.* (*bot.*) splitting up into double or treble ramifications. [DI (2), Gk. *tricha* three times and *tomos* cut].

DITRIGLYPH, [dī-trī'-glif], *n.* (*arch.*) a space between two columns, large enough for two triglyphs in the frieze, between the triglyphs that stand over the columns.

DITROCHEE, [dī-trō'-kē], *n.* a double trochee, a foot containing two trochees. [Gk. *ditrokhaios*].

DITTANDER, [dit-and'-er], *n.* pepperwort, *Lepidium latifolium*. [DITTANY].

DITTANY, [dit'-a-ni], *n.* (*bot.*) an aromatic plant, *Origanum dictamnus*, yielding a sweet-scented oil. [OFr. *ditan* from Gk. *diktamnon* from Mount *Dicte* in Crete].

DITTIED, [dit'-id], *adj.* sung, adapted to music.

DITTO, [dit'-ō], *n.* (contracted into *do.*), that which has been said before; the same thing. [It. *ditto* said].

DITTOGRAPHY, [dit-og'-raf-i], *n.* accidental repetition of a word or letter by a copyist. [Gk. *dittos* double and *graphia* writing].

DITTY, [dit'-i], *n.* a short simple song or poem to be sung. [OFr. *dité*].

DITTY-BOX, [dit'-i-boks'], *n.* a small box in which sailors keep various personal articles. [Unkn.].

DIURESIS, [dī'-yōō-rē'-sis], *n.* (*med.*) excessive discharge of urine. [DI (3) and Gk. *ouresis* urination].

DIURETIC (1) [dī'-yōō-rē'-tik], *n.* a diuretic medicine.

DIURETIC (2), [dī'-yōō-rē'-tik], *adj.* stimulating urination or excretion. [Gk. *diouretikos*].

DIURNA, [dī-urn'-a], *n.*(*pl.*) a family of insects,

Ephemerae, appearing only in the daytime. [L. *diurnus* daily].

DIURNAL (1), [dī-urn'-al], *n.* (*eccles.*) a service book containing the offices for the day.

DIURNAL (2) [dī-urn'-al], *adj.* belonging to the daytime; daily, performed in a day, occurring or recurring each day. [L. *diurnalis*].

DIURNALLY, [dī-urn'-al-i], *adv.* daily; every day.

DIURNALNESS, [dī-urn'-al-nes], *n.* the quality of being diurnal.

DIUTURNAL, [dī-yōō-turn'-al], *adj.* of considerable duration. [L. *diuturnus* long lasting].

DIUTURNITY, [dī'-yōō-turn'-it-i], *n.* long duration, lastingness. [L. *diuturnitas*].

DIVA, [dē'-va], *n.* a prima donna, a leading woman singer. [It. *diva* a goddess].

DIVAGATE, [dī'-va-gāt'], *v.i.* to wander about; to digress, stray, ramble. [L. *divagare*].

DIVAGATION, [dī'-va-gā'-shun], *n.* the act of divagating.

DIVALENT, [dī-vā'-lent], *adj.* (*chem.*) combining with two atoms of a radical, bivalent.

DIVALI, [di-vah'-lē], *n.* the feast of lanterns, the Hindu festival at the end of September. [Hind. *divali*].

DIVAN, [div-an'], *n.* an Oriental council of State (*esp.* Turkish); the chamber in which the Turkish State Council meets; a court of justice; a long, low, backless couch or raised seat fitted with cushions; a room open on one side to face a garden, lawn, etc.; a smoking-room; a cigar shop; a collection of Oriental lyric poems. [Pers. *diwan*].

DIVARICATE (1), [dī-va'-ri-kāt], *adj.* (*bot.*) branching off at a wide angle. [L. *divaricatus*].

DIVARICATE (2), [dī-va'-ri-kāt], *v.t. and i.* to fork, split up into branches, to branch off at an angle; to spread apart, open. [L. *divaricare*].

DIVARICATION, [dī-va'-ri-kā'-shun], *n.* the act of divaricating; that which divaricates; the state of being divaricated; the point of forking.

DIVE (1), [dīv], *n.* a plunge head first into water, with the arms held above the head; (*coll.*) an underground place of refreshment; a basement or cellar in which drinking, singing, etc., are carried on.

DIVE (2), [dīv], *v.i.* to perform a dive or series of dives; to sink down under water suddenly when swimming; to go under water in a specially constructed water-tight suit, etc.; to swoop down suddenly and quickly in the air from a height; to hurl oneself at, to dart down or into; to thrust one's hand rapidly into a receptacle; (*fig.*) to study rapidly and intensely; to submerge. [OE. *dyfan*].

DIVE-BOMBER, [dīv'-bom-er], *n.* an aeroplane designed to dive low in order to drop its bombs.

DIVELLENT, [dī-vel'-ent], *adj.* drawing asunder; separating, parting. [L. *divellens*].

DIVELLICATE, [dī-vel'-ik-āt], *v.t.* to pull in pieces, pluck apart. [DI (1) and L. *vellicare* to pluck].

DIVER, [dīv'-er], *n.* one who dives, *esp.* one who performs under-water tasks in a specially made diving dress, etc.; one of several species of water birds that dive, *esp.* a bird of the genus *Colymbus*.

DIVER

DIVERBERATION†, [dī-vur'-ber-ā'-shun], *n.* a beating or striking. [L. *diverberare* to strike].

DIVERGE, [dī-vurj'], *v.i.* to branch off along different courses at a particular point, to proceed in different directions; to separate; to deviate; to vary, differ; to depart from the stock form. [DI (1) and L. *vergere* to turn].

DIVERGEMENT, [dī-vurj'-ment], *n.* act of diverging.

DIVERGENCE, DEVERGENCE, [dī-vurj'-ents], *n.* the act of diverging; the amount anything diverges.

DIVERGENCY, [dī-vurj'-en-si], *n.* divergence.

DIVERGENT, [dī-vurj'-ent], *adj.* branching off in different directions, deviating, proceeding along different courses, forking in widening branches.

DIVERGINGLY [dī-vurj'-ing-li], *adv.* in a diverging way.

DIVERS, [dīv'-erz], *adj.* (*archaic*) different, various, several, sundry. [OFr. *divers*].

DIVERSE, [dī-vurs' di-vurs'], *adj.* different, varied, unlike.

DIVERSELY, [dī-vurs'-li], *adv.* in diverse fashion.

DIVERSIFIABLE, [di-vurs'-i-fī'-abl], *adj.* capable of being diversified.

DIVERSIFICATION, [dī-vurs'-i-fik-ā'-shun], *n.* the act of diversifying; the state of being diversified.

DIVERSIFORM, [dī-vurs'-i-fawm'], *adj.* of various forms or shapes.

DIVERSIFY, [dī-vurs'-i-fī], *v.t.* to make different, to give variety to. [MedL. *diversificare* to make unlike].

DIVERSILOQUENT†, [dī'-vers-il'-ō-kwent], *adj.* speaking in different ways. [DIVERSE and L. *loquens* speaking].

DIVERSION, [dī-vur'-shun], *n.* the act of diverting; that which diverts or distracts the attention pleasantly, relaxation, amusement, recreation; (*milit.*) a minor attack intended to divert an enemy from the point where the principal attack is to be made. [MedL. *diversio*].

DIVERSIONIST, [dī-vur'-shun-ist], *n.* one who attempts to create confusion behind the enemy's lines by sabotage, etc., when an attack is in progress.

DIVERSITY, [di-vur'-sit-i], *n.* considerable difference or differences, variety, unlikeness, the state of being diverse. [L. *diversitas*].

DIVERT, [dī-vurt'], *v.t.* to turn away from a fixed course, to change the direction of; to cause to move, or be employed in a different way; to direct the attention away from, to distract the thoughts; to entertain, to engage the mind or attention in pleasurable relaxation or recreation. [L. *divertere* to turn in different ways].

DIVERTER, [dī-vurt'-er], *n.* one who, or that which, diverts.

DIVERTICLE†, [dī-vurt'-ikl], *n.* a by-way; a branch, *esp.* of the intestine. [L. *diverticulum*].

DIVERTIMENTO, [div-ur'-tim-en'-tō], *n.* (*mus.*) a short, light, pleasant composition, vocal or instrumental. [It. *divertimento*].

DIVERTING, [dī-vurt'-ing], *adj.* amusing, entertaining.

DIVERTINGLY, [dī-vurt'-ing-li], *adv.* in diverting fashion.

DIVERTINGNESS, [dī-vurt'-ing-nes], *n.* tendency to divert; diverting nature.

DIVERTISSEMENT, [di-vāer'-tēs-mah(ng)], *n.* a short ballet or other entertainment, often introduced between the acts of a longer piece. [Fr. *divertissement*].

DIVERTIVE, [dī-vurt'-iv], *adj.* tending to divert, amusing, entertaining.

DIVEST, [dī-vest', di-vest'], *v.t.* to strip, to remove, to rid of; to dispossess, deprive of; (*leg.*) to take away; (*reflex.*) to shed; to give up. [OFr. *desvestir*].

DIVESTIBLE, [dī-vest'-ibl], *adj.* able to be divested.

DIVESTITURE, [dī-vest'-ich-er], *n.* the act of divesting; (*leg.*) surrender of property.

DIVESTMENT, [dī-vest'-ment], *n.* the act of divesting; the state of being divested.

DIVESTURE, [dī-ves'-cher], *n.* divestiture.

DIVET, see DIVOT.

DIVI, [div'-i], *n.* (*slang*) dividend paid to members of a co-operative society. [~ DIVIDEND].

DIVIDABLE, [di-vīd'-abl], *adj.* capable of being divided.

DIVIDE (1), [di-vīd'], *n.* that which divides; a watershed, a dividing ridge.

DIVIDE (2), [di-vīd'], *v.t.* to split up or mark out into parts; to separate into different groups, to classify; to share out; to split up into rival factions, to make discordant or at variance; to waver between two alternatives; to cut off from, to cause to be detached or separated from, to part; to take or ask for a vote on a motion under discussion; (*math.*) to find out how many times a number is contained in another; *v.i.* to become split up or separated, to part; to separate to take a vote on a motion; (*math.*) to be contained an exact number of times in another number. [L. *dividere* to force apart].

DIVIDED, [di-vīd'-id], *adj.* separated or split up into parts; parted, disunited, at variance; **d. consonant**, (*phon.*) a consonant formed by the tongue touching the palate in such a way that the flow of air passes on either side of the tongue.

DIVIDEDLY, [di-vīd'-id-li], *adv.* separately.

DIVIDEND, [div'-id-end], *n.* profits of a limited company proportionally divided among, and paid at certain periods to, proprietors and holders of shares; a share assigned to creditors out of the estate of a bankrupt; discount on purchases made, paid to members of a co-operative society out of trading profits; (*arith.*) the number to be divided by another. [L. *dividendum* required to be divided].

DIVIDER, [di-vīd'-er], *n.* one who, or that which, divides; (*pl.*) a pair of compasses with steel points for marking or measuring off small spaces.

DIVIDING, [di-vīd'-ing], *adj.* that divides.

DIVIDINGLY, [di-vīd'-ing-li], *adv.* by division.

DIVIDUAL, [di-vid'-yōō-al], *adj.* separate; shared or divided in common with others, divisible. [L. *dividuus*].

DIVIDUALLY, [di-vid'-yōō-al-i], *adv.* separately.

DIVIDUOUS, [di-vid'-yōō-us], *adj.* divisible. [L. *dividuus* divided].

DIVINATION, [div'-in-ā'-shun], *n.* the act of divining; a prophecy, a prediction; inspired guesswork. [L. *divinatio*].

DIVINATOR, [div'-in-āt-or], *n.* one who practises divination. [L. *divinator*].

DIVINATORY, [div-in-āt'-er-i], *adj.* relating to divination.

DIVINE (1), [di-vīn'], *n.* a theologian, one versed in divinity; (*coll.*) a clergyman. [OFr. *devin*].

DIVINE (2), [di-vīn'], *adj.* belonging to God, or a god; issuing from, or conferred by, God; as befits a god or God; heavenly, godlike; (*coll.*) wonderful, marvellous, extraordinarily good, superb. [L. *divinus* pertaining to a god].

DIVINE (3), [di-vīn'], *v.t. and i.* to conjecture or discover by intuition, to guess, to foretell; to foretell the future or make a revelation or decision by supernatural aid; to imagine. [L. *divinare* to foresee].

DIVINELY, [di-vīn'-li], *adv.* in divine fashion.

DIVINENESS, [di-vīn'-nes], *n.* the quality of being divine.

DIVINER, [di-vīn'-er], *n.* one who divines, *esp.* one who reveals the presence of subterranean sources of water, oil, etc., by means of a twig or rod held in the hand.

DIVINERESS, [di-vīn'-er-es], *n.* a female diviner.

DIVING, [dīv'-ing], *n.* the act of making a dive or dives; the performance of under-water work in special watertight suits or compartments.

DIVING-BELL, [dīv'-ing-bel'], *n.* a hollow vessel in which persons may be lowered into, and remain under, water for some time.

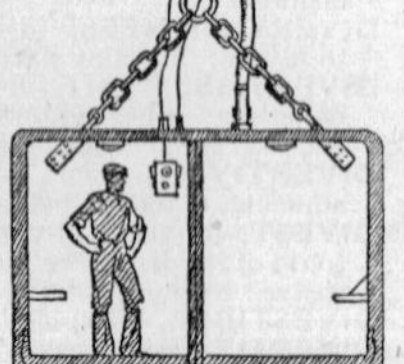

DIVING-BELL

DIVING-DRESS, [dīv'-ing-dres'], *n.* a special, weighted waterproof dress worn by divers.

DIVING-PIGEON, [dīv'-ing-pij'-un], *n.* the black guillemot, *Uria grylle.*

DIVING-SPIDER, [dīv'-ing-spīd'-er], *n.* the water-spider, *Argyroneta aquatica.*

DIVING-STONE, [dīv'-ing-stōn'], *n.* (*min.*) a variety of jasper.

DIVINIFIED, [di-vin'-i-fīd], *adj.* regarded as divine.

DIVINING-ROD, [di-vīn'-ing-rod'], *n.* a forked twig held in the hands to detect the presence of underground sources of water, oil, etc.

DIVINITY, [di-vin'-i-ti], *n.* the state or quality of being divine; a divine nature, force or power; a divine being, a god; the study of theology; **d. calf,** (*bookbinding*) dark-brown calf leather. [L. *divinitas*].

DIVINIZE, [div'-in-īz], *v.t.* to make divine, to deify.

DIVISIBILITY, [di-viz'-ib-il'-i-ti], *n.* the quality of being divisible.

DIVISIBLE, [di-viz'-ibl], *adj.* capable of division; (*math.*) capable of being divided exactly. [L. *divisibilis*].

DIVISIBLENESS, [di-viz'-ibl-nes], *n.* divisibility.

DIVISIBLY, [di-viz'-ib-li], *adv.* in a divisible fashion.

DIVISION, [di-vizh'-un], *n.* the act of dividing, state of being divided; that which divides, a partition; difference, dissension, discord; (*parl.*) separation of the members of a legislative or deliberative assembly for the purpose of voting, the act of taking a vote on a motion; that which is divided, a portion; a political, social, administrative, etc., unit; a class, separate group, special department, etc.; (*milit.*) the smallest formation containing all branches of troops capable of independent action, about 10,000 to 15,000 men; (*nav.*) part of a fleet, usually under a commander. [L. *divisio*].

DIVISIONAL, [di-vizh'-un-al], *adj.* pertaining to division, belonging to a division, dividing.

DIVISIONARY, [di-vizh'-un-er-i], *adj.* divisional.

DIVISIONER†, [di-vizh'-un-er], *n.* one who divides.

DIVISIVE, [di-vī'-siv], *adj.* able to make divisions, distinctions, etc.; tending to produce dissension.

DIVISOR, [di-vīz'-er], *n.* (*arith.*) the number by which another is divided; a factor. [L. *divisor*].

DIVORCE (1), [di-vaws'], *n.* legal dissolution of marriage; (*fig.*) separation or disunion, breaking of connexion between. [L. *divortium* separation].

DIVORCE (2), [di-vaws'], *v.t.* to obtain a divorce from; (*fig.*) to disunite, separate, break the connexion between.

DIVORCEABLE, [di-vaws'-abl], *adj.* capable of being divorced.

DIVORCEE, [di-vaws-ē'], *n.* a divorced person.

DIVORCEMENT, [di-vaws'-ment] *n.* the act or process of divorcing, the state of being divorced.

DIVORCER, [di-vaws'-er], *n.* one who divorces.

DIVORCIVE, [di-vaws'-iv], *adj.* tending to, or causing, divorce.

DIVOT, DIVET, [div'-ot], *n.* a sod, a piece of turf used for thatching or as fuel; (*golf*) a piece of turf dislodged by the head of a golf-club in hitting the ball. [Unkn.].

DIVULGATE, [di-vulg-āt'], *v.t.* to proclaim, to publish, to make known. [L. *divulgare* to divulge].

DIVULGATION, [di-vulg-ā'-shun], *n.* the act of divulging. [L. *divulgatio*].

DIVULGE, [di-vulj'], *v.t.* to reveal, to tell or make known (a secret, etc.); to disclose. [L. *divulgare* to publish abroad].

DIVULGEMENT, [di-vulj'-ment], *n.* divulgation.

DIVULGENCE, [di-vulj'-ents], *n.* divulgement.

DIVULGER, [di-vulj'-er], *n.* one who divulges.

DIVULSION, [di-vul'-shun], *n.* the act of tearing or pulling apart; the state of being torn or pulled apart. [L. *divulsio*].

DIVULSIVE, [di-vul'-siv], *adj.* tending to tear asunder or rend. [L. *divulsum*, *p.pt.* of *divellere* to tear apart].

DIXIE, [dik'-si], *n.* (*coll.*) a camp-kettle or stew-pot. [Hind. *degehi*].

DIZAIN, [diz-ān'], *n.* a poem or verse containing ten lines. [Fr. *dizain*].

DIZEN, [dīz'-en], *v.t.* to dress gaudily, to deck, to adorn. [~LGerm. *diesse* flax].

DIZZILY, [diz'-i-li], *adv.* in a dizzy manner.

DIZZINESS, [diz'-i-nes], *n.* the state of being dizzy.

DIZZY (1), [diz'-i], *adj.* giddy, with the head reeling, attacked by vertigo; bewildered, dazed, confused in mind, causing giddiness. [OE. *dysig* foolish].

DIZZY (2), [diz'-i], *v.t.* to make dizzy, to confuse. [OE. *dysigan* to be foolish].

DIZZYING, [diz'-i-ing], *adj.* whirling round; making dizzy.

DJERRID, [je'-rid], *n.* a blunt Turkish javelin, used in various forms of sport. [Arab. *jarid* palm branch].

DJIGGETAI, see DZIGGETAI.

DO (1), DOH, [dō], *n.* (*mus.*) the first note of the scale in the tonic sol-fa method of reading or singing music.

DO (2), [dōō], *n.* (*coll.*) a social entertainment, *esp.* on a rather elaborate scale; business, affair, happening, event; (*slang*) a fraud, swindle.

DO (3), [dōō], *v.t.* to perform; to be occupied with, engaged upon; to carry (an action, task or activity) to completion, to perform as work, to carry into effect (instructions, commands, mode of conduct, etc.); to affect (something) in some way, to make, to perform the work connected with, to work upon, *esp.* to cook or prepare food; to make use of, employ; to offer, bestow; to bring to disaster, to ruin; to deceive, to cheat; to visit as a tourist, see the sights of; to act (a play or rôle); to meet the needs or requirements of, to suit; to travel or traverse (a distance); (*p.pt.*) to complete, to finish; to cause the undoing, defeat, or ruin of; (*coll.*) to entertain, to treat; (*slang*) to serve (a sentence); to put, to bring to pass, to have; *v.i.* to act or behave; to succeed, to prosper; to be in a state or condition (of health or prosperity); to be suitable, to suffice; also used as an auxiliary verb in negative and interrogative sentences to indicate an urgent request or command, to express emphasis, to avoid the repetition of a verb,and for inversion; **well-to-d.,** prosperous, rich; **to d. away with,** to destroy, abolish; **to d. down,** to get the better of, cheat; **to d. for,** (*coll.*) to kill; to look after, attend to personally; **to d. in,** (*coll.*) to murder, kill; **to d. in the eye,** (*coll.*) to swindle, cheat; **to d. out,** to clean and make tidy; **to d. out of,** to prevent from getting, to defraud, cheat of; **to d. time,** (*slang*) to be in prison; **to d. to,** to treat; **to d. up,** to decorate anew, adorn; **to d. with,** to stand, tolerate, put up with; to be in need of, feel ready for; to manage with; **to have to d. with,** to have dealings with, be related to or concerned with; **to d. without,** to forgo. [OE. *don*].

DO (4), short form of DITTO.

DOAB, [dō'-ab], *n.* in India, a tract of land between two converging rivers. [Pers. *doab* two waters].

DOABLE, [dōō'-abl], *adj.* able to be done.

O-ALL, [dōō'-awl], *n.* a person who attends to everything.

OBBIN, [dob'-in], *n.* a pet name for a horse. [~ ROBIN].

OBBY, [dob'-i], *n.* (*dial.*) a fool, a childish old man; a sprite; a device or apparatus fitted to a loom for weaving small counts. [~ *Robbie*, *dim.* of *Robert*].

OBHASH†, [dob'-hash'], *n.* an East Indian interpreter. [Hind. *dubhashiya* man of two languages].

OCENT (1), [dō-sent'], *n.* a junior lecturer at a continental university. [G. *docent* from L. *docere* to teach].

OCENT (2), [dō'-sent], *adj.* teaching, instructing. [L. *docens*].

OCETAE, [do-sē'-tē], *n.(pl.)* a sect in the early Church who denied that Christ's body was the same as the human body. [Gk. *doketai* from *dokeo* I seem].

OCETIC, [do-sē'-tik], *adj.* pertaining to doceticism.

OCETICISM, [do-sē'-tis-izm], *n.* the teaching of the Docetae.

OCHMIAC, [dok'-mi-ak], *n.* a metrical foot of five syllables, a short, two longs, a short, and a long. [Gk. *dokhmiakos*].

OCIBILITY, [dō'-sib-il'-i-ti], *n.* docility.

OCIBLE, [dō'-sibl], *adj.* docile. [L. *docibilis*].

OCIBLENESS†, [dō'-sibl-nes], *n.* docility.

OCILE, [dō'-sīl], *adj.* easily managed, tractable, readily submissive to authority; eager to learn. [L. *docilis*].

OCILELY, [dō'-sīl-li], *adv.* in a docile manner.

OCILITY, [dō-sil'-i-ti], *n.* the quality of being docile. [L. *docilitas*].

OCIMASTIC, [dos'-i-mast'-ik], *adj.* assaying by tests, *esp.* ores or metals. [Gk. *dokimastikos* relating to examination].

OCIMASY, [dos-im'-a-si], *n.* the art of assaying metallic ores; the art of testing in materia medica. [Gk. *dokimasia*].

OCIMOLOGY, [dos'-im-ol'-o-ji], *n.* a dissertation on the art of assaying metals or on problems connected with obstetrics. [Gk. *dokimos* tested and *logos* speech].

OCK (1), [dok], *n.* (*bot.*) the name of several species of coarse plants of the genus *Rumex*. [OE. *docce*].

OCK (2), [dok], *n.* the short fleshy part of an animal's tail; a piece of leather harness over the stump of a horse's tail when cut short. [OIcel. *dokkr*].

OCK (3), [dok], *n.* an enclosed place in a criminal court where the prisoner stands for trial; an enclosure where ships are loaded, unloaded or repaired; **dry or graving docks,** docks from which the water can be pumped, leaving the ship on a row of keel blocks; **floating docks,** docks with hollow floating walls which can be raised or sunk, and with pumps to remove the water as in a dry dock. [Uncert.].

OCK (4), [dok], *v.t.* to cut off, to shorten (*esp.* a tail); to curtail, to cut down. [DOCK (2)].

OCK (5), [dok], *v.t. and i.* to enter or cause to enter a dock. [DOCK (3)].

OCKAGE, [dok'-ij], *n.* dock accommodation for a ship; dues payable for this.

OCKER, [dok'-er], *n.* a dock worker.

OCKET (1), DOCQUET†, [dok'-it], *n.* (*leg.*) a register or list of legal judgments; a summarized account of the contents at the foot of letters patent for the Great Seal; a list of court cases and litigants; a label tied to goods with directions for delivery or particulars of the contents; a memorandum attached to a document, summarizing its contents. [ME. *doket*].

OCKET (2), [dok'-it], *v.t.* to make an abstract of for entry in a book, to enter on a docket, to write out a docket or summary of contents, and affix it to a letter or parcel. [*Prec.*].

OCK-GLASS, [dok'-glahs], *n.* a large wineglass.

OCKIZATION, [dok'-iz-ā'-shun], *n.* the process of dockizing.

OCKIZE, [dok'-īz], *v.t.* to build docks along part of a river, harbour, etc.

OCK-MASTER, [dok'-mahst'-er], *n.* an overseer of a dock.

OCKYARD, [dok'-yahd], *n.* an establishment along a river-bank or sea-coast, fully equipped for the repairing or building of ships.

OCQUET, see DOCKET.

OCTOR (1), [dok'-ter], *n.* (*archaic*) a teacher, instructor, a learned man, *esp.* one of the learned Fathers of the Church, a medieval philosopher; a holder of the highest degree in any faculty of a university; (*pop.*) a physician or surgeon; a mechanical contrivance for adjusting or regulating; a fish of the genus *Acanthurus*, with sharp-edged spines near the tail; an artificial fly used for fishing; (*naut.*) a ship's cook; **Doctors' Commons,** originally the dining-hall, buildings and college of the Doctors of Civil Law in London and later the seat of a number of law courts; a former society of English Civil Lawyers, dissolved in 1857. [L. *doctor*].

DOCTOR (2), [dok'-ter], *v.t.* to treat medically; to repair; to adulterate, to tamper with, *esp.* by adding a drug; to falsify.

DOCTORAL, [dok'-ter-al], *adj.* pertaining to a doctor.

DOCTORALLY, [dok'-ter-al-i], *adv.* in the fashion of a doctor.

DOCTORATE, [dok'-ter-at], *n.* the degree of a doctor.

DOCTORESS, see DOCTRESS.

DOCTORING, [dok'-ter-ing], *n.* medical treatment; adulteration of liquids, falsification of facts.

DOCTORLY, [dok'-ter-li], *adj.* scholarly.

DOCTORSHIP, [dok'-ter-ship], *n.* the degree of doctor, the status of a doctor; great learning or scholarship; medical skill or care.

DOCTRESS, DOCTORESS, [dok'-tres], *n.* a woman physician; a woman holding a doctorate.

DOCTRINAIRE (1), [dok'-trin-āer'], *n.* an unpractical theorist; (*hist.*) one of a group of French politicians who in 1816 wished to set up a constitutional government in France. [Fr. *doctrinaire*].

DOCTRINAIRE (2), [dok'-trin-āer'], *adj.* seeking to apply theories irrespective of their practicability.

DOCTRINAL, [dok-trīn'-al], *adj.* pertaining to doctrine.

DOCTRINALLY, [dok-trīn'-al-i], *adv.* in a doctrinal fashion.

DOCTRINARIAN (1), [dok'-trin-āer'-i-an], *n.* doctrinaire.

DOCTRINARIAN (2), [dok'-trin-āer'-i-an], *adj.* doctrinaire.

DOCTRINARIANISM, [dok'-trin-āer'-i-an-izm], *n.* the programme of the Doctrinaires; unpractical, theorizing.

DOCTRINE, [dok'-trin], *n.* a thing taught, teaching; a belief, a principle taught as true; a set of accepted beliefs or principles in religion, politics, or science. [L. *doctrina* teaching].

DOCTRINISM, [dok'-trin-izm], *n.* obstinate belief in a particular doctrine.

DOCTRINIST, [dok'-trin-ist], *n.* one who wholeheartedly maintains a certain doctrine.

DOCUMENT (1), [dok'-yōō-ment], *n.* any writing or inscription, *esp.* one which may be used to verify or establish fact. [L. *documentum* proof, specimen].

DOCUMENT (2) [dok'-yōō-ment], *v.t.* to furnish or support with evidence from documents.

DOCUMENTAL, [dok'-yōō-ment'-al], *adj.* relating to documents.

DOCUMENTARY, [dok'-yōō-ment'-er-i], *adj.* pertaining to or supported by documents; **d. film,** a short film concerned solely with giving a realistic, accurate picture of some aspect of everyday life and work or technical process.

DOCUMENTATION, [dok'-yōō-men-tā'-shun], *n.* the act of documenting, the state of being documented. [MedL. *documentatio*].

DOD, (dodding, dodded), [dod], *v.t.* to clip, to lop (the top or head). [ME. *dodden*].

DODD, [dod], *n.* (*dial.*) a rounded eminence. [*Prec.*].

DODDED, [dod'-id], *adj.* lopped, clipped; (of sheep) without horns.

DODDER (1), [dod'-er], *n.* (*bot.*) a leafless parasitic plant of the genus *Cuscuta*. [ME. *doder*].

DODDER (2), [dod'-er], *v.i.* to totter, to tremble, to move in an unsteady fashion like one in a state of extreme mental or physical decay. [Uncert.].

DODDERED, [dod'-erd], *adj.* (of a tree) having the top lopped off, decayed through age.

DODDERER, [dod'-er-er], *n.* one who dodders, a senile semi-invalid.

DODDER-GRASS, [dod'-er-grahs'], *n.* (*bot.*) quaking grass, *Briza media*.

DODDERING, [dod'-er-ing], *adj.* tottering and foolish with extreme age or infirmity.

DODDERY, [dod'-er-i], *adj.* shaky, unsteady with age or infirmity; (*fig.*) foolish.

DODDYPOLL†, [dod'-i-pōl'], *n.* a dolt. [~DOTE].

DODECA-, *pref.* twelve. [Gk. *dodeka* twelve].

DODECAGON, [dō-dek'-a-gon], *n.* a polygon with twelve equal sides and angles. [DODECA and Gk. *gonia* angle].

DODECAHEDRAL, [dō'-dek-a-hē'-dral], *adj.* having twelve equal sides.

DODECAHEDRON, [dō'-dek-a-hē'-dron], *n.* a regular solid having twelve equal pentagonal bases. [DODECA and Gk. *hedra* base].

DODECAHEDRON

DODECANE, [dō-'dek-ān'], *n.* (*chem.*) a hydrocarbon of the paraffin group.

DODECAPETALOUS, [dō'-dek-a-pet'-al-us], *adj.* (*bot.*) possessing twelve petals. [DODECA and PETALOUS].

DODECARCHY, [dō'-dek-ahk-i], *n.* government by twelve. [DODECA and Gk. *arkhia* rule].

DODECASTYLE, [dō'-dek-a-stil'], *n.* (*arch.*) a portico having twelve columns in front. [DODECA and Gk. *stulos* column].

DODECASYLLABLE, [dō'-dek-a-sil'-abl], *n.* a verse or word containing twelve syllables. [DODECA and SYLLABLE].

DODGE (1), [doj], *n.* (*coll.*) a trick, deception, quibble, plan, tip; (*slang*) a gadget.

DODGE (2), [doj], *v.t. and i.* to get out of the way of, to elude by sudden rapid swerves or twists of the body; to shirk or escape by artifices or mean ingenious tricks; to twist and turn about to evade something; to shuffle, quibble; to shirk. [Unkn.].

DODGER, [doj'-er], *n.* one who dodges; an evasive rogue; (*naut.*) a sheltering screen on the bridge of a ship; (*U.S. slang*) a small printed handbill.

DODGY, [doj'-i], *adj.* full of dodges, artful, dishonest.

DODKIN, [dod'-kin], *n.* a small doit or Dutch coin of little value. [MDu. *duytkin*].

DODMAN, [dod'-man], *n.* a snail. [Unkn.].

DODO, [dō'-dō], *n.* the large flightless pigeon of Mauritius, *Didus ineptus*, extinct since 1681. [Portug. *doudo* simpleton].

DODO

DODONIAN, [dō-don'-i-an], *adj.* pertaining to Dodona in Epirus, the site of a famous oracle of Jupiter. [Gk. *Dodonaios*].

DOE, [dō], *n.* the female of the fallow deer, the rabbit, and certain other animals. [OE. *da*].

DOER, [dōō'-er], *n.* one who does; a man of action.

DOES, [duz], *third person sg. pres.ind.* of DO.

DOESKIN, [dō'-skin], *n.* the skin of a doe; a soft leather made from this; a compact twilled woollen cloth.

DOFF, [dof], *v.t.* to take off, to raise (the hat), to divest oneself of. [DO and OFF].

DOFFER, [dof'-er], *n.* a revolving cylinder in a carding-machine, for stripping the cotton from the cards.

DOG (1), [dog], *n.* a carnivorous quadruped of the genus *Canis*, existing in both a domesticated and wild state, of which there are many varieties, often used to denote the male of this species and certain similar animals; (*fig.*) a worthless, dishonest rascal, a cowardly, contemptuous rogue; (*coll.*) a fellow, a gallant, a gay young man-about-town, a blade; (*astron.*) one of the two constellations *Canis Major* or *Minor*; (*pl.*) the *Canes Venatici*, a constellation near the Great Bear; (*pl.*) a pair of andirons used to support logs on a fire; a mechanical grappling or clutching contrivance; **to go to the dogs**, to sink into degeneracy, to go to ruin; **to rain cats and dogs**, to rain extremely heavily; **to lead a d.'s life**, to lead a miserable, perpetually harassed existence; **hot d.**, (*U.S. slang*) a sandwich containing hot sausage meat; **the dogs**, (*slang*) greyhound racing. [OE. *docga*].

DOG (2), [dog], *v.t.* to follow or attend constantly and closely. [*Prec.*].

DOGAL, [dō'-gal], *adj.* belonging to a doge. [It. *dogale* ducal].

DOGANA, [dog-ah'-na], *n.* a custom-house. [It. *dogana*].

DOGARESSA, [dō'-ga-res'-a], *n.* the wife of a doge. [It. *dogaressa*].

DOGATE, [dō'-gāt], *n.* the rank and office of a doge. [It. *dogato*].

DOGBANE, [dog'-bān], *n.* (*bot.*) a plant of the genus *Apocynum* or *Cynoctonum*, yielding a medici juice.

DOG-BEE, [dog'-bē], *n.* a drone a humble-bee, a troublesome to dogs.

DOG-BELT, [dog'-belt], *n.* a strong belt worn rou the waist for hauling trucks in coal-mines.

DOGBERRY, [dog'-be'-ri], *n.* the berry of the d wood, *Cornus sanguinea*.

DOG-BISCUIT, [dog'-bis'-kit], *n.* a thick, h biscuit for dogs.

DOG-BOLT†, [dog'-bōlt], *n.* a blunt-headed arro (*fig.*) a contemptible fellow, a blackguard.

DOG-BRIER, [dog'-brī'-er], *n.* (*bot.*) the dog-ro *Rosa canina*.

DOGCART, [dog'-kaht], *n.* a light, high, two- or fo wheeled vehicle, drawn by one horse, for two perso with a box below for dogs.

DOG-COCKLE, [dog'-kokl'], *n.* the bivalve, *Pect culus glycimeris*.

DOG-COLLAR, [dog'-kol'-er], *n.* a collar for a d (*coll.*) a high stiff, white collar fastening at the ba as worn by clerics.

DOG-DAYS, [dog'-dāz'], *n.* †a period of forty da at the time when Sirius, the dog-star, rises and s with the sun; this period as comprising the hot part of the year, during July and August.

DOGE, [dōj], *n.* (*hist.*) chief magistrate of Venice a Genoa. [It. *doge* from L. *dux* leader].

DOG-EARED, [dog'-ēerd], *adj.* having the corn of the leaves turned down.

DOGEATE, [dōj'-āt], *n.* the rank or office of a do

DOGFANCIER, [dog'-fan'-si-er], *n.* a connoiss of dogs, one who breeds or rears dogs for sale.

DOG FIGHT, [dog'-fīt], *n.* (*aeron.*) a skirmish betwe fighter planes.

DOGFISH, [dog'-fish], *n.* a variety of small sha so called for following its prey in packs in the same manner as dogs.

DOGFISH

DOGFLY, [dog'-flī], *n.* a fly that attacks dogs.

DOG-FOX, [dog'-foks'], *n.* a male fox.

DOGGED, [dog'-id], *adj.* determined, resolu tenacious; (*archaic*) sullen, surly.

DOGGEDLY, [dog'-id-li], *adv.* in a dogged fashi

DOGGEDNESS, [dog'-id-nes], *n.* the quality being dogged.

DOGGER (1), [dog'-er], *n.* a two-masted Du fishing-smack. [Uncert.].

DOGGER (2), [dog'-er], *n.* (*min.*) a coarse variety ironstone. [Uncert.].

DOGGEREL (1), [dog'-er-il], *n.* fluent but fee verse, burlesque.

DOGGEREL (2), [dog'-er-il], *adj.* (of verse) triv inferior. [Unkn.].

DOGGERMAN, [dog'-er-man], *n.* a sailor in dogger.

DOGGINESS, [dog'-i-nes], *n.* the quality of rese bling a dog or being fond of dogs.

DOGGISH, [dog'-ish], *adj.* surly, morose.

DOGGISHNESS, [dog'-ish-nes], *n.* the quality being doggish.

DOGGO, [dog'-ō], *adv.* in such a manner as to esca attention. [Unkn.].

DOGGONE, [dog'-gon'], *adj.* (*U.S. slang*) c founded, wretched. [~GOD DAMNED.]

DOG-GRASS, [dog'-grahs'], *n.* (*bot.*) couch gra *Agropyrum repens*.

DOGGY, [dog'-i], *adj.* like a dog, devoted to do

DOGHEAD, [dog'-hed'], *n.* a gunlock hammer.

DOG-HEARTED, [dog'-haht'-id], *adj.* cruel, sull

DOG-HOLE, [dog'-hōl], *n.* a place fit only for do

DOGHOOD, [dog'-hōōd], *n.* the condition of be a dog.

DOG-HOUSE, [dog'-hows], *n* a kennel.

DOG-LATIN, [dog'-lat'-in], *n.* colloquial, n classical, barbarous Latin.

DOG-LEECH†, [dog'-lēch], *n.* a dog doctor; a qua

DOG-LIKE, [dog'-līk], *adj.* and *adv.* like, in fashion of, a dog.

DOGMA, [dog'-ma], *n.* a principle or maxim wh must not be disputed; that body of doctrine set fo by the Church as unquestionably true; opinions tenets propounded by a school of thought a accepted by its members. [Gk. *dogma* opinion].

DOG-MAD, [dog'-mad'], *adj.* mad as a dog, cra

DOGMATIC, [dog-mat'-ik], *adj.* pertaining religious dogma; dictatorial, admitting no argume [Gk. *dogmatikos*].

GMATICAL, [dog-mat'-ik-al], *adj.* dogmatic.
GMATICALLY, [dog-mat'-ik-a-li], *adv.* in a ɔgmatic manner; arrogantly.
GMATICALNESS, [dog-mat'-ikl-nes], *n.* the ıality of being dogmatical; positiveness.
GMATICS, [dog-mat'-iks], *n.(pl.)* the study of ligious dogma.
GMATISM, [dog'-mat-izm], *n.* the act of dogıatizing; a dogmatic state of mind, excessive ɔsitiveness of opinion; (*philos.*) a system of philoɔphy based entirely upon pure reason divorced om objective observation.
GMATIST, [dog'-mat-ist], *n.* a person who xpresses opinions and beliefs in a dogmatic way; a hilosopher who believes in dogmatism; a student r strong supporter of dogma.
GMATIZE, [dog'-mat-īz], *v.t. and i.* to assert ɔme opinion in an extremely emphatic manner as ıough admitting no doubt or question, to express a elief in an imperious way; to advance or formulate s a dogma. [Gk. *dogmatizo*].
GMATIZER, [dog'-mat-īz-er], *n.* one who dogıatizes.
GMATORY†, [dog'-mat-er-i], *adj.* dogmatical.
G-ROSE, [dog'-rōz], *n.* the wild rose, *Rosa canina.*
G'S-EAR, [dogz'-ēer], *n.* the turned-down, rinkled corner of a leaf in a book.
G'S-FENNEL, [dogz'-fen'-el], *n.* stinking mayeed, *Anthemis Cotula.*
GSHIP, [dog'-ship], *n.* the character of a dog.
GSHORES, [dog'-shawz], *n.(pl.)* pieces of wood sed as a brake or prop for a ship ready to be launched rom a building slip, and knocked away at the launchıg.
G-SICK, [dog'-sik], *adj.* sick as a dog.
GSKIN, [dog'-skin], *n.* the skin of a dog, the soft ather made from it or sheepskin.
G-SLEEP, [dog'-slēp], *adj.* uneasy, fitful sleep.
G'S-LETTER, [dogz'-let'-er], *n.* †the letter R, rom its trilled sound which was supposed to resemble he snarl of a dog. [L. *littera canina* canine letter].
G'S-MEAT, [dogz'-mēt], *n.* meat fit only for dogs, ffal.
G'S-MERCURY, [dogz'-murk'-yōō-ri], *n.* the ommon plant, *Mercurialis perennis.*
G'S-NOSE, [dogz'-nōz], *n.* a mixture of beer nd gin.
G'S-POISON, [dogz'-poizn], *n.* fool's-parsley, *Ethusa Cynapium.*
G'S-RUE, [dogz'-rōō], *n.* a plant, a variety of *crophularia.*
G'S-TAIL-GRASS, [dogz'-tāl-grahs'], *n.* a genus f perennial grasses, *Cynosurus cristatus*, having long viry roots, and hairy leaves.
G-STAR, [dog'-stah(r)], *n.* Sirius, the brightest of he stars in the constellation *Canis Major.*
G-STONES, [dog'-stōnz], *n.* (*bot.*) one of several pecies of the genus *Orchis.*
G'S-TONGUE, [dogz'-tung'], *n.* the hound's ongue, a plant of the genus *Cynoglossum.*
G'S-TOOTH, [dogz'-tōōth], *n.* the moth, *Hadena uasa.*
G'S-TOOTH-VIOLET, [dogz'-tōōth-vī'-ol-et], *n.* plant of the genus *Erythronium*, *esp. Erythonium lenscanis.*
G-THISTLE, [dog'-thisl], *n.* the thistle *Carduus rvensis.*
G-TIRED, [dog'-tī'-erd], *adj.* tired-out, very weary.
G-TOOTH, [dog'-tōōth], *n.* a canine tooth, a sharp-pointed tooth growing between the incisors and premolars; (*arch.*) a moulding consisting of four roughly triangular leaves meeting at a raised point in the centre, in the form of a series of raised points, much used in early English architecture; **d. spar**, a variety of mineral calcium carbonate having pointed, tooth-like crystals.

DOG-TOOTH MOULDING

G-TRICK, [dog'-trik], *n.* a spiteful trick.
G-TROT, [dog'-trot'], *n.* an easy trot, like that of a dog.
G-VANE, [dog'-vān], *n.* (*naut.*) a small vane made of thread, cork and feathers, placed on the weather gunwale.
DOG-VIOLET, [dog'-vī'-ol-et], *n.* the wild, scentless violet, *Viola canina.*
DOG-WATCH, [dog'-woch'], *n.* (*naut.*) one of two watches, from 4 to 6 p.m. and from 6 to 8 p.m.
DOG-WEARY, [dog'-wēer'-i], *adj.* dead-beat, tired-out.
DOG-WHELK, [dog'-welk], *n.* a univalve shell of the genus *Nassa*, commonly found on the British coast.
DOG-WOOD, [dog'-wŏŏd], *n.* a tree of the genus *Cornus*, particularly *Cornus sanguinea*, a common English shrub yielding dense clusters of white flowers.
DOH, [dō], *n.* the first note in the tonic sol-fa scale.
DOILY, DOYLEY, [doil'-i], *n.* a small ornamental piece of laced cloth, etc., placed on crockery, etc. [*Doyley*, the inventor].
DOINGS, [dōō'-ingz], *n.(pl.)* activities, things done; objects.
DOIT, [doit], *n.* a small valueless coin, a small Dutch copper coin worth about half a farthing. [Du. *duit*].
DOITED, [doit'-id], *adj.* foolish, mentally deranged, silly. [Unkn.].
DOLABRELLA, [dol'-ab-rel'-a], *n.* a genus of gastropods, with a shell which is shaped like a little hatchet. [L. from *dolabra* hatchet].
DOLABRIFORM, [dol-ab'-ri-fawm], *adj.* (*bot.*) having the shape of a hatchet. [L. *dolabra* hatchet and FORM].
DOLCE, [dol'-chi], *adv.* (*mus.*) softly, sweetly, and tenderly. [It. *dolce*].
DOLCEMENTE, [dol'-chim-en'-ti], *adv.* dolce. [It. *dolcemente*].
DOLDRUMS, [dol'-drŏŏmz], *n.* (*naut.*) a tropical zone between the regions of the trade-winds, where calms and variable winds prevail, with occasional squalls; (*fig.*) depression, the dumps. [Uncert.].
DOLE (1), [dōl], *n.* sorrow, lamentation. [L. *dolium*].
DOLE (2), [dōl], *n.* (*archaic*) a portion, share; fate, destiny; something distributed, *esp.* as a charitable gift in small scanty portions; a weekly payment made for a limited period to certain classes of the unemployed from funds contributed by the workman, his employer, and the state. [OE. *dal*].
DOLE (3), [dōl], *v.t.* to deal out in small portions, to distribute sparingly.
DOLEFUL, [dōl'-fŏŏl], *adj.* sad, sorrowful, melancholy. [DOLE (1) and FULL].
DOLEFULLY, [dōl'-fŏŏl-i], *adv.* in a doleful fashion.
DOLEFULNESS, [dōl'-fŏŏl-nes], *n.* the state of being doleful.
DOLERITE, [dol'-er-īt], *n.* (*min.*) a compact crystalline rock allied to the basaltic series, containing augite, felspar, and olivine. [Gk. *doleros* deceptive].
DOLESOME, [dōl'-sum], *adj.* doleful.
DOLESOMELY, [dōl'-sum-li], *adv.* in a dolesome fashion.
DOLESOMENESS, [dōl'-sum-nes], *n.* dolefulness.
DOLICHOCEPHALIC, [dol'-ik-ō-sef-al'-ik], *adj.* long-headed, having a skull whose length is at least one-fifth greater than its breadth. [Gk. *dolikhos* long and *kephale* head].
DOLICHOS, [dol'-ik-os], *n.* the hyacinth bean, *Mucuna pruriens*, a leguminous plant related to the kidney-bean, having long pods. [Gk. *dolikhos* long].
DOLICHURUS, [dol-ik'-yōō-rus], *n.* a dactylic hexameter containing a syllable too many. [Gk. *dolikhouros* long-tailed].
DOLIUM, [dol'-i-um], *n.* a genus of univalve molluscs, so called from their resemblance to a hogshead, or large wine-vessel. [L. *dolium* large jar].
DOLL (1), [dol], *n.* a child's toy representing a human or animal figure; (*coll.*) a girl or woman possessing an attractive appearance and a vacuous mind. [Pet form of *Dorothy*].
DOLL (2), [dol], *v.t. and reflex.* (*slang*) to dress in one's best or smartest clothes (used generally with *up*).
DOLLAR, [dol'-er], *n.* a silver or gold coin of the value of 100 cents, or nominally a little over four shillings in English money, which is the monetary unit in U.S.A., Canada, etc.; silver coins of approximately equal value current in Latin America, China, and other countries; originally the English name of the German silver thaler of three marks; (*slang*) five shillings. [Germ. *taler*].
DOLLMAN, see DOLMAN.
DOLLOP, [dol'-op], *n.* (*coll.*) a large quantity or lump, a big, shapeless mass. [Unkn.].
DOLL'S HOUSE, [dolz'-hows], *n.* a toy house suitable for dolls.
DOLLY (1), [dol'-i], *n.* a doll; a wooden implement in the form of a pronged stick used for beating and

stirring clothes in a wash-tub; an apparatus for stirring and washing ore; (*eng.*) a tapering steel bar having a hollow pointed end shaped to fit the head of a rivet, and held over the rivet while it is fastened; **d. shop,** a marine dealer's store, an inferior kind of pawn shop; **d. tub,** a wash-tub.

DOLLY (2), [dol'-i], *v.t.* to stir and beat clothes with a dolly.

DOLMAN, DOLLMAN, [dol'-man], *n.* a long outer garment in the form of a narrow-sleeved robe, worn by the Turks; a loose jacket with large hanging cape-like sleeves worn by ladies; the jacket of a hussar's uniform, worn like a cape or cloak. [Turk. *dolaman*].

DOLMEN, [dol'-men], *n.* a cromlech, a prehistoric stone chamber consisting of a large unhewn stone resting on top of several vertical stones. [Fr. *dolmen* from Corn. *doll* hole and *men* stone].

DOLOMITE, [dol'-om-īt], *n.* (*min.*) a semi-transparent crystalline mineral composed of carbonate of calcium and carbonate of magnesium. [M. *Dolomieu,* a French geologist].

DOLORIFEROUS†, [dol'-or-if'-er-us], *adj.* causing pain. [L. *dolor* pain and *ferre* to bear].

DOLORIFIC, [dol'-or-if'-ik], *adj.* that produces or expresses pain or grief. [MedL. *dolorificus*].

DOLOROSO, [dol'-or-ō'-sō], *adv.* (*mus.*) tenderly and pathetically. [It. *doloroso*].

DOLOROUS, [dol'-or-us], *adj.* distressing, sad, mournful. [OFr. *doleros*].

DOLOROUSLY, [dol'-or-us-li], *adv.* in a dolorous manner.

DOLOROUSNESS, [dol'-or-us-nes], *n.* the quality of being dolorous.

DOLOSE, [dol'-ōs], *adj.* deceitful; (*leg.*) fraudulent. [L. *dolosus*].

DOLOUR, [dol'-or], *n.* anguish, sorrow. [L. *dolor*].

DOLPHIN, [dol'-fin], *n.* a cetaceous animal of the genus *Delphinus*; a name applied to the fish, *Coryphæna hippuris,* the dorado, noted for its rapid changes of colour just before death; the name of a northern constellation; various implements or contrivances similar to a dolphin in shape, as a mooring post or buoy, the handle of a cannon; **d. striker,** (*naut.*) the vertical spar below the bowsprit. [Gk. *delphos* dolphin].

DOLPHIN

DOLPHINET†, [dol'-fin-et'], *n.* a female dolphin.

DOLPHIN-FLY, [dol'-fin-flī'], *n.* a louse very harmful to beans.

DOLT, [dōlt], *n.* a blockhead. [ME. *dold* dulled].

DOLTISH, [dōlt'-ish], *adj.* foolish, dull, stupid.

DOLTISHLY, [dōlt'-ish-li], *adv.* in a doltish fashion.

DOLTISHNESS, [dōlt'-ish-nes], *n.* stupidity.

DOM, [dom], *n.* a title given to certain dignitaries of the Roman Catholic Church, and Benedictine and Carthusian monks. [Portug. *dom* from L. *dominus* lord].

DOMABLE†, [dōm'-abl], *adj.* capable of being tamed. [LL. *domabilis* tamable].

DOMAIN, [dō-mān'], *n.* land under the rule or ownership of some particular person; territory, landed estates; dominions; (*fig.*) sphere of knowledge, work, influence, etc. [Fr. *domaine* from L. *dominicum* belonging to a lord].

DOMAL, [dōm'-al], *adj.* (*astrol.*) relating to a house. [MedL. *domalis*].

DOMANIAL, [dō-mā'-ni-al], *adj.* pertaining to domains.

DOME (1), [dōm], *n.* (*poet.*) a large imposing building, a palace; a rounded roof in the form of a hemisphere; anything having this shape; (*slang*) head. [L. *domus* house].

DOME (2), [dōm], *v.t.* to provide with a dome-shaped roof, to form into the shape of a dome.

DOMELIKE, [dōm'-līk], *adj.* dome-shaped, resembling a dome.

DOMESDAY, [dōōmz'-dā], *n.* doomsday; **D. Book,** a survey of the manors of England originally compiled in the reign of William I. [OE. *domesdæg* day of judgment].

DOME-SHAPED, [dōm'-shāpt], *adj.* having the shape of a dome.

DOMESMAN, [dōōmz'-man], *n.* (*archaic*) a judge or umpire.

DOMESTIC (1), [dom-est'-ik], *n.* a servant in a household.

DOMESTIC (2), [dom-est'-ik], *adj.* pertaining to the home, family or household; fond of home; ta[illegible] native, not foreign; internal, affecting or pertair[illegible] to one's own country. [L. *domesticus*].

DOMESTICABLE, [dom-est'-ik-abl], *adj.* able to domesticated.

DOMESTICALLY, [dom-est'-ik-a-li], *adv.* in domestic fashion.

DOMESTICANT†, [dom-est'-ik-ant], *adj.* dwelli[illegible] living in the same home. [L. *domesticans*].

DOMESTICATE, [dom-est'-ik-āt], *v.t.* to cause settle down into domestic life, to make in[illegible] ested in household life; to accustom to life w[illegible] human beings, to tame, to bring into the service man. [L. *domesticare* to dwell in a house].

DOMESTICATION, [dom-est'-ik-ā'-shun], *n.* act of domesticating, the condition of being dom[illegible] ticated.

DOMESTICITY, [do'-mes-tis'-i-ti], *n.* home life a[illegible] the love of it.

DOMETT, [dom'-it], *n.* a loose flannel of cotton a[illegible] wool, generally used for making shrouds. [Unkn.

DOMICAL, [dōm'-ik-al], *adj.* relating to, or sha[illegible] like, a dome.

DOMICILE (1), [dom'-is-īl], *n.* customary residen[illegible] home; (*leg.*) the place recognized for official purpo[illegible] as one's permanent residence; the fact of legally res[illegible] ing; (*comm.*) the place where a bill of exchange m[illegible] be paid. [Fr. from L. *domicilium* dwelling-place].

DOMICILE (2), [dom'-is-īl], *v.t.* to establish in a fix[illegible] residence, to cause to make a permanent home i[illegible] specified locality; (*comm.*) to render a bill of exchar[illegible] payable at a specified place.

DOMICILIARY, [dom'-is-il'-i-er-i], *adj.* pertain[illegible] to a domicile or residence; **d. visit,** an official visit a private dwelling for the purpose of searching inspecting it in accordance with the law.

DOMICILIATE, [dom'-is-il'-i-āt], *v.t.* to domicile

DOMICILIATED, [dom'-is-il'-i-āt-id], *adj.* domicil[illegible]

DOMICILIATION, [dom'-is-il'-i-ā'-shun], *n.* p[illegible] manent residence.

DOMIFY†, [dom'-i-fī], *v.t.* (*astrol.*) to divide (t[illegible] heavens) into twelve houses in order to form a ho[illegible] scope. [MedL. *domificare*].

DOMINANCE, [dom'-in-ants], *n.* the state of bei[illegible] dominant; authority, control.

DOMINANCY, [dom'-in-an-tsi], *n.* dominance.

DOMINANT (1), [dom'-in-ant], *n.* (*mus.*) the fi[illegible] note above the tonic; (*biol.*) an inheritable chara[illegible] teristic manifesting itself in most of the offspring.

DOMINANT (2), [dom'-in-ant], *adj.* ruling, preva[illegible] ing, having most influence, outstanding in imp[illegible] tance; (*mus.*) pertaining to the dominant or fi[illegible] above the tonic. [L. *dominans*].

DOMINATE, [dom'-in-āt], *v.t.* and *i.* to rule over, exercise great influence or authority over, to preva[illegible] to occupy a position which overlooks or commanc[illegible] [L. *dominatum, p.pt.* of *dominari* to rule over].

DOMINATION, [dom'-in-ā'-shun], *n.* the act dominating; (*pl.*) the fourth order of angels. [*dominatio*].

DOMINATIVE, [dom'-in-at-iv], *adj.* governin[illegible] imperious. [MedL. *dominativus*].

DOMINATOR, [dom'-in-āt-er], *n.* a ruling powe[illegible] [L. *dominator*].

DOMINEER, [dom'-in-ēer'], *v.i.* to rule, exerci[illegible] authority in a haughty overbearing manner; to a or express oneself in a lordly, imperious style. [D *domineren*].

DOMINEERING, [dom'-in-ēer'-ing], *adj.* overbea[illegible] ing, imperious.

DOMINICAL, [dom-in'-ikl], *adj.* relating to t[illegible] Lord, denoting or pertaining to Sunday; **d. yea[illegible]** the year as numbered from the birth of Christ; **[illegible] letter,** one of the first seven letters of the alphabe[illegible] symbolizing Sunday in an almanac. [LL. *domin[illegible] calis*].

DOMINICAN (1), [dom-in'-ik-an], *n.* a member [illegible] the order of preaching friars founded in 1215 by Spaniard, St. Domingo de Guzman, a Blackfria[illegible] [MedL. *Dominicus,* the Latin form of *Domingo*].

DOMINICAN (2), [dom-in'-ik-an], *adj.* belonging [illegible] the Dominicans. [*Prec.*].

DOMINICIDE†, [dom-in'-is-īd], *n.* one who murde[illegible] his master; the killing of a master. [LL. *dominicida*

DOMINIE, [dom'-in-i], *n.* (*Scots*) a schoolmaster.

DOMINION, [dom-in'-yun], *n.* supreme power [illegible] authority, control, rule, sovereignty; territori[illegible] under the rule of the king; (*pl.*) the self-governin[illegible] territories of the British Empire. [L. *dominiu[illegible]* lordship].

DOMINO, [dom'-in-ō], *n.* a cape or hood worn by

ıaster, a hood worn by a canon in cold weather; a ›ose cloak, with a hood and mask, worn as a disguise t masquerades, etc.; a person wearing one of these; small, flat, oblong piece of bone, ivory, wood, etc., aving one side black, the other white or black and ivided into equal halves, either of which may be lank or marked with from one to six spots; (*pl.*) a ame played with twenty-eight of these. [L. *domino*, *it.* of *dominus* lord].

•MITE, [dō'-mīt], *n.* (*min.*) a light grey species of rachyte. [*Puy de Dôme*, a place in Auvergne, France, here found].

•N (1), [don], *n.* a Spanish title equivalent to Mr.; *fig.*) an important person; a person of self-importance; ıe head, or a fellow or tutor of a college. [Sp. *don* om L. *dominus* lord].

•N (2), [don], *v.t.* to put on (articles of clothing). [DO nd ON].

•NAH, [dō'-na], *n.* (*slang*) a sweetheart; a woman. Sp. *doña* lady from L. *domina*].

•NARY, [dōn'-er-i], *n.* a gift. [L. *donarium*].

•NATE, [dō-nāt'], *v.t.* to give in charity, to present. L. *donatum*, *p.pt.* of *donare* to give].

•NATION, [dō-nā'-shun], *n.* the act of giving, ıat which is given, money for charitable purposes; *eg.*) the contract by which anything is freely trans- erred to the ownership of another. [L. *donatio*].

•NATISM, [dō'-nat-izm], *n.* the teaching of onatists.

•NATIST, [dō'-nat-ist], *n.* one of a sect of African chismatics of the fourth century, founded because f a dispute over the election of a bishop of Carthage. *Donatus*, a leader of the sect].

•NATISTIC, [dō-nat-ist'-ik], *adj.* relating to onatism.

•NATIVE (1), [dō'-nat-iv], *n.* a gift; (*eccles. leg.*) benefice given and collated to a person by the patron ithout presentation or institution by the ordinary. L. *donativum* an official gift].

•NATIVE (2), [dō'-nat-iv], *adj.* pertaining to a onative.

•NATOR, [dō-nāt'-or], *n.* a donor. [L. *donator*].

•NATORY, [dō'-nat-er-i], *n.* the receiver of a onation or gift. [MedL. *donatorius*].

•NE (1), [dun], *adj.* finished, performed; completely xhausted, dead beat; cooked sufficiently; (*slang*) ricked, duped; **not d.,** not in the best of taste; **o be d.,** to be ruined, exhausted; to be ready, nished; **to have d. with,** to give up, finish. [OE. *edon*, *p.pt.* of *don* DO].

•NE (2), [dun], *int.* agreed, settled. [*Prec.*].

•NEE, [dōn-ē'], *n.* the person to whom a gift is made. ~DONOR].

•NGA, [dong'-ga], *n.* (*South Africa*) a steep-sided hannel cut out by water. [Bantu *donga*].

›NIFEROUS†, [dōn-if'-er-us], *adj.* bearing gifts. L. *donum* gift and *ferre* to bear.]

›NJON, see DUNGEON (1).

›NKEY, [dong'-ki], *n.* the ass; (*coll.*) a stupid person; **. work,** (*slang*) hard unrewarded work. [Unkn.].

›NKEY-ENGINE, [dong'-ki-en'-jin], *n.* a small team-engine, as used on a ship for pumping or load- ıg.

›NKEY-PUMP, [dong'-ki-pump'], *n.* a pump perated by a donkey-engine.

›NKEY'S YEARS, [don'-kiz-yēerz'], *n.*(*pl.*) (*coll.*) considerable period of time.

›NNA, DONYA, [don'-a], *n.* the feminine Italian nd Portuguese equivalent of DON. [L. *domina*].

›NNISH, [don'-ish], *adj.* characteristic of a univer- ity don, pedantic.

›NNISM, [don'-izm], *n.* self-importance.

›NOR, [dō'-nor], *n.* one who makes a donation. L. *donator*].

›-NOTHING, [dōō'-nuth'-ing], *n.* a person who oes nothing.

›NSHIP, [don'-ship], *n.* the quality or rank of a entleman or knight.

›NYA, see DONNA.

›NZEL, [don'-zel], *n.* a prospective knight; a page. It. *donzello* bachelor].

›OB-GRASS, [dōōb'-grahs], *n.* (*bot.*) dub, *Cynodon Dactylon*, a perennial creeping grass. [Hind. *dub*].

›ODLE (1), [dōōdl], *n.* a simpleton. [LGerm. *dudeltopf*].

›ODLE (2), [dōōdl], *v.i.*, to scribble aimlessly and bsent-mindedly.

›OLIE, DOOLY, [dōōl'-i], *n.* a covered Indian itter of bamboo. [Hind. *doli*].

›OM (1), [dōōm], *n.* (*archaic*) judgment, judicial entence; fate; ruin; (*hist.*) a decree, statute; Judgment Day; **crack of d.,** the end of the world at the Day of Judgment. [OE. *dom*].

DOOM (2), [dōōm], *v.t.* to sentence to punishment, to condemn. [*Prec.*].

DOOMFUL, [dōōm'-fŏŏl], *adj.* pregnant with destruction, foreboding doom.

DOOM-PALM, see DOUM-PALM.

DOOMSDAY, [dōōmz'-dā], *n.* the Day of Judgment. [OE. *domesdæg*].

DOOMSMAN, [dōōmz'-man], *n.* a judge.

DOOR, [daw(r)], *n.* a sliding or hinged structure closing an entrance; (*fig.*) a means of approach to, that which gives access to; **next d.,** in the next house; **next d. to,** nearly, almost; **out of doors,** in the open air; **to lie at the d. of,** to be chargeable or attributable to; **to show a person the d.,** to ask or force a person to depart. [OE. *duru*].

DOOR-BELL, [daw'-bel'], *n.* a bell worked from outside a house to indicate the presence of a person wishing to enter, etc.

DOOR-CASE, [daw'-kās], *n.* the frame enclosing a door.

DOORING, [daw'-ring], *n.* a door-case.

DOORKEEPER, [daw'-kēp'-er], *n.* a porter; one who minds the entrance to a building.

DOOR-KNOCKER, [daw'-nok'-er], *n.* a knocker on a door used by one wishing to enter, etc.

DOORLESS, [daw'-les], *adj.* lacking a door.

DOORMAT, [daw'-mat], *n.* a mat placed inside an outer door, on which those entering may wipe their feet.

DOOR-NAIL, [daw'-nāl], *n.* a large-headed nail with which wooden doors were once studded for additional strength; **dead as a d.,** quite dead.

DOOR-PLATE, [daw'-plāt], *n.* a metal plate on the door of a house bearing the occupant's name.

DOOR-POST, [daw'-pōst], *n.* one of the uprights of a door-case.

DOOR-SILL, [daw'-sil], *n.* the sill under a door.

DOOR-STEAD, [daw'-sted'], *n.* a doorway.

DOOR-STEP, [daw'-step], *n.* a step immediately below the doorway of a house.

DOOR-STONE, [daw'-stōn], *n.* an oblong stone forming a door-step.

DOORWAY, [daw'-wā], *n.* an opening or entrance closed by a door.

DOOSUTI, [dus-ŏŏt'-i], *n.* a coarse cotton fabric manufactured in India. [Hind. *dosuta*].

DOPE (1), [dōp], *n.* a sluggish oily lubricant; a varnish with which the fabric of aeroplanes or the envelope of an airship is coated to increase tautness and air-tightness; (*coll.*) any drug, such as opium, taken as a narcotic, or used to drug horses, etc.; (*fig.*) anything intended to deceive or quieten; (*slang*) useful or necessary information; (*slang*) motor spirit; **to upset the d.,** to turn out otherwise than was anticipated. [Du. *doop* liquid].

DOPE (2), [dōp], *v.t. and i.* to treat with dope; (*coll.*) to doctor with dope, to drug; (*fig.*) to dupe, to deceive, to allay or soothe.

DOPER, [dōp'-er], *n.* one who drugs (a racehorse).

DOPPEL-GANGER, doppel-gänger, [dopl'-geng'-er], *n.* an apparition of a person not yet dead; a double. [Germ. *doppelgänger*].

DOPPER, [dop'-er], *n.* a dipper, a Dutch Baptist. [Du. *dooper*].

DOR, DORR, [daw(r)], *n.* the common black-beetle, *Geotrupes stercorarius.* [OE. *dora* humble-bee].

DORADO, [dor-ah'-dō], *n.* a southern constellation of six stars; a large fish of the genus *Coryphæna*, often erroneously called the dolphin. [Sp. *dorado* from L. *deauratus* gilded].

DORBIE, [daw'-bi], *n.* the dunlin, *Tringa alpina*. [Unkn.].

DORCAS, [daw'-kas], *n.* a society of charitably minded ladies who meet to make or provide garments for the poor. [*Dorcas*, the woman raised from the dead by St. Peter, Acts ix, 36].

DOR-HAWK, DORR-HAWK, [daw'-hawk], *n.* the nightjar, *Caprimulgus europæus*.

DORIAN (1), [daw'-ri-an], *n.* an inhabitant of Doris, a member of one of the three races which settled in Doris in Northern Greece, about the tenth century B.C.

DORIAN (2), [dawr'-i-an], *adj.* pertaining to Doris in Northern Greece, pertaining to the Dorians. [Gk. *Doros*].

DORIC (1), [dor'-ik], *n.* the Doric dialect of Greece; any broad, rough provincial dialect; the Doric order of architecture.

DORIC (2), [dor'-ik], *adj.* Dorian; (of dialect) unpolished, rough; **D. order,** (*arch.*) the oldest, strongest, and simplest of the three Grecian orders of architecture. [*Prec.*].

DORICISM, [dor'-is-izm], *n.* a Doric expression or phrase.

DORING, [daw'-ring], *n.* the catching of larks by means of a close net and a looking-glass. [Unkn.].

DORKING, [dawk'-ing], *n.* a breed of domestic fowl. [*Dorking*, in Surrey, where originally reared].

DORLACH, [daw'-lak], *n.* a bundle, a portmanteau. [Gael. *dorlach*].

DORMANCY, [daw'-man-si], *n.* the state of being dormant.

DORMANT, [daw'-mant], *adj.* sleeping, in a state of complete inactivity or torpidity; quiescent, at rest, not in use or action; (of a title) not claimed; (*her.*) asleep. [OFr. *dormant*].

DORMER, [daw'-mer], *n.* a bedroom; **d. window,** a vertical window projecting from a sloping roof. [L. *dormitorium* sleeping-room].

DORMER WINDOW

DORMITIVE (1), [dawm'-it-iv], *n.* a soporific. [OFr. *dormitif*].

DORMITIVE (2), [dawm'-it-iv], *adj.* inducing sleep.

DORMITORY, [dawm'-i-ter-i], *n.* a sleeping apartment for a number of people, one divided into several cubicles or containing many beds. [L. *dormitorium* sleeping-room].

DORMOUSE, [daw'-mows], *n.* a small, hibernating rodent related to the mouse and squirrel. [Uncert.].

DORMY, [daw'-mi], *adj.* (*golf*) as many holes up on one's opponent as there remain holes to play.

DORN, [dawn], *n.* the thornback skate, *Raia clavata*. [Germ. *dorn* a thorn].

DORNICK, DORNOCK, [dawn'-ik, -ok], *n.* a strong, figured linen fabric. [*Dornick*, or Tournay, in Flanders, where first made].

DORNIER, [dawn'-i-er], *n.* a German bombing aeroplane made by the firm bearing that name.

DOROTHY-PERKINS, [do'-ro-thi-pur'-kinz], *n.* a pink rambler rose. [Personal name].

DORR, see DOR.

DORR-HAWK, see DOR-HAWK.

DORSAL, [daw'-sal], *adj.* pertaining to, near, or on the back. [L. *dorsalis*].

DORSALLY, [daws'-a-li], *adv.* at or from the back.

DORSE, [daws], *n.* a young cod-fish. [LGerm. *dorsch*].

DORSEL (1), see DOSSAL.

DORSEL (2), DOSSEL†, [daw'-sel], *n.* a pannier for a beast of burden. [~DORSAL].

DORSI-, DORSO-, *pref.* back. [L. *dorsum* back].

DORSIBRANCHIATE, [daw'-si-brangk'-i-āt], *adj.* having gills on the back. [DORSI and BRANCHIATE].

DORSIFEROUS, [daw-sif'-er-us], *adj.* (*bot.*) (of ferns, etc.) bearing the organs of fertilization upon the back of the frond. [DORSI and L. *ferre* to bear].

DORSIFIXED, [daw'-si-fikst], *adj.* (*bot.*) fastened by the back. [DORSI and FIX].

DORSIGEROUS, [daw-sij'-er-us], *adj.* carrying its young upon the back. [DORSI and L. *gerere* to bear].

DORSIPAROUS, [daw-sip'-er-us], *adj.* (*bot.*) bearing seeds on the back of their leaves. [DORSI and L. *parus* bringing forth].

DORSISPINAL, [daw'-si-spī'-nal], *adj.* (*anat.*) pertaining to the spine and back.

DORSO-, see DORSI-.

DORSOVENTRAL, [daw'-sō-ven'-tral], *adj.* (*bot.*) differing in structure on the dorsal and ventral surfaces; (*anat.*) pertaining to the dorsal and ventral surfaces or parts.

DORSUM, [daw'-sum], *n.* (*anat.*) the back, the outer surface of an organ or part. [L. *dorsum* back].

DORY (1), [daw'-ri], *n.* an edible sea-fish, *Zeus faber*, known as the john dory. [Fr. *dorée* from L. *deaurata* gilded].

DORY (2), [daw'-ri], *n.* a small, flat-bottomed boat used in cod-fishing, etc. [Unkn.].

DOSAGE, [dōs'-ij], *n.* the act of dosing; the quantity of a single dose.

DOSE (1), [dōs], *n.* the quantity of medicine prescribed to be taken at one time; (*fig.*) a share or amount, a regular definite quantity; (*coll.*) a bout (of illness, etc.). [Gk. *dosis* gift].

DOSE (2), [dōs], *v.t.* to give a dose or series of doses to.

DOSIMETER, [dōs-im'-it-er], *n.* an apparatus measuring doses. [DOSE and METER].

DOSOLOGY, [dōs-ol'-o-ji], *n.* the study of medi with regard to doses and dosing. [DOSE and *logos* speech].

DOSS (1), [dos], *n.* (*slang*) a bed, *esp.* in a regist lodging-house; a sleep. [Unkn.].

DOSS (2), [dos], *v.i.* (*slang*) to sleep; to stay the n at a doss-house.

DOSSAL, DORSEL, DOSSEL, [dos'-al], *n.* (*ec* a richly ornamental cloth, hung behind the a or at the sides of the chancel; hangings of rich dra behind a chair. [MedL. *dossale*].

DOSSER, [dos'-er], *n.* one who sleeps at a doss-ho

DOSS-HOUSE, [dos'-hows], *n.* a cheap lodg house.

DOSSIER, [dos'-i-ā], *n.* a collection of paper documents on the same subject. [Fr. *dossier* lection of documents].

DOSSIL, [dos'-il], *n.* a wad of lint for pluggi wound; (*print.*) a cloth roll for wiping the i surface of a copper-plate. [OFr. *dosil* plug].

DOT (1), [dot], *n.* a very small, round point or m made with a pen, pencil, etc., *esp.* one used in punc tion; (*mus.*) a point placed after a rest or not indicate that its time value is to be increased by half; a speck, anything like a dot in size; (*coll.*) a child; the short symbol in signalling, Morse C etc.; **to be off one's d.,** (*slang*) to be crazy. *dott* speck].

DOT (2), [dō], *n.* a woman's marriage portio dowry. [Fr. *dot*].

DOT (3), (dotting, dotted), [dot], *v.t.* to mark a dot or dots; to trace out or draw with dots; to p a dot over (*i* or *j*) or after (a musical note or rest scatter about or cover with objects resembling from a distance; (*slang*) to hit, to strike; **to d. o i's,** to be extremely particular, exact, or scrupu [DOT (1)].

DOTAGE, [dōt'-ij], *n.* senility, the feebleness o age; folly, excessive fondness.

DOTAL, [dōt'-al], *adj.* relating to a dowry. (2)].

DOTARD, DOTTARD, [dōt'-erd], *n.* a pe feeble in mind and body because of old age.

DOTARDLY, [dōt'-erd-li], *adj.* like a dotard, fo and decrepit.

DOTATION, [dō-tā'-shun], *n.* the act of givi marriage portion to a woman; an endowment a charitable institution. [L. *dotatio*].

DOTE, [dōt], *v.i.* to behave or talk foolishly, to be weak-minded through old age; to adore bli **to d. on, upon,** to be infatuated with. [MLG *doten*].

DOTER, [dōt'-er], *n.* one who dotes.

DOTH, [duth], (*archaic*) *third person sg. pres* of DO.

DOTING, [dōt'-ing], *adj.* adoring, infatuated; w minded, senile.

DOTINGLY, [dōt'-ing-li], *adv.* in a doting fashi

DOTISH, [dōt'-ish], *adj.* stupid, childish, w minded.

DOTTARD, see DOTARD.

DOTTED, [dot'-id], *adj.* marked with a dot or **d. about,** scattered here and there.

DOTTEREL, DOTTREL, [dot'-er-el], *n.* a sp of plover much esteemed for its flesh, *Eudro morinellus*. [~DOTE].

DOTTLE, [dotl], *n.* a small plug of tobacco ash in a pipe after a smoke. [DOT (1)].

DOTTREL, see DOTTEREL.

DOTTY, [dot'-i], *adj.* marked with dots; (*slang*) crazy.

DOUANE, [dōō-ahn'], *n.* a custom-house, *esp* the Continent. [Fr. *douane* from Arab. *d* DIVAN].

DOUANIER, [dōō-ahn'-i-ā], *n.* a customs officia

DOUBLE (1), [dubl], *n.* twice the quantity or amo a person exactly similar in appearance to ano an easy running pace; (*cards*) an increase, us twice the amount, in points awarded or s decided upon by one of the players, on the stre of his hand; (*tennis*) two faults in succession serving; (*pl.*) a foursome at tennis; an acto singer who takes two parts in the same piece act of returning on one's tracks to baffle purs (*racing*) a bet on two horses in different races, winnings from one race together with the stake, carried forward and wagered upon the second (*darts*) a throw landing between the narrow s enclosed by the two outer circles of a dartboard

OUBLE (2), [dubl], *adj.* twice as much, as much gain (of quality, strength, amount, size, aspect, ppearance, etc.); for the use of two persons or things; erving two purposes; in pairs, having two similar arts, twofold; having two layers; acting in two ays; having two meanings, one of which is secret r underhand; (*mus.*) an octave lower in pitch. OFr. *double* from L. *duplus*].

OUBLE (3), [dubl], *adv.* doubly, two at a time, twice ver, in pairs.

OUBLE (4), [dubl], *v.t.* to make double; to bend o as to form two layers, to fold over; to play two arts in one piece; to clench (the fists); (*naut.*) to sail ompletely round a point so that the course of the hip is reversed; (*mus.*) to play the same melody as nother instrument, but an octave higher or lower n pitch; (*milit.*) to proceed at double-quick marching ime; (*billiards*) to pot a ball so that it rebounds from t least one cushion before entering the pocket; *ards*) to increase greatly the points possible to be ained or lost by an opponent, on the strength of ne's own hand; *v.i.* to become twice as much, to ncrease by as much again; to run; to twist and urn in one's course as one runs; to turn back upon ne's tracks to elude pursuers; **to d. up,** to cause a erson to bend right over in pain, etc.; (*fig.*) to cause person to collapse or crumple up; to collapse, to rumple up; (*betting*) to double the amount staked ach time until a win is recorded. [OFr. *doubler* from . *duplare*].

OUBLE-ACTING, [dubl'-akt'-ing], *adj.* (*mech.*) perating in two directions.

OUBLE-BANKED, [dubl'-bangkt'], *adj.* (*naut.*) aving two opposite oars for rowers on the same hwart or two men on the same oar.

OUBLE-BARRELLED, [dubl'-ba'-reld], *adj.* (of a un) furnished with two barrels; (*fig.*) having a two-old effect.

OUBLE-BASS, [dubl'-bās'], *n.* the largest of the tringed instruments of the violin family.

OUBLE-BITING, [dubl'-bīt'-ing], *adj.* cutting vith both sides.

OUBLE-BREASTED, [dubl'-brest'-id], *adj.* (of ackets, etc.) cut to have a double thickness in front vhen buttoned up, and capable of being fastened vith either flap outermost.

OUBLE-CROSS, [dubl'-kros'], *v.t.* to act treacher-usly towards, to swindle, to betray.

OUBLE-DEALER, [dubl'-dēl'-er], *n.* a deceitful erson who will make contrary professions to fit nmediate necessity.

OUBLE-DEALING, [dubl'-dēl'-ing], *n.* duplicity, reachery.

OUBLE-DECKER, [dubl'-dek'-er], *n.* a passenger ehicle having two levels of seating accommodation; *aeron.*) a biplane; a stand having seating accom-nodation on two levels or floors.

OUBLE-DECLUTCH, [dubl'-dē-kluch'], *v.i.* *motoring*) to let out the clutch both before leaving vhatever gear the car is already in, and going into eutral, and again before going from neutral gear into he next gear desired. [DOUBLE (2) and DECLUTCH].

OUBLE-DUTCH, [dubl'-duch'], *n.* (*coll.*) unintel-igible talk; anything unintelligible.

OUBLE-DYE, [dubl'-dī'], *v.t.* to dye twice.

OUBLE-DYED, [dubl'-dīd'], *adj.* having been yed twice; (*fig.*) deeply involved, habitually ractising, out-and-out.

OUBLE-EAGLE, [dubl'-ēgl], *n.* a gold coin worth wenty dollars.

OUBLE-EDGED, [dubl'-ejd], *adj.* having two dges; (*fig.*) having a two-fold effect.

OUBLE-ENTENDRE, [dōōbl'-ahn-tahn'-dr], *n.* tatement with two meanings, one of which is often mproper.

OUBLE-ENTRY, [dubl'-en'-tri], *n.* (*comm.*) a book-eeping system by which every transaction is entered wice, as a debt to one account, and a credit to nother.

OUBLE-FACED, [dubl'-fāst], *adj.* having or show-ng two faces; (*fig.*) insincere, hypocritical.

OUBLE-FIRST, [dubl'-furst'], *n.* a university egree with first-class honours in two sections of the xamination, or in two different subjects.

OUBLE-FLOWERED, [dubl'-flow'-erd], *adj.* (*hort.*) vith the stamens and pistils transformed into petals, hus having the number of petals doubled.

OUBLE-GILD, [dubl'-gild], *v.t.* to gild with a double oating.

OUBLE-GLOSTER, [dubl'-glos'-ter], *n.* a Glouces-er cheese of double thickness.

DOUBLE-HANDED, [dubl'-hand'-id] *adj.* having two handles; for use with both hands.

DOUBLE-HEADED, [dubl'-hed'-id], *adj.* having two heads.

DOUBLE-HEARTED, [dubl'-haht'-id], *adj.* treacherous, hypocritical.

DOUBLE-HUNG, [dubl'-hung'], *adj.* of window sashes, hung on ropes in such a way as to move up and down.

DOUBLE-LOCK, [dubl'-lok'], *v.t.* to lock twice; to fasten with double security.

DOUBLE-MANNED, [dubl'-mand'], *adj.* having twice the usual number of men.

DOUBLE-MEANING, [dubl'-mēn'-ing], *n.* a state-ment or phrase having two meanings, one usually indecent.

DOUBLE-MINDED, [dubl'-mīnd'-id], *adj.* of uncer-tain opinion, wavering.

DOUBLE-NATURED, [dubl'-nā'-cherd], *adj.* hav-ing a twofold nature.

DOUBLENESS, [dubl'-nes], *n.* the condition or quality of being double.

DOUBLE-PLEA, [dubl'-plē], *n.* (*leg.*) a defending plea which alleges two different matters in bar of the action.

DOUBLE-QUARREL, [dubl'-kwo'-rel], *n.* (*eccles. leg.*) a complaint to the archbishop against an inferior ordinary for delay of justice.

DOUBLE-QUICK, [dubl'-kwik'], *adj. and adv.* very quick(ly), at the speed of the double.

DOUBLE-SHADE, [dubl'-shād], *v.t.* to double the natural darkness of.

DOUBLE-SHINING, [dubl'-shīn'-ing], *adj.* shining with doubly increased lustre.

DOUBLE-SNIPE, [dubl'-snīp], *n.* the great snipe, *Gallinago major*.

DOUBLE-STAR, [dubl'-stah(r)], *n.* two stars so close together as to appear as one to the naked eye.

DOUBLE-STOP, [dubl'-stop], *v.i.* (*mus.*) to play chords on a violin on two or more stopped strings.

DOUBLET, [dub'-let], *n.* (*archaic*) a tight garment covering the upper part of the trunk; (*pl.*) a throw at dice of the same number on both dice; (*philol.*) one of several loan-words having a common origin, but entering a language at different periods or through different sources, having acquired a different form and often a separate meaning; two birds killed by one discharge from a double-barrelled gun; a com-bination of two simple lenses; an imitation gem con-sisting of two pieces of crystal with a colour or a small piece of a precious stone between them. [Fr. *doublet*].

DOUBLE-THROW, [dubl'-thrō], *adj.* (of a switch) operating in two ways.

DOUBLETON, [dubl'-ton], *n.* (*cards*) two cards only of a suit.

DOUBLE-TONGUED, [dubl'-tungd], *adj.* treacher-ous, back-biting.

DOUBLE-TONGUING, [dubl'-tung'-ing], *n.* (*mus.*) a method of playing rapidly repeated or staccato notes on the cornet or flute, by quickly alternating the tongue between the teeth and hard palate with a trilling effect.

DOUBLING, [dub'-ling], *n.* the act of one who doubles; a fold; (*her.*) the ornamental lining of a robe, etc.

DOUBLOON, [dub-lōōn'], *n.* a Spanish and South American gold coin of about the value of a guinea, so called as being originally double the value of a pistole. [Span. *doblon*].

DOUBLURE, [dubl'-yōō-er], *n.* lining; the orna-mental leather binding inside a book. [Fr. *doublure*].

DOUBLY, [dub'-li], *adv.* twice as much, to twice the extent.

DOUBT (1), [dowt], *n.* hesitancy or disinclination to believe, lack of conviction; state of being undecided; misgiving, uncertainty, suspicion; **to give the benefit of the d.,** to take a lenient view in the absence of proof. [OFr. *dute*, L. *dubitum*].

DOUBT (2), [dowt], *v.t.* to be disinclined to believe or recognize as true; to suspect, view with distrust; (*archaic*) to fear; *v.i.* to waver in opinion; to be undecided about and therefore disinclined to believe the truth of, *esp.* of religious doctrine; to be uncon-vinced; to think something to be unlikely. [OFr. *douter*, L. *dubitare* to be uncertain].

DOUBTABLE, [dowt'-abl], *adj.* capable of being doubted.

DOUBTER, [dowt'-er], *n.* a person who doubts.

DOUBTFUL, [dowt'-fōōl], *adj.* not proved or certain, not clear in meaning; undecided, not determined or resolute; disreputable.

DOUBTFULLY, [dowt'-fōōl-i], *adv.* in a doubtful way.
DOUBTFULNESS, [dowt'-fōōl-nes], *n.* the condition of being doubtful.
DOUBTINGLY, [dowt'-ing-li], *adv.* in a doubting way.
DOUBTIVE†, [dowt'-iv], *adj.* in doubt. [OFr. *doutif*].
DOUBTLESS (1), [dowt'-les], *adj.* (*rare*) confident, without fear or hesitation.
DOUBTLESS (2), [dowt'-les], *adv.* unquestionably; probably.
DOUBTLESSLY, [dowt'-les-li], *adv.* unquestionably, indubitably.
DOUC, [dōōk], *n.* a species of monkey found in Cochin China, *Semnopithecus nemaeus*. [Cochin *douc* monkey].
DOUCETS, [dow'-sets], *n.(pl.)* the testicles of a hart or stag. [Fr. *doucet* soft].
DOUCEUR, [dōō-sur'], *n.* a tip. [Fr. *douceur* sweetness].
DOUCHE (1), [dōōsh], *n.* a shower of water, or a stream of vapour, directed on some part of the body; a shower bath; (*fig.*) an unpleasant shock; **to throw a cold d. upon,** (*fig.*) to discourage. [Fr. *douche*].
DOUCHE (2), [dōōsh], *v.t.* to spray with a douche.
DOUCINE, [dōō-sēn'], *n.* (*arch.*) an ornamental moulding, concave above and convex below. [Fr. *doucine*].
DOUGH, [dō], *n.* a thick mass of flour or meal, kneaded ready for baking; (*slang*) money; **my cake is d.,** my plan has miscarried. [OE. *dah*].
DOUGH-BAKED, [dō'-bākt], *adj.* not properly baked.
DOUGHBOY, [dō'-boi], *n.* a boiled dumpling; (*U.S. slang*) an American soldier.
DOUGH-FACE, [dō'-fās], *n.* (*U.S.*) anyone easily influenced.
DOUGH-FACED, [dō'-fāst], *adj.* easily influenced.
DOUGH-KNEADED, [dō'-nēd'-id], *adj.* soft, like dough.
DOUGHNUT, [dō'-nut], *n.* a small, roundish, fried cake.
DOUGHTILY, [dowt'-i-li], *adv.* in a doughty manner.
DOUGHTINESS, [dowt'-i-nes], *n.* the quality of being doughty.
DOUGHTY, [dowt'-i], *adj.* (*archaic*) brave, valiant. [OE. *dyhtig*].
DOUGHY, [dō'-i], *adj.* like dough, soft, half-baked.
DOUKAR, [dōōk'-ah(r)], *n.* the dabchick. [Unkn.].
DOUKHOBORS, [dōōk'-ō-bawz], *n.(pl.)* a pacifist religious sect of Russian origin settled in Canada. [Russ. *doukhobor* spirit fighter].
DOUM (DOOM) PALM, [dowm' (dōōm) pahm], *n.* a variety of Egyptian palm, *Hyphena thebaica*, yielding an edible fruit, and having a trunk repeatedly branching in pairs. [Arab. *daum, dum.*]

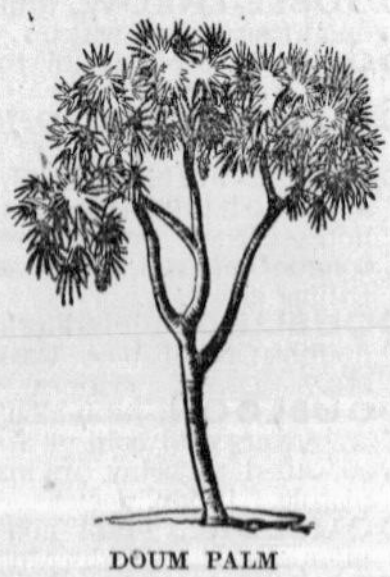
DOUM PALM

DOUR, [dōōer], *adj.* stern, obstinate. [L. *durus* hard].
DOURA, see DURRA.
DOURLY, [dōōer'-li], *adv.* in a dour fashion.
DOURNESS, [dōōer'-nes], *n.* the quality of being dour.
DOUROUCOLI, [dōō'-rōō-kol'-i], *n.* a South American monkey of the genus *Nyctipithecus*.
DOUSE, [dows], *v.t.* to plunge into water, to drench, squirt water on; (*naut.*) to slacken suddenly (a sail); (*coll.*) to put out (a light). [Unkn.].
DOUT, [dowt], *v.t.* to extinguish. [DO and OUT].
DOUTER, [dowt'-er], *n.* an extinguisher.
DOVE, [duv], *n.* one of the many species of pigeon; (*fig.*) the Holy Spirit; the emblem of innocence or peace; a term of endearment. [OE. *dufe*].
DOVE-COLOUR, [duv'-kul'-er], *adj.* purplish or pinkish grey.
DOVECOT, DOVECOTE, [duv'-kot], *n.* a wooden hutch on a pole, with roosting boxes for pigeons.
DOVE-HOUSE, [duv'-hows], *n.* a dovecot.
DOVEKIE, [duv'-ki], *n.* the black guillemot, *Uria grylle*, found in the Arctic. [Scots from DOVE].
DOVELET, [duv'-let], *n.* a young dove.
DOVELIKE, [duv'-lik], *adj.* innocent, meek.
DOVER, [dō'-ver], *v.i.* to sleep lightly, to doze off. [OE. *dofung* dotage].
DOVER'S-POWDER, [dō'-verz-pow'-der], *n.* a c pound of ipecacuanha, opium, and potassium s phate, used medicinally as a sedative and sudori [Dr. T. *Dover*, the inventor].
DOVES-FOOT, [duvz'-fōōt], *n.* the plant, *Gerani molle*.
DOVETAIL (1), [duv'-tāl], *n.* (*carp.*) a method fastening pieces of timber together, by pushing a wedge-shaped projection on one piece into a corresponding incision in another piece.

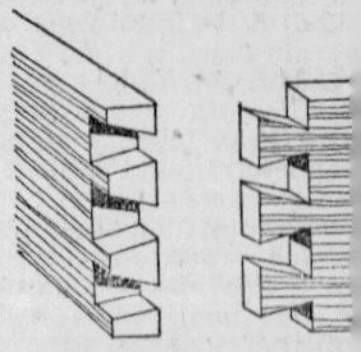
DOVETAILING JOINTS

DOVETAIL (2), [duv'-tāl], *v.t. and i.* to fasten together by means of dovetail joints; (*fig.*) to fit neatly and closely together.
DOVETAILING, [duv'-tāl-ing], *n.* a dovetail joint.
DOWABLE, [dow'-abl], *adj.* that may be endow entitled to a dower. [AFr. *douable*].
DOWAGER, [dow'-a-jer], *n.* a widow with a dow a titled woman whose husband has died. [O *douagere*].
DOWDILY, [dowd'-i-li], *adv.* in dowdy fashion.
DOWDINESS, [dow'-di-nes], *n.* the state or qua of being dowdy.
DOWDY (1), [dow'-di], *n.* a woman dressed ir slovenly fashion. [ME. *doudé* slut].
DOWDY (2), [dow'-di], *adj.* ill-dressed; inelegant.
DOWDYISH, [dow'-di-ish], *adj.* rather dowdy.
DOWEE, [dow'-ē], *n.* a woman having a dower. [*douée*].
DOWEL (1), [dow'-el], *n.* a pin or peg of metal, sto wood, etc., without a head, used in making joins a fastenings. [LGerm. *dovel* a plug].
DOWEL (2), (dowelling, dowelled), [dow'-el], to fasten by dowels.
DOWELLING, [dow'-el-ing], *n.* a method of fast ing by dowels.
DOWEL-PIN, [dow'-el-pin'], *n.* a dowel.
DOWER (1), [dow'-er], *n.* a part of a husband's est which falls to his widow for life, reverting to his he at her death; the property which a woman brings her husband in marriage; a gift made by a husba to a wife; endowment, gift; **d. house,** the ho reserved for the widow. [OFr. *douaire* from Med *dotarium*].
DOWER (2), [dow'-er], *v.t.* to provide with a dow to endow.
DOWERED, [dow'-erd], *adj.* having a dower.
DOWERLESS, [dow'-er-les], *adj.* without a dower
DOWERY, see DOWRY.
DOWLAS, [dow'-las], *n.* a coarse kind of cali [*Daoulas*, in Brittany, where first made].
DOWLE†, [dowl], *n.* the filament of a feather, dov the soft fur of animals or feathers of birds. [Uncer
DOWN (1), [down], *n.* the first plumage or s feathers of birds; any soft substance resembl this, the first hair appearing on a youth's face, hairy covering on certain plants, fruits, seeds, e [OIcel. *dunn*].
DOWN (2), [down], *n.* a tract of open, treeless, h land, mostly used as pasture. [OE. *dun* hill].
DOWN (3), [down], *n.* (*coll.*) a grudge; a reversa fortune. [DOWN (5)].
DOWN (4), [down], *adj.* descending; (*fig.*) deject (of a train, etc.), travelling away from the chief t minus, *esp.* London. [DOWN (5)].
DOWN (5), [down], *adv.* from a higher to a lower po tion, from a vertical to a horizontal position; to so place considered as being lower, as from a large c to a smaller place, from the source of a river to t mouth, to a place south of the speaker, etc.; in a l position, on the ground; below a level state, bel the horizon or surface, denoting loss of money; (*spo* indicating defeat or failure (also in a test or exami tion); from a higher to a lower social position, fr prosperity to misfortune; indicating decrease weakening; from earlier to later times; from t beginning; (*coll.*) on the spot, there and then; **to d. on,** to be strongly opposed to; **d. at heel,** deject shabby, poor; **d. in the mouth,** dispirited, miserab **a d.-and-out,** a person with no money or prospec **to be d. on one's luck,** to be in straitened circu stances; **d. with!** abolish, put an end to; **to be** (*sport*) to be behind, to be in arrears, to have lost mon [OE *of dune* from the hill].

DOWN (6), [down], *prep.* from a higher to a lower position on, in a descending direction in; away from (the speaker or a given point); along; from an earlier to a later time in. [*Prec.*].
DOWN (7), [down], *v.t.* (*coll.*) to bring, put, or knock down, to defeat; **to d. tools,** to cease work.
DOWNBEAR†, [down'-bāer], *v.t.* to bear down, to oppress.
DOWNBED, [down'-bed'], *n.* a bed of down.
DOWNCAST (1), [down'-kahst], *n.* a shaft for admitting air into a mine; (*geol.*) a downthrow.
DOWNCAST (2), [down'-kahst], *adj.* (of looks) directed downwards; dejected, dispirited.
DOWNCOME, [down'-kum], *n.* downfall, sudden fall.
DOWN-DRAUGHT, [down'-drahft], *n.* a downward current of air.
DOWN-EASTER, [down'-ēst'-er], *n.* a native of New England.
DOWNFALL, [down'-fawl], *n.* the act of descending; that which falls; (*fig.*) ruin, overthrow.
DOWNFALLEN, [down'-fawl'-en], *adj.* ruined, decrepit.
DOWNGRADE, [down'-grād], *n.* the downward path or trend.
DOWN-GYVED, [down'-jivd], *adj.* hanging loosely round the ankles.
DOWNHAUL, [down'-hawl], *n.* (*naut.*) a rope fastened to the upper corner of a sail to haul it down.
DOWNHEARTED, [down-haht'-id], *adj.* dispirited, dejected.
DOWNHILL (1), [down'-hil], *n.* declivity, the downward slope of a hill.
DOWNHILL (2), [down'-hil], *adj.* sloping downwards, descending the slope.
DOWNHILL (3), [down'-hil], *adv.* towards the bottom of a hill; (*fig.*) so as to decline or deteriorate, on the downward path.
DOWNINESS, [down'-i-nes], *n.* the condition of being downy.
DOWNLAND, [down'-land], *n.* hilly pasture land.
DOWN-LINE, [down'-līn], *n.* the railway line along which outward-bound trains from the main terminus travel.
DOWN-LOOKED†, [down'-lŏŏkt], *adj.* having a downcast look, having a guilty uncomfortable air, averting the gaze downwards.
DOWN-LYING, [down'-lī'-ing], *adj.* retiring to bed, lying at rest.
DOWNPOUR, [down'-paw(r)], *n.* a heavy continuous fall of rain, a deluge.
DOWN-QUILT, [down'-kwilt'], *n.* a quilt of eiderdown.
DOWNRIGHT (1), [down'-rīt], *adj.* plain, frank, direct, unceremonious; complete, utter.
DOWNRIGHT (2), [down'-rīt], *adv.* completely, utterly.
DOWNRIGHTLY, [down'-rīt'-li], *adv.* in a downright fashion.
DOWNRIGHTNESS, [down'-rīt-nes], *n.* the quality of being downright.
DOWNRUSH, [down'-rush], *n.* a sudden rushing down.
DOWNSET, [down'-set], *adj.* (*her.*) (of a fesse) broken so that both halves are not set on the same level.
DOWNSTAIRS (1), [down'-stāerz], *adj.* situated on a lower floor.
DOWNSTAIRS (2), [down-stāerz'], *adv.* to or on a lower floor.
DOWNSTREAM, [down'-strēm], *adv.* in the same direction as the flow of the stream.
DOWNTHROW, [down'-thrō], *n.* (*geol.*) the sinking of the strata where a fault occurs, the amount the strata sinks.
DOWN-TRAIN, [down'-trān], *n.* a train travelling away from the main terminus.

DOWNTHROW

DOWNTROD, [down'-trod'], *adj.* (*poet.*) downtrodden.
DOWNTRODDEN, [down'-trod'-en], *adj.* trampled or beaten down; (*fig.*) oppressed.
DOWNWARD (1), [down'-werd], *adj.* descending; (*fig.*) degenerate, leading to ruin. [OE. *adunweard*].
DOWNWARD (2), [down'-werd], *adv.* to a lower place, down; towards ruin or depravity.
DOWNWARDS, [down'-werdz], *adj. and adv.* downward.
DOWNWEED, [down'-wēd], *n.* (*bot.*) a downy, fluffy plant, the cottonweed.
DOWNY (1), [down'-i], *adj.* resembling downland.
DOWNY (2), [down'-i], *adj.* soft and fluffy like down; made of, or covered with down; (*slang*) artful, wily, alert.
DOWRY, DOWERY, [dow'-ri], *n.* the property or portion which a woman brings to her husband as a dower; (*fig.*) a natural gift or talent. [OFr. *douaire*].
DOWSE, [dows], *v.i.* to search for subterranean sources of water or mineral ores with a divining-rod. [Unkn.].
DOWSER, [dows'-er], *n.* one who seeks underground sources of water, or mineral deposits, with a divining-rod.
DOWSING, [dows'-ing], *n.* the art of discovering water or minerals by the divining-rod; **d.-rod,** a twig used by diviners.
DOXOLOGICAL, [dok'-sō-loj'-ik-al], *adj.* relating to doxology.
DOXOLOGIZE, [doks-ol'-oj-īz], *v.i.* to praise God, to utter a doxology.
DOXOLOGY, [doks-ol'-o-ji], *n.* a hymn of praise to God, *esp.* the short formula used at the end of canticles and psalms. [Gk. *doxologia* an utterance of praise].
DOXY (1), [dok'-si], *n.* a loose woman, a beggar's mistress. [Unkn.].
DOXY (2), [dok'-si], *n.* (*coll.*) an opinion, belief, doctrine. [(ORTHO)DOXY].
DOYEN, [dwa'-ya(ng)], *n.* the senior member of a profession or society. [Fr. *doyen* dean].
DOYLEY, see DOILY.
DOZE (1), [dōz], *n.* a short light sleep.
DOZE (2), [dōz], *v.i.* to slumber or sleep lightly for short periods, to drowse off into a light sleep. [Dan. *dosig* drowsy].
DOZEN, [duzn], *n.* a group of twelve; (*pl.*) (*coll.*) a great number; **baker's d.,** thirteen; **to talk nineteen to the d.,** (*coll.*) to talk incessantly and quickly. [OFr. *dozaine* from L. *duodecim* twelve].
DOZER, [dōz'-er], *n.* one who dozes.
DOZINESS, [dōz'-i-nes], *n.* the state of being dozy, drowsiness.
DOZY, [dōz'-i], *adj.* drowsy, half asleep.
DRAB (1), [drab], *n.* a slovenly woman; a prostitute, [Ir. *drabog* slattern].
DRAB (2), [drab], *n.* a kind of thick woollen cloth of a dun colour; a dull brownish grey colour. [Fr. *drap* cloth].
DRAB (3), [drab], *adj.* of a dull brown or dun colour; (*fig.*) dingy, dreary, monotonous. [*Prec.*].
DRABBET, [drab'-it], *n.* a drab twilled linen for smock-frocks. [*Prec.*].
DRABBISH, [drab'-ish], *adj.* rather drab-looking.
DRABBLE, [drabl], *v.t. and i.* to make wet and dirty by dragging through mud and water; to splash about and wade through mud and mire; (*angling*) to fish for barbel with a rod and line weighted with a bullet, so that the hook is drawn along the bottom. [LGerm. *drabbeln*].
DRABBLING, [drab'-ling], *n.* the act of one who drabbles.
DRABLER, [drab'-ler], *n.* (*naut.*) a small additional sail made fast to the bottom of a bonnet on a square sail.
DRACAENA, [dras-ē'-na], *n.* (*bot.*) a genus of evergreen plants of the order Liliaceae. [Gk. *drakaina*, *fem.* of *drakon* dragon].
DRACANTH, see TRAGACANTH.
DRACHM, [dram], *n.* a drachma; the eighth of a fluid ounce in apothecaries' weight, the sixteenth of an ounce in avoirdupois weight; (*fig.*) a minute amount or quantity. [Gk. *drakhme* an Attic coin or weight].
DRACHMA, [drak'-ma], *n.* the chief silver coin of the ancient Greeks; the modern Greek standard silver coin; an ancient Greek unit of weight. [*Prec.*].
DRACINA, DRACINE, [dras-ēn'(-a)], *n.* draconin.
DRACO, [drā'-kō], *n.* (*astron.*) a constellation of the northern hemisphere; (*zool.*) a genus of agamoid lizards, *esp. Draco volans*, a lizard found in Malay; a luminous gas over marshes. [Gk. *drakon* dragon].
DRACONIAN, [drak-ō'-ni-an], *adj.* (*leg.*) harsh, rigorous. [*Drakon*, an Athenian Greek who introduced a code of severe laws in 621 B.C.].
DRACONIC, [drak-on'-ik], *adj.* Draconian.
DRACONIN, DRACONINE, [drak'-on-in], *n.* the colouring matter in dragon's-blood, obtained from the palm, *Calamus Draco*, and from the tree, *Dracæna Draco*.
DRAFF, [draf], *n.* refuse, dregs, *esp.* of malt after the liquor has been drawn off; hog wash. [ME. *draf*].
DRAFFISH, [draf'-ish], *adj.* worthless like draff.
DRAFFY, [draf'-i], *adj.* draffish.
DRAFT (1), [drahft], *n.* the act of drawing; that which is drawn; a body of men selected for special service;

a written order authorizing payment by a banker, the act of drawing money with this; a preliminary outline or plan, a rough first copy. [DRAUGHT (1)].

DRAFT (2), [drahft], *v.t.* to select a body of men for special service; to make a rough copy of, to prepare plans for, to subject to later revision (a Parliamentary Bill).

DRAFT-HORSE, see DRAUGHT-HORSE.

DRAFT-OX, see DRAUGHT-OX.

DRAFTSMAN, see DRAUGHTSMAN.

DRAG (1), [drag], *n.* that which is dragged; a low cart or car, a heavy sledge, a four-wheeled coach drawn by two or four horses; a contrivance used for recovering objects under water; a heavy harrow; a strong-smelling substance dragged along a chosen course for the hounds to follow instead of chasing a fox; that which drags, the iron shoe of a brake; (*fig.*) a hindrance, a burden; (*billiards*) a method of striking the cue-ball so that it travels at a reduced speed; (*aeron.*) air resistance against an aeroplane when flying, reduction in power due to this.

DRAG (2), **(dragging, dragged)**, [drag], *v.t. and i.* to haul along with considerable effort; to break up land with a harrow; to allow (the feet) to trail along the ground; to use dredging or grappling instruments, nets, etc., to explore (a stretch of water) in search of some object; to trail along the ground, to pass very slowly, to be long drawn out; (*mus.*) to fail to keep up to time; **to d. on,** to be tedious and protracted; **to d. in,** to insert unnecessarily; **to d. up,** (*coll.*) to bring up (children) in a careless manner; **to d. anchor,** (*naut.*) to trail the anchor along the bottom when it has failed to hold. [Swed. *dragga*].

DRAGANT†, [drag-ant'], *n.* the gum tragacanth. [Gk. *tragakantha*].

DRAGEE, dragée, [drah'-zhā], *n.* a chocolate drop. [Fr. *dragée* from Gk. *tragemata* sweetmeats].

DRAGGLE, [dragl], *v.t. and i.* to make wet and dirty by dragging through mud; to be drawn along the ground or trailed through mud. [Unkn.].

DRAGGLE-TAIL, [dragl'-tāl], *n.* a slovenly woman, with muddy skirts.

DRAGGLE-TAILED, [dragl'-tāld], *adj.* sluttish, with muddy, trailing skirts.

DRAG-HUNT, [drag'-hunt], *n.* a hunt in which the hounds follow a drag.

DRAGMAN, [drag'-man], *n.* a fisherman who fishes with a drag-net.

DRAG-NET, [drag'-net'], *n.* a net drawn along the bottom of a stretch of water to catch fish, or along the ground to catch game.

DRAGOMAN, [drag'-ō-man], *n.* an interpreter, *esp.* in Arabic, Turkish, or Persian; a guide to foreigners in the East. [Arab. *targuman* interpreter].

DRAGON, [drag'-un], *n.* a fabulous monster, having the form of a serpent with wings, legs, and fiery breath; (*her.*) a representation of this monster; (*astron.*) the northern constellation, *Draco*; (*fig.*) a fierce, unapproachable, terrifying woman, *esp.* when the chaperon of a young girl; (*bot.*) the Mediterranean plant, *Arum Dracunculus*; (*zool.*) one of several species of lizards found in south-east Asia, the flying lizard of the East Indies, having wing-like processes along its sides; a variety of pigeon; a short musket or carbine with a dragon's head used by dragoons; (*bibl.*) name given to various animals in the Authorized Version; (*milit.*) a powerful tractor used in hauling artillery. [Fr. from Gk. *drakon* dragon].

DRAGONET, [drag'-un-et], *n.* one of several small sea-fishes of the family *Callionymidae*, the male of which is brilliantly coloured and possesses a large elongated dorsal fin. [Fr. *dragonet*].

DRAGON-FISH, [drag'-un-fish'], *n.* the dragonet.

DRAGON-FLY, [drag'-un-flī'], *n.* a brilliantly coloured insect of the order *Neuroptera*.

DRAGONISH, [drag'-un-ish], *adj.* resembling a dragon.

DRAGON-LIKE, [drag'-on-līk], *adj.* fiery and ferocious, like a dragon.

DRAGONNE, dragonné, [drag-on-ā'], *n.* (*her.*) the term for a beast with the hinder part of a dragon.

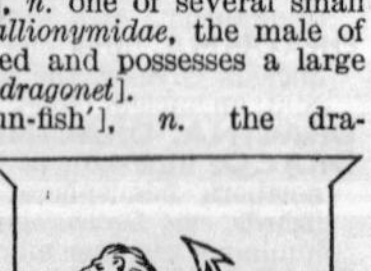
DRAGONNÉ

DRAGON'S-BLOOD, [drag'-unz-blŏŏd], *n.* a thick resinous juice obtained from certain tropical plants, reddish brown in colour, used for colouring purposes, and in process engraving.

DRAGON'S-HEAD, [drag'-unz-hed'], *n.* (*bot.*) one of several plants of the genus *Dracocephalum*; **dragon's-head and tail,** (*astron.*) the nodes of the planets, the head being the ascending and the tail the descending node.

DRAGON-SHELL, [drag'-un-shel'], *n.* (*zool.*) a species of limpet, *Cypræa stolida*.

DRAGON'S-MOUTH, [drag'-unz-mowth'], *n.* (*bot.*) the snapdragon, *Antirrhinum majus*.

DRAGON-TREE, [drag'-un-trē'], *n.* a tree-like plant of the lily family, *Dracæna Draco*, found in West Africa and the Canary Islands.

DRAGONWORT†, [drag'-un-wurt], *n.* (*bot.*) the tarragon, *Artemisia Dracunculus*; the bistort, *Polygonum Bistorta*.

DRAGOON (1), [drag-ōōn'], *n.* a mounted infantryman carrying the kind of carbine known as a dragon; a trooper belonging to certain cavalry regiments; a fierce person; a variety of pigeon. [DRAGON].

DRAGOON (2), [drag-ōōn'], *v.t.* to persecute or subject by armed forces; to compel to submit to, to force into. [*Prec.*].

DRAGOON-BIRD, [drag-ōōn'-burd], *n.* the Brazilian umbrella-bird, *Cephalopterus ornatus*.

DRAGOONER†, [drag-ōōn'-er], *n.* a dragoon.

DRAGSMAN, [dragz'-man], *n.* one who drives a drag; one who hangs on to a carriage to try to steal the luggage.

DRAIL, [drāl], *n.* a weighted hook and line, dragged through the water at the required depth in certain kinds of fishing. [DR(AG) and (TR)AIL].

DRAIN (1), [drān], *n.* a small artificial waterway, a pipe to carry water; (*pl.*) a system of pipes and culverts for removing sewage and waste-water, etc.; (*surg.*) a tube for drawing off morbid matter from a cavity discharging pus; (*fig.*) a persistent source of expenditure, a steady demand; a small quantity.

DRAIN (2), [drān], *v.t. and i.* to convey away excess water from land by cutting channels, laying pipes, etc.; (*surg.*) to clear of water by drains; to remove morbid matter from a discharging wound; to empty of liquor; (*fig.*) to empty, to exhaust, to deprive of (wealth, resources, strength); to furnish or provide with drains; to flow away slowly and gradually; **to d. to the dregs,** to empty completely; (*fig.*) to experience to the full. [OE. *dreahnian*].

DRAINABLE, [drān'-abl], *adj.* able to be drained.

DRAINAGE, [drān'-ij], *n.* the act, process, or system of draining, or of being drained; that which is drained away.

DRAINAGE-BASIN, [drān'-ij-bā'-sen], *n.* the territory drained by a river.

DRAINER, [drān'-er], *n.* a board on which articles are placed to drain; a colander.

DRAINING-PLOUGH, [drān'-ing-plow'], *n.* a plough used for cutting drains.

DRAINING-TILES, [drān'-ing-tīlz'], *n.(pl.)* tiles used in draining.

DRAINPIPE, [drān'-pīp], *n.* a pipe for drainage purposes.

DRAIN-TRAP, [drān'-trap'], *n.* a device preventing the escape of foul air from a drain, while admitting water.

DRAIN-TRAP

DRAKE (1), [drāk], *n.* the male of the duck [L Germ. *draak*].

DRAKE (2), [drāk], *n.* a species of *Ephemera*, or fly, used as bait in angling; †a former small type of cannon; a Viking warship. [OE. *draca* dragon].

DRAKE-STONE, [drāk'-stōn], *n.* a thin, flat stone to skim over water.

DRAM, [dram], *n.* a weight equivalent to one-eighth of an ounce (apothecaries' measure) or one-sixteenth of an ounce (avoirdupois); a liquid measure equal to one-eighth of a fluid ounce; a small amount of liquor a drop. [DRACHM].

DRAMA, [drah'-ma], *n.* a literary composition for stage performance, depicting the story in action and dialogue; a play; dramatic writing; theatrical art; a series of vivid passionate events. [Gk. *drama* deed, action].

DRAMATIC, [dram-at'-ik], *adj.* pertaining to the drama, in the form of a drama; resembling a drama in depicting vivid, passionate events; striking, arresting.

DRAMATICAL, [dram-at'-ik-al], *adj.* dramatic.

DRAMATICALLY, [dram-at'-ik-a-li], *adv.* in a dramatic way, in an unnatural manner.

DRAMATIS PERSONAE, [dram'-at-is-per-sō'-nē], *n.* the characters in a play. [L. *dramatis personae*].

DRAMATIST, [dram'-at-ist], *n.* a person who writes stage plays. [Gk. *drama dramatos* thing done].

DRAMATIZABLE, [dram'-at-īz'-abl], *adj.* capable of being dramatized.

DRAMATIZATION, [dram'-at-īz-ā'-shun], *n.* the process of dramatizing; that which is dramatized.

DRAMATIZE, [dram'-at-īz], *v.t.* to present in the form of a play.

DRAMATURGE, [dram'-at-urj], *n.* a playwright. [Gk. *dramatourgos*].

DRAMATURGIC, [dram'-at-urj'-ik], *adj.* relating to play-writing.

DRAMATURGIST, [dram'-at-urj'-ist], *n.* a dramatist.

DRAMATURGY, [dram'-at-urj'-i], *n.* the technique of writing and producing plays.

DRAMBUIE, [dram'-yōō'-e], *n.* (*prot.*) a whisky liqueur made in Scotland.

DRAM-DRINKER, [dram'-dringk'-er], *n.* (*coll.*) a heavy drinker of spirits.

DRANK, [drangk], *pret.* of DRINK. [OE. *dranc*].

DRAPE, [drāp], *v.t.* to cover with loose-hanging cloth, to clothe with some fabric so that it hangs in folds, to arrange artistically the folds of a covering. [OFr. *draper* from *drap* cloth].

DRAPED, [drāpd], *adj.* clothed in drapery.

DRAPER, [drāp'-er], *n.* a dealer in cloth and fabrics, a small shopkeeper dealing primarily in such commodities. [ME. *draper*].

DRAPERIED, [drāp' - er - id], *adj.* adorned with drapery.

DRAPERY, [drāp'-er-i], *n.* draping fabric, the folds or arrangement of something draped, the artistic treatment of drapings; †a draper's shop or stock. [OFr. *draperie*].

DRAPET, [drāp'-it], *n.* a coverlet. [It. *drappetto* little cloth].

DRASTIC, [dras'-tik], *adj.* vigorous, effective, thorough; severe but efficient and thorough-going (applied *esp.* to fierce purges or disciplinary action). [Gk. *drastikos*].

DRASTICALLY, [dras'-tik-a-li], *adv.* in drastic fashion.

DRAT, [drat], *int.* a mild, though low, expletive. [*God rot*].

DRAUGHT, [drahft], *n.* the act of drawing, the thing drawn, the drawing of liquid from a vessel, the amount of liquid swallowed without taking breath, a dose of medicine, a liquid purgative; the amount of water displaced by a ship, or the depth necessary to take her; an air-current coming from a small aperture; (*pl.*) a game for two, played on a board of sixty-four squares with twelve pieces a side; a piece used in this game. [OE. *draht*].

DRAUGHT-BOARD, [drahft'-bawd], *n.* the board used in the game of draughts.

DRAUGHT-COMPASSES, [drahft'-kum'-pas-iz], *n.* (*pl.*) compasses with adjustable points for making accurate plans.

DRAUGHT-HOOK, [drahft'-hŏŏk], *n.* an iron hook on the side of a gun-carriage, to which ropes are attached.

DRAUGHT-HORSE, DRAFT-HORSE, [drahft'-haws], *n.* a heavy horse used for pulling loads.

DRAUGHT-HOUSE, [drahft'-hows], *n.* a hut for waste matter.

DRAUGHTINESS, [drahft'-i-nes], *n.* the state of being draughty.

DRAUGHT(S)MAN, [drahft(s)'-man], *n.* a piece used in draughts.

DRAUGHT-OX, DRAFT-OX, [drahft'-oks], *n.* an ox employed for pulling loads, etc.

DRAUGHT-SCREEN, [drahft'-skrēn], *n.* a screen against draughts.

DRAUGHTSMAN, DRAFTSMAN, [drahfts'-man], *n.* one who drafts documents, books, works, Parliamentary Bills, etc.; a person who draws designs or plans for buildings, structures, etc.

DRAUGHTSMANSHIP, [drahfts'-man-ship], *n.* the practice and technique of a draughtsman.

DRAUGHTY, [drahft'-i], *adj.* unprotected from, full of, draughts of air.

DRAVIDIAN (1), [drav-id'-i-an], *n.* a member of the Dravidian race; the language spoken by this race.

DRAVIDIAN (2), [drav-id'-i-an], *adj.* relating to the supposed autochthonous inhabitants of India, now driven south by the Aryans. [Skt. *Dravida*, a region in the south of India].

DRAW (1), [draw], *n.* the process of drawing lots, the lot so drawn; a contest in which neither side is victorious; (*coll.*) an attraction, *esp.* a dramatic performance that attracts the public; the act of drawing a weapon, *esp.* a pistol.

DRAW (2), (drew, drawn), [draw], *v.t. and i.* to cause to move towards one, drag in one's direction, pull towards oneself, pull out of something by a steady movement; to pull back the string of a bow before discharging; to take (a sword) from its sheath; to attract towards oneself, to excite and focus (applause, etc.); to entice; to take money habitually from a source; to take in (breaths); (*fig.*) to get (ideas, feelings) from a thing, to form (a conclusion) from evidence; to take a ticket in a lottery, to pick something at random from several alternatives; to make a design, picture, or delineation with a pencil; to take out the entrails, to finish a contest with no advantage to either side; (*coll.*) to attract, be an attraction; to approach; **to d. back,** to retreat, hesitate at the last moment; **to d. down,** to incur, incite (anger, etc.); **to d. the line,** to show scruple, decline; **to d. the long bow,** to exaggerate, lie; **to d. out,** to encourage talk and confidences; **to d. round,** to gather round; **to d. the teeth of,** to render harmless; **to d. up,** to formulate, set out, make a detailed account of, make out (a legal document or commercial statement); to put into military formation; to come to a stop. [OE. *dragan*].

DRAWABLE, [draw'-abl], *adj.* able to draw or be drawn.

DRAWBACK, [draw'-bak'], *n.* an inconvenience or disadvantage in something otherwise desirable; import duty repaid on re-export.

DRAWBAR, [draw'-bah(r)], *n.* an iron rod connecting a locomotive with a tender or train.

DRAWBENCH, [draw'-bench'], *n.* a device for drawing strips of metal through a gauged opening.

DRAWBOLT, [draw'-bōlt], *n.* a coupling pin.

DRAW-BOY, [draw'-boi], *n.* a weaver's assistant.

DRAWBRIDGE, [draw'-brij], *n.* a bridge hinged at one end, so that it may be closed by being raised, *esp.* across the moat of a castle.

DRAWBRIDGE

DRAWEE, [draw-ē'], *n.* a person by whom a bill of exchange is payable.

DRAWER, [draw'-er], *n.* one who, or that which, draws; a lidless container sliding into a receptacle made for the purpose; the person drawing a cheque; (*pl.*) a legged undergarment.

DRAWGATE, [draw'-gāt], *n.* the door of a lock or sluice.

DRAW-GEAR, [draw'-gēer], *n.* harness used for drawing a wagon; railway couplings.

DRAWING, [draw'-ing], *n.* the act and technique of making a picture with pencil or brush; the picture so made.

DRAWING-BOARD, [draw'-ing-bawd'], *n.* a board on which to rest paper during drawing.

DRAWING-PAPER, [draw'-ing-pāp'-er], *n.* paper to draw on.

DRAWING-ROOM, [draw'-ing-rōōm'], *n.* a room for sociability and hospitality, a room for use after dinner; a court reception at which women are presented.

DRAW-KNIFE, [draw'-nīf], *n.* a kind of spokeshave.

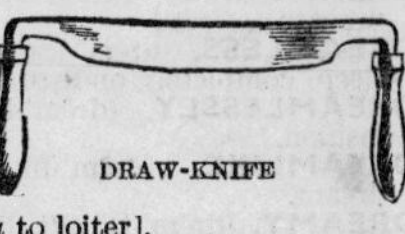
DRAW-KNIFE

DRAWL (1), [drawl], *n.* a drawling manner of speech.

DRAWL (2), [drawl], *v.t. and i.* to speak in a slow, lazy, monotonous way; to say (something) in this way. [OIcel. *dralla* to loiter].

DRAW-LATCH†, [draw'-lach], *n.* a thief or rogue.

DRAWLING, [drawl'-ing], *n.* the act or sound of speaking in a drawl.

DRAWLINGLY, [drawl'-ing-li], *adv.* in drawling fashion.

DRAWLINGNESS, [drawl'-ing-nes], *n.* a drawling manner of speech.

DRAW-LINK, [draw'-lingk], *n.* a link connecting railway carriages.

DRAWN, [drawn], *adj. and p.pt.* (of a contest) with victory to neither side; (of a weapon) out of its sheath; disembowelled; (of appearance) worn and tense. [OE. *dragen, p.pt.* of *dragan* to draw].

DRAW-NET, [draw'-net'], *n.* a net for catching large birds.

DRAWNWORK, [drawn'-wurk], *n.* a method of ornamenting linen by drawing out certain threads.

DRAW-PLATE, [draw'-plāt], *n.* a perforated steel plate used in making wire.

DRAW-WELL, [draw'-wel'], *n.* a well into which a bucket on a rope is lowered to fetch water.

DRAY, [drā], *n.* a low cart for heavy loads. [OE. *dræge* drag-net].

DRAYAGE, [drā'-ij], *n.* a charge for the use of a dray.

DRAY-HORSE, [drā'-haws], *n.* a cart-horse.

DRAYMAN, [drā'-man], *n.* a man in charge of a dray.

DRAY-PLOUGH, [drā'-plow], *n.* a plough used in heavy earth.

DRAZEL, [drāzl], *n.* a slut. [Uncert.].

DREAD (1), [dred], *n.* fearful apprehension, terror and anticipation, fear of something in the future. [ME. *drede*].

DREAD (2), [dred], *adj.* dreadful, awe-inspiring.

DREAD (3), [dred], *v.t. and i.* to feel terror of, to fear horribly, in anticipation; to be very apprehensive and afraid. [OE. *drædan*].

DREADABLE, [dred'-abl], *adj.* likely to be dreaded.

DREADER, [dred'-er], *n.* one who dreads.

DREADFUL, [dred'-fool], *adj.* inspiring dread; **penny d.**, a cheap lurid tale of awful bloody murders and fiendish villainies.

DREADFULLY, [dred'-fool-i], *adv.* in dreadful fashion.

DREADFULNESS, [dred'-fool-nes], *n.* the quality of being dreadful.

DREADLESS, [dred'-les], *adj.* fearless.

DREADLESSNESS, [dred'-les-nes], *n.* boldness.

DREADNOUGHT (1), [dred'-nawt], *n.* a type of powerful, heavily armoured battleship, first built by Gt. Britain in 1906, and afterwards adopted by other countries as the first warship to combine high speed and effective armour. [Named from the first ship of this class].

DREADNOUGHT (2), [dred'-nawt], *n.* a thick, long-piled cloth; a weather-proof made from this material.

DREAM (1), [drēm], *n.* the thought processes of the unconscious whilst the conscious mind is at rest, those parts of this process sufficiently disturbing to force themselves on the consciousness; an abstraction from realities, fantasy, baseless imagining; an improbable but preoccupying ambition, something far too pleasing to be real; (*pl.*) sleep in general. [OE. *dream* joy, revelry].

DREAM (2), [drēm], *v.t. and i.* to have dreams about; to have dreams in sleep, to see visions; to have aspirations, wild and wonderful ambitions; to imagine, to have baseless fancies.

DREAMER, [drēm'-er], *n.* one who dreams, an idealist, a wild visionary.

DREAMERY, [drēm'-er-i], *n.* the habit of day-dreaming.

DREAMFUL, [drēm'-fool], *adj.* full of dreams.

DREAMHOLE, [drēm'-hōl], *n.* a small window in a tower.

DREAMILY, [drēm'-i-li], *adv.* in dreamy fashion.

DREAMINESS, [drēm'-i-nes], *n.* the state of being dreamy.

DREAMINGLY, [drēm'-ing-li], *adv.* as if in a dream.

DREAMLAND, [drēm'-land], *n.* the world of unreality, sleep.

DREAMLESS, [drēm'-les], *adj.* without dreams; (of sleep) completely undisturbed.

DREAMLESSLY, [drēm'-les-li], *adv.* in dreamless fashion.

DREAMLIKE, [drēm'-līk], *adj.* unreal like a dream.

DREAMY, [drēm'-i], *adj.* like a dream, full of hazy content, unreal; given to dreams and fanciful ambitions.

DREAR, [drēer], *adj.* melancholy, gloomy, desolate. [DREARY].

DREARILY, [drēer'-i-li], *adv.* in dreary fashion.

DREARINESS, [drēer'-i-nes], *n.* the state of being dreary.

DREARISOME, [drēer'-i-sum], *adj.* inducing dreariness, wearisome.

DREARY, [drēer'-i], *adj.* depressingly gloomy, wearisome, dispiriting. [OE. *dreorig* bloody, woeful].

DREDGE (1), [drej], *n.* a mechanism for clearing or dragging ponds, rivers, etc., and fetching up things from the bottom. [OE. **drecg* from OE. *dragjn*].

DREDGE (2), [drej], *v.t. and i.* to drag, clear, fetch up with a dredge; to employ a dredge.

DREDGE (3), [drej], *v.t.* (*cookery*) to sprinkle with flour, sugar, etc. [ME. *dragie* from Gk. *tragema* sweetmeat].

DREDGE

DREDGER (1), [drej'-er], *n.* a ship used for dredging at sea.

DREDGER (2), [drej'-er], *n.* (*cookery*) a container with a perforated lid for sprinkling.

DREDGING-MACHINE, [drej'-ing-mash-ēn'], *n.* a machine for dredging.

DREE†, [drē], *v.t.* (*archaic*) to endure. [OE. *dreogan*].

DREGGINESS, [dreg'-i-nes], *n.* the condition of being dreggy.

DREGGISH, [dreg'-ish], *adj.* dreggy, fouled with dregs.

DREGGY, [dreg'-i], *adj.* full of dregs.

DREGS, [dregz], *n.(pl.)* sediment, *esp.* of wine, lees; (*fig.*) refuse, scum; criminals, the very poor. [OIcel. *dreggjar*].

DRENCH (1), [drench], *n.* a veterinary draught or purgative. [OE. *drenc* drink].

DRENCH (2), [drench], *v.t.* to soak, to make thoroughly sodden with liquid; to administer a draught to a horse or cow. [OE. *drencan* give to drink].

DRENCHER, [drench'-er], *n.* a funnel for giving a veterinary drench.

DRESDEN, [drez'-den], *n.* a variety of porcelain first manufactured in 1709 at Meissen. [*Dresden*, a German town].

DRESS (1), [dres], *n.* a garment; a one-piece, skirted outer garment worn by women; clothing in general; **full d.**, formal uniform; **evening d.**, special garments worn at dinner, and on certain social occasions; **morning d.**, garments worn on similar occasions earlier in the day; **d. circle**, the first tier of a theatre; **d. rehearsal**, the final rehearsal before a public performance, in which all takes place as if the public were present.

DRESS (2), [dres], *v.t.* to put clothes on to, to adorn, decorate, put in order; to draw up (troops) in straight lines; to arrange, to make smooth; to prepare and season with condiments; to clean, to bandage (a wound); *v.i.* to put on clothes, *esp.* to put on, wear evening dress; to wear, arrange, choose clothes; (*milit.*) to get into a straight line; **to d. down**, to rub a horse down; (*fig.*) to rebuke severely; **to d. up**, to deck oneself out specially for some occasion, to wear fancy dress. [OFr. *dresser*].

DRESSER (1), [dres'-er], *n.* one who dresses.

DRESSER (2), [dres'-er], *n.* a stand fitted with drawers and shelves for holding household utensils. [OFr. *dressour*].

DRESSING, [dres'-ing], *n.* the process of clothing, adorning; decoration, adornment; a sauce or seasoning for food (*esp.* green salads); lint and liniment applied to a wound; manure, fertilizer; starch used for stiffening; the cleaning of metals; (*arch.*) moulding round windows or doors; **a d. down**, a severe scolding and rebuking.

DRESSING-CASE, [dres'-ing-kās], *n.* a box to hold toilet articles.

DRESSING-GOWN, [dres'-ing-gown'] *n.* a gown worn, when necessary, over night attire.

DRESSING-ROOM, [dres'-ing-room'], *n.* a small room adjoining a bedroom, for dressing and undressing.

DRESSING-TABLE, [dres'-ing-tābl'], *n.* a table or stand containing mirrors and toilet utensils.

DRESSING-CASE

DRESSMAKER, [dres'-māk-er], *n.* one who makes dresses, *esp.* for a living, a women's garment maker or tailor.

DRESSY, [dres'-i], *n.* showy; inclined to overdress.

DREUL, [drool], *v.i.* to slaver, like a child. [Drivel].

DREW, [droo], *pret.* of DRAW. [ME. *drew*].

DREY, [drā], *n.* a squirrel's nest. [Uncert.].

DRIB†, [drib], *v.t. and i.* to lead on, go on little by little, to drip. [*Var.* of DRIP].

DRIBBLE, [dribl], *v.t. and i.* to spill out in a feeble trickle, *esp.* saliva from the mouth; to let fall in drips; to run with a football across the field, controlling it by frequent light kicks; to trickle out. [*Prec.*].
DRIBBLER, [drib′-ler], *n.* one who dribbles.
DRIBLET, [drib′-let], *n.* a small amount, *esp.* one of a series.
DRIER, [drī′-er], *n.* that which makes dry; a machine for drying hair, etc., by warm air; a substance employed to dry oil paints quickly.
DRIFT (1), [drift], *n.* the state or act of driving, the condition of being driven or moved irrespective of volition; *esp.* a slow current in the sea produced by wind, a similar movement of loose sand; (*naut.*) the rate at which such a current moves; a trend, slowly effective tendency in thought, conversation, etc.; the thing driven, *esp.* a heap of sand, snow, heaped up by the wind; (*arch.*) the horizontal, outward pressure of an arch; (*geol.*) a deposit; a South African ford. [ME. *drifte*].
DRIFT (2), [drift], *v.t. and i.* to cause to move, float along; to pile up into a drift; to float with the tide or wind; to move along without effort or control; (*fig.*) to move to some condition or situation gradually and unconsciously, to let oneself be carried along by events.
DRIFTAGE, [drift′-ij], *n.* (*naut.*) the amount by which a boat drifts off in bearing up against wind and water.
DRIFT-BOLTS, [drift′-bōlts], *n.(pl.)* bolts, usually made of steel, used to force out others.
DRIFTER, [drif′-ter], *n.* one who, or that which, drifts; a fishing vessel used for fishing with a drift-net.
DRIFTING, [drift′-ing], *n.* the act of drifting; the forming of a drift, the drift itself.
DRIFT-LAND, [drift′-land], *n.* sums paid by tenants for driving cattle through a manor.
DRIFTLESS, [drift′-les], *adj.* without drift.
DRIFT-NET, [drift′-net′], *n.* a floating or suspended fishing net permitted to float with the tide.
DRIFT-SAIL, [drift′-sāl], *n.* a sail dropped in the water to check the course of a ship in a storm.
DRIFT-SAND, [drift′-sand′], *n.* sand blown by the wind.
DRIFT-WAY, [drift′-wā], *n.* a road across a common for cattle; (*naut.*) the course of a ship drifting; (*mining*) a drift.
DRIFT-WIND, [drift′-wind], *n.* a wind causing drift.
DRIFT-WOOD, [drift′-wŏŏd], *n.* wood washed ashore.
DRIFTY, [drift′-i], *adj.* tending to produce drift.
DRILL (1), [dril], *n.* an instrument for piercing tough matter by a rapidly turning point. [Du. *dril* boring tool].
DRILL (2), [dril], *n.* a narrow furrow for planting seed; a machine for driving and sowing such furrows. [Uncert.].
DRILL (3), [dril], *n.* a rough twilled linen stuff. [Germ. *drillich* from L. *trilicem* thrice twilled].
DRILL (4), [dril], *n.* co-ordinated physical exercises performed by a body of persons; trial military manœuvres, practice or exercise of any kind. [DRILL (8)].
DRILL (5), [dril], *n.* a small baboon of Guinea [Native].
DRILL (6), [dril], *v.t. and i.* to bore a hole (in) with a drill. [DRILL (1)].
DRILL (7), [dril], *v.t.* to sow seed in drills or narrow furrows. [DRILL (2)].
DRILL (8), [dril], *v.t. and i.* to do drill or cause to do drill.
DRILL-BARROW, [dril′-ba′-rō], *n.* a mechanism for drilling and sowing.
DRILL-BOW, [dril′-bō], *n.* an instrument for spinning a drill with a cord.
DRILL-BOX, [dril′-boks′], *n.* a seed box.
DRILL-GRUBBER, [dril′-grub′-er], *n.* a tool for grubbing up earth.
DRILL-HARROW, [dril′-ha′-rō], *n.* a small harrow used for pulverizing the earth between the drills or rows, and destroying weeds.
DRILL-HUSBANDRY, [dril′-huz′-band-ri], *n.* the technique of sowing in drills.
DRILLING, [dril′-ing], *n.* drill used for garments. [Germ. *drillich*].

DRILL-BOW

DRILL-PLOUGH, [dril′-plow′], *n.* a plough for driving drills. [DRILL (2) and PLOUGH].
DRILL-PRESS, [dril′-pres′], *n.* a machine used in drilling holes in metal.
DRILL-SERGEANT, [dril′-sah′-jant], *n.* a sergeant who superintends drill and exercises.
DRILL-STOCK, [dril′-stok], *n.* the stock of a metal drill.
DRILY, [drī′-li], *adv.* in a dry manner (of speech).
DRINK (1), [dringk], *n.* liquid for drinking, liquid drunk, alcoholic liquor, *esp.* as a vice.
DRINK (2), [dringk], *v.t. and i.* to swallow liquid, to absorb, draw in deeply; (*fig.*) to accept credulously; to perform the action of consuming liquid; to consume alcoholic liquor, *esp.* habitually and to excess. [OE. *drincan*].
DRINKABLE, [dringk′-abl], *adj.* fit to drink.
DRINKABLENESS, [dringk′-abl-nes], *n.* the condition of being drinkable.
DRINKER (1), [dringk′-er], *n.* one who drinks; one who habitually drinks alcoholic liquors.
DRINKER (2), [dringk′-er], *n.* the moth, *Odonestis potatoria*.
DRINKING (1), [dringk′-ing], *n.* the act of one who drinks; the consumption of alcoholic liquor.
DRINKING (2), [dringk′-ing], *adj.* relating to the consumption of alcoholic liquor.
DRINKING-BOUT, [dringk′-ing-bowt′], *n.* a session of hard drinking.
DRINKING-FOUNTAIN, [dringk′-ing-fownt′-en], *n.* a public fountain of drinking-water.
DRINKING-HORN, [dringk′-ing-hawn′], *n.* a cup for drinking, made of a hollowed horn.
DRINKING-HOUSE, [dringk′-ing-hows′], *n.* a house for the sale and consumption of alcoholic liquor.
DRINKING-SONG, [dringk′-ing-song′], *n.* a song, generally in praise of alcoholic liquor, sung while getting drunk.
DRINKING-WATER, [dringk′-ing-waw′-ter], *n.* water fit to drink.
DRINKLESS, [dringk′-les], *adj.* without drink.
DRINK-MONEY, [dringk′-mun′-i], *n.* money given to buy liquor in which to toast the giver.
DRINK-OFFERING, [dringk′-of′-er-ing], *n.* a religious offering of liquor, a libation.
DRIP (1), [drip], *n.* one of a series of small drops, the sound made by the continuous falling of drops, a drip-stone.
DRIP (2), **(dripping, dripped)**, [drip], *v.t. and i.* to cause to fall in drops; to fall slowly in drops. [OE. *dryppan*].
DRIPPING, [drip′-ing], *n.* fat obtained from roasting or frying meat.
DRIPPING-EAVES, [drip′-ing-ēvz′], *n.(pl.)* (*arch.*) the projecting edges of the roof from which the rain drops.
DRIPPING-PAN, [drip′-ing-pan′], *n.* a pan for collecting the grease from cooking meat.
DRIP-STONE, [drip′-stōn], *n.* (*arch.*) a moulding over the heads of doorways and windows to throw off rain.
DRIP-TIP, [drip′-tip], *n.* the apex of a leaf, from which the rain drips off.
DRIVABLE, [drīv′-abl], *adj.* capable of being driven.

DRIP-STONE

DRIVE (1), [drīv], *n.* the state of being driven in a vehicle, a trip made for pleasure in a vehicle; a broad road made for driving up to a house, a carriage-way through a wood; the process of driving game towards the hunters or guns; the act of striking a ball with the whole bodily force and swing behind the blow, *esp.* the initial stroke from the tee in golf; vigour and energy of personality; the manner in which the power of an engine is employed; an intensive campaign of any sort.
DRIVE (2), **(drove, driven)**, [drīv], *v.t. and i.* to give motion to, to force into motion by a violent blow, by orders or threatenings, to force on or in by a smooth, violent blow, to set a ball in motion by a steady, square, strong stroke; to compel, control the motion of animals or vehicles, to cause (a machine) to move, to convey in a vehicle; (*fig.*) to compel, enforce to; to cut through, force a way through (with the implication of strong, steady effort); to be in control of the motion of an animal or vehicle; **to d. at**, to aim at in conversation; **to d. home**, to force right in; (*fig.*) to bring forcefully and definitely to the hearer. [OE. *drifan*].
DRIVEL (1), [driv′-el], *n.* stupid talk or writing.
DRIVEL (2), **(drivelling, drivelled)**, [driv′-el], *v.i.* to dribble, to trickle saliva from the mouth; to talk

or write in a rambling, feeble-minded fashion. [OE. *dreflian* to snivel].
DRIVELLER, [driv′-el-er], *n.* one who drivels, a silly, woolly-minded talker.
DRIVELLING (1), [driv′-el-ing], *n.* silly, rambling speech.
DRIVELLING (2), [driv′-el-ing], *adj.* that drivels; (*coll.*) nonsensical.
DRIVER, [drīv′-er], *n.* one who, or that which, drives; one who controls a vehicle or machine; that which imparts motion to something else; the wooden golf club used for driving from the tee; a drover.
DRIVING, [drīv′-ing], *n.* the controlling of a vehicle; the striking of a golf ball from the tee.
DRIZZLE (1), [drizl], *n.* fine, light rain.
DRIZZLE (2), [drizl], *v.t. and i.* to let fall in a fine, light spray; to rain in this fashion. [OE. *dreosan* to fall].
DRIZZLY, [driz′-li], *adj.* drizzling spasmodically.
DROFLAND, [drof′-land], *n.* an ancient due paid to drive through manor grounds to market. [OE. *draf* driving and LAND].
DROGHER, [drōg′-er], *n.* a small vessel trading in the West Indies. [Native].
DROGHING, [drōg′-ing], *n.* coastal trade off the West Indies.
DROGMAN, [drog′-man], *n.* a dragoman.
DROGUE, [drōg], *n.* a sea-anchor; a wind-sock; a device attached to a bomb to control the speed and direction of its descent; a square board on a harpoon line to check the speed of the whale. [DRAG (1)].
DROIL†, [droil], *n.* a drudge; drudgery, menial work. [Uncert.].
DROIT, [droit], *n.* a legal perquisite; **Droits of Admiralty**, rights of the Crown as to wrecks and prizes of war. [Fr. *droit*].
DROITURAL, [droit′-yōō-ral], *adj.* having legal right, as opposed to having right by possession. [Fr. *droiture*].
DROLL (1), [drōl], *n.* a waggish fellow, a clown.
DROLL (2), [drōl], *adj.* waggish, comical by virtue of an odd mock-seriousness. [Fr. *drôle*].
DROLL (3), [drōl], *v.t.* to mime with comical oddity.
DROLLER, [drōl′-er], *n.* one playing the droll.
DROLLERY, [drōl′-er-i], *n.* waggishness, droll antics.
DROLLING, [drōl′-ing], *n.* playing the droll.
DROLLINGLY, [drōl′-ing-li], *adj.* in droll fashion.
DROLLISH, [drōl′-ish], *adj.* fairly droll.
DROLLY, [drōl′-li], *adv.* in a droll fashion.
DROME, [drōm], *n.* (*coll.*) an aerodrome. [Short for AERODROME].
DROMEDARIAN, [drom′-id-āer′-i-an], *n.* one who rides a dromedary.
DROMEDARY, [drom′-id-er′-i], *n.* the Arabian one-humped riding camel, *Camelus dromedarius*. [LL. *dromedarius* from Gk. *dromas dromados* runner].

DROMEDARY

DROMOND, [drom′-ond], *n.* a fast, light galley with a single sail and one bank of oars, employed extensively by the Byzantine navy. [OF. from Gk. *dromos* race].
DRONE (1), [drōn], *n.* the male of the honey bee, with no function beyond the generative; (*fig.*) an idle, useless person; the low-pitched humming sound produced by the honey bee, any sound resembling this; one of the tubes of a bagpipe producing a deep, humming note. [OE. *dran*].
DRONE (2), [drōn], *v.t. and i.* to utter a deep, monotonous, humming sound; to live like a drone.
DRONE-FLY, [drōn′-flī], *n.* an insect of the genus *Eristalis*.
DRONGO, [dron′-gō], *n.* any of the king-crows of south-eastern Asia and Africa. [Malagasy *drongo*].
DRONING, [drōn′-ing], *n.* a deep rhythmical hum.
DRONISH, [drōn′-ish], *adj.* lazy, drone-like.
DRONISHLY, [drōn′-ish-li], *adv.* in dronish fashion.
DRONISHNESS, [drōn′-ish-nes], *n.* the state of being dronish.
DRONY, [drōn′-i], *adj.* dronish.
DROOL, [drōōl], *v.t. and i.* to let saliva trickle from the mouth. [DRIVEL].
DROOP (1), [drōōp], *n.* the state of drooping, hanging weakly, wilting.
DROOP (2), [drōōp], *v.t. and i.* to hang limply forward and down, to sag, let the head or top loll limply forward; (*fig.*) to languish, wilt, evince complete loss of spirit; to allow to hang limply. [OScand. *drupa*].
DROOPING, [drōōp′-ing], *adj.* in a droop, languishing, wilting.
DROOPINGLY, [drōōp′-ing-li], *adv.* in drooping fashion.
DROP (1), [drop], *n.* a small globule of liquid in suspension before falling, a measurement for small quantities of liquid, *esp.* medicine; (*fig.*) the smallest possible quantity of liquid, anything resembling in shape a globule of liquid, as certain sweets, ornaments, etc.; the vertical distance between two objects regarded as the distance to be fallen from the higher to the lower; a falling from a higher to a lower position; (*fig.*) a fall in position or rank, a sudden lowering in esteem, spirits; the movable china or metal plate over a keyhole; a lessening in quantity or degree; a falling contraption; a stage curtain; hinged platform; (*football*) a drop-kick. [OE. *dropa*].
DROP (2), (**dropping, dropped**), [drop], *v.t.* to let fall in drops; to let fall by releasing hold; (*coll.*) to set down someone from a vehicle; to cause to fall; (*fig.*) to give up, stop doing; to let fall; to lower the voice; (of animals) to give premature birth; *v.i.* to fall in drops; to fall, slip to a lower level; to be reduced in quantity, intensity, etc.; to cease to be thought of or discussed; **to d. a brick**, (*slang*) to commit a tactless blunder; **to d. in**, to call, visit casually; **to d. off**, to decline, to fall asleep; **to d. out of**, to cease to participate in; **to d. on**, to blame, take to task; **to let d.**, to utter (a remark) with real or assumed casualness. [OE. *dropian*].
DROPAX, [drō′-paks], *n.* a depilatory. [Gk. *dropax*].
DROP-CURTAIN, [drop′-kur′-tan], *n.* a drop-scene.
DROP-DRILL, [drop′-dril], *n.* a device that simultaneously manures and sows in drills.
DROP-KICK (1), [drop′-kik′], *n.* a kick in rugby football in which the ball is dropped and kicked as soon as it leaves the ground.
DROP-KICK (2), [drop′-kik′], *v.i.* to make a drop-kick.
DROPLET, [drop′-let], *n.* a small drop, *esp.* from sneezing.
DROPPING, [drop′-ing], *n.* the act of letting drop; that which drops; (*pl.*) the excrement of animals.
DROPPINGLY, [drop′-ing-li], *adv.* by drops.
DROP-SCENE, [drop′-sēn], *n.* a curtain or scenery on pulleys lowered to cut off part of the stage when desired.
DROPSICAL, [drop′-sikl], *adj.* relating to, suffering from, resembling, dropsy.
DROPSICALLY, [drop′-sik-a-li], *adv.* in dropsical fashion.
DROPSICALNESS, [drop′-sikl-nes], *n.* the condition or quality of being dropsical.
DROPSIED, [drop′-sid], *adj.* swollen with dropsy.
DROPSY, [drop′-si], *n.* (*med.*) a morbid gathering of watery fluid in the tissues or cavities of the body. [Gk. *hudrops*].
DROPWORT, [drop′-wurt], *n.* a perennial plant of the genus *Spiraea*; **water d.**, the plant, *Oenanthe crocata*.
DROSERA, [dros′-er-a], *n.* a genus of plants including the sundew. [Gk. *droseros* dewy].
DROSKY, [dros′-ki], *n.* an open four-wheeled Russian carriage with a bench for seating passengers. [Russ. *drozhki*].
DROSOMETER, [dros-om′-it-er], *n.* a device for measuring the fall of dew. [Gk. *drosos* dew and METER].
DROSS, [dros], *n.* rubbish, refuse; impurities thrown off by molten metal; (*fig.*) that which has no real worth. [OE. *dros*].
DROSSINESS, [dros′-i-nes], *n.* the condition of being drossy.
DROSSLESS, [dros′-les], *adj.* without dross.
DROSSY, [dros′-i], *adj.* consisting of dross, impure, worthless.
DROUGHT, [drowt], *n.* a long period of dry weather; extreme dryness of climate. [OE. *drugoth*].
DROUGHTINESS, [drowt′-i-nes], *n.* the state of being droughty.
DROUGHTY, DROUTHY, [drowt′-i], *adj.* dry, thirsty, in a state of drought.
DROUMY, [drōōm′-i], *adj.* very muddy, turgid. [Uncert.].

DROUTH, [drowth], *n.* drought, thirst. [*Var.* of DROUGHT].
DROUTHINESS, [drowth'-i-nes], *n.* droughtiness.
DROUTHY, see DROUGHTY.
DROVE (1), [drōv], *n.* a number of cattle or sheep driven along in a body. [OE. *draf*].
DROVE (2), [drōv], *pret.* of DRIVE (2). [OE. *draf, pret.* of *drifan* to drive].
DROVER, [drōv'-er], *n.* one who takes cattle or sheep to market in a drove.
DROWN, [drown], *v.t. and i.* to die or cause to suffocate to death by submersion in liquid; (*fig.*) to overwhelm, blot out; extinguish by overwhelming. [ONorw. *drukkna*].
DROWNER, [drown'-er], *n.* he who, or that which, drowns.
DROWSE (1), [drowz], *n.* a doze, a state of sluggishness.
DROWSE (2), [drowz], *v.t. and i.* to doze, to be in a sleepy, sluggish state; to make drowsy. [OE. *drusian* to be languid].
DROWSILY, [drowz'-i-li], *adv.* sleepily, sluggishly.
DROWSINESS, [drowz'-i-nes], *n.* the condition of being drowsy.
DROWSY, [drowz'-i], *adj.* sleepy, inclined to doze, torpid; tending to induce sleep.
DROWSY-HEADED, [drowz'-i-hed'-id], *adj.* of a sluggish disposition.
DRUB, (drubbing, drubbed), [drub], *v.t.* to beat with successive blows, belabour thoroughly, cudgel. [Swed. *drabba*].
DRUBBING, [drub'-ing], *n.* a cudgelling, a good beating.
DRUDGE (1), [druj], *n.* an ill-used menial, overworked with heavy, mean labour. [OE. *drycg*].
DRUDGE (2), [druj], *v.i.* to perform heavy menial labour like a drudge.
DRUDGERY, [druj'-er-i], *n.* the servile labour of a drudge.
DRUDGINGLY, [druj'-ing-li], *adv.* like a drudge.
DRUDGISM, [druj'-izm], *n.* the condition of a drudge.
DRUG (1), [drug], *n.* a medicine; a substance affecting the organs of the body and producing unnatural excitement or unconsciousness, etc. [Fr. *drogue*].
DRUG (2), (drugging, drugged), [drug], *v.t.* to mingle a drug with; to add a narcotic drug to (food); to cause to consume a drug in order to cause torpor, unconsciousness, or abnormal activity.
DRUGGER, [drug'-er], *n.* a drogher.
DRUGGERMAN, [drug'-er-man], *n.* a dragoman.
DRUGGET, [drug'-it], *n.* a coarse woollen cloth used as a cheap floor-covering, once of a finer quality, used in clothing. [OFr. *drouget*].
DRUGGIST, [drug'-ist], *n.* an apothecary.
DRUID, [droo'-id], *n.* a priest of the ancient pagan Celts; an Eisteddfod officer. [OCelt. *druid*].
DRUIDESS, [droo'-id-es], *n.* a woman Druid.
DRUIDIC, [droo-id'-ik], *adj.* Druidical.
DRUIDICAL, [droo-id'-ikl], *adj.* relating to Druids or Druidism.
DRUIDISM, [droo'-id-izm], *n.* the religious system and ceremonial of Druids.
DRUM (1), [drum], *n.* (*mus.*) an instrument consisting of a skin or parchment stretched tightly across the openings of a hollow (usually cylindrical) framework, played by beating with sticks; the resonant sound produced by this; anything resembling this in shape; (*anat.*) the membrane between the inner and outer ear; (*arch.*) the part of a column above the shaft.

DRUM

DRUM (2), [drum], *n.* a ridge produced by glacial drift. [Gael. *trum* ridge].
DRUM (3), (drumming, drummed), [drum], *v.t.* to beat on a drum, to beat on something resonant so that a drumming sound is produced; to thump rapidly and continuously with the fingers or heels; (*fig.*) to impart an idea or fact by frequent repetition; **to d. out,** to expel ceremoniously from the army to the beating of drums.
DRUMBLE, [drumbl], *v.i.* to drone, emit a drumming sound. [Echoic].
DRUMFIRE, [drum'-fier], *n.* heavy, continuous fire from a large number of guns directed upon one target.
DRUMFISH, [drum'-fish], *n.* one of several species of fish so called from their noise.
DRUMHEAD, [drum'-hed'], *n.* the parchment stretched over the head of a drum; **d. court-martial,** an emergency court-martial held in the field during active service.
DRUMLY†, [drum'-li], *adj.* troubled, gloomy, turbid. [Uncert.].
DRUM-MAJOR, [drum'-māj'-er], *n.* a senior band sergeant.
DRUMMER, [drum'-er], *n.* one who plays the drum; (*coll.*) a commercial traveller.
DRUMMOND-LIGHT, [drum'-ond-līt'], *n.* the limelight, so called from Captain *Drummond*, its inventor.
DRUMSTICK, [drum'-stik], *n.* a stick used to play the drum; (*coll.*) the lower part of a cooked chicken's leg.
DRUNK (1), [drungk], *n.* an intoxicated person, *esp.* one taken up by the police.
DRUNK (2), [drungk], *adj. and p.pt.* intoxicated with alcohol, inebriated; (*fig.*) overcome by some strong emotion or idea. [OE. *druncen, p.pt.* of *drincan*].
DRUNKARD, [drungk'-erd], *n.* a person seriously addicted to alcoholic liquors.
DRUNKEN, [drungk'-en], *adj.* inebriated; typical of, produced by, drunkenness; (*fig.*) at a perilous angle, liable to overbalance. [DRUNK].
DRUNKENLY, [drungk'-en-li], *adv.* in drunken fashion.
DRUNKENNESS, [drungk'-en-nes], *n.* the condition of being drunk.
DRUPACEOUS, [droo-pā'-shus], *adj.* (*bot.*) relating to drupes.
DRUPE, [droop], *n.* (*bot.*) a soft fleshy fruit containing a nutty kernel. [Gk. *druppa* a ripe olive].
DRUPEL, [droop'-el], *n.* (*bot.*) a small drupe.
DRUPELET, [droop'let[*n.* a drupel.
DRUSE, [drooz], *n.* (*geol.*) a rock cavity lined with crystals. [Czech *druza* crystallized ore].
DRUSED, [droozd], *adj.* drusy.
DRUSES, [drooz'-iz], *n.(pl.)* a Moslem heretical sect in Syria. [Ismail al-*Darazi*, the founder].
DRUSY, [drooz'-i], *adj.* covered with minute crystallizations.
DRY (1), [drī], *adj.* lacking moisture or liquid of any sort; having a low rainfall; (*coll.*) thirsty, wanting a drink; (of wine) not sweet; (*fig.*) boring, dull, uninteresting; **d. bread,** bread without butter; **d. goods,** non-perishable commodities; **d. work,** work inciting thirst; **d. bob,** one at Eton who plays cricket and football instead of rowing; **d. battery,** an electric battery composed of sealed cells containing absorbent matter. [OE. *dryge*].
DRY (2), [drī], *v.t. and i.* to make dry; to become dry; **to d. up,** to cease to provide something; (*coll.*) to cease talking; (of a speaker) to forget what to say. [OE. *drygan*].
DRYAD, [drī'-ad], *n.* a wood-nymph. [Gk. *druas druados*].
DRYASDUST, [drī'-as-dust], *n.* a pedant.
DRYBONE, [drī'-bōn], *n.* a silicate of zinc.
DRY-BONED, [drī'-bōnd], *adj.* fleshless.
DRY-CLEAN, [drī'-klēn], *v.t.* to clean (clothes, etc.) with chemicals without using water.
DRYER, [drī'-er], *n.* a drier.
DRY-EYED, [drī'-īd'], *adj.* tearless.
DRYFOOT, [drī'-foot], *adj.* without wetting the feet.
DRYING, [drī'-ing], *adj.* intended to free from moisture; freeing, becoming free, from moisture.
DRYING-OIL, [drī'-ing-oil'], *n.* linseed and other oils, heated with oxide of lead, and forming the basis of paints and varnishes.
DRYISH, [drī'-ish], *adj.* somewhat dry.
DRYLY, [drī'-li], *adv.* in dry fashion.
DRYNESS, [drī'-nes], *n.* the condition of being dry.
DRY-NURSE (1), [drī'-nurs], *n.* a nurse who attends to a child but does not suckle it; (*fig.*) an assiduous helper and adviser (usually in jeering sense).
DRY-NURSE (2), [drī-nurs'], *v.t.* (*fig.*) to look after with almost ridiculous assiduity.
DRY-POINT (1), [drī'-point], *n.* a needle used to make a mark on a copper plate in engraving, where acid is not used; a print from such engraving.
DRY-POINT (2), [drī'-point], *v.i.* to engrave with a dry-point. [DRY-POINT (1)].
DRY-RENT, [drī'-rent], *n.* (*leg.*) lease without a distress clause.
DRY-ROT, [drī'-rot'], *n.* the decaying of timber through the action of fungi.

DRY-RUB, [drī′-rub] *n.* a cleansing, or attempt at it, without soap or water.
DRYSALTER, [drī′-sawlt-er], *n.* one who trades in chemical preparations or salted foodstuffs.
DRYSALTERY, [drī-sawlt′-er-i], *n.* the trade of a drysalter.
DRYSHOD, [drī′-shod′], *adj.* dryfoot.
DRY-STOVE, [drī′-stōv], *n.* an apparatus for preserving the plants of hot climates, a sort of greenhouse.
DUAD, [dew′-ad′], *n.* a dyad.
DUAL, [dew′-al], *adj.* relating to the numeral two, double; (*gram.*) applied to the grammatical number by which certain languages express ‘ two of a thing.’ [L. *dualis* containing two].
DUALIN, [dew-al′-in], *n.* a form of dynamite composed of nitro-glycerin and nitre. [~DUAL].
DUALISM, [dew′-al-izm], *n.* the philosophic and religious doctrine of opposing forces in a twofold universe.
DUALIST, [dew′-al-ist], *n.* one who believes in dualism.
DUALISTIC, [dew-al-ist′-ik], *adj.* pertaining to dualism.
DUALITY, [dew-al′-i-ti], *n.* the state or quality of being dual. [LL. *dualitas*].
DUALIZE, [dew′-al-iz], *v.t.* to make dual.
DUAN, [dew′-an], *n.* a canto of an epic. [Gael. *duan*].
DUARCHY, [dew′-ahk-i], *n.* dyarchy.
DUB (1), [dub], *n.* a pond. [Uncert.].
DUB (2), (dubbing, dubbed), [dub], *v.t.* to make a person knight by laying a sword on the shoulder; to name, confer (a title or epithet) upon; to rub with grease. [OE. *dubbian*].
DUB (3), (dubbing, dubbed), [dub], *v.i.* (*slang*) to subscribe.
DUBASH, [dōō′-bash], *n.* an Indian interpreter. [Hind. *dobashi* man of two languages].
DUBBER, [dub′-er], *n.* an Indian leather vessel for holding oil. [Native].
DUBBIN, DUBBING, [dub′-in], *n.* a thick grease used for softening or waterproofing leather. [DUB (2)].
DUBIATE, [dew′-bi-āt], *v.i.* to feel doubt.
DUBIETY, [dew-bī′-e-ti], *n.* doubt. [L. *dubietas*].
DUBIOSITY, [dew′-bi-os′-i-ti], *n.* a doubtful matter. [L. *dubiosus*].
DUBIOUS, [dew′-bi-us], *adj.* doubtful, uncertain; questionable; having several interpretations. [L. *dubiosus*].
DUBIOUSLY, [dew′-bi-us-li], *adv.* in dubious fashion.
DUBIOUSNESS, [dew′-bi-us-nes], *n.* the state of being dubious.
DUBITABLE, [dew′-bit-abl], *adj.* dubious, to be doubted.
DUBITABLY, [dew′-bit-ab-li], *adv.* in dubitable fashion.
DUBITANCY, [dew′-bit-an-si], *n.* doubtfulness.
DUBITATE, [dew′-bit-āt], *v.i.* to have doubts, be in doubt, hesitate. [L. *dubitare*].
DUBITATION, [dew′-bit-ā′-shun], *n.* doubtfulness, uncertainty. [L. *dubitatio*].
DUBITATIVE, [dew′-bit-at-iv], *adj.* hesitant, doubtful, inclined to doubt. [L. *dubitativus*].
DUBITATIVELY, [dew′-bit-at-iv-li], *adv.* in dubitative fashion.
DUCAL, [dew′-kal], *adj.* relating to a duke. [L. *ducalis*].
DUCAT, [duk′-at], *n.* a medieval European gold coin. [LL. *ducatus* military command].
DUCATOON, [duk′-at-ōōn′], *n.* a former Dutch and Venetian silver coin. [It. *ducatone*].
DUCHESS, [duch′-es], *n.* a duke's wife, the female holder of a duchy. [LL. *ducissa*].
DUCHESSE, [dush-es′], *n.* a kind of satin; **d. lace,** a Brussels pillow-lace. [Fr. *duchesse* duchess].
DUCHY, [duch′-i], *n.* the dominions of a ruling duke. [LL. *ducatus* military command from L. *dux* leader].
DUCHY-COURT, [duch′-i-kawt′], *n.* the law-court of a duchy, *esp.* that of Lancaster.
DUCK (1), [duk], *n.* a coarse cotton or linen cloth. [Du. *doeck* linen cloth].
DUCK (2), [duk], *n.* a common broad-beaked waterfowl, *esp.* the female; the flesh of this prepared as food; (*coll.*) a likeable person; (*slang*) a score of nought at cricket; the act of ducking; **to play ducks and drakes,** to be absurdly wasteful; **like water off a duck's back,** without making the least impression; **like a d. to water,** naturally and confidently. [OE. *duce*].
DUCK (3), [duk], *v.t.* and *i.* to jerk down the head and upper body so as to dodge a blow, get out of sight, or present a smaller target; to plunge suddenly under water. [*Prec.*].
DUCK-ANT, [duk′-ant′], *n.* a species of termite found in Jamaica.
DUCK-BILL, [duk′-bil], *n.* the platypus *Ornithorhynchus*, an egg-laying amphibious Australasian mammal.
DUCK-BILLED, [duk′-bild], *adj.* having a bill resembling that of a duck.

DUCK-BILL

DUCKBOARD, [duk′-bawd], *n.* planking to form a path across muddy ground.
DUCKER, [duk′-er], *n.* a diving bird of the genus *Colymbus*.
DUCK-HAWK, [duk′-hawk] *n.* the marsh-harrier.
DUCKING, [duk′-ing], *n.* a severe wetting by being plunged into water.
DUCKING-STOOL, [duk′-ing-stōōl′], *n.* a stool or chair on the end of a long lever, in which nagging women were tied and ducked in water.
DUCK-LEGGED, [duk′-legd′], *adj.* possessing short legs, like a duck.
DUCKLING, [duk′-ling], *n.* a young duck.
DUCK-MOLE, [duk′-mōl], *n.* the duck-billed platypus.
DUCK'S-EGG, [duks′-eg], *n.* (*cricket*) a score of nought.
DUCK'S-FOOT, [duks′-fŏŏt], *n.* the plant, *Podophyllum peltatum*.
DUCK-SHOT, [duk′-shot′], *n.* ammunition used in shooting wild duck.
DUCK-WEED, [duk′-wēd], *n.* a plant of the genus *Lemna*, covering the surface of still water.
DUCT, [dukt], *n.* a tube, a covered channel carrying liquid; (*anat.*) a channel carrying glandular secretions in animal bodies; (*bot.*) a channel containing air or water. [L. *ductus* a leading].
DUCTILE, [dukt′-īl], *adj.* (of metals) able to be drawn out into a fine wire; (*fig.*) easily influenced. [L. *ductilis*].
DUCTILELY, [dukt′-il-li], *adv.* in ductile fashion.
DUCTILENESS, [dukt′-il-nes], *n.* the state of being ductile.
DUCTILIMETER, [dukt′-il-im′-it-er], *n.* an instrument for measuring the ductileness of metals. [DUCTILE and METER].
DUCTILITY, [dukt-il′-i-ti], *n.* ductileness.
DUCTLESS, [dukt′-les], *adj.* having no duct; **d. gland,** an endocrine gland.
DUD (1), [dud], *n.* a shell or bomb, etc., that lands but fails to explode; a defective (and so useless) instrument or object; a useless person; a bad coin or note. [~THUD].
DUD (2), [dud], *adj.* useless, defective, no good, ineffective.
DUDDER, [dud′-er], *v.t.* and *i.* to deafen, confuse, overwhelm with noise; to shudder. [Uncert.].
DUDE, [dewd], *n.* (*U.S. slang*) a dandy, a vulgar fop. [Unkn.].
DUDEEN, [dōō-dēn′], *n.* a small clay tobacco-pipe. [Ir. *dudeen*].
DUDGEON (1), [duj′-un], *n.* a handle to a dagger. [AFr. *digeon*].
DUDGEON (2), [duj′-un], *n.* sullen resentment, annoyance, anger. [Uncert.].
DUDS, [dudz], *n.* (*slang*) clothes; tattered garments, cheap clothing. [OScand. *duthi* swaddling clothes].
DUE (1), [dew], *n.* a sum to be paid, a sum legally payable; anything that should be given in justice or respect.
DUE (2), [dew], *adj.* (of debt, money) owing, requiring settlement, fitting, required by justice, etc.; appointed, promised for a certain time, expected in view of custom or promise; **d. to,** caused by, arising from. [Fr. *dû* from L. *debitum* owed].
DUE (3), [dew], *adv.* (used with points of the compass) exactly, precisely.
DUE-BILL, [dew′-bil], *n.* an acknowledgment of a debt.
DUEL (1), [dew′-el], *n.* a single combat between two persons, usually armed with similar weapons and fighting in accordance with pre-arranged rules until the death or injury of one of the contestants; (*fig.*) a battle of wits. [MedL. *duellum* fight].
DUEL (2), (duelling, duelled), [dew′-el], *v.i.* to fight a duel, practise duelling.
DUELLER, [dew′-el-er], *n.* one who fights a duel.

DUELLING, [dew'-el-ing], *n.* the custom of fighting duels.
DUELLIST, [dew'-el-ist], *n.* one skilled in duelling.
DUELLO, [dew-el'-ō], *n.* the rules of duelling. [It *duello*].
DUENNA, [dew-en'-a], *n.* a middle-aged woman who looks after the girls of a Spanish upper-class family; a chaperone. [Sp. *dueña* from L. *domina* mistress].
DUET, [dew-et'], *n.* (*mus.*) a piece for two performers. [It. *duetto*].
DUETTINO, [dew'-et-ē'-nō], *n.* a brief duet. [It. *duettino*].
DUETTIST, [dew-et'-ist], *n.* a performer in a duet.
DUETTO, [dew-et'-ō], *n.* a duet. [It. *duetto*].
DUFF (1), [duf], *n.* suet pudding. [DOUGH].
DUFF (2), [duf], *v.t.* (*slang*) to steal cattle by changing the branding mark; to doctor up old rubbish to look like new goods. [Uncert.].
DUFFEL, [duf'-el], *n.* a wool cloth with a heavy nap. [*Duffel*, in Belgium, where originally made].
DUFFER, [duf'-er], *n.* a clumsy, slow, heavy-witted person. [Unkn.].
DUFFING, [duf'-ing], *adj.* bogus; clumsily stupid.
DUG (1), [dug], *n.* the teat of female mammals. [Swed. *dægga* to suckle].
DUG (2), [dug], *pret. and p.pt.* of DIG.
DUGONG, [dew'-gong], *n.* the sea-cow, a mammal found in the Indian Ocean. [Malay *dugong*].

DUGONG

DUGOUT, [dug'-owt], *n.* a canoe made of a hollowed tree-trunk; a cavity dug out of the side of a trench for living quarters and shelter against shell-fire, etc.
DUIKER, [dī'-ker], *n.* a small antelope of South Africa, *Cephalophus grimmi*. [Du. *duiker* diver].
DUKE, [dewk], *n.* †a military leader; a member of the highest rank in the peerage; (*slang pl.*) fists. [OFr. *duc* from L. *dux* leader].
DUKEDOM, [dewk'-dom], *n.* the territory or rank of a duke.
DUKELING, [dewk'-ling], *n.* a petty duke.
DUKERY, [dewk'-er-i], *n.* a duke's residential estate; **the Dukeries**, a district in the English Midlands.
DULCAMARA, [dul'-kam-ah'-ra], *n.* (*bot.*) the woody nightshade, bittersweet, *Solanum Dulcamara*. [L. *dulcis* sweet and *amarus* bitter].
DULCET, [dul'-sit], *adj.* melodious, gentle. [OFr. *doucet*].
DULCIFICATION, [dul'-si-fik-ā'-shun], *n.* the act of dulcifying.
DULCIFIED, [dul'-si-fīd], *adj.* sweetened; **d. spirit**, a mixture of alcohol and mineral acids.
DULCIFLUOUS, [dul-sif'-lōō-us], *adj.* sweetly flowing. [L. *dulcis* and *fluere* to flow].
DULCIFY, [dul'-si-fī], *v.t.* to sweeten. [L. *dulcificare*].
DULCILOQUY, [dul-sil'-ok-wi], *n.* sweet or soft-toned fashion of speech. [L. *dulcis* sweet and *loqui* to speak].
DULCIMER, [dul'-sim-er], *n.* (*mus.*) an instrument consisting of metal wires or plates stretched horizontally across a sounding-board and played by striking with two little hammers. [OFr. *doulcimer*].
DULCINE, [dul'-sin], *n.* dulcose.
DULCOSE, [dul'-kōs], *n.* a kind of mannite produced in Madagascar.
DULIA, [dew'-li-a], *n.* the minor adoration given to saints and angels. [Gk. *douleia* servitude].
DULL (1), [dul], *adj.* slow-witted, obtuse, inept in comprehension, stupid; boring, commonplace; dim, cloudy, tarnished, unpolished; blunt; (*naut.*) without wind. [OE. *dol* stupid].
DULL (2), [dul], *v.t. and i.* to make dull, to become dull.
DULLARD (1), [dul'-erd], *n.* a stupid person.
DULLARDISM, [dul'-erd-izm], *n.* the condition of being a dullard.
DULL-BRAINED, [dul'-brānd], *adj.* stupid.
DULL-BROWED, [dul'-browd], *adj.* having a gloomy aspect.
DULL-DISPOSED, [dul'-dis-pōzd'], *adj.* inclined to dulness or sorrow.
DULL-EYED, [dul'-īd], *adj.* having a sleepy, unintelligent look.
DULL-HEAD, [dul'-hed'], *n.* a stupid person.
DULLISH, [dul'-ish], *adj.* rather dull.
DULL-SIGHTED, [dul'-sīt'-id], *adj.* having bad sight.
DULL-WITTED, [dul'-wit'-id], *adj.* stupid.
DULLY, [dul'-li], *adv.* in dull fashion.
DULNESS, [dul'-nes], *n.* the quality of being dull.
DULOCRACY, [dew-lok'-ra-si], *n.* the rule of slaves. [Gk. *doulos* slave and *kratia* rule].
DULSE, [duls], *n.* (*bot.*) the edible red seaweed, *Rhodymenia palmata*. [Gael. *duileasg*].
DULY, [dew'-li], *adv.* fitly, promptly.
DUMA, [dōōm'-a], *n.* the parliament of Imperial Russia from 1906-1917. [Russ. *duma* council].
DUMB, [dum], *adj.* incapable of articulation; silent, not speaking; (*fig.*) stupid, incapable of expressing an idea; **d. show**, mime without words. [OE. *dumb*].
DUMB-BARGE, [dum'-bahj'], *n.* a barge without sails.
DUMB-BELL, [dum'-bel], *n.* a bar with a heavy knob of iron at each end, held one in each hand during arm exercises.

DUMB-BELLS

DUMB-CAKE, [dum'-kāk], *n.* a cake formerly baked by superstitious maidens on St. Mark's Eve to discover their future husbands' identity.
DUMB-CANE, [dum'-kān], *n.* a West Indian plant, *Dieffenbachia Seguine*, which, when chewed, makes the tongue swell.
DUMBFOUND, [dum-fownd'], *v.t.* to strike dumb with amazement, to confound. [DUMB and (CON)FOUND].
DUMBLEDOR, [dumbl'-daw(r)], *n.* the humble-bee. [Uncert.].
DUMBLY, [dum'-li], *adj.* silently, as if dumb.
DUMBNESS, [dum'-nes], *n.* the condition of being dumb.
DUMB-SINGLES, [dum'-singlz], *n.(pl.)* kind of silk.
DUMB-WAITER, [dum'-wāt'-er], *n.* a framework of shelves, used for holding dishes, etc., and obviating the need for a servant at meals.
DUM-DUM, [dum'-dum], *n.* a soft-nosed bullet that expands when it hits anything. [*Dumdum*, the Indian arsenal, where first made].
DUMMERER, [dum'-er-er], *n.* a beggar who feigns dumbness.
DUMMY (1), [dum'-i], *n.* a bogus object; a model of a human being; an artificial teat for young children to suck; (*bridge*) the partner of the declarer, who, when play begins, exposes his hand on the table, and takes no part in the play; an actor without a speaking part; **tailor's d.**, a person with a dressy appearance, but little real worth; a tailor's model. [DUMB].
DUMMY (2), [dum'-i], *adj.* sham, bogus.
DUMOSE, [dew'-mōs], *adj.* covered with briars, bushy; (*bot.*) growing in a compact bush. [L. *dumus* bramble].
DUMOUS, [dew'-mus], *adj.* dumose.
DUMP (1), [dump], *n.* a heap of refuse, a place where refuse may be left; (*coll.*) a dirty, untidy place cluttered up with junk; (*milit.*) a deposit of supplies for future use.
DUMP (2), [dump], *n.* a shapeless mass, something thick and solid; a quoit made of rope; (*coll.*) a lumpish woman.
DUMP (3), [dump], *v.t. and i.* to unload roughly and casually by tipping out of a cart or basket, to deposit (refuse) on a rubbish heap; (*comm.*) to throw great quantities of goods on a foreign market at unprofitable prices; to descend abruptly with a bump. [Dan. *dumpe* to fall down].
DUMPINESS, [dump'-i-nes], *n.* the condition of being dumpy.
DUMPISHLY, [dump'-ish-li], *adv.* in dumpish fashion.
DUMPISHNESS, [dump'-ish-nes], *n.* the state of being dumpish.
DUMPLING, [dump'-ling], *n.* a ball of suet and dough, etc., boiled in water; **apple-d.**, an apple cooked in pastry.
DUMPS, [dumps], *n.* (*coll.*) low spirits, sullen depression.
DUMPTY, [dump'-ti], *n.* a large upholstered cushion used as a stool.

DUMPY (1), [dump′-i], *n.* a high hassock; a short-legged variety of hen; a short-handled umbrella.

DUMPY (2), [dump′-i], *adj.* short and podgy. [DUMP (2)].

DUN (1), [dun], *n.* a mound surmounted by a fortress. [Brit. *dun* hill].

DUN (2), [dun], *n.* a creditor, one who persistently demands to be paid. [DUN (5)].

DUN (3), [dun], *n.* a dull, greyish-brown colour; a variety of artificial fly for fishing. [DUN (4)].

DUN (4), [dun], *adj.* of the colour dun, drab. [OE. *dunn* dark brown].

DUN (5), (dunning, dunned), [dun], *v.t.* (of a creditor) to pester persistently for payment. [ME. *dunien* to clamour].

DUN (6), (dunning, dunned), [dun], *v.t.* (*U.S.*) to cure fish. [DUN (3)].

DUN-BIRD, [dun′-burd], *n.* the pochard duck, *Fuligula ferina*; the scaup, *Fuligula marila*.

DUNCE, [dunts], *n.* a dullard, who can learn nothing, a very stupid pupil. [*Duns* Scotus, whose followers were opposed to the study of the classics].

DUNCERY, [duns′-er-i], *n.* stupidity, the state of being a dunce.

DUNCISH, [duns′-ish], *adj.* like a dunce, stupid.

DUNCISHNESS, [duns′-ish-nes], *n.* the quality of being duncish.

DUN-COW, [dun′-kow′], *n.* the ray, *Raia fullonica*.

DUNDER, [dun′-der], *n.* lees, the fermented lees of cane-juice used in making rum. [Sp. *redundar* to overflow].

DUNDERHEAD, [dun′-der-hed′], *n.* a blockhead. [Unkn.].

DUNDERPATE, [dun′-der-pāt], *n.* a dunderhead.

DUN-DIVER, [dun′-dīv′-er], *n.* the goosander, *Mergus merganser*.

DUNDREARY, [dun-drēer′-i], *n.* (*usually pl.*) long sidewhiskers worn without a beard. [Lord *Dundreary*, character in a play by Tom Taylor].

DUNE, [dewn], *n.* a low hill of loose sand, close to the shore. [ODu. *duna*].

DUN-FISH, [dun′-fish], *n.* cod-fish cured by dunning.

DUNG (1), [dung], *n.* excrement. [OE. *dung*].

DUNG (2), [dung], *v.t. and i.* to manure with dung; to drop excrement.

DUNGAREE, [dung′-ger-ē′], *n.* cotton cloth used for sails and coarse working clothes; (*pl.*) overalls, etc., of this material. [Hind. *dungri*].

DUNG-BEETLE, [dung′-bētl], *n.* a beetle feeding on and (or) depositing its eggs in dung.

DUNGEON (1), † DONJON, [dun′-jun], *n.* (*originally*) the strongest tower of a castle; an underground prison-cell in a castle. [OFr. *donjon*].

DUNGEON (2), [dun′-jun], *v.t.* to confine in a dungeon.

DUNG-FORK, [dung′-fawk], *n.* a fork used for throwing dung and spreading it as manure.

DUNGHILL, [dung′-hil], *n.* a pile of dung; (*fig.*) a vile disgusting place.

DUNGING, [dung′-ing], *n.* manuring land.

DUNGMEER, [dung′-mēer], *n.* a pit where dung and weeds are mixed to rot and form manure.

DUNGY, [dung′-i], *adj.* smeared, tainted with dung.

DUNGYARD, [dung′-yahd], *n.* a yard where dung is deposited.

DUNLIN, [dun′-lin], *n.* (*ornith.*) the reddish sandpiper, *Tringa alpina*. [DUN (3)].

DUNLOP, [dun′-lop], *n.* a Scottish cheese. [*Dunlop*, in Ayrshire, where first made].

DUNNAGE, [dun′-ij], *n.* brushwood, branches, etc., placed under a ship's cargo to prevent damage by water, etc. [Unkn.].

DUNNE, [dun], *n.* the knot sandpiper, *Tringa canutus*. [Gael. *dunne*].

DUNNER, [dun′-er], *n.* a dun, or his agent.

DUNNING, [dun′-ing], *n.* the act of a creditor who presses to be paid; a method of curing cod.

DUNNISH, [dun′-ish], *adj.* of a somewhat dun colour.

DUNNOCK, [dun′-ok], *n.* the hedge-sparrow, *Accentor modularis*.

DUNNY, [dun′-i], *adj.* slow of hearing.

DUNT (1), [dunt], *n.* a hard thump; a blow sustained by aircraft on running into a vertical air current. [OE. *dynt*].

DUNT (2), [dunt], *n.* a giddiness sometimes affecting young sheep. [Uncert.].

DUO- (1), [dew′-ō], *pref.* two. [L. *duo* two].

DUO (2), [dew′-ō], *n.* a song in two parts; a duet; a variety act performed by two persons. [L. *duo* two].

DUODECENNIAL, [dew′-ō-des-en′-i-al], *adj.* occurring every twelve years, consisting of twelve years. [L. *duodecennium* period of twelve years].

DUODECIMAL (1), [dew′-o-des′-im-al], *n.*(*pl.*) a numerical system reckoning by twelves.

DUODECIMAL (2), [dew′-ō-des′-im-al], *adj.* reckoned in twelves, pertaining to twelve. [L. *duodecimus* twelfth].

DUODECIMALLY, [dew′-ō-des′-im-a-li], *adv.* in a duodecimal fashion.

DUODECIMO, [dew′-ō-des′-im-ō], *n.* a book, or the size of a book, in which the sheet is folded into twelve leaves. [L. *duodecimus* twelfth].

DUODECUPLE, [dew′-ō-dek′-yōō-pōōl], *adj.* in twelves.

DUODENA†, [dew′-ō-dēn′-a], *n.* (*leg.*) a jury of twelve.

DUODENAL, [dew′-ō-dēn′-al], *adj.* of, or relating to, the duodenum.

DUODENARY, [dew′-ō-dēn′-er-i], *adj.* in twelves. [L. *duodenarius* containing twelve].

DUODENITIS, [dew′-ō-dēn-it′-is], *n.* (*path.*) inflammation of the duodenum. [DUODENUM and Gk. *itis* denoting inflammation].

DUODENUM, [dew′-ō-dēn′-um], *n.* the upper end of the small intestine, leading into the stomach. [MedL. *duodenum*].

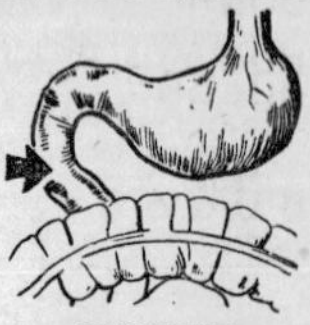

DUODENUM

DUOLITERAL, [dew′-ō-lit′-er-al], *adj.* biliteral.

DUOLOGUE, [dew′-ō-log], *n.* talk between two persons only. [DUO and Gk. *logos* speech].

DUP†, [dup], *v.t.* to open. [DO and UP].

DUPABILITY, [dewp′-a-bil′-i-ti], *n.* liability to be duped.

DUPABLE, [dewp′-abl], *adj.* easy to dupe.

DUPE (1), [dewp], *n.* one who is easily deceived. [Unkn.].

DUPE (2), [dewp], *v.t.* to deceive, trick.

DUPER, [dewp′-er], *n.* one who dupes.

DUPERY, [dewp′-er-i], *n.* the act of duping.

DUPION, [dew′-pi-on], *n.* a double cocoon, formed by two or more silkworms. [Fr. *doupion*].

DUPLE (1), [dewpl], *adj.* (*math.*) a figure in which the preceding term is double the consequent.

DUPLE (2), [dewpl], *adj.* (*mus.*) having two beats to the bar. [L. *duplus* double].

DUPLEX, [dew′-pleks], *adj.* twofold, having two parts, *esp.* of machinery, and in botany. [L. *duplex*].

DUPLICATE (1), [dew′-plik-āt], *n.* a replica.

DUPLICATE (2), [dew′-plik-āt], *adj.* being an identical copy of something; (*arith.*) in the ratio of one square to another.

DUPLICATE (3), [dew′-plik-āt], *v.t.* to make a copy identical with (the original), to repeat (an action, etc.) identically; to make copies of on a duplicator. [L. *duplicare* to double].

DUPLICATION, [dew′-plik-ā′-shun], *n.* the act of duplicating, the condition of being duplicated. [L. *duplicatio*].

DUPLICATIVE, [dew′-plik-at-iv], *adj.* relating to duplication, tending to duplicate.

DUPLICATOR, [dew′-plik-āt′-er], *n.* a machine for rapidly making numerous copies from a stencilled original.

DUPLICATURE, [dew′-plik-at-yōō-er], *n.* (*anat.*) the fold of a membrane.

DUPLICITY, [dew-plis′-i-ti], *n.* deceit, trickery, hypocrisy. [L. *duplicitas* state of being double].

DUPPER, [dup′-er], *n.* an Indian dubber of buffalo-hide. [Native].

DURABILITY, [dew′-ra-bil′-i-ti], *n.* the condition of being durable. [L. *durabilitas*].

DURABLE, [dew′-rabl], *adj.* able to withstand long and hard use, or exposure. [L. *durabilis*].

DURABLENESS, [dew′-rabl-nes], *n.* the quality of being durable.

DURABLY, [dew′-rab-li], *adv.* in durable fashion.

DURAIN, [dew′-rān], *n.* a compact coal of varied origin. [Unkn.].

DURALUMIN, [dyōōer-al′-yew-min], *n.* a tough alloy of aluminium. [L. *durus* hard and ALUMIN(IUM)].

DURAMEN, [dew-rā′-men], *n.* the wood in the centre of an exogenous tree. [L. *duramen* a hardened vine-branch].

DURANCE, [dew′-rants], *n.* imprisonment. [Fr. *durance*].

DURANT, [dew′-rant], *n.* a strong, glazed woollen fabric. [L. *durans* lasting].

DURATE, [dew-rah'-ti], *adj.* (*mus.*) harsh, not melodious. [It. *durate*].
DURATION, [dew-rā'-shun], *n.* period of existence or continuance. [L. *duratio*].
DURBAR, [dur'-bah(r)], *n.* a state levee in India held by the King as Emperor of India or by the Viceroy. [Hind. *durbar*].
DURDEN, [dur'-den], *n.* a sheltered copse. [Uncert.].
DURDUM, [dur'-dum], *n.* a great tumult. [Unkn.].
DURE†, [dew'-er], *v.i.* to endure. [L. *durare*].
DUREFUL, [dew'-er-fo͝ol], *adj.* long-lasting.
DURELESS, [dew'-er-les], *adj.* not lasting.
DURESS, [dew-res'], *n.* confinement, forcible compulsion; (*leg.*) compulsion by threat of bodily hurt. [OFr. *duresse*].
DURIAN, [dew'-ri-an], *n.* the fruit of *Durio zibethinus*.
DURING, [dew'-ring], *prep.* in the course of, through the existence or continuance of.
DURIO, [dew'-ri-ō], *n.* the East Indian tree bearing the durian. [Malay *duri* thorn].
DURITY, [dew'-ri-ti], *n.* hardness, strength. [L. *duritas*].
DURMAST, [dur'-mast'], *n.* an oak with downy leaves, sometimes known as *Quercus pubescens*. [Uncert.].
DUROY, [dew-roi'], *n.* a coarse woollen fabric common to the west of England. [Uncert.].
DURRA, DOURA, [do͝or'-a], *n.* (*bot.*) Indian millet, cultivated as a corn plant. [Arab. *durah*].
DURWAN, [dur-wahn'], *n.* a door-keeper. [Hind. *darwan*].
DUSE, [dews], *n.* an evil spirit, a goblin. [DEUCE].
DUSK (1), [dusk], *n.* the twilight at the end of the day.
DUSK (2), [dusk], *adj.* (*poet.*) dim, dusky. [OE. *dosc* dark, OScand. *dusk* fog].
DUSKILY, [dusk'-i-li], *adv.* in a dusky fashion.
DUSKINESS, [dusk'-i-nes], *n.* the condition of being dusky.
DUSKISH, [dusk'-ish], *adj.* tending to be dusky.
DUSKISHLY, [dusk'-ish-li], *adv.* in duskish mode.
DUSKISHNESS, [dusk'-ish-nes], *n.* the state of being dusky.

DURRA

DUSKY, [dusk'-i], *adj.* shadowy; of dark complexion.
DUST (1), [dust], *n.* powdery particles of matter; (*fig.*) a dead and crumbled body; **to bite the d.**, to be flung to the ground in combat; **to throw d. in the eyes of**, to deceive; **to kick up a d.**, (*slang*) to cause a disturbance, to protest. [OE. *dust*].
DUST (2), [dust], *v.t.* to brush or wipe the dust off; to sprinkle with powder.
DUSTBIN, [dust'-bin], *n.* a container for household refuse.
DUST-BRAND, [dust'-brand'], *n.* (*bot.*) a disease of plants.
DUST-CART, [dust'-kaht], *n.* a cart in which refuse is collected and removed.
DUSTER, [dust'-er], *n.* a cloth for wiping away dust; (*cooking*) a sprinkler.
DUSTHOLE, [dust'-hōl], *n.* a dump for refuse.
DUSTINESS, [dust'-i-nes], *n.* the condition of being dusty.
DUSTMAN, [dust'-man], *n.* a labourer who collects household refuse.
DUSTPAN, [dust'-pan'], *n.* a flat shovel into which dust may be easily brushed.
DUST-SHOT, [dust'-shot'], *n.* the smallest size of shot.
DUSTY, [dust'-i], *adj.* powdery; covered in dust; **not so d.**, (*slang*) fairly good.
DUSTY-FOOT, [dust'-i-fo͝ot'], *n.* a pedlar.
DUTCH (1), [duch], *n.* (*slang*) wife. [DUCHESS].
DUTCH (2), [duch], *n.*(*pl.*) the inhabitants of Holland; (*sing.*) their language. [MDu. *dutsch*].
DUTCH (3), [duch], *adj.* relating to Holland and its people; **D. courage**, false courage inspired by drink; (*coll.*) **double-D.**, incomprehensible.
DUTCHMAN, [duch'-man], *n.* an inhabitant of Holland.
DUTEOUS, [dew'-ti-us], *adj.* respectful, obedient.
DUTEOUSLY, [dew'-ti-us-li], *adv.* in duteous fashion.
DUTEOUSNESS, [dew'-ti-us-nes], *n.* the quality of being duteous.
DUTIABLE, [dew'-ti-able], *adj.* chargeable with customs duty.
DUTIED, [dew'-tid], *adj.* subject to customs duties.
DUTIFUL, [dew'-ti-fo͝ol], *adj.* submissive and respectful to one's superiors, attentive to one's (moral) duties.
DUTIFULLY, [dew'-ti-fo͝ol-i], *adv.* in dutiful fashion.
DUTIFULNESS, [dew'-ti-fo͝ol-nes], *n.* dutiful quality or conduct.
DUTY, [dew'-ti], *n.* moral or legal obligation to pursue some action; some task or action so performed; task or action obligatory upon some rank or office; a fitting expression of homage or respect; a particular task or set of tasks; indirect taxation payable on certain imports, exports, legal transactions, etc.; (*mech.*) the ratio of work done to fuel consumed; **to be on d.**, to be engaged in carrying out instructions. [OFr. *duete*].
DUUMVIR, [dew-um'-vur], *n.* one of two equal and joint officers. [L. *duumvir*].
DUUMVIRAL, [dew-um'-ver-al], *adj.* relating to a duumvir or duumvirate.
DUUMVIRATE, [dew-um'-ver-āt], *n.* the office held by duumvirs. [L. *duumviratus*].
DUX, [duks], *n.* a leader; (*mus.*) the chief subject in a fugue. [L. *dux* leader].
DWANG, [dwang], *n.* a mason's crow-bar. [Du. *dwang* force].
DWARF (1), [dwarf], *n.* (*myth.*) a small goblin living underground and often working metals; an undersized man, woman or other creature. [OE. *dweorg*].
DWARF (2), [dwarf], *adj.* abnormally small; **d. tree**, a tree whose branches shoot near the root.
DWARF (3), [dwarf], *v.t.* to make seem tiny or insignificant by comparison, to overshadow; to stunt or impede normal development in.
DWARFISH, [dwawf'-ish], *adj.* very small, smaller than is proper or normal, under-developed.
DWARFISHLY, [dwawf'-ish-li], *adv.* in a dwarfish fashion.
DWARFISHNESS, [dwawf'-ish-nes], *n.* the condition of being dwarfish.
DWELL, [dwel], *v.i.* to inhabit, reside or live in; **to d. on**, to pause at, ponder over, discuss at length, an idea, feeling, phrase. [OE. *dwellan* to lead astray].
DWELLER, [dwel'-er], *n.* one who dwells.
DWELLING, [dwel'-ing], *n.* a place to dwell in, the house in which one lives and sleeps.
DWINDLE, [dwindl], *v.i.* to grow less by wasting or shrinkage, grow smaller, to pass slowly into decay or oblivion. [OE. *dwinan*].
DYAD, [dī'-ad], *n.* a pair, something consisting of two equal parts; (*chem.*) element with atomic weight equalling two atoms of hydrogen. [Gk. *duas* (*duad-*) two].
DYADIC, [dī-ad'-ik], *adj.* relating to a dyad.
DYAK, [dī'-ak], *n.* a member of a people in Borneo. [Malay *dyak* savage].
DYARCHY, [dī'-ahk-i], *n.* government by two persons, forces or elements. [Gk. *duas* two and *arkhia* government, rule].
DYE (1), [dī], *n.* any substance for tinting fabrics, etc. [OE. *deag* colour].
DYE (2), (**dyes, dyeing, dyed**), [dī], *v.t. and i.* to tint or stain with a dye; to undergo change of colour by being dyed. [OE. *deagian*].
DYEING, [dī'-ing], *n.* the act, trade or occupation of a dyer.
DYER, [dī'-er], *n.* one whose trade is dyeing; **dyer's weed**, (*bot.*) a plant from which is obtained a yellow dye, *Reseda luteola*; **dyer's greenweed**, the plant, *Genista tinctoria*.
DYESTUFFS, [dī'-stufs], *n.*(*pl.*) substances employed in dyeing.
DYING, [dī'-ing], *adj.* passing in death, approaching death, an end; fading, losing colour, life, vigour, as at the approach of death. [DIE].
DYINGLY, [dī'-ing-li], *adv.* as if dying.
DYKE, see DIKE.
DYNACTINOMETER, [dīn'-ak-tin-om'-it-er], *n.* an instrument to test the actinic force of light and the action of lenses. [Gk. *dunamis* force, *aktis* a ray, and METER].
DYNAM, [dīn'-am], *n.* the unit of force required to raise one pound through one foot in one second. [Gk. *dunamis* force].
DYNAMETER, [dīn-am'-it-er], *n.* an instrument for measuring the magnifying power of a telescope. [Gk. *dunamis* force and METER].
DYNAMETRICAL, [dīn-a-met'-rik-al], *adj.* relating to a dynameter.

DYNAMIC, [dīn-am'-ik], *adj.* having power, energy; relating to force in motion; (*fig.*) having energy, force of personality, vigour; (*met.*) relating to dynamism. [Gk. *dunamikos*].
DYNAMICAL, [dīn-am'-ik-al], *adj.* relating to dynamics.
DYNAMICALLY, [dīn-am'-ik-a-li], *adv.* in dynamical fashion.
DYNAMICS, [dīn-am'-iks], *n.* the science dealing with energy and the movement of matter.
DYNAMISM, [dīn'-am-izm], *n.* philosophy basing the universe on the interplay of natural forces.
DYNAMITARD, [dīn'-a-mīt'-erd], *n.* an anarchist employing dynamite.
DYNAMITE (1), [dīn'-a-mīt], *n.* an explosive much used in blasting, consisting of nitro-glycerin stabilized by mixture with a porous substance. [Gk. *dunamis* force].
DYNAMITE (2), [dīn'-a-mīt], *v.t.* to blow up with dynamite.
DYNAMITER, [dīn'-a-mīt-er], *n.* one who endeavours to create terror and social disruption by acts of violence with dynamite.
DYNAMO, [dīn'-a-mō], *n.* a machine for changing mechanical into electrical energy. [Gk. *dunamis* force].
DYNAMOGRAPH, [dīn-am'-o-grahf], *n.* the recording made by a dynamometer. [DYNAMO and GRAPH].
DYNAMOMETER, [dīn'-a-mom'-it-er], *n.* an instrument for measuring the force of an engine; a dynameter.
DYNAST, [dīn'-ast], *n.* a member of a ruling family, a ruler by heredity. [Gk. *dunastes* ruler].
DYNASTIC, [dīn-ast'-ik], *adj.* relating to a dynasty, or the rule of dynasties.
DYNASTICAL, [dīn-ast'-ik-al], *adj.* dynastic.
DYNASTIDAN, [dīn-ast'-id-an], *n.* one of a group of large, foreign beetles, including the elephant beetle and the atlas beetle. [Gk. *dunastes* powerful one].
DYNASTY, [din'-ast-i], *n.* a continuous line of related and hereditary rulers. [Gk. *dunasteia* rule].
DYNE, [dīn], *n.* a unit of force; the force which will give one gramme an acceleration of one centimetre per second. [Fr. *dyne* from Gk. *dunamis* force].
DYS-, *pref.* bad. [Gk. *dus* bad].
DYSAESTHESIA, [dis'-ēs-thē'-zi-a], *n.* (*med.*) impaired feeling; a tendency to insensibility. [DYS and Gk. *aisthonomai* I perceive].
DYSCHROA, [dis'-krō-a], *n.* a discoloured condition of the skin. [DYS and Gk. *khroa* skin].
DYSCRASIA, [dis-krā'-zi-a], *n.* troubled condition of the bodily humours. [DYS and Gk. *krasis*].
DYSENTERIC, [dis'-en-te'-rik], *adj.* relating to, suffering from, dysentery.
DYSENTERY, [dis'-en-tri], *n.* inflammation of the mucous membrane of the large intestine, resulting in griping, diarrhoea and discharges of blood. [Gk. *dusenteria*].
DYSGENIC, [dis-jen'-ik], *adj.* having a detrimental biological effect. [DYS and (EU)GENIC].
DYSLOGISTIC, [dis'-loj-ist'-ik], *adj.* implying adverse criticism. [Gk. *duslogistos*].
DYSLOGISTICALLY [dis'-loj-ist'-ik-a-li], *adv.* in disapproving fashion.
DYSLOGY, [dis'-lo-ji], *n.* adverse criticism. [DYS and Gk. *logos* speech].
DYSLUITE, [dis'-lew-it], *n.* (*min.*) a brown spinel containing zinc, manganese and iron.
DYSMENIA, [dis-mēn'-i-a], *n.* dysmenorrhoea.
DYSMENORRHOEA, [dis'-men-or-ē'-a], *n.* abnormal or painful menstruation. [DYS, Gk. *men* month and *rheo* I flow].
DYSNOMY, [dis'-nom-i], *n.* a bad legal system. [DYS and Gk. *nomos* law].
DYSODILE, [dis'-o-dīl], *n.* a variety of greenish-grey or yellowish lignite which burns with a foul smell. [Gk. *dusodes* foul-smelling].
DYSOPSY, [dis-op'-si], *n.* bad eyesight. [DYS and Gk. *opsis* vision].
DYSOREXY, [dis'-o-rek-si], *n.* a want of appetite; an appetite for unhealthy things. [Gk. *dusorexia*].
DYSPATHY, [dis'-path-i], *n.* antipathy. [Gk. *duspatheia* lack of sensibility].
DYSPEPSIA, [dis-pep'-si-a], *n.* chronic indigestion, inability to digest foods owing to functional derangement. [Gk. *duspepsia*].
DYSPEPTIC (1), [dis-pept'-ik], *n.* a person subject to dyspepsia.
DYSPEPTIC (2), [dis-pept'-ik], *adj.* suffering from dyspepsia; (*fig.*) gloomy and bad-tempered.
DYSPHAGIA, [dis-fā'-ji-a], *n.* difficulty in swallowing. [DYS and Gk. *phagia* eating].
DYSPHONY, [dis'-fon-i], *n.* morbid difficulty in speaking; harshness of sound or speech. [Gk. *dusphonia*].
DYSPHORIA, [dis-faw'-ri-a], *n.* nervous impatience restlessness. [DYS and Gk. *phero* I bear].
DYSPNOEA, [disp-nē'-a], *n.* difficulty in breathing. [Gk. *duspnoia*].
DYSPNOIC, [disp-nō'-ik], *adj.* relating to, or suffering from, dyspnoea.
DYSTHETIC, [dis-the'-tik], *adj.* having a bad bodily condition. [Gk. *dusthesia*].
DYSTHYMIC, [dis-thim'-ik], *adj.* mentally, nervously depressed. [Gk. *dusthumos*].
DYSTOMIC, [dis-tom'-ik], *adj.* dystomous.
DYSTOMOUS, [dis'-tom-us], *adj.* (*min.*) difficult to cleave. [Gk. *dustomos*].
DYSURIA, [dis-yōō'-ri-a], *n.* dysury.
DYSURIC, [dis-yōō'-rik], *adj.* suffering from, relating to, disury.
DYSURY, [dis'-yōō-ri], *n.* a morbid condition of the urine; difficulty in passing water. [Gk. *dusouria*].
DYTISCUS, [dī-tis'-kus], *n.* a genus of water beetles. [Gk. *dutiskos* able to dive].
DZERON, [dze'-ron], *n.* a goat-antelope of the genus *Nemorrhædus*. [Mongolian *dseren*].
DZIGGETAI, DJIGGETAI, [dzig'-et-ī], *n.* the Asiatic wild ass, *Equus hemionus*. [Mongolian *tchikhitei* long-eared].

E

E (1), the fifth letter of the Latin and English alphabets.
E- (2), *pref.* out of, from, without. [L. *e, ex*].
EACH (1), [ēch], *adj.* every one of any group or number separately considered. [OE. *ælc, æghwylc*].
EACH (2), [ēch], *pron.* every one of any number or group considered separately. [*Prec.*].
EAGER, [ē'-ger], *adj.* impatient, anxious to act, excited by ardent desire; filled with a lively and alert spirit; earnest, keen. [OFr. *aigre* from L. *acer* sharp].
EAGERLY, [ē'-ger-li], *adv.* in an eager fashion.
EAGERNESS, [ē'-ger-nes], *n.* the quality of being eager.
EAGLE, [ēgl], *n.* a large bird of prey of the genus *Aquila*, having a strong curved beak and powerful wings and talons; any representation of this bird used as a sign, *esp.* as the standard of the Roman legionaries; an American gold coin worth ten dollars; a church reading-desk in the form of this bird; (*astron.*) a constellation of the northern hemisphere; (*coll.*) a golf-hole played in two strokes under bogey. [OFr. *aigle* from L. *aquila*].
EAGLE-EYED, [ēgl'-īd], *adj.* keen-sighted as an eagle; of penetrating discernment.
EAGLE-FLIGHTED, [ēgl'-flī'-tid], *adj.* soaring high as an eagle.
EAGLE-HAWK, [ēgl'-hawk], *n.* an Australian bird of prey, *Aquila audax*.
EAGLE-OWL, [ēgl'-owl], *n.* the European great horned-owl, *Bubo ignavus*.
EAGLE-PINIONED, [ēgl'-pin'-yund], *adj.* having or resembling eagle's wings.
EAGLE-RAY, [ēgl'-rā], *n.* the devil-fish, a large species of *Myliobatis*.
EAGLE-SIGHTED, [ēgl'-sī'-tid], *adj.* having acute eyesight.
EAGLE-STONE, [ēgl'-stōn], *n.* a hollow stone of argillaceous iron-ore usually holding pieces of another substance in it.
EAGLET, [ē'-glet], *n.* a young eagle.
EAGLE-WINGED, [ēgl'-wingd], *adj.* having the wings

of or like an eagle; swift and powerful in flight.

EAGLE-WOOD, [ēgl'-wŏŏd], *n.* a fragrant wood burnt as incense, *Aquilaria Agallocha.*

EAGRE, [ē'-ger], *n.* a sudden and exceptionally high tide in an estuary or river, a bore as in the Severn, etc. [Unkn.].

EAN†, [ēn], *v.t. and i.* to bring forth lambs. [YEAN].

EAR (1), [ēer], *n.* one of the two organs of hearing, particularly the external shell-like portion visible at the side of the head; **to be all ears,** to listen attentively; **to set by the ears,** to cause to quarrel; **to have an e. for music,** to be naturally musical. [OE. *eare*].

EAR (2), [ēer], *n.* a spike of corn; the seed receptacle of a cereal plant. [OE. *ear*].

EAR (3), [ēer], *v.t. and i.* to plough or till the land. [OE. *erian*].

EAR-ACHE, [ēer'-āk], *n.* pain in the internal part of the ear.

EAR-BORED, [ēer'-bawd], *adj.* having the lobes of the ears perforated.

EAR-CAP, [ēer'-kap], *n.* a cover for the ears as a protection against cold or injury.

EAR-COCKLE, [ēer'-kokl'], *n.* a disease in wheat, caused by the presence of spiral bacteria.

EAR-DROP, [ēer'-drop'], *n.* an ornament hanging from the ear.

EAR-DRUM, [ēer'-drum], *n.* (*anat.*) a membrane in the ear sensitive to sound vibrations.

EARED, [ēerd], *adj.* possessing ears.

EAR-ERECTING, [ēer'-i-rek'-ting], *adj.* pricking up the ears.

EAR-HOLE, [ēer'-hōl], *n.* the opening of the external ear.

EARING (1), [ēer'-ing], *n.* a ploughing of land. [EAR (2)].

EARING (2), [ēer'-ing], *n.* (*naut.*) a rope which reefs the corner of a sail.

EARL, [url], *n.* a rank or title in the British aristocracy next below that of marquis; a person bearing this rank; **E. Marshal,** head of the College of Arms, an hereditary title held by the Dukes of Norfolk, with the duty of directing national ceremonies. [OE. *eorl*].

EARLAP, [ēer'-lap'], *n.* the fold of flesh at the tip of the ear.

EARLDOM, [url'-dum], *n.* the title, jurisdiction, or dignity of an earl.

EARLESS, [ēer'-les], *adj.* lacking ears; deaf.

EARLINESS, [ur'-li-nes], *n.* the quality of being early.

EARLING, [ēer'-ling], *n.* a young lamb or kid. [YEARLING].

EARLOCK, [ēer'-lok'], *n.* a curl of hair close to the ear; a love-lock.

EARLY (1), [ur'-li], *adj.* in advance of the usual, expected, or specified time; occurring before the customary date, prior, forward, advanced; near the beginning of any particular period of time; **E. Closing Act,** one of the Shops Acts passed in 1912, ordering all shops, with certain exceptions, to close on one half-day a week.

EARLY (2), [ur'-li], *adv.* at the beginning of any particular period of time, soon, in good time; with the first in a procession or succession, among the leaders; betimes, premature. [OE. *ærlice*].

EARLY DOOR, [ur'-li-daw(r)], *n.* a theatre door and pay-box admitting the public at an extra charge to the cheaper priced seats some time before the performance commences; also (*pl.*).

EARMARK (1), [ēer'-mahk], *n.* a mark or notch for identification purposes on the ear of an animal; (*fig.*) a stamp or mark of identification, *esp.* on bullion to denote ownership.

EARMARK (2), [ēer'-mahk], *v.t.* to mark with an earmark; to reserve for a special purpose.

EARN, [urn], *v.t.* to acquire wages, honour or reward by hard work or performance; to deserve, acquire justly and fittingly. [OE. *earnian* to harvest].

EARNEST (1), [ur'-nist], *n.* a pledge or token of something more to come; payment of money as first instalment, as an indication of good faith; (*fig.*) a foretaste. [ME. *ernest* from ~ Heb. *erabon* pledge].

EARNEST (2), [ur'-nist], *adj.* determined, intent, zealous; serious-minded, governed by deep, sincere and consistent moral principles; **in e.,** serious, not joking. [OE. *eornost*].

EARNESTLY, [ur'-nist-li], *adv.* in an earnest fashion.

EARNEST-MONEY, [ur'-nist-mun'-i], *n.* money paid as a pledge of good faith.

EARNESTNESS, [ur'-nist-nes], *n.* the state of being earnest.

EARNING, [ur'-ning], *n.*(*pl.*) that which is earned by work, wages, reward. [OE. *earnung* merit].

EARPHONE, [ēer'-fōn], *n.* apparatus applied to the ears by which wireless and telephonic communications may be heard; a coil of plaited hair resembling this.

EARPICK, [ēer'-pik], *n.* an instrument for cleaning the ear.

EAR-PIERCING, [ēer'-pēers'-ing], *adj.* horribly penetrating; a shrill or sharp sound.

EAR-RING, [ēer'-ring], *n.* an ornament designed to hang from the lobe of the ear.

EAR-RINGED, [ēer'-ringd], *adj.* wearing ear-rings.

EARSHELL, [ēer'-shel'], *n.* a flattened ear-shaped univalve shell, a species of *Haliotis.*

EARSHOT, [ēer'-shot'], *n.* the distance within which sounds, *esp.* speech sounds, are audible.

EAR-SPLITTING, [ēer'-split'-ing], *adj.* extremely loud.

EARTH (1), [urth], *n.* the world inhabited by man considered as a planet in the universe, the globe; the hard surface of the globe as distinct from the sea, air, or heavens; dry ground, mould, soil, the substance and materials composing the land accessible to the ordinary man, the mixture of crumbled rock, rubble and decayed vegetation composing the crust of the globe; the hole, lair, or den of a fox, etc.; (*chem.*) an oxide of a light metal; (*elect.*) connexion with the earth completing a circuit; **to come back to e.,** to return to realities from idealism or a state of day-dreams; **to move heaven and e.,** to make prodigious efforts; **to run to e.,** (*fig.*) to track down. [OE. *eorthe*].

EARTH (2), [urth], *v.t. and i.* to surround or cover with earth; (*elect.*) to complete a circuit by connecting with the earth; to burrow.

EARTH-BAG, [urth'-bag'], *n.* a bag filled with earth, used for a barricade or trench in war.

EARTH-BANK, [urth'-bangk'], *n.* a bank or mound of earth.

EARTH-BATH, [urth'-bahth], *n.* a bath in dry soil or earth, as by a chicken.

EARTH-BOARD, [urth'-bawd], *n.* the mould-board of a plough.

EARTH-BORN, [urth'-bawn], *adj.* sprung from the soil; born on the earth, earthly.

EARTH-BOUND, [urth'-bownd], *adj.* firmly planted in the earth; prosaic.

EARTH-BRED, [urth'-bred'], *adj.* of humble rural stock.

EARTHEN, [urth'-en], *adj.* made of earth or of baked clay.

EARTHENWARE, [urth'-en-wāer'], *n.* domestic vessels made of baked clay, crockery, pottery.

EARTH-FALL, [urth'-fawl], *n.* (*geol.*) the collapse of a mound leaving a depression which fills with water.

EARTH-FLAX, [urth'-flaks'], *n.* a flax-like asbestos.

EARTH-HOUSE, [urth'-hows'], *n.* a natural chasm or split in rock or chalk converted into a subterranean dwelling-cave.

EARTHINESS, [urth'-i-nes], *n.* the quality of being earthy.

EARTHING, [urth'-ing], *n.* a connexion with the earth from a wireless set.

EARTHLINESS, [urth'-li-nes], *n.* the state of being earthly.

EARTHLING, [urth'-ling], *n.* an inhabitant of the earth, a mortal; a person with worldly ideas, a materialist.

EARTHLY, [urth'-li], *adj.* relating or belonging to the earth; solid, concrete, material.

EARTHLY-MINDED, [urth'-li-mīn'-did], *adj.* having a mind devoted chiefly to material interests.

EARTHLY-MINDEDNESS, [urth'-li-mīn'-did-nes], *n.* the quality of being earthly-minded.

EARTH-NUT, [urth'-nut], *n.* the chestnut-like tuber of a plant of the genus *Conopodium,* the pig-nut.

EARTH-PEA, [urth'-pē], *n.* a climbing leguminous plant.

EARTH-PLATE, [urth'-plāt], *n.* (*elect.*) a metal plate attached to electric apparatus to earth it.

EARTHQUAKE, [urth'-kwāk], *n.* a rocking, splitting or bursting of the earth's surface caused by subterranean volcanic activity.

EARTH-SHINE, [urth'-shīn], *n.* the light reflected from the earth on to that part of the new moon not exposed to the sun.

EARTH-SMOKE, [urth'-smōk], *n.* the plant *Fumaria officinalis.*

EARTHWARD, [urth'-werd], *adv.* towards the earth.

EARTHWORK, [urth'-wurk], *n.* (*eng.*) a cutting or

embankment of earth; a fortification of earth. [EARTH and WORK].

EARTHWORM, [urth'-wurm], *n.* the long tubular-shaped worm with a segmented body, that burrows in soil.

EARTHY, [urth'-i], *adj.* consisting of, similar to, or relating to earth; inhabiting the earth; gross, not refined.

EAR-TRUMPET, [ēer'-trum'-pet], *n.* an apparatus attached to the ear to aid the hearing.

EAR-WAX, [ēer'-waks'], *n.* cerumen, the waxy substance secreted by the glands of the ear, which collects in the outer passage.

EARWIG, [ēer'-wig], *n.* an insect of the genus *Forficula*, having horny forceps and wings folded under protective cases. [OE. *earwicga*].

EAR-WITNESS, [ēer'-wit'-nes], *n.* a person who is able to give testimony based on what was heard.

EASE (1), [ēz], *n.* an undisturbed or unrestricted state, freedom from constraint or exertion; comfort, quietness, pleasant peacefulness, freedom from pain, worry or other difficulties; **to stand at e.**, (*milit.*) to stand in a relaxed position, *esp.* with the legs apart and the hands behind the back. [OFr. *aise*].

EASE (2), [ēz], *v.t.* to free from constraint or restriction; to give more room to, to loosen; to relieve, assuage, give ease or comfort to; to facilitate; to slacken; **to e. off**, (*naut.*) to slacken a rope gradually; (*coll.*) to relax gradually. [*Prec.*].

EASEFUL, [ēz'-fŏŏl], *adj.* giving quiet, peaceful, characterized by rest.

EASEFULLY, [ēz'-fŏŏl-i], *adv.* in easeful manner.

EASEFULNESS, [ēz'-fool-nes], *n.* the quality of being easeful.

EASEL, [ēzl], *n.* an adjustable upright framework to support an artist's canvas or a blackboard. [Du. *ezel* ass, easel].

EASELESS, [ēz'-les], *adj.* having no ease.

EASEMENT, [ēz'-ment], *n.* that which affords ease; (*leg.*) any privilege, right, or convenience granted to one landowner in connexion with another's land or property. [OFr. *aisement*].

EASILY, [ēz'-i-li], *adv.* in an easy fashion.

EASINESS, [ēz'-i-nes], *n.* the condition of being easy.

EAST (1), [ēst], *n.* one of the four main points of the compass; the point on the horizon where the sun rises at the equinox; the countries situated in the eastern part of the globe, the Orient. [OE. *east*].

EAST (2), [ēst], *adj.* lying in, proceeding from the east.

EAST (3), [ēst], *adv.* towards the east.

EAST END, [ēst'-end'], *n.* the districts lying to the east, particularly of the city of London.

EASTER, [ēs'-ter], *n.* a spring festival of the Christian Church in commemoration of the resurrection of Christ; **E. dues**, the money of parishioners paid to their clergy as compensation for the tithe for personal labour; **E. eggs**, gifts of confectionery given at Easter; **E. offerings**, the collection taken for, or the payments made to, the incumbent on Easter Day; **E. term**, one of the four terms during which the high courts are in session, a school or university term extending for some thirteen weeks from the beginning of the year till Easter. [OE. *Eastre* from *Eostre* goddess of spring].

EASTERLING, [ēs'-ter-ling], *n.* a native of the East, *esp.* of Eastern Germany; a piece of money in circulation in the thirteenth century. [Du. *oesterling*]

EASTERLY, [ēs'-ter-li], *adj.* towards or coming from the east.

EASTERN, [ēs'-tern], *adj.* relating to the eastern part of the globe, oriental, being or dwelling in the East; towards the east. [OE. *easterne*].

EASTERNMOST, [ēs'-tern-mōst], *adj.* most easterly.

EASTERTIDE, [ēs'-ter-tīd], *n.* the week or period following Easter Sunday.

EASTING, [ēs'-ting], *n.* (*naut.*) a course set or covered in an easterly direction, the course east of any meridian.

EAST-SIDE, [ēst'-sīd], *n.* a district in New York lying east of Manhattan.

EASTWARD, [ēst'-werd], *adj.* towards the east.

EASY, [ē'-zi], *adj.* free from constraint or restriction, loose-fitting, loosened; comfortable, full of ease; slackened; not difficult; fluent; tolerant, not of strict morals; **shares are e.**, demand falls for specific shares; **honours are e.**, in bridge, an equal number of aces held by both sides during a no-trump hand. [OFr. *aisie*].

EASYCHAIR, [ē'-zi-chāer'], *n.* a soft arm-chair, designed for comfort.

EASY-GOING, [ē'-zi-gō'-ing], *adj.* casual, uncritical, tolerant.

EAT, (**ate, eaten**), [ēt], *v.t.* to take into the mouth, chew, and swallow; (*coll.*) to consume extravagantly; *v.i.* to take food into the system; **to e. away**, to remove gradually by gnawing, corrosion, etc.; **to e. into**, to bite into by slow acting agents such as acid; to waste by extravagance; **to e. one's heart out**, to keep a sorrow to oneself and brood over it, harming one's health; **to e. one's terms**, to qualify for the Bar by eating the traditional number of dinners in an Inn of Court; **to e. one's words**, to be forced to retract a statement. [OE. *etan*].

EATABLE, [ēt'-abl], *adj.* fit to be eaten.

EATABLES, [ēt'-ablz], *n.* (*pl.*) anything fit for or used as food.

EATAGE, [ēt'-ij], *n.* grazing grass, food for horses and cattle from the aftermath of the hay crop.

EATER, [ēt'-er], *n.* a person or thing that eats or corrodes.

EATING-HOUSE, [ēt'-ing-hows'], *n.* a cheap restaurant.

EATS, [ēts], *n.*(*pl.*) (*slang*) food.

EAU DE COLOGNE, [ō'-de-kol-ōn'], *n.* a perfume consisting of spirits of wine blended with fragrant oils, originally made at Cologne. [Fr. *eau de Cologne* water of Cologne].

EAU-DE-NIL, [ō'-de-nēl'], *n.* a dull-green colour, like the waters of the Nile. [Fr. *eau-de-nil*].

EAVES, [ēvz], *n.*(*pl.*) the edge of the roof of a building, overhanging the walls. [OE. *efese* edge].

EAVES-BOARD, [ēvz'-bawd], *n.* the board along the lower ends of the rafters to keep the slates flat.

EAVESDRIP, [ēvz'-drip], *n.* the dripping of water from the eaves.

EAVESDROP, (**eavesdropping, eavesdropped**), [ēvz'-drop'], *v.i.* to remain hidden while listening to the private conversation of others. [*Prec.*]

EAVESDROPPER, [ēvz'-drop'-er], *n.* one who eavesdrops.

EBB (1), [eb], *n.* the return of the tide to the sea; (*fig.*) falling off, decay. [OE. *ebba*].

EBB (2), [eb], *v.i.* to flow back; (*fig.*) to decline, fall off, decay. [OE. *ebbian*].

EBB-TIDE, [eb'-tīd], *n.* the receding tide.

EBIONITE, [eb'-yun-īt], *n.* the Jewish party in the early Church which considered Jesus an ordinary individual and upheld the Mosaic law. [Heb. *ebyon* poor].

EBLIS, [eb'-lis], *n.* the chief of the fallen angels; the Mohammedan name for Satan. [Arab. *iblis*].

E-BOAT, [ē'-bōt'], *n.* a kind of fast German torpedo-boat. [Germ. *E-boot*].

EBON, [eb'-on], *adj.* consisting of or resembling ebony; black. [Gk. *ebenos*].

EBONIST, [eb'-on-ist], *n.* a worker in ebony.

EBONITE, [eb'-on-īt], *n.* vulcanite, an insulating substance consisting of rubber and sulphur heated and fused together.

EBONIZE, [eb'-on-īz], *v.t.* to make black like ebony.

EBONY, [eb'-on-i], *n.* the hard, dark-coloured wood of various trees of the genus *Diospyros*; the quality of being black like this. [EBON].

EBOULEMENT, éboulement, [ā-bŏŏl'-mo(ng)], *n.* (*fort.*) the crumbling of a wall. [Fr. *éboulement*].

EBRACTEATE, [ē-brak'-ti-āt], *adj.* (*bot.*) having no bracts. [E (2) and BRACTEATE].

EBRIATE, [ē'-bri-āt], *adj.* intoxicated, drunk. [L. *ebriatum*, *p.pt.* of *ebriare* to make drunk].

EBRIETY, [ib-rī'-i-ti], *n.* intoxication. [L. *ebrietas*].

EBRILLADE, [eb-ril-ād'], *n.* a check to a horse by a sudden jerk of one rein if it refuses to turn. [Fr. *ébrillade*].

EBRIOSITY†, [e'-bri-os'-i-ti], *n.* habitual drunkenness. [L. *ebriositas*].

EBRIOUS, [ē'-bri-us], *adj.* drunk; inclined to drunkenness. [L. *ebrius*].

EBULLIENCE, [ib-ŏŏl'-yens], *n.* a boiling over; spontaneity, enthusiasm.

EBULLIENCY, [ib-ŏŏl'-yen-si], *n.* ebullience.

EBULLIENT, [ib-ŏŏl'-yent], *adj.* boiling over; bubbling with energy; exuberant. [L *ebulliens* bubbling].

EBULLITION, [eb'-yŏŏl-ish'-un], *n.* the act of boiling or bubbling up; (*fig.*) any sudden outburst. [L. *ebullitio*].

EBURNATION, [eb'-er-nā'-shun], *n.* (*med.*) a disease which consists in an abnormal deposition of osseous matter, causing the bones to thicken and the joints to stiffen. [~L. *eburnus* ivory].

EBURNEAN, [eb-ur'-ni-an], *adj.* made of ivory. [L. *eburnus*].
EBURNIFICATION†, [eb-ur'-ni-fik-ā'-shun], *n* the imparting of the appearance of ivory.
EBURNINE, [eb'-ur-nīn], *adj.* resembling or relating to ivory.
EC-, *pref.* out of. [Gk. *ek* out of].
ECARTE, écarté, [ā-kah'-tā], *n.* a game of cards for two. [Fr. *écarter* to discard].
ECAUDATE, [ē-kawd'-āt], *adj.* (*zool.*) having no tail; (*bot.*) without a stem.
ECBASIS, [ek'-ba-sis], *n.* (*rhet.*) treatment of things according to their events or consequences. [Gk. *ekbasis*].
ECBATIC, [ek-bat'-ik], *adj.* (*gram.*) signifying result as distinct from intention. [*Prec.*].
ECBLASTESIS, [ek'-blas-tē'-sis], *n.* (*bot.*) the production of buds owing to distorted inflorescences. [Gk. *ekblastesis* budding forth].
ECBOLE, [ek'-bo-li], *n.* (*rhet.*) a digression in a narrative introducing another speaking in his own words. [Gk. *ekbole*].
ECBOLIC (1), [ek-bol'-ik], *n.* an agent effecting abortion. [*Prec.*].
ECBOLIC (2), [ek-bol'-ik], *adj.* producing abortion.
ECCE HOMO, [ek'-si-hō'-mō], *n.* a picture or representation of Christ crowned with thorns. [L. *ecce homo* behold the man].
ECCENTRIC (1), [ek-sen'-trik], *n.* an eccentric individual; a circle which is not described from the same centre as another; a wheel with its axle not coaxial with the exact centre of the wheel.
ECCENTRIC (2), [ek-sen'-trik], *adj.* not having the same centre, deviating from the centre; odd, unconventional, slightly queer in the mind, having a peculiar character, abnormal. [Gk. *ekkentros* out of centre].
ECCENTRICAL, [ek-sen'-trik-al], *adj.* eccentric.
ECCENTRICALLY, [ek-sen'-trik-a-li], *adv.* in an eccentric fashion.
ECCENTRICITY, [ek'-sen-tris'-i-ti], *n.* the condition or quality of being eccentric.
ECCENTRIC-ROD, [ek-sen'-trik-rod'], *n.* the shaft imparting the motion of an eccentric wheel.
ECCENTRIC-STRAP, [ek-sen'-trik-strap'], *n.* the band grasping the circumference of an eccentric-wheel.
ECCENTRIC-WHEEL, [ek-sen'-trik-wēl'], *n.* a wheel with its axle not in the centre.
ECCHYMOSIS, [ek'-i-mō'-sis], *n.* (*med.*) inflamed blotches, bruises, or livid spots on the skin, caused by the effusion of extravasated blood. [Gk. *ekkhumosis* bruise].
ECCLESIA, [ek-lē'-zi-a], *n.* a political assembly of free citizens in Athens; a church. [Gk. *ekklesia* an assembly of citizens].
ECCLESIARCH, [ek-lē'-zi-ahk], *n.* a ruler of the Church. [ECCLESIA and Gk. *arkhe* rule].
ECCLESIASTES, [ek-lē'-zi-as'-tēz], *n.* the title of a book of the Old Testament ascribed to Solomon. [Gk. *ekklesiastes* member of the citizen assembly].
ECCLESIASTIC, [ek-lē'-zi-as'-tik], *n.* a clerk in holy orders, a cleric.
ECCLESIASTICAL, [ek-lē'-zi-as'-tikl], *adj.* relating to the Church.
ECCLESIASTICALLY, [ek-lē'-zi-as'-tik-a-li], *adv.* in an ecclesiastical fashion.
ECCLESIASTICUS, [ek-lē'-zi-as'-tik-us], *n.* one of the books of the Apocrypha.
ECCLESIOLATRY, [ek-lē'-zi-ol'-at-ri], *n.* excessive veneration for the Church. [ECCLESIA and Gk. *latreia* worship].
ECCLESIOLOGICAL, [ek-lē'-zi-ol-oj'-ik-al], *adj.* relating to ecclesiology.
ECCLESIOLOGIST, [ek-lē'-zi-ol'-oj-ist], *n.* a student of ecclesiology.
ECCLESIOLOGY, [ek-lē'-zi-ol'-o-ji], *n.* the history of church organization, church building and decoration. [ECCLESIA and Gk. *logos* speech].
ECCOPROTIC, [ek'-ō-prot'-ik], *n.* (*med.*) a medicine which purges gently. [EC and Gk. *kopros* dung].
ECCRINOLOGY, [ek'-rin-ol'-o-ji], *n.* (*physiol.*) the study of the secretions of the body. [Gk. *ekkrino* I separate and *logos* speech].
ECCRISIS†, [ek-ri'-sis], *n.* (*med.*) excretion. [~Gk. *ekkrino* I separate].
ECDEMIC, [ek-dem'-ik], *adj.* due to an exterior source, of foreign origin. [EK and Gk. *demos* the people].
ECDYSIS, [ek-dī'-sis], *n.* (*zool.*) the sloughing by snakes of the old skin; moulting. [Gk. *ekdusis*].
ECHAPPE, échappé, [ā-shap'-ā], *n.* a horse bred from a stallion and a mare of different breeds. [Fr. *échappé*].
ECHEANCE, [esh'-i-ahns], *n.* a specified day for cash settlement. [Fr. *échéance*].
ECHELLE†, échelle, [esh-el'], *n.* an arrangement of ribbons in the form of a ladder. [Fr. *échelle* ladder].
ECHELON échelon, [esh'-el-on], *n.* (*milit.*) troops stationed in depth, each formation stepped back with its front clear of the formation next to it. [Fr. *échelon*].
ECHIDNA, [ek-id'-na], *n.* the porcupine ant-eater, a spine-covered Australian mammal which lays eggs. [Gk. *ekhidna* viper].
ECHIDNIN, [ek-id'-nin], *n.* (*chem.*) the principle found in serpent-poison.
ECHIMYD, [ek'-i-mid], *n.* a South American rodent like a dormouse. [Gk. *ekhinos* hedgehog and *mus* mouse].

ECHIMYD

ECHINATE, [ek'-in-āt], *adj.* having prickles, like a hedgehog, bristled. [Gk. *ekhinos* hedgehog].
ECHINIDAN, [ek-in'-id-an], *n.* a species of the group of sea organisms including sea-urchins. [Gk. *ekhinos* hedgehog and *eidos* like].
ECHINITE, [ek'-in-it], *n.* (*geol.*) a fossil sea-urchin in chalk.
ECHINOCACTUS, [ek-ī'-no-kak'-tus], *n.* (*bot.*) a prickly South American flowering cactus. [Gk. *ekhinos* hedgehog and CACTUS].
ECHINOCOCCUS, [ek-ī'-nō-kok'-us], *n.* the larva of a tapeworm. [Gk. *ekhinos* hedgehog and COCCUS].
ECHINODERM, [ek-ī'-nō-durm'], *n.* (*zool.*) a species of the *Echinodermata*. [Gk. *ekhinos* hedgehog and *derma* skin].
ECHINOPS, [ek-in'-ops], *n.* (*bot.*) a genus of composite plants, of which the globe thistle is one. [Gk. *ekhinos* hedgehog and *opsis* appearance].
ECHINUS, (*pl.* **echini**), [ek-ī'-nus], *n.* the sea-urchin; (*bot.*) the prickly head of a plant; (*arch.*) an oval moulding, or cushion, beneath the capital of a Doric column. [Gk. *ekhinos* hedgehog].

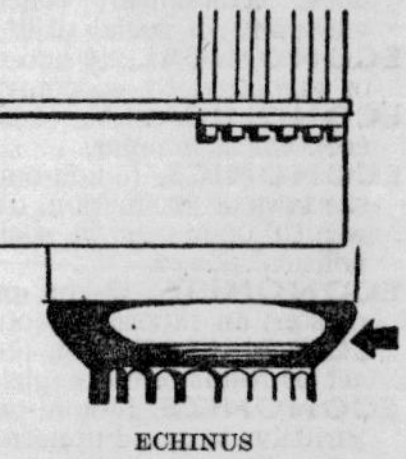
ECHINUS

ECHIODON, [ēk'-i-ō-don], *n.* a red fish that has no ventral fins, an eel.
ECHO (1), [ek'-ō], *n.* the repetition of a sound heard when its sound-waves are reflected from a solid surface; the repetition or imitation of a sound or speech; any imitation; (*bridge*) a conventional call indicating strength in a certain suit; (*arch.*) a vault or arch constructed to reflect sounds; (*mus.*) the repetition of a phrase in sequence. [Gk. *ekho*].
ECHO (2), [ek'-ō], *v.t. and i.* to make an echo; to copy or imitate.
ECHOIC, [ek-ō'-ik], *adj.* (*philol.*) of a word, intended to imitate the sound of the thing named, onomatopoeic. [ECHO].
ECHOISM, [ek'-ō-izm], *n.* the formation of words from sounds associated with the object indicated; onomatopoeia.
ECHOLESS, [ek'-ō-les], *adj.* without an echo.
ECHOMETER, [ek-om'-it-er], *n.* (*mus.*) an apparatus for measuring the duration of sounds together with their intervals and ratios; (*naut.*) an apparatus for taking soundings by means of wireless. [ECHO and METER].
ECHOMETRY, [ek-om'-it-ri], *n.* the measurement of the duration of sounds. [ECHO and Gk. *metria* measuring].
ECLAIR, éclair, [ā-klāer'], *n.* a finger-shaped piece of puff pastry filled with cream and coated with chocolate, etc. [Fr. *éclair*].
ECLAMPSIA, ECLAMPSY, [ek-lamp'-si-a], *n.* (*path.*) abnormal muscular spasms due to toxaemia during pregnancy; epileptic convulsions in which the patient imagines he sees flashes of light. [Gk. *eklampsis* brightness].
ECLAT, éclat, [ā-klah'], *n.* a burst of applause; acclamation, renown; **with é.,** with spectacular success. [Fr. *éclat* noise, clap].

ECLECTIC (1), [ek-lek′-tik], *n.* a philosopher who forms a system by combining elements considered most true in other systems; a believer in eclecticism.

ECLECTIC (2), [ek-lek′-tik], *adj.* accepting the principle or right of selection, choosing; given to selecting and collecting aesthetic and rational elements from different sources; incorporating what is considered the best and truest of the established discoveries of others. [Gk. *eklektikos* selecting].

ECLECTICALLY, [ek-lek′-tik-a-li], *adv.* in an eclectic manner.

ECLECTICISM, [ek-lek′-ti-sizm], *n.* the practice of an eclectic.

ECLIPSE (1), [ik-lips′], *n.* a total or partial interception of the light of the sun by the interposition of the moon between the earth and the sun, or of the moon by the shadow cast by the earth; (*fig.*) extinction, obscurity, complete relapse. [Gk. *ekleipsis*].

ECLIPSE (2), [ik-lips′], *v.t. and i.* to cut off the light from by an eclipse; (*fig.*) to obscure the fame or merit of, to dim or extinguish the brilliance of, to surpass.

ECLIPTIC (1), [ik-lip′-tik], *n.* (*astron.*) the apparent orbit traced by the sun in the heavens on its annual journey from west to east; (*geog.*) a great circle or line described on the globe, corresponding to this. [*Prec.*].

ECLIPTIC (2), [ik-lip′-tik], *adj.* relating to the ecliptic or to an eclipse.

ECLOGITE, [ek′-loj-īt], *n.* (*min.*) a garnet rock of the crystalline schist series mixed with hornblende. [Gk. *eklogos* selected].

ECLOGUE, [ek′-log], *n.* a short rural poem of idyllic character and conventional form. [Gk. *ekloge* selection].

ECMNESIA, [ek-nē′-zi-a], *n.* (*path.*) loss of memory concerning events occurring before a certain time or experience. [Gk. *ekmnesia* loss of memory].

ECOLOGY, OECOLOGY, [ē-kol′-o-ji], *n.* the study of organisms in relation to their surroundings. [Gk. *oikos* house and *logos* speech].

ECONOMIC, [ē′-kon-om′-ik], *adj.* relating to economics; economical; concerned with or from the viewpoint of social utility and productivity.

ECONOMICAL, [ē-kon-om′-ik-al], *adj.* relating to or regulated by economy; frugal, thrifty, saving.

ECONOMICALLY, [ē-kon-om′-ik-a-li], *adv.* in an economical manner.

ECONOMICS, [ē-kon-om′-iks], *n.(pl.)* the study of the laws of production, distribution and exchange of wealth operating in society and their relation to political power.

ECONOMIST, [ē-kon′-om-ist], *n.* an economical person; an expert in economics.

ECONOMIZATION, [ē-kon′-om-iz-ā′-shun], *n.* the act or result of economizing; saving.

ECONOMIZE, [ē-kon′-om-īz], *v.t. and i.* to expend thriftily; to avoid unnecessary expenses, to cut down expenditure.

ECONOMY, [ē′-kon-omi], *n.* the management of domestic resources or finances; a judicious management of finances, the practice of thrift; the careful or stringent organization of work and wages; the regular laws operating in natural organisms; the operation of laws of judicious management in relation to the affairs of a nation; (*theol.*) dispensation; the way in which a complex system, machine, or organization works. [Gk. *oikonomia* management of a household].

ECORCHE, écorché, [ā-kaw′-shā], *n.* (*art*) a model with the muscles exposed for the purpose of study. [Fr. *écorché*].

ECOSSAISE, écossaise, [ā-kos-āz′], *n.* (the music for) a Scottish country-dance. [Fr. *écossaise* Scottish].

ECOSTATE, [ek-ost′-āt], *adj.* (*bot.*) (of leaves) without a central rib. [E-(2) and COSTATE].

ECOUTES, écoutes, [ā-ko͞ots′], *n.(pl.)* (*fort.*) outposts, at equal distances from each other, in the form of small galleries leading from a covered parapet. [Fr. *écoute* listening].

ECPHASIS, [ek′-fas-is], *n.* an explicit declaration. [Gk. *ekphasis*].

ECPHLYSIS, [ek′-flī′-sis], *n.* (*med.*) an eruption on the skin. [Gk. *ekphlusis*].

ECPHONESIS, [ek′-fon-ē′-sis], *n.* (*rhet.*) a passionate exclamation in the course of an oration. [Gk. *ekphonesis*].

ECPHRACTIC, [ek-frak′-tik], *n.* (*med.*) a medicine removing viscid matter and obstruction; an aperient. [Gk. *ekphraktrikos*].

ECRASEUR, écraseur, [ā-kra-zur′], *n.* (*med.*) a surgical instrument excising diseased parts without haemorrhage. [~Fr. *écraser* to crush].

ECRU, écru, [ek-ro͞o′], *adj.* pale yellowish light brown, the colour of unbleached linen. [Fr. *écru* unbleached].

ECSTASY, EXTASY, [ek′-stas-i], *n.* an absorbing state of emotion involving intense feelings of exaltation, wonder, delight, a degree of delight strong enough to hold in abeyance the sense of reality; excessive enthusiasm, an intense feeling of pleasure. [Gk. *ekstasis* astonishment].

ECSTATIC, [ek-stat′-ik], *adj.* characterized by or causing ecstasy, rapturous. [Gk. *ekstatikos* unstable].

ECSTATICAL, [ek-stat′-ik-al], *adj.* ecstatic.

ECSTATICALLY, [ek-stat′-ik-a-li], *adv.* in ecstatic fashion.

ECTASIS, [ek′-ta-sis], *n.* (*rhet.*) the lengthening of a short syllable to a long. [Gk. *ektasis* stretching].

ECTHLIPSIS, [ek-thlip′-sis], *n.* (*gram.*) the elision of a final *m* and the preceding vowel when the next word begins with a vowel. [Gk. *ekthlipsis*].

ECTHYMA, [ek′-thi-ma], *n.* (*med.*) an eruption of pimples on the skin. [Gk. *ekthuma*].

ECTO-, *pref.* outside. [Gk. *ektos* outside].

ECTOBLAST, [ek′-tō-blast′], *n.* (*phys.*) the outer membranous wall of a cell. [ECTO and Gk. *blastos* germ].

ECTODERM, [ek′-tō-durm], *n.* an outer layer of the embryo; the outer layer of membrane of a cell. [ECTO and DERM].

ECTOPIA, [ek-tō′-pi-a], *n.* (*med.*) the displacement of an organ or member. [ECTO and ~Gk. *topos* place].

ECTOPLASM, [ek′-tō-plazm′], *n.* (*biol.*) the outer layer of protoplasm. [ECTO and PLASM].

ECTOZOA, [ek′-tō-zō′-a], *n.(pl.)* parasites that live on the external parts of other animals. [ECTO and Gk. *zoon* animal].

ECTROPICAL, [ek-trop′-ik-al], *adj.* beyond the tropics.

ECTROPION, [ek-trō′-pi-on], *n.* (*med.*) an everted condition of the eyelid by which the conjunctival surface becomes external. [EC and Gk. *tropion* turning].

ECTROTIC, [ek-trot′-ik], *adj.* (*med.*) relating to a preventive treatment; abortifacient. [Gk. *ektrotikos* relating to abortion].

ECTYLOTIC, [ek-tī-lot′-ik], *n.* (*med.*) a substance to reduce callosities of the skin. [EC and ~Gk. *tylos* callosity].

ECTYPAL, [ek-tīp′-al], *adj.* taken from the original.

ECTYPE, [ek′-tīp], *n.* a copy; (*arch.*) a cast in relief or embossed. [EC and TYPE].

ECTYPOGRAPHY, [ek′-tīp-og′-ra-fi], *n.* the art of etching with the lines in relief. [*Prec.* and Gk. *graphia* writing].

ECUMENICAL, OECUMENICAL, [ēk′-yo͝o-men′-ik-al], *adj.* general, universal (applied to the councils of the Catholic Church). [Gk. *oikoumenikos* universal].

ECUMENICITY, OECUMENICITY, [ēk′-yo͞o-men-is′-i-ti], *n.* the right of being called ecumenical.

ECZEMA, [ek′-sim-a], *n.* (*med.*) an eruption of small vesicles on the skin. [Gk. *ekzema*].

ECZEMATOUS, [ek-zē′-mat-us], *adj.* relating to eczema.

EDACIOUS, [ed-ā′-shus], *adj.* relating to, given to, eating; voracious. [L. *edax edacis*].

EDACIOUSLY, [ed-ā′-shus-li], *adv.* in a voracious manner.

EDACIOUSNESS, [ed-ā′-shus-nes], *n.* the condition of being edacious.

EDACITY, [ed-as′-i-ti], *n.* greediness.

EDDA, [ed′-a], *n.* an Old Icelandic compilation relating to the materials and conventions of Old Scandinavian poetry; an ancient collection of Old Scandinavian heroic and mythological poetry. [OIcel. *edda*].

EDDER (1), [ed′-er], *n.* flexible strips of wood binding hedge-stakes together. [OE. *eder* hedge].

EDDER (2), [ed′-er], *v.t.* to bind with edder.

EDDISH, †**EADISH**, [ed′-ish], *n.* the pasturing growth of grass that appears after mowing or reaping. [OE. *edisc*].

EDDOES, [ed′-ōz], *n.(pl.)* a species of edible tuber, resembling the potato, used as food by the natives of the Gold Coast. [Native].

EDDY (1), [ed′-i], *n.* circling movement of water or air deviating from the direction of the main current; a current of air, cloud, dust, etc., caught up in a spiral movement by the wind. [~OIcel. *itha*].

EDDY (2), (**eddies, eddied, eddying**), [ed′-i], *v.i.* to move like an eddy.

EDDY-WATER, [ed′-i-waw′-ter], *n.* (*naut.*) the water which falls back on the rudder of a moving ship.

EDDY-WIND, [ed′-i-wind′], *n.* wind thrown off from an obstruction.

EDELITE, [ăd'-el-īt], *n.* (*min.*) a silicate of alumina and lime. [~Germ. *edel* noble].
EDELWEISS, [ā'-del-vīs], *n.* (*bot.*) an Alpine plant, *Leontopodium alpinum.* [Germ. from *edel* noble and *weiss* white].
EDEMA, see OEDEMA.
EDEMATOSE, EDEMATOUS, see OEDEMATOUS.
EDEN, [ē'-den], *n.* in the Bible story, the Paradise of Adam and Eve immediately after creation; any delightful region. [Heb. *eden* delight].
EDENIC, [ē-den'-ik], *adj.* relating to or resembling Eden.
EDENTAL, [ē-dent'-al], *adj.* having no teeth.
EDENTATA, [ē'-den-tā'-ta], *n.(pl.)* (*zool.*) an order of animals having no front teeth. [E- (2) and ~L. *dens dentis* tooth].
EDENTATE, [ē-den'-tāt], *n.* an animal lacking front teeth.
EDENTATED, [ē'-den-tā'-tid], *adj.* (*zool.*) lacking teeth.
EDENTATION, [ē'-den-tā'-shun], *n.* lack of teeth.
EDENTULOUS, [ē-den'-chōōl-us], *adj.* toothless. [L. *edentulus* toothless].
EDGE (1), [ej], *n.* the extreme section or portion farthest from the centre, the margin; the sharp, sheared-off side of anything, *esp.* the sharp side of a cutting tool; a brink, lip, ledge; **to be on e.,** to be in a highly sensitive state, to be irritable; **to set one's teeth on e.,** to irritate acutely. [OE. *ecg*].
EDGE (2), [ej], *v.t. and i.* to provide with a sharp edge for cutting; to line, to hem, border; (*cricket*) to mishit the ball with the edge of the bat; **to e. away,** to move sideways carefully, little by little; **to e. into,** to move sideways into, to enter unobtrusively.
EDGE-BONE, [ej'-bōn'], *n.* the aitch bone.
EDGED, [ejd], *adj.* provided with an edge or border; sharp, keen.
EDGE-JOINT, [ej'-joint'], *n.* a corner.
EDGELESS, [ej'-les], *adj.* without an edge, not sharp; blunt.
EDGE-RAIL, [ej'-rāl'], *n.* the iron rail of a railway as laid on its edge.
EDGE-TOOL, [ej'-tōōl'], *n.* any sharp cutting instrument.
EDGEWAYS, [ej'-wāz], *adv.* edgewise.
EDGEWISE, [ej'-wīz], *adv.* with the edge upward or forward, in the direction of the edge. [EDGE and WISE].
EDGING, [ej'-ing], *n.* something forming the edge of a garment for ornament; a fringe, hem.
EDGY, [ej'-i], *adj.* having a sharp edge; with too hard an outline; easily provoked, with the nerves in an over-sensitive state.
EDIBLE, [ed'-ibl], *adj.* suitable for food. [LL. *edibilis* eatable].
EDIBLENESS, [ed'-ibl-nes], *n.* the quality of being edible.
EDICT, [ē'-dikt], *n.* a peremptory and authoritative order or command. [L. *edictum*].
EDICTAL, [ē-dikt'-al], *adj.* pertaining to an edict.
EDIFICANT†, [ed-if'-ik-ant], *adj.* building; constructing.
EDIFICATION, [ed'-if-ik-ā'-shun], *n.* the act of edifying, the condition of being edified; moral teaching. [L. *aedificatio* building].
EDIFICATORY, [ed'-i-fik-ā'-ter-i], *adj.* serving to edify.
EDIFICE, [ed'-i-fis], *n.* a large building. [L. *aedificium*].
EDIFICIAL, [ed'-i-fish'-al], *adj.* relating to an edifice.
EDIFIER, [ed'-i-fī-er], *n.* one who edifies.
EDIFY, [ed'-i-fī], *v.t.* to provide with instruction of a moral nature. [L. *aedificare* build].
EDIFYING, [ed'-i-fī-ing], *adj.* providing edification.
EDIFYINGLY, [ed'-i-fī'-ing-li], *adv.* in an edifying fashion.
EDIFYINGNESS, [ed'-i-fī'-ing-nes], *n.* the state of being edifying.
EDILE, [ē'-dīl], *n.* a magistrate in ancient Rome in charge of public buildings. [L. *aedilis*].
EDILESHIP, [ē'-dīl-ship], *n.* the office or period of office of an edile.
EDINGTONITE, [ed'-ing-ton-īt], *n.* (*min.*) a silicate of aluminium and barium. [*Edington*, a Scottish scientist].
EDIT, [ed'-it], *v.t.* to prepare for publication with critical apparatus; to censor or select for publication; to control the publication of. [L. *editum*, *p.pt.* of *edere*].
EDITION, [id-ish'-un], *n.* the format and issue of a book or newspaper, the total number of copies issued at one time; the re-publication of a book under the care of a different editor, or by a different press; a prototype, copy, replica; a reprint of a text with critical apparatus. [L. *editio*].
EDITOR, [ed'-it-er], *n.* one who edits.
EDITORIAL (1), [ed'-it-aw'-ri-al], *n.* an article by the editor, or written under his instructions, appearing in a newspaper.
EDITORIAL (2), [ed'-it-aw'-ri-al], *adj.* pertaining to editing or editors.
EDITORIALLY, [ed'-it-aw'-ri-al-i], *adv.* in the manner of an editor.
EDITORSHIP, [ed'-it-er-ship], *n.* the business and position of an editor.
EDITRESS, [ed'-it-res], *n.* a woman editor.
EDRIOPHTHALMATA, [ed'-ri-of-thal'-mat-a], *n.* (*pl.*) a division of crustaceans with sessile eyes in the sides of the head, including shrimps and prawns. [Gk. *hedra* seat and *ophthalmos* eye].
EDUCABILITY, [ed'-yewk-ab-il'-it-i], *n.* ability to be educated or trained.
EDUCABLE, [ed'-yŏŏ-kabl], *adj.* able to be educated.
EDUCAND, [ed'-yŏŏ-kand], *n.* the person educated.
EDUCATE, [ed'-yŏŏ-kāt'], *v.t.* to bring up, train; to develop the mind, character and body by planned discipline and instruction; to provide the money for a person's education. [L. *educare*].
EDUCATION, [ed'-yŏŏ-kā'-shun], *n.* the act of educating; the instruction and discipline employed to educate someone; the condition of being educated. [L. *educatio*].
EDUCATIONAL, [ed'-yŏŏ-kā'-shun-al], *adj.* relating to education; providing instruction.
EDUCATIONALIST, [ed'-yŏŏ-kā'-shun-al-ist], *n.* an expert on education.
EDUCATIONALLY, [ed'-yŏŏ-kā'-shun-al-i], *adv.* from the educational point of view, as regards education.
EDUCATOR, [ed'-yŏŏ-kā'-tor], *n.* a person who educates.
EDUCE, [i-dews'], *v.t.* to bring or draw out that which is inherent or latent; to infer, make a deduction. [L. *educere* to bring out].
EDUCIBLE, [i-dews'-ibl], *adj.* able to be educed.
EDUCT, [ē'-dukt], *n.* that which is educed; (*chem.*) matter extracted from a compound by analysis. [*Prec.*]
EDUCTION, [i-duk'-shun], *n.* the act of educing. [L. *eductio*].
EDUCTION-PIPE, [i-duk'-shun-pīp'], *n.* the exhaust-pipe through which steam escapes.
EDUCTOR, [i-duk'-tor], *n.* that which draws out.
EDULCORANT (1), [i-dul'-kor-ant], *n.* (*med.*) a medicine which purifies fluids by removing acids.
EDULCORANT (2), [i-dul'-kor-ant], *adj.* (*med.*) possessing the power to sweeten by removing acids. [LL. *edulcorans*].
EDULCORATE, [i-dul'-kor-āt], *v.t.* (*chem.*) to purify, sweeten; to free from acids and other soluble impurities. [L. *edulcorare* to sweeten].
EDULCORATION, [i-dul'-kor-ā'-shun], *n.* the act of edulcorating.
EDULCORATIVE, [i-dul'-kor-ā'-tiv], *adj.* having the quality of edulcorating.
EDULCORATOR, [i-dul'-kor-ā'-tor], *n.* a bottle for letting out small drops of a fluid one at a time.
EDWARDIAN (1), [ed-waw'-di-an], *n.* a person born or living during the reign of Edward VII.
EDWARDIAN (2), [ed-wawd'-i-an], *adj.* relating to Edward VII's reign.
EEL, [ēl], *n.* one of several varieties of snake-like, finless fresh and sea-water fishes. [OE. *æl*].

EEL

EELBUCK, [ēl'-buk], *n.* a basket for catching eels.
EEL-FARE, [ēl'-fāer], *n.* an elver, a young eel; a passage of eels travelling up-stream.
EEL-GRASS, [ēl'-grahs], *n.* a salt-water plant of the genus *Zostera.*
EEL-OIL, [ēl'-oil'], *n.* an oil extracted from roasted eels.
EEL-POT, [ēl'-pot'], *n.* a basket for catching eels.
EEL-POUT, [ēl'-powt], *n.* the burbot, *Lota vulgaris*, the viviparous blenny, a species of *Zoarces.*

EEL-POUT

EEL-PUNT, [ēl'-punt], *n.* a flat-bottomed boat from which eels are speared.
E'EN (1), [ēn], *n.* (*poet.*) a contraction for EVEN (1).
E'EN (2), [ēn], *adv.* (*poet.*) a contraction for EVEN (3).

E'ER, [āer], *adv.* (*poet.*) a contraction for EVER.
EERIE, EERY, [ēer'-i], *adj.* weird, frightening. [OE. *earg* cowardly].
EFFABLE, [ef'-abl], *adj.* explicable, speakable. [L. *effabilis*].
EFFACE, [i-fās'], *v.t.* to rub out, obliterate. [Fr. *effacer*].
EFFACEABLE, [i-fās'-abl], *adj.* capable of being effaced.
EFFACEMENT, [i'-fās'-ment], *n.* the act of effacing, the condition of being effaced.
EFFECT (1), [i-fekt'], *n.* any condition considered as a consequence in relation to an action; a consequence, result; show, ostentation; (*pl.*) goods, possessions, movable property; (*stage*) offstage or studio representation of sounds necessary to complete the realism of a scene. [L. *effectus* performance, result].
EFFECT (2), [i-fekt'], *v.t.* to cause to happen. [*Prec.*].
EFFECTIBLE, [i-fekt'-ibl], *adj.* practicable; feasible.
EFFECTION†, [i-fek'-shun], *n.* creation, production; (*geom.*) the construction of a proposition. [L. *effectio*].
EFFECTIVE (1), [i-fek'-tiv], *n.* one who is effective.
EFFECTIVE (2), [i-fek'-tiv], *adj.* capable of effecting or producing the result that is wanted; efficient, fit for action, competent; producing a strong and definite impression, showy, ostentatious. [L. *effectivus* productive].
EFFECTIVELY, [i-fek'-tiv-li], *adv.* in an effective fashion.
EFFECTIVENESS, [i-fek'-tiv-nes], *n.* the condition of being effective.
EFFECTLESS, [i-fekt'-les], *adj.* having no effect.
EFFECTOR, [i-fek'-ter], *n.* a person who effects; a creator.
EFFECTS, [i-fekts'], *n.*(*pl.*) goods, movable possessions; personal estate.
EFFECTUAL, [i-fek'-chōō'-al], *adj.* producing a desired effect; potent, valid.
EFFECTUALLY, [i-fek'-chōō-al-i], *adv.* in an effectual fashion.
EFFECTUALNESS, [i-fek'-chōō-al-nes], *n.* the quality of being effectual.
EFFECTUATE, [i-fek'-chōō-āt], *v.t.* to effect.
EFFECTUATION, [i-fek'-chōō-ā'-shun], *n.* the action of effectuating.
EFFECTUOUS†, [i-fek'-chōō-us], *adj.* effectual.
EFFEMINACY, [if-em'-in-a-si], *n.* the quality of being effeminate.
EFFEMINATE (1), [if-em'-in-at], *n.* an effeminate person.
EFFEMINATE (2), [if-em'-in-at], *adj.* having characteristics commonly ascribed to women, unmanly, feeble; voluptuous. [L. *effeminatus*].
EFFEMINATELY, [if-em'-in-at-li], *adv.* in an effeminate fashion.
EFFEMINATENESS, [if-em'-in-at-nes], *n.* the condition of being effeminate.
EFFEMINATING, [if-em'-in-āt-ing], *adj.* making, causing to appear, effeminate.
EFFEMINATION, [if-em'-in-ā'-shun], *n.* the state of being effeminate.
EFFENDI, [if-en'-di], *n.* a Turkish title of respect to officials and learned men. [Turk. *efendi* master].
EFFERENT, [ef'-er-ent], *adj.* (*anat.*) leading away from, conveying outwards. [L. *efferens*].
EFFERVESCE, [ef'-er-ves'], *v.t.* (of a liquid) to let off gas in the form of innumerable bubbles; to create bubbles, to froth; (*fig.*) (of a person) to be irrepressibly excited. [L. *effervescere* to bubble].
EFFERVESCENCE, [ef'-er-ves'-ents], *n.* the action of effervescing, the condition of being effervescent.
EFFERVESCENCY, [ef'-er-ves'-en-si], *n.* effervescence.
EFFERVESCENT (1), [ef'-er-ves'-ent], *n.* that which produces effervescence.
EFFERVESCENT (2), [ef'-er-ves'-ent], *adj.* giving out gas in bubbles, sparkling, gaseous.
EFFERVESCIBLE, [ef'-er-ves'-ibl], *adj.* able to effervesce.
EFFERVESCING, [ef'-er-ves'-ing], *adj.* bubbling; **e. draughts**, refreshing aerated drinks.
EFFETE, [ef-ēt'], *adj.* worn out, exhausted of vigour, barren, sterile. [L. *effetus* worn out].
EFFETENESS, [ef-ēt'-nes], *n.* the state or quality of being effete.
EFFICACIOUS, [ef'-ik-ā'-shus], *adj.* capable of producing an intended effect. [~L. *efficax* powerful].
EFFICACIOUSLY, [ef'-ik-ā'-shus-li], *adv.* in an efficacious fashion.
EFFICACIOUSNESS, [ef'-ik-ā'-shus-nes], *n.* the state of being efficacious.
EFFICACY, [ef'-ik-a-si], *n.* the power to produce a certain effect, effectiveness.
EFFICIENCY, [if-ish'-en-si], *n.* the condition of being efficient, competency; (*mech.*) the net amount of effective force.
EFFICIENT (1), [if-ish'-ent], *n.* a capable person, an effective; (*mech.*) the ratio of effective work to the total energy expended.
EFFICIENT (2), [if-ish'-ent], *adj.* producing effects, producing an intended result, effective, capable, competent. [L. *efficiens*].
EFFICIENTLY, [if-ish'-ent-li], *adv.* in an efficient fashion.
EFFIGIAL†, [ef-ij'-i-al], *adj.* relating to an effigy.
EFFIGIATE†, [ef-ij'-i-āt], *v.t.* to present a likeness.
EFFIGURATION, [ef-ig'-yōō-rā'-shun], *n.* (*bot.*) an outgrowth of the floral receptacle.
EFFIGY, [ef'-ij-i], *n.* a three dimensional image or likeness of a person. [L. *effigies* statue, likeness].
EFFLORESCE, [ef-lor-es'], *v.t.* (*bot.*) to blossom, to flower; (*chem.*) to become covered with whitish crystals due to chemical action. [L. *efflorescere*].
EFFLORESCENCE, [ef'-law-res'-ens], *n.* the process of efflorescing, the condition of being in blossom; the period of blossoming; (*med.*) a skin rash.
EFFLORESCENT, [ef-lor-es'-ent], *adj.* (*chem.*) efflorescing, or liable to effloresce.
EFFLUENCE, [ef'-lōō-ents], *n.* the process of flowing out.
EFFLUENT (1), [ef'-lōō-ent], *n.* a stream that flows out of a lake, etc.; a discharge of waste water from a factory, sewage tank, etc.
EFFLUENT (2), [ef'-lōō-ent], *adj.* flowing outwards. [EX and FLUENT].
EFFLUVIAL, [ef-lōō'-vi-al], *adj.* relating to, or consisting of, effluvia.
EFFLUVIUM, (*pl.* **effluvia**), [ef-lōō'-vi-um], *n.* exhalation; an obnoxious odour, *esp.* from putrefying substances. [LL. *effluvium* a flowing out].
EFFLUX, [ef'-luks], *n.* the act of flowing out, that which flows out; the passing of a period of time. [~L. *effluxum*, *p.pt.* of *effluere* to flow out].
EFFLUXION, [ef-luk'-shon], *n.* efflux.
EFFODIENT, [ef-ōd'-i-ent], *adj.* digging; accustomed to dig. [L. *effodiens*].
EFFOLIATION, [ef-ōl'-i-ā'-shun], *n.* (*bot.*) the deprivation of leaves. [E (2) and FOLIATION].
EFFORCE†, [ef-aws'], *v.t.* to force.
EFFORM, [ef-awm'], *v.t.* to fashion, shape.
EFFORT, [ef'-ert], *n.* an exertion of strength, a strenuous action or testing of power, a strain; an exertion of strength, in relation to a deliberate end in view, an endeavour, an attempt; (*coll.*) a feat, performance. [Fr. *effort*].
EFFORTLESS, [ef'-ert-les], *adj.* making no effort; requiring no effort.
EFFRANCHISE, see ENFRANCHISE.
EFFRONTERY, [i-frun'-ter-i], *n.* insolent boldness, impudence, audacity. [~L. *effrontis* shameless].
EFFULGE, [e-fulj'], *v.i.* to shine with dazzling radiance. [L. *effulgere*].
EFFULGENCE, [e-fulj'-ents], *n.* a radiance, a stream or flood of light, great lustre or brightness.
EFFULGENT, [e-fulj'-ent], *adj.* emitting a radiant light, brightly shining; (*fig.*) radiant.
EFFULGENTLY, [e-fulj'-ent-li], *adv.* in an effulgent manner.
EFFUMABILITY†, [e-fewm'-a-bil'-i-ti], *n.* the quality of being changed into vapour. [E- (2) and L. *fumus* smoke].
EFFUMABLE, [e-fewm'-abl], *adj.* capable of being converted into fumes or vapour.
EFFUSE (1), [i-fews'], *adj.* (*bot.*) (of efflorescence) spreading out loosely. [L. *effusus*].
EFFUSE (2), [i-fewz'], *v.t. and i.* to pour out, to shed, to gush out. [L. *effusum*, *p.pt.* of *effundere* to pour out].
EFFUSION, [i-few'-zhun], *n.* the act of pouring out; that which is poured out, a shedding; (*fig.*) fluent and tumultuous outpourings in speech, usually of a superficial character. [L. *effusio*].
EFFUSIVE, [i-few'-siv], *adj.* gushing, unrestrainedly lavish, demonstrative.
EFFUSIVELY, [i-few'-siv-li], *adv.* in effusive fashion.
EFFUSIVENESS, [i-few'-siv-nes], *n.* the quality of being effusive.

EFT†, [eft], *n.* a newt, a tailed amphibian of the genus *Triton*. [OE. *efete*].
EFTSOONS†, [eft-sōōnz'], *adv.* soon afterwards, in a short time. [OE. *eftsona* very soon].
EGAD†, [i-gad'], *int.* by gad.
EGALITARIAN, [i-gal'-i-tāer'-i-an], *adj.* of, or pertaining to, belief in total equality. [*Next*].
EGALITY†, [i-gal'-i-ti], *n.* equality. [Fr. *égalité*].
EGERAN, [ē'-jer-an], *n.* (*min.*) a sub-species of pyramidal garnet. [*Eger*, in Bohemia, where found].
EGEST, [i-jest'], *v.t.* to expel from the body, to cast or throw out; to void, as excrement. [L. *egestum*, *p.pt.* of *egerere* to bear out].
EGESTA, [i-jes'-ta], *n.*(*pl.*) excrements. [*Prec.*].
EGESTION, [i-jes'-chun], *n.* the voiding of excrement. [L. *egestio*].
EGG (1), [eg], *n.* the female germ-cell; the spherical or spheroidal body, covered with a membrane or shell, evolved by female birds, fishes, most reptiles and many other animals, and enclosing the germ from which a new animal may develop; (*slang*) a bomb dropped by an aircraft; **bad e.** a person with a bad character. [OScand. *egg*].
EGG (2), [eg], *v.t.* to incite, urge, provoke. [OScand. *eggja*].
EGGBIRD, [eg'-burd], *n.* the sooty tern, the West Indian tern, *Hydrochelidon fuliginosum*.
EGG-CUP, [eg'-kup], *n.* a cup, usually of china, for containing a boiled egg at table.
EGGER, [eg'-er], *n.* one of various species of moths, the lasiocampid moths. [Unkn.].
EGG-FLIP, [eg'-flip], *n.* a drink consisting of eggs beaten up in milk, beer, or whisky, sweetened and spiced.
EGGLER, [eg'-ler], *n.* a dealer in or a collector of eggs.
EGG-NOG, [eg'-nog'], *n.* egg-flip.
EGG-PLANT, [eg'-plahnt], *n.* the aubergine, *Solanum Melongena*, which bears an egg-shaped fruit, an East Indian plant used in cookery.
EGG-SHELL, [eg'-shel], *n.* the shell of an egg; a thin kind of transparent porcelain.
EGG-SLICE, [eg'-slis], *n.* a kitchen utensil with a very thin, flat head for removing omelettes or fried eggs from a pan.
EGG-SPOON, [eg'-spōōn], *n.* a small spoon for eating boiled eggs.
EGG-TOOTH, [eg'-tŏŏth], *n.* the knob on the sheath of the bill with which the unhatched bird breaks the shell from the inside.
EGG-WHISK, [eg'-wisk], *n.* a revolving hand-machine for beating up eggs.
EGIS, [ē'-jis], *n.* a shield; protection. [L. *aegis*].
EGLANDULOUS, [i-gland'-yōō-lus], *adj.* lacking glands.
EGLANTINE, [eg'-lan-tīn], *n.* the sweetbriar, *Rosa rubiginosa*. [Fr. *églantine*].
EGLOMERATE†, [i-glom'-er-āt], *v.t.* to unwind. [E (2) and GLOMERATE].
EGO, [eg'-ō], *n.* the self-conscious subject; the self in contrast with another person; the consciousness of the self and its development; (*psych.*) the part of the mind concerned with the perception of external reality and with adjusting responses to it. [L. *ego* I].
EGOCENTRIC, [eg'-ō-sen'-trik], *adj.* self-centred, egoistic, attempting to gain stability for the personality by concentrating on the satisfaction of personal desires, with indifference to the effect on others. [EGO and CENTRIC].
EGOCENTRICITY, [eg'-ō-sen-tris'-i-ti], *n.* the state of being egocentric.
EGOISM, [eg'-ō-izm], *n.* a state or habit of mind which sets the self in a position of first importance; consistent self-regard; the practice of selfishness as a creed. [EGO].
EGOIST, [eg'-ō-ist], *n.* a selfish, self-centred person; (*philos.*) an adherent of egoism.
EGOISTIC, [eg'-ō-is'-tik], *adj.* egoistical.
EGOISTICAL, [eg'-ō-is'-tik-al], *adj.* relating to egoism; derived from the ego.
EGOISTICALLY, [eg'-ō-is'-tik-al-i], *adv.* in an egoistic fashion.
EGOITY, [eg'-ō-i-ti], *n.* one's personality, identity.
EGOPHONY, [ēg-of'-on-i], *n.* (*path.*) a bleating sound, heard in auscultation, symptomatic of pleurisy. [Gr. *aix aigos* goat and *phone* sound].
EGOTHEISM, [ēg'-ō-thē'-izm], *n.* self-deification. [EGO and THEISM].
EGOTISM, [eg'-ot-izm], *n.* the habit of thinking too much about oneself and of inflicting on others the sense of one's own importance, self-conceit, self-pride, egoism. [EGO].
EGOTIST, [eg'-ō-tist], *n.* a person whose nature is tainted with egotism.
EGOTISTIC, [eg'-ō-tist'-ik], *adj.* egotistical.
EGOTISTICAL, [eg'-ō-tist'-ik-al], *adj.* characterized by egotism, deliberately affecting egotism, self-conceited, self-important.
EGOTISTICALLY, [eg'-ō-tist'-ik-a-li], *adv.* in an egotistical fashion.
EGOTIZE, [eg'-ō-tiz], *v.i.* to act as an egotist.
EGREGIOUS, [i-grē'-ji-us], *adj.* uncommonly bad. [L. *egregius* distinguished].
EGREGIOUSLY, [i-grē'-ji-us-li], *adv.* in an egregious fashion.
EGREGIOUSNESS, [i-grē'-ji-us-nes], *n.* the quality of being egregious.
EGRESS (1), [ē'-gres], *n.* the act of going away from or out of; the way out, exit. [L. *egressus* departure].
EGRESS (2), [ē-gres'], *v.i.* to go out, leave, depart.
EGRESSION, [i-gresh'-un], *n.* the act of going out from a place. [L. *egressio*].
EGRET, [ē'-gret], *n.* any of several lesser species of white heron, particularly the lesser white heron, *Ardea garzetta*; (*bot.*) the soft feathery tuft of seeds of composite plants such as the dandelion and thistle. [Fr. *aigrette*].

EGRET

EGRIOT†, [eg'-ri-ot], *n.* a kind of sour cherry. [Fr. *aigre* sour].
EGYPTIAN (1), [ē-jip'-shun], *n.* a native of Egypt; (*archaic*) a gipsy; drawing paper of a large size.
EGYPTIAN (2), [ē-jip'-shun], *adj.* relating to Egypt; **E. kale**, a variety of cabbage; **E. lotus**, a plant native to Egypt, *Nymphæa lotus*; **E. pebble**, a species of agate or jasper; **E. vulture**, a species of small, whitish vulture, protected as a town scavenger. [Gk. *Aiguptos* river Nile, Egypt].
EGYPTOLOGICAL, [ē-jip'-to-loj'-ik-al], *adj.* relating to Egyptology.
EGYPTOLOGIST, [ē'-jip-tol'-oj-ist], *n.* an expert in Egyptology.
EGYPTOLOGY, [ē'-jip-tol'-oj-i], *n.* the study of Egyptian antiquities. [EGYPT(IAN) and Gk. *logos* speech].
EH, [ā], *int.* denoting inquiry or slight surprise.
EIDAM, [ī'-dam], *n.* a variety of Dutch cheese with a red rind. [*Eidam*, a place in Holland, where made].
EIDER, [ī'-der], *n.* a sea-duck of the genus *Somateria*, living in the Arctic and sub-Arctic regions and noted for its fine down. [OIcel. *eider*].
EIDER-DOWN, [ī'-der-down], *n.* the fine, soft down of the eider-duck; a quilt stuffed with this.
EIDETIC, [ī-det'-ik], *adj.* (*psych.*) having, or referring to, the power of re-experiencing a visual impression with the clarity of an hallucination; pertaining to persistently recurring visual imagery. [Gk. *eidetikos* forming].

EIDER

EIDOGRAPH, [ī'-dō-graf], *n.* an instrument for reproducing plans or drawings, reduced or enlarged. [Gk. *eidos* form and GRAPH].
EIDOLON, [ī'-dol-on], *n.* a phantom, ghost, spectre. [Gk. *eidolon* image].
EIGHT (1), [āt], *n.* the cardinal number immediately following seven or preceding nine; the figure representing this number, 8; a rowing team of eight persons; **the Eights**, races between college crews of eight oarsmen at Oxford and Cambridge; **figure of e.**, movement of a skater on the ice following the lines of the figure 8; **to have had one over the e.**, (*slang*) to be drunk. [OE. *eahta*].
EIGHT (2), [āt], *adj.* one more than seven, one less than nine.
EIGHTEEN, [ā'-tēn], *n.* twice nine; ten and eight. [OE. *eahtatene*].
EIGHTEENMO, [ā'-tēn-mō], *n.* (*print.*) a size of a book in which a sheet is folded into eighteen leaves.
EIGHTEENTH (1), [ā'-tēnth], *n.* one of eighteen equal parts.

EIGHTEENTH (2), [ā'-tēnth], *adj.* coming next in order in a series after the seventeenth.

EIGHTFOLD, [āt'-fōld], *adj.* eight times the quantity. [EIGHT and FOLD].

EIGHTH (1), [āt'th], *n.* one of eight equal parts; the unit following the seventh in a series; (*mus.*) of an octave. [OE. *eahtotha*].

EIGHTH (2), [āt'-th], *adj.* next in order after the seventh, following seven others in a series.

EIGHTHLY, [āt'-thli], *adv.* in the eighth place.

EIGHTIETH (1), [ā'-ti-eth], *n.* one of eighty equal parts, following seventy-nine of a series.

EIGHTIETH (2), [ā'-ti-eth], *adj.* coming next in order after the seventy-ninth.

EIGHT-SCORE, [āt'-skaw(r)'], *n.* eight times twenty.

EIGHTSOME [āt'-sum], *n.* a Scottish reel for eight persons. [EIGHT and OE. *sum* one (of)].

EIGHTY (1), [ā'-ti], *n.* eight times ten. [OE. *eahtatig*].

EIGHTY (2), [ā'-ti], *adj.* eight times ten, four-score.

EIGNE (1), [ān], *n.* (*leg.*) the first-born or eldest son. [Fr. *âiné* first-born].

EIGNE (2), [ān], *adj.* (*leg.*) entailed; belonging to the eldest son.

EIKON, [ī'-kon], *n.* a likeness; an icon. [*Var.* of ICON].

EIRENICON, [ī-rēn'-ik-on], *n.* a plea for peace, *esp.* by an ecclesiastic. [Gk. *eirenikos* peaceful].

EISEL, [ēzl], *n.* vinegar. [OFr. *aisil*].

EISENKIESEL, [ī'-zen-kēzl'], *n.* (*min.*) quartz coloured red or yellow by iron oxide. [Germ. *eisen* iron and *kiesel* flint].

EISTEDDFOD, [ā-steth'-vod], *n.* a national assembly of Welsh poets, orators, musicians, etc., to compete for prizes. [Wel. *eisteddfod* session].

EIS-WOOL, [īs'-wōōl'], *n.* very fine wool being of the thickness of two threads and having a glossy texture. [Germ. *eis* ice].

EITHER (1), [ī'-THer, †ē'-THer], *pron.* one of two. [OE. *æghwæther*].

EITHER (2), [ī'-THer, ē'-THer], *adj.* one or other of a group or series, one or each of two.

EITHER (3), [ī'-THer, ē'-THer], *adv. correlative with* OR *and indicating the first of a series of alternatives, the others being indicated by* OR.

EJACULATE, [i-jak'-yōō-lāt], *v.t. and i.* to exclaim, to utter suddenly; (*physiol.*) to emit liquid. [L. *ejaculari* to throw out].

EJACULATION, [i-jak'-yōō-lā'-shun], *n.* that which is ejaculated; the act of ejaculating.

EJACULATIVE, [i-jak'-yōō-lā'-tiv], *adj.* ejaculatory.

EJACULATORY, [i-jak'-yōō-lā'-ter-i], *adj.* of or resembling an ejaculation.

EJECT (1), [ē'-jekt], *n.* that which is assumed by analogy with our own knowledge or experience to be known to or experienced by others, though not actually known to or experienced by ourselves.

EJECT (2), [i-jekt'], *v.t.* to remove suddenly, expel, discharge, dismiss. [~L. *ejectum*, *p.pt.* of *ejicere* expel].

EJECTION, [i-jek'-shun], *n.* the act of ejecting; the condition of being ejected.

EJECTIVE, [i-jek'-tiv], *adj.* relating to ejection or to an eject; tending to eject.

EJECTMENT, [i-jekt'-ment], *n.* an ejection, dispossession; (*leg.*) a writ or action for the recovery of land from which the owner has been ejected.

EJECTOR, [i-jek'-ter], *n.* a person who ejects or dispossesses another of his land; that which ejects; the device on a gun which ejects the cartridge.

EJOO, [ē'-jōō], *n.* the Gomuti palm, *Arenga saccharifera*, secreting palm sugar. [Malay *ejos*].

EJULATION†, [ē'-jōō-lā'-shun], *n.* a loud cry of pain or sorrow. [L. *ejulatio*].

EJURATION†, [ē'-jōō-rā'-shun], *n.* resignation. [L. *ejuratio*].

EKE (1), [ēk], *adv.* in addition, moreover. [OE. *eac*].

EKE (2), (eking, ekes, eked), [ēk], *v.t.* to add to; **to e. out,** to make to last by economy. [OE. *eacan* to increase].

EKING, [ēk'-ing], *n.* something added to increase.

EKKA, [ek'-a], *n.* a small Indian cart drawn by one horse or bullock. [Native].

ELABORATE (1), [i-lab'-or-at], *adj.* worked out with attention to detail, characterized by a complex form or pattern, complicated, laboured in design, loaded with ornamentation. [L. *elaboratum*, *p.pt.* of *elaborare*.]

ELABORATE (2), [i-lab'-or-āt], *v.t.* to work out with great pains and particular attention to detail, to make more elaborate. [L. *elaborare* to work out].

ELABORATELY, [i-lab'-or-at-li], *adv.* in an elaborate way.

ELABORATENESS, [i-lab'-or-at-nes], *n.* the state of being elaborate.

ELABORATION, [i-lab'-or-ā'-shun], *n.* the act of elaborating.

ELABORATIVE, [i-lab'-or-at-iv], *adj.* tending to elaborate; **e. faculty,** the faculty of seeing things in relation to each other.

ELABORATOR, [i-lab'-or-ā'-ter], *n.* one who elaborates.

ELABORATORY, [i-lab'-er-at-er-i], *adj.* elaborating.

ELAEIS, [e-lē'-is], *n.* the African oil-palm. [Gk. *elaia* olive-tree].

ELAEO-, *pref.* olive, olive oil. [Gk. *elaion*].

ELAEOCARPUS, [el'-ē-ō-kah'-pus], *n.* an East Indian tree, the fruit of which resembles that of the olive. [ELAEO and Gk. *karpos* fruit].

ELAEOLITE, [el-ē'-ō-līt], *n.* (*geol.*) a variety of lava stone of a greyish green, with bluish and reddish markings. [ELAEO and Gk. *lithos* stone].

ELAEOMETER, [el'-ē-om'-i-ter], *n.* an instrument for testing the purity of oils. [ELAEO and METER].

ELAEOPTENE, [el'-ē-op'-tēn], *n.* the liquid principle of a vegetable oil. [ELAEO and Gk. *ptenos* winged].

ELAIDATE, [el-ā'-id-āt], *n.* (*chem.*) a salt of elaidic acid.

ELAIDIC, [el-ā'-id-ik], *adj.* relating to elain or olein.

ELAIDIN, [el-ā'-id-in], *n.* a fatty substance made by the action of nitric acid upon certain oils.

ELAIN, [el-ā'-in], *n.* the liquid principle of oils and fats remaining after the removal of stearine. [*Var.* of OLEIN].

ELAIODIC, [el-ā-od'-ik], *adj.* derived from castor oil.

ELAIOMETER, [el'-ā-om'-i-ter], *n.* elaeometer.

ELAN, élan, [ā-lah(ng)'], *n.* impetuosity, high-spirited vigour. [Fr. *élan*].

ELANCE†, [ē-lahnts'], *v.t.* to throw, shoot; to dart. [Fr. *élancer*].

ELAND, [ē'-land], *n.* either of the two species of *Oreas* which are the largest of the South African antelopes. [Du. *eland* elk].

ELAND

ELANET, [ē'-lan-et], *n.* an insectivorous variety of kite. [~Gk. *elanos*].

ELAPHINE, [el'-a-fīn], *adj.* resembling or relating to a stag. [Gk. *elaphos* stag].

ELAPIDATION, [i-lap'-id-ā'-shun], *n.* a moving away of stones. [E and LAPIDATION].

ELAPSE, [i-laps'], *v.i.* to pass away silently. [L. *elapsum*, *p.pt.* of *elabi* to slip away].

ELAQUEATE†, [i-lak'-wi-āt], *v.t.* to disentangle. [L. *elaqueare*].

ELASMOBRANCHS, [i-las'-mo-brangks'], *n.(pl.)* the group of fishes including sharks and rays. [Gk. *elasmos* a metal plate and *bragkhia* gills].

ELASMOTHERIUM, [i-las'-mo-thēer'-i-um], *n.* an extinct race of pachydermatous mammalia. [Gk. *elasmos* metal plate and *ther* beast].

ELASTIC (1), [il-as'-tik], *n.* material manufactured in strips, composed of rubber and interwoven strands of silk, cotton, etc.; a strip of plain rubber, a rubber band.

ELASTIC (2), [il-as'-tik], *adj.* possessing resilience, having the power of returning to its original form after being stretched or extended; able to be stretched or expanded; springy, flexible; (*fig.*) adaptable. [Gk. *elastikos* spontaneous].

ELASTICAL, [il-as'-tikl], *adj.* elastic.

ELASTICALLY, [il-as'-tik-al-i], *adv.* in an elastic fashion.

ELASTICITY, [il-as-tis'-i-ti], *n.* the quality of being elastic.

ELASTIN, [il-as'-tin], *n.* the binding substance in elastic fibre.

ELATE (1), [il-āt'], *adj.* exhilarated, exultant, elated.

ELATE (2), [il-āt'], *v.t.* to make exhilarated, to raise the spirits of, to cause the emotional or mental level of experience to quicken. [~L. *elatum*, *p.pt.* of *efferre* to elevate].

ELATEDLY, [il-āt'-id-li], *adv.* in an elated manner.

ELATEDNESS, [il-āt'-id-nes], *n.* the condition of being elated.

ELATER, [il-āt'-er], *n.* (*bot.*) a tiny filament in certain plants, having elastic properties, and releasing the spores when ripe; (*entom.*) a genus of beetles able to jump into the air when placed on their backs. [Gk. *elater* driver].

ELATER

ELATERIN, [il-at'-er-in], *n.* the active principle of the juice of the squirting cucumber, *Ecballium Elaterium*, having powerful purgative properties. [Gk. *elaterion* driving].

ELATERITE, [i-lat'-er-īt], *n.* an elastic mineral pitch.

ELATERIUM, [il'-a-tēer'-i-um], *n.* a drug obtained from the juice of a species of *Ecballium*. [Gk. *elaterion* driving].

ELATERY, [el'-at-er-i], *n.* elasticity.

ELATINE, [el'-a-tī'-ni], *n.* (*bot.*) a genus of aquatic or marsh plants. [Gk. *elate* silver-fir].

ELATION, [il-ā'-shun], *n.* the state of being elated; pride, elevation of spirits. [L. *elatio*].

ELATOR, [il-ā'-ter], *n.* a person or thing that elates.

ELATROMETER, [el'-at-rom'-i-ter], *n.* an instrument for testing and measuring the density of air in the receiver of an air-pump. [Gk. *elater* driver and METER].

ELAXATION†, [il-aks-ā'-shun], *n.* the act of untying or unloosing. [L. *elaxatio*].

ELBOW (1), [el'-bō], *n.* the joint and bone formation between the forearm and upper arm; anything angular or bent like an elbow; **at the e.,** close by, near at hand; **out at e.,** shabby, reduced in circumstances. [OE. *elnboga*].

ELBOW (2), [el'-bō], *v.t. and i.* to use the elbows to push through a crowd, to push aside; to place inside an angle.

ELBOW-CHAIR, [el'-bō-chāer'], *n.* a chair with arm rests, an arm-chair.

ELBOW-GREASE, [el'-bō-grēs'], *n.* hard, continuous rubbing; power to work hard.

ELBOW-ROOM, [el'-bō-rŏŏm'], *n.* room for action.

ELBOW-TONGS, [el'-bō-tongz'], *n.*(*pl.*) crucible tongs having curved jaws.

ELCHEE, [el'-chē], *n.* an envoy. [Turk. *ilchi*].

ELD†, [eld], *n.* old age; antiquity. [OE. *eldo*].

ELDER (1), [el'-der], *n.* a small tree, *Sambucus nigra*, bearing white flowers having a pungent scent and dark purple berries. [OE. *ellern*].

ELDER (2), [el'-der], *n.* a person who is older, a senior in age, rank or experience; a person who held office by reason of age and experience in the early Christian Church; an administrative member of the Presbyterian Church; (*naut.*) one of the thirteen senior members of Trinity House who judge navigation cases; (*pl.*) those claiming authority by right of age. [OE. *eldra* older].

ELDER (3), [el'-der], *adj.* having lived a long time, born earlier, older. [*Prec.*].

ELDERBERRY, [el'-der-be'-ri], *n.* the fruit of the elder.

ELDERBERRY-WINE, [el'-der-be'-ri-wīn'], *n.* wine made from elderberries.

ELDER-GUN, [el'-der-gun'], *n.* a popgun made of elder-wood.

ELDERLINESS, [el'-der-li-nes], *n.* the condition of being elderly.

ELDERLY, [el'-der-li], *adj.* fairly old; advanced beyond middle age; approaching old age.

ELDERSHIP, [el'-der-ship], *n.* the office of a Presbyterian elder.

ELDER-WINE, [el'-der-wīn'], *n.* wine made from elderberries.

ELDEST, [el'-dest], *n. and adj.* oldest; the first born or oldest survivor of a family. [OE. *eldesta*].

ELDORADO, [el'-dō-rah'-dō], *n.* the country controlled by El Dorado, killed by the Spaniards in 1538; an imaginary land where the desires of the poor are satisfied with gold and plenty. [Span. *el dorado* the golden].

ELDRITCH, [el'-drich], *adj.* uncanny, hideous, ghastly. [Uncert.].

ELEATIC, [el'-ē-at'-ik], *adj.* relating to a sect of philosophers which explained the universe in terms of the unity of being. [*Elea*, a Greek colony in Italy].

ELECAMPANE, [el'-ē-kam'-pān], *n.* a composite plant with yellow flowers, *Inula Helenium*, of a pungent taste; a sweetmeat made from the root. [L. *Inula campana*].

ELECT (1), [il-ekt'], *n.* a person who is chosen, selected or set apart; (*theol.*) a person believed to be chosen by God for salvation.

ELECT (2), [il-ekt'], *adj.* selected, chosen, specially marked as the recipient of some privilege, elected to some office or position of rank but not yet installed; (*theol.*) believed to be chosen by God for salvation.

ELECT (3), [il-ekt'], *v.t. and i.* to pick out, choose by vote; to make a decision (to). [~L. *electum*, *p.pt.* of *eligere* to choose].

ELECTION, [il-ek'-shun], *n.* the act of electing, choice, selection, discrimination; (*theol.*) the state of being predestined to be granted salvation; **by-e.,** an election in one constituency, the seat of which has fallen vacant; **general e.,** a parliamentary election in every constituency at once. [L. *electio*].

ELECTIONEER, [il-ek'-shun-ēer'], *v.i.* to canvass for votes and do work for a candidate at an election.

ELECTIONEERING, [il-ek'-shun-ēer'-ing], *n.* the act of one who electioneers.

ELECTIVE, [il-ek'-tiv], *adj.* effected by choice; pertaining to the right of election; having the power of choice.

ELECTOR, [il-ek'-ter], *n.* a person who elects; a person who has the right to vote in election; (*hist.*) one of the German princes who elected the Holy Roman Emperor.

ELECTORAL, [il-ek'-ter-al], *adj.* relating to elections or electors.

ELECTORATE, [il-ek'-ter-āt], *n.* the office, authority or territory of an elector in the German Empire; the body of persons entitled to record votes.

ELECTORESS, [il-ek'-ter-es], *n.* an electress.

ELECTORIAL, [il-ek-taw'-ri-al], *adj.* relating to an election or elector.

ELECTORSHIP, [il-ek'-ter-ship], *n.* the function of an elector.

ELECTRESS, [il-ek'-tres], *n.* the wife or widow of a German Elector.

ELECTRIC (1), [il-ek'-trik], *n.* a non-conductor; any substance in which electricity can be generated by friction.

ELECTRIC (2), [il-ek'-trik], *adj.* pertaining to, producing or worked by electricity, electrical; **e. blue,** a brilliant blue of medium tone; **e. chair,** a chair used in America for electrocuting a criminal sentenced to death; **e. circuit,** the path in which electric energy is transmitted; **e. eel,** a South American fish of the genus *Gymnotus* capable of communicating a powerful electric shock; **e. field,** the area round an electrified body affected by the discharge of electricity; **e. ray,** a flat-fish of the genus *Torpedo*. [Gk. *elektron* amber].

ELECTRIC RAY

ELECTRICAL, [il-ek'-trik-al], *adj.* relating to electricity; (*fig.*) having a strong sudden effect on the mind or emotions.

ELECTRICALLY, [il-ek'-trik-al-i], *adv.* by electricity.

ELECTRICIAN, [il-ek-trish'-an], *n.* one who is expert in electricity, and deals with its practical applications.

ELECTRICITY, [il-ek-tris'-i-ti], *n.* a form of energy transmitted in waves, which produces accredited physical phenomena in heat, light, and sound; the science investigating and recording the operation of these phenomena.

ELECTRIFIABLE, [il-ek'-trif-ī'-abl], *adj.* capable of receiving and conducting electricity.

ELECTRIFICATION, [il-ek'-trif-ik-ā'-shun], *n.* the act of electrifying, the condition of being electrified.

ELECTRIFY, [il-ek'-tri-fī'], *v.t.* to charge with electricity; to adapt to an electric system of power; (*fig.*) to startle, surprise, to shock into a strong and sudden reaction.

ELECTRINE†, [il-ek'-trīn], *adj.* belonging to or resembling the properties of amber or electrum. [Gk. *elektrinos*].

ELECTRIZATION, [il-ek'-trīz-ā'-shun], *n.* electrification.

ELECTRIZE, [il-ek'-trīz], *v.t.* to electrify.

ELECTRIZERS, [il-ek-trīz'-ers], *n.*(*pl.*) plates of copper or silver and zinc prepared for medical purposes.

ELECTRO (1), [il-ek'-trō], *n.* (*print.*) an electrotype.

ELECTRO- (2), *pref.* pertaining to or produced by electricity. [Gk. *elektron* amber].

ELECTRO-BIOLOGIST, [il-ek'-trō-bī-ol'-oj-ist], *n.* a student of the science of electro-biology.
ELECTRO-BIOLOGY, [il-ek'-trō-bī-ol'-oj-i], *n.* the science of electric phenomena in connexion with living organisms.
ELECTRO-CHEMICAL, [il-ek'-trō-kem'-ikl], *adj.* relating to electro-chemistry.
ELECTRO-CHEMISTRY, [il-ek'-trō-kem'-is-tri], *n.* the study of electricity as an agent in chemical changes.
ELECTROCUTE, [il-ek'-trō-kewt'], *v.t.* to kill by electricity, *esp.* as a capital punishment for crime. [ELECTRO and (EXE)CUTE].
ELECTROCUTION, [il-ek'-trō-kew'-shun], *n.* death by electricity.
ELECTRODE, [il-ek'-trōd], *n.* one of the points at which an electric current passes from a conducting or producing circuit into another conducting medium. [ELECTRO and Gk. *hodos* track].
ELECTRO-DYNAMIC, [il-ek'-trō-dī-nam'-ik], *adj.* relating to electro-dynamics.
ELECTRO-DYNAMICS, [il-ek'-trō-dī-nam'-iks], *n.*(*pl.*) the study of the phenomena of electricity operating in active phases.
ELECTRO-ENGRAVING, [il-ek'-trō-en-grāv'-ing], *n.* an engraving by electricity.
ELECTRO-GILDING, [il-ek'-trō-gild'-ing], *n.* a method of gilding by electricity, electroplating.
ELECTROLIER, [il-ek'-trō-lēer'], *n.* a group of candle-shaped electric bulbs arranged to form a chandelier. [ELECTRO and (CHANDE)LIER].
ELECTROLOGY, [il-ek-trol'-oj-i], *n.* the study of electricity. [ELECTRO and Gk. *logos* speech].
ELECTROLYSE, [il-ek'-trol-īz], *v.t.* to decompose by electricity.
ELECTROLYSIS, [il-ek-trol'-is-is], *n.* chemical change or decomposition produced by electric energy. [ELECTRO and Gk. *lusis* a releasing].
ELECTROLYTE, [il-ek'-trol-īt], *n.* a compound able to be, or which has already been, decomposed by an electric current; the electrified solution in a secondary cell. [ELECTRO and Gk. *lutos* loosed].
ELECTRO-MAGNET, [il-ek'-trō-mag'-net], *n.* a magnet energized by a coil of wire carrying an electric current round it.
ELECTRO-MAGNETIC, [il-ek'-trō-mag-net'-ik], *adj.* relating to, producing, derived from, electro-magnetism.
ELECTRO-MAGNETISM, [il-ek'-trō-mag'-net-izm], *n.* the science which deals with the properties of electricity in producing and communicating a magnetic force.
ELECTRO-MEDICAL, [il-ek'-trō-med'-ikl], *adj.* relating to cure by electricity.
ELECTRO-METALLURGY, [il-ek'-trō-met-al'-ur'-ji], *n.* the branch of metallurgy which is concerned with the utilization of electricity in the various processes of depositing metals held in solution.
ELECTROMETER, [il-ek-trom'-it-er], *n.* an instrument by which electricity is measured.
ELECTROMETRICAL, [il-ek'-trō-met'-rik-al], *adj.* relating to an electrometer.
ELECTRO-MOTIVE, [il-ek'-trō-mō'-tiv], *adj.* producing motion by means of electricity.
ELECTROMOTOR, [il-ek'-trō-mō'-tor], *n.* a prime mover energized by electricity. [ELECTRO and MOTOR].
ELECTRON, [il-ek'-tron], *n.* the smallest possible charge of negative electricity; an alloy of gold and silver, electrum. [Gk. *elektron* amber].
ELECTRONIC, [ē-lek-tron'-ik], *adj.* (*phys.*) of, or pertaining to, electrons.
ELECTRONICS, [il-ek'-tron'-iks], *n.* the science which deals with the behaviour of electrons.
ELECTROPHONE, [il-ek'-trō-fōn], *n.* an instrument transmitting sound by electricity. [ELECTRO and Gk. *phone* sound].
ELECTROPHORUS, [il-ek-trof'-or-us], *n.* an apparatus for generating static electricity. [ELECTRO and Gk. *phoros* bearing].
ELECTROPHYSIOLOGY, [il-ek'-trō-fiz'-i-ol'-oj-i], *n.* the science of electric effects arising from physiological causes.
ELECTROPLATE (1), [il-ek'-trō-plāt'], *n.* metal articles coated with another metal, usually silver, by means of an electric process, silver-plate.
ELECTROPLATE (2), [il-ek'-trō-plāt], *v.t.* to coat with metal by means of electrolysis.
ELECTRO-POLAR, [il-ek'trō-pōl'-ar], *adj.* having electrical polarity.
ELECTROSCOPE, [il-ek'-tros-kōp], *n.* an instrument which tests the presence, nature, and intensity of electricity. [ELECTRO and Gk. *skopos* view].
ELECTROTHERAPEUTICS, [il-ek'-trō-the'-ra-pewt'-iks], *n.* the science of the treatment of disease by electricity.
ELECTROTHERAPY, [il-ek'-trō-the'-ra-pi], *n.* the cure of disease by electricity.
ELECTRO-THERMIC, [il-ek'-trō-thur'-mik], *adj.* relating to the production of heat phenomena by electricity.
ELECTROTYPE (1), [il-ek'-trō-tīp'], *n.* (*print.*) a plate used in printing having the representation protected by a thin coating of copper by electroplating. [ELECTRO and TYPE].
ELECTROTYPE (2), [il-ek'-trō-tīp'], *v.t.* to reproduce by the electrotype process.
ELECTROTYPIST, [il-ek'-trō-tī'-pist], *n.* one expert in making or printing from an electrotype.
ELECTRUM, [il-ek'-trum], *n.* amber; an alloy containing gold and silver. [Gk. *elektron*].
ELECTUARY, [il-ek'-chōō-a-ri], *n.* a sweetened medicine. [Gk. *ekleikho* I lick out].
ELEEMOSYNARY (1), [el'-i-ē-mos'-in-a-ri], *n.* one who lives on charity. [Gk. *eleemosune* charity].
ELEEMOSYNARY (2), [el'-i-ē-mos'-in-a-ri], *adj.* relating to charity.
ELEGANCE, [el'-ig-ants], *n.* the state of being elegant.
ELEGANCY, [el'-ig-an-si], *n.* elegance.
ELEGANT, [el'-ig-ant], *adj.* possessing grace, ease, refinement of speech and taste; having a neat, delicate and proportionate form with the surfaces smooth and refined and the colours blending harmoniously; delicately worked, refined and tasteful in conception. [Fr. *élégant* neat].
ELEGANTLY, [el'-ig-ant-li], *adv.* in an elegant way.
ELEGIAC (1), [el'-ij-ī'-ak], *n.* (usually *pl.*) elegiac verse.
ELEGIAC (2), [el'-ij-ī'-ak], *adj.* relating to, having a place in, suitable for, an elegy; expressing sorrow, mournful. [Gk. *elegiakos*].
ELEGIACAL, [el'-ij-ī'-akl], *adj.* elegiac.
ELEGIAST, [el-ē'-ji-ast], *n.* an elegist.
ELEGIST, [el'-ij-ist], *n.* a writer of elegies.
ELEGIT, [el-ē'-jit], *n.* (*leg.*) a writ of execution, on which a defendant's goods are taken and delivered to the plaintiff until the plaintiff's claim is settled. [L. *elegit* he chooses].
ELEGIZE, [el'-ij-īz], *v.t. and i.* to honour or celebrate with an elegy; to write an elegy.
ELEGY, [el'-ij-i], *n.* a poem or song expressive of sorrow or lamentation, a dirge. [Gk. *elegeia*].
ELEMENT, [el'-im-ent], *n.* one of the basic constituent parts of anything which cannot be separated into further uniform units, a substance or liquid in its simplest form; a necessary constituent, a component part; one of the four forces of nature, earth, air, fire, or water, in any form, in terms of which the ancients believed the whole world could be explained; (*pl.*) the rudiments, the basic principles of a system of thought, a plan, or an idea; the natural powers of the atmosphere *esp.* when roused in a tempest; **the Elements,** the bread and wine at Holy Communion. [L. *elementum*].
ELEMENTAL, [el'-im-entl'], *adj.* relating to elements, arising from first principles; primal, simple.
ELEMENTALISM, [el'-im-ent'-al-izm], *n.* the theory which relates the first principles motivating man and governing the world, to the forces and aspects of physical nature.
ELEMENTALLY, [el'-im-ent'-a-li], *adv.* in an elemental manner.
ELEMENTARINESS, [el'-im-ent'-er-i-nes], *n.* the quality of being elementary.
ELEMENTARITY, [el'-im-ent-a'-ri-ti], *n.* the condition of being basic.
ELEMENTARY, [el'-im-ent'-a-ri], *adj.* simple, undeveloped, rudimentary; containing or discussing first principles; dealing with elements; **e. school,** a state school for young children. [L. *elementarius*].
ELEMI, [el'-em-i], *n.* a resinous substance secreted by several trees, of a pungent odour, used in ointments and for toughening varnish. [Unkn.].
ELEMIN, [el'-em-in], *n.* the oil distilled from elemi.
ELENCHUS, (*pl.* **elenchi**), [el-engk'-us], *n.* a sophism; (*log.*) a syllogism which confutes an opponent in argument by forcing him to contradict himself. [Gk. *elenkhos* refutation].
ELEOT, [ē'-li-ot], *n.* a species of apple.
ELEPHANT, [el'-if-ant], *n.* a huge tusked quadruped, the largest of existing mammals; an outsize in drawing paper, being 28 by 23 inches; **e. beetle,** a beetle of the genus *Goliathus*; **white e.,** an albino type of elephant considered sacred in Siam; (*fig.*) an unprofit-

able possession or undertaking. [Gk. *elephas elephantos* elephant, ivory].

ELEPHANTIAC, [el'-if-an'-ti-ak], *adj.* relating to elephantiasis.

ELEPHANTIASIS, [el'-if-ant-ī'-as-is], *n.* (*med.*) a disease characterized by rapid or chronic thickening and inflammation of limbs or part of the body, particularly attacking the legs. [ELEPHANT and Gk. *asis* denoting condition].

ELEPHANTINE, [el'-if-an'-tīn], *adj.* relating to, or resembling, an elephant in bulk or action; huge, clumsy.

ELEPHANTOID, [el'-if-an'-toid], *adj.* like an elephant.

ELEUSINE, [el'-yōō-sī'-ni], *n.* (*bot.*) a genus of tropical grasses, one species of which, *Eleusine Coracano*, is cultivated as grain. [Gk. *Eleusis*, a Greek city].

ELEUSINIAN, [el'-yōō-sin'-i-an], *adj.* relating to the rites celebrated in honour of Ceres. [*Prec.*].

ELEUTHERIA, [el'-yōō-thēer'-i-a], *n.* *Croton Eleutheria*, a cascarilla, as gathered on the island of Eleuthera, one of the Bahamas. [Gk. *Eleutheria*].

ELEUTHEROMANIA, [el'-yōō-thēer'-ō-mā'-nia], *n.* fanatical passion for individual freedom. [Gk. *eleutheros* free and MANIA].

ELEUTHEROMANIAC (1), [el'-yōō-thēer'-ō-mā'-ni-ak], *n.* a person affected by eleutheromania.

ELEUTHEROMANIAC (2), [el'-yōō-thēer'-ō-mā-ni-ak], *adj.* insane with a desire for freedom.

ELEVATE, [el'-iv-āt], *v.t.* to raise from a lower position or state to a higher; to promote in rank; to improve morally or mentally; to delight, to cheer. [L. *elevare* to raise].

ELEVATED, [el'-iv-āt-id], *adj.* exalted, dignified; (*her.*) of wings, turned upward.

ELEVATION, [el'-iv-ā'-shun], *n.* the act of elevating; the state of being elevated; promotion in rank; that which is elevated; an emotional state of exaltation; a high moral or social status, dignity; (*arch.*) a scale drawing of one side of a building; (*astron.*) altitude of a heavenly body above the horizon; (*mus.*) raising of the pitch of a note to a sharper tone. [L. *elevatio*].

ELEVATOR, [el'-iv-ā-tor], *n.* a person or object which raises or lifts; a lift; a machine for conveying grain from the ground level to a higher floor in a granary; a grain storehouse; (*anat.*) any muscle with the function of raising; (*aeron.*) apparatus in the tail of an aeroplane for gaining altitude.

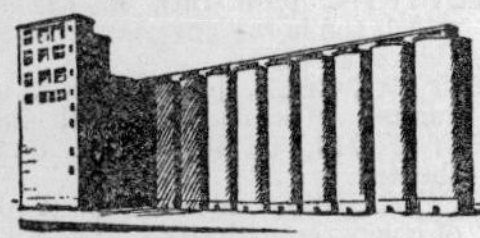
ELEVATOR

ELEVATORY (1), [el'-iv-ā'-to-ri], *n.* (*surg.*) an instrument used in trepanning, for lifting a depressed or fractured part of the skull.

ELEVATORY (2), [el'-iv-ā'-to-ri], *adj.* having power to raise.

ELEVEN (1), [il-ev'-en], *n.* a team composed of eleven players.

ELEVEN (2), [il-ev'-en], *adj.* one more than ten. [OE. *endlufon*].

ELEVENTH (1), [il-ev'-enth], *n.* one of eleven equal parts; (*mus.*) the interval of the octave above the fourth.

ELEVENTH (2), [il-ev'-enth], *adj.* next in order to tenth, forming one of eleven equal parts.

ELEVENTHLY, [il-ev'-enth-li], *adv.* in the eleventh place.

ELF, (*pl.* **elves**), [elf], *n.* (*myth.*) a small creature of the woods like a human dwarf and possessing supernatural or magic power; a weird or peculiar human being; a little or mischievous child. [OE. *elf*].

ELF-ARROW, [elf'-a'-rō], *n.* a flint arrow-head, popularly believed to have been made or shot by fairies.

ELF-BOLT, [elf'-bōlt], *n.* an elf-arrow.

ELF-CHILD, [elf'-chīld'], *n.* a child believed to have been left by the fairies in place of one stolen by them; a changeling.

ELFIN, [elf'-in], *adj.* pertaining to elves, fairylike. [ELF].

ELFISH, [elf'-ish], *adj.* relating to or resembling elves; as if done by an elf, mischievous; small.

ELF-LOCK, [elf'-lok'], *n.* hair twisted into a curl or lock, as if the work of mischievous fairies.

ELF-STRUCK, [elf'-struk], *adj.* bewitched, charmed.

ELFWORT, [elf'-wurt], *n.* (*bot.*) elecampane, *Inula Helenium*.

ELICIT, [il-is'-it], *v.t.* to draw out, to bring to light, to cause to become apparent. [L. *elicitum*, *p.pt.* of *elicere* to draw out].

ELICITATION, [il-is-it-ā'-shun], *n.* the act of eliciting.

ELIDABLE, [il-īd'-abl], *adj.* able to be elided.

ELIDE, [il-īd'], *v.t.* (*gram.*) to omit (a syllable, sound, etc.). [L. *elidere* force out].

ELIGIBILITY, [el'-ij-ib-il'-i-ti], *n.* the quality of being eligible.

ELIGIBLE, [el'-ij-ibl], *adj.* fit to be chosen, desirable; having the necessary qualifications. [L. *eligibilis*].

ELIGIBLENESS, [el'-ij-ibl-nes], *n.* the quality of being eligible.

ELIGIBLY, [el'-ij-ib-li], *adv.* in an eligible fashion.

ELIMATE†, [el'-im-āt], *v.i.* to polish; to smooth. [L. *elimare* to file].

ELIMINABLE [il-im'-in-abl], *adj.* able to be eliminated.

ELIMINANT, [il-im'-in-ant], *n.* that which is eliminated.

ELIMINATE, [il-im'-in-āt], *v.t.* to remove, exclude, obliterate; to throw out, expel. [L. *eliminare* to banish].

ELIMINATION, [il-im'in-ā'-shun], *n.* the act of eliminating; the condition of being eliminated.

ELINGUID†, [el-ing'-gwid], *adj.* tongue-tied, dumb. [E and L. *lingua* tongue].

ELIQUATION, [el'-ik-wā'-shun], *n.* (*chem.*) the act of separating one fusible substance from another by heat. [~L. *eliquare* to clarify].

ELISION, [il-izh'-un], *n.* (*gram.*) the act of eliding, the state of being elided. [L. *elisio*].

ELISOR, [il-īz'-or], *n.* (*leg.*) a deputy or a group of deputies appointed as a substitute for a jury. [OFr. *elisour* elector].

ELITE, élite, [ā-lēt'], *n.* a select body; the best of anything; the aristocracy, the smart set. [Fr. *élite* choice].

ELIXATION, [el'-iks'ā'-shun], *n.* extraction by boiling; digestion. [~L. *elixare*].

ELIXIR, [el'-ik-ser], *n.* a liquid of many ingredients formerly believed to transmute base metal into gold or to prolong life; a mixture of soluble substances and alcohol; a refined spirit or liquor; an invigorating drink. [Arab. *aliksir*].

ELIZABETHAN (1), [il-iz'-a-bē'-than], *n.* a person who lived in the Elizabethan era.

ELIZABETHAN (2), [il-iz'-a-bē'-than], *adj.* relating to Queen Elizabeth or her times (1558-1603).

ELK, [elk], *n.* (*zool.*) the largest of the deer, found in the north of Europe and America, and in Asia, the moose, *Alces machlis*. [OE. *elh*].

ELK-HOUND, [elk'-hound'], *n.* a shaggy-coated hunting dog of Scandinavian origin.

ELK-NUT, [elk'-nut'], *n.* the oil-nut.

ELK-WOOD, [elk'-wōōd'], *n.* the wood of the umbrella-tree.

ELK

ELL, [el], *n.* a measure of different lengths in different countries, used chiefly for measuring cloth, approximately an inch or two over a yard, an arm's length. [OE. *eln*].

ELLAGIC, [el-aj'-ik], *adj.* relating to gall-nuts. [Fr. *ellagique*].

ELLECK, [el'-ek], *n.* a sea-fish, the red gurnard. [Uncert.].

ELLIPSE, [il-ips'], *n.* a plane curved symmetrical figure longer than it is broad, an oval; (*geom.*) an oblique section of a cone. [*Next*].

ELLIPSE

ELLIPSIS, (*pl.* **ellipses**), [il-ip'-sis], *n.* omission, defect; (*gram.*) omission of word, phrase or thought having an implied presence and relation to the meaning of the sentence [Gk. *elleipsis* defect].

ELLIPSOGRAPH, [il-ip'-sō-graf], *n.* an instrument for drawing ellipses. [ELLIPSE and GRAPH].

ELLIPSOID, [il-ip'-soid], *n.* (*geom.*) an elliptical spheroid. [ELLIPSE and Gk. *oeides* like].

ELLIPSOIDAL, [il-ip-soid'-al], *adj.* relating to, resembling an ellipsoid.

ELLIPTIC, [il-ip'-tik], *adj.* relating to, having the form of an ellipse; having a part omitted; **e. compasses**, an instrument for describing an ellipse.

ELLIPTICAL, [il-ip'-tikl], *adj.* elliptic.

ELLIPTICALLY, [il-ip'-tik-a-li], *adv.* in an elliptical manner, in the form of an ellipse; having a part omitted.

ELLIPTICITY, [il'-ip-tis'-i-ti], *n.* the quality of being elliptical.

ELLIPTOGRAPH, [il-ip'-tō-graf], *n.* an ellipsograph.

ELLWAND, [el'-wond], *n.* a measuring rod the length of an ell.

ELM, [elm], *n.* a tree of the genus *Ulmus*, having serrated leaves, bark marked with long fissures and yielding valuable timber. [OE. *elm*].

ELMEN, [elm'-en], *adj.* pertaining to the elm.

ELMY, [el'-mi], *adj.* abounding in, covered with, elms.

ELOCULAR, [i-lok'-yōō-ler], *adj.* not divided by partitions. [E (2) and L. *loculus* small cell].

ELOCUTION, [el'-ō-kew'-shun], *n.* power of oral expression; manner of speaking or oral delivery; the art of speaking elegantly with clear delivery. [L. *elocutio*].

ELOCUTIONARY, [el'-ō-kew'-shun-er-i], *adj.* relating to elocution.

ELOCUTIONIST, [el'-ō-kew'-shun-ist], *n.* an expert in elocution.

ELOCUTIVE, [el'-ō-kew'-tiv], *adj.* possessing eloquent expression.

ELODES, [el-ō'-dēz], *n.* (*med.*) the sweating sickness. [Gk. *helodes* marshy].

ELOGIST, [el'-oj-ist], *n.* a person who speaks an elogium.

ELOGIUM, [el-ōj'-i-um], *n.* a speech of praise; an inscription of praise on a tombstone. [~Gk. *elegeion*].

ELOGY, [el'-oj-i], *n.* an elogium.

ELOHIM, [el-ō'-him], *n.*(*pl.*) a name of the Creator in the Hebrew Bible. [Heb. *elohim* God].

ELOHIST, [el-ō'-hist], *n.* one of the authors of certain parts of the Pentateuch in which the word ELOHIM is used.

ELOHISTIC, [el'-ō-his'-tik], *adj.* descriptive of those parts of the Pentateuch written by the Elohist.

ELOIN, [el-oin'], *v.t.* (*leg.*) to banish to a distance, to exile. [OFr. *eloiner*].

ELOINMENT, [el-oin'-ment], *n.* (*leg.*) banishment to a distance.

ELONGATE (1), [ē'-long-gāt], *adj.* long, thin, drawn-out; (*bot.*) remarkable for length as contrasted with its breadth.

ELONGATE (2), [ē'-long-gāt], *v.t.* to lengthen, stretch out, extend. [L. *elongare* to prolong].

ELONGATION, [ē-long-gā'-shun], *n.* the act of elongating; the condition of being elongated; (*astron.*) the distance of a planet from the sun, measured from the earth; (*surg.*) the extension, dislocation, or spraining of a muscle or ligament beyond its normal limits.

ELOPE, [i-lōp'], *v.i.* to run away with one's lover in order to marry without parental knowledge and consent. [OFr. *alouper*].

ELOPEMENT, [i-lōp'-ment], *n.* the act of eloping.

ELOQUENCE, [el'-ok-wents], *n.* the power of fluent speech which by its ease, force and brilliance of expression deeply affects the emotions of those who listen. [L. *eloquentia*].

ELOQUENT, [el'-ok-went], *adj.* possessing eloquence, having a brilliant and efficient control of words when addressing an audience; expressive in language; (*fig.*) affecting, moving.

ELOQUENTLY, [el'-ok-went-li], *adv.* in an eloquent fashion.

ELSE, [els], *adv.* as well, besides, in addition, as an extra; instead; otherwise, in different circumstances, if not. [OE. *elles*].

ELSEWHERE, [els'-wāer'], *adv.* at, to, in a different place. [OE. *elleshwær*].

ELTCHI, [el'-chi], *n.* elchee. [*Var.* of ELCHEE].

ELUCIDATE, [i-lew'-sid-āt], *v.t.* to throw light upon the meaning of, to explain, to illustrate. [L. *elucidare* to enlighten].

ELUCIDATION, [i-lew'-sid-ā'-shun], *n.* the act of elucidating, of throwing light on any obscurity.

ELUCIDATIVE, [i-lew'-sid-āt-iv], *adj.* tending to elucidate, making clear, explanatory.

ELUCIDATOR, [i-lew'-sid-ā'-ter], *n.* one who elucidates.

ELUCIDATORY, [i-lew'-sid-ā'-ter-i], *adj.* elucidative.

ELUDE, [il-ewd'], *v.t.* to evade, escape, to avoid capture by guile or dexterity; to escape being seen; (*fig.*) to evade definition in the mind. [L. *eludere*].

ELUDIBLE, [il-ew'-dibl], *adj.* able to be eluded.

ELUSION, [il-ew'-zhun], *n.* the act of eluding.

ELUSIVE, [il-ew'-siv], *adj.* tending to escape a physical or mental context; evasive, difficult to grasp; hard to remember.

ELUSIVENESS, [il-ew'-siv-nes], *n.* the quality of being elusive.

ELUSORINESS, [il-ew'-ser-i-nes], *n.* the quality of being elusory.

ELUSORY, [il-ew'-ser-i], *adj.* tending to elude. [L. *elusorius*].

ELUTRIATE, [il-ew'-tri-āt], *v.t.* to purify by decanting. [L. *elutriare* to wash out].

ELUTRIATION, [il-ew'-tri-ā'-shun], *n.* the act of elutriating.

ELUXATION, [el'-uks-ā'-shun], *n.* dislocation. [LL. *eluxatio*].

ELVAN, [el'-van], *adj.* relating to elves. [ELF].

ELVANS, [el'-vanz], *n.*(*pl.*) (*min.*) veins of a crystalline mixture and quartz forming in granite and fossiliferous slates in the west of England. [Unkn.].

ELVE-LOCK, [elv'-lok'], *n.* elf-lock.

ELVER, [el'-ver], *n.* a young eel. [EEL and FARE].

ELVES, [elvz], *n.* (*pl.* of ELF).

ELVISH, [el'-vish], *adj.* elfish.

ELVISHLY, [el'-vish-li], *adv.* in an elvish fashion.

ELYDORIC, [el'-id-o'-rik], *adj.* (of paint) consisting of oil mixed with water. [Gk. *elaion* oil and *hudor* water].

ELYSIAN, [i-liz'-i-an], *adj.* relating to or situated in Elysium; heavenly.

ELYSIUM, [el-iz'-ium], *n.* (*myth.*) the country beyond death inhabited by the souls of Greek heroes; (*fig.*) an imaginary country or emotional condition of extreme and continual happiness. [Gk. *Elusion*].

ELYTRIFORM, [el-it'-ri-fawm], *adj.* (*entom.*) in the form of a wing-sheath. [Gk. *elutron* sheath and FORM].

ELYTRIN, [el-it'-rin], *n.* (*chem.*) the substance of which the horny covering of insects is formed. [Gk. *elutron* sheath].

ELYTROCELE, [el'-it-rō-sēl'], *n.* a tumour in the vagina. [Gk. *elutron* sheath and *kele* tumour].

ELYTRON, [el'-it-ron], *n.* elytrum. [Gk. *elutron* sheath].

ELYTRUM, (*pl.* **elytra**), [el'-it-rum], *n.* the wing case of coleopterous insects. [*Prec.*].

ELZEVIR, [el'-zev-ēer], *n.* a copy of one of the editions of the classics published by the Elzevir family in Holland during the sixteenth and seventeenth centuries; (*print.*) a type resembling that used by this family.

EM (1), *pref.* a form of the prefix *en*, used before certain labial consonants.

EM (2), [em], (*print.*) a unit of measurement of width of type matter, being equal to the depth of the type used. [Derived from the letter M, which was originally as wide as it was deep].

'EM (3), [em], *pron.* (*coll.*) *var.* of THEM. [ME. *hem*].

EMACIATE, [i-mā'-shi-āt], *v.t. and i.* to reduce in weight, to cause the flesh to waste away; to become very thin. [L. *emaciare*].

EMACIATION, [i-mā'-si-ā'-shun], *n.* the act of emaciating; the state of being emaciated; an unnatural slimness due to under-nourishment.

EMACULATE†, [i-mak'-yōō-lāt], *v.t.* to remove spots or blemishes from. [L. *emaculatum*, *p.pt.* of *emaculare* to rid of blemishes].

EMANANT, [em'-an-ent], *adj.* issuing or flowing from a source. [L. *emanans*].

EMANATE, [em'-an-āt'], *v.i.* to issue, proceed, or spring from, to have its source in, start from. [L. *emanare* to flow from].

EMANATION, [em'-an-ā'-shun], *n.* the act of emanating; that which emanates, effluvium, efflux; **theory of e.**, the doctrine which regards all existence as derived from and part of the essence of God, and not created by Him from a void. [L. *emanatio*].

EMANATIST, [em'-an-at-ist], *n.* a believer in emanation.

EMANATIVE, [em'-an-at-iv], *adj.* that emanates.

EMANATORY, [em'-an-ā'-ter-i], *adj.* emanative.

EMANCIPATE, [im-an'-sip-āt], *v.t.* to release from a state of slavery, to declare to be free after taking the necessary action; to grant legal, moral, or political freedom to; (*Rom. leg.*) to free from parental control. [L. *emancipare* to declare free].

EMANCIPATION, [im-an'-sip-ā'-shun], *n.* the act of emancipating; the state of being emancipated.

EMANCIPATIONIST, [im-an'-sip-ā'-shun-ist], *n.* an advocate for the total abolition of religious, political and economic conditions of oppression.

EMANCIPATOR, [im-an'-sip-ā'-ter], *n.* one who emancipates.

EMANCIPIST, [im-an'-sip-ist], *n.* a convict who has served his sentence.

EMARGINATE (1), [im-ah'-jin-āt], *adj.* possessing indented edges, notched.

EMARGINATE (2), [im-ah'-jin-āt], *v.t.* to take away the margin or edge; to notch. [L. *emarginare* to remove the edge].

EMARGINATED, [im-ah'-jin-ā'-tid], *adj.* (*bot.*) having a notch at the apex of the leaf; (*min.*) having each edge of a crystal intersected by a plane.

EMARGINATELY, [im-ah'-jin-at-li], *adv.* in the form of notches.

EMARGINATION, [im-ah'-jin-ā'-shun], *n.* the act of emarginating; the state of being emarginated.

EMASCULATE, [i-mask'-yōō-lāt], *v.t.* to deprive of virility by castrating; (*fig.*) to make effeminate, to weaken, tone down. [L. *emasculare*].

EMASCULATION, [im-as'-kyōō-lā'-shun], *n.* the act of emasculating; the state of being emasculated.

EMASCULATORY, [im-as'-kyōō-lā'-ter-i], *adj.* tending to emasculate.

EMBALE, [em-bāl'], *v.t.* to make up into a bale; to pack. [EM (1) and BALE].

EMBALM, [em-bahm'], *v.t.* to preserve a dead body from decay by removing the internal organs and impregnating it with preservatives; (*fig.*) to preserve the memory of; to scent, to fill with fragrance. [Fr. *embaumer*].

EMBALMER, [em-bahm'-er], *n.* one who embalms.

EMBALMING, [em-bahm'-ing], *n.* the occupation of embalmer.

EMBALMMENT, [em-bahm'-ment], *n.* the act of embalming; a substance used to embalm. [EMBALM].

EMBANK, IMBANK†, [em-bangk'], *v.t.* to enclose with a bank; to build a bank alongside of. [EM (1) and BANK].

EMBANKMENT, [em-bangk'-ment], *n.* the act of embanking; the state of being embanked; a long artificial mound to form the limits of a river or along which a road or railway is built.

EMBAR, (**embarring, embarred**), [em-bah(r)'], *v.t.* to enclose or fasten with a bar; to shut in; to stop; to prevent.

EMBARGO, (*pl.* **embargoes**), [em-bah'-gō], *n.* a state order to prevent ships from entering or leaving a particular port; a prohibition of trade by government order; any imposition of restraint. [Span. *embargar*].

EMBARK, [em-bahk'], *v.t. and i.* to put on board a ship; to go on board ship; (*fig.*) to start, to participate in. [LL. *imbarcare*].

EMBARKATION, [em-bahk-ā'-shun], *n.* the act of embarking; that which is embarked.

EMBARKMENT†, [em-bahk'-ment], *n.* act of embarking.

EMBARRASS, [em-ba'-ras], *v.t.* to make a situation difficult, to render complex; to disconcert, to make nervous, to perplex; to hinder, obstruct; (*fig.*) to place in financial difficulties. [Fr. *embarrasser*].

EMBARRASSING, [em-ba'-ras-ing], *adj.* disconcerting, that embarrasses.

EMBARRASSINGLY, [em-ba'-ras-ing-li], *adv.* in an embarrassing manner.

EMBARRASSMENT, [em-ba'-ras-ment], *n.* the act of embarrassing; the state of being embarrassed; that which embarrasses; awkwardness, nervousness; financial difficulty.

EMBASSADE†, [em'-bas-ād], *n.* an embassy.

EMBASSAGE†, [em'-bas-ij], *n.* an embassy.

EMBASSY, [em'-bas-i], *n.* the official staff of an ambassador; the position of ambassador; the building in which an ambassador works and resides; a particular mission or business undertaken by a visiting ambassador; any message, mission or transaction undertaken by someone. [~L. *ambactia* service].

EMBATTLE (1), [em-batl'], *v.t.* to arrange in battle order. [OFr. *embataillier*].

EMBATTLE (2), [em-batl'], *v.t.* to provide with battlements. [EM (1) and OFr. *batailer*].

EMBATTLED, [em-batld'], *adj.* in battle order; (*her., arch.*) indented, like a battlement.

EMBATTLED

EMBAY, [em-bā'], *v.t.* to enclose in a bay; to landlock; to shut in within a bay; to surround.

EMBAYMENT, [em-bā'-ment], *n.* a bay; the act of forming into a bay.

EMBED, IMBED, (**embedding, embedded**), [im-bed'], *v.t.* to set firmly into other material; (*fig.*) to instil ineradicably into the mind; to lay, as in a bed.

EMBEDMENT, [em-bed'-ment], *n.* the act of embedding; the state of being embedded.

EMBELLISH, [em-bel'-ish], *v.t.* to adorn, decorate; to improve the appearance of, beautify, to make graceful or elegant; to add vivid details to; to furnish with illustrations. [~Fr. *embellir*].

EMBELLISHER, [em-bel'-ish-er], *n.* a person who embellishes.

EMBELLISHINGLY, [em-bel'-ish-ing-li], *adv.* so as to embellish.

EMBELLISHMENT, [em-bel'-ish-ment], *n.* the act of embellishing, the state of being embellished; anything that embellishes, adornment.

EMBER, IMBER†, [em'-ber], *n.* a smouldering cinder, the glowing pieces of coal, etc., in a dying fire. [OE. *æmerge* ashes].

EMBER-DAYS, [em'-ber-dāz'], *n.(pl.)* three days occurring periodically each season, and set aside by the Western Church for prayer and fasting. [OE. *ymbrenu* and DAY].

EMBER-GOOSE, [em'-ber-gōōs'], *n.* (*ornith.*) the great northern diver, *Colymbus glacialis*. [OScand. *emmer*].

EMBER-WEEK, [em'-ber-wēk'], *n.* a week in which ember-days fall.

EMBEZZLE, [em-bezl'], *v.t.* to misappropriate funds, goods, etc., placed in one's charge. [AFr. *enbesiler* fraudulently to do away with].

EMBEZZLEMENT, [em-bezl'-ment], *n.* the act of embezzling.

EMBEZZLER, [em-bez'-ler], *n.* a person who embezzles.

EMBITTER, [em-bit'-er], *v.t.* to make bitter; to arouse harsh feelings in; to exasperate.

EMBLAZE, [em-blāz'], *v.t.* to adorn with brilliant embellishment; to adorn with armorial figures; to display heraldic devices.

EMBLAZON, [em-blāzn'], *v.t.* to paint with heraldic devices; to depict (of armorial bearings, etc.); to decorate with brilliant colours; to celebrate, extol.

EMBLAZONER, [em-blāz'-on-er], *n.* one who emblazons.

EMBLAZONING, [em-blāz-on-ing], *n.* the act of adorning with heraldic devices.

EMBLAZONMENT, [em-blāz'-on-ment], *n.* an emblazoning; that which is emblazoned.

EMBLAZONRY, [em-blāz'-on-ri], *n.* blazonry, heraldic devices.

EMBLEM, [em'-blem], *n.* a concrete symbolization of some abstract thing; a sign or device standing as a symbol of something. [Gk. *emblema*].

EMBLEMATA, [em-blēm'-a-ta], *n.(pl.)* figures worked in precious metals decorating ancient vessels.

EMBLEMATIC, [em'-blem-at'-ik], *adj.* emblematical.

EMBLEMATICAL, [em'-blem-at'-ikl], *adj.* having the nature of or serving as an emblem, using emblems.

EMBLEMATICALLY, [em'-blem-at'-ik-al-i], *adv.* in an emblematic manner, by means of an emblem.

EMBLEMATICALNESS, [em'-blem-at'-ikl-nes], *n.* the quality of being emblematical.

EMBLEMATIST, [em-blem'-at-ist], *n.* a composer of emblems.

EMBLEMENTS, [embl'-ments], *n.(pl.)* (*leg.*) a tenant's produce and crops that he can claim even though his lease expires before harvest time. [OFr. *emblement*].

EMBLEMIZE, [em'-blem-iz], *v.t.* to represent by means of an emblem.

EMBLICA, [em'-blik-a], *n.* an Indian tree, the fruit and leaves of which are used in medicine as a purgative. [~Skr. *amalaka*].

EMBLOOM, [em-blōōm'], *v.t.* to cover with bloom.

EMBLOSSOM, [em-blos'-om], *v.t.* to cover with blossom.
EMBODIER, [em-bod'-i-er], *n.* one that embodies.
EMBODIMENT, [em-bod'-i-ment], *n.* the act of embodying; the condition of being embodied.
EMBODY, [em-bod'-i], *v.t.* to collect into a body; to invest with a material form, to represent in any medium, to incorporate, to include.
EMBOG, (**embogging, embogged**), [em-bog'], *v.t.* to sink in a bog; (*fig.*) to surround with perplexities.
EMBOGUE†, [em-bōg'], *v.i.* to discharge, as a river. [Uncert.].
EMBOGUING†, [em-bōg'-ing], *n.* the mouth of a river, where the water is discharged into the sea.
EMBOITEMENT, [em-boit'-ment], *n.* (*biol.*) the theory that the germ of each successive generation lies within its predecessor; (*milit.*) a tactic of closing up ranks as a protection for the front rank. [Fr. *emboîtement* a closing up].
EMBOLDEN, [em-bōld'-en], *v.t.* to make bold.
EMBOLDENER, [em-bōld'-en-er], *n.* a person who emboldens.
EMBOLISM, [em'-bol-izm], *n.* the regularization of time by the insertion of calculated periods such as days, months, or years; (*med.*) a clot of blood carried in the blood-stream which, when obstructing the flow of blood, may produce inflammation, gangrene, paralysis or death. [~Gk. *embolos* a wedge].
EMBOLISMAL, [em'-bol-iz'-mal], *adj.* embolismic.
EMBOLISMIC, [em'-bol-iz'-mik], *adj.* relating to embolism; inserted; clotted.
EMBOLITE, [em'-bol-īt], *n.* (*min.*) a grey-green ore compounded of chlorine, bromine and silver. [Gk. *embolion* intermediate].
EMBOLUS, [em'-bol-us], *n.* (*mech.*) something inserted or moving in another, as a wedge or a piston; (*med.*) the clot of blood in embolism. [Gk. *embolos* wedge].
EMBONPOINT, [on'-bon-pwa(ng)], *n.* superfluous fat, obesity. [Fr. from *en bon point* in good condition].
EMBORDER, [em-bawd'-er], *v.t.* to decorate with a border.
EMBOSOM, [em-bo͝ozm], *v.t.* to clasp to the bosom, to hold in one's arms close to the breast; (*fig.*) to shelter, to surround with, to shut in.
EMBOSS (1), [em-bos'], *v.t.* to cause parts of a surface to rise so as to form designs by hammering or from pressure with a die.
EMBOSS† (**2**), [em-bos'], *v.t.* to drive a quarry hard in hunting; to cover with foam. [OFr. *embose*].
EMBOSS† (**3**), [em-bos'], *v.t.* to enclose as in a box; to encase as in armour; to conceal in a thicket. [Uncert.].
EMBOSSED, [em-bost'], *adj.* having designs standing out in relief; (*bot.*) projecting from the centre of the surface like the boss of a round shield.
EMBOSSER, [em-bos'-er], *n.* a craftsman skilled in embossing.
EMBOSSING, [em-bos'-ing], *n.* the act of raising from a surface ornamental figures in relief; figures thus formed.
EMBOSSMENT, [em-bos'-ment], *n.* embossing.
EMBOTTLE, [em-botl'], *v.t.* to bottle.
EMBOUCHURE, [em-bo͞osh-yo͞oer'], *n.* the mouth of a river; the mouthpiece of a wind instrument; the manner of holding and controlling a mouthpiece with the lips, teeth, or tongue. [Fr. *embouchure*].
EMBOW, IMBOW†, [em-bō'], *v.t.* to bow, to vault.
EMBOWEL, (**embowelling, embowelled**), [em-bow'-el], *v.t.* to remove the entrails of; to enclose or embed in another substance. [OFr. *enboueler*].
EMBOWELLER, [em-bow'-el-er], *n.* a person who removes the bowels.
EMBOWELMENT, [em-bow'-el-ment], *n.* the act of removing the entrails.
EMBOWER, [em-bow'-er], *v.t.* and *i.* to cover with a bower, to shelter with plants; to take rest in a bower.
EMBOXED, [em-bokst'], *adj.* enclosed or placed in a box.
EMBRACE (1), [em-brās'], *n.* a holding or clasping of another person in one's arms against the breast, a hug, a clasp.
EMBRACE (2), [em-brās'], *v.t.* to hold and clasp in an embrace; to take, to seize eagerly, willingly, to avail oneself of; to comprehend, include; to encompass. [OFr. *embracer*].
EMBRACEABLE, [em-brās'-abl], *adj.* able to be embraced.
EMBRACEMENT, [em-brās'-ment], *n.* the act of embracing; the state of being contained.
EMBRACER, [em-brās'-er], *n.* (*leg.*) a person who attempts to influence a jury corruptly. [OFr. *embraceur* corrupter].
EMBRACERY, [em-brās'-er-i], *n.* (*leg.*) an attempt to influence a jury corruptly by bribery.
EMBRACIVE, [em-brās'-iv], *adj.* given to embracing.
EMBRAIL, [em-brāl'], *v.t.* to brail up.
EMBRANCHMENT, [em-brahnch'-ment], *n.* a forking apart of a river, a branching, ramification.
EMBRANGLE, IMBRANGLE†, [em-brang'-gl], *v.t.* to entangle; to perplex [EMBR(OIL) and (ENT)ANGLE].
EMBRASURE, [em-brā'-zher], *n.* (*arch.*) a recessed opening for a door or window in an interior having its sides cut back obliquely; (*fort.*) a recessed opening in a rampart in which guns or cannon are mounted. [OFr. *embraser*].

EMBRASURE

EMBRAVE, [em-brāv'], *v.t.* to embellish; to fill with courage.
EMBREATHEMENT†, [em-brēTH'-ment], *n.* inspiration, impregnation.
EMBRING-DAYS, [em'-bring-dāz'], *n.*(*pl.*) ember-days.
EMBRITTLE, [em-britl'], *v.t.* to make brittle.
EMBROCATE, [em'-brok-āt], *v.t.* (*med.*) to apply embrocation. [~Gk. *embrekho* I foment].
EMBROCATION, [em'-brok-ā'-shun], *n.* (*med.*) the act of embrocating; a lotion to be rubbed on a sprain.
EMBROGLIO, see IMBROGLIO.
EMBROIDER, [em-broid'-er], *v.t.* to decorate with designs picked out in different coloured threads; to ornament with needlework; (*fig.*) to add imaginative details to. [EM (1) and OFr. *broder* to work the edge of].
EMBROIDERER, [em-broid'-er-er], *n.* a person who embroiders.
EMBROIDERY, [em-broid'-er-i], *n.* the art of embroidering; work produced by embroidery; imaginative embellishments, *esp.* to a narrative.
EMBROIL, [em-broil'], *v.t.* to involve in trouble, to entangle with difficulties. [Fr. *embrouiller*].
EMBROILMENT, [em-broil'-ment], *n.* the act of embroiling; a state of entanglement, confusion.
EMBRONZE, [em-bronz'], *v.t.* to mould or cast in bronze.
EMBRUED, [em-bro͞od'], *adj.* (*her.*) represented as imbrued with blood. [IMBRUE].
EMBRUTE, [em-bro͞ot'], *v.t.* and *i.* to sink into brutishness; to cause to become brutish.
EMBRYO (1), [em'-bri-ō], *n.* the germ of an organism in the first stages of pre-natal development; an early stage of development in anything. [Gk. *embruon* new-born lamb].
EMBRYO (2), [em'-bri-ō], *adj.* relating to anything in an undeveloped state, rudimentary, incipient, unborn.
EMBRYO- (3), *pref.* relating to an embryo. [*Prec.*].
EMBRYOCTONY, [em'-bri-ok'-ton-i], *n.* (*surg.*) the killing of the foetus in the womb. [EMBRYO (3) and ~Gk. *kteino* I kill].
EMBRYOGENY, [em'-bri-oj'-en-i], *n.* the process of the generation and development of embryos; the science concerned with this. [EMBRYO (3) and Gk. *genes* born].
EMBRYOGRAPHY, [em'-bri-og'-ra-fi], *n.* a description of embryos. [EMBRYO (3) and Gk. *graphia* writing].
EMBRYOLOGY, [em'-bri-ol'-oj-i], *n.* the science concerned with the formation and development of embryos. [EMBRYO (3) and Gk. *logos* speech].
EMBRYON, [em'-bri-on], *n.* an embryo.
EMBRYONAL, [em'-bri-on'-al], *adj.* embryonic.
EMBRYONATED, [em'-bri-on-ā'-tid], *adj.* relating to or possessing an embryo; having the characteristics of an embryo.
EMBRYONIC, [em'-bri-on'-ik], *adj.* relating to or resembling an embryo; undeveloped, incipient.
EMBRYOTHLAST, [em'-bri-oth-last'], *n.* (*surg.*) an instrument for removing the fœtus during birth. [EMBRYO (3) and Gk. *thlao* I brush].
EMBRYOTOMY, [em'-bri-ot'-om-i], *n.* (*surg.*) the excision of the foetus from the womb to prevent possible mortality in delivery. [EMBRYO (3) and Gk. *tome* cutting].
EMBRYOUS, [em'-bri-us], *adj.* having the nature of an embryo.
EMEND, [im-end'], *v.t.* to amend; to correct (a mistake) or improve (a text). [L. *emendare*].

EMENDABLE, [im-end'-abl], *adj.* able to be amended.

EMENDATELY†, [im-end'-at-li], *adv.* without fault; correctly.

EMENDATION, [ē'-mend-ā'-shun], *n.* the act of emending; the alteration so made. [L. *emendatio*].

EMENDATOR, [ē'-mend-ā'-tor], *n.* a corrector of errors or faults in writings; a person who corrects or improves.

EMENDATORY, [ē'-mend-ā'-ter-i], *adj.* contributing to emendation, tending to improve.

EMERALD (1), [em'-er-ald], *n.* (*min.*) a precious stone of a brilliant green colour; a silicate and aluminate of glucinium; a green variety of corundum; (*fig.*) the colour of an emerald, a brilliant medium-toned green; (*print.*) a size of type between minion and nonpareil. [OFr. *emeraude* from Gk. *smaragdos*].

EMERALD (2), [em'-er-ald], *adj.* consisting of, having the colour of, an emerald.

EMERALD-COPPER, [em'-er-ald-kop'-er], *n.* (*min.*) copper silicate, in colour a beautiful emerald-green.

EMERALD-GREEN, [em'-er-ald-grēn'], *n.* a vivid light green pigment, produced from arsenate of copper for use in painting.

EMERGE, [im-urj'], *v.i.* to rise out of some enveloping medium, to come into view; to issue from, to proceed out of; to reappear after passing through a stage of obscurity or concealment. [L. *emergere*].

EMERGENCE, [im-urj'-ents], *n.* the act of emerging.

EMERGENCY, [im-urj'-en-si], *n.* a situation involving danger and a need for decisive action.

EMERGENT, [im-urj'-ent], *adj.* issuing, arising from.

EMERGENTLY, [im-urj'-ent-li], *adv.* in an emergent way.

EMERITED, [im-e'-rit-ed], *adj.* deserving merit for long and honourable public service.

EMERITUS, (*pl.* **emeriti**), [im-e'-rit-us], *n.* a person who has been granted a title or pension on retirement from public service, *esp.* a university professor. [L. *emeritus* veteran].

EMERODS†, [em'-er-odz], *n.*(*pl.*) haemorrhoids, painful, bleeding boils about the anus, piles. [OFr. *emmeroides*].

EMERSION, [im-ur'-shun], *n.* the process of emerging; emergence; (*astron.*) the reappearance of a heavenly body after an eclipse, or of a star which has been concealed by the sun's light. [~L. *emersum* emerged].

EMERY, [em'-er-i], *n.* a granular variety of corundum characterized by extreme hardness, used for grinding and polishing. [OFr. *emeril* from Gk. *smeris* emery powder].

EMERY-CLOTH, [em'-er-i-kloth'], *n.* cloth coated with emery powder and used for smoothing and polishing.

EMERY-PAPER, [em'-er-i-pā'-per], *n.* paper coated with emery powder, used for smoothing wood and polishing metals.

EMERY-WHEEL, [em'-er-i-wēl'], *n.* a wheel with the rim faced with emery for grinding and polishing purposes.

EMESIS, [em'-es-is], *n.* a vomiting. [Gk. *emesis*].

EMETIC (1), [im-et'-ik], *n.* (*med.*) a medicine which when taken internally causes vomiting.

EMETIC (2), [im-et'-ik], *adj.* causing vomiting. [Gk. *emetikos*].

EMETICALLY, [im-et'-ik-al-i], *adv.* in such a way as to induce vomiting.

EMETIN, [em'-et-in], *n.* a bitter white powder, obtained from the root of the ipecacuanha. [Gk. *emetos* vomiting].

EMETO-CATHARTIC, [im-et'-ō-kath-aht'-ik], *adj.* (*med.*) having the power to produce vomiting and purging simultaneously.

EMETOLOGY, [im'-et-ol'-oj-i], *n.* the study of vomiting and emetics. [Gk. *emetos* vomiting and *logos* speech].

EMETROPHIA, [im'-et-rof'-i-a], *n.* atrophy due to vomiting. [Gk. *emetos* vomiting and *atrophos* unnourished].

EMICANT†, [em'-ik-ant], *adj.* sparkling, flying off. [L. *emicans*, *pres.pt.* of *emicare* to flash forth].

EMICATION†, [em'-ik-ā'-shun], *n.* the action of sparkling; a flying off in small particles, as from heated iron or fermenting liquors. [L. *emicatio*].

EMICTION, [im-ik'-shun], *n.* the discharging of urine; urine when voided. [~L. *emictum*, *p.pt.* *emingere* to urinate].

EMICTORY (1), [im-ik'-ter-i], *n.* a medicine which induces a discharge of urine.

EMICTORY (2), [im-ik'-ter-i], *adj.* inducing a discharge of urine.

EMIGRANT (1), [em'-ig-rant], *n.* one who is emigrating or who has emigrated.

EMIGRANT (2), [em'-ig-rant], *adj.* emigrating or emigrated. [L. *emigrans*, *pres.pt.* of *emigrare*].

EMIGRATE, [em'-ig-rāt], *v.i.* to leave a native country to settle in another, to take up permanent residence and find work in another country. [L. *emigrare* to move out].

EMIGRATION, [em'-ig-rā'-shun], *n.* the act of emigrating.

EMIGRATIONAL, [em'-ig-rā'-shun-al], *adj.* relating to emigration.

EMIGRATIONIST, [em'-ig-rā'-shun-ist], *n.* a promoter of or advocate for emigration as a means for empire building or alleviating unemployment.

EMIGRATORY, [em'-ig-rā'-ter-i], *adj.* emigrating, accustomed to emigrate, as birds.

EMIGRE, **émigré**, [em'-ig-rā], *n.* an emigrant; a refugee, *esp.* from the French or Russian Revolutions. [Fr. *émigré*].

EMINENCE, [em'-in-ents], *n.* that which is high, the highest part, a part ascending from the common to a higher level of a surface; a hill; (*fig.*) superiority of rank; outstanding character or abilities, renown; the title of honour accorded to a cardinal.

EMINENCY, [em'-in-en-si], *n.* eminence.

EMINENT, [em'-in-ent], *adj.* exalted in rank, high in general esteem, famous, renowned, distinguished. [L. *eminens*, *pres.pt.* of *eminere* to stand out].

EMINENTLY, [em'-in-ent-li], *adv.* in an eminent fashion.

EMIR, [em'-ēer'], *n.* an independent Mohammedan ruler in Arabia, Asia, Africa; a male descendant of Mohammed. [Arab. *amir* commander].

EMISSARY (1), [em'-is-er-i], *n.* a special representative or messenger. [LL. *emissarius* one sent out].

EMISSARY (2), [em'-is-er-i], *adj.* spying.

EMISSION, [ē-mish'-un], *n.* the act of emitting; that which is discharged. [L. *emissio*].

EMISSIVE, [em-is'-iv], *adj.* having the power of emitting; relating to emission.

EMISSORY, [em'-is-er-i], *adj.* (*physiol.*) denoting those ducts which convey fluids to certain veins.

EMIT, (**emitting, emitted**), [im-it'], *v.t.* to send forth, eject, discharge, to cause to come forth; to issue, as notes and bills of credit, to print and send into circulation, as paper money. [L. *emittere* to send out].

EMMENAGOGUE, [em-en'-a-gōg], *n.* a medicine that facilitates the menstrual discharge. [Gk. *emmena* the menses and *agogos* drawing forth].

EMMENOLOGY, [em'-en-ol'-oj-i], *n.* a treatise on or a study of menstruation. [Gk. *emmena* the menses and *logos* speech].

EMMET, [em'-et], *n.* an ant. [OE. *æmete*].

EMMETROPIA, [em'-et-rop'-i-a], *n.* the normal condition of the lenses of the eye when the retina focuses parallel rays of light. [Gk. *emmetros* in measure and *ops* eye].

EMMEW, [em-mew'], *v.t.* to coop up, to enclose. [EM (1) and MEW].

EMOLLESCENCE, [im'-ol-es'-ents], *n.* (*chem.*) the condition of softening, that degree of softness in a body when it begins to melt before fusing. [L. *emollescere* grow soft].

EMOLLIATE, [im-ol'-i-āt], *v.t.* to soften, to render effeminate. [L. *emollire* to soften].

EMOLLIENT (1), [im-ol'-i-ent], *n.* (*med.*) an oily substance with soothing and softening properties.

EMOLLIENT (2), [im-ol'-i-ent], *adj.* having the power to soothe and make soft. [L. *emolliens*].

EMOLLITION, [em'-ol-ish'-un], *n.* the act of softening or relaxing.

EMOLUMENT, [im-ol'-yōō-ment], *n.* remuneration for services given while in office; fees, salary, profit, or advantage. [L. *emolumentum*].

EMOLUMENTAL, [im-ol'-yōō-ment'-al], *adj.* profitable.

EMOTION, [im-ō'-shun], *n.* strong instinctive feeling, an involuntary wave of such feeling, a stirring of one's inner nature by a mood, circumstance, or passion. [L. *emotum*, *p.pt.* of *emovere* to remove].

EMOTIONABLE, [im-ō'-shun-abl], *adj.* capable of having the emotions easily excited.

EMOTIONAL, [im-ō'-shun-al], *adj.* relating to the emotions; exciting or excited by emotion; possessing strong and deep emotions, being quick, subtle, powerful in emotional response.

EMOTIONALISM, [im-ō'-shun-al-izm], *n.* the habit of emphasizing the importance of free emotional response.

EMOTIONALLY, [imōsh'-un-al-i], *adv.* with regard to the emotions; with emotion.
EMOTIONLESS, [im-ō'-shun-les], *adj.* without emotion.
EMOTIONLESSNESS, [im-ō'-shun-les-nes], *n.* the character and condition of being without emotion.
EMOTIVE, [im-ō'-tiv], *adj.* characterized by emotion. [L. *emotum*, *p.pt.* of *emovere* to remove].
EMOTIVELY, [im-ō'-tiv-li], *adv.* in an emotive manner.
EMOTIVITY, [im'-ō-tiv'-i-ti], *n.* the capacity for or intensity of emotional response.
EMPALE, see IMPALE.
EMPALEMENT, see IMPALEMENT.
EMPANEL, IMPANEL, (**empanelling, empanelled**), [im-pan'-el], *v.t.* to form a list of jurors, to enrol as jurors. [OFr. *empaneller*].
EMPANOPLY, [em-pan'-op-li], *v.t.* to attire in full armour. [EM and PANOPLY].
EMPARK, [em-pahk'], *v.t.* to enclose with a fence, as a park.
EMPASM†, [em-pazm'], *n.* a powder sprinkled on any part of the person to counteract any offensive body odour. [Gk. *empasseo* I sprinkle on].
EMPATHY, [em'-path-i], *n.* (*psych.*) the power of subjective identification with an object or with another person during contact, having special reference to experience of a work of art. [Gk. *empatheia* feeling into].
EMPAWN, [em-pawn'], *v.t.* to give as a pledge.
EMPERIL†, see IMPERIL.
EMPEROR, [em'-per-or], *n.* the supreme male sovereign of an empire; the largest size of drawing paper measuring 66 inches by 47 inches; **e. butterfly**, the purple emperor, *Apatura iris*; **e. moth**, *Saturnia carpini*. [L. *imperator* ruler].
EMPHASIS, [em'-fas-is], *n.* any means, device, or method used to stress a part in relation to its context, eliciting its importance, significance, or meaning; accent on a word or syllable in speech; a more powerful or distinct element in the medium of a work of art rendering it more apparent than the rest; impressiveness of expression. [Gk. *emphasis* appearance, significance].
EMPHASIZE, [em'-fas-īz], *v.t.* to give emphasis to, to lay stress on, to accentuate, enhance, underline.
EMPHATIC, [em-fat'-ik], *adj.* expressing emphasis, forcible. [Gk. *emphatikos*].
EMPHATICAL, [em-fat'-ik-al], *adj.* emphatic.
EMPHATICALLY, [em-fat'-ik-al-i], *adv.* in an emphatic way.
EMPHATICALNESS, [em-fat'-ik-al-nes], *n.* the quality of being emphatic.
EMPHLYSIS, [em-flī'-sis], *n.* (*med.*) an eruption of vesicular pimples on the skin characterizing certain diseases. [EM (1) and Gk. *phlusis* pimple].
EMPHRACTIC (1), [em-frak'-tik], *n.* (*med.*) a substance which closes up the pores of the skin.
EMPHRACTIC (2), [em-frak'-tik], *adj.* (*med.*) having the power to close up the pores of the skin. [Gk. *emphraktikos*].
EMPHYMA, [em'-fim-a], *n.* a fleshy or encysted tumour. [EM (1) and Gk. *phuo* I produce].
EMPHYSEMA, [em-fi-sē'-ma], *n.* (*med.*) distension of a tissue due to air blocked up in the cellular tissues. [Gk. *emphusema* inflation].
EMPHYSEMATOUS, [em'-fi-sē'-mat-us], *adj.* (*med.*) relating to emphysema; swollen.
EMPHYTEUSIS, [em'-fit-ew'-sis], *n.* (in Roman law) a perpetual right to use a piece of land in a specified way, granted for payment of a yearly rent. [Gk. *emphuteusis* implanting].
EMPHYTEUTIC, [em'-fit-ew'-tik], *adj.* of the nature of emphyteusis, taken on hire.
EMPHYTEUTICARY†, [em'-fit-ew'-tik-er-i], *n.* a person who holds lands by emphyteusis.
EMPIRE (1), [em'-pīer], *n.* supreme power, complete sovereignty; dominion, wide territories ruled over by a supreme monarch; a group of states under the rule of an emperor, the largest unit of lands and peoples bound by one monarchical allegiance; **E. Day**, May 24, Queen Victoria's birthday, set aside for the celebration of the greatness of the British Empire. [Fr. *empire* from L. *imperium* command, power].
EMPIRE (2), [em'-pīer], *adj.* of, or relating to, an empire; a style in furniture or dress fashionable during the first French Empire.
EMPIRIC (1), [em-pi'-rik], *n.* a person relying on personal experience and observation for principles of practice and action, choosing to ignore the findings of science; a medical practitioner without scientific training, a charlatan, quack. [Gk. *empeirikos* experienced].
EMPIRIC (2), [em-pi'-rik], *adj.* empirical.
EMPIRICAL, [em-pi'-rik-al], *adj.* based on personal experience, or experiment and observation; known only from experience, without reference to the principles or facts put forward by scientists.
EMPIRICALLY, [em-pi'-rik-al-i], *adv.* in an empirical way.
EMPIRICISM, [em-pi'-ris-izm], *n.* the methods and point of view of an empiric.
EMPIRICIST, [em-pi'-ris-ist], *n.* an empiric.
EMPLACEMENT, [em-plās'-ment], *n.* position, site, ground; gun platform.
EMPLANE, [em-plān'], *v.t. and i.* to board or take on board an aeroplane. [EM (1) and PLANE].
EMPLASTER†, [em-plahs'-ter], *v.t.* to cover with plaster. [L. *emplastrare*].
EMPLASTIC†, [em-plas'-tik], *adj.* glutinous, sticky, suitable to be applied as a plaster. [Gk. *emplastikos*].
EMPLEAD†, see IMPLEAD.
EMPLECTON, [em-plek'-ton], *n.* (*arch.*) a mode of masonry in the construction of walls, with wrought stones to form the sides, and rubble in the interior. [Gk. *emplekton*].

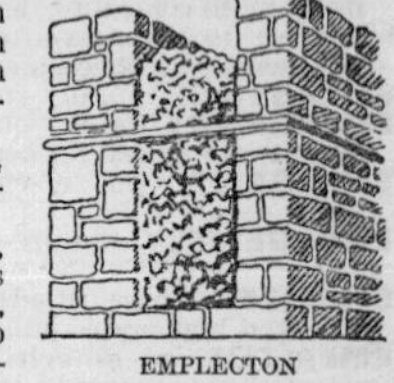
EMPLECTON

EMPLOY (1), [em-ploi'], *n.* employment, occupation, service.
EMPLOY (2), [em-ploi'], *v.t.* to make use of as an instrument, means, agent; to engage to do work for one, particularly in a weekly capacity; to give work, require workmen; to spend, occupy. [Fr. *employer* from L. *implicare* to fold up].
EMPLOYABILITY, [em-ploi'-ab-il'-i-ti], *n.* the quality of being employable.
EMPLOYABLE, [em-ploi'-abl], *adj.* able to be employed.
EMPLOYEE, [em-ploi'-ē], *n.* a person employed.
EMPLOYER, [em-ploi'-er], *n.* one who hires the service of others.
EMPLOYMENT, [em-ploi'-ment], *n.* the act of employing, the state of being employed; work, occupation, business.
EMPLOYMENT EXCHANGE, [em-ploi'-ment-eks-chānj'], *n.* one of the offices instituted by the Unemployed Workmen Act of 1905 for finding work for the unemployed and for paying out the money allotted by the government as unemployment benefit.
EMPLUME, [em-ploōm'], *v.t.* to decorate with plumes.
EMPLUNGE†, [em-plunj'], *v.t.* to plunge.
EMPOESTIC (1), [em-pēs'-tik], *n.* the art of embossing and riveting threads or plates of another metal in the raised surfaces. [Gk. *empoistike* embossing].
EMPOESTIC (2), [em-pēs'-tik], *adj.* of the character of empoestic work.
EMPOISON, IMPOISON, [em-poizn'], *v.t.* to poison, to taint with poison, to deprive of sweetness; (*fig.*) to embitter the mind of.
EMPOISONER, [em-poi'-zen-er], *n.* a person who administers poison.
EMPOISONMENT†, [em-poizn'-ment], *n.* the act of poisoning.
EMPORETIC†, [em'-por-et'-ik], *adj.* emporetical.
EMPORETICAL†, [em'-por-et'-ikl], *adj.* relating to merchandise or trade.
EMPORIUM, [em-paw'-ri-um], *n.* a trading centre; a large general shop stocking every kind of product. [Gk. *emporion* market].
EMPOWER, [em-pow'-er], *v.t.* to equip with power or authority, to authorize.
EMPRESS, [em'-pres], *n.* the wife of an emperor; a woman who rules an empire. [L. *imperatrix*].
EMPRESSMENT, [em-pres'-ment], *n.* display of eagerness, cordiality. [Fr. *empressement*].
EMPRISE, [em-prīz'], *n.* undertaking, romantic adventure. [OFr. *emprise*].
EMPROSTHOTONUS, [em'-pros-thot'-on-us], *n.* (*med.*) a spasmodic affection of the muscles of the trunk by which the body is drawn forward unnaturally. [Gk. *emprosthotonos*].
EMPTIER, [emp'-ti-er], *n.* one who, or that which empties.

EMPTINESS, [emp'-ti-nes], *n.* the state or quality of being empty.

EMPTION, [emp'-shun], *n.* the act of buying. [L. *emptio*].

EMPTIONAL, [emp'-shun-al], *adj.* able to be purchased.

EMPTY (1), [emp'-ti], *n.* (*coll.*) an empty bottle or receptacle.

EMPTY (2), [emp'-ti], *adj.* containing nothing, bare, without contents; without what it usually contains or is supposed to contain; (*fig.*) futile, worthless; meaningless; senseless, brainless; unsubstantial, poor. [OE. *æmtig* vacant].

EMPTY (3), [emp'-ti], *v.t.* and *i.* to make empty, to remove the contents of; to become empty; (*reflex.*) to discharge into. [OE. *æmtian* to be vacant].

EMPTY-HANDED, [emp'-ti-han'-did], *adj.* without gifts, booty or valuables.

EMPTY-HEADED, [emp'-ti-hed'-id], *adj.* silly and frivolous.

EMPTY-HEARTED, [emp'-ti-haht'-id], *adj.* without feeling and attachment.

EMPTYING, [emp'-ti-ing], *n.* the act of making empty; (*pl.*) the dregs of beer, etc.; (*U.S.*) yeast.

EMPTYSIS, [emp-tī'-sis], *n.* (*med.*) the spitting of blood owing to haemorrhage of the lungs. [Gk. *emptusis*].

EMPURPLE, IMPURPLE†, [em-purpl'], *v.t.* to make purple, stain with purple.

EMPUSE, [em-pewz'], *n.* a hobgoblin. [Gk. *empousa*].

EMPUZZLE, [em-puzl'], *v.t.* to puzzle sorely.

EMPYEMA, [em'-pī-ē'-ma], *n.* an accumulation of pus around the lungs, due to pleurisy. [Gk. *empuema*].

EMPYESIS, [em-pī-ē'-sis], *n.* a suppuration of pus. [Gk. *empuesis*].

EMPYREAL, [em-pī-rē'-al], *adj.* formed of the fiery elements; relating to the empyrean; heavenly.

EMPYREAN, [em'-pī-rē'-an], *n.* the highest heaven; the domain of fire; the dwelling-place of God; the pure sky, the open heavens. [Gk. *empuros* exposed to fire].

EMPYREUMA, [em'-pi-rōō'-ma], *n.* the acrid smoky taste and odour of animal or vegetable substances burned in close vessels. [Gk. *empureuma*].

EMPYREUMATIC, [em'-pi-rōō-mat'-ik], *adj.* having a burnt taste or smell.

EMPYREUMATICAL, [em'-pi-rōō-mat'-ikl], *adj.* empyreumatic.

EMPYREUMATIZE, [em'-pi-rōō-mat-īz], *v.t.* to impart an empyreuma to.

EMPYRICAL, [em-pi'-rikl], *adj.* relating to burning; combustible.

EMPYROSIS†, [em'-pi-rō'-sis], *n.* a conflagration. [Gk. *empurosis*].

EMU, [ē'-mew], *n.* a large flightless Australian bird of the genus *Dromæus*. [Uncert.].

EMUCID†, [im-ew'-sid], *adj.* rotten. [E-(2) and L. *mucidus* mouldy].

EMULATE, [em'-yŏŏ-lāt], *v.t.* to strive to equal or surpass, to rival enviously and strive to outdo. [L. *æmulari*].

EMULATION, [em'-yŏŏ-lā'-shun], *n.* the act of emulating; ambition to rival or surpass another. [L. *emulatio*].

EMULATIVE, [em'-yŏŏ-lat-iv], *adj.* tending to emulate, that emulates.

EMULATIVELY, [em'-yŏŏ-lāt'-iv-li], *adv.* in emulation.

EMU

EMULATOR, [em'-yŏŏ-lāt'-er], *n.* one who emulates, competitor, rival. [L. *emulator*].

EMULATRESS, [em'-yŏŏ-lāt'-res], *n.* a female emulator.

EMULGENT (1), [em-ulj'-ent], *n.* (*physiol.*) an emulgent vessel.

EMULGENT (2), [em-ulj'-ent], *adj.* draining or milking out, applied to the renal vessels. [L. *emulgens, pres.pt.* of *emulgere* to milk].

EMULOUS, [em'-yŏŏ-lus], *adj.* eager to emulate, striving to surpass or rival, eager to obtain. [L. *emulus*].

EMULOUSLY, [em'-yŏŏ-lus-li], *adv.* in emulous fashion.

EMULOUSNESS, [em'-yŏŏ-lus-nes], *n.* the quality of being emulous.

EMULSIC, [im-ul'-sik], *adj.* relating to emulsion.

EMULSIFY, [i-mul'-si-fī], *v.t.* to make into an emulsive fluid.

EMULSIN, [im-ul'-sin], *n.* a neutral ferment extracted from almonds.

EMULSION, [im-ul'-shun], *n.* a milky substance, the union of oil and water through the use of an alkali, especially a medical preparation of this sort; (*phot.*) a mixture of silver salts suspended in collodion, used for coating photographic plates, etc. [L. *emulsio*].

EMULSIVE, [im-ul'-siv], *adj.* relating to, resembling emulsion.

EMUNCTORY (1), [im-ungk'-ter-i], *n.* an organ by which waste matter may be discharged from the body.

EMUNCTORY (2), [im-ungk'-ter-i], *adj.* having an excretory function. [L. *emungere* to blow the nose].

EMU-WREN, [ē'-mew-ren'], *n.* an Australian bird of the genus *Stipiturus*.

EMYS, [ē'-mis], *n.* the freshwater tortoise. [Gk. *emus*].

EN- (1), *pref.* in; to make; to place into. [Gk. *en* in].

EN (2), [en], *n.* (*print.*) a unit of width equal to half an em. [The letter n originally half the width of m].

ENABLE, [en-ābl'], *v.t.* to allow, make able, to provide means to do something, to give suitable circumstances for something. [EN (1) and ABLE].

ENABLEMENT, [en-ābl'-ment], *n.* the act of enabling.

ENACT, [en-akt'], *v.t.* to decree; to make into a legal measure; to act, perform; to do, make to happen. [EN (1) and ACT].

ENACTING, [en-akt'-ing], *n.* a decreeing, performing.

ENACTIVE, [en-akt'-iv], *adj.* having competence to decree, making an enactment.

ENACTMENT, [en-akt'-ment], *n.* the act of enacting; that which is enacted.

ENACTOR, [en-akt'-er], *n.* one who enacts.

ENACTURE†, [en-ak'-chŏŏer], *n.* enactment.

ENALIOSAURIANS, [en-ā'-li-ō-saw'-ri-anz], *n.(pl.)* (*geol.*) extinct marine saurians of the orders *Sauropterygia* and *Ichthyopterygia*. [Gk. *enalios* marine and *sauros* lizard].

ENALLAGE, [en-al'-aj-i], *n.* the replacement of one grammatical form by another. [Gk. *enallage* change].

ENAMEL (1), [in-am'-el], *n.* a melted glass-like substance applied to the surface of objects, which, when cold, forms a hard, smooth, glossy, opaque surface; a kind of varnish producing an effect similar to this; any smooth, hard glazed covering, *esp.* that covering the crown of a tooth. [OFr. *esmail*].

ENAMEL (2), [in-am'-el], *adj.* made of, coated with enamel; resembling enamel.

ENAMEL (3), **(enamelling, enamelled)**, [in-am'-el], *v.t.* to coat with, or as if with, enamel; to work in enamels; (*fig.*) to adorn with varied and bright colouring.

ENAMELLAR, [in-am'-el-er], *adj.* resembling enamel.

ENAMELLER, [in-am'-el-er], *n.* a worker, designer in enamels.

ENAMELLING, [in-am'-el-ing], *n.* the art of laying on enamel.

ENAMORADO, [en-am'-or-ah'-dō], *n.* one obsessed by love. [Span. *enamorado*].

ENAMOUR, [en-am'-er], *v.t.* (usually *pass.*) to attract deeply, to inspire with love, to captivate. [OFr. *enamourer*].

ENANTHEMA, [en-an-thē'-ma], *n.* (*med.*) an eruption of the mucous membrane. [Gk. *enanthema*].

ENANTHESIS, [en-an-thē'-sis], *n.* an affection of the skin produced by some internal morbidity.

ENANTIOPATHY, [en-an'-ti-op'-ath-i], *n.* (*med.*) allopathy. [Gk. *enantiopathes* of contrary properties].

ENANTIOSIS, [en-an-ti-ō'-sis], *n.* a rhetorical figure in which is said the reverse of what is intended. [Gk. *enantios* opposite].

ENARCHED†, [en-ahcht'], *adj.* (*her.*) in the shape of an arch.

ENARMED†, [en-ahmd'], *adj.* (*her.*) having arms or attributes of a different colour to the body.

ENARRABLE†, [en-a'-rabl], *adj.* able to be narrated.

ENARRATION†, [en'-a-rā'-shun], *n.* a narration.

ENARTHRODIAL, [en'-ahth-rō'-di-al], *adj.* joining by the fitting of a ball into a socket.

ENARTHROSIS, [en'-ahth-rō'-sis], *n.* the articulation of joints by the fitting of a rounded end of bone into a socket. [Gk. *enarthrosis* jointing].

ENASCENT, [en-ās'-ent], *adj.* springing forth; about to be born. [L. *enascens*].

ENATE, [en-āt'], *adj.* growing from, born out of. [L. *enatus*].

ENAVIGATE†, [ē-nav'-ig-āt], *v.t.* to navigate, to steer out or in.

ENCAENIA, [en-sē'-ni-a], *n.(pl.)* commemorative

celebrations held on anniversaries, *esp.* those of foundations, consecrations, etc. [L. *encænia* feast of dedication].

ENCAGE, INCAGE, [en-kāj'], *v.t.* to shut up in a cage, to coop up.

ENCAMP, [en-kamp'], *v.t. and i.* to pitch camp, to take up an encamped position.

ENCAMPMENT, [en-kamp'-ment], *n.* the act of encamping, the place where an army or company is encamped; the camp itself.

ENCANTHIS, [en-kan'-this], *n.* a tumour in the internal corner of the eye. [EN- (1) and Gk. *kanthos* corner of the eye].

ENCAPSULATE, [en-kap'-syōō-lāt], *v.t.* to enclose in a capsule.

ENCARDION†, [en-kah'-di-on], *n.* the heart of a green vegetable. [EN- (1) and Gk. *kardia* heart].

ENCARNALIZE, [en-kah'-nal-īz], *v.t.* to debauch, to bring to sensuality; to embody.

ENCARPUS, [en-kah'-pus], *n.* (*arch.*) a festoon of flowers and fruit on a frieze. [L. *encarpa*].

ENCARPUS

ENCASE, INCASE†, [en-kās'], *v.t.* to put into a case or similar covering; to enclose in armour; to envelop, surround.

ENCASEMENT, [en-kās'-ment], *n.* the act of encasing; the state of being encased; the thing encasing.

ENCASH, [en-kash'], *v.t.* to turn into cash, to obtain ready money for (a draft, etc.).

ENCASHMENT [en-kash'-ment], *n.* the act of cashing.

ENCAUMA, [en-kaw'-ma], *n.* (*med.*) an ulcer of the cornea of the eye; the mark or vesicle produced by a burn. [Gk. *enkaio* I burn in].

ENCAUSTIC (1), [en-kaws'-tik], *n.* the method or process of encaustic painting; a tile so painted.

ENCAUSTIC (2), [en-kaws'-tik], *adj.* burnt in, pertaining to the art of painting with heated wax, or to the art of burning coloured designs into a tile. [Gk. *enkaustikos* burnt in].

ENCAVE, [en-kāv'], *v.t.* to enclose in, or as in, a cave.

ENCEINTE (1), [ah(n)-sant'], *n.* the enclosure surrounded by the main ramparts of a fortified place; the principal fortifications of a place. [Fr. *enceinte*].

ENCEINTE (2), [ah(n)-sant'], *adj.* (of human beings) pregnant. [Fr. *enceinte*].

ENCEPHAL-, *pref.* brain. [Gk. *enkephalos* brain].

ENCEPHALELCOSIS, [en-kef'-al-el-kō'-sis], *n.* ulceration of the brain. [ENCEPHAL and Gk. *elkosis* ulcer].

ENCEPHALGIA, [en'-kef-al'-ji-a], *n.* persistent intense headaches. [ENCEPH(AL) and Gk. *algos* pain].

ENCEPHALIC, [en'-kef-al'-ik], *adj.* (*med.*) relating to the brain. [Gk. *enkephalos* brain].

ENCEPHALITIS, [en'-kef-al-īt'-is], *n.* (*med.*) brain disease; **e. lethargica,** sleeping sickness. [ENCEPHAL and Gk. *itis* denoting inflammation].

ENCEPHALOCELE, [en-kef'-al-ō-sēl'], *n.* a tumour of the brain. [ENCEPHAL and Gk. *kele* tumour].

ENCEPHALOID, [en-kef'-al-oid], *adj.* resembling brain-matter, like the cellular brain-structure of a cancer. [ENCEPHAL and Gk. *oeides* like].

ENCEPHALON, [en-kef'-al-on], *n.* (*med.*) the brain-structure. [Gk. *enkephalos*].

ENCEPHALOTOMY, [en'-kef-al-ot'-om-i], *n.* dissection of the brain, surgical removal of part of the brain. [ENCEPHAL and Gk. *tome* cutting].

ENCEPHALOUS, [en-kef'-al-us], *adj.* (*zool.*) with a head. [Gk. *enkephalos*].

ENCHAFE, [en-chāf'], *v.t.* to chafe with the hands to produce warmth.

ENCHAIN, [en-chān'], *v.t.* to chain, bind with chains; (*fig.*) to enslave (by fascination), captivate. [OFr. *enchainer*].

ENCHAINMENT, [en-chān'-ment], *n.* the act of enchaining, the condition of being enchained.

ENCHAIRED, [en-chāerd'], *adj.* seated in state in a chair.

ENCHANT, [en-chahnt'], *v.t. and i.* to bewitch, influence, bind with a spell or incantation; (*fig.*) to fascinate in the highest degree, captivate; to make incantations. [OFr. *enchanter* from L. *incantare* to sing a charm over].

ENCHANTER, [en-chahnt'-er], *n.* one who enchants.

ENCHANTING, [en-chahnt'-ing], *adj.* delightful, charming, captivating.

ENCHANTINGLY, [en-chahnt'-ing-li], *adv.* in enchanting fashion.

ENCHANTMENT, [en-chahnt'-ment], *n.* the act of enchanting, the condition of being enchanted; a spell, incantation; (*fig.*) charm, ravishment, extraordinary attraction.

ENCHANTRESS, [en-chahnt'-res], *n.* a female enchanter; a delightful woman.

ENCHARAXIS, [en'-ka-rak'-sis], *n.* scarification. [Gk. *enkharaxis*].

ENCHARGE, [en-chahj'], *v.t.* to give in charge, commit to.

ENCHASE, [en-chās'], *v.t.* to set, encase in (usually a jewel in some precious metal); to chase, emboss. [Fr. *enchâsser*].

ENCHEQUERED, [en-chek'-erd], *adj.* chequered.

ENCHIRIDION, [en'-kī-rid'-i-on], *n.* a little book; an anthology of selected passages, a handbook. [Gk. *egkheiridion* handbook].

ENCHISEL, [en-chizl'], *v.t.* to cut with a chisel.

ENCHORIAL, [en-kaw'-ri-al], *adj.* enchoric.

ENCHORIC, [en-kaw'-rik], *adj.* common in a country, popular; **e. characters,** demotic characters, the popular simplified form of Egyptian hieroglyphics. [Gk. *egkhorios* native].

ENCHYMA, [en'-kim-a], *n.* (*med.*) an infusion. [Gk. *egkhuma*].

ENCHYMATOUS, [en-kim'-at-us], *adj.* relating to infusion.

ENCHYMONIA, [en'-kim-ōn'-ya], *n.* (*med.*) a spontaneous effusion of blood from some internal cause. [Gk. *egkhumonia*].

ENCHYMOSIS, [en'-kim-ōs'-is], *n.* the formation of enchymonia.

ENCINCTURE, [en-singk'-chōōer], *n.* a cincture. [EN- (1) and CINCTURE].

ENCINDERED, [en-sin'-derd], *adj.* burnt to a cinder.

ENCIRCLE, INCIRCLE†, [en-surkl'], *v.t.* to stand round or move round in a circle or so as to encompass.

ENCIRCLEMENT, [en-surkl'-ment], *n.* the act of encircling, the state of being encircled.

EN CLAIR, [ah(ng)-klāer'], *adj.* not in cipher. [Fr. *en clair*].

ENCLASP, INCLASP†, [en-klahsp'], *v.t.* to clasp round, to embrace firmly.

ENCLAVE, [en'-klāv], *n.* territory belonging to one country encircled by that of another. [EN-(1) and L. *clavus* a nail].

ENCLAVEMENT, [en-klāv'-ment], *n.* the process of making or condition of being an enclave.

ENCLITIC (1), [en-klit'-ik], *n.* (*gram.*) an enclitic particle.

ENCLITIC (2), [en-klit'-ik], *adj.* (*gram.*) attached to a word as an unaccented suffix. [Gk. *enklitikos*].

ENCLITICAL, [en-klit'-ikl], *adj.* (*gram.*) enclitic.

ENCLITICALLY, [en-klit'-ik-al-i], *adv.* in the manner of an enclitic.

ENCLITICS, [en-klit'-iks], *n.* (*gram.*) the study of enclitic particles.

ENCLOISTER, [en-klois'-ter], *v.t.* to shut up in a cloister, to seclude.

ENCLOSE, INCLOSE, [in-klōz'], *v.t.* to shut in, off; to surround and close in, to shut in a receptacle, to surround, frame; to put in, send along with something else.

ENCLOSER, INCLOSER, [in-klō'-zer], *n.* one who encloses.

ENCLOSURE, [en-klō'-zhur], *n.* the act of enclosing, state of being enclosed; the fencing in of common land for private ownership, land so fenced in; an open space enclosed by a barrier; something enclosed with a letter or package. [OFr. *enclos*].

ENCLOTHE, [en-klōTH'], *v.t.* to clothe.

ENCLOUDED, [en-klow'-did], *adj.* covered with clouds.

ENCOFFIN, [en-kof'-in], *v.t.* to seal in a coffin.

ENCOLLAR, [en-kol'-er], *v.t.* to encircle with a collar.

ENCOLPION, [en-kol'-pi-on], *n.* a pectoral cross. [Gk. *enkolpion*].

ENCOMIAST, [en-kō'-mi-ast], *n.* the writer or speaker of an encomium. [Gk. *enkomiastes*].

ENCOMIASTIC, [en-kō'-mi-as'-tik], *adj.* relating to an encomium.

ENCOMIASTICAL, [en-kō'-mi-as'-tikl], *adj.* encomiastic.

ENCOMIASTICALLY, [en-kō'-mi-as'-tik-al-i], *adv.* in encomiastic fashion.

ENCOMIUM, (*pl.* **encomiums**), [en-kō'-mium], *n.* a panegyric, a ceremonious eulogy. [Gk. *enkomion*].

ENCOMPASS, [en-kum'-pas], *v.t.* to surround, go round, encircle, to enclose on every side.

ENCOMPASSMENT, [en-kum'-pas-ment], *n.* act of encompassing, the condition of being encompassed.

ENCOPE, [en'-kop-i], *n.* (*med.*) an incision with a sharp instrument. [EN-(1) and Gk. *kope* a cutting].

ENCORE (**1**), [on'-kaw(r)'], *n.* a call of applause, a demand for the repetition of some admired performance; the repetition itself, or an additional item performed in response to applause.

ENCORE (**2**), [on'-kaw(r)'], *v.t. and i.* to demand the repetition of (a performance); to call "encore" in appreciation.

ENCORE (**3**), [on'-kaw(r)], *int.* again! once more! [Fr. *encore* again].

ENCOUNTER (**1**), [en-kown'-ter], *n.* an unexpected meeting; a hostile meeting, a conflict.

ENCOUNTER (**2**), [en-kown'-ter], *v.t.* to meet, *esp.* by chance or unexpectedly; to meet in conflict, battle; to come up against, to meet as an opponent or source of difficulty. [OFr. *encontrer* to meet from LL. *incontrare*].

ENCOURAGE, [en-ku'-rij], *v.t.* to inspire with courage, give confidence to, to foster, cause to arise, help to grow or spread. [Fr. *encourager*].

ENCOURAGEMENT, [en-ku'-rij-ment], *n.* the act of encouraging, that which encourages; a stimulus, an exhortation to be confident.

ENCOURAGER, [en-ku'-rij-er], *n.* one who encourages.

ENCOURAGING, [en-ku'-rij-ing], *adj.* offering encouragement, inspiring confidence.

ENCOURAGINGLY, [en-ku'-rij-ing-li], *adv.* in an encouraging fashion.

ENCRADLE, [en-krādl'], *v.t.* to put in a cradle.

ENCRIMSON, [en-krim'-zon], *v.t.* to colour crimson, to stain with crimson, to make wholly crimson.

ENCRINAL, [en-krīn'-al], *adj.* encrinic.

ENCRINIC, [en-krin'-ik], *adj.* pertaining to, containing, encrinites.

ENCRINITAL, [en-krin'-īt-al], *adj.* encrinic.

ENCRINITE, [en'-krin-īt], *n.* a fossil crinoid. [EN- (1) and Gk. *krinon* lily].

ENCRINITE

ENCRISPED, [en-krispt'], *adj.* thickly curled.

ENCROACH, [en-krōch'], *v.i.* (with *on* or *upon*) to go beyond one's just rights and invade the territory or privileges of another, to invade or go where one has no right, to usurp by slow degrees. [OFr. *encrocher* to seize].

ENCROACHER, [en-krō'-cher], *n.* a person or thing that encroaches.

ENCROACHINGLY, [en-krō'-ching-li], *adv.* by encroachment.

ENCROACHMENT, [en-krōch'-ment], *n.* the act of encroaching; that seized by encroaching; (*leg.*) taking more than is one's due. [OFr. *encrochement*].

ENCRUST, **INCRUST**, [in-krust'], *v.t.* to cover with or as with a crust, to become like a crust.

ENCRUSTMENT, [en-krust'-ment], *n.* the act of encrusting.

ENCUMBER, **INCUMBER**†, [in-kumb'-er], *v.t.* to cumber up, obstruct with unnecessary matter, to hamper, burden, impede. [Fr. *encombrer*].

ENCUMBRANCE, **INCUMBRANCE**†, [in-kum'-brans], *n.* that which encumbers; (*leg.*) a charge, mortgage upon property, a dependent person. [OFr. *encombrance*].

ENCUMBRANCER, [en-kum'-brans-er], *n.* (*leg.*) a person having a legal claim on an estate.

ENCURLED, [en-kurld'], *adj.* curled around.

ENCYCLIC (**1**), [en-sī'-klik], *n.* an encyclical. [Gk. *enkuklikos*].

ENCYCLIC (**2**), [en-sī'-klik], *adj.* encyclical.

ENCYCLICAL (**1**), [en-sik'-lik-al], *n.* a papal letter issued to the whole Roman Church. [Gk. *enkuklikos* in a circle].

ENCYCLICAL (**2**), [en-sik'-lik-al], *adj.* pertaining to encyclicals.

ENCYCLOPEDIA, **ENCYCLOPAEDIA**, [en-sī'-klō-pē'-di-a], *n.* a complete classified compendium of all knowledge or of some particular subject. [EN- (1) and Gk. *kuklos* circle and *paideia* education].

ENCYCLOPEDIACAL, **ENCYCLOPAEDIACAL**, [en-sī'-klō-pē'-di-akl], *adj.* encyclopedic.

ENCYCLOPEDIAN, [en-sī'-klō-pē'-di-an], *adj.* including or covering the whole field of learning.

ENCYCLOPEDIC, **ENCYCLOPAEDIC**, [en-sī'-klō-pē'-dik], *adj.* covering the whole field of knowledge or of a particular subject.

ENCYCLOPEDICAL, **ENCYCLOPAEDICAL**, [en-sī'-klō-pē'-dikl], *adj.* encyclopedic.

ENCYCLOPEDISM, **ENCYCLOPAEDISM**, [en-sī'-klō-pē'-dizm], *n.* the movement centred round Diderot and the French *Encyclopédie*; comprehensive knowledge.

ENCYCLOPEDIST, **ENCYCLOPAEDIST**, [en-sī'-klō-pē'-dist], *n.* the compiler of an encyclopedia; (*specif.*) one of the compilers of the French *Encyclopédie*.

ENCYSTED, [en-sis'-tid], *adj.* enclosed in a cyst.

ENCYSTIS, [en-sis'-tis], *n.* a collection of fluid matter in a cyst.

END (**1**), [end], *n.* the conclusion, finish, final point or part of a thing, extreme point, ultimate state, cessation, limit, close, last remaining part or thing, final part of a period of time; (*philos.*) the final purpose towards which will and action aim; (*fig.*) death; (*slang*) buttocks; **bitter e.**, conclusion, however unpleasant; **at a loose e.**, with nothing special to do; **to make ends meet**, to make do with a bare sufficiency; **wrong e. of the stick**, a mistake caused by confusing of opposites; **e. play**, the technique of play in the last stages of a game of chess. [OE. *ende*].

END (**2**), [end], *v.t. and i.* to finish, to bring to an end, to complete, to discontinue; to come to an end, to reach a termination, to result in, to conclude, to die. [OE. *endian*].

END-ALL, [end'-awl'], *n.* final aim, object.

ENDAMAGE, [en-dam'-ij], *v.t.* to damage, do injury to.

ENDAMAGEMENT, [en-dam'-ij-ment], *n.* damage.

ENDANGER, [en-dān'-jer], *v.t.* to expose to danger.

ENDANGERMENT, [en-dān'-jer-ment], *n.* the act of endangering; the state of being endangered.

ENDEAR, [en-dēer'], *v.t.* to make dear, to bind by ties of affection.

ENDEAREDNESS, [en-dēerd'-nes], *n.* the state of being endeared.

ENDEARING, [en-dēer'-ing], *adv.* gaining the affections.

ENDEARINGLY, [en-dēer'-ing-li], *adv.* in an endearing fashion.

ENDEARMENT, [en-dēer'-ment], *n.* the act of endearing; the state of being endeared; affection; a caress.

ENDEAVOUR (**1**), [en-dev'-er], *n.* an attempt to attain an object.

ENDEAVOUR (**2**), [en-dev'-er], *v.i.* to try, to make an attempt, to accomplish something. [EN- (1) and Fr. *devoir* duty].

ENDEAVOURER, [en-dev'-er-er], *n.* one who endeavours.

ENDECAGON, [en-dek'-ag-on], *n.* a plane figure having eleven sides and angles. [Gk. *hendeka* eleven and *gonia* angle].

ENDECAPHYLLOUS, [en'-dek-af'-il-us], *adj.* (*bot.*) having a compound leaf of eleven leaflets. [Gk. *hendeka* eleven and *phullon* leaf].

ENDEICTIC, [en-dīk'-tik], *adj.* exhibiting. [Gk. *endeiktikos*].

ENDEIXIS, [en-dīk'-sis], *n.* (*med.*) a symptom indicating the suitable remedy. [Gk. *endeixis*].

ENDEMIC (**1**), [en-dem'-ik], *n.* an endemic disease.

ENDEMIC (**2**), [en-dem'-ik], *adj.* (*med.*) local, affecting or usually found in one district or class; (*zool.*, *bot.*) peculiar to, or native to, a certain region. [EN- (1) and Gk. *demos* people].

ENDEMICAL, [en-dem'-ikl], *adj.* endemic.

ENDEMICALLY, [en-dem'-ik-al-i], *adv.* in endemic fashion.

ENDEMICITY, [en'-dem-is'-it-i], *n.* the quality of being endemic.

ENDEMIOLOGY, [en-dem'-i-ol'-oj-i], *n.* the medical science dealing with endemic diseases. [ENDEMIC and Gk. *logos* speech].

ENDENIZE†, [en-den'-īz], *v.t.* to naturalize.

ENDENIZEN, **INDENIZEN**†, [en-den'-izn], *v.t.* to naturalize. [EN- (1) and DENIZEN (1)].

ENDER, [end'-er], *n.* that which ends.

ENDERMATIC, [en-der-mat'-ik], *adj.* endermic.

ENDERMIC, [en-durm'-ik], *adj.* (*med.*) acting through the skin; applied to the skin after a blister. [EN- (1) and Gk. *derma* skin].

ENDING, [end′-ing], *n.* termination, conclusion; death; (*gram.*) inflexional suffix.
ENDIRON, see ANDIRON.
ENDIVE, [en′-div], *n.* a species of chicory, *Cichorium Endivia*, much used as a salad. [Fr. *endive*].
ENDLESS, [end′-les], *adj.* without end, everlasting; unlimited, infinite; (*coll.*) excessively long, interminable; **e. chain**, (*mech.*) a chain in which the ends are joined, and which revolves continuously over pulleys, etc.
ENDLESSLY, [end′-les-li], *adv.* so as to be endless, unceasingly.
ENDLESSNESS, [end′-les-nes], *n.* the quality of being endless.
ENDLONG, [end′-long′], *adv.* lengthwise, from end to end; on end, vertically. [ME. *endelong*].
ENDMOST, [end′-mōst], *adj.* farthest; placed at the end.
ENDO-, *pref.* within. [Gk. *endon* within].
ENDOCARDIAL, [en′-dō-kah′-di-al], *adj.* relating to the endocardium.
ENDOCARDITIS, [en′-dō-kah-dī′-tis], *n.* inflammation of the endocardium. [ENDOCARD(IUM) and Gk. *-itis* denoting inflammation].
ENDOCARDIUM, [en′-dō-kah′-di-um], *n.* (*anat.*) a membrane which lines the internal surface of the heart. [ENDO and Gk. *kardia* heart].
ENDOCARP, [en′-dō-kahp′], *n.* (*bot.*) inner layer of the lining of a seed-vessel. [ENDO and Gk. *karpos* fruit].
ENDOCHROME, [en′-dō-krōm], *n.* colouring matter in plants, *esp.* when other than green. [ENDO and CHROME].
ENDOCRINE (1), [en′-dō-krīn], *n.* an endocrine gland.
ENDOCRINE (2), [en′-dō-krīn], *adj.* (*anat.*) (of certain glands) ductless, secreting internally; (of secretions) secreted internally. [ENDO and Gk. *krino* I separate].
ENDOCTRINE, [en-dok′-trin], *v.t.* to train, to teach.
ENDOCYST, [en′-dō-sist], *n.* (*zool.*) the inner membrane of a polyzoon.
ENDODERM, [en′-dō-durm], *n.* (*anat.*, *biol.*) the inner lining of the alimentary canal, the inner germ-layer of an embryo; (*bot.*) the innermost layer of the cortex. [ENDO and Gk. *derma* skin].
ENDODERMIC, [en′-dō-durm′-ik], *adj.* relating to the endoderm.
ENDODONTITIS, [en′-dō-don-tī′-tis], *n.* (*med.*) inflammation of the internal membrane of the teeth. [ENDO, Gk. *odous odontos* tooth and *-itis* denoting inflammation].
ENDOGAMOUS, [en-dog′-am-us], *adj.* pertaining to endogamy.
ENDOGAMY, [en-dog′-a-mi], *n.* the restriction of marriage to members of the same tribe. [ENDO and Gk. *gamos* marriage].
ENDOGASTRITIS, [en′-dō-gas-trī′-tis], *n.* (*med.*) inflammation of the internal membrane of the stomach.
ENDOGEN, [en′-dō-jen], *n.* (*bot.*) a plant, such as a palm, which is supposed to grow from within and in which the stem cannot increase in thickness when the outside becomes hard. [ENDO and Gk. *genes* producing].
ENDOGENOUS, [en-doj′-en-us], *adj.* relating to endogens; growing from within, arising in the interior.
ENDOLYMPH, [en′-dō-limf], *n.* the fluid in the labyrinth of the ear. [ENDO and LYMPH].
ENDOMORPH, [en′-dō-mawf], *n.* (*min.*) a crystal of one mineral enclosed in another. [ENDO and Gk. *morphe* shape].
ENDOPARASITE, [en′-dō-pa′-ras-īt], *n.* an internal parasite.
ENDOPHAGY, [en-dof′-aj-i], *n.* cannibalism among members of the same tribe. [ENDO and Gk. *phago* I eat].
ENDOPHLOEUM, [en′-dō-flē′-um], *n.* (*bot.*) the inner bark of a tree. [ENDO and Gk. *phloios* bark].
ENDOPHYLLOUS, [en-dof′-il-us], *adj.* (*bot.*) (of leaves) evolved from within a sheath. [ENDO and Gk. *phullon* a leaf].
ENDOPLASM, [en′-dō-plazm], *n.* the inner layer of protoplasm.
ENDOPLAST, [en′-dō-plast], *n.* (*biol.*) a nucleated cell embedded in the protoplasm of the soft tissue of *Infusoria*. [ENDO and Gk. *plastos* formed].
ENDOPLEURA, [en′-dō-ploo′-ra], *n.* (*bot.*) the inner covering of a seed. [ENDO and Gk. *pleura* side].
ENDORHIZA, [en′-dō-rī′-za], *n.* (*bot.*) the enclosed radicle of the embryo of certain plants which does not increase in size, but develops rootlets from its sides or extremity. [ENDO and Gk. *rhiza* root].
ENDORHIZAL, [en′-dō-rīz′-al], *adj.* relating to the endorhiza.
ENDORSABLE, INDORSABLE, [in-daws′-abl], *adj.* able to be endorsed.
ENDORSE, INDORSE, [in-daws′], *v.t.* to write on the back of (a document), *esp.* to sign one's name on the back of a cheque, bill of exchange, etc., by way of ratification; (*fig.*) to confirm, to approve of, to sanction; (*U.S.*) to praise in an advertisement; to write on (a driving licence) so as to show that the owner has been convicted of a motoring offence. [MedL. *indorsare*].
ENDORSEE, INDORSEE, [en′-daw-sē′], *n.* the person for whom a document is endorsed.
ENDORSEMENT, INDORSEMENT, [en-daws′-ment], *n.* the art of endorsing, that which is written on the back of a document; (*fig.*) support, confirmation.
ENDORSER, INDORSER, [en-daws′-er], *n.* one who endorses.
ENDOSARC, [en′-dō-sahk′], *n.* endoplasm. [ENDO and Gk. *sarx sarkos* flesh].
ENDOSCOPE, [en′-dō-skōp′], *n.* an optical instrument for examining internal organs. [ENDO and Gk. *skopos* viewing].
ENDOSIS, [en-dō′-sis], *n.* the temporary cessation or subsidence of a fever. [Gk. *endosis*].
ENDOSKELETON, [en′-dō-skel′-it-on], *n.* the internal bony structure of vertebrates.
ENDOSMOMETER, [en′-dos-mom′-it-er], *n.* an instrument for measuring the force of endosmosmic action. [ENDO, Gk. *osmos* pushing and METER].
ENDOSMOSIS, [en′-dos-mō′-sis], *n.* the transmission of liquids or gases through a membranous or porous partition from the exterior to the interior. [ENDO and Gk. *osmos* pushing].
ENDOSMOSMIC, [en′-dos-mos′-mik], *adj.* endosmotic.
ENDOSMOTIC, [en′-dos-mot′-ik], *adj.* pertaining to endosmosis.
ENDOSPERM, [en′-dō-spurm], *n.* the nutritive tissue surrounding the embryo in many seeds.
ENDOSPERMIC, [en′-dō-spurm′-ik], *adj.* containing or relating to endosperm.
ENDOSPORE, [en′-dō-spaw(r)′], *n.* the inner coat of a spore.
ENDOSTEUM, [en-dos′-tē-um], *n.* the internal periosteum. [ENDO and Gk. *osteon* bone].
ENDOSTOME, [en′-dos-tōm], *n.* (*bot.*) the passage through the inner integument of a seed. [ENDO and Gk. *stoma* mouth].
ENDOTHELIUM, [en′-dō-thē′-li-um], *n.* (*anat.*) the lining of blood-vessels. [ENDO and Gk. *thele* nipple].
ENDOTHERMIC, [en′-dō-thurm′-ik], *adj.* producing heat during decomposition.
ENDOW, [en-dow′], *v.t.* to bestow money or property upon, *esp.* so as to provide continued financial support for (an institution, person, etc.); to provide with (gift, talent, quality, etc.). [EN- (1) and Fr. *douer* to bestow].
ENDOWER, [en-dow′-er], *n.* one who endows.
ENDOWMENT, [en-dow′-ment], *n.* the act of endowing, the state of being endowed; property or money given to endow a person or institution; natural talents or mental quality; **e. policy**, an insurance policy by which a fixed sum of money is payable at a certain date or upon the previous death of the holder.
ENDUE, INDUE†, [in-dyōō′], *v.t.* to invest or endow with, to bestow upon; (*archaic*) to put on, to clothe. [OFr. *enduire*].
ENDUEMENT†, [en-dew′-ment], *n.* that which is put on; endowment.
ENDURABLE, [en-dyōōer′-abl], *adj.* able to be endured.
ENDURABLENESS, [en-dyōōer′-abl-nes], *n.* the quality of being endurable.
ENDURABLY, [en-dyōōer′-ab-li], *adv.* in enduring fashion.
ENDURANCE, [en-dyōōer′-rants], *n.* the act of enduring, the power of enduring, fortitude.
ENDURE, [en-dyōōer′], *v.t. and i.* to bear with fortitude, to support without yielding, sinking or breaking up; to tolerate, undergo, suffer; to continue, to remain; to suffer without succumbing, to bear up under hardship, etc. [L. *indurare* to make hard].
ENDURING, [en-dyōōer′-ing], *adj.* permanent, long-lasting.

ENDURINGLY, [en-dyōōer'-ing-li], *adv.* in an enduring manner.
ENDURINGNESS, [en-dyōōer'-ing-nes], *n.* the quality of enduring.
ENDWAYS, [end'-wāz], *adv.* on end, with the end facing front.
ENDWISE, [end'-wīz], *adv.* endways.
ENECIA, [en-ē'-shi-a], *n.* (*med.*) a continued fever. [Gk. *enekes* long continued].
ENEID, see AENEID.
ENEMA, [en'-im-a], *n.* (*med.*) a liquid injected into the rectum. [Gk. *enema*].
ENEMY (1), [en'-em-i], *n.* a foe, antagonist, one who hates or endeavours to harm another as much as possible; a nation at war with another; the opposing armed forces or a section of them; a person strongly opposed to anything, an opponent; a force or factor harmful to another. [OFr. *enemi* from L. *inimicus* hostile].
ENEMY (2), [en'-em-i], *adj.* pertaining to an enemy, hostile.
ENERGETIC, [en'-er-jet'-ik], *adj.* full of energy, exhibiting great vigour, extremely active, forceful. [Gk. *energetikos*].
ENERGETICAL, [en'-er-jet'-ik-al], *adj.* energetic.
ENERGETICALLY, [en'-er-jet'-ik-a-li], *adv.* in an energetic fashion.
ENERGETICALNESS, [en'-er-jet'-ik-al-nes], *n.* the state of being energetic.
ENERGETICS, [en'-er-jet'-iks], *n.*(*pl.*) the science concerned with the principles and nature of physical energy.
ENERGIC, [en-ur'-jik], *adj.* energetic.
ENERGICO, [en-ur'-jik-ō], *adv.* (*mus.*) with energy and power, vigorously.
ENERGIZE, [en'-er-jīz], *v.t. and i.* to rouse to activity, to fill with energy, to make vigorous; to act with force and effect.
ENERGIZER, [en'-er-jīz-er], *n.* a person or thing that imparts energy.
ENERGUMEN, [en'-er-gew'-men], *n.* a person possessed of an extraordinary power, a fanatic. [Gk. *energoumenos* working].
ENERGY, [en'-er-ji], *n.* power, force which is able to effect change; the capacity to cause action or motion, inherent ability or strength; vigour, drive; (*mech.*) capacity to do effective work; (*phys.*) **conservation of e.**, the law expressing the belief that the capacity for energy in the material world remains constant regardless of the forms it takes. [Gk. *energeia* efficiency].
ENERVATE, [en'-er-vāt], *v.t.* to deprive of strength in any form, to sap the vigour of. [L. *enervare*].
ENERVATION, [en'-er-vā'-shun], *n.* the act of enervating; the state of being enervated.
ENERVATIVE, [en'-er-vā'-tiv], *adj.* enervating.
ENFACE, [en-fās'], *v.t.* to write or sign on the face of a bill or document.
ENFAMISH, [en-fam'-ish], *v.t.* to famish, to starve.
ENFEEBLE, [en-fēbl'], *v.t.* to render feeble. [OFr. *enfeblir*].
ENFEEBLEMENT, [en-fēbl'-ment], *n.* the act of enfeebling; the state of being enfeebled.
ENFEEBLER, [en-fē'-bler], *n.* a person or thing that enfeebles.
ENFEOFF, [en-fēf'], *v.t.* to invest with the fee of an estate, to give freehold property in fee simple or tail. [OFr. *enfeffer*].
ENFEOFFMENT, [en-fēf'-ment], *n.* the act of enfeoffing; the deed authorizing the investment with the fee of an estate.
ENFETTER, [en-fet'-er], *v.t.* to fetter.
ENFILADE (1), [en'-fil-ād'], *n.* (*milit.*) use of fire-power upon the enemy from a flank.
ENFILADE (2), [en'-fil-ād'], *v.t.* (*milit.*) to fire from a flank across the line of the enemy's advance or retreat. [~Fr. *enfiler*].
ENFOLD, INFOLD†, [en-fōld'], *v.t.* to envelop, to embrace, fold round.
ENFORCE, [en-faws'], *v.t. and i.* to compel obedience, to subdue opposition by force, to cause to take effect by forms of authority; to attempt by force. [OFr. *enforcer*].
ENFORCEABLE, [en-faws'-abl], *adj.* capable of being enforced.
ENFORCEDLY, [en-faws'-id-li], *adv.* by means of force.
ENFORCEMENT, [en-faws'-ment], *n.* the act of enforcing; the condition of being enforced; compulsion.
ENFORCER, [en-faws'-er], *n.* a person who enforces.
ENFOREST, [en-fo'-rist], *v.t.* to cover with a forest.
ENFORM, [en-fawm'], *v.t.* to form, mould, fashion, to give a form to.
ENFRAME, [en-frām'], *v.t.* to put a frame round, to put into a frame.
ENFRANCHISE, [en-fran'-chīz], *v.t.* to grant the right to vote; to release, to set free, emancipate; to grant the privileges of a free man; to convert into freehold. [OFr. *enfranchir*].
ENFRANCHISEMENT, [en-fran'-chiz-ment], *n.* the act of enfranchising; the condition of being enfranchised.
ENFRANCHISER, [en-fran'-chīz-er], *n.* a person who enfranchises.
ENGAGE, [en-gāj'], *v.t.* to bind by pledge or promise, to agree to preliminary conditions in a mutual contract, *esp.* to bind (oneself) to marry; to hire, to reserve for occupation or use; to occupy, use, employ; to secure, attach; *v.i.* to commence hostilities, to come to grips; to make a promise, to pledge oneself; to undertake; to take part in an enterprise. [Fr. *engager*].
ENGAGED, [en-gājd'], *adj.* betrothed, promised; employed, reserved, hired, in use; (*arch.*) **e. column**, a column half sunk in a wall.
ENGAGEDLY, [en-gāj'-id-li], *adv.* with charm; with attachment.
ENGAGEDNESS, [en-gāj'-id-nes], *n.* the state of being engaged.
ENGAGEMENT, [en-gāj'-ment], *n.* the act of engaging; the state of being engaged; that which engages; obligation, mutual arrangement; betrothal; occupation, employment, utilization; encounter between armed forces, battle.
ENGAGER, [en-gāj'-er], *n.* a person who enters into an engagement.
ENGAGING, [en-gāj'-ing], *n.* tending to attract the attention or the affections, pleasing.
ENGAGINGLY, [en-gāj'-ing-li], *adv.* in an engaging fashion.
ENGARLAND, [en-gah'-land], *v.t.* to decorate with garlands.
ENGARRISON, [en-ga'-ris-on], *v.t.* to provide with a garrison.
ENGASTRIMUTH, [en-gas'-trim-uth], *n.* a ventriloquist. [EN (1), Gk. *gaster* belly and *muthos* speech].
ENGENDER, [en-jen'-der], *v.t.* to create between the sexes, to breed; to stir up, rouse; to produce. [Fr. *engendrer* from L. *ingenerare* to produce].
ENGENDERER, [en-jen'-der-er], *n.* a person or object that engenders.
ENGILD, [en-gild'], *v.t.* to gild.
ENGINE, [en'-jin], *n.* one of many kinds of apparatus for converting sources of natural power such as heat, gas, steam, into mechanical energy, *esp.* a steam-engine, a locomotive; an instrument of war, a device. [L. *ingenium* character, capacity].
ENGINE-DRIVER, [en'-jin-drī'-ver], *n.* a person who controls a locomotive on a railway.
ENGINEER (1), [en'-jin-ēer'], *n.* an expert in engineering, a person trained in the scientific principles and possessing practical experience of constructing or supervising all kinds of engines and machines; a supervisor of the machinery in a ship; a member of a military corps that constructs fortifications, etc. [OFr. *engineor* from L. *ingeniator* a skilled man].
ENGINEER (2), [en'-jin-ēer'], *v.t. and i.* to direct and superintend the construction of anything as an engineer; to devise and carry out an intricate scheme or plan of action; to be engaged in engineering work.
ENGINEERING, [en'-jin-ēer'-ing], *n.* the science concerned with the principles, design, manufacture, and control of all types of engines and mechanical appliances; the profession of an engineer; **civil e.**, the science of designing and constructing bridges, railways, canals, roads, etc.; **military e.**, the construction of fortifications and the maintenance of lines of communication.
ENGINE-MAN, [en'-jin-man'], *n.* a man who controls an engine.
ENGINERY†, [en'-jin-er-i], *n.* engines in general; implements of war.
ENGINE-TURNING, [en'-jin-turn'-ing], *n.* a mode of metal engraving by machinery.
ENGIRD, [en-gurd'], *v.t.* to encircle with or like a girdle.
ENGIRDLE, [en-gurdl'], *v.t.* to surround with or as a girdle.
ENGLAND, [ing'-gland], *n.* the area of Great Britain not including Scotland and Wales; the British nation or country; formerly the land of the Angles as

ō (bone), ī (fine), ōō (food), ŏŏ (put), u (up), th (*th*ink), TH (*th*at), zh (azure), † = obsolete, ~ = related to.

distinguished from that of the Saxons. [OE. *Engla land* the land of the Angles].
ENGLANTE, englanté, [ah(ng)-glahn'-tā], *adj.* (*her.*) depicted with acorns. [Fr. *englanté*].

ENGLANTE

ENGLISH (1), [ing'-glish], *n.* the people of England; their language.
ENGLISH (2), [ing'-glish], *adj.* of or relating to England, its native inhabitants or their language. [OE. *englisc*].
ENGLISH (3), [ing'-glish], *v.t.* to translate into the English language.
ENGLISHMAN, [ing'-glish-man], *n.* a native of England.
ENGLISHRY, [ing'-glish-ri], *n.* the state of being English; people of English descent, particularly those living in Ireland.
ENGLOOM, [en-gloo͞m'], *v.t.* to make gloomy.
ENGLUT, (englutting, englutted), [en-glut'], *v.t.* to swallow up; to fill; to glut.
ENGORGE, [en-gawj'], *v.t.* to swallow with greediness, to eat with voracity. [Fr. *engorger*].
ENGORGEMENT, [en-gawj'-ment], *n.* the act of gorging; the state of being gorged, *esp.* of an organ of the body.
ENGOULED, [en-goo͝ld'], *adj.* (*her.*) describing crosses and other ordinaries when their extremities enter the mouths of animals. [Fr. *engouler* to swallow up].

ENGOULED

ENGRAFT, INGRAFT†, [in-grahft'], *v.t.* to insert, as a tree is grafted; (*fig.*) to introduce.
ENGRAIL, [en-grāl'], *v.t.* and *i.* (*her.*) to provide with an edge in the form of a series of small semicircles, to indent an edge. [OFr. *engresler*].
ENGRAILMENT, [en-grāl'-ment], *n.* (*her.*) the ring of dots or semicircles round the edges of a medal.
ENGRAIN, INGRAIN†, [in-grān'], *v.t.* to dye in the grain, to saturate.
ENGRAINED, [en-grānd'], *adj.* thorough, having a permanent tendency, completely impregnated or saturated.
ENGRASP, [en-grahsp'], *v.t.* to catch hold of in a grasp.
ENGRAVE, [en-grāv'], *v.t.* to cut lines in stone, metal or wood with a graver; to reproduce a pattern or picture by taking impressions from an inked metal plate in which the pattern or picture has been cut or etched in lines. [EN- (1) and GRAVE (2)].
ENGRAVEMENT, [en-grāv'-ment], *n.* the act of engraving; engraved work.
ENGRAVER, [en-grāv'-er], *n.* a person who engraves; a cutter of letters, figures or pictures in stone, metal, or wood.
ENGRAVERY, [en-grāv'-er-i], *n.* the work of an engraver.
ENGRAVING, [en-grāv'-ing], *n.* the art of an engraver; the art of cutting or etching patterns or pictures in a hard medium and taking impressions from the inked surface; a picture so made.
ENGROSS, INGROSS, [en-grōs'], *v.t.* to take up exclusively, monopolize; to corner the market in a product by buying up all available supplies in order to force up its price artificially; (*leg.*) to copy in clear writing for record purposes; to express formally in writing. [AFr. *engrosser*].
ENGROSSER, [en-grōs'-er], *n.* he who or that which exclusively occupies or monopolizes the whole; (*leg.*) one who engrosses documents.
ENGROSSING (1), [en-grōs'-ing], *n.* (*leg.*) a copy in legible characters.
ENGROSSING (2), [en-grōs'-ing], *adj.* all-absorbing, exclusively engaging the attention.
ENGROSSMENT, [en-grōs'-ment], *n.* the act of engrossing; (*leg.*) that which has been engrossed; the state of being engrossed.
ENGUARD, [en-gahd'], *v.t.* to guard.
ENGUICHE, enguiché, [ah(ng)-gē'-shā], *adj.* (*her.*) denoting a hunting-horn, when the rim about its mouth is a different colour from the rest. [OFr. *enguiché*].
ENGULF, INGULF†, [in-gulf'], *v.t.* to swallow up to overwhelm.
ENGULFMENT, INGULFMENT†, [in-gulf'-ment], *n.* the process of swallowing up; the state of being engulfed.
ENHANCE, [en-hahnts'], *v.t.* to raise, to advance; to increase, to heighten, to exaggerate. [OFr. *enhauncer*].
ENHANCED, [en-hahnst'], *adj.* (*her.*) denoting bearings raised higher on the field.
ENHANCEMENT, [en-hahnts'-ment], *n.* act of enhancing; the state of being enhanced.
ENHANCER, [en-hahnts'-er], *n.* a person who enhances.
ENHARBOUR†, [en-hah'-ber], *v.t.* to dwell in or inhabit.
ENHARDEN, [en-hahd'-en], *v.t.* to harden.
ENHARMONIC (1), [en'-hah-mon'-ik], *n.* (*mus.*) an interval smaller than a semitone.
ENHARMONIC (2), [en'-hah-mon'-ik], *adj.* (*mus.*) composed of enharmonic intervals.
ENHARMONICALLY, [en'-hah-mon'-ik-a-li], *adv.* in an enharmonic way; by means of enharmonic intonation.
ENHARMONION†, [en'-hah-mō'-ni-on], *n.* a part song; enharmonic music.
ENHEARTEN, [en-haht'-en], *v.t.* to give heart to, encourage.
ENHYDRIC, [en-hī'-drik], *adj.* (*min.*) enhydrous.
ENHYDRITE, [en-hī'-drīt], *n.* (*min.*) a mineral containing water.
ENHYDROUS, [en-hī'-drus], *adj.* (*min.*) containing or enclosing drops of water. [EN- (1) and HYDROUS].
ENIGMA, [en-ig'-ma], *n.* a puzzle, riddle; (*fig.*) a puzzling situation or circumstance; one who is difficult to understand. [Gk. *ainigma*].
ENIGMATIC, [en'-ig-mat'-ik], *adj.* pertaining to, or containing, an enigma; puzzling, mysterious.
ENIGMATICAL, [en'-ig-mat'-ik-al], *adj.* enigmatic.
ENIGMATICALLY, [en'-ig-mat'-ik-a-li], *adv.* in an enigmatic way.
ENIGMATIST, [en-ig'-mat-ist], *n.* a coiner of enigmas and puzzles.
ENIGMATIZE, [en-ig'-mat-īz], *v.t.* to devise enigmas or riddles.
ENIGMATOGRAPHY, [en'-ig-mat-og'-ra-fi], *n.* the art of making enigmas or solving them. [ENIGMA and Gk. *graphia* writing].
ENIGMATOLOGY, [en'-ig-mat-ol'-o-ji], *n.* enigmatography. [ENIGMA and Gk. *logos* speech].
ENISLE, [in-īl'], *v.t.* to make into or set on an island; (*fig.*) to set apart. [EN (1) and ISLE].
ENJAIL, [in-jāl'], *v.t.* to imprison.
ENJAMBEMENT, [en-jam'-ment], *n.* (*pros.*) the carrying over of a sentence or clause from one line of verse to the next.
ENJOIN, [en-join'], *v.t.* to lay down as a rule to be strictly carried out; to give orders or instructions for. [Fr. *enjoindre*].
ENJOINER, [en-join'-er], *n.* a person who enjoins.
ENJOINMENT, [en-join'-ment], *n.* a strict and urgent command.
ENJOY, [en-joi'], *v.t.* to use, possess or experience with joy; to have a right to the use of; (*archaic*) to have sexual relations with; **to e. oneself,** to find delight in what one is doing or the things or persons about one. [OFr. *enjoier*].
ENJOYABLE, [en-joi'-abl], *adj.* affording enjoyment.
ENJOYABLENESS, [en-joi'-abl-nes], *n.* the quality of being enjoyable.
ENJOYABLY, [en-joi'-ab-li], *adv.* in an enjoyable way.
ENJOYER, [en-joi'-er], *n.* a person who enjoys.
ENJOYMENT, [en-joi'-ment], *n.* delight, pleasure.
ENKERNEL, [en-kurn'-el], *v.t.* to form into kernels; to enclose in a kernel.
ENKINDLE, [en-kindl'], *v.t.* to set alight or on fire; (*fig.*) to put vigour or enthusiasm into.
ENLACE, INLACE†, [in-lās'], *v.t.* to embrace or enfold.
ENLACEMENT, [en-lās'-ment], *n.* the act of enlacing; the condition of being enlaced.
ENLARD, [en-lahd'], *v.t.* to lard; to cover with lard or grease.
ENLARGE, [en-larj'], *v.t.* to make bigger or more capacious, to add to; (*phot.*) to make a print larger than the negative of; to become bigger, more extensive, or capacious; **to e. upon,** to discuss very fully.
ENLARGEDLY, [en-lahj'-id-li], *adv.* diffusely; with enlargement.
ENLARGEDNESS, [en-lahj'-id-nes], *n.* the quality of being enlarged.

ENLARGEMENT, [en-lahj'-ment], *n.* the action of making larger, the condition of being larger; (*phot.*) a print larger than its negative.

ENLARGER, [en-lahj'-er], *n.* one who or that which enlarges; an amplifier; (*phot.*) an apparatus for enlarging.

ENLARGING, [en-lahj'-ing], *n.* enlargement; amplification.

ENLIGHTEN, [en-līt'-en], *v.t.* to impart knowledge to; to liberate from prejudice or superstition; (*poet.*) to illuminate.

ENLIGHTENED, [en-līt'-end], *adj.* elevated by, advanced in, knowledge; not barbarous in outlook.

ENLIGHTENER, [en-līt'-en-er], *n.* one who or that which imparts knowledge to the mind.

ENLIGHTENING, [en-līt'-en-ing], *adj.* that enlightens; illuminating.

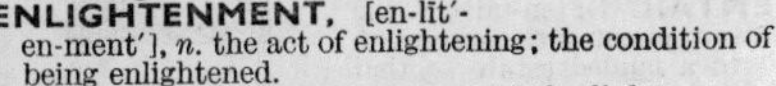

ENLARGER

ENLIGHTENMENT, [en-līt'-en-ment'], *n.* the act of enlightening; the condition of being enlightened.

ENLINK, [en-lingk'], *v.t.* to connect (by links).

ENLIST, [en-list'], *v.t. and i.* to receive as a member of a fighting force; to win or engage the active co-operation of; to join one of the fighting forces.

ENLISTMENT, [en-list'-ment], *n.* the act of enlisting.

ENLIVEN, [en-līv'-en], *v.t.* to put life or vigour into; to give gaiety or pleasant diversity to; to make cheerful.

ENLIVENER, [en-līv'-en-er], *n.* a person or thing that enlivens.

ENLIVENING, [en-līv'-en-ing], *adj.* the act of making lively.

ENLOCK, [en-lok'], *v.t.* to lock up.

ENMANCHE, enmanché, [on-mahn'-shā], *adj.* (*her.*) like a sleeve with long pendent ends. [Fr. *enmanché*].

ENMARBLE, [en-mahbl'], *v.t.* (*poet.*) to turn into marble; to make hard like marble.

ENMESH, [in-mesh'], *v.t.* to catch in a mesh, to entangle, entrap.

ENMESHMENT, [en-mesh'-ment], *n.* the action or process of enmeshing; the condition of being enmeshed.

ENMITY, [en'-mit-i], *n.* antagonistic feelings or actions, ill-will, opposition, hostility. [~OFr. *enemistie* from L. *inimicitia* hostility].

ENMOSSED, [en-most'], *adj.* overgrown with moss.

ENMURE, see IMMURE.

ENNEA-, *pref.* nine. [Gk. *ennea* nine].

ENNEACONTAHEDRAL, [en'-i-a-kon'-ta-hēd'-ral], *adj.* with ninety faces. [Gk. *enneakonta* ninety and *hedra* base].

ENNEAD, [en'-i-ad], *n.* a group or set of nine. [Gk. *enneas*].

ENNEAGON, [en'-i-a-gon], *n.* a polygon or plane figure with nine angles. [ENNEA and Gk. *gonia* angle].

ENNEAGON

ENNEAGONAL, [en'-i-ag'-on-al], *adj.* (*geom.*) having nine angles.

ENNEAGYNOUS, [en'-i-aj'-in-us], *adj.* (*bot.*) having nine pistils. [ENNEA and Gk. *gune* female].

ENNEAHEDRAL, [en'-i-a-hēd'-ral], *adj.* (*geom.*) with nine sides or faces. [ENNEA and Gk. *hedra* base].

ENNEANDROUS, [en'-i-an'-drus], *adj.* (*bot.*) with nine stamens. [ENNEA and Gk. *aner* (*andros*) male.

ENNEAPETALOUS, [en'-ē-a-pet'-al-us], *adj.* (*bot.*) having nine petals.

ENNEAPHYLLOUS, [en'-i-a-fil'-us], *adj.* (*bot.*) with nine leaflets composing a compound leaf. [ENNEA and Gk. *phullon* leaf].

ENNEASEPALOUS, [en'-i-a-sep'-al-us], *adj.* (*bot.*) with nine sepals.

ENNEASPERMOUS, [en'-i-a-spurm'-us], *adj.* (*bot.*) having nine seeds.

ENNEATIC, [en'-i-at'-ik], *adj.* enneatical.

ENNEATICAL, [en'-i-at'-ik-al], *adj.* ninth; **e. day**, every ninth day in the course of a disease; **e. year**, every ninth year in a human life. [~ENNEA].

ENNICHE, [en-nich'], *v.t.* to set in a niche.

ENNOBLE, [en-nōbl'], *v.t.* to elevate to the nobility; to impart noble qualities to.

ENNOBLEMENT, [en-nōbl'-ment], *n.* the act of ennobling; the condition of being ennobled.

ENNUI, [ahn-wē'], *n.* boredom, the feeling of being tired or uninterested in a thing. [Fr. *ennui*].

ENODAL, [ē-nōdl'], *adj.* having no nodes.

ENODATION, [ē'-nōd-ā'-shun], *n.* the act of untying knots; the solution of a difficulty.

ENODE (1), [ē-nōd'], *adj.* (*bot.*) free from knots. [L. *enodis*].

ENODE (2), [ē-nōd'], *v.t.* (*obs.*) to loose, untie, clear of knots; (*fig.*) to solve, unravel. [L. *enodare*].

ENOMOTARCH, [en-om'-ot-ahk], *n.* the commander of an enomoty. [Gk. *enomotarches*].

ENOMOTY, [en-om'-ot-i], *n.* (*hist.*) a band of picked Greek warriors bound by solemn oath sworn on a sacrifice; the smallest unit of the Spartan army. [Gk. *enomotia*].

ENOPTROMANCY, [en-op'-trō-man-si], *n.* divination by means of a mirror. [Gk. *enoptron* mirror and *manteia* divination].

ENORMITY, [in-awm'-i-ti], *n.* the state of being enormous; something that is enormous; an atrocious crime; a wicked act or behaviour. [Fr. *énormité*].

ENORMOUS, [in-aw'-mus], *adj.* of huge dimensions, vast, tremendous. [L. *enormis* abnormal].

ENORMOUSLY, [in-awm'-us-li], *adv.* to an enormous extent; very much.

ENORMOUSNESS, [in-awm'-us-nes], *n.* the quality of being enormous.

ENORTHOTROPE, [en-awth'-ō-trōp], *n.* a toy in the form of a card which, when rapidly revolved, transfers confused objects into various pictures or figures. [EN- (1), Gk. *orthos* erect and *tropos* turning].

ENOUGH (1), [i-nuf'], *n.* a fit and proper quantity, neither too much nor too little; the exact amount required.

ENOUGH (2), [i-nuf'], *adj.* neither too much nor too little, sufficient. [OE. *genoh*].

ENOUGH (3), [i-nuf'], *adv.* sufficiently, neither inadequately nor to excess.

ENOUNCE, [i-nownts'], *v.t. and i.* to utter, speak, pronounce. [Fr. *énoncer*].

ENOUNCEMENT, [i-nowns'-ment], *n.* enunciation; utterance.

ENOW† (1), [i-now'], *adj.* enough. [OE. *genoh genoge* enough].

ENOW† (2), [i-now'], *adv.* enough.

EN PASSANT, [ah(ng)-pas'-ah(ng)], *adv. phrase* (*chess*) in passing, used of the manner in which a pawn may take another but move directly forward. [Fr. *en passant* in passing].

EN PRISE, [ahn-prēz'], *adv.* (*chess*) liable to be taken. [Fr. *en prise*].

ENQUICKEN, [en-kwik'-en], *v.t.* to quicken.

ENQUIRE, see INQUIRE.

ENQUIRER, see INQUIRER.

ENQUIRY, see INQUIRY.

ENRACE, [en-rās], *v.t.* (*poet.*) to ascribe race or origin to.

ENRAGE, [en-rāj'], *v.t.* to rouse rage in, make angry. [OFr. *enrager*].

ENRAIL, [en-rāl'], *v.t.* to set upon the rails.

ENRANK, [en-rangk'], *v.t.* (*poet.*) to set in ranks.

ENRAPT, [en-rapt'], *adj.* enraptured, delighted to ecstasy.

ENRAPTURE, [en-rap'-cher], *v.t.* to make spellbound with delight.

ENRAVISH, [en-rav'-ish], *v.t.* (*poet.*) to enrapture.

ENRAVISHINGLY, [en-rav'-ish-ing-li], *adv.* in an enravishing manner.

ENRAVISHMENT, [en-rav'-ish-ment], *n.* a transport of delight; rapture.

ENREGIMENT, [en-rej'-i-ment], *v.t.* to marshal into a regiment; to make orderly.

ENREGISTER, [en-rej'-ist-er], *v.t.* to enrol, to enter in a register.

ENRHEUM, [en-rōōm'], *v.i.* to develop a cold. [EN- (1) and RHEUM].

ENRICH, [en-rich'], *v.t.* to make wealthy; to improve the quality of; to add richness to, make gorgeous or beautiful.

ENRICHER, [en-rich'-er], *n.* a person who enriches.

ENRICHMENT, [en-rich'-ment], *n.* the act of enriching or of acquiring riches; that which enriches; increase of quality or value.

ENRIDGE, [en-rij'], *v.t.* (*poet.*) to form into ridges.

ENRING, [en-ring'], *v.t.* to encircle; to deck with a ring.

ENRIPEN, [en-rīp'-en], *v.t.* to ripen.

ENROBE, [en-rōb'], *v.t.* to deck in rich attire.
ENROCKMENT, [en-rok'-ment], *n.* a mass of large stones thrown into water at random to form the foundation of piers, breakwaters, etc.
ENROL, [en-rōl'], *v.t.* to enter by name in a list, register, etc. [OFr. *enroller*].
ENROLLER, [en-rōl-er], *n.* one who enrols.
ENROLMENT, [en-rōl'-ment], *n.* the act of enrolling; the condition of being enrolled; that in which anything is enrolled.
ENROOT, [en-rōōt'], *v.t.* to fix by the root; to plant firmly.
ENS, [enz], *n.* an entity, *esp.* as an abstract idea. [LL. *ens* being].
ENSAMPLE (1), [en-sahmpl'], *n.* (*archaic*) an example or pattern. [OFr. *ensample*].
ENSAMPLE (2), [en-sahmpl'], *v.t.* (*archaic*) to show by example; to set an example.
ENSANGUINE, [en-sang'-gwin], *v.t.* to stain with blood.
ENSANGUINED, [en-sang'-gwind], *adj.* bloody, blood-stained.
ENSATE, [en'-sāt], *adj.* shaped like a sword. [~L. *ensis* sword].
ENSCHEDULE, [en-shed'-yōōl], *v.t.* to include in a schedule.
ENSCONCE, [en-skonts'], *v.t.* to set or stow in a safe place. [EN- (1) and SCONCE].
ENSEAL, [en-sēl'], *v.t.* to set a seal to; to seal up.
ENSEAM, [en-sēm'], *v.t.* to close up with a seam; mark as with a seam.
ENSEAR, [en-sēer'], *v.t.* to sear; to cauterize; (*poet.*) to dry up.
ENSEMBLE, [on-sombl'], *n.* the total effect or general appearance; two or more female garments designed to be worn together, usually a frock and coat; (*mus.*) any part of a musical composition in which all the performers are concerned. [Fr. *ensemble* together].
ENSHIELD, [en-shēld'], *v.t.* to shield; to protect; to cover.
ENSHRINE, [en-shrīn'], *v.t.* to set in a shrine; to preserve with great care and reverence.
ENSHRINEMENT, [en-shrīn'-ment], *n.* the act of enshrining; the condition of being enshrined.
ENSHROUD, [en-shrowd'], *v.t.* to veil or shroud.
ENSIFEROUS, [en-si'-fer-us], *adj.* bearing a sword. [L. *ensis* sword and *ferre* to bear].
ENSIFORM, [en'-si-fawm], *adj.* (*bot.*) being in the shape of a sword; **e. cartilage,** (*anat.*) a cartilage appended to the sternum. [L. *ensis* sword and FORM].
ENSIGN, [en'-sīn, en'-sin], *n.* any crest or symbol indicating the rank or office of the bearer; a flag of a regiment or country; (*U.S. navy*) an officer holding the lowest commissioned rank; †(*British army*) a second lieutenant. [OFr. *enseigne* from L. *insignium* badge].
ENSIGNCY, [en'-sīn-si], *n.* the rank of an ensign.
ENSIGNED, [en-sīnd'], *adj.* distinctively marked; (*her.*) distinguished by some significant ornament. [OFr. *ensignier* to mark with a sign].
ENSILAGE (1), [en'-sil'-ij], *n.* a way of preserving green fodder in a pit; fodder preserved in this way. [~SILO].
ENSILAGE (2), [en'-sil'-ij], *v.t.* to keep green fodder by ensilage.
ENSILE, [en-sīl'], *v.t.* to store in a sile or pit. [~SILE].
ENSKIED, [en-skīd'], *adj.* (*poet.*) set in the skies; (*fig.*) made immortal.
ENSLAVE, [en-slāv'], *v.t.* to reduce to slavery; to obtain the mastery over; to subject to one's will.
ENSLAVEDNESS, [en-slāv'-id-nes], *n.* the condition of being enslaved.
ENSLAVEMENT, [en-slāv'-ment], *n.* the action of enslaving; enslavedness.
ENSNARE, [en-snāer'], *v.t.* to trap in a snare; (*fig.*) to trick into a false position.
ENSNARL, [en-snahl'], *v.t.* (*poet.*) to entangle, ensnare. [EN- (1) and SNARL (3)].
ENSOUL, [en-sōl'], *v.t.* to provide with a soul, ascribe a soul to.
ENSPHERE, [en-sfēer'], *v.t.* to put in or surround with a sphere.
ENSTAMP, [en-stamp'], *v.t.* to mark as with a stamp; to impress.
ENSTATITE, [en'-stat-īt], *n.* (*min.*) a refractory silicate of magnesium and iron, ranging in colour from greyish-green to olive-green and brown. [Gk. *enstates* opponent].
ENSTEEP, [en-stēp'], *v.t.* to steep in water.
ENSTYLE, [en-stīl'], *v.t.* to call, style.
ENSUE, [en-sew'], *v.t. and i.* to occur as a consequence, follow as a result; †to endeavour to obtain. [~OFr. *ensuivre* to follow].
ENSUING, [en-sew'-ing], *adj.* following; resultant.
ENSURE, [en-shew(r)'], *v.t.* to make secure, insure.
ENSWATHE, [en-swāTH'], *v.t.* to wrap up as with a bandage or swathe.
ENSWATHEMENT, [en-swāTH'-ment], *n.* the act of enswathing; that which enswathes.
ENSWEEP, [en-swēp'], *v.t.* to sweep over.
ENTABLATURE, [en-tab'-la-chōōer], *n.* (*arch.*) that part of a structure which includes architrave, frieze and cornice. [Fr. *entablature*].

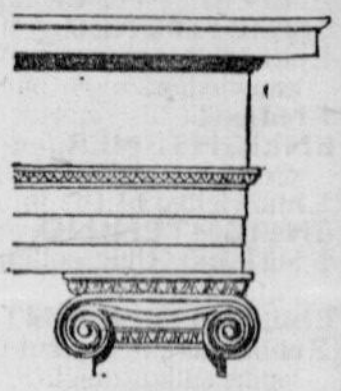

ENTABLATURE

ENTABLEMENT, [en-tābl'-ment], *n.* the slab on the top of a pedestal bearing a statue; entablature. [Fr. *entablement*].
ENTACKLE, [en-takl'], *v.t.* to provide with tackle.
ENTAIL (1), [en-tāl'], *n.* the settlement of the succession to a landed estate so that it cannot be bequeathed at will, but must be passed on in a specified order; an estate that is so settled.
ENTAIL (2), [en-tāl'], *v.t.* to bequeath by entail; to involve, to result inevitably in. [EN (1) and OFr. *tailler* to cut].
ENTAILMENT, [en-tāl'-ment], *n.* the act of entailing; the condition of being entailed.
ENTAME, [en-tām'], *v.t.* (*poet.*) to tame.
ENTANGLE, [en-tang'-gl], *v.t.* to cause to be caught in a mesh or net-like obstacle; (*fig.*) to obtain a steadily increasing influence over or control of. [EN- (1) and TANGLE].
ENTANGLEMENT, [en-tang'-gl-ment], *n.* the state of being entangled; perplexity; a wire barrier to impede the progress of an enemy.
ENTANGLER, [en-tang'-gler], *n.* person who entangles.
ENTASIA, [en-tāz'-i-a], *n.* (*med.*) a constrictive or tonic spasm. [Gk. *entasis* a straining].
ENTASIS, [en-tās'-is], *n.* (*arch.*) the swelling outline given to the shaft of a column to correct apparent concavity; (*med.*) entasia. [*Prec.*].
ENTASSMENT, [en-tas'-ment], *n.* a pile, heap; accumulation. [Fr. *entassement*].
ENTASTIC, [en-tas'-tik], *adj.* (*med.*) relating to entasia.
ENTE†, enté, [on'-tā], *n.* (*her.*) having one coat of arms engrafted on another. [Fr. *enté*, *p.pt.* of *enter* to graft].

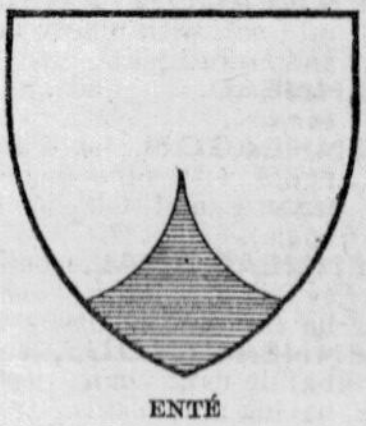

ENTÉ

ENTELECHY, [en-tel'-e-ki], *n.* (*philos.*) the realization of some potential form; developed, attained perfection. [Gk. *entelekheia* actuality].
ENTELLUS, [en-tel'-us], *n.* the Hindu sacred monkey, the hanuman or true langur, *Semnopithecus entellus*. [Gk. *entellos* order].
ENTENDER, [en-ten'-der], *v.t.* to make tender; to weaken, soften.
ENTENT†, see INTENT.
ENTENTE, [ahn-tahnt'], *n.* friendly understanding, *esp.* between nations; **E. cordiale,** the unofficial alliance established between Britain and France in the early 20th century. [Fr. *entente*].
ENTER, [ent'-er], *v.t.* to go or come in, pass inside; to penetrate, pierce; to become a member of; to write or record in a book; to take down the name of an entrant; to enrol as a member or prospective member; to break in (a horse); *v.i.* to go in, come in, pass inside, to come upon the stage; **to e. for,** to compete for; **to e. into,** to engage in, embark upon; to become a party to; to sympathize with, understand; to take part in; **to e. upon,** to begin to deal with; to assume possession of, to begin, embark upon. [OFr. *entrer*].
ENTERA, [en'-ter-a], *n.(pl.)* (*med.*) the intestines. [Gk. *entera*].
ENTERABLE, [en'-ter-abl], *adj.* capable of being entered.
ENTERADENOGRAPHY, [en'-ter-ad'-en-og'-ra-fi],

n. the scientific description of the intestinal glands. [ENTERA and ADENOGRAPHY].

ENTERADENOLOGY, [en′-ter-ad′-in-ol′-o-ji], *n.* the anatomical study of the intestinal glands. [ENTERA and ADENOLOGY].

ENTERALGIA, [en′-ter-al′-gi-a], *n.* (*med.*) pain in the intestines. [ENTERA and Gk. *algos* pain].

ENTERCLOSE, [en′-ter-klōz], *n.* (*arch.*) an intermediate passage between two rooms. [OFr. *entreclos*].

ENTERED, [en′-terd], *adj.* recorded; inserted in a list of members, etc.

ENTERIC, [en-te′-rik], *adj.* relating to the intestines. [Gk. *enterikos*].

ENTERING, [en′-ter-ing], *n.* the act of coming in or going in.

ENTERITIS, [en′-ter-ī′-is], *n.* inflammation of the intestines. [ENTERA and Gk. *itis* denoting inflammation].

ENTEROCELE, [en′-ter-ō-sēl′], *n.* (*med.*) a hernial tumour. [ENTERA and Gk. *kele* tumour].

ENTEROGASTROCELE, [en′-ter-ō-gas′-trō-sēl], *n.* abdominal hernia. [ENTERA, Gk. *gaster* stomach and *kele* tumour].

ENTEROLITE, [en′-ter-ō-līt′], *n.* intestinal calculus. [ENTERA and Gk. *lithos* stone].

ENTEROLOGY, [en′-ter-ol′-o-ji], *n.* the study of the bowels or internal parts of the body. [ENTERA and Gk. *logos* speech].

ENTEROMPHALOS, [en′-ter-om′-fal-us], *n.* an umbilical hernia. [ENTERA and Gk. *omphalos* navel].

ENTEROPATHY, [en′-ter-o′-pathi], *n.* (*med.*) disease of the intestines. [ENTERA and Gk. *pathos* suffering].

ENTEROTOMY, [en′-ter-ot′-o-mi], *n.* (*anat.*) dissection of the intestines; (*surg.*) incision of the intestines for the removal of strangulation, etc. [ENTERA and Gk. *tome* cutting].

ENTERPARLANCE†, [en′-ter-pah′-lants], *n.* conference; discussion. [AFr. *entreparlance*].

ENTERPRISE, [en′-ter-prīz], *n.* undertaking, task, adventure, *esp.* one of a bold or difficult nature; courageous and adventurous character; the ability to think out and make a start upon new schemes. [OFr. *entreprise*].

ENTERPRISER, [en′-ter-prīz-er], *n.* one who undertakes an enterprise, *esp.* a bold or dangerous one.

ENTERPRISING, [en′-ter-prīz-ing], *adj.* bold or venturesome in undertaking; having initiative.

ENTERPRISINGLY, [en′-ter-prīz-ing-li], *adv.* in an enterprising way.

ENTERTAIN, [en′-ter-tān′], *v.t. and i.* to provide hospitality (for); to provide light amusement (for) as by conversation, wit, etc.; to amuse; to give mental consideration to, to ponder. [Fr. *entretenir*].

ENTERTAINER, [en′-ter-tān′-er], *n.* person who entertains.

ENTERTAINING, [en′-ter-tān′-ing], *adj.* pleasant, amusing.

ENTERTAININGLY, [en′-ter-tān′-ing-li], *adv.* in an entertaining way.

ENTERTAININGNESS, [en′-ter-tān′-ing-nes], *n.* the quality of being entertaining.

ENTERTAINMENT, [en′-ter-tān′-ment], *n.* the act of entertaining; the condition of being entertained; amusement, an entertaining dramatic performance.

ENTERTISSUED, [en′-ter-tish′-yōōd], *adj.* (*poet.*) interwoven. [Fr. *entre* between and TISSUE].

ENTHEAL†, [en-thē′-al], *adj.* inspired by God; possessed by a deity. [~Gk. *entheos*].

ENTHEASTIC†, [en′-thi-as′-tik], *adj.* animated with the zeal and energy inspired by belief in some divine mission. [Gk. *entheastikos*].

ENTHEASTICALLY, [en′-thi-as′-tik-al-i], *adv.* in an entheastic way.

ENTHRAL, ENTHRALL, (enthralling, enthralled), [en-thrawl′], *v.t.* to enslave; to enchant; to interest intensely.

ENTHRALMENT, [en-thrawl′-ment], *n.* the act of enthralling; the condition of being enthralled.

ENTHRILL†, [en-thrill′], *v.t.* to pierce.

ENTHRONE, [en-thrōn′], *v.t.* to set on a throne; to invest with sovereign authority; to install as a bishop.

ENTHRONEMENT, [en-thrōn′-ment], *n.* act of enthroning; the condition of being enthroned.

ENTHRONIZATION, [en-thrōn′-ī-zā′-shun], *n.* enthronement.

ENTHRONIZE, [en-thrōn′-īz], *v.t.* to enthrone.

ENTHUNDER, [en-thund′-er], *v.i.* to make a loud noise like that of thunder.

ENTHUSE, [en-thewz′], *v.i.* (*coll.*) to be enthusiastic; to gush. [ENTHUS(IASM)].

ENTHUSIASM, [en-thew′-zi-azm], *n.* a keen zeal or admiration; religious fervour and exaltation. [Gk. *enthousiasmos* inspiration].

ENTHUSIAST, [en-thew′-zi-ast], *n.* an enthusiastic person.

ENTHUSIASTIC (1), [en-thew′-zi-as′-tik], *n.* an enthusiast.

ENTHUSIASTIC (2), [en-thew′-zi-as′-tik], *adj.* animated by intense zeal; zealous, eager, hearty.

ENTHUSIASTICALLY, [en-thew′-zi-as′-tik-al-i], *adv.* in an enthusiastic fashion.

ENTHYMEMATICAL, [en′-thim-em-at′-ik-al], *adj.* relating to or including an enthymeme.

ENTHYMEME, [en′-thi-mēm], *n.* (*log.*) a syllogism in which the major proposition is suppressed. [Gk. *enthumema*].

ENTICE, [en-tīs′], *v.t.* to tempt, *esp.* to evil, by exciting hopes or desires; to allure; to lead astray. [OFr. *enticier*].

ENTICEMENT, [en-tīs′-ment], *n.* the act of enticing; the condition of being enticed; that which entices.

ENTICER, [en-tīs′-er], *n.* a person or thing that entices.

ENTICING, [en-tīs′-ing], *adj.* having qualities that entice; alluring.

ENTICINGLY, [en-tīs′-ing-li], *adv.* in an enticing way.

ENTIRE (1), [en-tī′-er], *n.* anything that is unmixed; a blend of beer; porter sent straight from the brewery; an uncastrated animal.

ENTIRE (2), [en-tī′-er], *adj.* complete, having no flaw or imperfection; unbroken; uncastrated. [Fr. *entier*].

ENTIRELY, [en-tīer′-li], *adv.* wholly, fully; utterly.

ENTIRENESS, [en-tīer′-nes], *n.* the state of being entire.

ENTIRETY, [en-tīer′-ti], *n* the condition of being entire; the whole.

ENTITATIVE, [en′-tit-at-iv], *adj.* regarded as an entity.

ENTITLE, [en-titl′], *v.t.* to give a title or name to; to style; to give a claim or right to. [OFr. *entiteler*].

ENTITY, [en′-tit-i], *n.* a thing complete in itself, its actual existence as opposed to its qualities and attributes; something with a real existence of its own. [Fr. *entité*].

ENTO-, *pref.* within. [Gk. *entos* inside].

ENTOBLAST, [en′-tō-blahst], *n.* the nucleolus or little nucleus of a cell. [ENTO and Gk. *blastos* bud].

ENTOIL, [en-toil′], *v.t.* to trap with toils; to entangle.

ENTOMATOGRAPHY, [en′-tom-at-og′-ra-fi], *n.* the scientific study of insects. [ENTOMO and Gk. *graphia* writing].

ENTOMB, [en-tōōm′], *v.t.* to bury in a tomb; to shut as in a tomb.

ENTOMBMENT, [en-tōōm′-ment], *n.* the condition of being entombed; the act of laying (something) in a tomb.

ENTOMIC, [en-tom′-ik], *adj.* connected with insects.

ENTOMO-, *pref.* relating to insects. [Gk. *entomos* cut up].

ENTOMOID, [en′-tom-oid], *adj.* resembling an insect. [ENTOMO and Gk. *oeides* like].

ENTOMOLINE, [en-tom′-ol-īn], *n.* chitin; a chemical principle procured from the wings and elytra of beetles. [Gk. *entoma* insects].

ENTOMOLITE, [en′-tom-ol-īt], *n.* a fossilized insect. [ENTOMO and Gk. *lithos* stone].

ENTOMOLOGICAL, [en′-tom-o-loj′-ik-al], *adj.* relating to entomology.

ENTOMOLOGICALLY, [en′-tom-o-loj′-ik-al-i], *adv.* in an entomological way.

ENTOMOLOGIST, [en′-tom-ol′-oj-ist], *n.* one expert in entomology.

ENTOMOLOGIZE, [en′-tom-ol′-oj-īz], *v.i.* to collect insects for scientific observation.

ENTOMOLOGY, [en′-tom-ol′-oj-i], *n.* the science dealing with insects. [ENTOMO and Gk. *logos* speech].

ENTOMOPHAGOUS, [en′-tom-of′-ag-us], *adj.* eating, feeding on, insects. [ENTOMA and Gk. *phago* I eat].

ENTOMOPHILOUS, [en′-tom-of′-il-us], *adj.* (*bot.*) fertilized by insects. [ENTOMA and Gk. *philo* I love].

ENTOMOPHILY, [en′-tom-of′-il-i], *n.* (*bot.*) pollination by means of insects.

ENTOMOSTRACAN, [en′-tom-os′-trak-an], *n.* (*zool.*) a member of the lowest orders of the crustacea. [ENTOMO and Gk. *ostrakon* shell].

ENTOMOSTRACOUS, [en′-tom-os′-trak-us], *adj.* pertaining to the entomostracans.

ENTOMOTOMIST, [en'-tom-ot'-om-ist], *n.* one skilled in entomotomy.

ENTOMOTOMY, [en'-tom-ot'-o-mi], *n.* the dissection of insects. [ENTOMO and Gk. *tome* cutting].

ENTONIC, [en-ton'-ik], *adj.* strained, showing high tension. [Gk. *entonos*].

ENTOPHYTES, [en-tof'-īts], *n.(pl.)* (*bot.*) parasitic plants that grow on other plants or in animals. [ENTO and Gk. *phuton* plant].

ENTOPHYTIC, [en'-tof-it'-ik], *adj.* relating to entophytes.

ENTOPTIC, [en-top'-tik], *adj.* seen when the eyes are shut. [ENTO and OPTIC].

ENTORTILATION†, [en-taw'-til-ā'-shun], *n.* the act of turning or twisting into a circle. [~Fr. *entortiller* to twist].

ENTOSTHOBLAST, [en-tos'-thō-blahst], *n.* the nucleus or inner cell of the entoblast. [Gk. *entosthe* from within, and *blastos* bud].

ENTOTIC, [en-tot'-ik], *adj.* relating to the interior of the ear. [ENTO and OTIC].

ENTOURAGE, [ahn'-tōō-rahj'], *n.* the persons, circumstances, and things which together make up an individual's immediate surroundings; an immediate circle of servants and friends. [Fr. *entourage*].

EN-TOUT-CAS, [ahn'-tōō'-kah'], *n.* a contrivance that can be used as either an umbrella or a sunshade; a tennis-court for use in all weather. [Fr. *en tout cas* in any case].

ENTOZOAL, [en'-tō-zō'-al], *adj.* pertaining to the entozoa.

ENTOZOIC, [en'-tō-zō'-ik], *adj.* entozoal.

ENTOZOOLOGIST, [en'-tō-zō-ol'-oj-ist], *n.* one skilled in entozoology.

ENTOZOOLOGY, [en'-tō-zō-ol'-oj-i], *n.* the scientific study of entozoa. [ENTOZOA and Gk. *logos* speech].

ENTOZOON, (*pl.* **entozoa**), [en'-tō-zō'-on], *n.* a parasitic animal living inside another animal. [ENTO and Gk. *zoon* animal].

ENTR'ACTE, [on'-trakt'], *n.* the interval between the acts of a play; a performance given then. [Fr. *entr'acte*].

ENTRAIL, [en-trāl'], *v.t.* (*poet.*) to entwine, interlace, entangle. [OFr. *entreillier*].

ENTRAILS, [en'-trālz], *n.(pl.)* the internal parts of animal bodies, the bowels; (*fig.*) the internal parts or inside of anything. [OFr. *entrailles*].

ENTRAIN (1), [en-trān'], *v.t.* and *i.* to dispatch by train; to board a train.

ENTRAIN (2), [en-trān'], *v.t.* to draw on or after. [Fr. *entrainer*].

ENTRAMMEL, [en-tram'-el], *v.t.* to entangle.

ENTRANCE (1), [en'-trants], *n.* the act of one who enters; the right to be admitted; the action of an actor in coming on to the stage; a way in, a doorway; (*fig.*) a commencement or beginning. [OFr. *entrance*].

ENTRANCE (2), [en-trahnts'], *v.t.* to fill with delight or joyous fascination. [EN (1) and TRANCE].

ENTRANCEMENT, [en-trahns'-ment], *n.* the act of entrancing, the condition of one who is entranced; that which entrances.

ENTRANCING, [en-trahns'-ing], *adj.* delightfully fascinating, charming.

ENTRANT, [en'-trant], *n.* one who enters, a candidate.

ENTRAP, [en-trap'], *v.t.* to snare in a trap; to gain an advantage or ascendancy over by trickery.

ENTREAT, [en-trēt'], *v.t.* to make an urgent petition to, to implore; (*archaic*) to use, treat. [OFr. *entraiter*].

ENTREATABLE, [en-trēt'-abl], *adj.* able to be entreated.

ENTREATER, [en-trēt'-er], *n.* one who entreats.

ENTREATING, [en-trēt'-ing], *adj.* expressing an urgent appeal.

ENTREATINGLY, [en-trēt'-ing-li], *adv.* in an entreating way.

ENTREATIVE, [en-trēt'-iv], *adj.* pleading, imploring.

ENTREATY, [en-trēt'-i], *n.* an earnest petition; the act of one who entreats.

ENTRECOTE, **entrecôte**, [ahntr'-kōt], *n.* (*cookery*) a steak cut off the ribs. [Fr. *entrecôte*].

ENTREE, **entrée**, [ahn'-trā], *n.* right of access or entry; a light dish served between fish and meat courses. [Fr. *entrée* entry].

ENTREMETS, [ahntr'-mā], *n.(pl.)* subsidiary dishes between the main courses of a dinner. [Fr. *entremets* between the dishes].

ENTRENCH, **INTRENCH**, [en-trench'], *v.t.* to surround with a trench; to make and occupy a trench; (*fig.*) to make a stout resistance.

ENTRENCHMENT, [en-trench'-ment], *n.* the act of entrenching; the condition of being entrenched; a military trench or system of trenches.

ENTREPOT, **entrepôt**, [ahntr'-pō], *n.* a store, warehouse. [Fr. *entrepôt*].

ENTREPRENEUR, [ahntr'-prun-ur'], *n.* one who undertakes an artistic or commercial venture. [Fr. from *entreprendre* to undertake].

ENTRESOL, [ahntr'-sol], *n.* a small extra storey between the first and ground floors; the small window of such a storey. [Fr. *entresol*].

ENTROCHAL, [en'-trōk-al], *adj.* having entrochites.

ENTROCHITE, [en'-trōk-it], *n.* (*geol.*) the joint in the stem of a fossil sea-lily shaped like a wheel. [EN (1) and Gk. *trochos* wheel].

ENTROCHITE

ENTROPIUM, [en-trōp'-i-um], *n.* the turning of the eye-lashes inwards towards the eyes. [Gk. *entrepo* I turn inwards].

ENTROPY, [en'-trop-i], *n.* energy wasted by heating in an engine; a measurement of this. [EN (1) and Gk. *trope* change].

ENTRUST, **INTRUST**, [in-trust'], *v.t.* to commit to a person for safe keeping; to commit something to.

ENTRUSTMENT, [en-trust'-ment], *n.* the act of entrusting; that which is entrusted.

ENTRY, [en'-tri], *n.* the action or right of entering; a way in, a doorway; a memorandum or record written down; (*leg.*) the taking possession of property by entering it. [Fr. *entrée*].

ENTUNE, [en-tewn'], *v.t.* to chant or intone.

ENTWINE, **INTWINE**, [en-twīn'], *v.t.* and *i.* to twine or interlace; to twine round.

ENTWINEMENT, [en-twīn'-ment], *n.* an interweaving or twisting round.

ENTWIST, **INTWIST**, [en-twist'], *v.t.* and *i.* to interweave.

ENUBILATE, [i-new'-bil-āt], *v.t.* to clear of clouds or obscurity. [L. *enubilare*].

ENUBILOUS, [i-new'-bil-us], *adj.* clear, without mist or clouds.

ENUCLEATE, [i-new'-kli-āt], *v.t.* to extricate and make clear, to explain; to extract. [L. *enucleare*].

ENUCLEATION, [i-new'-kli-ā'-shun], *n.* the act of enucleating.

ENUMERATE, [i-new'-mer-āt], *v.t.* to reckon, count up or name one by one; to tell in detail. [L. *enumerare* to count].

ENUMERATION, [i-new'-mer-ā'-shun], *n.* the condition of being enumerated; the act of enumerating; a reckoning up; a detailed list or statement.

ENUMERATIVE, [i-new'-mer-at-iv], *adj.* connected with enumeration, summing up.

ENUMERATOR, [i-new'-mer-āt-er], *n.* one who enumerates.

ENUNCIABLE, [i-nun'-si-abl], *adj.* able to be enunciated.

ENUNCIATE, [i-nun'-si-āt], *v.t.* to proclaim, propound; to pronounce, to articulate. [L. *enuntiare* announce].

ENUNCIATION, [i-nun'-si-ā'-shun], *n.* the act of enunciating; the condition of being enunciated; the style or manner of enunciating; (*geom.*) a formal statement of a proposition.

ENUNCIATIVE, [i-nun'-si-a-tiv], *adj.* relating to enunciation.

ENUNCIATIVELY, [i-nun'-si-a-tiv-li], *adv.* in an enunciative manner.

ENUNCIATOR, [i-nun'-si-ā-ter], *n.* one who enunciates.

ENUNCIATORY, [i-nun'-si-a-ter-i], *adj.* enunciative.

ENURE, see INURE.

ENURESIS, [en'-yōō-rēs'-is], *n.* (*med.*) incontinence of urine. [Gk. *enouro* I urinate in].

ENVAPOUR, [en-vāp'-er], *v.t.* to enclose in vapour.

ENVASSAL, [en-vas'-al], *v.t.* to make a vassal.

ENVAULT, [en-vawlt'], *v.t.* to place in a vault.

ENVELOP, [en-vel'-op], *v.t.* to surround, cover up, hide; (*fig.*) to make almost unintelligible. [Fr. *envelopper*].

ENVELOPE, [en'-vel-ōp, on'-vel-ōp], *n.* a wrapping, outer covering; a paper cover for sending a letter in; the outer cover of the gas bag of a balloon or airship; (*bot.*) one of the reproductive organs of a plant, surrounding the stamens and pistils; (*fort.*) mound of earth thrown up to cover and protect some weak part of the fortifications. [Fr. *enveloppe*].

ENVELOPED, [en-vel'-opt], *adj.* (*her.*) entwined by a serpent, laurel, etc.

ENVELOPMENT, [en-vel'-op-ment], *n.* the act of enveloping; the condition of being enveloped; a wrapping; a complete covering.

ENVENOM, [en-ven'-om], *v.t.* to poison, impregnate with venom; (*fig.*) to embitter; to exasperate.

ENVERMEIL, [en-vur'-mil], *v.t.* (*poet.*) to impart a red colour to. [OFr. *envermeiller*].

ENVIABLE, [en'-vi-abl], *adj.* liable to excite envy; very desirable.

ENVIABLENESS, [en'-vi-abl-nes], *n.* the state of being enviable.

ENVIABLY, [en'-vi-ab-li], *adv.* in an enviable way.

ENVIED, [en'-vid], *adj.* made the object of envy.

ENVIER, [en'-vi-er], *n.* one who envies.

ENVIOUS, [en'-vi-us], *adj.* feeling envy; animated or motivated by envy.

ENVIOUSLY, [en'-vi-us-li], *adv.* in an envious fashion.

ENVIOUSNESS, [en'-vi-us-nes], *n.* the condition of being envious.

ENVIRON, [en-vī'-ron], *v.t.* to stand or be placed around, to encompass. [Fr. *environner*].

ENVIRONMENT, [en-vī'-ron-ment], *n.* the act of environing, the condition of being environed; surroundings, conditions in which one grows up or lives and which influence one's development.

ENVIRONNE, environné, [en-vi'-ron-ā], *adj.* (*her.*) set round, bound round. [Fr. *environné*].

ENVIRONS, [en-vī'-ronz], *n.*(*pl.*) the places and district in the immediate neighbourhood of a particular place; the suburbs, outskirts, surroundings.

ENVIRONNÉ

ENVISAGE, [en-viz'-ij], *v.t.* to imagine, visualize; to make a determined effort to deal with. [OFr. *envisager*].

ENVISAGEMENT, [en-viz'-ij-ment], *n.* the act of envisaging.

ENVOLUME, [en-vol'-yōōm], *v.t.* to include in or make part of a volume.

ENVOY (1), [en'-voi], *n.* a diplomatic representative next in rank to an ambassador. [Fr. *envoyé*].

ENVOY (2), [en'-voi], *n.* the concluding part, forming a kind of postscript to a poetical composition. [OFr. *envoyé*].

ENVOYSHIP, [en'-voi-ship], *n.* the office of an envoy.

ENVY (1), [en'-vi], *n.* a feeling of ill-will excited by grudging contemplation of another's good fortune; the object of such feeling. [OFr. *envie* from L. *invidia*].

ENVY (2), [en'-vi], *v.t.* to feel envy of, to cherish envious feelings against. [Fr. *envier* from L. *invidiare*].

ENWHEEL, [en-wēl'], *v.* (*poet.*) to encircle, encompass.

ENWIND, [en-wīnd'], *v.t.* to twine round something else.

ENWOMAN, [en-wŏŏm'-an], *v.t.* to make like a woman.

ENWOMB, [en-wōōm'], *v.t.* to hide, cover as in a womb.

ENWOVEN, [en-wōv'-en], *adj.* woven, interwoven.

ENWRAP, INWRAP, (enwrapping, enwrapped), [en-rap'], *v.t.* to envelop, enfold.

ENWRAPMENT, [en-rap'-ment], *n.* the state of being enwrapped; that which enwraps.

ENWREATHE, [en-rēTH'], *v.t.* to wreathe, to encompass with or as with a wreath or garland.

ENZONE, [en-zōn'], *v.t.* to confine as in a zone.

ENZOOTIC (1), [en'-zō-ot'-ik], *n.* a disease prevalent among the animals of a district at the same time, epizootic.

ENZOOTIC (2), [en'-zō-ot'-ik], *adj.* prevalent among the animals of a district. [EN (1) and Gk. *zoon* animal].

ENZYME, [en'-zīm], *n.* (*chem.*) a chemical ferment. [Gk. *enzumos* leavened].

EO-, *pref.* in the beginning. [Gk. *eos* dawn].

EOCENE, [ē'-ō-sēn], *adj.* (*geol.*) pertaining to the earliest division of the Tertiary strata. [EO and Gk. *kainos* new].

EOLITH, [ē'-ō-lith], *n.* a flint implement of the earliest age in human history. [EO and Gk. *lithos* stone].

EOLITHIC, [ē-ō-lith'-ik], *adj.* relating to the age of eoliths.

EOSIN, EOSINE, [ē'-ō-sin], *n.* a pink dyestuff used for staining objects for microscopic examination. [EO].

EOZOIC, [ē'-ō-zō'-ik], *adj.* (*geol.*) pertaining to rocks in which the first traces of organic life appear. [EO and Gk. *zoon* animal].

EOZOON, [ē'-ō-zō'-on], *n.* (*geol.*) a growth of calcite and serpentine once supposed to represent the earliest traces of organic life in the rocks of the earth. [*Prec.*].

EP-, EPI-, *pref.* on, upon, at, besides, in addition, on account of. [Gk. *epi*].

EPACT, [ē'-pakt'], *n.* the amount by which the solar exceeds the lunar year; the age of the moon on January 1. [Gk. *epakte*].

EPAGOGE, [ep'-ag-ōj'-i], *n.* (*rhet.*) a figure of speech in which universal propositions are proved by example. [Gk. *epagoge*].

EPAGOGIC, [ep'-ag-oj'-ik], *adj.* by epagoge, inductive.

EPALPATE, [ē-pal'-pāt], *adj.* (*entom.*) lacking feelers or palps. [E and L. *palpus* feeler].

EPANADIPLOSIS, [ep'-an'-ad-ip-lōs'-is], *n.* repetition; (*rhet.*) a figure of speech, in which a sentence ends with the same word with which it begins. [Gk. *epanadiplosis*].

EPANALEPSIS, [ep-an'-al-ep'-sis], *n.* (*rhet.*) a figure of speech by which the same word or clause is repeated in resuming the subject after a long parenthesis. [Gk. *epanalepsis*].

EPANODOS, [ep-an'-od-os], *n.* (*rhet.*) a figure of speech in which the second member of a sentence is an inversion of the first; a recapitulation of the chief points of a discourse after a digression. [Gk. *epanodos*].

EPANORTHOSIS, [ep'-an-aw-thōs'-is], *n.* (*rhet.*) a figure in which a speaker recalls a statement for the sake of refuting or intensifying it. [Gk. *epanorthosis*].

EPANTHOUS, [ep-an'-thus], *adj.* (*bot.*) growing upon flowers. [EP and Gk. *anthos* flower].

EPARCH, [ep'-ahk], *n.* the governor of a Greek province. [Gk. *eparkhos*].

EPARCHY, [ep'-ahk-i], *n.* a subdivision of modern Greece; †a Russian diocese in the Greek Orthodox Church. [Gk. *eparkhia* province].

EPAULE, [ep-awl'], *n.* (*fort.*) the shoulder of a bastion at the meeting of one of the faces and one of the flanks. [Fr. *épaule* shoulder].

EPAULETTE, EPAULET, [ep'-awl-et'], *n.* a piece of ornamentation on the shoulder of a uniform; **to win one's epaulettes,** to be promoted to the rank of officer. [Fr. *épaulette*].

EPAULETTED, [ep'-awl-et'-id], *adj.* provided with epaulettes.

EPEE, épée, [ep'-ā], *n.* a sharp-pointed sword for duelling, one with the point blunted for fencing. [Fr. *épée* sword].

EPAULETTE

EPEIRA, [ep-ī'-ra], *n.*(*pl.*) (*zool.*) an order of spiders including the garden spider, *Epeira diademata*. [EP and Gk. *eiros* wool].

EPENCEPHALIC, [ep'-en-kef-al'-ik], *adj.* belonging to the occipital part of the brain.

EPENCEPHALON, [ep'-en-kef'-al-on], *n.* anat.) the hindmost part or division of the brain. [EP and ENCEPHALON].

EPENTHESIS, [ep-en'-this-is], *n.* (*gram.*) the insertion of a letter or syllable in the middle of a word. [Gk. *epenthesis*].

EPENTHETIC, [ep'-en-thet'-ik], *adj.* (*gram.*) relating to epenthesis.

EPERGNE, [āp-āern'], *n.* a tall branched stand for holding flowers or fruit in the centre of a table. [Fr. *épargne* economy].

EPEXEGESIS, [ep'-ek-sij-ēs'-is], *n.* an additional explanation; additional words to make the meaning clearer. [EP and EXEGESIS].

EPEXEGETICAL, [ep'-ek-sij-et'-ik-al], *adj.* relating to epexegesis; explanatory.

EPEXEGETICALLY, [ep'-ek-sij-et'-ik-al-i], *adv.* in an epexegetical fashion.

EPHAH, [ē'-fa], *n.* a Hebrew dry measure. [Heb. *ephah*].

EPHEBUS, EPHEBE, [ef-ē'-bus, ef-ē'-bē], *n.* a young citizen in ancient Greece between 18 and 20 years old. [Gk. *ephebos*].

EPHEDRIN, EPHEDRINE, [ef'-ed-rin], *n.* (*med.*) a drug extracted originally from the Chinese plant Ma Huang, *Ephedra monostrachya*, and now also from other plants of the genus *Ephedra*.

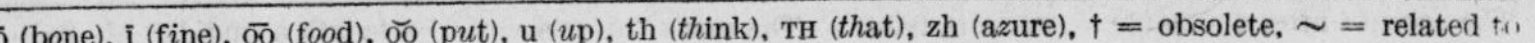

EPHELIS, (*pl.* **ephelides**), [ef-ēl'-is], *n.* a freckle. [Gk. *ephelis*].

EPHEMERA, (*pl.* **ephemerae**), [ef-ĕm'-er-a], *n.* an insect that lives only for a day; the order comprising such insects; (*fig.*) anything very short-lived. [Gk. *ephemeros* lasting a day].

EPHEMERAL, [ef-em'-er-al], *adj.* lasting only for a day, or a day or two; short-lived, transitory.

EPHEMERIS, (*pl.* **ephemerides**), [ef-em'-er-is], *n.* an astronomical almanac. [Gk. *ephemeris* journal].

EPHEMERIST, [ef-em'-er-ist], *n.* a person who studies the daily motions and positions of the planets; a diarist.

EPHEMERON, [ef-em'-er-on], *n.* anything, particularly an insect, that lives only for a day, or has a short, fleeting existence.

EPHESIAN (1), [i-fē'-zhun], *n.* an inhabitant of Ephesus; (*fig.*) a noisy, riotous fellow.

EPHESIAN (2), [i-fē'-zhun], *adj.* pertaining to Ephesus or its inhabitants.

EPHIALTES, [ef'-i-al'-tēz], *n.* the nightmare. [Gk. *ephialtes*].

EPHOD, [ē'-fod], *n.* a garment like an apron, worn by a Jewish priest; a vestment worn by any priest. [Heb. *ephod*].

EPHOR, (*pl.* **ephori**), [e'-faw(r)], *n.* (*hist.*) an overseer or magistrate in the Doric states. [Gk. *ephoros*].

EPHORALTY, [ef'-awr-al-ti], *n.* the office or period of office of an ephor.

EPHORI, *pl.* of EPHOR.

EPI-, see EP-.

EPIBLAST, [ep'-i-blahst], *n.* (*physiol.*) the outer wall of a cell, ectoderm. [EPI and Gk. *blastos* bud].

EPIC (1), [ep'-ik], *n.* a long poem, originally recited, describing the adventures and achievements of a hero or group of heroes; anything resembling this in scale or heroic character.

EPIC (2), [ep'-ik], *adj.* pertaining to, resembling an epic; heroic. [Gk. *epikos*].

EPICAL, [ep'-ik-al], *adj.* epic.

EPICALLY, [ep'-ik-al-i], *adv.* in an epic fashion.

EPICARP, [ep'-i-kahp], *n.* (*bot.*) the rind of fruits. [EPI and Gk. *karpos* fruit].

EPICEDE, [ep'-i-sēd], *n.* a funeral ode or dirge. [EPI and Gk. *kedos* funeral observance].

EPICEDIAL, [ep'-is-ēd'-i-al], *adj.* funereal, elegiac.

EPICEDIAN, [ep-is-ēd'-i-an], *adj.* epicedial.

EPICEDIUM, [ep-is-ēd'-i-um], *n.* a funereal ode or lament. [Gk. *epikedeion*].

EPICENE (1), [ep'-is-ēn], *n.* a person having characteristics and attributes of both sexes.

EPICENE (2), [ep'-is-ēn], *adj.* of the nature of both sexes; of vague and uncertain quality or character; (*gram.*) having common gender. [Gk. *epikoinos* promiscuous].

EPICENTRUM, EPICENTRE, [ep'-i-sen'-trum, ep'-i-sen'-ter], *n.* the centre of origin of an earthquake. [EPI and CENTRE].

EPICERASTIC, [ep'-i-ser-as'-tik], *adj.* (*med.*) soothing. [Gk. *epikerastikos* tempering].

EPICERIE, [ep-ēs'-er-i], *n.* groceries. [Fr. *épicerie*].

EPICHEIREMA, [ep'-i-kī-rēm'-a], *n.* (*logic*) a syllogism confirmed by an incidental proposition in either or both of the premises. [Gk. *epikheirema* an attempt].

EPICHORDIS, [ep'-i-kawd'-is], *n.* a membrane keeping the intestines in place, mesentery. [EPI and Gk. *khorde* gut, string].

EPICHORION, [ep'-i-kaw'-ri-on], *n.* the deciduous membrane enclosing the foetus. [EPI and Gk. *khorion* skin].

EPICLINAL, [ep'-i-klīn'-al], *adj.* (*bot.*) situated on the receptacle of a flower. [EPI and Gk. *kline* couch].

EPICOLIC, [ep'-i-kol'-ik], *adj.* pertaining to that part of the abdomen which lies over the colon. [EPI and COLON].

EPICOROLLINE, [ep'-i-ko'-ro-lin], *adj.* (*bot.*) situated on the corolla.

EPICRANIAL, [ep'-i-krān'-i-al], *adj.* (*anat.*) relating to the parts situated on the cranium.

EPICRANIUM, [ep'-i-krān-i-um], *n.* (*anat.*) the occipito-frontalis muscle; the skin covering the scalp.

EPICTETIAN, [ep'-ik-tēsh-an], *adj.* pertaining to Epictetus or his philosophy. [*Epictetus*, the Stoic philosopher].

EPICURE, [ep'-i-kyōōer], *n.* one who is fastidious and particular about what he eats and drinks, one who enjoys and thoroughly appreciates good food and drink. [*Epikouros*, a Greek philosopher who taught that the pleasures of the senses are the chief good in life].

EPICUREAN (1), [ep'-i-kyōōer-ē'-an], *n.* a follower of Epicurus; an epicure.

EPICUREAN (2), [ep'-i-kyōōer-ē'-an], *adj.* pertaining to Epicurus, his philosophy or followers; relating to an epicure or epicurism; possessing qualities that would delight an epicure.

EPICUREANISM, [ep'-i-kyōōer-ē'-an-izm], *n.* epicurism.

EPICURISM, [ep'-i-kyōōer-izm], *n.* the state or quality of being an epicure; the tastes and habits of an epicure.

EPICURIZE, [ep'-i-kyōōer-īz], *v.t.* to behave, feast like an epicure; to profess the philosophy of Epicurus.

EPICYCLE, [ep'-i-sīkl], *n.* a small circle with its centre situated and moving on the circumference of a larger circle. [EPI and Gk. *kuklos* circle].

EPICYCLIC, [ep'-i-sī'-klik], *adj.* relating to an epicycle.

EPICYCLIC GEAR, [ep'-i-sī'-klik-gēer'], *n.* (*mech.*) a change-speed gear consisting of three or more small cogged wheels arranged round and meshing with a larger and central wheel.

EPICYCLOID, [ep'-i-sī'-kloid], *n.* the curved path of a point situated on the circumference of an epicycle. [EPICYCLE and Gk. *oeides* like].

EPICYCLOIDAL, [ep'-i-sī'-kloid-al], *adj.* relating to or resembling an epicycloid.

EPICYCLIC GEAR

EPIDEICTIC, [ep'-i-dīk'-tik], *adj.* (*rhet.*) done for effect or to show off skill or power. [Gk. *epideiktikos*].

EPIDEMIC (1), [ep'-i-dem'-ik], *n.* the occurrence of a disease afflicting many people at once; anything common and temporary (opinion, state of affairs, etc.).

EPIDEMIC (2), [ep'-i-dem'-ik], *adj.* having the nature of an epidemic. [Gk. *epidemikos*].

EPIDEMICAL, [ep'-i-dem'-ik-al], *adj.* epidemic.

EPIDEMICALLY, [ep'-i-dem'-ik-al-i], *adv.* as an epidemic.

EPIDEMICALNESS, [ep'-i-dem'-ik-al-nes], *n.* the state of being epidemic.

EPIDEMIOLOGY, [ep'-i-dēm'-i-ol'-oj-i], *n.* the scientific study of epidemics. [EPIDEMIC and Gk. *logos* speech].

EPIDEMY†, [ep'-i-dem'-i], *n.* an epidemic.

EPIDENDRAL, [ep'-i-den'-dral], *adj.* living, growing on trees. [EPI and Gk. *dendron* tree].

EPIDERMAL, [ep'-i-durm'-al], *adj.* connected with the epidermis.

EPIDERMATOID, [ep'-i-durm'-a-toid], *adj.* resembling the epiderm. [EPIDERMIS and Gk. *oeides* like].

EPIDERMIC, [ep'-i-durm'-ik], *adj.* epidermal.

EPIDERMIDAL, [ep'-i-durm'-i-dal], *adj.* epidermic.

EPIDERMIS, [ep'-i-durm'-is], *n.* the cuticle or outer layer of skin on human beings and animals; (*bot.*) the outer covering of leaves and stems of plants. [Gk. *epidermis*].

EPIDERMOID, [ep'-i-durm'-oid], *adj.* resembling the epidermis. [EPIDERMIS and Gk. *oeides* like].

EPIDIASCOPE, [ep'-i-dī'-a-skōp'], *n.* a lantern with a system of reflecting mirrors for projecting an image of an opaque body on a screen and for projecting transparent lantern slides. [EPI, Gk. *dia* through and *skopos* viewer].

EPIDOTE, [ep'-id-ōt], *n.* a silicate of calcium, iron, and aluminium with manganese and cerium. [Fr. *épidote*].

EPIDOTIC, [ep'-id-ot'-ik], *adj.* pertaining to or containing epidote.

EPIGASTRIC, [ep'-i-gas'-trik], *adj.* pertaining to the upper part of the epigastrium.

EPIGASTRIUM, [ep'-i-gas'-tri-um], *n.* that part of the abdomen extending from the sternum towards the navel. [Gk. *epigastrion*].

EPIGASTROCELE, [ep'-i-gas'-trō-sēl], *n.* hernia in or near the epigastrium. [EPIGASTRIUM and Gk. *kele* tumour].

EPIGEAL, [ep'-i-jē'-al], *adj.* epigeous.

EPIGEE, [ep'-i-jē], *n.* (*astron.*) the point of the moon's orbit nearest the earth. [Gk. *epigeion*].

EPIGENE, [ep'-i-jēn], *adj.* (*geol.*) originating on the earth's surface; (*min.*) in a crystalline form not natural to a substance. [Gk. *epigenes*].

EPIGENESIS, [ep'-i-jen'-is-is], *n.* (*biol.*) a theory that every embryo or germ is formed as a new product and not merely developed in the reproductive process. [EPI and GENESIS].

EPIGENESIST, [ep'-i-jen'-is-ist], *n.* one who accepts epigenesis.

EPIGENOUS, [ep-ij'-en-us], *adj.* (*bot.*) living or growing on the surface.

EPIGEOUS, [ep-ij'-i-us], *adj.* growing on the surface of the earth, close to the ground; (*bot.*) having the cotyledons above ground.

EPIGLOTTIC, [ep'-i-glot'-ik], *adj.* pertaining to the epiglottis.

EPIGLOTTIS, [ep'-i-glot'-is], *n.* (*anat.*) a small cartilage serving to cover the top of the windpipe.

EPIGLOTTIS

EPIGONE, [ep'-i-gōn], *n.* a descendant, *esp.* an undistinguished descendant or follower of some great person. [Gk. *epigonoi* those born after].

EPIGRAM, [ep'-i-gram'], *n.* short poem or prose passage containing a neatly expressed satirical or witty thought; a pointed remark. [Gk. *epigramma*].

EPIGRAMMATIC, [ep'-i-gram-at'-ik], *adj.* relating to, skilful in epigrams; terse like an epigram.

EPIGRAMMATICAL, [ep'-i-gram-at'-ik-al], *adj.* epigrammatic.

EPIGRAMMATICALLY, [ep'-i-gram-at'-ik-al-i], *adv.* in an epigrammatic way.

EPIGRAMMATIST, [ep'-i-gram'-at-ist], *n.* one who is skilful at epigrams.

EPIGRAMMATIZE, [ep'-i-gram'-at-iz], *v.t.* to express epigrammatically; to compose an epigram on.

EPIGRAPH, [ep'-i-graf'], *n.* an engraved inscription; an inscription or quotation at the beginning of a book or section of a book. [Gk. *epigraphe*].

EPIGRAPHIC, [ep'-i-graf'-ik], *adj.* relating to epigraphs.

EPIGRAPHICS, [ep'-i-graf'-iks], *n.*(*pl.*) the study of epigraphs.

EPIGRAPHIST, [ep-ig'-raf-ist], *n.* an expert on epigraphs.

EPIGRAPHY, [ep-ig'-ra-fi], *n.* epigraphics.

EPIGYNOUS, [ep-ij'-in-us], *adj.* (*bot.*) growing on the ovary, as stamens of some plants. [EPI and Gk. *gune* female].

EPILEPSY, [ep'-i-lep'-si], *n.* (*med.*) a nervous affliction expressing itself from time to time by foaming at the mouth, convulsions, and unconsciousness, the falling sickness. [Gk. *epilepsia*].

EPILEPTIC (1), [ep'-i-lep'-tik], *n.* one suffering from epilepsy.

EPILEPTIC (2), [ep'-i-lep'-tik], *adj.* relating to, having, epilepsy.

EPILEPTICAL, [ep'-i-lep'-tik-al], *adj.* epileptic.

EPILEPTICS, [ep'-i-lep'-tiks], *n.*(*pl.*) medicines for epileptic patients.

EPILEPTOID, [ep'-i-lep'-toid], *adj.* resembling epilepsy. [EPILEPSY and Gk. *oeides* like].

EPILOGICAL, [ep'-i-loj'-ik-al], *adj.* relating to an epilogue.

EPILOGISTIC, [ep'-i-loj-is'-tik], *adj.* epilogical.

EPILOGUE, [ep'-i-log'], *n.* a short speech by one of the actors at the end of a play; (*rhet.*) the concluding summary of a discourse; any similar concluding section in a literary work. [Gk. *epilogos*].

EPILOGUIZE†, [ep-il'-og-īz], *v.t.* to recite an epilogue.

EPIMERAL, [ep'-i-mēer'-al], *adj.* (*zool.*) pertaining to the segment of an articulated animal above the limb joint. [EPI and Gk. *meros* part].

EPINASTY, [ep'-in-as-ti], *n.* (*bot.*) curvature due to more active growth on the upper side. [EPI and Gk. *nastos* squeezing].

EPINYCTIS, [ep'-i-nik'-tis], *n.* (*med.*) an eruption of the skin appearing only at night. [EPI and ~Gk. *nux* night].

EPIORNIS, [ep'-i-awn'-is], *n.* a huge fossil bird, found in Madagascar. [EPI and Gk. *ornis* bird].

EPIPEDOMETRY†, [ep'-i-pid-om'-it-ri], *n.* the measurement of figures standing on the same base. [Gk. *epipedos* plane and *metria* measurement].

EPIPERIPHERAL, [ep'-i-per-if'-er-al], *adj.* situated on the periphery.

EPIPETALOUS, [ep'-i-pet'-al-us], *adj.* (*bot.*) living, growing, on a petal.

EPIPHANY, [ip-if'-an-i], n. the manifestation of Christ to the Gentiles, represented by three Magi; the Christian festival of this kept on January 6. [Gk. *epiphaneia* manifestation].

EPIPHLOEUM, [ep'-i-flē'-um], *n.* (*bot.*) the corky covering of the bark next to the epidermis. [EPI and ~Gk. *phloos* bark].

EPIPHONEMA, [ep'-i-fon-ēm'-a], *n.* (*rhet.*) an abrupt exclamatory ejaculation in the course or at the conclusion of a discourse. [Gk. *epiphonema*].

EPIPHORA, [ep-if'-or-a], *n.* (*med.*) a disease in which the tears accumulate in the eye; (*rhet.*) the emphatic repetition of a word or phrase at intervals. [Gk. *epiphora*].

EPIPHRAGM, [ep'-i-fram'], *n.* (*zool.*) the operculum in shells of certain molluscs; (*bot.*) the tympanum in mosses. [Gk. *epiphragma*].

EPIPHYLLOSPERMOUS, [ep'-i-fil-ō-spurm'-us], *adj.* (*bot.*) bearing spores on the back of the leaves, as ferns. [EPI, Gk. *phullon* leaf and SPERM].

EPIPHYLLOUS, [ep-if'-il-us], *adj.* (*bot.*) growing upon a leaf. [EPI and Gk. *phullon* leaf].

EPIPHYSIS, (*pl.* **epiphyses**), [ep-if'-is-is], *n.* (*anat.*) part of a bone separated by a cartilage which becomes osseous; pineal gland. [Gk. *epiphusis*].

EPIPHYTAL, [ep-if'-īt-al], *adj.* relating to an epiphyte.

EPIPHYTE, [ep'-i-fīt'], *n.* a plant growing upon other plants but not parasitic. [EPI and Gk. *phuton* plant].

EPIPHYTIC, [ep'-i-fit'-ik], *adj.* epiphytal.

EPIPLEROSIS, [ep'-i-plēer-ōs'-is], *n.* (*med.*) excessive distension of the veins with blood. [Gk. *epiplerosis* overfilling].

EPIPLEXIS, [ep'-i-pleks'-is], *n.* (*rhet.*) a figure of speech in which the speaker endeavours to move his audience by a gentle rebuke. [Gk. *epiplexis*].

EPIPLOCE, [ep-ip'-los-i], *n.* (*rhet.*) a kind of climax. [Gk. *epiploke*].

EPIPLOIC, [ep'-i-plō'-ik], *adj.* pertaining to the caul or epiploon.

EPIPLOON, [ep'-i-plō'-on], *n.* (*med.*) the caul. [Gk. *epiploon*].

EPIPOLIC, [ep'-i-pol'-ik], *adj.* relating to epipolism.

EPIPOLISM, [ep-ip'-ol-izm], *n.* fluorescence. [Gk. *epipole* surface].

EPIPOLIZE, [ep-ip'-ol-īz], *v.t.* to bring about fluorescence in.

EPIRHEOLOGY, [ep'-i-ri-ol'-oj-i], *n.* the study of the effects of external influences on plants. [EPI, Gk. *rheos* stream and *logos* speech].

EPIRHIZOUS, [ep'-i-rīz'-us], *adj.* (*bot.*) situated, growing on a root. [EPI and Gk. *rhiza* root].

EPISCENIUM, [ep'-i-sēn'-i-um], *n.* (*antiq.*) the upper part of the scene in an ancient theatre. [Gk. *episkenion* scenery].

EPISCOPACY, [ep-isk'-op-as-i], *n.* the government of a church by bishops; the bishops in a body. [~Gk. *episkopos* guardian].

EPISCOPAL, [ep-isk'-ōp-al], *adj.* pertaining to or governed by bishops; a member of the Established Church of England.

EPISCOPALIA†, [ep-isk'-ōp-āl'-i-a], *n.*(*pl.*) payments formerly made by clergy to their diocesan bishops.

EPISCOPALIAN (1), [ep-isk'-ōp-āl'-i-an], *n.* an upholder of episcopacy; a member of a church governed by bishops; a member of the Established Church of England.

EPISCOPALIAN (2), [ep-isk'-ōp-āl'-i-an], *adj.* relating to, governed by, bishops; relating to the Church of England.

EPISCOPALIANISM, [ep-isk'-ōp-āl'-i-an-ism], *n.* the system of church government by bishops.

EPISCOPALLY, [ep-isk'-ōp-al-i], *adv.* in an episcopal way.

EPISCOPATE (1), [ep-isk'-ōp-āt], *n.* a bishopric; the office and rank of a bishop; the bishops as a body. [L. *episcopatus*].

EPISCOPATE† (2), [ep-isk'-ōp'-āt], *v.i.* to officiate as a bishop. [L. *episcopare*].

EPISCOPE, [ep'-i-skōp], *n.* an epidiascope. [EPI and Gk. *skopos* viewer].

EPISCOPY, [ep-isk'-op-i], *n.* the episcopal order; (*milit.*) survey, superintendence. [Gk. *episkopia* overseeing].

EPISODE, [ep'-is-ōd], *n.* an incidental narrative temporarily overshadowing the main story; one of a series of events; any unimportant occurrence; (*Gk. drama*) the action of a tragedy between two choric songs. [Gk. *epeisodion*].

EPISODIAL, [ep'-is-ōd'-i-al], *adj.* episodic.

EPISODIC, [ep'-is-od'-ik], *adj.* pertaining to, or

resembling, an episode; told in a series of short disjointed narratives.
EPISODICAL, [ep'-is-od'-ik-al], *adj.* episodic.
EPISODICALLY, [ep'-is-od'-ik-al-i], *adv.* in an episodic fashion.
EPISPASTIC (1), [ep'-i-spas'-tik], *n.* (*med.*) something that causes blistering.
EPISPASTIC (2), [ep'-i-spas'-tik], *adj.* (*med.*) blistering, vesicating. [Gk. *epispastikos* drawing out].
EPISPERM, [ep'-i-spurm], *n.* (*bot.*) the outer covering of a seed. [EPI and SPERM].
EPISPERMIC, [ep'-i-spurm'-ik], *adj.* relating to the episperm.
EPISTAXIS, [ep'-is-taks'-is], *n.* (*med.*) bleeding at the nose. [Gk. *epistaxis*].
EPISTEMOLOGICAL, [ep-ist'-im-ol-oj'-ik-al], *adj.* relating to the theory of knowledge.
EPISTEMOLOGY, [ep-ist'-im-ol'-oj-i], *n.* the study of the source, nature, and limitations of knowledge; the theory of knowledge. [Gk. *episteme* knowledge and *logos* speech].
EPISTERNAL, [ep'-i-stur'-nal], *adj.* relating to the anterior portion of the sternum, which in birds sustains the fork-bone.
EPISTERNUM, [ep'-i-stur'-num], *n.* the interclavicle. [EPI and STERNUM].
EPISTILBITE, [ep'-i-stil'-bīt], *n.* (*min.*) a white mineral composed of silica, alumina, calcium, and soda. [EPI and STILBITE].
EPISTLE, [i-pisl'], *n.* a letter; an apostolic letter forming one of the books of the New Testament; an extract from one of these, or some other portion of scripture not in the four gospels, appointed to be read at Holy Communion. [Gk. *epistole* message].
EPISTLER, EPISTOLLER, [i-pis'-ler], *n.* one who writes or reads out epistles.
EPISTOLARY, [i-pist'-ol-er-i], *adj.* relating to epistles or letter-writing.
EPISTOLET, [i-pist'-o-let], *n.* a short epistle.
EPISTOLIC, [ep'-ist-ol'-ik], *adj.* epistolical.
EPISTOLICAL, [ep'-ist-ol'-ik-al], *adj.* relating to epistles or letters.
EPISTOLIZE, [ep-ist'-ol-īz], *v.i.* to compose an epistle.
EPISTOLIZER, [ep-ist'-ol-īz-er], *n.* one who epistolizes.
EPISTOLLER, see EPISTLER.
EPISTOLOGRAPHIC, [ep-ist'-ol-o-graf'-ik], *adj.* connected with letter-writing.
EPISTOLOGRAPHY, [ep-ist'-ol-og'-raf-i], n. the art and practice of letter-writing.
EPISTROPHE, [ep-ist'-rof-i], *n.* (*rhet.*) a figure in which several consecutive sentences end with the same phrase. [Gk. *epistrophe*].
EPISTYLE, [ep'-i-stīl], *n.* (*arch.*) the main beam laid on top of the abacus of the capital of a column, architrave. [Gk. *epistulion*].
EPITAPH, [ep'-i-taf], *n.* a short memorial passage inscribed on a tomb or one suitable for such use. [Gk. *epitaphion* funeral oration].
EPITAPHIAN, [ep'-it-af'-i-an], *adj.* resembling an epitaph.
EPITAPHIC, [ep'-i-taf'-ik], *adj.* pertaining to an epitaph.
EPITAPHIST, [ep'-i-taf'-ist], *n.* one who writes epitaphs.
EPITASIS, [ep-it'-as-is], *n.* the part of the play which develops the plot, between protasis and catastrophe. [Gk. *epitasis*].
EPITHALAMIAL, [ep'-i-thal-ām'-i-al], *adj.* relating to an epithalamium.
EPITHALAMIC, [ep'-i-thal-am'-ik], *adj.* epithalamial.
EPITHALAMIUM, (*pl.* **epithalamia**), [ep'-i-thal-ām'-i-um], *n.* a poem or song celebrating a marriage. [Gk. *epithalamion*].
EPITHELIAL, [ep'-i-thēl'-i-al], *adj.* relating to the epithelium.
EPITHELIOMA, [ep'-i-thēl'-i-ōm'-a], *n.* a cancerous condition of the epithelium.
EPITHELIUM, [ep'-i-thēl'-i-um], *n.* (*anat.*) a thin covering of cells enveloping the mucous membrane; (*bot.*) a thin epidermis formed of young cells lining the inner cavities of plants. [EPI and Gk. *thele* teat].
EPITHEM, [ep'-i-them'], *n.* (*med.*) an external application for medicinal purposes. [Gk. *epithema* that which is placed upon].
EPITHET, [ep'-i-thet'], *n.* a descriptive phrase or word. [Gk. *epitheton*].
EPITHETIC, [ep'-i-thet'-ik], *adj.* relating to an epithet.
EPITHETICAL, [ep'-i-thet'-ik-al], *adj.* epithetic.
EPITHUMETIC, EPITHYMETIC, [ep'-i-thim-et'-ik], *adj.* pertaining to the desires and appetites. [Gk. *epithumetikos*].
EPITITHIDES, [ep'-i-tith'-id-ēz], *n.*(*pl.*) (*arch.*) mouldings at the top of a cornice. [~Gk. *epitithemi* I place on].

EPITITHIDES

EPITOME, [ep-it'-om-i], *n.* a brief recapitulation, an abridgement or summary in which nothing essential is omitted; (*fig.*) any similar miniature copy. [Gk. *epitome*].
EPITOMIST, [ep-it'-om-ist], *n.* one who writes epitomes.
EPITOMIZE, [ep-it'-om-īz], *v.t. and i.* to make an epitome of; to précis.
EPITOMIZER, [ep-it'-om-īz-er], *n.* an epitomist.
EPITONIC, [ep'-it-on'-ik], *adj.* stretched too far, overstrained. [EPI and TONIC (2)].
EPITRITE, [ep'-i-trīt], *n.* (*pros.*) a foot of three long syllables and one short, in any order. [Gk. *epitritos*].
EPITROPE, [ep-it'-rop-i], *n.* (*rhet.*) a figure by which a point is conceded to obtain an advantage later on. [Gk. *epitrope* concession.[
EPIZEUXIS, [ep'-i-zewks'-is], *n.* (*rhet.*) a figure in which a word is repeated vehemently. [Gk. *epizeuxis*].
EPIZOON, (*pl.* **epizoa**), [ep'-iz-ō'-on, ep'-iz-ō'-a], *n.* an external parasite, any crustacean of the orders *Copepoda* and *Pycnogonida*. [EPI and Gk. *zoon* animal].
EPIZOOTIC (1), [ep'-iz-ō-ot'-ik], *n.* a disease affecting many animals at once.
EPIZOOTIC (2), [ep'-iz-ō-ot'-ik], *adj.* relating to the epizoa or to an epizootic.
EPIZOOTY, [ep'-i-zō'-ot-i], *n.* an epizootic.
EPLICATE, [ē'-plik-āt], *adj.* not plaited. [E (2) and PLICATE].
EPOCH, [ē'-pok], *n.* an era in history; a period of time characterized by special events, movements, etc.; (*astron.*) heliocentric longitude of a planet at a given date; (*geol.*) one of the minor divisions of time. [Gk. *epokha* a check, stop].
EPOCHAL, [ēp'-ok-al], *adj.* pertaining to or marking an epoch.
EPOCH-MAKING, [ē'-pok-mā'-king], *adj.* marking the commencement of a new era; of outstanding importance and influence.
EPODE, [ep'-ōd], *n.* the third or last part of the ode following the strophe and antistrophe; any little verse or verses that follow one or more greater ones. [EP and ODE].
EPODIC, [ep-ōd'-ik], *adj.* pertaining to or like an epode.
EPONYM, [ep'-on-im], *n.* an historical or fabulous person from whose name the name of a race, family or place is derived. [Gk. *eponumos*].
EPONYMIC, [ep'-on-im'-ik], *adj.* eponymous.
EPONYMOUS, [ep-on'-im-us], *adj.* having a name from which a racial or family name is derived.
EPOPEE, [ep'-ōp-ē], *n.* an epic or epics in general. [Fr. *épopée* from Gk. *epopoeia*].
EPOPOEIA, [ep-op-ē'-a], *n.* the legend or subject matter of an epic poem. [*Prec.*].
EPOS, [ep'-os], *n.* a traditional epic of great antiquity. [Gk. *epos*].
EPROUVETTE, éprouvette, [ā-proov-et'], *n.* a device used in gunnery for testing the strength of explosives. [Fr. *éprouvette*].
EPSOMITE, [ep'-som-īt], *n.* hydrated sulphate of magnesium, commonly called Epsom salts. [*Epsom*, where first extracted from local water].
EPULARY, [ep'-yool-er-i], *adj.* relating to a banquet. [L. *epularis*].
EPULIS, [ep'-yoo-lis], *n.* (*med.*) a small swelling on the gums. [Gk. *epoulis*].
EPULOTIC (1), [ep'-yool-ot'-ik], *n.* (*med.*) an agent for drying up wounds or sores.
EPULOTIC (2), [ep'-yool-ot'-ik], *adj.* tending to dry up, cicatrize, and heal wounds and sores. [Gk. *epoulotikos*].
EPURATION, [ep'-yoo-rā'-shun], *n.* purification. [Fr. *épuration*].
EPURE, épure, [āp'-yooer'], *n.* (*arch.*) a large working plan. [Fr. *épure*].

EQUABILITY, [ek'-wa-bil'-i-ti], *n.* the quality of being equable.
EQUABLE, [ek'-wabl], *adj.* even, steady, uniform; not liable to sudden or excessive changes; not easily disturbed or upset. [L. *aequabilis* steady].
EQUABLENESS, [ek'-wabl-nes], *n.* the quality of being equable.
EQUABLY, [ek'-wab-li], *adv.* in an equable manner.
EQUAL (1), [ē'-kwal], *n.* a person of equal standing, capabilities, rank, age, etc.; a person of the same social standing.
EQUAL (2), [ē'-kwal], *adj.* the same in number, size, degree, etc.; of like amount, quality, etc.; uniform; evenly balanced; equable; **to be e. to**, to have necessary strength or ability for. [L. *aequalis*].
EQUAL (3), [ē'-kwal], *v.t.* to be equal to in number or quality; to come up to, be as good as; to be the same as in size, number, etc.
EQUALITY, [ēk-wol'-it-i], *n.* the condition of being equal. [OFr. *equalité*].
EQUALIZATION, [ē'-kwal-īz-ā'-shun], *n.* the act of equalizing; the state of being equalized.
EQUALIZE, [ē'-kwal-īz], *v.t.* to make even or equal.
EQUALIZER, [ē'-kwal-īz-er], *n.* one who or that which equalizes.
EQUALLY, [ē'-kwal-i], *adv.* in equal quantity or degree.
EQUALNESS, [ē'-kwal-nes], *n.* equality.
EQUANIMITY, [ek'-wan-im'-it-i], *n.* steadiness of disposition, composure of mind, outlook, etc.; calm courage. [L. *aequanimitas*].
EQUANIMOUS, [ek-wan'-im-us], *adj.* possessing the quality of equanimity.
EQUANT, [ē'-kwant], *n.* an imaginary circle used in Ptolemaic astronomy to adjust certain motions of the planets. [~ L. *aequans* equalling].
EQUATE, [ē-kwāt'], *v.t.* to look upon or refer to as equal, to make no distinction between. [L. *aequare* to make level].
EQUATION, [ē-kwā'-shun], *n.* the act of equating, the process of being equated; (*algebra*) a formal statement of equality. [~ L. *aequatio*].
EQUATIONAL, [ē-kwā'-shun-al], *adj.* relating to an equation.
EQUATIONALLY, [ē-kwā'-shun-al-i], *adv.* in the form of or by means of an equation.
EQUATOR, [ē-kwā'-tor], *n.* an imaginary line encircling the earth so that it is always equidistant from either pole; (*astron.*) the corresponding circle in the celestial sphere. [L. *aequator* an equalizer].
EQUATORIAL (1), [ĕk'-wat-aw'-ri-al], *n.* a telescope turning on an axle so as to follow the course of any heavenly body across the sky.
EQUATORIAL (2), [ĕk-wat-aw'-ri-al], *adj.* close to or relating to the equator.
EQUATORIALLY, [ĕk'-wat-aw'-ri-al-i], *adv.* so as to resemble, pertain to, or follow, the equator.
EQUERRY, [ek'-wer-i], *n.* a royal household officer in close attendance upon a royal personage; (*archaic*) a master of the royal stables. [Fr. *écurie*].
EQUESTRIAN (1), [ik-west'-ri-an], *n.* a horseman.
EQUESTRIAN (2), [ik-west'-ri-an], *adj.* pertaining to horsemanship; mounted, on horseback; **e. statue**, a statue of a person on horseback. [L. *equestris* of a horseman].
EQUESTRIANISM, [ik-west'-ri-an-izm], *n.* riding, horsemanship.
EQUESTRIENNE, [ik-west'-ri-en'], *n.* a woman equestrian.
EQUI-, *pref.* equal. [L. *aequus* equal].
EQUIANGULAR, [ē'-kwi-ang'-gew-ler], *adj.* (*geom.*) having equal angles.
EQUIBALANCE (1), [ē'-kwi-bal'-ants], *n.* equal balance.
EQUIBALANCE (2), [ē'-kwi-bal'-ants], *v.t.* to balance equally.
EQUICRURAL, [ē'-kwi-kroō'-ral], *adj.* with legs of equal length; isosceles. [L. *aequicrurus*].
EQUIDIFFERENT, [ē'-kwi-dif'-er-ent], *adj.* possessing equal differences; arithmetically proportional.
EQUIDISTANCE, [ē'-kwi-dis'-tants], *n.* the state of being equidistant, equal distance.
EQUIDISTANT, [ē'-kwi-dis'-tant], *adj.* equally distant.
EQUIDISTANTLY, [ē'-kwi-dis'-tant-li], *adv.* at an equal distance.
EQUIFORM, [ē'-kwi-fawm], *adj.* equal in form.
EQUIFORMITY, [ē'-kwi-fawm'-it-i], *n.* equalness of form, uniformity.
EQUILATERAL (1), [ē'-kwi-lat'-er-al], *n.* a figure with all its sides equal.
EQUILATERAL (2), [ē'-kwi-lat'-er-al], *adj.* having all sides equal.
EQUILIBRATE, [ē'-kwi-lib'-rāt], *v.t. and i.* to bring into a state of balance; to balance. [~L. *aequilibrare*].
EQUILIBRATION, [ē'-kwi-lib-rā'-shun], *n.* the act of keeping the balance even; the condition of being balanced.
EQUILIBRATOR, [ē'-kwi-lib'-rā-ter], *n.* a plane that balances an aeroplane.
EQUILIBRIST, [ē'-kwi-lib'-rist], *n.* one who performs feats of balancing. [Fr. *équilibriste*].
EQUILIBRITY, [ē'-kwi-lib'-ri-ti], *n.* the condition of being balanced.
EQUILIBRIUM, [ē'-kwi-lib'-ri-um], *n.* a state of poise, balance; the state of being kept at rest by equal but opposite forces; (*fig.*) a balance of power; equanimity. [L. *aequilibrium*].
EQUIMULTIPLE, [ē'-kwi-mul'-tipl], *n.* (*arith.*) any one of several numbers produced by multiplying several other numbers by the same number.
EQUINAL, [ek-wīn'-al], *adj.* equine.
EQUINE, [ek'-wīn], *adj.* relating to horses. [L. *equinus*].
EQUINECESSARY, [ē'-kwi-nes'-es-er-i], *adj.* required with equal urgency.
EQUINIA, [ek-win'-i-a], *n.* a disease called glanders chiefly affecting horses, but communicable to mankind. [EQUINE].
EQUINOCTIAL (1), [ē'-kwi-nok'-shal], *n.* equinoctial line.
EQUINOCTIAL (2), [ē'-kwi-nok'-shal], *adj.* relating to an equinox; **e. line**, the circle of the celestial sphere, corresponding to the terrestial equator, and having its plane perpendicular to the axis of the earth; **e. points**, the two points of intersection of the equator and the ecliptic. [L. *aequinoctialis*].
EQUINOCTIALLY, [ē'-kwi-nok'-shal-i], *adv.* towards the equinox.
EQUINOX, [ē'-kwi-noks'], *n.* the time when the sun passes over the equator, and day and night are of equal length; **spring, vernal, e.**, March 20; **autumnal e.**, September 22 or 23. [EQUI and L. *nox* night].
EQUINUMERANT†, [ē'-kwi-newm'-er-ant], *adj.* made up of the same number. [EQUI and L. *numerans* counting].
EQUIP, [ik-wip'], *v.t.* to furnish with what is necessary. [Fr. *équiper*].
EQUIPAGE, [ek'-wip-ij], *n.* the band of servants and officers attending a great person on a journey; travelling requisites.
EQUIPAGED, [ik-wip'-ijd], *adj.* provided with an equipage.
EQUIPEDAL, [e'-kwi-ped'-al], *adj.* with equal pairs of feet.
EQUIPENDENCY, [e'-kwi-pen'-den-si], *n.* the condition of being without bias.
EQUIPENDENT, [e'-kwi-pen'-dent], *adj.* in equipoise, without bias.
EQUIPMENT, [ik-wip'-ment], *n.* the act of equipping; condition of being equipped; that with which one is equipped, outfit, requisites.
EQUIPOISE (1), [e'-kwi-poiz], *n.* perfect balance; that which counterbalances; (*fig.*) equanimity.
EQUIPOISE (2), [e'-kwi-poiz], *v.t.* to counterbalance; (*fig.*) to keep in suspense.
EQUIPOLLENCE, [e'-kwi-pol'-ents], *n.* equality of force or meaning; that which is equipollent.
EQUIPOLLENT, [ē'-kwi-pol'-ent], *adj.* of equal force; equivalent.
EQUIPOLLENTLY, [ē'-kwi-pol'-ent-li], *adv.* with equal force.
EQUIPONDERANCE, [ē'-kwi-pond'-er-ants], *n.* the state of being equiponderant.
EQUIPONDERANT, [ē'-kwi-pon'-der-ant], *adj.* equal in weight.
EQUIPONDERATE, [ē'-kwi-pond'-er-āt], *v.t.* to be equal in weight to.
EQUIPOTENTIAL, [ē'-kwi-pōt-en'-shal], *adj.* (*phys.*) possessing at every point the same potential force.
EQUIROTAL, [ē'-kwi-rōt'-al], *adj.* having wheels of the same size. [EQUI and L. *rota* wheel].
EQUISETACEOUS, [ek'-wi-set-ā'-shus], *adj.* pertaining to the order *Equisetaceae*, such as the horsetails. [EQUISETUM].
EQUISETIC, [ek'-wi-sēt'-ik], *adj.* (*bot.*) relating to the genus *Equisetum*; **e. acid**, an acid obtained from a plant of this genus.
EQUISETIFORM, [ek'-wi-sēt'-i-fawm], *adj.* like horsetails.

EQUISETUM, [ek'-wi-sēt'-um], *n.* (*bot.*) the genus of plants including the horsetails. [L. *equisetum* horse-bristle].
EQUISONANCE, [ē'-kwi-sōn'-ants], *n.* (*mus.*, *archaic*) the concord of octaves. [L. *aequisonans* sounding equally].
EQUITABLE, [ek'-wit-abl], *adj.* according with justice and equity. [Fr. *équitable*].
EQUITABLENESS, [ek'-wit-abl-nes], *n.* the state of being equitable.
EQUITABLY, [ek'-wit-ab-li], *adv.* in an equitable fashion.
EQUITANCY, [ek'-wit-an-si], *n.* equestrianism.
EQUITANGENTIAL, [ē'-kwi-tan-jen'-shal], *adj.* (*geom.*) a curve whose tangent equals a constant line.
EQUITANT, [ek'-wit-ant], *adj.* (*bot.*) pertaining to leaves which overlap at their bases. [L. *equitans* riding].

EQUISETUM

EQUITATION, [ek'-wit-ā'-shun], *n.* skill in horsemanship. [L. *equitatio*].
EQUITY, [ek'-wit-i], *n.* the quality or condition of being just and unbiased; the principle of fair-mindedness and impartial unprejudiced judgment; (*leg.*) a judicial system supplementing and differing from Common Law. [L. *aequitas*].
EQUIVALENCE, [ik-wiv'-al-ents], *n.* the state of being equivalent.
EQUIVALENCY, [ik-wiv'-al-en-si], *n.* equivalence.
EQUIVALENT (1), [ik-wiv'-al-ent], *n.* that which is equivalent.
EQUIVALENT (2), [ik-wiv'-al-ent], *adj.* equal; (*chem.*) equal in combining value, producing the same result. [Fr. *équivalent*].
EQUIVALENTLY, [ik-wiv'-al-ent-li], *adv.* in an equal way.
EQUIVALVE (1), [ek'-wi-valv'], *n.* a bivalve in which the two valves are of equal size.
EQUIVALVE (2), [ek'-wi-valv'], *adj.* having equal valves.
EQUIVOCAL (1), [i-kwiv'-ok-al], *n.* an ambiguous word or expression.
EQUIVOCAL (2), [i-kwiv'-ok-al], *adj.* liable to be interpreted in more than one way, ambiguous; giving rise to suspicion or doubt. [L. *aequivocus* of equal voice].
EQUIVOCALLY, [i-kwiv'-ok-al-i], *adv.* in an equivocal fashion.
EQUIVOCALNESS, [ik-wiv'-okl-nes], *n.* the state of being equivocal.
EQUIVOCATE, [ik-wiv'-ok-āt], *v.i.* to use words of doubtful meaning; to use ambiguous expressions with a view to mislead; to lie; to quibble. [L. *aequivocare*].
EQUIVOCATION, [ik-wiv'-ōk-ā'-shun], *n.* the act or practice of equivocating.
EQUIVOCATOR, [ik-wiv'-ōk-āt'-er], *n.* a person who equivocates.
EQUIVOCATORY, [ik-wiv'-ōk-āt'-er-i], *adj.* of an equivocating character.
EQUIVOKE, [ek'-wi-vōk'], *n.* an equivocal term; an equivocation.
EQUIVOROUS, [ek-wiv'-aw-rus], *adj.* feeding on horseflesh. [EQUUS and L. *vorare* to devour].
EQUUS, [ek'-wus], *n.* (*zool.*) the family of ungulates containing horses, asses, and zebras. [L. *equus* horse].
ERA, [ēer'-a], *n.* a system of dating, starting from some selected event or point of time; epoch, period. [L. *aera* brass counters, method of calculation].
ERADIATE, [i-rād'-i-āt], *v.i.* to shoot out like rays of light.

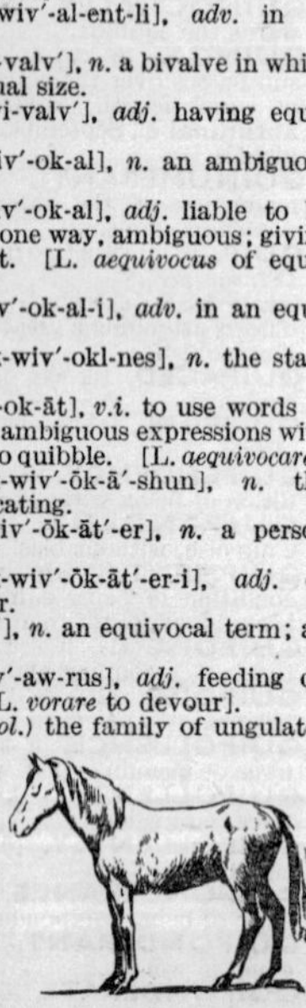

EQUUS

ERADIATION, [i-rād'-i-ā'-shun], *n.* sending forth, emission as of rays.
ERADICABLE, [i-rad'-ik-abl], *adj.* able to be eradicated.
ERADICATE, [i-rad'-ik-āt], *v.t.* to tear up by the roots; to wipe out, to extirpate. [L. *eradicare*].
ERADICATION, [i-rad'-ik-ā'-shun], *n.* the act of eradicating; the condition of being eradicated.
ERADICATIVE, [i-rad'-ik-at-iv], *adj.* able to eradicate.
ERASABLE, [i-rāz'-abl], *adj.* able to be erased.
ERASE, [i-rāz'], *v.t.* to scratch, or otherwise remove, from the surface on which it is written or cut; (*fig.*) to remove, wipe out. [~L. *erasum*, *p.pt.* of *eradere*].
ERASED, [i-rāzd'], *adj.* effaced; (*her.*) forcibly torn off, leaving the edges jagged and uneven.
ERASEMENT, [i-rāz'-ment], *n.* the act of erasing; the state of being erased.
ERASER, [i-rāz'-er], *n.* a person or thing that erases.
ERASION, [i-rā'-zhun], *n.* the act of erasing; the place where something has been erased.
ERASTIAN (1), [i-ras'-ti-an], *n.* one who adheres to the principles of Erastus. [*Erastus*, a sixteenth-century Swiss theologian].
ERASTIAN (2), [i-ras'-ti-an], *adj.* pertaining to Erastus or his teaching.
ERASTIANISM, [i-ras'-ti-an-izm], *n.* the doctrine which advocates the subjection of Church to State.
ERASURE, [i-rā'-zhur], *n.* the act of erasing; erasion, the place from which something has been erased.
ERATO, [er'-at-ō], *n.* (*myth.*) the muse of lyrics and love-poetry. [Gk. *Erato* the lovely one].
ERBIUM, [ur'-bi-um], *n.* the chemical element denoted by Er. [~*Ytterby*, in Sweden, where found].
ERE (1), [āer], *adv.* sooner; rather than. [OE. *ær*].
ERE (2), [āer], *prep.* before. [*Prec.*].
EREBUS, [er'-ib-us], *n.* the cavern between earth and hell; the nether regions. [L. *Erebus*].
ERECT (1), [i-rekt'], *adj.* vertically upright, standing up. [L. *erectus*].
ERECT (2), [i-rekt'], *adv.* in vertical position.
ERECT (3), [i-rekt'], *v.t.* to set up in an erect position; to elevate; to build. [~L. *erectum*, *p.pt.* of *erigere*].
ERECTABLE, [i-rekt'-abl], *adj.* able to be erected.
ERECTED, [i-rekt'-ed], *adj.* upright.
ERECTER, [i-rekt'-er], *n.* one who erects, a builder.
ERECTILE, [i-rekt'-il], *adj.* able to be erected; (*anat.*) in a state of rigidity.
ERECTION, [i-rek'-shun], *n.* the act of erecting; the condition of being erected; a thing erected, a building.
ERECTIVE, [i-rekt'-iv], *adj.* serving to erect.
ERECTLY, [i-rekt'-li], *adv.* in an erect position.
ERECTNESS, [i-rekt'-nes], *n.* the state of being erect.
ERECTOR, [i-rekt'-er], *n.* (*anat.*) a muscle that erects a part or organ; (*phot.*) a reversing lens.
ERELONG, [āer'-long'], *adv.* soon.
EREMACAUSIS, [ēer'-em-ak-aws'-is], *n.* a natural slow combustion in decaying organic compounds exposed to the air. [Gk. *erema* quietly and *kausis* burning].
EREMITAGE†, see HERMITAGE.
EREMITE, [e'-rim-it], *n.* a hermit. [L. *heremita*].
EREMITIC, [e'-rem-it'-ik], *adj.* eremitical.
EREMITICAL, [e'-rem-it'-ik-al], *adj.* relating to an eremite.
EREMITISM, [e'-rem-it-izm'], *n.* the way of life of a hermit.
ERENOW, [āer'-now'], *adj.* before now.
EREPTATION†, [e'-rept-ā'-shun], *n.* a creeping forth. [~L. *ereptare* to creep forth].
EREPTION, [i-rep'-shun], *n.* removal by force. [L. *ereptio*].
ERETHISM, [e'-rith-izm], *n.* (*med.*) morbid excitement or irritation of any organ or part. [Gk. *erethismos* irritation].
ERETHISTIC, [e'-rith-is'-tik], *adj.* pertaining to erethism.
EREWHILE, [āer'-wil'], *adv.* some time before. [ERE and WHILE].
ERF, [urf], *n.* a garden plot of about half an acre in South Africa. [Du. *erf*].
ERG, [urg], *n.* a unit of work equal to the amount performed by one dyne through one centimetre. [Gk. *ergon* work].
ERGO, [ur'-gō], *adv.* hence, therefore. [L. *ergo*].
ERGOMETER, [ur-gom'-it-er], *n.* an instrument for measuring the amount of work or energy. [ERG and METER].
ERGOT, [ur'-got], *n.* (*bot.*) a fungus causing a disease in rye and other cereals; this disease; a medicinal drug from this fungus. [Fr. *ergot*].
ERGOTED, [ur'-got-ed], *adj.* attacked by ergot.
ERGOTIN, [ur'-got-in], *n.* (*chem.*) a medicinal substance with bitter taste found in ergot.
ERGOTISM, [ur'-got-izm], *n.* a malady caused by ergot.
ERIACH, [ēer'-i-ak], *n.* (*leg.*, *Ir.*) a pecuniary fine which a murderer was formerly required to pay to the relatives of the victim. [Ir. *eriach*].
ERICA, [e'-rik-a], *n.* (*bot.*) the genus of plants that includes heather. [Gk. *ereike* heath].
ERICACEOUS, [e'-rik-ā'-shus], *adj.* relating to the ericas.

ERIGERON, [er-ij'-er-on], *n.* (*bot.*) a numerous genus of plants, including fleabane. [Gk. *erigeron* groundsel].

ERINACEOUS, [e'-rin-ā'-shus], *adj.* relating to hedgehogs. [L. *erinaceus*].

ERINEUM, [e-rin'-i-um], *n.* a growth or excrescence on leaves. [Gk. *erineos* woolly].

ERINYS, [e'-rin-is], *n.* (*myth.*) one of the Furies; (*fig.*) conscience. [Gk. *erinus*].

ERIODENDRON, [ē'-ri-ō-den'-dron], *n.* the wool- or silk-cotton tree, *Eriodendron anfractuosum.* [Gk. *erion* wool and *dendron* tree].

ERISTIC, [e-ris'-tik], *adj.* eristical.

ERISTICAL, [e-ris'-tik-al], *adj.* pertaining to controversy. [Gk. *eristikos*].

ERL-KING, [url'-king], *n.* (*Germ. myth.*) the king of the elves. [Germ. *Erl-König* a mistranslation of Dan. *ellerkonge* king of the elves].

ERMELIN†, [ur'-mal-in], *n.* ermine. [Fr. *hermeline*].

ERMINE, [ur'-min], *n.* the stoat, which in summer has a brown coat, and in winter in cold climates a white one, with a black tip on the tail; the winter fur of this animal, much used for the robes of judges and peers; (*her.*) a white field with black spots; (*fig.*) the office and duties of a judge of the High Court; (*poet.*) a symbol of purity and integrity. [OFr. *hermine*].

ERMINED, [ur'-mind], *adj.* (*her.*) white, marked with black spots of a peculiar shape.

ERMINED

ERMINES, [ur'-minz], *n.* (*pl.*) (*her.*) white spots on a black field.

ERMINOIS, [ur'-min-ois], *adj.* (*her.*) with black spots on a gold field. [OFr. *erminois*].

ERNE (1), [urn], *n.* an eagle, now especially the sea-eagle *Haliaetus albicilla.* [OE. *earn*].

ERNE† (2), [urn], *n.* a cottage; a hut; a place of retirement. [OE. *ærn* house].

ERODE, [i-rōd'], *v.t.* to gnaw away, to fret, to wear away slowly and gradually, to destroy by attrition, to corrode. [L. *erodere*].

ERODED, [i-rōd'-id], *adj.* (*bot.*) having an irregularly jagged edge.

ERODENT, [i-rōd'-ent], *n.* (*med.*) a caustic drug which eats away growths. [L. *erodens*].

EROSE, [i-rōz'], *adj.* (*bot.*) with small sinuses in the margin. [L. *erosus* eaten away].

EROSION, [i-rō'-zhun], *n.* the act of eroding; the state of being eroded; the destruction of the coast-line by the sea. [L. *erosum* eroded].

EROSIVE, [e-rōz'-iv], *adj.* capable of eroding.

EROSTRATE, [i-ros'-trāt], *adj.* having no beak. [E (2) and L. *rostrum* beak].

EROTEME, [e'-rōt-ēm], *n.* (*rhet.*) a question mark. [Gk. *erotema* question].

EROTESIS, [e'-rōt-ēs'-is], *n.* (*rhet.*) an assertion in the form of a question. [Gk. *erotesis*].

EROTETIC, [e'-rō-tet'-ik], *adj.* relating to erotesis; interrogatory.

EROTIC, [i-rot'-ik], *adj.* relating to love and sexual passion; sexually passionate, amorous. [Gk. *erotikos*].

EROTICAL, [i-rot'-ik-al], *adj.* erotic.

EROTOMANIA, [i-rōt'-ō-mān'-i-a], *n.* madness arising from erotic propensities; morbid excess of amorousness. [EROTIC and MANIA].

ERPETOLOGY, [ur'-pit-ol'-oj-i], *n.* the scientific study of reptiles; herpetology. [Gk. *herpeton* reptile and *logos* speech].

ERR, [ur], *v.i.* to make mistakes; to sin; †to wander from the right path. [L. *errare* to wander].

ERRABLE, [ur'-abl], *adj.* liable to err.

ERRAND, [e'-rand], *n.* a charge, mission; a short journey with a message, usually entrusted to an inferior. [OE. *ærende* message].

ERRAND-BOY, [e'-rand-boi'], *n.* a boy employed by a shop or firm to deliver goods, run messages, etc.

ERRANT (1), [e'-rant], *n.* a knight-errant.

ERRANT (2), [e'-rant], *adj.* travelling on no fixed course or definite mission; (*fig.*) wandering from the business in hand or from upright conduct; **knight-errant,** a medieval knight travelling about in search of adventure, one who performs a chivalrous act. [Fr. *errant*].

ERRANTRY, [e'-rant-ri], *n.* the mode of life of a knight errant.

ERRATIC (1), [i-rat'-ik], *n.* a rogue or vagabond; a wanderer; (*geol.*) a boulder carried by glacier ice from one formation to another.

ERRATIC (2), [i-rat'-ik], *adj.* wandering; roving; irregular, not pursuing a steady or settled course. [L. *erraticus*].

ERRATICAL, [i-rat'-ik-al], *adj.* erratic.

ERRATICALLY, [i-rat'-ik-al-i], *adv.* in an erratic manner.

ERRATICALNESS, [i-rat'-ik-al-nes], *n.* the state of being erratic.

ERRATUM, (*pl.* **errata**), [i-rā'-tum, i-rā'-ta], *n.* a slip or blunder in printing or writing. [L. *erratum* mistake].

ERRONEOUS, [i-rō'-ni-us], *adj.* incorrect, mistaken; (*poet.*) †wandering. [L. *erroneus* wandering].

ERRONEOUSLY, [i-rōn'-i-us-li], *adv.* in an erroneous fashion.

ERRONEOUSNESS, [i-rōn'-i-us-nes], *n.* the state of being erroneous.

ERROR, [e'-rer], *n.* the condition of erring; a deviation from the right way; mistake; fault; sin. [L. *error*].

ERRORIST, [e'-rer-ist], *n.* one who errs or encourages and spreads error.

ERSATZ, [āer-zats'], *adj.* artificial, substituted for a natural product. [Germ. *ersatz*].

ERSE, [urs], *n.* the Gaelic language spoken in Ireland and sometimes in the Scottish Highlands. [Scots *var.* of IRISH].

ERSH, [ursh], *n.* a stubble-field. [~EDDISH].

ERST, [urst], *adv.* formerly. [OE. *ærest*].

ERSTWHILE, [urst'-wīl'], *adv.* formerly; up till then. [ERST and WHILE].

ERUBESCENCE, [e'-rōōb-es'-ents], *n.* the state of being erubescent. [L. *erubescentia*].

ERUBESCENT, [e'-rōōb-es'-ent], *adj.* blushing. [L. *erubescens* growing red].

ERUBESCITE, [e'-rōōb-es'-īt], *n.* a copper ore containing sulphur and iron.

ERUCA, [e-rŏŏk'-a], *n.* the grub of the cabbage butterfly; the salad plant, *Eruca sativa,* whose seeds cause blisters. [L. *eruca* caterpillar].

ERUCT, [i-rukt'], *v.t. and i.* to eructate, belch. [L. *eructare*].

ERUCTATE, [i-ruk'-tāt], *v.t.* to belch wind. [L. *eructare*].

ERUCTATION, [e'-ruk-tā'-shun], *n.* the act of belching.

ERUDITE, [e'-rōōd-īt], *adj.* learned, scholarly. [L. *eruditus* informed].

ERUDITELY, [e'-rōōd-īt-li], *adv.* in an erudite fashion.

ERUDITENESS, [e'-rōōd-īt-nes], *n.* the state of being erudite.

ERUDITION, [ē'-rōōd-ish'-un], *n.* book-learning; scholarly knowledge. [L. *eruditio* instruction].

ERUGATE, [e'-rōōg-āt], *adj.* smoothed out, unwrinkled. [L. *erugatus*].

ERUMPENT, [i-rump'-ent], *adj.* (*bot.*) bursting forth, breaking out. [L. *erumpens*].

ERUPT, [i-rupt'], *v.i.* to break through, break out, burst forth. [~L. *eruptum, p.pt.* of *erumpere* break forth].

ERUPTED, [i-rupt'-ed], *adj.* forcibly ejected.

ERUPTION, [i-rup'-shun], *n.* the act of erupting; a volcanic upheaval; (*med.*) a rash or sore. [L. *eruptio*].

ERUPTIVE, [i-rup'-tiv], *adj.* bursting forth; liable to erupt; (*med.*) accompanied by an eruption on the skin. [Fr. *éruptif*].

ERUPTIVELY, [i-rup'-tiv-li], *adv.* in an eruptive way.

ERUPTIVENESS, [i-rup'-tiv-nes], *n.* the state of being eruptive.

ERUPTIVITY, [e'-rup-tiv'-it-i], *n.* eruptiveness.

ERVALENTA, [ur'-val-ent'-a], *n.* a food made of lentil flour.

ERVUM, [ur'-vum], *n.* (*bot.*) the lentil, *Lens esculenta.* [L. *ervum*].

ERYCINIA, [e'-ris-in'-i-a], *n.* a genus of beautiful lepidopterous insects. [L. *Erycinia* a name of Venus who was worshipped on Mount *Eryx* in Sicily].

ERYNGO, [e-ring'-gō], *n.* the genus of plants including the sea-holly, *Eryngium maritimum.* [Gk. *erungos*].

ERYSIMUM, [e-ris'-im-um], *n.* the genus of *Cruciferæ* including the treacle mustard and the hare's ear. [Gk. *erusimon* hedge-mustard].

ERYSIPELAS, [e'-ri-sip'-el-as], *n.* (*med.*) a feverish disease causing irritation and inflammation of the skin. [Gk. *erusipelas*].

ERYSIPELATOUS, [e'-ri-sip'-el-at-us], *adj.* erysipelous.

ERYSIPELOUS, [e'-ri-sip'-el-us], *adj.* eruptive; like or due to erysipelas.

ERYTHEMA, [e'-ri-thēm'-a], *n.* (*med.*) patchy inflammation of the skin. [Gk. *eruthema* redness].

ERYTHEMATIC, [e'-ri-them-at'-ik], *adj.* erythematous.
ERYTHEMATOUS, [e'-ri-them'-at-us], *adj.* relating to erythema.
ERYTHREAN, [e'-ri-thrē'-an], *adj.* red, reddish. [Gk. *eruthros*].
ERYTHRIN, [e'-ri-thrin], *n.* a dye stuff procured from the lichen, *Roccella fusiformis*. [Gk. *eruthros* red].
ERYTHRINA, [e'-ri-thrīn'-a], *n.* the coral-tree, *Erythrina Crista-galli*. [~Gk. *eruthros* red].
ERYTHRITE, [e'-ri-thrīt], *n.* (*min.*) a reddish hydrated arsenate of cobalt. [*Prec.*].
ERYTHRONIUM, [e'-ri-thrōn'-i-um], *n.* (*bot.*) the genus including the dog's-tooth violet. [Gk. *eruthronion*].
ERYTHROPHYLLIN, [e'-ri-throf'-i-lin], *n.* the red colouring in some leaves in autumn. [Gk. *eruthros* red and *phullon* leaf].
ERYTHROXYLUM, [e'-ri-throks'-il-um], *n.* (*bot.*) a genus of plants with red wood including *Erythroxylum Coca*, whose leaves yield cocaine. [Gk. *eruthros* red and *xulon* wood].
ESCALADE, [es'-kal-ād'], *n.* the act of scaling walls with ladders. [Fr. *escalade*].
ESCALATOR, [es'-ka-lā-ter], *n.* a staircase with an endless belt of steps which move whilst passengers stand on them. [Invented from ESCAL(ADE) and (ELEV)ATOR].
ESCALLONIA, [es'-kal-ōn'-i-a], *n.* a genus of evergreen shrubs found in the Andes. [*Escallon*, who first discovered them].
ESCALLOP, [es-kal'-op], *n.* a scallop. [OFr. *escalope* shell].
ESCALLOPEE, [es-kal'-op-ē], *adj.* (*her.*) covered with over-lapping escallops.
ESCALOPE, [es'-kal-op'], *n.* a dish consisting of a slice of lean veal, etc., fried with egg and breadcrumbs. [OFr. *escalope*].
ESCAMBIO, [es-kam'-bi-ō], *n.* a licence granted to transfer a bill of exchange to someone overseas. [Span. *escambio*].
ESCAPADE, [es'-kap-ād], *n.* any breaking loose from convention; rash and heedless action; (*horsemanship*) the movement of a horse when it kicks out with its hind legs. [Fr. *escapade*].
ESCAPE (1), [es-kāp'], *n.* the act of escaping; the state or fact of having escaped; a leakage; (*bot.*) a garden plant found growing wild.
ESCAPE (2), [es-kāp'], *v.t.* to avoid, evade, get away from; to issue unawares from; *v.i.* to get free; to get away safely; to find a way out. [OFr. *escaper*].
ESCAPEE, [es'-kāp-ē'], *n.* one who has escaped from detention, etc.
ESCAPEMENT, [es-kāp'-ment], *n.* the mechanism by which the action of the mainspring of a watch or the weights of a clock is regulated; the balance wheel.

ESCAPEMENT

ESCAPER, [es-kāp'-er], *n.* one who escapes.
ESCAPISM, [es-kāp'-izm], *n.* (*psych.*) the state or quality of being escapist.
ESCAPIST (1), [es-kāp'-ist], *n.* (*psych.*) one who takes refuge in other activities, *esp.* fantasy, to avoid facing disagreeable facts.
ESCAPIST (2), [es-kāp'-ist], *adj.* of, or pertaining to, an escapist.
ESCAPOLOGIST, [es'-kāp-ol'-oj-ist], *n.* a public performer who frees himself when chained, handcuffed, or shut up in a closed cell, etc.
ESCAR, ESKER, [es'-ker], *n.* (*geol.*) a ridge of gravel produced by the action of ice. [Ir. *eascra*].
ESCARBUNCLE, [es-kah'-bungkl], *n.* (*her.*) carbuncle, a central circular ornament with eight rays. [OFr. *escarbuncle*].
ESCARGATOIRE, [es-kah'-gat-wah(r)'], *n.* a nursery of edible snails. [Fr. *escargatoire*].
ESCARP (1), [es-kahp'], *n.* a steep bank or slope; (*fort.*) the side of the ditch immediately in front of and below the rampart. [Fr. *escarpe*].
ESCARP (2), [es-kahp'], *v.t.* to cut into a steep slope or escarp. [Fr. *escarper*].
ESCARPMENT, [es-kahp'-ment], *n.* a precipitous side of a hill; steep slope; escarp. [Fr. *escarpement*].
ESCARTELLED†, [es-kah'-teld], *adj.* (*her.*) with square notches at the edges. [OFr. *escartelé*].
ESCHALOT, [esh'-a-lot'], *n.* a shallot.
ESCHAR, [es'-ker], *n.* a piece of dead tissue, produced artificially by the application of caustics. [Gk. *eskhara* burn].
ESCHARA, [es'-ker-a], *n.* a kind of net-like coral. [Gk. *eskhara* burn].
ESCHAROTIC, [es'-ker-ot'-ik], *adj.* tending to form an eschar.
ESCHATOLOGICAL, [es'-kat-ol-oj'-ik-al], *adj.* relating to eschatology.
ESCHATOLOGIST, [es'-kat-ol'-oj-ist], *n.* a student of eschatology.
ESCHATOLOGY, [es'-kat-ol'-oj-i], *n.* the study of the last things, death, judgment, and the after-life. [Gk. *eskhatos* last and *logos* speech].
ESCHEAT (1), [es-chēt'], *n.* (*leg.*) lapsing of property to the crown or the lord of the manor when there are no heirs, or when it is forfeited; property thus lapsing. [OFr. *eschete*].
ESCHEAT (2), [es-chēt'], *v.t.* to confiscate; to hand over as an escheat; *v.i.* to lapse, fall to the crown or lord of the manor by escheat.
ESCHEATABLE, [es-chēt'-abl], *adj.* liable to be escheated.
ESCHEATAGE, [es-chēt'-ij], *n.* the right of succession to an escheat.
ESCHEATOR, [es-chēt'-er], *n.* (*hist.*) an official who took note of escheats to the king.
ESCHEW, [es-chew'], *v.t.* to shun; to refrain from. [OFr. *eschiver* to avoid].
ESCHEWAL, [es-chew'-al], *n.* eschewance.
ESCHEWANCE, [es-chew'-ants], *n.* the act of eschewing or shunning.
ESCHEWER, [es-chew'-er], *n.* one who eschews.
ESCHSCHOLTZIA, [esh-olt'-si-a], *n.* a Californian plant of the poppy family with deep yellow flowers. [*Eschscholtz*, a Russian botanist].
ESCORT (1), [es'-kawt], *n.* a person or body of persons or war machines accompanying another for purposes of protection or from courtesy. [Fr. *escorte*].
ESCORT (2), [es-kawt'], *v.t.* to accompany as an escort.
ESCOT† **(1)**, [es-kot'], *n.* scot; an old tax. [OFr. *escot*].
ESCOT† **(2)**, [es-kot'], *v.t.* to pay the account for; maintain. [OFr. *escoter*].
ESCOUADE, [es'-kōō-ād], *n.* a squad. [Fr. *escouade*].
ESCRIBED, [ē'-skrībd'], *adj.* (*geom.*) of a circle, having a circumference that passes through each of the apexes of a given triangle. [E (2) and SCRIBE (2)].
ESCRITOIRE, [es'-krit-wah(r)'], *n.* a kind of writing table, a desk. [Fr. *escritoire*].
ESCRITORIAL, [es'-krit-aw'-ri-al], *adj.* relating to an escritoire.
ESCROL, [es-krōl'], *n.* (*her.*) a scroll. [OFr. *escroele*].
ESCROW, [es-krō'], *n.* (*leg.*) a written undertaking held by a third person until the fulfilment of some condition. [AFr. *escrowe*].
ESCUAGE, [es'-kew-ij], *n.* (*feudal leg.*) tenure recompensed by the free military services of the tenant. [OFr. *escuage*].
ESCUDO, [es-kōō'-dō], *n.* a Portuguese coin worth about 2½d. [Portug. *escudo*].
ESCULAPIAN, [ēs-kyōō-lāp'-i-an], *adj.* medical; relating to the healing art. [L. *Æsculapius*, the god of healing].
ESCULENT (1), [es'-kyōō-lent], *n.* something that may be eaten.
ESCULENT (2), [es'-kyōō-lent], *adj.* eatable. [L. *esculentus*].
ESCULIN, [ēs'-kyōō-lin], *n.* an alkaloid procured from the horse-chestnut. [L. *Æsculus Hippocastanum* the learned name of the tree].
ESCUTCHEON, [es-kuch'-on], *n.* (*her.*) a shield with coat-of-arms; the place on the stern of a ship where the name is written; the movable cover of a keyhole; **a blot on one's e.**, a stain upon one's reputation. [ONFr. *escuchon*].

ESCUTCHEON

ESCUTCHEONED, [es-kuch'-ond], *adj.* with an escutcheon.
ESEMPLASTIC, [es'-em-plas'-tik], *adj.* making into a unity or into one. [ESO and Gk. *plastikos* moulding].
ESKER, see ESCAR.
ESKIMO (1), ESQUIMAU, (*pl.* **Esquimaux**), [es'-kim-ō], *n.* a member of a people inhabiting the extreme north of America and the Arctic islands; the language of this people. [Dan. *Eskimo* from American-Indian word].

ESKIMO (2), **ESQUIMAU**, [es-kim-ō], *adj.* relating to the Eskimos or their language.
ESNECY, [es'-nes-i], *n.* (*leg.*) the privilege of first choice after the division of an inheritance. [L. *aesnecia*].
ESO-, *pref.* within. [Gk. *eso* into, within].
ESOENTERITIS, [es'-ō-en'-ter-īt'-is], *n.* (*med.*) inflammation of the mucous membrane in the intestines. [ESO and ENTERITIS].
ESOGASTRITIS, [es'-ō-gas-trīt'-is], *n.* inflammation of the mucous membrane of the belly. [ESO and GASTRITIS].
ESOPHAGEAL, see OESOPHAGEAL.
ESOPHAGOTOMY, [es-of'-ag-ot'-om-i], *n.* the operation of making an incision into the oesophagus to remove a foreign body. [OESOPHAGUS and Gk. *tome* cutting].
ESOPHAGUS, see OESOPHAGUS.
ESOPIAN, [ē-sōp'-i-an], *adj.* resembling or pertaining to the fables of Æsop. [*Æsop*, an ancient Greek story-teller].
ESOTERIC, [ēs-ōt-er'-ik], *adj.* for the initiated only; confidential; secret. [Gk. *esoterikos*].
ESOTERICISM, [ēs-ōt-er'-is-izm], *n.* the practice of having different doctrines for the initiated and the uninitiated.
ESOTERY, [es-ōt'-er-i], *n.* esotericism; mystery; secrecy.
ESPADON, [es'-pad-on], *n.* a kind of long Spanish sword. [Span. *espadon*].
ESPAGNOLETTE, [es-pan'-yol-et'], *n.* the device that fastens a long casement window. [Fr. *espagnolette*].
ESPALIER, [es-pal'-i-er], *n.* lattice-work up which trees and shrubs are grown; a tree or shrub trained in this way. [Fr. *espalier*].
ESPARCET†, [es-pah'-set], *n.* variety of sainfoin. [Fr. *esparcet*].
ESPARTO, [es-pah'-tō], *n.* grass of the genera *Ampelodesma*, *Lygeum* and *Stipa*, growing in Spain and Algeria and manufactured into paper, ropes, etc. [Span. *esparto*].
ESPECIAL, [es-pesh'-al], *adj.* particular, special. [OFr. *especial*].
ESPECIALLY, [es-pesh'-al-i], *adv.* particularly.
ESPECIALNESS, [es-pesh'-al-nes], *n.* the state of being especial.
ESPERANCE, [es'-per-ants], *n.* (*poet.*) hope. [Fr. *espérance* hope].
ESPERANTIST, [es'-per-ant'-ist], *n.* a person who studies and uses Esperanto.
ESPERANTO, [es'-per-ant'-ō], *n.* an artificial language, based upon root-words common to the majority of Indo-European languages, and intended as a universal medium of communication. [*Esperanto* the hoping one, the pseudonym of the inventor, Dr. Zamenhof, a Polish physician].
ESPIAL, [es-pī'-al], *n.* the act of espying.
ESPIBAWN, [es'-pi-bawn], *n.* the ox-eye daisy. [Ir. *espibawn*].
ESPIEGLERIE, **espièglerie**, [esp-yāg'-ler-ē'], *n.* roguishness, playfulness. [Fr. *espièglerie*].
ESPIER, [es-pī'-er], *n.* one who espies.
ESPINEL†, [es'-pin-el], *n.* a variety of ruby spinel. [Fr. *espinelle*].
ESPIONAGE, [es'-pi-on-ahzh'], *n.* the practice of spying, or employment of spies. [Fr. *espionage*].
ESPIOTTE, [es'-pi-ot], *n.* a spear; a kind of rye. [Fr. *espiotte*].
ESPLANADE, [es'-plan-ād'], *n.* level space for walking, a public promenade; level space between the citadel of a fortress and the town. [Fr. *esplanade*].
ESPOUSAL, [es-pow'-zal], *n.* betrothal, marriage; (*fig.*) the act of enlisting in support of a cause, etc. [OFr. *espousailles*].
ESPOUSE (1), [es-powz'], *n.* spouse. [OFr. *espouse*].
ESPOUSE (2), [es-powz'], *v.t.* to marry, wed; to give in marriage; (*fig.*) to adopt, support. [OFr. *espouser*].
ESPOUSEMENT, [es-powz'-ment], *n.* espousal.
ESPOUSER, [es-pow'-zer], *n.* one who espouses.
ESPRESSIVO *see* EXPRESSIVO.
ESPRINGAL, [es-pring'-gal], *n.* an obsolete engine of war for throwing missiles. [OFr. *espringale*].
ESPRIT, [es'-prē'], *n.* liveliness, spirit; wit; **e. de corps**, loyalty to the community to which one belongs. [Fr. *esprit*].
ESPY, [es-pī'], *v.t.* to see, catch sight of. [OFr. *espier*].
ESQUIMAU, see ESKIMO.
ESQUIRE, [es-kwī'-er], *n.* a gentleman, squire; a courtesy distinction added after a gentleman's name. [OFr. *esquier*].
ESQUISSE, [es-kēs'], *n.* the first rough sketch of any work of art. [Fr. *esquisse*].
ESS, [es], *n.* the nineteenth letter of the alphabet, S; anything shaped like this.
ESSAY (1), [es'-ā], *n.* an attempt or experiment; a short didactic, argumentative, or discursive composition in prose or verse. [OFr. *essai*].
ESSAY (2), [es-ā'], *v.t.* to try, test; to attempt. [Fr. *essayer*].
ESSAYIST, [es'-ā-ist], *n.* one who writes essays.
ESSE, [es'-i], *n.* essential nature or being. [L. *esse* to be].
ESSENCE, [es'-ents], *n.* an entity, being; the distinctive qualities or nature of anything; indispensable element; extract obtained by distillation; scent, perfume. [Fr. *essence* from L. *essentia* being].
ESSENES, [es'-ēnz], *n.*(*pl.*) an ancient mystic and ascetic sect among the Jews. [Gk. *Essenoi*].
ESSENISM, [es'-ēn-izm], *n.* the tenets and practice of the Essenes.
ESSENTIAL (1), [i-sen'-shal], *n.* indispensable quality or element.
ESSENTIAL (2), [i-sen'-shal], *adj.* constituting the essence of; indispensable; characteristic; distinguishing. [L. *essentialis*].
ESSENTIALITY, [i-sen'-shi-al'-i-ti], *n.* the quality of being essential.
ESSENTIALLY, [i-sen'-shal-i], *adv.* in an essential fashion.
ESSENTIALNESS, [i-sen'-shal-nes], *n.* essentiality.
ESSERA, [es'-er-a], *n.* (*med.*) an irritant eruption on the skin. [L. *essera*].
ESSOIN (1), **ESSOIGN**, [es-oin'], *n.* (*leg.*) an excuse for not appearing in court. [OFr. *essoine*].
ESSOIN (2), [es-oin'], *v.t.* (*leg.*) to permit an excuse for non-appearance in court. [OFr. *essoinier*].
ESSOINER, [es-oin'-er], *n.* (*leg.*) one who satisfactorily excuses the absence of another.
ESSONITE, [es'-on-īt], *n.* (*min.*) the cinnamon-stone or yellow garnet. [Gk. *hesson* inferior to].
ESSORANT, [es'-aw-rant], *adj.* (*her.*) having wings spread as if about to fly. [OFr. *essorant*].
ESTABLISH, [es-tab'-lish], *v.t.* to settle on a fixed basis; to settle beyond dispute; to prove finally as true or valid; to set in a particular position. [OFr. *establissir*].
ESTABLISHED, [es-tab'-lisht], *adj.* instituted and recognized, *esp.* by the state.
ESTABLISHER, [es-tab'-lish-er], *n.* one who establishes.
ESTABLISHMENT, [es-tab'-lish-ment], *n.* the act of establishing; the condition of being established; that which is established; an institution, business house; a residence or household; **the E.**, Church of England.
ESTACADE, [es'-tak-ād'], *n.* (*milit.*) a fence of piles in the sea, river, or marsh to check an enemy. [Fr. *estacade*].
ESTAFETTE, [es-taf-et'], *n.* a mounted military courier. [Fr. *estafette*].
ESTAMINET, [es-tam'-in-ā], *n.* a cheap French restaurant, selling drinks. [Fr. *estaminet*].
ESTANCIA, [es-tahn'-si-a], *n.* a ranch in South America. [Span. *estancia*].
ESTATE, [es-tāt'], *n.* order; class; rank; condition; part of the body politic, with a share in the government; landed property; total collective assets and liabilities; **the Three Estates**, Lords Spiritual and Temporal, and the Commons; **the third e.**, the French bourgeoisie before the Revolution; **the fourth e.**, (*coll.*) the press; **real e.**, landed property; **personal e.**, movable property. [OFr. *estat*].
ESTEEM (1), [es-tēm'], *n.* high opinion, regard, respect.
ESTEEM (2), [es-tēm'], *v.t.* to have a high opinion of, respect; to consider, value. [Fr. *estimer*].
ESTEEMER, [es-tēm'-er], *n.* one who esteems.
ESTER, [es'-ter], *n.* (*chem.*) any compound of a class produced by the condensation of an alcohol and an acid. [Germ. invented word *Ester*].
ESTHESIOMETER, [es-thēz'-i-om'-et-er], *n.* a nerve needle. [Gk. *aisthesis* feeling and METER].
ESTIFEROUS, [es-tif'-er-us], *adj.* heat-producing. [L. *aestus* heat and *ferre* to bear].
ESTIMABLE, [es'-tim-abl], *adj.* deserving esteem. [Fr. *estimable*].
ESTIMABLENESS, [es'-tim-abl-nes], *n.* the state of being estimable.
ESTIMABLY, [es'-tim-ab-li], *adv.* in an estimable way.
ESTIMATE (1), [es'-tim-āt], *n.* approximate judgment of worth or size; rough calculation; contractor's statement of sum for which he will undertake a job; estimation.

ESTIMATE (2), [es'-tim-āt], *v.t.* to form an estimate of; calculate roughly. [L. *aestimare*].
ESTIMATION, [es'-tim-ā'-shun], *n.* the act of estimating; judgment of value, etc.; esteem. [OFr. *estimacion*].
ESTIMATIVE, [es'-tim-āt-iv], *adj.* having the power of comparing and adjusting values.
ESTIMATOR, [es'-tim-ā-tor], *n.* one who or that which estimates; a form of weighing-machine.
ESTIVAGE, [es'-tiv-ahj], *n.* a method of pressing cargoes into vessels. [Fr. *estivage*].
ESTOC, [es-tok'], *n.* a short sword worn by cavalrymen. [Fr. *estoc*].
ESTOILE, [es-toil'], *n.* (*her.*) a star with six waved points. [OFr. *estoile* star].

ESTOILE

ESTOILLEE, estoillée, [es-toi'-lā], *n.* (*her.*) a star with only four points. [OFr. *estoillée*].
ESTOP, [es-top'], *v.t.* (*leg.*) to hinder, bar from doing something. [OFr. *estoper*].
ESTOPPEL, [es-top'-el], *n.* (*leg.*) the fact of being precluded or barred from a certain action or statement by a previous action or statement of one's own. [OFr. *estoupail*].
ESTOUFFADE, [es-tōōf-ahd'], *n.* a method of stewing meat in a well-closed vessel. [OFr. *estouffade* a stifling].
ESTOVERS, [es-tō'-verz], *n.*(*pl.*) (*leg.*) necessaries; a reasonable allowance of lands or goods for the use of a tenant; **common of e.,** the right of taking wood from another's estate for use in the household, necessary repairs, etc. [OFr. *estovoir*].
ESTRADE, [es-trahd'], *n.* a slightly raised platform; a dais. [Fr. *estrade*].
ESTRANGE, [es-trānj'], *v.t.* to alienate, to destroy affection between. [OFr. *estranger*].
ESTRANGEDNESS, [es-trānj'-ed-nes], *n.* the condition of being estranged.
ESTRANGEMENT, [es-trānj'-ment], *n.* the act of estranging; the condition of being estranged.
ESTRAPADE, [es'-trap-ād'], *n.* (*horsemanship*) the movement of a restive horse, which rears and kicks violently. [Fr. *estrapade*].
ESTRAY (1), [es-trā'], *n.* a domestic animal, as a horse, ox, or sheep, which is found wandering or without an owner.
ESTRAY (2), [es-trā'], *v.i.* to stray. [OFr. *estrayer*].
ESTREAT, [es-trēt'], *v.t.* (*leg.*) to take out or copy the record of a fine, etc., and return to Court of Exchequer for prosecution. [AFr. *estrete* a record].
ESTREPEMENT, [es-trēp'-ment], *n.* (*leg.*) the spoiling or wasting of lands by a tenant. [AFr. *estrepement*].
ESTRIDGE, [es'-trij], *n.* the fine down of the ostrich lying under the feathers; †ostrich. [*Var.* of OSTRICH].
ESTUARINE, [es'-chōō-er-īn], *adj.* relating to an estuary.
ESTUARY, [es'-chōō-er-i], *n.* the expanding tidal mouth of a river. [L. *aestuarius* tidal].
ESTUATION†, [es'-chōō-ā'-shun], *n.* boiling; agitation. [~L. *aestuare* to boil].
ESURIENT, [i-sew'-ri-ent], *adj.* hungry; necessitous; grasping. [L. *esuriens*, *pres.pt.* of *esurire* to desire food].
ESURINE, [ēs'-yōō-rīn], *adj.* whetting the appetite. [~*Prec.*].
ETAERIO, [et-ēer'-i-ō], *n.* any aggregate fruit, as that of the strawberry or ranunculus. [~Gk. *hetairos* associate].

ÉTAGÈRE

ETAGERE, étagère, [āt'-ah-zhāer'], *n.* a dinner wagon [Fr. *étagère*].
ETAT-MAJOR, état-major, [āt'-ah-mah-zhaw(r)'], *n.* (*milit.*) the staff or staff office. [Fr. *état-major*].
ETCETERA, [et-set'-ra], *n.* and so on; and so forth; and the rest (usually written *etc.*); **etceteras,** extras, sundries, minor items. [L. *et caetera* and the rest].
ETCH (1), [ech], *n.* ground from which the crop has been taken; an aftercrop sown therein; eddish. [EDDISH].
ETCH (2), [ech], *v.t.* to produce pictures or designs by engraving a plate of metal with corrosives, and then taking prints from the plate; *v.i.* to practise the art of etching. [Du. *etsen*].
ETCHED, [echt], *adj.* marked on metal, glass, etc., by corrosion of an acid.
ETCHER, [ech'-er], *n.* an artist who makes etchings.
ETCHING, [ech'-ing], *n.* the process of etching; an impression taken from an etched plate.
ETCHING-GROUND, [ech'-ing-grownd'], *n.* the coating of wax or polish on the etching plate.
ETCHING-NEEDLE, [ech'-ing-nēdl'], *n.* a pointed steel instrument for tracing outlines on the etching ground.
ETEOSTIC, [ēt'-i-os'-tik], *n.* a chronogram. [Gk. *eteos* of the year and *stikhos* row].
ETERNAL, [i-turn'-al], *adj.* everlasting; perpetual; that always has been and always will be; without end; ceaseless, incessant; **the E.,** God; **the E. City,** Rome; **the e. triangle,** (*coll.*) two men and a woman or two women and a man whose relationships present a problem. [OFr. *éternal*].
ETERNALIST, [i-turn'-al-ist], *n.* one who believes the past existence of the world to be infinite in time.
ETERNALITY, [it-urn-al'-it-i], *n.* the quality of being eternal.
ETERNALIZE, [i-turn'-al-īz], *v.t.* to render eternal; to give endless duration to.
ETERNALLY, [i-turn'-al-i], *adv.* without beginning or end; perpetually, for ever; unchangeably.
ETERNITY, [i-turn'-it-i], *n.* the state of being eternal; infinite time; the future life; **the eternities,** the eternal truths. [Fr. *éternité*].
ETERNIZE, [i-turn'-īz], *v.t.* to eternalize.
ETESIAN, [it-ē'-zhun], *adj.* occurring regularly and annually; **e. winds,** north-westerly winds prevailing in the Levant for about forty days each summer. [L. *etesius* annual].
ETHAL, [ēth'-al], *n.* an oily substance procured from spermaceti. [~ETHER, which it resembles].
ETHANE, [ēth'-ān], *n.* ethyl hydride, a colourless, odourless and insoluble gas. [~ETHER].
ETHER, [ēth'-er], *n.* clear sky; upper regions of air beyond the clouds; (*chem.*) colourless, light, volatile and inflammable fluid produced by the action of acid on alcohol, and used as an anæsthetic; (*phys.*) a subtle material pervading space and filling up the gaps between particles of air and other matter, the medium for the transmission of light and radio waves. [Gk. *aither*].
ETHEREAL, [ith-ēer'-i-al], *adj.* airy; heavenly; delicate; spiritual.
ETHEREALISM, [ith-ēer'-i-al-izm], *n.* the quality of being ethereal.
ETHEREALITY, [ith-ēer'-i-al'-i-ti], *n.* etherealism.
ETHEREALIZE, [ith-ēer'-i-al-īz], *v.t.* to convert into ether; make ethereal.
ETHEREALLY, [ith-ēer'-i-al-i], *adv.* in an ethereal way.
ETHEREOUS, [ith-ēer'-i-us], *adj.* (*poet.*) made of ether; heavenly.
ETHERIA, [ēth-ēer'-i-a], *n.* (*zool.*) a genus of African bivalves, called river-oysters.
ETHERIFICATION, [ēth'-er-i-fik-ā'-shun], *n.* the process of making or producing ether.
ETHERIFORM, [ēth'-er-i-fawm], *adj.* presenting the appearance of ether.
ETHERISM, [ēth'-er-izm], *n.* the effects produced by the use of ether.
ETHERIZATION, [ēth'-er-īz-ā'-shun], *n.* the act or process of making ether; the medical administration of ether.
ETHERIZE, [ēth'-er-īz], *v.t.* to make into ether; to put under the influence of ether.
ETHEROGRAPHY, [ēth'-er-og'-ra-fi], *n.* a scientific description of the atmosphere. [ETHER and Gk. *graphia* writing].
ETHEROLE, [ēth'-er-ōl], *n.* light oil of wine, a colourless oily fluid. [ETHER and L. *oleum* oil].
ETHERO-SULPHURIC, [ēth'-er-ō-sul-few'-rik], *adj.* made up of ether and sulphur; **e. acid,** an acid prepared by passing the vapour of anhydrous sulphuric acid into pure alcohol kept cold.
ETHIC, [eth'-ik], *adj.* ethical. [Gk. *ethikos*].
ETHICAL, [eth'-ik-al], *adj.* relating to or treating of ethics; in accordance with an ethical code.
ETHICALLY, [eth'-ik-al-i], *adv.* in accordance with ethics.
ETHICS, [eth'-iks], *n.*(*pl.*) the science treating of morals. [ETHIC].

ETHIOP†, [ēth'-i-ŏp], *n.* an Ethiopian; a negro.
ETHIOPIAN (1), [ēth'-i-ōp'-i-an], *n.* a native of Ethiopia, an Abyssinian; †a negro. [*Ethiopia*].
ETHIOPIAN (2), [ēth'-i-ōp'-i-an], *adj.* pertaining to Ethiopia or the black races generally.
ETHIOPIC, [ēth'-i-ŏp'-ik], *adj.* Ethiopian. [L. *Aethiopicus*].
ETHMOID, [eth'-moid], *adj.* like a sieve; **e. bone**, (*anat.*) the perforated bone between the orbits of the eye that forms the roof of the nose. [Gk. *ethmoeides*].
ETHMOIDAL, [eth-moid'-al], *adj.* ethmoid.
ETHNARCH, [eth'-nahk], *n.* the ruler of a province. [Gk. *ethnarkhes*].
ETHNIC† **(1)**, [eth'-nik], *n.* a pagan.
ETHNIC (2), [eth'-nik], *adj.* pertaining to races or nations; pertaining to pagans, heathen. [Gk. *ethnikos*].
ETHNICAL, [eth'-nik-al], *adj.* ethnic.
ETHNICALLY, [eth'-nik-al-i], *adv.* racially, by race.
ETHNICISM, [eth'-nis-izm], *n.* heathendom.
ETHNOGRAPHER, [eth-nog'-ra-fer], *n.* one skilled in ethnography.
ETHNOGRAPHIC, [eth'-nō-graf'-ik], *adj.* ethnographical.
ETHNOGRAPHICAL, [eth'-nō-graf'-ik-al], *adj.* relating to ethnography.
ETHNOGRAPHY, [eth-nog'-ra-fi], *n.* the scientific study and description of human races. [Gk. *ethnos* race and *graphia* writing].
ETHNOLOGICAL, [eth'-nō-loj'-ik-al], *adj.* relating to ethnology.
ETHNOLOGICALLY, [eth'-nō-loj'-ik-al-i], *adv.* as regards ethnology.
ETHNOLOGIST, [eth-nol'-oj-ist], *n.* one skilled in ethnology.
ETHNOLOGY, [eth-nol'-oj-i], *n.* the science which deals with the races of mankind. [Gk. *ethnos* race and *logos* speech].
ETHOLOGICAL, [ēth'-o-loj'-ik-al], *adj.* relating to ethology.
ETHOLOGIST, [ēth-ol'-oj-ist], *n.* one skilled in ethology.
ETHOLOGY, [ēth-ol'-oj-i], *n.* the scientific study of the formation of character. [Gk. *ethos* disposition and *logos* speech].
ETHOS, [ēth'-os], *n.* general disposition, habitual character. [Gk. *ethos*].
ETHYL, [eth'-il, ēth'-il], *n.* (*chem.*) the base of any alcohol. [~ETHER].
ETIOLATE, [ēt'-i-ō-lāt], *v.t.* (*bot.*) to make pale by exclusion of light; (*med.*) to make pale through sickness or malnutrition, etc. [Fr. *étioler* to make into straw].
ETIOLATION, [ēt'-i-ō-lā'-shun], *n.* the act or process of becoming etiolated.
ETIOLIN, [ēt'-i-o-lin], *n.* (*bot.*) the yellow chlorophyll produced by etiolation.
ETIOLOGICAL, [ēt-i-ō-loj'-ik-al], *adj.* relating to etiology.
ETIOLOGY, [ēt'-i-ol'-o-ji], *n.* the study of the causes of disease. [Gk. *aitia* cause and *logos* speech].
ETIQUETTE, [et'-ik-et'], *n.* conventional rules of conduct. [Fr. *étiquette*].
ETNA, [et'-na], *n.* a small spirit stove for heating water, etc., with a reversed cone for the boiler. [Mount *Etna*, a volcano in Sicily].
ETNEAN, [et-nē'-an], *adj.* pertaining to the volcano, Mount Etna, in Sicily.
ETON, [ē'-ton], *adj.* belonging to or characteristic of Eton College; **E. coat**, a short tailless black jacket for boys; **E. collar**, a wide, spreading, stiff linen collar for boys; **E. crop**, a coiffure for women in which the hair is cut short as a boy's. [*Eton* College, near Windsor].
ETONIAN (1), [ēt-ōn'-i-an], *n.* a past or present pupil of Eton College. [*Prec.*].
ETONIAN (2), [ēt-ōn'-i-an], *adj.* of, or pertaining to, Eton or Etonians.
ETRUSCAN (1), [i-trusk'-an], *n.* a native of the ancient Italian district of Etruria. [L. *Etruscus*].
ETRUSCAN (2), [i-trusk'-an], *adj.* pertaining to Etruria; **E. vases**, beautifully designed vases found in Etruscan tombs.
ETUDE, étude, [ā-tewd'], *n.* (*mus.*) a piece of music intended as a technical exercise. [Fr. *étude* study].
ETUI, [et-wē'], *n.* a small case holding articles for personal use; a needle-case. [Fr. *étui* case].
ETYMOLOGICAL, [et'-im-o-loj'-ik-al], *adj.* relating to etymology.
ETYMOLOGICALLY, [et'-im-o-loj'-ik-a-li], *adv.* according to etymological principles.
ETYMOLOGICON, [et'-im-o-loj'-ik-on], *n.* a treatise on etymologies; a dictionary indicating etymologies. [Gk. *etumologikon*].
ETYMOLOGIST, [et'-im-ol'-oj-ist], *n.* one skilled in etymology.
ETYMOLOGIZE, [et'-im-ol'-oj-īz], *v.i.* to study etymology; to enquire into the origin of words.
ETYMOLOGY, [et'-im-ol'-o-ji], *n.* the (study of the) derivation and origin of words. [Gk. *etumologia*].
ETYMON, [et'-i-mon'], *n.* a primary or root-word from which others are derived. [Gk. *etumon* truth].
ETYPIC, [ē-tip'-ik], *adj.* not conforming to type. [E and TYPE].
EU-, *pref.* well. [Gk. *eu* well].
EUAEMIA, [yew-ēm'-i-a], *n.* a healthy state of the blood. [EU and Gk. *haima* blood].
EUAESTHESIA, [yew'-ēsth-ēz'-i-a], *n.* a healthy state of all the senses. [EU and Gk. *aisthesis* perception by the senses].
EUCALYPTOL, [yew'-ka-lip'-tol], *n.* essential of eucalyptus.
EUCALYPTUS, [yew'-ka-lip'-tus], *n.* (*bot.*) a numerous genus of plants of which one is the Australian gum-tree; oil of eucalyptus; **e. oil, oil of e.**, an oil prepared from these trees, useful as a disinfectant for colds, etc. [EU and Gk. *kaluptos* covered].
EUCHARIS, [yew'-ker-is], *n.* the genus of plants that includes the Amazon lilies. [Gk. *eukharis* charming].
EUCHARIST, [yew'-ker-ist], *n.* the sacrament of the Lord's Supper; the consecrated elements, *esp.* the bread. [Gk. *eukharistia* thanks].
EUCHARISTIC, [yew'-ker-ist'-ik], *adj.* expressing thanks; pertaining to the Eucharist; **E. Congress**, international meeting of Roman Catholics to venerate the Holy Sacrament.
EUCHARISTICAL, [yew'-ker-ist'-ik-al], *adj.* eucharistic.
EUCHLORIC, [yew-klo'-rik], *adj.* of a decidedly green colour; **e. gas**, euchlorine.
EUCHLORINE, [yew-klaw'-rēn], *n.* (*chem.*) a highly explosive green gas with bleaching properties, composed of chlorine and chloric oxide. [EU and CHLORINE].
EUCHOLOGY, [yew-kol'-o-ji], *n.* a formulary of prayers, the liturgy of the Greek Church. [Gk. *eukhologion*].
EUCHRE, [yew'-ker], *n.* a card game in which all cards below the sevens are left out. [Unkn.].
EUCHROITE, [yew'-krō-īt], *n.* (*chem.*) arseniate of copper. [~Gk. *eukhroos* fresh-looking].
EUCHYLIA, [yew-kil'-i-a], *n.* (*med.*) the healthy state of the chyle. [EU and CHYLE].
EUCLASE, [yew'-klāz], *n.* (*min.*) a brittle beryl, found in clear light-green crystals. [EU and Gk. *klasis* breaking].
EUCLIDEAN, [yew-klid'-i-an], *adj.* pertaining to Euclid; geometric; three-dimensional. [*Euclid*, Alexandrian mathematician].
EUCRASY, [yew'-kra-si], *n.* (*med.*) such a balance of qualities as to constitute health or soundness of body. [Gk. *eukrasia*].
EUCTICAL, [yewk'-tik-al], *adj.* connected with prayer. [Gk. *euktikos*].
EUDAEMONISM, [yew-dēm'-on-izm], *n.* the philosophy which holds that the production of happiness is the aim and measure of virtue; the moral obligation to make happiness. [Gk. *eudaimonia* happiness].
EUDIALITE, [yew-dī'-al-īt], *n.* (*min.*) a bright red silicate of zirconium with iron, manganese, lime and soda. [Gk. *eudialutos* soluble].
EUDIOMETER, [yew'-di-om'-it-er], *n.* an instrument for ascertaining the condition of the atmosphere, used in analysing gases. [Gk. *eudios* clear weather and METER].

EUDIOMETER

EUDIOMETRIC, [yew'-di-ō-met'-rik], *adj.* pertaining to a eudiometer.
EUDIOMETRICAL, [yew'-di-ō-met'-rik-al], *adj.* eudiometric.
EUDIOMETRY, [yew'-di-om'-it-ri], *n.* the art or practice of ascertaining the purity of the air or the composition of a gaseous mixture by means of the eudiometer.
EUGE, [yew'-ji], *int.* bravo! well done! [Gk. *euge*].

EUGENESIS, [yew-jen'-is-is], *n.* the condition of propagating freely and well.

EUGENIA, [yew-jēn'-i-a], *n.* (*bot.*) a tropical genus of 625 species, many of which yield edible fruits and spices. [Prince *Eugene* of Savoy].

EUGENIC, [yew-jen'-ik], *adj.* concerned with the improvement of the stock or race; tending to promote eugenics. [Gk. *eugenes* well born].

EUGENICS, [yew-jen'-iks], *n.(pl.)* the science which is concerned with the best means of producing a healthy stock.

EUGENIST, [yew'-jen-ist], *n.* a person who believes in the value of eugenics.

EUHARMONIC, [yew'-har-mon'-ik], *adj.* tending to produce harmony.

EUHEMERISM, [yew-hēm'-er-izm], *n.* the theory that myths are based on historic events and characters, and that gods are merely deified men. [*Euhemerus*, a Greek of the fourth century B.C.].

EUHEMERIST, [yew-hēm'-er-ist], *n.* one who believes in euhemerism.

EUHEMERISTIC, [yew'-hēm-er-ist'-ik], *adj.* tending to euhemerism.

EUHEMERISTICALLY, [yew-hēm'-er-ist'-ik-al-i], *adv.* in the manner of the followers of euhemerism.

EUHEMERIZE, [yew-hēm'-er-īz], *v.t.* to interpret myths by euhemerism.

EULOGIC, [yew-loj'-ik], *adj.* (*rare*) eulogical.

EULOGICAL, [yew-loj'-ik-al], *adj.* full of praise, commendatory.

EULOGICALLY, [yew-loj'-ik-al-i], *adv.* in a eulogical way.

EULOGIST, [yew'-loj-ist], *n.* one who writes or pronounces a eulogy.

EULOGISTIC, [yew-loj-ist'-ik], *adj.* full of praise, laudatory.

EULOGISTICALLY, [yew-loj-ist'-ik-al-i], *adj.* laudatorily; in a eulogistic manner.

EULOGIUM, [yew-lōj'-i-um], *n.* a eulogistic speech.

EULOGIZE, [yew'-loj-īz], *v.t.* to praise highly, commend, speak well of another.

EULOGY, [yew'-loj-i], *n.* a speech or written testimony greatly praising some person or thing; a panegyric; high commendation. [Gk. *eulogia*].

EUMENIDAE, [yew-men'-id-ē], *n.(pl.)* a family of hymenopterous insects, closely related to the wasps.

EUMENIDA

EUNICEAE, [yew-nīs'-i-ē], *n.(pl.)* (*zool.*) a group of annulose animals.

EUNOMY, [yew'-nom-i], *n.* an equal law, or a well-adjusted, equitable constitution of government. [Gk. *eunomia*].

EUNUCH, [yew'-nuk], *n.* a castrated man, formerly employed as a domestic officer of state by Eastern rulers. [Gk. *eunoukhos*].

EUNUCHATE, [yew'-nuk-āt], *v.t.* to castrate.

EUNUCHISM, [yew'-nuk-izm], *n.* the condition of a eunuch.

EUOMPHALUS, [yew-om'-fal-us], *n.* a fossil form of a whorled shell. [EU and Gk. *omphalos* the navel].

EUONYMIN, [yew-on'-im-in], *n.* a product obtained from the bark of the wahoo spindle-tree, *Euonymus atropurpureus*.

EUONYMUS, [yew-on'-im-us], *n.* (*bot.*) a genus of evergreen shrubs. [Gk. *euonumos* propitious].

EUOTOMOUS, [yew-ot'-om-us], *adj.* (*min.*) with distinct cleavages. [EU and Gk. *tome* cutting].

EUPATORINE, [yew-pat'-or-in], *n.* (*chem.*) an alkaloid derived from the hemp agrimony.

EUPATORIUM, [yew-pat-awr'-i-um], *n.* (*bot.*) a genus of composite plants, which includes the hemp agrimony, *Eupatorium cannabinum*. [Gk. *eupatorion* from *Eupator*, a surname of Mithridates who used this herb medicinally].

EUPEPSIA, [yew-pep'-si-a], *n.* good digestion. [Gk. *eupepsia*].

EUPEPSY, [yew-pep'-si], *n.* eupepsia.

EUPEPTIC, [yew-pep'-tik], *adj.* with a good digestion; (*fig.*) optimistic.

EUPHEMISM, [yew'-fem-izm], *n.* the use of a mild, pleasant word to express an unpleasant idea. [Gk. *euphemismos* well spoken].

EUPHEMISTIC, [yew'-fem-ist'-ik], *adj.* characterized by euphemism.

EUPHEMISTICALLY, [yew'-fim-ist'-ik-al-i], *adv.* in euphemistic fashion.

EUPHEMIZE, [yew'-fem-īz], *v.t.* to express in a euphemistic manner.

EUPHONIC, [yew-fon'-ik], *adj.* euphonious. [Fr. *euphonique*].

EUPHONICAL, [yew-fon'-ik-al], *adj.* euphonic.

EUPHONICON, [yew-fon'-ik-on], *n.* a type of upright piano; euphonon.

EUPHONIOUS, [yew-fōn'-i-us], *adj.* with euphony; of an agreeable sound.

EUPHONIOUSLY, [yew-fōn'-i-us-li], *adv.* in a euphonious way.

EUPHONISM, [yew'-fon'-izm], *n.* a well-sounding combination of sounds.

EUPHONIUM, [yew-fōn'-i-um], *n.* a bass instrument of the saxhorn type.

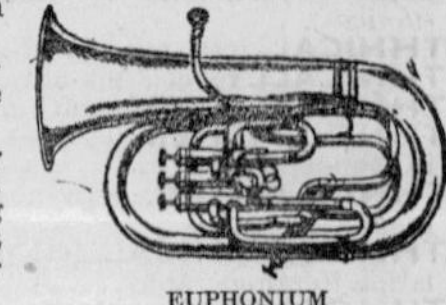
EUPHONIUM

EUPHONIZE, [yew'-fon-īz], *v.t.* to make euphonious.

EUPHONON, [yew'-fon-on], *n.* a musical instrument resembling an upright piano but with greater power and depth of tone.

EUPHONY, [yew'-fon-i], *n.* sweetness of sound; a smooth enunciation of sounds. [Gk. *euphonia*].

EUPHORBIA, [yew-faw'-bi-a], *n.* (*bot.*) a genus of plants of over 600 species, which includes the spurges. [Gk. *Euphorbos*, a physician].

EUPHORBIUM, [yew-faw'-bi-um], *n.* an inspissated sap which exudes from *Euphorbia resinifera*.

EUPHRASIA, [yew-frā'-zi-a], *n.* (*bot.*) a genus of plants of over 50 species, one of which is the herb eyebright. [Gk. *euphrasia* delight].

EUPHROE, [yew'-frō], *n.* (*naut.*) a thin bar of wood which suspends the ridge of an awning. [Du. *juffrouw*].

EUPHUISM, [yew'-few-izm], *n.* a precious, affected style of writing or speech. [Lyly's novel *Euphues*].

EUPHUIST, [yew'-few-ist], *n.* a person who writes or speaks in a precious, affected manner.

EUPHUISTIC, [yew'-few-ist'-ik], *adj.* characterized by euphuism; excessively refined in speech or writing.

EUPHUIZE, [yew'-few-īz], *v.i.* to talk in a euphuistic way.

EUPLASTIC, [yew-plas'-tik], *adj.* (*med.*) easily formed into an organic tissue. [Gk. *euplastos* easily moulded].

EUPLECTELLA, [yew'-plekt-el'-a], *n.* a genus of siliceous sponges including Venus's flower-basket. [Gk. *euplektos* well braided].

EUPNOEA, [yewp-nē'-a], *n.* (*path.*) ease of breathing. [Gk. *eupnoos*].

EURAFRICAN, [yew-raf'-rik-an], *n.* the child of an African and a European parent. [*Europe* and *Africa*].

EURASIAN, [yew-rā'-shi-an], *n.* the child of a European and an Asiatic parent. [*Europe* and *Asia*].

EUREKA, [yew-rē'-ka], *int.* equivalent to "Got it!" [Gk. *eureka* I have found (it)].

EURHYTHMICS, [yew-rith'-miks], *n.(pl.)* the art or practice of gracefully imitating music in bodily motions.

EURHYTHMY (1), [yew-rith'-mi], *n.* graceful, rhythmic movement. [Gk. *eurhuthmia* proportion].

EURHYTHMY (2), [yew-rith'-mi], *n.* symmetry, in architecture, painting and sculpture; (*med.*) regularity of pulsation. [Gk. *eurhuthmia*].

EURIPUS, (*pl.* **euripi**), [yew-rip'-us], *n.* the name of a Greek strait, applied now to any strait with violent or uncertain currents. [Gk. *Euripos*].

EURITE, [yew'-rīt], *n.* (*min.*) felspar or the white stone of Werner. [Gk. *eurutos* flowing plentifully].

EURITIC, [yew-rit'-ik], *adj.* composed of, or similar to, eurite.

EUROCLYDON, [yew-rok'-lid-on], *n.* a stormy wind, so called from a wind of that name mentioned in Acts xxvii, 14. [Gk. *Eurokludon*].

EUROMERICAN, [yew'-rō-mer'-ik-an], *adj.* the child of a European and an American parent. [*Europe* and *America*].

EUROPE, [yew'-rup], *n.* the geographic name given to the continent which stretches from the Atlantic to the Ural mountains. [Gk. *Europe*].

EUROPEAN (1), [yew'-rop-ē'-an], *n.* an inhabitant of Europe.

EUROPEAN (2), [yew'-rop-ē'-an], *adj.* connected with Europe.

EUROPEANIZE, [yew'-rop-ē'-an-īz], *v.t.* to make European.
EURUS, [yew'-rus], *n.* the classical name for the east wind. [Gk. *euros*].
EURYALE, [yew-rī'-al-i], *n.* (*bot.*) a genus of plants allied to the water-lily. [Gk. *Euruale*, name of a Gorgon].
EURYCEROUS, [yew-ris'-er-us], *adj.* having broad horns. [Gk. *eurukeros*].
EURYLAEMUS, [yew'-ril-ēm'-us], *n.* (*ornith.*) a genus of Indian birds including the broadbills. [Gk. *eurus* broad and *laimos* throat].
EUSEBIAN, [yew-sēb'-ian], *adj.* connected with Eusebius, bishop of Caesarea. [L. *Eusebianus*].
EUSKARIAN, [yew-skāer'-i-an], *n.* a Basque. [Basque *Euskara*].
EUSOL, [yew'-sol], *n.* (*chem.*) an antiseptic with a strong lime element prepared from bleaching powder. [Initial letters of *E*dinburgh *U*niversity *s*olution *o*f *l*ime].
EUSTACHIAN, [yew-stāsh'-an], *adj.* used of certain parts of the body first described by Eustachius; **e. tube**, a small duct running from a cavity of the ear into the back of the mouth. [*Eustachius* an Italian anatomist].
EUSTYLE, [yew'-stīl], *adj.* (*arch.*) a building where the columns are placed at 2¼ diameters apart. [Gk. *eustylos*].
EUTERPE, [yew-tur'-pi], *n.* the classical name for the Muse of music; (*bot.*) a genus of palms. [Gk. *Euterpe*].
EUTERPEAN, [yew-tur'-pi-an], *adj.* pertaining to Euterpe, or to music.
EUTHANASIA, [yew'-than-āz'-i-a], *n.* the practice or method of making death painless. [Gk. *euthanasia*].
EUTHERIA, [yew-thēer'-i-a], *n.(pl.)* (*zool.*) the main sub-class of the mammalia. [EU and Gk. *therion* a wild animal].
EUTROPHIC, [yew-tro'-fik], *n.* an agent which acts beneficially on the nutritive system.
EUTROPHY, [yew'-tro-fi], *n.* (*med.*) a healthy condition of the nutritive functions. [Gk. *eutrophia*].
EUTROPOUS, [yew'-trop-us], *adj.* (*bot.*) long-tongued; fertilized by means of long-tongued insects.
EUTYCHIAN, [yew-tik'-i-an], *n.* a member of a Christian sect of the fifth century, who believed that the divine and human natures of Christ, after their union, became one nature. [*Eutychius*, the founder of the sect].
EVACUANT (1), [i-vak'-ew-ant], *n.* (*med.*) a medicine that promotes evacuation; a purgative.
EVACUANT (2), [i-vak'-ew-ant], *adj.* (*med.*) emptying, promoting evacuation or purgation. [L. *evacuans*].
EVACUATE, [i-vak'-ew-āt], *v.t.* to empty out, to discharge, to rid of its contents; (*milit.*) to move troops away from; to remove from a dangerous area. [L. *evacuare*].
EVACUATION, [i-vak'-ew-ā-shun], *n.* the act or process of evacuation; matter which is evacuated; **e. area**, an area from which persons are to be evacuated. [LL. *evacuatio*].
EVACUATIVE, [i-vak'-ew-āt'-iv], *adj.* cathartic, purgative. [Fr. *évacuatif*].
EVACUEE, [ē-vak'-yew-ē'], *n.* one who has been evacuated.
EVADE, [i-vād'], *v.t.* to escape, elude; to avoid by dexterity, artifice, or trickery. [L. *evadere*].
EVADIBLE, [i-vād'-ibl], *adj.* that may be evaded or eluded.
EVAGATION, [ēv'-ag-ā'-shun], *n.* a wandering away; a digression. [L. *evagatio*].
EVAGINATE, [i-vag'-in-āt], *v.t.* (*med.*) to turn inside out, to unsheath. [L. *evaginare*].
EVAGINATION, [i-vag'-in-ā'shun], *n.* the act of evaginating. [L. *evaginatio*].
EVALUATE, [i-val'-ew āt], *v.t.* to determine the value of; to appraise. [Fr. *évaluer*].
EVALUATION, [i-val'-ew-ā'-shun], *n.* the act of evaluating; the result of such act. [Fr. *évaluation*].
EVANESCE, [ē'-van-es'], *v.i.* to fade or melt away, to disappear. [L. *evanescere*].
EVANESCENCE, [ē-van-es'-ents], *n.* a fading away, disappearance.
EVANESCENT, [ē-van-es'-ent], *adj.* that quickly vanishes; impermanent. [L. *evanescens*].
EVANESCENTLY, [ē-van-es'-ent-li], *adv.* in an evanescent way.
EVANGEL, [i-van'-jel], *n.* good tidings; one of the Four Gospels; Christianity. [Gk. *euangelion* glad tidings].
EVANGELIAN, [ē'-van-jēl'-ian], *adj.* offering thanks in token of gratitude on receiving good news.
EVANGELIC, [ē'-van-jel'-ik], *adj.* of, or pertaining to, the gospel, or to the Christian religion; Protestant. [LL. *evangelicus*].
EVANGELICAL (1), [ē'-van-jel'-ik-al], *n.* a Protestant; a member of the Evangelical party in the Church of England.
EVANGELICAL (2), [ē'-van-jel'-ik-al], *adj.* evangelic.
EVANGELICALISM, [ē'-van-jel'-ik-al-izm], *n.* the system or practice of Evangelicals.
EVANGELICALLY, [ē'-van-jel'-ik-al-i], *adv.* in an evangelical manner.
EVANGELICISM, [ē'-van-jel'-is-izm], *n.* Evangelicalism.
EVANGELISM, [i-van'-jel-izm], *n.* preaching the gospel.
EVANGELIST, [i-van'-jel-ist], *n.* a writer of one of the gospels; an evangelizing preacher of the gospel; a person authorized to preach. [L. *evangelista*].
EVANGELISTARY, [i-van'-jel-is'-ta-ri], *n.* a collection of passages from the gospels as lessons in divine service. [LL. *evangelistarium*].
EVANGELISTIC, [i-van'-jel-ist'-ik], *adj.* connected with an evangelist.
EVANGELIZATION, [i-van'-jel-ī-zā'-shun], *n.* propagating the Christian gospel.
EVANGELIZE, [i-van'-jel-iz], *v.t.* to preach the gospel to; to convert to Christianity and the gospel. [EcclesL. *evangelizare*].
EVANID†, [i-van'-id], *adj.* fleeting, transient, evanescent. [L. *evanidus*].
EVANISH, [i-van'-ish], *v.i.* to vanish away. [OFr. *esvanir*].
EVANISHMENT, [i-van'-ish-ment], *n.* the act of evanishing.
EVANITION, [ē'-van-ish'-un], *n.* the state of evanishment, disappearance. [OFr. *evanition*].
EVAPORABLE, [i-vāp'-or-abl], *adj.* that may be converted into vapour; capable of evaporation.
EVAPORATE, [i-vap'-or-āt], *v.t.* to change to vapour; *v.i.* to turn into vapour; (*fig.*) to disappear; to dissipate uselessly. [L. *evaporare*].
EVAPORATION, [i-vap'-or-ā'-shun], *n.* the act of evaporating; the condition of being evaporated; whatever is evaporated; the draining of the vaporable portion of a substance in a liquid form, in order to obtain it in a concentrated or a dry condition. [L. *evaporatio*].
EVAPORATIVE, [i-vap'-or-āt-iv], *adj.* of, or conducive to, evaporation. [L. *evaporativus*].
EVAPORATOR, [i-vap'-or-āt'-or], *n.* one who, or that which, evaporates; any apparatus for evaporating.
EVAPORIMETER, [i-vap'-or-im'-it-er], *n.* an instrument used to ascertain the quantity of a fluid evaporated in a given time.
EVASIBLE, [i-vāz'-ibl], *adj.* which can be evaded.
EVASION, [i-vā'-shun], *n.* escape; the act of evading; prevarication. [L. *evasio*].
EVASIVE, [i-vā'-siv], *adj.* tending to evade one, difficult to grasp; equivocal. [Fr. *évasif*].
EVASIVELY, [i-vās'-iv-li], *adv.* in an evasive way.

EVAPORIMETER

EVASIVENESS, [i-vās'-iv-nes], *n.* the quality of being evasive.
EVE (1), [ēv], *n.* the wife of Adam; personification of womankind.
EVE (2), [ēv], *n.* the latter part or close of the day; the evening before a holiday; the day before a saint's day; the time immediately preceding an event. [OE. *æfen*].
EVECTION, [i-vek'-shun], *n.* elevation; (*astron.*) a change of form in the lunar orbit, whereby its eccentricity is sometimes increased and sometimes diminished; **e. of heat**, the diffusion of heat by the motion of the heated particles of a fluid. [L. *evectio*].
EVEN (1), [ēv'-en], *n.* (*poet.*) evening. [OE. *æfen*].
EVEN (2), [ēv'-en], *adj.* level, smooth, flat; regular, rhythmical (of sounds); any whole multiple of two; (*fig.*) not easily ruffled or disturbed; monotonous; uneventful; **to be e. with**, to square accounts with; **e. money**, (*betting*) return of double the sum risked. [OE. *æfen* level, even, equal].
EVEN (3), [ēv'-en], *adv.* evenly; just as; at the same time as; according; expressing a strong assertion

and prefixed to words, etc., on which the emphatic character of the statement depends as, **he e. insulted him**; **e. though**, although. [EVEN (2)].

EVEN (4), [ēv'-en], *v.t.* to make even, to level, make smooth; to balance accounts; **to e. up**, balance; **to e. up on**, to requite. [EVEN (2)].

EVENER, [ēv'-en-er], *n.* one who, or that which, makes even.

EVENFALL, [ēv'-en-fawl'], *n.* the fall of the day, twilight.

EVEN-HANDED, [ēv'-en-hand'-id], *adj.* impartial, equitable, just.

EVEN-HANDEDLY, [ēv'-en-hand'-id-li], *adv.* in a just and impartial manner.

EVEN-HANDEDNESS, [ēv'-en-hand'-id-nes], *n.* the quality or condition of being even-handed.

EVENING, [ēv'-ning], *n.* the time between sunset and darkness; the time from the close of the afternoon until bedtime; **e. clothes**, **e. dress**, **e. suit**, the conventional clothes for wearing in public in the evening; **e. primrose**, a species of plant, *Œnothera biennis*, in which the flowers open at night; **e. star**, a planet seen in the west soon after sunset. [OE. *æfnung*].

EVENLY, [ēv'-en-li], *adv.* in an even manner; tranquilly.

EVENMINDED, [ēv'-en-mīnd'-id], *adv.* tranquil; unbiased.

EVENNESS, [ēv'-en-nes], *n.* the quality or state of being even.

EVENSONG, [ēv'-en-song'], *n.* (*eccles.*) the name of the church office read daily shortly before sunset, the sixth of the seven "canonical hours"; in the Church of England "Evening Prayer."

EVENT, [i-vent'], *n.* a happening; the result of an action, its outcome; an item in a programme; **in the e. of**, in case of; **at all events**, in any case. [L. *eventus* outcome].

EVEN-TEMPERED, [ēv'-en-temp'-erd], *adj.* having an equable temper.

EVENTERATE, [i-vent'-er-āt'], *v.t.* to disembowel. [E (2) and L. *venter* the belly]

EVENTFUL, [i-vent'-fool], *adj.* full of incidents; momentous.

EVENTIDE, [ēv'-en-tīd'], *n.* (*poet.*) evening.

EVENTILATE†, [i-vent'-il-āt], *v.t.* to submit to the action of wind; to fan; (*fig.*) to discuss, air one's opinions. [L. *eventilare* to fan].

EVENTILATION, [i-vent'-il-ā'-shun], *n.* the act of eventilating.

EVENTLESS, [i-vent'-les], *adj.* devoid of incident.

EVENTRATION, [ē-vent-rā'-shun], *n.* the action of opening the abdomen; an intestinal hernia. [Fr. *éventration*].

EVENTUAL, [i-vent'-yoo-al], *adj.* happening or likely to happen as a consequence or result of a series of incidents; contingent; ultimate. [Fr. *éventuel*].

EVENTUALITY, [i-vent'-yoo-al'-it-i], *n.* a possible event, one which may happen as a consequence.

EVENTUALLY, [i-vent'-yoo-al-i], *adv.* ultimately.

EVENTUATE, [i-vent'-yoo-āt], *v.i.* to happen; to result.

EVER, [ev'-er], *adv.* always; repeatedly; at any time; in any degree or condition; **e. and anon**, at one time and another; (*coll.*) **e. so**, very, in a great degree; **for e. and e.**, always; **for e. and a day**, eternally. [OE. *æfre*].

EVERGLADE, [ev'-er-glād'], *n.* a marshy land, with patches here and there covered with high grass, *esp.* the *Everglades* in Florida.

EVERGREEN (1), [ev'-er-grēn], *n.* a plant which has green leaves all the year round.

EVERGREEN (2), [ev'-er-grēn], *adj.* of a tree or plant which remains green all the year round; (*fig.*) always fresh and vigorous.

EVERLASTING, [ev'-er-lahst'-ing], *adj.* lasting for ever, eternal; durable; constantly recurring; repeated until one tires of it.

EVERLASTINGLY, [ev'-er-lahst'-ing-li], *adv.* eternally, perpetually, repeatedly.

EVERLASTINGNESS, [ev'-er-lahst'-ing-nes], *n.* the quality or state of being everlasting.

EVERMORE, [ev'-er-maw(r)'], *adv.* always, for ever, eternally.

EVERRICULUM, [ē'-ver-ik'-yoo-lum], *n.* (*surg.*) calculous particles removed by the operation of lithotomy. [L. *everriculum*].

EVERSION, [i-ver'-shun], *n.* overthrow; a turning outwards. [L. *eversio*].

EVERT, [i-vert'], *v.t.* (*fig.*) to overthrow; to turn outwards. [L. *evertere*].

EVERY, [ev'-er-i], *adj.* each one, all, each of a number singly or one by one; **e. now and then**, at intervals, from time to time; **e. time**, without exception. [ME. *everilch*].

EVERYBODY, [ev'-ri-bod'-i], *n* every person, all people (with *sg.* verb).

EVERYDAY, [ev'-ri-dā'], *adj.* happening every day, commonplace, usual.

EVERYMAN, [ev'-ri-man], *n.* the ordinary man, the "man in the street." [A character in a sixteenth-century morality play].

EVERYONE, [ev'-ri-wun], *n.* everybody.

EVERYTHING [ev'-ri-thing], *n.* all, each thing omitting nothing; the main thing.

EVERYWAY, [ev'-ri-wā'], *adv.* in all ways.

EVERYWHERE, [ev'-ri-wāer'], *adv.* in all places.

EVET, [ev'-et], *n.* (*zool.*) a newt. [OE. *efete*].

EVICT, [i-vikt'], *v.t.* to dispossess, turn a tenant out of property. [L. *evincere* to overcome].

EVICTION, [i-vik'-shun], *n.* act of evicting. [L. *evictio*].

EVIDENCE, [ev'-id-ents], *n.* testimony; information or facts which make evident; proof on the authority or sense, reason, or the witness of others; a witness; **to hear, call e.**, to listen to, ask for evidence; **circumstantial e.**, indirect evidence which is sufficient only for a judgment of probability; **King's e.**, information from a prisoner against his accomplices. [L. *evidentia*].

EVIDENT, [ev'-id-ent], *adj.* clear, visible, plain; obvious. [L. *evidens*].

EVIDENTIAL, [ev'-id-en'-shal], *adj.* of the nature of, affording, evidence.

EVIDENTIALLY, [ev'-id-en'-sha-li], *adv.* by means of evidence, in an evidential manner.

EVIDENTIARY, [ev'-id-en'-shar-i], *adj.* evidential.

EVIDENTLY, [ev'-id-ent'-li], *adv.* plainly, obviously, clearly.

EVIL (1), [ēv'-il], *n.* the bad; the harmful; physical disease; moral depravity. [OE. *yfel*].

EVIL (2), [ēv'-il], *adj.* bad; physically diseased; morally depraved. [OE. *yfel*].

EVIL-AFFECTED, [ēv'-il-af-ek'-tid], *adj.* unkindly, maliciously disposed.

EVIL-DOER, [ēv'-il-doo'-er], *n.* one who does evil; a sinner.

EVIL-EYE, [ēv'-il-ī'], *n.* a supposed magical power of fascinating, bewitching, or otherwise injuring, by the look.

EVIL-FAVOURED, [ēv'-il-fāv'-erd], *adj.* ill-favoured, repulsive, ugly.

EVILLY, [ēv'-il-i], *adv.* in an evil fashion.

EVIL-MINDED, [ēv'-il-mīnd'-id], *adj.* wicked, malicious.

EVILNESS, [ēv'-il-nes], *n.* wickedness; viciousness; depravity.

EVIL-SPEAKING, [ēv'-il-spēk'-ing], *n.* wicked talk; slander; defamation.

EVIL-STARRED, [ēv'-il-stahd'], *adj.* ill-starred, unfortunate.

EVINCE, [i-vints'], *v.t.* to show, make evident, exhibit; prove beyond doubt. [L. *evincere*].

EVINCEMENT†, [i-vins'-ment], *n.* the act of evincing; proof.

EVINCIBLE, [i-vins'-ibl], *adj.* that may be evinced; demonstrable.

EVINCIBLY, [i-vins'-ib-li], *adv.* in a manner to compel conviction.

EVINCIVE, [i-vins'-iv], *adj.* giving proof; tending to demonstrate.

EVIRATION, [ev-ir-ā'-shun], *n.* emasculation; the rendering a man effeminate. [L. *eviratio*].

EVISCERATE, [i-vis'-er-āt], *v.t.* to disembowel. [L. *eviscerare*].

EVITABLE, [ev'-it-abl], *adj.* avoidable. [L. *evitabilis*].

EVITATION, [ev'-i-tā'-shun], *n.* avoidance. [L. *evitatio*].

EVITERNAL†, [ev-it-ur'-nal], *adj.* eternal. [L. *aeviternus*].

EVOCATION, [ev'-ōk-ā'-shun], *n.* a calling forth, summoning. [L. *evocatio*].

EVOCATIVE, [ē-vok'-at-iv], *adj.* tending to evoke, reminiscent.

EVOCATOR, [ev'-ok-āt'-or], *n.* one who calls forth, a summoner. [L. *evocator*].

EVOKE, [i-vōk'], *v.t.* to call forth, summon; to produce (a reply, etc.). [L. *evocare*].

EVOLUTE, [ēv'-ol-ewt], *n.* (*math*) a curve which is determinant of another curve, its involute.

EVOLUTION, [ē'-vo-loo'-shun], *n.* the action, condition, or process of evolving, unfolding, developing; a series of things unfolded or developed; the development of higher forms of life from lower; the theory that such development is completely natural and any divine agency is an unnecessary postulate; **emergent e.**, the theory that an evolutionary movement can produce something entirely new and not in the initial state; (*biol.*) the theory that generation is the separate development of a pre-existent germ; (*geom.*) the unfolding of a curve, and making it describe an evolvent or involute; (*arith.*) the extraction of roots; (*milit.*) a manoeuvre to change the disposition of troops. [L. *evolutio* an unrolling, *esp.* of a book].

EVOLUTIONAL, [ē′-vo-lōō′-shun-al], *adj.* connected with evolution.

EVOLUTIONARY, [ē′-vo-lōō′-shun-ar-i], *adj.* of or pertaining to evolution.

EVOLUTIONISM, [ē′-vo-lōō′-shun-izm], *n.* belief in evolutionary theories.

EVOLUTIONIST, [ē′-vo-lōō′-shun-ist], *n.* one who advocates evolutionary theories; (*milit.*) one skilled in manoeuvres.

EVOLUTIVE, [ev-ol-ōō′-tiv], *adj.* pertaining to evolution.

EVOLVE, [i-volv′], *v.t.* to unfold, display, develop step by step; (*fig.*) to bring (an idea, etc.) to maturity; *v.i.* to unfold; to reach a better or more complex state by gradual process from a worse or simpler one. [L. *evolvere*].

EVOLVEMENT, [i-volv′-ment], *n.* an evolving.

EVOLVENT, [i-volv′-ent], *n.* (*math.*) the involute; the curve which results from the evolution of another curve, called the evolute. [L. *evolvens*].

EVOLVULUS, [i-volv′-yŏŏ-lus], *n.* (*bot.*) a genus of 80 species of the convolvulus order, which do not share the characteristic of that order of twining.

EVULGATION, [ēv′-ul-gā′-shun], *n.* the publishing of anything. [L. *evulgatio*].

EVULSION, [i-vul′-shun], *n.* the action of plucking or tearing-out by force. [L. *evulsio*].

EWE, [ew], *n.* female of the sheep; (*fig.*) **e. lamb,** a specially treasured possession; a person very dear to or valued by another. [OE. *eowu*].

EWE-NECKED, [ew′-nekt], *adj.* (of horses) having a thin, concave neck.

EWER, [yew′-er], *n.* a jug or pitcher, *esp.* a large one used in bedrooms, to hold water for washing. [AFr. *ewiere* water-vessel from OFr. *aiquiere* from L. *aquaria*].

EWER

EWRY, [yew′-ri], *n.* the scullery of a monastery; an officer in the royal household, responsible for the linen for the table, laying the cloth, and serving water in ewers after dinner.

EX-, *pref.* from off, drawn from; since, after; from out of, away from, forth from; former. [L. *ex*].

EXACERBATE, [eks-as′-er-bāt], *v.t.* to irritate; to increase the pain of, aggravate; (*fig.*) to exasperate, embitter. [L. *exacerbare*].

EXACERBATION, [eks′-as-er-bā′-shun], *n.* an exacerbating or a being exacerbated; the source of aggravation. [L. *exacerbatio*].

EXACERBESCENCE, [eks′-as-er-bes′-ents], *n.* increase of malignity or violence of a fever or disease. [L. *exacerbescens*].

EXACINATE, [eks-as′-in-āt], *v.t.* to extract the kernel or stones from. [MedL. *exacinare*].

EXACT (1), [igz-akt′], *adj.* finished off, complete; correct; accurate; precise; observing strict method, rule, or order; punctual. [L. *exactum*, *p.pt.* of *exigere* to drive out].

EXACT (2), [igz-akt′], *v.t.* to force from; to demand or extort by means of authority; to demand or require (attention). [L. *exactum*, *p.pt.* of *exigere* to drive out].

EXACTABLE, [igz-ak′-tabl], *adj.* that can be exacted.

EXACTER, [igz-ak′-ter], *n.* one who exacts payment, often excessively.

EXACTING, [igz-akt′-ing], *adj.* making severe or excessive demands; arduous, exhausting.

EXACTION, [igz-ak′-shun], *n.* the act of exacting; a tyrannous authoritative demand; extortion; that which is exacted; excessive service or tribute. [L. *exactio* a driving forth].

EXACTITUDE, [igz-akt′-i-tyōōd], *n.* exactness, correctness, accuracy.

EXACTLY, [igz-akt′-li], *adv.* in an exact manner; precisely; accurately; as a conversational interjection, quite so!

EXACTMENT, [igz-akt′-ment], *n.* an exaction.

EXACTNESS, [igz-akt′-nes], *n.* a being exact; accuracy; precision.

EXACTOR, [igz-akt′-or], *n.* a person who exacts; an officer who collects taxes, or customs; an extortioner; one who compels another to pay more than is legal; one who is very severe in his demands. [L. *exactor* one who drives forth].

EXACTRESS, [igz-akt′-res], *n.* a female exactor.

EXAERESIS, [egz-ēr′-es-is], *n.* (*surg.*) any operation which has as its objective the removal from the body of morbid parts. [EX and Gk. *airo* I take].

EXAGGERATE, [eg-zaj′-er-āt], *v.t.* to represent as greater than the reality; to over-emphasize, overstate; to increase and render abnormal; *v.i.* to use over-statement. [L. *exaggerare* to heap up].

EXAGGERATEDLY, [eg-zaj′-er-āt′-id-li], *adv.* in an exaggerated fashion.

EXAGGERATION, [eg-zaj′-er-ā′-shun], *n.* the act of exaggerating; an exaggerated remark. [L. *exaggeratio*].

EXAGGERATIVE, [eg-zaj′-er-āt′-iv], *adj.* marked by exaggeration.

EXAGGERATOR, [eg-zaj′-er-āt-er], *n.* a person who exaggerates. [LL. *exaggerator* one who heaps up].

EXAGGERATORY, [eg-zaj′-er-āt′-er-i], *adj.* containing or tending to exaggeration.

EXAGITATE†, [eg-zaj′-it-āt], *v.t.* to excite, rouse; to discuss. [L. *exagitare*].

EXAGITATION†, [eg-zaj′-it-ā′-shun], *n.* a rousing; a discussion. [L. *exagitatio*].

EXALBUMINOUS, [eks′-al-bew′-min-us], *adj.* (*bot.*) without albumen in the seed.

EXALT, [eg-zawlt′], *v.t.* to raise up high; to heighten in rank, to ennoble; to praise; (*alchemy*) to refine. [L. *exaltare*].

EXALTADOS, [egz-al-tahd′-ōz], *n.*(*pl.*) the advanced liberals in Spain in 1820. [Span. *exaltados*].

EXALTATION, [eg′-zawl-tā′-shun], *n.* the act of exalting; the state of being exalted; high spirits, elation; (*astron.*) the dignity and influence which a planet acquires in certain signs or parts of the zodiac; (*med.*) a morbid increase of action in an inflamed organ; **E. of the Cross,** a Christian festival observed on September 14. [L. *exaltatio*].

EXALTED, [eg-zawl′-tid], *adj.* lofty, elevated; of high rank; enraptured; inspired; (*alchemy*) refined, concentrated.

EXALTEDNESS, [eg-zawl′-tid-nes], *n.* the condition of being exalted.

EXALTER, [eg-zawl′-ter], *n.* one who, or that which, exalts.

EXALTMENT†, [eg-zawlt′-ment], *n.* the action of exalting, exaltation.

EXAM, [eg-zam′], *n.* examination. [Short form of EXAMINATION].

EXAMEN, [eg-zām′-en], *n.* an investigation, examination, scrutiny or enquiry. [L. *examen*].

EXAMINABILITY, [eg-zam′-in-ab-il′-i-ti], *n.* a being capable of examination.

EXAMINABLE, [eg-zam′-in-abl], *adj.* capable of being examined; (*leg.*) cognizable.

EXAMINANT, [eg-zam′-in-ant], *n.* a person examining. [L. *examinans*].

EXAMINATION, [eg-zam′-in-ā′-shun], *n.* investigation, careful inspection; a test by question and answer. [L. *examinatio*].

EXAMINATIONAL, [eg-zam′-in-ā′-shun-al], *adj.* of or pertaining to examinations.

EXAMINATOR, [eg-zam′-in-āt-er], *n.* one who examines. [LL. *examinator*].

EXAMINATORIAL, [eg-zam′-in-a-taw′-ri-al], *adj.* pertaining to an examiner or an examination.

EXAMINE, [eg-zam′-in], *v.t.* to inspect carefully and critically; to inquire into by interrogation; to test the knowledge or capacity of children and others by question and answer; to put to a test. [L. *examinare* to weigh accurately].

EXAMINEE, [eg-zam′-in-ē′], *n.* one subject to examination.

EXAMINER, [eg-zam′-in-er], *n.* a person who examines or inspects; one who marks examination papers; one who interrogates a witness or an offender; in chancery, two officers of that court who examine, on oath, the witnesses for the parties.

EXAMPLE, [eg-zahmpl′], *n.* a particular instance illustrating or dependent on rule or statement; someone or something to be imitated or the reverse; a precedent; a warning; **for e.,** by way of illustration, often abbreviated: e.g. (L. *exempli gratia*); **to make**

an e. of, to punish in order to deter others; **to set an e.,** to conduct oneself so as to be an object of imitation. [L. *exemplum*].

EXAMPLELESS†, [eg-zahmpl'-les], *adj.* unexampled.

EXANGIA, [eks-an'-ji-a], *n.(pl.)* (*med.*) diseases which cause dilatation of the blood-vessels. [EX and Gk. *angeion* blood-vessel].

EXANGULOUS, [eks-an'-gew-lus], *adj.* without corners. [EX and L. *angulus* corner].

EXANIMATE (1), [eks-an'-im-at], *adj.* lifeless; (*fig.*) disheartened. [L. *exanimare* to kill].

EXANIMATE (2), [eks-an'-im-āt], *v.t.* to deprive of life; (*fig.*) to discourage. [L. *exanimare* to kill].

EXANIMATION, [eks'-an-im-ā'-shun], *n.* death; (*fig.*) discouragement. [L. *exanimatio*].

EXANIMOUS, [eks-an'-im-us], *adj.* lifeless; discouraged.

EXANTHEMA, (*pl.* **exanthemata**), [eks'-an-thē'-ma], *n.* (*med.*) a febrile disease such as small-pox or measles, manifesting itself in a distinctive eruption on the skin, that takes a definite time to develop and die down. [Gk. *exanthema* an eruption].

EXANTHEMATIC, [eks-an'-them-at'-ik], *adj.* pertaining to exanthema.

EXANTHEMATOLOGY, [eks-an'-them-at-ol'-oji], *n.* a theoretical examination of exanthemata or eruptive fevers. [EXANTHEMA and Gk. *logos* speech].

EXANTHEMATOUS, [eks'-an-thēm'-at-us], *adj.* of, or pertaining to, exanthema; efflorescent.

EXANTHESIS, [eks-an-thēs'-is], *n.* eruption or feverish efflorescence of the skin. [Gk. *exanthesis*].

EXARCH, [eks'-ahk], *n.* a viceroy of the Byzantine emperors in Italy; in the Greek Church, a title assumed by certain bishops as primates over others, an inspector of the clergy appointed by the Eastern patriarchs. [Gk. *exarkhos* a ruler].

EXARCHATE, [eks'-ahk-āt], *n.* the office, dignity, or province of an exarch.

EXARCHY, [eks'-ahk-i], *n.* the province of an exarch. [Gk. *exarkhos* a leader].

EXAREOLATE, [eks-ahr-ē'-ol-āt], *adj.* not areolate; not spaced out. [EX and AREOLATE].

EXARILLATE, [eks-ar'-il-āt], *adj.* (*bot.*) without an aril.

EXARISTATE, [eks-ar'-is-tat], *adj.* having no arista, awn or beard.

EXARTERITIS, [eks-ah'-ter-īt'-is], *n.* (*path.*) severe inflammation of the external coat of arteries.

EXARTICULATION, [eks'-ah-tik-ew-lā'-shun], *n.* (*med.*) the dislocation of a joint; the removing of a limb or joint.

EXASPERATE, [egz-ahs'-per-āt], *v.t.* to rouse to anger; to aggravate a pain or disease; to provoke and infuriate. [L. *exasperare* to roughen].

EXASPERATER, EXASPERATOR, [egz-ahs'-per-āt'-er], *n.* a person who exasperates.

EXASPERATING, [egz-ahs'-per-ā-ting], *adj.* so as to exasperate.

EXASPERATINGLY, [egz-ahs'-per-ā-ting-li], *adv.* in an exasperating manner.

EXASPERATION, [egz-ahs'-per-ā'-shun], *n.* the action of exasperating or irritating; the state of being exasperated; provocation; rage; aggravation; exacerbation; extreme irritation. [L. *exasperatio*].

EXASPERATIVE, [egz-ahs'-per-āt'-iv], *adj* of a nature to exasperate.

EXASPERATOR, see EXASPERATER.

EXAUCTORATE†, [egz-awkt'-or-āt], *v.t.* to dismiss from office; to deprive of a church dignity or office. [L. *exauctorare* to dismiss from office].

EXAUCTORATION†, [egz-awk'-tor-ā'-shun], *n.* dismissal from service; deprivation; removal from a church dignity or office.

EXAUTHORIZE†, [eks-awth'-or-īz], *v.t.* to remove authority from.

EXCALCEATED, [eks-kal'-si-āt'-id], *adj.* with shoes removed. [L. *excalceare* to take off shoes].

EXCALEFACTION, [eks'-kal-if-ak'-shun], *n.* the action of warming; calefaction. [L. *excalefactio*].

EXCALEFACTORY, [eks'-kal-if-ak'-ter-i], *adj.* warming.

EXCAMBION, [eks-kam'-bi-on], *n.* (*Scots leg.*) exchange of lands. [MedL. *excambio*].

EXCANDESCENCE, [eks'-kand-es'-ents], *n.* a growing hot, a glowing. [L. *excandescere* to glow].

EXCANDESCENT, [eks'-kand-es'-ent], *adj.* white-hot. [L. *excandescens*].

EXCANTATION†, [eks'-kan-tā'-shun], *n.* a charming out or away.

EXCARNATE† **(1),** [eks-kah'-nāt], *v.t.* to divest of flesh or to deprive of a human body. [L. *excarnare*].

EXCARNATE (2), [eks-kah'-nāt], *adj.* not in the flesh.

EXCARNATION, [eks'-kah-nā'-shun], *n.* the rendering excarnate.

EXCATHEDRATE, [eks-kath-ēd'-rāt], *v.t.* (*eccles.*) to make an authoritative pronouncement *ex cathedra*.

EXCAVATE, [eks'-kav-āt], *v.t.* to dig a pit; to dig out; to unearth, *esp.* in archæological investigations. [L. *excavare* to make hollow].

EXCAVATION, [eks'-ka-vā'-shun], *n.* a pit; a digging; a digging out; anything revealed by digging, particularly an archæological site. [L. *excavatio*].

EXCAVATOR, [eks'-kav-āt'-er], *n.* a person who excavates; a machine used for excavating; a steam navvy; a dredger.

EXCECATION, [eks-ik-ā'-shun], *n.* a blinding; punishment by blinding.

EXCEED, [eks-ēd'], *v.t.* to overstep any limit; to surpass; (*coll.*) to drive a motor vehicle faster than the law permits; *v.i.* to go too far; to be guilty of excess; to be more or larger than. [L. *excedere* to exceed].

EXCEEDING (1), [ek-sēd'-ing], *adj.* in surpassing measure, extreme.

EXCEEDING (2)†, [ek-sēd'-ing], *adv.* exceedingly.

EXCEEDINGLY, [ek-sēd'-ing-li], *adv.* extremely, surpassingly.

EXCEL, [eks-el'], *v.t.* to go beyond; to exceed; to surpass; *v.i.* to have good qualities or to perform good or clever actions to an unusual degree; to be surpassingly clever or eminent. [L. *excellere*].

EXCELLENCE, [eks'-el-ents], *n.* superiority; notable proficiency; meritorious quality. [L. *excellentia*].

EXCELLENCY, [eks'-el-ens-i], *n.* a title of honour formerly used of kings, now given to ambassadors, governors, and other eminent persons. [L. *excellentia*].

EXCELLENT, [eks'-el-ent], *adj.* excelling; fine; surpassingly good of its kind. [L. *excellens*].

EXCELLENTLY, [eks'-el-ent-li], *adv.* in an excellent manner.

EXCELSIOR, [ek-sel'-si-or], *int.* higher! still higher! [L. *excelsior* higher].

EXCENTRAL, [ek-sen'-tral], *adj.* (*bot.*) out of the central, eccentric.

EXCEPT (1), [ek-sept'], *v.t.* leave out; *v.i.* to object. [L. *excipere* to take out].

EXCEPT (2), [ek-sept'], *prep.* exclusive of, but for, omitting, apart from, not including.

EXCEPT (3), [ek-sept'], *conj.* unless.

EXCEPTANT, [ek-sept'-ant], *adj.* taking or implying exception. [L. *exceptans*].

EXCEPTING, [ek-sept'-ing], *prep.* excluding, except.

EXCEPTION, [ek-sep'-shun], *n.* the action of excluding from a specified number; that which a rule does not include; objection; offence; (*leg.*) the denial of what is alleged; **bill of exceptions,** a statement of objections to the decision or instructions of a judge. [L. *exceptio*].

EXCEPTIONABLE, [ek-sep'-shun-abl], *adj.* open to objection.

EXCEPTIONABLENESS, [ek-sep'-shun-abl-nes], *n.* the quality of being open to objection.

EXCEPTIONAL, [ek-sep'-shun-al], *adj.* extraordinary, unusual; constituting an exception.

EXCEPTIONALLY, [ek-sep'-shun-a-li], *adv.* in an exceptional way; unusually; extraordinarily.

EXCEPTIONARY, [ek-sep'-shun-e-ri], *adj.* indicative of an exception.

EXCEPTIOUS, [ek-sep'-shus], *adj.* peevish; disposed or apt to cavil; cantankerous.

EXCEPTIOUSNESS, [ek-sep'-shus-nes], *n.* the quality of being exceptious.

EXCEPTIVE, [ek-sep'-tiv], *adj.* forming or including an exception.

EXCEPTLESS, [ek-sept'-les], *adj.* without exceptions.

EXCEPTOR, [ek-sep'-ter], *n.* a person who objects.

EXCEREBRATION, [eks'-e-rib-rā'-shun], *n.* the action of beating out the brains.

EXCERN†, [ek-sern'], *v.t.* to separate and give out through the pores or through small passages of the body; to strain out; to excrete. [L. *excernere* to sift].

EXCERPT (1), [eks'-erpt], *n.* a passage selected from a writing or book; a reprint of a paper in a technical publication. [L. *excerpere*].

EXCERPT (2), [eks-erpt'], *v.t.* to make an extract from, pick out, select.

EXCERPTION, [ek-serp'-shun], *n.* the action of excerpting, selecting; one or more extracts. [L. *excerptio*].

EXCERPTOR, [ek-serp'-ter], *n.* one who excerpts. [L. *excerptor*].

EXCESS (1), [ek-ses'], *n.* that which is beyond what is necessary; that which is beyond the common measure or due quantity; superabundance; any transgression of due limits; undue indulgence; intemperance; (*math.*) that by which one number or quantity exceeds another. [L. *excessus*].

EXCESS (2), [ek-ses'], *adj.* excessive, in excess of; **e. profits**, profits made in a stated period in excess of those made over a previous similar period. [*Prec.*].

EXCESS (3), [ek-ses'], *v.t.* to make an additional charge, *esp.* for any luggage over the weight ordinarily allowed.

EXCESSIVE, [ek-ses'-iv], *adj.* beyond any given, or the ordinary, measure, or proportion; beyond the bounds of justice, fitness, propriety, or utility; extravagant; unreasonable; vehement. [Fr. *excessif*].

EXCESSIVELY, [ek-ses'-iv-li], *adv.* in an extreme degree.

EXCESSIVENESS, [ek-ses'-iv-nes], *n.* the state or quality of being excessive.

EXCHANGE (1), [eks-chānj'], *n.* the act of exchanging, in which the thing received is claimed to be equivalent to the thing given; the act of giving up or resigning without contract one thing or state for another; the act of giving and receiving reciprocally; the thing given or the thing received in exchange; the form of exchanging one debt or credit for another, or settling by order, draft, or bill of exchange; foreign currency, or the place where it is bought; the place where the merchants, brokers, and bankers of a city meet to transact business at certain hours, sometimes abbreviated, *change*; the central telephone office of a particular district; **arbitration of e.**, the calculation of the profits of exchanges at different places; **bill of e.**, a written order directing one party to pay a sum of money to another; **course of e.**, the movement of price between two places. [LL. *excambium*].

EXCHANGE (2), [eks-chānj'], *v.t. and i.* to barter or give one thing in return for another; to surrender one thing, state or condition in return for another; to interchange; to deal in money by changing the currency of one country for the appropriate amount in the currency of another; to make an exchange. [LL. *excambiare*].

EXCHANGEABLE, [eks-chānj'-abl], *adj.* that can be exchanged; estimable by what could be got in exchange.

EXCHANGER, [eks-chānj'-er], *n.* a person who exchanges or practises exchange; a money-changer.

EXCHEQUER, [eks-chek'-er], *n.* a court of record, originally intended mainly for the collection and superintendence of the royal revenues, consisting afterwards of two divisions, one with jurisdiction in revenue matters, and the other a court of common law for the administration of justice; the Treasury; a treasury; **Chancellor of the E.**, the Finance Minister of Great Britain; **E. bill**, a bill for money or promissory bills issued by the Exchequer, as a floating debt. [OFr. *exchequier* from MedL. *scaccarium* a chessboard].

EXCIPIENT, [eks-ip'-i-ent], *n.* food introduced as a vehicle in administering a medicine, as breadcrumb, jelly, etc. [L. *excipiens*].

EXCISABLE, [eks-īz'-abl], *adj.* liable to excise duty.

EXCISE (1), [eks'-īz], *n.* a duty payable to the State on articles manufactured under licence; a licence to manufacture; that branch of the Inland Revenue which collects the duty. [MDu. *excijs*].

EXCISE (2), [eks'-īz], *v.t.* to levy excise duty on.

EXCISE (3), [eks-īz'], *v.t.* to cut out, cut away, or remove. [L. *excidere*].

EXCISEMAN, [eks'-iz-man], *n.* a collector of excise duty.

EXCISION, [ek-sizh'-un], *n.* the action of cutting out; what is cut out. [L. *excisio*].

EXCITABILITY, [ek-sīt'-ab-il'-it-i], *n.* capacity for being easily excited or stimulated to activity.

EXCITABLE, [ek-sīt'-abl], *adj.* easily excited. [L. *excitabilis*].

EXCITANT, [eks'-it-ant, eks-īt'-ant], *n.* that which produces or can produce increased action in a living body or organ; a stimulant. [L. *excitans*].

EXCITATION, [eks'-i-tā'-shun], *n.* the action of exciting. [L. *excitatio*].

EXCITATIVE, [eks-īt'-at-iv], *adj.* such as to excite. [Fr. *excitatif*].

EXCITATORY, [eks'-ī-tāt'-er-i], *adj.* such as to excite.

EXCITE, [eks-īt'], *v.t.* to rouse something into activity; to increase its activity; to stimulate, provoke. [L. *excitare*].

EXCITEMENT, [ek-sīt'-ment], *n.* the action of exciting; stimulation, specially to increased action; the state of being excited; that which excites or produces agitation.

EXCITER, [ek-sīt'-er], *n.* the agent or cause of excitement; (*med.*) a stimulant.

EXCITING, [ek-sīt'-ing], *adj.* producing excitement, thrilling, of absorbing interest.

EXCITINGLY, [ek-sīt'-ing-li], *adv.* in an exciting fashion.

EXCITIVE, [ek-sīt'-iv], *adj.* tending to excite.

EXCITO-MOTORY, [ek-sīt'-ō-mōt'-er-i], *adj.* (*anat.*) inducing muscular contraction or movement independently of volition.

EXCLAIM, [eks-klām'], *v.t. and i.* to utter a sudden sharp cry of surprise, to utter an ejaculation; **to e. against**, to accuse warningly, protest, blame; **to e. at**, to express surprise at. [L. *exclamare*].

EXCLAMATION, [eks'-kla-mā'-shun], *n.* outcry; clamour; vehement or emphatic utterance; a note by which emphatical utterance is marked, thus (!); (*gram.*) an interjection expressive of some emotion, as wonder. [L. *exclamatio*].

EXCLAMATIVE, [eks-kla'-mat-iv], *adj.* exclamatory.

EXCLAMATIVELY, [eks-klam'-at-iv-li], *adv.* exclamatorily.

EXCLAMATORILY, [eks-klam'-at-er-il-i], *adv.* in exclamatory fashion.

EXCLAMATORY, [eks-klam'-at-er-i], *adj.* full of exclamations, tending to exclaim.

EXCLUDE, [eks-klōōd'], *v.t.* to push or thrust out; to hinder from entering; to shut out; to debar; to hinder from participation or enjoyment; to except; not to comprehend or include. [L. *excludere*].

EXCLUSION, [eks-klōō'-zhun], *n.* the act of excluding, the thing excluded. [L. *exclusio*].

EXCLUSIONARY, [eks-klōō'-zhun-ar-i], *adj.* connected with exclusion.

EXCLUSIONISM, [eks-klōō'-zhun-izm], *n.* exclusivism.

EXCLUSIONIST, [eks-klōō'-zhun-ist], *n.* one who would exclude someone from a privilege.

EXCLUSIVE, [eks-klōō'-siv], *adj.* excluding, or tending to exclude, others; maintaining sole privilege; reserved for a few, unapproachable; **e. rights**, rights involving a lack of the same rights by others. [L. *exclusivus*].

EXCLUSIVELY, [eks-klōōs'-iv-li], *adv.* in an exclusive or superior manner; solely.

EXCLUSIVENESS, [eks-klōōs'-iv-nes], *n.* the quality or condition of being exclusive; the snobbish feeling or expression of superiority.

EXCLUSIVISM, [eks-klōōs'-iv-ism], *n.* adherence to some exclusive theory or practice.

EXCLUSORY, [eks-klōōs'-er-i], *adj.* tending to or aiming at exclusion.

EXCOGITATE, [eks-koj'-it-āt], *v.t.* to think out, devise. [L. *excogitare*].

EXCOGITATION, [eks'-koj-it-ā'-shun], *n.* the thinking out or devising of anything. [L. *excogitatio*].

EXCOMMUNICABLE, [eks'-kom-ewn'-ik-abl], *adj.* liable to excommunication.

EXCOMMUNICATE, [eks'-kom-ewn'-ik-āt], *v.t.* to exclude by authority and rite from Christian privileges and sacraments; to exclude officially, expel. [L. *excommunicare*].

EXCOMMUNICATION, [eks'-kom-ewn-ik-ā'-shun], *n.* the rite or act of excommunicating ecclesiastically, or expelling generally; **major e.**, complete ecclesiastical excommunication: **minor e.**, debarring officially from the sacraments. [L. *excommunicatio*].

EXCOMMUNICATORY, [eks'-ko-mewn'-ik-at'-er-i], *adj.* effecting excommunication.

EXCORIATE, [eks-ko'-ri-āt], *v.t.* to strip of a skin, rind, or bark; to flay. [L. *excoriare*].

EXCORIATION, [eks-ko'-ri-ā'-shun], *n.* the abrasion of the skin, the stripping off of a skin, rind or bark.

EXCORTICATE, [eks-kawt'-ik-āt], *v.t.* to strip off the bark of. [L. *excorticare*].

EXCORTICATION, [eks'-kawt-ik-ā'-shun], *n.* the process of excorticating.

EXCREMENT, [eks'-krem-ent], *n.* waste matter excreted and ejected from the body; ordure; dung. [L. *excrementum*].

EXCREMENTAL, [eks'-krem-ent'-al], *adj.* excreted or ejected.

EXCREMENTITIOUS, [eks'-krem-ent-ish'-us], *adj.* pertaining to, consisting of, or containing, excrement; excremental.

EXCRESCENCE, [eks-kres'-ents], *n.* a natural or abnormal protuberance or outgrowth; (*fig.*) an unnecessary development. [L. *excrescentia*].

EXCRESCENT, [eks-kres'-ent], *adj.* growing out of something else in an abnormal manner. [L. *excrescens*].

EXCRESCENTIAL, [eks'-kre-sen'-shal], *adj.* developing as an excrescence out of something.

EXCRETA, [eks-krēt'-a], *n.*(*pl.*) excreted matter or waste. [L. *excreta*].

EXCRETE, [eks-krēt'], *v.i.* to separate and expel, usually of waste matter from animal bodies. [L. *excernere* to sift out].

EXCRETION, [eks-krē'-shun], *n.* the action of excreting matter from the body; that which is excreted.

EXCRETIVE, [eks-krē'-tiv], *adj.* capable of excreting or causing excretion.

EXCRETORY (1), [eks-krēt'-er-i], *n.* (*anat.*) duct or vessel for the reception and expulsion of waste matter from an animal body.

EXCRETORY (2), [eks-krēt'-er-i], *adj.* serving to excrete.

EXCRUCIATE†, [eks-kroosh'-i-āt], *v.t.* to torture physically or mentally; (*fig.*) to give great pain to. [L. *excruciare*].

EXCRUCIATING, [eks-kroosh'-i-āt'-ing], *adj.* causing intense physical or mental pain; very distressing.

EXCRUCIATINGLY, [eks-kroosh'-i-āt'-ing-li], *adv.* in an excruciating fashion; (*coll.*) very.

EXCRUCIATION, [eks-kroosh'-i-ā'-shun], *n.* torture, anguish; the giving of such pain. [L. *excruciatio*].

EXCULPABLE, [eks-kulp'-abl], *adj.* which may be exculpated and freed from blame.

EXCULPATE, [eks'-kulp-āt], *v.t.* to free from blame or guilt.

EXCULPATION, [eks-kul-pā'-shun], *n.* a clearing from blame or guilt; the grounds for such a clearing.

EXCULPATORY, [eks-kulp'-at-er-i], *adj.* tending to clear of blame or guilt.

EXCURRENT, [eks'-kur-ent], *adj.* running or flowing out; (*bot.*) protruding at the top. [L. *excurrens*].

EXCURSE, [eks-kurs'], *v.i.* to digress. [L. *excursum*, *p.pt.* of *excurrere* to run forth].

EXCURSION, [eks-kur'-shun], *n.* deviation or wandering from a prescribed course; a digression; a ramble; a brief tour; a trip for health or pleasure; **e. train**, a train for excursionists at a reduced fare. [L. *excursio*].

EXCURSIONIST, [eks-kur'-shun-ist], *n.* one who is on an excursion; a tripper or an organizer of trips.

EXCURSIVE, [eks-kurs'-iv], *adj.* tending to digress.

EXCURSIVELY, [eks-kurs'-iv-li], *adv.* in an excursive fashion.

EXCURSIVENESS, [eks-kur'-siv-nes], *n.* a tendency to be excursive.

EXCURSUS, [eks-kurs'-us], *n.* a supplemental treatise or appendix on some important point referred to in the main work. [L. *excursus*].

EXCUSABLE, [eks-kewz'-a-bl], *adj.* deserving excuse; pardonable. [L. *excusabilis*].

EXCUSABLENESS, [eks-kews'-abl-nes], *n.* the state of being able to be excused or forgiven.

EXCUSABLY, [eks-kews'-abli], *adv.* in an excusable fashion, so as to allow of forgiveness.

EXCUSATOR†, [eks'-kews-āt'-or], *n.* a person who makes or conveys an excuse. [L. *excusator*].

EXCUSATORY, [eks-kews'-at-er-i], *adj.* tending to excuse.

EXCUSE (1), [eks-kews'], *n.* the action of excusing; a plea offered in extenuation of a fault or irregularity; a pretext. [Fr. *excuse*].

EXCUSE (2), [eks-kewz'], *v.t.* to try to clear someone of blame; to overlook a fault, to accept an excuse; to free from an obligation; to ask pardon for a breach of etiquette either actual or contemplated; **e. me**, a polite formula prefixed as an extenuation to a breach of manners or strict etiquette; a polite or ironical way of disputing a statement. [L. *excusare*].

EXCUSELESS, [eks-kews'-les], *adj.* without excuse, inexcusable.

EXCUSS†, [eks-kus'], *v.t.* to shake off; to decipher; to seize and detain by law. [L. *excussum*, *p.pt.* of *excutere* to shake out].

EXEAT, [eks'-i-at], *n.* formal permission given either to an undergraduate to leave college, or to a priest to leave his diocese. [L. *exeat* let him go out].

EXECRABLE, [ek'-sek-rabl], *adj.* worthy to be execrated; abominable; hateful. [L. *execrabilis* accursed].

EXECRABLENESS, [ek'-sek-rabl-nes], *n.* the condition of being execrable.

EXECRABLY, [ek'-sek-rab-li], *adv.* in an execrable manner.

EXECRATE, [eks'-ek-rāt], *v.t.* to detest or to express detestation; *v.i.* to curse. [L. *execrari* to curse].

EXECRATION, [eks'-ek-rā'-shun], *n.* detestation, and its expression in words; the object execrated; cursing. [L. *execratio*].

EXECRATORY, [eks'-ek-rāt'-or-i], *adj.* of or pertaining to execration; cursing.

EXECUTABLE, [ek-sek'-ewt-abl], *adj.* capable of execution.

EXECUTANT, [eg-zek'-ew-tant], *n.* the agent; one who executes or performs, *esp.* a musician. [Fr. *exécutant*].

EXECUTE, [eks'-ik-ewt], *v.t.* to carry out; of an artist or musician, to perform; to inflict capital punishment on; (*leg.*) to put into effect any legal provision; to fulfil the provisions of a will or instrument conveying property from one person to another. [L. *exsecutum*, *p.pt.* of *exsequi* to follow out].

EXECUTION, [eks'-i-kew'-shun], *n.* the performance of any act; the putting into practice of a previously calculated policy or line of conduct; the performance of a piece of music; the exercise of technique in sculpture or painting; a killing after capital sentence; the fulfilling of the provisions of a legal enactment or document. [L. *exsecutio*].

EXECUTIONER, [eks'-i-kew'-shun-er], *n.* one who executes; the man who executes a sentence of capital punishment.

EXECUTIVE (1), [eg-zek'-ew-tiv], *n.* the administrative side of a government; any administrative body; (*U.S.*) a member of a business organization who is allowed to exercise his own initiative.

EXECUTIVE (2), [eg-zek'-ew-tiv], *adj.* concerned with carrying out policies rather than planning them.

EXECUTIVELY, [eg-zek'-ew-tiv-li], *adv.* in a fashion concerned with execution; so far as concerns execution.

EXECUTOR (1), [eg-zek'-ew-ter], *n.* one who carries out a plan or policy; one appointed by a testator to execute his will. [L. *executor*].

EXECUTOR† **(2)**, [eg-zek'-ew-tor], *n.* an executioner. [L. *executor*].

EXECUTORIAL, [eg-zek'-ew-tawr'-i-al], *adj.* pertaining to an executor.

EXECUTORSHIP, [eg-zek'-ew-ter-ship'], *n.* the office of the executor of a will.

EXECUTORY, [eg-zek'-ewt-er-i], *adj.* connected with the carrying out of commands, laws, etc.; in operation.

EXECUTRIX, [eg-zek'-ewt-riks], *n.* a female executor. [MedL. *executrix*].

EXEDRA, [eks'-id-ra, eks-ēd'-ra], *n.* (*antiq.*) a hall for conversation; a recess; a vestibule. [L. *exedra*].

EXEDRA

EXEGESIS, [eks-i-jēs'-is], *n.* an elucidatory note, *esp.* on the scriptures; elucidation. [Gk. *exegesis*].

EXEGETE, [eks'-i-jēt], *n.* an elucidator, writer of notes; one who expounds. [Gk. *exegetes* an interpreter].

EXEGETIC, [eks-i-jet'-ik], *adj.* exegetical.

EXEGETICAL, [eks-i-jet'-ik-al], *adj.* explanatory.

EXEGETICALLY, [eks-i-jet'-ik-al-i], *adj.* by way of elucidation.

EXEGETICS, [eks-i-jēt'-iks], *n.*(*pl.*) the art or study of biblical interpretation.

EXEGETIST, [eks-i-jēt'-ist], *n.* an exegete.

EXEMPLAR, [eg-zemp'-lah(r)], *n.* a model to be followed and imitated; a specimen. [ME. *exemplaire* from OFr. *exemplaire*].

EXEMPLARILY, [eg-zemp'-lar-il-i], *adv.* in exemplary fashion.

EXEMPLARINESS, [eg-zemp'-lar-i-nes], *n.* the quality of being exemplary.

EXEMPLARITY, [eg-zemp-la'-rit-i], *n.* exemplary conduct; exemplary nature.

EXEMPLARY, [eg-zemp'-lar-i], *adj.* worthy to be imitated; serving for a warning; commendable. [LL. *exemplaris*].

EXEMPLIFIABLE, [eg-zemp'-li-fī'-abl], *adj.* capable of being illustrated by example.

EXEMPLIFICATION, [eg-zemp'-lif-i-kā'-shun], *n.* the act of exemplifying; illustrating by examples. [MedL. *exemplificatio*].
EXEMPLIFY, [eg-zemp'-lif-ī], *v.t.* to illustrate with examples; to take an attested copy of. [MedL. *exemplificare*].
EXEMPT (1), [eg-zempt'], *adj.* exempted, excused from the performance of any duty. [L. *exemptum*, *p.pt.* of *eximere* to take out].
EXEMPT (2), [eg-zempt'], *v.t.* to excuse from the performance of any duty. [Fr. *exempter*].
EXEMPTIBLE, [eg-zempt'-ibl], *adj.* able to be exempted.
EXEMPTION, [eg-zemp'-shun], *n.* an exempting; a being exempt; immunity. [L. *exemptio*].
EXEMPTIVE, [eg-zemp'-tiv], *adj.* tending to exempt.
EXENTERATE, [ek-sent'-er-āt], *v.t.* to take out the entrails of, disembowel. [L. *exenterare*].
EXEQUATUR, [eks-ek-wāt'-ur], *n.* the document recognizing a consul or commercial agent issued by the government to which he comes accredited, and authorizing him to exercise his powers. [L. *exequatur* let him perform].
EXEQUIAL, [ek-sēk'-wi-al], *adj.* pertaining to funerals. [L. *exequialis*].
EXEQUIES, [eks'-ek-wiz], *n.(pl.)* funeral rites. [L. *exequiae*].
EXERCISABLE, [eks'-er-sīz'-abl], *adj.* which may be exercised or performed.
EXERCISE (1), [eks'-er-sīz], *n.* a putting in use or practice; exertion of the body for health, strength, or dexterity; performance; practice for the acquisition of skill; drill; a task appointed one to perform; act of divine worship; a lesson for practice; (*mus.*) any composition calculated to improve the voice or fingers. [L. *exercitium*].
EXERCISE (2), [eks'-er-sīz], *v.t.* to use; to cause something to move or function, often in order to keep it in good order or healthy; to perplex; to discipline; *v.i.* to engage in bodily activity with the purpose of keeping healthy.
EXERCITATION, [eks-er-sit-ā'-shun], *n.* exercise, practice. [L. *exercitatio*].
EXERCITOR, [eks-ur'-sit-or], *n.* the person, owner, or freighter, who has a right to the profits of a trading vessel. [L. *exercitor*].
EXERGUE, [eks'-erg, egz'-erg], *n.* the space below the design on a medal or coin intended to hold the date or other inscription. [Fr. *exergue*].
EXERT, [egz-urt'], *v.t.* to bring into active operation; **to e. oneself,** to use effort, to strive. [L. *exertum*, *exsertum*, *p.pt.* of *exserere* to put out].
EXERTION, [eg-zur'-shun], *n.* the act of exerting or exercising something; the output of force; great physical activity.
EXERTIVE, [eg-zur'-tiv], *adj.* rousing into activity.
EXES, [eks'-es], *n.(pl.)* (*slang*) expenses.
EXEUNT, [eks'-i-unt], *v.i.* they go, a stage direction. [L. *exeunt* they go out].
EXFOETATION, [eks-fēt-ā'-shun], *n.* (*med.*) imperfect foetation in some organ exterior to the uterus. [EX and L. *fetare*].
EXFOLIATE, [eks-fōl'-i-āt], *v.i.* to split off in scales; to peel off. [LL. *exfoliare* to strip the leaves off].
EXFOLIATION, [eks-fōl'-i-ā'-shun], *n.* a peeling off in scales; act of exfoliating. [Fr. *exfoliation*].
EXFOLIATIVE, [eks-fōl'-i-āt'-iv], *adj.* that has the power to cause exfoliation. [Fr. *exfoliatif*].
EXHALABLE, [eks-hāl'-abl], *adj.* able to be exhaled.
EXHALANT, EXHALENT, [eks-hāl'-ent], *adj.* exhaling. [L. *exhalans*].
EXHALATION, [eks'-hal-ā'-shun], *n.* an exhaling; that which is exhaled; a mist, vapour, effluvium. [L. *exhalatio*].
EXHALE, [eks-hāl'], *v.t.* to give off, emit a vapour; *v.i.* to breathe out. [L. *exhalare*].
EXHALENT, see EXHALANT.
EXHAUST (1), [eg-zawst'], *n.* an exhaust-pipe; the exhausted gases escaping through it; *e. gas*, fumes produced by burnt petrol, etc., and emitted through an exhaust.
EXHAUST (2), [eg-zawst'], *v.t.* to draw out or drain off the whole of; to empty by drawing off; to use or expend the whole of; to consume completely; to tire out; to treat of, as a subject, so completely as to leave nothing unsaid. [L. *exhaustum*, *p.pt.* of *exhaurire*].
EXHAUSTED, [eg-zawst'-id], *adj.* empty; used up; finished; that has lost its virtue, or strength; tired out; completely dealt with.
EXHAUSTER, [eg-zawst'-er], *n.* one who exhausts, that which exhausts.
EXHAUSTIBILITY, [eg-zawst'-ib-il'-it-i], *n.* capacity of being exhausted.
EXHAUSTIBLE, [eg-zawst'-ibl], *adj.* that can be exhausted.
EXHAUSTING, [eg-zawst'-ing], *adj.* causing exhaustion; wearying.
EXHAUSTION, [eg-zaws'-chun], *n.* the act of exhausting; the condition of being exhausted; (*math.*) a method of proving the equality of two magnitudes by a *reductio ad absurdum*; (*log.*) a method of proving a point by demonstration of the absurdity of every other possible hypothesis.
EXHAUSTIVE, [eg-zawst'-iv], *adj.* that which exhausts; thorough.
EXHAUSTIVELY, [eg-zawst'-iv-li], *adv.* in an exhaustive manner; thoroughly.
EXHAUSTIVENESS, [eg-zawst'-iv-nes], *n.* the quality of being exhaustive; thoroughness.
EXHAUSTLESS, [eg-zawst'-les], *adj.* that cannot be exhausted; boundless; tireless.
EXHAUST-PIPE, [eg-zawst'-pīp], *n.* the pipe in an engine through which the exhausted gases escape.
EXHEREDATION, [eks'-her-ed-ā'-shun], *n.* (*leg.*) the action of disinheriting. [L. *exheredatio*].
EXHIBIT (1), [egz-ib'-it], *n.* anything displayed; (*leg.*) a sworn deed produced in court as evidence.
EXHIBIT (2), [eg-zib'-it], *v.t.* to show, display; to display publicly in an exhibition; to manifest signs of. [L. *exhibere* to show, show forth].
EXHIBITANT, [eg-zib'-it-ant], *n.* (*leg.*) one who makes an exhibit.
EXHIBITION, [eks'-i-bish'-un], *n.* the act of exhibiting or showing; display; the producing of papers before a tribunal in proof of facts; that which is exhibited; a public show, *esp.* of art or manufacture, natural products, etc.; allowance of meat and drink; a bursary to a student in an English university; (*med.*) administration. [L. *exhibitio*].
EXHIBITIONER, [eks'-i-bish'-un-er], *n.* one who receives an annual grant for his support in a school or college, as a student.
EXHIBITIONISM, [eks'-i-bish'-un-izm], *n.* (*psych.*) a psychological condition causing the sufferer to exhibit the genital organs; a tendency to perform acts which draw attention to one.
EXHIBITIONIST, [eks-i-bish'-un-ist], *n.* a person who exhibits at an exhibition; one subject to exhibitionism.
EXHIBITIVE, [eg-zib'-it-iv], *adj.* indicative. [MdL. *exhibitivus*].
EXHIBITOR, [eg-zib'-it-or], *n.* one whose exhibit is included in any exhibition. [L. *exhibitor*].
EXHIBITORY, [eg-zib'-it-or-i], *adj.* showing, displaying; pertaining to display. [L. *exhibitori(us)*].
EXHILARANT (1), [egz-il'-er-ant], *n.* a medicine that exhilarates.
EXHILARANT (2), [eg-zil'-er-ant], *adj.* exciting mirth or pleasure, exhilarating. [L. *exhilarans*].
EXHILARATE, [eg-zil'-er-āt], *v.t.* to make cheerful, to enliven, to invigorate. [L. *exhilarare*].
EXHILARATING, [eg-zil'-er-āt-ing], *adj.* enlivening, invigorating.
EXHILARATINGLY, [eg-zil'-er-āt-ing-li], *adv.* in an exhilarating fashion.
EXHILARATION, [egz-il'-ar-ā'-shun], *n.* the act of exhilarating; the state of being exhilarated; the means employed in exhilarating. [LL. *exhilaratio*].
EXHILARATIVE, [eg-zil'-er-āt'-iv], *adj.* tending to cause exhilaration.
EXHORT, [eg-zawt'], *v.t.* to urge to good conduct; to warn, admonish; to entreat. [L. *exhortari*].
EXHORTATION, [egz'-aw-tā'-shun], *n.* the art or practice of exhorting to laudable deeds; a form of words intended to incite and encourage; warning, admonition. [L. *exhortatio*].
EXHORTATIVE, [eg-zawt'-at-iv], *adj.* tending to exhortation. [L. *exhortativus*].
EXHORTATOR, [egz'-aw-tā'-tor], *n.* a person who exhorts. [LL. *exhortator*].
EXHORTATORY, [egz'-aw-tā'-tor-i], *adj.* tending to exhort. [LL. *exhortatorius*].
EXHORTER, [eg-zawt'-er], *n.* one who exhorts.
EXHUMATE, [eks-ewm'-āt], *v.t.* to exhume. [L. *exhumare*].
EXHUMATION, [eks-ew-mā'-shun], *n.* process of exhuming. [Fr. *exhumation*].
EXHUME, [eks-hewm'], *v.t.* to dig up, disinter (*esp.* a body that has been buried). [Fr. *exhumer* from MedL. *exhumare*].

EXIGEANT, [eks-ē-zhah(ng)′], *adj.* exacting. [Fr. *exigeant*].

EXIGENCE, [eks′-ij-ents], *n.* the quality or process of being exigent; urgency. [L. *exigentia*].

EXIGENCY, [eks′-ij-en-si], *n.* exigence; any circumstances demanding immediate attention, a crisis. [L. *exigentia*].

EXIGENT, [eks′-i-jent], *adj.* urgent, pressing. [L. *exigens*].

EXIGIBLE, [eks′-ij-ibl], *adj.* that may be charged or demanded.

EXIGUITY, [eks′-ig-ew′-it-i], *n.* scantiness. [Fr. *exiguité* from L. *exiguitas*].

EXIGUOUS, [eg-zig′-yōō-us], *adj.* scanty, very small, insufficient. [L. *exiguus*].

EXIGUOUSNESS, [ek-zig′-yew-us-nes], *n.* paucity, insufficiency.

EXILE (1), [eg′-zīl, ek′-sīl], *n.* banishment or absence from one's native land; the place to which one then retires. [L. *exilium*].

EXILE (2), [eg′-zīl, ek′-sīl], *n.* one banished or absent from his own country. [L. *exul*].

EXILE (3), [eg′-zīl, ek′-sīl], *v.t.* to banish, to exclude a person from his own country, or from his customary surroundings.

EXILEMENT, [eks-īl′-ment], *n.* banishment.

EXILIAN, [eg-zil′-i-an], *adj.* exilic.

EXILIC, [ek-sil′-ik, eg-zil′-ik], *adj.* of, or pertaining to, exile, *esp.* the Jewish exile in Babylon.

EXILITY, [eks-il′-iti], *n.* thinness, meagreness; (*fig.*) unsubstantial quality. [L. *exilitas*].

EXIMIOUS, [eks-im′-i-us], *adj.* distinguished, eminent. [L. *eximius*].

EXINTINE, [eks-int′-ēn], *n.* (*bot.*) a membrane growing between the extine and the intine in the pollen of the yew, juniper, cypress, etc. [A term coined by the botanist Fritzsche].

EXIST, [eg-zist′], *v.i.* to be; to have material being: to occur; to continue in being; (*coll.*) to live poorly. [L. *exsistere*].

EXISTENCE, [eg-zist′-ents], *n.* a state of being; occurrence; life; **mere e.,** continuance of life without pleasure or purpose. [OFr. *existence*].

EXISTENT, [eg-zist′-ent], *adj.* that exists. [L. *existens*].

EXISTENTIAL, [eg′-zis-ten′-shal], *adj.* connected with existence; (*log.*) predicating existence. [LL. *existentialis*].

EXISTIBLE, [eg-zist′-ibl], *adj.* capable of existing.

EXIT (1), [eks′-it], *n.* the departure of an actor from the stage; any departure; a door or outlet.

EXIT (2), [eks′-it], *v.i.* to make one's departure; (*fig.*) to die. [L. *exit* he departs].

EXITIAL†, [eg-zish′-al], *adj.* destructive to life. [L. *exitialis* destructive].

EXITIOUS†, [eg-zish′-us], *adj.* exitial. [L. *exitiosus* destructive].

EXITUS, [eks′-it-us], *n.* issue; (*leg.*) the yearly rent or profits of land. [L. *exitus*].

EX-LEX, [eks′-leks], *n.* an outlaw. [L. *ex* out and *lex* law].

EX-LIBRIS, [eks-lib′-ris], *n.* the motto customary on a book-plate; the book-plate. [L. *ex libris* out of the books].

EXO-, *pref.* outside. [Gk. *exo*].

EXOCOETUS, [ekz-o-sēt′-us], *n.* the genus comprising the flying-fishes. [EXO and Gk. *koite* a bed].

EXOCOETUS

EXOCULATION, [eks′-ok-ew-lā′-shun], *n.* a putting out of an eye, blinding.

EXODE, [eks′-ōd], *n.* in Greek drama, the dénouement; in Roman drama, a kind of farce, which consisted of a recitation of facetious verses by a buffoon after the tragedy was ended. [Fr. *exode* from LL. *exodium*].

EXODIC, [ek-sod′-ik], *adj.* pertaining to an exodus or an exode.

EXODUS, [eks′-od-us], *n.* the title of the second book of the Old Testament which records the departure from Egypt of the Israelites; (*fig.*) any departure. [Gk. *exodus*].

EX-OFFICIAL, [eks′-of-ish′-al], *adj.* the result of office or authority.

EX-OFFICIO, [eks′-o-fish′-i-ō], *adj.* official, in virtue of, or because of, office or authority; **e. member,** one who is a member of a committee in virtue of some other office.

EXOGAMOUS, [eks-og′-am-us], *adj.* relating to exogamy. [EXO and Gk. *gamos* marriage].

EXOGAMY, [eks-og′-am-i], *n.* a tribal convention which compels all tribesmen to marry wives from other tribes. [EXO and Gk. *gamos* marriage].

EXOGASTRITIS, [eks′-ō-gast-rīt′-is], *n.* (*med.*) a form of gastritis where the external membrane of the stomach is inflamed. [EXO and GASTRITIS].

EXOGEN, [eks′-o-jen], *n.* (*bot.*) a plant in which the stem is formed by successive growths on the outside of the wood. [Fr. *exogène*].

EXOGENOUS, [ek-soj′-en-us], *adj.* (*bot.*) with the wood augmented by annual external accretions.

EXOMIS, [ek-sōm′-is], *n.* (*Rom. antiq.*) a garment without sleeves worn by slaves. [Gk. *exomis*].

EXOMOLOGESIS, [ek-som′-ol-o-jēs′-is], *n.* public oral confession. [Gk. *exomologesis*].

EXOMPHALOS, [eks-om′-fal-us], *n.* (*med.*) umbilical hernia; a navel rupture. [EX and Gk. *omphalos* the navel].

EXON, [eks′-on], *n.* the ordinary title of the four chief officers of the yeomen of the royal guard.

EXONERATE, [eg-zon′-er-āt], *v.t.* to free from blame or obligation. [L. *exonerare*].

EXONERATION, [eg-zon′-er-ā′-shun], *n.* an exonerating; the grounds for this. [L. *exoneratio*].

EXONERATIVE, [eg-zon′-er-āt′-iv], *adj.* tending to exonerate.

EXOMIS

EXOPHAGY, [ek-sof′-aj-i], *n.* that cannibalism which is confined to eating those who are not of the same tribe. [EXO and Gk. *phago* I eat].

EXOPHTHALMIA, [eks-of-thal′-mi-a], *n.* (*med.*) abnormal protrusion, from disease, of the eyeball, so that the eyelid cannot cover it. [EXO and Gk. *ophthalmos* the eye].

EXOPHYLLOUS, [eks-of′-il-us], *adj.* (*bot.*) without a further leaf to ensheathe it. [EXO and Gk. *phullon* leaf].

EXOPODITE, [ek-sop′-ō-dīt], *n.* (*zool.*) one of the two secondary joints into which the limb of a crustacean is divided. [EXO and Gk. *pous podos* foot].

EXORABLE, [eks′-or-abl], *adj.* that can be moved by prayer. [L. *exorabilis*].

EXORBITANCE, [eg-zaw′-bi-tants], *n.* the quality of being exorbitant, excessive, or exceeding due bounds; extravagance; excess.

EXORBITANCY, [eg-zaw′-bi-tan-si], *n.* the characteristic of being exorbitant.

EXORBITANT, [eg-zaw′-bi-tant], *adj.* making excessive demands; exceedingly large. [L. *exorbitans*].

EXORBITANTLY, [eg-zaw′-bi-tant-li], *adv.* in an exorbitant fashion, excessively.

EXORCISE, [eks′-aw-sīz], *v.t.* to perform an exorcism; (*fig.*) to dispel or banish. [LL. *exorcizare*].

EXORCISER, [eks′-aw-sīz-er], *n.* one who claims to cast out evil spirits.

EXORCISM, [eks′-aw-sizm], *n.* the expulsion of an evil spirit by religious rite. [Eccles. Gk. *exorkismos*].

EXORCIST, [eks′-aw-sist], *n.* one who exorcises. [Gk. *exorkistes*].

EXORDIAL, [egz-awd′-i-al], *adj.* having the character of an exordium.

EXORDIUM, [egz-awd′-i-um], *n.* the introductory part of a discourse or a composition; the beginning. [L. *exordium*].

EXORHIZAE, [eks-ō-rī′-zē], *n.(pl.)* (*bot.*) those plants whose roots shoot out directly from the base of the embryo; exogens. [EXO and Gk. *rhiza* root].

EXORHIZOUS, [eks-ō-rī′-zus], *adj.* of, or pertaining to, the exorhizae.

EXORNATION, [eks-aw-nā′-shun], *n.* ornamenting; the ornament. [L. *exornatio*].

EXOSKELETON, [eks-ō-skel′-i-ton], *n.* (*anat.*) the external skeleton.

EXOSMOSE, [eks-os′-mōs], *n.* (*physiol.*) the transfusion or outward flow of a gas or fluid in a living body through a porous membrane. [EXO and Gk. *osmos* pushing].

EXOSMOTIC, [eks-os-mot′-ik], *adj.* of or pertaining to exosmose.

EXOSSEOUS, [eks-os′-i-us], *adj.* having no bones. [L. *exossis* boneless].

EXOSTEMMA, [eks-ō-stem′-a], *n.* (*bot.*) a genus of

trees and shrubs related to the cinchona. [EXO and Gk. *stemma* a crown].

EXOSTOME, [eks'-o-stōm], *n.* (*bot.*) the outermost of the perforations which constitute the foramen of the ovule of a plant. [EXO and Gk. *stoma* a mouth].

EXOSTOSIS, [eks-os-tōs'-is], *n.* (*anat.*) an unnatural protuberance of a bone; (*bot.*) a disease in which knots form in the wood. [Gk. *exostosis* an outgrowth of bone].

EXOTERIC, [eks-ō-te'-rik], *adj.* external; of doctrines, rites, etc., such as are taught to the uninitiate; (*fig.*) popular. [Gk. *exoterikos*].

EXOTERICAL, [eks-ō-te'-rik-al], *adj.* exoteric.

EXOTERICISM, [eks-ō-te'-ris-izm], *n.* exoteric teaching, the habit of so teaching.

EXOTIC (1), [eg-zot'-ik], *n.* a plant, word, etc., of foreign origin.

EXOTIC (2), [eg-zot'-ik], *adj.* having foreign characteristics; not yet naturalized; foreign-looking. [Gk. *exotikos*].

EXOTISM, [egz'-ot-izm], *n.* the condition of being exotic. [Fr. *exotisme*].

EXPAND, [eks-pand'], *v.t. and i.* to spread out; to enlarge upon a statement; to grow larger, develop; to become communicative; **expanded metal,** sheet metal slit and stretched into lattice work sheets and used in making reinforced concrete. [L. *expandere*].

EXPANSE, [eks-pants'], *n.* a wide extent.

EXPANSIBILITY, [eks-pans'-i-bil'-it-i], *n.* capacity of being expanded.

EXPANSIBLE, [eks-pans'-ibl], *adj.* that may be expanded.

EXPANSIBLENESS, [eks-pans'-ibl-nes], *n.* expansibility.

EXPANSIBLY, [eks-pans'-ib-li], *adv.* in an expansible fashion.

EXPANSILE, [eks-pans'-il], *adj.* tending to expansion.

EXPANSION, [eks-pan'-shun], *n.* the process of expanding; the state of being expanded; distention, extent. [L. *expansio*].

EXPANSIONIST, [eks-pan'-shun-ist], *adj.* of, or pertaining to, (territorial) expansion.

EXPANSIVE, [eks-pan'-siv], *adj.* tending to expand, capable of expansion; (*fig.*) genial, unreserved.

EXPANSIVELY, [eks-pans'-iv-li], *adv.* in an expansive fashion.

EXPANSIVENESS, [eks-pans'-iv-nes], *n.* capacity for, or tendency to, expansion; (*fig.*) geniality.

EXPATIATE, [eks-pā'-shi-āt], *v.i.* to dilate upon, usually in speech or writing. [L. *expatiari*].

EXPATIATION, [eks-pā'-shi-ā'-shun], *n.* the process of expatiating.

EXPATIATIVE, [eks-pā'-shi-at-iv], *adj.* tending to expatiate.

EXPATIATOR, [eks-pā'-shi-āt-er], *n.* one who expatiates.

EXPATIATORY, [eks-pā'-shi-at-er-i], *adj.* expatiating.

EXPATRIATE (1), [eks-pāt'-ri-at], *n.* an exile, *esp.* one who has severed all ties with his native land.

EXPATRIATE (2), [eks-pāt-ri-at], *adj.* of, or pertaining to, an expatriate; expatriated.

EXPATRIATE (3), [eks-pā'-tri-āt], *v.t.* to banish from one's country. [LL. *expatriare*].

EXPATRIATION, [eks-pā-tri-ā'-shun], *n.* banishment.

EXPECT, [ek-spekt'], *v.t.* to wait for; to look for as likely to happen; to calculate on being done; to anticipate; *v.i.* to wait; to suppose. [L. *exspectare*].

EXPECTANCE, [ek-spek'-tants], *n.* the state of waiting for anything.

EXPECTANCY, [ek-spek'-tan-si], *n.* a being expectant; that which is expected. [L. *expectantia*].

EXPECTANT, [ek-spek'-tant], *adj.* waiting, looking out; **e. mother,** a pregnant woman.

EXPECTANTLY, [eks-pek'-tant-li], *adv.* with expectation.

EXPECTATION, [eks'-pekt-ā'-shun], *n.* the act of expecting; the state of being expected; that which is expected; an awaiting, looking forward to good to come. [L. *expectatio*].

EXPECTATIVE, [ek-spekt'-at-iv], *adj.* anticipatory; expectant. [LL. *expectativus*].

EXPECTINGLY, [ek-spekt'-ing-li], *adv.* in an expectant fashion.

EXPECTORANT (1), [eks-pek'-ter-ant], *n.* (*med.*) an expectorant medicine.

EXPECTORANT (2), [eks-pek'-ter-ant], *adj.* that promotes expectoration.

EXPECTORATE, [ek-spekt'-er-āt], *v.t.* to cough up (phlegm, etc.); *v.i.* to eject phlegm; to spit. [L. *expectorare*].

EXPECTORATION, [ek-spekt'-er-ā'-shun], *n.* the act of expectorating.

EXPECTORATIVE, [ek-spekt'-er-rā-tiv], *adj.* pertaining to expectoration.

EXPEDIENCE, [ek-spē'-di-ents], *n.* expediency. [Fr. *expédience*].

EXPEDIENCY, [ek-spē'-di-en-si], *n.* fitness for effecting a purpose; propriety under particular circumstances. [Fr. *expédience*].

EXPEDIENT (1), [ek-spē'-di-ent], *n.* a means to an end; a means devised in an emergency.

EXPEDIENT (2), [ek-spē-di-ent], *adj.* serviceable for a purpose, useful; proper in the circumstances. [L. *expediens*].

EXPEDIENTIAL, [ek-spē'-di-en'-shal], *adj.* based on, dictated by, considerations of expediency or advantage.

EXPEDIENTLY, [ek-spē'-di-ent-li], *adv.* in an expedient manner.

EXPEDITATE, [eks-ped'-i-tāt], *v.t.* (*leg.*) to cut out the balls or claws of a dog's forefeet for preservation of the king's game. [MedL. *expeditare*] .

EXPEDITE (1), [eks'-pi-dīt], *adj.* speedy; expeditious; easy; active; unencumbered.

EXPEDITE (2), [eks'-pi-dīt], *v.t.* to hasten; to facilitate; to accelerate. [L. *expedire*].

EXPEDITELY, [eks'-pi-dīt'-li], *adv.* in an expeditious manner.

EXPEDITION, [eks'-pi-dish'-un], *n.* haste; a journey undertaken, *esp.* for exploration; the collective body on an expedition. [L. *expeditio*].

EXPEDITIONARY, [eks'-pi-dish'-un-ar-i], *adj.* connected with a military expedition.

EXPEDITIOUS, [eks-pi-dish'-us], *adj.* accomplished, done, with expedition or dispatch.

EXPEDITIOUSLY, [eks-pi-dish'-us-li], *adv.* in an expeditious fashion.

EXPEDITIOUSNESS, [eks-pi-dish'-us-nes], *n.* celerity.

EXPEDITIVE†, [eks-ped'-i-tiv], *adj.* expeditory.

EXPEDITORY†, [eks-ped'-it-er-i], *adj.* expeditious, tending to expedition.

EXPEL, [eks-pel'], *v.t.* to drive out, to compel to leave; to eject, banish; to compel to leave school in disgrace. [L. *expellere*].

EXPELLABLE, [eks-pel'-abl], *adj.* capable of being expelled.

EXPEND, [eks-pend'], *v.t. and i.* to lay out, spend; to use; to consume, use up; to be laid out, used, consumed. [L. *expendere*].

EXPENDABLE, [eks-pend'-abl], *adj.* that may be expended; (*milit.*) (of personnel or equipment) not sufficiently essential for the future conduct of a war to be rescued from the enemy at all costs.

EXPENDITURE, [eks-pend'-i-cher], *n.* the act of spending; anything expended (as money, time, energy, etc.).

EXPENSE, [ek-spents'], *n.* that which is expended; cost; disbursement; price paid; (*Scots leg.*) (*pl.*) costs of a law suit. [LL. *expensa*].

EXPENSIVE, [ek-spens'-iv], *adj.* involving expense; costly.

EXPENSIVELY, [ek-spens'-iv-li], *adv.* in an expensive manner.

EXPENSIVENESS, [ek-spens'-iv-nes], *n.* the quality of being expensive; costliness.

EXPERIENCE (1), [eks-pēer'-i-ents], *n.* the ascertained result of a series of trials or experiments; observation of a fact or of the same facts or events happening in like circumstances; what one has felt and learned by enjoying or suffering; being well versed in anything; often an experiencing, a suffering; (*coll.*) a disastrous or disturbing occasion in life in general, sexual relationship, etc.; **e. table,** a table of normal expectation of life used by the insurance companies in assessing their policies. [L. *experientia*].

EXPERIENCE (2), [eks-pēer'-i-ents], *v.t.* to have experience of; to undergo, suffer; to meet with.

EXPERIENCED, [eks-pēer'-i-enst], *adj.* versed, practised; knowing.

EXPERIENTIALISM, [eks-pēer'-i-en'-shal-izm], *n.* the doctrine which derives all our ideas from experience, or would refer all knowledge to the test of experience.

EXPERIENTIALIST, [eks-pēer'-i-en'-shal-ist], *n.* a supporter of experientialism.

EXPERIMENT (1), [eks-pe'-rim-ent], *n.* investigation

by trial and error, *esp.* scientific investigation. [L. *experimentum*].

EXPERIMENT (2), [eks-pe'-ri-ment], *v.i.* to make an experiment or experiments.

EXPERIMENTAL, [eks-pe'-ri-ment'-al], *adj.* connected with experiment; founded on experiment; derived from experience.

EXPERIMENTALISM, [eks-pe'-ri-ment'-al-ism], *n.* empiricism.

EXPERIMENTALIST, [eks-pe'-ri-ment'-al-ist], *n.* one who devotes himself to experimental research in science; one who tries new schemes; an empiricist.

EXPERIMENTALIZE, [eks-pe'-ri-ment'-al-īz], *v.i.* to perform experiments.

EXPERIMENTALLY, [eks-pe'-ri-ment'-al-i], *adv.* in an experimental fashion.

EXPERIMENTARIAN, [eks-pe'-ri-ment-āer'-ian], *n.* one in the habit of making experiments.

EXPERIMENTATION, [eks-pe'-ri-ment-ā'-shun], *n.* the making of experiments.

EXPERIMENTATIVE, [eks-pe'-ri-ment'-at-iv], *adj.* tending to make experiments.

EXPERIMENTER, [eks-pe'-ri-ment'-er], *n.* one who experiments.

EXPERIMENTIST, [eks-pe'-ri-ment-ist], *n.* an experimenter.

EXPERT (1), [eks'-pert], *n.* a person specially trained and qualified in any department of science or art; one who professes to have such special qualification.

EXPERT (2), [eks'-pert], *adj.* possessing skill or knowledge in any work or branch of knowledge; skilful, dexterous; **e. work**, work skilfully done. [L. *expertus*].

EXPERTLY, [eks-pert'-li], *adv.* in an expert way.

EXPERTNESS, [eks-pert'-nes], *n.* the quality or condition of being expert.

EXPIABLE, [eks'-pi-abl], *adj.* capable of being expiated. [L. *expiabilis*].

EXPIATE, [eks'-pi-āt], *v.t.* to atone for; to make amends for. [L. *expiare*].

EXPIATION, [eks'-pi-ā'-shun], *n.* the act of expiating, or the means employed; atonement. [L. *expiatio*].

EXPIATOR, [eks'-pi-āt'-er], *n.* one who expiates. [L. *expiator*].

EXPIATORY, [eks-pi-āt'-er-i], *adj.* tending to expiate. [L. *expiatorius*].

EXPIRATION, [eks-pi-rā'-shun], *n.* the physical movement of breathing out; the last emission of breath, death; (*fig.*) the end. [L. *expiratio*].

EXPIRATORY, [eks-pi'-rat-or-i], *adj.* pertaining to the process of expiration.

EXPIRE, [eks-pier'], *v.t.* to breathe out from the lungs; *v.i.* to die down, to die out; to emit the last breath; to die; to come to an end. [L. *expirare*].

EXPIRING, [eks-pier'-ing], *adj.* breathing out air; dying; uttered when dying.

EXPIRY, [eks-pier'-i], *n.* expiration; end; death.

EXPISCATE†, [eks-pis'-kāt], *v.t.* to fish out; (*fig.*) to find out by careful enquiry. [L. *expiscari*].

EXPLAIN, [eks-plān], *v.t.* to make plain or intelligible; to justify by giving reasons; to excuse; *v.i.* to give explanations; **to e. away**, to attempt to prove that a statement or situation was misunderstood. [L. *explanare*].

EXPLAINABLE, [eks-plān'-abl], *n.* capable of explanation.

EXPLANATION, [eks-plan-ā'-shun], *n.* the action of explaining, or the means employed; an excuse; a justification; any reason or cause. [L. *explanatio*].

EXPLANATORINESS, [eks-plan'-at-er-i-nes], *n.* the quality of being explanatory.

EXPLANATORY, [eks-plan'-at-er-i], *n.* serving to explain.

EXPLETIVE, [eks-plēt'-iv], *n.* (*gram.*) a particle which rounds out the sense of a sentence; an exclamation, oath. [L. *expletivus* tending to fill out].

EXPLETIVELY, [eks-plēt'-iv-li], *adv.* in an expletive fashion.

EXPLETORY, [eks'-plēt-er-i], *adj.* serviceable for filling up.

EXPLICABLE, [eks-plik'-abl], *adj.* that can be explained. [L. *explicabilis*].

EXPLICABLENESS, [eks-plik'-abl-nes], *n.* the quality of admitting of explanation.

EXPLICATE, [eks'-plik-āt], *v.t.* to explain anything complicated; to develop an argument. [L. *explicare* to unfold].

EXPLICATION, [eks-plik-ā'-shun], *n.* the action of explicating, or the complicated reasoning involved. [L. *explicatio*].

EXPLICATIVE, [eks'-plik-āt-iv], *adj.* explicatory. [L. *explicativus*].

EXPLICATOR†, [eks'-plik-āt-er], *n.* one who explicates. [L. *explicator*].

EXPLICATORY, [eks'-plik-āt'-er-i], *adj.* serving to explicate, explanatory.

EXPLICIT (1), [eks-plis'-it], *n.* the phrase used to mark the end of a book or section in a manuscript or printed work. [MedL. *explicit* here ends].

EXPLICIT (2), [eks-plis'-it], *adj.* distinctly stated, not merely implied; express; outspoken. [L. *explicare*].

EXPLICITLY, [eks-plis'-it-li], *adv.* in an explicit fashion.

EXPLICITNESS, [eks-plis'-it-nes], *n.* the quality of being explicit; outspokenness.

EXPLODE, [eks-plōd'], *v.t. and i.* to burst or expand with violence and a loud report; to utter a burst of laughter; to cause to burst; to prove to be fallacious; to demonstrate as absurd. [L. *explodere, explaudere* to drive off (an actor) by hissing and clapping].

EXPLODER, [eks-plōd'-er], *n.* one who, or that which, causes an explosion; **magneto e.**, a portable electrical apparatus used to detonate high-explosive charges.

EXPLOIT (1), [eks'-ploit], *n.* a notable heroic or adventurous deed or achievement. [OFr. *esploit*].

EXPLOIT (2), [eks-ploit'], *v.t.* to turn, often unfairly, to use and profit; to use selfishly; to make an unfair use of (another's services). [Fr. *exploiter*].

EXPLOITATION, [eks-ploit-a'-shun], *n.* the act of exploiting; the condition of being exploited. [Fr. *exploitation*].

EXPLOITER, [eks-ploit'-er], *n.* one who exploits.

EXPLORATION, [eks-plaw-rā'-shun], *n.* the act of exploring; close and thorough search; travel for purposes of investigation; preliminary theoretic discussion before putting any policy into action. [L. *exploratio*].

EXPLORATIVE, [eks-plaw'-rat-iv], *adj.* concerned with exploration.

EXPLORATORY, [eks-plor'-āt-er-i], *adj.* pertaining to exploration; preliminary, tentative. [L. *exploratorius*].

EXPLORE, [eks-plaw(r)'], *v.t. and i.* to search and examine with care; to travel for purposes of investigation; to investigate; to discuss; (*surg.*) to probe (a wound). [L. *explorare*].

EXPLORER, [eks-plawr'-er], *n.* one who explores; an instrument used to explore a cavity in a tooth; an instrument for sounding in mines or water; (*surg.*) an instrument for probing a wound; (*elect.*) a device to ascertain leakage in a dynamo.

EXPLORING, [eks-plawr'-ing], *adj.* engaged in, or fond of, exploring.

EXPLOSION, [eks-plō'-zhun], *n.* a bursting with violence and a loud report; the firing of gunpowder, dynamite, etc.; any loud burst of sound; a relieving of the feelings in any sudden violent manner. [L. *explosio*].

EXPLOSIVE (1), [eks-plō'-ziv], *n.* the substance whose sudden expansion causes an explosion; the motive principle in the firing of shells, etc.; **high e.**, explosive with a high explosive coefficient.

EXPLOSIVE (2), [eks-plō'-ziv], *adj.* tending to explode or burst with noise and violence; irascible; coming in sudden eruptive bursts, as of laughter.

EXPLOSIVELY, [eks-plō'-ziv-li], *adv.* in an explosive fashion.

EXPONENT, [eks-pōn'-ent], *n.* a person who, or that which, expounds or explains; (*alg.*) a number placed above a quantity on the right hand, to indicate how often that quantity is to be multiplied by itself. [L. *exponens*].

EXPONENTIAL, [eks'-pōn-en'-shal], *adj.* relating to, or involving, exponents; **e. curve**, one whose nature is defined by means of an exponential equation; **e. equation**, an equation which contains an exponential quantity; **e. quantity**, a quantity whose exponent is variable.

EXPORT (1), [eks'-pawt], *n.* the act of exporting; merchandise conveyed from one country to another; **invisible e.**, export of services involving no transfer of goods; the yearly value of such exports.

EXPORT (2), [eks'-pawt, eks-pawt'], *v.t.* to send out of a country by way of trade. [L. *exportare*].

EXPORTABLE, [eks-pawt'-abl], *adj.* that can be exported.

EXPORTATION, [eks-paw-tā'-shun], *n.* the act of exporting; †the conveying of persons out of a country. [L. *exportatio*].

EXPORTER, [eks-pawt'-er], *n.* an export trader.

EXPOSAL, [eks-pōz'-al], *n.* exposure; setting forth

EXPOSE, [eks-pōz], *v.t.* to remove the covering or protection from, to reveal, to make defenceless; to lay open to (some danger or influence); to make public, unmask, declare the villainy of. [Fr. *exposer*].

EXPOSE, exposé, [eks-pōz'-ā], *n.* an explanatory analysis; an exposing of something discreditable. [Fr. *exposé*].

EXPOSED, [eks-pōzd'], *adj.* open; open to attack; open to the severity of the weather.

EXPOSEDNESS, [eks-pōz'-id-nes], *n.* the condition of being exposed.

EXPOSITION, [eks-pō-zish'-un], *n.* the act of exposing, laying open, or exhibiting; an exhibition, explanation, elucidation or interpretation. [L. *expositio*].

EXPOSITIVE, [eks-pos'-it-iv], *adj.* expository, explanatory. [L. *expositivus*].

EXPOSITOR, [eks-poz'-it-er], *n.* a person who, or book which, expounds. [L. *expositor*].

EXPOSITORY, [eks-poz'-it-er-i], *adj.* serving to set forth the meaning.

EXPOSTULATE, [eks-pos'-tyŏŏ-lāt], *v.i.* to reason seriously (with a person) on some impropriety of conduct or words, to remonstrate; to protest. [L. *expostulare*].

EXPOSTULATION, [eks-pos'-tyŏŏ-lā'-shun], *n.* act of expostulating; remonstrance; protest. [L. *expostulatio*].

EXPOSTULATOR, [eks-pos'-tyŏŏ-lā'-ter], *n.* a person who expostulates.

EXPOSTULATORY, [eks-pos'-tyŏŏ-lā'-ter-i], *adj.* characterized by expostulation.

EXPOSURE, [eks-pō'-zhur], *n.* the act of exposing, or laying open, whether to the action of the elements or, figuratively, to public knowledge; the being so exposed; (*phot.*) the period of time light is allowed to operate on a sensitive emulsion.

EXPOUND, [eks-pownd'], *v.t.* to lay open the meaning of; to explain; to interpret. [OFr. *expondre* from L. *exponere*].

EXPRESS (1), [eks-pres'], *n.* a specially fast messenger or way of conveyance; a fast train which does not stop at intermediate stations.

EXPRESS (2), [eks-pres'], *adj.* clear, definite, precise, explicit; exactly resembling; intended or sent for a particular purpose. [L. *expressum*, *p.pt.* of *exprimere* to crush].

EXPRESS (3), [eks-pres'], *v.t.* to press out; to utter or set forth in words or symbols; to make manifest; to depict; to signify; to make (one's thoughts or feelings) manifest; (*refl.*) to explain one's opinions correctly. [OFr. *expresser*].

EXPRESSAGE, [eks-pres'-ij], *n.* fee for an article sent by express.

EXPRESSED, [eks-prest'], *adj.* pressed out; uttered, or set forth, in words, symbols, or pictures.

EXPRESSIBLE, [eks-pres'-ibl], *adj.* capable of being expressed.

EXPRESSION, [eks-presh'-un], *n.* the act of expressing; the act or method of giving utterance or form; artistic style or method; the modulation of the voice, the mood or phrasing of a musical performance; a turn of phrase, a phrase or idiom; the general look of a person's face, *esp.* as expressing his mood or character. [L. *expressio*].

EXPRESSIONAL, [eks-presh'-un-al], *adj.* pertaining to expression.

EXPRESSIONISM, [eks-presh'-un-izm], *n.* (*art*) that quality of modern artists whereby they seek to avoid a realistic technique and to express their meaning symbolically, seeking to bring out the meaning by suggestion rather than by naturalistic representation.

EXPRESSIONIST, [eks-presh'-un-ist], *n.* one who belongs to a non-realistic, modern school in art.

EXPRESSIONLESS, [eks-presh'-un-les], *adj.* without expression, inexpressive.

EXPRESSIVE, [eks-pres'-iv], *adj.* serving to express; full of feeling and character (of the face, voice or of a work of art); vivid. [Fr. *expressif*].

EXPRESSIVELY, [eks-pres'-iv-li], *adv.* in an expressive fashion.

EXPRESSIVENESS, [eks-pres'-iv-nes], *n.* the quality of being expressive.

EXPRESSIVO, ESPRESSIVO, [eks'-pres-ēv'-ō, es'-pres-ēv'-ō], *adv.* (*mus.*) with great expression or passion. [It. *espressivo*].

EXPRESSLY, [eks-pres'-li], *adv.* in direct, plain terms; unequivocally; intentionally.

EXPRESSNESS, [eks-pres'-nes], *n.* the quality of being express.

EXPROMISSION, [eks-prom-ish'-un], *n.* (*leg.*) the taking of a new debtor for an old.

EXPROMISSOR, [eks-prom'-is-or], *n.* (*leg.*) one who takes on the obligation of the debt of another. [L. *expromissor*].

EXPROPRIATE, [eks-prō'-pri-āt], *v.t.* to take (property) away from. [L. *expropriare*].

EXPROPRIATION, [eks'-prō-pri-ā'-shun], *n.* the act of expropriating, depriving of property.

EXPULSION, [eks-pul'-shun], *n.* the act of expelling; the state of being expelled; banishment; dismissal. [L. *expulsio*].

EXPULSIVE, [eks-pul'-siv], *adj.* tending or serving to expel. [Fr. *expulsif*].

EXPUNCTION, [eks-pungk'-shun], *n.* the act of expunging; condition of being expunged. [L. *expunctio*].

EXPUNGE, [ex-punj'], *v.t.* to wipe out, erase. [L. *expungere*].

EXPURGATE, [eks'-per-gāt], *v.t.* to purify; to remove offensive matter from a book; to remedy a fault of conduct. [L. *expurgare*].

EXPURGATION, [eks'-per-gā'-shun], *n.* the action of expurgating. [L. *expurgatio*].

EXPURGATOR, [eks'-per-gāt'-er], *n.* a person who expurgates.

EXPURGATORIAL, [eks-per'-ga-taw'-ri-al], *adj.* tending to expurgate.

EXPURGATORY, [eks-per'-gat-er-i], *adj.* pertaining to expurgation; (*eccles.*) expurgatorial.

EXQUISITE (1), [eks'-kwiz-it], *n.* a dandy; a precious person.

EXQUISITE (2), [eks'-kwiz-it], *adj.* choice; refined, delicate; highly finished; excellent; of keen delicacy of discrimination; acutely felt. [L. *exquisitum*, *p.pt.* of *exquirere* to seek out].

EXQUISITELY, [eks'-kwiz-it-li], *adv.* in an exquisite fashion.

EXQUISITENESS, [eks'-kwiz-it-nes], *n.* the quality of being exquisite.

EXSANGUINATE, [ek-sang'-gwin-āt], *v.t.* to drain of blood. [L. *exsanguinare*].

EXSANGUINE, [eks-ang'-win], *adj.* bloodless, anaemic.

EXSANGUINITY, [eks-ang-gwin'-it-i], *n.* a state of bloodlessness; anaemia.

EXSCIND, [eks-ind'], *v.t.* to cut out, *esp.* matter from a book, or a clause from legislation. [L. *exscindere*].

EXSCRIPTURAL, [ek-skrip'-chŏŏ-ral], *adj.* not to be found in the Scriptures.

EXSECT, [eks-ekt'], *v.t.* to cut out. [L. *exsectum*, *p.pt.* of *exsecare*].

EXSECTION, [eks-ek'-shun], *n.* a cutting out or away. [L. *exsectio*].

EXSERT, [eks-ert'], *adj.* exserted. [L. *exsertum* *p.pt.* of *exserere*].

EXSERTED, [eks-ert'-id], *adj.* stretched forth or out; protruding.

EXSERTILE, [eks-ert'-il], *adj.* capable of being exserted, thrust out. [Fr. *exsertile*].

EXSICCANT, [eks-ik'-ant], *adj.* drying; having the power or quality of drying up. [L. *exsiccans*].

EXSICCATA, [ek-sik-āt'-a], *n.* a collection of dried plants. [L. *exsiccata* dried things, from *exsiccare* to dry out].

EXSICCATE, [eks'-ik-āt], *v.t.* to dry; remove all moisture from. [L. *exsiccare*].

EXSICCATION, [eks-ik-ā'-shun], *n.* the act or operation of drying; thorough dryness. [L. *exsiccatio*].

EXSICCATIVE, [eks-ik'-at-iv], *adj.* tending to produce dryness. [MedL. *exsiccativus*].

EXSPUTORY, [eks-pewt'-er-i], *adj.* that is spat out.

EXSTIPULATE, [ek-stip'-yŏŏ-lāt], *adj.* (*bot.*) without stipules.

EXSUCCOUS, [ek-suk'-us], *adj.* destitute of juice, sapless. [L. *exsuccus*].

EXSUCTION, [ek'-suk'-shun], *n.* the action of sucking out.

EXSUFFLATION†, [eks'-uf-lā'-shun], *n.* the action of blowing out; (*eccles.*) a form of exorcism. [L. *exsufflatio*].

EXSUSCITATE†, [eks-us'-it-āt], *v.t.* to rouse up; to excite. [L. *exsuscitare*].

EXTANT, [eks-tant', eks'-tant], *adj.* still in existence. [L. *ex(s)tans*].

EXTASY, see ECSTASY.

EXTEMPORAL, [eks-temp'-er-al], *adj.* done or said without previous preparation. [L. *extemporalis*].

EXTEMPORALLY, [eks-temp'-er-al-i], *adv.* in an unpremeditated manner.

EXTEMPORANEOUS, [eks-temp'-er-ān'-i-us], *adj.* without premeditation; extempore. [LL. *extemporaneus*].

EXTEMPORANEOUSLY, [eks-temp'-er-ān'-i-us-li], *adv.* in an extemporaneous manner.

EXTEMPORANEOUSNESS, [eks-temp'-er-ān'-i-us-nes], *n.* the quality of being extemporaneous.

EXTEMPORARILY, [eks-temp'-er-ar-il-i], *adv.* in an extemporary manner.

EXTEMPORARY, [eks-temp'-er-ar-i], *adj.* unpremeditated, without previous preparation.

EXTEMPORE, [eks-temp'-er-i], *adv.* without previous study or meditation; without notes; on the spur of the moment. [L. *ex tempore* out of the time].

EXTEMPORINESS, [eks-temp'-er-in-es], *n.* an extemporary condition.

EXTEMPORIZATION, [eks-temp'-er-īz-ā'-shun], *n.* the action of extemporizing.

EXTEMPORIZE, [eks-temp'-er-īz], *v.i.* to do something without preparation.

EXTEND, [eks-tend'], *v.t. and i.* to reach or stretch out; to lengthen; to make last longer; to make larger, cause to have wider influence or to be more inclusive; to be stretched out; to be capable of stretching out; to last, continue, endure. [L. *extendere*].

EXTENDANT†, [eks-tend'-ant], *adj.* stretched out; (*her.*) having the wings expanded.

EXTENDEDLY, [eks-tend'-id-li], *adv.* in an extended fashion.

EXTENDER, [eks-tend'-er], *n.* he who, or that which, extends.

EXTENDIBLE, [eks-tend'-ibl], *adj.* able to be extended.

EXTENSIBILITY, [eks-tens'-ib-il'-it-i], *n.* the capability of being extended.

EXTENSIBLE, [eks-tens'-ibl], *adj.* capable of being extended or enlarged. [Fr. *extensible*].

EXTENSIBLENESS, [eks-tens'-ibl-nes], *n.* extensibility; the quality of being extensible.

EXTENSILE, [eks-ten'-sīl], *adj.* able to be extended or stretched out.

EXTENSION, [eks-ten'-shun], *n.* the act of extending; the state of being extended; the amount extended; a branch or addition; continuation in time; widening; enlargement; continuation; (*phys.*) that property of a body by which it occupies a portion of space in each of its three dimensions—length, breadth, and thickness; (*comm.*) a written engagement on the part of creditors, allowing a debtor further time for the payment of his debts; (*surg.*) the operation of straightening a limb that has been bent or dislocated; (*log.*) the range of the application of a term in contrast to its comprehension; **university e.,** system which provides university teaching to adult students not actually members of a university. [L. *extensio*].

EXTENSIONAL, [eks-ten'-shun-al], *adj.* having extension.

EXTENSIVE, [eks-ten'-siv], *adj.* wide in extent; comprehensive. [L. *extensivus*].

EXTENSIVELY, [eks-ten'-siv-li], *adv.* to a wide extent; comprehensively.

EXTENSIVENESS, [eks-ten'-siv-nes], *n.* an extensive character; comprehensiveness.

EXTENSOR, [eks-tens'-er], *n.* (*anat.*) a muscle whose function is to extend or straighten any part of the body. [LL. *extensor*].

EXTENT, [eks-tent'], *n.* the space over which, or degree to which, anything is extended; scope; limit; (*leg.*) an inventory of lands; a writ of execution against the body, lands, and goods of a debtor. [AFr. *extente*].

EXTENUATE, [eks-ten'-yōō-āt], *v.t. and i.* to make thin or tenuous, diminish; to excuse or minimize a fault; to practise extenuation. [L. *extenuare*].

EXTENUATING, [eks-ten'-yōō-āt-ing], *adj.* that extenuates.

EXTENUATINGLY, [eks-ten'-yōō-āt-ing-li], *adv.* in an extenuating way.

EXTENUATION, [eks-ten'-yōō-ā'-shun], *n.* the act of extenuating; an excuse. [L. *extenuatio*].

EXTENUATOR, [eks-ten'-yōō-āt-er], *n.* one who extenuates.

EXTENUATORY, [eks-ten'-yōō-āt-er-i], *adj.* having the function of extenuating.

EXTERIOR (1), [eks-tēer'-i-er], *n.* the outside, *esp.* of a building; a picture of the outside of a building.

EXTERIOR (2), [eks-tēer'-i-er], *adj.* visible; external; on the outside; foreign; extrinsic. [L. *exterior*].

EXTERIORITY, [eks-tēer-i-o'-rit-i], *n.* outwardness, superficies.

EXTERIORLY, [eks-tēer'-i-er-li], *adv.* outwardly, superficially.

EXTERMINATE, [eks-tur'-min-āt], *v.t.* †to drive beyond the frontiers; to destroy completely; to extirpate. [L. *exterminare*].

EXTERMINATION, [eks-tur'-mi-nā'-shun], *n.* the act of exterminating; total destruction. [L. *exterminatio*].

EXTERMINATOR, [eks-tur'-min-āt-er], *n.* he who, or that which, exterminates. [L. *exterminator*].

EXTERMINATORY, [eks-tur'-min-āt'-er-i], *adj.* tending to exterminate.

EXTERN (1), [eks-turn'], *n.* outward part; one who is attached to, but does not reside in, an establishment, as a day student or a visiting doctor at a hospital; an outsider.

EXTERN (2), [eks-turn'], *adj.* external; non-resident. [L. *externus* outward].

EXTERNAL (1), [eks-turn'-al], *n.* some external person or thing, a non-resident; (*pl.*) outward appearance; (*fig.*) inessential aspects.

EXTERNAL (2), [eks-turn'-al], *adj.* outward; visible; connected with foreign nations; (*fig.*) inessential, incidental; **e. evidence,** evidence obtained from independent sources; **e. nature,** the outward universe as distinct from man. [L. *externus* outward].

EXTERNALITY, [eks-turn-al'-it-i], *n.* the state or quality of being external.

EXTERNALIZATION, [eks-turn'-al-i-zā'-shun], *n.* act or process of embodying in outward form.

EXTERNALLY, [eks-turn'-al-i], *adv.* in an external manner; from the outside; outwardly.

EXTERNAT, [eks-turn'-ah'], *n.* a day school. [Fr. *externat*].

EXTERRANEOUS, [eks-te-rān'-i-us], *adj.* originating abroad. [LL. *exterraneus*].

EXTERRITORIAL, [eks'-te-rit-aw'-ri-al], *adj.* outside the jurisdiction of the country; extraterritorial.

EXTERSION†, [eks-tur'-shun], *n.* the action of rubbing or wiping out.

EXTINCT, [eks-tingkt'], *adj.* quenched, extinguished, no longer alive or active. [L. *extinctum*, *p.pt.* of *extinguere*].

EXTINCTION, [eks-tingk'-shun], *n.* the act of extinguishing; the state of being extinct. [L. *extinctio*].

EXTINE, [eks'-tīn], *n.* (*bot.*) the outer membrane of the pollen grain. [~L. *extimus* outermost].

EXTINGUISH, [eks-ting'-gwish], *v.t.* to put out, quench, destroy, suppress; to obscure by superior splendour, to eclipse; to reduce to silence. [L. *extinguere*].

EXTINGUISHABLE, [eks-ting'-gwish-abl], *adj.* capable of being extinguished.

EXTINGUISHER, [eks-ting'-gwish-er], *n.* that which extinguishes; a hollow conical cap with which to put out the light of a candle; (*fig.*) a gloomy person who casts a shadow over others' happiness.

EXTINGUISHMENT†, [eks-ting'-gwish-ment], *n.* the act of extinguishing; extinction; (*leg.*) the extinction or annihilation of a right by its being merged in another.

EXTIRPABLE, [eks-tur'-pabl], *adj.* capable of being extirpated.

EXTIRPATE, [eks'-tur-pāt], *v.t.* to root out, destroy; (*surg.*) to remove completely. [L. *extirpare*].

EXTIRPATION, [eks'-tur-pā'-shun], *n.* the act of extirpating, rooting out, or completely destroying. [L. *extirpatio*].

EXTIRPATOR, [eks'-tur-pāt'-er], *n.* one who extirpates. [L. *extirpator*].

EXTOL, [eks-tōl'], *v.t.* to praise highly, magnify, laud. [L. *extollere* lift up].

EXTOLLER, [eks-tōl'-er], *n.* a person who extols.

EXTORSIVE, [eks-taw'-siv], *adj.* serving, tending to extort.

EXTORSIVELY, [eks-taw'-siv-li], *adv.* in an extorsive fashion.

EXTORT, [eks-tawt'], *v.t.* to force from a person or thing; to obtain by undue pressure. [L. *extortum*, *p.pt.* of *extorquere*].

EXTORTION, [eks-taw'-shun], *n.* oppressive or illegal exaction; that which is so exacted. [L. *extortio*].

EXTORTIONARY, [eks-taw'-shun-ar-i], *adj.* pertaining to, or exercising, extortion.

EXTORTIONATE, [eks-taw'-shun-at], *adj.* characterized by extortion.

EXTORTIONER, [eks-taw'-shun-er], *n.* a person who practises extortion.

EXTRA- (1), [eks'-tra], *pref.* outside of, beyond the usual, in excess. [L. *extra* on the outside, without].

EXTRA (2), [eks'-tra], *n. and adj.* in addition; more than; something added on beyond the agreed upon, or customary, charge; a perquisite; a supernumerary.
EXTRA (3), [eks'-tra], *adj.* in addition; more than normal.
EXTRA (4), [eks'-tra], *adv.* additionally, especially, particularly.
EXTRA-CONSTELLARY, [eks'-tra-kons-tel'-ar-i], *adj.* (*astron.*) of those stars not included in any constellation.
EXTRA-COSMICAL, [eks'-tra-koz'-mik-al], *adj.* outside the cosmos or universe.
EXTRA-CRANIAL, [eks'-tra-krān'-i-al], *adj.* (*anat.*) outside the skull.
EXTRACT (1), [eks'-trakt], *n.* something which is extracted; a passage taken from a book; (*chem.*) a solution containing one or more substances removed from a mixture by means of a solvent.
EXTRACT (2), [eks-trakt'], *v.t.* to draw out by force or persuasion; to take out or select a part from. [L. *extractum, p.pt.* of *extrahere*].
EXTRACTABLE, [eks-trakt'-abl], *adj.* that may be extracted; suitable for quotation or extracting.
EXTRACTIFORM, [eks-trak'-ti-fawm], *adj.* (*chem.*) with the nature or appearance of an extract.
EXTRACTION, [eks-trak'-shun], *n.* the act or process of extracting, *esp.* the pulling of a tooth; an extract; racial or family descent; the eliciting (of information). [MedL. *extractio*].
EXTRACTIVE, [eks-trak'-tiv], *adj.* capable of being extracted; of the nature of an extract; concerned with obtaining natural productions. [L. *extractivus*].
EXTRACTOR, [eks-trak'-ter], *n.* the person who, or that which, extracts; (*surg.*) forceps or instrument for extracting, used in midwifery, lithotomy, and dentistry.

EXTRACTOR (FORCEPS)

EXTRADICTIONARY†, [eks'-tra-dik'-shun-er-i], *adj.* beyond expression in words. [L. *extra dictionem* outside the mode of expression].
EXTRADITABLE, [eks'-tra-dīt'-abl], *adj.* liable to extradition.
EXTRADITE, [eks'-tra-dīt], *v.t.* to surrender someone to a foreign country in conformity with the terms of an extradition treaty.
EXTRADITION, [eks'-trad-ish'-un], *n.* surrender, by one government to another, of fugitives from justice. [Fr. *extradition*].
EXTRADOS, [eks-trăd'-os], *n.* (*arch.*) the upper or exterior curve of an arch. [Fr. *extrados*].
EXTRADOTAL, [eks-trad-ōt'-al], *adj.* forming no part of a dowry.
EXTRAFOLIACEOUS, [eks'-tra-fō-li-ā'-shus], *adj.* (*bot.*) separated from the leaves, or inserted in a different place from them.
EXTRAFORANEOUS, [eks'-tra-for-ān'-i-us], *adj.* outdoor.
EXTRAGENEOUS, [eks-tra-jē'-ni-us], *adj.* of a different kind; foreign. [EXTRA (1) and L. *genus*].
EXTRAJUDICIAL, [eks'-tra-jōō-dish'-al], *adj.* (*leg.*) outside the ordinary course of legal procedure.
EXTRAJUDICIALLY, [eks'-tra-jōō-dish'-al-i], *adv.* in an extrajudicial manner.
EXTRALIMITARY, [eks'-tra-lim'-it-ar-i], *adj.* beyond the limits or bounds.
EXTRALOGICAL, [eks'-tra-loj'-ik-al], *adj.* beyond the limits of logic.
EXTRAMISSION†, [eks'-tra-mish'-un], *n.* a sending outwards, emission.
EXTRAMUNDANE, [eks'-tra-mun'-dān], *adj.* beyond the bounds of this world; (*fig.*) remote.
EXTRAMURAL, [eks'-tra-myōōer'-al], *adj.* outside the walls of a city; relating to the external teaching of a university.
EXTRANEITY, [eks-tran-ē'-it-i], *n.* the state or condition of being extraneous.
EXTRANEOUS, [eks-trān'-i-us], *adj.* foreign; not connected with, external to; not essential; not germane, unrelated. [L. *extraneus*].
EXTRANEOUSLY, [eks-trān'-i-us-li], *adv.* in an extraneous manner.
EXTRANEOUSNESS, [eks-trān'-i-us-nes], *n.* the state or quality of being extraneous.
EXTRA-OCULAR, [eks'-tra-ok'-yōō-lar], *adj.* (*entom.*) of those antennae inserted on the outsides of the eyes.
EXTRA-OFFICIAL, [eks'-tra-of-ish'-al], *adj.* outside the limits of official duty.
EXTRAORDINARILY, [eks'-tr(a)-awd'-in-ar-il-i], *adv.* in an extraordinary manner.
EXTRAORDINARINESS, [eks'-tr(a)-awd'-in-ar-i-nes], *n.* the quality of being extraordinary.
EXTRAORDINARY, [eks'-tr(a)-awd'-in-ar-i], *adj.* out of the ordinary; unusual; outstanding, brilliant; strange; rare; of a person employed on special service, as **ambassador e.** [L. *extraordinarius*].
EXTRAPAROCHIAL, [eks'-tra-par-ōk'-i-al], *adj.* outside the limits of a parish.
EXTRAPHYSICAL, [eks'-tra-fis'-ik-al], *adj.* outside the province of physics.
EXTRAPOLATION, [eks'-tra-pol-ā'-shun], *n.* (*math.*) the calculation, from the known terms in a series, of those which are unknown.
EXTRAPROFESSIONAL, [eks'-tra-prof-esh'-un-al], *adj.* foreign to a profession; outside the ordinary limits of professional duty.
EXTRA-PROVINCIAL, [eks'-tra-prov-in'-shal], *adj.* outside the limits of a province.
EXTRA-REGULAR, [eks'-tra-reg'-yōō-lar], *adj.* not comprehended within a rule or set of rules. [EXTRA (1) and REGULAR].
EXTRA-SOLAR, [eks'-tra-sō'-lar], *adj.* outside the bounds of the solar system.
EXTRA-SPECTRAL, [eks'-tra-spek'-tral], *adj.* beyond the visible spectrum.
EXTRA-TERRESTRIAL, [eks'-tra-te-rest'-ri-al], *adj.* beyond the earth and its atmosphere.
EXTRATERRITORIAL, [eks'-tra-te'-ri-taw'-ri-al], *adj.* outside a local jurisdiction; **e. waters,** the open sea beyond the territorial limit.
EXTRATERRITORIALITY, [eks'-tra-te'-rit-taw'-ri-al'-it-i], *n.* the state of being outside any local jurisdiction; immunity from a country's laws.
EXTRATROPICAL, [eks'-tra-trop'-ik-al], *adj.* beyond the tropics; outside the tropics, either north or south.
EXTRAVAGANCE, [eks-tra'-vag-ants], *n.* irregularity; excess; lavish wastefulness of one's money or means; outlandishness in behaviour or opinions. [Fr. *extravagance*].
EXTRAVAGANCY, [eks-tra'-vag-an-si], *n.* the quality of being extravagant.
EXTRAVAGANT, [eks-trav'-ag-ant], *adj.* exceeding due limits; excessive, immoderate; wasteful of one's resources; exaggerated. [Fr. *extravagant*].
EXTRAVAGANTLY, [eks-tra'-vag-ant-li], *adv.* in an extravagant manner.
EXTRAVAGANTNESS, [eks-tra'-vag-ant-nes], *n.* extravagance.
EXTRAVAGANTS, [eks-tra'-vag-ants], *n.(pl.)* (*eccles.*) a number of decretal epistles or constitutions of the popes, not at first incorporated with the rest, but inserted later in the canon law. [MedL. *extravagans pres.pt.* of *extravagari* to stray.]
EXTRAVAGANZA, [eks-tra'-va-gan'-za], *n.* (*mus.*) a musical composition distinguished by its absurdity and irregularity; any wild, capricious flight of fancy. [It. *estravaganza*].
EXTRAVAGATE, [eks-tra'-vag-āt], *v.t.* to stray. [MedL. *extravagari*].
EXTRAVASATE, [eks-trav'-as-āt], *v.t.* (*med.*) to let or force out of the proper vessels. [EXTRA (1) and L. *vas* vessel].
EXTRAVASATION, [eks'-tra-va-sā'-shun], *n.* (*med.*) the action of letting out of its proper vessel any fluid of the body, *esp.* the blood, through rupture or injury.
EXTRAVASCULAR, [eks'-tra-vas'-kyōō-lar], *adj.* outside the vascular system.
EXTRAVERT, see EXTROVERT.
EXTREME (1), [eks-trēm'], *n.* the furthest limit, extremity, utmost possible degree; (*math.*) the first or last terms of a proportion; (*log.*) the subject and predicate of the conclusion of a syllogism.
EXTREME (2), [eks-trēm'], *adj.* outermost, furthest off, most pressing; worst or best that can exist or be supposed; very highest; having uncompromising opinions; drastic; **the e. penalty,** capital punishment; **e. unction,** unction administered to one at the point of death. [L. *extremus*].
EXTREMELESS, [eks-trēm'-les], *adj.* infinite.
EXTREMELY, [eks-trēm'-li], *adv.* in an extreme degree; very.
EXTREMENESS, [eks-trēm'-nes], *n.* violent nature.
EXTREMISM, [eks-trēm'-izm], *n.* the holding of extreme opinions.

EXTREMIST, [eks-trēm'-ist], *n.* a supporter of extreme doctrines or action; a revolutionist.

EXTREMITY, [eks-trem'-it-i], *n.* the utmost point or bound; the utmost or highest degree; extreme or utmost distress; the end; [*pl.*) the hands and feet. [Fr. *extrémité*].

EXTRICABLE, [eks'-trik-abl], *adj.* that may be extricated.

EXTRICATE, [eks'-trik-āt], *v.t.* to unravel; to disentangle; (*chem.*) to liberate. [L. *extricare*].

EXTRICATION, [eks'-trik-ā'-shun], *n.* the action of extricating, disentangling.

EXTRINSIC, [eks-trin'-sik], *adj.* external, outward, not contained in, or belonging to, a body, foreign; inessential. [LL. *extrinsecus*].

EXTRINSICAL, [eks-trin'-sikl], *adj.* extrinsic.

EXTRINSICALITY, [eks-trin'-sik-al'-it-i], *n.* the condition of being extrinsic.

EXTRINSICALLY, [eks-trin'-sik-al-i], *adv.* in an extrinsic fashion.

EXTRINSICALNESS, [eks-trin'-sik-al-nes], *n.* the state or condition of being extrinsical.

EXTRORSAL, [eks-traw'-sal], *adj.* in an outward direction.

EXTRORSE, [eks-traws'], *adj.* (*bot.*) opening away from the centre of the flower head. [L. *extrorsus*].

EXTROVERSION, [eks'-tro-ver'-shun], *n.* a turning or being turned outwards; (*path.*) a malformation of the bladder; (*psych.*) the state of a mind not prone to introspection.

EXTROVERT, EXTRAVERT, [eks'-trov-ert], *n.* (*psych.*) a person mentally unaccustomed to turning the thoughts inwards upon himself, one averse to introspection. [EXTRA (1) and L. *vertere* to turn].

EXTRUDE, [eks-trōōd'], *v.t.* to thrust, press or force out; to expel. [L. *extrudere*].

EXTRUSION, [eks-trōō'-zhun], *n.* the action of extruding. [L. *extrusio*].

EXTRUSIVE, [eks-trōōs'-iv], *adj.* that tends to extrude or be extruded.

EXTUBERANCE†, [eks-tew'-ber-ants], *n.* the quality of swelling out.

EXTUBERANCY, [eks-tew'-ber-an-si], *n.* a swelling, a protuberant part.

EXTUBERATE, [eks-tew'-ber-āt], *v.i.* to swell, become protuberant. [L. *extuberare*].

EXUBERANCE, [eg-zew'-ber-ants], *n.* rich, luxuriant growth; overflowing fulness of feeling or expression; a superabundance of vitality. [L. *exuberantia*].

EXUBERANCY, [eg-zew'-ber-an-si], *n.* exuberance.

EXUBERANT, [eg-zew'-ber-ant], *adj.* abundant, over-abundant, overflowing. [L. *exuberans*].

EXUBERANTLY, [eg-zew'-ber-ant-li], *adv.* in an exuberant manner.

EXUBERATE, [eg-zew'-ber-āt], *v.i.* to be exuberant. [L. *exuberare*].

EXUDATION, [eks'-yōō-dā'-shun], *n.* the action of exuding fluid matter through pores; matter exuded. [LL. *exudatio*].

EXUDE, [eg-zewd'], *v.t.* to discharge slowly; *v.i.* to ooze out; to pass off through the pores as sweat or through corresponding organs or incisions in animals and plants. [L. *exudare*].

EXULCERATE†, [eks-ul'-ser-āt], *v.t.* to cause ulcers on; to exacerbate or anger; *v.i.* to become an ulcer or ulcerous. [L. *exulcerare*].

EXULCERATION, [eks-ul'-ser-ā'-shun], *n.* the beginning of ulceration; a sore; (*fig.*) exacerbation. [L. *exulceratio*].

EXULCERATIVE†, [eks-ul'-ser-at-iv], *adj.* having a tendency to produce ulcers. [Fr. *exulceratif*].

EXULCERATORY, [eks-ul'-ser-ā'-te-ri], *adj.* exulcerative.

EXULT, [eg-zult'], *v.i.* to rejoice greatly or excessively; to triumph. [L. *exultare* to leap up].

EXULTANCE, [eg-zult'-ants], *n.* exultancy. [LL. *exultantia*].

EXULTANCY, [eg-zult'-an-si], *n.* exultant condition; rapture, triumph. [LL. *exultantia*].

EXULTANT, [eg-zult'-ant], *adj.* rejoicing triumphantly. [L. *exultans*].

EXULTANTLY, [eg-zult'-ant-li], *adv.* in an exultant fashion.

EXULTATION, [egz'-ul-tā'-shun], *n.* joy at success; intense delight; triumph. [L. *exultatio*].

EXULTINGLY, [eg-zult'-ing-li], *adv.* in an exulting fashion.

EXUNGULATE, [eks-ung'-gew-lāt], *v.t.* to pare off superfluous parts such as nails. [LL. *exungulare* to lose a hoof].

EXUVIABLE, [eg-zew'-vi-abl], *adj.* capable of being exuviated or shed. [Fr. *exuviable*].

EXUVIAE, [eg-zew'-vi-ē], *n.*(*pl.*) the cast-off skins, shells, or coverings of animals. [L. *exuviae* garments stripped off].

EXUVIAL, [eg-zew'-vi-al], *adj.* of the nature of exuviae.

EXUVIATE, [eg-zew'-vi-āt], *v.i.* to cast off, slough, shed.

EXUVIATION, [eg-zew'-vi-ā'-shun], *n.* the act or process of exuviating or sloughing off.

EYALET, [ī'-al-et], *n.* an administrative area in the Turkish Republic, presided over by a pasha, as viceroy; a vilayet. [Turk. *eyalet*].

EYAS, [ī'-as], *n.* a young hawk recently taken from the nest. [OFr. *niais*].

EYAS-MUSKET, [ī'-as-mus'-ket], *n.* a very young, unfledged, male sparrow-hawk.

EYE (1), [ī], *n.* the organ of sight, the eyeball with its nerves; the visible part of the eye; the eyesight; power of observation; an object thought to resemble an eye in form, as the hole in a needle, the bud on a plant, a small catch on clothes for a hook; **to keep one's e. on,** to watch; **to make a person open his eyes wide,** to surprise him; **to open a person's eyes to something,** to make him aware of it; **to make eyes at,** to ogle; **to have an e. for,** to know how to judge; to notice; **to do in the e.,** (*coll.*) to spoil; to cheat; **all my e.,** (*coll.*) nonsense; **up to the eyes in it,** extremely busy; **with half an e.,** with slight effort easily; **sheep's eyes,** amorous glances.

EYE (2), [ī], *v.t.* to fix the eyes on; look fixedly at; regard narrowly.

EYEBALL, [ī'-bawl], *n.* the globular organ of sight.

EYE-BATH, [ī'-bahth], *n.* a small glass vessel shaped to facilitate douching the eye.

EYE-BOLT, [ī'-bōlt], *n.* (*naut.*) a bar of iron, having an eye at one end, formed to be screwed into the deck or sides of a ship for fastening ropes.

EYE-BOLT

EYEBRIGHT, [ī'-brīt], *n.* (*bot.*) a popular name for the small white wild flower, euphrasy.

EYEBROW, [ī'-brow], *n.* the hairy arch which overhangs the eye.

EYEBROW-PENCIL, [ī'-brow-pen'-sil], *n.* a cosmetic pencil for darkening the eyebrows.

EYED, [īd], *adj.* having eyes or eye-like markings.

EYE-DROP, [ī'-drop], *n.* (*coll.*) a tear.

EYE-FLAP, [ī'-flap], *n.* one of the two leather eye-shades or blinkers, on a horse's harness.

EYE-GLANCE, [ī'-glahnts], *n.* the glance from an eye; a rapid glance.

EYEGLASS, [ī'-glahs], *n.* a lens to assist the sight; the glass next the eye in an optical instrument; (*pl.*) a pair of lenses arranged to clip upon the bridge of the nose.

EYEHOLE, [ī'-hōl], *n.* a peep-hole.

EYELASH, [ī'-lash], *n.* the hair fringing the eyelid; a single hair of the fringe.

EYELESS, [ī'-les], *adj.* without eyes.

EYELET, [ī'-let], *n.* eyelet-hole. [OFr. *oeillet* little eye].

EYELETEER, [ī-let-ēer'], *n.* a small pointed instrument employed in piercing eyelet-holes.

EYELET-HOLE, [ī'-let-hōl'], *n.* a small hole or perforation to receive a lace or small rope or cord; the metal ring which lines this hole.

EYELID, [ī'-lid], *n.* the upper or lower movable cover of skin that serves as a protection to the front of the eyeball.

EYE-OPENER, [ī'-ō'-pen-er], *n.* (*coll.*) a revelation, an unmasking; an early drink.

EYEPIECE, [ī'-pēs], *n.* in a telescope or microscope, the lens or combination of lenses with which the image is seen and magnified.

EYEPIT, [ī'-pit], *n.* the socket of the eye.

EYER, [ī'-er], *n.* a person who eyes another.

EYE-SERVANT, [ī'-sur'-vant], *n.* a servant who does his duty only when watched.

EYE-SERVICE, [ī'-sur'-vis], *n.* service done only under the eye of an overseer.

EYESHOT, [ī'-shot], *n.* range of vision.

EYESIGHT, [ī'-sīt], *n.* the sight of the eye; vision; the range of vision.

EYESORE, [ī'-saw(r)], *n.* anything ugly or offensive to the eye.

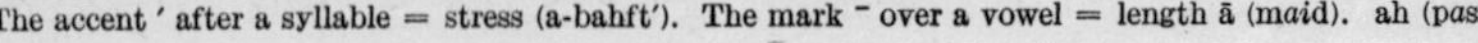

EYE-SPLICE, [ī'-splīs], *n.* (*naut.*) a kind of eye or circle formed by splicing the end of a rope into itself.

EYE-SPOT, [ī'-spot], *n.* a spot resembling an eye as on a peacock's tail feather.

EYE-SPLICE

EYE-STONE, [ī'-stōn], *n.* a little calcareous stone, employed in taking substances from between the lid and ball of the eye.

EYESTRINGS, [ī'-stringz], *n.*(*pl.*) (*anat.*) the strings or muscles and tendons of the eye.

EYE-TOOTH, [ī'-tōōth], *n.* (*anat.*) one of the upper canine teeth; **to cut one's eye-teeth,** to grow up; **to draw (someone's) eye-teeth),** to take the conceit out of (someone).

EYE-WASH, [ī'-wosh], *n.* a lotion for bathing the eyes; (*coll.*) humbug, deception, fraudulent pretences.

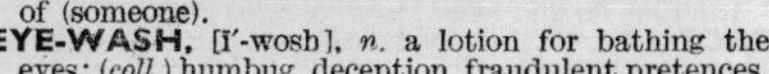

EYEWATER, [ī'-waw-ter], *n.* a lotion for the eyes; (*slang*) gin.

EYE-WITNESS, [ī'-wit-nes], *n.* one who sees a thing happen.

EYNE†, [īn], *n.*(*pl.*) eyes.

EYOT, [ā'-ot], *n.* a small island in a river or lake. [OE. *igeoth*].

EYRA, [īer'-a], *n.* the little cat of Central and South America, *Felis eyra.* [Native].

EYRA CAT

EYRANT, [īer'-ant], *n.* a bird of prey in its nest.

EYRE, [āer], *n.* (*leg.*) circuit; a court of itinerant justices. [OFr. *eire* journey].

EYRIE, see AERIE.

EZAN, [e'-zan], *n.* the call to prayer chanted by the Muslim muezzin. [Arab. *azan*].

F

F, [ef], the sixth letter of the Latin, English, and other alphabets.

FAAM, FAHAM, [fahm], *n.* an orchid, *Angraecum fragrans,* the leaves of which are valued as a stomachic and for pulmonary consumption, or as a substitute for China tea.

FAAP, [fahp], *n.* name for the garfish, *Belone vulgaris.*

FABA, [fā'-ba], *n.* learned name for the broad bean, *Vicia Faba.* [L. *faba* bean].

FABACEOUS, [fab-ā'-shus], *adj.* bean-like, pertaining to beans. [L. *fabaceus*].

FABIAN (1), [fā'-bi-an], *n.* a member of the Fabian Society.

FABIAN (2), [fā'-bi-an], *adj.* wearing out an enemy by a policy of caution and waiting; **F. Society,** a society of socialists employing such a policy for the propagation of socialism. [L. *Fabianus*].

FABLE (1), [fābl], *n.* a story, usually of a supernatural or improbable character, *esp.* a short story in which animals are represented as speaking and acting like human beings in order to convey a moral; myth, legend; idle tale; lie, untruth, falsehood; anything which is merely supposed to exist; the plot of a play or epic poem. [L. *fabula*].

FABLE (2), [fābl], *v.i.* (*poet.*) to tell fictitious stories.

FABLED, [fābld], *adj.* celebrated in fables, legendary.

FABLER, [fā'-bler], *n.* one who tells fictitious tales; one who invents or narrates fables; a romancer.

FABLIAU, (*pl.* **fabliaux**), [fab'-li-ō], *n.* in early French poetry, a short metrical tale, usually of a topical nature. [Fr. *fabliau*].

FABRIC, [fab'-rik], *n.* structure, frame; texture, tissue; woven material; edifice, construction, building. [L. *fabrica*].

FABRICANT, [fab'-rik-ant], *n.* one who fabricates; manufacturer. [L. *fabricans*].

FABRICATE, [fab'-rik-āt], *v.t.* to make, construct, put together by art and labour, to manufacture; to forge; to state falsely, invent (facts). [L. *fabricare*].

FABRICATION, [fab'-rik-ā'-shun], *n.* the act or process of fabricating; manufacture; forgery; that which is fabricated; a falsehood. [L. *fabricatio*].

FABRICATOR, [fab'-rik-ā'-ter], *n.* a person who fabricates. [L. *fabricator*].

FABRILE†, [fab'-rīl], *adj.* pertaining to handicraft or a craftsman. [L. *fabrilis*].

FABULIST, [fab'-yōō-list], *n.* an inventor of fables. [Fr. *fabuliste*].

FABULIZE, [fab'-yōō-līz], *v.i.* to make up or relate fables.

FABULOSITY, [fab'-yōō-los'-it-i], *n.* the quality of being fabulous. [L. *fabulositas*].

FABULOUS, [fab'-yōō-lus], *adj.* celebrated in fable; fictitious, legendary; unreal, incredible, absurd, exaggerated, excessive; **the f. age,** that in which a people's history was conceived of and accepted in terms of myth and legend. [L. *fabulosus*].

FABULOUSLY, [fab'-yōō-lus-li], *adv.* in a fabulous way.

FABULOUSNESS, [fab'-yōō-lus-nes], *n.* fabulosity.

FACADE, façade, [fas-ahd'], *n.* the front view of a building, the face of a building looking out into the street or any open space. [Fr. *façade*].

FACE (1), [fās], *n.* the front of the head, visage; look, expression; the front of anything; the surface that presents itself to the view; the plane surface of a solid; outward aspect; the dial of a watch or clock; coolness, effrontery; **f. to f.,** confronted; **f. to f. with,** confronted with; **in f. of,** opposite to; in spite of; **to fly in the f. of,** to flout openly; **to show one's f.,** to make an appearance; **to one's f.,** in one's hearing; **to look in the f.,** to confront squarely; **to set one's f. against,** to oppose; **to make, pull, a f.,** to distort the features, grimace; **to wear, pull, a long f.,** to look gloomy or discontented; **to have (the) f. to,** to be pert or shameless enough to; **to lose f.,** to be openly shamed, to suffer a loss in dignity; **to save (one's) f.,** to avoid being openly shamed, preserve one's dignity; **on the f. of it,** to judge by outward appearances; **f. value,** surface value, nominal value. [Fr. *face* from LL. *facia*].

FACE (2), [fās], *v.t.* to meet, confront firmly or defiantly; to oppose; to stand with the face or front surface towards; to undergo; not to be dismayed by; to cover the outer surface of; to attach facings to; to dress the surface of; *v.i.* to be turned; **to f. out,** to carry through boldly in the face of difficulty; to meet unashamedly, to brave unblushingly.

FACE-ACHE, [fās'-āk'], *n.* neuralgia; (*slang*) a mildly abusive appellation.

FACE-AGUE, [fās'-ā'-gew], *n.* severe facial neuralgia, tic-douloureux.

FACE-CLOTH, [fās'-kloth'], *n.* a cloth laid upon the face of a corpse; a cloth, usually of flannel, used for washing the face.

FACE-CREAM, [fās'-krēm'], *n.* a greasy preparation for application to the face, for the purpose of softening or otherwise preserving or improving the skin.

FACED, [fāst], *adj.* having a face; having the surface treated or covered.

FACE-GUARD, [fās'-gahd'], *n.* a protective guard for the face.

FACE-HAMMER, [fās'-ham'-er], *n.* a flat-faced hammer.

FACELESS, [fās'-les], *adj.* having no face.

FACE-LIFT, [fās'-lift'], *n.* face-lifting.

FACE-LIFTING, [fās'-lif'-ting], *n.* an operation carried out by beauty specialists to tighten the skin, smooth out wrinkles, get rid of a double chin, etc.

FACE-PAINTER, [fās'-pānt'-er], *n.* one who paints portraits; (*coll.*) one who applies paint to the face.

FACE-PAINTING, [fās-pānt'-ing], *n.* the act or art of portrait-painting.

FACER, [fā'-ser], *n.* a sharp blow in the face; a serious difficulty; a ticklish problem.

FACET, [fas'-et], *n.* one of the small surfaces of a cut gem; one side of any many-sided object; one segment of the compound eye of an insect; (*arch.*) the flat surface between the flutings of a column; (*glass-making*) an iron implement thrust into the mouth of a bottle to enable the worker to carry it to the annealing-tower. [Fr. *facette*].

FACETED, [fas'-et-ed], *adj*. with facets.

FACETIAE, [fas-ē'-shi-ē], *n.(pl.)* pleasantries, jests; obscene books. [L. *facetiae* witticisms].

FACETIOUS, [fas-ē'-shus], *adj*. waggish, addicted to pleasantries. [L. *facetus*].

FACETIOUSLY, [fas-ē'-shus-li], *adv*. in a facetious manner.

FACETIOUSNESS, [fas-ē'-shus-nes], *n*. the condition of being facetious.

FACIA, see FASCIA.

FACIAL (1), [fāshl], *n*. a treatment of face-massage.

FACIAL (2), [fāshl], *adj*. pertaining to the face; **f. angle**, (*anthrop.*) the angle formed by a line drawn from the nostril to the ear with a line drawn from the nostril to the forehead. [MedL. *facialis*].

FACIALLY, [fā'-shal-i], *adv*. in a facial way.

FACIES, [fā'-shi-ēz], *n*. outer appearance; (*anat.*) face; (*geol.*) appearance, general aspect of any period, among rocks and their contents. [L. *facies*].

FACILE, [fas'-il, fas'-il], *adj*. easily performed or won; fluent, ready; glib; compliant, yielding. [L. *facilis*].

FACILENESS, [fas'-il-nes, fas'-il-nes], *n*. quality of being facile.

FACILITATE, [fas-il'-it-āt], *v.t.* to make easy, or less difficult; to help forward.

FACILITATION, [fas-il'-it-ā'-shun], *n*. the process of facilitating.

FACILITIES, [fas-il'-it-iz], *n.(pl.)* means by which anything is made easier; convenient opportunities.

FACILITY, [fas-il'-it-i], *n*. ease, absence of difficulty; readiness, aptitude, fluency, dexterity; opportunity. [L. *facilitas*].

FACING, [fā'-sing], *n*. an outer layer or covering of different material; (*pl.*) cuffs and collar of a soldier's uniform, coloured differently from the rest; trimmings of a garment; turning movements in military drill; **to put a soldier through his facings**, to test his smartness in drill.

FACINGLY, [fā'-sing-li], *adv*. after the manner of facing.

FACINOROUS, [fas-in'-er-us], *adj*. (*rare*) criminal, atrociously wicked. [L. *facinorosus*].

FACON DE PARLER, façon de parler, [fas'-o(ng)-de-pahr'-lā], *n*. manner of speaking; a conventional formula. [Fr. *façon de parler*].

FACSIMILE (1), [fak-sim'-il-i], *n*. a perfectly accurate reproduction, as of handwriting. [L. *facere* to make and *simile* like, similar, a similar thing].

FACSIMILE (2), [fak-sim'-il-i], *v.t.* to make a facsimile of.

FACSIMILIST, [fak-sim'-il-ist], *n*. a person who makes facsimiles.

FACT, [fakt], *n*. something performed, or that has occurred, deed, act, event; something certainly known to be true, to exist or to have occurred; something assumed as a basis for inferences, or brought forward as a truth; **a matter of f.**, something pertaining to the sphere of fact, not mere conjecture or inference; **as a matter of f., in f.**, in reality, actually, really; **in point of f.**, as a matter of fact; **the f. of the matter**, the truth about the matter. [L. *factum* that which is done, deed].

FACTION, [fak'-shun], *n*. a turbulent minority; a troublesome clique in a party; over-prevalence of party spirit; dissension; partisan strife. [L. *factio*].

FACTIONAL, [fak'-shun-al], *adj*. of or pertaining to a faction or factions.

FACTIONARY, [fak'-shun-a-ri], *n*. one belonging to a faction.

FACTIONIST, [fak'-shun-ist], *n*. one who promotes faction; a factionary.

FACTIOUS, [fak'-shus], *adj*. connected with a faction; tending to promote dissension. [L. *factiosus*].

FACTIOUSLY, [fak'-shus-li], *adv*. in a factious way.

FACTIOUSNESS, [fak'-shus-nes], *n*. the quality of being factious; behaviour in the spirit of faction.

FACTITIOUS, [fak-tish'-us], *adj*. produced by art as distinct from nature; artificial, sham. [L. *facticius* artificial].

FACTITIOUSLY, [fak-tish'-us-li], *adv*. artificially, in a factitious way.

FACTITIOUSNESS, [fak-tish'-us-nes], *n*. the state of being factitious.

FACTITIVE, [fak'-tit-iv], *adj*. **f. verb**, (*gram.*) a verb which expresses the act of changing the character of, or imparting a specific character to, the object. [L. *factitare* to do repeatedly].

FACTOR, [fak'-ter], *n*. a proxy or representative; a middleman; any circumstance, influence, etc., which helps towards a certain result; (*arith.*) one of two numbers which when multiplied together produce a third, the product. [L. *factor* a doer].

FACTORAGE, [fak'-tor-ij], *n*. commission paid to a factor.

FACTORIAL, [fak-taw'-ri-al], *adj*. relating to a factory; (*math.*) pertaining to factors.

FACTORIZE, [fak'-tor-iz], *v.t.* (*math.*) to reduce to factors; (*U.S.*) to attach the goods of a debtor in the hands of a third person.

FACTORSHIP, [fak'-tor-ship], *n*. the business or office of a factor.

FACTORY, [fak'-ter-i], *n*. a merchant's foreign trading depot; building where commodities are manufactured; **F. Acts**, acts regulating working conditions.

FACTOTUM, [fak-tō'-tum], *n*. a man of all work; servant discharging all sorts of duties. [L. *factotum* from *fac* do and *totum*, *neut.* of *totus* all].

FACTUAL, [fak'-chōō-al], *adj*. relating to, concerned with facts; real.

FACTUALLY, [fak'-chōō-al-i], *adv*. in a factual manner.

FACTUM, [fak'-tum], *n*. a statement of facts; a concise review of the main points of a case in law. [L. *factum* deed].

FACTURE, [fak'-chur], *n*. (*rare*) the process of making anything; workmanship. [Fr. *facture*].

FACULA, (*pl.* **faculae**), [fak'-yōō-la], *n*. (*astron.*) a spot on the sun's surface which looks brighter than the rest. [L. *facula* a little torch].

FACULAR, [fak'-yōō-ler], *adj*. relating to faculae.

FACULOUS, [fak'-yōō-lus], *adj*. pertaining to or having faculae.

FACULTATIVE, [fak'-ōōl-tā'-tiv], *adj*. of a faculty; optional. [Fr. *facultatif*].

FACULTY, [fak'-ōōl-ti], *n*. special aptitude; proficiency; natural function; one of the main divisions of knowledge comprised in the studies at a University; the body of teachers of one such division; (*leg.*) dispensation, authorization by law; (*eccles.*) dispensation to do something accorded by the chancellor of a diocese; **the four f.'s**, Divinity, Law, Medicine, Arts; **the f.**, (*coll.*) the medical profession. [L. *facultas*].

FACUNDITY, [fak-und'-it-i], *n*. eloquence, fluency of speech. [L. *facunditas*].

FAD, [fad], *n*. a whim; a crotchet; a craze; pet notion. [Unkn.].

FADDINESS, [fad'-in-es], *n*. the quality of being faddy.

FADDISH, [fad'-ish], *adj*. inclined to be faddy.

FADDISHNESS, [fad'-ish-nes], *n*. the quality of being faddish.

FADDIST, [fad'-ist], *n*. a person given to fads.

FADDLE, [fadl], *v.t.* to fondle, pet, caress; *v.i.* to trifle, toy. [Unkn.].

FADDY, [fad'-i], *adj*. given to fads; fussy; over-fastidious; crotchety.

FADE (1), [fahd], *adj*. flat, insipid. [Fr. *fade*].

FADE (2), [fād], *v.t.* to cause to lose its colour; (*wirel.*) to diminish the volume in transmission, to cause one item to disappear against another; **to f. in**, (*cinema*) to cause a picture to become gradually clearer; (*wirel.*) to increase strength of volume gradually; **to f. out**, (*cinema*) to cause a picture to become gradually less distinct until it disappears altogether; (*wirel.*) to diminish strength of volume gradually; **f. unit**, (*wirel.*) instrument to control the number or combination of microphones in circuit at one time; *v.i.* to droop, to lose youth, bloom or vigour; to wane; to become paler or dimmer in colour, or more indistinct; to become fainter, to die away gradually; to become inaudible; (*cinema*) to cause a picture to become gradually clearer or less distinct; (*wirel.*) of signals, to vary and lose strength, *esp.* periodically. [OFr. *fader*].

FADELESS, [fād'-les], *adj*. unfading; not liable to fade.

FADGE, [faj], *n*. a bundle of sticks, leather, etc.; a bale or load of cloth, wool, etc. [Uncert.].

FADING, [fād'-ing], *n*. withering, drooping; loss of freshness or colour; (*wirel.*) decrease in volume, whether intentional or accidental.

FADINGLY, [fād'-ing-li], *adv*. in a fading way.

FADINGNESS, [fād'-ing-nes], *n*. the quality of being liable to fade.

FAE-BERRY, [fā'-be'-ri], *n*. a name for the gooseberry. [Uncert.].

FAECAL, FECAL, [fēkl], *adj*. composed of dregs or sediment; excremental. [L. *faex* dregs].

FAECES, FECES, [fē'-sēz], *n.(pl.)* waste matter, excrement; sediment after infusion or distillation. [L. *faeces*, *pl.* of *faex* dregs].

FAECULA, [fē′-kyŏŏ-la], *n.* fetid matter; vegetable sediment. [L. *faecula*].
FAERIE (1), [fāer′-i], *n.* enchantment; fairyland. [ME. *faerie* enchantment].
FAERIE (2), [fāer′-i], *adj.* of or relating to the fairies or fairyland; fanciful, imaginary.
FAFFLE†, [fafl], *v.i.* to stutter; to flap in the wind (of a sail). [Uncert.].
FAG (1), [fag], *n.* painful toil; trying, tedious work; fatigue, weariness; junior boy at a public school who performs certain services for a senior; (*slang*) cigarette. [Unkn.].
FAG (2), (fagging, fagged), [fag], *v.t.* to labour painfully; to fatigue, tire, exhaust; (of a senior boy at a public school) to employ a junior as a fag; (of a junior) to perform certain tasks for a senior; **to f. out,** (*cricket*) to field.
FAG-END, [fag′-end′], *n.* a tedious conclusion; a cigarette end.
FAGGERY, [fag′-er-i], *n.* drudgery for another; the system of fagging at public schools.
FAGGING, [fag′-ing], *n.* the performance of certain duties for a senior by a junior at a public school.
FAGGOT (1), FAGOT†, [fag′-ot], *n.* a bundle of sticks bound together; a bundle of metal rods; a savoury rissole of chopped and seasoned liver. [Fr. *fagot*].

FAGGOT

FAGGOT (2), [fag′-ot], *v.t. and i.* to make faggots (of).
FAGGOT-VOTE, [fag′-ot-vōt′], *n.* a vote fraudulently obtained by temporarily transferring sufficient property to a person otherwise not qualified to vote.
FAGGOT-VOTER, [fag′-ot-vō′-ter], *n.* one using a faggot-vote.
FAGIN, FAGINE, [fā′-jin], *n.* a product obtained from the nuts of the common beech. [L. *fagus* beech].
FAGOT†, see FAGGOT.
FAGOTTO, [fag-ot′-ō], *n.* the bassoon. [It. *fagotto*].
FAHAM, see FAAM.
FAHLERZ, [fahl′-āertz′], *n.* grey copper ore, tetrahedrite. [Ger. *fahl* yellowish and *erz* ore].
FAHRENHEIT (1), [fa′-ren-hīt], *n.* a thermometer, used chiefly in England, with a freezing-point at 32° and boiling-point at 212°. [The German inventor *Fahrenheit*].
FAHRENHEIT (2), [fa′-ren-hīt], *adj.* reckoned according to the system invented by Fahrenheit.
FAIENCE, FAYENCE, [fah-yonts′], *n.* a kind of glazed porcelain embellished with painted designs. [Fr. *Faience* Faenza, the town in Italy where this kind of porcelain is said to have been first manufactured].
FAIL (1), [fāl], *n.* (*rare*) failure; **without f.,** for certain, quite definitely. [OFr. *faile*].
FAIL (2), [fāl], *v.t.* to disappoint, to let down; to desert; to cause to fail in an examination, to declare unsuccessful; *v.i.* to be inadequate, not to suffice, to run short; to grow feeble, lose strength; to be wanting, lack, come short; neglect; omit; to be unsuccessful, *esp.* in an examination; to become insolvent. [OFr. *faillir*].
FAILING (1), [fā′-ling], *n.* a defect, shortcoming, imperfection, weakness.
FAILING (2), [fā′-ling], *prep.* in the lack of, without.
FAILINGLY, [fā′-ling-li], *adv.* through or by failing.
FAILLE, [fah′-ē], *n.* a strong, ribbed Flemish silk. [Fr. *faille*].
FAILURE, [fāl′-yur], *n.* a failing; deficiency; cessation of supply; omission; non-performance; decay, or defect from decay; lack of success; a person who fails, is unsuccessful; insolvency.
FAIN (1), [fān], *adj.* ready, willing; **f. to,** obliged to, having no alternative but to. [OE. *fægen* glad].
FAIN (2), [fān], *adv.* gladly, willingly.
FAIN (3), FAINS, [fān(z)], *v.i.* school children's formula, claiming exemption from some unwelcome task for those who say it first, as **fains I, batting first.** [Unkn.].
FAINEANT (1), fainéant, [fā-nā-o(ng)′], *n.* an idler; official who does nothing, *esp.* as applied to some weak French kings of the Merovingian line, who were completely dominated by their ministers. [Fr. *fainéant*].
FAINEANT (2), fainéant, [fā-nā-o(ng)′], *adj.* idle, sluggish.
FAINT (1), [fānt], *n.* swoon, fainting fit; **in a dead f.,** completely unconscious.
FAINT (2), [fānt], *adj.* feeble, not vigorous or effective, nervous, unenterprising; giddy, dizzy, about to swoon; lacking in vividness, dull, insipid; vague, indistinct; **ruled f.,** term applied to paper ruled with faint lines. [OFr. *feint* feigned].
FAINT (3), [fānt], *v.i.* to feel sick, giddy or weak; to become weak; to fall unconscious in a swoon.
FAINT-HEART, [fānt′-haht′], *n.* a coward.
FAINT-HEARTED, [fānt′-hah′-tid], *adj.* fearful, timid; discouraged; easily depressed or yielding to fear.
FAINT-HEARTEDLY, [fānt′-hah′-tid-li], *adv.* in a faint-hearted way.
FAINT-HEARTEDNESS, [fānt′-hah′-tid-nes], *n.* the quality of being faint-hearted.
FAINTING, [fānt′-ing], *n.* the act of swooning, loss of consciousness.
FAINTISH, [fānt′-ish], *adj.* somewhat faint.
FAINTISHNESS, [fānt′-ish-nes], *n.* the condition of being faintish.
FAINTLY, [fānt′-li], *adv.* in a faint way.
FAINTNESS, [fānt′-nes], *n.* the condition of being faint.
FAINTY, [fānt′-i], *adj.* sickly; weak, feeble; languid.
FAIR (1), [fāer], *n.* a periodical gathering for sale of articles of various kinds, often accompanied by side-shows and other entertainments; **a day too late for the f., a day after the f.,** too late for some important occasion. [OFr. *feire* from L. *feria* holiday].
FAIR (2), [fāer], *n.* (*poet., archaic*) women; a woman.
FAIR (3), [fāer], *adj.* lovely, beautiful; fresh, clean, clear; fine, dry, bright, sunny; favourable, promising; just, equitable, unprejudiced; moderately good, passable, not bad; light-coloured; having light-coloured hair or complexion; plausible, specious; **f. and square,** above board, without finesse; **a f. copy,** a clean and perfect copy transcribed from a rough one; **the f. sex,** women; **to be in a f. way to,** to be likely to. [OE. *fæger*].
FAIR (4), [fāer], *adv.* justly, honestly; courteously; directly; **to bid f. to,** to appear likely to.
FAIR-FACED, [fāer′-fāst′], *adj.* with a fair face; fair-spoken with intent to deceive.
FAIRILY, [fāer′-il-i], *adv.* in a fairy-like fashion.
FAIRING (1), [fāer′-ing], *n.* gift bought at a fair; a thin cake made of sugar and butter, a jumble. [FAIR (1)].
FAIRING (2), [fāer′-ing], *n.* the process of making the surface of an aeroplane smooth and stream-like; something added to the structure of an aeroplane in order to achieve a smooth and stream-like surface.
FAIRISH, [fāer′-ish], *adj.* reasonably good; moderately fair.
FAIR ISLE, [fāer′-īl′], *adj.* denoting knitted articles made in *Fair Isle* in the Shetlands.
FAIRLEAD, [fāer′-lēd′], *n.* (*naut.*) the strip of board or block which keeps a rope in its place so that it may run clear.
FAIRLY, [fāer′-li], *adv.* in a fair manner; clearly; nearly, almost; moderately, reasonably.
FAIRMINDED, [fāer′-mīnd′-id], *adj.* unbiased, impartial.
FAIRNESS, [fāer′-nes], *n.* the quality of being fair; justice; impartiality.
FAIR-SEEMING, [fāer′-sē′-ming], *adj.* of (deceptively) fair appearance.
FAIR-SPOKEN, [fāer′-spō′-ken], *adj.* using fair words; plausible, specious.
FAIRWAY, [fāer′-wā], *n.* the navigable channel of a river; the smooth stretch of trimmed turf between rough and hazards, from green to green, on a golf course.
FAIRWEATHER, [fāer′-weTH′-er], *adj.* only fitted or of use for easy circumstances, not to be relied on in trouble or difficulty.
FAIRY (1), [fāer′-i], *n.* a small supernatural being conceived to have a human form and exercise magical powers; (*slang*) a male pervert. [OFr. *faerie* fairyland].
FAIRY (2), [fāer′-i], *adj.* pertaining to fairies or fairyland; fairy-like, dainty, lovely, delicate, small.
FAIRY-BEADS, [fāer′-i-bēdz′], *n.(pl.)* the joints and plates of fossil crinoids, also called St. Cuthbert's beads.
FAIRYDOM, [fāer′-i-dom], *n.* the domain of the fairies, fairyland.
FAIRY-FINGERS, [fāer′-i-fing′-gerz], *n.* a name for the foxglove, *Digitalis purpurea.*
FAIRYHOOD, [fāer′-i-hŏŏd], *n.* the condition of being a fairy.
FAIRYISM, [fāer′-i-izm], *n.* belief in fairies.

FAIRY-LAMP, [fāer'-i-lamp'], *n.* a small lamp employed for illuminations.
FAIRYLAND, [fāer'-i-land'], *n.* the domain or abode of the fairies.
FAIRY-LIKE, [fāer'-i-līk'], *adj.* after the manner of fairies; dainty, ethereal, resembling a fairy.
FAIRY-RINGS, [fāer'-i-ringz'], *n.(pl.)* circles of darker green grass caused by fungi, but popularly supposed to be caused by the dancing of the fairies.
FAIRY-STONES, [fāer'-i-stōnz], *n.(pl.)* popular name for fossil echinoderms.
FAIRY-TALE, [fāer'-i-tāl], *n.* a tale about fairies; a fib, preposterous story.
FAITH, [fāth], *n.* confidence, trust; belief, *esp.* in religious doctrines; a system of religious belief; the accepting of divine truth without actual proof; warrant; promise, undertaking; sincerity; loyalty, fidelity; **Defender of the F.,** title conferred upon Henry VIII by the Pope in 1521 and borne by sovereigns of England ever since; **in good f.,** sincerely, with honest intent; **bad f.,** deceit; **Punic f.,** treachery. [ME. *feith*, ~OFr. *fei*].
FAITHFUL, [fāth'-fool], *adj.* loyal, constant, keeping faith; reliable, accurate; not false or deceitful; **the f.,** true believers, *esp.* of Islam.
FAITHFULLY, [fāth'-fool-i], *adv.* in a faithful way.
FAITHFULNESS, [fāth'-fool-nes], *n.* the condition of being faithful.
FAITH-HEALING, [fāth'-hē'-ling], *n.* the practice of attempting to cure sickness by faith rather than medical aid.
FAITHLESS, [fāth'-les], *adj.* lacking faith; disloyal; not true to one's promise or vow; fickle.
FAITHLESSLY, [fāth'-les-li], *adv.* in a faithless way.
FAITHLESSNESS, [fāth'-les-nes], *n.* the condition of being faithless.
FAITHWORTHY, [fāth'-wur'-THi], *adj.* that can be relied upon, trustworthy.
FAKE (1), [fāk], *n.* sham, an imitation, a piece of faking, a cooked report; (*naut.*) one round of a coil of rope.
FAKE (2), [fāk], *v.t.* to make a sham copy of, to touch up so as to raise the apparent value of. [Uncert.].
FAKEMENT, [fāk'-ment], *n.* a makeshift; a sham, or shoddy substitute.
FAKER, [fā'-ker], *n.* one who fakes; a cheat.
FAKIR, [fak'-ēer'], *n.* a Hindu or Mohammedan ascetic beggar, looked upon as a very holy man. [Arab. *faqir* poor man].
FAKIRISM, [fak'-ēer-izm], *n.* the practice of begging as a religious exercise.
FALANGE, [fal-an'-gi], *n.* the Spanish fascist party. [Span. *falange*].
FALANGIST (1), [fal-an'-gist], *n.* a member of the Falange.
FALANGIST (2), [fal-an'-gist], *adj.* of or pertaining to the Falange or the Falangists.
FALCADE, [fal-kād'], *n.* the movement of a horse when he throws himself on his haunches two or three times in very quick curvets. [Fr. *falcade*].
FALCATE, [fal'-kāt], *adj.* curved like a sickle, as the moon; (*bot.*) hooked. [L. *falcatus*].
FALCATED, [fal'-kā-tid], *adj.* falcate.
FALCATION, [fal-kā'-shun], *n.* a curve in the form of a sickle.
FALCHION, [fawl'-chun], *n.* a short sword with a curved blade. [OFr. *fauchon*].
FALCIFORM, [fal'-sif-awm], *adj.* in the form of a sickle; like a reaping-hook.
FALCON, [fawkn, fawlkn], *n.* a bird of prey, allied to the hawk, formerly trained and much used for hunting game; a kind of light cannon. [OFr. *faucon*].

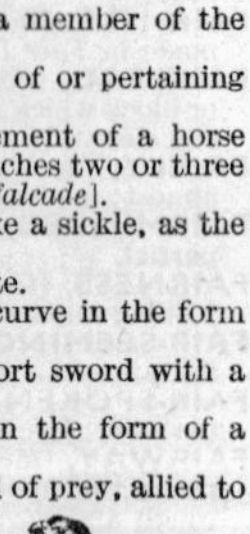

FALCON

FALCONER, [fawk'-on-er, fawlk'-on-er], *n.* one who breeds and trains falcons; one who hunts with falcons.
FALCONET, [fawk'-on-et, fawlk'-on-et], *n.* a pygmy falcon of the genus *Hierax*; a kind of small cannon.
FALCON-GENTLE, [faw(l)kn'-jentl'], *n.* the female of the gos-hawk, *Accipiter palumbarius*.
FALCONINE, [faw(l)k'-on-īn], *adj.* relating to falcons.
FALCONRY, [fawk'-on-ri, fawlk'-on-ri], *n.* the art of training falcons; the sport of hunting with falcons.
FALCULA, [fal'-kyoo-la], *n.* (*zool.*) a sharp-pointed claw curved like a sickle. [L. *falcula* little sickle].
FALCULATE, [fal'-kyoo-lāt], *adj.* in the form of a falcula.
FALDAGE, [fawld'-ij], *n.* a privilege formerly reserved to themselves by several English lords of setting up folds for sheep in any fields within their manors, the better to manure them. [MedL. *faldagium*].
FALDSTOOL, [fawld'-stool], *n.* a folding stool like a camp-stool; the armless chair used by a bishop, when not in his own cathedral; a kneeling stool; a small desk at which the litany is read. [MedL. *faldistolium*].

FALDSTOOL

FALERNIAN (1), [fal-ur'-ni-an], *n.* the wine from Falerno in Italy, much praised by the ancients.
FALERNIAN (2), [fal-ur'-ni-an], *adj.* pertaining to Falerno or the wine made there. [The *Ager Falernus* in Campania].
FALL (1), [fawl], *n.* the act of falling, drop; quantity of rain, etc., that falls; surrender; a succumbing to temptation; a lessening in value, drop in prices; a cataract of water; a wrestling match; a throw in wrestling; (*U.S.*) autumn; **the f., the f. of man,** the sin of Adam; **to try a f. with,** (*fig.*) to pit oneself against.
FALL (2), (falling, fell, fallen), [fawl], *v.i.* to drop, descend unhindered from a high to a low level; to collapse, to come down; to lose high office; (of lambs) to be born; (of the face) to express dismay; to sink to a lower level, diminish in value; to be killed in battle; to sin, yield to temptation, (of women) to lose chastity; to hang down; to abate, ebb, grow milder, less buoyant; to come by chance, alight upon; to pass into a specified condition, become; to occur; to be uttered; **to f. away,** to withdraw (friendship, support, allegiance, etc.), desert; to decay, disappear; **to f. back,** to retreat; **to f. back upon,** to withdraw to, have recourse to; **to f. flat,** to fail to produce the desired effect, fail to evoke laughter; **to f. foul of,** (*naut.*) to collide with; to quarrel with, to get on the wrong side of; **to f. for,** to be captivated, attracted by; to fall in love with; to be deceived by; **to f. in,** to collapse inwards, give way; to come to an end, lapse; (*milit.*) to take up correct position in the ranks, get into line; **to f. in with,** to come across by chance; to acquiesce in, comply with; **to f. off,** to diminish, grow less in quantity or quality; (*naut.*) of a ship, not to answer the helm; **to f. on,** to attack; **to f. out,** to happen, turn out; to disagree, quarrel; (*milit.*) to leave one's position in the ranks; **to f. short,** to be insufficient, to run out; **to f. through,** to come to naught. [OE. *feallan*].
FALLABLE, [fawl'-abl], *adj.* inclined, liable to fall.
FALLACIOUS, [fal-ā'-shus], *adj.* founded on fallacy; deceptive and misleading; producing disappointment; false; compounded of fallacies.
FALLACIOUSLY, [fal-ā'-shus-li], *adv.* in a fallacious way.
FALLACIOUSNESS, [fal-ā'-shus-nes], *n.* the condition of being fallacious.
FALLACY, [fal'-as-i], *n.* deceptive appearance; a sophism; a misleading argument which sounds plausible. [L. *fallacia*].
FAL-LALS, [fal'-lalz'], *n.(pl.)* showy trifles; gewgaws. [Unkn.].
FALLEN, [fawl'-en], *adj.* abandoned; degraded.
FALLIBILITY, [fal'-ib-il'-it-i], *n.* the quality of being fallible.
FALLIBLE, [fal'-ibl], *adj.* inclined, liable to err; liable to deceive, unreliable. [LL. *fallibilis*].
FALLIBLY, [fal'-ib-li], *adv.* in a fallible way.
FALLING, [fawl'-ing], *n.* (*path.*) prolapse.
FALLING-AWAY, [fawl'-ing-a-wā'], *n.* the renunciation of one's faith, apostasy.
FALLOPIAN, [fal-ō'-pi-an], *adj.* pertaining to, discovered by, Fallopio; **f. tubes,** the oviducts of mammals. [*Fallopio* an Italian anatomist].
FALLOW (1), [fal'-ō], *n. and adj.* ploughed and harrowed but left uncropped for a season; (*fig.*) of the mind, uncultivated, untrained; **to lie f.,** to remain uncultivated. [ME. *fallowe*].
FALLOW (2), [fal'-ō], *adj.* brownish-yellow, dun. [OE. *falo*].
FALLOW (3), [fal'-ō], *v.t.* to plough and harrow land without cropping it.

FALLOW-CROP, [fal'-ō-krop'], *n.* a crop obtained from fallow ground.
FALLOW-DEER, [fal'-ō-dēer'], *n.* a species of deer, smaller than the red deer, of a yellowish-brown colour, common in England, *Cervus dama.* [FALLOW (2) and DEER].
FALLOW-FINCH, [fal'-ō-finch'], *n.* a small bird, sometimes called the wheatear, *Saxicola oenanthe.*
FALLOWNESS, [fal'-ō-nes], *n.* the state of lying untilled or fallow.
FALLOWSNATCH, [fal'-ō-snach'], *n.* a name for the fallow-finch.
FALL-TRAP, [fawl'-trap'], *n.* a trap with a door which falls and imprisons whatever has trodden on it.
FALSE (1), [fawls], *adj.* not true; wrong, incorrect, mistaken; deceitful, lying, treacherous, unfaithful, disloyal, deceptive, misleading, sham, spurious, artificial; **f. quantity,** an inaccurate vowel-length; **f. position,** an awkward position that may lead to misunderstanding, or necessitate action against one's principles; **f. pretences,** misrepresentations made with intent to deceive. [L. *falsus*].
FALSE (2), [fawls], *adv.* **to play someone f.,** to betray, deceive, let down.
FALSE-FACE, [fawls'-fās'], *n.* another name for a mask.
FALSE-FACED, [fawls'-fāst'], *adj.* deceitful, hypocritical.
FALSE-HEARTED, [fawls'-hah'-tid], *adj.* shallow, insincere, perfidious.
FALSE-HEARTEDNESS, [fawls'-hah'-tid-nes], *n.* insincerity; perfidiousness; treachery.
FALSEHOOD, [fawls'-hŏod], *n.* an untruth, lie; (*rare*) the quality of being false.
FALSELY, [fawls'-li], *adv.* in a false way.
FALSENESS, [fawls'-nes], *n.* the quality of being false.
FALSETTE, [fawl-set'], *adj.* falsetto.
FALSETTO (1), [fawl-set'-ō], *n.* a high male voice, resembling the female voice in pitch; forced shrill voice above the natural pitch. [It. *falsetto*].
FALSETTO (2), [fawl-set'-ō], *adj.* of the quality of falsetto, shrill, forced, squeaky.
FALSIFIABLE, [fawl'-sif-ī'-abl], *adj.* that can be falsified.
FALSIFICATION, [fawl'-sif-ik-ā'-shun], *n.* the act or process of falsifying; the condition of being falsified.
FALSIFIER, [fawl'-sif-ī-er], *n.* one who falsifies.
FALSIFY, [fawl'-sif-ī], *v.t.* to give a false impression of or appearance to, misrepresent, distort; to prove to be false; to disappoint; to alter fraudulently, tamper with. [LL. *falsificare*].
FALSITY, [fawls'-it-i], *n.* the condition of being false; a false assertion.
FALTER, [fawl'-ter], *v.i.* to be unsteady, stumble, totter, move uncertainly and with hesitation; to speak hesitantly, stammer, speak in a broken voice; to hesitate, waver, flinch, lose confidence. [ME. *falteren*].
FALTERING, [fawl'-ter-ing], *adj.* hesitating; speaking with an uncertain trembling utterance.
FALTERINGLY, [fawl'-ter-ing-li], *adv.* in a faltering way.
FALUNS, [fah'-lunz], *n.(pl.)* (*geol.*) a series of Miocene deposits. [Fr. *faluns*].
FALX, [falks], *n.* (*anat.*) a membranous process shaped like a sickle; as *falx cerebri,* a process of the dura mater. [L. *falx* sickle].
FAMA, [fā'-ma], *n.* the goddess of rumour; **f. clamosa,** (*Scots leg.*) a widespread rumour alleging immoral conduct on the part of a clergyman, church office-bearer, or member, as a ground of prosecution. [L. *fama*].
FAME, [fām], *n.* rumour, report; good repute; reputation; renown, celebrity. [L. *fama*].
FAMED, [fāmd], *adj.* famous, renowned.
FAMELESS, [fām'-les], *adj.* undistinguished, without renown.
FAMILIAR (1), [fam-il'-yar], *n.* a certain official in a Pope's or Roman Catholic bishop's household; a demon attending on a witch, magician, etc., a familiar spirit.
FAMILIAR (2), [fam-il'-yar], *adj.* relating to the family, private, domestic; intimate, closely acquainted; well known; common, current, usual; well versed in, conversant; impudent, presumptuous, over-free, over-cordial. [L. *familiaris*].
FAMILIARISM, [fam-il'-yar-izm], *n.* a conversational turn of speech, a colloquialism.
FAMILIARITY, [fam-il'-i-ar'-it-i], *n.* close acquaintance, intimacy; accurate knowledge; intimate gesture, caress; unceremoniousness, informality; impudence, presumption. [L. *familiaritas*].
FAMILIARIZATION, [fam-il'-yar-īz-ā'-shun], *n.* the act or process of making or becoming familiar.
FAMILIARIZE, [fam-il'-yar-iz], *v.t.* to make familiar.
FAMILIARLY, [fam-il'-yar-li], *adv.* in a familiar way.
FAMILY, [fam'-il-i], *n.* the members of a household, parents, children, domestics, etc.; a group of parents and children; a set of relations; one's children, or other relatives; the descendants of a common ancestor; group of people of same stock; group of objects having features in common; **f. baker, butcher, etc.,** a baker, etc., supplying private families as opposed to large organizations, etc.; **f. hotel,** a hotel catering for, and with special terms for, families; **f. likeness,** a rather vague resemblance often observable between relations; **f. man,** a man with a family or with domestic proclivities; **in the f. way,** pregnant. [L. *familia* household].
FAMINE, [fam'-in], *n.* desperate scarcity of food in a district; shortage, dearth of food or water; starvation. [Fr. *famine*].
FAMISH, [fam'-ish], *v.t.* to reduce to extreme hunger; *v.i.* to be reduced to extreme hunger; **to be famishing, famished,** (*coll.*) to feel very hungry. [~L. *fames* hunger].
FAMISHING, [fam'-ish-ing], *adj.* starving; perishing by hunger; (*coll.*) very hungry.
FAMISHMENT, [fam'-ish-ment], *n.* the condition of famishing, starvation.
FAMOUS, [fā'-mus], *adj.* renowned, celebrated, usually in a good sense; (*coll.*) excellent, fine. [L. *famosus*].
FAMOUSLY, [fā'-mus-li], *adv.* in a famous manner; (*coll.*) very well.
FAMOUSNESS, [fā'-mus-nes], *n.* the condition of being famous.
FAMULIST, [fam'-yŏŏ-list], *n.* a subordinate member of a college at Oxford; a servant.
FAMULUS, [fam'-yŏŏ-lus], *n.* one who assists a magician. [L. *famulus* servant].
FAN (1), [fan], *n.* a machine for winnowing corn; a device, usually folding, for cooling the face by winnowing the air; anything spread out like a fan; a device that rotates to provide a current of air for the purpose of cooling or ventilation; a small sail of a windmill for keeping the main sails across the wind; (*naut.*) a propeller, screw. [OE. *fann* from L. *vannus* basket for winnowing].

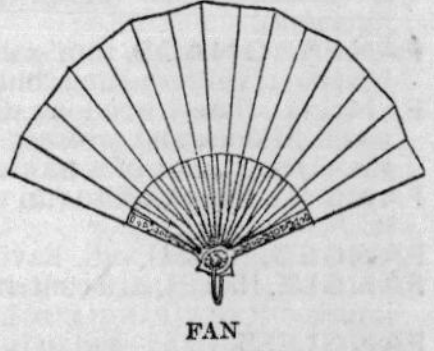
FAN

FAN (2), [fan], *n.* (*slang*) an ardent admirer or devotee; **f. mail,** admiring letters written by fans to a celebrity. [Short form of FANATIC].
FAN (3), [fan], *v.t.* to winnow, blow the chaff away from; to move (the air) with a fan; to cool (oneself) by means of a fan; to kindle a flame by making a current of air as with a fan; to blow gently on; to spread out in a shape like a fan; **to f. the flame,** to increase the excitement, feed the anger or indignation, etc.
FANAL, [fānl], *n.* a beacon, *esp.* in a lighthouse. [L. *fanalis*].
FANATIC (1), [fan-at'-ik], *n.* a person filled with extreme ardour for something; person filled with excessive and usually mistaken enthusiasm, *esp.* in religious matters.
FANATIC (2), [fan-at'-ik], *adj.* affected with or prompted by excessive and exclusive zeal, *esp.* religious zeal; animated by or proceeding from fanaticism. [L. *fanaticus* pertaining to a temple, inspired].
FANATICAL, [fan-at'-ikl], *adj.* fanatic.
FANATICALLY, [fan-at'-ik-al-i], *adv.* in a fanatical manner.
FANATICALNESS, [fan-at'-ikl-nes], *n.* the quality of being fanatical.
FANATICISM, [fan-at'-is-izm], *n.* the violent zeal of a fanatic.
FAN-BLAST, [fan'-blahst'], *n.* a blast produced by a fan.
FANCIED, [fan'-sid], *adj.* imaginary; favoured, preferred.
FANCIER, [fan'-si-er], *n.* a connoisseur; one who has a fancy for something.

FANCIFUL, [fan'-sif-o͝ol], *adj.* dictated by fancy; fantastical; whimsical.

FANCIFULLY, [fan'-sif-o͝ol-i], *adv.* in a fanciful way.

FANCIFULNESS, [fan'-sif-o͝ol-nes], *n.* the quality or condition of being fanciful.

FANCILESS, [fan'-sil-es], *adj.* lacking fancy.

FAN-CRICKET, [fan'-krik'-it], *n.* a name for the mole-cricket, *Gryllotalpa vulgaris.*

FANCY (1), [fan'-si], *n.* baseless belief, delusion; imagination, faculty of calling up mental images; supposition; whim, caprice; inclination, taste, liking; **the f.,** those who have a fancy for a certain pastime, *esp.* boxing enthusiasts. [Short form of FANTASY].

FANCY (2), [fan'-si], *adj.* not plain or simple, decorative, elaborate; whimsical, extravagant; based on imagination rather than fact; **f. dog, pigeon, etc.,** a dog, etc., bred to special points of excellence; **f. dress,** masquerade costume; **f. work,** embroidery, ornamental needlework; **at a f. price,** preposterously dear.

FANCY (3), [fan'-si], *v.t.* to have a liking, predilection for; to picture to oneself, imagine, conceive, think of; to be inclined to think, to suppose, to breed; with attention to special points; (*coll.*) to have a good opinion of, be conceited about.

FANCY-FREE, [fan'-si-frē'], *adj.* not in love, heart-whole.

FANCY-GOODS, [fan'-si-go͝odz'], *n.(pl.)* decorative fabrics and oddments of various kinds, as ribbons, silks, etc., as distinct from those plain and useful.

FANCY-MONGER, [fan'-si-mung'-ger], *n.* one who deals in tricks of the fancy.

FANCY-SICK, [fan'-si-sik'], *adj.* mentally distempered.

FANDANGO, [fan-dang'-gō], *n.* an old Spanish national dance, in which the dancers beat time with castanets. [Span. *fandango*].

FANE, [fān], *n.* a temple; a place consecrated to religion. [L. *fanum*].

FANFARE, [fan'-fāer], *n.* a short flourish of trumpets, as on a knight's entry into the lists, etc.; a lively piece of music performed on hunting-horns; a bravado. [Fr. *fanfare*].

FANFARON, [fan'-fahr-on], *n.* a swaggering bully; a braggart who blows his own trumpet. [Fr. *fanfaron*].

FANFARONADE, [fan'-fahr-on-ād'], *n.* ostentation; bragging; vain boasting; bluster. [Fr. *fanfaronnade*].

FANG (1), [fang], *n.* a long sharp tooth, *esp.* the canine tooth in dogs and wolves; venom-tooth of a snake; the pronged root of a tooth. [OE. *fang*].

FANG (2), [fang], *v.t.* to run water into a pump to start it. [FANG (1)].

FANGED, [fangd], *adj.* having fangs.

FANGLE, [fangl], *n.* a contrivance; a novelty; a knick-knack. [(NEW)FANGLE(D)].

FANGLESS, [fang'-les], *adj.* having no fangs.

FANGOT, [fang'-got], *n.* a quantity of wares, as raw silk, etc., varying from one to about three cwts.

FANION, [fan'-yon], *n.* a marking flag used by surveyors; (*milit.*) a small flag carried with the baggage. [Fr. *fanion*].

FANLIGHT, [fan'-lit], *n.* a window shaped like an extended fan, over a door.

FANNEL, [fanl], *n.* a banner; a splint. [L. *fanula*].

FANNER, [fan'-er], *n.* a winnowing-machine; one who, or that which, fans.

FAN-NERVED, [fan'-nurvd'], *adj.* (*bot., entom.*) with the nerves or nervures disposed like a fan.

FANNING-MILL, [fan'-ing-mil'], *n.* a machine for separating grain from chaff and dirt.

FANLIGHT

FANON, [fan'-on], *n.* a napkin; an embroidered scarf worn on the left arm of a Roman Catholic priest at Mass; a church banner. [Fr. *fanon* from L. *fano* flag].

FAN-PALM, [fan'-pahm'], *n.* a palm with fan-shaped leaves, normally the talipot palm, *Corypha umbraculifera,* of Ceylon.

FANTAIL, [fan'-tāl], *n.* a pigeon with a fan-shaped tail; a species of Australian bird; a gas-burner which emits a fan-like flame.

FANTAILED, [fan'-tāld'], *adj.* having a fan-shaped tail.

FANTAN, [fan'-tan'], *n.* a Chinese game played with coins and a bowl; a card game. [Chin. *fan-tan*].

FANTASIA, [fan-taz-ē'-a], *n.* free musical composition in which the composer follows his fancy rather than any particular musical form. [It. *fantasia*].

FANTASIED, [fan'-taz-id], *adj.* fanciful; fancy-fashioned.

FANTASSIN, [fan-tas'-in], *n.* a foot-soldier. [Fr. *fantassin*].

FANTAST, [fan'-tast], *n.* a person who indulges in fantasies. [Gk. *phantastes* a boaster].

FANTASTIC (1), [fan-tas'-tik], *n.* an extravagant, whimsical person; a fop.

FANTASTIC (2), [fan-tas'-tik], *adj.* extravagant; whimsical; preposterous. [Gk. *phantastikos* showing to the mind].

FANTASTICAL, [fan-tas'-tikl], *adj.* fantastic.

FANTASTICALLY, [fan-tas'-tik-a-li], *adv.* in a fantastical way.

FANTASTICALNESS, [fan-tas'-tikl-nes], *n.* the quality of being fantastical.

FANTASY, PHANTASY, [fan'-taz-i], *n.* fancy; a dream; hallucination, illusion. [Gk. *phantasia* a making visible].

FANTEE, [fan'-tē], *n.* a member of a West African negro tribe so styled; the language of this tribe; **to go f.,** to live like a native, go native.

FANTOCCINI, [fan-to-chē'-ni], *n.(pl.)* puppets, marionettes; dramatic representations in which puppets are used as performers. [It. *fantoccini* little children].

FAN-TRACERY, [fan'-trā'-ser-i], *n.* (*arch.*) elaborate and delicate carved work on a vaulted roof in the form of a fan.

FAR (1), [fah(r)], *n.* a remote place; a high, great degree.

FAR (2), [fah(r)], *adj.* remote, distant, not close at hand; **a f. cry,** a long way; **few and f. between,** rare.

FAR (3), [fah(r)], *adv.* at a distance, a long way off; by a great interval, by much; to a great distance; **f. and away,** very much; **f. be it from me,** I would on no account; I have not the audacity, or inclination to; **f. gone,** advanced; in an advanced state of drunkenness, disease, or insanity, etc.; **to go f.,** to do much, progress, be successful, get on. [OE. *feorr*].

FAR† (4), [fah(r)], *n.* a coarse kind of buckwheat grown on poor lands in the south of Europe. [L. *far*].

FARAD, [fa'-rad], *n.* the unit of electrical capacity. [*Faraday,* the scientist].

FARADAIC, [fa'-rad-ā'-ik], *adj.* susceptible to, or producing, induction; inductive.

FARADIC, [fa-rad'-ik], *adj.* faradaic.

FARADIZATION, [fa'-ra-dī-zā'-shun], *n.* a method of treating disease by the application of electric currents. [*Faraday* who discovered it].

FARANDAMS, [fa'-ran-damz], *n.* a fabric of wool and silk. [Uncert.].

FARANDINE, FERRANDINE†, [fa'-ran-dīn], *n.* a sort of cloth made partly of silk and partly of wool, much used for clothes in the seventeenth century. [Unkn.].

FARANDOLE, [fa-ran-dōl'], *n.* a Spanish dance, popular in the south of France. [Fr. *farandole*].

FARAWAY, [fah(r)'-a-wā], *adj.* remote; distant; (*fig.*) dreamy.

FAR-BROUGHT, [fah(r)'-brawt'], *adj.* brought from afar; (*fig.*) far-fetched.

FARCE, [fahs], *n.* dramatic work, solely intended to promote laughter; comedy of the more uproarious kind; such plays in general; absurd proceeding; mockery; travesty. [OFr. *farce* stuffing].

FARCEMEAT, [fahs'-mēt], *n.* stuffing used for game and other meats as a seasoning; forcemeat. [Fr. *farce* stuffing and MEAT].

FARCICAL, [fah'-sikl], *adj.* pertaining or appropriate to a farce, ridiculous.

FARCICALITY, [fah'-sik-al'-it-i], *n.* the state or quality of being farcical.

FARCICALLY, [fah'-sik-al-i], *adv.* in a farcical way.

FARCICALNESS, [fah'-sikl-nes], *n.* farcicality.

FARCIN, [fah'-sin], *n.* farcy. [Fr. *farcin*].

FARCING, [fah'-sing], *n.* edible mixed stuffing.

FARCY, [fah'-si], *n.* a disease of horses affecting the skin and blood-vessels and allied to glanders. [Fr. *farcin*].

FARDAGE, [fah'-dij], *n.* a former term for dunnage. [Fr. *fardage*].

FARDEL (1), [fahdl], *n.* a bundle. [OFr. *fardel*].

FARDEL (2), [fahdl], *v.t.* to pack up in bundles.

FARDEL-BAG, [fahdl'-bag'], *n.* the third stomach of a ruminating animal, where green food lies till it is chewed again.

FARDEL-BOUND, [fahdl'-bound'], *adj.* costive, used to describe a condition in cattle and sheep in which the fardel-bag is overgorged and inflamed, and food is retained in its folds.

FARE (1), [fäer], *n.* the price of a passenger's conveyance, passage-money; the person conveyed for this. [OE. *fær* journey].

FARE (2), [fäer], *n.* food, provisions. [OE. *faru* journey].

FARE (3), [fäer], *v.i.* to travel, journey, go; to get on; to happen, turn out. [OE. *faran*].

FARE (4), [fäer], *v.i.* to be entertained, be fed; to feed.

FAREWELL (1), [fäer'-wel'], *n.* good wishes on parting, leave-taking.

FAREWELL (2), [fäer'-wel'], *int.* good-bye! adieu! [FARE (3) and WELL (3)].

FAR-FETCHED, [fah(r)'-fecht'], *adj.* not naturally deduced or introduced; forced; strained, unlikely.

FARINA, [fa-rē'-na], *n.* the pollen of plants; the flour of any kind of corn or starchy root, such as the potato; starch. [L. *farina* flour].

FARINACEOUS, [fa-rin-ā'-shus], *adj.* consisting of, or containing, farina or flour; mealy; floury. [L. *farinaceus*].

FARINACEOUSLY, [fa-rin-ā'-shus-li], *adv.* in a floury manner.

FARINOSE, [fa'-rin-ōs], *adj.* producing farina; covered with farina.

FARL, [fahl], *n.* a thin oatmeal cake made round, cut into thirds or quarters, and then baked. [ME. *fardel* quarter].

FARM (1), [fahm], *n.* a group of fields and buildings devoted to agriculture and dairy-produce. [OFr. *ferme* from MedL. *firma* fixed payment].

FARM (2), [fahm], *v.t.* to till, cultivate, grow; to care for, for a fixed sum of money; to take proceeds of, after paying a fixed sum of money; *v.i.* to be a farmer; **to f. out,** to let out the labour of, for hire; to let out proceeds in return for a fixed sum.

FARMABLE, [fahm'-abl], *adj.* that can be farmed.

FARMER, [fahm'-er], *n.* one who earns his living by tilling the soil, breeding stock, etc.; one who farms.

FARMERY, [fahm'-er-i], *n.* the buildings around a farm.

FARMHOUSE, [fahm'-hows'], *n.* a house belonging to a farm.

FARMING, [fahm'-ing], *n.* the pursuit, occupation of a farmer.

FARM-LABOURER, [fahm'-lā'-ber-er], *n.* a man employed on a farm.

FARMOST, [fah'-mōst], *adj.* most distant.

FARMSTEAD, [fahm'-sted], *n.* the buildings about a farm.

FARMYARD, [fahm'-yahd], *n.* the yard close to the farm-buildings.

FARNESS, [fah'-nes], *n.* remoteness.

FARO, [fäer'-ō], *n.* an old game of hazard played with cards. [The name *Pharaoh*].

FARRAGINOUS, [fa-raj'-in-us], *adj.* made of various materials; mixed.

FARRAGO, [fa-rā'-gō], *n.* a mixture of various materials; a medley; hodge-podge. [L. *farrago* hodge-podge].

FAR-REACHING, [fah'-rē'-ching], *adj.* extending far, carrying many consequences.

FARRIER, [fa'-ri-er], *n.* a shoe-smith, one who shoes horses; a horse-doctor; the non-commissioned officer whose duty it is to look after the horses of a cavalry regiment. [L. *ferrarius*].

FARRIERY, [fa'-ri-er-i], *n.* the trade of a farrier.

FARROW (1), [fa'-rō], *n.* a litter of young pigs. [OE. *fearh* a young pig].

FARROW (2), [fa'-rō], *v.t.* to produce, give birth to (pigs); *v.i.* to give birth to young pigs.

FARSE, [fahs], *n.* a translation from the Latin of the epistle for the day, read in some churches before the Reformation. [L. *farsa*].

FAR-SIGHTED, [fah'-sī'-tid], *adj.* able to see a great distance; foreseeing remote issues.

FAR-SIGHTEDNESS, [fah'-sī'-tid-nes], *n.* the quality of being far-sighted.

FARTHER, [fah'-THer], *adj. and adv.* more far, more remote. [*Var.* of FURTHER].

FARTHERMOST, [fah'-THer-mōst], *adj.* most remote, farthest.

FARTHEST, [fah'-THest], *adj.* most remote, most distant.

FARTHING, [fah'-THing], *n.* the fourth part of a penny; a small bronze coin worth this amount. [OE. *feorthing*].

FARTHINGALE, [fah'-THing-gāl], *n.* a hoop petticoat, a petticoat spread out by hoops formed of whalebone. [~OFr. *verdugale* from Span. *verdugado*].

FASCES, [fas'-ēz], *n.(pl.)* a bundle of rods bound together round an axe, in Roman times carried by the lictors before some high magistrate, the emblem of the Fascists in Italy. [L. *Fasces*].

FASCETS, [fas'-its], *n.(pl.)* iron implements used for conveying the bottles to the annealing oven in glass-making. [Uncert.].

FASCIA, FACIA, [fa'-shi-a], *n.* a band, fillet, stripe; (*anat.*) a thin fibrous sheath; (*arch.*) long flat surface under the eaves of a house, or more often a shop, on which the name of the shopkeeper, etc., is usually placed. [L. *fascia*].

FASCIA

FASCIAL, [fa'-shi-al], *adj.* relating to the fasces. [L. *fascialis*].

FASCIATED, [fa'-shi-ā-tid], *adj.* (*bot.*) bound with a band; growing in a close bundle.

FASCIATION, [fa'-shi-ā'-shun], *n.* (*bot.*) the quality or condition of being compressed or growing into one. [Fr. *fasciation* from L. *fasciare* to swathe].

FASCICLE, [fas'-ikl], *n.* (*bot.*) a small bundle; a close cluster; an instalment of a book, etc. [L. *fasciculus*].

FASCICLED, [fas'-ikld], *adj.* gathered together in a fascicle.

FASCICULAR, [fas-ik'-yōō-lar], *adj.* growing in clusters; gathered together in a bundle.

FASCICULARLY, [fas-ik'-yōō-ler-li], *adv.* in the shape of bundles.

FASCICULATE, [fas-ik'-yōō-lāt], *adj.* (*bot.*) growing together in bunches.

FASCICULATED, [fas-ik'-yōō-lāt-id], *adj.* (*bot.*) fasciculate.

FASCICULATELY, [fas-ik'-yōō-lāt-li], *adv.* in a fasciculated way.

FASCICULE, [fas'-ik-yōōl], *n.* a tuft. [L. *fasciculus*].

FASCICULUS, [fas-ik'-yōō-lus], *n.* (*bot.*) a little bundle; bunch; cluster. [L. *fasciculus*].

FASCINATE, [fas'-in-āt], *v.t.* to exercise a powerful influence over; to charm, attract; to deprive of will-power, so that the victim is unable to resist, escape, etc. [L. *fascinare*].

FASCINATING, [fas-in-ā'-ting], *adj.* entrancing; captivating.

FASCINATINGLY, [fas'-in-āt-ing-li], *adv.* in fascinating fashion.

FASCINATION, [fas-in-ā'-shun], *n.* the act of fascinating; the quality of attracting or enchanting others; charm; attractiveness. [L. *fascinatio*].

FASCINATOR, [fas'-in-ā-ter], *n.* a person who fascinates. [L. *fascinator*].

FASCINE, [fas-in'], *n.* a long faggot bound with withes, used for engineering and military purposes; **f. dwelling,** a prehistoric dwelling built upon layers of sticks sunk beneath the surface of a lake. [L. *fascina*].

FASCIOLARIA, [fas'-i-ōl-äer'-i-a], *n.* the genus of gastropods of which the tulip-shells are members.

FASCISM, [fash'-izm], *n.* the political creed of the Fascists. [It. *Fascismo*].

FASCIST, [fash'-ist], *n.* a member of the Nationalist anti-Communist, and quasi-syndicalist movement in Italy, which arose after the first World War under the dictatorship of Benito Mussolini; a member of an anti-Communist party with similar aims in any other country; in England, a sympathiser with a similar movement founded by Sir Oswald Mosley. [It. *fascista*].

FASH, [fash], *v.t.* to vex; annoy; trouble; bother; upset. [OFr. *fascher*].

FASHION (1), [fash'-un], *n.* form; shape; pattern; style; manner; the prevailing mode of dress; the prevailing custom or usage; **after a f.,** somehow, anyhow, not well. [AFr. *fachon* from L. *factio*].

FASHION (2), [fash'-un], *v.t.* to shape, make.

FASHIONABLE, [fash'-un-abl], *adj.* following the prevailing mode or usage; stylish, smart; characteristic of, approved by, people of fashion.

FASHIONABLENESS, [fash'-un-abl-nes], *n.* the quality of being fashionable.

FASHIONABLY, [fash'-un-ab-li], *adv.* in a fashionable way.

FASHIONER, [fash'-un-er], *n.* one who fashions.

FASHIONIST, [fash'-un-ist], *n.* a stickler for fashion.

FASHIONLESS, [fash'-un-les], *adj.* lacking fashion.

FASHION-MONGER, [fash'-un-mung'-ger], *n.* one who assiduously studies and follows the fashion.

FASHION-MONGERING, [fash'-un-mung'-ger-ing], *n.* a slavish devotion to fashion.

FASHIOUS, [fash'-us], *adj.* irritating, vexatious. [OFr. *fascheux*].

FAST (1), [fahst], *n.* the act of fasting; the time appointed for fasting. [ME. *faste*].

FAST (2), [fahst], *adj.* firm, secure; firmly attached, steady; unfading; fixed; rapid, quick; inducing rapid motion; dissipated. [OE. *fæst*].

FAST (3), [fahst], *adv.* firmly, securely, fixedly; tightly; soundly (of sleep); rapidly, quickly.

FAST (4), [fahst], *v.i.* to abstain from eating, *esp.* as a religious observance; to go without food. [OE. *fæstan*].

FAST-DAY, [fahst'-dā'], *n.* a day appointed for a fast; in Scotland, a day originally of fasting as a preparation for communion.

FASTEN, [fah'-sen], *v.t. and i.* to attach, fix, tie, bind; to become or be capable of becoming fastened or fixed; **to f. off,** to secure a thread with a knot, etc.; **to f. on,** to seize upon, single out for emphasis (*esp.* in order to pick a quarrel, or criticize). [OE. *fæstnian*].

FASTENER, [fahs'-(e)n-er], *n.* that which fastens (garments).

FASTENING, [fah'-sen-ing], *n.* anything that fastens.

FASTEN'S-EEN, [fahst'-enz-ēn'], *n.* Shrove Tuesday. [OE. *fæstenes efn* the eve of fasting].

FAST-HANDED, [fahst'-han'-did], *adj.* close-fisted; mean.

FASTI, [fas'-tī], *n.* the Roman calendar, which announced the days for festivals, courts, etc. [L. *fasti*].

FASTIDIOUS, [fas-tid'-i-us], *adj.* squeamish; particular; hard to please. [L. *fastidiosus*].

FASTIDIOUSLY, [fas-tid'-i-us-li], *adv.* in a fastidious way.

FASTIDIOUSNESS, [fas-tid'-i-us-nes], *n.* the quality or state of being fastidious.

FASTIGIATE, [fas-tij'-i-āt], *adj.* (*bot.*) tapering to a point; cone-shaped.

FASTIGIUM, [fas-tij'-i-um], *n.* the apex, or ridge of a house, gable or pediment. [L. *fastigium*].

FASTIGIUM

FASTING, [fahst'-ing], *n.* the act of one who fasts.

FASTISH, [fahst'-ish], *adj.* somewhat fast.

FASTNESS, [fahst'-nes], *n.* a stronghold, a fortified place; the quality of being fast.

FAT (1), [fat], *n.* an oily substance that makes up the fat parts of animal bodies; the fat part of anything; (*fig.*) the best, choicest part of anything; (*print.*) copy easy and profitable for the compositor; (*theatre*) the part of a role that shows off an actor to best advantage; (*chem.*) a compound of glycerin with an acid; **the f. is in the fire,** there's going to be trouble soon; **to live on the f. of the land,** to live in comfort and prosperity; **f. lime,** nearly pure lime, that slakes easily. [OE. *fætt*].

FAT (2), [fat], *n.* a measure of nine bushels; another name for a vat. [*Var.* of VAT].

FAT (3), [fat], *adj.* corpulent, obese; well fed; plump; thick, substantial, heavy; prosperous, thriving; oily, greasy; fertile, rich, fruitful; sticky; bituminous; (*print.*) easy to set up, and well paid; (*fig.*) dull, stupid, slow, sluggish; **a f. lot,** (*coll.*) a great deal, usually used sarcastically for hardly any; **to cut up f.,** to leave a lot of money. [OE. *fætt*].

FAT (4), [fat], *v.t.* to fatten, feed up, to make fat; to cover, smear with fat; *v.i.* to grow fat. [OE. *fættian*].

FATAL, [fātl], *adj.* causing death or ruin, deadly, disastrous; fated, fateful. [L. *fatalis* decreed by fate, deadly].

FATALISM, [fā'-tal-izm], *n.* the doctrine or belief that all events are predetermined by the arbitrary decrees of God or fate; submission to all that happens as predetermined.

FATALIST, [fā'-tal-ist], *n.* one who believes in fatalism.

FATALISTIC, [fā-tal-ist'-ik], *adj.* like a fatalist; involving fatalism.

FATALISTICALLY, [fā'-tal-ist'-ik-al-i], *adv.* in a fatalistic fashion.

FATALITY, [fat-al'-it-i], *n.* the inevitable course of events; subjection to fate; supremacy of fate; predetermined disaster; calamity; death by accident, war, or violence of any kind. [LL. *fatalitas*].

FATALLY, [fā'-tal-i], *adv.* so as to prove fatal; so as to cause death.

FATALNESS, [fā'-tal-nes], *n.* the state or quality of being fatal; fatality.

FAT-BRAINED, [fat'-brānd'], *adj.* slow-witted, dull of apprehension.

FATE (1), [fāt], *n.* the power that orders events beforehand from eternity; destiny, fortune; that which must inevitably happen; that which is predestined; one's ultimate appointed condition; calamity, death, destruction; **the Fates,** (*myth.*) the three goddesses supposed by the ancients to preside over the destinies of men. [L. *fatum*].

FATE (2), [fāt], *v.t.* to preordain, predestine.

FATED, [fā'-tid], *adj.* destined, *esp.* to disaster.

FATEFUL, [fāt'-fool'], *adj.* having fatal power; producing fatal events; unalterable, irrevocable.

FATEFULLY, [fāt'-fool-i], *adv.* in a fateful way.

FATEFULNESS, [fāt'-fool-nes], *n.* the quality of being fateful.

FAT-HEAD, [fat'-hed], *n.* dolt, stupid fellow.

FAT-HEADED, [fat'-hed'-id], *adj.* (*coll.*) having a fat head; crassly stupid.

FAT-HEN, [fat'-hen'], *n.* popular name for the plant white goosefoot, *Chenopodium album*, and several others.

FATHER (1), [fah'-THer], *n.* male parent, begetter; ancestor, progenitor; originator, creator, designer; early leader; one who deserves filial respect and veneration; doyen; mode of addressing a priest or confessor; **the F.,** the First Person of the Trinity; **the Holy F.,** the Pope; **F. of the faithful,** a title of a Caliph; **the F. of lies,** the devil, Satan; **Fathers of the Church,** the early Christian writers; **the Pilgrim Fathers,** those who sailed over to settle in America in the *Mayflower* in 1620; **Conscript Fathers,** members of the Roman Senate. [OE. *fæder*].

FATHER (2), [fah-THer], *v.t. and i.* to beget; to be a father to; to behave like a father to; to treat with paternal care, cherish as a father; **to f. on,** to ascribe paternity to.

FATHERHOOD, [fah-THer-hood], *n.* the condition of being a father; the character or authority of a father.

FATHER-IN-LAW, [fah'-THer-in-law], *n.* the father of a person's husband or wife.

FATHERLAND, [fah'-THer-land'], *n.* the land of one's fathers; one's native country.

FATHER-LASHER, [fah'-THer-lash'-er], *n.* a small fish, the sea bull-head, *Cottus scorpius*, related to the river bull-head or miller's thumb, *Cottus gobio*.

FATHERLESS, [fah'-THer-les], *adj.* having no father living; without a known author.

FATHERLESSNESS, [fah'-THer-les-nes], *n.* the state of being fatherless.

FATHERLINESS, [fah'-THer-li-nes], *n.* fatherly kindness; the benevolent feelings appropriate to a father.

FATHER-LONGLEGS, [fah'-THer-long'-legz], *n.* name for the crane-fly, *Tipula oleracea*, or daddy-longlegs.

FATHERLY, [fah'-THer-li], *adj.* paternal; like a father; kind, affectionate; protective.

FATHERSHIP, [fah'-THer-ship], *n.* the state or dignity of being a father.

FATHOM (1), [faTHm], *n.* a nautical and mining measure of depth, 6 ft.; measure of wood 6 ft. square of any length; (*fig.*) depth, profundity; penetration. [OE. *fæthm*].

FATHOM (2), [faTHm], *v.t.* to sound, measure (water); (*fig.*) to get to the bottom of; penetrate; understand; solve; (*archaic*) embrace, encompass with the arms. [OE. *fæthmian* to embrace].

FATHOMABLE, [faTH'-um-abl], *adj.* able to be fathomed.

FATHOMLESS, [faTH'-um-les], *adj.* that cannot be fathomed.

FATIDICAL, [fat-id'-ikl], *adj.* (*rare*) interpreting fate or destiny; prophetic. [L. *fatidicus*].

FATIDICALLY, [fat-id'-ik-al-i], *adv.* in a fatidical way.

FATIGUE (1), [fat-ēg'], *n.* exhaustion, weariness after exertion of some kind; (of metal) weakness after blows or strain; a task or exertion causing weariness; duties carried out by soldiers, in addition to military routine. [Fr. *fatigue*].

FATIGUE (2), [fat-ēg'], *v.t.* to make weary; (of metal) to weaken by repeated blows or strain. [L. *fatigare*].

FATIGUELESS, [fat-ēg'-les], *adj.* untiring, unwearied.

FATIGUING, [fat-ēg'-ing], *adj.* exhausting, tiring.

FATIGUINGLY, [fat-ēg'-ing-li], *adv.* in a fatiguing fashion.

FATIMITES, [fat'-im-its], *n.(pl.)* a dynasty of Eastern rulers descended from Fatima, the daughter of Mohammed, and ruling over a large part of Northern Africa and Syria, 909-1175. [*Fatima*].

FATISCENCE, [fat-is'-ents], *n.* (*geol.*) a gap or opening; the condition of being fatiscent.

FATISCENT, [fat-is'-ent], *adj.* having chinks or clefts. [L. *fatiscens*].

FATLING, [fat'-ling], *n.* a young animal fattened for the table; any fat animal.

FATLUTE, [fat'-lōōt], *n.* a preparation of linseed oil and pipeclay for filling joints.

FATLY, [fat'-li], *adv.* coarsely, grossly; greasily.

FATNESS, [fat'-nes], *n.* the condition of being fat; richness; fruitfulness; abundance.

FATTED, [fat'-id], *adj.* fattened.

FATTEN, [fatn], *v.t.* to make fat, *esp.* for slaughtering; to make more fertile; *v.i.* to grow fat.

FATTENER, [fat'-en-er], *n.* one who, or that which, fattens.

FATTINESS, [fat'-in-es], *n.* the quality of being fatty.

FATTISH, [fat'-ish], *adj.* rather fat.

FATTY (1), [fat'-i], *n.* familiar and somewhat contemptuous mode of addressing a corpulent person.

FATTY (2), [fat'-i], *adj.* greasy, like or consisting of fat; having unhealthy deposits of fat.

FATUITOUS, [fat-yōō'-it-us]; *adj.* weak in mind; silly; fatuous; illusory.

FATUITY, [fat-yōō'-it-i], *n.* weakness of intellect; foolishness. [L. *fatuitas*].

FATUOUS, [fat'-yōō-us], *adj.* silly, foolish, fatuitous. [L. *fatuus*].

FATUOUSLY, [fat'-yōō-us-li], *adv.* in a fatuous way.

FATUOUSNESS, [fat'-yōō-us-nes], *n.* the quality of being fatuous.

FAT-WITTED, [fat'-wit'-id], *adj.* stupid.

FAUBOURG, [fō'-bōōerg], *n.* an outlying district or suburb in French cities, or what was originally such. [Fr. *faubourg*].

FAUCAL, [fawkl], *adj.* guttural; uttered deep in the throat; pertaining to the fauces.

FAUCES, [faw'-sēz], *n.(pl.)* the upper portion of the throat, the passage from the root of the tongue to the gullet. [L. *fauces*].

FAUCET, [faw'-set], *n.* a tap; a tube inserted in a cask for extracting the liquid. [Fr. *fausset*].

FAUGH, [faw], *int.* expressing contempt, disgust, or abhorrence.

FAULT (1), [fawlt], *n.* blemish, imperfection; failing, error; offence, wrongdoing; (*geol.*) a displacement of the strata; (*hunting*) the loss of the scent; (*tennis*) failure to serve the ball over the net and into the proper court; **to find f. with**, to criticize adversely, nag. [OFr. *faute*].

FAULT (2), [fawlt], *v.t. and i.* (*geol.*) to displace strata; to show a displacement of strata; (*tennis*) to serve a fault.

FAULTED, [fawlt'-id], *adj.* (*geol.*) having a fault, displaced.

FAULTER, [fawlt'-er], *n.* one who defaults, an offender.

FAULTFINDER, [fawlt'-fīnd'-er], *n.* one given to finding fault.

FAULTFUL, [fawlt'-fŏŏl], *adj.* full of mistakes; faulty.

FAULTILY, [fawlt'-il-i], *adv.* in a faulty way.

FAULTINESS, [fawlt'-i-nes], *n.* the condition or quality of being faulty.

FAULTLESS, [fawlt'-les], *adj.* with no fault or blemish.

FAULTLESSLY, [fawlt'-les-li], *adv.* in a faultless way.

FAULTLESSNESS, [fawlt'-les-nes], *n.* freedom from faults or blemishes.

FAULTY, [fawl'-ti], *adj.* having faults; imperfect; defective; wrong; inaccurate.

FAUN, [fawn], *n.* a Latin woodland deity, having a tail and horns. [L. *Faunus*].

FAUN

FAUNA, [fawn'-a], *n.(pl.)* the animal life of any district or geological period. [L. *Fauna* a Roman goddess].

FAUNISTIC, [fawn-ist'-ik], *adj.* pertaining to fauna or to a faunist.

FAUSSE-BRAYE, [fōs'-brā], *n.* (*fort.*) a mound of earth cast up around a rampart. [Fr. *fausse-braie*].

FAUTEUIL, [fō'-til, fō-tu(r)-ē], *n.* an arm-chair; a seat in the stalls at the theatre. [Fr. *fauteuil* arm-chair].

FAUVETTE, [fō-vet'], *n.* the garden warbler *Sylvia hortensis*. [Fr. *fauvette*].

FAUX PAS, [fō'-pah'], *n.* a false step; a tactless remark or action. [Fr. from *faux* false and *pas* step].

FAVEOLATE, [fav-ē'-ō-lāt], *adj.* (*bot.*) resembling a honeycomb.

FAVILLOUS, [fav-il'-us], *adj.* consisting of or relating to ashes; resembling ashes. [L. *favilla* ashes].

FAVONIAN, [fav-ōn'-yan], *adj.* relating to the west wind. [L. *Favonius* the west wind].

FAVOSE, [fav-ōs'], *adj.* resembling a honeycomb. [L. *favus* honeycomb].

FAVOSITES, [fav-ō-sī'-tez], *n.* a fossil coral with a minute honeycomb structure. [L. *favus* honeycomb].

FAVOUR (1), [fā'-vur], *n.* goodwill; an act of goodwill; undue kindness; preference; partiality; something worn or given as a sign of favour; **to curry f.**, to insinuate oneself into the good graces of someone; **in f. of**, in support of; to the account of; **without fear or f.**, boldly and impartially. [L. *favor*].

FAVOUR (2), [fā'-vur], *v.t.* to show goodwill towards; to prefer; to treat with undue kindness; to support, help; to facilitate; to prove advantageous to.

FAVOURABLE, [fā'-vur-abl], *adj.* showing favour or goodwill; propitious; conducive; kindly, friendly. [L. *favorabilis*].

FAVOURABLENESS, [fā'-vur-abl-nes], *n.* the quality of being favourable.

FAVOURABLY, [fā'-vur-ab-li], *adv.* in a favourable way.

FAVOUREDNESS, [fā'-vurd-nes], *n.* the state of being well- or ill-favoured.

FAVOURER, [fā'-ver-rer], *n.* person who, or that which favours.

FAVOURING, [fā'-vur-ing], *adj.* wishing well to; promoting; showing partiality to.

FAVOURINGLY, [fā'-vur-ing-li], *adv.* in a partial way, so as to favour.

FAVOURITE (1), [fā'-vur-it], *n.* a person or thing regarded with especial favour; the competitor generally expected to win. [OFr. *favorit* favoured].

FAVOURITE (2), [fā'-vur-it], *adj.* held in particular favour or esteem, most preferred.

FAVOURITISM, [fā'-vur-it-izm], *n.* the habit of having, and discriminating to, the advantage of, favourites; bias, partiality.

FAVOURLESS, [fā'-vur-les], *adj.* not looked on with favour; unpatronized.

FAVUS, [fā'-vus], *n.* a disease of the scalp causing incrustations resembling a honeycomb. [L. *favus* honeycomb].

FAWN (1), [fawn], *n.* a young deer, a fallow deer of the first year; a light yellowish-brown. [OFr. *faon*].

FAWN (2), [fawn], *adj.* of the colour of a fawn, light yellowish-brown.

FAWN (3), [fawn], *v.i.* to bring forth, give birth to, a fawn.

FAWN (4), [fawn], *v.i.* (of animals) to show delight or affection by wagging the tail, pawing, etc.; to cringe, flatter servilely in order to gain favour. [OE. *fagenian* to be glad].

FAWNER, [fawn'-er], *n.* one who fawns.

FAWNING, [fawn'-ing], *n.* servile cringing and flattery; gross flattery to obtain favours.

FAWNINGLY, [fawn'-ing-li], *adv.* in a servile manner.

FAY (1), [fā], *n.* name for a fairy. [OFr. *fae*].

FAY (2), [fā], *v.t.* to fit two pieces of wood closely together, in shipbuilding; *v.i.* to fit together very closely. [OE. *fegan*].

FAYALITE, [fā'-yal-it], *n.* a mineral composed of silicate of iron with other bases. [*Fayal* in the Azores where discovered].

FAYENCE, see FAIENCE.

FAYING, [fā-ing], *n.* (*naut.*) the joining of two pieces so closely that no intervening space occurs.

FEABERRY, [fē'-be-ri], *n.* a name for the gooseberry. [Uncert.].

FEAL (1), [fēl], *n.* turf, as used for making dikes or fences.

FEAL (2), [fēl], *adj.* faithful; **f. and leal**, faithful and loyal to the feudal lord; **f. homages**, faithful vassals. [OFr. *feal* faithful].

FEALTY, [fē'-al-ti], *n.* the loyalty of a feudal vassal to his lord. [OFr. *feaulté* fidelity].

FEAR (1), [fēer], *n.* mental distress in the presence of real or imagined danger; terror, cowardice; apprehension for the future; worry, anxiety; a grave probability that the unpleasant will occur; profound and submissive respect. [OE. *fær*].

FEAR (2), [fēer], *v.t.* to be afraid of; to revere, hold in

awe; to shrink from; to have an uneasy anticipation of; *v.i.* to be afraid. [OE. *færan* to fear].
FEARFUL, [fēer'-fōōl], *adj.* filled with fear, frightened, timid; anxious; terrible, inspiring fear; (*coll.*) annoying, extreme.
FEARFULLY, [fēer'-fōōl-i], *adv.* in a fearful fashion; (*coll.*) very.
FEARFULNESS, [fēer'-fōōl-nes], *n.* condition of being fearful.
FEARLESS, [fēer'-les], *adj.* without fear; intrepid.
FEARLESSLY, [fēer'-les-li], *adv.* in a fearless way.
FEARLESSNESS, [fēer'-les-nes], *n.* the quality of being fearless.
FEARNOUGHT, [fēer'-nawt], *n.* a thick woollen material for lining port-holes in ships, and other purposes.
FEARSOME, [fēer'-sum], *adj.* inspiring fear and awe, terrible, appalling.
FEARSOMELY, [fēer'-sum-li], *adv.* in a fearsome manner.
FEARSOMENESS, [fēer'-sum-nes], *n.* the state or quality of being fearsome.
FEASIBILITY, [fē-zib-il'-it-i], *n.* the quality of being feasible.
FEASIBLE, [fē'-zibl], *adj.* that may be done, practicable. [OFr. *faisible*].
FEASIBLENESS, [fē'-zibl-nes], *n.* feasibility.
FEASIBLY, [fē'-zib-li], *adv.* possibly, practicably.
FEAST (1), [fēst], *n.* a religious festival of rejoicing; joyful anniversary; a banquet, a sumptuous meal; (*fig.*) a plentiful and enjoyable quantity of anything; something very gratifying to the senses or mind; **movable f.,** a religious festival that has no fixed date. [OFr. *feste*].
FEAST (2), [fēst], *v.t.* to regale; to pass, spend, in feasting; *v.i.* to take part in, partake of, a feast; to fare sumptuously, regale oneself.
FEAST-DAY, [fēst'-dā'], *n.* a day of feasting; a festival, holiday.
FEASTER, [fēst'-er], *n.* one who fares sumptuously or entertains magnificently.
FEASTING, [fēst'-ing], *n.* eating sumptuously; rejoicing as at a feast.
FEAST-RITE, [fēst'-rīt], *n.* a rite or custom observed at feasts.
FEAT, [fēt], *n.* an act or deed, *esp.* one demanding extraordinary strength, skill, or courage. [OFr. *feit* from L. *factum* a deed].
FEATHER (1), [feTH'-er], *n.* an appendage consisting of a quill, shaft, and two sets of barbs, growing with many others on a bird's skin, as fur on a beast; a plume; plumage; something like, light as, a feather; **birds of a f.,** people of the same kind; **to show the white f.,** to behave like, be, a coward; **a f. in one's cap,** a deed one is proud of and which will raise one's standing with other people. [OE. *fether*].
FEATHER (2), [feTH'-er], *v.t.* to cover, line, adorn, with feathers; (*rowing*) to turn (the oar) so that it passes through the air edgeways; (*shooting*) to shoot the feathers off (a bird) without killing; *v.i.* to move like a feather; to turn the oar so that it passes through the air edgeways; (*hunting*) of a hound, to quiver while seeking a scent; **to f. one's nest,** to get rich, enrich oneself. [OE. *fitherian*].
FEATHER-BED, [feTH'-er-bed'], *n.* a mattress stuffed with feathers.
FEATHER-BOARDING, [feTH'-er-bawd'-ing], *n.* weather-boarding in which the edge of one board overlaps that of the next, like the feathers of a bird.

FEATHER-BOARDING

FEATHER-BRAINED, [feTH'-er-brānd'], *adj.* heedless, irresponsible.
FEATHERED, [feTH'-erd], *adj.* furnished, covered with, feathers; winged; smoothed.
FEATHER-EDGE, [feTH'-er-ej], *n.* an edge of a board that is thinner than the other.
FEATHER-EDGED, [feTH'-er-ejd'], *adj.* with one edge thinner than the other.
FEATHERFEW, [feTH'-er-few'], *n.* name for the feverfew, *Matricaria Parthenium.* [Uncert.].
FEATHER-FLOWERS, [feTH'-er-flow'-erz], *n.(pl.)* flowers made of feathers.
FEATHERFOIL, [feTH'-er-foil'], *n.* name for the water-violet, *Hottonia palustris.* [FEATHER (1) and ME *foil* leaf].
FEATHER-GRASS, [feTH'-er-grahs'], *n.* a kind of grass with narrow, single-flowered spikelets, *Stipa pennata.*
FEATHERINESS, [feTH'-er-i-nes], *n.* the state or quality of being feathery.
FEATHERING (1), [feTH'-er-ing], *n.* the act of turning the blade of an oar or scull to the horizontal as it leaves the water; (*pl.*) (*arch.*) ornamental cusps formed by the junction of small arcs.
FEATHERING (2), [feTH'-er-ing], *adj.* (*mech.*) acting in the same way as an oar when feathering.
FEATHERLESS, [feTH'-er-les], *adj.* without feathers; unfledged.
FEATHER-MAN, [feTH'-er-man], *n.* a man who deals in feathers.
FEATHER-SHOT, [feTH'-er-shot'], *n.* a popular name for copper, from the shape it assumes when dropped molten into cold water.
FEATHER-SPRAY, [feTH'-er-sprā'], *n.* the feathery spray cast up by the cut-water of a boat when sailing rapidly.
FEATHERSTAR, [feTH'-er-stah(r)'], *n.* name for the common crinoid, *Antedon rosaceus.*
FEATHERSTITCH, [feTH'-er-stich'], *n.* a kind of embroidery in which the stitches are made in a series of branching zigzags.
FEATHER-VEINED, [feTH'-er-vānd'], *adj.* (*bot.*) having veins branching off from the midrib like the parts of a feather.
FEATHERWEIGHT, [feTH'-er-wāt'], *n.* anything very light; a jockey weighing not more than 4 st. 7 lb.; a boxer weighing not more than 9 st.
FEATHERY, [feTH'-er-i], *adj.* covered with feathers; looking like feathers.
FEATLY, [fēt'-li], *adv.* neatly; skilfully.
FEATNESS, [fēt'-nes], *n.* neatness; adroitness.
FEATURE (1), [fē'-chur], *n.* a part of the face; characteristic; trait; part that arrests attention. [OFr. *faiture*].
FEATURE (2), [fē'-chur], *adj.* **f. film,** the main film of a cinema programme.
FEATURE (3), [fē'-chur], *v.t.* to characterize, be the distinctive mark of; to show the prominent points of; to show on the cinema screen.
FEATURED, [fē'-churd], *adj.* having a certain cast of feature; shaped; figured in a film.
FEATURELESS, [fē'-chur-les], *adj.* without distinctive features.
FEATURELY, [fē'-chur-li], *adj.* good-featured; rather good-looking.
FEBRICULA, [feb-rik'-yōō-la], *n.* a slight fever of no specified type, lasting only a short time. [L. *febricula*].
FEBRICULOSE, [feb-rik'-yōō-lōs], *adj.* (*med.*) febrile, feverish. [L. *febriculosus*].
FEBRICULOSITY, [feb-rik'-yōō-los'-it-i], *n.* (*med.*) the state of being febriculose.
FEBRIFACIENT, [feb'-ri-fā'-shent], *adj.* inducing, bringing on, fever. [L. *febris* fever and *faciens* making].
FEBRIFEROUS, [feb-rif'-er-us], *adj.* inducing fever. [L. *febris* fever and *ferre* to bear].
FEBRIFIC, [feb-rif'-ik], *adj.* inducing fever; feverish. [Fr. *febrifique*].
FEBRIFUGAL, [feb'-rif-ewgl'], *adj.* possessing the quality of curing fever.
FEBRIFUGE, [feb'-rif-ewj'], *n.* a medicine that cures fever. [Fr. *fébrifuge*].
FEBRILE, [fe'-brīl], *adj.* pertaining to, or indicating, fever; feverish. [L. *febrilis*].
FEBRONIANISM, [feb-rō'-ni-an-izm], *n.* a heresy in the R.C. Church maintaining certain ecclesiastical liberties against papal claims. [Justinus *Febronius*, the assumed name of von Hontheim of Treves].
FEBRUARY, [feb'-rōō-a-ri], *n.* the second month of the year; **fair maids of F.,** a name for snowdrops. [L. *februarius*].
FEBRUATION, [feb'-rōō-ā'-shun], *n.* expiation by purification; purification. [L. *februatio*].
FECAL, see FAECAL.
FECES, see FAECES.
FECIAL, see FETIAL (1).
FECIT, [fē'-sit], *v.* a word inscribed on a monument, building or other work after the name of the man who carried out the work or designed it. [L. *fecit* he made].
FECKLESS, [fek'-les], *adj.* reckless, careless.
FECKLESSNESS, [fek'-les-nes], *n.* the quality of being feckless.
FECKLY, [fek'-li], *adv.* efficiently, effectually.
FECULA, [fek'-yōō-la], *n.* the sediment of vegetable substances, *esp.* starch; sediment, dregs. [L. *faecula* crust of wine].

FECULENCE, [fek'-yōō-lents], *n*. the state of being feculent; feculent matter. [L. *faeculentia* dregs].
FECULENCY, [fek'-yōō-len-si], *n*. feculence.
FECULENT, [fek'-yōō-lent], *adj*. fetid, muddy. [L. *faeculentus*].
FECULUM, [fek'-yōō-lum], *n*. a dry, dusty substance procured from plants.
FECUND, [fē'-kund, fek'-und], *adj*. fruitful; fertile; prolific. [L. *fecundus*].
FECUNDATE, [fē'-kun-dāt, fek'-un-dāt], *v.t.* to make fruitful or prolific; to impregnate; to fertilize. [L. *fecundare*].
FECUNDATION, [fē'-kun-dā'-shun, fek'-un-dā'-shun], *n*. the act of making fruitful or prolific; impregnation; fertilization.
FECUNDITY, [fē-kun'-dit-i, fek-un'-dit-i], *n*. fruitfulness; fertility. [L. *fecunditas*].
FED, [fed], *pret. and p.pt.* of FEED; **f. up**, sated, having had more than enough (of), sick (of). [ME. *fedde*].
FEDELINI, [fe'-de-lē'-ni], *n*. a paste-like pipe. [It. *fedelini*].
FEDERACY, [fed'-er-as-i], *n*. a federation.
FEDERAL (1), [fed'-er-al], *n*. a supporter of the federal principle in the constitution of the United States; a member of a federal state.
FEDERAL (2), [fed'-er-al], *adj*. relating to the political system by which several internally independent states unite under a central government for the management of interests or affairs that concern them all, such as foreign policy; (*U.S. hist.*) of the Northern party in the Civil War; in favour of central government; (*theol.*) relating to, founded on, the doctrine of Covenants. [Fr. *fédéral*].
FEDERALISM, [fed'-er-al-izm], *n*. the principles of the federalists; federal union as a political policy or theory. [Fr. *fédéralisme*].
FEDERALIST, [fed'-er-al-ist], *n*. one who supports the doctrine of federal union, *esp*. of the United States of America. [Fr. *fédéraliste*].
FEDERALIZE, [fed'-er-al-īz], *v.t.* to unite, league (independent states) together under a federal government.
FEDERATE (1), [fed'-er-āt], *adj*. joined in confederacy, united under a federal government.
FEDERATE (2), [fed'-er-āt], *v.t. and i.* to unite under a federal government. [L. *foederare* to establish by treaty].
FEDERATION, [fed'-er-ā'-shun], *n*. the act of federating; the state of being federated; a group of independent states united under a federal government; a league or confederation. [L. *foederatio*].
FEDERATIVE, [fed'-er-at-iv], *adj*. relating to federation; federal.
FEE (1), [fē], *n*. a feudal benefice; inherited estate; sum payable to a public officer, a physician, lawyer, etc., for his services; entrance-money for a club, society, examination, etc.; (*pl*.) amount payable each term to a school or college. [ME. *fee*].
FEE (2), [fē], *v.t.* to pay a fee to, to hire.
FEEBLE, [fēbl], *adj*. weak; unstable; infirm; irresolute; dim, indistinct. [OFr. *feble* from L. *flebilis* lamentable].
FEEBLE-MINDED, [fēbl'-mīnd'-id], *adj*. of weak intellect; deficient in intelligence.
FEEBLE-MINDEDNESS, [fēbl'-mīnd'-id-nes], *n*. the condition of being feeble-minded.
FEEBLENESS, [fēbl'-nes], *n*. the condition of being feeble.
FEEBLISH, [fēbl'-ish], *adj*. not very strong, rather feeble.
FEEBLY, [fē'-bli], *adv*. in a feeble way.
FEED (1), [fēd], *n*. the act of feeding, of taking or giving food; green crops; horse's allowance of food; fodder; a meal; the fuelling, feeding, of a machine; the apparatus that does this; the charge of a gun; the man who in a comedy act supplies the comedian with cues, etc.; **to be off one's f.**, to have no appetite.
FEED (2), (**fed**), [fēd], *v.t.* to supply with food; to satisfy, gratify; serve as food for; to keep supplied; to supply with material; *v.i.* to eat, take food; to graze. [OE. *fedan*].
FEEDER, [fē'-der], *n*. one who or that which feeds; feeding apparatus in a machine; a feeding-bottle for a child; a child's bib; a tributary of a larger river; the person who throws the ball to the striker in such games as rounders.
FEEDING, [fē'-ding], *adj*. that supplies with food, or material; (*slang*) annoying, tiresome, that makes one fed up; **a f. storm**, a storm that constantly increases in intensity.
FEED-PIPE, [fēd'-pīp'], *n*. the pipe that supplies a machine with material.
FEED-PUMP, [fēd'-pump'], *n*. a pump supplying a machine with material.
FEE-FARM, [fē'-fahm'], *n*. land held without homage, fealty, or other condition except as stipulated in the feoffment.
FEEL (1), [fēl], *n*. sense of touch; sensation characteristic of something; intuitive understanding.
FEEL (2), [fēl], *v.t.* to perceive, become aware of, by touch; to handle, explore, test by touch; to experience; to be affected, moved by; to be conscious of; *v.i.* to produce a sensation of being; to have the sense of touch; to be physically or emotionally aware; **to f. for someone**, to have sympathy with someone; **to f. in one's bones**, to have a deep conviction; **to f. one's way**, to grope one's way, go carefully. [OE. *felan*].
FEELER, [fēl'-er], *n*. an organ found on the heads of certain insects; (*fig*.) a remark uttered tentatively in order to sound the opinions of others, a hint.

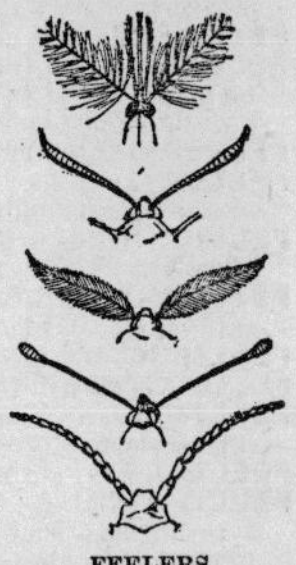
FEELERS

FEELER-GAUGE, [fēl'-er-gāj'], *n*. wires of varying and known thickness used for determining the size of extremely small spaces or apertures in mechanical engines, etc., by insertion.
FEELING, [fēl'-ing], *n*. the act of perceiving or exploring by touch; the sense of touch; physical sensation, as of pleasure or pain; emotion; tenderness; sensibility; sentiment; emotional effect produced by a work of art.
FEELINGLY, [fēl'-ing-li], *adv*. in a feeling manner, sympathetically.
FEE-SIMPLE, [fē'-simpl'], *n*. an estate held by a person in his own right, freehold, absolute property.
FEET, [fēt], *pl*. of FOOT (1). [OE. *fēt*].
FEE-TAIL, [fē'-tāl'], *n*. an estate entailed to the possessor's heirs, and thus held with limitation.
FEETLESS, [fēt-les], *adj*. having no feet.
FEEZE, [fēz], *v.t.* to turn or twist as when driving a screw; to screw. [OE. *fesian* to drive].
FEHMGERICHT, see VEHMGERICHT.
FEHMIC, see VEHMIC.
FEIGN, [fān], *v.t.* to invent, fabricate; pretend, sham; imagine; forge; *v.i.* to sham, pretend; dissimulate. [ME. *feinen* from OFr. *feindre* from L. *fingere* to form].
FEIGNED, [fānd], *adj*. pretended; false; counterfeited; **f. issue**, (*leg*.) an action brought merely for the sake of trying a question of right.
FEIGNEDLY, [fā'-ned-li], *adv*. in pretence; insincerely.
FEIGNEDNESS, [fānd'-nes], *n*. the condition of being feigned.
FEIGNING, [fān'-ing], *n*. deception; pretence.
FEIGNINGLY, [fān'-ing-li], *adv*. with false appearance; insincerely.
FEINT (1), [fānt], *n*. a sham attack intended to outwit an opponent; false show; pretence. [Fr. *feinte*].
FEINT (2), [fānt], *adj*. **f. lines**, faintly marked lines on paper to guide the writing. [*Var*. of FAINT (2)].
FEINT (3), [fānt], *v.i.* to make a sham attack in order to deceive an enemy or opponent.
FELDSPAR, see FELSPAR.
FELDSPATHIC, [feld-spath'-ik], *adj*. relating to felspar; consisting of felspar.
FELDSPATHOSE, [feld-spath'-ōs], *adj*. containing felspar.
FELICIDE, [fēl'-is-īd], *n*. a killer of cats. [L. *felis* cat and *cida* murderer].
FELICIFIC, [fel-is-if'-ik], *adj*. producing, promoting, happiness. [L. *felicificus*].
FELICITATE, [fel-is'-it-āt], *v.t.* to congratulate; (*rare*) to make glad. [L. *felicitare*].
FELICITATION, [fel-is-it-ā'-shun], *n*. the act of felicitating, congratulation.
FELICITATOR, [fel-is'-it-ā-ter], *n*. one who felicitates.
FELICITOUS, [fel-is'-it-us], *adj*. very happy; fortunate; ingenious; most appropriate.
FELICITOUSLY, [fel-is'-it-us-li], *adv*. in a felicitous way.
FELICITOUSNESS, [fel-is'-it-us-nes], *n*. the condition of being felicitous.
FELICITY, [fel-is'-it-i], *n*. the state of being intensely happy; contentment; blissfulness; appropriateness, tact. [L. *felicitas*].

FELID, [fē'-lid], *n.* a member of the cat family of animals, the *Felidae*.
FELINE (1), [fē'-lin], *n.* a member of the cat family of animals.
FELINE (2), [fē'-līn], *adj.* pertaining to cats or the cat family; cat-like; catty. [L. *felinus*].
FELINITY, [fē-lin'-it-i], *n.* the quality of being feline; cattishness.
FELL (1), [fel], *n.* the hide of an animal; a hem laid level with the cloth. [OE. *fel*].
FELL (2), [fel], *n.* a mountain side; a barren or rocky hill. [~OIcel. *fiall*].
FELL (3), [fel], *adj.* cruel; fierce; ruthless; savage. [OFr. *fel*].
FELL (4), [fel], *v.t.* to cause to fall; to bring down (*esp.* trees) by cutting or striking. [OE. *fellan*].
FELL (5), [fel], *v.t.* to sew a hem laid level with the cloth. [Uncert.].
FELLABLE, [fel'-abl], *adj.* suitable for being felled.
FELLAH, (*pl.* **fellahin**), [fel'-ah, fel'-ah-hēn], *n.* member of the peasant or labouring class in Egypt. [Arab. *fellah* ploughman].
FELLER (1), [fel'-er], *n.* one who fells trees.
FELLER (2), [fel'-er], *n.* a kind of hemming device used in a sewing-machine.
FELLIC, [fel'-ik], *adj.* pertaining to, from, bile. [L. *fel* gall].
FELLIFLUOUS, [fel-if'-lōō-us], *adj.* flowing with gall or bile. [LL. *fellifluus*].
FELLINIC, [fel-in'-ik], *adj.* fellic.
FELLMONGER, [fel'-mung'-ger], *n.* a dealer in skins.
FELLNESS, [fel'-nes], *n.* the quality of being fell; ruthlessness.
FELLOE, see FELLY.
FELLOW, [fel'-ō], *n.* a partner, or sharer in anything; a person associated with another; a comrade; an accomplice; an equal; an inferior; an uncultured person; a man or boy, a chap; member of the governing body of some universities; member of various learned and professional societies; a graduate holding certain grants on condition of research. [OE. *feolaga*].
FELLOW-FEELING, [fel'-ō-fēl'-ing], *n.* a feeling in common, sympathy.
FELLOWSHIP, [fel'-ō-ship], *n.* the state of being fellows; comradeship; sharing; participation; a group of people bound by some common aim or belief; the rank of a Fellow of a University, or learned professional society; (*coll.*) the examination that must be passed before one can become a Fellow of the Royal College of Surgeons.
FELLY, FELLOE, [fel'-i, fel'-ō], *n.* one of the curved strips joined together to form the rim of a wheel, to which the tyre is fixed; the rim of a wheel. [OE. *felg*].
FELO-DE-SE, [fē'-lō-di-sē'], *n.* suicide by one of sound mind. [LL. *felo de se* murderer of himself].
FELON (1), [fel'-on], *n.* a criminal; a ruffian; one who has committed felony. [OFr. *felon*].
FELON (2), [fel'-on], *n.* a whitlow. [Uncert.].
FELON (3), [fel'-on], *adj.* cruel; evil; treacherous; murderous. [FELON (1)].
FELONIOUS, [fel-ō'-ni-us], *adj.* wicked; worthy of a felon; (*leg.*) done with the deliberate purpose of committing a crime.
FELONIOUSLY, [fel-ō'-ni-us-li], *adv.* in a felonious way.
FELONIOUSNESS, [fel-ō'-ni-us-nes], *n.* the quality or condition of being felonious.
FELONRY, [fel'-on-ri], *n.* felons in general.
FELONY, [fel'-on-i], *n.* (*leg.*) one of the most serious kind of crimes or offences, regarded as more serious than a misdemeanour. [Fr. *felonie*].
FELSITE, [fel'-sīt], *n.* an igneous rock composed of felspar and quartz. [Ger. *fels* rock].
FELSPAR, FELDSPAR, [fel'-spah(r), feld-spah(r)], *n.* a widely distributed group of minerals consisting of anhydrous aluminium silicates, combined with potassium, calcium, sodium, or barium, and forming a constituent part of many igneous and metamorphic rocks. [Germ. *feldspath*].
FELSPATHIC, [fel-spath'-ik], *adj.* relating to felspar.
FELSPATHOSE, [fel-spath'-ōs], *adj.* consisting of, containing, felspar.
FELSTONE, [fel'-stōn'], *n.* a rock composed of quartz and felspar. [Germ. *felsstein*].
FELT (1), [felt], *n.* a compact tough fabric, made by rolling and pressing together wool, size, etc., much used for making hats. [OE. *felt*].
FELT (2), [felt], *v.t.* to cover with felt; to mat together; make into felt; *v.i.* to become matted, as felt.
FELT (3), [felt], *pret. and p.pt.* of FEEL (2).
FELTER, [felt'-er], *v.t.* to compress together like felt.
FELT-GRAIN, [felt'-grān'], *n.* (*carp.*) the grain of cut timber, transverse to the annular rings.
FELTING, [felt'-ing], *n.* the act or process of making felt; felt.
FELTRE, [felt'-er], *n.* a variety of felt-made cuirass. [OFr. *feltre*].
FELTWORT, FELWORT, [fel(t)'-wurt], *n.* a name for the mullein, *Verbascum Thapsus*; a native gentian. *Gentiana Amarella*.
FELUCCA, [fel-uk'-a], *n.* a sailing vessel with oars used in the Mediterranean. [Arab. *felucca*].

FELUCCA

FELWORT, see FELTWORT.
FEMALE (1), [fē'-māl], *n.* a female person or animal; person or animal of the sex that bears offspring; (*vulg.*) woman.
FEMALE (2), [fē'-māl], *adj.* of the sex that bears offspring; pertaining to, of, women; (of screws, etc.) made so as to fit together with the corresponding "male" part; (*bot.*) fruit-bearing, having a pistil and ovary but no stamens. [L. *femella* a woman].
FEMALIZED, [fē'-māl-īzd], *adj.* made female.
FEME, [fam], *n.* (*leg.*) a woman; **f. covert**, a married woman; **f. sole**, an unmarried woman, widow, or woman of independent means. [AFr. *feme* woman].
FEMERELL, [fem'-er-el], *n.* an opening, lantern or louvre on the roof of a kitchen to let out smoke or to let in air. [L. *fumariolum*].
FEMICIDE, [fem'-is-īd], *n.* the killing of a woman. [L. *femina* woman and *cidium* murder].
FEMINAL†, [fem'-inl], *adj.* relating to a woman. [OFr. *feminal*].
FEMINALITY, [fem-in-al'-it-i], *n.* (*rare*) the quality of being feminal, female nature.
FEMINEITY, [fem-in-ē'-it-i], *n.* the quality of being feminine, womanliness.
FEMININE, [fem'-in-in], *adj.* pertaining to the female sex, pertaining to women; characteristic of or befitting a woman; womanly; (*gram.*) of the gender or form proper to females; **f. caesura**, (*pros.*) a caesura that does not immediately follow a stress; **f. ending**, (*pros.*) an ending having the last accent in the line on the penultimate syllable; **f. rhyme**, (*pros.*) a rhyme consisting of a stressed syllable followed by an unstressed syllable. [L. *femininus*].
FEMININELY, [fem'-in-in-li], *adv.* in a feminine way.
FEMININENESS, [fem'-in-in-nes], *n.* the condition or quality of being feminine.
FEMININISM, [fem'-in-in-izm], *n.* a feminine idiom or turn of phrase; a tendency towards effeminacy.
FEMININITY, [fem'-in-in'-it-i], *n.* the quality of being feminine.
FEMINIST, [fem'-in-ist], *n.* an advocate of women's claims to equal privileges with men, etc.
FEMINITY, [fem-in'-it-i], *n.* femininity. [OFr. *feminité*].
FEMINIZE, [fem'-in-īz], *v.t.* to make feminine or effeminate.
FEMORAL, [fem'-or-al], *adj.* relating to the thigh.
FEMUR, [fē'-mur], *n.* the thigh or thigh-bone. [L. *femur*].
FEN, [fen], *n.* low marshy land; a bog or marsh. [OE. *fenn*].
FENBERRY, [fen'-be'-ri], *n.* name for the cranberry, *Vaccinium Oxycoccus*.
FENCE (1), [fents], *n.* the art of swordsmanship; hedge, wall, barrier, enclosing a field, *esp.* one made of wood; a guard or guide on some kinds of machine; (*slang*) a receiver of stolen goods; **master of f.**, a skilful swordsman; (*fig.*) a brilliant debater; **to sit on the f.**, not to take sides; **to come down on the right side of the f.**, to join the winning side. [(DE)FENCE].
FENCE (2), [fents], *v.t.* to screen, protect; to enclose with a fence; to fortify; *v.i.* to fight man against man with swords; to repel, keep out; to jump fences; (*slang*) to receive stolen goods.
FENCEFUL, [fents'-fool], *adj.* offering or affording defence.
FENCELESS, [fents'-les], *adj.* without a fence, unenclosed.
FENCE-MONTH, [fents'-munth'], *n.* the close-time for fish or game.

FENCER, [fen'-ser], *n.* person who fences or teaches fencing; a maker of fences.
FENCIBLE†, [fen'-sibl], *n.* a soldier enlisted for home defence. [~DEFENSIBLE].
FENCING, [fen'-sing], *n.* the art of self-defence with a sword; a barrier or railing, *esp.* of wood, fences; material suitable for fences; **f. cully**, (*slang*) one who stores stolen goods; **f. ken**, (*slang*) a store for stolen goods.
FEN-CRICKET, [fen'-krik'-it], *n.* the mole-cricket, a species of *Gryllotalpa*.
FEND, [fend], *v.i.* to repel; keep (off); provide (for). [(DE)FEND].
FENDER, [fend'-er], *n.* a protective frame round a hearth; a protection from injury by collision, etc.

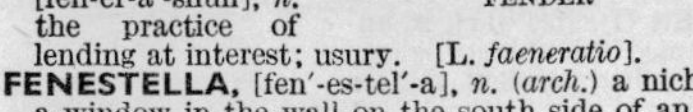
FENDER

FEN-DUCK, [fen'-duk'], *n.* name for the shoveller duck, *Spatula clypeata*.
FENERATION†, [fen-er-ā'-shun], *n.* the practice of lending at interest; usury. [L. *faeneratio*].
FENESTELLA, [fen'-es-tel'-a], *n.* (*arch.*) a niche like a window in the wall on the south side of an altar. [L. *fenestella*].
FENESTER, [fen'-est-er], *n.* an opening that serves as a window. [L. *fenestra*].
FENESTRAL, [fen-est'-ral], *adj.* relating to windows. [OFr. *fenestral*].
FENESTRATE, [fen'-est-rāt], *adj.* perforated with holes like windows. [L. *fenestrare*].
FENESTRATED, [fen'-es-trā'-tid], *adj.* having or marked with windows, or with anything resembling windows.
FENESTRATION, [fen'-es-trā'-shun], *n.* architectural arrangement as regards windows; (*bot.*, *zool.*) the condition of being fenestrate.
FENGITE, see PHENGITE.
FEN-GOOSE, [fen'-gōōs'], *n.* a name for the greylag goose, *Anser ferus*.
FENIAN, [fē'-ni-an], *n.* a member of a revolutionary organization formed to overthrow English rule and set up a native republic in Ireland. [OIr. *fene* inhabitant of Ireland].
FENIANISM, [fē'-ni-an-izm], *n.* the political tenets of the Fenians.
FENKS, [fengks], *n.* the refuse of blubber of whales. [Unkn.].
FENLANDER, [fen'-land-er], *n.* an inhabitant of the fen country.
FENMAN, [fen'-man], *n.* one who lives in a fen country.
FENNEC, [fen'-ek], *n.* the zerda, a small North African fox with large ears, *Canis zerda*. [Arab. *fanek*].
FENNEL, [fen'-el], *n.* a sweet-smelling umbelliferous plant with finely divided leaves, *Foeniculum vulgare*. [OE. *finule*].
FENNEL-FLOWER, [fen'-el-flow'-er], *n.* a plant of the genus *Nigella*, also called love-in-a-mist.
FENNY, [fen'-i], *adj.* marshy; having fens.
FENT, [fent], *n.* an opening or slit left in a garment, as at the throat or sleeve, to let it slip easily off and on. [Fr. *fente*].
FENUGREEK, FENUGREC, [fen'-yōō-grēk], *n.* a leguminous plant related to clover. [L. *faenum graecum*].
FEOD, see FEUD (2).
FEODARY, [few'-da-ri], *adj.* held according to the laws of feudal tenure.
FEOFF, see FIEF.
FEOFFEE, [fēf-ē'], *n.* one who is enfeoffed. [AFr. *feoffé*].
FEOFFMENT, [fēf'-ment], *n.* the grant of a fief. [AFr. *feoffement*].
FEOFFOR, [fēf'-ur], *n.* person who grants a fief. [AFr. *feoffour*].
FERACIOUS, [fer-ā'-shus], *adj.* fruitful, prolific, yielding abundantly.
FERACITY, [fer-as'-it-i], *n.* (*rare*) the quality of being feracious; fruitfulness; fecundity. [L. *feracitas*].
FERAE NATURAE, [fēer'-ē-nat-yōōer'-ē], *adj.* (*leg.*) term applied to wild animals like deer, as distinct from domestic, such as horses, cows, pigs, sheep and poultry. [L. *ferae naturae* of a wild nature].
FERAL (1), [fēer'-al], *adj.* fatal, deadly. [L. *feralis* pertaining to the dead].
FERAL (2), [fēer'-al], *adj.* wild, untamed; uncultivated; escaped from a domesticated condition. [~L. *fera* wild beast].
FER-DE-LANCE, [fāer'-de-lahnts'], *n.* the poisonous lance-headed pit-viper of South America and the West Indies, *Lachesis lanceolatus*. [Fr. *fer-de-lance* lance-head].
FERETORY, [fer'-et-or-i], *n.* a shrine for holding the relics when carried in processions. [L. *feretrum* a receptacle for carrying].
FERGUSONITE, [fur'-gus-on-īt], *n.* a species of mineral, consisting chiefly of tantalic acid and yttrium, with calcium, iron, uranium, etc. [Robert *Ferguson*].
FERIAE, [fēer'-i-ē], *n.*(*pl.*) feast-days in ancient Rome during which there was suspension of work. [L. *feriae*].
FERIAL, [fēer'-i-al], *adj.* relating to holidays, *esp.* formerly in Scotland to non-court days. [MedL. *ferialis*].
FERINE, [fēer'-īn], *adj.* not domestic, untamed; savage. [L. *ferinus*].
FERINELY, [fer-īn'-li], *adv.* after the manner of wild animals.
FERINENESS, [fer-īn'-nes], *n.* the quality of being ferine; savageness.
FERINGHEE, [fer-ing'-gē], *n.* a Hindu term for Europeans generally used in a derogatory sense. [Pers. *Faranji* a Frank].
FERLY, [fur'-li], *n.* (*prov.*) a marvel or wonder; something strange; astonishment. [OE. *færlic* sudden].
FERMENT (1), [fur'-ment], *n.* that which causes fermentation, leaven; fermentation; (*fig.*) agitation, uproar, excitement. [L. *fermentum*].
FERMENT (2), [fur-ment'], *v.t.* to leaven; (*fig.*) to stir up, agitate, excite; *v.i.* to undergo fermentation; to effervesce. [L. *fermentare*].
FERMENTABILITY, [fur-ment'-ab-il'-it-i], *n.* capacity for being fermented.
FERMENTABLE, [fur-ment'-abl], *adj.* capable of being fermented.
FERMENTATION, [fur'-men-tā'-shun], *n.* a chemical process in which much effervescence takes place, induced by the presence of yeast or enzymes; (*fig.*) agitation, turmoil, tumult. [L. *fermentatio*].
FERMENTATIVE, [fur-ment'-at-iv], *adj.* inducing, or consisting in, fermentation.
FERMENTATIVENESS, [fur-ment'-at-iv-nes], *n.* the quality or state of being fermentative.
FERMENTESCIBLE, [fur'-ment-es'-ibl], *adj.* capable of being fermented.
FERMETURE, [fur'-me-chōōer], *n.* the device by which the breech of a gun is shut. [Fr. *fermeture*].
FERMILLET†, [fur'-mil-et], *n.* an ornamental buckle or clasp. [OFr. *fermillet*].
FERN, [furn], *n.* a large flowerless cryptogamous plant with feathery fronds. [OE. *fearn*].
FERNERY, [furn'-er-i], *n.* a place where ferns are grown.
FERN-OWL, [furn'-owl], *n.* a name for the European goatsucker or night-jar, *Caprimulgus europæus*.
FERNTICLES, [furn'-tiklz'], *n.*(*pl.*) (*prov.*) freckles on the skin, in appearance like the seeds of fern. [ME. *ferntyklle*].
FERNY, [fur'-ni], *adj.* abounding in ferns.
FEROCIOUS, [fer-ō'-shus], *adj.* fierce, brutal, savage.
FEROCIOUSLY, [fer-ō'-shus-li], *adv.* in a ferocious way.
FEROCIOUSNESS, [fer-ō'-shus-nes], *n.* the quality or condition of being ferocious.
FEROCITY, [fer-os'-it-i], *n.* the state or quality of being ferocious. [L. *ferocitas*].
FERRANDINE, see FARANDINE.
FERRARA, [fer-ah'-ra], *n.* a broadsword of very good quality. [*Ferrara* an Italian swordsmith].
FERRATE, [fe'-rāt], *n.* (*chem.*) a substance produced when ferric acid is combined with a base.
FERREOUS, [fe'-rē-us], *adj.* containing, pertaining to, or made of, iron. [L. *ferreus*].
FERRET (1), [fe'-ret], *n.* a small partially domesticated variety of pole-cat used to chase rabbits and rats from their holes. [OFr. *furet*].
FERRET (2), [fe'-ret], *n.* a kind of narrow tape made of woollen thread or sometimes of cotton or silk. [It. *fioretti* small flowers; floss-silk].
FERRET (3), [fe'-ret], *v.i.* to hunt with ferrets; (*fig.*) to make a conscientious search; **to f. out**, to discover after a persistent search.
FERRETER, [fe'-ret-er], *n.* one who ferrets something out.
FERRETTO, [fe-ret'-ō], *n.* copper calcined with

brimstone or white vitriol, used for colouring glass. [It. *ferretto*].
FERRIAGE, [fe'-ri-ij], *n.* the fare due to be paid at a ferry.
FERRIC, [fe'-rik], *adj.* relating to, belonging to, iron in its quadrivalent state.
FERRIFEROUS, [fe-rif'-er-us], *adj.* yielding iron. [L. *ferrum* iron and *ferre* to bear].
FERRILITE, [fe'-ril-īt], *n.* Rowley rag, a trap rock containing oxide of iron. [L. *ferrum* iron and Gk. *lithos* stone].
FERRIS-WHEEL, [fe'-ris-wēl'], *n.* a giant vertical revolving wheel at a fair, with passenger-cars on its periphery. [*Ferris* an American engineer].
FERROCALCITE, [fe'-rō-kal'-sīt], *n.* calcite containing carbonate of iron.
FERRO-CONCRETE, [fe'-rō-kon'-krēt], *n.* concrete reinforced with iron.
FERROCYANATE, [fe'-rō-sī'-an-āt], *n.* a combination of ferrocyanic acid with a base.
FERROCYANIC, [fe'-rō-sī-an'-ik], *adj.* made of, pertaining to, ferrocyanogen.
FERROCYANIDE, [fe'-rō-sī'-an-id], *n.* a combination of a cyanide with cyanide of iron.
FERROCYANOGEN, [fe'-rō-si-an'-oj-en], *n.* a compound of iron with cyanogen.
FERROTYPE, [fe'-rō-tīp'], *n.* a positive photograph taken on a sensitized iron plate.
FERROUS, [fe'-rus], *adj.* containing, pertaining to iron in its divalent state.
FERRUGINATED, [fe-rōō'-jin-ā-tid], *adj.* of the colour of, or having properties of, the rust of iron.
FERRUGINOUS, [fe-rōō'-jin-us], *adj.* containing iron or iron rust; of the colour of iron rust. [L. *ferrugineus*].
FERRUGO, [fe-rōō'-gō], *n.* a disease of plants, commonly called rust, due to the presence of minute fungi. [L. *ferrugo* rust].
FERRULE, [fer'-ewl], *n.* a metal cap or tip strengthening the end of a stick, tube or umbrella shaft; a metal band strengthening a joint. [ME. *verrel* from OFr. *virelle* from MedL. *viriola*].
FERRUMINATION, [fe-rōō'-min-ā'-shun], *n.* the act of cementing together; the soldering or uniting of metals. [L. *ferruminatio*].
FERRY (1), [fe'-ri], *n.* a boat used as a floating bridge; the place of passage where one may be rowed across water; the right of ferrying across; **f. pilot**, one who flies an aircraft to its base of operations.
FERRY (2), [fe'-ri], *v.t. and i.* to cross or carry across a river in a boat or ferry. [OE. *ferian*].
FERRY-BOAT, [fe'-ri-bōt'], *n.* a boat for conveying passengers or goods across a ferry.
FERRYMAN, [fe'-ri-man], *n.* a man who keeps or works a ferry.
FERTILE, [fur'-tīl], *adj.* productive; rich in resources; inventive; prolific. [L. *fertilis*].
FERTILELY, [fur'-til-li], *adv.* in a fertile way.
FERTILENESS, [fur'-til-nes], *n.* the quality or condition of being fertile.
FERTILITY, [fur-til'-it-i], *n.* fertileness. [L. *fertilitas*].
FERTILIZATION, [fur'-til-īz-ā'-shun], *n.* the act or process of rendering fertile; impregnation.
FERTILIZE, [fur'-til-īz], *v.t.* to render fertile or fruitful; to enrich; to pollinate.
FERTILIZER, [fur'-til-īz-er], *n.* that which fertilizes; manure.
FERULA, [fe'-ryōōl-a], *n.* a ferule, a genus of plants containing the giant fennel. [L. *ferula*].
FERULACEOUS, [fe'-ryōōl-ā'-shus], *adj.* pertaining to reeds or canes. [L. *ferulaceus*].
FERULE, [fe'-ryōōl], *n.* the giant fennel; a flat rod (*orig.* made from this) for punishing children; **to be under the f.**, to be under a teacher, to be at school. [L. *ferula* the giant fennel, a rod].
FERVENCY, [fur'-ven-si], *n.* the state or quality of being fervent; ardour; zeal.
FERVENT, [fur'-vent], *adj.* hot, glowing; ardent, zealous, passionate. [L. *fervens*].
FERVENTLY, [fur'-vent-li], *adv.* in a fervent way.
FERVENTNESS, [fur'-vent-nes], *n.* the state of being fervent.
FERVESCENT, [fur-ves'-ent], *adj.* growing, becoming hot. [L. *fervescens*].
FERVID, [fur'-vid], *adj.* †hot, glowing; burning; ardent. [L. *fervidus*].
FERVIDLY, [fur'-vid-li], *adv.* in a fervid way.
FERVIDNESS, [fur'-vid-nes], *n.* the state of being fervid.
FERVOUR, [fur'-ver], *n.* great heat; ardour, warm devotion; zeal. [L. *fervor*].
FESCENNINE, [fes'-en-in], *adj.* gay, satirical and licentious; **f. verses**, one of the earliest forms of Italian poetry. [L. *Fescenninus* relating to Fescennia, a city in Etruria].
FESCUE, [fes'-kew], *n.* a small straw formerly used to point out letters to children when learning to read; **f. grass**, a species of the genus *Festuca*, the stem of which was used as a pointer. [OFr. *festu* a straw].
FESSE, FESS, [fes], *n.* (*her.*) a broad band crossing the shield horizontally and occupying a third of it; one of the nine honourable ordinaries, and representing the girdle of a knight; **f.-point**, (*her.*) the middle point of an escutcheon. [L. *fascia* band].

FESSE

FESTAL, [festl], *adj.* belonging, suitable, to a feast; joyous. [OFr. *festal*].
FESTALLY, [fes'-tal-i], *adv.* in a festive way.
FESTER (1), [fes'-ter], *n.* an inflamed tumour or sore, containing purulent matter. [OFr. *festre* from L. *fistula*].
FESTER (2), [fes'-ter], *v.i.* to suppurate, grow septic; to corrupt; to rankle.
FESTINATE†, [fes'-tin-at], *adj.* speedy; hurried. [L. *festinare* to hurry].
FESTIVAL (1), [fes'-tiv-al], *n.* a feast; a festive celebration; a day of religious rejoicing.
FESTIVAL (2), [fes'-tiv-al], *adj.* pertaining or appropriate to a feast; gay, joyous. [MedL. *festivalis*].
FESTIVE, [fes'-tiv], *adj.* pertaining or appropriate to a feast; merry. [L. *festivus*].
FESTIVELY, [fes'-tiv-li], *adv.* in a festive way.
FESTIVITY, [fes-tiv'-it-i], *n.* feasting; joyous celebration as at a feast; a festival. [L. *festivitas*].
FESTIVOUS, [fes'-tiv-us], *adj.* relating to a feast, joyous. [L. *festivus*].
FESTOON (1), [fes-tōōn'], *n.* a garland of flowers, etc., suspended so as to hang in a loop and with the ends hanging down; a sculptured ornament in imitation of such a garland; the curve on the cutting edge of a falcon's beak; **f. moth**, the species *Limacodes testudo*. [OFr. *feston*].
FESTOON (2), [fes-tōōn'], *v.t.* to form in festoons, to adorn with festoons.
FESTUCA, [fes-tew'-ka], *n.* a genus of ninety species of grasses; fescue grass. [L. *festuca* stalk].
FETATION, [fē-tā'-shun], *n.* the formation of a fœtus; conception.
FETCH (1), [fech], *n.* a dodge; a trick; an artifice; **f. of the sea**, the distance of a coast from the closest weather-shore. [FETCH (3)].
FETCH (2), [fech], *n.* a wraith, apparition. [Unkn.].
FETCH (3), [fech], *v.t.* to go for and bring back a person or thing; to cause to come; to bring in, realize; (*coll.*) to charm, captivate; **to f. and carry**, to run errands, to perform the duties of a servant; **to f. a sigh**, to heave a sigh; **to f. someone a blow**, to deal someone a blow. [OE. *feccan*].
FETCH-CANDLE, [fech'-kandl'], *n.* a light like a moving candle seen at night and believed to bode death.
FETCHER, [fech'-er], *n.* a person who fetches.
FETCHING, [fech'-ing], *adj.* alluring, attractive.
FETE, fête, [fāt], *n.* a festival or holiday; a kind of fair held in a charitable cause. [Fr. *fête*].
FETED, fêted, [fā'-tid], *adj.* honoured with a fête; made a fuss of.
FETIAL (1), FECIAL, [fēsh'-al], *n.* (*Rom. antiq.*) one of twenty priests whose duties were concerned with the ceremonial declaration of war or peace. [L. *fetialis*].
FETIAL (2), [fēsh'-al], *adj.* **f. law**, international law concerning the declaration of war or peace. [L. *fetialis*].
FETICH, see FETISH.
FETICHE, see FETISH.
FETICIDE†, see FOETICIDE.
FETID, see FOETID.
FETIFEROUS, see FOETIFEROUS.
FETISH, FETICH, FETICHE, [fet'-ish, fē'-tish], *n.* an inanimate object believed to be inhabited by spirits, and therefore worshipped by savages; (*fig.*) any object of excessive devotion or veneration. [Fr. *fétiche*].
FETISHISM, [fet'-ish-izm, fē'-tish-izm], *n.* the worship of a fetish; the system of fetishes; ju-ju.

FETISHISTIC, [fet'-ish-is'-tik, fē'-tish-is'-tik], *adj.* relating to fetishism.
FETIVA, [fet'-iv-a], *n.* a written verdict by a Mohammedan judge. [Arab. *fatwa*].
FETLOCK, [fet'-lok], *n.* the tuft of hair that grows behind the pastern joints of horses; the part where it grows. [ME. *fetlak*].

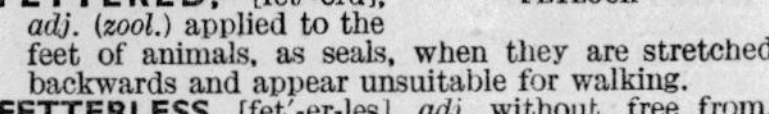
FETLOCK

FETLOCKED, [fet'-lokt], *adj.* having a fetlock.
FETOR, see FOETOR.
FETTER (1), [fet'-er], *n.* a shackle restraining the feet; anything that confines or restrains. [OE. *feter*].
FETTER (2), [fet'-er], *v.t.* to chain, shackle (*esp.* the feet); to confine, put under restraint.
FETTERED, [fet'-erd], *adj.* (*zool.*) applied to the feet of animals, as seals, when they are stretched backwards and appear unsuitable for walking.
FETTERLESS, [fet'-er-les], *adj.* without, free from, fetters.
FETTERLOCK, [fet'-er-lok], *n.* a shackle or fetter for a horse's fetlock.
FETTLE (1), [fetl], *n.* fine condition; fitness [ME. *fetlen* to make ready].
FETTLE (2), [fetl], *n.* (*dial.*) a basket handle; a girdle; a bandage. [OE. *fetel*].
FETUS, see FOETUS.
FEU (1), [few], *n.* a tenure on the condition that the tenant performs certain services or makes certain payments; (*in Scotland*) disposal of land for building on condition of paying a stipulated annual rent. [OFr. *fiu*].
FEU (2), [few], *v.t.* to let in feu; to lease. [OFr. *fiu*].
FEUAR, [few'-ar], *n.* a tenant of real estate on payment of feu-duty.
FEUD (1), [fewd], *n.* a fierce and deadly quarrel between two families, persons or groups of persons. [OFr. *fede* from OHGerm. *fehida* hostility].
FEUD (2), **FEOD**†, [fewd], *n.* a fief; land held on condition of man-service. [MedL. *feudum*].
FEUDAL, [fewdl], *adj.* relating to feuds or fiefs; consisting of feuds or fiefs; **the f. system**, the social system in medieval Europe, by which vassals held their lands from the lord superior on condition of military service when required. [MedL. *feudalis*].
FEUDALISM, [few'-dal-izm], *n.* the feudal system.
FEUDALIST, [few'-dal-ist], *n.* an authority on feudalism.
FEUDALISTIC, [few'-dal-ist'-ik], *adj.* pertaining to feudalism.
FEUDALITY, [few-dal'-it-i], *n.* the condition or quality of being feudal; feudal constitution. [Fr. *feudalité*].
FEUDALIZATION, [few'-dal-īz-ā'-shun], *n.* the act or process of feudalizing.
FEUDALIZE, [few'-dal-īz], *v.t.* to make feudal, to reduce to a feudal tenure.
FEUDALLY, [few'-dal-i], *adv.* in the feudal way.
FEUDARY (1), [few'-da-ri], *n.* a former officer in a court of wards. [MedL. *foedarius*].
FEUDARY (2), [few'-da-ri], *adj.* held from a superior.
FEUDATORY, [few'-dat-or-i], *n.* vassal who holds his lands of a superior on condition that he gives military service when required. [MedL. *feudatarius*].
FEUDIST, [few'-dist], *n.* one who writes on feudal law.
FEUILLAGE, [fur-yahzh], *n.* a collection or bunch of leaves. [Fr. *feuillage*].
FEUILLEMORT, **FEUILLEMORTE**, [fu(r')-i-mawt'], *n.* the colour of dead leaves; yellowish-brown. [Fr. *feuillemorte*].
FEUILLETON, [fur'-y-ton], *n.* the space in a French journal devoted to light literature or criticism; in an English journal, a serial story. [Fr. *feuilleton*].
FEUILLETONIST, [fur'-yet-on-ist], *n.* a writer on light topics; a writer of light criticism or serial stories.
FEVER, [fē'-ver], *n.* morbid condition of the system characterized by high temperature; one of various diseases characterized by a rise in temperature; a state of great nervous excitement; **f. heat**, abnormally high temperature of the body, as in a fever; (*fig.*) high pressure of work, great speed or excitement. [OE. *fefor*].
FEVERFEW, [fē'-ver-few'], *n.* a febrifuge; the plant *Matricaria Parthenium*, and other species of the same genus. [L. *febrifugia*].
FEVERISH, [fē'-ver-ish], *adj.* slightly fevered; showing, indicating fever; excited, nervous, agitated.
FEVERISHLY, [fē'-ver-ish-li], *adv.* in a feverish way.
FEVERISHNESS, [fē'-ver-ish-nes], *n.* the quality of being feverish.
FEVEROUS, [fē'-ver-us], *adj.* infected with fever; restless; excited.
FEVER-ROOT, [fē'-ver-rōōt'], *n.* a name for the plant, *Triosteum perfoliatum*.
FEVER-SORE, [fē'-ver-saw(r)'], *n.* a sore caused by fever.
FEVER-WORT, [fē'-ver-wurt'], *n.* the plant, *Erythraea Centaurium*, sometimes called the fever-root.
FEW (1), [few], *n.* a small number; not many; **the f.**, the minority; **a good f.**, (*coll.*) a good many; quite a number.
FEW (2), [few], *adj.* not many; a small number of; **every f. days, hours, etc.**, once in every group, or at intervals, of a few days, hours, etc.; **some f.**, quite a good number of. [OE. *feawe*].
FEWNESS, [few'-nes], *n.* a small quantity; paucity.
FEY, [fā], *adj.* doomed to die, dying; epithet applied when a person acts in a remarkably light-hearted, happy way, popularly supposed to be a prelude to death. [OE. *fæge*].
FEZ, [fez], *n.* a tall brimless red cap. [Turk. *fes*].
FIACRE, [fē-ahkr'], *n.* a French hackney-carriage. [Fr. *fiacre*].
FIANCE, fiancé, [fē-ahn'-sā], *n.* a betrothed man, the man to whom one is betrothed. [Fr. *fiancé*].
FIANCEE, fiancée, [fē-ahn'-sā], *n.* a betrothed woman, the woman to whom one is betrothed. [Fr. *fiancée*].
FIANNA FAIL, [fē'-an-a-fawl'], *n.* the name of the Irish political party led by Eamon de Valera. [Ir. *fianna fail*].
FIAR, [fē'-ar], *n.* a freeholder as distinguished from a life-renter; the owner of a fee-simple. [Uncert.].
FIARS, [fē'-arz], *n.(pl.)* (*Scots leg.*) average prices of grain in each county for the current year determined by the sheriff as a rule for fixing certain rates. [OFr. *fuar* from LL. *forum* price].
FIASCO, [fē-as'-kō], *n.* any signal failure; an attempt that comes to nothing. [It. *fiasco* bottle].
FIAT, [fī'-at], *n.* an order to do something; a decree; **f. money**, in America, inconvertible paper-money made legal tender by government decree. [L. *fiat* let it be done].
FIB (1), [fib], *n.* a trivial falsehood; a harmless inexactitude. [Uncert.].
FIB (2), (**fibbing, fibbed**), [fib], *v.i.* to tell trivial falsehoods.
FIBBER, [fib'-er], *n.* person who tells fibs.
FIBRE, [fī'-ber], *n.* thread-like filament in plants and animals; (*comm.*) the raw material in textile manufacture; **f. needle**, a gramophone needle made of bamboo. [L. *fibra*].
FIBRED, [fī'-berd], *adj.* (played) with fibres.
FIBRELESS, [fī'-ber-les], *adj.* without fibres.
FIBRIFORM, [fī'-brif-awm], *adj.* like a fibre in shape.
FIBRIL, [fī'-bril], *n.* a small fibre; a slender thread.
FIBRILLAE, [fī-bril'-ē], *n.(pl.)* (*bot.*) the absorbent hairs covering the roots of young plants.
FIBRILLATED, [fī'-bril-ā'-tid], *adj.* (*bot.*) having fibrillae.
FIBRILLOSE, [fī'-bril-ōs], *adj.* made up of, or covered with, fibres.
FIBRILLOUS†, [fī'-bril-us], *adj.* fibrillose.
FIBRIN, [fī'-brin], *n.* coagulable lymph found in animals and vegetables, distinguishable by its disposition to form into extremely delicate filaments; gluten.
FIBRINATION, [fī'-brin-ā'-shun], *n.* (*med.*) excessive formation of fibrin.
FIBRINOUS, [fī'-brin-us], *adj.* containing, of the nature of, fibrin.
FIBROCELLULAR, [fī'-brō-sel'-yŏŏ-ler], *adj.* composed of fibrous and cellular tissues.
FIBROID, [fī'-broid], *adj.* like fibre. [FIBRE and Gk. *oeides* like].
FIBROIN, [fī'-brō-in], *n.* the substance that forms the chief constituent of silk, cobwebs, etc.
FIBROLINE, [fī'-brō-lēn], *n.* yarn made from the waste in spinning.
FIBROMA, [fī-brō'-ma], *n.* (*pathol.*) a fibrous tumour.
FIBROMUSCULAR, [fī'-brō-mus'-kyŏŏ-ler], *adj.* composed of muscular and connective tissue.
FIBROSE, [fī'-brōs], *adj.* fibrous.

FIBROSIS, [fi-brō'-sis], *n.* morbid growth of fibroid matter.

FIBROSITIS, [fī'-brō-sī'-tis], *n.* inflamed condition of fibres.

FIBROUS, [fī'-brus], *adj.* consisting of, or containing, fibres.

FIBROUSNESS, [fī'-brus-nes], *n.* the state or quality of being fibrous.

FIBROVASCULAR, [fī'-brō-vas'-kyōō-ler], *adj.* composed of ducts and woody fibres.

FIBSTER, [fib'-ster], *n.* a fibber, one who tells trivial falsehoods.

FIBULA, [fib'-yōō-la], *n.* (*anat.*) the outer and smaller bone of the leg. [L. *fibula* a brooch].

FIBULAR, [fib'-yōō-lah(r)], *adj.* pertaining to the fibula.

FICARIA, [fī-kāer'-ia], *n.* learned name for the pilewort or little celandine, *Ranunculus Ficaria.*

FICHU, [fē'-shōō], *n.* a piece of silk or lace, etc., draped on the front of a dress. [Fr. *fichu*].

FICKLE, [fikl], *adj.* changeable, vacillating, inconstant. [OE. *ficol*].

FICKLENESS, [fikl'-nes], *n.* the quality or state of being fickle.

FICO, [fē'-kō], *n.* a scornful snap of the fingers. [It. *fico* fig].

FICTILE, [fik'-tīl], *adj.* moulded or mouldable into form by the potter; of pottery. [L. *fictilis*].

FICTILENESS, [fik'-tīl-nes], *n.* the quality or state of being fictile.

FICTION, [fik'-shun], *n.* an invented statement or narrative; that type of literature which tells imaginary stories; anything based on imagination; **legal f.,** an accepted falsehood or inaccuracy by which the raising of an awkward or irrelevant issue is avoided. [L. *fictio*].

FICTIONAL, [fik'-shunl], *adj.* based on fiction.

FICTIONIST, [fik'-shun-ist], *n.* a writer of fiction; a novelist.

FICTITIOUS, [fik-tish'-us], *adj.* invented; imagined; unreal; not true, or genuine; assumed, pretended; occurring in fiction; regarded as, or relating to, a legal fiction. [L. *ficticius*].

FICTITIOUSLY, [fik-tish'-us-li], *adv.* in a fictitious way.

FICTITIOUSNESS, [fik-tish'-us-nes], *n.* the quality or state of being fictitious.

FICTIVE, [fik'-tiv], *adj.* pertaining to fiction; false, imagined. [Fr. *fictif*].

FICTIVELY, [fik'-tiv-li], *adv.* in a fictive way.

FID, [fid], *n.* (*naut.*) a conical wooden pin used as a splicing tool; a bar of wood or iron put through a hole to hold a spar in place. [Unkn.].

FIDALGO, [fid-al'-gō], *n.* a Portuguese nobleman. [Portug. *fidalgo*].

FIDDLE (1), [fidl], *n.* a familiar or derogatory name for a violin; general term for an instrument of the family that comprises the violin, viola, violoncello and double-bass; (*naut.*) a wooden device fitted to tables to prevent things from sliding off; **as fit as a f.,** in good health; **to play second f.,** to take a subordinate part; **a face as long as a f.,** a gloomy expression; **to hang up one's f. when one comes home,** to be amusing abroad but dull at home. [ME. *fithele*].

FIDDLE (2), [fidl], *v.i.* to play the fiddle or violin; to make aimless, fidgety movements; to waste time.

FIDDLEBLOCK, [fidl'-blok'], *n.* (*naut.*) a long block having two sheaves in the same plane.

FIDDLE-BOW, [fidl'-bō'], *n.* the stringed bow by means of which the fiddle is played.

FIDDLE-DE-DEE, [fidl'-dē-dē'], *int.* rubbish! nonsense!

FIDDLE-FADDLE (1), [fidl'-fadl'], *n.* trivial talk; petty matters; trifles.

FIDDLE-FADDLE (2), [fidl'-fadl'], *adj.* trifling; petty; trivial; nonsensical.

FIDDLE-FISH, [fidl'-fish'], *n.* a name for the monkfish, *Rhina squatina.*

FIDDLE-HEAD, [fidl'-hed'], *n.* an ornament on a ship's prow, shaped off like the head of a fiddle, and taking the place of the figure-head.

FIDDLER, [fidl'-er], *n.* one who plays on a fiddle; a violinist; a small American crab with a large claw and a short one, of the genus *Portunus.* [OE. *fithelere*].

FIDDLEBLOCK

FIDDLE-STICK, [fidl'-stik], *n.* the bow of a fiddle; **fiddle-sticks!** (*int.*) rubbish! nonsense!

FIDDLE-STRING, [fidl'-string'], *n.* one of the guts or strings of a fiddle.

FIDDLE-WOOD, [fidl'-wōōd'], *n.* a tropical American tree of the genus *Citharoxylum,* yielding durable timber. [Mistranslation of Fr. *bois fidèle* true wood].

FIDDLING, [fidl'-ing], *adj.* trifling in a fussy way; fidgety; petty; trivial.

FIDELITY, [fid-el'-it-i], *n.* the state or quality of being faithful; strict adherence to fact or truth; accuracy of detail; exact conformity with the original. [L. *fidelitas*].

FIDGET (1), [fij'-et], *n.* toying fussiness; mental uneasiness or nervousness; a restless person; **the fidgets,** a fit of restlessness or anxiety. [Uncert.].

FIDGET (2), (**fidgeting, fidgeted**), [fij'-et], *v.t.* to make restless or nervy; to get on the nerves of; to disturb, upset; *v.i.* to make restless, spasmodic movements; to fuss; to be anxious or nervous.

FIDGETINESS, [fij'-et-in-es], *n.* the quality of being fidgety.

FIDGETY, [fij'-et-i], *adj.* moving restlessly about; uneasy.

FIDICULA, [fid-ik'-yōō-la], *n.* a miniature lute. [L. *fidicula*].

FIDUCIAL, [fī'-dew'-shal], *adj.* confident; undoubting; of the nature of a trust; **f. line, point,** a line, etc., assumed, or taken on trust, as a fixed basis of comparison. [L. *fiducialis*].

FIDUCIALLY, [fī'-dew'-shal-i], *adv.* with confidence; on trust.

FIDUCIARY (1), [fī-dew'-sha-ri], *n.* one who holds something in trust; a trustee.

FIDUCIARY (2), [fī-dew'-sha-ri], *adj.* confident; undoubting; held or given in trust. [L. *fiduciarius*].

FIE, [fī], *int.* expression of disapproval or disgust. [Fr. *fi*].

FIEF, FEOFF, [fēf], *n.* a fee; a feud; an estate held of a superior in return for military service. [OFr. *fief* from MedL. *foedum*].

FIELD (1), [fēld], *n.* a tract of land, usually enclosed and used for agricultural purposes; a stretch of land rich in some mineral product; the ground where a battle is fought; the open country; the background of shields, flags, coins, etc.; area of observation or operation; scope, range; province, realm, department (of knowledge, study, etc.); ground on which games are played; the participants or competitors in outdoor sports, except the favourite; the fielding side in cricket; **to take the f.,** to commence hostilities. [OE. *feld*].

FIELD (2), [fēld], *v.t.* (baseball, cricket, etc.) to stop a ball and return it to the bowler or pitcher; *v.i.* to act as fielder, while the other side is batting.

FIELD-ALLOWANCE, [fēld'-al-ow-ants], *n.* a special allowance made to officers and warrant officers while on field duty, for the extra expense of food, equipment, etc.

FIELD AMBULANCE, [fēld'-am'-byōō-lants], *n.* an army unit of medical equipment, personnel, etc., for emergency treatment of wounded on a battlefield.

FIELD-ARTILLERY, [fēld'-ah-til'-er-i], *n.* artillery to co-operate with infantry in the field.

FIELD-BATTERY, [fēld'-bat'-er-i], *n.* a battery composed of field-guns.

FIELD-BED, [fēld'-bed'], *n.* a portable or collapsible campbed.

FIELD BOOK, [fēld'-bōōk'], *n.* a book used in surveying, for setting down the angles, distances, etc.

FIELD-CLUB, [fēld'-klub'], *n.* a club devoted to open-air nature study.

FIELD-COLOURS, [fēld'-kul'-urz], *n.*(*pl.*) small flags, used for marking out the ground for squadrons and battalions.

FIELD-CORNET, [fēld'-kaw'-net], *n.* a magistrate in South Africa.

FIELD-DAY, [fēld'-dā'], *n.* (*milit.*) a day when troops are drawn out for review in field exercises and manoeuvres; a day when all take the field; (*fig.*) a day marked by some celebration or display beyond the ordinary.

FIELD-DUCK, [fēld'-duk'], *n.* name for the little bustard, *Otis tetrax.*

FIELDER, [fēld'-er], *n.* (*cricket*) one who fields.

FIELDFARE, [fēld'-fāer'], *n.* a migratory bird of the thrush family, *Turdus pilaris,* coming to Britain during the winter. [ME. *feldefare*].

FIELD-GLASS, [fēld'-glahs'], *n.* the lens of an eyepiece that is nearest the object; (*pl.*) a binocular telescope; a large opera-glass.

FIELD-GUN, [fēld'-gun'], *n.* (*milit.*) a gun to be used on the battlefield as distinct from a siege-gun.

FIELD-MARSHAL, [fēld'-mahsh'-al], *n.* (*milit.*) the highest rank of officer.

FIELD-MOUSE, [fēld'-mows], *n.* a small rodent of the genus *Microtus*.

FIELD-OFFICER, [fēld'-of'-is-er], *n.* (*milit.*) an officer of, or senior to, the rank of major.

FIELD-PIECE, [fēld'-pēs], *n.* (*milit.*) a piece of field-artillery, a field-gun.

FIELD-PREACHER, [feld'-prē'-cher], *n.* a person who preaches in the open air.

FIELDSMAN, [fēldz'-man], *n.* (*cricket*) a fielder.

FIELD-SPORTS, [fēld'-spawtz'], *n.*(*pl.*) open-air sports, as shooting, fishing, and hunting.

FIELD-WORKS, [fēld'-wurks'], *n.*(*pl.*) (*milit.*) works thrown up in the siege or defence of a place.

FIEND, [fēnd], *n.* devil; evil spirit; Satan, the Devil; a very wicked or cruel person; (*coll.*) devotee, addict. [OE. *feond* enemy].

FIENDFUL, [fēnd'-fŏŏl], *adj.* fiendish, full of fiendish practices.

FIENDFULLY, [fēnd'-fŏŏl-i], *adv.* in a fiendlike way.

FIENDISH, [fēnd'-ish], *adj.* like a fiend, cruel, devilish, malicious.

FIENDISHLY, [fēnd'-ish-li], *adv.* in a fiendish way.

FIENDISHNESS, [fēnd'-ish-nes], *n.* the state of being fiendish.

FIENDLIKE, [fēnd'-līk'], *adj.* like a fiend.

FIERCE, [fēers], *adj.* cruel, brutal, savage, ferocious; uncontrolled, violent; strong, intense. [OFr. *fiers* from L. *ferus* wild].

FIERCELY, [fēers'-li], *adv.* in a fierce way.

FIERCENESS, [fēers'-nes], *n.* quality or condition of being fierce.

FIERI FACIAS, [fī'-er-i-fā'-shi-as], *n.* (*leg.*) a writ of execution requiring a sheriff to levy in behalf of one who has been awarded a debt or damages. [L. *fieri facias* cause it to be done].

FIERILY, [fīer'-il-i], *adv.* in a fiery manner.

FIERINESS, [fīer'-in-es], *n.* the condition of being fiery.

FIERY, [fīer'-i], *adj.* burning, full of flames; carrying or containing fire; like fire; hot, glowing, red; (*fig.*) impetuous; quick-tempered, vehement; passionate; ardent; (of horses) high-spirited; (*min.*) inflammable. [FIRE (1)].

FIERY-CROSS, [fīer'-i-kros'], *n.* a cross charred and dipped in blood, sent round in the Scottish Highlands to summon the clans to war.

FIESTA, [fē-es'-ta], *n.* a festivity, a holiday, merry-making. [Span. *fiesta* feast].

FIFE (1), [fīf], *n.* a kind of small shrill flute used chiefly in martial music. [Uncert.].

FIFE (2), [fīf], *v.i.* to play a fife.

FIFE-MAJOR, [fīf'-mā'-jor], *n.* in former times, the non-commissioned officer in charge of the fifers of a battalion.

FIFER, [fīf'-er], *n.* one who plays a fife.

FIFE-RAIL, [fīf'-rāl'], *n.* (*naut.*) the rail round a ship's mast with belaying pins.

FIFE-RAIL

FIFTEEN (1), [fif-tēn'], *n.* the cardinal number next after fourteen; a team of Rugby football players; **the F.**, the Jacobite rebellion of 1715.

FIFTEEN (2), [fif-tēn'], *adj.* one more than fourteen. [OE. *fiftene*].

FIFTEENTH (1), [fif-tēnth'], *n.* a fifteenth part; (*mus.*) the interval of the double octave.

FIFTEENTH (2), [fif-tēnth'], *adj.* the fifth after the tenth; forming one part in fifteen.

FIFTH (1), [fifth], *n.* a fifth part; one of five equal parts; (*mus.*) an interval of three tones and a semitone.

FIFTH (2), [fifth], *adj.* the ordinal number corresponding to five; the next after fourth; **f. wheel**, something superfluous; **F. Monarchy**, the last of the five great empires; **F. Monarchy men**, seventeenth-century fanatics expecting the immediate coming of Christ. [OE. *fifta*].

FIFTH COLUMN, [fifth-kol'-um], *n.* the body of traitors within a given area or country. [From the Spanish Civil War of 1936-9 when four columns of troops threatened Madrid and the *fifth column* consisted of the secret sympathizers inside the city].

FIFTH COLUMNIST, [fifth-kol'-um-ist], *n.* a member of the fifth column.

FIFTHLY, [fifth-li], *adv.* fifth in order, in the fifth place.

FIFTIETH, [fif'-ti-eth], *adj.* the first after the forty-ninth; the ordinal of fifty; forming one part in fifty.

FIFTY (1), [fif'-ti], *n.* the cardinal number next after forty-nine; **the fifties**, the decade in a century between the years 50 and 60; **f.-f.**, (*coll.*) equal sharing; **to go f.-f.**, to share equally.

FIFTY (2), [fif'-ti], *adj.* five times ten; one more than forty-nine. [OE. *fiftig*].

FIG, [fig], *n.* the fig-tree, *Ficus carica*; the soft, pear-shaped many-seeded fruit of the fig-tree; a thing of no worth; a spongy excrescence which grows on the feet of some horses; a piece of tobacco; abbreviation of *figure*; **under one's vine and f.-tree**, safely at home. [OFr. *fige* from L. *ficus*].

FIG-APPLE, [fig'-apl'], *n.* a variety of apple.

FIG-CAKE, [fig'-kāk], *n.* a concoction of figs and almonds pressed into round cakes.

FIG-EATER, [fig'-ē'-ter], *n.* the beccafico or garden warbler, a kind of *Sylvia*.

FIG-GNAT, [fig'-nat'], *n.* *Culex ficarius*, a gnat that destroys figs.

FIGHT (1), [fīt], *n.* the act of fighting; struggle; contest; battle; combat; conflict; ability, inclination to fight; pugnacity; **prize f.**, a pugilistic contest; **stand-up f.**, a formal, open combat; **free f.**, a fight without clearly defined sides; **to put up a good f.**, to fight pluckily; **to show f.**, to show readiness to fight. [OE. *gefeoht*, ME. *fiht*].

FIGHT (2), (**fighting, fought**), [fīt], *v.t.* to have a fight with or about; *v.i.* to engage in a fight; **to f. it out**, to settle (a dispute) by fighting; **to f. shy of**, to avoid, keep aloof from. [OE. *feohtan*].

FIGHTER, [fī'-ter], *n.* person who fights; a combatant; a warrior; an aeroplane designed to attack other aeroplanes; a person who does not give in easily.

FIGHTER-BOMBER, [fīt'-er-bom'-er], *n.* (*aeron.*) an aeroplane combining the capabilities of a fighter and a bomber.

FIGHTING, [fī'-ting], *adj.* trained or designed to fight; engaged in war or combat; **a f. chance**, a possibility of success if every effort is made.

FIGHTING-FISH, [fī'-ting-fish'], *n.* a small fresh-water fish, *Betta pugnax*, plentiful in Siam, remarkable for its pugnacity.

FIGHTING-TOP, [fī'-ting-top'], *n.* a circular gun-platform fixed to the mast of a battleship.

FIG-LEAF, [fig'-lēf'], *n.* the leaf of a fig-tree; a device for covering the sexual organs in statuary, etc.

FIG-MARIGOLD, [fig'-ma'-rig-ōld], *n.* a variety of *Mesembryanthemum*, a succulent plant, resembling houseleek.

FIGMENT, [fig'-ment], *n.* an invention; a fiction; anything feigned or imagined. [L. *figmentum*].

FIG-PECKER, [fig'-pe'-ker], *n.* the garden-warbler or fig-eater. [Translation of It. *beccafico*].

FIG-SHELL, [fig'-shel'], *n.* a univalve shell of the genus *Pyrula*, which is shaped like a fig or pear.

FIGULATE†, [fig'-yŏŏ-lāt], *adj.* figuline, made of potter's clay; moulded; shaped. [L. *figulare* to shape in the way of a potter].

FIGULINE (1), [fig'-yŏŏ-lin], *n.* potter's clay.

FIGULINE (2), [fig'-yŏŏ-lin], *adj.* fictile, made of earthenware. [L. *figulinus*].

FIGURABILITY, [fig'-ur-ab-il'-it-i], *n.* the state of being figurable.

FIGURABLE, [fig'-yooer-abl], *adj.* capable of being fashioned into a fixed shape; describable.

FIGURAL, [fig'-yooer-al], *adj.* depicted by figure or delineation. [OFr. *figural*].

FIGURANT, [fig'-yooer-ant], *n.* a male ballet-dancer, member of a ballet. [Fr. *figurant*].

FIGURANTE (1), [fig'-yooer-ant], *n.* a female ballet-dancer, member of a ballet-company. [Fr. *figurante*].

FIGURANTE (2), (*pl.* **figuranti**), [fig'-yooer-an'-tā], *n.* figurant or figurante (1); a ballet-dancer. [It. *figurante*].

FIGURATE, [fig'-yooer-āt], *adj.* of, or according to, a determinate form. [L. *figurare* to fashion].

FIGURATED, [fig'-yooer-ā'-tid], *adj.* of, possessing a determinate form.

FIGURATELY, [fig'-yooer-at-li], *adv.* in a figurate way.

FIGURATION, [fig'-yooer-ā'-shun], *n.* the act or process of giving figure or determinate form; determination to a certain form; (*mus.*) a mixture of concords and discords or ornamental treatment. [L. *figuratio*].

FIGURATIVE, [fig'-yooer-at-iv], *adj.* representing something else; representing by resemblance, parable

ō (bone), ī (fine), ōō (food), ŏŏ (put), u (up), th (*th*ink), TH (*th*at), zh (azure). † = obsolete. ~ = related to.

or symbol; not literal or direct; abounding in figures of speech; flowery. [LL. *figurativus*].

FIGURATIVELY, [fig'-yōoer-rat-iv-li], *adv.* metaphorically, not literally.

FIGURATIVENESS, [fig'-yōoer-at-iv-nes]. *n.* the quality of being figurative.

FIGURE (1), [fig'-ur], *n.* outer shape or appearance; form; the human form, bodily shape; a representation of the human form; a statue; image, likeness; a person as actually seen, or as contemplated mentally; an emblem, type; an illustration, descriptive diagram, or drawing; a horoscope; a numerical symbol; a movement or series of movements in skating; a set of steps in, division of, a dance; (*geom.*) a space enclosed by lines or surfaces; (*log.*) a particular form of syllogism; (*gram.*) a permissible deviation from the ordinary construction; (*mus.*) a short series of notes producing a single impression, a phrase; (*rhet.*) a recognized mode of expression, in which words are used in some abnormal sense for the sake of emphasis, variety, etc.; **at a low (high) f.**, cheap, (dear); **to cut a f.**, to make an impression. [L. *figura*].

FIGURE (2), [fig'-ur], *v.t.* to represent pictorially, or diagrammatically; to decorate, embellish with a pattern; to be a symbol of; *v.i.* to appear; to be conspicuous; **to f. out**, to work out; to give results in figures; **to f. up**, to reckon up, calculate the amount of; **to f. oneself**, to imagine.

FIGURE-CASTER, [fig'-ur-kahst'-er], *n.* one who casts horoscopes; a pretender to astrology.

FIGURED, [fig'-urd], *adj.* adorned with figures; having a pattern or design; figurative.

FIGURE-HEAD, [fig'-ur-hed'], *n.* the figure, statue, or bust on the projecting part of a ship's prow; a person occupying an eminent position but possessing no real authority.

FIGURE-MAKER, [fig'-ur-mā'-ker], *n.* one who makes figures; a modeller; one who practises the art of moulding; a maker of anatomical models for artists.

FIGURE-OF-EIGHT, [fig'-ur-of-āt'], *n.* a knot made in the form of an 8; a skating figure in the form of a large 8.

FIGURE-STONE, [fig'-ur-stōn'], *n.* a kind of soapstone used for figure-carving.

FIGURE-WEAVING, [fig'-ur-wē'-ving], *n.* the process or act of weaving patterns or designs as in damask.

FIGURIAL, [fig-yōō'-ri-al], *adj.* represented by a figure or figures.

FIGURINE, [fig'-yōō-rēn], *n.* a statuette. [Fr. *figurine*].

FIGURIST, [fig'-yōō-rist], *n.* one expert at figures.

FIGWORT, [fig'-wurt'], *n.* a plant of the genus *Scrophularia*.

FILACEOUS, [fil-ā'-shus], *adj.* consisting of threads.

FILAGREE, see FILIGREE.

FILAMENT, [fil'-am-ent], *n.* a slender thread or fibre, such as is found in animal and vegetable tissues, as well as some mineral structures; (*bot.*) the long thread-like part which supports the anther; a fine wire used in electric light bulbs. [L. *filare* to spin].

FILAMENTARY, [fil'-am-ent'-a-ri], *adj.* pertaining to, of the nature of, a filament.

FILAMENTOUS, [fil'-am-ent'-us], *adj.* like a thread.

FILANDERS, [fil-an'-derz], *n.*(*pl.*) an intestinal disease in hawks. [OFr. *filandres* threads (of wool for spinning)].

FILAR, [fī'-lah(r)], *adj.* having threads.

FILATORY, [fil'-at-or-i], *n.* a machine for spinning threads. [MedL. *filatorium*].

FILATURE, [fil'-a-chooer], *n.* the process of reeling silk from cocoons; the reel so used; a place where it is done. [Fr. *filature*].

FILBERT, [fil'-bert], *n.* the fruit of the cultivated hazel, differing from the cobnut by the fact that the husk projects beyond the point of the nut, *Corylus Avellana*. [Fr. *noix de Filbert*, St. Philibert's nut].

FILCH, [filch], *v.t.* to steal (*esp.* some petty object). [Uncert.].

FILCHER, [filch'-er], *n.* one who commits a petty theft.

FILCHINGLY, [filch'-ing-li], *adv.* by petty theft or pilfering.

FILE (1), [fīl], *n.* a steel instrument with roughened surface for smoothing or reducing hard objects; (*slang*) a sly, artful person. [OE. *fil*, *feol*].

FILE (2), [fīl], *n.* stiff wire on which papers, documents, etc., are threaded for keeping; a hooked wire on which documents may be kept for reference; a cardboard box or folder for a similar purpose; papers so kept. [L. *filum* thread].

FILE (3), [fīl], *n.* a row of people or things one behind the other; (*milit.*) a row of soldiers ranged one behind the other; (*chess*) a line of squares reaching from player to player; **in f.**, (*milit.*) drawn up or marching in a line, one behind the other; **Indian, single f.**, a single line of men in file; **rank and f.**, (*milit.*) soldiers who are not commissioned or warrant officers; (*fig.*) the lower classes; the general body as distinct from the leaders. [FILE (6)].

FILE (4), [fīl], *v.t.* to reduce, smooth, with a file. [FILE (1)].

FILE (5), [fīl], *v.t.* to put on a file; to keep in a file; to place among public records; to send (a message) by cable. [FILE (2)].

FILE (6), [fīl], *v.t.* to command to march in file; *v.i.* to march in file. [Fr. *filer*].

FILE† (7), [fīl], *v.t.* to defile, sully, stain or spot. [OE. *afylan*, ME. *fulen*].

FILE-CUTTER, [fīl'-kut'-er], *n.* a person who makes files.

FILE-FISH, [fīl'-fish], *n.* a tropical sea-fish of the genus *Balistes*, having a dorsal fin with a file-like edge.

FILE-FISH

FILE-LEADER, [fīl'-lēd'-er], *n.* (*milit.*) the soldier at the head of a file.

FILEMOT (1), **FOLIOMORT**†, [fil'-mot], *n.* a yellowish-brown colour, the colour of a faded leaf. [Fr. *feuille morte* dead leaf].

FILEMOT (2), [fil'-mot], *adj.* of the colour of a withered leaf, yellowish-brown.

FILER, [fī'-ler], *n.* one who files.

FILET, [fē'-lā], *n.* a kind of net having a fine rectangular mesh. [Fr. *filet*].

FILIAL, [fil'-i-al], *adj.* pertaining to a son or daughter; becoming, proper to, expected from, a son or daughter; (*fig.*) related as a child or offspring. [LL. *filialis*].

FILIALLY, [fil'-i-al-i], *adv.* in filial fashion.

FILIATE, [fil'-i-āt], *v.t.* to affiliate. [MedL. *filiare* to bear a child].

FILIATION, [fil-i-ā'-shun], *n.* the state of being a son or daughter, the relationship of a child to its parents; the fact of being a descendant of; genealogical relationship; the development of new branches or subsidiary organizations. [MedL. *filiatio*].

FILIBEG, FILLIBEG, PHILIBEG, [fil'-ib-eg], *n.* the kilt. [Gael. *feileadh-beag* small fold].

FILIBUSTER (1), [fil'-ib-us-ter], *n.* a pirate, a freebooter, a buccaneer, a military adventurer who unlawfully attacks the possessions of a foreign state; (*U.S.*) a political obstructionist. [Span. *filibustero* from Du. *vrijbuiter*].

FILIBUSTER (2), [fil'-ib-us-ter], *v.i.* to act as, behave like, a filibuster.

FILIBUSTERISM, [fil'-ib-us'-ter-izm], *n.* the practices of the filibusters.

FILICAL, [fil'-ikl], *adj.* pertaining to the ferns. [L. *filix* a fern].

FILICALES, [fil'-ik-ā'-lez], *n.*(*pl.*) (*bot.*) the order of *Pteridophyta*, including the true ferns.

FILICES, [fil'-is-ēz], *n.*(*pl.*) the ferns. [L. *filices*, *pl.* of *filix* a fern].

FILICIFORM, [fil-is'-if-awm], *adj.* fern-shaped.

FILICOID (1), [fil'-ik-oid], *n.* a plant resembling a fern. [L. *filix* fern and Gk. *oeides* like].

FILICOID (2), [fil'-ik-oid], *adj.* like a fern.

FILIFORM, [fil'-if-awm], *adj.* like a thread.

FILIGRANE, [fil'-ig-rān], *n.* filigree. [It. *filigrana*].

FILIGREE, FILAGREE, [fil'-ig-rē], *n.* fine ornamental open-work in gold and silver, so delicate as to resemble lacework; (*fig.*) fine delicate work of any kind. [FILIGRANE].

FILIGREED, [fil'-ig-rēd], *adj.* ornamented with filigree work.

FILINGS, [fī'-lingz], *n.*(*pl.*) minute fragments or particles accumulated by filing.

FILL (1), [fil], *n.* that which fills; a full supply or amount a due. [OE. *fyllo*].

FILL (2), [fil], *v.t. and i.* to put into a receptacle, etc., such a quantity as to leave little or no space in it unoccupied; to stuff, to pack, to crowd; to make full, to occupy a space completely; to perform the duties of an office or position; to appoint someone to (a vacant post); (*naut.*) to cause to swell out (of sails); to provide with abundant supplies of; to become full; **to f. in**, to complete by inserting some necessary information required; to level out a hollow, etc.; **to f. out**, to become distended; (*coll.*) to become plump or fatter; **to f. up**, to make completely full; to complete by adding necessary information in the appropriate spaces; to become full; **to f. the bill**, (*coll.*) to meet the case or requirements satisfactorily. [OE. *fyllan*].

FILLE-DE-CHAMBRE, [fē'-de-shawmbr'], *n.* a chambermaid. [Fr. *fille de chambre*].

FILLER (1), [fil'-er], *n.* one who, or that which, fills; a vessel or tube used in filling bottles, casks, etc.; (*motoring*) the narrow opening by which a petrol or oil tank, etc., is filled.

FILLER (2), [fil'-āer'], *n.* a Hungarian unit of currency, the hundredth part of a pengo. [Hung. *filler*].

FILLET (1), [fil'-et], *n.* a small band of ribbon tied round the hair; a portion of fish that has been filleted; a thick, fleshy portion of meat, *esp.* the undercut of a sirloin of beef, or the thick part round the loins; the fleshy part of a leg of veal, tied round with string in a roll; (*pl.*) the loins of a horse; (*arch.*) a narrow band separating two mouldings, or between the flutes of a column; (*her.*) a horizontal band across a chief, one fourth its width; (*carp.*) a narrow strip of wood or scantling; (*print.*) a narrow line made upon the cover of a book. [Fr. *filet* from L. *filum* thread].

FILLET (2), [fil'-et], *v.t.* to bind or adorn with a head-band or ribbon; to remove the bones from (fish or meat) and slice.

FILLIBEG, see FILIBEG.

FILLING, [fil'-ing], *n.* that which is used to fill or stop up a cavity, *esp.* in a tooth.

FILLING-STATION, [fil'-ing-stā'-shun], *n.* a place where petrol is sold for use in motor vehicles.

FILLIP (1), [fil'-ip], *n.* a flick or sharp jerk of the finger when released suddenly from the thumb, which has been pressing upon it; an incentive, a stimulus, an incitement; a light blow or tap; a trifle, something of small account. [Imitative].

FILLIP (2), [fil'-ip], *v.t.* and *i.* to strike with a fillip; to spin (a coin) with a fillip; to give a fillip to.

FILLISTER, [fil'-is-ter], *n.* a plane used for cutting a longitudinal groove or rabbet; the longitudinal groove in a window-sash into which the glass fits. [Unkn.].

FILLY, [fil'-i], *n.* a female foal, a young mare; (*fig.*) a high-spirited young girl. [OIcel. *fylja*].

FILM (1), [film], *n.* a thin layer, coating, or skin; a fine, slender gossamer-like thread; (*phot.*) a flexible sheet or ribbon of cellulose or similar substance, sensitized on one surface; a reel or spool of this on which a cinematograph picture is photographed; any of the separate screen items composing a cinema entertainment; **U. f.**, a film passed by the censor as being suitable for children under sixteen years of age; **A. f.**, a film to which persons under the age of sixteen years are not admitted, unless accompanied by an adult. [OE. *filmen* a membrane].

FILM (2), [film], *v.t.* and *i.* to cover with a film; (*phot.*) to make a film of, to photograph; to become clouded over with a film; to make films.

FILM-ACTOR, [film'-ak'-ter], *n.* an actor engaged in acting for the screen as opposed to the stage.

FILMINESS, [film'-in-es], *n.* the condition of being filmy.

FILM-PACK, [film'-pak'], *n.* a set of films arranged in a container, and capable of being inserted into, or withdrawn from, a camera in daylight.

FILM-STAR, [film'-stah(r)'], *n.* a film-actor or actress who has achieved a pre-eminent position in the profession.

FILM-STUDIO, [film'-stew'-di-ō], *n.* a permanent building in which cinema films are made.

FILM-TEST, [film'-test'], *n.* a series of photographs taken to discover whether a person is suitable for acting on the films or in a particular film.

FILMY, [film'-i], *adj.* resembling a film in nature or appearance, clouded over with a film.

FILOPLUME, [fil'-ō-ploōm], *n.* a hair-like feather, a slender feather without vane. [L. *filum* thread and *pluma* feather].

FILOSE, [fil'-ōs], *adj.* (*zool.*) ending in a thread-like process.

FILOSELLE, [fil'-os-el], *n.* floss silk. [Fr. *filoselle*].

FILTER (1), [fil'-ter], *n.* a substance or apparatus used for ridding liquids of impurities or solid matter; an apparatus for purifying air, or for making water fit to drink; a plate of coloured glass, celluloid, etc., through which light is passed to alter its colour, intensity, or character; (*motoring*) a wire gauze to prevent dirt from the petrol tank, etc., passing into the engine; (*wirel.*) a circuit along which a limited number of frequencies only may pass. [MedL. *filtrum* a strainer].

FILTER (2), [fil'-ter], *v.t.* and *i.* to strain or purify by passing through a filter or porous substance; to rid of impurities or solid matter; (of light) to modify by passing through a filter; to trickle as through a filter; (*fig.*) to pass or be received slowly and intermittently as through a filter.

FILTERABLE, [fil'-ter-abl], *adj.* that may be filtered; **f. virus**, a microbe large enough to be isolated by filtering.

FILTER-BED, [fil'-ter-bed'], *n.* a reservoir with an artificial lining of some porous substance through which water, sewage, etc., may be filtered.

FILTERING, [fil'-ter-ing], *n.* the act of straining, purifying, or modifying by means of a filter; **f. cup**, a pneumatic apparatus used to demonstrate the pressure of the atmosphere upon water.

FILTER-PAPER, [fil'-ter-pā'-per], *n.* porous paper used for filtering liquids.

FILTH, [filth], *n.* foul, unclean matter; anything that defiles; dirt, dust, mud, etc.; (*fig.*) obscenity, indecency; (*coll.*) trash, rubbish. [OE. *fylth*].

FILTHILY, [filth'-il-i], *adv.* in a filthy fashion.

FILTHINESS, [filth'-in-es], *n.* the condition of being filthy.

FILTHY, [fil'-thi], *adj.* foul, unclean, dirty, abounding in filth; obscure, indecent; depraved; (*coll.*) vile, very bad; **f. lucre**, money.

FILTRATE (1), [fil'-trāt], *n.* the liquid which has been run through a filter.

FILTRATE (2), [fil'-trāt], *v.t.* to filter.

FILTRATION, [fil-trā'-shun], *n.* the act or process of filtering.

FIMBLE, [fimbl], *n.* the male hemp plant. [Du. *femel* female, formerly applied to what is now termed the male hemp].

FIMBRIA, [fim'-bria], *n.* a fringe; (*bot.*) the denticulated ring of the operculum of mosses; (*anat.*) the fringe-like termination of the Fallopian tube. [L. *fimbria*].

FIMBRIATE (1), [fim'-bri-āt], *adj.* (*bot.*, *zool.*) edged with fringe-like processes. [L. *fimbriatus*].

FIMBRIATE (2), [fim'-bri-āt], *v.t.* to furnish with a border or fringe.

FIMBRIATED, [fim'-bri-ā-tid], *adj.* fimbriate; (*her.*) decorated as an ordinary, with a narrow border of another tincture.

FIMBRICATE, [fim'-brik-āt], *adj.* fimbriate.

FIMETARIOUS, [fim-et-āer'-i-us], *adj.* flourishing among dung. [L. *fimetum* dung-hill].

FIMETIC, [fim-et'-ik], *adj.* pertaining to, or resembling, dung.

FIN (1), [fin], *n.* a flat ribbed projecting organ of locomotion of a fish or cetacean; a similar flat projection attached to the vertical part of the tail of an aeroplane or to an airship for balancing or steering purposes; (*slang*) the hand. [OE. *finn*].

FIN (2), **(finning, finned)**, [fin], *v.t.* to cut up (a chub).

FINABLE, [fīn'-abl], *adj.* liable to a fine or penalty.

FINAL (1), [fī'-nal], *n.* the concluding stage, that which is final, the last heat, round, or match in a knock-out competition or event; (*pl.*) the final examination for a University degree, diploma, or certificate.

FINAL (2), [fī'-nal], *adj.* pertaining to the end, last, concluding, ultimate; conclusive, decisive, determining; **f. clause**, (*gram.*) a clause expressing purpose; **f. newspaper**, (*coll.*) the last edition of a newspaper published during the day. [L. *finalis*].

FINALE, [fin-ah'-li], *n.* (*mus.*) the last movement in a symphony, concerto, sonata, etc.; the last song or chorus of an act of an opera; that which concludes or finishes, the end, the close. [It. *finale*].

FINALIST, [fīn'-al-ist], *n.* a competitor who has reached the final of a competition, tournament, race, etc.

FINALITY, [fīn-al'-it-i], *n.* the quality of being final, conclusiveness; that which is final. [L. *finalitas*].

FINALLY, [fī'-nal-i], *adv.* lastly, in conclusion; completely.

FINANCE (1), [fī-nants', fin-ants'], *n.* the science of managing money matters, *esp.* public money or revenue; (*pl.*) funds, wealth, monetary resources. [OFr. *finance* the act of settling a debt].

FINANCE (2), [fī-nants', fin-ants'], *v.t.* to find the capital for, to furnish with the necessary money or funds.

FINANCIAL, [fī-nan'-shal, fin-an'-shal], *adj.* pertaining to finance or to money matters.

FINANCIALLY, [fī-nan'-shal-i, fin-an'-shal-i], *adv.* as regards money matters, from the point of view of finance.

FINANCIER, [fi-nan'-si-er, fin-an'-si-er], *n.* one skilled or versed in finance; a person engaged in large-scale monetary dealings. [Fr. *financier*].

FINBACK, [fin'-bak'], *n.* a kind of whale, the rorqual.

FINCH, [finch], *n.* one of a large family of small perching birds, of the *Fringillidae*. [OE. *finc*].

FINCHED, [fincht], *adj.* marked or spotted on the back. [Unkn.].

FIND (1), [find], *n.* a discovery, *esp.* one of a peculiarly satisfying or important nature; an unexpected and profitable acquisition.

FIND (2), [find], *v.t. and i.* to discover, to perceive that which was hidden or lost; to discover by experiment, trial, experience, study; to detect; to provide, furnish with; (*leg.*) to judge, to decide and declare; to obtain, to get hold of; to discover game; (*leg.*) to give a verdict, to decide in favour of, or against; **to f. a true bill**, (*leg.*) to establish grounds of accusation; **to f. oneself**, (of health, etc.) to be, to fare; **to f. a ship's trim**, (*naut.*) to discover how a ship sails best; **to f. one's way**, to make one's way. [OE. *findan*].

FINDABLE, [find'-abl], *adj.* discoverable, that may be found.

FINDER, [find'-er], *n.* one who, or that which, finds; a small lens attached to a camera in which can be seen an image of the object or scene to be photographed; a small telescope attached to a larger one for sighting purposes.

FIND-FAULT, [find'-fawlt'], *n.* a censurer, a carping critic.

FINDING, [find'-ing], *n.* that which is found; (*leg.*) decision reached by a judge, jury, arbitrator, etc.; (*pl.*) conclusions arrived at by a commission or tribunal of enquiry.

FINDON, see FINNAN.

FINE (1), [fin], *n.* a payment of a sum of money imposed by law as punishment for an offence; payment made by a person renewing a lease; (*feudal leg.*) sum of money paid by a vassal or tenant to his overlord; an old method of conveyance by a collusive or fictitious action; **in f.**, finally, in short. [OFr. *fin* end, settlement].

FINE (2), [fin], *adj.* slender, small, thin; rare; minute; delicately wrought, displaying dexterous workmanship; polished, refined, finished; delicate, not coarse; sharp, keen; elegant, ornate, handsome; accomplished, skilful, extremely good; superb, splendid, striking, excellent, compelling admiration; well developed, in excellent condition, having few defects; free from impurities, pure; nice, bright, not raining; subtle, requiring discrimination; acute, keen, discriminating; ostentatious, showy; **one of these f. days**, upon some future unspecified occasion; **f. arts**, arts cultivated for their aesthetic not utilitarian qualities; **f. chemicals**, chemicals made in small quantities, and refined to a high degree of purity. [Fr. *fin*].

FINE (3), [fin], *adv.* finely, very well; **to cut it f.**, (*coll.*) to allow oneself a bare minimum or hardly enough.

FINE (4), [fin], *v.t.* to impose a fine upon, to punish by a fine.

FINE (5), [fin], *v.t. and i.* to become more pure or clear; to become finer in texture, quality, etc.; to purify, to refine.

FINE-CUT, [fin'-kut], *adj.* cut fine.

FINE-DRAW, [fin'-draw], *v.t.* to sew together or mend so that the join or mending is not noticeable; to draw out to a high degree of thinness or fineness.

FINE-DRAWN, [fin'-drawn'], *adj.* having the edges joined or sewn in such a way as to be unnoticeable; drawn out very finely; over-subtle, requiring keen discrimination.

FINE-FINGERED, [fin'-fing'-gerd], *adj.* skilful and dexterous in workmanship.

FINELY, [fin'-li], *adv.* in a fine fashion.

FINENESS, [fin'-nes], *n.* the quality of being fine.

FINER, [fin'-er], *n.* one who refines.

FINERY (1), [fin'-er-i], *n.* that which is fine; splendour or elaborateness of personal attire; resplendent array.

FINERY (2), [fin'-er-i], *n.* a hearth used in the manufacture of steel from pig-iron, or in making cast-iron malleable. [Fr. *finerie*].

FINE-SPOKEN, [fin'-spōk'-en], *adj.* using fine phrases or words.

FINE-SPUN, [fin'-spun], *adj.* spun out to a high degree of fineness, delicate; (*fig.*) elaborated with excessive subtlety.

FINESSE (1), [fin-es'], *n.* subtlety of action, diplomatic management, tact, dexterity; artfulness, cunning; (*cards*) an attempt to take a trick with a low card, while holding a high one in that suit, in order to make an extra trick. [Fr. *finesse*].

FINESSE (2), [fin-es'], *v.t. and i.* to act with finesse, to use finesse; (*cards*) to make a finesse; to deal with by finesse; (*whist*) to play as a finesse.

FINESSER, [fin-es'-er], *n.* one who finesses.

FINESTILL, [fin'-stil'], *v.t.* to distil spirit from molasses, treacle, or some saccharine preparation.

FINE-STUFF, [fin'-stuf'], *n.* the second coat of plaster for the walls of a room, consisting of finely sifted lime and water.

FIN-FISH, [fin'-fish'], *n.* a fin-backed whale.

FIN-FOOT, [fin'-fōōt'], *n.* a family of tropical birds characterized by webbed feet, of which the *Heliornis fulica* is the most familiar species.

FIN-FOOTED, [fin'-fōōt'-id], *adj.* web-footed.

FINGER (1), [fing'-ger], *n.* one of the five digits in which the hand terminates, *esp.* any one of these other than the thumb; the breadth of one of these; part of a glove into which a finger fits; anything shaped like a finger; a small slender projection from a fruit or plant; a similar shaped projecting piece of machinery; a long thin slice; one of the pointers of a clock or watch; **not to lift a f.**, to make no attempt to help; **to have a f. in the pie**, to have a share in; **to lay a f. on**, to harm, to injure; **to have at one's f. ends**, to have certain knowledge ready for immediate use; to be thoroughly conversant with. [OE. *finger*].

FINGER (2), [fing'-ger], *v.t.* to hold, touch, or handle with the fingers; (*mus.*) to play an instrument with the fingers, to play a passage using a particular fingering; to indicate, on the music itself, the fingering to be used; (*coll.*) to pilfer, to take or accept illegally.

FINGER-ALPHABET, [fing'-ger-alf'-ab-et], *n.* various signs or positions of the fingers and hands representing the different letters of the alphabet, and used by deaf and dumb persons in conversing.

FINGER AND TOE, [fing'-ger-and-tō'], *n.* anbury, a disease attacking various roots, chiefly turnips, and caused by the slime-fungus, *Plasmodiophora Brassicae*.

FINGERBOARD, [fing'-ger-bawd'], *n.* the board at the neck of a violin, guitar, or the like, where the fingers are pressed against the strings; a keyboard.

FINGER-BOWL, [fing'-ger-bōl'], *n.* a small bowl containing water in which the fingers may be dipped after dessert at the dinner-table.

FINGERBREADTH, [fing'-ger-bredth'], *n.* the sixteenth part of a foot.

FINGERED, [fing'-gerd], *adj.* having fingers; (*bot.*) digitate; **light-f. gentry**, (*coll.*) pickpockets.

FINGER-FISH, [fing'-ger-fish'], *n.* the star-fish.

FINGER-FLOWER, [fing'-ger-flow'-er], *n.* the foxglove.

FINGERGLASS, [fing'-ger-glahs'], *n.* a finger-bowl.

FINGER-GRASS, [fing'-ger-grahs'], *n.* a grass of the genus *Digitaria*.

FINGERING (1), [fing'-ger-ing], *n.* the act or method of playing a musical instrument with the fingers, the use of the proper finger in playing each note of a musical composition; the written instructions on the music as to the proper fingers to use in playing each note; the act of touching or handling with the fingers.

FINGERING (2), **FINGRAM**†, [fing'-ger-ing], *n.* a loose-twisted fine kind of wool. [Fr. *fin grain* fine grain].

FINGER-LANGUAGE, [fing'-ger-lang'-wij], *n.* the deaf and dumb alphabet.

FINGERLING, [fing'-ger-ling], *n.* a young salmon, the parr.

FINGER-MARK, [fing'-ger-mahk'], *n.* a mark or impression made by the finger.

FINGER-NAIL, [fing'-ger-nāl'], *n.* the thin layer of horny substance at the tip of the finger.

FINGERNUT, [fing'-ger-nut'], *n.* a butterfly nut.

FINGERPLATE, [fing'-ger-plāt'], *n.* a plate fixed to the door, near the handle, to protect the paint from finger-marks.

FINGERPOST, [fing'-ger-pōst'], *n.* a sign-post at crossroads, etc., *esp.* one whose signs end in the representation of a finger.

FINGERPRINT, [fing'-ger-print'], *n.* an impression taken from, or left by, the ball of the finger, used to identify criminals.

FINGERSTALL, [fing'-ger-stawl'], *n.* a cover or protection for the finger when hurt.

FINGERSTONE, [fing'-ger-stōn'], *n.* a fossil resembling an arrow; a belemnite.

FINGER-TIP CONTROL, [fing'-ger-tip'-kon-trōl'], *n.* arrangement of controls of a motor-car in the centre of the steering wheel.

FINGRAM†, see FINGERING (2).

FINIAL, [fin′-i-al], *n.* (*arch.*) an ornamental projection surmounting a gable, pinnacle, etc. [L. *finis* end].

FINICAL, [fin′-ikl], *adj.* extremely fastidious, fussy, too particular about unimportant details; containing a superfluity of highly finished, elaborate detail. [Uncert.].

FINIAL

FINICALLY, [fin′-ik-al-i], *adv.* in a finical fashion.

FINICALNESS, [fin′-ik-al-nes], *n.* the quality of being finical.

FINICKING, [fin′-ik-ing], *adj.* finical, affectedly refined, over-precise, *esp.* about trifling details; paltry, mean, insignificant.

FINICKY, [fin′-ik-i], *adj.* finicking, fussy.

FINING, [fī′-ning], *n.* the process of refining or purifying; a solution, generally of gelatine, used for clarifying wines.

FINING-POT, [fī′-ning-pot′], *n.* a receptacle in which metals are refined.

FINIS, [fin′-is], *n.* the end, conclusion. [L. *finis*].

FINISH (1), [fin′-ish], *n.* the concluding stage, end, close; final attention, care, or preparation to make as perfect as possible; that which completes or makes perfect; the style in which a thing is finished; **to fight to a f.,** to fight until a decisive result is reached.

FINISH (2), [fin′-ish], *v.t.* and *i.* to bring to an end, to complete, to cease, to conclude; to come to the end of; to make as perfect as possible; to kill, to destroy, to put an end to; to come to an end, to terminate; (*coll.*) to be discharged; **to f. with,** to cease to have further dealings or relations with. [ME. *finishen* from L. *finire* to finish].

FINISHED, [fin′-isht], *adj.* complete, perfect, highly wrought, consummate.

FINISHER, [fin′-ish-er], *n.* one who, or that which, finishes, a workman or machine that performs the final processes in the manufacture of an article.

FINISHING, [fin′-ish-ing], *adj.* completing, giving a finish to, ending.

FINITE, [fī′-nīt], *adj.* limited, having a fixed boundary, bounded; (*math.*) that has ends determinable; (*gram.*) (of a part of a verb) limited as regards number and person. [L. *finitum*, *p.pt.* of *finire* to limit].

FINITELESS, [fī′-nīt-les], *adj.* infinite.

FINITELY, [fī′-nīt-li], *adv.* to a limited degree.

FINITENESS, [fī′-nīt-nes], *n.* the condition of being finite.

FINITUDE, [fī′-ni-choōd], *n.* finiteness.

FINLESS, [fin′-les], *adj.* without fins.

FINLET, [fin′-let], *n.* a small fin.

FINLIKE, [fin′-līk], *adj.* resembling a fin.

FINN, [fin], *n.* a native of Finland. [OE. *Finnas* Finns].

FINNAN, FINDON, [fin′-an], *n.* a haddock cut open, salted, and smoke-dried over a special fire. [*Findhorn*, a Scottish river or a fishing village on the river].

FINNED, [find], *adj.* provided with fins.

FINNER, [fin′-er], *n.* a fin-backed whale, a rorqual.

FINNIC, [fin′-ik], *adj.* pertaining to the Finns, their language, or the group of languages to which it belongs.

FINNIKIN, [fin′-ik-in], *n.* a pigeon having a mane-like crest. [Unkn.].

FINNISH (1), [fin′-ish], *n.* the language of the Finns.

FINNISH (2), [fin′-ish], *adj.* pertaining to the Finns or their language.

FINNOC, PHINOC, [fin′-ok], *n.* (*Scots*) the white trout, *Salmo trutta*. [Gael. *fionnag*].

FINNY, [fin′-i], *adj.* provided with fins.

FINOCHIO, [fin-ok′-i-ō], *n.* sweet fennel, *Fœniculum dulce*. [It. *finocchio*].

FINOS, [fēn′-os], *n.*(*pl.*) second quality merino wool. [Span. *finos*, *pl.* of *fino* fine].

FINSCALE, [fin′-skāl], *n.* a river fish, the rudd, *Leuciscus erythrophthalmus*.

FINSEN LIGHT, [fin′-sen-līt′], *n.* a special electric light used in ultra-violet ray treatment of disease. [The Danish doctor, N. *Finsen*].

FIN-TOED, [fin′-tōd], *adj.* web-footed.

FIN-WHALE, [fin′-wāl], *n.* a rorqual; any species of the genus *Balaenoptera*.

FIN-WHALE

FIORD, [fē′-awd], *n.* a deeply indented, narrow, and rock-bound inlet in the coast, formed by ice action, as on the west coast of the Scandinavian peninsula. [Norw. *fjord*].

FIORIN, [fē′-or-in], *n.* the white bent-grass, *Agrostis alba*. [Ir. *fiorthan* long coarse grass].

FIORITE, [fi-aw′-rīt], *n.* (*min.*) a glassy incrustation formed from siliceous deposits in volcanic areas. [Santa *Fiora* where first found].

FIORITURA, [fē′-o-ri-tyoōer′-a], *n.* (*mus.*) a florid embellishment. [It. *fioritura*].

FIR, [fur], *n.* any of several species of cone-bearing trees of various genera, chiefly *Abies* and *Pinus*, highly valued for their timber; the wood of these trees. [ME. *firre*].

FIRE (1), [fīer], *n.* the active principle of combustion, characterized by flame, smoke and heat; a quantity of fuel burning in a hearth or enclosed space to provide heat, or by way of celebration; a conflagration, burning of a building, etc.; discharge of fire-arms; a state of combustion; (*fig.*) light, lustre; strong feeling, fervour, ardent zeal or passion; spirit, animation; **to set f. to,** to cause to burn; **to play with f.,** to meddle in dangerous things; **to catch f.,** to start to burn; **to set the Thames on f.,** to accomplish some startling exploit; **to go through f. and water,** to endure all manner of risks, dangers, or hardships; **out of the frying pan into the f.,** from an unpleasant situation to one still more unenviable; **on f.,** burning, in a state of ignition; wildly excited or eager; **under f.,** exposed to shooting; **to open f.,** to begin shooting; **between two fires,** attacked from two sides. [OE. *fyr*].

FIRE (2), [fīer], *v.t.* and *i.* to set on fire, to light; to supply with fuel; to apply heat to; to cauterize; to bake (bricks), to dry (tea); (*fig.*) to direct a continual stream (of questions, etc.); to rouse, to stir violently, to inflame; (*slang*) to dismiss from a post or from service; to become ignited; to discharge fire-arms; **to f. away,** (*coll.*) to begin, to go ahead; **to f. up,** to burst into sudden violent anger; **to f. off,** to cause to cease burning (a kiln).

FIRE-ALARM, [fīer′-al-ahm′], *n.* an apparatus for giving the alarm in case of fire.

FIRE-ARM, [fīer′-ahm], *n.* a weapon from which a missile is discharged by the ignition of an explosive.

FIREBACK, [fīer′-bak′], *n.* the iron plate at the back of a fireplace; a variety of East Indian pheasant of the genus *Euplocamus*.

FIRE-BALL, [fīer′-bawl′], *n.* a large explosive meteor; a ball of lightning; (*milit.*) a receptacle filled with combustibles and hurled among the enemy.

FIRE-BALLOON, [fīer′-bal-oōn′], *n.* a balloon filled with rarefied air, heated by a fire at its mouth.

FIRE-BARREL, [fīer′-ba′-rel], *n.* a hollow cylinder filled with explosives and used in fireships.

FIRE-BARS, [fīer′-bahz′], *n.*(*pl.*) the iron bars of a grate or furnace to support the fuel.

FIREBASKET, [fīer′-bahs′-ket], *n.* a small portable grate for a bedroom; the grate in a fireplace.

FIRE-BAVIN, [fīer′-bav′-in], *n.* a bundle of dry brush-wood readily ignited.

FIREBLAST, [fīer′-blahst′], *n.* a disease attacking plants causing them to appear scorched and withered.

FIREBOARD, [fīer′-bawd′], *n.* a chimney-board placed in front of a fireplace in summer.

FIRE-BOMB, [fīer′-bom′], *n.* an incendiary bomb.

FIREBOX, [fīer′-boks′], *n.* the part of a boiler in which the fuel is burnt.

FIREBRAND, [fīer′-brand′], *n.* a piece of wood kindled or on fire; an incendiary; (*fig.*) one who inflames the minds of others and incites them to revolt; a trouble-maker.

FIREBRICK, [fīer′-brik′], *n.* a brick that will not disintegrate under the action of intense heat.

FIRE-BRIGADE, [fīer′-brig-ād′], *n.* an organized body of men, properly equipped and trained for dealing with outbreaks of fire.

FIRE-BRUSH, [fīer′-brush′], *n.* a brush used for sweeping the hearth.

FIRE-BUCKET, [fīer′-buk′-it], *n.* a bucket in which to carry water for extinguishing fire.

FIRE-BUG, [fīer′-bug′], *n.* a firefly.

FIRECLAY, [fīer′-klā′], *n.* clay used in making firebricks.

FIRECOCK, [fīer′-kok′], *n.* a cock or spout from which water may be drawn to put out a fire.

FIRE-COMPANY, [fīer′-kum′-pan-i], *n.* a fire-brigade; a company that issues insurance against fire.

FIRE-CONTROL, [fīer′-kon-trōl′], *n.* the system by which the guns of a ship can be controlled from one central position.

FIRE-CRACKERS, [fīer′-krak′-erz], *n.*(*pl.*) fireworks ignited for amusement.

FIRECREST, [fier'-krest'], *n.* the wren, *Regulus ignicapillus*, with a brightly coloured crest.
FIREDAMP, [fier'-damp'], *n.* an explosive gas occurring in coal-mines.
FIREDOG, [fier'-dog'], *n.* an andiron, a piece of metal supporting burning fuel on an open hearth.
FIRE-DRILL, [fier'-dril'], *n.* practice in fire-fighting for the members of a fire-brigade; practice in the routine to be observed in case of fire.
FIRE-EATER, [fier'-ē'-ter], *n.* a performer who claims to eat fire; a hot-headed, quick-tempered, contentious person.
FIRE-ENGINE, [fier'-en'-jin], *n.* a vehicle for transporting firemen and equipment to an outbreak of fire, and provided with an engine for pumping water at high pressure to a considerable height, through hoses.
FIRE-ESCAPE, [fier'-es-kāp'], *n.* a contrivance for enabling persons to escape from the upper part of a building on fire; an iron staircase on the outside of a building, to be used in case of fire.
FIRE - EXTINGUISHER, [fier'-eks-ting'-gwish-er], *n.* a portable metal receptacle containing a chemical liquid for extinguishing an outbreak of fire.
FIRE-EYED, [fier'-id'], *adj.* having angry eyes, with glowing eyes.
FIRE-FLAIR, [fier'-flāer'], *n.* the sting ray, *Trygon pastinaca*.
FIREFLY, [fier'-flī'], *n.* a winged insect emitting a phosphorescent light; a luminous beetle of the *Elateridae* or *Lampyridae*.
FIRE-GUARD (1), [fier'-gahd'], *n.* a framework placed in front of a fireplace to prevent small children from approaching too near a fire.
FIRE-GUARD (2), [fier'-gahd'], *n.* a fire-watcher or body of fire-watchers.
FIRE-HOOK, [fier'-ho͝ok'], *n.* a large hook for pulling down burning buildings.
FIREHOSE, [fier'-hōz'], *n.* a hose through which water is pumped at high pressure by a fire-engine, for putting out a fire.
FIRE-INSURANCE, [fier'-in-sho͞oer'-ants], *n.* an indemnity against loss from fire.
FIRE-IRONS, [fier'-iernz'], *n.(pl.)* metal implements for use in tending a domestic fire.
FIRE-KILN, [fier'-kiln'], *n.* an oven or place for baking bricks, etc.
FIRE-LEAF, [fier'-lēf], *n.* an incendiary leaf-shaped object dropped from raiding aircraft. [FIRE (1) and LEAF (1)].
FIRELESS, [fier'-les], *adj.* devoid of fire or a fire.
FIRELIGHT, [fier'-līt'], *n.* the light given off from the fire.
FIRE-LIGHTER, [fier'-lī'-ter], *n.* a combustible substance with which a fire may be kindled.
FIRELOCK, [fier'-lok'], *n.* an old-fashioned musket in which powder was ignited by sparks produced by percussion or friction of a steel and flint in the gun-lock.
FIREMAN, [fier'-man], *n.* a person specially trained for dealing with outbreaks of fire; a stoker.
FIRE-NEW, [fier'-new'], *adj.* brand-new.
FIRE-OFFICE, [fier'-of'-is], *n.* the office of a fire-insurance company.
FIRE-OPAL, [fier'-ō'-pal], *n.* a variety of opal reflecting a vivid flame-coloured light.
FIRE-PAN, [fier'-pan'], *n.* a pan for holding fire, a brazier; the priming part of a gun.
FIREPLACE, [fier'-plās'], *n.* a small recess in the wall at the bottom of a chimney, in which a fire may be lighted, together with the ornamental structure or piece of furniture built above and at each side of this.
FIRE-PLUG, [fier'-plug'], *n.* the valve in a water-main to which the firehose is connected.
FIRE-POLICY, [fier'-pol'-is-i], *n.* an insurance policy against loss or damage by fire.
FIRE-POT, [fier'-pot'], *n.* a crucible, the receptacle for a fire in a furnace or stove.
FIREPROOF, [fier'-pro͞of'], *adj.* proof against fire, non-inflammable and heat-resisting.
FIREPROOF CURTAIN, [fier'-pro͞of'-kurt'-an], *n.* a safety curtain made of some fire-resisting material, lowered before, or during an interval of, a theatrical performance.
FIRER, [fier'-er], *n.* one who fires.
FIRE-RAISING, [fier'-rā'-zing], *n.* arson, incendiarism.
FIRE-SCREEN, [fier'-skrēn'], *n.* a movable screen placed before a fire as a shield against the heat; a protection against fire.
FIRESHIP, [fier'-ship'], *n.* a ship containing lighted combustibles, sent among enemy ships to ignite them.
FIRE-SHOVEL, [fier'-shuv'-el], *n.* a shovel for placing coal on a fire or removing cinders.
FIRESIDE, [fier'-sīd], *n.* that part of a room near the fireplace, hearth; *(fig.)* home, home-life; **f.-talk,** an informal broadcast address.
FIRE-SPOTTER, [fier'-spot'-er], *n.* one detailed to watch for fires caused by raiding aircraft.
FIRE-STEP, [fier'-step'], *n.* *(fort.)* the raised step in a trench on which a soldier stands to fire over the parapet.
FIRE-STICK, [fier'-stik'], *n.* a lighted stick or brand; one of two pieces of wood rubbed together to produce fire.
FIRE-STONE, [fier'-stōn'], *n.* a fireproof stone, a hearthstone; any of several varieties of sandstone, granite, etc.; *(archaic)* iron pyrites.
FIRETAIL, [fier'-tāl'], *n.* the redstart, *Ruticilla phœnicurus*.
FIRETRAP, [fier'-trap'], *n.* a building offering no adequate protection or means of escape in the event of fire.
FIRE-WALKING, [fier'-wawk'-ing], *n.* a religious rite of walking barefoot over white-hot stones, the feet of those taking part in the ceremony being apparently unharmed by the ordeal.
FIRE-WARD, [fier'-wawd], *n.* a fire-warden.
FIRE-WARDEN, [fier'-wawd'-en], *n.* the official responsible for supervising fire-fighting operations.
FIRE-WATCHER, [fier'-woch-er], *n.* one detailed to guard against fires caused by raiding aircraft.
FIREWATER, [fier'-waw'-ter], *n.* *(coll.)* strong spirits.
FIRE-WEED, [fier'-wēd'], *n.* a plant springing up rapidly where brushwood has been burned, *Plantago media* or *Epilobium angustifolium*.
FIREWOOD, [fier'-wo͝od'], *n.* wood for fuel, *esp.* when chopped into small sticks.
FIREWORKS, [fier'-wurks'], *n.(pl.)* preparations of gunpowder, sulphur, and other inflammable materials, packed in cardboard cylinders or containers, and discharged by the lighting of a small fuse; *(slang)* startling and disturbing occurrences.
FIRE-WORSHIP, [fier'-wur'-ship], *n.* the worship of fire, *esp.* as embodied in the sun.
FIRE-WORSHIPPER, [fier'-wur'-ship-er], *n.* one who worships fire.
FIRING, [fier'-ing], *n.* the discharge of fire-arms; fuel; the action of setting on fire, or subjecting to heat in order to bake.
FIRING-LINE, [fier'-ing-līn'], *n.* the line of trenches and soldiers nearest to those of the enemy.
FIRING-PARTY, [fier'-ing-pah'-ti], *n.* the group of soldiers selected for the special duty of shooting a condemned soldier or spy or of discharging a salute over the grave of a soldier.
FIRKIN, [fur'-kin], *n.* a small cask or barrel; a measure, the fourth part of a barrel, approximately 9 gallons. [ME. *ferdekyn*, Du. *vierde* fourth].
FIRLOT, [fur'-lot], *n.* an old measure of capacity, the fourth part of a boll; a vessel used in measuring this quantity. [OIcel. *fjorthi hlotr* fourth part].
FIRM (1), [furm], *n.* an association of two or more persons in partnership for conducting the affairs of a business organization; the name or title under which a company operates. [It. *firma* signature].
FIRM (2), [furm], *adj.* solid, compact, resisting, resolute, steadfast; unflinching; steady, fixed, stable; strong, determined; *(comm.)* not subject to sudden variations, not tending to drop. [L. *firmus*].
FIRM (3), [furm], *adv.* firmly.
FIRM (4), [furm], *v.t. and i.* to fix, to make firm; to become firm.
FIRMAMENT, [furm'-a-ment], *n.* the sky, the heavens. [L. *firmamentum* support].
FIRMAMENTAL, [furm'-a-ment'-al], *adj.* relating to the firmament, celestial.
FIRMAN, [fur'-man], *n.* an edict issued by an Oriental ruler. [Pers. *ferman*].
FIRMLY, [furm'-li], *adv.* in firm fashion.
FIRMNESS, [furm'-nes], *n.* the condition of being firm.
FIRST (1), [furst], *n.* the beginning; one who, or that which, is first in number or quality; a first place or prize in a contest, a first class in an examination; *(mus.)* the highest part of a piece of music written for different voices, the instrument playing the highest part of an orchestral work.
FIRST (2), [furst], *adj.* beginning a series; taking place, performing something before anything or anyone else; foremost in position, preceding all others in a

series; earliest; principal, chief, leading; taking precedence over all others; original; **f. thing,** as early as possible. [OE. *fyrst*].

FIRST (3), [furst], *adv.* before anything else in time, place, rank, consideration, etc.; before something may take place; for the first time; (*coll.*) rather, preferably.

FIRST-AID, [furst'-ād'], *n.* immediate simple treatment given to an injured person.

FIRST-BORN (1), [furst'-bawn'], *n.* the eldest child.

FIRST-BORN (2), [furst'-bawn'], *adj.* eldest.

FIRST-CLASS (1), [furst'-klahs'], *adj.* of the best quality, of the highest standard; (*coll.*) splendid, excellent, tremendous.

FIRST-CLASS (2), [furst'-klahs'], *adv.* (*coll.*) excellently, very well; by first-class accommodation.

FIRST-FLOOR, [furst'-flaw(r)'], *adj.* relating to the floor immediately above the ground floor.

FIRST-FOOT, [furst'-fŏŏt'], *n.* (*Scots*) the first caller to enter a house on New Year's Day.

FIRST-FRUITS, [furst'-frōōts'], *n.* the first harvest products collected in any season, *esp.* when offered for religious purposes; (*fig.*) the first results, effects; (*eccles. hist.*) a payment equivalent to the first year's revenue made by each holder of a benefice or remunerative office.

FIRST-HAND, [furst'-hand'], *adj.* direct; **at f.,** without the intervention of an intermediary.

FIRSTLING, [furst'-ling], *n.* the first to be produced, the first result, effect, etc.; the first-born of an animal.

FIRSTLY, [furst'-li], *adv.* in the first place.

FIRST-MOVER, [furst'-mōō'-ver], *n.* the prime mover; the original propelling power.

FIRST NIGHT, [furst'-nīt], *n.* the first performance in the run of a play, etc.

FIRST-NIGHTER, [furst'-nīt'-er], *n.* (*coll.*) a person who makes a practice of attending first performances of plays.

FIRST-RATE (1), [furst'-rāt'], *n.* a ship of war of the largest and most powerful class.

FIRST-RATE (2), [furst'-rāt'], *adj.* of the highest degree of excellence, pre-eminent; (*nav.*) belonging to the largest and most powerful class.

FIRST-RATE (3), [furst'-rāt'], *adv.* excellently, extremely well.

FIRST-WATER, [furst'-waw'-ter], *n.* the finest quality.

FIRTH, [furth], *n.* a long narrow inlet stretching into the coast. [OIcel. *fjorthr*].

FISC, [fisk], *n.* a state or public treasury, that of the Roman Republic, or the Crown Treasury of Scotland. [L. *fiscus* purse].

FISCAL (1), [fis'-kal], *n.* a high legal official, a Public Prosecutor; (*Scots*) the Procurator-fiscal.

FISCAL (2), [fis'-kal], *adj.* relating to the public revenue; **Procurator-f.** (*Scots*) the public prosecutor for cases involving the less serious crimes.

FISH (1), [fish], *n.* a cold-blooded finned creature dwelling in water and equipped with gills by which it breathes; any creature living entirely in water; the edible flesh of such creatures; (*fig.*) a person; a torpedo; **a f. out of water,** a person obviously ill at ease with his surroundings; **to have other f. to fry,** (*coll.*) to have something else to attend to; **a pretty kettle of f.,** (*coll.*) a nice mix-up; **to drink like a f.,** to indulge to excess in alcoholic beverages; **to cry stinking f.,** to indulge in self-depreciation. [OE. *fisc*].

FISH (2), [fish], *n.* a flat piece of wood or iron fastened to another to strengthen it or used to join two rails of a railway line. [Fr. *fiche* a fixing].

FISH (3), [fish], *v.t. and i.* to catch, or try to catch fish; (*fig.*) to angle for, to seek to obtain by indirect means or artifices, hints, etc.; to search for various animals living in water; to try to catch fish in; to seek to catch; **to f. the anchor,** (*naut.*) to secure the anchor to the gunwale after catting; **to f. in troubled waters,** to endeavour to reap personal gain from unsettled conditions. [OE. *fiscian*].

FISH (4), [fish], *v.t.* to strengthen or join by means of a fish or fish-plate.

FISHABLE, [fish'-abl], *adj.* able to be fished in.

FISH-BALL, [fish'-bawl'], *n.* a fried dish of shredded fish and potato served in the form of a cake.

FISH-BASKET, [fish'-bahs'-ket], *n.* a basket in which fish are carried, a creel.

FISHBEAM, [fish'-bēm'], *n.* a beam of timber, convex on the underside.

FISH-BLOCK, [fish'-blok'], *n.* a block to lift the flukes of an anchor to the gunwale.

FISH-BOLT, [fish'-bōlt'], *n.* a bolt used to secure two fishplates.

FISH-CAKE, [fish'-kāk'], *n.* a fried cake consisting of chopped fish and mashed potatoes.

FISH-CARVER, [fish'-kah'-ver], *n.* a broad knife for serving fish at a dinner-table, a fish-slice.

FISH-CURER, [fish'-kyōōer'-rer], *n.* one employed in curing fish.

FISH-DAVIT, [fish'-dav'-it], *n.* a strong spar used for fishing the anchor.

FISHER, [fish'-er], *n.* one who fishes; a species of the weasel family, the fisher marten, black fox or pekan, *Mustela pennanti*; an animal that catches fish; a fishing-boat.

FISHERBOAT, [fish'-er-bōt'], *n.* a fishing-boat.

FISHERMAN, [fish'-er-man], *n.* a person who catches fish; a skilful angler; a fishing-boat.

FISHERY, [fish'-er-i], *n.* the occupation of catching fish, the fishing industry; a place where fish are caught; (*leg.*) legal permission or authority to fish in certain waters.

FISH-FAG, [fish'-fag'], *n.* a fish-wife.

FISH-FLY, [fish'-flī'], *n.* a bait used in catching fish.

FISHGARTH, [fish'-gahth'], *n.* a weir or enclosure for trapping or preserving fish.

FISHGIG, [fish'-gig'], *n.* a weighted pole equipped with barbed points used for striking fish.

FISH-GLUE, [fish'-glōō'], *n.* glue made by boiling the skins and bones of fish.

FISH-HAWK, [fish'-hawk'], *n.* the osprey.

FISH-HOOK, [fish'-hŏŏk'], *n.* a barbed hook for catching fish.

FISHINESS, [fish'-i-nes], *n.* the quality of being fishy.

FISHING, [fish'-ing], *n.* the art or practice of catching fish; legal authority or permission to catch fish in particular waters; a stretch of water over which such rights are held.

FISHING-BOAT, [fish'-ing-bōt'], *n.* a boat used for fishing.

FISHING-FROG, [fish'-ing-frog'], *n.* a large-headed spinous-finned sea-fish, the angler, *Lophius piscatorius*.

FISHING-LINE, [fish'-ing-līn'], *n.* a line to which is attached a fish-hook for catching fish.

FISHING-NET, [fish'-ing-net'], *n.* a net used for catching fish.

FISHING-ROD, [fish'-ing-rod'], *n.* a pliable rod to which is attached a line and hook for angling.

FISHING-TACKLE, [fish'-ing-takl'], *n.* implements used by fishermen when fishing.

FISH-JOINT, [fish'-joint'], *n.* the fastening of two rails end to end by means of a fishplate.

FISH-KETTLE, [fish'-ketl'], *n.* a large oval kitchen utensil in which fish may be boiled whole.

FISH-KNIFE, [fish'-nīf'], *n.* a blunt knife with a broad flat tapering blade used for eating fish; a fish-carver.

FISH-LADDER, [fish'-lad'-er], *n.* a contrivance for assisting fish to ascend a weir or other fall on their way upstream.

FISH-MAW, [fish'-maw'], *n.* the air-bladder of a fish.

FISH-MEAL, [fish'-mēl'], *n.* dried fish ground to a fine powder.

FISHMONGER, [fish'-mung'-ger], *n.* one who sells fish.

FISH-OIL, [fish'-oil'], *n.* oil obtained from fish.

FISH-PASTE, [fish'-pāst'], *n.* a savoury paste made of fish or shellfish, eaten on bread and butter.

FISHPLATE, [fish'-plāt'], *n.* the steel plate by which the rails are joined end to end on a railway line.

FISHPLATE

FISH-POND, [fish'-pond'], *n.* a pond in which fishes are reared.

FISH-POT, [fish'-pot'], *n.* a wicker receptacle in which crabs, lobsters, etc., may be caught.

FISH-ROOM, [fish'-rōōm'], *n.* an apartment in a ship, used for keeping salt-fish in storage.

FISH-ROYAL, [fish'-roi'-al], *n.* (*leg.*) the sturgeon and the whale, to which the sovereign is entitled when caught within the boundaries of the kingdom.

FISH-SAUCE, [fish'-saws'], *n.* a sauce to be eaten with fish; a sauce made from fish.

FISH-SKIN, [fish'-skin'], *n.* the skin of a fish, the hard skin of certain species of shark, used for polishing; **f. disease,** (*med.*) ichthyosis, a disease in which the skin becomes hard and scaly.

FISH-SLICE, [fish'-slīs], *n.* a fish-carver.

FISH-SOUND, [fish'-sownd'], *n.* the swimming bladder of a fish.

FISH-SPEAR, [fish'-spēer'], *n.* a spear for stabbing fish.
FISH-STRAINER, [fish'-strā'-ner], *n.* a metal colander provided with handles for removing fish from the fish-kettle; a perforated dish to drain off water from fish.
FISH-TACKLE, [fish'-takl'], *n.* (*naut.*) tackle used in fishing the anchor.
FISH-TAIL, [fish'-tāl'], *adj.* in the shape of the tail of a fish; **f. burner**, a gas-burner producing a flat flame of this shape; **f. wind**, a wind that continually changes direction.
FISH-TROWEL, [fish'-trow'-el], *n.* a fish-carver.
FISH-WEIR, [fish'-wēer'], *n.* a fishgarth.
FISH-WIFE, (fish'-wif'], *n.* a woman who hawks fish; (*fig.*) a vulgar woman.
FISHY, [fish'-i], *adj.* consisting of, or full of, fish; like fish; resembling the smell of a fish; cold, glassy and vacant; (*coll.*) dubious, questionable.
FISSI-, *pref.* divided, cleft. [L. *fissus*, *p.pt.* of *findere* to split].
FISSICOSTATE, [fis'-i-kos'-tāt], *adj.* with the ribs divided. [FISSI and L. *costa* rib].
FISSILE, [fis'-īl], *adj.* capable of being split; dividing readily and naturally. [L. *fissilis*].
FISSILINGUAL, [fis'-i-ling'-gwal], *adj.* having a divided tongue.
FISSILITY, [fis-il'-i-ti], *n.* the quality of being fissile.
FISSION, [fish'-un], *n.* a cleaving or breaking up into parts; the process by which cells and certain simple organisms spontaneously split up into two independent new creatures. [L. *fissio*].
FISSIPARISM, [fis-ip'-a-rizm], *n.* reproduction by fission.
FISSIPAROUS, [fis-ip'-a-rus], *adj.* reproducing by fission.
FISSIPAROUSLY, [fis-ip'-a-rus-li], *adv.* in a fissiparous fashion.
FISSIPED (1), [fis'-i-ped'], *n.* a fissiped animal.
FISSIPED (2), [fis'-i-ped'], *adj.* having the toes separated. [FISSI and L. *pes pedis* foot].
FISSIROSTRAL, [fis'-i-ros'-tral], *adj.* (*ornith.*) having a deep cleft bill. [FISSI and L. *rostrum* beak].
FISSURE (1), [fish'-er], *n.* a cleft, split; (*anat.*) a natural deep narrow opening in an organ, a narrow depression dividing the anterior and middle lobes of the cerebrum; (*path.*) a crack in a bone or other tissue; (*her.*) the fourth part of the bend sinister. [L. *fissura* a cleft].
FISSURE (2), [fish'-er], *v.t. and i.* to cleave, split open, form a fissure in.
FISSURELLA, [fish'-yōō-rel'-a], *n.* the genus of the keyhole limpets. [L. *fissurella* fissure].
FIST (1), [fist], *n.* the hand when clenched and with the fingers bent over to touch the palm; (*coll.*) handwriting, the hand. [OE. *fyst*].
FIST (2), [fist], *v.t.* to strike with the fist, to grasp, seize.
FISTIC, [fist'-ik], *adj.* pertaining to, involving the use of, the fists, referring to boxing.
FISTICUFFS, [fist'-i-kufs'], *n.*(*pl.*) blows, a fight with the fists. [FIST and CUFF].
FIST-LAW, [fist'-law'], *n.* rule, law or justice founded on physical might.
FISTUCA, [fis-tew'-ka], *n.* a pile-driver, rammer. [L. *fistuca*].
FISTULA, [fis'-chōō-la], *n.* (*path.*) an abnormal channel or opening between two organs, or between an organ and the skin, caused by the discharge of pus from an ulcer; a slender winding ulcer; an organ resembling a pipe in certain insects; (*eccles.*) the tube through which the Pope partakes of the consecrated wine; (*mus.*) an ancient pipe-like instrument. [L. *fistula* pipe].
FISTULAR, [fis'-chōō-ler], *adj.* pertaining to a fistula; shaped like a fistula, pipe-like, tubular.
FISTULARIA, [fis'-chōō-lāer'-i-a], *n.* the tobacco-pipe fish.
FISTULATE†, [fis'-chōō-lāt], *v.t. and i.* to make hollow and cylindrical; to develop into a fistula. [L. *fistulare*].
FISTULIFORM, [fis'-chōō-li-fawm], *adj.* in the form of a pipe or tube. [FISTULA and FORM].
FISTULOSE, [fis'-chōō-lōs], *adj.* fistular.
FISTULOUS, [fis'-chōō-lus], *adj.* pertaining to a fistula; resembling a pipe or reed; containing long, narrow, hollow cylinders. [L. *fistulosus*].
FIT (1), [fit], *n.* a sudden and violent derangement of the nerves due to disease and often accompanied by convulsions, nervous spasms, and insensibility; a seizure, paroxysm; any sudden violent bout; nn impulsive whim, a fancy of the moment; any impulsive intermittent exertion. [ME. *fitt* strife].
FIT (2), [fit], *n.* (*archaic*) a group of verses in a poem or song, a canto. [OE. *fitt*].
FIT (3), [fit], *n.* the way in which a thing fits; a thing that fits; adjustment, *esp.* of dress to the body.
FIT (4), [fit], *adj.* appropriate, suitable, worthy; agreeable or adapted to some purpose; seemly, becoming; competent, in a proper state; ready, healthy, in sound mental and physical condition; well-trained. [ME. *fitte* an equal, match].
FIT (5), (**fitting, fitted**), [fit], *v.t.* to be of the right proportions or dimensions for; to suit, conform to; to adjust or fashion to the proper size or dimensions; to prepare, to make competent to undertake; to supply with what is necessary, suitable, or desired; to try an incomplete garment on for adjustment if necessary; to qualify, to make to conform with; *v.i.* to suit exactly; to conform to the proportions or contours of something else; to be proper, becoming or seemly; **to f. out**, to furnish, to equip; **to f. up**, to get ready, to provide with necessary or suitable furnishings, equipment, etc. [ME. *fitten*].
FITCH (1), see VETCH.
FITCH (2), [fich], *n.* the polecat; a brush made of the hair of the fitch; the fur or hair of the polecat. [MDu. *fisse*].
FITCHE, fitché, [fich'-ē], *adj.* (*her.*) sharpened to a point at the lower extremity (of a cross). [Fr. *fiché* fixed].

FITCHÉ

FITCHET, [fich'-it], *n.* the fitchew.
FITCHEW, [fich'-ōō], *n.* the polecat. [OFr. *fichau*].
FITCHY, [fich'-i], *adj.* (*her.*) fitché.
FITFUL, [fit'-fōōl], *adj.* intermittent, spasmodic, impulsive and irregular; changeful.
FITFULLY, [fit'-fōōl-i], *adv.* by fits, in a fitful manner.
FITFULNESS, [fit'-fōōl-nes], *n.* the quality of being fitful.
FITLY, [fit'-li], *adv.* in a fit fashion.
FITMENT, [fit'-ment], *n.* an article of furniture; a fitting.
FITNESS, [fit'-nes], *n.* the state or quality of being fit.
FIT-OUT, [fit'-owt'], *n.* (*coll.*) equipment.
FITTER, [fit'-er], *n.* one who fits; a tailor who fits and tries on clothes; a mechanic or engineer who adjusts or assembles the fittings of a machine.
FITTING (1), [fit'-ing], *n.* the act of one who, or that which, fits; (*pl.*) necessary or suitable fixtures, furniture or equipment; the detachable parts of a machine.
FITTING (2), [fit'-ing], *adj.* suitable, proper, becoming, appropriate.
FITTINGLY, [fit'-ing-li], *adv.* in a fitting manner.
FITTINGNESS, [fit'-ing-nes], *n.* suitableness, appropriateness.
FITTING-UP, [fit'-ing-up'], *n.* the act of equipping with things suitable or necessary.
FITZ-, *pref.* the son of; used only in proper names. [AFr. *fitz* from L. *filius* son].
FIVE (1), [fīv], *n.* the number between four and six; a playing card, etc., marked with five spots; that which comprises five things.
FIVE (2), [fīv], *adj.* one more than four, one less than six. [OE. *fif*].
FIVE-FINGER, [fīv'-fing'-ger], *n.* (*bot.*) the cinquefoil, *Potentilla reptans*; the oxlip, *Primula elatior*.
FIVEFOLD (1), [fīv'-fōld'], *adj.* five times repeated; having five component parts.
FIVEFOLD (2), [fīv'-fōld], *adv.* to a degree five times as great, by five times.
FIVELEAF, [fīv'-lēf'], *n.* (*bot.*) cinquefoil, *Potentilla reptans*.
FIVER, [fīv'-er], *n.* (*coll.*) a five-pound note issued by the Bank of England.
FIVES, [fīvz], *n.* a game played in a walled court by two or four persons, in which a small, hard ball is struck against the walls by the hands or a bat. [Unkn.].
FIVES-BALL, [fīvz'-bawl'], *n.* the small hard ball used in playing fives.
FIVES-COURT, [fīvz'-kawt'], *n.* the walled court in which the game of fives is played.
FIX (1), [fiks], *n.* (*coll.*) a predicament, an awkward situation.
FIX (2), [fiks] *v.t.* to fasten, secure in position; to set,

place; to cause to be firmly implanted in; to direct firmly, help, concentrate; to catch and hold; to cause to remain unchanged, to establish in a permanent, unalterable form; to determine, settle; to arrange, decide, appoint; to attribute, lay to the responsibility of; to ascertain, determine exactly; (*coll.*) to adjust, put right; to attend to; (*chem.*) to make solid, non-fluid; (*phot.*) to give permanency to, to secure against change or fading; to preserve; *v.i.* to settle, become firm or set; to congeal; **to f. up,** to arrange; to decide on; to settle, smooth out; (*coll.*) to make arrangements for, find lodgings, attire, etc., for. [L. *fixum*, *p.pt.* of *figere*].

FIXABLE, [fiks'-abl], *adj.* capable of being fixed.

FIXATION, [fiks-ā'-shun], *n.* the act of fixing, the state of being fixed; (*psych.*) an affection abnormal in degree or kind. [MedL. *fixatio*].

FIXATIVE (1), [fiks'-at-iv], *n.* anything used for fixing; a gummy composition for fixing the hair in the required position.

FIXATIVE (2), [fiks'-at-iv], *adj.* tending to fix.

FIXED, [fikst], *adj.* unwavering, steady; determined, settled, definitely decided; made fast, established in permanent form; not subject to fluctuation; stationary; inflexible, rigid, unalterable, firmly adhering to; (*chem.*) solidified.

FIXEDLY, [fiks'-id-li], *adv.* in a fixed manner.

FIXEDNESS, [fiks'-id-nes], *n.* the quality of being fixed.

FIXER, [fiks'-er], *n.* one who, or that which, fixes.

FIXIDITY, [fiks-id'-i-ti], *n.* fixedness.

FIXING, [fiks'-ing], *n.* the act of anyone or anything that fixes.

FIXITY, [fiks'-i-ti], *n.* permanence, the state of being fixed.

FIXTURE, [fiks'-cher], *n.* that which is permanently attached to something as a necessary part of it; (*pl., leg.*) fittings or accessories attached to a building or land so as to form part of the real property, not removable at will by the occupier; (*coll.*) one who, or that which, seems to have become established as a permanent feature of some place; an appointment, event, or engagement of a sporting nature for a specified future date; the means of fixing. [FIX and (MIX)-TURE].

FIZGIG, [fiz'-gig], *n.* a firework emitting a series of rapid explosions; a kind of harpoon; a high-spirited, frivolous young lady. [FIZZ and GIG].

FIZZ (1), [fiz], *n.* a spluttering or hissing sound; effervescence; that which fizzes; (*coll.*) champagne; a wine or drink that effervesces strongly.

FIZZ (2), [fiz], *v.i.* to make a quick bubbly hissing sound; to effervesce. [Imitative].

FIZZLE (1), [fizl], *n.* the act of fizzling; (*coll.*) a failure, fiasco.

FIZZLE (2), [fizl], *v.i.* to fizz feebly; **to f. out,** to extinguish itself by a series of diminishing explosions; (*fig.*) to end feebly. [Echoic].

FLABBERGAST, [flab'-er-gahst], *v.t.* (*coll.*) to confound, to astonish completely. [Uncert.].

FLABBILY, [flab'-i-li], *adv.* in a flabby fashion.

FLABBINESS, [flab'-i-nes], *n.* the condition of being flabby.

FLABBY, [flab'-i], *adj.* wanting firmness; limp, soft and yielding; hanging loose; (*fig.*) weak. [Low Germ. *flabbe* hanging lip].

FLABELLATE, [flab'-el-āt], *adj.* (*bot.*) in the shape of a fan. [L. *flabellare* to fan].

FLABELLATION, [flab'-el-ā'-shun], *n.* (*surg.*) the act of fanning.

FLABELLIFORM, [flab-el'-i-fawm], *adj.* fan-shaped. [FLABELLUM and FORM].

FLABELLUM, [flab'-el-um], *n.* a fan, *esp.* a ceremonial fan of state; a fan-shaped appendage or organ. [L. *flabellum* a fan].

FLACCID, [flak'-sid], *adj.* flabby; soft and yielding, loose, limp; (*fig.*) weak, lacking in energy or force. [L. *flaccidus*].

FLACCIDITY, [flak-sid'-i-ti], *n.* flaccidness.

FLACCIDLY, [flak'-sid-li], *adv.* in a flaccid fashion.

FLACCIDNESS, [flak'-sid-nes], *n.* the condition of being flaccid.

FLACKIE, [flak'-i], *n.* a heap of straw for protecting a horse's back when carrying a basket, etc. [Unkn.].

FLAG (1), [flag], *n.* (*bot.*) any of several plants, growing in marshy places, having long, thin, flat leaves; a plant of the genus *Iris*; the reed-like *Acorus Calamus*, the sweet flag; the blade of a plant; a kind of rough grass. [ME. *flagge*].

FLAG (2), [flag], *n.* a large flat slab of stone used for paving; a flag-stone; (*pl.*) a pavement of flag-stones. [OScand. *flag*].

FLAG (3), [flag], *n.* a piece of bunting or other similar cloth usually containing a distinctive emblem in colours and attached to a pole or halyard; **black f.,** the emblem of piracy; a former signal of smallpox cases; a signal of the execution of a prisoner; **red f.,** a danger signal; the symbol of defiance or challenge; the Communist or Socialist flag; **yellow f.,** a signal of quarantine and infectious illness; **white f.,** a signal of surrender, parley, or truce; **to strike the f.,** (*fig*) to surrender. [Uncert.].

FLAG (4), [flag], *n.* the quill-feathers on a bird's wing. [Uncert.].

FLAG (5), (flagging, flagged), [flag], *v.t. and i.* to droop, to stand limply; to grow spiritless or enervated; to abate, to diminish. [ME. *flacken*].

FLAG (6), [flag], *v.t.* to decorate with flags; to signal to with flags.

FLAG (7), [flag], *v.t.* to pave with flags.

FLAG-CAPTAIN, [flag'-kap'-tin], *n.* the captain of a flagship.

FLAG-DAY, [flag'-dā'], *n.* a day on which street-collectors give a small flag or imitation flower in return for contributions towards some specific charitable organization.

FLAGELLANT, [flaj'-el-ant], *n.* one who scourges himself in religious discipline; (*pl.*) a fanatical sect originating in Italy, A.D. 1260, who believed in flagellation as a punishment for sin. [L. *flagellans*].

FLAGELLATE (1), [flaj'-el-āt], *adj.* (*biol.*) possessing a flagellum or flagella; having the shape of a flagellum.

FLAGELLATE (2), [flaj'-el-āt], *v.t.* to whip, to scourge, to flog. [L. *flagellare*].

FLAGELLATION, [flaj'-el-ā-shun], *n.* the act of scourging. [L. *flagellatio*].

FLAGELLATOR, [flaj'-el-ā'-tor], *n.* one who flagellates.

FLAGELLIFORM, [flaj-el'-i-fawm], *adj.* shaped like a whip-thong. [FLAGELLUM and FORM].

FLAGELLUM, (*pl.* **flagella**), [flaj-el'-um], *n.* (*biol.*) a long flexible appendage of a cell, shaped like a whip-thong, and darting about rapidly; (*bot.*) a creeping shoot, a whip-like process. [L. *flagellum* whip].

FLAGEOLET (1), [flaj'-ō-let'], *n.* a wood-wind instrument resembling a pipe, and provided with six holes. [Fr. *flageolet*].

FLAGEOLET (2), [flaj'-ō-let'], *n.* a variety of kidney-bean. [Fr. *flageolet*].

FLAGGINESS, [flag'-i-nes], *n.* the quality of being flaggy.

FLAGGING, [flag'-ing], *n.* the act of paving with flag-stones; a pavement of flag-stones; flag-stones.

FLAGGY (1), [flag'-i], *adj.* weak, flexible, insipid, flaccid, flabby.

FLAGGY (2), [flag'-i], *adj.* relating to flag-stones.

FLAGGY (3), [flag'-i], *adj.* (*bot.*) overgrown with flags.

FLAGITATION, [flaj'-it-ā'-shun], *n.* the act of demanding in a violent and importunate manner. [L. *flagitatio*].

FLAGITIOUS, [flaj-ish'-us], *adj.* deeply criminal, grossly wicked, guilty of atrocious crimes, disgraceful. [L. *flagitiosus* shameful].

FLAGITIOUSLY, [flaj-ish'-us-li], *adv.* in a flagitious manner.

FLAGITIOUSNESS, [flaj-ish'-us-nes], *n.* extreme wickedness and cruelty.

FLAG-LIEUTENANT, [flag'-lef-ten'-ant], *n.* the adjutant assisting a flag-officer.

FLAGMAN, [flag'-man], *n.* one who signals with flags.

FLAG-OFFICER, [flag'-of'-is-er], *n.* a naval officer in command of a squadron; the commodore of the squadron of a yacht-club, distinguished by flying his own flag.

FLAGON, [flag'-un], *n.* a large vessel with handle, lid, and narrow mouth, used for wine, *esp.* at Holy Communion; a large flattened bottle. [OFr. *flagon*].

FLAGRANCY, [flā'-gran-si], *n.* the quality of being flagrant, enormity, glaring, obtrusive nature. [L. *flagrantia* burning, ardour].

FLAGRANT, [flā'-grant], *adj.* glaringly evil, notorious, scandalous, obvious; unqualified. [L. *flagrans* burning].

FLAGRANTLY, [flā'-grant-li], *adv.* in a flagrant fashion.

FLAG-SHIP, [flag'-ship'], *n.* the ship in which the commander of a squadron sails, and on which his flag is flown.

FLAG-STAFF, [flag'-stahf'], *n.* the staff from which a flag is hung.

FLAG-STONE, [flag'-stōn'], *n.* a large flat stone used in paving.

FLAGWAGGING, [flag′-wag′-ing], *n.* (*coll.*) hand signalling with flags; (*fig.*) bellicose, bluff, boastful talk.
FLAG-WORM, [flag′-wurm′], *n.* a grub living among sedges and flags, a green gentle.
FLAIL, [flāl], *n.* a wooden implement for threshing grain by hand. [OFr. *flaiel*].

FLAIL

FLAIR, [flāer], *n.* intuitive appreciation or discernment, natural aptitude or gift. [Fr. *flair*].
FLAIR-TINKER, [flāer′-tingk′-er], *n.* the skate, *Raia batis*.
FLAK, [flak], *n.* anti-aircraft fire; **f. boat**, a small German vessel equipped with anti-aircraft guns; **f. tower**, a tower equipped with anti-aircraft guns. [Germ. *flak* from *flugzeugabwehrkanonen* anti-aircraft guns].
FLAKE (1), [flāk], *n.* a small light mass of anything that floats about in the air, as snow, wool, etc.; a thin, light, flat piece of some substance that scales or peels off. [OIcel. *flaki*].
FLAKE (2), [flāk], *n.* a kind of scaffold or platform made of hurdles and used for drying fish; (*naut.*) a platform hung over the side for caulking a ship. [OIcel. *flake* hurdle].
FLAKE (3), [flāk], *v.t. and i.* to form into flakes, to separate or peel off into flakes; to cover with flakes; to fall in flakes.
FLAKE-WHITE, [flāk′-wīt], *n.* a white pigment obtained from white lead in a flaky or scaly form.
FLAKINESS, [flāk′-i-nes], *n.* the condition of being flaky.
FLAKY, [flāk′-i], *adj.* composed of flakes; breaking off in flakes.
FLAM, [flam], *v.t.* to deceive by means of lies, to delude, to trick, to hoax. [Unkn.].
FLAMBE, flambé, [flam′-bā], *adj.* (of pottery) ornamented with splashes of coloured glaze. [Fr. *flambé*].
FLAMBEAU, (*pl.* **flambeaux**), [flahm′-bō], *n.* a large ceremonial torch. [Fr. *flambeau*].
FLAMBOYANCY, [flam-boi′-an-si], *n.* ornateness, floridness, showy elaborateness.
FLAMBOYANT, [flam-boi′-ant], *adj.* (*arch.*) denoting a French Gothic style with flame-like wavings in its tracery; (*fig.*) florid to excess, showy, over-ornate. [Fr. *flamboyant* flaming].
FLAME (1), [flām], *n.* luminous heat or blaze rising from a burning body, or any inflammable gas in a state of glowing visible combustion; anything resembling this in its fierce brightness or glow, anything of a fiery red or yellow colour; (*fig.*) ardour, heat of passion or other strong emotion; vigour and keenness of thought, glow of imagination; (*coll.*) a sweetheart, one beloved. [L. *flamma*].
FLAME (2), [flām], *v.i.* to blaze, to give off flames in burning; to emit a fiery glow or flame-like luminosity, to flare, to show or appear as a blaze of colour; to blush vividly; to break out in violence of passion or excitement. [L. *flammare*].
FLAME-COLOURED, [flām′-kul′-erd], *adj.* of the colour of a flame, vivid fiery red.
FLAME-FLOWER, [flām′-flow′-er], *n.* the red-hot poker plant.
FLAMEN, [flām′-en], *n.* (*Rom. antiq.*) a priest devoted to some particular god. [L. *flamen*].
FLAME-THROWER, [flām′-thrō′-er], *n.* (*milit.*) an apparatus for discharging blazing liquid or flame on to the enemy lines.
FLAMING, [flām′-ing], *adj.* blazing, emitting flames; very bright, lurid, glaring; passionate, ardent.
FLAMINGLY, [flām′-ing-li], *adv.* extremely brightly; in a flaming fashion.
FLAMINGO, [flam-ing′-gō], *n.* a genus of birds, *Phœnicopterus*, with very long necks and legs, and palmated feet, and, when in full plumage, of a vivid red colour. [Portug. *flamengo*].
FLAMINICAL†, [flam-in′-ik-al], *adj.* relating to a Roman flamen.
FLAMMABILITY†, [flam′-a-bil′-i-ti], *n.* inflammability.
FLAMMABLE†, [flam′-abl], *adj.* inflammable.
FLAMMIFEROUS, [flam-if′-er-us], *adj.* causing flame. [L. *flamma* flame and *ferre* to bear].
FLAMMIVOMOUS, [flam-iv′-om-us], *adj.* belching forth flames, as a volcano. [L. *flamma* flame and *vomere* to vomit].
FLAMY, [flām′-i], *adj.* like a flame in nature or colour.

FLAN, [flan], *n.* a shallow tart of pastry filled with fruit, treacle, etc. [Fr. *flan*].
FLANCH, [flanch], *n.* (*her.*) one of the honourable ordinaries in the form of an arched line drawn from the corners of the chief and curving towards the centre of the shield; (*mech.*) a flange. [OFr. *flanche*].

FLANCH

FLANCONNADE, [flangk′-on-ād], *n.* (*fencing*) a sort of thrust in the flank or side. [Fr. *flanconade*].
FLANDERS-BRICK, [flahn′-derz-brik′], *n.* a brick for cleaning knives, etc.
FLANERIE, flânerie, [flahn′-er-ē′], *n.* loafing, idleness. [Fr. *flânerie*].
FLANEUR, flâneur, [flan-ur′], *n.* a lounger, idler. [Fr. *flâneur*].
FLANG, [flang], *n.* a double-pointed pick used by miners. [Unkn.].
FLANGE (1), [flanj], *n.* a projecting edge, rib, or rim on a wheel, girder, pipe, etc.; a tool employed in making flanges. [OFr. *flanche*].
FLANGE (2), [flanj], *v.t.* to provide with a flange.
FLANGE-RAIL, [flanj′-rāl′], *n.* a rail provided with a flange.
FLANK (1), [flangk], *n.* the fleshy part of an animal or human being between the ribs and the hip; the side of a mountain, hill, building, etc.; (*fort.*) that part of a bastion which reaches from the curtain to the face; (*milit.*) the side of an army or body of troops; (*pl.*) a wrench or other harm done to the back of a horse; **f. movement**, (*milit.*) a movement made in order to turn the enemy's flank. [OFr. *flanc*].
FLANK (2), [flangk], *v.t. and i.* to command or be situated at the flank of; to attack the flank of; to place troops at the flank of; to secure, guard, or protect on the flank; to border, to touch, to be placed on the side. [Fr. *flanquer*].
FLANKARDS†, [flangk′-ahdz], *n.(pl.)* the knots or knobs in the flanks of a deer. [OFr. (*nœuds*) *flancards*].
FLANKER, [flangk′-er], *n.* (*fort.*) a fortification projecting so as to protect the flank or to command the enemy flank; (*pl.*) skirmishers posted on the flanks of an army on the march.
FLANNEL (1), [flan′-el], *n.* a soft plain woollen cloth of loose texture; a piece of flannel used for polishing or cleaning; (*pl.*) clothes made of flannel, particularly trousers worn for games or as informal attire. [OFr. *flaine* blanket].
FLANNEL (2), [flan′-el], *adj.* made of flannel.
FLANNELETTE, [flan′-el-et′], *n.* a cotton fabric, similar in texture to fine flannel.
FLANNELLED, [flan′-eld], *adj.* dressed in flannel.
FLANNELLY, [flan′-el-i], *adj.* like flannel.
FLAP, [flap], *n.* a slight sharp blow with a broad flat object; a noise made by anything flapping; anything broad and flexible, fastened at one end or side, and wrapping over and covering some aperture; a thin membranous substance covering the eyes and gills of fishes; the soft flexible brim of a hat, or a hanging portion of a garment; (*coll.*) excitement. [Du. *flap* blow].
FLAP (2), [flap], *v.t. and i.* to give a light slap with a broad, flat, flexible object; to move (some broad flat object) rapidly up and down, to beat (as a bird's wings); to cause to flap or flutter; to move lightly and loosely up and down or to and fro, often with a sharp light recurring sound; to fall or hang down as a flap. [*Prec.*].
FLAPDOODLE, [flap′-doodl′], *n.* (*coll.*) nonsense, rubbish, humbug.
FLAP-DRAGON†, [flap′-drag′-on], *n.* snapdragon, a dish of burning brandy and raisins; one of the raisins eaten in this way.
FLAP-EARED, [flap′-ēerd′], *adj.* having broad, loose, pendulous ears.
FLAP-JACK, [flap′-jak′], *n.* a broad pancake; a lady's flat powder compact containing a powder-puff and powder.
FLAP-MOUTHED, [flap′-mowTHd′], *adj.* having loose, hanging, flabby lips.
FLAPPED, [flapt], *adj.* struck with something broad and flat.
FLAPPER, [flap′-er], *n.* one who, or that which, flaps; a fly-whisk, the flexible striking part of a flail, a broad

flat object used for striking, and making a noise to scare away birds; the flipper or broad fin of a seal, etc.; a young wild duck or partridge; (*coll.*) a young girl; **f. bracket,** a pillion seat on a motor-cycle.

FLARE (1), [flāer], *n.* unsteady, fitful glare of light of brief duration and rapidly increasing intensity or size; a combustible substance which, when ignited, emits a brief dazzling glare of light, used as a signal or in flashlight photography, or by aircraft to illuminate targets; (*fig.*) ostentation; a sudden display of temper; **f.-path,** a lighted track to enable aircraft to land at night.

FLARE (2), [flāer], *v.i.* to blaze up with or emit a flare or flash; (of a candle, lamp, etc.) to burn up too high; (of a skirt, sides of a ship); to spread or swell outwards as a bowl, etc.; **to f. up,** to blaze up suddenly; to fly suddenly into a passionate display of temper. [Norw. *flara* to blaze].

FLARING, [flāer'-ing], *adj.* emitting a flare or series of flares; swelling or curving outwards; (*fig.*) showy, gaudy, presenting a glaring display.

FLARINGLY, [flāer'-ing-li], *adv.* in a flaring fashion.

FLASH (1), [flash], *n.* a sudden instantaneous blaze or gleam of light; a very brief moment, a twinkling, an instant, the time occupied by a flash; thieves' slang; vulgar ostentation; a rapid stream of water suddenly released, a device for releasing this; sudden inspiration, a brief outburst of brilliance, anger, etc.; pieces of black velvet worn at the back of the collar by the Royal Welch Fusiliers; similar marks used by other regiments; (*cinema*) a short portion of a cinema film; a preliminary brief announcement of an item of news; **f. in the pan,** a sudden show of brilliance, etc., that quickly goes out.

FLASH (2), [flash], *adj.* showy, vulgarly ostentatious, smart; counterfeit; (*slang*) wide-awake, cute; pertaining to a class of thieves, dishonest rogues, sharpers, etc.; **f. steam,** (*eng.*) steam which is reheated to an extremely high temperature for high-speed engines.

FLASH (3), [flash], *v.t. and i.* to emit a flash or a series of flashes; to burst into, or reflect as, a sudden instantaneous gleam of light; to light up, to gleam; to pass like a flash; to expand molten glass into a sheet; (*fig.*) to break out or burst forth with sudden brilliance or striking manifestation; to occur suddenly, to pass rapidly through the mind; to emit in flashes; to direct a light suddenly upon an object; to cause to flare up; (*fig.*) to direct a sudden fleeting glance, smile, etc., at; to transmit rapidly by wireless, telephony, signalling apparatus, etc.; to cause to travel with the speed of a flash; to protect against inclement weather by covering (a roof) with lead, slates, etc.; (*coll.*) to display in a showy manner. [Unkn.].

FLASH-BACK, [flash'-bak'], *n.* (*cinema*) a sudden switch-over to an earlier point in the story.

FLASH-BOARD, [flash'-bawd'], *n.* a contrivance for stopping or controlling flow of water in a mill-stream.

FLASHER, [flash'-er], *n.* one who, or that which, flashes; a shallow wit; a boiler in which water is rapidly converted into steam.

FLASHES, [flash'-iz], *n.(pl.)* a type of electric lamp giving an intermittent light, much used for illuminating electric signs.

FLASH-HOUSE, [flash'-hows'], *n.* a house where thieves, criminals, and vicious persons reside; a brothel.

FLASHILY, [flash'-i-li], *adv.* in a flashy fashion.

FLASHINESS, [flash'-i-nes], *n.* the condition of being flashy.

FLASHING, [flash'-ing], *n.* the act of that which, or of one who, flashes; the process of covering colourless glass with a thin layer of coloured glass, the process of heating and expanding glass into a sheet; pieces of lead or other material lapping over portions of roofs or walls, to prevent rain from entering.

FLASHLIGHT, [flash'-lit'], *n.* an intermittent light, or one that flashes; a lamp used for signalling by means of flashes; an electric torch, operated by a dry battery within the frame of the torch, which can be switched off and on as required; a brief dazzling light used in taking certain kinds of photographs.

FLASHPOINT, [flash'-point'], *n.* the lowest temperature at which vapour from an oil or spirit will ignite.

FLASHY, [flash'-i], *adj.* cheap, showy but worthless, possessing a shallow brilliance, vulgarly ostentatious.

FLASK, [flahsk], *n.* a small flattened bottle, often protected by leather, etc., for wine, spirits, oil, or other liquid; a narrow-necked flat-bottomed glass vessel with bulging sides for water, etc.; a frame holding sand used as a mould in casting. [LL. *flasca*].

FLASKET, [flask'-it], *n.* a long shallow basket; a small flask. [OFr. *flasquet*].

FLAT (1), [flat], *n.* a floor or storey in a house; a suite of rooms on one floor arranged as, and constituting, a separate, complete dwelling-place. [OE. *flet* ground, floor].

FLAT (2), [flat], *n.* that which is flat, the flat side or part of anything, a flat level surface; a shoal or shallow; (*arch.*) that part of the covering of a house laid horizontally; (*paint.*) a surface painted without gloss; (*min.*) a horizontal stratum or vein; stage scenery set on a wooden frame, and pushed on the stage into position; (*horse-racing*) flat level ground without hedges or ditches; (*mus.*) a semitone below a natural; (*coll.*) one who is easily duped, a gullible fool.

FLAT (3), [flat], *adj.* having an even, level surface, and usually horizontal; lacking sharp relief, only slightly raised from the adjacent surface; prostrate, levelled to, or stretched out on, the ground; (*paint.*) without relief, not suggesting distance; uniform; lying in a plane surface, having no prominent contours; dull, dispirited; monotonous, lacking interesting variation; having lost its sparkle or freshness; unqualified, peremptory, downright, absolute; (*mus.*) out of tune because of a drop in pitch; (*phon.*) pronounced or made with a more or less level tongue; (*golf*) having the head jointed to the shaft at a wide angle (of a club); **that's f.,** that is final and admitting of no exception. [OScand. *flatr*].

FLAT (4), [flat], *adv.* prone, so as to be flat; resting against and touching at all points; entirely, directly, completely; without interest; (*coll.*) bluntly, definitely; **to fall f.,** to fail to produce the intended effect; **to go f. out,** (*coll.*) to travel as quickly as possible, to strain every nerve in order to achieve something.

FLAT (5), [flat], *v.t. and i.* to make flat; to become flat.

FLATFISH, [flat'-fish], *n.* a fish with a flat body, which, when fully grown, swims on its side and has both eyes on one side, as the flounder, halibut, etc.

FLATFOOTED, [flat-foot'-id], *adj.* having flat-soled feet with little or no arched instep.

FLATHEAD (1), [flat'-hed'], *n.* a fish of the genus *Ceratodus.*

FLATHEAD (2), [flat'-hed'], *n.* a snake native to North America.

FLAT-IRON, [flat'-iern], *n.* an implement used for ironing clothes, and consisting of a heavy, flat, smooth-bottomed piece of metal provided with a handle.

FLATLET, [flat'-let], *n.* a small self-contained flat.

FLATLING (1), [flat'-ling], *adj.* lying flat.

FLATLING (2), [flat'-ling], *adv.* (*archaic*) in a flat position.

FLAT-LONG†, [flat'-long], *adj.* prostrate, with the flat sides touching.

FLATLY, [flat'-li], *adv.* in a flat manner; plainly, positively, frankly.

FLAT-HEAD

FLATNESS, [flat'-nes], *n.* the state or quality of being flat; (*wirel.*) low degree of selectivity in a wireless receiver.

FLAT-RACE, [flat'-rās'], *n.* a race run on reasonably level ground, without obstacles to be jumped.

FLAT-SPOT, [flat'-spot'], *n.* (*motoring*) a temporary lack of response of the carburetter to acceleration.

FLATTEN, [flatn], *v.t. and i.* to make flat or level and less thick; to depress, to dispirit; (*mus.*) to lower the pitch of; (*fig.*) to crush, to overwhelm with dismay; (*naut.*) to make (a sail) set flat; to become flat; **f. out,** (*aeron.*) to cause an aeroplane to assume a more or less horizontal position after climbing or falling.

FLATTER (1), [flat'-er], *n.* one who, or that which, makes a thing flat.

FLATTER (2), [flat'-er], *v.t. and i.* to praise falsely or insincerely, to pay artful compliments; to give too favourable an impression or representation of; (*reflex.*) to obtain self-satisfaction from the fact, to feel convinced of one's ability to do a certain thing; to please, to gratify. [ME. *flateren* from OFr. *flaterie* flattery].

FLATTERABLE, [flat'-er-abl], *adj.* susceptible to flattery.

FLATTERER, [flat'-er-er], *n.* one who flatters.

FLATTERESS, [flat'-er-es], *n.* a female flatterer.

FLATTERING, [flat'-er-ing], *adj.* that flatters, sycophantic, uttering false praise; representing too favourably; pleasing to pride or vanity.

FLATTERINGLY, [flat'-er-ing-li], *adv.* in a flattering fashion.

FLATTERY, [flat'-er-i], *n.* false or excessive praise, insincere compliment. [OFr. *flaterie*].

FLATTIE, [flat′-i], *n.* (*slang*) a policeman. [FLAT (FOOT)].

FLATTING, [flat′-ing], *n.* the process of making flat; a mode of painting, in which the paint, being mixed with turpentine, leaves the work without gloss; a method of preserving gilding unburnished by treating it with size; rolling out metals by cylindrical pressure.

FLATTISH, [flat′-ish], *adj.* rather flat.

FLATULENCE, [flat′-yo͞o-lents], *n.* (*med.*) windiness caused by gases generated in a weak stomach and intestines; (*fig.*) emptiness, vanity.

FLATULENCY, [flat′-yo͞o-len-si], *n.* flatulence.

FLATULENT, [flat′-yo͞o-lent], *adj.* affected with, or causing, flatulence; (*fig.*) empty, without substance. [LL. *flatulentus* from L. *flatus* blowing].

FLATULENTLY, [flat′-yo͞o-lent-li], *adv.* in a flatulent fashion.

FLATWISE, [flat′-wīz], *adj.* with the flat surface uppermost.

FLAUNT (1), [flawnt], *n.* a proud display or parade.

FLAUNT (2), [flawnt], *v.t. and i.* to make a brave show; to wave or move proudly; to display showily and objectionably; to flourish or parade offensively; to boast of. [Uncert.].

FLAUNTER, [flawnt′-er], *n.* one who, or that which, flaunts.

FLAUNTING, [flawnt′-ing], *adj.* making an ostentatious display, waving or moving proudly.

FLAUNTINGLY, [flawnt′-ing-li], *adv.* in a flaunting manner.

FLAUTIST, [flawt′-ist], *n.* a person who plays the flute. [It. *flautista*].

FLAVESCENT, [flā-ves′-ent], *adj.* becoming golden-yellow, yellowish. [L. *flavescens*].

FLAVICOMOUS, [flā-vik′-om-us], *adj.* having yellow hair. [L. *flavus* yellow and *coma* hair].

FLAVINE, [flā′-vēn], *n.* a vegetable extract which imparts an olive yellow colour to cloth. [L. *flavus* yellow].

FLAVOROUS, [flā′-ver-us], *adj.* of an agreeable flavour.

FLAVOUR (1), [flā′-ver], *n.* fragrance, scent; taste, savour, relish, that quality of a substance which arouses a distinctive sensation in the organs of taste and smell; (*fig.*) strong suggestion, distinctive atmosphere. [OFr. *flaveur*].

FLAVOUR (2), [flā′-ver], *v.t.* to season, to give a flavour to; (*fig.*) to give a distinctive quality or atmosphere to.

FLAVOURED, [flā′-verd], *adj.* having a distinctive flavour.

FLAVOURING, [flā′-ver-ing], *n.* substance added to give flavour to anything; a slight but distinctive flavour.

FLAVOURLESS, [flā′-ver-les], *adj.* having no flavour.

FLAVOURSOME, [flā′-ver-sum], *adj.* rich in flavour, possessing a marked flavour.

FLAW (1), [flaw], *n.* a defect, blemish, disfigurement; a break, crack; a fault, error; that which detracts from the excellence or correctness of anything; (*leg.*) a fallacy, omission, misrepresentation, etc., which makes a legal document invalid. [ME. *flawe* flake of snow, OIcel. *flaga* slab].

FLAW (2), [flaw], *n.* a sudden gust, a squall, a brief storm; (*fig.*) a sudden commotion or agitation. [Norw. *flage* gust of wind].

FLAW (3), [flaw], *v.t.* to break, to crack, to produce a flaw in.

FLAWLESS, [flaw′-les], *adj.* free from flaws, perfect, faultless, unblemished.

FLAWY (1), [flaw′-i], *adj.* full of flaws, faulty, imperfect.

FLAWY (2), [flaw′-i], *adj.* gusty.

FLAX, [flaks], *n.* (*bot.*) an annual plant, *Linum usitatissimum*, the stalks of which yield a fibre which is used for making linen, cambric, lace, etc., and from which linseed oil is made; the fibrous part of the plant when broken and cleaned. [OE. *fleax*].

FLAX

FLAX-COMB, [flaks′-kōm′], *n.* a hackle used for preparing or dressing flax.

FLAX-DRESSER, [flaks′-dres′-er], *n.* a cleaner of flax.

FLAXEN, [flaks′-en], *adj.* made of, or like flax; of the colour of flax; pale yellow. [OE. *fleaxen*].

FLAXEN-HAIRED, [flaks′-en-hāerd′], *adj.* having hair of a pale yellow colour.

FLAX-LILY, [flaks′-lil′-i], *n.* New Zealand flax, a lily-like plant, *Phormium tenax*, the fibre of which is used for textile weaving.

FLAX-MILL, [flaks′-mil′], *n.* a factory where flax is spun.

FLAX-SEED, [flaks′-sēd′], *n.* the seed of flax, linseed.

FLAXTAIL, [flaks′-tāl′], *n.* the reed-mace, *Typha latifolia.*

FLAX-WENCH, [flaks′-wench′], *n.* a woman who spins flax.

FLAXY, [flaks′-i], *adj.* like flax, flaxen.

FLAY, [flā], *v.t.* to strip the skin from; to beat severely; (*fig.*) to plunder ruthlessly; to attack or criticize unmercifully. [OE. *flean*].

FLAYER, [flā′-er], *n.* one who flays off the skin.

FLAY-FLINT, [flā′-flint′], *n.* a miser, skinflint.

FLEA, [flē], *n.* a small blood-sucking insect of the genus *Pulex*, possessing a troublesome bite; a small insect resembling a flea. [OE. *fleah*].

FLEA-BANE, [flē′-bān′], *n.* any of several species of plants which are supposed to drive away fleas.

FLAXTAIL

FLEA-BEETLE, [flē′-bētl′], *n.* any of several varieties of leaping beetles, very destructive to plants.

FLEA-BITE, [flē′-bīt′], *n.* the bite of a flea, the small red spot on the skin caused by this; (*coll.*) a trifle, something of no account.

FLEA-BITTEN, [flē′-bitn′], *adj.* bitten by a flea; (*coll.*) poor, dingy, shabby.

FLEA-HOPPER, [flē′-hop′-er], *n.* a garden pest attacking beans.

FLEAK, [flēk], *n.* a small lock. [Unkn.].

FLEAKING, [flēk′-ing], *n.* a covering of reeds used in the thatching of houses. [Unkn.].

FLEAM, PHLEME†, [flēm], *n.* (*vet.*) a sharp-pointed instrument used for bleeding cattle. [OFr. *flieme*].

FLEA-WORT, [flē′-wurt′], *n.* (*bot.*) a plant of the genus *Cineraria*; a plantain, *Plantago Psyllium*, producing mucilaginous seeds, used medicinally.

FLECHE, flèche, [flāsh], *n.* (*arch.*) a tall slender spire of a Gothic church, usually placed over the spot where the transept crosses the nave. [Fr. *flèche* arrow].

FLECK (1), [flek], *n.* the flounder, *Pleuronectes flesus.*

FLECK (2), [flek], *n.* a spot, streak, speck, a small patch or particle. [~OIcel. *flekkr* spot].

FLECK (3), [flek], *v.t.* to spot, to streak or speck, to variegate; to dapple. [OIcel. *flekka* to spot].

FLECKED, [flekt], *adj.* spotted, variegated, marked with flecks.

FLECKER, [flek′-er], *v.t.* to fleck.

FLECKLESS, [flek′-les], *adj.* unspotted, immaculate.

FLECTION, see FLEXION.

FLED, [fled], *pret. and p.pt.* of FLEE. [ME. *fledde*].

FLEDGE, [flej], *v.t. and i.* (of a bird) to grow feathers; to rear until it has grown feathers; to provide with feathers; **fully fledged**, (*fig.*) properly qualified. [~OE. *flycgan* to fly].

FLEDGELING, [flej′-ling], *n.* a young bird just fledged; (*fig.*) a young inexperienced person.

FLEE, [flē], *v.t. and i.* to run away as quickly as possible, to retreat with all speed; (*fig.*) to avoid, to hasten (from); to depart, to pass away, depart in haste from, shun. [OE. *fleon*].

FLEECE (1), [flēs], *n.* the woolly coat or covering of a sheep, *esp.* when detached whole by shearing; (*fig.*) any similar soft, downy covering. [OE. *fleos*].

FLEECE (2), [flēs], *v.t.* to shear the wool from (a sheep), to furnish with a fleece, to spread over as a fleece; (*fig.*) to strip, to rob, to plunder by crooked dealing or extortion.

FLEECELESS, [flēs′-les], *adj.* without a fleece.

FLEECER, [flēs′-er], *n.* (*coll.*) one who fleeces, a sharper, trickster.

FLEECY, [flēs′-i], *adj.* covered with wool or a fleece, woolly, soft.

FLEER (1), [flēer], *n.* a derisive word or laugh, a look or grimace in mockery.

FLEER (2), [flēer], *v.i.* to mock, grin, grimace derisively, to jeer, flout. [~Norw. *flera*].

FLEERER, [flēer′-er], *n.* one who fleers.

FLEERING, [flēer′-ing], *adj.* mocking, derisive, contemptuous.

FLEERINGLY, [flēer′-ing-li], *adv.* in a fleering fashion.

FLEET (1), [flēt], *n.* a creek, small stream, a bay. [OE. *fleot*].

FLEET (2), [flēt], *n.* a number of vessels sailing or collected together in pursuit of some common aim; (*nav.*) a large body of warships under one command; unit; a navy; (*fig.*) a collection of vehicles usually under one ownership and used for a common purpose. [OE. *fleot* ship].

FLEET (3), [flēt], *adj.* swift of pace, moving rapidly and lightly, speedy.

FLEET (4), [flēt], *v.t. and i.* to fly swiftly and lightly, to hasten silently, to flit; to while away, to cause to pass swiftly and imperceptibly; (*naut.*) to move, *esp.* cables, tackle, etc. [OE. *fleotan* to float].

FLEET-DIKE, [flēt'-dik'], *n.* an embankment built as a protection against inundation.

FLEET-FOOTED, [flēt'-fŏŏt'-id], *adj.* swift of foot; able to run very quickly.

FLEETING, [flēt'-ing], *adj.* passing away quickly and easily, hastening swiftly and imperceptibly.

FLEETINGLY, [flēt'-ing-li], *adv.* in a fleeting fashion.

FLEETLY, [flēt'-li], *adv.* swiftly, rapidly.

FLEETNESS, [flēt'-nes], *n.* the quality of being fleet.

FLEMING, [flem'-ing], *n.* a native of Flanders. [MDu. *vlamming*].

FLEMISH (1), [flem'-ish], *n.* the quivering of a hound's tail and body when he is finding the trail. [Uncert.].

FLEMISH (2), [flem'-ish], *adj.* pertaining to Flanders, its inhabitants or language; **f. horse,** (*naut.*) a rope for the feet at the yardarms of the topsail yards. [MDu. *Vlaemisch*].

FLEMISH (3), [flem'-ish], *v.i.* (of a hound) to cause the body and tail to quiver when scenting the trail. [Unkn.].

FLENSE, FLENCH, FLINCH, [flents, flench, flinch], *v.t.* to cut the blubber out of (a whale). [Du. *vlenzen*].

FLESH (1), [flesh], *n.* the soft tissue covering the bones of an animal body; the edible muscular tissue and fat of certain animals; the pulpy soft part of fruit or vegetables; the physical human body; the sensual nature, bodily cravings, carnality; human nature, mankind; **one's own f. and blood,** one's relatives, kindred; **in the f.,** as a living person or thing; **proud f.,** rapidly growing granulated tissue forming over a wound. [OE. *flæsc*].

FLESH (2), [flesh], *v.t.* to whet the appetite of (a hawk or hound) for hunting, by feeding it with the game it has taken; to thrust into flesh (a sword); to remove small pieces of flesh from a hide whch has just been stripped; to make fat; (*fig.*) to initiate or harden to bloodshed.

FLESHBROTH, [flesh'-broth'], *n.* a soup made by stewing meat in water.

FLESHBRUSH, [flesh'-brush'], *n.* a stiff brush with which the skin is rubbed to encourage circulation.

FLESH-CLOGGED, [flesh'-klogd'], *adj.* encumbered with surplus flesh.

FLESH-COLOURED, [flesh'-kul'-erd], *adj.* of the colour of flesh, pale pinkish.

FLESHED, [flesht], *adj. and p.pt.* fat, fleshy; initiated or accustomed to bloodshed or fighting.

FLESHER (1), [flesh'-er], *n.* (*Scots*) a butcher.

FLESHER (2), [flesh'-er], *n.* the red-backed shrike, *Lanius collurio*.

FLESHFLY, [flesh'-flī'], *n.* a fly laying its eggs in flesh, upon which its larva feeds. [ME. *fleschflie*].

FLESH-GLOVE, [flesh'-gluv'], *n.* a glove having a rough bristly surface, and used for rubbing the skin to help circulation.

FLESHHOOD, [flesh'-hŏŏd], *n.* one's fleshly condition.

FLESHHOOK, [flesh'-hŏŏk'], *n.* a hook on which meat is hung; a hook used to take meat, when cooked, from the pot.

FLESHHOOK

FLESHINESS, [flesh'-i-nes], *n.* the condition of being fleshy.

FLESHING, [flesh'-ing], *n.* the act of whetting the appetite (of a hound, hawk, etc.) for hunting by a taste of the game killed; the act of cleaning hides of fat and flesh; (*pl.*) close-fitting flesh-coloured tights.

FLESHLESS, [flesh'-les], *adj.* lacking flesh, lean, bony.

FLESHLINESS, [flesh'-li-nes], *n.* the state of being fleshy; sensuality.

FLESHLING†, [flesh'-ling], *n.* one intent on carnal pleasure, a sensualist.

FLESHLY, [flesh'-li], *adj.* (*archaic*) pertaining to the flesh; pertaining to the physical body and its attributes; carnal, sensual. [OE. *flæsclic*].

FLESHLY-MINDED, [flesh'-li-mind'-id], *adj.* given to carnal pursuits or pleasures.

FLESHMEAT, [flesh'-mēt'], *n.* the edible flesh of animals.

FLESHMENT, [flesh'-ment], *n.* the act of fleshing; (*fig.*) eagerness produced by an early success.

FLESHMONGER, [flesh'-mung'-ger], *n.* one who deals in flesh, a butcher; †a pimp.

FLESH-POT, [flesh'-pot'], *n.* a vessel in which flesh is cooked; (*fig.*) a luxury greatly desired.

FLESH-WOUND, [flesh'-wōōnd'], *n.* a superficial wound which injures the flesh only, and does not affect an internal organ or bone.

FLESHY, [flesh'-i], *adj.* consisting of flesh; like flesh; fat, corpulent; bodily, corporeal; pulpy.

FLETCH, [flech], *v.t.* to provide (an arrow) with feathers. [Fr. *flèche* arrow].

FLETCHER, [flech'-er], *n.* (*archaic*) a maker or seller of arrows. [OFr. *flechier*].

FLEUR-DE-LIS, (*pl.* **fleurs-de-lis**), [flur'-de-lē(s)'], *n.* (*bot.*) the flower of a plant of the genus *Iris*; (*her.*) the representation of a lily. [Fr. *fleur-de-lis* flower of the lily].

FLEUR-DE-LIS

FLEURET, [flur-et'], *n.* a small flower used in ornamental work. [Fr. *fleurette*].

FLEURETTEE, fleurettée, [flur-et'-ā], *adj.* ending or edged with a fleur-de-lis. [Fr. *fleureté*].

FLEURY, FLORY, [flur'-i], *adj.* (*her.*) decorated with, ending in, fleurs-de-lis. [Fr. *fleuri* covered with flowers].

FLEW, [flōō], *pret.* of FLY. [OE. *fleah*].

FLEWED, [flōōd], *adj.* deep-mouthed, having prominent chaps.

FLEWS, [flōōz], *n.*(*pl.*) the large chaps of a deep-mouthed dog. [Unkn.].

FLEX (1), [fleks], *n.* flexible insulated wire to carry electricity to a lamp-socket or other electrical equipment. [FLEX(IBLE)].

FLEX (2), [fleks], *v.t. and i.* to bend (as of joints, limbs); (*geol.*) to fold (as of strata). [L. *flexum*, *p.pt.* of *flectere* to bend].

FLEXIBILITY, [fleks'-ib-il'-i-ti], *n.* flexibleness, pliability, the quality of being flexible. [L. *flexibilitas*].

FLEXIBLE, [fleks'-ibl], *adj.* pliant, easily bent; expressive, supple, (of a voice) modulating easily; pliable, compliant, able to be influenced by, and readily adapting oneself to, new influences or circumstances; easily persuaded; versatile, not fixed. [L. *flexibilis*].

FLEXIBLENESS, [fleks'-ibl-nes], *n.* the quality of being flexible.

FLEXIBLY, [fleks'-ib-li], *adv.* in a flexible fashion.

FLEXICOSTATE, [fleks'-i-kos'-tāt], *adj.* having bent ribs. [FLEX (2) and L. *costa* rib].

FLEXILE, [fleks'-īl], *adj.* easily bent, pliable. [L. *flexilis*].

FLEXION, FLECTION, [flek'-shun], *n.* the act of bending; the state of being bent; that which is bent, a fold; (*anat.*) the bending of a joint or limb by the flexor muscles; (*gram.*) inflexion; (of a voice) modulation or modification of the sound or tone. [L. *flexio*].

FLEXOR, [fleks'-er], *n.* (*anat.*) a muscle that bends a limb or joint, as opposed to an extensor. [~FLEX (2)].

FLEXUOSE, [fleks'-yew-ōs], *adj.* flexuous. [L. *flexuosus* tortuous].

FLEXUOSITY, [fleks'-yew-os'-i-ti], *n.* the quality of being flexuous.

FLEXUOUS, [fleks'-yew-us], *adj.* bending, curving, winding, tortuous; (*fig.*) wavering. [L. *flexuosus*].

FLEXURE, [flek'-sher], *n.* the act of bending or curving; a bend, curve, fold; the condition of being bent or curved; (*geol.*) bending of strata under great pressure. [L. *flexura*].

FLIBBERTIGIBBET, [flib'-er-ti-jib'-it], *n.* a flighty, restless person, displaying no concentration, and unable to settle down to any one thing. [Invented].

FLICK (1), [flik], *n.* a smart light jerk or snap, as with a whip, the fingers, etc.; an extremely quick, jerky turn of the wrist in making certain kinds of strokes at cricket, in playing the back-hand shot at table-tennis, or in delivering a cricket-ball. [Imitative].

FLICK (2), [flik], *n.* (*slang*) a cinematograph film; (*pl.*) a cinematograph performance. [~FLICKER (2)].

FLICK (3), [flik], *v.t.* to strike lightly and smartly with a quick, jerky movement; to jerk rapidly and smartly. [FLICK (1)].

FLICKER (1), [flik'-er], *n.* a wavering, fitful gleam of light; unsteady, intermittent light that continually disappears and reappears with lightning rapidity; a fluttering, or rapid, agitated, flapping movement.

FLICKER (2), [flik'-er], *v.i.* to burn with a flicker; to flutter, to quiver, to waver. [OE. *flicorian*].

FLICKERING, [flik'-er-ing], *adj.* that flickers.

FLICKERINGLY, [flik'-er-ing-li], *adv.* in a flickering fashion.

FLICKERMOUSE, see FLITTERMOUSE.

FLIER, FLYER, [flī'-er], *n.* one who flies or flees.

FLIGHT (1), [flīt], *n.* the action of flying, movement or progression through the air by natural or mechanical means; a journey or voyage through the air; the manner of flying, the path described in moving through the air; migration of birds; distance flown; a number of creatures or things flying together, a volley (of missiles); a unit or formation of aeroplanes; birds born in the same season; a series of stairs, hurdles, locks, terraces, etc.; (*fig.*) the process of passing away or elapsing; (*archery*) a contest in long-distance shooting; an arrow used in such a contest; (*cricket*) control or variation of the trajectory of the delivery of a cricket-ball; **in the first f.**, in the highest class or topmost rank. [OE. *flyht*].

FLIGHT (2), [flīt], *n.* the act of fleeing, hasty departure or retreat, running away; **to put to f.**, to defeat and cause to flee. [ME. *fliht*].

FLIGHT (3), [flīt], *v.t.* to shoot (birds) when flying together in a flight; to provide (an arrow) with feathers; (*cricket*) to deliver (a cricket-ball) at different heights and trajectories, so that it describes different paths through the air. [FLIGHT (1)].

FLIGHT-COMMANDER, [flīt'-kom-ahnd'-er], *n.* an officer of the Royal Air Force above a flight-lieutenant.

FLIGHTED, [flī'-tid], *adj.* (of an arrow) furnished with feathers; (*cricket*) cunningly varied in speed and trajectory through the air.

FLIGHT-FEATHER, [flīt'-feTH'-er], *n.* a quill-feather in the wing of a bird.

FLIGHTILY, [flīt'-i-li], *adv.* capriciously, in a flighty fashion.

FLIGHTINESS, [flīt'-i-nes], *n.* the state of being flighty.

FLIGHT-LIEUTENANT, [flīt'-lef-ten'-ant], *n.* a rank in the Royal Air Force corresponding to captain in the army.

FLIGHT-SERGEANT, [flīt'-sahj-ant], *n.* the rank next above sergeant in the R.A.F.

FLIGHT-SHOT, [flīt'-shot'], *n.* the distance which an arrow flies, a bow-shot.

FLIGHTY, [flīt'-i], *adj.* capricious, volatile, giddy, fickle, inconstant, fanciful.

FLIMSILY, [flim'-zi-li], *adv.* in a flimsy fashion.

FLIMSINESS, [flim'-zi-nes], *n.* the state of being flimsy.

FLIMSY (1), [flim'-zi], *n.* (*coll.*) that which is flimsy; a thin sheet of paper, carbon, or transfer paper; paper used by newspaper reporters, newspaper copy; (*slang*) a banknote; a telegram.

FLIMSY (2), [flim'-zi], *adj.* light, fragile, without strength or substance, weak, having no solidity, of loose or unsubstantial texture or nature; weak, shallow, poor, ill thought-out, trivial, incapable of bearing or withstanding close investigation. [Unkn.].

FLINCH (1), [flinch], *v.i.* to shrink back in fear or pain, to wince, to draw back from, to fail to stand up to. [OFr. *flenchir* to turn aside, to bend].

FLINCH (2), see FLENSE.

FLINCHINGLY, [flinsh'-ing-li], *adv.* in a flinching fashion.

FLINDERMOUSE, see FLITTERMOUSE.

FLINDERS, [flin'-derz], *n.*(*pl.*) splinters. [~Du. *flenter* rags].

FLINDERSIA, [flin-dur'-si-a], *n.* a genus of twelve species of Australian evergreen trees, related to the satin-wood, with a timber similar to mahogany. [Matthew *Flinders*, the navigator].

FLING (1), [fling], *n.* a throw, a cast, a sudden violent, agitated movement, *esp.* of the limbs; (*fig.*) a taunt, sneer, gibe; a period of complete self-indulgence or gratification of one's desires or impulses, a bout of pleasure; **Highland f.**, a Scottish dance characterized by rapid energetic movements of the legs and arms in time to music.

FLING (2), (**flung**), [fling], *v.t.* to cast, to throw with an energetic or violent movement, to hurl; to move (a limb, head, etc.) in a hasty, vigorous, impulsive manner; to scatter; to spread, to give out, to send forth; (of troops, etc.) to bring or send rapidly into action at a certain point; (*reflex.*) to hurl or propel oneself vigorously or violently into a certain position; (*fig.*) to enter into, to take up, with great enthusiasm and impulsive determination; *v.i.* to rush away, depart, to go, to hurl oneself in violent, impetuous manner, to kick (of a horse), to plunge; **to f. in one's teeth**, to reproach or taunt with; **to f. caution to the winds**, to abandon all care or discretion; **to f. out**, (*fig.*) to fly into a sudden outburst of angry abuse, invective, etc. [ME. *flingen*].

FLINGER, [fling'-ger], *n.* one who flings.

FLINT (1), [flint], *n.* an opaque dark grey or brown variety of quartz, consisting mainly of silica, and struck against steel or iron to produce fire; a piece of flint used to produce a spark in a tinderbox, musket, etc.; a small piece or pebble of flint; an ancient tool or weapon made from flint; anything hard, unyielding or untouched by the gentler feelings or emotions; **to skin a f.**, to be extremely miserly; **to wring water from a f.**, to perform an extremely difficult task. [OE. *flint*].

FLINT (2), [flint], *adj.* made of flint, resembling flint.

FLINT-GLASS, [flint'-glahs'], *n.* a species of lustrous, crystalline glass, originally made from calcined flints, and extensively used for domestic purposes, and in the manufacture of optical lenses.

FLINT-HEARTED, [flint'-haht'-id], *adj.* having a hard, pitiless, unfeeling heart.

FLINTINESS, [flint'-i-nes], *n.* the quality of being flinty, or extremely hard.

FLINT-KNAPPER, [flint'-nap'-er], *n.* person who breaks up flints for use in road-making.

FLINT-LOCK, [flint'-lok'], *n.* an ancient type of musket-lock in which a flint strikes on a steel pan to produce a spark for igniting the powder.

FLINTY, [flint'-i], *adj.* consisting of, resembling, flint, abounding in flint; hard, unfeeling.

FLIP (1), [flip], *n.* a drink consisting of a mixture of milk, egg, spirits, or wines, sweetened with sugar, and served hot or cold. [FLIP (3)].

FLIP (2), [flip], *n.* a slight quick stroke, a flick; (*gunnery*) recoil of a gun-barrel when fired; (*slang*) a short flight in an aeroplane.

FLIP (3), [flip], *v.t. and i.* to flick, to jerk, to toss with the thumb or finger-nail; to move jerkily; to make a flip or flick. [Uncert.].

FLIP-DOG, [flip'-dog'], *n.* an iron used to heat flip.

FLIP-FLAP, [flip'-flap'], *n.* (*coll.*) a somersault; a kind of firework, a cracker.

FLIPPANCY, [flip'-an-si], *n.* the state or quality of being flippant.

FLIPPANT, [flip'-ant], *adj.* frivolous in mind and speech, wanting in proper seriousness, gravity or respect, pert, displaying a too casual light-heartedness. [Uncert.].

FLIPPANTLY, [flip'-ant-li], *adv.* in a flippant fashion.

FLIPPANTNESS, [flip'-ant-nes], *n.* flippancy.

FLIPPER, [flip'-er], *n.* a limb of a reptile, animal, etc., used for swimming, as of a turtle, penguin, seal, etc.; (*slang*) the hand.

FLIRT (1), [flurt], *n.* a sudden brisk jerky movement, a flick; a person who plays at courtship with as many of the opposite sex as will respond to his or her attentions or advances, a coquette.

FLIRT (2), [flurt], *v.t. and i.* to move about with a sudden, jerky motion; to endeavour to engage the amorous attentions of the opposite sex in a cavalier way, without serious intentions, to play at courtship; to trifle, to toy or dally; to flick, to propel with a sudden, brisk, jerky movement (*esp.* by suddenly releasing the finger-nail from under the thumb or vice versa), to move with a sharp, quick action; **to f. (a fan)**, to open and close smartly. [Unkn.].

FLIRTATION, [flurt-ā'-shun], *n.* the act or practice of flirting, coquetry, a pleasant, light-hearted love affair, not to be taken too seriously.

FLIRTATIOUS, [flurt-ā'-shus], *adj.* fond of flirting.

FLIRTING, [flurt'-ing], *adj.* coquettish, given to flirting.

FLIRTINGLY, [flurt'-ing-li], *adv.* in a flirting fashion.

FLISK, [flisk], *n.* (*Scots*) a comb with large teeth; a whisk made of twigs or horsehair; a flick, a flip; a whim. [Echoic].

FLIT (1), [flit], *n.* a change of residence, *esp.* when unexpected and secret.

FLIT (2), (**flitting, flitted**), [flit], *v.i.* to fly quickly and softly from place to place, to dart about through the air; to move about quickly and quietly; (*fig.*) (of fancies, dreams, etc.) to pass lightly in rapid succession; to remove to another place of residence, often implying a secret forced change of dwelling to avoid payment of debts, etc. [OScand. *flytja*].

FLITCH, [flich], *n.* the side of a pig, salted and cured; a halibut steak; a square chunk of blubber; a long

piece of wood cut from the outside edge of a tree-trunk. [OE. *flicce*].
FLITE, [flit], *v.i.* to wrangle, scold. [OE. *flitan*].
FLITTER, [flit'-er], *v.i.* to flutter.
FLITTERCHACK, [flit'-er-chak'], *n.* the ring ouzel.
FLITTERMOUSE, FLICKERMOUSE, FLINDER-MOUSE, [flit'-er-mows'], *n.* the pipistrelle bat, a bat. [FLITTER and MOUSE].

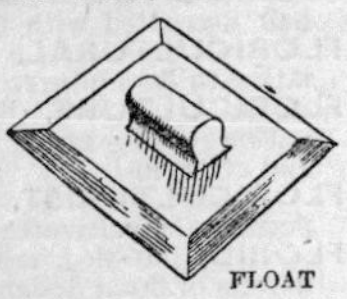
FLITTERMOUSE

FLITTERN-BARK, [flit'-ern-bahk'], *n.* a young oak.
FLITTINESS, [flit'-i-nes], *n.* the quality of being flitty.
FLITTING, [flit'-ing], *n.* a flying about swiftly and quietly from place to place; a removal from one dwelling place to another.
FLITTINGLY, [flit'-ing-li], *adv.* in a flitting fashion.
FLIVVER, [fliv'-er], *n.* (*slang*) a cheap or old-fashioned motor-car. [Invented].
FLIX, [fliks], *n.* the underfur of various four-footed animals, the down of a beaver. [Unkn.].
FLOAT (1), [flōt], *n.* that which floats, the cork or quill of an angling line serving to support the bait and indicate the presence of a fish on the hook; a raft; a large flat-bottomed boat; one of the pieces of cork on the edge of a fishing-net to prevent it from sinking; the air-bladder of a fish that supports it in the water; the board fastened to the paddle-wheels of steamers and undershot water-wheels, by which they transmit power; a hollow ball serving to indicate the level of water in a cistern, etc., by floating on the surface; a broad, shallow, low-built cart for conveying milk, livestock, and other heavy articles; a low platform on wheels on which is grouped a tableau in a procession; a wooden trowel for smoothing plaster on walls; a smoothing file; (*stage*) the footlights; (*geol.*) masses of ore washed down from their original position; (*aviation*) an enclosed, hollow, watertight compartment enabling a seaplane to float on water. [~OE. *flot* floating, *flota* a ship].

FLOAT

FLOAT (2), [flōt], *v.t.* to set afloat (a ship); to bear upon the surface, to support, to allow to float; to cause to float; to cover with water; (*comm.*) to start, to put into circulation, to set going; *v.i.* to be supported on or near the surface of water or other liquid, either drifting gently or at rest; to glide through or be carried along through the air without making any effort to move; to become afloat (of a ship); (*fig.*) to hover, pass through or move about in an aimless, effortless manner as though floating. [OE. *flotian*].
FLOATABLE, [flōt'-abl], *adj.* able to be floated, that allows a vessel to float upon it.
FLOATAGE, [flōt'-ij], *n.* the state of floating; that which floats, flotsam; the right to take anything found floating; ability to float; the parts of a ship above the water-line.
FLOATATION, see FLOTATION.
FLOAT-BOARD, [flōt'-bawd'], *n.* a board fastened to the rim of a water-wheel or paddle-wheel.
FLOATER, [flōt'-er], *n.* one who, or that which, floats; (*coll.*) a security to be paid to the bearer, a stock-certificate, bond, etc., recognized and accepted as a security.
FLOAT-FISHING, [flōt'-fish'-ing], *n.* angling by means of a float, bottom-fishing.
FLOAT-GRASS, [flōt'-grahs'], *n.* a name given to several kinds of marsh grass, *esp. Glyceria*.
FLOATING (1), [flōt'-ing], *n.* the act of one who or that which floats; the state of being buoyed up on or near the surface of water or other liquid.
FLOATING (2), [flōt'-ing], *adj.* supported on or near the surface of water or other liquid, either at rest or drifting gently; suspended or gliding through the air; pertaining to sea-cargoes; movable, shifting, unattached, fluctuating, variable; (*comm.*) unfunded; **f. bridge**, a bridge consisting of logs of timber, having a plank floor; a bridge of boats, pontoons, rafts, etc., used for conveying troops across narrow channels; the floating part of a swing bridge; a large steam ferry-boat; **f. dock**, a dock constructed of steel compartments, and capable of being submerged to admit a vessel, then raised and converted into a dry dock; **f. harbour**, a breakwater formed of large masses of floating timber fastened together; **f. kidney**, a kidney liable to displacement; **f. light**, a heavy boat or lightship, moored to sunken rocks or shoals, and bearing a light as a beacon to shipping; a buoy equipped with a light which serves as a warning of rocks, shallow water, etc.; **f. policy**, (*comm.*) an insurance policy having no specified application at first; **f. rib**, one of the lower, movable ribs, not fastened to the breast-bone.
FLOATINGLY, [flōt'-ing-li], *adv.* in a floating manner.
FLOATSAM, see FLOTSAM.
FLOAT-STONE, [flōt'-stōn'], *n.* quartz of spongy texture, which floats on the surface of water; stone used by bricklayers for smoothing the surfaces of bricks.
FLOATY, [flō'-ti], *adj.* buoyant, light, having a shallow draft (of a ship).
FLOCCILLATION, [flok'-sil-ā'-shun], *n.* the picking of bedclothes by a patient, a disturbing symptom in certain acute diseases. [~L. *floccus* tuft of wool].
FLOCCOSE, [flok'-ōs], *adj.* (*bot.*) tufted, covered with little tufts like wool, woolly. [LL. *floccosus* woolly].
FLOCCOSELY, [flok'-ōs-li], *adv.* in a floccose manner.
FLOCCULE, [flok'-ewl], *n.* a small flock of wool or anything resembling this; a cloudy, flaky substance formed in precipitation.
FLOCCULENCE, [flok'-yōō-lents], *n.* the state of being flocculent.
FLOCCULENT, [flok'-yōō-lent], *adj.* woolly, coalescing and adhering in flocks or flakes, fluffy, tufted with flocks.
FLOCCULOSE, [flok'-yōō-lōs], *adj.* woolly, tufty, fluffy.
FLOCCULOUS, [flok'-yōō-lus], *adj.* flocculose.
FLOCCULUS, [flok'-yōō-lus], *n.* a small curly tuft of hair; (*astron.*) a dense vaporous mass in the sun's atmosphere; (*anat.*) a small rounded projection situated on the lower side of the cerebellum.
FLOCCUS, (*pl.* **flocci**), [flok'-us], *n.* (*zool.*) the long tuft of hair which is found at the end of the tails of the mammalia; the down of unfledged birds. [L. *floccus* a tuft of wool].
FLOCK (1), [flok], *n.* a lock or tuft of wool; (*pl.*) cotton or woollen waste used for stuffing mattresses, and in upholstery; (*coll.*) fine particles of wool used in making flock-paper; (*pl.*) a flaky, fibrous precipitate forming light, loose masses in solution. [L. *floccus*].
FLOCK (2), [flok], *n.* an assemblage, collection, or company of anything, *esp.* a number of sheep or other smaller domestic animals, housed and pasturing together and under one ownership; a group under one guardian; the Christian Church considered in relation to Christ; the congregation of a church; **flocks and herds**, sheep and cattle. [OE. *flocc*].
FLOCK (3), [flok], *v.t.* to stuff or coat with flocks; to treat the surface of glass so that it acquires a rough, woolly finish.
FLOCK (4), [flok], *v.i.* to crowd together so as to form a large company or flock; (of birds) to assemble together, *esp.* in preparation for a flight.
FLOCK-BED, [flok'-bed'], *n.* a bed stuffed with coarse wool or wool refuse.
FLOCKLY†, [flok'-li], *adv.* in the manner of a flock.
FLOCKMASTER, [flok'-mahst'-er], *n.* the owner or shepherd of flocks of sheep.
FLOCK-PAPER, [flok'-pā'-per], *n.* a kind of wall-paper resembling cloth, made of flock or cloth cut up very finely and dusted on to the paper.
FLOCKY, [flok'-i], *adj.* abounding with flocks or locks, resembling flock.
FLOE, [flō], *n.* a large mass of floating ice. [Icel. *flo* layer].
FLOG, [flog], *v.t. and i.* to whip, to beat hard, to thrash with a stick, rod, whip, etc.; to flap in a noisy violent manner; to urge on by beating; **to f. a dead horse**, to seek to revive a well-worn, thoroughly discussed point of controversy, to waste one's energy in unavailing effort; **to f. the water**, to cast a fly continually over a stream in certain kinds of fishing. [~L. *flagellare*].
FLOGGING, [flog'-ing], *n.* corporal punishment by beating or thrashing with a rod, whip, lash, etc.
FLONG, [flong], *n.* paper prepared for making moulds in the process of stereotyping. [Fr. *flan*].
FLOOD (1), [flud], *n.* a large body of water, rising and flowing over land not usually covered with water; the incoming tide; a great amount of water or other liquid, a copious quantity of water discharged in torrential fashion; profuse weeping; (*archaic*) any considerable stretch of water; (*fig.*) a great outpouring

or outburst, profuse flow; **the F.,** the inundation described in Genesis, of which Noah and his family were the sole survivors; **at the f.,** (*fig.*) at the highest or most favourable point. [OE. *flod*].

FLOOD (2), [flud], *v.t.* to cover with a flood, to inundate, to discharge a great amount of water into, to cause to be under water; to overflow; (*fig.*) to fill to excess, to swamp, to overwhelm; *v.i.* to brim over; to be at the flood; (*med.*) to be afflicted with uterine haemorrhage.

FLOOD-GATE, [flud'-gāt'], *n.* a sluice or gate that can be opened to allow excess water or floodwater to escape, or shut to prevent water from escaping; the lower gates of a lock.

FLOODING, [flud'-ing], *n.* inundation, overflowing in such quantities as to cause that to be under water which is not normally covered by water; (*med.*) uterine haemorrhage.

FLOOD-LIGHT, [flud'-līt'], *v.t.* to illuminate the exterior of a building by flood-lighting.

FLOOD-LIGHTING, [flud'-līt'-ing], *n.* lighting up of the exterior of a building usually by powerful, concealed electric lights which direct strong beams of light upon the building in the manner of a search-light, giving uniform illumination and absence of shadow.

FLOOD-MARK, [flud'-mahk'], *n.* high-water mark.

FLOODOMETER, [flud-om'-it-er], *n.* an instrument which measures the height of a flood. [FLOOD and METER].

FLOOD-TIDE, [flud'-tīd'], *n.* the tide when rising, or coming in.

FLOODWATER, [flud'-wawt'-er], *n.* water brought or left by floods.

FLOOK, see FLUKE (1).

FLOOR (1), [flaw(r)], *n.* the flat surface, usually horizontal, forming the bottom of a building, room, or passage, and on which one walks, a storey of a building; the upper side of the bottom of a structure, the base, the lowest ground surface; the main area of a hall etc., lowest in position; **to take the f.,** to begin to dance; to address a meeting. [OE. *flor*].

FLOOR (2), [flaw(r)], *v.t.* to furnish with a floor or floors; to strike to the ground; (*coll.*) to confound, to defeat or silence; (*slang*) to answer successfully.

FLOORAGE, [flaw'-rij], *n.* amount of floor space, floor area.

FLOOR-CLOTH, [flaw(r)'-kloth'], *n.* a piece of soft woollen fabric, capable of absorbing water readily, used for washing floors.

FLOORER, [flaw'-rer], *n.* a knock-down blow; (*fig.*) a very difficult or awkward question to answer, a baffling situation, an extremely discomfiting piece of news.

FLOORING, [flaw'-ring], *n.* the floor of a room, building or passage; materials from which floors are made.

FLOORLESS, [flaw(r)'-les], *adj.* without a floor.

FLOOR POLISHER, [flaw(r)'-pol-ish-er], *n.* one who, or that which, polishes floors; a preliminary ball at a reduced price to "polish the floor" for the ensuing grand ball.

FLOOR-WALKER, [flaw(r)'-wawk'-er], *n.* a supervising attendant in a large stores for advising customers.

FLOP (1), [flop], *n.* the act of flopping; a dull thud made by one who, or that which, flops; (*slang*) a complete failure.

FLOP (2), [flop], *adv.* with a flop.

FLOP (3), (flopping, flopped), [flop], *v.t.* to throw or set down heavily and clumsily; to let down the brim of a hat; *v.i.* (*coll.*) to plump down suddenly, heavily, and limply; to move heavily and clumsily; to flap about; (*slang*) to fail miserably. [~FLAP].

FLOPPINESS, [flop'-i-nes], *n.* the state of being floppy.

FLOPPY, [flop'-i], *adj.* inclined to flop, slack, flaccid, lacking in smartness; loose, careless, clumsy, limp.

FLORA, [flaw'-ra], *n.* the plant life found in, and characteristic of, a specific region or period; a book containing a systematic catalogue or description of such plants; (*class. myth.*) the goddess of flowers. [L. *Flora*, the goddess of flowers].

FLORAL, [flaw'-ral], *adj.* of or pertaining to flora; pertaining to flowers; **f. envelope,** (*bot.*) the calyx and corolla which envelop the inner part of a flower; **f. zone,** a particular area with its characteristic plant life. [L. *floralis*].

FLORALLY, [flaw'-ra-li], *adv.* with flowers, in a floral manner.

FLOREATED, see FLORIATED.

FLORENCE, [flor'-ents], *n.* the English name for Firenze, a city in Italy; a variety of wine; a sort of cloth; the gold florin (worth 6 shillings) of Edward III's reign; **f. flask,** a glass bottle with a long neck; **f. oil,** an olive oil made at Florence and sold in flasks. [*Florence* an Italian city].

FLORENTINE (1), [flo'-ren-tīn], *n.* a native of Florence; a kind of silk cloth; a kind of large meat pie baked in a dish.

FLORENTINE (2), [flo'-ren-tīn], *adj.* pertaining to Florence; **f. fresco,** a kind of painting for decorating walls, first used at Florence; **f. iris,** a large pale blue variety of iris. [L. *Florentinus* pertaining to Florence].

FLORESCENCE, [flor-es'-ents], *n.* process of bursting into flower or blossoming; the flowering season. [L. *florescens pres.pt.* of *florescere* to burst into flower].

FLORET, [flo'-ret], *n.* a small flower; (*bot.*) one of the small separate flowers forming the head of composite flowers. [OFr. *florete*].

FLORIAGE†, [flaw'-ri-ij], *n.* blossom.

FLORIATED, FLOREATED, [flaw'-ri-ā-tid], *adj.* decorated with floral designs.

FLORICAN, [flaw'-rik-an], *n.* an Indian bustard of the genus *Sypheotides*. [Unkn.].

FLORICOMOUS, [flaw'-rik-ōm'-us], *adj.* having the hair decorated with flowers. [LL. *floricomus*].

FLORICULTURAL, [flaw'-ri-kul'-cher-al], *adj.* relating to floriculture.

FLORICULTURE, [flaw'-ri-kul'-cher], *n.* the cultivation of flowering plants. [L. *flos floris* flower and CULTURE].

FLORICULTURIST, [flaw'-ri-kul'-cher-ist], *n.* a person who cultivates flowers.

FLORID, [flo'-rid], *adj.* †decorated or covered with flowers or floral designs, flowery; highly embellished, elaborately ornate, lavishly decorated with ornament; bright in colour, of a lively red; showy, vulgarly ostentatious. [L. *floridus*].

FLORIDITY, [flo-rid'-i-ti], *n.* the quality of being florid.

FLORIDLY, [flo'-rid-li], *adv.* in a florid fashion.

FLORIDNESS, [flo'-rid-nes], *n.* the quality of being florid.

FLORIFEROUS, [flaw-rif'-er-us], *adj.* yielding flowers. [L. *florifer*].

FLORIFICATION, [flaw'-ri-fik-ā'-shun], *n.* the act of flowering.

FLORIFORM, [flaw'-ri-fawm], *adj.* having the form of a flower. [L. *flos floris* flower and FORM].

FLORILEGIUM, [flaw'-ri-lē'-ji-um], *n.* a collection of flowers, a treatise on flowers; an anthology. [~L. *florilegus*].

FLORIN, [flo'-rin], *n.* a current British silver coin worth 2 shillings; a gold coin of the time of Edward III worth 6 shillings; † a gold coin minted at Florence, and bearing that city's badge, a lily, on one side. [ME. *florin* from Ital. *fiorino* little flower].

FLORIPAROUS, [flaw-rip'-a-rus], *adj.* (*bot.*) putting forth flowers. [L. *flos floris* flower and *parere* to bear].

FLORIST, [flo'-rist], *n.* one who cultivates flowers, a dealer in flowers, a nurseryman.

FLOROON, [flor-ōōn'], *n.* a border decorated with flowers. [Fr. *fleuron*].

FLORUIT, [flo'-rōō-it], *n.* the period when a person lived. [L. *floruit* he flourished].

FLORY, see FLEURY.

FLORY-BOAT, [flaw'-ri-bōt'], *n.* a boat used to convey passengers from a steamer to the landing-place at low tide.

FLOSCULAR, [flos'-kyōō-ler], *adj.* (*bot.*) having a composite flower, consisting of tubular florets or floscules.

FLOSCULE, [flos'-kyōōl], *n.* (*bot.*) a floret of a composite bloom. [L. *flosculus*].

FLOSCULOUS, [flos'-kyōō-lus], *adj.* floscular.

FLOS-FERRI, [flos'-fe'-rī], *n.* the branching species of aragonite. [L. *flos ferri* flower of iron].

FLOSS (1), [flos], *n.* short rough fibres of silk forming a kind of outer shell round the cocoon of a silkworm; silk spun from this; soft fluffy matter resembling this, a group of hanging styles in the flower of maize, a silky substance in the husks of certain plants as the bean. [Fr. (*soie*) *floche* floss silk].

FLOSS (2), [flos], *n.* a fluid glass floating on iron in a furnace, and produced by a vitrification of oxides and earths. [Germ. *flosz*].

FLOSS-SILK, [flos'-silk'], *n.* portions of untwisted silk broken off in reeling silk from the cocoons, spun into a soft, fluffy, coarse yarn, and used in embroidery.

FLOSSY, [flos'-i], *adj.* composed of or like floss.

FLOT, [flot], *n.* (*geol.*) ore at definite levels in the strata, or lying between the beds. [Unkn.].

FLOTANT, [flō'-tant], *adj.* (*her.*) floating in the air or in water. [OFr. *flotant*].

FLOTATION, FLOATATION, [flō-tā'-shun], *n.* the act of floating; the science dealing with floating bodies; the launching of a limited company, the state of keeping afloat. [Fr. *flotation*].

FLOTILLA, [flō̆t-il'-a], *n.* a fleet of small vessels; a group of destroyers, submarines, or other small warships under a single command. [Span. *flotilla*].

FLOTSAM, FLOATSAM†, [flot'-sum], *n.* (*leg.*) goods lost by shipwreck, and found floating on the sea. [OFr. *flotaison* a floating].

FLOUNCE (1), [flownts], *n.* a sudden quick jerky movement of the body, a tossing of the head or a limb.

FLOUNCE (2), [flownts], *n.* a narrow piece of material in the form of silk, lace, cloth, etc., sewn by its upper edge round the edge of a skirt or dress as an ornament, and with its lower edge hanging loose. [~FROUNCE].

FLOUNCE (3), [flownts], *v.t.* to adorn or furnish with a flounce or flounces. [FLOUNCE (2)].

FLOUNCE (4), [flownts], *v.i.* to toss oneself about in a jerky, spasmodic, agitated manner, to struggle, to fling about the limbs and body; to plunge about. [~MSwed. *flunsa* to dip].

FLOUNDER (1), [flown'-der], *n.* the small flat-fish, *Pleuronectes flesus*, found in estuaries and harbours and up rivers. [~Swed. *flundra*].

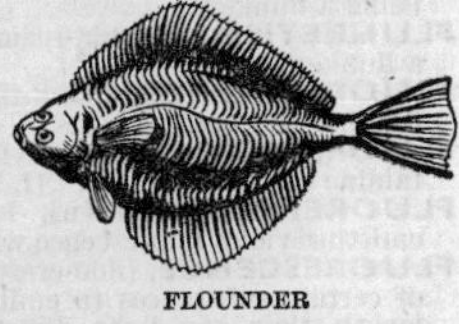
FLOUNDER

FLOUNDER (2), [flown'-der], *v.i.* to stumble or stagger along with difficulty, as through mud or water; (*fig.*) to stumble, blunder or proceed with difficulty in a confused manner. [Unkn.].

FLOUR (1), [flow(r)], *n.* the meal of wheat or other grain ground to a fine powder, and sifted to separate the coarser elements; any fine soft powder resembling this. [ME. *flour*].

FLOUR (2), [flow(r)], *v.t.* to reduce to flour; to sprinkle or cover with flour.

FLOUR-BOX, [flow(r)'-boks'], *n.* a tin box pierced with holes, used for sifting or sprinkling flour.

FLOUR-DREDGER, [flow(r)'-drej'-er], *n.* a perforated tin case used for sprinkling flour on meat, etc.

FLOUR-DRESSER, [flow(r)'-dres'-er], *n.* a cylinder used for dressing flour.

FLOURISH (1), [flu'-rish], *n.* brandishing, drawing or waving anything with an elaborate sweeping gesture; a piece of showy embellishment in speech or writing, showy parade of rhetoric; an ornamental bold fanciful curved stroke in handwriting, printing or engraving; (*mus.*) a passage of decorative notes added for the sake of effect or as a prelude; a fanfare of trumpets, etc., to herald the arrival of an eminent visitor.

FLOURISH (2), [flu'-rish], *v.t.* to decorate with flowery ornament, to embellish with flourishes; to draw, brandish, wave, or move with an elaborate sweeping gesture; *v.i.* to prosper, succeed, to be in a healthy vigorous condition; to live, to be at the height of one's activity; to indulge in florid rhetoric; to brag; to make bold fanciful flowing strokes in writing; (*mus.*) to improvise or add passages of elaborate ornament; to sound a fanfare. [ME. *florisshen*].

FLOURISHER, [flu'-rish-er], *n.* a person who flourishes.

FLOURISHING, [flu'-rish-ing], *adj.* thriving, successful, in sound, healthy condition.

FLOURISHINGLY, [flu'-rish-ing-li], *adv.* in a flourishing manner.

FLOUR-MILL, [flow(r)'-mil'], *n.* a mill where corn is ground.

FLOURY, [flow(r)'-i], *adj.* covered with flour; like flour; consisting of, relating to, flour.

FLOUT (1), [flowt], *n.* a jeer, scoff, insult.

FLOUT (2), [flowt], *v.t. and i.* to treat with contempt, to mock at, to ignore disdainfully; to behave in an insulting manner. [~Du. *fluiten* to play the flute, to mock].

FLOUTER, [flowt'-er], *n.* one who flouts.

FLOUTINGLY, [flowt'-ing-li], *adv.* in a flouting manner.

FLOW (1), [flō], *n.* that which flows, a stream; the act of flowing; the quantity or volume that flows; the rise of a tide; (*fig.*) an uninterrupted sequence or supply.

FLOW (2), [flō], *v.i.* to move along with a smooth continuous motion; to run freely, to gush; (of blood) to circulate; to melt and run as a liquid; to move in a steady stream; to proceed readily and effortlessly; (of the tide) to rise, to come in; to be poured out in copious amounts; to fall in loose profuse masses, to hang in loose folds; (*fig.*) to spring, issue, to emanate in continual profuseness. [OE. *flowan*].

FLOWAGE, [flō'-ij], *n.* the state or act of flowing.

FLOWER (1), [flow'-er], *n.* the brightly coloured leaves or petals forming the head of a plant; any of certain herbaceous plants producing these; (*bot.*) the reproductive organs of a seed-plant; the ornamental representation of a flower; (*fig.*) an adornment, an embellishment; the finest part; the prime of life; the state or period of blooming; (*pl.*) (*chem.*) fine powdery deposits remaining after sublimation; scum or growth formed in fermentation. [L. *flos floris* flower].

FLOWER (2), [flow'-er], *v.t.* to cause to produce flowers; to embellish with figures of flowers; *v.i.* to produce a flower, to blossom.

FLOWERAGE, [flow'-er-ij], *n.* the condition of being in flower; flowers.

FLOWER-BEARING, [flow'-er-bāer'-ing], *adj.* producing flowers.

FLOWERBED, [flow'-er-bed'], *n.* a plot in a garden, in which flowers are cultivated.

FLOWER-DE-LUCE, [flow'-er-de-lōōs'], *n.* an iris; the fleur-de-lis. [~FLEUR-DE-LIS].

FLOWERED, [flow'-erd], *adj.* formed into flowers; embellished with figures of flowers.

FLOWERER, [flow'-er-er], *n.* a flowering plant.

FLOWERET, [flow'-er-et], *n.* a small flower; a floret.

FLOWER-FENCE, [flow'-er-fents'], *n.* a tropical bush, with prickly branches and vivid flowers, *Poinciana pulcherrima*.

FLOWER-GARDEN, [flow'-er-gahdn'], *n.* a garden devoted primarily to the cultivation of flowers as distinct from food crops.

FLOWER-GENTLE†, [flow'-er-jentl'], *n.* (*bot.*) a variety of amaranth, *Amaranthus tricolor*.

FLOWER-GIRL, [flow'-er-gurl'], *n.* a woman who sells flowers in the streets or markets.

FLOWERHEAD, [flow'-er-hed'], *n.* a method of inflorescence in which all the florets are attached directly to the main stem without stalk, and combine to form a compact cluster.

FLOWERINESS, [flow'-er-i-nes], *n.* the condition of being flowery.

FLOWERING, [flow'-er-ing], *adj.* producing flowers; phanerogamous; cultivated for the flower; **f. ash**, the manna-ash, *Fraxinus ornus*; **f. fern**, the king fern, *Osmunda regalis*; **f. rush**, the aquatic plant, *Butomus umbellatus*.

FLOWER-LEAF, [flow'-er-lēf'], *n.* a petal.

FLOWERLESS, [flow'-er-les], *adj.* without flowers.

FLOWERLESSNESS, [flow'-er-les-nes], *n.* lack of flowers.

FLOWERMAKER, [flow'-er-mā'-ker], *n.* one who makes artificial flowers.

FLOWERPOT, [flow'-er-pot'], *n.* an earthenware or china pot in which certain plants are grown.

FLOWER-SERVICE, [flow'-er-sur'-vis], *n.* a special church service at which gifts of flowers for the sick are received.

FLOWER-SHOW, [flow'-er-shō'], *n.* a horticultural display or exhibition at which flowers and ornamental plants are shown in competition for prizes.

FLOWERY, [flow'-er-i], *adj.* full of, covered with, flowers, composed of flowers, resembling flowers; florid, full of elaborate ornamentation.

FLOWING, [flō'-ing], *adj.* that flows; fluent; waving in loose folds; curving smoothly and naturally; proceeding readily and without effort.

FLOWINGLY, [flō'-ing-li], *adv.* in a flowing fashion.

FLOWINGNESS, [flō'-ing-nes], *n.* the quality of being flowing.

FLOW-LINE, [flō'-līn'], *n.* (*geol.*) a line in igneous rock marking the path of flow when molten.

FLOWN†, [flōn], *adj.* swollen, exalted; having colours which readily merge into one another. [FLOW].

FLU, [flōō], *n.* (*coll.*) influenza. [~INFLUENZA].

FLUCTUANT, [fluk'-chōō-ant], *adj.* wavering, unsteady, undulating, variable; floating. [L. *fluctuans*].

FLUCTUATE, [fluk'-chōō-āt], *v.t. and i.* to rise and fall, or move backwards and forwards, periodically; (*fig.*) to vary, to vacillate, to change repeatedly and irregularly; to cause to vary. [L. *fluctuare* to move like a wave].

FLUCTUATING, [fluk'-chōō-āt-ing], *adj.* unsteady, wavering, variable.

FLUCTUATION, [fluk'-chōō-ā'-shun], *n.* the act of fluctuating. [L. *fluctuatio*].

FLUE (1), [flōō], *n.* a pipe or shaft for conveying hot air, gas, smoke, etc.; a small chimney or branch of a chimney; a tube conveying heat to water in a boiler; (*mus.*) the mouthpiece of an organ pipe. [Uncert.].

FLUE (2), [flōō], *n.* a loose, fluffy mass of particles of some downy substance or dust. [~Flem. *vluwe*].

FLUE (3), [flōō], *n.* a variety of fishing-net. [~Du. *flouw*].

FLUE (4), [flōō], *v.t.* to expand, to splay. [Unkn.].

FLUELLIN†, [flōō-el'-in], *n.* (*bot.*) any of several varieties of Speedwell or *Veronica*. [Corruption of *Llewelyn*].

FLUELLITE, [flōō'-el-īt], *n.* the fluoride of aluminium. [~FLUORINE].

FLUENCY, [flōō'-en-si], *n.* the quality of being fluent. [L. *fluentia*].

FLUENT (1), [flōō'-ent], *n.* (*math.*) a constantly varying quantity in fluxions.

FLUENT (2), [flōō'-ent], *adj.* having a ready command and flow of words, voluble, glib; spoken easily, rapidly, and without hesitation; flowing, smoothly, and continuous; proceeding readily and naturally without effort; (*archaic*) fluid, mobile. [L. *fluens*].

FLUENTIAL, [flōō-en'-shal], *adj.* (*math.*) relating to a fluent.

FLUENTLY, [flōō'-ent-li], *adv.* in a fluent manner.

FLUE-PIPE, [flōō'-pīp'], *n.* the pipe of an organ or similar musical instrument in which the sound is produced by a flow of air against the mouthpiece.

FLUE-WORK, [flōō'-wurk'], *n.* the range of flue-pipes in an organ.

FLUEY, [flōō'-i], *adj.* downy; fluffy.

FLUFF (1), [fluf], *n.* a light soft downy substance; soft fur; the first growth of hair on the face; a woolly mass of dust particles. [~FLUE (2)].

FLUFF (2), [fluf], *v.t. and i.* to spread or shake out into a soft, fluffy mass; (*slang*) to bungle, foozle, to perform in a careless, unskilful way; (*theatre*) to bungle a part imperfectly learned; to float, move, or settle like fluff; to become fluffy.

FLUFFINESS, [fluf'-i-nes], *n.* the state of being fluffy.

FLUFFY, [fluf'-i], *adj.* consisting of, relating to, or resembling, fluff; covered with fluff, down, or soft fine hair; (*slang*) drunk; liable to bungle a theatrical part.

FLUGELMAN, see FUGLEMAN.

FLUID (1), [flōō'-id], *n.* a liquid or gaseous substance, a substance that cannot permanently resist forces tending to change its shape.

FLUID (2), [flōō'-id], *adj.* flowing, liquid or gaseous; (*fig.*) mobile, yielding readily to forces tending to change it, not set; fluent, flowing easily and gracefully. [L. *fluidus*].

FLUIDIFY, [flōō-id'-i-fī], *v.t.* to make fluid.

FLUIDITY, [flōō-id'-i-ti], *n.* the quality or state of being fluid; a fluid substance. [Fr. *fluidité*].

FLUIDIZE, [flōō'-id-īz], *v.t.* to make fluid.

FLUIDNESS, [flōō'-id-nes], *n.* fluidity.

FLUKE (1), FLOOK, [flōōk], *n.* the broad flattened triangular tip of the shank of an anchor; the barbed head of a harpoon, arrow, lance, etc.; the lobe of the tail of a whale. [Uncert.].

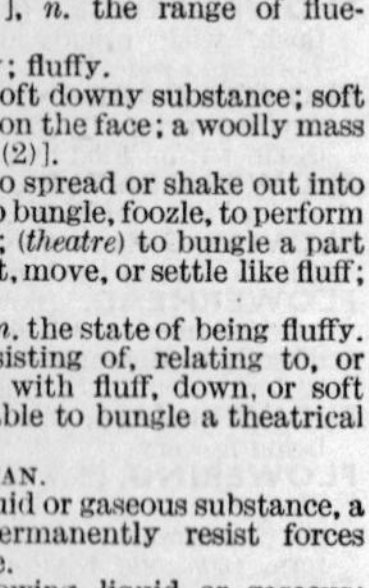

FLUKE

FLUKE (2), [flōōk], *n.* a flat-fish, *esp.* the flounder or megrim; a parasitic animal of the genus of flat-worms causing liver-rot in sheep; a kind of kidney potato. [OE. *floc*].

FLUKE (3), [flōōk], *n.* (*coll.*) a lucky unintentional scoring shot at billiards or other games; (*fig.*) a happy piece of luck or good-fortune, a chance successful stroke. [Unkn.].

FLUKE (4), [flōōk], *v.t. and i.* (*coll.*) to make a fluke or a series of flukes; to score by means of a fluke; to gain by a fluke. [*Prec.*].

FLUKILY, [flōōk'-i-li], *adv.* luckily, by a lucky chance.

FLUKINESS, [flōōk'-i-nes], *n.* the quality of being fluky.

FLUKY (1), [flōōk'-i], *adj.* (*coll.*) lucky, chance, accidentally successful, of the nature of a fluke.

FLUKY (2), [flōōk'-i], *adj.* attached by flukes.

FLUME (1), [flōōm], *n.* the passage for the water that drives a mill-wheel; any artificial channel down which water may be directed for industrial purposes; a deep ravine through which a stream flows. [ME. *flume* from OFr. *flum* river].

FLUME (2), [flōōm], *v.t. and i.* to construct a flume; to convey by a flume.

FLUMINOUS†, [flōō'-min-us], *adj.* possessing many rivers. [~L. *flumen* river].

FLUMMERY, [flum'-eri], *n.* a sour jelly made by boiling oatmeal with the husks; a kind of flavoured blancmange; (*fig.*) nonsense, idle, vapid talk; empty flattery. [Unkn.].

FLUMMOX, [flum'-oks], *v.t.* (*slang*) to bewilder, disconcert, confound, floor. [Unkn.].

FLUMP, [flump], *v.t. and i.* to fall heavily and with a dull thud, to flop; to throw down heavily. [Echoic].

FLUNG, [flung], *pret. and p.pt.* of FLING.

FLUNKEY, [flungk'-i], *n.* a man-servant in livery, a footman, a lackey; (*fig.*) a toady. [Uncert.].

FLUNKEYDOM, [flungk'-i-dum], *n.* the state of being a flunkey.

FLUNKEYISM, [flungk'-i-izm], *n.* the character of a flunkey.

FLUOBORIC, [flōō'-ō-bor'-ik], *adj.* composed of fluorine and boron.

FLUOR, [flōō'-er], *n.* any variety of mineral containing calcium fluoride. [L. *fluor* a flowing].

FLUORENE, [flōō'-or-ēn], *n.* a coal-tar product, emitting violet fluorescence when impure.

FLUORESCENCE, [flōō-er-es'-ents], *n.* the property of certain substances to emit light of longer wave-length than the light directed upon them. [Fr. *fluorescence*].

FLUORESCENT, [flōō'-er-es'-ent], *adj.* possessing or exhibiting fluorescence.

FLUORESCIN, [flōō'-or-es'-in], *n.* a dye-stuff exhibiting green fluorescence.

FLUORIC, [flōō-or'-ik], *adj.* pertaining to or obtained from fluor; (*chem.*) pertaining to fluorine.

FLUORIDE, [flōō'-er-īd], *n.* a compound of fluorine and a metallic base.

FLUORINE, [flōō'-er-ēn], *n.* an element usually in the form of a greenish-yellow gas, and occurring always in combination with metals. [~FLUOR].

FLUORITE, [flōō'-er-īt], *n.* fluor-spar.

FLUOROSCOPE, [flōō'-er-ō-skōp'], *n.* an apparatus used to detect or illustrate fluorescence. [FLUOR and SCOPE].

FLUOROSCOPY, [flōō-er-os'-kop-i], *n.* the examination of a substance by fluorescence. [FLUOR and Gk. *skopos* watcher].

FLUOROTYPE, [flōō'-er-ō-tīp'], *n.* a photographic process in which salts of fluoric acid are employed to sensitize the paper. [FLUOR(IDE) and TYPE].

FLUOROUS†, [flōō'-er-us], *adj.* containing or derived from fluor.

FLUORSPAR, [flōō'-er-spah(r)'], *n.* (*min.*) calcium fluoride, a transparent mineral of various tints, common in Derbyshire; Blue John.

FLUOSILICATE, [flōō'-ō-sil'-ik-āt], *n.* a salt of fluosilicic acid. [FLUOR and SILICATE].

FLUOSILICIC, [flōō'-ō-sil-is'-ik], *adj.* derived from fluorine and silicon. [FLUOR and SILICIC].

FLURRY (1), [flu'-ri], *n.* a sudden gust of wind; a sudden commotion, agitation, or bustle, restless hurry and confusion; the convulsive movements of a dying whale. [Echoic].

FLURRY (2), [flu'-ri], *v.t.* to bewilder, to agitate, to fluster by restless unceasing bustle.

FLUSH (1), [flush], *n.* a flock of birds suddenly started in flight; a sudden rush of water or other liquid, the stream from a mill-wheel; a sudden flow of blood to the face; redness induced by this, a ruddy glow of colour; a sudden blooming or sprouting; a sudden impulsive feeling of elation; a feverish attack; height of vigour or freshness; abundance.

FLUSH (2), [flush], *n.* (*cards*) a hand containing only cards of the same suit; a run of cards of the same suit. [*Next*].

FLUSH (3), [flush] *adj.* brimming, full; level, forming one even surface on the same plane; (*coll.*) well supplied with money, prosperous; plentiful; lavish; **f. deck**, (*naut.*) a deck having a continuous level floor from stem to stern.

FLUSH (4), [flush], *adj.* made up of cards of the same suit.
FLUSH (5), [flush], *adv.* in a flush manner, so as to form one even surface on the same plane.
FLUSH (6), [flush], *v.t.* to cleanse by a sudden rush of water or other liquid; to suffuse with a ruddy glow; (*pass.*) to be wildly elated at or with; *v.i.* to fly up suddenly in startled fashion; to flow suddenly, quickly and in a large volume; (of blood) to rush to the skin; to become filled with a sudden flow of water; to blush, to become suddenly red; to send forth sprouts or shoots; (*fig.*) to glow. [ME. *flusen* to fly about quickly].
FLUSH (7), [flush], *v.t.* to make flush or level.
FLUSHER (1), [flush'-er], *n.* the red-backed shrike, *Lanius collurio.* [Unkn.].
FLUSHER (2), [flush'-er], *n.* one who, or that which, flushes sewers.
FLUSHING, [flush'-ing], *n.* blushing.
FLUSHINGLY, [flush'-ing-li], *adv.* in a flushing fashion.
FLUSHNESS, [flush'-nes], *n.* the state of being flush.
FLUSTER (1), [flus'-ter], *n.* the state of being flustered, agitation, confusion.
FLUSTER (2), [flus'-ter], *v.t. and i.* to agitate and confuse, to make hot and bothered; to be confused and nervously agitated; to be excited or muddled with drink; to bustle, to fuss. [~Icel. *flaustra* to be flustered].
FLUSTRA, [flus'-tra], *n.* (*biol.*) the sea-mat, a variety of polyzoon. [L. *flustra*].
FLUTE (1), [flōōt], *n.* a musical wind-instrument consisting of a wooden pipe containing holes to be covered by the fingers or keys, and played by blowing across an oval-shaped hole in the side of the instrument; an organ-stop producing a sound similar to that of this instrument; a flautist in an orchestra; a narrow vertical furrow or channel along the shaft of a column; an object resembling a flute in shape. [Fr. *flûte*].
FLUTE (2), [flōōt], *n.* a long vessel or boat, with flat ribs or floor timbers; a warship, not fully equipped, and used for transport. [Du. *fluit*].
FLUTE (3), [flōōt], *v.t. and i.* to play the flute, to sing in flute-like tones; to play (an air) on a flute; to sound as a flute; to form flutes in. [OFr. *fleuter*].
FLUTED, [flōōt'-id], *adj.* channelled, grooved, decorated with flutes; flute-like.
FLUTER, [flōōt'-er], *n.* a flutist; one who makes flutes in columns; a tool for making flutes on columns.
FLUTE-STOP, [flōōt'-stop'], *n.* a range of pipes in an organ, designed to imitate the timbre or quality of the flute.
FLUTINA, [flōōt-ē'-na], *n.* a kind of accordion.
FLUTING, [flōōt'-ing], *n.* (*arch.*) fluted work; a shallow groove in a column, or in a lady's ruffle; (*mus.*) the action of playing the flute.

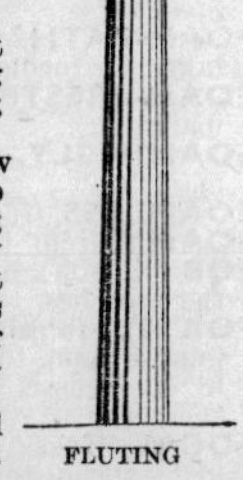
FLUTING

FLUTIST, [flōōt'-ist], *n.* a flautist.
FLUTTER (1), [flut'-er], *n.* the act of fluttering; the condition of being nervously agitated and excited; (*coll.*) a small gamble.
FLUTTER (2), [flut'-er], *v.t.* to throw into a state of mental agitation, to cause to throb, to disturb, perturb; *v.i.* to move or flap the wings quickly and nervously; to make short flights flapping the wings in this way; to vibrate with a rapid irregular motion, to flap rapidly and continually; to throb faintly, quickly, and unevenly; to be in a state of confused nervous bustle or excitement. [OE. *floterian*].
FLUTTERER, [flut'-er-er], *n.* one who flutters; one who acts in a nervously excited and clumsy way.
FLUTTERINGLY, [flut'-er-ing-li], *adv.* in a fluttering fashion.
FLUTY, [flōōt'-i], *adj.* having the sound or timbre of a flute.
FLUVIAL, [flōō'-vi-al], *adj.* belonging to rivers; living in a river. [L. *fluvialis*].
FLUVIALIST, [flōō'-vi-al-ist], *n.* one who explains geological phenomena as due to river action.
FLUVIATIC, [flōō'-vi-at'-ik], *adj.* existing in rivers, pertaining to rivers. [L. *fluviaticus*].
FLUVIATILE, [flōō'-vi-at-il], *adj.* growing or living in rivers; made by river action; pertaining to a river. [L. *fluviatilis*].
FLUVIOMARINE, [flōō'-vi-ō-ma-rēn'], *adj.* (of deposits) formed by river-currents at the bottom of the sea, estuarine. [L. *fluvius* river and MARINE].
FLUX (1), [fluks], *n.* the act or state of flowing, fluidity, an excessive discharge of morbid matter, blood, etc., from the body; the flowing in of a tide; that which flows; (*fig.*) an excessive stream of words or talk; a continuous flow of people; (*phys.*) the amount flowing over a certain area in a specified time; (*math.*) continual motion (of a point); (*metal.*) any substance mixed with a metal or mineral to promote fusion; (*magn.*) the total number of lines of force found in any given part of a magnetic circuit or field. [L. *fluxus*].
FLUX (2), [fluks], *v.t. and i.* to flow; to issue from the body as a flux; to fuse, melt; (*med.*) to cause a flux in; to melt by using a flux.
FLUXATION†, [fluks-ā'-shun], *n.* the act of flowing.
FLUXIBILITY, [fluks'-ib-il'-i-ti], *n.* the quality of being fluxible.
FLUXIBLE, [fluks'-ibl], *adj.* that may be melted or fused.
FLUXIBLENESS, [fluks'-ibl-nes], *n.* fluxibility.
FLUXILITY, [fluks-il'-iti], *n.* fluxibility.
FLUXION, [fluk'-shun], *n.* (*archaic*) the act of flowing; an abnormal flow of liquid to any part of the body; that which flows; a flux; (*math.*) the rate of increase in magnitude of a variable quantity; (*pl.*) the Newtonian calculus. [L. *fluxio*].
FLUXIONAL, [fluk'-shun-al], *adj.* relating to fluxions.
FLUXIONARY, [fluk'-shun-er-i], *adj.* variable.
FLUXIONIST, [fluk'-shun-ist], *n.* one versed in fluxions.
FLY (1), [flī], *n.* a small two-winged flying insect of many kinds, *esp.* one of the genus *Musca*; (*zool.*) a member of the order of dipterous insects; an artificial imitation of such an insect, fastened to a fish-hook to attract fish; a disease injurious to plants caused by insects; (*print.*) a person or mechanical device that removes the printed sheets from a press; **f. in the ointment,** a drawback. [OE. *fleoge, flyge*].
FLY (2), [flī], *n.* the act of flying; a flight or journey through the air; a four-wheeled hackney carriage drawn by one horse; a strip of cloth covering and enclosing a row of buttons on a garment; a canvas flap covering and overlapping the entrance to a tent; that edge of a flag, pennant, etc., farthest away from the staff; the width of a flag, ensign, etc., from the staff to the edge most remote from it; (*pl.*) the place above the stage of a theatre from which scenery is moved; (*baseball*) the flight of a ball before touching the ground; a piece of apparatus for controlling the speed of a machine or clockwork contrivance.
FLY (3), (flew, flown), [flī], *v.t.* to cause to fly; to navigate or control during flight; to hang up (a flag) from a mast or staff; to flee from; to jump by leaping from one foot and alighting on the other; *v.i.* to move through the air by wings or by mechanical means; to rise up in the air, and be borne by the wind; to float in the air; to move rapidly through the air; to soar over with a rapid forceful leap; to stream out or flutter in the wind; to hasten as rapidly as possible; to travel at an extremely quick rate; to flee; to move with a sudden rapid and violent motion; **to f. at,** (*fig.*) to attack fiercely, to abuse or rate soundly; **to f. into,** to develop (a rage, temper) quickly and violently; **to f. out at,** to burst into a passion or storm of abuse against; **to let f.,** to shoot, aim, hurl; **as the crow flies,** in a straight or direct line; **to f. in the face of,** to flout; **to f. high,** to be ambitious. [OE. *fleogan*].
FLYAWAY, [flī'-a-wā'], *adj.* flighty, capricious; (of garments, etc.) streaming loosely.
FLY-BITTEN, [flī'-bitn'], *adj.* marked by spots resembling, or made by, the bites of flies.
FLY-BLISTER, [flī'-blis'-ter], *n.* (*med.*) a blister produced by the dried Spanish flies or cantharides.
FLY-BLOW (1), [flī'-blō'], *n.* the egg or larva of a fly laid in flesh; the state of being fly-blown.
FLY-BLOW (2), [flī'-blō'], *v.t.* to taint or corrupt by depositing eggs in.
FLY-BLOWN, [flī'-blōn'], *adj.* corrupted or tainted with fly-blow; (*fig.*) discredited, sullied.
FLYBOAT, [flī'-bōt'], *n.* a canal boat carrying passengers; a large flat-bottomed Dutch vessel.
FLY-BOOK, [flī'-bŏŏk'], *n.* a book or container in which artificial flies used in angling are kept.
FLY-CATCHER, [flī'-kach'-er], *n.* any of various perching birds of the genus *Muscicapa* that feed on

flies; any of certain American tyrant-birds feeding on flies; a plant whose leaves form a hollow rounded trap for flies, which it feeds on when caught in this way; a trap or piece of paper coated with some adhesive substance for catching flies.

FLYER, see FLIER.

FLY-FISHING, [flī'-fish'-ing], *n.* the art or practice of catching fish by means of flies fastened to the fish-hook.

FLY-FLAP, [flī'-flap'], *n.* something with which to drive away or kill flies.

FLYING (1), [flī'-ing], *n.* the act or practice of one who, or that which, flies, aviation.

FLYING (2), [flī'-ing], *adj.* that flies; hasty, hurried, of short duration; hanging free, streaming out in the air; resembling anything that flies, vigorous and rapid; speedy, very fast; **with f. colours,** with distinction; **f. squad,** a special branch of the police equipped with high-powered motor-cars or motor-cycles, for the pursuit of criminals; **f. handicap,** (*sport*) a short informal impromptu tournament; (*billiards*) a knock-out competition in which a fixed small number of points have to be scored.

FLYING-ARTILLERY, [flī'-ing-ah-til'-er-i], *n.* horse artillery trained to act with cavalry; a corps trained to execute rapid short manoeuvres.

FLYING-BOAT, [flī'-ing-bōt], *n.* (*aeron.*) an aeroplane so constructed that the fuselage can rest directly on the water.

FLYING-BRIDGE, [flī'-ing-brij'], *n.* a bridge of pontoons; a large flat-bottomed boat fastened to a rope, and made to pass like a ferry-boat from one side of a river to the other; the topmost bridge on a ship.

FLYING-BUTTRESS, [flī'-ing-but'-res], *n.* (*arch.*) a buttress usually in the form of a sloping arch, the base of which stands away from the wall it is supporting.

FLYING-CAMP, [flī'-ing-kamp'], *n.* a body of troops kept moving from one place to another, and practically independent of the main base.

FLYING-COLUMN, [flī'-ing-kol'-um], *n.* a flying-camp.

FLYING-CORPS, [flī'-ing-kaw(r)'], *n.* the former name of the Royal Air Force.

FLYING-FISH, [flī'-ing-fish'], *n.* a fish of the genus *Exocœtus* which is able to sustain itself in the air for a time by means of its long pectoral fins.

FLYING-BUTTRESS

FLYING-FOX, [flī'-ing-foks'], *n.* the fruit-eating bat of the genus *Pteropus.*

FLYING-GURNARD, [flī'-ing-gurn'-erd], *n.* a fish of the genus *Dactylopterus,* with large pectoral fins, by which it is able to sustain itself in flight in the air for a short period.

FLYING-JIB, [flī'-ing-jib'], *n.* (*naut.*) a light sail set immediately in front of the jib.

FLYING-JUNCTION, [flī'-ing-jungk'-shun], *n.* a railway junction in which one line crosses over another by means of a long bridge built with ramps.

FLYING-LEMUR, [flī'-ing-lē'-mer], *n.* the cobego, an insect-eating animal of the genus *Galeopithecus* with a flying membrane extending from behind the throat to the toes and the tip of the tail.

FLYING-MACHINE, [flī'-ing-ma-shēn'], *n.* an aeroplane.

FLYING-OFFICER, [flī'-ing-of'-is-er], *n.* a rank in the Royal Air Force immediately below that of flight-lieutenant.

FLYING-PARTY, [flī'-ing-pah'-ti], *n.* (*milit.*) a detachment of men employed as skirmishers.

FLYING-PHALANGER, [flī'-ing-fal'-an-jer], *n.* a marsupial quadruped of the genus *Petaurus,* having a membrane extending from the toes of the forefoot to the hind foot, with which it supports itself when leaping.

FLYING-PINION, [flī'-ing-pin'-yun], *n.* a device in a chiming clock to regulate the speed of the clock when the striking weight descends.

FLYING-SQUID, [flī'-ing-skwid'], *n.* the sea-arrow, a cephalopod of the genus *Ommastrephes.*

FLYING-SQUIRREL, [flī'-ing-skwi'-rel], *n.* a squirrel with an extensible skin on each side, reaching from the forelegs to the hind legs, by which it is supported when leaping.

FLYING-START, [flī'-ing-staht'], *n.* a start to a race, competition, etc., in which the competitors approach the starting line on the move, and are officially started as they pass over it; (*fig.*) an auspicious commencement resulting in an early advantage or considerable rapid progress.

FLY-LEAF, [flī'-lēf'], *n.* a leaf of blank paper at the beginning and end of a book; a printed circular contained on a single sheet.

FLYMAN, [flī'-man'], *n.* the driver of a hackney fly; a scene-shifter in the flies of a theatre.

FLY-NET, [flī'-net'], *n.* a net to protect food, animals, etc., from flies.

FLY-NUT, [flī'-nut'], *n.* a screw nut with wings, a butterfly nut.

FLY-OVER, [flī'-ō'-ver], *n.* a method of avoiding crossroads, etc., whereby one road or set of rails crosses over another by means of a shallow bridge built up with ramps which connect with the lower road.

FLYPAPER, [flī'-pā'-per], *n.* a paper coated with a sticky or poisonous substance, and hung up to catch flies.

FLY-POWDER, [flī'-pow'-der], *n.* an oxide of arsenic, which, mixed with sugar and water, is used to poison flies.

FLY-RAIL, [flī'-rāl'], *n.* an arm of a table which can be drawn out to support the hinged leaf.

FLY-SHEET, [flī'-shēt'], *n.* a handbill or circular printed on a single sheet.

FLY-SHUTTLE, [flī'-shutl'], *n.* a shuttle worked by machinery.

FLY-SPECK, [flī'-spek'], *n.* the excrement of an insect, *esp.* the common house-fly.

FLY-TRAP, [flī'-trap'], *n.* a plant that traps and eats small insects and flies; **Venus's f.,** *Dionæa muscipula,* a plant related to the sundew.

FLY-WATER, [flī'-waw'-ter], *n.* a solution of arsenic for killing flies.

FLY-WHEEL, [flī'-wēl'], *n.* a heavy, rimmed revolving wheel used to control the speed of a machine.

FOAL (1), [fōl], *n.* the young of a horse, ass or other related animal. [OE. *fola*].

FOAL (2), [fōl], *v.t. and i.* to give birth to a foal.

FOAL-FOOT, [fōl'-fŏŏt'], *n.* the coltsfoot plant.

FOALING, [fōl'-ing], *n.* the act of bringing forth a foal.

FOAL-TEETH, [fōl'-tēth'], *n.(pl.)* the first teeth of a horse.

FOAM (1), [fōm], *n.* the white frothy collection of small bubbles forming on the surface of liquids in a state of fermentation, effervescence or agitation; anything resembling this; (*poet.*) the sea. [OE. *fam*].

FOAM (2), [fōm], *v.i.* to form or produce foam; to emit thick saliva or profuse perspiration resembling foam; to run in the form of foam (of liquids); **to f. at the mouth,** (*fig.*) to be in a furious rage. [OE. *famigan*].

FOAM-BATH, [fōm'-bahth'], *n.* a bath of foam taken for medicinal purposes or to cleanse the skin.

FOAM-CRESTED, [fōm'-krest'-id], *adj.* crested with foam.

FOAMINGLY, [fōm'-ing-li], *adv.* in a foaming manner.

FOAMLESS, [fōm'-les], *adj.* without foam.

FOAMY, [fōm'-i], *adj.* covered with, or like, foam.

FOB (1), [fob], *n.* a small pocket in the waistband of the breeches. [~LGerm. *fobke* little pocket].

FOB (2), (fobbing, fobbed), [fob], *v.t.* (*archaic*) to impose upon, to cheat; **to f. off,** to delude or put off by an excuse, pretence, or trick. [~ME. *fobbere* cheater].

FOCAL, [fōkl], *adj.* relating to a focus; **f. length** (*opt.*) the distance between the centre of a lens and the point where the rays meet.

FOCALIZE, [fō'-kal-īz], *v.t.* to focus.

FOCAL-PLANE SHUTTER, [fōkl'-plān'-shut'-er], *n.* (*phot.*) a shutter blind with a slit which moves rapidly across the front of a plate or film.

FOCIMETER, [fō-sim'-it-er], *n.* an instrument by which focal distances are measured. [FOCUS and METER].

FOCIMETRY, [fō-sim'-it-ri], *n.* the measurement of focal distances.

FOCKE-WULF, [fok'-er-vŏŏlf], *n.* the name of certain German aircraft, *esp.* a four-engined, long-range bomber. [*Focke-Wulf* the maker's name].

FOCOSO, [fō-kō'-sō], *adj.* (*mus.*) spiritedly, in lively, animated manner. [It. *focoso*].

FO'C'SLE, [fōksl], *n.* the forecastle of a ship.

FOCUS (1), (*pl.* **foci**), [fō'-kus], *n.* (*phys.*) a point in which rays of light, heat, sound, etc., meet after being reflected or refracted; adjustment or position required to produce a sharply defined image; focal length or distance; (*fig.*) the centre of convergence, point where anything is gathered to a head, area of greatest activity; (*geom.*) one of the points having properties of a special kind in relation to a curve; **in f.**, (*phot.*) correctly adjusted so that the image is sharply defined; (*fig.*) undistorted; **virtual f.**, a point in which rays would meet if produced backwards. [L. *focus* hearth, home].

FOCUS (2), (**focusing, focused**), [fō'-kus], *v.t. and i.* to bring to a focus; to adjust so as to produce a sharply defined image of an object, to bring into focus; (*fig.*) to concentrate; to converge.

FODDER (1), [fod'-er], *n.* food for horses, cattle or sheep, *esp.* dried food such as hay, straw, etc. [OE. *fodor*].

FODDER (2), [fod'-er], *v.t.* to feed or supply with fodder.

FODDERER, [fod'-er-er], *n.* one who fodders cattle.

FODIENT, [fō'-di-ent], *adj.* digging. [L. *fodiens*].

FOE, [fō], *n.* an enemy, adversary; an antagonist; an opponent; that which is injurious or hostile to anything. [OE. *fah*].

FOEHN, [furn], *n.* a dry, hot wind of the Northern Alps. [Germ. *föhn*].

FOETAL, [fētl], *adj.* relating to the foetus.

FOETATION, [fē-tā'-shun], *n.* pregnancy, development of a foetus.

FOETICIDE, FETICIDE†, [fēt'-is-īd], *n.* criminal abortion.

FOETID, FETID, [fē'-tid], *adj.* having an offensive smell. [L. *foetidus*].

FOETIFEROUS, FETIFEROUS, [fē-tif'-er-us], *adj.* bearing offspring. [L. *foetifer*].

FOETOR, FETOR, [fē'-ter], *n.* any foul odour. [L. *foetor*].

FOETUS, FETUS, [fē'-tus], *n.* the young of viviparous animals before birth, and of oviparous ones in the shell, after the embryo has developed. [L. *foetus* a bringing forth].

FOG (1), [fog], *n.* a dense mass of low-lying watery vapour, smoke particles, etc., reducing or obliterating visibility; (*phot.*) a blurred condition of a photographic print or negative; (*fig.*) a state of perplexity, bewilderment or confusion of the mind. [Uncert.].

FOG (2), [fog], *n.* long grass unpastured and left untouched during winter; **winter f.**, the grass *Agrostis canina*, the brown bent; **Yorkshire f.**, the grass *Holcus lanatus*. [ME. *fogge* rank grass].

FOG (3), (**fogging, fogged**), [fog], *v.t.* to surround or envelop with fog; (*phot.*) to make blurred and cloudy; (*fig.*) to perplex, to baffle, to throw into a state of mental confusion; *v.i.* to become foggy; (*phot.*) to cloud over; to place fog-signals on a railway line. [FOG (1)].

FOG (4), (**fogging, fogged**), [fog], *v.t.* to leave with the long grass standing; to feed on fog. [FOG (2)].

FOG-BANK, [fog'-bangk'], *n.* a dense mass of fog at sea, resembling land at a distance.

FOGBOUND, [fog'-bownd], *adj.* hindered or brought to a halt by fog.

FOG-BOW, [fog'-bō'], *n.* a kind of white rainbow of light caused by the sun's rays shining on the particles of fog.

FOGEY, FOGY, [fō'-gi], *n.* an elderly, fussy, old-fashioned person, out of contact and sympathy with what is modern. [Unkn.].

FOGEYDOM, [fō'-gi-dum], *n.* the state or condition of a fogey.

FOGGILY, [fog'-i-li], *adv.* in a foggy manner.

FOGGINESS, [fog'-i-nes], *n.* the state of being foggy

FOGGY (1), [fog'-i], *adj.* pertaining to, clouded with, or resembling fog; (*phot.*) clouded, blurred; (*fig.*) obscure, baffling; confused, mystified.

FOGGY (2), [fog'-i], *adj.* abounding in the grass known as fog.

FOGHORN, [fog'-hawn], *n.* a powerful siren blown to give warning of a ship's position or approach in a fog.

FOG-LAMP, [fog'-lamp'], *n.* a lamp fitted to the front of a motor vehicle, emitting a ray which penetrates fog, and which is usually turned outwards towards the edge of the kerb.

FOG-SIGNAL, [fog'-sig'-nal], *n.* any audible warning signal used in the event of fog.

FOGY, see FOGEY.

FOH, [fō], *int.* an exclamation of contempt or disgust.

FOIBLE, [foibl], *n.* an unworthy feature in one's character, a small failing; an idiosyncrasy. [OFr. *foible* feeble].

FOIL (1), [foil], *n.* a small rounded leaf-like space between the cusps in window tracery; a plate of metal beaten out into an extremely thin sheet; a thin leaf of metal placed under precious stones to heighten their brilliancy; a thin coating of tin and quicksilver laid on the back of a sheet of glass to make a mirror; (*fig.*) anything of another colour or different quality, which serves to set off another thing to advantage by contrast. [OFr. *foil* from L. *folium*].

FOIL

FOIL (2), [foil], *n.* the track or trail of game when pursued; (*fig.*) defeat, check, failure, *esp.* when on the point of success; **to run upon the f.**, to foil the scent.

FOIL (3), [foil], *n.* a light rapier or tapering sword used as a thrusting weapon in fencing, and tipped with a leather-covered button. [Uncert.].

FOIL (4), [foil], *v.t.* (*arch.*) to decorate or provide with a foil; to back or cover with foil; (*fig.*) to set off by contrast as a foil.

FOIL (5), [foil], *v.t. and i.* to frustrate, to defeat; to repulse, to beat off; (*hunting*) to cross and recross so as to obliterate or confuse the scent; to spoil the trail. [~OFr. *fouler*].

FOILABLE, [foil'-abl], *adj.* that may be foiled.

FOILED, [foild], *adj.* (*arch.*) having foils.

FOILER, [foil'-er], *n.* one who foils another.

FOILING (1), [foil'-ing], *n.* (*arch.*) ornamentation or tracery in the form of foils.

FOILING (2), [foil'-ing], *n.* the track or trail of a deer in passing.

FOIL-STONE, [foil'-stōn'], *n.* a sham jewel.

FOIN† **(1)**, [foin], *n.* a lunge, push or thrust in fencing.

FOIN† **(2)**, [foin], *v.i.* to make a foin. [ME. *foinen* from L. *fuscina* fish-spear].

FOININGLY, [foin'-ing-li], *adv.* in a pushing fashion.

FOISON, [foi'-zon], *n.* abundance. [OFr. from L. *fusio* a pouring].

FOIST, [foist], *v.t.* to insert secretly or wrongfully, to palm off (something bad) in an underhand way. [Du. *vuisten* to take in the fist].

FOKKER, [fok'-er], *n.* a variety of fighting aeroplane. [A. H. *Fokker*, a Dutch aviator].

FOLD (1), [fōld], *n.* a bend or part of some flexible material that is doubled over; a crease, hollow, or mark made by such bending over or folding; a layer; (*geol.*) a bend or dip in stratification, a hollow in the ground. [OE. *fald*].

FOLD (2), [fōld], *n.* a pen or enclosure for sheep; a flock of sheep in such an enclosure; (*fig.*) the Church, the flock of believers, a religious congregation. [OE. *falod*].

FOLD (3), [fold], *v.t. and i.* to lay or bend one part of (something flexible) over another, to double over or up; to wrap round, to wind, to coil; to envelop; to embrace; to close or bend back over another part, to be capable of being folded; **to f. one's arms**, to cross one's arms over the breast with the elbows bent. [OE. *faldan*].

FOLD (4), [fōld], *v.t.* to enclose in a fold, to pen; to manure land by enclosing sheep in folds upon it.

FOLDAGE, [fōld'-ij], *n.* the right of folding sheep; the folding of leaves one over another.

FOLDER, [fōld'-er], *n.* an instrument used in folding paper; folding eyeglasses; a container for papers; a time-table, advertisement, or other document that folds up.

FOLDING (1), [fōld'-ing], *n.* a fold; the act of doubling one part of a substance over another; the penning of sheep or cattle.

FOLDING (2), [fōld'-ing], *adj.* that folds or can be folded.

FOLDING-BED, [fōld'-ing-bed'], *n.* a small collapsible camp-bed.

FOLDING-DOOR, [fōld'-ing-daw(r)'], *n.* a door consisting of two leaves hung on opposite side-posts, and meeting in the middle, without intervening space, when closed.

FOLDING-JOINT, [fōld'-ing-joint'], *n.* a joint made like that of a hinge.

FOLDING-MACHINE, [fōld'-ing-ma-shēn'], *n.* a machine that folds printed matter.

FOLDING-SCREEN, [fōld'-ing-skrēn'], *n.* an upright portable screen that can be folded up.
FOLDING-STOOL, [fōld'-ing-stōōl'], *n.* a small stool which folds up in scissor-like fashion.
FOLDLESS, [fōld'-les], *adj.* without a fold or folds.
FOLD-YARD, [fōld'-yahd'], *n.* a yard in which cattle are penned.
FOLIACEOUS, [fō'-li-ā'-shus], *adj.* relating to, or like, foliage. [L. *foliaceus*].
FOLIAGE (1), [fō'-li-ij], *n.* the leaves of a plant, leaves collectively; decoration or ornamentation in the form of leaves; **f. leaf,** an actual leaf itself as distinct from petal, sepal, etc.; **f. plant,** a plant raised primarily for its foliage. [OFr. *foillage*].
FOLIAGE (2), [fō'-li-ij], *v.t.* to ornament with leaf-like decoration.
FOLIAR, [fō'-li-er], *adj.* pertaining to, or resembling, a leaf.
FOLIATE (1), [fō'-li-āt], *adj.* resembling a leaf; provided with a leaf or leafage; **f. curve,** (*geom.*) a curve of the second order in the form of a leaf. [L. *foliatus* leaved].
FOLIATE (2), [fō'-li-āt], *v.t.* to beat into a leaf or thin plate; to spread (a mirror) over with a coat of tin and quicksilver; to decorate with foils or foliage; to number the leaves or folios of a book, as distinct from the pages; *v.i.* to split into leaves. [*Prec.*].
FOLIATED, [fō'-li-ā-tid], *adj.* spread or covered with a thin plate or foil; (*min.*) consisting of plates or thin layers; (*arch.*) adorned with foils; (*zool.*) shaped like a leaf; (*her.*) consisting of leaves; (*mus.*) decorated with slurred notes.
FOLIATION, [fō'-li-ā'-shun], *n.* the act of springing into leaf, the state of being in leaf; the process of beating into foil, or covering with foil; a leaf-like process; (*geol.*) the quality of splitting into thin layers or laminae; decoration or tracery in the form of foils; the numbering of the folios of a book.
FOLIATURE, [fō'-li-chōōer], *n.* foliage, a mass of leaves; representation of leaves as ornamentation. [LL. *foliatura*].
FOLIER, [fō'-li-er], *n.* goldsmith's foil used to heighten the effect of precious stones.
FOLIIFEROUS, [fō-li-if'-er-us], *adj.* bearing leaves. [L. *folium* leaf and *ferre* to bear].
FOLIO (1), [fō'-li-ō], *n.* a sheet of paper folded once; a book of the largest size, formed by folding the sheets of paper once; (*print.*) a leaf of a printed book; the page number of a book; (*comm.*) the right- and left-hand pages of an account-book, bearing the same number, and used for both sides of an account; (*leg.*) seventy-two or ninety words of manuscript, being the unit employed for estimating the length of a document. [L. *folio*, *ablative* of *folium* leaf].
FOLIO (2), [fō'-li-ō], *adj.* having the paper folded once only.
FOLIO (3), [fō'-li-ō], *v.t.* to number the leaves on one side only, to page.
FOLIOLATE, [fō'-li-ol-āt], *adj.* pertaining to, or having, leaflets or folioles.
FOLIOLE, [fō'-li-ōl], *n.* a leaflet of a compound leaf; (*zool.*) a small appendage resembling a leaf in form. [LL. *foliolum*].
FOLIOMORT, see FILEMOT.
FOLIOSE, [fō'-li-ōs], *adj.* covered with leaves, leafy. [L *foliosus*].
FOLIOT†, [fo'-li-ot], *n.* a sort of goblin. [Uncert.].
FOLIOUS, [fō'-li-us], *adj.* leafy, abounding in, or resembling, leaves.
FOLK, [fōk], *n.* people in general; a nation, a race; a particular class or division of people; (*pl.*) relatives, relations. [OE. *folc*].
FOLK-ETYMOLOGY, [fōk'-et'-im-ol'-o-ji], *n.* the popular but usually inaccurate derivation of a word.
FOLKLAND, [fōk'-land], *n.* (*hist.*) public land held by customary right. [OE. *folcland*].
FOLK-LORE, [fōk'-law(r)'], *n.* legendary traditions, popular beliefs, sayings, and customs prevailing among a people; the study of these.
FOLKMOTE, FOLKMOOT, [fōk'-mōt'], *n.* (*hist.*) general assembly of all classes of freemen of a town or district. [OE. *folc-gemot*].
FOLKRIGHT†, [fōk'-rīt], *n.* (*hist.*) the common law of England. [OE *folc-riht*].
FOLKSONG, [fōk'-song'], *n.* a popular traditional song and air.
FOLKSPEECH, [fōk'-spēch'], *n.* the traditional dialect of the common people.
FOLKTALE, [fōk'-tāl'], *n.* a popular traditional tale usually containing legendary or mythical features.
FOLLIA, [fol'-i-a], *n.* (*mus.*) a kind of composition which consists of variations on a given air. [Span. *follia*].
FOLLICLE, [fol'-ikl], *n.* (*bot.*) a pod opening on the ventral side; a vessel distended with air; a little bag or secreting recess in animal bodies, serving as a gland; (*entom.*) cocoon. [L. *folliculus* little bag].
FOLLICULAR, [fol-ik'-yōō-ler], *adj.* in the form of a follicle, pertaining to a follicle, consisting of, or containing, follicles.
FOLLICULATE, [fol-ik'-yōō-lat], *adj.* (*bot.*) folliculated.
FOLLICULATED, [fol-ik'-yōō-lā'-tid], *adj.* (*bot.*) having a follicle; (*entom.*) contained in a cocoon.
FOLLICULOUS, [fol-ik'-yōō-lus], *adj.* containing, or consisting of, follicles; resembling a follicle.
FOLLOW (1), [fol'-ō], *n.* the act of following; (*coll.*) a small second helping of food; **f. on,** (*cricket*) a second innings taken immediately after the first by a side which has failed to score the requisite number of runs in the first innings; **f. through,** (*billiards*) a stroke in which the ball continues in approximately the same straight line after striking a ball as before; (*sport*) the continuation and completion of the swing of a stroke after impact.
FOLLOW (2), [fol'-ō], *v.t.* to go or come after; to accompany; to pursue; to occur after; to succeed; to be next in order; to be engaged or employed in (a particular profession or career); to pursue with the eye, to watch; to imitate, to be a disciple or adherent of; (*fig.*) to obey, to endeavour to carry out; to keep in touch with, to make a study of, to devote part of one's leisure to; to understand clearly, to pay close attention to, to grasp the stages of (an argument, exposition, etc.); *v.i.* to come after; to happen later; to result, to happen as a natural sequence or course; **to f. suit,** (*cards*) to play a card of the same suit as the one led; (*fig.*) to do likewise; **to f. on,** (*coll.*) to come at some later time; (*cricket*) to take the second innings immediately after the first in consequence of not having scored a sufficient number of runs in the first innings (of a side which does not bat first); **to f. through,** (*billiards*) to play a stroke so that the cue-ball continues in approximately the same straight line after striking another ball; (*sport*) to continue and complete the swing or motion of a stroke after the ball has been hit; **to f. up,** to pursue steadily and persistently; to carry out to a conclusion, to investigate thoroughly, to emphasize by repetition of an action; (*football*) to keep near the player with the ball so as to render help or continue a movement. [OE. *folgian*].
FOLLOWER, [fol'-ō-er], *n.* one who follows, a disciple; a retainer, an attendant, a subordinate; a supporter; (*coll.*) a courter, a lover; (*machinery*) a plate or block applying pressure in a press; a sheet of parchment added to the first or indenture sheet.
FOLLOWING (1), [fol'-ō-ing], *n.* the act of one who follows; body of followers, a crowd of supporters.
FOLLOWING (2), [fol'-ō-ing], *adj.* that follows, next after, succeeding; (of wind) moving in the same direction as the course of a ship, a runner in a race, etc.; mentioned next.
FOLLY, (*pl.* **follies**), [fol'-i], *n.* a foolish act, utterance, or piece of behaviour; want of sense, stupidity, foolishness or weakness of mind; a costly, impractical, unsuccessful structure. [OFr. *folie*].
FOMENT, [fō-ment'], *v.t.* to apply warm lotions or poultices, to bathe in warm liquid; (*fig.*) to excite, to stir up, to cherish, to encourage. [LL. *fomentare*].
FOMENTATION, [fō'-men-tā'-shun], *n.* the act of fomenting; the lotion, poultice, etc., applied; (*fig.*) incitement, stirring up. [L. *fomentatio*].
FOMENTER, [fō-men'-ter], *n.* one who foments.
FOMES, (*pl.* **fomites**), [fō'-mēz], *n.* a porous substance that absorbs contagious matter. [L. *fomes* touchwood].
FOND, [fond], *adj.* vain, credulous, misguided; foolishly tender and doting; loving, affectionate; (*archaic*) foolish, silly; **to be f. of,** to relish highly, to like, to derive pleasure from; to regard with great affection. [ME. *fonned* infatuated, *p.pt.* of *fonnen* to dote].
FONDANT, [fon'-dant], *n.* a kind of sweetmeat made of moulded sugar. [Fr. *fondant*].
FONDLE, [fondl], *v.t. and i.* to caress, to stroke or play with lovingly or tenderly, to cuddle. [*Prec.*].
FONDLER, [fondl'-er], *n.* one who fondles
FONDLING, [fondl'-ing], *n.* a person or thing fondled, a pet, a darling.
FONDLY, [fond'-li], *adv.* in a fond manner, foolishly, misguidedly; lovingly.

FONDNESS, [fond'-nes], *n.* the condition of being fond. [ME. *fonnednesse*].

FONDU, [fon'-dew'], *n.* a mode of printing calico, paper-hangings, etc., in which the colours are in bands which blend imperceptibly one with the other. [Fr. *fondu*, *p.pt.* of *fondre* to melt].

FONT (1), [font], *n.* a receptacle for containing the holy water used in baptism; the reservoir or container of an oil-lamp; (*poet.*) fountain, spring. [OE. *font* from L. *fons*].

FONT

FONT (2), see FOUNT (2).

FONTAL, [fon'-tal], *adj.* relating to a fount or source, baptismal.

FONTANEL, FONTANELLE, [fon'-tan-el'], *n.* (*anat.*) a space covered with membrane between, and at an angle to, the parietal bones in the skull of an infant. [Fr. *fontanelle*].

FONTANGE, [fon-tahnzh'], *n.* a tall head-dress fashionable in France in the seventeenth and eighteenth centuries. [Mme *Fontanges*, a mistress of Louis XIV].

FOOD, [fōōd], *n.* that which can be eaten or absorbed by an animal or plant as nutriment; solid edible matter; a particular kind of nourishment; (*fig.*) that which provides intellectual nourishment, or stimulates and develops the mind and soul, matter to be reflected upon, discussed, or assimilated mentally. [OE. *foda*].

FOOD-CONTROLLER, [fōōd'-kon-trōl'-er], *n.* a person appointed to organize the rationing and distribution of supplies of food in time of emergency.

FOODFUL, [fōōd'-fŏŏl], *adj.* supplying food; full of food, nourishing, nutritious.

FOODLESS, [fōōd'-les], *adj.* lacking food or provisions.

FOODSTUFF, [fōōd'-stuf], *n.* an article commonly regarded as food.

FOOL (1), [fōōl], *n.* a madman, an imbecile, idiot; a stupid, silly person, of no wisdom or intelligence; a dupe, a butt; a clown, jester or buffoon, often half-witted or pretending to be mad, formerly kept in a noble household to make jokes, and provide the household with amusement; (*coll.*) a light-hearted, mischievous, irresponsible person who makes people laugh by his antics and remarks; **fool's paradise**, (*fig.*) a state of happiness founded on illusion and vain, imaginary hopes; **All Fools' day**, April 1; **April f.**, a person hoaxed on this day. [OFr. *fol* from L. *follis* bellows filled with air].

FOOL (2), [fōōl], *n.* a dish consisting of fruit stewed, pounded to a juicy pulp and mixed with cream, milk, custard, etc. [Uncert.].

FOOL (3), [fōōl], *v.t. and i.* to hoax, dupe, make a fool of, to deceive; to act like a fool.

FOOL-BORN, [fōōl'-bawn'], *adj.* foolish from birth.

FOOLEN, [fōōl'-en], *n.* the space between the high-water mark and the foot of the wall built on the bank to guard against the river's occasional overflow. [Unkn.].

FOOLERY, [fōōl'-er-i], *n.* foolish behaviour, habitual folly; an act of folly, a foolish thing, idea, etc.

FOOL-HAPPY, [fōōl'-hap'-i], *adj.* lucky by nature.

FOOLHARDILY, [fōōl'-hahd'-i-li], *adv.* in a foolhardy way.

FOOLHARDINESS, [fōōl'-hahd'-i-nes], *n.* courage without sense or judgment; rashness.

FOOLHARDY, [fōōl'-hahd'-i], *adj.* taking or involving unnecessary, foolish risks. [OFr. *fol hardi*].

FOOLISH, [fōōl'-ish], *adj.* mentally deranged, weak in intellect; silly, stupid; exhibiting little or no intelligence, forethought, or judgment, rash, indiscreet, ill-advised; (*Bible*) sinful, impious.

FOOLISHLY, [fōōl'-ish-li], *adv.* in a foolish fashion.

FOOLISHNESS, [fōōl'-ish-nes], *n.* folly.

FOOL-PROOF, [fōōl'-prōōf'], *adj.* (*coll.*) (*esp.* of machinery) so made that even the most stupid or inexperienced person can work it safely.

FOOLSCAP, [fōōlz'-kap], *n.* close-fitting cap, resembling a cock's comb in shape, furnished with bells, and formerly worn by a jester or professional fool; a dunce's cap; a size of paper, about 17 inches by 14, originally water-marked with a fool's cap.

FOOL'S-PARSLEY, [fōōlz'-pahs'-li], *n.* (*bot.*) an umbelliferous plant, *Æthusa Cynapium*, resembling parsley, and commonly thought to be poisonous.

FOOL-STONES, [fōōl'-stōnz], *n.* (*bot.*) a kind of orchid.

FOOL-TRAP, [fōōl'-trap], *n.* a trap for catching fools.

FOOT (1), (*pl.* **feet**), [fŏŏt], *n.* that end of the leg on which an animal stands and walks; anything like this in shape or function; the part of a stocking or boot which receives this; the lower part, the base; the lower edge of a sail; footing; step; infantry soldiers; a lineal measure of 12 inches, approximating to the length of a man's foot; the shortest unit of the metre of a verse; pace; **cubic f.**, a cube with a side of 1 square foot, containing 1,728 cubic inches; **square f.**, a square whose side is 1 foot, containing 144 square inches; **at one's feet**, captive or captivated; **to fall on one's feet**, to have good luck; **to find one's feet**, to gain experience; **to set on f.**, to originate; **to put one's f. down**, to demur, act with decision; **to put one's f. in it**, to act tactlessly; **to put one's best f. foremost**, (*coll.*) to do one's utmost. [OE. *fot*].

FOOT (2), [fŏŏt], *v.t.* to walk; to supply a new foot to (stockings); **to f. the bill**, to pay; **to f. a measure**, to dance.

FOOTBALL, [fŏŏt'-bawl], *n.* an inflated, round, or egg-shaped ball of thin rubber, cased in leather, and kicked by the feet; the team games played with it.

FOOT-BATH, [fŏŏt'-bahth'], *n.* a small bath in which to wash the feet.

FOOTBOARD, [fŏŏt'-bawd'], *n.* a board which acts as a support for the feet; the step running alongside a railway-coach; the sloping board on which a coachman or motorist supports his feet when driving; the board at the foot of a bed.

FOOTBOY, [fŏŏt'-boi], *n.* a male attendant or messenger.

FOOT-BRAKE, [fŏŏt'-brāk], *n.* a brake, *esp.* on a motor-car, that is operated by the foot.

FOOT-BREADTH, [fŏŏt'-bredth'], *n.* the width of the foot.

FOOT-BRIDGE, [fŏŏt'-brij'], *n.* a bridge for foot-passengers.

FOOT-CLOTH, [fŏŏt'-kloth], *n.* the covering of a horse, which reaches down to his heels.

FOOTED, [fŏŏt'-id], *adj.* having feet or a foot.

FOOTER, [fŏŏt'-er], *n.* (*slang*) football.

FOOTFALL, [fŏŏt'-fawl], *n.* the sound of a footstep.

FOOT-FAULT (1), [fŏŏt'-fawlt], *n.* (*tennis*) an illegal service, on account of the position of the server's feet when striking the ball.

FOOT-FAULT (2), [fŏŏt'-fawlt], *v.t.* to penalize for committing a foot-fault; *v.i.* to commit a foot-fault.

FOOT-GUARDS, [fŏŏt'-gahdz'], *n.(pl.)* (*milit.*) the five infantry regiments which form part of the household troops.

FOOT-HALT, [fŏŏt'-hawlt], *n.* a disease of sheep.

FOOTHOLD, [fŏŏt'-hōld], *n.* that which offers a secure position for the feet; (*fig.*) a support, a stable position.

FOOTHOT†, [fŏŏt'-hot'], *adv.* (*hunting*) in hot haste, closely.

FOOTING, [fŏŏt'-ing], *n.* the act of setting down the feet; foothold; firm foundation; basis, status or condition; tread, step; **to pay one's f.**, to discharge a fee or obligation on gaining admission to a club, society, trade, etc.

FOOT-IRON, [fŏŏt'-īern'], *n.* a fetter for the ankle; a spiked iron fixed to the foot for climbing poles, etc.; a carriage step.

FOOTLE (1), [fōōtl], *n.* (*coll.*) nonsense, twaddle. [Unkn.].

FOOTLE (2), [fōōtl], *v.i.* to talk or act foolishly.

FOOTLESS, [fŏŏt'-les], *adj.* without feet; (*fig.*) uninhabited.

FOOTLICKER, [fŏŏt'-lik'-er], *n.* a flatterer, one who panders ignobly to another.

FOOTLIGHTS, [fŏŏt'-līts], *n.(pl.)* the row of lights along the front of a stage, level with the actors' feet; (*fig.*) the actor's profession.

FOOTLING, [fōōtl'-ing], *adv.* trifling, foolish.

FOOTMAN, [fŏŏt'-man], *n.* a foot-soldier; a liveried attendant.

FOOT-MANTLE, [fŏŏt'-mantl'], *n.* a garment for keeping the gown clean when riding.

FOOTMARK, [fŏŏt'-mahk], *n.* a footprint; (*fig.*) a trace.

FOOTMUFF, [fŏŏt'-muf'], *n.* a bag lined with fur, for keeping the feet warm in winter.

FOOTNOTE, [fŏŏt′-nōt], *n.* a note or comment at the foot of a page.

FOOTPACE, [fŏŏt′-pās], *n.* walking pace; a raised portion of a floor; a dais; the first wide step in the sanctuary of a church.

FOOTPAD, [fŏŏt′-pad′], *n.* a highway robber who goes on foot.

FOOT-PASSENGER, [fŏŏt′-pas′-in-jer], *n.* one who journeys on foot, a pedestrian.

FOOTPATH, [fŏŏt′-pahth], *n.* a path for pedestrians only.

FOOTPLATE, [fŏŏt′-plāt], *n.* a carriage step; the platform on a locomotive on which the driver and fireman stand.

FOOTPLOUGH, [fŏŏt′-plow], *n.* a swing plough.

FOOT-POST, [fŏŏt′-pōst′], *n.* a postman or messenger who travels on foot.

FOOT-POUND, [fŏŏt′-pownd], *n.* the unit of work, the work required to raise 1 lb. through 1 foot.

FOOTPRINT, [fŏŏt′-print], *n.* the print or mark of a foot.

FOOT-RACE, [fŏŏt′-rās], *n.* a race on foot.

FOOT-ROPE, [fŏŏt′-rōp], *n.* (*naut.*) the rope along a yard on which men stand when reefing; that part of the bolt-rope to which the foot of the sail is attached.

FOOT-ROT, [fŏŏt′-rot], *n.* a disease of the feet of sheep and cattle.

FOOTRULE, [fŏŏt′-rōōl′], *n.* a ruler 12 inches long.

FOOTS, [fŏŏts], *n.(pl.)* the waste or sediment, dregs.

FOOTSCRAPER, [fŏŏt′-skrāp′-er], *n.* an iron scraper at an outside door, for removing dirt and mud from the feet.

FOOT-SHACKLES, [fŏŏt′-shaklz′], *n.(pl.)* fetters for the feet.

FOOTSCALD, [fŏŏt′-skawld′], *n.* inflammation of the underside of a horse's foot.

FOOT-SOLDIER, [fŏŏt′-sōl′-jer], *n.* a soldier who fights on foot; an infantryman.

FOOTSORE, [fŏŏt′-saw(r)], *adj.* having sore feet, tired with walking.

FOOTSTALK, [fŏŏt′-stawk], *n.* (*bot.*) a petiole, a stem supporting the leaf; anything similar to this.

FOOTSTALL, [fŏŏt′-stawl], *n.* the pedestal of a figure; a woman's stirrup.

FOOTSTEP, [fŏŏt′-step], *n.* a step of the foot; a footfall; a footmark; the sound made by a person walking; the area covered by the foot; (*fig.*) a mark, indication; **to follow in a person's footsteps,** to follow an example or precedent.

FOOTSTICK, [fŏŏt′-stik], *n.* (*print.*) a bevelled piece of wood or iron fixed at the foot of the page to lock up the type.

FOOTSTOOL, [fŏŏt′-stōōl], *n.* a stool on which to rest the feet when sitting; (*fig.*) a person who is used ignominiously by another.

FOOTSURE, [fŏŏt′-shōōer], *adj.* sure of foot.

FOOT-VALVE, [fŏŏt′-valv], *n.* (*eng.*) a valve placed between the condenser and air-pump in a steam-engine.

FOOT-WALING, [fŏŏt′-wāl′-ing], *n.* the inside planks or wood lining of a vessel, covering the floor-timbers.

FOOTWARMER, [fŏŏt′-wahm′-er], *n.* any appliance for warming the feet.

FOOTWAY, [fŏŏt′-wā], *n.* a footpath.

FOOTWEAR, [fŏŏt′-wāer], *n.* boots, shoes, sandals, etc.

FOOTWORN, [fŏŏt′-wawn], *adj.* worn by the feet; footsore.

FOOZLE (1), [fōōzl], *n.* a failure, a bungle.

FOOZLE (2), [fōōzl], *v.t.* to bungle, act clumsily; (*golf*) to spoil a stroke, fluff. [Unkn.].

FOP, [fop], *n.* a dandy, coxcomb. [ME. *foppe*].

FOPDOODLE†, [fop′-dōōdl′], *n.* a fop; (*coll.*) nonsense.

FOPLING, [fop′-ling], *n.* a young fop, a petty affected fellow.

FOPPERY, [fop′-er-i], *n.* affectation.

FOPPISH, [fop′-ish], *adj.* affected, like a fop.

FOPPISHLY, [fop′-ish-li], *adv.* in foppish fashion.

FOPPISHNESS, [fop′-ish-nes], *n.* the quality of being foppish, affectation.

FOR (1), [faw(r)], *prep.* in the place of, instead of; as being; towards; for the sake of; on account of; in favour of; towards the obtaining of; by reason of; through a certain space; through a certain time; in quest of; in order to obtain; in spite of, notwithstanding. [OE. *for*].

FOR (2), [faw(r)], *conj.* because, seeing that, since; on this account that.

FOR- (3), [faw(r)], *pref.* forward, through; out beyond; thoroughly, to excess; to a wrong end. [OE. *fer for*.

FORAGE (1), [fo′-rij], *n.* food for horses and cattle; search by soldiers for provisions, plundering. [OFr. *fourage*].

FORAGE (2), [fo′-rij], *v.t.* to provide forage for; to plunder for forage; *v.i.* to search for forage; (*fig.*) to rummage.

FORAGE-CAP, [fo′-rij-kap′], *n.* (*milit.*) a peaked, coloured undress infantry cap.

FORAGER, [fo′-rij-er], *n.* one who forages.

FORAGING, [fo′-rij-ing], *n.* the act of searching for forage.

FORAMEN, (*pl.* **foramina**), [fo-rā′-men], *n.* (*anat.*) a hole, an opening in a bone for a vessel to pass through; (*bot.*) the orifice of an ovule. [L. *foramen*].

FORAMINATED, [fo-ram′-in-ā′-tid], *adj.* having a foramen; perforated.

FORAGE-CAP

FORAMINIFERA, [fo′-ram-in-if′-er-a], *n.(pl.)* (*zool.*) a group of protozoa enclosed in fragile calcareous shells with small perforations. [FORAMEN and L. *ferre* to bear].

FORAMINIFEROUS, [fo′-ram-in-if′-er-us], *adj.* of or pertaining to the foraminifera.

FORAMINOUS, [fo-ram′-in-us], *adj.* perforated, with foramina. [L. *foraminosus*].

FORAMINULE, [fo-ram′-in-ewl], *n.* a type of small foramen.

FORASMUCH, [for-az-much′], *conj.* seeing that, considering that.

FORAY (1), [fo′-rā], *n.* a raid, a plundering expedition.

FORAY (2), [fo′-rā], *v.t. and i.* to make a foray upon. [ME. *forraien*].

FORBEAR (1), see FOREBEAR.

FORBEAR (2), [for-bāer′], *v.t.* to abstain from; to treat indulgently and leniently; *v.i.* to hold one's self in check; to refrain; to hold back; to be patient. [OE. *forberan*].

FORBEARANCE, [for-bāer′-ants], *n.* the act of forbearing; abstinence, patience and understanding, leniency, self-control.

FORBEARINGLY, [for-bāer′-ing-li], *adv.* in a forbearing fashion.

FORBID, (**forbidding, forbade, forbidden**), [for-bid′], *v.t.* to order not to do; to refuse entry; to prevent; to prohibit; *v.i.* to utter a prohibition. [OE. *forbeodan*].

FORBIDDANCE†, [for-bid′-ants], *n.* prohibition.

FORBIDDEN, [for-bid′-en], *adj.* not allowed, prohibited.

FORBIDDENLY, [for-bid′-en-li], *adv.* in an unlawful way.

FORBIDDER, [for-bid′-er], *n.* one who forbids.

FORBIDDING, [for-bid′-ing], *adj.* awesome; repulsive.

FORBIDDINGLY, [for-bid′-ing-li], *adv.* in forbidding fashion.

FORBIDDINGNESS, [for-bid′-ing-nes], *n.* the quality of being forbidding.

FOR-BY, [faw-bi′], *prep.* (*Scots*) near to, adjacent. [ME. *forbi*].

FORCE (1), [faws], *n.* power or energy exerted so as to issue in change or movement; physical or moral pressure or constraint; compulsory power; moral power to convince the mind; validity, legality; a body of troops; one of the fighting services; a body organized for action; necessity; (*leg.*) any unlawful violence to person or property; **mechanical force,** any cause which tends to alter a body's state of rest or of uniform motion in a straight line; **brute f.,** sheer physical violence; **the F.,** the police force. [Fr. *force* from L. *fortis*].

FORCE (2), [faws], *n.* a waterfall. [OIcel. *fors*]

FORCE (3), [faws], *v.t.* to constrain by the exertion of force; to overpower by strength; to draw or push by force; to compel; to take by force; to violate; to overstrain; to distort; to cause to ripen prematurely; *v.i.* to use violence; to lay stress on; to strive; **to f. from,** to wrest from; **to f. a smile,** to compel the features to assume a smile unwillingly. [ME *forcen* from L. *fortiare*].

FORCE (4), [faws], *v.t.* to stuff, to season meat; to farce. [Fr. *farcir*].

FORCEABLE, [faws′-abl], *adj.* that may be forced.

FORCED, [fawst], *adj.* performed by means of external force; not spontaneous, unnatural, overstrained, compulsory.

FORCEDLY, [faws'-id-li], *adv.* in a forced fashion.
FORCEDNESS, [faws'-id-nes], *n.* the condition of being forced.
FORCEFUL, [faws'-fo͝ol], *adj.* full of force; forcible; effective; of a strong or overbearing personality.
FORCEFULLY, [faws'-fo͝ol-i], *adv.* in a forceful manner.
FORCEFULNESS, [faws'-fo͝ol-nes], *n.* the state or quality of being forceful.
FORCELESS, [faws'-les], *adj.* devoid of force.
FORCE MAJEURE, [faws'-mah-zhur'], *n.* power exerted by a strong state over a weaker one; coercion. [Fr. *force majeure* superior strength].
FORCEMEAT, [faws'-mēt], *n.* meat chopped finely and highly seasoned, as a stuffing.
FORCEPS, [faw'-seps], *n.* a pair of pincers or small tongs, *esp.* as used in surgery, dentistry, etc.; (*zool.*) an organ resembling these in shape or function. [L. *forceps* pincers].
FORCE-PUMP, [faws'-pump], *n.* a pump from which water is forced out under pressure of a plunger.
FORCER, [faws'-er], *n.* a person or thing that forces.
FORCIBLE, [faws'-ibl], *adj.* effected by force or compulsion; powerful; convincing.
FORCIBLENESS, [faws'-ibl-nes], *n.* the quality of being forcible.
FORCIBLY, [faws'-ib-li], *adv.* in a forcible fashion.
FORCING, [faws'-ing], *n.* the action of a person or thing that forces; (*hort.*) the art of raising plants, etc., by the use of artificial heat; the fining of wines by a speedy process; (*fig.*) any hastening of development, *esp.* of a child's mind.
FORCING-HOUSE, [faws'-ing-hows'], *n.* (*hort.*) a hot-house.
FORCING-PIT, [faws'-ing-pit'], *n.* (*hort.*) a sunken pit for holding the fermenting materials used to produce bottom heat for forcing plants.
FORCIPATED, [faw'-si-pā'-tid], *adj.* constructed and working like a pair of pincers.
FORCIPATION, [faw'-si-pā'-shun], *n.* a method of punishment by pinching with forceps.
FORD (1), [fawd], *n.* a shallow place where a river or other mass of water may be crossed by wading. [OE. *ford*].
FORD (2), [fawd], *v.t.* to cross by a ford.
FORDABLE, [fawd'-abl], *adj.* that can be forded.
FORDO, (**fordid, fordone**), [faw-do͞o'], *v.t.* to destroy, ruin, undo. [FOR (3) and DO].
FORDONE, [faw-dun'], *adj.* wearied, exhausted.
FORE (1), [faw(r)], *n.* the front; **to the f.**, into prominence, prominent.
FORE (2), [faw(r)], *adj.* situated in front of.
FORE (3), [faw(r)], *adv.* before, in front; **f. and aft**, (*naut.*) from one end to the other of a ship. [OE. *fore*].
FORE- (4), *pref.* before, in front of; at the front part of; before in time, antedating; prior.
FORE (5), [faw(r)], *int.* a warning cry to move out of the way, at golf.
FOREARM (1), [fawr'-ahm], *n.* (*anat.*) the arm between elbow and wrist.
FOREARM (2), [fawr-ahm'], *v.t.* to arm beforehand; to prepare in advance for.
FOREBEAR, FORBEAR, [faw'-bāer], *n.* an ancestor, forefather.
FOREBODE, [faw-bōd'], *v.t.* to foretell or prognosticate; to feel a strong inward sense of something future. [OE. *forebodian*].
FOREBODEMENT, [faw-bōd'-ment], *n.* the act of foreboding; a foreboding.
FOREBODER, [faw-bōd'-er], *n.* a person who forebodes.
FOREBODING, [faw-bōd'-ing], *n.* a prediction, presage; a presentiment, *esp.* of ill; dread.
FOREBODINGLY, [faw-bōd'-ing-li], *adv.* in a foreboding manner.
FORE-BOW, [faw(r)'-bō'], *n.* the front part of a saddle.
FORE-BRACE, [faw(r)'-brās'], *n.* (*naut.*) a rope working from the fore yard-arm to alter the foresail.
FORE-CABIN, [faw(r)'-kab'-in], *n.* a cabin situated in the fore part of the ship.

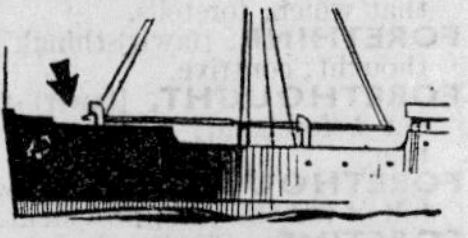
FORECASTLE

FORECAST (1), [faw(r)'-kahst], *n.* a prediction of future events; a weather prediction; an estimate.
FORECAST (2), [faw-kahst'], *v.t.* to estimate beforehand; to foresee; to predict, foretell; to estimate.
FORECASTLE, [fōksl], *n.* (*naut.*) that part of the upper deck of a ship forward of the foremast; the forward part of a merchant vessel under the deck, where the seamen eat and sleep.
FORECLOSE, [faw(r)-klōz'], *v.t.* (*leg.*) to preclude; to cut off a mortgager from the power of redeeming mortgaged goods; to close prematurely. [ME. *forclosen* from OFr. *forclos*].
FORECLOSURE, [faw(r)-klō'-zher], *n.* the action of foreclosing.
FORECOURSE, [faw(r)'-kaws], *n.* (*naut.*) the foresail on a full-rigged ship.
FORECOURT, [faw(r)'-kawt], *n.* a court in front of, or near, the entrance to a building.
FOREDATE, [faw(r)-dāt'], *v.t.* to antedate.
FOREDECK, [faw(r)'-dek], *n.* (*naut.*) the fore part of a ship's deck.
FOREDOOM, [faw(r)-do͞om'], *v.t.* to condemn in advance.
FOREDOOR, [faw(r)'-daw'-er], *n.* a door in the front of a building.
FORE-EDGE, [faw(r)'-ej], *n.* the front or outer edge of a book; **f.-painting**, decoration of the front and top edges of a book with colour.
FORE-END, [faw(r)'-end], *n.* the front.
FOREFATHER, [faw(r)'-fah'-THer], *n.* an ancestor, progenitor.
FOREFEELING, [faw(r)'-fēl'-ing], *n.* a presentiment.
FOREFINGER, [faw(r)'-fing-ger], *n.* that finger next the thumb.
FOREFOOT, [faw(r)'-fo͝ot], *n.* one of the front feet of a quadruped; (*naut.*) a piece of timber which terminates the keel at the fore-end.
FOREFRONT, [faw(r)'-frunt], *n.* the principal or foremost part of anything, prominence.
FOREGO, (**foregoing, foregone, forewent**), [faw(r)-gō'], *v.t.* to go before; to precede. [OE. *foregan*].
FOREGOER, [faw(r)'-gō-er], *n.* a person who goes before another.
FOREGONE, [faw(r)'-gon], *adj.* past; determined beforehand; certain, settled.
FOREGROUND, [faw(r)'-grownd], *n.* that part of anything nearest the spectator; the part of a picture representing this; (*fig.*) a conspicuous position.
FORE-HAMMER, [faw(r)'-ham'-er], *n.* a sledge-hammer.
FOREHAND (1), [faw(r)'-hand], *n.* the part of a horse in front of the rider; the chief part; (*tennis*) a forehand stroke or shot.
FOREHAND (2), [faw(r)'-hand], *adj.* done sooner than is customary; done beforehand, forward; (*tennis*) executed with the palm of the hand facing the front, the ball being taken on the right-hand side of a right-handed player.
FOREHANDED, [faw(r)'-hand'-id], *adj.* seasonable; well off.
FOREHEAD, [fo'-red, faw(r)'-hed], *n.* the front part of the face above the eyes; (*fig.*) impudence; confidence. [OE. *forheafod*].
FOREHOODS, [faw(r)'-ho͝odz], *n.* (*pl.*) (*naut.*) those planks placed most forward in shipbuilding.
FORE-HOOK, [faw(r)'-ho͝ok], *n.* (*naut.*) a piece of timber laid across the stem to strengthen the fore part.
FOREIGN, [fo'-rin], *adj.* not belonging to; of another nation; alien; not to the purpose; strange. [OFr. *forain*].
FOREIGNER, [fo'-rin-er], *n.* a person belonging to a foreign country; an alien; a stranger.
FOREIGNNESS, [fo'-rin-nes], *n.* the state of being foreign.
FOREJUDGE, [faw(r)'-juj'], *v.t.* to prejudge, to give judgment before hearing the facts and proof; (*leg.*) to expel from a court for malpractice, etc.
FOREJUDGMENT, [faw(r)-juj'-ment], *n.* judgment determined beforehand.
FOREKNOW, (**foreknew**), [faw(r)-nō'], *v.t.* to know beforehand.
FOREKNOWABLE, [faw(r)-nō'-abl], *adj.* capable of being known beforehand.
FOREKNOWINGLY, [faw(r)-nō'-ing-li], *adv.* in a foreknowing manner.
FOREKNOWLEDGE, [faw(r)'-nol'-ej], *n.* knowledge of an event before it happens; prescience.
FOREL, FORREL, [fo'-ril], *n.* a case or covering in which a book is kept; a thin kind of parchment. [OFr. *forrel*].
FORELAND, [faw(r)'-land], *n.* a cape, headland promontory.

FORELAY, [faw(r)-lā'], *v.t.* to contrive before the event; to lie in wait for.
FORELEADER, [faw(r)'-lēd'-er], *n.* one who leads the advance; a chief captain.
FORELEG, [faw(r)'-leg], *n.* one of the front legs of a quadruped.
FORELEND, [faw(r)-lend'], *v.t.* to give or lend before.
FORELOCK, [faw(r)'-lok], *n.* the lock of hair that grows from the fore part of the head; a flat piece of iron driven through the end of a bolt to keep it in position; **to take time by the f.**, to seize an opportunity.
FOREMAN, [faw(r)'-man], *n.* the chief man; the principal juror and spokesman of a jury; a supervisor, overseer.
FOREMAST, [faw(r)'-mahst], *n.* (*naut.*) the mast nearest the bow.
FOREMASTMAN, [faw(r)'-mahst'-man], *n.* (*naut.*) an able seaman, so called from being berthed before the mainmast.
FORE-MEANT, [faw(r)-ment'], *adj.* premeditated, deliberate.
FOREMENTIONED, [faw(r)'-men'-shund], *adj.* previously referred to.
FOREMOST, [faw(r)'-mōst], *adj.* first in place; first in dignity or importance; most prominent, chief. [OE. *formest*].
FOREMOTHER, [faw(r)'-muTH'-er], *n.* a female ancestor, a progenitrix.
FORENAME, [faw(r)'-nām], *n.* a Christian name preceding the surname.
FORENOON, [faw(r)'-nōōn], *n.* the earlier part of the day from sunrise to noon; the morning.
FORENSAL, [fo-ren'-sal], *adj.* forensic.
FORENSIC, [fo-ren'-sik], *adj.* of the law court; **f. medicine**, medical jurisprudence. [L. *forensis* relating to the forum].
FORE-ORDAIN, [faw(r)'-aw-dān'], *v.t.* to ordain beforehand; to predestinate.
FORE-ORDINATION, [faw(r)'-aw-di-nā'-shun], *n.* the act of fore-ordaining; the state of being fore-ordained.
FOREPEAK, [faw(r)'-pēk], *n.* (*naut.*) that part of a vessel in the angle of the bow.
FOREPLANE, [faw(r)'-plān], *n.* (*carp.*) the plane used immediately after the saw and axe.
FORE-POSSESSED, [faw(r)'-poz-est'], *adj.* holding formerly in possession.
FOREPROMISED, [faw(r)'-prom'-ist], *adj.* promised previously.
FORE-RANK, [faw(r)'-rank'], *n.* the front, foremost rank.
FOREREACH, [faw-rēch'], *v.t.* to gain upon; (*naut.*) to go ahead on a wind and move up to windward of.
FOREREADING, [faw(r)'-rēd'-ing], *n.* a previous reading.
FORERUN, (**forerunning, foreran**), [faw-run'], *v.t.* to precede, go before.
FORERUNNER, [faw(r)'-run-er], *n.* a messenger sent on ahead; a harbinger, a prognostic, predecessor; (*naut.*) the piece of rag that marks the end of the stray part of the log-line.
FORESAIL, [faw(r)'-sal], *n.* (*naut.*) in square-rigged vessels the forecourse; in fore-and-aft-rigged vessels the staysail; in schooners the gaff-sail on the foremast.
FORESAY, (**foresays, foresaid**), [faw(r)-sā'], *v.t.* to say beforehand, predict, presage.
FORESCENT, [faw(r)'-sent], *n.* anticipation.
FORE-SCUTTLE, [faw(r)'-skutl], *n.* (*naut.*) the hatch which leads to the forecastle.
FORESEE, (**foresaw, foreseen**), [faw(r)-sē'], *v.t. and i.* to see beforehand, to have foreknowledge of; to have foresight; to anticipate. [OE. *foreseon*].
FORESEER, [faw(r)-sēer'], *n.* a person who foresees.
FORESEIZE, [faw(r)-sēz'], *v.t.* to get beforehand.
FORESHADOW, [faw(r)-shad'-ō], *v.t.* to typify beforehand, prefigure; to give a previous account of.
FORESHEET, [faw(r)'-shēt], *n.* (*naut.*) the rope by which the foresail is worked; (*pl.*) the inner part of a boat's bow forward of the bow-oar's thwart.
FORESHIP, [faw(r)'-ship], *n.* the fore part of a ship. [OE. *forscip*].
FORESHORE, [faw(r)'-shaw(r)], *n.* the shelving part of the seashore, between the high and low water marks.
FORESHORTEN, [faw(r)-shaw'-ten], *v.t.* (*art*) to represent objects as they appear in perspective.
FORESHORTENING, [faw(r)-shawt'-ning], *n.* the effect of perspective upon lines or planes receding from the observer.
FORESHOW, (**foreshown**), [faw(r)-shō'], *v.t.* to show beforehand, to foreshadow. [OE. *foresceawian*].
FORESIDE, [faw(r)'-sīd], *n.* the front side.
FORESIGHT (**1**), [faw(r)'-sīt], *n.* the foremost of the two sites of a gun; the muzzle-sight.
FORESIGHT (**2**), [faw(r)'-sīt], *n.* the action of foreseeing what will happen; provident care, prudence, caution, intelligent anticipation.
FORESIGHTED, [faw(r)'-sīt'-id], *adj.* manifesting foresight.
FORESIGHTFUL, [faw(r)-sīt'-fōōl], *adj.* full of foresight.
FORESIGNIFY, [faw(r)-sig'-ni-fī], *v.t.* to signify beforehand.
FORESKIN, [faw(r)'-skin], *n.* (*anat.*) the skin covering the glans of the penis.
FORESKIRT, [faw(r)'-skurt], *n.* the loose and pendulous front part of a coat.
FORESLEEVE, [faw(r)'-slēv], *n.* that part of a sleeve from the wrist to the elbow.
FORESPEAK, [faw(r)-spēk'], *v.t.* to speak beforehand; to bespeak in advance.
FORESPEECH, [faw(r)'-spēch], *n.* a preface.
FORESPOKEN†, [faw-spōk'-en], *adj.* before mentioned.
FOREST (**1**), [fo'-rest], *n.* an extensive wood, a large stretch of land covered with trees; an uncultivated tract of woodland and heath; (*hist.*) an unenclosed royal hunting-ground; a large number of tree-like objects, closely clustered. [OFr. *forest*].
FOREST (**2**), [fo'-rest], *adj.* belonging to a forest; sylvan.
FOREST (**3**), [fo'-rest], *v.t.* to plant with trees.
FORESTAFF, [faw(r)'-staf], *n.* the cross-staff.
FORESTAGE, [fo'-rest-ij], *n.* an ancient service rendered by foresters to the king; the right of foresters to remove wood from the forest.
FORESTAL, [fo'-rest-al], *adj.* of or pertaining to a forest.
FORESTALL, [faw(r)-stawl'], *v.t.* to act before another and thus frustrate his intention; to anticipate. [ME. *forstallen* to buy up goods on their way to market].
FORESTALLER, [faw(r)-stawl'-er], *n.* a person who forestalls.
FORESTAY, [faw(r)'-stā], *n.* (*naut.*) a stout rope reaching from the foremast head of a ship towards the bow to support the mast.
FORESTAYSAIL, [faw(r)-stā'-sal], *n.* (*naut.*) a triangular sail which slides up and down the forestay.
FORESTER, [fo'-rest-er], *n.* an officer who is in charge of a forest; an inhabitant of a forest; one skilled in forestry; a member of the Ancient Order of Foresters; the zygænid moth, *Ino statices*. [OFr. *forestier*].
FOREST-FLY, [fo'-rest-flī'], *n.* a species of fly, *Hippobosca equina*, very troublesome to horses, and abounding in the New Forest.
FOREST-MARBLE, [fo'-rest-mahbl'], *n.* (*min.*) an oolitic limestone full of dark-coloured shells, and taking a fine polish. [Wychwood *Forest*, Oxfordshire, where it is found].
FOREST-OAK, [fo'-rest-ōk'], *n.* beef-wood, an Australian tree of the genus *Casuarina*.
FORESTRY, [fo'-rest-ri], *n.* the art of cultivating forests; forests collectively.
FORET, [fo'-rā], *n.* a drill for boring the touch-hole of a gun. [Fr. *foret*].
FORETACKLE, [faw(r)'-takl'], *n.* (*naut.*) the tackle on the foremast of any ship.
FORETASTE (**1**), [faw(r)'-tāst], *n.* a taste beforehand; anticipation; enjoyment in advance.
FORETASTE (**2**), [faw(r)-tāst'], *v.t.* to taste beforehand; to anticipate.
FORETEACH, [faw(r)-tēch'], *v.t.* to teach beforehand.
FORETELL, (**foretold**), [faw-tel'], *v.t.* to tell beforehand; predict, prophesy.
FORETELLER, [faw(r)-tel'-er], *n.* a person who, or that which, foretells.
FORETHINK, [faw(r)-thingk'], *v.t.* to anticipate in thought; contrive.
FORETHOUGHT, [faw(r)'-thawt], *n.* a thinking out beforehand; prudence, caution, wise anticipation.
FORETHOUGHTFUL, [faw(r)'-thawt'-fōōl], *adj.* full of forethought; provident.
FORETIME, [faw(r)'-tīm], *n.* the past; former times.
FORETOKEN, [faw(r)-tō'-ken], *n.* a warning token. [OE. *foretacn*].

FORE-TOOTH, [faw(r)'-tōōth], *n.* a front tooth.
FORETOP, [faw(r)'-top], *n.* the hair on the fore part of the head; that part of a head-dress that is towards the front; the top of a periwig; the platform at the head of the foremast.
FORETOPGALLANT, [faw(r)'-top-gal'-ant], *n.* (*naut.*) the mast above the fore-topmast.
FORETOPMAN, [faw(r)'-top'-man], *n.* (*naut.*) a sailor stationed in the foretop.
FORETOPMAST, [faw(r)'-top'-mahst], *n.* (*naut.*) the mast which rises from the head of the foremast, and is surmounted by the fore-topgallant mast.
FORETOPSAIL, [faw(r)'-top'-sal], *n.* the sail above the topsail.
FOREVER (1), [for-ev'-er], *n.* eternity.
FOREVER (2), [for-ev'-er], *adv.* for ever.
FOREVOUCHED, [faw(r)'-vowcht'], *adj.* vouched for before.
FOREWARD, [faw(r)'-wud], *n.* the first line of an army, the van.

FORETOPGALLANT

FOREWARN, [faw(r)-wawn'], *v.i.* to warn beforehand.
FOREWIND, [faw(r)'-wind], *n.* a favourable wind.
FOREWISH, [faw(r)-wish'], *v.t.* to wish in advance.
FOREWOMAN, [faw(r)'-wōōm'-an], *n.* a female supervisor or overseer.
FOREWORD, [faw(r)'-wurd'], *n.* a preface; a note or preface before the introduction.
FOREYARD, [faw(r)'-yahd], *n.* (*naut.*) the lowest yard on the foremast.
FORFEIT (1), [faw'-fit], *n.* something risked, and liable to be lost if one fails; anything so lost, a small penalty; (*pl.*) a parlour game, whose interest lies in the exaction of mock penalties. [OFr. *forfet*].
FORFEIT (2), [faw'-fit], *v.t.* to be deprived of through breach of conditions; to lose in consequence of any act; to surrender, often voluntarily. [ME. *forfeten*].
FORFEITABLE, [faw'-fit-abl], *adj.* subject to forfeiture.
FORFEITER, [faw'-fit-er], *n.* a person who forfeits.
FORFEITURE, [faw'-fich-er], *n.* the act of forfeiting; the thing which is forfeited. [OFr. *forfeture*].
FORFEND, [faw-fend'], *v.t.* to avert, keep off, prevent. [ME. *forfenden*].
FORFEX, [faw'-feks], *n.* pair of scissors; (*zool.*) a scissor-like appendage. [L. *forfex*].
FORFICATE, [faw'-fi-kāt], *adj.* (*zool.*) resembling a pair of scissors in shape. [L. *firfex forficis* scissors].
FORFICULA, [faw-fik'-yōō-la], *n.* (*entom.*) the genus of orthopterous insects among which are the earwigs. [L. *forficula* small scissors].
FORGATHER, [faw-gaTH'-er], *v.i.* to assemble; to meet and talk together.
FORGE (1), [fawj], *n.* a furnace or workshop in which iron or other metal is heated in order to be hammered into form; a smithy; a blacksmith's furnace; the manufacture of metals. [OFr. *forge*].
FORGE (2), [fawj], *v.t.* to soften and work metal; to produce by such a process; (*fig.*) to mould and form with effort and difficulty; to counterfeit, fabricate; **to f. ahead**, to move forward in spite of opposition; to make notable progress. [OFr. *forgier*].
FORGEMAN, [fawj'-man], *n.* a coachsmith in charge of the forge, and having a hammerman under him.
FORGER, [fawj'-er], *n.* a person who forges; one guilty of forging signatures, documents, paper money, etc.
FORGERY, [fawj'-er-i], *n.* the act of forging; that which is forged.
FORGET, (**forgetting, forgot**), [fer-get'], *v.t.* to lose the remembrance of something, to fail to recall to mind; to neglect, sometimes intentionally; to leave behind inadvertently; to leave unnoticed by accident; *v.i.* to fail to remember; **to f. oneself**, to omit to behave with due self-respect. [OE. *forgetan*].
FORGETFUL, [fer-get'-fōōl], *adj.* liable to forget, neglectful, inattentive.
FORGETFULLY, [fer-get'-fōōl-i], *adv.* in forgetful fashion.
FORGETFULNESS, [fer-get'-fōōl-nes], *n.* the quality of being forgetful; a failure of memory.
FORGETIVE, [fawj'-et-iv], *adj.* inventive, creative. [2 Henry IV, IV, iii, by W. Shakespeare].
FORGET-ME-NOT, [fer-get'-mi-not'], *n.* a small blue flower of the genus *Myosotis*. [Transl of OFr. *ne m'oubliez mye*].
FORGETTABLE, [fer-get'-abl], *adj.* that may be forgotten.
FORGETTER, [fer-get'-er], *n.* a person who forgets.
FORGETTINGLY, [fer-get'-ing-li], *adv.* in a forgetful manner.
FORGING, [fawj'-ing], *n.* the action of beating heated metal into shape; forged work; a counterfeiting.
FORGIVABLE, [fer-giv'-abl], *adj.* pardonable.
FORGIVE, [fer-giv'], *v.t.* to pardon; to remit, *esp.* of a debt, to overlook a fault; to treat someone as though he had not offended; *v.i.* habitually to disregard injuries, slights, etc. [OE. *forgifan*].

FORGET-ME-NOT

FORGIVENESS, [fer-giv'-nes], *n.* the action of forgiving; the character of being habitually forgiving; a token that one is forgiven.
FORGIVING, [fer-giv'-ing], *adj.* merciful, willing or always ready to forgive.
FORGIVINGNESS, [fer-giv'-ing-nes], *n.* the quality of being forgiving.
FORGO, (**forgone, forwent**), [faw'-gō'], *v.t.* to refrain from, go without; to abstain from something pleasurable or profitable. [OE. *forgan*].
FORINSECAL†, [fo-rin'-sik-al], *adj.* foreign, alien; from another land.
FORISFAMILIATE, [fo'-ris-fam-il'-i-āt], *v.i.* (*leg.*) to resign any further claim on the paternal estate; *v.t.* to separate from the family and further claim on the paternal estate. [MedL. *forisfamiliare*].
FORISFAMILIATION, [fo'-ris-fam-il'-i-ā'-shun], *n.* the action of forisfamiliating.
FORK (1), [fawk], *n.* an implement with a handle and two or more prongs, used for various purposes; a pronged utensil, implement, or instrument; the branch caused by the meeting of two roads or two rivers. [OE. *forca*].
FORK (2), [fawk], *v.t.* to use a fork for or upon; to make to bifurcate; to loosen with a fork; *v.i.* to divide into two branches; **to f. in**, to dig in; **to f. out**, (*slang*) to pay out money.
FORKBEARD, [fawk'-bēerd'], *n.* a fish of the cod family, *Phycis blennoides*; a species of rockling of the genus *Motella* or *Raniceps*.
FORK-CHUCK, [fawk'-chuk'], *n.* a fitting used on a turning-lathe.
FORKEDLY, [fawk'-id-li], *adv.* in a forked manner.
FORKEDNESS, [fawk'-id-nes], *n.* the condition of being forked.
FORKHEAD, [fawk'-hed'], *n.* the barbed head of an arrow; the double head of a knuckle-joint.
FORKINESS, [fawk'-i-nes], *n.* the quality of being forked.
FORKLESS, [fawk'-les], *adj.* without a fork.
FORK LUNCH, [fawk'-lunch'], *n.* a light lunch that requires no knife to cut it. [Transl. of Germ. *gabelfrühstück*].
FORKTAIL, [fawk'-tāl'], *n.* a salmon in the fourth year of its growth; the kite, a bird of the genus *Milvus*; a drongo or king-crow, a bird of the genus *Micrurus*.
FORKY, [fawk'-i], *adj.* shaped like a fork.
FORLORN, [for-lawn'], *adj.* forsaken, helpless, bereft, wretched; desolate, neglected; **a f. hope**, a very faint hope; (*milit.*) a detachment of men appointed to perform some task of great peril and uncertainty; any desperate enterprise undertaken as a last hope. [OE. *forloren*].
FORLORNLY, [faw-lawn'-li], *adv.* in a forlorn fashion.
FORLORNNESS, [faw-lawn'-nes], *n.* the condition of being forlorn.
FORM (1), [fawm], *n.* shape, external appearance; the human body; good health, good spirits; a state in which one displays one's abilities to the full; the essential structure or plan of anything; kind, type, in which anything is manifested; the grouping or arrangement of particular things in a pattern or to serve a purpose; mould; formula; artistic expression, shape, style; established conventional practice, etiquette; an official document prescribing the plan of an answer to a request for information; a long bench; a class in a school; the lair or sleeping-place of a hare; (*philos.*) the system of essential characteristics which dominates and shapes matter and development; (*philol.*) a particular representation or modifi-

cation of a word, base, etc.; (*racing, etc.*) an estimate of the potentialities of racehorses, sports-teams, etc., with a view to forecasting the results of some future contest. [L. *forma*].

FORM (2), [fawm], *v.t.* to make, to give shape to, to mould; to give direction to the character of, to educate; to plan, to arrange; to settle; to contrive; to make up; to frame; to combine; to establish; to compile; to constitute; (*gram.*) to create, build up; *v.i.* to take a form. [L. *formare*].

FORMAL, [faw'-mal], *adj.* in accordance with form or established mode; methodical; strictly ceremonious; done in due form; having the form without the substance; depending on customary forms; essential, proper; corresponding strictly to some set pattern. [L. *formalis*].

FORMALDEHYDE, [faw-mal'-di-hīd'], *n.* (*chem.*) methyl alcohol partially oxidized. [FORM(IC) and ALDEHYDE].

FORMALIN, [fawm'-a-lin], *n.* an aqueous solution of formaldehyde.

FORMALISM, [fawm'-al-izm], *n.* habitual observance of external forms to the neglect of spiritual realities.

FORMALIST, [fawm'-al-ist], *n.* a person who insists excessively on forms in art or religion; one who works to a formula.

FORMALITY, [fawm-al'-i-ti], *n.* the rigid observance of forms; precise conformity to customary modes; conventionality; an official regulation, or the compliance with it; a matter of form.

FORMALIZATION, [fawm'-al-iz-ā'-shun], *n.* the action of formalizing.

FORMALIZE, [fawm'-al-īz], *v.t.* to form, to make formal; *v.i.* to behave formally.

FORMALLY, [fawm'-al-i], *adv.* in a formal fashion, officially.

FORMAT, [fawm'-at], *n.* the form or style in which a book is produced. [Fr. *format*].

FORMATE, [fawm'-āt], *n.* a salt of formic acid.

FORMATION, [fawm-ā'-shun], *n.* the action of forming; the manner in which a thing is formed, arrangement; a group of aeroplanes flying in a fixed order; (*geol.*) a group of strata united by community of age, origin, or composition. [L. *formatio*].

FORMATIVE (1), [fawm'-at-iv], *n.* (*gram.*) an element helping to form a word.

FORMATIVE (2), [fawm'-at-iv], *adj.* having the power of forming and of regulating development; serving to form. [L. *formativus*].

FORME, [fawm], *n.* (*print.*) a collection of type set up, locked in a chase, and ready to be printed. [FORM (1)].

FORMED, [fawmd], *adj.* arranged; matured, perfected by training; definite, decided.

FORMER (1), [fawm'-er], *n.* the person who, or thing which, forms; anything which determines the shape of a product; a support on which electrical coils are wound.

FORMER (2), [fawm'-er], *adj.* preceding in time, earlier, nearer the beginning; the first mentioned; in days gone by, one-time. [ME. *formere*].

FORMERLY, [fawm'-er-li], *adv.* in times past, of old.

FORMIC, [fawm'-ik], *adj.* of, or pertaining to, ants; **f. acid**, a fatty acid obtained originally from red ants, but now artificially produced. [L. *formica* ant].

FORMICANT, [fawm'-ik-ant], *adj.* crawling like an ant; (*med.*) (of the pulse) very slow. [L. *formicans*].

FORMICARY, [fawm'-ik-er-i], *n.* an ant-hill. [LL. *formicarius*].

FORMICATE, [fawm'-ik-āt], *v.i.* to crawl like ants; to be covered with multitudinous creatures, to swarm with. [L. *formicare*].

FORMICATION, [fawm'-ik-ā'-shun], *n.* (*med.*) a sensation of ants creeping on the skin.

FORMIDABILITY, [fawm'-id-ab-il'-i-ti], *n.* the quality of being formidable.

FORMIDABLE, [fawm'-id-abl], *adj.* inspiring, or such as to inspire, fear; difficult; large and awe-inspiring. [L. *formidabilis*].

FORMIDABLENESS, [fawm'-id-abl-nes], *n.* the state of being formidable.

FORMIDABLY, [fawm'-id-ab-li], *adv.* in a formidable manner.

FORMLESS, [fawm'-les], *adj.* without determinate form; amorphous.

FORMLESSLY, [fawm'-les-li], *adv.* in formless fashion.

FORMLESSNESS, [fawm'-les-nes], *n.* the quality of being formless.

FORMULA, (*pl.* **formulae, formulas**), [fawm'-yōō-la], *n.* a precise form of words; a prescribed form; any rule of thumb, enabling one to act without reasoning; any oft-repeated phrase; (*eccles.*) a formal statement of accepted doctrine or belief; (*med.*) a prescription; (*math.*) a general expression for solving certain cases or problems; (*chem.*) a set of symbols representing the constituents of a compound body. [L. *formula*].

FORMULARIZATION, [fawm'-yōō-ler-iz-ā'-shun], *n.* the action of formularizing; a formularized expression.

FORMULARIZE, [fawm'-yōō-ler-īz], *v.t.* to generalize into a formula; to formulate.

FORMULARY (1), [fawm'-yōō-ler-i], *n.* a book made up of stated and prescribed forms, as of oaths, declarations, prayers, etc.; a prescribed form.

FORMULARY (2), [fawm'-yōō-ler-i], *adj.* prescribed. ritual, according to formula. [L. *formularius*].

FORMULATE, [fawm'-yōō-lāt], *v.t.* to express in a formula; to express in clear definite terms.

FORMULISM, [fawm'-yōō-lizm], *n.* the study of formulae; action governed purely by formulae.

FORMULIST, [fawm'-yōō-list], *n.* one who studies formulae; a believer in formulism.

FORMULIZATION, [fawm'-yōō-liz-ā'-shun], *n.* reduction to a precise, abstract formula or set of formulae.

FORMULIZE, [fawm'-yōō-līz], *v.t.* to formulate.

FORMULIZED, [fawm'-yōō-līzd], *adj.* reduced to a formula.

FORNICATE, [fawn'-ik-āt], *v.i.* to commit fornication. [EcclesL. *fornicari* to visit a brothel].

FORNICATED, [fawn'-ik-āt-id], *adj.* arched; (*bot.*) arching over. [L. *fornicatum*].

FORNICATION, [fawn'-ik-ā'-shun], *n.* sexual intercourse between unmarried persons; idolatry; (*arch.*) an arching; the forming of a vault. [EcclesL. *fornicatio*].

FORNICATOR, [fawn'-ik-ā'-ter], *n.* a person guilty of fornication. [EcclesL. *fornicator*].

FORNICATRESS, [fawn'-ik-ā'-tres], *n.* an unmarried female guilty of fornication.

FORNIX, [fawn'-iks], *n.* the excavated part of a shell beneath the umbo; the upper part of the shell of the oyster; (*anat.*) a triangular lamina which extends into each lateral ventricle of the brain. [L. *fornix* an arch].

FORRADER, [fo'-rad-er], *adv.* (*slang*) more advanced, more forward. [FORWARD].

FORREL, see FOREL.

FORSAKE, [fer-sāk'], *v.t.* to abandon, leave entirely; to withdraw from; to cease. [OE. *forsacan*].

FORSAKEN, [fer-sāk'-en], *adj.* deserted, abandoned, left destitute, desolate.

FORSAKENLY, [fer-sāk'-en-li], *adv.* in a forsaken manner.

FORSAKENNESS, [fer-sāk'-en-nes], *n.* the state of being forsaken.

FORSOOTH, [fer-sōōth'], *adv.* in truth, indeed, no doubt. [ME. *for sothe*].

FORSPEND, [faw-spend'], *v.t.* to spend entirely; to wear out, exhaust.

FORSWEAR, [faw-swāer'], *v.t.* to renounce or disown upon oath; to abjure; *v.i.* to swear falsely; (*reflex.*) to perjure oneself.

FORSWEARER, [faw-swāer'-er], *n.* a person who forswears.

FORSWORNNESS, [faw-swawn'-nes], *n.* the condition of being forsworn.

FORSYTHIA, [faw-sī'-thi-a], *n.* (*bot.*) a spring-flowering shrub bearing bright yellow sprays of blossom. [W. *Forsyth*, an English botanist].

FORT, [fawt], *n.* a fortified building or position from which to resist an enemy. [Fr. *fort*].

FORTALICE, [fawt'-a-lis], *n.* an outwork; a small fort; a fortress. [OFr. *fortelesce*].

FORTE (1), [fawt], *n.* the quality in which one excels; one's strong point. [Fr. *fort* strong].

FORTE (2), [fawt'-i], *adv.* (*mus.*) loudly, with force. [It. *forte*].

FORTED, [fawt'-id], *adj.* guarded by forts.

FORTH, [fawth], *adv.* forwards, onwards in time, place or order; away; out into view; **so far f.**, to that degree or extent. [OE. *forth*].

FORTHCOMING, [fawth'-kum'-ing], *adj.* about to appear; in the near future; available; (*fig.*) communicative; generous.

FORTHGOING, [fawth'-gō'-ing], *n.* a going forth; an utterance; a proceeding from.

FORTH-ISSUING, [fawth'-ish'-yōō-ing], *adj.* coming forward into view.

FORTHRIGHT (1), [fawth'-rīt], *adj.* direct, straightforward, downright. [ME. *forth riht*].

FORTHRIGHT (2), [fawth'-rīt], *adv.* at once, straightway. [ME. *forth rihte*].

FORTHWITH, [fawth'-wiTH'], *adv.* without delay.
FORTIETH (1), [faw'-ti-eth], *n.* one of forty equal parts. [OE. *feowertigotha*].
FORTIETH (2), [faw'-ti-eth], *adj.* the first after the thirty-ninth; one part in forty.
FORTIFIABLE, [fawt'-i-fī'-abl], *adj.* capable of being fortified.
FORTIFICATION, [faw'-ti-fi-kā'-shun], *n.* the act of fortifying; (*pl.*) the works erected to fortify a place; a place fortified. [L. *fortificatio*].
FORTIFIER, [faw'-ti-fī-er], *n.* a person who fortifies.
FORTIFY, [faw'-ti-fī], *v.t.* to make stronger; (*milit.*) to strengthen and secure against enemy attack by forts or batteries; to strengthen liquor with alcohol; to confirm, corroborate; *v.i.* to raise defence works. [L. *fortificare*].
FORTISSIMO, [faw-tis'-i-mō], *adv.* (*mus.*) with the greatest strength or loudness. [It. *fortissimo*].
FORTITUDE, [fawt'-i-tewd], *n.* patience combined with strength of mind and courage to face or to suffer adversity. [L. *fortitudo*].
FORTITUDINOUS, [fawt'-i-tewd'-in-us], *adj.* having fortitude.
FORTLET, [fawt'-let], *n.* a little fort.
FORT-MAJOR, [fawt'-mā'-jer], *n.* the officer in command of a fort in the absence of the governor.
FORTNIGHT, [fawt'-nīt], *n.* a period of two weeks. [OE. *feowertyne niht* fourteen nights].
FORTNIGHTLY, [fawt'-nīt-li], *adv. and adj.* (appearing or occurring) every fortnight.
FORTRESS, [fawt'-res], *n.* a fortified town or place; a fort; any place of defence or security. [OFr. *forteresse*].
FORTUITISM, [faw-tew'-it-izm], *n.* belief in chance as the chief determining force in life and nature.
FORTUITIST, [faw-tew'-it-ist], *n.* an adherent of fortuitism.
FORTUITOUS, [faw-tew'-it-us], *adj.* that happens by chance, accidental.
FORTUITOUSLY, [faw-tew'-it-us-li], *adv.* in fortuitous fashion.
FORTUITOUSNESS, [faw-tew'-it-us-nes], *n.* the quality of being fortuitous.
FORTUITY, [faw-tew'-i-ti], *n.* fortuitousness, chance.
FORTUNATE, [faw'-tew-nat, faw'-chŏŏ-nat], *adj.* lucky; bringing or boding good luck or success, auspicious. [L. *fortunatus*].
FORTUNATELY, [faw'-tew-nat-li, faw'-chŏŏ-nat-li], *adv.* successfully; by good fortune, luckily.
FORTUNATENESS, [faw'-tew-nat-nes, faw'-chŏŏ-nat-nes], *n.* the quality of being fortunate.
FORTUNE (1), [faw'-chewn], *n.* chance, luck; the good or ill that befalls one, one's lot; good luck, success; considerable private means; great wealth. [L. *fortuna*].
FORTUNE (2), [faw'-chewn], *v.t.* to furnish with a fortune; *v.i.* to chance, happen.
FORTUNE-BOOK, [faw'-chewn-bŏŏk'], *n.* a book that may be consulted to discover one's fortune.
FORTUNED, [faw'-chewnd], *adj.* having fortune.
FORTUNE-HUNTING, [faw'-chewn-hunt'-ing], *n.* the seeking of a fortune, *esp.* by a suitable marriage.
FORTUNELESS, [faw'-chewn-les], *n.* without fortune.
FORTUNE-TELLER, [faw'-chewn-tel'er], *n.* a person who professes to tell one's future.
FORTY (1), [faw'-ti], *n.* the sum of four tens; **the Roaring Forties,** the stormy region of the Atlantic Ocean between 40 degrees and 50 degrees north latitude; **the F.-five,** the Jacobite rising of 1745.
FORTY (2), [faw'-ti], *adj.* four times ten; **f. winks,** a short nap in the daytime. [OE. *feowertig*].
FORTYFOLD, [faw'-ti-fōld'], *adj.* forty times.
FORUM, [faw'-rum], *n.* the market-place in Roman cities; a place of common judgment or justice; (*fig.*) a place or occasion of open discussion. [L. *forum*].
FORWARD (1), [faw'-wud], *n.* one who plays in the front line in football, polo, or hockey; (*pl.*) pioneers.
FORWARD (2), [faw'-wud], *adj.* onward; in the front part of; in advance of something else; progressive; early, unusually advanced in development; quick to mature; too ready, bold, presumptuous. [OE. *foreweard*].
FORWARD (3), [faw'-wud], *adv.* towards what is in front, onward; (*fig.*) progressively; into notice; (*naut.*) in the front end of a ship; **carriage f.,** payment for carriage on delivery. [OE. *on foreweardan* in a forward position].
FORWARD (4), [faw'-wud], *v.t.* to advance, help onward; to send on, transmit; to re-direct and re-post a letter, etc.; (*bookbinding*) to attach a plain cover to a sewn book, making it ready for the finisher.
FORWARD (5), [faw'-wud], *imper.* (*milit.*) advance!
FORWARDER, [faw'-wud-er], *n.* a person who forwards; (*bookbinding*) a workman who forwards the boarding or rough part of a book.
FORWARDING, [faw'-wud-ing], *n.* the action of sending goods or letters on.
FORWARDLY, [faw'-wud-li], *adv.* in a forward fashion.
FORWARDNESS, [faw'-wud-nes], *n.* the quality of being forward.
FORWARDS, [faw'-wudz], *adv.* forward.
FORWENT, [faw-went'], *pret.* of FORGO.
FORWORN, [faw-wawn'], *adj.* tired out.
FORZANDO, [fawt-san-dō], *adv.* (*mus.*) loudly and abruptly. [It. *forzando*].
FOSSA, [fos'-a], *n.* a small carnivore of Madagascar, *Cryptoprocta ferox*, related both to the cats and civets. [L. *fossa*].
FOSSE, [fos], *n.* a ditch; (*anat.*) a depression in a bone. [L. *fossa*].
FOSSETTE, [fos-et'], *n.* a dimple; a slight depression. [Fr. *fossette*].
FOSSICK, [fos'-ik], *v.i.* (*coll.*) to rummage, to hunt about for odds and ends; (*Australian*) to seek gold in the waste of old diggings. [E. dial., *fossick* to bustle about].
FOSSICKER, [fos'-ik-er], *n.* one who fossicks gold.
FOSSIL (1), [fosl'], *n.* (*geol.*) the form of the body of a plant or animal petrified and preserved in the strata of the earth's surface; (*fig.*) any person or thing out of harmony with the present; an old-fashioned fogey.
FOSSIL (2), [fosl'], *adj.* having the character of a fossil. [L. *fossilis* able to be dug up].
FOSSILIFEROUS, [fos'-il-if'-er-us], *adj.* fossil-bearing. [FOSSIL and L. *ferre* to bear].
FOSSILIFICATION, [fos-il'-i-fi-kā'-shun], *n.* the act of fossilifying; a fossilized state.
FOSSILIFY, [fos-il'-i-fī], *v.t. and i.* to turn into a fossil.
FOSSILISM, [fos'-il-izm], *n.* the science of fossils; palæontology.
FOSSILIST, [fos'-il-ist], *n.* a person learned in the study of fossils.
FOSSILITY, [fos-il'-i-ti], *n.* the quality of a fossil.
FOSSILIZATION, [fos'-il-īz-ā'-shun], *n.* the act of fossilizing.
FOSSILIZE, [fos'-il-īz], *v.t.* to reduce to a fossil or fixed state; *v.i.* to be converted into a fossil or fixed state.
FOSSILOLOGY, [fos'-il-ol'-o-ji], *n.* the science of fossils. [FOSSIL and Gk. *logos* speech].
FOSSORIAL, [fos-aw'-ri-al], *adj.* adapted for digging or burrowing. [L. *fossorius*].
FOSSULATE, [fos'-yŏŏ-lāt], *adj.* having long and narrow hollows. [L. *fossula* a small depression].
FOSSWAY, [fos'-wā], *n.* one of the main Roman military highways of England, with a ditch on each side.

FOSSWAY

FOSTER (1), [fos'-ter], *adj.* connected through nursing or rearing. [OE. *fostor*].
FOSTER (2), [fos'-ter], *v.t.* to nourish, nurse, rear; (*fig.*) to encourage, cherish.
FOSTERAGE, [fos'-ter-ij], *n.* the rearing of the child of another.
FOSTER-BROTHER, [fos'-ter-bruTH'-er], *n.* a brother by nursing though not by birth.
FOSTER-CHILD, [fos'-ter-chīld'], *n.* a child nursed and reared by one who is not its parent.
FOSTER-DAM, [fos'-ter-dam'], *n.* a nurse, a foster-mother.
FOSTER-DAUGHTER, [fos'-ter-daw'-ter], *n.* a daughter by nursing, but not by birth.
FOSTER-EARTH, [fos'-ter-urth'], *n.* earth in which a plant grows, though not its native soil.
FOSTERER, [fos'-ter-er], *n.* a person who fosters; one who takes the place of a parent.
FOSTER-FATHER, [fos'-ter-fah'-THer], *n.* the man who takes the place of a father in bringing up a child.
FOSTERLING, [fos'-ter-ling], *n.* a foster-child.
FOSTER-MOTHER, [fos'-ter-muTH'-er], *n.* a woman who acts as mother to another's child; (*fig.*) an instrument or contrivance used in rearing chickens.
FOSTER-PARENT, [fos'-ter-pāer'-ent], *n.* a foster-father or foster-mother.

FOSTER-SISTER, [fos'-ter-sis'-ter], *n.* a sister by nursing, though not by birth.
FOSTER-SON, [fos'-ter-sun'], *n.* a boy nursed and brought up as a son by foster-parents.
FOSTRESS, [fos'-tres], *n.* a woman who fosters.
FOTHER (1), [foTH'-er], *n.* a cart-load of material; an enormous quantity; a weight of 21 cwt. used for lead. [OE. *fother*].
FOTHER (2), [foTH'-er], *v.t.* (*naut.*) to endeavour to stop a leak in the bottom of a ship, while afloat, by letting down under the bottom a sail filled with yarn and oakum, to be sucked into the crack. [~Du. *voederen*, ~LGerm. *fodern*].
FOUGADE†, [fōō-gahd'], *n.* (*milit.*) a fougasse. [Fr. *fougade*].
FOUGASSE†, [fōō-gas'], *n.* (*milit.*) a mortar or mine charged with small stones, iron, etc., and fired by gunpowder. [AFr. *fougasse*].
FOUGHT, [fawt], *pret and p.pt.* of FIGHT.
FOUL (1), [fowl], *n.* (*naut.*) a slight collision; (*sport*) a breach of the rules of a game, an unlawful blow, tackle, stroke, or action.
FOUL (2), [fowl], *adj.* ugly; dirty, muddy; offensive; wicked, abominable; obscene; (*naut.*) having the ship's bottom covered with weeds and barnacles; (of ropes and cordage) entangled, jammed; (of weather) squally; (*sport*) against the rules; (*slang*) uncomfortable, disagreeable; unsatisfactory; **f. play**, violence; **by fair means or f.**, without scruple. [OE. ful].
FOUL (3), [fowl], *v.t.* to make foul; to collide with; (*sport*) to commit a foul upon; *v.i.* to become foul; to become entangled, to collide; (*sport*) to commit a foul. [OE. *fulian*].
FOULARD, [fōō'-lahd], *n.* a light dress-material of silk or silk and cotton; a silk kerchief. [Fr. *foulard*].
FOUL BROOD, [fowl'-brōōd'], *n.* a disease affecting the larvae of bees.
FOUL-FACED, [fowl'-fāst'], *adj.* having an ugly or revolting face.
FOUL-FEEDING, [fowl'-fēd'-ing], *adj.* eating grossly.
FOUL-FISH, [fowl'-fish], *n.* a fish at the time of spawning.
FOULLY, [fowl'-li], *adv.* in a foul fashion.
FOUL-MOUTHED, [fowl'-mowTHd], *adj.* habitually indulging in bad language.
FOULNESS, [fowl'-nes], *n.* the quality of being foul.
FOUL-SPOKEN, [fowl'-spōk'-en], *adj.* foul-mouthed.
FOUMART, [fōō'-maht], *n.* the polecat. [ME. *fulmart*].
FOUND (1), [fownd], *v.t.* to lay the basis of; to begin the building or construction of; to establish; to endow; to originate; to fix firmly; *v.i.* to rest. [L. *fundare*].
FOUND (2), [fownd], *v.t.* to cast; to form by melting a metal and pouring it into a mould. [Fr. *fondre* to melt].
FOUND (3), *pret. and p.pt.* of FIND.
FOUNDATION, [fown-dā'-shun], *n.* the act of founding; that part of a structure which rests on or below the ground; the base, groundwork or sub-structure on which anything rests; basis; origin; reason; an endowment appropriated to support an institution; an endowed institution; **f. stone**, a stone laid with ceremony to celebrate the founding of a building. [L. *fundatio*].
FOUNDATIONER, [fown-dā'-shun-er], *n.* a student who is supported from the funds of an endowed school.
FOUNDATIONLESS, [fown-dā'-shun-les], *adj.* without foundations.
FOUNDER (1), [fownd'-er], *n.* a person who founds anything; an endower of an institution. [OFr. *fondeor*].
FOUNDER (2), [fownd'-er], *n.* a man who founds metal. [FOUND (2)].
FOUNDER (3), [fownd'-er], *v.t.* to cause internal inflammation and soreness in the feet of a horse; *v.i.* to fill with water and sink, as a ship; to fail, to miscarry; to trip up; to fall through soreness in the feet; to give way, collapse. [OFr. *fondrer*].
FOUNDEROUS, [fownd'-er-us], *adj.* such as causes anything to founder or collapse.
FOUNDLING, [fownd'-ling], *n.* a deserted child of unknown parents. [ME. *fundeling*].
FOUNDRESS, [fownd'-res], *n.* a woman who is a founder.
FOUNDRY, [fownd'-ri], *n.* the process of casting metals; the place where metals are cast. [AFr. *fonderie*].
FOUNDRYMAN, [fownd'-ri-man], *n.* a workman employed in a foundry.
FOUNT (1), [fownt], *n.* a spring, source, fountain. [AFr. *funt*].
FOUNT (2), [fownt], *n.* (*typ.*) a set of type of a uniform size and design.
FOUNTAIN, [fownt'-in], *n.* a spring or source; a spout of water issuing from a pipe, a series of these contrived as an ornament; a jet of drinking-water; a receptacle or reservoir for holding liquids; (*fig.*) source or inspiration; **soda f.**, an apparatus or bar for supplying soft drinks. [AFr. *funtaine*].
FOUNTAIN-HEAD, [fownt'-en-hed'], *n.* source; (*fig.*) ultimate origin.
FOUNTAINLESS, [fownt'-en-les], *adj.* destitute of fountains.
FOUNTAIN-PEN, [fownt'-en-pen], *n.* a pen with a reservoir that can be filled with ink which flows to the nib as the pen is used.
FOUNTFUL, [fownt'-fōōl], *adj.* having many fountains.
FOUR (1), [faw(r)], *n.* the cardinal number next after three; a four-oared boat; (*pl.*) races rowed in such boats; (*pl.*) (*milit.*) a formation for marching four deep; **on all fours**, on hands and knees. [OE. *feower*].
FOUR (2), [faw(r)], *adj.* of the cardinal number next after three; **to the f. winds**, in all directions; to the remotest parts of the world; **the f. corners**, the limits, entire scope of anything.
FOUR-ALE, [faw(r)-āl], *n.* ale formerly sold at fourpence per quart; **f. bar**, the public bar.
FOURBE, [fōōerb], *n.* a tricking fellow; a cheat. [Fr. *fourbe*].
FOURBISSEUR, [fōōerb'-is-ur'], *n.* a sword-cutler. [Fr. *fourbisseur*].
FOURCHETTE, [fōōer'-shet'], *n.* (*surg.*) a small fork-shaped instrument used in operations on the tongue; the furcula of a bird. [Fr. *fourchette* fork].
FOUR-FLUSHER, [faw(r)'-flush'-er], *n.* (*U.S. slang*) a deceiver, humbug.
FOURFOLD, [faw(r)'-fōld], *adj.* quadruple, made up of four parts.
FOUR-FOOTED, [faw(r)'-fōōt-id], *adj.* with four feet, quadruped.
FOURGON, [fōōer'-gon], *n.* an ammunition wagon, a luggage wagon. [Fr. *fourgon*].
FOUR-HANDED, [faw(r)'-hand'-id], *adj.* having four hands, designed for four persons; played by four persons.
FOUR-HORSE, [faw(r)'-haws], *adj.* having four horses.
FOURIERISM, [fōōer'-i-er-izm], *n.* a socialistic scheme of society propounded by C. *Fourier* the French Socialist, 1772-1837.
FOUR-IN-HAND, [faw(r)'-in-hand'], *n.* a vehicle with four horses driven by one man.
FOUR-LEGGED, [faw(r)'-leg'-id], *adj.* with four legs, quadruped.
FOURLING, [faw(r)'-ling], *n.* one of quadruplets.
FOURNEAU†, [fōōer'-nō], *n.* (*milit.*) the chamber of a mine in which the powder is placed. [Fr. *fourneau* oven].
FOURPENCE, [faw(r)'-pents], *n.* a third of a shilling.
FOURPENNY, [faw(r)'-pen-i], *adj.* costing or worth fourpence; **f. piece**, an old English silver coin worth fourpence.
FOUR-POSTER, [faw(r)'-pōst'-er], *n.* a large square bedstead with upright pillars at each corner, and often a canopy.
FOUR-POUNDER, [faw(r)'-pownd'-er], *n.* a gun throwing shot of 4 lb. weight.
FOURRIER, [fōōer'-i-er], *n.* a harbinger. [Fr. *fourrier*].
FOURSCORE, [faw(r)'-skaw(r)], *adj.* four times twenty, eighty.
FOUR-SEATER, [faw(r)'-sēt'-er], *n.* a motor-car to seat four people.
FOURSOME, [faw(r)'-sum], *n.* a game or dance in which four persons take part in two opposing pairs; (*golf*) a game in which there are two players on each side who play the ball alternately; **mixed f.**, one with a man and a woman on each side.
FOUR-SQUARE, [faw(r)'-skwāer'], *adj.* with sides and four angles equal; square.
FOUR-STROKE, [faw(r)'-strōk], *adj.* (*mech.*) having a cycle of four strokes (of an internal combustion engine).
FOURTEEN (1), [faw(r)'-tēn], *n.* the sum of four and ten; the symbol for this sum.
FOURTEEN (2), [faw(r)'-tēn], *adj.* of fourteen.

FOURTEENTH (1), [faw(r)'-tēnth], *n.* one of fourteen equal parts; (*mus.*) an interval extending to the octave of the seventh.
FOURTEENTH (2), [faw(r)'-tēnth], *adj.* equal to a fourteenth; the ordinal of fourteen.
FOURTH (1), [fawth], *n.* one who makes up a party to four; a quarter; (*mus.*) an interval composed of two tones and a semitone. [OE. *feortha*].
FOURTH (2), [fawth], *adj.* the ordinal of four; immediately following the third.
FOURTHLY, [fawth'-li], *adv.* in the fourth place.
FOUR-WHEELED, [faw(r)'-wēld'], *adj.* having or running on four wheels.
FOUR-WHEELER, [faw(r)'-wēl'-er], *n.* a four-wheeled vehicle.
FOVEA, [fō'-vi-a], *n.* (*anat.*, *zool.*, *bot.*) a small pit. [L. *fovea*].
FOVEATE, [fō'-vi-āt], *adj.* foveolated.
FOVEOLATED, [fō'-vi-ō-lā'-tid], *adj.* (*bot.*, *zool.*) with little depressions or pits.
FOVILLA, [fō-vil'-a], *n.* (*bot.*) the fine fertilizing substance found in the pollen of flowers. [MdL. *fovilla*].
FOWL (1), [fowl], *n.* a bird, *esp.* an edible bird, poultry; a cock or hen; the flesh of such birds. [OE. *fugol*].
FOWL (2), [fowl], *v.i.* to shoot or snare wildfowl. [OE. *fuglian*].
FOWLER, [fowl'-er], *n.* a sportsman who snares or shoots wildfowl.
FOWL-GRASS, [fowl'-grahs'], *n.* the meadow grass, *Poa trivialis*.
FOWLING, [fowl'-ing], *n.* the art or practice of snaring or shooting wildfowl.
FOWLING-NET, [fowl'-ing-net], *n.* a net for fowling.
FOWLING-PIECE, [fowl'-ing-pēs'], *n.* a light shotgun for shooting wildfowl.
FOX (1), [foks], *n.* a small reddish-brown animal of the genus *Vulpes*, hunted for sport, etc.; the fur of this animal; (*fig.*) a sly cunning fellow; (*naut.*) a small strand of rope, made by twisting rope-yarns together; a fish, the dusky skulpin, *Callionymus lyra*. [OE. *fox*].
FOX (2), [foks], *v.t.* to deceive, hoax; to intoxicate, befuddle; to discolour paper; to repair boots and shoes by renewing the upper leather; *v.i.* (of beer) to turn sour in fermenting; to pretend, simulate.
FOX-BAT, [foks'-bat'], *n.* a fruit-bat or flying-fox.
FOX-BRUSH, [foks'-brush'], *n.* the bushy tail of the fox.
FOX-CASE, [foks'-kās'], *n.* a fox's pelt.
FOX-CHASE, [foks'-chās'], *n.* the hunting of a fox with hounds.
FOX-EARTH, [foks'-urth'], *n.* the burrow of the fox.
FOXED, [fokst], *adj.* stained, as timber; spotted or discoloured, as paper; soured, as beer; repaired, as boots.
FOX-EVIL, [foks'-ē'-vil], *n.* (*path.*) alopecia, a disease in which the hair falls off.
FOXGLOVE, [foks'-gluv], *n.* a medicinal plant, with flowers resembling the fingers of a glove, *Digitalis purpurea*. [OE. *foxes glofa*].

FOXGLOVE

FOXGRAPE, [foks'-grāp], *n.* a kind of grape.
FOXHOUND, [foks'-hownd], *n.* a type of hound used in fox-hunting.
FOXHUNT, [foks'-hunt], *n.* the hunting of a fox with hounds.
FOXHUNTER, [foks'-hunt'-er], *n.* one who hunts the fox.
FOXHUNTING (1), [foks'-hunt'-ing], *n.* the sport of hunting the fox with hounds.
FOXHUNTING (2), [foks'-hunt'-ing], *adj.* of, or pertaining to, foxhunting; (*coll.*) (of one of the upper classes) not at home in town life, roisterous and a little gross.
FOXINESS, [foks'-i-nes], *n.* the quality of being foxy.
FOXISH, [foks'-ish], *adj.* like a fox, crafty, cunning.
FOXLIKE, [foks'-līk], *adj.* foxish.
FOX-SHARK, [foks'-shahk], *n.* the thrasher shark, *Alopecias vulpes*.
FOX-SLEEP, [foks'-slēp], *n.* simulated sleep.
FOXTAIL, [foks'-tāl], *n.* (*bot.*) a species of grass of the genus *Alopecurus*.
FOX-TAILED, [foks'-tāld], *adj.* resembling the tail of a fox.
FOX-TERRIER, [foks-te'-ri-er], *n.* a terrier originally used to drive the fox into the open.
FOX-TRAP, [foks'-trap], *n.* a snare for catching foxes.
FOX-TROT, [foks'-trot], *n.* a series of short steps made by a horse when changing its pace; a ballroom dance; music suitable for this.
FOXY, [foks'-i], *adj.* of, or pertaining to, foxes; wily; having a dun, fox-like colour; sour; tasting like the foxgrape; †austere; marked with brown stains.
FOY, [foi], *n.* a parting feast, drink, or social entertainment. [Du. *fooi*].
FOYBLE, [foibl], *n.* the pointed half of a sword-blade. [Fr. *foyble*].
FOYER, [fwah'-yā, foi'-er], *n.* a large lobby or anteroom in a theatre; any anteroom used for waiting. [Fr. *foyer*].
FRACAS, [frak'-ah], *n.* an uproar, a noisy quarrel, a brawl. [Fr. *fracas* a crash].
FRACID, [fras'-id], *adj.* over-ripe; rotten from over-ripeness. [L. *fracidus*].
FRACTED, [frak'-tid], *adj.* (*her.*) disjointed as if broken.
FRACTILE, [frak'-tīl], *adj.* of, or pertaining to, breakage; (*geol.*) denoting fracture.
FRACTION, [frak'-shun], *n.* the act of breaking; the state of being broken; a fragment; a very small quantity, degree, etc.; (*math.*) one or more of aliquot parts into which a whole number is divided; **decimal f.**, a fraction in which the unit is divided by 10 or a power of 10 and in which the denominator is a power of 10 and is not stated; **vulgar f.**, a fraction in which the unit is divided by any number; **compound f.**, a fraction of a fraction. [L. *fractio*].
FRACTIONAL, [frak'-shun-al], *adj.* belonging to or containing a fraction or fractions; (*chem.*) denoting the separation, by heating, etc., of various substances which have different boiling points, etc.
FRACTIONARY, [frak'-shun-er-i], *adj.* fractional.
FRACTIONATED, [frak'-shun-āt-id], *adj.* (*chem.*) separated by fractional crystallization, distillation or precipitation into different constituents.
FRACTIONIZED, [frak'-shun-īzd], *adj.* broken up into fractions.
FRACTIOUS, [frak'-shus], *adj.* apt to break out in a passion; unruly; cross; fretful, peevish, quarrelsome. [FRACTION].
FRACTIOUSLY, [frak'-shus-li], *adv.* in a fractious fashion.
FRACTIOUSNESS, [frak'-shus-nes], *n.* the condition of being fractious.
FRACTURE (1), [frak'-cher], *n.* a breaking, *esp.* one caused by violence; a crack; (*surg.*) the breaking of a bone; (*philol.*) diphthongization of certain Old English vowels, when followed by certain consonantal combinations; (*min.*) the manner in which a mineral breaks, and by which its texture is displayed; the surface as it appears when broken; **simple f.**, a fracture in which the bone is merely divided; **compound f.**, a fracture in which the bone is broken and the skin is lacerated. [L. *fractura*].
FRACTURE (2), [frak'-cher], *v.t.* to break; *v.i.* to be liable to break.
FRAGILE, [fraj'-īl], *adj.* easily broken, delicate, brittle. [L. *fragilis*].
FRAGILELY, [fraj'-il-li], *adv.* in a fragile fashion.
FRAGILENESS, [fraj'-īl-nes], *n.* the condition of being fragile.
FRAGILITY, [fraj-il'-i-ti], *n.* fragileness; frailty.
FRAGMENT, [frag'-ment], *n.* a part broken off; a small detached portion; an unfinished work of art. [L. *fragmentum*].
FRAGMENTAL, [frag-ment'-al], *adj.* fragmentary.
FRAGMENTARY, [frag-ment'-er-i], *adj.* consisting of fragments; **f. rocks**, (*geol.*) rocks formed of the fragments of other rocks, as conglomerates, sandstones, etc.
FRAGMENTED, [frag-ment'-id], *adj.* broken into fragments.
FRAGOR†, [frā'-gor], *n.* a loud sudden sound; the report of an explosion; a crash. [L. *fragor*].
FRAGRANCE, [frā'-grants], *n.* the quality of being fragrant. [L. *fragrantia*].
FRAGRANCY, [frā'-gran-si], *n.* fragrance.
FRAGRANT, [frā'-grant], *adj.* diffusing an agreeable odour; sweet smelling; (*fig.*) fresh and sweet. [L. *fragrans*].
FRAGRANTLY, [frā'-grant-li], *adv.* in a fragrant manner.
FRAIL (1), [frāl], *n.* a rush basket in which figs, raisins, etc., are packed; a rush for weaving baskets; a certain quantity of raisins, about 75 lb. [OFr. *frayel*].
FRAIL (2), [frāl], *adj.* delicate, fragile; deficient in

strength, weak; weak of will; (formerly) not chaste. [OFr. *fraile*].

FRAILLY, [frāl'-li], *adv.* in a frail fashion.

FRAILNESS, [frāl'-nes], *n.* the state of being frail.

FRAILTY, [frāl'-ti], *n.* weakness in resisting temptation; infirmity; a foible.

FRAISE (1), [frāz], *n.* a ruff; (*fort.*) a defence consisting of pointed stakes driven into the rampart in a horizontal or inclined position. [AFr. *fraise*].

FRAISE (2), [frāz], *v.t.* to fortify with a fraise; to defend with a row of pikes on all sides.

FRAISED, [frāzd], *adj.* (*fort.*) fortified with a fraise.

FRAMABLE, [frām'-abl], *adj.* capable of being framed.

FRAME (1), [frām], *n.* a fabric or structure designed to surround and support; the skeleton structure round which a thing is built; form, system, shape; skeleton, the bony structure of a human or animal body; background; temper or disposition of mind; a forcing box for plants, with a sloping glass top; a loom on which linen, silk, etc., is stretched for quilting or embroidering; a machine or loom for making lace, knitting stockings, etc.; (*print.*) a stand to support the cases in which the types are distributed; (*founding*) a kind of ledge, enclosing a board, which, when filled with wet sand, serves as a mould for castings; **f. aerial,** an aerial, wound on a flat frame, and adapted for directional reception; **f. up,** (*coll.*) a false charge.

FRAME (2), [frām], *v.t.* to surround and support with a frame; to serve as a frame or background to; to fit together, construct; to shape; to devise (a policy); to compose (a sentence, law); to adapt; (*slang*) to contrive someone's defeat by a trick, to compromise falsely; *v.i.* to contrive, progress; to be active and in correct adjustment. [OE. *framian*].

FRAME-BRIDGE, [frām'-brij'], *n.* a bridge so framed as to secure the greatest possible strength.

FRAME-HOUSE, [frām'-hows], *n.* a framework of timber covered with boards; a half-timbered house.

FRAMER, [frām'-er], *n.* a person who frames.

FRAME-SAW, [frām'-saw], *n.* a saw stretched and kept rigid in a hand-frame.

FRAMEWORK, [frām'-wurk], *n.* the frame which supports or encloses a thing; the skeleton; the understructure; (*fig.*) organization.

FRAMING-CHISEL, [frām'-ing-chizl'], *n.* a chisel with a socket shank used for cutting mortises.

FRAMING-CHISEL

FRANC, [frangk], *n.* a French coin, the monetary unit of France, worth 100 centimes; the corresponding coin of Belgium and Switzerland. [Fr. *franc*].

FRANCHISE, EFFRANCHISE, [fran'-chīz], *n.* a privilege, immunity, or right granted by a prince or sovereign to an individual or to a number of persons; the district or jurisdiction to which such a privilege or immunity extends; citizenship; the right to vote in a public election, *esp.* in a parliamentary election. [Fr. *franchise* freedom].

FRANCHISEMENT†, [fran'-chīz-ment], *n* enfranchisement; a privilege.

FRANCIC, [frangk-ik], *adj.* Frankish.

FRANCISATION, [frans'-i-zā'-shun], *n.* the action of entering a vessel on the French register.

FRANCISCA, [fran-sis'-ka], *n.* an ancient battle-axe used by the Franks. [MedL. *francisca*].

FRANCISCAN (1), [fran-sis'-kan], *n.* a friar of the order of St. Francis of Assisi. [St. *Francis*, the founder of the order, 1182-1226].

FRANCISCAN (2), [fran-sis'-kan], *adj.* of, or pertaining to, St. Francis of Assisi or to the Franciscans.

FRANCO-, *pref.* Frankish; French. [LL. *Francus*].

FRANCOLIN, [frangk'-o-lin], *n.* a bird somewhat like a partridge. [It. *francolino*].

FRANCOLITE, [frangk'-o-līt], *n.* (*min.*) a variety of apatite found at Wheal Franco in Devonshire. [Wheal *Franco*, and Gk. *lithos* stone].

FRANCOPHILE, [frangk'-ō-fīl], *n.* a lover of France and all things French. [FRANCO and Gk. *philos* lover].

FRANCOPHOBE, [frangk'-ō-fōb], *n.* one who dreads French influences; one who hates the French or what is French. [FRANCO and Gk. *phobos* fear].

FRANC-REAL, [frangk'-rē'-al], *n.* a kind of baking pear.

FRANC-TIREUR, [frah(ng)'-tē-rur'], *n.* a combatant who lacks military status; a guerrilla fighter. [Fr. *franc tireur*].

FRANGIBILITY, [fran'-ji-bil'-i-ti], *n.* the quality of being frangible.

FRANGIBLE, [fran'-jibl], *adj.* easily broken. [L *frangibilis*].

FRANGIBLENESS, [fran'-jibl-nes], *n.* frangibility

FRANGIPANI, FRANGIPANE, [fran-ji-pah'-ni], *n.* a kind of rich pastry; a perfume prepared from the red jasmine. [Fr. *frangipani*].

FRANK (1), [frangk], *n.* an Eastern term for a West-European; a member of a Germanic people who overran, and gave their name to, France. [OE. *Franca*].

FRANK (2), [frangk], *n.* a signature exempting from postage; any letter or parcel so exempted. [FRANK (4)].

FRANK (3), [frangk], *adj.* free and open in manner and speech; sincere; candid. [Fr. *franc* free].

FRANK (4), [frangk], *v.t.* to render free; to be responsible for a person's expenses; to exempt a letter from postage by means of a frank. [FRANK (3)].

FRANKALMOIGNE, [frangk'-al-moin], *n.* (*leg.*) a tenure by which a religious corporation holds lands on condition of praying for the soul of the donor. [FRANK (3) and AFr. *almoine* alms].

FRANK-CHASE, [frangk'-chās], *n.* (*leg.*) the liberty to hunt in a forest.

FRANKENSTEIN, [frangk'-en-stīn], *n.* one who creates a thing or situation he is afterwards unable to control; a thing or situation so created. [Count *Frankenstein* in a novel by Mary Shelley (1818)].

FRANK-FEE, [frangk'-fē'], *adj.* (*leg.*) holding land in fee simple.

FRANKFOLD, [frangk'-fōld], *n.* (*leg.*) the right to fold sheep; foldage.

FRANKFORT-BLACK, [frangk'-furt-blak'], *n.* a jet-black pigment used in copperplate printing, made by burning vine-branches, grape-stones, etc.

FRANKFURTER, [frangk'-furt'-er], *n.* a small smoked German sausage. [*Frankfurt*, in Germany].

FRANK-HEARTED, [frangk'-haht'-id], *adj.* having a candid, open disposition.

FRANK-HEARTEDNESS, [frangk'-haht'-id-nes], *n.* the condition of being frank-hearted.

FRANKINCENSE, [frangk'-in-sents], *n.* gum-olibanum, a resinous substance that gives off a fragrant smell when burning, and obtained from *Boswelli Carteri* of Hadramaut and Somaliland. [OFr. *franc encens* incense of high quality].

FRANKING, [frangk'-ing], *n.* the act of exempting from postage by a frank; (*carp.*) window-sashes.

FRANKISH, [frangk'-ish], *adj.* pertaining to the Franks.

FRANKLIN, [frangk'-lin], *n.* an old English freeholder, *esp.* one who held his lands direct of the crown; a yeoman. [AFr. *fraunkelayn*].

FRANKLINIC, [frangk-lin'-ik], *adj.* (*elect.*) excited by friction. [Benjamin *Franklin*, the American writer and politician 1706-1790].

FRANKLINITE, [frangk'-lin-īt], *n.* (*min.*) a mineral containing iron, zinc, and manganese. [*Franklin*, in New Jersey].

FRANKLY, [frangk'-li], *adv.* in a frank fashion; candidly.

FRANKNESS, [frangk'-nes], *n.* the quality of being frank.

FRANK-PLEDGE, [frangk'-plej], *n.* (*leg.*) a feudal pledge for the behaviour of freemen, *esp.* the responsibility of every member of a tithing for the conduct of the other members.

FRANK-SERVICE, [frangk'-sur'-vis], *n.* (*leg.*) service rendered by freemen.

FRANK-TENEMENT, [frangk'-ten'-i-ment], *n.* (*leg.*) the holding of land by a freeman.

FRANTIC, [fran'-tik], *adj.* violently excited, disordered, wild; distraught, temporarily mad; (*coll.*) in a hurry; disturbing. [OFr. *frenetike*].

FRANTICALLY, [fran'-tik-al-i], *adv.* in frantic fashion.

FRANTICNESS, [fran'-tik-nes], *n.* the condition of being frantic.

FRAP, (frapping, frapped), [frap], *v.i.* (*naut.*) to pass a rope or line round anything to keep it together; to secure and strengthen by binding with ropes crossing each other. [OFr. *fraper*].

FRAPPE, frappé, [frap'-ā], *adj.* iced, cooled. [Fr. *frappé*].

FRASLING, [fraz'-ling], *n.* the perch, *Perca fluviatilis*. [Unkn.].

FRATERNAL, [frat-urn'-al], *adj.* brotherly; pertaining to brothers; very friendly. [L. *fraternus*].

FRATERNALLY, [frat-urn'-al-i], *adv.* in fraternal fashion.

FRATERNITY, [frat-urn'-i-ti], *n.* the state of being brothers; brotherhood; a company of men associated

for a common interest; men of the same class or profession. [Fr. *fraternité*].
FRATERNIZATION, [frat'-ern-iz-ā'-shun], *n.* the action of fraternizing.
FRATERNIZE, [frat'-ern-iz], *v.i.* to associate together as brothers or in friendly intimacy. [MedL. *fraternizare*].
FRATERY, [frā'-ter-i], *n.* the refectory of a monastery. [L. *frater* brother].
FRATRICIDAL, [frat'-ri-sīd'-al], *adj.* of, or pertaining to, fratricide.
FRATRICIDE, [frat'-ri-sīd], *n.* one who wilfully kills his brother; the murder thus committed. [L. *fratricida*].
FRAU, [frow], *n.* the German title for a married woman. [Germ. *Frau* lady, Mrs.].
FRAUD, [frawd], *n.* a trick or subterfuge by which the right or interest of another is injured; a stratagem intended to obtain some undue advantage; a cheat, an impostor; cheating, imposition, deceit. [Fr. *fraude*].
FRAUDFUL, [frawd'-fōōl], *adj.* fraudulent.
FRAUDFULLY, [frawd'-fōōl-i], *adv.* in a fraudulent manner.
FRAUDLESS, [frawd'-les], *n.* without fraud.
FRAUDLESSLY, [frawd'-les-li], *adv.* without fraud.
FRAUDLESSNESS, [frawd'-les-nes], *n.* freedom from fraud.
FRAUDULENCE, [frawd'-yōō-lents], *n.* fraudulency.
FRAUDULENCY, [frawd'-yōō-len-si], *n.* the quality of being fraudulent.
FRAUDULENT, [frawd'-yōō-lent], *adj.* committing fraud; addicted to fraud; obtained by fraud; dishonest. [L. *fraudulentus*].
FRAUDULENTLY, [frawd'-yōō-lent-li], *adv.* in a fraudulent fashion.
FRAUDULENTNESS, [frawd'-yōō-lent-nes], *n.* the quality of being fraudulent.
FRAUGHT, [frawt], *adj.* freighted, laden; (*fig.*) stored; full of. [ME. *fraghten*].
FRAULEIN, **fräulein**, [froi'-līn], *n.* in Germany, an unmarried woman. [Germ. *Fräulein* Miss].
FRAUNHOFER LINES, [frown'-hō-fer-līnz'], *n.*(*pl.*) (*opt.*) the dark lines in the spectrum. [*Fraunhofer*, the German optician, 1787-1826].
FRAXININ, [fraks'-in-in], *n.* (*chem.*) a substance obtained from the bark of the common ash. [L. *fraxinus* the ash].
FRAY (1), [frā], *n.* a brawl; the thick of a fight; (*fig.*) any struggle. [ME. *frai*].
FRAY (2), [frā], *v.t.* (*archaic*) to frighten. [AFFRAY].
FRAY (3), [frā], *v.t.* to wear into loose ends by rubbing, to ravel; (*fig.*) to try the temper; to rub the velvet off the new antlers of a deer; *v.i.* to become ravelled. [Fr. *frayer* to rub].
FRAYING, [frā'-ing], *n.* a ravelling or its result; the peel of a deer's horn.
FRAZIL, [fraz'-il], *n.* ice formed in small circular crystals; anchor ice. [CanFr. *frazil*].
FRAZZLE (1), [frazl], *n.* a shred, tatter; **to reduce to a f.**, to make thoroughly weary; **to beat to a f.**, to beat thoroughly.
FRAZZLE (2), [frazl], *v.t.* to fray, reduce to tatters; *v.i.* to become frayed; (*slang*) to be worn out, nervous. [Unkn.].
FREAK (1), [frēk], *n.* a sudden, non-rational change of mind; a capricious humour; an abnormality, a monstrosity; (*slang*) an eccentric or curiously ugly person. [Uncert.].
FREAK (2), [frēk], *adj.* unusual, abnormal.
FREAK (3), [frēk], *v.t.* to fleck, variegate. [Milton, "Lycidas" 144].
FREAKED, [frēkt], *adj.* streaked, flecked.
FREAKISH, [frēk'-ish], *adj.* full of freaks; capricious; unusual.
FREAKISHLY, [frēk'-ish-li], *adv.* in a freakish manner.
FREAKISHNESS, [frēk'-ish-nes], *n.* the quality of being freakish.
FRECKLE (1), [frekl], *n.* a brown spot on the skin caused by the action of the sun's rays; any small spot or discoloration. [~ME. *frakin* a spot].
FRECKLE (2), [frekl], *v.t.* to cover with freckles; *v.i.* to become freckled; to be liable to freckles.
FRECKLED, [frekld], *adj.* marked with freckles.
FRECKLEDNESS, [frekld'-nes], *n.* the condition of being freckled.
FRECKLY, [frek'-li], *adv.* covered with freckles.
FREE (1), [frē], *adj.* able to move; unhindered by close restraint; enjoying liberty; not enslaved, not imprisoned or confined; self-determining; released from obligations, exempt; unrestricted; unconstrained or uncontrolled by rule or convention; unattached; unreserved; liberal, lavish; outspoken; ready, abundant; with no price to be paid, gratis; not engaged, unoccupied; (*chem.*) uncombined; **f. hand**, liberty of action; **f. lance**, an unattached journalist or politician; **f. verse**, verse not conforming to a recognized pattern; **f. wheel**, a wheel driven by a gear in which the driven member may freely outrun the driving member; **F. Church**, a dissenting Scottish body; (*pl.*) the Nonconformist churches. [OE. *freo*].
FREE (2), [frē], *adv.* freely.
FREE (3), [frē], *v.t.* to rid, liberate, set free.
FREE-AGENCY, [frē'-ā'-jen-si], *n.* the condition of acting freely.
FREE-BENCH, [frē'-bench'], *n.* (*leg.*) the dowry of a widow in a copyhold.
FREEBOARD, [frē'-bawd], *n.* (*naut.*) the part of a vessel's hull that rises from the waterline; a strip of ground extending for not more than thirty inches along the outer side of a fence.
FREEBOOTER, [frē-bōōt'-er], *n.* a pirate; a person or a ship out for plunder. [Du. *vrijbuiter* robber].
FREEBOOTERY, [frē'-bōōt'-er-i], *n.* piracy.
FREEBOOTY, [frē'-bōōt'-i], *n.* plunder taken by freebooters.
FREEBORN, [frē'-bawn], *adj.* born free.
FREEDMAN, [frēd'-man], *n.* one who has been a slave and is now freed.
FREEDOM, [frē'-dom], *n.* the state of being free; liberty; exemption from slavery, servitude or confinement; franchise; immunity; ease or facility of doing anything; frankness; licence; improper familiarity; **f. of a city**, admission to citizenship with participation in its privileges. [OE. *freodom*].
FREE-FIGHT, [frē'-fīt'], *n.* a haphazard general fight or struggle.
FREE-FOOTED, [frē'-fōōt'-id], *adj.* not subject to any restraint in marching.
FREE-GRACE, [frē'-grās], *n.* grace dispensed at one's good pleasure; **f. or for nothing**, without cost or effort.
FREE-HAND, [frē'-hand], *adj.* (*art*) drawn without the use of instruments.
FREE-HANDED, [frē'-hand'-id], *adj.* generous, liberal.
FREE-HEARTED, [frē'-haht'-id], *adj.* open-hearted, generous.
FREE-HEARTEDLY, [frē'-haht'-id-li], *adv.* in free-hearted fashion.
FREE-HEARTEDNESS, [frē'-haht'-id-nes], *n.* the quality of being free-hearted.
FREEHOLD, [frē'-hōld], *n.* the land or tenement which is held in fee-simple, fee-tail, or for term of life; estate or appointment thus held.
FREEHOLDER, [frē'-hōld'-er], *n.* one who possesses a freehold.
FREE LIVER, [frē'-liv'-er], *n.* a person who indulges his appetites freely.
FREE LIVING, [frē'-liv'-ing], *adj.* given to full gratification of the appetites; (*zool.*) not parasitic.
FREE LOVE, [frē'-luv'], *n.* the doctrine that sexual relations should not be limited by marriage; the practice of that doctrine.
FREELY, [frē'-li], *adv.* in a free manner.
FREEMAN, [frē'-man], *n.* one who is personally free; a full member of a state; one on whom the freedom of a city or town has been conferred. [OE. *freoman*].
FREEMARTIN, [frē'-maht'-in], *n.* an imperfect female calf, twin with a male and incapable of breeding. [Unkn.].
FREEMASON, [frē'-mā'-son], *n.* a member of an ancient and secret fraternity, originally an association of masons or builders in stone, now a mutual assistance society.
FREEMASONRY, [frē-mā'-son-ri], *n.* the spirit and institutions of freemasons.
FREE-MINDED, [frē'-mīnd'-id], *n.* free from care or perplexity.
FREENESS, [frē'-nes], *n.* the state of being free.
FREER, [frē'-er], *n.* a liberator.
FREE-REED, [frē'-rēd'], *n.* the metal tongue arranged at one end over a slit in metal, by which the sound is made in a mouth organ, harmonium, etc.
FREESIA, [frē'-zi-a], *n.* (*bot.*) a South African bulbous plant of the iris family, with white or pale coloured racemes of flowers. [MdL. *freesia*].
FREE-SOCAGE, [frē'-sŏk'-ij], *n.* (*leg.*) common socage; free tenure of lands.
FREE-SPOKEN, [frē'-spōk'-en], *adj.* speaking without seemly reserve, embarrassingly frank.
FREE-SPOKENNESS, [frē-spōk'-en-nes], *n.* the quality of being free-spoken.
FREESTONE, [frē'-stōn], *n.* a building stone which,

having no grain, can be cut in any direction; oolitic sandstone.

FREETHINKER, [frē′-thingk′-er], *n.* one who rejects the teachings of the churches in religious matters; a deist or rationalist.

FREETHINKING, [frē′-thingk′-ing], *n.* rationalism; deism; irreligion.

FREETHOUGHT, [frē′-thawt′], *n.* rationalism, atheism, agnosticism.

FREE-TONGUED, [frē′-tungd′], *adj.* free-spoken.

FREE TRADE, [frē′-trād′], *n.* (*econ.*) trade or commerce exempt from Government control.

FREE TRADER, [frē′-trād′-er], *n.* an exponent of free trade.

FREE-WARREN, [frē′-wor′-en], *n.* (*leg.*) a royal privilege or right of killing animals and fowls in a warren.

FREE-WILL (1), [frē′-wil′], *n.* the philosophic belief that one's will is entirely self-determined; **of one's own f.,** voluntarily.

FREE-WILL (2), [frē′-wil′], *adj.* spontaneous, voluntary; appertaining to the philosophic doctrine of free-will.

FREE-WOMAN, [frē′-wŏŏm′-an], *n.* a woman enjoying full rights as citizeness of a state.

FREEZABLE, [frēz′-abl], *adj.* capable of being frozen.

FREEZE, (froze, frozen), [frēz], *v.t.* to congeal (a liquid) into a solid state; to kill by cold; to chill; (*fig.*) to quench the vigour of; to forbid or prevent the free circulation of (currency, credits, etc.); **to f. off,** to snub, get rid of; *v.i.* to be congealed by cold; to be chilled; (*coll.*) to feel the cold. [OE. *freosan*].

FREEZER, [frēz′-er], *n.* a freezing apparatus, a refrigerator.

FREEZING-MIXTURE, [frēz′-ing-miks′-cher], *n.* a mixture of two or more substances, which, in combining, absorb heat from contiguous bodies and thus produce intense cold.

FREEZING-POINT, [frēz′-ing-point′], *n.* the temperature at which a fluid *esp.* water, freezes.

FREIGHT (1), [frāt], *n.* load, goods loaded for transport; monetary recompense for carrying goods; transport of goods; (*fig.*) load, burden; **f. train,** a goods train. [ME. *freyght*].

FREIGHT (2), [frāt], *v.t.* to load with goods for transport; to hire for this purpose.

FREIGHTAGE, [frāt′-ij], *n.* freight; charge for freight.

FREIGHTER, [frāt′-er], *n.* a man who freights a ship; one who transports goods by rail; a ship that does not primarily carry passengers.

FREMESCENT, [frem-es′-ent], *adj.* complaining loudly. [L. *fremescens*].

FRENATE, [frē′-nāt], *adj.* having a frenum.

FRENCH (1), [french], *n.* the French language or people.

FRENCH (2), [french], *adj.* of, or pertaining to, France and her inhabitants. [OE. *Frencisc*].

FRENCH-BEAN, [french′-bēn′], *n.* the common kidney bean, *Phaseolus vulgaris.*

FRENCH-BERRY, [french′-be′-ri], *n.* the Avignon berry, the berry of *Rhamnus infectorius* used in making a yellow dye.

FRENCH BREAD, [french′-bred′], *n.* a fancy bread made of fine flour.

FRENCH-CHALK, [french′-chawk′], *n.* a hardened talc of a pearly-white or greyish colour, used for drawing lines on cloth, and for various dusting purposes when powdered.

FRENCH-FAKE, [french′-fāk′], *n.* a way of coiling a rope by laying it in straight lines placed side by side.

FRENCH GREY, [french′-grā′], *n.* a blue-grey colour.

FRENCH-HORN, [french′-hawn′], *n.* a musical wind-instrument of brass or silver, with a range of three octaves.

FRENCH-HORN

FRENCHIFY, [french′-i-fī], *v.t.* to make French.

FRENCH-LEAVE, [french′-lēv′], *n.* departure, a holiday, taken without permission.

FRENCH-LIKE, [french′-līk], *adv.* in French fashion.

FRENCHMAN, [french′-man], *n.* a native of France; a French ship; a red-legged variety of partridge.

FRENCH-PIE, [french′-pī′], *n.* the great spotted woodpecker, *Picus major.*

FRENCH-POLISH (1), [french′-pol′-ish], *n.* a spirit polish for wooden furniture.

FRENCH-POLISH (2), [french′-pol′-ish], *v.t.* to give a high finish to furniture with french-polish.

FRENCH-POLISHER, [french′-pol′-ish-er], *n.* one who french-polishes for a living.

FRENCH-ROLL, [french′-rōl′], *n.* a light kind of milk-bread.

FRENCH-ROOF, [french′-rŏŏf′], *n.* a type of mansard roof.

FRENCH-WHITE, [french′-wīt′], *n.* a form of finely pulverized talc.

FRENCH-WINDOW, [french′-win′-dō], *n.* a glass door opening on to a garden or balcony.

FRENCHWOMAN, [french′-wŏŏm-an], *n.* a woman of French origin.

FRENULUM, [frēn′-yŏŏ-lum], *n.* (*entom.*) the bristle by which many of the lepidoptera lock together their fore and hind wings. [L. *frenulum* a little bridle].

FRENUM, [frēn′-um], *n.* a ligament. [L. *frenum* a bridle].

FRENZIED, [fren′-zid], *adj.* affected with frenzy, distraught; wildly excited.

FRENZY (1), PHRENSY†, [fren′-zi], *n.* mental disturbance, uncontrollable rage or mania; any great excitement, delirious fury. [OFr. *frensie*].

FRENZY (2), PHRENSY†, [fren′-zi], *v.t.* to fill with frenzy.

FREQUENCY, [frē′-kwen-si], *n.* regular or repeated occurrence; (*phys.*) the rate of such occurrence. [L. *frequentia*].

FREQUENT (1), [frē′-kwent], *adj.* oft repeated; regularly repeated; plentiful. [L. *frequens*].

FREQUENT (2), [fri-kwent′], *v.t.* to resort to often; to be often in the society of. [L. *frequentare*].

FREQUENTAGE, [fri-kwent′-ij], *n.* the habit of frequenting.

FREQUENTATION, [frē′-kwen-tā′-shun], *n.* frequentage.

FREQUENTATIVE, [fri-kwent′-a-tiv], *adj.* (*gram.*) (of verbs) signifying the frequent repetition of an action. [L. *frequentativus*].

FREQUENTER, [fri-kwent′-er], *n.* one who frequents.

FREQUENTLY, [frē′-kwent-li], *adv.* often.

FREQUENTNESS, [frē′-kwent-nes], *n.* the quality of occurring frequently.

FRESCADE, [fres-kād′], *n.* a cool walk; a shady place. [Fr. *frescade*].

FRESCO, [fres′-kō], *n.* a method of painting durably on fresh plaster, the colours often being mixed with the white of an egg; a picture so painted; **al f.,** in the open air. [It. *fresco* cool].

FRESH, [fresh], *adj.* not used, not worn out; strong; blooming; recently made or grown; (of horses) lively; not faded; in a good state; not forgotten or obliterated; not salt; brisk and cool; having new vigour; invigorating; healthy; (*coll.*) slightly intoxicated; (*U.S. slang*) cheeky; **f. way,** (*naut.*) the increased velocity of a vessel. [OE. *fersc*].

FRESH-BLOWN, [fresh′-blōn′], *adj.* (of flowers) newly blown.

FRESHEN, [fresh′-en], *v.t. and i.* to make fresh; to refresh; to grow fresh.

FRESHENER, [fresh′-(e)n-er], *n.* that which refreshes; a refreshing drink; (*journ.*) a fresh handling of a story.

FRESHER, [fresh′-er], *n.* (*slang*) a freshman.

FRESHERDOM, [fresh′-er-dum], *n.* (*slang*) freshmen as a whole.

FRESHES, [fresh′-iz], *n.(pl.)* the intermingling of fresh water with salt water in rivers or bays; a flood; a freshet. [OFr. *freschet*].

FRESHET, [fresh′-et], *n.* a clear brook; the flooding of a river by heavy rains or melted snow. [OFr. *freschet*].

FRESH-LOOKING, [fresh′-lŏŏk′-ing], *adj.* with a clear fresh appearance or complexion.

FRESHLY, [fresh′-li], *adv.* in a fresh manner; newly, recently.

FRESHMAN, [fresh′-man], *n.* a newcomer; a student in his first year at the university.

FRESHMANSHIP, [fresh′-man-ship], *n.* the condition of being a freshman.

FRESHNESS, [fresh′-nes], *n.* the quality of being fresh.

FRESHWATER, [fresh′-waw′-ter], *adj.* formed or living in fresh water; accustomed to sail on fresh water only; raw, unskilled; **f. sailor,** a poor fair-weather sailor.

FRESH-WATERED, [fresh′-waw′-terd], *adj.* recently watered; supplied with fresh water.

FRET (1), [fret], *n.* a criss-cross pattern of ornament; a piece of wood cut to a fine ornamental pattern by sawing out the interstices; the cut made by a fine saw or any similar action; (*med.*) herpes; (*mus.*) the raised pattern which assists fingering on the guitar; (*her.*) a series of interlacing narrow bands. [ME. *frette* an ornament of interlaced wire].

FRET

FRET (2), [fret], *n.* a frayed state of nerves; irritation; uneasiness; (*geol.*) the worn side of a river bank. [FRET (4)].

FRET (3), (fretting, fretted), [fret], *v.t.* to pattern with a fret; (*arch.*) to decorate a vault, etc., in relief. [OFr. *freter* to interlace].

FRET (4), (fretting, fretted), [fret], *v.t. and i.* to eat away; to wear away a passage by erosion; to stir up; to worry, cause agitation to, irritate; to be uneasy and agitated, to grieve, repine. [OE. *fretan* to eat].

FRETFUL, [fret'-fŏŏl], *adj.* inclined to fret, restlessly irritable, peevish.

FRETFULLY, [fret'-fŏŏl-i], *adv.* in a fretful manner.

FRETFULNESS, [fret'-fŏŏl-nes], *n.* the condition of being fretful.

FRET-SAW, [fret'-saw'], *n.* a light saw used for fret cutting and fretwork.

FRETTED, [fret'-id], *adj.* decorated with fretwork; (*her.*) interlaced with narrow bands.

FRETTER, [fret'-er], *n.* one who, or that which, frets.

FRETTING, [fret'-ing], *n.* the act of one who frets.

FRETTY, [fret'-i], *adj.* decorated with fretwork; (*her.*) fretted.

FRETWORK, [fret'-wurk], *n.* interlaced ornament; ornamental woodwork in which the pattern has been cut out by a thin fine saw; work decorated with frets.

FRET-SAW

FRIABILITY, [frī'-a-bil'-i-ti], *n.* the condition of being friable.

FRIABLE, [frī'-abl], *adj.* crumbling easily; pulverizable. [L. *friabilis*].

FRIABLENESS, [frī'-abl-nes], *n.* friability.

FRIAR, [frī'-er], *n.* a member of a religious mendicant order; (*print.*) a patch on a page which has not received the ink properly. [OFr. *frere* brother].

FRIAR-LIKE, [frī'-er-līk], *adj.* like a friar; of or pertaining to friars.

FRIARLY, [frī-er-li], *adv.* in the manner of a friar.

FRIAR'S BALSAM, [frī'-erz-bawl'-sam], *n.* compound tincture of benzoin, a popular medical application for wounds.

FRIAR'S-COWL, [frī-erz-kowl'], *n.* the plant, *Arum maculatum*, so called from its resemblance to a cowl; the cuckoo-pint.

FRIAR'S-LANTERN, [frī'-erz-lan'-tern] *n.* will-o'-the-wisp.

FRIARY, [frī'-er-i], *n.* a convent of friars; the life led by friars.

FRIATION, [frī'-ā'-shun], *n.* the action of crumbling.

FRIBBLE (1), [fribl], *n.* a frivolous, contemptible fellow.

FRIBBLE (2), [fribl], *v.i.* to spend one's time in foolish frivolity. [Symbolic].

FRIBBLER, [frib'-ler], *n.* a person who fribbles.

FRICANDEAU, [frik'-an-dō], *n.* a thick slice of veal stewed with vegetables. [Fr. *fricandeau*].

FRICASSEE, [frik'-a-sē'], *n.* a dish of meat and vegetables cut small and stewed in a thick gravy. [Fr. *fricassée*].

FRICATIVE (1), [frik'-a-tiv], *n.* (*phon.*) a fricative consonant.

FRICATIVE (2), [frik'-a-tiv], *adj.* (*phon.*) (of a consonant sound) produced by the friction of the breath passing through a narrow passage in the mouth, as in *f* or *s*. [L. *fricativus*].

FRICTION, [frik'-shun], *n.* the act of rubbing the surface of one body against that of another; attrition, abrasion; (*fig.*) the clash of two personalities; (*mech.*) the resistance offered to a moving body by the surface on which it moves; (*med.*) the act of rubbing any part of the surface of the body to promote circulation. [L. *frictio*].

FRICTIONAL, [frik'-shun-al], *adj.* connected with, caused by, friction.

FRICTION-BALLS, [frik'-shun-bawlz'], *n.(pl.)* the small balls used in ball-bearings.

FRICTION-CLUTCH, [frik'-shun-kluch'], *n.* (*eng.*) a clutch in which one member is driven through friction.

FRICTION-CONES, [frik'-shun-kōnz'], *n.(pl.)* (*eng.*) the conical-shaped members of a friction-clutch.

FRICTIONLESS, [frik'-shun-les], *adj.* without friction.

FRICTION-ROLLERS, [frik'-shun-rōl'-erz], *n.(pl.)* small metal cylinders used for lessening friction in rotary motion.

FRICTION-WHEEL, [frik'-shun-wēl'], *n.* (*eng.*) a wheel moved by frictional contact.

FRIDAY, [frī'-dā], *n.* the sixth day of the week; **Good F.,** the last Friday before Easter, commemorating the death of Christ. [OE. *frigedæg* from *Frig*, wife of Odin and DAY].

FRIED, [frīd], *pret. and p.pt.* of FRY.

FRIEND, [frend], *n.* one who is attached to another by ties of affection, an intimate companion; one who assists another; an acquaintance; a member of the sect of Quakers; a colleague. [OE. *freond*].

FRIENDED, [frend'-id], *adj.* befriended.

FRIENDLESS, [frend'-les], *adj.* without friends.

FRIEND-LIKE, [frend'-līk], *adj.* in the manner of a friend.

FRICTION-WHEEL

FRIENDLILY, [frend'-li-li], *adv.* in a friendly manner.

FRIENDLINESS, [frend'-li-nes], *n.* the quality of being friendly.

FRIENDLY (1), [frend'-li], *adj.* having the disposition of a friend; sympathetic, courteous, kind; disposed to peace; favourable; propitious; **f. society,** a mutual aid society, whose contributions provide sickness and other benefits for its members.

FRIENDLY (2), [frend'-li], *adv.* in a friendly fashion.

FRIENDSHIP, [frend'-ship], *n.* the relationship of friends; friendly affection. [OE. *freondscipe*].

FRIESIAN, [frēz'-i-an], *adj.* (of cattle) of the Friesland breed.

FRIEZE (1), [frēz, frīz], *n.* a kind of coarse woollen material with a nap, made in Ireland. [~Fr. *friser* to curl].

FRIEZE (2), [frēz], *n.* (*arch.*) that part of the entablature of a column which is between the architrave and cornice, and is generally ornamented; a decorative band, sometimes of wallpaper, placed immediately below the ceiling or cornice. [Fr. *frise*].

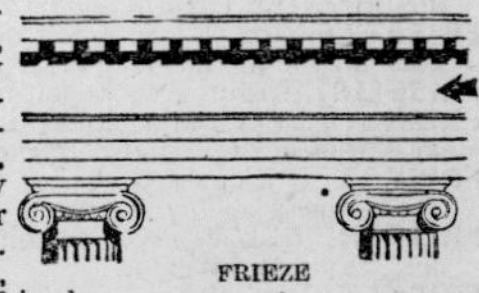

FRIEZE

FRIEZE (3), [frēz], *v.i.* to curl. [Fr. *friser*].

FRIEZED, [frēzd], *adj.* shaggy with nap.

FRIEZE-LIKE, [frēz'-līk], *adj.* in the manner of a frieze.

FRIEZE-PANEL, [frēz'-pan'-el], *n.* the upper half of a six-panelled door.

FRIEZE-RAIL, [frēz'-rāl], *n.* a picture-rail below the frieze.

FRIGATE, [frig'-at], *n.* (*naut.*) a large sailing vessel; a ship of war rating next below a ship of the line, and originally carrying her guns on the main-deck and on a raised quarter-deck and forecastle. [It. *fregata*].

FRIGATE-BIRD, [frig'-at-burd'], *n.* a large and rapacious tropical seabird, *Fregatus aquila*; the man-of-war bird.

FRIGATE-BUILT, [frig'-at-bilt], *adj.* built with a raised quarterdeck and forecastle in the manner of frigates.

FRIGATOON, [frig-at-ōōn'], *n.* (*naut.*) a Venetian ship, with a square stern, and a mainmast and mizenmast only.

FRIGHT (1), [frīt], *n.* sudden fear, violent terror; (*coll.*) any person or thing of a shocking or curious appearance. [OE. *fyrhto*].

FRIGHT (2), [frīt], *v.t.* to frighten.

FRIGHTEN, [frīt'-en], *v.t.* to fill with fear, to scare, terrify.

FRIGHTENABLE, [frīt'-en-abl], *adj.* that may be frightened.

FRIGHTFUL, [frīt'-fōōl], *adj.* fearful, terrible, dreadful, shocking; (*coll.*) unconventional; badly dressed; appalling.
FRIGHTFULLY, [frīt'-fōōl-i], *adv.* in a frightful manner; (*coll.*) very.
FRIGHTFULNESS, [frīt'-fōōl-nes], *n.* the quality or act of being frightful.
FRIGHTLESS, [frīt'-les], *adj.* free from fright.
FRIGID, [frij'-id], *adj.* so cold as to be almost frozen; wanting warmth of affection; wanting zeal, wanting animation or life; stiff, formal; aloof, indifferent; wanting feeling; forbidding; sexually impotent; **f. zone,** the parts of the earth between the polar circles and the poles. [L. *frigidus*].
FRIGIDITY, [frij-id'-i-ti], *n.* the state of being frigid.
FRIGIDLY, [frij'-id-li], *adv.* in a frigid fashion.
FRIGIDNESS, [frij'-id-nes], *n.* frigidity.
FRIGORIFIC, [frig'-er-if'-ik], *adj.* producing cold. [L. *frigorificus*].
FRILL (1), [fril], *n.* a fringe; a loose, protruding edging along the seam of a garment; a ruffle; anything resembling this, *esp.* when used as ornament; (*pl.*) (*fig.*) affected airs, mannerisms; meretricious ornament; elaboration. [Unkn.].
FRILL (2), [fril], *v.t.* to decorate with a frill; *v.i.* to form into a frill; to ruffle.
FRILLING, [fril'-ing], *n.* frilled edges; the act of putting frills on to anything.
FRINGE (1), [frinj], *n.* an ornamental bordering of hanging threads or tassels; anything resembling this, *esp.* if broken or uneven; a border, margin, outer edge; a border of hair worn over the forehead; (*fig.*) the initial stages of anything. [OFr. *frenge*].
FRINGE (2), [frinj], *v.t.* to decorate with a fringe; to form a fringe to.
FRINGELESS, [frinj'-les], *adj.* without a fringe.
FRINGE-LIKE, [frinj'-līk], *adj.* resembling a fringe.
FRINGEMAKER, [frinj'-māk'-er], *n.* one who makes fringes.
FRINGE-TREE, [frinj'-trē'], *n.* (*bot.*) a small American tree, the snowdrop tree, the flowers of which hang down like a fringe, *Chionanthus virginica*.
FRINGILLA, [frin-jil'-a], *n.* a genus of finches which includes the chaffinch, *Fringilla cœlebs* and the brambling, *Fringilla montifringilla*. [L. *fringilla*].
FRINGILLACEOUS, [frin'-jil-ā'-shus], *adj.* of, or pertaining to, the finches.
FRINGING, [frinj'-ing], *n.* a border, fringe.
FRINGY, [frinj'-i], *adj.* having a fringe.
FRIPPER, [frip'-er], *n.* a vendor of frippery.
FRIPPERY, [frip'-er-i], *n.* †old clothes; tawdry, meretricious finery; showy trifles; (*fig.*) empty rhetoric. [Fr. *friperie*].
FRISETTE, [friz-et'], *n.* a row of small artificial curls worn on the forehead. [Fr. *frisette*].
FRISEUR, [fris-ur'], *n.* a hairdresser. [Fr. *friseur*].
FRISK (1), [frisk], *n.* a caper; a lively frolic; a fit of boisterous gaiety. [OFr. *frisque*].
FRISK (2), [frisk], *v.t. and i.* to caper, frolic, gambol; (*fig.*) to hoax; (*slang*) to search (someone).
FRISKER, [frisk'-er], *n.* a person who frisks; a whimsical, capricious person.
FRISKET, [fris'-kit], *n.* (*print.*) the light frame which holds a sheet of paper to the tympan to be laid on the forme for the impression. [Fr. *frisquette*].
FRISKFUL, [frisk'-fōōl], *adj.* frisky, lively; capricious.
FRISKILY, [frisk'-i-li], *adv.* in a frisky fashion.
FRISKINESS, [frisk'-i-nes], *n.* the state of being frisky.
FRISKY, [frisk-'i] *adj.* given to frisking; frolicsome; lively.
FRISLET, [fris'-let], *n.* a small ruffle.
FRIT (1), [frit], *n.* the material of which glass is made after it has been calcined, but before fusion; the material for glazing pottery. [It. *fritta* fry].
FRIT (2), **(fritting, fritted)** [frit], *v.t.* to make into frit, to calcine.
FRITH (1), [frith], *n.* firth; a narrow inlet of the sea. [OIcel. *fjorthr*].
FRITH (2), [frith], *n.* a wooded place; a piece of land covered with brushwood. [OE. *fyrhth(e)*].
FRITILLARY, [frit-il'-er-i], *n.* a genus of liliaceous plants, including the crown imperial, *Fritillaria imperialis*; any of several species of British butterflies, the wings of which are coloured like the mottled petals of the plant. [MedL. *fritillaria*].
FRITTER (1), [frit'-er], *n.* a pancake of batter, often containing a slice of fruit or meat. [Fr. *friture*].
FRITTER (2), [frit'-er], *v.t. and i.* to cut into small pieces; to cut into small pieces and fry; **to f. away,** (*fig.*) to waste, squander aimlessly and futilely.
FRIVOL, (frivolling, frivolled), [friv'-ol], *v.i.* to act frivolously, to trifle.
FRIVOLITY, [friv-ol'-i-ti], *n.* frivolousness, idle trifling.
FRIVOLOUS, [friv'-ol-us], *adj.* of little worth or consequence; trifling, silly, empty; superficial without depth of character. [L. *frivolus*].
FRIVOLOUSLY, [friv'-ol-us-li], *adv.* in a frivolous fashion.
FRIVOLOUSNESS, [friv'-ol-us-nes], *n.* the state of being frivolous.
FRIZEL, [friz'-el], *n.* the steel plate that takes the blow of the snaphance in a flint-lock. [FRIZZLE (1)].
FRIZZ (1), [friz], *n.* a crisped lock of hair; fuzzy curls.
FRIZZ (2), [friz], *n.* the sputtering noise made in frying. [FRIZZLE].
FRIZZ (3), [friz], *v.t.* to curl or crisp; to form the nap of cloth into little hard burrs. [Fr. *friser*].
FRIZZLE (1), [frizl], *v.t. and i.* to sputter; to fry, toast, or grill with a sputtering sound; (*fig.*) to be baked by the sun. [Echoic].
FRIZZLE (2), [frizl], *v.i.* to curl the hair into frizzes. [Fr. *friser*].
FRIZZLER, [friz'-ler], *n.* one who or that which frizzles.
FRIZZY, [friz'-i], *adj.* frizzed.
FRO, [frō], *adv.* from, away, backwards; **to and f.** alternately forwards and backwards. [OIcel. *fra*].
FROCK (1), [frok], *n.* a long outer garment; a woman's dress; a child's dress; a garment indicative of their order, worn by monks and priests. [Fr. *froc*].
FROCK (2), [frok], *v.t.* to clothe in a frock; to make a priest or monk of.
FROCK-COAT, [frok'-kōt'], *n.* a half-length skirted coat for men, worn with a top-hat.
FROCKED, [frokt], *adj.* clothed in a frock.
FROCKLESS, [frok'-les], *n.* without a frock.
FROE, see FROW.
FROEBELISM, [frur'-bel-izm], *n.* a system of education for young children whereby they learn mainly through play; kindergarten education. [*Froebel*, the German educationalist, 1782-1852].
FROG (1), [frog], *n.* a tailless amphibian of the genus *Rana*; a tender horn that grows in the middle of the sole of a horse's foot; a set of points at a railway junction; (*coll.*) a Frenchman, from the idea that the French live mainly on frogs; **frog-march,** the punishment of being carried face downwards by four men each holding an arm or a leg. [OE. *frocga*].
FROG (2), [frog], *n.* a cloak button, the attachment to the belt by which the sword is held; a braided coat fastening on uniforms; a small barrel-shaped silk ornament with tassels, used in the decoration of clothes. [Uncert.].
FROGBIT, [frog'-bit], *n* (*bot.*) the water plant, *Hydrocharis Morsus-ranæ*.
FROG-FISH, [frog'-fish], *n.* the angler or fishing-frog.
FROGGED, [frogd], *adj.* adorned with braided decoration on the front of the coat.
FROGGERY, [frog'-er-i], *n.* a place where many frogs are collected together.
FROGGY (1), [frog'-i], *n.* (*coll.*) a Frenchman. [FROG (1)].

FROG

FROGGY (2), [frog'-i], *adj.* resembling or containing frogs.
FROGHOPPER, [frog'-hop'-er], *n.* (*entom.*) a small leaping insect, *Aphrophora spumaria*, which lives on plants, and whose larvæ are found on leaves in a frothy liquid called cuckoo-spit.
FROGMOUTH, [frog'-mowth], *n.* (*ornith.*) any species of the family of wide-mouthed birds related to the goatsuckers and the oil-bird.
FROG-SHELL, [frog'-shel], *n.* any species of tropical shell of the genus *Ranella*.
FROG-SPAWN, [frog'-spawn], *n.* the ova or spawn of frogs.
FROISE, [froiz], *n.* a pancake containing bacon. [Uncert.].
FROLIC (1), [frol'-ik], *n.* a joyful, light-hearted game; a romp; a merrymaking; an excursion, picnic, or light entertainment.
FROLIC (2), [frol'-ik], *adj.* gay, merry, light-hearted. [Du. *vroolijk*].
FROLIC (3), [frol'-ik], *v.i.* to engage in a frolic; to indulge in merry, light-hearted play.
FROLICFUL, [frol'-ik-fōōl], *adj.* frolicsome.

FROLICSOME, [frol'-ik-sum], *adj.* full of frolics; sportive; full of fun and high spirits.
FROLICSOMELY, [frol'-ik-sum-li], *adv.* in a frolicsome way.
FROLICSOMENESS, [frol'-ik-sum-nes], *n.* the quality of being frolicsome.
FROM, [from], *prep. expressing* motion away; subtraction; exclusion; difference; continued action; point of origin; out of; starting at; leaving behind; by reason of; since; **f. time to time**, occasionally. [OE. *from*].
FROMWARD†, [from'-wud], *adv.* away from.
FROND, [frond], *n.* (*bot.*) the leaf-like organ of a fern or similar plant, which bears the reproductive cells; any leaf, or leaf-like object. [L. *frons frondis*].
FRONDAGE, [frond'-ij], *n.* foliage; the collective mass of fronds.
FRONDE, [frawnd], *n.* (*hist.*) a French party opposed to the Court during the minority of Louis XIV; a bitter political opposition. [Fr. *fronde* a sling].
FRONDESCE, [frond-es'], *v.i.* to put forth leaves or fronds. [L. *frondescere*].
FRONDESCENCE, [frond-es'-ents], *n.* (*bot.*) the time of the year when each plant unfolds its leaves; the act of putting forth leaves.
FRONDESCENT, [frond-es'-ent], *adj.* putting forth leaves or fronds. [L. *frondescens*].
FRONDEUR, [frawnd-ur'], *n.* (*hist.*) a member of the Fronde.
FRONDIFEROUS, [frond-if'-er-us], *adj.* having fronds. [L. *frondifer*].
FRONDOSE, [frond'-ōs], *adj.* bearing leaves or fronds. [L. *frondosus*].
FRONDOUS, [frond'-us], *adj.* leafy.
FRONS, [fronz], *n.* (*anat.*) that section of the skull between the orbits and the vertex. [L. *frons* front].
FRONT (1), [frunt], *n.* the forehead; the forepart of anything; the foremost rank, the van; the area of military operations; a position directly before the face of a person; a set of false hair or curls worn on the forepart of the head; a dickey or separate shirt-front; the face of a building; a promenade along the sea, above the shore; **to come to the f.**, to achieve eminence. [L. *frons frontis* forehead].
FRONT (2), [frunt], *adj.* first; advanced, prominent, eminent; (*of sounds*) palatal; **f. page news**, important or sensational news.
FRONT (3), [frunt], *v.t.* to oppose face to face; to stand in front of or against; to face; to supply with a front; (*phon.*) to pronounce further forward in the mouth; *v.i.* to have the face in a certain direction.
FRONTAGE, [frunt'-ij], *n.* the front part of a building; the side of a piece of land that abuts on a road or river; the building line.
FRONTAGER, [frunt'-ij-er], *n.* the owner of the property adjoining or opposite.
FRONTAL (1), [frunt'-al], *n.* something worn on the forehead as a guard or ornament; (*eccles.*) a hanging ornamental panel in front of an altar; (*arch.*) a little pediment or front piece over a small door or window; (*med.*) a medicament to be applied to the forehead.

FRONTAL

FRONTAL (2), [frunt'-al], *adj.* in front; (*anat.*) connected with the forehead or brow; (*milit.*) (of an attack) from the front.
FRONTED, [frunt'-id], *adj.* having a front.
FRONTIER (1), [frunt'-i-er], *n.* that part of a country bordering on another country, (*pl.*) (*fig.*) the extreme limits. [Fr. *frontière*].
FRONTIER (2), [frunt'-i-er], *adj.* lying on the border; (*Canadian*) connected with pioneer days.
FRONTIERSMAN, [frunt'-ēerz-man], *n.* a settler on the frontier; a backwoodsman.
FRONTINIAC, [front-in'-yak], *n.* a kind of French wine. [*Frontignan* in France, where produced].
FRONTISPIECE, [frunt'-is-pēs], *n.* (*arch.*) the main façade of a building; (*print.*) the illustration or ornamental design facing the title-page of a book. [Fr. *frontispice*].
FRONTLESS, [frunt'-les], *adj.* without a front; without shame or modesty.
FRONTLET, [frunt'-let], *n.* a band worn on the forehead; (*ornith.*) the stiff bristly margin of the head behind the bill of birds; the narrow strip of cloth, silk, or metal completing the frontal of an altar.
FRONTON, [frunt'-on], *n.* (*arch.*) a pediment; a triangular ornament over the principal entrance of a building. [Fr. *fronton*].
FRONTWARD, [frunt'-wud], *adv.* towards the front.
FRONTWARDS, [frunt'-wudz], *adv.* frontward.
FRORE, [fraw(r)], *adj.* intensely cold, frozen, frosted. [OE. *froren* frozen].
FROST (1), [frost], *n.* that temperature of the air, at or below 32 degrees Fahrenheit, which causes freezing of water; frozen dew or moisture; (*fig.*) frigidity; (*coll.*) complete failure. [OE. *forst*].
FROST (2), [frost], *v.t.* to nip with frost; to give the appearance of being covered with hoar frost; to roughen the surface of metal or glass; (*fig.*) to chill.
FROST-BITE (1), [frost'-bīt], *n.* a gangrenous condition set up by continued exposure to extreme cold.
FROST-BITE (2), [frost'-bīt], *v.t.* to nip with frost; to produce frost-bite in.
FROST-BITTEN, [frost'-bit'-en], *adj.* nipped by the frost; suffering from frost-bite.
FROSTBLITE, [frost'-blīt], *n.* (*bot.*) a plant, the white goosefoot, *Chenopodium album*.
FROST-BOUND, [frost'-bownd], *adj.* confined by frost.
FROSTED, [frost'-id], *adj.* having been subjected to frost; covered with hoar-frost; (of glass or metal) roughened.
FROSTILY, [frost'-i-li], *adv.* in a frosty manner.
FROSTINESS, [frost'-i-nes], *n.* the condition of being frosty.
FROSTING, [frost'-ing], *n.* a preparation of loaf-sugar, resembling hoar-frost, for covering a cake; a light covering of white paint or alum solution dabbed on glass, to render it opaque.
FROSTLESS, [frost'-les], *adj.* without frost.
FROST-NAIL, [frost'-nāl'], *n.* a nail driven into a horseshoe, to prevent the horse from slipping on ice.
FROST-WORK, [frost'-wurk], *n.* patterns traced by frost on flat surfaces; patterns resembling these.
FROSTY, [frost'-i], *adj.* freezing, or containing frost; ice-cold; resembling hoar-frost; (of the hair) hoary; (*fig.*) chill, frigid.
FROTH (1), [froth], *n.* foam; the bubbles caused on liquids by fermentation or agitation, similar bubbles forming in saliva; (*fig.*) any empty show of wit or eloquence; light, unsubstantial matter. [OIcel. *frotha*].
FROTH (2), [froth], *v.t.* to form froth on; to beat to a froth; (*fig.*) to talk superficially; *v.i.* to form a froth, foam.
FROTHILY, [froth'-i-li], *adv.* in a frothy manner.
FROTHINESS, [froth'-i-nes], *n.* the condition of being frothy.
FROTHLESS, [froth'-les], *adj.* having no froth.
FROTH-SPIT, [froth'-spit], *n.* a white froth on the leaves of plants, cuckoo-spit.
FROTHY, [froth'-i], *adj.* full of, or covered with, froth; (*fig.*) insubstantial, empty.
FROU-FROU, [frōō'-frōō'], *n.* the rustling of silk. [Fr. *frou-frou*].
FROUNCE (1), [frownts], *n.* a wrinkle, plait, or curl; an ornament of dress; a mass of pimples in the palate of a horse; a disease in hawks. [OFr. *fronce*].
FROUNCE (2), [frownts], *v.t.* to frizz the hair; to gather into frounces; *v.i.* to become wrinkled; to frown. [Fr. *froncer*].
FROW (1), FROE, [frō], *n.* a tool for cleaving laths or splitting staves. [Unkn.].

FROW

FROW (2), [frow], *n.* a Dutch or German woman; a housewife. [Du. *vrouw*, Germ. *Frau*].
FROWARD, [frō'-ard], *adj.* perverse, wayward, disobedient, sinful.
FROWARDLY, [frō'-ard-li], *adv.* in a froward way.
FROWARDNESS, [frō'-ard-nes], *n.* the quality of being froward.
FROWER, [frō'-er], *n.* a sharp-edged cleaving tool, a frow.
FROWN (1), [frown], *n.* a knitting of the brows in displeasure or concentration; a look denoting displeasure or censure.
FROWN (2), [frown], *v.i.* to contract the brows in a frown; to look gloomy; **to f. on**, to regard with displeasure, be opposed to. [ME. *frounen* from OFr. *froignier*].
FROWNING, [frown'-ing], *adj.* exhibiting or wearing a frown; gloomy and forbidding.

FROWNINGLY, [frown'-ing-li], *adv.* in a frowning manner.
FROWST (1), [frowst], *n.* a close stuffy atmosphere in a room, fug.
FROWST (2), [frowst], *v.i.* to lounge in an over-heated room. [Unkn.].
FROWSY, FROWZY, [frow'-zi], *adj.* fusty, ill-smelling; untidy, bedraggled, slatternly. [Unkn.].
FROWY, [frō'-i], *adj.* musty, foetid, stale.
FROWZY, see FROWSY.
FROZEN, [frōz'-en], *adj.* congealed by cold; extremely cold, icy; cold in affection; frigid; repressed. [FREEZE].
FROZENNESS, [frōz'-en-nes], *n.* condition of being frozen.
FRUCTED, [frukt'-id], *adj.* (*her.*) having fruit. [L. *fructus* fruit].
FRUCTESCENCE, [frukt-es'-ents], *n.* (*bot.*) the time of bearing fruit. [L. *fructescens* bearing fruit].
FRUCTIFEROUS, [frukt-if-'er-us], *adj.* producing or bearing fruit. [L. *fructifer*].
FRUCTIFICATION, [frukt'-i-fi-kā'-shun], *n.* (*bot.*) the act or the process of fructifying; the group of organs employed in the reproduction of a plant.
FRUCTIFY, [frukt'-i-fī], *v.t.* to make fruitful, to fertilize; *v.i.* to bear fruit, become fruitful. [Fr. *fructifier*].
FRUCTOSE, [frukt'-ōs], *n.* sugar present in ripe fruit and honey; fruit-sugar. [~L. *fructus* fruit].
FRUCTUARY, [frukt'-yōō-er-i], *n.* a person who has right to the produce of anything. [L. *fructuarius*].
FRUCTUOUS, [frukt'-yōō-us], *adj.* fruitful, fertile; (*fig.*) advantageous. [OFr. *fructuous*].
FRUGAL, [frōō'-gal], *adj.* careful in the use of means, goods, or food; thrifty; meagre; poor; living poorly. [L. *frugalis*].
FRUGALITY, [frōō-gal'-i-ti], *n.* the quality of being frugal.
FRUGALLY, [frōō'-gal-i], *adv.* in a frugal manner.
FRUGALNESS, [frōō'-gal-nes], *n.* frugality.
FRUGGAN, [frug'-an], *n.* (*dial.*) the rod with which ashes in the oven are stirred. [~Fr. *fourgon* poker].
FRUGIFEROUS, [frōō-jif'-er-us], *adj.* fruit-bearing; fruitful. [L. *frugifer*].
FRUGIVOROUS, [frōō-jiv'-er-us], *adj.* eating fruits. [L. *frux frugis* fruit and *vorare* to devour].
FRUIT (1), [frōōt], *n.* the produce of a tree or other plant; the seed of plants, the part that contains the seed; that which is produced, offspring; (*fig.*) effect, consequence; reward. [OFr. *fruit*].
FRUIT (2), [frōōt], *v.i.* to produce fruit.
FRUITAGE, [frōōt'-ij], *n.* fruit collectively; product. [OFr. *fruitage*].
FRUITARIAN, [frōōt-āer'-i-an], *n.* one who eats mainly fruit.
FRUIT-BEARER, [frōōt'-bāer'-er], *n.* that which bears fruit.
FRUIT-BEARING, [frōōt'-bāer'-ing], *adj.* fruit-producing.
FRUIT-BUD, [frōōt'-bud], *n.* the bud which produces fruit.
FRUIT-CAKE, [frōōt'-kāk], *n.* a cake containing several kinds of dried fruits.
FRUITERER, [frōōt'-er-er], *n.* a person who deals in fruit.
FRUITERY, [frōōt'-er-i], *n.* fruit collectively; a fruit-loft.
FRUIT-FLY, [frōōt'-flī], *n.* a small black fly harmful to fruit-trees in the spring season.
FRUITFUL, [frōōt'-fōōl], *adj.* productive of fruit, offspring, or profit; useful; effective, successful.
FRUITFULLY, [frōōt'-fōōl-i], *adv.* in a fruitful fashion.
FRUITFULNESS, [frōōt'-fōōl-nes], *n.* the state of being fruitful.
FRUITINESS, [frōōt'-i-nes], *n.* the quality of being fruity.
FRUITING, [frōōt'-ing], *adj.* bearing fruit.
FRUITION, [frōō-ish'-un], *n.* pleasurable realization, enjoyment; the pleasure derived from use or possession or the maturing of an idea or scheme. [L. *fruitio*].
FRUITIVE, [frōō'-it-iv], *adj.* enjoying; arising from fruition.
FRUIT-KNIFE, [frōōt'-nīf], *n.* a knife for cutting fruit.
FRUITLESS, [frōōt'-les], *adj.* not bearing fruit; unprofitable; barren, useless; unproductive; unsuccessful; abortive.
FRUITLESSLY, [frōōt'-les-li], *adv.* in a fruitless fashion.
FRUITLESSNESS, [frōōt'-les-nes], *n.* the quality of being fruitless.
FRUITLET, [frōōt'-let], *n.* a little fruit; a single small fruit from a cluster or head.
FRUIT-LOFT, [frōōt'-loft], *n.* an attic storeroom for fruit.
FRUIT-PIGEON, [frōōt'-pij'-un], *n.* the largest species of pigeon, which feeds on fruit.
FRUIT SALAD, [frōōt-sal'-ad], *n.* a compote of mixed fruit.
FRUIT SUGAR, [frōōt'-shōōg'-ar], *n.* a sugar present in ripe fruit.
FRUIT-TIME, [frōōt'-tīm], *n.* the time of fruit-gathering.
FRUIT-TREE, [frōōt'-trē], *n.* a tree which bears edible fruit.
FRUITY, [frōōt'-i], *adj.* like fruit; having the flavour of fruit; ripe; (*slang*) suggestive, salacious; (*slang*) (of a voice) over-rich in quality.
FRUMENTACEOUS, [frōō'-men-tā'-shus], *adj.* made of, or like, grain. [L. *frumentaceus*].
FRUMENTARIOUS, [frōō'-men-tāer'-ius], *adj.* of or pertaining to grain. [L. *frumentarius*].
FRUMENTATION, [frōō'-men-tā'-shun], *n.* (*Rom. antiq.*) a generous gift of corn made to the people in ancient Rome. [L. *frumentatio*].
FRUMENTY, [frōō'-men-ti], *n.* a dish made of wheat boiled in milk. [OFr. *fromentée*].
FRUMP, [frump], *n.* a plain and dowdy woman. [Unkn.].
FRUMPER, [frump'-er], *n.* one who mocks or jeers; a scoffer. [Unkn.].
FRUMPISH, [frump'-ish], *adj.* old-fashioned; sneering; like a frump.
FRUMPY, [frump'-i], *adj.* like a frump.
FRUSH (1), [frush], *n.* the frog in a horse's foot; a discharge of morbid matter from it. [Uncert.].
FRUSH (2), [frush], *adj.* brittle. [OFr. *fruissier*].
FRUSTRABLE, [frus'-trabl], *adj.* capable of frustration.
FRUSTRATE (1), [frus'-trāt], *adj.* frustrated. [L. *frustratus*].
FRUSTRATE (2), [frus-trāt'], *v.t.* to hinder; to render of no avail; to baffle, thwart, foil, baulk. [L. *frustrari* deceive].
FRUSTRATION, [frus-trā'-shun], *n.* the act of frustrating; the state of being frustrated.
FRUSTRATIVE, [frus'-trat-iv], *adj.* tending to frustrate.
FRUSTRATORY, [frus'-trat-er-i], *adj.* that frustrates.
FRUSTULE, [frus'-tewl], *n.* the siliceous two-valved shell of a diatom. [LL. *frustulum*].
FRUSTUM, (*pl.* **frusta**), [frus'-tum], *n.* (*geom.*) that part of a solid next the base, formed by cutting off the top parallel to the base; the part of any solid between two planes; (*arch.*) the section of the shaft of a column. [L. *frustum* a piece broken off].

FRUSTUM

FRUTESCENT, [frōōt-es'-ent], *adj.* shrubby, in the manner of a shrub.
FRUTEX, [frōōt'-eks], *n.* a shrub. [L. *frutex*].
FRUTICOSE, [frōōt'-i-kōs], *adj.* branching in the manner of a shrub; pertaining to shrubs; shrubby.
FRUTICOUS, [frōōt'-i-kus], *adj.* fruticose.
FRUTICULOSE, [frōōt-ik'-yōō-lōs], *adj.* fruticose.
FRY (1), [frī], *n.* the small young, *esp.* of fish; **small f.**, insignificant persons; children. [OIcel. *frio* seed].
FRY (2), [frī], *n.* fried food; the edible inwards of a pig or a lamb. [FRY (3)].
FRY (3), [frī], *v.t.* to cook with fat in a pan over the fire; *v.i.* to cook in a frying-pan in fat; (*fig.*) to seethe with passion; to scorch. [Fr. *frire*].
FRYER, [frī'-er], *n.* a frying-pan; a person who fries.
FRYING-PAN, [frī'-ing-pan'], *n.* a shallow pan for frying food.
FUB, (**fubbing, fubbed**), [fub], *v.t.* to cheat, to fob off. [FOB].
FUBBY, [fub'-i], *adj.* plump, chubby.
FUBSY, [fub'-si], *adj.* fubby.
FUCATE, [few'-kāt], *adj.* not in its natural colours; having defects masked by paint; counterfeit. [L. *fucatus*].
FUCHSIA, [few'-sha], *n.* (*bot.*) an ornamental shrub with pendulous flowers. [L. *Fuchs*, a German botanist].
FUCHSIN, [fōōk'-sin], *n.* a dye of fuchsia red, obtained from a salt of rosanaline.
FUCIVOROUS, [few-siv'-er-us], *adj.* subsisting on seaweeds. [L. *fucus* rock lichen and *vorare* to devour].

FUCOID (1), [few'-koid], *n.* a fossil marine plant bearing the markings of seaweed.

FUCOID (2), [few'-koid], *adj.* of the nature of, relating to, seaweed. [L. *fucus* rock-lichen and Gk. *oeides* like].

FUCOIDAL, [few-koid'-al], *adj.* fucoid.

FUCUS, (*pl.* **fuci**), [few'-kus], *n.* a kind of seaweed; a dye formed from it. [L. *fucus* rock-lichen].

FUDDLE (1), [fudl], *n.* a muddle; a state of besotted confusion.

FUDDLE (2), [fudl], *v.t.* to confuse by means of drink; (*fig.*) to confuse the thoughts of; *v.i.* to get drunk. [Unkn.].

FUDDLER, [fud'-ler], *n.* a person who becomes fuddled.

FUDGE (1), [fuj], *n.* a made-up story; a soft, crumbly sweetmeat; stop-press news. [Uncert.].

FUDGE (2), [fuj], *v.t.* to fake, fabricate.

FUDGE (3), [fuj], *int.* stuff and nonsense!

FUEL (1), [few'-el], *n.* any combustible material which feeds a fire; firing; (*fig.*) anything that inflames the mind; **to add f. to the flames,** to aggravate, keep a passion raging. [OFr. *fouaille*].

FUEL (2), (**fuelling, fuelled**), [few'-el], *v.t.* to supply with fuel; *v.i.* to get provision of fuel.

FUELLER, [few'-el-er], *n.* one who or that which fuels.

FUELLING, [few'-el-ing], *n.* the act of providing with fuel; material used for fuel.

FUERO, [fōō-āer'-ō], *n.* a charter of privileges; a statute. [Span. *fuero*].

FUFF (1), [fuf], *n.* a puff; a whiff; a burst of bad temper. [Echoic].

FUFF (2), [fuf], *v.i.* to puff.

FUFFY, [fuf'-i], *adj.* light and soft; huffy, touchy.

FUG, [fug], *n.* (*coll.*) a hot dense atmosphere; stuffy heat. [Unkn.].

FUGACIOUS, [few-gā'-shus], *adj.* fleeting, transitory. [L. *fugax fugacis* apt to fly].

FUGACIOUSNESS, [few-gā'-shus-nes], *n.* the quality of being fugacious.

FUGACITY, [few-gas'-i-ti], *n.* fugaciousness.

FUGAL, [fewg'-al], *adj.* of or pertaining to fugues.

FUGATO, [fewg-ah'-tō], *n.* a musical composition resembling the fugue. [It. *fugato*].

FUGGY, [fug'-i], *adj.* stuffy, badly ventilated.

FUGH, [few], *int.* an exclamation of disgust or abhorrence. [FAUGH].

FUGILE, [few'-jīl], *n.* (*med.*) a gathering in the ear.

FUGITIVE (1), [few'-ji-tiv], *n.* one who flees from danger, captivity, or justice; a deserter.

FUGITIVE (2), [few'-ji-tiv], *adj.* fleeing; fleeting, swiftly passing, volatile, evanescent; escaping from justice; connected with fugitives. [L. *fugitivus* running away].

FUGITIVELY, [few'-ji-tiv-li], *adv.* in a fugitive manner.

FUGITIVENESS, [few'-ji-tiv-nes], *n.* the condition of being fugitive.

FUGLEMAN, FLUGELMAN, [f(l)ewgl'-man], *n.* a trained soldier giving a lead to the company during drill; one whose example is followed by others. [Germ. *flügelmann*].

FUGUE, [fewg], *n.* (*mus.*) a composition in contrapuntal form developing a first theme, an answering theme, and counter subjects according to the acknowledged devices of counterpoint. [L. *fuga* flight].

FUGUIST, [fewg'-ist], *n.* one who composes fugues.

FUHRER, führer, [few'-rer], *n.* a leader, dictator, *esp.* applied to Adolf Hitler, Chancellor and Leader of Nazi Germany. [Germ. *Führer*].

FULCRATE, [ful'-krāt], *adj.* provided with fulcrums; **f. stem,** (*bot.*) a stem whose branches bend and come to rest on the earth.

FULCRUM, (*pl.* **fulcra, fulcrums**), [ful'-krum], *n.* (*bot.*) the part of a plant which serves to defend or support it; (*mech.*) the support on which a lever rests; (*fig.*) any means to an end. [L. *fulcrum* bed-post].

FULFIL, (**fulfilling, fulfilled**), [fōōl-fil'], *v.t.* to accomplish; to carry out, to complete; to perform what is required, to discharge (a duty). [OE. *fullfyllan*].

FULFILLER, [fōōl-fil'-er], *n.* a person who fulfils.

FULFILLING, [fōōl-fil'-ing], *n.* fulfilment.

FULFILMENT, [fōōl-fil'-ment], *n.* accomplishment; satisfaction, realization in experience of spiritual or psychological potentialities.

FULGENCY, [ful'-jen-si], *n.* radiancy, effulgence.

FULGENT, [ful'-jent], *adj.* radiant, dazzling, bright with light. [L. *fulgens*].

FULGENTLY, [ful'-jent-li], *adv.* in a fulgent way.

FULGOR†, [ful'-ger], *n.* radiance. [L. *fulgor*].

FULGOROUS†, [ful'-ger-us], *adj.* brilliant, flashing.

FULGURATION, [ful'-gyōō-rā'-shun], *n.* (*metal.*) the quickly passing film of light occurring across a drop of fused gold or silver, signifying the expulsion of the last element of vitreous lead or copper. [L. *fulguratio* lightning].

FULGURITE, [ful'-gyōō-rīt], *n.* a tube of vitrified matter discovered in sand, supposed to be formed by lightning striking the ground; any mineral with marks of fusion.

FULIGINOSITY, [few'-lij-in-os'-i-ti], *n.* the quality of being fuliginous.

FULIGINOUS, [few-lij'-in-us], *adj.* consisting of, or resembling, soot; smoky, dusky. [L. *fuliginosus*].

FULIGINOUSLY, [few-lij'-in-us-li], *adv.* in a fuliginous manner.

FULL (1), [fōōl], *n.* the highest or utmost degree or state of any quality, attribute, or characteristic; **in f.,** fully, completely; **to the f.,** completely.

FULL (2), [fōōl], *adj.* having no space empty, containing as much as capacity permits; crowded; having eaten as much food as possible, sated; well-provided, abounding in, having plenty; occupied with, intently concerned with; overwhelmed by emotion; having reached the highest degree or state of some quality, process, or characteristic; resonant; plump; roomy; stretched out, extended; **in f. cry,** hard on the scent of the hunted; **f. dress,** elaborate ceremonial uniform. [OE. *full*].

FULL (3), [fōōl], *adv.* completely, to the maximum extent.

FULL (4), [fōōl], *v.t. and i.* to make a dress or garment more ample; to become full, to possess fulness.

FULL (5), [fōōl], *v.t.* to cleanse and thicken cloth after weaving. [OE. *fullian*].

FULLAGE†, [fōōl'-ij], *n.* money paid for fulling cloth. [OFr. *foullage*].

FULL-AGED, [fōōl'-ājd'], *adj.* of mature age.

FULL-ARMED, [fōōl'-ahmd'], *adj.* armed to the teeth.

FULL-BLOWN, [fōōl'-blōn], *adj.* fully expanded; (*fig.*) past maturity.

FULL-BOTTOMED, [fōōl'-bot'-omd], *adj.* having a large bottom, as a wig worn by a K.C.

FULL-BUTT, [fōōl'-but'], *adv.* meeting directly, and with violence, head-on.

FULL-DRIVE, [fōōl'-drīv'], *adv.* at full speed.

FULLER (1), [fōōl-er], *n.* a person whose business consists in fulling cloth. [OE. *fullere*].

FULLER (2), [fōōl'-er], *n. and v.t.* a set-hammer for forming grooves in iron; to form a groove with a fuller. [Unkn.].

FULLER'S EARTH, [fōōl'-erz-urth'], *n.* a kind of soft clay which absorbs grease, used in fulling cloth and as a dusting powder.

FULLER'S-THISTLE, [fōōl'-erz-thisl'], *n.* the plant, *Dipsacus fullonum*, a teasel.

FULLER'S-WEED, [fōōl'-erz-wēd'], *n.* fuller's-thistle.

FULLERY, [fōōl'-er-i], *n.* the place or the works where cloth was fulled.

FULL-EYED, [fōōl'-īd'], *adj.* having wide-open, prominent eyes.

FULL FACE, [fōōl'-fās'], *adj. and adv.* (of a portrait) with the sitter directly facing the camera or artist.

FULL-FACED, [fōōl'-fāst'], *adj.* with a full broad-boned or plump face.

FULL-GROWN, [fōōl'-grōn'], *adj.* mature in development, grown to full size.

FULL-HEARTED, [fōōl'-haht'-id], *adj.* in high spirits, elated; courageous; generous.

FULLING-MILL, [fōōl-ing-mil'], *n.* a mill for processing cloths by fulling.

FULL-LENGTH, [fōōl'-length'], *adj.* extending the whole length, stretched out to the full.

FULLNESS, see FULNESS.

FULL-ORBED, [fōōl'-awbd'], *adj.* having the disk fully illuminated and displayed.

FULL-PITCHER, [fōōl'-pich'-er], *n.* (*cricket*) a ball that pitches inside the batting crease, or that hits the stumps without previously touching the ground.

FULL-RIGGED, [fōōl'-rigd'], *adj.* set with square-rig on all three masts.

FULL-RIGGED

FULL-STOP, [fōōl'-stop'], *n.* the period (.) used in punctuation, *esp.* to denote the end of a sentence.

FULL-SWING (1), [fōōl-swing'], *n.* the highest speed, activity and efficiency.

FULL-SWING (2), [fōōl'-swing'], *adv.* at the highest pitch of organized movement, at full speed.

FULLY, [fŏŏl-i], *adv.* to the full, in full manner; entirely.
FULMAR, [fŏŏl'-mah(r)], *n.* a sea-bird resembling the gull, the petrel *Fulmarus glacialis*, native of the Arctic. [OIcel. *full* foul and *mar* sea-mew].
FULMINANT, [ful'-min-ant], *adj.* thundering; (*med.*) developing extremely quickly. [L. *fulminans*].
FULMINATE (1), [ful'-min-āt], *n.* (*chem.*) a highly combustible compound of fulminic acid with a base, detonated by percussion, heat, or friction.
FULMINATE (2), [ful-min-āt'], *v.t.* to cause to explode, detonate; *v.i.* to explode loudly, to detonate; to flash; to utter vehement denunciations. [L. *fulminare* to lighten].
FULMINATING, [ful'-min-āt-ing], *adj.* thundering; exploding loudly and violently, detonating; threatening vehemently; (*med.*) fulminant; **f. powder**, an explosive containing nitre, carbonate of potash, and sulphur.
FULMINATION, [ful-min-ā'-shun], *n.* the act of fulminating; a chemical explosion; violent threats or censure. [L. *fulminatio*].
FULMINATORY, [ful'-min-āt'-er-i], *adj.* characterized by, or given to, fulmination.
FULMINEOUS, [ful-min'-i-us], *adj.* of or resembling thunder.
FULMINIC, [ful'-min-ik], *adj.* explosive; **f. acid**, an acid forming unstable explosive salts.
FULNESS, FULLNESS, [fŏŏl'-nes], *n.* the condition of being full.
FULSOME, [fŏŏl'-sum], *adj.* patently insincere, servile, disgusting, gross, over-fat.
FULSOMELY, [fŏŏl'-sum-li], *adv.* in a fulsome way.
FULSOMENESS, [fŏŏl'-sum-nes], *n.* the condition of being fulsome.
FULVID, [ful'-vid], *adj.* fulvous. [MedL. *fulvidus*].
FULVOUS, [ful'-vus], *adj.* tawny. [L. *fulvus*].
FUM, [fum], *n.* a fabulous bird, the guardian phœnix of China; the fung. [Chin. *hwang*].
FUMADO, [fewm-ah'-dō], *n.* a smoked pilchard. [Sp. *fumado* smoked].
FUMAGE†, [fewm'-ij], *n.* a tax on chimneys, hearth-money, mentioned as being enforced in the Domesday Book. [MedL. *fumagium*].
FUMARATE, [fewm'-er-āt], *n.* a salt of fumaric acid.
FUMARIC, [fewm-āer'-ik], *adj.* resembling, or obtained from, fumitory.
FUMAROLE, [fewm'-er-ōl], *n.* a natural hole from which smoke rises in a volcano or sulphur-mine. [L. *fumariolum*].
FUMATORIUM, [fewm'-at-aw'-ri-um], *n.* a room, cupboard, or place where articles are fumigated.
FUMATORY, [fewm'-at-er-i], *n.* a fumatorium.
FUMBLE, [fumbl], *v.t. and i.* to manage awkwardly, bungle; to fail to pick up something cleanly, to make awkward clumsy movements. [Unkn.].
FUMBLER, [fum'-bler], *n.* a person who fumbles.
FUMBLING, [fumbl'-ing], *adj.* groping, controlling the hands awkwardly.
FUMBLINGLY, [fumbl'-ing-li], *adv.* in a fumbling way.
FUME (1), [fewm], *n.* pungent smoke, strong bitter smell, acidulous vapour, exhalation; a hot blast of air; outbreak of rage, violent turmoil of emotion; †a slight witticism; excessive flattery. [L. *fumus*].
FUME (2), [fewm], *v.t.* to dry in smoke; to give a smoky finish or colour to a wood surface; to disinfect with vapour, fumigate; †to flatter excessively; *v.i.* to give off fumes, to smoke, to pass off in the form of vapour; to be in a rage, to be in a turmoil of emotion, to fret, chafe, fidget in irritation.
FUMELESS, [fewm'-les], *adj.* without fumes.
FUMET†, [fewm'-et], *n.* the dung of deer, etc.; the smell of high game, fumette. [Fr. *fumet*].
FUMETTE, [fewm-et'], *n.* the smell of high game, or of stale meat when cooking. [Fr. *fumette*].
FUMEWORT, [fewm'-wurt], *n.* fumitory.
FUMID†, [fewm'-id], *adj.* fuming, smoky. [L. *fumidus*].
FUMIDITY, [fewm'-id-i-ti], *n.* smokiness.
FUMIDNESS, [fewm'-id-nes], *n.* fumidity.
FUMIFEROUS†, [fewm-if'-er-us], *adj.* making smoke. [FUME (1) and L. *ferre* to bear].
FUMIGANT, [fewm'-i-gant], *adj.* fume-producing. [L. *fumigans*].
FUMIGATE, [fewm'-i-gāt], *v.t.* to disinfect by smoke or vapour. [L. *fumigare*].
FUMIGATION, [fewm'-i-gā'-shun], *n.* the act of fumigating. [L. *fumigatio*].
FUMIGATORY, [fewm'-i-gāt'-er-i], *adj.* having the power of fumigating.
FUMILY, [fewm'-i-li], *adv.* in a fuming fashion.
FUMINGLY, [fewm'-ing-li], *adv.* in a fuming way.
FUMISHNESS, [fewm'-ish-nes], *n.* chafing, fretfulness.
FUMITORY, [fewm'-i-ter-i], *n.* a herb plant of the genus *Fumaria*. [OFr. *fumeterre* from MedL. *fumus terrae* the smoke of the earth].
FUMOUS, [fewm'-us], *adj.* full of smoky fumes or vapours. [L. *fumosus*].
FUMY, [fewm'-i], *adj.* full of fumes, fumous.
FUN (1), [fun], *n.* matter for laughter, sport, cause or source of merriment; amusement, spontaneous entertainment, jollity. [~ME. *fonnen* to be foolish].
FUN† **(2)**, [fun], *v.i.* to cause fun, to be amusing.
FUNAMBULATE, [few-nam'-byŏŏ-lāt], *v.t.* to walk on a rope. [L. *funis* rope and *ambulare* to walk].
FUNAMBULATION, [few-nam'-byŏŏ-lā'-shun], *n.* tight-rope walking.
FUNAMBULATORY, [few-nam'-byŏŏ-lāt'-er-i], *adj.* given to performing on a tight-rope.
FUNAMBULIST, [few-nam'-byŏŏ-list], *n.* a performer on a tight-rope.
FUNCTION (1), [fungk'-shun], *n.* the activity, or line of progress, pertaining to a person or object which is peculiarly vital to its nature; the action or vitality natural to a physiological or biological organ; specially designed activity; the series of duties attached to a particular office; something carried out or performed; a gathering of people under official control; a ceremony; a large social gathering; (*math.*) a quantity related to another having corresponding values. [L. *functio* performance].
FUNCTION (2), [fungk'-shun], *v.i.* to act, to fulfil in action characteristic powers of work or vitality.
FUNCTIONAL, [fungk'-shun-al], *adj.* relating to, or affecting, functions but not structure; having a practical purpose in action.
FUNCTIONALIZE, [fungk'-shun-al-iz], *v.t.* to appoint to certain functions.
FUNCTIONALLY, [fungk'-shun-al-i], *adv.* by means of the functions, in relation to the functions.
FUNCTIONARY, [fungk'-shun-er-i], *n.* a public official; anyone entrusted to perform a duty.
FUNCTIONLESS, [fungk'-shun-les], *adj.* having no function.
FUND (1), [fund], *n.* a stock, store, *esp.* a sum of money; money loaned to the government and constituting a national debt; (*pl.*) capital, cash resources; government securities. [L. *fundus* basis].
FUND (2), [fund], *v.t.* to provide a fund for paying interest; to add to a fund.
FUNDABLE, [fund'-abl], *adj.* able to be funded.
FUNDAMENT, [fund'-a-ment], *n.* the seat of the body; the buttocks, the anus. [L. *fundamentum*].
FUNDAMENTAL (1), [fund'-a-ment'-al], *n.* basic principle, radical element, a component of the groundwork of a system, an essential.
FUNDAMENTAL (2), [fund'-a-ment'-al], *adj.* relating to, or connected with, the basic principles or foundations of anything, primary, radical, essential; **f. bass**, (*mus.*) the lowest note sustaining a chord.
FUNDAMENTALISM, [fund'-a-ment'-al-izm], *n.* a firm belief in the necessity to resort to considered fundamental principles as a guidance to thought and action; *esp.* entire acceptance of the truth and reality of the story of the Creation in the Old Testament.
FUNDAMENTALIST, [fund'-a-ment'-al-ist], *n.* a person whose attitude is based on fundamentalism.
FUNDAMENTALITY, [fund'-a-ment-al'-i-ti], *n.* that which is fundamental.
FUNDAMENTALLY, [fund'-a-ment'-al-i], *adv.* in a fundamental way.
FUNDED, [fund'-id], *adj.* invested in state securities; deposited in a fund from which payments or interest are drawn; **f. debt**, public debt in the form of securities issued for a term of years.
FUND-HOLDER, [fund'-hōld'-er], *n.* a person who owns property in the public funds.
FUNDI, [fund'-i], *n.* a species of *Paspalum*, grown in W. Africa as a grain.
FUNDLESS, [fund'-les], *adj.* having no capital, destitute of funds.
FUNEBRAL, [few-nē'-bral], *adj.* connected with, or relating to, a funeral; funereal. [L. *funebris*].
FUNEBRIAL, [few-nē'-bri-al], *adj.* funebral.
FUNERAL (1), [few'-ner-al], *n.* burial of the dead with ceremonial rites; a procession attending the corpse on the way to the cemetery. [L. *funeralia*].
FUNERAL (2), [few'-ner-al], *adj.* relating to a funeral.
FUNEREAL, [few-nēer'-i-al], *adj.* suitable for, or relating to, a funeral; mournful. [L. *funereus*].
FUNEREALLY, [few-nēer'-i-al-i], *adv.* in a funereal way.

FUNEST†, [fewn-est'], *adj.* doleful, mournful. [L. *funestus*].

FUNGACEOUS, [fung-gā'-shus], *adj.* relating to the fungi.

FUNGAL (1), [fung'-gal], *n.* a fungus.

FUNGAL (2), [fung'-gal], *adj.* belonging to the fungi.

FUNGI, [fung'-gī], *n.(pl.)* of FUNGUS.

FUNGIA, [fun'-ji-a], *n.* a genus of corals, resembling a mushroom in form.

FUNGIBLES, [fun'-jiblz], *n.(pl.)* *(leg.)* in Scotland, goods that are mutually interchangeable in the execution of a contract. [MedL. *fungibilis*].

FUNGIC, [fun'-jik], *adj.* obtained from fungi; **f. acid**, an acid extracted from certain fungi.

FUNGICIDE, [fun'-ji-sīd], *n.* a preparation for killing fungi.

FUNGIFORM, [fung'-gi-fawm], *adj.* having the shape of a mushroom.

FUNGIN, [fun'-jin], *n.* the substance forming the fleshy part of a mushroom.

FUNGITE, [fun'-jit], *n.* a variety of fossil coral.

FUNGIVOROUS, [fun-jiv'-er-us], *adj.* feeding on fungi.

FUNGOID, [fung'-goid], *adj.* having the characteristics of a mushroom. [L. *fungus* mushroom and Gk. *oeides* like].

FUNGOLOGIST, [fung-gol'-o-jist], *n.* one who studies fungi.

FUNGOLOGY, [fung-gol'-o-ji], *n.* the study of fungi. [L. *fungus* mushroom and Gk. *logos* speech].

FUNGOSITY, [fung-gos'-i-ti], *n.* fleshy growth resembling fungus, soft excrescence.

FUNGOUS, [fung'-gus], *adj.* having the characteristics of a fungus, spongy, of mushroom growth and structure. [L. *fungosus* spongy].

FUNGUS, (*pl.* **fungi, funguses**), [fung'-gus, fung'-gi, fung'-gus-iz], *n.* one of a class of flowerless plants comprising the mushrooms, toadstools and those cellular plants formed as mould, mildew, etc.; *(med.)* a spongy growth on a wound, proud-flesh; an affection of the skin caused by vegetable parasites. [L. *fungus* mushroom].

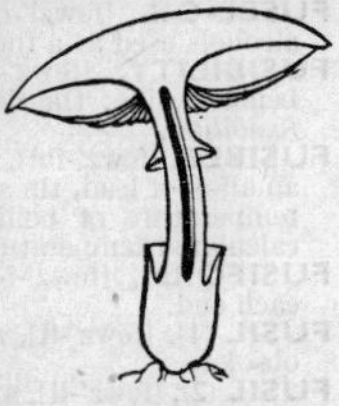

FUNGUS

FUNICLE, [few'-nikl], *n.* a small cord or fibre; *(bot.)* a little stalk by which the seed is joined to the placenta. [L. *funiculus* a little rope].

FUNICULAR, [few-nik'-yōō-ler], *adj.* joined by, worked by, a rope; pertaining to cords or fibres; **f. railway**, a railway consisting of two carriages connected by a system of metal cables running over pulley wheels, so weighted that the carriage descending causes the other to ascend. [L. *funiculus* a little rope].

FUNIS, [few'-nis], *n.* *(anat.)* the umbilical cord. [L. *funis* cord].

FUNK† **(1)**, [fungk], *n.* an offensive smell, stench. [Unkn.].

FUNK (2), [fungk], *n.* *(slang)* fear, timidity, a coward; **blue f.**, a state of utter terror. [Unkn.].

FUNK (3), [fungk], *v.t.* and *i.* *(slang)* to fear, to be afraid of, to be frightened by; to act as a coward, to feel fear.

FUNKY, [fungk'-i], *adj.* frightened, nervously timid in manner.

FUNNEL, [funl], *n.* a metal chimney or smoke-stack usually in a cylindrical form; a conical metal bowl tapering down to a tube in the bottom, and used for transferring liquid into a container with a narrow neck. [ME. *fonel* from L. *infundibulum* instrument for pouring into].

FUNNELLED, [fun'-eld], *adj.* provided with, or like, a funnel.

FUNNILY, [fun'-i-li], *adv.* in a funny way; **f. enough**, peculiar as it may seem.

FUNNIMENT, [fun'-i-ment], *n.* drollery, horseplay.

FUNNINESS, [fun'-i-nes], *n.* the quality of being funny.

FUNNING (1), [fun'-ing], *n.* drollery.

FUNNING (2), [fun'-ing], *adj.* joking.

FUNNY (1), [fun'-i], *n.* a light, clinker-built rowing-boat. [Uncert.].

FUNNY (2), [fun'-i], *adj.* laughable, full of fun; queer; peculiar; having the appearance of dishonesty.

FUNNYBONE, [fun'-i-bōn], *n.* the part of the elbow sensitive to knocks.

FUR (1), [fur], *n.* the short, closely set hair growing on the skin, and forming the protective coat of certain animals; animals growing this; such animal skin prepared for use as a coat, collar or cuff ornaments or lining; a coating or deposit of morbid matter collecting on the tongue; a chalky deposit left when undistilled water is boiled; *(her.)* one of a group of spots on a coat of arms representing a tone of colour or texture; **to make the f. fly**, to provoke enmity or actual hostilities. [OFr. *forre, fuerre* scabbard].

FUR (2), **(furring, furred)**, [fur], *v.t.* and *i.* to line, trim, cover with fur; to cover, coat with a morbid deposit; to level a surface by covering with thin strips of wood or casing to take plaster; to form a coating, to become furred.

FURACIOUS, [few-rā'-shus], *adj.* having a tendency to thieve, thievish. [L. *furari* to steal].

FURBELOW (1), [fur'-bel-ō], *n.* the seaweed, *Laminaria bulbosa*; the moth, *Scoliopteryx libatrix*.

FURBELOW (2), [fur'-bel-ō], *n.* a pleated flounce attached to a gown or petticoat. [~Fr. *falbala*].

FURBELOW (3), [fur'-bel-ō], *v.t.* to provide with a furbelow.

FURBISH, [fur'-bish], *v.t.* to rub or scour to brightness, to polish; **to f. up**, to clean up, smarten up, polish up. [ME. *forbischen* from OFr. *fourbir* to polish].

FURBISHABLE, [fur'-bish-abl], *adj.* able to be furbished.

FURBISHER, [fur'-bish-er], *n.* a person or thing that furbishes.

FURCATE (1), [fur'-kāt], *adj.* forked, furcated. [L. *furca* a fork].

FURCATE (2), [fur'-kāt], *v.t.* and *i.* to fork, to cause to divide.

FURCATED, [fur-kāt'-id], *adj.* forked; dividing like the prongs of a fork.

FURCATION, [fur-kā'-shun], *n.* the process of furcating; a branching like a fork.

FURCULA, [fur'-kyōō-la], *n.* *(ornith.)* a forked bone, the shoulder-girdle of a bird, which is formed by the united clavicles; the merrythought or wishbone. [L. *furcula* a little fork].

FURCULAR, [fur'-kyōō-ler], *adj.* fork-shaped.

FURFUR, [fur'-fur], *n.* *(path.)* scurf, dandruff; scales like bran being a sediment in the urine. [L. *furfur* bran].

FURFURACEOUS, [fur'-few-rā'-shus], *adj.* scaly; scurfy, resembling bran. [LL. *furfuraceus*].

FURFURAMIDE, [fur'-fur-a-mīd], *n.* *(chem.)* a white crystalline substance, the product of furfurol when treated with ammonia.

FURFURATION†, [fur'-fur-ā'-shun], *n.* the shedding of the skin of the head in the form of scurf.

FURFURINE, [fur'-fur-in], *n.* *(chem.)* a vegeto-alkali, formed by boiling furfuramide with a solution of caustic potash or by submitting furfuramide to heat.

FURFUROL, [fur'-fur-ol], *n.* *(chem.)* an oil obtained from distillation of bran, starch, etc.

FURIBONDO, [fewr'-i-bon'-dō], *adv.* *(mus.)* with furious energy. [It. *furibondo*].

FURIOSITY, [fewr'-i-os'-i-ti], *n.* madness, fury.

FURIOSO, [fewr'-i-ō'-sō], *adv.* *(mus.)* with great energy. [It. *furioso*].

FURIOUS, [fewr'-i-us], *adj.* raging; boisterous; rushing with impetuosity; transported with passion, frenzied; mad with rage, savagely angry. [L. *furiosus* full of rage].

FURIOUSLY, [fewr'-i-us-li], *adv.* in a furious fashion.

FURIOUSNESS, [fewr'-i-us-nes], *n.* the state of being furious.

FURL (1), [furl], *n.* the action of one who furls; that which is furled.

FURL (2), [furl], *v.t.* to fold, to roll up, as a sail; to roll up closely, to fold up compactly. [Uncert.].

FURLONG, [fur'-long], *n.* a measure of distance, the eighth of a mile, 40 poles, 220 yards. [OE. *furlang* the length of a furrow].

FURLOUGH (1), [fur'-lō], *n.* leave of absence granted to rank and file in the armed forces. [~Du. *verlop* permission].

FURLOUGH (2), [fur'-lō], *v.t.* to allow to go on furlough.

FURMETY, [furm'-i-ti], *n.* frumenty.

FURNACE, [fur'-nis], *n.* any enclosed fireplace for concentrating combustible matter to generate heat at high temperatures, a firebox. [OFr. *fornais* from L. *fornax*].

FURNIMENT†, [furn'-i-ment], *n.* furniture, fittings. [OFr. *fourniment*].

FURNISH, [furn'-ish], *v.t.* to supply with anything necessary, to equip, to fit up, to stock, to supply, *esp.* to fill (a house) with furniture and fittings. [OFr. *furnir* to provide].

FURNISHER, [furn'-ish-er], *n.* a person who furnishes; a shopkeeper who deals in furniture.

FURNISHMENT, [furn'-ish-ment], *n.* a supply, the act of furnishing.

FURNITURE, [fur'-nich-er], *n.* articles of equipment, those movable articles of domestic utility and convenience having a place in the rooms or apartments of a house; articles with a functional value constituting the equipment of a ship; full armour and equipment for horse and man, accoutrements; (*arch.*) brasswork of a house; (*print.*) a device for clamping pages together and fixing a uniform margin. [Fr. *fourniture*].

FUROR, [few'-raw(r)], *n.* rage, anger. [L. *furor*].

FURORE, [few'-raw(r)], *n.* an outburst of enthusiasm; an excited disturbance; a sensation. [It. *furore* rage].

FURRIER, [fu'-ri-er], *n.* a dealer in, or dresser of, furs.

FURRIERY, [fu'-ri-er-i], *n.* furs in general; trade of a furrier.

FURRING, [fur'-ring], *n.* the process or act of one who, or that which, furs; anything deposited as fur; that which is used to fur; (*naut.*) doubling planks on the side of a ship.

FURROW (1), [fu'-rō], *n.* the trench or channel in the ground made by a plough to receive the seed; a rut, long groove, cart-rut; a wrinkle on the face. [OE. *furh*].

FURROW (2), [fu'-rō], *v.t.* to make furrows in, to make grooves in, to plough; to cause deep wrinkles.

FURROW-DRAIN, [fu'-rō-drān], *n.* a deep open channel made by a plough for draining purposes.

FURROW-FACED, [fu'-rō-fāst'], *adj* having a tired, wrinkled face.

FURROW-WEED, [fu'-rō-wēd'], *n.* a weed on ploughed land.

FURROWY, [fu'-rō-i], *adj.* full of furrows, with furrows.

FURRY, [fur'-ri], *adj.* covered with fur; dressed in fur; consisting of or resembling fur; **f. dance**, a festival dance through the streets of Helston, Cornwall, which takes place on the 8th May.

FURTHER (1), [fur'-THer], *adj.* farther, more distant, more remote; additional, more, besides what is done or spoken of, etc. [OE. *furthra*].

FURTHER (2), [fur'-THer], *adv.* to a greater distance or degree; besides, also, moreover. [OE. *furthor*].

FURTHER (3), [fur'-THer], *v.t.* to bring to a higher, more forward stage of development, progress, or maturity; to promote, to help forward. [OE. *fyrthrian* to advance].

FURTHERANCE, [fur'-THER-ants], *n.* the act of advancing; the distance advanced.

FURTHERER, [fur'-THer-er], *n.* a person who furthers.

FURTHERMORE, [fur'-THer-maw(r)], *adv.* moreover, besides, in addition.

FURTHERMOST, [fur'-THer-mōst], *adj.* remotest, farthermost. [FURTHER and MOST].

FURTHEST (1), [fur'-THest], *adj.* most remote, most distant either in time or place.

FURTHEST (2), [fur'-THest], *adv.* at, or to, the greatest distance.

FURTIVE, [fur'-tiv], *adj.* covert, stealthy; secret, surreptitious. [L. *furtivus* stolen, secret].

FURTIVELY, [fur'-tiv-li], *adv.* in a furtive way.

FURTIVENESS, [fur'-tiv-nes], *n.* the quality of being furtive.

FURUNCLE, [few'-rungkl], *n.* (*med.*) a small inflammatory tumour, a boil. [L. *furunculus* petty thief].

FURUNCULOSIS, [fur-rungk'-ew-lōs'-is], *n.* (*med.*) a disease characterized by extensive boils. [FURUNCLE and Gk. *-osis* denoting condition].

FURY, [fyōōer'-i], *n.* violent emotional agitation, rage, frenzy; a violent person; (*myth.*) a goddess of vengeance. [L. *furia* rage].

FURY-LIKE, [fewr'-i-līk], *adj.* raging, furious.

FURZE, [furz], *n.* a thorny, matted, branched evergreen shrub of the genus *Ulex*, having yellow flowers, and spines instead of leaves; gorse, whin. [OE. *fyrs*].

FURZECHAT, [furz'-chat], *n.* a species of bird, the whinchat.

FURZELING, [furz'-ling], *n.* a species of bird, the Dartford warbler, *Melizophilus undatus*.

FURZEN, [furz-en], *adj.* covered with furze, furzy.

FURZY, [furz'-i], *adj.* covered, overgrown with, furze.

FUSAIN, [few'-zān], *n.* a dull, easily powdering coal of homogeneous botanical origin with a firm structure, used as a charcoal crayon. [Fr. *fusain*].

FUSAROLE, [few'-zer-ōl], *n.* (*arch.*) a semicircular, beaded form of moulding placed beneath the echinus or quarter-round of Doric, Ionic, or Corinthian columns. [It. *fusaruolo* spindle whorl].

FUSAROLE

FUSCATION†, [fus-kā'-shun], *n.* a darkening.

FUSCINE, [fus'-sin], *n.* a brownish matter extracted from empyreumatic oil. [L. *fuscus* dark].

FUSCITE, [fus'-sīt], *n.* (*min.*) crystallized pyrargillite.

FUSCOUS, [fus'-kus], *adj.* dark in colour, brownish black. [L. *fuscus* swarthy].

FUSE (1), FUZE, [fewz], *n.* a tube filled with explosive or ignitable matter used as a protective device when dynamiting; a device to explode a shell; (*elect.*) a safety device consisting of fusible metal, inserted into an electric circuit, which melts when the current exceeds a specific power. [L. *fusus* spindle].

FUSE (2), [fewz], *v.t. and i.* to melt, to liquefy by heat; to cause to mingle together, to unite as by melting together; to be melted; to be liquefied, to become blended. [L. *fusus*, *p.pt.* of *fundere* to melt].

FUSEE (1), FUZEE, [few-zē'], *n.* the grooved conical wheel of a watch or clock, round which the chain is wound. [Fr. *fusée* from ~L. *fusus* spindle].

FUSEE (2), [few-zē'], *n.* a small neat musket; a match with a head that glows for a long time, used by smokers for igniting tobacco out of doors. [Fr. *fusée* a spindleful].

FUSELAGE, [few'-zil-ahzh'], *n.* the body part of an aeroplane.

FUSEL-OIL, [fewzl'-oil'], *n.* a crude form of mixed alcohols used as a fuel.

FUSIBILITY, [fewz'-i-bil'-i-ti], *n.* the quality of being fusible; the degree of fusible capacity. [Fr. *fusibilité*].

FUSIBLE, [fewz'-ibl], *adj.* able to be fused; **f. metal**, an alloy of lead, tin and bismuth, which melts at the temperature of boiling water, or at a specifically calculated temperature.

FUSIFORM, [fewz'-i-fawm], *adj.* (*bot.*) tapering to each end.

FUSIL (1), [fewz'-il], *n.* a light flint-lock musket now obsolete.

FUSIL (2), [fewz'-il], *n.* (*her.*) a figure so named from its spindle shape. [L. *fusellum* little spindle].

FUSILE, [fewz'-īl], *adj.* capable of being melted by heat; flowing, as a liquid. [L. *fusilis*].

FUSILIER, FUSILEER, [fewz'-il-ēer'], *n.* in olden days, a soldier belonging to a regiment armed with fusils; now sometimes applied to riflemen.

FUSILLADE (1), [fewz'-il-ād'], *n.* a sustained discharge of fire-arms [Fr. *fusillade*].

FUSILLADE (2), [fewz'-il-ād'], *v.t.* to attack by a fusillade.

FUSION, [few'-zhun], *n.* the process of melting by heat; the condition of being melted; the act of blending; a coalition. [L. *fusio* a pouring out].

FUSS (1), [fus], *n.* an excited, nervous, and anxious state of mind, commotion, a tumult, bustle; unnecessary ado about trifles, angry complaint. [Unkn.].

FUSS (2), [fus], *v.i.* to make a fuss, to become nervously excited; to make much of trivialities.

FUSSILY, [fus'-i-li], *adv.* in a fussy way.

FUSSINESS, [fus'-i-nes], *n.* the condition of being fussy.

FUSSY, [fus'-i], *adj.* making a fuss, finicky over detail; fidgety.

FUST (1), [fust], *n.* (*arch.*) the shaft of a column. [L. *fustis* staff].

FUST (2), [fust], *n.* a strong musty smell, a stale smell. [OFr. *fust* cask].

FUST (3), [fust], *v.i.* to become mouldy, to become stale so as to smell. [FUST (2)].

FUSTANELLA, [fust'-a-nel'-a], *n.* the modern Greek's white kilt or stiff short skirt finishing at the knees. [Gk. *phoustani*].

FUSTED, [fust'-id], *adj.* ill-smelling, covered with mildew.

FUST

FUSTERIC, [fust'-er-ik], *n.* the yellow dye obtained from the fustet or fustic tree.

FUSTET, [fust'-et], *n.* young fustic, a Mexican tree, the sumach, *Rhus coriaria*, the leaves of which are used for tanning and for obtaining a yellow dye. [Fr. *fustet*].

FUSTIAN (1), [fust'-i-an], *n.* a kind of twilled cloth, corduroy; (*fig.*) a bombastic style of writing, turgid with adjectives and phrases. [OFr. *fustaigne*].
FUSTIAN (2), [fust'-i-an], *adj.* made of fustian; (*fig.*) bombastic in style.
FUSTIANIST, [fust'-i-an-ist], *n.* a person who writes in a bombastic style.
FUSTIC, [fust'-ik], *n.* the wood of a tropical American tree which yields a dingy yellow dye, *Chlorophora tinctoria*. [Pers. *pistah*].
FUSTIGATE, [fust'-i-gāt], *v.t.* to cudgel. [L. *fustigare*].
FUSTIGATION, [fust'-i-gā'-shun], *n.* a cudgelling or thrashing. [L. *fustigatio*].
FUSTILARIAN†, [fust'-il-āer'-i-an], *n.* a frowsy, stale-smelling, fat person, a low fellow.
FUSTILUG†, [fust'-i-lug'], *n.* a gross, fat, frowsy person, a fustilarian.
FUSTINESS, [fust'-i-nes], *n.* the state or quality of being fusty.
FUSTY, [fust'-i], *adj.* smelling stale, mouldy; (*fig.*) old-fashioned, pedantic, bookish.
FUSURE†, [few'-zher], *n.* a fusion. [L. *fusura* founding].
FUTCHEL, [fuch'-el], *n.* the timber beam along the bottom of a carriage supporting the axle-bar. [Unkn.].
FUTHORC, FUTHARC, [fōō'-THawk, fōō'-THahk], *n.* the Runic alphabet, so called from the first six letters, *f, u, th, o, r, k.*
FUTILE, [few'-tīl], *adj.* ineffectual, trifling, fruitless; superficial, worthless, inept. [L. *futilis*].
FUTILELY, [few'-tīl-li], *adv.* in a futile fashion.
FUTILENESS, [few'-tīl-nes], *n.* the quality of being futile.
FUTILITY, [few-til'-i-ti], *n.* futileness; a futile act. [L. *futilitas*].
FUTTOCK, [fut'-ok], *n.* (*naut.*) one of the lower timbers passing across the keel underneath the deck; **f. plates,** iron plates in a ship's top with sockets for the dead-eyes; **f. shrouds,** the small, short shrouds above the futtock plates. [Uncert.].
FUTURE (1), [few'-cher], *n.* the time which lies ahead; events that will occur; (*pl.*) (*comm.*) goods paid for at their price when the deal was made and not at their later price at the time of delivery.
FUTURE (2), [few'-cher], *adj.* occurring after the present, happening afterwards, having an existence in time later than the present; following life; **f. perfect,** (*gram.*) expressing the past in relation to an assumed future; **f. tense,** a modification of the verb expressing time to come. [L. *futurus*].
FUTURELESS, [few'-cher-les], *adj.* having a grim, comfortless future, without hope.
FUTURELY, [few'-cher-li], *adv.* in time to come.
FUTURISM, [few'-cher-izm], *n.* faith in the fulfilment of the prophecies made in the Bible; a movement in art rejecting convention and based on the free exploitation of line and colour according to non-realist vision, founded in Italy in the early years of the 20th century.
FUTURIST (1), [few'-cher-ist], *n.* an advocate of futurism, relating to futurism.
FUTURIST (2), [few'-cher-ist], *adj.* futuristic.
FUTURISTIC, [few'-cher-ist'-ik], *adj.* pertaining to, characteristic of, the futurists, *esp.* in art.
FUTURITION, [few'-cher-ish'-un], *n.* the state of being hereafter, existence in the future. [MedL. *futuritio*].
FUTURITY, [few-chew'-ri-ti], *n.* future time, time to come; the state of being yet to come; **f. stakes,** stakes raced for some time after competitors are nominated.
FUZE, see FUSE (1).
FUZEE, see FUSEE (1).
FUZZ (1), [fuz], *n.* a mass of fluff, a small tangle of fibre, hairs, threads. [Uncert.].
FUZZ (2), [fuz], *v.t.* to cover with fine particles.
FUZZ-BALL, [fuz'-bawl], *n.* a puff ball, a variety of *Lycoperdon* or *Bovista*.
FUZZLE, [fuzl], *v.t.* to inebriate. [Uncert.].
FUZZY, [fuz'-i], *adj.* fluffy; blurred.
FUZZY-WUZZY, [fuz'-i-wuz-i], *n.* slang name for a member of one of the savage tribes of the Sudan. [FUZZY].
FYKE, [fīk], *n.* (*U.S.*) a long bag-net used for catching fish. [Du. *fuik*].
FYLFOT, [fil'-fot], *n.* a symbol used as decoration in the Middle Ages, the swastika. [Uncert.].
FYRD†, [fēerd], *n.* the English army in Anglo-Saxon times. [OE. *fyrd*].

G

G, [jē], the seventh letter and the fifth consonant of the English alphabet; (*mus.*) the sign of the treble clef; **G-man,** (*U.S.*) a Federal Government police-agent.
GAB (1), [gab], *n.* (*coll.*) idle chatter, talkativeness; **the gift of the g.,** the ability to speak fluently and at great length.
GAB (2), (gabbing, gabbed), [gab], *v.i.* to chatter, prattle, to talk volubly and pointlessly. [~Du. *gabberen* to chatter].
GABARAGE†, [gab'-er-ij], *n.* rough packing cloth; formerly wrappers in which Irish goods were packed. [Unkn.].
GABARDINE, see GABERDINE.
GABBLE (1), [gabl], *n.* loud, rapid incoherent talk; inarticulate sounds rapidly uttered.
GABBLE (2), [gabl], *v.t. and i.* to chatter, jabber; to talk rapidly, loudly, and in confused manner; to utter rapidly, indistinctly and incoherently. [Echoic].
GABBLER, [gab'-ler], *n.* one who gabbles.
GABBRO, [gab'-rō], *n.* an igneous rock mainly composed of felspar and augite, and resembling granite. [It. *gabbro*].
GABBRONITE, [gab'-ron-īt], *n.* a yellow variety of scapolite similar to gabbro.
GABELLE, GABEL, [gab-el'], *n.* a tax, *esp.* a tax on salt imposed in France before the Revolution. [Fr. *gabelle* from Arab. *qabala*].
GABERDINE, [gab'-er-dēn'], *n.* a long coarse coat *esp.* as traditionally worn by Jews, a thin woollen material with a fine parallel rib. [OFr. *gauvardine*, ~MHGerm. *wallevart* a pilgrimage].
GABION, [gā'-bi-on], *n.* (*fort.*) a cylindrical basket of wicker-work or other material, filled with earth and used as a temporary defence, or to block a harbour mouth. [It. *gabbione* from LL. *gabia* cage].
GABIONNADE, [gā'-bi-on-ād'], *n.* an obstruction or protective work made of gabions. [Fr. *gabionnade*].
GABLE, [gābl], *n.* the triangular top part of the end wall of a building; the end wall of a building, having a top of this shape; a piece of architecture in this form. [OFr. *gable* from OIcel. *gafl*].
GABLE-END, [gābl'-end'], *n.* an end wall of a building, terminating in a gable. 
GABLET, [gāb'-let], *n.* a small ornamental gable built as a canopy. [AFr. *gablet*].

GABLE

GABLE-WINDOW, [gābl'-win-dō], *n.* a window in a gable.
GABY, [gā'-bi], *n.* a silly, foolish person, a simpleton. [Unkn.].
GAD (1), [gad], *n.* the tip of a spear or arrow-head; a pointed mining chisel or wedge; a spear; a measuring rod, a measure of length; a rod, bar, or ingot of metal; (*hist.*) a metal spike. [OIcel. *gaddr*].
GAD (2), (gadding, gadded), [gad], *v.i.* to wander about aimlessly in pursuit of pleasure or diversion; (*archaic*) (of a plant) to straggle. [~OE. *gædeling* companion].
GADABOUT, [gad'-ab-owt], *n.* a person fond of gadding.
GADDER, [gad'-er], *n.* a gadabout.
GADDINGLY, [gad'-ing-li], *adv.* in a gadding fashion.

GADDISH, [gad'-ish], *adj.* inclined to gad about.
GADELLE, [gad-el'], *n.* a French variety of currant. [Fr. *gadelle*].
GADFLY, [gad'-flī'], *n.* the horse-fly, the sting of which is often maddening to animals; a gadder; (*fig.*) a person who annoys or torments.
GADGET, [gaj'-et], *n.* (*coll.*) an ingenious contrivance or appliance, a cunning mechanical device. [Unkn.].
GADHELIC (1), [gad-el'-ik], *n.* (*philol.*) the language spoken by the Gaels. [Ir. *Gaedheal* Gael].
GADHELIC (2), [gad-el'-ik], *adj.* (*philol.*) pertaining to the Gaels or their language.
GADI, [gad'-i], *n.* the state-throne of an Indian ruler; (*fig.*) sovereign power or office. [Hind. *gaddi* cushion].
GADIDAE, [gad'-id-ē], *n.(pl.)* (*zool.*) the group of fishes including the cod-fish, haddock, etc. [Gk. *gados*].
GADLING, [gad'-ling], *n.* one of the small metal spikes on the knuckles of leather or mail gauntlets.
GADOID (1), [gad'-oid], *n.* a member of the cod-fish family. [Gk. *gados* cod and *oeides* like].
GADOID (2), [gad'-oid], *adj.* pertaining to the cod-fishes.
GADOLINITE, [gad'-ol-in-īt], *n.* a black silicate of yttrium, iron, glucinum, etc. [J. *Gadolin*, the mineralogist].
GADOLINIUM, [gad'-ol-in'-i-um], *n.* the chemical element Gd, present in gadolinite.
GADROON, [gad-rōōn'], *n.* (*arch.*) one of the small rounded protuberances forming an ornamental edge or border on gold and silver articles, or in architecture, etc. [Fr. *godron*].
GADUS, [gad'-us], *n.* the genus of fishes including the cod. [Gk. *gados* cod].
GADWALL, [gad'-wawl], *n.* the migratory duck, *Anas streperus*. [Unkn.].
GAEKWAR, GAIKWAR, [gī'-kwah(r)], *n.* the title of the ruler of Baroda. [Marathi *gaekwar* cow-herd].
GAELIC (1), [gā'-lik], *n.* the Celtic language spoken by the Gaels of Scotland, Ireland, and the Isle of Man. [Scots Gael. *Gaidheal*].
GAELIC (2), [gā'-lik], *adj.* pertaining to the Gaels or to their language; *esp.* pertaining to the Scottish Gaels.
GAFF (1), [gaf], *n.* a light barbed fishing spear; a stick fitted with an iron hook for landing salmon, etc.; (*naut.*) a boom or yard used to extend the top portion of certain fore-and-aft sails. [Fr. *gaffe* a boat-hook].
GAFF (2), [gaf], *n.* (*slang*) an inferior type of theatre or place of entertainment. [Unkn.].
GAFF (3), [gaf], *n.* (*slang*) nonsense, foolish talk; **to blow the g.** (*slang*) to reveal a secret. [Uncert.].
GAFFE, [gaf], *n.* a blunder, indiscretion, an embarrassing mistake. [Fr. *gaffe*].
GAFFER, [gaf'-er], *n.* an old rustic; an elderly fellow; a boss, foreman, overlooker. [Contraction of GODFATHER OR GRANDFATHER].
GAFFLE†, [gafl], *n.* an artificial spur, put on fighting cocks; a steel lever to bend crossbows. [Du. *gaffel*].
GAG (1), [gag], *n.* something thrust into, or placed over, a person's mouth to prevent him from speaking or crying out; (*surg.*) a device for keeping the mouth open as wide as possible during an operation; (*parl.*) a closure of a debate; (*theatre*) an impromptu remark introduced as an addition to, or substitution for, the author's script by an actor; (*slang*) a joke, funny story; a wheeze, excuse; a hoax, lie.
GAG (2), (**gagging, gagged**), [gag], *v.t.* to silence forcibly by means of a gag; (*fig.*) to deny freedom of speech or expression to; (*slang*) to deceive, hoax; *v.i.* to add or substitute one's own remarks in acting. [ME. *gaggen* to suffocate].
GAGA, [gag'-ah], *adj.* (*slang*) gibbering incoherently; crazy, mad, deranged. [Imitative].
GAGE (1), [gāj], *n.* a pledge, something given as a security; something thrown down as a challenge; a challenge. [Fr. *gage*].
GAGE (2), see GAUGE.
GAGE (3), [gāj], *v.t.* to pledge, offer as security. [Fr. *gager*].
GAGER, [gāj'-er], *n.* one who gages.
GAGGER, [gag'-er], *n.* one who gags; a lifter used by founders, in the form of a light T-shaped piece of iron.
GAGGLE (1), [gagl], *n.* a group or flock of geese. [~OIcel. *gaggl*].
GAGGLE (2), [gagl], *v.i.* (of geese) to cackle.
GAIETY, [gā'-et-i], *n.* the state or quality of being gay, merriment, cheerfulness; (*pl.*) that which is gay, festivities. [Fr. *gaieté*].
GAIKWAR, see GAEKWAR.
GAILY, [gā'-li], *adv.* in a gay manner.
GAIN (1), [gān], *n.* the act or process of gaining; that which is gained, profit, earnings, rewards. [OFr. *gain, gaain*].
GAIN (2), [gān], *n.* (*carp.*) a groove in a piece of wood. [Uncert.].
GAIN (3), [gān], *v.t.* to obtain, to acquire (something advantageous); to obtain by industry, to earn; to acquire as an addition, increase, profit, or reward; to obtain by merit, superiority, success; to win; to reach, attain; (of a watch, etc.) to increase in rate by; to save (time); *v.i.* to benefit, to derive advantage from; to improve; to increase; (of a clockwork mechanism) to work at a faster rate than is accurate; **to g. on, upon,** to overtake; to outdistance; to encroach upon; **to g. ground,** to move faster than; (*fig.*) to make progress; **to g. time,** to secure the delay or putting-off of something; **to g. the wind,** (*naut.*) to reach the windward side of another ship. [ME. *gainen* from OIcel. *gagn* advantage and OFr. *gaaigner* to reap profit from cultivation].
GAINABLE, [gān'-abl], *adj.* capable of being gained.
GAIN-CONTROL, [gān'-kon-trōl'], *n.* (*wirel.*) the volume-control on a wireless receiver.
GAINER, [gān'-er], *n.* one who gains.
GAINFUL, [gān'-fōōl], *adj.* profitable, advantageous; eager for gain.
GAINFULLY, [gān'-fōōl-i], *adv.* in a gainful manner.
GAINFULNESS, [gān'-fōōl-nes], *n.* profit, advantage.
GAININGS, [gān'-ingz], *n.(pl.)* that which is gained, earnings, profits, winnings.
GAINLESS, [gān'-les], *adj.* providing no gain.
GAINLESSNESS, [gān'-les-nes], *n.* the quality of being gainless.
GAINLY†, [gān'-li], *adj.* comely, graceful, shapely. [ME. *geinlich* from OIcel. *gegn*].
GAINSAY, [gān-sā'], *v.t.* to contradict, to deny what another says, to dispute. [ME. *gainseien* from OIcel. *gegn* against, and SAY].
GAINSAYER, [gān'-sā'-er], *n.* one who gainsays.
GAIR-FOWL, [gāer-fowl'], *n.* the gare-fowl.
GAIT (1), [gāt], *n.* manner of walking or moving. [GATE (2)].
GAIT (2), [gāt], *n.* (*dial.*) a single sheaf of corn tied near the top. [Unkn.].
GAIT (3), [gāt], *v.t.* to stack (corn) in simple sheaves instead of stooks. [*Prec.*].
GAITED, [gāt'-id], *adj.* walking with a particular gait.
GAITER (1), [gāt'-er], *n.* a covering of leather or cloth fitting over the ankle and the leg below the knee. [Fr. *guêtre*].
GAITER † (2), [gāt'-er], *n.* the dogwood, *Cornus sanguinea*; the spindle-tree, *Euonymus europæus*. [Uncert.].
GAITER (3), [gāt'-er], *v.t.* to dress or furnish with gaiters.
GAL, [gal], *n.* (*slang*) a girl. [GIRL].
GALA, [gā'-la, gah'-la], *n.* an occasion for merry-making, feasting and entertainment, a festival, *esp.* one in which competitions, races, etc., are held. [It. *gala*].
GALACTAGOGUE, [ga-lak'-ta-gog], *n.* a medicine which encourages the secretion of milk. [GALACTO and Gk. *agogos* leading].
GALACTIA, [ga-lak'-ti-a], *n.* (*med.*) an excessive or morbid flow of milk. [Gk. *gala galaktos* milk].
GALACTIC, [ga-lak'-tik], *adj.* lactic; pertaining to the Milky Way. [Gk. *galaktikos* milky].
GALACTIN, [ga-lak'-tin], *n.* a vegetable substance extracted from the sap of the cow-tree of tropical America, *Brosimum Galactodendron*; the element in milk causing coagulation; a gelatinous substance said to be found in milk.
GALACTITE†, [ga-lak'-tīt], *n.* a precious white-stone; natrolite, the milk-stone. [Gk. *galaktites*].
GALACTO-, *pref.* milk. [Gk. *gala galaktos* milk].
GALACTOCELE, [ga-lak'-tō-sēl'], *n.* a tumour in the breast during lactation, due to an obstruction in the mammary glands. [GALACTO and Gk. *kele* tumour].
GALACTODENDRON, [ga-lak'-tō-den'-dron], *n.* the cow-tree or milk-tree. [GALACTO and Gk. *dendron* a tree].
GALACTOMETER, [gal'-ak-tom'-it-er], *n.* an instrument for measuring the specific gravity of milk. [GALACTO and METER].
GALACTOPHAGIST, [gal'-ak-tof'-aj-ist], *n.* one whose chief food is milk.
GALACTOPHAGOUS, [gal'-ak-tof'-ag-us], *adj.* living on milk. [Gk. *galaktophagos*].
GALACTOPHOROUS, [gal'-ak-tof'-er-us], *adj.* yielding milk. [Gk. *galaktophoros*].

GALACTOPOIETIC, [gal'-ak-tō-poi-et'-ik], *adj.* tending to make or produce milk. [GALACTO and Gk. *poietikos* making].
GALACTORRHOEA, [gal'-ak-to-rē'-a], *n.* (*med.*) an excessive secretion of milk. [GALACTO and Gk. *rhoia* flowing].
GALA DRESS, [gā'-la-, gah'-la-dres'], *n.* a bright-coloured, fancy costume worn at a gala.
GALAGO, [ga-lā'-gō], *n.* an African genus of small, long-tailed lemurs. [Native].
GALAH, [ga-lah'], *n.* a variety of Australian cockatoo. [Native].
GALALITH, [gal'-a-lith], *n.* a hard, incombustible substance made from milk. [Gk. *gala* milk and *lithos* stone].
GALANGAL, see GALINGALE.
GALANTHUS, [ga-lan'-thus], *n.* the snowdrop genus of plants. [Gk. *gala* milk and *anthos* flower].
GALANTINE, [gal'-an-tēn'], *n.* a dish of veal, chicken, or other white meat, boned, minced, tied up, boiled, and served cold. [Fr. *galantine*].
GALANTY-SHOW, [gal-an'-ti-shō'], *n.* a silhouette display in which the shadows of moving puppets are thrown on to a screen; (*coll.*) a lavish spectacular ceremony or theatrical performance.

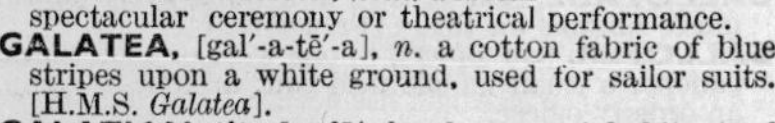

GALAGO

GALATEA, [gal'-a-tē'-a], *n.* a cotton fabric of blue stripes upon a white ground, used for sailor suits. [H.M.S. *Galatea*].
GALATIAN (1), [ga-lā'-shun], *n.* an inhabitant of Galatia, in Asia Minor.
GALATIAN (2), [ga-lā'-shun], *adj.* pertaining to Galatia.
GALAXY, [gal'-ak-si], *n.* the Milky Way, a luminous girdle composed of myriads of stars, individually indistinguishable, stretching across the heavens; (*fig.*) an assemblage of outstanding persons or things, a spectacular array. [Gk. *galaxias*].
GALBAN, [gal'-ban], *n.* galbanum.
GALBANUM, [gal'-ban-um], *n.* a thick resinous juice or gum obtained from a species of *Ferula*, used medicinally. [~Gk. *khalbane*].
GALE (1), [gāl], *n.* a violent blustery wind; (*poet.*) a gentle breeze. [Uncert.].
GALE (2), [gāl], *n.* a periodical money payment. [OE. *gagel*].
GALE (3), [gāl], *n.* the bog-myrtle, *Myrica Gale.* [~GAVEL].
GALEA, [gā'-li-a], *n.* (*bot., zool.*) a structure or process resembling a helmet in shape or function. [L. *galea* leather-helmet].
GALEATE, [gā'-li-āt], *adj.* (*bot., zool.*) galeated. [L. *galeatus* helmeted].
GALEATED, [gā'-li-āt-id], *adj.* (*bot., zool.*) covered with a structure resembling a helmet in shape or function; shaped like a helmet; wearing a helmet.
GALEENY, [ga-lē'-ni], *n.* a guinea-fowl. [Span. *gallina* (*morisca*) Moorish hen].
GALEGA, [ga-lē'-ga], *n.* goat's rue, a genus of leguminous plants. [MdL. *galega*].
GALENA, [ga-lē'-na], *n.* native sulphide of lead. [Gk. *galene*].
GALENIC, [gā-lē'-nik], *adj.* pertaining to Galen or to his methods; relating to remedies consisting of vegetable substances or herbs. [*Galen* the famous Greek physician].
GALENISM, [gā-len-izm], *n.* the teaching of Galen.
GALENIST, [gā'-len-ist], *n.* a disciple of Galen.
GALERICULATE, [gal'-er-ik'-yoo-lāt], *adj.* covered or furnished as with a cap. [L. *galericulum* a little cap].
GALERITE, [gal-ēer'-īt], *n.* a fossil sea-urchin. [L. *galerum* cap].
GALETTE, [ga-let'], *n.* a flat French cake of bread or pastry. [Fr. *galette*].
GALILEAN (1), [gal'-i-lē'-an], *n.* a native of Galilee; one of an anti-Roman sect among the Jews called after Judas, a Galilean. [Gk. *Galilaia* Galilee].
GALILEAN (2), [gal'-i-lē'-an], *adj.* pertaining to Galilee.
GALILEAN (3), [gal'-i-lē'-an], *adj.* pertaining to *Galileo*, the Italian mathematician and physicist; **G. telescope,** a telescope invented by Galileo, having a concave lens in the eyepiece.
GALILEE, [gal'-i-lē], *n.* (*eccles. antiq.*) a porch or chapel, usually situated at the west end of a church. [*Galilee* in Palestine].
GALIMATIAS, GALLIMATIAS, [gal'-i-mat'-i-as], *n.* confused nonsensical talk; gibberish. [Fr. *galimatias*].
GALINGALE, GALANGAL, [gal'-ing-gāl], *n.* a sedge, the sweet cyperus, *Cyperus longus*; the aromatic roots of an Asiatic plant, *Alpinia officinarum.* [~*Arab khalanjan*].
GALIONGEE, [gal-yon-jē'], *n.* a Turkish sailor. [Turk. *qalyunji*].
GALIOT, see GALLIOT.
GALIPOT, [gal'-i-pot], *n.* a white viscid resin issuing from, and hardening upon, fir-trees. [Fr. *galipot*].
GALIUM, [gā'-li-um], *n.* bed-straw, a large genus of plants, of which certain species are used to curdle milk. [Gk. *galion*].
GALL (1), [gawl], *n.* the bile, a bitter yellowish-green liquid secreted in the glandular substance of the liver; the gall-bladder; (*fig.*) bitterness of mind, rancour, malignity. [~OE. *gealla*, ~OIcel. *gall*].
GALL (2), [gawl], *n.* a hard round growth on trees, *esp.* oaks, caused by insects; **oak-g.,** a gall used in making ink, dyeing, in medicine, etc. [L. *galla* gall-nut].
GALL (3), [gawl], *n.* a painful swelling or blister, *esp.* on a horse; a sore or wound on the skin caused by rubbing; (*fig.*) something maddeningly irritating. [~OE. *gealla* sore place].
GALL (4), [gawl], *v.t.* to chafe or break the skin by rubbing; (*fig.*) to irritate, chagrin, exasperate; to harass; *v.i.* to become sore or chafed; to rankle. [GALL (3)].

GALL

GALLANT (1), [gal-ant'] *n.* a smart, dashing young man, a fine gentleman; a lady's man; a suitor, a lover.
GALLANT (2), [gal'-ant], *adj.* brave, high-spirited, noble; chivalrous; stately, imposing; having a fine appearance; (*parl.*) applied to a member of parliament who is also an officer in the forces. [Fr. *galant*].
GALLANT (3), [gal'-ant], *adj.* courtly, extremely polite, attentive and courteous to ladies; relating to love, amorous. [GALLANT (2)].
GALLANT (4), [gal'-ant, gal-ant'], *v.t. and i.* to escort; to pay excessive attention to; to flirt with; to play the gallant.
GALLANTLY, [gal'-ant-li], *adv.* in a gallant manner.
GALLANTNESS, [gal'-ant-nes], *n.* the quality of being gallant.
GALLANTRY, [gal'-an-tri], *n.* bravery, daring, courage; a brave deed; courageous bearing; polite deference to ladies, courtliness of behaviour; a polite compliment, a courteous act or speech; love affairs. [Fr. *galanterie*].
GALLA-OX, [gal'-a-oks'], *n.* an Abyssinian ox, having large horns curving upward like a lyre.
GALLATE, [gal'-āt], *n.* a salt of gallic acid.
GALL-BLADDER, [gawl'-blad'-er], *n.* the small, pear-shaped membranous sac on the underside of the liver, to receive the bile.
GALL-DUCTS, [gawl'-dukts'], *n.*(*pl.*) the ducts which convey the bile.
GALLEAS, see GALLIAS.
GALLEON, [gal'-i-on], *n.* a large sailing ship with three or four decks, formerly used by the Spaniards. [Span. *galeon*].
GALLERIED, [gal'-er-id], *adj.* provided with galleries.
GALLERY, [gal'-er-i], *n.* a narrow balcony, partly open in front, on the outside of a building; a long narrow passage built into, or projecting from, the walls of a room, at some height from the ground, and partly open on the side that faces inwards; a long narrow semi-covered court or cloister, open at one side; a long, narrow passage or corridor; a narrow underground communicating passage or corridor in a mine, etc.; a raised structure projecting some distance from the back and side walls above the floor of a hall, etc., supported by pillars or brackets, and forming a kind of second storey; the uppermost and cheapest seats in a theatre; (*fig.*) the part of the audience occupying these seats; a building or room which contains a collection or display of works of

GALLEON

art; (*tennis*) openings beneath the side pent-house on each side of the net; **to play to the g.,** to make a vulgar spectacular display likely to please the popular taste. [Fr. *galerie*].

GALLEY, [gal'-i], *n.* an ancient war vessel propelled by oars; a low, flat-built vessel with one deck, driven by oars and sails; a large rowing-boat or pleasure boat; the kitchen of a ship; (*print.*) an oblong frame in which lines of type are placed, a galley proof. [ME. *galeie* from MedL. *galea*].

GALLEY-FOIST, [gal'-i-foist'], *n.* a barge of state; the Lord Mayor's barge.

GALLEY-PROOF, [gal'-i-prōōf'], *n.* (*print.*) a proof taken straight from the galley, before the printed matter is made up into pages or columns.

GALLEY-SLAVE, [gal'-i-slāv'], *n.* a criminal condemned to work at the oar on board a galley.

GALLEY-WORM, [gal'-i-wurm'], *n.* a myriapod, from its innumerable legs which resemble the oars of a galley as they move.

GALL-FLY, [gawl'-flī'], *n.* an insect which causes galls on plants or trees.

GALLIAMBIC (1), [gal'-i-am'-bik], *n.* galliambic verse.

GALLIAMBIC (2), [gal'-i-am'-bik], *adj.* (*class. pros.*) composed in feet of four syllables, consisting of two short syllables followed by two long. [L. *galliambus* song of the priests of Cybele].

GALLIARD, [gal'-i-ahd], *n.* a lively dance in triple time for two persons; (*archaic*) a gay young fellow. [OFr. *gaillard* gay, merry].

GALLIAS, GALLEAS†, [gal'-i-as], *n.* a low three-masted warship propelled mainly by oars. [It. *galeaza*].

GALLIC (1), [gal'-ik], *adj.* pertaining to Gaul or the Gauls; pertaining to France or the French. [L. *Gallicus* of the Gauls].

GALLIC (2), [gawl'-ik], *adj.* pertaining to galls or oak-apples; derived from galls; **g. acid,** an acid obtained in fine white needles from gall-nuts. [GALL (2)].

GALLICAN (1), [gal'-ik-an], *n.* a member of the French Roman Catholic party resisting complete Papal control.

GALLICAN (2), [gal'-ik-an], *adj.* pertaining to Gaul or France; (*eccles.*) pertaining to the national Roman Catholic Church of France; pertaining to the Gallicans. [L. *Gallicanus* of Gaul].

GALLICANISM, [gal'-ik-an-izm], *n.* the doctrines and principles of the Gallicans.

GALLICISM, [gal'-is-izm], *n.* a French idiom, word, or turn of phrase.

GALLICIZE, [gal'-is-īz], *v.t.* to put into the French idiom; to make French.

GALLIGASKINS, [gal'-i-gas'-kinz], *n.(pl.)* leggings or wide breeches; a kind of large open hose. [~Fr. *garguesque* from It. *grechesca* Greek].

GALLIMATIAS, see GALIMATIAS.

GALLIMAUFRY, [gal'-i-maw'-fri], *n.* a hash, a confused collection, a hotchpotch. [Fr. *galimafrée* stew].

GALLINACEOUS, [gal-in-ā'-shus], *adj.* pertaining to the family of birds including the domestic fowl, pheasant, partridge, grouse, etc. [L. *gallinaceus* of domestic poultry].

GALLINAZO, [gal'-in-ā'-zō], *n.* a species of American vulture. [Span. *gallinaza* from L. *gallina* hen].

GALLING, [gawl'-ing], *adj.* fretting, vexing, annoying, irritating, rankling.

GALLINIPPER, [gal'-i-nip'-er], *n.* a large mosquito. [Uncert.].

GALLINULE, [gal'-in-ewl], *n.* the water-hen, *Gallinula chloropus,* a bird related to the coot. [LL. *gallinula* a small hen].

GALLIO, [gal'-i-ō], *n.* a person who refuses to attend to things that do not strictly concern him; a happy-go-lucky easy-going person. [*Gallio* the Roman proconsul of Achaia, Acts, xviii, 17].

GALLIOT, GALIOT, [gal'-i-ot], *n.* a small, swift Mediterranean galley or brigantine driven by sails or oars; a single-masted Dutch fishing-vessel. [OFr. *galiote*].

GALLIPOLI-OIL, [gal-ip'-o-li-oil'], *n.* an inferior kind of olive-oil from Gallipoli.

GALLIPOT, [gal'-i-pot], *n.* a glazed earthenware pot. [GALLEY and POT].

GALLIUM, [gal'-i-um], *n.* the soft, greyish-white metallic element Ga. [L. *gallus* cock, a translation of the first name of its discoverer, Lecoq de Boisbaudran].

GALLIVANT, [gal'-i-vant'], *v.i.* to gad about; to flirt or idle with members of the opposite sex. [GALLANT].

GALLIVAT, [gal'-i-vat], *n.* a large two-masted Eastern boat having triangular sails. [Portug. *galeota*].

GALLIWASP, [gal'-i-wosp'], *n.* a small West Indian lizard. [Unkn.].

GALLIZATION, [gal'-īz-ā'-shun], *n.* a process in wine-making by which the quality is improved and the quantity increased, by the addition of water and sugar. [Dr. *Gall* its inventor].

GALLIZE, [gal'-īz], *v.t.* to treat with the process of gallization.

GALLOMANIA, [gal'-ō-mā'-ni-a], *n.* an irrational enthusiasm for the French or for what is French. [L. *Gallus* Gaul and MANIA].

GALLON, [gal'-un], *n.* a measure of capacity equivalent to four quarts. [AFr. *galon*].

GALLOON, GALOON, [ga-lōōn'], *n.* a narrow, close braid of silk, gold or silver thread, for edging or trimming garments. [Fr. *galon* lace].

GALLOP (1), [gal'-op], *n.* the fastest moving pace of a horse, etc., in which both forelegs or hind legs touch the ground together, and all four legs are in the air at some period of the stride; a quick ride at this pace. [OFr. *galop*].

GALLOP (2), [gal'-op], *v.t. and i.* to move, ride or run at a gallop; to progress at a rapid pace; to hurry; to cause to gallop. [Fr. *galoper*].

GALLOPADE, [gal'-op-ād], *n.* a rapid lively dance; music suitable for this. [Fr. *galopade*].

GALLOPER, [gal'-op-er], *n.* one who, or that which, gallops; a small mobile field-gun; an aide-de-camp, an orderly officer.

GALLOWAY, [gal'-ō-wā], *n.* a hardy species of horse of a small size, originally bred in Galloway, in Scotland; one of a breed of cattle native to Galloway.

GALLOWGLASS, [gal'-ō-glahs'], *n.* an ancient Irish heavily-armed foot-soldier. [Ir. *galloglach*].

GALLOWS, [gal'-ōz], *n.* a wooden structure provided with a crossbeam from which criminals are hanged, any object or structure resembling this; a gallows-bird; (*pl.*) (*dial.*) trouser-braces. [OE. *galga*].

GALLOWS-BIRD, [gal'-ōz-burd'], *n.* one who deserves, or is destined for, the gallows.

GALLOWS-BITTS, [gal'-ōz-bitz'], *n.* (*naut.*) a frame of timber on the bitts at the main and fore hatchways forming a support or store for spare topmasts, yards, and booms.

GALLOWS-FREE, [gal'-ōz-frē'], *adj.* not in danger of hanging on the gallows.

GALLOWS-TOPS, [gal'-ōz-tops'], *n.(pl.)* (*naut.*) a crosspiece of timber placed at the top of the gallows-bitts.

GALLOWS-TREE, [gal'-ōz-trē'], *n.* a gallows.

GALL-STONE, [gawl'-stōn], *n.* a concretion formed in the gall-bladder or duct.

GALLY, [gawl'-i], *adj.* resembling gall.

GALOON, see GALLOON.

GALOOT, [ga-lōōt'], *n.* (*slang*) an uncouth person, a lout. [Unkn.].

GALOP (1), [gal'-op], *n.* a quick lively dance in two-four time; music suitable for this. [Fr. *galop*].

GALOP (2), [gal'-op], *v.i.* to dance a galop. [OFr. *galoper*].

GALORE (1), GOLORE, [ga-law(r)'], *n.* (*rare*) abundance, a great amount or number, plenty.

GALORE (2), GOLORE, [ga-law(r)'], *adv.* in abundance, in great quantities. [Ir. *go lear* enough].

GALOSH, see GOLOSH.

GALUMPH, [ga-lumf'], *n.* to dance about joyfully and triumphantly. [Invented by Lewis Carroll, from GALLOP and TRIUMPH].

GALVANIC, [gal-van'-ik], *adj.* (*elect.*) pertaining to, produced by, galvanism; producing electricity by galvanism; (*fig.*) convulsive, produced by a sudden burst of energy or effort.

GALVANISM, [gal'-van-izm], *n.* electricity produced by chemical action; that aspect of the science of electricity dealing with this; remedial treatment by this kind of electricity. [*Galvani,* its discoverer].

GALVANIST, [gal'-van-ist], *n.* a student of galvanism.

GALVANIZE, [gal'-van-īz], *v.t.* to treat by means of galvanism; to coat with a covering of metal, originally by galvanic action; (*fig.*) to startle, stir, shock, into energetic action.

GALVANIZED, [gal'-van-īzd], *adj.* electrified by galvanism; coated with metal; **g. iron,** iron plates coated with zinc to prevent rusting.

GALVANO-, *pref.* galvanism, galvanic. [*Galvani,* its discoverer].

GALVANOGRAPHY, [gal'-van-og'-ra-fi], *n.* a method of making plates for copperplate engraving by means of the electrotype process. [GALVANO and Gk. *graphia* writing].

GALVANOLOGIST, [gal'-van-ol'-oj-ist], *n.* one skilled in galvanology.

GALVANOLOGY, [gal'-van-ol'-oj-i], *n.* the science of galvanic electricity; a treatise on galvanism. [GALVANO and Gk. *logos* speech].

GALVANOMETER, [gal'-van-om'-it-er], *n.* an instrument for measuring the strength of a galvanic current of electricity. [GALVANO and METER].

GALVANOMETER

GALVANOPLASTIC, [gal'-van-ō-plas'-tik], *adj.* pertaining to galvanoplasty. [GALVANO and PLASTIC].

GALVANOPLASTY, [gal'-van-ō-plas'-ti], *n.* the process of coating a substance with metal by means of galvanic action.

GALVANOSCOPE, [gal'-van-ō-skōp'], *n.* an instrument for detecting the presence of a galvanic current of electricity. [GALAVNO and SCOPE].

GAM, [gam], *n.* a school of whales; an exchange of social visits by whaling-ships at sea. [~Icel. *gamen* sport].

GAMA-GRASS, [gah'-ma-grahs'], *n.* a tall fertile grass of the Southern States of North America, *Tripsacum dactyloides.*

GAMBA, [gam'-ba], *n.* a viola-da-gamba, a kind of large violin resembling the violoncello; an organ-stop producing a tone similar to that of a viol. [LL. *gamba* leg].

GAMBADO (1), [gam-bā'-dō], *n.* one of a pair of leather leggings or boots fastened to a saddle, to encase the legs and feet of a rider. [~It. *gamba* leg].

GAMBADO (2), [gam-bā'-dō], *n.* a leap or spring of a horse; a caper or fantastic bound. [~It. *gambata* gambol].

GAMBESON, [gam'-bis-un], *n.* (*hist.*) a stuffed protective doublet of leather or padded cloth. [OFr. *gambaison*].

GAMBETTA, [gam-bet'-a], *n.* the redshank, *Totanus calidris.* [It. *gambetta* from *gamba* leg].

GAMBIER, [gam'-bi-er], *n.* catechu, an extract from a species of *Uncaria*, used as a dyeing and tanning substance. [Malay *gamber*].

GAMBIST, [gam'-bist], *n.* a player on the gamba.

GAMBIT, [gam'-bit], *n.* an opening move in the game of chess in which a pawn or minor piece is sacrificed for a possible subsequent advantage; (*fig.*) an opening move in a piece of strategy, transaction, etc. [It. *gambetto* a tripping-up].

GAMBLE (1), [gambl], *n.* the act of gambling; something dependent upon chance.

GAMBLE (2), [gambl], *v.i.* to play games of chance for money, *esp.* for high stakes; to risk money in financial speculation; (*fig.*) to base action upon some fortuitous uncertain event. [~ME. *gamenen* to play].

GAMBLER, [gam'-bler], *n.* one who gambles habitually.

GAMBLING, [gam'-bling], *n.* the playing of games of chance for money.

GAMBLING-HOUSE, [gam'-bling-hows'], *n.* a place used for gambling.

GAMBOGE, [gam'-bōzh', gam'-bōōzh'], *n.* the gum-resin of *Garcinia morella*, used as a yellow pigment and also medicinally. [MdL. *gambogium* from *Cambodia* in Indo-China].

GAMBOL (1), [gam'-bel], *n.* a skipping or leaping about in frolic, the rhythmical bodily expression of high spirits. [It. *gambata* a caper].

GAMBOL (2), (**gambolling, gambolled**), [gam'-bel], *v.i.* to frisk, frolic, caper, to dance and skip about.

GAMBREL, [gam'-brel], *n.* a stick with a hooked end, used by butchers for hanging up meat; a horse's hock. [OFr. **gamberel*].

GAMBROON, [gam-brōōn'], *n.* a twilled linen cloth used for linings. [*Gambroon* a town on the Persian Gulf].

GAME (1), [gām], *n.* amusement, sport, pastime, play; a sporting contest played according to certain rules; a single round, part, or match of such a contest; the scoring of a definite number of points constituting this; the state of a game; (*pl.*) (*antiq.*) public athletic, musical, or dramatic contests as a recreation, spectacle, or celebration; a joke, jest, prank; intention, object, aim; trick, artful scheme; business, undertaking; wild animals or birds that are hunted in the chase or sports of the field; the edible flesh of such animals or birds; (*fig.*) an object of pursuit, quarry; **the g. is not worth the candle**, the reward does not justify the effort spent or risks incurred; **to play the g.**, to act or behave in an honest, decent manner; **to have a g. with**, to fool; **to be on one's g.**, to play well; **to make g. of**, to mock, to laugh at. [OE. *gamen* amusement, sport].

GAME (2), [gām], *adj.* plucky, courageous; eager ready, willing.

GAME (3), [gām], *adj.* injured, crippled, lame, disabled. [Uncert.].

GAME (4), [gām], *v.i.* to gamble; (*archaic*) to play, sport. [OE. *gamenian*].

GAMEBAG, [gām'-bag], *n.* a receptacle used for carrying game when killed.

GAMECOCK, [gām'-kok], *n.* a fighting-cock.

GAME-EGG, [gām'-eg], *n.* an egg laid by a game-fowl.

GAMEFUL, [gām'-fōōl], *adj.* sportive, jesting, playful.

GAMEKEEPER, [gām'-kēp'-er], *n.* a person employed to look after game.

GAME-LAWS, [gām'-lawz], *n.*(*pl.*) laws for the protection or preservation of game.

GAME-LICENCE, [gām'-lī'-sents], *n.* a licence granting legal permission to kill or sell game.

GAMELY, [gām'-li], *adv.* in a game manner.

GAMENESS, [gām'-nes], *n.* the quality of being game.

GAME-PRESERVE, [gām'-pri-zurv'], *n.* a tract of land used as a breeding, rearing, or dwelling-place for game.

GAME-PRESERVER, [gām'-pri-zurv'-er], *n.* a holder of a game-preserve.

GAMESOME, [gām'-sum], *adj.* gay, sportive, playful, merry, frolicsome.

GAMESOMELY, [gām'-sum-li], *adv.* in a gamesome fashion.

GAMESOMENESS, [gām'-sum-nes], *n.* the quality of being gamesome.

GAMESTER, [gām'-ster], *n.* a person addicted to gaming, a gambler; (*pl.*) (*billiards*) two opponents who have scored the same number of points at some stage of a game.

GAMETE, [gam-ēt'], *n.* (*biol.*) a sexual reproductive cell uniting with another to produce a zygote. [Gk. *gamete* wife.]

GAME-TENANT, [gām'-ten'-ant], *n.* one who rents the right to fish or shoot game over a particular estate.

GAMETOGENESIS, [gam'-et-ō-jen'-is-is], *n.* reproduction through gametes. [GAMETE and GENESIS].

GAMIC, [gam'-ik], *adj.* sexual. [Gk. *gamikos* pertaining to marriage].

GAMIN, [gam'-a(ng)], *n.* a mischievous ragged urchin of the streets. [Fr. *gamin*].

GAMING, [gām'-ing], *n.* gambling.

GAMING-HOUSE, [gām'-ing-hows'], *n.* a house where gaming is carried on.

GAMING-TABLE, [gām'-ing-tābl'], *n.* a table used for various gambling games.

GAMMA, [gam'-a], *n.* the third letter of the Greek alphabet γ; a common European moth, *Plusia gamma*, so called from its wing-markings.

GAMMADION, [gam-ā'-di-on], *n.* a swastika. [Gk. *gammadion*].

GAMMER, [gam'-er], *n.* an old woman. [GRANDMOTHER].

GAMMERSTANG, [gam'-er-stang], *n.* (*prov.*) a tall and awkward girl; a loose woman. [GAMMER and STANG].

GAMMOCK, [gam'-ok], *n.* a game, jest, lark, fun. [Uncert.].

GAMMON (1), [gam'-un], *n.* the lower part of a flitch of bacon, containing the hind leg; a cured ham. [ONFr. *gambon*].

GAMMON (2), [gam'-un], *n.* victory at backgammon by which all one's men are withdrawn from the board before one's opponent has withdrawn any. [ME. *gamen* game].

GAMMON (3), [gam'-un], *n.* (*naut.*) the lashing of rope securing the bowsprit. [Unkn.].

GAMMON (4), [gam'-un], *n.* a hoax, deception. [GAMMON (2)].

GAMMON (5), [gam'-un], *v.t.* to cure bacon. [GAMMON (1)].

GAMMON (6), [gam'-un], *v.t.* to defeat (an opponent) at backgammon by making a gammon. [GAMMON (2)].

GAMMON (7), [gam'-un], *v.t.* (*naut.*) to secure the bowsprit to the stem by lashings of ropes. [GAMMON (3)].

GAMMON (8), [gam'-un], *v.t. and i.* to hoax, deceive, to dupe; to pretend, dissemble. [GAMMON (4)].
GAMMON (9), [gam'-un], *int.* nonsense, humbug, rubbish.
GAMMY, [gam'-i], *adj.* (*coll.*) crippled, lamed, deformed, injured. [GAME (3)].
GAMOGENESIS, [gam'-ō-jen'-is-is], *n.* sexual reproduction. [Gk. *gamos* marriage and GENESIS].
GAMOPETALOUS, [gam'-ō-pet'-al-us], *adj.* (*bot.*) with the petals united towards the base. [Gk. *gamos* marriage and PETALOUS].
GAMOSEPALOUS, [gam'-ō-sep'-al-us], *adj.* (*bot.*) having the sepals joined together. [Gk. *gamos* marriage and SEPALOUS].
GAMP, [gamp], *n.* a loose, large, badly rolled umbrella; (*coll.*) any umbrella. [Mrs. Sarah *Gamp*, in " Martin Chuzzlewit " by Dickens].
GAMUT, [gam'-ut], *n.* †(*mus.*) the lowest note of the medieval scale, being G below middle C; †the complete medieval scale of twenty notes; any scale used at some particular period in history; the range of a voice or instrument; (*fig.*) scope, compass, range, scale. [MedL. *gamma ut* from *gamma* the name of the symbol representing the lowest note of the medieval scale and *ut* the first of the six notes of the hexachord].
GAMY, [gām'-i], *adj.* having the taste of game, high.
GANCH†, [ganch], *n.* to execute by dropping or fixing upon sharp stakes or hooks; to gash or rend with the tusk (of a boar). [Fr. *gancher*].
GANDER, [gan'-der], *n.* the male of the goose; (*fig.*) a fool, a stupid blockhead. [OE. *gandra*].
GANG, [gang], *n.* a squad, a band, a group of persons associated together for some particular, common purpose; a set, clique; a complete set of tools for some particular process. [OE. *gang* the act of going].
GANG-BOARD, [gang'-bawd], *n.* a board or plank used as a ship's gangway; a plank laid along the bottom of a racing craft; a narrow platform on the inside of the gunwales, serving as a means of communication between the quarter-deck and forecastle.
GANG-DAYS, [gang'-dāz], *n.*(*pl.*) the days in Rogation week when the clergy and leading parishioners formerly made a tour of the parish boundary.
GANGE, [ganj], *v.t.* to bind that portion of a fishing line nearest the hook in order to strengthen it. [Unkn.].
GANGER, [gang'-er], *n.* the foreman of a gang of labourers or platelayers.
GANGETIC, [gan-jet'-ik], *adj.* pertaining to the Ganges. [L. *Gangeticus*].
GANGING, [ganj'-ing], *n.* the process of strengthening a fishing line by binding it with thread, or thin wire.
GANGLIAC, [gang'-gli-ak], *adj.* relating to, or resembling, a ganglion.
GANGLIFORM, [gang'-gli-fawm'], *adj.* resembling a ganglion in shape. [GANGLI(ON) and FORM].
GANGLIOFORM, [gang'-gli-ō-fawm'], *n.* gangliform.
GANGLION, (*pl.* **ganglia**), [gang'-gli-on], *n.* (*anat*) a nucleus of nerve-cells, a centre from which nerve-cells radiate; (*med.*) an encysted tumour or sac usually on a tendon or sinew; (*fig.*) a meeting point of several converging forces or branches of activity. [Gk. *ganglion* a swelling].
GANGLIONARY, [gang'-gli-on-er-i], *adj.* consisting of ganglia.
GANGLIONATED, [gang'-gli-on-āt-id], *adj.* furnished with ganglia.
GANGLION-CELL, [gang'-gli-on-sel'], *n.* a single cell of a mass of nerve-cells.
GANGLIONIC, [gang'-gli-on'-ik], *adj.* pertaining to, composed of, ganglia.
GANGREL, [gang'-grel], *n.* a vagabond, a vagrant, a beggar. [GANG].
GANGRENATE†, [gang'-grin-āt], *v.t. and i.* to cause a gangrene in; to become infected with gangrene.
GANGRENE (1), [gang'-grēn], *n.* mortification affecting a considerable area of animal tissue; (*fig.*) a decaying force. [Gk. *gangraina*].
GANGRENE (2), [gang'-grēn], *v.t. and i.* to cause gangrene in; to become mortified.
GANGRENESCENT, [gang'-grin-es'-ent], *adj.* turning gangrenous, tending to mortification.
GANGRENOUS, [gang'-grin-us], *adj.* of the nature of, affected by, gangrene.
GANG-SAW, [gang'-saw], *n.* a mechanical saw with two or more blades operating simultaneously.
GANGSTER, [gang'-ster], *n.* an armed member of a criminal gang, unhesitatingly resorting to violence to perpetrate some crime or avoid capture.
GANGUE, [gang], *n.* (*mining*) the substance which contains the ore of metals. [Germ. *gang* a vein of ore].
GANGWAY, [gang'-wā], *n.* a board or movable bridge placed between a ship and the landing-stage, by which persons may embark or disembark; the opening in the bulwarks of a ship into which this fits; a passage, road, way of approach; a passage separating blocks of seats in a hall, theatre, etc.; (*parl.*) a passage across the House of Commons separating the front benches from the back benches.
GANIL, [gan'-il], *n.* a variety of brittle limestone. [Fr. *ganil*].
GANISTER, [gan'-is-ter], *n.* a hard siliceous rock used in making fire-proof bricks and linings for furnaces. [Unkn.].
GANJA, [gan'-ja], *n.* an intoxicating drink made from Indian hemp. [Hind. *ganjha*].
GANNET, [gan'-et], *n.* a large sea-bird, the solan-goose, *Sula bassana*. [OE. *ganot*].
GANOID (1), [gan'-oid], *n.* a ganoid fish.
GANOID (2), [gan'-oid], *adj.* (of a scale) smooth, hard, shining, and enamel-like; (of fishes) having hard, enamel-like scales of bone. [Gk. *ganos* splendour and *oeides* like].

GANNET

GANTLET, see GAUNTLET (1).
GANTLOPE, see GAUNTLET (2).
GANTRY, GAUNTRY, [gan'-tri], *n.* a framework of two upright members some distance apart, spanned by a horizontal piece, *esp.* one crossing several sets of railway lines and bearing signals, or carrying a travelling crane; a wooden stand mounted on four legs, used for supporting barrels. [OFr. *gantier*].
GANYMEDE, [gan'-i-mēd], *n.* a cupbearer; (*astron.*) the largest satellite of Jupiter. [Gk. *Ganumedes* Jove's cupbearer].
GANZA, [gan'-za], *n.* a wild goose. [MdL. *ganza*].
GAOL (1), **JAIL**, [jāl], *n.* a prison; confinement in prison. [OFr. *jaiole*].
GAOL (2), **JAIL**, [jāl], *v.t.* to put into gaol.
GAOL-BIRD, [jāl'-burd'], *n.* a hardened criminal.
GAOLER, JAILER, [jāl'-er], *n.* the head of a gaol; a prison warder.
GAOLERESS, [jāl'-er-es], *n.* a female gaoler.
GAOL-FEVER, [jāl'-fē'-ver], *n.* typhus fever, so called because it was formerly widespread amongst prisoners.
GAP, [gap], *n.* a hole, breach, opening in anything; a gorge, an opening in a range of mountains or hills; an interval, vacant place, a blank space, a deficiency caused by a break in the sequence. [OIcel. *-gap* chasm].
GAPE (1), [gāp], *n.* the act of gaping, a vacant stare accompanied by an opening of the mouth; a yawn; (*zool.*) the width of the mouth when opened to its fullest extent; (*pl.*) a disease attacking young poultry and causing the birds to gape continually; (*coll.*) a yawning fit; (*fig.*) an opening.
GAPE (2), [gāp], *v.i.* to stare in open-mouthed astonishment or stupidity; (of a bird) to open the mouth wide for food; to yawn; (of the earth) to open in a fissure; **to g. at**, to gaze in amazement at. [OIcel. *gapa* to yawn].
GAPER, [gāp'-er], *n.* one who gapes; a bivalve mollusc of the genus *Mya*; a seafish, the comber, *Serranus cabrilla*.
GAPING, [gāp'-ing], *n.* the act of one who gapes.
GAPINGLY, [gāp'-ing-li], *adv.* in a gaping manner.
GAPPY, [gāp'-i], *adj.* with gaps, interrupted, not continuous.
GAP-TOOTHED, [gap'-tōōtht'], *adj.* having the teeth irregularly set, with intervening gaps.
GAR, [gah(r)], *n.* a garfish. [OE. *gar* spear].
GARAGE (1), [ga'-rahj, ga-rahzh'], *n.* a building in which motor vehicles are kept when not in use; an establishment where motor vehicles may be housed, repaired, overhauled, etc., and at which petrol and motor accessories may be purchased. [Fr. *garage*].
GARAGE (2), [ga'-rahj, ga-rahzh'], *v.t.* to put away in a garage.
GARANCIN, [ga'-ran-sin], *n.* an extract of madder used in dyeing. [Fr. *garancine*].

GARB (1), [gahb], *n.* mode or style of dress, attire, *esp.* distinctive type of dress of a class, occupation, etc. [It. *garbo* grace].
GARB (2), [gahb], *n.* (*her.*) a sheaf of grain. [OHGerm. *garba*].
GARB (3), [gahb], *v.t. and reflex.* to dress, attire, clothe.
GARBAGE, [gahb'-ij], *n.* refuse, offal; (*fig.*) sordid rubbish. [Uncert.].
GARBLE, [gahbl], *v.t.* to separate the fine or valuable parts from the coarse or useless; to pick out the useful parts from; to give a distorted version or impression of. [Arab. *gharbala* to sift].
GARBLER, [gah'-bler], *n.* a person who garbles.
GARBOARD, [gah'-bawd], *n.* (*naut.*) a row of planks or steel plates laid next to the keel on the outside of a ship. [Du. *gaarboord*].
GARCINIA, [gah-sin'-i-a], *n.* a genus of tropical African or Asiatic trees, some of the species of which yield gamboge. [L. *Garcin*, the naturalist].
GARDANT, [gahd'-ant], *adj.* (*her.*) full-faced and looking right forward to face the beholders. [OFr. *gardant*].
GARDE-BRAS, [gahd'-brah'], *n.* (*antiq.*) a piece of armour fastened to the elbow-plates as an arm-guard. [Fr. *garde-bras*].
GARDEN (1), [gahdn], *n.* a plot of land devoted to the cultivation of flowers, fruits, and plants, usually laid out with paths, and frequently attached to a house; (*pl.*) a public enclosure for the cultivation of flowers, trees, etc., serving as a place of recreation or rest; a richly fertile and well-cultivated region; the school of Epicurus; **hanging g.**, a garden built in terraces; **market g.**, a large garden in which fruit, flowers or vegetables are grown for sale; **to lead up the g.**, (*slang*) to befool, deceive. [AFr. *gardin*].
GARDEN (2), [gahdn], *adj.* pertaining to a garden, cultivated in a garden.
GARDEN (3), [gahdn], *v.i.* to cultivate a garden, to work in a garden.
GARDEN-CITY, [gahdn'-sit'-i], *n.* a town built in a harmonious style of architecture, usually containing wide, tree-lined roads, and having ample provision for gardens for the houses.
GARDENER, [gahd'-ner], *n.* one whose occupation is to cultivate a garden; a person interested in gardening.
GARDEN-FRAME, [gahdn'-frām'], *n.* a forcing-frame for plants.
GARDEN-GLASS, [gahdn'-glahs'], *n.* a bell-shaped glass vessel to protect tender plants.
GARDENIA, [gah-dēn'-i-a], *n.* a tropical and subtropical shrub cultivated in conservatories for its yellow and white, fragrant flowers. [A. *Garden*, the American botanist].

GARDENIA

GARDENING, [gahdn'-ing], *n.* the art of cultivating a garden.
GARDEN-MOULD, [gahdn'-mōld'], *adj.* mould suitable for a garden.
GARDEN-PARTY, [gahdn'-pah'-ti], *n.* a social gathering held in the open, on the lawn of a garden or park.
GARDEN-PLOT, [gahdn'-plot'], *n.* a tract of ground laid out and cultivated as a garden.
GARDEN-STUFF, [gahdn'-stuf'], *n.* the produce of a garden.
GARDEN-SUBURB, [gahdn'-sub'-urb], *n.* a residential quarter on the outskirts of a town, with tree-lined avenues, and adequate provision for gardens.
GARDEN-TUB, [gahdn'-tub'], *n.* a large tub filled with soil in which ornamental shrubs, etc., are grown.
GARDEN-WHITE, [gahdn'-wīt'], *n.* a variety of butterfly.
GARDON†, [gahd'-un], *n.* the ide, a fish, *Leuciscus idus*, related to the roach. [Fr. *gardon*].
GARE†, [gah(r)], *n.* coarse wool found on the legs of sheep. [AFr. *gare*].
GARE-FOWL, [gāer'-fowl'], *n.* the great auk. [OIcel. *geir-fugl*].
GARFISH, GUARDFISH, [gah'-fish, gahd-fish], *n.* a slender sea-fish of the genus *Belone*, with long beak-like jaws. [ME. *garfissh* from OE. *gar* spear].

GARFISH

GARGANEY, [gah'-gan-ā], *n.* a sea-duck related to the teal, *Querquedula circia*. [Germ. *garganey*].
GARGANTUAN, [gah-gan'-tew-an], *adj.* prodigious, of extremely large proportions. [*Gargantua* the giant with a great appetite, who is the hero of " Gargantua and Pantagruel " by Rabelais].
GARGET, [gah'-get], *n.* a diseased, swollen condition of the throats of cattle and hogs; inflammation of the udders in cows or sheep. [OFr. *gargate* throat].
GARGIL†, GARGOL, [gah'-gil], *n.* a disease affecting the throats and heads of cattle and hogs; a disease causing inflammation of the udders in cows. [OFr. *gargouille*].
GARGLE (1), [gahgl], *n.* the act of gargling; any antiseptic liquid preparation used for washing the mouth and throat.
GARGLE (2), [gahgl], *v.t. and i.* to cleanse the mouth and throat with a liquid preparation, while breathing out steadily and forcefully, so that the liquid is constantly agitated, and is not swallowed. [Fr. *gargouiller*].
GARGOL, see GARGIL.
GARGOYLE, [gah'-goil], *n.* a projecting rain-spout of the gutter of a building, *esp.* one carved in the form of a grotesque figure. [OFr. *gargouille* throat].
GARIBALDI, [ga'-ri-bawl'-di], *n.* a loose blouse of some vivid cerise material; a kind of hat; **g. biscuit**, a biscuit containing a layer of currants. [*Garibaldi*, 1807-82].
GARISH, [gāer'-ish], *adj.* gaudy, showy, extravagantly gay, glaringly bright. [~ME. *gauren* to stare].
GARISHLY, [gāer'-ish-li], *adv.* in a garish fashion.
GARISHNESS, [gāer'-ish-nes], *n.* the quality of being garish.
GARLAND (1), [gah'-land], *n.* a wreath or chaplet of flowers, branches, leaves, etc., worn round the head or neck, or hung round any object; anything resembling or representing this; a band or wreath worn as a mark of success or merit; a vessel or band containing shot; (*fig.*) a sign of victory or success. [OFr. *garlande*].
GARLAND (2), [gah'-land], *v.t.* to adorn or wreathe with a garland.
GARLANDAGE, [gah'-land-ij], *n.* a decoration formed of garlands.
GARLANDRY, [gah'-land-ri], *n.* decoration or ornament in the form of garlands.
GARLIC, [gah'-lik], *n.* a bulbous culinary plant *Allium sativum*, allied to the onion, and possessing a strong taste and smell. [OE. *garleac* spear-leek].
GARLICKY, [gah'-lik-i], *adj.* like or containing garlic.
GARLIC-PEAR, [gah'-lik-pāer'], *n.* the American tree, *Cratæva gynandra*, the fruit of which has a similar smell to that of garlic.
GARLIC-SNAIL, [gah'-lik-snāl'], *n.* a species of the helix family, *Zonites alliarius*, exuding an odour like that of garlic.
GARMENT (1), [gah'-ment], *n.* an article of clothing; a covering which serves to clothe anything; (*pl.*) dress, attire, clothes. [OFr. *garniment*].
GARMENT (2), [gah'-ment], *v.t.* (*poet.*) to clothe, array, dress.
GARNER (1), [gah'-ner], *n.* a store-house, *esp.* for grain; a collection. [L. *granarium* granary].
GARNER (2), [gah'-ner], *v.t.* to store up as in a garner.
GARNERAGE, [gah'-ner-ij], *n.* a garner.
GARNET, [gah'-net], *n.* a variously coloured siliceous stone, crystallizing in the cubical system; the deep-red variety of this, cut as a gem. [ME. *gernet*, *garnet* from MedL. *granatum*].
GARNISH (1), [gah'-nish], *n.* ornament, decoration; articles served with food to garnish it; literary adornment.
GARNISH (2), [gah'-nish], *v.t.* to decorate, adorn, embellish; to make a dish of food more attractive by serving a sauce, relish, etc., with it; (*leg.*) to serve notice preventing a person from paying money, etc., due to someone who in turn owes to another. [Fr. *garnir*].
GARNISHED, [gah'-nisht], *adj.* (*her.*) adorned with devices of a particular tincture.
GARNISHEE (1), [gah'-nish-ē], *n.* (*leg.*) one who is prevented from paying over money, etc., due to a person who in turn owes money, by an order obtained by the latter's creditor.
GARNISHEE (2), [gah'-nish-ē], *v.t.* to seize funds or property due to a debtor at the instigation of the latter's creditor.
GARNISHER, [gah'-nish-er], *n.* (*leg.*) one who garnishes.
GARNISHING, [gah'-nish-ing], *n.* anything that garnishes.

ō (bone), ī (fine), ōō (food), ŏŏ (put), u (up), th (*th*ink), TH (*th*at), zh (azure), † = obsolete, ~ = related to.

GARNISHMENT, [gah'-nish-ment], *n.* ornament, embellishment; (*leg.*), a warning given to a party to appear in court, or to withhold payment of money to another.

GARNITURE, [gah'-nich-er], *n.* ornamental appendages, decoration, dress. [Fr. *garniture*].

GAROTTE, see GARROTTE.

GAROUS†, [gāer'-us], *adj.* like garum.

GARPIKE, [gah'-pīk'], *n.* the garfish.

GARRAN, see GARRON.

GARRET, [ga'-ret], *n.* an attic, a small room at the top of the house. [OFr. *garite* a watchtower].

GARRETED, [ga'-ret-id], *adj.* provided with garrets.

GARRETEER, [ga'-ret-ēer'], *n.* one who dwells in a garret; a poor author.

GARRETING, [ga'-ret-ing], *n.* chips of stone inserted into the mortar of rough joints of masonry as a method of pointing; the act of pointing in this way. [Uncert.].

GARRET-MASTER, [ga'-ret-mahst'-er], *n.* a person who makes articles of furniture, etc., which he sells direct to dealers.

GARRISON (1), [ga'-ris-un], *n.* a body of troops quartered in a fortress or fortified town for its defence; a fortress or fortified town defended in this way. [OFr. *garison* defence].

GARRISON (2), [ga'-ris-un], *v.t.* to provide with a garrison; to occupy as a garrison; to send (troops) as a garrison.

GARRISON-ARTILLERY, [ga'-ris-un-ah'-til'-er-i], *n.* heavy artillery firing large-calibre shells.

GARRISON-TOWN, [ga'-ris-un-town'], *n.* a town occupied by a garrison.

GARRON, GARRAN, [ga'-ron], *n.* a small poor breed of Irish or Highland horses. [Gael. *gearran*].

GARROT (1), [ga'-rot], *n.* (*surg.*) a small cylinder of wood used to tighten the circular band by which the artery of a limb is compressed; (*antiq.*) a lever by which a crossbow is wound. [Fr. *garrot*].

GARROT (2), [ga'-rot], *n.* a sea-duck of the genus *Clangula*. [Fr. *garrot*].

GARROTTE (1), GAROTTE, [ga-rot'], *n.* a means of execution in Spain and Portugal by strangulation, originally with a cord, now by means of a spiked iron collar, the point of which penetrates to the spine when tightened; strangulation by means of a cord wound tightly round the victim's neck. [Span. *garrotte* stick].

GARROTTE (2), [ga-rot'], *v.t.* to strangle with a garotte, *esp.* preparatory to robbing.

GARROTTER, [ga-rot'-er], *n.* a robber who strangles his victims by means of a garrotte.

GARROTTING, [ga-rot'-ing], *n.* punishment by strangulation; throttling by means of the garrotte.

GARRULITY, [ga-rōō'-li-ti], *n.* the quality of being garrulous. [L. *garrulitas*].

GARRULOUS, [gar'-yōō-lus], *adj.* talkative, inclined to discourse at great length upon topics of slight interest or importance; (of a stream) babbling, incessantly rippling. [L. *garrulus* talkative].

GARRULOUSLY, [gar'-yōō-lus-li], *adv.* in a talkative fashion.

GARRULOUSNESS, [gar'-yōō-lus-nes], *n.* the quality of being garrulous.

GARRYA, [ga'-ri-a], *n.* an American genus of evergreen flowering shrubs, of which one species, *Garrya elliptica*, bears long catkins. [M. *Garry*, the botanist].

GARTER (1), [gah'-ter], *n.* an elastic band worn round the leg to keep the stocking in position; the highest order of knighthood in Great Britain, instituted by Edward III; the badge of the order; membership of this order; (*her.*) the half of a bend; **G. King of Arms,** the principal herald of the College of Arms of England. [OFr. *gartier*].

GARTER (2), [gah'-ter], *v.t.* to fasten with a garter; to invest with the Order of the Garter.

GARTER-FISH, [gah'-ter-fish], *n.* a fish having a long thin body, the scabbard-fish, *Lepidopus caudatus*.

GARTER-SNAKE, [gah'-ter-snāk'], *n.* a non-venomous striped snake of the American genus *Eutania*.

GARTH, [gahth], *n.* a yard, a court, an enclosed lawn; a weir for catching fish. [OIcel. *garthr*].

GARUM, [gāer'-um], *n.* a sauce, prized by the Romans, made of small marinated fish. [Gk. *garon*].

GARVIE, [gah'-vi], *n.* the sprat. [Unkn.].

GAS (1), [gas], *n.* one of various elastic air-like substances, *esp.* that obtained from coal and used for heating and illumination; nitrous oxide gas when used as an anaesthetic in dentistry; any poisonous chemical used in modern warfare; (*min.*) fire-damp mixed with air and forming an explosive mixture; (*U.S.*) gasoline; (*coll.*) idle talk; **to step on the g.,** (*slang*) to accelerate; **g. proof,** impervious to poison gas. [Invented by Van Helmont, the Belgian chemist].

GAS (2), (gassing, gassed), [gas], *v.t.* to poison or kill by the fumes of gas; *v.i.* (*coll.*) to gossip.

GAS-ALARM, [gas'-a-lahm], *n.* a warning of the presence of poison-gas.

GAS-ATTACK, [gas'-a-tak'], *n.* an attack with poison gas.

GAS-BAG, [gas'-bag], *n.* a bag for holding gas; (*slang*) a talkative person, a gossip.

GAS-BRACKET, [gas'-brak'-it], *n.* a fixed or jointed gas-pipe with a burner, attached to a wall, etc.

GAS-BUOY, [gas'-boi], *n.* a buoy illuminated by gas.

GAS-BURNER, [gas'-burn'-er], *n.* the jet fitted at the end of a gas-pipe, from which the flame appears.

GAS-COAL, [gas'-kōl'], *n.* coal from which gas is made.

GAS-COKE, [gas'-kōk'], *n.* coke obtained as a by-product in the manufacture of gas.

GASCON, [gas'-kon], *n.* a native of Gascony in France; a boaster. [Fr. *Gascon*].

GASCONADE (1), [gas'-kon-ād'], *n.* boastful, blustering, bragging talk. [Fr. *gasconnade*].

GASCONADE (2), [gas'-kon-ād'], *v.i.* to boast, brag, bluster.

GASCONADER, [gas'-kon-ād'-er], *n.* a great boaster, a braggart.

GAS-CONDENSER, [gas'-kon-dens'-er], *n.* an apparatus used for purifying coal-gas from tar.

GAS-COOKER, [gas'-kŏŏk'-er], *n.* a stove in which the heat for cooking is supplied by gas.

GAS-CURTAIN, [gas'-kurtn'], *n.* a thick curtain put up to keep out poison gas.

GASEITY, [gas-ē'-it-i], *n.* the condition of being gaseous.

GASELIER, [gas'-el-ēer'], *n.* a gas chandelier.

GAS-ENGINE, [gas'-en'-jin], *n.* an engine driven by gas.

GASEOUS, [gā'-si-us], *adj.* in the form of gas, like gas.

GASEOUSNESS, [gā'-si-us-nes], *n.* the condition of being gaseous.

GAS-FIRE, [gas'-fīer'], *n.* a fire burning gas as fuel.

GAS-FITTER, [gas'-fit'-er], *n.* a workman who installs gas-fittings.

GAS-FITTINGS, [gas'-fit'-ingz], *n.(pl.)* pipes, brackets, jets, etc., necessary for the use of gas for heating and lighting purposes.

GAS-GAUGE, [gas'-gāj'], *n.* a device to test gas pressure.

GAS-GOVERNOR, [gas'-guv'-ern-er], *n.* an apparatus for regulating the flow of gas.

GASH (1), [gash], *n.* a narrow, deep and long cut; a cleft.

GASH (2), [gash], *v.t.* to make a gash in. [OFr. *garscher*].

GAS-HELMET, [gas'-hel'-mit], *n.* a hood for the protection of babies against poison-gas.

GAS-HOLDER, [gas'-hōld-er], *n.* a reservoir or storage-tank for gas.

GASIFICATION, [gas'-if-ik-ā'-shun], *n.* the act of gasifying.

GASIFORM, [gas'-i-fawm], *adj.* having the form of gas.

GASIFY, [gas'-i-fī], *v.t.* *and* *i.* to turn into gas; to manufacture gas from.

GAS-JET, [gas'-jet'], *n.* a jet on the end of a gas-pipe, a gas-burner.

GASKET, [gas'-ket], *n.* (*naut.*) a flat plaited cord or canvas strip with which a furled sail is tied to a yard; a piece of plaited hemp, etc., used for packing the piston of a steam engine or stopping up a joint; a copper-asbestos joint. [It. *gaschetta* rope-end].

GASKIN, [gas'-kin], *n.* the rear thigh of a horse. [Uncert.].

GAS-LAMP, [gas'-lamp'], *n.* a lamp which burns gas.

GAS-LIGHT, [gas'-līt'], *n.* light produced by burning coal-gas; a lamp burning gas; **g. plates,** (*phot.*) sensitized photographic plates which can be developed in subdued artificial light.

GAS-LIQUOR, [gas'-lik'-er], *n.* ammoniacal liquid used in condensing or purifying gas.

GAS-MAINS, [gas'-mānz'], *n.(pl.)* the principal pipes which carry the gas from the gas-works.

GASMAN, [gas'-man], *n.* a man employed by a gas company either to make gas or to collect money due for gas used.

GAS-MANTLE, [gas'-mantl'], *n.* a small gauze-like net of cotton fabric fitted to a gas-burner, and becoming incandescent when heated by the flame.

GAS-MASK, [gas'-mahsk'], *n.* a respirating apparatus worn over the face and head as a protection against the inhaling of poisonous gas.

GAS-MASK

GAS-METER, [gas'-mē'-ter], *n.* a mechanical contrivance for measuring and recording the quantity of gas consumed.

GASOGENE, see GAZOGENE.

GASOLINE, [gas'-ō-lēn], *n.* an inflammable product obtained from the refining of crude petroleum, and used for heating and lighting; (*U.S.*) petrol.

GASOMETER, [gas-om'-it-er], *n.* (*coll.*), a reservoir or storage tank for gas; (*chem.*) an apparatus for holding or measuring a quantity of gas. [GAS and METER].

GASOMETRIC, [gas'-ō-met'-rik], *adj.* relating to gasometry.

GASOMETRY, [gas-om'-et-ri], *n.* the science, art, or practice of measuring gases.

GASP (1), [gahsp], *n.* a sudden convulsive effort to catch one's breath; **at the last g.,** at the limit of one's powers or strength.

GASP (2), [gahsp], *v.t. and i.* to breathe by a series of gasps, to fight for breath, to catch the breath in fear or amazement; to utter in a gasp. [ME. *gaspen* from OIcel. *geispa* to yawn].

GASPER, [gahsp'-er], *n.* (*slang*) a cigarette, *esp.* of inferior quality.

GASPING, [gahsp'-ing], *adj.* that gasps, convulsive, laborious and spasmodic.

GASPINGLY, [gahsp'-ing-li], *adv.* in a gasping fashion.

GAS-PIPE, [gas'-pīp'], *n.* a pipe along which gas is conveyed.

GAS-RATTLE, [gas'-ratl'], *n.* a rattle employed to sound a local gas-alarm.

GAS-REGULATOR, [gas'-reg'-yōō-lāt'-er], *n.* a gas-governor.

GAS-RETORT, [gas'-ri-tawt'], *n.* a vessel which holds the material from which gas is to be made.

GAS-RING, [gas'-ring'], *n.* a metal ring pierced with holes through which gas is burnt for cooking purposes.

GAS-SHELL, [gas'-shel'], *n.* an explosive shell containing poison-gas or chemicals emitting deadly fumes.

GASSING, [gas'-ing], *n.* the process of singeing lace or thread over a gas flame in order to remove the hairy filaments.

GASSOUL, [gas'-ōōl], *n.* a mineral soap exported from Morocco. [Native].

GAS-STOVE, [gas'-stōv'], *n.* a cooking-stove heated by burning gas.

GASSY, [gas'-i], *adj.* gaseous; full of gas; (*coll.*) talkative.

GAS-TANK, [gas'-tangk], *n.* a tank used for holding gas.

GAS-TAR, [gas'-tah(r)'], *n.* the bituminous product that distils over in the manufacture of coal-gas.

GASTEROPOD, GASTROPOD, [gas'-ter-o-pod], *n.* a member of the class of gasteropoda.

GASTEROPODA, GASTROPODA, [gas'-ter-op'-o-da], *n.(pl.)* the class of univalve molluscs moving by means of a muscular organ situated in the region of the stomach, and including snails, slugs, whelks, limpets, etc. [GASTRO and Gk. *pous podos* foot].

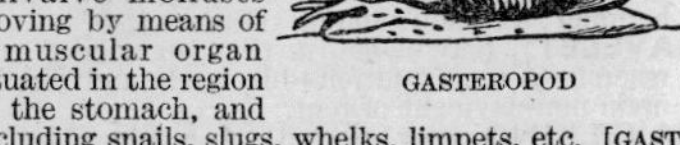

GASTEROPOD

GASTEROPODOUS, GASTROPODOUS, [gas'-ter-op'-o-dus], *adj.* pertaining to the gasteropoda.

GAS-TIGHT, [gas'-tīt'], *adj.* proof against gas.

GASTRAL, [gas'-tral], *adj.* gastric.

GASTRALGIA, [gas-tral'-ja], *n.* (*med.*) acute intermittent pain in the stomach. [GASTR(O) and Gk. *algos* pain].

GASTRIC, [gas'-trik], *adj.* belonging to the stomach; **g. juice**, a thin clear acid secretion from glands in the stomach, which aids digestion; **g. fever**, typhoid fever.

GASTRICISM, [gas'-tris-izm], *n.* a gastric disease; a theory that almost all diseases are due to a disordered condition of the stomach.

GASTRILOQUIST, [gas-tril'-o-kwist], *n.* a ventriloquist. [Cf. VENTRILOQUIST].

GASTRILOQUY, [gas-tril'-o-kwi], *n.* ventriloquism.

GASTRITIS, [gas-trīt'-is], *n.* chronic acute inflammation of the stomach. [GASTR(O) and *itis* denoting inflammation].

GASTR(O)-, *pref.* stomach, belly. [Gk. *gaster* stomach].

GASTROCELE, [gas'-trō-sēl'], *n.* rupture of the stomach. [GASTRO and Gk. *kele* tumour].

GASTRO-CEPHALITIS, [gas'-trō-sef'-al-īt'-is], *n.* (*med.*) chronic inflammation of the stomach and brain.

GASTROCNEMIUS, [gas'-trōk-nē'-mi-us], *n.* the chief muscle in the calf of the leg. [Gk. *gastroknemia* calf of the leg].

GASTRODYNIA, [gas'-trō-din'-i-a], *n.* gastralgia. [GASTRO and Gk. *odune* pain].

GASTRO-ENTERITIS, [gas'-trō-en'-ter-īt'-is], *n.* (*med.*) chronic inflammation of the stomach and intestines.

GASTROLOGY, [gas-trol'-oj-i], *n.* the science or art of cookery. [GASTRO and Gk. *logos* speech].

GASTRO-MALACIA, [gas'-trō-mal-ā'-sha], *n.* (*med.*) a softening of the stomach. [GASTRO and Gk. *malakia* softness].

GASTROMANCY, [gas'-trō-man'-si], *n.* divination by means of the belly. [GASTRO and Gk. *manteia* divination].

GASTRONOME, [gas'-trō-nōm'], *n.* an epicure, one who enjoys and appreciates good food and cookery. [Fr. *gastronome*].

GASTRONOMER, [gas-tron'-om-er], *n.* a gastronome.

GASTRONOMIC, [gas'-trō-nom'-ik], *adj.* relating to gastronomy.

GASTRONOMIST, [gas-tron'-om-ist], *n.* one fond of good living, an epicure.

GASTRONOMY, [gas-tron'-om-i], *n.* the art of gratifying the stomach by good food and cooking. [Gk. *gastronomia*].

GASTROPHILE, [gas'-tro-fīl'], *n.* a gastronome. [GASTRO and Gk. *philos* lover].

GASTROPOD, see GASTEROPOD.

GASTROPODA, see GASTEROPODA.

GASTROPODOUS, see GASTEROPODOUS.

GASTRORAPHY, [gas-tror'-a-fi], *n.* (*surg.*) the operation of sewing up wounds made in the abdomen. [Gk. *gastrorraphia*].

GASTROSCOPY, [gas-tros'-ko-pi], *n.* (*med.*) a medical examination of the abdomen. [GASTRO and Gk. *skopia* viewing].

GASTROSTOMY, [gas-tros'-to-mi], *n.* the operation of making an opening in the stomach by which food may be introduced directly into the system. [GASTRO and Gk. *stoma* mouth].

GASTROTOMY, [gas-trot'-om-i], *n.* the operation of cutting into or opening the abdomen. [GASTRO and Gk. *tomia* cutting].

GASTRO-VASCULAR, [gas'-trō-vas'-kyōō-ler], *adj.* pertaining both to the abdominal receptacle and to a vessel.

GASTRULA, [gas'-trōōl-a], *n.* a cup-shaped embryo with two layers of cell in its wall. [MdL. *gastrula*].

GAS-WATER, [gas'-waw'-ter], *n.* water through which coal-gas has been passed during the process of purification.

GAS-WORKS, [gas'-wurks'], *n.(pl.)* the works where coal-gas is manufactured for heating and lighting.

GAT (1), [gat], *n.* a channel or strait between sand-banks. [OIcel. *gat* passage].

GAT (2), [gat], *n.* (*U.S.*) a Gatling gun; (*coll.*) a gun. [GAT(LING)].

GATE (1), [gāt], *n.* a structure usually in the form of an open framework, swinging on hinges, fastened by a catch or lock, and used to open or close the entrance to an enclosure, a drive, etc., or to bar progress along a path; a gateway; a structure to regulate or stop the flow of water through a lock, dock, etc.; the number of persons assembled to watch a sporting contest; the total amount of money paid by such spectators. [OE. *geat*].

GATE (2), [gāt], *n.* a road, street, way. [OIcel. *gata* road].

GATE (3), [gāt], *v.t.* to prohibit students or schoolboys from leaving their colleges, schools, or grounds after a certain hour. [GATE (1)].

GATEAU, [gat'-ō], *n.* a fancy cake. [Fr. *gâteau* cake].

GATE-BILL, [gāt'-bil], *n.* a record of fines imposed on Oxford and Cambridge undergraduates who return to college after hours.
GATE-CRASH, [gāt'-krash'], *v.t. and i.* to gain admittance to a social gathering as an intruder without invitation or ticket of admission.
GATE-CRASHER, [gāt'-krash'-er], *n.* one who gate-crashes.
GATED, [gāt'-id], *adj.* provided with gates; confined to college or school.
GATE-HOUSE, [gāt'-hows'], *n.* a house built adjacent to, or over, a gate giving entrance to an enclosure, city, etc.
GATEKEEPER, [gāt'-kēp'-er], *n.* a person in charge of a gate.
GATE-LEGGED TABLE, [gāt'-legd'-tābl'], *n.* a table having legs which fold inwards into a confined space, and a top whose end leaves fold downwards, when not in use.
GATEMAN, [gāt'-man], *n.* a gatekeeper; a person collecting the levy at a toll-gate, or gate-money paid by spectators.
GATE-MONEY, [gāt'-mun'-i], *n.* money taken as charge for admission to an enclosure in which is being held a sporting contest, etc.
GATE-POST, [gāt'-pōst'], *n.* one of the two posts on either side of an opening closed by a gate.
GATE-VEIN, [gāt'-vān'], *n.* the portal vein.
GATEWAY, [gāt'-wā], *n.* an opening in a wall, hedge, etc., closed by a gate; (*fig.*) a means of access.
GATHER (1), [GATH'-er], *n.* a small pleat or fold in cloth, etc., made by drawing a thread through the material.
GATHER (2), [GATH'-er], *v.t.* to bring together, to collect; to pick, pluck; to acquire, accumulate; to muster, summon up; to store up gradually in the mind; to infer, conclude; to pleat, to draw together into small folds by means of a thread; to increase in; to contract, pucker; *v.i.* to assemble, come together; to increase; to generate pus or morbid matter; to come to a head; **to g. way,** (*naut.*) to start moving so as to be capable of being steered. [OE. *gaderian*].
GATHERABLE, [GATH'-er-abl], *adj.* able to be gathered.
GATHERER, [GATH'-er-er], *n.* one who, or that which, gathers.
GATHERING, [GATH'-er-ing], *n.* the act of one who gathers; an assembly, a meeting; a congregation, collection; the proper arrangement of the sheets making up a book; a definite number of sheets folded once and connected together in the binding; a swelling generating pus.
GATLING, [gat'-ling], *n.* a rapid-firing American machine-gun. [Dr. R. J. *Gatling*, its inventor].
GAUB (1), [gawb], *n.* an Indian tree, *Diospyros embryopteris*, producing a sticky pulp used for caulking boats. [Hind. *gab*].
GAUB (2), [gawb], *n.* (*naut.*) the back-rope leading inboard from the martingale. [Unkn.].
GAUCHE, [gōsh], *adj.* clumsy, awkward, lacking in tact. [Fr. *gauche* left-hand].
GAUCHERIE, [gōsh'-er-ē'], *n.* awkwardness, clumsiness, want of tact. [Fr. *gaucherie*].
GAUCHO, [gow'-chō], *n.* a native of the South American pampas, of mixed Spanish and Indian descent. [Span. *gaucho*].
GAUD, [gawd], *n.* a trinket, a showy knick-knack; (*pl.*) gaieties, ostentatious ceremonial. [L. *gaudere* to rejoice].
GAUDERY, [gawd'-er-i], *n.* empty finery, showy ornaments.
GAUDILY, [gawd'-i-li], *adv.* in a gaudy fashion.
GAUDINESS, [gawd'-i-nes], *n.* the state of being gaudy.
GAUDY (1), [gawd'-i], *n.* a feast, entertainment, *esp.* an annual commemorative dinner or reunion at a college. [L. *gaudium* joy].
GAUDY (2), [gawd'-i], *adj.* showy, gay, unpleasantly brilliant, too highly coloured; overburdened with ornament. [GAUDY (1)].
GAUFFER, see GOFFER (1).
GAUFFERING, see GOFFERING.
GAUFFRE, see GOFFER (1).
GAUGE (1), GAGE, [gāj], *n.* a standard measure, *esp.* the width of a bullet, the distance between the rails of a railway; (*naut.*) the position of one vessel with respect to another and also to the wind; the number of feet to which a ship sinks in the water; an instrument for measuring the force, quantity, height, volume, etc., of such constantly varying things as wind, rain, steam-pressure, etc.; an instrument for testing the size and shapes of tools, instruments, etc., and for making them conform to standard requirements; (*carp.*) an instrument used in marking a line at any given width, parallel to the straight edge of a board, plank, etc.; (*print.*) a strip used for regulating the width of the margin, or the length of a page; (*type-founding*) a notched piece of hard wood or metal used to adjust the shape and dimensions of various kinds of letters; (*fig.*) a means of estimating, a criterion; **to have the weather g. of,** (*naut.*) to lie to windward of; (*fig.*) to have the advantage over. [AFr. *gauge*].
GAUGE (2), GAGE, [gāj], *v.t.* to measure the force, quantity, volume, etc., by means of a gauge; to measure exactly anything made to standard requirements; to cause to conform to standard dimensions; to determine the capacity of (a vessel); to mark off; (*fig.*) to estimate; judge. [AFr. *gauger*].
GAUGEABLE, [gāj'-abl], *adj.* capable of being gauged.
GAUGER, [gāj'-er], *n.* one who gauges; an excise officer employed in gauging casks of liquor.
GAUGING, [gāj'-ing], *n.* the act of one who gauges; **g. rod, rule,** an instrument used to determine the capacity of a cask of liquor.
GAUL, [gawl], *n.* a native of Gaul; (*coll.*) a Frenchman. [Fr. *Gaule*].
GAULEITER, [gow'-līt-er], *n.* the governor of a district in Germany or German-occupied territory. [Germ. *gauleiter* from *gau* region and *leiter* leader].
GAULISH (1), [gawl'-ish], *n.* the language of the Gauls.
GAULISH (2), [gawl'-ish], *adj.* pertaining to Gaul, or to the Gauls.
GAULT, [gawlt], *n.* the clay found between the Upper and Lower Greensands. [Unkn.].
GAUM, [gawm], *v.t.* to smear with some sticky material. [Uncert.].
GAUNT, [gawnt], *adj.* lean, thin, emaciated; grim, austere. [~Norw. *gand* a thin person].
GAUNTLET (1), [gawnt'-let], *n.* (*hist.*) a leather glove covered with small steel plates, worn to protect the hand; a strong, large glove with a wide mouth; **to fling down the g.,** to issue a challenge. [Fr. *gantelet*].
GAUNTLET (2), GANTLET†, GANT(E)LOPE†, [gawnt'-let], *n.* a naval or military punishment, in which the offender was compelled to run between two lines of men armed with rods, who struck him as he passed; **to run the g.,** to undergo this form of punishment; (*fig.*) to be liable to hostile attacks or criticism. [Earlier GANTELOPE from Swed. *gatlopp*, influenced by GAUNTLET (1)].
GAUNTLETED, [gawnt'-let-id], *adj.* wearing a gauntlet.
GAUNTLY, [gawnt'-li], *adv.* in a gaunt fashion.
GAUNTNESS, [gawnt'-nes], *n.* the quality of being gaunt.
GAUNTRY, see GANTRY.
GAUR, [gow'-er], *n.* the Indian wild ox, *Bos gaurus*. [Hind. *gaur*].
GAUSS, [gows], *n.* (*magn.*) the unit of strength of a magnetic field. [K. *Gauss*, the German physicist].
GAUZE, [gawz], *n.* a very thin, slight, transparent stuff, of silk, linen, cotton, wire, etc.; a slight haze; **g. wire cloth,** a kind of open cloth made of copper brass, or iron wire. [Fr. *gaze*].
GAUZY, [gawz'-i], *adj.* like gauze, thin, light, transparent.
GAVEL (1), [gav'-el], *n.* toll, rent, customary payment to an overlord. [OE. *gafol*].
GAVEL (2), [gav'-el], *n.* a small quantity of corn, cut and awaiting binding into a sheaf. [ONFr. *gavel*].
GAVEL (3), [gav'-el], *n.* a small hammer or mallet used by a chairman at a meeting; an auctioneer's hammer; a mason's maul. [Uncert.].
GAVELET†, [gav'-el-et], *n.* (*leg.*) an ancient custom whereby a tenant forfeits his lands and tenements upon non-payment of rent.
GAVELKIND, [gav'-el-kīnd], *n.* a tenure by which land is bequeathed in equal portions among the sons or heirs, upon the death of the tenant.
GAVELMAN, [gav'-el-man], *n.* a tenant liable to pay gavel.
GAVELOCK, [gav'-el-ok], *n.* an iron crowbar; a javelin; a dart, a spear used for throwing. [OE. *gafeluc*].
GAVERHALE, [gav'-er-hāl'], *n.* the jack snipe. [Unkn.].
GAVIAL, [gā'-vi-al], *n.* an Asiatic variety of crocodile,

Gavialis gangeticus, with a long narrow muzzle. [Fr. *gavial* from Hind. *ghariyal*].

GAVILAN, [gav'-il-an], *n.* a variety of hawk. [Unkn.].

GAVOTTE, [gav-ot'], *n.* a stately dance danced to music written in common time; music suitable for this dance. [Provenc. *gavoto* from *Gavot* a native of the country round Gap in the Alps].

GAWK, [gawk], *n.* an awkward, clumsy, stiff-jointed person. [Uncert.].

GAWKY (1), [gawk'-i], *n.* a gawky person.

GAWKY (2), [gawk'-i], *adj.* stiff-jointed, clumsy, awkward, ungainly.

GAWN, [gawn], *n.* a small tub or ladling vessel, usually having a long handle. [GALLON].

GAY, [gā], *adj.* lively, cheerful, vivacious, light-hearted; fond of pleasure and gaiety; bright; showy, brilliant. [Fr. *gai*].

GAYAL, [gī'-yal], *n.* the Indian ox, *Bos frontalis*. [Hind. *gayal*].

GAYNESS, [gā'-nes], *n.* the quality of being gay.

GAYSOME, [gā'-sum], *adj.* full of gaiety, very gay.

GAZE (1), [gāz], *n.* a continued, steady, thoughtful look; **at g.**, (*her.*) full-faced.

GAZE (2), [gāz], *v.i.* to look steadily, thoughtfully and continuedly. [ME. *gasen* ~Swed. *gasa*].

GAZEBO, [gaz-ē'-bō], *n.* a balcony, turret, window or building with a wide outlook; a summer-house. [Unkn.].

GAZEHOUND, [gāz'-hownd'], *n.* a hound that hunts by the sight.

GAZELLE, [gaz-el'], *n.* a genus, *Gazella*, of small, swift antelopes with large, gentle black eyes and a dark triangular marking on the forehead. [Arab. *ghazal*].

GAZELLE

GAZELLINE, [gaz-el'-īn], *adj.* related to the gazelle.

GAZER, [gāz'-er], *n.* one who gazes.

GAZETTE (1), [gaz-et'], *n.* (*hist.*) a news-sheet, a periodical journal of current happenings; an official publication, printed by government authority, in which public appointments, promotions, bankruptcies, and other public notices are recorded. [It. *gazetta*].

GAZETTE (2), [gaz-et'], *v.t.* to publish in the "Gazette."

GAZETTEER, [ga'-zet-ēer'], *n.* an official Government journalist who writes for the "Gazette"; a geographical dictionary. [It. *gazzettiere*].

GAZING-STOCK, [gāz'-ing-stok'], *n.* an object of public curiosity or contempt.

GAZOGENE, GASOGENE, [gaz'-o-jēn, gas'-o-jēn], *n.* an apparatus for making aerated water. [Fr. *gazogène*].

GAZON†, [gaz'-on], *n.* (*fort.*) pieces of turf used for lining parapets and faces of earthworks. [Fr. *gazon* turf].

GEAN, [gēn], *n.* the wild cherry, *Prunus avium*. [Fr. *guigne*].

GEAR (1), [gēer], *n.* harness, trappings; tools, implements necessary to perform some operation; (*archaic*) equipment, clothes; (*naut.*) rigging; (*machinery*) a piece of machinery consisting of a combination of toothed wheels for transmitting motion, and for regulating the rate of revolution or movement of the part driven in relation to the driving part; **high g.**, a mechanical contrivance whereby the driving part of machinery moves relatively slowly compared with the driven part; **low g.**, a mechanical contrivance which causes the driving part of machinery to move relatively quickly compared with the driven part; **out of g.**, (*fig.*) not proceeding smoothly and easily. [ME. *gere* equipment from OIcel. *gervi*].

GEAR (2), [gēer], *v.t.* to harness, equip; to put into gear; *v.i.* to be connected in the gearing system (with).

GEAR-BOX, [gēer'-boks'], *n.* the case in which the gearing mechanism is encased.

GEAR-CUTTER, [gēer'-kut'-er], *n.* a manufacturer of gears for machinery; a machine for making gear-wheels.

GEARING, [gēer'-ing], *n.* the act of fitting a machine with gears; the manner in which the gears work; the arrangement of gears in a piece of machinery.

GEARLESS, [gēer'-les], *adj.* having no gears.

GEAR-WHEEL, [gēer'-wēl], *n.* a wheel with cogs, forming part of a gearing system.

GECKO, [gek'-ō], *n.* a family of small, nocturnal insectivorous wall-lizards with suckers on their feet. [Malay *gekoq*].

GECKO

GED, [ged], *n.* the pike. [OIcel. *gedda*].

GEE (1), [jē], *int.* a word of encouragement or command to a horse.

GEE (2), [jē], *int.* (*U.S.*) an exclamation of astonishment, appreciation, delight, etc.

GEE-GEE, [jē'-jē], *n.* a word for a horse used in speaking to children.

GEESE, [gēs], *n.(pl.)* of GOOSE.

GEEST, [gēst], *n.* alluvial matter of ancient formation on the surface of land. [Germ. *geest*].

GEEZ, [gēz], *n.* the ancient language of Abyssinia. [Native].

GEEZER, [gēz'-er], *n.* (*coll.*) an old woman or man. [GUISER].

GEGENSCHEIN, [gā'-gen-shīn'], *n.* (*astron.*) counter glow, a faint luminous spot in the zodiacal band. [Germ. *gegenschein* opposite shining].

GEHENNA, [ge-hen'-a], *n.* hell; a place of torture or torment. [EcclesL. *gehenna* from Heb. *Ge-hinnom* the valley of Hinnom, near Jerusalem, where children were once sacrified to Moloch].

GEIR-EAGLE†, [gēer'-ēgl'], *n.* a small vulture of the genus *Neophron*. [Du. *gier* vulture].

GEISHA, [gā'-sha], *n.* a Japanese dancing and singing girl. [Jap. *geisha*].

GEISSLER-TUBE, [gīs'-ler-tyōōb'], *n.* a sealed tube containing rarefied gas which is made incandescent by passing a current of electricity through it, used in lighting shop-windows, etc. [H. *Geissler*, the German physicist].

GEITONOGAMY, [gī'-ton-og'-ami], *n.* pollination from another flower on the same plant. [Gk. *geiton* neighbour and *gamia* marriage].

GEL, [jel], *n.* (*chem.*) a colloid which has hardened and set into a jelly. [GELATINE].

GELABLE, [jel'-abl], *adj.* that may be frozen or congealed. [L. *gelabilis*].

GELASTIC, [jel-as'-tik], *adj.* laughable. [Gk. *gelastikos*].

GELATIGENOUS, [jel'-at-ij'-in-us], *adj.* yielding gelatine. [GELATINE and Gk. *genes* producing].

GELATIN, see GELATINE.

GELATINATE, [jel-at'-in-āt], *v.t.* to convert into gelatine; *v.i.* to be transformed into gelatine.

GELATINATION, [jel-at'-in-ā'-shun], *n.* the act of gelatinating; the state of being gelatinated.

GELATINE, GELATIN, [jel'-at-ēn, jel'-at-in], *n.* a deep yellow, brittle, translucent substance which can be melted, obtained by boiling certain animal tissues in hot water; **vegetable g.**, a substance found in gluten; **blasting g.**, a highly explosive compound containing nitro-glycerin. [It. *gelatina*].

GELATINIFORM, [jel'-at-in'-i-fawm], *adj.* having the form of gelatine. [GELATINE and FORM].

GELATINOID, [jel-at'-in-oid], *adj.* like gelatine. [GELATINE and Gk. *oeides* like].

GELATINOUS, [jel-at'-in-us], *adj.* relating to, consisting of, gelatine; of the nature of jelly.

GELD (1), [geld], *n.* (*hist.*) a tax formerly paid by English landowners to the crown. [OE. *gield*, *geld*, *gyld*].

GELD (2), [geld], *v.t.* to castrate, emasculate. [OIcel. *gelda*].

GELDABLE, [geld'-abl], *adj.* capable of being gelded.

GELDER-ROSE, see GUELDER-ROSE.

GELDING, [geld'-ing], *n.* the act of castrating; a castrated animal, *esp.* a horse. [OIcel. *geldingr*].

GELID, [jel'-id], *adj.* icy cold; (*fig.*) frigidly aloof. [L. *gelidus*].

GELIDITY, [jel-id'-i-ti], *n.* the quality of being gelid.

GELIDLY, [jel'-id-li], *adv.* in a gelid manner.

GELIDNESS, [jel'-id-nes], *n.* gelidity.

GELIGNITE, [jel-ig'-nīt], *n.* gelatine dynamite, a highly-explosive substance used for blasting. [GEL(ATINE)] and L. *ignis* fire].

GEM (1), [jem], *n.* a precious stone, *esp.* when cut and polished; a precious or semi-precious stone on which is engraved a design; anything of outstanding quality, worth or beauty; (*fig.*) the best, choicest. [Fr. *gemme* from L. *gemma* a bud].

GEM (2), (**gemming, gemmed**), [jem], *v.t.* to adorn with gems.

GEMARA, [gem-ah'-ra], *n.* the second part of the

Talmud, consisting of a commentary on the Mishna, or first part. [Arab. *gemara* completion].

GEMEL, [jem'-el], *n.* (*hist.*) a kind of double ring worn on the finger; a hinge; (*pl.*) (*her.*) bars arranged in couples. [Fr. from L. *gemellus* twin].

GEMELS

GEMELLIPAROUS†, [jem'-el-ip'-er-us], *adj.* giving birth to twins. [L. *gemellus* twin and *parere* to bring forth].

GEMINATE (1), [jem'-in-āt], *adj.* (*bot.*) (of leaves) issuing in pairs from the same point; twin. [L. *geminatus*].

GEMINATE (2), [jem'-in-āt], *v.t.* to double, to pair. [*Prec.*].

GEMINATION, [jem'-in-ā'-shun], *n.* (*gram.*) the doubling of a letter or consonant sound. [L. *geminatio*].

GEMINI, [jem'-i-nī], *n.* (*astron.*) the constellation Castor and Pollux; the third sign of the zodiac. [L. *gemini*, *pl.* of *geminus* twin].

GEMINOUS, [jem'-in-us], *adj.* double, in pairs, twin. [L. *geminus*].

GEMMA, (*pl.* **gemmae**), [jem'-a], *n.* (*bot.*) a leaf-bud; (in mosses, etc.), a small cellular nodule reproducing a new plant; (*zool.*) a bud-like development which separates and becomes a new animal organism. [L. *gemma* a bud].

GEMMACEOUS, [jem-ā'-shus], *adj.* relating to, or resembling, leaf-buds.

GEMMATE (1), [jem'-āt], *adj.* (*bot.*) reproducing by buds. [L. *gemmatus*].

GEMMATE (2), [jem'-āt], *v.i.* (*bot.*) to reproduce itself by buds. [L. *gemmare*].

GEMMATION, [jem-ā'-shun], *n.* (*bot.*) the process of reproduction by gemmae; budding-time; the way in which the leaf is enveloped in the bud; the arrangement of the buds upon the stalk; (*zool.*) reproduction by budding off.

GEMMEOUS, [jem'-ē-us], *adj.* relating to, or like, gems; **g. dragonet,** the sea-fish dusky skulpin, *Callionymus lyra*. [L. *gemmeus*].

GEMMHO, [gem'-ō], *n.* the inverse of the megohm.

GEMMIFEROUS, [jem-if'-er-us], *adj.* producing or reproducing by means of buds or gemmae. [L. *gemmifer*].

GEMMINESS, [jem'-i-nes], *n.* the quality of being gemmy.

GEMMIPARITY, [jem'-i-pa'-ri-ti], *n.* the quality of being gemmiparous.

GEMMIPAROUS, [jem-ip'-er-us], *adj.* reproducing by budding; pertaining to the process of budding. [L. *gemma* bud and *parere* to bring forth].

GEMMOSITY†, [jem-os'-i-ti], *n.* gemminess. [L. *gemmosus* full of gems].

GEMMULE, [jem'-yōōl], *n.* (*biol.*) the point of growth in the embryo; (*zool.*) a small bud-like growth among lower animals which separates and grows into a new individual. [L. *gemmula*].

GEMMULIFEROUS, [jem'-yōōl-if'-er-us], *adj.* producing gemmules. [GEMMULE and L. *ferre* to bear.]

GEMMY, [jem'-i], *adj.* full of gems; set with gems; glittering.

GEMSBOK, [gemz'-bok], *n.* a large South African antelope, *Oryx gazella*, having straight horns. [Du. *gemsbok*].

GEMSHORN, [gemz'-hawn], *n.* an organ-stop resembling a flute or horn in quality. [Germ. *gemshorn* chamois horn].

GEN (1), [jen], *n.* an Eastern manna from the camel's-thorn, *Alhagi camelorum*. [Native].

GEN (2), [jen], *n.* (R.A.F. *slang*) (reliable) information. [INTELLIGENCE].

GENA, [jē'-a], *n.* (*anat.*) the cheek. [L. *gena*].

GENAPPE, [ji-nap'], *n.* a smooth worsted yarn used in the manufacture of fringes, braid, etc. [*Genappe* in Belgium, where originally made].

GENDARME, [zhahn'-dahm], *n.* a member of a body of soldiers in France, performing police duties, and maintaining public safety and order. [Fr. from *gens d'armes* men-at-arms].

GENDARMERIE, [zhahn-dahm'-er-ē], *n.* the collective body of gendarmes. [Fr. *gendarmerie*].

GENDER (1), [jen'-der], *n.* a grammatical classification of nouns and pronouns sometimes corresponding to that of sex. [ME. *gendre* kind from OFr. *genre*].

GENDER (2), [jen'-der], *v.t.* (*archaic*) to engender. [OFr. *gendrer*, *genrer*].

GENE, [jēn], *n.* (*biol.*) a factor determining hereditary characteristics. [Gk. *genes* producing, born of].

GENEALOGICAL, [jē'-ni-al-oj'-ik-al], *adj.* pertaining to genealogy, showing genealogy; **g. tree,** a diagram representing the origin and descent of a family by means of a tree with branches. [Gk. *genealogikos*].

GENEALOGICALLY, [jē'-ni-al-oj'-ik-al-i], *adv.* in a genealogical fashion.

GENEALOGIST, [jē'-ni-al'-oj-ist], *n.* one who studies genealogy.

GENEALOGIZE, [jē'-ni-al'-oj-īz], *v.t. and i.* to relate or trace the pedigree of; to study genealogies.

GENEALOGY, [jē'-ni-al'-o-ji], *n.* a history of the descent of a person or family from the earliest known ancestor, a pedigree; an account or diagrammatic representation of this; the way in which animals, plants, etc., have evolved from primitive types; the making of pedigrees, the study of the descent of persons or families. [Gk. *genealogia*].

GENEARCH, [jen'-i-ahk], *n.* the head of a tribe or family. [Gk. *genearkhos*].

GENERA, [jen'-er-a], *n.pl.* of GENUS.

GENERABLE, [jen'-er-abl], *adj.* capable of being generated. [L. *generabilis*].

GENERAL (1), [jen'-er-al], *n.* a class or group considered collectively; *orig.*, the commander of an army, now the designation of the officer next in rank below a field-marshal, and also (*pop.*) of a lieutenant-general and major-general; the head of certain religious organizations, as the Salvation Army, Jesuits, etc.; one skilful in manoeuvring and marshalling his resources; a general maid; (*archaic*) the general public; (*pl.*) generalities.

GENERAL (2), [jen'-er-al], *adj.* not confined to any particular section, aspect or part; relating to a whole class, involving all or many parts of a whole; referring to, affecting, or applicable to, a large number of instances; summarizing all aspects; widespread, prevalent, common; usual; chief; miscellaneous; vague, indistinct; considered as a whole; (*milit.*) above the rank of colonel (of an officer or rank); (*coll.*) complete, utter; **g. meeting,** a meeting all members are invited to attend; **g. election,** an election held at the same time in every constituency throughout the country; **G. Council,** a council summoned by the Pope, at which all Catholic bishops are requested to be present; **as a g. rule,** usually; **in g.,** on the whole; **G. Headquarters,** the headquarters of the Commander-in-Chief; **G. Hospital,** a military hospital; (in certain cities) a hospital which does not specialize in any particular type of malady. [L. *generalis*].

GENERALISSIMO, [jen'-er-al-is'-i-mō], *n.* the chief commander of the combined forces of allies. [It. *generalissimo*].

GENERALITY, [jen'-er-al'-i-ti], *n.* the quality of being general; that which is general; a general statement; the greater part. [L. *generalitas*].

GENERALIZABLE, [jen'-er-al-īz'-abl], *adj.* able to be generalized.

GENERALIZATION, [jen'-er-al-īz-ā'-shun], *n.* the act of generalizing; an inference or deduction of general applicability; a statement which seeks to summarize all aspects; the process of becoming widespread.

GENERALIZE, [jen'-er-al-īz], *v.t.* to infer or express in general terms; to depict the general aspect of; to cause to be widespread; *v.i.* to make general inferences from specific examples or facts; to extend from the particular to the general; to represent the general appearance or aspect of anything.

GENERALLY, [jen'-er-al-i], *adv.* in a general fashion; usually, as a rule; without being specific; widely, commonly.

GENERALNESS, [jen'-er-al-nes], *n.* the quality of being general.

GENERALSHIP, [jen'-er-al-ship], *n.* the rank or dignity of a general; skill in military tactics, strategy and leadership; ability to manage or direct.

GENERANT, [jen'-er-ant], *n.* that which generates; (*math.*) a point, line, or surface, which, as it moves, forms a line, surface, or solid. [L. *generans*].

GENERATE, [jen'-er-āt], *v.t.* to procreate, to reproduce a similar being or individual; to produce, to cause the presence of; (*fig.*) to bring about; (*math.*) to produce or form (a line, surface, or solid) as it moves. [L. *generare*].

GENERATING, [jen'-er-āt'-ing], *adj.* producing; **g. station,** an electric power-house.

GENERATION, [jen'-er-ā'-shun], *n.* the act of generating; a single distinct step or grade in the line of descent; all the persons who form such a stage; relations, kindred; a period of time, approximately thirty years, which, as a general rule, marks off each stage in the line of descent; people considered as belonging to, or naturally associated with, such a period; **the rising g.,** the younger members of a period or age. [L. *generatio*].
GENERATIVE, [jen'-er-at-iv], *adj.* having the power of generating, pertaining to generation.
GENERATOR, [jen'-er-āt'-er], *n.* one who, or that which, generates; an apparatus for generating gas, electricity, steam, etc. [L. *generator*].
GENERATRIX, [jen'-er-a-triks], *n.* (*math.*) a generant; a dynamo. [L. *generatrix*].
GENERIC, [jen-e'-rik], *adj.* pertaining to, or comprising, a genus or class; common to all members of a genus; general.
GENERICAL, [jen-e'-rik-al], *adj.* generic.
GENERICALLY, [jen-e'-rik-al-i], *adv.* in a generic manner.
GENERICALNESS, [jen-e'-rik-al-nes], *n.* the quality of being generic.
GENEROSITY, [jen-er-os'-i-ti], *n.* the quality of being generous; liberality, magnanimity, open-handedness. [L. *generositas*].
GENEROUS, [jen'-er-us], *adj.* (*archaic*) of noble birth; liberal, munificent; of noble nature, magnanimous, large-hearted; freely given, abundant, plentiful; large, big; rich; deep, full; (of wine) strong, invigorating. [L. *generosus* of noble birth].
GENEROUSLY, [jen'-er-us-li], *adv.* in generous fashion.
GENEROUSNESS, [jen'-er-us-nes], *n.* generosity; magnanimity
GENESIOLOGY, [jen-ē'-si-ol'-oj-i], *n.* the science which deals with generation. [GENESIS and Gk. *logos* speech].
GENESIS, [jen'-es-is], *n.* the origin, birth, beginning, the way in which anything came into being; the first book of the Old Testament, which tells of the creation of the world. [Gk. *genesis*].
GENET (1), [jen'-et], *n.* a variety of civet-cat; the fur from this animal; cat-skin made to resemble this fur. [Arab. *jarnait*].

GENET

GENET (2), see JENNET.
GENETHLIAC, [jen-eth'-li-ak], *n.* a birthday poem; one who calculates nativities; (*pl.*) the science which claims to foretell a person's future life from the position of the planets at birth; a horoscope. [Gk. *genethliakos* pertaining to one's birth].
GENETIC, [jen-et'-ik], *adj.* arising from, caused by, or relating to, the genesis of a thing. [GENESIS].
GENETICAL, [jen-et'-ik-al], *adj.* genetic.
GENETICALLY, [jen-et'-ik-al-i], *adv.* in a genetic manner, according to genetics.
GENETICS, [jen-et'-iks], *n.*(*pl.*) the study of heredity.
GENEVA, [jen-ē'-va], *n.* a spirit distilled from grain, flavoured with juniper-berries; gin, hollands; the juniper. [Du. *genever* from L. *juniperus* juniper].
GENEVAN (1), [jen-ē'-van], *n.* an inhabitant of Geneva; a Calvinist.
GENEVAN (2), [jen-ē'-van], *adj.* pertaining to Geneva. [*Geneva* the town in Switzerland].
GENEVANISM, [jen-ē'-van-izm], *n.* Calvinism.
GENEVESE, [jen'-ev-ēz'], *n.* a native of Geneva, the people of Geneva.
GENEVRETTE, [jen'-ev-ret], *n.* a wine made from fermented juniper berries. [Fr. *genevrette*].
GENIAL (1), [jē'-ni-al], *adj.* cheerful, kindly, affably good-natured; (of climate) pleasant, mild, warm; (*rare*) exhibiting genius; (*archaic*) pertaining to generation or marriage. [L. *genialis*].
GENIAL (2), [jen-ī'-al], *adj.* pertaining to the chin. [Gk. *geneion* chin].
GENIALITY, [jē'-ni-al'-i-ti], *n.* the state or quality of being genial. [L. *genialitas*].
GENIALLY, [jē'-ni-al-i], *adv.* in a genial fashion.
GENIALNESS, [jē'-ni-al-nes], *n.* geniality.
GENICULATE (1), [jen-ik'-yōō-lāt], *adj.* (*bot., zool.*) jointed, having knots, bent like a knee. [L. *geniculatus*].
GENICULATE (2), [jen-ik'-yōō-lāt], *v.t.* to joint, to bend into knee-shaped joints. [*Prec.*].
GENICULATED, [jen-ik'-yōō-lāt'-id], *adj.* geniculate.
GENICULATION, [jen-ik'-yōō-lā'-shun], *n.* the state of being geniculated. [LL. *geniculatio*].
GENIE, [jē'-ni], *n.* an Arabian sprite or goblin. [L. *genius* tutelary spirit].
GENIOGLOSSE, [jen-ī'-og-los], *n.* a tongue muscle connected with the chin and hyoid bone. [MdL. *genioglossus*].
GENIPAP, [jen'-i-pap], *n.* a tropical American fruit, *Genipa americana*. [Native].
GENISTA, [jen-is'-ta], *n.* a genus of 80 species of leguminous shrubs with yellow and, less frequently, white flowers. [L. *genista* broom].
GENITAL, [jen'-it-al], *adj.* relating to, connected with, generation. [L. *genitalis*].
GENITALS, [jen'-it-alz], *n.*(*pl.*) the external organs of procreation.
GENITIVAL, [jen'-it-īv'-al], *adj.* pertaining to, having the form of, or derived from, the genitive.
GENITIVE, [jen'-it-iv], *adj.* (*gram.*) **g. case,** a grammatical form of nouns, pronouns or adjectives indicating origin, source, ownership, possession, etc. [L. *genitivus* belonging to birth].
GENITOR, [jen'-it-or], *n.* a male parent. [L. *genitor* begetter].
GENITURE†, [jen'-ich-er], *n.* procreation, birth; offspring; the seed of generation in animals; (*astrol.*) horoscope. [L. *genitura* begetting].
GENIUS, (*pl.* **geniuses**), [jē'-ni-us], *n.* spiritual atmosphere, traditional associations, mood, or feeling conjured up by the essential nature of anything; natural aptitude or capacity of mind for a particular thing; talent or natural ability of the highest order, unsurpassed intellectual, creative, and expressive power; a person displaying such talent or power; (*myth.*) the spirit presiding over a place, or influencing the life and actions of a person; (*fig.*) a person wielding a powerful influence over the life of another; **g. loci,** traditional atmosphere or group of associations native to a place; presiding spirit of a place. [L. *genius*].
GENNET, see JENNET.
GENOA CAKE, [jen'-ō-a-kāk'], *n.* a rich fruit-cake containing glacé cherries. [*Genoa* in Italy].
GENOESE (1), (*pl.* **Genoese**), [jen'-ō-ēz'], *n.* an inhabitant of Genoa.
GENOESE (2), [jen'-ō-ēz'], *adj.* pertaining to Genoa. [*Genoa*, in Northern Italy].
GENOUILLERE, genouillère, [zhen-ōō-yāer'], *n.* a metal cap for protecting the knees; (*fort.*) the part of the parapet of a battery under the embrasure. [Fr. *genouillère*].
GENRE, [zhahnr], *n.* type, species, style; a style of painting or writing depicting scenes or subjects in everyday life. [Fr. *genre*].
GENRO, [gen-rō', gen'-rō], *n.*(*pl.*) Japanese "elder statesmen." [Jap. *genro*].
GENS, [jenz], *n.* in ancient Rome, a tribe, a group of related families having a common ancestor, name, and customs. [L. *gens*].
GENT, [jent], *n.* (*coll.*) gentleman. [GENTLEMAN].
GENTEEL, [jen-tēl'], *adj.* stylish, elegant, graceful; having the manners, bearing, and behaviour of a well-bred person; mincing, affecting a mode of life, or deportment considered suitable for, or typical of, the upper classes. [Fr. *gentil*].
GENTEELLY, [jen-tēl'-li], *adv.* in a genteel fashion.
GENTEELNESS, [jen-tēl'-nes], *n.* the quality of being genteel.
GENTIAN, [jen'-shan], *n.* one of the 300 species of plants belonging to the genus *Gentiana* possessing bitter roots and bright flowers. [L. *gentiana* from Gentius, king of Illyria].
GENTIAN-BITTER, [jen'-shan-bit'-er], *n.* a medicinal tonic obtained from the roots of the gentian.
GENTIANIN, [jen'-shan-in], *n.* (*chem.*) an organic acid obtained by dissolving powdered gentian root in water.
GENTILE (1), [jen'-tīl], *n.* a non-Jew; (*archaic*) a heathen.
GENTILE (2), [jen'-tīl], *adj.* not a member of the Jewish nation; (*archaic*) pertaining to a nation or tribe. [L. *gentilis* belonging to one family].
GENTILEDOM, [jen'-tīl-dom], *n.* the non-Jewish world; the state of being a Gentile.
GENTILISH†, [jen'-tīl-ish], *adj.* like a Gentile; heathenish.
GENTILISM, [jen'-til-izm], *n.* paganism.
GENTILITIAL, [jen'-til-ish'-al], *adj.* pertaining to a nation or people; relating to a gens.

GENTILITIOUS, [jen'-til-ish'-us], *adj.* gentilitial. [L. *gentilitius*].

GENTILITY, [jen-til'-i-ti], *n.* (*archaic*) gentle birth; the manners, behaviour, and mode of life of well-bred persons; affected refinement. [L. *gentilitas* relationship].

GENTILIZE, [jen'-til-īz], *v.t.* to deprive of Jewish character; *v.i.* to live or behave like a Gentile.

GENTLE (1), [jentl], *n.* the maggot of the bluebottle fly, a species of *Calliphora*, used as a fishing bait.

GENTLE (2), [jentl], *adj.* well-bred; mild, kindly, tender; peace-loving, placid; moderate, slight; soft, soothing; not excessive; not rough or rapid; gradual; docile, quiet; (*her.*) having the right to bear arms; (*archaic*) courteous, well-mannered. [L. *gentilis* belonging to the same family].

GENTLE (3), [jentl], *v.t.* to break in (a horse).

GENTLEFOLK, [jentl'-fōk], *n.(pl.)* persons of good or noble breeding and family.

GENTLEHOOD, [jentl'-hood], *n.* the position or condition of being gentle.

GENTLEMAN, [jentl'-man], *n.* a chivalrous, well-mannered person; a well-born person belonging to the upper classes of society; a man of means and leisure; (*hist.*) a man who has the right to bear arms, although not a nobleman; (*hist.*) a man of high birth and breeding attached to the court, or to the household of a person of high rank; (*leg.*) a person of independent means; a courteous form of address; **gentleman's agreement,** a tacit agreement. [ME. *gentil man*].

GENTLEMAN-AT-ARMS, [jentl'-man-at-ahmz'], *n.* a member of the sovereign's bodyguard on state occasions.

GENTLEMAN-COMMONER, [jentl'-man-kom'-on-er], *n.* the highest class of commoner at Oxford University.

GENTLEMAN-FARMER, [jentl'-man-fahm'-er], *n.* in England, a gentleman farming his own or leased land; (*U.S.*) a man of independent means who farms for pleasure or diversion.

GENTLEMANHOOD, [jentl'-man-hood], *n.* the position or qualities of a gentleman.

GENTLEMANLIKE, [jentl'-man-līk], *adj.* gentlemanly.

GENTLEMANLINESS, [jentl'-man-li-nes], *n.* the quality of being gentlemanly.

GENTLEMANLY, [jentl'-man-li], *adj.* characteristic or worthy of a gentleman.

GENTLEMANSHIP, [jentl'-man-ship], *n.* the conduct or status of a gentleman.

GENTLEMAN-USHER, [jentl'-man-ush'-er], *n.* one who is usher to a person of high rank.

GENTLENESS, [jentl'-nes], *n.* the quality of being gentle.

GENTLEWOMAN, [jentl'-woom'-an], *n.* a lady, a woman of good family or breeding; a woman who waits upon one of high rank.

GENTLEWOMANLINESS, [jentl'-woom-an-li-nes], *n.* the quality of being gentlewomanly.

GENTLEWOMANLY, [jentl'-woom-an-li], *adj.* resembling or befitting a gentlewoman.

GENTLY, [jent'-li], *adv.* in a gentle manner.

GENTOO (1), [jen'-tōō], *n.* a Hindoo, *esp.* a Telugu-speaking Hindoo living in the south of the Peninsula. [Portug. *Gentio* a Gentile].

GENTOO (2), [jen'-tōō], *n.* the penguin *Pygosceles tæniata*, inhabiting the Falkland Islands. [Unkn.].

GENTRY, [jen'-tri], *n.* untitled people of good birth and high social position; type of people, class of folks; (*archaic*) birth, *esp.* high birth. [OFr. *genterise*].

GENUAL, [jen'-yōō-al], *adj.* relating to the knee. [L. *genu* knee].

GENUFLECT, [jen'-yōō-flekt'], *v.i.* to bend the knee in worship. [MedL. *genuflectere*].

GENUFLECTORY, [jen'-yōō-flek'-ter-i], *adj.* relating to genuflexion.

GENUFLEXION, GENUFLECTION, [jen'-yōō-flek'-shun], *n.* the bending of the knee in reverence. [MedL. *genuflexio*].

GENUINE, [jen'-yōō-in], *adj.* real, valid, authentic; honest, not assumed or counterfeit; belonging to the original stock, pure-bred. [L. *genuinus* native, innate].

GENUINELY, [jen'-yōō-in-li], *adv.* in a genuine fashion.

GENUINENESS, [jen'-yōō-in-nes], *n.* the quality of being genuine.

GENUS, (*pl.* **genera**), [jē'-nus, jen'-er-a], *n.* (*bot.*, *zool.*) a group of species possessing certain distinctive structural characters in common; (*logic*) a class made up of several species, each distinguished slightly from the others; kind, sort, class. [L. *genus*].

GEO-, *pref.* the earth. [Gk. *ge*, *geo*-].

GEOCENTRIC, [jē'-ō-sen'-trik], *adj.* regarded as seen or reckoned from the centre of the earth; having the earth for centre. [GEO and CENTRIC].

GEOCENTRICAL, [jē'-ō-sen'-trik-al], *adj.* geocentric.

GEOCENTRICALLY, [jē'-ō-sen'-trik-al-i], *adv.* in a geocentric fashion.

GEOCYCLIC, [jē'-ō-sī'-klik], *adj.* relating to the revolution of the earth; encircling the earth periodically. [GEO and CYCLIC].

GEODE, [jē'-ōd], *n.* a rounded stone containing a small cavity lined with crystals; the hollow crystal-lined centre of such a stone. [Gk. *geodes* earth-like].

GEODESIC (1), [jē'-ō-dē'-sik], *n.* a line of which each part is the smallest distance between the points limiting it.

GEODESIC (2), [jē'-ō-dē'-sik], *adj.* pertaining to, produced by, geodesy.

GEODESICAL, [jē'-ō-dē'-sik-al], *adj.* geodesic.

GEODESY, [jē-od'-esi], *n.* the science of measuring the earth, or surveying any large portion of it. [Gk. *geodaisia*].

GEODETIC, [jē'-ō-dē'-tik], *adj.* geodesic.

GEODETICAL, [jē'-ō-dē'-tik-al], *adj.* geodetic.

GEODIC, [jē-ōd'-ik], *adj.* pertaining to, resembling, a geode.

GEODIFEROUS, [jē'-ō-dif'-er-us], *adj.* bearing geodes. [GEODE and L. *ferre* to bear].

GEODYNAMICS, [jē'-ō-dī-nam'-iks], *n.(pl.)* the study of the forces acting on the earth's surface. [GEO and DYNAMICS].

GEOGNOSTIC, [jē'-og-nos'-tik], *adj.* relating to geognosy; geological. [GEO and Gk. *gnostos* one who knows].

GEOGNOSTICAL, [jē'-og-nos'-tik-al], *adj.* geognostic.

GEOGNOSY, [jē-og'-nos-i], *n.* the science of the constitution and structure of the earth, and of the arrangement and distribution of its strata; the geology of a particular locality. [GEO and Gk. *gnosis* knowledge].

GEOGONIC, [jē'-ō-gon'-ik], *adj.* relating to geogony.

GEOGONY, [jē-og'-on-i], *n.* the study of the structure of the earth. [GEO and Gk. *gonia* production].

GEOGRAPHER, [jē-og'-raf-er], *n.* one who studies or writes about geography.

GEOGRAPHIC, [jē'-ō-graf'-ik], *adj.* pertaining to geography. [Gk. *geographikos*].

GEOGRAPHICAL, [jē'-ō-graf'-ik-al], *adj.* geographic; **g. mile,** a measure of length equivalent to one degree of longitude on the equator.

GEOGRAPHICALLY, [jē'-ō-graf'-ik-al-i], *adv.* in a geographical manner, from the point of view of geography.

GEOGRAPHY, [jē-og'-ra-fi], *n.* the science which deals with the description of the earth's surface, its physical features, peoples, products, climate, etc., and their arrangement and distribution; the arrangement and relative position of the different parts of a place, building, etc.; a book about geography. [Gk. *geographia*].

GEOLATRY, [jē-ol'-at-ri], *n.* earth-worship. [GEO and Gk. *latreia* worship].

GEOLOGICAL, [jē-ol-oj'-ik-al], *adj.* relating to geology.

GEOLOGIST, [jē-ol'-oj-ist], *n.* a student of geology.

GEOLOGIZE, [jē-ol'-oj-īz], *v.t. and i.* to study geology; to make geological investigations; to study the geology of.

GEOLOGY, [jē-ol'-oj-i], *n.* the science which deals with the structure of the earth's crust, with its rocks and their contents, the successive changes these have undergone, and the causes thereof; the geological features of a district; a book about geology. [GEO and Gk. *logos* speech].

GEOMANCER, [jē'-ō-man'-ser], *n.* a student of geomancy.

GEOMANCY, [jē'-ō-man-si], *n.* divination by figures formed on the ground when a handful of earth is thrown down, or by figures made by a succession of dots jotted down haphazardly upon paper. [GEO and Gk. *manteia* divination].

GEOMANTIC, [jē'-ō-man'-tik], *adj.* of, relating to, geomancy.

GEOMETER, [jē-om'-it-er], *n.* one skilled in geometry; (*entom.*), any one of the looper moths, so called from the peculiar manner of walking of the caterpillars. [Gk. *geometres* one who measures land].

GEOMETRIC, [jē'-ō-met'-rik], *adj.* geometrical; **g. spider,** a spider whose web is of symmetrical shape. [Gk. *geometrikos*].

GEOMETRICAL, [jē'-ō-met-rik-al], *adj.* pertaining to, according to, the principles of geometry; constructed by geometry; regular, symmetrical, made up of figures and shapes used in geometry; **g. progression,** progression in which the quantities increase by a common multiplier or decrease by a common divisor.

GEOMETRICALLY, [jē'-ō-met'-rik-al-i], *adv.* in accordance with geometry.

GEOMETRICIAN, [jē'-om-et-rish'-un], *n.* one learned in geometry.

GEOMETRIZE, [jē-om'-et-rīz], *v.t. and i.* to use geometrical principles; to perform geometrically.

GEOMETRY, [jē-om'-et-ri], *n.* that part of mathematics which deals with points, lines, surfaces, and solids; a book about geometry. [Gk. *geometria* measurement of the earth].

GEOMORPHOLOGY, [jē'-ō-mawf-ol'-oj-i], *n.* the study of the arrangement, forms, and shape of the crust of the earth. [GEO and MORPHOLOGY].

GEONOMY, [jē-on'-om-i], *n.* the science of the physical laws of the earth. [GEO and Gk. *nomia* arrangement].

GEOPHAGISM, [jē-of'-ag-izm], *n.* the custom or practice of eating earth. [GEO and Gk. *phago* I eat].

GEOPHAGIST, [jē-of'-ag-ist], *n.* a person suffering from geophagy.

GEOPHAGY, [jē-of'-ag-i], *n.* a morbid tendency or desire to eat earth.

GEOPHONE, [jē'-ō-fōn], *n.* an apparatus used to detect subterranean sounds in mining, etc. [GEO and Gk. *phone* voice].

GEOPHYSICAL, [jē'-ō-fiz'-ik-al], *adj.* pertaining to geophysics. [GEO and PHYSICAL].

GEOPHYSICS, [jē'-ō-fiz'-iks], *n.* the science dealing with the physical principles, causes, or forces involved in, or affecting, the structure of the earth. [GEO and PHYSICS].

GEOPONIC, [jē'-ō-pon'-ik], *adj.* pertaining to agriculture. [Gk. *geoponos* husbandman].

GEOPONICAL, [jē'-ō-pon'-ik-al], *adj.* geoponic.

GEOPONICS, [jē'-ō-pon'-iks], *n.(pl.)* agriculture, husbandry.

GEORAMA, [jē'-ō-rahm'-a], *n.* a hollow sphere which displays from its interior a complete geographical view of the earth's surface. [GEO and Gk. *orama* view].

GEORGE, [jawj], *n.* a jewelled figure of St. George on horseback, together with the dragon, worn by Knights of the Garter; (*slang*) a half-crown; **G. noble,** a gold coin of Henry VIII with a george on the reverse, worth 6s. 8d.; **St. George's cross,** a vertical and horizontal bar of red, intersecting in their centres. [Gk. *Georgios* the name of a Cappadocian saint who was martyred].

GEORGE NOBLE

GEORGETTE, [jawj-et'], *n.* a thin, light, partially transparent silk and cotton fabric. [Mme *Georgette*, a French dressmaker].

GEORGIAN (1), [jaw'-ji-an], *n.* a native or the language of Georgia in the Caucasus, or Georgia, U.S.A.

GEORGIAN (2), [jaw'-ji-an], *adj.* pertaining to Georgia in the Caucasus or to Georgia, U.S.A.

GEORGIAN (3), [jaw'-ji-an], *adj.* belonging to the reigns of the Georges, kings of England.

GEORGIC (1), [jawj'-ik], *n.* a poetical composition on rural husbandry, one of the books of Virgil's poem upon husbandry.

GEORGIC (2), [jawj'-ik], *adj.* pertaining to agricultural and rural affairs. [Gk. *georgikos*].

GEORGICAL, [jawj'-ik-al], *adj.* georgic.

GEOSELENIC, [jē'-ō-sel-ĕn'-ik], *adj.* pertaining to both the earth and the moon. [GEO and Gk. *selene* moon].

GEOSTATIC, [jē'-ō-stat'-ik], *adj.* pertaining to the pressure of the earth. [GEO and STATIC].

GEOSTATICS, [jē'-ō-stat'-iks], *n.(pl.)* the statics of rigid bodies.

GEOSTROPHIC, [jē'-ō-strof'-ik], *adj.* (*meteor.*) dependent on the earth's rotation. [GEO and Gk. *strophikos* turning].

GEOTECTONIC, [jē'-ō-tek-ton'-ik], *adj.* pertaining to the structure of the earth's crust; structural. [GEO and Gk. *tektonikos* skilled in building].

GEOTHERMIC, [jē'-ō-thurm'-ik], *adj.* pertaining to the central heat of the earth. [GEO and THERMIC].

GEOTHERMOMETER, [jē'-ō-thur-mom'-it-er], *n.* an instrument for recording the degree of heat in the earth at different places, *esp.* in artesian wells, mines, etc. [GEO and THERMOMETER].

GEOTROPISM, [jē-ot'-rop-izm], *n.* the tendency of parts of plants to turn towards the centre of the earth (positive geotropism) or away from the centre of the earth (negative geotropism). [GEO and Gk. *trope* turning].

GERAH, [jēer'-ah], *n.* a Hebrew coin and weight equivalent to the twentieth part of a shekel. [Heb. *gerah*].

GERANIUM, [jer-ā'-ni-um], *n.* one of a large genus of plants having lobed leaves and red, pink or white flowers; any of several species of *Pelargonium*. [Gk. *geranion* the crane's bill plant].

GERANIUM

GERATOLOGY, [je'-rat-ol'-oj-i], *n.* the investigation of the phenomena of deterioration and decay, *esp.* of the dying-out of a species of animals. [Gk. *geras geratos* old age and *logos* speech].

GERBILLE, [jer'-bil], *n.* a rodent having a long tufted tail. [MdL. *gerbillus*].

GERENT, [je'-rent], *n.* a governor, ruler, director, manager, one who holds some official position. [L. *gerens*].

GERFALCON, GYRFALCON, JERFALCON, [jer'-faw(l)k-on], *n.* a large falcon found in the northern regions. [OFr. *gerfaucon*].

GERM (1), [jurm], *n.* the origin of an embryo, the rudimentary form of an organism from which a new similar individual being can develop; a microbe, *esp.* one which helps to cause disease; (*fig.*) the primitive, undeveloped form from which anything springs or grows. [L. *germen* bud, sprout].

GERM (2), [jurm], *v.i.* (*fig.*) to bud, sprout, take root; to form.

GERMAN (1), [jur'-man], *n.* a native of Germany; the German language; **High G.,** the standard literary language in Germany; **Low G.,** the German dialects other than High German. [L. *Germanus*].

GERMAN (2), [jur'-man], *adj.* pertaining to Germany, the German people or language; made in, characteristic of, Germany; **G. text,** black letter; **G. measles,** a mild infectious disease resembling measles. [L. *Germanus*].

GERMAN (3), [jur'-man], *adj.* having the same grandparents; born of the same parents. [L. *Germanus*].

GERMANDER, [jer-man'-der], *n.* one of the labiate, aromatic plants of the genus *Teucrium*. [MedL. *germandra*].

GERMANE, [jer-mān'], *adj.* related, appropriate, pertinent. [GERMAN (3)].

GERMANIC (1), [jer-man'-ik], *n.* the language of the Teutonic people, *esp.* in its earliest stage.

GERMANIC (2), [jer-man'-ik], *adj.* pertaining to Germany or to the Germans; relating to the Teutonic peoples. [L. *Germanicus*].

GERMANISM, [jur'-man-izm], *n.* a German idiom; a German quality or characteristic; love of and devotion towards Germany and that which is German.

GERMANIUM, [jer-mā'-ni-um], *n.* a greyish-white metallic element, Ge, occurring in the mineral argyrodite. [L. *Germanus* German].

GERMANIZATION, [jur'-man-iz-ā'-shun], *n.* the act of Germanizing; the state of becoming Germanized.

GERMANIZE, [jur'-man-iz], *v.t. and i.* to make German.

GERMAN-MILLET, [jur'-man-mil'-et], *n.* a grass which yields an edible grain, *Sitaria germanica*.

GERMANOMANIA, [jur'-man-ō-mā'-ni-a], *n.* excessive, unreasoning devotion to that which is German. [GERMAN and MANIA].

GERMANOPHILE, [jur-man'-ō-fīl], *n.* a lover or fervent admirer of the Germans or of that which is German. [GERMAN and Gk. *philos* lover].

GERMANOPHOBIA, [jur'-man-ō-fō'-bi-a], *n.* hatred of Germans or of that which is German. [GERMAN and PHOBIA].

GERMAN-PASTE, [jur'-man-pāst'], *n.* a food for certain kinds of cage-birds, consisting of hempseed, pea-meal, lard, and honey.
GERMAN-SAUSAGE, [jur'-man-sos'-ij], *n.* a large sausage containing meat partly cooked and highly flavoured.
GERMAN-SILVER, [jur'-man-sil'-ver], *n.* an alloy containing copper, zinc, and nickel.
GERMAN-TINDER, [jur'-man-tin'-der], *n.* a sponge-like substance made from a kind of fungus, and used as tinder.
GERM-CELL, [jurm'-sel], *n.* a reproductive cell.
GERMEN, [jurm'-en], *n.* (*bot.*) a seed-vessel, ovary. [L. *germen*].
GERMICIDAL, [jurm'-i-sīd'-al], *adj.* able to, or tending to, destroy germs.
GERMICIDE (1), [jurm'-i-sīd], *n.* a substance by which germs, *esp.* disease germs, can be destroyed. [GERM and L. *cida* murderer].
GERMICIDE (2), [jurm'-i-sīd], *adj.* able to kill germs, *esp.* disease germs.
GERMINAL, [jurm'-in-al], *adj.* pertaining to, of the nature of, a germ; (*fig.*) in an undeveloped, rudimentary stage. [MdL. *germinalis*].
GERMINANT, [jurm'-in-ant], *adj.* sprouting, germinating. [L. *germinans*].
GERMINATE, [jurm'-in-āt], *v.t.* and *i.* to sprout, bud, shoot, to begin to develop; to cause to do this. [L. *germinare*].
GERMINATION, [jurm'-in-ā'-shun], *n.* the process of germinating; the state or period of germinating. [L. *germinatio*].
GERMINATIVE, [jurm'-in-at-iv], *adj.* pertaining to germination, able to germinate, causing germination.
GERMON, [jurm'-on], *n.* a variety of tunny fish. [Fr. *germon*].
GERM-PLASM, [jurm'-plazm'], *n.* (*biol.*) that part of the nucleus of a germ-cell transmitted unchanged from generation to generation.
GEROCOMY, [jer-ok'-om-i], *n.* the science dealing with the treatment of old people. [Gk. *gerokomia*].
GERONTOCRACY, [jer'-on-tok'-ra-si], *n.* government by old men. [Gk. *geron gerontos* old man and *kratia* government].
GEROPIGA, [jer-op-ē'-ga], *n.* a compound of unfermented grape-juice and colouring matter, preserved in brandy and sugar, and used to give an artificial strength and colour to port wine. [Portug. *geropiga*].
GERRY, see JERRY.
GERRYMANDER (1), [je'-ri-man'-der], *n.* unfair manipulation, wangling, *esp.* of electoral districts in politics. [Elbridge *Gerry*, a governor of Massachusetts, who unfairly divided a county into electoral divisions].
GERRYMANDER (2), [je'-ri-man'-der], *v.t.* to manipulate unfairly, to wangle, *esp.* of an electoral district.
GERSDORFFITE, [gāerz'-dawf-īt], *n.* a compound of nickel, arsenic, and sulphur. [Von *Gersdorff* the owner of the mine where it was first found].
GERUND, [je'-rund], *n.* the verbal noun in Latin, having the nature of a noun but expressing the action of a verb; the English verbal noun ending in *-ing*. [L. *gerundium*].
GERUNDIAL, [je-run'-di-al], *adj.* pertaining to, or resembling, a gerund.
GERUNDIVE (1), [je-rund'-iv], *n.* the verbal adjective formed from the gerund, resembling a passive participle, and used to indicate necessity, etc. [LL. *gerundivus*].
GERUNDIVE (2), [je-rund'-iv], *adj.* pertaining to a gerund.
GERVAS, [jur'-vas], *n.* a tropical South American plant, the leaves of which are sold as tea, or used to adulterate tea. [Native].
GESSO, [jes'-ō], *n.* gypsum, or plaster of Paris, prepared for use in sculpture and painting; a surface of this. [It. *gesso* from L. *gypsum* plaster].
GEST, [jest], *n.* a tale or story; (*archaic*) an exploit, noble deed. [L. *gesta* deeds].
GESTAPO, [ges'-tah'-pō], *n.* the Nazi Secret Police; any organization resembling this. [Germ. *gestapo* from *Ge(heime) Sta(ats) Po(lizei)*secret state police].
GESTATION, [jest-ā'-shun], *n.* the act of carrying or the state of being carried in the womb; period of pregnancy. [L. *gestatio*].
GESTATORIAL, [jest'-a-taw'-ri-al], *adj.* **g. chair,** the chair in which the Pope is borne on certain ceremonial occasions. [L. *gestatorius* for carrying].
GESTATORY, [jest'-a-ter-i], *adj.* that may be carried or worn; pertaining to carrying. [L. *gestatorius* for carrying].
GESTIC, [jest'-ik], *adj.* pertaining to dancing or bodily movement. [L. *gestus* gesture].
GESTICULATE, [jest-ik'-yōō-lāt], *v.t.* and *i.* to make rapid brisk movements of the arms or body as a means of emphasis or vivid expression when speaking, or as a means of communication in place of speech; to express by gesture. [L. *gesticulare*].
GESTICULATION, [jes'-tik-yōō-lā'-shun], *n.* the act of gesticulating, forceful gesture. [L. *gesticulatio*].
GESTICULATOR, [jest-ik'-yōō-lāt'-er], *n.* a person who gesticulates.
GESTICULATORY, [jest-ik'-yōō-lāt'-er-i], *adj.* pertaining to gesticulation, representing by gesture.
GESTURAL, [jes'-cher-al], *adj.* pertaining to gesture.
GESTURE (1), [jes'-cher], *n.* a movement of the limbs or body, expressing an idea, feeling, etc., or to emphasize what is being said, a facial movement or grimace used in such a way; an action performed to convey an impression or to suggest a particular attitude. [MedL. *gestura*].
GESTURE (2), [jes'-cher], *v.t.* and *i.* to make gestures; to express by means of gesture.
GESTURELESS, [jes'-cher-les], *adj.* without gestures.
GESTUREMENT†, [jes'-cher-ment], *n.* gesture.
GET (1), [get], *n.* (of animals) offspring; the output of a coal-mine during a certain period.
GET (2), (getting, got), [get], *v.t.* to acquire possession of, to procure, obtain, receive; to have or possess; to succeed in doing something or bringing something about; to score; to beget; to catch; to put in a certain condition; to persuade to do, to prevail on, to induce; to be put into communication with; (*prov.*) to be referred to as; (*coll.*) to understand; *v.i.* to become, to grow; to arrive at any place; to accomplish something, to succeed in achieving something; to undergo an experience; to earn, make money; to be compelled or obliged; **to g. about,** to resume normal activity; to visit many places; **to g. along,** to depart; to prosper, to manage; **to g. at,** to obtain access to; to come into contact with; to reach; to grasp, understand; to attack; to drive at; to find out, to discover; **to g. away,** to leave; to escape; **to g. away with,** to succeed in making off with; to pass off successfully, to avoid due retribution; to escape discovery in connexion with; **to g. down to,** to concentrate whole-heartedly upon; **to g. home,** to find its mark; **to g. in,** to enter; to be elected; to succeed in gaining admission to a theatre, etc.; to gather; **to g. in with,** to associate with; **to g. into,** to enter; to put on, don; to involve oneself in; **to g. off,** to dismount, alight from; to succeed in avoiding punishment for a person; to escape; **to g. off with,** to be punished leniently; (*slang*) to flirt with, to have an affair with; **to g. on,** to advance, to make progress; to depart; to establish friendly relations with, to agree; to be successful; **to be getting on,** to fare; to reach an advanced stage of life, to become old; (of the hour) to be late; **to be getting on for,** (*coll.*) to approach, to be nearly; **to g. on to,** (*coll.*) to approach (someone) about, to speak to (someone) by telephone; **to g. on with,** to agree with, to be on friendly terms with; to continue with, to start and make progress with; **to g. over,** to surmount; to recover from (a shock, illness, etc.); **to g. out,** to extract, to draw from; (*coll.*) to draw up, to work out; to produce, make; (*cricket*) to be dismissed; to dismount, alight; **to g. out of,** to escape, avoid; to alight from, come out of; **to g. round,** to cajole, to win the good favour or opinion of; to overcome, surmount; **to g. together,** to collect; to meet, assemble; **to g. up,** to arise from bed; to stand on one's feet from a sitting or lying position; to study, cram; to develop; to array, adorn oneself; to decorate, to ornament; to start, organize; to launder; **to g. up to,** to involve oneself in (mischief, etc.); to scheme; **to g. through,** to penetrate or to pass through; to succeed in an examination or test; to finish, to accomplish; **to g. hold of,** to grasp; to find, to meet; **to g. away from,** to avoid, to leave behind; **to g. back,** to return, to retreat; **to g. back to,** to resume; **to g. across with,** (*coll.*) to fall into disfavour; **to g. there,** to succeed; **to tell someone where he gets off,** (*coll.*) to give a person a piece of one's mind, to put him in his proper place. [OIcel. *geta*].
GETABLE, [get'-abl], *adj.* that may be obtained.
GET-AT-ABLE, [get-at'-abl], *adj.* accessible, that can be approached or reached.

GETAWAY, [get'-a-wā], *n.* (*slang*) escape; departure.

GETTER, [get'-er], *n.* one who begets; one who gets.

GETTERING, [get'-er-ing], *n.* (*wirel.*) a process of burning up any air remaining in a thermionic valve after exhaustion by igniting a small piece of magnesium inside the valve. [Unkn.].

GETTING, [get'-ing], *n.* acquisition, gain; the act of one who gets.

GET-UP, [get'-up], *n.* the way in which a person is dressed, clothes; general appearance.

GEUM, [jē'-um], *n.* a hardy genus of plants related to the rose, and including the herb-bennet. [L. *geum* herb-bennet].

GEW-GAW, [gew'-gaw'], *n.* a showy, worthless trifle, a bauble, a knick-knack. [ME. *giuegoue*].

GEYSER, [gē'-zer, gā'-zer], *n.* a natural jet of hot water and steam rising to a considerable height from a hot spring; a metal cylinder in which water is heated quickly by means of lighted gas, etc. [*Geysir*, the name of a geyser in Iceland].

GHAST, [gahst], *adj.* (*archaic*) ghastly.

GHASTLINESS, [gahst'-li-nes], *n.* the condition of being ghastly.

GHASTLY, [gahst'-li], *adj.* horrible, terrifying; deathlike, pale, like a corpse; (*coll.*) dreadful, shocking; frightful. [OE. *gastlic* spiritual and OE. *gæstlic* terrible].

GHAT, ghât, GHAUT, [gawt], *n.* a mountain pass; either of two ranges of mountains along the east and west side of southern India; a flight of stairs descending to a river, and used as a landing-place. [Hind. *ghaut* landing-place].

GHAZI, [gah'-zē], *n.* a Mohammedan fanatic; a title of honour awarded to national heroes in Turkey. [Arab. *ghazi*].

GHEBER, see GUEBRE.

GHEE, [gē], *n.* in the East Indies, clarified butter made from the milk of buffaloes. [Hind. *ghi*].

GHERKIN, [gur'-kin], *n.* a small cucumber commonly used for pickling. [~Du. *gurkje*].

GHETTO, [get'-ō], *n.* the Jewish quarter in a city; (*coll.*) a place frequented by large numbers of Jews. [It. *ghetto* a quarter in Italian cities to which Jews were confined].

GHIBELLINE, [gib'-el-ēn], *n.* a member of the Italian political party supporting the Emperor in opposition to the Pope. [It. *Ghibellino* from Germ. *Waiblingen*, one of the estates of the Germanic Emperors].

GHOST, [gōst], *n.* the soul, the spiritual essence of life; the spirit of a dead person appearing before the living in visible form, a spectre, phantom; a shadow, a pale, unsubstantial, emaciated image of a person's former self; an unknown person who does literary and artistic work for another who takes the credit for it; (*fig.*) shadowy recollections of times past; the spirit of man or God; **to give up the g.,** to die; **the g. walks,** (*theatrical slang*) salaries are paid. [OE. *gast* spirit, the *h* being introduced by early printers].

GHOST-DANCE, [gōst'-dahnts'], *n.* a ritual dance among North American Indians.

GHOSTLIKE, [gōst'-līk], *adj.* resembling a ghost; ghastly.

GHOSTLINESS, [gōst'-li-nes], *n.* the quality of being ghostly.

GHOSTLY, [gōst'-li], *adj.* spiritual, relating to the soul; holy; pertaining to a ghost; like a ghost, shadowy, unsubstantial; frequented by ghosts, suggesting the presence of ghosts. [OE. *gastlic*].

GHOST-MOTH, [gōst'-moth'], *n.* the moth *Hepialus humuli*.

GHOST-STORY, [gōst'-staw'-ri], *n.* a tale about ghosts.

GHOST-WORD, [gōst'-wurd], *n.* a word which is not a genuine word at all.

GHOUL, [gōōl], *n.* a demon in Eastern countries supposed to frequent burial places and devour corpses; (*fig.*) a fiendish monster. [Arab. *ghul*].

GHOULISH, [gōōl'-ish], *adj.* like a ghoul; fiendish, cruelly horrible.

GHYLL, [gil], *n.* a ravine, gully. [GILL (4)].

GIALLOLINO, [jal-ō-lē'-nō], *n.* a fine yellow pigment, Naples yellow. [It. *giallolino*].

GIANT (1), [jī'-ant], *n.* a fabulous being in human form possessing extraordinary bulk, stature, and strength; a person of exceptional height and size; a peculiarly large plant or animal; a person outstanding in merit or genius. [OFr. *geant*].

GIANT (2), [jī'-ant], *adj.* of extraordinary dimensions or proportions, enormous.

GIANT-FENNEL, [jī'-ant-fen'-el], *n.* one of the largest of the temperate herbaceous plants, *Ferula communis*.

GIANTISM, [jī'-ant-izm], *n.* an abnormal bodily condition in man and animals resulting in excessive and usually misproportioned growth, due to abnormal secretion of the pituitary gland.

GIANT-LIKE, [jī'-ant-līk], *adj.* gigantic; huge, tremendous.

GIANTSHIP, [jī'-ant-ship], *n.* the state, quality, or character of a giant.

GIANT-STRIDE, [jī'-ant-strīd'], *n.* a pole surmounted by a revolving wheel from which a number of ropes hang, a person holding one of these ropes being thus able to take huge strides as the wheel revolves.

GIAOUR, [jow(r)], *n.* the Turkish name for an unbeliever, *esp.* for a Christian. [Pers. *gaur*].

GIB (1), [jib, gib], *n.* hooked gristle developing on the lower jaw of the male salmon after the spawning season; a wedge-shaped piece of metal used to hold part of a machine in place. [Uncert.].

GIB (2), [gib], *n.* a male-cat, *esp.* when castrated; (*coll.*) an old woman. [*Gilbert*].

GIBBER, [jib'-er], *v.i.* to chatter away in a rapid incoherent manner; to jabber. [Imitative].

GIBBERISH, [jib'-er-ish], *n.* rapid, incoherent, inarticulate talk; a language unintelligible to the hearer or reader.

GIBBET (1), [jib'-et], *n.* a gallows, a post with a projecting arm at the top from which the body of an executed person was hung in chains; the projecting beam of a crane, to which the pulley is fixed. [OFr. *gibet*].

GIBBET (2), **(gibbeting, gibbeted),** [jib'-et], *v.t.* to hang on a gibbet; (*fig.*) to exhibit to public contempt or ridicule.

GIBBON, [gib'-on], *n.* a long-armed, tailless, small ape of the genus *Hylobates*. [Fr. *gibbon*].

GIBBOSE, [gib'-ōs], *adj.* gibbous.

GIBBOSITY, [gib-os'-i-ti], *n.* the quality of being gibbous; a protuberance.

GIBBOUS, [gib'-us], *adj.* protuberant, bulging, convex; hump-backed; (of the moon, planets) greater than half but less than full. [L. *gibbosus* humped].

GIBBET

GIBBOUSLY, [gib'-us-li], *adv.* in a gibbous manner.

GIBBOUSNESS, [gib'-us-nes], *n.* gibbosity.

GIB-CAT, [gib'-kat'], *n.* a tom-cat, *esp.* when castrated.

GIBE (1), [jīb], *n.* a scoff, taunt, sneer, a derisive reference.

GIBE (2), [jīb], *v.i.* to utter a gibe or gibes, to sneer; **to g. at,** to deride. [Unkn.].

GIBEL, [gēb'-el], *n.* a small freshwater fish, the Prussian carp, *Carassius gibelio*. [Germ. *gibel*, *giebel*].

GIBEONITE, [gib'-i-on-īt], *n.* an inhabitant of Gibeon; a menial of the lowest rank. [*Gibeon*, Joshua ix, 17].

GIBER, [jīb'-er], *n.* one who gibes.

GIBINGLY, [jīb'-ing-li], *adv.* in gibing fashion.

GIBLET, [jib'-let], *adj.* made of giblets.

GIBLETS, [jib'-lets], *n.*(*pl.*) the edible, but not relished, parts of poultry, as the gizzard, liver, etc., usually removed before cooking. [OFr. *gibelotte* stew].

GIB-STAFF, [jib'-stahf'], *n.* a staff used to gauge water, or to push a boat; a staff used in fighting beasts on the stage.

GIBUS, [jīb'-us], *n.* an opera-hat, a top-hat with a collapsible crown which can be folded up. [*Gibus*, its inventor].

GID, [gid], *n.* a brain-disease in sheep. [GIDDY].

GIDDILY, [gid'-i-li], *adv.* in a giddy fashion.

GIDDINESS, [gid'-i-nes], *n.* the quality of being giddy; vertigo.

GIDDY (1), [gid'-i], *adj.* dizzy, having the impression that stationary objects are reeling about; tending to cause vertigo; thoughtless, irresponsible, foolish; light-headed, flighty; hectic, frivolous. [OE. *gydig* insane].

GIDDY-BRAINED, [gid'-i-brānd'], *adj.* careless; thoughtless, frivolous, flighty.

GIDDY-HEAD, [gid'-i-hed'], *n.* a thoughtless, frivolous person.

GIDDY-HEADED, [gid'-i-hed'-id], *adj.* heedless, unsteady, foolish.

GIDDY-PACED, [gid'-i-pāst'], *adj.* moving irregularly and spasmodically.

GIDYA, [gid'-ya], *n.* an Australian hardwood tree, *Acacia homalophylla*, a variety of mimosa; a native spear made from the wood of this tree. [Native].

GIFT (1), [gift], *n.* that which is given, a present, donation; a natural endowment or talent, an inherent aptitude or particular ability; the act of giving; the right of giving; (*leg.*) voluntary transference to the possession of others without equivalent or reasonable return; (*slang*) an easy thing, a cinch. [OIcel. *gift*].

GIFT (2), [gift], *v.t.* to endow with a particular talent or aptitude.

GIFTED, [gift'-id], *adj.* having a special specified gift, talented, naturally skilled.

GIFTEDNESS, [gift'-id-nes], *n.* the quality of being gifted.

GIFT-HORSE, [gift'-haws'], *n.* a horse that is given as a gift; (*fig.*) a favourable opportunity or chance.

GIG (1), [gig], *n.* a small harpoon; a line provided with a number of hooks set back to back, and drawn through a shoal of fish. [FISHGIG].

GIG (2), [gig], *n.* a light, two-wheeled carriage; a light, slender, speedy ship's boat; a racing boat of similar design; a rotary cylinder fitted with wire teeth, for teazing woollen cloth; (*pl.*) swellings on the inside of a horse's lips. [Uncert.].

GIG (3), (**gigging, gigged**), [gig], *v.i.* to fish with a gig.

GIGANTEAN, [jī-gan'-tē-an], *adj.* gigantic. [L. *giganteus*].

GIGANTESQUE, [jī-gan-tesk'], *adj.* gigantic, characteristic of a giant.

GIGANTIC, [jī-gan'-tik], *adj.* like a giant, enormous, colossal, stupendous, immense. [Gk. *gigantikos*].

GIGANTICALLY, [jī-gan'-tik-al-i], *adv.* in a gigantic fashion.

GIGANTOLOGY, [jī'-gan-tol'-oj-i], *n.* a dissertation on giants. [Gk. *gigas gigantos* giant and *logos* speech].

GIGANTOMACHY, [jī'-gan-tom'-ak-i], *n.* (*class.*) the contest between the giants and the gods; strife between giant forces. [Gk. *gigantomakhia* giant-battle].

GIGGLE (1), [gigl], *n.* a nervous, partly repressed, ill-controlled burst of laughter.

GIGGLE (2), [gigl], *v.i.* to utter a giggle or series of giggles. [Imitative].

GIGGLER, [gig'-ler], *n.* one who giggles.

GIG-LAMPS, [gig'-lamps'], *n.(pl.)* (*coll.*) spectacles.

GIGLET, GIGLOT, [gig'-lot], *n.* a high-spirited, light-hearted, irresponsible girl. [Uncert.].

GIGMAN, [gig'-man], *n.* a respectable narrow-minded middle-class bourgeois (one who keeps a gig). [Invented by Carlyle].

GIGMANITY, [gig-man'-i-ti], *n.* conventional respectability; the class of gigmen as a whole.

GIG-MILL, [gig'-mil'], *n.* a device for producing a nap on cloth by means of teazles or wire-cards; the factory in which this is done.

GIGOLO, [jig'-ol-ō], *n.* a hired male dancing partner, a lounge lizard. [Fr. *gigolo*].

GIGOT, [jig'-ot], *n.* (*dial.*) a leg of mutton. [Fr. *gigot*].

GIGUE, [zhēg], *n.* a brisk old-fashioned dance; a lively tune to which this was performed. [OFr. *gigue*].

GILA-MONSTER, [hē-la-mons'-ter], *n.* a large poisonous North American lizard. [*Gila*, a river in the United States of America].

GILD (1), see GUILD.

GILD (2), [gild], *v.i.* to cover with a veneer of gold or gold-leaf; to colour with gold paint or any similar substance; to brighten and give a lustre to; to adorn, add beauty to; **to g. the pill**, to make an unpleasant thing more palatable. [OE. *gyldan*].

GILDED, [gild'-id], *adj.* covered or adorned with gilt, having a golden colour; **G. Chamber**, the House of Lords; **g. youth**, smart rich young men of social standing.

GILDER, [gild'-er], *n.* one who gilds.

GILDING, [gild'-ing], *n.* the act or process of one who gilds; gold, gold leaf, gold paint, or dust lain on a substance to gild it; a gilt appearance; adornment.

GILL (1), [gil], *n.* the organ of respiration in fishes and water animals; the flap that hangs below the beak of a fowl; the flesh under the chin; the ridges or plates on the underside of the head of fungus. [ME. *gylle* ~ODan. *gælle* ~OSwed. *gel*].

GILL (2), [jil], *n.* a measure equivalent to a quarter pint liquid measure; a vessel holding this amount. [ML. *gillo* a cooling vessel].

GILL (3), [gil], *n.* a ravine, a narrow valley with steep sides, a gully; a narrow stream. [OIcel. *gil* glen].

GILL (4), [jil], *n.* a girl, sweetheart, a lass. [*Gillian* from L. *Juliana*].

GILLAROO, [gil'-er-ōō], *n.* a variety of trout, *Salmo stomachicus*. [Ir. *giolla ruadh* red fellow].

GILL-COVER, [gil'-kuv'-er], *n.* a gill-flap.

GILL-FLAP, [gil'-flap'], *n.* a membrane fastened to the posterior edge of the gill-lid, closing the gill-opening.

GILL-FLIRT, [jil'-flurt'], *n.* a coquettish woman.

GILLIAN, [jil'-i-an], *n.* a girl; a sweetheart; a flirt. [L. *Juliana*].

GILLIE, [gil'-i], *n.* an outdoor attendant or servant in the Highlands, accompanying a sportsman on a fishing or hunting expedition. [Gael. *gille* servant].

GILL-LID, [gil'-lid'], *n.* the covering of the gill.

GILL-OPENING, [gil'-ōp'-ning], *n.* the aperture of the gill.

GILLYFLOWER, [jil'-i-flow'-er], *n.* one of several British flowers whose scent is similar to that of a clove; the clove-pink, *Dianthus Caryophyllus*; the white stock, *Matthiola incana*, the wallflower, *Cheiranthus Cheiri*. [~ME. *gilofre*, *gelofer* from OFr. *girofle*].

GILPIN, [gil'-pin], *n.* the coal-fish, *Gadus virens*.

GILT, [gilt], *n.* gold leaf, paint, dust or plate used for gilding; (*fig.*) attractiveness, lustre, surface beauty. [GILD].

GILT-EDGED, [gilt'-ejd'], *adj.* having the edges gilded; (*fig.*) extremely favourable or valuable; (*comm.*) sound, safe, reliable; **g. security**, originally Government stock, now any stock resembling this in its soundness.

GILT-HEAD, [gilt'-hed], *n.* the conner, a sea-fish of the wrasse family, *Crenilabrus melops*; one of the sea-breams, *Pagrus auratus*.

GILT-TAIL, [gilt'-tāl'], *n.* a worm having a yellow tail.

GIM†, [jim], *adj.* neat, spruce, well dressed, smart. [JIMP].

GIMBALS, [jim'-balz], *n.(pl.)* two brass rings moving within each other, each perpendicular to its plane, used in suspending a mariner's compass, barometer, etc., in a horizontal position; a gemel ring. [GEMEL].

GIMCRACK (1), [jim'-krak], *n.* a superficially attractive, worthless object; a trifling, showy toy. [~ME. *gibecrake* a kind of inlaid work].

GIMCRACK (2), [jim'-krak], *adj.* empty, trifling, showy, cheap, of the nature of a gimcrack.

GIMCRACKERY, [jim-krak'-er-i], *n.* useless ornaments, worthless show, tawdry trifles.

GIMLET (1), [gim'-let], *n.* a boring tool consisting of a slender piece of steel terminating in a pointed spiral, and provided with a cross-handle set at right-angles; **g. eyed**, having a sharp, penetrating gaze. [ME. *gymlot* from OFr. *guimbelet*].

GIMLET (2), [gim'-let], *v.t.* to bore with, or as with, a gimlet.

GIMMAL, [jim'-al], *n.* (*antiq.*) a kind of finger-ring which may be made into a double ring. [GEMEL].

GIMMEL RINGS, [jim'-el-rings], *n.* two or three ornamental metal rings fastened within each other. [GEMEL].

GIMMEL RINGS

GIMMER, [jim'-er], *n.* a gimbal. [GIMMAL].

GIMP (1), [gimp], *n.* a trimming or edging of twisted cord, silk, etc., stiffened by wire; a fishing-line bound with wire to make it stronger. [Du. *gimp*].

GIMP (2), see JIMP.

GIN (1), [jin], *n.* a spirit drink distilled from grain or malt and flavoured with juniper berries; **g. palace**, a public-house with a spirit licence. [Fr. *genièvre* from L. *juniperus* juniper].

GIN (2), [jin], *n.* a mechanical contrivance of various kinds; a snare, a trap for catching game; a kind of three-legged, triangular crane with a single movable leg; (*mining*) a kind of hoist or pump; a machine used to remove cotton from the seeds; †a trick, trap or ruse. [ENGINE].

GIN (3), [jin], *n.* an aboriginal woman of Australia. [Native].

GIN (4), (**ginning, ginned**), [jin], *v.t.* to snare, entrap; to clear (cotton) of its seed by means of a machine. [GIN (2)].

GIN-FIZZ, [jin'-fiz'], *n.* a drink consisting of soda-water, gin, and lemon.

GINGAL, JINGAL, [jing'-gawl], *n.* a large musket, used in India and China, and fired generally from a rest; a light gun mounted on a swivel. [Hind. *janjal*].
GINGER (1), [jin'-jer], *n.* a tropical aromatic plant, *Zingiber officinale*; the hot spicy root of this plant; (*coll.*) energy, spirit, liveliness. [OE. *gingifer*].
GINGER (2), [jin'-jer], *adj.* (*coll.*) (of hair) bright red.
GINGER (3), [jin'-jer], *v.t.* to flavour with ginger; to dose (a horse) with ginger; (*coll.*) to liven up, to stir to increased activity.
GINGERADE, [jin'-jer-ād'], *n.* an aerated drink having a ginger taste.
GINGER-ALE, [jin'-jer-āl'], *n.* a golden, sparkling aerated beverage flavoured with ginger.
GINGER-BEER, [jin'-jer-bēer'], *n.* an aerated drink made from ginger, cream of tartar, sugar, and yeast.
GINGERBREAD, [jin'-jer-bred'], *n.* a kind of cake containing treacle, sweetened, and flavoured with ginger, formerly made into varied and fanciful shapes and frequently gilded; **g. tree,** a West African bread-fruit tree, *Parinarium macrophyllum*; the doum palm, *Hyphæne thebaica*; **g. work,** vulgarly flamboyant, carved or ornamental work; **to take the gilt off the g.,** to disillusion. [ME. *gingebrar* from OFr. *gingembras* preserved ginger].
GINGER-CORDIAL, [jin'-jer-kaw'-di-al], *n.* a mild spirituous beverage flavoured with ginger.
GINGERLY (1), [jin'-jer-li], *adj.* careful, cautious; delicate. [OFr. *genzor* delicate].
GINGERLY (2), [jin'-jer-li], *adv.* in a cautious, gingerly way.
GINGER-POP, [jin'-jer-pop'], *n.* ginger-beer.
GINGER-WINE, [jin'-jer-win'], *n.* a brown fermented drink containing ginger.
GINGERY, [jin'-jer-i], *adj.* resembling ginger; spicy, pungent; of a light reddish-brown colour; (*fig.*) irascible, hot-tempered.
GINGHAM, [ging'-am], *n.* a striped or chequered cotton or linen cloth made from dyed yarn; (*coll.*) a large umbrella. [Malay *ginggang* striped cotton].
GINGILI, [jin'-jil-i], *n.* the oil yielded by an East Indian plant, *Sesamum indicum*; the plant itself. [Hind. *jinjali*].
GINGING, [jing'-ging], *n.* (*mining*)) the lining of a mineshaft, built as a support. [Unkn.].
GINGIVAL, [jin-jī'-val], *adj.* relating to the gums. [L. *gingiva* gums].
GINGIVITIS, [jin'-jiv-īt'-is], *n.* (*med.*) inflammation of the gums. [L. *gingiva* the gums and Gk. *itis* denoting inflammation].
GINGKO, [gingk'-ō], *n.* a Japanese or Chinese tree producing fan-shaped leaves and a yellow fruit. [Jap. *gingko*].
GINGLE, see JINGLE.
GINGLYMOID, [jing'-glim-oid], *adj.* like a hinge. [GINGLYMUS and Gk. *oeides* like].
GINGLYMOIDAL, [jing'-glim-oid'-al], *adj.* ginglymoid.
GINGLYMUS, [jing'-glim-us], *n.* (*anat.*) a hinge-like joint permitting movement in two directions only. [Gk. *ginglumos* hinge-joint].
GIN-HORSE, [jin'-haws'], *n.* a horse that works a mill.
GIN-HOUSE, [jin'-hows'], *n.* a place where cotton is ginned.
GINK, [gingk], *n.* (*U.S. slang*) fellow, chap, person. [Unkn.].
GINNING, [jin'-ing], *n.* the process by which cotton is separated from its seeds.
GINNY-CARRIAGE, [jin'-i-ka'-rij], *n.* a small strong carriage for conveying materials on a railroad.
GINSENG, [jin'-seng], *n.* a Chinese or North American plant of the genus, *Aralia* or *Panax*; the root of this plant, used medicinally. [Chin. *jenshen* man-image].
GIN-SLING, [jin'-sling'], *n.* an iced drink of gin and sweetened water, flavoured in various ways.
GIP, [gip], *v.t.* to clean (fish) in readiness for salting and smoking. [Unkn.].
GIPPO, [jip'-ō], *n.* (*coll.*) a gipsy, an Egyptian. [GIPSY].
GIPSY (1), GYPSY, [jip'-si], *n.* a member of a wandering race of people of Indian origin; the gipsy language, Romany; (*fig.*) a dark-featured person; a fickle, untrustworthy person of erratic habits. [ME. *Egypcien* from LL. *Aegyptianus*, the gipsies being wrongly supposed to have come from Egypt].
GIPSY (2), [jip'-si], *adj.* relating to, or resembling, the gipsies; **g. bonnet,** a woman's bonnet with large ear-flaps; **g. flower,** the wild scabious; **g. table,** a light portable three-legged round table.
GIPSY-CART, [jip'-si-kaht'], *n.* the roofed van in which gipsy families live and travel.
GIPSYDOM, [jip'-si-dum], *n.* the world of gipsies; gipsy life; the state of a gipsy.
GIPSYISM, [jip'-si-izm], *n.* a gipsy expression or custom.
GIPSY-MOTH, [jip'-si-moth'], *n.* a large species of European moth.
GIPSYWORT, [jip'-si-wurt], *n.* the plant, *Lycopus europæus.*
GIRAFFE, [ji-raf'], *n.* a long-necked, four-legged, hooved animal with a spotted skin and a small, narrow head, the camelopard. [Arab. *zarafa, zorafa*].
GIRANDOLE, [ji'-ran-dōl], *n.* any of various circular objects; a bracket chandelier; a large kind of branched candlestick; a series of fireworks arranged to form a wheel; a revolving water-jet; a pendant in the form of a large central stone set round with smaller ones. [It. *girandola*].
GIRASOL, GIRASOLE, [ji'-ras-ol], *n.* the fire-opal, a precious stone. [It. *girasole*].
GIRD† (1), [gurd], *n.* a twitch or pang; a sudden spasm or jerk; a gibe, a sarcastic taunt. [GIRD (3)].
GIRD (2), [gurd], *v.t.* to bind round with a flexible substance such as a belt, etc., *esp.* at the waist; to fasten by a girdle; to surround, encircle; to invest, endue; (*fig.*) (*reflex.*) to prepare; **to g. up one's loins,** to prepare oneself for vigorous action. [OE. *gyrdan*].
GIRD (3), [gurd], *v.i.* **to g. at,** to reproach, deride, find fault with, sneer at. [ME. *girden* to strike].
GIRDER, [gurd'-er], *n.* a strong beam of wood or steel, used in building and engineering as a main support.
GIRDING, [gurd'-ing], *n.* a covering; girders; preparation; a fastening or binding by means of a belt.
GIRDLE (1), [gurdl], *n.* a belt, cord or band used to encircle the waist, and confine the clothing; (*fig.*) that which surrounds or encompasses; (*anat.*) a ring-like bony support for the limbs where they join the trunk; (*bot.*) a circular incision through the bark of a tree; (*arch.*) a circular band or fillet round the shaft of a column; a line separating two faces of a precious stone. [OE *gyrdel*].

GIRDLE

GIRDLE (2), [gurdl], *n.* a round metal plate on which cakes may be baked over a fire. [GRIDDLE].
GIRDLE (3), [gurdl], *v.t.* to bind with a girdle; to make a circular incision through the bark of a tree; (*fig.*) to surround, encompass.
GIRDLER, [gurd'-ler], *n.* one who, or that which, girdles; a maker of girdles.
GIRDLING, [gurd'-ling], *n.* a method of killing trees by cutting circles round them with a hatchet.
GIRL, [gurl], *n.* a female child; a young or unmarried female; a maidservant; a female member of a business staff, company, etc.; (*coll.*) a fiancée, sweetheart. [OE. *gyrlle*].
GIRLHOOD, [gurl'-hŏŏd], *n.* the period of being a girl.
GIRLIE, [gurl'-i], *n.* (*coll.*) a term of affection for a girl. [GIRL].
GIRLISH, [gurl'-ish], *adj.* of or like a girl.
GIRLISHLY, [gurl'-ish-li], *adv.* in a girlish fashion.
GIRLISHNESS, [gurl'-ish-nes], *n.* the quality of being a girl.
GIRN, [gurn], *v.i.* to grumble, complain or growl perpetually. [GRIN (2)].
GIRNEL, [gurn'-el], *n.* a receptacle for grain. [GARNER].
GIRONDIST, GIRONDIN, [zhi-ron'-dist, zhi-ron'-dan(g)], *n.* one of the moderate Republican party in the French Revolution, called the Gironde. [Fr. *Gironde* the French department of which Bordeaux is the capital].
GIROUETTE, [zhi-rōō-et'], *n.* a weathercock; (*fig.*) a person constantly changing his opinions and principles. [Fr. *girouette*].
GIRT (1), [gurt], *n.* girth. [GIRTH (1)].
GIRT (2), [gurt], *adj.* (*naut.*) (of a ship) moored so taut as to be unable to turn or swing with the tide or wind. [GIRD].
GIRT (3), [gurt], *v.t. and i.* to gird; to fasten with a girth; to measure the girth of. [GIRT (1)].
GIRTH (1), [gurth], *n.* the band or strap passing under the belly of a horse or other beast of burden, by which a saddle, load, etc., is made fast; measurement round that which is more or less circular or spherical.

circumference, distance round the middle; (*fig.*) that which surrounds or encompasses. [ME. *gerth* ~OIcel. *gjorth*].

GIRTH (2), [gurth], *v.t.* to put on girths, to fasten by means of a girth; **to g. up,** to tighten the girths.

GIRT-LINE, [gurt'-līn'], *n.* (*naut.*) a rope used to lift up the rigging to the masthead.

GISMONDINE, [giz-mond'-in], *n.* a silicate of aluminium and calcium found near Rome. [*Gismondi*, an Italian mineralogist].

GIST, [jist], *n.* the main point of a question or argument; the essence; (*leg.*) the foundation or essential point of an action. [OFr. *giste*].

GITE†, [zhēt], *n.* a place where one may sleep or obtain lodging. [Fr. *gîte*].

GITTERN, [git'-ern], *n.* a cithern, an instrument of the guitar variety. [OFr. *guiterne*].

GIUSTO, [jŏŏs'-tō], *adj.* (*mus.*) in steady strict time. [It. *giusto*].

GIVE (1), [giv], *n.* resilience, springiness, elasticity.

GIVE (2), (gave, given), [giv], *v.t.* to convey to the possession of another without requiring a recompense, provide with; to afford; to award as punishment; to pronounce a verdict; to deliver into the temporary possession of; to deal, deliver; to dedicate, sacrifice; to impart, communicate; to deliver as a pledge; to deliver over something in return or exchange for something else; to pay; to read, recite, sing; to assign, allot; to arrange, present, provide; to portray, represent; to produce, yield; to emit, utter; to perform some bodily movement indicating an emotional state; to concede, allow; to announce, pronounce; to offer; to include, show; to attribute; *v.i.* to make donations; to break down under pressure; to be resilient, to yield slightly to pressure; **to g. away,** to transfer unconditionally; to sacrifice; to disclose; **to g. back,** to restore; to repay; to retreat, retire; **to g. forth,** to proclaim; **to g. in,** to hand in; to acknowledge oneself beaten; **to g. best to,** to acknowledge the superiority of; **to g. out,** to distribute; to announce; to come to an end; **to g. over,** to deliver up; to refrain completely from; **to g. up,** to abandon, renounce; to relinquish; to regard as beyond hope of recovery, etc.; to confess oneself beaten by something or someone; **to g. oneself up to,** to devote oneself to; **to g. one's word,** to promise faithfully; **to g. it to,** to punish severely; **to g. a horse, man, his head,** to allow to proceed without restraint; **to g. a piece of one's mind,** to say just what one thinks about a certain thing; **to g. way,** to yield; **to g. way to,** to abandon oneself to; **to g. ground,** to retreat; **to g. tongue,** to bay as a hound; **to g. rise to,** to cause, start; **to g. place to,** to be succeeded by. [OE. *giefan* ~OIcel. *gefa*].

GIVE (3), see GYVE (1).

GIVEABLE, [giv'-abl], *adj.* able to be given.

GIVE AND TAKE, [giv'-en-tāk'], *n.* the mutual making and receiving of concessions; compromise.

GIVEN, [giv'-en], *adj.* specified, agreed, stated; taken for granted; **g. to,** fond of, addicted to.

GIVER, [giv'-er], *n.* one who gives.

GIVING, [giv'-ing], *n.* the act of one who gives.

GIZZARD, [giz'-erd], *n.* the muscular second stomach of a bird in which the food is ground; (*coll.*) the throat; **to stick in one's g.,** to be unpalatable. [OFr. *guisier*].

GLABRATE, [glab'-rāt], *adj.* glabrous. [L. *glabratus*].

GLABROUS, [glab'-rus], *adj.* without hair or down, bald. [L. *glaber* without hair].

GLACE, glacé, [glas'-i], *adj.* having a shiny, highly polished surface; covered with sugar, iced. [Fr. *glacé*].

GLACIAL, [glā'-shal], *adj.* pertaining to, like, ice; due to ice, consisting of ice; pertaining to glaciers; the geological era during which the northern hemisphere was largely under ice. [L. *glacialis*].

GLACIALIST, [glā'-shal-ist], *n.* one who refers certain geological phenomena to the action of ice; one who studies glaciology.

GLACIATE, [glā'-si-āt], *v.t.* to cover with ice, to freeze; to polish by the action of ice; to produce a frosted surface upon. [L. *glaciare*].

GLACIATION, [glā'-si-ā'-shun], *n.* the state of being covered by glaciers; the condition of being acted upon by ice or glaciers; the action of ice.

GLACIER, [glas'-i-er], *n.* a mass of frozen snow formed on mountains, and slowly moving down towards the valleys along a definite track, until it reaches a point at which it gradually melts. [Fr. *glacier*].

GLACIER-TABLE, [glas'-i-er-tābl'], *n.* a large block of stone carried down and left standing by a glacier.

GLACINE, [glas'-ēn], *n.* a partly transparent substance resembling cellophane. [GLACIAL].

GLACIOLOGY, [glā'-si-ol'-oji], *n.* the study of the geological action of ice or of glaciers. [GLACIER and Gk. *logos* speech].

GLACIS, [gla'-si], *n.* a gentle slope; a sloping bank; (*fort.*) the parapet of the covered way, sloping down to the ground and exposed to gunfire. [Fr. *glacis*].

GLAD (1), [glad], *adj.* pleased, agreeably satisfied, relieved; happy, willing; joyful, affording pleasure; †cheerful; **g. rags,** (*slang*) one's best or smartest attire; evening dress; **to give the g. eye to,** to cast inviting, amorous glances at. [OE. *glæd*].

GLAD (2), (gladding, gladded), [glad], *v.t.* (*archaic*) to make glad. [OE. *gladian*].

GLADDEN, [glad'-en], *v.t. and i.* to make glad; to become glad.

GLADE, [glād], *n.* an open space, clearing or avenue in a forest. [Uncert.].

GLADIATE, [glad'-i-āt], *adj.* sword-shaped. [L. *gladius* sword].

GLADIATOR, [glad'-i-āt'-er], *n.* (*Rom. antiq.*) a swordsman; one who fought in an arena to provide entertainment; (*fig.*) a warrior, a contentious debater. [L. *gladiator*].

GLADIATORIAL, [glad'-i-a-taw'-ri-al], *adj.* relating to gladiators.

GLADIATORSHIP, [glad'-i-āt'-er-ship], *n.* the art or practice of a gladiator.

GLADIOLE, [glad'-i-ōl], *n.* the British sword-lily, a gladiolus.

GLADIOLUS, [glad-i-ōl'-us], *n.* a genus of 90 species of sword-lilies or corn-flags. [L. *gladiolus* a small sword].

GLADIUS, [glad'-i-us], *n.* the internal bone of cuttle-fish; the sword-fish. [L. *gladius* sword].

GLADLY, [glad'-li], *adv.* willingly, with gladness.

GLADNESS, [glad'-nes], *n.* the quality of being glad.

GLADSOME, [glad'-sum], *adj.* radiating gladness, inspiring with gladness. [ME. *gladsum*].

GLADSOMELY, [glad'-sum-li], *adv.* in gladsome fashion.

GLADSOMENESS, [glad'-sum-nes], *n.* the condition of being gladsome.

GLADSTONE, [glad'-ston], *n.* a four-wheeled carriage for two persons; **g. bag,** a light leather bag opening along the middle and secured with a clasp. [W. E. *Gladstone*, 1809-98].

GLADWYN, [glad'-win], *n.* the purple iris, *Iris foetidissima*. [OE. *glædene*].

GLAGOL, [glag'-ol], *n.* the glagolitic alphabet. [Slav. *glagol* word].

GLAGOLITIC, [glag'-ol-it'-ik], *adj.* relating to the Slavonic alphabet.

GLAIR (1), [glāer], *n.* the white of an egg used as varnish; any substance resembling the white of an egg in character or appearance. [Fr. *glaire*].

GLAIR (2), [glāer], *v.t.* to paint with glair.

GLAIREOUS, [glāer'-i-us], *adj.* glairous.

GLAIROUS, [glāer'-us], *adj.* like, painted with, glair.

GLAIRY, [glāer'-i], *adj.* glairous.

GLAIVE†, [glāv], *n.* a sword; a lance; a bill; a spear; a weapon resembling a halberd. [Fr. *glaive* from L. *gladius* sword].

GLAMOROUS, [glam'-er-us], *adj.* possessing glamour, attracting by glamour.

GLAMOUR, [glam'-er], *n.* allure, charm, a deceptive and fascinating quality about a person or place that attracts in spite of the reality, a seductive fascination. [Scots].

GLANCE (1), [glahnts], *n.* a brief look, a hasty or furtive look; an oblique impact deflecting the course of the object; a swift flash of brightness; (*cricket*) a stroke on the leg side by which the course of the ball is slightly diverted. [GLANCE (3)].

GLANCE (2), [glahnts], *n.* a bright mineral sulphide. [Germ. *glanz* lustre].

GLANCE (3), [glahnts], *v.t.* (*coll.*) to glimpse; (*cricket*) to deflect a ball on the leg side; *v.i.* to cast a glance; to strike obliquely so as to be deflected; to flash, flicker briefly; to reflect bright light. [Uncert.].

GLANCE (4), [glahnts], *v.t.* to burnish, polish. [Du. *glanzen*].

GLANCINGLY, [glahn'-sing-li], *adj.* by glancing.

GLAND (1), [gland], *n.* one of many animal organs extracting substances from the blood and turning them into vital chemical fluids; (*bot.*) a secretory organ in plants. [Fr. *glande*].

GLAND (2), [gland], *n.* a device for holding a packing tight on a piston-rod. [~Scand. *glaund* iron clamp].

GLANDERED, [gland'-erd], *adj.* suffering from glanders.
GLANDEROUS, [gland'-er-us], *adj.* glandered.
GLANDERS, [gland'-erz], *n.* (*med.*) a contagious and malignant disease affecting the mucous membrane in horses and communicable to man. [OFr. *glandres*].
GLANDIFEROUS, [gland-if'-er-us], *adj.* bearing acorns or nuts.
GLANDIFORM, [gland'-i-fawm], *adj.* shaped like a nut.
GLANDULAR, [gland'-yōō-ler], *adj.* relating to the glands; (*bot.*) covered with gland-tipped hairs.
GLANDULARLY, [gland'-yōō-ler-li], *adv.* from the glandular aspect.
GLANDULATION, [gland'-yōō-lā'-shun], *n.* (*bot.*) the arrangement and form of the secretory organs in plants.
GLANDULE, [gland'-ewl], *n.* a small gland; a little tumour. [L. *glandula*].
GLANDULIFEROUS, [gland'-yōō-lif'-er-us], *adj.* having glands.
GLANDULOUS, [gland'-yōō-lus], *adj.* glandular.
GLANS, [glanz], *n.* (*anat.*) the rounded protuberance forming the end of the penis. [L. *glans* acorn].
GLARE (1), [glāer], *n.* a brightness that blinds and strains the eyes; (*fig.*) annoying publicity or prominence; a fierce stare.
GLARE (2), [glāer], *v.i.* to give out a blinding, harsh light; to blaze with vulgar brightness; to stare fiercely and angrily. [ME. *glaren* to shine].
GLAREOUS, [glāer'-i-us], *adj.* growing in gravel.
GLARINESS, [glāer'-i-nes], *n.* glaringness.
GLARING, [glāer'-ing], *adj.* blazing brightly, blinding; vulgar, garish; obvious to anyone, patent.
GLARINGLY, [glāer'-ing-li], *adv.* in glaring fashion; (*fig.*) obviously.
GLARINGNESS, [glāer'-ing-nes], *n.* the quality of being glaring.
GLARY, [glāer'-i], *adj.* glaring.
GLASS (1), [glahs], *n.* a brittle translucent substance made by the fusion of silicates with alkalis; an object made of this substance, *esp.* a drinking vessel made of this; the capacity or contents of such a vessel; a mirror; a magnifying lens, an optical instrument; a barometer; a sand-clock; (*pl.*) spectacles, binoculars; **ground g.**, glass so roughened as to lose its transparency. [OE. *glæs*].
GLASS (2), [glahs], *adj.* made of glass; brittle, transparent.
GLASS (3), [glahs], *v.t.* to cover with glass.
GLASSBENDER, [glahs'-bend'-er], *n.* one who moulds and shapes glass.
GLASSBLOWER, [glahs'-blō'-er], *n.* one who shapes and moulds glass by blowing.
GLASSCLOTH, [glahs'-kloth], *n.* a soft cloth for polishing glass.
GLASS-COACH, [glahs'-kōch'], *n.* a coach panelled with glass.
GLASS-CRAB, [glahs'-krab], *n.* the larva of a crab once mistaken for a species.
GLASSCUTTER, [glahs'-kut'-er], *n.* a workman employed in glasscutting; a tool used for cutting glass.
GLASSCUTTING, [glahs'-kut'-ing], *n.* the craft of cutting glass into patterns or sizes.
GLASSFUL, [glahs'-fōōl], *n.* the quantity of liquid that fills a glass.
GLASS-FURNACE, [glahs'-fur'-nis], *n.* a furnace for fusing silicate into glass.
GLASSGAUL, [glahs'-gawl], *n.* the saline crust on molten glass.
GLASS-GAZING, [glahs'-gāz'-ing], *n.* crystal-gazing; the vanity of pausing before mirrors.
GLASS-GRINDER, [glahs'-grīnd'-er], *n.* one whose trade is to cut and ornament glass.
GLASSHOUSE, [glahs'-hows], *n.* a hot-house, a conservatory; a factory where glass is made; an establishment where glass is sold; (*fig.*) a state of very insecure self-satisfaction; (*slang*) a military prison.
GLASSILY, [glahs'-i-li], *adv.* in glassy fashion.
GLASSINESS, [glahs'-i-nes], *n.* the quality of being glassy.
GLASSITES, [glahs'-īts], *n.*(*pl.*) a religious sect founded in Scotland, in 1725. [John *Glass* or *Glas*, the founder].
GLASSLIKE, [glahs'-līk], *adj.* resembling glass, smooth and very still.
GLASSMETAL, [glahs'-met'-al], *n.* molten glass.
GLASS-MOSAIC, [glahs'-mō-zā'-ik], *n.* a mosaic made of pieces of coloured glass.
GLASS-PAINTING, [glahs'-pānt'-ing], *n.* the craft of painting on glass.
GLASS-PAPER, [glahs'-pā'-per], *n.* paper covered with pulverized glass, used for smoothing wood.
GLASS-POT, [glahs'-pot], *n.* a container used in melting glass.
GLASS-SNAKE, [glahs'-snāk], *n.* the brittle lizard, *Ophisaurus paljasi*.
GLASS-SOAP, [glahs'-sōp], *n.* black oxide of manganese.
GLASSWARE, [glahs'-wāer], *n.* vessels and ornaments made from glass.

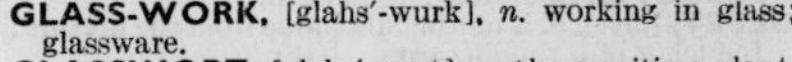
GLASS-SNAKE

GLASS-WORK, [glahs'-wurk], *n.* working in glass; glassware.
GLASSWORT, [glahs'-wurt], *n.* the maritime plant, *Salicornia herbacea*, used in glassmaking because of the soda it contains. [GLASS and OE. *wyrt* plant].
GLASSY, [glahs'-i], *adj.* smooth, cold, and expressionless as glass; resembling glass; still and without feeling.
GLAUBERITE, [glaw'-ber-īt], *n.* sulphate of sodium and calcium [J. *Glauber*, 1604-1668, its discoverer].
GLAUBER'S SALT, [glaw'-ber-sawlt'], *n.* sulphate of sodium, a powerful aperient. [J. *Glauber*, 1604-1668].
GLAUCESCENCE, [glaw-ses'-ents], *n.* the quality of being glaucescent.
GLAUCESCENT, [glaw-ses'-ent], *adj.* bluish-green, with a sea-green sheen. [Gk. *glaukos* gleaming].
GLAUCODOTE, [glaw'-ko-dōt], *n.* a mineral containing cobalt, arsenic, sulphur, and iron.
GLAUCOLITE, [glaw'-kō-līt], *n.* a silicate of lime and alumina. [Gk. *glaukos* gleaming and *lithos* stone].
GLAUCOMA, [glaw-kō'-ma], *n.* a disease of the eyeball, marked by a blue-green tinge of the pupil. [Gk. *glaukoma*].
GLAUCOMATOUS, [glaw-kōm'-at-us], *adj.* relating to glaucoma.
GLAUCONITE, [glaw'-kon-īt], *n.* a hydrous silicate of potassium and iron found in greensand, and common over many parts of the sea-bed.
GLAUCOUS, [glaw'-kus], *adj.* greenish-blue; (*bot.*) with a bluish bloom. [Gk. *glaukos* gleaming].
GLAZE (1), [glāz], *n.* a glassy surface imparted to earthenware, paper, etc.; a thin wash of varnish over paint; a vitreous, glossy surface applied to anything; a coating of jelly over cold meat; a shiny film; pottery coated with a smooth vitreous surface.
GLAZE (2), [glāz], *v.t. and i.* to cover with glass; to coat or cover with a glaze; to impart a glaze to pottery; to become glassy and expressionless. [ME. *glasen*].
GLAZED, [glāzd], *adj.* coated with jelly; provided with glass windows; **g. frost**, a frost following quickly on a thaw, a silver thaw.
GLAZER, [glāz'-er], *n.* one whose trade is to glaze pottery; a glazing tool; a knife-polisher.
GLAZIER, [glāz'-i-er], *n.* one who cuts, fits, and trades in window-glass.
GLAZING, [glāz'-ing], *n.* the act of applying a glaze or fitting window-glass; the substance used to glaze pottery; a thin coat of varnish applied over paint.
GLAZY, [glāz'-i], *adj.* showing a glaze.
GLEAD, see GLEDE.
GLEAM (1), [glēm], *n.* a transitory glint or beam of light; the reflection from polished metal or glass; (*fig.*) a sudden slight showing of understanding or some other desirable quality. [OE. *glæm* radiance].
GLEAM (2), [glēm], *v.i.* to emit or reflect light; to glow brightly, flash; (*fig.*) (of a quality) to show itself, become evident. [ME. *glemen*].
GLEAMING, [glēm'-ing], *adj.* shining brightly, reflecting the light, glowing.
GLEAMY, [glēm'-i], *adj.* giving out or reflecting light.
GLEAN, [glēn], *v.t. and i.* to gather up scattered ears of corn ignored by the reapers; to gather up unconsidered leavings; (*fig.*) to obtain, discover, by thorough and diligent search. [ME. *glenen*].
GLEANER, [glēn'-er], *n.* one who gleans.
GLEANING, [glēn'-ing], *n.* the act of one who gleans; some trifle so gathered.
GLEBE, [glēb], *n.* (*eccles.*) land attached to a living and held by the incumbent; †soil. [L. *gleba* lump of earth].
GLEBE-HOUSE, [glēb'-hows], *n.* a clergyman's house built on glebe-land.
GLEBOUS, [glēb'-us], *adj.* gleby.
GLEBY, [glēb'-i], *adj.* earthy, muddy.
GLEDE, GLEAD, [glēd], *n.* the kite, *Milvus ictinus*; the buzzard, *Buteo vulgaris*. [OE. *glida* kite].

GLEDGE, [glej], *v.i.* (*Scots*) to squint, to leer in side-long fashion. [Uncert.].

GLEE, [glē], *n.* mirthful jollity, joyous gaiety; (*mus.*) a part-song for three or more voices, usually unaccompanied. [OE. *gleo* music].

GLEEFUL, [glē'-fōōl], *adj.* full of glee displaying mirthful pleasure; inspiring glee.

GLEEFULLY, [glē-fōōl-i], *adv.* in a gleeful fashion.

GLEEK† (1), [glēk], *n.* a game played by three persons with forty-four cards. [OFr. *glic*].

GLEEK† (2), [glēk], *n.* a scoffing taunt. [Uncert.].

GLEEMAN, [glē'-man], *n.* a strolling musician. [OE. *gleo-man*].

GLEESOME, [glē'-sum], *adj.* gleeful.

GLEET, [glēt], *n.* a morbid discharge from the urethra; the ichor of a running sore. [OFr. *glete*].

GLEETY, [glēt'-i], *adj.* like pus, watery and foul.

GLEN, [glen], *n.* a narrow valley in the hills. [OIr. *glenn*].

GLENE, [glēn], *n.* the eye-socket, the eyeball. [Gk. *glene*].

GLENGARRY, [glen-ga'-ri], *n.* a boat-shaped Highland cap, with narrow sloping sides and a depressed crown, having two streamers of ribbon at the back and a cockade at the side. [*Glengarry*, in Scotland].

GLENOID, [glēn'-oid], *adj.* (of a socket, etc.) receiving the head of a bone to form a joint. [GLENE and Gk. *oeides* like].

GLENOIDAL, [glēn-oid'-al], *adj.* glenoid.

GLIADIN, [glī'-a-din], *n.* a viscid yellow substance obtained from gluten. [Gk. *glia* glue].

GLIB, [glib], *adj.* over-facile of speech, fluent, plausible but unconvincing. [~Du. *glibberig* slippery].

GLIBLY, [glib'-li], *adv.* in glib fashion.

GLIBNESS, [glib'-nes], *n.* the quality of being glib.

GLIDE (1), [glīd], *n.* a gliding movement, progression by gliding; an easy descent; a smooth incline for gliding.

GLIDE (2), [glīd], *v.i.* to slide smoothly down an incline, to progress easily and noiselessly; (of persons) to move smoothly and silently without effort; to float easily over water; (*aeron.*) to plane down or along without using the engine, or in a glider. [OE. *glidan*].

GLIDER, [glīd'-er], *n.* an engineless aircraft progressing by gliding on air-currents.

GLIDINGLY, [glīd'-ing-li], *adv.* by, as if by, gliding.

GLIM, [glim], *n.* (*dial.*) a light, lamp. [GLEAM].

GLIMMER (1), [glim'-er], *n.* a very faint gleam, a fitful flicker of light; (*fig.*) a faint and infrequent flicker of intelligence, etc.

GLIMMER (2), [glim'-er], *v.i.* to shine feebly and fitfully, to flicker. [ME. *glimeren* to shine].

GLIMMERING, [glim'-er-ing], *n.* a glimmer; (*fig.*) a faint comprehension.

GLIMPSE (1), [glimps], *n.* a brief sight, fleeting vision, a fugitive visual impression of something; a glimmer.

GLIMPSE (2), [glimps], *v.t.* to catch sight of briefly and incompletely, to perceive in a glimpse or glimpses. [ME. *glimsen* to shine].

GLINT (1), [glint], *n.* a faint, brief, and intermittent flash; a gleam of suppressed anger or amusement in the eye.

GLINT (2), [glint], *v.i.* to flash briefly, flicker brightly and intermittently; to shine with a faint gleam. [ME. *glenten* to shine].

GLISSADE (1), [glis-ahd'], *n.* a downhill upright glide over snow or ice in alpine climbing; a sidelong glide in dancing. [Fr. *glissade* a slide].

GLISSADE (2), [glis-ahd'], *v.i.* to execute a glissade.

GLISSAUN, [glis'-own], *n.* the coal-fish, *Gadus virens*.

GLIST, [glist], *n.* mica. [GLISTEN].

GLISTEN, [glis'-en], *v.i.* to glitter, to gleam with a bright reflection, to sparkle with reflected light. [OE. *glisnian*].

GLISTENINGLY, [glis'-en-ing-li], *adv.* in glistening fashion.

GLISTER (1), [glist'-er], *n.* a gleam, sparkle.

GLISTER (2), [glist'-er], *v.i.* to gleam, sparkle. [ME. *glisteren*].

GLISTERING, [glist'-er-ing], *adj.* sparkling.

GLISTERINGLY, [glist'-er-ing-li], *adv.* in glistering fashion.

GLITTER (1), [glit'-er], *n.* sparkle, brightness; (*fig.*) colourful, blazing splendour.

GLITTER (2), [glit'-er], *v.i.* to shine brightly, sparkle with light; (*fig.*) to blaze with splendour, make a dazzling show. [ME. *gliteren*].

GLITTERING, [glit'-er-ing], *adj.* sparkling, gleaming, splendid; falsely brilliant.

GLITTERINGLY, [glit'-er-ing-li], *adv.* in glittering fashion.

GLOAM, [glōm], *v.i.* to begin to grow dusk.

GLOAMING, [glōm'-ing], *n.* (*poet.*) twilight, dusk. [Scots].

GLOAT, [glōt], *v.i.* to feel or display unpleasant exultation in or over something; to take extreme pleasure in another's misfortune. [OIcel. *glotta* to smile scornfully].

GLOATINGLY, [glōt'-ing-li], *adv.* in gloating fashion.

GLOBATE, [glōb'-āt], *adj.* having the shape of a globe, spherical, spheroidal. [L. *globatus*].

GLOBATED, [glōb'-āt-id], *adj.* globate.

GLOBE, [glōb], *n.* a sphere, a ball; the earth; a spherical model of the earth; anything shaped like a ball; an orb; a spherical glass vessel. [L. *globus*].

GLOBE-AMARANTH, [glōb'-am'-er-anth], *n.* a flower of the amaranth order, *Gomphrena globosa*.

GLOBE-DAISY, [glōb'-dā'-zi], *n.* a plant of the genus *Globularia*.

GLOBE-FISH, [glōb'-fish] *n.* the fish *Tetron lagocephalus*, so called because of its ability to inflate itself into a globe.

GLOBE-FISH

GLOBE-FLOWER, [glōb'-flow'-er], *n.* the plant *Trollius europæus*, bearing globular blooms.

GLOBE-THISTLE, [glōb'-thisl], *n.* a plant of the genus *Echinops*.

GLOBE-TROTTER, [glōb'-trot'-er], *n.* an inveterate world traveller, a continual sightseer.

GLOBOID, [glōb'-oid], *adj.* globous.

GLOBOSE, [glōb'-ōs], *adj.* globous.

GLOBOSITY, [glōb-os'-i-ti], *n.* the quality of being globose.

GLOBOUS, [glōb'-us], *adj.* like a globe, globular.

GLOBULAR, [glob'-yōō-ler], *adj.* having the shape of a globe, ball-shaped, spherical. [L. *globulus*].

GLOBULARIA, [glob'-yōō-lāer'-i-a], *n.* (*bot.*) a genus of plants that bear flowers in globose heads.

GLOBULARLY, [glob'-yōō-ler-li], *adv.* in relation to globular form.

GLOBULARNESS, [glob'-yōō-ler-nes], *n.* the state of being globular.

GLOBULE, [glob'-ewl], *n.* a minute spherical particle of liquid, a drop; a blood corpuscle. [L. *globulus*].

GLOBULIN, [glob'-yōōl-in], *n.* the protein constituent of haemoglobin; (*bot.*) vegetable vesicular granules.

GLOBULOUS, [glob'-yōōl-us], *adj.* relating to a globule; globular.

GLOBULOUSNESS, [glob'-yōōl-us-nes], *n.* the condition of being globulous.

GLOBUS-HYSTERICUS, [glōb'-us-his-ter'-ik-us], *n.* an hysterical sensation as of a ball in the throat.

GLOBY, [glōb'-i], *adj.* relating to, resembling a globe.

GLOCHIDIATE, [glok-id'-i-āt], *adj.* relating to the larvae of freshwater mussels.

GLOCKENSPIEL, [glok'-en-shpēl], *n.* a musical instrument played by striking a series of hanging metal bars with a hammer. [Germ. *glockenspiel* bell-play].

GLOME, [glōm], *n.* a rounded bloom in flowers. [L. *glomus*].

GLOMERATE (1), [glom'-er-āt], *adj.* accumulated, rolled together; **g. gland**, a gland giving immediately into a duct. [L. *glomeratus*].

GLOMERATE (2), [glom'-er-āt], *v.t.* to gather together in a mass, to collect into a ball. [L. *glomerare*].

GLOMERATION, [glom'-er-ā'-shun], *n.* matter formed into a ball; the act of glomerating. [L. *glomeratio*].

GLOMEROUS, [glom'-er-us], *adj.* collected into a spherical mass.

GLOMERULE, [glom'-er-yōōl], *n.* a cluster of small organisms or of short-stalked flowers.

GLOOM (1), [glōōm], *n.* darkness, absence of light; despondency, dejection; conditions conducive to melancholy and depression. [OE. *glom* twilight].

GLOOM (2), [glōōm], *v.i.* to become or to look gloomy. [ME. *glommen* to frown].

GLOOMILY, [glōōm'-i-li], *adv.* in gloomy fashion.

GLOOMINESS, [glōōm'-i-nes], *n.* the state of being gloomy; conditions inducing gloom.

GLOOMY, [glōōm'-i], *adj.* dark, obscure, shadowed; depressed, despondent, pessimistic; hopeless, dismal.

GLORIA, [glaw'-ri-a], *n.* (*eccles.*) a doxology commencing with the word *gloria*. [L. *gloria* glory].

GLORIFICATION, [glaw'-ri-fi-kā'-shun], *n.* the act

of glorifying; the condition of being glorified. [L. *glorificatio*].

GLORIFY, [glaw'-ri-fī], *v.t.* to magnify and worship, give praise and glory (*esp.* to God); to exalt beyond reason; to praise and laud some rather sorry act or person; to make more glorious, enhance, redecorate splendidly. [ME. *glorifien* from L. *glorificare*].

GLORIOLE, [glaw'-ri-ōl], *n.* a nimbus, halo round the head of a saint, etc. [L. *gloriola*].

GLORIOUS, [glaw'-ri-us], *adj.* splendid, full of glory; overwhelmingly beautiful, illustrious, majestic, triumphant; (*coll.*) very amusing, completely satisfactory. [L. *gloriosus*].

GLORIOUSLY, [glaw'-ri-us-li], *adv.* in glorious fashion.

GLORIOUSNESS, [glaw'-ri-us-nes], *n.* the quality of being glorious.

GLORY (1), [glaw'-ri], *n.* radiant, heavenly splendour; pomp, magnificent majesty; triumph; illustrious renown; praise and worship in the highest; pride, extreme arrogance; brilliant beauty, wonderful loveliness; the peak of splendour and renown; a nimbus. [L. *gloria*].

GLORY (2), [glaw'-ri], *v.i.* to exult, rejoice in; to boast.

GLORY-HOLE, [glaw'-ri-hōl], *n.* (*coll.*) a cupboard where everything is allowed to be in disorder. [Unkn.].

GLORYINGLY, [glaw'-ri-ing-li], *adv.* in glorying fashion.

GLORY-OF-THE-SNOW, [glaw'-ri-ov-THe-snō'], *n.* the plant, *Chionodoxa*.

GLORY-PEA, [glaw'-ri-pē], *n.* an Australian variety of *Clianthus*.

GLOSS (1), [glos], *n.* a comment on, explanation of, some difficulty in a text; a translation of a word or short phrase; (*fig.*) an excuse, an explanation of deplorable conduct. [L. *glossa* a word needing explanation].

GLOSS (2), [glos], *n.* a smooth sheen, a bright, reflecting surface; (*fig.*) a false surface lustre. [OIcel. *glossi* a blaze].

GLOSS (3), [glos], *v.t.* to make a gloss on; to put as a gloss for; to extenuate, explain (bad conduct). [GLOSS (1)].

GLOSS (4), [glos], *v.t.* to impart a gloss to, make shiny. [GLOSS (2)].

GLOSSARIAL, [glos-āer'-i-al], *adj.* relating to a glossary.

GLOSSARIST, [glos'-er-ist], *n.* a writer of glosses.

GLOSSARY, [glos'-er-i], *n.* a vocabulary of foreign or difficult words occurring in a text. [L. *glossarium*].

GLOSSATOR, [glos-āt'-or], *n.* one who glosses. [MedL. *glossator*].

GLOSSER, [glos'-er], *n.* the author of a gloss.

GLOSSILY, [glos'-i-li], *adv.* in glossy fashion.

GLOSSINESS, [glos'-i-nes], *n.* the state of being glossy; the gloss on a surface.

GLOSSITIS, [glos-īt'-is], *n.* (*med.*) inflammation of the tongue. [Gk. *glossa* tongue and *itis* denoting inflammation].

GLOSSO-, *pref.* tongue. [Gk. *glossa* tongue].

GLOSSOCELE, [glos'-ō-sēl], *n.* a swelling of the tongue. [GLOSSO and Gk. *kele* swelling].

GLOSSOGRAPHER, [glos-og'-ra-fer], *n.* one who writes glosses, or a glossary.

GLOSSOGRAPHY, [glos-og'-ra-fi], *n.* the writing of glosses, or of a glossary. [GLOSSO and Gk. *graphia* writing].

GLOSSOHYAL, [glos-o-hī'-al], *adj.* lingual. [GLOSSO and HYOID].

GLOSSOLOGIST†, [glos-ol'-oj-ist], *n.* one versed in glossology.

GLOSSOLOGY†, [glos-ol'-oj-i], *n.* linguistic science. [GLOSSO and Gk. *logos* speech].

GLOSSOTOMY, [glos-ot'-om-i], *n.* (*anat.*) dissection of the tongue. [GLOSSO and Gk. *tome* cutting].

GLOSSY, [glos'-i], *adj.* having a smooth, highly polished surface.

GLOTTAL, [glot'-al], *adj.* relating to the glottis.

GLOTTIC, [glot'-ik], *adj.* glottal.

GLOTTIS, [glot'-is], *n.* the opening between the vocal cords in the larynx. [Gk. *glottis*].

GLOTTIS

GLOVE (1), [gluv], *n.* a covering for the hand, *esp.* one with separate compartments for the fingers; **with the gloves off**, in deadly earnest; **to throw down the g.**, to challenge to a duel. [OE. *glof*].

GLOVE (2), [gluv], *v.t.* to cover with a glove.

GLOVE-BAND, [gluv'-band], *n.* a band round the wrist of a glove for holding it in place.

GLOVER, [gluv'-er], *n.* a merchant or maker of gloves.

GLOVE-STRETCHERS, [gluv'-strech'-erz], *n.(pl.)* a device for stretching and opening out the fingers of a glove.

GLOW (1), [glō], *n.* red-heat, combustion at great heat but with neither flames nor smoke; a steady, rich, distant luminosity; (*fig.*) a bodily feeling of warmth and satisfaction; a feeling of intense embarrassment, a blush; ardent enthusiasm, fervour; intensity of colour.

GLOW (2), [glō], *v.i.* to give off, emit, a glow; to feel a bodily glow; to feel mental vigour or enthusiasm; to blaze with colour; (of the cheeks) to redden. [OE. *glowan*].

GLOWER, [glow'-er], *v.i.* to scowl, to gaze sullenly and ominously. [ME. *gloren* to glare].

GLOWING, [glō'-ing], *adj.* shining with heat, in a glow; (*fig.*) ardent, enthusiastic; vivid, flamboyant, vehement.

GLOWINGLY, [glō'-ing-li], *adv.* in glowing fashion.

GLOW-LAMP, [glō'-lamp], *n.* an incandescent lamp.

GLOW-WORM, [glō'-wurm], *n.* the female of a beetle, *Lampyris noctiluca*, which emits a glow in the dark.

GLOXINIA, [glok-sin'-i-a], *n.* a tropical American plant of the genus *Sinningia*. [B. *Gloxin*, a German botanist].

GLOXINIA

GLOZE (1), [glōz], *n.* a gloss; flattery, deceit, palliation.

GLOZE (2), [glōz], *v.i.* **g. over**, to explain away, palliate. [Fr. *gloser*].

GLOZER, [glōz'-er], *n.* a flatterer, one who glozes over.

GLOZING, [glōz'-ing], *n.* specious palliation, deceitful and facile explanation.

GLUCIC, [glōō'-sik], *adj.* relating to, obtained from, glucose. [Gk. *glukus* sweet].

GLUCINA, [glōō'-sīn'-a], *n.* oxide of glucinum.

GLUCINUM, [glōō-sin'-um], *n.* beryllium. [Gk. *glukus* sweet].

GLUCOHAEMIA, [glōō'-kō-hē'-mi-a], *n.* a morbid condition marked by a large proportion of glucose in the urine. [Gk. *glukus* sweet and *haima* blood].

GLUCOSE, [glōō'-kōs], *n.* a form of sugar made by acting upon starch with sulphuric acid; diabetic sugar. [Gk. *glukus* sweet].

GLUCOSIDE, GLUCOSID, [glōō'-kos-īd], *n.* a compound producing glucose by fermentation.

GLUE (1), [glōō], *n.* a highly sticky, viscous gelatine made by boiling hides, bones, etc.; any strong adhesive. [OFr. *glu* birdlime].

GLUE (2), [glōō], *v.t.* to fasten together with glue, to cause to adhere to; (*fig.*, *pass.*) to be constantly associated with, to fix the attention firmly upon.

GLUE-BOILER, [glōō'-boil'-er], *n.* a maker of glue.

GLUER, [glōō'-er], *n.* one who glues.

GLUEY, [glōō'-i], *adj.* sticky, adhesive, like glue.

GLUEYNESS, [glōō'-i-nes], *n.* the property of being gluey.

GLUISH, [glōō'-ish], *adj.* like glue.

GLUM, [glum], *adj.* dully sullen, silently bad-tempered or depressed, morose. [GLOOM].

GLUMACEOUS, [glōōm-ā'-shus], *adj.* with glumes.

GLUMAL, [glōōm'-al], *adj.* having a glume, relating to glumes.

GLUME, [glōōm], *n.* a small bract having a flower in the axil; the husk or chaff of grain. [L. *gluma*].

GLUMLY, [glum'-li], *adv.* in glum fashion.

GLUMNESS, [glum'-nes], *n.* the condition or quality of being glum.

GLUMOUS, [glōōm'-us], *adj.* having glumes, having a common glume.

GLUT (1), [glut], *n.* a superabundance of anything; a quantity too great for consumption.

GLUT (2), (**glutting, glutted**), [glut], *v.t.* to gobble greedily, stuff down food; to surfeit, feed to the full; to flood the market with a superabundance of a commodity [L. *glutire* to swallow].

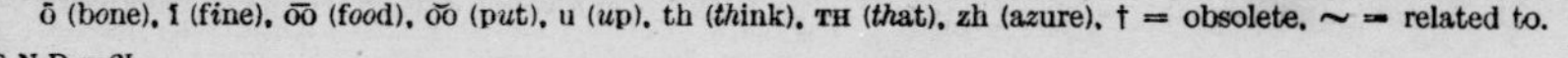

ō (bone), ī (fine), ōō (food), ŏŏ (put), u (up), th (*th*ink), TH (*th*at), zh (azure), † = obsolete, ~ = related to.

GLUTAEUS, [gloo͞-tē′-us], *n.* one of the buttock muscles. [Gk. *gloutos* buttock].
GLUTEAL, [gloo͞-tē′-al], *adj.* relating to the buttock muscles.
GLUTEN [gloo͞′-ten], *n.* a greyish viscid, albuminous substance. [L. *gluten* glue].
GLUTINATE, [gloo͞′-tin-āt], *v.t.* to glue; (*med.*) to constipate. [L. *glutinare*].
GLUTINATION, [gloo͞′-tin-ā′-shun], *n.* act of gluing; (*med.*) constipation. [L. *glutinatio*].
GLUTINATIVE†, [gloo͞′-tin-at-iv], *adj.* tenacious; (*med.*) astringent.
GLUTINOSE, [gloo͞′-tin-ōz], *adj.* glutinous. [L. *glutinosus*].
GLUTINOSITY, [gloo͞′-tin-os′-i-ti], *n.* glutinousness.
GLUTINOUS, [gloo͞′-tin-us], *adj.* sticky, viscous, resembling glue; (*bot.*) smeared with viscous moisture.
GLUTINOUSNESS, [gloo͞′-tin-us-nes], *n.* the condition of being glutinous.
GLUTTON, [glut′-on], *n.* one who over-eats grossly; (*fig.*) one who indulges excessively in anything, without being sated; (*zool.*) the wolverine, *Gulo luscus*. [L. *gluto*].
GLUTTONISH, [glut′-on-ish], *adj.* gluttonous.
GLUTTONIZE, [glut′-on-īz], *v.i.* to behave like a glutton.
GLUTTON-LIKE, [glut′-on-līk], *adj.* resembling a glutton.
GLUTTONOUS, [glut′-on-us], *adj.* grossly greedy, given to gluttony.
GLUTTONOUSLY, [glut′-on-us-li], *adv.* in gluttonous fashion.
GLUTTONY, [glut′-on-i], *n.* the gross appetite and behaviour of a glutton.
GLYCERIDE, [glis′-er-īd], *n.* an ether of glycerin.
GLYCERIN(E), [glis′-er-in], *n.* a sweet viscous liquid extracted from fats, used in medicine and the manufacture of explosives, etc. [Gk. *glukeros* sweet].
GLYCEROL, [glis′-er-ōl], *n.* glycerin.
GLYCOCOLL, [glīk′-o-kol], *n.* an amido-acetic acid. [Gk. *glukus* sweet and *kolla* glue].
GLYCOGEN, [glī′-kō-jen], *n.* (*chem.*) a carbohydrate present in animal tissues.
GLYCOGENESIS, [glī′-ko-jen′-is-is], *n.* the formation of glucose in the body. [Gk. *glukus* sweet and GENESIS].
GLYCOL, [glik′-ol, glī′-kol], *n.* a group of viscous, sweet-tasting alcohols, *esp.* ethylene glycol.
GLYCONIAN, [glī-kō′-ni-an], *adj.* glyconic.
GLYCONIC (1), [glī-kon′-ik], *n.* (*pros.*) a classical metrical form of four feet. [*Glukon*, a Greek poet].
GLYCONIC (2), [glī-kon′-ik], *adj.* written in glyconics.
GLYCOSURIA, [glī-kō-syoo͞er′-i-a], *n.* (*med.*) the presence of sugar in urine owing to excess of sugar in the blood. [Gk. *glukus* sweet and *ouron* urine].
GLYCYRRHIZIN, [glīs-i-riz′-in], *n.* a sweet substance extracted from the root of liquorice.
GLYPH, [glif], *n.* (*arch.*) a vertical ornamental fluting; (*archae.*) a figure carved in relief. [Gk. *gluphe* carving].
GLYPHIC, [glif′-ik], *adj.* carved in relief.
GLYPHOGRAPH, [glif′-ō-graf], *n.* an etched plate or etching made by glyphography.
GLYPHOGRAPHER, [glif-og′-raf-er], *n.* one skilled or working in glyphography.
GLYPHOGRAPHY, [glif-og′-ra-fi], *n.* a process for transforming etching into relief for printing, by means of electrotyping.
GLYPTIC, [glip′-tik], *adj.* relating to carving, *esp.* to engravings on ivory or precious stones. [Gk. *gluptikos* carving].
GLYPTICS, [glip′-tiks], *n.* the art of engraving figures on jewels.
GLYPTODON, [glip′-to-don], *n.* an extinct creature of the armadillo family, having fluted teeth. [Gk. *gluptos* carved and *odous odontos* tooth].

GLYPTODON

GLYPTOGRAPHY, [glip-tog′-ra-fi], *n.* the study or practice of glyptics.
GLYPTOTHECA, [glip′-tō-thē′-ka], *n.* a museum or gallery of sculpture. [Gk. *gluptos* carved and *theke* repository].
GMELINITE, [mē′-lin-īt], *n.* a whitish mineral of silica, alumina, lime, and soda. [C. A. *Gmelin*, the chemist].
GNAPHALIUM, [naf-ā′-li-um], *n.* a composite genus of 150 species of plants including the cudweeds.
GNARL (1), KNARL†, [nahl], *n.* a knot in wood, *esp.* on the trunk of a tree. [~OIcel. *gnerr*].
GNARL (2), [nahl], *v.i.* to snarl, growl. [Echoic].
GNARLED, KNARLED†, [nahld], *adj.* knotted, covered with gnarls; (*fig.*) rugged, lined, weather-beaten of appearance and complexion.
GNARLY, [nah′-li], *adj.* gnarled.
GNARR, [nah(r)], *v.i.* to snarl like a dog. [Echoic].
GNARRY, [nah′-ri], *adj.* gnarled.
GNASH, [nash], *v.t.* to grind the teeth together with rage or strong emotion. [Echoic].
GNASHINGLY, [nash′-ing-li], *adv.* by gnashing.
GNAT, [nat], *n.* any of the small two-winged insects of the family *Culex*. [OE. *gnæt*].
GNATHIC, [nath′-ik], *adj.* relating to the jaw. [Gk. *gnathos* jaw].
GNATHISM, [nath′-izm], *n.* a projection of the lower jaw; classification by jaw-structure.
GNATHITIS, [nath-īt′-is], *n.* (*med.*) inflammation of the jaw. [Gk. *gnathos* jaw and *itis* denoting inflammation].
GNATHONIC, [nath-on′-ik], *adj.* parasitical. [*Gnatho*, a character in Terence's " Eunuchs "].
GNAT-WORM, [nat′-wurm], *n.* the larva of a gnat.
GNAW, [naw], *v.t. and i.* to wear away by scratching with the teeth or by biting; to bite up (food) like an animal; (*fig.*) to wear away; to torment continually. [OE. *gnagan*].
GNAWER, [naw′-er], *n.* one who, or that which, gnaws; a rodent.
GNAWINGLY, [naw′-ing-li], *adv.* by gnawing.
GNEISS, [nīs], *n.* (*min.*) laminated granite. [Germ. *gneiss*].
GNEISSOID, [nīs′-oid], *adj.* like, consisting of, gneiss. [GNEISS and Gk. *oeides* like].
GNEISSOSE, [nīs′-ōz], *adj.* resembling gneiss in structure.
GNOME (1), [nōm], *n.* a mythical subterranean supernatural dwarf, usually represented as guarding buried treasure; a dwarfish person resembling such a being. [Fr. *gnome*].
GNOME (2), [nōm], *n.* a moral aphorism. [Gk. *gnome* intelligence].
GNOMIC, [nōm-ik], *adj.* aphoristic, didactic, sententious. [Gk. *gnomikos*].
GNOMICAL, [nōm′-ik-al], *adj.* gnomic.
GNOMIOMETRICAL, [nōm′-i-ō-met′-rik-al], *adj.* related to the measurement of angles. [GNOMON and METRICAL].
GNOMOLOGY, [nōm-ol′-o-ji], *n.* a collection of aphorisms. [GNOME (2) and Gk. *logos* speech].
GNOMON, [nōm′-on], *n.* the rod of a sundial by whose shadow the time is shown; a perpendicular shaft used in astronomical observations; the index of the hour circle of a globe; part of a parallelogram. [Gk. *gnomon* a judge, a T-square].
GNOMONIC, [nōm-on′-ik], *adj.* relating to gnomons or sundials. [Gk. *gnomonikos*].
GNOMONICAL, [nōm-on′-ik-al], *adj.* gnomonic.
GNOMONICALLY, [nōm-on′-ik-al-i], *adv.* by gnomonics.
GNOMONICS, [nōm-on′-iks], *n.(pl.)* the principles of the sundial; the art of telling time by shadows.
GNOMONOLOGY, [nōm-on-ol′-o-ji], *n.* the study of the principles of the sundial. [GNOMON and Gk. *logos* speech].
GNOSIS, [nōs′-is], *n.* mystical knowledge obtained by direct spiritual ecstasy and experience. [Gk. *gnosis* knowledge].
GNOSTIC (1), [nos′-tik], *n.* a believer in gnosticism, *esp.* a member of the second century gnostic heresy.
GNOSTIC (2), [nos′-tik], *adj.* relating to gnosis and to gnosticism. [Gk. *gnostikos* knowing].
GNOSTICISM, [nos′-ti-sizm], *n.* belief in gnosis and its implications, *esp.* the philosophy built up from the combination of Christian mysticism and platonic speculation.
GNU, [new], *n.* a wildebeest, an antelope of the genus *Connochœtes*. [Hottentot *gnu*].
GO (1), [gō], *n.* movement, performance; undertaking, occurrence; endeavour, action; spirit, energy; bargain, deal; **on the g.,** active; **all the g.,** much in vogue.
GO (2), (went, gone), [gō], *v.i.* to move, walk; to proceed away from the speaker, to depart; to be educated in a place; (of machinery) to work, function; to break down, cease to function; to disappear, to cease to be present; to die; to carry on, happen, take place; to become, change to; to behave in a particular manner; to be available for; to lead to; (of wagers,

etc.) to undertake, contract to achieve something; to be sold; to be put; **to g. about,** (*naut.*) to tack; **to g. at,** to undertake furiously; **to g. back on,** to withdraw, back down; **to g. down,** to sink; to leave a university; **to g. in for,** to devote oneself to; **to g. into,** to investigate, undertake; **to g. off,** to explode; to decline, decay; to take place; **to g. on,** to continue; **to g. out,** to become extinguished; to endeavour eagerly and with all one's efforts; to become unfashionable; **to g. over,** to study; to correct, criticize; **to g. through with,** to persist, endure; **to g. with,** to harmonize. [OE. *gan*].

GOA-CEDAR, [gō'-ah-sē'-der], *n.* a variety of cypress, *Cupressus lusitanica.*

GOAD (1), [gōd], *n.* a sharp instrument for driving animals; (*fig.*) a pressing incentive. [OE. *gad* point of a weapon].

GOAD (2), [gōd], *v.t.* to drive with a goad; (*fig.*) to gall, prick on; to incite, provoke, enrage.

GOAF, [gōf], *n.* the space between pillars from which coal has been worked out; gob. [OIcel. *golf* floor].

GO-AHEAD, [gō'-a-hed'], *adj.* active, pushing, ambitious.

GOAL (1), [gōl], *n.* aim, final purpose, ambition; the two posts between which the ball has to be driven in various team-games, the score obtained by so driving the ball; the mark set up at the end of a race track, the winning post. [ME. *gol* boundary].

GOAL (2), [gōl], *v.i.* to act as goalkeeper.

GOALIE, [gōl'-i], *n.* (*coll.*) a goalkeeper.

GOALKEEPER, [gōl'-kēp'-er], *n.* the player guarding the goal in football and hockey.

GOAL-LINE, [gōl'-līn], *n.* the line between the goal-posts, which is extended in either direction to mark the terminal boundary of the playing-field.

GOAL-POSTS, [gōl'-pōsts], *n.(pl.)* the posts between which the ball must be driven in order to score.

GOAT, [gōt], *n.* a hollow-horned, bearded ruminant of the genus *capra*; one of the signs of the zodiac; (*fig.*) an unrestrained old lecher; **to get one's g.,** to make angry; **to act the g.,** to act in a foolish, excited fashion. [OE. *gat*].

GOATCHAFER, [gōt'-chāf-er], *n.* a beetle, *Melolontha solstitialis.*

GOATEE, [gōt-ē'], *n.* a short, straggling, goat-like beard.

GOATHERD, [gōt'-hurd], *n.* one in charge of a herd of goats.

GOATISH, [gōt'-ish], *adj.* like a goat, lecherous.

GOATISHLY, [gōt'-ish-li], *adv.* in goatish fashion.

GOATISHNESS, [gōt'-ish-nes], *n.* the state of being goatish.

GOATLING, [gōt'-ling], *n.* a two-year-old goat.

GOAT-MARJORAM, [gōt'-mah'-jer-am], *n.* a plant, goat's-beard.

GOAT-MILKER, [gōt'-milk'-er], *n.* the night-jar, a bird of the genus *Caprimulgus,* so called from its supposed practice of sucking goats.

GOAT-MILKER

GOAT-MOTH, [gōt'-moth], *n.* a great British moth, *Cossus ligniperda.*

GOAT'S-BEARD, [gōtz'-bēerd], *n.* a plant of the genus *Tragopogon,* goat-marjoram.

GOATSKIN, [gōt'-skin], *n.* the skin of a goat.

GOATS-RUE, [gōtz'-rōō], *n.* a leguminous plant of the genus *Galega.*

GOATS-THORN, [gōtz'-thawn], *n.* a plant of the genus *Astragalus.*

GOATSUCKER, [gōt'-suk'-er], *n.* a goat-milker.

GOB, [gob], *n.* (*prov.*) a large bite of food; (*slang*) the mouth; (*vulg.*) a globule of saliva; (*U.S.*) a sailor; (*mining*) the waste matter used for filling up a goaf. [OFr. *gobe* mouthful].

GOBANG, [gō'-bang], *n.* a Japanese game played on a board with sixteen squares a side, the object being to get five counters in a row. [Chin. *k'ipan* chess-board].

GOBBET, [gob'-et], *n.* a lump of food or spittle fresh from the mouth; a small portion of something, *esp.* a passage set for translation or comment in an examination. [ME. *gobet*].

GOBBING, [gob'-ing], *n.* the mining of gob.

GOBBLE (1), [gobl], *n.* a gobbling sound or action.

GOBBLE (2), [gobl], *v.t. and i.* to bolt down food; to eat rapidly and noisily. [Fr. *gober* to swallow].

GOBBLE (3), [gobl], *v.i.* to utter a noise as a turkey. [GABBLE (2)].

GOBBLE-GUT, [gobl'-gut], *n.* a glutton, greedy eater.

GOBBLER (1), [gob'-ler], *n.* one who gobbles. [GOBBLE (2)].

GOBBLER (2), [gob'-ler], *n.* a young turkey. [GOBBLE (3)].

GOBBO, [gob'-ō], *n.* the fruit of *Hibiscus esculentus,* used in soups.

GOBELIN (1), [gob'-el-a(ng)], *n.* a rich and fine tapestry originally made by the brothers Gobelin in fifteenth-century Paris.

GOBELIN (2), [gob'-el-a(ng)], *adj.* made by, relating to, or similar to, the work of the brothers Gobelin.

GOBEMOUCHE, [gòb'-mōōsh], *n.* a gabbling gossip. [Fr. *gobemouche*].

GO-BETWEEN, [gō'-bi-twēn], *n.* an intermediary; a disreputable agent, pander.

GOBLET, [gob'-let], *n.* a drinking vessel, *esp.* one without handles and with a pedestal base. [Fr. *gobelet*].

GOBLIN, [gob'-lin], *n.* an ugly, malicious spirit, a grotesque sprite, a bogey. [OFr. *gobelin*].

GOBY, [gō'-bi], *n.* small fish of the genus *Gobius,* with suckers on the ventral fins. [Gk. *kobios*].

GO-BY, [gō'-bī], *n.* (*coll.*) a purposeful avoidance, a deliberate passing-over or ignoring.

GO-CART, [gō'-kaht], *n.* a wheeled framework in which children learn to walk; a perambulator.

GOBLET

GOD, [god], *n.* a powerful supernatural being controlling an aspect of the universe, a male deity; the creator of the universe; (*fig.*) one of superhuman qualities or stature; an idolized ideal, an object of worship; **God's acre,** a churchyard. [OE. *god*].

GODCHILD, [god'-chīld], *n.* a child sponsored at baptism. [ME. *godchild*].

GODDAUGHTER, [god'-daw-ter], *n.* a female godchild. [OE. *goddohter*].

GODDESS, [god'-es], *n.* a female divinity; an idolized woman.

GODDESS-LIKE, [god'-es-līk], *adj.* like a goddess.

GODET, [gō'-dā], *n.* a triangular piece of material inserted to widen a garment. [Fr. *godet*].

GODETIA, [gō-dē'-sha], *n.* a showy annual garden flower. [*Godet,* a Swiss botanist].

GODFATHER (1), [god'-fah'-ᴛʜer], *n.* the male sponsor at baptism.

GODFATHER (2), [god'-fah'-ᴛʜer], *v.t.* to act as godfather to.

GODFEARING, [god'-fēer-ing], *adj.* pious, obedient to God's will.

GODFORSAKEN, [god'-faw-sāk'-en], *adj.* abandoned, desolate.

GODHEAD, [god'-hed], *n.* the divinity of a god or of God.

GODHOOD, [god'-hŏŏd], *n.* godhead.

GODLESS, [god'-les], *adj.* impious, irreligious, atheistical.

GODLESSLY, [god'-les-li], *adv.* in godless fashion.

GODLESSNESS, [god'-les-nes], *n.* the condition of being godless.

GODLIKE, [god'-līk], *adj.* like a god, almost divine.

GODLIKENESS, [god'-līk-nes], *n.* the quality of being godlike.

GODLILY, [god'-li-li], *adv.* in godly fashion.

GODLINESS, [god'-li-nes], *n.* the quality of being godly, holiness.

GODLING, [god'-ling], *n.* a petty god.

GODLY, [god'-li], *adj.* pious, religious, God-fearing.

GODMOTHER, [god'-muᴛʜ-er], *n.* the female sponsor at baptism.

GODOWN, [gō'-down], *n.* a store or warehouse in the Far East. [Malay *godong*].

GODPARENT, [god'-pāer-ent], *n.* a sponsor at baptism.

GODROON, [god'-rōōn], *n.* (*arch.*) a reversed fluting. [Fr. *godron* plait].

GODS, [godz], *n.(pl.)* (*coll.*) the audience in the gallery of a theatre.

GODSEND, [god'-send], *n.* a sudden, unexpected, and extremely welcome piece of good fortune, an opportune stroke of luck. [GOD and ME. *sonde* message].

GODSHIP, [god'-ship], *n.* godhead, divinity.

GODSMITH, [god'-smith], *n.* one who makes idols.

GODSON, [god'-sun'], *n* a male godchild.

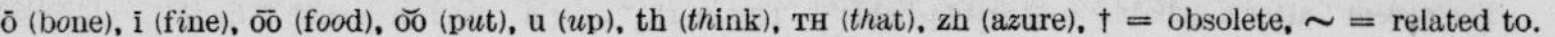

GOD-SPEED, [god'-spēd], *n.* good luck, a wish for success.
GODWARD, [god'-wud], *adv.* towards God.
GODWIT, [god'-wit], *n.* an edible coastal snipe. [Uncert.].
GOER, [gō'-er], *n.* one who goes; a fast horse; (*slang*) an active, ambitious person.
GOFER, [gōf'-er], *n.* a thin wafer-like cake of batter, baked between iron plates which imprint a honey-comb pattern upon it. [Fr. *gaufre* honeycomb].
GOFFER (1), GAUFFER, GAUFFRE, [gōf'-er], *n.* a fluted border in garments, an edging of frills or pleats. [Fr. *gauffre* pleat].
GOFFER (2), [gōf'-er], *v.t.* to gather cloth in pleats.
GOFFERING, GAUFFERING, [gōf'-er-ing], *n.* goffer work; act of gathering in pleats.
GO-GETTER, [gō'-get'-er], *n.* (*U.S.*) a person of energy and successful determination. [GO and GET].
GOGGLE (1), [gogl], *n.* a popping, stupid, surprised stare.
GOGGLE (2), [gogl], *v.i.* to roll the eyes in amazement or terror, to stare with stupid, popping eyes. [~Ir. *gog* nod].
GOGGLED, [gogld], *adj.* staring, goggle-eyed; wearing goggles.
GOGGLE-EYE, [gogl'-i], *n.* a silly, popping eye.
GOGGLE-EYED, [gogl'-īd], *adj.* having goggle-eyes, popping the eyes in astonishment.
GOGGLES, [goglz], *n.*(*pl.*) spectacles guarded with projecting metal rims forming cylindrical tubes, worn in motor-racing, etc.; (*med.*) an instrument used to adjust a squint; (*coll.*) ordinary spectacles.
GOGLET, [gog'-let], *n.* a porous earthenware vessel for cooling liquids. [Portug. *gorgoleta*].
GOIDELIC, [goi-del'-ik], *adj.* Gaelic. [OIr. *goidel*].
GOING (1), [gō'-ing], *n.* the act of progressing; departure; travelling conditions, state or character of the road; pregnancy.
GOING (2), [gō'-ing], *adj.* in working order; prospering.
GOITRE, [goit'-er], *n.* bronchocele of the thyroid, a pathological condition accompanied by swelling in the fore-part of the neck. [Fr. *goitre*].
GOITRED, [goit'-erd], *adj.* afflicted with goitre.
GOITROUS, [goit'-rus], *adj.* relating to, suffering from, goitre.
GOLA, [gō'-la], *n.* (*arch.*) the crown of the cornice. [L. *gula*].
GOLCONDA, [gol-kond'-a], *n.* a fabulous repository of enormous treasure. [*Golconda*, a fortress and treasure house of the Nizam of Hyderabad].
GOLD (1), [gōld], *n.* a soft, heavy, yellow precious metal, the chemical element Au; coins made of this; the yellow colour resembling that of the metal; (*fig.*) wealth, riches, money; purchasing power, material prosperity; worth, virtues; (*archery*) the gilt bull's-eye of the target; **g. rush**, a rush to stake out claims on a newly discovered goldfield; **g. standard**, the legal fixing of a currency at an equivalent in gold. [OE. *gold*].
GOLD (2), [gōld], *adj.* made of, resembling gold; golden.
GOLDBEATER, [gōld'-bēt'-er], *n.* a craftsman who hammers gold into leaf.
GOLDBEATING, [gōld'-bēt'-ing], *n.* the craft of the goldbeater.
GOLDCLOTH, [gōld'-kloth], *n.* cloth of gold thread.
GOLDCREST, [gōld'-krest], *n.* the golden-crested wren, *Regulus cristatus*.
GOLD-DIGGER, [gōld'-dig'-er], *n.* (*slang*) an adventuress who wheedles money out of rich but stupid males.
GOLD-DUST, [gōld'-dust], *n.* particles of gold sifted from the ore.
GOLDEN, [gōld'-en], *adj.* made of gold, resembling gold in colour; (*fig.*) valuable, promising; virtuous; happy; **g. calf**, a false material idol; **g. age**, the period of perfection; **g. opportunity**, the best possible chance for something; **g. syrup**, refined, yellow, edible treacle; **g. wedding**, the fiftieth anniversary of one's wedding; **g. number**, the number of a year as used in reckoning Easter.
GOLDEN-CUP, [gōld'-en-kup], *n.* the plant, *Caltha palustris*, the marsh marigold.
GOLDEN-EYE, [gōld'-en-ī], *n.* the northern diving-duck, *Clangula glaucion*, so called from its plumage.
GOLDENROD, [gōld'-en-rod], *n.* a perennial yellow-flowered plant of the genus, *Solidago*.
GOLDFIELD, [gōld'-fēld], *n.* a tract of land rich in gold-bearing ore.
GOLDFINCH, [gōld'-finch], *n.* the gold-winged song-bird, *Carduelis elegans*.
GOLDFISH, [gōld'-fish], *n.* a small Far-Eastern fish of the carp family with golden scales.
GOLDFOIL, [gōld'-foil], *n.* gold beaten into thin sheets, used chiefly for decoration.
GOLDHAMMER, [gōld'-ham'-er], *n.* a bird, the yellow bunting.
GOLDILOCKS, [gōld'-i-loks], *n.* a child with golden hair; the buttercup, *Ranunculus auricomus*. [GOLD and LOCK (1)].
GOLDING, [gōld'-ing], *n.* a species of hop.
GOLD LEAF, [gōld'-lēf'], *n.* gold beaten into very thin sheets.
GOLDLESS, [gōld-les], *adj.* without gold or money.
GOLDNEY, [gōld'-ni], *n.* the gilthead.
GOLD PLATE, [gōld'-plāt'], *n.* a coating of gold plated on another metal; articles so plated; silver gilt.
GOLDSINNY, [gōld'-sin-i], *n.* a sea-fish of the genus *Crenilabrus* (*cornubicus*); **Jago's g.**, *Crenilabrus rupestris*.
GOLDSMITH, [gōld'-smith], *n.* a worker in gold, a trader in gold work.
GOLDTHREAD, [gōld'-thred], *n.* the yellow-rooted flower *Coptis trifolia*.
GOLF (1), [golf], *n.* a game in which a ball has to be struck successively into 9 or 18 holes along a specially laid-out course, by means of long clubs. [Uncert.].
GOLF (2), [golf], *v.i.* to play golf.
GOLF-CLUB, [golf'-klub], *n.* a club used in striking the ball in golf; an association for the purpose of playing golf; the links and buildings held by such an association.
GOLFER, [golf'-er], *n.* one who plays golf.
GOLF-LINKS, [golf'-lingks'], *n.*(*pl.*) land laid out for golf.
GOLIARD, [gol'-yahd], *n.* a wandering medieval jester. [OFr. *goliard*].
GOLIATH-BEETLE, [go-lī'-ath-bētl'], *n.* a tropical beetle of great size.
GOLLIWOG, [gol'-i-wog], *n.* a grotesque black, pop-eyed doll; (*coll.*) a fuzzy-haired person. [Invented].
GOLLY, [gol'-i], *int.* (*coll.*) good God! [AmerNegro corruption of GOD].
GOLORE, see GALORE.
GOLOSH, GALOSH, [gol-osh'], *n.* a rubber over-shoe for keeping out damp. [Fr. *galoche*].
GOLUPTIOUS, [gol-up'-shus], *adj.* (*slang*) scrumptious. [~ VOLUPTUOUS].
GOMBEEN, [gom'-bēn], *n.* (*Ir.*) moneylending. [Ir. *gaimbin* interest].
GOMBEEN-MAN, [gom'-bēn-man], *n.* (*Ir.*) a money-lender.
GOMBROON, [gom'-brōōn], *n.* a white variety of Persian porcelain. [*Gombroon*, on the Persian Gulf, where it was made].
GOME, [gōm], *n.* black cart-wheel grease. [OIcel. *gaumr*].
GOMELIN, [gom'-el-in], *n.* a starch used in cotton weaving. [Fr. *gommeline*].
GOMPHIASIS, [gom-fī'-as-is], *n.* (*med.*) a morbid loosening of the teeth. [Gk. *gomphiasis* tooth-ache].
GOMPHOSIS, [gom-fō'-sis], *n.* (*anat.*) an immovable articulation of the bones. [Gk. *gomphosis* a nailing together].
GOMUTI, [gom-ōōt'-i], *n.* a Malay palm from whose fibres ropes are made, and from whose sap sugar and palm wine are extracted. [Malay *gumuti*].
GON, [gon], *suff.* angled. [Gk. *-gonos*].
GONAD, [gon'-ad'], *n.* a reproductive gland. [Gk. *gone* generation].
GONAGRA, [gon-ag'-ra], *n.* (*path.*) gout in the leg joints. [Gk. *gonu* knee].
GONALGIA, [gon-al'-ji-a], *n.* (*path.*) morbid pain in the knee. [Gk. *gonu* knee and *algos* pain].
GONDOLA, [gon'-do-la], *n.* a long, narrow flat-bottomed Venetian boat with a high, curving prow and stern; the car of an airship. [Uncert.].

GONDOLA

GONDOLIER, [gon'-do-lēer'], *n.* one who propels a gondola.
GONDOLINO, [gon'-do-lē'-nō], *n.* a gondola for racing. [It. *gondolino*].
GONE, [gon], *p.pt.* of GO. [OE. *gān*].
GONER, [gon'-er], *n.* (*slang*) one inevitably doomed or ruined; one on the point of destruction or defeat.

GONFALON, [gon'-fal-on], *n.* a banner with several streamers, hanging from a crosspiece; the banner of the medieval Papacy; the square pennon of a lance. [Fr. from It. *gonfalone* banner].

GONFALON

GONFALONIER, [gon'-fal-on-ēer'], *n.* a standard-bearer; the chief magistrate of medieval Florence.

GONG (1), [gong], *n.* a metal disk with a raised rim, giving out a sonorous sound when struck. [Malay *gong*].

GONG (2), [gong], *v.t.* (*coll.*) to strike on a gong; (*coll.*) to summon a car exceeding the speed-limit to stop.

GONIATITES, [gon'-i-a-tī'-tēz], *n.* (*pl.*) lobed ammonites.

GONIDIA, [gon-id'-i-a], *n.*(*pl.*) the cells composing the thallus of lichens.

GONIOMETER, [gon-i-om'-it-er], *n.* an instrument for measuring the angles of solids, or for measuring the angle of rotation in a wireless direction-finder. [Gk. *gonia* angle and METER].

GONOCOCCUS, [gon'-ō-kok'-us], *n.* (*path.*) the micrococcus which causes gonorrhoea. [Gk. *gone* seed and COCCUS].

GONORRHOEA, [gon'-er-rē'-a], *n.* a contagious venereal disease symptomized by inflammation of the urethra and a morbid discharge. [Gk. *gone* seed and *rhoia* flow].

GONORRHOEAL, [gon'-er-rē'-al], *adj.* pertaining to gonorrhoea.

GOOD (1), [gŏŏd], *n.* a merit, a moral quality, a virtue; an advantage, benefit, profit; (*pl.*) material possessions, wealth, property; merchandise, articles of use or commerce, *esp.* other than livestock; **to deliver the goods**, to carry out one's promise; **to make g.**, to compensate for (loss of), to succeed in life. [OE. *god* a good thing].

GOOD (2), [gŏŏd], *adj.* having worth; possessing merit or desirability; suitable for its purpose; pleasant; tending to promote health, comfort, etc.; virtuous, pious, having high moral standards; well-behaved; competent, skilled, talented; in sound condition; valid, standing; true, remaining unsuperseded; capable of supplying, maintaining, undertaking; thorough, adequate, satisfactory; **to be as g. as one's word**, to keep one's promise. [OE. *god*].

GOODBYE (1), [gŏŏd-bī'], (*int.*) farewell! as a greeting given on parting. [*good* (*day, night, etc.*) and (*God*) *be with you* (or *ye*)].

GOODBYE (2), [gŏŏd-bī'], *n.* a farewell.

GOOD-FELLOWSHIP, [gŏŏd-fel'-ō-ship], *n.* conviviality, sentimentally hearty companionship.

GOOD-FOLK, [gŏŏd'-fōk], *n.*(*pl.*) fairies.

GOOD-HUMOURED, [gŏŏd-hew'-merd], *adj.* cheerful, good-tempered.

GOOD-HUMOUREDLY, [gŏŏd-hew'-merd-li], *adv.* in a good-humoured way.

GOODISH, [gŏŏd'-ish], *adj.* (*coll.*) considerable, fair.

GOODLINESS, [gŏŏd'-li-nes], *n.* the quality of being goodly.

GOODLY, [gŏŏd'-li], *adj.* pleasing, handsome, agreeable; moderately large.

GOODMAN, [gŏŏd'-man], *n.* a householder, husband, master of a house.

GOOD-NATURED, [gŏŏd-nā'-cherd], *adj.* agreeable, naturally kindly of temper.

GOOD-NATUREDLY, [good-nā'-cherd-li], *adv.* in a good-natured way.

GOOD-NATUREDNESS, [gŏŏd-nā'-cherd-nes], *n.* the state of being good-natured.

GOODNESS, [gŏŏd'-nes], *n.* the quality of being good; holiness, moral worth; excellence of quality; that which does good, *esp.* nourishment.

GOODS-TRAIN, [gŏŏdz'-trān], *n.* a train carrying only merchandise.

GOOD-TEMPERED, [gŏŏd-tem'-perd], *adj.* of level temper, not easily angered.

GOODWIFE, [gŏŏd'-wif], *n.* the mistress of a household.

GOODWILL, [gŏŏd'-wil], *n.* benevolence, kindly approval; (*leg.*) that value of a business lying in its name, reputation and trade.

GOODWOMAN, [gŏŏd'-wŏŏm-an], *n.* a goodwife.

GOODY, [gŏŏd'-i], *n.* a sweetmeat; a person who is prim and narrow-minded; †an old woman.

GOODY-GOODY (1), [gŏŏd'-i-gŏŏd'-i], *n.* a goody-goody person.

GOODY-GOODY (2), [gŏŏd'-i-gŏŏd'-i], *adj.* primly pious, weakly moral, smugly narrow-minded; namby-pamby; (*U.S.*) good.

GOOF, [gōōf], *n.* (*slang*) a simpleton. [Invented].

GOOFY, [gōōf'-i], *adj.* (*slang*) silly with sentimental love; simple-minded, foolish.

GOOGLE, [gōōgl], *v.i.* (*cricket*) to bowl googlies.

GOOGLY, [gōōg'-li], *n.* (*cricket*) an off-break bowled with a leg-break action, or the reverse. [Unkn.].

GOOR, [gaw(r)], *n.* palm-sugar. [Hind. *goor*].

GOOSANDER, [gōōs-and'-er], *n.* a large diving bird of the genus *Mergus*. [Unkn.].

GOOSE, (*pl.* **geese**), [gōōs, gēs], *n.* a web-footed bird of the genus *Anser*, *esp.* the domestic variety; (*coll.*) a silly person; a tailor's iron; **to cook someone's g.**, to frustrate or deal with someone. [OE. *gos*].

GOOSEBERRY, [gŏŏz'-ber-i], *n.* the juicy, edible berry of the shrub *Ribes Grossularia*; the shrub itself; **to play the g.**, (*coll.*) to hamper a flirtation by unwelcome intrusion. [GOOSE and BERRY].

GOOSEBERRY-FOOL, [gŏŏz'-ber-i-fōōl'], *n.* a succulent dish made from pulped gooseberries and cream.

GOOSEBERRY-TOMATO, [gŏŏz'-ber-i-tom-ah'-tō], *n.* the fruit of *Physalis peruviana*.

GOOSECAP, [gōōs'-kap], *n.* (*coll.*) a ninny.

GOOSE-CORN, [gōōs'-kawn], *n.* a kind of rush, *Juncus squarrosus*.

GOOSE-FLESH, [gōōs'-flesh], *n.* a prickly roughening of the skin in cold or fear.

GOOSEFOOT, [gōōs'-fŏŏt], *n.* a plant of the genus *Chenopodium*.

GOOSE-GIRL, [gōōs'-gurl], *n.* a girl employed to look after geese.

GOOSEGRASS, [gōōs'-grahs], *n.* a trailing, burr-bearing weed, *Galium Aparine*.

GOOSEGRAY, [gōōs'-grā], *n.* the plant, *Potentilla anserina*.

GOOSE-HERD, [gōōs'-hurd], *n.* a tender of geese.

GOOSENECK, [gōōs'-nek], *n.* (*naut.*) the iron point of a boom.

GOOSEQUILL, [gōōs'-kwil], *n.* a pen made from the quill of a goose.

GOOSERY, [gōōs'-er-i], *n.* a yard for geese; (*coll.*) silliness.

GOOSE-STEP, [gōōs'-step], *n.* a kind of German military marching step in which the legs are raised parallel to the ground at each step, without bending the knees.

GOOSETONGUE, [gōōs'-tung], *n.* the sneeze-wort, *Achillea Ptarmica*.

GOOSEWING, [gōōs'-wing], *n.* (*naut.*) the projecting lower corner of a sail when furled; the position when fore and aft sails are set on opposite sides.

GOPHER, [gōf'-er], *n.* the prairie squirrel, a small burrowing American rodent. [Fr. *gaufre* honeycomb].

GORAL, [gaw'-ral], *n.* a horned Himalayan ruminant, related to the antelope. [Native].

GORAMY, see GOURAMI.

GORCOCK, [gaw'-kok], *n.* the male of the red grouse. [Unkn.].

GOR-CROW, [gaw'-krō], *n.* the carrion crow. [OE. *gor* dung].

GORDIAN, [gaw'-di-an], *adj.* **to cut the G. knot**, to get out of a difficulty by drastic and direct means. [*Gordius*, King of Phrygia, who tied a complicated knot that Alexander cut with his sword].

GORDIUS, [gaw'-di-us], *n.* the hair-worm, from its habit of twisting itself into knots. [*Prec.*].

GORE (1), [gaw(r)], *n.* human blood, *esp.* from a wound; clotted blood. [OE. *gor* dung].

GORE (2), [gaw(r)], *n.* a wedge-shaped piece of material let into a garment to make it wider; an heraldic abatement. [OE. *gar* spear, triangular plot of land].

GORE (3), [gaw(r)], *v.t.* to let a gore into a garment.

GORE (4), [gaw(r)], *v.t.* to pierce with the tusks or horns, to stab with sharp points. [OE. *gar* spear].

GORGE (1), [gawj], *n.* the throat, food-passage; a narrow, deep valley between rocks; a narrow way through fortifications. [Fr. *gorge* throat].

GORGE (2), [gawj], *n.* a gross meal; the act of gorging. [GORGE (3)].

GORGE (3), [gawj], *v.t. and i.* to eat heavily and greedily, to cram to repletion. [GORGE (1)].

GORGED, [gawjd], *adj.* stuffed, crammed; (*her.*) (of animals) having a collar.

GORGE-HOOK, [gawj'-hŏŏk], *n.* a double fish-hook.

GORGEOUS, [gawj-us], *adj.* richly splendid, heavily

and resplendently magnificent; (*coll.*) very excellent, marvellous. [OFr. *gorgias*].

GORGEOUSLY, [gawj'-us-li], *adv.* in gorgeous fashion.

GORGEOUSNESS, [gawj'-us-nes], *n.* the quality of being gorgeous.

GORGET, [gawj'-et], *n.* throat armour; an ornamental neck-plate derived from this; a kind of ruff; a coloured patch on the throat of a bird. [OFr. *gorgete*].

GORGET

GORGON, [gaw'-gon], *n.* (*class. myth.*) one of three hideous woman-like creatures whose hair consisted of snakes, and whose eyes petrified all who saw them; (*fig.*) an alarmingly fierce elderly female. [Gk. *gorgos* terrible].

GORGONEION, [gaw-gon-ē'-on], *n.* (*arch.*) a representation of the head of a gorgon.

GORGONIA, [gaw-gō'-ni-a], *n.* a flexible coral growing in shrub formations. [MdL. *gorgonia* coral].

GORGONIAN, [gaw-gō'-ni-an], *adj.* resembling, related to, a gorgon.

GORGONIZE, [gaw'-gon-īz], *v.t.* to petrify, turn to stone.

GORGONZOLA, [gaw'-gon-zō'-la], *n.* a highly flavoured cheese made originally in Lombardy. [*Gorgonzola*, near Milan].

GOR-HEN, [gaw(r)'-hen], *n.* the female of the red grouse. [Unkn.].

GORILLA, [go-ril'-a], *n.* a great anthropoid ape found in the Congo. [Native].

GORING, [gaw(r)'-ing], *n.* a pricking, laceration.

GORM, [gawm], *n.* the surface shine on varnish. [Unkn.].

GORMAND, see GOURMAND.

GORMANDISM, [gaw'-mand-izm], *n.* delight in good food.

GORMANDIZE, [gaw-mand-īz], *v.i.* to take pleasure in food.

GORMANDIZER, [gaw'-mand-īz-er], *n.* a gourmand.

GORSE, [gaws], *n.* a spiny, yellow-flowered bush of the genus *Ulex*; a cluster of, or area covered by, such plants. [OE. *gorst*].

GORSECHAT, [gaws'-chat], *n.* the whinchat, *Pratincola rubetra*.

GORSEDD, [gaw'-seTH], *n.* a session or meeting of Welsh bards or Druids. [Wel. *gorsedd*].

GORSY, [gaws'-i], *adj.* thick with gorse.

GORY, [gaw'-ri], *adj.* covered with gore, bloody; (*fig.*) murderous.

GOSH, [gosh], *int.* a mild expletive. [~GOD].

GOSHAWK, [gos'-hawk], *n.* the powerful, short-winged bird, *Astur palumbarius*, formerly used in hawking. [OE. *goshafoc*].

GOSLING, [goz'-ling], *n.* a young goose. [OE. *gos* goose].

GOSPEL (1), [gos'-pel], *n.* any of the first four books of the New Testament, giving the life and teachings of Christ; the teachings of Christ; a statement of some absolute and holy truth; the book of a sacred doctrine. [OE. *godspel*].

GOSPEL (2), [gos'-pel], *adj.* sacred and inviolable.

GOSPEL-GOSSIP, [gos'-pel-gos'-ip], *n.* one over-zealous in preaching to his friends.

GOSPELLER, [gos'-pel-er], *n.* an evangelist; the priest or deacon reading the gospel for the day.

GOSSAMER, [gos'-a-mer], *n.* a light substance formed of filmy strands of cobweb found floating or caught in bushes; anything very light, filmy, and insubstantial. [ME. *gossomer* goose-summer].

GOSSAMERY, [gos'-a-mer-i], *adj.* flimsy, like gossamer.

GOSSAN, [gos'-an], *n.* iron oxide found in mineral lodes. [Cornish].

GOSSIP (1), [gos'-ip], *n.* one who gossips, an old busybody; unfounded personal anecdotes and rumours about others bandied about in conversation, *esp.* ill-natured and spiteful tittle-tattle. [OE. *godsibb* sponsor].

GOSSIP (2), [gos'-ip], *v.i.* to chat casually and intimately; to spread spiteful and ill-natured rumours about the private concerns of others.

GOSSIPRY, [gos'-ip-ri], *n.* gossipy talk.

GOSSIPY, [gos'-ip-i], *adj.* of the nature of gossip; fond of gossiping.

GOSSOON, [gos-ōōn'], *n.* a loutish lad. [Fr. *garçon* boy].

GOSSYPIUM, [go-sip'-i-um], *n.* a genus of malvaceous plants including cotton. [Gk. *gossupion* cotton tree].

GOTH, [goth], *n.* a member of a Germanic people who overran much of the Roman Empire; (*fig.*) a barbarous person. [Gk. *Gothos*].

GOTHA, [gō'-ta], *n.* a long-distance German bombing plane. [*Gotha*, in Thuringia, Germany].

GOTHAMITE, [got'-am-īt], *n.* a person of a similar turn of mind to the wise men of Gotham.

GOTHIC (1), [goth'-ik], *n.* Gothic architecture; the language of the Goths.

GOTHIC (2), [goth'-ik], *adj.* relating to, derived from, the Goths; (*arch.*) in the late medieval style of pointed arches; (*typog.*) having the heavy, complex characters as in modern German; (*fig.*) barbarous; vulgarly austere.

GOTHICALLY, [goth'-ik-al-i], *adv.* in the Gothic manner.

GOTHICISM, [goth'-is-izm], *n.* affectation of the Gothic.

GOTHICIZE, [goth'-is-īz], *v.t. and i.* to make Gothic; to affect the Gothic style.

GOUACHE, [gwash], *n.* an artistic technique in which the paint is mixed with gum. [Fr. *gouache*].

GOUDA, [gow'-da], *n.* a Dutch cheese. [*Gouda*, in Holland].

GOUGE (1), [gowj], *n.* a concave-bladed chisel used for cutting grooves. [Fr. *gouge*].

GOUGE

GOUGE (2), [gowj], *v.t. and i.* to make grooves with a gouge; to prise out as if with a gouge; to force out the eye with the thumb.

GOUGE-SLIPS, [gowj'-slips], *n.(pl.)* hones for sharpening gouges.

GOULARD, [gōō'-lahd], *n.* lead lotion, used in inflammation. [*Goulard*, a French doctor].

GOULASH, [gōō'-lash], *n.* a rich spiced stew of meat and vegetables; (*bridge*) a re-deal in which the hands are not shuffled, but left arranged in order of suits. [Hung. *gulyas-hus* herdsman's meat].

GOURA, [gōō'-ra], *n.* a genus of great pigeons; the crowned Papuan pigeon. [Native].

GOURAMI, GORAMY, [gōō'-ra-mi], *n.* an East Indian edible fish. [Native].

GOURD, [gōoerd], *n.* any of several plants of the order *Cucurbitaceae*; the rounded fruit of such plants; a drinking vessel made from the dried hollowed husk of this. [Fr. *gourde*].

GOURDINESS, [gōoerd'-i-nes], *n.* a bulbous swelling on the leg of a horse.

GOURD-WORM, [gōoerd'-wurm], *n.* the liver-fluke, a worm infesting the liver of animals.

GOURDY, [gōoerd'-i], *adj.* morbidly swollen; like a gourd in appearance.

GOURMAND, GORMAND, [gōoer'-mahn(g)], *n.* a glutton. [Fr. *gourmand*].

GOURMET, [gōoer'-mā], *n.* one with a delicate and fastidious delight in food. [Fr. *gourmet*].

GOUT (1), [gowt], *n.* a morbid painful inflammation of the joints produced by an excess of uric acid. [Fr. *goutte* drop].

GOUT (2), [gōō], *n.* appreciative taste. [Fr. *goût*].

GOUTILY, [gowt'-i-li], *adv.* in gouty fashion.

GOUTINESS, [gowt'-i-nes], *n.* the state of being gouty; gouty diseases.

GOUTWEED, [gowt'-wēd], *n.* the plant, *Ægopodium Podagraria*.

GOUTY, [gowt'-i], *adj.* suffering from, arising from gout.

GOVERN, [guv'-ern], *v.t. and i.* to rule, guide, direct, control, have authority over; to determine; to check, curb, restrain; (*gram.*) to cause a subordinate word to adopt a certain case, etc.; to modify the sense or force of a statement. [Fr. *gouverner*].

GOVERNABLE, [guv'-ern-abl], *adj.* amenable to government.

GOVERNANCE, [guv'-ern-ants], *n.* (*archaic*) control, sway, authority.

GOVERNESS, [guv'-ern-es], *n* a private instructress of young children.

GOVERNING, [guv'-ern-ing], *adj.* controlling, ruling, prevailing; exercising government.

GOVERNMENT, [guv'-ern-ment], *n.* the act or power of governing; power, dominion, rule; the governing machinery or body of a state; the state itself. [Fr. *gouvernement*].

GOVERNMENTAL, [guv'-ern-ment'-al], *adj.* relating to government or to the Government.
GOVERNOR, [guv'-ern-er, guv'-ner], *n.* one who governs; one who exercises the supreme authority of a state in part of its territory; a member of the governing body of an institution; (*mech.*) a device for regulating the speed or motion of a machine; (*slang*) father, chief, boss, sir. [OFr. *governeor*].
GOVERNOR-GENERAL, [guv'-er-ner-jen'-er-al'], *n.* the principal governor of a subject territory; a viceroy.
GOVERNORSHIP, [guv'-ern-er-ship], *n.* the office of a governor.
GOWAN, [gow'-an], *n.* (*Scots*) a daisy. [Uncert.].
GOWDIE, [gowd'-i], *n.* (*Scots*) the grey gurnard, *Trigla gurnardus*. [GOLD].
GOWK, [gowk], *n.* the cuckoo; (*coll.*) a clumsy, gaping adolescent. [~OIcel. *gaukr*].
GOWN (1), [gown], *n.* a loose, body-length garment; a one-piece woman's dress; an academic robe; the official robe of an alderman, barrister, etc. [OFr. *goune*].
GOWN (2), [gown], *v.t.* to clothe in a gown.
GOWNSMAN, [gownz'-man], *n.* one in residence at a university.
GRAB (1), [grab], *n.* a sudden, clutching snatch; a mechanical device for clutching up rubble, etc.
GRAB (2), [grab], *n.* a small, two-masted Malabar trading vessel. [Uncert.].
GRAB (3), (**grabbing, grabbed**), [grab], *v.t.* to snatch, to seize hold of hastily and forcefully, to make a grab at. [~Swed. *grabba*].
GRABBER, [grab'-er], *n.* one who, or that which, grabs.
GRABBLE, [grabl], *v.i.* to scrabble.
GRACE (1), [grās], *n.* pleasing symmetry, poise, dignity; polished elegance, felicity, tasteful disposition; goodwill; clemency; suavity; kindness, respite, unobliged allowance of extra time for the fulfilment of an obligation; God's mercy or permission; the state of enjoying Divine favour; a declaration of thanksgiving made at meal-times; a decree granting a privilege; (*mus.*) an ornamental flourish; (*myth.*) one of the goddesses of the arts. [OFr. *grace*].
GRACE (2), [grās], *v.t.* to give grace, charm, or attractiveness to.
GRACE-CUP, [grās'-kup], *n.* the loving-cup shared after grace.
GRACEFUL, [grās'-fōōl], *adj.* displaying grace, elegant of movement, balanced, easy and pleasing in motion.
GRACEFULLY, [grās'-fōōl-i], *adv.* in graceful fashion.
GRACEFULNESS, [grās'-fōōl-nes], *n.* the quality of being graceful.
GRACELESS, [grās'-les], *adj.* lacking grace; beyond grace.
GRACELESSLY, [grās'-les-li], *adv.* in graceless fashion.
GRACELESSNESS, [grās'-les-nes], *n.* the state of being graceless.
GRACILE, [gras'-il], *adj.* slender, delicate. [L. *gracilis*].
GRACILITY, [gras-il'-i-ti], *n.* slenderness. [L. *gracilitas*].
GRACIOUS, [grā'-shus], *adj.* exhibiting grace; dispensing grace; kindly condescending, nobly forgiving; favourable. [OFr. *gracious*].
GRACIOUSLY, [grā'-shus-li], *adv.* in gracious fashion.
GRACIOUSNESS, [grā'-shus-nes], *n.* the quality of being gracious.
GRACKLE, GRAKLE, [grakl], *n.* a glossy black Indian bird allied to the starlings. [L. *graculus* jackdaw].
GRADATE, [grad-āt'], *v.t.* to arrange in grades; to arrange colours so that one gradually merges into another; *v.i.* to merge in gradation.
GRADATION, [grad-ā'-shun], *n.* a series of stages of advance, a gradual progression or changing by imperceptible degrees; a regular grading in order; (*philol.*) a change of vowel caused by difference of accent or tone; (*mus.*) a diatonic progression of chords. [L. *gradatio*].
GRADATIONAL, [grad-ā'-shun-al], *adj.* pertaining to gradation.
GRADATIONED, [grad-ā'-shund], *adj.* in gradation.
GRADATORY (1), [grad-āt'-er-i], *n.* (*arch.*) a flight of steps leading from the cloisters into the church.
GRADATORY (2), [grad-āt'-er-i], *adj.* gradational.
GRADE (1), [grād], *n.* a stage in a classification; a degree of rank, quality, class, educational proficiency, etc.; (*biol.*) a variation effected by crossbreeding; a gradient; (*philol.*) one of the possible ways in which the vowel of a base may vary. [L. *gradus* step].
GRADE (2), [grād], *v.t.* to put into grades, to classify; to crossbreed.
GRADELY (1), [grād'-li], *adj.* (*dial.*) graceful, attractive, pleasant. [ME. *graythely*].
GRADELY (2), [grād'-li], *adv.* (*dial.*) decently, nicely, in handsome fashion.
GRADIENT (1), [grād'-i-ent], *n.* a slope or incline; the measurement or inclination of this.
GRADIENT (2), [grād'-i-ent], *adj.* walking, moving; (*her.*) shown as walking. [L. *gradiens*].
GRADINE, [grād'-in], *n.* a sculptor's chisel; the low tiers of an amphitheatre; the ledge at the back of an altar. [It. *gradino*].
GRADUAL (1), [graj'-yōō-al], *n.* the antiphon, formerly sung on the steps of the altar; a book containing musical settings of parts of the Mass. [L. *graduale*].
GRADUAL (2), [graj'-yōō-al], *adj.* proceeding step by step, happening slowly and by degrees; sloping gently. [Fr. *graduel*].
GRADUALLY, [graj'-yōō-al-i], *adv.* slowly, by degrees.
GRADUATE (1), [grad'-yōō-at], *n.* one who has graduated at a university. [MedL. *graduatus*].
GRADUATE (2), [grad'-yōō-āt], *v.t. and i.* to arrange in grades, to take a degree at a university, *esp.* the Bachelor's degree; to mark with graduations.

GRADINE

GRADUATED, [grad'-yōō-āt-id], *adj.* marked with graduations.
GRADUATESHIP, [grad'-yōō-at-ship], *n.* the state of being a graduate.
GRADUATION, [grad'-yōō-ā-shun], *v.i.* the act of graduating; classification, a regular progression in degree; a mark indicating measure, *esp.* on a medicine bottle; the state of being so marked. [L. *graduatio*].
GRADUATOR, [grad'-yōō-āt-er], *n.* an instrument for dividing lines into regular sections. [LL. *graduator*].
GRADUS, [grād'-us], *n.* a list of Latin synonyms with the quantities marked, used by schoolboys in writing Latin verse. [L. *gradus* (*ad Parnassum*) steps to Parnassus].
GRAECISM, [grē'-sizm], *n.* the affectation of Greek style or idiom.
GRAECIZE, [grē'-sīz], *v.t. and i.* to make Greek; to affect the classical.
GRAFF†, [grahf], *n.* a ditch. [~MDu. *grave*].
GRAFFITO, [graf-ē'-tō], *n.* a scribbling on a wall, *esp.* when ancient. [It. *graffito*].
GRAFT (1), [grahft], *n.* a shoot from a plant transplanted into another, to form a new growth; a piece of living tissue used to replace injured or defective tissue; (*coll.*) payments made as a bribe; unfair influence or manipulation, political jobbery; (*dial.*) a spadeful. [~OFr. *graffe*].
GRAFT (2), [grahft], *v.t.* to transfer as a horticultural or surgical graft; to join one thing to another so that they merge; *v.i.* (*coll.*) to practise graft.
GRAFTING, [grahft'-ing], *n.* the act of making a horticultural or surgical graft; the part so grafted.
GRAIL (1), [grāl], *n.* the vessel in which Joseph of Arimathea collected Christ's blood; a priceless object of vain quest. [OFr. *graal*].
GRAIL (2), [grāl], *n.* (*eccles.*) a gradual. [OFr. *grael*].
GRAIN (1), [grān], *n.* plant-seed, cereal produce; a small round body; the smallest possible quantity of anything; smallest unit of troy and apothecaries' measure; starch particles in a photographic negative; the fibres of wood; the direction in which the fibres run; **against the g.**, repugnant to nature. [L. *granum*].
GRAIN (2), [grān], *v.t.* to rub down to small particles; to impart a granular surface to; to paint so as to represent the grain of wood.
GRAINAGE, [grān'-ij], *n.* tumours in the legs of horses.
GRAINED, [grānd], *adj.* rough, having a grain.
GRAINER, [grān'-er], *n.* a tanning liquid consisting of pigeons' dung and water; a tanner's knife; a tool for graining.
GRAINING, [grān'-ing], *n.* the process of surfacing in tanning; the arrangement of the grain in wood; the artificial reproduction of this.
GRAIN-MOTH, [grān'-moth], *n.* the insect, *Tinea granella*, whose larvae feed on stored grain.
GRAINS (1), [grānz], *n.(pl.)* the husks of grain.
GRAINS (2), [grānz], *n.* a barbed harpoon. [OIcel. *grein* fork].
GRAINSTAFF, [grān'-stahf], *n.* a quarter-staff.
GRAIN-TIN, [grān'-tin], *n.* tin melted with charcoal.
GRAINY, [grān'-i], *adj.* having a grain; full of grains.

GRAIP, [grāp], *n.* a wide-pronged fork. [OIcel. *greip*].
GRAKLE, see GRACKLE.
GRALLATORES, [gral′-a-taw′-rēz], *n.(pl.)* long-legged wading birds, such as the heron. [L. *grallator* a walker on stilts].
GRALLATORIAL, [gral′-a-taw′-ri-al], *adj.* relating to the grallatores.
GRALLIC, [gral′-ik], *adj.* related to the grallatores.
GRALLOCH (1), [gral′-ok], *n.* the intestines of a stag. [Gael. *grealach*].
GRALLOCH (2), [gral′-ok], *v.i.* to disembowel a stag.
GRAM, see GRAMME.
GRAMA, [grahm′-a], *n.* pasture grass in the west of the United States of America. [Span. *grama*].
GRAMARYE, [gram′-er-i], *n.* necromancy. [ME. *gramery* learning].
GRAMERCY, [gram-ur′-si], *int.* goodness me! [Fr. *grand-merci* great thanks].
GRAMINACEOUS, [gram′-in-ā′-shus], *adj.* relating to grasses. [L. *gramen* grass].
GRAMINEAL, [gra-min′-i-al], *adj.* gramineous.
GRAMINEOUS, [gra-min′-i-us], *adj.* like grass.
GRAMINIFOLIOUS, [gram′-in-i-fōl′-i-us], *adj.* bearing gramineous leaves. [L. *gramen* grass and *folium* leaf].
GRAMINIVOROUS, [gram′-in-iv′-er-us], *adj.* feeding wholly on plants. [L. *gramen* grass and *vorare* to devour].
GRAMMALOGUE, [gram′-a-log], *n.* a word symbolized by a logogram. [Gk. *gramma* letter and *logos* word].
GRAMMAR, [gram′-er], *n.* the study and history of the forms of a language; the rules governing the forms of words in their relations to each other, and their arrangement as members of a sentence; a treatise on this subject; (*fig.*) the rudiments of a subject. [OFr. *gramaire*].
GRAMMARIAN, [gram-āer′-i-an], *n.* one versed in the study of grammar.
GRAMMAR SCHOOL, [gram′-ar-skōōl], *n.* an endowed secondary day school, founded originally to instruct boys in classical grammar.
GRAMMATIC, [gram-at′-ik], *adj.* grammatical. [Gk. *grammatikos*].
GRAMMATICAL, [gram-at′-ik-al], *adj.* conforming to the rules of grammar; relating to grammar.
GRAMMATICALLY, [gram-at′-ik-al-i], *adv.* in grammatical fashion, according to grammar.
GRAMMATICALNESS, [gram-at′-ik-al-nes], *n.* the quality of being grammatical.
GRAMMATICASTER, [gram-at′-i-kast′-er], *n.* a pedant.
GRAMMATICISM, [gram-at′-is-izm], *n.* a small point of grammar.
GRAMMATICIZE, [gram-at′-is-īz], *v.t.* to make grammatical; *v.i.* to discuss points of grammar.
GRAMMATITE, [gram′-a-tīt], *n.* tremolite.
GRAMME, GRAM, [gram], *n.* metric unit of weight, equal to one cubic centimetre of water, or 15·432 grains. [Gk. *gramma* small weight].
GRAMOPHONE, [gram′-a-fōn], *n.* a machine for reproducing sounds by means of a needle, connected to a vibrating plate, and moving across a revolving grooved disk. [Gk. *gramma* letter and *phone* sound].
GRAMPUS, [gram′-pus], *n.* the spouting whale, *Orca gladiator*. [~OFr. *graspeis* from L. *crassus piscis* fat fish].

GRAMPUS

GRANADILLA, [gran′-a-dil′-a], *n.* the fruit of the passion-flower, [Span. from *granada* pomegranate].
GRANARY, [gran′-er-i], *n.* a storehouse for grain, a barn; a place rich in grain. [L. *granarium*].
GRAND (1), [grand], *n.* a grand piano; (*U.S. slang*) a thousand dollars.
GRAND (2), [grand], *adj.* great; splendid, magnificent distinguished; important, haughty; lofty, majestic, large and inspiring; (*slang*) extremely good. very enjoyable. [ME. *grand* from L. *grandis*].
GRANDAM, [gran′-dam], *n.* a grandmother.
GRAND-AUNT, [grand′-ahnt], *n.* the sister of a grandparent.
GRANDCHILD, [grand′-chīld], *n.* a son's or daughter's child.
GRANDDAUGHTER, [grand′-daw-ter], *n.* a son's or daughter's daughter.
GRAND DUCHESS, [grand′-duch′-es], *n.* the female holder of a Grand Duchy; the wife of a Grand Duke.
GRAND DUCHY, [grand′-duch′-i], *n.* a Continental exalted rank of duke; the honour or possessions attached to this.
GRAND DUKE, [grand′-dewk′], *n.* the holder of a Grand Duchy.
GRANDEE, [grand-ē′], *n.* a Spanish noble; a great and illustrious noble. [Span. *grande*].
GRANDE-GARDE, [grawnd′-gahd], *n.* armour protecting the heart and left shoulder. [Fr. *grande-garde*].
GRANDEUR, [grand′-yer], *n.* splendour, glory, magnificence; noble elevation, greatness; breadth of conception. [Fr. *grandeur*].
GRANDFATHER, [grand′-fah′-THer], *n.* a parent's father; **g. clock**, a tall pendulum clock standing on the floor.
GRANDILOQUENCE, [grand-il′-o-kwents], *n.* pomposity of speech, bombast. [L. *grandiloquus*].
GRANDILOQUENT, [grand-il′-o-kwent], *adj.* boastful, pompous of speech, having a lofty and exaggerated style. [L. *grandiloquus*].
GRANDILOQUOUS, [grand-il′-o-kwus], *adj.* grandiloquent.
GRANDIOSE, [grand′-i-ōs], *adj.* pretentiously imposing, bombastic. [Fr. *grandiose*].
GRANDIOSITY, [grand′-i-os′-i-ti], *n.* the state of being grandiose.
GRANDLY, [grand′-li], *adv.* in grand style.
GRANDMOTHER, [grand′-muTH-er], *n.* the mother of a parent.
GRANDNEPHEW, [grand′-nev′-ew], *n.* the grandson of a brother or sister.
GRANDNESS, [grand′-nes], *n.* the quality of being grand.
GRANDNIECE, [grand′-nēs′], *n.* the granddaughter of a brother or sister.
GRANDPARENT, [grand′-pāer′-ent], *n.* a parent's parent.
GRANDSIRE, [grand′-sīer], *n.* grandfather.
GRANDSON, [grand′-sun′], *n.* a son's or daughter's son.
GRANDSTAND, [grand′-stand], *n.* the principal stand on a racecourse or similar arena.
GRAND-UNCLE, [grand′-ungkl′], *n.* a grandparent's brother.
GRANGE, [grānj], *n.* a small country house joined to farm-buildings and granaries; the house of a small country gentleman. [AFr. *graunge*].
GRANGER, [grānj′-er], *n.* a farmer's bailiff.
GRANGERISM, [grānj′-er-izm], *n.* the practice of grangerizing.
GRANGERIZE, [grānj-er-īz], *v.t.* to illustrate a book by inserting pictures, cuttings, etc., after publication. [James *Granger*, author of the "Biographical History of England."].
GRANIFEROUS, [gran-if′-er-us], *adj.* having grain-like seeds, producing grain. [L. *granifer*].
GRANIFORM, [gran′-i-fawm], *adj.* shaped like, formed in, grains.
GRANILITE, [gran′-i-līt], *n.* a granitic rock. [L. *granum* grain and Gk. *lithos* stone].
GRANITE (1), [gran′-it], *n.* a hard, igneous rock, of granular texture. [It. *granito*].
GRANITE (2), [gran′-it], *adj.* made of granite; (*fig.*) very hard, inflexible.
GRANITELL, [gran′-it-el], *n.* a kind of granite containing only quartz and felspar.
GRANITIC, [gran-it′-ik], *adj.* relating to granite.
GRANITICAL, [gran-it′-ik-al], *adj.* granitic.
GRANITIFICATION, [gran′-it-i-fi-kā′-shun], *n.* formation into granite.
GRANITIFORM, [gran-it′-i-fawm], *adj.* like granite.
GRANITOID, [gran′-it-oid], *adj.* like, related to granite.
GRANIVOROUS, [gran-iv′-er-us], *adj.* feeding on grain.
GRANNOM (1), [gran′-om], *n.* (*prov.*) a grandmother.
GRANNOM (2), [gran′-om], *n.* a kind of water-fly; an imitation of it for fly-fishing.
GRANNY, [gran′-i], *n.* childish abbreviation of grandmother.
GRANOLITHIC, [gran′-ō-lith′-ik], *n.* concrete composed of cement and granite.
GRANOPHYRE, [gran′-ō-fier], *n.* (*min.*) a porphyritic rock similar to granite. [Germ. *granophyr*].
GRANT (1), [grahnt], *n.* something granted; a sum of money granted to enable the pursuit of some specified object or study; (*leg.*) an assignment by deed.
GRANT (2), [grahnt], *v.t.* to allow, permit, concede a

favour or request; to confer on, award, allot to, assign; to concede a point; to assume for argument's sake; (*leg.*) to make a legal assignment. [OFr. *graunter*].

GRANTABLE, [grahnt'-abl], *adj.* able to be granted.

GRANTEE, [grahnt-ē'], *n.* (*leg.*) a person to whom a grant is made.

GRANTER, [grahnt'-er], *n.* a person who grants.

GRANTH, [granth], *n.* the sacred book of the Sikhs. [Skr. *grantha* trying].

GRANTOR, [grahnt'-or], *n.* (*leg.*) one who assigns.

GRANULAR, [gran'-yŏŏ-ler], *adj.* consisting of grains; grained, of rough texture.

GRANULARITY, [gran'-yŏŏ-la'-rit-i], *n.* the state or quality of being granular.

GRANULARLY, [gran'-yŏŏ-ler-li], *adv.* in granular style.

GRANULARY, [gran'-yŏŏ-ler-i], *adj.* granular.

GRANULATE, [gran'-yŏŏ-lāt], *v.t.* *and i.* to rub to grains; to roughen; to form granules of metal by pouring through a sieve into water, while molten; to become grained, rough of surface.

GRANULATED, [gran'-yŏŏ-lāt-id], *adj.* consisting of grains; granular.

GRANULATION, [gran'-yŏŏ-lā'-shun], *n.* the act of granulating; (*med.*) granular formation on the surface of a wound.

GRANULE, [gran'-ewl], *n.* a tiny granular particle. [LL. *granulum* small grain].

GRANULIFEROUS, [gran'-yŏŏ-lif'-er-us], *adj.* having grains, containing granules.

GRANULIFORM, [gran'-yŏŏ-li-fawm], *adj.* of granular structure.

GRANULOUS, [gran'-yŏŏl-us], *adj.* grained; consisting of granules.

GRAPE, [grāp], *n.* the fruit of the vine; the vine itself; (*coll.*) wine; grape-shot; (*pl.*) (*med.*) morbid growths on the leg of a horse. [OFr. *grape*].

GRAPE-FRUIT, [grāp'-frōōt], *n.* a large round, lemon-coloured, tropical citrus fruit.

GRAPE-HYACINTH, [grāp'-hī'-a-sinth], *n.* the dark blue hyacinth, *Muscari racemosum.*

GRAPELESS, [grāp'-les], *adj.* without grapes.

GRAPERY, [grāp'-er-i], *n.* a vinery.

GRAPESHOT, [grāp'-shot], *n.* a round of small shot fired simultaneously from a cannon, a primitive kind of shrapnel.

GRAPESTONE, [grāp'-stōn], *n.* the pip of a grape.

GRAPE-VINE, [grāp'-vīn], *n.* the vine on which grapes grow.

GRAPE-WORT, [grāp'-wurt], *n.* a poisonous plant, the baneberry, *Actaea spicata.*

GRAPH (1), [graf], *n.* a linear diagram to express mathematical relationships, and based on two graduated scales. [GRAPHIC].

GRAPH (2), [graf], *n.* a gelatine slab for copying.

GRAPHIC, [graf'-ik], *adj.* relating to, expressed in, writing; relating to, expressed in, drawing, or by visual means; (*fig.*) very vivid, realistic; (*science*) diagrammatic. [Gk. *graphikos*].

GRAPHICAL, [graf'-ik-al], *adj.* graphic.

GRAPHICALLY, [graf'-ik-al-i], *adv.* in graphic fashion.

GRAPHICALNESS, [graf'-ik-al-nes], *n.* the quality of being graphic.

GRAPHICNESS, [graf'-ik-nes], *n.* graphicalness.

GRAPHICS, [graf'-iks], *n.* the art of drawing; the art of calculating stresses, etc., by means of graphs and geometrical plans.

GRAPHIOLOGY, [graf-i-ol'-oj-i], *n.* the art of writing. [Gk. *grapho* I draw and *logos* speech].

GRAPHITE, [graf'-īt], *n.* a form of carbon, used as pencil lead.

GRAPHIUM, [graf'-i-um], *n.* a stylus for writing on wax.

GRAPHO-, *pref.* writing, drawing. [Gk. *grapho* I draw].

GRAPHOLITE, [graf'-ō-līt], *n.* a kind of slate, from which writing-slates are made. [GRAPHO and Gk. *lithos* stone].

GRAPHOLOGY, [graf-ol'-oj-i], *n.* the art of divining character by handwriting; the art of calculating by graphs. [GRAPHO and Gk. *logos* speech].

GRAPHOMETER, [graf-om'-it-er], *n.* a mathematical instrument for measuring the degrees of an angle. [GRAPHO and METER].

GRAPHOTYPE, [graf'-ō-tīp], *n.* a substitute for wood engraving using compressed chalk and a special ink which remains in relief when the chalk intervals are brushed away. [GRAPHO and TYPE].

GRAPNEL, [grap'-nel], *n.* an anchor with radiating flukes, used for grappling an enemy, or in emergency mooring. [ME. *grapenel* from OFr. *grapin*].

GRAPNEL

GRAPPLE (1), [grapl], *n.* a grappling-iron; a seizure with a grapple; a firm grip, hug; a fight at close quarters, a wrestle. [OFr. *grappil* grapnel].

GRAPPLE (2), [grapl], *v.t.* *and i.* to seize with a grappling-iron; to seize in a strong, clutching hold; (*naut.*) to come close to for boarding; to wrestle closely, to engage hand-to-hand; (*fig.*) to get to grips with.

GRAPPLING-IRON, [grap'-ling-iern'], *n.* a grapnel.

GRAPTOLITE, [grap'-to-līt], *n.* a fossil marine zoophyte or fossil hydrozoon, with its cells grouped round a stem; a stone bearing marks resembling writing. [MdL. *graptolithus*].

GRAPTOLITIC, [grap-tō-lit'-ik], *adj.* relating to graptolites.

GRAPY, [grāp'-i], *adj.* like grapes.

GRASP (1), [grahsp], *n.* a firm grip, clasp, hold; a firm handshake; control, power; mental capacity, comprehension, intellectual understanding; ability of getting, reach.

GRASP (2), [grahsp], *v.t.* *and i.* to seize in one's grasp, to clasp firmly, to clutch; to comprehend, understand; to grab. [ME. *graspen*].

GRASPABLE, [grahsp'-abl], *adj.* that may be grasped.

GRASPER, [grahsp'-er], *n.* he who, that which, grasps.

GRASPING, [grahsp'-ing], *adj.* meanly avaricious, insatiably eager for gain.

GRASPINGLY, [grahsp'-ing-li], *adv.* in grasping fashion.

GRASPINGNESS, [grahsp'-ing-nes], *n.* the quality of being grasping.

GRASS (1), [grahs], *n.* low-growing, green herbage covering the ground; (*bot.*) any plant of the monocotyledonous group of the *Gramineæ*; ground covered with such herbage. [OE. *græs*].

GRASS (2), [grahs], *v.t.* to sow with grass; to put to pasture; to bring to the ground; to shoot down an animal; to land a fish.

GRASS-BLADE, [grahs'-blād], *n.* a leaf of grass.

GRASS-CLOTH, [grahs'-kloth], *n.* an Eastern fabric made from fibres of ramie.

GRASSCUTTER, [grahs'-kut-er], *n.* one employed to cut grass; an Indian servant who collects fodder; a lawn-mower.

GRASS-GREEN (1), [grahs'-grēn'], *n.* the green of grass.

GRASS-GREEN (2), [grahs'-grēn'], *adj.* of a grassy greenness.

GRASS-GROWN, [grahs'-grōn], *adj.* overgrown with grass.

GRASSHOPPER, [grahs'-hop-er], *n.* a small, short-antennaed insect related to the locust, commonly found in long grass. [ME. *græshoppere*].

GRASSHOPPER

GRASSINESS, [grahs'-i-nes], *n.* the condition of being grassy.

GRASSING, [grahs'-ing], *n.* the act of bleaching by spreading out in the open air.

GRASS-LAND, [grahs'-land], *n.* a district largely covered with grass; land permanently under grass.

GRASSLESS, [grahs'-les], *adj.* without grass.

GRASS-OIL, [grahs'-oil], *n.* volatile oil extracted from certain scented Eastern grasses.

GRASS-PLOT, [grahs'-plot], *n.* a plot grown with grass.

GRASS-SNAKE, [grahs'-snāk], *n.* the harmless British snake, *Tropidontus natrix.*

GRASS-TREE, [grahs'-trē], *n.* the Australian plant, *Xanthorrhœa*, with grass-like foliage.

GRASS-WIDOW, [grahs'-wid'-ō], *n.* a woman whose husband is absent from her.

GRASS-WIDOWER, [grahs'-wid'-ō-er], *n.* a husband whose wife is absent from him.

GRASS-WRACK, [grahs'-rak], *n.* the eel-grass, *Zostera marina*, growing in shallow sea-water.

GRASSY, [grahs′-i], *adj.* covered with, abounding in, grass; relating to grass.

GRATE (**1**), [grāt], *n.* a metal frame fronted with iron bars, and used for holding fuel in the fireplace; a grating. [ME. *grate* from LL. *grata*].

GRATE (**2**), [grāt], *v.t. and i.* to scrape on or with a rough surface; to scrape and rub into small fragments, to grind to powder; to produce an excruciating noise by the harsh friction of rough objects; to produce irritation or pain by harsh sound; (*fig.*) to produce an unpleasant impression upon. [OFr. *grater*].

GRATEFUL, [grāt′-fōōl], *adj.* feeling or expressing gratitude; welcome, gratifying, pleasing. [L. *gratus* pleasing].

GRATEFULLY, [grāt′-fōōl-i], *adv.* in grateful fashion.

GRATEFULNESS, [grāt′-fōōl-nes], *n.* the quality of being grateful.

GRATER, [grāt′-er], *n.* a rough-surfaced instrument for grating substances.

GRATICULATION, [grat-ik′-yōō-lā′-shun], *n.* the division of a design into squares in order to reproduce it in enlargement or diminishment. [Fr. *graticulation*].

GRATICULE, [grat′-ik-yewl], *n.* a piece of glass covered with very fine parallel rulings or scratches, *esp.* as used in the eyepiece of a microscope, etc., as a measuring scale.

GRATIFICATION, [grat′-i-fi-kā′-shun], *n.* a feeling of pleasurable satisfaction; the act of gratifying; that which gratifies; the state of being gratified. [L. *gratificatio*].

GRATIFIER, [grat′-i-fī-er], *n.* one who, or that which, gratifies.

GRATIFY, [grat′-i-fī], *v.t.* to please, satisfy, make content; to indulge some desire. [L. *gratificari* to do favour to].

GRATIFYINGLY, [grat′-i-fī-ing-li], *adv.* in gratifying fashion.

GRATIN, [grat′-a(ng)], *n.* a grated surface of bread-crumbs, cheese, etc., topping certain dishes. [Fr. *grater* to scrape].

GRATING (**1**), [grāt′-ing], *n.* a grille, a frame of parallel or intersecting bars used as the covering of a window, etc.; (*opt.*) a close framework of parallel wires to diffract spectra. [GRATE (1)].

GRATING (**2**), [grāt′-ing], *adj.* producing a harsh, unpleasant sound, irritating, jarring. [GRATE (2)].

GRATINGLY, [grāt′-ing-li], *adv.* in grating fashion.

GRATIS, [grāt′-is], *adv.* free of charge. [L. *gratiis* by favour].

GRATITUDE, [grat′-i-tewd], *n.* thankfulness for benefits received, full appreciation of the kindness of a benefactor. [LL. *gratitudo*].

GRATUITOUS, [grat-ew′-it-us], *adj.* free, unrecompensed, performed freely, obtained or given without payment; uncalled for, unsought, unnecessary; (*leg.*) benefiting one of the parties only. [L. *gratuitus*].

GRATUITOUSLY, [grat-ew′-it-us-li], *adv.* in gratuitous fashion.

GRATUITOUSNESS, [grat-ew′-it-us-nes], *n.* the state of being gratuitous.

GRATUITY, [grat-ew′-it-i], *n.* something given without obligation, a tip; a gift made to soldiers at the end of their service. [LL. *gratuitas*].

GRATULATE, [grat′-yōō-lāt], *v.t. and i.* to congratulate; (*rare*) to manifest pleasure or joy. [L. *gratulari*].

GRATULATION, [grat′-yōō-lā′-shun], *n.* congratulation. [L. *gratulatio*].

GRATULATORY, [grat′-yōō-lat-er-i], *adj.* congratulatory.

GRAVAMEN, [grav-ā′-men], *n.* the fundamental, substantial part (of a charge, accusation, matter, problem); (*eccles.*) a grievance laid before the Upper House of Convocation by the Lower. [LL. *gravamen* trouble].

GRAVE (**1**), [grāv], *n.* a hole dug in the ground for the burial of a corpse; a mound, etc., marking this; a tomb, monumental place of sepulture; (*fig.*) death, mortality; that which causes death. [OE. *græf*].

GRAVE (**2**), [grāv], *adj.* heavy, momentous, of weighty importance, ominous; serious; solemn, heavily anxious; austere, occupied with solemn and weighty matters; (*mus.*) low-pitched, heavy. [L. *gravis*].

GRAVE (**3**), [grahv], *adj.* (*gram.*) low-pitched, indicating a more open sound; of, or pertaining to, the symbol (`) used to denote this. [Fr. *grave*].

GRAVE (**4**), [grāv], *v.t. and i.* to engrave, to carve; (*fig.*) to impress deeply on. [OE. *grafan* dig].

GRAVE (**5**), [grāv], *v.t.* to clean a ship's hull, and apply fresh pitch and tar to it. [OFr. *grave* beach].

GRAVE-CLOTHES, [grāv′-klōTHz], *n.* cerements, winding sheets.

GRAVE-DIGGER, [grāv′-dig′-er], *n.* one who digs graves.

GRAVEL (**1**), [grav′-el], *n.* a mixture of sand and small stones used to make paths, surface roads, etc.; (*med.*) a collection of small concretions in the bladder. [OFr. *gravele*].

GRAVEL (**2**), (**gravelling, gravelled**), [grav′-el], *v.t.* to cover a road with gravel; (*fig.*) to disconcert, catch out, nonplus.

GRAVELESS, [grāv′-les], *adj.* left unburied.

GRAVELLING, [grav′-el-ing], *n.* a sprinkling with gravel; a covering of gravel.

GRAVELLY, [grav′-el-i], *adj.* abounding in gravel.

GRAVEL-PIT, [grav′-el-pit], *n.* a place from which gravel is dug.

GRAVELY, [grāv′-li], *adv.* in grave fashion.

GRAVEN†, [grāv′-en], *adj.* carved, sculptured.

GRAVENESS, [grāv′-nes], *n.* the quality of being grave.

GRAVEOLENT, [grav-ē′-ō-lent], *adj.* smelling strongly and offensively. [L. *graveolens*].

GRAVER, [grāv′-er], *n.* an engraver's chisel; one who engraves.

GRAVES (**1**), [grahv], *n.* a common white Bordeaux wine. [From the gravelly soil in which the vines are grown].

GRAVES (**2**), see GREAVES (2).

GRAVESTONE, [grāv′-stōn], *n.* a tombstone, a monument over a grave.

GRAVEYARD, [grāv′-yahd′], *n.* a churchyard, a cemetery.

GRAVID, [grav′-id], *adj.* pregnant, heavy with child. [L. *gravidus* loaded].

GRAVIED, [grāv′-id], *adj.* covered with gravy.

GRAVIGRADE, [grav′-i-grād], *adj.* walking ponderously. [L. *gravis* heavy and *gradus* step].

GRAVIMETER, [grav-im′-it-er], *n.* an instrument for determining specific gravities. [L. *gravis* heavy and METER].

GRAVIMETRIC, [grav′-i-met′-rik], *adj.* measured by weight.

GRAVING (**1**), [grāv-ing], *n.* engraving, carving. [GRAVE (4)].

GRAVING (**2**), [grāv′-ing], *n.* the act of cleaning a ship's hull in dry dock. [GRAVE (5)].

GRAVITATE, [grav′-i-tāt], *v.t.* (*phys.*) to move according to gravity; to sink, fall; (*fig.*) to move naturally, tend by nature in a certain direction. [*Next*].

GRAVITATION, [grav′-i-tā′-shun], *n.* the force exercised by gravity; movement impelled by gravity; the act of gravitating.

GRAVITATIONAL, [grav′-it-ā′-shun-al], *adj.* of, or pertaining to, gravity.

GRAVIMETER

GRAVITY, [grav′-i-ti], *n.* seriousness; a grave mien, solemnity; seriousness of mind and character; danger, serious consequences; (*phys.*) the natural attraction of bodies; the gravimetric proportion of substances to an equal volume of water. [L. *gravitas*].

GRAVURE, [grav-yōōer′], *n.* short form of PHOTOGRAVURE.

GRAVY, [grāv′-i], *n.* the juice from roasting meat; a sauce consisting largely of such juice. [ME. *grave* dressing for meats].

GRAY, see GREY.

GRAYLING, [grā′-ling], *n.* the freshwater fish, *Thymallus vulgaris*, of the trout family, and having long dorsal fins; a butterfly the undersides of the wings of which are grey. [GREY].

GRAYWACKE, [grā′-wak-er], *n.* a kind of dark sandstone. [~Germ. *grauwacke*].

GRAZE (**1**), [grāz], *n.* a slight scratch or contusion caused by a light passing touch; a very slight contact in passing. [GRAZE (3)].

GRAZE (**2**), [grāz], *n.* pasture. [GRAZE (4)].

GRAZE (**3**), [grāz], *v.t.* to touch lightly during passage, to scrape lightly across; to cause a graze in. [Uncert.].

GRAZE (**4**), [grāz], *v.t. and i.* to feed on growing herbage; to put out to grass; to allot land for use as pasture; to pasture. [OE. *grasian*].

GRAZER, [grāz′-er], *n.* a creature that grazes.

GRAZIER, [grāz′-i-er], *n.* one who grazes cattle.

GRAZING, [grāz′-ing], *n.* pasturage.

GRAZIOSO, [grat′-si-ō′-sō], *adv.* (*mus.*) elegantly, with refinement. [It. *grazioso*].

GREASE (**1**), [grēs], *n.* animal fat obtained by melting; the fat produced by cooking meat; oily matter used in the lubrication of machines; wool that has not been washed; (*med.*) inflammation of a horse's fetlock; **g.-paint**, greasy, heavy make-up used by actors. [OFr. *graisse*].

GREASE (2), [grēz], *v.t.* to coat with grease, lubricate with grease, put grease on; (*slang*) to tip, bribe.

GREASER, [grēs'-er], *n.* one who lubricates machinery; (*U.S. slang*) a South or Central American.

GREASILY, [grēz'-i-li], *adv.* in greasy fashion.

GREASINESS, [grēz'-i-nes], *n.* the condition of being greasy.

GREASY, [grēz'-i, grēs'-i], *adj.* containing grease, smeared with grease; slimy, slippery; (*fig.*) difficult to keep hold of; (*coll.*) smarmy, obsequious; (*naut.*) (of weather) dirty.

GREAT, [grāt], *adj.* large, big in amount, size, extent, number; of excelling qualities, having talents and mental or moral stature much above the average; exceedingly distinguished; (of nations) powerful, holding wide and strong rule; of high social rank; sublime, important; (*slang*) fine, splendid. [OE. *great*].

GREAT CIRCLE, [grāt'-surkl], *n.* a circle whose plane passes through the centre of the sphere on which it is described; (*naut.*) a circle whose arc represents the shortest distance between two places on the globe.

GREATCOAT, [grāt'-kōt], *n.* a heavy military overcoat.

GREAT-GRANDFATHER, [grāt'-gran'-fah-THER], *n.* the father of one's grandfather or grandmother.

GREAT-GRANDMOTHER, [grāt'-gran'-muTH-er], *n.* the mother of one's grandfather or grandmother.

GREAT-GRANDSON, [grat'-gran'-son], *n.* the son of one's grandson or granddaughter.

GREATHEARTED, [grāt'-haht'-id], *adj.* very generous, noble, magnanimous.

GREATLY, [grāt'-li], *adv.* to a great extent, in great degree, style.

GREATNESS, [grāt'-nes], *n.* the quality of being great.

GREATS, [grāts], *n.* the School of Philosophy and the Classics at Oxford; **modern G.**, a variation of this in which Economics, etc., can be taken in place of Classics.

GREAVES (1), [grēvz], *n.(pl.)* metal armour for the leg between knee and ankle. [OFr. *greve*].

GREAVES (2), **GRAVES (2)**, [grēvz], *n.(pl.)* the sediment of tallow used as fish-bait. [~LGerm. *greven*].

GREBE, [grēb], *n.* a tailless diving bird of the genus *Podiceps*. [Fr. *grèbe*].

GREBE

GRECIAN (1), [grēsh'-an], *n.* †a Greek; a member of the highest form at Christ's Hospital; a scholar of ancient Greek.

GRECIAN (2), [grē'-shan], *adj.* Hellenic, relating to ancient Greece.

GRECIANIZE, [grē'-shan-īz], *v.t.* to Grecize.

GRECISM, [grēs'-izm], *n.* a Greek idiom or turn of phrase.

GRECIZE, [grēs'-īz], *v.t. and i.* to put into Greek style or idiom; to affect the Greek; to make Greek.

GREE, [grē], *n.* (*Scots*) a step; pre-eminence. [OFr. *gré*].

GREED, [grēd], *n.* avarice, covetousness, excessive desire to obtain; gluttony. [GREEDY].

GREEDILY, [grēd'-i-li], *adv.* with greed.

GREEDINESS, [grēd'-i-nes], *n.* the state of being greedy.

GREEDY, [grēd'-i], *adj.* covetous, avaricious, over-eager to obtain and possess; inclined to gluttony. [OE. *grædig*].

GREEDY-GUTS, [grēd'-i-guts'], *n.* a glutton.

GREEK (1), [grēk], *n.* a native of Greece; the language of Greece.

GREEK (2), [grēk], *adj.* relating to Greece, its inhabitants, culture, customs, etc.; relating to the Orthodox Church. [OE. *Grec* from Gk. *Graikos*].

GREEN (1), [grēn], *n.* the colour of grass and foliage; (*pl.*) vegetable leaves cooked for food, *esp.* young cabbage; a common plot of grassy ground in the middle of a town; a plot of smooth grass in certain sports; the smooth turf round the hole in golf; the green badge of Irish Republicanism; (*fig.*) the vigorous prime of youth.

GREEN (2), [grēn], *adj.* of a colour between yellow and blue; made up of fresh vegetables; (of a salad) consisting of leaf vegetables only; of a sickly complexion, jaundiced; (*fig.*) violently jealous; unripened, unmatured, unseasoned; (*fig.*) callow, inexperienced, credulous; verdant, richly flourishing; **g. belt**, a stretch of land around a town in which building is forbidden by the local authority. [OE. *grene*].

GREEN (3), [grēn], *v.t.* to make green; (*fig.*) to deceive, dupe; *v.i.* to become green.

GREEN-BACK, [grēn'-bak], *n.* (*coll.*) an American banknote; a green variety of frog.

GREENERY, [grēn'-er-i], *n.* a mass of leafy plants; a place abounding in green plants.

GREEN-EYED, [grēn'-īd], *adj.* jealous.

GREENFINCH, [grēn'-finch], *n.* the green-plumed finch, the green linnet.

GREENFLY, [grēn'-flī], *n.* the green aphis.

GREENGAGE, [grēn'-gāj], *n.* a sweet green plum. [Sir William *Gage*, who introduced it into England in the 18th century].

GREENGROCER, [grēn'-grōs'-er], *n.* one who trades in vegetables or fruit.

GREENHAND, [grēn'-hand], *n.* a greenhorn.

GREENHEART, [grēn'-haht], *n.* a West Indian hard-wood tree.

GREENHORN, [grēn'-hawn], *n.* (*coll.*) a raw novice.

GREENHOUSE, [grēn'-hows], *n.* a glass building, sometimes heated, used to foster delicate plants or produce fruit out of season.

GREENING, [grēn'-ing], *n.* the green-gilled oyster; a growing green.

GREENISH, [grēn'-ish], *adj.* tending to greenness.

GREENISHNESS, [grēn'-ish-nes], *n.* the quality of being greenish.

GREENLAND, [grēn'-land], *n.* the name of an Arctic territory, N.E. of North America, used to denote animals and plants from this region; **G. falcon**, the white falcon, *Falco caudicans*; **G. whale**, the Arctic right whale. [Swed. *Grönland* green land].

GREENLANDER, [grēn'-land-er], *n.* an inhabitant of Greenland.

GREENLET, [grēn'-let], *n.* a small, green-plumaged American song-bird.

GREENNESS, [grēn'-nes], *n.* the condition of being green.

GREENOCKITE, [grēn'-ok-īt], *n.* sulphide of cadmium.

GREENROOM, [grēn'-rōōm], *n.* the waiting and social room behind the stage of a theatre for the use of the players.

GREENSAND, [grēn'-sand], *n.* glauconite; a formation between chalk and wealden clay.

GREENSHANK, [grēn'-shangk], *n.* the green-legged sandpiper.

GREEN-STALL, [grēn'-stawl], *n.* a barrow from which vegetables are sold.

GREENSTICK, [grēn'-stik], *n.* a fracture occurring in young children in which the bones are bent.

GREENSTONE, [grēn'-stōn], *n.* jade; nephrite.

GREENSTUFF, [grēn'-stuf], *n.* green vegetables or grass used for food or fodder.

GREENSWARD, [grēn'-swawd], *n.* grassland.

GREENWEED, [grēn'-wēd], *n.* dyer's weed, *Genista tinctoria*.

GREENWOOD, [grēn'-wōōd], *n.* green, leafy woodland.

GREENY, [grēn'-i], *adj.* greenish.

GREET (1), [grēt], *v.i.* to weep, wail, mourn. [OE. *greotan*].

GREET (2), [grēt], *v.t.* to address when meeting; to receive or meet by making some gesture or form of salutation, to welcome; to express or feel an emotion at. [OE. *gretan* to approach].

GREETING, [grēt'-ing], *n.* a salutation on meeting, a welcome.

GREFFIER, [gref'-i-er], *n.* a notary in the Channel Islands. [Fr. *greffier*].

GREGAL, [grē'-gal], *adj.* like a flock.

GREGARIAN, [grig-āer'-i-an], *adj.* in, relating to, a herd; gregarious.

GREGARINES, [greg'-er-īnz], *n.(pl.)* a group of parasitic protozoa.

GREGARIOUS, [grig-āer'-i-us], *adj.* relating to a flock; living in herds, flocks, or communities; (*bot.*) growing in clusters; (*fig.*) fond of company, sociable. [L. *gregarius* belonging to a flock].

GREGARIOUSLY, [grig-āer'-i-us-li], *adv.* in a flock.

GREGARIOUSNESS, [grig-āer'-i-us-nes], *n.* the quality of being gregarious.

GREGORIAN, [greg-aw'-ri-an], *adj.* (of a chant, tones, etc.) relating to, introduced by, Pope Gregory I; (of a calendar or epoch) devised or introduced by Pope Gregory XIII.

GREGORY-POWDER, [greg'-er-i-pow'-der], *n.* an aperient compounded of rhubarb and magnesia. [Dr. J. *Gregory*, its inventor].

GREMIAL, [grēm'-i-al], *n.* (*eccles.*) the apron worn by bishops at Mass or Ordination. [L. *gremium* bosom].

GREMLIN, [grem'-lin], *n.* (R.A.F. *slang*) an imp or goblin alleged to be responsible for mysterious faults in an aeroplane. [G(OBLIN) and (*F*)*remlin*, the name of a brewer in whose bottles the imps were supposed to hide].

GRENADE, [gren-ād'], *n.* a hand bomb thrown at short range; a small spherical fire-extinguisher. [Span. *granada* pomegranate].

GRENADIER, [gren'-ad-ēer'], *n.* a soldier throwing grenades; (*hist.*) a member of the right flank company of a battalion; a member of the Grenadier Guards; (*zool.*) the South African weaver bird; a member of the *Macrouridæ*, a class of sea-fish. [Fr. *grenadier*].

GRENADINE (1), [gren'-ad-ēn], *n.* a larded and glazed fricassee of veal; a scented carnation. [Fr. *grenadin*].

GRENADINE (2), [gren'-ad-ēn], *n.* a heavy syrup made from pomegranates; a light dress material; a red dye. [Fr. *grenadine*].

GRENATITE, [gren'-a-tīt], *n.* (*min.*) staurolite. [Fr. *grenat* garnet].

GRESSORIAL, [gres-aw'-ri-al], *adj.* (*zool.*) (of birds) having three toes in front and one at the back. [L. *gressor* walker].

GREY (1), GRAY, [grā], *n.* the colour of ashes; a grey horse; (*pl*). the 2nd Dragoons.

GREY (2), GRAY, [grā], *adj.* of a colour between black and white, ashy; overcast, cloudy, sunless; (*fig.*) gloomy; sombre, dismal, dreary; hopeless; dull, lustreless, colourless. [OE. *græg*].

GREY (3), GRAY, [grā], *v.t.* to make or become grey.

GREYBEARD, [grā'-bēerd], *n.* an old man; an earthenware liquor jug; a straggling lichen.

GREYFRIAR, [grā'-frier], *n.* a member of the Order of Franciscans; **Greyfriars**, a convent of this order.

GREY-GOOSE, [grā'-gōōs], *n.* the greylag goose.

GREYHEN, [grā'-hen'], *n.* the female black-grouse.

GREYHOUND, [grā'-hownd], *n.* a slender, very swift breed of dog, now bred and specialized for racing; **ocean g.**, (*fig.*) a speedy liner. [OE. *grighund*].

GREYISH, [grā'-ish], *adj.* somewhat grey.

GREYLAG, [grā'-lag], *n.* the migrating goose, *Anser cinereus*.

GREYNESS, [grā'-nes], *n.* the quality of being grey.

GREYSTONE, [grā'-stōn], *n.* a felspar and augite rock.

GREYWETHER, [grā'-weTH-er], *n.* sarsen stone, found scattered on chalk downs.

GRICE†, [gris], *n.* a young bear. [OIcel. *griss*].

GRID, [grid], *n.* a grating; a gridiron; a network of wires between filament and plate of a wireless valve; a network to distribute electricity. [GRID(IRON)].

GRIDDLE, [gridl], *n.* an iron baking-plate; a mining sieve. [AFr. *gridil*].

GRIDDLE-CAKE, [gridl'-kāk], *n.* an oatmeal cake cooked on a griddle.

GRIDE, [grīd], *v.i.* to grate against harshly. [Uncert.].

GRIDELIN, [grid'-el-in], *n.* a greyish violet colour. [Fr. *gris de lin* grey of flax].

GRIDIRON, [grid'-ī-ern], *n.* an iron frame for grilling over a fire; an instrument of torture resembling this, on which victims were roasted; (*railways*) a set of parallel rails for shunting; (*elect.*) a network of power cables; a framework over a stage from which are worked drop scenes, etc. [ME. *gredire*].

GRID-LEAK, [grid'-lēk], *n.* (*elect.*) a high resistance joined from grid to filament to allow the escape of electrons.

GRIEF, [grēf], *n.* misfortune; sorrow, woe; a cause of sorrow; mental distress. [OFr. *grief*].

GRIEVABLE, [grēv'-abl], *adj.* lamentable.

GRIEVANCE, [grēv'-ants], *n.* a ground of complaint; some injury giving ground for complaint. [OFr. *grevance*].

GRIEVANCE-MONGER, [grēv'-ants-mung'-ger], *n.* one continually harping on a grievance.

GRIEVE, [grēv], *v.t. and i.* to distress with grief; to feel sorrow, lament, bewail. [OFr. *grever*].

GRIEVINGLY, [grēv'-ing-li], *adv.* sorrowfully.

GRIEVOUS, [grēv'-us], *adj.* woeful, causing grief or great distress, lamentable. [OFr. *grevous*].

GRIEVOUSLY, [grēv'-us-li], *adv.* in grievous fashion.

GRIEVOUSNESS, [grēv'-us-nes], *n.* the quality of being grievous.

GRIFFIN, [grif'-in], *n.* a heraldic monster, a composite of lion and eagle; (*coll.*) a fierce and ugly woman. [OFr. *grifoun*].

GRIFFIN-LIKE, [grif'-in-līk], *adj.* like a griffin.

GRIFFON, [grif'-on], *n.* a small, rough-haired hunting dog. [GRIFFIN].

GRIG, [grig], *n.* a sand-eel; a grasshopper; a small variety of poultry. [Uncert.].

GRILL (1), [gril], *n.* a framework of metal bars; a gridiron; (*philately*) a kind of postal cancellation; a grill-room. [OFr. *grail*].

GRILL (2), [gril], *v.t. and i.* to cook or be cooked on a grill; to subject or be subjected to extreme heat; (*U.S.*) to put through a thorough and violent cross-examination; (*philately*) to stamp with a grill.

GRIFFON

GRILLADE, [grē-yahd'], *n.* food broiled on a gridiron. [Fr. *grillade*].

GRILLAGE, [gril'-ij], *n.* a frame of timbers supporting a building in crumbling soil.

GRILLE, [gril], *n.* a crosswork of bars over an aperture, a grating. [Fr. *grille*].

GRILLED, [grild], *adj.* cooked on a grill; made very hot.

GRILLER, [gril'-er], *n.* an apparatus for grilling.

GRILL-ROOM, [gril'-rōōm], *n.* a room in a restaurant where food is publicly cooked on a grill.

GRILSE, [grils], *n.* a salmon in its second year. [AFr. *grillez*].

GRIM, [grim], *adj.* sternly fierce, ominous, cruel; horrifying, terrible; (*slang*) very unpleasant. [OE. *grim*].

GRIMACE (1), [grim-ās'], *n.* a horrifying or humorous facial contortion. [Fr. *grimace* wrinkle].

GRIMACE (2), [grim-ās'], *v.i.* to make a grimace.

GRIMACED, [grim-āst'], *adj.* distorted.

GRIMALKIN, [grim-awl'-kin], *n.* a female cat. [*Graymalkin*, cf. "Macbeth" I. i. 8, by Shakespeare].

GRIME (1), [grīm], *n.* thick, coated, ingrained dirt; ingrained soot; general filth and dirtiness. [ME. *grim*].

GRIME (2), [grīm], *v.t.* to cover or coat with grime.

GRIMILY, [grīm'-i-li], *adv.* in grimy fashion.

GRIMINESS, [grīm'-i-nes], *n.* the condition of being grimy.

GRIMLY, [grim'-li], *adv.* in grim fashion.

GRIMNESS, [grim'-nes], *n.* the quality of being grim.

GRIMY, [grīm'-i], *adj.* covered with grime, filthy, sooty.

GRIN (1), [grin], *n.* a distorted smile; a broad smile showing the teeth.

GRIN (2), **(grinning, grinned)**, [grin], *v.i.* to smile showing the teeth, to smile crudely or with cruel delight. [OE. *grennian* to bare the teeth].

GRIND (1), [grīnd], *n.* the act of grinding; tedious, laborious work, wearisome, difficult study; a tedious and gruelling race.

GRIND (2), **(ground)**, [grīnd], *v.t. and i.* to reduce to powder or fragments by friction and pressure; to shape, sharpen, roughen, or make smooth by friction; to grit the teeth together; (*fig.*) to oppress; (*coll.*) to turn the handle of a barrel organ; to toil tediously at a difficult task. [OE. *grindan*].

GRINDER, [grīnd'-er], *n.* one who, that which, grinds; a molar.

GRINDERY, [grīnd'-er-i], *n.* equipment for a leather-worker; a shop where this is sold; a place for grinding tools.

GRINDSTONE, [grīnd'-stōn], *n.* a revolving disk of hard sandstone used for grinding; (*fig.*) tedious and laborious work.

GRINGO, [gring'-gō], *n.* an insulting Mexican slang term for an American or Englishman. [Uncert.].

GRINNINGLY, [grin'-ing-li], *adv.* with grins.

GRIP (1), [grip], *n.* the act of gripping; a hold, clutch, grasp, *esp.* a wrestling hold; a thing meant to be gripped; the handle of something; a hand-bag; (*fig.*) grasp, power of intellectual mastery and understanding; psychological control of oneself and situations; **to get to grips**, to tackle. [OE. *gripe*].

GRIP (2), **(gripping, gripped)**, [grip], *v.t. and i.* to clutch firmly, hold tightly; (*fig.*) to hold strongly the attention and interest; to seize; to grasp. [OE. *grippan*].

GRIPE (1), [grīp], *n.* colic; (*pl.*) (*naut.*) hooks and ropes for suspending a boat from the davits; the timber at the fore-end of the keel; (*mech.*) a brake on a wheel; †the act of griping or clutching.

GRIPE (2), [grīp], *v.t.* to distress with colic pains in the bowels; †to seize, clutch, grasp. [~GRIP.]

GRIPEFUL, [grip'-fŏŏl], *adj.* tending to, causing, gripe.

GRIPER, [grip'-er], *n.* an extortioner.

GRIPEWATER, [grip'-wawt-er], *n.* a fluid medicine to relieve gripes.

GRIPING, [grip'-ing], *adj.* causing colic pains.

GRIPINGLY, [grip'-ing-li], *adv.* in griping fashion.

GRIPPE, [grip], *n.* influenza. [Fr. *grippe*].

GRIPPER, [grip'-er], *n.* that which grips.

GRIQUA, [grē'-kah], *n.* a Dutch-Negro half-caste; a native of Griqualand. [Native].

GRISAILLE, [griz-a'-i], *n.* a painting in grey monochrome, to simulate sculpture in relief. [Fr. *grisaille*].

GRISEOUS, [griz'-i-us], *adj.* grizzled. [Fr. *gris* grey].

GRISETTE, [griz-et'], *n.* a French working-girl, *esp.* a dressmaker. [Fr. *grisette* a grey dress].

GRISKIN, [gris'-kin], *n.* a loin of pork; a little pig. [~OIcel. *griss*].

GRISLINESS, [griz'-li-nes], *n.* the quality of being grisly.

GRISLY, [griz'-li], *adj.* fear-inspiring, horrifying. [OE. *grislic*].

GRISON, [grē'-son], *n.* a South American animal related to the weasel. [Fr. *grison*].

GRISON

GRIST (1), [grist], *n.* ground corn; corn about to be ground. [OE. *grist* grinding].

GRIST (2), [grist], *n.* the thickness of rope. [Unkn.].

GRISTLE, [grisl], *n.* animal cartilage, *esp.* in food. [OE. *gristel*].

GRISTLINESS, [gris'-li-nes], *n.* the condition of being gristly.

GRISTLY, [gris'-li], *adj.* containing gristle.

GRIST-MILL, [grist'-mil], *n.* a mill for grinding grain.

GRIT (1), [grit], *n.* stone-dust, gravel, small fragments of stone; (*geol.*) hard sandstone; (*fig.*) something small that impedes action; (*coll.*) pluck, courageous endurance. [OE. *greot*].

GRIT (2), (**gritting, gritted**), [grit], *v.t. and i.* to grind together, *esp.* the teeth; to produce a grating noise by friction; to grate, to grind through impediments caused by grit, etc.

GRITSTONE, [grit'-stōn], *n.* a gritty sandstone.

GRITTINESS, [grit'-i-nes], *n.* the condition of being gritty.

GRITTY, [grit'-i], *adj.* containing, full of, grit.

GRIZZLE (1), [grizl], *n.* a grey horse; (*rare*) a grey object. [OFr. *grisel* a man with grey hair].

GRIZZLE (2), [grizl], *v.i.* to cry, whimper in a sullen, fretting way; to grumble. [Unkn.].

GRIZZLED, [grizld], *adj.* grey; marked with grey.

GRIZZLY, [griz'-li], *n.* a large and ferocious North American bear.

GROAN (1), [grōn], *n.* a deep, moaning sound of sorrow, pain, or distress; the creaking of timber under stress; (*fig.*) a deep complaint.

GROAN (2), [grōn], *v.i.* to utter a groan or groans; to speak with a groan; (of timber) to creak; (*fig.*) to suffer and complain under oppression. [OE. *granian*].

GROANFUL, [grōn'-fŏŏl], *adj.* mournful; full of groans.

GROAT, [grōt], *n.* a former fourpenny piece; a small medieval coin of the Netherlands, etc. [MDu. *groot*].

GROATS, [grōts], *n.(pl.)* hulled grain. [OE. *grot* coarse meal].

GROBIAN, [grōb'-i-an], *n.* a clumsy, stupid person. [Germ. *grobian*].

GROCER, [grōs'-er], *n.* a dealer in dry stores and household necessities. [ME. *grosser* spice dealer from OFr. (*marchant*) *grossier* wholesale (merchant)].

GROCERY, [grōs'-er-i], *n.* the business of a grocer; (*pl.*) the goods he sells. [OFr. *grosserie*].

GROG, [grog], *n.* rum diluted with water. [*Grogram*, a nickname of Admiral Vernon who wore breeches of grogram].

GROG-BLOSSOM, [grog'-blos'-um], *n.* the rich facial redness of the tippler.

GROGGERY, [grog'-er-i], *n.* a grog-shop.

GROGGINESS, [grog'-i-nes], *n.* the state of being groggy.

GROGGY, [grog'-i], *adj.* unsteady on the feet, staggering, shaky; not firm, strong or well made. [GROG].

GROGRAM, [grog'-ram], *n.* a coarse material made of silk and mohair. [Fr. *gros grain* coarse cloth].

GROG-SHOP, [grog'-shop], *n.* a shop where spirits are sold.

GROIN, [groin], *n.* that part of the body where the thighs join the abdomen; (*arch.*) the intersection of two arches; (*math.*) the intersection of two cylinders. [ME. *grynde*].

GROIN

GROINED, [groind], *adj.* (*arch.*) with an angular curve formed by the intersection of two arches.

GROLIERESQUE, [grōl'-yāer-esk'], *adj.* after the style of Grolier, a famous French designer of book bindings.

GROMMET, GRUMMET, GROMET, [grom'-et], *n.* (*naut.*) a rope ring. [Fr. *grommet*].

GROMWELL, [grom'-wel], *n.* a blue-flowered plant, resembling borage, of the genus *Lithospermum*. [~OFr. *gromil*].

GROOM (1), [grŏŏm], *n.* a man-servant or stable-hand in charge of the horses; a bridegroom; one of several officials in the Royal Household; †a boy or manservant. [ME. *grome*].

GROOM (2), [grŏŏm], *v.t.* to rub down, brush, and comb a horse; to keep one's clothes and person neat and tidy, to smarten up.

GROOMSMAN, [grŏŏmz'-man], *n.* person who attends the bridegroom, the best man. [GROOM and MAN].

GROOVE (1), [grōōv], *n.* a furrow or elongated hollow cut by a tool; a shaft or pit sunk into the earth; a narrow channel running spirally round the bore of a gun; **to get into a g.,** to become set in habits. [Du. *groef*, *groeve*].

GROOVE (2), [grōōv], *v.t.* to cut a groove in, to furrow.

GROOVER, [grōōv'-er], *n.* a person who makes grooves.

GROOVING, [grōōv'-ing], *n.* the act or process of making grooves.

GROPE, [grōp], *v.t. and i.* to search for one's way by touch, as though blind; to feel for points of guidance; (*fig.*) to work cautiously towards a settlement of doubts or difficulties; to fumble. [OE. *grapian*].

GROPINGLY, [grōp'-ing-li], *adv.* in a groping fashion.

GROS, [grō], *n.* a stout fabric with a base of silk; **g. de Naples,** a heavy silken material. [Fr. *gros*].

GROSBEAK, GROSSBEAK, [grōs'-bēk], *n.* a bird with a large, broad beak, related to the bullfinch, *Pyrrhula*. [Fr. *grosbec*].

GROSCHEN, [gro'-shen], *n.* a former German silver coin, worth approximately 1d.; (*coll.*) a ten-pfennig piece; the hundredth part of a schilling. [Germ. *groschen*].

GROSS (1), [grōs], *n.* bulk, mass, main body; twelve dozen; **in g.,** (*leg.*) taken in the entire and not as an adjunct; **villein in g.,** a slave owned by the lord of the manor.

GROSS (2), [grōs], *adj.* thick, bulky, stout, fat; coarse, ill-mannered; vulgar, obscene, disgusting; clumsy, awkward, unskilful; total, including everything; (*leg.*) wanton, inexcusable; patently obvious. [Fr. *gros*].

GROSSBEAK, see GROSBEAK.

GROSS-HEADED, [grōs'-hed'-id], *adj.* stupid.

GROSSIFICATION, [gros'-if-i-kā'-shun], *n.* (*bot.*) the expansion of the ovary following impregnation. [GROSS and L. *facere* to make].

GROSSLY, [grōs'-li], *adv.* in gross fashion.

GROSSNESS, [grōs'-nes], *n.* the quality of being gross.

GROT, [grot], *n.* (*poet.*) a grotto, cave. [It. *grotta*].

GROTESQUE (1), [grō-tesk'], *n.* a style of creative expression concentrating on the quaint and incongruous; any work containing such elements; a grotesque person.

GROTESQUE (2), [grō-tesk'], *adj.* (of art, ornamentation, etc.) characterized by combinations of incongruities, fantastic images, and bizarre extravagances; ludicrous, incongruous, fantastic, absurd. [It. *grottesca* (*pittura*) grotesque (painting)].

GROTESQUELY, [grō-tesk'-li], *adv.* in a grotesque way.

GROTESQUENESS, [grō-tesk'-nes], *n.* the quality of being grotesque.

GROTTO, (*pl.* **grottoes, grottos**), [grot'-ō], *n.* a cavern in the earth, a cave with a decorative interior; a miniature shrine built of shells. [It. *grotta*].

GROTTO-WORK, [grot'-ō-wurk], *n.* ornamental work, similar to that in a grotto.

GROUCH (1), [growch], *n.* grumble; (*U.S. slang*) a person perpetually grumbling.

GROUCH (2), [growch], *v.i.* to grumble. [GRUDGE].

GROUND (1), [grownd], *n.* the earth, soil, land; the surface of the earth; an area, piece of land, *esp.* a field for athletics or sports; the surface used as a background in painting; the dominant colour in a colour scheme; foundation, set of conditions determining development; intellectual basis for an argument, reason, etc.; (*pl.*) an estate surrounding a house; (*pl.*) undissolved particles at the bottom of a vessel containing liquid, dregs, sediment; (*etching*) a composition spread over the metal plate as a protection against acid; (*mus.*) a composition having a recurring pattern of bass notes as an accompaniment to a continually developing melodic line; **g. staff**, the mechanics, etc., responsible for maintenance of aircraft on the ground; **to break g.**, to initiate a movement; **to gain, lose g.**, to advance or retreat from a point of advantage; **down to the g.**, (*coll.*) entirely, absolutely. [OE. *grund*].

GROUND (2), [grownd], *adj.* reduced to powder by grinding; having the surface prepared, smoothed, or roughened by grinding. [GRIND].

GROUND (3), [grownd], *v.t.* to place on the ground; to base, to pound; to educate in basic principles; to provide with a main outline; (*elect.*) to earth; (*naut.*) to cause to run aground; *v.i.* (*naut.*) to run aground.

GROUNDAGE, [grownd'-ij], *n.* a mooring tax based on the amount of space occupied by a vessel in port.

GROUND-ANGLING, [grownd'-ang'-gling], *n.* the act of fishing without a float, using a weight resting on the bottom a few inches from the hook.

GROUND-ASH, [grownd'-ash], *n.* a sapling of ash; a switch cut from a young ash-plant.

GROUND-BAILIFF, [grownd'-bā'-lif], *n.* a chief foreman of mines.

GROUNDBAIT, [grownd'-bāt], *n.* bait dropped to the bottom of the water to attract the fish.

GROUND-BASS, [grownd'-bās], *n.* (*mus.*) a bass of a few bars recurring as a pattern for accompaniment.

GROUND-DOVE, [grownd'-duv], *n.* a dove that spends most of its time on the ground.

GROUNDEDLY, [grownd'-id-li], *adv.* upon firm principles.

GROUNDER, [grownd'-er], *n.* (*cricket*) a ball that hits the ground after being struck before rising to be caught; (*baseball*) a ball struck so as to roll along the ground; (*slang*) a knock-down punch.

GROUND-FLOOR, [grownd'-flaw(r)'], *n.* the floor of a building level with the ground.

GROUND-GAME, [grownd'-gām], *n.* running game such as hares and rabbits.

GROUND-GRU, [grownd'-grōō], *n.* ground-ice forming at the bottom of a river.

GROUND-HOG, [grownd'-hog], *n.* an American marmot, the aard-vark.

GROUND-ICE, [grownd'-īs], *n.* anchor ice, ice at the bottom of the water.

GROUNDING, [grownd'-ing], *n.* the act of placing on, or coming down to, the ground; the act of preparing a surface as a ground; the prepared surface; a background; thorough instruction in the first principles of a subject; (*elect.*) the act of making an earth-connexion; (*golf*) the act of touching the ground just behind the ball with one's club.

GROUND-IVY, [grownd'-ī'-vi], *n.* the plant *Nepeta glechoma*, which grows along the ground.

GROUND-LANDLORD, [grownd'-land'-lawd], *n.* the owner of land who receives rent from the owners of buildings standing on it.

GROUNDLESS, [grownd'-les], *adj.* without reason, unfounded.

GROUNDLESSLY, [grownd'-les-li], *adv.* without ground or reason.

GROUNDLESSNESS, [grownd'-les-nes], *n.* the quality of being groundless.

GROUNDLING, [grownd'-ling], *n.* a member of the audience who stood in the pit of an Elizabethan theatre; (*fig.*) a person of little taste; one of several fishes that keep close to the ground, as the black goby or spiny loach.

GROUNDNUT, [grownd'-nut], *n.* the South American earth-nut, *Bunium esculentum*; the pea-nut, *Arachis hypogæa*.

GROUND-OAK, [grownd'-ōk], *n.* a sapling of oak.

GROUND PINE, [grownd'-pīn'], *n.* (*bot.*) a British labiate plant, *Ajuga chamæpitys*, resembling a pine in habit.

GROUND-PLAN, [grownd'-plan], *n.* (*arch.*) the horizontal plan of the ground storey of a building.

GROUND-PLANE, [grownd'-plān], *n.* the situation of the original plane drawn in perspective in relation to the horizon.

GROUND-PLOT, [grownd'-plot], *n.* the ground on which a building stands, the ground-plan.

GROUND-RENT, [grownd'-rent], *n.* the rent paid to the ground-landlord for the privilege of building on his land.

GROUND-ROOM, [grownd'-rōōm], *n.* a room situated on the ground-floor.

GROUNDS, [growndz], *n.*(*pl.*) dregs, lees, sediment; reasons, pretexts, causes.

GROUNDSEL (1), **GRUNDSEL**, [grownd'-sel], *n.* the composite plant, *Senecio vulgaris*, having yellow flowers. [OE. *grundeswelge* ground swallower].

GROUNDSEL† (2), [grownd'-sel], *n.* the timber of a building, placed immediately above the ground. [GROUND and SILL].

GROUNDSMAN, [growndz'-man], *n.* the man responsible for preparing the turf in a cricket field or sports ground.

GROUND SPEED, [grownd'-spēd], *n.* (*aviation*) speed of aircraft measured in terms of its position relative to the ground.

GROUND-SQUIRREL, [grownd'-skwir'-el], *n.* a species of *Tamias*, a chipmunk.

GROUND-SWELL, [grownd'-swel], *n.* a broad, heavy swell of the sea continuing after the wind has fallen.

GROUND-TACKLE, [grownd'-takl], *n.* the gear necessary to anchor a vessel.

GROUNDWORK, [grownd'-wurk], *n.* the work which forms the foundation of anything, basis.

GROUP (1), [grōōp], *n.* a collection or assemblage of components, a cluster; a number of persons having the same views or objects; an aggregation of objects or organisms related to, or resembling, each other, and together forming a distinct entity or subdivision; (*mus.*) a series of notes joined by the same line; (*paint., sculp.*) a collection of figures or images related to one another to form an artistic whole; (*pl.*) the sections of the Buchmanite movement. [It. *gruppo*].

GROUP (2), [grōōp], *v.t. and i.* to form into a group; to cluster, to cause to come together; to classify, to arrange in groups.

GROUP CAPTAIN, [grōōp'-kap'-tin], *n.* a commissioned rank in the Air Force of the same status as captain in the Navy and colonel in the Army.

GROUPER, [grōōp'-er], *n.* a person who groups; one of various kinds of fishes related to the sea bass; a Buchmanite.

GROUPING, [grōōp-ing], *n.* the arrangement of the objects of a picture or piece of sculpture.

GROUSE (1), [grows], *n.* a group of several varieties of wild fowl shot as game, including the ptarmigan, *Lagopus mutus*, and the red grouse, *Lagopus scoticus*. [Unkn.].

GROUSE

GROUSE (2), [grows], *v.t.* (*slang*) to grumble. [Unkn.].

GROUSER, [grows'-er], *n.* (*slang*) a person who grouses.

GROUSE-SHOOTING, [grows'-shōōt'-ing], *n.* the shooting of driven red grouse during a season which begins on August 12.

GROUT (1), [growt], *n.* coarse meal, grain when peeled; sediment, dregs. [OE. *grut*].

GROUT (2), [growt], *n.* coarse liquid mortar for filling in joints, etc., in brickwork. [Unkn.].

GROUT (3), [growt], *v.t.* to fill in with grout.

GROUTING, [growt'-ing], *n.* the process of filling in defective brickwork with grout; the grout thus filled in; plaster for ceilings.

GROVE, [grōv], *n.* a small shady wood; an avenue of trees. [OE. *graf*].

GROVEL, (**grovelling, grovelled**), [grovl], *v.i.* to fawn (on someone) for favours or from fear, to be abject, to crawl on the earth; (*fig.*) to debase oneself. [ME. *grovelinge* on the face].

GROVELLER, [grov'-el-er], *n.* a person who grovels.

GROVELLING, [grov'-el-ing], *adj.* servile, abject, without dignity, debased.

GROVELLINGLY, [grov'-el-ing-li], *adv.* in grovelling fashion.

GROW, (grew, grown), [grō], *v.t.* to cultivate, to raise; **to g. on,** to gain control over; **to g. out of,** to pass beyond, become too old for; **to g. up,** to develop to a mature stage; *v.i.* to increase in size; to flourish, to be produced; to be changed in condition, characteristics, features, etc.; to increase extensively or intensively, in quantity or quality. [OE. *growan*].

GROWABLE, [grō'-abl], *adj.* able to be grown.

GROWER, [grō'-er], *n.* a person whose business is the cultivation of plants and produce; that which grows.

GROWL (1), [growl], *n.* a low roar of anger, fear, or hostility; an angry murmur, snarl; a menacing rumble.

GROWL (2), [growl], *v.i.* to utter a growl or growls; to grumble; to snarl. [AFr. *grouler* to make the cry of a crane].

GROWLER, [growl'-er], *n.* a snarling cur; a person who growls, a grumbler; a North American perch, *Grystes salmonoides*, so called from the growl it gives when lifted out of the water; (*slang*) an old-fashioned horse-drawn cab with four wheels; a small iceberg.

GROWLING (1), [grow-ling], *n.* the act of one who growls.

GROWLING (2), [growl'-ing], *adj.* emitting or accompanied by growls.

GROWLINGLY, [growl'-ing-li], *adv.* in a growling fashion.

GROWN, [grōn], *adj.* fully developed, mature. [GROW].

GROWTH, [grōth], *n.* the act of growing; the stage of development attained by an organism; increase, natural progress, development; cultivation; anything produced by growing; increase in size or numbers; **new g.,** (*path.*) a core of morbid tissue, a cancer. [~OIcel. *grothi*].

GROYNE, [groin], *n.* a breakwater built across a beach to resist the erosion of the sea. [GROIN].

GRUB (1), [grub], *n.* the larva of an insect; (*coll.*) a dwarf; a dirty small boy; (*cricket*) a ball that fails to rise when bowled. [ME. *grubbe*].

GRUB (2), [grub], *n.* food, tuck. [Uncert.].

GRUB (3), (grubbing, grubbed), [grub], *v.i.* to dig up; to grope in dust or dirt; to toil as a drudge, to work at tedious jobs; **to g. up,** to dig up by the roots. [ME. *grubben, grobben* to dig].

GRUB-AXE, [grub'-aks], *n.* a pick used for grubbing for roots.

GRUBBER, [grub'-er], *n.* a person who grubs; an implement to stir up soil and clear out weeds.

GRUBBINESS, [grub'-i-nes], *n.* the condition of being grubby.

GRUBBING-HOE, [grub'-ing-hō'], *n.* an implement for grubbing up trees, shrubs, etc.

GRUBBLE†, [grubl], *v.i.* to feel in the dark; to grope amongst dirt. [GRABBLE].

GRUBBY, [grub'-i], *adj.* dirty, slovenly, full of grubs.

GRUB-STAKE, [grub'-stāk], *n.* (*U.S. slang*) the mining outfit and provisions supplied to a prospector in return for a percentage of the profits from working the mine.

GRUB-STREET, [grub'-strēt], *n.* a street frequented in the 17th century by jobbing literary men; authors living by hack work. [*Grub Street* now Milton Street, Moorfields, London].

GRUDGE (1), [gruj], *n.* a feeling of envy, resentment, secret hostility to another person; a reason or pretext for bearing ill-will.

GRUDGE (2), [gruj], *v.t.* to show envy and resentment at; to envy a person some advantage; *v.i.* †to murmur, complain. [ME. *grucchen, grugge*].

GRUDGER, [gruj'-er], *n.* a person who grudges.

GRUDGING, [gruj'-ing], *adj.* ungenerous, mean, niggardly; ungracious, reluctant.

GRUDGINGLY, [gruj'-ing-li], *adv.* in a grudging fashion.

GRUEL (1), [groo͞'-el], *n.* a thin porridge of meal boiled in water; **to get one's g.,** to be severely punished, or killed. [OFr. *gruel*].

GRUEL (2), (gruelling, gruelled), [groo͞'-el], *v.t.* (*slang*) to treat harshly, to make undergo a severe experience.

GRUELLING (1), [groo͞'-el-ing], *n.* (*slang*) an exhausting punishment or defeat, a harsh handling.

GRUELLING (2), [groo͞'-el-ing], *adj.* harsh, exhausting.

GRUESOME, [groo͞'-sum], *adj.* evoking horror, horrible, terrible. [ME. *gruwen* to shiver].

GRUESOMELY, [groo͞'-sum-li], *adv.* in a gruesome fashion.

GRUESOMENESS, [groo͞'-sum-nes], *n.* the condition or quality of being gruesome.

GRUFF, [gruf], *adj.* of a rough surly manner; ungracious, abruptly impatient; hoarse, deep in tone. [Scots *grof* coarse].

GRUFFISH, [gruf'-ish], *adj.* slightly gruff; grumpy.

GRUFFLY, [gruf'-li], *adv.* in a gruff fashion.

GRUFFNESS, [gruf'-nes], *n.* the quality of being gruff.

GRU-GRU, [groo͞'-groo͞], *n.* the grub of a tropical coleopterous insect, cooked and eaten as a great delicacy; the macaw-palm, a species of *Acrocomia*. [Uncert.].

GRUM, [grum], *adj.* gloomy, morose, surly; gruff. [Dan. *grum* cruel].

GRUMBLE, [grumbl], *v.i.* to mutter complaints, to murmur with discontent, to growl; to rumble. [Fr. *grommeler*].

GRUMBLER, [grum'-bler], *n.* a person who grumbles.

GRUME, [groo͞m], *n.* (*med.*) a thick fluid or liquid; a clot, as of blood. [LL. *grumus* pile of earth].

GRUMLY, [grum'-li], *adv.* in a grum way.

GRUMMET, see GROMMET.

GRUMNESS, [grum'-nes], *n.* the state of being grum.

GRUMOSE, [groo͞'-mōs], *adj.* (*bot.*) having clusters; (*med.*) clotted.

GRUMOUS, [groo͞'-mus], *adj.* (*bot.*) grumose.

GRUMOUSNESS, [groo͞'-mus-nes], *n.* the condition of being grumose.

GRUMPILY, [grump'-i-li], *adv.* (*coll.*) in a grumpy fashion.

GRUMPINESS, [grump'-i-nes], *n.* the state of being grumpy.

GRUMPY, [grump'-i], *adj.* irritable, surly, bad-tempered. [Echoic].

GRUNDEL, [grundl], *n.* a fish, the groundling [~Du. *grondel*].

GRUNDSEL, see GROUNDSEL.

GRUNDYISM, [grund'-i-izm], *n.* ridiculous emphasis on respectable conventions, excessive prudery [Mrs. *Grundy*, a character referred to in the play "Speed the Plough," 1798, by T. Morton].

GRUNT (1), [grunt], *n.* a coarse, forced, throaty ejaculation; a deep guttural sound, as of a hog.

GRUNT (2), [grunt], *v.t. and i.* to make a grunt or series of grunts. [OE. *grunnettan*].

GRUNTER, [grunt'-er], *n.* a person or animal that grunts; a species of gurnard, so called from the grunting noise it makes.

GRUNTINGLY, [grunt'-ing-li], *adv.* with grunting.

GRUNTLING, [grunt'-ling], *n.* a young hog.

GRUYERE, Gruyère, [grwē'-yāer, groo͞-yāer'], *n.* a kind of cheese made of skim milk, with many holes. [*Gruyère*, a district in Switzerland].

GRYPOSIS, [grī-pō'-sis], *n.* (*med.*) an ingrowing of the nails. [Gk. *grypos* bent].

GRYSBOK, [grīs'-bok], *n.* a small grey African antelope, *Nanotragus melanotis*. [Du. *grijs* grey and *bok* buck].

GUACHARO, [gwah-chah'-rō], *n.* the oil-bird, *Steatornis caripensis*, a South American nocturnal bird allied to the nightjars. [Span. *guacharo*].

GUAIACOL, [gwī'-a-kol], *n.* a sharp-smelling liquid distilled from guaiacum and creosote and used in treating consumption.

GUAIACUM, [gwī'-a-kum], *n.* a genus of tropical American trees, the wood of one species, *Guaiacum officinale*, being lignum vitae; the resin of this tree used medicinally. [Span. *guayaco*].

GUAN, [gwahn], *n.* a South American game-bird of the genus *Penelope*, allied to the curassows. [Native].

GUANACO, [gwah-nah'-kō], *n.* a South American llama of the genus *Auchenia*. [Peruvian *huanacu*].

GUANCHOS, [gwahn'-chōz], *n.*(*pl.*) the original natives of the Canary Islands.

GUANIFEROUS, [gwan-if'-er-us], *adj.* bearing guano. [GUANO and L. *ferre* to bear].

GUANIN, [gwahn'-in], *n.* (*chem.*) a nitrogenous compound, allied to uric acid, and found in guano.

GUANO, [gwah'-nō], *n.* a rich manure, composed of the dung of sea-birds. [Peruvian *huanu* dung].

GUARACHA, [gwa-rah'-chah], *n.* a Spanish dance in which the dancer accompanies himself on the guitar. [Span. *guaracha*].

GUARANA, [gwah-rah'-na], *n.* Brazilian cocoa made from certain seeds, and used both as food and a tonic. [Native].

GUARANTEE (1), [ga-ran-tē'], *n.* an agreement to conclude or observe strictly some arrangement or contract; the pledge or security, handed over in support of this; the person accepting a surety; the person offering the surety. [GUARANTY].

GUARANTEE (2), [ga-ran-tē′], *v.t.* to take on the office of a guarantor for, to give security for; to protect against losses, to indemnify; to give a specific guarantee that; to promise, undertake.

GUARANTEED, [ga-ran-tēd′], *adj.* warranted; covered by guarantee.

GUARANTOR, [ga′-ran-tor′], *n.* a person who gives a guarantee.

GUARANTY, [ga′-ran-ti], *n.* an undertaking in writing to be responsible for the liabilities of another person; a promise to observe a right or agreement; a basis of security, pledge. [AFr. *guarantie* thing warranted].

GUARD (1), [gahd], *n.* a means of defence; a state of watchful caution; a posture of defence; a body of men keeping watch against attack or danger; a sentry; an armed escort in charge of prisoners, etc.; an official in charge of a railway train; metal bar or shield on a sword hilt to protect the fencer's hand; a wire frame shielding a fireplace; a watch-chain; a ring worn above a wedding ring; (*pl.*) regiments of household troops whose duty it was to protect the King's person; **off one's g.**, unprepared, defenceless; **to take g.**, (*cricket*) to place the bat according to the umpire's directions in a position to defend the wicket. [OFr. *guarde*, *garde* watching].

GUARD (2), [gahd], *v.t. and i.* to protect, act as guard for; to restrain by watching; to be on the defensive; (*fencing*) to take up a posture of defence; **to g. against**, to prevent by taking precautions. [OFr. *guarder*].

GUARDABLE, [gahd′-abl], *adj.* able to be protected.

GUARDANT, [gahd′-ant], *adj.* (*her.*) looking out from the field as though guardian. [Fr. *gardant*].

GUARD-BOAT, [gahd′-bōt], *n.* a boat acting as a means of communication for a fleet at anchor; an official harbour-boat.

GUARD-BOOK, [gahd′-bŏŏk], *n.* a book or portfolio with patent binding to take extra leaves.

GUARDED, [gahd′-id], *adj.* defended; discreet, circumspect.

GUARDEDLY, [gahd′-id-li], *adv.* in a guarded way.

GUARDEDNESS, [gahd′-id-nes], *n.* the quality of being guarded.

GUARDFISH, see GARFISH.

GUARDFUL†, [gahd′-fŏŏl], *adj.* wary, cautious.

GUARD-HOUSE, [gahd′-hows], *n.* a building inhabited by the guard, or in which military prisoners are detained.

GUARDIAN (1), [gahd′-i-an], *n.* a person who guards, a defender, custodian, or warder; (*leg.*) a person appointed to the legal custody of the estate, welfare, and upbringing of a minor, or person legally incapable of managing his affairs.

GUARDIAN (2), [gahd′-i-an], *adj.* protecting, acting as a guardian.

GUARDIANSHIP, [gahd′-i-an-ship], *n.* the office of a guardian; protection.

GUARDLESS, [gahd′-les], *adj.* without a guard.

GUARD-ROOM, [gahd′-room], *n.* a guard-house.

GUARDSHIP, [gahd′-ship], *n.* care, protection.

GUARD-SHIP, [gahd′-ship′], *n.* a warship stationed in a harbour, to protect a port and accommodate seamen waiting to join their ships.

GUARDSMAN, [gahdz′-man], *n.* a soldier or officer of the household troops.

GUAVA, [gwah′-va], *n.* a tree of the myrtle family, *Psidium Guajava*, with a small pear-shaped fruit. [Span. *guayaba*].

GUAYULE, [gwah-yōōl′], *n.* a Mexican plant resembling the aster, the secretion of which is used as a rubber substitute. [Native].

GUBERNATORIAL, [gew′-ber-na-taw′-ri-al], *adj.* belonging to government, or to a governor. [L. *gubernator* steersman].

GUDGEON (1), [guj′-un], *n.* a small freshwater fish allied to the carp, *Gobio fluviatilis*; (*fig.*) a dupe; **sea g.**, the black goby or rock-fish. [Fr. *goujon*].

GUDGEON (2), [guj′-un], *n.* a pivot or collar at the end of an axle; a pin fixing the piston-rod to the connecting rod; a socket in which the rudder turns; a pin securing two stone blocks together. [OFr. *gojon* sculptor's chisel].

GUEBRE, GHEBER, [geb′-er], *n.* a fire-worshipper. [Pers. *gabr*].

GUELDER-ROSE, GELDER-ROSE†, [geld′-er-rōz′], *n.* the snowball tree, *Viburnum Opulus*, having large globular, white clusters of flowers. [Fr. *rose de gueldre*].

GUELF, GUELPH, [gwelf], *n.* a member of a militant political party in Italy during the Middle Ages, supporters of the Pope against the German emperors; ancestor of the Georges, Kings of England. [It. *Guelfo*].

GUELPHIC, [gwelf′-ik], *adj.* relating or belonging to the Guelphs.

GUENON, [gē′-non], *n.* a long-tailed African monkey of the genus *Cercopithecus*. [Fr. *guenon* she-monkey].

GUERDON (1), [ger′-don], *n.* a reward. [OFr. *guerdon*].

GUERDON (2), [ger′-don], *v.t.* to reward. [OFr. *guerredoner*].

GUERDONABLE, [ger′-don-abl], *adj.* meriting reward.

GUEREZA, [ger-ē′-za], *n.* the black and white Abyssinian monkey, *Colobus guereza*. [Native].

GUERILLA, see GUERRILLA.

GUERITE†, [ge′-rit], *n.* (*fort.*) a small loop-holed tower generally situated on the point of a bastion, as a sentry post; a sentry-box. [Fr. *guérite*].

GUERNSEY, [gurn′-zi], *n.* a thick jersey; a breed o dairy cattle, giving very rich milk, first bred in Guernsey. [*Guernsey*, one of the Channel Islands].

GUERRILLA, GUERILLA, [ger-il′-a], *n.* a form of war carried on by armed bands making sporadic attacks and raids without centralized leadership; a member of such a band. [Span. *guerrilla* little war].

GUESS (1), [ges], *n.* judgment without real evidence, a conjecture.

GUESS (2), [ges], *v.t. and i.* to make a guess; to make a guess as to; to surmise, consider likely; to discover by a guess. [ME. *gessen* to suppose].

GUESSABLE, [ges′-abl], *adj.* able to be guessed.

GUESSER, [ges′-er], *n.* a person who guesses.

GUESSINGLY, [ges′-ing-li], *adv.* by means of guesses.

GUESSWORK, [ges′-wurk], *n.* a conjecture or opinion arrived at by guessing; work dependent on, or done by, guesses.

GUEST, [gest], *n.* a visitor or a friend entertained in the house or invited to a meal by another; a lodger paying for accommodation at a hotel; **g. night**, a night on which guests are received. [OE. *gest* stranger, visitor].

GUEST-CHAMBER, [gest′-chām′-ber], *n.* an apartment used exclusively for accommodating guests.

GUEST-HOUSE, [gest′-hows], *n.* a house providing accommodation for paying guests.

GUEST-ROPE, [gest′-rōp], *n.* (*naut.*) a rope used to steady a boat being towed astern; a rope for steadying boats coming alongside.

GUESTWISE, [gest′-wīz], *adv.* as a guest.

GUFFAW (1), [guf-aw′], *n.* a loud vulgar laugh. [Echoic].

GUFFAW (2), [guf-aw′], *v.i.* to utter a guffaw.

GUGGLE (1), [gugl], *n.* a gurgle. [Echoic].

GUGGLE (2), [gugl], *v.t.* to gurgle.

GUHR, [gōōer], *n.* a loose earthy deposit left by water, found in rocks and crevices. [Germ. *guhr* fermentation].

GUICHET, [gē′-shā], *n.* a grating over the opening of a ticket-office. [Fr. *guichet*].

GUIDABLE, [gīd-abl], *adj.* able to be guided.

GUIDAGE†, [gīd′-ij], *n.* reward given a guide; fee paid for guidance. [Fr. *guidage* guiding].

GUIDANCE, [gīd′-ants], *n.* the act of guiding, instruction.

GUIDE (1), [gīd], *n.* a person who helps another by showing him the way or by directing him to a place; a person who conducts visitors or sightseers; a person accepted as a moral preceptor; that which directs; a book containing directions or practical knowledge; a guide-book; a member of the Girl Guides. [OFr. *guide*].

GUIDE (2), [gīd], *v.t.* to direct, to conduct another on the way; to give physical support or moral example to; to control the activity of a person or country; to instruct; to superintend. [OFr. *guider*].

GUIDE-BARS, [gīd′-bahz], *n.(pl.)* (*mech.*) the bars supporting and steadying sliding blocks.

GUIDE-BLOCKS, [gīd′-bloks], *n.(pl.)* (*mech.*) blocks sliding upon guide-bars.

GUIDE-BOOK, [gīd′-bŏŏk], *n.* a book describing places and routes.

GUIDELESS, [gīd′-les], *adj.* lacking a guide.

GUIDE-POST, [gīd′-pōst], *n.* a signpost at the fork of a road.

GUIDE-RAIL, [gīd′-rāl], *n.* an auxiliary rail to keep wheels on a line.

GUIDE-ROPE, [gīd′-rōp], *n.* a rope to control and steady the motion of a rope carrying a suspended load.

GUIDON, [gid'-on], *n.* (*milit.*) a pennant or cavalry flag with an indented fly; the trooper carrying this flag. [Fr. *guidon*].

GUILD, GILD, [gild], *n.* (*hist.*) an association of craftsmen following the same craft, formed during the Middle Ages to protect the members' interests and supervise the standard of work; an incorporated society; **g. socialism,** a form of socialism based on guilds; **g. socialist,** an exponent of this. [ME. *gild* payment, brotherhood].

GUILD-BROTHER, [gild'-bruᴛʜ'-er], *n.* a member of the same guild.

GUILDER, [gild'-er], *n.* an old Dutch gold coin; a Dutch silver coin worth about 1s. 8d. [Du. *gulden*].

GUILDHALL, [gild'-hawl'], *n.* the hall in which the meetings of a guild were held; a town-hall; the great assembly-hall of the Corporation of London.

GUILDRY, [gild'-ri], *n.* a guild.

GUILE, [gīl], *n.* wiliness, craft, duplicity. [OFr. *guile*].

GUILEFUL, [gīl'-fool], *adj.* wily, crafty, treacherous.

GUILEFULLY, [gīl'-fool-i], *adv.* in a guileful way.

GUILEFULNESS, [gīl'-fool-nes], *n.* the quality of being guileful.

GUILELESS, [gīl'-les], *adj.* without guile.

GUILELESSLY, [gīl'-les-li], *adv.* in a guileless way.

GUILELESSNESS, [gīl'-les-nes], *n.* the quality of being guileless.

GUILLEMET, [gē'-mā], *n.* a quotation mark; inverted commas (" "). [*Guillemet*, its inventor].

GUILLEMOT, [gil'-i-mot], *n.* a web-footed sea-bird of the auk family, *Uria troile*. [Fr. *guillemot*].

GUILLEMOT

GUILLEVAT, [gil'-i-vat], *n.* a vat for fermenting liquors.

GUILLOCHE, [gil-osh'], *n.* (*arch.*) an ornamental border of intertwined bands or ribbons running in a wavy series parallel to the edge. [Fr. *guilloche*].

GUILLOTINE (1), [gil'-ō-tēn], *n.* an instrument for decapitating persons, consisting of a wide and heavy knife-blade running down two grooved posts towards the head-rest; a machine for cutting sheets of paper evenly; a surgical cutting-instrument. [Dr. J. I. *Guillotin*, who urged its use during the French Revolution].

GUILLOTINE (2), [gil'-o-tēn], *v.t.* to behead by means of the guillotine; to cut with a guillotine.

GUILLS, [gilz], *n.* the plant, *Chrysanthemum segetum*, the corn marigold. [Unkn.].

GUILT, [gilt], *n.* the fact or consciousness of having committed a crime or offence, criminality, culpability; (*leg.*) violation of criminal law; (*theol.*) sin. [OE. *gylt*].

GUILTILY, [gilt'-i-li], *adv.* in a guilty way.

GUILTINESS, [gilt'-i-nes], *n.* the quality of being guilty.

GUILTLESS, [gilt'-les], *adj.* free from guilt, blameless.

GUILTLESSLY, [gilt'-les-li], *adv.* in a guiltless way.

GUILTLESSNESS, [gilt'-les-nes], *n.* the quality of being guiltless.

GUILTY, [gilt'-i], *adj.* pertaining to guilt, arising from, expressing guilt, responsible, blameworthy; having committed a crime. [OE. *gyltig*].

GUINEA, [gin'-i], *n.* a gold coin, formerly current in Great Britain, worth 21s., and first coined in gold brought from Guinea; a nominal value of 21s. [Portug. *Guiné*, a country on the west coast of Africa].

GUINEA-CORN, [gin'-i-kawn'], *n.* *Sorghum vulgare*, plane millet.

GUINEA-FOWL, [gin'-i-fowl'], *n.* the galeeny, *Numida meleagris*, a West African game-bird.

GUINEA-GRASS, [gin'-i-grahs], *n.* an African fodder plant, *Panicum maximum*.

GUINEA-PEPPER, [gin'-i-pep'-er], *n.* a species of *Capsicum*; the fruit of certain West African plants.

GUINEA-PIG, [gin'-i-pig'], *n.* a small domesticated variety of *Cavia cutleri*; (*coll.*) one who receives a guinea as a fee for his services; **g. director,** one paid for the use of his name on a board of directors.

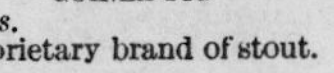

GUINEA-PIG

GUINEA-WORM, [gin'-i-wurm], *n.* the parasitic worm afflicting man and cattle, *Dracunculus medinensis*.

GUINNESS, [gin'-is], *n.* a proprietary brand of stout. [*Guinness*, the brewer].

GUIPURE, [gē-pyōōer'], *n.* a kind of large-patterned lace in imitation of antique, gimp. [Fr. *guipure*].

GUISE, [gīz], *n.* a masking of external appearance; style of dress and manner; disguise, pretence. [OFr. *guise* from OHG. *wisa*].

GUISER, [gīz'-er], *n.* a person in disguise; a mummer at Christmas time; (*slang*) a bloke, geezer.

GUITAR, [gi-tah(r)'], *n.* a lute with a flat back and six strings, played with the fingers stopping the strings against a fretted finger-board. [Span. *guitarra*].

GUITARIST, [gi-tah'-rist], *n.* player on a guitar.

GULAR, [gew'-ler], *adj.* of, or relating to, the throat. [L. *gula* throat].

GULCH, [gulch], *n.* a ravine; a deep bed formed and filled by a torrent. [ME. *gulchen* to gulp].

GULDEN, [gōōld'-en], *n.* a silver florin, originally of gold, worth 2s., formerly current in Austria-Hungary; the Dutch guilder. [MHG. *guldin* made of gold].

GULES, [gyōōlz], *n.* (*her.*) the colour red. [OFr. *goules, geules*].

GUITAR

GULF, [gulf], *n.* a large deep bay; a tongue of water set deep in the land; a deep place in the earth, an abyss; an impassable barrier; a whirlpool. [OFr. *goulfe*].

GULF-STREAM, [gulf'-strēm], *n.* a broad warm current crossing the Atlantic Ocean, from the Gulf of Mexico.

GULFWEED, [gulf'-wēd], *n.* a tropical seaweed pimpled with air-bladders of the genus *Sargassum*.

GULFY, [gulf'-i], *adj.* full of gulfs.

GULL (1), [gul], *n.* any of the several species of sea-bird, with long wings, webbed feet, and a square tail. [Cornish *gwilan, gullan*].

GULL (2), [gul], *n.* a trick; a person easily cheated, a dupe. [Uncert.].

GULL (3), [gul], *v.t.* to cheat, dupe, deceive, swindle. [GULL (2)].

GULL-CATCHER†, [gul'-kach'-er], *n.* a person who dupes silly people.

GULLER†, [gul'-er], *n.* a swindler, a cheat.

GULLET, [gul'-et], *n.* the passage by which food enters the stomach; a small channel or gutter for conveying water. [OFr. *goulet* little throat].

GULLIBILITY, [gul'-i-bil'-i-ti], *n.* the quality of being gullible.

GULLIBLE, [gul'-ibl], *adj.* able to be deceived or duped easily, credulous.

GULLIED, [gul'-id], *adj.* having a groove worn by water.

GULLY (1), [gul'-i], *n.* a channel or hollow worn by water; a manufactured water channel, a gutter; a position on the cricket field between slips and point; a large knife; an iron tram-plate. [Fr. *goulet* bottle-necked opening].

GULLY (2), [gul'-i], *v.t.* to form a gully in, to furrow with water.

GULLY-HOLE, [gul'-i-hōl], *n.* an opening in a street, covered with a grating, where gutters empty into the sewer.

GULP (1), [gulp], *n.* the action of gulping, a swallow; the noise made at the back of the throat when swallowing; a large mouthful, as much as is swallowed at once.

GULP (2), [gulp], *v.t.* to swallow noisily and quickly; to swallow convulsively and greedily; to check as if by swallowing back; (*fig.*) to take in, to accept with credulous ease. [ME. *gulpen, gloppen*].

GULY, [gewl'-i], *adj.* coloured red.

GUM (1), [gum], *n.* the firm flesh round the jaws, in which the teeth are imbedded. [OE. *goma* palate].

GUM (2), [gum], *n.* one of various sticky, soluble resins exuded from trees; any sticky substance for use as an adhesive; a transparent sweetmeat made of coloured gelatine; **chewing g.,** a sticky sweet with a rubbery texture made of chicle coated with sugar and flavoured; **g. arabic,** a gum extracted from *Acacia senegal* and *Acacia scorpioides*; **g. tree,** the eucalyptus. [L. *gummi*].

GUM (3), (**gumming, gummed**), [gum], *v.t. and i.* to smear with gum; to stick, join, fasten, stiffen with gum; to give off gum, as a plum tree in an unhealthy condition. [GUM (2)].

GUMBO, [gum'-bō], *n.* a preparation made out of the young capsules of a tropical herb, okra, *Hibiscus* *esculentus*, seasoned with salt and pepper, stewed and served with melted butter; a soup thickened with these capsules. [Native].

GUM-BOIL, [gum'-boil], *n* a boil on the gum.

GUMBOOTS, [gum'-bōōts], *n.(pl.)* rubber boots with high leggings, worn as a protection from mud or water; waders.

GUM-DRAGON, [gum'-drag'-on], *n.* tragacanth, a gum with medicinal properties.

GUMDROP, [gum'-drop], *n.* a sweet made in small drops from sweetened gum arabic.

GUM-ELASTIC, [gum'-i-last'-ik], *n.* rubber. [MdL. *gummi elasticum*].

GUM-JUNIPER, [gum'-jōōn'-i-per], *n.* a tree, the sandarac.

GUMLAH, [gum'-la], *n.* a large Indian earthenware jar for water. [Hind. *gamla*].

GUMMA, (*pl.* **gummata**), [gum'-a, gum'-a-ta], *n.* (*path.*) a syphilitic tumour containing gummy matter. [L. *gumma* a gum].

GUMMIFEROUS, [gum-if'-er-us], *adj.* producing gum. [GUM and L. *ferre* to bear].

GUMMINESS, [gum'-i-nes], *n.* the quality of being gummy.

GUMMING, [gum'-ing], *n.* an exudation of gum from cherry or plum trees in an unhealthy condition; the act of smearing gum on a surface.

GUMMOSITY†, [gum-os'-i-ti], *n.* gumminess.

GUMMOUS, [gum'-us], *adj.* gummy. [L. *gummosus*].

GUMMY, [gum'-i], *adj.* relating to, consisting of, gum; covered with gum.

GUMPTION, [gump'-shun], *n.* shrewd sense, practical common sense. [Scots *gumption*].

GUM-RASH, [gum'-rash], *n.* (*med.*) red gum strophulus, a rash appearing on the gums of a teething infant.

GUM-RESIN, [gum'-rez'-in], *n.* a mixture of gum and resin partially soluble in water or alcohol.

GUM-TRAGACANTH, [gum-trag'-a-kanth], *n.* a kind of gum used in medicine, obtained from an Asiatic plant, *Astragalus*.

GUM-TREE, [gum'-trē], *n.* any species of *Eucalyptus*; **to be up a g.**, (*coll.*) to be in a desperate quandary.

GUN, [gun], *n.* a mounted tube of metal from which explosives are fired; a fire-arm; a member of a shooting party; a tool for forcing thick grease into joints or bearings; **to blow great guns**, (*naut.*) to blow a gale; **to stick to one's guns**, to hold to one's opinions in a vigorous argument. [ME. *gunne*].

GUN-BARREL, [gun'-ba'-rel], *n.* the barrel of a gun.

GUNBOAT, [gun'-bōt], *n.* a small vessel of light draught, armed with heavy guns.

GUN-CARRIAGE, [gun'-ka'-rij], *n.* a wheel-carriage for carrying and transporting cannon.

GUN-COTTON, [gun'-kot-en], *n.* a high explosive obtained by saturating cotton, cellulose, or any vegetable fibre with nitro-sulphuric acid.

GUN-FIRE, [gun'-fīer], *n.* (*milit., naut.*) the firing of guns to announce the time; discharge of guns.

GUNMAN, [gun'-man], *n.* an armed bandit.

GUN-METAL, [gun'-met'-al], *n.* an alloy of copper and tin with a dark khaki-green colour; a metal used in cheap manufacture resembling this.

GUNNAGE, [gun'-ij], *n.* the number of guns on one ship.

GUNNEL, [gunl], *n.* the butter-fish, *Centronotus gunnellus*, a kind of blenny found in the Atlantic. [Unkn.].

GUNNEL

GUNNER (1), [gun'-er], *n.* a person who operates a gun; an artilleryman; (*naut.*) a warrant-officer in charge of the ship's ordnance.

GUNNER (2), [gun'-er], *n.* the sea-bream.

GUNNERY, [gun'-er-i], *n.* the science of artillery, ballistics; the firing of guns.

GUNNING, [gun'-ing], *n.* the shooting of game.

GUNNY, [gun'-i], *n.* a coarse sackcloth made out of jute. [Hind. *goni* sacking].

GUNPOWDER, [gun'-powd'-er], *n.* an explosive mixture of granulated nitre, sulphur, and charcoal; **g. tea**, a green tea of high quality.

GUN-REACH, [gun'-rēch], *n.* gunshot.

GUN-ROOM, [gun'-rōōm], *n.* a room in which fire-arms are stored; (*naut.*) the junior officers' mess-room.

GUNSHOT, [gun'-shot], *n.* the range of a gun.

GUN-SHY, [gun'-shī], *adj.* liable to take fright at the noise of shooting.

GUNSMITH, [gun'-smith], *n.* a maker and repairer of small fire-arms.

GUNSMITHERY, [gun'-smith'-er-i], *n.* the business of a gunsmith; the art of making and repairing small fire-arms.

GUNSTICK, [gun'-stik], *n.* a ramrod.

GUNSTOCK, [gun'-stok], *n.* the stock or wood acting as a support in which the barrel of a gun is fixed.

GUNSTONE†, [gun'-stōn], *n.* a round stone formerly used for cannon shot.

GUN-TACKLE, [gun'-takl], *n.* the ropes and blocks attached to each side of a gun-carriage.

GUNTER, [gun'-ter], *n.* (*naut.*) a movable topmast; a sail carried by this; **Gunter's chain**, a chain of 100 links, 66 feet long, used for land measurement; **Gunter's line**, a calulating instrument for multiplying and dividing; **Gunter's scale**, a two-foot rule used in surveying and navigation. [E. *Gunter*, the inventor, 1581-1626].

GUNWALE, [gun'-el], *n.* (*naut.*) the upper edge of timber running round an open boat's side; uppermost wale of a ship, the strake immediately below the bulwarks.

GUNYAH, [gun'-yah], *n.* a rough hut in the bush. [Native].

GURGITATION, [gur'-ji-tā'-shun], *n.* a violent surging or boiling up of a liquid. [L. *gurgitatio*].

GURGLE (1), [gurgl], *n.* a bubbling sound as of rippling liquid.

GURGLE (2), [gurgl], *v.i.* to flow in a broken current making bubbling sounds; to make a throaty gurgle or series of gurgles. [OFr. *gorguler*].

GURJUN, [gur'-jun], *n.* an Indian balsam obtained from several species of *Dipterocarpus*. [Native].

GURKHA, [gōōer'-ka], *n.* a province in Nepal; a member of a warlike Rajput race that settled there late in the eighteenth century; a member of a native Indian regiment from this province.

GURLY, [gurl'-i], *adj.* boisterous, stormy. [Scots *gurly*].

GURNARD, [gurn'-erd], *n.* a gurnet. [OFr. *gornard*, *gornart*].

GURNET, [gurn'-et], *n.* a small sea-fish of the genus *Trigla*, having a large head and six feelers growing from the breast. [GURNARD].

GURRAH, [gur'-ra], *n.* a coarse Indian muslin; an Indian earthenware jar. [Hind. *garha*].

GURRY (1), [gu'-ri], *n.* a small fort. [Hind. *garhi*].

GURRY (2), [gu'-ri], *n.* (*prov.*) offal.

GURU, [gōō'-rōō], *n.* an Indian teacher. [Skr. *guru* venerable].

GUSH (1), [gush], *n.* a sudden flood of fluid from an enclosed space, such as a channel or container; (*fig.*) a spate of effusive phrases; an outburst of insincere emotion or sentimentality.

GUSH (2), [gush], *v.i.* to flood suddenly, stream out; to flow in an unrestrained, vigorous and copious stream; to talk effusively; to be extravagantly emotional, enthusiastic or sentimental. [ME. *guschen*, *gosshe*].

GUSHER, [gush'-er], *n.* one who, or that which, gushes, *esp.* an oil-well that flows abundantly when first tapped.

GUSHING, [gush'-ing], *adj.* that gushes, flowing copiously; effusive; overpoweringly emotional or demonstrative.

GUSHINGLY, [gush'-ing-li], *adv.* in a gushing way.

GUSHY, [gush'-i], *adj.* gushing.

GUSSET (1), [gus'-et], *n.* any piece of cloth or material, usually of a triangular shape, let into a garment to enlarge it; a piece of chain-mail inserted in the armour suit as a joint under the armpit; an iron brace for supporting corners; (*her.*) a triangular abatement on a coat of arms. [OFr. *gousset*].

GUSSET (2), (**gussetting, gussetted**), [gus'-et], *v.t.* to insert a gusset into.

GUST† **(1)**, [gust], *n.* the sense of tasting; the pleasure of tasting, relish, gratification, enjoyment, gusto. [L. *gustus* tasting].

GUST (2), [gust], *n.* a sudden squall, a violent and sudden blast of wind; (*fig.*) a violent outburst of passion. [OIcel. *gustr*].

GUSTABLE†, [gust'-abl], *adj.* able to be tasted; pleasant to the taste. [L. *gustabilis*].

GUSTATORY, [gust'-at-er-i], *adj.* (*anat.*) relating to the sense of taste.

GUSTILY, [gust'-i-li], *adv.* in gusty fashion.

GUSTO, [gust'-ō], *n.* relish, enjoyment, zest. [It. *gusto*].

GUSTY, [gust'-i], *adj.* subject to gusts of wind, squally; (*fig.*) passionate.

GUT (1), [gut], *n.* (*anat.*) that part of the alimentary canal extending from the pylorus to the anus; the bowels, the intestines, entrails; a narrow channel in a river, a narrow passage in a street; a thin cord prepared from a sheep's intestines, and used as a string for musical instruments, etc., catgut; the intestine of a silkworm used for making fishing casts; (*pl.*) stamina, will-power; courage and determination; strength, body, substance. [OE. *guttas* entrails].

GUT (2), (gutting, gutted), [gut], *v.t.* to remove the guts from, eviscerate; (*fig.*) to remove everything inside, *esp.* of a building by fire; to plunder; to get the essential substance of a book; *v.i.* to eat greedily.

GUTTA, (*pl.* **guttae**), [gut'-a], *n.* (*arch.*) a small ornament resembling a rounded head of a peg, used in the Doric entablature. [L. *gutta* drop].

GUTTA

GUTTA-PERCHA, [gut'-a-purch'-a], *n.* the hardened, elastic milky juice of several varieties of trees found chiefly in the Malay Peninsula. [Malay *gatah* gum and *percha* tree].

GUTTATE, [gut'-āt], *adj.* (*zool., bot.*) spotted, speckled. [L. *guttare* to drip].

GUTTATED, [gut'-āt-id], *adj.* speckled, sprinkled with drops.

GUTTEE, see GUTTY (2).

GUTTER (1), [gut'-er], *n.* an open channel for carrying away water, *esp.* a metal trough at the edge of a roof for drainage; the edge of the roadway next to the pavement, forming a channel down which rainwater runs; (*print.*) the space between the sides of two pairs of mated pages; (*fig.*) the most degraded or dirty stage in the social scale; **g. press**, cheap scurrilous newspapers. [ME. *gotere* from OFr. *gutiere*].

GUTTER (2), [gut'-er], *v.t.* and *i.* to provide with a gutter; to form into a series of small channels or furrows; (of a candle) to run down one side with melted wax.

GUTTER-BLOOD, [gut'-er-blud], *n.* a person of low birth.

GUTTER-BRACKET, [gut'-er-brak'-it], *n.* a bracket for supporting and fixing a gutter to the roof.

GUTTERING, [gut'-er-ing], *n.* the action of making gutters; a forming into hollows or channels; a system of gutters.

GUTTER-SNIPE, [gut'-er-snīp'], *n.* a slum child, a street arab; (*U.S. slang*) a kerbstone broker.

GUTTIFEROUS, [gut-if'-er-us], *adj.* (*bot.*) giving off gum or resin. [GUTTA and L. *ferre* to bear].

GUTTLE, [gutl], *v.t.* to eat greedily. [Uncert.].

GUTTURAL (1), [gut'-er-al], *n.* (*phon.*) a guttural consonant or vowel.

GUTTURAL (2), [gut'-er-al], *adj.* relating to the throat; (*phon.*) formed in, or at the back of, the throat; (of speech) harsh, rasping, as though uttered from the back of the throat. [L. *guttur* throat].

GUTTURALLY, [gut'-er-al-i], *adv.* in a guttural way.

GUTTURALNESS, [gut'-er-al-nes], *n.* the quality of being guttural.

GUTTURIZE, [gut'-er-īz], *v.t.* (*phon.*) to produce in the throat.

GUTTY (1), [gut'-i], *n.* (*coll.*) a gutta-percha golf-ball.

GUTTY (2), GUTTEE, [gut'-i], *adj.* (*her.*) sprinkled with drops. [OFr. *goute*].

GUTWORT, [gut'-wurt], *n.* an African plant of the genus *Globularia*, used as a violent purgative.

GUY (1), [gī], *n.* (*naut.*) a rope attached to anything to guide or steady it. [OFr. *guie* guide].

GUY (2), [gī], *n.* an effigy of Guy Fawkes; any absurd effigy; a badly dressed person; a person who is ridiculed. [*Guy* Fawkes, hanged for attempting to blow up the Houses of Parliament in 1605].

GUY (3), [gī], *v.t.* to steady by means of a rope. [OFr. *guier*].

GUY (4), [gī], *v.t.* to ridicule by representing in grotesque effigy; (*fig.*) to mock, imitate derisively. [GUY (2)].

GUZZLE, [guzl], *v.t.* and *i.* to swallow liquor greedily; to eat or drink in noisy, gluttonous fashion. [~OFr. *gosillier* gulp].

GUZZLER, [guz'-ler], *n.* person who guzzles.

GWINIAD, GWYNIAD, [gwin'-i-ad], *n.* a freshwater fish, *Coregonus clupeoides*, the powan. [Wel. *gwyn* white].

GYBE (1), [jīb], *n.* the act or process of gybing.

GYBE (2), [jīb], *v.t.* and *i.* (*naut.*) (of a boom or sail) to swing from one side to another when running before the wind; to cause to gybe. [JIB].

GYLE, [gīl], *n.* the quantity of one brewing of ale or beer; a vat in which fermenting takes place. [Du. *gijlen* to ferment].

GYM, [jim], *n.* (*coll.*) a gymnasium. [GYM(NASIUM)].

GYMKHANA, [jim-kah'-na], *n.* a meeting for an athletic display, *esp.* for races. [Hind. *gendkhana* racket-court].

GYMNASIUM, (*pl.* **gymnasiums**), [jim-nā'-zi-um], *n.* a hall or building specially equipped for performing physical exercises; (in Germany) a school for the higher branches of literature and science. [L. *gymnasium*].

GYMNAST, [jim'-nast], *n.* a person expert in gymnastic exercises. [Gk. *gumnastes* trainer of athletes].

GYMNASTIC, [jim-nast'-ik], *adj.* relating to physical exercises; (*fig.*) agile, quick-thinking.

GYMNASTICAL, [jim-nast'-ik-al], *adj.* gymnastic.

GYMNASTICALLY, [jim-nast'-ik-al-i], *adv.* in a gymnastic way.

GYMNASTICS, [jim-nast'-iks], *n.(pl.)* the art of teaching exercises designed to promote a healthy and perfectly developed body; gymnastic feats; feats of agility.

GYMNIC, [jim'-nik], *adj.* gymnical.

GYMNICAL, [jim'-nikl], *adj.* relating to, or performing, physical exercises.

GYMNO-, [jim'-nō], *pref.* naked, uncovered. [Gk. *gumnos*].

GYMNOCARPOUS, [jim'-nō-kah'-pus], *adj.* (*bot.*) having exposed fruit. [GYMNO and Gk. *karpos* fruit].

GYMNOGENS, [jim'-nō-jenz'], *n.(pl.)* (*bot.*) plants with exposed seeds. [GYMNO and Gk. *genes* producing].

GYMNOGYNOUS, [jim-noj'-in-us], *adj.* (*bot.*) having a naked ovary. [GYMNO and Gk. *gune* female].

GYMNORHINAL, [jim'-nō-rīn'-al], *adj.* (*zool.*) possessing unfeathered nostrils. [GYMNO and Gk. *rhis* nostril].

GYMNOSOPHIST, [jim-nos'-o-fist], *n.* an Indian ascetic, so called by the Greeks from his habit of living naked. [Gk. *gumnosophistes*].

GYMNOSOPHY, [jim-nos'-o-fi], *n.* the ascetic doctrines of the gymnosophists.

GYMNOSPERM, [jim'-nō-spurm], *n.* (*bot.*) a plant that bears naked seeds, as the conifers. [GYMNO and SPERM].

GYMNOSPERMOUS, [jim'-nō-spurm'-us], *adj.* (*bot.*) having naked seeds.

GYMNOSPORE, [jim'-nō-spaw(r)], *n.* (*bot.*) a naked spore. [GYMNO and SPORE].

GYMNOTUS, [jim-nō'-tus], *n.* a genus of apodal fishes with eel-shaped bodies, able to give off an electric discharge. [GYMNO and Gk. *notos* back].

GYNAECEUM, [ji-nē'-si-um], *n.* (Gk. *antiq.*) women's apartments in a house; (*bot.*) female organs in a plant. [Gk. *gunaikeion* belonging to women].

GYNANDRIA, [jī-nan'-dri-a], *n.(pl.)* (*bot.*) plants whose stamens and pistil are united. [Gk. *gune* woman and ~*aner andros* man].

GYNANDRIAN, [ji-nan'-dri-an], *adj.* gynandrous.

GYNANDROUS, [ji-nan'-drus], *adj.* possessing stamens united with the carpels in the pistils.

GYNARCHY, [jin'-ahk-i], *n.* government by women. [Gk. *gune* woman and *arkhia* rule].

GYNECIAN, [ji-nē'-si-an], *adj.* pertaining to women. [GYNAECEUM].

GYNECOCRACY, [jī'-nik-ok'-ra-si], *n.* government by women. [Gk. *gunaikrokratia*].

GYNECOLOGY, [jī'-nik-ol'-o-ji], *n.* (*med.*) the study of the diseases of women. [Gk. *gunaikos* female and *logos* speech].

GYNEOLATRY, [jī'-ni-ol'-a-tri], *n.* the worship of woman. [Gk. *gune* woman and *latreia* worship].

GYNERIUM, [jī-nēer'-i-um], *n.* the plant, *Gynerium argenteum*, pampas grass.

GYNO-, *pref.* woman, female. [Gk. *gune*].

GYNOBASIC, [jī'-nō-bās'-ik], *adj.* (*bot.*) lateral, as the style in labiate plants. [GYNO and BASIC].

GYNOPHORE, [jī'-nō-faw(r)], *n.* (*bot.*) the pedicle carrying the carpels. [GYNO and ~Gk. *phero* I bear].

GYP, [jip], *n.* (*coll.*) a college servant at Cambridge or Durham Universities. [Uncert.].

GYPSEOUS, [jip'-si-us], *adj.* resembling gypsum. [L. *gypseus*].

GYPSIFEROUS, [jip-sif'-er-us], *adj.* producing gypsum. [GYPSUM and L. *ferre* to bear].

GYPSOGRAPHY, [jip-sog'-ra-fi], *n.* the art of

engraving on gypsum. [GYPSUM and Gk. *graphia* writing].
GYPSOPHILA, [jip-sof′-i-la], *n.* a genus of 50 species of garden flowers having sprays of white or pink flowers. [Gk. *gupsos* chalk and *philos* lover].
GYPSOPLAST, [jip′-sō-plast], *n.* a cast in plaster-of-Paris. [GYPSUM and Gk. *plasso* I fashion].
GYPSUM, [jip′-sum], *n.* sulphate of lime, which when burnt, yields plaster-of-Paris. [L. *gypsum*].
GYPSY, see GIPSY (1).
GYRAL, [jier′-al], *adj.* moving in a circular track.
GYRATE, [jier-āt′], *v.i.* to revolve round a central point, as a tornado, to whirl round. [L. *gyrare*].
GYRATION, [jier-ā′-shun], *n.* the act or process of gyrating; (*zool.*) a whorl of a spiral shell.
GYRATORY, [jier′-at-er-i], *adj.* revolving, moving in a circle.
GYRE (1), [jier], *n.* a circular motion, or a circle described by a moving body, a gyration. [Gk. *guros* ring].
GYRE (2), [jier], *v.i.* to gyrate.
GYRFALCON, see GERFALCON.
GYRO-, *pref.* relating to gyration. [Gk. *guros* ring].
GYROIDAL, [jier-oid′-al], *adj.* arranged or moving in a spiral. [GYRO and Gk. *oeides* like].
GYROMANCY, [jier′-ō-man-si], *n.* divination by walking round in a circle till dizziness produces a fall, the direction of the body being supposed to be full of significance. [GYRO and Gk. *manteia* divination].
GYRON, [jier′-on], *n.* (*her.*) a triangular subordinary, one-eighth of the coat of arms, having an angle at the fess point and the opposite side at the escutcheon edge. [Fr. *giron* from OH Germ. *gero* gusset].

GYRON

GYRONNY, [jier′-on-i], *adj.* (*her.*) separated into gyrons. [Fr. *gironné*].
GYROPTER, [jier-opt′-er], *n.* a flying machine with revolving planes. [GYRO and Gk. *pteron* wing].
GYROSCOPE, [jier′-ō-skōp], *n.* a heavy stabilising flywheel which tends to remain stationary when revolving. [GYRO and SCOPE].
GYROSE, [jier-ōs′], *adj.* (*bot.*) bent at the top like a crook.
GYROSTAT, [jier′-ō-stat], *n.* a form of gyroscope with the flywheel fixed in a rigid case. [GYRO and Gk. *statos* standing].
GYRUS, [jier′-us], *n.* (*anat.*) a convolution.
GYVE (1), GIVE, [jiv], *n.* a fetter, shackle or handcuff. [AFr. *guives*].
GYVE (2), [jiv], *v.t.* to shackle or bind with gyves.

H

H, [āch], the eighth letter of the English alphabet.
HA, [hah], *int.* an exclamation of surprise, joy, grief, or laughter.
HAAR, HARR, HOAR, [hah(r)], *n.* a cold sea-mist. [OIcel. *harr* hoar].
HABEAS CORPUS, [hā′-bi-as-kaw′-pus], *n.* (*leg.*) a writ issued to present a prisoner before justices, in order to determine the legality of his arrest and retention in custody. [L. *habeas corpus* thou shalt have the body].
HABENDUM, [hab-end′-um], *n.* (*leg.*) the clause in a deed defining the estate or interest granted. [L. *habendum* to be had].
HABERDASHER, [hab′-er-dash′-er], *n.* a dealer in drapery and small articles connected with dress-wear. [ME. *haberdashere*].
HABERDASHERY, [hab′-er-dash′-er-i], *n.* the goods sold by a haberdasher; the business of a haberdasher.
HABERDINE†, [hab′-er-dēn], *n.* stock-fish, cod salted and dried in the sun. [Du. *abberdaan*].
HABERGEON, [hab′-er-jun], *n.* a short coat of chain-armour from neck to waist, without sleeves. [OFr. *haubergeoun*].
HABILABLE†, [ha-bil′-abl], *adj.* capable of being clothed.
HABILIMENT, [ha-bil′-i-ment], *n.* dress, a garment, clothing. [Fr. *habillement*].
HABILITORY†, [ha-bil′-i-ter-i], *adj.* wearing clothes.
HABIT (1), [hab′-it], *n.* the ordinary condition or disposition of mind or body; a tendency acquired through frequent repetition; normal behaviour; an action or tendency which has become instinctive; practice, custom; dress, garment, an article of clothing or uniform, *esp.* as distinctive of a class; a wide skirt for women who ride on horseback. [L. *habitus* condition].
HABIT (2), [hab′-it], *v.t.* to dress, clothe; †to inhabit. [L. *habitare*].
HABITABILITY, [hab′-it-a-bil′-i-ti], *n.* habitableness.
HABITABLE, [hab′-it-abl], *adj.* capable of being dwelt in. [L. *habitabilis*].
HABITABLENESS, [hab′-it-abl-nes], *n.* the quality of being habitable.
HABITABLY, [hab′-it-ab-li], *adv.* in a habitable fashion.
HABITANCY, [hab′-it-an-si], *n.* legal settlement; permanent residence.
HABITANT, [hab′-it-ant], *n.* an inhabitant, *esp.* a French Canadian. [Fr. *habitant*].
HABITAT, [hab′-it-at], *n.* the natural environment of an animal or a plant; the region where anything takes place. [L. *habitat* he inhabits].
HABITATION, [hab′-it-ā′-shun], *n.* the act of inhabiting; place of abode, residence; natural locality or environment. [L. *habitatio*].
HABIT-SHIRT, [hab′-it-shurt′], *n.* a thin covering of muslin, etc., worn over the neck and breast.
HABITUAL, [ha-bich′-ōō-al], *adj.* formed or acquired by habit, frequent, usual, normal, customary; having a specific tendency which recurs. [LL. *habitualis*].
HABITUALLY, [ha-bich′-ōō-al-i], *adv.* in an habitual manner.
HABITUALNESS, [ha-bich′-ōō-al-nes], *n.* the condition of being habitual.
HABITUATE, [ha-bich′-ōō-āt], *v.t.* to accustom, make used to. [L. *habituare*].
HABITUATION, [ha-bich′-ōō-ā′-shun], *n.* the state of being habituated; act of habituating.
HABITUDE, [hab′-i-tewd], *n.* customary manner or mode; habit. [L. *habitudo* condition].
HABITUE, habitué, [ha-bit′-yōō-ā], *n.* a person who frequents a place, a regular attender. [Fr. *habitué*].
HACHURE, [ah-shew′-er], *n.* the method of shading by short lines, to indicate a mountain on maps. [Fr. *hachure* cutting].
HACIENDA, [(h)as′-i-en′-da], *n.* a stock-raising farm; an estate or establishment of various kinds in the country. [Span. *hacienda*].
HACK (1), [hak], *n.* the action of hacking; a cut, gash, or notch, crudely made; a kick on the shin. [HACK (6)].
HACK (2), [hak], *n.* a horse kept for hire, *esp.* as a mount; a horse put to all kinds of work; a horse of poor breeding; a decrepit horse; (*fig.*) a writer employed in work of poor quality or of no creative intention. [Span. *haca* nag].
HACK (3), [hak], *n.* a mining tool, a mattock. [Germ. *hacke*].
HACK (4), [hak], *n.* a sort of frame, a rack for food; a pile of bricks not yet fired. [OE. *hæc*].
HACK (5), [hak], *adj.* fit for a hack; hired out; overworked; requiring more persistence than intellect.
HACK (6), [hak], *v.t. and i.* to chop with an axe; to gash, notch, or cut clumsily; to kick the shins; to break up clods of earth; to trim a hedge; to rack the chest by coughing. [OE. *haccian*].
HACK (7), [hak], *v.t. and i.* to let out on hire; to engage to do hack work; to ride a hack; to work as a literary hack. [HACK (2)].
HACKBERRY, see HAGBERRY.
HACKBOLT, [hak′-bōlt], *n.* the great shearwater, *Puffinus major*.
HACKBUT, HAQUEBUT, [hak′-but], *n.* an arquebus. [Du. *haakbus*].

The accent ′ after a syllable = stress (a-bahft′). The mark ¯ over a vowel = length ā (*maid*). ah (*pass*).

HACKEE, [hak'-ē], *n.* the American chipmunk, *Tamias striatus.* [Echoic].

HACKERY, [hak'-er-i], *n.* an Indian cart drawn by oxen. [Hind. *chhakra*].

HACKET, [hak'-et], *n.* the kittiwake, *Rissa tridactyla.*

HACKING, [hak'-ing], *adj.* harsh and dry, as a cough racking.

HACKLE (1), [hakl], *n.* the long, brilliant plumage on the neck of certain birds, as a cock or peacock; an artificial fly made of these feathers, used by fishermen. [OE. *hacele* cloak].

HACKLE (2), [hakl], *n.* a stickleback, a fish of the genus *Gasterosteus.*

HACKLE (3), [hakl], *n.* a comb used for treating flax. [ME. *hakell, hekele*].

HACKLE (4), [hakl], *v.t.* to prepare flax with a hackle.

HACKLER, [hakl'-er], *n.* a person who hackles flax.

HACKLET, HAGLET, [hak'-let], *n.* the shearwater.

HACKLY, [hak'-li], *adj.* rough, broken crudely; (*min.*) having short, sharp points on the surface.

HACKMATACK, [hak'-ma-tak], *n.* the tamarack or American larch, *Larix americana.* [NAmer. Indian. *hackmatack*].

HACKNEY (1), [hak'-ni], *n.* a horse hired out as a hack; a hackney-coach. [ME. *hakenei*, OFr. *haquenee* pad-horse].

HACKNEY (2), [hak'-ni], *adj.* let out on hire.

HACKNEY (3), [hak'-ni], *v.t.* to make commonplace or trite by over-use.

HACKNEY-COACH, [hak'-ni-kōch'], *n.* a four-wheeled horse-drawn carriage for hire.

HACKNEY-COACH

HACKNEYED, [hak'-nid], *adj.* commonplace, much used, trite.

HACKNEYMAN, [hak'-ni-man], *n.* a man who lets out horses and carriages for hire; a jobmaster.

HACQUETON, [hak'-ton], *n.* the stuffed and quilted jacket worn under a coat of mail. [OFr. *hacqueton*].

HAD, [had], *pret. and p.pt.* of HAVE. [OE. *hæfde*].

HADDOCK, [had'-ok], *n.* the sea fish, *Gadus æglefinus*, eaten as a food. [Unkn.].

HADE (1), [hād], *n.* (*mining*) a deviation from the vertical of a fault or vein. [Uncert.].

HADE (2), [hād], *v.i.* to incline from the vertical.

HADES, [hā'-dēz], *n.* the region believed to be inhabited by the dead, the underworld, hell. [Gk. *Hades* Pluto, god of the lower world].

HADING, [hā'-ding], *n.* a hade.

HADITH, [had'-ith], *n.* the body of oral tradition concerning Mohammed. [Arab. *hadith* tale].

HADJ, [haj], *n.* a pilgrimage to Mecca undertaken by Moslems. [Arab. *hajj*].

HADJI, [haj'-ē], *n.* a Moslem who has performed his hadj. [Arab. *hajji*].

HAEMA-, *pref.* blood. [Gk. *haima*].

HAEMACYTE, [hē'-ma-sīt], *n.* a blood corpuscle. [HAEMA and Gk. *kutos* vessel].

HAEMADYNAMOMETER, [hē'-ma-di'-nam-om'-it-er], *n.* an instrument for determining blood pressure. [HAEMA and DYNAMOMETER].

HAEMAL, [hē'-mal], *adj.* pertaining to the blood.

HAEMATEMESIS, [hē'-ma-tem'-es-is], *n.* (*med.*) vomiting of blood from the stomach. [HAEMATO and Gk. *emeo* I vomit].

HAEMATIC, [hē-mat'-ik], *adj.* (*med.*) relating to, resembling, acting on, the blood. [Gk. *haimatikos*].

HAEMATIN, HEMATIN, [hē'-ma-tin], *n.* (*chem.*) the colouring principle in blood.

HAEMATITE, HEMATITE, [hē'-ma-tīt], *n.* an iron ore, red or brown ferric oxide, red ochre. [Gk. *haimatites* bloodlike].

HAEMATO-, *pref.* relating to or consisting of blood. [Gk. *haimato* from *haima* blood].

HAEMATOCELE, [hē'-ma-tō-sēl], *n.* (*med.*) a tumour containing blood. [HAEMATO and Gk. *kele* tumour].

HAEMATOID, [hē'-ma-toid], *adj.* of the appearance of blood. [HAEMATO and Gk. *oeides* like].

HAEMATOLOGY, [hē'-ma-tol'-o-ji], *n.* the science of the blood. [HAEMATO and Gk. *logos* speech].

HAEMATOSIN, [hē'-ma-tō'-sin], *n.* haematin. [Gk. *haima haimatos* blood].

HAEMATOSIS, [hē'-ma-tō'-sis], *n.* formation into blood; oxygenation of the blood in the lungs. [HAEMATO and Gk. *osis* denoting condition].

HAEMATOXYLIN, [hē'-ma-toks'-il-in], *n.* (*chem.*) a crystalline substance, the colouring principle of logwood. [HAEMATO and Gk. *xulon* wood].

HAEMATOZOA, [hē'-ma-tō-zō'-a], *n.(pl.)* entozoa in the blood. [HAEMATO and Gk. *zoa* animals].

HAEMATURIA, [hē'-ma-tyōōer'-i-a], *n.* (*med.*) haemorrhagic discharge from the urinary organs. [MdL. *haematuria*].

HAEMIC, [hē'-mik], *adj.* belonging to, relating to, the blood.

HAEMO-, *pref.* short form of HAEMATO-.

HAEMOCHROME, [hē'-mō-krōm], *n.* haemoglobin. [HAEMO and CHROME].

HAEMOGLOBIN, [hē'-mō-glōb'-in], *n.* (*physiol.*) a red fluid substance in the red corpuscles of the blood, which takes in and distributes the oxygen. [HAEMO and GLOBE].

HAEMOPHILIA, [hē'-mō-fil'-i-a], *n.* (*med.*) an hereditary disease marked by a tendency to excessive haemorrhage. [HAEMO and Gk. *philia* tendency to].

HAEMOPHTHALMIA, [hē'-mof-thal'-mi-a], *n.* effusion of blood in the eye, the symptom of pink-eye. [HAEMO and OPHTHALMIA].

HAEMOPTYSIS, [hē-mop'-ti-sis], *n.* (*med.*) a coughing up of blood from the lungs. [HAEMO and Gk. *ptusis* spitting].

HAEMORRHAGE, HEMORRHAGE, [hem'-er-ij], *n.* (*med.*) discharge of blood from a blood vessel, *esp.* when violent. [G. *haimorrhagia*].

HAEMORRHAGIC, [hem'-er-aj'-ik], *adj.* relating to haemorrhage.

HAEMORRHOIDAL, [hem'-er-oid'-al], *adj.* relating to haemorrhoids.

HAEMORRHOIDS, HEMORRHOIDS, [hem'-er-oidz], *n.(pl.)* piles. [L. *haemorrhoida*].

HAEMOSTASIS, [hē'-mō-stā'-sis], *n.* (*med.*) a stoppage or checking of bleeding. [HAEMO and Gk. *stasis* stoppage].

HAEMOSTATICAL, [hē'-mō-stat'-ik-al], *adj.* checking haemorrhage. [HAEMO and Gk. *statikos* checking].

HAFFETS, [haf'-etz], *n.(pl.)* (*dial.*) the temples; the side of the head, the cheek. [OE. *healfheafod* half-head].

HAFFLE, [hafl], *v.i.* (*dial.*) to speak unintelligibly; to prevaricate by mumbling.

HAFIZ, [hah'-fiz], *n.* a person who knows the Koran by heart. [Pers. *hafiz*].

HAFNIUM, [haf'-ni-um], *n.* the chemical element Hf, found with zirconium. [L. *Hafnia* Copenhagen].

HAFT (1), [hahft], *n.* a handle or shaft fitted to a tool. [OE. *hæft*].

HAFT (2), [hahft], *v.t.* to fit with a haft.

HAG (1), [hag], *n.* an ugly, dirty, vindictive old woman; a witch. [ME. *hagge*].

HAG (2), [hag], *n.* a patch of firm ground in a bog; the stepped edge of a hole cut out of peat in a bog; a soft patch in a bog. [~OIcel. *högg* cut, gap].

HAG (3), [hag], *n.* a fish parasite allied to the lamprey, the hagfish.

HAG (4), (**hagging, hagged**), [hag], *v.t.* to harass; to irritate, to make cross, vex. [HAG (1)].

HAGBERRY, HACKBERRY, [hag'-be'-ri], *n.* a tree of the genus *Celtis*, allied to the elm, with edible fruit; the bird-cherry, *Prunus Padus.* [~Dan. *haeggebaer*].

HAGDEN, HAGDOWN, [hag'-den], *n.* the great shearwater; the hackbolt. [Unkn.].

HAGFISH, [hag'-fish], *n.* the hag, *Myxine glutinosa*, a parasite feeding on the entrails of fishes. [Uncert.].

HAGGARD (1), [hag'-erd], *n.* an untrained hawk.

HAGGARD (2), [hag'-erd], *adj.* hollow-eyed and tired-looking, worn out, drawn, pinched, gaunt; (*falconry*) wild. [Fr. *hagard*].

HAGGARDLY, [hag'-erd-li], *adv.* in a haggard fashion.

HAGGED, [hag'-id], *adj.* lean, ugly, like a hag.

HAGGIS, [hag'-is], *n.* a Scottish dish made of certain internal organs of a sheep chopped up and mixed with oatmeal and suet, highly seasoned with spices and onions, and boiled in a sheep's stomach-bag. [ME. *hageys*].

HAGGISH, [hag'-ish], *adj.* like a hag; ugly, dirty, vindictive.

HAGGISHLY, [hag'-ish-li], *adv.* in the manner of a hag.

HAGGLE, [hagl], *v.i.* to argue, wrangle, bargain, *esp.* over a money payment. [Uncert.].

HAGGLER, [hagl'-er], *n.* a person who haggles.

HAGIARCHY, [hag'-i-ahk-i], *n.* government by saints; the order of saints. [HAGIO and Gk. *arkhia* rule].

HAGIO-, [hag'-i-ō], *pref.* holy, sacred. [Gk. *hagios*].

HAGIOGRAPHA, [hag'-i-og'-ra-fa], *n.* (*bibl.*) those Old Testament books not grouped under the Law and the Prophets. [Gk. *hagiographa* holy writings].

HAGIOGRAPHER, [hag'-i-og'-raf-er], *n.* a writer in the Hagiographa; a writer of a hagiography.

HAGIOGRAPHICAL, [hag'-i-ō-graf'-ikal], *adj.* pertaining to hagiography or to the Hagiographa.

HAGIOGRAPHY, [hag'-i-og'-ra-fi], *n.* the study of the lives of saints; an anthology of saints' biographies. [HAGIO and Gk. *graphia* writing].

HAGIOLATRY, [hag'-i-ol'-a-tri], *n.* the extreme worship of saints. [HAGIO and Gk. *latrea* worship].

HAGIOLOGIST, [hag'-i-ol'-o-jist], *n.* one versed in hagiology.

HAGIOLOGY, [hag'-i-ol'-o-ji], *n.* a study of the lives of saints; a collection of writings recording the lives and traditional legends of the saints. [HAGIO and Gk. *logos* speech].

HAGIOSCOPE, [ha'-gi-ō-skōp'], *n.* (*arch.*) an oblique opening in a church to enable those in the side aisle to catch a glimpse of the altar. [HAGIO and SCOPE].

HAGLET, see HACKLET.

HAG-RIDDEN, [hag'-rid-en], *adj.* controlled by a tyrannous female; afflicted with nightmare.

HAGSHIP, [hag'-ship], *n.* the state or status of a hag.

HAGTAPER, [hag'-tā'-per], *n.* (*dial.*) a plant, the mullein, *Verbascum Thapsus*. [HAG and TAPER].

HAH, [hah], *int.* an exclamation of surprise, triumph or effort.

HAHA, [ha'-hah, haw'-haw], *n.* a low boundary fence or wall sunk between slopes.

HAIK (1), HEYKE, [hāk], *n.* a medieval cloak, similar to a huke. [Uncert.].

HAIK (2), HYKE, [hīk], *n.* a length of cloth worn by an Arab as an outer garment. [Arab. *hayk*].

HAIL (1), [hāl], *n.* frozen rain, a shower of this; anything which strikes sharply in rapid succession. [OE. *hagol*].

HAIL (2), [hāl], *n.* the action of greeting; a salutation, call; the range of hearing a shout. [HAIL (4)].

HAIL (3), [hāl], *v.t. and i.* to hurl a rapid succession of; to shower down hail. [HAIL (1)].

HAIL (4), [hāl], *v.t.* to shout or say " hail " as a greeting, to salute, welcome; to address in an official capacity; to attract the attention of by shouting or waving; to signal; **to h. from,** to come from. [OIcel. *heilla*].

HAIL (5), [hāl], *int.* a cry of greeting or salutation. [OIcel. *heill*].

HAIL-FELLOW, [hāl'-fel'-ō], *n.* an intimate companion; **h. well met,** on familiar terms.

HAILSTONE, [hāl'-stōn], *n.* a frozen raindrop falling in a small, hard pellet.

HAILSTORM, [hāl'-stawm], *n.* a storm of hail.

HAILY, [hāl'-i], *adj.* accompanied by, consisting of, hail.

HAIR, [hāer], *n.* one of the many fine, threadlike filaments that grow from the skin of an animal or human being; the whole growth of such filaments covering the scalp of a human being; a fine fibre growing from the surface of a stem, stalk, or leaf; a thread like wire; **to keep one's h. on,** (*slang*) to remain calm; **to make one's h. stand on end,** to horrify; **not to turn a h.,** to remain composed, to show no sign of fear; **to split hairs,** to argue over trivial details or over-subtle distinctions. [OE. *hær*].

HAIRBELL, [hāer'-bel], *n.* the flower, *Campanula rotundifolia*, the bluebell of Scotland.

HAIRBREADTH, [hāer'-bredth], *adj.* very narrow.

HAIR-BROOM, [hāer'-broom], *n.* a broom with the head set with hair.

HAIR-BRUSH, [hāer'-brush], *n.* a brush used for the hair.

HAIR-CLOTH, [hāer'-kloth], *n.* a textile woven chiefly of horsehair.

HAIRDRESSER, [hāer'-dres'-er], *n.* a barber.

HAIRED, [hāerd], *adj.* provided with hair.

HAIR-GRASS, [hāer'-grahs], *n.* a grass of the genus *Aira*, having very fine leaves.

HAIRINESS, [hāer'-i-nes], *n.* the condition of being hairy.

HAIR-LACE, [hāer'-lās], *n.* a fillet for binding a woman's hair.

HAIRLESS, [hāer'-les], *adj.* without hair; bald.

HAIRLINE, [hāer'-līn], *n.* a line made of hair; a hair stroke, a very thin line.

HAIR-NET, [hāer'-net], *n.* a fine net for keeping a woman's hair in place.

HAIR-OIL, [hāer'-oil], *n.* perfumed oil for dressing and setting the hair.

HAIR-PENCIL, [hāer'-pen'-sil], *n.* a brush made of very fine hair used in water-colour painting.

HAIR-PIN, [hāer'-pin], *n.* a two-pronged pin used in keeping the hair in place; **h. bend,** a dangerous sharp bend in a road which almost doubles back on itself.

HAIR-POWDER, [hāer'-pow'-der], *n.* a fine perfumed powder of pulverized starch formerly used for sprinkling the hair of the head or wig.

HAIR-SALT, [hāer'-sawlt], *n.* the mineral epsomite, found as fine fibres.

HAIRSBREADTH, [hāerz'-bredth], *n.* the breadth of a hair; a minute distance.

HAIR-SLIDE, [hāer'-slīd], *n.* a clip made of metal, tortoise-shell, etc., to keep women's hair in place.

HAIR-SPACE, [hāer'-spās], *n.* (*typ.*) the thinnest printer's space between two type-set words.

HAIR-SPLITTING (1), [hāer'-split'-ing], *n.* the making of over-subtle distinctions in argument, quibbling.

HAIR-SPLITTING (2), [hāer'-split'-ing], *adj.* characterized by quibbling.

HAIRSPRING, [hāer'-spring], *n.* a very fine spring on the balance-wheel of a watch.

HAIRSTROKE, [hāer'-strōk], *n.* the thin upward stroke of the pen in copy-book handwriting.

HAIRTAIL, [hāer'-tāl], *n.* a tropical fish of the genus *Trichiurus*, without caudal fin.

HAIRWORM, [hāer'-wurm], *n.* a genus of slender freshwater worms, resembling a long hair.

HAIRY, [hāer'-i], *adj.* covered with, relating to, or resembling hair; **h. heeled,** (*slang*) ill-mannered.

HAKE, [hāk], *n.* a sea-fish, *Merluccius vulgaris*, of coarse flesh, allied to the cod. [ME. *hake*, ~OE. *haca* hook].

HAKE

HAKIM, [hah'-kim], *n.* an Indian philosopher or a physician. [Arab. *hakim* wise].

HALATION, [ha-lā'-shun], *n.* a blurring caused by strong light reflected from the back in a developed negative.

HALBERD, [hal'-berd, hawl'-berd], *n.* an obsolete military weapon combining the blade of a battle-axe with a spear-head mounted on a long handle. [MHGerm. *halmbarte*].

HALBERDIER, [hal'-(haw-') berd-ēer'], *n.* a soldier armed with a halberd.

HALCYON (1), [hal'-si-on], *n.* the kingfisher bird; a wood kingfisher of the genus *Halcyon*. [Gk. *alkuon*].

HALCYON (2), [hal'-si-on], *adj.* relating to the kingfisher; calm, peaceful, happy; **h. days,** the fourteen days divided by the winter solstice, believed in folk-lore always to be accompanied by fine weather, to enable the kingfisher to breed peacefully; (*fig.*) a time of exceeding happiness, peace and prosperity.

HALBERD

HALE (1), [hāl], *adj.* sound in body, healthy, robust, vigorous; **h. and hearty,** healthy, fit. [OE. *hal*].

HALE (2), [hāl], *v.t.* to haul, to drag along, pull. [Fr. *haler*].

HALENESS, [hāl'-nes], *n.* the condition of being hale.

HALF (1), (*pl.* **halves**), [hahf], *n.* one of two equal parts into which a thing may be divided; one of two complementary portions, weights, values, *esp.* when of the same size; **better h.** (*coll.*) a wife; **by halves,** not thoroughly. [OE. *half*].

HALF (2), [hahf], *adj.* consisting of, equal to, a half; incomplete, imperfect.

HALF (3), [hahf], *adv.* in part, to the extent of a half; imperfectly; **not h.,** (*coll.*) rather.

HALF-AND-HALF, [hahf'-and-hahf'], *n.* a mixture of two components in equal quantities, *esp.* of stout and ale; an insincere person, a compromiser.

HALF-BACK, [hahf'-bak'], *n.* a player who takes up a position behind the forwards at football.

HALF-BLOOD, [hahf'-blud], *n.* a blood relationship through one parent; a person related in this way;

a person whose parents are of two different races, a half-breed.
HALF-BLOODED, [hahf'-blud'-id], *adj.* having parents of different breeds; partly high-born and partly low-born.
HALF-BLUE, [hahf'-bloo'], *n.* a colour awarded at Oxford or Cambridge for minor sports; a representative who has won this.
HALF-BOUND, [hahf'-bownd], *adj.* (*bookbinding*) bound with leather only on the back and corners.
HALF-BRED, [hahf'-bred], *adj.* of mixed breeding; imperfectly bred.
HALF-BREED (1), [hahf'-brēd'], *n.* a person whose parents are of mixed races, *esp.* of white and black races.
HALF-BREED (2), [hahf'-brēd'], *adj.* half-blooded; hybrid.
HALF-BROTHER, [hahf'-bruTH'-er], *n.* a brother by one parent only.
HALF-CASTE (1), [hahf'-kahst'], *n.* a person born of a white parent and a coloured parent.
HALF-CASTE (2), [hahf'-kahst], *adj.* of mixed race.
HALF-COCK, [hahf'-kok], *n.* the position of the trigger of a gun when retained by the first notch.
HALF-CROWN, [hahf-krown'], *n.* a silver coin worth 2s. 6d.; a sum of money having this value.
HALF-DEAD, [hahf'-ded'], *adj.* almost dead; tired and exhausted.
HALF-DOLLAR, [hahf'-dol'-er], *n.* an American silver coin worth 50 cents; (*coll.*) half-a-crown.
HALFER, [hahf'-er], *n.* a person who possesses only half; a male fallow-deer gelded.
HALF-FACE, [hahf'-fās'], *adv.* in profile.
HALF-HEARTED, [hahf'-haht'-id], *adj.* unenthusiastic, not resolute, having mixed sympathies.
HALF-HEARTEDLY, [hahf'-haht'-id-li], *adv.* in a half-hearted manner.
HALF-HEARTEDNESS, [hahf'-haht'-id-nes], *n.* the quality of being half-hearted.
HALF-HITCH, [hahf'-hich], *n.* a kind of hitch formed by looping the rope, string, or thread, and drawing the end through the loop.
HALF-HOLIDAY, [hahf'-hol'-i-dā], *n.* a holiday from work or school, commencing at noon or one o'clock.
HALF-LENGTH (1), [hahf'-length'], *n.* a half-length portrait.
HALF-LENGTH (2), [hahf'-length], *adj.* (of a portrait) taking in only the top half of the body.
HALF-MARK, [hahf'-mahk'], *n.* an old coin worth 6s. 8d. sterling.
HALF-MAST, [hahf'-mahst'], *adv.* (of a flag) lower than the masthead, in sign of mourning.
HALF-MOON, [hahf'-moon], *n.* the moon when only half of its face can be seen; anything in the shape of this; an egg-shaped fish found in the Pacific Ocean; (*fort.*) an outwork at a salient angle whose gorge is in the form of a half-disk.
HALF-MOURNING, [hahf'-mawn'-ing], *n.* a mode of dress of black relieved by grey or white, worn during the period between full mourning and normal dress.
HALF-NELSON, [hahf'-nel'-son], *n.* a hold in wrestling with one arm held under the opponent's armpit while facing his rear, and the hands pressing on the nape of his neck.
HALF-NOTE, [hahf'-nōt], *n.* (*mus.*) a minim, a semitone.
HALF-PAST, [hahf'-pahst'], *adv.* half an hour past.
HALF-PAY (1), [hahf'-pā'], *n.* reduced pay given to a retired officer.
HALF-PAY (2), [hahf'-pā'], *adj.* retired on half-pay.
HALFPENNY (1), (*pl.* **halfpence**), [hāp'-ni], *n.* a British copper coin worth half a penny.
HALFPENNY (2), [hāp'-ni], *adj.* of the value of half a penny; cheap, trivial, worthless.
HALF-PIKE, [hahf'-pīk'], *n.* a half-sized pike.
HALF-PRICE, [hahf'-prīs'], *adv.* and *adj.* at a reduced charge.
HALF-RATER, [hahf'-rāt'-er], *n.* a small racing yacht half a sail-ton in size.
HALF-ROUND, [hahf'-rownd], *n.* a semicircular section, *esp.* of a moulding.
HALF-SEAS, [hahf'-sēz], *adj.* (*naut.*) halfway across the sea; **h.-over**, (*slang*) almost drunk.
HALF-SHIFT, [hahf'-shift], *n.* (*mus.*) a move of the hand upward on a violin to the second position.
HALF-SIGHTED, [hahf'-sīt'-id], *adj.* of weak discernment.
HALF-SISTER, [hahf'-sis'-ter], *n.* a sister by one parent only.
HALF-SOVEREIGN, [hahf'-sov'-rin], *n.* (a gold coin worth) ten shillings.
HALF-STRAINED, [hahf'-strānd], *adj.* half-bred; imperfect.
HALF-SWORD, [hahf'-sawd], *n.* a fight within the range of half the length of a sword; a close fight.
HALF-TIMBERED, [hahf'-tim'-berd], *adj.* (*arch.*) having the main supports of a wall in timber, and the remaining parts filled in with brick, stone, and plaster.
HALF-TIMER, [hahf'-tīm'-er], *n.* a pupil who spent half a day at school and half a day working for wages.
HALF-TITLE, [hahf'-titl], *n.* a short title of a book printed usually on the leaf preceding the title-page.
HALF-TONE, [hahf'-tōn], *n.* a process block obtained by photographing the drawing or other object through a glass screen covered with a network of fine lines.
HALFWAY (1), [hahf'-wā], *adj.* equally distant from the extremes.
HALFWAY (2), [hahf'-wā'], *adv.* in the middle, at half the distance from each end.
HALF-WIT, [hahf'-wit], *n.* a simpleton, an imbecile, a fool.
HALF-WITTED, [hahf'-wit'-id], *adj.* mentally deficient, foolish.
HALF-YEARLY (1), [hahf'-yur'-li], *adj.* occurring every half-year.
HALF-YEARLY (2), [hahf'-yur'-li], *adv.* twice a year, at intervals of half a year.
HALIBUT, HOLIBUT†, [hal'-i-but], *n.* the edible fish, *Hippoglossus vulgaris*, the largest of the flat-fishes. [ME. *hali* holy and BUTT].
HALICORE, [hal'-i-kaw(r)], *n.* (*zool.*) the dugong. [Gk. *hals* sea and *kore* maiden].
HALIDOM†, [hal'-i-dum], *n.* a small holy relic carried for luck. [OE. *haligdom*].
HALIEUTIC, [hal'-i-ew'-tik], *adj.* pertaining to fishing. [Gk. *halieutikos*].
HALION, [hal'-yun], *n.* a sea-fish, the skipper, *Scomberesox saurus*.
HALIOTIS, [hal'-i-ō'-tis], *n.* an ear-shell, a univalve sea-shell from certain species of which is obtained mother-of-pearl. [Gk. *hals* sea and *ous otos* ear].
HALIOTOID, [hal'-i-ot-oid], *adj.* (*zool.*) ear-shaped. [Gk. *haliotis* ear-shell and *oeides* like].
HALITOSIS, [hal-i-tō'-sis], *n.* (*med.*) bad breath. [L. *halitus* breath].
HALITUOUS, [ha-lit'-yoo-us], *adj.* (*med.*) like breath; vaporous. [L. *halitus* breath].
HALL, [hawl], *n.* formerly, the large chamber or apartment used as a living-room in a feudal court or castle; the spacious dining-room in a palace, castle, etc.; the apartment, corridor or passage into which the entrance opens; a mansion, large residence; a large public building used for municipal administrative purposes, assemblies or social functions; a college. [OE. *heall*].
HALL-DOOR, [hawl'-daw(r)'], *n.* the front-door.
HALLELUJAH, HALLELUIAH, [hal'-i-loo'-ya], *int.* a word of praise used in religious worship as a shout, peal or refrain. [Heb. *hallelu-yah* praise ye Jehovah].
HALLIARD, see HALYARD.
HALL-MARK (1), [hawl'-mahk], *n.* a small embossed mark stamped on gold or silver or plate, *esp.* at Goldsmiths' Hall, as an official guarantee of quality; (*fig.*) any sign of distinction or characteristic of quality.
HALL-MARK (2), [hawl'-mahk], *v.t.* to stamp gold or silver or plate with the official hall-mark; (*fig.*) to provide with a guarantee of high quality.
HALLO, [ha-lō', hu-lō'], *int.* an introductory remark when meeting someone; a call for attention. [Echoic].
HALLOO (1), [ha-loo'], *n.* a cry to attract the attention of someone in the distance; a call to hounds at a hunt. [ME. *halow* call].
HALLOO (2), [ha-loo'], *v.t.* and *i.* to stimulate a pack of hounds to the chase; to shout halloos; to shout.
HALLOW, [hal'-ō], *v.t.* to set apart for sacred use; to consecrate; to reverence or regard as sacred; to render holy. [OE. *halga* saint].
HALLOWEEN, [hal'-ō-ēn'], *n.* the eve of All-Saints' Day, falling on October 31. [HALLOW and E(V)EN].
HALLOWMASS†, [hal'-ō-mas], *n.* the religious ceremony of All-Saints' Day.
HALLUCINATION, [hal-ew'-si-nā'-shun], *n.* the effect of a temporarily deranged mind by which the senses create and present an object to themselves which in reality does not exist; the object of such a subjective perception. [L. *hallucinari*].

HALLUCINATORY, [hal-ew'-si-nā'-ter-i], *adj.* resembling, or pertaining to, an hallucination.

HALLUX, (*pl.* **halluces**), [hal'-uks], *n.* (*anat.*) the big toe in mammals; the hind toe in birds. [L. *allex*].

HALM, see HAULM.

HALMA, [hal'-ma], *n.* a game for two or four players on a board of 256 squares. [Gk. *halma* a leaping].

HALO, [hā'-lō], *n.* a luminous circle surrounding the sun or moon; a ring of light or a white, gold or silver disk encircling the head of Christ, a saint, etc., in paintings; (*fig.*) glory or attractiveness associated with a romantic ideal, act. etc.; (*path.*) a ring of colour surrounding a nipple. [Gk. *halos* threshing floor on which a ring was worn by the oxen's hooves].

HALO

HALOGEN, [hal'-ō-jen], *n.* (*chem.*) one of the chemical elements allied to chlorine. [Gk. *hals* salt and *genes* born of].

HALOGENOUS, [hal-oj'-in-us], *adj.* relating to, of the nature of, a halogen.

HALOID, [hal'-oid], *adj.* (*chem.*) resembling a salt; **h. salt,** a salt formed by the reaction of a halogen to a metal. [Gk. *hals* salt and *oeides* like].

HALOPHYTE, [hal'-ō-fīt], *n.* a plant living in salt soil or salt water. [Gk. *hals* salt and *phuton* plant].

HALT† (**1**), [hawlt], *n.* lameness, a limp. [HALT (4)].

HALT (**2**), [hawlt], *n.* a temporary stoppage of any act of work or movement; a pause; a place to stop at, a stage on a journey or route where buses, trams, etc., stop to pick up passengers; a small wayside station on a main railway line to which a regular service is not maintained. [Fr. *halte*].

HALT (**3**), [hawlt], *adj.* lame, crippled, having a limp. [OE. *halt, healt*].

HALT (**4**), [hawlt], *v.i.* to be lame, to walk with a limp; (*fig.*) to be unable to make up one's mind, to hesitate; to speak falteringly or in disconnected phrases; to argue illogically; to be faulty in metre. [OE. *haltian, healtian*].

HALT (**5**), [hawlt], *v.t. and i.* (*milit.*) to bring a body of troops to a halt by a command; to cease walking, marching, moving or any activity for the time being. [HALT (2)].

HALTER (**1**), [hawl'-ter], *n.* a short rope for leading a horse; a rope ending in a slip noose for hanging criminals. [OE. *hælftre*].

HALTER (**2**), [hawl'-ter], *v.t.* to put a halter on; to bind with a halter.

HALTERES, [hal-tēer'-ēz], *n.* (*entom.*) the pair of club-like filaments in flies in place of the second pair of wings. [Gk. *halteres* dumb-bells].

HALTING, [hawlt'-ing], *adj.* stumbling, limping, faltering, hesitating.

HALTINGLY, [hawlt'-ing-li], *adv.* in halting fashion.

HALVE, [hahv], *v.t.* to divide into two equal parts; to lessen to a half; to offer or take an equal share; **to h. a hole or match,** (*golf*) to complete the hole or match in equal strokes; **to go halves,** to share equally. [ME. *halven*].

HALYARD, HALLIARD, [hal'-yahd], *n.* (*naut.*) a rope for hoisting flags or sails up the mast. [ME. *halier* carrier and YARD].

HAM, [ham], *n.* the inner or hind part of the thigh; the thigh of an animal, *esp.* of a pig, salted and dried in smoke; a portion or dish of slices of this meat; **a h. actor,** (*slang*) a bad actor in a stiff and stilted style. [OE. *hamm, homm*].

HAMADRYAD, [ham'-a-drī'-ad], *n.* (*myth.*) a wood-nymph believed to live in a tree and die with it; (*zool.*) the Indian king cobra, *Naja bungarus*; the Arabian baboon, *Cynocephalus hamadryas.* [Gk. *hamadruas*].

HAMATE, [hā'-māt], *adj.* hooked, or set with hooks. [L. *hamatus*].

HAMBLE†, [hambl], *v.t.* to maim a dog's foot. [OE. *hamelian*].

HAMBURG, [ham'-burg], *n.* a small breed of domestic fowl; a species of grape. [*Hamburg*, in Germany].

HAMBURGER, [ham'-burg-er], *n.* a steak usually cooked or eaten with onions; a kind of breakfast sausage.

HAME, [hām], *n.* one of the curved bars fitted with a loop by which the trace is fastened to the collar of a horse. [ME. *hame*].

HAMIFORM, [hā'-mi-fawm], *adj.* shaped like a hook. [L. *hamus* hook and FORM].

HAMITE, [hā'-mīt], *n.* a fossil cephalopod with a shell shaped like a hook. [L. *hamus* hook].

HAMITIC, [ham-it'-ik], *adj.* relating to Ham or his descendants; negroid. [*Ham*, Noah's son].

HAMLET, [ham'-let], *n.* a small village; a little group of cottages in the country. [AFr. *hamelet*].

HAMMAM, HUMMUM, [ham'-am], *n.* a Turkish bath. [Arab. *hammam*].

HAMMER (**1**), [ham'-er], *n.* a tool for striking, beating, or driving in by blows, having a wooden handle to which is fitted crosswise a short thick head of metal; anything which resembles this in function; one of the mechanical felted heads of a piano action; the striking device of a bell; an auctioneer's mallet; a heavy piece of machinery for crushing, beating, etc.; the percussion head of a gun-lock released by the trigger; **to come under the h.,** to be sold by auction; **to go at it h. and tongs,** to set about anything with great energy. [OE. *hamor*].

HAMMER (**2**), [ham'-er], *v.t.* to beat, strike, drive with a hammer; to strike, punch repeatedly; (*coll.*) to defeat crushingly; to declare a Stock Exchange member a defaulter; *v.i.* to wield a hammer; **to h. into,** (*fig.*) to fix in the mind by forceful repetition; **to h. out,** (*fig.*) to force a solution to a problem by assiduous application.

HAMMERABLE, [ham'-er-abl], *adj.* that may be beaten into shape with a hammer.

HAMMER-AXE, [ham'-er-aks'], *n.* an implement whose head combines a hammer and an axe.

HAMMERBEAM, [ham'-er-bēm'], *n.* (*arch.*) a short beam projecting from the top of a wall instead of a tie-beam.

HAMMERCLOTH, [ham'-er-kloth], *n.* the cloth which covers the box containing the repair outfit of a coach or carriage.

HAMMER-DRESSED, [ham'-er-drest'], *adj.* (of a stone) dressed with a pick or pointed hammer.

HAMMERER, [ham'-er-er], *n.* a worker with a hammer.

HAMMERHEAD, [ham'-er-hed], *n.* the metal head of a hammer; a species of shark, *Zygæna malleus*; an African bird, the umbre, *Scopus umbretta*.

HAMMERLESS, [ham'-er-les], *adj.* without a hammer.

HAMMER-LOCK, [ham'-er-lok], *n.* a hold in wrestling in which the opponent's arm is bent and held behind his back.

HAMMERMAN, [ham'-er-man], *n.* a hammerer, a smith.

HAMMERHEAD

HAMMER-TOE, [ham'-er-tō'], *n.* (*med.*) a deformed toe with the joint abnormally bent.

HAMMOCK, [ham'-ok], *n.* a hanging bed or open mattress, usually of canvas or network, suspended by cords from hooks; **h. chair,** a folding chair with a canvas seat and back. [Span. *hamaca*].

HAMOSE, [hā'-mōs], *adj.* hamous.

HAMOUS, [hā'-mus], *adj.* (*bot.*) having the end hooked. [L. *hamus* hook].

HAMPER (**1**), [ham'-per], *n.* a large basket with a lid, used for carrying food, vegetables, etc. [~HANAPER].

HAMPER (**2**), [ham'-per], *n.* a fetter or shackle; (*naut.*) obstructive but necessary objects. [HAMPER (3)].

HAMPER (**3**), [ham'-per], *v.t.* to impede, hinder, obstruct, cramp. [ME. *hampren*].

HAMSHACKLE, [ham'-shakl], *v.t.* to fasten the head of an animal to one of its forelegs with a rope.

HAMSTER, [ham'-ster], *n.* a large rat of the genus *Cricetus*, having two cheek-pouches for holding grain. [OHGerm. *hamistro, hamastro*].

HAMSTRING (**1**), [ham'-string], *n.* one of the tendons behind the knee; a large tendon behind the hock of a horse.

HAMSTRING (**2**), [ham'-string], *v.t.* to lame by severing a hamstring, to hough; (*fig.*) to put out of action.

HAMULAR, [ham'-yoo-ler], *adj.* resembling a small hook.

HAMULATE, [ham'-yoo-lāt], *adj.* (*bot.*) ending in a small hook.

HAMULUS, [ham'-yoo-lus], *n.* a small hook or hook-like appendage. [L. *hamulus* small hook].

HANAPER, [han'-a-per], *n.* a basket for holding money or official documents. [OFr. *hanapier*].

HANCE, [hants], *n.* (*arch.*) the greatest part of an elliptical arch of several centres. [Uncert.].

HAND (1), [hand], *n.* the end portion of the arm below the wrist, comprising the palm and its back, the thumb, and four fingers; an approximate unit of measurement being the width of this; agency; skill, workmanship, artistry; a workman, a manual labourer; style of work, artistic touch; position or direction at the side to right or left; penmanship, handwriting; the indicator of the hours, minutes or seconds on a clock face; the number of cards dealt to a player as his share; (*fig.*) (*pl.*) authority, custody, jurisdiction; **at h.,** nearby, handy; **an old h.,** an experienced person; **at first h.,** with the authority of an original; **from h. to mouth,** in poor circumstances; **h. in glove,** intimate, closely associated; **to wait on h. and foot,** to attend assiduously; **in h.,** in the process of completion; **the upper h.,** advantage; **to feed out of one's h.,** (*fig.*) to obey one; **to get out of h.,** to get out of control; **to have in h.,** to have in reserve; **off h.,** on the spur of the moment; haughty, indifferent; **to play into another's hands,** to surrender an advantage either accidentally or deliberately; **to take a h.,** to join in; **to win hands down,** to win easily. [OE. *hand*].

HAND (2), [hand], *v.t.* to give, pass, offer with the hand; to transmit, transfer, to convey into another's keeping; **to h. down,** to transmit as an inheritance; **to h. in,** to deliver; **to h. on,** to pass on its way; **to h. out,** to distribute; **to h. over,** to give up to the care or possession of another; **to h. it to someone,** (*slang*) to give due credit, acknowledge as superior.

HANDBAG, [hand'-bag], *n.* a small light bag for carrying on the wrist or in the hand.

HANDBALL, [hand'-bawl], *n.* a game in which the ball is hit by the hand against a wall.

HAND-BARROW, [hand'-ba'-rō], *n.* a barrow with two wheels and a pair of handles at one end, a costermonger's barrow.

HANDBELL, [hand'-bel], *n.* a small portable bell rung by the hand.

HANDBILL, [hand'-bil], *n.* an instrument for pruning trees; a loose sheet containing some announcement, and given out by hand.

HANDBOOK, [hand'-bo͝ok], *n.* a book serving as a guide to a particular subject, a manual.

HANDBRACE, [hand'-brās], *n.* a boring tool into which a bit is fitted for drilling.

HAND-BRAKE, [hand'-brāk], *n.* a brake on a vehicle, worked by a hand lever.

HANDBREADTH, [hand'-bredth], *n.* the breadth of the hand; a space equal to this.

HANDCART, [hand'-kaht], *n.* a small cart pushed or drawn by hand.

HANDCUFF (1), [hand'-kuf], *n.* an iron manacle for the wrists consisting of a horseshoe-shaped ring connected by a bar which fits into a lock.

HANDCUFF (2), [hand'-kuf], *v.t.* to put handcuffs on.

HANDBRACE

HANDED, [hand'-id], *adj.* having hands; having a specified number of players; **heavy-h.,** clumsily forceful; severe.

HANDFAST (1), [hand'-fahst], *n.* confirmation of an engagement to marry, betrothal.

HANDFAST (2), [hand'-fahst], *adj.* engaged, betrothed.

HANDFAST (3), [hand'-fahst], *v.t.* to pledge oneself to marry, to betroth by the traditional handclasp. [OE. *handfæstan*].

HANDFUL, [hand'-fo͝ol], *n.* a quantity containing as much as the hand will grasp or contain; a small quantity or number; (*slang*) a lively young child or horse difficult to control. [OE. *handfull*].

HAND-GALLOP, [hand'-gal'-op], *n.* a slow and easy gallop.

HANDGEAR, [hand'-gēer], *n.* the handles of the working gear of a machine started or controlled by hand; (*naut.*) the emergency helm and steering gear.

HAND-GLASS, [hand'-glahs], *n.* a frame of glass used for protecting and fostering plants; a small portable mirror.

HAND-GRENADE, [hand'-gren-ād'], *n.* (*milit.*) a small bomb thrown by hand.

HANDGRIP, [hand'-grip], *n.* a grasp of the hand; a hilt. [OE. *handgripe*].

HANDICAP (1), [hand'-i-kap], *n.* a penalty, obstacle, or drawback imposed on a competitor in a sporting contest, etc., to place him on an equal footing with the rest of the competitors; a race or contest under these conditions; (*fig.*) any abnormal disability or disadvantage. [Uncert.].

HANDICAP (2), (handicapping, handicapped), [hand'-i-kap], *v.t.* to allot a handicap to; to be a disadvantage to.

HANDICAPPER, [hand'-i-kap'-er], *n.* a person who allots handicaps to competitors.

HANDICRAFT, [hand'-i-krahft], *n.* skilled and artistic hand work; manual occupation. [OE. *handcræft* skill of hand].

HANDICRAFTSMAN, [hand'-i-krahfts-man], *n.* a man occupied or skilled in handicrafts.

HANDILY, [hand'-i-li], *adv.* in a handy manner.

HANDINESS, [hand'-i-nes], *n.* the quality of being handy.

HANDIWORK, [hand'-i-wurk], *n.* work, *esp.* skilled artistic work done by hand; something due to some specified agency.

HANDKERCHIEF, [hangk'-er-chēf], *n.* a square of cotton, silk, linen, etc., used for wiping the nose, face or hands.

HANDLE (1), [handl], *n.* that part of a tool or utensil gripped by the hand to simplify lifting, carrying, wielding, etc.; **to give a h. to,** to provide with an excuse or opportunity for attack. [OE. *handle*].

HANDLE (2), [handl], *v.t.* to touch, feel, wield, move with the hands; to control, manage, work on with the hands, to manipulate; to cope with, control, to direct the movements of; to treat, to behave towards; to deal in. [OE. *handlian*].

HANDLE-BAR, [handl'-bah(r)], *n.* the steering apparatus of a bicycle.

HANDLER, [handl'-er], *n.* a person who handles.

HANDLESS, [hand'-les], *adj.* without a hand; (*fig.*) clumsy.

HANDLINE, [hand'-līn], *n.* a fishing-line without a rod.

HANDLING, [handl'-ing], *n.* the act of one who handles; the way in which anything is handled, treatment, skill in dealing with.

HANDLOOM, [hand'-lo͞om], *n.* a loom operated by hand.

HANDMAID, [hand'-mād], *n.* a female servant; a kind of moth; (*fig.*) anything subordinate to and helping something else.

HANDMAIDEN, [hand'-mādn], *n.* a handmaid.

HAND-MICROPHONE, [hand'-mī'-krōf-ōn], *n.* a portable microphone, *esp.* as used by speakers; a telephone mouthpiece and receiver that can be held with one hand.

HANDMILL, [hand'-mil], *n.* a small mill worked by the hand, for grinding coffee.

HAND-ORGAN, [hand'-awg'-an], *n.* a hurdy-gurdy.

HANDPRESS, [hand'-pres], *n.* a press worked by hand.

HANDRAIL, [hand'-rāl], *n.* a rail that may be gripped for support, *esp.* on a staircase.

HANDRAILER, [hand'-rāl-er], *n.* a support for a handrail.

HANDSAW, [hand'-saw], *n.* a saw worked with one hand.

HANDSCREEN, [hand'-skrēn], *n.* a screen held in the hand for protection.

HANDSCREW, [hand'-skro͞o], *n.* a lifting jack.

HANDSEL (1), [hand'-sel], *n.* a gift as a token of good luck; (*archaic*) a first sale; a first payment, deposit; (*leg.*) a handshake in presence of witnesses to confirm or conclude a bargain. [OIcel. *handsal*].

HANDSEL (2), (handselling, handselled), [hand'-sel], *v.t.* to offer a handsel to; to inaugurate.

HANDSOME, [han'-sum], *adj.* good-looking, of well-proportioned features; shapely; generous, ample, abundant, liberal; magnificent; †handy, convenient; well-bred. [ME. *handsom* easy to handle].

HANDSOMELY, [han'-sum-li], *adv.* in a handsome fashion.

HANDSOMENESS, [han'-sum-nes], *n.* the quality of being handsome.

HANDSPIKE, [hand'-spīk], *n.* a bar used as a lever for moving heavy objects.

HANDSTAFF, [hand'-stahf], *n.* †a javelin; the handle of a flail.

HAND-WINGED, [hand'-wingd], *adj.* having membranes on the hands, like the bats.

HANDWRITING, [hand'-rīt-ing], *n.* that which is written by the hand; style of writing.

HANDY (1), [hand'-i], *adj.* dexterous, expert with the hands, manually adroit; near, close to hand; convenient, suitable for handling, useful.

HANDY (2), [hand'-i], *adv.* nearby, close at hand.

HANDYBILLY†, [hand'-i-bil'-i], *n.* (*naut.*) a small jigger purchase for assistance in hoisting.

HANDY-DANDY, [hand'-i-dand'-i], *n.* a child's game in which the participants send an article round the ring, hide it among themselves, and then challenge one to guess where it is.

HANDYMAN, [hand'-i-man], *n.* a man with a knowledge of practical things, a jack-of-all-trades; a seaman.

HANG (1), [hang], *n.* the way a thing hangs; the way the component parts of anything are interdependent on one another; the knack; the way a mechanism works; the meaning, significance; **to get the h. of**, to understand, grasp.

HANG (2), (**hanged, hung**), [hang], *v.t.* to fasten or attach something to a high point of support placed above it, to suspend by a cord, etc.; to suspend game or meat till fit to eat; to cover with decorations which are suspended from point to point; to put to death by suspending by the neck, causing strangulation; to support on hinges; to paste wallpaper to the wall; *v.i.* to be suspended, to dangle; to fall or drop into a form, as clothes round the body; to be deprived of life by swinging with a rope pulled tightly round the throat: **to h. about**, or **around**, to frequent, haunt; to keep close to; to loiter, idle; **to h. back**, to hesitate to act; to remain behind; **to h. fire**, to delay, to be slow in maturing; **to h. out**, (*slang*) to live, frequent a place; **to h. together**, to be closely associated; to take a practical form; to have all the parts in working order; **to h. up**, to delay, retard, postpone progress; **to h. upon someone's words**, to be attentive to the point of adoration; **to h. the head**, to incline the head forward in shame; **to let go h.**, to be ostentatiously indifferent to. [OE. *hangian* and OE. *hon*].

HANGAR, [hang'-er], *n.* a shed for housing aircraft. [Fr. *hangar*].

HANGDOG, [hang'-dog], *adj.* miserable, sullen, dejected.

HANGER (1), [hang'-er], *n.* the object or support from which a thing is hung; that which hangs or is suspended; a short curved broadsword hung from the belt of a naval officer; one who hangs.

HANGER (2), [hang'-er], *n.* a wood on the slope of a hill. [OE. *hangra*].

HANGER-ON, [hang'-er-on'], *n.* a person who persists in associating with another in expectation of favours, a parasite.

HANGING (1), [hang'-ing], *n.* the action of that which hangs; the state of being hanged or hung; the object which is hung; (*pl.*) a piece of fabric or a curtain used in interior decoration.

HANGING (2), [hang'-ing], *adj.* being in a state of suspension; **h. gardens**, gardens laid out in terraces, or characterized by creeping and climbing plants; **h. valve**, a hinged metal plate used as a form of protection.

HANGMAN, [hang'-man], *n.* a public executioner.

HANGNAIL, [hang'-nāl], *n.* a loose piece of skin which hangs from the cuticle covering a finger-nail.

HANGNEST, [hang'-nest], *n.* a bird of the genus *Icterus*, which hangs its nest from a tree.

HANG-NET, [hang'-net'], *n.* a net with a wide mesh.

HANG-OUT, [hang'-owt], *n.* (*slang*) a place to live or lodge in.

HANG-OVER, [hang'-ō-ver], *n.* (*slang*) uncomfortable after-effects of intoxication.

HANK, [hangk], *n.* a coil or loop; a skein of yarn, string, etc., of a particular length; (*naut.*) one of several wooden rings attached to a stay to secure the luff of the fore-and-aft sails. [OIcel. *hanki* clasp].

HANKER, [hangk'-er], *v.i.* to long for with a keen desire, to yearn for, crave for. [Unkn.].

HANKERING, [hangk'-er-ing], *n.* a yearning, craving, longing.

HANKERINGLY, [hangk'-er-ing-li], *adv.* in a hankering fashion.

HANKLED†, [hangkld], *adj.* twisted, entangled.

HANKY, [hangk'-i], *n.* (*coll.*) a handkerchief.

HANKY-PANKY, [hangk'-i-pangk'-i], *n.* trickery, mischievous deceit, deceptive action.

HANSARD, [han'-sahd], *n.* the official printed record of speeches, debates, and proceedings in the Houses of Parliament. [Luke *Hansard*, printer of these reports in the eighteenth and nineteenth centuries].

HANSE, [hans'-er], *n.* a league or guild of merchants in medieval Europe; **H. towns**, certain cities of Germany, associated in the Middle Ages for the protection of their commercial interests. [OHGerm. *hansa*].

HANSEATIC, [han'-si-at'-ik], *adj.* relating to the Hanse towns.

HANSOM, [han'-sum], *n.* a light two-wheeled cab for two passengers, with the driver mounted on a raised seat behind. [J. A. *Hansom*, 1803-1882, its inventor].

HANSOM

HANUMAN, [han'-ōō-mahn'], *n.* the monkey god of the Hindus; an Indian species of monkey, the true langur, *Semnopithecus entellus*. [Hind. *hanuman*].

HAP (1), [hap], *n.* that which happens by chance, fortune, luck. [OIcel. *happ*].

HAP (2), (**happing, happed**), [hap], *v.i.* to happen, chance.

HAPAX LEGOMENON, (*pl.* **hapax legomena**), [hap'-aks-li-gom'-en-on], *n.* (*philol.*) a word, form, idiom, etc., which apparently occurs only once. [Gk. *hapax legomenon* once said].

HAPHAZARD (1), [hap'-haz'-erd], *n.* chance, accident.

HAPHAZARD (2), [hap'-haz'-erd], *adj.* accidental, random, unmethodical.

HAPLESS, [hap'-les], *adj.* luckless, unfortunate, unlucky.

HAPLY†, [hap'-li], *adv.* by chance, perhaps.

HA'P'ORTH, [hā'-puth], *n.* (*slang*) a halfpennyworth.

HAPPEN, [hap'-en], *v.t.* to come to pass, to take place; to do anything by chance; **to h. on**, to find by chance; **to h. to**, to occur to; to enter into or become involved in the life of. [ME. *hapenen*].

HAPPILY, [hap'-i-li], *adv.* in a happy manner; luckily.

HAPPINESS, [hap'-i-nes], *n.* the state of being happy, good fortune; joy.

HAPPY, [hap'-i], *adj.* joyful, contented, cheerful, pleased with life; pleased with success, good fortune and participation in what is considered good, beautiful and kind; well-adapted to a purpose, suitable, apt; bringing about or indicating joy and delight. [ME. *happi*].

HAPPY-GO-LUCKY, [hap'-i-gō'-luk'-i], *adj.* carefree, indifferent to obligations, thoughtless and lighthearted.

HAQUEBUT, see HACKBUT.

HARA-KIRI, HARI-KARI, [hah'-ra-kēer'-i], *n.* a Japanese way of committing suicide by slitting the abdomen. [Jap. *hara* belly and *kiri* cut].

HARANGUE (1), [ha-rang'], *n.* an inciting speech made to a crowd; a public speech, *esp.* one with deliberately popular and emotional appeal, a tirade; a stilted speech admonitory in purpose. [Fr. *harangue*].

HARANGUE (2), [ha-rang'], *v.t. and i.* to address by means of an harangue; to pronounce an harangue.

HARANGUER, [ha-rang'-er], *n.* a person who harangues.

HARASS, [ha'-ras], *v.t.* to weary, to annoy or exhaust by repetitions or persistence; to worry, distract. [OFr. *harasser*].

HARASSER, [ha'-ras-er], *n.* a person who harasses.

HARASSMENT, [ha'-ras-ment], *n.* the act of harassing; the state of being harassed.

HARBINGER (1), [hah'-bin-jer], *n.* a precursor, forerunner; formerly, an army officer who went on ahead to provide lodgings. [~OFr. *herbergeor* provider of lodgings].

HARBINGER (2), [hah'-bin-jer], *v.t.* to herald, to be the harbinger of.

HARBOUR (1), [hah'-ber], *n.* a natural or artificial small bay or stretch of water on the coast-line, giving shelter and smooth anchorage to boats; a sheltered place, refuge, haven. [OIcel. *herbergi* lodging].

HARBOUR (2), [hah'-ber], *v.t.* to shelter; to provide a secret refuge for, conceal; to keep in the mind; to track to its hiding place; *v.i.* to lodge, to take cover; to come to rest in a harbour.

HARBOURAGE, [hah'-ber-ij] *n.* a place of shelter; refuge, cover.

HARBOUR-BAR, [hah'-ber-bah(r)'], *n.* a shoal at the mouth of a harbour.

HARBOUR-DUES, [hah'-ber-dewz'], *n.(pl.)* fees charged for anchorage in a harbour.

HARBOURER, [hah'-ber-er], *n.* a person who harbours.

HARBOURLESS, [hah'-ber-les], *adj.* without a harbour; destitute of shelter or a lodging.

HARBOUR-MASTER, [hah'-ber-mahst'-er], *n.* an officer who superintends the mooring of ships, etc., at a port.

HARD (1), [hahd], *n.* a landing beach; (*slang*) hard labour.

HARD (2), [hahd], *adj.* firm, not easily penetrated or pressed, solid, unyielding; harsh, unfeeling, exacting; unjust; painful, distressing, uncomfortable, difficult; involving intense mental effort, complex; full of force, vigorous, powerful; severe; lacking resonance; laborious, strenuous; bitter, angry, unpleasant; **h. and fast**, rigid, inflexible; **h. food**, corn fodder; **h. luck**, bad fortune, unlucky failure; **h. of hearing**, deaf; **h. water**, water containing an abnormal amount of lime or chalk, in which soap dissolves with difficulty; **h. up**, having little or no money. [OE. *heard*].

HARD (3), [hahd], *adv.* close, near; to the point of hardness; strenuously, with great vigour; severely, sorely; laboriously, painfully, with difficulty; excessively, immoderately; **it will go h.**, it will be serious. [OE. *heard*].

HARDBAKE, [hahd'-bāk], *n.* a toffee almond-cake; almond toffee.

HARDBEAM, [hahd'-bēm], *n.* the hornbeam tree, *Carpinus Betulus*.

HARDBITTEN, [hahd'-bit-en], *adj.* stubborn, tough; of a coarse but capable character.

HARD-BOILED, [hahd'-boild], *adj.* (of an egg) boiled till the yolk and white are solid; (*slang*) callous, brutally efficient.

HARD-BOUND, [hahd'-bownd], *adj.* tight; slow.

HARD-CORE, [hahd'-kaw(r)], *n.* rubble put down to form the foundation of a road; residuum.

HARD COURT, [hahd'-kawt], *n.* a tennis court with a playing surface of shale, wood, or asphalt.

HARD-EARNED, [hahd'-urnd], *adj.* earned with much labour, *esp.* for a low rate of pay.

HARDEN, [hahdn], *v.t.* to make hard or harder, to solidify; to make hardy; to make insensitive, callous, obstinate; *v.i.* to become hard or harder, to grow solid; to become insensitive, callous; (*commercial*) (of prices) to remain stable at a high level; **to h. off**, to expose seedlings gradually to the cold. [OIcel. *harthna*].

HARDENED, [hahd'-end], *adj.* confirmed.

HARDENER, [hahd'-ner], *n.* he who, or that which, hardens.

HARDENING, [hahdn'-ing], *n.* the act of making hard or hardy; that which hardens.

HARDFACED, [hahd'-fāst], *adj.* having a harsh and stern expression.

HARDFAVOURED, [hahd'-fā'-verd], *adj.* hard-faced.

HARDFEATURED, [hahd'-fē'-cherd], *adj.* hard-faced.

HARDFISTED, [hahd'-fist'-id], *adj.* close-fisted, covetous, miserly.

HARDFOUGHT, [hahd'-fawt], *adj.* vigorously contested.

HARDGOTTEN, [hahd'-got'-en], *adj.* earned, obtained with difficulty.

HARDHANDED, [hahd'-hand'-id], *adj.* severe, oppressive.

HARDHEADED, [hahd'-hed'-id], *adj* unsentimental; practical; selfishly realistical.

HARDHEARTED, [hahd'-haht'-id], *adj.* merciless, cruel; unfeeling.

HARDHEARTEDLY, [hahd'-haht'-id-li], *adv.* in a hardhearted fashion.

HARDHEARTEDNESS, [hahd'-haht'-id-nes], *n.* the quality of being hardhearted.

HARDIHOOD, [hahd'-i-hŏŏd], *n.* boldness, insolent daring, effrontery; hardiness.

HARDILY, [hahd'-i-li], *adv.* in hardy fashion.

HARDINESS, [hahd'-i-nes], *n.* the quality of being hardy.

HARDISH, [hahd'-ish], *adj.* fairly hard.

HARD LABOUR, [hahd'-lā'-ber], *n.* the most rigorous form of ordinary imprisonment.

HARDLY, [hahd'-li], *adv.* with difficulty, only just; barely; harshly, fiercely, strenuously.

HARDMOUTHED, [hahd'-mowᴛʜd], *adj.* (of a horse) insensible to the bit; (*fig.*) obstinate; foul-mouthed.

HARDNESS, [hahd'-nes], *n.* the quality of being hard.

HARDOCK, [hahd'-ok], *n.* the plant, *Arctium Lappa*, burdock.

HARD-PAN, [hahd'-pan], *n.* a hard subsoil containing a large proportion of gravel or clay.

HARD PRESSED, [hahd'-prest'], *adj.* in severe difficulties, encompassed and almost overwhelmed by the enemy.

HARDS, [hahdz], *n.(pl.)* the refuse of flax or wool. [OE. *heordan*].

HARDSET, [hahd'-set'], *adj.* solidified, set in a firm jelly; (*fig.*) determined, obstinate.

HARDSHELL, [hahd'-shel], *adj.* having a hard shell; (*coll.*) rigid and uncompromising.

HARDSHIP, [hahd'-ship], *n.* arduous conditions of living, privation, discomfort; unfair treatment, unjust deprivation; any particular example of this.

HARD TACK, [hahd'-tak'], *n.* ship's biscuit.

HARD-VISAGED, [hahd'-viz'-ijd], *adj.* harsh-faced.

HARDWARE, [hahd'-wāer], *n.* ironmongery.

HARDWAREMAN, [hahd'-wāer-man] *n.* a maker of, or dealer in, hardware.

HARDWON, [hahd'-wun'], *adj.* achieved with difficulty.

HARDWOOD, [hahd'-wŏŏd], *n.* close-grained wood; deciduous timber.

HARDWORKING, [hahd'-wurk'-ing], *adj.* industrious.

HARDY, [hahd'-i], *adj.* able to endure hardship, tough, robust; bold, audacious; (of plants) resisting frost and bad weather. [Fr. *hardi*].

HARE (1), [hāer], *n.* a long-eared rodent of the genus *Lepus*. [OE. *hara*].

HARE (2), [hāer], *v.i.* (*slang*) to run very fast, *esp.* in flight.

HARE-AND-HOUNDS, [hāer'-and-howndz'], *n.* a paper-chase.

HAREBELL, [hāer'-bel], *n.* the plant, *Campanula rotundifolia*, bearing blue, bell-shaped flowers.

HAREBELL

HAREBRAINED, [hāer'-brānd], *adj.* empty-headed, careless.

HAREHEARTED, [hāer'-haht'-id], *adj.* rabbit-hearted, white-livered.

HAREHOUND, [hāer'-hownd], *n.* a hound used in hunting hares.

HARELD, [ha'-reld], *n.* the duck, *Harelda glacialis*. [Uncert.].

HARELIP, [hāer'-lip], *n.* (*med.*) a deformity of the lip, in which the upper lip is cleft.

HAREM, [hah-rēm', hāer'-em], *n.* the part of a Moslem house in which wives and concubines are secluded; the wives and concubines of a potentate. [Arab. *harim* forbidden place].

HARENGIFORM, [ha-ren'-ji-fawm], *adj.* having the shape of a herring. [Fr. *hareng* herring and FORM].

HAREPIPE, [hāer'-pīp], *n.* a snare for hares.

HARICOT, [ha'-ri-kō], *n.* a savoury hash containing kidney beans; the kidney bean, *Phaseolus vulgaris*. [Fr. *haricot*].

HARI-KARI, see, HARA-KIRI.

HARIOLATION, [ha'-ri-o-lā'-shun], *n.* prophecy. [L. *hariolatio*].

HARISH, [hāer'-ish], *adj.* rather like a hare.

HARK, [hahk], *v.t and i.* to listen, hear; **to h. back**, to return to the point from which one started; to refer repeatedly to what is past. [ME. *herkien*].

HARL, [hahl], *n.* the fibre of flax; the barb of a feather. [ME. *herle*].

HARLEQUIN, [hah'-li-kwin], *n.* a fantastic masked character in Italian comedy and pantomime, the lover of Columbine. [OFr. *harlequin*].

HARLEQUINADE, [hah'-li-kwi-nād], *n.* the scene in which Harlequin appears; frolics and buffoonery.

HARLOT, [hah'-lot], *n.* a prostitute. [ME. *herlot* a vagabond].

HARLOTRY, [hah'-lot-ri], *n.* the trade and manners of a harlot.

HARM (1), [hahm], *n.* injury, ill, damage. [OE. *hearm*].

HARM (2), [hahm], *v.t.* to do harm to. [OE. *hearmian*].

HARMATTAN, [hah-mat'-an], *n.* a hot sandy wind blowing westward from the Sahara during winter. [Native].

HARMEL, [hah'-mel], *n.* the wild Syrian rue. [Arab. *harmal*].

HARMFUL, [hahm'-fŏŏl], *adj.* hurtful, causing harm.

HARMFULLY, [hahm'-fŏŏl-i], *adv.* in harmful fashion.

HARMFULNESS, [hahm'-fŏŏl-nes], *n.* the quality of being harmful.

HARMLESS, [hahm'-les], *adj.* doing no harm, unable or unwilling to hurt; inoffensive.
HARMLESSLY, [hahm'-les-li], *adv.* in harmless fashion.
HARMLESSNESS, [hahm'-les-nes], *n.* the quality of being harmless.
HARMONIC (1), [hah-mon'-ik], *n.* (*mus.*) an additional and superimposed frequency set up when a note is played; (*pl.*) (*wirel.*) secondary frequencies of an oscillating circuit.
HARMONIC (2), [hah-mon'-ik], *adj.* relating to harmony; harmonious; (*arith.*) with reciprocals in arithmetical progression. [Gk. *harmonikos*].
HARMONICA, [hah-mon'-ik-a], *n.* a musical instrument consisting of a series of rounded glass plates rubbed or struck; a kind of mouth-organ. [L. *harmonicus* harmonic].

HARMONICA

HARMONICAL, [hah-mon'-ik-al], *adj.* harmonic.
HARMONICALLY, [hah-mon'-ik-al-i], *adv.* in harmonic fashion.
HARMONICS, [hah-mon'-iks], *n.*(*pl.*) (*mus.*) the science of harmony.
HARMONIOUS, [hah-mō'-ni-us], *adj.* in harmony, melodious; (*fig.*) justly proportioned and agreeably combined, congruous, suitable, well adapted to each other.
HARMONIOUSLY, [hah-mō'-ni-us-li], *adv.* in harmonious fashion.
HARMONIOUSNESS, [hah-mō'-ni-us-nes], *n.* the condition of being harmonious.
HARMONIST, [hah'-mon-ist], *n.* (*mus.*) one skilled in harmonics or in the writing of harmony; one who reconciles apparent literary and religious inconsistencies.
HARMONISTIC, [hah'-mon-ist'-ik], *adj.* relating to a harmonist and his work.
HARMONIUM, [hah-mō'-ni-um], *n.* a small organ with a keyboard and free metal reeds, played by pedals operated by the feet. [L. *harmonia* harmony].
HARMONIZE, [hah'-mon-īz], *v.t.* *and i.* to bring into harmony; to be harmonious; to get on well together.
HARMONIZER, [hah'-mon-īz-er], *n.* one who, that which, harmonizes.
HARMONOMETER, [hah'-mon-om'-it-er], *n.* a device for measuring the harmonic relations of sounds. [Gk. *harmonia* harmony and METER].
HARMONY, [hah'-mon-i], *n.* just proportion of the parts or qualities of a thing so as to produce an aesthetic whole; (*mus.*) musical concord, the combination of different notes into a chord; music characterized by combinations and progressions of chords; the art of composing such music, and the rules governing its composition; music or pleasing sounds in general; concord, peaceful agreement; a combining of several narratives to produce a complete account. [Gk. *harmonia*].
HARMOTOME, [hah'-mo-tōm], *n.* a cross-stone. [Gk. *harmos* joint and *tome* cutting].
HARN, [hahn], *n.* (*Scots*) coarse linen. [OE. *hærnes*].
HARNESS (1), [hah'-nes], *n.* the trappings of a horse, by which it is driven, and by which it draws; †the armour and accoutrements of a man; **double h.,** marriage; **to die in h.,** to die still working. [OFr. *harneis* armour].
HARNESS (2), [hah'-nes], *v.t.* to put in harness; to tie to some work; to bring under control for practical use; †to equip with armour. [OFr. *harneschier*].
HARNESS-CASK, [hah'-nes-kahsk'], *n.* a ship's cask for keeping salted meat ready for use.
HARNESSER, [hah'-nes-er], *n.* a person who harnesses.
HARNESS-MAKER, [hah'-nes-māk'-er], *n.* a maker of horses' harness.
HARNESS-TUB, [hah'-nes-tub'], *n.* a harness-cask.
HARP (1), [hahp], *n.* (*mus.*) an instrument consisting of strings stretched over a triangular frame, and played by plucking with the fingers. [OE. *hearpe*].

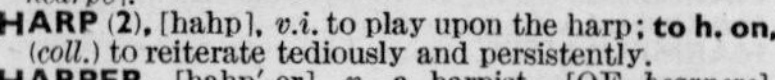
HARP

HARP (2), [hahp], *v.i.* to play upon the harp; **to h. on,** (*coll.*) to reiterate tediously and persistently.
HARPER, [hahp'-er], *n.* a harpist. [OE. *hearpere*].
HARPING-IRON, [hahp'-ing-īern'], *n.* a harpoon.
HARPINGS, [hahp'-ingz], *n.*(*pl.*) battens or strakes on the bow of a ship to give extra strength. [Uncert.].
HARPIST, [hahp'-ist], *n.* one who plays the harp.
HARPOON (1), [hah-pōōn'], *n.* a fish-spear, a barbed throwing-spear used in whale-hunting. [OFr. *harpon* grappling-iron].
HARPOON (2), [hah-pōōn'], *v.t.* to spear with a harpoon.
HARPOONER, [hah-pōōn'-er], *n.* a man who uses a harpoon.
HARP-SHELL, [hahp'-shel], *n.* the harp-shaped shell of the genus *Harpa.*
HARPSICHORD, [hahp'-si-kawd], *n.* (*mus.*) an old-fashioned keyboard instrument in which the strings are plucked by quills. [Fr. *harpechorde*].
HARPY, [hahp'-i], *n.* (*Gk. myth.*) a filthy creature with the head and breasts of a woman and the wings and claws of a bird; (*fig.*) a cruel woman. [Fr. *harpie*].
HARR, see HAAR.
HARRIDAN, [ha'-ri-dan], *n.* a fierce and filthy old woman, an old prostitute, a hag. [Unkn.].
HARRIER (1), [ha'-ri-er], *n.* a dog used for hunting hares; a cross-country runner. [HARE].
HARRIER (2), [ha'-ri-er], *n.* a small fierce hawk of the genus *Circus.* [HARRY].
HARROVIAN (1), [ha-rōv'-i-an], *n.* a pupil of Harrow School. [MdL. *Harrovia* Harrow].
HARROVIAN (2), [ha-rōv'-i-an], *adj.* of, or pertaining to, Harrow or Harrovians.
HARROW (1), [ha'-rō], *n.* a toothed agricultural instrument for levelling ploughed land and breaking soil. [ME. *harowe*].

HARRIER

HARROW (2), [ha'-rō], *v.t.* to smooth, break up ground with a harrow; (*fig.*) to torment the feelings; to move to horror and distress.
HARROWER, [ha'-rō-er], *n.* one who harrows.
HARROWING (1), [ha'-rō-ing], *n.* a ravaging, wounding, and distressing.
HARROWING (2), [ha'-rō-ing], *adj.* causing horror and distress, moving to mental anguish, that harrows.
HARRY, [ha'-ri], *v.t.* to ravage, despoil; (*fig.*) to worry and disturb, to pester. [OE. *hergian*].
HARSH, [hahsh], *adj.* rough, coarse of texture; discordant of sound; inharmonious, aesthetically unpleasing; crude; unfeeling, severe; rigorous, savagely stern; angry and bitter. [ME. *harsk* rough].
HARSHLY, [hahsh'-li], *adv.* in harsh fashion.
HARSHNESS, [hahsh'-nes], *n.* the quality of being harsh.
HART, [haht], *n.* a stag from its sixth year. [OE. *heort*].
HARTAL, [haht'-al], *n.* the closing of shops in India in civil disobedience campaigns. [Hind. *hath* market and *talna* stop].
HARTEBEEST, [haht'-i-bēst], *n.* a large reddish South African antelope of the genus *Bubalis.* [Afrik. *hartebeest*].
HARTSHORN, [hahts'-hawn], *n.* ammonium carbonate distilled from the horns of stags.
HART'S-TONGUE, [hahts'-tung], *n.* a narrow-leaved fern of the genus *Scolopendrium.*
HARTWORT, [haht'-wurt], *n.* the plant. *Tordylium maximum.*
HARUM-SCARUM, [hāer'-um-skāer'-um], *adj.* flighty, irresponsible, madcap. [Scots].
HARUSPEX, [ha'-rus-pex], *n.* one who makes divinations from the entrails of animals. [L. *haruspex*].
HARUSPICY, [ha-rōō'-spi-si], *n.* the art of divination by inspecting the entrails of animals. [*Prec.*].
HARVEST (1), [hah'-vest], *n.* the gathering in of crops; the season when crops are gathered; the crops so gathered in; the fruits of labour or action. [OE. *hærfest*].
HARVEST (2), [hah'-vest], *v.t.* to gather in crops, to garner; to store up what has been gathered or gained.
HARVESTER, [hah'-vest-er], *n.* one who gathers a harvest; a reaping machine; a harvest-mite.
HARVEST FESTIVAL, [hah'-vist-fest'-iv-al], *n.* a church festival at which, to celebrate the gathering of the harvest, flowers and fruit are brought to church as a thankoffering.

HARVEST-HOME, [hah'-vest-hōm'], *n.* the festivities at the completion of harvest; a religious thanksgiving service at the time of harvest.
HARVEST-LADY, [hah'-vest-lā'-di], *n.* the second reaper in a row.
HARVEST-LORD, [hah'-vest-lawd'], *n.* the first reaper in a row.
HARVESTMAN, [hah'-vest-man], *n.* a labourer who helps to gather in the harvest.
HARVEST-MITE, [hah'-vest-mīt'], *n.* a small tick, found in grass-stalks, which burrows under the skin, the harvest-bug, *Trombidium holosericeum.*
HARVEST-MOON, [hah'-vest-mōōn'], *n.* the moon near the autumnal equinox.
HARVEST-MOUSE, [hah'-vest-mows'], *n.* a small field-mouse nesting amongst corn stalks.
HAS, [haz], *3rd person pres.ind. sg.* of HAVE.
HAS-BEEN, [haz'-bēn], *n.* (*coll.*) a person who has passed his heyday.
HASH (1), [hash], *n.* a stew of vegetables and reheated meat; (*fig.*) a mess, a muddle, a complete mismanagement of something. [Fr. *hâchis*].
HASH (2), [hash], *v.t.* to make into a hash; (*fig.*) to make an utter mess of. [Fr. *hâcher*].
HASHISH, [hash'-ēsh], *n.* a preparation of Indian hemp used as a stimulating or narcotic drug. [Arab. *hashish*].
HASLETS, [haz'-lets], *n.(pl.)* the edible entrails of an animal, *esp.* of a pig. [OFr. *hastelet*].
HASP (1), [hahsp], *n.* a clasp, a catch for closing a door, book, etc.; a metal flag for hanging over a staple; a spindle for thread; a hank of yarn, etc. [OE. *hæpse*].
HASP (2), [hahsp], *v.t.* to close, hold with a hasp.
HASSOCK, [has'-ok], *n.* a tussock of grass; a stuffed, solid cushion for kneeling. [OE. *hassoc*].
HASTATE, [has'-tāt], *adj.* (*bot.*) spear-shaped. [L. *hasta* a spear].
HASTATED, [has-tāt'-id], *adj.* hastate.
HASTE (1), [hāst], *n.* speed, quickness of motion; an endeavouring to accomplish something in the shortest possible time; precipitancy, rashness caused by efforts to accomplish quickly. [OFr. *haste*].
HASTE (2), [hāst], *v.t. and i.* to make to hurry, to cause to be done in the quickest possible time; to hurry, to move or do quickly. [OFr. *haster*].
HASTELER, [hast'-ler], *n.* a turnspit. [AFr. **hasteler*].
HASTEN, [hāsn], *v.t. and i.* to make to haste, to speed up, to cause to happen at the earliest possible time; to be in haste, to act with speed, hurry. [HASTE].
HASTIFORM, [hast'-i-fawm], *adj.* hastate. [L. *hasta* spear and FORM].
HASTILY, [hāst'-i-li], *adv.* in hasty fashion.
HASTINESS, [hāst'-i-nes], *n.* the quality of being hasty.
HASTING, [hāst'-ing], *adj.* ripening early.
HASTINGS, [hāst'-ingz], *n.(pl.)* peas that ripen early.
HASTY, [hāst'-i], *adj.* exhibiting haste, in too great haste; rash; quick-tempered. [OFr. *hastif*].
HASTY-PUDDING, [hāst'-i-pŏŏd'-ing], *n.* a kind of thin batter made of flour and water or milk.
HAT, [hat], *n.* a brimmed covering for the head, *esp.* one made of hardish material and retaining a definite shape; **to talk through one's h.,** (*coll.*) to talk complete nonsense. [OE. *hætt*].
HAT-BAND, [hāt'-band], *n.* a band round the crown of a hat.
HAT-BOX, [hat'-boks], *n.* a box for hats.
HAT-BRUSH, [hat'-brush], *n.* a brush for hats.
HAT-CASE, [hat'-kās], *n.* a hat-box.
HATCH (1), [hach], *n.* a movable covering above a hole, *esp.* (*naut.*) in the deck of a ship; (*naut.*) a hatchway; a door with an open space above or below a wicket; the upper or lower part of a divided door; the flood-gate of a weir. [OE. *hæc* grating].
HATCH (2), [hach], *n.* the process of hatching eggs; the brood hatched at one time. [HATCH (3)].
HATCH (3), [hach], *v.t. and i.* to produce young from eggs by incubation; (*fig.*) to plan and develop secretly; to be in process of incubation. [ME. *hacchen*].
HATCH (4), [hach], *v.t.* to mark or shade with very fine cross lines; to decorate with fine, close lines. [Fr. *hâcher* to chop].
HATCH-BOAT, [hach'-bōt], *n.* a half-decked fishing boat.
HATCHEL, [hach'-el], *v.t.* to heckle, irritate, harry. [~HACKLE].
HATCHELLER, [hach'-el-er], *n.* a heckler.
HATCHER, [hach'-er], *n.* one who hatches.
HATCHERY, [hach'-er-i], *n.* a place for hatching fish.
HATCHET, [hach'-et], *n.* a light chopping axe held in one hand; a tomahawk; **to bury the h.,** to make peace. [Fr. *hachette* little chopper].
HATCHET-FACE, [hach'-et-fās], *n.* a thin, narrow face with prominent features.
HATCHING, [hach'-ing], *n.* the process of shading by fine crossed lines; the decoration produced in this way. [HATCH (4)].
HATCHMENT, [hach'-ment], *n.* (*her.*) the escutcheon of a deceased person, painted on wood and hung by his tomb. [ME. *atcheament* achievement].

HATCHMENT

HATCHWAY, [hach'-wā], *n.* (*naut.*) an opening from the deck to the interior of the vessel.
HATE (1), [hāt], *n.* extreme ill-feeling, violent hostility, loathing, detestation; (*coll.*) a furious artillery bombardment for no tactical reason. [ME. *hate*].
HATE (2), [hāt], *v.t. and i.* to loathe, detest, abominate, feel hate towards. [OE. *hatian*].
HATEFUL, [hāt'-fōōl], *adj.* arousing hatred, provoking ill-will, detestable.
HATEFULLY, [hāt'-fōōl-i], *adv.* in hateful fashion.
HATEFULNESS, [hāt'-fōōl-nes], *n.* the quality of being hateful.
HATER, [hāt'-er], *n.* one who hates.
HATLESS, [hat'-les], *adj.* without a hat.
HAT-PIN, [hat'-pin], *n.* a pin to attach a hat to the hair.
HATRED, [hā'-tred], *n.* hate, strong and enduring ill-will. [ME. *hatereden*].
HATTED, [hat'-id], *adj.* wearing a hat.
HATTER, [hat'-er], *n.* a maker of, or dealer in, hats.
HATTERIA, [hat-ēer'-i-a], *n.* the sphenodon lizard of New Zealand.
HAT-TRICK, [hat'-trik'], *n.* (*cricket*) the taking of three wickets by successive balls; the act of scoring three goals during a game of football, hockey, etc.; (*coll.*) a triple success.
HAUBERK, [haw'-berk], *n.* a coat made of chain mail, or made of cloth surfaced with metal rings or plates. [OFr. *hauberc* from OHGerm. *halsberc* neck protection].
HAUGH, [haw], *n.* a river flat. [OE. *halh* corner].
HAUGHTILY, [haw'-ti-li], *adv.* in haughty fashion.
HAUGHTINESS, [haw'-ti-nes], *n.* the quality of being haughty.
HAUGHTY, [haw'-ti], *adj.* insolently proud, arrogant, supercilious. [OFr. *halt, haut* high].
HAUL (1), [hawl], *n.* the act of hauling; a catch of fish; booty, profits, acquisitions.
HAUL (2), [hawl], *v.t. and i.* to pull, heave, drag along or up with effort; (*naut.*) to bring a vessel close to the wind; (*naut.*) to alter the course of a ship; **to h. over the coals,** to reprimand severely. [Fr. *haler*].
HAULAGE, [hawl'-ij], *n.* the act of hauling; the force employed in hauling.
HAULER, [hawl'-er], *n.* one who hauls.
HAULIER, [hawl'-i-er], *n.* one employed in hauling; a carter; one hauling coal to the foot of a mine-shaft.
HAULM, HAUM, HALM, [hawlm], *n.* the stubble of grain; straw; a plant stalk. [OE. *healm*].
HAUNCH, [hawnch], *n.* that part of the body including the upper thigh, the hip, and the buttock; (*arch.*) the part of an arch beneath the crown. [OFr. *hanche*].
HAUNCHED, [hawncht], *adj.* possessing haunches.
HAUNT (1), [hawnt], *n.* a resort, a place constantly frequented by a person; the lair of an animal.
HAUNT (2), [hawnt], *v.t.* to visit frequently, *esp.* to frequent as a ghost or apparition; to pester by continual visits; to follow, seek importunately; to trouble the mind continually; to be associated with. [Fr. *hanter*].
HAUNTED, [hawnt'-id], *adj.* subject to supernatural manifestations.
HAUNTER, [hawnt'-er], *n.* one that haunts.
HAURIANT, [haw'-ri-ant], *adj.* (*her.*) (of fishes) drawn perpendicularly. [L. *haurians*].
HAURL, [hawl], *v.t.* to drag along the ground; to rough-cast, mixing lime and gravel. [Unkn.].
HAUSTELLATE, [haws'-tel-āt], *adj.* possessing a sucker or haustellum.

HAUSTELLUM, [haws-tel′-um], *n.* the sucker of certain insects. [L. *haustellum*].
HAUSTORIUM, [haws-taw′-ri-um], *n.* (*bot.*) a sucker. [~L. *haustor* drawer].
HAUTBOY, [ō′-boi], *n.* a wood-wind musical instrument with a double reed, the oboe. [Fr. *hautbois*].
HAUTEUR, [ō-tur′], *adj.* genteel haughtiness. [Fr. *hauteur*].
HAUT-GOUT, [ō′-gōō′], *n.* excessive seasoning. [Fr. *haut gout*].
HAUTIN, [hawt′-in], *n.* a sea-fish sometimes found in fresh water, *Coregonus oxyrhynchus.* [Fr. *hautin*].
HAVANA, [hav-a′-na], *n.* the name of the capital of Cuba, used to designate cigars, etc., produced there.
HAVE, (has, had), [hav], *v.t.* to possess, own; to possess as a function or characteristic; to experience; to encounter, meet with; to declare, assert; to dupe; to outwit; to take; to consume; to be obliged, compelled; **to h. at,** to attack. [~OE. *habban*].
HAVEN, [hā′-ven], *n.* a harbour; (*fig.*) refuge, place of safe retirement. [OE. *hæfen*].
HAVERCAKE, [hav′-er-kāk′], *n.* (*Scots*) oatcake. [ME. *haver* oats].
HAVERSACK, [hav′-er-sak], *n.* a wallet or small sack for provisions etc., during marching or travelling, carried slung on the back or by the side. [Germ. *hafersack* oat sack].
HAVILDAR, [hav′-il-dah(r)], *n.* a native sergeant in the Indian Army. [Pers. *hawaldar* holder of duty].
HAVOC, [hav′-ok], *n.* devastation, untold damage, extensive, indiscriminate harm; a type of American military aircraft. [AFr. *havoc* from OFr. *havot* plunder].
HAW (1), [haw], *n.* (*archaic*) an enclosure; the yard of a house. [OE. *haga*].
HAW (2), [haw], *n.* a hawthorn berry. [OE. *haga*].
HAW (3), [haw], *n.* the membranous third eyelid of a horse or dog; (*pl.*) inflammation of this. [Unkn.].
HAW (4), [haw], *n.* a loud, silly, uncertain laugh; an affected, inarticulate noise of embarrassment or nervousness. [Echoic].
HAW (5), [haw], *v.i.* to utter a haw or series of haws in speaking. [HAW (4)].
HAWFINCH, [haw′-finch], *n.* the large-beaked British finch, *Coccothraustes vulgaris.*
HAW-HAW, [haw′-haw′], *n.* stupid guffaw. [Echoic].
HAWK (1), [hawk], *n.* any of the smaller members of the falcon family, *esp.* the long-tailed, short-winged, hunting falcon; (*fig.*) a sharper, trickster, swindler. [OE. *heafoc*].
HAWK (2), [hawk], *n.* a noise made in clearing the throat. [HAWK (6)].
HAWK (3), [hawk], *n.* a farming fork with the prongs bent at right angles. [Unkn.].
HAWK (4), [hawk], *n.* a plasterer's carrying board, consisting of a rectangular flat board with a handle fitted underneath. [Unkn.].

HAWK

HAWK (5), [hawk], *v.i.* to hunt with the hawk, to practise falconry; to swoop down on its prey in flight. [HAWK (1)].
HAWK (6), [hawk], *v.t. and i.* to cough up phlegm; to clear the throat thickly. [Echoic].
HAWK (7), [hawk], *v.t. and i.* to take round and insistently offer for sale from door to door, to cry for sale in the streets; (*fig.*) to circulate, spread. [HAWKER].
HAWK-BELL, [hawk′-bel], *n.* a bell worn by trained falcons.
HAWKBIT, [hawk′-bit], *n.* a plant of the genus *Leontodon.*
HAWK-EAGLE, [hawk′-ēgl], *n.* a bird of the genus *Nisaëtus.*
HAWKER (1), [hawk′-er], *n.* one practising falconry.
HAWKER (2), [hawk′-er], *n.* a pedlar who hawks his wares, *esp.* in a cart or barrow. [ME. *hokkerye* huckster's trade].
HAWK-EYED, [hawk′-īd], *adj.* keen-eyed and vigilant.
HAWKMOTH, [hawk′-moth], *n.* a large quick-darting, hovering moth of the family *Sphingidæ.*
HAWK-NOSED, [hawk′-nōsd], *adj.* having a hooked nose.
HAWK-OWL, [hawk′-owl], *n.* an owl that hunts by daylight.
HAWKSBEARD, [hawks′-bēerd], *n.* a plant of the genus *Crepis.*
HAWKWEED, [hawk′-wēd], *n.* a yellow-flowered plant of the genus *Hieracium.*
HAWSE, [hawz], *n.* (*naut.*) the hawseholes of a ship; the part of the bows where the hawseholes are situated. [~OIcel. *hals* bow of a ship].
HAWSEHOLE, [hawz′-hōl], *n.* (*naut.*) a hole in a ship's bows through which the anchor cables are let out and hauled in.
HAWSER, [hawz′-er], *n.* (*naut.*) a mooring rope or steel cable with a right-handed twist. [~OFr. *halcier* to raise].
HAWTHORN, [haw′-thawn], *n.* the spiny tree, *Cratægus oxyacantha,* related to the rose, the may-tree. [OE. *haguthorn*].
HAY (1), [hā], *n.* cut grass dried for fodder; grass grown for this purpose; **to make h. of,** to make a mess of. [OE. *hieg, heg*].
HAY (2), [hā], *n.* a figure in many country-dances; a variety of country-dance. [OFr. *haye*].
HAYBAND, [hā′-band], *n.* a rope of hay.
HAYBOX, [hā′-boks], *n.* a box packed with hay, in which food may be maintained at cooking heat.
HAYCOCK, [hā′-kok], *n.* a pile of hay ready for carting.
HAY-FEVER, [hā′-fē′-ver], *n.* an irritating persistent catarrh caused by the inhalation of pollen or dust.
HAYFIELD, [hā′-fēld], *n.* a field in which hay is grown.
HAYFORK, [hā′-fawk], *n.* a fork for moving hay.
HAY-KNIFE, [hā′-nīf], *n.* a knife for cutting hay from the stack.
HAYLOFT, [hā′-loft], *n.* a loft for storing hay.
HAYMAKER, [hā′-māk-er], *n.* a man or machine that makes hay; (*slang*) a vigorous unscientific blow.
HAYMAKING, [hā′-māk-ing], *n.* the act of cutting grass and leaving it to dry into hay.
HAYMOW, [hā′-mō], *n.* a haystack; a cutting of hay stored in a barn.
HAYRICK, [hā′-rik], *n.* a haystack.
HAY-SEED, [hā′-sēd′], *n.* grass-seed; (*slang*) a simple rustic.
HAYSTACK, [hā′-stak], *n.* a stacked mass of hay.
HAYTEDDER, [hā′-ted′-er], *n.* a machine that scatters the cut grass for hay.
HAYWARD, [hā′-wahd], *n.* a parish officer inspecting the hedges and fences.
HAYWIRE, [hā′-wier′], *adj.* (*U.S.*) **to go h.,** to run riot, behave in a wild and unmanageable fashion.
HAZARD (1), [haz′-erd], *n.* a risk, chance, gamble; a danger, a perilous daring; a gambling game played with dice; a shot in billiards in which one of the balls is played into a pocket; (*tennis*) a winning opening in a tennis court; **losing h.,** (*billiards*) an in-off shot; **winning h.,** (*billiards*) a pot. [OFr. *hasard* game of dice].
HAZARD (2), [haz′-erd], *v.t.* to expose to risks, endanger; to venture.
HAZARDABLE, [haz′-erd-abl], *adj.* that may be hazarded.
HAZARDER, [haz′-erd-er], *n.* a person who hazards.
HAZARDOUS, [haz′-erd-us], *adj.* dangerous, risky; highly speculative.
HAZARDOUSLY, [haz′-erd-us-li], *adv.* in hazardous fashion.
HAZARDOUSNESS, [haz′-erd-us-nes], *n.* the quality or state of being hazardous.
HAZE (1), [hāz], *n.* a thin smoke, a faint obscurity of the atmosphere, a light mist; (*fig.*) a state of mental cloudiness. [Unkn.].
HAZE (2), [hāz], *v.t. and i.* to make hazy; to put in a haze; to be or become misty.
HAZE (3), [hāz], *v.t.* to rag mildly, to make unpleasant sport of. [OFr. *haser* to vex].
HAZEL (1), [hāzl], *n.* the tree, *Corylus Avellana,* with edible nuts; the colour of these nuts, light brown. [OE. *hæsel*].
HAZEL (2), [hāzl], *adj.* made of hazel-wood; tasting of the hazelnut; of a hazel colour, light brown.
HAZEL-EARTH, [hāzl′-urth], *n.* a sort of red loam.
HAZELLY, [hāz′-el-i], *adj.* of a hazel colour.
HAZELNUT, [hāzl′-nut], *n.* the nut of the hazel.
HAZILY, [hāz′-i-li], *adv.* in hazy fashion.

HAZEL

HAZINESS, [hāz′-i-nes], *n.* mistiness, the condition of being hazy; (*fig.*) a state of mental confusion.

HAZY, [hāz'-i], *adj.* obscured by haze, misty; (*fig.*) confused, not clear, dim, vague.

HE, [hē], *3rd person sg. masc. pron., nom. case.* [OE. *he*].

HEAD (1), [hed], *n.* the part of the body containing the brain, mouth, nose, ears, and eyes; anything resembling this, the topmost or foremost part of a thing; the side of a coin bearing the ruler's portrait; the source, fount, top of a thing; the froth on the top of a liquid, the pustulent top of a pimple or boil; an individual person or animal; a leader, the foremost person of a group; the principal master of a school; the senior of a group; the position of seniority, the rank of leadership; a division of a thesis or statement; aptitude, intelligence; **to bring to a h.,** to bring to its climax; **to give someone his h.,** to release from restraint. [OE. *heafod*].

HEAD (2), [hed], *adj.* chief, principal, senior.

HEAD (3), [hed], *v.t. and i.* to lead, be at the head of; to provide with a head; (*football*) to strike or propel the ball with the head; to make way against wind or stream; **to h. off,** to divert; **to h. for,** to go towards; to be about to meet with.

HEADACHE, [hed'-āk], *n.* a dull pain in the head.

HEADACHY, [hed'-āk-i], *adj.* having a headache; prone to, or causing, headaches.

HEADBAND, [hed'-band], *n.* the band at each end of a book; a band worn round the head.

HEADBOROUGH, [hed'-ber-er], *n.* the chief of a tithing. [ME. *hedborwe*].

HEADCHEESE, [hed'-chēz], *n.* brawn; pressed swine's trotters.

HEAD-DRESS, [hed'-dres], *n.* an elaborate covering or decoration worn on the head.

HEADED, [hed'-id], *adj.* having a head; relating to intelligence and understanding.

HEADER, [hed'-er], *n.* a dive head-foremost; a brick laid at right-angles to the face of a wall; a striking of a football with the head.

HEADFAST, [hed'-fahst], *n.* (*naut.*) a rope at the head of a ship for fastening it.

HEADFRAME, [hed'-frām], *n.* the framework carrying the winding wheels of a mine.

HEAD-GARGLE, [hed'-gahgl], *n.* a disease attacking cattle.

HEADGEAR, [hed'-gēer], *n.* hats, head-coverings.

HEAD-HUNTER, [hed'-hunt'-er], *n.* a savage belonging to a tribe which practises head-hunting.

HEAD-HUNTING, [hed'-hunt'-ing], *n.* the practice of decapitating enemies, and smoking and preserving their heads.

HEADILY, [hed'-i-li], *adv.* in heady fashion.

HEADINESS, [hed'-i-nes], *n.* the quality of being heady.

HEADING, [hed'-ing], *n.* the act of one who heads; the title, headwords, at the top of a page of writing; a brick laid at right-angles to the face of a wall.

HEADLAMP, [hed'-lamp], *n.* either of two bright driving-lights on the front of a car.

HEADLAND, [hed'-land], *n.* a steep, jutting promontory; a strip of unploughed land at the edge of a field.

HEADLESS, [hed'-les], *adj.* without a head.

HEADLIGHT, [hed'-līt], *n.* a directing light fixed to the front of a vehicle.

HEADLINE, [hed'-līn], *n.* the bold heading across the top of a newspaper, or at the beginning of a new subject; (*naut.*) a rope used to fasten a sail to the yard.

HEADLONG (1), [hed'-long], *adj.* head first, impetuous.

HEADLONG (2), [hed'-long], *adv.* head-foremost, precipitately, impetuously [ME. *hedlinge*].

HEAD-MAIN, [hed'-mān'], *n.* the principal canal of an irrigating system.

HEADMAN, [hed'-man], *n.* the chief man of a village, tribe, or party; a foreman.

HEADMARK, [hed'-mahk], *n.* an outstanding characteristic.

HEADMASTER, [hed'-mahst'-er], *n.* the chief master of a school.

HEADMISTRESS, [hed'-mis'-tres], *n.* the chief mistress of a school.

HEADMONEY, [hed'-mun'-i], *n.* a poll-tax; an award for bringing in a prisoner, dead or alive.

HEADMOST, [hed'-mōst], *adj.* foremost.

HEADNOTE, [hed'-nōt], *n.* a note printed at the top of a page.

HEAD-ON (1), [hed'-on'], *adj.* coming from opposite directions; **h. collision,** a collision between vehicles coming from opposite directions.

HEAD-ON (2), [hed'-on'], *adv.* from opposite directions.

HEAD-PENCE, [hed'-pens], *n.* headmoney.

HEADPIECE, [hed'-pēs], *n.* a helmet; a decoration at the head of a page; (*slang*) the head, the intelligence.

HEADQUARTERS, [hed'-kwaw'-terz], *n.(pl.)* the residence or station of the commander-in-chief of an army; the central office of any business or organization.

HEADREST, [hed'-rest], *n.* a support for the head at the back of a chair.

HEAD-SEA, [hed'-sē], *n.* sea rolling contrary to a ship's course.

HEADSHIP, [hed'-ship], *n.* the position or office of head.

HEADSMAN, [hedz'-man], *n.* an executioner who decapitates.

HEADSPRING, [hed'-spring], *n.* the principal spring, source.

HEADSTALL, [hed'-stawl], *n.* leading harness, harness without a bit.

HEADSTOCK, [hed'-stok], *n.* the part of a lathe holding the spindle.

HEADSTONE, [hed'-stōn], *n.* the keystone of an arch; the stone at the head of a grave.

HEADSTRONG, [hed'-strong], *adj.* stubbornly self-willed, impetuously obstinate.

HEADTIRE, [hed'-tier], *n.* headgear.

HEAD VOICE, [hed'-vois], *n.* a light high-pitched tone of voice.

HEADWAY, [hed'-wā], *n.* progress in a forward direction, *esp.* against opposition; the forward motion of a ship; the space between the head and the ceiling or door-top.

HEAD-WIND, [hed'-wind], *n.* a wind blowing against one's course.

HEADWORD, [hed'-wurd], *n.* a word in bold type forming a heading.

HEADWORK, [hed'-wurk], *n.* work requiring mental effort; ornamental carving round the keystone of an arch.

HEAD-WORKMAN, [hed'-wurk'-man], *n.* the chief workman.

HEADY, [hed'-i], *adj.* intoxicating; inflaming; conducive to neglect of judgment; rashly headstrong.

HEAL, [hēl], *v.t. and i.* to restore to health, to cure injury or sickness; to become healthy or sound; (of wounds) to grow a new skin. [OE. *hælan*].

HEALABLE, [hēl'-abl], *adj.* possible to be healed.

HEALD, [hēld], *n.* heddle. [OE. *hefeld*].

HEALER, [hēl'-er], *n.* one who heals, *esp.* by non-medical means.

HEALING, [hēl'-ing], *adj.* that heals.

HEALINGLY, [hēl'-ing-li], *adv.* in healing fashion.

HEALTH, [helth], *n.* the state of being free from sickness, disorder, injury, or disease; bodily condition; something inducing good bodily condition; a toast drunk to someone's prosperity and well-being. [OE. *hælth*].

HEALTHFUL, [helth'-fōōl], *adj.* conducive to good health; healthy.

HEALTHFULLY, [helth'-fōōl-i], *adv.* in healthful fashion.

HEALTHFULNESS, [helth'-fōōl-nes], *n.* the condition of being healthful.

HEALTHILY, [helth'-i-li], *adv.* in healthy fashion.

HEALTHINESS, [helth'-i-nes], *n.* the condition of being healthy.

HEALTHLESS, [helth'-les], *adj.* unhealthy.

HEALTHLESSNESS, [helth'-les-nes], *n.* the condition of being healthless.

HEALTHY, [helth'-i], *adj.* enjoying good health; conducive to good health; displaying good health; (*fig.*) wholesome.

HEAM, [hēm], *n.* the caul of an animal. [Uncert.].

HEAP (1), [hēp], *n.* a pile or mound of things; (*slang*) (*pl.*) a large quantity, a great number. [OE. *heap* troop].

HEAP (2), [hēp], *v.t. and i.* to pile up into a heap; to accumulate in great quantities; to fill up with a heap or heaps. [OE. *heapian*].

HEAPY, [hēp'-i], *adj.* heaped up.

HEAR, [hēer], *v.t. and i.* to perceive sounds with the ear; to listen to; to learn; to grant, answer (a request); (*leg.*) to attend to, judge; **to h. from,** to receive a communication from. [OE. *heran*].

HEARABLE, [hēer'-abl], *adj.* possible to be heard.

HEARER, [hēer'-er], *n.* one who hears.

HEARING, [hēer'-ing], *n.* the faculty of perceiving sound; attention, a chance of speaking; earshot; (*leg.*) the judgment of a case.

HEARKEN, [hahk'-en], *v.i.* to listen; to attend to. [OE. *heorcnian*].

HEARKENER, [hahk'-en-er], *n.* one who hearkens.

HEARSAY, [hēer'-sā], *n.* something heard said, rumour.
HEARSE, [hurs], *n.* vehicle carrying a corpse to the grave; a framework bearing the pall. [OFr. *herce* harrow].
HEARSE-CLOTH, [hurs'-kloth], *n.* a pall.
HEARSELIKE, [hurs'-līk], *adj.* like a hearse, funereal.
HEART, [haht], *n.* that organ of the body propelling the blood through the veins by its pulsations; (*fig.*) the seat of the emotions and affections; courage, ardour, enthusiasm; the temperament; the centre, core of anything; the crux, the vital part of a thing; anything resembling the heart in shape; (*pl.*) (*cards*) the suit marked by red heart-shaped figures; **to take to h.,** to take very seriously; **to eat one's h. out,** to pine away in secret; **h. to h.,** intimate; **to take h.,** to be encouraged, cheer up. [OE. *heorte*].
HEARTACHE, [haht'-āk], *n.* sorrow, grief.
HEARTBREAK, [haht'-brāk], *n.* intense sorrow.
HEARTBROKEN, [haht'-brōk'-en], *adj.* overwhelmed by sorrow or disappointment.
HEARTBURN, [haht'-burn], *n.* acidity of the stomach producing a tingling sensation in the throat.
HEARTBURNING, [haht'-burn'-ing], *n.* secret hatred and envy.
HEART-COCKLE, [haht'-kokl], *n.* the bivalve mollusc, *Isocardia cor.*
HEARTEASE, [haht'-ēz], *n.* peace of mind.
HEARTEN, [haht'-en], *v.t. and i.* to encourage, cheer up.
HEARTFELT, [haht'-felt], *adj.* felt deeply.
HEARTH, [hahth], *n.* the stone or bricks on which household fires are made; the floor of a furnace; (*fig.*) the home, domestic life and comfort. [OE. *heorth*].
HEARTHBROOM, [hahth'-brōōm], *n.* a broom with which the hearth may be swept.
HEARTHMONEY, [hahth'-mun'-i], *n.* a tax formerly levied on hearths.
HEARTHRUG, [hahth'-rug], *n.* a rug lying in front of the hearth.
HEARTHSTONE, [hahth'-stōn], *n.* the stone forming the hearth; a soft stone or pumice used to clean the hearth and other stone surfaces.
HEARTILY, [haht'-i-li], *adv.* in hearty fashion.
HEARTINESS, [haht'-i-nes], *n.* the quality of being hearty.
HEARTLESS, [haht'-les], *adj.* pitiless; lacking enthusiasm or courage.
HEARTLESSLY, [haht'-les-li], *adv.* in heartless fashion.
HEARTLESSNESS, [haht'-les-nes], *n.* the quality of being heartless.
HEARTLET, [haht'-let], *n.* a small heart.
HEARTRENDING, [haht'-rend'-ing], *adj.* moving to the deepest grief and pity.
HEART'S-BLOOD, [hahts'-blud], *n.* life-blood; (*fig.*) life itself.
HEARTSEASE, [hahts'-ēz], *n.* the wild pansy, *Viola tricolor*; any of several other varieties of pansy.
HEART-SICK, [haht'-sik], *adj.* deeply grieved, distressed.
HEARTSOME, [haht'-sum], *adj.* heartening, gladsome.
HEARTSTRINGS, [haht'-stringz], *n.* the profoundest feelings.
HEART-WHEEL, [haht'-wēl], *n.* the cam wheel.
HEART-WHOLE, [haht'-hōl], *adj.* unmoved by sexual love.
HEART-WOOD, [haht'-wŏŏd], *n.* the hard growth in the centre of a tree.
HEARTY (1), [haht'-i], *n.* (*slang*) a student who prefers sport and social life to intellectual pursuits.
HEARTY (2), [haht'-i], *adj.* healthy, in fine physical condition, vigorous, strong; proceeding from good condition; good-hearted, sincere; brutishly philistine.
HEAT (1), [hēt], *n.* a form of energy connected with molecular activity; a condition of matter characterized by high temperature, warmth; a sensation produced by contact with, or exposure to, high temperature; the burning taste of certain spices; periodic sexual excitement in animals; strong emotion, passion, wrath; (*athletics*) a preliminary eliminating contest. [OE. *hætu*].
HEAT (2), [hēt], *v.t. and i.* to impart heat to; to rouse, stir; to become hot. [OE. *hætan*].
HEAT-APOPLEXY, [hēt'-ap'-o-plek'-si], *n.* sunstroke.
HEATED, [hēt'-id], *adj.* that has been made warm or hot; (*fig.*) passionate, with acrimony.
HEATER, [hēt'-er], *n.* a machine or apparatus for heating something.
HEATH, [hēth], *n.* a stretch of open, uncultivated land, *esp.* if covered with heather; any pinkish-flowered shrub of the genus *Erica.* [OE. *hæth*].
HEATH-CLAD, [hēth'-klad], *adj.* grown over with heather.
HEATH-COCK, [hēth'-kok], *n.* the male of the black grouse.
HEATHEN (1), [hē'-THen], *n.* (*sg. and collect.*) (*O.T.*) anyone not observing the Jewish religion; any non-Christian; anyone not observing one of the major religions; a totemist, an animistic savage; (*fig.*) a rough, barbarous person. [OE. *hæthen*].
HEATHEN (2), [hē'-THen], *adj.* pertaining to, or characteristic of, a heathen; impious; (*coll.*) uncultured and unenlightened.

HEATH-COCK

HEATHENDOM, [hē'-THen-dum], *n.* the heathen parts of the world; the state of being heathen. [OE. *hæthendom*].
HEATHENISH, [hē'-THen-ish], *adj.* idolatrous, barbarous, relating to the heathen. [OE. *hæthenisc*].
HEATHENISHLY, [hē'-THen-ish-li], *adv.* in heathenish fashion.
HEATHENISHNESS, [hē'-THen-ish-nes], *n.* the condition of being heathenish.
HEATHENISM, [hē'-THen-izm], *n.* the state of being heathen.
HEATHENIZE, [hē'-THen-īz], *v.t.* to make heathen.
HEATHENRY, [hē'-THen-ri], *n.* heathendom.
HEATHER, [heTH'-er], *n.* the plant, *Calluna vulgaris*, or the plant, *Erica cinerea*, related to the heath; a stretch of land covered with this. [ME. *hathir*].
HEATHERBELL, [heTH'-er-bel'], *n.* the plant, *Erica tetralix*, or its flower; the plant, *Erica cinerea*.
HEATHERY, [heTH'-er-i], *adj.* prolific in heather.
HEATH-PEA, [hēth'-pē], *n.* the edible wild vetch.
HEATHPOUT, [hēth'-powt], *n.* the heath-cock.
HEATHY, [hēth'-i], *adj.* covered with heath.
HEATING (1), [hēt'-ing], *n.* the apparatus for keeping warm a building; the means for raising the temperature of anything.
HEATING (2), [hēt'-ing], *adj.* that heats.
HEAT-SPOT, [hēt'-spot], *n.* a small pimple supposed to be produced by heat.
HEAT-WAVE, [hēt'-wāv], *n.* a spell of excessive heat.
HEAUME, [hōm], *n.* a heavy medieval tilting helmet. [Fr. *heaume*].
HEAVE (1), [hēv], *n.* the act of heaving; a swelling, upward movement; a retching; (*geol.*) displacement caused by a fault in the stratum; a wrestling throw.
HEAVE (2), [hēv], *v.t.* to raise, swing up with effort; to move, drag heavily and laboriously; to throw; (*naut.*) to haul; (*naut.*) to move by hauling a rope, to move (a ship); *v.i.* to rise in long, high waves; to rise and fall deeply and regularly; to swell; to retch, vomit; (*naut.*) to haul a rope; (of a ship) to proceed, move; **to h. to,** to stop a ship's progress. [~OE. *hebban*].
HEAVEN, [hev'-en], *n.* the abode of God or of the gods, the place to which the blessed soul goes after death; the sky, the firmament; (*pl.*) the universe; (*fig.*) a place or state of extreme joy and blessedness; the highest fulfilment of hope and desire. [OE. *heofon*].
HEAVEN-BORN, [hev'-en-bawn], *adj.* born of, or at the instigation of, the gods.
HEAVEN-BUILT, [hev'-en-bilt], *adj.* divinely built.
HEAVEN-DIRECTED, [hev'-en-di-rek'-tid], *adj.* divinely guided.
HEAVENLINESS, [hev'-en-li-nes], *n.* the quality of being heavenly.
HEAVENLY, [hev'-en-li], *adj.* relating to heaven; having the joys of heaven; highly delightful, divine, adorable. [OE. *heofonlic*].
HEAVENLY-MINDED, [hev'-en-li-mīnd'-id], *adj.* thinking about holy things.
HEAVENLY-MINDEDNESS, [hev'-en-li-mīnd'-id-nes], *n.* the quality of being heavenly-minded.
HEAVENWARD, [hev'-en-wud], *adv.* towards heaven.
HEAVER, [hēv'-er], *n.* one who shifts heavy objects; (*naut.*) a lever for heaving rope.
HEAVES, [hēvz], *n.* broken wind, an asthmatic affliction of horses.
HEAVILY, [hev'-i-li], *adv.* in heavy fashion.

HEAVINESS, [hev'-i-nes], *n.* the quality of being heavy.
HEAVING (1), [hēv'-ing], *n.* the act of one who, or that which, heaves.
HEAVING (2), [hēv'-ing], *adj.* that heaves.
HEAVISIDE, [hev'-i-sīd], *n.* the name of a physicist, Oliver *Heaviside*, used to denote a layer of particles in the upper atmosphere from which wireless waves are reflected back to earth.
HEAVY (1), [hev'-i], *adj.* having weight, ponderous; of oppressive weight; crushing, wearisome, burdensome; excessive, too great, considerable; powerful, of the largest class; forceful, violent, severe; thundery, overcast; depressing, grievous; depressed; solid, rich, indigestible; (of troops) elaborately armed and equipped; thick, muddy, clinging; over-elaborate; over-serious, boring, dull; not spontaneous, produced with effort; graceless, clumsy; torpid, lifeless, without energy; pregnant; pompous. [OE. *hefig*].
HEAVY (2), [hēv'-i], *adj.* affected with heaves.
HEAVY-HANDED, [hev'-i-hand'-id], *adj.* oppressive; clumsy; tactless.
HEAVY-HEADED, [hev'-i-hed'-id], *adj.* sleepy; dull.
HEAVY-LADEN, [hev'-i-lād'-en], *adj.* heavily burdened.
HEAVY-SPAR, [hev'-i-spah(r)'], *n.* barytes; sulphate of baryta.
HEAVY-WEIGHT, [hev'-i-wāt], *n.* a boxer weighing more than 11 stone 4 lb., *esp.* one over 12 stone 7 lb. in weight; an animal or person of the largest class.
HEBDOMAD, [heb'-dō-mad], *n.* a group of seven; a week. [Gk. *hebdomas* seventh].
HEBDOMADAL, [heb-dom'-ad-al], *adj.* weekly.
HEBDOMADARY, [heb-dom'-a-der-i], *adj.* hebdomadal.
HEBDOMATICAL, [heb'-do-mat'-ik-al], *adj.* weekly.
HEBE, [hē'-bi], *n.* (*slang*) a barmaid. [Gk. *Hebe*, Goddess of Youth].
HEBETANT, [heb'-i-tant], *adj.* blunting, making dull. [L. *hebetans*].
HEBETATE, [heb'-i-tāt], *v.t.* to dull mentally, to stupefy. [L. *hebetare*].
HEBETATION, [heb-i-tā'-shun], *n.* the act of hebetating; the state of being dulled or blunted. [L. *hebetatio*].
HEBETUDE, [heb'-i-tewd], *n.* stupidity, dulness. [L. *hebetudo*].
HEBRAIC, [hē-brā'-ik], *adj.* relating to the Hebrews. [Gk. *hebraikos*].
HEBRAICALLY, [hē-brā'-ik-al-i], *adv.* in Hebrew fashion.
HEBRAISM, [hē'-brā-izm], *n.* Judaism; Hebrew ideology; a Hebrew word or turn of phrase.
HEBRAIST, [hē'-brā-ist], *n.* a student of the Hebrew language, religion, and culture; a follower of Hebraism.
HEBRAISTIC, [hē'-brā-ist'-ik], *adj.* relating to Hebraism.
HEBRAIZE, [hē'-brā-īz], *v.t. and i.* to translate into Hebrew, to make or become Hebraic. [Gk. *hebraizo*].
HEBREW (1), [hē'-brōō], *n.* an Israelite; a Jew; the language of the Israelites. [ME. *Hebreu* from Aramaic *Hebrai*].
HEBREW (2), [hē'-brōō], *adj.* relating to the Hebrews.
HECATOMB, [hek'-a-tōōm], *n.* a sacrifice of a hundred oxen; a wholesale slaughter or sacrifice, a massacre. [Gk. *hekatombe*].
HECK, [hek], *n.* a rack for holding fodder; a loom frame for taking the warp. [OE. *hæc* gate].
HECKLE, [hekl], *v.t.* to dress flax; to harass a speaker with taunts, interjections, and difficult questions. [ME. *heckelen*].
HECKLER, [hek'-ler], *n.* one who heckles.
HECKYMAL, [hek'-i-mal], *n.* the blue tit, *Parus obscurus*. [Unkn.].
HECTARE, [hek'-tāer], *n.* a hundred ares. [Fr. *hectare*].
HECTIC, [hek'-tik], *adj.* consumptive, feverish; agitated, excited; wildly exciting. [Gk. *hektikos*].
HECTICALLY, [hek'-tik-al-i], *adv.* in hectic fashion.
HECTO-, *pref.* hundred. [Gk. *hekaton*].
HECTOCOTYLUS, [hek'-tō-kot'il-us], *n.* the copulative tentacle of the octopus and certain related animals. [HECTO and Gk. *kotule* small cup].
HECTOGRAM, HECTOGRAMME, [hek'-tō-gram'], *n.* a hundred grammes. [HECTO and GRAMME].
HECTOGRAPH (1), [hek'-tō-grahf], *n.* a device for duplicating from a gelatine slab. [HECTO and GRAPH].
HECTOGRAPH (2), [hek'-tō-grahf], *v.t.* to duplicate by means of a hectograph.
HECTOLITRE, [hek'-tō-lē-ter], *n.* a hundred litres. [HECTO and LITRE].
HECTOMETRE, [hek'-tō-mē-ter], *n.* a hundred metres. [HECTO and METRE].
HECTOR, [hek'-ter], *v.t. and i.* to bully, scold, browbeat; to bluster, swashbuckle. [*Hector*, the Trojan warrior and son of Priam, from his character as depicted in medieval romances].
HECTORISM, [hek'-ter-izm], *n.* bullying, swashbuckling, browbeating.
HECTORLY, [hek'-ter-li], *adj.* hectoring.
HECTOSTERE, [hek'-tō-stēer'], *n.* a solid measure equivalent to a hundred cubic metres. [HECTO and STERE].
HEDDLE, [hedl], *n.* an eyed wire through which the warp is threaded in weaving. [OE. *hefeld*].
HEDERACEOUS, [hed'-er-ā'-shus], *adj.* relating to, resembling, ivy. [L. *hedera* ivy].
HEDERAL, [hed'-er-al], *adj.* hederaceous.
HEDERATED, [hed'-er-āt'-id], *adj.* ivied.
HEDERIFEROUS, [hed'-er-if'-er-us], *adj.* bearing ivy. [L. *hedera* ivy and *ferre* to bear].
HEDGE (1), [hej], *n.* a barrier or boundary of closely planted shrubs or bushes set in line and trimmed; a thickset row or line of anything; (*fig.*) that which restricts or shuts off. [OE. *hecg*].
HEDGE (2), [hej], *v.t. and i.* to surround with a hedge; to surround, shut in, restrict; (*betting*) to place secondary stakes in order to cover one's losses if the main gamble fails; to construct or trim a hedge; to hesitate or moderate so as to avoid committing oneself.
HEDGE-BILL, [hej'-bil], *n.* a bill used for trimming hedges.
HEDGE-BORN, [hej'-bawn], *adj.* of low or illegitimate birth.
HEDGE-CREEPER, [hej'-krēp'-er], *n.* a furtive, creeping vagabond.
HEDGE-GARLIC, [hej'-gah'-lik], *n.* the cruciferous plant, *Sisymbrium Alliaria*.
HEDGEHOG, [hej'-hog], *n.* the insectivorous mammal *Erinaceus europæus*, notable for its covering of quills; (*coll.*) a grumpy person, (*milit.*) a position which can be defended from all sides.

HEDGEHOG

HEDGEHOG-THISTLE, [hej'-hog'-thisl'], *n.* any plant of the genus *Echinocactus*.
HEDGE-HYSSOP, [hej'-his'-op], *n.* a bitter herb of the genus *Gratiola* or *Scutellaria minor*.
HEDGELESS, [hej'-les], *adj.* without hedges.
HEDGE-MARRIAGE, [hej'-ma'-rij], *n.* a clandestine marriage.
HEDGE-MUSTARD, [hej'-mus'-terd], *n.* the cruciferous plant, *Sisymbrium officinale*.
HEDGE-PARSLEY, [hej'-pahs'-li], *n.* either of the two plants *Torilis Anthriscus* and *Æthusa Cynapium*.
HEDGE-PARSON, [hej'-pahs'-on], *n.* a disreputable and ill-conditioned priest.
HEDGEPIG, [hej'-pig], *n.* a young hedgehog.
HEDGER, [hej'-er], *n.* a maker or trimmer of edges.
HEDGEROW, [hej'-rō], *n.* a hedge; a row of small trees set in a hedge.
HEDGE-SCHOOL, [hej'-skōōl], *n.* a primitive open-air school.
HEDGE-SPARROW, [hej'-spa'-rō], *n.* the grey and brown passerine bird, *Accentor modularis*.
HEDGEVINE, [hej'-vīn], *n.* virgin's bower, *Clematis Vitalba*.
HEDONIC, [hē-don'-ik], *adj.* hedonistic. [Gk. *hedonikos*].
HEDONISM, [hē'-don-izm], *n.* (*eth.*) the theory that pleasure is the chief good and final cause; devotion to cultivated pleasure. [Gk. *hedone* pleasure].
HEDONIST, [hē'-don-ist], *n.* an adherent of hedonism; one constantly engaged in the pursuit of pleasure.
HEDONISTIC, [hē'-don-ist'-ik], *adj.* relating to, following, hedonism.
HEDYPHANE, [hē'-di-fān], *n.* an oxide of lead and lime. [Gk. *hedus* sweet and *phanes* seeming].
HEED (1), [hēd], *n.* watchful care, attention, obedience.
HEED (2), [hēd], *v.t. and i.* to pay attention to, observe, have care. [OE. *hedan*].
HEEDFUL, [hēd'-fōōl], *adj.* taking heed, watchful, obedient.
HEEDFULLY, [hēd'-fōōl-i], *adv.* in heedful fashion.

HEEDFULNESS, [hēd'-fŏŏl-nes], *n.* the quality of being heedful.
HEEDLESS, [hēd'-les], *adj.* careless, disobedient, inattentive, disregardful.
HEEDLESSLY, [hēd'-les-li], *adv.* in heedless fashion.
HEEDLESSNESS, [hēd'-les-nes], *n.* the quality of being heedless.
HEE-HAW (1), [hē'-haw'], *n.* the bray of the donkey. [Echoic].
HEE-HAW (2), [hē'-haw'], *v.i.* to utter hee-haws.
HEEL (1), [hēl], *n.* the back part of the foot behind and below the ankle; the raised piece supporting this in a shoe; the part of any footgear covering this; the hock or hoof of an animal; a heel-shaped end part of an implement; the bottom of a glass; the tail end of a thing; **head over heels**, completely over; **down at heel**, shabby, ragged; **to take to one's heels**, to run away. [OE. *hela*].
HEEL (2), [hēl], *n.* the heeling, list of a ship. [HEEL (4)].
HEEL (3), [hēl], *v.t.* to provide with a heel; (*football*) to kick with the heel; (*hort.*) to cover over with loose earth preparatory to planting. [HEEL (1)].
HEEL (4), [hēl], *v.t.* and *i.* to tilt over to the side, to list, to reel over; to cause to do this. [OE. *heldan* to bend].
HEELBALL, [hēl'-bawl], *n.* a mixture of wax and lampblack used for polishing leather, etc.
HEEL-PIECE, [hēl'-pēs], *n.* the projection forming the heel of a shoe; a tailpiece.
HEEL-TAP, [hēl'-tap], *n.* the last drops of liquid left in a glass after drinking; the layer of leather on the heel of a boot.
HEFT, [heft], *v.t.* to lift; to estimate approximately the weight of by holding. [HEAVE].
HEFTILY, [hef'-ti-li], *adv.* in hefty fashion.
HEFTINESS, [hef'-ti-nes], *n.* the quality of being hefty.
HEFTY, [hef'-ti], *adj.* (*coll.*) strong, muscular, big and of powerful physique. [HEFT].
HEGELIAN (1), [hā-gē'-li-an], *n.* a disciple of Hegel.
HEGELIAN (2), [hā-gē'-li-an], *adj.* relating to Hegel's philosophy.
HEGELIANISM, [hā-gē'-li-an-izm], *n.* the idealist philosophy of Hegel.
HEGEMONIC, [hē'-gi-mon'-ik], *adj.* relating to a hegemony; exercising a hegemony. [Gk. *hegemonikos* leading].
HEGEMONICAL, [hē'-gi-mon'-ik-al], *adj.* hegemonic.
HEGEMONY, [hē-gem'-on-i], *n.* the political supremacy of one state amongst a group or confederacy. [Gk. *hegemonia*].
HEGIRA, [hej'-ir-a], *n.* the flight of Mohammed from Mecca in A.D. 622, this being taken as the beginning of the Mohammedan era. [Arab. *hijra* separation].
HEIFER, [hef'-er], *n.* a cow that has not yet calved. [OE. *heahfore*].
HEIGH, [hā], *int.* an exclamation of exhortation or to attract attention.
HEIGH-HO, [hā'-hō'], *int.* an expression of surprise or weariness.
HEIGHT, [hīt], *n.* the condition of being high; the extent to which anything is high, the altitude, vertical extent; (*fig.*) the summit, peak, highest degree of a thing; a high place, a mountain, high hill. [OE. *hiehthu*].
HEIGHTEN, [hīt'-en], *v.t.* and *i.* to make higher, augment; (*fig.*) to intensify, enhance; to become higher; to become more intense or more coloured.
HEINOUS, [hā'-nus], *adj.* wicked, hateful, worthy of punishment; atrocious, detestable. [OFr. *haïnos*].
HEINOUSLY, [hā'-nus-li], *adv.* in heinous fashion.
HEINOUSNESS, [hā'-nus-nes], *n.* the quality of being heinous.
HEIR, [āer], *n.* one who succeeds to the property of another; one who is entitled or appointed by will to succeed to property on the death of the holder; the successor to anything; one to whom some attribute, ideal, etc., is bequeathed. [OFr. *heir*].
HEIR-APPARENT, [āer'-a-pa'-rent], *n.* one who, failing his own death, is bound to succeed.
HEIR-AT-LAW, [āer'-at-law'], *n.* the natural heir of another.
HEIR-BY-CUSTOM, [āer'-bī-kus'-tom], *n.* an heir by gavelkind or borough English.
HEIRDOM, [āer'-dum], *n.* the state of being an heir; succession by right or by will.
HEIRESS, [āer'-es], *n.* a female heir.
HEIRLESS, [āer'-les], *adj.* without an heir.
HEIRLOOM, [āer'-lōōm], *n.* something inherited, *esp.* an inherited chattel that cannot be alienated.
HEIR-PRESUMPTIVE, [āer'-pri-zump'-tiv], *n.* one who is heir failing a birth into a more direct line of succession.
HEIRSHIP, [āer'-ship], *n.* the status or rights of an heir.
HELCOID, [hel'-koid], *adj.* ulcerated, ulcerous. [Gk. *helkos* ulcer and *oeides* like].
HELCOLOGY, [hel-kol'-o-ji], *n.* the study of ulceration. [Gk. *helkos* ulcer and *logos* speech].
HELD, [held], *pret.* and *p.pt.* of HOLD. [OE. *heold*].
HELIAC, [hē'-li-ak], *adj.* heliacal. [Gk. *heliakos*].
HELIACAL, [hē-lī'-ak-al], *adj.* solar, relating to the sun.
HELIACALLY, [hē-lī'-ak-al-i], *adv.* in heliacal fashion.
HELIANTHEMUM, [hē'-li-an'-thi-mum], *n.* (*bot.*) the genus including the rock-rose.
HELIANTHUS, [hē'-li-an'-thus], *n.* (*bot.*) the genus including the sunflower. [Gk. *helios* sun and *anthos* flower].
HELICAL, [hel'-ik-al], *adj.* spiral, pertaining to a helix; **h. gear**, a gearing with the teeth so cut that if extended they would form a spiral or helix about the axis of the wheel. [L. *helix helicis* a spiral].
HELICIFORM, [hel-is'-i-fawm], *adj.* in the shape of a helix. [HELIX and FORM].
HELICOID, [hel'-ik-oid], *adj.* in the form of a helix, spiral. [Gk. *helikoeides*].
HELICOIDAL, [hel'-ik-oid-al], *adj.* helicoid.

HELICAL GEAR

HELICON, [hel'-ik-on], *n.* (*mus.*) a brass wind-instrument resembling a large French horn. [Gk. *helikon* spiral].
HELICONIAN, [hel'-i-kō'-ni-an], *adj.* relating to Mount Helicon, or to the Muses.
HELICOPTER, [hel'-i-kop'-ter], *n.* a flying machine with horizontal rotors above it, by means of which it can ascend and descend vertically. [HELIX and Gk. *pteron* wing].
HELIO-, *pref.* relating to the sun. [Gk. *helios* sun].
HELIOCENTRIC, [hē'-li-ō-sen'-trik], *adj.* relating to the sun as centre of the universe. [HELIO and CENTRIC].
HELIOGRAM, [hē'-li-ō-gram], *n.* a message flashed heliographically. [HELIO and Gk. *gramma* writing].
HELIOGRAPH, [hē'-li-ō-grahf], *n.* a device for transmitting messages by flashing a mirror or polished surface; an instrument for measuring the intensity of sunlight; a method of engraving by exposing a chemically treated plate to sunlight. [HELIO and GRAPH].
HELIOGRAPHIC, [hē'-li-ō-graf'-ik], *adj.* relating to a heliograph.
HELIOGRAPHICALLY, [hē'-li-ō-graf'-ik-al-i], *adv.* by means of the heliograph.

HELIOGRAPH

HELIOGRAPHY, [hē'-li-og'-ra-fi], *n.* signalling by means of the heliograph. [HELIO and Gk. *graphia* writing].
HELIOLATER, [hē'-li-ol'-a-ter], *n.* a sun worshipper.
HELIOLATRY, [hē'-li-ol'-a-tri], *n.* sun worship. [HELIO and Gk. *latreia* worship].
HELIOLOGY, [hē'-li-ol'-o-ji], *n.* the study of the sun. [HELIO and Gk. *logos* speech].
HELIOMETER, [hē'-li-om'-it-er], *n.* an instrument for measuring the diameter of the sun, or the angular distance between stars. [HELIO and METER].
HELIOPHILOUS, [hē'-li-of'-i-lus], *adj.* loving the sun. [HELIO and Gk. *philos* love].
HELIOSCOPE, [hē'-li-ō-skōp'], *n.* a device for protecting the eyes during solar observation. [HELIO and SCOPE].
HELIOSIS, [hē'-li-ō'-sis], *n.* sunstroke. [Gk. *heliosis*].
HELIOSTAT, [hē'-li-ō-stat'], *n.* a mechanically operated rotating mirror for directing a sunbeam continually along one path. [HELIO and Gk. *statos* placed].
HELIO-THERAPY, [hē'-li-ō-the'-ra-pi], *n.* sunshine treatment.
HELIOTROPE (1), [hē'-li-ō-trōp], *n.* a plant of the genus *Heliotropum*, with pale purple flowers that turn towards the sun; the scent of this flower; a light purple colour; a kind of heliograph. [Gk. *heliotropion*].

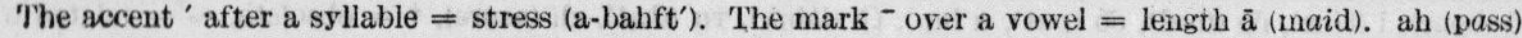

HELIOTROPE (2), [hē'-li-ō-trōp], *adj.* having the colour or scent of the heliotrope.
HELIOTROPIC, [hē'-li-ō-trop'-ik], *adj.* turning towards the light.
HELIOTROPISM, [hē'-li-ot'-rop-izm], *n.* the tendency of plants to turn towards the sun.
HELISPHERIC, [hel'-i-sfe'-rik], *adj.* helispherical.
HELISPHERICAL, [hel'-i-sfe'-rik-al], *adj.* turning spirally round a sphere. [HELIX and SPHERICAL].
HELIUM, [hē'-li-um], *n.* a non-inflammable gas, the element He, used for supporting airships, etc. [Gk. *helios* sun].
HELIX, (*pl.* **helices**), [hēl'-iks], *n.* a spiral line, a coil, a convolution; the rim of the external ear; a genus of snails; (*math.*) a curve on a rounded surface which forms a straight line when the surface is spread flat. [Gk. *helix* coil].
HELL, [hel], *n.* the eternal abode of the damned, according to the Christian religion; (*fig.*) extreme pain, discomfort, and distress; a haunt of vice. [OE. *hel*].
HELL-BROTH, [hel'-broth], *n.* a witches' brew; an unpleasant concoction.
HELL-CAT, [hel'-kat], *n.* a violent and evil-tempered woman.
HELLEBORE, [hel'-i-baw(r)], *n.* the Christmas rose; a medicinal drug extracted from this; a poisonous plant of the same genus. [Gk. *helleboros*].
HELLEBORINE, [hel'-i-baw-rēn'], *n.* a British orchid. [Gk. *helleborine*].
HELLENE, [hel'-ēn], *n.* a Greek. [Gk. *Hellene*].
HELLENIAN, [hel-ē'-ni-an], *adj.* Hellenic.
HELLENIC, [hel-ē'-nik], *adj.* relating to ancient Greece, its people and language. [Gk. *Hellenikos*].
HELLENISM, [hel'-en-izm], *n.* Greek culture, or the affectation of it; a Greek turn of phrase; Greek nationality. [Gk. *hellenismos*].
HELLENIST, [hel'-en-ist], *n.* a devotee of Hellenism; a Greek Jew.
HELLENISTIC, [hel'-en-ist'-ik], *adj.* relating to the kingdoms and culture of the Asiatic Greeks, *esp.* to the successors of Alexander in Asia Minor.
HELLENISTICALLY, [hel'-en-ist'-ik-al-i], *adv.* in Hellenistic fashion.
HELLENIZE, [hel'-en-īz], *v.t.* *and i.* to make Greek; to become Greek. [Gk. *hellenizo*].
HELL-HAG, [hel'-hag], *n.* a hell-cat.
HELLHOUND, [hel'-hownd], *n.* a horrible and wicked person; a demoniacal dog.
HELLISH, [hel'-ish], *adj.* relating to, resembling, hell; (*coll.*) extremely unpleasant.
HELLISHLY, [hel'-ish-li], *adv.* in hellish fashion.
HELLISHNESS, [hel'-ish-nes], *n.* the quality of being hellish.
HELLO, [he-lō'], *int.* an exclamation expressing greeting.
HELLWARD, [hel'-wud], *adv.* towards hell.
HELM (1), [helm], *n.* a helmet. [OE. *helm*].
HELM (2), [helm], *n.* the tiller, steering wheel or steering mechanism of a vessel; management, control, leadership of anything. [OE. *helma*].
HELMED, [helmd], *adj.* helmeted.
HELMET, [hel'-met], *n.* a metal cap or hat worn as head-armour; protective headgear worn by police, firemen, certain troops, people in hot climates, etc.; the muzzle-like protection worn over the face in fencing; (*her.*) a representation of a helmet bearing the crest in a coat of arms; the top of a retort. [OFr. *healmet*].
HELMETED, [hel'-met-id], *adj.* having a helmet on.
HELMINTH, [hel'-minth], *n.* an intestinal worm. [Gk. *helmins*].
HELMINTHAGOGUE, [hel-minth'-a-gog], *n.* (*med.*) a purgative against intestinal worms. [HELMINTH and Gk. *agogos* drawing out].
HELMINTHIC (1), [hel-minth'-ik], *n.* (*med.*) helminthagogue.
HELMINTHIC (2), [hel-minth'-ik], *adj.* relating to intestinal worms.
HELMINTHOID, [hel-minth'-oid], *adj.* worm-shaped. [HELMINTH and Gk. *oeides* like].
HELMINTHOLOGIC, [hel-minth'-o-loj'-ik], *adj.* helminthological.
HELMINTHOLOGICAL, [hel-minth'-o-loj'-ik-al], *adj.* relating to helminthology.
HELMINTHOLOGIST, [hel'-minth-ol'-oj-ist], *n.* a student of helminthology.
HELMINTHOLOGY, [hel'-minth-ol'-o-ji], *n.* the scientific study of intestinal worms. [HELMINTH and Gk. *logos* speech].
HELMLESS, [helm'-les], *adj.* lacking a helm.
HELMSMAN, [helmz'-man], *n.* one who controls the helm.
HELOSIS, [hēl-ō'-sis], *n.* (*med.*) a turning back of the eyelid. [Gk. *eilo* I roll and *osis* denoting condition].
HELOT, [hel'-ot], *n.* (*Gk. antiq.*) a member of the autochthonous race of Sparta whom the Spartans subjected and oppressed; (*fig.*) a slave-like subject. [Gk. *Heilos*].
HELOTISM, [hel'-ot-izm], *n.* the condition of a helot.
HELOTRY, [hel'-ot-ri], *n.* the status of a helot; helots as a class.
HELP (1), [help], *n.* aid, assistance, succour; the act of helping; one who, or that which, helps; a domestic servant. [OE. *help*].
HELP (2), [help], *v.t.* *and i.* to aid, succour, assist; to co-operate with in achieving some end; to assist financially; to serve, pass food to; (usually with **can't**) to avoid, prevent. [OE. *helpan*].
HELPER, [help'-er], *n.* one who helps.
HELPFUL, [help'-fōōl], *adj.* helping, assisting, obliging.
HELPFULNESS, [help'-fōōl-nes], *n.* the quality of being helpful.
HELPING, [help'-ing], *n.* a portion of food served to one person.
HELPLESS, [help'-les], *adj.* unable to help oneself, in need of help.
HELPLESSLY, [help'-les-li], *adv.* in helpless fashion.
HELPLESSNESS, [help'-les-nes], *n.* the condition of being helpless.
HELPMATE, [help'-māt], *n.* a helpmeet.
HELPMEET, [help'-mēt], *n.* a helper, friend; wife.
HELTER-SKELTER, [hel'-ter-skel'-ter], *adv.* in confused, noisy haste. [Echoic].
HELVE (1), [helv], *n.* a handle, a haft. [OE. *helfe*].
HELVE (2), [helv], *v.t.* to provide with a helve.
HELVE-HAMMER, [helv'-ham'-er], *n.* a heavy hammer used in manufacturing wrought iron.
HELVETIC, [hel-vet'-ik], *adj.* Swiss. [L. *Helvetia*].
HELVIN, [hel'-vin], *n.* a yellowish crystalline mineral, a silicate of glucinum and manganese. [L. *helvus* pale bay].
HEM (1), [hem], *n.* the edge of cloth folded over and sewn down; the decorative border of a garment. [OE. *hem*].
HEM (2), (**hemming, hemmed**), [hem], *v.t.* to make a hem round; **to h. in,** to surround closely on all sides.
HEM (3), [hem], *int.* a sound expressing hesitation, nervousness.
HE-MAN, [hē'-man'], *n.* (*slang*) a virile domineering male, usually of low intelligence but muscular physique.
HEMATIN, see HAEMATIN.
HEMATITE, see HAEMATITE.
HEMI-, *pref.* half. [Gk. *hemi*].
HEMICHORDATE, [hem'-i-kawd'-āt], *adj.* (*zool.*) intermediate in structure between vertebrates and invertebrates. [HEMI and Gk. *khorde* a string].
HEMICRANIA, [hem'-i-krā'-ni-a], *n.* a pain situated only in one side of the head. [L. *hemicrania*].
HEMICYCLE, [hem'-i-sīkl], *n.* a semicircle; a semicircular area. [Gk. *hemicyclion*].
HEMIHEDRAL, [hem'-i-hē'-dral], *adj.* (of a crystal) having half the usual number of faces. [HEMI and Gk. *hedra* base].
HEMIOPIA, [hem'-i-ō'-pi-a], *n,* (*med.*) defective vision in which objects are only partially seen. [HEMI and Gk. *ops* the eye].
HEMIPLEGIA, [hem-i-plēj'-i-a], *n.* (*med.*) a paralysis affecting one side of the body. [HEMI and Gk. *plege* a blow].
HEMIPTERA, [hem-ip'-ter-a], *n.*(*pl.*) (*entom.*) an order of insects, having a sucking proboscis. [HEMI and Gk. *pteron* wing].
HEMIPTERAL, [hem-ip'-ter-al], *adj.* hemipterous.
HEMIPTEROUS, [hem-ip'-ter-us], *adj.* relating to the hemiptera.
HEMISPHERE, [hem'-i-sfēer], *n.* a half-sphere; half of the earth's surface; (*anat.*) one of the halves of the brain. [Gk. *hemisphairion*].
HEMISPHERIC, [hem'-i-sfe'-rik], *adj.* hemispherical.
HEMISPHERICAL, [hem'-i-sfe'-rik-al], *adj.* having the form of a hemisphere.
HEMISTICH, [hem'-i-stik], *n.* (*pros.*) a half-line of verse. [Gk. *hemistikhion*].
HEMISTICHAL, [hem-is'-tik-al], *adj.* relating to a hemistich.
HEMITROPIC, [hem'-i-trop'-ik], *adj.* (of crystals) half turned. [HEMI and Gk. *tropos* turn].

HEMLOCK, (hem'-lok], *n.* the poisonous herb, *Conium maculatum*; the poison made from this herb. [OE. *hymlice*].

HEMLOCK-SPRUCE, [hem'-lok-sprōōs'], *n.* the coniferous tree, *Tsuga canadensis.*

HEMMER, [hem'-er], *n.* a person who hems; the hemming apparatus of a sewing-machine.

HEMMING, [hem'-ing], *n.* a hem; the making of a hem.

HEMORRHAGE, see HAEMORRHAGE.

HEMORRHOIDS see HAEMORRHOIDS.

HEMP, [hemp], *n.* a herbaceous plant of the genus *Cannabis*; a narcotic drug obtained from this plant; coarse cloth and rope woven from the fibres of this and several similar plants. [OE. *hænep*].

HEMLOCK

HEMPEN, [hemp'-en], *adj.* made of hemp.

HEMP-NETTLE, [hemp'-netl'], *n.* the plant, *Galeopsis Tetrahit.*

HEMPSEED, [hemp'-sēd], *n.* the seed of hemp.

HEMPY, [hemp'-i], *adj.* resembling hemp.

HEMSTITCH (1), [hem'-stich], *n.* a hem made by hemstitching.

HEMSTITCH (2), [hem'-stich], *v.t.* to decorate the border of a woven material by pulling out groups of adjacent threads, and gathering the cross-threads into groups so as to leave a row of gaps between the gatherings. [HEM and STITCH].

HEN, [hen], *n.* the female of any bird, the female of the domestic fowl; (*coll.*) a prim, fussy middle-aged man. [OE. *henn*].

HENATHEISM, [hen'-a-thē'-izm], *n.* worship of one god as superior to the rest of the deities. [Gk. *heis henos* one and THEISM].

HENBANE, [hen'-bān], *n.* the poisonous herb, *Hyoscyamus niger.* [HEN and BANE].

HENBIT, [hen'-bit], *n.* the labiate plant, *Lamium amplexicaule*, a dead nettle; the speedwell, *Veronica hederifolia.*

HENCE, [hents], *adv.* away from this place; from this time; from this; as a result of this, for this reason. [ME. *hennes*].

HENCEFORTH, [hens-fawth'], *adv.* from this time onward. [~OE. *heonan forth*].

HENCEFORWARD, [hens'-faw'-wōōd], *adv.* henceforth.

HENCHMAN, [hench'-man], *n.* a close and trusted follower or retainer. [ME. *henxtman* page of honour].

HEN-COOP, [hen'-kōōp], *n.* a coop for fowls.

HENDECAGON, [hen-dek'-a-gon], *n.* (*geom.*) a plane figure having eleven sides. [Gk. *hendeka* eleven and *gonia* angle].

HENDECASYLLABLE, [hen'-dek-a-sil'-abl], *n.* (*pros.*) a metrical form employing a line of eleven syllables. [Gk. *hendeka* eleven and SYLLABLE].

HENDIADYS, [hen-dī'-a-dis], *n.* a figure of speech in which the sense of a noun and adjective is emphatically expressed by two nouns. [MedL. *hendiadys*].

HENDRIVER, [hen'-drīv'-er], *n.* a hen-harrier.

HENEQUEN, [hen'-i-ken], *n.* sisal hemp, *Agave rigida.* [Span. *henequen*].

HEN-HARRIER, [hen'-ha'-ri-er], *n.* the hawk, *Circus cyaneus.*

HEN-HEARTED, [hen'-haht'-id], *adj.* cowardly.

HEN-HOUSE, [hen'-hows'], *n.* a shed or hut for fowls.

HEN-MOULD, [hen'-mōld'], *n.* a black, spongy mould.

HENNA, [hen'-a], *n.* the white-flowered Asiatic shrub, *Lawsonia inermis*; the reddish nail-tint and hair shampoo made from this. [Arab. *hinna*].

HENNERY, [hen'-er-i], *n.* a fowl-run.

HENOTIC, [hen-ot'-ik], *adj.* reconciling. [Gk. *henotikos*].

HEN-PARTY, [hen'-pah-ti], *n.* (*coll.*) a party for women only.

HENPECKED, [hen'-pekt], *adj.* nagged by one's wife.

HENROOST, [hen'-rōōst], *n.* a place in which poultry roost; **to rob the henroosts,** to take over accumulated wealth.

HENRY, [hen'-ri], *n.* (*elect.*) the international inductive unit. [Joseph *Henry*, the American physicist, 1797-1878].

HENTING, [hent'-ing], *n.* (*prov.*) the furrow ending the ridge. [Uncert.].

HENWIFE, [hen'-wīf], *n.* a woman tending poultry.

HEPAT-, HEPATO-, *pref.* relating to the liver. [~Gk. *hepar* the liver].

HEPATIC (1), [hi-pat'-ik], *n.* a liverwort.

HEPATIC (2), [hi-pat'-ik], *adj.* relating to the liver; of a brownish, livery colour. [Gk. *hepatikos*].

HEPATICA, [hi-pat'-i-ka], *n.* the European anemone, *Anemone triloba*, having three-lobed leaves. [L. *hepatica*].

HEPATITIS, [hep'-a-tī'-tis], *n.* inflammation of the liver. [HEPAT and Gk. *itis* denoting inflammation].

HEPATIZATION, [hep'-a-tīz-ā'-shun], *n.* hardening of the lung tissue till it resembles the liver in texture

HEPATIZE, [hep'-a-tīz], *v.t.* to induce hepatization in.

HEPATO-, see HEPAT-.

HEPATOCELE, [he-pat'-ō-sēl], *n.* a tumour of the liver. [HEPATO and Gk. *kele* tumour].

HEPATOGASTRIC, [hep'-a-tō-gas'-trik], *adj.* pertaining to the liver-stomach relationship [HEPATO and GASTRIC].

HEPATORRHOEA, [hep'-a-to-rē'-a], *n.* a morbid excretion of bile. [HEPATO and Gk. *rhoia* flow].

HEPATOSCOPY, [hep'-a-tos'-ko-pi], *n.* divination by the liver; (*surg.*) examination of the liver. [HEPATO and Gk. *skopos* view].

HEPTA-, *pref.* seven. [Gk. *hepta*].

HEPTACHORD, [hep'-ta-kawd'], *n.* (*mus.*) a major seventh; a series of seven consecutive notes; an instrument having seven strings. [Gk. *heptakhordos* seven-stringed].

HEPTADE, [hep'-tād], *n.* a group of seven. [Gk. *heptas heptados*].

HEPTAGLOT, [hep'-ta-glot], *n. and adj.* (a person) speaking seven languages. [HEPTA and Gk. *glotta* a tongue].

HEPTAGON. [hep'-ta-gon], *n.* (*geom.*) a plane figure of seven sides and seven angles; (*fort.*) a place with seven defensive bastions. [Gk. *heptagonos*].

HEPTAGON

HEPTAGONAL, [hep-tag'-on-al], *adj.* in the form of a heptagon.

HEPTAGYNIA, [hep'-ta-jin'-i-a], *n.* (*pl.*) (*bot.*) plants having seven styles. [HEPTA and Gk. *gune* woman].

HEPTAGYNIAN, [hep'-ta-jin'-i-an], *adj.* heptagynous.

HEPTAGYNOUS, [hep-taj'-in-us], *adj.* (*bot.*) having seven styles.

HEPTAHEDRON, [hep'-ta-hē'-dron], *n.* a seven-faced solid. [HEPTA and Gk. *hedra* base]

HEPTAHEXAHEDRAL, [hep'-ta-heks'-a-hē'-dral], *adj.* having forty-two faces arranged in groups of sixes and sevens. [HEPTA and HEXAHEDRAL].

HEPTAMERIDE, [hep-tam'-er-id], *n.* a thing divisible into seven parts. [HEPTA and Gk. *meros* part].

HEPTAMETER, [hep-tam'-it-er], *n.* (*pros.*) a line of verse containing seven feet. [HEPTA and METER].

HEPTANGULAR, [hep-tang'-gyōō-ler], *adj.* of seven angles. [HEPTA and ANGULAR].

HEPTAPHYLLOUS, [hep-taf'-il-us], *adj.* (*bot.*) of seven leaves. [HEPTA and Gk. *phullon* leaf].

HEPTARCH, [hep'-tahk], *n.* a ruler in a heptarchy. [HEPTA and Gk. *arkhos* ruler].

HEPTARCHIC, [hep-tahk'-ik], *adj.* relating to a heptarchy.

HEPTARCHY, [hep'-tahk-i], *n.* government by seven rulers; the period in Anglo-Saxon history when England was divided into seven kingdoms. [HEPTA and Gk. *arkhia* kingdom].

HEPTASPERMOUS, [hep'-ta-spurm'-us], *adj.* (*bot.*) having seven seeds. [HEPTA and Gk. *sperma* seed].

HEPTASYLLABIC, [hep'-ta-sil-ab'-ik], *adj.* of seven syllables. [HEPTA and SYLLABIC].

HEPTATEUCH, [hep'-ta-tewk], *n.* the first seven books of the Bible. [HEPTA and Gk. *teukhos* book].

HER (1), [hur], *adj.* belonging, relating to a particular female. [OE. *hire*].

HER (2), [hur], *pron., acc. and dat.* of SHE. [OE. *hire*].

HERALD (1), [he'-rald], *n.* one who makes public announcements on behalf of a potentate; an officer entrusted with the granting or withdrawing of armorial bearings; anyone announcing anything, *esp.* for the first time; a forerunner; an anticipation. [OFr. *herallt*].

HERALD (2), [he'-rald], *v.t.* to proclaim as a herald, to announce.

HERALDIC, [he-rald'-ik], *adj.* relating to heraldry.

HERALDICALLY, [he-rald'-ik-al-i], *adv.* according to heraldry.

HERALDRY, [he'-rald-ri], *n.* the art and study of armorial bearings; heraldic devices; the position of herald. [OFr. *heralderie*].

HERALDSHIP, [he'-rald-ship], *n.* the office of a herald.

HERB, [hurb], *n.* a low-growing seasonal plant; a plant possessing aromatic or medical qualities; (*poet.*) grass. [L. *herba*].

HERBACEOUS, [hurb-ā'-shus], *adj.* relating to herbs; dying in winter like a herb; covered with or resembling herbs; not woody. [L. *herbaceus* grassy].

HERBAGE, [hurb'-ij], *n.* herbs, pasturage, plants growing in fields; the juicy tops of herbs; (*leg.*) the right of grazing. [Fr. *herbage*].

HERBAGED, [hurb'-ijd], *adj.* grown over with grass.

HERBAL (1), [hurb'-al], *n.* a book or pamphlet on medicinal herbs.

HERBAL (2), [hurb'-al], *adj.* relating to herbs. [L. *herbalis*].

HERBALIST, [hurb'-al-ist], *n.* one skilled in the use of herbs; a dealer in herbs.

HERBARIAN, [hurb-āer'-i-an], *n.* a herbalist.

HERBARIUM, [hurb-āer'-i-um], *n.* a collection of dried plants; a room or building in which this is housed. [L. *herbarium*].

HERBARY, [hurb-er-i], *n.* a herbarium.

HERBLET, [hurb'-let], *n.* a little herb.

HERBESCENT, [hurb-es'-ent], *adj.* growing with herbs.

HERBIFEROUS, [hurb-if'-er-us], *adj.* bearing herbs. [HERB and L. *ferre* to bear].

HERBIVORA, [hurb-i'-ver-a], *n.*(*pl.*) graminivorous mammals. [HERB and L. *vorare* to devour].

HERBIVOROUS, [hurb-iv'-er-us], *adj.* feeding on herbage.

HERBLESS, [hurb'-les], *adj.* without herbage.

HERBORIST, [hurb'-er-ist], *n.* a herbalist.

HERBORIZATION, [hurb'-er-īz-ā'-shun], *n.* the collecting of herbs; the collection of plants.

HERBORIZE, [hurb'-er-īz], *v.i.* to study and collect herbs.

HERBOUS, [hurb'-us], *adj.* having herbs.

HERB-WOMAN, [hurb'-wŏŏm'-an], *n.* a woman selling aromatic herbs.

HERBY, [hurb'-i], *adj.* herbous.

HERCULEAN, [hur'-kew-lē'-an], *adj.* relating to Hercules, resembling him in size and strength; tremendously laborious, requiring a Hercules. [L. *Herculeus*].

HERCULES, [hur'-kew-lēz], *n.* (*class. myth.*) a hero notable for his strength; a man of immense physical strength and size. [L. *Hercules*].

HERCULES-BEETLE, [hur'-kew-lēz-bētl'], *n.* the great, long-pincered South American beetle, *Dynastes hercules*.

HERCYNIAN, [hur-sin'-i-an], *adj.* relating to the Harz forest in Central Germany. [L. *Hercynia*].

HERD (1), [hurd], *n.* a large group of gregarious animals living and moving together; a large group of domestic animals of one breed, and usually under one ownership; (*fig.*) a crowd of sheep-like human beings. [OE. *heord*].

HERD (2), [hurd], *n.* a herdsman. [OE. *herde, hierde*].

HERD (3), [hurd], *v.t. and i.* to gather, drive together into a herd; to come together in a herd; to huddle together in a close mass.

HERD-BOOK, [hurd'-bŏŏk], *n.* a book of the pedigrees of stud cattle.

HERD INSTINCT, [hurd'-in-stingkt], *n.* the tendency to crowd together, act, feel, and think as a herd.

HERDMAN, [hurd'-man], *n.* a herdsman.

HERDS-GRASS, [hurdz'-grahs], *n.* the best kinds of grass, for prize sheep and cattle.

HERDSMAN, [hurdz'-man], *n.* one who looks after a domestic herd.

HERE, [hēer], *adv.* at this place; towards this place; **h. and there**, thinly scattered. [OE. *her*].

HEREABOUT, [hēer'-a-bowt], *adv.* hereabouts.

HEREABOUTS, [hēer'-a-bowtz], *adv.* somewhere near this place.

HEREAFTER (1), [hēer-ahft'-er], *n.* the next life.

HEREAFTER (2), [hēer-ahft'-er], *adv.* after the present, later on; after death, in the next world. [OE. *hersæfter*].

HEREAT, [hēer-at'], *adv.* at this, when this occurred.

HEREAWAY, [hēer'-a-wā], *adv.* hereabouts.

HEREBY, [hēer'-bī], *adv.* near this, near here; as a result of this, by this.

HEREDIPETY, [he'-ri-dip'-i-ti], *n.* inheritance hunting. [L. *heredipeta*].

HEREDITABILITY, [hi-red'-it-a-bil'-i-ti], *n.* the condition of being inheritable.

HEREDITABLE, [hi-red'-it-abl], *adj.* possible to be inherited. [L. *hereditabilis*].

HEREDITAMENT, [hi-red'-it-a-ment], *n.* (*leg.*) hereditable property. [L. *hereditamentum*].

HEREDITARIAN, [hi-red'-it-āer'-i-an], *n.* one who studies heredity.

HEREDITARILY, [hi-red'-it-er-i-li], *adv.* by inheritance.

HEREDITARY, [hi-red'-it-er-i], *adj.* descending by inheritance; inherited; derived from one's ancestors. [L. *hereditarius*].

HEREDITY, [hi-red'-i-ti], *n.* the ability of organisms to transmit characteristics to their offspring; the process by which this transmission takes place. [L. *hereditas*].

HEREFORD, [he'-ri-ford], *n.* the name of a breed of red and white cattle. [*Hereford*, an English county].

HEREIN, [hēer'-in, hēer-in'], *adv.* in this. [OE. *herinne*].

HEREINAFTER, [hēer'-in-ahft'-er], *adv.* afterwards, after this, henceforward, in this document.

HEREINBEFORE, [hēer-in'-bi-faw(r)'], *adv.* (*leg.*) previously in the document; above.

HEREINTO, [hēer-in'-tōō], *adv.* into this.

HEREOF, [hēer-ov'], *adv.* of this.

HEREON, [hēer-on'], *adv.* on this.

HEREOUT, [hēer-owt'], *adv.* out of this.

HERESIARCH, [hi-rez'-i-ahk], *n.* a leader in heresy. [L. *haeresiarcha*].

HERESIOGRAPHER, [hi-rez'-i-og'-raf-er], *n.* a chronicler of heresies.

HERESIOGRAPHY, [hi-rez'-i-og'-ra-fi], *n.* a book or pamphlet on heresy. [HERESY and Gk. *graphia* writing].

HERESY, [he'-res-i], *n.* a doctrine or religious belief contrary to the teachings of the Church, *esp.* of the Christian Church; a theory contrary to that officially approved. [L. *haeresis*].

HERETIC, [he'-ret-ik], *n.* a believer in a heresy, one who will not subscribe to official doctrine. [L. *haereticus*].

HERETICAL, [hi-ret'-ik-al], *adj.* relating to, believing in, heresy; contrary to official doctrine.

HERETICALLY, [hi-ret'-ik-al-i], *adv.* in heretical fashion.

HERETICATE, [hi-ret'-ik-āt], *v.t.* to declare heretical. [MedL. *haereticare*].

HERETO, [hēer'-tōō'], *adv.* hereunto, to this.

HERETOFORE, [hēer'-tōō-faw(r)], *adv.* hitherto; before this.

HEREUNTO, [hēer'-un-tōō], *adv.* to this.

HEREUPON, [hēer'-up-on'], *adv.* upon this, at this.

HEREWITH, [hēer'-with'], *adv.* with this, at this time, now.

HERIOT, [he'-ri-ot], *n.* (*leg.*) a feudal due payable on a tenant's death to his overlord. [OE. *heregeatwe* military equipment].

HERIOTABLE, [he'-ri-ot-abl], *adj.* liable to heriot.

HERISSON, [he'-ris-on], *n.* (*milit.*) a revolving bar clustered with projecting spikes, used to obstruct a passage. [Fr. *hérisson* hedgehog].

HERITABLE, [he'-rit-abl], *adj.* possible to be inherited. [Fr. *héritable*].

HERITABLY, [he'-rit-ab-li], *adv.* by inheritance.

HERITAGE, [he'-rit-ij], *n.* that which is inherited; (*Scots leg.*) real estate. [OFr. *heritage*].

HERITOR, [he'-rit-or], *n.* one who inherits. [Fr. *héritier*].

HERLING, [hur'-ling], *n.* (*Scots*) the sea-trout, *Salmo trutta*. [Unkn.].

HERLING

HERMAPHRODISM, [her-maf'-rō-dizm], *n.* the state of being hermaphrodite.

HERMAPHRODITE (1), [her-maf'-rō-dīt], *n.* (*biol.*) an organism containing both fertilizing and generative organs; a person or animal with indeterminate sexual organs, or with those of both sexes. [Gk. *Hermaphroditos*].

HERMAPHRODITE (2), [her-maf'-rō-dīt], *adj.* hermaphroditic.

HERMAPHRODITIC, [her-maf'-rō-dit'-ik], *adj.* having the organs of both sexes; relating to a hermaphrodite.

HERMAPHRODITICAL, [her-maf'-rō-dit'-ik-al], *adj.* hermaphroditic.

HERMAPHRODITISM, [her-maf′-rō-dīt′-izm], *n.* hermaphrodism.

HERMENEUTIC, [her-men-ew′-tik], *adj.* interpretative. [Gk. *hermeneutikos*].

HERMENEUTICAL, [her-men-ew′-tik-al], *adj.* hermeneutic.

HERMENEUTICS, [her-men-ew′-tiks], *n.(pl.)* the interpretation of the Scriptures.

HERMES, [hur′-mēz], *n.* (*myth.*) the messenger of the gods; (*fig.*) a swift, fluent person. [Gk. *Hermes*].

HERMETIC, [her-met′-ik], *adj.* air-tight, sealed so securely as to forbid the passage of air; †alchemistic. [LL. *hermeticus*].

HERMETICAL, [her-met′-ik-al], *adj.* hermetic.

HERMETICALLY, [her-met′-ik-al-i], *adv.* so as to be air-tight.

HERMIT, [hur′-mit], *n.* one living alone in seclusion in order to pursue his religious life undisturbed, an anchorite; (*fig.*) one who shuns human society; a variety of humming-bird. [L. *eremita*].

HERMITAGE, EREMITAGE†, [hur′-mit-ij], *n.* the dwelling of a hermit. [ME. *hermitage*].

HERMITARY, [hur′-mit-er-i], *n.* a hermitage.

HERMIT-CRAB, [hur′-mit-krab′], *n.* a soft-bodied, decapod crab inhabiting a discarded mollusc shell.

HERMITICAL, [hur-mit′-ik-al], *adj.* relating to a hermit.

HERMODACTYL, [hur′-mō-dak′-til], *n.* a Turkish species of colchicum used as a cathartic. [HERMES and DACTYL].

HERN†, see HERON.

HERNIA, [hur′-ni-a], *n.* (*med.*) the protrusion of an internal organ, owing to displacement, through the side of its protective wall. [L. *hernia* rupture].

HERNIAL, [hur′-ni-al], *adj.* relating to hernia.

HERNIOTOMY, [hur′-ni-ot′-o-mi], *n.* surgical operation of cutting for dangerous hernia. [HERNIA and Gk. *tome* cutting].

HERNSHAW†, see HERONSHAW.

HERO, [hēer′-ō], *n.* one of more than mortal stature venerated by a primitive people for warlike prowess or social benefits; one of excelling valour, one outstandingly brave and victorious in war; one idolized as a model of prowess and virtue; the leading male character in a story or drama. [Gk. *heros*].

HEROIC, [hi-rō′-ik], *adj.* possessing, displaying, the qualities of a hero; (of actions) daring and brave; on a great scale; (of representations in art) larger than life; relating to epic poetry; (*pros.*) written in the classical hexameter, the French Alexandrine or English pentameter; **h. couplets,** (*pros.*) rhymed couplets of ten syllables and five regular stresses. [Gk. *heroikos*].

HEROICALLY, [hi-rō′-ik-al-i], *adv.* in heroic fashion.

HEROICALNESS, [hi-rō′-ik-al-nes], *n.* the quality of being heroic.

HEROICNESS, [hi-rō′-ik-nes], *n.* heroicalness.

HEROI-COMIC, [hi-rō′-i-kom′-ik], *adj.* combining the heroic and the ludicrous.

HEROI-COMICAL, [hi-rō′-i-kom′-ik-al], *adj.* heroi-comic.

HEROIN, [he′-rō-in], *n.* a dangerous derivative of morphine. [HERO].

HEROINE, [he′-rō-in], *n.* a female hero; the principal young female character of a story or drama. [Gk. *heroine*].

HEROISM, [he′-rō-izm], *n.* the qualities displayed by a hero, extreme bravery. [Fr. *héroisme*].

HEROIZE, [he′-rō-īz], *v.t. and i.* to make a hero of; to ape the hero.

HERON, HERN†, [he′-ron], *n.* the large wading bird, *Ardea cinerea*, distinguished by its long legs, neck, and beak. [OFr. *hairon*].

HERONRY, [he′-ron-ri], *n.* a colony of herons.

HERONSBILL, [he′-ronz-bil], *n.* a plant of the genus *Erodium.*

HERONSHAW, HERNSHAW†, [he′-ron-shaw], *n.* a young heron. [OFr. *heronceau*].

HEROSHIP, [hēer′-ō-ship], *n.* the status or condition of a hero.

HERO-WORSHIP, [hēer-ō-wur′-ship], *n.* the worship of a hero; the excessive idolization of someone.

HERPES, [hur′-pēz], *n.* (*path.*) a skin disease marked by clusters of vesicles. [Gk. *herpes*].

HERPETIC, [hur-pet′-ik], *adj.* relating to herpes. [Fr. *herpétique*].

HERPETOID, [hur′-pet-oid], *adj.* snake-like; sauroid. [Gk. *herpeton* creeping thing and *oeides* like].

HERPETOLOGIC, [hur′-pet-ol-oj′-ik], *adj.* relating to herpetology.

HERPETOLOGICAL, [hur′-pet-ol-oj′-ik-al], *adj.* herpetologic.

HERPETOLOGIST, [hur′-pet-ol′-oj-ist], *n.* one studying herpetology.

HERPETOLOGY, [hur′-pet-ol′-o-ji], *n.* the scientific study of reptiles. [Gk. *herpeton* creeping thing and *logos* speech].

HERR, [hāer], *n.* the German title for a man, Mr. [Germ. *herr* gentleman, Mr.].

HERRING, [he′-ring], *n.* the edible marine shoal-fish, *Clupea harengus*; any of several fish resembling this; **red h.,** (*fig.*) an irrelevant fact or suggestion introduced to divert attention from the point at issue; **h.-pond,** (*coll.*) the North Atlantic Ocean. [OE. *hæring*].

HERRING-BONE, [he′-ring-bōn′], *n.* a herring's spine; a pattern resembling this; (*arch.*) a method of bricklaying in which courses are laid in alternate diagonals; a cross-stitch.

HERRNHUTER, [hāern′-hōōt′-er], *n.* one of a sect of German Moravians. [*Herrnhut*, near Bautzen in Germany, where they first settled].

HERS, [hurz], *pron.* belonging to her. [ME. *hires*].

HERSCHELITE, [hur′-shel-īt], *n.* a silicate of alumina with soda and potash. [Sir J. *Herschel*, 1792-1871, its discoverer].

HERSE, [hurs], *n.* a grated portcullis with spikes at the base; a portable framework covered with barbed wire for blocking trenches in an emergency; a military formation for moving in semi-open order. [HEARSE].

HERSELF, [hur-self′], *pron.* emphatic and reflexive form of HER. [OE. *hire selfum*].

HERTZIAN, [hurtz′-i-an], *adj.* relating to the etheric wave movements investigated by Hertz. [H. *Hertz*, 1857-1894, the German physicist].

HESITANCY, [hez′-i-tan-si], *n.* hesitation. [L. *haesitantia*].

HESITANT, [hez′-i-tant], *adj.* hesitating, doubtful. [L. *haesitans*].

HESITANTLY, [hez′-i-tant-li], *adv.* in hesitant fashion.

HESITATE, [hez′-i-tāt], *v.i.* to pause doubtfully; to falter; to be unwilling to. [L. *haesitare*].

HESITATING, [hez′-i-tāt-ing], *adj.* doubtful, undecided.

HESITATINGLY, [hez′-i-tāt′-ing-li], *adv.* in hesitating fashion.

HESITATION, [hez-i-tā′-shun], *n.* the act or state of hesitating; indecision, unwillingness; a speech defect. [L. *haesitatio*].

HESITATIVE, [hez′-it-at-iv], *adj.* tending to hesitate.

HESITATOR, [hez′-i-tāt-or], *n.* a person who hesitates.

HESPER, [hes′-per], *n.* the planet Venus. [Gk. *hesperos* evening].

HESPERIAN, [hes-pēer′-i-an], *adj.* western, relating to the west. [*Prec.*].

HESPERIDES, [hes-pe′-rid-ēz], *n.(pl.)* (*Gk. myth.*) sisters guarding the golden apples given by Ge to Hera on her marriage with Zeus. [Gk. *hesperos*].

HESPERORNIS, [hes′-per-awn′-is], *n.* a prehistoric toothed bird. [Gk. *hesperos* western and *ornis* bird].

HESSIAN, [hesh′-an], *n.* a coarse cloth made from jute or hemp; a high boot. [*Hesse*, in Germany].

HESSIAN-FLY, [hes′-ian-flī′], *n.* a small fly, *Cecidomyia destructor*, whose larvae destroy wheat.

HEST, [hest], *n.* a command. [OE. *hæs*].

HESYCHAST, [hes′-i-kast], *n.* a mystic. [Gk. *hesuches* quiet].

HETAIRISM, [het-ī′-er-izm], *n.* communal marriage. [Gk. *hetaira* superior prostitute].

HETER(O)-, *pre.* irregular, different, of another kind. [Gk. *heteros*].

HETERARCHY, [het′-er-ahk′-i], *n.* rule by an alien. [HETER and Gk. *arkhaia* rule].

HETEROCERCAL, [het′-er-ō-surkl′], *adj.* having the upper fork of the tail extending beyond the lower. [HETERO and Gk. *kerkos* tail].

HETEROCHROMOUS, [het′-er-ō-krōm′-us], *adj.* variously coloured. [HETERO and Gk. *khroma* colour].

HETEROCLITE (1), [het′-er-ō-klīt], *n.* (*gram.*) an irregularly declined noun.

HETEROCLITE (2), [het′-er-ō-klīt], *adj.* abnormal, unusual; (*gram.*) irregularly declined. [Gk. *heteroklitos*].

HETEROCLITIC, [het′-er-ō-klit′-ik], *adj.* (*gram.*) declining irregularly; abnormal.

HETEROCLITICAL, [het′-er-ō-klit′-ik-al], *adj.* (*gram.*) heteroclitic.

HETEROCLITOUS, [het′-er-ok′-lit-us], *adj.* heteroclitic.

HETERODACTYL, [het'-er-ō-dak'-til], *adj.* having a deformity in the arrangement or number of the fingers. [HETERO and DACTYL].
HETERODONT, [het'-er-ō-dont'], *adj.* having teeth of various kinds. [HETER and Gk. *odous odontos* tooth].
HETERODOX, [het'-er-ō-doks], *adj.* unorthodox, heretical. [Gk. *heterodoxos*].
HETERODOXNESS, [het'-er-ō-doks-nes], *n.* heterodoxy.
HETERODOXY, [het'-er-ō-dok'-si], *n.* heterodox opinions; the holding of such opinions. [Gk. *heterodoxia*].
HETERODYNE, [het'-er-ō-dīn], *n.* (*wirel.*) a beat note due to differences in frequency between the transmitted waves and those created in the receiver, with which they are combined. [HETERO and DYNE].
HETEROGAMOUS, [het'-er-og'-am-us], *adj.* having irregular or varying sexual organs and means of generation. [HETERO and Gk. *gamos* marriage].
HETEROGENEAL, [het'-er-ō-jē'-ni-al], *adj.* heterogeneous.
HETEROGENEITY, [het'-er-ō-jen-ē'-i-ti], *n.* the condition of being heterogeneous.
HETEROGENEOUS, [het'-er-ō-jē'-ni-us], *adj.* of dissimilar kind; consisting of unrelated parts; unable to be compared; (*math.*) having no common measure. [Gk. *heterogenes*].
HETEROGENEOUSLY, [het'-er-ō-jē'-ni-us-li], *adv.* in heterogeneous fashion.
HETEROGENEOUSNESS, [het'-er-ō-jē'-ni-us-nes], *n.* heterogeneity.
HETEROGENESIS, [het'-er-ō-jen'-is-is], *n.* (*biol.*) production of an organism from a dissimilar parent. [HETERO and GENESIS].
HETEROGENY, [het'-er-oj'-en-i], *n.* heterogenesis.
HETEROGRAPHY, [het'-er-og'-ra-fi], *n.* unorthodox spelling. [HETERO and Gk. *graphia* writing].
HETEROLOGOUS, [het'-er-ol'-og-us], *adj.* of different type. [HETERO and Gk. *logos* speech].
HETEROMEROUS, [het'-er-om'-er-us], *adj.* (*chem.*) of dissimilar composition; (*entom.*) having differently articulated legs. [HETERO and Gk. *meros* part].
HETEROMORPHIC, [het'-er-ō-mawf'-ik], *adj.* of unusual or varying shape or form. [HETERO and Gk. *morphe* form].
HETEROMORPHISM, [het'-er-ō-mawf'-izm], *n.* the existence of different or abnormal forms.
HETERONOMOUS, [het'-er-on'-om-us], *adj.* under alien rule; (*biol.*) liable to divergence of form. [HETERO and Gk. *nomos* law].
HETERONOMY, [het'-er-on'-ō-mi], *n.* subjection to some law, *esp.* other than reason; government by another; (*philos.*) the subjection of the will to circumstances; (*biol.*) deviation from type. [HETERO and Gk. *nomos* law].
HETERONYM, [het'-er-ō-nim], *n.* a word similar in spelling to another but different in meaning and pronunciation. [Gk. *heteronumos*].
HETERO-OUSIAN, [het'-er-ō-ow'-zi-an], *adj.* of a different essence. [HETERO and Gk. *ousia* essence].
HETEROPATHY, [het'-er-op'-a-thi], *n.* allopathy. [HETERO and Gk. *patheia* suffering].
HETEROPHYLLOUS, [het'-er-of'-il-us], *adj.* (*bot.*) having differently shaped leaves on the same stem. [HETERO and Gk. *phullon* leaf].
HETEROPOD, [het'-er-ō-pod], *n.* a mollusc having a fin-like muscular lamina. [HETER and Gk. *pous podos* foot].
HETEROSCIAN, [het'-er-os'-i-an], *n.* an inhabitant of either of the temperate zones, so called on account of the noon shadows falling in opposite directions. [Gk. *heteroskios* diversely shadowed].
HETEROSEXUAL, [het'-er-ō-sek'-shōō-al], *adj.* normally sexual, sexually attracted by the opposite sex. [HETER and SEXUAL].
HETEROSITE, [het'-er-ō-sīt], *n.* a grey or bluish mineral, turning violet on exposure.
HETEROTOMOUS, [het'-er-ot'-om-us], *adj.* (*min.*) having a different cleavage. [HETERO and Gk. *tome* cutting].
HETMAN, [het'-man], *n.* a cossack leader; a Polish commander. [Polish *hetman*].
HEUGH, [hew], *n.* a deep ravine; a sheer descent. [OE. *hoh*].
HEULANDITE, [hew'-land-īt], *n.* (*min.*) a siliceous mineral occurring in metalliferous veins. [H. *Heuland*, an English mineralogist].
HEURISTIC, [hew-rist'-ik], *adj.* leading to knowledge by discovery; (of a method of teaching) avoiding direct instruction in favour of self-educative discovery. [Gk. *heurisko* I find].
HEVEA, [hē'-vi-a], *n.* the tree from which is obtained Para rubber, *Hevea brasiliensis*.
HEW, (hewn), [hew], *v.t. and i.* to chop, cut with heavy strokes; to carve or shape in this way. [OE. *heawan*].
HEWER, [hew'-er], *n.* one who hews.
HEWN, [hewn], *p.pt.* of HEW.
HEX-, HEXA-, *pref.* six, relating to six. [Gk. *hex*].
HEXACHORD, [heks'-a-kawd], *n.* (*mus.*) a diatonic scale of six notes; a major sixth. [Gk. *hexakhordos*].
HEXACTINELLID, [heks'-ak-ti'-nel-id], *adj.* relating to the *Hexactinellidae*, a group of sponges with six spines. [HEX and Gk. *aktis* ray].
HEXAD, [heks'-ad], *n.* a series containing six numbers. [Gk. *hexas*].
HEXADACTYLOUS, [heks'-a-dak'-til-us], *adj.* having six fingers. [HEXA and DACTYL].
HEXAGON, [heks'-a-gon], *n.* a plane figure having six (equal) sides. [Gk. *hexagonos*].
HEXAGONAL, [heks-ag'-on-al], *adj.* like a hexagon, six-sided.
HEXAGRAM, [heks'-a-gram'], *n.* (*geom.*) a plane figure obtained by the intersection of two equilateral triangles to form a regular hexagon. [HEXA and Gk. *gramma* writing].
HEXAGYNIAN, [heks'-a-jin'-i-an], *adj.* (*bot.*) possessing six styles.
HEXAGYNOUS, [heks-aj'-in-us], *adj.* hexagynian.

HEXAGON

HEXAHEDRAL, [heks'-a-hē'-dral], *adj.* like a hexahedron.
HEXAHEDRON, [heks'-a-hē'-dron], *n.* (*geom.*) a regular six-sided solid. [Gk. *hexaedros*].
HEXAHEMERON, [heks'-a-hē'-mer-on], *n.* a period of six days; the progress of the creation. [HEXA and Gk. *hemera* day].
HEXAMETER, [heks-am'-it-er], *n.* (*pros.*) the classical heroic metre of six feet; any metrical line of six feet. [Gk. *hexametros*].
HEXAMETRIC, [heks-a-met'-rik], *adj.* written in hexameters.
HEXAMETRICAL, [heks-a-met'-rik-al], *adj.* hexametric.
HEXANDRIAN, [heks-an'-dri-an], *adj.* hexandrous.
HEXANDROUS, [heks-an'-drus], *adj.* (*bot.*) possessing six stamens.
HEXANGULAR, [heks-ang'-gyŏŏ-ler], *adj.* having six angles. [HEX and ANGULAR].
HEXAPETALOUS, [heks'-a-pet'-al-us], *adj.* (*bot.*) having six petals. [HEXA and PETAL].
HEXAPHYLLOUS, [heks-af'-il-us], *adj.* (*bot.*) possessing six leaves. [HEXA and Gk. *phullon* leaf].
HEXAPLA, [heks'-ap-la], *n.* Origen's sixfold parallel text of the Scriptures. [Gk. *hexapla* sixfold].
HEXAPLAR, [heks'-ap-ler], *adj.* in six parallel columns.
HEXAPOD, [heks'-a-pod], *adj.* (*zool.*) having six feet. [HEXA and Gk. *pous podos* foot].
HEXASTICH, [heks'-a-stik], *n.* (*pros.*) a stanza of six lines. [HEXA and Gk. *stikhos* line of verse].
HEXASTYLE, [heks'-a-stil], *n.* (*arch.*) a building having six pillars in front. [Gk. *hexastulos*].
HEXASYLLABLE, [heks'-a-sil'-abl], *n.* a word containing six syllables. [HEXA and SYLLABLE].
HEXATEUCH, [heks'-a-tewk], *n.* the first six books of the Bible. [HEXA and Gk. *teuchos* book].
HEXOCTAHEDRON, [heks'-ok-ta-hē'-dron], *n.* a solid having 48 regular faces. [HEX and Gk. *octahedron*].
HEYDAY, [hā'-dā], *n.* acme, height, period of greatest prosperity or activity. [HIGH DAY].
HEYKE, see HAIK (1).
HI, [hī], *int.* a call to attract attention.
HIATUS, [hī-ā'-tus], *n.* a gap, space, lacuna; (*gram.*) the unelided pronunciation of two adjacent vowels. [L. *hiatus* yawn].
HIBERNACLE, [hī-burn'-akl], *n.* (*bot.*) the leaf budding in winter. [L. *hibernaculum*].
HIBERNAL, [hī-burn'-al], *adj.* wintry; relating to winter sleep. [L. *hibernalis*].
HIBERNATE, HYBERNATE†, [hī'-ber-nāt], *v.i.* to pass the winter in sleep; to retire into warm inactivity during the winter. [L. *hibernare* to spend the winter].

HIBERNATION, [hī'-ber-nā'-shun], *n.* the practice or condition of hibernating. [L. *hibernatio*].
HIBERNIAN (1), [hī-bur'-ni-an], *n.* a member of the Irish people. [L. *Hibernia* Ireland].
HIBERNIAN (2), [hī-bur'-ni-an], *adj.* Irish.
HIBERNIANISM, [hī-bur'-ni-an-izm], *n.* an Irishism.
HIBERNICISM, [hī-bur'-ni-sizm], *n.* an Irishism.
HIBERNICIZE, [hī-bur'-ni-sīz], *v.t. and i.* to make or become Irish.
HIBERNIZATION, [hī'-ber-nīz-ā'-shun], *n.* hibernation.
HIBERNIZE, [hī'-ber-nīz], *v.t.* to hibernate.
HIBERNO-CELTIC, [hī-bur'-nō-kelt'-ik], *n.* Erse.
HIBISCUS, [hi-bis'-kus], *n.* the cultivated mallow, the rose-mallow. [Gk. *hibiskos*].
HICCATEE, [hik-a-tē'], *n.* a freshwater tortoise found in Central America. [Native].
HICCOUGH (1), [hik'-up], *n.* a sudden involuntary drawing together of the diaphragm, resulting in a coughing sound; the sound so produced. [ME. *hickock*].
HICCOUGH (2), [hik'-up], *v.t. and i.* to utter a hiccough or series of hiccoughs; to speak with a hiccough.
HICKORY, [hik'-er-i], *n.* an American hardwood tree of the genus *Carya*; the wood from this tree. [Native].
HICKWALL, [hik'-wawl], *n.* the hickway.
HICKWAY, [hik'-wā], *n.* (*prov.*) a species of woodpecker, *Picus minor*. [Uncert.].
HIDAGE†, [hīd'-ij], *n.* a tax levied on every hide of land. [MedL. *hidagium*].
HIDALGO, [hid-al'-gō], *n.* a Spanish gentleman of noble descent. [Span. *hidalgo*].
HIDDEN (1), [hidn], *adj.* secret, mysterious, not plain or obvious. [*Next*].
HIDDEN (2), [hidn], *p.pt.* of HIDE (3).
HIDDENLY, [hidn'-li], *adv.* in hidden fashion.
HIDE (1), [hīd], *n.* the skin of a beast, *esp.* when flayed off; (*fig.*) the human skin; (*coll.*) insolence; thickness of skin. [OE. *hyd*].
HIDE (2), [hīd], *n.* a measure of land of between 50 and 100 acres. [OE. *higid*].
HIDE (3), [hīd], *v.t. and i.* to conceal, secret; to place out of view; to keep from being known or understood; to withhold; to go into concealment. [OE. *hydan*].
HIDE (4), [hīd], *v.t.* to flay; (*coll.*) to thrash.
HIDEBOUND, [hīd'-bownd], *adj.* rigidly conservative, obstinately conventional; (of an animal) having too close a hide.
HIDEOSITY, [hid'-i-os'-i-ti], *n.* hideousness.
HIDEOUS, [hid'-i-us], *adj.* very ugly; revolting, terrifyingly repulsive. [OFr. *hidous*].
HIDEOUSLY, [hid'-i-us-li], *adv.* in hideous fashion.
HIDEOUSNESS, [hid'-i-us-nes], *n.* the quality of being hideous.
HIDEOUT, [hīd'-owt], *n.* a safe retreat or hiding place.
HIDER, [hīd'-er], *n.* one who hides.
HIDEROPE, [hīd'-rōp], *n.* a rope made of hide.
HIDING (1), [hīd'-ing], *n.* concealment. [HIDE (3)].
HIDING (2), [hīd'-ing], *n.* a flogging, beating. [HIDE (4)].
HIDROSIS, [hī-drō'-sis], *n.* sweat; (*med.*) excessive sweating. [Gk. *hidros* sweat].
HIDROTIC, [hī-drot'-ik], *adj.* tending to encourage sweating. [Gk. *hidrotikos*].
HIE, [hī], *v.i.* to go in haste. [OE. *higian*].
HIEMAL, [hī'-em-al], *adj.* wintry. [L. *hiemalis* wintry].
HIEMATION, [hī'-em-ā'-shun], *n.* the act of wintering. [L. *hiematio*].
HIER-, HIERO-, *pref.* sacred; relating to priesthood. [Gk. *hieros*].
HIERARCH, [hīer'-ahk], *n.* a chief priest; a priest-king. [Gk. *hierarkhes*].
HIERARCHAL, [hīer'-ahk-al], *adj.* hierarchic.
HIERARCHIC, [hīer'-ahk-ik], *adj.* relating to a hierarch or a hierarchy.
HIERARCHICAL, [hīer-ahk'-ik-al], *adj.* hierarchal.
HIERARCHISM, [hīer'-ahk-izm], *n.* hierarchic government; the theory of priestly rule.
HIERARCHY, [hīer'-ahk-i], *n.* an order of angels or other sacred persons; an order of priests; the organization of such an order; government by a body of persons graded so that each rank directly controls that immediately inferior to it; a graded system of organization, *esp.* ecclesiastical. [Gk. *hierarkhia*].
HIERATIC, [hīer-at'-ik], *adj.* priestly; **h. script,** an ancient Egyptian form of writing, being a modified form of hieroglyphics. [Gk. *hieratikos*].
HIERO-, see HIER-.
HIEROCRACY, [hīer-ok'-ra-si], *n.* priestly government. [HIERO and Gk. *kratia* rule].
HIEROGLYPH, [hīer'-ō-glif], *n.* a character in the picture writing of the ancient Egyptians; a character in any picture-script; (*fig.*) an incomprehensible symbol.
HIEROGLYPHIC (1), [hīer'-ō-glif'-ik], *n.* a hieroglyph; (*pl.*) writing in hieroglyphic characters.
HIEROGLYPHIC (2), [hīer'-ō-glif'-ik], *adj.* written in picture-script or hieroglyphs. [Gk. *hierogluphikos*].

HIEROGLYPHICS

HIEROGLYPHICAL, [hīer'-ō-glif'-ik-al], *adj.* hieroglyphic.
HIEROGLYPHICALLY, [hīer'-ō-glif'-ik-al-i], *adv.* in hieroglyphics.
HIEROGLYPHIST, [hīer-og'-li-fist], *n.* one with a knowledge of hieroglyphics.
HIEROGRAM, [hīer'-ō-gram], *n.* a sacred written symbol. [HIERO and Gk. *gramma* something written].
HIEROGRAMMATIC, [hīer'-ō-gram-at'-ik], *adj.* relating to hierograms.
HIEROGRAMMATIST, [hīer'-ō-gram'-at-ist], *n.* one versed in hierograms.
HIEROGRAPHER, [hīer-og'-ra-fer], *n.* one versed in hierography.
HIEROGRAPHIC, [hīer'-ō-graf'-ik], *adj.* relating to hierography. [Gk. *hierographikos*].
HIEROGRAPHICAL, [hīer'-ō-graf'-ik-al], *adj.* hierographic.
HIEROGRAPHY, [hīer-og'-ra-fi], *n.* a description of holy things, *esp.* of religions. [HIERO and Gk. *graphia* writing].
HIEROLATRY, [hīer-ol'-at-ri], *n.* the worship of saints. [HIERO and Gk. *latreia* worship].
HIEROLOGIC, [hīer'-ō-loj'-ik], *adj.* hierological.
HIEROLOGICAL, [hīer'-ō-loj-ik-al], *adj.* relating to hierology.
HIEROLOGIST, [hīer-ol'-oj-ist], *n.* one versed in hierology.
HIEROLOGY, [hīer-ol'-o-ji], *n.* sacred literature and tradition. [Gk. *hierologia* sacred language].
HIEROMANCY, [hīer'-ō-man'-si], *n.* divination by the inspection of sacrificial or holy objects. [HIERO and Gk. *manteia* divination].
HIEROPHANT, [hīer'-ō-fant], *n.* one who initiates into the mysteries. [Gk. *hierophantes*].
HIEROPHANTIC, [hīer'-ō-fant'-ik], *adj.* relating to the office of a hierophant.
HIEROSCOPY, [hīer-os'-kop-i], *n.* hieromancy. [HIERO and Gk. *skopos* viewing].
HIGGLE, [higl], *v.i.* to haggle over small transactions, to drive a mean bargain. [HAGGLE].
HIGGLEDY-PIGGLEDY, [higl'-di-pigl'-di], *adv.* in complete disorder, jumbled together haphazardly. [Symbolic].
HIGGLER, [hig'-ler], *n.* one who higgles.
HIGH (1), [hī], *adj.* lofty, elevated, extending a good distance upwards; of a certain altitude; at a good or specified distance above the ground; exalted, of important status or position; proud, haughty; chief, principal; very good; sublime, noble; advanced developed; extreme in opinion; intense, of an outstanding degree; exaggerated in colour or sound, shrill, sharp; (of food) beginning to decay; (of explosives) powerful and rapid in action; **h. sea,** the sea some distance from land; **h. tea,** a meat tea. [OE. *heh, heah*].
HIGH (2), [hī], *adv.* highly, to a high extent, level or degree.
HIGHBALL, [hī'-bawl], *n.* a whisky and soda. [U.S. slang].
HIGH-BLOWN, [hī'-blōn], *adj.* swollen with pride.
HIGHBORN, [hī'-bawn], *adj.* of noble birth.
HIGHBRED, [hī'-bred], *adj.* of noble stock; well-bred.
HIGHBROW (1), [hī'-brow], *n.* one of intellectual interests, without patience or desire to show toleration of the culturally inferior.
HIGHBROW (2), [hī'-brow], *adj.* relating to a highbrow, his interests, and tastes.
HIGH-CHURCH, [hī'-church'], *adj.* Anglican ritualistic.
HIGH-CHURCHISM, [hī'-church'-izm], *n.* the belief in or practice of elaborate ritual, traditionalism and Anglicanism.
HIGH-CHURCHMAN, [hī'-church'-man], *n.* one believing in High-Churchism.
HIGH-COLOURED, [hī'-kul'-erd], *adj.* bright, vivid, florid.
HIGHDAY, [hī'-dā'], *n.* a holiday, a festival.

HIGHFALUTIN', [hī'-fal-ōōt'-in], *adj.* pretentious, absurdly bombastic, high-sounding.
HIGH-FED, [hī'-fed], *adj.* pampered, overfed.
HIGH-FLIER, [hī'-flī-er], *n.* an extremely ambitious person; one tending to go to extremes; the Purple Emperor butterfly.
HIGHFLOWN, [hī'-flōn], *adj.* proudly ambitious; bombastic.
HIGH-FLUSHED, [hī'-flusht], *adj.* much elated.
HIGH-FLYING, [hī'-flī-ing], *adj.* over-ambitious.
HIGH-HANDED, [hī'-hand'-id], *adj.* overbearing, arbitrary.
HIGH-HAT, [hī'-hat'], *n.* and *adj.* (*U.S.*) a top hat; **to be h.**, to be arrogant.
HIGH-HEARTED, [hī'-haht'-id], *adj.* full of courage.
HIGH-HUNG, [hī'-hung], *adj.* hung high.
HIGHLAND (1), [hī'-land], *n.* any hilly or mountainous district; **Highlands**, the elevated region of the north and north-west of Scotland.
HIGHLAND (2), [hī'-land], *adj.* relating to the Highlands.
HIGHLANDER, [hī'-land-er], *n.* a native of the Scottish Highlands; a soldier of a Highland regiment.
HIGHLANDISH, [hī'-land-ish], *adj.* of highland character.
HIGHLANDMAN, [hī'-land-man], *n.* a highlander.
HIGH-LIFE, [hī'-līf], *n.* the life of the rich and pretentious.
HIGHLIGHT, [hī'-līt], *n.* the brightest part of a painting, etc.; the best, or outstanding part of a performance.
HIGH-LIVED, [hī'-livd], *adj.* relating to high life.
HIGHLOWS, [hī'-lōz], *n.(pl.)* laced boots reaching just above the ankle.
HIGHLY, [hī'-li], *adv.* to or at a height; extremely; with esteem; very favourably; well. [OE. *healice*].
HIGH-METTLED, [hī'-metld], *adj.* high-spirited; high-hearted.
HIGH-MINDED, [hī'-mīnd'-id], *adj.* nobly minded; haughty.
HIGHNESS, [hī'-nes], *n.* height, the state or extent of being high; title of respect given to princes and princesses of royal blood. [OE. *heahness*].
HIGH-PRESSURE, [hī'-presh'-er], *adj.* driven by high pressure of steam, etc., without a condenser; (*fig.*) done with great speed and energy.
HIGH-PRIEST, [hī'-prēst'], *n.* chief priest.
HIGH-PRIESTSHIP, [hī'-prēst'-ship], *n.* office or status of a high-priest.
HIGH-PRINCIPLED, [hī'-prin'-sipld], *adj.* high-minded, honourable.
HIGH-PROOF, [hī'-prōōf], *adj.* highly rectified.
HIGH-REACHING, [hī'-rēch'-ing], *adj.* very ambitious.
HIGH-REPENTED, [hī'-ri-pent'-id], *adj.* deeply repented.
HIGHROAD, [hī'-rōd], *n.* main road; (*fig.*) the quickest and most direct way.
HIGH-SOULED, [hī'-sōld], *adj.* of lofty ideals.
HIGH-SOUNDING, [hī'-sownd'-ing], *adj.* highfalutin'; lofty in word.
HIGH-SPIRITED, [hī'-spi'-rit-id], *adj.* vivacious, full of daring and ardency; full of vigour.
HIGH-STEPPER, [hī'-step'-er], *n.* a high stepping horse; (*slang*) a female of great sexual attractiveness, and decided social aspirations.
HIGH-STOMACHED, [hī'-stum'-akt], *adj.* proud, haughty.
HIGHT, [hīt], *adj.* (*archaic*) named. [ME. *hight*].
HIGH-TIDE, [hī'-tīd'], *n.* the highest level to which a tide rises; the time of this maximum rising; the state of tidal water at this time; (*fig.*) the fullest extent of anything.
HIGH-TIME, [hī'-tīm], *adj.* full time, time for action.
HIGH-TONED, [hī'-tōnd], *adj.* of high moral feeling; elevated, honourable.
HIGH-WATER, [hī'-waw-ter], *n.* high-tide.
HIGH-WATER MARK, [hī'-waw'-ter-mahk'], *n.* a mark showing the highest limit reached by a tide; (*fig.*) the highest point of development, the acme.
HIGHWAY, [hī'-wā], *n.* a public road; (*fig.*) the best and quickest way to something.
HIGHWAYMAN, [hī'-wā-man], *n.* a (sometimes mounted) bandit who held up and robbed travellers on country roads.
HIGH-WROUGHT, [hī'-rawt'], *adj.* excited, overwrought; highly finished.
HIGTAPER, [hig'-tā'-per], *n.* the mullein, *Verbascum Thapsus*.
HIJACKER, [hī'-jak-er], *n.* (*U.S. slang*) a parasitical criminal robbing bootleggers of their liquor, etc.

HIKE (1), [hīk], *n.* a long country walk, taken for pleasure. [Dial. *hike*].
HIKE (2), [hīk], *v.i.* to go on a hike; to tramp.
HIKER, [hīk'-er], *n.* a devotee of hiking; a tramp.
HILAR, [hī'-ler], *adj.* relating to a hilum.
HILARIOUS, [hil-āer'-i-us], *adj.* very merry, boisterously gay; exciting great merriment. [Gk. *hilaros* cheerful].
HILARIOUSLY, [hil-āer'-i-us-li], *adv.* in hilarious fashion.
HILARITY, [hil-a'-ri-ti], *n.* the state of being hilarious. [L. *hilaritas*].
HILARY, [hil'-er-i], *n.* the January legal term; the university term from Christmas to Easter. [St. *Hilarius*, bishop of Poitiers, whose festival is on January 13].
HILDING, [hild'-ing], *n.* (*archaic*) a base and deceitful person. [~OE. *heldan* to bend].
HILL (1), [hil], *n.* a smallish natural elevation on the surface of the earth; an artificial hillock or mound. [OE. *hyll*].
HILL (2), [hil], *v.t.* and *i.* to make a hill of; to bank up earth about plants; to surround with hills; to go to the hills.
HILL-FORT, [hil'-fawt], *n.* a prehistoric fortification built on a hill.
HILLINESS, [hil'-i-nes], *n.* the quality of being hilly.
HILLO, [hi-lō'], *int.* a cry to attract attention.
HILLOCK, [hil'-ok], *n.* a small hill, mound.
HILLSIDE, [hil'-sīd], *n.* the side of a hill.
HILLTOP, [hil'-top], *n.* the crest of a hill.
HILLY, [hil'-i], *adj.* having many hills.
HILSAH, [hil'-sah], *n.* an edible fish found in the Ganges. [Hind. *hilsa*].
HILT (1), [hilt], *n.* the handle of a sword, dagger, pick, etc.; **up to the h.**, utterly, completely. [OE. *hilt*].
HILT (2), [hilt], *v.t.* to add a hilt to.
HILTED, [hilt'-id], *adj.* furnished with a hilt.
HILUM, [hī'-lum], *n.* the scar on a bean or other seed where it was attached to the placenta. [L. *hilum* trifle].
HIM, [him], *personal pron. objective case* of HE. [OE. *him*].
HIMSELF, [him-self'], *pron. 3rd person sg., masc. used reflexively, or emphatically for the personal pronoun*; **by h.**, alone; **he is h. again** he has recovered. [OE. *him selfum*].

HILT

HIMYARITE, [him'-yer-īt], *n.* a member of an ancient Semitic tribe of south-west Arabia. [*Himyar*, a legendary king of Yemen in south-west Arabia].
HIMYARITIC (1), [him'-yer-it'-ik], *n.* the language of the Himyarites.
HIMYARITIC (2), [him'-yer-it'-ik], *adj.* relating to the Himyarites.
HIN, [hin], *n.* a Hebrew liquid measure equivalent to about six quarts. [Heb. *hin*].
HIND (1), [hīnd], *n.* a female red deer. [OE. *hind*].
HIND (2), [hīnd], *n.* a farm servant; a peasant, a rustic; (*Scots*) a skilled farm labourer in charge of two horses. [OE. *hina*].
HIND (3), [hīnd], *adj.* posterior; situated behind. [ME. *hind*].
HINDBERRY, [hīnd'-be'-ri], *n.* the wild raspberry.
HINDBOW, [hīnd'-bō], *n.* the part of a saddle that projects behind, the cantle.
HINDER (1), [hīnd'-er], *adj.* that is at the rear or at the back, posterior. [OE. *hinder*].
HINDER (2), [hin'-der], *v.t.* to prevent; to delay, to thwart, partially or completely. [OE. *hindrian*].
HINDERER, [hind'-er-er], *n.* a person who, or that which, hinders.
HINDERMOST, [hind'-er-mōst], *adj.* farthest behind, hindmost.
HINDI (1), [hin'-dē'], *n.* the dialect spoken in northern India.
HINDI (2), [hin'-dē'], *adj.* pertaining to northern India, or to the dialect spoken there. [Hind. *Hindi* Indian].
HINDMOST, [hīnd'-mōst], *adj. superl.* of HIND (3), farthest behind.

HINDRANCE, [hin'-drants], *n.* the act of hindering; one who, or that which, hinders; obstacle.
HINDU (1), [hin-dōō'], *n.* a non-Moslem Aryan inhabitant of northern India; any believer in Hinduism; a native of Hindustan. [Pers *Hindu* Indian].
HINDU (2), [hin-dōō'], *adj.* of, or pertaining to, the Hindus.
HINDUISM, [hin'-dōō-izm], *n.* the religion of the Hindus.
HINDUSTANI (1), [hin'-dōōs-tah'-ni], *n.* a native inhabitant of Hindustan; the most widespread language of India, Urdu, being a variety of Hindi mixed with Persian, etc. [HINDU and Pers. *stan* place].
HINDUSTANI (2), [hin'-dōōs-tah'-ni], *adj.* pertaining to Hindustan.
HINGE (1), [hinj], *n.* a joining device by which one or both of two objects so connected may move in relation to the other; (*fig.*), a pivot, the point on which anything turns. [ME. *henge*].
HINGE (2), [hinj], *v.t. and i.* to fasten or connect with a hinge; (*fig.*) to turn or depend on.
HINK†, [hingk], *n.* (*prov.*) a reaping hook.
HINNY (1), [hin'-i], *n.* the offspring of a she-ass and a stallion. [L. *hinnus*].
HINNY (2), [hin'-i], *v.t.* to neigh. [Fr. *hennir*].
HINT (1), [hint], *n.* a suggestion or allusion; a faint intimation; a short useful item of advice. [~OE. *hentan* seize].
HINT (2), [hint], *v.t. and i.* to intimate, suggest
HINTERLAND, [hin'-ter-land], *n.* land behind a stretch of coast, or river-bank; the region served by a port. [Germ. *hinterland* behind-land].
HINTINGLY, [hint'-ing-li], *adv.* in a hinting way.
HIP (1), [hip], *n.* the projection made by the side of the pelvis and the top end of the thigh bone, the haunch; (*arch.*) the sloping and projecting edge of a roof; **on the h.,** at a disadvantage; **h. and thigh,** utterly, remorselessly. [OE. *hype*].
HIP (2), [hip], *n.* the fruit of the dog-rose. [OE. *heope*].
HIP (3), HYP†, [hip], *n.* (*slang*) melancholy, despondency. [HYPOCHONDRIA].
HIP (4), [hip], *int.* the exclamation twice given as a signal for a general cheer.
HIP (5), HYP†, (hipping, hipped), [hip], *v.t.* to depress in spirits. [HIP (3)].
HIP-BATH, [hip'-bahth], *n.* a bath to be sat in.
HIP-BELT, [hip'-belt], *n.* hip-girdle.
HIP-BONE, [hip'-bōn], *n.* the haunch-bone.
HIP DISEASE, [hip'-di-zēz'], *n.* disease of the hip-joint.
HIP-GIRDLE, [hip'-gurdl], *n.* a sword-belt about the waist, catching up on the right hip and slanting towards the left side.
HIP-GOUT, [hip'-gowt], *n.* gout of the hip, sciatica.
HIPPARION, [hip-āer'-i-on], *n.* a prehistoric ancestor of the horse having lateral toes on each side of the foot. [Gk. *hipparion* pony].
HIPPED, [hipt], *adj.* (*coll.*) depressed, melancholy.
HIPPIATRIC, [hip'-i-at'-rik], *adj.* relating to hippiatry. [Gk. *hippiatrikos*].
HIPPIATRY, [hip'-i-at-ri], *n.* veterinary surgery for horses; farriery.
HIPPIC, [hip'-ik], *adj.* relating to horses. [Gk. *hippikos*].
HIPPO (1), [hip'-ō], *n.* (*coll.*) a hippopotamus. [HIPPO(POTAMUS)].
HIPPO- (2), *pref.* horse. [Gk. *hippos* horse].
HIPPOCAMPUS, (*pl.* **hippocampi**), [hip'-ō-kamp'-us], *n.* the sea-horse, a small fish with a head and neck like those of a horse, and a tapering prehensile tail; (*myth.*) a sea-horse with a long tail, usually represented as drawing the chariot of a sea-god. [Gk. *hippokampos*].
HIPPOCENTAUR, [hip'-ō-sen'-taw(r)], *n.* a fabulous creature, half man, half horse. [HIPPO and CENTAUR].
HIPPOCRAS, [hip'-o-kras], *n.* a spiced wine, strained and used medicinally. [OFr. *ipocras* from *Hippocrates*, the ancient Greek physician].
HIPPOCRATIC, [hip'-ō-krat'-ik], *adj.* pertaining to Hippocrates; relating to the ashen appearance of the human face shortly before death; **H. oath,** the medical oath. [*Hippocrates*, the Greek physician, who first described it].
HIPPOCRATISM, [hip-ok'-rat-izm], *n.* the teaching of Hippocrates.
HIPPOCREPIAN, [hip'-ō-krēp'-i-an], *adj.* like a horseshoe in shape. [HIPPO and Gk. *krepis* shoe].
HIPPODROME, [hip'-ō-drōm], *n.* a circus or arena for horseshows, riding displays, etc.; (*hist.*) a course for horse or chariot races in ancient Greece and Rome; a theatre. [Gk. *hippodromos*].
HIPPOGRIFF, HIPPOGRYPH, [hip'-ō-grif], *n.* a fabulous monster, a mixture of horse and griffin. [Fr. *hippogriffe*].
HIPPOLITH, [hip'-o-lith], *n.* a stone found in a horse's stomach or intestines. [HIPPO and Gk. *lithos* stone].
HIPPOLOGICAL, [hip'-ol-oj'-ik-al], *adj.* of, or pertaining to, hippology.
HIPPOLOGIST, [hip-ol'-oj-ist], *n.* a student of hippology.
HIPPOLOGY, [hip-ol'-o-ji], *n.* the scientific study of horses. [HIPPO and Gk. *logos* speech].
HIPPOPATHOLOGY, [hip'-ō-path-ol'-o-ji], *n.* medical science as relating to horses. [HIPPO and PATHOLOGY].
HIPPOPHAGOUS, [hip-of'-a-gus], *adj.* eating horse-flesh. [HIPPO and Gk. *phago* I eat].
HIPPOPHAGY, [hip-of'-a-ji], *n.* the practice of feeding on horseflesh.
HIPPOPHILE, [hip'-ō-fīl], *n.* one who loves horses. [HIPPO and Gk. *philos* loving].
HIPPOPOTAMUS, [hip'-ō-pot'-am-us], *n.* the African river horse, *Hippopotamus amphibius.* [Gk. *hippopotamos*].

HIPPOPOTAMUS

HIPPURIC, [hip-ew'-rik], *adj.* procured from the urine of horses. [HIPPO and URIC].
HIPPURITE, [hip'-yōō-rīt], *n.* an extinct bivalve mollusc found in chalk. [Gk. *hippouris* horse-tailed].
HIP-ROOF, [hip'-rōōf], *n.* (*arch.*) a roof with ends slanting back at the same angle as the adjacent sides.
HIPSHOT, [hip'-shot], *adj.* with a dislocated hip.
HIRABLE, [hīer'-abl], *adj.* able to be hired.
HIRCIN, [hur'-sin], *n.* a fatty matter present in mutton suet. [L. *hircinus* pertaining to a he-goat].
HIRCINE, [hur'-sīn], *adj.* pertaining to a he-goat; like a goat. [*Prec.*].
HIRCINOUS, [hur'-sin-us], *adj.* rank-smelling like a goat.
HIRE (1), [hīer], *n.* the act of hiring; the payment made to hire something; the rights or benefits acquired by hiring something. [OE. *hyr* wages].
HIRE (2), [hīer], *v.t.* to obtain services or temporary possession and use of something in exchange for payment; to lend out in exchange for payment; to bribe, engage under promise of monetary payment. [OE. *hyrian*].
HIRELESS, [hīer'-les], *adj.* without hire.
HIRELING, [hīer'-ling], *n.* a paid supporter or follower; one who, or that which, is hired. [OE. *hyrling*].
HIRER, [hīer'-er], *n.* one who hires or lets out on hire.
HIRSUTE, [hur-sewt'], *adj.* hairy. [L. *hirsutus*].
HIRSUTENESS, [hur'-sewt-nes], *n.* the quality of being hirsute.
HIRUDINAL†, [hi-rōō'-din-al], *adj.* pertaining to, resembling, a leech. [L. *hirudo* leech].
HIS, [hiz], *pronominal adj. and possessive pron., 3rd person, masc.* belonging or pertaining to him. [OE. *his*].
HISK, [hisk], *v.i.* to breathe with difficulty. [Unkn.].
HISPANICISM, [his-pan'-is-izm], *n.* a Spanish idiom or turn of phrase. [L. *Hispania* Spain].
HISPID, [his'-pid], *adj.* bristly; rough, with stiff hairs [L. *hispidus*].
HISS (1), [his], *n.* a prolonged sibilant sound sometimes indicating annoyance, disapproval, etc.; any similar sound produced mechanically; the noise made by a snake or cat when alarmed.
HISS (2), [his], *v.t. and i.* to emit a hiss; to show disapproval by such a sound. [ME. *hissen*].
HISSING, [his'-ing], *n.* the act of one who, or that which, hisses; the sound thus produced, *esp.* when indicating disapproval.
HISSINGLY, [his'-ing-li], *adv.* with a hissing noise.
HIST, [hist], *int.* hush, be quiet. [Echoic].
HISTO-, *pref.* tissue. [Gk. *histos*].
HISTOGENETIC, [his'-tō-jen-et'-ik], *adj.* forming tissue. [HISTO and GENETIC].
HISTOGENY, [his-toj'-en-i], *n.* the formation of tissue. [HISTO and Gk. *genes* born of].
HISTOGRAPHY, [his-tog'-ra-fi], *n.* the description of organic tissue. [HISTO and Gk. *graphia* writing].

HISTOLOGICAL, [his'-tō-loj'-ik-al], *adj.* relating to histology.
HISTOLOGIST, [his-tol'-oj-ist], *n.* one versed in histology.
HISTOLOGY, [his-tol'-o-ji], *n.* the scientific study of organic tissue. [HISTO and Gk. *logos* speech].
HISTOLYSIS, [his-tol'-is-is], *n.* dissolution of organic tissue. [HISTO and Gk. *lusis* loosening].
HISTONOMY, [his-ton'-om-i], *n.* the study of the formation of organic tissues. [HISTO and Gk. *nomos* law].
HISTORIAN, [his-taw'-ri-an], *n.* one versed in history.
HISTORIC, [his-to'-rik], *adj.* pertaining to, recorded in, history; momentous, memorable, famous [L. *historicus*].
HISTORICAL, [his-to'-rik-al], *adj.* true to history; historic; according to history; displaying the whole development of something step by step.
HISTORICALLY, [his-to'-rik-al-i], *adv.* in an historical fashion.
HISTORIETTE, [his'-to-ri-et'], *n.* a short history or story. [Fr. *historiette*].
HISTORIOGRAPHER, [his'-to-ri-og'-ra-fer], *n.* a writer of history; an official recorder of historical events.
HISTORIOGRAPHICAL, [his-to'-ri-ō-graf'-ik-al], *adj.* pertaining to historiography.
HISTORIOGRAPHY, [his'-to-ri-og'-ra-fi], *n.* the art of writing history; written history. [L. *historiographus* a writer of history].
HISTORY, [his'-ter-i], *n.* the narrative of events recorded chronologically; the study of human activities and events arising from them, from the earliest times, *esp.* the study of past times and events; the whole course of development of anything, an account of this. [L. *historia*].
HISTORY-PIECE, [his'-ter-i-pēs'], *n.* a pictorial representation of a historical event.
HISTRION, [his'-tri-on], *n.* an actor, stage-player. [L. *histrio*].
HISTRIONIC, [his'-tri-on'-ik], *adj.* pertaining to actors or acting; dramatic; theatrical. [L. *histrionicus*].
HISTRIONICAL, [his'-tri-on'-ik-al], *adj.* histrionic.
HISTRIONICALLY, [his'-tri-on'-ik-al-i], *adv.* in a histrionic fashion.
HISTRIONISM, [his'-tri-on-izm], *n.* stage-playing.
HIT (**1**), [hit], *n.* a blow, stroke, etc., that hits its mark; a stroke of success, *esp.* if unexpected; a happy or witty remark, *esp.* in sarcasm, a taunt, dig; (*coll.*) a popular success; **to make a h. with,** to impress favourably.
HIT (**2**), (**hitting, hit**), [hit], *v.t.* to strike, knock, come in sharp contact with; **to h. on,** to find, *esp.* unexpectedly; **to h. off,** to imitate exactly; **to h. it,** (*slang*) to depart; to guess right; **to h. it off with,** (*coll.*) to get on well with. [OE. *hyttan*].
HITCH (**1**), [hich], *n.* a jerky motion; a limp; a temporary dislocation of arrangements; a kind of knot used by sailors.
HITCH (**2**), [hich], *v.t.* to move with a jerk or jerks; to fasten by something that catches on; **to h. up,** to pull up sharply. [ME. *hicchen* to remove].
HITCH-HIKE, [hich'-hīk'], *v.i.* (*coll.*) to travel by road obtaining lifts where possible. [Unkn.].
HITCHING, [hich'-ing], *n.* a fastening in a horse's harness.
HITHE, HYTHE, [hīTH], *n.* a landing-place; a small harbour or haven.
HITHER (**1**), [hiTH'-er], *adj.* lying on this side, nearer. [OE. *hider*].
HITHER (**2**), [hiTH'-er], *adv.* to this place, in this direction; **h. and thither,** on an uncertain, varying course. [OE. *hider*]
HITHERMOST, [hiTH'-er-most], *adj.* nearest in this direction.
HITHERSIDE, [hiTH'-er-sīd], *n.* the side nearest the speaker.
HITHERTO, [hiTH'-er-tōō'], *adv.* up to this time; up till now; †up to this place.
HITHERWARD†, [hiTH'-er-wud], *adv.* hither, in this direction.
HIT-OR-MISS, [hit'-or-mis], *adj.* careless, haphazard.
HITTER, [hit'-er], *n.* one who hits, *esp.* one who hits hard.
HITTITE, [hit'-īt], *n.* a member or the language of an ancient kingdom extending from Lydia into Palestine. [Heb. *Khittim*].
HIVE (**1**), [hīv], *n.* a box in which bees are kept; (*fig.*) a place swarming with busy people. [OE. *hyf*].
HIVE (**2**), [hīv], *v.t. and i.* to collect bees into a hive; to store up honey in a hive; (*fig.*) to make a comfortable home.
HIVE-BEE, [hīv'-bē], *n.* the honey-bee, *Apis mellifica.*
HIVELESS, [hīv'-les], *adj.* having no hive.
HIVER, [hīv'-er], *n.* one who gathers bees into a hive.
HIVES, [hīvz], *n.(pl.)* a rash on the skin, *esp.* chicken-pox. [Unkn.].
HO, [hō], *int.* a cry to attract attention.
HOAR (**1**), [haw(r)], *n.* a white, powdery coating of frost, rime.
HOAR (**2**), see HAAR.
HOAR (**3**), [haw(r)], *adj.* greyish-white; white-haired; (*fig.*) venerable and ancient. [OE. *har*].
HOAR †(**4**), [haw(r)], *v.i.* to become hoary.
HOARD (**1**), [hawd], *n.* a secret and guarded store of treasure; an accumulation, a secret collection; store, fund. [OE. *hord*].
HOARD (**2**), [hawd], *v.t. and i.* to gather together in secret, store away. [OE. *hordian*].
HOARDER, [hawd'-er], *n.* one who hoards, a miser.
HOARDING (**1**), [hawd'-ing], *n.* the act of making a hoard. [HOARD (2)].
HOARDING (**2**), [hawd'-ing], *n.* a high wooden fence; such a fence erected or used for exhibiting posters. [Uncert.].
HOAR-FROST, [haw(r)'-frost'], *n.* white frost.
HOARHOUND, see HOREHOUND.
HOARINESS, [haw(r)'-i-nes], *n.* the quality of being hoary.
HOARSE, [haw(r)s], *adj.* husky in speech; harsh-sounding. [OE. *has*].
HOARSELY, [haw(r)s'-li], *adv.* in a hoarse voice.
HOARSENESS, [haw(r)s'-nes], *n.* the condition of being hoarse.
HOAR-STONE, [haw(r)'-stōn], *n.* an ancient stone, sometimes designating a boundary. [OE. *hār* white and STONE].
HOARY, [haw'-ri], *adj.* greyish-white in colour; white-haired; (*fig.*) venerable, ancient, of long standing. [ME. *hori*].
HOATZIN, [hō'-at-sin], *n.* a tropical South American bird of the genus *Opisthocomus*, of which the young have a claw on the thumb and first finger of the wing by which they are able to climb trees. [Native].
HOAX (**1**), [hōks], *n.* a deceiving trick or statement; a practical joke. [HOCUS].
HOAX (**2**), [hōks], *v.t.* to deceive or trick; to play a practical joke upon.
HOAXER, [hōks'-er], *n.* a person who hoaxes.
HOB (**1**), [hob], *n.* a hub, the nave of a wheel; the flat part of a grate, at the side, where kettles, etc., are placed to be kept warm; the shoe on a sledge-runner. [Uncert.].
HOB (**2**), [hob], *n.* an imp; a fairy; a clown. [~ROB from ROBIN].
HOBBISM, [hob'-izm], *n.* the teaching of Hobbes. [T. *Hobbes*, 1588-1679, the English philosopher].
HOBBIST, [hob'-ist], *n.* a disciple of Hobbes.
HOBBLE (**1**), [hobl], *n.* a lame, stumbling walk; the shackle used for hobbling.
HOBBLE (**2**), [hobl], *v.t. and i.* to check a horse, etc., by tying two of its legs together with a length of rope; to limp or stumble along laboriously and painfully. [ME. *hobelen*].
HOBBLEDEHOY, [hobl'-di·hoi], *n.* a clumsy, ill-mannered youth. [Unkn.].
HOBBLER, [hob'-ler], *n.* a retainer who, by his tenure, was to maintain a hobby or horse for military service. [OFr. *hobeler*].
HOBBLINGLY, [hob'-ling-li], *adv.* with a hobbling gait.
HOBBY (**1**), [hob'-i], *n.* †a nag; a hobby-horse; an occupation for one's leisure; a fad. [ME. *hobin* nag].
HOBBY (**2**), [hob'-i], *n.* a small hawking falcon, *Falco subbuteo.* [OFr. *hobé*].
HOBBY-HORSE, [hob'-i-haws], *n.* a children's toy consisting of a stick with the head of a horse at one end; a rocking horse; a morris-dancer wearing the head of a horse; a hobby; a pet theme.
HOBGOBLIN, [hob'-gob'-lin], *n.* an imp; an alarming apparition; a bogey. [HOB (2) and GOBLIN].
HOBIT, [hob'-it], *n.* a small mortar. [~Germ. *haubitz*].
HOBLIKE, [hob'-līk], *adj.* like a hob, clownish. [HOB (2)].
HOBNAIL, [hob'-nāl], *n.* a nail with a thick head used for the soles of boots.
HOBNAILED, [hob'-nāld], *adj.* having hobnails; **h. liver,** a liver covered with small projections, as a result of cirrhosis of the liver.
HOBNOB (**1**), [hob'-nob'], *n.* (*slang*) a friendly chat.

HOBNOB (2), (**hobnobbing, hobnobbed**), [hob'-nob'], *v.i.* to be very friendly; to converse amicably. [~ME. *hab nab* come what may].
HOBO, [hō'-bō], *n.* (*U.S.*) a tramp; a professional vagabond. [Unkn.].
HOBSON-JOBSON, [hob'-sun-job'-sun], *n.* native excitement in India during the religious ceremonies of Moharram.
HOCK (1), [hok], *n.* the joint between the true knee and the fetlock in the hind leg of a horse, the hough. [HOUGH].
HOCK (2), [hok], *n.* a German white wine. [HOCK(AMORE) from Germ. *Hochheimer* wine of Hochheim].
HOCK (3), [hok], *n.* **in h.**, (*slang*) in pawn, in prison or in debt. [Du. *hok*].
HOCK (4), [hok], *v.t.* to hough; to hamstring.
HOCK (5), [hok], *v.t.* (*U.S. slang*) to pawn; to pledge as a security. [HOCK (3)].
HOCKAMORE†, [hok'-a-maw(r)], *n.* hock.
HOCKEY (1), [hok'-i], *n.* a game played between two teams of eleven, with a small hard ball driven by curved sticks. [Uncert.].
HOCKEY (2), [hok'-i], *adj.* belonging to the game of hockey.
HOCKHERB, [hok'-hurb], *n.* a kind of mallow.
HOCKLE†, [hokl], *v.t.* (*prov.*) to mow. [Uncert.]
HOCK-TIDE, [hok'-tīd], *n.* the Monday and Tuesday in the second week after Easter, formerly feast-days to celebrate the defeat of the Danes by Ethelred. [Unkn.].
HOCUS (1), [hō'-kus], *n.* a drugged draught.
HOCUS (2), [hō'-kus], *v.t.* to dupe, swindle, hoax; to doctor the drink of, drug. [HOCUS-POCUS].
HOCUS-POCUS, [hō'-kus-pō'-kus], *n.* meaningless jargon employed by a conjurer while performing a trick, to distract attention; silly mystification; nonsense; swindling, underhand work. [Uncert.].
HOD, [hod], *n.* a wooden trough on a long handle for carrying mortar and bricks over the shoulder. [ME. *hodd*, ~MDu. *hodde* basket].

HOD

HODDEN, [hod'-en], *n.* (*Scots*) coarse undyed woollen material; **h. grey**, the mixed black and white woollen cloth used for the kilts of the London Scottish. [Unkn.].
HODGE, [hoj], *n.* (*coll.*) an agricultural labourer. [*Hodge*, a character in the 16th-century comedy "Gammer Gurton's Needle"].
HODGE-PODGE, HOTCH-POTCH, [hoj'-poj', hoch-poch'], *n.* a mixture, medley, miscellany. [HOTCH POT].
HODGE-PUDDING†, [hoj'-pōōd'-ing], *n.* a pudding of many and various ingredients.
HODIERNAL, [hō'-di-ur'-nal], *adj.* of, pertaining to, today. [L. *hodiernus*].
HODMAN, [hod'-man], *n.* a man who carries a hod; a bricklayer's assistant.
HODMANDOD, [hod'-man-dod], *n.* a snail. [Uncert.].
HODOGRAPH, [ho'-dō-graf], *n.* a velocity curve invented by Sir W. R. Hamilton; a machine for measuring or testing the pace of horses. [Gk. *hodos* path and GRAPH].
HODOMETER, [ho-dom'-it-er], *n.* a device for measuring the distance travelled by a wheeled vehicle. [Gk. *hodos* path and METER].
HOE (1), [hō], *n.* a garden tool for weeding and loosening the earth. [Fr. *houe*].
HOE (2), [hō], *n.* a promontory. [OE. *hoh*].
HOE (3), [hō], *n.* a species of small shark, the spur dog-fish, *Acanthias vulgaris*.
HOE (4), [hō], *v.t. and i.* to use a hoe for weeding or turning the surface of the soil. [HOE (1)].
HOE-CAKE, [hō'-kāk], *n.* a cake made of Indian meal baked before the fire.

HOE

HOG (1), [hog], *n.* a castrated boar; a pig; (*fig.*) a coarse, inconsiderate, or filthy person; (*naut.*) a brush for cleaning the ship's bottom when it is under water; **to go the whole h.**, to do something very thoroughly; **a road h.**, a motorist inconsiderate of other road users. [OE. *hogg*].
HOG (2), (**hogging, hogged**), [hog], *v.t. and i.* to arch like the back of a hog; to act or eat like a hog; to clean a ship's bottom with a hog.
HOGBACKED, [hog'-bakt] *adj.* shaped like a hog's back.
HOGCOTE, [hog'-kōt], *n.* a pigsty.
HOGGED, [hogd], *adj.* ridged like a hog's back.
HOGGEREL, [hog'-er-el], *n.* a young sheep of the second year.
HOGGER-PUMP, [hog'-er-pump], *n.* the upper pump in the sinking pit of a mine.
HOGGERS, [hog'-erz], *n.(pl.)* footless stockings worn by coal-miners when in the pit. [Uncert.].
HOGGERY, [hog'-er-i], *n.* a place for rearing hogs; a herd of hogs; (*fig.*) conduct characteristic of a hog.
HOGGET, [hog'-et], *n.* a sheep of the second year; a colt of a year old; a young boar of the second year.
HOGGISH, [hog'-ish], *adj.* like a hog; swinish, greedy, filthy.
HOGGISHLY, [hog'-ish-li], *adv.* in a hoggish way.
HOGGISHNESS, [hog'-ish-nes], *n.* the quality of being hoggish.
HOG-HERD, [hog'-hurd], *n.* a keeper of hogs.
HOGMANAY, [hog'-man-ā], *n.* (*Scots*) New Year's Eve; the festivities then held. [OFr. *hoguinané*].
HOG-PEN, [hog'-pen], *n.* a sty for hogs.
HOG-PLUM, [hog'-plum], *n.* a tropical tree of the genus *Spondias*, bearing a fruit resembling a plum.
HOG-REEVE, [hog'-rēv], *n.* a parish officer whose business was to adjudicate regarding the trespasses of swine.
HOG-RINGER, [hog'-ring'-er], *n.* one who puts rings in the snouts of swine.
HOGSCORE, [hog'-skaw(r)], *n.* a distance-line drawn across the rink in the game of curling.
HOGSHEAD, [hogz'-hed], *n.* a large cask; a liquid measure equal to 52½ imperial gallons, or 54 gallons of beer or cider.
HOG-SHEARING, [hog'-shēer'-ing], *n.* a great fuss about nothing.
HOGSKIN, [hog'-skin], *n.* leather made from the skins of swine.
HOGSTEER, [hog'-stēer], *n.* a wild boar of the third year.
HOGSTY, [hog'-stī], *n.* an enclosure or shed for hogs.
HOGWASH, [hog'-wosh], *n.* kitchen refuse made into swill for swine; (*fig.*) silly talk.
HOGWEED, [hog'-wēd], *n.* cow-parsnip, *Heracleum Sphondylium*.
HOIDEN, see HOYDEN.
HOIST (1), [hoist], *n.* the act of hoisting; a lift, an apparatus for hoisting.
HOIST (2), [hoist], *v.t.* to raise, heave up, *esp.* by means of tackle. [ME. *hyse*, *hoise*, ~MDu. *hyssen*].
HOISTWAY, [hoist'-wā], *n.* a hole in a ship's deck through which goods may be hoisted up from the hold.
HOIT† (1), [hoit], *n.* a spoilt, ill-mannered, awkward child.
HOIT† (2), [hoit], *v.i.* to romp; to limp. [Uncert.].
HOITING†, [hoit'-ing], *n.* a riotous gathering.
HOITY-TOITY, [hoi'-ti-toi'-ti], *int. and adj.* a cry of protest, *esp.* at arrogance; touchy, arrogant.
HOKEY-POKEY, [hō'-ki-pō'-ki], *n.* a kind of cheap ice-cream. [HOCUS-POCUS].
HOKUM, [hō'-kum], *n.* (*U.S. slang*) the plot of a play; business imposed on the dialogue; a film scenario such as would satisfy the less critical minded; hocus-pocus, nonsense. [Unkn.].
HOLARCTIC, [hol-ahk'-tik], *adj.* (*zool.*) inhabiting or belonging to the Arctic region. [Gk. *holos* whole and ARCTIC].
HOLD (1), [hōld], *n.* the action of holding; manner or power of holding; that by which one may hold on; that which contains or receives something, a socket; (*fig.*) power, control; mental grip, understanding; influence; **to get h. of**, to obtain; (*slang*) to force an interview with; **h. up**, stoppage, delay, *esp.* of traffic. [OE. (*ge*)*heald*, (*ge*)*hald*].
HOLD (2), [hōld], *n.* the space below deck in a ship, for storing cargo. [Du. *hol* hole].
HOLD (3), (**held**), [hōld], *v.t.* to seize with and retain by the hand; to cling to, grasp; to catch; to retain; to possess, own; to occupy; to be in charge of; to defend, *esp.* successfully; to maintain, support; to proffer, present; to keep inviolate, abide by; to contain, to be capable of containing; to retain pending use, to have in preparation; to restrain, keep from escaping; to control, dominate; to be a match

for; to attract and retain the attention or interest of; to retain in the mind; to believe, to possess as an opinion; to deem; to decide; to organize, institute, etc.; *v.i.* to withstand strain; to be or remain valid, to last; to continue to do or to be; **to h. forth,** to talk at length, harangue; **to h. on,** to persevere, to keep on going; **to h. one's own,** to be the equal of one's opponents; **to h. out,** to proffer; to present; to defend amid difficulties; **to h. over,** to threaten with; to postpone; **to h. to,** to abide by; to compel to abide by; **to h. water,** (*fig.*) (of an idea, statement, etc.) to be sound and valid; (*naut.*) to stop a rowing-boat by holding the oars vertical in the water; **to h. with,** to approve of; **to h. up,** to rob on a road or railway; to delay. [OE. *healdan*].

HOLDALL, [hōld'-awl], *n.* a large bag for conveniently carrying all manner of things.

HOLDBACK, [hōld'-bak], *n.* a hindrance, impediment, drag.

HOLDER, [hōld'-er], *n.* one who, or that which, holds; a tenant; a receptacle.

HOLDER-FORTH, [hōld'-er-fawth'], *n.* one who discourses at length.

HOLDFAST, [hōld'-fahst], *n.* something to which one may hold on; that which holds fast, a clamp, a support, etc.

HOLDING, [hōld'-ing], *n.* the action of one who holds; land or property owned.

HOLE (1), [hōl], *n.* a cavity, a depression in a solid surface; an empty space; a socket; an excavation; the lair, den, or burrow of an animal; a small mean house or lodging; an unpleasant place; a break, gap, or rent, a perforation; an opening, an orifice; (*fig.*) a flaw, inaccuracy; (*golf*) the cup cut in the green into which the players try to hit the ball; a point scored in a holing game; (*slang*) a difficult situation, a scrape; **to make a h. in,** to reduce, consume; **to pick holes in,** to make adverse criticism of. [OE. *hol*].

HOLE (2), [hōl], *v.t. and i.* to make a hole in, hollow out; to make a tunnel through; to put, strike, or drive into a hole.

HOLE-AND-CORNER, [hōl'-and-kawn'-er], *adj.* (*coll.*) underhand, secret.

HOLEWORT, [hōl'-wurt], *n.* the moschatel, *Adoxa moschatellina.*

HOLEY, [hōl'-i], *adj.* having holes; full of holes.

HOLIBUT, see HALIBUT.

HOLIDAY (1), [hol'-i-di], *n.* an ecclesiastical feast day, a religious festival; a day of festivity, rest or recreation when work temporarily ceases; a period of rest from work and duty, a vacation; **Bank H.,** a general national holiday in England appointed by Act of Parliament. [OE. *haligdæg* holy day].

HOLIDAY (2), [hol'-i-di], *adj.* belonging to, or befitting, a holiday.

HOLIDAY (3), [hol'-i-di], *v.i.* to take a holiday.

HOLIDAY-MAKER, [hol'-i-di-māk'-er], *n.* someone on holiday; a tripper.

HOLILY, [hōl'-i-li], *adv.* in a holy manner.

HOLINESS, [hōl'-i-nes], *n.* the quality of being holy; **His H.,** the Pope's title.

HOLING-AXE, [hōl'-ing-aks'], *n.* an axe for cutting holes in posts.

HOLLA (1), HOLLOA†, [ho-la'], *int.* a call of greeting or to attract attention. [Fr. *holà!* ho there!].

HOLLA† (2), [hol'-a], *v.t. and i.* (*slang*) to shout loudly or suddenly.

HOLLAND, [hol'-and], *n.* a kind of coarse linen, or linen and cotton mixture, unbleached and usually dyed brown. [*Holland*, where first made].

HOLLANDER, [hol'-and-er], *n.* an inhabitant of Holland, a Dutchman.

HOLLANDISH, [hol'-and-ish], *adj.* resembling Holland.

HOLLANDS, [hol'-andz], *n.* gin made in Holland. [Du. *hollandsch* (*genever*) Dutch gin].

HOLLOA, see HOLLA.

HOLLOW (1), [hol'-ō], *n.* a depression, wide groove, shallow cavity; a little valley. [OE. *holh*].

HOLLOW (2), [hol'-ō], *adj.* having a cavity or depression in the surface; (of eyes) deep-set; (of the face) lean; not solid, having an outer hulk or husk but nothing inside; re-echoing, resonant; (*fig.*) insubstantial, vain, unauthenticated; (of laughter) mirthless, unreal.

HOLLOW (3), [hol'-ō], *v.t.* to render hollow; to make a hollow in.

HOLLOW-EYED, [hol -ō-īd'], *adj.* having sunken eyes.

HOLLOW-HEARTED, [hol'-ō-haht'-id], *adj.* shallow; insincere.

HOLLOWLY, [hol'-ō-li], *adv.* in a hollow way.

HOLLOWNESS, [hol'-ō-nes], *n.* the quality of being hollow.

HOLLOW SQUARE, [hol'-ō-skwāer], *n.* a company of soldiers drawn up in the form of a square with a vacant space in the middle.

HOLLOW-TONED, [hol'-ō-tōnd], *adj.* sounding as if coming from a cavity; re-echoing.

HOLLOW-WARE, [hol'-ō-wāer], *n.* utensils that are hollow in shape.

HOLLY, [hol'-i], *n.* an evergreen tree of the genus *Ilex*, with dark-green prickly leaves and scarlet berries. [OE. *hole(g)n*].

HOLLYHOCK, [hol'-i-hok], *n.* a tall plant related to the mallow, *Althæa rosea.* [ME. *holihoc* holy mallow].

HOLLYHOCK

HOLM, [hōm], *n.* a low, flat river bank; a small island, *esp.* in an estuary or river. [OE. *holm*].

HOLM-OAK, [hōm'-ōk], *n.* the evergreen oak, *Quercus Ilex.* [†*holm* holly and OAK].

HOLO-, *pref.* entire, whole; (*geol.*) relating to the most recent strata. [Gk. *holos*].

HOLOARTHRITIC, [hol'-ō-ahth-rit'-ik], *adj.* (*med.*) suffering from gout in every joint. [HOLO and ARTHRITIC].

HOLOBAPTIST, [hol'-ō-bap'-tist], *n.* one who believes in or practises baptism by immersion. [HOLO and BAPTIST].

HOLOBLASTIC, [hol'-ō-blast'-ik], *adj.* (*bot.*) completely germinal. [HOLO and Gk. *blastos* bud].

HOLOCAUST, [hol'-ō-kawst], *n.* a sacrifice by fire; massacre, mass destruction. [Fr. *holocauste*].

HOLOCEPHALOUS, [hol'-ō-kef'-al-us], *adj.* (*anat.*) having an undivided skull. [HOLO and Gk. *kephale* head].

HOLOCRYPTIC, [hol'-ō-kript'-ik], *adj.* undecipherable. [HOLO and CRYPTIC].

HOLOGRAPH, [hol'-ō-graf], *n.* a document entirely in the handwriting of the signatory. [HOLO and GRAPH].

HOLOGRAPHIC, [hol'-ō-graf'-ik], *adj.* pertaining to a holograph; written throughout by the author, *esp.* as testator.

HOLOHEDRAL, [hol'-ō-hē'-dral], *adj.* (of a crystal) perfectly symmetrical according to its type. [HOLO and Gk. *hedra* side].

HOLOMETABOLA, [hol'-ō-met-ab'-ol-a], *n.(pl.)* (*entom.*) insects subject to complete metamorphosis. [HOLO and Gk. *metabole* change].

HOLOMETER, [hol-om'-it-er], *n.* an instrument able to take all kinds of measures. [HOLO and METER].

HOLOPHANEROUS, [hol'-ō-fan'-er-us], *adj.* (*entom.*) completely visible. [HOLO and Gk. *phaneros* visible].

HOLOSERICEOUS, [hol'-ō-ser-is'-i-us], *adj.* (*bot.*) completely covered with a silky down. [HOLO and L. *sericeus* silken].

HOLOTHURIAN, [hol'-ō-thew'-ri-an], *n.* an animal of the family *Holothuria*, which includes the sea-cucumbers, sea-slugs, and trepang. [MdL. *holothuria* marine polypi].

HOLPEN†, [hō(l)p'-en], *p.pt.* of HELP (2).

HOLSTER, [hōl'-ster], *n.* a leather pistol case, hung from the belt or saddle-bow. [Swed. *holster* sheath, case].

HOLSTERED, [hōl'-sterd], *adj.* furnished with holsters.

HOLT (1), [hōlt], *n.* a grove, a small wood or thicket. [OE. *holt*].

HOLT (2), [hōlt], *n.* a burrow. [Unkn.].

HOLSTER

HOLY (1), [hō'-li], *n.* a holy place; **H. of Holies,** the inmost sanctuary of the Jewish temple or tabernacle; any holy place; (*slang*) an inaccessible sanctum.

HOLY (2), [hō'-li], *adj.* sacred; spiritually noble and pure; blessed by the Church; connected with religion; saint-like, pious; (*slang*) great. [OE. *halig*].

HOLY-DAY, [hō'-li-dā'], *n.* a religious feast or fast; a day in the Church's calendar.
HOLY GHOST, [hōl'-i-gōst'], *n.* the third person of the Trinity, the comforter bequeathed by Christ after his resurrection.
HOLYSTONE (1), [hō'-li-stōn], *n.* (*naut.*) a soft stone used to scour the decks.
HOLYSTONE (2), [hō'-li-stōn] *v.t.* to scour with holystone.
HOMAGE, [hom'-ij], *n.* the ritual act by which one declares oneself the vassal of another or pays allegiance to him; (*fig.*) deference, respect; an expression of these. [OFr. *homage*].
HOMAGEABLE, [hom'-ij-abl], *adj.* liable to pay homage.
HOMAGER, [hom'-ij-er], *n.* one who does homage.
HOMBURG, [hom'-burg], *n.* a soft, felt, brimmed hat for men. [*Homburg*, in Germany, where first worn].
HOME (1), [hōm], *n.* the house of one's birth and nurture or that belonging to one's parents; the house or apartment where one lives; a house where one is welcomed as a member of the family; one's habitual haunt; household, family-circle; the contents, *esp.* furniture, of a house; mother-country; the town, city, etc., where one was born; the place or state in which one finds happiness and satisfaction; the point of departure, to which one will ultimately return; the goal of one's endeavour; an asylum or institute where the sick and poor are cared for; a small private hospital; the lair of an animal; the place where anything is found or fostered; the goal or base in a game; **at h.**, receiving visitors; **at h. with**, at one's ease with; **nothing to write h. about**, not exciting or unusual. [OE. *ham*].
HOME (2), [hōm], *adj.* pertaining to one's home or to one's native country; internal; appropriate.
HOME (3), [hōm], *adv.* towards home; accurately, right on to the mark, as far as possible; movingly; with rational force.
HOME-BIRD, [hōm'-burd], *n.* (*coll.*) a person who loves to be at home.
HOMEBORN, [hōm'-bawn], *adj.* born at home, native.
HOMEBOUND, [hōm'-bownd], *adj.* on the way home.
HOMEBRED, [hōm'-bred], *adj.* bred at home, native.
HOMECOMING, [hōm'-kum'-ing], *n.* return to or arrival at home, or one's native land.
HOME-FARM, [hōm'-fahm], *n.* the farm attached to the dwelling-house of the occupier of an estate.
HOMEFELT, [hōm'-felt], *adj.* felt in the heart, private, intimate.
HOME GUARD, [hōm'-gahd'], *n.* a body of part-time soldiers enrolled for defence against invasion; a member of this body. [HOME (1) and GUARD (1)].
HOMEKEEPING, [hōm'-kēp'-ing], *adj.* remaining at home.
HOMELAND, [hōm'-land], *n.* native land.
HOMELESS, [hōm'-les], *adj.* having no home.
HOMELESSNESS, [hōm'-les-nes], *n.* the state of being homeless.
HOMELIKE, [hōm'-līk], *adj.* like home; homely; informal.
HOMELILY, [hōm'-li-li], *adv.* in homely manner.
HOMELINESS, [hōm'-li-nes], *n.* the quality of being homely.
HOME-LOT, [hōm'-lot], *n.* an enclosure on or near which a dwelling-house stands.
HOMELY, [hōm'-li], *adj.* like home; informal, friendly; lacking polish; familiar, everyday; (*U.S.*) plain-looking.
HOMELYN, [hōm'-lin], *n.* the spotted ray, *Raia maculata*.
HOMEMADE, [hōm'-mād'], *adj.* (as if) made at home.
HOMER (1), [hōm'-er], *n.* a Hebrew liquid measure equal to 75 gallons, a similar dry measure equal to 32 pecks. [Heb. *homer* heap].
HOMER (2), [hōm'-er], *n.* a homing pigeon.
HOMERIC, [hō-me'-rik], *adj.* pertaining to the Greek poet Homer or to his poetry; resembling his poetry; epic. [Gk. *Homerikos*].
HOME RULE, [hōm'-rōōl'], *n.* autonomy, independent and local government without outside control or interference.
HOMESICK, [hōm'-sik], *adj.* miserable with the longing to be at home.
HOMESICKNESS, [hōm'-sik'-nes], *n.* the state of being homesick, nostalgia.
HOMESPEAKING, [hōm'-spēk'-ing], *n.* vigorous, straightforward, and efficacious speaking.
HOMESPUN (1), [hōm'-spun], *n.* cloth of hand-woven yarn.
HOMESPUN (2), [hōm'-spun], *adj.* woven by hand in the home; (*fig.*) simple, honest, inelegant.
HOMESTALL, [hōm'-stawl], *n.* a homestead.
HOMESTEAD, [hōm'-sted], *n.* a farm with the surrounding buildings and land.
HOMEWARD, [hōm'-wud], *adv.* in the direction of home. [OE. *hamweard*].
HOMICIDAL, [hom'-i-sīd-al], *adj.* pertaining to homicide; like homicide; murderous.
HOMICIDE, [hom'-i-sīd], *n.* the killing of one man by another; a person who kills another. [L. *homicida*].
HOMILETIC, [hom-il-et'-ik], *adj.* pertaining to sermons or preaching. [Gk. *homiletikos*].
HOMILETICAL, [hom-il-et'-ik-al], *adj.* homiletic.
HOMILETICS, [hom-il-et'-iks], *n.(pl.)* the art of preaching; religious oratory.
HOMILIST, [hom'-il-ist], *n.* a preacher.
HOMILY, [hom'-i-li], *n.* a sermon, moral discourse, instructive lecture. [Gk. *homilia*].
HOMINY, [hom'-in-i], *n.* a meal prepared from Indian corn, boiled maize. [Native].
HOMMOCK, see HUMMOCK.
HOMO-, *pref.* the same, of the same sort. [Gk. *homos*].
HOMOCARPOUS, [ho'-mō-kahp'-us], *adj.* (*bot.*) with all the fruits of the florets alike. [HOMO and Gk. *karpos* fruit].
HOMOCENTRIC, [ho'-mō-sen'-trik], *adj.* with the same centre. [HOMO and CENTRE].
HOMOCERCAL, [ho'-mō-surkl'], *adj.* having both tail lobes equal; symmetrical. [HOMO and Gk. *kerkos* tail].
HOMOCHROMOUS, [ho-mok'-rom-us], *adj.* (*bot.*) with all the florets of the same colour. [HOMO and Gk. *khroma*].
HOMODONT, [hom'-ō-dont, hō'-mō-dont], *adj.* (*zool.*) having all the teeth alike. [HOMO and Gk. *odous odontos* tooth].
HOMODROMOUS, [ho'-mō-drōm'-us], *adj.* pointing or going in the same direction. [HOMO and Gk. *dromos* running].
HOMOEO-, *pref.* the same, like. [Gk. *homoios*].
HOMOEOPATHIC, [ho'-mi-ō-path'-ik], *adj.* relating to homoeopathy.
HOMOEOPATHICALLY, [hō'-mi-ō-path'-ik-al-i], *adv.* according to the methods of homoeopathy.
HOMOEOPATHIST,]hō'-mi-op'-ath-ist], *n.* one who practises or believes in homoeopathy.
HOMOEOPATHY, [hō'-mi-op'-ath-i], *n.* a medical system founded upon the idea that a disease or illness can be cured by frequent doses of very small quantities of some drug producing symptoms similar to those of the illness or disease. [Gk. *homoiopatheia* like feeling].
HOMOEOZOIC, [hō'-mi-ō-zō'-ik], *adj.* containing forms of life of the same kind. [HOMOEO and Gk. *zoon* animal].
HOMOGAMOUS, [hom-og'-am-us], *adj.* (*bot.*) having stamens and pistils which ripen together; pertaining to, or being in a state of, homogamy. [HOMO and Gk. *gamos* marriage].
HOMOGAMY, [hom-og'-am-i], *n.* (*bot.*) self-fertilization of a flower or plant.
HOMOGENEAL, [hom-ō-jē'-ni-al], *adj.* homogeneous.
HOMOGENEITY, [hom'-ō-jen-ē'-i-ti] *n.* the state of being homogeneous.
HOMOGENEOUS, [hom'-ō-jē'-ni-us], *adj.* alike, similar; uniform; of the same kind, of like parts throughout; (*math.*) commensurable. [MedL. *homogeneus*].
HOMOGENEOUSLY, [hom'-ō-jē'-ni-us-li], *adv.* in a homogeneous way.
HOMOGENEOUSNESS, [hom'-ō-jē'-ni-us-nes], *n.* homogeneity.
HOMOGENESIS, [hom'-ō-jen'-is-is], *n.* (*biol.*) sexual reproduction in which succeeding generations resemble the parent type. [HOMO and GENESIS].
HOMOGRAPH, [hom'-ō-graf], *n.* one of a pair or series of words alike in spelling but different in meaning. [HOMO and GRAPH].
HOMOGRAPHIC, [hom'-ō-graf'-ik], *adj.* (of spelling) in which each sound is denoted by an individual symbol.
HOMOIOUSIAN (1), [hom'-oi-ow'-sian], *n.* one who accepts the homoiousian doctrine.

HOMOIOUSIAN (2), [hom'-oi-ow'-si-an], *adj.* (*theol.*) pertaining to or accepting the doctrine that the Second Person of the Trinity is of like, but not the same substance with, the Father. [Gk. *homoiousios* of like substance].
HOMOLOGATE, [hom-ol'-og-āt], *v.t.* (*leg.*) to ratify. [LL. *homologare* to agree].
HOMOLOGICAL, [hom'-ō-loj'-ik-al], *adj.* relating to homology; with parts corresponding.
HOMOLOGIZE, [hom-ol'-oj-īz], *v.t.* to make homologous; *v.i.* to be, homologous.
HOMOLOGIZED, [hom-ol'-oj-īzd], *adj.* made, shown to be, homologous.
HOMOLOGOUS, [hom-ol'-og-us], *adj.* corresponding in character, position, proportion, value, structure, etc. [Gk. *homologos* agreeing].
HOMOLOGUE, [hom'-ol-og], *n.* that which is homologous to something; the same organ in origin or structure in different animals. [*Prec.*].
HOMOLOGY, [hom-ol'-oj-i], *n.* the quality of being homologous; (*biol.*) affinity of structure, though not of form or function. [Gk. *homologia*].
HOMOMORPHOUS, [hom'-ō-mawf'-us], *adj.* alike in form; (*bot.*) having flowers all of the same type; (*zool.*) having the larva like the imago. [HOMO and Gk. *morphe* shape].
HOMONYM, [hom'-ō-nim], *n.* one of a pair or series of words identical in sound but different in meaning and source. [Gk. *homonumos* having the same name].
HOMONYMIC, [hom'-ō-nim'-ik], *adj.* homonymous.
HOMONYMOUS, [hom-on'-im-us], *adj.* possessing the same name; like, or that are, homonyms; ambiguous.
HOMONYMOUSLY, [hom-on'-im-us-li], *adv.* in a homonymous manner.
HOMONYMY, [hom-on'-im-i], *n.* the quality of being homonymous. [Gk. *homonumia*].
HOMOOUSIAN, [hom'-ō-ow'-zi-an], *adj.* pertaining to or believing in the doctrine that the First and Second Persons of the Trinity are of one and the same substance. [Gk. *homoousios* consubstantial].
HOMOPHONE, [hom'-ō-fōn], *n.* a letter or symbol representing the same sound as another; a homonym. [Gk. *homophonon*].
HOMOPHONIC, [hom'-ō-fon'-ik], *adj.* homophonous.
HOMOPHONOUS, [hom-of'-on-us], *adj.* having the same sound; (*mus.*) monodic; unisonant. [Gk. *homophonos*].
HOMOPHONY, [hom-of'-on-i], *n.* the quality of being homophonic. [Fr. *homophonie*].
HOMOPLASTIC, [hom'-ō-plast'-ik], *adj.* (*biol.*) similarly formed or analogous, but of different origin. [HOMO and PLASTIC].
HOMOPTERA, [hom-op'-ter-a], *n.*(*pl.*) (*entom.*) a class of insects with forewings usually like the hind wings. [HOMO and Gk. *ptera* wings].
HOMOSEXUAL, [hom'-ō-sek'-shōō-al], *adj.* possessing a sexual propensity for persons of one's own sex. [HOMO and SEXUAL].
HOMOTAXIAL, [hom'-ō-taks'-i-al], *adj.* having likeness of order.
HOMOTAXIS, [hom'-ō-taks'-is], *n.* likeness of order; contemporaneity. [HOMO and Gk. *taxis* arrangement].
HOMOTONOUS, [hom-ot'-on-us], *adj.* of the same tenor; equable. [HOMO and Gk. *tonos* tone].
HOMOTROPAL, [hom-ot'-rop-al], *adj.* (*bot.*) turned in the same direction as the body to which they belong. [HOMO and Gk. *tropos* turning].
HOMOTYPE, [hom'-ō-tīp], *n.* (*biol.*) a part which has the same type of structure as another. [HOMO and TYPE].
HOMUNCULAR, [hom-ungk'-yōō-ler], *adj.* relating to a homunculus.
HOMUNCULUS, [hom-ungk'-yōō-lus], *n.* a dwarf or mannikin. [L. *homunculus* little man].
HONE (1), [hōn], *n.* a whetstone; a stone of a fine grain used for sharpening blades. [OE. *han* stone].
HONE (2), [hōn], *v.t.* to sharpen by means of a hone.
HONEST, [on'-est], *adj.* to be trusted, not given to immoral or illegal actions; fair-minded, impartial; frank, sincere; not given to lying or dissimulation; legally or conscientiously earned or done; clean, fresh, and respectable in appearance; virtuous, truthful, decent; †(of a woman) chaste. [L. *honestus*].
HONESTLY, [on'-est-li], *adv.* in an honest fashion.
HONESTY, [on'-es-ti], *n.* the quality of being honest; the garden plant with silvery pods, *Lunaria biennis*. [OFr. *honesté*].
HONEY (1), [hun'-i], *n.* a sweet, yellow, glutinous substance that bees make from the nectar of flowers; (*fig.*) anything very sweet or delightful; (*coll.*) darling. [OE. *hunig*].
HONEY (2), [hun'-i], *adj.* pertaining to, or productive of, honey.
HONEY-BAG, [hun'-i-bag], *n.* the sac or receptacle for honey in a honey-bee.
HONEY-BEAR, [hun'-i-bāer], *n.* the Indian sloth-bear, *Melursus ursinus*, the kinkajou.
HONEY-BEE, [hun'-i-bē], *n.* a bee, *Apis mellifica*, kept for its honey.
HONEY-BUZZARD, [hun'-i-buz'-erd], *n.* a hawk, *Pernis apivorus*, that feeds on the grubs of bees and other insects.
HONEYCOMB (1), [hun'-i-kōm], *n.* a structure of hexagonal wax cells made by bees to contain honey or larvae; any perforated object resembling this in its pattern. [OE. *hunigcamb*].
HONEYCOMB (2), [hun'-i-kōm], *v.t.* to perforate excessively; to riddle with holes or passages.
HONEYCOMBED, [hun'-i-kōmd], *adj.* full of holes like a honeycomb.
HONEYDEW, [hun'-i-dew], *n.* a sweet substance secreted mainly by aphides on leaves of plants; a sweetish tobacco; ambrosia.
HONEY-EATER, [hun'-i-ēt'-er], *n.* a South Pacific group of birds characterized by a long extensile tongue.
HONEYED, [hun'-id], *adj.* covered with honey; (*fig.*) sweet; ingratiating, flattering.
HONEYEDNESS, [hun'-id-nes], *n.* the quality of being honeyed.

HONEY-EATER

HONEY-FLOWER, [hun'-i-flow'-er], *n.* an evergreen plant of the genus *Melianthus*.
HONEYGUIDE, [hun'-i-gīd], *n.* a bird of the genus *Indicator*, supposed by its motions and cries to indicate the nests of bees.
HONEY-HARVEST, [hun'-i-hah'-vest], *n.* the gathering of honey; collected honey.
HONEYLESS, [hun'-i-les], *adj.* without honey.
HONEY-LOCUST, [hun'-i-lō'-kust], *n.* a sub tropical tree of the genus *Gleditschia*, which has a thorny stem.
HONEYMOON (1), [hun'-i-mōōn], *n.* the holiday spent by the bridal pair immediately after marriage. [HONEY (1) and MOON (1)].
HONEYMOON (2), [hun'-i-mōōn], *v.i.* to take or spend a honeymoon.
HONEY-MOUTHED, [hun'-i-mowTHd], *adj.* soft-spoken; of flattering speech.
HONEYSTALK, [hun'-i-stawk], *n.* clover-flower.
HONEYSUCKLE, [hun'-i-sukl], *n.* a climbing plant of the genus *Lonicera*, with beautiful, fragrant yellow flowers; **Australian h.**, a plant of the genus *Banksia*; **French h.**, a plant of the genus *Hedysarum*. [ME. *hunisuccle*].
HONEY-SWEET, [hun'-i-swēt], *adj.* sweet as honey; honeyed. [OE. *hunigswete*].
HONEY-TONGUED, [hun'-i-tungd], *adj.* soft-spoken.
HONEYWORT, [hun'-i-wurt], *n.* a European plant related to borage with flowers very attractive to bees.
HONG, [hong], *n.* an Eastern trading factory or warehouse. [Cantonese *hong*].
HONITON, [hun'-i-ton], *n.* a hand-made lace from Honiton. [*Honiton*, in Devonshire].
HONORARIUM, [on-er-āer'-i-um], *n.* a voluntary payment for services rendered; gratuity. [L. *honorarium* (*donum*) a gift in return for an honour received].
HONORARY, [on'-er-er-i], *adj.* pertaining to, or denoting, honour; conferred as an honour, but neither producing profit nor involving obligations; holding a post of this kind; morally but not legally binding. [L. *honorarius*].
HONORIFIC, [on-er-if'-ik], *adj.* conferring honour; expressing honour. [L. *honorificus*].
HONOUR (1), [on'-er], *n.* a complex virtue or idea compounded of truth, purity, courage, and generosity of spirit; high-mindedness; self-respect; elevation of character; deference or veneration; high reverence and esteem; the just recognition of someone's merit; glory, renown, good repute; that which does credit to, or confers, respect; a special distinction gained;

a token symbolizing this; high rank, exalted position; courtesy rendered; (*pl.*) acts expressing reverence or admiring affection; acts of hospitality; a specialized university degree; (*leg.*) a group of manors held by one lord, jurisdiction over these; (*golf*) the right of making the first stroke off the tee; (*bridge*) playing-cards above the ten; †(of a woman) chastity, reputation for chastity; †(of a man) sensitiveness to disgrace or affront; **a debt of h.,** a debt which is morally but not legally due to be paid; **h. bright,** indeed, truly; **to do the honours,** to act as host or hostess; **to have the h.,** to be allowed. [AFr. *honour*].

HONOUR (2), [on'-er], *v.t.* to bestow honour upon; to esteem, respect; (of a debt) to pay according to agreement; (of a promise) to keep.

HONOURABLE, [on'-er-abl], *adj.* worthy to be honoured; having and being moved by principles of honour, noble, high-minded; based upon or appealing to principles of honour; bestowing honour; a courtesy title given to the children of barons, to the younger sons or eldest daughter of a viscount, to the younger sons of earls or to the wife of such a person; used as an epithet of courtesy when one member of the House of Commons or similar governing body refers to another; used in addressing a High Court Judge, a Judge of the High Court of Scotland or a Royal Maid of Honour; **Right H.,** a phrase used in the title of earls, viscounts, and barons, Privy Councillors, Lords Justices, Lords of Appeal, the Lord Mayor of London, the Lord Provost of Edinburgh, and the Chairman of the London County Council; **Most H.,** the style of a marquis or member of the Order of the Bath. [OFr. *honorable*].

HONOURABLENESS, [on'-er-abl-nes], *n.* the condition of being honourable.

HONOURABLY, [on'-er-ab-li], *adv.* in an honourable way.

HONOURER, [on'-er-er], *n.* a person who honours.

HONOUR-POINT, [on'-er-point], *n.* (*her.*) the point immediately above the centre of the shield, which divides the top part into two equal portions.

HOOCH, [hōōch], *n.* (*U.S. slang*) spirits, alcoholic liquor, *esp.* when synthetic. [Alaskan Indian].

HOOD (1), [hŏŏd], *n.* a soft brimless covering for the head and neck, attached to or separate from a cloak; an academic cowl worn hanging at the back from the neck, and denoting the degree and university of the wearer; anything resembling a hood in shape; the collapsible cover on a motor-car, etc. [OE. *hod*].

HOOD (2), [hŏŏd], *v.t.* to cover as with a hood; to supply with a hood. [HOOD (1)].

HOODED, [hŏŏd'-id], *adj.* covered with, wearing, a hood; (*bot.*) hollowed in the form of a hood; (*zool.*) having a crest or markings like a hood.

HOODIE, [hŏŏd'-i], *n.* (*Scots*) the hooded crow.

HOODLUM, [hōōd'-lum], *n.* (*U.S. slang*) a rowdy youth; a hooligan. [Unkn.].

HOODMAN-BLIND†, [hŏŏd'-man-blīnd'], *n.* blind-man's buff.

HOOD-MOULDING, [hŏŏd'-mōld'-ing], *n.* (*arch.*) the upper moulding over an arch; the drip-stone.

HOODWINK, [hŏŏd'-wingk], *v.t.* to bind or partly cover the eyes of a horse; to deceive, mislead, trick.

HOOF (1), (*pl.* **hoofs, hooves**), [hōōf], *n.* the horny protection to the underneath of the feet of horses, swine, or other animals; (*slang*) a human foot. [OE. *hof*].

HOOF (2), [hōōf], *v.t.* (*slang*) **to h. out,** to eject violently; to dismiss from employment; **to h. it,** to walk.

HOOFBOUND, [hōōf'-bownd], *adj.* having a painful contraction of the hoof causing lameness.

HOOFED, [hōōft], *adj.* having hoofs.

HOOK (1), [hŏŏk], *n.* a piece of metal bent in the shape of letter J, often having the shorter prong sharpened, used for catching, hanging, fastening, etc.; a bent metal contrivance fitting into a metal loop or eye to fasten a garment; a short chopping tool, with a curved blade, for lopping branches, etc.; a stroke in golf or cricket in which the ball is hit sharply to the left; a blow in boxing with the arm bent; **h. up,** (*wirel.*) a temporary connexion enabling radio programmes to be transmitted simultaneously from several stations; **by h. or by crook,** somehow or other; **to sling one's h.,** (*slang*) to depart. [OE. *hoc*].

HOOK (2), [hook], *v.t.* and *i.* to shape or be shaped like a hook; to catch or fasten with a hook; to be attached or attachable by a hook or hooks; to make a hook stroke at golf, cricket or boxing; (*Rugby football*) to take up the position of hooker; (*fig.*) to beguile, seduce; (*slang*) to steal.

HOOKAH, [hŏŏk'-ah], *n.* a long Oriental tobacco pipe, in which the smoke is made to pass through water. [Arab. *huqqah* bowl].

HOOKAH

HOOKED, [hŏŏkt], *adj.* bent or curved like a hook; having hooks.

HOOKEDNESS, [hŏŏk'-id-nes], *n.* the state of being hooked.

HOOKER (1), [hŏŏk'-er], *n.* a Dutch two-masted fishing-boat; a fishing-smack. [Du. *hoeker*].

HOOKER (2), [hŏŏk'-er], *n.* one who hooks; the player in Rugby football whose duty it is to try to win possession of the ball with his foot, when it is put into the scrummage.

HOOKNOSED, [hŏŏk'-nōzd], *adj.* having a hooked or aquiline nose.

HOOKPIN, [hŏŏk'-pin], *n.* a tool used by carpenters in making floors and roofs.

HOOKWORM, [hŏŏk'-wurm], *n.* a parasitic worm, *Ankylostoma*, infesting the intestines in hot climates. [HOOK (1) and WORM (1)].

HOOKY, [hŏŏk'-i], *adj.* having hooks; like a hook.

HOOLIGAN, [hōō'-li-gan], *n.* a rough boy; a ruffian, a rowdy vandal. [*Houlihan*, the name of a noisy family in an Irish music-hall song].

HOOP (1), [hōōp], *n.* a ring of wood, bone, metal, etc.; one of the circular horizontal pieces on a cask to keep the vertical laths together; a whalebone or wooden ring at one time worn under petticoats to extend them; a large wooden or metal ring trundled along the ground by children; the rounded metal arch through which a croquet-ball is struck. [OE. *hop*].

HOOP (2), [hōōp], *n.* a shout. [HOOP (4)].

HOOP (3), [hōōp], *v.t.* to encircle with a hoop. [HOOP (1)].

HOOP (4), [hōōp], *v.i.* to utter a wheezy cry as when suffering from whooping-cough; to shout. [OFr. *houper*].

HOOPER, [hōōp'-er], *n.* a person who hoops casks and barrels.

HOOPING-COUGH, see WHOOPING-COUGH.

HOOP-IRON, [hōōp'-ī'-ern], *n.* a thin strip of iron for hooping casks.

HOOP-LA, [hōōp'-lah], *n.* a popular game at fairs in which wooden rings are tossed at an array of various objects to encircle and so win them.

HOOPOE, [hōōp'-ōō], *n.* a crested bird of the genus *Upupa*. [Echoic].

HOOPOE

HOOSH, [hōōsh], *n.* a mixed stew. [Uncert.].

HOOT (1), [hōōt], *n.* the cry of an owl; a shout of contempt, dislike or derision; the shrill note emitted by a hooter.

HOOT (2), [hōōt], *v.t.* and *i.* to utter a hoot. [ME. *houten*, ~ MSwed. *huta*].

HOOTER, [hōōt'-er], *n.* one who, or that which, hoots; a steam whistle; a horn sounded by steam or compressed air as a signal; a siren.

HOOVE, [hōōv], *n.* a cattle disease in which the stomach is distended from eating an excess of green fodder. [Uncert.].

HOP (1), [hop], *n.* the plant, *Humulus Lupulus*, of which the female plant bears green cones which when ripened are used in brewing to give a bitter flavour. [MDu. *hoppe*].

HOP (2), [hop], *n.* a jump achieved on one leg; a small jump; (*slang*) a dance; (*aeron.*) a stage in a long-distance flight. [HOP (4)].

HOP (3), **(hopping, hopped),** [hop], *v.t.* to impregnate with hop cones; *v.i.* to gather hops. [HOP (1)].

HOP (4), **(hopping, hopped),** [hop], *v.i.* to jump on one leg; to dance about; to progress by a series of short leaps, to bounce, skip; **to h. it,** (*slang*) to depart quickly, *esp.* by stealth. [OE. *hoppian*].

HOP

HOP-BACK, [hop'-bak], *n.* a vat for straining hops. [HOP (1) and BACK (2)].

HOP-BIND, [hop'-bīn,], *n.* hop-bine.

HOP-BINE, [hop'-bīn], *n.* the twining stem of the hop plant. [HOP (1) and BINE].

HOPDOG, [hop'-dog], *n.* the pale tussock moth, *Dasychira pudibunda.*

HOPE (1), [hōp], *n.* confident expectation that something longed for will come; the state of mind entertaining such expectation; someone or something that inspires such expectation or upon which success depends; likelihood. [OE. *hopa*].

HOPE (2), [hōp], *n.* an inlet or small bay in the coast; enclosed land surrounded by fen or wasteland; a little enclosed valley. [OE. *hop*].

HOPE (3), [hōp], *v.i.* to desire and expect that something will come to pass; to be hopeful, to trust, desire. [OE. *hopian*].

HOPEFUL, [hōp'-fŏŏl], *adj.* full of hope; hoping; promising.

HOPEFULLY, [hōp'-fŏŏl-i], *adv.* in a hopeful manner.

HOPEFULNESS, [hōp'-fŏŏl-nes], *n.* the condition of being hopeful.

HOPELESS, [hōp'-les], *adj.* without hope; desponding; desperate; incurable.

HOPELESSLY, [hōp'-les-li], *adv.* in a hopeless way.

HOPELESSNESS, [hōp'-les-nes], *n.* the quality of being hopeless.

HOPGARDEN, [hop'-gahd'-en], *n.* a field planted with hops.

HOPINGLY, [hōp'-ing-li], *adv.* hopefully; with hope.

HOPKILN, [hop'-kiln], *n.* a kiln for drying hops; oast-house.

HOPLITE, [hop'-līt], *n.* a heavy infantryman of ancient Greece. [Gk. *hoplites*].

HOPPER, [hop'-er], *n.* one who hops; a funnel or trough by which grain passes into a mill; any similar gadget; an animal that hops; a picker of hops; a barge or railway truck which empties its contents through its bottom.

HOPPER-BOY, [hop'-er-boi], *n.* a rake that moves in a circle drawing meal over an opening, through which it falls.

HOPPERS, [hop'-erz], *n.* a game in which those playing it hop.

HOPPET, [hop'-et], *n.* a hand-basket; a large basket or cage for lowering men and materials into an excavation or mine. [Uncert.].

HOP-PICKER, [hop'-pik'-er], *n.* a person who picks hops; a machine for picking hops.

HOPPLE, [hopl], *v.t.* to hobble (an animal). [~MDu. *hoppelen*].

HOPPLES, [hoplz], *n.(pl.)* thongs for hoppling horses or other animals.

HOPPO, [hop'-ō], *n.* a Chinese overseer of commerce; the Chinese board of customs and revenue. [Chin. *hoopoo*].

HOP-POCKET, [hop'-pok'-it], *n.* a large sack, holding from $1\frac{1}{2}$ to 2 cwt. of hops.

HOP-POLE, [hop'-pōl], *n.* the pole up which hops are trained.

HOPPY, [hop'-i], *adj.* tasting of, or like, hops.

HOP-SCOTCH, [hop'-skoch], *n.* a children's game in which one hops along on one leg, at the same time pushing forward a small slab of stone, brick, etc., into numbered squares. [HOP (2) and SCOTCH (1)].

HOP-VINE, [hop'-vīn], *n.* hop-bine.

HOP-YARD, [hop'-yahd], *n.* a hop-garden.

HORAL, [haw'-ral], *adj.* pertaining to an hour. [L. *horalis*].

HORARY, [hawr'-er-i], *adj.* pertaining to an hour or the hours; hourly; for an hour. [L. *horarius*].

HORATIAN, [ho-rā'-shun], *adj.* pertaining to Horace or his verse; written in the style of Horace. [L. *Horatianus*].

HORDE (1), [hawd], *n.* a nomadic warlike tribe; a great, barbarian host; a large, jostling mob; a vast herd or collection of animals; *(pl.) (coll.)* crowds, swarms. [Turk. *orda* camp].

HORDE (2), [hawd], *v.i.* to wander about as nomads; to gather as in a horde.

HORDEIN, [haw'-dē-in], *n.* a substance like starch, found in barley. [L. *hordeum* barley].

HORDEOLUM, [haw-dē'-ō-lum], *n.* a small tumour on the eyelid, so called as resembling a barleycorn. [L. *hordeolum*].

HOREHOUND, HOARHOUND, [haw(r)'-hownd], *n.* *Marrubium vulgare,* a labiate plant, the bitter juice of which is used as a remedy for coughs. [OE. *har* white and *hune* the name of a plant].

HORIZON, [ho-rī'-zon], *n.* the line at which earth and sky seem to meet and beyond which it is not possible to see; *(fig.)* the limit of one's intellectual perception or experience. [Gk. *horizon*].

HORIZONTAL (1), [ho'-riz-on'-tal], *n.* something level or horizontal.

HORIZONTAL (2), [ho'-riz-on'-tal], *adj.* at right-angles with the vertical; parallel with the horizon; flat, level; **h. bars,** two bars fixed horizontally a few feet above the floor and used in gymnastic exercises. [Fr. *horizontal*].

HORIZONTALITY, [ho'-riz-on-tal'-i-ti], *n.* the quality of being horizontal.

HORIZONTALLY, [ho'-riz-on'-ta-li], *adv.* in a horizontal direction or position.

HORMONE, [haw'-mōn], *n.* *(physiol.)* one of various endocrine secretions which stimulate organs of the body. [Gk. *hormon* urging].

HORN (1), [hawn], *n.* one of the hard, sharp, curved projections on the heads of cattle and other animals; anything resembling this, a tusk or bony snout; the hard substance composing this; an object made of or resembling this; a projection, cusp; the end of a crescent, *esp.* of the new moon; a musical wind-instrument originally manufactured of horn but now of metal; a wind-operated instrument used to utter a note of warning, a hooter, siren; **the h. of plenty,** the cornucopia, any source of wealth and well-being; **French h.,** a musical instrument of the trumpet type; **English h.,** a tenor oboe; **hunting-h.,** a shrill-toned instrument blown during a hunt as a guide to the hunters; **h.-eyed,** short-sighted, purblind; **to take the bull by the horns,** to face a problem audaciously. [OE. *horn*].

HORN (2), [hawn], *adj.* of horn, made of horn.

HORN (3), [hawn], *v.t.* to remove the horns from cattle; to provide with horns; to strike or gore with the horns.

HORNBAR, [hawn'-bah(r)], *n.* the crossbar of a carriage.

HORNBEAK, [hawn'-bēk], *n.* the garfish, *Belone vulgaris.*

HORNBEAM, [hawn'-bēm], *n.* a deciduous tree, *Carpinus Betulus,* somewhat like a beech, with a wood of horny toughness. [HORN (1) and OE. *beam* tree].

HORNBILL, [hawn'-bil], *n.* a tropical bird of the family *Bucerotidæ,* with a large horny growth on head and bill.

HORNBLENDE, [hawn'-blend], *n.* a mineral consisting of silica, magnesia, lime, iron, and alumina, found in igneous rocks. [Germ.].

HORNBLENDE-SCHIST, [hawn'-blend-shist'], *n.* a schist having hornblende as its chief mineral constituent.

HORNBLOWER, [hawn'-blō'-er], *n.* person who blows a horn.

HORNBOOK, [hawn'-bŏŏk], *n.* a sheet of paper inscribed on one side with the alphabet, etc., backed with wood and covered with a thin sheet of transparent horn, used formerly to give a child its first lessons; a primer.

HORN-BUG, [hawn'-bug], *n.* the stag-beetle.

HORN-DISTEMPER, [hawn'-dis-tem'-per], *n.* a disease of cattle in which the internal substance of the horn is affected.

HORNED, [hawnd], *adj.* furnished with antlers or horns; having horny or horn-like projections; crescent-shaped; having a horny surface.

HORNER (1), [hawn'-er], *n.* *(rare)* one who works or deals in horn; a person who blows a horn.

HORNER (2), [hawn'-er], *n.* the sand-eel, *Ammodytes lanceolatus.* [Uncert.].

HORNET, [hawn'-et], *n.* a large species of wasp, *Vespa crabro,* whose sting gives severe pain; *(fig.)* an irritating or oppressive person. [~ OE. *hyrnet*].

HORNFISH, [hawn'-fish], *n.* the garfish, mackerel guide, or sea-needle, *Belone vulgaris.* [OE. *hornfisc*].

HORNFOOT, [hawn'-fŏŏt], *adj.* hoofed.

HORNING, [hawn'-ing], *n.* *(Scots leg.)* **Letters of h.,** a summons demanding the payment of a debt or debts by a fixed date under penalty of outlawry.

HORNISH, [hawn'-ish], *adj.* hard like horn.

HORNITO, [hawn-ē'-tō], *n.* an oven-shaped mound found near volcanoes. [Span. *hornito* little oven].

HORN-NUT, [hawn'-nut], *n.* a water-plant with floating leaves, *Trapa natans.*

HORN-OWL, [hawn'-owl], *n.* an owl with tufted feathers like horns on its head.

HORNPIPE, [hawn'-pīp], *n.* †a former wooden reed instrument; an energetic dance originally performed to an accompaniment on this; music to accompany such a dance.

HORN-SHAVINGS, [hawn'-shāv'-ingz], *n.(pl.)* scrapings from the horns of deer.

HORN-SILVER, [hawn'-sil'-ver], *n.* a chloride of silver, cerargyrite.

HORN-SLATE, [hawn'-slāt], *n.* a kind of siliceous rock.

HORN-OWL

HORNSTONE, [hawn'-stōn], *n.* a brittle flinty kind of quartz.

HORNWORK, [hawn'-wurk], *n.* articles made of horn; (*fort.*) an outwork of two half-bastions linked by a curtain.

HORNWORT, [hawn'-wurt], *n.* a water-plant, *Ceratophyllum demersum.*

HORNWRACK, [hawn'-rak], *n.* a kind of coralline of the genus *Flustra.*

HORNY, [hawn'-i], *adj.* made of horn; hard like horn.

HOROGRAPHY, [haw-rog'-ra-fi], *n.* the science of reckoning time, *esp.* by sundials; the art of making sundials. [Fr. *horographie*].

HOROLOGE, [ho'-rō-lōj], *n.* an instrument that indicates the hours. [OFr. *horologe*].

HOROLOGICAL, [ho'-rō-loj'-ik-al], *adj.* relating to horology; showing the hours.

HOROLOGIST, [ho-rol'-oj-ist], *n.* one skilled in horology.

HOROLOGY, [ho-rol'-o-ji], *n.* the technique of measuring time or making timepieces.

HOROMETRICAL, [ho'-rō-met'-rik-al], *adj.* pertaining to horometry.

HOROMETRY, [ho-rom'-et-ri], *n.* the art or practice of measuring the hours. [Gk. *hora* hour and *metria* measurement].

HOROSCOPE, [ho'-rō-skōp], *n.* an observation of the position of the stars and planets at some particular moment, *esp.* at a child's birth, in order to foretell its future; a diagram showing this. [Gk. *horoskopos* watching the hours].

HOROSCOPIC, [ho'-rō-skop'-ik], *adj.* of, or relating to, a horoscope or to horoscopy.

HOROSCOPICAL, [ho'-rō-skop'-ik-al], *adj.* horoscopic.

HOROSCOPIST, [ho'-ros-kop'-ist], *n.* a student of horoscopy.

HOROSCOPY, [ho-ros'-kop-i], *n.* skill in casting horoscopes.

HORRENT, [ho'-rent], *adj.* (*rare, poet.*) bristly. [L. *horrens*].

HORRIBLE, [ho'-ribl], *adj.* causing, or liable to cause, horror; dreadful; shocking; (*coll.*) not at all pleasant, tiresome. [L. *horribilis*].

HORRIBLENESS, [ho'-ribl-nes], *n.* the quality of being horrible.

HORRIBLY, [ho'-rib-li], *adv.* in a horrible fashion; (*coll.*) very.

HORRID, [ho'-rid], *adj.* liable to excite horror; frightful; very offensive or disgusting; (*coll.*) irritating, annoying, disagreeable. [L. *horridus* bristling].

HORRIDLY, [ho'-rid-li], *adv.* in a horrid fashion.

HORRIDNESS, [ho'-rid-nes], *n.* the quality of being horrid.

HORRIFIC, [ho-rif'-ik], *adj.* horrible, frightening. [L. *horrificus*].

HORRIFY, [ho'-ri-fī], *v.t.* to fill with horror; (*coll.*) to shock. [L. *horrificare*].

HORRIPILATION, [ho'-rip-i-lā'-shun], *n.* the feeling that one's hair is standing on end through fear or illness. [L. *horripilatio*].

HORRISONANT, [ho'-ri-sōn-ant], *adj.* horrible in sound. [L. *horrere* to bristle and *sonare* to sound].

HORRISONOUS†, [ho'-ri-sōn'-us], *adj.* emitting a terrible sound. [L. *horrisonus*].

HORROR, [ho'-rer], *n.* a powerful feeling of fear or loathing; that which excites this feeling; (*coll.*) an unpleasant sight; a tiresome or disagreeable person; (*pl.*) extreme terror, *esp.* in delirium tremens; **h. film,** (*cinema*) a film dealing with terrifying subjects and licensed for showing to adults only. [OFr. *horrour*].

HORROR-STRICKEN, [ho'-rer-strik'-en], *adj.* smitten with terror, horrified.

HORS, [aw(r)], *prep.*, out of; **h. de combat,** wounded, disabled; **h. d'oeuvre,** a small dish or relish served usually at the beginning of a meal, consisting of salted or flavoured fish or meat and vegetables, normally served cold. [Fr. *hors*].

HORSE (1), [haws], *n.* a large, hoofed quadruped, commonly domesticated and used for pulling, carrying and riding upon; an adult male of the species, a stallion; (*zool.*) any member of the large family *Equidæ*; cavalry; something resembling a horse; **clothes h.,** a wooden frame on which clothes are hung for drying and airing; **vaulting h.,** a piece of gymnastic apparatus used for jumping exercises, consisting of a long, stuffed, leather-coated trunk, supported on four wooden legs. [OE. *hors*].

HORSE (2), [haws], *adj.* pertaining to a horse; strong and large as a horse.

HORSE (3), [haws], *v.t.* to furnish with a horse or horses; (*coll.*) to baffle. [OE. *horsian*].

HORSEBACK, [haws'-bak], *n.* a horse's back; **on h.,** mounted, in the saddle.

HORSEBANE, [haws'-bān], *n.* the plant, *Œnanthe Phellandrium.*

HORSE-BEAN, [haws'-bēn], *n.* a small bean used for feeding horses; the tick bean, a variety of *Faba vulgaris.*

HORSE-BLOCK, [haws'-blok], *n.* a block or step to assist persons in mounting and dismounting from a horse.

HORSE-BOAT, [haws'-bōt], *n.* a boat used for conveying horses over water.

HORSEBOX, [haws'-boks], *n.* a railway or road van constructed to carry horses.

HORSE-BOY, [haws'-boi], *n.* a boy who assists a groom, a stable-boy.

HORSEBREAKER, [haws'-brāk-er], *n.* one employed in breaking in horses.

HORSE-CHESTNUT, [haws'-ches'-nut], *n.* the tree, *Æsculus Hippocastanum*; its fruit.

HORSECLOTH, [haws'-kloth], *n.* a blanket to cover a horse's back; a saddle-cloth.

HORSECOPER, [haws'-kōp-er], *n.* a horsedealer, *esp.* a dishonest one.

HORSE-CUCUMBER, [haws'-kew'-kum-ber], *n.* a variety of large green cucumber.

HORSEDEALER, [haws'-dēl-er], *n.* a dealer in horses.

HORSE-DOCTOR, [haws'-dok'-ter], *n.* a veterinary surgeon.

HORSE-DRENCH, [haws'-drench'], *n.* a medicinal dose for a horse.

HORSE-EMMET, [haws'-em'-et], *n.* the horse-ant, *Formica rufa.*

HORSE-FACED, [haws'-fāst'], *adj.* (*coll.*) having a long face like a horse.

HORSEFLESH, [haws'-flesh'], *n.* the edible flesh of a horse; horses collectively.

HORSEFLY, [haws'-flī], *n.* a fly that stings horses, *Hippobosca equina*; the gad-fly.

HORSEFLY

HORSEFOOT, [haws'-fŏŏt], *n.* the plant colts-foot, *Tussilago Farfara.*

HORSE-GRAM, [haws'-gram], *n.* the plant, *Dolichos biflorus.*

HORSEHAIR (1), [haws'-hāer], *n.* the hair of a horse's mane or tail, used for upholstering.

HORSEHAIR (2), [haws'-hāer], *adj.* made of, stuffed with, horsehair.

HORSE-HOE, [haws'-hō], *n.* a large hoe drawn by horses.

HORSE-HOOF, [haws'-hŏŏf], *n.* coltsfoot.

HORSE-JOCKEY, [haws'-jok'-i], *n.* a man who rides in horseraces, a jockey.

HORSEKEEPER, [haws'-kēp-er], *n.* one who keeps or looks after horses.

HORSEKNACKER, [haws'-nak'-er], *n.* one who buys old, worn-out horses, to kill them and dispose of their carcases.

HORSE LATITUDES, [haws'-lat'-it-ewdz], *n.(pl.)* the calm area to the north of the north-east trade-winds. [Unkn.].

HORSE-LAUGH, [haws'-lahf], *n.* a loud boisterous laugh; guffaw.

HORSE-LEECH, [haws'-lēch], *n.* a large kind of leech; a veterinary surgeon.

HORSELESS, [haws'-les], *adj.* having no horse.

HORSE-LITTER, [haws'-lit'-er], *n.* a litter hung on poles between two horses.
HORSELOAD, [haws'-lōd], *n.* a load fit for a horse.
HORSELY†, [haws'-li], *adj.* pertaining to a horse; characteristic of a horse.
HORSE-MACKEREL, [haws'-mak'-er-el], *n.* any of the larger varieties of mackerel.
HORSEMAN, [haws'-man], *n.* a rider on horseback; a kind of carrier-pigeon.
HORSEMANSHIP, [haws'-man-ship], *n.* the art of riding a horse, or of training and managing horses.
HORSE MARINE, [haws'-ma-rēn'], *n.* a fictitious rating, mentioned jocularly to hint at disbelief on the part of the speaker.
HORSE-MARTEN, [haws'-mah-tin], *n.* a species of large bee.
HORSE-MASTERSHIP, [haws'-mahst'-er-ship], *n.* skill in the management of a horse.
HORSEMEAT, [haws'-mēt], *n.* food for horses; fodder.
HORSEMILL, [haws'-mil], *n.* a mill that is worked by a horse.
HORSE-MILLINER, [haws'-mil'-in-er], *n.* one who furnishes ribbons and other decorations for horses.
HORSE MINT, [haws'-mint], *n.* any of various wild mints with a pungent odour.
HORSEPLAY, [haws'-plā], *n.* rough boisterous play; noisy romping.
HORSEPOND, [haws'-pond], *n.* a pond for watering or washing horses.
HORSE-POWER, [haws'-pow'-er], *n.* a unit for measuring power standardized as the power needed to lift 550 lb. one foot per second.
HORSERACE, [haws'-rās], *n.* a race run by horses.
HORSE-RADISH, [haws'-rad'-ish], *n.* a cruciferous plant with a hot, pungent root, *Cochlearia Armoracia*.
HORSE-SENSE, [haws'-sents], *n.* practical common sense.
HORSESHOE (1), [haws'-shōō'], *n.* an iron shoe for horses; anything of the same shape.
HORSESHOE (2), [haws'-shōō'], *adj.* shaped like a horseshoe.
HORSESHOEING, [haws'-shōō'-ing], *n.* the act or business of shoeing horses.
HORSE-STINGER, [haws'-sting'-ger], *n.* the dragon-fly.
HORSE-TAIL, [haws'-tāl], *n.* the tail of a horse, used as a Turkish standard, or badge of rank; (*bot.*) the genus *Equisetum* of flowerless plants.
HORSE-WAY, [haws'-wā], *n.* a way over which horses may travel.
HORSE-WHIM, [haws'-wim], *n.* a machine worked by a horse, and used for raising the ore from a mine-shaft.
HORSEWHIP (1), [haws'-wip], *n.* a long whip used in driving a team of horses.
HORSEWHIP (2), (**horsewhipping, horse-whipped**), [haws'-wip], *v.t.* to flog severely, *esp.* with a horsewhip.
HORSEWOMAN, [haws'-wŏŏm-an], *n.* a woman rider; a woman skilled in managing horses.
HORSY, [haws'-i], *adj.* interested in, accustomed to, horses; having the appearance of a person with such interests and habits.
HORTATION, [hawt-ā'-shun], *n.* admonition; exhortation. [L. *hortatio*].
HORTATIVE, [hawt'-at-iv], *adj.* exhorting, admonishing, encouraging. [L. *hortativus*].
HORTATORY, [hawt'-at-er-i], *adj.* hortative. [L. *hortatorius*].
HORTICULTURAL, [hawt'-i-kul'-cher-al], *adj.* of, or relating to, horticulture.
HORTICULTURE, [hawt'-i-kul-cher], *n.* the art of growing flowers and fruits; the craft of making and keeping a garden. [L. *hortus* garden and CULTURE].
HORTICULTURIST, [hawt'-i-kul'-cher-ist], *n.* one skilled in horticulture.
HOSANNA, [hō-zan'-a], *int.* a cry of adoration. [Heb. *hoshana* save, we pray].
HOSE (1), [hōz], *n.(pl.)* socks and stockings; †a garment fitting the legs, *esp.* long, close-fitting trousers. [OE. *hosa* leg-covering].
HOSE (2), [hōz], *n.* a long tube for conveying water, usually made of rubber or leather. [Du. *hoos*].
HOSEPIPE, [hōz'-pīp], *n.* a hose.
HOSE-REEL, [hōz'-rēl], *n.* a hosepipe; a round frame or reel on which a hosepipe is wound for storage
HOSIER, [hō'-zher], *n.* a dealer in hosiery.
HOSIERY, [hō'-zher-i], *n.* the lighter articles of men's clothing, as socks, collars, underwear; the trade dealing in these articles; a factory where they are made.
HOSPICE, [hos'-pis], *n.* a travellers' house of rest kept by monks; a home for the sick and poor. [Fr. *hospice*].
HOSPITABLE, [hos'-pit-abl], *adj.* liberal in entertaining guests; affording shelter and hospitality. [Fr. *hospitable*].
HOSPITABLENESS, [hos'-pit-abl-nes], *n.* the quality of being hospitable.
HOSPITABLY, [hos'-pit-ab-li], *adv.* in a hospitable fashion.
HOSPITAL, [hos'-pit-al], *n.* an institution where sick and injured persons are received and attended to; a charitable institution for the sick, poor, or aged, or for travellers; a school. [L. *hospitale* a guest-house].
HOSPITALISM, [hos'-pit-al-izm], *n.* the modern hospital system.
HOSPITALITY, [hos'-pit-al'-i-ti], *n.* generous entertainment of guests; entertainment provided for guests either on a friendly or commercial basis; cheerful willingness to receive guests. [Fr. *hospitalité*].
HOSPITALLER, [hos-pit'-al-er], *n.* an inmate of a charitable institution providing food, care, and lodging for the sick, poor and aged; a member of the order of St. John of Jerusalem, which, in the Middle Ages, protected Christian pilgrims to Palestine, and now is engaged in ambulance work. [OFr. *hospitalier*].
HOSPODAR, [hos'-pō-dah(r)], *n.* the former title of the governors of Moldavia and Wallachia when these were part of the Turkish Empire. [Rumanian *hospodar*].
HOST (1), [hōst], *n.* (*archaic*) an army; (*fig.*) a great number. [L. *hostis* enemy].
HOST (2), [hōst], *n.* one who receives guests; an innkeeper; (*biol.*) a plant or animal on which a parasite lives. [OFr. *hoste*].
HOST (3), [hōst], *n.* (*eccles.*) the consecrated wafer of the Eucharist. [L. *hostia* victim of a sacrifice].
HOSTAGE, [host'-ij], *n.* a member of one of two warring states, armies, etc., handed over to, or seized by, the other as a pledge of good faith; (*fig.*) a security. [OFr. *ostage*].
HOSTEL, [hos'-tel], *n.* a hall of residence for members of a particular society, group or institution; †an inn. [OFr. *hostel*].
HOSTELLER, [hos'-tel-er], *n.* (*rare*) an innkeeper; one who frequents a hostel; a student in a hostel attached to a university.
HOSTELRY, [hos'-tel-ri], *n.* an hotel, inn. [ME. *hostellerie*].
HOSTESS, [hōst'-es], *n.* (one paid to act as) a female host; the host's wife; a female innkeeper.
HOSTILE, [hos'-tīl], *adj.* of, or pertaining to, an enemy; inimical, opposing; showing unfriendliness and dislike, opposed to. [Fr. *hostile*].
HOSTILELY, [hos'-tīl-li], *adv.* in a hostile way.
HOSTILITY, [hos-til'-i-ti], *n.* animosity, hatred, enmity, opposition; the feeling or expression of these; (*pl.*) acts of war. [Fr. *hostilité*].
HOSTLER, see OSTLER.
HOT (1), [hot], *adj.* having heat to such an extent as may be felt; giving a sense of burning in the mouth; (of food) newly cooked; (*fig.*) eager and impetuous; intense and vigorous; (*slang*) brilliant, extremely clever or good, expert; (of music) elaborately syncopated and rhythmical; (*slang*) hectic, uncomfortably dangerous; sexually aroused; (of scent) strong and well marked; **to be h. on the track**, to be on the heels of the quarry; **to be h. on**, (*coll.*) to be very fond of, addicted to; **to get h.**, to be very near the place where something is hidden, to be very near guessing the right answer; **h. air**, pointless and unbusinesslike talk; **h. dog** (*U.S.*) a hot sausage sandwich; **h. water**, (*coll.*) trouble, difficulties, a scrape. [OE. *hat*].
HOT (2), [hot], *adv.* in a hot manner; so as to render hot; hotly, severely; **to blow h. and cold**, to hesitate, waver.
HOT-BED, [hot'-bed], *n.* (*hort.*) a layer of fermenting manure covered with earth, used to encourage the growth of seeds and plants; (*fig.*) a place where something evil is fostered and unusually rife.
HOT-BLAST, [hot'-blahst'], *n.* a current of warm air forced into a furnace.
HOT-BLOODED, [hot'-blud'-id], *adj.* passionate; irritable.
HOT-BRAINED, [hot'-brānd], *adj.* excitable; hot-headed.
HOT-BULB, [hot'-bulb'], *n.* (in an oil fuel engine) a small heated chamber at one end of the cylinder in

which the piston moves, where the oil fuel is compressed, vaporized, and heated so that it explodes; a hot-spot.

HOTCH-POT, [hoch'-pot], *n.* (*leg.*) the gathering together of the property of someone who has died intestate so that it may be equally distributed among the heirs. [Fr. *hochepot*].

HOTCH-POTCH, see HODGE-PODGE.

HOT-COCKLES, [hot'-koklz'], *n.* a game in which someone is blindfolded and has to guess who strikes him.

HOTEL, [hō-tel'], *n.* a large inn of a superior kind. [Fr. *hôtel*].

HOT-FOOT, [hot'-fōōt], *adv.* in great haste.

HOT-HEADED, [hot'-hed'-id], *adj.* excitable, impetuous, stupidly rash.

HOTHOUSE, [hot'-hows], *n.* an artificially heated glasshouse in which tender or exotic plants are reared.

HOTLY, [hot'-li], *adv.* ardently, vehemently.

HOT-MOUTHED, [hot'-mowTHd], *adj.* wilful, headstrong.

HOTNESS, [hot'-nes], *n.* the condition of being hot.

HOTPOT, [hot'-pot], *n.* a stew of various meats and vegetables baked in a casserole.

HOT-PRESS (1), [hot'-pres], *n.* a machine for giving a gloss to linen or paper by pressing it between hot metal plates.

HOT-PRESS (2), [hot'-pres], *v.t.* to put through a hot-press.

HOT-SHORT, [hot'-shawt], *adj.* (of iron) brittle when hot.

HOT-SPIRITED, [hot'-spir'-it-id], *adj.* having a lively spirit.

HOT-SPOT, [hot'-spot'], *n.* (in an oil fuel engine) a heated point or chamber where the oil is vaporized.

HOTSPUR, [hot'-spur], *n.* a rash, quick-tempered person; a kind of pea of early growth. [Nickname of Sir H. Percy, of Shakespeare's play "Henry IV"].

HOTSPURRED, [hot'-spurd], *adj.* rash, headstrong.

HOTTENTOT (1), [hot'-en-tot], *n.* a member of a native South African race; the language of this people; (*fig.*) an ill-mannered, uncultured person. [Du. *Hottentot*].

HOTTENTOT (2), [hot'-en-tot], *adj.* of, or relating to, the Hottentots.

HOTTENTOTISM, [hot'-en-tot-izm], *n.* a form of stammering.

HOT-WALL, [hot'-wawl], *n.* a wall containing flues for hot air, used to hasten the growth of fruit-trees.

HOUDAH, HOWDAH, [how'-dah], *n.* a seat on an elephant's back. [Pers. *haudah*].

HOUDAH

HOUGH (1), [hock], *n.* the joint between the knee and fetlock on the back legs of a quadruped; the back of the human knee. [OE. *hoh* heel].

HOUGH (2), [hock], *v.t.* to hamstring. [HOUGH (1)].

HOUND (1), [hownd], *n.* a dog, *esp.* a large dog or a hunting dog; one of the pursuers in a paper-chase; (*pl.*) a hunt; (*coll.*) a blackguard; a bounder. [OE. *hund*].

HOUND (2), [hownd], *v.t.* to pursue vigorously and unremittingly; to incite.

HOUND-FISH, [hownd'-fish], *n.* a fish belonging to the shark family.

HOUNDS, [howndz], *n.(pl.)* (*naut.*) the projections at the masthead to hold up the trestle trees.

HOUND'S-TONGUE, [howndz'-tung'], *n.* the plant, *Cynoglossum officinale*, so called from the texture of its leaves.

HOUR, [ow'-er], *n.* the twenty-fourth part of a day and a night, 60 minutes; an occasion; an opportunity; a vaguely conceived period of time; the time; the present moment; a distance that can be travelled in one hour; (*astron.*) 15 degrees of longitude; (*pl.*) personifications of the hours in Roman mythology; (*eccles.*) prayers said at the canonical hours; (*pl.*) a period fixed for the transaction of business; **canonical hours,** (*eccles.*) seven periods of the day appointed for prayer; **the eleventh h.,** the last moment; **his h. has come,** his death is imminent; he has now his greatest chance. [L. *hora*].

HOUR-ANGLE, [ow'-er-ang'-gl], *n.* (*astron.*) the angular distance of a heavenly body to the east or west of a meridian.

HOUR-CIRCLE, [ow'-er-surkl], *n.* a meridian. [So called because there are usually 24 of them marked on a globe].

HOUR-GLASS, [ow'-er-glahs], *n.* a device for measuring intervals of time by running sand between two glass bulbs.

HOUR-GLASS

HOUR-HAND, [ow'-er-hand], *n.* the hand of a watch or clock which shows the hour.

HOURI, [hōō(e)r'-i], *n.* a female inhabitant of the Mohammedan paradise; (*fig.*) a voluptuous, fascinating woman. [Pers. *huri*].

HOURLY (1), [ow'-er-li], *adj.* occurring or done every hour; lasting an hour; continual.

HOURLY (2), [ow'-er-li], *adv.* every hour; continually; frequently.

HOUR-PLATE, [ow'-er-plāt], *n.* the dial of a watch or clock.

HOUSAGE, [howz'-ij], *n.* a charge made for housing goods.

HOUSE (1), [hows], *n.* a building designed for human habitation; a dwelling-place; an hotel, tavern or boarding-house; a boarding-house attached to a public-school; its inmates; one of several artificial divisions in which the pupils are grouped in a day-school, in imitation of the boarding-house system in public-schools; a hall or college attached to a university; the members of such a hall or college; any educational institution providing residence for its members; a household, a family, domestic circle; lineage, *esp.* an ancient or noble family; the lair, shell, nest of an animal, insect, bird, etc.; a commercial firm; a theatre or other hall of entertainment; the audience in such a place; a religious establishment for nuns, monks, etc.; the inmates of such an establishment; a building for the meeting of a large deliberative or legislative body; the House of Commons; the members of such a body; **h. of ill fame,** a brothel; **the H.,** the Stock Exchange, London; Christ Church, Oxford; Peterhouse, Cambridge; the workhouse; **like a h. on fire,** with extreme rapidity; **as safe as houses,** very safe indeed; **to make a h.,** (of a legislative or deliberative assembly, etc.), to have sufficient members present to constitute a quorum; to arrange for this to happen; **to bring the h. down,** to provoke storms of laughter or applause from the audience. [OE. *hus*].

HOUSE (2), [howz], *v.t.* and *i.* to provide with a house or houses; to give food and lodging to; to offer or find room for; to store; (*carp.*) to fit into a socket or joint. [OE. *husian*].

HOUSE-AGENT, [hows'-ā'-jent], *n.* one employed to let or sell household property.

HOUSEBOAT, [hows'-bōt], *n.* a covered boat for living in; a barge or pontoon with a wooden house built on it.

HOUSEBOTE, [hows'-bōt], *n.* the repair of a house; the wood a tenant may demand in order to repair his dwelling. [HOUSE (1) and OE. *bot* profit].

HOUSEBREAKER, [hows'-brāk'-er], *n.* a daytime thief or burglar; one who pulls down buildings.

HOUSEBREAKING, [hows'-brāk'-ing], *n.* burglary by day; the act of pulling down a house or building.

HOUSECARL, [hows'-kahl], *n.* a member of the bodyguard of a Teutonic king or nobleman in the ninth and tenth centuries. [OE. *huscarl*].

HOUSE-CAT, [hows'-kat], *n.* a domesticated cat living in the house.

HOUSED, [howzd], *adj.* provided with, settled in, a house; covered with housings.

HOUSE-DOG, [hows'-dog], *n.* a dog trained to guard a house.

HOUSE-FLAG, [hows'-flag], *n.* a ship's flag indicating to which commercial house it belongs.

HOUSE-FLY, [hows'-flī], *n.* the common dipterous insect, *Musca domestica*.

HOUSEFUL, [hows'-fōōl], *n.* as many people as the house will hold.

HOUSEHOLD (1), [hows'-hōld], *n.* the members of one family, together with servants, etc., living under one roof; a home, domestic establishment; **the h. of the faith,** Christians generally. [ME. *houshold*].

HOUSEHOLD (2), [hows'-hōld], *adj.* of, or pertaining to, a household, *esp.* to the Royal Household; **h. word,** a word of everyday usage; **H. troops,** the regiments of Guards brigade whose duty it is to guard the Sovereign.

HOUSEHOLDER, [hows'-hōld'-er], *n.* one who occupies a house.
HOUSEKEEPER, [hows'-kēp'-er], *n.* the mistress of a household, who organizes it, feeds its inmates, etc.; a hired servant who manages a household.
HOUSEKEEPING, [hows'-kēp'-ing], *n.* the science or act of keeping house.
HOUSEL, [howzl], *n.* (*archaic, eccles.*) the consecrated elements at the Eucharist; the administration or reception of the Eucharist. [OE. *husl*].
HOUSELEEK, [hows'-lēk], *n.* a plant of the genus, *Sempervivum*, growing on walls and roofs.
HOUSELESS, [hows'-les], *adj.* having no house.
HOUSELINE, [hows'-lin], *n.* (*naut.*) a small line composed of three strands, used for seizings.
HOUSELING, HOUSLING, [howz'-ling], *adj.* pertaining to the Eucharist; sacramental.
HOUSEMAID, [hows'-mād], *n.* a female domestic servant.
HOUSEMAID'S KNEE, [hows'-mādz-nē'], *n.* an affection of the knee produced by much kneeling.
HOUSE-PARTY, [hows'-pah'-ti], *n.* a number of guests entertained for several days, usually at a country residence.
HOUSE-PHYSICIAN, [hows'-fiz-ish'-an], *n.* a junior physician residing in a hospital.
HOUSEPROUD, [hows'-prowd'], *adj.* taking a great interest in the clean and orderly appearance of one's house and furniture.
HOUSEROOM, [hows'-rōōm], *n.* accommodation in the house.
HOUSE-SPARROW, [hows'-spa'-rō], *n.* the common sparrow.
HOUSE-STEWARD, [hows'-stew'-erd], *n.* a person who manages the domestic affairs of an establishment.
HOUSE-SURGEON, [hows'-sur'-jon], *n.* a junior surgeon residing in a hospital.
HOUSE-TAX, [hows'-taks], *n.* a tax on houses.
HOUSE-WARMING, [hows'-wahm'-ing], *n.* a party given by occupants of a new house to celebrate their arrival.
HOUSEWIFE, HUSSIF, [hows'-wif', huz'-if], *n.* the mistress of a household; a female domestic economist; a small case for holding needles, thread, etc. [ME. *huswif*].
HOUSEWIFELY, [hows'-wif'-li], *adj.* befitting, pertaining to, a housewife.
HOUSEWIFERY, [hows'-wif'-er-i, huz'-if-ri], *n.* the occupation or business of a housewife; domestic economy.
HOUSEWRIGHT, [hows'-rīt], *n.* a builder of houses.
HOUSING (1), [howz'-ing], *n.* the act of furnishing with a house or houses; sheltering, accommodation; (*carp.*) the joint or socket made to receive a piece of timber; the covering which receives part of a machine.
HOUSING (2), [howz'-ing], *n.* a saddle cloth, *esp.* when large and of a decorative nature; (*pl.*) trappings. [OFr. *houce*].
HOUSLING, see HOUSELING.
HOVE, [hōv], *p.t.* of HEAVE.
HOVEL (1), [hov'-el], *n.* a hut, shelter, a mean, sordid, and squalid dwelling; (*arch.*) a niche; (*pottery*) the conical covering of a porcelain kiln. [ME. *hovel*].
HOVEL (2), (**hovelling, hovelled**), [hovl], *v.t.* to shelter in a hovel; (*pottery*) to provide with a hovel; to make in the conical shape of a hovel.
HOVELLER, [hov'-el-er], *n.* a boatman who hires his boat and services out for odd jobs; his boat. [Uncert.].
HOVELLING, [hov'-el-ing], *n.* a hoveller's work.
HOVER (1), [hov'-er], *n.* the act of hovering.
HOVER (2), [hov'-er], *v.i.* (of a bird, etc.) to hang poised in the air without forward motion; **to h. about**, (of persons) to loiter near; (*fig.*) to hesitate, show irresolution. [ME. *hoveren*].
HOVER-GROUND, [hov'-er-grownd], *n.* light soil.
HOVERINGLY, [hov'-er-ing-li], *adv.* in a hovering way.
HOW (1), [how], *n.* a hill; a hillock; a mound, a barrow. [~OScand. *haugr* mound].
HOW (2), [how], *n.* the means, manner, method. [HOW (3)].
HOW (3), [how], *interrogative adv.* in what manner? by what method or means?; to what extent?; **and how,** (*U.S.*) *a meaningless phrase expressing emphasis.* [OE. *hu*].
HOW (4), [how], *relative adv.* in what manner, by what method or means; to what extent; that; **for all you know h.,** with your utmost endeavour. [OE. *hu*].
HOW (5), [how], *adv. of degree introducing exclamatory phrases,* to what degree. [OE. *hu*].
HOWBEIT†, [how-bē'-it], *adv.* nevertheless. [HOW, BE and IT].
HOWDAH, see HOUDAH.
HOWDIE, [how'-di], *n.* (*Scots*) a midwife. [Unkn.].
HOW-D'YE-DO, [how'-di-dōō], *n.* (*coll.*) a mix-up, fix, awkward state of affairs.
HOWEVER (1), [how-ev'-er], *adv.* by whatever means or method, in whatever manner, to whatever degree; †although.
HOWEVER (2), [how-ev'-er], *conj.* nevertheless.
HOWITZER, [how'-it-ser], *n.* a short gun of high trajectory and low muzzle velocity. [Germ. *haubitze*].
HOWKER, [how'-ker], *n.* a Dutch sailing ship with two masts. [Du. *hoeker*].
HOWL (1), [howl], *n.* a loud long wailing cry, a yell, wail, moan; a loud outburst of laughter or tears. [HOWL (2)].
HOWL (2), [howl], *v.i.* to utter a howl or series of howls; to yell, wail; (*coll.*) to laugh very heartily. [ME. *houlen* ~Du. *huilen*].
HOWLER, [how'-ler], *n.* a South American monkey of the genus *Alouatta*; one who howls; (*slang*) a bad mistake, glaring blunder.
HOWLET, see OWLET.
HOWLING (1), [howl'-ing], *n.* the act of uttering howls.
HOWLING (2), [howl'-ing], *adj.* uttering howls; (*slang*) excessive, glaring; **h. wilderness,** a very wild and dangerous wilderness.
HOWSOEVER †(1), [how-sō-ev'-er], *conj.* however, nevertheless, notwithstanding.
HOWSOEVER (2), [how'-sō-ev'-er], *adv.* in what way or manner so ever.
HOY (1), [hoi], *n.* a small coasting vessel. [MDu. *hoei*].
HOY (2), [hoi], *int.* a cry uttered to attract attention; (*naut.*) a cry used to call aloft. [Echoic].
HOYDEN, HOIDEN, [hoid'-en], *n.* a lively, boisterous girl. [Unkn.].
HUB, [hub], *n.* the boss at the centre of a wheel; (*fig.*) a centre of activity. [Uncert.].
HUBBLE-BUBBLE, [hubl'-bubl'], *n.* a pipe in which the smoke is drawn through water with a bubbling sound; a hookah; a hubbub. [Echoic].
HUBBUB, [hub'-ub], *n.* confused noise; din, uproar. [Echoic].
HUBBUBBOO, [hub-ub-ōō'], *n.* din, howling. [HUBBUB].
HUBBY, [hub'-i], *n.* affectionate *dim.* of HUSBAND.
HUBRISTIC, [hew-brist'-ik], *adj.* insolently proud. [Gk. *hubristikos*].
HUCK (1), [huk], *n.* a variety of German river trout. [Uncert.].
HUCK (2), [huck], *n.* the hip. [Uncert.].
HUCKABACK, [huk'-a-bak], *n.* a coarse kind of linen with raised figures on it, used for towels. [Unkn.].
HUCKLE, [hukl], *n.* the hip. [HUCK (2)].
HUCKLEBACKED, [hukl'-bakt], *adj.* round-shouldered.
HUCKLEBERRY, [hukl'-be'-ri], *n.* an American plant of the genus *Gaylussacia*, whortleberry. [~Dial. *hurtleberry* from WHORTLEBERRY].
HUCKLEBONE, [hukl'-bōn], *n.* the hip-bone; haunch-bone.
HUCKSTER, [huk'-ster], *n.* a vendor of small goods; a hawker. [MDu. *heukster*].
HUCKSTERAGE, [huk'-ster-ij], *n.* petty traffic.
HUCKSTRESS, [huk'-stres], *n.* a female huckster.
HUD, [hud], *n.* a husk. [Uncert.].
HUDDLE (1), [hudl], *n.* a promiscuous mass or crowd.
HUDDLE (2), [hudl], *v.t. and i.* to push, throw, drive into a promiscuous heap or crowd; **to h. through,** to perform (a task, etc.) in a hurried fashion; **to h. on,** (of clothes) to put on in a hurried and untidy fashion; **to h. together,** to gather close together in a hurried unceremonious fashion. [Uncert.].
HUDDLER, [hudl'-er], *n.* (*rare*) someone who huddles.
HUDIBRASTIC, [hew'-di-bras'-tik], *adj.* in the style of *Hudibras*, satirical, mock-heroic, displaying coarse and merciless wit. [*Hudibras*, a poem by Samuel Butler, 1612-1680].
HUE (1), [hew], *n.* tint or colour; shade. [OE. *heow, hiew*].
HUE (2), [hew], *n.* **h. and cry,** an outcry of pursuit; widely expressed and noisy disapproval; †a proclamation demanding the apprehension of a felon. [OFr. *hu* a shout].
HUED, [hewd], *adj.* coloured; with a hue.
HUEL, [hew'-el], *n.* a mine. [Corn. *huel*].
HUELESS, [hew'-les], *adj.* having no colour.

HUER, [hew'-er], *n.* (Cornish pilchard fishing) a man keeping watch on a cliff to warn those below when a shoal of fish approaches. [OFr. *huer* to cry].
HUFF (1), [huf], *n.* a sulky mood, sulkiness; (*draughts*) the act of huffing.
HUFF (2), [huf], *v.t. and i.* to behave in a bullying insolent fashion; to cause to sulk by rude behaviour; (*draughts*) to take one of an opponent's pieces from the board if he fails to take one of one's own when the chance occurs; †to blow. [ME. *huffen* to blow].
HUFFER, [huf'-er], *n.* one who huffs.
HUFFILY, [huf'-i-li], *adv.* in a huffy manner.
HUFFINESS, [huf'-i-nes], *n.* the state of being huffy.
HUFFING, [huf'-ing], *n.* petulance; peevish anger.
HUFFISH, [huf'-ish], *adj.* petulant; inclined to take offence; bullying.
HUFFISHLY, [huf'-ish-li], *adv.* in a huffish way.
HUFFISHNESS, [huf'-ish-nes], *n.* the condition of being huffish.
HUFFY, [huf'-i], *adj.* petulant; inclined to take offence.
HUG (1), [hug], *n.* a close or loving embrace; a special grip in wrestling.
HUG (2), (**hugging, hugged**), [hug], *v.t.* to embrace warmly and closely; to move in a direction closely parallel to; (*fig.*) to cherish, refuse to be parted from. [Uncert.].
HUGE, [hewj], *adj.* enormous; very big; gigantic. [OFr. *ahuge*].
HUGELY, [hewj'-li], *adv.* to a huge degree.
HUGENESS, [hewj'-nes], *n.* the condition of being huge.
HUGEOUS, [hewj'-yus], *adj.* (*facetious*) huge.
HUGEOUSLY, [hewj'-yus-li], *adv.* (*facetious*) hugely.
HUGEOUSNESS, [hewj'-yus-nes], *n.* the condition of being hugeous.
HUGGER-MUGGER (1), [hug'-er-mug'-er], *n.* secrecy; confusion. [Unkn.].
HUGGER-MUGGER (2), [hug'-er-mug'-er], *adj.* secret; confused.
HUGGER-MUGGER (3), [hug'-er-mug'-er], *adv* in a muddled fashion.
HUGUENOT, [hew'-gen-ō], *n.* a sixteenth-century French Protestant. [Fr. *Huguenot*].
HUGUENOTISM, [hew'-gen-ot-izm], *n.* the principles of French Protestantism of the sixteenth and seventeenth centuries.
HUH, [huh], *int.* an exclamation of disgust or disdain.
HUIA, [hōō'-i-a], *n.* the New Zealand bird, *Heteralocha acutirostris*. [Echoic].
HUITIEME, huitième, [wēt'-i-em], *n.* a sequence of eight at piquet. [Fr. *huitième* eighth].
HUKE, [hewk], *n.* a hooded cape or cloak worn in late medieval times. [OFr. *huque*].
HULA, [hōō'-la], *n.* a native dance by women of Hawaii. [Native].
HULK, [hulk], *n.* the body of an old, dismantled ship; a clumsy, unwieldy ship; (*fig.*) a large ungainly person. [OE. *hulc*].
HULKING, [hulk'-ing], *adj.* large; clumsy, unwieldy.
HULL (1), [hul], *n.* a seed-pod, a shell of a fruit, vegetable, etc.; the outer part of a match-box, etc. [OE. *hulu*].
HULL (2), [hul], n. the body of a ship or boat; the space below deck. [Uncert.].
HULL (3), [hul], *v.t.* to remove (seeds) from their pod. [HULL (1)].
HULL (4), [hul], *v.t.* to strike the hull of a ship. [HULL (2)].

HULL

HULLABALOO, [hul'-a-ba-lōō], *n.* outcry, clamour, hue and cry. [Echoic].
HULLED, [huld], *adj.* (of seeds, peas, etc.) with the husk or hull removed.
HULLER, [hul'-er], *n.* a machine for hulling seeds.
HULLO, [hul-ō'], *int.* a word of greeting, a cry of surprise.
HULLY, [hul'-i], *adj.* having husks or hulls.
HUM (1), [hum], *n.* the act of humming; a buzzing sound; a continuous, steady but indistinct noise; (*coll.*) an unpleasant odour.
HUM (2), [hum], *n* (*slang*) a humbug; a hoax. [HUMBUG].
HUM (3), (**humming, hummed**), [hum], *v.t.* to make a prolonged musical sound of nasal quality, by vibrating the vocal chords and keeping the lips closed; to sing with the lips closed; to make a steady buzzing sound; **to make things h.**, to excite lively activity; **to h. along**, to proceed at a rapid, even pace; **to h. and haw**, to utter short ejaculations expressive of doubt, hesitation, or embarrassment. [ME. *hummen*].
HUMAN, [hew'-man], *adj.* of, or pertaining to, mankind; resembling, consisting of, men, women, or children; sympathetic and understanding; pathetic, touching. [L. *humanus*].
HUMANE, [hew-mān'], *adj.* tender and sympathetic; merciful; understanding; pertaining to humanism; polite, cultured, civilized; **h. killer**, a device for the painless slaughtering of cattle. [HUMAN].
HUMANELY, [hew-mān'-li], *adv.* in a humane way
HUMANENESS, [hew-mān'-nes], *n.* the quality of being humane.
HUMANIFIED, [hew-man'-i-fīd], *adj.* become, or made, human.
HUMANISM, [hew'-man-izm], *n.* learning or an intellectual outlook concerned with such studies as are connected with human culture, *esp.* classical culture; a view of knowledge which ranks the study of man, his passions, thoughts, and works as of first consideration.
HUMANIST, [hew'-man-ist], *n.* one who adopts the outlook, ethics, and ideals of humanism; *esp.* a Renaissance scholar having such an outlook. [Fr. *humaniste*].
HUMANISTIC, [hew'-man-ist'-ik], *adj.* relating to humanists or humanism.
HUMANITARIAN (1), [hew-man'-it-āer'-i-an], *n.* one who professes or practises humanitarian principles; one who doubts or rejects the Divine Nature of Christ.
HUMANITARIAN (2), [hew-man'-it-āer'-i-an], *adj.* merciful, having regard to, and striving to mitigate or eliminate, pain and suffering in human beings or animals.
HUMANITARIANISM, [hew-man'-it-āer'-i-an-izm], *n* the religious doctrine of humanitarians; devotion to the good of humanity.
HUMANITY, [hew-man'-i-ti], *n.* the human race; the quality of being human; the quality of being humane; a humane act; human nature; (in Scots universities) the study of Latin; (*pl.*) the study of literature, *esp.* classical literature. [L. *humanitas*].
HUMANIZATION, [hew'-man-iz-ā'-shun], *n.* the act or process of humanizing.
HUMANIZE, [hew'-man-iz], *v.t. and i.* to make humane; to make human; to become humane.
HUMANIZED, [hew'-man-īzd], *adj.* **h. milk**, cow's milk treated so as to resemble human milk.
HUMANKIND, [hew'-man-kīnd], *n.* mankind, humanity.
HUMANLY, [hew'-man-li], *adv.* in a human way.
HUMANNESS, [hew'-man-nes], *n.* the quality of being human.
HUMATION†, [hew-mā'-shun], *n.* interment; burial. [L. *humatio*].
HUMBLE (1), [humbl], *adj.* meek and unassuming; modest; cringing, obsequious; of lowly origin or birth; not belonging to the upper classes; poor, unpretentious; unimportant. [OFr. *humble*].
HUMBLE (2), [humbl], *v.t.* to abase, humiliate.
HUMBLE-BEE, [humbl'-bē], *n.* a bumble-bee, a bee of the genus *Bombus*. [ME. *hombulbe*].
HUMBLE-MOUTHED, [humbl'-mowTHd], *adj* meek; unassertive.
HUMBLENESS, [humbl'-nes], *n.* the quality of being humble.
HUMBLE-PIE, UMBLE-PIE, [(h)umbl'-pī'], *n.* † a pie made of the entrails of deer; **to eat h.**, to suffer humiliation; to offer a humiliating apology. [UMBLES and HUMBLE].
HUMBLE-PLANT, [humbl'-plahnt], *n.* a variety of sensitive plant.
HUMBLER, [hum'-bler], *n.* one who, or that which, humbles.
HUMBLING, [hum'-bling], *adj.* liable to, able to, humble.
HUMBLY, [hum'-bli], *adv.* in a humble way.
HUMBUG (1), [hum'-bug], *n.* a hoax, a sham; empty, insincere talk; deliberate mis-statement; a pretentious, hypocritical person; a specious rogue; a peppermint sweetmeat. [Uncert.].
HUMBUG (2), (**humbugging, humbugged**), [hum-bug], *v.t.* to dupe, delude.
HUMDRUM, [hum'-drum], *adj.* tedious and dull; uneventful.
HUMEFIED, [hew'-mi-fīd], *adj.* moistened.
HUMERAL (1), [hew'-mer-al], *n.* (*eccles.*) the humeral veil.
HUMERAL (2), [hew'-mer-al], *adj.* (*anat.*) of, or

pertaining to, the shoulder; **h. veil,** (*eccles.*) the scarf worn by the priest or subdeacon when holding the paten on which the host is placed. [LL. *humeralis*].

HUMERUS, [hew'-mer-us], *n.* (*anat.*) the bone of the arm from shoulder to forearm [L. *humerus* shoulder].

HUMET, [hew-met'], *n.* (*her.*) an ordinary cut short at the extremities. [Uncert.].

HUMHUM, [hum'-hum], *n.* a plain, coarse, cotton cloth, made in India [Unkn.].

HUMIC, [hew'-mik], *adj.* produced from humus by the action of an alkali. [L *humus* ground, earth].

HUMID, [hew'-mid], *adj.* damp, moist. [L. *humidus*].

HUMIDIFY, [hew-mid'-i-fī], *v.t.* to make humid.

HUMIDITY, [hew-mid'-i-ti], *n.* the quality of being humid.

HUMIDNESS, [hew'-mid-nes], *n.* humidity.

HUMERUS

HUMILIATE, [hew-mil'-i-āt], *v.t.* to lower the pride of, humble; to hurt the feelings of; to disgrace. [L. *humiliare*].

HUMILIATING, [hew'-mil-i-āt'-ing], *adj.* causing humiliation.

HUMILIATION, [hew'-mil-i-ā'-shun], *n.* the act of humiliating; the condition of having been humiliated; a feeling of defeat or mortification. [L. *humiliatio*].

HUMILITY, [hew-mil'-i-ti], *n.* the quality of being humble. [L. *humilitas*].

HUMITE, [hew'-mīt], *n.* a kind of chondrodite. [Sir A. *Hume*].

HUMMEL (1), [hum'-el], *adj.* (*Scots*) (of stags and cattle) that have no horns. [~LGerm. *hummel* animal without horns].

HUMMEL (2), (hummelling, hummelled), [hum'-el], *v.t.* (*Scots*) to separate awn from the barley. [*Prec.*].

HUMMELLER, [hum'-el-er], *n.* an instrument or machine for hummelling barley.

HUMMER, [hum'-er], *n.* one who hums.

HUMMING (1), [hum'-ing], *n.* the sound of anything that hums.

HUMMING (2), [hum'-ing], *adj.* that hums.

HUMMING-BIRD, [hum'-ing-burd], *n.* a member of the family of American birds, the *Trochilidæ*, which have a brilliant plumage, and produce a humming noise with their rapidly vibrating wings.

HUMMING-BIRD

HUMMING-TOP, [hum'-ing-top], *n.* a hollow top with a hole at the side which makes it hum when spinning.

HUMMOCK, HOMMOCK, [hum'-ok], *n.* a hillock. [Uncert.].

HUMMOCKED, [hum'-okt], *adj.* abounding in hummocks.

HUMMOCKY, [hum'-ok-i], *adj.* having hummocks.

HUMMUM, see HAMMAM.

HUMORAL, [hew'-mer-al], *adj.* of, or pertaining to, the four humours, at one time supposed to control the health.

HUMORALISM, [hew'-mer-al-izm], *n.* (*med.*) the doctrine that diseases are caused by the condition of the humours.

HUMORALIST, [hew'-mer-al-ist], *n* a believer in humoral pathology.

HUMORESQUE, [hew'-mer-esk'], *n.* a composition of a whimsical nature.

HUMORISM, [hew'-mer-izm], *n.* facetiousness; humorousness; humoralism.

HUMORIST, [hew'-mer-ist], *n.* a person given to making jokes; a person who always sees the funny side of things; a professional purveyor of humour. [MedL. *humorista*].

HUMORISTIC, [hew'-mer-ist'-ik], *adj.* facetious; humorous.

HUMORLESS, see HUMOURLESS.

HUMOROUS, [hew'-mer-us], *adj.* funny, amusing, laughable; having a sense of humour; †whimsical; †dominated by one of the four humours. [L. *humorosus* wet].

HUMOROUSLY, [hew'-mer-us-li], *adv.* in a humorous way.

HUMOROUSNESS, [hew'-mer-us-nes], *n.* the quality of being humorous.

HUMOUR (1), [hew'-mer], *n.* temperament; passing inclination, whim; ability to enjoy the ludicrous; fun, comicality, laughable absurdity, jesting; the liquids of the eye; †vapour; †one of the four liquids, supposed in medieval times to be in the human body, which, by the proportions in which they were present, were supposed to determine a person's temperament and character; **out of h.,** depressed, annoyed. [OFr. *humor*].

HUMOUR (2), [hew'-mer], *v.t.* to indulge the whims of; to bring to a happier or more pliant disposition by tact and diplomacy; to manipulate to one's own ends and wishes by careful treatment.

HUMOURLESS, HUMORLESS, [hew'-mer-les], *adj.* lacking humour.

HUMOURSOME, HUMORSOME, [hew'-mer-sum], *adj.* capricious; influenced by the humour of the moment.

HUMOURSOMELY, HUMORSOMELY, [hew'-mer-sum-li], *adv.* in a humoursome way.

HUMOUS, [hew'-mus], *adj.* found in, or derived from, vegetable mould.

HUMP (1), [hump], *n.* a lump or protuberance; the lump on the backs of certain animals; the lump on a person's back due to deformity of the spine; a knoll; (*slang*) a fit of melancholy. [~Du. *homp*].

HUMP (2), [hump], *v.t* to stoop so as to arch the back into a hump; (*slang*) to depress in spirits.

HUMPBACK, [hump'-bak], *n.* a back with a hump; a person having such a back; a whale of the genus *Megapterus*.

HUMPBACKED, [hump'-bakt], *adj.* having a back with a hump.

HUMPED, [humpt], *adj.* with a hump.

HUMPH, [humf], *int.* a snort of contempt or dissatisfaction. [Echoic].

HUMPLESS, [hump'-les], *adj.* having no hump.

HUMPY, [hump'-i], *adj.* having humps.

HUMSTRUM, [hum'-strum], *n.* a hurdy-gurdy. [Echoic].

HUMULIN, [hewm'-yōō-lin], *n.* the narcotic principle in hops.

HUMULUS, [hewm'-yōō-lus], *n.* the hop genus of plants. [L. *humulus* hop].

HUMUS, [hew'-mus], *n.* vegetable mould forming soil. [L. *humus* ground, soil].

HUN, [hun], *n.* one of the Asiatic invaders of Europe in the fourth century; (*fig.*) a vandal, a destructive person; (*coll.*) a German, a German soldier.

HUNCH (1), [hunch], *n.* a hump on the back; a thick slice; (*U.S. slang*) a suspicion, notion. [Uncert.].

HUNCH (2), [hunch], *v.t.* to stoop and arch the back; **to h. up,** (the shoulders) to draw them together so as to make a hump on the back.

HUNCHBACK, [hunch'-bak'], *n.* a back that is hunched up or humped, as in a person suffering from spinal curvature; a person so afflicted.

HUNCHBACKED, [hunch'-bakt'], *adj.* humpbacked.

HUNDRED (1), [hun'-dred], *n.* one more than ninety-nine; a great many; †a former subdivision of an English county. [OE. *hundred*].

HUNDRED (2), [hun'-dred], *adj.* being one more than ninety-nine; (*pl.*) very many; **a h. and one,** very many.

HUNDREDER, [hun'-dred-er], *n.* one who lives in a hundred; a juror from a hundred.

HUNDREDTH (1), [hun'-dredth], *n.* one of a hundred equal parts, a hundredth part; the hundredth member of a series; **Old H.,** the name of a well-known hymn tune.

HUNDREDTH (2), [hun'-dredth], *adj.* the ordinal of a hundred; the next after the ninety-ninth.

HUNDREDWEIGHT, [hun'-dred-wāt], *n.* eight stone, or 112 lb. avoirdupois; (*U.S.*) 100 lb.

HUNGARY-WATER, [hung'-ger-i-waw'-ter], *n.* distilled water prepared from infused rosemary-flowers.

HUNG-BEEF, [hung'-bēf], *n.* beef, slightly salted, and hung up to cure by drying.

HUNGER (1), [hung'-ger], *n.* lack of food; the physical pain and weakness arising from lack of food; famine; a craving for food; (*fig.*) any great craving or desire. [OE. *hungor*].

HUNGER (2), [hung'-ger], *v.i.* to lack food and nourishment; **to h. for, h. after,** to crave violently for. [*Prec.*].

HUNGERBITTEN, [hung'-ger-bit'-en], *adj.* famished.

HUNGERED†, [hung'-gerd], *adj.* famished; hungry.

HUNGER-MARCH, [hung'-ger-mahch], *n.* a journey made on foot to the capital or seat of government by the unemployed as a protest against their condition.

HUNGER-MARCHER, [hung′-ger-mahch′-er], *n.* one who participates in a hunger-march.

HUNGER-ROT, [hung′-ger-rot′], *n.* a disease in sheep brought on by poor feeding.

HUNGER-STARVED, [hung′-ger-stahvd], *adj.* famished, starved with hunger.

HUNGER-STRIKE, [hung′-ger-strīk], *n.* a refusal to eat, *esp.* when adopted to express protest.

HUNGRILY, [hung′-gri-li], *adv.* in a hungry way.

HUNGRY, [hung′-gri], *adj.* lacking food; ready and eager to eat; (*fig.*) earnestly and keenly desiring, craving for; (of a look) lean, avid. [OE. *hungrig*].

HUNK, [hungk], *n.* a large slice or chunk. [~Flem. *hunke*].

HUNKERS, [hungk′-erz], *n.*(*pl.*) the back of the thighs, the hams. [Scots *hunker* to squat].

HUNKS, [hungks], *n.* a mean man; a niggard, a miser. [Unkn.].

HUNKY-DORY, [hungk′-i-daw′-ri], *adj.* (*U.S. slang*) excellent, thoroughly good. [Unkn.].

HUNT (1), [hunt], *n.* the act of hunting; an association of persons who indulge in hunting; the area over which they hunt; a body of persons, hounds, and horses engaged in hunting; (*fig.*) a vigorous search.

HUNT (2), [hunt], *v.t. and i.* to chase wild animals and kill them, *esp.* to chase foxes, hares, stags, etc., with hounds and horses; to follow the chase; to act as master of the hounds; to chase, drive away, pursue; to search intensely for; (of machinery) to oscillate abnormally. [OE. *huntian*].

HUNTER, [hunt′-er], *n.* one who hunts; a horse ridden for foxhunting; a watch in a hinged case protecting the glass.

HUNTING, [hunt′-ing], *n.* the act of one who hunts; the chase; abnormal oscillation or eccentric rotation in machinery.

HUNTING-BOX, [hunt′-ing-boks], *n.* a small house lived in during the hunting season.

HUNTING-CROP, [hunt′-ing-krop], *n.* a whipstock with a loop at one end and a handle at the other.

HUNTING-HORN, [hunt′-ing-hawn], *n.* a horn used by huntsmen.

HUNTING-HORN

HUNTRESS, [hunt′-res], *n.* a woman who hunts.

HUNTSMAN, [hunts′-man], *n.* a hunter; the man in charge of a pack of hounds.

HUNTSMANSHIP, [hunts′-man-ship], *n.* the art of hunting; skill in hunting.

HURDIES, [hurd′-iz], *n.*(*pl.*) buttocks; hips. [Unkn.].

HURDLE (1), [hurdl], *n.* a light wooden oblong framework, used to make a temporary fence or barrier, or for jumping over in a race; a similar structure on which a condemned man was lashed and dragged to the place of execution; (*pl.*) hurdle race, hurdle racing. [OE. *hyrdel*].

HURDLE (2), [hurdl], *v.t. and i.* to make hurdles; to enclose with hurdles; to jump over hurdles in a hurdle race.

HURDLER, [hurd′-ler], *n.* a maker of hurdles; one who runs in hurdle races.

HURDS, [hurdz], *n.*(*pl.*) the coarse part of flax or hemp; tow; hards. [OE. *heordan*].

HURDY-GURDY, [hurd′-i-gurd′-i], *n.* a rustic stringed instrument now obsolete; a barrel-organ. [Echoic].

HURKARU, [hur′-ka-rōō], *n.* a Hindu messenger or courier. [Hindi *harkara*].

HURL (1), [hurl], *n.* the action of hurling.

HURL (2), [hurl], *v.t. and i.* to throw with great force; to hurtle; to play at hurling. [ME. *hurlen*].

HURLBONE, [hurl′-bōn], *n.* a bone in the buttock of a horse. [WHIRLBONE].

HURLER, [hurl′-er], *n.* one who hurls; a player in a game of hurling.

HURLEY, [hurl′-i], *n.* a name for hockey; shinty; a hockey stick.

HURLING, [hurl′-ing], *n.* the act of one who hurls; the Irish form of hockey; a Cornish traditional ball game.

HURLWIND, [hurl′-wind], *n.* a whirlwind.

HURLY, [hur′-li], *n.* commotion, hurly-burly. [OFr. *hurlee* loud noise].

HURLY-BURLY, [hur′-li-bur′-li], *n.* tumult; bustle; commotion.

HURRAH (1), [hōō-rah′], *n.* a cry of "hurrah!"

HURRAH (2), [hōō-rah′], *v.i.* to shout "hurrah!"

HURRAH (3), [hōō-rah′], *int.* a shout of triumph and delight.

HURRICANE (1), [hu′-rik-an], *n.* a cyclonic storm in the South Atlantic; a very violent wind; a type of fighter plane; (*fig.*) a vehement outburst. [Sp. *huracan*].

HURRICANE (2), [hu′-rik-an], *adj.* like a hurricane, violent, vigorous.

HURRIED, [hu′-rid], *adj.* moving with haste; done in a hurry.

HURRIEDLY, [hu′-rid-li], *adv* in a hurried way.

HURRIEDNESS, [hu′-rid-nes], *n.* the condition of being hurried.

HURRIER, [hu′-ri-er], *n.* a person who hurries.

HURRY (1), [hu′-ri], *n.* the act of hurrying; bustling, busy speed; a chute from which a ship is loaded with coal; (*mus.*) violin tremolo used to accompany violent or rapid action on stage or screen; **in a h.,** eager and impatient; readily. [~Swed. *hurr*].

HURRY (2), [hu′-ri], *v.t. and i.* to do or go quickly; to hasten; to cause to hasten; to send hastily; to do, or cause to be done, with increased speed; to bustle, flurry, hasten unnecessarily; **to h. up,** to accelerate.

HURRYINGLY, [hu′-ri-ing-li], *adv.* in a hurrying way.

HURRY-SCURRY, [hu′-ri-sku′-ri], *adv.* in confused haste.

HURST, [hurst], *n.* a wood; a thicket; a wood on a hill. [OE. *hyrst*].

HURT (1), [hurt], *n.* a whortleberry. [HURTLEBERRY].

HURT (2), [hurt], *n.* pain, injury, damage.

HURT (3), [hurt], *v.t. and i.* to cause pain to; to damage, injure; (*fig.*) to wound the feelings of; to come to harm; **it won't h.,** (*coll.*) it does not matter. [OFr. *hurter* to knock against].

HURTER, HURTOIR, [hurt′-er, hurt′-wah(r)], *n.* (*fort.*) a piece of wood at the lower end of a platform, to prevent the wheels of gun-carriages from damaging the parapet. [Fr. *heurtoir* buffer].

HURTFUL, [hurt′-fōōl], *adj.* causing hurt, harmful, injurious.

HURTFULLY, [hurt′-fōōl-i], *adv.* in a hurtful way.

HURTFULNESS, [hurt′-fōōl-nes], *n.* the quality of being hurtful.

HURTLE (1), [hurtl], *n.* a collision; a crash as of violent impact.

HURTLE (2), [hurtl], *v.i.* to fly, to rush or be projected through the air with great violence; (*archaic*) to crash, collide. [ME. *hurtlen*].

HURTLEBERRY, see WHORTLEBERRY.

HURTLESS, [hurt′-les], *adj.* harmless; without hurt

HURTOIR, see HURTER.

HUSBAND (1), [huz′-band], *n.* a married man, the spouse of a woman; †the steward or manager of an estate. [OE. *husbonda* householder].

HUSBAND (2), [huz′-band], *v.t.* to manage with skill and economy; (of a man) to marry; (of a woman) to provide with a husband; †to cultivate (ground, produce, etc.).

HUSBANDABLE, [huz′-band-abl], *adj.* that may be husbanded.

HUSBANDAGE, [huz′-band-ij], *n.* commission to the ship's agent for managing the ship's business.

HUSBANDHOOD, [huz′-band-hōōd], *n.* the condition of being a husband.

HUSBANDLESS, [huz′-band-les], *adj.* without a husband.

HUSBANDLIKE, [huz′-band-līk], *adj.* like, or fitting for, a husband.

HUSBANDMAN, [huz′-band-man], *n.* a farmer; one who tills the ground.

HUSBANDRY, [huz′-band-ri], *n.* farming, agriculture; thrift, good management.

HUSBANDSHIP, [huz′-band-ship], *n.* husbandhood.

HUSH (1), [hush], *n.* a silence.

HUSH (2), [hush], *v.t.* to make or become calm and silent; to soothe; to bring to an end; **to h. up,** to keep from public knowledge and discussion. [Echoic].

HUSH-HUSH, [hush′-hush′], *adj.* very secret.

HUSHION, [hōōsh′-un], *n.* (*Scots*) a stocking without a foot. [Uncert.].

HUSHMONEY, [hush′-mun′-i], *n.* money paid to secure silence.

HUSH-MUSH, [hush′-mush], *n.* a state of cautious silence. [HUSH].

HUSK (1), [husk], *n.* the dry outer covering of some seeds and fruits, the skin, rind, pod; (*fig.*) the dull framework of some subject. [ME. *huske*].

HUSK (2), [husk], *v.t.* to strip the husk from.

HUSKED, [huskt], *adj.* having husks; stripped of husks.

HUSKILY, [husk′-i-li], *adv.* in a husky tone.

HUSKINESS, [husk′-i-nes], *n.* the quality of being husky.

HUSKING, [husk′-ing], *n.* the act of removing husks; (*U.S.*) a party of people engaged in this operation.

HUSKY (1), [hus′-ki], *n.* an Eskimo; his language; an Eskimo dog. [ESKIMO].

HUSKY (2), [hus′-ki], *adj.* having a hoarse dry rasping quality in the speech. [DialE. *hask*, *husk* hoarse].

HUSKY (3), [hus′-ki], *adj.* covered with a husk; like a husk; (*coll.*) strong, vigorous, having a rough but forceful personality.

HUSSAR, [hōoz-ah(r)′], *n.* a member of the Hungarian light cavalry; a member of certain regiments of light cavalry of other nations. [Hungarian *huszar*].

HUSSIF, see HOUSEWIFE.

HUSSITE, [hus′-īt], *n.* a follower of John Huss, the Bohemian religious reformer. [J. *Huss*, 1373-1415].

HUSSY, [huz′-i], *n.* a roguish, pert or impudent girl; a woman of dubious reputation. [HUSSIF].

HUSTINGS, [hust′-ingz], *n.(pl.)* a court of the City of London, at one time also held in other English boroughs and cities; the platform where the dignitaries of this court sat in the Guildhall; a platform on which parliamentary candidates were nominated and from which they addressed meetings; the proceedings of an election. [OE. *husting* a council].

HUSTLE (1), [husl], *n.* rapid, decisive, and vigorous action; restless activity.

HUSTLE (2), [husl], *v.t. and i.* to jostle, push quickly and unceremoniously; to hurry, bustle; to push, push oneself forward; to get a move on, to get things done quickly. [Uncert.].

HUSTLER, [hus′-ler], *n.* a man of energy, who gets things done quickly.

HUT (1), [hut], *n.* a small wooden building; a cabin; a hovel. [Fr. *hutte*].

HUT (2), (**hutting, hutted**), [hut], *v.t. and i.* to inhabit a hut; to provide with a hut or huts.

HUTCH (1), [huch], *n.* a bin or box in which flour or grain is kept; a trough for kneading dough; a truck in which the hewn coal is carried from the pit face to the shaft of a mine; a trough where ore is washed; a wooden cage or box where small tame animals may be kept; (*coll.*) a cottage, a small house. [OFr. *huche*].

HUTCH (2), [huch], *v.t.* to wash ore in a hutch; to store in a hutch; to keep live animals in a hutch.

HUT-CIRCLE, [hut′-surkl], *n.* (*archæ.*) a circular ridge of earth or stones indicating the site of a prehistoric hut.

HUTIA, [hōo′-tia], *n.* the West Indian hog-rat, a species of *Capromys*. [Native].

HUTMENT, [hut′-ment], *n.* a group of huts; a camp or settlement.

HUX, [huks], *v.t.* to fish for pike with hooks and lines attached to floating bladders. [Uncert.].

HUZZA†, [hōoz′-ah′], *int.* a shout of joy and triumph.

HYACINTH, [hī′-a-sinth], *n.* (*Gk. myth.*) a legendary blue flower which sprang from the blood of the youth Hyacinthus who was killed by Apollo; (*bot.*) one of the group of familiar bulbous plants that flower with numerous bell-shaped blossoms set in a conical spike; (*min.*) a dark orange-coloured variety of zircon; (*Gk. antiq.*) a blue sapphire-like jewel. [Gk. *huakinthos*].

HYACINTHINE, [hī′-a-sin′-thīn], *adj.* like a hyacinth; of the colour of hyacinths.

HYADES, [hī′-ad-ēz], *n.(pl.)* a group of five stars in the head of Taurus, supposed to bring rain when they rose with the sun. [Gk. *Huades*].

HYAENA, see HYENA.

HYALESCENCE, [hī′-al-es′-ents], *n.* the process of becoming transparent like glass. [Gk. *hualos* glass].

HYALINE (1), [hī′-al-īn], *n.* (*poet.*) something resembling glass.

HYALINE (2), [hī′-al-in], *adj.* resembling glass, vitreous. [Gk. *hualinos*].

HYALITE, [hī′-al-īt], *n.* a kind of colourless opal. [Fr. *hyalite*].

HYALO-, *pref.* glass. [Gk. *hualos*].

HYALOGRAPHY, [hī-al-og′-ra-fi], *n.* the art of writing on glass. [HYALO and Gk. *graphia* writing].

HYALOID, [hī′-al-oid], *adj.* like glass, glassy. [HYALO and Gk. *oeides* like].

HYALOMELAN†, [hī′-al-om′-el-an], *n.* a kind of tachylite. [HYALO and Gk. *melas* black].

HYALOPHANE, [hī-al′-ō-fān], *n.* a kind of orthoclase containing baryta; a barium felspar. [HYALO and Gk. *phanes* showing].

HYBERNATE, see HIBERNATE.

HYBODONT, [hī′-bō-dont], *n.* a shark having teeth with humpy crowns. [Gk. *hubos* hump and *odous odontos* tooth].

HYBRID (1), [hī′-brid], *n.* a plant or animal which is a crossbreed from different species; a word made up of elements drawn from different languages; anything of mixed origin. [L. *hibrida* the offspring of a domestic sow and a wild boar].

HYBRID (2), [hī′-brid], *adj.* possessing the nature of a hybrid; of mixed parentage; fashioned of mixed elements.

HYBRIDISM, [hī′-brid-izm], *n.* the condition of being hybrid; crossbreeding.

HYBRIDITY, [hī-brid′-i-ti], *n.* hybridism.

HYBRIDIZATION, [hī′-brid-īz-ā′-shun], *n.* the act of hybridizing; crossbreeding.

HYBRIDIZE, [hī′-brid-iz], *v.t. and i.* to produce hybrids, interbreed.

HYBRIDOUS, [hī′-brid-us], *adj.* hybrid.

HYDATID, [hī′-dat-id], *n.* (*path.*) a cyst, containing watery fluid; the bladder-worm stage of certain tapeworms. [Gk. *hudatis* watery vesicle].

HYDATISM, [hī′-dat-izm], *n.* (*med.*) sound caused by an effusion of fluid from a bodily cavity.

HYDATOID, [hī′-dat-oid], *adj.* resembling water. [Gk. *hudatoeides* like water].

HYDRA, [hī′-dra], *n.* (*Gk. myth.*) the nine-headed serpent slain by Hercules; any legendary serpent; (*zool.*) any of a group of freshwater polyps, any part of which, when severed from the whole, develops into a complete polyp; (*astron.*) a southern constellation supposed to represent a serpent; (*fig.*) an evil which always reappears despite every effort to exterminate it. [Gk. *hudra* water serpent].

HYDRAGOGUE, [hī′-dra-gog], *n.* a medicine that causes a watery discharge. [HYDRO and Gk. *ago* I lead].

HYDRA-HEADED, [hī′-dra-hed′-id], *adj.* having many heads; (*fig.*) difficult to get rid of.

HYDRANGEA, [hī-drān′-ja], *n.* a kind of shrub of the *Saxifragaceæ*, whose flowers, white, pink, and blue, blossom in large clusters. [MdL. *hydrangea*].

HYDRANT, [hī′-drant], *n.* a pipe to which a hose may be attached, to draw water from a main. [HYDRO].

HYDRARGYLLITE, [hī-drah′-jil-īt], *n.* hydrate of alumina; wavellite. [HYDRO and Gk. *argillos* clay].

HYDRARGYRUM, [hī-drah′-jir-um], *n.* mercury or quicksilver, the chemical element Hg. [HYDRO and Gk. *argyros* silver].

HYDRATE (1), [hī′-drāt], *n.* (*chem.*) a compound of which the OH radicle is a constituent.

HYDRATE (2), [hī′-drāt], *v.t.* (*chem.*) to make a hydrate of; to combine with water.

HYDRATED, [hī′-drāt′-id], *adj.* (*chem.*) combined with water.

HYDRAULIC, [hī-dro′-lik], *adj.* of, or pertaining to, the properties of water or other liquids when conveyed through a pipe; operating by the passage of water through a pipe; connected with, worked by, or containing, water; tending to harden or solidify in water. [Gk. *hudraulikos*].

HYDRAULICALLY, [hī-dro-′-lik-al-i], *adv.* by means of water-power or hydraulics.

HYDRAULICON, [hī-dro′-lik-on], *n.* an ancient musical instrument worked by water, a water organ. [Gk. *hudraulikon* (*organon*) hydraulic (organ)].

HYDRAULICS, [hī-dro′-liks], *n.* the science of the motive power of liquids.

HYDRENTEROCELE, [hī-dren′-ter-ō-sēl′], *n.* (*med.*) an intestinal hernia, with water in the sac. [HYDRO, ENTERA and Gk. *kele* tumour].

HYDRIAD, [hī′-dri-ad], *n.* a water nymph. [Gk *hudrias*].

HYDRIC, [hī′-drik], *adj.* (*chem.*) pertaining to hydrogen. [HYDROGEN].

HYDRIDE, [hī′-drīd], *n.* (*chem.*) a compound of hydrogen and a metal or some other radical.

HYDRIODIC, [hī-dri-od′-ik], *adj.* (*chem.*) made up of hydrogen and iodine. [HYDR(OGEN) and IOD(INE)].

HYDRO (1), [hī′-drō], *n.* a hydropathic.

HYDRO- (2), *pref.* water. [Gk. *hudor*].

HYDRO-AEROPLANE,′ [hī′-drō-āer′-ō-plān], *n.* a seaplane. [HYDRO (2) and AEROPLANE].

HYDROBAROMETER, [hī′-drō-ba-rom′-it-er], *n.* an instrument for determining the depth of the sea by registering pressure. [HYDRO (2) and BAROMETER].

HYDROBROMIC, [hī′-drō-brōm′-ik], *adj.* (*chem.*) consisting of hydrogen and bromine. [HYDRO(GEN) and BROM(INE)].

HYDROCARBON, [hī′-drō-kahb′-on], *n.* a compound consisting of hydrogen and carbon. [HYDRO-(GEN) and CARBON].

HYDROCELE, [hī′-drō-sēl], *n.* (*med.*) dropsy of the testicle; water on the testicle. [HYDRO (2) and Gk. *kele* tumour].

HYDROCEPHALIC, [hī'-drō-sef-al'-ik], *adj.* relating to, affected with, hydrocephalus.

HYDROCEPHALUS, [hī'-drō-sef'-al-us], *n.* (*med.*) dropsy of the brain; water on the brain. [HYDRO (2) and Gk. *kephale* head].

HYDROCHLORIC, [hī'-drō-klo'-rik], *adj.* (*chem.*) consisting of chlorine and hydrogen. [HYDRO(GEN) and CHLOR(INE)].

HYDROCYANIC, [hī'-drō-sī-an'-ik], *adj.* consisting of hydrogen and cyanogen. [HYDRO(GEN) and CYAN(OGEN)].

HYDRODYNAMIC, [hī'-drō-dī-nam'-ik], *adj.* relating to the dynamics of fluids. [HYDRO (2) and DYNAMIC].

HYDRODYNAMICS, [hī'-drō-dī-nam'-iks], *n.* the dynamics of liquids. [HYDRO (2) and DYNAMICS].

HYDRO-ELECTRIC, [hī'-drō-i-lek'-trik], *adj.* pertaining to electricity generated by water-power. [HYDRO (2) and ELECTRIC].

HYDRO-EXTRACTOR, [hī'-drō-eks-trak'-ter], *n.* a device for separating water from solids by centrifugal action. [HYDRO (2) and EXTRACT (2)].

HYDROFLUORIC, [hī'-drō-flōō-or'-ik], *adj.* (*chem.*) composed of fluorine and hydrogen. [HYDRO(GEN) and FLUOR(INE)].

HYDROGEN, [hī'-drō-jen], *n.* a highly inflammable gas, the chemical element H. [Fr. *hydrogène*].

HYDROGENATE, [hī-droj'-en-āt], *v.t.* to combine with hydrogen.

HYDROGENIZE, [hī-droj'-en-īz], *v.t.* to hydrogenate.

HYDROGENOUS, [hī-droj'-en-us], *adj.* relating to, containing, hydrogen.

HYDROGNOSY, [hī-drog'-no-si], *n.* the study of waters on or beneath the surface. [HYDRO (2) and Gk. *gnosis* knowledge].

HYDROGRAPHER, [hī-drog'-raf-er], *n.* one who draws maps of the sea, lakes, or other waters; a chart-maker. [HYDRO (2) and Gk. *graphia* writing].

HYDROGRAPHIC, [hī'-drō-graf'-ik], *adj.* pertaining to hydrography.

HYDROGRAPHICAL, [hī'-drō-graf'-ik-al], *adj.* hydrographic.

HYDROGRAPHY, [hī-drog'-ra-fi], *n.* the science that treats of the waters of the earth; the technique of measuring and making maps of these. [HYDRO (2) and Gk. *graphia* writing].

HYDROID, [hī'-droid], *adj.* like a hydra. [HYDRA and Gk. *oeides* like].

HYDROKINETICS, [hī'-drō-kin-et'-iks], *n.* the study of the movements of liquids. [HYDRO(2) and KINETICS].

HYDROLOGICAL, [hī'-drō-loj'-ik-al], *adj.* relating to hydrology.

HYDROLOGY, [hī-drol'-o-ji], *n.* the scientific study of water. [HYDRO (2) and Gk. *logos* speech].

HYDROLYSIS, [hī-drol'-is-is], *n.* decomposition by water. [HYDRO (2) and Gk. *lusis* dissolving].

HYDROMANCY, [hī'-drō-man-si], *n.* divination by means of water. [HYDRO (2) and ~Gk. *manteia* divination].

HYDROMANIA, [hī'-drō-mā'-ni-a], *n.* a craving, usually morbid, for water. [HYDRO (2) and MANIA].

HYDROMECHANICS, [hī'-drō-mi-kan'-iks], *n.* the study of the use of liquids as driving power for machinery. [HYDRO (2) and MECHANICS].

HYDROMEL, [hī'-drō-mel], *n.* a liquor made of honey and water. [L. *hydromel*].

HYDROMETEOR, [hī'-drō-mē'-ti-or], *n.* a watery phenomenon in the air. [HYDRO (2) and METEOR].

HYDROMETER, [hī-drom'-it-er], *n.* an instrument for measuring the specific gravity of liquids, or the velocity of water. [HYDRO (2) and METER].

HYDROMETER

HYDROMETRIC, [hī'-drō-met'-rik], *adj.* relating to hydrometry.

HYDROMETRICAL, [hī'-drō-met'-rik-al], *adj.* relating to hydrometry.

HYDROMETRY, [hī-drom'-et-ri], *n.* the measuring of the specific gravity of liquids, and the strength of spirituous liquors. [HYDRO (2) and Gk. *metria* measurement].

HYDROMOTOR, [hī'-drō-mō'-ter], *n.* a machine for propelling ships by jets of water. [HYDRO (2) and MOTOR].

HYDROPATHIC (1), [hī'-drō-path'-ik], *n.* a hotel with special facilities for those taking a water-cure.

HYDROPATHIC (2), [hī'-drō-path'-ik], *adj.* relating to hydropathy.

HYDROPATHIST, [hī-drop'-ath-ist], *n.* a doctor practising hydropathy.

HYDROPATHY, [hī-drop'-a-thi], *n.* (*med.*) a German medical cure by water; the water-cure. [Germ. *hydropathie*].

HYDROPHANE, [hī'-drō-fān], *n.* (*min.*) a variety of opal which becomes transparent when immersed in water. [HYDRO (2) and Gk. *phainomai* I appear].

HYDROPHANOUS, [hī-drof'-an-us], *adj.* becoming transparent when wetted.

HYDROPHIDES, [hī-drof'-id-ēz], *n.(pl.)* the water-snakes. [HYDRO (2) and Gk. *ophis* snake].

HYDROPHILOUS, [hī'-dro'-fil-us], *adj.* (*bot.*) depending on moisture for fertilization. [HYDRO (2) and Gk. *philos* lover].

HYDROPHOBIA, [hī'-drō-fō'-bi-a], *n.* (*path.*) difficulty in swallowing water and intense dread of it, *esp.* as a symptom of rabies; rabies, a form of madness attacking dogs, etc., or caused by a bite from a rabid animal. [Gk. *hudrophobia*].

HYDROPHOBIC, [hī'-drō-fōb'-ik], *adj.* relating to hydrophobia.

HYDROPHONE, [hī'-drō-fōn], *n.* an instrument for detecting by sound the approach of submarines. [HYDRO (2) and Gk. *phone* sound].

HYDROPHORE, [hī'-drō-faw(r)], *n.* an instrument for obtaining water from any given depth. [Gk. *hudrophoros* water-carrying].

HYDROPHTHALMIA, [hī'-drof-thal'-mi-a], *n.* (*med.*) a morbid watery condition of the eye. [HYDRO (2) and OPHTHALMIA].

HYDROPHYTE, [hī'-drō-fīt], *n.* a water-plant. [HYDRO (2) and Gk. *phuton* plant].

HYDROPHYTIC, [hī'-drō-fit'-ik], *adj.* pertaining to a hydrophyte. [*Prec.*].

HYDROPHYTOLOGY, [hī'-drō-fīt-ol'-o-ji], *n.* the study of water-plants. [HYDROPHYTE and Gk. *logos* speech].

HYDROPIC, [hī-drop'-ik], *adj.* affected with dropsy, dropsical. [OFr. *idropique*].

HYDROPICAL, [hī-drop'-ik-al], *adj.* hydropic.

HYDROPLANE, [hī'-drō-plān], *n.* a rudder controlling the vertical movement of a submarine; a plane or board fixed to a motor-boat by which it can skim over the surface of the water; a motor-boat having such an attachment; an aeroplane fitted with floats, a seaplane. [HYDRO (2) and PLANE].

HYDROPLANE

HYDROPONICS, [hī'-drō-pon'-iks], *n.* the art of growing plants by feeding them on chemical solutions without using soil.

HYDROPSY, [hī'-drop-si], *n.* (*path.*) a morbid collection of watery fluid in the body, dropsy. [OFr. *idropesie*].

HYDROPULT, [hī'-drō-pult], *n.* a force-pump worked by one hand.

HYDROSCOPE, [hī'-drō-skōp], *n.* a water-clock. [Gk. *hudroskopos* seeking water].

HYDROSPHERE, [hī'-drō-sfēer], *n.* the atmospheric moisture that envelops the globe; the waters of the earth. [HYDRO (2) and SPHERE].

HYDROSTAT, [hī'-drō-stat], *n.* an electrical mechanism by which the presence of water may be detected; a safety-valve on steam-boilers. [HYDRO and Gk. *statos* placed].

HYDROSTATIC, [hī'-drō-stat'-ik], *adj.* concerning the equilibrium of liquids; employing the pressure of water as a driving force; pertaining to any aquatic animal furnished with air-bladders.

HYDROSTATICAL, [hī'-drō-stat'-ik-al], *adj.* hydrostatic.

HYDROSTATICALLY, [hī'-drō-stat'-ik-al-i], *adv.* according to the principles of hydrostatics.

HYDROSTATICS, [hī'-drō-stat'-iks], *n.(pl.)* the science treating of the equilibrium of fluids. [HYDRO (2) and STATICS].

HYDROSULPHURIC, [hī'-drō-sul-fewr'-ik], *adj.* (*chem.*) composed of hydrogen and sulphur. [HYDRO(GEN) and SULPHURIC].

HYDROTELLURIC, [hī'-drō-tel-ewr'-ik], *adj.* (*chem.*) composed of hydrogen and tellurium. [HYDRO(GEN) and TELLURIC].

HYDROTHERAPY, [hī'-drō-the'-ra-pi], *n.* the treatment of disease by water. [HYDRO (2) and THERAPY].

HYDROTHERMAL, [hī'-drō-thur'-mal], *adj.* relating to hot springs. [HYDRO (2) and THERMAL].

HYDROTHORAX, [hī'-drō-thaw'-raks], *n.* (*med.*) dropsy of the chest. [HYDRO (2) and THORAX].

HYDROTIC, [hī-drot'-ik], *adj.* bringing about a discharge of water or phlegm.
HYDROTROPIC, [hī'-drō-trōp'-ik], *adj.* affected by hydrotropism. [HYDRO (2) and Gk. *tropos* turning].
HYDROTROPISM, [hī-drō'-trop-izm], *n.* a tendency to grow towards or away from moisture.
HYDROUS, [hī'-drus], *adj.* (*chem.*) containing or compounded of water. [Gk. *hudor* water].
HYDROXIDE, [hī-drok'-sīd], *n.* (*chem.*) an oxide of a metal combined with water; a metallic hydrate. [HYDRO (2) and OXIDE].
HYDROXYL, [hī-droks'-il], *n.* (*chem.*) the OH radicle, which combines with a metallic radicle to form a hydrate. [HYDR(OGEN) and OX(YGEN) and Gk. *hule* matter].
HYDROZOA, [hī'-drō-zō'-a], *n.*(*pl.*) minute organisms between plant and animal, living in water. [HYDRO (2) and Gk. *zoa*, *pl.* of *zoon* animal].
HYDRUS, [hī'-drus], *n.* a legendary sea-serpent; a genus of snakes, the *Hydrophis*. [L. *hydrus*].
HYENA HYAENA, [hī-ē'-na], *n.* a flesh-eating quadruped of the genus, *Hyænidæ*, allied to the dog-tribe, and noted for its repulsive habits; (*fig.*) a cruel or repulsive person. [L. *hyaena*].

HYENA

HYETAL, [hī'-i-tal], *adj.* regarding rainfall. [Gk. *huetos* rain].
HYETO-, *pref.* rain. [Gk. *huetos*].
HYETOGRAPH, [hī'-et-ō-graf], *n.* a rainfall chart.
HYETOGRAPHY, [hī-et-og'-ra-fi], *n.* the study of the rainfall. [HYETO and Gk. *graphia* writing].
HYETOLOGY, [hī'-et-ol'-o-ji], *n.* the science that treats of rainfall. [HYETO and Gk. *logos* speech].
HYETOMETER, [hī'-et-om'-it-er], *n.* an instrument for measuring rainfall, a raingauge. [HYETO and METER].
HYGEIAN, [hī'-jē'-an], *adj.* pertaining to health or hygiene.
HYGIENE, [hī'-jēn], *n.* the theory and practice of the maintenance of public and private health. [Gk. *hugieine* (*tekhne*) the art of health].
HYGIENIC, [hī-jēn'-ik], *adj.* pertaining to hygiene; in accordance with good hygiene; sanitary, wholesome, healthy.
HYGIENICALLY, [hī-jēn'-ik-al-i], *adv.* in a hygienic fashion.
HYGIENISM, [hī'-jēn-izm], *n.* the practice of hygiene.
HYGIENIST, [hī'-jēn-ist], *n.* one versed in the study and practice of hygiene.
HYGRO-, *pref.* damp, moist. [Gk. *hugros*].
HYGROLOGY, [hī-grol'-o-ji], *n.* the scientific study of humidity. [HYGRO and Gk. *logos* speech].
HYGROMETER, [hī-grom'-it-er], *n.* a device for measuring the moisture of the atmosphere. [HYGRO and METER].
HYGROMETRIC, [hī'-grō-met'-rik], *adj.* relating to hygrometry.
HYGROMETRICAL, [hī'-grō-met'-rik-al], *adj.* hygrometric.
HYGROMETRY, [hī-grom'-et-ri], *n.* the measuring of the moisture of the air. [HYGRO and Gk. *metria* measurement].
HYGROPHYTE, [hī'-grō-fīt], *n.* (*bot.*) a plant which depends on moisture in order to thrive. [HYGRO and Gk. *phuton* plant].
HYGROPHYTIC, [hī'-grō-fit'-ik], *adj.* pertaining to a hygrophyte.
HYGROSCOPE, [hī'-grō-skōp], *n.* an instrument to show the variation in the quantity of moisture in the air. [HYGRO and Gk. *skopos* watcher].
HYGROSCOPIC, [hī'-grō-skop'-ik], *adj.* taking in moisture from the atmosphere; relating to a hygroscope.
HYGROSCOPICITY, [hī'-grō-skop-is'-i-ti], *n.* (*bot.*) susceptibility as regards absorption or giving off of moisture.
HYGROSTATICS, [hī'-grō-stat'-iks], *n.* the science that compares or measures degrees of moisture. [HYGRO and STATICS]
HYKE, see HAIK (2).
HYLAEOSAURUS, [hī'-lē-ō-saw'-rus], *n.* a dinosaur whose fossil remains were discovered in the Wealden rocks. [Gk. *hulaios* pertaining to forests and *sauros* lizard].
HYLARCHICAL, [hī-lahk'-ik-al], *adj.* ruling, presiding over, matter. [Gk. *hule* matter and *arkhos* ruler].
HYLIC, [hī'-lik], *adj.* (*philos.*) material as opposed to spiritual. [Gk. *hulikos*].
HYLICIST, [hī'-lis-ist], *n.* (*philos.*) one who assigns a material basis to being.
HYLISM, [hī'-lizm], *n.* the doctrine that derives evil from matter.
HYLO-, [hī'-lō], *pref.* matter. [Gk. *hule*].
HYLOBATE, [hī'-lō-bāt], *n.* one of various kinds of long-armed anthropoid apes or gibbons. [L. *hylobates* walker of the woods].
HYLOIST, [hī'-lō-ist], *n.* a person who believes matter to be God.
HYLOPATHISM, [hī-lop'-ath-izm], *n.* the doctrine ascribing sentiency to matter. [HYLO and Gk. *pathos* suffering].
HYLOTHEISM, [hī'-lō-thē'-izm], *n.* the theory which relates any deity to a material source. [HYLO and THEISM].
HYLOZOIC, [hī'-lō-zō'-ik], *adj.* relating to hylozoism.
HYLOZOISM, [hī'-lō-zō'-izm], *n.* the theory that all matter has life; materialism. [HYLO and Gk. *zoe* life].
HYLOZOIST, [hī'-lō-zō'-ist], *n.* a materialist.
HYMEN, [hī'-men], *n.* (*anat.*) the virginal membrane at the head of the vagina, the maidenhead; (*bot.*) the fine pellicle surrounding a flower in bud; (*myth.*) the god of marriage; marriage. [Gk. *humen* membrane].
HYMENEAL, [hī'-men-ē'-al], *adj.* relating to marriage or to the hymen.
HYMENEAN, [hī'-men-ē'-an], *adj.* hymeneal.
HYMENOGENY, [hī'-men-oj'-en-i], *n.* the production of membranes from liquids in contact. [HYMEN and Gk. *genes* born of].
HYMENOPTERA, [hī'-men-op'-ter-a], *n.*(*pl.*) (*entom.*) the highest order of insects, those with four membranous wings. [Gk. *humenopteros* membrane-winged].
HYMENOPTERAL, [hī'-men-op'-ter-al], *adj.* pertaining to hymenoptera, having four membranous wings.
HYMENOPTEROUS, [hī'-men-op'-ter-us] *adj.* hymenopteral.
HYMENOTOMY, [hī'-men-ot'-o-mi], *n.* (*surg.*) the cutting or dissection of membranes. [HYMEN and Gk. *tome* cutting].
HYMN (1), [him], *n.* a song of praise, usually in a religious service. [L. *hymnus*].
HYMN (2), [him], *v.t. and i.* to give praise, celebrate in hymns; to sing a hymn.
HYMNAL (1), [him'-nal], *n.* a collection of hymns for worship, a hymn-book.
HYMNAL (2), [him'-nal], *adj.* relating to hymns.
HYMNARY, [him'-ner-i], *n.* a hymnal. [LL. *hymnarium*].
HYMN-BOOK, [him'-bŏŏk], *n.* a hymnal.
HYMNIC, [him'-nik], *adj.* relating to, resembling, hymns.
HYMNIST, [him'-nist], *n.* one who composes hymns.
HYMNODIST, [him'-nod-ist], *n.* a student or writer of hymns.
HYMNODY, [him'-no-di], *n.* hymnology; singing of hymns. [Gk. *humnodia*].
HYMNOGRAPHER, [him-nog'-raf-er], *n.* a writer about hymns; composer of hymns. [Gk. *humnographos* writing hymns].
HYMNOLOGIST, [him-nol'-oj-ist], *n.* a student of hymns; a composer of hymns.
HYMNOLOGY, [him-nol'-o-ji], *n.* the study of hymns; a collection of hymns. [Gk. *humnologia*].
HYODONT, [hī'-ō-dont], *adj.* possessing teeth resembling those of a pig. [Gk. *hus* pig and *odous odontos* tooth].
HYOID, [hī'-oid], *adj.* (*anat.*) having a U-shaped bone at the base of the tongue. [Gk. *huoeides* having a shape like the letter U].
HYOSCINE, [hī'-o-sēn], *n.* (*med.*) a poisonous alkaloid of henbane used as a local anaesthetic. [Gk. *huoskuamos* henbane].
HYOSCYAMINE, [hī'-o-sī'-a-min], *n.* an alkaloid extracted from henbane. [*Next*].
HYOSCYAMUS, [hī'-ō-sī'-a-mus], *n.* henbane. [Gk. *huoskuamos*].
HYP†, see HIP (3).
HYPAETHRAL, [hī-pē'-thral], *adj.* (*arch.*) open to the sky. [Gk. *hupaithros*].
HYPALLAGE, [hī-pal'-a-ji], *n.* (*rhet.*) a figure of speech in which the attributes expressed in one set

of words are interchanged with those of another set [Gk. *hupallage* exchange].

HYPER-, *pref.* in excess of; going beyond; above. [Gk. *huper*].

HYPERACUTE, [hī-per-a-kewt'], *adj.* unusually acute.

HYPERAEMIA, [hī'-per-ē'-mi-a], *n.* (*med.*) excess of blood. [HYPER and Gk. *haima* blood].

HYPERAESTHESIA, [hī'-per-es-thē'-zi-a], *n.* (*med.*) excess of sensitiveness of the nerves. [HYPER and AESTHESIA].

HYPERBATIC, [hī'-per-bat'-ik], *adj.* relating to, or characterized by, hyperbaton. [Gk. *huperbatikos*].

HYPERBATON, [hī-pur'-bat-on], *n.* (*gram.*) inversion of the natural order of words and sentences. [Gk. *huperbatos* transposed].

HYPERBOLA, [hī-pur'-bol-a], *n.* (*geom.*) a curve in which the plane is at a greater angle to the base than that made by the side of the cone. [Gk. *huperbole* excess].

HYPERBOLA

HYPERBOLE, [hī-pur'-bol-i], *n.* (*gram.*) a figure of speech which expresses more or less than the truth by understatement or overstatement; an exaggerated statement. [Gk. *huperbole* excess].

HYPERBOLIC, [hī'-per-bol'-ik], *adj.* relating to, resembling, hyperbole; exaggerating; (*geom.*) relating to a hyperbola. [Gk. *huperbolikos*].

HYPERBOLICAL, [hī'-per-bol'-ik-al], *adj.* relating to, of the nature of, hyperbole.

HYPERBOLICALLY, [hī'-per-bol'-ik-al-i], *adv.* in a hyperbolic way.

HYPERBOLIFORM, [hī'-per-bol'-i-fawm], *adj.* (*geom.*) resembling a hyperbola in form. [HYPERBOLE and FORM].

HYPERBOLISM, [hī-pur'-bol-izm], *n.* the use of hyperbole; an example of this.

HYPERBOLIST, [hī-pur'-bol-ist], *n.* a person who uses hyperboles.

HYPERBOLIZE, [hī-pur'-bol-īz], *v.t. and i.* to exaggerate, to use hyperboles.

HYPERBOLOID, [hī-pur'-bol-oid], *n.* (*geom.*) a solid shape whose perimeter is formed by the revolution of a hyperbola about its axis. [HYPERBOLA and Gk. *oeides* like].

HYPERBOREAN (1), [hī'-per-baw'-ri-an], *n.* an inhabitant of the northern regions; (*Gk. myth.*) a member of a people believed to live in perpetual youth and happiness on the edge of the world.

HYPERBOREAN (2), [hī'-per-baw'-ri-an], *adj.* northern; bitterly cold. [Gk. *huperboreos* of a northern region].

HYPERCATALECTIC, [hī'-per-kat'-al-ek'-tik], *adj.* (*pros.*) having an extra syllable or two at the end. [HYPER and CATALECTIC].

HYPERCATALEXIS, [hī'-per-kat'-al-ek'-sis], *n.* (*pros.*) the state of being hypercatalectic. [HYPER and Gk. *katalexis* end].

HYPERCRITIC, [hī'-per-krit'-ik], *n.* a person who is overcritical. [HYPER and CRITIC].

HYPERCRITICAL, [hī'-per-krit'-ik-al], *adj.* overcritical, excessively severe in judgment.

HYPERCRITICALLY, [hī'-per-krit'-ik-al-i], *adv.* in a hypercritical way.

HYPERCRITICISM, [hī'-per-krit'-is-izm], *n.* oversevere criticism.

HYPERDULIA, [hī'-per-dew'-li-a], *n.* (*R.C.*) the superior form of veneration paid to the Blessed Virgin. [MedL. *hyperdulia*].

HYPERDYNAMIC, [hī'-per-dī-nam'-ik], *adj.* (*med.*) unduly active; (*fig.*) extremely vital. [HYPER and DYNAMIC].

HYPEREMESIS, [hī'-per-em'-is-is], *n.* (*med.*) excessive vomiting. [HYPER and EMESIS].

HYPERICUM, [hī-pe'-rik-um], *n.* the genus of plants having clusters of yellow flowers, and including the St. John's wort. [Gk. *hupereikon* excessive health].

HYPERINOSIS, [hī'-per-i-nō'-sis], *n.* (*med.*) morbid excess of fibrin in the blood. [HYPER and Gk. *is inos* fibre].

HYPERKINESIS, [hī'-per-kī-nē'-sis], *n.* irregular action. [HYPER and Gk. *kinesis* movement].

HYPERMETER, [hī-pur'-mit-er], *n.* (*pros.*) a metrical line containing too many syllables. [Gk. *hupermetros* over the measure].

HYPERMETRICAL, [hī'-per-met'-rik-al], *adj.* (*pros.*) of, or relating to, hypermeter; having a redundant syllable.

HYPERMETROPIA, [hī'-per-met-rō'-pi-a], *n.* (*opt.*) long sight. [Gk. *hupermetros* over the measure and *ops* eye].

HYPERMETROPIC, [hī'-per-met-rop'-ik], *adj.* (*opt.*) long-sighted.

HYPERORTHODOXY, [hī'-per-awth'-ō-dok-si], *n.* an excessive insistence on orthodoxy. [HYPER and ORTHODOXY].

HYPERPEPSIA, [hī'-per-pep'-si-a], *n.* (*path.*) an excessive secretion of neutral chlorides in the gastric juices. [HYPER and Gk. *pepsis* digestion].

HYPERPHASIA, [hī'-per-fā'-zi-a], *n.* difficulty in controlling the organs of speech [HYPER and Gk. *phasis* speaking].

HYPERPHYSICAL, [hī'-per-fiz'-ik-al], *adj.* beyond material limits, supernatural. [HYPER and PHYSICAL].

HYPERPIESIA, [hī'-per-pī-ēz-i-a], *n.* (*med.*) abnormally high blood pressure. [HYPER and Gk. *piesis* pressure].

HYPERPYREXIA, [hī'-per-pī-rek'-si-a], *n.* (*path.*) abnormally high temperature. [HYPER and MdL. *pyrexia* fever].

HYPERSARCOSIS, [hī'-per-sahk-ō'-sis], *n.* (*path.*) proud flesh. [HYPER and Gk. *sarx* flesh].

HYPERSENSITIVE, [hī'-per-sen'-sit-iv], *adj.* extremely sensitive. [HYPER and SENSITIVE].

HYPERSTHENE, [hī'-per-sthēn], *n.* a mineral of iron and magnesium of the hornblende group. [HYPER and Gk. *sthenos* strength].

HYPERSTHENIA, [hī'-per-sthē'-ni-a], *n.* abnormal excitement of vital phenomena. [HYPER and Gk. *sthenos* strength].

HYPERTENSION, [hī'-per-ten'-shun], *n.* an extreme state of tension. [HYPER and TENSION].

HYPERTHYROID, [hī'-per-thī'-roid], *adj.* (*psych.*) relating to, derived from, over-activity of the thyroid gland. [HYPER and THYROID].

HYPERTHYROIDISM, [hī'-per-thī'-roid-izm], *n.* (*path.*) a condition caused by over-activity of the thyroid gland, Graves' disease.

HYPERTROPHIED, [hī-pur'-trō-fid], *adj.* (*path.*) morbidly enlarged; (*fig.*) over-developed.

HYPERTROPHY, [hī-pur'-trō-fi], *n.* (*med.*) a morbid enlargement of an organ or part of an organism. [HYPER and Gk. *trophe* nourishment].

HYPHA, (*pl.* **hyphae**), [hī'-fa], *n.* (*bot.*) the matter forming the mycelium of a fungus. [Gk. *huphe* web].

HYPHEN (1), [hī'-fen], *n.* a short, horizontal dash connecting words or syllables. [Gk. *huph hen* under one (head)].

HYPHEN (2), [hī'-fen], *v.t.* to hyphenate.

HYPHENATE, [hī'-fen-āt], *v.t.* to connect by a hyphen.

HYPHENATED, [hī'-fen-āt'-id], *adj.* joined by a hyphen.

HYPNOID, [hip'-noid], *adj.* of, or relating to, hypnosis. [Gk. *hupnos* sleep and *oeides* like].

HYPNOLOGY, [hip-nol'-o-ji], *n.* the study of sleep. [Gk. *hupnos* sleep and *logos* speech].

HYPNOSIS, [hip-nō'-sis], *n.* a deep sleep, artificially induced, in which the sleeper is sensitive to external suggestions; a hypnotic state. [Gk. *hupnos* sleep].

HYPNOTIC (1), [hip-not'-ik], *n.* a medicine or drug that induces sleep, soporific; a person who is easily hypnotized.

HYPNOTIC (2), [hip-not'-ik], *adj.* inducing sleep, narcotic, soporific; relating to hypnosis or to hypnotism. [Gk. *hupnotikos* sleepy].

HYPNOTISM, [hip'-not-izm], *n.* an artificially induced state of sleep; the theory and practice of inducing sleep by hypnosis; (*fig.*) the power to render a person fascinated or open to suggestion.

HYPO (1), [hī'-pō], *n.* hyposulphite of soda, used for fixing photographic prints and negatives. [HYPO-(SULPHITE)].

HYPO- (2), *pref.* beneath. [Gk. *hupo*].

HYPOBOLE, [hī-pob'-o-li], *n.* (*rhet.*) the inclusion in an argument of possible objections to it, together with their refutation. [Gk. *hupoballo* I suggest].

HYPOCAUST, [hī'-pō-kawst], *n.* a sunken heating chamber to warm a hothouse; the hot-air chamber under a Roman bath. [Gk. *hupokauston* burnt below].

HYPOCHONDRIA, [hī'-pō-kon'-dri-a], *n.* chronic nervous and mental disorder characterized by depression, melancholy, and excessive concern for health. [Gk. *hupokhondria* the upper parts of the stomach].

HYPOCHONDRIAC (1), [hī'-pō-kon'-dri-ak], *n.* a person who suffers from hypochondria.

HYPOCHONDRIAC (2), [hī'-pō-kon'-dri-ak], *adj.*

relating to hypochondria. [Gk. *hupokhondriakos*].

HYPOCHONDRIACAL, [hī'-pō-kon-drī'-ak-al], *adj.* hypochondriac.

HYPOCHONDRIACALLY, [hī'-pō-kon-drī'-ak-al-i], *adv.* in a hypochondriacal fashion.

HYPOCHONDRIACISM, [hī'-po-kon-drī'-as-izm], *n.* hypochondriasis.

HYPOCHONDRIASIS, [hī'-pō-kon-drī'-as-is], *n.* (*med.*) hypochondria.

HYPOCHONDRIUM, [hī'-pō-kon'-dri-um], *n.* (*anat.*) the region below the short ribs and above the abdomen. [Gk. *hupokhondrion*].

HYPOCHROMAT, [hī'-pō-krō'-mat], *n.* one unable to distinguish between colours. [HYPO (2) and Gk. *khroma khromatos* colour].

HYPOCORISTIC, [hī'-pō-ko-rist'-ik], *adj.* pertaining to a nickname or a euphemism. [Gk. *hupokoristikos*].

HYPOCRATERIFORM, [hī'-pō-krā-ter'-i-fawm], *adj.* (*bot.*) resembling a salver. [Gk. *hupokraterion* salver and FORM].

HYPOCRISY, [hip-ok'-ra-si], *n.* the practice of disguising one action or statement by simulating another which is believed to be more acceptable, dissimulation; pretended goodness or sincerity. [ME. *ipocrisie* from Gk. *hupokrisis* an acting on the stage].

HYPOCRITE, [hip'-ō-krit], *n* a person who uses hypocrisy. [ME. *ipocrite* from Gk. *hupokrites* actor].

HYPOCRITICAL, [hip'-ō-krit'-ik-al], *adj.* relating to hypocrisy; practising hypocrisy. [Gk. *hupokritikos*].

HYPOCRITICALLY, [hip'-ō-krit'-ik-al-i], *adv.* in a hypocritical fashion.

HYPODERMIC (1), [hī'-pō-durm'-ik], *n.* a drug injected under the skin; the act of making such an injection.

HYPODERMIC (2), [hī'-pō-durm'-ik], *adj.* beneath the skin; **h. syringe,** a syringe to inject drugs, etc., beneath the skin. [HYPO and DERM].

HYPOGASTRIC, [hī'-pō-gas'-trik], *adj.* (*anat.*) pertaining to the hypogastrium. [HYPO and GASTRIC].

HYPOGASTRIUM, [hī'-pō-gas'-tri-um], *n.* (*anat.*) the middle part of the abdomen. [Gk. *hupogastrion* belly].

HYPOGASTROCELE, [hī'-pō-gas'-trō-sēl], *n.* (*med.*) a hernia in the hypogastrium. [Gk. *hupogastrion* and *kele* tumour].

HYPOGEAN, [hī'-pō-jē'-an], *adj.* beneath the ground. [HYPO and Gk. *ge* the soil].

HYPOGENE, [hī'-pō-jēn], *adj.* (*geol.*) (of rocks) formed under the surface. [HYPO and Gk. *genes* born of].

HYPOGEUM, [hī'-pō-jē'-um], *n.* (*arch.*) that part of a building lying beneath the ground; an underground vault. [Gk. *hupogeios* underground].

HYPOGLOSSAL, [hī'-pō-glos'-al], *adj.* (*anat.*) under the tongue, *esp.* of the large nerve there. [HYPO and Gk. *glossa* tongue].

HYPOGNATHOUS, [hī-pog'-nath-us], *adj.* (*zool.*) with the lower mandible extending beyond the upper. [HYPO and Gk. *gnathos* jaw].

HYPOGYNOUS, [hī-poj'-in-us], *adj.* (*bot.*) growing from beneath the pistils or ovary. [HYPO and Gk. *gune* woman].

HYPOPHOSPHITE, [hī'-pō-fos'-fīt], *n.* (*chem.*) a compound of hypophosphorous acid. [HYPO and PHOSPHITE].

HYPOPHOSPHOROUS, [hī'-pō-fos'-fer-us], *adj.* (*chem.*) pertaining to an acid of phosphorus.

HYPOPHYSIS, [hī-pof'-is-is], *n.* (*anat.*) the pituitary body of the brain. [Gk. *hupophusis* offshoot].

HYPOSTASIS, [hī-pos'-tas-is], *n.* (*philos.*) the reality or basis behind all being; (*theol.*) any one of the persons of the Trinity; (*med.*) an excess of blood. [Gk. *hupostasis* substance].

HYPOSTATIC, [hī'-pō-stat'-ik], *adj.* (*philos.*) relating to an hypostasis, fundamental; **h. union,** (*theol.*) the union of distinct natures, as human and divine, in one person, as exemplified in Jesus Christ. [Gk. *hupostatikos*].

HYPOSTATIZE, [hī-pos'-tat-īz], *v.t.* to look upon (an abstract idea) as a distinct substance or as a person having a real existence.

HYPOSTROPHE, [hī-pos'-tro-fi], *n.* (*path.*) a relapse in illness, return of a disease. [Gk. *hupostrophe* turning back].

HYPOSTYLE, [hī'-pō-stīl], *n.* (*arch.*) anything supported by pillars; a colonnade. [Gk. *hupostulos*].

HYPOTAXIS, [hī'-pō-tak'-sis], *n.* (*gram.*) a subordinate or dependent construction. [HYPO and Gk. *tasso* I place].

HYPOTENUSE, [hī-pot'-en-yōōs], *n.* (*geom.*) that side of a right-angled triangle which faces and closes the right angle. [Gk. *hupoteinousa* (*gramme*) a subtending line].

HYPOTHEC, [hī'-pō-thek], *n.* (*Scots leg.*) the security which a creditor has over goods belonging to a debtor. [Gk. *hupotithemi* I pledge].

HYPOTHECARY, [hī-poth'-ek-er-i], *adj.* (*Scots leg.*) relating to a hypothec, in acknowledgment of a debt. [L. *hypothecarius*].

HYPOTHECATE, [hī-poth'-ik-āt], *v.t.* (*leg.*) to pledge as security for a debt. [LL. *hypothecare*].

HYPOTHECATION, [hī-poth'-ik-ā'-shun], *n.* the act of hypothecating. [LL. *hypothecatio*].

HYPOTHECATOR, [hī-poth'-ik-āt'-er], *n.* (*leg.*) a person who hypothecates, a mortgagor.

HYPOTHESIS, (*pl.* **hypotheses**), [hī-poth'-is-is], *n.* an assumption adopted as a basis for argument and which, though admitted, is not backed by a proof of its correctness. [Gk. *hupothesis* foundation].

HYPOTHETIC, [hī'-poth-et'-ik], *adj.* assumed for the sake of argument, hypothetical. [Gk. *hupothetikos*].

HYPOTHETICAL, [hī'-poth-et'-ik-al], *adj.* hypothetic.

HYPOTHETICALLY, [hī'-poth-et'-ik-al-i], *adv.* in a hypothetical manner.

HYPOTHYROIDISM, [hī-pō-thī'-roid-izm], *n.* (*med.*) a condition of morbid underactivity of the thyroid gland. [HYPO (2) and THYROID].

HYPOTYPOSIS, [hī'-pō-tī-pō'-sis], *n.* (*rhet.*) vivid presentation of a scene, event, etc., so as to give the reader or listener an impression almost as clear as that of an eye-witness. [Gk. *hupotuposis* outline].

HYPOZOIC, [hī'-pō-zō'-ik], *adj.* (*geol.*) lying under strata containing organic remains. [HYPO and Gk. *zoe* life].

HYPPISH, [hip'-ish], *adj.* (*slang*) affected with hypochondria; miserable.

HYPSOMETER, [hip-som'-it-er], *n.* an instrument which registers altitudes by measuring atmospheric pressure. [Gk. *hupsos* height and METER].

HYPSOMETRY, [hip-som'-it-ri], *n.* the technique of measuring altitudes. [Gk. *hupsos* height and *metria* measuring].

HYPURAL, [hī-pew'-ral], *adj.* placed under the tail. [HYPO and Gk. *oura* tail].

HYRAX, [hī'-raks], *n.* one of several African species of small mammals having hoofs resembling those of the guinea-pig. [Gk. *hurax* shrewmouse].

HYSON, [hī'-sun], *n.* a variety of green tea from China. [Chin. *hyson* blooming spring].

HYSSOP, [his'-op], *n.* a kind of mint, *Hyssopus officinalis*; the popular name of various aromatic herbs. [Gk. *hussopos*].

HYSTERANTHOUS, [his-ter-an'-thus], *adj.* (*bot.*) (of plants) whose leaves appear after the blossom. [Gk. *husteros* later and *anthos* flower].

HYSTERECTOMY, [his'-ter-ek'-to-mi], *n.* excision of the womb. [Gk. *hustera* womb and *ektome* cutting out].

HYSTERESIS, [his-ter-ē'-sis], *n.* (*phys.*) the time-lag between the magnetic force itself and its effects. [Gk. *husteros* later].

HYSTERIA, [his-tēer'-i-a], *n.* a nervous disorder characterized by wild behaviour, shrieking, or giggling fits and excessive emotional excitement; (*fig.*) wild excitement. [Gk. *hustera* womb].

HYSTERIC, [his-te'-rik], *adj.* hysterical. [Gk. *husterikos* relating to the womb].

HYSTERICAL, [his-te'-rik-al], *adj.* pertaining to, affected by, hysteria; (*fig.*) excessively emotional.

HYSTERICALLY, [his-te'-rik-al-i], *adv.* in a hysterical fashion.

HYSTERICS, [his-te'-riks], *n.* a fit of hysteria.

HYSTERIFORM (1), [his-te-ri-fawm], *adj.* (*med.*) resembling or pertaining to hysteria. [HYSTERIA].

HYSTERIFORM (2), [his-te'-ri-fawm], *adj.* resembling or of the genus *Hysterium* of fungi.

HYSTERITIS, [his'-ter-ī'-tis], *n.* (*med.*) inflammation of the uterus. [Gk. *hustera* womb and *itis* denoting inflammation].

HYSTEROID, [his'-te-roid], *adj.* resembling hysteria. [HYSTERIA and Gk. *oeides* like].

HYSTERON-PROTERON, [his'-ter-on-prot'-er-on], *n.* (*gram.*) an inverting of the logical or usual form of an expression. [Gk. *husteron proteron* latter former].

HYSTEROTOMY, [his'-ter-ot'-o-mi], *n.* (*med.*) an incision made in the womb. [Gk. *hustera* womb and *tome* cutting].

HYTHE, see HITHE.

I

I (1), [i], the ninth letter and third vowel of the English and related alphabets.

I (2), [ī], *pron., 1st. per. sg. nom.* of the personal pronoun. [OE. *ic*].

IAMB, [ī'-amb'], *n.* an iambus.

IAMBIC (1), [ī-am'-bik], *n.* an iambic foot or verse; (*pl.*) verses containing, or composed of, iambic feet.

IAMBIC (2), [ī-am'-bik], *adj.* consisting of iambuses; composing in iambuses. [Gk. *iambikos*].

IAMBICALLY, [ī-am'-bĭk-al-i], *adv.* in the fashion of iambics.

IAMBUS, [ī-am'-bus], *n.* (*pros.*) a metrical foot consisting of a short syllable followed by a long or an unaccented syllable followed by an accented. [Gk. *iambos*].

IATRICAL, [i-at'-rik-al], *adj.* pertaining to medicine or physicians, medical. [Gk. *iatrikos*].

IATROLEPTIC, [ī'-a-trō-lept'-ik], *adj.* (*med.*) healing by rubbing the skin with remedial preparations. [Gk. *iatros* physician and *aleipho* I anoint].

IBERIAN (1), [ī-bēer'-i-an], *n.* an inhabitant of Iberia, *i.e.* Spain, Portugal and the Pyrenees; the language of Iberia; (*anthrop.*) a member of the prehistoric neolithic race of Western Europe, North Africa, and Britain.

IBERIAN (2), [ī-bēer'-i-an], *adj.* pertaining to Iberia or the Iberians. [L. *Iberia*].

IBEX, [ī'-beks], *n.* a mountain wild goat of the genus *Capra*. [L. *ibex*].

IBID, [ib'-id], *adv.* abbreviation of IBIDEM.

IBIDEM, [ib-ī'-dem], *adv.* in the same place, on the same page, etc.; from the same author, work, part, etc. [L. *ibidem*].

IBIS, [ī'-bis], *n.* a genus of wading birds related to the storks, one species of which was worshipped in Egypt. [Gk. *ibis*].

IBEX

ICARIAN, [ik-āer'-i-an], *adj.* disastrously ambitious or venturesome. [*Icarus*, son of Daedalus, who, in escaping from Crete, soared too near the sun and fell into the sea, as the wax securing his artificial wings melted].

ICE (1), [is], *n.* frozen water; an ice-cream; **to cut no i.,** to fail to impress; **to break the i.,** to overcome natural reserve or formal politeness; to take the first steps in any enterprise; **on thin i.,** on delicate ground. [OE. *is*].

ICE (2), [is], *v.t.* to freeze; to chill with ice; to cover with ice or icing.

ICE AGE, [is'-āj], *n.* (*geol.*) an epoch in which ice-fields and glaciers covered much of the surface of the earth.

ICE-ANCHOR, [is'-angk'-er], *n.* a large grapnel for securing ships to the ice.

ICE-AXE, [is'-aks], *n.* an axe used for cutting footholds, etc., in the ice.

ICEBELT, [is'-belt], *n.* the border of ice along the Arctic shores.

ICEBERG, [is'-burg], *n.* a huge mass of floating ice, partially submerged. [~Dan. *iisbierg*, Du. *ijsberg*].

ICE-BIRD, [is'-burd], *n.* the glaucous gull; the little auk; the Indian nightjar, *Caprimulgus asiaticus*.

ICEBLINK, [is'-blingk], *n.* a shining whiteness on the horizon caused by the reflection of light from the ice.

ICE-BOAT, [is'-bōt], *n.* an ice-breaker; a light boat equipped with runners for sailing over ice.

ICEBOUND, [is'-bownd], *adj.* hemmed in and brought to a standstill by ice.

ICE-BOX, [is'-boks], *n.* (*coll.*) a refrigerator.

ICE-BREAKER, [is'-brāk'-er], *n.* a steamer strongly built for the purpose of forcing a way through floating ice.

ICE-CAP, [is'-kap], *n.* a permanent sheet of ice covering the top of a mountain; land round the North or South Poles, etc.

ICE-CHISEL, [is'-chizl], *n.* a long-handled, socketed chisel for cutting holes in ice, or splitting blocks of ice.

ICE-CREAM, [is'-krēm'], *n.* a flavoured and sweetened mixture of frozen cream or custard.

ICE-FIELD, [is'-fēld], *n.* a wide region of ice.

ICE-FLOE, [is'-flō], *n.* a large mass of floating ice.

ICE-FOOT, [is'-fŏŏt], *n.* a solid barrier of ice formed along the coast in Arctic and Antarctic regions.

ICE-HOUSE, [is'-hows], *n.* a storehouse for ice.

ICELANDER, [is'-land-er], *n.* a native of Iceland.

ICELANDIC (1), [is-land'-ik], *n.* the language of Iceland.

ICELANDIC (2), [is-land'-ik], *adj.* pertaining to Iceland.

ICELAND MOSS, [is'-land-mos'], *n.* a north European lichen, *Cetraria islandica*, used medicinally and as food.

ICELAND-SPAR, [is'-land-spah(r)'], *n.* a transparent variety of calcite.

ICEMAN, [is'-man], *n.* a person skilled in travelling over ice.

ICEMANSHIP, [is'-man-ship], *n.* skill in journeying upon ice.

ICEPACK, [is'-pak], *n.* a large, solid body formed by masses of broken floating ice packed tightly together.

ICE-PAIL, [is'-pāl], *n.* a pail containing ice in which wine, etc., is cooled.

ICE-PLANT, [is'-plahnt], *n.* a variety of *Mesembryanthemum*, whose leaves seem to be covered with frost.

ICE PUDDING, [is'-pŏŏd'-ing], *n.* a pudding made of ice-cream.

ICE-SHEET, [is'-shēt], *n.* a layer of ice spread over a great area of land, *esp.* that believed to have covered a large part of the northern hemisphere during the Ice Age.

ICE-SPAR, [is'-spah(r)], *n.* ryacolite, a greyish translucent mineral with a vitreous lustre, consisting mainly of silica.

ICHABOD, [ik'-a-bod], *int.* exclamation of regret, from the name given by the daughter-in-law of Eli to her son. [1 Samuel iv, 21].

ICHNEUMON, [ik-new'-mon], *n.* a small Eastern brownish-coloured carnivore of the genus *Herpestes*, feeding on the eggs of crocodiles; **i. fly,** a parasitic hymenopterous insect laying its eggs on the larvae of other insects. [Gk. *ikhneumon* tracker].

ICHNOGRAPHIC, [ik'-nō-graf'-ik], *adj.* ichnographical.

ICHNOGRAPHICAL, [ik'-nō-graf'-ik-al], *adj.* relating to ichnography; describing a ground plan.

ICHNOGRAPHY, [ik-nog'-raf-i], *n.* (*arch.*) a horizontal section of a building, etc., a ground plan. [Gk. *ikhnographia*].

ICHNOLITE, [ik'-nō-līt], *n.* a fossil footprint. [Gk. *ikhnos* track and *lithos* stone].

ICHNOLOGY, [ik-nol'-oj-i], *n.* the scientific study of fossil footprints. [Gk. *ikhnos* track and *logos* speech].

ICHOR, [ī'-kaw(r)], *n.* (*Gk. myth.*) an ethereal fluid, corresponding to blood, in the veins of the gods; (*path.*) a thin watery discharge of matter from a wound or sore. [Gk. *ikhor*].

ICHOROUS, [ī'-ker-us], *adj.* resembling ichor; thin; serous.

ICHTHY(O)-, [ik'-thi(ō)], *pref.* pertaining to fish. [Gk. *ikhthus* fish].

ICHTHYIC, [ik'-thē-ik], *adj.* of, or resembling, a fish.

ICHTHYODORULITE, [ik'-thi-o-do'-ryŏŏ-līt], *n.* a fossil fish-spine. [ICHTHYO and Gk. *doru* spear and *lithos* stone].

ICHTHYOGRAPHY, [ik'-thi-og'-raf-i], *n.* a dissertation on fishes. [ICHTHYO and Gk. *graphia* writing].

ICHTHYOID (1), [ik'-thi-oid], *n.* a fish-like vertebrate.

ICHTHYOID (2), [ik'-thi-oid], *adj.* resembling or allied to a fish. [ICHTHYO and Gk. *oeides* like].

ICHTHYOLATRY, [ik'-thi-ol'-a-tri], *n.* worship of a god represented as a fish. [ICHTHYO and Gk. *latreia* worship].

ICHTHYOLITE, [ik'-thi-ō-līt], *n.* a fossil fish or its impression. [ICHTHYO and Gk. *lithos* stone].

ICHTHYOLOGICAL, [ik'-thi-ō-loj'-ik-al], *adj.* relating to ichthyology.

ICHTHYOLOGIST, [ik'-thi-ol'-oj-ist], *n.* one versed in ichthyology.

ICHTHYOLOGY, [ik'-thi-ol'-oj-i], *n.* the scientific study of fishes. [ICHTHYO and Gk. *logos* speech].
ICHTHYOPHAGIST, [ik'-thi-of'-aj-ist], *n.* one who lives on fish.
ICHTHYOPHAGOUS, [ik'-thi-of'-ag-us], *adj.* living on fish, fish-eating. [Gk. *ikhthuophagos*].
ICHTHYOPHAGY, [ik'-thi-of'-aj-i], *n.* the habit of eating fish. [Gk. *ikhthuophagia* a diet of fish].
ICHTHYOPHTHALMITE, [ik'-thi-of-thal'-mīt], *n.* apophyllite, fish-eye stone. [ICHTHYO and Gk. *ophthalmos* eye].
ICHTHYORNIS, [ik'-thi-awn'-is], *n.* a genus of fossil-toothed birds. [ICHTHYO and Gk. *ornis* bird].
ICHTHYOSAURUS, [ik'-thi-ō-saw'-rus], *n.* an extinct marine animal having an immense head, tapering body and four paddle-like limbs. [ICHTHYO and Gk. *sauros* lizard].

ICHTHYOSAURUS

ICHTHYOSIS, [ik'-thi-ō'-sis], *n.* (*path.*) a skin disease in which the part affected becomes hard, dry and scaly. [ICHTHYO and Gk. *osis* denoting condition].
ICHTHYOTOMY, [ik'-thi-ot'-om-i], *n.* the dissection of fishes. [ICHTHYO and Gk. *tomos* cutting].
ICICLE, [is'-ikl], *n.* a slender, tapering pendant of ice formed by the freezing of dripping or slowly running water. [OE. *is-gicel*].
ICILY, [īs'-i-li], *adv.* in an icy way.
ICINESS, [īs'-i-nes], *n.* the quality of being icy.
ICING, [is'-ing], *n.* powdered sugar mixed with the white of an egg, milk, and some flavouring substance, used as a covering for cakes.
ICON, [ī'-kon], *n.* a representation of some holy person in painting or metallic low relief, honoured as a sacred object, *esp.* in the Eastern Orthodox Church. [Gk. *eikon*].
ICONO-, *pref.* relating to an image. [Gk. *eikon* image].
ICONOCLASM, [ī-kon'-ō-klazm], *n.* the breaking of images or sacred objects; (*fig.*) the destruction of popular beliefs, customs, etc., commonly regarded with reverence. [ICONO and Gk. *klasma* breaking].
ICONOCLAST, [ī-kon'-ō-klast], *n.* a breaker of images or idols; (*eccles. hist.*) one who wished to abolish images and pictures in the Eastern Christian churches in the 8th and 9th centuries; (*fig.*) a destroyer of beliefs, institutions, etc., generally considered as sacrosanct. [Gk. *eikonoklastes*].
ICONOCLASTIC, [ī-kon'-ō-klast'-ik], *adj.* breaking images; (*fig.*) overthrowing traditional institutions, beliefs, etc.
ICONOGRAPHY, [ī'-kon-og'-raf-i], *n.* the representation of objects or persons by portraits, figures, images, etc.; the art of illustration; the study of the portraits, statues, etc., of a particular person. [Gk. *eikonographia* description].
ICONOLATER, [ī'-kon-ol'-at-er], *n.* a worshipper of images.
ICONOLATRY, [ī'-kon-ol'-at-ri], *n.* the worship of images. [Gk. *eikonolatreia*].
ICONOLOGY, [ī'-kon-ol'-oj-i], *n.* the study of icons. [ICONO and Gk. *logos* speech].
ICONOMACHY, [ī'-kon-om'-ak-i], *n.* strong opposition to the use of religious images. [ICONO and Gk. *makhe* battle].
ICONOMETER, [ī'-kon-om'-it-er], *n.* (*phot.*) a view-finder through which the object to be photographed is seen directly, and not as a reflected image; (*surveying*) an instrument used in finding the size and distance of an object. [ICONO and METER].
ICONOSTASIS, [ī'-kon-os'-tas-is], *n.* (*Gk. Church*) an ornamental altar screen embellished with icons. [ICONO and Gk. *stasis* standing].
ICOSAHEDRAL, [ī'-ko-sa-hē'-dral], *adj.* having twenty sides or faces.
ICOSAHEDRON, [ī'-ko-sa-hē'-dron], *n.* a solid bounded by twenty planes. [Gk. *eikosaedron*].
ICOSANDRIAN, [ī'-kos-an'-dri-an], *adj.* (*bot.*) having twenty or more stamens in the calyx. [Gk. *eikosi* twenty and *aner andros* man].
ICTERIC (1), [ik-te'-rik], *n.* a cure for jaundice; a person suffering from jaundice.
ICTERIC (2), [ik-te'-rik], *adj.* pertaining to, similar to jaundice; suffering from, remedial against jaundice. [Gk. *ikterikos*].
ICTERINE, [ik'-ter-īn], *adj.* yellow; **I. warbler**, the tree warbler, *Hypolais icterina*.
ICTERITIOUS, [ik'-ter-ish'-us], *adj.* suffering from jaundice; (*fig.*) biased. [MedL. *icteritia* jaundice].
ICTIC, [ik'-tik], *adj.* sudden, abrupt, sharp.
ICTUS, [ik'-tus], *n.* (*pros.*) rhythmical accentuation. [L. *ictus* a blow, stroke].
ICY, [ī'-si], *adj.* covered with, consisting of, resembling, ice; extremely cold; (*fig.*) indifferent, aloof.
ID, [id], *n.* (*psychol.*) the total of instinctive impulses in the individual. [L. *id* it].
IDEA, [ī-dē'-a], *n.* that which exists in the mind as a result of mental activity, a mental conception; a notion; a vague impression, fancy, feeling; opinion; thought; plan, intention; principle behind anything; (*Gk. philos.*) the universal, eternal, immaterial pattern of which all material things are but imperfect copies; (*modern philos.*) the immediate object of thought, understanding or perception; absolute truth which lies behind the existence of all phenomena. [Gk. *idea* form, kind, ideal pattern].
IDEAL (1), [ī-dē'-al], *n.* a conception of supreme excellence, *esp.* when set up in the mind as a standard to be aspired to; anything or anyone who exemplifies such a conception; something which exists only in the mind.
IDEAL (2), [ī-dē'-al], *adj.* existing only as an idea; realized only in the imagination; best conceivable, typifying or realizing one's notion of supreme excellence, perfect; representing an idea. [LL. *idealis* of an idea].
IDEALESS, [ī-dē'-a-les], *adj.* without ideas.
IDEALISM, [ī-dē'-al-izm], *n.* (*philos.*) the theory that resolves the universe into ideas as the only existences or objects of perception; the tendency to form ideals or to idealize; ideal treatment in art or literature.
IDEALIST, [ī-dē'-al-ist], *n.* one who bases his conduct and mode of thought upon ideals; one who concerns himself with ideals, an impractical visionary; an artist or writer treating his subjects from an ideal point of view; (*philos.*) an upholder of idealism.
IDEALISTIC, [ī'-dē-al-ist'-ik], *adj.* pertaining to, based upon, characterized by, idealism.
IDEALITY, [ī'-dē-al'-i-ti], *n.* the quality of being ideal; that which is ideal; the faculty or power of idealizing.
IDEALIZATION, [ī'-dē-al-īz-ā'-shun], *n.* the act of idealizing, the state of being idealized; an idealized representation or treatment of anything.
IDEALIZE, [ī-dē'-al-īz], *v.t. and i.* to make ideal, to treat from an ideal point of view; to form ideals.
IDEALLY, [ī-dē'-al-li], *adv.* in an ideal fashion.
IDEALOGUE, [ī-dē'-al-og], *n.* an idealist; an impractical dreamer.
IDEATE, [ī-dē'-āt], *v.t. and i.* to form an idea of, to imagine; to form ideas.
IDEATION, [ī'-dē-ā'-shun], *n.* the act of forming ideas.
IDEATIONAL, [ī'-dē-ā'-shun-al], *adj.* relating to ideation.
IDEE FIXE, idée fixe, [ē'-dā-fēks'], *n.* an obsession. [Fr. *idée fixe*].
IDEM, [ī'-dem], *n.* the same book, author, name, reference, etc. [L. *idem* the same].
IDENTICAL, [ī-dent'-ik-al], *adj.* the very same; exactly alike. [MedL. *identicus*].
IDENTICALLY, [ī-dent'-ik-al-i], *adv.* in identical fashion.
IDENTICALNESS, [ī-dent'-ik-al-nes], *n.* the quality of being identical.
IDENTIFIABLE, [ī-dent'-i-fī'-abl], *adj.* able to be identified.
IDENTIFICATION, [ī-dent'-i-fi-kā'-shun], *n.* the act of identifying; the state of being identified; **i. card, disk**, etc., a card, disk, etc., to prove one's identity.
IDENTIFY, [ī-dent'-i-fī], *v.t.* to establish the identity of, to prove to be a particular thing or person; (*reflex.*) to associate oneself closely (with). [LL. *identificare*].
IDENTITY, [ī-dent'-i-ti], *n.* the fact or state of being a given person or thing; the quality of being identical. [LL. *identitas*].
IDEO-, *pref.* kind, idea. [Gk. *idea* form].
IDEOGRAM, [id'-ē-ō-gram], *n.* an ideograph. [IDEO and Gk. *gramma* something written].
IDEOGRAPH, [id'-ē-ō-graf], *n.* a character used in writing, in certain languages as Chinese, which symbolizes the idea of an object or the object itself, and is not merely an orthographical representation of a speech sound. [IDEO and GRAPH].
IDEOGRAPHIC, [id'-ē-ō-graf'-ik], *adj.* representing

or expressing ideas or things directly by figures or ideographs.

IDEOLOGICAL, [īd'-ē-ō-loj'-ik-al], *adj.* relating to ideology.

IDEOLOGIST, [īd'-ē-ol'-oj-ist], *n.* one who studies ideology.

IDEOLOGY, [īd'-ē-ol'-oj-i], *n.* the science of ideas; the theory deriving all ideas from sensations; impractical, ideal speculation; (*pol.*) a set of ideas or theories governing a political, religious, or economic system. [IDEO and Gk. *logos* speech].

IDEOPRAXIST, [īd'-ē-ō-praks'-ist], *n.* one who in his work or actions puts into practice an idea. [IDEO and Gk. *praxis* doing].

IDES, [idz], *n.*(*pl.*) (*Rom. hist.*) the 15th of March, May, July, and October, and the 13th of other months, being one of the three days in each month of the Roman calendar used in reckoning dates. [L. *idus*].

IDIO-, *pref.* one's own, distinct, individual. [Gk. *idios*].

IDIOCRACY, [id'-i-ok'-ras-i], *n.* personal or private government. [IDIO and Gk. *kratia* rule].

IDIOCRATIC, [id'-i-ō-krat'-ik], *adj.* relating to idiocracy.

IDIOCRATICAL, [id'-i-ō-krat'-ik-al], *adj.* idiocratic.

IDIOCY, [id'-i-o-si], *n.* the state of being an idiot, extreme mental defectiveness; extremely stupid behaviour. [Gk. *idioteia* private life, lack of education].

IDIOGRAPH, [id'-i-ō-graf], *n.* a private signature or trade-mark. [IDIO and GRAPH].

IDIOM, [id'-i-um], *n.* a special turn of phrase, expression, grammatical construction, etc., characteristic of a particular language; the language of a particular people or country; a dialect; the essential spirit or nature of a language. [Gk. *idioma*].

IDIOMATIC, [id'-i-ō-mat'-ik], *adj.* peculiar to a language; exhibiting the idioms of a language; full of, characterized by, idioms; of the nature of an idiom. [Gk. *idiomatikos*].

IDIOMATICALLY, [id'-i-ō-mat'-ik-al-i], *adv.* in an idiomatic fashion.

IDIOMORPHIC, [id'-i-ō-mawf'-ik], *adj.* having its own distinctive form. [IDIO and Gk. *morphe* shape].

IDIOMORPHOUS, [id'-i-ō-mawf'-us], *adj.* idiomorphic.

IDIOPATHIC, [id'-i-ō-path'-ik], *adj.* (of a disease) not produced or arising from another disease. [IDIO and PATHIC].

IDIOPATHICALLY, [id'-i-ō-path'-ik-al-i], *adv.* in the fashion of an idiopathic disease.

IDIOPATHY, [id'-i-op'-ath-i], *n.* (*path.*) a morbid condition not caused by a preceding disease. [IDIO and Gk. *patheia* suffering].

IDIOSYNCRASY, [id'-i-ō-singk'-ras-i], *n.* a peculiarity of mental constitution, temperament or character; a characteristic and individualistic mannerism or mode of expression; (*med.*) the physical constitution of a particular individual. [Gk. *idiosugkrasia*].

IDIOSYNCRATIC, [id'-i-ō-singk-rat'-ik], *adj.* peculiar to a particular individual or thing. [IDIO and Gk. *sugkratikos* mixing].

IDIOT, [id'-i-ot], *n.* an imbecile, an extremely mentally defective person; (*coll.*) an utter fool. [Gk. *idiotes* a private individual, an uneducated person].

IDIOTCY, [id'-i-ot-si], *n.* the state of being an idiot.

IDIOTIC, [id'-i-ot'-ik], *adj.* like, characteristic of, relating to, an idiot; senseless, extremely stupid. [Gk. *idiotikos*].

IDIOTICALLY, [id'-i-ot'-ik-al-i], *adv.* in idiotic fashion.

IDIOTICON, [id'-i-ot'-ik-on], *n.* a dictionary of words found only in a dialect. [Gk. *idiotikon*].

IDIOTISH†, [id'-i-ot-ish], *adj.* like an idiot, senseless.

IDIOTISM, [id'-i-ot-izm], *n.* an idiom; idiocy. [Gk. *idiotismos* a common or vulgar fashion].

IDIOTIZE, [id'-i-ot-īz], *v.t. and i.* to become idiotic; to make a fool of. [Gk. *idiotizo* I put into the common tongue].

IDLE (1), [īdl], *adj.* unemployed, doing nothing; inactive, not in use; lazy, unwilling to work; unprofitable, vain; frivolous, unimportant; unfounded. [OE. *idel*].

IDLE (2), [īdl], *v.i.* to remain idle, to waste time.

IDLENESS, [īdl'-nes], *n.* the state or quality of being idle. [OE. *idelness*].

IDLER, [id'-ler], *n.* one who wastes his time in idleness.

IDLE-WHEEL, [īdl'-wēl], *n.* a cogged wheel placed between two other wheels which cannot be geared directly, in order to transmit motion.

IDLY, [id'-li], *adv.* in idle fashion.

IDO, [ē'-dō], *n.* an artificial world language after the manner of Esperanto.

IDOCRASE, [ī'-dō-krās], *n.* a translucent silicate of lime and aluminium, displaying double refraction. [Gk. *eidos* form and *krasis* mixing].

IDOL, [ī'-dol], *n.* a visible image, statue, etc., of an unseen deity or object of worship; a false god; a person or object devoutly admired or adored; the extreme favourite; a false idea, belief or method of reasoning. [Gk. *eidolon* image].

IDOLATER, [ī-dol'-at-er], *n.* a worshipper of idols; a devout admirer. [Gk. *eidololatres*].

IDOLATRESS, [ī-dol'-at-res], *n.* a female idolater.

IDOLATRIZE, [ī-dol'-at-rīz], *v.t.* to make an idol of; (*fig.*) to worship as a god.

IDOLATROUS, [ī-dol'-at-rus], *adj.* of the nature of idolatry, practising idolatry.

IDOLATROUSLY, [ī-dol'-at-rus-li], *adv.* in idolatrous fashion.

IDOLATRY, [ī-dol'-at-ri], *n.* the worship of idols, images or false gods; (*fig.*) extravagant admiration. [Gk. *eidololatreia*].

IDOLIZATION, [ī'-dol-īz-ā'-shun], *n.* the act of idolizing.

IDOLIZE, [ī'-dol-īz], *v.t.* to make an idol of; to worship blindly.

IDOLIZER, [ī'-dol-īz-er], *n.* a person who idolizes.

IDOLOCLAST, [ī-dol'-ō-klast], *n.* a destroyer of idols. [Gk. *eidolon* idol and *klastes* breaker].

IDOLUM, (*pl.* **idola**), [ī-dōl'-um], *n.* a mental image or idea; a false conception or argument. [L. *idolum*].

IDRIALITE, [ī'-dri-a-līt], *n.* a bituminous substance from the quicksilver mines of Idria. [*Idria* in Austria and Gk. *lithos* stone].

IDYLL, IDYL, [ī'-dil, id'-il], *n.* a short simple poem, *esp.* one describing everyday life amid natural or pastoral surroundings, and tinged with a flavour of romance; a similar prose composition; an incident or scene providing an admirable subject for such a poem. [Gk. *eidullion* little picture].

IDYLLIC, [ī-dil'-ik], *adj.* of the nature of an idyll; suitable for an idyll; charmingly picturesque and rural.

IF, [if], *conj.* supposing that; provided that; even though, although; whether. [OE. *gif*].

I'FAITH†, [i-fāth'], *int.* truly, indeed. [IN and FAITH].

IGLOO, [ig'-lōō], *n.* the dome-shaped dwelling of an Eskimo, built of blocks of frozen snow. [Eskimo *igloo*].

IGLOO

IGNEOUS, [ig'-ni-us], *adj.* pertaining to, consisting of, like, fire; (*geol.*) produced by the action of fire or volcanic activity. [L. *igneus*].

IGNESCENT, [ig-nes'-ent], *adj.* emitting sparks when struck; (*fig.*) easily roused. [L. *ignescens*].

IGNIFEROUS, [ig-nif'-er-us], *adj.* producing fire. [L. *ignifer*].

IGNIFLUOUS†, [ig-nif'-lōō-us], *adj.* flowing with fire. [LL. *ignifluus*].

IGNIPOTENT, [ig-nip'-ot-ent], *adj.* ruling over fire. [L. *ignipotens*].

IGNIS FATUUS, [ig'-nis-fat'-yōō-us], *n.* phosphorescence appearing at night over marshy places, due to the decomposition of organic matter under water, will-o'-the-wisp. [L. *ignis fatuus* foolish fire].

IGNITE, [ig-nīt'], *v.t. and i.* to kindle, set on fire; (*chem.*) to heat until combustion takes place; to take fire. [L. *ignitum*, *p.pt.* of *ignire*].

IGNITIBLE, [ig-nīt'-ibl], *adj.* able to be ignited.

IGNITION, [ig-nish'-un], *n.* the act of igniting; the state of being ignited; the means of firing the explosive mixture in the cylinder of an internal combustion engine. [MedL. *ignitio*].

IGNIVOMOUS, [ig-niv'-om-us], *adj.* vomiting fire. [LL. *ignivomus*].

IGNOBILITY, [ig'-nō-bil'-i-ti], *n.* ignobleness.

IGNOBLE, [ig-nōbl'], *adj.* of mean character, dishonourable, base, despicable; (*archaic*) of low birth. [L. *ignobilis*].

IGNOBLENESS, [ig-nōbl'-nes], *n.* the quality of being ignoble.

IGNOBLY, [ig-nōb'-li], *adv.* in ignoble fashion.

IGNOMINIOUS, [ig'-nō-min'-i-us], *adj.* contemptible, base, dishonourable, disgraceful, inglorious. [L. *ignominiosus*].
IGNOMINIOUSLY, [ig'-nō-min'-i-us-li], *adv.* in ignominious fashion.
IGNOMINIOUSNESS, [ig'-nō-min'-i-us-nes], *n.* ignominy.
IGNOMINY, [ig'-no-min-i], *n.* public disgrace, degradation; shameful, base conduct. [L. *ignominia*].
IGNORAMUS, [ig'-ner-ā'-mus], *n.* an ignorant person. [L. *ignoramus* we do not know].
IGNORANCE, [ig'-ner-ants], *n.* lack of general knowledge or experience; lack of particular knowledge of some specific thing. [L. *ignorantia*].
IGNORANT, [ig'-ner-ant], *adj.* uneducated, lacking general knowledge; proceeding or resulting from ignorance; uninformed, unaware of some particular thing. [L. *ignorans*].
IGNORANTLY, [ig'-ner-ant-li], *adv.* without knowledge.
IGNORE, [ig-naw(r)'], *v.t.* to take no notice of, to disregard deliberately, to pretend not to know; to refuse to recognize or consider; (*leg.*) (of a grand jury) to reject a bill for want of evidence. [L. *ignorare*].
IGNOSCIBLE†, [ig-nos'-ibl], *adj.* pardonable. [L. *ignoscibilis*].
IGUANA, [ig-wah'-na], *n.* any of a large family of American lizards, distinguished by their short, thick, non-protractile tongues, and crested backs. [Span. *iguana*].
IGUANODON, [ig'-wan'-ō-don], *n.* a large extinct herbivorous lizard. [IGUANA and Gk. *odous odontos* tooth].
IHLANG-IHLANG, [i-lang'-i-lang'], *n.* a perfume obtained from the oil of the flowers of the Malayan plant, *Cananga odoratum*; the plant itself. [Malay *ihlang-ihlang* flower of flowers].
IL-, *pref.* form of negative prefix IN-, used before *l*. [L. *il-* for *in-* when followed by *l*].
ILEAC, [il'-i-ak], *adj.* pertaining to the ileum.
ILEUM, [il'-i-um], *n.* (*anat.*) the lower portion of the small intestine. [ILIUM].
ILEUS, [il'-i-us], *n.* ileac passion, a colic caused by a stoppage in the intestines. [Gk. *ileos*, *eileos* eolic].
ILEX, [ī'-leks], *n.* the evergreen or holm-oak, *Quercus ilex*. [L. *ilex*].
ILIAC, [il'-i-ak], *adj.* pertaining to the ilium; pertaining to the ileum; **i. region,** the region of the abdomen between the ribs and the hips; **i. passion,** a severe form of colic or stoppage in the small intestine. [L. *iliacus*].
ILIAD, [il'-i-ad'], *n.* an epic poem, generally attributed to Homer, describing the events of the siege of Troy. [L. *Ilias Iliadis*].
ILIUM, (*pl.* **ilia**), [il'-i-um], *n.* (*anot.*) the upper partly-flattened portion of the hip-bone. [L. *ilium* the flanks].
ILK, [ilk], *adj.* same; **of that i.,** denotes that a person's surname is the same as that of his estate or of the clan of which he is the head. [OE. *ilca*].
ILL (1), [il], *n.* wickedness, misfortune, ailment; an unpleasant happening.
ILL (2), [il], *adj.* sick, indisposed, suffering from a disease; evil, wicked; producing evil, hostile, harmful; unfavourable; bad, poor; irritable; troublesome. [OIcel. *illr*].
ILL (3), [il], *adv.* not well, badly, poorly; faultily, not rightly; unfavourably; inadequately; with difficulty; **i. at ease,** uncomfortable.
ILL-ADVISED, [il'-ad-vīzd'], *adj.* injudicious, rash.
ILL-ADVISEDLY, [il'-ad-vīz'-id-li], *adv.* in an ill-advised fashion.
ILL-AFFECTED, [il'-a-fekt'-id], *adj.* unfriendly, hostile, viewing with disapproval.
ILLATION, [i-lā'-shun], *n.* inference; that which is deduced or inferred. [L. *illatio*].
ILLATIVE, [i-lāt'-iv], *adj.* pertaining to, of the nature of, containing, an inference; that may be deduced; (*gram.*) expressing or introducing an inference. [LL. *illativus*].
ILLATIVELY, [i-lāt'-iv-li], *adv.* by inference.
ILLAUDABLE, [i-lawd'-abl], *adj.* not meriting praise. [LL. *illaudabilis*].
ILLAUDABLY, [i-lawd'-ab-li], *adv.* in an illaudable fashion.
ILL-BLOOD, [il'-blud'], *n.* ill-feeling, animosity, unfriendliness.
ILL-BRED, [il'-bred], *adj.* badly brought up, discourteous, displaying a complete lack of good manners.
ILL-BREEDING, [il'-brēd'-ing], *n.* want of good breeding, absence of good manners, discourtesy.
ILL-CONDITIONED, [il'-kon-dish'-und], *adj.* having a nasty or wicked disposition; in bad physical condition.
ILLEGAL, [i-lē'-gal], *adj.* unlawful. [MedL. *illegalis*].
ILLEGALITY, [il'-ē-gal'-i-ti], *n.* unlawfulness.
ILLEGALIZE, [i-lē'-gal-īz], *v.t.* to make illegal.
ILLEGALLY, [i-lē'-gal-i], *adv.* in illegal fashion.
ILLEGALNESS, [i-lē'-gal-nes], *n.* illegality.
ILLEGIBILITY, [i-lej'-i-bil'-i-ti], *n.* the quality of being illegible.
ILLEGIBLE, [i-lej'-ibl], *adj.* unable to be read. [IL and LEGIBLE].
ILLEGIBLENESS, [i-lej'-ibl-nes], *n.* illegibility.
ILLEGIBLY, [i-lej'-ib-li], *adv.* in an illegible fashion.
ILLEGITIMACY, [il'-i-jit'-im-as-i], *n.* the condition of being illegitimate.
ILLEGITIMATE (1), [il'-i-jit'-im-at], *n.* an illegitimate child.
ILLEGITIMATE (2), [il'-i-jit'-im-at], *adj.* unlawful, irregular; bastard, born out of wedlock; illogical, incorrectly inferred. [L. *illegitimus*].
ILLEGITIMATE (3), [il'-i-jit'-im-āt], *v.t.* to render or declare illegitimate.
ILLEGITIMATELY, [il'-i-jit'-im-at-li], *adv.* in an illegitimate fashion.
ILLEGITIMATION, [il'-i-jit'-im-ā'-shun], *n.* the act of declaring or making illegitimate; illegitimacy.
ILLEISM, [il'-i-izm], *n.* the inordinate use in writing of the pronoun *he* when the writer is speaking of himself in the third person, or of another person. [L. *ille* he].
ILLEVIABLE†, [i-lē'-vi-abl], *adj.* unable to be levied or collected. [IL and LEVIABLE].
ILL-FAME, [il'-fām'], *n.* bad repute; **house of i.** a brothel.
ILL-FATED, [il'-fāt'-id], *adj.* doomed to misfortune; resulting in misfortune.
ILL-FAVOURED, [il'-fāv'-erd], *adj.* ugly.
ILL-GOT, [il'-got], *adj.* ill-gotten.
ILL-GOTTEN, [il'-gotn'], *adj.* obtained by wrong-doing.
ILL-HUMOUR, [il'-hew'-mer], *n.* irritability, anger, moroseness.
ILLIBERAL, [i-lib'-er-al], *adj.* not generous, stingy; narrow-minded, intolerant; not enlightened or refined. [L. *illiberalis* mean].
ILLIBERALITY, [i-lib'-er-al'-i-ti], *n.* the quality of being illiberal.
ILLIBERALIZE, [i-lib'-er-al-īz], *v.t.* to render illiberal.
ILLIBERALLY, [i-lib'-er-al-i], *adv.* in an illiberal fashion.
ILLICIT, [i-lis'-it], *adj.* prohibited, illegal. [L. *illicitus*].
ILLICITLY, [i-lis'-it-li], *adv.* in an illicit fashion.
ILLICITNESS, [i-lis'-it-nes], *n.* the condition of being illicit.
ILLIMITABILITY, [i-lim'-it-a-bil'-i-ti], *n.* illimitableness.
ILLIMITABLE, [i-lim'-it-abl], *adj.* that cannot be limited, boundless, unrestricted. [IL and LIMITABLE].
ILLIMITABLENESS, [i-lim'-it-abl-nes], *n.* the condition of being illimitable.
ILLIMITABLY, [i-lim'-it-ab-li], *adv.* in an illimitable fashion.
ILLIMITATION, [i-lim'-it-ā'-shun], *n.* the state of being unlimited. [IL and LIMITATION].
ILLIMITED, [i-lim'-it-id], *adj.* not limited.
ILLIMITEDNESS, [i-lim'-it-id-nes], *n.* illimitation.
ILLINITION, [il'-in-ish'-un], *n.* a thin coating of foreign matter or minerals; a rubbing in of ointment; the ointment rubbed in. [LL. *illinire* to smear].
ILLISION, [i-lizh'-un], *n.* the action of dashing or striking against. [L. *illisio*].
ILLITERACY, [i-lit'-er-as-i], *n.* the state of being illiterate.
ILLITERATE (1), [i-lit'-er-at], *n.* an illiterate person, *esp.* one unable to read or write.
ILLITERATE (2), [i-lit'-er-at], *adj.* unlearned, uneducated, lacking knowledge of literature or letters; unable to read or write. [L. *illiteratus*].
ILLITERATENESS, [i-lit'-er-at-nes], *n.* illiteracy.
ILL-JUDGED, [il'-jujd'], *adj.* unwise, foolish.
ILL-MANNED, [il'-mand'], *adj.* (*naut.*) not properly manned.
ILL-MANNERED, [il'-man'-erd], *adj.* badly behaved, rude.
ILL-NATURE, [il'-nā'-cher], *n.* maliciousness, bad temper.
ILL-NATURED, [il-nā'-cherd], *adj.* malicious, spiteful, morose.
ILL-NATUREDLY, [il-nā'-cherd-li], *adv.* in an ill-natured fashion.

ō (bone), ī (fine), ōō (food), ŏŏ (put), u (up), th (think), TH (that), zh (azure), † = obsolete, ~ = related to.

ILL-NATUREDNESS, [il-nā′-cherd-nes], *n.* the quality of being ill-natured.
ILLNESS, [il′-nes], *n.* the state of being ill, indisposition; a particular kind of disease or sickness.
ILLOGICAL, [i-loj′-ik-al], *adj.* irrational, not based on correct reasoning, not reasonable. [IL and LOGICAL].
ILLOGICALLY, [i-loj′-ik-al-i], *adv.* in an illogical fashion.
ILLOGICALNESS, [i-loj′-ik-al-nes], *n.* the condition of being illogical.
ILL-OMENED, [il-ō′-mend], *adj.* attended or fraught with misfortune, inauspicious.
ILL-STARRED, [il′-stahd], *adj.* unfortunate, ill-omened.
ILL-TEMPERED, [il′-tem′-perd], *adj.* cross, morose.
ILL-TIMED, [il′-tīmd], *adj.* coming at the wrong time, tactless.
ILL-TREAT, [il′-trēt′], *v.t.* to treat in a cruel, brutal fashion.
ILL-TURN, [il′-turn′], *n.* an unkind act.
ILLUDE†, [il-ewd′], *v.t.* to deceive, trick. [L. *illudere*].
ILLUME, [i-lōōm′], *v.t.* to illumine.
ILLUMINABLE, [i-lōōm′-in-abl], *adj.* able to be illuminated.
ILLUMINANT (1), [i-lōōm′-in-ant], *n.* anything which illuminates.
ILLUMINANT (2), [i-lōōm′-in-ant], *adj.* giving light, illuminating. [L. *illuminans*].
ILLUMINATE, [i-lōōm′-in-āt], *v.t.* to light up, to make light; to adorn with bright lights and coloured lamps; to decorate (a manuscript) with brightly coloured ornamental initial letters and miniature illustrations; (*fig.*) to enlighten, make clear. [L. *illuminare*].
ILLUMINATI, [i-lōōm′-in-ā′-tī, i-lōōm′-in-ah′-tē], *n.* (*pl.*) persons pretending to be specially enlightened, *esp.* any of several religious societies, priding themselves on their supposed enlightenment as to certain beliefs. [L. *illuminati*, *pl.* of *illuminatus* enlightened].
ILLUMINATING, [i-lōōm′-in-āt-ing], *n.* the act of one who illuminates manuscripts and books.
ILLUMINATION, [i-lōōm′-in-ā′-shun], *n.* the act of illuminating; the state of being illuminated; (*pl.*) a special display of bright lights and coloured lamps; (*fig.*) divine inspiration; intellectual enlightenment; a decorated initial letter in a manuscript or book. [L. *illuminatio*].

ILLUMINATION

ILLUMINATIVE, [i-lōōm′-in-at-iv], *adj.* that illuminates.
ILLUMINATOR, [i-lōōm′-in-āt-er], *n.* a person or thing that illuminates or gives light; one whose profession is to illuminate manuscripts. [L. *illuminator*].
ILLUMINE, [i-lōōm′-in], *v.t.* to light up; to throw light upon; to make a meaning clear. [L. *illuminare*].
ILLUMINISM, [i-lōōm′-in-izm], *n.* the opinions or practice of the illuminati.
ILLUMINIST, [i-lōōm′-in-ist], *n.* a follower, disciple, or adherent of illuminism.
ILLUMINIZE, [i-lōōm′-in-īz], *v.t.* to initiate into the doctrines of the illuminati.
ILL-USE, [il′-yōōz′], *v.t.* to ill-treat; to misuse.
ILLUSION, [i-lōō′-zhun], *n.* that which appears to the eye other than it actually is; anything that conveys a deceptive impression to the senses; a delusion, a mistaken belief. [L. *illusio* a mocking].
ILLUSIONISM, [i-lōō′-zhun′-izm], *n.* a theory that the external world consists entirely of illusions.
ILLUSIONIST, [i-lōō′-zhun-ist], *n.* one who believes in illusionism; a conjurer.
ILLUSIVE, [i-lōō′-siv], *adj.* deceptive. [L. *illusum*, *p.pt.* of *illudere* to mock].
ILLUSIVELY, [i-lōō′-siv-li], *adv.* in illusive fashion.
ILLUSIVENESS, [i-lōō′-siv-nes], *n.* the quality of being illusive.
ILLUSORINESS, [i-lōō′-zer-i-nes], *n.* the quality of being illusory.
ILLUSORY, [i-lōō′-zer-i], *adj.* deceptive; produced by, or consisting of, an illusion, not real. [LL. *illusorius* mocking].
ILLUSTRATE, [il′-us-trāt], *v.t.* to make more clear by giving examples; to bring out the force or truth of by performing some action, or producing supporting evidence; to provide with pictures and drawings. [L. *illustrare* to explain].
ILLUSTRATED, [il′-us-trāt′-id], *adj.* containing pictures or drawings.
ILLUSTRATION, [il′-us-trā′-shun], *n.* an example or instance which illustrates something; a drawing or picture in a book, etc.; the act of illustrating. [L. *illustratio*].
ILLUSTRATIVE, [il′-us-trat-iv], *adj.* that illustrates.
ILLUSTRATIVELY, [il′-us-trat-iv-li], *adv.* in an illustrative way.
ILLUSTRATOR, [il′-us-trāt′-er], *n.* one who illustrates, *esp.* one who draws illustrations. [LL. *illustrator*].
ILLUSTRATORY, [il′-us-trāt-er-i] *adj.* that illustrates.
ILLUSTRIOUS, [il-us′-tri-us], *adj.* renowned, celebrated, eminent, noble. [L. *illustris*].
ILLUSTRIOUSLY, [il-us′-tri-us-li], *adv.* in illustrious fashion.
ILLUSTRIOUSNESS, [il-us′-tri-us-nes], *n.* the quality of being illustrious.
ILL-WILL, [il′-wil′], *n.* enmity, malice, spite.
ILLYRIAN, [il-i′-rian], *adj.* relating to Illyria. [*Illyria*, in Yugoslavia].
ILMENITE, [il′-men-īt], *n.* (*min.*) an oxide of iron and titanium. [The *Ilmen* mountains in Russia, where it was first found].
IM-, *pref.* form of the Latin prefix IN- used before *b*, *m*, and *p*. [L. *im*].
IMAGE (1), [im′-ij], *n.* a material representation of a person, in the form of a statue, carved figure, painting, etc.; an idol; a person who is extraordinarily like someone else; a figure of speech; a likeness, semblance; picture, embodiment; a mental picture, an idea, concept; (*optics*) an impression produced on the eye of some object reflected in a mirror or on to a screen through a lens. [L. *imago*].
IMAGE (2), [im′-ij], *v.t.* to make or form an image of; to mirror in the mind; to imagine; to reflect, present a faithful picture of.

IMAGE

IMAGEABLE, [im′-ij-abl], *adj.* that may be imaged or imagined.
IMAGELESS, [im′-ij-les], *adj.* without image.
IMAGERY, [im′-ij-ri], *n.* images, statues, carvings, effigies, etc.; (*rhet.*) figures of speech and their use figurative description. [Fr. *imagerie*].
IMAGE-WORSHIP, [im′-ij-wur′-ship], *n.* the worship of images or idols.
IMAGINABLE, [i-maj′-in-abl], *adj.* that may be imagined, conceivable. [LL. *imaginabilis*].
IMAGINABLY, [i-maj′-in-ab-li], *adv.* in an imaginable fashion.
IMAGINAL, [i-maj′-in-al], *adj.* (*entom.*) pertaining to the imago of an insect.
IMAGINARY, [i-maj′-in-er-i], *adj.* existing only in imagination, not real. [L. *imaginarius*].
IMAGINATION, [i-maj′-in-ā′-shun], *n.* the ability of the mind to call up images which vividly recreate some past experience, or to form mental pictures of some object not present; the power of the mind to create images or form concepts of things which have not been or cannot be experienced; a mental image, a phantasy of the mind; a fanciful notion. [L. *imaginatio*].
IMAGINATIVE, [i-maj′-in-at-iv], *adj.* displaying, proceeding from, imagination; having no foundation in reality; possessing a powerful imagination. [LL *imaginativus*].
IMAGINATIVENESS, [i-maj′-in-at-iv-nes], *n.* the quality of being imaginative.
IMAGINE, [i-maj′-in], *v.t.* to form a mental image of; to fancy, conjecture, suppose. [L. *imaginari*]
IMAGINER, [i-maj′-in-er], *n.* one who imagines.
IMAGIST (1), [im′-aj-ist], *n.* one of a group of twentieth-century poets who placed special emphasis on the employment of imagery.
IMAGIST (2), [im′-aj-ist], *adj.* of, or pertaining to, the imagists or their theories.
IMAGO, (*pl.* **imagines, imagoes**), [i-mā′-gō, *pl.* i-mā′-jin-ēz, i-mā′-gōz], *n.* (*entom.*) the adult or completely developed state of an insect. [L. *imago* image].

IMAM, IMAUM, [i-mahm'], *n.* the officer in charge of a Mohammedan mosque; a Mohammedan prince, chief, or religious leader. [Arab. *imam* leader].

IMBAND, [im-band'], *v.t.* to form into a band or bands.

IMBANK, see EMBANK.

IMBATHE, [im-bāTH'], *v.t.* to bathe all over.

IMBECILE (1), [im'-bi-sēl], *n.* a mentally deficient person; (*coll.*) a fool, idiot.

IMBECILE (2), [im'-bi-sēl], *adj.* feeble-minded, mentally deficient; (*coll.*) foolish, silly. [Fr. *imbécile*].

IMBECILITATE, [im'-bi-sil'-it-āt], *v.t.* make imbecile.

IMBECILITY, [im'-bi-sil'-i-ti], *n.* the state of being imbecile; an imbecile act. [L. *imbecillitas*].

IMBED, see EMBED.

IMBENCHING, [im-bench'-ing], *n.* a raised work resembling a bench.

IMBER, see EMBER.

IMBIBE, [im-bīb'], *v.t.* to drink in, to absorb into the system (liquid nourishment); to inhale; to soak up, to take in (moisture); (*fig.*) to assimilate mentally; (*coll.*) to indulge in alcoholic beverages. [L *imbibere*].

IMBIBER, [im-bīb'-er], *n.* a person or thing that imbibes.

IMBIBITION, [im'-bib-ish'-un], *n.* the act of imbibing. [L. **imbibitio*].

IMBITTER, see EMBITTER.

IMBITTERER, [im-bit'-er-er], *n.* that which, or one who, embitters.

IMBOSOM, [im-bŏoz'-um], *v.t.* to hold in the bosom; to caress; to surround.

IMBOUND, [im-bownd'], *v.t.* to shut in.

IMBOW, see EMBOW.

IMBRANGLE, see EMBRANGLE.

IMBREED, see INBREED.

IMBRICATE (1), [im'-brik-āt], *adj.* (*nat. hist.*) composed of overlapping scales. [L. *imbricatus* shaped like a tile].

IMBRICATE (2), [im'-brik-āt], *v.t. and i.* to overlap like tiles; to arrange so as to overlap in this way. [L. *imbricare*].

IMBRICATED, [im'-brik-āt'-id], *adj.* composed of parts overlapping like tiles; arranged so as to overlap like tiles.

IMBRICATION, [im'-brik-ā'-shun], *n.* the act of imbricating; the state of being imbricated.

IMBROGLIO, EMBROGLIO, [im-brō'-li-ō], *n.* a confused, complicated state of affairs; a perplexing muddle of ideas. [It. *imbroglio* entanglement].

IMBROWN, [im-brown'], *v.t.* to make brown, obscure.

IMBRUE, [im-brōō'], *v.t.* to stain, drench, soil (in blood, etc.). [OFr. *embreuver* to moisten].

IMBRUEMENT, [im-brōō'-ment], *n.* the act of imbruing; the condition of being imbrued.

IMBRUTE, [im-brōōt'], *v.t.* to bring to the state of a brute; *v.i.* to sink to the condition of a brute.

IMBUE, [im-bew'], *v.t.* to soak, saturate; to dye, stain; (*fig.*) to fill, inspire or instil with. [L. *imbuere*].

IMBUEMENT, [im-bew'-ment], *n.* the act of imbuing, the state of being imbued.

IMBURSE, [im-burs'], *v.t.* to supply with money; to put in a purse. [MedL. *imbursare*].

IMBURSEMENT, [im-burs'-ment], *n.* the act of imbursing.

IMITABILITY, [im'-it-a-bil'-i-ti], *n.* the quality of being imitable.

IMITABLE, [im'-it-abl], *adj.* able to be imitated.

IMITATE, [im'-it-āt], *v.t.* to copy exactly, to follow in manner of conduct or behaviour, to act like; to reproduce closely; to make something intended to resemble closely something else; to mimic; to counterfeit; to resemble. [L. *imitari*].

IMITATION, [im'-it-ā'-shun], *n.* the act of imitating; that which imitates; a counterfeit, a copy intended to be taken for the real thing; a likeness, copy; burlesque. [L. *imitatio*].

IMITATIVE, [im'-it-at-iv], *adj.* formed after a model; reproducing, copying, that imitates; tending or content to imitate something or someone else. [LL. *imitativus*].

IMITATIVELY, [im'-it-at-iv-li], *adv.* so as to imitate.

IMITATIVENESS, [im'-it-at-iv-nes], *n.* the quality of being imitative.

IMITATOR, [im'-it-āt-er], *n.* one who imitates. [L. *imitator*].

IMMACULATE, [i-mak'-yŏŏ-lat], *adj.* spotless; extremely neat and fashionable, faultless; pure, undefiled by sin, irreproachable; (*zool.*) without markings; (of the conception of the Virgin Mary) devoid of original sin. [L. *immaculatus* unspotted].

IMMACULATELY, [i-mak'-yŏŏ-lat-li], *adv.* in an immaculate fashion.

IMMACULATENESS, [i-mak'-yŏŏ-lat-nes], *n.* the quality of being immaculate.

IMMALLEABLE, [i-mal'-i-abl], *adj.* not able to be hammered out.

IMMANACLE, [i-man'-akl], *v.t.* to put manacles on, to fetter.

IMMANATION, [im'-an-ā'-shun], *n.* a flowing in [IM and L. *manare* to flow].

IMMANENCE, [im'-an-ents], *n.* the condition of being immanent, inherence.

IMMANENCY, [im'-an-en-si], *n.* immanence.

IMMANENT, [im'-an-ent], *adj.* inherent; (*theol.*) (of God) present throughout the whole universe. [L. *immanens*].

IMMARCESCIBLE, [im'-ah-ses'-ibl], *adj.* never fading, undying, everlasting. [IM and L. *marcescere* to fade].

IMMARGINATE, [i-mah'-jin-āt], *adj.* without a border or margin.

IMMASK†, [i-mahsk'], *v.t.* to cover with or as with a mask.

IMMATERIAL, [im'-a-tēer'-i-al], *adj.* not consisting of matter, spiritual, possessing no bodily form; unimportant. [MedL. *immaterialis*].

IMMATERIALISM, [im'-a-tēer'-i-al-izm], *n.* the doctrine that denies the independent existence of matter, and claims that all things exist only as ideas in the mind.

IMMATERIALIST, [im'-a-tēer'-i-al-ist], *n.* one who supports immaterialism.

IMMATERIALITY, [im'-a-tēer'-i-al'-i-ti], *n.* the state of being immaterial.

IMMATERIALIZE, [im'-a-tēer'-i-al-īz], *v.t.* to make immaterial.

IMMATERIALLY, [im'-a-tēer'-i-al-i], *adv.* in an immaterial fashion.

IMMATERIALNESS, [im-a-tēer'-i-al-nes], *n* the condition of being immaterial.

IMMATURE, [im'-a-tyōōer'], *adj.* not ripe, not fully formed, not thoroughly developed. [L. *immaturus*].

IMMATURELY, [im'-a-tyōōer-li], *adv.* in an immature fashion.

IMMATURENESS, [im'-a-tyōōer'-nes], *n.* immaturity.

IMMATURITY, [im'-a-tyōōer -i-ti], *n.* the condition of being immature.

IMMEABILITY, [im'-ē-a-bil'-i-ti], *n.* lack of power to flow through a channel. [IM and L. *meabilis* passable].

IMMEASURABILITY, [i-mezh'-er-a-bil'-i-ti], *n.* immeasurableness.

IMMEASURABLE, [i-mezh'-er-abl], *adj.* unable to be measured, enormous.

IMMEASURABLENESS, [i-mezh'-er-abl-nes], *n.* the quality of being immeasurable.

IMMEASURABLY, [i-mezh'-er-ab-li], *adv.* to an immeasurable degree.

IMMEDIACY, [i-mē'-di-as-i], *n.* the state or quality of being immediate.

IMMEDIATE, [i-mē'-di-at], *adj.* with nothing intervening; instant, without loss of time or delay; present at this or that particular moment; very near; standing next to, nearest; adjacent, in close proximity; direct, next in succession. [L. *immediatus*].

IMMEDIATELY, [i-mē'-di-at-li], *adv.* at once, without delay; directly; proximately, without anything intervening.

IMMEDIATENESS, [i-mē'-di-at-nes], *n.* immediacy.

IMMEDICABLE, [i-med'-ik-abl], *adj.* that cannot be healed or cured. [L. *immedicabilis*].

IMMEMORABLE, [i-mem'-er-abl], *adj.* not worth remembering. [L. *immemorabilis*].

IMMEMORIAL, [im'-em-aw'-ri-al], *adj.* exceedingly old, extremely ancient, beyond memory or record. [MedL. *immemorialis*].

IMMEMORIALLY, [im'-em-aw'-ri-al-i], *adv.* from time beyond memory.

IMMENSE, [i-ments'], *adj.* vast, huge, colossal; (*coll.*) splendid. [L. *immensus*].

IMMENSELY, [i-mens'-li], *adv.* to an immense degree; (*coll.*) exceedingly.

IMMENSENESS, [i-mens'-nes], *n.* the quality of being immense.

IMMENSITY, [i-men'-si-ti], *n.* immenseness; infinity, the infinite universe. [L. *immensitas*].

IMMENSURABILITY, [i-men'-sher-a-bil-i-ti], *n.* the quality of being immensurable.

IMMENSURABLE, [i-men'-sher-abl], *adj.* incapable of being measured. [LL. *immensurabilis*].

IMMENSURATE†, [i-men'-sher-at], *adj.* unmeasured. [LL. *immensuratus*].

IMMERGE, [i-murj'], *v.t. and i.* to plunge into a liquid; to sink down, to become immersed. [L. *immergere*].
IMMERSE, [i-murs'], *v.t.* to plunge or dip deep into liquid; **to be immersed in**, to be engrossed by, to have one's whole attention absorbed by. [L. *immersum*, *p.pt.* of *immergere* to plunge into].
IMMERSION, [im-ur'-shun], *n.* the act of immersing; the condition of being immersed; baptism by covering the whole body with water; (*astron.*) the disappearance of a celestial body behind, or in the shadow of, another. [L. *immersio*].
IMMESH, see ENMESH.
IMMIGRANT (1), [im'-i-grant], *n.* one who immigrates.
IMMIGRANT (2), [im'-i-grant], *adj.* coming to live in a foreign country. [L. *immigrans*].
IMMIGRATE, [im'-i-grāt], *v.t. and i.* to come to live in a foreign country permanently; to bring as a settler into a foreign country. [L. *immigrare*].
IMMIGRATION, [im'-i-grā'-shun], *n.* the act of immigrating; the entrance into a country of bodies of immigrants.
IMMINENCE, [im'-in-ents], *n.* the quality of being imminent. [LL. *imminentia*].
IMMINENT, [im'-in-ent], *adj.* impending, close at hand, about to take place. [L. *imminens* overhanging].
IMMINENTLY, [im'-in-ent-li], *adv.* in an imminent fashion.
IMMINGLE, [i-ming'-gl], *v.t.* to mingle or mix closely with.
IMMISCIBILITY, [i-mis'-i-bil'-i-ti], *n.* the quality of being immiscible.
IMMISCIBLE, [i-mis'-ibl], *adj.* incapable of being mixed. [L. *immiscibilis*].
IMMITIGABLE, [i-mit'-ig-abl], *adj.* impossible to mitigate. [L. *immitigabilis*].
IMMITIGABLY, [i-mit'-ig-ab-li], *adv.* in an immitigable way.
IMMIX, [i-miks'], *v.t.* to mix or mingle closely, to intermingle. [L. *immixtus*, *p.pt.* of *immiscere*].
IMMIXTURE, [i-miks'-cher], *n.* the act of mixing, the state of being mixed; (*fig.*) the fact of being mixed up with.
IMMOBILE, [i-mō'-bil], *adj.* unable to move or be moved, fixed; stationary, motionless. [L. *immobilis*].
IMMOBILITY, [im'-ō-bil'-i-ti], *n.* the condition or quality of being immobile. [L. *immobilitas*].
IMMOBILIZE, [i-mō'-bil-iz], *v.t.* to make immobile; to make (a body of troops) incapable of being mobilized; to keep fixed or stationary; to withdraw from circulation. [Fr. *immobiliser*].
IMMODERATE, [i-mod'-er-at], *adj.* excessive, extravagant, extreme, lacking in moderation. [L. *immoderatus*].
IMMODERATELY, [i-mod'-er-at-li], *adv.* to an immoderate extent.
IMMODERATENESS, [i-mod'-er-at-nes], *n.* the condition of being immoderate.
IMMODERATION, [i-mod'-er-ā'-shun], *n.* lack of moderation. [L. *immoderatio*].
IMMODEST, [i-mod'-est], *adj.* improper, lewd; lacking modesty; arrogant, forward. [L. *immodestus*].
IMMODESTLY, [i-mod'-est-li], *adv.* in an immodest way.
IMMODESTY, [i-mod'-est-i], *n.* the quality of being immodest. [L. *immodestia*].
IMMOLATE, [im'-ō-lāt], *v.t.* to kill as a sacrifice; (*fig.*) to surrender, allow to be destroyed as a sacrifice. [L. *immolare* to sprinkle a victim with meal].
IMMOLATION, [im'-ō-lā'-shun], *n.* the act of sacrificing; the state of being sacrificed; a sacrifice. [L. *immolatio*].
IMMOLATOR, [im'-ō-lāt'-er], *n.* one who immolates. [L. *immolator*].
IMMOMENTOUS, [im'-ō-ment'-us], *adj.* unimportant.
IMMORAL, [i-mo'-ral], *adj.* not moral, inconsistent with moral rectitude; having no moral principles; licentious, vicious, unchaste; obscene.
IMMORALITY, [im'-or-al'-i-ti], *n.* the quality of being immoral; licentiousness; an immoral action.
IMMORALLY, [i-mo'-ral-i], *adv.* in an immoral way.
IMMORTAL (1), [i-maw'-tal], *n.* a person who is immortal; one whose fame and glory is everlasting.
IMMORTAL (2), [i-maw'-tal], *adj.* living for ever, not subject to death; imperishable, eternal; remembered and renowned for ever. [L. *immortalis*]
IMMORTALITY, [im'-aw-tal'-i-ti], *n.* the quality of being immortal. [L. *immortalitas*].
IMMORTALIZATION, [i-maw'-tal-iz-ā'-shun], *n.* the act of immortalizing; the condition of being immortalized.
IMMORTALIZE, [i-maw'-tal-iz], *v.t.* to make immortal, to cause to be renowned for ever.
IMMORTALLY, [i-maw'-tal-i], *adv.* for ever, perpetually, everlastingly; (*coll.*, *archaic*) exceedingly.
IMMORTELLE, [im'-aw-tel'], *n.* any of several genera of flowers, including *Helichrysum*, *Ammobium*, *Helipterum*, and *Antennaria*, the petals of which retain their colour and shape when dried. [Fr. *immortelle*].
IMMORTIFICATION, [i-maw'-ti-fi-kā'-shun], *n.* failure to subject or submit the body and passions to fasting, penance, etc. [L. *immortificatio*].
IMMOVABILITY, [i-mōōv'-a-bil'-i-ti], *n.* the quality of being immovable.
IMMOVABLE, [i-mōōv'-abl], *adj.* not able to be moved; unalterable, steadfast, unshakable; motionless; (*leg.*) that cannot be removed or taken away.
IMMOVABLENESS, [i-mōōv'-abl-nes], *n.* immovability.
IMMOVABLES, [i-mōōv'-ablz], *n.(pl.)* (*leg.*) property that cannot be removed or taken away.
IMMOVABLY, [i-mōōv'-ab-li], *adv.* in an immovable fashion.
IMMUNE, [i-mewn'], *adj.* safe, not likely to be harmed. [L. *immunis* exempt from a public service].
IMMUNITY, [i-mewn'-i-ti], *n.* the quality of being immune; (*leg.*) exemption from obligation, liability, tax, etc. [L. *immunitas* freedom from public service].
IMMUNIZATION, [im'-yōōn-iz-ā'-shun], *n.* the act of immunizing; the state of being made immune.
IMMUNIZE, [im'-yōōn-iz], *v.t.* to make immune.
IMMUNOLOGY, [im'-yōōn-ol'-oj-i], *n.* (*med.*) the study of factors producing immunity from disease, infection, etc. [IMMUNE and Gk. *logos* speech].
IMMURE, ENMURE†, [i-mew'-er], *v.t.* to shut up, to imprison; (*reflex.*) to shut oneself up, to remain in seclusion. [MedL. *immurare*].
IMMUREMENT, [i-mew'-er-ment], *n.* the act of immuring; the state of being immured.
IMMUTABILITY, [i-mewt'-a-bil'-i-ti], *n.* the quality of being immutable. [L. *immutabilitas*].
IMMUTABLE, [i-mewt'-abl], *adj.* steadfastly the same, not alterable, fixed. [L. *immutabilitas*].
IMMUTABLENESS, [i-mewt'-abl-nes], *n.* immutability.
IMMUTABLY, [i-mewt'-ab-li], *adv.* in an unchangeable fashion.
IMP (1), [imp], *n.* a little demon, a mischievous sprite; (*coll.*) a mischievous child. [OE. *impa* a young tree].
IMP (2), [imp], *v.t.* to extend or repair by inserting or adding something; to introduce feathers into a bird's wing to repair or strengthen it; to enlarge. [OE. *impian* to graft].
IMPACT (1), [im'-pakt], *n.* collision, a striking or impinging against, violent contact. [L. *impactus*].
IMPACT (2), [im-pakt'], *v.t.* to press or pack closely together, to drive firmly in. [L. *impactum*, *p.pt.* of *impingere* to impinge].
IMPAINT†, [im-pānt'], *v.t.* to adorn with colours, to paint upon something, to portray in colours.
IMPAIR, [im-pāer'], *v.t.* to weaken, sap, to make worse, to lessen in quantity or excellence. [OFr. *empeirer*].
IMPAIRER, [im-pāer'-er], *n.* a person or thing that impairs.
IMPAIRMENT, [im-pāer'-ment], *n.* the condition of being impaired; the act of impairing.
IMPALE, EMPALE, [im-pāl'], *v.t.* to put to death by fixing on an upright sharp stake, to transfix; (*her.*) to place side by side on one shield, divided by a vertical line down the centre; †to enclose, surround with palings. [MedL. *impalare*].
IMPALEMENT, EMPALEMENT, [im-pāl'-ment], *n.* the act or punishment of impaling; the state of being impaled; (*her.*) the representation of two coats of arms on one shield, divided by a vertical line. [OFr. *empalement*].

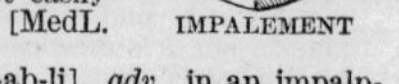
IMPALEMENT

IMPALPABILITY, [im-palp'-a-bil'-i-ti], *n.* the quality of being impalpable.
IMPALPABLE, [im-palp'-abl], *adj.* not able to be felt or experienced by touch; (*fig.*) not easily grasped by the mind. [MedL. *impalpabilis*.]
IMPALPABLY, [im-palp'-ab-li], *adv.* in an impalpable way.

IMPALSY, [im-pawl'-zi], *v.t.* to afflict with palsy.
IMPALUDISM, [im-pal'-yōōd-izm], *n.* a malarial disease common in marshy regions. [IM and L. *pallus* marsh].
IMPANATE (1), [im-pā'-nāt], *adj.* embodied and included in bread. [MedL. *impanatus*].
IMPANATE (2), [im-pā'-nāt], *v.t.* to embody or include in bread. [MedL. *impanare*].
IMPANATION, [im'-pan-ā'-shun], *n.* the presence and union of Christ's material body in and with the bread at the Eucharist. [MedL. *impanatio*].
IMPANEL, see EMPANEL.
IMPARADISE, [im-pa'-ra-dīs], *v.t.* to make supremely happy; to make a paradise of.
IMPARIDIGITATE, [im-pa'-ri-dij'-it-āt], *adj.* with an uneven number of toes or fingers on each limb. [L. *impar* unequal and DIGITATE].
IMPARIPINNATE, [im-pa'-ri-pin'-āt], *adj.* (of a pinnate leaf) having an odd leaflet at the end. [MdL. *imparipinnatus*].
IMPARISYLLABIC, [im-pa'-ri-sil-ab'-ik], *adj.* (*Gk., L. gram.*) (of nouns) having more syllables in the oblique cases than in the nominative. [L. *impar* unequal and SYLLABIC].
IMPARITY†, [im-pa'-ri-ti], *n.* unequalness, disproportion. [LL. *imparitas*].
IMPARK, [im-pahk'], *v.t.* (of land) to enclose as, turn into, a park; (of animals) to enclose or confine in a park. [OFr. *emparquer*].
IMPART, [im-paht'], *v.t.* to bestow; to make known, tell. [L. *impartire*].
IMPARTANCE, [im-paht'-ants], *n.* impartation.
IMPARTATION, [im-paht-ā'-shun], *n.* the act of imparting, communication.
IMPARTER, [im-paht'-er], *n.* one who imparts.
IMPARTIAL, [im-pah'-shal], *adj.* not prejudiced, fair, just, disinterested.
IMPARTIALITY, [im-pah'-shi-al'-i-ti], *n.* the quality of being impartial.
IMPARTIALLY, [im-pah'-shal-i], *adv.* in an impartial way.
IMPARTIBILITY, [im-paht'-i-bil'-i-ti], *n.* the quality of being impartible.
IMPARTIBLE, [im-paht'-ibl], *adj.* not capable of being partitioned, indivisible. [LL. *impartibilis*].
IMPARTMENT, [im-paht'-ment], *n.* the act of imparting; whatever is imparted.
IMPASSABLE, [im-pahs'-abl], *adj.* that cannot be passed over or crossed.
IMPASSABLENESS, [im-pahs'-abl-nes], *n.* the condition of being impassable.
IMPASSABLY, [im-pahs'-ab-li], *adv.* in an impassable manner.
IMPASSE, [im-pahs', am-pahs'], *n.* a deadlock, stalemate; a road or passage closed at one end. [Fr. *impasse*].
IMPASSIBILITY, [im-pas'-i-bil'-i-ti], *n.* the state or quality of being impassible. [L. *impassibilitas*].
IMPASSIBLE, [im-pas'-ibl], *adj.* incapable of suffering, insensitive to pain; that cannot be injured; incapable of feeling or passion. [L. *impassibilis*].
IMPASSIBLENESS, [im-pas'-ibl-nes], *n.* impassibility.
IMPASSION, [im-pash'-un], *v.t.* to stir to strong feeling or passion. [It. *impassionare*].
IMPASSIONABLE, [im-pash'-un-abl], *adj.* readily stirred to passion or strong feeling.
IMPASSIONATE (1), [im-pash'-un-at], *adj.* impassioned.
IMPASSIONATE (2), [im-pash'-un-at], *adj.* (*archaic*) dispassionate, free from passion. [MedL. *impassionatus*].
IMPASSIONED, [im-pash'-und], *adj.* displaying passion, animated, passionate, fiery.
IMPASSIVE, [im-pas'-iv], *adj.* unemotional, unmoved by feeling or passion; calm and unruffled; incapable of suffering, insensitive to pain.
IMPASSIVELY, [im-pas'-iv-li], *adv.* in an impassive fashion.
IMPASSIVENESS, [im-pas'-iv-nes], *n.* the quality of being impassive.
IMPASSIVITY, [im'-pas-iv'-i-ti], *n.* impassiveness.
IMPASTATION, [im'-past-ā'-shun], *n.* the act of impasting; the formation of a paste.
IMPASTE, [im-pāst'], *v.t.* to make into a paste; to cover or enclose with a paste; to lay colours on thickly and boldly in painting. [It. *impastare*].
IMPASTO, [im-past'-ō], *n.* the applying of colour in thick layers in painting; a style of painting in which the colours are laid on thickly.
IMPATIENCE, [im-pā'-shents], *n.* lack of ability to endure delay, opposition, restraint, or other annoying things, irritability; restless desire to engage in activity. [L. *impatientia*].
IMPATIENS, [im-pā'-shi-enz], *n.* the genus of plants comprising the balsams, so called from the explosive way in which they discharge their seeds. [L. *impatiens* impatient].
IMPATIENT, [im-pā'-shent], *adj.* displaying or indicating impatience, restive, irritable. [L. *impatiens*].
IMPATIENTLY, [im-pā'-shent-li], *adv.* in an impatient way.
IMPATRONIZE†, [im-pat'-ron-īz], *v.t.* to put in possession of; to take possession of; (*reflex.*) to become master of. [It. *impatronire*].
IMPAVID, [im-pav'-id], *adj.* fearless, undaunted. [L. *impavidus*].
IMPAVIDLY, [im-pav'-id-li], *adv.* fearlessly.
IMPAWN, [im-pawn'], *v.t.* to deposit as security, to put in pawn; (*fig.*) to pledge, to plight.
IMPAYABLE, [im-pā'-abl], *adj.* that cannot be paid; beyond price; (*coll.*) incomparable. [Fr. *impayable*].
IMPEACH, [im-pēch'], *v.t.* to charge or accuse, *esp.* of high treason or similar crime; to call in question, discredit; to implicate, inform against. [OFr. *empechier* to hinder].
IMPEACHABLE, [im-pēch'-abl], *adj.* that may be impeached.
IMPEACHER, [im-pēch'-er], *n.* a person who impeaches.
IMPEACHMENT, [im-pēch'-ment], *n.* the act of impeaching; the condition of being impeached; censure, disparagement. [OFr. *empechement*].
IMPEARL, [im-purl'], *v.t.* to form into, or make like, pearls; to adorn with pearls. [Fr. *emperler*].
IMPECCABILITY, [im-pek'-a-bil'-i-ti], *n.* the quality of being impeccable. [MedL. *impeccabilitas*].
IMPECCABLE, [im-pek'-abl], *adj.* sinless, not liable to do wrong; irreproachable. [LL. *impeccabilis*].
IMPECCANCY, [im-pek'-an-si], *n.* impeccability. [L. *impeccantia*].
IMPECCANT, [im-pek'-ant], *adj.* impeccable. [IM and L. *peccans* sinning].
IMPECUNIOSITY, [im'-pik-ewn'-i-os'-i-ti], *n.* the condition of being impecunious.
IMPECUNIOUS, [im'-pik-ewn'-i-us], *adj.* penniless; poor, poverty-stricken. [IM and L. *pecuniosus* rich].
IMPEDANCE, [im-pēd'-ants], *n.* (*elect.*) resistance, arising from self-induction, offered by a coil of wire to an alternating current of electricity passing through it.
IMPEDE, [im-pēd'], *v.t.* to hinder, hamper, bar the progress or free movement of, obstruct. [L. *impedire* to entangle].
IMPEDIMENT, [im-ped'-im-ent], *n.* the cause of a defective or indistinct articulation; obstacle, hindrance. [L. *impedimentum*].
IMPEDIMENTA, [im-ped'-im-ent'-a], *n.* baggage, luggage. [L. *impedimenta*].
IMPEDIMENTAL, [im-ped'-im-ent'-al], *adj.* obstructing.
IMPEDITIVE, [im-ped'-it-iv], *adj.* obstructive.
IMPEL, (impelling, impelled), [im-pel'], *v.t.* to drive or urge forward; to constrain, stir to action, cause to do something. [L. *impellere*].
IMPELLENT (1), [im-pel'-ent], *n.* that which impels.
IMPELLENT (2), [im-pel'-ent], *adj.* driving forward, urging on, that impels. [L. *impellens*].
IMPELLER, [im-pel'-er], *n.* the thing or person that impels.
IMPEND, [im-pend'], *v.i.* to hang over, to threaten, to be about to take place. [L. *impendere*].
IMPENDENCE, [im-pend'-ents], *n.* the state of impending.
IMPENDENCY, [im-pend'-en-si], *n.* impendence.
IMPENDENT, [im-pend'-ent], *adj.* impending. [L. *impendens*].
IMPENDING, [im-pend'-ing], *adj.* threatening, approaching, about to take place.
IMPENETRABILITY, [im-pen'-i-tra-bil'-i-ti], *n.* the quality of being impenetrable.
IMPENETRABLE, [im-pen'-it-rabl], *adj.* unable to be penetrated or pierced; unable to be solved or understood, inscrutable; insensible to ideas, feelings, influences; unable to be seen or passed through; (*philos.*) not admitting the presence of two substances in the same place at the same time. [L. *impenetrabilis*].
IMPENETRABLENESS, [im-pen'-it-rabl-nes], *n.* impenetrability.
IMPENETRABLY, [im-pen'-it-rab-li], *adv.* in an impenetrable way.

IMPENETRATE, [im-pen'-i-trāt], *v.t.* to penetrate or pierce deeply to sink down into.

IMPENITENCE, [im-pen'-it-ents], *n.* absence of repentance, refusal or inability to be penitent. [LL. *impoenitentia*].

IMPENITENCY, [im-pen'-it-en-si], *n.* impenitence.

IMPENITENT (1), [im-pen'-it-ent], *n.* a person who is unrepentant.

IMPENITENT (2), [im-pen'-it-ent], *adj.* unrepentant. [L. *impoenitens*].

IMPENITENTLY, [im-pen'-it-ent-li], *adv.* in an impenitent way.

IMPENNATE, [im-pen'-āt], *adj.* having short, unfeathered wings, as penguins.

IMPENNOUS†, [im-pen'-us], *adj.* having no wings. [IM and L. *penna* feather, wing].

IMPERATIVE (1), [im-pe'-rat-iv], *n.* (*gram.*) the imperative mood, that form of the verb used to indicate a command; a word, sentence, etc., expressing a command.

IMPERATIVE (2), [im-pe'-rat-iv], *adj.* authoritative, commanding; absolutely necessary, vital; (*gram.*) expressing a command. [LL. *imperativus*].

IMPERATIVELY, [im-pe'-rat-iv-li], *adv.* in an imperative fashion.

IMPERATOR, [im-per-āt'-or], *n.* a title given to a victorious general under the Roman Republic; emperor, supreme lord. [L. *imperator*].

IMPERATORIAL, [im-pe'-rat-aw'-ri-al], *adj.* pertaining to, like, an imperator or emperor. [L. *imperatorius*].

IMPERCEPTIBILITY, [im'-per-sept'-i-bil'-i-ti], *n.* the quality of being imperceptible.

IMPERCEPTIBLE, [im'-per-sept'-ibl], *adj.* unable to be perceived or discerned; extremely small or gradual, unnoticeable. [L. *imperceptibilis*].

IMPERCEPTIBLENESS, [im'-per-sept'-ibl-nes], *n.* imperceptibility.

IMPERCEPTIBLY, [im'-per-sept'-ib-li], *adv.* in an imperceptible way.

IMPERCEPTIVE, [im'-per-sept'-iv], *adj.* not perceiving, without perception.

IMPERCIPIENT, [im'-per-sip'-i-ent], *adj.* not perceiving, lacking power to perceive.

IMPERFECT, [im-per'-fekt], *adj.* not perfect, defective, faulty; deficient in some respect, incomplete; (*leg.*) not legally binding; (*mus.*) indicating a diminished fourth, fifth, or triad; **i. tense,** (*gram.*) a tense used to express action continuing and not complete; **i. cadence,** (*mus.*) a cadence not ending on the chord of the tonic. [L. *imperfectus*].

IMPERFECTION, [im'-per-fek'-shun], *n.* the state of being imperfect; a defect, shortcoming. [L. *imperfectio*].

IMPERFECTLY, [im-per'-fekt-li], *adv.* in an imperfect fashion.

IMPERFECTNESS, [im-per'-fekt-nes], *n.* the condition of being imperfect.

IMPERFORABLE, [im-per'-fer-abl], *adj.* unable to be perforated.

IMPERFORATE, [im-per'-fer-at], *adj.* having no perforation; (*anat.*) having no opening, with the normal openings closed; (of postage stamps) not having a perforated edge.

IMPERFORATED, [im-per'-fer-āt'-id], *adj.* imperforate.

IMPERFORATION, [im-per'-fer-ā'-shun], *n.* the condition of being imperforate.

IMPERIAL (1), [im-pēer'-i-al], *n.* a tuft of beard cultivated beneath the lower lip, after the fashion of Napoleon III; the outside seat on a diligence; a Russian gold coin formerly current; a particular size of paper (30 inches by 22 inches) or roofing slate (2½ feet by 2 feet).

IMPERIAL (2), [im-pēer'-i-al], *adj.* pertaining to an empire or to an emperor; pertaining to Great Britain or to the British Empire; standardized throughout the whole of Great Britain; like or befitting an emperor, commanding, majestic. [L. *imperialis*].

IMPERIALISM, [im-pēer'-i-al-izm], *n.* the doctrine that seeks to weld the different possessions of a state or empire into a closely bound whole; the increasing of the power and extent of an empire however and wherever possible; rule by an emperor.

IMPERIALIST, [im-pēer'-i-al-ist], *n.* a supporter of an emperor or imperial government; an advocate of imperialism.

IMPERIALITY, [im-pēer'-i-al'-i-ti], *n.* imperial personages, members of the imperial family.

IMPERIALIZE, [im-pēer'-i-al-īz], *v.t.* to render imperial, to cause to be part of an empire; to imbue with imperialist principles.

IMPERIALLY, [im-pēer'-i-al-i], *adv.* in an imperial way; from the point of view of imperialism.

IMPERIL, EMPERIL†, (imperilling, imperilled) [im-pe'-ril], *v.t.* to endanger, to place in peril.

IMPERILMENT, [im-pe'-ril-ment], *n.* the act of imperilling; the state of being imperilled.

IMPERIOUS, [im-pēer'-i-us], *adj.* domineering, overbearing, dictatorial; urgent; irresistible; (*archaic*) commanding, majestic, lofty. [L. *imperiosus* possessing power].

IMPERIOUSLY, [im-pēer'-i-us-li], *adv.* in an imperious way.

IMPERIOUSNESS, [im-pēer'-i-us-nes], *n.* the quality of being imperious.

IMPERISHABLE, [im-pe'-rish-abl], *adj.* not subject to decay; enduring for ever, eternal.

IMPERISHABLENESS, [im-pe'-rish-abl-nes], *n.* the quality of being imperishable.

IMPERISHABLY, [im-pe'-rish-ab-li], *adv.* in an imperishable way.

IMPERIUM, [im-pēer'-i-um, im-pe'-ri-um], *n.* sovereign authority, supreme command. [L. *imperium*].

IMPERMANENCE, [im-per'-man-ents], *n.* want of permanence, transitoriness.

IMPERMANENT, [im-per'-man-ent], *adj.* not permanent, transitory.

IMPERMEABILITY, [im-perm'-ē-a-bil'-i-ti], *n.* impermeableness.

IMPERMEABLE, [im-perm'-ē-abl], *adj.* not permitting the passage of a fluid, not allowing liquid to penetrate or soak in; impassable. [L. *impermeabilis*].

IMPERMEABLENESS, [im-perm'-ē-abl-nes], *n.* the condition of being impermeable.

IMPERMEABLY, [im-perm'-ē-ab-li], *adv.* in an impermeable way.

IMPERMISSIBLE, [im'-per-mis'-ibl], *adj.* not allowed.

IMPERSCRIPTIBLE, [im-per-skript'-ibl], *adj.* not based on written authority. [IM and L. *perscriptum*, *p.pt.* of *perscribere* to write down].

IMPERSONAL, [im-per'-son-al], *adj.* having no personality or individuality; having no personal significance, from the point of view of no particular person; (*gram.*) (of verbs) used only in the third person singular without a subject. [LL. *impersonalis*].

IMPERSONALITY, [im-per'-son-al'-i-ti], *n.* the quality of being impersonal.

IMPERSONALLY, [im-per'-son-al-i], *adv.* in an impersonal way.

IMPERSONATE, [im-per'-son-āt], *v.t.* to embody, manifest in tangible or material form; to represent in one's person; to pretend to be someone else, to mimic. [IM and L. *persona* person].

IMPERSONATION, [im-per'-son-ā'-shun], *n.* the act of impersonating; the manner of acting the part of a character in a play; the imitation of another person.

IMPERSONATIVE, [im-per'-son-at-iv], *adj.* able to impersonate; relating to impersonation.

IMPERSONATOR, [im-purs'-on-āt-er], *n.* one who impersonates.

IMPERSPICUITY, [im-per'-spik-ew'-i-ti], *n.* the quality of being imperspicuous.

IMPERSPICUOUS, [im'-per-spik'-yōō-us], *adj.* obscure, not clear, not easily seen. [L. *imperspicuus*].

IMPERTINENCE, [im-per'-tin-ents], *n.* the quality of being impertinent, presumptuousness; an impertinent act or speech; irrelevancy.

IMPERTINENCY, [im-per'-tin-en-si], *n.* impertinence.

IMPERTINENT, [im-per'-tin-ent], *adj.* rude, unmannerly, disrespectful; irrelevant; inappropriate, out of place. [L. *impertinens*].

IMPERTINENTLY, [im-per'-tin-ent-li], *adv.* in an impertinent fashion.

IMPERTURBABILITY, [im'-per-turb'-a-bil'-i-ti], *n.* the quality of being imperturbable.

IMPERTURBABLE, [im'-per-turb'-abl], *adj.* not liable to be disturbed, ruffled, or excited; cool, collected. [LL. *imperturbabilis*].

IMPERTURBATION, [im-per-turb-ā'-shun], *n.* freedom from agitation, coolness. [L. *imperturbatio*].

IMPERTURBED, [im'-per-turbd'], *adj.* calm, unmoved, unruffled.

IMPERVIABILITY, [im-per'-vi-a-bil'-i-ti], *n.* imperviableness.

IMPERVIABLE, [im-per'-vi-abl], *adj.* impervious, impenetrable.

IMPERVIABLENESS, [im-per'-vi-abl-nes], *n.* imperviousness.

IMPERVIOUS, [im-per'-vi-us], *adj.* not to be penetrated or passed through, proof against; (*fig.*) insensible to, heedless of, not open to influence by. [L. *impervius*].

IMPERVIOUSLY, [im-per'-vi-us-li], *adv.* in an impervious way.

IMPERVIOUSNESS, [im-per'-vi-us-nes], *n.* the quality of being impervious.

IMPETIGINOUS, [im'-pi-tij'-in-us], *adj.* resembling impetigo. [L. *impetiginosus*].

IMPETIGO, [im'-pi-tī'-gō], *n.* a skin disease characterized by an eruption, usually in clusters, of yellow-scaled pustules. [L. *impetigo*].

IMPETRATE, [im'-pet-rāt], *v.t.* to obtain by petition or entreaty. [L. *impetrare*].

IMPETRATION, [im'-pet-rā'-shun], *n.* the act of impetrating. [L. *impetratio*].

IMPETRATIVE, [im'-pet-rāt'-iv], *adj.* obtaining by entreaty or petition. [L. *impetrativus*].

IMPETRATORY, [im'-pet-rāt'-er-i], *adj.* impetrative.

IMPETUOSITY, [im-pet'-yōō-os'-i-ti], *n.* the quality of being impetuous; an impetuous act or speech.

IMPETUOUS, [im-pet'-yōō-us], *adj.* rushing violently; rash, hasty; vehement, dashing, passionate; inclined to act on sudden impulse. [L. *impetuosus*].

IMPETUOUSLY, [im-pet'-yōō-us-li], *adv.* in an impetuous way.

IMPETUOUSNESS, [im-pet'-yōō-us-nes], *n.* the quality of being impetuous.

IMPETUS, [im'-pet-us], *n.* the force with which a body moves, depending upon its weight and rate of movement, momentum; a driving force, a spur. [L. *impetus* attack].

IMPEYAN, [im'-pi-an], *adj.* denoting a Himalayan pheasant, *Lophophorus impeyanus*, found in Chamba. [Sir Elijah *Impey*, Chief Justice of Bengal].

IMPI, [im'-pi], *n.* a regiment or large organized body of Zulu warriors. [Zulu *impi*].

IMPIETY, [im-pī'-et-i], *n.* the condition or quality of being impious; an impious act or speech. [L. *impietas*].

IMPIGNORATE, [im-pig'-nor-āt], *v.t.* to pledge or pawn, to mortgage. [MedL. *impignorare*].

IMPINGE, [im-pinj'], *v.i.* to fall or dash against, to strike, to come into contact with. [L. *impingere*].

IMPINGEMENT, [im-pinj'-ment], *n.* the act of impinging.

IMPINGENT, [im-pinj'-ent], *adj.* impinging, striking, falling against. [L. *impingens*].

IMPIOUS, [im'-pi-us], *adj.* irreverent, profane, wicked, ungodly. [L. *impius*].

IMPIOUSLY, [im'-pi-us-li], *adv.* in an impious way.

IMPIOUSNESS, [im'-pi-us-nes], *n.* impiety.

IMPISH, [imp'-ish], *adj.* like an imp, mischievous.

IMPISHLY, [imp'-ish-li], *adv.* in impish fashion.

IMPISHNESS, [imp'-ish-nes], *n.* the state or quality of being impish.

IMPLACABILITY, [im-plak'-a-bil'-i-ti], *n.* the quality of being implacable. [LL. *implacabilitas*].

IMPLACABLE, [im-plak'-abl], *adj.* not to be appeased, relentless, inexorable. [L. *implacabilis*].

IMPLACABLENESS, [im-plak'-abl-nes], *n.* implacability.

IMPLACABLY, [im-plak'-ab-li], *adv.* in an implacable way.

IMPLACENTAL, [im'-pla-sent'-al], *adj.* lacking placenta.

IMPLANT, [im-plahnt'], *v.t.* to set or plant deeply, to insert; (*fig.*) to instil, inculcate, impress. [Fr. *implanter*].

IMPLANTATION, [im'-plahnt-ā'-shun], *n.* the act of implanting; that which is implanted.

IMPLANTED, [im-plahnt'-id], *adj.* set or fixed firmly.

IMPLATE, [im-plāt'], *v.t.* to sheathe, cover.

IMPLAUSIBILITY, [im-plawz'-i-bil'-i-ti], *n.* implausibleness.

IMPLAUSIBLE, [im-plawz'-ibl], *adj.* not plausible, not giving the impression of truth, unlikely.

IMPLAUSIBLENESS, [im-plawz'-ibl-nes], *n.* the quality of being implausible.

IMPLAUSIBLY, [im-plawz'-ib-li], *adv.* in an implausible way.

IMPLEACH, [im-plēch'], *v.t.* to interweave, entwine.

IMPLEDGE, [im-plej'], *v.t.* to pledge, pawn.

IMPLEMENT (1), [im'-pli-ment], *n.* a tool, instrument, machine, etc., for carrying out some task; (*Scots leg.*) accomplishment, fulfilment of an agreement, promise, etc. [L. *implere* fulfil].

IMPLEMENT (2), [im'-pli-ment'], *v.t.* to accomplish, complete, give effect to; (*Scots leg.*) to fulfil, carry out.

IMPLEMENTAL, [im'-pli-ment'-al], *adj.* used as, or serving as, an implement.

IMPLETION, [im-plē'-shun], *n.* the act of filling; the condition of being full. [LL. *impletio*].

IMPLICATE (1), [im'-pli-kat], *n.* that which is implied.

IMPLICATE (2), [im'-pli-kāt], *v.t.* to enfold, entangle; to imply, to indicate or suggest a certain inference; to show to be connected with. [L. *implicare*].

IMPLICATION, [im'-pli-kā'-shun], *n.* the act of implicating; the state of being implicated; something implied; the act of implying. [L. *implicatio*].

IMPLICATIVE, [im-plik'-at-iv], *adj.* tending to implicate or imply.

IMPLICATIVELY, [im-plik'-at-iv-li], *adv.* in an implicative way.

IMPLICIT, [im-plis'-it], *adj.* implied though not definitely stated; absolute, complete, unquestioning. [L. *implicitus*].

IMPLICITLY, [im-plis'-it-li], *adv.* in an implicit way.

IMPLICITNESS, [im-plis'-it-nes], *n.* the quality of being implicit.

IMPLIED, [im-plīd'], *adj.* understood, intended to be inferred.

IMPLIEDLY, [im-plīd'-li], *adv.* by implication.

IMPLODE, [im-plōd'], *v.t.* (*phon.*) to produce a stop consonant without breathing out audibly in the normal way after the sound is made; *v.i.* to be produced in this way. [IM and (EX)PLODE].

IMPLORATION, [im-plaw-rā'-shun], *n.* earnest entreaty. [L. *imploratio*].

IMPLORATORY, [im-plaw'-rat-er-i], *adj.* imploring.

IMPLORE, [im-plaw(r)'], *v.t.* to beg earnestly; to entreat, beseech. [L. *implorare*].

IMPLORER, [im-plaw'-rer], *n.* one who implores.

IMPLORING, [im-plaw'-ring], *adj.* beseeching, begging earnestly.

IMPLORINGLY, [im-plaw'-ring-li], *adv.* in an imploring fashion.

IMPLOSIVE (1), [im-plōz'-iv], *n.* an implosive consonant.

IMPLOSIVE (2), [im-plōz'-iv], *adj.* (*phon.*) (of a stop consonant) formed by imploding.

IMPLUME†, [im-plōōm'], *adj.* implumous. [L. *implumis*].

IMPLUMOUS†, [im-plōōm'-us], *adj.* without plumes.

IMPLUNGE, [im-plunj'], *v.t.* to plunge, immerse.

IMPLUVIUM, [im-plōō'-vi-um], *n.* a cistern in the hall of a Roman house, in which the rain-water from the roof was collected. [L. *impluvium*].

IMPLY, [im-plī'], *v.t.* to suggest, signify, to have a certain intended meaning not directly expressed; to hint, intend to suggest; to necessitate as a logical conclusion. [OFr. *emplier*].

IMPOCKET, [im-pok'-it], *v.t.* to pocket.

IMPOISON, see EMPOISON.

IMPOLDER, [im-pōl'-der], *v.t.* (of a tract of low-lying land) to reclaim from the sea or river. [Du. *impolderen*].

IMPOLICY, [im-pol'-i-si], *n.* inexpedient policy or conduct, unwisdom.

IMPOLITE, [im'-pol-īt'], *adj.* not polite ; rude, uncivil. [L. *impolitus*].

IMPOLITELY, [im-pol-īt'-li], *adv.* in an impolite way.

IMPOLITENESS, [im'-pol-īt'-nes], *n.* the quality of being impolite; an impolite act or speech.

IMPOLITIC, [im-pol'-it-ik], *adj.* not wise, inexpedient, imprudent.

IMPOLITICLY, [im-pol'-it-ik-li], *adv.* in an impolitic way.

IMPONDERABILITY, [im-pon'-der-a-bil'-i-ti], *n.* the state of being imponderable.

IMPONDERABLE (1), [im-pon'-der-abl], *n.* an imponderable body or thing.

IMPONDERABLE (2), [im-pon'-der-abl], *adj.* unable to be weighed; having no apparent or virtual weight, extremely light; (*fig.*) incalculable.

IMPONDERABLENESS, [im-pon'-der-abl-nes], *n.* imponderability.

IMPONDEROUS, [im-pon'-der-us], *adj.* without perceptible weight.

IMPONDEROUSNESS, [im-pon'-der-us-nes], *n.* the condition of being imponderous.

IMPONENT (1), [im-pōn'-ent], *n.* one who, or that which, imposes.

IMPONENT (2), [im-pōn'-ent], *adj.* that imposes. [L. *imponens*].

IMPORT (1), [im'-pawt], *n.* that which is imported; (*pl.*) goods brought into a country; meaning, implication; importance, consequence.

IMPORT (2), [im-pawt'], *v.t.* to bring in, *esp.* to bring into a country in the course of international trade; to introduce from an external or foreign source; to mean, imply; to be of importance to. [L. *importare*].

IMPORTABLE, [im-pawt'-abl], *adj.* able to be imported; (*fig.*) unbearable, intolerable.

IMPORTANCE, [im-pawt'-ants], *n.* the quality or state of being important; the reason why a particular thing is important. [MedL. *importantia*].

IMPORTANT, [im-pawt'-ant], *adj.* eminent, influential, notable; of considerable consequence or significance; momentous, vital; essential; pompous. [MedL. *importans*].

IMPORTANTLY, [im-pawt'-ant-li], *adv.* in an important way.

IMPORTATION, [im'-pawt-ā'-shun], *n.* the act or practice of importing; that which is imported.

IMPORTER, [im-pawt'-er], *n.* one who imports goods into a country.

IMPORTUNACY, [im-paw'-chōōn'-as-i], *n.* importunity.

IMPORTUNATE, [im-paw'-chōōn-at], *adj.* persistently and annoyingly entreating, demanding with tiresome pertinacity; insistent, continual, pestering. [L. *importunus* inopportune].

IMPORTUNATELY, [im-paw'-chōōn-at-li], *adv.* in an importunate fashion.

IMPORTUNATENESS, [im-paw'-chōōn-at-nes], *n.* importunity.

IMPORTUNE, [im'-paw-chōōn, im-paw'-chōōn], *v.t.* to weary with persistent begging or demands; to pester with entreaties. [MedL. *importunari*].

IMPORTUNER, [im-paw'-chōōn-er], *n.* one who importunes.

IMPORTUNITY, [im'-paw-chōōn'-i-ti], *n.* the quality of being importunate. [L. *importunitas*].

IMPOSABLE, [im-pōz'-abl], *adj.* able to be imposed.

IMPOSABLENESS, [im-pōz'-abl-nes], *n.* the quality of being imposable.

IMPOSE, [im-pōz'], *v.t.* to force to accept; to inflict; to levy, exact; to trick into accepting; (*print.*) to arrange (pages) for printing, and prepare the forme for press; *v.i.* to impress; **to i. on, upon,** to dupe, take a mean advantage of. [Fr. *imposer* to place].

IMPOSER, [im-pōz'-er], *n.* one who imposes.

IMPOSING (1), [im-pōz-'ing], *n.* (*print.*) the arrangement of the pages of a sheet in proper order, and preparation of the forme for printing.

IMPOSING (2), [im-pōz'-ing], *adj.* striking, compelling attention, commanding.

IMPOSINGLY, [im-pōz'-ing-li], *adv.* in an imposing way.

IMPOSINGNESS, [im-pōz'-ing-nes], *n.* the state or quality of being imposing.

IMPOSITION, [im'-poz-ish'-un], *n.* the act of imposing; that which is imposed, a tax, toll, duty; a task set as a punishment for misbehaviour in school; a deception; (*eccles.*) the laying on of hands by a bishop, etc., in ordination or confirmation. [L. *impositio*].

IMPOSSIBILITY, [im-pos'-i-bil'-i-ti], *n.* the state of being impossible; anything that is impossible. [L. *impossibilitas*].

IMPOSSIBLE, [im-pos'-ibl], *adj.* not possible; (*coll.*) insufferable, outrageous.

IMPOST (1), [im'-pōst], *n.* a tax or duty imposed by authority; (*racing*) the weight carried by a horse as a handicap in a race. [MedL. *impostum*].

IMPOST (2), [im'-pōst], *n.* (*arch.*) the moulding on the top of a pillar or pier from which an arch springs. [AFr. *imposte*].

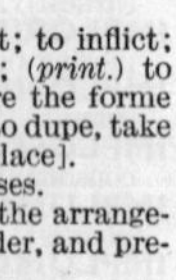

IMPOST

IMPOSTOR, [im-post'-er], *n.* one who attempts to trick people into believing that he is some other person, a cheat, fraud. [LL. *impostor*].

IMPOSTUMATE†, [im-pos'-chōōm-āt], *v.i.* to form an abscess; *v.t.* to affect with an abscess. [APOSTEMATE].

IMPOSTUMATION†, [im-pos'-chōōm-ā'-shun], *n.* the act of impostumating; an abscess.

IMPOSTUME†, [im-pos'-chōōm], *n.* an abscess, a festering sore. [OFr. *empostume*].

IMPOSTURE, [im-pos'-cher], *n.* a swindle, hoax, deception. [LL. *impostura*].

IMPOT, [im'-pot'], *n.* (*schoolboy slang*) an imposition. [IMPOSITION].

IMPOTENCE, [im'-pot-ents], *n.* the condition of being impotent. [L. *impotens* powerless].

IMPOTENCY, [im'-pot-en-si], *n.* impotence.

IMPOTENT, [im'-pot-ent], *adj.* weak, feeble, lacking physical strength; (of males) unable to perform the sexual act; helpless, unable to do anything. [L. *impotens*].

IMPOTENTLY, [im'-pot-ent-li], *adv.* in an impotent way.

IMPOUND, [im-pownd'], *v.t.* to shut up (cattle) in a pound; to confine as in a pound; to hold in security, to seize by legal authority.

IMPOVERISH, [im-pov'-er-ish], *v.t.* to make poor; to exhaust the resources or fertility of; to weaken; to make less attractive. [OFr. *empoverir*].

IMPOVERISHER, [im-pov'-er-ish-er], *n.* the thing or person that impoverishes.

IMPOVERISHMENT, [im-pov'-er-ish-ment], *n.* the act of impoverishing; the condition of being impoverished.

IMPRACTICABILITY, [im-prak'-tik-a-bil'-i-ti], *n.* the quality of being impracticable; that which is impracticable.

IMPRACTICABLE, [im-prak'-tik-abl], *adj.* that cannot be done, unable to be carried out, unworkable; (of persons) intractable, difficult to manage; (of roads) impassable, in very bad condition.

IMPRACTICABLENESS, [im-prak'-tik-abl-nes], *n.* the quality of being impracticable.

IMPRACTICABLY, [im-prak'-tik-ab-li], *adv.* in an impracticable fashion.

IMPRECATE, [im'-pri-kāt], *v.t.* to invoke (an evil), to pray that a misfortune fall on. [L. *imprecari*].

IMPRECATION, [im'-pri-kā'-shun], *n.* the act of imprecating; a curse, a misfortune imprecated. [L. *imprecatio*].

IMPRECATORY, [im'-pri-kāt'-er-i], *adj.* of the nature of an imprecation.

IMPRECISION, [im'-pri-sizh'-un], *n.* lack of precision.

IMPREGNABILITY, [im-preg'-na-bil'-i-ti], *n.* impregnableness.

IMPREGNABLE, [im-preg'-nabl], *adj.* able to withstand any attack; proof against pressure, persuasion, or temptation. [~Fr. *imprenable*].

IMPREGNABLENESS, [im-preg'-nabl-nes], *n.* the quality of being impregnable.

IMPREGNABLY, [im-preg'-nab-li], *adv.* in an impregnable fashion.

IMPREGNATE (1), [im-preg'-nāt], *adj.* rendered pregnant; filled, saturated.

IMPREGNATE (2), [im'-preg-nāt], *v.t.* to make pregnant, fertilize; to fill, imbue, instil; to saturate, spread throughout. [L. *impraegnare*].

IMPREGNATION, [im-preg-nā'-shun], *n.* the act of impregnating; the state of being impregnated; that which impregnates.

IMPRESARIO, [im'-pres-ah'-ri-ō], *n.* a manager, organizer, and producer of concerts and dramatic and operatic performances, etc. [It. *impresario* one who undertakes].

IMPRESCRIPTIBILITY, [im'-pri-skript'-i-bil'-i-ti], *n.* the condition of being imprescriptible.

IMPRESCRIPTIBLE, [im'-pri-skript'-ibl], *adj.* that cannot be lost or impaired or bound by prescription; unchallengeable, inviolable.

IMPRESS (1), [im'-pres], *n.* the act of impressing; a mark or impression; a seal, imprint, likeness; the result of some powerful influence or force.

IMPRESS (2), [im-pres'], *v.t. and i.* to mark by applying pressure, to imprint; to fix deeply in a person's mind, to show forcibly; to strike the mind forcibly, affect powerfully; to evoke a strong feeling of commendation or approval. [L. *impressum*, *p.pt.* of *imprimere*].

IMPRESS (3), [im-pres'], *v.t.* to force into public service, *esp.* to compel to serve in the army or navy; to seize for public service; (*fig.*) to enforce the assistance of, introduce as a help. [IM and PRESS (3)].

IMPRESSIBILITY, [im-pres'-i-bil'-i-ti], *n.* the quality of being impressible.

IMPRESSIBLE, [im-pres'-ibl], *adj.* that may be impressed, susceptible to impression.

IMPRESSIBLY, [im-pres'-ib-li], *adv.* in an impressible way.

IMPRESSION, [im-presh'-un], *n.* the act of impressing; the state of being impressed; a mark or stamp made by pressure; the effect upon anything produced by some external agency or influence; a notion, a rather vague feeling; a printed copy; (*print.*) the number of copies of a book, etc., printed for a single issue; a reprint of a book without additions or alterations; **to be under an i.,** to think, believe. [L. *impressio*].

IMPRESSIONABILITY, [im-presh'-un-a-bil'-i-ti], *n.* the quality of being impressionable.

IMPRESSIONABLE, [im-presh'-un-abl], *adj.* readily sensitive to impressions. [Fr. *impressionnable*].

IMPRESSIONISM, [im-presh'-un-izm], *n.* the artistic doctrine which maintains that a painter should attempt to convey the general impression immediately produced on the mind or feelings by an object, rather than reproduce a detailed objective representation of it; the application of this theory in art and literature.

IMPRESSIONIST (1), [im-presh'-un-ist], *n.* a painter or writer who carries into practice the doctrine of impressionism.

IMPRESSIONIST (2), [im-presh'-un-ist], *adj.* of, or pertaining to, impressionism or its exponents.

IMPRESSIONISTIC, [im-presh'-un-ist'-ik], *adj.* impressionist; based on impressions rather than on detailed study or comparisons.

IMPRESSIVE, [im-pres'-iv], *adj.* creating a deep impression, striking, stirring.

IMPRESSIVELY, [im-pres'-iv-li], *adv.* in an impressive fashion.

IMPRESSIVENESS, [im-pres'-iv-nes], *n.* the quality of being impressive.

IMPRESSMENT, [im-pres'-ment], *n.* the act of impressing for public service.

IMPREST (1), [im'-prest], *n.* a sum of money forwarded to a person to enable him to perform some State business or duties. [OFr. *emprest* a loan].

IMPREST† (2), [im-prest'], *v.t.* to advance, lend; to forward a sum of money to. [MedL. *impraestare*].

IMPRIMATUR, [im-prīm-āt'-ur], *n.* a licence to print a book, *esp.* one granted by the Roman Catholic Church; (*fig.*) sanction, approval. [L. *imprimatur* let it be imprinted].

IMPRIMIS, [im-prīm'-is], *adv.* first of all. [L. *imprimis*].

IMPRINT (1), [im'-print], *n.* that which is imprinted, an impression; the name of the printer or publisher of a book, with the place and date of printing or publication, printed either at the front or the end of a book; (*fig.*) a feature impressed upon something, trace. [OFr. *empreinte*].

IMPRINT (2), [im-print'], *v.t.* to stamp, to make, produce or mark by pressure; to press, print; (*fig.*) to fix clearly in the mind. [OFr. *empreinter*].

IMPRISON, [im-priz'-on], *v.t.* to confine in a prison, to shut up. [OFr. *emprisoner*].

IMPRISONER, [im-priz'-on-er], *n.* a person who imprisons.

IMPRISONMENT, [im-priz'-on-ment], *n.* the act of imprisoning; the state of being imprisoned; period of detention. [OFr. *emprisonnement*].

IMPROBABILITY, [im-prob'-a-bil'-i-ti], *n.* the quality of being improbable.

IMPROBABLE, [im-prob'-abl], *adj.* not likely to be true. [L. *improbabilis*].

IMPROBABLY, [im-prob'-ab-li], *adv.* in an improbable way.

IMPROBATION, [im'-prob-ā'-shun], *n.* (*Scots leg.*) an action brought to prove a document to be false or forged, or to set aside a deed on this account.

IMPROBITY, [im-prōb'-i-ti], *n.* want of probity, dishonesty. [L. *improbitas*].

IMPROFICIENCE†, [im'-prō-fish'-ents], *n.* improficiency.

IMPROFICIENCY, [im'-prō-fish'-en-si], *n* lack of proficiency.

IMPROGRESSIVE, [im'-prō-gres'-iv], *adj.* not progressive.

IMPROMPTU (1), [im-promp'-chōō], *n.* anything done or made impromptu.

IMPROMPTU (2), [im-promp'-chōō], *adj.* performed on the spur of the moment without previous preparation, extempore, improvised. [Fr. *impromptu*].

IMPROMPTU (3), [im-promp'-chōō], *adv.* without previous preparation.

IMPROPER, [im-prop'-er], *adj.* not proper, unsuitable; irregular, incorrect; indecent; **i. fraction**, (*arith.*) a fraction whose numerator is greater than its denominator.

IMPROPERLY, [im-prop'-er-li], *adv.* in an improper way.

IMPROPRIATE (1), [im-prō'-pri-āt], *adj.* having been appropriated as private property; having been placed in the hands of a layman.

IMPROPRIATE (2), [im-prō'-pri-āt], *v.t.* to transfer, annex, or appropriate an ecclesiastical benefice for private use; to place ecclesiastical property in the hands of a clergyman. [MedL. *impropriare*].

IMPROPRIATION, [im-prō'-pri-ā'-shun], *n.* the act of impropriating; that which is impropriated.

IMPROPRIATOR, [im-prō'-pri-āt-er], *n.* a person to whom a benefice is impropriated.

IMPROPRIETY, [im'-prō-prī'-i-ti], *n.* the quality or condition of being improper; an improper act, speech, feature, etc. [L. *improprietas*].

IMPROSPEROUS†, [im-pros'-per-us] *adj.* not prosperous, unlucky. [L. *improsper*].

IMPROVABILITY, [im-prōōv'-a-bil'-i-ti], *n.* improvableness.

IMPROVABLE, [im-prōōv'-abl], *adj.* that may be improved.

IMPROVABLENESS, [im-prōōv'-abl-nes], *n.* the condition of being improvable.

IMPROVABLY, [im-prōōv'-ab-li], *adv.* in a way that admits of improvement.

IMPROVE, [im-prōōv'], *v.t.* to make more valuable or better; to use to advantage; *v.i.* to become better. [AFr. *emprouver*].

IMPROVEMENT, [im-prōōv'-ment], *n.* the act of improving; the state of being improved; that which constitutes an increase in value or good qualities. [AFr. *emprouvement*].

IMPROVER, [im-prōōv'-er], *n.* one who or that which improves, an apprentice.

IMPROVIDENCE, [im-prov'-id-ents], *n.* the quality of being improvident. [L. *improvidentia*]

IMPROVIDENT, [im-prov'-id-ent], *adj.* thriftless, wanting in foresight, not given to making provision for the future.

IMPROVIDENTLY, [im-prov'-id-ent-li], *adv.* in an improvident fashion.

IMPROVING, [im-prōōv'-ing], *adj.* that improves.

IMPROVINGLY, [im-prōōv'-ing-li], *adv.* in a fashion to improve.

IMPROVISATION, [im'-prov-iz-ā'-shun, im-prov'-iz-ā'-shun], *n.* the act of improvising; whatever is improvised.

IMPROVISATOR, [im'-prov-īz-āt'-er, im-prov'-iz-āt'-er], *n.* one who improvises.

IMPROVISE, [im'-prov-īz], *v.t. and i.* to compose and perform on the spur of the moment without previous preparation; to rig up in a makeshift way, to construct a rough or approximate copy of an object out of any materials or other objects at hand. [It. *improvisare*].

IMPROVISO†, [im-prov-īz'-ō], *adj.* extempore, without preparation. [It. *improviso*].

IMPRUDENCE, [im-prōōd'-ents], *n.* the quality of being imprudent; that which is imprudent. [L. *imprudentia*].

IMPRUDENT, [im-prōōd'-ent], *adj.* rash indiscreet, not prudent. [L. *imprudens*].

IMPRUDENTLY, [im-prōōd'-ent-li], *adv.* in an imprudent way.

IMPUBERAL, [im-pew'-ber-al], *adj.* not at puberty, immature. [L. *impubes*].

IMPUBERTY, [im-pew'-ber-ti], *n.* the condition of not having arrived at the state of puberty.

IMPUDENCE, [im'-pyōō-dents], *n.* the quality of being impudent. [L. *impudentia*].

IMPUDENT, [im'-pyōō-dent], *adj.* wanting modesty, shameless, rude, cheeky. [L. *impudens*].

IMPUDENTLY, [im'-pyōō-dent-li], *adv.* in an impudent way.

IMPUDICITY, [im'-pyōō-dis'-i-ti], *n.* immodesty, shamelessness. [Fr. *impudicité*].

IMPUGN, [im-pewn'], *v.t.* to attack in argument; to call in question. [L. *impugnare* to attack].

IMPUGNABLE, [im-pewn'-abl], *adj.* able to be questioned.

IMPUGNER, [im-pewn'-er], *n.* one who impugns.

IMPUISSANCE, [im-pwēs'-ahnts], *n.* feebleness, impotence. [Fr. *impuissance*].

IMPUISSANT, [im-pwēs'-ant], *adj.* impotent, powerless. [Fr. *impuissant*].

IMPULSE, [im'-puls], *n.* the act of impelling, a thrust, push; a sudden emotional urge to action; a large force applied or lasting for an extremely short time. [L. *impulsus*].

IMPULSION, [im-pul'-shun], *n.* the act of impelling; the state of being impelled; impetus; effect produced by impelling; an impulse. [L. *impulsio*].

IMPULSIVE, [im-puls'-iv], *adj.* able or tending to impel; liable to act on impulse without considering the possible consequences; based on an impulse. [MedL. *impulsivus*].

IMPULSIVELY, [im-puls'-iv-li], *adv.* in an impulsive way.

IMPULSIVENESS, [im-puls'-iv-nes], *n.* the quality of being impulsive.

IMPUNITY, [im-pewn'-i-ti], *n.* exemption or freedom from penalty, punishment, injury, or loss; **with i.**, without fear of the consequences. [L. *impunitas*].

IMPURE, [im-pyōōer'], *adj.* not pure; dirty; unhallowed; obscene, unchaste; mixed with some foreign matter or elements; adulterated.

IMPURELY, [im-pew′-er-li], *adv.* in an impure fashion.
IMPURENESS, [im-pew′-er-nes], *n.* the condition of being impure.
IMPURITY, [im-pew′-er-i-ti], *n.* the quality or state of being impure; that which is impure, a foreign element that adulterates. [L. *impuritas*].
IMPURPLE, see EMPURPLE.
IMPUTABILITY, [im-pewt′-a-bil′-i-ti], *n.* the condition of being imputable.
IMPUTABLE, [im-pewt′-abl], *adj.* able to be imputed, charged, or attributed.
IMPUTABLENESS, [im-pewt′-abl-nes], *n.* imputability.
IMPUTATION, [im′-pewt-ā′-shun], *n.* the act of imputing, attribution, *esp.* of something bad, to a person; the accusation made against a person; (*theol.*) the attribution of the guilt of Adam and the righteousness of Christ to all Christians. [LL. *imputatio*].
IMPUTATIVE, [im-pewt′-at-iv], *adj.* by imputation, imputed. [LL. *imputativus*].
IMPUTATIVELY, [im-pewt′-at-iv-li], *adv.* in an imputative way.
IMPUTE, [im-pewt′], *v.t.* to attribute, ascribe to (*esp.* something bad); to lay to the blame of; (*theol.*) to attribute to as being natural or spiritual descendants of. [L. *imputare* to reckon].
IMPUTER, [im-pewt′-er], *n.* one who imputes.
IMPUTRESCIBLE, [im′-pyōō-tres′-ibl], *adj.* not subject to decay or corruption, incorruptible.
IN (1), [in], *n.*(*pl.*) (*polit.*) the party in the office; **the ins and outs**, the full details, complexities, etc.
IN (2), [in], *adj.* interior, internal.
IN (3), [in], *adv.* within, inside, into; along, close to; into the bargain; (of a fire) burning, alight; (*pol.*) holding office; (*cricket*) taking one's innings, batting; arrived at a place; **i. for**, committed to; about or certain to receive; entered or applied for; (*coll.*) due for; **i. with**, on friendly terms with. [OE. *in, inn*].
IN (4), [in], *prep.* inside of, within; partly or completely enclosed by; during; at the end of; by means of, through the medium of; because of; by way of; having regard to; *also used to express state, condition, place, time, manner, action, limitation, method of arrangement.* [OE. *in*].
IN- (5), *pref.* not. [L. *in-*].
IN- (6), *pref.* in, upon; into, against, towards. [L. *in*].
INABILITY, [in′-a-bil′-i-ti], *n.* incapacity, lack of ability.
INABSTINENCE, [in-ab′-stin-ents], *n.* want of abstinence.
INABSTRACTED†, [in′-ab-strakt′-id], *adj.* not abstracted.
INABUSIVELY, [in′-a-bews′-iv-li], *adv.* without abuse.
INACCESSIBILITY, [in′-ak-ses′-i-bil′-i-ti], *n.* the quality of being inaccessible.
INACCESSIBLE, [in-ak-ses′-ibl], *adj.* out-of-the-way, remote, difficult to get at; unattainable; extremely reserved or aloof. [LL. *inaccessibilis*].
INACCESSIBLENESS, [in′-ak-ses′-ibl-nes], *n.* inaccessibility.
INACCESSIBLY, [in′-ak-ses′-ib-li], *adv.* in an inaccessible way.
INACCURACY, [in-ak′-yōō-ra-si], *n.* the quality of being inaccurate; a mistake.
INACCURATE, [in-ak′-yōō-rat], *adj.* not accurate, incorrect, wrong.
INACCURATELY, [in-ak′-yōō-rat-li], *adv.* in an inaccurate way.
INACQUIESCENT, [in-ak′-wi-es′-ent], *adj.* not acquiescing.
INACTION, [in-ak′-shun], *n.* want of action; inertness; state of doing nothing.
INACTIVE, [in-akt′-iv], *adj.* not active, indisposed to exertion or effort; quiescent, dormant; indolent; out of work, unemployed; not operating.
INACTIVELY, [in-akt′-iv-li], *adv.* in an inactive way.
INACTIVITY, [in′-ak-tiv′-i-ti], *n.* the state or period of being inactive.
INADAPTABLE, [in′-a-dapt′-abl], *adj.* that may not be adapted; lacking adaptability.
INADAPTATION, [in-ad′-apt-ā′-shun], *n.* want of adaptation.
INADEQUACY, [in-ad′-i-kwa-si], *n.* the quality of being inadequate.
INADEQUATE, [in-ad′-i-kwat], *adj.* not adequate, not equal to the purpose, not competent.
INADEQUATELY, [in-ad′-i-kwat-li], *adv.* in an inadequate fashion.
INADEQUATENESS, [in-ad′-i-kwat-nes], *n.* inadequacy.
INADEQUATION, [in′-ad-i-kwā′-shun], *n.* lack of exact correspondence.
INADHERENT, [in′-ad-hēer′-ent], *adj.* not adherent.
INADHESION, [in′-ad-hē′-zhun], *n.* lack of adhesion.
INADMISSIBILITY, [in′-ad-mis′-i-bil′-i-ti], *n.* the quality of being inadmissible.
INADMISSIBLE, [in′-ad-mis′-ibl], *adj.* that cannot be admitted.
INADVERTENCE, [in′-ad-vert′-ents], *n.* the quality of being inadvertent; anything done inadvertently, an oversight.
INADVERTENCY, [in′-ad-vert′-en-si], *n.* inadvertence.
INADVERTENT, [in-ad-vert′-ent], *adj.* heedless, not paying proper attention; unintentional, due to an accidental error or miscalculation. [IN (5) and ADVERTENT].
INADVERTENTLY, [in′-ad-vert′-ent-li], *adv.* in an inadvertent way.
INAFFECTATION, [in′-af-ek-tā′-shun], *n.* unaffectedness.
INAJA, [in-a-jah′], *n.* the lofty Brazilian palm, *Maximiliana regia*, having leaves forty feet in length. [Tupi *inaja*].
INALIENABILITY, [in-ā′-li-en-a-bil′-i-ti], *n.* the quality of being inalienable.
INALIENABLE, [in-ā′-li-en-abl], *adj.* that may not be alienated.
INALIENABLENESS, [in-ā′-li-en-abl-nes], *n.* inalienability.
INALIENABLY, [in-ā′-li-en-ab-li], *adv.* in an inalienable way.
INALTERABILITY, [in-awl′-ter-a-bil′-i-ti], *n.* the quality of being unalterable.
INALTERABLE, [in-awl′-ter-abl], *adj.* unalterable.
INAMIABLE, [in-ā′-mi-abl], *adj.* not amiable, unfriendly.
INAMORATO, INAMORATA, [in-am′-o-rah′-tō (-ta)], *n.* a lover, a beloved man (woman). [It. *inamorato(ta)*].
IN-AND-IN, [in′-and-in′], *adv.* from the same stock.
INANE (1), [in-ān′], *n.* the limitless void.
INANE (2), [in-ān′], *adj.* silly, brainless, vacant, frivolous. [L. *inanis* empty].
INANIMATE, [in-an′-im-at], *adj.* without life or animation; (*fig.*) inactive. [LL. *inanimatus*].
INANIMATED, [in-an′-im-āt′-id], *adj.* inanimate.
INANIMATION, [in-an′-im-ā′-shun], *n.* the state of being inanimate.
INANITION, [in′-a-nish′-un], *n.* exhaustion from lack of nourishment. [L. *inanitio* emptiness].
INANITY, [in-an′-i-ty], *n.* the quality of being inane; an inane remark or act. [L. *inanitas* emptiness].
INANTHERATE, [in-an′-ther-at], *adj.* without anthers.
INAPPEASABLE, [in′-a-pēz′-abl], *adj.* not to be appeased or satisfied.
INAPPELLABLE, [in′-a-pel′-abl], *adj.* not able to be appealed against. [IN (5) and L. *appellare* to address].
INAPPETENCE, [in-ap′-it-ents], *n.* lack of desire, *esp.* sexual desire. [APPETENCE].
INAPPETENCY, [in-ap′-it-en-si], *n.* inappetence.
INAPPETENT, [in-ap′-it-ent], *adj.* lacking desire, *esp.* sexual desire.
INAPPLICABILITY, [in-ap′-lik-a-bil′-i-ti], *n.* the quality of being inapplicable.
INAPPLICABLE, [in-ap′-lik-abl], *adj.* not applicable; unsuitable.
INAPPLICABLY, [in-ap′-lik-ab-li], *adv.* in an inapplicable way.
INAPPLICATION, [in-ap′-lik-ā′-shun], *n.* want of application; unsuitableness.
INAPPOSITE, [in-ap′-ō-zit], *adj.* not apposite, irrelevant, out of place.
INAPPOSITELY, [in-ap′-ō-zit-li], *adv.* in an inapposite way.
INAPPRECIABLE, [in-a-prē′-shyabl], *adj.* imperceptible, negligible, not appreciable.
INAPPRECIABLY, [in′-a-prē′-shyab-li], *adv.* in an inappreciable way.
INAPPRECIATIVE, [in′-a-prē′-shyat-iv], *adj.* not appreciative.
INAPPREHENSIBLE, [in-ap′-ri-hens′-ibl], *adj.* not intelligible or understandable. [LL. *inapprehensibilis*].
INAPPREHENSIVE, [in-ap′-ri-hens′-iv], *adj.* not apprehensive.
INAPPROACHABLE, [in-a-prōch′-abl], *adj.* unapproachable; (*fig.*) frigid, unfriendly.

INAPPROPRIATE, [in'-a-prō'-pri-at], *adj* not appropriate, unsuitable.
INAPPROPRIATELY, [in'-a-prō'-pri-at-li], *adv.* in an inappropriate way.
INAPPROPRIATENESS, [in'-a-prō'-pri-at-nes], *n.* the quality of being inappropriate.
INAPT, [in-apt'], *adj.* unskilful, clumsy; incongruous, out of place.
INAPTITUDE [in-apt'-it-ewd], *n* the quality of being inapt.
INAPTLY, [in-apt'-li], *adv.* in an inapt fashion.
INAPTNESS, [in-apt'-nes], *n.* inaptitude.
INARABLE, [in-a'-rabl], *adj.* not arable.
INARCH, [in-ahch'], *v.t.* to graft, without separation from the parent tree, into a near-by stock.
INARM, [in-ahm'], *v.t.* to fold in the arms, to embrace.
INARTICULATE, [in'-ah-tik'-yōō-lat], *adj.* (*anat.*) not jointed or articulated; (of speech) not clear or distinct, jumbled and gabbled; unable to speak or express oneself clearly and fluently [L. *inarticulatus*].
INARTICULATELY, [in'-ah-tik'-yōō-lat-li], *adv.* in an inarticulate way.
INARTICULATENESS, [in'-ah-tik'-yōō-lat-nes], *n.* the quality of being inarticulate.
INARTICULATION, [in'-ah-tik'-yōō-lā'-shun], *n.* inarticulateness.
INARTIFICIAL, [in'-ah-ti-fish'-al], *adj.* natural, not artificial, unaffected; inartistic, unskilful. [L. *inartificialis*].
INARTIFICIALLY, [in'-ah-ti-fish'-al-i], *adv.* in an inartificial way.
INARTISTIC, [in'-ah-tist'-ik], *adj.* lacking in artistry; inelegant; lacking a taste for or appreciation of the arts.
INARTISTICALLY, [in'-ah-tist'-ik-al-i], *adv.* in an inartistic way.
INASMUCH, [in'-az-much'], *adv.* **i. as,** seeing that, because, since; in so far as.
INATTENTION, [in'-a-ten'-shun], *n.* want of attention, failure to pay attention or concentrate; lack of courtesy or consideration.
INATTENTIVE, [in'-a-tent'-iv], *adj.* not paying attention; heedless; negligent.
INATTENTIVELY, [in'-a-tent'-iv-li], *adv.* in an inattentive way.
INAUDIBILITY, [in-awd'-i-bil'-i-ti], *n.* the condition of being inaudible.
INAUDIBLE, [in-awd'-ibl], *adj.* unable to be heard. [L. *inaudibilis*].
INAUDIBLENESS, [in-awd'-ibl-nes], *n.* inaudibility.
INAUDIBLY, [in-awd'-ib-li], *adv.* in an inaudible fashion.
INAUGURAL, [in-awg'-yōō-ral], *adj.* pertaining to inauguration, given on entering into office or at an opening ceremony. [Fr. *inaugural*].
INAUGURATE, [in-awg'-yōō-rāt], *v.t.* to install or induct into office with suitable ceremonies; to introduce or commence formally, to start; to open formally to the public by a special ceremony. [L. *inaugurare* to take omens from the flight of birds].
INAUGURATION, [in-awg'-yōō-rā'-shun], *n.* the act of inaugurating; the condition of being inaugurated. [L. *inauguratio*].
INAUGURATOR, [in-awg'-yōō-rāt'-er], *n.* one who inaugurates.
INAUGURATORY, [in-awg'-yōō-rāt'-er-i], *adj.* inaugural.
INAURATE (1), [in-aw'-rāt], *adj.* covered with gold or gilt. [L. *inauratus*].
INAURATE† **(2),** [in-aw'-rāt], *v.t.* to gild [L. *inaurare*].
INAUSPICIOUS, [in'-aws-pish'-us], *adj.* ill-omened, ill-starred, unfortunate.
INAUSPICIOUSLY, [in'-aws-pish'-us-li], *adv.* in an inauspicious way.
INAUSPICIOUSNESS, [in'-aws-pish'-us-nes], *n.* the quality of being inauspicious.
INAUTHORITATIVE, [in'-aw-tho'-rit-at-iv], *adj.* lacking authority.
INBEING, [in'-bē-ing], *n.* essential, intrinsic nature.
INBOARD, [in'-bawd], *adj.* within the ship, towards the centre of the ship.
INBOND, [in-bond'], *adj.* (of a brick) laid lengthwise across a wall.

INBOND

INBORN, [in'-bawn], *adj.* innate, inherent instinctive.
INBREAKING, [in'-brāk-ing], *n.* a breaking into, forcible intrusion into
INBREATHE [in-brēTH'], *v.t.* to inhale.
INBRED, [in'-bred], *adj.* innate, inherent, natural; bred from the mating of individuals sprung from common ancestors.
INBREED, IMBREED†, [in-brēd'], *v.t.* to breed in-and-in; to implant or engender within.
INBURST, [in'-burst], *n.* a bursting in.
INCA, [ingk'-a], *n.* the king of, or a member of the royal family of, Peru before it was conquered by the Spaniards. [Peruvian *inca* ruler].
INCAGE, see ENCAGE.
INCALCULABLE, [in-kal'-kyōō-labl], *adj.* unable to be calculated, untold; unable to be foretold or forecast; volatile, fickle.
INCALCULABLENESS, [in-kal'-kyōō-labl-nes], *n.* the quality of being incalculable.
INCALCULABLY, [in-kal'-kyōō-lab-li], *adv.* in an incalculable way.
INCANDESCE, [in'-kand-es'], *v.t.* to cause to incandesce; *v.i.* to become incandescent, to emit light when strongly heated. [L. *incandescere*].
INCANDESCENCE, [in'-kand-es'-ents], *n.* the condition of being incandescent.
INCANDESCENT, [in'-kand-es'-ent], *adj.* glowing with a white heat, emitting light because of its high temperature; luminous, shining; (*fig.*) burning, passionate. [L. *incandescens*].
INCANTATION, [in'-kant-ā'-shun], *n.* a magical formula chanted or recited, a spell. [L. *incantatio*].
INCANTATORY, [in'-kant-āt'-er-i], *adj.* pertaining to, of the nature of, an incantation.
INCANTON, [in-kant'-on], *v.t.* to unite or form into a canton.
INCAPABILITY, [in-kāp'-a-bil'-i-ti], *n.* the quality of being incapable.
INCAPABLE, [in-kāp'-abl], *adj.* not capable, unable; helpless; incompetent; (*leg.*) disqualified or barred from.
INCAPABLENESS, [in-kāp'-abl-nes], *n.* incapability.
INCAPABLY, [in-kāp'-ab-li], *adv* in an incapable way.
INCAPACIOUS, [in'-kap-ā'-shus], *adj.* of small size or content, narrow, tiny; unable to understand or grasp with the mind. [~L. *incapax incapacis*].
INCAPACIOUSNESS, [in'-kap-ā'-shus-nes], *n.* the state of being incapacious.
INCAPACITATE, [in'-kap-as'-it-āt], *v.t.* to render unfit or incapable of, to disable; (*fig.*) to disqualify, bar.
INCAPACITATION, [in'-kap-as'-it-ā'-shun], *n.* the act of incapacitating; the condition of being incapacitated.
INCAPACITY, [in'-kap-as'-i-ti], *n.* want of capacity, inability, incompetence; (*leg.*) disqualification.
INCARCERATE, [in-kah'-ser-āt], *v.t.* to shut up in a prison. [MedL. *incarcerare*].
INCARCERATION, [in-kah'-ser-ā'-shun], *n.* the act of incarcerating; the state or period of being incarcerated; (*path.*) strangulation of a hernia. [L. *incarceratio*].
INCARN, [in-kahn'], *v.t. and i.* to cover over or fill up with flesh; to heal over, to become covered with flesh. [L. *incarnare* to make flesh].
INCARNADINE (1), [in-kahn'-ad-īn], *adj.* flesh-coloured; blood-red. [It. *incarnadino*].
INCARNADINE (2), [in-kahn'-ad-in], *v.t.* to make red, to dye blood-red.
INCARNATE (1), [in-kahn'-at], *adj.* invested with or embodied in flesh, in bodily form; personified. [L. *incarnatus*].
INCARNATE (2), [in-kahn'-āt], *v.t.* to embody in flesh, to take on bodily form; to express in concrete form. [*Prec.*].
INCARNATION, [in'-kahn-ā'-shun], *n.* the act of incarnating; the assumption of a human body and personality; the personification of an abstract quality; (*surg.*) the process of healing wounds and filling the part affected with new flesh. [LL. *incarnatio*].
INCARNATIVE (1), [in-kahn'-at-iv], *n.* an incarnative medicine
INCARNATIVE (2), [in-kahn'-at-iv], *adj.* causing new flesh to grow, healing. [MedL. *incarnativus*].
INCASE, see ENCASE.
INCATENATION, [in'-kat-en-ā'-shun], *n.* a linking together, a harnessing with chains. [MedL. *incatenatio*].
INCAUTION, [in-kaw'-shun], *n.* want of caution, rashness.

INCAUTIOUS, [in-kaw'-shus], *adj.* not cautious, indiscreet, rash.

INCAUTIOUSLY, [in-kaw'-shus-li], *adv.* in an incautious fashion.

INCAUTIOUSNESS, [in-kaw'-shus-nes], *n.* the quality of being incautious, rashness.

INCAVATED, [in'-kav-āt'-id], *adj.* hollowed out, bent round or in.

INCAVATION, [in'-kav-ā'-shun], *n.* the act of making hollow; a hollow.

INCAVERN, [in-kav'-ern], *v.t.* to shut up in a cavern.

INCAVO, [in-kā'-vō], *n.* the sunken part of an intaglio. [It. *incavo*].

INCENDIARISM, [in-send'-i-er-izm], *n.* arson, the act of wilfully setting fire to property; (*fig.*) an inflaming of passions, agitation to violence or disaffection.

INCENDIARY (1), [in-send'-i-er-i], *n.* one who indulges in incendiarism; an incendiary bomb.

INCENDIARY (2), [in-send'-i-er-i], *adj.* pertaining to, given to, the malicious burning of property; capable of causing a fire; (*fig.*) tending to excite disaffection, violence or sedition. [L. *incendiarius* causing burning].

INCENSANT, [in-sens'-ant], *adj.* (*her.*) in an angry posture.

INCENSE (1), [in'-sents], *n.* fragrant odours or smoke arising from aromatic herbs, spices, etc., burned in religious rites; the materials thus burned; any fragrant odour; (*fig.*) flattery, homage. [OFr. *encens* from L. *incensus* burnt].

INCENSE (2), [in-sents'], *v.t.* to perfume, fumigate with incense; to burn or offer incense to; to scent; to enrage, to make furious. [OFr. *encenser* from L. *incensus*, *p.pt.* of *incendere* to set on fire].

INCENSEMENT, [in-sens'-ment], *n.* the act of incensing; the state of being incensed.

INCENSORY, [in-sen'-ser-i], *n.* the vessel in which incense is burned. [MedL. *incensorium*].

INCENSURABLE, [in-sen'-sher-abl], *adj.* not deserving censure.

INCENTIVE (1), [in-sent'-iv], *n.* a stimulus, spur, incitement.

INCENTIVE (2), [in-sent'-iv], *adj.* tending to stimulate or stir up. [L. *incentivus*].

INCENTIVELY, [in-sent'-iv-li], *adv.* in a manner to incite.

INCEPT, [in-sept'], *v.t.* (*biol.*) to absorb as an organism; *v.i.* to fulfil the conditions required for a first degree, thus qualifying for a higher degree (at Cambridge University). [L. *inceptum*, *p.pt.* of *incipere* to begin].

INCEPTION, [in-sep'-shun], *n.* commencement, start. [L. *inceptio*].

INCENSORY

INCEPTIVE, [in-sept'-iv], *adj.* beginning, commencing, initial; (*gram.*) expressing the beginning of an action. [L. *inceptum*, *p.pt.* of *incipere* to begin].

INCEPTIVELY, [in-sept'-iv-li], *adv.* in an inceptive way.

INCEPTOR, [in-sept'-er], *n.* one who has taken or who is about to take a first degree at Cambridge or Oxford University. [L. *inceptor*].

INCEREMONIOUS†, [in'-se-ri-mō'-ni-us], *adj.* unceremonious.

INCERTITUDE, [in-sert'-it-ewd], *n.* uncertainty, doubtfulness; insecurity. [Fr. *incertitude*].

INCESSABLY, [in-ses'-ab-li], *adv.* unceasingly. [L. *incessabilis*].

INCESSANCY, [in-ses'-an-si], *n.* the quality of being incessant.

INCESSANT, [in-ses'-ant], *adj.* unceasing, continual, endless. [LL. *incessans*].

INCESSANTLY, [in-ses'-ant-li], *adv.* without ceasing, continually.

INCESSANTNESS, [in-ses'-ant-nes], *n.* the quality of being incessant.

INCEST, [in'-sest], *n.* sexual intercourse within the prohibited degrees of relationship. [L. *incestus*].

INCESTUOUS, [in-sest'-yōō-us], *adj.* guilty of incest, of the nature of incest. [L. *incestuosus*].

INCESTUOUSLY, [in-sest'-yōō-us-li], *adv.* in an incestuous way.

INCH (1), [inch], *n.* a twelfth of a foot; (of rain) a quantity sufficient to cover a surface to the depth of an inch; a small amount, distance, etc.; (*pl.*) height, stature; **by inches, i. by i.**, gradually; **every i.**, completely, entirely. [OE. *ynce* from L. *uncia* a twelfth part].

INCH (2), [inch], *n.* in Scotland, a small island; a detached hillock. [Gael. *innis* island].

INCH (3), [inch], *v.t.* to calculate or measure the number of inches in; to drive or cause to move by small degrees; *v.i.* to move by inches.

INCHED, [incht], *adj.* containing inches.

INCHEST, [in-chest'], *v.t.* to place into a chest.

INCHMEAL, [inch'-mēl], *adv.* by inches, gradually. [INCH and OE. *mæl* measure].

INCHOATE (1), [in-kō'-āt], *adj.* just begun, in an early stage; unfinished. [L. *inchoatus*].

INCHOATE (2), [in'-kō-āt], *v.t. and i.* to begin, start, initiate.

INCHOATELY, [in-kō'-āt-li], *adv.* in an inchoate manner.

INCHOATION, [in'-kō-ā'-shun], *n.* commencement, beginning. [LL. *inchoatio*].

INCHOATIVE, [in-kō'-at-iv], *adj* (*gram.*) expressing the beginning of an action; initial, rudimentary, introductory. [LL. *inchoativus*].

INCHPIN†, [inch'-pin'], *n.* the sweetbread of a deer.

INCIDENCE, [in'-sid-ents], *n.* the fact of falling upon; the manner of falling upon; range, extent to which a thing affects anything; direction in which a line or moving body strikes or falls upon another; **angle of i.**, the angle which a ray of light, line, etc., falling on a surface, makes with a perpendicular to that surface. [Fr. *incidence*].

INCIDENCY†, [in'-sid-en-si], *n.* an incident; incidence; the quality of being liable to occur to.

INCIDENT (1), [in'-sid-ent], *n.* that which happens, an event; a single particular happening considered as separate and complete in itself; a subordinate episode in a literary composition; (*leg.*) a privilege, right, obligation attaching to, or inseparably connected with, an office, estate, etc.; **i. officer**, a person deputed to take charge of an individual incident caused by the dropping of a bomb.

INCIDENT (2), [in'-sid-ent], *adj.* liable to happen to, naturally belonging to, connected with; (*phys.*) striking or falling on; (*leg.*) attached to, attendant on. [L. *incidens*].

INCIDENTAL (1), [in'-sid-ent'-al], *n.* that which is incidental.

INCIDENTAL (2), [in'-sid-ent'-al], *adj.* attendant on, liable to happen in; (of expenses) incurred in addition to the main expense; occasional, subordinate, by the way; (of music) intended to go with a spoken play.

INCIDENTALLY, [in'-sid-ent'-al-i], *adv.* in an incidental fashion; by the way.

INCIDENTALNESS, [in'-sid-ent'-al-nes], *n.* the quality of being incidental.

INCINERATE, [in-sin'-er-āt], *v.t.* to burn to ashes. [MedL. *incinerare*].

INCINERATION, [in-sin'-er-ā'-shun], *n.* a burning to ashes. [MedL. *incineratio*].

INCINERATOR, [in-sin'-er-āt'-er], *n.* a furnace for burning refuse; a cremation furnace.

INCIPIENCE, [in-sip'-i-ents], *n.* the quality of being incipient; start, beginning.

INCIPIENCY, [in-sip'-i-en-si], *n.* incipience.

INCIPIENT, [in-sip'-i-ent], *adj.* beginning, commencing, in the earliest stages. [L. *incipiens*].

INCIPIENTLY, [in-sip'-i-ent-li], *adv.* in an incipient way.

INCIPIT, [in'-sip-it], *n.* the opening words of a manuscript employed to identify it. [L. *incipit* it begins].

INCIRCLE, see ENCIRCLE.

INCISE, [in-sīz'], *v.t.* to make a cut in; to carve, engrave. [L. *incisum*, *p.pt.* of *incidere*].

INCISED, [in-sīzd'], *adj.* cut, gashed; (*bot.*, *zool.*) regularly and deeply indented along the margin.

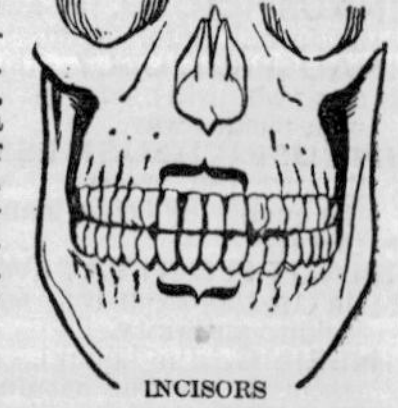

INCISORS

INCISION, [in-sizh'-un], *n.* the act of incising; a cut, *esp.* one made for surgical purposes; (*bot.*, *zool.*) a deep marginal indentation. [L. *incisio*].

INCISIVE, [in-sīs'-iv], *adj.* cutting sharply into; (*fig.*) sharp, piercing, trenchant, sarcastic. [MedL. *incisivus*].

INCISOR, [in-sīz'-er], *n.* any of those front teeth occurring between the canine teeth, in the upper or lower jaws of mammals. [MedL. *incisor*].

INCISORIAL, [in'-sīz-aw'-ri-al], *adj.* incisory.

INCISORY, [in-sīz'-er-i], *adj.* sharp, able to cut, incisive.

INCISURE, [in-sizh'-er], *n.* an incision. [L. *incisura*].

INCITANT (1), [in-sīt'-ant], *n.* anything which incites.

INCITANT (2), [in-sīt'-ant], *adj.* arousing, inciting. [L. *incitans*].

INCITATION, [in'-sīt-ā'-shun], *n.* the act of inciting; incitement, incentive. [L. *incitatio*].

INCITATIVE†, [in-sīt'-at-iv], *adj.* tending to incite.

INCITE, [in-sīt'], *v.t.* to stir up, stimulate, rouse. [L. *incitare*].

INCITEMENT, [in-sīt'-ment], *n.* the act of inciting; the condition of being incited; that which incites, a stimulus.

INCITER, [in-sīt'-er], *n.* the person or thing that incites.

INCITINGLY, [in-sīt'-ing-li], *adv.* so as to incite.

INCIVILITY, [in'-siv-il'-i-ti], *n.* rudeness, want of courtesy; an act of rudeness. [LL. *incivilitas*].

INCIVILIZATION, [in'-siv-il-īz-ā'-shun], *n.* barbarous condition.

INCIVISM, [in'-siv-izm], *n.* neglect of duty as a citizen, *esp.* want of loyalty to the principles of the French Revolution. [Fr. *incivisme*].

INCLASP, see ENCLASP.

INCLEARING, [in-klēer'-ing], *n.* the amount payable by a bank on bills, cheques, etc., offered through a clearing-house.

INCLEMENCY, [in-klem'-en-si], *n.* lack of clemency; harshness; severity of weather. [L. *inclementia*].

INCLEMENT, [in-klem'-ent], *adj.* (of weather) severe, cold, rough, stormy; †harsh, cruel. [L. *inclemens*].

INCLEMENTLY, [in-klem'-ent-li], *adv.* in an inclement way.

INCLINABLE, [in-klīn'-abl], *adj.* leaning, tending; willing to comply with, favourable to. [OFr. *enclinable*].

INCLINABLENESS†, [in-klīn'-abl-nes], *n.* the state of being inclinable.

INCLINATION, [in'-klin-ā'-shun], *n.* the act of inclining, a sloping; the state of being inclined, a slanting position; the amount of deviation from the horizontal; favourable disposition towards, a feeling that one would like to or that one ought to; fondness, partiality; tendency; the dip of the magnetic needle; (*geom.*) the angle made by two lines or planes which meet, or which would meet if produced. [L. *inclinatio*].

INCLINATORILY†, [in-klīn'-at-er-i-li], *adv.* obliquely.

INCLINATORY†, [in-klīn'-at-er-i], *adj.* leaning or inclining.

INCLINE (1), [in'-klīn], *n.* a slope, gradient, inclined plane.

INCLINE (2), [in-klīn'], *v.t.* to cause to slant or deviate from a horizontal position, to tilt; to bow, bend downwards; to direct; *v.i.* to lean, slope or slant; to tend, to be disposed, prone or liable; **to be or feel inclined to**, to feel as if one ought or one would like to. [L. *inclinare*].

INCLINED, [in-klīnd'], *adj.* slanting, deviating from the horizontal; tending to, having a leaning towards; favourable towards.

INCLINER, [in-klīn'-er], *n.* a person who, or thing which, inclines.

INCLINOMETER, [in'-klin-om'-it-er], *n.* an instrument used for measuring the direction and intensity of the earth's magnetic force. [INCLINE (1) and METER].

INCLIP, (**inclipping, inclipped**), [in-klip'], *v.t.* to grasp, enclose, embrace.

INCLOSE, [in-klōz'], *v.t.* to enclose, *esp.* common or waste land. [ENCLOSE].

INCLOSER, see ENCLOSER.

INCLOSURE, [in-klō'-zher], *n.* enclosure, *esp.* the fencing off of common and waste land.

INCLOUD†, [in-klowd'], *v.t.* to surround with cloud, to obscure.

INCLUDE, [in-klo͞od'], *v.t.* to comprise, comprehend, contain as part of the whole; to consider as a constituent part of, to mention as being a necessary feature of. [L. *includere* to shut up].

INCLUDED, [in-klo͞od'-id], *adj.* (*bot.*) not projecting; shut up, confined.

INCLUDIBLE, [in-klo͞od'-ibl], *adj.* able to be included.

INCLUDING, [in-klo͞od'-ing], *adj.* counting, reckoning in, together with.

INCLUSION, [in-klo͞o'-zhun], *n.* the act of including; the state of being included. [L. *inclusio* a shutting up].

INCLUSIVE, [in-klo͞o'-siv], *adj.* including, together with; including both extremes mentioned; reckoning in everything. [MedL. *inclusivus*].

INCLUSIVELY [in-klo͞o'-siv-li], *adv.* so as to include everything or all things mentioned.

INCOAGULABLE, [in'-kō-ag'-yo͞ol-abl], *adj.* unable to be coagulated.

INCOALESCENCE, [in'-kō-al-es'-ents], *n.* lack of coalescence.

INCOERCIBLE, [in'-kō-urs'-ibl], *adj.* unable to be coerced.

INCOEXISTENCE, [in'-kō-egz-ist'-ents], *n.* the state of not existing together.

INCOG, [in-kog'], *adv.* incognito.

INCOGITABLE, [in-koj'-it-abl], *adj.* inconceivable, not to be thought of or about. [LL. *incogitabilis*].

INCOGITANT, [in-koj'-it-ant], *adj.* thoughtless, inconsiderate. [L. *incogitans*].

INCOGITANTLY, [in-koj'-it-ant-li], *adv.* thoughtlessly.

INCOGITATIVE, [in-koj'-it-at-iv], *adj.* unthinking, thoughtless; unable to think.

INCOGNITA, [in-kog'-nit-a], *n.* a lady travelling under an assumed name. [It. *incognita*].

INCOGNITO (1), [in-kog'-nit-ō], *n.* a person who endeavours to keep secret his identity; an assumed name adopted to conceal identity.

INCOGNITO (2), [in-kog'-nit-ō], *adj.* adopting or travelling under an assumed name. [It. *incognito*].

INCOGNITO (3), [in-kog'-nit-ō], *adv.* under an assumed name, or title seldom used.

INCOGNIZABLE, [in-kog'-niz-abl], *adj.* unable to be recognized or distinguished.

INCOGNIZANCE, [in-kog'-niz-ants], *n.* lack of knowledge, failure to recognize, unawareness.

INCOGNIZANT, [in-kog'-niz-ant], *adj.* unaware, unconscious of; in ignorance of.

INCOGNOSCIBLE, [in-kog-nos'-ibl], *adj.* unknowable.

INCOHERENCE, [in'-kō-hēer'-ents], *n.* the state or quality of being incoherent; an incoherent statement, idea, etc.

INCOHERENCY, [in'-kō-hēer'-en-tsi], *n.* incoherence.

INCOHERENT, [in'-kō-hēer'-ent], *adj.* disconnected, disjointed, not proceeding by a logical progression, inconsistent.

INCOHERENTLY, [in'-kō-hēer'-ent-li], *adv.* in an incoherent way.

INCOINCIDENCE, [in'-kō-in'-sid-ents], *n.* want of coincidence, lack of agreement.

INCOINCIDENT, [in'-kō-in'-sid-ent], *adj.* not coinciding, not the same as.

INCOMBUSTIBILITY, [in'-kom-bust'-i-bil'-i-ti], *n.* the quality of being incombustible.

INCOMBUSTIBLE, [in'-kom-bust'-ibl], *adj.* unable to be burnt. [MedL. *incombustibilis*].

INCOMBUSTIBLENESS, [in'-kom-bust'-ibl-nes], *n.* incombustibility.

INCOMBUSTIBLY, [in'-kom-bust'-ib-li], *adv.* so as to withstand combustion.

INCOME, [in'-kum], *n.* the total amount of money periodically accruing to a person in the form of wages, interest, profit, rent, etc.

INCOMER, [in'-kum'-er], *n.* a resident who was not born in the district, a settler; a successor.

INCOME TAX, [in'-kum-taks'], *n.* tax levied on annual income, earned or unearned.

INCOMING (1), [in'-kum-ing], *n.* the act of coming in, arrival; (*pl.*) income.

INCOMING (2), [in'-kum'-ing], *adj.* coming in; succeeding; (of profit, payment) falling due, resulting; settling in from abroad; (of a period of time) about to start.

INCOMMENSURABILITY, [in'-kom-en'-sher-a-bil'-i-ti], *n.* the quality of being incommensurable.

INCOMMENSURABLE, [in'-kom-en'-sher-abl], *adj.* not comparable with, having no common standard for comparative measurement; unworthy to be compared with; (*math.*) (of two quantities) having no common measure.

INCOMMENSURABLENESS, [in'-kom-en'-sher-abl-nes], *n.* incommensurability.

INCOMMENSURABLY, [in'-kom-en'-sher-ab-li], *adv.* in an incommensurable way.

INCOMMENSURATE, [in'-kom-en'-sher-at], *adj.* incommensurable; disproportionate, not equivalent, unequal.

INCOMMENSURATELY, [in'-kom-en'-sher-at-li], *adv.* in an incommensurate manner.
INCOMMISCIBLE, [in'-kom-is'-ibl], *adj.* that cannot be mixed together. [L. *incommiscibilis*].
INCOMMODATION, [in-kom'-ō-dā'-shun], *n.* inconvenience, annoyance.
INCOMMODE, [in'-kom-ōd'], *v.t.* to inconvenience, to cause discomfort or trouble to, to annoy. [L. *incommodare*].
INCOMMODIOUS, [in'-kom-ō'-di-us], *adj.* inconvenient, troublesome; not sufficiently spacious, uncomfortably small.
INCOMMODIOUSLY, [in'-kom-ō'-di-us-li], *adv.* in an incommodious way.
INCOMMODIOUSNESS, [in'-kom-ō'-di-us-nes], *n.* the condition of being incommodious.
INCOMMODITY, [in'-kom-od'-i-ti], *n.* incommodiousness; that which is incommodious. [L. *incommoditas*].
INCOMMUNICABILITY, [in'-kom-ewn'-ik-a-bil'-i-ti], *n.* the quality of being incommunicable.
INCOMMUNICABLE, [in'-kom-ewn'-ik-abl], *adj.* unable to be communicated or imparted to others.
INCOMMUNICABLENESS, [in'-kom-ewn'-ik-abl-nes], *n.* incommunicability.
INCOMMUNICABLY, [in'-kom-ewn'-ik-ab-li], *adv.* in an incommunicable way.
INCOMMUNICATIVE, [in'-kom-ewn'-ik-at-iv], *adj.* not communicative, disinclined to impart information; not disposed to converse freely.
INCOMMUNICATIVELY, [in'-kom-ewn'-ik-at-iv-li], *adv.* in an incommunicative way.
INCOMMUTABILITY, [in'-kom-ewt'-a-bil'-i-ti], *n.* the quality of being incommutable.
INCOMMUTABLE, [in'-kom-ewt'-abl], *adj.* that may not be commuted, unalterable; not able to be exchanged. [L. *incommutabilis*].
INCOMMUTABLENESS, [in'-kom-ewt'-abl-nes], *n.* the quality of being incommutable.
INCOMMUTABLY, [in'-kom-ewt'-ab-li], *adv.* in an incommutable way.
INCOMPACT, [in'-kom-pakt'], *adj.* not compact, loose.
INCOMPACTED, [in'-kom-pakt'-id], *adj.* incompact.
INCOMPARABLE, [in-kom'-per-abl], *adj.* not able to be compared (with); beyond comparison, matchless, unrivalled. [L. *incomparabilis*].
INCOMPARABLENESS, [in-kom'-per-abl-nes], *n.* the quality of being incomparable.
INCOMPARABLY, [in-kom'-per-ab-li], *adv.* in an incomparable way.
INCOMPASS, see ENCOMPASS.
INCOMPATIBILITY, [in'-kom-pat'-i-bil'-i-ti], *n.* the quality or condition of being incompatible.
INCOMPATIBLE, [in'-kom-pat'-ibl], *adj.* not compatible, mutually opposed, incongruous; inconsistent with; continually at variance; irreconcilable; (of benefices) unable to be held at the same time.
INCOMPATIBLENESS, [in'-kom-pat'-ibl-nes], *n.* incompatibility.
INCOMPATIBLY, [in'-kom-pat'-ib-li], *adv.* in an incompatible manner.
INCOMPETENCE, [in-kom'-pit-ents], *n.* the state or quality of being incompetent.
INCOMPETENCY, [in-kom'-pit-en-si], *n.* incompetence; (*leg.*) incapacity or disability.
INCOMPETENT, [in-kom'-pit-ent], *adj.* lacking the necessary qualifications or ability; useless, unsatisfactory, totally inefficient; (*leg.*) without proper qualifications or authority, incapable. [LL. *incompetens*].
INCOMPETENTLY, [in-kom'-pit-ent-li], *adv.* in an incompetent fashion.
INCOMPLETE, [in'-kom-plēt], *adj.* not complete, unfinished; having some part missing.
INCOMPLETELY, [in'-kom-plēt'-li], *adv.* in an incomplete way.
INCOMPLETENESS, [in'-kom-plēt'-nes], *n.* the state of being incomplete.
INCOMPLETION, [in'-kom-plē'-shun], *n.* incompleteness.
INCOMPLEX, [in-kom'-pleks], *adj.* simple, not complex, straightforward.
INCOMPLIANCE, [in'-kom-plī'-ants], *n.* failure to comply with; the quality of being incompliant.
INCOMPLIANT, [in'-kom-plī'-ant], *adj.* not yielding to the wishes of others, unamenable, unaccommodating; incompatible.
INCOMPLIANTLY, [in'-kom-plī'-ant-li], *adv.* in an incompliant manner.
INCOMPOSITE, [in-kom'-pŏz-it], *adj.* not composite, simple.
INCOMPOSSIBLE, [in'-kom-pos'-ibl], *adj.* not possible to be or subsist with something else, not possible together. [L. *incompossibilis*].
INCOMPREHENSIBILITY, [in-kom'-pri-hens'-i-bil'-i-ti], *n.* the quality of being incomprehensible.
INCOMPREHENSIBLE, [in-kom'-pri-hens'-ibl], *adj.* that cannot be understood, unintelligible; boundless, infinite. [L. *incomprehensibilis*].
INCOMPREHENSIBLENESS, [in'-kom-pri-hens'-ibl-nes], *n.* incomprehensibility.
INCOMPREHENSIBLY, [in'-kom-pri-hens'-ib-li], *adv.* in an incomprehensible way.
INCOMPREHENSION, [in'-kom-pri-hen'-shun], *n.* failure to understand, lack of comprehension.
INCOMPREHENSIVE, [in'-kom-pri-hens'-iv], *adj.* not comprehensive, not including everything; not understanding.
INCOMPREHENSIVENESS, [in'-kom-pri-hens'-iv-nes], *n.* the quality of being incomprehensive.
INCOMPRESSIBILITY, [in'-kom-pres'-i-bil'-i-ti], *n.* the quality of being incompressible.
INCOMPRESSIBLE, [in'-kom-pres'-ibl], *adj.* unable to be compressed.
INCOMPUTABLE, [in'-kom-pewt'-abl], *adj.* that cannot be computed.
INCONCEIVABILITY, [in'-kon-sēv'-a-bil'-i-ti], *n.* the quality of being inconceivable.
INCONCEIVABLE, [in'-kon-sēv'-abl], *adj.* unimaginable, that cannot be conceived; (*coll.*) extremely unlikely.
INCONCEIVABLENESS, [in'-kon-sēv'-abl-nes], *n.* inconceivability.
INCONCEIVABLY, [in'-kon-sēv'-ab-li], *adv.* in an inconceivable way.
INCONCINNITY, [in'-kon-sin'-i-ti], *n.* incongruity; want of propriety, inappropriateness. [L. *inconcinnitas*].
INCONCLUSIVE, [in'-kon-klōō'-siv], *adj.* not conclusive; indecisive.
INCONCLUSIVELY, [in'-kon-klōō'-siv-li], *adv* in an inconclusive fashion.
INCONCLUSIVENESS, [in'-kon-klōō'-siv-nes], *n.* the state of being inconclusive.
INCONDENSABILITY, [in'-kon-den'-sa-bil'-i-ti], *n.* the quality of being incondensable.
INCONDENSABLE, [in'-kon-dens'-abl], *adj.* that cannot be condensed.
INCONDENSABLENESS, [in' - kon - dens' - abl-nes], *n.* incondensability.
INCONDITE, [in-kond'-it], *adj.* badly constructed, ill-arranged; crude, unpolished. [L. *inconditum*].
INCONFORMABLE, [in'-kon-fawm'-abl], *adj.* not conforming; unwilling to conform.
INCONFORMITY, [in'-kon-fawm'-i-ti], *n.* want of conformity or correspondence; nonconformity.
INCONFUSED, [in'-kon-fewzd'], *adj.* not confused, distinct, unmixed.
INCONFUSION†, [in'-kon-few'-zhun], *n.* distinctness, absence of confusion.
INCONGEALABLE, [in'-kon-jĕl'-abl], *adj.* not congealable.
INCONGEALABLENESS, [in'-kon-jĕl'-abl-nes], *n.* the quality of being incongealable.
INCONGENIAL, [in'-kon-jē'-ni-al], *adj.* uncongenial.
INCONGENIALITY, [in'-kon-jē'-ni-al'-i-ti], *n.* lack of congeniality.
INCONGRUENCE, [in-kong'-grōō-ents], *n.* incongruity.
INCONGRUENT, [in-kong'-grōō-ent], *adj.* not congruent, unsuitable, not fitting. [L. *incongruens*].
INCONGRUITY, [in'-kong-grōō'-i-ti], *n.* want of congruity, inappropriateness, inconsistency; that which is incongruous.
INCONGRUOUS, [in-kong'-grōō-us], *adj.* unsuitable, inappropriate; inconsistent. [L. *incongruus*].
INCONGRUOUSLY, [in-kong'-grōō-us-li], *adv.* in an incongruous way.
INCONSECUTIVE, [in'-kon-sek'-yōō-tiv], *adj.* not consecutive.
INCONSECUTIVELY, [in'-kon-sek'-yōō-tiv-li], *adv.* in an inconsecutive fashion.
INCONSECUTIVENESS, [in'-kon-sek'-yōō-tiv-nes], *n.* the quality of being inconsecutive.
INCONSEQUENCE, [in-kon'-si-kwents], *n.* the quality of being inconsequent; that which is inconsequent.
INCONSEQUENT, [in-kon'-si-kwent], *adj.* not

consequent, disconnected, irrelevant, illogical. [L. *inconsequens*].

INCONSEQUENTIAL, [in-kon'-si-kwen'-shal], *adj.* inconsequent; of no importance.

INCONSEQUENTIALITY, [in-kon'-si-kwen'-shi-al'-i-ti], *n.* the quality of being inconsequential.

INCONSEQUENTIALLY, [in-kon'-si-kwen'-shal-i], *adv.* in an inconsequential fashion.

INCONSIDERABLE, [in'-kon-sid'-er-abl], *adj.* not worthy of consideration, unimportant, trifling; small.

INCONSIDERABLENESS, [in'-kon-sid'-er-abl-nes], *n.* the quality of being inconsiderable.

INCONSIDERABLY, [in'-kon-sid'-er-ab-li], *adv.* in an inconsiderable degree or way.

INCONSIDERATE, [in'-kon-sid'-er-at], *adj.* rash, indiscreet; indifferent to the feelings or wishes of others, thoughtless.

INCONSIDERATELY, [in'-kon-sid'-er-at-li], *adv.* in an inconsiderate fashion.

INCONSIDERATENESS, [in'-kon-sid'-er-at-nes], *n.* the quality of being inconsiderate.

INCONSIDERATION, [in'-kon-sid-er-ā'-shun], *n.* lack of consideration. [LL. *inconsideratio*].

INCONSISTENCY, [in'-kon-sist'-en-si], *n.* the state of being inconsistent; that which is inconsistent, a discrepancy.

INCONSISTENT, [in'-kon-sist'-ent], *adj.* not consistent, incompatible; not uniform, irreconcilable, logically opposed; illogically or haphazardly variable or changeable.

INCONSISTENTLY, [in'-kon-sist'-ent-li], *adv.* in an inconsistent fashion.

INCONSOLABLE, [in'-kon-sōl'-abl], *adj.* not to be consoled or comforted.

INCONSOLABLY, [in'-kon-sōl'-ab-li], *adv.* in an inconsolable fashion.

INCONSONANCE, [in-kon'-son-ants], *n.* disagreement, lack of harmony.

INCONSONANCY, [in-kon'-son-an-si], *n.* inconsonance.

INCONSONANT, [in-kon'-son-ant], *adj.* disagreeing, inharmonious.

INCONSONANTLY, [in-kon'-son-ant-li], *adv.* in an inconsonant way.

INCONSPICUOUS, [in'-kon-spik'-yōō-us], *adv.* not conspicuous, not strikingly noticeable. [L. *inconspicuus*].

INCONSPICUOUSLY, [in'-kon-spik'-yōō-us-li], *adv.* in an inconspicuous way.

INCONSPICUOUSNESS, [in-kon-spik'-yōō-us-nes], *n.* the state or quality of being inconspicuous.

INCONSTANCY, [in-kon'-stan-si], *n.* the quality of being inconstant. [L. *inconstantia*].

INCONSTANT, [in-kon'-stant], *adj.* fickle, unfaithful; prone to change, variable; irregular. [L. *inconstans*].

INCONSTANTLY, [in-kon'-stant-li], *adv.* in an inconstant way.

INCONSUMABLE, [in'-kon-sewm'-abl], *adj.* that cannot be consumed; not intended for consumption. [IN (5) and CONSUMABLE].

INCONSUMABLY, [in'-kon-sewm'-ab-li], *adv.* so as to be inconsumable.

INCONSUMMATE†, [in-kon'-sum-at], *adj.* not finished, incomplete. [L. *inconsummatus*].

INCONTESTABLE, [in'-kon-test'-abl], *adj.* undeniable, undisputed, unquestionable. [Fr. *incontestable*].

INCONTESTABLY, [in'-kon-test'-ab-li], *adv.* in an incontestable way.

INCONTINENCE, [in-kon'-tin-ents], *n.* the state or quality of being incontinent. [L. *incontinentia*].

INCONTINENT (1), [in-kon'-tin-ent], *adj.* lacking self-control or restraint; given to unrestrained sexual indulgence; unable to restrain the natural discharges. [L. *incontinens*].

INCONTINENT (2), [in-kon'-tin-ent], *adv.* (*archaic*) straightway, instantly. [LL. *incontinenti* (*tempore*) without interruption].

INCONTINENTLY (1), [in-kon'-tin-ent-li], *adv.* in an incontinent fashion.

INCONTINENTLY (2), [in-kon'-tin-ent-li], *adv.* immediately, suddenly.

INCONTROLLABLE, [in'-kon-trōl'-abl], *adj.* unable to be controlled. [IN (5) and CONTROLLABLE].

INCONTROLLABLY, [in'-kon-trōl'-ab-li], *adv.* in an incontrollable way.

INCONTROVERTIBLE, [in-kon'-trō-vurt'-ibl], *adj.* indisputable, that cannot be argued about. [IN (5) and CONTROVERTIBLE].

INCONTROVERTIBLY, [in-kon'-trō-vurt'-ib-li], *adv.* in an incontrovertible fashion.

INCONVENIENCE (1), [in'-kon-vēn'-yents], *n.* the state or quality of being inconvenient; that which is inconvenient; discomfort, awkwardness. [LL. *inconvenientia*].

INCONVENIENCE (2), [in'-kon-vēn'-yents], *v.t.* to put to inconvenience, to trouble.

INCONVENIENCY, [in'-kon-vēn'-yen-si], *n.* inconvenience.

INCONVENIENT, [in'-kon-vēn'-yent], *adj.* not convenient, troublesome, causing discomfort or embarrassment, awkward; (*archaic*) unsuitable. [L. *inconveniens*].

INCONVENIENTLY, [in'-kon-vēn'-yent-li], *adv.* in an inconvenient way.

INCONVERSABLE, [in'-kon-vurs'-abl], *adj.* reticent, not talkative, taciturn. [IN (5) and CONVERSABLE].

INCONVERSANT, [in'-kon-vurs'-ant], *adj.* ignorant of, unfamiliar with. [IN (5) and CONVERSANT].

INCONVERTIBILITY, [in'-kon-vurt'-i-bil'-i-ti], *n.* the quality of being inconvertible.

INCONVERTIBLE, [in'-kon-vurt'-ibl], *adj.* not convertible, unable to be changed into, or exchanged for, something else; (*esp.* of paper money) unable to be converted into coin. [LL. *inconvertibilis*].

INCONVICTEDNESS†, [in'-kon-vikt'-id-nes], *n.* the state of being not convicted or convinced. [IN (5) and CONVICT (2)].

INCONVINCIBLE, [in'-kon-vins'-ibl], *adj.* unable to be convinced. [IN (5) and CONVINCIBLE].

INCO-ORDINATION, [in'-kō-awd'-in-ā'-shun], *n.* lack of co-ordination. [IN (5) and CO-ORDINATION].

INCORPORATE (1), [in-kaw'-per-at], *adj.* not having a material body, spiritual. [L. *incorporatus*].

INCORPORATE (2), [in-kaw'-per-at], *adj.* united in a body or corporation; formally established as a corporation. [LL. *incorporatus*].

INCORPORATE (3), [in-kaw'-per-āt], *v.t.* to embody; to adopt into, to include and make a homogeneous part of; to blend into a uniform mass; to make a member of a corporation or society; to form into a legal corporation; *v.i.* to unite, mix or blend so as to form one substance. [LL. *incorporare*].

INCORPORATION, [in-kaw'-per-ā'-shun], *n.* the act of incorporating; the condition of being incorporated; association in a corporate body; (*philol.*) the combination of different parts of speech or formative elements to make one word. [L. *incorporatio*].

INCORPORATIVE, [in-kaw'-per-at-iv], *adj.* tending to incorporate, that incorporates.

INCORPOREAL, [in'-kaw-paw'-ri-al], *adj.* not in bodily form, spiritual, having no material shape or structure; pertaining to immaterial beings; (*leg.*) having no tangible existence itself, but inseparably connected with some actual physical thing. [L. *incorporeus*].

INCORPOREALISM†, [in'-kaw-paw'-ri-al-izm], *n.* belief in the existence of incorporeal substance or matter.

INCORPOREALITY, [in'-kaw-paw'-ri-al'-i-ti], *n.* incorporeity.

INCORPOREALLY, [in'-kaw-paw'-ri-al-i], *adv.* in an incorporeal way.

INCORPOREITY, [in'-kaw-per-ē'-i-ti], *n.* the quality of being incorporeal, immateriality. [MedL. **incorporeitas*].

INCORRECT, [in'-ker-ekt], *adj.* not correct, not conforming to rule or a recognized standard or custom; wrong, inaccurate; untrue. [L. *incorrectus* uncorrected].

INCORRECTLY, [in'-ker-ekt'-li], *adv.* in an incorrect way.

INCORRECTNESS, [in'-ker-ekt'-nes], *n.* the state or quality of being incorrect; something that is incorrect.

INCORRIGIBILITY, [in-ko'-rij-i-bil'-i-ti], *n.* the quality or state of being incorrigible.

INCORRIGIBLE, [in-ko'-rij-ibl], *adj.* unable to be corrected, reformed or improved. [L. *incorrigibilis*].

INCORRIGIBLENESS, [in-ko'-rij-ibl-nes], *n.* incorrigibility.

INCORRIGIBLY, [in-ko'-rij-ib-li], *adv.* to an incorrigible extent.

INCORRODIBLE, [in-ker-ōd'-ibl], *adj.* unable to be corroded. [IN (5) and CORRODIBLE].

INCORRUPT, [in'-ker-upt'], *adj.* sound, untainted, not decayed or corrupt; unable to be bribed. [L. *incorruptus*].

INCORRUPTIBILITY, [in'-ker-upt'-i-bil'-i-ti], *n.* incorruptibleness.

INCORRUPTIBLE, [in'-ker-upt'-ibl], *adj.* everlasting, not subject to decay; unable to be bribed. [L. *incorruptibilis*].

INCORRUPTIBLENESS, [in'-ker-upt'-ibl-nes], *n.* the quality of being incorruptible.

INCORRUPTIBLY, [in'-ker-upt'-ib-li], *adv.* in an incorruptible way.

INCORRUPTION, [in'-ker-up'-shun], *n.* immunity from decay. [L. *incorruptio*].

INCORRUPTIVE†, [in'-ker-upt'-iv], *adj.* incorruptible. [LL. *incorruptivus*].

INCORRUPTNESS, [in'-ker-upt'-nes], *n.* the quality of being incorrupt.

INCRASSATE (1), [in-kras'-at], *adj.* (*bot.*) swollen, fattened. [L. *incrassatus*].

INCRASSATE (2), [in-kras'-āt], *v.t.* to thicken. [L. *incrassare*].

INCRASSATION, [in'-kras-ā'-shun], *n.* the act of thickening; the condition of growing thicker.

INCRASSATIVE† (1), [in-kras'-at-iv], *n.* (*med.*) a preparation that thickens the blood.

INCRASSATIVE† (2), [in-kras'-at-iv], *adj.* tending to make thicker.

INCREASABLE, [in-krēs'-abl], *adj.* able to be increased.

INCREASABLENESS, [in-krēs'-abl-nes], *n.* the quality of being increasable.

INCREASE (1), [in'-krēs], *n.* growth, augmentation; the fact of becoming larger, more numerous or extensive; the amount by which anything is increased; (*archaic*) offspring; crops.

INCREASE (2), [in-krēs'], *v.t.* to make greater, to extend, enlarge; to intensify, aggravate, augment; to make more numerous, multiply; *v.i.* to become larger, greater or more numerous, to multiply; to grow, advance in. [OFr. *encreistre*].

INCREASER, [in-krēs'-er], *n.* one who, or that which, increases.

INCREASINGLY, [in-krēs'-ing-li], *adv.* to an increasing extent.

INCREATE, [in'-krē-āt'], *adj.* not created, uncreated. [MedL. *increatus*].

INCREATED, [in'-krē-āt'-id], *adj.* uncreated.

INCREDIBILITY, [in-kred'-i-bil'-i-ti], *n.* the quality of being incredible. [L. *incredibilitas*].

INCREDIBLE, [in-kred'-ibl], *adj.* not credible, unbelievable; (*coll.*) tremendous; extraordinary. [L. *incredibilis*].

INCREDIBLENESS, [in-kred'-ibl-nes], *n.* incredibility.

INCREDIBLY, [in-kred'-ib-li], *adv.* in an incredible manner, to an incredible extent; (*coll.*) extraordinarily.

INCREDULITY, [in'-kred-ew'-li-ti], *n.* the quality of being incredulous. [LL. *incredulitas*].

INCREDULOUS, [in-kred'-yo͞o-lus], *adj.* sceptical, unwilling to believe; indicating lack or absence of belief. [LL. *incredulus*].

INCREDULOUSLY, [in-kred'-yo͞o-lus-li], *adv.* in an incredulous fashion.

INCREDULOUSNESS, [in-kred'-yo͞o-lus-nes], *n.* the state of being incredulous.

INCREMENT, [in'-krim-ent], *n.* the act of increasing, increase; an addition; the amount by which a thing is increased; (*math.*) the regular increase of a variable quantity. [L. *incrementum*].

INCRESCENT, [in-kres'-ent], *adj.* increasing, having the shape of the moon in its first quarter. [L. *increscens*].

INCRIMINATE, [in-krim'-in-āt], *v.t.* to charge with a crime; to render a person liable to be accused of a crime, to implicate in a charge of crime or guilt. [MedL. *incriminare*].

INCRIMINATORY, [in-krim'-in-at-er-i], *adj.* tending to incriminate, that incriminates.

INCRUST, see ENCRUST.

INCRUSTATION, [in'-krust-ā'-shun], *n.* the act of incrusting; the state of being incrusted; a crust or coating; a mosaic or inlaid covering, the arrangement of stone-like molecules on a surface acted on by lime-impregnated water. [LL. *incrustatio*].

INCUBATE, [in'-kyo͞o-bāt], *v.t. and i.* to sit upon eggs in order to hatch them out, to hatch artificially; (*fig.*) to ponder over; (*med.*) (of a disease) to undergo the stage of incubation. [L. *incubare*].

INCUBATION, [in'-kyo͞o-bā'-shun], *n.* the act or process of incubating; (*path.*) the stage or period of an infectious disease occurring between the time of infection and the first appearance of symptoms. [L. *incubatio*].

INCUBATOR, [in'-kyo͞o-bāt'-er], *n.* a heated apparatus for hatching eggs artificially; an apparatus for cultivating bacteria; an apparatus for rearing children prematurely born. [L. *incubator*].

INCUBATOR

INCUBOUS, [in'-kyo͞o-bus], *adj.* (*bot.*) having the upper part of each leaf covering the lower part of the leaf next above it.

INCUBUS, [in'-kyo͞o-bus], *n.* a nightmare; a demon believed to haunt and oppress women when asleep; a troublesome obsession or encumbrance. [LL. *incubus*].

INCULCATE, [in'-kul-kāt], *v.t.* to impress forcibly upon the mind of someone else. [L. *inculcare* to ram down].

INCULCATION, [in'-kul-kā'-shun], *n.* the process of inculcating. [LL. *inculcatio*].

INCULCATOR, [in'-kul-kāt'-er], *n.* a person who inculcates. [LL. *inculcator*].

INCULPABLE, [in-kulp'-abl], *adj.* free from censure, innocent. [LL. *inculpabilis*].

INCULPABLENESS, [in-kulp'-abl-nes], *n.* freedom from blame.

INCULPABLY, [in-kulp'-ab-li], *adv.* in a blameless manner.

INCULPATE, [in'-kulp-āt], *v.t.* to censure, lay a charge against; to implicate in an accusation. [MedL. *inculpare*].

INCULPATION, [in'-kulp-ā'-shun], *n.* censure, the act of inculpating.

INCULPATORY, [in-kulp'-at-er-i], *adj.* tending to inculpate.

INCULT, [in-kult'], *adj.* (*archaic*) uncultivated, not tilled; (*fig.*) rough, uncouth. [L. *incultus*].

INCULTIVATED†, [in-kult'-iv-āt'-id], *adj.* not cultivated; uncultured.

INCULTIVATION, [in'-kult-iv-ā'-shun], *n.* lack of cultivation.

INCUMBENCY, [in-kumb'-en-si], *n.* the holding of an ecclesiastical office, *esp.* a benefice; the period during which it is held; an ecclesiastical office.

INCUMBENT (1), [in-kumb'-ent], *n.* (*eccles.*) a person who holds a benefice; (*rare*) one who holds any office.

INCUMBENT (2), [in-kumb'-ent], *adj.* lying or resting upon; obligatory, as a duty; (*bot.*) (of a cotyledon) with a radicle folded along its back; (*entom.*) (of wings) lying folded along the back of an insect when at rest; **i. upon,** required of. [L. *incumbens*].

INCUMBENTLY, [in-kumb'-ent-li], *adv.* in an incumbent way.

INCUMBER†, see ENCUMBER.

INCUMBRANCE†, see ENCUMBRANCE.

INCUNABULA, [in'-kyo͞o-nab'-yo͞o-la], *n.*(*pl.*) the earliest part or first stages of anything; books printed in the earliest stages of printing, *i.e.* before 1500. [L. *incunabula* swaddling-clothes].

INCUR, [in-kur'], *v.t.* to become liable to, to bring upon oneself. [L. *incurrere* to run into].

INCURABILITY, [in-kewr'-a-bil'-i-ti], *n.* the condition of being incurable.

INCURABLE (1), [in-kewr'-abl], *n.* a person afflicted with an incurable disease.

INCURABLE (2), [in-kewr'-abl], *adj.* that cannot be cured or remedied.

INCURABLENESS, [in-kewr'-abl-ness], *n.* incurability.

INCURABLY, [in-kewr'-ab-li], *adv.* in an incurable way.

INCURIOSITY, [in-kewr'-i-os'-i-ti], *n.* want of curiosity, lack of interest.

INCURIOUS, [in-kewr'-i-us], *adj.* not curious or inquisitive; not interested in; not arousing curiosity; (*archaic*) carelessly indifferent, negligent. [L. *incuriosus*].

INCURIOUSLY, [in-kewr'-i-us-li], *adv.* in an incurious way.

INCURIOUSNESS, [in-kewr'-i-us-nes], *n.* incuriosity.

INCURRABLE, [in-kur'-abl], *adj.* possible to be incurred.

INCURRENCE, [in-ku'-rents], *n.* the act of incurring.

INCURSION, [in-kur'-shun], *n.* an attack, a sudden invasion, raid. [L. *incursio*].

INCURSIVE, [in-kurs'-iv], *adj.* making an incursion, raiding.
INCURVATE (1), [in-kurv'-āt], *adj.* curved inwards. [L. *incurvatus*].
INCURVATE (2), [in-kurv'-āt], *v.t.* to curve inwards. [L. *incurvare*].
INCURVATION, [in'-kurv-ā'-shun], *n.* the act of incurvating; the state of being incurvated; a bend inwards. [L. *incurvatio*].
INCURVE, [in-kurv'], *v.t. and i.* to curve inwards.
INCURVED, [in-kurvd'], *adj.* bent inwards.
INCUS, [ingk'-us], *n.* the middle of the three small bones of the inner ear which receive vibrations sent by the hammer. [L. *incus* anvil].
INCUSE (1), [in-kewz'], *n.* an impression or mark stamped on a coin.
INCUSE (2), [in-kewz'], *adj.* stamped, marked by a die or hammer. [L. *incusus*].
INCUSE (3), [in-kewz'], *v.t.* to impress or stamp with a die. [L. *incusum*, *p.pt.* of *incudere*].
INCUT, [in-kut'], *adj.* (*print.*) inserted in a page in the space left for it, *esp.* of type matter or block.
IND, [ind], *n.* (*archaic, poet.*) India.
INDABA, [in-dah'-ba], *n.* a native assembly or council among the South African Bantu tribes. [Bantu *indaba* business].
INDEBTED, [in-det'-id], *adj.* owing money; under an obligation, extremely grateful. [OFr. *endetter*].
INDEBTEDNESS, [in-det'-id-nes], *n.* the condition of being indebted; debt.
INDECENCY, [in-dē'-sen-si], *n.* the quality of being indecent; an indecent action or expression, an impropriety.
INDECENT, [in-dē'-sent], *adj.* not decent, unbecoming, indecorous; obscene, lewd. [L. *indecens*].
INDECENTLY, [in-dē'-sent-li], *adv.* in an indecent way.
INDECIDUATE, [in'-di-sid'-yōō-at], *adj.* not deciduate.
INDECIDUOUS, [in'-di-sid'-yōō-us], *adj.* not deciduous, evergreen.
INDECIPHERABLE, [in'-di-sī'-fer-abl], *adj.* unable to be deciphered; illegible.
INDECISION, [in-di-sizh'-un], *n.* want of decision, hesitation.
INDECISIVE, [in'-di-sīs'-iv], *adj.* inconclusive, not deciding one way or another; irresolute.
INDECISIVELY, [in'-di-sīs-iv-li], *adv.* in an indecisive fashion.
INDECISIVENESS, [in'-di-sīs'-iv-nes], *n.* the quality or state of being indecisive.
INDECLINABLE, [in'-di-klīn'-abl], *adj.* (*gram.*) that cannot be declined, uninflected. [L. *indeclinabilis* unchangeable].
INDECLINABLY, [in'-di-klīn'-ab-li], *adv.* in an indeclinable way.
INDECOMPOSABLE, [in'-dē-kom-pōz'-abl], *adj.* unable to be decomposed.
INDECOMPOSABLENESS, [in'-dē-kom-pōz'-abl-nes], *n.* the quality of being indecomposable.
INDECOROUS, [in'-dek'-er-us], *adj.* not in good taste, unseemly. [L. *indecorus*].
INDECOROUSLY, [in'-dek'-er-us-li], *adv.* in an indecorous way.
INDECOROUSNESS, [in'-dek'-er-us-nes], *n.* the quality of being indecorous.
INDECORUM, [in'-dik-aw'-rum], *n.* the quality of being indecorous, impropriety; an indecorous act or speech.
INDEED (1), [in-dēd'], *adv.* in reality; as a matter of fact; certainly, in truth, let it be granted; *used also for emphasis.*
INDEED (2), [in-dēd'], *int.* used to express various emotions as surprise, indignation, etc.
INDEFATIGABILITY, [in'-di-fat'-ig-a-bil'-i-ti], *n.* the quality of being indefatigable.
INDEFATIGABLE, [in'-di-fat'-ig-abl], *adj.* unable to be wearied or tired out; tireless. [L. *indefatigabilis*].
INDEFATIGABLENESS, [in'-di-fat'-ig-abl-nes], *n.* indefatigability.
INDEFATIGABLY, [in'-di-fat'-ig-ab-li], *adv.* in an indefatigable way.
INDEFEASIBILITY, [in'-di-fēz'-i-bil'-i-ti], *n.* the quality of being indefeasible.
INDEFEASIBLE, [in'-di-fēz'-ibl], *adj.* that cannot be set aside, forfeited, or declared void.
INDEFEASIBLY, [in'-di-fēz'-ib-li], *adv.* in an indefeasible way.
INDEFECTIBLE, [in'-di-fekt'-ibl], *adj.* not liable to defect, failure, or decay; perfect.
INDEFENSIBILITY, [in'-di-fens'-i-bil'-i-ti], *n.* the quality of being indefensible.
INDEFENSIBLE, [in'-di-fens'-ibl], *adj.* that cannot be defended; unjustifiable, inexcusable.
INDEFENSIBLY, [in'-di-fens'-ib-li], *adv.* in an indefensible fashion.
INDEFENSIVE, [in'-di-fens'-iv], *adj.* defenceless.
INDEFINABLE, [in'-di-fīn'-abl], *adj.* that cannot be defined, indescribable.
INDEFINABLY, [in'-di-fīn'-ab-li], *adv.* in an indefinable way.
INDEFINITE, [in-def'-in-it], *adj.* not clearly defined, vague; not expressly stated or specified; (*gram.*) (of *adj.*, *pron.*) not indicating precisely the number, place, person, etc., to which they refer; (of *v.*) not stating whether an action is complete or continuous.
INDEFINITELY, [in-def'-in-it-li], *adv.* in an indefinite way.
INDEFINITENESS, [in-def'-in-it-nes], *n.* the quality of being indefinite, vagueness.
INDEFINITUDE†, [in'-di-fin'-it-ewd], *n.* indefiniteness.
INDEHISCENCE, [in'-di-his'-ents], *n.* the quality of being indehiscent.
INDEHISCENT, [in'-di-his'-ent], *adj.* (*bot.*) (of seed-vessels) not splitting open when ripe.
INDELIBERATE, [in'-di-lib'-er-at], *adj.* not deliberate.
INDELIBERATELY, [in'-di-lib'-er-at-li], *adv.* not deliberately.
INDELIBILITY, [in'-del-i-bil'-i-ti], *n.* the quality of being indelible.
INDELIBLE, [in-del'-ibl], *adj.* that cannot be effaced or rubbed out; producing an inerasable mark; that cannot be wiped out or lived down. [L. *indelibilis*].
INDELIBLY, [in-del'-ib-li], *adv.* in an indelible way.
INDELICACY, [in-del'-ik-a-si], *n.* the quality of being indelicate; an indelicate act or speech.
INDELICATE, [in-del'-ik-at], *adj.* not delicate, offensive to decency, coarse.
INDELICATELY, [in-del'-ik-at-li], *adv.* in an indelicate way.
INDEMNIFICATION, [in-dem'-ni-fi-kā'-shun], *n.* the act of indemnifying; that which indemnifies; the state of being indemnified.
INDEMNIFY, [in-dem'-ni-fī], *v.t.* to safeguard against, render immune from (loss, damage, etc.); to free from (liability or responsibility); to compensate for. [L. *indemnis* uninjured].
INDEMNITOR, [in-dem'-nit-or], *n.* one who indemnifies another.
INDEMNITY, [in-dem'-ni-ti], *n.* security or compensation against loss or damage; the amount paid or demanded as compensation; exemption or immunity from liability or responsibility. [LL. *indemnitas*].
INDEMONSTRABLE, [in'-di-mon'-strabl], *adj.* that cannot be proved or established.
INDENIZEN†, see ENDENIZEN.
INDENT (1), [in-dent', in'-dent], *n.* a notch or cut in the margin of anything; an indenture; an official demand or application for goods; (*comm.*) an order for goods.
INDENT (2), [in'-dent], *n.* a depression, dent, hollow made by a blow.
INDENT (3), [in-dent'], *v.t.* to cut the edge of into a series of tooth-like points; to make sharp recesses in; to separate (a document written out in duplicate) into corresponding halves by means of a jagged or zigzag line; to write out in duplicate; (*print.*) to begin farther in from the margin than the remainder of that particular section; *v.i.* to draw upon (stores, etc.) by making out an official order or application (together with a duplicate copy to be kept). [Fr. *endenter* to notch].
INDENT (4), [in-dent'], *v.t.* to make a dent in; to imprint, mark by pressure.
INDENTATION, [in'-dent-ā'-shun], *n.* the act of indenting, the condition of being indented; a tooth-shaped cut in the edge of anything; a recess or narrow opening in a coast-line, etc.; that which is indented.

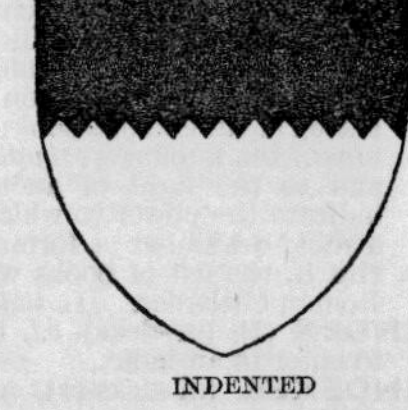
INDENTED

INDENTED, [in-dent'-id], *adj.* notched, cut into indentations; having a zigzag edge; (*her.*) toothed,

ō (bone), ī (fine), ōō (food), ŏŏ (put), u (up), th (think), TH (that), zh (azure), † = obsolete, ~ = related to.

notched; (of a document) having a jagged edge where it was separated from its duplicate; bound by an indenture.

INDENTEDLY, [in-dent'-id-li], *adv.* with indentations.

INDENTION, [in-den'-shun], *n.* (*print.*) the act of indenting a line; the space so left; indentation.

INDENTURE (1), [in-den'-cher], *n.* an indentation, a notch; a document drawn up in duplicate, and cut, by means of a jagged line, into corresponding halves; a deed, contract, etc., between two or more parties, *esp.* one which binds an apprentice to his employer; an official, authoritative deed, certificate, etc. [OFr. *endenteure*].

INDENTURE (2), [in-den'-cher], *v.t.* to bind by an indenture, to draw up a formal contract or deed with.

INDEPENDENCE, [in'-di-pend'-ents], *n.* the condition or quality of being independent.

INDEPENDENCY, [in'-di-pend'-en-si], *n.* independence; Congregationalism.

INDEPENDENT (1), [in'-di-pend'-ent], *n.* a person who supports no particular political party, etc.; one who maintains that every religious congregation of Christians constitutes a complete independent church.

INDEPENDENT (2), [in'-di-pend'-ent], *adj.* not dependent on or subject to the authority of others; not conditional upon something; unconstrained, not influenced by others; (of an income) of such proportions that the possessor has no need to earn his living; (of a person) possessing such an income; self-supporting, able to maintain oneself; unwilling to accept help or advice; irrespective (of); relating to Congregationalism.

INDEPENDENTLY, [in'-di-pend'-ent-li], *adv.* in an independent way.

INDESCRIBABLE, [in'-di-skrīb'-abl], *adj.* that cannot be described.

INDESCRIPTIVE, [in'-di-skript'-iv], *adj.* not descriptive.

INDESIGNATE, [in-dez'-ig-nāt], *adj.* with no indication of quantity, indefinite.

INDESTRUCTIBILITY, [in'-dis-trukt'-i-bil'-i-ti], *n.* the quality of being indestructible.

INDESTRUCTIBLE, [in'-dis-trukt'-ibl], *adj.* that cannot be destroyed.

INDESTRUCTIBLENESS, [in'-dis-trukt'-ibl-nes], *n.* indestructibility.

INDESTRUCTIBLY, [in'-dis-trukt'-ib-li], *adv.* in an indestructible way.

INDETERMINABLE, [in'-di-ter'-min-abl], *adj.* that cannot be determined or fixed.

INDETERMINABLY, [in'-di-ter'-min-ab-li], *adv.* in an indeterminable way.

INDETERMINATE, [in'-di-ter'-min-at], *adj.* not fixed, uncertain; indefinite, vague; (*math.*) possessing no fixed or calculable value; (*math.*) capable of an infinite number of solutions.

INDETERMINATELY, [in'-di-ter'-min-at-li], *adv.* in an indeterminable way.

INDETERMINATENESS, [in'-di-ter'-min-at-nes], *n.* the quality of being indeterminate.

INDETERMINATION, [in'-di-ter-min-ā'-shun], *n.* lack of determination, vacillation, irresoluteness; indeterminateness.

INDETERMINED, [in'-di-ter'-mind], *adj.* not determined.

INDETERMINISM, [in'-di-ter'-min-izm], *n.* (*philos.*) the doctrine that human action is largely free and not predestined.

INDEVOTION, [in'-di-vō'-shun], *n.* lack of devotion.

INDEVOUT, [in'-di-vowt'], *adj.* not devout, irreverent.

INDEVOUTLY, [in'-di-vowt'-li], *adv.* in an indevout manner.

INDEX (1), (*pl.* **indices, indexes**), [in'-deks, (*pl.*) in'-di-sēz], *n.* that which indicates anything, *esp.* a pointer on a dial or graduated scale; an alphabetical list of topics, persons mentioned, etc., in a book together with the pages on which they occur, usually placed at the end of a book; (*fig.*) an indication, guide; (*anat.*) the forefinger; (*math.*) a number placed above and to the right of another number or letter to indicate the power to which it is raised or to denote a root; a number or formula expressing some ratio; **the I.,** the list of books which may not be read by Roman Catholics. [L. *index*].

INDEX (2), [in'-deks], *v.t.* to provide with an index; to enter in an index.

INDEXER, [in'-deks-er], *n.* a person who compiles an index.

INDEXICAL, [in-deks'-ikl], *adj.* pertaining to, in the form of, an index.

INDEXICALLY, [in-deks'-ik-al-i], *adv.* in the manner or form of an index.

INDEX-NUMBER, [in'-deks-num'-ber], *n.* a percentage number used as a means of measuring the average variation of wages, price of commodities, etc.

INDEXTERITY, [in'-deks-te'-ri-ti], *n.* clumsiness.

INDIAMAN, [in'-di-a-man'], *n.* a large ship engaged in trade with the East or West Indies.

INDIAMAN

INDIAN (1), [in'-di-an], *n.* a native of India or the East Indies; an aboriginal of North or South America, or of the West Indies; the language of the aboriginal inhabitants of America; **Red I.,** a North-American aboriginal.

INDIAN (2), [in'-di-an], *adj.* pertaining to India or the East Indies; pertaining to an Indian; made in India; **I. berry,** *Anamirta cocculus*; **I. club,** a long, slender, bottle-shaped, wooden club swung in the hands in certain gymnastic exercises; **I. corn,** maize, *Zea Mays*; **I. cress,** the nasturtium, a plant of the genus *Tropæolum*; **I. date,** the tamarind tree, *Tamarindus indica*; **I. fig,** the prickly pear, *Opuntia vulgaris*; the banyan tree; **I. file,** single file; **I. ink,** a black writing or drawing ink made of lampblack and animal glue; **I. madder,** a vegetable substance used for dyeing; **I. reed,** *Canna indica*; **I. summer,** a spell of fine, warm weather occurring towards the end of autumn; (*fig.*) a sudden revival of youthful vigour and feeling in old age; **I. tobacco,** a species of lobelia; **I. turnip,** an araceous plant, *Arum Draconium*, yielding a head of red berries; **I. yam,** *Dioscorea trifida*.

INDIANITE, [in'-di-an-īt], *n.* a grey variety of anorthite, obtained from the Carnatic, in India.

INDIANIZE, [in'-di-an-īz], *v.t.* to make Indian in character.

INDIA-PAPER, [in'-di-a-pā'-per], *n.* a soft, fine, pale-yellow paper manufactured in China, used for impressions of engravings; a very thin opaque paper used for printing books.

INDIA-RUBBER, [in'-di-a-rub'-er], *n.* a substance obtained from the curdled or hardened juice of certain tropical plants; a small piece of this used for erasing pencil marks.

INDICANT, [in'-dik-ant], *n.* (*med.*) that which indicates the remedial treatment to be carried out. [L. *indicans*].

INDICATE, [in'-dik-āt], *v.t.* to point out, show; to make known, convey, express; to suggest, imply; to reveal, betoken. [L. *indicare*].

INDICATION, [in'-dik-ā'-shun], *n.* the act of indicating, the condition of being indicated; that which indicates, a sign, token.

INDICATIVE (1), [in-dik'-at-iv], *n.* (*gram.*) the indicative mood.

INDICATIVE (2), [in-dik'-at-iv], *adj.* that indicates; **i. mood,** (*gram.*) that mood of the verb used to express a statement of fact, or to ask a question implying a fact.

INDICATIVELY, [in-dik'-at-iv-li], *adv.* in an indicative way.

INDICATOR, [in'-dik-āt'-er], *n.* that which, or a person who, indicates, *esp.* a needle or finger on a dial, which registers some specific information; (*chem.*) a substance added to two reacting substances to indicate a chemical reaction.

INDICATORY, [in-dik'-at-er-i, in-dik-āt'-er-i], *adj.* serving to indicate.

INDICAVIT, [in'-dik-ā'-vit], *n.* (*leg.*) a writ of prohibition by a patron whose incumbent is sued for tithes by another clergyman, by which the suit may be heard in a secular court. [L. *indicavit* he has indicated].

INDICIUM, [in-dis'-i-um], *n.* a sign, indication. [L. *indicium*].

INDICOLITE, [in'-dik-ō-līt], *n.* (*min.*) an indigo-blue kind of tourmalin. [Gk. *indikon* indigo and *lithos* stone].

INDICT, [in-dīt'], *v.t.* to charge with a crime, accuse formally. [OFr. *enditer*].

INDICTABLE, [in-dīt'-abl], *adj.* that may be indicted; exposing to indictment.

INDICTEE, [in'-dīt-ē'], *n.* one who is indicted.

INDICTER, [in-dīt'-er], *n.* a person who indicts.

INDICTION, [in-dik'-shun], *n.* a proclamation, declaration; a decree of the Roman Emperors determining a valuation on which the assessment of the land-tax was based every 15 years; the tax paid under this decree; a financial cycle of 15 years used in marking dates. [L. *indictio*].

INDICTIVE†, [in-dikt'-iv], *adj.* proclaimed, announced. [L. *indictivus*].

INDICTMENT, INDITEMENT†, [in-dīt'-ment], *n.* the act of indicting; a formal written charge or accusation; the document containing this.

INDIFFERENCE, [in-dif'-er-ents], *n.* the state of being indifferent, unconcern; apathy; unimportance.

INDIFFERENCY, [in-dif-er-en-si], *n.* indifference.

INDIFFERENT, [in-dif'-er-ent], *adj.* displaying no active feeling towards; unconcerned, not interested in; apathetic; unmoved by; unimportant; neither good nor bad, commonplace; mediocre; (*elect.*) neutral; (*archaic*) impartial. [L. *indifferens* similar].

INDIFFERENTISM, [in-dif'-er-ent-izm], *n.* indifference, *esp.* in religious or political matters.

INDIFFERENTIST, [in-dif'-er-ent-ist], *n.* one who claims to be indifferent to matters of religion or politics.

INDIFFERENTLY, [in-dif'-er-ent-li], *adv.* in an indifferent way.

INDIGENCE, INDIGENCY†, [in'-dij-ents-(i)], *n.* the state of being indigent, extreme want. [L. *indigentia*].

INDIGENE, [in'-dij-ēn], *n.* a native. [L. *indigena*].

INDIGENOUS, [in-dij'-en-us], *adj.* native, belonging naturally to. [LL. *indigenus*].

INDIGENT, [in'-dij-ent], *adj.* lacking means of subsistence, extremely poor. [L. *indigens*].

INDIGENTLY, [in'-dij-ent-li], *adv.* in an indigent manner.

INDIGESTED, [in'-di-jest'-id], *adj.* not digested, not properly sorted out or assimilated mentally; undigested.

INDIGESTIBLE, [in'-di-jest'-ibl], *adj.* that may not be easily digested.

INDIGESTIBLY, [in'-di-jest'-ib-li], *adv.* in an indigestible manner.

INDIGESTION, [in'-di-jes'-chun], *n.* improper digestion of food, dyspepsia; the state of being undigested. [LL. *indigestio*].

INDIGN, [in-dīn'], *adj.* (*archaic*) shameful, dishonourable. [L. *indignus*].

INDIGNANT, [in-dig'-nant], *adj.* inflamed with righteous anger at some injustice or insult. [L. *indignans*].

INDIGNANTLY, [in-dig'-nant-li], *adv.* in an indignant fashion.

INDIGNATION, [in'-dig-nā'-shun], *n.* strong feeling of resentful anger, tinged with disgust. [L. *indignatio*].

INDIGNITY, [in-dig'-ni-ti], *n.* an insult, affront, or uncivil action intended to humiliate or discredit. [L. *indignitas* unworthiness].

INDIGO (1), [in'-dig-ō], *n.* a deep blue dye, obtained from the indigo plant; the indigo plant. [Gk. *indikon* Indian].

INDIGO (2), [in'-dig-ō], *adj.* deep blue.

INDIGOGEN, [in'-dig-ō-jen], *n.* white indigo obtained by treating indigo with a deoxidizing body. [INDIGO (1) and Gk. *genes* producing].

INDIGOMETER, [in'-dig-om'-it-er], *n.* an instrument for testing the strength of indigo. [INDIGO (1) and METER].

INDIGOTIC, [in'-dig-ot'-ik], *adj.* pertaining to indigo.

INDIGOTIN, [in'-dig-ō-tin], *n.* the blue colouring matter present in indigo.

INDIRECT, [in'-dī-rekt'], *adj.* not direct; roundabout, devious; implied rather than stated; not first-hand; dishonest, unfair; **i. tax** a tax levied on commercial goods, etc., in which the consumer pays both for the article and the tax; **i. speech,** (*gram.*) reported speech; **i. object,** (*gram.*) the object affected in turn by an action which primarily affects a direct object.

INDIRECTION, [in'-dī-rek'-shun], *n.* a roundabout course or action; a dishonest practice.

INDIRECTLY, [in'-di-rekt'-li], *adv.* in an indirect fashion.

INDIRECTNESS, [in'-dī-rekt'-nes], *n.* the condition of being indirect.

INDISCERNIBLE (1), [in'-di-sern'-ibl], *n.* an indiscernible thing.

INDISCERNIBLE (2), [in'-di-sern'-ibl], *adj.* that may not be discerned, imperceptible.

INDISCERNIBLENESS, [in'-di-sern'-ibl-nes], *n.* the quality of being indiscernible.

INDISCERNIBLY, [in'-di-sern'-ib-li], *adv.* so as not to be discerned.

INDISCERPTIBILITY, [in'-di-serpt'-i-bil'-i-ti], *n.* the condition of being indiscerptible.

INDISCERPTIBLE, [in'-di-serpt'-ibl], *adj.* that may not be split up into its separate parts.

INDISCIPLINABLE, [in-dis'-i-plin-abl], *adj.* unable to be disciplined.

INDISCIPLINE, [in-dis'-i-plin], *n.* lack of discipline.

INDISCOVERABLE, [in'-dis-kuv'-er-abl], *adj.* that may not be discovered.

INDISCREET, [in'-dis-krēt'], *adj.* not discreet, imprudent, ill-advised.

INDISCREETLY, [in'-dis-krēt'-li], *adv.* in an indiscreet way.

INDISCREETNESS, [in'-dis-krēt'-nes], *n.* the condition of being indiscreet.

INDISCRETE, [in'-dis-krēt'], *adj.* not split up into separate distinct parts. [L. *indiscretus*].

INDISCRETION, [in'-dis-kresh'-un], *n.* want of discretion; an indiscreet act. [LL. *indiscretio*].

INDISCRIMINATE, [in'-dis-krim'-in-at], *adj.* not displaying discrimination, promiscuous, making no attempt to select or distinguish.

INDISCRIMINATELY, [in'-dis-krim'-in-at-li], *adv.* in an indiscriminate way.

INDISCRIMINATING, [in'-dis-krim'-in-āt'-ing], *adj.* indiscriminative.

INDISCRIMINATION, [in'-dis-krim'-in-ā'-shun], *n.* lack of discrimination.

INDISCRIMINATIVE, [in'-dis-krim'-in-at-iv], *adj.* exercising no discrimination.

INDISPENSABILITY, [in'-dis-pen'-sa-bil'-i-ti], *n.* the quality of being indispensable.

INDISPENSABLE, [in'-dis-pen'-sabl], *adj.* that may not be done without, absolutely necessary; not able to be annulled or disregarded.

INDISPENSABLENESS, [in'-dis-pen'-sabl-nes], *n.* indispensability.

INDISPENSABLY, [in'-dis-pen'-sab-li], *adv.* in an indispensable way.

INDISPOSE, [in'-dis-pōz'], *v.t.* to disincline, to make unwilling; to render unfit for or incapable of; to make unwell.

INDISPOSED, [in'-dis-pōzd'], *adj.* disinclined; ill, unwell; unfriendly.

INDISPOSEDNESS, [in'-dis-pōzd'-nes], *n.* the condition of being indisposed.

INDISPOSITION, [in'-dis-poz-ish'-un], *n.* slight illness, ill health; aversion, unwillingness.

INDISPUTABLE, [in'-dis'-pewt-abl], *adj.* undoubted, not admitting of dispute.

INDISPUTABLENESS, [in'-dis'-pewt-abl-nes], *n.* the quality of being indisputable.

INDISPUTABLY, [in'-dis'-pewt-ab-li], *adv.* undoubtedly.

INDISSOCIABILITY, [in'-di-sō'-sha-bil'-i-ti], *n.* the quality of being indissociable.

INDISSOCIABLE, [in'-di-sō'-shabl], *adj.* that may not be dissociated or separated. [L. *indissociabilis*].

INDISSOLUBILITY, [in'-di-sol'-yōō-bil'-i-ti], *n.* the quality of being indissoluble.

INDISSOLUBLE, [in'-di-sol'-yōōbl, in-dis'-ol-yōōbl], *adj.* that may not be dissolved; indestructible; permanent, that may not be broken. [L. *indissolubilis*].

INDISSOLUBLENESS, [in'-di-sol'-yōōbl-nes, in-dis'-ol-yōōbl-nes], *n.* the state of being indissoluble.

INDISSOLUBLY, [in'-di-sol'-yōōb-li, in-dis'-ol-yōōb-li], *adv.* in an indissoluble way.

INDISTINCT, [in'-dis-tingkt'], *adj.* not distinct or clear, vague, dim, faint, confused.

INDISTINCTION, [in'-dis-tingk'-shun], *n.* inability to distinguish between; lack of distinctness or distinctiveness.

INDISTINCTLY, [in'-dis-tingkt'-li], *adv.* in an indistinct way.

INDISTINCTNESS, [in'-dis-tingkt'-nes], *n.* the quality of being indistinct.

INDISTINGUISHABLE, [in'-dis-ting'-gwish-abl], *adj.* that may not be distinguished.

INDISTURBANCE, [in'-dis-turb'-ants], *n.* absence of disturbance, calm.

INDITE, [in-dīt'], *v.t.* to compose; to put into words, to write. [OFr. *enditer*].

INDITEMENT†, see INDICTMENT.

INDIUM, [in'-di-um], *n.* a soft, silver-white metallic element, In, found with zinc. [L. *indicum* indigo].

INDIVERTIBLE, [in'-di-vurt'-ibl], *adj.* that may not be diverted.

INDIVIDUAL (1), [in'-di-vid'-yōō-al], *n.* a single person, animal, thing, etc.; a single member of a class; (*coll.*) a person.

INDIVIDUAL (2), [in'-di-vid'-yōō-al], *adj.* single,

separate; distinctive, readily distinguishable, peculiar; relating to, or characteristic of, one person, animal, or thing. [MedL. *individualis*].

INDIVIDUALISM, [in'-di-vid'-yōō-al-izm], *n.* self-centredness, egoism; social doctrine advocating the limitation of state control or organization of society in favour of individual freedom of action; (*philos.*) the theory that only individuals have an independent existence, any large mass being merely an aggregate of individuals.

INDIVIDUALIST, [in'-div-id'-ew-al-ist], *n.* a supporter of individualism; a person who displays marked individual traits; one who prefers to work on his own rather than to co-operate.

INDIVIDUALISTIC, [in'-div-id'-ew-al-ist'-ik], *adj.* pertaining to, of the nature of, individualism.

INDIVIDUALITY, [in'-di-vid'-yōō-al'-i-ti], *n.* the sum of those distinctive personal traits or qualities which render an individual strikingly different from others; the fact of having a separate existence as an individual.

INDIVIDUALIZATION, [in'-di-vid'-yōō-al-īz-ā'-shun], *n.* the act of individualizing; the condition of being individualized.

INDIVIDUALIZE, [in'-di-vid'-yōō-al-īz], *v.t.* to make individual, characterize; to consider individually.

INDIVIDUALLY, [in'-di-vid'-yōō-al-i], *adv.* one by one, singly; as a separate, distinct individual.

INDIVIDUATE, [in'-di-vid'-yōō-āt], *v.t.* to individualize; to make into an individual entity. [MedL. *individuare*].

INDIVIDUATION, [in'-di-vid'-yōō-ā'-shun], *n.* the act of individuating, the state of being individualized. [MedL. *individuatio*].

INDIVISIBILITY, [in'-di-viz'-i-bil'-i-ti], *n.* the quality of being indivisible.

INDIVISIBLE (1), [in'-di-viz'-ibl], *n.* an indivisible quantity or thing.

INDIVISIBLE (2), [in'-di-viz'-ibl], *adj.* that may not be divided, infinitely small.

INDIVISIBLENESS, [in'-di-viz'-ibl-nes], *n.* the quality of being indivisible.

INDIVISIBLY, [in'-di-viz'-ib-li], *adv.* so as to be indivisible.

INDIVISION, [in'-di-vizh'-un], *n.* the condition of being undivided. [LL. *indivisio*].

INDO-, [in'-dō], *pref.* Indian. [Gk. *Indo-*].

INDOCILE, [in-dō'-sīl], *adj.* not docile, intractable, unruly.

INDOCILITY, [in'-dō-sil'-i-ti], *n.* the quality of being indocile.

INDOCTRINATE, [in-dok'-trin-āt], *v.t.* to fill the mind with a particular doctrine or set of principles; to teach.

INDOCTRINATION, [in-dok'-trin-ā'-shun], *n.* the act of indoctrinating.

INDO-EUROPEAN (1), [in'-dō-yōōer'-ō-pē'-an], *n.* a group of related languages including most of those spoken in Europe and part of Asia; the original language from which these have evolved; a member of a race speaking one of these languages.

INDO-EUROPEAN (2), [in'-dō-yōōer'-ō-pē'-an], *adj.* pertaining to Indo-European.

INDOLENCE, [in'-dol-ents], *n.* the quality of being indolent.

INDOLENT, [in'-dol-ent], *adj.* idle, slothful; (*path.*) giving no pain. [LL. *indolens*].

INDOLENTLY, [in'-dol-ent-li], *adv.* in an indolent fashion.

INDOMITABLE, [in-dom'-it-abl], *adj.* that cannot be subdued, untamable, unyielding. [LL. *indomitabilis*].

INDONESIAN, [in'-dō-nē'-shan], *adj.* of the East Indian islands. [INDO and Gk. *nesos* island].

INDOOR, [in'-daw(r)], *adj.* within the house, situated, performed, suitable for, inside a house.

INDOORS, [in-dawz'], *adv.* inside a house.

INDORSABLE, see ENDORSABLE.

INDORSE, see ENDORSE.

INDORSEE, see ENDORSEE.

INDORSEMENT, see ENDORSEMENT.

INDORSER, see ENDORSER.

INDRAUGHT, [in'-drahft], *n.* the act of drawing in; an inward current of water or air.

INDRAWN, [in'-drawn], *adj.* drawn in.

INDRI, [in'-dri], *n.* the largest of the lemurs, *Indris brevicaudata.* [Malagasy *indri* behold !].

INDUBIOUS, [in-dew'-bi-us], *adj.* certain, not doubtful.

INDUBITABLE, [in-dewb'-it-abl], *adj.* undoubted, absolutely certain. [L. *indubitabilis*].

INDUBITABLENESS, [in-dewb'-it-abl-nes], *n.* the quality of being indubitable.

INDUBITABLY, [in-dewb'-it-ab-li], *adv.* undoubtedly.

INDUCE, [in-dews'], *v.t.* to persuade, prevail upon; to bring on, occasion; to infer by reasoning from particular instances to general principles; (*elect.*) to bring about by induction. [L. *inducere* to lead in].

INDUCEMENT, [in-dews'-ment], *n.* that which induces, a means of persuasion, incentive.

INDUCER, [in-dews'-er], *n.* a person or thing that induces.

INDUCIBLE, [in-dews'-ibl], *adj.* that may be induced.

INDUCT, [in-dukt'], *v.t.* to install formally and ceremoniously into office, *esp.* into an ecclesiastical office; to place in, conduct to a position or seat. [L. *inductum*, *p.pt.* of *inducere* to lead in].

INDUCTANCE, [in-dukt'-ants], *n.* (*elect.*) the setting up of a magnetic field or flux by induction when an electric current is passed continuously through a conductor or circuit, the coefficient of self-induction.

INDUCTILE, [in-dukt'-īl], *adj.* not ductile.

INDUCTILITY, [in'-dukt-il'-i-ti], *n.* the quality of being inductile.

INDUCTION, [in-duk'-shun], *n.* the act of inducting into office; method of reasoning from particular instances to general principles; an example of this reasoning; a statement, fact, etc., brought forward to bear out a general statement; (*elect.*) the production of an electrical or magnetic force in a circuit or conductor without direct contact; that part of the piston's stroke in an internal combustion engine which draws the gas from the carburettor; **i. coil,** an apparatus for producing a flow of electricity by induction, or for transforming intermittent currents of low voltage into currents of high voltage; **i. pipe,** a pipe through which gas or steam is admitted to the cylinder. [L. *inductio* a leading into].

INDUCTIONAL, [in-duk'-shun-al], *adj.* relating or due to induction.

INDUCTIVE, [in-dukt'-iv], *adj.* pertaining to, using induction; inducing; (*elect.*) produced by, producing electricity by, induction. [L. *inductivus*].

INDUCTIVELY, [in-dukt'-iv-li], *adv.* by means of induction or inference.

INDUCTOR, [in-dukt'-er], *n.* one who inducts a person into office; that part of an electrical apparatus which sets up induction. [L. *inductor* a leader-in].

INDUE† see ENDUE.

INDULGE, [in-dulj'], *v.t.* to satisfy wholeheartedly one's longing for; to pamper, yield to every wish of; (*eccles.*) to grant an indulgence; *v.i.* (*coll.*) to drink heavily; **to i. in,** to allow oneself the pleasure of having. [L. *indulgere* to be kind].

INDULGENCE, [in-dulj'-ents], *n.* the act of indulging one's desires; forbearance, kindliness; a favour, *esp.* the offer of certain religious liberties or privileges granted as a favour to Nonconformists by Charles II and James II; (*R.C. Church*) the remission of temporal punishment granted through the Church to a penitent. [L. *indulgentia*].

INDULGENCY, [in-dulj'-en-si], *n.* indulgence.

INDULGENT, [in-dulj'-ent], *adj.* showing indulgence; that indulges; inclined to overlook faults, etc., too easily. [L. *indulgens*].

INDULGENTIAL†, [in'-dulj-en'-shal], *adj.* pertaining to the indulgences of the Roman Catholic Church.

INDULGENTLY, [in-dulj'-ent-li], *adv.* in an indulgent way.

INDULGER, [in-dulj'-er], *n.* one who indulges.

INDULINE, [in'-dyōō-lin], *n.* (*chem.*) a group of dye-stuffs related to aniline, yielding blue, black, and grey dyes. [~INDIGO].

INDULT, [in'-dult], *n.* (*R.C. Church*) a special decree or licence issued by the Pope allowing something not normally sanctioned. [L. *indultum* permission].

INDUMENT, [in'-dyōō-ment], *n.* (*zool.*) the plumage of birds; (*bot.*) any hairy covering; a garment. [L. *indumentum*].

INDUNA, [in-dōōn'-a], *n.* the chief of an impi; a subordinate officer or councillor of a Zulu, or other native South African, chief. [Zulu *induna*].

INDUPLICATE, [in-dew'-plik-āt], *adj.* (*bot.*) (of a leaf, petal, etc.) with the edges bent towards the axis but not overlapping.

INDURATE, [in'-dyōō-rāt], *v.t. and i.* to harden; (*fig.*) to make or become callous. [L. *indurare*].

INDURATION, [in'-dyōō-rā'-shun], *n.* the act of hardening; the state of being hardened. [MedL. *induratio*].

INDUSIAL, [in-dew'-zi-al], *adj.* consisting of the larva-cases of certain insects.

INDUSIUM, (*pl.* **indusia**), [in-dew'-si-um], *n.* (*bot.*) a hairy cup enclosing a stigma; the cover of the sori in ferns; (*entom.*) the case or covering of certain larvæ. [L. *indusium* tunic].

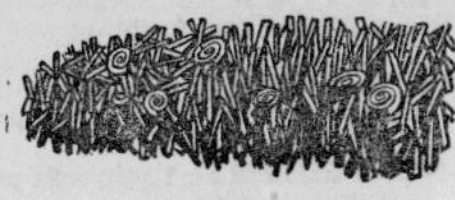
INDUSIUM

INDUSTRIAL (1), [in-dus'-tri-al], *n.* a person engaged in industry; (*pl.*) industrial shares.

INDUSTRIAL (2), [in-dus'-tri-al], *adj.* pertaining to, characterized by, engaged in, industry; prepared specially for use in industry; **i. school**, a school to which neglected children or young delinquents are sent to learn a trade.

INDUSTRIALISM, [in-dus'-tri-al-izm], *n.* employment in industrial pursuits or occupations; a social system characterized by this.

INDUSTRIALIST, [in-dus'-tri-al-ist], *n.* one engaged in industry; an industrial worker or magnate.

INDUSTRIALIZE, [in-dus'-tri-al-iz], *v.t.* to make industrial.

INDUSTRIALLY, [in-dus'-tri-al-i], *adv.* from the point of view of industry.

INDUSTRIOUS, [in-dus'-tri-us], *adj.* hard-working, assiduous, showing zealous application to one's work. [L. *industriosus*].

INDUSTRIOUSLY, [in-dus'-tri-us-li], *adv.* in an industrious fashion.

INDUSTRY, [in'-dus-tri], *n.* the quality of being industrious; work devoted to the production of resources or wealth, *esp.* organized labour engaged in the production of manufactures; a particular branch of trade or manufacture. [L. *industria*].

INDUVIAE, [in-dew'-vi-ē'], *n.(pl.)* (*bot.*) the withered leaves that remain on the stem of some plants. [L. *induviae* clothes].

INDWELL, [in-dwel'], *v.i.* to dwell, inhabit.

INDWELLER, [in-dwel'-er], *n.* an inhabitant.

INDWELLING, [in-dwel'-ing], *n.* the act of dwelling within, residence, *esp.* the dwelling of the Holy Spirit within the soul.

INEARTH, [in-urth'], *v.t.* to inter.

INEBRIANT (1), [in-ē'-bri-ant], *n.* an intoxicant.

INEBRIANT (2), [in-ē'-bri-ant], *adj.* intoxicating. [L. *inebrians*].

INEBRIATE (1), [in-ē'-bri-at], *n.* an intoxicated person; a habitual drunkard.

INEBRIATE (2), [in-ē'-bri-at], *adj.* drunken, intoxicated. [L. *inebriatus*].

INEBRIATE (3), [in-ē'-bri-āt], *v.t.* to intoxicate, to make drunk; (*fig.*) to excite or intoxicate the mind. [L. *inebriare*].

INEBRIATION, [in-ē'-bri-ā'-shun], *n.* the act of inebriating; the state of being intoxicated. [L. *inebriatio*].

INEBRIETY, [in'-ē-brī'-i-ti], *n.* habitual drunkenness; intoxication.

INEBRIOUS, [in-ē'-bri-us], *adj.* drunken.

INEDIBLE, [in-ed'-ibl], *adj.* not fit for eating.

INEDITED, [in-ed'-it-id], *adj.* unpublished; published without being edited. [L. *ineditus* not made known].

INEFFABILITY, [in-ef'-a-bil'-i-ti], *n.* the quality of being ineffable.

INEFFABLE, [in-ef'-abl], *adj.* unspeakable, indescribable. [L. *ineffabilis*].

INEFFABLENESS, [in-ef'-abl-nes], *n.* ineffability.

INEFFABLY, [in-ef'-ab-li], *adv.* in an ineffable way.

INEFFACEABLE, [in'-i-fās'-abl], *adj.* that may not be effaced.

INEFFACEABLY, [in'-i-fās'-ab-li], *adv.* in an ineffaceable way.

INEFFECTIVE, [in'-i-fekt'-iv], *adj.* useless, having no effect; not producing the right effect; incompetent.

INEFFECTIVELY, [in'-i-fekt'-iv-li], *adv.* in an ineffective way.

INEFFECTIVENESS, [in'-i-fekt'-iv-nes], *n.* the state of being ineffective.

INEFFECTUAL, [in'-i-fek'-chōō-al], *adj.* ineffective, unsuccessful, unavailing, abortive.

INEFFECTUALITY, [in'-i-fek'-chōō-al'-i-ti], *n.* the state of being ineffectual.

INEFFECTUALLY, [in'-i-fek'-chōō-al-i], *adv.* in an ineffectual way.

INEFFECTUALNESS, [in'-i-fek'-chōō-al-nes], *n.* ineffectuality.

INEFFERVESCENCE, [in-ef'-er-ves'-ents], *n.* absence of effervescence.

INEFFERVESCENT, [in-ef'-er-ves'-ent], *adj.* not effervescing.

INEFFERVESCIBILITY, [in-ef'-er-ves'-i-bil'-i-ti], *n.* the state of being ineffervescible.

INEFFERVESCIBLE, [in-ef'-er-ves'-ibl], *adj.* not capable of effervescing.

INEFFICACIOUS, [in-ef'-ik-ā'-shus], *adj.* not efficacious.

INEFFICACIOUSLY, [in-ef'-ik-ā'-shus-li], *adv.* in an inefficacious way.

INEFFICACIOUSNESS, [in-ef'-ik-ā'-shus-nes], *n.* the quality of being inefficacious.

INEFFICACY, [in-ef'-ik-as-i], *n.* lack of efficacy. [LL. *inefficacia*].

INEFFICIENCY, [in'-i-fish'-en-si], *n.* the quality of being inefficient.

INEFFICIENT, [in'-if-ish'-ent], *adj.* not efficient, unable to perform something satisfactorily; not in sound working order.

INEFFICIENTLY, [in'-i-fish'-ent-li], *adv.* in an inefficient way.

INELABORATE, [in'-i-lab'-er-at], *adj.* not elaborate, simple.

INELASTIC, [in'-i-last'-ik], *adj.* not elastic; (*fig.*) unyielding, unadaptable.

INELASTICITY, [in'-i-las-tis'-i-ti], *n.* the quality of being inelastic.

INELEGANCE, [in-el'-i-gants], *n.* want of elegance, clumsiness; that which is inelegant.

INELEGANCY, [in-el'-i-gan-si], *n.* inelegance.

INELEGANT, [in-el'-i-gant], *adj.* wanting in elegance; uncouth, awkward.

INELEGANTLY, [in-el'-i-gant-li], *adv.* in an inelegant way.

INELIGIBILITY, [in-el'-ij-i-bil'-i-ti], *n.* the quality of being ineligible.

INELIGIBLE, [in-el'-ij-ibl], *adj.* not eligible; unworthy.

INELIGIBLY, [in-el'-ij-ib-li], *adv.* in an ineligible way.

INELOQUENT, [in-el'-ō-kwent], *adj.* not eloquent.

INELOQUENTLY, [in-el'-ō-kwent-li], *adv.* in an ineloquent manner.

INELUCTABLE, [in'-i-lukt'-abl], *adj.* from which one may not escape, unavoidable, struggled against in vain. [L. *ineluctabilis*].

INELUDIBLE, [in'-i-lewd'-ibl], *adj.* that cannot be eluded.

INEMBRYONATE, [in-em'-bri-on-āt], *adj.* having no embryo.

INENARRABLE†, [in'-en-a'-rabl], *adj.* that cannot be narrated, unspeakable. [L. *inenarrabilis*].

INENCHYMA, [in-eng'-ki-ma], *n.* (*bot.*) fibrocellular tissue. [~Gk. *is inos* fibre and *egkhuma* infusion].

INEPT, [in-ept'], *adj.* stupid, fatuous; not apt. [L. *ineptus* unsuited].

INEPTITUDE, [in-ept'-it-ewd], *n.* the condition of being inept; an inept act or speech. [L. *ineptitudo*].

INEPTLY, [in-ept'-li], *adv.* in an inept fashion.

INEPTNESS, [in-ept'-nes], *n.* the quality of being inept.

INEQUABLE, [in-ek'-wabl], *adj.* uneven, not steady or uniform. [L. *inaequabilis*].

INEQUALITY, [in'-ē-kwol'-i-ti], *adj.* lack of equality, disparity; unevenness; tendency to vary; lack of uniformity; (*astron.*) variation in the motion of a heavenly body.

INEQUIDISTANT, [in-ēk'-wi-dist'-ant], *adj.* not equidistant.

INEQUILATERAL, [in-ēk'-wi-lat'-er-al], *adj.* with unequal sides.

INEQUITABLE, [in-ek'-wit-abl], *adj.* not equitable, unfair.

INEQUITY, [in-ek'-wit-i], *n.* unfairness.

INEQUIVALVE, [in-ēk'-wi-valv], *adj.* having valves unequal in size.

INEQUIVALVULAR, [in-ēk'-wi-valv'-yōō-ler], *adj.* inequivalve.

INERADICABLE, [in'-i-rad'-ik-abl], *adj.* that may not be eradicated.

INERADICABLY, [in'-i-rad'-ik-ab-li], *adv.* so as to be ineradicable.

INERM, [in-erm'], *adj.* (*bot.*) without prickles or thorns. [L. *inermis* unarmed].

INERMOUS, [in-erm'-us], *adj.* (*bot.*) inerm.

INERRABILITY, [in-e'-ra-bil'-i-ti], *n.* the quality of being inerrable.

INERRABLE, [in-e'-rabl], *adj.* that cannot err, infallible. [L. *inerrabilis*].

INERRABLENESS, [in-e'-rabl-nes], *n.* inerrability.

INERRABLY, [in-e'-rab-li], *adv.* infallibly.

INERRANT, [in-e'-rant], *adj.* incapable of error.
INERRATIC, [in'-i-rat'-ik], *adj.* travelling along a fixed course.
INERT, [in-ert'], *adj.* unable to move itself or resist motion; sluggish, lifeless; (*science*) displaying no activity. [L. *iners* unskilled].
INERTIA, [in-er'-sha], *n.* (*phys.*) that property of matter by which when in rest it remains still and unchanged, and when in motion continues to move uniformly along a straight line, unless some external force is applied to it; sluggishness, inactivity. [L. *inertia* unskilfulness].
INERTION, [in-er'-shun], *n.* inertness.
INERTLY, [in-ert'-li], *adv.* in an inert way.
INERTNESS, [in-ert'-nes], *n.* the quality of being inert; inertia.
INERUDITE, [in-e'-rōō-dīt], *adj.* unlearned, not scholarly. [L. *ineruditus*].
INESCAPABLE, [in'-es-kāp'-abl], *adj.* from which one may not escape.
INESCUTCHEON, [in'-es-kuch'-un], *n.* (*her.*) a small shield placed within a shield.

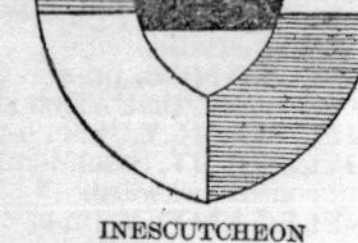
INESCUTCHEON

INESSENTIAL (1), [in'-i-sen'-shal], *n.* that which is inessential.
INESSENTIAL (2), [in'-i-sen'-shal], *adj.* not essential, not vitally necessary.
INESTIMABLE, [in-est'-im-abl], *adj.* that may not be estimated; invaluable.
INESTIMABLY, [in-est'-im-ab-li], *adv.* in an inestimable way.
INEVASIBLE, [in'-i-vāz'-ibl], *adj.* unable to be evaded.
INEVIDENT, [in-ev'-id-ent], *adj.* not evident, obscure.
INEVITABILITY, [in-ev'-it-a-bil'-i-ti], *n.* the quality of being inevitable.
INEVITABLE, [in-ev'-it-abl], *adj.* unavoidable, bound to come or follow. [L. *inevitabilis*].
INEVITABLENESS, [in-ev'-it-abl-nes], *n.* inevitability.
INEVITABLY, [in-ev'-it-ab-li], *adv.* in an inevitable way.
INEXACT, [in'-egz-akt'], *adj.* not exact or precise.
INEXACTITUDE, [in'-egz-akt'-it-ewd], *n.* inexactness; something that is inexact.
INEXACTNESS, [in-egz-akt'-nes], *n.* inexactitude.
INEXCUSABLE, [in'-eks-kewz'-abl], *adj.* not to be excused, unpardonable.
INEXCUSABLENESS, [in'-eks-kewz'-abl-nes], *n.* the quality of being inexcusable.
INEXCUSABLY, [in'-eks-kewz'-ab-li], *adv.* in inexcusable fashion.
INEXECUTABLE, [in-ek'-si-kewt'-abl], *adj.* that may not be executed.
INEXECUTION, [in'-ek-si-kew'-shun], *n.* failure to do something.
INEXERTION, [in'-eg-zer'-shun], *n.* inertia, failure or inability to exert oneself.
INEXHALABLE, [in-eg-zāl'-abl], *adj.* not evaporable, unable to be exhaled.
INEXHAUSTED, [in'-egz-awst'-id], *adj.* not exhausted.
INEXHAUSTIBLE, [in'-egz-awst'-ibl], *adj.* that cannot be exhausted.
INEXHAUSTIBLENESS, [in'-egz-awst'-ibl-nes], *n.* the quality of being inexhaustible.
INEXHAUSTIBLY, [in'-egz-awst'-ib-li], *adv.* in an inexhaustible way.
INEXHAUSTIVE, [in'-egz-awst'-iv], *adj.* not exhaustive.
INEXISTENCE, [in'-egz-ist'-ents], *n.* non-existence.
INEXISTENT, [in'-egz-ist'-ent], *adj.* non-existent.
INEXORABILITY, [in-eks'-er-a-bil'-i-ti], *n.* the quality of being inexorable.
INEXORABLE, [in-eks'-er-abl], *adj.* relentless, not to be shaken from one's purpose, or its course; unmoved by entreaty. [L. *inexorabilis*].
INEXORABLENESS, [in-eks'-er-abl-nes], *n.* inexorability.
INEXORABLY, [in-eks'-er-ab-li], *adv.* in an inexorable way.
INEXPANSIBLE, [in'-eks-pan'-sibl], *adj.* unable to expand or be expanded.
INEXPECTANT, [in'-eks-pekt'-ant], *adj.* not expectant.
INEXPECTATION, [in'-eks-pekt-ā'-shun], *n.* the condition of having no expectation.
INEXPEDIENCE, [in'-eks-pē'-di-ents], *n.* inexpediency.
INEXPEDIENCY, [in'-eks-pē'-di-en-si], *n.* the state of being inexpedient.
INEXPEDIENT, [in'-eks-pē'-di-ent], *adj.* not expedient, not wise or profitable in view of circumstances, impolitic.
INEXPEDIENTLY, [in'-eks-pē'-di-ent-li], *adv.* in an inexpedient way.
INEXPENSIVE, [in'-eks-pen'-siv], *adj.* not expensive; not extravagant.
INEXPERIENCE, [in'-eks-pēer'-i-ents], *n.* lack of experience, or of knowledge by experience.
INEXPERIENCED, [in'-eks-pēer'-i-enst], *adj.* lacking experience.
INEXPERT, [in-eks'-pert], *adj.* not expert, unskilled.
INEXPERTNESS, [in-eks'-pert-nes], *n.* the quality of being inexpert.
INEXPIABLE, [in-eks'-pi-abl], *adj.* that may not be expiated or atoned for; implacable.
INEXPIABLY, [in-eks'-pi-ab-li], *adv.* in inexpiable fashion.
INEXPLICABILITY, [in-eks'-plik-a-bil'-i-ti], *n.* the quality of being inexplicable.
INEXPLICABLE, [in-eks-plik'-abl], *adj.* that cannot be explained, unaccountable. [L. *inexplicabilis*].
INEXPLICABLENESS, [in-eks-plik'-abl-nes], *n.* inexplicability.
INEXPLICABLY, [in-eks-plik'-ab-li], *adv.* in an inexplicable way.
INEXPLICIT, [in'-eks-plis'-it], *adj.* not explicit, not clearly stated or expressed.
INEXPLORABLE, [in'-eks-plawr'-abl], *adj.* unable to be explored.
INEXPLOSIVE, [in'-eks-plō'-ziv], *adj.* not able or tending to explode.
INEXPOSURE, [in'-eks-pō'-zher], *n.* unexposed state.
INEXPRESSIBLE (1), [in'-eks-pres'-ibl], *n.(pl.)* (*coll., archaic*) trousers.
INEXPRESSIBLE (2), [in'-eks-pres'-ibl], *adj.* that may not be expressed, indescribable.
INEXPRESSIBLY, [in'-eks-pres'-ib-li], *adv.* in an inexpressible fashion.
INEXPRESSIVE, [in'-eks-pres'-iv], *adj.* not expressing anything.
INEXPRESSIVENESS, [in'-eks-pres'-iv-nes], *n.* the quality of being inexpressive.
INEXPUGNABLE, [in'-eks-pug'-nabl], *adj.* impregnable, invincible, not to be taken by assault or force. [L. *inexpugnabilis*].
INEXTENSIBLE, [in'-eks-ten'-sibl], *adj.* that may not be extended.
INEXTINCT, [in'-eks-tingkt'], *adj.* not extinct or extinguished.
INEXTINGUISHABLE, [in'-eks-ting'-gwish-abl], *adj.* that cannot be extinguished.
INEXTIRPABLE, [in'-eks-turp'-abl], *adj.* unable to be rooted out. [L. *inexstirpabilis*].
INEXTRICABLE, [in-eks'-trik-abl], *adj.* from which one may not be extricated; unable to be disentangled or straightened out. [L. *inextricabilis*].
INEXTRICABLENESS, [in-eks'-trik-abl-nes], *n.* the quality of being inextricable.
INEXTRICABLY, [in-eks'-trik-ab-li], *adv.* in an inextricable way.
INFALL, [in'-fawl], *n.* a raid or inroad; the point at which water flows into a reservoir, etc.
INFALLIBILITY, [in-fal'-i-bil'-i-ti], *n.* the quality of being infallible, *esp.* in regard to faith and morals, as claimed by Roman Catholics for the Church as a whole, and for the Pope, when speaking officially upon matters of doctrine.
INFALLIBLE, [in-fal'-ibl], *adj.* incapable of error; always right; that cannot go wrong; unfailing. [L. *infallibilis*].
INFALLIBLENESS, [in-fal'-ibl-nes], *n.* infallibility.
INFALLIBLY, [in-fal'-ib-li], *adv.* in an infallible way.
INFAMIZE, [in'-fam-iz], *v.t.* to render infamous, defame.
INFAMOUS, [in'-fam-us], *adj.* notoriously wicked or evil, having a very bad reputation; shameful, vile; (*leg.*) deprived of citizenship because convicted of certain crimes. [MedL. *infamosus*].
INFAMOUSLY, [in'-fam-us-li], *adv.* in an infamous way.
INFAMY, [in'-fam-i], *n.* the quality of being infamous; public disgrace; infamous behaviour; (*leg.*) loss of citizenship through crime. [L. *infamia* dishonour].

INFANCY, [in'-fan-si], *n.* the state or period of being an infant; legal minority; the rudimentary stages of anything. [L. *infantia* inability to speak].

INFANT (1), [in'-fant], *n.* a young child; (*leg.*) a minor, a person under the age of 21 years. [L. *infans*].

INFANT (2), [in'-fant], *adj.* pertaining to infancy or to infants.

INFANTA, [in-fant'-a], *n.* (formerly in Spain and Portugal) a daughter of the king and queen. [Span. *infanta*].

INFANTE, [in-fant'-ā], *n.* (formerly in Spain and Portugal) any son of the king and queen, other than the heir to the throne. [Span. *infante*].

INFANTICIDAL, [in-fant'-i-sīd'-al], *adj.* relating to infanticide.

INFANTICIDE, [in-fant'-i-sīd], *n.* the murder of an infant, *esp.* of a newly-born child; the murderer of an infant. [LL. *infanticidium*].

INFANTILE, [in'-fant-īl], *adj.* belonging to, affecting, infants; rudimentary; childish; **i. paralysis**, an infectious disease, poliomyelitis, which often causes paralysis. [LL. *infantilis*].

INFANTILISM, [in-fant'-il-izm], *n.* (*path.*) a morbid condition in which one remains mentally or physically an infant.

INFANTINE, [in'-fant-īn], *adj.* infantile.

INFANTLY, [in'-fant-li], *adv.* in a childlike or childish manner.

INFANTRY, [in'-fant-ri], *n.* foot-soldiers. [It. *infanteria*].

INFATUATE, [in-fat'-yōō-āt], *v.t.* to deprive of sound judgment; to cause to fall madly in love with. [L. *infatuare*].

INFATUATION, [in-fat'-yŏŏ-ā'-shun], *n.* the act of infatuating; the state of being infatuated; fierce unreasoning passion.

INFAUST, [in-fawst'], *adj.* unfortunate. [L. *infaustus*].

INFEASIBILITY, [in'-fēz-i-bil'-i-ti], *n.* the quality of being infeasible.

INFEASIBLE, [in-fēz'-ibl], *adj.* not feasible.

INFEASIBLENESS, [in-fēz'-ibl-nes], *n.* infeasibility.

INFECT, [in-fekt'], *v.t.* to taint or pollute with disease germs; to communicate a disease to; (*fig.*) to imbue with, to communicate to, by example. [L. *infectum*, *p.pt.* of *inficere* to dip into].

INFECTER, [in-fekt'-er], *n.* a thing or person that infects.

INFECTIBLE, [in-fekt'-ibl], *adj.* that may be infected.

INFECTION, [in-fek'-shun], *n.* the act of infecting; the state or process of being infected with disease; that which infects; (*fig.*) mental or moral influence readily communicated and assimilated; contamination. [L. *infectio*].

INFECTIOUS, [in-fek'-shus], *adj.* that infects; readily transmitted through the air, etc., without need of actual contact; caught by proximity to a source of infection; (*fig.*) catching, easily communicated and imparted indirectly and unobtrusively.

INFECTIOUSLY, [in-fek'-shus-li], *adv.* in an infectious way.

INFECTIOUSNESS, [in-fek'-shus-nes], *n.* the condition of being infectious.

INFECTIVE, [in-fekt'-iv], *adj.* infectious.

INFECUND, [in'-fek-und'], *adj.* unfruitful, barren. [L. *infecundus*].

INFECUNDITY, [in'-fek-und'-i-ti], *n.* unfruitfulness, barrenness. [L. *infecunditas*].

INFEFTMENT, [in-feft'-ment], *n.* (*Scots leg.*) the symbolical act of putting one in possession of an hereditament. [ENFEOFFMENT].

INFELICITOUS, [in'-fel-is'-it-us], *adj.* unhappy; inappropriate, unfortunate.

INFELICITY, [in'-fel-is'-i-ti], *n.* the quality of being infelicitous; an infelicitous act or remark. [L. *infelicitas*].

INFELONIOUS, [in-fel-ō'-ni-us], *adj.* not felonious.

INFER, (**inferring, inferred**), [in-fur'], *v.t.* to deduce, conclude; to imply, give the impression of. [L. *inferre*].

INFERABLE, [in'-fer-abl], *adj.* that may be inferred.

INFERENCE, [in'-fer-ents], *n.* the act of inferring; that which is inferred; implication. [MedL. *inferentia*].

INFERENTIAL, [in'-fer-en'-shal], *adj.* ascertained by inference.

INFERENTIALLY, [in'-fer-en'-shal-i], *adv.* in an inferential manner.

INFERIAE, [in-fēer'-i-ē], *n.(pl.)* pagan Roman sacrifices to the souls of the dead. [L. *inferiae*].

INFERIOR (1), [in-fēer'-i-er], *n.* a person who is inferior.

INFERIOR (2), [in-fēer'-i-er], *adj.* lower in position, place, or quality; below something else; poor, mediocre; low in rank, status, or value, humble, subordinate; (*astron.*) situated within the earth's orbit; (*print.*) placed on a lower level than the normal line of print; **i. to**, not so good as; subordinate to. [L. *inferior*].

INFERIORITY, [in-fēer'-i-o'-riti], *n.* the state of being inferior; **i. complex**, (*psych.*) a morbid mental condition characterized by a marked feeling of inferiority and lack of self-confidence.

INFERNAL (1), [in-furn'-al], *n.* an inhabitant of hell or the lower regions.

INFERNAL (2), [in-furn'-al], *adj.* pertaining to hell or the lower regions; fiendish, diabolical; (*coll.*) confounded, deuced; **i. machine**, an explosive bomb or machine. [L. *infernalis*].

INFERNALLY, [in-furn'-al-i], *adv.* (*coll.*) in an infernal manner, to an infernal degree.

INFERNO, [in-furn'-ō], *n.* hell; (*fig.*) anything resembling hell. [It. *inferno*].

INFERRIBLE, [in-fur'-ibl], *adj.* inferable.

INFERTILE, [in-fur'-tīl], *adj.* not fertile, arid.

INFERTILITY, [in'-fer-til'-i-ti], *n.* the quality of being infertile.

INFEST, [in-fest'], *v.t.* to trouble greatly, to overrun, to swarm on in troublesome manner. [L. *infestare* to attack].

INFESTATION, [in'-fest-ā'-shun], *n.* the act of infesting; the state of being infested. [LL. *infestatio*].

INFESTIVITY, [in'-fest-iv'-i-ti], *n.* lack of festivity.

INFEUDATION, [in'-few-dā'-shun], *n.* the act of putting one in possession of an estate in fee; the granting of tithes to laymen. [MedL. *infeudatio*].

INFIBULATION, [in-fib'-yŏŏ-lā'-shun], *n.* the act of securing with a clasp, *esp.* the fastening of the sexual organs in this way to prevent intercourse. [L. *infibulare*].

INFIDEL (1), [in'-fid-el], *n.* one who does not believe in religion, a heathen, atheist; (*hist.*) one who does not believe in Christianity; (among Moslems or Jews) one who believes in some other religion; an unbeliever.

INFIDEL (2), [in'-fid-el], *adj.* unbelieving, heathen; practising a false religion. [L. *infidelis* unfaithful].

INFIDELITY, [in'-fid-el'-i-ti], *n.* want of faith or belief, *esp.* in Christianity; unfaithfulness, *esp.* of a husband or wife. [L. *infidelitas*].

INFIELD, [in'-fēld], *n.* the portion of a farm which is manured and kept in crop; farm-land immediately surrounding the farm buildings; (*cricket*) that part of the field near the wicket; one who fields near the wicket; (*baseball*) the space enclosed by the base lines.

INFILTER, [in-fil'-ter], *v.t.* to infiltrate.

INFILTERED, [in-fil'-terd], *adj.* infiltrated.

INFILTRATE, [in-fil'-trāt], *v.t. and i.* to cause to filter through; to filter through, permeate.

INFILTRATION, [in'-fil-trā'-shun], *n.* the act of infiltrating; the state of being infiltrated; an infiltrated substance.

INFINITE (1), [in'-fin-it], *n.* that which is infinite; the supreme deity; (*math.*) an infinite quantity.

INFINITE (2), [in'-fin-it], *adj.* boundless, unlimited; immeasurable; innumerable; (*gram.*) not limited by number and person; (*math.*) having no limit. [L. *infinitus*].

INFINITELY, [in'-fin-it-li], *adv.* to an infinite extent.

INFINITENESS, [in'-fin-it-nes], *n.* the quality of being infinite.

INFINITESIMAL (1), [in'-fin-it-es'-im-al], *n.* an infinitely small quantity.

INFINITESIMAL (2), [in'-fin-it-es'-im-al], *adj.* too small to be measured or calculated, infinitely small.

INFINITESIMALLY, [in'-fin-it-es'-im-al-i], *adv.* in an infinitesimal manner, to an infinitesimal degree.

INFINITIVAL, [in'-fin-it-īv'-al], *adj.* belonging to the infinitive.

INFINITIVE (1), [in-fin'-it-iv], *n.* (*gram.*) the infinitive form of the verb.

INFINITIVE (2), [in-fin'-it-iv], *adj.* (*gram.*) pertaining to that form of the verb expressing its mere action without limitation of person, number, tense, or voice. [L. *infinitivus* indefinite].

INFINITUDE, [in-fin'-it-ewd], *n.* the quality of being infinite; an infinite number, quantity or size.

INFINITY, [in-fin'-i-ti], *n.* the quality of being infinite; that which is infinite; (*math.*) an infinite quantity; infinite space, time or distance. [L. *infinitas*].

INFIRM, [in-furm'], *adj.* not strong physically, weak, decrepit, *esp.* through age; irresolute, halting; unsound mentally or morally. [L. *infirmus* not firm].

INFIRMARY, [in-furm'-er-i], *n.* a hospital; the

sick-room of a public institution, school, monastery, etc. [MedL. *infirmaria*].

INFIRMATIVE, [in-furm'-at-iv], *adj.* tending to weaken or render invalid. [Fr. *infirmatif*].

INFIRMITY, [in-furm'-i-ti], *n.* the state of being infirm; a particular form of weakness; a moral defect. [L. *infirmitas*].

INFIRMLY, [in-furm'-li], *adv.* in an infirm fashion.

INFIRMNESS, [in-furm'-nes], *n.* the condition of being infirm.

INFIX (1), [in'-fiks], *n.* (*gram.*) a formative or modifying element introduced into the body of a word.

INFIX (2), [in-fiks'], *v.t.* to fix firmly in; (*fig.*) to implant strongly in the mind; (*gram.*) to introduce (an infix) into the body of a word. [OFr. *infixer*].

INFLAME, [in-flām'], *v.t. and i.* to suffuse with a fiery glow; to make or become hot, red, swollen and tender; (*rare*) to kindle, set or become on fire; (*fig.*) to excite to strong anger, passion or indignation. [L. *inflammare*].

INFLAMER, [in-flām'-er], *n.* the person or thing that inflames.

INFLAMMABILITY, [in'-flam-a-bil'-i-ti], *n.* the quality of being inflammable.

INFLAMMABLE, [in-flam'-abl], *adj.* readily catching fire, easily combustible; (*fig.*) highly excitable, hot-tempered, easily roused. [Fr. *inflammable*].

INFLAMMABLENESS, [in-flam'-abl-nes], *n.* inflammability.

INFLAMMABLY, [in-flam'-ab-li], *adv.* in an inflammable way.

INFLAMMATION, [in'-flam-ā'-shun], *n.* the act of inflaming; the state of being inflamed; (*path.*) redness and swelling, accompanied by pain, febrile symptoms, and an increase of heat in the affected part. [L. *inflammatio*].

INFLAMMATORY, [in-flam'-at-er-i], *adj.* tending to inflame or cause inflammation; accompanied by inflammation.

INFLATABLE, [in-flāt'-abl], *adj.* able to be inflated.

INFLATE, [in-flāt'], *v.t.* to cause to swell, to distend with air or gas; (*fig.*) to make haughty and overbearing; (*comm.*) to raise artificially beyond the normal or natural level; to increase the amount of money, *esp.* paper money, in circulation. [L. *inflare*].

INFLATED, [in-flāt'-id], *adj.* blown up or distended with air or gas; (*fig.*) turgid, bombastic; swollen with pride or vanity; (*comm.*) increased beyond the natural limits.

INFLATION, [in-flā'-shun], *n.* the act of inflating; the state of being inflated. [L. *inflatio*].

INFLECT, [in-flekt'], *v.t.* to bend inwards, to curve; (*gram.*) to vary the endings of a word in order to express differences of number, case, tense, etc.; (*mus.*) to modulate (the voice). [L. *inflectere*].

INFLECTED, [in-flekt'-id], *adj.* bent inwards; (*gram.*) exhibiting inflexion.

INFLECTION, see INFLEXION.

INFLECTIONAL, see INFLEXIONAL.

INFLECTIVE, [in-flekt'-iv], *adj.* that inflects; (*gram.*) modified by inflexion.

INFLEXED, [in-flekst'], *adj.* (*bot.*) bent inwards.

INFLEXIBILITY, [in-fleks'-i-bil'-i-ti], *n.* the quality of being inflexible.

INFLEXIBLE, [in-fleks'-ibl], *adj.* that may not be bent, rigid; (*fig.*) not to be turned aside, relentless, unyielding, unbending; immovably fixed. [L. *inflexibilis*].

INFLEXIBLENESS, [in-fleks'-ibl-nes], *n.* inflexibility.

INFLEXIBLY, [in-fleks'-ib-li], *adv.* in an inflexible way.

INFLEXION, INFLECTION, [in-flek'-shun], *n.* the act of inflecting; the state of being inflected; (*gram.*) variation in the endings of words which inflect; an inflected form; a termination used to inflect modulation. [L. *inflexio*].

INFLEXIONAL, INFLECTIONAL, [in-flek'-shun-al], *adj.* (*gram.*) pertaining to or exhibiting inflexion.

INFLICT, [in-flikt'], *v.t.* to deal to, to cause to suffer, (a blow, wound, etc.); to impose (something unpleasant). [L. *inflictum*, *p.pt.* of *infligere* strike].

INFLICTER, [in-flikt'-er], *n.* one who inflicts.

INFLICTION, [in-flik'-shun], *n.* the act of inflicting; that which is inflicted. [LL. *inflictio*].

INFLICTIVE, [in-flikt'-iv], *adj.* tending to inflict.

INFLORESCENCE, [in'-flor-es'-ents], *n.* (*bot.*) the method of flowering of a plant; the arrangement of the flowers on the stalks; the whole mass of flowers blossoming on a plant; the process of blossoming. [MdL. *inflorescentia*].

INFLOW (1), [in'-flō], *n.* the process of flowing in; that which flows in.

INFLOW (2), [in-flō'], *v.i.* to flow in.

INFLUENCE (1), [in'-flōō-ents], *n.* any power, force or agency producing an effect in such a way that its action is not apparent; the effect so produced; control or authority indirectly manifested; power of affecting action, thought, etc.; a thing or person exercising such power; (*astrol.*) the effect exerted upon human life and destiny by the stars. [Fr. *influence*].

INFLUENCE (2), [in'-flōō-ents], *v.t.* to exert influence upon, to affect or persuade by one's influence.

INFLUENT (1), [in'-flōō-ent], *n.* a stream or tributary flowing into a river.

INFLUENT (2), [in'-flōō-ent], *adj.* flowing in. [L. *influens*].

INFLUENTIAL, [in'-flōō-en'-shal], *adj.* that influences; possessing and able to exert strong influence, powerful.

INFLUENTIALLY, [in'-flōō-en'-shal-i], *adv.* in an influential way.

INFLUENZA, [in'-flōō-en'-za], *n.* an infectious and contagious epidemic disease, characterized by catarrh accompanied by fever and exhaustion. [It. *influenza* influence].

INFLUX, [in'-fluks], *n.* the act of flowing in, *esp.* of a tributary or stream into a river; the place where this occurs; the constant flow of anything, *esp.* in large quantities, into a place. [LL. *influxus*].

INFLUXION, [in-fluk'-shun], *n.* an inflow or influx. [LL. *influxio*].

INFOLD†, see ENFOLD.

INFORM, [in-fawm'], *v.t.* to fill, inspire; to pervade; to communicate some knowledge or fact to, to acquaint with; **to i. against**, to bring a charge against, to communicate facts resulting in a charge being made against. [L. *informare* to give form to].

INFORMAL, [in-fawm'-al], *adj.* not in the usual, customary, or recognized form; without formality or ceremony; familiar.

INFORMALITY, [in'-fawm-al'-it-i], *n.* the quality of being informal; that which is informal.

INFORMALLY, [in-fawm'-al-i], *adv.* in an informal way.

INFORMANT, [in-fawm'-ant], *n.* one who gives information. [L. *informans*].

INFORMATION, [in'-fawm-ā'-shun], *n.* the act of informing; something told, knowledge of a fact or facts communicated or learnt; news; knowledge; (*leg.*) a charge or accusation made to a magistrate or a court instead of a formal indictment. [L. *informatio*].

INFORMATIVE, [in-fawm'-at-iv], *adj.* that informs, instructive; (*leg.*) pertaining to, of the nature of, an information.

INFORMATIVELY, [in-fawm'-at-iv-li], *adv.* so as to provide information; for information and not for publication.

INFORMATORY, [in-fawm'-at-er-i], *adj.* containing information.

INFORMED, [in-fawmd'], *adj.* possessing information; enlightened; educated.

INFORMER, [in-fawm'-er], *n.* one who informs; one who informs against another, *esp.* one who habitually does this.

INFRA (1), [in'-fra], *adj.* below, underneath; further down or on; **i. dig.**, beneath one's dignity. [L. *infra*].

INFRA- (2), *pref.* below. [L. *infra*].

INFRACOSTAL, [in'-fra-kost'-al], *adj.* below the ribs. [INFRA (2) and L. *costa* rib].

INFRACTION, [in-frak'-shun], *n.* violation, infringement; breach. [L. *infractio*].

INFRACTOR, [in-frakt'-er], *n.* a violator. [MedL. *infractor*].

INFRAHUMAN, [in'-fra-hew'-man], *adj.* below the human level.

INFRALAPSARIAN (1), [in'-fra-laps-āer'-i-an], *n.* a Calvinist who maintains that God's election of the chosen ones came after, and was due to, the fall of man. [INFRA (2) and L. *lapsus* fall].

INFRALAPSARIAN (2), [in'-fra-laps-āer'-i-an], *adj.* pertaining to the infralapsarians or their beliefs.

INFRAMAXILLARY, [in'-fra-maks'-il-er-i], *adj.* beneath the jaw. [INFRA (2) and L. *maxilla* jawbone].

INFRAMEDIAN, [in'-fra-mē'-di-an], *adj.* between the median and the deep-sea zone of the ocean.

INFRANGIBLE, [in-franj'-ibl], *adj.* that cannot be broken or violated.

INFRAORBITAL, [in'-fra-awb'-it-al], *adj.* (*anat.*) beneath the orbit of the eye.

INFRAPOSITION, [in'-fra-poz-ish'-un], *n.* the state of being placed or situated beneath something else.

INFRA-RED, [in′-fra-red′], *adj.* (*phys.*) relating to the invisible rays beyond the red rays of the spectrum; **i. photography,** photography by the use of infra-red rays.

INFRASCAPULAR, [in′-fra-skap′-yōō-ler], *adj.* (*anat.*) under the shoulder-blade. [INFRA (2) and L. *scapula* shoulder-blade].

INFREQUENCY, [in-frē′-kwen-si], *n.* the state of being infrequent, rarity. [L. *infrequentia*].

INFREQUENT (1), [in-frē′-kwent], *adj.* not frequent, rare, sparse. [L. *infrequens*].

INFREQUENT (2), [in′-fri-kwent′], *v.t.* to keep away from, forsake.

INFREQUENTLY, [in-frē′-kwent-li], *adv.* not frequently, rarely.

INFRINGE, [in-frinj′], *v.t.* to break, violate, transgress, to commit a breach of. [L. *infringere*].

INFRINGEMENT, [in-frinj′-ment], *n.* the act of infringing; a breach, an offence against the rules or the law; that which infringes.

INFRINGER, [in-frinj′-er], *n.* one who infringes.

INFRUCTUOSE, [in-frukt′-yōō-ōs], *adj.* not bearing fruit, barren; (*fig.*) unprofitable. [L. *infructuosus*].

INFULA, [in′-fyōō-la], *n.* (*Rom. antiq.*) a fillet worn as a badge of priestly, sacrificial, or royal consecration; the ribbons hanging from the back of a mitre. [L. *infula*].

INFUMATE, [in′-fyōōm-āt′], *v.t.* to smoke, to dry or cure by smoking. [L. *infumare*].

INFUNDIBULAR, [in′-fund-ib′-yōō-ler], *adj.* shaped like a funnel. [L. *infundibulum* funnel].

INFUNDIBULIFORM, [in′-fund-ib′-yōō-li-fawm], *adj.* funnel-shaped.

INFURCATION†, [in′-furk-ā′-shun], *n.* a forked extension. [IN (6) and L. *furca* fork].

INFURIATE, [in-few′-ri-āt], *v.t.* to make furious, enrage, madden. [MedL. *infuriare*].

INFUSE, [in-fewz′], *v.t.* to pour into; to steep or soak in liquid, to extract its properties; (*fig.*) to cause to enter, to inspire with. [L. *infusum*, *p.pt.* of *infundere* to pour into].

INFUSER, [in-fewz′-er], *n.* one who, or that which, infuses; a vessel used in infusing.

INFUSIBILITY, [in′-fewz-i-bil′-i-ti], *adj.* the quality of being infusible.

INFUSIBLE (1), [in-fewz′-ibl], *adj.* that may not be fused or melted.

INFUSIBLE (2), [in-fewz′-ibl], *adj.* that may be poured into.

INFUSION, [in-few′-zhun], *n.* the act of infusing; that which is infused; liquid in which plants or vegetable substances have been infused; (*fig.*) introduction; blend. [L. *infusio*].

INFUSIVE, [in-fewz′-iv], *adj.* able to infuse or be infused.

INFUSORIA, [in′-fewz-aw′-ri-a], *n.*(*pl.*) a class of microscopic motile protozoa present in liquids, *esp.* in infusions of animal or vegetable matter. [MdL. *infusorius*].

INFUSER

INFUSORIAL, [in′-fewz-aw′-ri-al], *adj.* pertaining to, containing, infusoria; **i. earth,** tripoli powder, a siliceous deposit composed of fossil diatoms.

INFUSORIAN, [in′-fewz-aw′-ri-an], *n.* a member of the *Infusoria*.

INFUSORY, [in-fewz′-er-i], *adj.* infusorial.

INGATE, [in′-gāt], *n.* an entrance; an aperture in a mould for pouring in metal.

INGATHERING, [in′-gaTH′-er-ing], *n.* harvesting; a gathering in, collection.

INGEMINATE, [in-jem′-in-āt], *v.t.* to repeat, reiterate, to say again. [L. *ingeminare*].

INGEMINATION, [in-jem′-in-ā′-shun], *n.* (*archaic*) the act of ingeminating, repetition.

INGENERABLE, [in-jen′-er-abl], *adj.* that cannot be engendered or generated. [MedL. *ingenerabilis*].

INGENERATE (1), [in-jen′-er-āt], *adj.* innate, inbred, inborn. [L. *ingeneratus*].

INGENERATE (2), [in-jen′-er-āt], *v.t.* to generate or produce within, to engender. [L. *ingenerare*].

INGENIOUS, [in-jē′-ni-us], *adj.* clever, artful; possessing originality; good at inventing or contriving things; artfully contrived. [L. *ingeniosus*].

INGENIOUSLY, [in-jē′-ni-us-li], *adv.* in an ingenious way.

INGENIOUSNESS, [in-jē′-ni-us-nes], *n.* the condition of being ingenious.

INGENUE, ingénue, [an-zhā-new′], *n.* a simple, innocent, unsophisticated girl; an actress playing such a part. [Fr. *ingénue*].

INGENUITY, [in′-ji-new′-i-ti], *n.* the quality of being ingenious. [L. *ingenuitas* nobility].

INGENUOUS, [in-jen′-yōō-us], *adj.* frank, sincere, candid; simple, innocent, guileless; (*hist.*) free-born, of noble birth. [L. *ingenuus*].

INGENUOUSLY, [in-jen′-yōō-us-li], *adv.* in an ingenuous fashion.

INGENUOUSNESS, [in-jen′-yōō-us-nes], *n.* the quality of being ingenuous.

INGEST, [in-jest′], *v.t.* to take in, introduce into the stomach. [L. *ingestum*, *p.pt.* of *ingerere*].

INGESTION, [in-jes′-chun], *n.* the act of ingesting. [L. *ingestio*].

INGESTIVE, [in-jest′-iv], *adj.* pertaining to ingestion.

INGLE (1), [ing′-gl], *n.* a fire burning on a hearth; a fireplace. [Gael. *aingeal* fire].

INGLE† (2), [ing′-gl], *n.* a boy-favourite, a young boy kept for unnatural purposes. [Unkn.].

INGLENOOK, [ingl′-nŏŏk′], *n.* a chimney corner.

INGLORIOUS, [in-glaw′-ri-us], *adj.* not bringing honour, shameful, ignominious; unrenowned, not celebrated. [L. *ingloriosus*].

INGLORIOUSLY, [in-glaw′-ri-us-li], *adv.* in an inglorious fashion.

INGLORIOUSNESS, [in-glaw′-ri-us-nes], *n.* the condition of being inglorious.

INGLUVIES, [in-glōō′-vi-ēz], *n.* the crop or craw of a bird; the first stomach of a ruminating animal. [L. *ingluvies*].

INGOING (1), [in′-gō-ing], *n.* entrance; a sum paid by a new tenant for fittings, fixtures, etc., on taking up his tenancy.

INGOING (2), [in′-gō′-ing], *adj.* entering, going in.

INGOT, [ing′-got], *n.* unwrought gold, silver, or other metal, cast in a mould. [IN (6) and OE. *goten*, *p.pt.* of *geotan* to pour].

INGRAFT†, see ENGRAFT.

INGRAFTER†, [in-grahft′-er], *n.* a person who engrafts.

INGRAFTMENT†, [in-grahft′-ment], *n.* the act of engrafting; that which is engrafted.

INGRAIN (1), [in-grān′], *adj.* dyed in the grain; dyed in the yarn with fast colours before manufacture; (*fig.*) innate, inborn.

INGRAIN† (2), see ENGRAIN.

INGRAINED, [in-grānd′], *adj.* firmly fixed in, and complete, impregnating every part; deeply rooted, inveterate, inborn.

INGRATE (1), [in′-grāt], *n.* an ungrateful person.

INGRATE (2), [in′-grāt], *adj.* (*archaic*) ungrateful. [L. *ingratus*].

INGRATEFUL†, [in-grāt′-fōōl], *adj.* ungrateful; unpleasant.

INGRATIATE, [in-grā′-shi-āt], *v. reflex.* to worm one's way into favour, to get into the good graces of another person. [It. *ingratiare*].

INGRATIATING, [in-grā′-shi-āt′-ing], *adj.* seeking to curry favour, winning.

INGRATITUDE, [in-grat′-it-ewd], *n.* want of gratitude.

INGRAVESCENT, [in′-grav-es′-ent], *adj.* (*med.*) (of a disease) becoming worse or more severe. [L. *ingravescens*].

INGREDIENT, [in-grē′-di-ent], *n.* that which goes to make up a compound, a component part. [L. *ingrediens*].

INGRESS, [in′-gres], *n.* the act of going in; a means of entrance; (*leg.*) power or right of entrance. [L. *ingressus*].

INGRESSION, [in-gresh′-un], *n.* entrance. [L. *ingressio*].

INGROSS†, see ENGROSS.

INGROWING, [in′-grō′-ing], *adj.* growing inwards, (*esp.* of a nail) growing into the flesh.

INGROWTH, [in′-grōth], *n.* the act of growing inwards; a growth into the flesh of a nail.

INGUINAL, [ing′-gwin-al], *adj.* relating to the groin. [L. *inguinalis*].

INGULF†, see ENGULF.

INGULFMENT†, see ENGULFMENT.

INGURGITATE, [in-gurj′-it-āt], *v.t. and i.* to swallow up greedily; (*fig.*) to engulf; to gorge, guzzle. [L. *ingurgitare*].

INGURGITATION, [in-gurj′-it-ā′-shun], *n.* the act of ingurgitating. [LL. *ingurgitatio*].

INHABIT, [in-hab'-it], *v.t.* to live or dwell in, to occupy as a residence; (*fig.*) to be present in. [L. *inhabitare*].

INHABITABLE, [in-hab'-it-abl], *adj.* that may be lived in.

INHABITANCY, [in-hab'-it-an-si], *n.* the fact of inhabiting; status as an inhabitant.

INHABITANT, [in-hab'-it-ant], *n.* one who lives in a certain place, etc., a resident. [L. *inhabitans*].

INHABITATION, [in-hab'-it-ā'-shun], *n.* the act of inhabiting; the state of being inhabited; a dwelling-place, habitation.

INHABITER, [in-hab'-it-er], *n.* an inhabitant.

INHABITRESS, [in-hab'-it-res], *n.* a female inhabitant.

INHALANT (1), [in-hāl'-ant], *n.* a medicine to be taken by inhalation.

INHALANT (2), [in-hāl'-ant], *adj.* inhaling, breathing in. [L. *inhalans*].

INHALATION, [in'-hal-ā'-shun], *n.* the act of inhaling; that which is inhaled.

INHALE, [in-hāl'], *v.t. and i.* to breathe in, to draw into the lungs; to do this habitually with tobacco smoke. [L. *inhalare*].

INHALER, [in-hāl'-er], *n.* one who inhales; an apparatus for inhaling medicated vapours, a respirator.

INHALER

INHARMONIC, [in'-hah-mon'-ik], *adj.* not harmonic, dissonant, inharmonious.

INHARMONIOUS, [in'-hah-mō'-ni-us], *adj.* not harmonious, discordant.

INHARMONIOUSLY, [in'-hah-mō'-ni-us-li], *adv.* in an inharmonious way.

INHARMONY, [in-hah'-mun-i], *n.* want of harmony, discord.

INHAUL, [in'-hawl'], *n.* (*naut.*) a rope used for hauling in the lower corner of a boomsail.

INHERE, [in-hēer'], *v.i.* to exist in as a natural and permanent feature, to form an intrinsic part of; to be vested in; to be naturally implied in. [L. *inhaerere* to stick in].

INHERENCE, [in-hēer'-ents], *n.* the state of being inherent. [MedL. *inhaerentia*].

INHERENCY, [in-hēer'-en-si], *n.* inherence.

INHERENT, [in-hēer'-ent], *adj.* natural to, existing in as an essential, inseparable element; vested in. [L. *inhaerens*].

INHERENTLY, [in-hēer'-ent-li], *adv.* in an inherent way.

INHERIT, [in-he'-rit], *v.t.* to receive from an ancestor or former possessor, as an heir; to acquire from a predecessor as a gift; to derive, possess as a hereditary characteristic; to gain, obtain; *v.i.* to become an heir, to take possession as heir. [OFr. *enheriter*].

INHERITABILITY, [in-he'-rit-a-bil'-i-ti], *n.* the condition of being inheritable.

INHERITABLE, [in-he'-rit-abl], *adj.* that may be inherited; able or entitled to inherit. [OFr. *inheritable*].

INHERITABLY, [in-he'-rit-ab-li], *adv.* by inheritance, so as to be inheritable.

INHERITANCE, [in-he'-rit-ants], *n.* the act of inheriting; that which is inherited or possessed as a birthright; (*biol.*) the transmission of hereditary characteristics. [OFr. *enheritance*].

INHERITOR, [in-he'-rit-or], *n.* one who inherits as an heir.

INHERITRESS, [in-he'-rit-res], *n.* a female who inherits as an heiress.

INHERITRIX, [in-he'-ri-triks], *n.* an inheritress.

INHESION, [in-hē'-zhun], *n.* inherence. [LL. *inhaesio*].

INHIBIT, [in-hib'-it], *v.t.* to prohibit, prevent, *esp.* (*eccles. leg.*) to forbid a priest to carry out ecclesiastical duties; to hinder, delay, check; (*psych.*) to keep in check by inhibition. [L. *inhibitum*, *p.pt.* of *inhibere* restrain].

INHIBITION, [in'-hib-ish'-un], *n.* the act of inhibiting, a formal prohibition; (*psych.*) an unconscious force forbidding what would otherwise be an impulse or urge; (*eccles. leg.*) a court order forbidding further proceedings in an inferior court; an official order inhibiting a clergyman; (*Scots leg.*) a writ preventing a person from alienating his heritable estate by debt; (*physiol.*) deliberate or involuntary temporary stopping or restraining of the functions of a structure or organism. [OFr. *inhibicion*].

INHIBITORY, [in-hib'-it-er-i], *adj.* that inhibits, of the nature of an inhibition. [MedL. *inhibitorius*].

INHOSPITABLE, [in-hos'-pit-abl], *adj.* affording no hospitality; bleak, cheerless. [MedL. *inhospitabilis*].

INHOSPITABLENESS, [in-hos'-pit-abl-nes], *n.* the quality of being inhospitable.

INHOSPITABLY, [in-hos'-pit-ab-li], *adv.* in an inhospitable way.

INHOSPITALITY, [in-hos'-pit-al'-iti], *n.* inhospitableness. [L. *inhospitalitas*].

INHUMAN, [in-hew'-man], *adj.* void of human or humane feelings or qualities, brutal, savage; pertaining to that which is not human. [L. *inhumanus*].

INHUMANITY, [in'-hew-man'-i-ti], *n.* the quality of being inhuman; an inhuman act. [L. *inhumanitas*].

INHUMANLY, [in-hew'-man-li], *adv.* in an inhuman way.

INHUMATION, [in-hew-mā'-shun], *n.* burial in the ground, interment.

INHUME, [in-hewm'], *v.t.* to bury in the ground, to inter. [L. *inhumare*].

INIA, [in'-ya], *n.* the freshwater dolphin of the Amazon. [Native].

INIMAGINABLE†, [in'-im-aj'-in-abl], *adj.* unimaginable.

INIMICAL, [in-im'-ik-al], *adj.* hostile; unfavourable, injurious. [LL. *inimicalis*].

INIMICALLY, [in-im'-ik-al-i], *adv.* in an inimical way.

INIMITABILITY, [in-im'-it-a-bil'-i-ti], *n.* the quality of being inimitable.

INIMITABLE, [in-im'-it-abl], *adj.* that cannot be imitated, unique, without rival. [L. *inimitabilis*].

INIMITABLY, [in-im'-it-ab-li], *adv.* in an inimitable way.

INION, [in'-yon], *n.* (*anat.*) the ridge of the occiput. [Gk. *inion* nape of the neck].

INIQUITOUS, [in-ik'-wit-us], *adj.* wicked, sinful, unjust.

INIQUITOUSLY, [in-ik'-wit-us-li], *adv.* in an iniquitous way.

INIQUITY, [in-ik'-wit-i], *n.* the quality of being iniquitous, injustice, sin; iniquitous conduct. [L. *iniquitas*].

INIRRITABLE, [in-i'-rit-abl], *adj.* that may not be irritated.

INITIAL (1), [in-ish'-al], *n.* an initial letter; (*pl.*) the first letter of the Christian name(s) and surname of a person; (*mus.*) any of the limited choice of notes on which the melody of a plain-song may begin.

INITIAL (2), [in-ish'-al], *adj.* pertaining to, constituting, or occurring at, the beginning; first, incipient, earliest. [L. *initialis*].

INITIAL (3), **(initialling, initialled)**, [in-ish'-al], *v.t.* to write one's initials on.

INITIALLY, [in-ish'-al-i], *adv.* at the beginning, in the first place.

INITIATE (1), [in-ish'-i-at], *n.* one who has been initiated.

INITIATE (2), [in-ish'-i-at], *adj.* having been initiated. [L. *initiatus*].

INITIATE (3), [in-ish'-i-āt], *v.t.* to originate, start, set on foot; to admit into some society, etc., *esp.* with appropriate rites and ceremonies; to instruct in the first principles of anything. [L. *initiare*].

INITIATION, [in-ish'-i-ā'-shun], *n.* the act or ceremony of initiating; the state of being initiated. [L. *initiatio*].

INITIATIVE (1), [in-ish'-i-at-iv], *n.* the initial move, first step; the right of making the first move; the lead; ability to transcend routine and tradition and initiate things; enterprise; (*parl.*) the right of introducing legislation.

INITIATIVE (2), [in-ish'-i-at-iv], *adj.* serving to initiate.

INITIATOR, [in-ish'-i-āt-or], *n.* one who initiates.

INITIATORY, [in-ish'-i-āt'-er-i], *adj.* that initiates, introductory.

INJECT, [in-jekt'], *v.t.* to cause to enter by pressure, to force in (fluid) as by a syringe, etc.; to fill (a bodily cavity or tissue) by this means. [L. *injectum*, *p.pt.* of *injicere* to throw in].

INJECTION, [in-jek'-shun], *n.* the act of injecting, *esp.* a liquid by means of a syringe, etc.; a medicinal preparation to be injected. [L. *injectio*].

INJECTOR, [in-jekt'-er], *n.* an apparatus used for injecting; a device for forcing water into the boiler of a steam-engine.

INJECTOR

INJUDICIAL, [in'-jōō-dish'-al], *adj.* not in accordance with legal forms or procedure.

INJUDICIOUS, [in'-jōō-dish'-us], *adj.* unwise, not displaying judgment, ill-advised.

INJUDICIOUSLY, [in'-jōō-dish'-us-li], *adv.* in an injudicious way.

INJUDICIOUSNESS, [in'-jōō-dish'-us-nes], *n.* the condition of being injudicious.

INJUNCTION, [in-jungk'-shun], *n.* the act of enjoining; that which is enjoined; an order, command, instruction; (*leg.*) a writ restraining a person from committing a wrong against, or infringing the rights of, another person. [LL. *injunctio*].

INJURE, [in'-jer], *v.t.* to do harm to, to wrong; to hurt, do physical injury to. [INJURY].

INJURED, [in'-jerd], *adj.* wronged, offended; expressing a sense of wrong, injustice, or hurt; damaged, hurt.

INJURER, [in'-jer-er], *n.* one who injures.

INJURIOUS, [in-jōōer'-i-us], *adj.* unjust, causing injury; tending or intended to injure; (of language) slanderous; detrimental. [L. *injuriosus*].

INJURIOUSLY, [in-jōōer'-i-us-li], *adv.* in an injurious way.

INJURIOUSNESS, [in-jōōer'-i-us-nes], *n.* the state of being injurious.

INJURY, [in'-jer-i], *n.* any wrong done to a man's person, rights, reputation, or goods; physical hurt or damage; moral or mental hurt. [L. *injuria*].

INJUSTICE, [in-just'-is], *n.* a wrong, an unjust act; unfairness. [L. *injustitia*].

INK (1), [ingk], *n.* a bluish-black or other coloured fluid used in writing; a thick black or coloured paste used for printing; a black liquid emitted by a squid and related animals when in danger or attacked. [Gk. *enkauston* purple ink used by Greek and Roman emperors].

INK (2), [ingk], *v.t.* to mark or trace over with ink.

INK-BAG, [ingk'-bag], *n.* a bladder-shaped sac in the cuttle-fish and other related fishes, in which its ink is stored.

INK-BOTTLE, [ingk'-botl], *n.* a bottle for holding ink.

INKER, [ingk'-er], *n.* (*print.*) a roller used to smear type with ink.

INKHOLDER, [ingk'-hōld'-er], *n.* an ink-bottle.

INK-HORN, [ingk'-hawn], *n.* a small vessel formerly made of horn, and used for holding ink.

INKINESS, [ingk'-i-nes], *n.* the state of being inky.

INKING-ROLLER, [ingk'-ing-rōl'-er], *n.* (*print.*) a roller for inking printing types.

INKING-TABLE, [ingk'-ing-tābl'], *n.* (*print.*) the flat surface or slab smeared with ink by the inking roller.

INKLE, [ingkl], *n.* a kind of broad linen tape; the linen thread from which this is made. [Uncert.].

INKLING, [ingk'-ling], *n.* a hint, intimation, a vague notion or suspicion. [Uncert.].

INKMAKER, [ingk'-māk'-er], *n.* one who makes ink.

IN-KNEED, [in'-nēd], *adj.* knock-kneed.

IN-KNIT†, (in-knitting, in-knitted), [in-nit'], *v.t.* to knit together or in.

IN-KNOT, (in-knotting, in-knotted), [in-not'], *v.t.* to fasten with a knot.

INK-POT, [ingk'-pot], *n.* a small (lipped) vessel containing ink.

INKSTAND, [ingk'-stand], *n.* a stand for ink-pots, usually provided also with a ledge for pens.

INK-STONE, [ingk'-stōn], *n.* a kind of iron sulphate used in making ink; a flat smooth slab of stone on which indian ink is manufactured.

INK-WELL, [ingk'-wel'], *n.* an ink-pot fitting a hole in a desk.

INKY, [ingk'-i], *adj.* consisting of, marked or covered with, ink; black as ink.

INLACE, see ENLACE.

INLAID, [in-lād'], *adj.* laid into the surface of a thing, *esp.* so as to form a decorative pattern.

INLAND (1), [in'-land], *n.* the interior part of a country.

INLAND (2), [in'-land], *adj.* remote from the sea; situated in the interior of a country; carried on within a country; **i. revenue,** revenue derived from taxes and duties imposed inside the country.

INLAND (3), [in'-land], *adv.* in or towards the interior of a country.

INLANDER, [in'-land-er], *n.* one who dwells inland.

INLAW†, [in'-law], *v.t.* (*hist.*) to restore to the protection and authority of the law. [OE. *inlagian*].

IN-LAWS, [in-lawz'], *n.(pl.)* (*coll.*) one's relations by marriage.

INLAY (1), [in'-lā], *n.* inlaid work.

INLAY (2), (inlaid), [in-lā'], *v.t.* to insert pieces of hard material into differently coloured, or different kinds of, material so as to form an ornamental pattern; to lay or embed into the surface of something else so as to form one continuous level upper surface; (*print.*) to insert a page, plate, etc., of a book into a space cut to receive it in a larger and stronger sheet.

INLAYER, [in-lā'-er], *n.* one who inlays.

INLAYING, [in-lā'-ing], *n.* the act of one who inlays; inlaid work.

INLET, [in'-let], *n.* a small opening or creek in the coast-line or in the bank of a river or lake; a means of entrance; anything inserted or let in.

INLIER, [in'-li-er], *n.* (*geol.*) an outcrop entirely surrounded by younger rock.

INLY, [in'-li], *adv.* deeply, inwardly, sincerely. [OE. *innlice*].

INMATE, [in'-māt], *n.* an inhabitant of a house, asylum, or institution, an occupant.

INMOST, [in'-mōst], *adj.* deepest or farthest within; most private or secret.

INN, [in], *n.* a house providing bedroom accommodation and catering for travellers, a hotel; **Inns of Court,** four incorporated societies of lawyers in London, to join which provides the exclusive means of qualifying for the bar; the buildings belonging to these societies. [OE. *inn*].

INNATE, [in-āt'], *adj.* native, inborn, inherent, instinctive. [L. *innatus*].

INNATELY, [in-āt'-li], *adv.* in an innate way.

INNATENESS, [in-āt'-nes], *n.* the condition of being innate.

INNAVIGABLE, [i-nav'-ig-abl], *adj.* not navigable.

INNAVIGABLY, [i-nav'-ig-ab-li], *adv.* in a way not to be navigable.

INNER (1), [in'-er], *n.* the ring, on a target, immediately surrounding the bull's-eye; a shot hitting within this area.

INNER (2), [in'-er], *adj.* farther in, inside, interior, inward; nearer the centre. [OE. *innera, inra*].

INNERMOST, [in'-er-mōst], *adj.* farthest inward, deepest, inside, inmost.

INNER-TUBE, [in'-er-tewb'], *n.* a tube of rubber placed inside a tyre and inflated.

INNERVATE, [i-nurv'-āt], *v.t.* to give nervous energy to, to act as a tonic on (the nerves).

INNERVATION, [in'-erv-ā'-shun], *n.* a condition of weakness; act of strengthening; nervous action or influence.

INNERVE, [i-nurv'], *v.t.* to animate, to give nerve to, to invigorate.

INNHOLDER†, [in'-hōld'-er], *n.* an innkeeper.

INNINGS, [in'-ingz], *n.* the turn of a particular side to bat in cricket; the turn of one player to bat; (*pl.*) lands recovered from the sea.

INNKEEPER, [in'-kēp'-er], *n.* a person who keeps an inn; a person who holds a licence to sell alcoholic liquor in a particular house.

INNOCENCE, [in'-ō-sents], *n.* the quality of being innocent. [L. *innocentia* blamelessness].

INNOCENCY†, [in'-ō-sen-si], *n.* innocence.

INNOCENT (1), [in'-ō-sent], *n.* an idiot, a person without sense of responsibility; an ingenuous person.

INNOCENT (2), [in'-ō-sent], *adj.* innocuous, harmless; free from guilt or sin; having no intentions of doing harm; lawful; guileless, ingenuous; ignorant, simple and inexperienced in the ways of the world. [L. *innocens*].

INNOCENTLY, [in'-ō-sent-li], *adv.* in an innocent way.

INNOCUOUS, [i-nok'-yōō-us], *adj.* harmless in effect; inoffensive. [L. *innocuus*].

INNOCUOUSLY, [i-nok'-yōō-us-li], *adv.* in an innocuous way.

INNOCUOUSNESS, [i-nok'-yōō-us-nes], *n.* the quality of being innocuous.

INNOMINATE, [in-nom'-in-āt], *adj.* not having a name, unnamed; **i. bone,** (*anat.*) the hip-bone or pelvic bone; **i. veins,** the brachycephalic veins. [L. *innominatus*].

INNOVATE, [in'-ō-vāt], *v.i.* to introduce new things or methods into established practice. [L. *innovare*].

INNOVATION, [in'-ō-vā'-shun], *n.* the act or process

of innovating; that which is newly introduced, a novelty. [L. *innovatio*].
INNOVATOR, [in'-ō-vāt'-er], *n.* an introducer of changes.
INNOXIOUS, [i-nok'-shus], *adj.* harmless in effects, free from crime, innocuous. [L. *innoxius*].
INNOXIOUSLY, [i-nok'-shus-li], *adv.* in an innoxious way.
INNOXIOUSNESS, [i-nok'-shus-nes], *n.* the quality of being innoxious.
INNUENDO, [in-yōō-en'-dō], *n.* a suggestive allusion; an indirect reference of a malicious character; an insinuation. [L. *innuendo* by pointing].
INNUIT, [in'-yōō-it], *n.* an Eskimo. [Native].

INNUIT

INNUMERABILITY, [i-newm'-er-a-bil'-i-ti], *n.* the quality of being innumerable.
INNUMERABLE, [i-newm'-er-abl], *adj.* not able to be counted, countless. [L. *innumerabilis*].
INNUMERABLENESS, [i-newm'-er-abl-nes], *n.* innumerability.
INNUMERABLY, [i-newm'-er-ab-li], *adv.* without number.
INOBSERVANCE, [in'-ob-zurv'-ants], *n.* want of observance, inattention.
INOBSERVANT, [in'-ob-zurv'-ant], *adj.* not observant, inattentive.
INOCCUPATION, [in-ok-yōō-pā'-shun], *n.* lack of occupation.
INOCULABLE, [in-ok'-yōō-labl], *adj.* able to be inoculated; able to communicate disease by inoculation.
INOCULATE, [in-ok'-yōō-lāt], *v.t.* (*bot.*) to insert a bud or shoot into another plant or tree so that it may grow on the new stock; (*med.*) to introduce the weakened germ or virus of a specific disease into a person's system so as to set up its antitoxins or antibodies. [L. *inoculare*].
INOCULATION, [in-ok'-yōō-lā'-shun], *n.* the act of inoculating.
INOCULATOR, [in-ok'-yōō-lāt'-er], *n.* a person who inoculates.
INOCULUM, [in-ok'-yōō-lum], *n.* (*path.*) the virus used in inoculation. [MdL. *inoculum*].
INODORATE†, [in-ō'-der-āt], *adj.* inodorous.
INODOROUS, [in-ō'-der-us], *adj.* without scent. [L. *inodorus*].
INOFFENSIVE, [in'-o-fens'-iv], *adj.* giving no offence, harmless, innocent; having no positive characteristics.
INOFFENSIVELY, [in'-o-fens'-iv-li], *adv.* in an inoffensive way.
INOFFENSIVENESS, [in'-o-fens'-iv-nes], *n.* the condition of being inoffensive.
INOFFICIOUS, [in'-o-fish'-us], *adj.* ignoring the demands of duty; contrary to duty; having neither office nor authority. [L. *inofficiosus*].
INOPERABLE, [in-op'-er-abl], *adj.* (*med.*) not able to be operated upon; that does not operate. [IN (5) and Fr. *opérable*].
INOPERATIVE, [in-op'-er-at-iv], *adj.* having no force or effect.
INOPPORTUNE, [in-op'-er-tewn], *adj.* not opportune, untimely.
INOPPORTUNELY, [in-op'-er-tewn-li], *adv.* in an inopportune way.
INORDINACY, [in-awd'-in-a-si], *n.* inordinateness.
INORDINATE, [in-awd'-in-at], *adj.* irregular; excessive, extravagant. [L. *inordinatus* disorderly].
INORDINATELY, [in-awd'-in-at-li], *adv.* in an inordinate way.
INORDINATENESS, [in-awd'-in-at-nes], *n.* the quality of being inordinate.
INORGANIC, [in'-aw-gan'-ik], *adj.* not organic, not possessing parts in a functioning or developing relationship; (*chem.*) consisting of inanimate matter; dealing with all substances other than the carbon compounds.
INORGANICAL, [in'-aw-gan'-ik-al], *adj.* inorganic.
INORGANICALLY, [in'-aw-gan'-ik-al-i], *adv.* in an inorganic fashion.
INORGANIZATION, [in-aw'-gan-īz-ā'-shun], *n.* lack of organization.
INORGANIZED, [in-aw'-gan-īzd], *adj.* not organized.
INORNATE, [in'-aw-nāt'], *adj.* not ornate, simple.
INOSCULATE, [in-os'-kyōō-lāt], *v.t.* to join; *v.i.* to unite parts of a body or organism by their ends; to intertwine, to form one whole by blending, to amalgamate. [IN (6) and L. *osculare* to provide with an opening].
INOSCULATION, [in-os'-kyōō-lā'-shun], *n.* the process of inosculating; the state of being inosculated.
IN-PLAYER, [in'-plā'-yer], *n.* the server at rackets.
INPUT, [in'-pōōt], *n.* (*elect.*) the current taken in by or put into an electrical apparatus.
INQUEST, [in'-kwest], *n.* a judicial inquiry held with a jury present for the purpose of establishing facts; **coroner's i.,** such an inquiry into the circumstances of a death. [MedL. *inquesta*].
INQUIETUDE, [in-kwī'-et-ewd], *n.* disturbed state of body or mind, restlessness, uneasiness. [LL. *inquietudo*].
INQUIRABLE, [in-kwīer'-abl], *adj.* open to inquiry.
INQUIRE, ENQUIRE, [in-kwīer'], *v.t. and i.* to ask; to ask questions about; **to i. after,** to ask about the state of someone's health; **to i. into,** to investigate. [L. *inquirere*].
INQUIRENDO, [in'-kwi-ren'-dō], *n.* (*leg.*) authority given to someone to inquire into something for the sovereign's advantage. [L. *inquirendo* by inquiring].
INQUIRER, ENQUIRER, [in-kwīer'-er], *n.* a person who makes inquiry.
INQUIRING, [in-kwīer'-ing], *adj.* given to inquiry, curious.
INQUIRINGLY, [in-kwīer'-ing-li], *adv.* in an inquiring way.
INQUIRY, ENQUIRY, [in-kwīer'-i], *n.* the act of inquiring; a single question; an official investigation of facts.
INQUISITION, [in'-kwiz-ish'-un], *n.* an official inquiry, investigation; (*R.C.*) the medieval ecclesiastical tribunal established to discover and punish heretics; any aggressive or rigorous examination. [L. *inquisitio* seeking].
INQUISITIONAL, [in'-kwiz-ish'-un-al], *adj.* relating to an examination; pertaining to or resembling the Inquisition.
INQUISITIVE, [in-kwiz'-it-iv], *adj.* having a desire to increase one's knowledge, curious to know; curious about other people's business, prying. [LL. *inquisitivus* inquiring].
INQUISITIVELY, [in-kwiz'-it-iv-li], *adv.* in an inquisitive way.
INQUISITIVENESS, [in-kwiz'-it-iv-nes], *n.* the quality of being inquisitive.
INQUISITOR, [in-kwiz'-it-or], *n.* a person who inquires, *esp.* officially; a member of the Inquisition. [L. *inquisitor*].
INQUISITORIAL, [in-kwiz'-it-aw'-ri-al], *adj.* relating to inquiry, or to the Inquisition; searching; prying.
INQUISITORIALLY, [in-kwiz'-it-aw'-ri-al-i], *adv.* in the manner of an inquisitor.
INRIGGED, [in'-rigd], *adj.* having rowlocks on the gunwale.
INRO, [in'-rō], *n.* a small Japanese box for holding sweets, carried on the belt. [Jap. *inro*].
INROAD, [in'-rōd], *n.* a sudden aggressive advance into an enemy's country; attack, invasion; encroachment.
INRUSH, [in'-rush], *n.* the act of rushing in.
INSALIVATE, [in-sal'-iv-āt], *v.t.* to mingle food with saliva in mastication.
INSALIVATION, [in-sal'-iv-ā'-shun], *n.* the act of insalivating.
INSALUBRIOUS, [in'-sal-ew'-bri-us], *adj.* unhealthy, unwholesome. [L. *insalubris*].
INSALUBRITY, [in'-sal-ew'-brit-i], *n.* the quality of being insalubrious.
INSALUTARY, [in-sal'-yōō-ter-i], *adj.* unwholesome; injurious to health. [L. *insalutaris*].
INSANE, [in-sān'], *adj.* mad, not of a sound mind, mentally deranged; apparently mad. [L. *insanus*].
INSANELY, [in-sān'-li], *adv.* in an insane way.
INSANENESS, [in-sān'-es], *n.* insanity.
INSANITARY, [in-san'-it-er-i], *adj.* not sanitary, unhealthy, likely to carry infection.
INSANITATION, [in-san'-it-ā'-shun], *n.* unwholesome sanitary arrangements.
INSANITY, [in-san'-i-ti], *n.* the condition of being insane.
INSATIABILITY, [in-sā'-sha-bil'-i-ti], *n.* the quality of being insatiable.
INSATIABLE, [in-sā'-shabl], *adj.* impossible to be satisfied or appeased. [L. *insatiabilis*].
INSATIABLENESS, [in-sā'-shabl-nes], *n.* insatiability.
INSATIABLY, [in-sā'-shab-li], *adv.* in an insatiable way.

INSATIATE, [in-sā'-shi-at], *adj.* never satisfied, insatiable. [L. *insatiatus*].

INSATIATELY, [in-sā'-shi-at-li], *adv.* in an insatiate way.

INSATURABLE, [in-sach'-ōō-rabl], *adj.* impossible to be saturated. [L. *insaturabilis*].

INSCRIBABLE, [in-skrīb'-abl], *adj.* able to be inscribed.

INSCRIBABLENESS, [in-skrīb'-abl-nes], *n.* the condition of being inscribable.

INSCRIBE, [in-skrīb'], *v.t.* to write on, to engrave letters, symbols, or figures upon; to write down; to record in a register; (*geom.*) to draw a figure within another. [L. *inscribere*].

INSCRIBER, [in-skrīb'-er], *n.* a person who inscribes.

INSCRIPTION, [in-skrip'-shun], *n.* the act of inscribing; that which is inscribed; the lettering on a coin, scroll, roll of honour, etc.; a written dedication in the front of a book. [L. *inscriptio*].

INSCRIPTIVE, [in-skript'-iv], *adj.* having the nature of an inscription.

INSCROLL, [in-skrōl'], *v.t.* to inscribe a scroll. [IN (6) and SCROLL].

INSCRUTABILITY, [in-skrōōt'-a-bil'-i-ti], *n.* the quality of being inscrutable.

INSCRUTABLE, [in-skrōōt'-abl], *adj.* impossible to understand or unravel; enigmatic; impenetrable. [L. *inscrutabilis*].

INSCRUTABLENESS, [in-skrōōt'-abl-nes], *n.* inscrutability.

INSCRUTABLY, [in-skrōōt'-ab-li], *adv.* in an inscrutable way.

INSCULPTURED, [in-skulp'-cherd], *adj.* engraved.

INSECT, [in'-sekt], *n.* (*entom.*) one of the small arthropod animals, often winged, having a body in three sections, viz. head, thorax and abdomen, set on six legs arranged in three pairs; (*fig.*) a contemptible mean person. [L. *insectum (animal)* animal cut into].

INSECTARIUM, [in'-sekt-āer'-i-um], *n.* a house or room for keeping a collection of living insects.

INSECTED, [in'-sekt-id], *adj.* segmented like an insect.

INSECTICIDE, [in-sekt'-i-sīd], *n.* a preparation for killing insects. [INSECT and L. *cida* killer].

INSECTIFUGE, [in-sekt'-i-fewj], *n.* a preparation for driving off insects. [INSECT and L. *fugare* to put to flight].

INSECTILE, [in-sekt'-īl], *adj.* resembling insects.

INSECTION, [in-sek'-shun], *n.* the act or process of cutting into, incision. [L. *insectio*].

INSECTIVORA, [in'-sekt-iv'-er-a], *n.(pl.)* an order of mammals that eat insects.

INSECTIVORE, [in-sekt'-i-vaw(r)], *n.* a mammal that eats insects. [INSECT and L. *vorare* to devour].

INSECTIVOROUS, [in'-sekt-iv'-er-us], *adj.* feeding on insects.

INSECTOLOGY, [in'-sekt-ol'-o-ji], *n.* the study of insects and their habits, *esp.* as affecting the health and property of men. [INSECT and Gk. *logos* speech].

INSECURE, [in'-si-kew'-er], *adj.* open to peril or danger; unsafe; not effectively protected; having inadequate support or strength; unreliable.

INSECURELY, [in'-si-kew'-er-li], *adv.* in an insecure way.

INSECURITY, [in'-si-kyōōer'-it-i], *n.* the condition of being insecure.

INSEMINATE, [in-sem'-in-āt], *v.t.* to sow, plant; impregnate. [L. *inseminare*].

INSEMINATION, [in-sem'-in-ā'-shun], *n.* the act of inseminating.

INSENSATE, [in-sen'-sāt], *adj.* unable to take in experience through the senses; wanting sensibility; stupid, irrational, senseless. [LL. *insensatus*].

INSENSATELY, [in-sen'-sāt-li], *adv.* in an insensate fashion.

INSENSIBILITY, [in-sen'-si-bil'-i-ti], *n.* lack of sensibility, the quality of being insensible.

INSENSIBLE, [in-sen'-sibl], *adj.* unable to partake of sensory experience; senseless, unconscious; incapable or devoid of sympathetic feeling or emotion, passionless; having no power of intellectual perception, irrational; imperceptible. [L. *insensibilis*].

INSENSIBLENESS, [in-sens'-ibl-nes], *n.* insensibility.

INSENSIBLY, [in-sens'-ib-li], *adv.* imperceptibly; gradually.

INSENSITIVE, [in-sens'-it-iv], *adj.* not sensitive, incapable of experiencing particular sensations or emotions.

INSENSITIVENESS, [in-sen'-sit-iv-nes], *n.* the state of not being sensitive.

INSENSUOUS, [in-sen'-shōō-us], *adj.* not sensuous.

INSENTIENT, [in-sen'-shi-ent], *adj.* not having perception, inanimate.

INSEPARABILITY, [in-sep'-er-a-bil'-i-ti], *n.* the quality of being inseparable.

INSEPARABLE, [in-sep'-er-abl], *adj.* not capable of being separated, joined firmly together; always accompanying one another; (*gram.*) not existing as an independent word. [LL. *inseparabilis*].

INSEPARABLENESS, [in-sep'-er-abl-nes], *n.* inseparability.

INSEPARABLY, [in-sep'-er-ab-li], *adv.* in an inseparable way.

INSERT, [in-surt'], *v.t.* to set or place in or among, to introduce into something else. [L. *insertum*, *p.pt.* of *inserere*].

INSERTED, [in-surt'-id], *adj.* (*bot.*) growing from or attached to.

INSERTION, [in-sur'-shun], *n.* the act of inserting; the state of being inserted; the thing, *esp.* a word or printed matter, inserted; a piece of lace, embroidery, etc., inserted in some other material. [L. *ins*[illegible]*tio*].

INSESSORES, [in'-ses-aw'-rēz], *n.(pl.)* (*ornith.*) [illegible]erching birds.

INSESSORIAL, [in'-ses-aw'-ri-al], *adj.* (*ornith.*) relating to perchers; perching.

INSET (1), [in'-set], *n.* an insertion; something set in, *esp.* a leaf or batch of leaves inserted in a book; a small picture, map, etc., set within a larger.

INSET (2), (insetting, insetted), [in-set'], *v.t.* to insert, to place in, to infix.

INSEVERABLE, [in-sev'-er-abl], *adj.* not able to be severed.

INSHADED, [in-shād'-id], *adj.* marked with different shades, sketched in by means of cross-hatching.

INSHEATHE, [in-shēTH'], *v.t.* to place or cover in a sheath.

INSHELL, [in-shel'], *v.t.* to hide or place in a shell.

INSHELTER, [in-shel'-ter], *v.t.* to place in a shelter.

INSHIP, (inshipping, inshipped), [in-ship'], *v.t.* to place in a ship; to embark.

INSHORE (1), [in'-shaw(r)], *adj.* situated near the shore.

INSHORE (2), [in'-shaw(r)], *adv.* near the shore.

INSICCATION†, [in'-sik-ā'-shun], *n.* the process of drying in. [IN (6) and L. *siccare* to dry].

INSIDE (1), [in'-sīd], *n.* the inner part, surface, edge, etc., the interior; a passenger in the inside of a vehicle; (*slang*) stomach.

INSIDE (2), [in'-sīd], *adj.* placed on the inner side, within, having a position on the inside; secret, privileged.

INSIDE (3), [in-sīd'], *prep.* on the inner side, within.

INSIDER, [in-sīd'-er], *n.* a person in the secret; a person having inside knowledge; a person having access to a particular class or group.

INSIDIOUS, [in-sid'-i-us], *adj.* working, gaining access, or progressing, imperceptibly; intended to deceive or ensnare by stealth, treacherous. [L. *insidiosus*].

INSIDIOUSLY, [in-sid'-i-us-li], *adv.* in an insidious way.

INSIDIOUSNESS, [in-sid'-i-us-nes], *n.* the condition of being insidious.

INSIGHT, [in'-sīt], *n.* the mental faculty of sharp discernment, clear perception; an intuitive grasp of a situation.

INSIGNIA, [in-sig'-ni-a], *n.(pl.)* symbols, tokens, ribands, badges of office or honour; distinguishing marks. [L. *insignia*].

INSIGNIFICANCE, [in'-sig-nif'-ik-ants], *n.* the quality of being insignificant.

INSIGNIFICANCY†, [in'-sig-nif'-ik-an-si], *n.* insignificance.

INSIGNIFICANT, [in'-sig-nif'-ik-ant], *adj.* having no sense or meaning; unimpressive, unimposing; unimportant, trivial, contemptible.

INSIGNIFICANTLY, [in'-sig-nif-'ik-ant-li], *adv.* in an insignificant way.

INSIGNIFICATIVE†, [in'-sig-nif'-ik-at-iv], *adj.* having no external signs indicative of importance.

INSINCERE, [in'-sin-sēer'], *adj.* not expressing real feeling or thought, not sincere, hypocritical, false.

INSINCERELY, [in'-sin-sēer'-li], *adv.* in an insincere way.

INSINCERITY, [in'-sin-se'-ri-ti], *n.* the quality of being insincere.

INSINUATE, [in-sin'-yōō-āt], *v.t. and i.* to penetrate, creep in, worm oneself in gradually and imperceptibly; to draw attention to one's good qualities cunningly; to suggest by allusion or indirect reference, to hint, imply. [L. *insinuare* to wind in].

INSINUATING, [in-sin'-yōō-āt-ing], *adj.* that insinuates, characterized by insinuation.
INSINUATINGLY, [in-sin'-yōō-āt'-ing-li], *adv.* in an insinuating fashion.
INSINUATION, [in-sin'-yōō-ā'-shun], *n.* the act of insinuating; that which is insinuated, a suggestion, hint, implication. [L. *insinuatio*].
INSINUATIVE, [in-sin'-yōō-at-iv], *adj.* given to working for favour, insinuating.
INSINUATOR, [in-sin'-yōō-āt'-er], *n.* a person who insinuates.
INSIPID, [in-sip'-id], *adj.* without a well-defined flavour, tasteless; (*fig.*) dull, spiritless, pointless. [LL. *insipidus*].
INSIPIDITY, [in'-sip-id'-i-ti], *n.* the quality of being insipid.
INSIPIDLY, [in-sip'-id-li], *adv.* in an insipid way.
INSIPIDNESS, [in-sip'-id-nes], *n.* insipidity.
INSIPIENCE, [in-sip'-i-ents], *n.* foolishness, lack of wisdom. [L. *insipientia*].
INSIPIENT†, [in-sip'-i-ent], *adj.* wanting sense or wisdom. [L. *insipiens*].
INSIST, [in-sist'], *v.t. and i.* to persist in; to urge as a command, to demand with urgency, to emphasize in argument; to assert. [L. *insistere* to pursue].
INSISTENCE, [in-sist'-ents], *n.* the act of insisting; the quality of being insistent.
INSISTENT, [in-sist'-ent], *adj.* emphatic, imperative; predominant, commanding. [L. *insistens*].
INSOBRIETY, [in'-sō-brī'-i-ti], *n.* lack of sobriety.
INSOCIABLE, [in-sō'-shabl], *adj.* not sociable.
INSOCIABLY, [in-sō'-shab-li], *adv.* unsociably.
INSOLATE, [in'-sol-āt], *v.t.* to expose to the sun's rays, *esp.* in order to dry. [L. *insolare*].
INSOLATION, [in'-sol-ā'-shun], *n.* the act of insolating. [L. *insolatio*].
INSOLE, [in'-sōl], *n.* the inner sole of footwear.
INSOLENCE, [in'-sol-ents], *n.* the quality of being insolent; insulting behaviour, impertinence. [L. *insolentia*].
INSOLENT, [in'-sol-ent], *adj.* haughtily contemptuous, insulting, arrogantly rude.
INSOLENTLY, [in'-sol-ent-li], *adv.* in an insolent way.
INSOLIDITY, [in'-sol-id'-i-ti], *n.* lack of solidity.
INSOLUBILITY, [in-sol'-yōō-bil'-i-ti], *n.* the condition of being insoluble.
INSOLUBLE, [in-sol'-yōōbl], *adj.* not able to be dissolved; that cannot be solved. [L. *insolubilis* unable to be set loose].
INSOLUBLENESS, [in-sol'-yōōbl-nes], *n.* insolubility.
INSOLUBLY, [in-sol'-yōōb-li], *adv.* in an insoluble way.
INSOLVABLE, [in-solv'-abl], *adj.* not able to be solved; †that cannot be paid or discharged.
INSOLVENCY, [in-solv'-en-si], *n.* the state of being insolvent, bankruptcy.
INSOLVENT (1), [in-solv'-ent], *n.* a person who is insolvent.
INSOLVENT (2), [in-solv'-ent], *adj.* not able to pay debts, bankrupt; relating to bankruptcy.
INSOMNIA, [in-som'-ni-a], *n.* sleeplessness.
INSOMUCH, [in'-sō-much'], *adv.* in as far as, to such a degree.
INSOUCIANCE, [in-sōō'-si-ants], *n.* indifference expressed freely and easily, unconcern. [Fr. *insouciance*].
INSOUCIANT, [in-sōō'-si-ant], *adj.* indifferent, careless, unconcerned. [Fr. *insouciant*].
INSPAN, (inspanning, inspanned), [in-span'], *v.t.* to yoke (oxen, etc.). [Du. *inspannen*].
INSPECT, [in-spekt'], *v.t.* to look into; to examine carefully, *esp.* as an official; to superintend. [L. *inspectum*, *p.pt.* of *inspicere*].
INSPECTED, [in-spekt'-id], *adj.* examined closely, viewed with care.
INSPECTION, [in-spek'-shun], *n.* the act of inspecting; scrutiny, official examination. [L. *inspectio*].
INSPECTIVE, [in-spekt'-iv], *adj.* given to inspecting. [L. *inspectivus*].
INSPECTOR, [in-spekt'-er], *n.* one who inspects, *esp.* an official whose duty it is to inspect and send in reports; a police-officer ranking immediately above a sergeant.
INSPECTORATE, [in-spekt'-er-at], *n.* a body of official inspectors; inspectorship.
INSPECTORIAL, [in'-spekt-aw'-ri-al], *adj.* relating to an inspector.
INSPECTORSHIP, [in-spekt'-er-ship], *n.* the office of inspector; the period of office of an inspector.
INSPEXIMUS, [in-speks'-im-us], *n.* (*leg.*) a charter, commencing with this word, which confirms the grants afforded by an earlier one. [L. *inspeximus* we have inspected].
INSPIRABLE, [in-spīer'-abl], *adj.* capable of being inspired.
INSPIRATION, [in'-spi-rā'-shun], *n.* the act of breathing in; the act of inspiring; the state of being inspired; the simultaneous fusion of intense intellectual and emotional activity which controls one's creative, visionary power; that which, or one who, inspires; an intuitional impulse, an original idea; divine guidance. [L. *inspiratio*].
INSPIRATIONAL, [in'-spi-rā'-shun-al], *adj.* having the power to inspire; relating to inspiration.
INSPIRATIONISM, [in'-spi-rā'-shun-izm], *n.* the theory that everything is inspired by God.
INSPIRATIONIST, [in'-spi-rā'-shun-ist], *n.* one who believes in inspirationism.
INSPIRATOR, [in'-spi-rāt-er], *n.* an apparatus for sucking in air or vapour. [L. *inspirator*].
INSPIRATORY, [in-spīer'-at-er-i], *adj.* relating to the inhaling of air into the lungs.
INSPIRE, [in-spīer'], *v.t.* to draw air into the lungs, to breathe in; to influence a person to attain a state of controlled excitement; to instil into the mind; to fill with creative power; to communicate divine power. [L. *inspirare*].
INSPIRED, [in-spīerd'], *adj.* moved by inspiration.
INSPIRER, [in-spīer'-er], *n.* one who inspires.
INSPIRING, [in-spīer'-ing], *adj.* that inspires or tends to inspire, animating.
INSPIRIT, [in-spi'-rit], *v.t.* to infuse spirit into, to give new life to, to animate, stimulate.
INSPISSATE, [in'-spis-āt], *v.t.* to thicken, *esp.* a fluid, by boiling, evaporation, etc. [L. *inspissare*].
INSPISSATION, [in'-spis-ā'-shun], *n.* the process of inspissating.
INSTABILITY, [in'-sta-bil'-i-ti], *n.* lack of stability; shakiness; inconstancy; fickleness; irresolution. [L. *instabilitas*].
INSTABLE, [in-stābl'], *adj.* unstable.
INSTABLENESS, [in-stābl'-nes], *n.* instability.
INSTALL, [in-stawl'], *v.t.* to place in office, invest with a rank, with formal ceremony; to establish in a place or seat; to place in position ready for use. [MedL. *installare* to introduce].
INSTALLATION, [in'-stal-ā'-shun], *n.* the act of installing; apparatus fitted in position and ready for use. [MedL. *installatio*].
INSTALMENT, [in-stawl'-ment], *n.* part payment of a debt made regularly until the whole is paid off; part of a whole, appearing serially or supplied periodically until complete; †installation.
INSTANCE (1), [in'-stants], *n.* a particular example, occurrence, an illustrative fact; suggestion, request; **for i.,** as an example. [L. *instantia* presence].
INSTANCE (2), [in'-stants], *v.t.* to mention as an example or illustration.
INSTANCY, [in'-stan-si], *n.* insistency, urgency.
INSTANT (1), [in'-stant], *n.* a point of time, exact moment, particular second; an extremely brief period of time.
INSTANT (2), [in'-stant], *adj.* pressing, urgent; admitting no delay, immediate; present; current. [L. *instans*].
INSTANTANEITY, [in'-stant-a-nē'-i-ti], *n.* the quality of being instantaneous.
INSTANTANEOUS, [in'-stant-ā'-ni-us], *adj.* occurring or done in an instant, immediate; at some particular instant.
INSTANTANEOUSLY, [in'-stant-ā'-ni-us-li], *adv.* in an instant; without a second wasted.
INSTANTANEOUSNESS, [in'-stant-ā'-ni-us-ness], *n.* instantaneity.
INSTANTER, [in-stant'-er], *adv.* without delay, immediately. [L. *instanter*].
INSTANTLY, [in'-stant-li], *adv.* at once, immediately.
INSTAR (1), [in'-stah(r)], *n.* (*zool.*) a stage in development; the form of an invertebrate after each stage. [L. *instar* shape].
INSTAR (2), (instarring, instarred), *v.t.* to adorn or stud with stars or brilliants.
INSTATE, [in-stāt'], *v.t.* to set or place in a particular position; to establish, install. [IN and STATE].
INSTAURATION, [in'-staw-rā'-shun], *n.* the process of renovating, restoration, renewal, repair. [L. *instauratio*].
INSTEAD, [in-sted'], *adv.* in place of, substitute for.
INSTEEP†, [in-stēp'], *v.t.* to steep or soak, to immerse.

INSTEP, [in'-step], *n.* the top curved side of the human foot at the base of the shinbone: that which covers this part in a stocking, boot or shoe. [Uncert.].

INSTIGATE, [in'-sti-gāt], *v.t.* to incite, to set or urge on; to stir up, foment, provoke. [L. *instigare*].

INSTIGATINGLY, [in'-sti-gāt'-ing-li], *adv.* in the way of instigation.

INSTEP

INSTIGATION, [in'-sti-gā'-shun], *n.* the act of instigating; incitement; provocation. [L. *instigatio*].

INSTIGATOR, [in'-sti-gāt'-er], *n.* a person who instigates.

INSTIL, INSTILL, (instilling, instilled), [in-stil'], *v.t.* to pour in by drops; to infuse slowly but firmly into the mind. [L. *instillare*].

INSTILLATION, [in'-stil-ā'-shun], *n.* the act of instilling; that which is instilled.

INSTILLER, [in-stil-'er], *n.* a person who instils.

INSTILMENT, [in-stil'-ment], *n.* instillation.

INSTINCT (1), [in'-stingkt], *n.* intuition, natural inclination; (*psych.*) a natural urge compelling a more or less definite mode of behaviour, a congenital impulse towards specific immediate ends, a pattern of conduct derived from a congenital organization of energy. [L. *instinctus* impulse].

INSTINCT (2), [in-stingkt'], *adj.* filled with; possessing by nature; animated by. [L. *instinctus*].

INSTINCTIVE, [in-stingkt'-iv], *adj.* prompted by, arising from instinct; intuitional.

INSTINCTIVELY, [in-stingkt'-iv-li], *adv.* in an instinctive manner.

INSTIPULATE, [in-stip'-yōō-lāt], *adj.* (*bot.*) without stipules.

INSTITUTE (1), [in'-stit-ewt], *n.* a settled or established principle, law, or order; a society with some scientific, educational, or recreational purpose; an organization giving a social service paid for by public money; the building housing such a society or organization; (*pl.*) a book of fundamental principles of law or medicine. [L. *institutum*].

INSTITUTE (2), [in'-stit-ewt], *v.t.* to set up, establish, found; to set functioning, commence proceedings; to install, appoint, invest. [L. *institutum*, *p.pt.* of *instituere*].

INSTITUTION, [in'-stit-ew'-shun], *n.* the act of instituting; the state of being instituted; something which has been instituted; custom or established order; a scientific, educational, etc., organization or society set up to provide a public service; the building which is the headquarters for such work; (*coll.*) something or someone regarded as a noteworthy, accepted public feature. [L. *institutio*].

INSTITUTIONAL, [in'-stit-ew'-shun-al], *adj.* relating to an institution; instituted by authority.

INSTITUTIONARY, [in'-stit-ew'-shun-er-i], *adj.* relating to a legal institute; rudimentary.

INSTITUTIST†, [in'-stit-ewt-ist], *n.* a writer of elementary rules and instructions.

INSTITUTIVE, [in'-stit-ewt'-iv], *adj.* pertaining to an institute; depending on institution.

INSTITUTOR, [in'-stit-ewt-er], *n.* a person who institutes; a founder; an instructor. [L. *institutor*].

INSTREAM, [in-strēm'], *v.t.* to flow in.

INSTRUCT, [in-strukt'], *v.t.* to impart knowledge or information to, to teach, train, educate; to give orders to, command; (*leg.*) to direct and authorize. [L. *instructum*, *p.pt.* of *instruere*].

INSTRUCTION, [in-struk'-shun], *n.* the act of instructing; teaching, information, knowledge imparted to another person; direction, order, command. [L. *instructio*].

INSTRUCTIONAL, [in-struk'-shun-al], *adj.* containing instruction.

INSTRUCTIVE, [in-strukt'-iv], *adj.* serving to instruct, containing information.

INSTRUCTIVELY, [in-strukt'-iv-li], *adv.* in an instructive fashion.

INSTRUCTIVENESS, [in-strukt'-iv-nes], *n.* the quality of being instructive.

INSTRUCTOR, [in-strukt'-er], *n.* a teacher, one appointed to instruct others.

INSTRUCTRESS, [in-strukt'-res], *n.* a female instructor.

INSTRUMENT (1), [in'-strōōm-ent], *n.* something used as an aid to a job of work, a tool, implement, *esp.* for delicate operations as in surgery; a contrivance designed to produce musical sounds when played; (*fig.*) a person acting as an agent or tool of another; (*leg.*) a formal document or deed. [L. *instrumentum*].

INSTRUMENT (2), [in'-strōōm-ent], *v.t.* (*mus.*) to score for instruments, orchestrate.

INSTRUMENTAL, [in'-strōōm-ent'-al], *adj.* acting as a means to an end; produced by or for a musical instrument or instruments; due to, made by, an instrument; (*gram.*) expressing means of performance.

INSTRUMENTALIST, [in'-strōōm-ent'-al-ist], *n.* a person who plays a musical instrument.

INSTRUMENTALITY, [in'-strōōm-ent-al'-i-ti], *n.* means, agency by which something is accomplished.

INSTRUMENTALLY, [in'-strōōm-ent'-al-i], *adv.* by means of an instrument; with musical instruments.

INSTRUMENTATION, [in'-strōōm-ent-ā'-shun], *n.* (*mus.*) the arrangement of a composition for musical instruments, orchestration; the use of instruments in surgery, science, etc.

INSUAVITY, [in-swav'-i-ti], *n.* unpleasantness.

INSUBJECTION, [in'-sub-jek'-shun], *n.* insubordination.

INSUBMISSION, [in'-sub-mish'-un], *n.* want of submission.

INSUBORDINATE, [in'-sub-awd'-in-at], *adj.* defying discipline or authority, disobedient, rebellious.

INSUBORDINATION, [in'-sub-awd'-in-ā'-shun], *n.* the state of being insubordinate, disobedience.

INSUBSTANTIAL, [in'-sub-stan'-shal], *adj.* having no substance, not real.

INSUBSTANTIALITY, [in'-sub-stan'-shi-al'-i-ti], *n.* the quality of being insubstantial.

INSUFFERABLE, [in-suf'-er-abl], *adj.* not to be suffered or endured, intolerable, detestable.

INSUFFERABLY, [in-suf'-er-ab-li], *adv.* in an insufferable manner.

INSUFFICIENCY, [in'-suf-ish'-en-si], *n.* the quality of being insufficient; an insufficient amount, lack.

INSUFFICIENT, [in'-suf-ish'-ent], *adj.* not sufficient, inadequate. [L. *insufficiens*].

INSUFFICIENTLY, [in'-suf-ish'-ent-li], *adv.* in an insufficient fashion.

INSUFFLATE, [in'-su-flāt], *v.t.* to blow air into the body, *esp.* into the lungs; to fill with air; to breathe upon, *esp.* in order to fill with the Holy Spirit. [L. *insufflare*].

INSUFFLATION, [in'-su-flā'-shun], *n.* the act of insufflating. [L. *insufflatio*].

INSUFFLATOR, [in'-su-flāt'-er], *n.* (*med.*) a respiratory apparatus.

INSULAR, [in'-syōō-ler], *adj.* belonging to, of the nature of, an island; (*fig.*) separate, narrow-minded, out of touch with the main movement of ideas, affairs, etc. [L. *insularis*].

INSULARITY, [in'-syōō-la'-ri-ti], *n.* the quality of being insular.

INSULARLY, [in'-syōō-ler-li], *adv.* in insular fashion.

INSULATE, [in'-syōō-lāt], *v.t.* to make into an island; to place in an isolated position, to separate from surroundings, lines or means of communication; (*elect.*) to isolate by means of a non-conducting substance. [L. *insula* island].

INSULATION, [in'-syōō-lā'-shun], *n.* the act of insulating; state of being insulated, *esp.* by a non-conductor; that which insulates.

INSULATOR, [in'-syōō-lāt'-or], *n.* a non-conductor; a device consisting of some substance which does not readily conduct electricity, for insulating.

INSULATOR

INSULIN, [in'-syōō-lin], *n.* (*med.*) a preparation from the pancreas of sheep, etc., used in the treatment of diabetes. [L. *insulae* islands].

INSULT (1), [in'-sult], *n.* a word, act, or gesture which offends the feelings, dignity or sense of honour; an abuse, affront. [L. *insultus*].

INSULT (2), [in-sult'], *v.t.* to offer an insult or insults to, to affront, offend. [L. *insultare*].

INSULTABLE, [in-sult'-abl], *adj.* able to be insulted.

INSULTER, [in-sult'-er], *n.* a person who insults.

INSULTING, [in-sult'-ing], *adj.* that conveys or expresses an insult, insolent.

INSULTINGLY, [in-sult'-ing-li], *adv.* in an insulting manner.

INSUPERABILITY, [in-sew'-per-a-bil'-i-ti], *n.* the quality of being insuperable.

INSUPERABLE, [in-sew'-per-abl], *adj.* unable to be overcome or surmounted. [L. *insuperabilis*].

INSUPERABLENESS, [in-sew'-per-abl-nes], *n.* insuperability.

INSUPERABLY, [in-sew'-per-ab-li], *adv.* to an insuperable degree.

INSUPPORTABLE, [in'-su-pawt'-abl], *adj.* not capable of being supported; intolerable.

INSUPPORTABLENESS, [in'-su-pawt'-abl-nes], *n.* the quality of being insupportable.

INSUPPORTABLY, [in'-su-pawt'-ab-li], *adv.* to an insupportable degree.

INSUPPRESSIBLE, [in'-su-pres'-ibl], *adj.* not to be suppressed.

INSUPPRESSIBLY, [in'-su-pres'-ib-li], *adv.* so as not to be suppressed.

INSUPPRESSIVE, [in'-su-pres'-iv], *adj.* not suppressive; insuppressible.

INSURABLE, [in-shōōer'-abl], *adj.* capable of being insured against loss or damage.

INSURANCE, [in-shōōer'-ans], *n.* the state of being insured; the act of insuring; a contract to make good a specified loss on certain conditions in return for a stipulated premium; the premium itself.

INSURANT, [in-shōōer'-ant], *n.* the holder of an insurance policy.

INSURE, [in-shōōer'], *v.t.* to contract to pay or receive under specified conditions in return for a stated premium a sum of money at a prescribed date, or indemnification against stipulated liabilities, or compensation for injury to or loss (of life, health, goods, profits, employment, prospects, etc.). [ENSURE].

INSURER, [in-shōōer'-er], *n.* a person who insures.

INSURGENCY, [in-surj'-en-si], *n.* the state of being insurgent, insurrection.

INSURGENT (1), [in-surj'-ent], *n.* a person who is in revolt, a revolutionary, rebel.

INSURGENT (2), [in-surj'-ent], *adj.* rising against established authority in an endeavour to usurp it, participating in rebellion; surging. [L. *insurgens*].

INSURMOUNTABLE, [in'-ser-mownt'-abl], *adj.* not to be surmounted or overcome.

INSURMOUNTABLY, [in'-ser-mownt'-ab-li], *adv.* to an insurmountable degree.

INSURRECTION, [in'-ser-ek'-shun], *n.* the act of rising up against authority; a spasmodic revolt against those in power, rebellion. [L. *insurrectio*].

INSURRECTIONAL, [in'-ser-ek'-shun-al], *adj.* insurrectionary.

INSURRECTIONARY, [in'-ser-ek'-shun-er-i], *adj.* relating to, or participating in, insurrection.

INSURRECTIONIST, [in'-ser-ek'-shun-ist], *n.* a person who favours or engages in insurrection.

INSUSCEPTIBILITY, [in'-su-sept'-i-bil'-i-ti], *n.* absence of susceptibility.

INSUSCEPTIBLE, [in'-su-sept'-ibl], *adj.* not susceptible; unaffected, insensible.

INSWINGER, [in'-swing-er], *n.* (*cricket*) a ball which swings in towards the wicket from the off side.

INTACT, [in-takt'], *adj.* uninjured, untouched, unharmed; entire, unimpaired. [L. *intactus*].

INTAGLIATED, [in-ta'-li-āt-id], *adj.* carved, engraved or stamped on. [It. *intagliare* to incise].

INTAGLIO, [in-ta'-li-ō], *n.* a design, figure, or pattern which has been cut or engraved into a hard surface; a jewel with an incised design. [It. *intaglio*].

INTAKE, [in'-tāk], *n.* a tract of enclosed land, *esp.* reclaimed from a marsh; the inlet of a pipe; the point where a tube narrows; the ventilation shaft of a mine.

INTANGIBILITY, [in-tanj'-i-bil'-i-ti], *n.* the quality of being intangible.

INTANGIBLE, [in-tanj'-ibl], *adj.* not able to be sensed by the touch, not tangible; (*fig.*) not able to be understood; indefinite, vague.

INTANGIBLENESS, [in-tanj'-ibl-nes], *n.* intangibility.

INTANGIBLY, [in-tanj'-ib-li], *adv.* in an intangible fashion.

INTASTABLE, [in-tāst'-abl], *adj.* tasteless.

INTEGER, [in'-ti-jer], *n.* a complete, undivided whole; (*math.*) a whole number. [L. *integer* entire].

INTEGRAL (1), [in'-ti-gral], *n.* an entirety, a whole, a totality.

INTEGRAL (2), [in'-ti-gral], *adj.* having all the component parts, entire, whole, complete; necessary, indispensable in order to be complete; (*math.*) relating to, consisting of, integers. [LL. *integralis*].

INTEGRALIST (1), [in'-teg-ral-ist], *n.* a member of the Brazilian Fascist party. [INTEGRAL (2)].

INTEGRALIST (2), [in'-teg-ral-ist], *adj.* of, or pertaining to, the integralists or their theories.

INTEGRALLY, [in'-ti-gral-i], *adv.* as an integral part; wholly, completely.

INTEGRANT, [in'-ti-grant], *adj.* helping to form a whole; necessary to completeness, constituent, component. [L. *integrans*].

INTEGRATE (1), [in'-ti-grāt], *adj.* made up of parts; whole, entire, complete.

INTEGRATE (2), [in'-ti-grāt], *v.t.* to form parts into a whole, to complete, to make entire; to give the total. [L. *integrare* to renew].

INTEGRATION, [in'-ti-grā'-shun], *n.* the act of integrating; the state of being integrated.

INTEGRITY, [in-teg'-ri-ti], *n.* the state of being complete or unimpaired, wholeness, entireness; (*fig.*) the controlled realization of all the component aspects of one's personality; moral soundness, uprightness; honesty. [L. *integritas*].

INTEGUMENT, [in-teg'-yōō-ment], *n.* that which naturally covers anything, *esp.* the outer shell, skin, rind, envelope. [L. *integumentum*].

INTEGUMENTARY, [in-teg'-yōō-ment'-er-i], *adj.* relating to, composed of, integuments.

INTELLECT, [in'-tel-ekt], *n.* the faculty of thinking, the ability to reason; the power of perceiving or knowing through the mind; an intellectual person. [L. *intellectus* discernment].

INTELLECTION, [in'-tel-ek'-shun], *n.* the act of understanding or thinking.

INTELLECTIVE, [in'-tel-ekt'-iv], *adj.* having power to understand; pertaining to the intellect.

INTELLECTIVELY, [in'-tel-ekt'-iv-li], *adv.* with intellection.

INTELLECTUAL (1), [in'-tel-ek'-chōō-al], *n.* an intellectual person.

INTELLECTUAL (2), [in'-tel-ek'-chōō-al], *adj.* relating to, appreciated by, created by, exercised by, the intellect; able to follow or create a difficult line of reasoning; tending to devote oneself to mental activity. [L. *intellectualis*].

INTELLECTUALISM, [in'-tel-ek'-chōō-al-izm], *n.* the exercise of the intellect for the sake of acquiring knowledge; the practice of theories; the theory that knowledge can lead to truth only when the intellect is entirely free of emotional interference; belief in the primary importance of the intellect.

INTELLECTUALIST, [in'-tel-ek'-chōō-al-ist], *n.* a person devoted to intellectual culture; a supporter of intellectualism.

INTELLECTUALITY, [in'-tel-ek'-chōō-al'-i-ti], *n.* the quality of being intellectual; intellectual power.

INTELLECTUALIZE, [in'-tel-ek'-chōō-al-iz], *v.t.* to treat intellectually; to render intellectual; to idealize.

INTELLECTUALLY, [in'-tel-ek'-chōō-al-i], *adv.* in an intellectual manner.

INTELLIGENCE, [in-tel'-ij-ents], *n.* the faculty of understanding, involving the power to respond quickly and easily, though not necessarily at a high level of intellectuality, to new situations, commonsense with a good basis of intellectual control, sagacity; information; communicated information, news; an intelligent person. [L. *intelligentia*].

INTELLIGENCER†, [in-tel'-ij-en-ser], *n.* a person who, or that which, conveys intelligence; a spy.

INTELLIGENT, [in-tel'-ij-ent], *adj.* possessing intelligence; able to reason and understand; having a quick or acute intellect, clever; displaying high intelligence. [L. *intelligens*].

INTELLIGENTIAL, [in-tel'-ij-en'-shal], *adj.* of, or relating to, the intellect, intellectual; spiritual.

INTELLIGENTLY, [in-tel'-ij-ent-li], *adv.* in an intelligent way.

INTELLIGENTSIA, [in-tel'-ij-ent'-si-a], *n.(pl.)* the educated and intellectual classes.

INTELLIGIBILITY, [in-tel'-ij-i-bil'-i-ti], *n.* the quality of being intelligible.

INTELLIGIBLE, [in-tel'-ij-ibl], *adj.* able to be understood; (*philos.*) clear to the mental understanding only. [L. *intelligibilis*].

INTELLIGIBLENESS, [in-tel'-ij-ibl-nes], *n.* intelligibility.

INTELLIGIBLY, [in-tel'-ij-ib-li], *adv.* in an intelligible manner.

INTEMPERANCE, [in-tem'-per-ants], *n.* lack of control or moderation; excess, extravagance; over-indulgence, *esp.* in drinking, habitual drunkenness. [L. *intemperantia*].

INTEMPERANT†, [in-tem'-per-ant], *n.* an intemperate person. [L. *intemperans*].
INTEMPERATE, [in-tem'-per-at], *adj.* immoderate, unrestrained, extravagant; over-indulgent, *esp.* in intoxicating drink. [L. *intemperatus*].
INTEMPERATELY, [in-tem'-per-at-li], *adv.* in an intemperate manner.
INTEMPERATENESS, [in-tem'-per-at-nes], *n.* the state of being intemperate.
INTENABLE, [in-ten'-abl], *adj.* untenable.
INTEND, [in-tend'], *v.t.* to hold a thought which has a practical end in view, in the mind, to mean, to design, to purpose. [L. *intendere* to extend].
INTENDANCY, [in-tend'-an-si], *n.* the office or status of an intendant; the district under his charge.
INTENDANT, [in-tend'-ant], *n.* a superintendent, a head administrative official. [Fr. *intendant*].
INTENDED, [in-tend'-id], *n.* (*coll.*) an affianced lover.
INTENDEDLY, [in-tend'-id-li], *adv.* intentionally, purposely.
INTENDER, [in-tend'-er], *n.* a person who intends.
INTENDMENT, [in-tend'-ment], *n.* (*archaic*) intention; (*leg.*) the exact meaning of a legal instrument.
INTENSATIVE, [in-ten'-sat-iv], *adj.* intensive.
INTENSE, [in-tents'], *adj.* having a specific quality to a marked or extreme degree; extreme, keen, deep, violent, excessive; highly or deeply emotional; (of feeling) concentrated, wrought to a high pitch. [L. *intensus*].
INTENSELY, [in-tents'-li], *adv.* in an intense manner, to an intense degree.
INTENSENESS, [in-tents'-nes], *n.* the quality of being intense.
INTENSIFICATION, [in-tents'-i-fi-kā-shun], *n.* the act of making intense or more intense.
INTENSIFIER, [in-tents'-i-fī-er], *n.* the agent which intensifies.
INTENSIFY, [in-tens'-i-fī], *v.t.* to make more intense; (*phot.*) to increase the contrast in a negative by chemical means.
INTENSION, [in-ten'-shun], *n.* the act of making more tense or intense; the state of being more tense or intense; (*logic*) the sum of attributes implied in a term. [L. *intensio*].
INTENSITY, [in-tents'-i-ti], *n.* the quality of being intense; the degree to which anything is intense.
INTENSIVE, [in-ten'-siv], *adj.* concentrated, intense; relating to, characterized by intensity; admitting of intensification; relating to concentrated work; (*gram.*) giving emphasis, expressing intensity; (*med.*) progressively increasing in force.
INTENSIVELY, [in-ten'-siv-li], *adv.* in an intensive fashion.
INTENT (1), ENTENT†, [in-tent'], *n.* purpose, aim, intention, motive. [L. *intentus* an extending].
INTENT (2), [in-tent'], *adj.* having the mind concentrated on some object or action; having firmly and fully concentrated the attention on; fixed, earnest, diligent. [L. *intentum, intensum, p.pt.* of *intendere* to apply oneself].
INTENTION, [in-ten'-shun], *n.* that which is intended, design, purpose, end, aim; (*eccles.*) closeness of application or particular fixedness of attention to accomplish something; (*philos.*) idea, concept; (*surg.*) a method of curative treatment. [L. *intentio* application].
INTENTIONAL, [in-ten'-shun-al], *adj.* intended, premeditated, done designedly.
INTENTIONALLY, [in-ten'-shun-al-i], *adv.* in an intentional manner.
INTENTIONED, [in-ten'-shund], *adj.* having intentions; meant, deliberate.
INTENTIVENESS, [in-tent'-iv-nes], *n.* the quality of being intensive, close attention.
INTENTLY, [in-tent'-li], *adv.* in an intent manner.
INTENTNESS, [in-tent'-nes], *n.* the quality of being intent.
INTER (1), (**interring, interred**), [in-tur'], *v.t.* to bury. [LL. *interrare*].
INTER- (2), *pref.* among, between; *expressing a relationship*. [L. *inter*].
INTERACT (1), [in'-ter-akt'], *n.* the interval between two acts of a play; the performance given during this interval. [~Fr. *entr'acte*].
INTERACT (2), [in'-ter-akt'], *v.i.* to act and react upon each other.
INTERACTION, [in'-ter-ak'-shun], *n.* the process of interacting, reciprocal action.
INTERACTIVE, [in'-ter-akt'-iv], *adj.* interacting.
INTERAGENT, [in'-ter-ā'-jent], *n.* an intermediate agent, an intermediary.
INTERARTICULAR, [in'-ter-ah-tik'-yōō-ler], *adj.* (*anat.*) lying between the joints or articulations.
INTERAULIC, [in'-ter-aw'-lik], *adj.* between royal courts. [INTER (2) and L. *aula* court].
INTERAXAL, [in'-ter-aks'-al], *adj.* relating to, situated in, the interaxis.
INTERAXILLARY, [in'-ter-ak-sil'-er-i], *adj.* (*bot.*) placed within the axils of leaves.
INTERAXIS, [in'-ter-aks'-is], *n.* (*arch.*) the space between the axes in columnar erections.
INTERBLEND, [in'-ter-blend'], *v.t.* to blend with each other.
INTERBREED, [in'-ter-brēd'], *v.t.* to crossbreed.
INTERCALARY, [in'-ter-kal'-er-i], *adj.* inserted or interpolated between others; (of a period of time) added to the calendar; having such a period added. [L. *intercalarius*].
INTERCALATE, [in'-ter-kal-āt'], *v.t.* to insert between or among, interpolate; to add a period to the calendar. [L. *intercalare*].
INTERCALATION, [in'-ter-kal-ā'-shun], *n.* the act of intercalating. [L. *intercalatio*].
INTERCEDE, [in'-ter-sēd], *v.i.* to plead, to mediate. [L. *intercedere* to go between].
INTERCEDER, [in'-ter-sēd'-er], *n.* a person who intercedes.
INTERCELLULAR, [in'-ter-sel'-yōō-ler], *adj.* (*bot.*) lying between or among the cells.
INTERCEPT, [in'-ter-sept'], *v.t.* to seize, halt a person or object on its journey from one point to another, to prevent from arriving at its destination; to hinder the progress of, obstruct; to interrupt a communication with; (*math.*) to mark off between two points or lines. [L. *interceptum, p.pt.* of *intercipere*].
INTERCEPTER, [in'-ter-sept'-er], *n.* a person who intercepts.
INTERCEPTION, [in'-ter-sep'-shun], *n.* the act of intercepting; obstruction, hindrance.
INTERCEPTOR, [in'-ter-sept'-er], *n.* one who intercepts; **i. plane**, an aeroplane designed to intercept enemy planes, a fighter plane.
INTERCEREBRAL, [in'-ter-se'-ri-bral], *adj.* between the parts of the brain.
INTERCESSION, [in'-ter-sesh'-un], *n.* the act of interceding, reconciliatory mediation, entreaty on behalf of another; a prayer offering this. [L. *intercessio* a going between].
INTERCESSIONAL, [in'-ter-sesh'-un-al], *adj.* relating to, containing, intercession.
INTERCESSOR, [in'-ter-ses'-er], *n.* one who intercedes; a bishop administering a see until a new bishop is elected. [L. *intercessor*].
INTERCESSORIAL, [in'-ter-ses-aw'-ri-al], *adj.* relating to an intercessor, or to intercession.
INTERCESSORY, [in'-ter-ses'-er-i], *adj.* that intercedes.
INTERCHAIN, [in'-ter-chān], *v.t.* to chain together.
INTERCHANGE (1), [in'-ter-chānj], *n.* mutual exchange; alternate succession. [OFr. *entrechange*].
INTERCHANGE (2), [in'-ter-chānj'], *v.t. and i.* to give and take mutually, to exchange with each other; to put one in place of the other; to cause to take each other's place alternately; to follow alternately.
INTERCHANGEABILITY, [in'-ter-chānj'-a-bil'-i-ti], *n.* interchangeableness.
INTERCHANGEABLE, [in'-ter-chānj'-abl], *adj.* able to be interchanged.
INTERCHANGEABLENESS, [in'-ter-chānj'-abl-nes], *n.* the quality of being interchangeable.
INTERCHANGEABLY, [in'-ter-chānj'-ab-li], *adv.* in an interchangeable fashion.
INTERCHANGEMENT†, [in'-ter-chānj'-ment], *n.* exchange, an interchange.
INTERCHAPTER, [in'-ter-chapt'-er], *n.* an interpolated chapter.
INTERCLAVICLE, [in'-ter-klav'-ikl], *n.* (*anat.*) the ligament situated between the clavicles.
INTERCLAVICULAR, [in'-ter-klav-ik'-yōō-ler], *adj.* lying between the clavicles.
INTERCOLLEGIATE, [in'-ter-kol-ē'-ji-at], *adj.* taking place between colleges.
INTERCOLONIAL, [in'-ter-kol-ō'-ni-al], *adj.* taking place between colonies.
INTERCOLUMNAR, [in'-ter-kol-um'-ner], *adj.* (*arch.*) placed between columns.
INTERCOLUMNIATION, [in'-ter-kol-um'-ni-ā'-shun], *n.* (*arch.*) the space between the columns of a colonnade.
INTERCOMMUNICABLE, [in'-ter-kom-ewn'-ik-abl], *adj.* suitable for intercommunication.
INTERCOMMUNICATE, [in'-ter-kom-ewn'-ik-āt],

v.i. to hold intercourse together; (of rooms) to lead into one another.

INTERCOMMUNICATION, [in'-ter-kom-ewn'-ik-ā'-shun], *n.* the act of intercommunicating, reciprocal communication.

INTERCOMMUNION, [in'-ter-kom-ewn'-yun], *n.* mutual communion.

INTERCOMMUNITY, [in'-ter-kom-ewn'-i-ti], *n.* the quality of being common to many, or of having things in common.

INTERCOMPARISON, [in'-ter-kom-pa'-ris-on], *n.* mutual comparison.

INTERCONNECT, [in'-ter-kon-ekt'], *v.t. and i.* to join together; to be linked together.

INTERCONTINENTAL, [in'-ter-kon'-tin-ent'-al], *adj.* occurring between continents.

INTERCONVERTIBLE, [in'-ter-kon-vurt'-ibl], *adj.* capable of being interchanged.

INTERCOSTAL, [in'-ter-kost'-al], *adj.* (*anat.*) lying between the ribs; (*bot.*) occurring between the veins.

INTERCOURSE, [in'-ter-kaws], *n.* a social relationship of reciprocal dealings; communion; fellowship, mutual communication; sexual connexion. [OFr. *entrecours*].

INTERCROSS, [in'-ter-kros'], *v.t.* to cross mutually; to cause lines to cross each other; to crossbreed.

INTERCURRENCE, [in'-ter-ku'-rents], *n.* the state of being intercurrent; a passing or running between.

INTERCURRENT, [in'-ter-ku'-rent], *adj.* occurring between, intervening; (*med.*) recurring periodically.

INTERCUTANEOUS†, [in'-ter-kew-tā'-ni-us], *adj.* occurring within or under the skin. [L. *intercutaneus*].

INTERDENTIL, [in'-ter-dent'-il], *n.* (*arch.*) the space between two dentils.

INTERDEPENDENCE, [in'-ter-di-pend'-ents], *n.* mutual dependence.

INTERDEPENDENT, [in'-ter-di-pend'-ent], *adj.* depending upon each other, mutually dependent.

INTERDICT (1), [in'-ter-dikt], *n.* an official demand or decree prohibiting something, *esp.* one forbidding participation in the Church ceremonies. [L. *interdictum*].

INTERDICT (2), [in'-ter-dikt], *v.t.* to forbid or prohibit by authority; to place under an interdict; to debar, prevent.

INTERDICTION, [in'-ter-dik'-shun], *n.* the act of interdicting; prohibition. [L. *interdictio*].

INTERDICTIVE†, [in'-ter-dikt'-iv], *adj.* interdictory, prohibiting.

INTERDICTORY, [in'-ter-dikt'-er-i], *adj.* that interdicts; relating to, of the nature of, an interdict.

INTERDIGITAL, [in'-ter-dij'-it-al], *adj.* between the fingers.

INTERDIGITATE, [in'-ter-dij'-it-āt], *v.i.* to join with one another by intertwining like the fingers of both hands when interlocked.

INTERDIGITATION, [in'-ter-dij'-it-ā'-shun], *n.* the act of interdigitating; the state of being interdigitated.

INTEREQUINOCTIAL, [in'-ter-ek'-wi-nok'-shal], *adj.* occurring between the vernal and autumnal equinoxes.

INTEREST (1), [in'-ter-est], *n.* state of mind or emotion strong enough to control and focus the attention; concern, preoccupation; the thing which engages the attention; advantage, benefit; consequence, importance; a group of people sharing the same business or political aims; a premium paid for use of money; a share, a legal or financial claim; something added.

INTEREST (2), [in'-ter-est], *v.t.* to awaken interest in, to engage the attention, to excite the curiosity; to induce to take part in. [L. *interest* it concerns].

INTERESTED, [in'-trest-id], *adj.* having or taking an interest in something; exhibiting interest; personally concerned in and thus liable to be biased; influenced for private reasons.

INTERESTEDLY, [int'-er-est-ed-li], *adv.* with interest.

INTERESTING, [in'-trest-ing], *adj.* arousing interest, engaging the attention of curiosity; (*coll.*) pregnant.

INTERESTINGLY, [in'-trest-ing-li], *adv.* in an interesting fashion.

INTERFACIAL, [in'-ter-fā'-shal], *adj.* (*geom., min.*) included between the faces of two planes.

INTERFEMORAL, [in'-ter-fem'-er-al], *adj.* lying between the thighs.

INTERFENESTRATION, [in'-ter-fen'-es-trā'-shun], *n.* (*arch.*) the spatial design of windows in a building.

INTERFERE, [in'-ter-fēer'], *v.i.* to interpose; to intervene in another's business, to meddle; to come into collision as a horse's feet while in motion; (*phys.*) to modify each other, to interact; **to i. with,** to hinder, impede; to molest, pester; to prevent. [INTER (2) and L. *ferire* to strike].

INTERFERENCE, [in'-ter-fēer'-ents], *n.* the act of interfering; meddling, unwarranted intervention; hindrance; (*phys.*) the interaction of two currents of heat, light, or sound, etc., waves; (*wirel.*) the jamming of a wave-length.

INTERFERENTIAL, [in'-ter-fer-en'-shal], *adj.* (*phys.*) relating to light and sound waves in terms of interference.

INTERFERER, [in'-ter-fēer'-er], *n.* a person who interferes.

INTERFERING, [in'-ter-fēer'-ing], *adj.* that interferes, meddlesome.

INTERFERINGLY, [in'-ter-fēer'-ing-li], *adv.* in an interfering manner.

INTERFEROMETER, [in'-ter-fēer-om'-it-er], *n.* (*phys.*) an instrument for measuring light waves by means of interference phenomena.

INTERFLOW, [in'-ter-flō], *v.i.* to flow into each other.

INTERFLUENT, [in'-ter-flōō'-ent], *adj.* flowing together or between.

INTERFLUOUS, [in'-ter-flōō'-us], *adj.* interfluent.

INTERFOLD, [in'-ter-fōld'], *v.t.* to fold into each other.

INTERFOLIACEOUS, [in'-ter-fō'-li-ā'-shus], *adj.* (*bot.*) being placed between opposite leaves, but occurring alternately with them.

INTERFOLIATE, [in'-ter-fō'-li-āt], *v.t.* to interleave.

INTERFRETTED, [in'-ter-fret'-id], *adj.* (*her.*) interlaced.

INTERFRONTAL, [in'-ter-frunt'-al], *adj.* (*anat.*) situated between the frontal bones; being at the front.

INTERFUSE, [in'-ter-fewz'], *v.t. and i.* to blend, intermix, mix together. [L. *interfusum*, *p.pt.* of *interfundere* to pour between].

INTERFUSED, [in'-ter-fewzd'], *adj.* poured between; intermixed.

INTERFUSION, [in'-ter-few'-zhun], *n.* the act of interfusing; the condition of being interfused. [L. *interfusio*].

INTERGLACIAL, [in'-ter-glā'-shal], *adj.* (*geol.*) relating to, or coming between, glacial periods.

INTERGLANDULAR, [in'-ter-gland'-yōō-ler], *adj.* occurring between glands.

INTERGLOBULAR, [in'-ter-glob'-yōō-ler], *adj.* taking place between globules.

INTERGRADATION, [in'-ter-grad-ā'-shun], *n.* the act of passing through a series of grades or tones; the state of being graded or toned.

INTERGROWTH, [in'-ter-grōth'], *n.* the act of growing together; the state of having grown together; that which has grown together.

INTERIM (1), [in'-ter-im], *n.* intermediate period, time intervening. [L. *interim* in the meantime].

INTERIM (2), [in'-ter-im], *adj.* relating to, occurring in an interim; temporary, in the meantime.

INTERIOR (1), [in-tēer'-i-er], *n.* the inside of anything, *esp.* of a room or body; the inland part of a country; the state department dealing with home affairs.

INTERIOR (2), [in-tēer'-i-er], *adj.* placed, lying, in the inside of anything, internal, inner; relating to the inside of a house; remote from boundaries or coasts. [L. *interior*].

INTERIORLY, [in-tēer'-i-er-li], *adv.* internally.

INTERJACENCY, [in'-ter-jā'-sen-si], *n.* the quality of being interjacent.

INTERJACENT, [in'-ter-jā'-sent], *adj.* intermediate, intervening. [L. *interjacens*].

INTERJACULATE, [in'-ter-jak'-yōō-lāt], *v.t.* to ejaculate when others are talking, to interject. [INTER (2) and L. *jaculare* throw].

INTERJECT, [in'-ter-jekt'], *v.t.* to throw between; to insert; to interrupt a conversation with. [L. *interjectum*, *p.pt.* of *interjicere* to throw in].

INTERJECTION, [in'-ter-jek'-shun], *n.* the act of interjecting; a word expressing some sudden emotion or passion; a sudden exclamation, ejaculation. [L. *interjectio*].

INTERJECTIONAL, [in'-ter-jek'-shun-al], *adj.* relating to, of the nature of, an interjection.

INTERJECTIONALLY, [in'-ter-jek'-shun-al-i], *adv.* by way of an interjection.

INTERJECTORY, [in'-ter-jekt'-er-i], *adj.* interjectional.

INTERJOIST, [in'-ter-joist'], *n.* an opening between two joists.

INTERJUNCTION†, [in'-ter-jungk'-shun], *n.* a mutual joining.

INTERKNIT, (**interknitting, interknitted**), [in'-ter-nit'], *v.t.* to knit together, interweave.

INTERLACE, [in'-ter-lās'], *v.t. and i.* to twist together, interweave, to put or insert one thing with another; to be interwoven. [Fr. *entrelacer*].

INTERLACEMENT, [in'-ter-lās'-ment], *n.* the act of interlacing; that which is interlaced. [Fr. *entrelacement*].

INTERLAMINATED, [in'-ter-lam'-in-ā-tid], *adj.* (*geol.*) inserted between plates.

INTERLARD, [in'-ter-lahd'], *v.t.* to mix with alternate layers of fat; to interpose; to intersperse, mix.

INTERLAY, [in'-ter-lā'], *v.t.* to lay between.

INTERLEAF, [in'-ter-lēf'], *n.* a blank leaf set in between other leaves.

INTERLEAVE, [in'-ter-lēv'], *v.t.* to insert a blank leaf or leaves in a book and bind them up with the other leaves.

INTERLINE, [in'-ter-līn'], *v.t.* to print in alternate lines; to insert between the printed lines.

INTERLINEAL, [in'-ter-lin'-i-al], *adj.* interlinear.

INTERLINEAR, [in'-ter-lin'-i-er], *adj.* written, inserted or printed between lines. [MedL. *interlinearis*].

INTERLINEARY, [in'-ter-lin'-i-er-i], *n.* a book that has insertions between the lines.

INTERLINEATION, [in'-ter-lin-i-ā'-shun], *n.* the act of interlining; the word or words interlined.

INTERLINK, [in'-ter-lingk'], *v.t.* to link together.

INTERLOBULAR, [in'-ter-lob'-yōō-ler], *adj.* (*anat.*) lying between lobes or lobules.

INTERLOCATION, [in'-ter-lōk-ā'-shun], *n.* interposition, a placing between; that which is placed between.

INTERLOCK, [in'-ter-lok'], *v.i.* to lock, embrace, clasp, join together by means of alternate projections; to connect signals so that the action of one is dependent on the functioning of another.

INTERLOCUTION, [in'-ter-lo-kew'-shun], *n.* conference; conversation, dialogue. [L. *interlocutio*].

INTERLOCUTOR, [in'-ter-lok'-yōō-ter], *n.* a person who speaks in dialogue; the compère of a concert party.

INTERLOCUTORY, [in'-ter-lok'-yōō-ter-i], *adj.* relating to, consisting of, dialogue; (*leg.*) intermediate, not final or definite but limited to the earliest stages.

INTERLOCUTRESS, [in'-ter-lok'-yōō-tres], *n.* a female interlocutor.

INTERLOPE†, [in'-ter-lōp'], *v.i.* to act as an interloper; to take advantage of one's position as mediator to further one's interests. [INTER (2) and OIcel. *hlaupa* to run].

INTERLOPER, [in'-ter-lōp'-er], *n.* a person who interferes in another's business, an intruder.

INTERLUCENT†, [in'-ter-lōō'-sent], *adj.* shining between.

INTERLUDE, [in'-ter-lōōd], *n.* a short performance between the acts of a morality play; a one-act play performed between two acts of the main play; the interval between two acts; an interval, an intervening period; a series of incidents occurring as by-play between the main events; (*mus.*) a short passage played by instruments, to link up two stanzas. [MedL. *interludium*].

INTERLUNAR, [in'-ter-lōōn'-er], *adj.* relating or belonging to the time when the moon, about the change, is invisible.

INTERMARRIAGE, [in'-ter-ma'-rij], *n.* marriage between persons of different races, tribes, castes, families, etc.

INTERMARRY, [in'-ter-ma'-ri], *v.i.* to marry, *esp.* of persons of different races, tribes, castes, etc.

INTERMAXILLARY, [in'-ter-maks-il'-er-i], *adj.* (*anat.*) lying between the jawbones.

INTERMEDDLE, [in'-ter-medl'], *v.i.* to meddle in the affairs of others, to interfere.

INTERMEDDLER, [in'-ter-med'-ler], *n.* a person who intermeddles.

INTERMEDDLESOME, [in'-ter-medl'-sum], *adj.* inclined to intermeddle.

INTERMEDIACY, [in'-ter-mē'-di-a-si], *n.* the state of being intermediate; mediation.

INTERMEDIAL†, [in'-ter-mē'-di-al], *adj.* lying between, intervenient.

INTERMEDIARY (1), [in'-ter-mē'-di-er-i], *n.* an intermediary object or person.

INTERMEDIARY (2), [in'-ter-mē'-di-er-i], *adj.* standing in relation to two or more objects without the interposition of any one of them; lying between, intermediate; acting as agent or go-between. [L. *intermedius*].

INTERMEDIATE (1), [in'-ter-mē'-di-at], *n.* an examination to be taken between matriculation and a final degree; an intermediate object.

INTERMEDIATE (2), [in'-ter-mē'-di-at], *adj.* situated in the middle between extremes; situated or occurring between two things or points of time; interposed. [L. *intermedius*].

INTERMEDIATE (3), [in'-ter-mē'-di-āt], *v.i.* to intervene, to be an intermediary.

INTERMEDIATELY, [in'-ter-mē'-di-at-li], *adv.* in an intermediate position.

INTERMEDIATION, [in'-ter-mē-di-ā'-shun], *n.* the act of intermediating, intervention.

INTERMEDIATOR, [in'-ter-mē'-di-āt-er], *n.* a person who intermediates.

INTERMEDIUM, [in'-ter-mē'-di-um], *n.* intermediate space; agency, the means of transmission. [L. *intermedium*].

INTERMENT, [in-tur'-ment], *n.* burial.

INTERMETACARPAL, [in'-ter-met'-a-kahp'-al], *adj.* (*anat.*) situated between the metacarpal bones.

INTERMEZZO, [in'-ter-met'-sō], *n.* an interlude; (*mus.*) a short piece played between acts, or linking the movements of a symphony, etc. [It. *intermezzo*].

INTERMIGRATION, [in'-ter-mī-grā'-shun], *n.* reciprocal migration.

INTERMINABLE, [in-tur'-min-abl], *adj.* endless, without limit; tediously prolonged, boring. [LL. *interminabilis*].

INTERMINABLENESS, [in-tur'-min-abl-nes], *n.* the condition of being interminable.

INTERMINABLY, [in-tur'-min-ab-li], *adv.* in an interminable way.

INTERMINATION†, [in'-ter-min-ā'-shun], *n.* the action of threatening; a menace or threat. [L. *interminatio*].

INTERMINGLE, [in'-ter-ming'-gl], *v.t.* to blend, mix or mingle together; *v.i.* to be mixed or blended.

INTERMISSION, [in'-ter-mish'-un], *n.* cessation for a time, respite, interval, pause, interlude. [L. *intermissio*].

INTERMISSIVE, [in'-ter-mis'-iv], *adj.* relating to an intermission; intermittent. [L. *intermissivus*].

INTERMIT, (**intermitting, intermitted**), [in'-ter-mit'], *v.t.* to cause to cease for a time; *v.i.* to cease for a time, to pause. [L. *intermittere*].

INTERMITTENT, [in'-ter-mit'-ent], *adj.* ceasing at intervals; alternately weak or strong, active or quiescent. [L. *intermittens*].

INTERMITTENTLY, [in'-ter-mit'-ent-li], *adv.* in intermittent fashion.

INTERMITTINGLY, [in'-ter-mit'-ing-li], *adv.* intermittently.

INTERMIX, [in'-ter-miks'], *v.t. and i.* to intermingle, mix together.

INTERMIXTURE, [in'-ter-miks'-cher], *n.* a mass formed by mixture, a compound, blend.

INTERMODILLION, [in'-ter-mo-dil'-yon], *n.* (*arch.*) the space between two modillions.

INTERMONTANE, [in'-ter-mon'-tān], *adj.* between mountains.

INTERMUNDANE, [in'-ter-mund'-ān], *adj.* placed or present between worlds.

INTERMURAL, [in'-ter-myōōer'-al], *adj.* situated between walls.

INTERMUSCULAR, [in'-ter-mus'-kyōō-ler], *adj.* (*anat.*) occurring between muscles.

INTERMUTATION, [in'-ter-mew-tā'-shun], *n.* interchange.

INTERN (1), [in-turn'], *n.* (*U.S.*) a pupil at a boarding-school; a house-surgeon in a hospital.

INTERN (2), [in-turn'], *v.t.* to imprison, confine in custody, *esp.* aliens in time of war, political opponents, prisoners of war. [Fr. *interner*].

INTERNAL, [in-turn'-al], *adj.* pertaining to, present in, the inside of anything; inner, inward; relating to, derived from, the nature of anything, intrinsic; relating to, concerned with, the home affairs of a country; **i. combustion engine**, an engine driven by the recurrent explosions of gas in air chambers. [L. *internus*].

INTERNALITY, [in'-ter-nal'-i-ti], *n.* the quality of being internal.

INTERNALLY, [in-turn'-al-i], *adv.* in the inside, inwardly.

INTERNATIONAL (1), [in'-ter-nash'-un-al], *n.* a player representing his country in any sport; an international body for the propagation of socialism, *esp.* the **First I.** (1864), **Second I.** (1889) and **Third I.** (1919).

INTERNATIONAL (2), [in'-ter-nash'-un-al], *adj.* relating to, affecting, common to, carried on between, different nations.

INTERNATIONALE, [in'-ter-nash'-un-ahl'], *n.* a song adopted as the anthem of the international socialist movement and (1919-44) the national anthem of the U.S.S.R. [Fr. *Internationale*].

INTERNATIONALISM, [in'-ter-nash'-un-al-izm], *n.* political doctrine stressing the universal brotherhood of men, *esp.* of the workers of the world.

INTERNATIONALIST, [in'-ter-nash'-un-al-ist], *n.* a believer in the power and validity of internationalism; one expert in international law.

INTERNATIONALIZE, [in'-ter-nash'-un-al-īz], *v.t.* to render international.

INTERNATIONALLY, [in'-ter-nash'-un-al-i], *adv.* with an international significance.

INTERNECINE, [in'-ter-nē'-sīn], *adj.* mutually destructive, deadly. [L. *internecinus*].

INTERNEE, [in'-tern-ē'], *n.* one who is or has been interned.

INTERNEURAL, [in'-ter-new'-ral], *adj.* situated between the neural processes.

INTERNMENT, [in-turn'-ment], *n.* the act of interning; the state of being interned; **i. camp,** a camp in which aliens, political prisoners, or prisoners of war are interned.

INTERNODAL, [in'-ter-nōd'-al], *adj.* (*bot.*) situated between nodes, joints, etc.

INTERNODE, [in'-ter-nōd'], *n.* (*bot.*) the space or part of a stem between two joints of a plant.

INTERNUNCIAL, [in'-ter-nun'-shal], *adj.* relating to an internuncio; transmitting nervous impressions.

INTERNUNCIO, [in'-ter-nun'-shō], *n.* a messenger between two parties; a lesser papal representative. [It. *internunzio*].

INTEROCEANIC, [in'-ter-ō'-shi-an'-ik], *adj.* joining, extending between, two oceans.

INTEROCULAR, [in'-ter-ok'-yōō-ler], *adj.* situated between the eyes.

INTERORBITAL, [in'-ter-aw'-bit-al], *adj.* between the orbits.

INTEROSCULANT, [in'-ter-os'-kyōō-lant], *adj.* (*bot., zool.*) related through certain affinities.

INTEROSCULATE, [in'-ter-os'-kyōō-lāt], *v.i.* (*bot.*) to be intermixed; to have specific characteristics in common.

INTEROSSEAL, [in'-ter-os'-i-al], *adj.* interosseous.

INTEROSSEOUS, [in'-ter-os'-i-us], *adj.* (*anat.*) taking place or situated between bones. [INTER (2) and L. *os* bone].

INTERPELLATE, [in'-ter-pel'-āt, in-tur'-pel-āt], *v.t.* to question formally the confidence of a government. [L. *interpellare* to interrupt].

INTERPELLATION, [in'-ter-pel-ā'-shun, in-tur'-pel-ā'-shun], *n.* the act or process of interpellating; a question interrupting a parliamentary debate. [L. *interpellatio*].

INTERPENETRATE, [in'-ter-pen'-i-trāt], *v.t.* to penetrate mutually, pervade each other.

INTERPENETRATION, [in'-ter-pen'-i-trā'-shun], *n.* the act of interpenetrating.

INTERPETIOLAR, [in'-ter-pet'-i-ō-ler], *adj.* (*bot.*) situated between petioles.

INTERPHALANGEAL, [in'-ter-fa-lanj'-i-al], *adj.* (*anat.*) between the phalanges of the hand or foot.

INTERPILASTER, [in'-ter-pil-ast'-er], *n.* (*arch.*) the space between two pilasters.

INTERPLACE, [in'-ter-plās'], *v.t.* to place between.

INTERPLANETARY, [in'-ter-plan'-et-er-i], *adj.* placed or occurring between planets.

INTERPLAY, [in'-ter-plā'], *n.* action and reaction of two sides, elements, factors, etc., upon one another, reciprocation.

INTERPLEAD, [in'-ter-plēd'], *v.i.* (*leg.*) to discuss some point, incidentally happening, which concerns a third party.

INTERPLEADER, [in'-ter-plēd'-er], *n.* (*leg.*) a person who interpleads; a suit pleaded between two parties on a matter of claim or right, to determine to which of them payment, etc., is due from a third party.

INTERPLEDGE, [in'-ter-plej'], *v.t.* to pledge mutually.

INTERPOLAR, [in'-ter-pōl'-er], *adj.* placed or occurring between the poles, *esp.* of an electric cell or battery.

INTERPOLATE, [in-tur'-pol-āt], *v.t.* to insert words or passages in a book or manuscript, to corrupt a text; (*math.*) to insert intermediate terms in a series. [L. *interpolare*].

INTERPOLATION, [in-tur'-pol-ā'-shun], *n.* the act of interpolating; the state of being interpolated; that which is interpolated. [L. *interpolatio*].

INTERPOLATOR, [in-tur'-pol-āt'-er], *n.* a person who interpolates. [L. *interpolator*].

INTERPOSAL†, [in'-ter-pōz'-al], *n.* interposition.

INTERPOSE, [in'-ter-pōz'], *v.t. and i.* to place, put between, insert; to put forward suddenly or unexpectedly an offer, objection, etc.; to butt in with a remark, interruption, etc.; to come between, intervene; to interrupt.

INTERPOSER, [in'-ter-pōz'-er], *n.* a person who interposes.

INTERPOSIT†, [in'-ter-poz'-it], *n.* a place of deposit for commercial goods, a depôt. [L. *interpositum*, *p.pt.* of *interponere* to place between].

INTERPOSITION, [in'-ter-poz-ish'-un], *n.* the act of interposing; intervention; anything interposed. [L. *interpositio*].

INTERPRET, [in-tur'-prit], *v.t. and i.* to explain the significance of, give the meaning of, elucidate; to represent in practical fashion by artistic means; to translate; to take to mean, regard; to act as interpreter. [L. *interpretari*].

INTERPRETABLE, [in-tur'-prit-abl], *adj.* able to be interpreted.

INTERPRETATION, [in-tur'-prit-ā'-shun], *n.* the act or power of interpreting; the way in which anything is interpreted; significance, meaning; reading. [L. *interpretatio*].

INTERPRETATIVE, [in-tur'-prit-at-iv], *adj.* that interprets, explanatory, pertaining to interpretation.

INTERPRETATIVELY, [in-tur'-prit-at-iv-li], *adv.* in an interpretative way.

INTERPRETER, [in-tur'-prit-er], *n.* one who interprets; one employed in translating foreign languages orally and instantaneously.

INTERPRETERSHIP, [in-tur'-prit-er-ship], *n.* the office and duties of an interpreter.

INTERPROVINCIAL, [in'-ter-prov-in'-shal], *adj.* taking place between provinces.

INTERPUNCTUATION, [in'-ter-pungk'-tew-ā'-shun], *n.* punctuation within the sentence.

INTERRACIAL, [in'-ter-rā'-shal], *adj.* taking place between races.

INTERRADIAL, [in'-ter-rā'-di-al], *adj.* lying between radii.

INTERREGAL, [in'-ter-rē'-gal], *adj.* taking place between kings.

INTERREGNUM, [in'-ter-reg'-num], *n.* the time between two reigns, governments, or ministries; interval, break. [L. *interregnum*].

INTERREIGN, [in'-ter-rān'], *n.* interregnum.

INTERRELATION, [in'-ter-ri-lā'-shun], *n.* mutual relation.

INTERRELATIONSHIP, [in'-ter-ri-lā'-shun-ship], *n.* mutual relationship.

INTERREX, [in'-ter-reks'], *n.* a person who governs during an interregnum, regent. [INTER (2) and L. *rex* king].

INTERROGATE, [in-te'-ro-gāt], *v.t. and i.* to question, inquire, cross-examine. [L. *interrogare*].

INTERROGATION, [in-te'-ro-gā'-shun], *n.* the act of interrogating; a question; **note of i.,** a punctuation mark (?) denoting a question. [L. *interrogatio*].

INTERROGATIVE (1), [in'-ter-og'-at-iv], *n.* an interrogative pronoun or word.

INTERROGATIVE (2), [in'-ter-og'-at-iv], *adj.* relating to, denoting, a question; expressed in the form of a question, inquiring. [L. *interrogativus*].

INTERROGATIVELY, [in'-ter-og'-at-iv-li], *adv.* in an interrogative way.

INTERROGATOR, [in-te'-ro-gāt'-er], *n.* a questioner.

INTERROGATORY (1), [in'-ter-og'-at-er-i], *n.* a question or inquiry; a formal series of questions to be answered on oath as part of the preliminaries before a trial.

INTERROGATORY (2), [in'-ter-og'-at-er-i], *adj.* relating to, containing, expressing, a question. [L. *interrogatorius*].

INTERRUPT, [in'-ter-upt'], *v.t.* to cause to stop by breaking in upon, to hinder by intervention; to obstruct, block; to break the continuity of, to cut off. [L. *interruptum*, *p.pt.* of *interrumpere*].

INTERRUPTED, [in'-ter-upt'-id], *adj.* not continuous; broken; intermitted.

INTERRUPTEDLY, [in'-ter-upt'-id-li], *adv.* in an interrupted way.

INTERRUPTER, [in'-ter-upt'-er], *n.* a person who interrupts.

INTERRUPTION, [in'-ter-up'-shun], *n.* the act of

interrupting; the state of being interrupted; that which interrupts. [L. *interruptio*].
INTERRUPTIVE, [in'-ter-upt'-iv], *adj.* liable to interrupt.
INTERRUPTIVELY, [in'-ter-upt'-iv-li], *adv.* by interruption.
INTERSCAPULAR, [in'-ter-skap'-yōō-ler], *adj.* (*anat.*) situated between the shoulder blades, *esp.* of the feathers of birds.
INTERSCIND†, [in'-ter-sind'], *v.t.* to cut off. [INTER (2) and L. *scindere* to cut].
INTERSECT, [in'-ter-sekt'], *v.t. and i.* to divide by cutting or passing across; to cut, cross; to cross each other. [L. *intersecare*].
INTERSECTION, [in'-ter-sek'-shun], *n.* the act of intersecting; the point or line in which two lines or planes intersect. [L. *intersectio*].
INTERSECTIONAL, [in'-ter-sek'-shun-al], *adj.* of or relating to intersection.
INTERSEGMENTAL, [in'-ter-seg-ment'-al], *adj.* relating to segments.
INTERSEPTAL, [in'-ter-sept'-al], *adj.* (*anat.*) situated between septa. [INTER (2) and L. *septum* midriff].
INTERSERTION†, [in-ter-sur'-shun], *n.* an insertion. [L. *intersertio*].
INTERSOCIAL, [in'-ter-sō'-shal], *adj.* mutually social.
INTERSONANT, [in'-ter-sōn'-ant], *adj.* sounding between. [L. *intersonans*].
INTERSPACE (1), [in'-ter-spās], *n.* a space situated between.
INTERSPACE (2), [in-ter-spās'], *v.t.* to put spaces between.
INTERSPECIFIC, [in'-ter-spe-sif'-ik], *adj.* existing between species.
INTERSPERSE, [in'-ter-spurs'], *v.t.* to scatter or set here and there; to diversify. [L. *interspersus* strewn].
INTERSPERSION, [in'-ter-spur'-shun], *n.* the act of interspersing, the condition of being interspersed.
INTERSPINOUS, [in'-ter-spīn'-us], *adj.* (*anat.*) situated between spines.
INTERSTATE, [in'-ter-stāt'], *adj.* situated, existing, or occurring between estates.
INTERSTELLAR, [in'-ter-stel'-er], *adj.* passing between, situated among, the stars.
INTERSTELLARY, [in'-ter-stel'-er-i], *adj.* interstellar.
INTERSTICE, [in-tur'-stis], *n.* a small space between things closely set, an intervening space; a chink, narrow gap. [L. *interstitium*].
INTERSTITIAL, [in'-ter-stish'-al], *adj.* relating to or containing interstices.
INTERSTRATIFIED, [in'-ter-strat'-i-fīd], *adj.* (*geol.*) alternated with other strata.
INTERTANGLE, [in'-ter-tang'-gl], *v.t.* to intertwist, to tangle inextricably.
INTERTENTACULAR, [in'-ter-ten-tak'-yōō-ler], *adj.* lying between tentacles.
INTERTERRITORIAL, [in'-ter-te'-ri-taw'-ri-al], *adj.* taking place between territories.
INTERTEXTURE, [in'-ter-teks'-cher], *n.* the act of interweaving; the condition of being interwoven.
INTERTIDAL, [in'-ter-tīd'-al], *adj.* taking place between the tides.
INTERTIE, [in'-ter-tī'], *n.* (*carp.*) a short, horizontal timber between two posts to tie them together.
INTERTISSUED, [in'-ter-tish'-ewd], *adj.* made with joint tissue, interwoven. [OFr. *entretissu*].
INTERTRANSPICUOUS, [in'-ter-tran-spik'-yōō-us], *adj.* transpicuous between.
INTERTRIBAL, [in'-ter-trīb'-al], *adj.* taking place, existing, between tribes.
INTERTRIGO, [in'-ter-trī'-gō], *n.* (*path.*) inflammation of the skin due to chafing. [L. *interterigo*].
INTERTROPICAL, [in'-ter-trop'-ik-al], *adj.* lying within the tropics.
INTERTWINE, [in'-ter-twīn'], *v.t. and i.* to twine together; to be intertwisted.
INTERTWINEMENT, [in'-ter-twīn'-ment], *n.* the process of intertwining; the condition of being intertwined.
INTERTWININGLY, [in'-ter-twīn'-ing-li], *adv.* in an intertwining way.
INTERTWIST, [in'-ter-twist'], *v.t.* to twist together.
INTERTWISTINGLY, [in'-ter-twist'-ing-li], *adv.* by intertwisting or being intertwisted.
INTERVAL, [in'-ter-val], *n.* a space between; the extent of separation or difference; an intervening amount of time, a period between two fixed periods; a pause between two acts of a play; intermission, interlude; (*mus.*) the difference of pitch between two notes. [L. *intervallum*].
INTERVALE, [in'-ter-vāl'], *n.* (*U.S.*) a tract of low ground between hills.
INTERVALLIC, [in'-ter-val'-ik], *adj.* relating to, characterized by, intervals.
INTERVARY, [in'-ter-vāer'-i], *v.t.* to vary between themselves.
INTERVEINED, [in'-ter-vānd'], *adj.* intersected, as with veins.
INTERVENE, [in'-ter-vēn'], *v.i.* to take place, occur, come between; to lie between; to prevent, to be interposed; to interfere; (*leg.*) to become a party to an action. [L. *intervenire*].
INTERVENIENT, [in'-ter-vēn'-i-ent], *adj.* coming between, that intervenes. [L. *interveniens*].
INTERVENTION, [in'-ter-ven'-shun], *n.* the act of intervening; interposition; mediation. [L. *interventio*].
INTERVENTRICULAR, [in'-ter-ven-trik'-yōō-ler], *adj.* (*anat.*) taking place between ventricles.
INTERVERTEBRAL, [in'-ter-ver'-ti-bral], *adj.* (*anat.*) being between the vertebrae.
INTERVIEW (1), [in'-ter-vew], *n.* a meeting between persons or groups to discuss a specified question; *esp.* a meeting between a reporter and a person who is to be the subject of an article. [~Fr. *entrevue*].
INTERVIEW (2), [in'-ter-vew], *v.t.* to have an interview with.
INTERVIEWER, [in'-ter-vew-er], *n.* a person who interviews, a newspaper reporter who specializes in interviewing.
INTERVISIBLE, [in'-ter-viz'-ibl], *adj.* (of two stations, points, etc.) that can be seen each from the other.
INTERVOCALIC, [in'-ter-vō-kal'-ik], *adj.* occurring between vowels.
INTERVOLVE, [in'-ter-volv'], *v.t.* to coil one within another; to roll up together. [INTER (2) and L. *volvere* to roll].
INTERWEAVE, (interwove, interwoven), [in'-ter-wēv'], *v.t.* to twine or weave together, to intermingle.
INTERWORK, [in'-ter-wurk'], *v.t.* to work together.
INTERWREATHE, [in'-ter-rēTH'], *v.t.* to wreathe together.
INTESTABLE, [in-test'-abl], *adj.* (*leg.*) disqualified from making a will. [L. *intestabilis*].
INTESTACY, [in-test'-a-si], *n.* the condition of dying intestate.
INTESTATE (1), [in-test'-āt], *n.* a person who dies without making a will.
INTESTATE (2), [in-test'-āt], *adj.* leaving no will; not disposed of by will. [L. *intestatus*].
INTESTINAL, [in-test'-in-al], *adj.* relating to the intestines.
INTESTINE (1), [in-test'-in], *n.* the part of the alimentary canal situated beneath the stomach, the bowel, gut.
INTESTINE (2), [in-test'-in], *adj.* internal, existing within, *esp.* inside a country, domestic. [L. *intestinus*].
INTEXTINE, [in-teks'-tīn], *n.* (*bot.*) an inner membrane or coating of the pollen grain. [L. *intus* within and EXTINE].
INTEXTURED†, [in-teks'-cherd], *adj.* inwrought, woven in.
INTIMACY, [in'-tim-a-si], *n.* the condition of being intimate; close familiarity, sexual intercourse.
INTIMATE (1), [in'-tim-at], *n.* a close friend, a constant associate.
INTIMATE (2), [in'-tim-at], *adj.* relating to the private and deepest recesses of mind and feelings; closely associated, having an intense or continuous emotional relationship as friends; private, personal; joined in sexual intercourse.
INTIMATE (3), [in'-tim-āt'], *v.t.* to announce, make known, declare; to hint, suggest, imply. [LL. *intimare*].
INTIMATELY, [in'-tim-at-li], *adv.* in an intimate way.
INTIMATION, [in'-tim-ā'-shun], *n.* the act of intimating; an announcement. [LL. *intimatio*].
INTIMIDATE, [in-tim'-id-āt], *v.t.* to make afraid, to terrorize; to coerce. [MedL. *intimidare*].
INTIMIDATION, [in-tim'-id-ā'-shun], *n.* the act of intimidating; the condition of being intimidated.
INTIMIDATORY, [in-tim'-id-āt'-er-i], *adj.* that intimidates.
INTIMITY, [in-tim'-i-ti], *n.* intimacy; inwardness, seclusion. [L. *intimus* innermost].
INTINE, [in'-tīn], *n.* (*bot.*) the inner coat of the pollen grain. [L. *intus* within].
INTITULE, [in-tit'-yōōl], *v.i.* to entitle. [LL. *intitulare*].
INTO, [in'-tōō], *prep. expressing movement towards an*

inner point, denoting passage from outside to inside, or from one state to another.
INTOED, [in'-tōd'], *adj.* having the toes turned in.
INTOLERABLE, [in-tol'-er-abl], *adj.* that cannot be tolerated or endured. [L. *intolerabilis*].
INTOLERABLENESS, [in-tol'-er-abl-nes], *n.* the condition of being intolerable.
INTOLERABLY, [in-tol'-er-ab-li], *adv.* in an intolerable way.
INTOLERANCE, [in-tol'-er-ants], *n.* the quality of being intolerant. [L. *intolerantia*].
INTOLERANT, [in-tol'-er-ant], *adj.* not able or refusing to endure; not able to tolerate difference of opinion, impatient of opposing beliefs, bigoted. [L. *intolerans*].
INTOLERANTLY, [in-tol'-er-ant-li], *adv.* in an intolerant way.
INTOLERATION, [in'-tol-er-ā'-shun], *n.* lack of tolerance, bigotry.
INTOMB, [in-tōōm'], *v.t.* to place in a tomb.
INTONATE, [in'-ton-āt], *v.i.* to sound musical notes, to modulate the voice, to intone. [L. *intonare*].
INTONATION, [in'-tōn-ā'-shun], *n.* the act of intoning; modulation of the voice; fluctuation of the pitch of the voice; (*mus.*) the production of musical tones; the introductory phrase in plain-song.
INTONE, [in-tōn'], *v.t. and i.* to utter in a singing tone with fluctuating pitch of the voice, to recite in a sing-song manner, to chant; to practise intonation. [L. *intonare* to resound].
INTORSION, [in-taw'-shun], *n.* (*bot.*) the act of winding or twisting. [L. *intortio*].
INTORT†, [in-tawt'], *v.t.* to curl, twist, wind. [L. *intortum*, *p.pt.* of *intorquere* to twist].
INTOXICANT (1), [in-toks'-ik-ant], *n.* anything intoxicating, *esp.* an intoxicating liquor.
INTOXICANT (2), [in-toks'-ik-ant], *adj.* that intoxicates. [L. *intoxicans*].
INTOXICATE, [in-toks'-ik-āt], *v.t.* to make drunk; (*fig.*) to excite the senses to an abnormal emotional pitch. [MedL. *intoxicare* to affect with poison].
INTOXICATEDNESS, [in-toks'-ik-āt'-id-nes], *n.* the state of being intoxicated.
INTOXICATING, [in-toks'-ik-āt'-ing], *adj.* tending to produce intoxication.
INTOXICATION, [in-toks'-ik-ā'-shun], *n.* the condition of being intoxicated; the act of intoxicating.
INTRA-, *pref.* within. [L. *intra*].
INTRACTABILITY, [in-trakt'-a-bil'-i-ti], *n.* the quality of being intractable.
INTRACTABLE, [in-trakt'-abl], *adj.* ungovernable, stubborn, not amenable to discipline; awkward, difficult. [L. *intractabilis*].
INTRACTABLENESS, [in-trakt'-abl-nes], *n.* intractability.
INTRACTABLY, [in-trakt'-ab-li], *adv.* in an intractable way.
INTRACTILE, [in-trakt'-il], *adj.* not extensible.
INTRADOS, [in-trā'-dos], *n.* (*arch.*) the interior line or curve of an arch. [INTRA and Fr. *dos* back].
INTRAFOLIACEOUS, [in'-tra-fō'-li-ā'-shus], *adj.* (*bot.*) growing on the under side of a leaf.
INTRAMUNDANE, [in'-tra-mun'-dān], *adj.* within the world.
INTRAMURAL, [in'-tra-mew'-ral], *adj.* within the walls, as of a city.
INTRANQUILLITY, [in'-tran-kwil'-i-ti], *n.* lack of tranquillity, unquietness.

INTRADOS

INTRANSIENT, [in-tran'-si-ent], *adj.* not transient.
INTRANSIGENT (1), [in-tran'-si-jent], *n.* an intransigent person.
INTRANSIGENT (2), [in-tran'-si-jent], *adj.* refusing to be reconciled, uncompromising in hostility. [Span. *intransigente*].
INTRANSITIVE (1), [in-tran'-si-tiv], *n.* an intransitive verb.
INTRANSITIVE (2), [in-tran'-si-tiv], *adj.* (*gram.*) not governing a direct object, expressing an action limited to the agent. [L. *intransitivus*].
INTRANSITIVELY, [in-tran'-si-tiv-li], *adv.* in an intransitive way.
INTRANSMISSIBLE, [in'-trans-mis'-ibl], *adj.* not transmissible.
INTRANSMUTABILITY, [in'-trans-mewt'-a-bil'-i-ti], *n.* the quality of being intransmutable.
INTRANSMUTABLE, [in'-trans-mewt'-abl], *adj.* not capable of being transmuted or changed.
INTRANT, [in'-trant], *n.* a person who enters on some office. [L. *intrans*].
INTRENCH, see ENTRENCH.
INTRENCHANT†, [in-trench'-ant], *adj.* not able to be divided.
INTREPID, [in-trep'-id], *adj.* not to be frightened, without fear; undaunted, brave. [L. *intrepidus*].
INTREPIDITY, [in'-trep-id'-i-ti], *n.* the quality of being intrepid.
INTREPIDLY, [in-trep'-id-li], *adv.* in an intrepid way.
INTRICACY, [in'-trik-a-si], *n.* the quality of being intricate.
INTRICATE, [in'-trik-at], *adj.* difficult to disentangle, involved, complicated. [L. *intricare* to entangle].
INTRICATELY, [in'-trik-at-li], *adv.* in an intricate way.
INTRICATENESS, [in'-trik-at-nes], *n.* intricacy.
INTRIGUANT, [an-trē-gahn(g)'], *n.* an intriguer. [Fr. *intriguant*].
INTRIGUE (1), [in'-trēg], *n.* a secret plot or machination; a secret love-affair. [Fr. *intrigue*].
INTRIGUE (2), [in-trēg'], *v.t.* to puzzle, mystify; to fascinate, to attract by its unusualness or subtle complexity; *v.i.* to participate in, or originate, an intrigue. [Fr. *intriguer*].
INTRIGUER, [in-trēg'-er], *n.* a person who intrigues.
INTRIGUING, [in-trēg'-ing], *adj.* practising intrigue; that intrigues.
INTRIGUINGLY, [in-trēg'-ing-li], *adv.* in an intriguing way.
INTRINSIC, [in-trin'-sik], *adj.* relating to the essential nature, inherent; genuine; real. [L. *intrinsecus* inwardly].
INTRINSICAL, [in-trin'-sik-al], *adj.* intrinsic.
INTRINSICALLY, [in-trin'-sik-al-i], *adv.* in an intrinsic way.
INTRO-, *pref.* within. [L. *intro* to the inside].
INTROCESSION, [in'-trō-sesh'-un], *n.* (*med.*) a depression, a tendency to collapse on itself. [MdL. *introcessio*].
INTRODUCE, [in'-trō-dews'], *v.t.* to lead, bring, usher in; to present, cause to make the acquaintance of; to present formally for debate; to bring up in conversation; to bring into a particular position; to place or put in, to inaugurate, initiate; to add, give. [L. *introducere*].
INTRODUCER, [in'-trō-dews'-er], *n.* a person who introduces.
INTRODUCTION, [in'-trod-uk'-shun], *n.* the act of introducing; the state of being introduced; that which introduces something, a preliminary statement, a preface; an elementary text book. [L. *introductio*].
INTRODUCTIVE, [in'-trō-dukt'-iv], *adj.* introductory.
INTRODUCTIVELY, [in'-trō-dukt'-iv-li], *adv.* in an introductive way.
INTRODUCTORILY, [in'-trō-dukt'-er-i-li], *adv.* in an introductory way.
INTRODUCTORY, [in'-trō-dukt'-er-i], *adj.* serving to introduce something, opening. [L. *introductorius*].
INTROFLEXED, [in'-trō-flekst'], *adj.* bent inward.
INTROGRESSION, [in'-trō-gresh'-un], *n.* entrance. [L. **introgressio*].
INTROIT, [in'-trō-it], *n.* (*R.C. Church*) the verses of Scripture sung as the priest enters within the altar-rails to celebrate Mass. [L. *introitus* entrance].
INTROMISSION, [in'-trō-mish'-un], *n.* the act of intromitting.
INTROMIT, [in'-trō-mit'], *v.t.* to permit to enter, admit; to place or put in; *v.i.* (*Scots leg.*) to meddle with the effects of another. [L. *intromittere* to send in].
INTROMITTENT, [in'-trō-mit'-ent], *adj.* that intromits.
INTROMITTER, [in-trō-mit'-er], *n.* a person who intromits.
INTRORECEPTION, [in'-trō-ri-sep'-shun], *n.* the act of admitting into or within.
INTRORSE, [in-traws'], *adj.* (*bot.*) facing inwards, turned towards the axis. [L. *introrsus*].
INTROSPECT, [in'-trō-spekt'], *v.i.* to give oneself up to introspection, to look inwards. [L. *introspectum*, *p.pt.* of *introspicere*].
INTROSPECTION, [in'-trō-spek'-shun], *n.* the act

of observing one's own thoughts and feelings; self-inspection, self-analysis.

INTROSPECTIVE, [in'-trō-spekt'-iv], *adj.* relating to, based on, given to, introspection.

INTROSUSCEPTION, [in'-trō-su-sep'-shun], *n.* (*biol.*, *path.*) reception within; intussusception. [INTRO and L. *susceptio* a taking in].

INTROVERSION, [in'-trō-vur'-shun], *n.* the act of introverting; the condition of being introverted.

INTROVERSIVE, [in'-trō-vurs'-iv], *adj.* turning inwards; introspective.

INTROVERT (1), [in'-trō-vurt'], *n.* an introspective person who tends to alter external reality in his imagination to make it correspond more closely with his own ideas and desires.

INTROVERT (2), [in'-trō-vurt'], *v.t.* to turn inwards. [INTRO and L. *vertere* to turn].

INTROVERTIVE, [in'-trō-vurt'-iv], *adj.* introversive.

INTRUDE, [in-trōōd'], *v.t.* and *i.* to push, thrust in; to enter without permission; to encroach; trespass; to associate with people without invitation; (*geol.*) to penetrate by force into, or between, different strata. [L. *intrudere*].

INTRUDER, [in-trōōd'-er], *n.* a person who intrudes.

INTRUSION, [in'-trōō'-zhun], *n.* the act of intruding; an instance of this; the state of being intruded. [MedL. *intrusio*].

INTRUSIVE, [in-trōōs'-iv], *adj.* tending to intrude; that intrudes; (*geol.*) formed by intrusion.

INTRUSIVELY, [in-trōōs'-iv-li], *adv.* in an intrusive way.

INTRUSIVENESS, [in-trōōs'-iv-nes], *n.* the condition of being intrusive.

INTRUST, see ENTRUST.

INTUBATE, [in'-tewb-āt], *v.t.* (*med.*) to insert a tube.

INTUITION, [in'-tew-ish'-un], *n.* a faculty of consciousness directed by unreasoning feeling or instinct, characterized by immediate perception; that which is so apprehended. [MedL. *intuitio*].

INTUITIONAL, [in'-tew-ish'-un-al], *adj.* relating to intuition.

INTUITIONALISM, [in'-tew-ish'-un-al-izm], *n.* the doctrine maintaining that the perception of truth is by intuition.

INTUITIONISM, [in'-tew-ish'-un-izm], *n.* the doctrine that the perception of the reality of external objects is by intuition.

INTUITIONIST, [in'-tew-ish'-un-ist], *n.* an adherent of intuitionism.

INTUITIVE, [in-tew'-it-iv], *adj.* perceived or perceiving intuition. [MedL. *intuitivus*].

INTUITIVELY, [in-tew'-it-iv-li], *adv.* in an intuitive way.

INTUITIVENESS, [in-tew'-it-iv-nes], *n.* the state of being intuitive.

INTUITIVISM, [in-tew'-it-iv-izm], *n.* intuitionalism.

INTUMESCE, [in'-tew-mes'], *v.i.* to swell; to expand with heat. [L. *intumescere*].

INTUMESCENCE, [in'-tew-mes'-ents], *n.* the process of swelling; a swelling; the state of being swollen.

INTUMESCENCY, [in'-tew-mes'-en-si], *n.* intumescence.

INTUMESCENT, [in'-tew-mes'-ent], *adj.* swelling up. [L. *intumescens*].

INTUMULATED†, [in-tew'-mew-lāt'-id], *adj.* entombed. [L. *intumulare*].

INTUSSUSCEPTION, [in'-tus-us-ep'-shun], *n.* the taking in of one part of the intestine by an adjacent part; the conversion of foreign matter into tissue by an organism. [L. *intus* within and *susceptio* acceptance].

INTWINE, see ENTWINE.

INTWIST, see ENTWIST.

INULIN, [in'-yōō-lin], *n.* (*chem.*) the starchy matter extracted from the root of elecampane, *Inula*. [L *inula*].

INUMBRATE†, [in-um'-brāt], *v.t.* to shade. [L. *inumbrare*].

INUNCTION, [in-ungk'-shun], *n.* the act of anointing. [L. *inunctio*].

INUNCTUOSITY, [in-ungk'-tew-os'-i-ti], *n.* absence of greasiness or oiliness.

INUNDANT, [in-un'-dant], *adj.* flooding, overflowing. [L. *inundans*].

INUNDATE, [in'-un-dāt], *v.t.* to flood; to overflow; (*fig.*) to overwhelm. [L. *inundare*].

INUNDATION, [in'-un-dā'-shun], *n.* the act of inundating; a flood, deluge. [L. *inundatio*].

INURBANE, [in'-ur-bān'], *adj.* inelegant, uncivil, uncouth, unpolished.

INURBANELY, [in'-ur-bān'-li], *adv.* in an inurbane way.

INURBANENESS, [in'-ur-bān'-nes], *n.* incivility.

INURBANITY, [in'-ur-ban'-i-ti], *n.* inurbaneness.

INURE, ENURE, [in-yōōer'], *v.t.* and *i.* to expose to the discipline of use or practice, to harden, accustom; (*leg.*) to become operative. [IN (6) and Fr. *œuvre* work].

INUREMENT, [in-yōōer'-ment], *n.* the act of inuring.

INURN, [in-urn'], *v.t.* to put in a crematory urn; to bury.

INUTILE, [in-ew'-til], *adj.* useless, having no purpose. [L. *inutilis*].

INUTILITY, [in'-ew-til'-i-ti], *n.* uselessness. [L. *inutilitas*].

INUTTERABLE, [in-ut'-er-abl], *adj.* that cannot be uttered, beyond description.

INUUS, [in'-yōō-us], *n.* the Barbary ape, *Macacus inuus*. [L. *Inuus* the god Pan].

INVADE, [in-vād'], *v.t.* to enter a country with hostile intentions; to attack, to seize upon; (*fig.*) to encroach upon; to swarm into. [L. *invadere* to enter].

INVADER, [in-vād'-er], *n.* a person who invades.

INVAGINATE, [in-vaj'-in-āt], *v.t.* to put into a sheath; to introvert.

INVAGINATION, [in-vaj'-in-ā'-shun], *n.* the act of invaginating; (*med.*) intussusception.

INVALETUDINARY†, [in-val'-i-tewd'-in-er-i], *adj.* lacking good health. [L. *invaletudinarius*].

INVALID (1), [in'-val-ēd], *n.* a person who is sick or in poor health.

INVALID (2), [in-val'-id], *adj.* not valid; null, having no legal cogency. [L. *invalidus* weak].

INVALID (3), [in'-val-ēd], *adj.* suffering from bad health, ill, weak, infirm; used by, suitable for an ailing person. [L. *invalidus*].

INVALID (4), [in'-val-ēd, in-val-ēd'], *v.t.* to make an invalid, *esp.* to draft out of active service for reasons of ill-health or wounds.

INVALIDATE, [in-val'-id-āt], *v.t.* to destroy the validity of, deprive of legal force.

INVALIDATION, [in-val'-id-ā'-shun], *n.* the act of invalidating; the condition of being invalidated.

INVALIDHOOD, [in'-val-ēd-hōōd], *n.* the state of being an invalid; the time during which one is an invalid.

INVALIDISM, [in'-val-ēd-izm], *n.* invalidhood.

INVALIDITY, [in'-val-id'-i-ti], *n.* the state of being not valid.

INVALIDLY, [in-val'-id-li], *adv.* without validity.

INVALIDNESS, [in-val'-id-nes], *n.* invalidity.

INVALUABLE, [in-val'-yōō-abl], *adj.* that cannot be valued, very precious, priceless.

INVALUABLY, [in-val'-yōō-ab-li], *adv.* in an invaluable way.

INVAR, [in'-vah(r)], *n.* an alloy of nickel and steel, valuable for its invariability when subject to marked changes of temperature. [INVAR(IABLE)].

INVARIABILITY, [in-vāer'-i-a-bil'-i-ti], *n.* the quality of being invariable.

INVARIABLE, [in-vāer'-i-abl], *adj.* not variable; constant, unalterable; (*math.*) fixed.

INVARIABLENESS, [in-vāer'-i-abl-nes], *n.* invariability.

INVARIABLY, [in-vāer'-i-ab-li], *adv.* in invariable fashion, regularly.

INVARIED, [in-vāer'-id], *adj.* unvaried.

INVASION, [in-vā'-zhun], *n.* the act of invading; the state of being invaded; an aggressive intrusion, hostile incursion. [LL. *invasio*].

INVASIVE, [in-vās'-iv], *adj.* relating to, characterized by, invasion; aggressive.

INVECTED, [in-vekt'-id], *adj.* (*her.*) jagged, engrailed; reversed so that the arches are the right way up. [L. *invectus* brought in].

INVECTIVE, [in-vekt'-iv], *n.* vehement and reviling language, abuse. [MedL. *invectiva* (*oratio*)].

INVECTIVELY, [in-vekt'-iv-li], *adv.* abusively.

INVEIGH, [in-vā'], *v.i.* to attack with invective, to rail against with bitterness. [L. *invehi*, *pass.* of *invehere* to carry into].

INVEIGHER, [in-vā'-er], *n.* a person who inveighs.

INVEIGLE, [in-vēgl'], *v.t.* to persuade or coax by means of artful cajolery, to entice, wheedle, lure. [OFr. *aveugler* to blind].

INVEIGLEMENT, [in-vēgl'-ment], *n.* the act of inveigling, enticement.

INVEIGLER, [in-vēg'-ler], *n.* a person who inveigles.

INVEILED†, [in-vāld'], *adj.* covered with a veil.

INVENDIBLE, [in-vend'-ibl], *adj.* not saleable.

INVENT, [in-vent′], *v.t.* to devise something original; to fabricate; make up. [L. *inventum*, *p.pt.* of *invenire* to find].
INVENTFUL, [in-vent′-fŏŏl], *adj.* full of invention, original in ideas.
INVENTIBLE, [in-vent′-ibl], *adj.* that may be invented.
INVENTIBLENESS, [in-vent′-ibl-nes], *n.* the condition of being inventible.
INVENTION, [in-ven′-shun], *n.* the act of inventing; the state of being invented; that which is invented, an original contrivance; a fiction, lie, fabrication; the faculty or ability to invent things; the act of finding. [L. *inventio*].
INVENTIVE, [in-vent′-iv], *adj.* able to invent; having an ingenious turn of mind, quick at contriving new things.
INVENTIVELY, [in-vent′-iv-li], *adv.* in an inventive way.
INVENTIVENESS, [in-vent′-iv-nes], *n.* facility in inventing.
INVENTOR, [in-vent′-er], *n.* a person who invents; a discoverer of new principles or applications, a constructor of original mechanical devices. [L. *inventor*].
INVENTORIALLY, [in′-vent-aw′-ri-al-i], *adv.* in the form or manner of an inventory.
INVENTORY, [in′-vent-ri], *n.* a list or a catalogue, *esp.* of goods or chattels; things named in such a list. [MedL. *inventorium*].
INVERACITY, [in′-ver-as′-i-ti], *n.* lack of veracity.
INVERMINATION, [in-vurm′-in-ā′-shun], *n.* the state of being infested with worms in the intestines. [IN (6) and L. *verminatio* disease due to worms].
INVERNESS, [in′-ver-nes′], *n.* the name of a Scottish town used to denote a man's cloak formerly fashionable.
INVERSE (1), [in-vurs′], *n.* the condition of being inverted; that which is the exact opposite of something else.
INVERSE (2), [in-vurs′], *adj.* contrary, reversed, opposite, inverted; **i. proportion**, (*math.*) an increase in one quantity to the extent another decreases; **i. ratio**, (*math.*) the ratio of the reciprocals of two quantities. [L. *inversus*].
INVERSELY, [in-vurs′-li], *adv.* in an inverse way.
INVERSION, [in-vur′-shun], *n.* the act of inverting; the state of being inverted; something inverted; change of order or position into its opposite. [L. *inversio*].
INVERSIVE, [in-vurs′-iv], *adj.* relating to, characterized by, inversion; that inverts.
INVERT (1), [in′-vurt′], *n.* (*arch.*) an inverted arch; one whose sex is inverted; **i. sugar**, a compound of laevulose and dextrose.
INVERT (2), [in-vurt′], *v.t.* to turn upside down; to place in a contrary position or order, to reverse, transpose; (*gram.*) to reverse the normal order of words; (*math.*) to transpose the antecedent and consequent terms of a proposition; (*mus.*) to raise the lower note of an interval an octave in pitch; (*psychol.*) to reverse (the sex of). [L. *invertere*].
INVERTEBRAL†, [in-vurt′-i-bral], *adj.* invertebrate.
INVERTEBRATA, [in-vurt′-i-brāt′-a], *n.(pl.)* a division of animals comprising all those which have no backbone or spinal column. [IN (5) and L. *vertebra* backbone].
INVERTEBRATE (1), [in-vurt′-i-brāt], *n.* an invertebrate animal.
INVERTEBRATE (2), [in-vurt′-i-brat], *adj.* (*zool.*) lacking a spinal column or backbone.
INVERTEDLY, [in-vurt′-id-li], *adv.* in an inverted fashion.
INVERTIBLE†, [in-vurt′-ibl], *adj.* able to be inverted.
INVEST, [in-vest′], *v.t.* to array, dress, clothe, *esp.* decorate, with the dress or symbols of rank or office; to surround; to lay siege to; to lay out a sum of money with a view to obtaining a subsequent profit on it. [L. *investire*].
INVESTIGABLE, [in-vest′-ig-abl], *adj.* able to be investigated. [L. *investigabilis*].
INVESTIGATE, [in-vest′-ig-āt], *v.t.* to examine into with care; to make a systematic inquiry into. [L. *investigare* to trace].
INVESTIGATION, [in-vest′-ig-ā′-shun], *n.* the act of investigating; research, inquiry. [L. *investigatio*].
INVESTIGATIVE, [in-vest′-ig-at-iv], *adj.* relating to, dealing with, investigation.
INVESTIGATOR, [in-vest′-ig-āt-er], *n.* a person who investigates. [L. *investigator*].
INVESTIGATORY, [in-vest′-ig-āt′-er-i], *adj.* relating to investigation.
INVESTITURE, [in-vest′-ich-er], *n.* the act or right of investing with a rank, etc.; the formal occasion when a person is so invested; the state of being invested with. [MedL. *investitura*].
INVESTIVE, [in-vest′-iv], *adj.* that invests.
INVESTMENT, [in-vest′-ment], *n.* the act of investing money; money so invested; something in which one may invest money; the act of laying siege to; dress, array; investiture.
INVESTOR, [in-vest′-or], *n.* a person who invests money.
INVETERACY, [in-vet′-er-a-si], *n.* the quality of being inveterate.
INVETERATE, [in-vet′-er-at], *adj.* firmly established by long custom, confirmed, out-and-out; obstinate; of long standing. [L. *inveteratus*].
INVETERATELY, [in-vet′-er-at-li], *adv.* in an inveterate fashion.
INVETERATENESS, [in-vet′-er-at-nes], *n.* inveteracy.
INVETERATION†, [in-vet′-er-ā′-shun], *n.* the process of becoming inveterate. [L. *inveteratio*].
INVEXED, [in-vekst′], *adj.* (*her.*) arched, concaved.
INVIDIOUS, [in-vid′-i-us], *adj.* likely to arouse ill-will, provoke envy, or give offence; envious. [L. *invidiosus*].
INVIDIOUSLY, [in-vid′-i-us-li], *adv.* in an invidious way.
INVIDIOUSNESS, [in-vid′-i-us-nes], *n.* the condition of being invidious.
INVIGILANCE, [in-vij′-il-ants], *n.* lack of vigilance.
INVIGILATE, [in-vij′-il-āt], *v.i.* to supervise candidates taking an examination. [L. *invigilare* to watch over].
INVIGILATION, [in-vij′-il-ā′-shun], *adj.* the act of invigilating.
INVIGILATOR, [in-vij′-il-āt-er], *n.* a person who invigilates.
INVIGORATE, [in-vig′-er-āt], *v.t.* to impart vigour to, to make strong, to refresh in mind or body, to stimulate. [L. **invigorare*].
INVIGORATION, [in-vig′-er-ā′-shun], *n.* the act of invigorating; the condition of being invigorated.
INVILLAGED†, [in-vil′-ijd], *adj.* made into a village.
INVINCIBILITY, [in-vin′-si-bil′-i-ti], *n.* the condition of being invincible.
INVINCIBLE, [in-vin′-sibl], *adj.* not able to be conquered or subdued; insuperable. [L. *invincibilis*].
INVINCIBLENESS, [in-vin′-sibl-nes], *n.* invincibility.
INVINCIBLY, [in-vin′-sib-li], *adv.* in an invincible way.
INVIOLABILITY, [in-vī′-ol-a-bil′-i-ti], *n.* the state of being inviolable.
INVIOLABLE, [in-vī′-ol-abl], *adj.* not to be violated, broken, or damaged. [L. *inviolabilis*].
INVIOLABLENESS, [in-vī′-ol-abl-nes], *n.* inviolability.
INVIOLABLY, [in-vī′-ol-ab-li], *adv.* in an inviolable way.
INVIOLACY, [in-vī′-ō-la-si], *n.* the state of being inviolate.
INVIOLATE, [in-vī′-ol-at], *adj.* not violated, unprofaned, preserved unharmed or unimpaired, unbroken. [L. *inviolatus*].
INVIOLATED, [in-vī′-ol-āt-id], *adj.* inviolate.
INVIOLATELY, [in-vī′-ol-at-li], *adv.* in an inviolate way.
INVIOLATENESS, [in-vī′-ol-at-nes], *n.* the quality of being inviolate.
INVIOUS†, [in′-vi-us], *adj.* untrodden. [L. *invius*].
INVIOUSNESS, [in′-vi-us-nes], *n.* the condition of being invious.
INVISIBILITY, [in′-viz-i-bil′-i-ti], *n.* the condition of being invisible.
INVISIBLE, [in-viz′-ibl], *adj.* not able to be seen, imperceptible. [L. *invisibilis*].
INVISIBLENESS, [in-viz′-ibl-nes], *n.* invisibility.
INVISIBLY, [in-viz′-ib-li], *adv.* in an invisible way.
INVITATION, [in′-vit-ā′-shun], *n.* the act of inviting; a request for a visit, etc.; a proposal that invites. [L. *invitatio*].
INVITATORY, [in-vīt′-at-er-i], *adj.* that invites.
INVITE, [in-vīt′], *v.t.* to request the company of, to ask a person to come to a social gathering; to request; to encourage; to solicit; to provoke, ask for. [L. *invitare*].
INVITER, [in-vīt′-er], *n.* a person who invites.
INVITING, [in-vīt′-ing], *adj.* alluring, tempting.
INVITINGLY, [in-vīt′-ing-li], *adv.* in an inviting way.
INVITINGNESS, [in-vīt′-ing-nes], *n.* the condition of being inviting.

INVITRIFIABLE, [in-vit'-ri-fī'-abl], *adj.* not able to be made into glass.

INVOCATION, [in'-vō-kā'-shun], *n.* the act of invoking, *esp.* God or some supernatural being; the prayer or words expressing this. [L. *invocatio*].

INVOCATORY, [in-vok'-at-er-i], *adj.* that invokes; relating to invocation.

INVOICE (1), [in'-vois], *n.* a detailed list of goods delivered, together with their prices, sent to their purchaser. [OFr. *envoi* that which is sent].

INVOICE (2), [in'-vois], *v.t.* to make an invoice of, to enter in an invoice.

INVOKE, [in-vōk'], *v.t.* to address in prayer, summon aid from; to call upon; to beg for solemnly, implore; to conjure up. [L. *invocare*].

INVOLUCEL, [in-vol'-yo͞o-sel], *n.* (*bot.*) a whorl of bracts, a secondary involucre as in umbelliferous plants. [L. *involucellum* a small envelope].

INVOLUCRAL, [in'-vol-ew'-kral], *adj.* (*bot.*) belonging to an involucre.

INVOLUCRATE, [in'-vol-ew'-krat], *adj.* involucral.

INVOLUCRE, [in'-vol-ewk'-er], *n.* (*anat.*) a covering of membrane; (*bot.*) a group of bracts enclosing buds or the leaves at the base of the flowers. [L. *involucrum* case].

INVOLUNTARILY, [in-vol'-un-ter-i-li], *adv.* in an involuntary way.

INVOLUNTARINESS, [in-vol'-un-ter-i-nes], *n.* the state of being involuntary.

INVOLUNTARY, [in-vol'-un-ter-i], *adj.* not arising from the functioning of the will-power, instinctive; unwilling, without intention. [L. *involuntarius*].

INVOLUTE (1), [in'-vol-ewt], *n.* (*geom.*) a curve traced out by the end of a string unwinding itself from another curve, in the plane of this latter curve.

INVOLUTE

INVOLUTE (2), [in'-vol-o͞ot], *adj.* involved; (*bot.*) possessing edges curved inwards or rolled under; (*zool.*) curving spirally. [L. *involutum*, *p.pt.* of *involvere* roll up].

INVOLUTED, [in'-vol-o͞ot'-id], *adj.* involute.

INVOLUTION, [in'-vol-o͞o'-shun], *n.* the act of involving; the condition of being involved; that which is involved or involute; (*gram.*) the addition of clauses complicating the construction of a sentence; (*math.*) the raising of a quantity to any given power; (*biol.*) degeneration, atrophy. [L. *involutio*].

INVOLVE, [in-volv'], *v.t.* to entangle; to overwhelm with intricate details or complications; to be placed inextricably in a position; to cause to happen as a necessity, to entail; †to envelop. [L. *involvere* to roll up].

INVOLVED, [in-volvd'], *adj.* complicated, intricate, complex to the point of being obscure; difficult to unravel or sort out.

INVOLVEMENT, [in-volv'-ment], *n.* the act of involving; the condition of being involved.

INVULNERABILITY, [in-vul'-ner-a-bil'-i-ti], *n.* the quality of being invulnerable.

INVULNERABLE, [in-vul'-ner-abl], *adj.* that cannot be wounded, damaged or assailed [L. *invulnerabilis*].

INVULNERABLENESS, [in-vul'-ner-abl-nes], *n.* invulnerability.

INVULNERABLY, [in-vul'-ner-ab-li], *adv.* in an invulnerable way.

INVULTUATE, [in-vul'-tew-at], *v.t.* to make an image of a person in wax, so as to have power to practise witchcraft on the person so represented. [MedL. *invultuare*].

INWALL, [in-wawl'], *v.t.* to enclose with a wall.

INWARD (1), [in'-wud], *adj.* placed or existing on the inside, inner, internal; progressing towards the interior; spiritual, subjective. [OE. *innanweard* within].

INWARD (2), [in'-wud], *adv.* towards the inside; in the imagination or the mind.

INWARDLY, [in'-wud-li], *adv.* in the inner parts; privately, intimately; in the inner self.

INWARDNESS, [in'-wud-nes], *n.* the condition of being inward; inner significance or nature.

INWARDS, [in'-udz], *n.(pl.)* the inner parts of an animal, the viscera, bowels, entrails.

INWEAVE, [in-wēv'], *v.t.* to weave together; to intertwine by weaving.

INWICK, [in'-wik], *n.* (*curling*) a cannon off another stone resulting in a commanding position close to the tee. [Uncert.].

INWIT†, [in'-wit], *n.* conscience. [OE. *inwitt(e)*].

INWORK†, [in-wurk'], *v.t. and i.* to work within, or on the inside.

INWORKING†, [in'-wurk-ing], *n.* internal operation; the functioning of the spirit.

INWORN, [in'-wawn], *adj.* worn in; habitual.

INWRAP, see ENWRAP.

INWREATHE, [in-rēTH'], *v.t.* to encircle with a wreath.

INWROUGHT, [in-rawt'], *adj.* having a pattern wrought or worked in; worked in as a design; interwoven.

INYALA, [in-yah'-la], *n.* a South African harnessed antelope or bushbuck, *Tragelaphus angasi*. [Native].

IO, [ī-ō'], *int. expressing joy or triumph.* [Gk. *io*].

IODATE, [ī'-o-dāt], *n.* a salt of iodic acid.

IODIC, [ī-od'-ik], *adj.* containing, related to, iodine; **i. acid,** an acid composed of iodine, oxygen, and hydrogen, HIO_3.

IODIDE, [ī'-o-dīd], *n.* a compound of iodine with another element.

IODINE, [ī'-o-dēn, ī'-o-dīn], *n.* a non-metallic element with important medical and chemical uses, extracted from seaweed. [Gk. *ioeides* like the violet].

IODISM, [ī'-o-dizm], *n.* iodine poisoning.

IODIZE, [ī'-o-dīz], *n.* to permeate with iodine.

IODOFORM, [ī-ō'-dō-fawm], *n.* an antiseptic containing iodine.

IODYRITE, [ī-ō'-di-rīt], *n.* iodide of silver.

IOLITE, [ī'-o-līt], *n.* a bluish mineral containing alumina, silica, and magnesia. [Gk. *io* violet and *lithos* stone].

ION, [ī'-on], *n.* (*phys.*) an electrically charged atom or collection of atoms. [Gk. *ienai* to go].

IONIAN, [ī-ō'-ni-an], *adj.* relating to Ionia, its inhabitants, dialect, and culture. [Gk. *Ionios*].

IONIC (1), [ī-on'-ik], *adj.* Ionian; (*pros.*) (of metrical feet) containing two long and two short syllables; **I. order,** (*arch.*) that style characterized by flutings and scrolled capitals. [Gk. *ionikos*].

IONIC

IONIC (2), [ī-on'-ik], *adj.* of, pertaining, or relating to, an ion or ions. [ION].

IONIZATION, [ī'-on-īz-ā'-shun], *n.* the act of ionizing; the state of being ionized.

IONIZE, [ī'-on-īz], *v.t.* to charge a liquid or gas with ions.

IOTA, [ī-ō'-ta], *n.* the Greek letter *i*; (*fig.*) a very small quantity, jot, tittle. [Gk. *iota*].

I O U, [ī'-ō'-yo͞o'], *n.* a writing acknowledging a debt or loan. [*I owe you*].

IPECACUANHA, [ip'-ik-ak-yo͞o-an'-a], *n.* a South American plant, an extract of whose root is used as an emetic, etc. [Native].

IPOMOEA, [ip'-o-mē'-a], *n.* a large genus of twining plants related to the *Convolvuli*. [Gk. *ips* worm and *homoios* like].

IRACUND, [īer'-a-kund], *adj.* ill-tempered. [L. *iracundus*].

IRADE, [i-rah'-de], *n.* a Turkish written decree. [Arab. *iradah* will].

IRAKI (1), [i-rahk'-i], *n.* a native of Irak, formerly Mesopotamia.

IRAKI (2), [i-rahk'-i], *adj.* of, or pertaining to, Irak or Irakis. [Arab. *Iraqi*].

IRANIAN (1), [ī-rā'-ni-an], *n.* a Persian; the Iranian group of languages.

IRANIAN (2), [ī-rā'-ni-an], *adj.* Persian; (*philol.*) pertaining to that division of Indo-European including Zend and Old Persian. [Pers. *Iran* Persia].

IRASCIBILITY, [i-ras'-i-bil'-i-ti], *n.* the condition of being irascible.

IRASCIBLE, [i-ras'-ibl], *adj.* irritable, quickly angered. [L. *irascibilis*].

IRASCIBLENESS, [i-ras'-ibl-nes], *n.* irascibility.

IRASCIBLY, [i-ras'-ib-li], *adv.* in irascible fashion.

IRATE, [ī-rāt'], *adj.* angered, enraged. [L. *iratus*].

IRE, [īer], *n.* rage, angry resentment. [L. *ira*].

IREFUL, [īer'-fo͝ol], *adj.* full of anger.

IREFULLY, [īer'-fo͝ol-i], *adv.* in ireful fashion.

IREFULNESS, [īer'-fo͝ol-nes], *n.* the condition of being ireful.

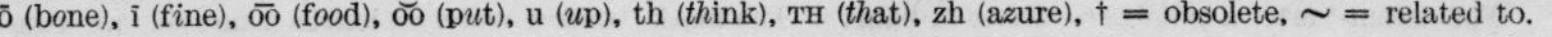

IRENICAL, [ī-ren′-ik-al], *adj.* pacific, peaceful. [Gk. *eirenikos*].

IRENICON, [ī-ren′-ik-on], *n.* (*eccles.*) a message to promise peace and goodwill between churches. [Gk. *eirenikon*].

IRIAN, [īer′-i-an], *adj.* (*med.*) pertaining to the iris.

IRIDACEOUS, [īer′-i-dā′-shus], *adj.* (*bot.*) belonging to the order *Iridaceae.*

IRIDESCENCE, [i′-ri-des′-ents], *n.* the state of being iridescent.

IRIDESCENT, [i′-ri-des′-ent], *adj.* shining with the colours of the rainbow; reflecting light in differing colours and intensities. [Gk. *iris iridos* rainbow].

IRIDIN, [īer′-i-din], *adj.* iridescent.

IRIDIUM, [i-rid′-i-um], *n.* the element Ir, a heavy silvery metal found with platinum. [Gk. *iris iridos* rainbow].

IRIDOSMINE, [i′-rid-os′-mēn], *n.* osmide of iridium.

IRIS, [īer′-is], *n.* the coloured area surrounding the pupil of the eye; (*bot.*) a genus of plants with blade-shaped leaves, and brightly coloured flowers; an iridescent colouring; a rainbow; the diaphragm of a camera, etc. [Gk. *iris* rainbow].

IRIS

IRISATED, [īer′-is-āt′-id], *adj.* iridescent.

IRISCOPE, [īer′-is-kōp], *n.* a device for exhibiting the prismatic colours. [IRIS and Gk. *skopos* watcher].

IRISED, [īer′-ist], *adj.* irisated; having an iris round the pupil.

IRISH (1), [īer′-ish], *n.* the people of Ireland; the native language of Ireland. [OE. *Iras* the Irish from Erse *Eire*].

IRISH (2), [īer′-ish], *adj.* relating to Ireland, its people, language, customs, and characteristics; **I. stew,** a boiled hash of mutton, potatoes, and onions.

IRISHISM, [īer′-ish-izm], *n.* an Irish idiom.

IRISHIZE, [īer′-ish-īz], *v.t.* to make Irish.

IRISHMAN, [īer′-ish-man], *n.* a native of Ireland.

IRISHRY, [īer′-ish-ri], *n.* the Irish.

IRITE, [īer′-īt], *n.* an insoluble mineral containing iridium, osmium, iron, chromium, and manganese.

IRITIS, [īer-īt′-is], *n.* (*med.*) morbid inflammation of the iris. [IRIS and Gk. *itis* denoting inflammation].

IRK, [urk], *v.t.* (*archaic*) to worry, tire, annoy; to irritate, fret. [ME. *irken* to weary].

IRKSOME, [urk′-sum], *adj.* that irks, wearisome, vexatious.

IRKSOMELY, [urk′-sum-li], *adv.* in irksome fashion.

IRKSOMENESS, [urk′-sum-nes], *n.* the condition of being irksome.

IRON (1), [īern], *n.* the element Fe, a malleable, hard, tough metal; a tool made of this, *esp.* one with a flat surface, heated and used to smooth and fold linen, etc.; a stirrup; an iron-headed golf club; (*fig.*) something very hard, ruthless, and unyielding; (*pl.*) chains, fetters; **to strike while the i. is hot,** to act promptly and at the right moment. [OE. *iren*].

IRON (2), [īern], *adj.* made of iron, resembling iron; (*fig.*) very hard, ruthless, unyielding; **i. rations,** rations to be retained for use in an emergency.

IRON (3), [īern], *v.t.* to smooth linen with an iron; to furnish with iron parts; to fit iron on the heel of a shoe; to put into fetters.

IRONBARK, [īern′-bahk], *n.* a variety of *Eucalyptus.*

IRONBOUND, [īern′-bownd], *adj.* bound, belted, with iron; (*fig.*) ruthless, unyielding; savagely rocky.

IRONCLAD, [īern′-klad], *n.* an armoured warship.

IRONER, [īern′-er], *n.* one who, or that which, irons.

IRONFOUNDER, [īern′-fownd′-er], *n.* one who casts iron.

IRONFOUNDRY, [īern′-fownd′-ri], *n.* a place where iron is melted and cast.

IRONGREY, [īern′-grā′], *adj.* of the hard grey colour of newly broken iron.

IRONHEARTED, [īern′-haht′-id], *adj.* ruthless, inflexible, unpitying.

IRONIC, [ī-ron′-ik], *adj.* ironical. [Gk. *eironikos*].

IRONICAL, [ī-ron′-ik-al], *adj.* relating to irony, said in irony.

IRONICALLY, [ī-ron′-ik-al-i], *adv.* in ironical fashion.

IRONING, [īern′-ing], *n.* the process of smoothing linen with a heated iron; clothes, etc., to be ironed.

IRONIST, [īeron′-ist], *n.* one fond of or using irony.

IRON-LIQUOR, [īern′-lik′-er], *n.* acetate of iron.

IRONMASTER, [īern′-mahst′-er], *n.* the owner of an ironfoundry.

IRONMONGER, [īern′-mung′-ger], *n.* a dealer in metal goods.

IRONMONGERY, [īern′-mung′-ger-i], *n.* metal goods; the trade of an ironmonger.

IRONMOULD, [īern′-mōld], *n.* a stain made by iron rust.

IRON-SICK, [īern′-sik], *adj.* (*naut.*) with rusted and corroded bolts and rivets.

IRONSIDE, [īern′-sīd], *n.* a member of Cromwell's cavalry; a fierce, humourless person.

IRONSMITH, [īern′-smith], *n.* one who works in iron.

IRONSTONE, [īern′-stōn], *n.* impure iron-ore.

IRONWARE, [īern′-wāer], *n.* ironmongery.

IRONWOOD, [īern′-wōōd], *n.* an exceptionally hard wood obtained from various trees of India, Australia, N. and S. America.

IRONWORK, [īern′-wurk], *n.* an iron structure; objects made of iron; (*pl.*) a place where iron is smelted.

IRONY (1), [īer′-on-i], *n.* a satiric mode of speaking in which words are used with an intention exactly opposite to their meaning; (*fig.*) a result precisely opposite in effect from what might have been expected from its cause. [Gk. *eironeia*].

IRONY (2), [īern′-i], *adj.* containing, resembling iron.

IRRADIANCE, [i-rā′-di-ants], *n.* the condition of being irradiant.

IRRADIANCY, [i-rā′-di-an-si], *n.* irradiance.

IRRADIANT, [i-rā′-di-ant], *adj.* radiating light, brightly gleaming. [L. *irradians*].

IRRADIATE, [i-rā′-di-āt], *v.t.* to shine upon, illumine with beams of light; to make bright, light up; to give out, pour forth; (*phys.*) to subject to radiation; (*fig.*) to explain, enlighten about. [L. *irradiare*].

IRRADIATION, [i-rā′-di-ā′-shun], *n.* the process of irradiating; the condition of being irradiated; a beam of light; (*opt.*) apparent magnification of a bright body against darkness.

IRRADICATE, [i-rad′-ik-āt], *v.t.* (*rare*) to root in firmly. [IN (6) and L. *radicare* to take root].

IRRATIONAL (1), [i-rash′-un-al], *n.* (*math.*) an irrational number or quantity.

IRRATIONAL (2), [i-rash′-un-al], *adj.* unreasoning; not rational or logical, contrary to sense; (*math.*) incapable of expression by integer or vulgar fraction. [L. *irrationalis*].

IRRATIONALITY, [i-rash′-un-al′-i-ti], *n.* the condition of being irrational.

IRRATIONALLY, [i-rash′-un-al-i], *adv.* in an irrational fashion.

IRREALIZABLE, [i-rē′-al-īz-abl], *adj.* not able to be realized.

IRREBUTTABLE, [i′-ri-but′-abl], *adj.* not to be rebutted.

IRRECEPTIVE, [i′-ri-sept′-iv], *adj.* not receptive.

IRRECIPROCAL, [i′-ri-sip′-rō-kal], *adj.* not reciprocal.

IRRECLAIMABLE, [i′-ri-klām′-abl], *adj.* impossible to be reclaimed.

IRRECLAIMABLY, [i′-ri-klām′-ab-li], *adv.* in irreclaimable fashion.

IRRECOGNIZABLE, [i-rek′-og-nīz′-abl], *adj.* not recognizable.

IRRECONCILABLE, [i′-rek-on-sīl′-abl], *adj.* not able to be reconciled; hopelessly incompatible.

IRRECONCILABLENESS, [i′-rek-on-sīl′-abl-nes], *n.* the condition of being irreconcilable.

IRRECONCILABLY, [i′-rek-on-sīl′-ab-li], *adv.* in irreconcilable fashion.

IRRECONCILED, [i-rek′-on-sīld], *adj.* not reconciled.

IRRECONCILEMENT, [i-rek′-on-sīl′-ment], *n.* the condition of being unreconciled or irreconcilable.

IRRECORDABLE, [i′-ri-kawd′-abl], *adj.* not able to be recorded.

IRRECOVERABLE, [i′-ri-kuv′-er-abl], *adj.* impossible to recover or be recovered, beyond recovery.

IRRECOVERABLENESS, [i′-ri-kuv′-er-abl-nes], *n.* the condition of being irrecoverable.

IRRECOVERABLY, [i′-ri-kuv′-er-ab-li], *adv.* in an irrecoverable way.

IRRECUSABLE, [i′-ri-kewz′-abl], *adj.* not to be refused. [LL. *irrecusabilis*].

IRREDEEMABILITY, [i′-ri-dēm′-a-bil′-i-ti], *n.* the condition of being irredeemable.

IRREDEEMABLE, [i′-ri-dēm′-abl], *adj.* not to be redeemed; not to be converted into cash.

IRREDEEMABLENESS, [i′-ri-dēm′-abl-nes], *n.* irredeemability.

IRREDEEMABLY, [i'-ri-dēm'-ab-li], *adv.* beyond redemption.
IRREDENTISM, [i'-ri-dent'-izm], *n.* the political belief that demands the inclusion in the state of all the people and areas by whom and in which its language is spoken.
IRREDENTIST (1), [i'-ri-dent'-ist], *n.* a believer in irredentism. [It. *irredentista*].
IRREDENTIST (2), [i-ri-dent'-ist], *adj.* of, or pertaining to, irredentism or irredentists.
IRREDUCIBLE, [i'-ri-dews'-ibl], *adj.* not to be reduced, already brought to the lowest possible level, form, or degree.
IRREDUCIBLENESS, [i'-ri-dews'-ibl-nes], *n.* the condition of being irreducible.
IRREDUCIBLY, [i'-ri-dews'-ib-li], *adv.* beyond reduction.
IRREFLECTIVE, [i'-ri-flekt'-iv], *adj.* unreflecting.
IRREFRAGABILITY, [i'-ri-frag'-a-bil'-i-ti], *n.* the state of being irrefragable.
IRREFRAGABLE, [i'-ri-frag'-abl], *adj.* beyond dispute, unanswerable, irrefutable. [L. *irrefragabilis*].
IRREFRAGABLENESS, [i'-ri-frag'-abl-nes], *n.* irrefragability.
IRREFRAGABLY, [i'-ri-frag'-ab-li], *adv.* in irrefragable fashion.
IRREFRANGIBLE, [i'-ri-franj'-ibl], *adj.* inviolable, unbreakable.
IRREFUTABLE, [i'-ri-fewt'-abl, i-ref'-yŏŏt-abl], *adj.* impossible to refute.
IRREFUTABLY, [i'-ri-fewt'-ab-li, i-ref'-yŏŏt-ab-li], *adv.* beyond refutation.
IRREGENERACY, [i'-ri-jen'-er-a-si], *n.* unregeneracy.
IRREGULAR (1), [i-reg'-yŏŏ-ler], *n.* a member of a loosely organized, casually disciplined body of troops outside the regular army.
IRREGULAR (2), [i-reg'-yŏŏ-ler], *adj.* not regular; unsymmetrical, not evenly ordered ; out of form and order; not conforming to rule or general type; contrary to normal practice or standards; unlawful. [MedL. *irregularis*].
IRREGULARIST, [i-reg'-yŏŏ-ler-ist], *n.* one who vaunts irregularity.
IRREGULARITY, [i-reg'-yŏŏ-la'-ri-ti], *n.* the state of being irregular; that which is irregular. [MedL. *irregularitas*].
IRREGULARLY, [i-reg'-yŏŏ-ler-li], *adv.* in irregular fashion.
IRRELATIVE, [i-rel'-at-iv], *adj.* unrelated; not relative.
IRRELATIVELY, [i-rel'-at-iv-li], *adv.* in irrelative fashion.
IRRELEVANCY, [i-rel'-iv-an-si], *n.* the state of being irrelevant; that which is irrelevant.
IRRELEVANT, [i-rel'-iv-ant], *adj.* not relevant, inapplicable, beside the point.
IRRELEVANTLY, [i-rel'-iv-ant-li], *adv.* in irrelevant fashion.
IRRELIEVABLE, [i'-ri-lēv'-abl], *adj.* not to be relieved.
IRRELIGION, [i'-ri-lij'-un], *n.* contempt of religion, want of reverence. [L. *irreligio*].
IRRELIGIONIST, [i'-ri-lij'-un-ist], *n.* one who lacks or despises religion.
IRRELIGIOUS, [i'-ri-lij'-us], *adj.* without or despising religion; impious. [L. *irreligiosus*].
IRRELIGIOUSLY, [i'-ri-lij'-us-li], *adv.* in irreligious fashion.
IRRELIGIOUSNESS, [i'-ri-lij'-us-nes], *n.* the condition of being irreligious.
IRREMEDIABLE, [i'-ri-mēd'-i-abl], *adj.* impossible to be remedied or repaired. [L. *irremediabilis*].
IRREMEDIABLENESS, [i'-ri-mēd'-i-abl-nes], *n.* the condition of being irremediable.
IRREMEDIABLY, [i'-ri-mēd'-i-ab-li], *adv.* in irremediable fashion.
IRREMISSIBLE, [i'-ri-mis'-ibl], *adj.* impossible to be pardoned, inexcusable. [L. *irremissibilis*].
IRREMISSIBLENESS, [i'-ri-mis'-ibl-nes], *n.* the state of being irremissible.
IRREMISSIBLY, [i'-ri-mis'-ib-li], *adv.* to an irremissible degree.
IRREMISSIVE, [i'-ri-mis'-iv], *adj.* not to be remitted.
IRREMOVABILITY, [i'-ri-mŏŏv'-a-bil'-i-ti], *n.* the state of being irremovable.
IRREMOVABLE, [i'-ri-mŏŏv'-abl], *adj.* impossible to be removed.
IRREMOVABLY, [i'-ri-mŏŏv'-ab-li], *adv.* in irremovable fashion.
IRREMOVAL, [i'-ri-mŏŏv'-al], *n.* non-removal.
IRREMUNERABLE, [i'-ri-mewn'-er-abl], *adj.* impossible to be rewarded.
IRREPARABILITY, [i-rep'-er-a-bil'-i-ti], *n.* the state of being irreparable.
IRREPARABLE, [i-rep'-er-abl], *adj.* impossible to be rectified or repaired. [L. *irreparabilis*].
IRREPARABLENESS, [i-rep'-er-abl-nes], *n.* irreparability.
IRREPARABLY, [i-rep'-er-ab-li], *adv.* in irreparable fashion.
IRREPEALABILITY, [i'-ri-pēl'-a-bil'-i-ti], *n.* irrepealableness.
IRREPEALABLE, [i'-ri-pēl'-abl], *adj.* impossible to be repealed.
IRREPEALABLENESS, [i'-ri-pēl'-abl-nes], *n.* the state of being irrepealable.
IRREPEALABLY, [i'-ri-pēl'-ab-li], *adv.* beyond repeal.
IRREPENTANCE, [i'-ri-pent'-ants], *n.* lack of repentance.
IRREPLACEABLE, [i'-ri-plās'-abl], *adj.* impossible to replace.
IRREPLEVIABLE, [i'-ri-plēv'-i-abl], *adj.* (*leg.*) that cannot be replevied.
IRREPREHENSIBLE, [i-rep'-ri-hents'-ibl], *adj.* not to be blamed. [LL. *irreprehensibilis*].
IRREPREHENSIBLENESS, [i'-rep'-ri-hents'-ibl-nes], *n.* the condition of being irreprehensible.
IRREPREHENSIBLY, [i-rep'-ri-hents'-ib-li], *adv.* in irreprehensible fashion.
IRREPRESENTABLE, [i-rep'-ri-zent'-abl], *adj.* impossible to represent.
IRREPRESSIBLE, [i'-ri-pres'-ibl], *adj.* impossible to repress, beyond control.
IRREPRESSIBLY, [i'-ri-pres'-ib-li], *adv.* in irrepressible fashion.
IRREPROACHABLE, [i'-ri-prōch'-abl], *adj.* blameless, beyond reproach.
IRREPROACHABLENESS, [i'-ri-prōch'-abl-nes], *n.* the state of being irreproachable.
IRREPROACHABLY, [i'-ri-prōch'-ab-li], *adv.* in irreproachable fashion.
IRREPRODUCIBLE, [i-rē'-prō-dews'-ibl], *adj.* impossible to reproduce.
IRREPROVABLE, [i'-ri-prŏŏv'-abl], *adj.* that cannot be reproved; faultless.
IRREPROVABLY, [i'-ri-prŏŏv'-ab-li], *adv.* in irreprovable fashion.
IRREPTITIOUS, [i'-rep-tish'-us], *adj.* secretly entering.
IRRESISTANCE, [i'-ri-zist'-ants], *n.* passive obedience.
IRRESISTIBILITY, [i'-ri-zist'-i-bil'-i-ti], *n.* the state of being irresistible.
IRRESISTIBLE, [i'-ri-zist'-ibl], *adj.* impossible to be resisted, overpowering, overwhelming; irrefutable. [LL. *irresistibilis*].
IRRESISTIBLENESS, [i'-ri-zist'-ibl-nes], *n.* irresistibility.
IRRESISTIBLY, [i'-ri-zist'-ib-li], *adv.* in irresistible fashion.
IRRESISTLESS, [i'-ri-zist'-les], *adj.* irresistible.
IRRESOLUBLE, [i'-ri-zol'-yŏŏbl], *adj.* indissoluble; that may not be resolved. [L. *irresolubilis*].
IRRESOLUBLENESS, [i'-ri-zol'-yŏŏbl-nes], *n.* the condition of being irresoluble.
IRRESOLUTE, [i-rez'-ol-ōōt], *adj.* lacking resolution, hesitant, vacillating.
IRRESOLUTELY, [i-rez'-ol-ōōt-li], *adv.* in irresolute fashion.
IRRESOLUTENESS, [i-rez'-ol-ōōt-nes], *n.* the state of being irresolute.
IRRESOLUTION, [i-rez'-ol-ōō'-shun], *n.* irresoluteness; an irresolute state of mind.
IRRESOLVABILITY, [i'-ri-zolv'-a-bil'-i-ti], *n.* the state of being irresolvable.
IRRESOLVABLE, [i'-ri-zolv'-abl], *adj.* unable to be resolved, analysed, or solved.
IRRESOLVABLENESS, [i'-ri-zolv'-abl-nes], *n.* irresolvability.
IRRESPECTIVE (1), [i'-ri-spekt'-iv], *adj.* without reference to, without taking account of, independent of.
IRRESPECTIVE (2), [i'-ri-spekt'-iv], *adv.* irrespectively.
IRRESPECTIVELY, [i'-ri-spekt'-iv-li], *adv.* without regard to, without account of.
IRRESPIRABLE, [i'-ri-spīer'-abl, i-res'-pir-abl], *adj.* impossible to breathe. [LL. *irrespirabilis*].
IRRESPONSIBILITY, [i'-ri-spon'-si-bil'-i-ti], *n.* the state of being irresponsible; an irresponsible attitude of mind.
IRRESPONSIBLE, [i'-ri-spon'-sibl], *adj.* not responsible; having no sense of responsibility or no capacity for bearing responsibility, unreliable, unable to

appreciate properly the consequences of one's actions.
IRRESPONSIBLY, [i'-ri-spon'-sib-li], *adv.* in irresponsible fashion.
IRRESPONSIVE, [i'-ri-spon'-siv], *adj.* not responsive; not responding.
IRRESTRAINABLE, [i'-ri-strān'-abl], *adj.* impossible to restrain.
IRRESUSCITABLE, [i'-ri-sus'-it-abl], *adj.* impossible to be resuscitated.
IRRESUSCITABLY, [i'-ri-sus'-it-ab-li], *adv.* beyond resuscitation.
IRRETENTIVE, [i'-ri-tent'-iv], *adj.* not retentive, unable to retain ideas.
IRRETRACEABLE, [i'-ri-trās'-abl], *adj.* impossible to retrace.
IRRETRIEVABLE, [i'-ri-trēv'-abl], *adj.* impossible to retrieve, beyond recovery, irremediable.
IRRETRIEVABLENESS, [i'-ri-trēv'-abl-nes], *n.* the condition of being irretrievable.
IRRETRIEVABLY, [i'-ri-trēv'-ab-li], *adv.* in irretrievable fashion.
IRREVEALABLE, [i'-ri-vēl'-abl], *adj.* impossible to be revealed.
IRREVEALABLY, [i'-ri-vēl'-ab-li], *adv.* in irrevealable fashion.
IRREVERENCE, [i-rev'-er-ents], *n.* the state of being irreverent; irreverent behaviour or speech. [L. *irreverentia*].
IRREVERENT, [i-rev'-er-ent], *adj.* impious, irreligious, without reverence, disrespectful. [L. *irreverens*].
IRREVERENTLY, [i-rev'-er-ent-li], *adv.* in irreverent fashion.
IRREVERSIBLE, [i'-ri-vurs'-ibl], *adj.* impossible to reverse or be reversed; impossible to annul.
IRREVERSIBLENESS, [i'-ri-vurs'-ibl-nes], *n.* the quality of being irreversible.
IRREVERSIBLY, [i'-ri-vurs'-ib-li], *adv.* in irreversible fashion.
IRREVOCABILITY, [i-rev'-ok-a-bil'-i-ti], *n.* the state of being irrevocable.
IRREVOCABLE, [i-rev'-ok-abl], *adj.* beyond recall, unalterable. [L. *irrevocabilis*].
IRREVOCABLENESS, [i-rev'-ok-abl-nes], *n.* irrevocability.
IRREVOCABLY, [i-rev'-ok-ab-li], *adv.* in irrevocable fashion.
IRRIGATE, [i'-rig-āt], *v.t.* to provide (land) with water, *esp.* by a system of artificial canals, etc.; (*med.*) to keep a wound moist by a constant spray of water. [L. *irrigare*].
IRRIGATION, [i'-rig-ā'-shun], *n.* the act of irrigating; the condition of being irrigated. [L. *irrigatio*].
IRRIGATOR, [i'-rig-āt-er], *n.* one who, or that which, irrigates. [L. *irrigator*].
IRRIGUOUS, [i-rig'-yōō-us], *adj.* watered, moistened. [L. *irriguus*].
IRRISION, [i-rizh'-un], *n.* mockery. [L. *irrisio*].
IRRITABILITY, [i'-rit-a-bil'-i-ti], *n.* the state of being irritable.
IRRITABLE, [i'-rit-abl], *adj.* easily irritated, nervously petulant; inflamed, excited. [L. *irritabilis*].
IRRITABLENESS, [i'-rit-abl-nes], *n.* irritability.
IRRITABLY, [i'-rit-ab-li], *adv.* in irritable fashion.
IRRITANCY (1), [i'-rit-an-si], *n.* the condition of being irritated; an irritant.
IRRITANCY (2), [i'-rit-an-si], *n.* (*leg.*) annulment.
IRRITANT (1), [i'-rit-ant], *n.* an irritant substance, action, or circumstance.
IRRITANT (2), [i'-rit-ant], *adj.* producing irritation. [L. *irritans*].
IRRITANT (3), [i'-rit-ant], *adj.* rendering null and void. [L. *irritans*].
IRRITATE (1), [i'-rit-āt], *v.t.* to anger, provoke, exasperate by petty slights and small annoyances; to cause morbid itching or excitement in a part of the body; (*physiol.*) to stimulate to activity. [L. *irritare*].
IRRITATE (2), [i'-rit-āt], *v.t.* (*Scots leg.*) to make null and void. [L. *irritare*].
IRRITATING, [i'-ri-tāt-ing], *adj.* that irritates; annoying.
IRRITATINGLY, [i'-ri-tāt-ing-li], *adv.* in irritating fashion.
IRRITATION, [i'-rit-ā'-shun], *n.* the act of irritating; the state of being irritated; an itching, a disturbing excitation; (*fig.*) a state of mind in which small things excite and infuriate; that which irritates. [L. *irritatio*].
IRRITATIVE, [i'-rit-at-iv], *adj.* producing, marked by, irritation.
IRRITATORY, [i'-rit-āt'-er-i], *adj.* tending to irritate; stimulating.
IRRUPTION, [i-rup'-shun], *n.* a violent bursting in, a furious, overwhelming invasion. [L. *irruptio*].
IRRUPTIVE, [i-rupt'-iv], *adj.* rushing in violently, bursting upon.
IRRUPTIVELY, [i-rupt'-iv-li], *adv.* in irruptive fashion.
IS, [iz], *3rd person sg. pres. ind.* of BE.
ISABELLA, [iz'-a-bel'-a], *n.* a dull brownish-yellow colour. [Uncert.].
ISABELLINE, [iz'-a-bel'-īn], *adj.* of the colour of isabella.
ISAGOGIC, [ī'-sa-goj'-ik], *adj.* isagogical.
ISAGOGICAL, [ī'-sa-goj'-ik-al], *adj.* introductory. [Gk. *eisagoge* introduction].
ISAGOGICS, [ī'-sa-goj'-iks], *n.(pl.)* the historical and literary study of the Bible.
ISAGON, [ī'-sa-gon], *n.* a geometrical figure having equal angles. [Gk. *isos* equal and *gonia* an angle].
ISANDROUS, [ī-san'-drus], *adj.* (*bot.*) having stamens equal in number to the petals. [Gk. *isos* equal and *aner andros* male].
ISANTHOUS, [ī-san'-thus], *adj.* having regular flowers. [Gk. *isos* equal and *anthos* flower].
ISATIN, [ī'-sat-in], *n.* a reddish crystalline substance obtained from oxide of indigo. [Gk. *isatis* woad].
ISATIS, [ī'-sat-is], *n.* a genus of cruciferous herbs producing woad. [Gk. *isatis* woad].
ISCHIAGRA, [is'-ki-ag'-ra], *n.* (*med.*) a gout affecting the hips. [Gk. *iskhion* hip-bone and *agra* seizure].
ISCHIAL, [is'-ki-al], *adj.* relating to the hip-bone.
ISCHIALGIA, [is'-ki-al'-ji-a], *n.* sciatica. [Gk. *iskhion* hip-bone and *algos* pain].
ISCHIATIC, [is'-ki-at'-ik], *adj.* relating to the hip-joint or to sciatica. [Gk. *iskhiatikos*].
ISCHNOPHONIA, [isk'-nō-fō'-ni-a], *n.* a weakness of voice. [Gk. *iskhnophonos*].
ISCHNOPHONY, [isk-nof'-o-ni], *n.* ischnophonia; stammering.
ISCHURETIC (1), [isk'-yōō-ret'-ik], *n.* (*med.*) a medicine or drug for alleviating ischury.
ISCHURETIC (2), [isk'-yōō-ret'-ik], *adj.* (*med.*) alleviating ischury.
ISCHURY, [isk'-yōō-ri], *n.* (*path.*) morbid retention of urine. [Gk. *iskho* I keep back and *ouron* urine].
ISENERGIC, [ī'-sen-urj'-ik], *adj.* of equal energy. [Gk. *isos* equal and ENERGIC].
ISERINE, [ī'-ser-in], *n.* isometric titanic iron. [Germ. *eisen* iron].
ISHMAELITE, [ish'-māl-īt], *n.* a social outcast, a hater of humanity. [*Ishmael*, Genesis XVI, 11].
ISINGLASS, [ī'-sing-glahs], *n.* a gelatinous substance prepared from the bladders and viscera of certain fishes, and used in the manufacture of glues and jellies. [ODu. *huizenblas* sturgeon's bladder].
ISLAM, [iz'-lahm], *n.* the religion of Mahomet; the countries under Mohammedan rule or religion. [Arab. *salam* safety].
ISLAMIC, [iz-lam'-ik], *adj.* relating to Islam.
ISLAMISM, [iz'-lam-izm], *n.* Mohammedanism.
ISLAMITIC, [iz'-lam-it'-ik], *adj.* relating to Islam or Islamism.
ISLAMIZE, [iz'-lam-īz], *v.t.* to convert to Islamism.
ISLAND (1), [ī'-land], *n.* a piece of land completely surrounded by water; anything, *esp.* cellular tissue, completely isolated; a refuge for pedestrians in the middle of a roadway. [OE. *igland*].
ISLAND (2), [ī'-land], *adj.* pertaining to islands, found on, living on, an island.
ISLAND (3), [ī'-land], *v.t.* to make into an island, to isolate; to set with islands; to insulate.
ISLANDED, [ī'-land-id], *adj.* made into an island, surrounded; dotted with islands.
ISLANDER, [ī'-land-er], *n.* one who inhabits an island.
ISLE, [īl], *n.* (*poet.*) an island. [OFr. *isle*].
ISLESMAN, [īlz'-man], *n.* a native of the Hebrides; an islander.
ISLET, [ī'-let], *n.* a little island.
ISM, [izm], *n.* a theory, science, *esp.* one supposed to be difficult, impractical, or eccentric. [Gk. *ismos*].
ISO-, *pref.* equal. [Gk. *isos*].
ISOBAR, [ī'-sō-bah(r)], *n.* a line on a map joining places of similar barometric pressure. [Gk. *isobaros* weighing the same].
ISOBARIC, [ī'-sō-ba-rik], *adj.* consisting of isobars.
ISOBAROMETRIC, [ī'-sō-ba'-rō-met'-rik], *adj.* having equal barometric pressure.
ISOBATHYTHERM, [ī'-sō-bath'-i-thurm], *n.* an imaginary line on a vertical section of the sea con-

necting the points of equal temperature. [ISO and Gk. *bathus* deep and *therme* heat].

ISOCHEIM, [ī'-sō-kīm], *n.* an isochimenal line. [ISO and Gk. *kheima* winter].

ISOCHEIMAL, [ī'-sō-kīm'-al], *adj.* isochimenal.

ISOCHIMENAL, [ī'-sō-kīm'-in-al], *adj.* of the same average winter temperature; **i. line,** a line on a map joining places of the same average winter temperature.

ISOCHROMATIC, [ī'-sō-krō-mat'-ik], *adj.* of the same colour.

ISOCHRONAL, [ī-sok'-ron-al], *adj.* isochronous.

ISOCHRONISM, [ī-sok'-ron-izm], *n.* temporal coincidence, the condition of taking place in equal times.

ISOCHRONOUS, [ī-sok'-ron-us], *adj.* of equal time, happening in the same space of time. [ISO and Gk. *khronos* time].

ISOCHROUS, [ī-sok'-rus], *adj.* of uniform colour. [ISO and Gk. *khroa* colour].

ISOCLINAL, [ī'-sō-klīn'-al], *adj.* pertaining to places where the magnetic needle has similar inclination. [ISO and Gk. *klino* I lean].

ISOCLINIC, [ī'-sō-klin'-ik], *adj.* isoclinal.

ISODIAMETRIC, [ī'-sō-dī-a-met'-rik], *adj.* of equal diameter.

ISODOMON, [ī-sod'-om-on], *n.* (*arch.*) a method of construction employing stones of uniform length and thickness layered in parallel courses, with the join of one pair of blocks exactly in the centre of the blocks above and below. [ISO and Gk. *domos* layer].

ISODONT, [ī'-sō-dont], *adj.* with uniform teeth. [ISO and Gk. *odous odontos* tooth].

ISODYNAMIC, [ī'-sō-dī-nam'-ik], *adj.* of equal force.

ISOGENY, [ī-soj'-i-ni], *n.* the state of having arisen from the same origin. [ISO and Gk. *genes* born of].

ISOGEOTHERMAL, [ī'-sō-jē'-ō-thurm'-al], *adj.* relating to imaginary lines in vertical sections of the earth, connecting points of like temperature. [ISO and Gk. *ge* earth and *therme* heat].

ISOGNATHOUS, [ī'-sō-nā'-thus], *adj.* having molar teeth alike in both jaws. [ISO and Gk. *gnathos* a jaw].

ISOGON, [ī'-sō-gon], *n.* a figure having equal angles. [ISO and Gk. *gonia* angle].

ISOGONIC, [ī'-sō-gon'-ik], *adj.* pertaining to places where the magnetic needle has similar declination.

ISOHEL, [ī'-sō-hel], *n.* a line on a map joining places having similar sunshine. [ISO and Gk. *helios* sun].

ISOHYETAL, [ī'-sō-hī'-i-tal], *n.* a line on a map connecting places with equal rainfall. [ISO and Gk. *huetos* moisture].

ISOGON

ISOLATE (1), [ī'-sol-āt], *adj.* in isolation, isolated.

ISOLATE (2), [ī'-sol-āt], *v.t.* to set apart, cut off, make separate; (*chem.*) to separate an element from a compound; (*med.*) to put into quarantine, remove (an infectious case) from contact with others; (*elect.*) to insulate. [It. *isolare*].

ISOLATION, [ī'-sol-ā'-shun], *n.* the state of being isolated; the act of isolating.

ISOMERIC, [ī'-sō-me'-rik], *adj.* (*chem.*) (of compounds) having similar elements in similar proportion but possessing different properties. [ISO and Gk. *meros* part].

ISOMERISM, [ī-som'-er-izm], *n.* the quality of being isomeric.

ISOMETRIC, [ī'-sō-met'-rik], *adj.* of equal measure.

ISOMORPHISM, [ī'-sō-mawf'-izm], *n.* the condition of being isomorphous.

ISOMORPHOUS, [ī'-sō-mawf'-us], *adj.* possessing different elements but similar crystalline form. [ISO and Gk. *morphe* shape].

ISONOMY, [ī-son'-o-mi], *n.* one law for all. [ISO and Gk. *nomos* law].

ISOPATHY, [ī-sop'-a-thi], *n.* the cure of disease by the same disease or its virus. [ISO and Gk. *pathos* suffering].

ISOPERIMETRICAL, [ī'-sō-pe'-ri-met'-rik-al], *adj.* with equal perimeters.

ISOPERIMETRY, [ī'-sō-pe-rim'-i-tri], *n.* the technique of constructing dissimilar figures with equal perimeters.

ISOPOD, [ī'-sō-pod], *n.* any species of that group of the crustacea having seven similar and equal pairs of legs. [ISO and Gk. *pous podos* foot].

ISOPODOUS, [ī-sop'-od-us], *adj.* relating to, resembling, an isopod.

ISOSCELES, [ī-sos'-i-lēz], *adj.* (*geom.*) (of a triangle) having two equal sides. [Gk. *isoskeles* equal-legged].

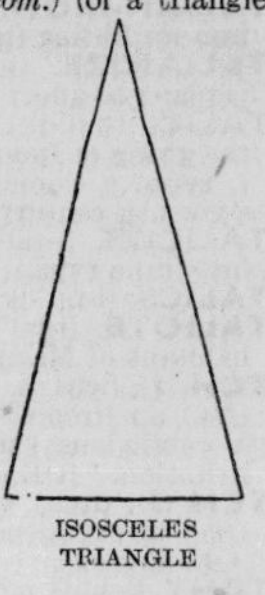

ISOSCELES TRIANGLE

ISOSEISMAL, [ī'-sō-sīz'-mal], *n.* the line on a map connecting places where the shock of an earthquake was of equal intensity. [ISO and Gk. *seismos* earthquake].

ISOSTACY, [ī-sos'-ta-si], *n.* stability due to equality of pressure; a theory concerning the earth's centre based on this principle. [ISO and Gk. *stasis* station].

ISOSTEMONOUS, [ī'-sō-stem'-on-us], *adj.* (*bot.*) having the same number of stamens as petals. [ISO and Gk. *stemon* thread].

ISOTHERAL, [ī'-sō-ther'-al], *adj.* of the same average summer temperature.

ISOTHERE, [ī'-sō-thēer], *n.* a line on a map connecting places having the same average summer temperature. [ISO and Gk. *theros* summer].

ISOTHERM, [ī'-sō-thurm], *n.* a line on a map joining places of the same thermometer readings. [ISO and Gk. *therme* heat].

ISOTHERMAL, [ī'-sō-thurm'-al], *adj.* of equal heat; **i. lines,** lines on a map joining places of similar temperature.

ISOTONIC, [ī'-sō-ton'-ik], *adj.* of equal tone.

ISOTOPE, [ī'-sō-tōp], *n.* (*chem.*) one of two or more states of an element, chemically identical, but differing in their atomic weight. [ISO and Gk. *topos* place].

ISRAELITE, [iz'-rel-īt], *n.* an inhabitant of Biblical Israel; a Jew, *esp.* an orthodox Jew. [Heb. *yisrael* one who strives with God, Jacob].

ISRAELITIC, [iz'-rel-it'-ik], *adj.* Israelitish.

ISRAELITISH, [iz'-rel-īt'-ish], *adj.* Jewish; relating to Israel.

ISSUABLE, [ish'-yōō-abl], *adj.* possible, permissible to be issued.

ISSUANCE, [ish'-yōō-ants], *n.* the act of issuing; that which is issued.

ISSUANT, [ish'-yōō-ant], *adj.* (*her.*) issuing out of.

ISSUE (1), [ish'-yōō], *n.* the act of issuing; that which is issued or which issues; a flow, bursting out; the place or time of flowing; publications sent out at one particular time; children, offspring; the point arising from a situation, depending upon certain events; the main point of an argument; the result, outcome. [OFr. *issue*].

ISSUE (2), [ish'-yōō], *v.t. and i.* to give or send out, publish, circulate; to distribute; to come forth, flow from, emerge; to spring from, be derived or descended from; to result in.

ISSUELESS, [ish'-yōō-les], *adj.* without children.

ISSUER, [ish'-yōō-er], *n.* one who issues.

-IST, [ist], *suff.* implying adherence to a particular doctrine or the practice of a particular habit.

ISTHMIAN, [isth'-mi-an], *adj.* relating to an isthmus.

ISTHMUS, [isth'-mus], *n.* a strip of land linking two continental masses or a peninsula with the mainland; a narrow strip joining two larger parts. [Gk. *isthmos*].

ISTLE, [ist'-li], *n.* a Mexican plant-fibre used for making cord. [Mexican *ixtli*].

IT (1), [it], *n.* the ideal, the acme of perfection; (*U.S. slang*) personal charm, attractiveness.

IT (2), [it], *n.* (*coll.*) Italian vermouth. [IT(ALIAN)].

ISTHMUS

IT (3), [it], *3rd person sg. neut. pron. used to signify anything impersonal or non-human.* [OE. *hit*].

ITACOLUMITE, [it'-a-kol'-yōō-mīt], *n.* a granular, quartzose, talcomicaceous slate, the matrix of Brazilian diamonds. [*Itacoluma*, a Brazilian mountain].

ITALIAN (1), [i-tal'-yan], *n.* a native of Italy; the language of Italy.

ITALIAN (2), [i-tal'-yan], *adj.* relating to Italy and its people. [L. *Italianus*].

ITALIANATE, [i-tal′-yan-āt], *adj.* affecting the manners and culture of Italy.
ITALIAN-IRON, [i-tal′-yan-īern′], *n.* a smoothing iron for fluting frills.
ITALIANIZE, [i-tal′-yan-īz], *v.t. and i.* to make Italian; to affect the Italian.
ITALIC, [i-tal′-ik], *adj.* relating to ancient Italy or to the group of Indo-European languages spoken there; **i. type,** a sloping type first used in Venice in the sixteenth century. [L. *Italicus* of Italy].
ITALICIZE, [i-tal′-is-īz], *v.t.* to emphasize by putting into italic type.
ITALICS, [i-tal′-iks], *n.(pl.)* italic type or characters.
ITALIOTE, [i-tal′-i-ōt], *n.* an Italian Greek, an inhabitant of Magna Graecia. [Gk. *Italiotes*].
ITCH (1), [ich], *n.* an irritation of the skin, a tickling; (*fig.*) an irrepressible urge to do something; (*med.*) a contagious skin disease accompanied by violent irritation. [OE. *gicce*].
ITCH (2), [itch], *v.i.* to feel a violent skin irritation; (*fig.*) to experience an itch; (*med.*) to have the itch. [OE. *giccean*].
ITCHY, [ich′-i], *adj.* itching, tickling, feeling irritation.
ITEM (1), [ī′-tem], *n.* a particular article or detail of a list; a particular selected from many; a part of a programme, agenda, etc. [L. *item* likewise].
ITEM (2), [ī′-tem], *adv.* also, likewise. [L. *item*].
ITEMIZE, [ī′-tem-īz], *v.t.* to set out in items; to instance item by item.
ITERANT, [it′-er-ant], *adj.* repeating. [L. *iterans*].
ITERATE, [it′-er-āt], *v.t.* to repeat, to say again. [L. *iterare*].
ITERATION, [it′-er-ā′-shun], *n.* repetition; the act of repeating; something repeated. [L. *iteratio*].
ITERATIVE, [it′-er-at-iv], *adj.* repetitive.
ITINERACY, [it-in′-er-a-si], *n.* itinerancy.
ITINERANCY, [it-in′-er-an-si], *n.* the state of being itinerant.
ITINERANT (1), [it-in′-er-ant], *n.* one who wanders from place to place, a tramp.
ITINERANT (2), [it-in′-er-ant], *adj.* moving from place to place; wandering without fixed headquarters. [L. *itinerans*].
ITINERANTLY, [it-in′-er-ant-li], *adv.* in itinerant fashion.
ITINERARY (1), [it-in′-er-er-i], *n.* route, way of going from place to place; an account of this, a guide book for travellers. [L. *itinerarium*].
ITINERARY (2), [it-in′-er-er-i], *adj.* relating to a journey. [L. *itinerarius*].
ITINERATE, [it-in′-er-āt], *v.i.* to wander from place to place without fixed abode. [L. *itinerari*].
ITS, [its], *pron. possessive* of IT (3).
ITSELF, [it-self′], *pron.* the *emphatic form* of IT (3): the *reflexive* of IT (3)].
ITTNERITE, [it′-ner-it], *n.* a hard mineral containing silica, alumina, and soda. [*Ittner*, its discoverer].
IVIED, [ī′-vid], *adj.* covered with ivy.
IVIGAR, [iv′-i-ger], *n.* the sea-urchin, *Echinus miliaris*. [Unkn.].
IVORY (1), [ī′-ver-i], *n.* the hard, white, bony substance composing the tusks of the elephant, hippopotamus, walrus, and narwhal; a whitish colour; (*pl.*) (*slang*) teeth; piano-keys. [OFr. *ivurie*].
IVORY (2), [ī′-ver-i], *adj.* made of ivory; of an ivory colour.
IVORY-TURNER, [ī′-ver-i-turn′-er], *n.* one who works in ivory.
IVY, [ī′-vi], *n.* the glossy-leaved, climbing, evergreen plant, *Hedera Helix*. [OE. *ifig*].
IXIOLITE, [iks′-i-ō-līt], *n.* a mineral resin found in bituminous coal. [Swed. *ixiolith*].
IZARD, (iz′-erd], *n.* the chamois of the Pyrenees. [Fr. *isard*].
IZZARD, [iz′-ard], *n.* the letter Z. [~*zed* the letter Z].

J

J, [jā], the tenth letter in the English alphabet.
JAB, [jab], *v.t.* to dig with a stick, to poke roughly. [Unkn.].
JABBER (1), [jab′-er], *n.* a stream of rapid, semi-intelligible talk, voluble chatter.
JABBER (2), [jab′-er], *v.t. and i.* to utter rapidly or indistinctly; to talk rapidly or indistinctly, to chatter. [Imitative].
JABBERER, [jab′-er-er], *n.* one who jabbers.
JABBERING, [jab′-er-ing], *n.* the act of one who jabbers; indistinct chatter.
JABBERINGLY, [jab′-er-ing-li], *adv.* in a jabbering manner.
JABIRU, [jab′-i-rōō], *n.* a wading bird of the genus *Mycteria*, allied to the storks, found in equatorial America. [Braz. *jabiru*].
JABORANDI, [jab′-er-an-di], *n.* the small leaves of a plant of the genus *Pilocarpus* when in a dry condition and prepared for medicinal purposes. [Braz. *jaburandi*].
JABOT, [zhab′-ō], *n.* a frill or bow on the front of a bodice or shirt. [Fr. *jabot*].
JACAMAR, [jak′-a-mah(r)], *n.* a tropical bird of the genus *Galbula*, allied to the kingfisher, living on insects. [Braz. *jacamar*].
JACANA, [jak′-a-nah], *n.* one of the ten species of *Parra*, the American tropical birds which walk on the leaves of water-plants. [Braz. *jacana*].
JACARANDA, [jak-a-ran′-da], *n.* a numerous genus of South American hardwood trees with scented wood. [Braz. *jacaranda*].
JACCHUS, [jak′-us], *n.* the common marmoset, *Hapale jacchus*. [L. *jacchus*].
JACENT†, [jā′-sent], *adj.* lying at length, recumbent. [L. *jacens*].
JACINTH, [jā′-sinth, jas′-inth], *n.* a transparent reddish-orange oxide of zirconium used as a semi-precious stone. [OFr. *jacinte* from Gk. *huakinthos*].
JACK (1), [jak], *n.* a rank and file sailor, jack tar; a cheeky young fellow; the knave in a suit of cards; a contrivance for turning a spit; an apparatus for lifting heavy weights, *esp.* for raising the wheel of a motor-car off the ground; a bootjack; a young pike; a small white ball used as a mark in the game of bowls; a wooden frame supporting wood to be sawn; (*naut.*) a short spar or yard; the flag-staff in the bows of a ship; the flag flown from this staff; **before you can say J. Robinson,** in a fraction of a second; **cheap-j.,** hawker, pedlar; **every man j.,** the whole company; **j.-o'-lantern,** will-o'-the-wisp; **J. of all trades,** a person who can cope with any kind of practical job, an odd-job man; **j.-in-the-box,** the plant, *Hermandia sonora*; a child's toy consisting of a doll on a spring which jumps out of a box when the lid is opened; **J. Frost,** a personification of frost; **Union J.,** the national flag of the British Isles. [ME. *Jakke*, *Jankyn*, *dim.* of JOHN].
JACK (2), [jak], *n.* bread-fruit eaten by East Indian natives. [Malay *chakka*]
JACK (3), [jak], *v.t.* to lift with a jack. [JACK (1)].
JACK-A-DANDY†, [jak′-a-dan′-di], *n.* a foppish fellow.
JACKAL, [jak′-awl], *n.* an animal, *Canis aureus*, resembling a dog, with the colour and bushy tail of a fox, found in North Africa; (*fig.*) a menial. [Pers. *shagal*].

JACKAL

JACK-A-LENT†, [jak′-a-lent], *n.* a stupid fellow, originally a stuffed puppet, thrown at in Lent.
JACKANAPES, [jak′-a-nāps], *n.* a monkey; a mischievous boy; a conceited fop. [Unkn.].
JACKAROO, [jak′-a-rōō], *n.* (*slang*) in the Australian bush, a novice or new hand, generally known as a jackaroo squatter. [JACK (1) and (KANG)AROO].
JACKASS, [jak′-as′], *n.* a male ass or donkey; a blockhead, dolt; **laughing j.,** the laughing kingfisher found in Australia, *Dacelo gigantea*. [JACK (1) and ASS].

JACK-BOOT, [jak'-bōōt'], *n.* a large boot which extends above the knees as protection in deep water.

JACKDAW, [jak'-daw], *n.* a British bird, the daw, *Corvus monedula.* [JACK (1) and DAW].

JACKET, [jak'-it], *n.* a short coat; an outer covering, with sleeves, to protect the torso. [OFr. *jaquet*].

JACKETED, [jak'-it-id], *adj.* wearing a jacket.

JACK-FLAG, [jak'-flag'], *n.* a flag hoisted on a jack.

JACK-IN-OFFICE, [jak'-in-of'-is], *n.* an overbearing minor official.

JACK JOHNSON, [jak'-jon'-sun], *n.* (*slang*) a shell fired from one of the heavy German guns in the war of 1914-18. [*Jack Johnson*, a negro boxer nicknamed "Black Smoke"].

JACK-BOOT

JACK-KNIFE, [jak'-nīf], *n.* a large clasp-knife for the pocket.

JACK-PLANE, [jak'-plān], *n.* a plane for preparing rough wood.

JACKPOT, [jak'-pot'], *n.* a pool at the card game of poker.

JACK-PUDDING†, [jak'-pōōd'-ing], *n.* a fool, a buffoon, a merry andrew.

JACKS, [jaks], *n.*(*pl.*) wooden wedges, used in coal-mining.

JACKSAW, [jak'-saw], *n.* a bird, the goosander, *Mergus merganser*, which has a bill with a sawlike edge. [JACK (1) and SAW].

JACK-SCREW, [jak'-skrōō], *n.* a lifting jack operated by a screw, used for stowing cotton in a ship's hold or raising heavy weights. [JACK (1) and SCREW]

JACK-SNIPE, [jak'-snīp], *n.* a species of small snipe, *Gallinago gallinula.*

JACKSTAYS, [jak'-stāz], *n.*(*pl.*) (*naut.*) ropes or strips of wood or iron stretched along a ship's yard to bind the sails to. [JACK (1) and STAY].

JACK-STRAW†, [jak'-straw], *n.* a man of straw, or worth nothing. [*Jack Straw*, leader of the peasants' revolt of 1381].

JACK TAR, [jak'-tah(r)'], *n.* (*coll.*) a sailor of the Royal Navy.

JACK-TOWEL, [jak'-tow'-el], *n.* a long towel looped round a roller.

JACKYARD, [jak'-yahd], *n.* (*naut.*) the extending boom at the foot of a gaff-topsail in fore and aft rigged craft. [JACK (1) and YARD].

JACOBEAN, [jak'-ō-bē'-an], *adj.* belonging or relating to the reign of James I. [L. *Jacobaeus*].

JACOBIN (1), [jak'-ō-bin], *n.* a monk of the order of St. Dominic; a member of a revolutionary party in the French Revolution which met in a Jacobin convent to decide on programme and tactics; a kind of pigeon with its neck feathers formed like a hood. [MedL. *Jacobinus*].

JACOBIN (2), [jak'-ō-bin], *adj.* Jacobinical.

JACOBINICAL, [jak'-ō-bin'-ik-al], *adj.* pertaining to the Jacobins; holding revolutionary principles; Jacobin.

JACOBINISM, [jak'-ō-bin-izm], *n.* Jacobin principles based on the belief in the necessity of overthrowing the established government by force.

JACOBINIZE, [jak'-ō-bin-īz], *v.t.* to influence with Jacobinism.

JACOBITE, [jak'-ob-īt], *n.* a follower of James II after he had abdicated; an adherent of the party believing in the rightness of the cause of his descendants in claiming the throne of England. [L. *Jacobus* James].

JACOBITICAL, [jak'-ob-it'-ik-al], *adj.* pertaining to the Jacobites or their principles.

JACOBITISM, [jak'-ob-īt-izm], *n.* the political principles of the Jacobites.

JACOB'S-LADDER, [jā'-kobz-lad'-er], *n.* a plant having blue flowers, *Polemonium cæruleum*; (*naut.*) a rope ladder with wooden steps for climbing rigging.

JACOB'S-STAFF†, [jā'-kobz-stahf'], *n.* a pilgrim's staff; a staff concealing a dagger; a cross staff, a kind of astrolabe.

JACOBUS, [jak-ō'-bus], *n.* a gold coin minted in the reign of James I. [L. *Jacobus* James].

JACONET, [jak'-on-et], *n.* a light, soft, open textured muslin. [Hind. *Jagannath* a town in Bengal].

JACQUARD, [jak'-ahd], *n.* a contrivance fitted to a loom consisting of a belt of cards which form openings for the movement of the shuttle between the warp threads in conformity with a prearranged pattern. [M. *Jacquard* the inventor].

JACQUERIE, [zhak'-er-ē'], *n.* the peasants' rebellion in France in 1358. [Fr. *Jacques* James or peasant].

JACTATION, [jak-tā'-shun], *n.* the act of throwing; bragging. [L. *jactatio*].

JACTITATION, [jak'-tit-ā'-shun], *n.* (*med.*) a delirious tossing of the body, restlessness; vain boasting; (*leg.*) a false pretension to marriage. [MedL. *jactitatio*].

JADE (1), [jād], *n.* a badly bred, aged or worn-out horse, a nag; an ill-kempt woman old before her time with work, worry, bad temper, or immoral habits. [Unkn.].

JADE (2), [jād], *n.* a green mineral silicate of magnesium, calcium, and sodium, used, when cut, for ornaments. [Span. (*piedra de*) *ijada* stone to cure pains in the side].

JADE (3), [jād], *v.t. and i.* to make exhausted by overwork; to become tired and weary. [JADE (1)].

JADISH, [jād'-ish], *adj.* having the characteristics of a jade, vicious, unchaste.

J'ADOUBE, [zha-dōōb'], *interj.* a phrase used in chess by a player who fingers a piece he has not definitely decided to move. [Fr. *j'adoube* I adjust].

JAEGER (1), [yā'-ger], *n.* (*prot.*) a proprietary name for a pure woollen material and range of clothing.

JAEGER (2), see JAGER.

JAFFA, [jaf'-a], *adj.* relating to, grown in, Jaffa, *esp.* of a sweet, large, thick-skinned variety of orange. [*Jaffa* a town in Palestine].

JAG (1), [jag], *n.* a projection with a sharp, ragged edge; notch, tooth; a slit or tear in material. [Unkn.].

JAG (2), (**jagging, jagged**), [jag], *v.t.* to cut, tear or slit so that a ragged edge is left. [*Prec.*].

JAGER, JAEGER, [yāg-er], *n.* a sea-bird of predatory habits, of the family *Laridae*, the great skua. [Germ. *jäger* hunter].

JAGGED, [jag'-id], *adj.* having an uneven edge, notched.

JAGGEDNESS, [jag'-id-nes], *n.* the state of being jagged.

JAGGER, [jag'-er], *n.* a brass wheel or mould with a notched edge for cutting cakes or pastry into patterns or shapes.

JAGGER

JAGGERY, [jag'-er-i], *n.* a coarse brown sugar obtained by inspissation from palm sap. [Hind. *shakkas* sugar].

JAGGY, [jag'-i], *adj.* set with teeth, notched, uneven.

JAGHIR, [jah-hēer'], *n.* an annual assignment of land or a share in the produce granted to an individual in India, generally for military purposes. [Hind. *jagher*].

JAGHIRDAR, [jah-urd'-ah(r)], *n.* the holder of a jaghir.

JAGUAR, [jag'-yōō-ah(r)], *n.* the largest of the American carnivores, with a dappled brown and yellow fur, belonging to the cat family, *Felis onca.* [Braz. *yaguara*].

JAH, [jah, yah], *n.* Jehovah. [Heb. *Yahweh*].

JAHVIST, see YAHWIST.

JAIL, GAOL, [jāl], *n.* a building for the detention and confinement of people convicted of crime, a prison; **j. fever**, typhus fever. [OFr. *jaole*].

JAILBIRD, [jāl'-burd], *n.* a prisoner; a person who has been confined in prison, *esp.* more than once. [JAIL and BIRD].

JAILER, see GAOLER.

JAINISM, [jān'-izm], *n.* the Indian religion founded by Vardhamana Mahavira about 500 B.C. based on the belief that all matter is animated by soul. [Skr. *jaina* of a conqueror].

JAKES†, [jāks], *n.* a lavatory. [Unkn.].

JALAP, [jal'-ap], *n.* the root of *Ipomœa Purga*, a plant used as a cathartic. [*Xalapa*, a town in Mexico].

JALAPIN, [jal'-ap-in], *n.* the purgative principle of jalap.

JALOUSIE, [zhal'-ōō-zē], *n.* a blind of sloping wooden slats; a Venetian blind. [Fr. *jalousie* jealousy].

JAM (1), [jam], *n.* a conserve of fruits boiled with sugar and left to stand in jars till firm and cold. [Uncert.].

JAM (2), [jam], *n.* a state of being squeezed together; that which is squeezed together, a forcibly compact mass or body, a crush. [JAM (3)].

JAM (3), [jam], *v t.* to press, to crowd, to squeeze tight into a small space; to form or force into a compact mass or body; to block movement; to become wedged. [~CHAMP].

JAMAICA PEPPER, [ja-mā'-ka-pep'-er], *n.* allspice, *Pimenta officinalis.*

JAMB, [jam], *n.* the sidepiece or post of a door or fireplace. [Fr. *jambe*].

JAMBE, [zhahmb], *n.* a piece of leg armour. [Fr. *jambe* leg].

JAMBOK, [sham'-bok], *n.* a strip of hide used as a whip in South Africa. [Du. *sjambok*].

JAMBONE, [jam'-bōn], *n.* a player who has to lay his cards on the table at euchre. [Uncert.].

JAMBOREE, [jam-bo-rē'], *n.* a jolly gathering, a spree, a great concourse of boy scouts. [Uncert.].

JAMDANI, [jam'-dan-e'], *n.* a kind of patterned cotton cloth. [Pers. *jamdani*].

JAMEWAR, [jam'-i-wah(r)], *n.* a cloth of goat's hair made in Kashmir. [Kashmir *jamiwar*].

JAMMY, [jam'-i], *adj.* covered with jam; sticky like jam. [JAM (1)].

JANE, [jān], *n.* a kind of fabric, jean. [OFr. *Janne*].

JANGADA, [jan-gah'-da], *n.* a large raft of timber fitted with a sail and used for fishing on the Amazon. [Span. *jangada*].

JANGLE (1), [jang'-gl], *n.* a noise made by different discordant sounds, a clash of noises. [JANGLE (2)].

JANGLE (2), [jang'-gl], *v.t. and i.* to make a noise with the different sounds out of tune, particularly of bells ringing; to make a harsh noise; to talk all at once noisily. [OFr. *jangler*].

JANGLER, [jang'-gler], *n.* a wrangling, noisy fellow.

JANGLING, [jang'-gling], *n.* a noisy dispute; a wrangling.

JANISSARY, JANIZARY, [jan'-is-er-i], *n.* a soldier of the Turkish infantry, disbanded in 1826, formed originally of Christian youths taken prisoners as a bodyguard of the Sultan. [Turk. *yenitsheri* new soldiers].

JANITOR, [jan'-it-or], *n.* a doorkeeper, porter. [L. *janitor*].

JANITRIX, [jan'-it-riks], *n.* a female doorkeeper. [L. *janitrix*].

JANNOCK, [jan'-ok], *adj.* (*dial.*) excellent, trusty, right. [Unkn.].

JANSENISM, [jan'-sen-izm], *n.* the doctrine embodying the principles of *Jansen*, bishop of Ypres (died 1638), who maintained the doctrine of the perverseness of man's natural will in opposition to the R.C. authorities.

JANSENIST, [jan'-sen-ist], *n.* a supporter of Jansenism.

JANTU, [jahn-tōō'], *n.* a machine used in India to raise water in irrigation. [Hind. *jantu*].

JANUARY, [jan'-yoo-er-i], *n.* the first month of the year, according to the present computation as settled by Act of Parliament in 1752. [L. *Januarius* belonging to Janus].

JANUS, [jā'-nus], *n.* an ancient Roman god credited with the faculty of looking both ways, front and back, into the future and the past, and represented as having two faces to his head. [L. *Janus*].

JANUS-FACED, [jā'-nus-fāst'], *adj.* having two faces; double-dealing. [*Prec.*].

JAP (1), [jap], *n.* (*coll.*) a Japanese.

JAP (2), [jap], *adj.* relating to, coming from, Japan.

JAPAN (1), [jap-an'], *n.* the name of certain islands lying off the coast of China in the Far East; the hard varnish or lacquer used to cover and decorate woodwork by the Japanese; work in this varnish. [Chin. *Jeh-pun* rising sun].

JAPAN (2), [jap-an], *adj.* relating to Japan. [*Prec.*].

JAPAN (3), (**japanning, japanned**), [jap-an'], *v.t.* to cover with a hard coat of black varnish, to lacquer. [JAPAN (2)].

JAPAN-EARTH, [jap-an'-urth'], *n.* catechu.

JAPANESE (1), [jap'-an-ēz'], *n.* a native of Japan; the language of Japan.

JAPANESE (2), [jap'-an-ēz'], *adj.* relating to Japan or its inhabitants.

JAPANESE-PAPER, [jap'-an-ēz'-pā'-per], *n.* a form of fine tough tissue-paper used as an absorbent by dentists.

JAPANNER, [jap-an'-er], *n.* a person who varnishes in the manner of the Japanese.

JAPE (1), [jāp], *n.* a comic trick; a joke, a jest. [OFr. *jape*].

JAPE (2), [jāp], *v.i.* to joke, to jest. [OFr. *japer*].

JAPHETIC, [jaf-et'-ik], *adj.* relating to Japheth, son of Noah; Aryan as distinguished from Semitic.

JAPONICA, [jap-on'-ik-a], *n.* the Japanese quince, *Cydonia japonica*. [MdL. *japonica* Japanese].

JAR (1), [jah(r)], *n.* a harsh discordant sound, a crude discord of rattling sounds; a sudden shock and its after-effects on the nerves caused by collision of two bodies; a physical impact causing shock; an unexpected obstruction to accepted ideas, mental disturbance; (*fig.*) quarrelsome debate, contention. [JAR (3)].

JAR (2), [jah(r)], *n.* a glass or earthenware pot having no spout at the rim, generally cylindrical and upright. [Arab. *jarrah* jar].

JAR (3), (**jarring, jarred**), [jah(r)], *v.t. and i.* to shake, to cause to tremble by sharp impact, to upset the functional equilibrium of a person, body, or mechanism; to cause mental disturbance, to obstruct the flow of normal ideas; to give out a discordant sound, to be inconsistent; to be a cause of contention; to work as an irritant on a person's nerves. [Uncert.].

JARARAKA, [ja'-ra-rah'-ka], *n.* a very dangerous poisonous snake of the West Indies and South America, *Bothrops lanceolatus*. [Braz. *jararaca*].

JARDINIERE, jardinière, [zhah'-dēn-yāer'], *n.* an ornamental flower-stand. [Fr. *jardinière*].

JARGON, [jah'-gon], *n.* technical terminology that is unintelligible to the inexpert reader or listener; muddled incantatory speech, gibberish. [OFr. *jargon* prattle].

JARGONELLE, [jah'-gon-el'], *n.* a variety of pear that ripens early. [Fr. *jargonelle*].

JARGONIZE, [jah'-gon-iz], *v.i.* to speak jargon.

JARGOON, [jah-gōōn'], *n.* a translucent colourless or green variety of zirconium, the heaviest gem. [Arab. *yargun* having the colour of gold].

JARL, [yahl], *n.* a leader; an earl, chieftain. [OScand. *jarl* earl].

JARRAH, [ja'-ra], *n.* the hard and enduring wood of *Eucalyptus marginata*. [Australian *jerrhyl*].

JARRING, [jah'-ring], *adj.* harshly discordant; disturbing to the nerves. [JAR (1)].

JARRINGLY, [jah'-ring-li], *adv.* in a jarring manner.

JARVEY, [jah'-vi], *n.* (*slang*) a driver of an Irish cab, a cab-driver. [*Jarvis* a surname].

JASEY, [jā'-zi], *n.* a comic name for a worsted wig; a wig. [~JERSEY].

JASMINE, JESSAMINE, [jas'-min], *n.* (*bot.*) a plant of the genus *Jasminum*, a climbing shrub with delicate and fragrant white or yellow flowers. [Pers. *yasmin*].

JASPER, [jas'-per], *n.* an opaque variety of quartz found in different colours and capable of being highly polished. [Gk. *iaspis* bright chalcedony].

JASPERATED, [jas'-per-ā'-tid], *adj.* mixed with jasper.

JASPERY, [jas'-per-i], *adj.* resembling, having the qualities of, jasper.

JASPIDEAN†, [jas-pid'-i-an], *adj.* like jasper, consisting of jasper, jaspideous. [~L. *iaspis iaspidis* jasper].

JASPIDEOUS, [jas-pid'-i-us], *adj.* jaspidean.

JAUNDICE (1), [jawn'-dis], *n.* a disease due to chronic secretion of bile and a generally disordered liver characterized by yellow pigment forming in the whites of the eyes and under the skin, the patient feeling very weak and sick; (*fig.*) jealousy. [OFr. *jaunice* from L. *galbinus* yellow].

JAUNDICE (2), [jawn'-dis], *v.t.* to cause to become jealous, to distort the power of judgment of. [*Prec.*].

JAUNT (1), [jawnt], *n.* a trip taken for pleasure, a short journey, tour or excursion. [Uncert.].

JAUNT (2), [jawnt], *v.i.* to take a short pleasure trip, to go for a day's outing. [*Prec.*].

JAUNTILY, [jawn'-ti-li], *adv.* in a jaunty manner.

JAUNTINESS, [jawn'-ti-nes], *n.* the quality of being jaunty.

JAUNTING-CAR, [jawn'-ting-kah(r)'], *n.* a low light car, with seats back to back at right angles to the axle, used in Ireland.

JAUNTY, [jawn'-ti], *adj.* expressing or feeling free and easy confidence, sprightly in bearing.

JAUP, [jawp], *v.t.* (*Scots*) to dash and splash back, to bespatter with water or mud. [Uncert.].

JAVANESE (1), [jah'-van-ēz], *n.* a native of Java, or the language.

JAVANESE (2), [jah'-van-ēz'], *adj.* relating to Java.

JAVELIN, [jav'-el-in], *n.* a short light spear with a barbed head, a dart. [Fr. *javeline*].

JAW (1), [jaw], *n.* the bones in which the teeth are fixed; the mouth; anything like the jaw, such as a crushing or gripping device in machinery; (*naut.*) the inner end of a boom or gaff; (*slang*) talk, continuous talking; (*coll.*) formal reproof not respected as being without vigour. [Uncert.].

JAW (2), [jaw], *v.t. and i.* (*slang*) to reprove, to scold, to lecture; to talk rapidly, to be garrulous, to hold forth. [*Prec.*].

JAWBONE, [jaw'-bōn], *n.* one of the bones of the

jaw containing the teeth and forming the framework of the mouth. [JAW (1) and BONE].

JAWBREAKER, [jaw'-brā'-ker], *n.* (*slang*) a word of difficult pronunciation [JAW (1) and BREAKER].

JAWED, [jawd], *adj.* having a form like the jaws, having jaws.

JAW-LEVER, [jaw'-lē'-ver], *n.* an instrument for forcing open the mouth and administering medicine to cattle. [JAW (1) and LEVER].

JAWROPE, [jaw'-rōp], *n.* (*naut.*) the rope that secures the jaws of the gaff to the mast. [JAW (1) and ROPE (1)].

JAY, [jā], *n.* a chattering bird of the crow family, *Garrulus glandarius*; (*fig.*) a loose woman, a harlot. [OFr. *jaie* from MedL. *gaius*].

JAY

JAZERANT, see JESSERANT.

JAZZ (1), [jaz], *n.* syncopated ragtime music being a loose form of composition usually consisting of sixteen or thirty-two bars derived from negro spirituals and developed in a popular form as an accompaniment for dancing during the war of 1914-18. [U.S. *jazz*].

JAZZ (2), [jaz], *adj.* relating to, consisting of, jazz.

JAZZ (3), [jaz], *v.t.* to dance to jazz music; to transcribe into a syncopated form.

JAZZY, [jaz'-i], *adj.* resembling, having the characteristics of, jazz.

JEALOUS, [jel'-us], *adj.* experiencing feelings of envy and enmity towards another person who is believed to be damaging one's importance or to be usurping objects or affections or spoiling one's success; afraid of and hostile to a rival in love or friendship; envious; eagerly vigilant, solicitous. [OFr. *gelos* from LL. *zelosus* zealous].

JEALOUSLY, [jel'-us-li], *adv.* in a jealous manner, with jealousy.

JEALOUSNESS, [jel'-us-nes], *n.* the state of being jealous.

JEALOUSY, [jel'-us-i], *n.* the emotional condition aroused by the envious and hostile recognition of another's success in matters in which personal success is desired; eager vigilance. [OFr. *gelosie*].

JEAMES†, [jēmz], *n.* a flunky, footman, or lackey of the old style. [A satirical form of the name *James*, given to a footman by Thackeray].

JEAN, [jēn], *n.* a twilled cotton cloth; (*pl.*) overalls. [ME. *Gene* Genoa].

JEDCOCK, [jed'-kok'], *n.* the jack-snipe.

JEDDART, [jed'-aht], *n.* rough justice, so called after the custom obtaining at Jedburgh, Scotland, where a criminal was hanged first and tried afterwards.

JEEP, [jēp], *n.* (*U.S.*) a small high-powered open military car used for transport of personnel, etc. [G.P. initials of *general purpose* car].

JEER (1), [jēr], *n.* a sneering remark; derision, mockery.

JEER (2), [jēr], *v.t. and i.* to make rude and contemptuous remarks, to sneer at someone, to mock derisively. [Unkn.].

JEERER, [jēer'-er], *n.* a person who jeers, a scoffer, a railer.

JEERING, [jēer'-ing], *adj.* mocking, derisive.

JEERINGLY [jē'-ring-li], *adv.* in a jeering manner.

JEFFERSONITE, [jef'-er-son-īt'], *n.* a dark-green foliated variety of augite. [*Jefferson*, U.S. President, 1801-1809].

JEHAD, JIHAD, [ji-hahd'], *n.* a holy war waged by Mohammedans against unbelievers; (*fig.*) a crusade for or against a doctrine. [Arab. *jehad* war].

JEHOVAH, [ji-hō'-va], *n.* the God of Israel, Yahweh, the name given to God by the Old Testament writers. [Heb. *Yahweh* God].

JEHOVIST, [ji-hō'-vist], *n.* the author of the Jehovistic portion of the Old Testament. [*Prec.*].

JEHOVISTIC, [ji'-hō-vis'-tik], *adj.* relating to, containing the name, Jehovah.

JEHU, [jē'-hew], *n.* a skilful or reckless driver. [2 Kings, ix, 20].

JEJUNE, [ji-jewn'], *adj.* empty, void of interest; meagre, barren, unproductive. [L. *jejunus* barren].

JEJUNELY, [ji-jewn'-li], *adv.* in a jejune manner.

JEJUNENESS, [ji-jewn'-nes], *n.* the quality of being jejune.

JEJUNUM, [ji-jōōn'-um], *n.* (*anat.*) the small intestine between the duodenum and the ileum, because it is said to be found nearly empty after death. [JEJUNE].

JELL, [jel], *v.i.* (of jelly) to set.

JELLIED, [jel'-id], *adj.* brought to the consistency of jelly; thickened with jelly; prepared in or with jelly.

JELLIFY, [jel'-if-i], *v.t.* to make into a jelly; *v.i.* to become gelatinous.

JELLY, [jel'-i], *n.* an edible substance of uniform colour and consistency obtained either by boiling animal matter such as bones and flesh in water, straining and allowing the liquid to cool, or by boiling down fruit and sugar and allowing the juice when strained to cool. [~L. *gelatum*, *p.pt.* of *gelare* to freeze].

JELLYBAG, [jel'-i-bag'], *n.* the conical bag through which jelly is strained. [JELLY and BAG].

JELLYFISH, [jel'-i-fish], *n.* a sea animal, formless almost colourless and slow in the water, a medusa or similar animal resembling a jelly in consistency and transparency. [JELLY and FISH].

JELLYGRAPH, [jel'-i-graf], *n.* a duplicating machine using a tray of rubbery jelly. [JELLY and Gk. *graphia* writing].

JEMADAR, [jem'-a-dah(r)'], *n.* a native lieutenant in the Indian army. [Pers. *jama* aggregate and *dar* holder].

JEMMY† (1), [jem'-i], *adj.* smart, spruce, well dressed. [~The personal name *James* or *Jimmy*].

JEMMY (2), JIMMY, [jem'-i], *n.* a small crowbar used by burglars; a baked sheep's head. [*Var.* of *James*].

JENNET, GENET, GENNET, [jen'-it], *n.* a small Spanish horse; the offspring of a stallion and a female donkey. [OFr. *genette*].

JENNETING, [jen'-it-ing], *n.* a species of early apple. [Fr. *Jeannet*].

JENNY, [jen'-i], *n.* a machine for spinning which takes a number of threads simultaneously; (*billiards*) a losing hazard in which the object ball is situated near the side cushion on the same side of the table into which the cue ball goes. [*Jenny*, a woman's name].

JENTLING, [jent'-ling], *n.* the blue chub, a species of *Leuciscus* found in the Danube.

JEMMY

JEOFAIL†, [jef-āl'], *n.* (*leg.*) a recognized oversight in pleading or other proceeding. [AFr. *jeo fail* I make a mistake].

JEOPARDER, [jep'-er-der], *n.* person who dares danger.

JEOPARDIZE, [jep'-er-dīz], *v.t.* to expose to jeopardy, to place in danger.

JEOPARDOUS†, [jep'-er-dus], *adj.* exposed to danger.

JEOPARDOUSLY†, [jep'-er-dus-li], *adv.* with risk.

JEOPARDY, [jep'-er-di], *n.* exposure to loss or injury, peril, danger. [OFr. *jeu parti* even game].

JEQUIRITY, [ji-kwi'-ri-ti], *n.* an Indian shrub, *Abrus precatorius*, the red and black seeds of which are used in medicine and as beads. [SAmer. *jekiriti*].

JERBOA, [jer-bō'-a], *n.* a small African rodent, *Dipus jaculus*, having long hind legs. [Arab. *yarbu* loins].

JERBOA

JEREMIAD, [jer'-i-mī'-ad], *n.* lamentation or complaining tirade, specially over supposed modern decadence. [*Jeremiah*, the name of the Hebrew prophet].

JERFALCON, see GERFALCON

JERID, [je-rēd'], *n.* a blunt javelin used for practice and at tournaments in the Near East. [Arab. *jarid*].

JERK (1), [jurk], *n.* a sharp quick pull or tug, a sudden brief movement, a jolt; a brief sharp contraction of a muscle, a nervous twitch or spasm. [Unkn.].

JERK (2), [jurk], *v.t. and i.* to perform any action with a jerk, to give a sudden sharp pull, twitch, or jolt to; to progress in jolts and jerks.

JERKED, [jurkt], *adj.* cut into strips or pieces, as beef, and dried in the sun. [Peruvian *ccharqui* cured meat].

JERKER, [jurk'-er], *n.* a person who strikes with a quick, smart blow; (*U.S.*) a shaker.

JERKILY, [jurk'-i-li], *adv.* in a jerky manner.

JERKIN (1), [jurk'-in], *n.* a man's leather jacket; a short waistcoat cut close to the body. [Uncert.].

JERKIN (2), [jurk'-in], *n.* the male of the gerfalcon species.

JERKINESS, [jurk'-i-nes], *n.* the quality of being jerky.

JERKY, [jurk'-i], *adj* characterized by jerks.

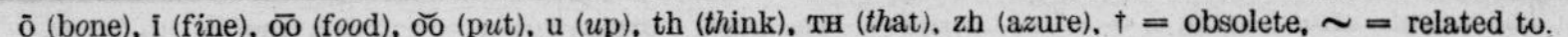

JEROBOAM, [je'-ro-bō'-am], *n.* a large metal bowl; a large earthenware bottle for holding wine; a large bottle of champagne. [Heb. *Jeroboam* strong man].

JERQUER†, [jurk'-er], *n.* a clerk in the customs. [Uncert.].

JERQUING†, [jurk'-ing], *n.* the searching of a ship by a customs officer.

JERRY (1), **GERRY**, [je'-ri], *n.* (*slang*) a German soldier or airman.

JERRY (2), **GERRY**, [je'-ri], *n.* (*slang*) a chamber pot. [Short form of *Jeremiah*].

JERRY-BUILDER, [je'-ri-bil'-der], *n.* an unscrupulous builder of cheap, ugly, insubstantial houses with poor material.

JERSEY, [jur'-zi], *n.* one of the Channel Islands; a close-fitting, knitted jacket or jumper; a Jersey cow.

JERUSALEM ARTICHOKE, [jer-ōō'-sal-em-ah'-ti-chōk], *n.* a sunflower, *Helianthus tuberosus*, or its edible root. [It. *girasole* sunflower].

JERUSALEM PONY, [jer-ōō'-sal-em-pō'-ni], *n.* (*slang*) a donkey.

JERVIN, [jur'-vin], *n.* an alkaloid extracted from the root of white hellebore, *Veratrum album*. [Sp. *jervin*].

JESS, [jes], *n.* a short strap round the legs of a hawk, whereby it is held and let fly. [OFr. *ges*].

JESSAMINE, see JASMINE.

JESSAMY, [jes'-am-i], *adj.* resembling jasmine in perfume. [~JASMINE].

JESSE, [jes'-i], *n.* a large branching candlestick used in churches, so called from its spreading out like the genealogical tree of Jesse; a stained glass window representing Jesse's pedigree. [*Jesse*, the father of David].

JESSED, [jest], *adj.* (*her.*) with jesses on.

JESSERANT, **JAZERANT**, [jes'-er-ant], *n.* a jacket armoured with thin slips of steel sewn on to the canvas and stitched inside the garment. [OFr. *jesserant*].

JEST (1), [jest], *n.* a joke; raillery, banter; some act intended to excite laughter; **in j.**, not in earnest. [L. *gesta* deeds].

JEST (2), [jest], *v.i.* to make jokes; not to be in earnest. [*Prec.*].

JEST-BOOK, [jest'-bŏŏk], *n.* a book composed of jests.

JESTER, [jest'-er], *n.* a person who jests; †a teller of heroic stories, †an attendant in absurd livery kept for making jests.

JESTFUL, [jest'-fŏŏl], *adj.* full of jests; given to jesting.

JESTING, [jest'-ing], *adj.* that jests.

JESTINGLY, [jest'-ing-li], *adv.* in jest.

JESTING-STOCK, [jest'-ing-stok'], *n.* a laughing-stock.

JESUIT, [jes'-yōō-it], *n.* a member of the Society of Jesus, founded by Ignatius Loyola in 1534; (*coll.*) a crafty person, an intriguer, a casuist; **Jesuit's bark**, cinchona; **Jesuit's drops**, friar's balsam. [Fr. *Jésuite*].

JESUITED, [jez'-yōō-it-id], *adj.* of Jesuit principles.

JESUITESS, [jez'-yōō-it-es'], *n.* one of an order of nuns established on the principles of the Jesuits, suppressed by Pope Urban VIII.

JESUITIC, [jez'-yōō-it'-ik], *adj.* Jesuitical.

JESUITICAL, [jez'-yōō-it'-ik-al], *adj.* of, or pertaining to, the Jesuits; (*coll.*) crafty, prevaricating, cunning, designing.

JESUITICALLY, [jez'-yōō-it'-ik-al-i], *adv.* in a Jesuitical manner.

JESUITISM, [jez'-yōō-it-izm], *n.* the principles and practices of the Jesuits; craftiness, intrigue, cunning.

JESUITRY, [jez'-yōō-it-ri], *n.* Jesuitism.

JESUS, [jē'-zus], *n.* a Jewish personal name, given to the second person of the Trinity; an outsize in paper; **the Society of J.**, the Jesuits.

JET (1), [jet], *n.* a hard, black, velvety form of lignite; a set of beads or ornaments of it; a deep glossy black. [OFr. *jaiet*].

JET (2), [jet], *n.* a single column of liquid or gas forced from a narrow opening; a spirt; any narrow passage through which liquid or gas is forced. [~JET (4)].

JET (3), [jet], *adj.* of jet, of a jet-black colour. [JET (1)].

JET (4), [jet], *v.t.* and *i.* to emit in a single stream; to spurt. [Fr. *jeter*].

JET-BLACK, [jet'-blak'], *adj.* of the colour of jet, the deepest, purest black.

JETSAM, [jet'-sam], *n.* goods thrown overboard to lighten a vessel in distress; such goods washed up; **flotsam and j.**, articles washed ashore; (*fig.*) the waifs and strays of society. [~JETTISON].

JETTEE†, see JETTY.

JETTINESS, [jet'-i-nes], *n.* the quality of being jet-black.

JETTISON, [jet'-is-on], *v.t.* to throw goods overboard so as to lighten a ship; (*fig.*) to forgo, abandon. [~AFr. *getteson*].

JETTON, [jet'-on], *n.* a counter; a brass check. [OFr. *jeton* from *jeter* to throw].

JETTY (1), **JETTEE**†, [jet'-i], *n.* a small pier; a projection. [OFr. *getee*].

JETTY (2), [jet'-i], *adj.* made of jet; jet-black.

JEW (1), [jōō], *n.* a member of the Hebrew branch of the Semitic race; (*slang*) a shamelessly extortionate bargainer. [OFr. *giu*].

JEW (2), [jōō], *v.t.* (*coll.*) to cheat, outwit, dupe. [*Prec.*].

JEW-BAITING, [jōō'-bā'-ting], *n.* goading and persecution of Jews.

JEWEL (1), [jōō'-el], *n.* an ornament of dress, usually containing a precious stone; a precious stone; anything highly valued or dear to one; (*naut.*) **j. blocks**, two small blocks, suspended at the extremity of the main and foretopsail yards; **j. case**, a casket or safe for holding jewels. [AFr. *jouel*].

JEWEL (2), [jōō'-el], *v.t.* to adorn or set with jewels; (*fig.*) to decorate brightly. [*Prec.*].

JEWEL-BOX, [jōō'-el-boks'], *n.* a small lined box or nest of boxes or drawers for keeping jewels.

JEWEL-HOUSE, [jōō'-el-hows'], *n.* a number of rooms in the Wakefield Tower of the Tower of London where the Crown Jewels are kept.

JEWELLER, [jōō'-el-er], *n.* one who deals in or sets jewels.

JEWELLER'S PUTTY, [jōō'-el-erz-put'-i], *n.* oxide of tin.

JEWELLERY, **JEWELRY**, [jōō'-el-ri], *n.* jewels in general; the jewel trade.

JEWEL-LIKE, [jōō'-el-lik'], *adj.* resembling a jewel; brilliant.

JEWELRY, see JEWELLERY.

JEWESS, [jōō'-es], *n.* a woman of the Hebrew race.

JEWFISH, [jew'-fish], *n.* one of various edible exotic fish, *esp.* of the *Serranidae*. [JEW (1) and FISH (1)].

JEWISH, [jōō'-ish], *adj.* of, or pertaining to, a Jew or to Jewry.

JEWISHLY, [jōō'-ish-li], *adv.* in the manner of a Jew.

JEWISHNESS, [jōō'-ish-nes], *n.* the condition of being Jewish.

JEWRY, [jōōer'-i], *n.* the land of the Jews; the district inhabited by the Jews in a town, the ghetto; the Jews collectively; the Jewish religion. [AFr. *juerie*].

JEW'S-EAR, [jōōz'-ēer], *n.* (*bot.*) a kind of edible fungus shaped like an ear.

JEW'S-HARP, [jōōz'-hahp'], *n.* a small harp-shaped musical instrument, with a spring or metal tongue, which, if placed between the teeth, and struck by the finger, gives modulated sounds.

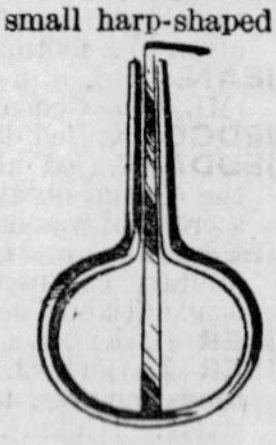

JEW'S-HARP

JEW'S-MALLOW, [jōōz'-mal'-ō], *n.* a plant, *Corcorus capsularis*, grown in abundance about Aleppo, and used as a pot-herb.

JEW'S-MYRTLE, [jōōz'-murtl'], *n.* the butcher's broom, *Ruscus aculeatus*.

JEZEBEL, [jez'-i-bel], *n.* name of the infamous queen of Ahab, king of Israel; a vicious temptress; **painted J.**, a vicious woman, who is superficially respectable and artificially beautiful. [*Jezebel*, wife of Ahab].

JEZHAIL, see JUZAIL.

JHEEL, [jēl], *n.* lake, pond. [Hind. *jhil*].

JIB (1), [jib], *n.* (*naut.*) the foremost sail of a ship, extending from the outer end of the jib-boom; the extended arm of a crane; **flying-j.**, a sail sometimes set upon a boom rigged out beyond the jib-boom; **middle j.**, a similar sail set between the jib and flying-jib. [Uncert.].

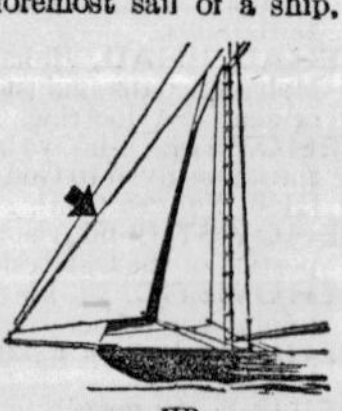
JIB

JIB (2), [jib], *v.t.* and *i.* (of a jib) to swing over, to pull round in tacking. [*Prec.*].

JIB (3), [jib], *v.i.* to stop, (of a horse) to shy; to move restively back and forth; (*fig.*) **to j. at**, to hesitate at, raise objections to. [*Prec.*].

JIBBER, [jib'-er], *n.* a horse that jibs.

JIB-BOOM, [jib'-bōōm'], *n.* (*naut.*) the continuation

of the bowsprit; **flying j.**, a boom extended beyond the jib-boom by means of two boom irons.

JIB-DOOR, [jib′-daw(er)], *n.* a door that stands flush with the wall, without dressings or mouldings.

JIBE, [jib], *v.t. and i.* to taunt, sneer, make unkind fun of. [~GIBE].

JIB-HEADER, [jib′-hed′-er], *n.* (*naut.*) a triangular fore-and-aft topsail.

JIBOYA, [jib-ō′-ya], *n.* a large South American boa-constrictor. [Braz. *jiboya*].

JIB-TOPSAIL, [jib-topsl′], *n.* (*naut.*) the headsail in fore-and-aft vessels which extends between the topmast head and the end of the jib-boom.

JICKAJOG, [jik′-a-jog′], *n.*(*coll.*) a push, jog. [Symbol].

JIFFY, [jif′-i], *n.* (*coll.*) a very short space of time.

JIG (1), [jig], *n.* a brisk dance or tune, usually in 6/8 time. [Fr. *gigue*].

JIG (2), [jig], *n.* a guide for a machine or other tool in repetitive work. [Unkn.].

JIG (3), [jig], *v.t.* to jerk; *v.i.* to dance a jig; to move jerkily. [JIG (1)].

JIGGER (1), [jig′-er], *n.* a person who dances jigs; a potter's wheel; a miner who cleans ore in a sieve; a machine for holding the cable when it is hauled into the ship by the windlass; (*naut.*) a small mizen abaft the sternpost; (*coll.*) any small mechanical device; (*golf*) iron-headed club.

JIGGER (2), [jig′-er], *n.* the sand-flea, a minute insect which lays its eggs underneath the skin of men and animals. [~CHIGOE].

JIGGERED, [jig′-erd], *adj.* suffering from the burrowing of the jigger; (*coll.*) worn out, spoilt, broken.

JIGGERY-POKERY, [jig′-er-i-pō′-ker-i], *n.* (*coll.*) humbug, underhand scheming, wire pulling. [Unkn.].

JIGGING, [jig′-ing], *n.* the dancing of jigs; (*mining*) the process of sorting ore by passing it through a wire-bottomed sieve.

JIGGISH, [jig′-ish], *adj.* in a jig-like manner, light, frivolous.

JIGGLE, [jigl], *v.t. and i.* to move up and down. [~JIG (1)].

JIG-JOG, [jig′-jog′], *n.* a jolting motion; a jog-trot. [~JOG].

JIG-MAKER, [jig′-mā′-ker], *n.* one who makes jigs.

JIG-SAW, [jig′-saw], *n.* a saw for cutting fretwork; **j. puzzle**, a picture pasted on thin board and cut into interlocking pieces to be fitted into one another.

JIHAD, see JEHAD.

JILL, [jil], *n.* (*coll.*) a young woman. [*Jill*, a female name].

JILLET, [jil′-et], *n.* a flirt; a jilt. [~JILL].

JILL-FLIRT, [jil′-flurt], *n.* a light, frivolous young woman; a flirt.

JILT (1), [jilt], *n.* a young woman who dismisses her lover; a coquette. [~JILLET].

JILT (2), [jilt], *v.t.* to discard a lover. [*Prec.*].

JIM CROW, [jim′-krō′], *n.* (*U.S.*) (*coll.*) a negro; a lookout appointed to watch for the approach of hostile aircraft. [*Jim, dim.* of James, and CROW (1)].

JIM-JAMS, [jim′-jamz], *n.* (*coll.*) depression; delirium tremens. [Unkn.].

JIMMY, see JEMMY (2).

JIMP, GIMP, [jimp], *adj.* neat, elegant in shape; handsome; scanty in measure. [Uncert.].

JIMSON, [jim′-son], *n.* (*bot.*) (*U.S.*) the thorn-apple, *Datura Stramonium.* [~*Jamestown* an American place-name].

JINGAL, see GINGAL.

JINGLE (1), GINGLE, [jingl], *n.* a clinking sound, as of little bells or pieces of metal knocking together; that which jingles; a little bell or rattle; correspondence of sound in rhymes; a covered two-wheeled public cart used in the south of Ireland. [Echoic].

JINGLE (2), GINGLE, [jingl], *v.t.* to cause to jingle; *v.i.* to sound like a jingle. [*Prec.*].

JINGO, [jing′-gō], *n.* an exclamation of surprise; anyone who advocates a warlike policy or brags of his country's readiness to fight. [Uncert.].

JINGOISM, [jing′-gō-izm], *n.* militaristic spirit.

JINGOISTIC, [jing-gō-ist′-ik], *adj.* expressing or resembling jingoism.

JINK, [jink], *n.* the act of turning quickly; **high jinks**, merrymaking. [Unkn.].

JINN, [jin], *n.* a demon; a sprite of Mohammedan demonology. [Arab. *jinn*].

JINRICKSHA, [jin′-rik′-shaw], *n.* a light man-drawn carriage; a rickshaw. [Jap. *jin* man, *riki* power and *sha* car].

JIRGA, [jur′-ga], *n.* an Afghan assembly of head men. [Pushtu *jirga*].

JITNEY, [jit′-ni], *n.* (*U.S. slang*) a five-cent piece; a motor-car running for hire over a certain route. [Unkn.].

JITTERBUG, [jit′-er-bug], *n.* (*coll.*) one who dances to jazz music with spasmodic energy; (*coll.*) an alarmist. [*Next*].

JITTERS, [jit′-erz], *n.*(*pl.*) (*U.S.*) shudderings; a feeling of nervous alarm.

JITTERY, [jit′-er-i], *adj.* panicky; shaking.

JIU-JITSU, see JU-JITSU.

JO, [jō], *n.* a sweetheart, darling. [~JOY].

JOB (1), [job], *n.* a piece of work; anything to be done whether of more or less importance; an undertaking professedly for the public good but really for one's own; occupation, profession, employment, post; **to make a good j. of it**, do a thing well; **j. lots**, odd lots; **odd j.**, an isolated piece of work; **a good j.**, fortunate; **to be on the j.**, (*coll.*) to be doing one's best, to be very busy. [Unkn.].

JOB (2), [job], *v.t.* to use personal influence in public appointments; to hire out; to act as broker in; *v.i.* to undertake small pieces of work, work casually; to act as a small broker; to let or hire. [*Prec.*].

JOB (3), [job], *v.t.* to strike or stab with a sharp instrument. [~JAB].

JOBATION, [jō-bā′-shun], *n.* (*coll.*) a long tedious reproof. [*Job* the Patriarch].

JOBBER, [job′-er], *n.* one who does odd jobs; a dealer in stock-exchange securities; one who uses a public office for private gain.

JOBBERNOWL, [job′-er-nowl′], *n.* (*slang*) a blockhead. [Fr. *jobard* a dupe and OE. *hnol* head].

JOBBERY, [job′-er-i], *n.* intriguing for private profit, *esp.* in public transactions.

JOBBING, [job′-ing], *n.* doing odd jobs.

JOBMASTER, [job′-mah′-ster], *n.* a person who lets out horses and carriages; a livery-stable keeper.

JOB'S COMFORTER, [jōbz′-kum′-fort-er], *n.* a friend whose commiserations serve only to augment one's grief. [Job, xvi, 2].

JOB'S-TEARS, [jōbz′-tēerz], *n.* an Eastern cereal, *Coix lachryma.*

JOCKEY (1), [jok′-i], *n.* the rider of a racehorse; a man trained for that purpose; **J. Club**, the club of owners that controls horseracing; a perfume. [Scots personal name *Jock*].

JOCKEY (2), [jok′-i], *v.t. and i.* to use unfair means, to outwit; to jostle by riding against one; **j.** (a person) **into doing something**, persuade or urge him into it; **to j. for position**, to try to obtain an advantage by questionable means. [*Prec.*].

JOCKEYISM, [jok′-i-izm], *n.* the habits and customs of jockeys.

JOCKEYSHIP, [jok′-i-ship], *n.* the art or practice of the jockey.

JOCKO, [jok′-ō], *n.* the chimpanzee; (*coll.*) a monkey. [Fr. *jocko*].

JOCOSE, [jō-kōs′], *adj.* given to joking; facetious, merry. [L. *jocosus*].

JOCOSELY, [jō-kōs′-li], *adv.* in a merry manner.

JOCOSENESS, [jō-kōs′-nes], *n.* the quality of being jocose; merriness.

JOCULAR, [jok′-yōō-ler], *adj.* given to joking; waggish; merry; bantering; not in earnest. [L. *jocularis*].

JOCULARITY, [jok′-yōō-la′-ri-ti], *n.* merriment, jesting, fun, waggishness.

JOCULARLY, [jok′-yōō-ler-li], *adv.* in a jocular fashion.

JOCULATOR, [jok′-yoo-lā-tor], *n.* a jester or minstrel. [L. *joculator*].

JOCULATORY, [jok′-yōō-lā′-ter-i], *adj.* jocular, droll.

JOCUND, [jok′-und], *adj.* gay, sportive, merry, lighthearted, sprightly. [LL. *jocundus*].

JOCUNDITY, [jok-und′-i-ti], *n.* the condition of being jocund.

JOCUNDLY, [jok′-und-li], *adv.* in a jocund fashion.

JOCUNDNESS, [jok′-und-nes], *n.* the quality of being jocund; jocundity.

JODHPURS, [jod′-perz], *n.*(*pl.*) a kind of tight-legged riding breeches which reach to the ankles. [*Jodhpur* a state in India].

JOEY (1), [jō′-i], *n.* a fourpenny piece. [*Joseph* Hume the philanthropist].

JOEY (2), [jō′-i], *n.* a parrot. [*Joseph*].

JOEY (3), [jō′-i], *n.* a young kangaroo; a young animal or child. [Native Australian *joè.*]

JOG (1), [jog], *n.* a slight, sudden push, often intended to attract the attention; a nudge. [Symbolic].

JOG (2), (**jogging, jogged**), [jog], *v.t.* to give a slight push to, to nudge; (*fig.*) to arouse the attention, to remind; *v.i.* to ride or move at a slow trot; to

proceed slowly; (*fig.*) **to j. along**, to continue steadily with one's way of life or occupation. [*Prec.*].
JOGGER, [jog'-er], *n.* one who, or that which, jogs.
JOGGLE (1), [jogl], *n.* jolt. [~JOG].
JOGGLE (2), [jogl], *n.* (*building, carp.*) a notch in a joint; (*eng.*) a kink or set in sheet metal. [*Prec.*].
JOGGLE (3), [jogl], *v.t.* to jolt, to jar, to shake; to give a sudden slight push to; *v.i.* to shake, to move in jolts. [*Prec.*].
JOGGLE (4), [jogl], *v.t.* to join by the use of a joggle.
JOG-TROT (1), [jog'-trot], *n.* a slow regular pace; (*fig.*) a slow, monotonous but steady progress.
JOG-TROT (2), [jog'-trot], *adj.* at a jog-trot pace; (*fig.*) monotonously regular; humdrum.
JOHANNES, [jō-han'-ez], *n.* an old Portuguese gold coin.
JOHANNINE, [jō-han'-īn], *adj.* pertaining to St. John.
JOHANNISBERGER, [jō-han'-is-burg'-er], *n.* a hock from Johannisberg on the Rhine.
JOHANNITE, [jō'-han-īt], *n.* (*min.*) a sulphate of uranium and copper. [Archduke *Johann*].
JOHN, [jon], *n.* a man's name; **J.-a-dreams**, a dreamy fellow; **J. Barleycorn**, whisky, etc.; **J. Bull**, typical Englishman; **J. Doe**, a proper name used *exempli causa* in legal parlance; **j. dory**, the dory; **J. Collins**, a delectable drink of gin, lemon, and soda. [OFr. *Johan*, Heb. *Yokhanan*]

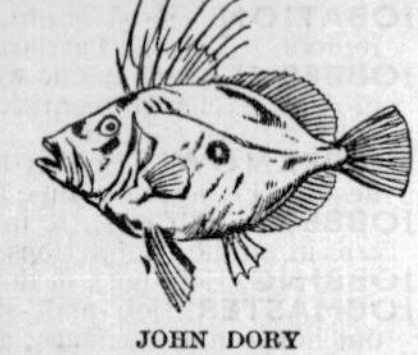
JOHN DORY

JOHNNY, [jon'-i], *n.* (*slang*) a silly but amiable young man.
JOHNSONESE, [jon'-son-ēz'], *n.* a ponderous style of verbal expression. [Dr. Samuel *Johnson*, the eighteenth century lexicographer].
JOHNSONIAN, [jon'-sō'-ni-an], *adj.* pertaining to Dr. Johnson or his style.
JOIE DE VIVRE, [zhwa'-de-vēvr'], *n.* gusto; zest. [Fr. *joie de vivre*].
JOIN (1), [join], *n.* the act of joining; a junction, joint, seam.
JOIN (2), [join], *v.t.* to fasten together; to connect not at one point only but along a whole line of juxtaposition; to unite; to adjoin; (*fig.*) to combine; to unite oneself with; *v.i.* to be in contact, combine; **to j. battle**, to begin the actual fighting, to fight; **to j. forces with**, to unite with; **to j. up**, to enlist in one of the services. [Fr. *joindre* from L. *jungere*].
JOINDER, [join'-der], *n.* the act of joining; (*leg.*) any coupling of two parties in an action. [Fr. *joindre*].
JOINER (1), [join'-er], *n.* a carpenter.
JOINER (2), [join'-er], *v.t. and i.* to practise joinery; to botch up.
JOINERY, [join'-er-i], *n.* the craft or product of a joiner; woodwork.
JOINT (1), [joint] *n.* the place where two or more things join; any constituent part of a jointed whole; a juncture which admits of motion of the parts as in the body or in a machine; a part so joined; the joining of two or more bones, a hinge; one of the parts into which a butcher divides a carcase for cooking purposes; (*geol.*) a fissure dividing rock masses into blocks; (*bot.*), the place at which leaf or branch is joined to the stem; (*U.S. slang*) a low drinking house; any building, house, or institution; **out of j.**, (of a bone) dislocated; (of the times) unhappy, disorderly; **to put one's nose out of j.**, to supplant one in favour of another, to outshine one. [OFr. *joint*].
JOINT (2), [joint], *adj.* shared by two or more.
JOINT (3), [joint], *v.t.* to provide with joints; to unite by joints; to cut or divide a carcase into joints and quarters; to form the edges of boards so that they may fit closely together; to fit closely.
JOINTED, [joint'-id], *adj.* with joints, not in a continuous, unbroken line.
JOINTEDLY, [joint'-id-li], *adv.* connectedly.
JOINTER, [joint'-er], *n.* a plane used by carpenters in making joints; a metal bar for joining stones; a mason's tool used in pointing.
JOINT-HEIR, [joint'-āer], *n.* an heir who has a joint interest with another.
JOINTING, [joint'-ing], *n.* the making of a joint; **j. plane**, a jointer; **j. rule**, a straight edge used by bricklayers for accurate manipulation of the jointer.
JOINTLESS, [joint'-les], *adj.* having no joints.
JOINTLY, [joint'-li], *adv.* together; unitedly; in concert; in conjunction.
JOINTRESS, JOINTURESS, [joint'-res], *n.* a woman who holds a jointure.
JOINT-STOCK, [joint'-stok'], *n.* (*comm.*) stock contributed by a number of people in company; **j. company, j. bank**, a company or bank where the stock is divided into shares which are transferable by each owner without the consent of the other holders.
JOINT-STOOL, [joint'-stōōl], *n.* a stool made up of parts inserted in each other.
JOINT-TENANCY, [joint'-ten'-an-si], *n.* the holding of an estate jointly.
JOINT-TENANT, [joint'-ten'-ant], *n.* a person who owns an estate by joint-tenancy.
JOINTURE, [join'-cher], *n.* (*leg.*) an estate settled on a married woman for her lifetime. [Fr. *jointure*].
JOINTURESS, see JOINTRESS.
JOIST, [joist], *n.* one of the parallel timbers to which the boards of a floor or the laths of a ceiling are fastened. [OFr. *giste*].
JOKE (1), [jōk], *n.* a funny, humorous, or witty phrase, anecdote, or trick, a jest; something not serious or in earnest, done for fun; any thing or person meriting laughter; **no j.**, earnest, a serious matter; **practical j.**, a trick played on a person so as to raise a laugh or to annoy or tease; **to crack a j.**, to make a joke. [L. *jocus*].
JOKE (2), [jōk], *v.i.* to make jokes; to jest, to make fun.
JOKER, [jō'-ker], *n.* one who jokes; a jester; the fifty-third card in a pack used in some games; (*U.S.*) a snag in an act or legal agreement.
JOKESOME, [jōk'-sum], *adj.* characterized by jokes, facetious.
JOKINGLY, [jō'-king-li], *adv.* in a joking manner.
JOLE, [jōl], *n.* jaw, jowl. [~JOWL].
JOLLIFICATION, [jol'-i-fik-ā'-shun], *n.* merry-making; a merry party.
JOLLIFY, [jol'-i-fī], *v.t.* to make merry.
JOLLILY, [jol'-i-li], *adv.* in a jolly fashion.
JOLLINESS, [jol'-i-nes], *n.* the condition of being jolly; jollity.
JOLLITY, [jol'-it-i], *n.* the condition of being jolly; merriment; joviality; revelry. [OFr. *jolite*].
JOLLY (1), [jol'-i], *n.* (*coll.*) a marine.
JOLLY (2), [jol'-i], *adj.* lively, cheerful, gay; full of life and mirth; expressing mirth or inspiring it; plump and cheerful in appearance; fond of jollity; (*coll.*) slightly drunk; splendid, enjoyable, agreeable. [OFr. *joli*].
JOLLY (3), [jol'-i], *adv.* in a jolly fashion, merrily; (*coll.*) extremely, very.
JOLLY (4), [jol'-i], *v.t.* to treat with good humour; (*coll.*) to flatter, cajole; to chaff; to pester; *v.i.* to cheer, make merry. [JOLLY (2)].
JOLLY-BOAT, [jol'-i-bōt'], *n.* (*naut.*) a ship's boat. [Uncert.].
JOLT (1), [jōlt], *n.* a sudden jerk or jar; (*fig.*) a shock, jerk to the mind.
JOLT (2), [jōlt], *v.t.* to shake with sudden jerks, to jar, to jog; *v.i.* to move along bumping. [Unkn.].
JOLTER, [jōlt'-er], *n.* one who, or that which, jolts.
JOLTER-HEAD, [jōlt'-er-hed'], *n.* dunce, dolt. [Unkn.].
JOLTINGLY, [jōlt'-ing-li], *adv.* in a jolting manner.
JONAH, [jō'-na], *n.* the name of a Hebrew prophet; any one who, like him, brings bad luck. [*Jonah*, the Hebrew prophet].
JONATHAN, [jon'-ath-an], *n.* one of a male pair of close friends; a dessert apple. [*Jonathan*, 2 Sam. i, 26].
JONQUIL, [jong'-kwil], *n.* a variety of narcissus. [Fr. *jonquille*, ~L. *juncus* a rush].
JORAM, see JORUM.
JORDAN, [jaw'-dan], *n.* (*coll.*) a chamber-pot. [River *Jordan* in Palestine].
JORDAN ALMOND, [jaw'-dan-ah'-mond], *n.* a fine variety of cultivated almond. [Fr. *jardin* garden and ALMOND].
JORDANITE, [jaw'-dan-īt], *n.* (*chem.*) sulph-arsenate of silver. [Dr. *Jordan*, its discoverer].
JORUM, JORAM, [jaw'-rum], *n.* a large drinking-vessel; a bowl of drink; a large quantity; a dose. [King *Joram*, 2 Kings viii, 16].
JOSEPH, [jō'-zif], *n.* a long, buttoned, riding-woman's cloak with a cape; a thin unsized paper; **J's. coat**, (*bot.*) a cultivated variety of *Amaranthus tricolor* with variegated leaves. [*Joseph*, one of the twelve sons of Jacob, who had a coat of many colours, Genesis xxxvii, 3].
JOSEPH AND MARY, [jō'-zif-and-māer'-i], *n.* (*bot.*)

the lungwort. [St. *Joseph*, husband of the Virgin *Mary*].

JOSH, [josh], *n.* (*slang*) a hoax. [Unkn.].

JOSS, [jos], *n.* a Chinese idol. [Portug. *deos* god, L. *deus*].

JOSS-BLOCK, [jos'-blok'], *n.* (*dial.*) a block used for mounting a horse. [Unkn.].

JOSSER, [jos'-er], *n.* (*slang*) a fellow, an old or peculiar person. [Unkn.].

JOSS-HOUSE, [jos'-hows'], *n.* a Chinese temple. [JOSS and HOUSE].

JOSS-STICK, [jos'-stik], *n.* a thin odoriferous stick which the Chinese burn before their idols.

JOSTLE (1), [josl], *n.* a rough push, such as one gets in a crowd; a jog.

JOSTLE (2), [josl], *v.t. and i.* to push against, to elbow, hustle. [~JOUST].

JOT (1), [jot], *n.* an iota, a tittle, a negligible quantity. [Gk. *iota* the letter *i*].

JOT (2), [jot], *v.t.* to make a written note of. [*Prec.*].

JOTTING, [jot'-ing], *n.* a brief note.

JOTUN, [yot'-un], *n.* one of a race of giants in Scandinavian mythology. [ONorse *jotunn*].

JOULE, [jowl], *n.* (*phys.*) the electrical unit of work. [Dr. *Joule*, an English physicist].

JOULEMETER, [jowl'-mē'-ter], *n.* (*phys.*) a meter for measuring in joules.

JOUNCE, [jownts], *v.t. and i.* to jolt. [Unkn.].

JOURNAL, [jurn'-al], *n.* a daily record of events: a diary, a day-book; the book in which this record is kept; a daily newspaper; any periodical or magazine; (*mech.*) the neck of the bearing portion of the shaft in machinery; a passage or small conduit in the interior of a piece of machinery. [OFr. *jornal* from L. *diurnalis*].

JOURNAL

JOURNALESE, [jur'-nal-ēz'], *n.* a style of writing such as occurs in journals, highly coloured, loose, and full of stock phrases. [*Prec.*].

JOURNALISM, [jur'-nal-izm], *n.* the keeping of a journal; writing for journals; the profession of producing journals.

JOURNALIST, [jur'-nal-ist], *n.* the writer of a journal or diary; one who writes for or edits a journal.

JOURNALISTIC, [jur'-nal-ist-'ik], *adj.* pertaining to, or resembling, journals or journalism.

JOURNALIZE, [jur'-nal-iz], *v.t.* to record in a journal; *v.i.* to write a diary; to be a journalist.

JOURNEY (1), [jur'-ni], *n.* a route or the traversing of a route from one place to another; the round of a commercial traveller or delivery van. [OFr. *jornee* day's work].

JOURNEY (2), [jur'-ni], *v.i.* to travel, usually for some considerable distance or with some difficulty. [*Prec.*].

JOURNEYER, [jurn'-i-er], *n.* one who journeys, a traveller.

JOURNEYMAN, [jur'-ni-man], *n.* †a workman hired from day to day and no longer bound to serve for years; an artisan who has learnt his craft; an indifferent performer.

JOURNEY-WEIGHT, [jur'-ni-wāt], *n.* fifteen pounds' weight of coined gold or sixty pounds' weight of coined silver.

JOURNEY-WORK, [jur'-ni-wurk'], *n.* work done by a journeyman.

JOUST (1), [jowst], *n.* an encounter, properly a tournament; a festivity.

JOUST (2), [jowst], *v.i.* to engage in a joust, to tilt; to be festive. [OFr. *juster* from L. *juxtare* to approach].

JOVE, [jōv], *n.* a name of Jupiter, the supreme deity of the Romans; (*coll.*) **by J.!** (*to register surprise*) good gracious! [L. *Jovis* Jupiter].

JOVIAL, [jō'-vi-al], *adj.* cheerful, merry (so used because of the supposed influence of the planet Jupiter). [*Prec.*].

JOVIALIST†, [jō'-vi-al-ist], *n.* one of jovial temperament.

JOVIALITY, [jō'-vi-al'-i-ti], *n.* the condition of being jovial.

JOVIALLY, [jō'-vi-al-i], *adv.* in a jovial fashion.

JOVIALNESS, [jō'-vi-al-nes], *n.* the quality of being jovial; conviviality.

JOVIAN, [jō'-vi-an], *adj.* pertaining to Jove or to the planet Jupiter; god-like, majestic. [~JOVE].

JOWL, [jowl], *n.* the cheek; the jaw; a heavy and pendulous chin; the head of a fish; **cheek by j.**, close together, head to head. [OE. *ceafl* jaw].

JOWLER, [jow'-ler], *n.* a hunting dog with a large jowl.

JOY (1), [joi], *n.* a feeling of quiet continuous exaltation, inward happiness; gladness, exhilaration, delight; an object promoting such a feeling; **a j. ride**, a ride for pleasure. [OFr. *joie* from L. *gaudium* joy].

JOY (2), [joi], *v.t.* to give happiness to, to gladden; *v.i.* to rejoice, be glad, exult. [OFr. *joir* from L. *gaudere* rejoice].

JOYANCE, [joi'-ants], *n.* (*poet.*) gaiety. [~JOY].

JOY-BELLS, [joi'-belz'], *n.*(*pl.*) church bells rung to celebrate some happy event.

JOYFUL, [joi'-fōōl], *adj.* full of joy, happy, glad; bringing joy.

JOYFULLY, [joi'-fōōl-i], *adv.* in a joyful fashion.

JOYFULNESS, [joi'-fōōl-nes], *n.* the state of being joyful; great gladness.

JOYLESS, [joi'-les], *adj.* miserable; causing misery.

JOYLESSLY, [joi'-les-li], *adv.* in a joyless manner.

JOYLESSNESS, [joi'-les-nes], *n.* the state of being miserable.

JOYOUS, [joi'-us], *adj.* joyful, giving joy, gay. [AFr. *joyous*].

JOYOUSLY, [joi'-us-li], *adv.* in a joyous fashion.

JOYOUSNESS, [joi'-us-nes], *n.* the condition of being joyous.

JOYSTICK, [joi'-stik], *n.* the control lever of an aeroplane.

JUBA, [jōō'-ba], *n.* a kind of negro dance accompanied by clapping of hands, striking of the thighs and singing a refrain in which the word *Juba* occurs frequently. [Negro *juba*].

JUBATE, [jōō'-bāt], *n.* (*zool.*) having a mane or fringe of hair. [L. *jubatus*].

JUBE, jubé, [jōō'-bā], *n.* (*eccles.*) a rood-loft. [L. *Jube*, first word of prayer said from the rood-loft before the reading of the gospel].

JUBILANT, [jōō'-bil-ant], *adj.* rejoicing, uttering sounds of triumph, exultant. [~L. *jubilans*].

JUBILATION, [jōō'-bil-ā'-shun], *n.* triumphant rejoicing; exultation. [L. *jubilatio*].

JUBILEE, [jōō'-bil-ē], *n.* a festival of emancipation among the Jews proclaimed by the sound of a trumpet and held every fifty years to commemorate their deliverance out of Egypt; (*eccles.*) a year of plenary indulgence celebrated every twenty-fifth year at Rome or at times specially appointed; any festive season or occasion; fiftieth anniversary of a notable event; **silver j.**, twenty-fifth anniversary; **diamond j.** sixtieth anniversary, *esp.* of Queen Victoria's commemoration in 1897. [L. *jubilaeus* (*annus*) year of jubilee, ~Heb. *yobel* ram's horn trumpet].

JUDAIC, [jōō-dā'-ik], *adj.* Jewish. [Gk. *Ioudaikos*].

JUDAICAL, [jōō-dā'-ik-al], *adj.* pertaining to the Jews.

JUDAICALLY, [jōō-dā'-ik-al-i], *adv.* in the manner of the Jews.

JUDAISM, [jōō'-dā-izm], *n.* Jewish religion and its practices; (*hist.*) special revenue paid by Jews. [Gk. *Ioudaios* a Jew].

JUDAIZATION, [jōō'-dā-iz-ā'-shun], *n.* the act of judaizing.

JUDAIZE, [jōō'-dā-iz], *v.t.* to convert to Judaism; to overrun with Jews or Jewish ideas; *v.i.* to conform to Jewish doctrines and modes of thought and action.

JUDAIZER, [jōō'-dā-iz-er], *n.* one who promotes Judaism or turns Jew.

JUDAS, [jōō'-das], *n.* an abominable traitor. [*Judas*, the disciple who betrayed Christ].

JUDAS-HOLE, [jōō'-das-hōl'], *n.* a peep-hole.

JUDAS-TREE, [jōō'-das-trē'], *n.* (*bot.*) a leguminous tree, *Cercis siliquastrum*, traditionally the tree on which Judas hanged himself.

JUDCOCK, [jud'-kok'], *n.* the jack-snipe. [Unkn.].

JUDGE (1), [juj], *n.* an officer of the crown appointed to preside over a court of justice and to hear and decide causes, civil or criminal; an arbiter, a person chosen to settle a dispute; one competent to appreciate, and to decide merit or worth in any given direction; person appointed to estimate success in a competition or contest. [Fr. *juge* from L. *judex*].

JUDGE (2), [juj], *v.t.* to hear and determine a case in a law-court; to examine and pass sentence on; to try; to pass severe sentence upon; to reckon; to consider; *v.i.* to act the judge; to pass sentence; to distinguish; to consider. [Fr. *juger* from L. *judicare*].

JUDGE-ADVOCATE, [juj'-ad'-vōk-at], *n.* (*leg.*) a legal official acting at a court-martial.

JUDGE-MADE, [juj'-mād], *adj.* (*leg.*) based on previous interpretations of statute law.
JUDGEMENT, see JUDGMENT.
JUDGER, [juj'-er], *n.* one who judges or estimates or who is qualified to do so.
JUDGESHIP, [juj'-ship], *n.* the office or function of a judge.
JUDGMENT, JUDGEMENT, [juj'-ment], *n.* a judging; the legal sentence of a judge; a divinely inflicted penalty; the ultimate trial of the human race by God; any authoritative decision; criticism, censure; personal capacity for sound discrimination; discernment, appreciation. [OFr. *jugement*].
JUDGMENT DAY, [juj'-ment-dā'], *n.* the last day, doomsday.
JUDGMENT DEBT, [juj'-ment-det'], *n.* a security debt, legalized by the order of a judge, under which execution can be issued at any time.
JUDGMENT-HALL, [juj'-ment-hawl'], *n.* a hall in which courts of justice are held.
JUDGMENT-SEAT, [juj'-ment-sēt'], *n.* the seat of a judge; judgeship; tribunal.
JUDICA, [jōō'-dik-a], *n.* Passion Sunday, the fifth Sunday in Lent; (*R.C.*) the service on that day which begins with the Latin words *Judica me*.
JUDICABLE, [jōō'-dik-abl], *adj.* able to be tried and judged.
JUDICATIVE, [jōō'-dik-at-iv], *adj.* capable of judging.
JUDICATORY, [jōō'-dik-āt'-er-i], *n.* a court; a body of judges; a judicial system. [LL. *judicatorius*].
JUDICATURE, [jōō'-dik-a-cher], *n.* the power of jurisdiction; the body of judges or the judicial system of a country. [MedL. *judicatura*].
JUDICIAL, [jōō-dish'-al], *adj.* pertaining to judgment or courts of justice; judge-like. [L. *judicialis*].
JUDICIALLY, [jōō-dish'-al-i], *adv.* in a judicial manner.
JUDICIARY (1), [jōō-dish'-er-i], *n.* the judges collectively; that department of government which is concerned in the trial and determination of causes.
JUDICIARY (2), [jōō-dish'-er-i], *adj.* judicial; of, or pertaining to, a court of law. [L. *judiciarius*].
JUDICIOUS, [jōō-dish'-us], *adj.* having or exercising sound judgment, wise, discerning; well-timed; clever. [Fr. *judicieux*].
JUDICIOUSLY, [jōō-dish'-us-li], *adv.* in a judicious fashion.
JUDICIOUSNESS, [jōō-dish'-us-nes], *n.* the quality of being judicious; discrimination; habit of acting only after due consideration.
JUDO, [jōō'-dō], *n.* an advanced form of ju-jitsu. [Jap. *judo*].
JUDY, [jōō'-di], *n.* the traditional wife of Punch, the puppet; (*slang*) a woman. [*Judy*, a woman's name].
JUG (1), [jug], *n.* any deep pouring vessel; (*slang*) **stone j.**, prison; **in j.**, in gaol. [Unkn.].
JUG (2), [jug], *n.* a bird's note. [Echoic].
JUG (3), [jug], *v.t.* to stew in a covered jar, *esp.* a hare; (*slang*) to put into gaol. [JUG (1)].
JUGAL, [jōō'-gal], *adj.* (*anat.*) pertaining to the cheek. [L. *jugalis*].
JUGATE, [jōō'-gāt], *adj.* jugated. [L. *jugatum*, *p.pt.* of *jugare* to join together].
JUGATED, [jōō'-gā-tid], *adj.* (*bot.*) with the leaflets in pairs.
JUGFUL, [jug'-fōōl], *adj.* the contents of a jug; the quantity that a jug will hold.
JUGGERNAUT, [jug'-er-nawt], *n.* a title of the Hindu god, Vishnu; the image of this god at Orissa which, mounted on its chariot at certain seasons, was taken in procession when thousands contended for the honour of dragging the vehicle and many devotees threw themselves under its wheels to be crushed; a relentless inhuman force which destroys blindly anything that comes its way. [Hind. *Jagganath* lord of the universe].
JUGGINS, [jug'-inz], *n.* (*slang*) a simple dupe. [*Juggins*, a surname].
JUGGLE (1), [jugl], *n.* a piece of juggling; an imposture; a manipulation.
JUGGLE (2), [jugl], *v.i.* to perform tricks of manual dexterity; **to j. with**, to manipulate, to perform tricks with; also (*fig.*). [OFr. *jogler* from L. *joculari* to jest].
JUGGLER, [jug'-ler], *n.* one who gives exhibitions of jugglery; (*fig.*) a deceiver, a trickster. [OFr. *jogleor* from L. *joculator*].
JUGGLERY, [jug'-ler-i], *n.* manual dexterity; trickery. [OFr. *juglerie*].
JUGGLING, [jug'-ling], *n.* sleight-of-hand; the juggler's trade; trickery in general.
JUGGLINGLY, [jug'-ling-li], *adv.* in a juggling or deceptive manner.
JUGO-SLAV, see YUGOSLAV.
JUGULAR (1), [jug'-yōō-ler], *n.* the jugular vein.
JUGULAR (2), [jug'-yōō-ler], *adj.* pertaining to the neck or throat; **j. veins**, the large veins in the throat. [MedL. *jugularis*].
JUGULATE, [jug'-yōō-lāt], *v.t.* to kill, strangle; to apply a desperate remedy to, check. [L. *jugulatum*, *p.pt.* of *jugulare* to cut the throat of].
JUICE, [jōōs], *n.* sap, the liquid part of vegetable matter; (*fig.*) the essential part of anything; (*slang*) any motive power, electricity, petrol, etc. [L. *jus* soup].
JUICELESS, [jōōs'-les], *adj.* without juice.
JUICINESS, [jōōs'-i-nes], *n.* the quality of having much juice, succulence.
JUICY, [jōōs'-i], *adj.* full of juice, succulent; (*slang*) full of rather questionable interest, racy, suggestive.
JU-JITSU, JIU-JITSU, [jōō-jit'-sōō], *n.* Japanese wrestling. [Jap. *jujutsu*].
JUJU, [jōō'-jōō], *n.* African magic; a charm or taboo connected with this; animism. [Uncert.].
JUJUBE, [jōō'-jōōb], *n.* (*bot.*) a shrub of the genus *Zizyphus*, or its fruit; a lozenge of gum arabic and sugar. [MedL. *jujuba*].
JULEP, [jōōl'-ep], *n.* a sweet liquid forming a foundation for medicines; a drink consisting of spirituous liquor, water, and sugar with a seasoning of mint. [Pers. *gul* rose and *ab* water].
JULIAN, [jōō'-li-an], *adj.* pertaining to Julius Caesar, usually of his calendar, superseded in England in 1752 by the Gregorian. [L. *julianus*].
JULIENNE, [zhōōl-i-en'], *n.* a clear meat soup with finely shredded vegetables. [Fr. *Julienne*].
JULIS, [jōō'-lis], *n.* a small fish, the rainbow wrasse. *Coris julis*.
JULUS, [jōō'-lus], *n.* (*bot.*) a catkin; (*zool.*) a myriapod with more than thirty rings and many eyes crowded together in a cluster. [L. *Julus*].

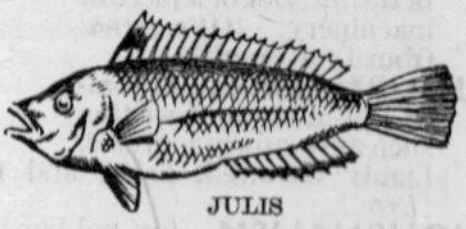
JULIS

JULY, [jōō-lī'], *n.* the seventh month of the year, named after Julius Caesar. [OFr. *Jule* from L. (*mensis*) *Julius*].
JUMART, [jōō'-maht], *n.* supposititious offspring of a mare by a bull or a cow by a horse. [Fr. *jumart*].
JUMBLE (1), [jumbl], *n.* an obviously confused collection of heterogeneous objects; **j. sale**, a sale of cast-off goods for charity.
JUMBLE (2), [jumbl], *n.* a thin, hollow, cylindrical, crisp, sweet cake.
JUMBLE (3), [jumbl], *v.t.* to mix, confuse; to send to a jumble sale; *v.i.* to act or think confusedly. [Echoic].
JUMBLEMENT, [jumbl'-ment], *n.* a jumbling; a confused mixture.
JUMBLER, [jumb'-ler], *n.* one who jumbles.
JUMBLINGLY, [jumb'-ling-li], *adv.* confusedly.
JUMBO, [jum'-bō], *n.* a name for an elephant; (*fig.*) anything large or clumsy. [*Jumbo*, a former famous elephant in the London Zoo].
JUMP (1), [jump], *n.* sudden motion upwards, a leap, spring, bound; a nervous start; a sudden acceleration or change of direction in any ordered progress or motion; (*geol.*) a fault; (*slang*) a lucky chance.
JUMP (2), [jump], *v.t.* to jump over; to make to jump; (of a male animal) to cover; to omit; (of a nerve) to throb, to start nervously; to interrupt an ordered sequence, to be erratic; **to j. at**, to seize eagerly; **to j. into**, to rush into; **to j. on**, to blame instantly; **to j. with**, to agree with, correspond to; **to j. a claim**, to take possession of a piece of land or claim; (*coll.*) **to j. to it**, to hurry; *v.i.* to make or take a jump, to leap, spring, bound. [Echoic].
JUMPER (1), [jump'-er], *n.* one who, or that which, jumps; the maggot of the cheese-fly; one of a Welsh Methodist sect from their practice of jumping about in excitement at worship; (*coll.*) a ticket-inspector on a public conveyance; (*naut.*) a rope to prevent the yard jumping; **counter-j.**, a shop-assistant.
JUMPER (2), [jump'-er], *n.* a sailor's loose tunic; a blouse reaching over the top of the skirt. [Fr. *jupon* skirt].
JUMPINESS, [jump'-i-nes], *n.* the condition of being jumpy, erratic, nervously on edge.
JUMPY, [jump'-i], *adj.* nervous; erratic.

JUNCOUS, [jung'-kus], *adj.* (*bot.*) connected with, or resembling, rushes. [L. *juncosus*].

JUNCTION, [jungk'-shun], *n.* the act of joining; the state of being joined, union, coalition, meeting; the place or point of union, the join; meeting point of two or more sets of railway lines. [L. *junctio*].

JUNCTURE, [jungk'-cher], *n.* a joining; union; the line or point at which two bodies are joined; point of time, critical moment, position of affairs. [L. *junctura*].

JUNE, [jo͞on], *n.* the sixth month of the year. [OFr. *juin* from L. (*mensis*) *Junius*].

JUNGLE, [jungl], *n.* wild, waste, heavily overgrown, trackless ground in tropical countries; (*fig.*) anything through which it is hard to find one's way. [Hind. *jangal*].

JUNGLE-FEVER, [jungl'-fē'-ver], *n.* a remittent tropical fever; malaria.

JUNGLE-FOWL, [jungl'-fowl'], *n.* the game-bird of the jungle from which domestic poultry developed.

JUNGLE-FOWL

JUNGLY, [jungl'-i], *adj.* covered with jungle.

JUNIOR (1), [jo͞on'-i-or], *n.* a person who is younger in years or practice, subordinate.

JUNIOR (2), [jo͞on'-i-or], *adj.* younger in years or practice; of the younger of two brothers, or son with the same name as his father; subordinate; of less standing. [L. *junior*].

JUNIORITY, [jo͞on'-i-o'-ri-ti], *n.* the state of being junior or subordinate to.

JUNIPER, [jo͞on'-ip-er], *n.* (*bot.*) an evergreen tree bearing dark, purple berries, the oil of which is used in medicines and in flavouring gin. [L. *juniperus*].

JUNK (1), [jungk], *n.* pieces of old cable or cordage put to secondary uses; hard, salt beef; the source of spermaceti in the sperm-whale; (*slang*) cast-off, broken things. [Unkn.].

JUNK (2), [jungk], *n.* a large flat-bottomed vessel with one to three pole masts with flat matting sails used in China Seas. [Malay *jong*].

JUNK

JUNKER, [yo͝ong'-ker], *n.* a Prussian or North German landed aristocrat. [Germ. *junker*].

JUNKERS, [yo͝ongk-erz], *n.* the name of various types of German aircraft. [*Junkers* the maker].

JUNKET (1), [jungk'-it], *n.* soft curds; a blithe entertainment. [AFr. *jonquette* rush basket].

JUNKET (2), [jungk'-it], *v.i.* to attend a junketing.

JUNKETING, [jungk'-it-ing], *n.* a merry entertainment.

JUNK-RING, [jungk'-ring'], *n.* a steam-tight packing round the piston of a steam-engine.

JUNO, [jo͞o'-nō], *n.* (*Roman myth.*) the stately wife of Jupiter and Queen of Heaven; a queenly, full and statuesque figure; (*astron.*) one of the minor planets. [L. *Juno*].

JUNTA, JUNTO, [jun'-ta, jun'-tō], *n.* the Spanish Grand Council; a secret political convention; a small secret and unofficial council, a cabal. [Sp. *junta*].

JUPITER, [jo͞o'-pit-er], *n.* (*Roman myth.*) the supreme deity, Jove; (*astron.*) the largest of the planets. [L. *Jupiter*].

JUPON, [jo͞o'-pon], *n.* a close-fitting tunic or surcoat. [Fr. *jupon*].

JURAL, [jo͞oer'-al], *adj.* pertaining to rights or law. [~L. *jus juris* law].

JURASSIC, [jo͞o-ras'-ik], *adj.* of the geological character of the Jura Mountains; pertaining to the division of the secondary rocks formed by the lias and oolites. [Fr. *jurassique*].

JURAT, [jo͞o'-rat], *n.* a municipal officer or a magistrate in certain corporations. [MedL. *juratus* sworn man].

JURATORY, [jo͞oer-at-er-i], *adj.* involving an oath. [L. *juratorius*].

JURIDICAL, [jo͞o-rid'-ik-al], *adj.* of, or pertaining to, a judge or justice. [~L. *juridicus*].

JURIDICALLY, [jo͞o-rid'-ik-al-i], *adv.* in a juridical manner.

JURISCONSULT, [jo͞oer'-is-kon'-sult], *n.* an official legal authority in any system of law based on the Roman. [L. *jurisconsultus*].

JURISDICTION, [jo͞oer'-is-dik'-shun], *n.* authority or power to try causes; the district or sphere where such a right runs; the trying of causes; (*more generally*), administration, realm, government, province. [L. *jurisdictio*].

JURISDICTIONAL, [jo͞oer'-is-dik'-shun-al], *adj.* pertaining to jurisdiction.

JURISDICTIVE, [jo͞oer'-is-dik'-tiv], *adj.* (*rare*) having legal power or jurisdiction.

JURISPRUDENCE, [jo͞oer'-is-pro͞o'-dents], *n.* knowledge of the practice and history of laws, rights, usages, and so forth; study in this. [L. *jurisprudentia*].

JURISPRUDENT, [jo͞oer'-is-pro͞o'-dent], *adj.*, versed in the science of law.

JURISPRUDENTIAL, [jo͞oer'-is-pro͞o-den'-shal], *adj.* pertaining to jurisprudence.

JURIST, [jo͞oer'-ist], *n.* one versed in law; a student of, writer on, law, particularly civil or international law. [MedL. *jurista*].

JUROR, [jo͞oer-or], *n.* a juryman, or anyone with similar functions; one who swears an oath. [AFr. *jurour*].

JURY, [jo͞oer'-i], *n.* a sworn body of men and women, peers of the accused, who must pronounce a verdict on the facts of a cause from the evidence adduced in court after direction by a judge; any body of judges, umpires, etc. [OFr. *jurée*].

JURY-BOX, [jo͞oer'-i-boks'], *n.* a jury's enclosed seats.

JURYMAN, [jo͞oer'-i-man], *n.* a member of a jury.

JURYMAST, [jo͞oer'-i-mahst], *n.* (*naut.*) a temporary mast. [Uncert.].

JUSSI, [ho͞os'-i], *n.* a dress fabric made in Manila. [Tagalog *husi*].

JUSSIVE, [jus'-iv], *adj.* conveying or containing a command or order; (*gram.*) connected with the imperative mood or sense of any verb. [L. *jussus*].

JUST (1), [just], *adj.* righteous; in conformity with abstract, ideal right, one's rights as a man or as a citizen, or to the rules, principles, and practice of a juridical system or administration; equitable, due, impartial, proper; in conformity with what is good, or fitting, or recognized as such; honest, fair, sporting; in conformity with any limit; of a correct, equivalent, or equal size, amount or extent. [Fr. *juste* from L. *justus*].

JUST (2), [just], *adv.* exactly; nearly, barely; almost; a short time before; (*coll.*) quite, simply. [*Prec.*].

JUSTICE, [jus'-tis], *n.* the ideal principle determining what is fitting and right; the quality of being just, justness; rectitude in the dealings of men one with another; honesty; accordance with truth and fact; just desert; (*leg.*) jurisdiction; a due punishment; a person commissioned to hold courts, or to try and decide controversies and administer justice; a judge; **J. of the Peace**, an unpaid local magistrate. [L. *justitia*].

JUSTICESHIP, [just'-is-ship], *n.* the office or rank of a justice.

JUSTICIABLE, [just-ish'-i-abl], *adj.* proper to be examined in a court of justice.

JUSTICIAR, [just-ish'-i-er], *n.* an administrator of justice; a lord chief justice. [MedL. *justiciarius*].

JUSTICIARY, [just-ish'-i-er-i], *n.* the High Court in Scotland, of supreme jurisdiction in all criminal cases; a justiciar, a judge.

JUSTI-COAT, [just'-ik-ōt], *n.* a close-fitting short coat, a waistcoat with sleeves. [Fr. *juste au corps* close to the body].

JUSTIFIABLE, [just'-i-fī-abl], *adj.* that can be justified; defensible, excusable. [Fr. *justifiable*].

JUSTIFIABLENESS, [just'-i-fī'-abl-nes], *n.* the quality of being justifiable.

JUSTIFIABLY, [just'-i-fī'-ab-li], *adv.* so as to be justifiable; in a justifiable manner; rightly.

JUSTIFICATION, [just'-i-fik-ā'-shun], *n.* the act of justifying; vindication, defence; (*theol.*) acceptance of a sinner as righteous through the merits of Christ. [LL. *justificatio*].

JUSTIFICATIVE, [just'-i-fik-at-iv], *adj.* justifying; justificatory; that has power to justify.

JUSTIFICATORY, [just'-i-fik-āt'-er-i], *adj.* vindicatory, defensory.

JUSTIFIER, [just'-i-fīer], *n.* one who justifies; (*print.*) an agent or instrument for type-spacing.

JUSTIFY, [just'-i-fī], *v.t.* to prove; to show to be just, right, allowable, excusable, reasonable; to exculpate,

exonerate; to adjust; (*print.*) to space out (type). [Fr. *justifier* from L. *justificare*].
JUSTIFYING, [just'-i-fī-ing], *adj.* (*theol.*) that may absolve from guilt.
JUSTLE, [jusl], *v.i.* to jostle, to push. [~JOSTLE (2)].
JUSTLY, [just-li], *adv.* in a just manner; rightly.
JUSTNESS, [just'-nes], *n.* the quality of being just; rectitude; uprightness; correctness, accuracy.
JUT (1), [jut], *n.* a sharp, well-defined projection.
JUT (2), [jut], *v.i.* to project sharply, strikingly. [~JET (3)].
JUTE (1), [jōōt], *n.* an important vegetable fibre serving as coarse hemp for canvas, ropes, etc.; the Bengal trees from which it is derived, *Corchorus capsularis* and *C. olitorius*. [Bengali *jhoto*].
JUTE (2), [jōōt], *n.* a member of one of the Low German invading tribes which settled in Kent and Hampshire. [L. *Juta*].
JUTTINGLY, [jut'-ing-li], *adv.* so as to project sharply.
JUTTY†, [jut'-i], *n.* a pier, jetty. [~JETTY].
JUT-WINDOW, [jut'-wind'-ō], *n.* a projecting window.
JUVENESCENCE, [jōō'-ven-es'-ents], *n.* the process of becoming young.
JUVENESCENT, [jōō-ven-es'-ent], *adj.* immature, growing into young manhood. [L. *juvenescens*].
JUVENILE (1), [jōō'-ven-īl], *n.* an official or opprobrious term for a youth; a juvenile offender; a book for children.
JUVENILE (2), [jōō'-ven-īl], *adj.* young, youthful, pertaining to or suited to youth; adolescent; a **j. offender**, a guilty person, not yet of age, tried in a special court and liable to special penalties. [L. *juvenilis*].
JUVENILENESS, [jōō'-ven-īl-nes], *n.* the quality of being juvenile; youthfulness.
JUVENILIA, [jōō-ven-il'-i-a], *n.(pl.)* books written or works of art executed in youth. [L. *juvenilia*].
JUVENILITY, [jōō-ven-il'-i-ti], *n.* juvenile condition; youthfulness. [L. *juvenilitas*].
JUWANZA, [jōō-wan'-za], *n.* (*bot.*) the tree *Alhagi camelorum*, camel's thorn.
JUXTAPOSE, [juks'-ta-pōz], *v.t.* to place side by side. [Fr. *juxtaposer*].
JUXTAPOSITION, [juks'-ta-pōz-i-shun], *n.* the state of being placed side by side. [Fr. *juxtaposition*].
JUZAIL, JEZHAIL, [jew-zāl', jez-āl'], *n.* a heavy rifle used by the Afghans. [Afghan *jezhail*].

K

K, [kā], the eleventh letter of the English alphabet.
KAAMA, [kah'-ma], *n.* a South African antelope, *Bubalis caama*. [Sechuana].

KAAMA

KABBALA, see CABALA.
KABOOK, [ka-bōōk'], *n.* a clay ironstone found in Ceylon. [Native].
KABYLE, [kab-īl'], *n.* a Berber farmer living in the highlands of Algeria; the dialect of these people, a form of Berber. [Arab. *Qabail*, (*pl.*) of *qabilah* tribe.]
KADDISH, [kad'-ish], *n.* a Jewish prayer of thanksgiving and praise in the daily service; a mourning prayer said by a son for his father. [Aramaic *qaddish* holy one].
KADI, see CADI.
KAFFIR, KAFIR, CAFFRE, [kaf'-er], *n.* a member of the chief native race in South-East Africa, a branch of the Bantus, *esp.* one living between Natal and Cape Province; their language; a native of Kafiristan in Afghanistan; (*pl.*) South African mining shares. [Arab. *kafir* infidel].
KAFFIR-BOOM, [kaf'-er-bōōm'], *n.* the South African tree, *Erythrina Caffra*, yielding a very light wood.
KAFILA, [kaf'-il-a], *n.* a camel caravan. [Arab. *qafilah* caravan].
KAFIR, see KAFFIR.
KAFTAN, see CAFTAN.
KAGO, [kah'-gō], *n.* a Japanese palanquin. [Jap. *kaugo*].
KAGU, [kah'-gōō], *n.* a bird related to the cranes, found in New Caledonia, *Rhinocetus jubatus*; a bird related to the hemipodes found in Madagascar, *Mesites variegatus*. [Native].
KAIL (1), see KAYLE.
KAIL (2), see KALE.
KAIMAKAM, CAIMACAM, [kī'-mak-ahm], *n.* a Turkish title for a lieutenant or deputy. [Arab. *qa'im maqam* deputy].
KAINITE, [kā'-nīt], *n.* a mineral consisting of magnesium sulphate and potassium chloride; a fertilizer made of this. [Gk. *kainos* new].
KAINOZOIC, see CAINOZOIC.
KAISER, [kī'-zer], *n.* the title taken by the sovereigns of the Holy Roman Empire, in imitation of the ancient Roman Caesars, and in 1871 adopted by William, King of Prussia, as first Emperor of the new German Empire. [Germ. form of CAESAR].
KAKA, [kah'-ka], *n.* the parrot, *Nestor meridionalis*, of New Zealand. [Maori *kaka*].
KAKAPO, [kah'-kah-pō], *n.* the owl parrot, *Stringops habroptilus*, of New Zealand. [Maori *kaka* parrot and *po* night].

KAKAPO

KAKEMONO, [kah'-kem-ō'-nō], *n.* a Japanese hanging picture, unrolling vertically and usually painted on silk. [Jap. *kake* to hang and *mono* thing].
KAKI, [kah'-ki], *n.* the Chinese date, *Diospyros Kaki*. [Jap. *kaki*].
KAKISTOCRACY, [kak'-is-tok'-ras-i], *n.* rule by the worst elements of a community. [Gk. *kakistos* worst and *kratia* rule].
KAKODYL, see CACODYL.
KALA, [kah'-la], *n.* destiny, death. [Skr. *kala*].
KALA-AZAR, [kal'-a-az'-ah(r)], *n.* a tropical infectious protozoan disease. [Assamese *kala-azar*].
KALE, KAIL, [kāl], *n.* a curly-leafed cabbage of the genus *Brassica*, cole, colewort. [Scots form of COLE].
KALEIDOSCOPE, [kal-ī'-dō-skōp], *n.* an optical instrument, usually in the form of a tube containing reflecting surfaces, having an eye-hole at one end, and, at the other, pieces of coloured glass, forming constantly changing symmetrical figures as the tube is turned or shaken; (*fig.*) a constantly changing scene of colour. [Gk. *kalos* beautiful, *eidos* form, and SCOPE].
KALEIDOSCOPIC, [kal-ī'-dō-skop'-ik], *adj.* of, pertaining to, or resembling, a kaleidoscope; rapidly changing in colour or appearance.
KALENDS, see CALENDS.
KALEVALA, [ka-li-va-lah'], *n.* a collection of ancient Finnish epics. [Finnish *kalevala* land of heroes].
KALEYARD, [kāl'-yahd], *n.* a Scottish kitchen garden; **k. school**, a group of authors writing sentimentally, and with extensive use of dialect, about humble Scottish domestic life.
KALI (1), [kah'-lē], *n.* the Hindu goddess of death and destruction. [Skr. *kali* black].
KALI (2), [kā'-li], *n.* a species of glasswort, *Salicornia*, the ashes of which yield soda ash. [Arab. *qali*].
KALIF, see CALIPH.
KALIGENOUS, [kal-ij'-en-us], *adj.* producing alkalis. [Arab. *qali* and Gk. *genes* producing].
KALINITE, [ka'-lin-īt], *n.* alum, hydrated sulphate of potassium and aluminium. [~ALKALINE].

KALIUM, [kā'-li-um], *n.* (*chem.*) the element potassium. [~KALI (2)].

KALMIA, [kal'-mi-a], *n.* (*bot.*) a genus of American evergreen shrubs of the heath order. [~ *Kalm*, a Swedish botanist].

KALMUCK, [kal'-muk'], *n.* a kind of shaggy cloth like bearskin; a coarse cotton fabric made in Prussia; a Mongolian tribe living between the Volga and Western China; the dialect of this people. [Russ. *Kalmiki*].

KALONG, [kah'-long], *n.* the Malay fox-bat, *Pteropus edulis*. [Native].

KALPA, [kal'-pa], *n.* in the Hindu chronology, the period of 4,320,000,000 years which occurs between one destruction of the world and the next. [Skr. *kalpa*].

KALSOMINE, see CALCIMINE.

KAM, see CAM (2).

KAMA, [kah'-ma], *n.* the Hindu god of love; sexual passion. [Skr. *kama* love].

KAMARBAND, see CUMMERBUND.

KAME, [kām], *n.* (*geol.*) a high, steep, ridge-like deposit of post-glacial gravel found at the lower end of certain large valleys, an esker. [~COMB].

KAMERAD, [kam'-er-ahd'], *n.* the word said to be used by German soldiers when surrendering. [Germ. *kamerad* from Fr. *camarade* comrade].

KAMICHI, [kam'-ich-i], *n.* a variety of bird in the swamps of Guiana and Brazil, *Palamedes cornuta*. [Fr. *kamichi*].

KAMIS, [kam'-is], *n.* an embroidered shirt worn by male Mohammedans. [Arab. *qamis*].

KAMPONG, [kam-pong'], *n.* a Malay village or compound. [Malay *kampong*].

KAMSIN, see KHAMSIN.

KANAKA, [kan-ak'-a, kan'-ak-a], *n.* a native of the South Sea Islands, *esp.* one brought under contract to Australia as a native labourer. [Hawaiian *kanaka* man].

KANGAROO, [kang'-ga-rōō'], *n.* a herbivorous marsupial mammal of the genus *Macropus*, native to Australia, having short weak forelegs and long powerful hind legs, by which it travels in a series of leaps, using its long thick tail as a support when standing or sitting erect; (*pl.*) (*Stock Exchange*) West Australian mining shares; a method of procedure in the House of Commons by which the Chairman of a committee can choose the amendments to be discussed; **brush k.,** a wallaby, any small species of *Macropus*; **rock k.,** any species of *Petrogale*; **tree k.,** any species of *Dendrolagus*. [Native].

KANGAROO-APPLE, [kang'-ga-rōō'-apl'], *n.* the plant, *Solanum aviculare*; its fruit.

KANGAROO-GRASS, [kang'-ga-rōō'-grahs'], *n.* the tall Australian grass, *Anthistiria australis*.

KANGAROO-RAT, [kang'-ga-rōō'-rat'], *n.* a small species of marsupial animals, *esp.* one of the genus *Potorous* or *Bettongia*; a North American rodent.

KANTEN, [kan'-ten], *n.* the seaweed, *Fucus cartilaginosus*. [Unkn.].

KANTIAN (1), [kan'-ti-an], *n.* a follower of Kant. [~*Kant*, the German philosopher].

KANTIAN (2), [kan'-ti-an], *adj.* relating to the philosophical system of Kant.

KANTISM, [kant'-izm], *n.* a Kantian doctrine or theory; Kantian criticism.

KANTIST, [kant'-ist], *n.* a follower of Kant.

KAOLIN, [kā'-ol-in], *n.* a fine white clay, being a hydrous aluminium silicate obtained from decomposed granite rock, used medicinally and in the manufacture of porcelain, china clay. [Chin. *kao-ling* high mountain, the name of the mountain where originally obtained].

KAPITIA, [kap-it'-i-a], *n.* a resinous variety of lacquer, obtained from Ceylon. [Native].

KAPOK, [kāp'-ok], *n.* a soft, light, downy, oily fibre obtained from the silk-cotton tree, *Eriodendron anfractuosum*. [Malay *kapoq*].

KAPUT, [kap-ŏŏt'], *adj.* (*slang*) finished, all in. [Germ. *kaput*].

KARAGAN, [ka'-ra-gan], *n.* the Tartar fox, *Vulpes karagan*. [Turk. *karagan* from *kara* black].

KARAITE, [kāer'-a-īt], *n.* a member of a Jewish sect holding a literal interpretation of the Scriptures, and rejecting traditional rabbinical interpretation. [Heb. *qara* to read].

KARATAS, [ka'-rat-as], *n.* a plant found in South America and the West Indies, being related to the pine-apple. [Native].

KARMA, [kah'-ma], *n.* (*Indian philos.*) the total effect of a person's acts in one life which decides his fate in his next state of existence; fate, destiny. [Skr. *karma* deed].

KARMATHIANS, [kah-mā'-thi-anz.], *n.*(*pl.*) a Mohammedan rationalistic sect, founded by one *Karmat* in the ninth century.

KAROB, [ka'-rob], *n.* the twenty-fourth part of a grain. [Unkn.].

KAROO, [ka-rōō'], *n.* a South African barren tableland or dry plateau. [Hottentot *Karrusa* dry].

KAROSS, CAROSS, [ka-ros'], *n.* a South African native cloak or rug of animal skin with the hair or fur left on. [S. African *kaross*].

KARRI, [ka'-ri], *n.* an Australian variety of eucalyptus tree; the hard, red wood of this tree. [Native].

KARYOPLASM, [ka'-ri-ō-plazm], *n.* (*biol.*) the protoplasm of the nucleus of a cell. [Gk. *karuon* nut and PLASM].

KATABATIC, [kat-ab-at'-ik], *adj.* (*meteor.*) due to the downward flow of air. [Gk. *katabatikos*].

KATABOLISM, [kat-ab'-ol-izm], *n.* the process by which complex organic compounds of living bodies are broken up into simpler ones. [Gk. *katabole* throwing down].

KATYDID, [kā'-ti-did], *n.* a North American tree-grasshopper of a greenish colour, so called from the peculiar sound made by its wing covers. [Echoic].

KAURI, [kow'-ri], *n.* a conifer belonging to the genus *Agathis*. [Maori *kauri*].

KAVA, [kah'-va], *n.* a Polynesian intoxicating drink from the roots of the shrub *Macropiper latifolium*. [Native].

KAVASS, [kav-as'], *n.* a Turkish constable or armed servant. [Turk. *qawwas* bow-maker].

KAYAK, [kī'-ak], *n.* a covered Eskimo canoe having an opening in the middle to receive the person using the boat. [Eskimo *kayak*].

KAYAK

KAYLE, KAIL, [kāl], *n.* (usually *pl.*) skittles, ninepins; the game played with these. [~MDu. *keghel*, *kegel*].

KEA, [kā'-a], *n.* the New Zealand parrot, *Nestor notabilis*, which attacks sheep. [Maori *kea*].

KEBLAH, see KIBLAH.

KECK, [kek], *v.i.* to retch, as in an effort to vomit; to heave. [Imitative].

KECKLE, [kekl], *v.t.* to wind old rope round a cable to prevent or protect its surface from being chafed; to cackle. [Unkn.].

KECKLING, [kek'-ling], *n.* (*naut.*) old rope wound round cables to keep them from chafing.

KECKS, see KEX.

KECKY†, [kek'-i], *adj.* resembling kex.

KEDGE (1), [kej], *n.* a small anchor used for mooring or warping a ship. [~KEDGE (3)].

KEDGE (2), [kej], *adj.* (*prov.*) brisk, lively, in high spirits. [Unkn.].

KEDGE (3), [kej], *v.i.* to move a ship by winding in a hawser which is fastened to a small anchor dropped at some distance from the ship, to warp a ship. [Uncert.].

KEDGEREE, [kej'-er-ē'], *n.* a spiced dish of stewed fish, rice and eggs. [Hind. *khichri*].

KEDGY, [kej'-i], *adj.* merry, in good spirits. [~CADGY].

KEEK, [kēk], *v.i.* to peep; to spy. [~MDu. *kieken*].

KEEL (1), [kēl], *n.* the lowest set of plates or timbers in a ship's structure, extending from stem to stern, upon which the framework of the ship is built; (*bot.*) a central ridge-like projection along the back of a leaf, petal, etc.; **false k.,** a second keel bolted under the main keel; **sliding k.,** a centre-board working in a trunk along the line of the keel so as to deepen it when necessary. [OIcel. *kjolr*].

KEEL (2), [kēl], *n.* a flat-bottomed coal barge, as used on the Tyne; the quantity of coal carried in one of these; a boat, ship. [MDu. *kiel*].

KEEL (3), [kēl], *v.t.* to turn up the keel of so as to show the bottom of; **to k. over,** to capsize.

KEELAGE, [kēl'-ij], *n.* duty required from a ship at certain harbours.

KEEL-BOAT, [kēl'-bōt], *n.* a large flat-bottomed American river-boat; a yacht equipped with a keel in place of a centre board.

KEELED, [kēld], *adj.* (*bot.*, *zool.*) having a central ridge-like projection along the back.

KEELER, [kēl'-er], *n.* a small shallow tub, *esp.* for salting mackerel. [~OE. *celan* to cool].

KEEL-HAUL, [kēl'-hawl], *v.t.* to hang to the yard-arm, drop over the side of the ship, and haul under the keel to the other side as a punishment; (*fig.*) to rebuke or punish severely. [Du. *kielhalen*].

KEEL-HAULING, [kēl′-hawl′-ing], *n.* the punishment of dragging a culprit under the bottom of a vessel by ropes from the yard-arms on each side.

KEELING, [kēl′-ing], *n.* a cod fish. [Uncert.].

KEELIVINE, [kēl′-iv-in], *n.* a black-lead pencil or coloured pencil. [Unkn.].

KEELLESS, [kēl′-les], *adj.* (*nat. hist.*) devoid of a keel; (*poet.*) unvisited by ships.

KEELMAN, [kēl′-man], *n.* a man who works on a keel or barge, *esp.* a lighterman on the River Tyne.

KEELSON, KELSON, [kēl′-son], *n.* set of timbers or plates placed above and parallel to the keel, and by which the keel is bolted to the floor-timbers. [KEEL (1), second element unknown].

KEEN (1), [kēn], *n.* bitter lamentation and wailing set up by the Irish upon the death of some person, or over a corpse. [Ir. *caoine* dirge].

KEEN (2), [kēn], *adj.* sharp, having a fine cutting edge; sensitive, highly developed; strong, poignant, intense; biting, severe; incisive, sharp, acute; piercing; eager, zealous, enthusiastic, devoted; shrewd, searching; desirous of; hard and closely contested; strong, well marked; **to be k. on,** to be anxious to, to desire eagerly; to have a strong affection for. [OE. *cene*].

KEEN (3), [kēn], *v.i.* to lament loudly and bitterly for the dead. [KEEN (1)].

KEENER, [kēn′-er], *n.* a professional mourner in Ireland.

KEENLY, [kēn′-li], *adv.* in a keen fashion.

KEENNESS, [kēn′-nes], *n.* the condition of being keen.

KEEN-WITTED, [kēn′-wit′-id], *adj.* sharp-witted, discerning, smart at repartee.

KEEP (1), [kēp], *n.* care; the act of keeping; the fact or condition of being kept; that which keeps or supports, maintenance, food, sustenance, attention and lodging necessary to keep anyone or anything, money or other recompense required in return for this; the innermost and most strongly fortified tower of a castle, the donjon; **for keeps,** (*coll.*) for ever. [KEEP (2)].

KEEP (2), (kept), [kēp], *v.t.* to retain in one's possession, to hold either permanently or temporarily; to continue to hold; to cause to remain, to deposit in a particular place for convenience, security, etc.; to fulfil, abide by; to celebrate; to maintain, provide means of sustenance and residence for, *esp.* to maintain for personal use or enjoyment; to manage, be in charge of; to maintain in proper order, preserve a record of; to defend from attack; to detain; to preserve; to continue to (*with another v.*); to have in stock for sale; *v.i.* to remain in a certain (*esp.* good) condition; to stay in a certain place; to continue; to remain; **to k. at,** to continue to, to stick to; to compel to remain at; **to k. from,** to withhold, conceal from; to prevent access to, to prevent doing; **to k. away from,** not to go near; **to k. to,** to stick to; **to k. away,** to prevent from approaching close to; **to k. back,** to restrain, repress; to conceal, withhold; **to k. in,** to detain (*esp.* after normal hours at school), to compel to stay; to restrain; **to k. off,** to abstain from; to ward off; **to k. on,** to continue to; to retain in employment; not to take off; **to k. out,** to prevent from entering; to take no part in, to avoid; **to k. up,** not to let slide or lapse; to maintain; to continue, to preserve; to remain unsubdued; to prevent from falling (*esp.* of courage or spirits); **to k. up with,** to progress at the same rate as; **to k. down,** to suppress; **to k. an eye on,** (*coll.*) to look after; **to k. one's eyes open,** (*coll.*) to be on the alert for, to observe carefully. [OE. *cepan*].

KEEPER, [kēp′-er], *n.* one who keeps or guards, a custodian, protector; an attendant in charge of a lunatic; an employee responsible for the care and upkeep of a park or other enclosure; one who is in charge; a ring worn above another to keep it from slipping off the finger; a clasp.

KEEPERSHIP, [kēp′-er-ship], *n.* the position of keeper.

KEEPING, [kēp′-ing], *n.* the act of holding or retaining; protection, guardianship; observance; preservation; completing and maintaining in proper condition; just proportion.

KEEPING-ROOM, [kēp′-ing-rōōm′], *n.* the sitting-room or living-room.

KEEPSAKE, [kēp′-sāk], *n.* a token of remembrance, a memento.

KEESHOND, [kās′-hond], *n.* a variety of Dutch dog like a chow. [Du. *keeshond*].

KEEVE (1), KIVE, [kēv], *n.* a large tub or vat for fermenting liquors; a bleaching tub; a receptacle for washing ore. [OE. *cyf*].

KEEVE (2), KIVE, [kēv], *v.t.* to set in a keeve for fermentation.

KEG, [keg], *n.* a small barrel. [~Icel. *kaggi*].

KEIR, see KIER.

KEITLOA, [kāt′-lō-a], *n.* a South African variety of rhinoceros. [Sechuana *khetlwa*].

KELKEL, [kel′-kel], *n.* a dried and salted slice of sole. [Unkn.].

KELL, [kel], *n.* (*prov.*) a caul; a shroud; a thin membrane; a covering of gossamer. [~CAUL].

KELP, [kelp], *n.* ashes of seaweed used in the manufacture of iodine; the seaweed itself, *esp.* the large seaweeds burned because of their valuable ashes. [ME. *culp*].

KELPIE, [kelp′-i], *n.* (*Scots*) an imaginary sprite or demon haunting lakes or rivers. [Uncert.].

KELSON, see KEELSON.

KELT (1), [kelt], *n.* a spent salmon or sea-trout after spawning, and before returning to the sea. [Unkn.].

KELT (2), [kelt], *n.* a kind of homespun material of native black and white wool. [Scots *kelt*].

KELT (3), see CELT (1).

KELTER, KILTER, [kelt′-er, kilt′-er], *n.* good health, fine order. [Uncert.].

KELTIE, [kelt′-i], *n.* the gull, *Rissa tridactyla*. [Unkn.].

KEMP, [kemp], *n.* the coarse hairs in wool, which lower its quality. [OIcel. *kampr* beard].

KEMPS, [kempz], *n.* the plantain, *Plantago media*. [~Swed. *kampa*].

KEN (1), [ken], *n.* range of vision; range of knowledge or experience. [KEN (2)].

KEN (2), (kenning, kenned), [ken], *v.t.* †(*and dial*) to know; to recognize; to see. [OE. *cennan* to make known].

KENDAL-GREEN, [kendl′-grēn′], *n.* a green woollen cloth manufactured originally at Kendal, dyed with a mixture of woad and dyer's greenweed. [*Kendal*, in Westmorland].

KENNEL (1), [ken′-el], *n.* a hut for a dog; a dwelling-hole of other animals; a pack of hounds; a band or troop of animals; a mean dwelling-place. [NFr. *kenel*].

KENNEL (2), [ken′-el], *n.* gutter, open drain or watercourse of a street. [~CANAL].

KENNEL (3), (kennelling, kennelled), [ken′-el], *v.t.* to confine or put into a kennel or kennels; *v.i.* to live in a kennel.

KENNING, [ken′-ing], *n.* knowledge, knowing; one of the highly metaphorical phrases used in Old Norse poetry to describe a simple thing. [OIcel. *kenna til* to name after].

KENOSIS, [ken-ō′-sis], *n.* (*theol.*) the laying aside by Christ of part of his divinity, when he came on earth as a human being. [Gk. *kenosis* emptying].

KENOTRON, [ken-ō′-tron], *n.* (*wirel.*) a double-electrode valve whose bulb is virtually a vacuum.

KENT-BUGLE, [kent′-bewgl′], *n.* a keyed bugle, named after the Duke of Kent.

KENTISH, [kent′-ish], *adj.* belonging to Kent; **K. fire,** prolonged applause or demonstration of dissent; **K. man,** a person living in any other part of Kent but East Kent, as opposed to **Man of Kent,** one living in East Kent; **K. rag,** a limestone of the lower greensand found in Kent. [*Kent*, the English county].

KENTLE, see QUINTAL.

KENTLEDGE, [kent′-lej], *n.* pig-iron used for ballast, and laid on the floor of a ship. [Uncert.].

KEPI, képi, [ke′-pē], *n.* a flat-topped French military cap, having a horizontal peak. [Germ. Swiss *käppi*, *dim.* of *kappe* cap].

KERAMIC, see CERAMIC.

KERARGYRITE, see CERARGYRITE.

KERASINE, [ke′-ras-īn], *adj.* horny, resembling horn. [Gk. *keras* a horn].

KERATIN, [ke′-rat-in], *n.* the principal constituent of hair and horn. [Gk. *keras* a horn].

KERATITIS, [ke′-rat-it′-is], *n.* chronic inflammation of the cornea. [Gk. *keras* horn and *itis* denoting inflammation].

KEPI

KERATONYXIS, [ke′-rat-on-iks′-is], *n.* (*opt.*) the operation of couching with a needle through the cornea of the eye to break the opaque mass of a cataract. [Gk. *keras* horn and *nuxis* pricking].

KERATOSE (1), [ke'-rat-ōs], *n.* horn-like substance of which part of the skeleton of certain sponges consists.

KERATOSE (2), [ke'-rat-ōs], *adj.* horny.

KERB, [kurb], *n.* the edge of the pavement of a street, a raised path,etc.; **on the k.**,Stock-Exchange business transacted in the street, *esp.* after the exchange has closed. [~CURB (1)].

KERBSTONE, [kurb'-stōn], *n.* one of the stones forming the kerb; **k. broker**, a broker who is not a member of the Stock Exchange.

KERCHIEF (1), [kur'-chēf], *n.* a cloth worn by women to cover the head; a scarf. [OFr. *couvrechief* head-covering].

KERCHIEF (2), [kur'-chēf], *v.t.* to cover with a kerchief.

KERF, [kurf], *n.* the slit, channel, or notch made by a saw, axe, or other cutting instrument; the place at which a tree or branch has been cut; that which is cut off, a cutting. [OE. *cyrf* something cut off].

KERMES, [kur'-mēz], *n.* the female of the insect *Coccus ilicis*, the dried bodies of which are used in making a crimson dye; the bright red dye obtained from the dried bodies of this insect; kermes-mineral. [Arab. *qirmiz*].

KERMES-MINERAL, [kur'-mēz-min'-er-al], *n.* a crimson-coloured mineral, antimony trisulphide.

KERMESS(E), KERMIS, [kur'-mes'], *n.* a periodical fair in the Netherlands, originally held on a Church anniversary. [Du. *kermis* from *kerkmisse* Church mass].

KERN (1), [kurn], *n.* (*hist.*) a light-armed Irish infantry-man; an Irish peasant. [Ir. *ceithern* a band of soldiers, a soldier].

KERN (2), [kurn], *n.* (*print.*) that part of a type extending beyond the body or shank of the type. [Fr. *carne* the nib of a quill pen].

KERN (3), [kurn], *v.i.* to harden, to seed, to develop the grains in the ear, to corn. [ME. *kerne*].

KERN-BABY, [kurn'-bā'-bi], *n.* an image adorned with corn, and carried before reapers to the harvest-home.

KERNEL, [kurn'-el], *n.* the seed of a fruit, *esp.* when enclosed within a hard husk or shell; a grain of wheat or other grassy plant; †a hard rounded swelling or concretion in the flesh, a swollen gland; (*fig.*) the essential point, the central part of anything. [OE. (Kentish) *cernel* a little corn].

KERNELLED, [kurn'-eld], *adj.* possessing a kernel.

KERNELLY, [kurn'-el-i], *adj.* full of kernels, like kernels.

KEROSENE, [ke'-rōs-ēn], *n.* oil for illumination obtained from petroleum. [Gk. *keros* wax].

KERRIA, [ke'-ri-a], *n.* (*bot.*) jew's mallow, or Japanese rose, *Kerria japonica*. [William *Kerr*, the English botanist].

KERRY, [ke'-ri], *n.* the name of an Irish county used to denote a large breed of terrier or a breed of dairy cattle.

KERSEY, [kurz'-i], *n.* a coarse, closely woven, ribbed variety of woollen cloth. [*Kersey* in Suffolk, where once made].

KERSEYMERE, [kurz'-i-mēer], *n.* a fine twilled woollen cloth, cashmere. [Corruption of CASHMERE].

KESTREL, [kes'-trel], *n.* the windhover, *Falco tinnunculus*, a small migratory falcon. [OFr. *quercerelle*].

KETCH, [kech], *n.* a small two-masted vessel having a short mizzen-mast. [~CATCH (1)].

KETCHUP, [kech'-up], *n.* a cold sauce containing mushrooms, tomatoes, or walnuts. [Malay *kechup*].

KETONE, [kē'-tōn], *n.* (*chem.*) a member of a group of organic compounds, of which acetone is a member, produced in distilling organic acids and by oxidation of a secondary alcohol. [Germ. *keton*, ~ACETONE].

KETTLE, [ketl], *n.* a metal vessel, provided with a spout and handle, used for boiling liquids; **a pretty k. of fish**, (*coll.*) a nice mess. [OE. *cetel*, OScand. *ketill*].

KETTLEDRUM, [ketl'-drum], *n.* a drum made of copper and having a parchment head; an afternoon tea-party.

KETTLE-HOLDER, [ketl'-hōld'-er], *n.* small piece of cloth to protect the hand when grasping the heated handle of a kettle.

KETTLE-PINS, [ketl'-pinz], *n.*(*pl.*) ninepins, skittles.

KEUPER, [koi'-per], *n.* (*geol.*) the upper portion of the Triassic system, including marls, sandstones, and clays.

KEVEL (1), [kev'-el], *n.* (*naut.*) a large cleat for belaying ropes. [ONFr. *keville*].

KEVEL† (2), [kev'-el], *n.* a young gazelle. [Senegalese].

KEX, KECKS, [keks], *n.* the dried hollow stalks of certain umbelliferous plants. [ME. *keks*].

KEY (1), [kē], *n.* a small metal instrument with one end shaped to fit the wards of a lock, and by which the bolt of a lock may be moved backwards and forwards; a strategic position from which one may dominate; a representation of a key as a symbol of office or authority; (*mus.*) a system of related notes, consisting of a particular note together with its scale, on which the whole, or a portion, of a composition is based; pitch; tone, medium, style; (*fig.*) that which serves to explain anything, a set of answers to a series of problems or questions, a translation; that which resembles a key in shape or function, an instrument for winding up a watch, a contrivance for screwing or unscrewing a bolt, a wedge of wood fastened across the grain to prevent warping, a wedge for securing a joint, the first layer of plaster over the laths of a wall, which serves to bind the rest; (*arch.*) the central stone of an arch, binding it together; a small button or lever depressed by the fingers in working a telegraphic instrument or typewriter; (*mus.*) a lever on a musical instrument depressed by the fingers, causing a padded hammer to strike against the strings of a pianoforte, or opening the valves or holes of a wind instrument, the piece of wood in the neck of string instruments by which the strings are tuned to the required pitch; (*fig.*) that which opens up or unlocks; (*theol.*, *pl.*) the spiritual power or authority of the Pope or priests as being representatives of Christ upon earth; a winged fruit, as the sycamore; **latch k.**, the key opening the main door of a house; **master, skeleton-k.**, a key so constructed as to be capable of opening a number of locks; **House of Keys**, one of the two assemblies of the Manx legislature; **k. industry**, an industry essential to other industries which could not exist without supplies of its manufactures; **k. signature**, (*mus.*) a sign, consisting of an arrangement of sharps and flats, indicating the key of a musical composition; **gold k.**, the symbol of office of the Lord Chamberlain; **power of the keys**, authority of the Pope or clergy to grant or withhold privilege; **k. move**, (*chess*) the opening move in the solution of a problem. [OE. *cæg*].

KEY (2), [kē], *n.* a low-lying island, reef, or ridge of rocks near the surface of the water. [Span. *cayo* shoal].

KEY (3), see QUAY.

KEY (4), [kē], *v.t.* to lock or secure with or attach to a key; (*mus.*) to tune to a particular pitch; to vary the wording of (an advertisement inserted in different publications) in such a way that the advertiser can identify the corresponding replies; **to k. up**, to rouse to a state of nervous excitement. [KEY (1)].

KEYAGE, see QUAYAGE.

KEYBOARD, [kē'-bawd], *n.* the complete series of keys on a piano, organ, typewriter, etc.

KEYBOLT, [kē'-bōlt], *n.* a bolt secured by a cotter instead of a nut.

KEYED, [kēd], *adj.* furnished with a key; secured or fastened by a key; having a keystone.

KEYHOLE, [kē'-hōl], *n.* the hole in a lock for the key.

KEYLESS, [kē'-les], *adj.* able to be wound up without a key.

KEYNOTE, [kē'-nōt], *n.* (*mus.*) the tonic note of a particular key; (*fig.*) the predominant or prevailing tone, motive, or feature.

KEY-RING, [kē'-ring], *n.* a split ring on which a bunch of keys may be carried.

KEYSTONE, [kē'-stōn], *n.* the central stone of an arch serving to bind the other stones together; (*fig.*) principal element, basis, that round which all else is built.

KHABAR, [kab'-ah(r)], *n.* news. [Hind. *khabar*].

KHADDAR, [kad'-ah(r)], *n.* a variety of native home-spun cloth in India. [Hindu *khaddar*].

KHAKI (1), [kah'-ki], *n.* dull yellowish-brown twilled fabric used for the regulation field-service military uniform.

KHAKI (2), [kah'-ki], *adj.* dull yellowish-brown, resembling the colour of the ground or sun-parched grass. [Hind. *khaki* dust-coloured].

KHAMSIN, KAMSIN, [kam'-sēn], *n.* a hot southerly wind blowing in Egypt for about fifty days, at a certain season of the year. [Arab. *khamsun* fifty].

KHAN (1), [kahn], *n.* title given to rulers, governors, or high officials in Central Asia, formerly applied to princes and chieftains. [Pers. *khan* lord].

KHAN (2), [kahn], *n.* an unequipped eastern inn or caravanserai. [Arab. *khan* inn].
KHANATE, [kahn'-āt], *n.* district ruled or governed by a khan.
KHANSAMAH, [kahn'-sam-ah], *n.* a native butler or steward in an Anglo-Indian house. [Pers. *khansaman* lord of stores].
KHEDDAH, [ked'-a], *n.* an enclosure used in the capture of wild elephants. [Hind. *kheda*].
KHEDIVE, [ked-ēv'], *n.* the title assumed by the Turkish Viceroys in Egypt from 1867 until the establishment of the independent kingdom of Egypt in 1922. [Pers. *khadiv*].
KHEDIVIAL, [ked-iv'-i-al], *adj.* of, or pertaining to, the Khedive.
KHIDMUTGAR, [kid'-mut-gah(r)], *n.* a man-servant who waits at table. [Pers. *khidmatgar*].
KHUTBAH, [kut'-ba], *n.* an oration or public prayer offered in the Moslem mosques every Friday. [Arab. *khutbah* from *khatabah* to preach].
KIBBLE, [kibl], *n.* an iron bucket for raising ore from a mine, a well-bucket. [Germ. *kübel* tub].
KIBE, [kīb], *n.* an ulcerated chilblain, *esp.* one on the heel. [Unkn.].
KIBED, [kībd], *adj.* affected with broken chilblains on the heel.
KIBITKA, [kib-it'-ka], *n.* a Russian vehicle with a covered hoop-shaped hood; a circular Tartar tent of lattice work covered with strong felt. [Russ. *kibitka*].
KIBITZER, [ki-bitz'-er], *n.* (*U.S.*) a looker-on who professes to know more about the matter in hand than do the participants. [Yiddish].
KIBLAH, KEBLAH, [kib'-lah], *n.* the point towards which Mohammedans turn their faces in prayer, being the direction in which lies the sacred shrine at Mecca. [Arab. *qiblah* from *qabala* to lie opposite].
KIBOSH, [kī'-bosh], *n.* (*slang*) stuff and nonsense; **to put the k. on,** to put a stop to, to spoil. [Unkn.].
KIBY, [kīb'-i], *adj.* suffering from kibes.
KICK (1), [kik], *n.* a blow with the foot; the act of kicking; one who kicks; the recoil of a gun; (*coll.*) a bite, snap; (*slang*) a thrill, feeling of acute satisfaction; a sixpence; **to get the k.,** (*slang*) to be dismissed from a post; **k. off,** the start of a football match; **k. about,** an informal game of football. [KICK (2)].
KICK (2), [kik], *v.t.* to strike with the foot; to strike on account of a sharp recoil; to achieve by kicking; *v.i.* to strike or thrust out violently with the foot or feet; (of a gun) to recoil; (*cricket, etc.*) to rear up sharply beyond the normal rebound; (*fig.*) to object strongly, to resist; **to k. against,** to be strongly opposed to, to resent; **to k. off,** to remove by kicking; (*football*) to start or resume the game by kicking the ball from the centre of the ground; **to k. out,** (*slang*) to eject forcibly, to cause to leave, to dismiss from a post or position; **to k. up,** to create, raise, cause, stir up; **to k. against the pricks,** to resist vainly something that rankles but must be endured; **to k. the beam,** to cause the lighter end of a balance to rise and hit the beam; (*coll.*) to weigh; **to k. the bucket,** (*slang*) to die; **to k. one's heels,** (*coll.*) to remain needlessly inactive, to waste one's time in impatient idleness; **to k. over the traces,** to break loose from some imposed restraint. [ME. *kiken*].
KICKER, [kik'-er], *n.* one who kicks; (*U.S.*) one who continually disparages or depreciates.
KICKSHAW, [kik'-shaw], *n.* a light dainty dish, a tasty delicacy; a vain, superficially attractive object or ornament, a knick-knack. [Fr. *quelque chose* something].
KICKSIES, [kik'-siz], *n.(pl.)* (*slang*) the wide-bottomed pearl-buttoned trousers of costermongers.
KICK-UP, [kik'-up], *n.* (*slang*) a row, shindy; a hilarious party.
KID (1), [kid], *n.* a young goat or antelope; the skin or flesh of a young goat or antelope; leather made from the skin of a kid; (*astron.*) a group of three stars in the constellation Auriga, reputed to herald impending storms; (*slang*) a child, a young, inexperienced person. [ME. *kid*].
KID (2), [kid], *n.* a faggot, a bundle of furze, brushwood, etc. [Unkn.].
KID (3), [kid], *n.* (*naut.*) a small wooden tub or vessel. [Uncert.].
KID (4), [kid], *n.* (*slang*) a hoax, swindle. [Unkn.].
KID (5), **(kidding, kidded),** [kid], *v.i.* to bring forth young, as a goat.
KID (6), [kid], *v.t.* to make into a bundle or faggot.
KID (7), [kid], *v.t. and i.* to hoax, swindle.
KIDDER, [kid'-er], *n.* (*coll.*) a Kidderminster carpet.
KIDDERMINSTER, [kid'-er-mins'-ter], *n.* a kind of carpet made up of two cloths of different colours woven together to form a pattern. [*Kidderminster*, where made].
KIDDLE, [kidl], *n.* a wicker fish-weir, used with nets, for catching fish in rivers. [OFr. *quidel*].
KIDDOW, [kid'-ō], *n.* the guillemot. [Unkn.].
KIDDY, [kid'-i], *n.* (*coll.*) a small child.
KIDLING, [kid'-ling], *n.* a young kid.
KIDNAP, [kid'-nap], *v.t.* to steal and carry off (a child), to seize and forcibly carry away any person against his will. [KID (1) and *nap* from NAB].
KIDNAPPER, [kid'-nap-er], *n.* one who kidnaps.
KIDNEY, [kid'-ni], *n.* one of two long, flattened, glandular organs, situated in the back part of the abdominal cavity in mammals, reptiles and birds, which secrete urine from the blood and help to remove other waste products; anything like a kidney; (*fig.*) type, class, disposition. [Uncert.].
KIDNEY-BEAN, [kid'-ni-bēn'], *n.* name given to two varieties of bean, the dwarf French bean, *Phaseolus vulgaris*, and the scarlet runner, *Phaseolus multiflorus*.
KIDNEY-SHAPED, [kid'-ni-shāpt'], *adj.* having the shape of a kidney.
KIDNEY-VETCH, [kid'-ni-vech'], *n.* the plant, *Anthyllis vulneraria*.
KIEF, [kēf], *n.* drowsiness or stupor induced by inhaling Indian hemp. [Arab. *kaif* pleasurable ease].
KIEFEKIL, [kē'-fek-il], *n.* a kind of clay, meerschaum. [Uncert.].
KIE-KIE, [kē'-kē'], *n.* a climbing shrub found in New Zealand. [Maori *kie-kie*].
KIER, KEIR, [kēer], *n.* a vat in which textiles are boiled during bleaching. [~OIcel. *ker* vessel].
KIESELGUHR, [kē'-zel-gōōer], *n.* a fine white diatomaceous earth used in the manufacture of dynamite. [Germ. *kiesel* gravel and *guhr* earthy powder].
KILDERKIN, [kil'-der-kin], *n.* a cask containing sixteen gallons of ale or eighteen of beer; a measure of this amount. [~MDu. *kinderkin*].
KILERG, [kil'-erg], *n.* a unit of work equivalent to a thousand ergs. [KILO and ERG].
KILL (1), [kil], *n.* the act of killing; that which is killed. [KILL (2)].
KILL (2), [kil], *v.t.* to cause the death of; to blast; to slaughter; to destroy or weaken the vitality of; (*fig.*) to destroy, put an end to, suppress; to cause (time) to pass as quickly as possible; to destroy the effect of; to overwhelm, crush; (*coll.*) to produce a profound impression on; (*football*) to trap (the ball) with the foot so that it stops dead; (*tennis*) to smash or put away in such a manner that it may not be returned; to veto, defeat (a bill); to cause the failure of by adverse criticism; (*print.*) to suppress, omit; *v.i.* to cause death; to slaughter; **to k. with kindness,** to overwhelm with kindness. [ME. *killen*].
KILLADAR, [kil'-ad-ah(r)], *n.* the governor of an Indian fort. [Arab. *qila* fort and Pers. *dar* holder].
KILLAS, [kil'-as], *n.* a clay-slate. [Cornish].
KILLDEER, [kil'-dēer], *n.* the largest North American ring-plover, *Aegialitis vociferus*. [Echoic].
KILLER, [kil'-er], *n.* one who kills; a murderer; a butcher; an implement used for slaughtering animals; a voracious dolphin feeding on seals and whales, the grampus, *Orca gladiator*.
KILLICK, see KILLOCK.
KILLING (1), [kil'-ing], *n.* the act of slaughtering, destruction of life.
KILLING (2), [kil'-ing], *adj.* that kills, deadly; (*coll.*) exhausting; extremely amusing; winningly attractive.
KILLINITE, [kil'-in-īt], *n.* a pale-green mineral formed by the weathering or decomposition of spodumene. [*Killiney Bay*, near Dublin, Ireland].
KILLJOY, [kil'-joi], *n.* a gloomy, depressing person, a wet blanket.
KILLOCK, KILLICK, [kil'-ok], *n.* a large stone used on small vessels for an anchor, a small anchor. [Uncert.].
KILMARNOCK, [kil-mahn'-ok], *n.* a tam-o'-shanter. [*Kilmarnock*, in Scotland].
KILN, [kiln], *n.* a furnace or oven for drying, burning, baking or hardening. [OE. *cyln* from L. *culina*].
KILN-DRY, [kiln'-drī], *v.t.* to dry as in a kiln.
KILO-, *pref.* a thousand. [Gk. *khilioi* thousand].
KILODYNE, [kil'-ō-dīn], *n.* a thousand dynes. [KILO and DYNE].

KILOGRAM, KILOGRAMME, [kil'-ō-gram], *n.* a thousand grammes, or about 2¼ lb. avoirdupois. [KILO and GRAMME].

KILOGRAMMETRE, [kil'-ō-gram'-mē-ter], *n.* the energy required to raise a kilogram through one metre. [KILOGRAM and METRE].

KILOLITRE, [kil'-ō-lē'-ter], *n.* a thousand litres. [KILO and LITRE].

KILOMETRE, [kil'-ō-mē'-ter], *n.* a thousand metres. [KILO and METRE].

KILOWATT, [kil'-ō-wot'], *n.* (*elect.*) a thousand watts. [KILO and WATT].

KILT (1), [kilt], *n.* a short pleated skirt, usually of tartan cloth. [KILT (2)].

KILT (2), [kilt], *v.t.* to tuck up (as a skirt, etc.); to gather in vertical pleats. [~Dan. *kilte* to tuck up].

KILTER, see KELTER.

KILTIE, [kilt'-i], *n.* a soldier belonging to a kilted regiment.

KIMMER, [kim'-er], *n.* (*Scots*) a female neighbour, a young handsome girl.

KIMMERIDGE-CLAY, [kim'-er-ij-klā'], *n.* an oolitic clay obtainable at *Kimmeridge*, in the Isle of Purbeck.

KIMONO, [kim-ō'-nō], *n.* a long loose-fitting outer robe with wide sleeves, worn by the Japanese; a kind of dressing-gown. [Jap. *kimono*].

KIN, [kin], *n.* family, group of persons related by descent or consanguinity; relatives; relationship. [OE. *cynn* kind, race].

KILT

KINAESTHESIS, [kin'-es-thē'-sis], *n.* (*psych.*) awareness of muscular effort behind bodily movement. [Gk. *kino* I move and Gk. *aisthesis* perception].

KINAESTHETIC, [kin'-ēs-thet'-ik], *adj.* pertaining to kinaesthesis.

KINCOB, [kin'-kob], *n.* a rich Indian fabric embroidered with gold or silver thread-work. [Pers. *kinkhab*].

KIND (1), [kīnd], *n.* sort, variety, class, type; essential character, natural disposition; natural products as opposed to money; (*archaic*) race, species; way, manner; (*eccles.*) one of the elements in the ceremony of Holy Communion. [OE. *gecynd* nature].

KIND (2), [kīnd], *adj.* naturally disposed to do good to or help others, and make them happy; benevolent, considerate, indulgent; proceeding from goodness of heart; also used in various formal or polite phrases with little or no significance. [OE. *gecynde* natural].

KINDERGARTEN, [kind'-er-gah-ten], *n.* an infant school. [Germ. *kindergarten*].

KIND-HEARTED, [kīnd'-haht'-id], *adj.* benevolent.

KINDLE, [kindl], *v.t.* to set fire to, light; (*fig.*) to illuminate, cause to glow; to provoke, incite; *v.i.* to take fire; (*fig.*) to glow, shine; to become excited, to flare up. [~OIcel. *kynda*].

KINDLER, [kind'-ler], *n.* one who, or that which, kindles.

KINDLESS, [kīnd'-less], *adj.* unkind.

KINDLINESS, [kīnd'-li-nes], *n.* the state of being kindly; a kindly act or deed.

KINDLING, [kind'-ling], *n.* the act of setting fire to or of becoming inflamed; fuel for lighting a fire.

KINDLY (1), [kīnd'-li], *adj.* benevolent and sympathetic; expressing or displaying kindness of heart; †natural. [OE. *gecyndelic*].

KINDLY (2), [kīnd'-li], *adv.* in a kind manner. [OE. *gecyndelice*].

KINDNESS, [kīnd'-nes], *n.* the quality of being kind; a kind deed or act.

KINDRED (1), [kin'-dred], *n.* relationship by blood or birth, now loosely including relationship by marriage; group of persons related by blood; kinsfolk. [OE. *cynnræden*].

KINDRED (2), [kin'-dred], *adj.* belonging to the same family, related by blood or birth; congenial, having similar qualities of properties; related, allied.

KIND-SPOKEN, [kīnd'-spōk'-en], *adj.* kindly spoken or speaking.

KINE, [kīn], *n.* (*poet.*) cows, cattle. [ME. *kin* from OE. *cy*, (*pl.*) of *cu* cow].

KINEMA, see CINEMA.

KINEMATIC, KINEMATICAL, [kin'-im-at'-ik-(al)], *adj.* pertaining to kinematics. [Gk. *kinema* motion].

KINEMATICS, [kin'-im-at'-iks], *n.*(*pl*) (*phys.*) the science dealing with pure motion, irrespective of the force producing it or the mass moved.

KINEMATOGRAPH, see CINEMATOGRAPH.

KINEMATOGRAPHY, see CINEMATOGRAPHY.

KINESIPATHY, [kin'-es-ip'-ath-i], *n.* the treatment of disease by muscular movement or gymnastic exercises. [Gk. *kinesis* motion and *pathos* suffering].

KINETIC, [kin-et'-ik, kī-net'-ik], *adj.* (*phys.*) pertaining to or due to motion. [Gk. *kinetikos* moving].

KINETICS, [kin-et'-iks, kī-net'-iks], *n.*(*pl.*) (*phys.*) that branch of dynamics which deals with the motions of bodies considered in relation to the forces acting upon them.

KING (1), [king], *n.* the male sovereign of a nation, the monarch, usually succeeding by hereditary right; one who holds a position of influence in a certain sphere; (*fig.*) the chief, the supreme example; (*cards*) a card bearing a picture of a king and generally ranking in value above a queen; the principal piece in chess; (*draughts*) a piece that has been crowned by having a similar piece placed on it, and which may move either backwards or forwards; **k. of beasts,** the lion; **k. of birds,** the eagle; **K. of Kings,** God; a title of certain Eastern monarchs; **k. fern,** the royal fern, *Osmunda regalis*; **K. of Arms,** one of the three chief officers of the College of Arms below the Earl Marshal, and being Garter, Norroy and Clarenceux for England, and Lyon for Scotland; **King's Bench,** the division of the High Court of Justice presided over by the Lord Chief Justice; **king's clover,** the melilot, *Melilotus officinalis*; **King's Counsel,** barristers appointed as counsel to the Crown, appointed by patent, wearing a silk gown, sitting within the bar of the court, always assisted by a junior counsel, and taking precedence over other barristers; **King's evidence,** evidence given by an accomplice in a crime against his fellow criminals; **king's evil,** the scrofula, supposed to be cured by the touch of a king; **king's spear,** the plant, *Asphodelus albus*; **king's yellow,** a compound of sulphur and arsenic. [OE. *cyning*].

KING (2), [king], *v.t. and i.* to make a king; to rule as, or occupy a position comparable with that of, a king. [*Prec.*].

KING-APPLE, [king'-apl], *n.* a large red variety of apple.

KINGBIRD, [king'-burd], *n.* the American tyrant fly-catcher, *Tyrannus pipiri*, a kind of bird of paradise..

KING-CRAB, [king'-krab'], *n.* a large animal of the genus *Limulus*, having an upper shell shaped like a broad horseshoe, and a lower shell rather like that of a crab.

KINGCRAFT, [king'-krahft], *n.* the art of ruling as a king.

KINGCUP, [king'-kup], *n.* the marsh marigold, *Caltha palustris*.

KINGDOM, [king'-dom], *n.* the state, authority, or power of a king; the territory ruled over by a king, the realm; the rule of God in heaven or upon earth; (*nat. hist.*) one of the three main divisions of nature; **k. come,** heaven, the life hereafter. [~OE. *cynedom*].

KINGFISH, [king'-fish], *n.* the name given to various edible fishes distinguished by their size, appearance, etc.

KINGFISHER, [king'-fish-er], *n.* the halcyon, a bird of the genus *Alcedo*, distinguished by its long beak and brightly coloured plumage, dwelling near streams and rivers, and feeding on fish.

KINGFISHER

KINGHOOD, [king'-hŏŏd], *n.* condition of being a king.

KINGLESS, [king'-les], *adj.* without king.

KINGLET, [king'-let], *n.* a puppet king; the golden-crested wren.

KINGLIKE, [king'-lik], *adj.* like a king, kingly, regal, majestic.

KINGLINESS, [king'-li-nes], *n.* the quality of being kingly.

KINGLING, [king'-ling], *n.* an insignificant, petty king.

KINGLY, [king'-li], *adj* pertaining to a king; becoming, or as befits, a king; regal, majestic, noble; worthy of a king; *adv.* in the manner of a king.

KING-PIN, [king'-pin'], *n.* the main bolt in a machine or structure; (*fig.*) a leading figure. [KING and PIN (1)].

KINGPOST, [king'-pōst], *n.* (*carp.*) the main perpendicular beam supporting the ridge of a roof, and running from the horizontal tie-beam to the apex of the roof; (*aeron.*) the strut to which the bracing wires are secured.

KINGSHIP, [king'-ship], *n.* the state of being a king.

KINGSTONE, [king'-stōn], *n.* the angel fish, or monk fish, a species of *Rhina*.

KINGWOOD, [king'-wo͝od], *n.* a Brazilian hardwood, having a violet colouring and used in making cabinets, etc.

KINK (1), [kingk], *n.* a short twist, bend or curl in a rope, hair, wire, etc., at which it is doubled upon itself; (*fig.*) a mental or moral twist, oddity, or irregularity. [~Du. *kink* a twist].

KINK (2), [kingk], *v.t.* and *i.* to twist or curl so as to form a kink in. [*Prec.*].

KINKAJOU, [kingk'-a-jo͞o], *n.* a species of *Cercoleptes*, a nocturnal animal allied to the racoon, having short legs and a long tail, dwelling in trees, and being very partial to honey. [Native].

KINKLE (1), [kingkl], *n.* a small kink, twist, or curl in the hair, etc.

KINKLE (2), [kingkl], *v.t. and i.* to form into kinkles.

KINKY, [kingk-i], *adj.* full of kinks.

KINLESS, [kin'-les], *adj.* without kinsfolk or relatives.

KINNIKINIK, [kin'-i-kin'-ik], *n.* a mixture of dried leaves and bark of various plants smoked by the North American Indians in place of tobacco. [Native].

KINO, [kē'-nō], *n.* an astringent substance obtained from the stem of *Pterocarpus Marsupium* and other trees, being the thickened dried juice of these trees. [African].

KINOPLASM, [kin'-ō-plazm, kī'-nō-plazm], *n.* (*biol.*) that part of protoplasm concerned with movement. [Gk. *kino* I move and PLASM].

KINSFOLK, [kinz'-fōk], *n.*(*pl.*) persons of the same family, relatives.

KINSH, [kinsh], *n.* a lever for raising stones. [Unkn.].

KINSHIP, [kin'-ship], *n.* blood relationship; (*fig.*) affinity, close connexion or similarity, likeness in temperament.

KINSMAN, [kinz'-man], *n.* a male relation, *esp.* one related by blood or birth. [KIN and MAN].

KINSWOMAN, [kinz'-wo͝om'-an], *n.* a female relation, *esp.* one related by blood or birth.

KIOSK, [kē-osk'], *n.* a Turkish or Persian open summer-house, consisting usually of a light structure, often pillared and equipped with a balustrade; a light, open, ornamental building resembling this, in Western Europe, used as a bandstand, refreshment place, or newspaper stall. [Turk. *kiushk* pavilion].

KIP (1), [kip], *n.* the hide of young cattle, *esp.* when used for leather. [Unkn.].

KIP (2), **(kipping, kipped)**, [kip], *v.i.* (*slang*) to sleep, to go to bed. [~Du. *kippe* a mean dwelling].

KIPE, [kīp], *n.* a basket for catching fish. [OE. *cype* a basket].

KIPPER (1), [kip'-er], *n.* a male salmon during spawning time; a herring or mackerel cleaned, dried, smoked, and salted; (*slang*) a person. [~OE. *cypera*].

KIPPER (2), [kip'-er], *v.t.* (of a herring or mackerel) to cure by cleaning, drying, smoking, and salting. [*Prec.*].

KIPSKIN, [kip'-skin], *n.* the tanned hide of young cattle, used as leather.

KIRBEH, [kur'-bā], *n.* a water-skin. [Arab. *kirbeh*].

KIRIMON, [ki'-rim-on], *n.* one of the two Japanese Imperial crests, three leaves of the paulownia tree beneath three budding stems. [Jap. *kiri* the paulownia tree and *mon* crest].

KIRK, [kurk], *n.* (*dial.*) a church; the **K.**, the **Auld K.**, the (Established) Church of Scotland; **K. session**, the lowest court of the Established Church of Scotland, composed of the minister and lay elders. [OScand. *kirkja*].

KIROUMBO, [ki-ro͞om'-bō], *n.* a bird of the genus *Leptosoma*. [*Kiroumbo*, an island near Madagascar].

KIRSCHWASSER, [kēersh'-vas'-er], *n.* an intoxicating spirit made in Germany from the fermented juice and crushed stones of cherries. [Germ. *kirsch* cherry and *wasser* water].

KIRTLE, [kurtl], *n.* a woman's gown, skirt or petticoat; a man's short tunic extending as far as the knees or just below. [OE. *cyrtel*].

KIRTLED, [kurtld], *adj.* wearing a kirtle.

KISH, [kish], *n.* a large woven basket used for carrying turf in Ireland. [Ir. *cis*].

KISMET, [kiz'-met], *n.* fate or destiny. [Arab. *qismat*].

KISS (1), [kis], *n.* a pressure or salute given with the lips as a sign of reverence or homage, or as a caress of love and affection; (*fig.*) a gentle touch, pressure or contact; name given to a small sweet or sugared confection; (*billiards*) a stroke in which the ball struck hits the object ball a second time, a contact between moving balls at billiards or bowls. [*Next*].

KISS (2), [kis], *v.t.* to give a kiss to, to salute or caress with the lips; (*fig.*) to touch lightly, to caress gently (*billiards*) to strike a second time; *v. reflex.* to kiss each other; **to k. the dust, ground,** to be overthrown or slain; **to k. the rod,** to bow to discipline and punishment. [OE. *cyssan*].

KISS-CURL, [kis'-kurl], *n.* a small curl on the temple or forehead.

KISSER, [kis'-er], *n.* one who kisses; (*slang*) the mouth.

KISSING-COMFIT, [kis'-ing-kum'-fit], *n.* a perfumed sweet to sweeten the breath.

KISSING-CRUST, [kis'-ing-krust'], *n.* the soft part of the crust of a loaf where it has touched another loaf during baking.

KISS-ME-QUICK, [kis'-mi-kwik'], *n.* a small old-fashioned bonnet worn on the back of the head, a curl in front of the ear.

KIST, [kist], *n.* (*dial.*) a chest, coffer, strong-box; a coffin. [OScand. *kista*].

KISTVAEN, [kist'-vān], *n.* a sepulchral chamber made of flat stones in the form of a chest. [Wel. *cist faen* stone chest].

KIT (1), [kit], *n.* a small round wooden tub usually having a handle; receptacle in which a soldier, sailor or airman carries his outfit and personal belongings; box or bag in which a workman's tools are carried; the outfit or personal equipment of a soldier, sailor or airman; set of tools required in some particular occupation; special attire, equipment, or outfit for sport, travelling, etc. [MDu. *kitte* wooden vessel].

KIT (2), [kit], *n.* a small violin. [Unkn.].

KIT-BAG, [kit'-bag'], *n.* a long bag in which a soldier, sailor, or airman carries his kit; a leather travelling-bag for carrying personal equipment or attire.

KITCAT, [kit'-kat'], *n.* a Whig political and literary club founded in London in 1703, which met at the pie-house of Christopher Cat, from which the club took its name; **k. portrait,** a small, less than half-length, portrait including the upper part of the body and the hands, so called from the portraits of the club members done in this size.

KITCHEN (1), [kich'-en], *n.* the room or part of a house or building in which the cookery is done. [OE. *cycene* from L. *coquina*].

KITCHEN (2), [kich'-en], *adj.* pertaining to a kitchen; **k. garden,** a plot of ground in which vegetables are raised for the table; **k. stuff,** fat, dripping, or waste-products of the kitchen; vegetables or produce to be cooked in the kitchen.

KITCHENER, [kich'-en-er], *n.* a cooking range; the person in charge of the kitchen of a monastery.

KITCHENETTE, [kich'-en-et'], *n.* a small combined kitchen and pantry.

KITCHENMAID, [kich'-en-mād'], *n.* a female servant who does the rougher work of a kitchen.

KITCHEN-MIDDEN, [kich'-en-mid'-en], *n.* a refuse heap from a dwelling of primitive man containing bones of animals, shells, stone implements, etc. [~Dan. *kjökkenmodding* rubbish heap].

KITE, [kīt], *n.* a bird of prey of the hawk family distinguished by its long forked tail, long wings, and short legs; a flying toy or contrivance consisting of a light wooden framework covered with paper or other light material, steadied by a tail, having a long length of string attached to it, by which the flier retains control over it when it is carried aloft by the wind; (*comm.*) an accommodation bill or bill of exchange; (*fig.*) a rapacious person, one who preys upon others; **to fly the k.,** to throw out a feeler to test public opinion upon some matter. [OE. *cyta*].

KITE

KITE-BALLOON, [kīt'-bal-o͞on'], *n.* a captive observation balloon used for obtaining recordings of scientific information.

KITE-FLYING, [kīt'-flī'-ing], *n.* (*comm.*) the act or practice of dealing in accommodation paper for the purpose of raising money.

KITEFOOT, [kīt'-fo͝ot], *n.* a kind of tobacco plant.

KITH, [kith], *n.* (*archaic*) friends, acquaintances; **k. and kin,** close friends and relations, often implying only relatives or family. [OE. *cyththu* knowledge, native land].

KITLING, [kit'-ling], *n.* a kitten. [~OIcel. *ketlingr*].

KITTEN (1), [kitn], *n.* a young cat. [~OFr. *chitoun*].

KITTEN (2), [kitn], *v.i.* to bring forth, give birth to, kittens.

KITTENISH, [kitn'-ish], *adj.* playful, like a kitten, frisky, lively.

KITTIWAKE, [kit'-i-wāk], *n.* a three-toed variety of seagull, *Rissa tridactyla*, so called from its cry. [Echoic].

KITTLE (1), [kitl], *adj.* difficult to manage, awkward to handle, ticklish. [*Var.* of TICKLE].

KITTLE (2), [kitl], *v.i.* (*prov.*) to have kittens.

KITTLISH, [kit'-lish], *adj.* ticklish, difficult, awkward.

KITTY, [kit'-i], *n.* a pet name for a kitten; the pool of stakes to which the players of certain card-games contribute in turn; the common fund out of which certain communal expenses of a party are paid.

KIVE, see KEEVE.

KIWI, [kē'-wē], *n.* the apteryx, a New Zealand flightless bird with a long curved beak, and no tail; (*aeron. slang*) a member of the Royal Air Force not actually engaged in flying. [Maori native name].

KIWI

KLEPHT, [kleft], *n.* a Greek bandit or brigand, originally one of a band of Greeks who would not be ruled by the Turks after their conquest of Greece, and who asserted their independence in the mountains. [MdGk. *klephtes* robber].

KLEPTOMANIA, [klept'-ō-mā'-ni-a], *n.* a form of mental disease or disorder expressing itself in an irresistible urge to steal. [Gk. *kleptes* thief and MANIA].

KLEPTOMANIAC, [klept'-ō-mān'-i-ak'], *n.* one suffering from kleptomania.

KLICK†, see CLICK (1).

KLIPSPRINGER, [klip'-spring'-er], *n.* an antelope of the genus *Oreotragus*. [Afrikaans *klip* rock and SPRINGER].

KLOOF, [kloōf], *n.* a narrow gorge or ravine. [Du. *kloof* cleft].

KNACK, [nak], *n.* a trick, dodge; special dexterity, knowledge or manipulative skill required to do something, the trick of knowing how to do something and being able to do it well; gift, art, talent. [Uncert.].

KNACKER (1), [nak'-er], *n.*(*pl.*) two pieces of wood or bone held between the fingers, and played by striking them together; a castanet. [Swed. *knacka* to crack].

KNACKER (2), [nak'-er], *n.* one who buys worn-out horses for slaughter, and cuts the carcases up for dogs' meat; one who buys up old houses or ships to be broken up for scrap. [Uncert.].

KNACKY, [nak'-i], *adj.* having a knack, cunning, clever, ingenious.

KNAG, [nag], *n.* a short knob or stump projecting from the trunk of a tree, a peg, hook; a knot in the grain of wood. [ME. *knagge*].

KNAGGY, [nag'-i], *adj.* knotty, rough, knobby, gnarled, abounding in knags.

KNAP (1), [nap], *n.* the top, summit of a hill, a hillock. [OE. *cnæp*].

KNAP (2), (knapping, knapped), [nap], *v.t. and i.* to strike smartly; to break, crack in pieces or snap by a sharp blow; to tap or knock off; to bite. [~Du. *knappen* to snap].

KNAPPER, [nap'-er], *n.* a maker of flint flakes, a stone-breaker; a hammer used in shaping and breaking flints.

KNAPSACK, [nap'-sak'], *n.* a small bag or wallet of canvas or leather, used for carrying food, clothing, and personal belongings, slung over the shoulder or strapped to the back. [LGerm. *knapsack* food-bag].

KNAPWEED, [nap'-wēd], *n.* a plant of the genus *Centaurea*, a hardy weed having a purple flower. [~KNOP and WEED].

KNAR, [nah(r)], *n.* a knarl. [ME. *knarre*].

KNARL†, see GNARL (1).

KNARLED†, see GNARLED.

KNARRY, [nah'-ri], *adj.* knotty.

KNAVE, [nāv], *n.* a dishonest person, a rogue, rascal, a base fellow; (*cards*) the lowest court-card, the jack, ranking between the queen and ten, and bearing a picture of a page; †a boy, a servant-lad. [OE. *cnafa* boy].

KNAVERY, [nāv'-er-i], *n.* dishonesty, petty villainy, fraud, sharp tricks or practices.

KNAVISH, [nāv'-ish], *adj.* worthy of a knave, dishonest, roguish, underhand, rascally.

KNAVISHLY, [nāv'-ish-li], *adv.* in a knavish fashion.

KNAVISHNESS, [nāv'-ish-nes], *n.* the quality of being knavish.

KNAWEL, [naw'-el], *n.* a plant of the genus *Scleranthus*, knotgrass. [Germ. *knauel*].

KNEAD, [nēd], *v.t.* to work into a soft yielding mass by pressing out and squeezing together with the hands; to make soft or supple by similar movements with the hands; (*fig.*) to mould, fashion. [OE. *cnedan*].

KNEADABLE, [nēd'-abl], *adj.* able to be kneaded.

KNEADING, [nēd'-ing], *n.* the act of working into dough, or any similar movement of the hands.

KNEADING-TROUGH, [nēd'-ing-trof'], *n.* a trough or tray in which dough is kneaded.

KNEE (1), [nē], *n.* the joint, together with the part surrounding it, of the thigh and the lower leg bones of a human being; a joint resembling or corresponding to this, as the heel of a bird, joint in the foreleg of a horse; a bent or angular piece of timber or metal resembling in shape a bent knee, *esp.* one used for connecting the beams of a ship; **to bow the k.,** to submit, yield, acknowledge defeat; **to bend the k. to,** to pray to. [OE. *cneo*].

KNEE (2), [nē], *v.t.* to strike, knock with the knee; to stretch out of shape, lose the crease, at the knee.

KNEE-BREECHES, [nē'-brich'-iz], *n.*(*pl.*) breeches fastening just below the knee.

KNEECAP, [nē'-kap'], *n.* a small, flat, heart-shaped bone, the patella, situated at the fore-part of the knee-joint; a cover or protection for the knee.

KNEED, [nēd], *adj.* having knees; (*bot.*) bent or having a joint or angle like the knee; baggy at the knees.

KNEE-DEEP, [nē'-dēp], *adj.* up to the knees.

KNEE-HIGH, [nē'-hī], *adj.* rising to the knees.

KNEEHOLE DESK, [nē'-hōl-desk], *n.* a desk with an opening in the front shaped to admit the knees and legs.

KNEE-HOLLY, [nē'-hol'-i], *n.* (*bot.*) butcher's broom, *Ruscus aculeatus*.

KNEEHOLM, [nē'-hōm], *n.* knee-holly.

KNEEJOINT, [nē'-joint], *n.* the joint of the knee, a hinged joint resembling that of the knee.

KNEEL, (kneeling, knelt), [nēl], *v.i.* to go down on one's bended knees so that the weight of the body is supported by the knees as they rest upon the ground. [OE. *cneowlian*].

KNEELER, [nēl'-er], *n.* one who kneels; a hassock or cushion on which to kneel.

KNEELINGLY, [nēl'-ing-li], *adv.* in a posture of kneeling.

KNEEPAN, [nē'-pan'], *n.* the kneecap.

KNEE-PIECE, [nē'-pēs], *n.* a protective covering for the knee; a bent piece of timber used to connect beams in shipbuilding; (*arch.*) a rafter bent down in the form of an angle.

KNEE-STOP, [nē'-stop'], *n.* a lever operated by the knee of the performer on an organ to diminish or increase gradually the volume of sound.

KNEE-TIMBER, [nē'-tim'-ber], *n.* timber used in making knees because it is naturally bent.

KNEE-TRIBUTE, [nē'-trib'-yoōt], *n.* tribute paid by kneeling.

KNELL (1), [nel], *n.* the sound of a church bell tolling, *esp.* of one rung at a funeral or to announce a death or disaster; (*fig.*) an omen of death or ending; **to sound the k. of,** to indicate or announce the ending of. [OE. *knell*].

KNELL (2), [nel], *v.t.* to summon or call by a knell; *v.i.* to toll as at a death or funeral, to sound mournfully. [OE. (Kentish) *cnellan*].

KNEW, [new], *pret.* of KNOW.

KNICKERBOCKERS, [nik'-er-bok'-erz], *n.*(*pl.*) loose breeches gathered in under the knee. [Washington Irving's Dutchman, Diedrich *Knickerbocker*, the imaginary author of the *History of New York*].

KNICKERS, [nik'-erz], *n.*(*pl.*) short loose-fitting breeches fastened below the knees, short loose-fitting trousers ending at the knee; a woman's undergarment covering the upper part of the legs. [~*Prec.*].

KNICK-KNACK, [nik'-nak'], *n.* a trifle, toy, a small, dainty, attractive, ornamental article or object.

KNIFE (1), [nīf], *n.* an instrument for cutting, usually consisting of a short handle to which is fastened a blade with a sharp cutting edge; the cutting blade of a machine; **war to the k.,** relentless, unyielding, merciless fighting or hostility; **to have one's k. in a person,** to owe him a perpetual grudge, to adopt a hostile, unfriendly attitude towards. [OE. *cnif*].

KNIFE (2), [nif], *v.t.* to stab or cut with a knife so as to wound or kill.

KNIFEBOARD, [nif'-bawd], *n.* a piece of wood on which knives are cleaned; name given to two long benches placed together lengthwise on the top of an early form of omnibus.

KNIFE-BOY, [nif'-boi], *n.* a scullery lad whose job it is to clean the knives.

KNIFE-EDGE, [nif'-ej'], *n.* a sharp edge of steel serving as the axis of a balance; the edge of a knife; (*fig.*) anything very sharp.

KNIFEGRINDER, [nif'-grind'-er], *n.* one who sharpens knives for a living.

KNIFE-REST, [nif'-rest], *n.* a small stand for keeping carving knife and fork from dirtying the tablecloth.

KNIGHT (1), [nit], *n.* a non-hereditary title of honour conferred by the sovereign, which entitles the possessor to use the title *Sir* before his name; †one admitted to a certain military rank, the recipients of the honour being usually of noble birth; name of a rank conferred upon certain of its distinguished members by several organizations; (*fig.*) a brave, courteous, chivalrous person, *esp.* a lady's champion; (*chess*) name of a piece bearing a horse's head; **K. Bachelor,** the lowest class of knights consisting of those who are not members of any order of knighthood; **K. Banneret,** formerly a knight, distinguished on the battlefield by having the pointed fly of his pennon cut off, who ranked higher than other knights; **K.-errant,** one who travelled in search of adventures to show his military prowess, gallantry and chivalry; (*fig.*) a courteous, valorous champion of causes, etc.; **knight's fee,** the amount of land owned, possession of which entailed knight-service; **K. of the Shire,** (*hist.*) the representative of a shire or county in parliament; **k. of the road,** a highwayman. [OE. *cniht* boy].

KNIGHT (2), [nit], *v.t.* to create a knight.

KNIGHTAGE, [nit'-ij], *n.* the body of knights; a book containing a list and account of those who are knights.

KNIGHT-ERRANTRY, [nit'-e'-rant-ri], *n.* the practice, conduct or behaviour of a knight-errant; an act worthy of a knight-errant.

KNIGHT-HEAD, [nit'-hed], *n.* (*naut.*) one of two pieces of timber in a ship rising on each side of the stem, and supporting the bowsprit between them.

KNIGHTHOOD, [nit'-hood], *n.* the rank, dignity, and character of a knight; the body of knights, the orders of knights.

KNIGHT-LIKE, [nit'-lik], *adj.* resembling a knight.

KNIGHTLINESS, [nit'-li-nes], *n.* the quality of being knightly.

KNIGHTLY, [nit'-li], *adj.* pertaining to a knight; becoming or worthy of a knight, chivalrous, brave, courteous.

KNIGHT-SERVICE, [nit'-sur'-vis], *n.* military service due from a knight as a condition of holding lands, a tenure of lands held on condition of military service.

KNIT, (**knitting, knitted**), [nit], *v.t.* to weave or connect (yarn, wool, etc.), by a series of interlocking loops and knots made with long eyeless needles; to fashion or make (a fabric) in this way; to cause to grow together, to join, fasten closely together; to draw together, contract; to unite or link closely; to make compact; *v.i.* to practise knitting; to grow together closely, to unite, to become compact or welded together into a whole; **to k. up,** to fasten up dropped stitches in knitting; to become closely bound with. [OE. *cnyttan* to knot].

KNITTABLE, [nit'-abl], *adj.* able to be knitted.

KNITTER, [nit'-er], *n.* one who, or that which, knits.

KNITTING, [nit'-ing], *n.* the act or work of one who knits; the thing that is knitted.

KNITTLE, [nitl], *n.* (*naut.*) a small line of yarn used for hammock clues, etc.

KNIT-WEAR, [nit'-wāer], *n.* knitted garments.

KNOB, [nob], *n.* a small hard rounded protuberance on a stick, branch, etc.; a hard rounded boss or stud used as a handle, etc.; a small lump of coal, sugar; a hillock, mound; (*arch.*) a rounded carved boss-like projection at the junction of vaulting, etc. [ME. *knobbe*].

KNOBBED, [nobd], *adj.* containing or studded with knobs.

KNOBBINESS, [nob'-i-nes], *n.* the quality of being knobby.

KNOBBLE, [nobl], *n.* a small knob.

KNOBBLY, [nob'-li], *adj.* full of knobbles, knobby.

KNOBBY, [nob'-i], *adj.* full of, containing, knobs; rough, knotty; resembling a knob.

KNOBKERRIE, [nob'-ke'-ri], *n.* a round-topped stick employed as a weapon by African natives. [Afrikaans *knobkirie*].

KNOB-KERRIE

KNOBSTICK, [nob'-stik], *n.* a stick provided with a heavy knobbed head; (*slang*) a blackleg, one who refuses to support an organized strike.

KNOCK, [nok], *v.t.* to strike, rap, deliver a sharp blow to, beat; to drive against; (*fig.*) to produce a striking impression upon, to startle, flabbergast; *v.i.* to strike a blow with something hard or heavy, *esp.* to rap on a door with the knocker or the knuckle in order to attract attention or indicate one's presence; to bump or rattle heavily because of some mechanical defect; **to k. about,** to batter; to travel about, *esp.* to visit many places in a haphazard idle way; **to k. down,** to fell; to sell at a reduced price; (of auctioneers) to assign to a bidder at an auction by a knock with the hammer; **to k. on,** (*rugby*) to strike the ball forward with the hand or arm; **to k. off,** to force off or away by striking; to cease work; to complete hurriedly; **to k. out,** to force out or remove by striking; to eliminate from a competition; to render temporarily unconscious; **to k. together,** to improvise, to construct in rough and ready fashion; **to k. up,** to hit in an upward direction, to put out of joint (a finger, etc.) by a sharp blow; (*tennis*) to practise tennis shots; to construct roughly and hastily; to arouse by knocking; to exhaust, wear out, make unwell by excessive toil or exertion; **to k. on the head,** to put an end to, defeat, thwart; **to k. the bottom out of,** to demolish, prove (an argument) false. [OE. *cnocian*].

KNOCKABOUT (1), [nok'-a-bowt'], *n.* rough, slapstick, noisy farce.

KNOCKABOUT (2), [nok'-a-bowt'], *adj.* rough, slapstick, boisterous, noisy, violent; suitable for hard wear and rough travelling.

KNOCKDOWN, [nok'-down], *adj.* (of a blow) that fells or strikes to the ground, of such force as to knock down; so constructed as to be easily taken to pieces again; (*fig.*) overwhelming; **k. price,** the lowest price that will be accepted by the seller.

KNOCKER, [nok'-er], *n.* one who, or that which, knocks; a metal striker or kind of a hammer hinged to a door, which is struck against a metal plate to announce one's presence or attract attention.

KNOCK-KNEE, [nok'-nē'], *n.* a deformity in which the legs bend inwards, and the knees knock against each other in walking.

KNOCK-KNEED, [nok'-nēd], *adj.* with knees that knock against each other in walking; weak, feeble.

KNOCK-ON, [nok'-on'], *n.* (*rugby football*) an infringement of the rules caused by propelling the ball forward with the hand or fist.

KNOCK-OUT (1), [nok'-owt], *n.* an auction sale in which the bids are arranged beforehand by the dealers in attendance, who later resell privately amongst themselves the articles previously acquired; (*boxing*) a punch or blow delivered with such force as to prevent one's opponent from continuing the fight after the timekeeper has counted ten; a knock-out competition; (*fig.*) a striking success, conquest.

KNOCK-OUT (2), [nok'-owt], *adj.* felling, stunning, bringing about a knock-out; pertaining to, of the nature of, a knock-out auction sale; of an eliminating tournament or competition in which a single defeat means retirement from the competition or tournament.

KNOCK-UP, [nok'-up], *n.* (*tennis*) a few preliminary practice shots before the start of a match or game; a bout of practice as opposed to a game.

KNOLL (1), [nōl], *n.* †the top of a hill; a rounded hillock or mound. [OE. *cnoll*].

KNOLL (2), [nōl], *v.t. and i.* to knell, to toll, to sound (of a bell). [~KNELL (1)].

KNOLLER, [nōl'-er], *n.* one who tolls a bell.

KNOP, [nop], *n.* a rounded top, a knob, boss. [~Du. *knop* button].

KNOPPED†, [nopt], *adj.* provided with knops.

KNOPPER, [nop'-er], *n.* a kind of gall-nut or excrescence, formed by an insect on the flower-cups of the oak, used in tanning and dyeing. [Germ. *knopper* oak-gall].

KNOSP, [nosp], *n.* (*arch.*) an ornament in the form of a flower-bud. [Germ. *knospe* bud].

KNOT (1), [not], *n.* the tying, intertwining, or entangling of one or more ropes, threads, cords, etc., tightly for the purpose of fastening, etc.; a bow or tie worn as an ornament; a specific quantity of thread or yarn; (*fig.*) a difficulty, an intricate problem, an awkward tangle or complication; the meeting-point of a number of converging lines, etc.; a bend, tie, link, that which unites; a hard thickened excrescence or protuberance, a nodule or protuberant joint of a plant; a hard mass in a tree trunk where a branch joins it, a hard rounded cross-grained mass in a sawn piece of wood; a figure consisting of a number of interlacing lines; a knob, boss, or stud; a small group of people gathered closely together; (*naut.*) a division of the log-line, marked by a knotted string fastened to it, serving to measure the rate of a vessel's motion, and so arranged that the number of knots which run off the reel in half a minute shows the number of nautical miles the vessel sails in an hour; also loosely used as a nautical mile. [OE. *cnotta*].

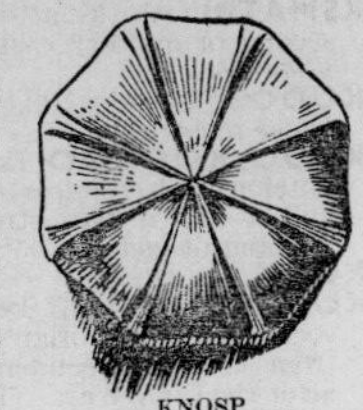
KNOSP

KNOT (2), [not], *n.* the red-breasted sand piper, *Tringa canutus*, a bird related to the plover. [OScand. *Knutr*, ~personal name *Canute*].

KNOT (3), (knotting, knotted), [not], *v.t.* to tie a knot or a series of knots in, to fasten with a knot; to form of protuberances or knots in; to entangle; to unite closely; *v.i.* to tie knots; to knit thread, etc., into a kind of fringe; to become knotty.

KNOTGRASS, [not'-grahs], *n.* a common British weed, *Polygonum aviculare*, so called from the joints on its stems; name given to several other plants having jointed stems.

KNOTLESS, [not'-les], *adj.* without knots.

KNOTTED, [not'-id], *adj.* full of knots; tied into knots; entangled, complicated; containing hard round protuberances or excrescences.

KNOTTINESS, [not'-i-nes], *n.* the quality of being knotty.

KNOTTING, [not'-ing], *n.* the act of tying or forming into a knot or knots; the knitting of thread, etc., into a kind of fringe-work formed by a series of knots; the act of painting over the knots in wood with a preparation of red lead, the preparation used for this.

KNOTTY, [not'-i], *adj.* full of knots; (*fig.*) perplexing, puzzling, difficult; hard, rugged.

KNOUD, [nowd], *n.* the grey gurnard, *Trigla gurnardus*. [Unkn.].

KNOUT (1), [nowt], *n.* a whip or scourge. [Russ. *knut*].

KNOUT (2), [nowt], *v.t.* to flog or whip with the knout.

KNOW, (knew, known), [nō], *v.t.* to be aware of or familiar with, to possess accurate information or knowledge as to; to have experience of, to be conversant with; to understand, to have in the mind a clear notion of; to have learnt, to have assimilated into the mind so that it forms part of one's mental equipment; to be acquainted with; to recognize by remembrance, perception, or description as being something or someone; to be able to distinguish between; to have sexual relations with; *v.i.* to be certain, to be informed; **to k. of,** to have heard about; to possess information about; **to k. what's what, to k. a thing or two, etc.,** to enjoy a certain degree of common sense or worldly wisdom. [OE. *cnawan*].

KNOWABLE, [nō'-abl], *adj.* that may be known; recognizable; easy to become acquainted with.

KNOWABLENESS, [nō'-abl-nes], *n.* the quality of being knowable.

KNOWER, [nō'-er], *n.* one who knows.

KNOWING, [nō'-ing], *adj.* astute, clever, cunning, shrewd, wily, enlightened, well-informed, skilful, intelligent.

KNOWINGLY, [nō'-ing-li], *adv.* with knowledge, deliberately, consciously; in a knowing manner.

KNOWINGNESS, [nō'-ing-nes], *n.* the quality of being knowing.

KNOWLEDGE, [nol'-ij], *n.* clear and certain mental perception, understanding, the fact of being aware of something; experience of, acquaintance or familiarity with, information of; learning, erudition, that which is known, facts learned or acquired by study of; (*leg.*) cognizance, recognition; sexual intercourse. [ME. *knoweleche*].

KNOWLEDGEABLE, [nol'-ij-abl], *adj.* well-informed, clever, erudite, learned; intelligent, skilful.

KNOWN, [nōn], *adj.* recognized, admitted, understood, proved. [*P.pt.* of KNOW].

KNUBS, [nubz], *n.*(*pl.*) waste silk produced in winding off from the cocoon, afterwards carded and spun. [LGerm. *knubbe* knob].

KNUCKLE (1), [nukl], *n.* the joint of a finger, protruding noticeably at the back of the hand when clenched; the corresponding joint in the leg of a quadruped together with the surrounding muscular parts, *esp.* considered as a joint of meat; **near the k.,** (*coll.*) verging on indecency. [~MDu. *knokel*].

KNUCKLE (2), [nukl], *v.t. and i.* to strike or rub with the knuckles; **to k. down to,** to settle down to steady work at; **to k. under,** to yield, submit.

KNUCKLE-BONE, [nukl'-bōn], *n.* a bone of the knuckles, the protruding end of a joint of a bone in the fingers; the knuckle of an animal, a joint of meat consisting of a leg-bone with the knuckle; a small bone from the limb of a sheep, etc.; (*pl.*) a game played with these bones.

KNUCKLED, [nukld], *adj.* having knuckles, having protuberances like knuckles.

KNUCKLEDUSTER, [nukl'-dust'-er], *n.* a metal protection or bar worn over the knuckles by certain roughs in fighting, and often studded with projecting knobs or points to render a blow from the fist more formidable.

KNUCKLE-JOINT, [nukl'-joint], *n.* (*machinery*) a grooved joint shaped like a knuckle.

KNURL (1), [nurl], *n.* a small rounded protuberance, a knot.

KNURL (2), see NURL.

KNURR, KNUR, [nur], *n.* hard, round protuberance or knob on the trunk of a tree; a wooden ball used in the game of knurr and spell. [~MDu. *knorre*].

KOA, [kō'-a], *n.* a species of *Acacia* native to Hawaii. [Native].

KOALA, [kōō-ah'-la], *n.* the bear-like Australian marsupial rodent. *Phascolarctus cinereus* [Native].

KOALA

KOB, [kob], *n.* an African antelope of the genus *Cobus*. [Native].

KOBA, [kō'-ba], *n.* the kob. [*Prec.*].

KOBANG, [kō'-bang'], *n.* a gold Japanese coin in circulation up to 1870, of oblong shape. [Jap. *ko-ban* little division].

KOBIL†, see COBLE.

KOBOLD, [kob'-old], *n.* a household spirit or elf; a gnome or goblin frequenting mines. [Germ. *kobold*]

KODAK, [kō'-dak], *n.* a patented type of small portable camera taking pictures on a roll of sensitized film. [Trade name of the Eastman *Kodak* Co.].

KOFF, [kof], *n.* a small two-masted Dutch vessel. [Du. *kof*].

KOFTGARI, [koft'-ga-rē'], *n.* a kind of ornamental steel-work containing a pattern inlaid with gold. [Pers. *koftgari* beaten-work].

KOHL, [kōl], *n.* powdered antimony, a black pigment used in the East as a cosmetic. [Arab. *koh'l*].

KOHL-RABI, [kōl'-rah-bi], *n.* an edible cabbage having a globular, turnip-shaped stem. [Germ. *kohlrabi* from It. *cavoli rape* kale-turnip].

KOKRA-WOOD, [kok'-ra-wŏŏd'], *n.* the wood of the Burmese tree, *Aporosa dioica*, used in making flutes. [Native].

KOLA, [kō'-la], *n.* a tropical West African tree of the genus *Cola*, which bears a fruit whose seeds contain caffeine, and cocoa; a drink prepared from the seeds of this fruit. [Native].

KOLARIAN (1), [kol-āer'-i-an], *n.* a member of the primitive native tribes of the foot-hills and woods outside Bengal. [Unkn.]

KOLARIAN (2), [kol-āer'-i-an], *adj.* pertaining to the Kolarians.

KOLINSKY, [kol-in'-ski], *n.* the Siberian mink, *Mustela sibirica*. [Russ. *kolinsky* from *Kola* in N.W. Russia].

KOLLYRITE, see COLLYRITE.

KONISCOPE, [kon'-i-skōp], *n.* an apparatus for measuring the quantity of dust in the atmosphere. [Gk. *konis* dust and SCOPE].

KONISTRA, [kon'-is-tra], *n.* the place for the orchestra in a Greek theatre. [Gk. *konistra*].
KOODOO, see KUDU.
KOPECK, see COPECK.
KOPJE, [kop'-i], *n.* (*S. Afr.*) a hillock or large mound, a small round-topped hill. [Du. *kopje*].
KORAN, [ko-rahn', kaw'-ran], *n.* the sacred book of the Mohammedan religion, containing the revelations alleged to have been made by God to Mohammed.
KOSHER, [kōsh'-er], *adj.* pure, clean, right, fulfilling the requirements of the Jewish sacred law. [Heb. *kasher*].
KOTH, [koth], *n.* a slimy earth, erupted by some volcanoes of South America. [Native].
KOTO, [kō'-tō], *n.* a musical instrument with thirteen silk strings, played in Japan. [Jap. *koto*].
KOTWAL, [kot'-wahl], *n.* the ruling magistrate or head constable of an Indian town. [Hind. *kotwal*].
KOUL, [kowl], *n.* (*East Indies*) a promise or contract; (*Persia*) a soldier in a noble corps. [Native].
KOUMISS, [kōō'-mis], *n.* a spirituous liquor made among the Tartars by fermenting mare's milk, similar fermented drink prepared from skimmed cow's milk. [Tartar *kumiz*].
KOURBASH, [kŏŏer'-bash], *n.* a whip made from the hide of a rhinoceros or hippopotamus, and used as a means of punishment in Turkey, Egypt, and the Sudan. [Turk. *qirbach* whip].
KOUSSO, [kōōs'-ō], *n.* the dried blossom of the Abyssinian tree, *Hagenia abyssinica*, used for medicinal purposes. [Abyssinian *kousso*].
KOW-TOW (1), [kow'-tow'], *n.* the Chinese custom of touching the ground with the forehead as a mark of reverence or deep respect. [Chin. *k'o* knock and *to'u* the head].
KOW-TOW (2), [kow'-tow'], *v.i.* to perform the kowtow; (*fig.*) **to k. to,** to fawn on, to treat with servile, complaisant deference. [*Prec.*].
KRAAL (1), [krahl], *n.* a native village in South Africa consisting usually of a collection of huts surrounded by a fence or mud walls, and containing a cattle enclosure in the centre of it. [Du. *kraal*].
KRAAL (2), [krahl], *v.t.* to enclose in a kraal.
KRAIT, [krit], *n.* the venomous Indian snake, *Bungarus candidus*. [Hind. *karait*].
KRAKEN, [krahk'-en], *n.* a mythical giant monster of the northern seas. [Norw. *kraken*].
KRANTZ, [krantz], *n.* a steep overhanging wall of rock encompassing a mountain peak or narrow gorge. [Afrikaans *krantz*].
KRASIS, [krā'-sis], *n.* Eucharistic wine mixed with water. [Gk. *krasis*].
KREASOTE†, see CREOSOTE.
KREMLIN, [krem'-lin], *n.* the citadel of a Russian town, *esp.* the ancient citadel of Moscow. [Russ. *kreml* citadel].
KRENG, [kreng], *n.* the carcase of a whale after the blubber has been stripped off, and the whalebone and jawbone removed. [Du. *kreng*].
KREUTZER, [kroit'-ser], *n.* a coin, worth one farthing, formerly in circulation in Austria and Germany. [Germ. *kreuzer* from *kreuz* cross].
KRIEGSPIEL, [krēg'-shpēl], *n.* a game played by military general staffs, in which pieces representing army units are manoeuvred on a map. [Germ. *krieg* war and *spiel* game].
KRIS, [kris], *n.* a Malay dagger having a wavy blade. [Malay *kris*].
KRISHNA, [krish'-na], *n.* a Hindu man-god, one of the incarnations of Vishnu. [Hind. *krisna*].
KROMESKY, [krō-mesk'-i], *n.* a croquette consisting of minced meat rolled up in a rasher of bacon, and then cooked. [Russ. *kromochki*].
KRONE, [krō'-ner], *n.* a Scandinavian silver coin worth approximately 1s. 1½d.; a former German 10 mark gold piece; a former Austrian silver coin. [Germ. *krone*, Dan. *krone*, Swed. *krona*].
KROO, [krōō], *n.* a member of a negro tribe of the Guinea coast in West Africa. [Native].
KRULLER, [krul'-er], *n.* a cake curled or crisped, and boiled in fat. [~CURL].

KRIS

KRYOMETER, [krī-om'-it-er], *n.* a thermometer for recording exceptionally low temperatures. [Gk. *kruos* frost and METER].
KRYPTON, [krip'-ton], *n.* a rare gaseous constituent of the atmosphere, the chemical element Kr. [Gk. *kruptos* hidden].
KSHATRIYA, [kshat'-rē-ya], *n.* a member of the second or military caste among the Hindoos. [Skr. *kshatriya*].
KUDOS, [kew'-dos], *n.* (*slang*) fame, credit, glory. [Gk. *kudos* renown].
KUDU, KOODOO, [kōō'-dōō], *n.* the large African antelope, *Strepsiceros kudu*, with corkscrew horns, and a brown skin streaked with white markings. [Hottentot *kudu*].
KUFIC, see CUFIC.
KU-KLUX-KLAN, [kew'-kluks'-klan'], *n.* a secret society in U.S.A., originally started to prevent negroes from gaining ascendency in the Southern States after the Civil War. [Invented word].
KUKRI, [kŏŏk'-ri], *n.* a knife with a curved blade, which is broader at its extremity than at the handle, used by Gurkhas. [Hind. *kukri*].
KULAK, [kōō'-lak], *n.* a former well-to-do Russian peasant farmer. [Russ. *kulak* fist].
KULTURKAMPF, [kŏŏl-tōōer'-kampf'], *n.* a late 19th-century German political struggle between the Government and the Catholics. [Germ. *kulturkampf* culture struggle].
KUMBUK, [kum'-buk], *n.* an Indian tree whose bark produces a black dye. [Native].
KUMMEL, kümmel, [kim'-el], *n.* a German liqueur made from caraway seeds and cumin. [Germ. *kümmel*].
KUMQUAT, see CUMQUAT.
KUNKUR, [kungk'-er], *n.* an Indian nodular limestone. [Hind. *kankar*].
KUOMINTANG, [kwō'-min-tang'], *n.* the nationalist radical party in China. [Chin. *kuomintang* people's national party].
KUPFERNICKEL, [kŏŏp'-fer-nikl'], *n.* nicolite, an ore of nickel of a copper colour, copper-nickel. [Germ. *kupfer* copper and *nickel* nickel].
KUPFERSCHIEFER, [kup'-fer-shē'-fer], *n.* a black bituminous shale containing a large proportion of copper. [Germ. *kupfer* copper and *schiefer* slate].
KURD, [kurd], *n.* a native of Kurdistan.
KURDISH (1), [kurd'-ish], *n.* the language of the Kurds.
KURDISH (2), [kurd'-ish], *adj.* of, or pertaining to, the Kurds or their language.
KURKEE, [kur'-kē], *n.* a coarse sort of blanket. [Unkn.].
KURSAAL, [kŏŏer'-sahl], *n.* a large building at a watering place, used for public recreation, amusement, and entertainment. [Germ. *kur* cure and *saal* room].
KUTCH, see CUTCH.
KVASS, [kvas], *n.* a thin Russian beer brewed from rye. [Russ. *kvas*].
KYANG, [kyang], *n.* the Tibetan wild horse, *Equus kyang*. [Tibetan *rkyang*].
KYANIZE, [kī'-an-iz], *v.t.* to prevent the rotting of wood by immersing it in a solution of corrosive sublimate. [*Kyan*, the inventor of the process].
KYE, [kī], *n.(pl.)* cattle.
KYLE, [kīl], *n.* a narrow channel or strait separating two islands or an island from the mainland. [ONorw. *kil*].
KYLIN, [kī'-lin], *n.* a grotesque animal figure found in Japanese and Chinese pottery. [Chin. *ch'i lin* from *ch'i* male and *lin* female].
KYLLOSIS, [kil-ō'-sis], *n.* club-foot. [Gk. *kullosis*].
KYLOE, [kī'-lō], *n.* one of a breed of small Highland black cattle with long horns. [Uncert.].
KYMOGRAPH, [kī'-mō-graf], *n.* an instrument for recording on a graph in a wave-form variations in pressure, tone, etc. [Gk. *kuma* wave and GRAPH].
KYPOO, [kip'-ōō], *n.* an astringent extract made in Ceylon similar to catechu. [Native].
KYRIE, [kier'-i-ā], *n.* a musical setting of the *Kyrie eleison*.
KYRIE ELEISON, [kier'-i-ā-el-ā'-is-on], *n.* a Greek religious petition or invocation used *esp.* at the beginning of the mass and as a response; a musical setting of this, *esp.* when forming the opening movement of a mass. [Gk. *kurie eleison* "Lord have mercy"].
KYRIOLOGIC, [ki'-ri-ō-loj'-ik], *adj.* relating to simple hieroglyphics. [Gk. *kuriologos* speaking literally].
KYRIOLOGICAL, [ki'-ri-ō-loj'-ik-al], *adj.* kyriologic.

L

L, [el], the twelfth letter of the English alphabet.

LA† **(1), [lah, law],** *int.* (*archaic*) look, behold.

LA (2), [lah], *n.* (*mus.*) the sixth note in the tonic sol-fa scale.

LAAGER (1), [lah'-ger], *n.* a defensive camp formed by a ring of waggons. [Afrik. *lager*].

LAAGER (2), [lah'-ger], *v.i.* to make a laager.

LAB, [lab], *n.* (*coll.*) laboratory.

LABARUM, [lab'-er-um], *n.* a cavalry standard of the Romans, *esp.* one surmounted by the monogram of Christ, and used by Constantine the Great. [L. *labarum*].

LABEFACTION, [lab'-i-fak'-shun], *n.* the process of weakening or loosening; decay. [L. *labefactio*].

LABEL (1), [lā'-bel], *n.* a strip of paper or cardboard attached to anything as an identification tab, *esp.* for parcels, luggage, exhibits; (*fig.*) a brief term or phrase describing and summarizing; (*arch.*) a moulding projecting over doors and windows, a drip-stone; (*astron.*) a brass rule for measuring altitudes; (*her.*) a fillet with pendants added by a son while his father is still alive. [OFr. *label*].

LABEL

LABEL (2), (labelling, labelled), [lā'-bel], *v.t.* to fasten a label to; to apply a descriptive tag to.

LABEL-CUTTER, [lā'-bel-kut'-er], *n.* a mechanical device for cutting labels in large quantities; a person employed to cut labels.

LABELLUM, [la-bel'-um], *n.* (*bot.*) the lip-shaped lower petal of orchids and other plants. [L. *labellum* a little lip].

LABIAL (1), [lā'-bi-al], *n.* (*phon.*) a labial consonant or vowel.

LABIAL (2), [lā'-bi-al], *adj.* relating to the lips; (*phon.*) articulated by the lips. [L. *labialis*].

LABIALISM, [lā'-bi-al-izm], *n.* labial pronunciation; the habit of labializing.

LABIALIZE, [lā'-bi-al-īz], *v.t.* (*phon.*) to make labial in quality.

LABIALLY, [lā'-bi-al-i], *adv.* by means of the lips.

LABIATE, [lā'-bi-āt], *adj.* resembling or having lips; (*bot.*) (of an irregular corolla) divided into two parts to resemble lips; belonging to the *Labiatæ*, herbaceous plants including dead-nettles, lavender, etc.

LABIATED, [lā'-bi-āt-id], *adj.* labiate.

LABILE, [lā'-bīl], *adj.* liable to err; (*chem.*) unstable. [L. *labilis*].

LABIODENTAL (1), [lā'-bi-ō-dent'-al], *n.* a labiodental sound.

LABIODENTAL (2), [lā'-bi-ō-dent'-al], *adj.* (*phon.*) pronounced with the lips and teeth. [L. *labium* lip and DENTAL].

LABIUM, (*pl.* **labia**), [lā'-bi-um], *n.* (*anat.*) the outer fold of the external female genital organs; the inside lip of a univalve shell; (*bot.*) the lip of a labiate plant. [L. *labium* lip].

LABORATORY, [lab'-er-at-er-i, lab-o'-rat-er-i], *n.* a room or building equipped with apparatus and set apart for experimental work in the sciences. [MedL. *laboratorium* workshop].

LABORIOUS, [la-baw'-ri-us], *adj.* taking great pains, caring for detail and accuracy at the expense of speed; slow and somewhat clumsy in practical matters; attained by or requiring much labour. [L. *laboriosus*].

LABORIOUSLY, [la-baw'-ri-us-li], *adv.* in a laborious way.

LABORIOUSNESS, [la-baw'-ri-us-nes], *n.* the quality of being laborious.

LABOUR (1), [lā'-ber], *n.* work, *esp.* done to earn a living; manual work; prolonged and severe mental or physical exertion; the class of men and women who earn their living by being employed by others, the working class, *esp.* manual workers; the section of this class organized into trade unions, the Labour Party; the pangs of childbirth; **hard l.,** a form of punishment for convicted criminals, formerly involving heavy work. [L. *labor*].

LABOUR (2), [lā'-ber], *v.t.* to repeat with pointless detail and emphasis; *v.i.* to engage in labour, work very hard; to toil strenuously, strive, *esp.* to accomplish something; to progress with difficulty; to experience the pains of childbirth. [L. *laborare*].

LABOURED, [lā'-berd], *adj.* characterized by extreme effort in the execution; clumsy, over-worked in style.

LABOURER, [lā'-ber-er], *n.* a person who labours, *esp.* a manual worker or farm-hand.

LABOUR-EXCHANGE, [lā'-ber-eks-chānj'], *n.* a branch office of the Ministry of Labour.

LABOUR-FRONT, [lā'-ber-frunt], *n.* labour as organized in National Socialist Germany. [Translation of Germ. *arbeitsfront*].

LABOURING, [lā'-ber-ing], *adj.* earning a living by manual labour.

LABOURITE, [lā-'ber-īt], *n.* a member of the Parliamentary Labour Party.

LABOURLESS, [lā'-ber-les], *adj.* not laborious.

LABOUR-SAVING, [lā'-ber-sāv'-ing], *adj.* designed or adapted to save work and conserve energy.

LABOURSOME, [lā'-ber-sum], *adj.* (*archaic*) laborious; (of a ship) apt to labour.

LABRADOR, [la'-bra-daw(r)'], *n.* the name of a peninsula in British North America, used to denote various products of this region, as cloth, dog, duck, etc.

LABRADORITE, [lab'-ra-daw'-rīt], *n.* (*min.*) a variety of iridescent limestone felspar. [*Labrador*].

LABRET, [lā'-bret], *n.* an ornament worn by primitive peoples through a pierced lip.

LABROSE, [lā'-brōs], *adj.* having thick lips. [L. *labrosus*].

LABRUM, [lā'-brum], *n.* (*entom.*) the upper lip of insects. [L. *labrum* lip].

LABURNIC, [la-burn'-ik], *adj.* of the nature of, derived from, laburnum.

LABURNUM, [la-burn'-um], *n.* a small tree of the genus *Cytisus*, having large hanging racemes of yellow flowers. [L. *laburnum*].

LABYRINTH, [lab'-i-rinth], *n.* a complicated arrangement of passages and paths, with one exit extremely difficult to find, a maze; (*fig.*) anything resembling this in its intricacy; (*anat.*) the cavity of the internal ear. [Gk. *laburinthos*].

LABYRINTHIAN, [lab'-i-rinth'-i-an], *adj.* labyrinthine.

LABYRINTHIC, [lab'-i-rinth'-ik], *adj.* labyrinthine. [Gk. *laburinthikos*].

LABYRINTHIFORM, [lab'-i-rinth'-i-fawm], *adj.* having the intricate form of a labyrinth.

LABYRINTHINE, [lab'-i-rinth'-īn], *adj.* resembling a labyrinth, winding, intricate.

LAC (1), [lak], *n.* a resinous substance secreted by *Coccus lacca*, which yields a fine red dye. [Hind. *lakh*].

LAC (2), LAKH, [lak], *n.* in India, 100,000 (rupees). [Hind. *lakh*].

LACCIC, [lak'-sik], *adj.* consisting of, resembling, lac, or produced from it.

LACCINE, [lak'-sin], *n.* a colouring substance found in shellac.

LAC-DYE, [lak'-dī'], *n.* lac prepared for dyeing.

LACE (1), [lās], *n.* a decorative fabric of delicate mesh or network with the threads plaited, knotted and turned to make patterns; a string or leather thong used for fastening, *esp.* shoes, etc.; a dash of brandy or gin in hot coffee; **point l.,** lace made with a single thread. [OFr. *laz* noose].

LACE (2), [lās], *v.t. and i.* to fasten by means of a lace; to decorate with lace; to mix a dash of brandy or gin with coffee, etc.

LACE-BARK, [lās'-bahk], *n.* the bark of two West Indian trees of the genus *Lagetta*.

LACE-CORAL, [lās'-kor'-al], *n.* a coral of the fenestella group.

LACE-FRAME, [lās'-frām], *n.* a frame or machine on which lace is made.

LACEMAN, [lās'-man], *n.* a dealer in lace.

LACERABLE, [las'-er-abl], *adj.* able, or liable to be torn. [LL. *lacerabilis*].

LACERATE (1), [las'-er-āt], *v.t.* to tear, rend. (*fig.*) to affect the feelings painfully. [L. *lacerare*].
LACERATE (2), [las'-er-āt], *adj.* lacerated.
LACERATED, [las'-er-āt-id], *adj.* torn, rent; (*fig.*) deeply grieved or wounded.
LACERATION, [las-er-ā'-shun], *n.* the act of lacerating; the condition of being lacerated; the hole made by rending; that which is lacerated. [L. *laceratio*].
LACERTA, [la-surt'-a], *n.* (*zool.*) a lizard. [L. *lacerta* lizard].
LACERTIAN, [la-sur'-shan], *adj.* (*zool.*) pertaining to lizards.
LACERTILIAN, [la'-sur-til'-i-an], *adj.* lacertian.
LACERTINE, [la-surt'-īn], *adj.* resembling a lizard, lacertian.
LACET, [la-set'], *n.* lace made with inserted tape or braid.

LACERTA

LACEWING, [lās'-wing], *adj.* having lace-like wings; **l. flies,** (*entom.*) the *Chrysopides*, insects with such wings.
LACE-WINGED, [lās'-wingd'], *adj.* having wings like lace.
LACHES, [lash'-iz], *n.* (*leg.*) negligence; inexcusable delay in making a claim. [OFr. *laschesse*].
LACHRYMA CHRISTI, [lak'-ri-ma-krist'-i], *n.* a sweet, rich wine from a monastery on the lower slopes of Mount Vesuvius. [L. *lachryma Christi* tear of Christ].
LACHRYMAL, [lak'-rim-al], *adj.* relating to tears; secreting tears; tending to stimulate tears. [MedL. *lacrimalis*].
LACHRYMARY, [lak'-rim-er-i], *adj.* containing tears.
LACHRYMATION, [lak-rim-ā'-shun], *n.* a burst of tears, weeping. [L. *lacrimatio*].
LACHRYMATORY (1), [lak'-rim-at-er-i], *n.* a vase or a bottle found in the tombs of the ancients, supposed to contain tears, but used for perfumes and ointments.
LACHRYMATORY (2), [lak'-rim-at-er-i], *adj.* relating to, stimulating, tears.
LACHRYMOSE, [lak'-rim-ōs], *adj.* given to habitual weeping; tearful. [L. *lacrimosus*].
LACHRYMOSELY, [lak'-rim-ōs-li], *adv.* in lachrymose fashion.
LACING, [lās'-ing], *n.* a method of fastening with a lace drawn through eyelet holes; a cord used in this.
LACINIA, [la-sin'-i-a], *n.* (*bot.*) a slash or jag in a leaf or petal; (*entom.*) the point of the maxilla in insects. [L. *lacinia* lappet].
LACINIATE, [la-sin'-i-āt], *adj.* (*bot.*) fringed, having jagged projections.
LACINIATED, [la-sin'-i-āt-id], *adj.* laciniate.
LACK (1), [lak], *n.* deficiency, shortage; absence; need, poverty. [~LGerm. *lak*].
LACK (2), [lak], *v.t. and i.* to be short of, to be without, to want; to be needy.
LACKADAISICAL, [lak'-a-dāz'-ik-al], *adj.* affectedly indifferent or listless, dreamily absent-minded. [LACK-A-DAY].
LACKADAISICALLY, [lak'-a-dāz'-ik-al-i], *adv.* in a lackadaisical manner.
LACK-A-DAY, [lak'-a-dā], *int.* expressing sorrow, melancholy, etc.
LACKBRAIN, [lak'-brān], *n.* a person who has no brains.
LACKER, [lak'-er], *n.* a person who lacks.
LACKEY (1), [lak'-i], *n.* a manservant who wears livery or uniform; a footman; (*fig.*) a servile follower; a fawning hypocrite. [Fr. *laquais*].
LACKEY (2), [lak'-i], *v.t.* to perform the duties of a lackey for; (*fig.*) to fawn round.
LACK-LUSTRE, [lak'-lust'-er], *adj.* deficient in lustre or brightness, dull, dim.
LAC-LAKE, [lak'-lāk], *n.* a kind of lac dye.
LACONIC, [la-kon'-ik], *adj.* expressing much in few words, concise, pithy. [Gk. *Lakonikos* Spartan-like].
LACONICAL, [la-kon'-ik-al], *adj.* laconic.
LACONICALLY, [la-kon'-ik-al-i], *adv.* in a laconic way.
LACONICISM, [la-kon'-is-izm], *n.* a concise style; a pithy phrase or expression.
LACONISM, [lak'-on-izm], *n.* laconicism.
LACOUM, [lah'-kōōm], *n.* the sweet Turkish delight, *rahat lacoum.* [Turk. *lacoum*].
LACQUER (1), [lak'-er], *n.* a varnish made of shellac which dries with a hard, bright polished surface. [Fr. *lacre* sealing-wax].
LACQUER (2), [lak'-er], *v.t.* to cover or coat with lacquer.
LACQUERER, [lak'-er-er], *n.* a person who varnishes with lacquer.
LACROSSE, [la-kros'], *n.* a game played with a rubber ball which is caught in a net-like racket, and thrown through a goal. [Fr. *la crosse* the hooked stick].
LACTARINE, [lak'-ta-rin], *n.* a preparation of casein from milk, used by calico-printers. [L. *lactarius* milky].
LACTATE, [lak'-tāt], *n.* (*chem.*) a salt of lactic acid.
LACTATION, [lak-tā'-shun], *n.* the act of giving suck; the time of suckling; the secreting of milk.
LACTEAL (1), [lak'-ti-al], *n.* (*anat.*) one of the lymphatic vessels conveying chyle.
LACTEAL (2), [lak'-ti-al], *adj.* resembling, relating to milk; conveying chyle. [L. *lacteus* milky].
LACTEAN, [lak'-ti-an], *adj.* lacteous.
LACTEOUS, [lak'-ti-us], *adj.* consisting of milk; milky. [L. *lacteus*].
LACTESCENCE, [lak-tes'-ents], *n.* the condition of being lactescent; (*bot.*) liquid flowing from a plant when wounded.
LACTESCENT, [lak-tes'-ent], *adj.* turning to milk; secreting milk or a milky juice. [L. *lactescens*].
LACTIC, [lak'-tik], *adj.* relating to, derived from, milk; (*chem.*) formed from sour milk, as lactic acid.
LACTIFEROUS, [lak-tif'-er-us], *adj.* secreting milk or white juice. [L. *lactifer*].
LACTIFUGE, [lak'-ti-fewj], *n.* (*med.*) a medicine to check or diminish the secretion of milk. [L. *lac* milk and *fugare* to put to flight].
LACTINE, [lak'-tin], *n.* (*chem.*) sugar obtained by evaporating the whey of milk.
LACTOMETER, [lak-tom'-it-er], *n.* an instrument for measuring the proportion of cream in milk. [L. *lac* milk and METER].
LACTOSCOPE, [lak'-to-skōp], *n.* an instrument for ascertaining the purity of milk by its opacity. [L. *lac* milk and SCOPE].
LACTOSE, [lak'-tōs], *n.* (*chem.*) sugar of milk.
LACUNA, (*pl.* **lacunae**), [la-kew'-na], *n.* a gap, vacant space. [L. *lacuna* pit].
LACUNAL, [la-kew'-nal], *adj.* relating to or having lacunae.
LACUNAR, [la-kew'-ner], *n.* (*arch.*) a ceiling consisting of panels formed by hollow chambers or cells. [L. *lacunar*].
LACUNOSE, [la-kew'-nōs], *adj.* furrowed or pitted; having many cavities. [L. *lacunosus*].
LACUSTRAL, [la-kus'-tral], *adj.* lacustrine.
LACUSTRINE, [la-kus'-trīn], *adj.* relating to lakes. [L. *lacus* lake].
LAD, [lad], *n.* a boy, young man, youth; (*coll.*) a man of rather dashing and irresponsible habits. [ME. *ladde*].
LADANUM, [lad'-an-um], *n.* the resinous secretion from the leaves of *Cistus creticus* and *Cistus ladaniferus.* [L. *ladanum*].
LADDER (1), [lad'-er], *n.* a portable device for climbing, consisting of two equal and parallel side pieces connected firmly by a series of rungs set equidistantly; a break in the mesh of silk stockings, etc., which resembles this; (*fig.*) a means of ascending in the world; **accommodation l.,** a light railed staircase for the use of senior naval officers; **Jacob's l.,** (*naut.*) a rope ladder, not fitted with ratlines, abaft the topgallant masts; a garden plant, *Polemonium cæruleum.* [OE. *hlædder*].
LADDER (2), [lad'-er], *v.t. and i.* to cause a ladder to appear in silk stockings.
LADDIE, [lad'-i], *n.* a little lad; (*slang*) old man.
LADE, (**lading, laden**), [lād], *v.t.* to store freight in a vehicle or vessel; to load; to scoop out with a ladle. [OE. *hladan* to load].
LADEN, [lād'-en], *adj.* loaded to capacity; (*fig.*) burdened, oppressed. [OE. *hladen*].
LA(H)-DI-DA(H), [lah'-di-dah'], *adj.* (*slang*) affectedly upper-class; foppish, affected.
LADING, [lād'-ing], *n.* cargo, freight.
LADLE (1), [lādl], *n.* a deep spoon with a long handle for scooping out or serving liquids; the tank attached to a mill-wheel which receives the water turning the wheel. [OE. *hlædel*].
LADLE (2), [lādl], *v.t.* to scoop out or serve with a ladle; **to l. out,** (*fig.*) to hand round freely.
LADLEFUL, [lādl'-fōōl], *n.* the capacity of a ladle.
LADY, [lā'-di], *n.* a female of refined manners, good taste and sympathetic understanding, a gentlewoman; a female of aristocratic breeding or title; a female with sufficient invested capital to live without working for

her living; any female; the mistress of a house; a title afforded to a female whose husband is a titled person ranking below a duke, or whose father holds a rank higher than viscount; **lady's slipper,** the flower *Cypripedium*; **lady's smock,** the flower *Cardamine pratensis*; **young l.,** a lady-love. [OE. *hlæfdige* mistress of a household].

LADYBIRD, [lā'-di-burd'], *n.* (*entom.*) a small flying beetle of the genus *Coccinella*, generally of a brilliant red or yellow colour and black-spotted.

LADYBIRD

LADY-CHAPEL, [lā'-di-chap'-el], *n.* a chapel dedicated to the Virgin Mary.

LADYCOW, [lā'-di-kow'], *n.* a ladybird.

LADY-DAY, [lā'-di-dā'], *n.* the day of the Annunciation of the Virgin Mary, March 25th, a quarter day.

LADY-FERN, [lā'-di-furn'], *n.* (*bot.*) the fern, *Lastrea Filix-fœmina*.

LADY-HELP, [lā'-di-help'], *n.* a superior kind of domestic servant.

LADY-IN-WAITING, [lā'-di-in-wāt'-ing], *n.* a lady of the court whose duty it is to attend on the queen.

LADYISM, [lā'-di-izm], *n.* the behaviour of a lady.

LADY-KILLER, [lā'-di-kil'-er], *n.* a man who fancies he has an irresistible way with women.

LADYLIKE, [lā'-di-līk'], *adj.* like a lady in manners; well-bred; soft, delicate, effeminate.

LADY-LOVE, [lā'-di-luv'], *n.* the woman a man is in love with, a sweetheart or mistress.

LADYSHIP, [lā'-di-ship], *n.* the rank or title of a lady; a titled lady.

LADY'S MAID, [lā'-diz-mād'], *n.* a woman employed as a lady's personal servant.

LADY'S MAN, [lā'-diz-man'], *n.* a man who seeks the society of women to pay them attentions.

LAEVULOSE, [lē'-vyōō-lōs], *n.* (*chem.*) a fruit sugar the crystals of which refract polarized light to the left. [~L. *laevus* left].

LAG (1), [lag], *n.* a convict, *esp.* one who has been in prison more than once. [Uncert.].

LAG (2), [lag], *n.* a boiler cover or jacket; a barrel stave. [Swed. *lagg*].

LAG (3), [lag], *n.* retardation, lapse in time, *esp.* when the effect of a force makes itself felt after its initial action. [LAG (6)].

LAG (4), [lag], *v.t.* to send to prison. [LAG (1)].

LAG (5), [lag], *v.t.* to cover a boiler with lags. [LAG (2)].

LAG (6), [lag], *v.i.* to fall behind, to linger, loiter. [Uncert.].

LAGAN, [lag'-an], *n.* wreckage of a ship or cargo at the bottom of the sea. [OFr. *lagan*].

LAGER, [lah'-ger], *n.* a German beer stored some months before being drunk. [Germ. *lager* storehouse].

LAGGARD, [lag'-erd], *n.* a person who falls behind; a loiterer, an idler.

LAGGING, [lag'-ing], *n.* a non-conducting covering; (*slang*) a term of imprisonment.

LAGGINGLY, [lag'-ing-li], *adv.* in a lagging way.

LAGOON, [la-gōōn'], *n.* a shallow stretch of water near the sea or a river. [It. *laguana* bog].

LAGOPHTHALMY, [lag'-of-thal'-mi], *n.* (*path.*) a morbid affliction which prevents the eye from closing. [Gk. *lagophthalmos* hare-eyed].

LAGOPODOUS, [lag-op'-od-us], *adj.* having thickly furred or feathered feet. [Gk. *lagos* hare and *pous podos* foot].

LAGOSTOMA, [lag-os'-tom-a], *n.* hare-lip. [Gk. *lagos* hare and *stoma* mouth].

LAICAL, [lā'-ik-al], *adj.* relating to the laity.

LAICIZE, [lā'-is-iz], *v.t.* to throw open to the laity; to secularize.

LAID, [lād], *adj.* (of paper) having a ribbed watermark.

LAIN, [lān], *p.pt.* of LIE. [OE. (*ge*)*legen*].

LAIR, [lāer], *n.* a place to rest in; the bed of a wild beast; a den. [OE. *leger* bed].

LAIRAGE, [lāer'-ij], *n.* a receiving depot for cattle.

LAIRD, [lāerd], *n.* a Scottish landowner. [Scots *laird* lord].

LAIRDSHIP, [lāerd-ship], *n.* the rank of a laird; a laird's domain.

LAISSEZ-FAIRE, [le'-sā-fāer'], *n.* a policy of non-interference in industry by the state and a reliance on competition based on individual initiative. [Fr. *laissez-faire* leave alone].

LAITHE, [lāTH], *n.* a seafish, the pollack, *Gadus pollachius*.

LAITY, [lā'-i-ti], *n.* the people other than the clergy.

LAKE (1), [lāk], *n.* a stretch of water enclosed by land; **l. dwellings,** prehistoric houses built on piles in lakes. [L. *lacus* pool].

LAKE (2), [lāk], *n.* a deep red pigment consisting of a luminous earth, with a colouring made from cochineal. [Fr. *laque*].

LAKELET, [lāk'-let], *n.* a little lake.

LAKH, see LAC (2).

LAKY, [lāk'-i], *adj.* resembling or pertaining to a lake or lakes; full of lakes.

LALLATION, [lal-ā'-shun], *n.* pronunciation of the letter *r* like *l*. [L. *lallatio*].

LAM, (lamming, lammed), [lam], *v.t.* (*slang*) to beat, to thrash, baste. [OIcel. *lamja*].

LAMA, [lah'-ma], *n.* a Tibetan Buddhist priest. [Tibetan *blama*].

LAMAISM, [lah'-ma-izm], *n.* the form of Buddhism practised in Tibet and Mongolia in which the priests are taken to be incarnations of Buddhas.

LAMANTIN, [la-mant'-in], *n.* a manatee or sea-cow. [Fr. *lamantin*].

LAMASERY, [lah-mah'-ser-i], *n.* a Tibetan monastery where lamas live. [Fr. *lamaserie*].

LAMB (1), [lam], *n.* a young sheep; the edible cooked flesh of this; a child. [OE. *lamb*].

LAMB (2), [lam], *v.i.* to bring forth a lamb or lambs.

LAMB-ALE, [lam'-āl], *n.* a feast at lamb-shearing.

LAMBDACISM, [lam'-da-sizm], *n.* lallation. [Gk. *lambdakismos*].

LAMBDOIDAL, [lam-doid'-al], *adj.* in the form of the Greek lambda (Λ, λ). [Gk. *lambda* letter *l* and *oeides* like].

LAMBENCY, [lam'-ben-si], *n.* the condition of being lambent.

LAMBENT, [lam'-bent], *adj.* moving lightly, playing on the surface, touching lightly, flickering. [L. *lambens*].

LAMBKIN, [lam'-kin], *n.* a small lamb.

LAMBLIKE, [lam'-līk], *adj.* like a lamb, gentle, mild.

LAMBREQUIN, [lam'-bre-kin], *n.* a scarf forming the covering of a helmet; drapery over a door or window; (*her.*) a scroll or rolled drapery enclosing the sides and back of a helmet. [Fr. *lambrequin*].

LAMBSKIN, [lam'-skin], *n.* the prepared skin and fleece of the lamb.

LAMB'S-WOOL, [lamz'-wōōl], *n.* wool from lambs; hot ale, mixed with sugar and the pulp of roasted apples, and spiced with nutmeg.

LAME (1), [lām], *adj.* disabled in a limb, *esp.* in the legs or feet; not smooth in movement; poor, not convincing. [OE. *lam*(*a*) lame].

LAME (2), [lām], *v.t.* to make lame.

LAMELLA, (*pl.* **lamellae**), [la-mel'-a], *n.* (*nat. hist.*) a thin plate or scale. [L. *lamella*].

LAMELLAR, [la-mel'-er], *adj.* (*zool.*) composed of lamellae.

LAMELLARLY, [la-mel'-er-li], *adv.* in lamellae.

LAMELLATE, [lam'-el-āt], *adj.* furnished with, composed of, lamellae.

LAMELLATED, [lam'-el-āt'-id], *adj.* lamellate.

LAMELLIBRANCH, [la-mel'-i-brangk'], *n.* (*zool.*) a lamellibranchiate mollusc. [LAMELLA and Gk. *bragkhia* gills].

LAMELLIBRANCHIATE, [la-mel'-i-brangk'-i-āt], *adj.* (*zool.*) (of molluscs) characterized by lamellate gills.

LAMELLICORN, [la-mel'-i-kawn], *adj.* (*entom.*) characterized by antennae ending in a lamellate club. [LAMELLA and L. *cornu* horn].

LAMELLIFEROUS, [lam'-el-if'-er-us], *adj.* characterized by a lamellar or foliated structure. [LAMELLA and L. *ferre* to bear].

LAMELLIFORM, [la-mel'-i-fawm], *adj.* having the form of a lamella. [LAMELLA and FORM].

LAMELLIROSTRAL, [la-mel'-i-ros'-tral], *adj.* having the beak edged with numerous lamellae, as the swan. [LAMELLA and L. *rostrum* beak].

LAMELY, [lām'-li], *adv.* in lame fashion.

LAMENESS, [lām'-nes], *n.* the state of being lame.

LAMENT (1), [la-ment'], *n.* the expressing aloud of a deeply felt sorrow; a funeral elegy.

LAMENT (2), [la-ment'], *v.t. and i.* to express deep sorrow at or for, to grieve for; to deplore; to utter a lament, mourn. [L. *lamentare*].

LAMENTABLE, [lam'-ent-abl], *adj.* to be lamented, grievous; mournful, pitiful; of extremely poor quality.

LAMENTABLENESS, [lam'-ent-abl-nes], *n.* the condition of being lamentable.

LAMENTABLY, [lam'-ent-ab-li], *adv.* in a lamentable way.

LAMENTATION, [lam'-ent-ā'-shun], *n.* the act of lamenting; an expression of sorrow; (*pl.*) (*O.T.*) a book of Scripture, embodying the lamentations of Jeremiah. [L. *lamentatio*].

LAMENTER, [la-ment'-er], *n.* person who laments.

LAMENTING, [lam-ent'-ing], *n.* lamentation.

LAMENTINGLY, [la-ment'-ing-li], *adv.* with lamentation.

LAMETTA, [la-met'-a], *n.* foil or wire of gold, silver or brass. [It. *lametta*].

LAMIA, [lā'-mi-a], *n.* (*myth.*) a sorceress, a witch. [Gk. *lamia* vampire].

LAMINA, (*pl.* **laminae**), [lam'-in-a], *n.* a thin plate, layer or scale. [L. *lamina*].

LAMINABLE, [lam'-in-abl], *adj.* able to be laminated.

LAMINAR, [lam'-in-er], *adj.* arranged in, or consisting of, laminae.

LAMINATE (1), [lam'-in-āt], *adj.* laminated.

LAMINATE (2), [lam'-in-āt], *v.t. and i.* to form into, cover with, laminae.

LAMINATED, [lam'-in-āt-id], *adj.* consisting of, arranged in, laminae.

LAMINATION, [lam'-in-ā'-shun], *n.* the condition of being laminated; the process of laminating; (*elect.*) a thin plate of soft iron used in an armature.

LAMINIFEROUS, [lam'-in-if'-er-us], *adj.* having a laminar structure. [LAMINA and L. *ferre* to bear].

LAMISH, [lām'-ish], *adj.* somewhat lame.

LAMMAS, [lam'-as], *n.* August 1, as the day of first-fruits, the feast celebrated on this day. [OE. *hlafmæsse*, *hlammæsse*].

LAMMERGEYER, [lam'-er-gi'-er], *n.* a large vulture of the genus *Gypaetus*. [Germ. *lämmer* lambs and *geier* vulture].

LAMP, [lamp'], *n.* a contrivance for giving light, by burning oil or gas or consuming electricity, usually fitted with a shade; (*fig.*) a means of enlightenment. [Gk. *lampas*].

LAMPADIST, [lam'-pad-ist], *n.* the winner of a lampadrome. [Gk. *lampadistes*].

LAMPADROME, [lam'-pa-drōm], *n.* in ancient Greece, a torch race. [Gk. *lampas* torch and *dromos* course].

LAMPAS (1), [lam'-pas], *n.* a fleshy swelling in the gums and palate of a horse. [Fr. *lampas*].

LAMPAS (2), [lam'-pas], *n.* a flowered patterned silk. [Fr. *lampas*].

LAMPBLACK, [lamp'-blak], *n.* a fine soot from the condensation of the smoke of burning oil, pitch, etc.; a jet black pigment from this.

LAMPERN, [lamp'-urn], *n.* the young of the river lamprey. [OFr. *lamprion*].

LAMPION, [lamp'-i-on], *n.* a small oil lamp fitted with coloured glass, used for open-air illumination. [It. *lampione*].

LAMPLESS, [lamp'-les], *adj.* without a lamp.

LAMPLIGHT, [lamp'-lit], *n.* the light given by a lamp.

LAMPLIGHTER, [lamp'-lit'-er], *n.* a person employed to light street lamps.

LAMPOON (1), [lam-pōōn'], *n.* a literary composition of a crude, personal, satirical nature. [Fr. *lampon* drinking song].

LAMPOON (2), [lam-pōōn'], *v.t.* to attack, satirize publicly in a lampoon.

LAMPOONER, [lam-pōōn'-er], *n.* a person who writes a lampoon.

LAMPOONIST, [lam-pōōn'-ist], *n.* a lampooner.

LAMPOONRY, [lam-pōōn'-ri], *n.* the practice of lampooning.

LAMP-POST, [lamp'-pōst'], *n.* a stout metal pillar supporting a lamp used to light the streets.

LAMPREY, [lam'-pri], *n.* an eel-like, vertebrate fish having a round mouth by which it fastens itself to rocks, etc. [Fr. *lamproi*].

LAMPSHADE, [lamp'-shād], *n.* a covering fitted to a lamp in order to concentrate or diffuse the light.

LAMP-SHELL, [lamp'-shel], *n.* a brachiopod.

LAMP-SOCKET, [lamp'-sok'-et], *n.* a fitment for holding an electric bulb.

LANA, [lā'-na], *n.* the close-grained wood of the genipap tree, *Genipa americana*. [Native].

LANARKITE, [lan'-erk-it], *n.* sulphate and carbonate of lead in small laminar crystals. [*Lanarkshire*, where found].

LANATE, [la'-nāt], *adj.* (*bot.*) covered with thick curly wool-like hair. [L. *lanatus*].

LANATED, [la'-nāt-id], *adj.* lanate.

LANCASTER, [lang'-kas-ter], *n.* a type of British four-engined bomber. [*Lancaster*, the county town of Lancashire].

LANCASTERIAN, [lang'-kas-tēer'-i-an], *adj.* relating to the system of supplementing teachers by monitors, introduced into schools by Joseph Lancaster. [J. *Lancaster*, 1778-1838].

LANCASTRIAN (1), [lan(g)-kas'-tri-an], *n.* an adherent, or member, of the House of Lancaster; a native of Lancashire.

LANCASTRIAN (2), [lan(g)-kas'-tri-an], *adj.* belonging to Lancashire or Lancaster; connected with the House of Lancaster.

LANCE (1), [lahnts], *n.* a weapon consisting of a long shaft with a sharp metal head; a thin sharp-pointed surgical instrument, a lancet. [L. *lancea* a light spear].

LANCE (2), [lahnts], *v.t.* to impale with a lance; (*surg.*) to make an incision in with a lancet.

LANCE-CORPORAL, [lahnts'-kaw'-per-al], *n.* (*milit.*) a private soldier acting as a corporal.

LANCELET, [lahnts'-let], *n.* (*zool.*) a small species of the protochordates, *Branchiostoma lanceolatum*.

LANCEOLAR, [lahn'-si-ō-ler], *adj.* (*bot.*) tapering toward each end. [L. *lanceola* small lance].

LANCEOLATE, [lahn'-si-ō-lāt], *adj.* (*bot.*) tapering toward the outer extremity. [L. *lanceolatus* lance-shaped].

LANCEOLATED, [lahn'-si-ō-lāt'-id], *adj.* lanceolate.

LANCER, [lahn'-ser], *n.* a cavalry soldier armed with a lance; (*pl.*) a kind of dance with set figures; the music for this. [OFr. *lanceor*].

LANCET, [lahn'-set], *n.* a thin, sharp surgical instrument for making incisions in flesh; (*arch.*) a narrow window or arch with a pointed top. [Fr. *lancette*].

LANCET WINDOW

LANCEWOOD, [lahnts'-wood], *n.* a flexible tough wood obtained from certain species of the South American genus *Duguetia*; a fishing rod made of this wood.

LANCIFORM, [lahn'-si-fawm], *adj.* in the form of a lance. [LANCE and FORM].

LANCINATE, [lan'-sin-āt], *v.t.* to tear, to lacerate. [L. *lancinare*].

LANCINATING, [lan'-sin-āt-ing], *adj.* (of pain) piercing, stabbing.

LANCINATION, [lan'-sin-ā'-shun], *n.* the process of tearing.

LAND (1), [land], *n.* the solid dry surface of the earth; a portion of this; a recognized region or specific area of the earth, a country, etc.; soil, ground, earth, *esp.* arable soil; a specific area of land owned as an estate; **to see how the l. lies**, to sound a person; to explore the state or facts of a situation. [OE. *land*].

LAND (2), [land], *v.t.* to set, place on shore; to take from a transport vehicle and set down; to bring a fish to the bank; (*coll.*) to strike a blow; to establish a desired relationship with; to place, set; to win; *v.i.* to come to rest on or by the land, to disembark; to arrive at a place. [OE. *leudan*].

LAND-AGENT, [land'-ā'-jent], *n.* a person who manages land for the owner; one who deals in landed property.

LANDAMMAN, [land'-am-an], *n.* the chief magistrate of certain Swiss cantons. [Germ. Swiss *landamman*].

LAND ARMY, [land'-ah'-mi], *n.* a body of women formed under Government supervision to work on the land.

LANDAU, [land'-aw], *n.* a four-wheeled horse-drawn carriage with a roof that folds back in two sections. [*Landau*, in Bavaria, where first made].

LANDAU

LANDAULET, [land'-aw-let'], *n.* a type of motor-car with a landau body.

LAND-BREEZE, [land'-brēz], *n.* a current of air blowing from the land toward the sea.

LAND-CRAB, [land'-krab], *n.* a crab mainly frequenting land, *esp.* one of the genus, *Gecarcinus*.

LANDE, [lahnd], *n.* a large extent of wild or sterile land, a heath. [Fr. *lande*].

LANDED, [land'-id], *adj.* possessing an estate in land; composed of real estate or land; disembarked; (*slang*) in a difficult situation.

LANDER, [land'-er], *n.* a person who lands; the miner working at the mouth of a shaft to superintend the unloading of the bucket containing ore.

LANDFALL, [land'-fawl], *n.* an unexpected transfer of landed property by the death of a landowner; a landslide; (*naut.*) the first land sighted after a voyage.

LAND-FLOOD, [land'-flud], *n.* a flooding of land.

LAND-FORCE, [land'-faws], *n.* (*milit.*) a military force serving on land.

LAND-GIRL, [land'-gurl'], *n.* a woman employed, *esp.* in wartime, to cultivate the land.

LANDGRAVE, [land'-grāv], *n.* a count in Germany holding special territorial judicial powers. [MHGerm. *lantgrave*].

LANDGRAVIATE, [land-grāv'-i-āt], *n.* the province held, or administered, by a landgrave. [MedL. *landgraviatus*].

LANDGRAVINE, [land'-grav-ēn'], *n.* the wife of a landgrave. [Germ. *landgräfin*].

LANDHOLDER, [land'-hōld'-er], *n.* a freeholder; a landowner; a tenant holding land.

LANDING, [land'-ing], *n.* the act of one who lands; the place for setting on shore or for stepping on to; an intermediate stage between two flights of stairs; a passage at the top of a flight of stairs from which rooms are reached; **l. net**, a net fastened to the end of a long handle, and used by fishermen for landing heavy fish caught by rod and line; **l.-stage**, a pier to which passenger boats are secured, a jetty; a platform built over the water on to which passengers step from a boat.

LAND-JOBBER, [land'-job'-er], *n.* one who speculates in land

LANDLADY, [land'-lā'-di], *n.* a female landlord; the wife of a landlord; the manageress of an inn; a woman who owns or manages a boarding-house.

LANDLESS, [land'-les], *adj.* destitute of land.

LANDLOCK, [land'-lok], *v.t.* to enclose by land.

LANDLOPER, [land'-lōp-er], *n.* a tramp, a vagrant. [LAND and Du. *loopen* to run].

LANDLORD, [land'-lawd], *n.* the owner of land or houses; the master or manager of an inn or tavern; the proprietor of a lodging-house.

LANDLORDISM, [land'-lawd-izm], *n.* land-ownership with its rights, interests and influence; the collective class of landlords.

LANDLUBBER, [land'-lub'-er], *n.* (*naut.*) a landsman, a person with no knowledge of or skill in nautical matters.

LANDMARK (1), [land'-mahk], *n.* a salient characteristic or mark serving to indicate the boundary of land; an object that serves as a guide to a locality; a notable stage or episode; a boundary line.

LANDMARK (2), [land'-mahk], *v.t.* to provide with a landmark.

LAND-MINE, [land'-mīn], *n.* (*milit.*) a mine capable of employment against troops, etc.; (*coll.*) a bomb dropped by means of a parachute.

LANDOCRACY, [land-ok'-ra-si], *n.* the social class whose ownership of land gives them a collective power. [LAND and Gk. *kratia* rule].

LANDOWNER, [land'-ōn-er], *n.* the proprietor of land, landlord.

LANDOWNING, [land'-ōn-ing], *adj.* that owns (large areas of) land.

LANDRAIL, [land'-rāl], *n.* the corncrake, *Crex pratensis*.

LANDSCAPE, [land'-skāp], *n.* a region of countryside with its trees, contours and vegetation as seen by an observer, a prospect; the representation of this in a pictorial art medium, a picture of scenery; the branch of painting and drawing specializing in this. [Du. *landschap*].

LANDSCAPE-GARDENER, [land'-skāp-gahd'-ner], *n.* one who aims to lay out grounds, parks, and gardens, so as to produce a natural effect.

LANDSCAPE-PAINTER, [land'-skāp-pānt'-er], *n.* an artist specializing in landscapes.

LAND-SHARK, [land'-shahk], *n.* a person who cheats sailors ashore.

LANDSLIDE, [land'-slīd], *n.* a fall of a mass of land due to undermining or erosion, a landslip; (*fig.*) a serious electoral defeat of a political party.

LANDSLIP, [land'-slip], *n.* a small landslide.

LANDSMAN, [landz'-man], *n.* one who lives and works on land; (*naut.*) one who is a novice on board ship.

LAND-SPRING, [land'-spring], *n.* a spring of water which runs only after heavy rains.

LAND-STEWARD, [land'-stew'-erd], *n.* a person who has charge of a landed property.

LANDSTURM, [land'-shtōōrm], *n.* the German or Swiss militia; the final reserve of men under sixty. [LAND and Germ. *sturm* storm].

LAND-SURVEYING, [land'-sur-vā'-ing], *n.* the art of measuring and mapping out land, *esp.* landed estates.

LAND-SURVEYOR, [land'-ser-vā'-er], *n.* a person trained to measure and draw plans of landed estates, etc.

LAND-TAX, [land'-taks], *n.* a tax assessed on land and buildings.

LAND-TAXER, [land'-taks'-er], *n.* a person who advocates the taxing of land-values.

LAND-TURN†, [land'-turn], *n.* a land breeze.

LAND-VALUE, [land'-val'-yōō], *n.* (*econ.*) the value of land, *esp.* as a basis for taxation or rating.

LAND-WAITER, [land'-wā'-ter], *n.* a customs officer whose duty is to attend to landed goods.

LANDWARD, [land'-wood], *adv.* in the direction of the coast, towards the land.

LANDWEHR, [lant'-vāer], *n.* in Germany and Switzerland, troops composed of men still pursuing civil occupations who are called out as militia in times of national emergency. [MdGerm. *landwehr* land defence].

LAND-WIND, [land'-wind], *n.* a wind blowing from the land.

LANDWORKER, [land'-wurk'-er], *n.* a person who works on the land, an agricultural labourer.

LANE, [lān], *n.* a narrow way or passage, *esp.* in the country; a country by-road; a narrow street; a passage between lines of people. [OE. *lane*].

LANGATE, [lan'-gāt], *n.* a linen roller for wounds. [Unkn.].

LANGITE, [lang'-īt], *n.* (*min.*) a hydrated sulphate of copper, resembling brochantite. [*von Lang*, its discoverer].

LANGRAGE†, [lang'-grij], *n.* iron fragments or shot for damaging sails and rigging of enemy ships. [Unkn.].

LANGSETTLE, [lang'-setl], *n.* a long bench fitted with a high back.

LANGSHAN, [lang'-shan], *n.* a breed of black poultry, introduced originally from China, notable for their feathered feet. [*Langshan*, a district near Shanghai in China].

LANG SYNE, [lang-sīn'], *n.* (*Scots*) long ago. [Scots *lang syne* long since].

LANGUAGE, [lang'-gwij], *n.* the complete set of articulate sounds and sound combinations used as the means of verbal communication, *esp.* by a particular nation, people or race; the graphical representation of this; any mode of expression, style; the characteristic terminology of a science, etc.; the inarticulate cries of animals; any method of expressing thoughts and feelings; **bad l.**, profanity, swearing. [OFr. *language*].

LANGUAGED, [lang'-gwijd], *adj.* possessing a language; expert in language.

LANGUENTE, [lang'-gōō-ent'-ā], *adv.* (*mus.*) in a languishing manner. [It. *languente*].

LANGUET, [lang'-gwet], *n.* anything tongue-shaped. [Fr. *languette* small tongue].

LANGUID, [lang'-gwid], *adj.* listless, indisposed to exertion; slow, lifeless, half-hearted. [L. *languidus* faint].

LANGUIDLY, [lang'-gwid-li], *adv.* in a languid style.

LANGUIDNESS, [lang'-gwid-nes], *n.* the condition of being languid.

LANGUISH, [lang'-gwish], *v.i.* to become languid, to lose health and vigour; to grow weak, wane; to undergo a prolonged experience of emotional and mental disturbance due to lack of objective interests; to experience an enervating attack of melancholy. [Fr. *languir*].

LANGUISHING, [lang'-gwish-ing], *adj.* that languishes, fading; wistful and tender.

LANGUISHINGLY, [lang'-gwish-ing-li], *adv.* in a languishing fashion.

LANGUISHMENT, [lang'-gwish-ment], *n.* the state of languishing; languor; heartache, the pangs of amorous longing.

LANGUOR, [lang'-ger], *n.* the condition of being languid; lassitude, listlessness; a state of dreamy inaction, due to excessive introversion. [L. *languor*].

LANGUOROUS, [lang'-ger-us], *adj.* displaying or inducing languor.

LANGUR, [lang-gōōr'], *n.* a monkey of the genus *Semnopithecus*. [Hind. *langur*].

LANIARD, see LANYARD.

LANIARY (**1**), [lā'-ni-er-i], *n.* a canine tooth.

LANIARY (**2**), [lā'-ni-er-i], *adj.* (of teeth) fit for tearing or lacerating. [L. *laniarius* relating to a butcher].

LANIATE, [lā'-ni-āt], *v.t.* to tear in pieces. [L. *laniare*].

LANIFEROUS, [lan-if'-er-us], *adj.* bearing or producing wool, fleecy. [L. *lanifer*].

LANGUR

LANIGEROUS, [lan-ij'-er-us], *adj.* bearing or producing wool. [L. *lana* wool and *gerere* to carry].

LANK, [langk], *adj.* lean, thin and long; loose and drooping; (of hair) straight and limp. [OE. *hlanc* lean].

LANKILY, [langk'-i-li], *adv.* in a lanky manner.

LANKINESS, [langk'-i-nes], *n.* the condition of being lanky; slenderness.

LANKLY, [langk'-li], *adv.* in a lank fashion.

LANKNESS, [langk'-nes], *n.* the condition of being lank.

LANKY, [langk'-i], *adj.* having a lean figure, tall and thin.

LANNER, [lan'-er], *n.* a species of falcon, *Falco feldeggi*, *esp.* the female bird. [OFr. *lanier* cowardly].

LANNERET, [lan'-er-et'], *n.* the male lanner, which is smaller than the female.

LANOLIN, [lan'-ō-lin], *n.* a grease obtained from wool; an ointment made from this. [L. *lana* wool and *oleum* oil].

LANSQUENET, [lan'-sken-et], *n.* a pikeman; a mercenary soldier; formerly, a German foot-soldier; a German card game. [Germ. *landsknecht* foot soldier].

LANTERN, LANTHORN†, [lan'-tern], *n.* a portable lamp usually consisting of a metal case or frame set with horn or glass, and enclosing a flame fed by grease or oil; the chamber at the top of a lighthouse, housing the lights; (*arch.*) an open-sided structure or frame at the top of a church, etc., to provide light or ventilation; (*mech.*) a lantern pinion; **l. fly**, (*entom.*) a South American insect emitting a light from its head. [L. *lanterna*].

LANTERN-JAWED, [lan'-tern-jawd'], *adj.* having a square-formed jaw framing a lean, hollow-cheeked face.

LANTERN PINION, [lan'-tern-pin'-yon], *n.* a cog-wheel in the form of an open cylinder the sides of which consist of staves set equidistantly into the circular ends.

LANTHANUM, [lan'-tha-num], *n.* the rare metallic element La, allied to cerium. [Gk. *lanthano* I lie hidden].

LANTHORN†, see LANTERN.

LANUGINOUS, [lan-ew'-jin-us], *adj.* covered with down or fine soft hair. [L. *lanuginosus*].

LANTERN PINION

LANYARD, LANIARD, [lan'-yahd], *n.* (*naut.*) a short piece of rope made fast to anything to secure it; a length of cord looped round the shoulder in artillery uniform. [~Fr. *lanière*].

LAODICEAN, [lā-ō-di-sē'-an], *adj.* like the Christians of Laodicea, lukewarm in religion or other matters. [Rev. iii, 14-16].

LAP (**1**), [lap], *n.* an overhanging piece of material or garment; the space between the knees and the waist available as a seat or support when one is seated; a revolving metal wheel covered with leather for burnishing metal; one circuit of a racing track; a measured stage in a line of progress; (*fig.*) bosom, heart. [OE. *lappa* skirt].

LAP (**2**), [lap], *n.* a licking with the tongue; the sound thus made.

LAP (**3**), (**lapping, lapped**), [lap], *v.t.* and *i.* to fold over, to wrap; to surround; to place something so that it partially covers another; to fold or turn back; to overlap; to be a lap ahead of. [LAP (1)].

LAP (**4**), (**lapping, lapped**), [lap], *v.t.* and *i.* to lick up with the tongue; to make a noise like this; **to l. up**, to swallow or assimilate eagerly and readily. [OE. *lapian*].

LAPDOG, [lap'-dog], *n.* a small pet dog. [LAP (1) and DOG].

LAPEL, [la-pel'], *n.* the continuation of the coat collar turned back in the form of a flap. [LAP (1)].

LAPELLED, [la-peld'], *adj.* having lapels.

LAPFUL, [lap'-fōōl], *n.* the capacity of a lap.

LAPIDARIAN†, [lap'-id-āer'-i-an], *adj.* having an expert knowledge of stones; engraved on stone. [~L. *lapidarius* stone worker].

LAPIDARY (**1**), [lap'-id-er-i], *n.* one engaged in the polishing and cutting of stones; a connoisseur of precious stones; a treatise on precious stones. [L. *lapidarius*].

LAPIDARY (**2**), [lap'-id-er-i], *adj.* relating to stones; relating to the art of cutting and polishing precious stones; apt for engraving on stone as an inscription; **l. wheel**, the lathe for cutting and polishing precious stones.

LAPIDATE, [lap'-id-āt], *v.t.* to stone. [L. *lapidare*].

LAPIDATION, [lap'-id-ā'-shun], *n.* the act of stoning to death. [L. *lapidatio*].

LAPIDEOUS, [lap-id'-i-us], *adj.* like stone, stony. [L. *lapidius*].

LAPIDIFICATION, [lap-id'-if-ik-ā'-shun], *n.* petrification.

LAPIDIFY, [lap-id'-i-fī], *v.t.* and *i.* to turn into stone. [L. *lapis* stone and *ficere* to make].

LAPIDIST, [lap'-id-ist], *n.* a lapidary.

LAPILLI, [lap-il'-ī], *n.*(*pl.*) small fragments of lava erupted from a volcano. [L. *lapillus* small stone].

LAPILLIFORM, [lap-il'-i-fawm], *adj.* having the form of small stones.

LAPIS, [lap'-is], *n.* a method of printing by stone on calico with the aid of indigo; **l. lydius**, touchstone, a variety of siliceous slate. [L. *lapis* a stone].

LAPIS LAZULI, [lap'-is-laz'-yōō-lī], *n.* a light-blue, semi-precious stone, a silicate of soda, lime, and alumina, with a sulphide. [L. *lapis* stone and MedL. *lazuli*, *gen. sg.* of *lazulum* azure].

LAP-JOINT, [lap'-joint], *adj.* overlapping, as the clinker joint in boatbuilding.

LAPP, [lap], *n.* a native of Lapland.

LAPPER, [lap'-er], *n.* person who laps.

LAPPET, [lap'-et], *n.* a loose flap or fold, *esp.* on a woman's cap or head-dress. [LAP (1)].

LAPSABLE, [laps'-abl], *adj.* liable to lapse.

LAPSE (**1**), [laps], *n.* a sliding or imperceptible passing; that which has thus passed by, a period of time; a slip, mistake; a failing in duty, an omission; deviation from strict principles of conduct, morality, or truth; (*eccles.*) failure of authority to allot a benefice within six months of vacancy; (*leg.*) a legacy rendered inoperative owing to the legatee's death. [L. *lapsus* a fall].

LAPSE (**2**), [laps], *v.i.* to pass by degrees, to glide, slip, slide; to fail to maintain a certain standard of morality, to err, to sin; (*leg.*) to cease to be valid; to pass to another. [L. *lapsare* to slide].

LAPSED, [lapst], *adj.* fallen; passed to another; (*leg.*) (of a legacy, etc.) inoperative because the right or claim to it has passed to another.

LAPSIDED†, see LOPSIDED.

LAPSTONE, [lap'-stōn], *n.* a cobbler's stone held in the lap.

LAPUTAN, [la-pew'-tan], *adj.* fantastic, visionary, extravagantly absurd. [*Laputa*, the flying island in "Gulliver's Travels" by J. Swift].

LAPWING, [lap'-wing], *n.* the crested peewit or green plover, *Vanellus cristatus*. [OE. *hleapewince*].

LAPWING

LAPWORK, [lap'-work], *n.* work in which one part overlaps another.

LAR, (*pl.* **lares**), [lah(r), lāer'-ēz], *n.* (*Rom. antiq.*) a household god. [L. *lar*].

LARBOARD (**1**), [lah'-bawd], *n.* (*naut.*) the left side of a ship when looking from the stern towards the bows. [~ME. *ladde-bord*].

LARBOARD (**2**), [lah'-bawd], *adj.* relating to, placed on, the larboard.

LARCENER, [lah'-sen-er], *n.* a thief.

LARCENIST, [lah'-sen-ist], *n.* a larcener.

LARCENOUS, [lah'-sen-us], *adj.* having the features of theft; thieving.

LARCENY, [lah'-sen-i], *n.* theft, stealing, *esp.* on a minor scale. [~OFr. *larrecin*].

LARCH, [lahch], *n.* a conifer of the genus *Larix.* [Germ. *lärche*].
LARD (1), [lahd], *n.* pig fat, *esp.* that taken from the abdomen, refined by melting, and used in cooking. [OFr. *lard* bacon].
LARD (2), [lahd], *v.t.* to smear or cover with lard; to cover with pieces of bacon fat before cooking; (*fig.*) to enrich, embellish; to overdecorate.
LARDER, [lahd'-er], *n.* a room or place where provisions, meat, etc., are kept; a pantry. [OFr. *lardier*].
LARDY, [lahd'-i], *adj.* resembling, containing, affected by, lard.
LARGE (1), [lahj], *adj.* big, great in size, bulk, quantity; spacious; numerous, copious; ample, broad; having broad ideas, liberal; generous, magnanimous; comprehensive. [OF. *large*].
LARGE (2), [lahj], *adv.* in a large manner.
LARGE-HANDED, [lahj'-hand'-id], *adj.* generous, liberal.
LARGE-HANDEDNESS, [lahj'-hand'-id-nes], *n.* liberality.
LARGE-HEARTED, [lahj'-haht'-id], *adj.* liberal, generous, magnanimous; tolerant; charitable.
LARGE-HEARTEDNESS, [lahj'-haht'-id-nes], *n.* the quality of being large-hearted.
LARGELY, [lahj'-li], *adv.* to a large degree or extent.
LARGE-MINDED, [lahj'-mind'-id], *adj.* magnanimous, generous; tolerant.
LARGENESS, [lahj'-nes], *n.* the quality of being large.
LARGESSE, [lah'-jes'], *n.* a present, a gift; alms thrown to a crowd. [OFr. *largesse* generousness].
LARGETTO, [lah-get'-ō], *n.* a movement or piece to be played larghetto.
LARGHETTO, [lah-get'-ō], *adv.* (*mus.*) rather slowly. [It. *larghetto*].
LARGISH, [lahj'-ish], *adv.* somewhat large.
LARGO (1), [lah'-gō], *n.* (*mus.*) a movement or piece in largo time.
LARGO (2), [lah'-gō], *adv.* (*mus.*) in broad, slow and measured time. [It. *largo* broad].
LARIAT, [la'-ri-at], *n.* a long rope with a slip noose for picketing horses, or for use as a lasso. [Span. *la reata* the rope].
LARK (1), [lahk], *n.* a genus of small birds including the skylark, *Alauda arvensis*, remarkable for their lively sweet song. [OE. *laferce*].
LARK (2), [lahk], *n.* a practical joke, a bit of fun, a frolic. [Uncert.].
LARK (3), [lahk], *v.i.* to participate in a lark; to indulge in tricks; to frolic. [LARK (2)].
LARK (4), [lahk], *v.t.* to catch larks. [LARK (1)].
LARKINESS, [lahk'-i-nes], *n.* the quality of being larky, playfulness.
LARK'S-HEEL, [lahks'-hēl], *n.* (*bot.*) the Indian cress, a species of *Tropæolum.*
LARKSPUR, [lahk'-spur], *n.* (*bot.*) a plant of the genus *Delphinium*, with a spur-shaped calyx.
LARKY, [lahk'-i], *adj.* sportive.
LARMIER, [lah'-mi-er], *n.* (*arch.*) the corona or dripstone. [Fr. *larmier*].
LARRIKIN, [la'-ri-kin], *n.* (*Australian slang*) a rough, a tough, a hooligan, a rowdy. [Uncert.].
LARRUP, [la'-rup], *v.t.* (*vulg.* or *dial.*) to thrash, to beat or flog. [~Du. *larpen*].
LARVA, (*pl.* **larvae**), [lah'-va], *n.* (*entom.*) a fly, moth, butterfly, etc., in its caterpillar, grub, or maggot stage; a fish, frog, etc., in the corresponding stage. [L. *larva* ghost].
LARVAL, [lahv'-al], *adj.* relating to the larva stage.
LARVIFORM, [lahv'-i-fawm], *adj.* resembling a larva in shape. [LARVA and FORM].
LARVIPAROUS, [lahv-ip'-er-us], *adj.* producing larvae; produced as larvae. [LARVA and L. *parere* to bring forth].
LARYNGEAL, [la-rin'-ji-al], *adj.* relating to the larynx.
LARYNGEAN, [la-rin'-ji-an], *adj.* laryngeal.
LARYNGISMUS, [la'-rin-jis'-mus], *n.* (*path.*) a spasmodic closure of the larynx. [MdL. *laryngismus*].
LARYNGITIS, [la'-rin-jī'-tis], *n.* inflammation of the larynx. [LARYNX and Gk. *itis* denoting inflammation].
LARYNGOPHONY, [la'-rin(g)-gof'-o-ni], *n.* (*med.*) examination of the sound of the voice by the stethoscope. [LARYNX and Gk. *phonia* sound].
LARYNGOSCOPE, [la-ring'-gō-skōp], *n.* (*med.*) an instrument fitted with reflecting mirrors for examining the larynx and throat. [LARYNX and Gk. *skopos* view].
LARYNGOSCOPIST, [la'-ring-gos'-ko-pist], *n.* an expert with the laryngoscope.
LARYNGOSCOPY, [la'-ring-gos'-kop-i], *n.* the technique of using the laryngoscope; the employment of this.
LARYNGOTOMY, [la'-ring-got'-o-mi], *n.* (*surg.*) the operation of cutting into the larynx.
LARYNX, [la'-ringks], *n.* (*anat.*) the cartilaginous cavity of the upper part of the windpipe at the back of the throat, containing the vocal cords. [Gk. *larunx*].
LASCAR, [las'-kah(r)], *n.* a native East Indian employed as a sailor. [Pers. *lashkar* army].
LASCIVIOUS, [la-siv'-i-us], *adj.* slyly and powerfully sexual, lustful; wanton; exciting lust. [LL. *lasciviosus*].
LASCIVIOUSLY, [la-siv'-i-us-li], *adv.* in a lascivious way.
LASCIVIOUSNESS, [la-siv'-i-us-nes], *n.* the quality of being lascivious.
LASH (1), [lash], *n.* a thong, *esp.* one forming part of a whip; a stroke given with a whip or anything flexible; (*fig.*) severe satire, a cutting retort; a single eyelash. [ME. *lasch*].
LASH (2), [lash], *v.t.* to strike with a whip, to flog; to cause to move rapidly in the manner of a wielded whip; to fasten tightly with the coils of a rope; (*fig.*) to scourge with censure, satirize vehemently; (*fig.*) to excite to violence; to dash violently against; *v.i.* to lunge out violently with legs or arms; to attack violently; (of rain) to beat down heavily.
LASHER, [lash'-er], *n.* one who lashes; a vent in a weir; **father-l.**, the small fish, *Cottus scorpius.*
LASHING (1), [lash'-ing], *n.* a piece of rope for making fast one thing to another; (*pl.*) a great deal of anything, a large portion.
LASHING (2), [lash'-ing], *n.* a beating, castigation or chastisement.
LASKETS, [las'-ketz], *n.(pl.)* (*naut.*) small lines, like hoops, sewn to a sail to which is fastened a bonnet or extension. [Uncert.].
LASS, [las], *n.* a female child; a young woman, a girl; a sweetheart. [ME. *lasse*].
LASSIE, [las'-i], *n.* (*Scots*) a young lass; a small girl.
LASSITUDE, [las'-it-ewd], *n.* faintness, weariness in body or mind. [L. *lassitudo*].
LASSO (1), [las-ōō'], *n.* a long strip of leather or length of rope with a running noose at one end, used by cowboys to catch cattle. [Span. *lazo*].
LASSO (2), [las-ōō'], *v.t.* to catch by means of a lasso.
LAST (1), [lahst], *n.* that which is last; the end. [LAST (4)].
LAST (2), [lahst], *n.* a model of the human foot, made of metal or wood, on which shoes are made by the cobbler. [OE. *last* sole of the foot].
LAST (3), [lahst], *n.* a load, a cargo; a specific weight or measure. [OE. *hlæst* burden].
LAST (4), [lahst], *adj.* occurring at the end of a series, coming after all the others, hindmost; latest; final, conclusive; most recent; sole; immediately prior to the present event, or to any specified fact, etc.; the least likely or desirable. [OE. *latost*].
LAST (5), [lahst], *adv.* on the last occasion; in the end, finally.
LAST (6), [lahst], *v.i.* to continue in time, to endure, to continue unimpaired; **to l. out**, to maintain strength; to hold out. [OE. *læstan*].
LASTING, [lahst'-ing], *adj.* permanent, continuing, durable.
LASTINGLY, [lahst'-ing-li], *adv.* to a lasting degree.
LASTINGNESS, [lahst'-ing-nes], *n.* the condition of being lasting, durability.
LASTLY, [lahst'-li], *adv.* in the last place, finally.
LAT, [laht], *n.* an Indian pillar. [Hindi *lat* pole].
LATAKIA, [lat'-a-kē'-a], *n.* a fine Syrian tobacco. [*Latakia*, a Syrian port].
LATCH (1), [lach], *n.* a movable catch for a door or gate; a small lock supplementing the main lock on an outside door. [Uncert.].
LATCH (2), [lach], *v.t.* to fasten with a latch.
LATCHES, [lach'-iz], *n.(pl.)* (*naut.*) laskets.
LATCHET† (1), [lach'-it], *n.* a leather shoelace. [OFr. *lachet* thong].
LATCHET (2), [lach'-it], *n.* the sapphirine gurnard, *Trigla hirundo.* [Uncert.].
LATCH-KEY, [lach'-kē'], *n.* a small door-key.
LATE (1), [lāt], *adj.* arriving after the expected or settled time, tardy, behindhand; appearing after the normal season, backward; taking place near the end of a period; existing not long ago, just prior to the present; having just previously come to an end; former; deceased; recent. [OE. *læt* slow].
LATE (2), [lāt], *adv.* after the expected or designated

time; towards the end of a particular period or season; at or to a late hour of the night.
LATEEN, [lat-ēn'], *n.* (*naut.*) a triangular sail, extended by a long yard, used on small boats; a boat bearing such a sail. [Fr. (*voile*) *latine* latin (sail)].

LATEEN

LATELY, [lāt'-li], *adv.* not long ago, recently, of late.
LATENCY, [lā'-ten-si], *n.* the quality of being latent.
LATENESS, [lāt'-nes], *n.* the condition of being late.
LATENT, [lā'-tent], *adj.* concealed, lying dormant, present but not visible; **l. heat,** the heat given off or absorbed by a body in changing its state. [L. *latens*].
LATENTLY, [lā'-tent-li], *adv.* in latent fashion.
LATERAL, [lat'-er-al], *adj.* pertaining to, situated at, or proceeding from the side. [L. *lateralis*].
LATERALITY, [lat'-er-al'-i-ti], *n.* the condition of being lateral.
LATERALIZE, [lat'-er-al-iz], *v.t.* to render lateral in position.
LATERALLY, [lat'-er-al-i], *adv.* in a lateral manner or direction.
LATERIFOLIOUS, [lat'-er-i-fō'-li-us], *adj.* (*bot.*) growing on the side of a leaf at the base. [L. *latus* side and FOLIOUS].
LATERITE, [lat'-er-īt], *n.* (*min.*) a red ferruginous rock found in India, brick-stone. [~L. *later* brick].
LATERITIOUS, [lat'-er-ish'-us], *adj.* of a brick colour. [L. *lateritius*].
LATEST, [lāt'-est], *adj.* most recent. [OE. *latost*].
LATEX, [lā'-teks], *n.* (*bot.*) the milky juice of certain plants; vegetable milk. [L. *latex* liquid].
LATH, [lahth], *n.* a thin strip of wood, *esp.* one used to form a support for tiles or plaster; a strip of wood used for trellis-work or Venetian blinds. [Uncert.].
LATHE (1), [lāTH], *n.* an administrative division of the county of Kent. [OE. *læth* estate].
LATHE (2), [lāTH], *n.* a turner's machine tool which spins round the material to be cut. [Uncert.].
LATHER (1), [lah'-THer], *n.* froth made by rubbing soap in water; a foam of sweat exuded by a horse. [OE. *leathor* soda].
LATHER (2), [lah'-THer], *v.t. and i.* to cover with lather; to form lather.
LATHI, [lah'-ti], *n.* a long stick loaded with iron used by the Indian police to quell native riots. [Hind. *lathi* stick].
LATHSPLITTER, [lahth'-split'-er], *n.* a person employed in splitting wood into laths.
LATHWORK, [lahth'-wurk], *n.* a base formed of laths for receiving plaster, tiles, etc.
LATHY, [lahth'-i], *adj.* thin; long and slender.
LATI-, *pref.* broad. [L. *latus*].
LATICIFEROUS, [lat'-i-sif'-er-us], *adj.* (*bot.*) producing latex. [L. *latex* latex and *ferre* to bear].
LATICLAVE, [lat'-i-klāv], *n.* the broad purple stripe on the tunic, distinguishing a Roman senator. [LATI and L. *clavus* stripe].
LATICOSTATE, [lat'-i-kost'-āt], *adj.* (*zool.*) broad-ribbed. [LATI and L. *costa* rib].
LATIDENTATE, [lat'-i-dent'-āt], *adj.* (*zool.*) broad-toothed. [LATI and DENTATE].
LATIFOLIATE, [lat'-i-fō'-li-āt], *adj.* latifolious.
LATIFOLIOUS, [lat'-i-fō'-li-us], *adj.* (*bot.*) having broad leaves.
LATIN (1), [lat'-in], *n.* the language of the ancient Romans; a member of one of the Latin races.
LATIN (2), [lat'-in], *adj.* relating to Latium, or to the Latins; relating to, written in, Latin; **L. Church,** the Roman Catholic Church; **L. race,** a race whose members speak a language derived from Latin; **Ecclesiastical L.,** Latin as used by the R.C. Church; **Low L.,** medieval Latin. [L. *Latinus*].
LATINISM, [lat'-in-izm], *n.* a Latin idiom.
LATINIST, [lat'-in-ist], *n.* one versed in Latin.
LATINITY, [lat-in'-i-ti], *n.* Latin style; the Latin tongue or idiom. [L. *latinitas*].
LATINIZE, [lat'-in-iz], *v.t. and i.* to give Latin form or terminations to; to use words or phrases borrowed from the Latin; to make Latin in character.
LATIPENNATE, [lat'-i-pen'-āt], *adj.* (*ornith.*) characterized by broad wings. [LATI and PENNATE].
LATIROSTRAL, [lat'-i-ros'-tral], *adj.* latirostrous.
LATIROSTROUS, [lat'-i-ros'-trus], *adj.* (*ornith.*) characterized by a broad beak. [LATI and L. *rostrum* beak].
LATISEPTAL, [lat'-i-sept'-al], *adj.* (*bot.*) bearing a broad septum. [LATI and SEPTUM].
LATISH, [lāt'-ish], *adj.* somewhat late.
LATITATION, [lat'-it-ā'-shun], *n.* the condition of being hidden, a lying concealed. [L. *latitatio*].
LATITUDE, [lat'-it-ewd], *n.* a distance from the equator; scope, extent; freedom from restrictions, *esp.* on thought; (*astron.*) the distance of a heavenly body from the ecliptic. [L. *latitudo* breadth].
LATITUDINAL, [lat'-it-ewd'-in-al], *adj.* relating to latitude; in the direction of latitude.
LATITUDINARIAN (1), [lat'-it-ewd-in-āer'-i-an], *n* a person of latitudinarian outlook.
LATITUDINARIAN (2), [lat'-it-ewd-in-āer'-i-an], *adj.* not restricted, liberal, broad-minded in views and principles; (*theol.*) refusing to restrict oneself to a literal interpretation of religious dogma, tending towards unorthodoxy or laxity of belief.
LATITUDINARIANISM, [lat'-it-ewd-in-āer'-i-an-izm], *n.* a latitudinarian outlook towards religious belief or dogma.
LATITUDINOUS, [lat'-it-ewd'-in-us], *adj.* having latitude, extensive.
LATRIA, [la-trī'-a], *n.* (*theol.*) supreme worship, as that paid to God. [Gk. *latreia* service].
LATRINE, [la-trēn'], *n.* a camp lavatory. [L. *latrina*].
LATROBITE, [la-trōb'-it], *n.* (*min.*) a Labrador variety of red anorthite. [The Rev. J. C. *Latrobe* its discoverer].
LATTEN†, [lat'-en], *n.* an alloy of zinc and copper, a fine brass used for crosses and memorial plates. [OFr. *laton*].
LATTER, [lat'-er], *adj.* taking place in the second half; happening after something else; last mentioned of two. [OE. *lætra* later].
LATTERLY, [lat'-er-li], *adv.* lately, of late, in time not long past; towards the end of a specified time.
LATTER-MATH, [lat'-er-mahth'], *n.* (*dial.*) the aftermath.
LATTICE (1), [lat'-is], *n.* a network of thin strips of wood or laths set obliquely; a window with diamond-shaped panes held secure by lead strips crossing diagonally; (*her.*) figure in the form of a lattice. [OFr. *lattis*].
LATTICE (2), [lat'-is], *v.t.* to cover or furnish with a lattice.
LATTICED, [lat'-ist], *adj.* in the form of a lattice; furnished with a lattice.
LAUD (1), [lawd], *n.* praise, eulogy; (*pl.*) the prayer of praise in divine worship, usually recited at dawn; a song of praise. [L. *laus laudis*].
LAUD (2), [lawd], *v.t.* to praise; to celebrate.
LAUDABILITY, [lawd'-a-bil'-i-ti], *n.* the quality of being laudable.
LAUDABLE, [lawd'-abl], *adj.* worthy of praise. [L. *laudabilis*].
LAUDABLENESS, [lawd'-abl-nes], *n.* laudability.
LAUDABLY, [lawd'-ab-li], *adv.* in laudable fashion.
LAUDANUM, [lod'-an-um], *n.* opium prepared in spirits, tincture of opium. [MdL. *laudanum*].
LAUDATION, [lawd-ā'-shun], *n.* the act of praising; the state of being praised; eulogy, praise. [L. *laudatio*].
LAUDATIVE, [lawd'-at-iv], *adj.* expressing praise. [L. *laudativus*].
LAUDATORILY, [lawd'-at-er-i-li], *adv.* in a laudatory manner.
LAUDATORY (1), [lawd'-at-er-i], *n.* that which praises.
LAUDATORY (2), [lawd'-at-er-i], *adj.* containing praise; tending to praise; eulogistic. [LL. *laudatorius*].
LAUGH (1), [lahf], *n.* the act of laughing; the sound thus uttered.
LAUGH (2), [lahf], *v.i.* to utter a sound or sounds expressive of a nervous or reflexive response attendant upon a feeling of happiness, amusement, etc., and accompanied by a grin and shaking of the body; to be pleased and gratified; to give expression to good humour; to embody prosperity and gay content; **to l. at,** to ridicule; to take no heed of; **to l. off,** to turn away in pleasantry a remark threatening to be embarrassing; **to l. in someone's face,** to defy someone openly. [OE. *hlæhhan*].
LAUGHABLE, [lahf'-abl], *adj.* causing laughter; ludicrous, ridiculous.
LAUGHABLENESS, [lahf'-abl-nes], *n.* the quality of being laughable.
LAUGHABLY, [lahf'-ab-li], *adv.* in a laughable manner.

LAUGHER, [lahf′-er], *n.* a person who laughs.
LAUGHING-GAS, [lahf′-ing-gas′], *n.* nitrous oxide, used as an anaesthetic in dentistry.
LAUGHING HYENA, [lahf′-ing-hī-ē′-na], *n.* the spotted hyena.
LAUGHING JACKASS, [lahf′-ing-jak′-as], *n.* an Australian bird allied to the kingfisher, with a harsh guffawing cry.
LAUGHINGLY, [lahf′-ing-li], *adv.* in a laughing manner.
LAUGHING-STOCK, [lahf′-ing-stok′], *n.* an object of derision.
LAUGHTER, [lahf′-ter], *n.* sound of laughing; convulsive merriment. [OE. *hleahtor*].
LAUGHTERLESS, [lahf′-ter-les], *adj.* without laughter.
LAUMONTITE, [law′-mont-īt], *n.* (*min.*) a zeolite, composed of hydrated silicate of alumina and lime. [G. de *Laumont* its discoverer].
LAUNCE, [lawnts], *n.* a sand-eel of the genus *Ammodytes*; **sable l.,** the capelin. [Uncert.].
LAUNCH (1), [lawnch], *n.* the act of launching a boat; the movement of a boat as it is launched; a boat, usually driven by motor, used for pleasure or patrolling purposes; the largest boat carried by a warship. [Span. *lancha* pinnace].
LAUNCH (2), [lawnch], *v.t.* to throw, hurl through the air; to cause to move; to initiate, set going, start; to cause to glide into the water, *esp.* a new ship for the first time; *v.i.* to glide into the water; **l. out,** (*fig.*) to begin a new set of operations on a large scale. [ME. *launchen* from OFr. *lancher*].
LAUNDER, [lawnd′-er], *v.t.* to wash, dry, and iron dirty clothes or linen. [OFr. *lavander*].
LAUNDERER, [lawnd′-er-er], *n.* one who launders clothes.
LAUNDRESS, [lawnd′-res], *n.* a woman who launders clothes for a living.
LAUNDRY, [lawn′-dri], *n.* the establishment, place, or room where clothes are washed; clothes and other articles to be washed. [OFr. *lavanderie*].
LAURA, [law′-ra], *n.* a hermitage; a community of detached cells inhabited by monks. [Gk. *laura* alley].
LAUREATE (1), [lo′-ri-at, law′-ri-at], *n.* a person crowned with laurel.
LAUREATE (2), [lo′-ri-at, law′-ri-at], *adj.* crowned with laurel; **poet l.,** a poet appointed for life to an official position in the Royal Household and expected to write suitable poetry on state occasions. [L. *laureatus*].
LAUREATESHIP, [lo′-ri-at-ship, law′-ri-at-ship], *n.* the office of poet laureate.
LAUREATION, [lo′-ri-ā′-shun], *n.* the conferring of a degree in certain universities.
LAUREL, [lo′-rel], *n.* a bay tree, one of several species of evergreen shrubs, the leaves of which were used in ancient Greece to make wreaths of honour and success; (*pl.*) (*fig.*) the reward of success, honours; **garden l.,** a shrub of the genus *Prunus*. [L. *laurus*].
LAURELLED, [lo′-reld], *adj.* crowned with laurel, honoured, rewarded for success.
LAURESTINUS, see LAURUSTINUS.
LAURIFEROUS, [lawr-if′-er-us], *adj.* producing or bringing laurel. [L. *laurus* laurel and *ferre* to bear].

LAUREL

LAURIN, [law′-rin], *n.* (*chem.*) a crystalline fatty substance found in the berries of the laurel.
LAURITE, [law′-rīt], *n.* a sulphide of ruthenium and osmium found with platinum. [Mrs. *Laura* Joy after whom it was named].
LAURUSTINUS, LAURESTINUS, [law′-rus-tī′-nus], *n.* an ornamental evergreen shrub with pink-white blossoms, *Viburnum tinus*. [L. *laurus* laurel and *tinus* plant].
LAUTU, [law′-tōō], *n.* a band of twisted cotton ornamented with feathers, worn round the head of the Inca of Peru as a royal badge. [Native].
LAVA, [lah′-va], *n.* rock matter which issues molten from a volcano; **l. millstone,** a hard basaltic stone found near the Rhine. [It. *lava*].
LAVABO, [la-vā′-bō], *n.* a ritual washing of hands; a lavatory basin. [L. *lavabo* I shall wash].
LAVAGE, [lā′-vij], *n.* (*med.*) internal washing, *esp.* of a therapeutic nature. [Fr. *lavage*].
LAVA-LIKE, [lah′-va-līk′], *adj.* resembling lava.
LAVATION, [lav-ā′-shun], *n.* the act of washing or cleansing. [L. *lavatio*].
LAVATORY, [lav′-at-er-i], *n.* a place for washing; a room fitted with wash-basins and conveniences; a privy. [L. *lavatorium*].
LAVE, [lāv], *v.t. and i.* to wash, to bath, to bathe. [OE. *lafian*].
LAVENDER (1), [lav′-en-der], *n.* (*bot.*) a fragrant, pale, purple-flowered plant, *Lavendula vera*; the perfume characteristic of the plant; a light purple colour; **l. water,** a perfume made from lavender. [OFr. *lavendre*].
LAVENDER (2), [lav′-en-der], *adj.* relating to the lavender plant, its scent or colour.
LAVER (1), [lā-ver], *n.* a washing utensil, a large basin. [OFr. *laveoir*].
LAVER (2), [lā′-ver], *n.* a red edible seaweed of the genus *Porphyra*. [L. *laver*].
LAVEROCK, [lav′-er-ok], *n.* the skylark, *Alauda arvensis*. [OE. *laferce*].

LAVEROCK

LAVISH (1), [lav′-ish], *adj.* extremely liberal, very generous; extravagant, wasteful; ample, abundant. [OFr. *lavache* downpour].
LAVISH (2), [lav′-ish], *v.t.* to give with excessive generosity; to spend extravagantly, squander.
LAVISHLY, [lav′-ish-li], *adv.* to a lavish degree.
LAVISHNESS, [lav′-ish-nes], *n.* the quality of being lavish.
LAW, [law], *n.* the body of rules governing the conduct, affairs and relationships of the members of a nation or community, as established and administered by authority; any one of these rules; the system of legal operation, jurisprudence; the study of this; the body of rules and customs relating to social behaviour and procedure, *esp.* as established by tradition; an abstract statement formulating the general relationship of a fact to its context; a definition expressing the specific sequence of events peculiar to a given activity under certain conditions. [OE. *lagu*].
LAW-ABIDING, [law′-ab-ī′-ding], *adj.* having a conscientious regard for the law.
LAWBREAKER, [law′-brāk′-er], *n.* person who violates the law.
LAW COURT, [law′-kawt], *n.* a court where the law is administered; (*pl.*) the public building in London used for this purpose.
LAWFUL, [law′-fŏŏl], *adj.* allowed by, in accordance with, the law; legitimate, acknowledged or constituted by law, rightful.
LAWFULLY, [law′-fŏŏl-i], *adv.* in lawful fashion.
LAWFULNESS, [law′-fŏŏl-nes], *n.* the condition of being lawful.
LAWGIVER, [law′-giv′-er], *n.* one who prescribes laws.
LAWGIVING, [law′-giv′-ing], *adj.* making or enacting laws.
LAWLESS, [law′-les], *adj.* not subject to or governed by law; contrary to law; unruly, undisciplined.
LAWLESSLY, [law′-les-li], *adv.* in a lawless way.
LAWLESSNESS, [law′-les-nes], *n.* the condition of being lawless.
LAWMAKER, [law′-māk′-er], *n.* one who makes and enacts laws.
LAWMAKING, [law′-māk′-ing], *adj.* legislative.
LAW-MERCHANT, [law′-merch′-ant], *n.* (*hist.*) the body of special laws concerned with and regulating international trading.
LAWMONGER, [law′-mung′-ger], *n.* a pettifogger.
LAWN (1), [lawn], *n.* a stretch of more or less flat ground, covered with grass and kept closely mown; (*poet.*) an open space in a wood, a glade. [OFr. *launde*].
LAWN (2), [lawn], *n.* a fine linen or cambric, *esp.* used for bishops' sleeves. [*Laon*, a French town].
LAWNMOWER, [lawn′-mō′-er], *n.* a machine for cutting the grass on a lawn.
LAWN TENNIS, [lawn′-ten′-is], *n.* a game played on a specially marked-out lawn or court, in which a small white, felt-covered rubber ball is hit to and fro over a net by opposing players by means of racquets.
LAWNY, [lawn′-i], *adj.* of the nature of lawn.
LAW-STATIONER, [law′-stā′-shun-er], *n.* a person or firm specializing in the stationery required by legal practitioners.
LAWSUIT, [law′-sewt], *n.* an action at law.
LAW-WRITER, [law′-rī′-ter], *n.* a clerk employed as a copyist by a lawyer.

LAWYER, [law'-yer], *n.* one expert in legal knowledge and procedure who practises law; a legal adviser, *esp.* a solicitor; (*dial.*) a long, thorny, climbing bramble.
LAWYER-LIKE, [law'-yer-lik'], *adj.* like a lawyer.
LAWYERLY, [law'-yer-li], *adj.* in the manner of a lawyer.
LAX (1), [laks], *n.* (smoked) salmon. [OE. *leax* salmon].
LAX (2), [laks], *n.* (*med.*) relaxed condition of the bowels, diarrhoea.
LAX (3), [laks], *adj.* loose, slack, not taut; not strict, free, *esp.* in morals; careless; loose in the bowels. [L. *laxus*].
LAXATIVE (1), [laks'-at-iv], *n.* a medicine for curing constipation, a purgative.
LAXATIVE (2), [laks'-at-iv], *adj.* loosening the bowels, purging. [L. *laxativus*].
LAXATIVENESS, [laks'-at-iv-nes], *n.* the condition of being loose.
LAXITY, [laks'-i-ti], *n.* looseness; inexactness; absence of strict morals. [L. *laxitas*].
LAXLY, [laks'-li], *adv.* in a lax way, loosely.
LAXNESS, [laks'-nes], *n.* the condition of being lax.
LAY (1), [lā], *n.* a short narrative poem; a lyrical poem; a song or ballad. [OFr. *lai*].
LAY (2), [lā], *n.* that which is laid; the position in which a person or object is found; (*naut.*) the direction in which the strands of a rope are twisted; share of profit. [LAY (4)].
LAY (3), [lā], *adj.* relating to the laity, non-ecclesiastical; not belonging to a specific profession, non-specialist. [Gk. *laikos*].
LAY (4), (laid), [lā], *v.t.* to put down, set, cause to lie in a particular place or be in a particular condition; to place in order, *esp.* eating utensils; to prepare a table; to cause to settle; to make subside or disappear; to beat, strike down; to produce (eggs); to propose odds for a wager; to impose as a tax, etc.; to charge with; to present; to assert, as a claim; to contrive; (*naut.*) to place in dock; *v.i.* to produce eggs; to make a bet; **to l. about**, to fight with wild and reckless vigour; **to l. aside**, to discontinue; **to l. by the heels**, to place in custody; **to l. down**, to resign, relinquish; **to l. down the law**, to be dogmatic; **to l. off**, (*slang*) to cease; (*naut.*) to cause a ship to move farther away; to suspend temporarily from work; **to l. out**, to plan; to expend; to render insensible by a blow; to prepare (a body) for the grave; **to l. to**, (*naut.*) to bring a ship into a stationary position; **to l. up**, to store; to confine to bed. [OE. *lecgan*].
LAY-BROTHER, [lā'-bruTH'-er], *n.* a person received into a convent of monks without taking holy orders.
LAY-BY, [lā'-bī], *n.* a railway siding.
LAY-CLERK, [lā'-klahk], *n.* a layman who reads the responses in the church service.
LAY-DAYS, [lā'-dāz], *n.*(*pl.*) a certain number of days allowed to load or unload cargo.
LAY-ELDER, [lā'-eld'-er], *n.* (Presbyterian Church) an elder who is not a member of the ministry.
LAYER (1), [lā'-er], *n.* person who lays, *esp.* odds; a bird that lays eggs.
LAYER (2), [lā'-er], *n.* a section of a substance, placed upon another, a stratum; (*hort.*) an undetached shoot laid underground to enable it to take root.
LAYER (3), [lā'-er], *v.t.* (*hort.*) to bend a branch or stem of a plant so that it is covered by earth and able to take root.
LAYERING, [lā'-er-ing], *n.* (*hort.*) propagation by layers.
LAYETTE, [lā-et'], *n.* a new-born baby's outfit; †a powder tray. [Fr. *layette* a small chest].
LAY-FIGURE, [lā'-fig'-er], *n.* an artist's model made of wood, etc., in imitation of the human body; (*fig.*) a puppet, a nonentity.
LAYING, [lā'-ing] *n.* the first coat of plaster on laths; the act or period of producing eggs; the eggs laid at one sitting; method of twisting the strands of a rope.
LAYLAND, [lā'-land], *n.* fallow land.
LAYMAN, [lā'-man], *n.* a man who is not a clergyman; a man with no professional skill or status, a non-specialist.
LAY-OFF, [lā'-of], *n.* temporary period of unemployment for a worker during a slack season.
LAY-OUT, [lā'-owt], *n.* a plan of buildings, etc.; a ground plan; a rough draft of an advertisement design.
LAY-OVER, [lā'-ō'-ver], *n.* an extra cloth used in restaurants for covering a stained table-cloth.
LAYSHAFT, [lā'-shahft], *n.* a subsidiary shaft of a machine, etc., operating independently of the main motor.
LAYSTALL, [lā'-stawl], *n.* a heap of manure; a place where dung is laid; a place for housing milch cows.
LAZAR†, [laz'-er], *n.* a diseased beggar, a person infected with leprosy or other pestilence; †a leper. [*Lazarus*, Luke xvi, 20].
LAZARET, [laz'-er-et], *n.* lazaretto.
LAZARETTO, [laz'-er-et'-ō], *n.* a hospital for diseased beggars or lepers; a place of quarantine. [It. *lazaretto*].
LAZAR-HOUSE, [laz'-er-hows'], *n.* a lazaretto.
LAZARISTS, [laz'-er-ists], *n.*(*pl.*) Lazarites.
LAZARITES, [laz'-er-īts], *n.*(*pl.*) (*R.C.*) an order of priests established by St. Vincent de Paul in 1632. [St. *Lazare*, a R.C. college in Paris].
LAZAR-LIKE, [laz'-er-līk'], *adj.* lazarly.
LAZARLY, [laz'-er-li], *adj.* affected by sores; leprous.
LAZE, [lāz], *v.t.* *and i.* to waste time in idleness; to indulge in the minimum of exertion.
LAZILY, [lāz'-i-li], *adv.* in a lazy way.
LAZINESS, [lāz'-i-nes], *n.* the condition of being lazy.
LAZULITE, [laz'-yōō-līt], *n.* (*min.*) a blue-coloured mineral composed of aluminium and magnesium phosphates. [L. *lazulus*].
LAZY, [lā'-zi], *adj.* unwilling to work, not disposed to exert oneself, slothful; **l. bed**, (*hort.*) a bed in which potatoes may be left to lie near the surface with soil lightly covering them; **l.-bones**, a lazy person; **l. tongs**, a series of collapsible scissor-like bars opening out in a criss-cross pattern to grasp an object. [Uncert.].
LAZZARONE, [lats'-er-ō'-ni], *n.* one of the unemployed beggar class of Naples. [It. *lazzarone* beggar].
LEA, [lē], *n.* a meadow or pasture, a stretch of country free from trees. [OE. *leah* field].
LEACH (1), [lēch], *n.* a tub in which wood ashes are leached; the ashes being leached.
LEACH (2), LETCH, [lēch], *v.t.* *and i.* to wash by a process of percolating; to separate alkali from ashes by percolation; to dissolve. [OE. *leccan* to water].
LEAD (1), [led], *n.* the heavy metallic element Pb, a lump of this used for taking soundings at sea, a plummet; a small stick of plumbago used in pencils; (*print.*) thin strip of metal used to separate lines of type; (*pl.*) sheets of lead for covering roofs; roofs so covered; **red l.**, oxide of lead; **white l.**, carbonate of lead; **to swing the l.**, to sham, malinger. [OE. *lead*].
LEAD (2), [lēd], *n.* a strap, chain or cord for leading a dog, etc.; a watercourse, *esp.* an artificial one leading to a mill; the privilege of leading off in a game; the card played first; the principal role in a play or film; the actor or actress who plays this; the distance a competitor in a race is in front of his nearest rival; the action of leading; the position or right of leading, command; direction, guide, cue; (*elect.*) a length of wire acting as a conductor of current.
LEAD (3), [led], *adj.* made of lead.
LEAD (4), [led], *v.t.* to cover with lead; to fit or stop with lead; (*print.*) to insert thin metal strips between lines of type. [LEAD (1)].
LEAD (5), [lēd], *v.t.* to conduct, guide, *esp.* by the hand; to act as head, controller, or principal agent in; to bring; to convey; to persuade to act in a certain way; to cause; to incline; to spend, pass; to cause to spend; to be at the head of; (*milit.*) to command; (*cards*) to play as the first card; *v.i.* to proceed in front and show the way; to act as chief, conductor, or principal; to be ahead of all other competitors; to go; **to l. off**, to make the first move in a game; **to l. out of**, to give on to; **to l. to**, to result in; **to l. up to**, to approach indirectly; to provide opportunity for. [OE. *lædan*].
LEAD-ARMING, [led'-ahm'-ing], *n.* a lump of wax or fat fitted into the lower end of a sounding-lead to ascertain the nature of the bottom.
LEADED, [led'-id], *adj.* (*print.*) (of type) fitted with or set in lead; separated by leads.
LEADEN, [led'-en], *adj.* made of lead; (*fig.*) heavy, dull; unenergetic, inert.
LEADEN-HEARTED, [led'-en-haht'-id], *adj.* having no feeling; depressed, sorrowful.
LEADEN-HEELED, [led'-en-hēld'], *adj.* moving slowly.
LEADEN-STEPPING, [led'-en-step'-ing], *adj.* walking slowly.
LEADER, [lēd'-er], *n.* a person who leads; the horse at the head of a team; the principal player in each section of an orchestra; a tributary branch of ore; a principal article in a newspaper, stating its attitude, an editorial; the top bud of a branch or plant, the most recent growth or shoot from a branch; the principal driving wheel in a machine; a tendon; (*leg.*) a senior counsel.

LEADERETTE, [lĕd'-er-et'], *n.* a short leading article or paragraph written by an editor.
LEADERSHIP, [lĕd'-er-ship], *n.* the office of a leader; direction.
LEAD-GLANCE, [led'-glahns], *n.* an ore from which lead is extracted.
LEADHILLITE, [led'-hil-īt], *n.* (*min.*) a mineral composed of sulphate and carbonate of lead. [*Leadhills*, in Scotland].
LEAD-IN, [lēd'-in'], *n.* (*wirel.*) a conductor connecting an aerial to a receiving set.
LEADING (1), [led'-ing], *n.* strips of lead used for building purposes, *esp.* in casement windows.
LEADING (2), [lēd'-ing], *n.* guidance, direction.
LEADING (3), [lēd'-ing], *adj.* that leads; chief, principal, most important.
LEADING ARTICLE, [lēd'-ing-aht'-ikl], *n.* any one of a regular series of articles in a newspaper, devoted primarily to expressing editorial opinion.
LEADINGLY, [lēd'-ing-li], *adv.* in a leading way.
LEADING QUESTION, [lēd'-ing-kwes'-chun], *n.* (*leg.*) a question which suggests the answer required.
LEADING-REIN, [lēd'-ing-rān'], *n.* a control rein held by a riding instructor and connected to the bit of the pupil's horse.
LEADING-STRINGS, [lēd'-ing-stringz'], *n.*(*pl.*) strings by which children are supported when beginning to walk; **in l.,** unable to act for oneself.
LEAD-MILL, [led'-mil], *n.* a circular plate of lead used for grinding or roughing precious stones.
LEAD-PENCIL, [led'-pen'-sil], *n.* a slender stick of black-lead encased in a wood covering, and used for drawing or writing.
LEAD POISONING, [led'-poiz'-on-ing], *n.* (*path.*) a form of poisoning caused by the introduction of lead into the system.
LEADSMAN, [ledz'-man], *n.* (*naut.*) the sailor appointed to take soundings.
LEAD-WOOL, [led'-wŏŏl], *n.* uncarded wool, used in plumbing for plugging pipe joints.
LEADY, [led'-i], *adj.* pertaining to, containing, or like, lead.
LEAF (1), (*pl.* **leaves**), [lēf], *n.* (*bot.*) one of the thin, flat growths from the stem of a plant; anything resembling this in shape or thinness; a sheet of a book, etc., corresponding to two pages; the insertable or folding flap of a table top; a thin sheet of pressed metal; **to turn over a new l.,** to mend one's ways. [OE. *leaf*].
LEAF (2), [lēf], *v.i.* to produce leaves.
LEAFAGE, [lēf'-ij], *n.* leaves collectively, foliage.
LEAF-BRIDGE, [lēf'-brij], *n.* a drawbridge constructed with a movable platform on each side.
LEAF-BUD, [lēf'-bud], *n.* a bud containing a leaf and not a flower.
LEAF-CROWNED, [lēf'-krownd], *adj.* crowned with leaves.
LEAFED, [lēft], *adj.* having leaves.
LEAF-FAT, [lēf'-fat], *n.* (*anat.*) fat arranged in thin layers.
LEAFINESS, [lēf'-i-nes], *n.* the quality of being leafy.
LEAFING, [lēf'-ing], *n.* the process of developing leaves.
LEAF INSECT, [lēf'-in'-sekt], *n.* an insect which resembles a leaf in appearance.

LEAF INSECT

LEAF-LARD, [lēf'-lahd], *n.* lard in the form of leaf-fat.
LEAFLESS, [lēf'-les], *adj.* bare of leaves.
LEAFLET, [lēf'-let], *n.* a small pamphlet, a handbill of unstitched pages; (*bot.*) a little leaf, one of the divisions of a compound leaf, a foliole.
LEAF-METAL, [lēf'-met'-al], *n.* a leafy metallic preparation for imparting a brilliant gloss to substances.
LEAF-MOULD, [lēf'-mōld'], *n.* humus formed by decayed leaves.
LEAFSCAR, [lēf'-skah(r)], *n.* the mark or wound on the stem left by the fallen leaf.
LEAFSTALK, [lēf'-stawk], *n.* the stalk bearing a leaf.
LEAFY, [lēf'-i], *adj.* bearing numerous leaves, full of leaves.
LEAGUE (1), [lēg], *n.* a measure of length, equal in England to three miles. [LL. *leuga*].
LEAGUE (2), [lēg], *n.* an organized alliance of individuals, states, etc., for the protection or furtherance of common interests; the collective body of such persons, states, etc., *esp.* a group of sports clubs in competition for championships. [Fr. *ligue*].
LEAGUE (3), [lēg], *v.t. and i.* to form into a league; to unite together in a league.
LEAGUE OF NATIONS, [lēg'-ov-nā'-shuns], *n.* an association of nations to bring about international peace and co-operation.
LEAGUER (1), [lēg'-er], *n.* a person who belongs to a league.
LEAGUER (2), [lēg'-er], *n.* a camp of besiegers. [Du. *leger* camp].
LEAK (1), [lēk], *n.* a crack or hole in a container or vessel which allows liquid, gas, etc., to escape or enter improperly; the water, gas, etc., which is thus let in or out; (*elect.*) an escape of electricity owing to imperfect insulation.
LEAK (2), [lēk], *v.i.* (of water, gas, etc.) to enter or escape through a leak; **to l. out,** (*fig.*) to become known gradually, unintentionally, or irregularly. [OIcel. *leka*].
LEAKAGE, [lēk'-ij], *n.* the process of leaking; the quantity lost or entering through a leak; (*fig.*) an improper disclosure of information; (*comm.*) loss not accounted for.
LEAKINESS, [lēk'-i-nes], *n.* the condition of being leaky.
LEAKY, [lēk'-i], *adj.* that leaks, full of leaks.
LEAL†, [lēl], *adj.* loyal, faithful, true; **land of the l.,** heaven. [OFr. *leal*].
LEAM, [lēm], *n.* a light, flame, a ray. [OE. *leoma*].
LEAMER†, [lēm'-er], *n.* a nut fully ripe.
LEAN (1), [lēn], *n.* that part of meat or flesh which is free from fat. [LEAN (3)].
LEAN (2), [lēn], *n.* a slope, inclination; divergence from the perpendicular. [LEAN (4)].
LEAN (3), [lēn], *adj.* having or consisting of little fat; having relatively little flesh on the body, thin; (*fig.*) poor, unproductive. [OE. *hlæne*].
LEAN (4), (**leant**), [lēn], *v.t. and i.* to deviate from the perpendicular, to incline; to incline towards; to rest against, support oneself on; to be partial to, to be disposed to; (*fig.*) to rely upon. [OE. *hlænan*].
LEAN-FACED, [lēn'-fāst], *adj.* having a thin face; (*typ.*) (of letters) not of full breadth.
LEANING, [lēn'-ing], *n.* the act or state of one who leans, inclination, predisposition.
LEANLY, [lēn'-li], *adv.* in lean fashion, poorly.
LEANNESS, [lēn'-nes], *n.* the quality of being lean.
LEAN-TO, [lēn'-tōō'], *n.* a shed with a roof sloping against a wall.
LEAN-WITTED, [lēn'-wit'-id], *adj.* of limited intelligence.
LEAP† (1), [lēp], *n.* (*prov.*) a basket; an osier creel. [OE. *leap*].
LEAP (2), [lēp], *n.* a jump, bound, a spring into the air; the height or length of this; (*fig.*) a sudden upward trend.
LEAP (3), (**leapt**), [lēp], *v.t. and i.* to make a leap or leaps, to jump, to spring into the air; to spring over by a leap; to cause to jump; **to l. at,** to accept eagerly. [OE. *hleapan*].
LEAPER, [lēp'-er], *n.* a person who leaps; a horse which is a steeplechaser.
LEAP-FROG, [lēp'-frog'], *n.* a game in which each of the players leaps over the stooping backs of the others in turn.
LEAPINGLY, [lēp'-ing-li], *adv.* by leaps.
LEAP-YEAR, [lēp'-yēer], *n.* a year of 366 days formed by adding an extra day to February.
LEARN, (**learned, learnt**), [lurn], *v.t. and i.* to acquire knowledge of; to commit to memory; to develop skill or technique in by practice; to gain knowledge; to understand, experience; to endeavour by practice to become. [OE. *leornian*].
LEARNABLE, [lurn'-abl], *adj.* able to be learnt.
LEARNED, [lurn'-id], *adj.* possessing learning acquired by study; erudite; containing and showing learning; relating to learning and study.
LEARNEDLY, [lurn'-id-li], *adv.* in learned fashion.
LEARNEDNESS, [lurn'-id-nes], *n.* condition of being learned.
LEARNER, [lurn'-er], *n.* a person who is learning, a novice.
LEARNING, [lurn'-ing], *n.* the act of studiously acquiring knowledge; knowledge, information, scholarship, the whole body of knowledge possessed by a scholar. [OE. *leornung*].
LEARY†, [lēer'-i], *n.* an old mine-working. [Uncert.].
LEASABLE, [lēs'-abl], *adj.* able to be leased.
LEASE (1), [lēs], *n.* a letting of land or tenements for

a term of years; the contract for such letting; any tenure, term, period or time. [AFr. *laes*].
LEASE (2), [lēs], *n.* the place at which the warp threads cross in weaving. [LEASH].
LEASE (3), [lēs], *v.t.* to let or hold on lease. [OFr. *lesser* to leave].
LEASEHOLD (1), [lēs'-hōld], *n.* a tenure held by lease.
LEASEHOLD (2), [lēs'-hōld], *adj.* held on a lease.
LEASEHOLDER, [lēs'-hōld'-er], *n.* a tenant under a lease, lessee.
LEASE-LEND, [lēs'-lend'], *adj.* used to denote a policy or goods originating from the provisions of the American Lease and Lend Act.
LEASH (1), [lēsh], *n.* a thong, strap, etc., by which a dog or hawk is held close; a set of three hounds, whippets, hares, etc.; a brace and a half. [OFr. *lesse*].
LEASH (2), [lēsh], *v.t.* to hold fast by means of a leash.
LEASING, [lēz'-ing], *n.* (*dial.*) falsehood, lies. [OE. *leasung* deceit].
LEASOW†, [lē'-sō], *n.* a pasture. [OE. *læswe*].
LEAST (1), [lēst], *n.* the least amount, the smallest in measurement or estimation; **not in the l.,** not a bit; **at l.,** nevertheless, not less than.
LEAST (2), [lēst], *adj.* smallest. [OE. *læsest læst*].
LEAST (3), [lēst], *adv.* in the smallest or lowest degree or extent, below all others.
LEASTWAYS, [lēst'-wāz], *adv.* leastwise.
LEASTWISE, [lēst'-wiz], *adv.* (*coll.*) anyhow, at least.
LEAT, [lēt], *n.* an open watercourse to or from a mill. [OE. *gelæt* cross-roads].
LEATHER (1), [leTH'-er], *n.* the skin of animals prepared for use by tanning; the fleshy part of a dog's ear; (*slang*) the skin of a human being; a football. [OE. *lether*].
LEATHER (2), [leTH'-er], *adj.* consisting of leather.
LEATHER (3), [leTH'-er], *v.t.* to beat, thrash, *esp.* with a leather belt.
LEATHERBACK, [leTH'-er-bak], *n.* the turtle *Sphargis coriacea.*
LEATHER-CLOTH, [leTH'-er-kloth'], *n.* leatherette.
LEATHER-COAT, [leTH'-er-kōt'], *n.* a species of apple with a tough peel.

LEATHERBACK

LEATHER-DRESSER, [leTH'-er-dres'-er], *n.* a person employed in dressing leather or preparing hides.
LEATHERETTE, [leTH'-er-et'], *n.* a substitute for leather, imitation leather.
LEATHER-JACKET, [leTH'-er-jak'-it], *n.* an Australian tree, *Eucalyptus resinifera*; the larva of the daddy-longlegs or crane-fly.
LEATHERN, [leTH'-ern], *adj.* made of leather.
LEATHERSELLER, [leTH'-er-sel'-er], *n.* a dealer in leather.
LEATHERWOOD, [leTH'-er-wŏŏd'], *n.* (*bot.*) a North American plant, *Dirca palustris*, with a tough bark used as rope and for baskets.
LEATHERY, [leTH'-er-i], *adj.* like leather, tough.
LEAVE (1), [lēv], *n.* permission; temporary freedom granted by permission, *esp.* holiday from work or duty for a member of the armed forces; departure, farewell; (*billiards*) the position in which the balls are left after a stroke or break; **French-l.,** absence from duty without permission. [OE. *leaf*].
LEAVE (2), (left), [lēv], *v.t.* to depart from; to terminate residence in or association with; to abandon, desert; to let lie, to let stay; to forget to pick up or carry away; to possess at one's death; to bequeath; to make responsible for, to entrust; to deposit; to render, cause to become; to forbear; to refer; (*arith.*) to cause to remain over; *v.i.* to desist; to depart; **to l. off,** to cease to wear; to cease; **to l. out,** to omit. [OE. *læfan*]
LEAVED, [lēvd], *adj.* having leaves.
LEAVEN (1), [lev'-en], *n.* a substance that makes dough rise, yeast, barm; (*fig.*) anything which effects fresh activity through modification. [L. *levamen* that which raises].
LEAVEN (2), [lev'-en], *v.t.* to mix or raise with leaven; (*fig.*) to imbue; to modify, temper.
LEAVENING, [lev'-en-ing], *n.* the process of mixing with leaven; that which leavens.
LEAVENOUS, [lev'-en-us], *adj.* containing leaven.
LEAVER, [lēv'-er], *n.* a person who leaves.
LEAVES, [lēvz], *n.(pl.)* of LEAF.
LEAVE-TAKING, [lēv'-tāk'-ing], *n.* formal termination of a meeting, parting compliments.
LEAVINGS, [lēv'-ingz], *n.(pl.)* things left or cast away; relics; refuse.
LEAVING-SHOP, [lēv'-ing-shop'], *n.* a pawnbroker's shop.
LEBENSRAUM, [lāb'-enz-rowm], *n.* territory viewed by a power as belonging to its indispensable economic domain. [Germ. *lebensraum* from *leben* life and *raum* space].
LECHER (1), [lech'-er], *n.* a man habitually indulging in lewdness. [OFr. *lecheur* rake].
LECHER (2), [lech'-er], *v.i.* to indulge in lechery.
LECHEROUS, [lech'-er-us], *adj.* immoderately given to sexual indulgence, lustful; provoking lust.
LECHEROUSLY, [lech'-er-us-li], *adv.* in a lecherous manner.
LECHEROUSNESS, [lech'-er-us-nes], *n.* the quality of being lecherous, lust.
LECHERY, [lech'-er-i], *n.* lecherous behaviour, lewdness.
LECITHIN, [les'-ith-in], *n.* (*physiol.*) a waxy constituent of nervous tissue and yolk of egg, possessing therapeutic properties. [Gk. *lekothos* yolk].
LECOTROPAL, [li-kot'-rop-al], *adj.* having the shape of a horseshoe. [Gk. *lekos* dish and *tropos* turn].
LECTERN, [lek'-tern], *n.* a reading desk for supporting heavy books; *esp.* one used in church; in Scotland, the precentor's desk. [LL. *lectrum*].
LECTION, [lek'-shun], *n.* a variant in a manuscript or book; (in divine service) a reading of a scriptural text. [L. *lectio* reading].
LECTIONARY, [lek'-shun-er-i], *n.* a service-book containing the appropriate scripture passages to be read in church; a table indicating such passages. [EcclesL. *lectionarium*].
LECTOR, [lek'-ter], *n.* a lecturer in a continental university; †a bible clerk. [L. *lector* a reader].
LECTURE (1), [lek'-cher], *n.* an informative discourse on a particular subject delivered before an audience; a formal reproof, reprimand. [Fr. *lecture*].
LECTURE (2), [lek'-cher], *v.t. and i.* to instruct by means of lectures; to reprove; to deliver a lecture.
LECTURER, [lek'-cher-er], *n.* one who lectures, *esp.* a university or college teacher.
LECTURESHIP, [lek'-cher-ship], *n.* the office of lecturer.
LED, [led], *pret. and p.pt.* of LEAD.
LED-CAPTAIN†, [led'-kap'-tin], *n.* a sycophant.
LEDGE, [lej], *n.* a narrow shelf; a narrow extended projection from any surface, *esp.* from a cliff, rock, etc.; (*arch.*) a small moulding. [ME. *legge* bar].

LEDGE

LEDGER, [lej'-er], *n.* (*bookkeeping*) a book in which the main debit and credit items are entered in summary form; (*arch.*) a horizontal, supporting piece of timber used in scaffolding; a horizontal slab of stone. [~OE. *lecgan* to lay].
LEDGER-LINE, [lej'-er-lin'], *n.* a fishing-line with a sinker near the hook; (*mus.*) a line added above or below the staff to accommodate notes falling outside the range. [*Prec.*].
LEDGY, [lej'-i], *adj.* having many ledges.
LED-HORSE, [led'-haws], *n.* a packhorse ; a spare horse.
LEE (1), [lē], *n.* (*naut.*) the protected side of the quarter towards which the wind blows; shelter.
LEE (2), [lē], *adj.* (*naut.*) situated on the side farthest from the wind; **l. board,** a plank fixed to the lee side of a flat-bottomed boat, and acting as a counter-support when boat is close hauled; **l. anchor,** the anchor to leeward of a ship. [OE. *hleo* shelter].
LEECH (1), [lēch], *n.* a species of blood-sucking worm, *Hirudo medicinalis*, used for blood-letting; any species of the family of worms, *Hirudinea*; a doctor. [OE. *læce*].
LEECH (2), [lēch], *n.* (*naut.*) the flying edge of a sail. [Du. *lijk* bolt-rope].
LEECH (3), [lēch], *v.t.* to apply a leech to, for the purpose of blood-letting.
LEECHCRAFT, [lēch'-krahft], *n.* medical treatment; the art of healing.
LEECHEE, see LITCHI.
LEEFANGE, [lē'-fanj], *n.* (*naut.*) an iron bar along which the sheets of fore and aft sails traverse. [Uncert.].
LEEFUL†, [lē'-fŏŏl], *adj.* lawful, proper, permissible. [ME. *leveful*].

LEEK, [lēk], *n.* a vegetable allied to the onion, *Allium Porrum*, the national emblem of Wales; **to eat the l.**, to retract with humiliation. [OE. *leac*].

LEEMOST, [lē'-mōst], *adj.* farthest to leeward.

LEEP, [lēp], *v.t.* to wash with manure and water. [Hind. *lipna*].

LEER (1), **LEHR**, [lēer], *n.* an annealing furnace for cooling off molten glass during manufacture. [Ukn.].

LEER (2), [lēer], *n.* a furtive, sidelong grin. [OE. *hleor* cheek].

LEER (3), [lēer], *v.i.* to look with a leer.

LEERINGLY, [lēer'-ing-li], *adv.* in leering fashion.

LEERY, [lēer'-i], *adj.* characterized by leering; (*slang*) sly.

LEEK

LEES, [lēz], *n.*(*pl.*) dregs at the bottom of liquor. [Fr. *lie*].

LEET (1), [lēt], *n.* (*hist.*) a manorial court of record formerly held annually. [AFr. *lete*].

LEET (2), [lēt], *n.* a sea-fish, the pollack. [Unkn.].

LEET (3), [lēt], *n.* (*Scots*) a list of candidates eligible for an office. [OFr. *eslite*].

LEEWARD (1), [lōō'-erd, lē'-wŏŏd], *n.* (*naut.*) the lee side.

LEEWARD (2), [lōō'-erd, lē'-wŏŏd], *adj.* relating to, placed in, the lee side.

LEEWARD (3), [lōō'-erd, lē'-wŏŏd], *adv.* towards the lee.

LEEWARDLY, [lōō'-erd-li, lē'-wŏŏd-li], *adv.* in a leeward direction.

LEEWAY, [lē'-wā], *n.* the lateral movement of a ship drifting to leeward; (*fig.*) loss of progress or time, arrears of work.

LEFT (1), [left], *n.* the left side, position or direction; (*pol.*) the party or group of parties characterized by advanced radical or socialistic principles, so called as occupying a position on the left-hand side of the speaker or president in a legislative assembly.

LEFT (2), [left], *adj.* relating to, connected with, that side of the body in which the heart is normally situated, indicating a position or direction corresponding with this side. [OE. *left* weak].

LEFT (3), [left], *adv.* towards the left side.

LEFT-HAND (1), [left'-hand], *n.* the left side.

LEFT-HAND (2), [left'-hand], *adj.* situated on the left side; performed with the left hand.

LEFT-HANDED, [left'-hand'-id], *adj.* using the left hand more naturally than the right; (of a marriage) morganatic; awkward, clumsy; **l. compliment**, a compliment which has an ambiguous derogatory meaning.

LEFT-HANDEDNESS,]left'-hand'-id-nes], *n.* the quality of being left-handed.

LEFT-HANDER, [left'-hand'-er], *n.* a left-handed person, *esp.* a cricketer who adopts a left-handed stance; a blow with the left hand.

LEFT-OVER (1), [left'-ō'-ver], *n.* anything not used up.

LEFT-OVER (2), [left'-ō'-ver], *adj.* not used up.

LEFTWARD, [left'-wud], *adv.* to the left.

LEFT WING, [left'-wing'], *n.* *and adj.* that element in a state or a political party which tends more to the left than do the rest.

LEG (1), [leg], *n.* one of the limbs, consisting of the parts between hip and ankle, by means of which an animal supports itself; clothing which covers this; that part of anything which acts as a support; the thigh part of a leg of a beast or fowl, prepared as food; any side of a triangle other than the base; (*cricket*) the area of the field at the batsman's back; (*naut.*) a tack to windward; **on one's last legs**, about to die or come to an end; **to pull someone's l.**, to impose on a person for a joke. [OIcel. *leggr*].

LEG (2), (**legging, legged**), [leg], *v.i.* (*slang*) to use one's legs, *esp.* to run away or hurry.

LEGACY, [leg'-a-si], *n.* a bequest left by will; (*fig.*) that which has been bequeathed; a consequence. [OFr. *legacie* office of legate].

LEGACY-HUNTER, [leg'-a-si-hunt'-er], *n.* a person who intrigues with a view to obtaining legacies.

LEGAL, [lē'-gal], *adj.* connected with, relating to, or according to law, lawful; created by law; required by law; **l. offence**, an act defined by statute as unlawful and punishable. [L. *legalis*].

LEGALISM, [lē'-gal-izm], *n.* respect for, or adherence to, the law; excessive respect for complicated legal forms and procedure.

LEGALIST, [lē'-gal-ist], *n.* one who relies strictly on the law; one who delights in legalism.

LEGALITY, [li-gal'-i-ti], *n.* the quality of being legal, lawfulness.

LEGALIZE, [lē'-gal-īz], *v.t.* to make lawful.

LEGALLY, [lē'-gal-i], *adv.* according to law.

LEGATE, [leg'-at], *n.* the pope's ambassador to a foreign prince or state. [L. *legatus*].

LEGATEE, [leg'-at-ē'], *n.* the person to whom a legacy is bequeathed.

LEGATESHIP, [leg'-at-ship], *n.* the office of legate.

LEGATINE, [leg'-at-īn], *adj.* relating to, or proceeding from, a legate.

LEGATION, [leg-ā'-shun], *n.* the staff of the minister of a foreign country sent abroad on diplomatic work; their official residence or headquarters abroad. [L. *legatio* embassy].

LEGATO, [leg-ah'-tō], *adv.* (*mus.*) smoothly and evenly. [It. *legato*].

LEG-BAIL, [leg'-bāl'], *n.* escape from custody; french-leave; (*cricket*) bail on the leg side.

LEG-BYE, [leg'-bī], *n.* (*cricket*) a run scored off the batsman's leg.

LEGEND, [lej'-end], *n.* †a chronicle of the life of a saint; a traditional story, usually of oral origin, with thematic material of an imaginatively fantastic and marvellous nature; a story based more on fancy than on fact; an inscription on a shield, medal or coin. [L. *legenda* things to be read].

LEGENDARY (1), [lej'-end-er-i], *n.* a collection of legends.

LEGENDARY (2), [lej'-end-er-i], *adj.* having the nature and form of legend; romantic, fabulous. [MedL. *legendarius*].

LEGER (1), [lej'-er], *n.* a leaden weight used in bottom fishing in a fast stream.

LEGER† **(2)**, [lej'-er], *adj.* small in size or weight.

LEGERDEMAIN, [lej'-er-de-mān'], *n.* sleight of hand; a deceptive conjuring trick which depends on clever manipulation. [Fr. *léger de main* light of hand].

LEGGED, [legd, leg'-id], *adj.* having legs.

LEGGERS, [leg'-erz], *n.*(*pl.*) men employed in conducting a barge through a canal tunnel, by pushing against the walls with their legs.

LEGGING, [leg'-ing], *n.* a leather cover for the leg fastened by buttons or straps; a long supple gaiter.

LEGGY, [leg'-i], *adj.* having long legs; weedy.

LEGHORN, [leg'-hawn, le-gawn'], *n.* a Tuscan plait of smooth straw for making bonnets and hats; a bonnet or hat made of this; a breed of poultry. [*Leghorn*, in Italy].

LEGIBILITY, [lej'-i-bil'-i-ti], *n.* the condition of being legible.

LEGIBLE, [lej'-ibl], *adj.* capable of being read; clear and distinct; easily decipherable. [LL. *legibilis*].

LEGIBLENESS, [lej'-ibl-nes], *n.* legibility.

LEGIBLY, [lej'-i-bli], *adv.* in a legible style.

LEGION, [lē'-jun], *n.* a major Roman military unit consisting of 3,000 to 6,000 men together with a force of cavalry; any large body of troops; a great number of people, multitude, *esp.* in organized order; **British L.**, an association for the protection of the interests of ex-service men who served in the First World War; **Foreign L.**, a corps of volunteers recruited by the French army from foreigners for service abroad; **L. of Honour**, a French order founded by Napoleon I, awarded for meritorious military or civil activities. [L. *legio legionis*].

LEGIONARY (1), [lē'-jun-er-i], *n.* a member of a legion.

LEGIONARY (2), [lē'-jun-er-i], *adj.* relating to, consisting of a legion or legions; countless, innumerable. [L. *legionarius*].

LEGIONNAIRE, [lē'-jun-āer], *n.* a member of a legion, *esp.* the Foreign Legion. [Fr. *légionnaire*].

LEGISLATE, [lej'-is-lāt], *v.i.* to make or enact a law or laws.

LEGISLATION, [lej-is-lā'-shun], *n.* the procedure of legislating. [LL. *legislatio*].

LEGISLATIVE, [lej'-is-lat-iv], *adj.* appointed to legislate; relating to legislation; done by legislation.

LEGISLATIVELY, [lej'-is-lat-iv-li], *adv.* in a legislative form.

LEGISLATOR, [lej'-is-lāt'-er], *n.* person who makes laws; a member of a legislature. [L. *legislator* one who proposes a law].

LEGISLATORSHIP, [lej'-is-lāt'-er-ship], *n.* the office of legislator.

LEGISLATRESS, [lej'-is-lā-tres], *n.* a female legislator.

LEGISLATRIX, [lej'-is-lā-triks], *n.* a legislatress.
LEGISLATURE, [lej'-is-lā-cher], *n.* the assembly in a state invested with power to make, amend or repeal laws.
LEGIST, [lē'-jist], *n.* a person skilled in law. [Fr. *légiste*].
LEGITIMACY, [li-jit'-im-a-si], *n.* the quality or fact of being legitimate.
LEGITIMATE (1), [li-jit'-im-at], *adj.* born in lawful wedlock; lawful, rightful, legal; reasonable, just, proper; having the status and rights of a lawful heir to the throne. [L. *legitimus*].
LEGITIMATE (2), [li-jit'-im-āt], *v.t.* to make legitimate; to declare to be legitimate.
LEGITIMATELY, [li-jit'-im-at-li], *adv.* in legitimate fashion.
LEGITIMATENESS, [li-jit'-im-at-nes], *n.* legitimacy.
LEGITIMATION, [li-jit'-im-ā'-shun], *n.* the act of rendering legitimate.
LEGITIMATIZE, [li-jit'-im-at-iz], *v.t.* to make legitimate.
LEGITIMISM, [li-jit'-im-izm], *n.* the principles advocated by legitimists.
LEGITIMIST, [li-jit'-im-ist], *n.* one in favour of an hereditary monarchy; a supporter of the Bourbons in France.
LEGITIMIZE, [li-jit'-im-īz], *v.t.* to legitimate.
LEGLESSNESS, [leg'-les-nes], *n.* the condition of having no legs.
LEG-PULL, [leg'-pōōl], *n.* a deception of a person for the sake of a joke.
LEGUME, [leg'-yōōm], *n.* (*bot.*) a fruit which splits into two halves and has the seeds attached to the ventral suture, as the bean, pea, etc.; the pod of such plants. [Fr. *légume*].
LEGUMIN, [li-gew'-min], *n.* an albumin extracted from leguminous plants; vegetable casein.
LEGUMINACEOUS, [leg-ewm'-in-ā'-shus], *adj.* of, or pertaining to, the family of plants, the *Leguminosæ*, which have pod-like seeds or legumes. [L. *legumen* pod].
LEGUMINOUS, [li-gew'-min-us], *adj.* pertaining to, of the nature of, a legume.
LEHR, see LEER (1).
LEIOTRICHOUS, [li-ot'-rik-us], *adj.* smooth-haired [Gk. *leios* smooth and *thrix* hair].
LEIPOTHYMIC, [līp'-o-thīm'-ik], *adj.* (*med.*) fainting; prone to swooning. [Gk. *leipo* I leave and *thumos* soul].
LEISTER, [lēs'-ter], *n.* a fishing spear with three prongs for catching salmon. [OIcel. *ljostr*].
LEISURABLE, [lezh'-er-abl], *adj.* able to take leisure.
LEISURABLY, [lezh'-er-ab-li], *adv.* at leisure.
LEISURE, [lezh'-er], *n.* freedom from occupation; time free from employment. [OFr. *leisir*].
LEISURED, [lezh'-erd], *adj.* of, possessing, or displaying, leisure.
LEISURELY, [lezh'-er-li], *adj.* performed at leisure or at one's ease; rather slow and deliberate.
LEIT-MOTIV, [līt'-mō-tēf'], *n.* (*mus.*) the principal theme. [MdGerm. *leitmotiv*].
LEMAN, [lem'-an], *n.* a lover, a sweetheart; a mistress. [ME. *leofman* dear one].
LEMMA, (*pl.* **lemmata**), [lem'-a], *n.* (*math.*) a proposition postulated or demonstrated for use in the demonstration of some other proposition; a headline or headword; the argument of a literary work. [Gk. *lemma* something taken for granted].
LEMMING, [lem'-ing], *n.* (*zool.*) a migratory rodent of the genus *Lemmus*. [Lap. *loumek*].
LEMNIAN, [lem'-ni-an], *adj.* relating to, coming from, the Isle of Lemnos.
LEMNISCATE, [lem-nis'-kāt], *n.* (*math.*) a curve forming a figure 8. [L. *lemniscus* hanging ribbon].
LEMON (1), [lem'-un], *n.* a yellow-skinned acidulous fruit; the tree that bears this, *Citrus Limonum*; (*U.S. slang*) an unattractive girl; a swindle, a catch; **salt of l.,** potash mixed with oxalic acid; **l. grass,** a species of *Andropogon*. [Arab. *laimun*].
LEMON (2), [lem'-on], *adj.* having the colour or characteristics of a lemon; made with lemon.
LEMONADE, [lem-on-ād'], *n.* a drink consisting of lemon juice mixed with water and sweetened; a bottled drink made of a flavoured soda-water. [Fr. *limonade*].
LEMON SOLE, [lem'-on-sōl], *n.* a trade name for certain edible fish of the family *Pleuronectes*. [Fr. *limande*].
LEMON SQUASH, [lem'-on-skwosh'], *n.* a drink made of the juice of squeezed lemons and water or soda-water, sweetened.
LEMUR, [lē'-mur], *n.* a nocturnal mammal allied to the monkeys and insectivores, having a long bushy tail. [L. *lemures* ghosts].

LEMUR

LEMURES†, [lem'-yōō-rēz], *n.*(*pl.*) ghosts or spectres among the ancient Romans. [L. *lemures*].
LEMURIAN, [li-mew'-ri-an], *adj.* lemurine.
LEMURIFORM, [li-mew'-ri-fawm], *adj.* resembling the lemur.
LEMURINE, [lem'-yōō-rīn], *adj.* relating to or resembling the lemurs.
LEMUROID, [lem'-yōō-roid], *adj.* lemurine.
LEND, (lent), [lend], *v.t.* to transfer to a person for use over a limited period; to contribute, tend to add; to loan money out at interest; (*reflex.*) to be adaptable for use as. [OE. *lænan*].
LENDABLE, [lend'-abl], *adj.* able to be lent.
LENDER, [lend'-er], *n.* one who lends; one engaged in lending money.
LENDING, [lend'-ing], *n.* the act of making a loan; that which is lent or furnished.
LENDING LIBRARY, [lend'-ing lī'-brer-i], *n.* a library that lends out books.
LENGTH, [lengkth], *n.* measurement from end to end or from one point to another; duration, total measurement of time taken by a completed action or activity; extent, size, range; **at l.,** after a time; for a long time; in detail, fully. [OE. *lengthu*].
LENGTHEN, [lengkth'-en], *v.t. and i.* to make longer; to become longer.
LENGTHILY, [lengkth'-i-li], *adv.* in a lengthy manner, at great length.
LENGTHINESS, [lengkth'-i-nes], *n.* the quality of being lengthy.
LENGTHWISE, [lengkth'-wīz], *adv.* in the direction of the length.
LENGTHY, [lengkth'-i], *adj.* long; full and detailed, diffuse.
LENIENCY, [lē'-ni-en-si], *n.* the quality of being lenient.
LENIENT, [lē'-ni-ent], *adj.* not severe, mild, merciful, tolerant; †emollient. [L. *leniens*].
LENIENTLY, [lē'-ni-ent-li], *adv.* in lenient fashion.
LENIFY, [len'-i-fī, lē'-ni-fī], *v.t.* to render calm; to alleviate. [L. *lenis* gentle and *ficare* to make].
LENINISM, [len'-in-izm], *n.* the social, political and philosophical principles of Lenin; the doctrine of the unity of theory and practice as elaborated by Lenin; the theory and the tactics of the proletarian revolution, *esp.* the dictatorship of the proletariat.
LENINIST (1), [len'-in-ist], *n.* a follower or advocate of Lenin's doctrine or principles.
LENINIST (2), [len'-in-ist], *adj.* relating to, derived from, Lenin or his doctrines.
LENINITE, [len'-in-īt], *n.* a Leninist.
LENITIVE (1), [len'-it-iv, lē'-nit-iv], *n.* (*med.*) a medicine alleviating pain, and soothing excitement or irritation.
LENITIVE (2), [len'-it-iv, lē'-nit-iv], *adj.* having the power to mitigate, soften, assuage; emollient. [MedL. *lenitivus*].
LENITY, [len'-i-ti], *n.* the quality of being lenient, clemency.
LENO, [lē'-nō], *n.* a kind of cotton gauze. [Fr. *linon*].
LENS, [lenz], *n.* a piece of glass specially ground so as to modify, in some particular way, the course of rays of light passing through it; an objective; (*anat.*) that part of the eye having a similar function. [L. *lens* lentil].
LENT (1), [lent], *n.* the 40 days from Ash Wednesday to Easter Day observed by Christians as a time of fasting and abstinence. [OE. *lencten*, *lengten* spring].
LENT (2), [lent], *pret. and p.pt.* of LEND.
LENTAMENTE, [lent'-am-ent'-i], *adv.* (*mus.*) slowly. [It. *lentamente*].
LENTANDO, [lent-and'-ō], *adv.* (*mus.*) slower and slower. [It. *lentando*].
LENTEN, [lent'-en], *adj.* belonging to, or used in Lent; (*fig.*) sparing, meagre. [OE. *lencten*].
LENTICULAR, [lent-ik'-yōō-ler], *adj.* resembling a lentil; having the form of a double-convex lens; in or of the lens of the eye. [LL. *lenticularis*].

LENTICULARLY, [lent-ik'-yōō-ler-li], *adv.* in the form of a double-convex lens or lentil.
LENTIFORM, [lent'-i-fawm], *adj.* lenticular.
LENTIGINOUS, [lent-ij'-in-us], *adj.* having freckles, spotted; scurfy. [LL. *lentiginosus*].
LENTIGO, [len-tī'-gō], *n.* (*med.*) a freckly affliction of the skin. [L. *lentigo*].
LENTIL, [len'-til], *n.* a leguminous plant, *Lens esculenta*, and its seed. [Fr. *lentille*].
LENTISK, [lent'-isk], *n.* the mastic tree, *Pistacia lentiscus*. [L. *lentiscus*].
LENT-LILY, [lent'-lil'-i], *n.* a daffodil.
LENTO, [len'-tō], *adv.* (*mus.*) slowly. [It. *lento*].
LENTOID, [lent'-oid], *adj.* formed like a lens. [L. *lens* pulse and Gk. *oeides* like].
LENTOUS, [len'-tus], *adj.* clammy; tenacious. [L. *lentus* slow].
LENZINITE, [len'-sin-īt], *n.* (*min.*) halloysite, a hydrated silicate of aluminium, resembling coal. [Dr. J. G. *Lenz*].
LEO, [lē'-ō], *n.* the Lion, the fifth sign of the Zodiac. [L. *leo* lion].
LEONERO, [lē'-ō-nāer'-ō], *n.* a breed of dogs trained for puma-hunting.
LEONID, [lē'-ō-nid], *n.* a meteor thought to come from the constellation Leo. [L. *leo* lion].
LEONINE (1), [lē'-on-in], *adj.* relating to (Pope) Leo; **l. verse,** elegiac verse characterized by internal rhyme, the word before the caesura rhyming with the end word.
LEONINE (2), [lē'-ō-nīn], *adj.* resembling a lion. [L. *leoninus*].
LEONINELY, [lē'-ō-nīn'-li], *adv.* in a leonine manner.
LEOPARD, [lep'-erd], *n.* a spotted carnivore of the cat group, *Felis pardus*; **American l.,** the jaguar, *Felis onca*; **snow l.,** the ounce, *Felis ancia*; **leopard's bane,** a plant of the genus *Doronicum*. [L. *leopardus*].

LEOPARD

LEOPARD-CAT, [lep'-erd-kat'], *n.* a small wild cat, *Felis bengalensis*.
LEOPARDESS, [lep'-erd-es'], *n.* a female leopard.
LEOPARD MOTH, [lep'-erd-moth'], *n.* a large white moth marked with black spots, the larva of which eats into timber.
LEPCHA, [lep'-cha], *n.* a member of a race of people inhabiting Sikkim and parts of Tibet. [Native].
LEPER, [lep'-er], *n.* a person affected with leprosy. [OFr. *lepre* from Gk. *lepra*].
LEPIDO-, *pref.* scaly. [Gk. *lepis lepidos* scale].
LEPIDODENDRON, [lep'-i-dō-den'-dron], *n.* a genus of fossil plants having a scaly stem. [LEPIDO and Gk. *dendron* tree].
LEPIDOID, [lep'-id-oid], *adj.* having bright scales of bone, ganoid. [LEPIDO and Gk. *oeides* like].
LEPIDOLITE, [lep'-id-ō-lit], *n.* (*min.*) a lilac-coloured species of mica from which lithium and rubidium salts are extracted. [LEPIDO and Gk. *lithos* stone].
LEPIDOMELANE, [lep'-i-dō-mel-ān'], *n.* (*min.*) a black mica containing more iron than magnesium. [LEPIDO and Gk. *melas melanos* black].
LEPIDOPTERA, [lep'-id-op'-ter-a], *n.*(*pl.*) (*entom.*) an order of insects, comprising the moths and butterflies, and having four wings covered with microscopic scales. [LEPIDO and Gk. *pteron* wing].
LEPIDOPTERAL, [lep'-id-op'-ter-al], *adj.* lepidopterous.
LEPIDOPTEROUS, [lep'-id-op'-ter-us], *adj.* belonging to the lepidoptera.
LEPIDOSIREN, [lep'-id-ō-sī'-ren], *n.* the South American mud-fish, *Lepis paradoxa*. [LEPIDO and SIREN].
LEPIS, [lep'-is], *n.* a small membranous scale. [L. *lepis*].
LEPORINE, [lep'-er-in], *adj.* relating to, or resembling, the hare. [L. *leporinus*].
LEPRA, [lē'-pra], *n.* (*med.*) a scaly affliction of the skin; leprosy; psoriasis. [Gk. *lepra*].
LEPRECHAUN, [lep'-ra-kawn], *n.* a benevolent brownie in the shape of an old man. [Ir. *lupracan* small-bodied].
LEPROSY, [lep'-ro-si], *n.* an infectious disease attacking the skin, caused by the *Bacillus lepræ*.
LEPROUS, [lep'-rus], *adj.* infected with leprosy.
LEPROUSLY, [lep'-rus-li], *adv.* in leprous fashion.
LEPROUSNESS, [lep'-rus-nes], *n.* condition of being leprous.

LEPTODACTYL, [lep'-tō-dak'-til], *n.* (*zool.*) having slender toes. [Gk. *leptos* small and DACTYL].
LEPTOLOGY, [lep-tol'-o-ji], *n.* a tedious dissertation on trifling things. [Gk. *leptos* small and *logos* speech].
LEPTON, (*pl.* **lepta**), [lep'-ton], *n.* a Greek coin worth one-hundredth of a drachma. [Gk. *lepton*].
LEPTORRHINE, [lep'-tō-rīn], *adj.* (*zool.*) having a slender nose. [Gk. *leptos* small and *rhis rhinos* nose].
LESBIAN (1), [lez'-bi-an], *n.* a female sexual invert.
LESBIAN (2), [lez'-bi-an], *adj.* pertaining to female sexual inversion. [Sappho of *Lesbos*].
LESE-MAJESTE, lèse-majesté, [lēz-mazh'-es-tā], *n.* high treason. [[Fr. *lèse majesté*].
LESION, [lē'-zhun], *n.* damage, wound, injury; (*med.*) pathological change in tissue. [L. *lesio*].
LESIONAL, [lē'-zhun-al], *adj.* relating to, characterized by, a lesion.
LESS (1), [les], *n.* a smaller portion or amount; the inferior or younger.
LESS (2), [les], *adj.* smaller in size or amount, not so much; fewer; not so long; not so important; **no l. a person than,** no other person than.
LESS (3), [les], *adv.* in a lower degree, to a smaller extent. [OE. *læs*].
LESS (4), [les], *prep.* deducting.
LESSEE, [les-ē'], *n.* the person who holds a lease.
LESSEN, [les'-en], *v.t. and i.* to make less; to become less.
LESSER, [les'-er], *adj.* less, smaller.
LESSON, [les'-on], *n.* a set piece of instruction in a subject given by a teacher during a single period; the period so allotted; instructions, facts, etc., to be learnt for such a period; anything learned, *esp.* through bitter experience; example, warning; a portion of Scripture read in divine service; (*pl.*) instruction necessary for one's education. [OFr. *leçon*].
LESSOR, [les'-er], *n.* one who grants a lease.
LEST, [lest], *conj.* for fear that; in case, that . . . not. [OE. *thy læs the* by that the less that].
LET (1), [let], *n.* a retarding, hindrance, stoppage; (*lawn tennis, rackets, etc.*) an accidental obstruction of the game. [LET (3)].
LET (2), [let], *n.* (*coll.*) a letting, renting, lease. [LET (4)].
LET† (3), (letting, let), [let], *v.i.* to hinder, prevent, to thwart. [OE. *lettan*].
LET (4), (letting, let), [let], *v.t.* to leave; not to disturb or interfere with; to grant temporary possession and use of in return for rent, to lease; to allow to escape (blood); to allow, permit; (*imper.*) *expressing command or wish*; **to l. alone,** to say nothing of; **to l. down,** to break a promise or fail to fulfil an obligation; **to l. in,** to introduce into a piece of material to lengthen or widen it; **to l. off,** to discharge; to excuse from punishment; **to l. on,** to reveal a secret; **to l. out,** to make bigger by untacking a hem or tuck; to disclose. [OE. *lætan*].
LETCH, see LEACH (2).
LETHAL, [lē'-thal], *adj.* deadly, mortal, fatal. [L. *lethalis*].
LETHALITY, [lē-thal'-i-ti], *n.* the property of being lethal.
LETHARGIC, [li-thah'-jik], *adj.* inclined to, affected with, lethargy; dull, apathetic. [Gk. *lethargikos*].
LETHARGICAL, [li-thah'-jik-al], *adj.* lethargic.
LETHARGICALLY, [li-thah'-jik-al-i], *adv.* in a lethargic way.
LETHARGICALNESS, [li-thah'-jik-al-nes], *n.* the condition of being lethargic.
LETHARGY, [leth'-ah-ji], *n.* a heavy, unnatural state of mental or physical drowsiness; dulness, inaction; oblivion; torpidity. [Gk. *lethargia*].
LETHE, [lē'-thē], *n.* (*Gk. myth.*) one of the rivers of the nether world, a draught of whose water induced oblivion in dead souls; oblivion, forgetfulness. [Gk. *lethe*].
LETHEAN, [lē-thē'-an], *adj.* promoting forgetfulness.
LETHIFEROUS, [lē-thif'-er-us], *adj.* bringing death; deadly. [LETHE and L. *ferre* to bear].
LET-OFF, [let'-of], *n.* the act of excusing; an unexpected escape from punishment or retribution.
LETT, [let], *n.* a native of Latvia. [Germ. *Lette* from native name].
LETTER (1), [let'-er], *n.* a written or carved symbol representing a speech sound or sounds; a printed type; a written communication sent to a person by post or messenger, an epistle; (*pl.*) literature, literary learning, erudition; any of various legal documents or official certificates; **the l. of the law,** the literal meaning of the law; **letters patent,** an official

document granting some legal right or privilege. [L. *littera* letter of the alphabet].

LETTER (2), [let'-er], *v.t.* to draw, mark, or form letters on.

LETTER-BOARD, [let'-er-bawd'], *n.* (*typ.*) a board on which pages of type are laid out for distribution; a board for docketing visitors' letters, a letter rack.

LETTER-BOX, [let'-er-boks'], *n.* the receptacle in which letters are posted or delivered.

LETTER-CARD, [let'-er-kahd'], *n.* a postcard that can be folded and sealed.

LETTER-CARRIER, [let'-er-ka'-ri-er], *n.* a person who delivers letters, a postman.

LETTERED, [let'-erd], *adj.* engraved, marked with letters; educated, cultured; belonging to learning.

LETTER-FOUNDER, [let'-er-fownd'-er], *n.* a type-founder.

LETTERING, [let'-er-ing], *n.* the act of drawing or painting letters; the letters printed, painted or drawn; the style in which they are executed.

LETTERLESS, [let'-er-les], *adj.* having no letters; illiterate, uncultured.

LETTER-LOCK, [let'-er-lok'], *n.* a lock that can be opened only by a specific combination of letters.

LETTER-PERFECT, [let'-er-pur'-fekt], *adj.* reproducing the words with absolute accuracy.

LETTERPRESS, [let'-er-pres'], *n.* (*typ.*) printed words or letters, *esp.* as distinct from the processes of lithography or photogravure.

LETTER-WEIGHT, [let'-er-wāt'], *n.* a heavy object, often patterned or decorated, for holding down letters.

LETTERWOOD, [let'-er-wŏŏd'], *n.* a beautiful wood found in Guiana, used for cabinet work and veneering, *Brosimum Aubletii*.

LETTER-WRITER, [let'-er-rī'-ter], *n.* person who writes letters; an instrument for copying letters; †a book to teach letter-writing.

LETTIC, [let'-ik], *adj.* relating to the Letts or their language.

LETTISH (1), [let'-ish], *n.* the language of the Letts.

LETTISH (2), [let'-ish], *adj.* relating to the Letts or their language.

LETTSOMITE, [let'-som-īt], *n.* (*min.*) a hydrated sulphate of copper and aluminium. [W. G. *Lettsom*, the mineralogist].

LETTUCE, [let'-is], *n.* vegetable plant of the genus *Lactuca*, whose leaves are used as a salad. [Fr. *laitue*].

LEU, (*pl.* **lei**), [lā], *n.* the Rumanian unit of currency. [Rumanian *leu*].

LEUCAEMIA, [lōō-sē'-mi-a], *n.* leucocythaemia. [MdL. *leucaemia*].

LEUCAETHIOPIC, [lōō'-sē-thi-op'-ik], *adj.* relating to an albino, or to leucopathy. [LEUCO and Gk. *Aithiops* an Ethiopian].

LEUCIN, [lōō'-sin], *n.* a white pulverulent substance extracted from muscular fibre. [~Gk. *leukos* white].

LEUCITE, [lōō'-sīt], *n.* (*min.*) a dull glassy silicate of potassium and aluminium, found in volcanic lava. [Germ. *leucit*].

LEUCITIC, [lōō-sit'-ik], *adj.* relating to, containing, leucite.

LEUCO-, *pref.* white. [Gk. *leukos*].

LEUCOCYTE, [lōō'-kō-sīt], *n.* a white corpuscle in the blood stream. [LEUCO and Gk. *kutos* container].

LEUCOCYTHAEMIA, [lōō'-kō-sī-thē'-mi-a], *n.* (*path.*) a disease characterized by excessive increase of white corpuscles in the blood stream, and producing a general anaemic condition. [LEUCOCYTE and Gk. *haima* blood].

LEUCODERMA, [lōō'-kō-durm'-a], *n.* (*med.*) a skin disease causing white patches on the skin. [LEUCO and Gk. *derma* skin].

LEUCOL, [lōō'-kol], *n.* a coal-tar product.

LEUCOMA, [lōō-kō'-ma], *n.* (*path.*) an affection of the eye characterized by opacity of the cornea. [Gk. *leukoma* something whitened].

LEUCOPATHY, [lōō-kop'-ath-i], *n.* (*med.*) albinism. [LEUCO and Gk. *pathos* suffering].

LEUCOPHLEGMACY, [lōō'-kō-fleg'-ma-si], *n.* (*path.*) a dropsical condition of body. [LEUCO and Gk. *phlegma* inflammation].

LEUCOPHLEGMATIC, [lōō'-kō-fleg-mat'-ik], *adj.* (*path.*) affected with leucophlegmacy.

LEUCORRHOEA, [lōō'-kō-rē'-a], *n.* (*path.*) a disease characterized by a white mucous discharge from the lining of the uterus or of the vaginal canal; the whites. [LEUCO and Gk. *rhoia* flow].

LEUCOSIS, [lōō-kō'-sis], *n.* (*med.*) a state of pallor. [LEUCO and Gk. *osis* expressing condition].

LEUCOUS, [lōō'-kus], *adj.* white.

LEV, (*pl.* **leva**), [lev], *n.* the monetary unit of Bulgaria. [Bulgarian *lev*].

LEVANT (1), [li-vant'], *n.* the eastern coasts of the Mediterranean Sea. [Fr. *levant* the place where the sun rises].

LEVANT (2), [li-vant'], *adj.* eastern.

LEVANT (3), [li-vant'], *v.i.* to disappear without paying one's debts. [Span. *levantar el campo* to decamp].

LEVANTER (1), [li-vant'-er], *n.* a strong easterly wind on the North African coast. [LEVANT (1)].

LEVANTER (2), [li-vant'-er], *n.* (*coll.*) a bookmaker who decamps to escape paying the money he owes. [LEVANT (3)].

LEVANTINE (1), [li-vant'-īn], *n.* a native of the Levant; a kind of silk cloth.

LEVANTINE (2), [li-vant'-īn], *adj.* coming from, pertaining to, the Levant.

LEVATOR, [li-vā'-ter], *n.* (*anat.*) a muscle that raises some part of the body; (*surg.*) an instrument for raising depressed bone, an elevator. [LL. *levator* that which raises].

LEVEE (1), [lev'-i, le-vē'], *n.* a dyke formed by alluvial deposits; an artificial river bank; a wharf. [Fr. *levée* a lifting up].

LEVEE (2), [lev'-i, le-vē'], *n.* a reception by a prince or ruler held in the morning; a royal reception at which only men are presented. [Fr. *lever* to rise].

LEVEL (1), [lev'-el], *n.* a horizontal even surface or plane; a flat section of ground; a height identical with something specified; the normal height; a similar state of morals, intellect, etc.; a standard; (*mech.*) an instrument capable of indicating an exact horizontal line, used for testing whether a surface is level; **on the l.**, (*slang*) honest, genuine. [OFr. *level*].

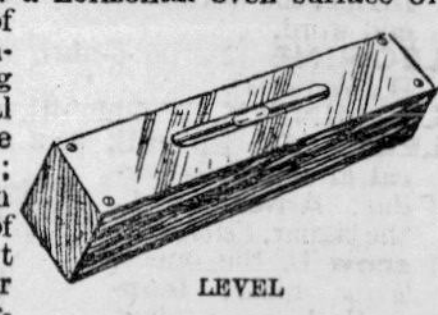

LEVEL

LEVEL (2), [lev'-el], *adj.* even, of equal height, having a flat horizontal surface; constant in power; equal in quality, rank or degree; well-balanced; impartial, sober; (of a note, stress, etc.) having a constant pitch or force; **one's l. best**, one's utmost.

LEVEL (3), (**levelling, levelled**), [lev'-el], *v.t.* to make level; to form a straight line between the sight and a target, to aim; to raze to the ground; (*fig.*) to make equal; (*philol.*) to combine under a single sound.

LEVEL-HEADED, [lev'-el-hed'-id], *adj.* possessing common sense; thoughtful, judicious, controlled in a crisis.

LEVELLER, [lev'-el-er], *n.* person who levels; a believer in equal rights and status for all, *esp.* a member of the radical party in the Parliamentary army of the English Civil War which advocated a primitive communist programme.

LEVELLING, [lev'-el-ing], *n.* the act of making level; the art of measuring elevations of objects.

LEVER (1), [lē'-ver], *n.* a bar of rigid substance working on a fulcrum or prop to raise or dislodge a weight by pressure on the free end; any device or contrivance functioning similarly; (*fig.*) a means of bringing pressure to bear upon. [OFr. *levere*].

LEVER (2), [lē'-ver], *v.t. and i.* to dislodge or lift by using a lever.

LEVERAGE, [lē'-ver-ij], *n.* an arrangement of levers; the principle of a lever; the mechanical advantage gained by its use; (*fig.*) a means of effecting.

LEVERET, [lev'-er-et], *n.* a hare in its first year; †a paramour, mistress. [OFr. *levrete* hare].

LEVERWOOD, [lē'-ver-wŏŏd'], *n.* the North American tree, *Ostrya virginica*.

LEVIABLE, [lev'-i-abl], *adj.* capable of being levied or assessed and collected; taxable.

LEVIATHAN, [li-vī'-a-than], *n.* a sea monster; (*fig.*) anything huge or monstrous. [Heb. *levyathan*].

LEVIGABLE, [lev'-ig-abl], *adj.* able to be levigated. [L. *levigabilis*].

LEVIGATE, [lev'-ig-āt], *v.t.* to grind, to reduce to a fine powder. [L. *levigare* to smooth].

LEVIGATION, [lev'-ig-ā'-shun], *n.* the act of levigating. [L. *levigatio*].

LEVIN†, [lev'-in], *n.* a flash of lightning; the rays of the sun. [ME. *leven*].

LEVIRATE, [lev'-ir-āt], *n.* the ancient Hebrew custom which required a man to marry the widow of a brother who died without issue. [L. *levir* husband's brother].

LEVITATE, [lev'-it-āt], *v.t. and i.* (to cause) to float or rise in the air; to become buoyant. [L. *levitas* lightness].

LEVITATION, [lev'-it-ā'-shun], *n.* the act of levitating or state of being levitated.

LEVITE, [lē'-vīt], *n.* a member of the tribe or family of Levi; an assistant to the Jewish priests; a priest; (*coll.*) a Jew. [Heb. *Levi*].

LEVITICAL, [li-vit'-ik-al], *adj.* connected with, belonging to, the Levites; priestly; **l. degrees,** the degrees of affinity within which marriage was forbidden in Leviticus.

LEVITICALLY, [li-vit'-ik-al-i], *adv.* after the manner of the Levites.

LEVITY, [lev'-i-ti], *n.* lightness of weight, tendency to be buoyant; (*fig.*) lightness of temper or conduct, inconstancy; want of proper seriousness, irresponsibility, frivolity. [L. *levitas*].

LEVOGYRATE, [lē'-vō-jī'-rāt], *adj.* turning or turned to the left. [L. *laevus* left and GYRATE].

LEVY (1), [lev'-i], *n.* the imposition of a tax by decree; the tax so imposed; conscription for military service; the troops thus raised. [Fr. *levée*].

LEVY (2), [lev'-i], *v.t. and i.* to impose a levy; to raise troops by conscription; to raise money by a levy; **to l. war,** to declare and commence war; **to l. a fine,** to institute proceedings to establish one's title to lands, etc.

LEW, [lōō], *adj.* tepid, weak; pale, wan. [Uncert.].

LEWD, [lōōd], *adj.* obscene, licentious, indecent; †uneducated, ignorant. [OE. *læwede* lay].

LEWDLY, [lōōd'-li], *adv.* in a lewd way.

LEWDNESS, [lōōd'-nes], *n.* the state of being lewd.

LEWIS (1), [lōō'-is], *n.* a device for raising large stones having thin wedges of iron dovetailed into the stone; son of a freemason. [Unkn.].

LEWIS (2), [lōō'-is], *v.t.* to fasten by means of a lewis.

LEWIS GUN, [lōō'-is-gun], *n.* a type of light automatic machine gun. [Col. *Lewis*, the inventor].

LEWISITE, [lōō'-is-īt], *n.* a liquid, vesicant poison-gas, containing arsenic, and having a characteristic odour of geraniums. [Prof. *Lewis*, the inventor].

LEXICAL, [leks'-ik-al], *adj.* relating to a lexicon or lexicography.

LEXICOGRAPHER, [leks'-i-kog'-ra-fer], *n.* one who makes a dictionary. [Gk. *lexikographos*].

LEXICOGRAPHIC, [leks'-i-kō-graf'-ik], *adj.* relating to lexicography.

LEXICOGRAPHICAL, [leks'-i-kō-graf'-ik-al], *adj.* lexicographic.

LEXICOGRAPHY, [leks'-i-kog'-ra-fi], *n.* the art or practice of compiling dictionaries.

LEXICOLOGIST, [leks'-i-kol'-oj-ist], *n.* an expert in lexicology.

LEXICOLOGY, [leks'-i-kol'-o-ji], *n.* the science dealing with the derivation, signification, and history of words. [Gk. *lexicon* word and *logos* speech].

LEXICON, [leks'-i-kon], *n.* a dictionary, *esp.* a Greek or Semitic dictionary. [Gk. *lexikon*].

LEXIGRAPHIC, [leks'-i-graf'-ik], *adj.* relating to lexigraphy.

LEXIGRAPHY, [leks-ig'-ra-fi], *n.* the art or practice of definition; a method of writing in which each symbol stands for a complete word.

LEY, see LYE.

LEYDEN JAR, [lā'-den-jah(r)'], *n.* a glass jar lined with tinfoil, used to accumulate static electricity. [*Leyden*, in Holland].

LEY FARMING, [lā'-fah'-ming], *n.* (*agric.*) pastoral farming on land previously cropped.

LI, [lē], *n.* a Chinese unit of length approximating to 633 yards; Chinese unit of weight equal to three-fifths of a grain [Chin. *li*].

LIABILITY, [lī'-a-bil'-i-ti], *n.* the quality or fact of being liable; that, *esp.* a sum of money, for which one is liable.

LIABLE, [lī'-abl], *adj.* responsible for, bound, obliged in law or equity; apt, inclined, subject. [~Fr. *lier* to bind].

LIABLENESS, [lī'-abl-nes], *n.* the condition of being liable.

LIAISON, [li-ā'-zon], *n.* a working relationship between two parties, usually of a semi-official nature; a bond of union, association; state of intimacy, *esp.* of an illicit sexual nature; co-ordination between allies or military units. [Fr. *liaison*].

LEYDEN JAR

LIANA, [li-ah'-na], (*bot.*) any tropical climbing plant. [Fr. *liane*].

LIAR, [lī'-er], *n.* a person who tells lies. [ME. *liere*].

LIARD, [lē'-ah(r)], *n.* a French farthing. [OFr. *liard*].

LIAS, [lī'-as], *n.* (*geol.*) an argillaceous limestone immediately below the oolitic series of rocks; a blue limestone rock. [Fr. *liais* limestone of a fine grain].

LIASSIC, [lī-as'-ik], *adj.* relating to the lias formation.

LIBATION, [lī-bā'-shun], *n.* a liquid sacrifice to the gods; the wine so sacrificed; (*coll.*) a drink. [L. *libatio*].

LIBATORY, [lī'-bat-er-i], *adj.* consisting of libations, pertaining to libation. [L. *libatorius*].

LIBEL (1), [lī'-bel], *n.* a statement in writing judged to harm the reputation of a person; a misrepresentation of a person's merits; (*leg.*) any book, writing or representation which, being published, exposes unjustifiably a person to defamation; (*leg.*) the written declaration of the charges made by a plaintiff. [L. *libellus* little book].

LIBEL (2), (libelling, libelled), [lī'-bel], *v.t.* to defame by means of a libel; (*pop.*) to misrepresent a person's merits or nature; (*leg.*) to bring a libel against.

LIBELLANT, [lī'-bel-ant], *n.* one who libels; (*leg.*) one who brings forward a libel against another.

LIBELLER, [lī'-bel-er], *n.* person who libels; a lampooner.

LIBELLOUS, [lī'-bel-us], *adj.* constituting a libel, defamatory; habitually publishing libels.

LIBELLOUSLY, [lī'-bel-us-li], *adv.* in libellous fashion.

LIBER, [lī'-ber], *n.* (*bot.*) the inner bark of exogens consisting of a layer of woody tissue; the phloem. [L. *liber* bark].

LIBERAL (1), [lib'-er-al], *n.* an adherent of a political party so called, standing for free and enlightened development and modification of institutions within a democratic framework, and basing its programme on a principle of reform.

LIBERAL (2), [lib'-er-al], *adj.* giving freely, generous, ample; abundant, plentiful; having broad interests and sympathies, tolerant; enlightened, advanced; (*pol.*) connected with the Liberal party. [L. *liberalis* of freedom].

LIBERALISM, [lib'-er-al-izm], *n.* (*pol.*) the theory and practice of the Liberal party.

LIBERALIST, [lib'-er-al-ist], *n.* a person who advocates liberalism.

LIBERALISTIC, [lib'-er-al-ist'-ik], *adj.* tending to be of the nature of liberalism.

LIBERALITY, [lib'-er-al'-i-ti], *n.* the quality of being liberal; a particular act of generosity, a donation. [L. *liberalitas*].

LIBERALIZATION, [lib'-er-al-īz-ā'-shun], *n.* the act of liberalizing; the condition of being liberalized.

LIBERALIZE, [lib'-er-al-īz], *v.t.* to render liberal or catholic in outlook.

LIBERALLY, [lib'-er-al-i], *adv.* in liberal fashion, generously.

LIBERATE, [lib'-er-āt], *v.t.* to set free, release; to set in motion; (*chem.*) to allow to escape. [L. *liberare*].

LIBERATION, [lib'-er-ā'-shun], *n.* the act of liberating; release. [L. *liberatio*].

LIBERATIONISM, [lib'-er-ā'-shun-izm], *n.* the doctrine that the Church should be disestablished.

LIBERATIONIST, [lib-er-ā'-shun-ist], *n.* a person who believes in liberationism.

LIBERATOR, [lib'-er-āt-er], *n.* a person who liberates, *esp.* a leader who sets his people free from tyranny; a type of heavy American bomber. [L. *liberator*].

LIBERTARIAN (1), [lib'-er-tāer'-i-an], *n.* a person of libertarian views.

LIBERTARIAN (2), [lib'-er-tāer'-i-an], *adj.* (*philos.*) upholding the doctrine that in human experience opportunities occur for the exercise of free will.

LIBERTARIANISM, [lib'-er-tāer'-i-an-izm], *n.* the principles of the libertarians.

LIBERTICIDAL, [lib'-er-ti-sīd'-al], *adj.* destroying liberty.

LIBERTICIDE, [lib'-er-ti-sīd], *n.* destruction of liberty; a destroyer of liberty. [LIBERTY and L. *cida* murderer].

LIBERTINAGE, [lib'-er-tin-ij], *n.* the behaviour of a libertine, libertinism.

LIBERTINE (1), [lib'-er-tēn], *n.* a person who spends his life in habitual licentiousness and debauchery; †a man free from legal restraint. [L. *libertinus* a free man].

LIBERTINE (2), [lib'-er-tēn], *adj.* devoid of moral restraint; licentious, lecherous, dissolute.

LIBERTINISM, [lib'-er-tin-izm], *n.* the theory of the necessity for unrestrained behaviour; loose living.

LIBERTY, [lib'-er-ti], *n.* freedom; the state of being free in one's personal life; absence of undesired restrictive forces governing the life of a community; permission, privilege; an area offering freedom and certain rights; an instance of bad manners, offensive behaviour; **civil l.,** life free from artificial restraint; participation by the civilian members of a nation in communal life at its best; (*pol.*) the fruitful interaction of state and social and personal functions on a plane of economic equality; **at l.,** not in use; unoccupied; free from captivity. [L. *libertas*].

LIBETHENITE, [lib-eth'-in-īt], *n.* (*min.*) a hydrated phosphate of copper. [*Libethen*, in Hungary, where discovered].

LIBIDINAL, [lib-id'-in-al], *adj.* connected with, characterized by, libido.

LIBIDINIST, [lib-id'-in-ist], *n.* a licentious lecher.

LIBIDINOUS, [lib-id'-in-us], *adj.* having or implying an immoderate desire for indulgence in lust, lewd, sensual; exciting lust. [L. *libidinosus*].

LIBIDINOUSLY, [lib-id'-in-us-li], *adv.* in a libidinous manner.

LIBIDINOUSNESS, [lib-id'-in-us-nes], *n.* the condition of being libidinous.

LIBIDO, [lib-ī'-dō], *n.* (*psych.*) the basic emotional power in a human being. [L. *libido* lust].

LIBRA, [lī'-bra], *n.* the seventh sign in the Zodiac, the Scales; a pound weight. [L. *libra* pair of scales].

LIBRARIAN, [lī-brāer'-i-an], *n.* a person employed to look after a library. [L. *librarius* secretary].

LIBRARIANSHIP, [lī-brāer'-i-an-ship], *n.* the office or vocation of librarian.

LIBRARY, [lī'-brer-i], *n.* a collection of books; a collection of books for public use or loan; the building or room in which such a collection is housed; a series of books forming a homogeneous category. [L. *librarium* book-case].

LIBRATE, [lī-brāt'], *v.t.* to tremble as a pair of scales before it attains balance, to oscillate; to poise. [L. *librare* to weigh].

LIBRATION, [lī-brā'-shun], *n.* the act of balancing or of librating; the state of being balanced; (*astron.*) a vibratory or oscillating motion.

LIBRATORY, [lī-brāt'-er-i], *adj.* characterized by vibration.

LIBRETTIST, [li-bret'-ist], *n.* the writer of a libretto.

LIBRETTO, (*pl.* **libretti**), [li-bret'-ō], *n.* the words or text of a musical play or opera; the book containing them. [It. *libretto* little book].

LIBYAN (1), [lib'-i-an], *n.* a native of Libya, a North African province.

LIBYAN (2), [lib'-i-an], *adj.* of or relating to Lybia.

LICENCE, [lī'-sents], *n.* leave, permission from an authority, frequently required to be paid for; a certificate giving such official permission; irregular behaviour, unrestrained conduct; justifiable deviation from accepted rules. [L. *licentia* freedom].

LICENCELESS, [lī'-sents-les], *adj.* having no licence.

LICENSABLE, [lī'-sens-abl], *adj.* that may be licensed.

LICENSE, [lī'-sens], *v.t.* to authorize, to grant a licence for something.

LICENSED, [lī'-senst], *adj.* authorized by licence; **l. victualler,** a publican licensed to sell food and drinks.

LICENSEE, [lī'-sen-sē'], *n.* the holder of a licence, *esp.* for the sale of alcoholic drinks.

LICENSER, [lī'-sen-ser], *n.* the official who issues licences.

LICENTIATE (1), [lī-sen'-shi-at], *n.* a person holding a licence, *esp.* a recognized professional practitioner; a Presbyterian qualified to preach. [L. *licentiare* to permit].

LICENTIATE (2), [lī-sen'-shi-āt], *v.t.* to give licence to.

LICENTIATION, [lī-sen'-shi-ā'-shun], *n.* the act of permitting.

LICENTIOUS, [lī-sen'-shus], *adj.* indulging in unrestrained gratification of sensual appetites, *esp.* of lust, immoral, dissolute; regardless of rules or custom, irregular. [L. *licentiosus*].

LICENTIOUSLY, [lī-sen'-shus-li], *adv.* in a licentious way.

LICENTIOUSNESS, [lī-sen'-shus-nes], *n.* the condition of being licentious.

LICHEN

LICHEN, [lī'-ken], *n.* (*bot.*) one of a class of cryptogamic thallophytes in which the individual plant consists of a fungus and an alga living symbiotically; (*med.*) a skin disease of an eruptive character. [Gk. *leikhen*].

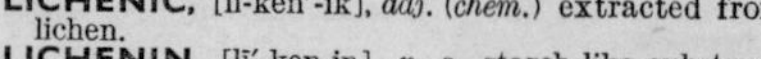

LICHENIC, [lī-ken'-ik], *adj.* (*chem.*) extracted from lichen.

LICHENIN, [lī'-ken-in], *n.* a starch-like substance extracted from Iceland moss.

LICHENOID, [lī'-ken-oid], *adj.* resembling, or relating to, a lichen. [LICHEN and Gk. *oeides* like].

LICHENOGRAPHY, [lī'-ken-og'-ra-fi], *n.* the scientific description of lichens. [LICHEN and Gk. *graphia* writing].

LICHENOLOGY, [lī'-ken-ol'-o-ji], *n.* the science concerned with lichens. [LICHEN and Gk. *logos* speech].

LICHENOUS, [lī'-ken-us], *adj.* of, or like, lichen.

LICHGATE, LYCHGATE, [lich'-gāt], *n.* a porch or covered gateway at the entrance of a churchyard under which the coffin is laid while part of the burial service is being read. [OE. *lic* body and GATE].

LICITNESS†, [lis'-it-nes], *n.* lawfulness.

LICK (1), [lik], *n.* the act of licking; an inadequate wash; a taste, morsel; a daub; (*coll.*) a swift speed.

LICK (2), [lik], *v.t.* to draw the tongue over; to moisten with the tongue; (*fig.*) (of flames, etc.) to touch lightly, quickly and eagerly; (*coll.*) to flog; to defeat; to run; **to l. the dust,** to be slain or triumphed over; **to l. someone's boots,** to play the toady to someone; **to l. into shape,** to improve, educate. [OE. *liccian*].

LICKERISH, LIQUORISH†, [lik'-er-ish], *adj.* of vigorous bodily appetites; greedy; nice about food; lecherous. [OFr. *licherous*].

LICKERISHLY, [lik'-er-ish-li], *adv.* in lickerish fashion.

LICKERISHNESS, [lik'-er-ish-nes], *n.* the quality of being lickerish.

LICKEROUS, [lik'-er-us], *adj.* lickerish. [OFr. *lecheros*].

LICKING, [lik'-ing], *n.* the act of one who licks; a lick; (*coll.*) a severe beating.

LICKSPITTLE, [lik'-spitl], *n.* a servile flatterer, a toady.

LICORICE, see LIQUORICE.

LICTOR, [lik'-ter], *n.* (*Rom. hist.*) an officer who carried the fasces before a Roman magistrate. [L. *lictor*].

LID, [lid], *n.* a movable cover to close a vessel or receptacle; the cover of the eye, eyelid; **to put the l. on,** (*coll.*) to finish. [OE. *hlid*].

LIDDED, [lid'-id], *adj.* having a lid.

LIDLESS, [lid'-les], *adj.* without a lid.

LIDO, [lē'-dō, lī'-dō], *n.* an outdoor bathing pool with a terrace for sunbathing; a place of entertainment. [The *Lido*, a Venetian bathing beach].

LIE (1), [lī], *n.* an intentional falsehood, a violation of truth; a false appearance; **a white l.,** a justifiable untruth. [OE. *lyge*].

LIE (2), [lī], *n.* the way anything lies; state of affairs. [LIE (4)].

LIE (3), [lī], *v.i.* to utter a lie or lies; to present a false appearance. [OE. *leogan*].

LIE (4), (lay, lain), [lī], *v.i.* to assume a recumbent position, to recline; to lean or press on; to be situate; to remain, to be; to be spread out motionless, *esp.* in death; (*leg.*) to be sustainable; **to l. low,** to remain in hiding; **to l. at one's door,** to appertain to; **to l. in,** to be in childbed, to stay in bed late; **to l. up,** to be ill in bed; **to l. with,** to have sexual intercourse with; **to l. off,** (*naut.*) to ride at anchor off. [OE. *licgan*].

LIEBERKUHN, [lē'-ber-kōōn], *n.* an annular reflector fitted round the nose of a microscope to reflect the rays passing through the glass slide. [*Lieberkuhn*, its inventor].

LIEF† (1), [lēf], *adj.* dear, beloved; willing. [OE. *leof*].

LIEF (2), [lēf], *adv.* gladly, willingly.

LIEGE (1), [lēj], *n.* a feudal lord with vassals; a vassal holding a fee by which he is bound to perform certain services to his lord. [OFr. *liege*].

LIEGE (2), [lēj], *adj.* connected by feudal rights and duties; relating to homage.

LIEGEMAN, [lēj'-man], *n.* a vassal.

LIEN, [lēn, lē'-en], *n.* (*leg.*) a right to hold the property of another until the satisfaction of a claim. [Fr. *lien*].

LIENTERIC, [lī'-en-ter-'ik], *adj.* pertaining to a lientery.

LIENTERY, [lī'-en-ter-i], *n.* (*med.*) a diarrhoea in which the contents of the alimentary canal are discharged undigested. [Gk. *leienteria*].

LIEU, [lew], *n.* place, stead. [Fr. *lieu*].

LIEUTENANCY, [lef-ten'-an-si], *n.* the rank of

lieutenant; the possession of this rank; the holders of this rank, as a body.

LIEUTENANT, [lef-ten'-ant], *n.* a deputy, substitute; a principal assistant; an officer acting for another; (*milit.*) a junior officer or rank next below a captain; (*nav.*) an officer or rank next below a lieutenant-commander. [LIEU and TENANT].

LIEUTENANT-COLONEL, [lef-ten'-ant-kur'-nel], *n.* (*milit.*) an officer of the rank next below colonel.

LIEUTENANT-COMMANDER, [lef-ten'-ant-kom-ahnd'-er], *n.* (*nav.*) an officer holding the rank next below commander.

LIEUTENANT-GENERAL, [lef-ten'-ant-jen'-er-al], *n.* (*milit.*) an officer holding the rank next below general.

LIEUTENANT-GOVERNOR, [lef-ten'-ant-guv'ern-er], *n.* a subsidiary or assistant governor.

LIEUTENANTSHIP, [lef-ten'-ant-ship], *n.* the position of lieutenant.

LIFE, (*pl.* **lives**), [līf], *n.* that condition of an animal or plant organism in which it is capable of performing its natural functions; the source from, or principle, by, which it achieves this condition; organisms that have achieved this condition; present state or manner of existence, spiritually or materially; the time from birth to death; period of existence; human affairs and experience; the general state of man, *esp.* with reference to his social relations, social activity; spirit, animation; vitality, energy; joyous living, supreme felicity; inspiration, moving spirit; a person; a biography; the subject of an insurance policy; **l. assurance,** a contract for the payment of a specific sum of money upon a person's death or upon reaching a certain age; **to see l.,** to enjoy at first-hand the world and its excitements; **for dear l.,** with all one's might; **as large as l.,** unmistakable; **for l.,** until one is dead; (of a legal sentence) for twenty years. [OE. *lif*].

LIFEBELT, [līf'-belt'], *n.* a special belt to support the body in water.

LIFEBLOOD, [līf'-blud], *n.* the blood necessary for life; (*fig.*) that which constitutes or provides strength and energy.

LIFEBOAT, [līf'-bōt], *n.* a specially built boat for saving persons from shipwreck; a small boat on a large ship, for use in case of emergency.

LIFEBUOY, [līf'-boi], *n.* a lifebelt.

LIFE-ESTATE, [līf'-es-tāt'], *n.* an estate that continues during the life of the owner.

LIFEGIVING, [līf'-giv'-ing], *adj.* giving life or animation; invigorating.

LIFEGUARD, [līf'-gahd], *n.* the safety device attached to machinery, vehicles, etc., to prevent serious accidents; a bodyguard of soldiers; (*pl.*) those regiments forming part of the King's bodyguard in England; a member of one of these.

LIFE-HISTORY, [līf'-his'-ter-i], *n.* the complete cycle of the development of an organism; the story of this.

LIFEHOLD, [līf'-hōld], *n.* land held by lease for life.

LIFE INTEREST, [līf'-int'-er-est], *n.* (*leg.*) an interest or claim valid only during one's lifetime.

LIFE-JACKET, [līf'-jak-et], *n.* a jacket of buoyant material for support in the water.

LIFELESS, [līf'-les], *adj.* destitute of life; dead; inanimate; dull, uninspiring.

LIFELESSLY, [līf'-les-li], *adv.* in a lifeless fashion.

LIFELESSNESS, [līf'-les-nes], *n.* the condition of being lifeless.

LIFELIKE, [līf'-līk], *adj.* resembling life or reality; resembling closely its living original.

LIFELINE, [līf'-līn], *n.* a rope for rescue work, *esp.* at sea; one of the lines on the palm of the hand.

LIFELONG, [līf'-long], *adj.* throughout life.

LIFE-PEERAGE, [līf'-pēer'-ij], *n.* a peerage granted only for one life.

LIFE-PRESERVER, [līf'-pri-zurv'-er], *n.* an apparatus for preserving lives in cases of shipwreck or fire; a stick weighted at one end; a bludgeon.

LIFER, [līf'-er], *n.* (*slang*) a prisoner undergoing penal servitude for life; a life sentence.

LIFE-RENT, [līf'-rent], *n.* a rent that continues during a person's lifetime.

LIFE-ROCKET, [līf'-rok'-it], *n.* the rocket carrying a lifeline.

LIFE-SAVING (1), [līf'-sāv-ing], *n.* the saving of life, *esp.* from immediate hazards.

LIFE-SAVING (2), [līf'-sāv-ing], *adj.* applicable or pertaining to life-saving.

LIFE-SIZE, [līf'-sīz'], *adj.* of a drawing, etc., of the same magnitude as the original it represents.

LIFETIME, [līf'-tīm], *n.* duration of the life of an individual; the time anything lasts.

LIFT (1), [lift], *n.* the act of lifting, a heave; the result of lifting, a rise; an upward spring; a rise in status or salary; an act of assistance; a hoist for carrying persons or goods from floor to floor; a piece of packing designed to increase height, as an under-strip of leather in a shoe heel; free transport in a private vehicle.

LIFT (2), [lift], *v.t.* to raise, elevate, hoist; (*sport*) to direct upwards; (*fig.*) to raise in dignity, rank, etc.; to dig up; (*slang*) to steal; *v.i.* (of mist, etc.) to rise, disperse. [OIcel. *lypta*].

LIFTABLE, [lift'-abl], *adj.* that may be lifted.

LIFTER, [lift'-er], *n.* a person or thing that lifts; (*slang*) a thief.

LIFTING-BRIDGE, [lift'-ing-brij'], *n.* a drawbridge which lifts.

LIGAMENT, [lig'-a-ment], *n.* a tie, band; (*anat.*) a strong fibrous connecting band in the body. [L. *ligamentum*].

LIGAMENT

LIGAMENTAL, [lig'-a-ment-al], *adj.* resembling, pertaining to, a ligament; binding together.

LIGAMENTOUS, [lig'-a-ment'-us], *adj.* ligamental.

LIGATE, [lī-gāt'], *v.t.* to tie with a ligature. [L. *ligare* to bind].

LIGATION, [li-gā'-shun], *n.* the act of binding; state of being bound; the place where a thing is bound.

LIGATURE, [lig'-a-cher], *n.* anything that ties; the act of tying; a thing that is tied; (*surg.*) a thread used to tie up a blood-vessel, etc., to prevent excessive bleeding; (*mus.*) a line connecting several notes; a character made up of two letters joined together. [L. *ligatura*].

LIGGER, [lig'-er], *n.* (*prov.*) a horizontal pole in a scaffold; a bedcover; a kilt. [N. dial. *lig* to lie].

LIGHT (1), [līt], *n.* the cause of visibility, the brightness emanating from the sun; a source of this; a lamp, a window, window-pane, or aperture; the degree or strength of the light; day, the dawn; (*fig.*) moral, spiritual or intellectual illumination, knowledge, revelation; a point of view; manner in which a situation strikes one; (*phys.*) that form of radiation measurable by a spectroscope; (*paint.*) the representation of the illumination of a subject; **ancient lights,** the right to prevent obstruction of light; **l. year,** distance travelled by light in one year; **to stand in one's l.,** to obstruct one's interests; **to come to l.,** to be revealed, transpire; **to throw l. upon,** to make clear, explain. [OE. *leoht*].

LIGHT (2), [līt], *adj.* not dark or shadowed, bright; pale.

LIGHT (3), [līt], *adj.* not heavy; below the just or legal weight; not heavily armed; carrying only what is light; nimble, active, dainty; slight, without force; (of soil) loose, sandy; (of food) easy to digest; not deep, gentle; (*fig.*) easy to bear or to perform; graceful and elegant; gay; frivolous; unchaste; of little importance or value, trivial; **to make l. of,** to minimize the importance or the difficulty of. [OE. *leoht*].

LIGHT (4), [līt], *adv.* in light fashion.

LIGHT(5), (**lit**), [līt], *v.t.* to cause to emit light; to set fire to; to supply light to, upon or for; *v.i.* to begin to emit light; to be capable of emitting light; (*fig.*) to show signs of animation; **to l. up,** to brighten. [OE. *lihtan*].

LIGHT (6), [līt], *v.i.* to alight, land; **to l. on,** find by chance. [OE. *lihtan*].

LIGHT-ARMED, [līt'-ahmd], *adj.* armed only with light weapons.

LIGHTABLE, [līt'-abl], *adj.* that may be lighted.

LIGHTEN (1), [līt'-en], *v.t.* to afford light to, illuminate; *v.i.* (of lightning) to flash; to increase in luminosity. [LIGHT (1)].

LIGHTEN (2), [līt'-en], *v.t.* to make lighter; to relieve, cheer. [LIGHT (3)].

LIGHTER (1), [līt'-er], *n.* one who makes a light; a device for producing a flame. [LIGHT (1)].

LIGHTER (2), [līt'-er], *n.* a large, open flat-bottomed boat used in loading and unloading ships. [Du. *lichter*].

LIGHTERAGE, [līt'-er-ij], *n.* the act of unloading or the price for unloading, ships into lighters.

LIGHTERMAN, [līt'-er-man], *n.* a boatman of a lighter.

LIGHT-FINGERED, [līt'-fing'-gerd], *adj.* deft; thievish.

LIGHT-FOOTED, [līt-fŏŏt'-id], *adj.* light of foot, nimble, active.

LIGHT-HANDED, [līt-hand'-id], *adj.* deft; not unkind, harsh or emphatic; not carrying anything heavy; (*naut.*) without a full complement of crew.

LIGHT-HEADED, [līt-hed'-id], *adj.* thoughtless, heedless, not responsible; delirious.

LIGHT-HEADEDLY, [līt'-hed'-ed-li], *adv.* in light-headed fashion.

LIGHT-HEADEDNESS, [līt'-hed'-id-nes], *n.* the condition of being light-headed.

LIGHT-HEARTED, [līt'-haht'-id], *adj.* free of grief and anxiety; cheerful, merry, gay.

LIGHT-HEARTEDLY, [līt'-haht'-id-li], *adv.* in light-hearted fashion.

LIGHT-HEARTEDNESS, [līt'-haht'-id-nes], *n.* the condition of being light-hearted.

LIGHTHOUSE, [līt'-hows'], *n.* a tower or building emitting a powerful light to direct navigation or aviation at night; a beacon; **l. keeper,** one in charge of a lighthouse.

LIGHTING, [līt'-ing], *n.* illumination; a system or appurtenances for the illumination of a building, stage, etc.

LIGHTISH, [līt'-ish], *adj.* fairly light.

LIGHT-LEGGED, [līt'-legd], *adj.* swift of foot, nimble.

LIGHTLESS, [līt'-les], *adj.* destitute of light; sightless.

LIGHTLY, [līt'-li], *adv.* in a light fashion.

LIGHT-MINDED, [līt'-mīnd'-id], *adj.* frivolous.

LIGHTNESS, [līt'-nes], *n.* the quality of being light.

LIGHTNING, [līt'-ning], *n.* a flash, or succession of flashes, of light due to the discharge of atmospheric electricity; **like l.,** very quickly. [LIGHTEN (1)].

LIGHTNING-CONDUCTOR, [līt'-ning-kon-dukt'-er], *n.* a metal conductor so placed on a building as to attract atmospheric electricity and conduct it harmlessly to earth.

LIGHTNING-GLANCE, [līt'-ning-glahnts'], *n.* a quick glance.

LIGHTNING-ROD, [līt'-ning-rod'], *n.* a lightning-conductor.

LIGHT-O'-LOVE, [līt'-o-luv'], *n.* a light woman, prostitute.

LIGHT-ROOM, [līt'-rōōm], *n.* a small compartment on a warship with double-glass windows to admit light into the powder magazine.

LIGHTS, [līts], *n.(pl.)* the lungs of cattle and pigs, *esp.* when used as food. [LIGHT (3)].

LIGHTSHIP, [līt'-ship], *n.* a vessel anchored near a shoal or dangerous rocks, bearing lights as a warning.

LIGHTSHIP

LIGHTSOME, [līt'-sum], *adj.* gay; nimble; dainty.

LIGHTSOMENESS, [līt'-sum-nes], *n.* the quality of being lightsome.

LIGHT-SPIRITED, [līt'-spir'-it-id], *adj.* cheerful.

LIGHTWEIGHT, [līt'-wāt], *adj.* of small weight; (of a boxer) no more than 9 stone 9 lb. in weight; slight, trifling.

LIGN-ALOES, [līn'-al'-ōz], *n.* aloes-wood, *Aquillaria agallocha.*

LIGNEOUS, [lig'-ni-us], *adj.* made of wood; resembling wood. [L. *ligneus*].

LIGNI-, *pref.* wood, of wood. [L. *lignum*].

LIGNIFEROUS, [lig-nif'-er-us], *adj.* producing wood. [L. *lignum* wood and *ferre* to bear].

LIGNIFICATION, [lig'-ni-fi-kā'-shun], *n.* the process of becoming ligneous; the state of being ligneous.

LIGNIFORM, [lig'-ni-fawm], *adj.* of the form, or appearance, of wood. [L. *lignum* wood and FORM].

LIGNIFY, [lig'-ni-fī], *v.t.* to turn into wood, make ligneous; *v.i.* to become wood. [L. *lignum* wood and *ficere* to make].

LIGNIN, [lig'-nin], *n.* woody fibre.

LIGNIPERDOUS, [lig'-ni-per'-dus], *adj.* (of insects) destroying wood. [LIGNI and L. *perdere* to destroy].

LIGNITE, [lig'-nīt], *n.* brown coal retaining the texture of the wood from which it originated.

LIGNITIC, [lig-nit'-ik], *adj.* containing or like lignite.

LIGNOSE (1), [lig'-nōs], *n.* wood fibre combined with nitro-glycerine as an explosive.

LIGNOSE (2), [lig'-nōs], *adj.* ligneous.

LIGNUM-VITAE, [lig'-num-vī'-tē], *n.* the extremely hard, dark-coloured, close-grained wood of the tropical American tree, *Guaiacum officinale*; the wood of the *Metrosideros buxifolia*, a New Zealand climber. [L. *lignum vitae* wood of life].

LIGULATE, [lig'-yōō-lāt], *adj.* (*bot.*) like a strap; having ligules.

LIGULATED, [lig'-yōō-lāt-id], *adj.* ligulate.

LIGULE, [lig'-yōōl], *n.* (*bot.*) the flat part of the leaf of a grass; a strap-shaped ray or petal. [L. *ligula* little tongue].

LIGURITE, [lig'-yōō-rīt], *n.* a transparent kind of sphene of a pea-green colour, a semi-precious stone. [*Liguria*, the Italian town].

LIKE (1), [līk], *n.* that which resembles something else; a copy; (*coll.*) **the likes of,** people like. [LIKE (3)].

LIKE (2), [līk], *n.* that which one likes, preference. [LIKE (4)].

LIKE (3), [līk], *adj.* equal in quality, quantity or degree; resembling, similar, of corresponding kind or nature; in keeping with. [OE. *ge-lic*].

LIKE (4), [līk], *adv.* in the same manner; likely; (*dial.*) **l. enough,** probably. [OE. *ge-lice*].

LIKE (5), [līk], *v.t.* to be pleased with, attracted to, fond of; to enjoy; to approve; to be accustomed to; to want, wish, will. [OE. *lician*].

LIKEABLE, [līk'-abl], *adj.* that one can like, amiable.

LIKEABLENESS, [līk'-abl-nes], *n.* the quality of being likeable.

LIKELIHOOD, [līk'-li-hōōd], *n.* the quality of being likely; probability.

LIKELINESS, [līk'-li-nes], *n.* likelihood.

LIKELY (1), [līk'-li], *adj.* resembling reality; such as may reasonably be expected; probable; suitable; pleasing.

LIKELY (2), [līk'-li], *adv.* probably.

LIKE-MINDED, [līk'-mīnd'-id], *adj.* of similar views or temperament, in agreement.

LIKEN, [līk'-en], *v.t.* to represent as like; to make like; to compare.

LIKENESS, [līk'-nes], *n.* the quality of being like, resemblance; a portrait, photograph, *esp.* a successful one; (*archaic*) appearance.

LIKEWISE, [līk'-wīz], *adv.* similarly, also, moreover.

LIKIN, [lēk'-ēn], *n.* (*econ.*) a Chinese transport tax. [Chin. *likin*].

LIKING, [līk'-ing], *n.* feeling of being attracted by; inclination, taste.

LILAC, [lī'-lak], *n.* a sweet-smelling flowering shrub, of the genus *Syringa*; its colour, a faintly pink purple. [Pers. *lilah*].

LILACIN, [lil'-as-in], *n.* the bitter principle of the lilac; syringa.

LILIACEOUS, [lil'-i-ā'-shus], *adj.* pertaining to the lily family.

LILIED, [lil'-id], *adj.* decorated with, having, lilies; white, pale.

LILLIPUTIAN (1), [lil'-i-pew'-shan], *n.* an inhabitant of Lilliput, where everything was diminutive. [*Lilliput*, a fabulous country in "Gulliver's Travels" by J. Swift].

LILLIPUTIAN (2), [lil'-i-pew'-shan], *adj.* of Lilliput; diminutive.

LILO, [lī'-lō], *n.* (*prot.*) an inflatable rubberized mattress.

LILT (1), [lilt], *n.* a smooth, rhythmic, melodious characteristic quality in a song or in a speaking voice; a song exhibiting this.

LILT (2), [lilt], *v.i.* to sing or say with a lilt. [ME. *lulte*].

LILY, [lil'-i], *n.* a bulbous flowering plant of the genus *Lilium* or of certain allied genera; (*fig.*) pallor; chastity; mourning; **l. of the mountain,** *Polygonatum multiflorum*; **l. of the valley,** the plant *Convallaria majalis.* [OE. *lilie*].

LILY-HANDED, [lil'-i-hand'-id], *adj.* with delicate white hands.

LILY-LIVERED, [lil'-i-liv'-erd], *adj.* cowardly, fearful.

LILY-PAD, [lil'-i-pad'], *n.* the leaf of the waterlily.

LILY-WHITE, [lil'-i-wīt], *adj.* white as a lily.

LIMACEOUS, [lī'-mā'-shus], *adj.* pertaining to, resembling, slugs. [L. *limax* slug].

LIMATION, [lī-mā'-shun], *n.* a polishing up; a filing to perfection. [L. *limatio*].

LIMATURE, [līm'-ach-er], *n.* metal filings. [LL. *limatura*].

LIMA-WOOD, [lē'-ma-wōōd'], *n.* a Brazil wood, marketed in Lima, used to dye a red and peach colour.

LIMB (1), [lim], *n.* any corporeal member, as the arm, leg, wing, etc.; the branch of a tree; (*fig.*) a member or section of any organization; (*coll.*) a mischievous child; **life and l.,** the whole being. [OE. *lim*].

LIMB (2), [lim], *n.* the edge or border of a surface; (*astron.*) the edge of the disk of the sun and moon; (*bot.*) the border of a monopetalous corolla; (*math.*) the graduated edge of a sextant or similar instrument. [L. *limbus*].

LIMBATE, [lim'-bāt], *adj.* (*bot.*) bordered, having one colour edged by another. [LL. *limbatus*].
LIMBECK, [lim'-bek], *n.* (*poet.*) an alembic; a still. [ALEMBIC].
LIMBED, [limd], *adj.* having limbs.
LIMBER (1), [lim'-ber], *n.* (*milit.*) the detachable front part of a gun-carriage. [Unkn.].
LIMBER (2), [lim'-ber], *adj.* flexible, pliant; lithe. [Unkn.].
LIMBER (3), [lim'-ber], *v.t.* to attach the limber to (a gun); to prepare to move a gun.
LIMBER (4), [lim'-ber], *v.i.* to loosen up the limbs.
LIMBERNESS, [lim'-ber-nes], *n.* the quality of being limber.
LIMBILITE, [lim'-bil-īt], *n.* (*min.*) a mineral thought to be decomposed chrysolite. [*Limbourg*, in Belgium].
LIMBO, LIMBUS, [lim'-bō, lim'-bus], *n.* the region intermediate between heaven and hell; any intermediate, ambiguous position; neglect, oblivion. [L. *limbus* border].
LIME (1), [līm], *n.* (*chem.*) quicklime, oxide of calcium obtained by burning limestone; a viscous substance used for catching birds, birdlime. [OE. *lim*].
LIME (2), [līm], *n.* the linden-tree, of the genus *Tilia*. [OE. *lind*].
LIME (3), [līm], *n.* the tree, *Citrus medica*; its lemon-like fruit; lime-juice. [Arab. *limah*].
LIME (4), [līm], *v.t.* to smear birdlime on; to snare.
LIMEBURNER, [līm'-burn'-er], *n.* a man who burns limestone to obtain the lime.
LIME-HOUND, [līm'-hownd], *n.* a lyam-hound, a hunting dog; a bloodhound.
LIME-JUICE, [līm'-jōōs], *n.* a drink made from the fruit of the lime, a specific against scurvy.
LIMEKILN, [līm'-kiln], *n.* a kiln in which limestone is burnt and reduced to lime.
LIMELIGHT, [līm'-līt], *n.* the light given off by a cylinder of lime heated to incandescence; **in the l.,** on the front part of the stage; (*fig.*) in the public eye.
LIMEN, [lī'-men], *n.* (*psych.*) the threshold of the conscious mind or self, the dividing line between the conscious and subconscious. [L. *limen* threshold].
LIME-PIT, [līm'-pit], *n.* a pit where lime is dug or slaked.
LIMERICK, [lim'-er-ik], *n.* a verse of five lines, invented by Edward Lear, the first and second lines rhyming with the fifth, and the shorter third with the shorter fourth.
LIME-SINK, [līm'-sink], *n.* a rounded hole or pit in limestone districts.
LIMESTONE, [līm'-stōn], *n.* (*geol.*) a rock whose chief constituent is carbonate of lime.
LIME-TREE (1), [līm'-trē], *n.* a tree of the genus *Tilia* with deciduous leaves and fragrant hanging blossoms. [LIME (2)].
LIME-TREE (2), [līm'-trē], *n.* the tree, *Citrus medica*, prized for its green lemon-like fruit. [LIME (3)].
LIME-TWIG, [līm'-twig], *n.* a twig smeared with birdlime.
LIME-WASH, [līm'-wash], *n.* a mixture of lime and water, used for whitening walls.
LIME-WATER, [līm'-waw'-ter], *n.* a solution of calcium hydroxide used medicinally.
LIMEWORT, [līm'-wurt], *n.* (*bot.*) any of certain viscid plants so styled.
LIMINAL, [lī'-min-al], *adj.* (*psych.*) pertaining to the limen.
LIMING, [līm'-ing], *n.* the act of employing lime, or treating with lime.
LIMIT (1), [lim'-it], *n.* a boundary, edge, terminus; restriction; the utmost extent; any external surface defining or constitutive of shape; the utmost possible; (*coll.*) something or someone utterly intolerable. [L. *limes limitis*].
LIMIT (2), [lim'-it], *v.t.* to set a boundary to; to restrain, restrict.
LIMITABLE, [lim'-it-abl], *adj.* that may be limited.
LIMITARIAN (1), [lim'-it-āer'-i-an], *n.* (*theol.*) one holding limitarian views.
LIMITARIAN (2), [lim'-it-āer'-i-an], *adj.* (*theol.*) believing that only the chosen can be saved.
LIMITARY, [lim'-it-er-i], *adj.* placed at the limit, as a guard; restrained within limits; confining. [L. *limitaris*].
LIMITATION, [lim'-it-ā'-shun], *n.* the act of limiting; state of being limited; that which limits, depreciates or qualifies; (*leg.*) the period limited by statute within which an action may be brought. [L. *limitatio*].
LIMITED, [lim'-it-id], *adj.* narrow, circumscribed, restricted; **l. liability,** in a joint-stock company, liability of the shareholders to the nominal value of their shares; **l. monarchy,** a kingdom in which the sovereign must keep within the bounds of the constitution.
LIMITEDLY, [lim'-it-id-li], *adv.* in a limited manner.
LIMITEDNESS, [lim'-it-id nes], *n.* the state of being limited.
LIMITER, (lim'-it-er], *n.* a person who, or that which, limits.
LIMITLESS, [lim'-it-les], *adj.* without limit, immense.
LIMITROPHE, [lim'-i-trōf], *adj.* situated on or near a frontier. [L. *limitrophus*].
LIMMER, [lim'-er], *n.* a person of bad character. [Unkn.].
LIMN, [lim], *v.t.* to illuminate (letters or manuscripts); to draw, paint, describe in glowing colours. [ME. *limnen* from Fr. *enluminer*].
LIMNER, [lim'-ner], *n.* one who limns.
LIMNETIC, [lim-net'-ik], *adj.* living in fresh water. [Gk. *limne* lake].
LIMNING, [lim'-ning], *n.* the act of one who limns; vivid description.
LIMNITE, [lim'-nīt], *n.* (*min.*) bog iron ore, a hydrated form of limonite. [Gk. *limne* lake].
LIMNOLOGY, [lim-nol'-o-ji], *n.* the scientific study of lakes, ponds, marshes and dew-ponds. [Gk. *limne* lake, marsh and *logos* speech].
LIMONITE, [lim'-on-īt], *n.* (*min.*) brown iron ore, an amorphous hydrated oxide of iron. [Gk. *limne* lake].
LIMOSIS, [lī-mō'-sis], *n.* a ravenous appetite. [Gk. *limos* hunger and *osis* expressing condition].
LIMOUS, [līm'-us], *adj.* muddy, slimy. [L. *limus*].
LIMOUSINE, [lim'-ŏŏz-ēn], *n.* a covered motor-car in which the driver's seat is divided from the back seats by a glass partition. [Fr. from *Limousin* a French province].

LIMOUSINE

LIMP (1), [limp], *n.* a lameness; the act of limping. [LIMP (3)].
LIMP (2), [limp], *adj.* wanting firmness and stiffness, flaccid; (of fabric) unstiffened; (*fig.*) characterless, without energy; **l. binding,** a binding in which no millboard is used. [~OIcel. *limpa* lameness].
LIMP (3), [limp], *v.i.* to walk lamely and unevenly; (of verse) to have a faulty rhythm. [MHighGerm. *limpan*].
LIMPET, [lim'-pet], *n.* (*zool.*) a univalve mollusc of the genus *Patella*, sticking to rocks. [OE. *lempedu*].
LIMPID, [lim'-pid], *adj.* crystal-clear, pellucid; (*fig.*) lucid, easy. [Fr. *limpide*].
LIMPIDITY, [lim-pid'-i-ti], *n.* the quality of being limpid.
LIMPIDLY, [lim'-pid-li], *adv.* in limpid fashion.
LIMPIDNESS, [lim'-pid-nes], *n.* limpidity.
LIMPING, [limp'-ing], *adj.* halting, lame.
LIMPINGLY, [limp'-ing-li], *adv.* in a limping manner.
LIMPKIN, [limp'-kin], *n.* the courlan.
LIMPLY, [limp'-li], *adv.* in limp fashion.
LIMPNESS, [limp'-nes], *n.* the quality of being limp.
LIMY, [līm'-i], *adj.* viscous; like, or having the qualities of, lime; containing lime.
LIN†, see LINN.
LINAGE, see LINEAGE.
LINARITE, [lin'-er-īt], *n.* (*min.*) hydrated sulphate of lead and copper. [*Linares* in Spain, where supposedly found].
LINCH, [linch], *n.* (*dial.*) a ledge of rock or ground; a rectangular projection; a boundary strip, baulk. [OE. *hlinc*].
LINCHPIN, [linch'-pin], *n.* a pin or peg to keep a wheel in its place on the axle. [~OE. *lynis* axle-tree].
LINCOLN-GREEN, [lingk'-un-grēn'], *n.* the colour of a bright green material formerly made at Lincoln.
LINCRUSTA, [lin-krust'-a], *n.* (*prot.*) a compound of cellulose paper and pulverized cork soaked with oil and resin, used for floor cloth and for covering ceilings, etc.
LINCTUS, [lingk'-tus], *n.* a thick soothing throat medicine. [L. *linctus* a licking].
LINDEN, [lin'-den], *n.* a lime-tree. [OE. *lind*].
LINE† (1), [līn], *n.* flax. [OE. *lin*].
LINE (2), [līn], *n.* a slender string or cord; a thread-like stroke or trace; such a mark used to trace out a limit or point of division; a narrow furrow in the brow, palm, etc.; a row, a series in regular succession, *esp.* of written words, persons, etc.; a fleet of merchant ships; a railroad; a railway company; a verse; lineage; outline, lineament; a trench or rampart; a series of

adjoining fortified defensive positions; the twelfth part of an inch; disposition; method; course; direction; occupation, branch of employment; (*coll.*) a series of specified goods; (*coll.*) a short letter, a brief note; a telephone wire; (*math.*) that which has length without breadth or thickness; (*geog.*) the equator; **l. of battle,** the disposition of an army or fleet; **ship of the l.,** a ship of war; **to draw the l. at,** to refuse to contemplate, object to; **to toe the l.,** to obey. [L. *linea* linen thread].

LINE (3), [līn], *v.t.* to mark with lines; to form into lines; to form a line along.

LINE (4), [līn], *v.t.* to cover on the inside with another layer of material; (of an animal) to cover, impregnate. [LINE (1)].

LINEAGE, LINAGE, [lin'-i-ij], *n.* a course of descent; descendants; family; a method of payment for newspaper contributions at so much per line. [OFr. *lignage*].

LINEAL, [lin'-i-al], *adj.* linear; in a direct line from an ancestor. [L. *linealis*].

LINEALITY, [lin'-i-al'-i-ti], *n.* the quality of being lineal.

LINEALLY, [lin'-i-al-i], *adv.* by direct descent.

LINEAMENT, [lin'-i-a-ment], *n.* distinguishing outline of a body or figure, *esp.* of the face; (*pl.*) features; (*fig.*) distinguishing features of the character. [L. *lineamentum*].

LINEAR, [lin'-i-er], *adj.* pertaining to a line; consisting of lines; in a straight direction; like a line; (*bot.*) narrow and long; **l. perspective,** that which regards only the positions, magnitudes and forms of objects. [L. *linearis*].

LINEARLY, [lin'-i-er-li], *adv.* in a linear manner.

LINEATE, [lin'-i-āt], *adj.* traversed, marked by lines. [L. *lineatus*].

LINEATION, [lin'-i-ā'-shun], *n.* a dividing with linear marks; the manner of doing this. [L. *lineatio*].

LINED, [lind], *adj.* marked with lines or wrinkles.

LINE ENGRAVING, [līn'-en-grāv'-ing], *n.* a form of engraving by means of fine lines on a surface of metal, etc.

LINEN (1), [lin'-in], *n.* cloth woven from flax; articles or garments made of this; underclothing; tablecloths; bed-clothes. [OE. *linen*].

LINEN (2), [lin'-in], *adj.* made of linen.

LINEN-DRAPER, [lin'-in-drāp'-er], *n.* a tradesman who deals in linens, calicoes, etc., and articles made of these.

LINER, [līn'-er], *n.* a large passenger vessel belonging to a regular line of ships.

LINESMAN, [līnz'-man], *n.* a soldier of the line; a man employed in attending to railway lines; a judge who watches the boundary lines at tennis or football.

LINE-UP, [line'-up], *n.* a deploying of opposing forces as a preliminary to battle.

LING (1), [ling], *n.* an edible sea-fish related to the cod, *Molva vulgaris.* [ME. *lenge*].

LING (2), [ling], *n.* the common heath, *Calluna vulgaris.* [OIcel. *lyng*].

LINGAM, [ling'-gam], *n* the phallus among the Hindus. [Hind. *lingam*].

LING-BIRD, [ling'-burd], *n.* the common meadow-pipit, *Anthus pratensis.*

LINGEL, [linggl], *n.* (*dial.*) a thong or latchet; a waxed thread. [AFr. *lengle*].

LINGER, [ling'-ger], *v.t.* to protract; *v.i.* to delay, to remain long; to walk or proceed slowly, loiter. [~OE. *lengan* to prolong].

LINGERER, [ling'-ger-er], *n.* one who lingers.

LINGERIE, [lan'-zher-ē], *n.* women's fine underclothes. [Fr. *lingerie*].

LINGERING, [ling'-ger-ing], *adj.* that lingers; protracted; tardy.

LING

LINGERINGLY, [ling'-ger-ing-li], *adv.* in a lingering fashion.

LINGISM, [ling'-izm], *n.* a system of physical exercises performed rhythmically to music. [*Ling* their Swedish inventor].

LINGO, [ling'-gō], *n.* language, jargon; (in contempt) a foreign language; a dialect. [Provenc. *lingo, lengo*].

LINGUA-, LINGUO-, *pref.* relating to the tongue. [L. *lingua* tongue].

LINGUA FRANCA, [ling'-gwa-frangk'-a], *n.* the international language of the Levant, a mixture of Italian, Arabic, Greek, etc.; any language of similar usage or usefulness. [It. *lingua franca* language of the Franks].

LINGUAL (1), [ling'-gwal], *n.* a lingual sound as *l, d,* etc.

LINGUAL (2), [ling'-gwal], *adj.* of, or pertaining to, the tongue; (*phon.*) formed by the tongue.

LINGUIFORM, [ling'-gwi-fawm], *adj.* shaped like a tongue.

LINGUIST, [ling'-gwist], *n.* a person skilled in foreign languages.

LINGUISTIC, [ling-gwist'-ik], *adj.* pertaining to languages.

LINGUISTICS, [ling-gwist'-iks], *n.*(*pl.*) the scientific study of language, its nature and development.

LINGUO-, see LINGUA-.

LINGUODENTAL (1), [ling'-gwō-dent'-al], *n.* (*phon.*) a linguodental consonant.

LINGUODENTAL (2), [ling'-gwō-dent'-al], *adj.* (*phon.*) formed by the combined use of the tongue and teeth. [LINGUO and DENTAL].

LINGY (1), [ling'-i], *adj.* heathery, covered with ling.

LINGY (2), [linj'-i], *adj.* (*dial.*) supple, active, strong. [OFr. *linge*].

LINHAY, [lin'-ā], *n.* a farm shed with a lean-to roof. [~OE. *hlinian* to lean].

LINIMENT, [lin'-i-ment], *n.* a medicated liquid for rubbing into the skin to relieve pain or strain; an embrocation. [L. *linimentum*].

LINING, [lin'-ing], *n.* the covering of the inner surface of anything; (*fig.*) anything resembling this.

LINK (1), [lingk], *n.* a ring or loop forming part of a chain; anything doubled and closed like this; a device for fastening shirt cuffs, a cuff-link; (*fig.*) a person or thing that bridges a gap; a connexion; (*mach.*) a short connecting rod; a measure of 7.92 inches. [OE. *hlencan*].

LINK (2), [lingk], *n.* a torch made of tow and pitch. [Unkn.].

LINK (3), [lingk], *n.* (usually *pl.*) grassy undulating ground near the sea; a golf course. [OE. *hlinc* slope].

LINK (4), [lingk], *v.t.* to unite or connect as with a link; *v.i.* to be coupled, go arm in arm; **to l. arms,** to put one's arm in another's. [LINK (1)].

LINKBOY†, [lingk'-boi'], *n.* a boy employed to carry a torch to light people along the streets.

LINKMAN†, [lingk'-man], *n.* a linkboy.

LINN, LIN†, [lin], *n.* a pool made by a waterfall; a waterfall. [~OE. *hlynn* torrent and ~Wel. *llyn* pool].

LINNAEAN, [lin-ē'-an], *adj.* (*nat. hist.*) pertaining to the classification evolved by Linné, the celebrated Swedish naturalist. [*Linnaeus,* latinized form of *Linné*].

LINNET, [lin'-it], *n.* the small song-bird, *Linota cannabina.* [OFr. *linette* flax].

LINOCUT, [lī'-nō-kut'], *n.* a drawing cut in relief on a linoleum block; the print taken from this. [LINO(LEUM) and CUT (1)].

LINOLEUM, [lin-ō'-li-um], *n.* a shiny washable covering for floors, of compacted linseed oil on a canvas base. [L. *linum* flax and *oleum* oil].

LINOTYPE, [lī'-nō-tīp], *n.* (*print.*) a type-setting machine in which the matter is cast in lines as it is set. [LINE OF TYPE].

LINNET

LINSANG, [lin'-sang], *n.* a genus of richly coloured carnivores allied to the civets. [Javanese *linsang*].

LINSEED, [lin'-sēd], *n.* the seed of the flax plant; **l. cake,** the hard mass left after the oil has been pressed out of flax-seed; **l. meal,** ground linseed; **l. oil,** oil pressed from flax-seed. [OE. *lin* flax and SEED].

LINSEY, [lin'-zi], *n.* linsey-woolsey.

LINSEY-WOOLSEY, [lin'-zi-wool'-zi], *n.* a coarse fabric of wool and cotton or linen; a garment of this; (*fig.*) an incongruous mixture; confusion, jargon. [OE. *lin* flax and WOOL].

LINSTOCK†, [lin'-stok], *n.* a pointed staff holding a lighted match, used chiefly in firing cannon. [Du. *lontstok* match stick].

LINT, [lint], *n.* (*surg.*) linen specially prepared for dressing wounds. [ME. *linnet*].

LINTEL, [lin'-tel], *n.* the horizontal timber or stone piece over a door or casement. [OFr. *lintel* threshold].

LINTIE, [lin'-ti], *n.* (*Scots dial.*) the linnet.

LINT-WHITE (1), [lint'-wit'], *n.* the linnet. [OE. *linet-hwige*].

LINT-WHITE (2), [lint'-wīt], *adj.* as white as lint or linen.
LINY, [lī'-ni], *adj.* marked with lines or wrinkles.
LION, [lī'-on], *n.* the large, carnivorous, tawny-coloured wild cat, *Felis leo*; (*fig.*) any strong or powerful person; a celebrity; (*astron.*) the constellation Leo; **lion's share,** the largest share. [OFr. *lion*].
LIONCEL, [lī'-on-sel], *n.* (*her.*) a little lion [OFr. *lioncel*].
LIONESS, [lī'-on-es], *n.* a female lion.
LION-HEART, [lī'-on-haht], *n.* a man of great courage.
LION-HEARTED, [lī'-on-haht'-id], *adj.* having great courage.
LION-HUNTER, [lī'-on-hunt'-er], *n.* one who hunts lions; one who seeks the company of celebrities.
LIONISM, [lī'-on-izm], *n.* the act of lionizing; the state of being lionized.
LIONIZE, [lī'-on-īz], *v.t.* to treat as a celebrity; *v.i.* to visit the places of interest, to go sightseeing.
LIP (1), [lip], *n.* the upper or the lower red fleshy edge of the mouth; any edge or rim; (*zool.*) one of the two opposite divisions of a labiate coral; (*coll.*) impudence; **to hang on someone's lips,** to listen intently to someone. [OE. *lippa*].
LIP (2), (**lipping, lipped**), [lip], *v.t.* to kiss; to utter.
LIPAROCELE, [lip-a'-ro-sēl], *n.* (*path.*) a fatty tumour in the scrotum. [Gk. *liparos* oily and *kele* hernia].
LIP-DEVOTION, [lip'-di-vō'-shun], *n.* worship only in words.
LIP-GOOD, [lip'-good], *adj.* good only in profession.
LIPHAEMIA, [lip-hē-mi-a], *n.* (*med.*) poorness, deficiency of blood. [Gk. *leipo* I am lacking and *haima* blood].
LIP-LABOUR, [lip'-lāb'-er], *n.* empty words.
LIPOGRAM, [lip'-ō-gram], *n.* a composition from which a certain letter is wholly omitted. [Gk. *leipo* I am lacking and *gramma* letter].
LIPOHAEMIA, [lip-ō-hē'-mi-a], *n.* (*path.*) a fatty condition of the blood. [Gk. *lipos* fat and *haima* blood].
LIPOMA, [lip-ō'-ma], *n.* (*path.*) a fatty tumour. [Gk. *lipos* fat and *oma* a swelling].
LIPP, [lip], *n.* an edible fish much esteemed in the Crimea. [Unkn.].
LIPPED, [lipt], *adj.* with lips, having a raised or rounded edge like a lip; (*bot.*) labiate.
LIPPER, [lip'-er], *n.* a rippling, slight ruffling. [Echoic].
LIPPIE, see LIPPY.
LIPPITUDE, [lip'-i-tewd], *n.* soreness of eyes; bleariness. [L. *lippitudo*].
LIPPY, LIPPIE, [lip'-i], *n.* the fourth part of a peck; a measure holding this amount. [LEAP].
LIP-READER, [lip'-rēd'-er], *n.* one who practises lip-reading.
LIP-READING, [lip'-rēd'-ing], *n.* the art or practice of following what is said by observing the movements of the speaker's lips.
LIP-SERVICE, [lip'-ser'-vis], *n.* a disingenuous profession.
LIPSTICK, [lip'-stik'], *n.* a cosmetic in the shape of a stick for reddening the lips.
LIP-WISDOM, [lip'-wiz'-dom], *n.* wisdom that lies in speech only.
LIQUABLE†, [lik'-wabl], *adj.* that may be liquefied or liquated. [L. *liquabilis*].
LIQUATE, [lik'-wāt], *v.t.* to liquefy; to separate metals or the constituents of an alloy when cooling from the molten state. [L. *liquare*].
LIQUATION, [lik-wā'-shun], *n.* the act of liquating. [L. *liquatio*].
LIQUEFACIENT, [lik'-wi-fā'-shi-ent], *adj.* serving to liquefy. [L. *liquefaciens*].
LIQUEFACTION, [lik'-wi-fak'-shun], *n.* the act of liquefying; the state of being liquefied. [L. *liquefactio*].
LIQUEFIABLE, [lik'-wi-fī'-abl], *adj.* that can be liquefied.
LIQUEFIER, [lik'-wi-fī-er], *n.* one who, or that which, liquefies.
LIQUEFY, [lik'-wi-fī], *v.t.* and *i.* to make liquid; to become liquid. [L. *liquefacere*].
LIQUESCENT, [lik-wes'-ent], *adj.* in process of melting, becoming fluid. [L. *liquescens*].
LIQUEUR, [lik-yoōer'], *n.* a strong, distilled, aromatic spirit; **l. brandy,** fine brandy. [Fr. *liqueur*].
LIQUID (1), [lik'-wid], *n.* any liquid substance, a watery material; (*phon.*) a sonant or consonant such as *l* or *r*.
LIQUID (2), [lik'-wid], *adj.* flowing, fluid; in a state intermediate between the solid and the gaseous; (of a fluid) that runs freely, not stiff; bright, gleaming, clear; (of assets, etc.) easily changed into money [L. *liquidus*].
LIQUIDAMBAR, [lik'-wid-am'-ber], *n.* the genus of the North American sweet gum tree, *Liquidambar styraciflua*.
LIQUIDATE, [lik'-wid-āt], *v.t.* and *i.* to settle, pay, clear off, as a debt; (*comm.*) to wind up, as a bankrupt estate, to determine the debts and assets of; to go into bankruptcy; to destroy or stamp out. [L. *liquidare*].
LIQUIDATION, [lik'-wid-ā'-shun], *n.* the act of liquidating; the state of being liquidated.
LIQUIDATOR, [lik'-wid-āt'-er], *n.* the person who effects a liquidation.
LIQUIDITY, [lik-wid'-i-ti], *n.* liquidness.
LIQUIDLY, [lik'-wid-li], *adv.* in a liquid fashion.
LIQUIDNESS, [lik'-wid-nes], *n.* the quality of being liquid.
LIQUOR, [lik'-er], *n.* a fluid; liquid for drinking, *esp.* when alcoholic; the liquid product of any operation; **in l.,** intoxicated. [OFr. *licur*].
LIQUORICE, LICORICE, [lik'-er-is], *n.* the perennial plant, *Glycyrrhiza glabra*, the dried juice of which is used medicinally and as a sweetmeat. [AFr. *licorys* from Gk. *glukus* sweet and *rhiza* root].
LIQUORISH, see LICKERISH.
LIRA, (*pl.* **lire**), [lēer'-a], *n.* an Italian coin and monetary unit. [It. *lira*].
LIRIPIPE, LIRIPOOP, [lī'-ri-pīp, li'-ri-pōop], *n.* (*hist.*) the tail of an academic hood. [MedL. *liripipium*].
LIROCONE, [lī'-rō-kōn], *adj.* (*min.*) in the form of a whitish powder. [Gk. *leiros* pale and *konia* dust].
LIROCONITE, [li-rok'-on-īt], *n.* a hydrated phosphate of aluminium and copper, occurring in bluish-green crystals.
LISBON, [liz'-bon], *n.* a sweet heavy wine exported from Lisbon.
LISP (1), [lisp], *n.* a speech impediment resulting in the mispronunciation of *s* or *z* as *th*. [OE. *wlisp*].
LISP (2), [lisp], *v.t.* and *i.* to speak with a lisp; to speak imperfectly, as a child; to utter with a lisp. [OE. *wlispian*].
LISPER, [lisp'-er], *n.* a person who lisps.
LISPINGLY, [lisp'-ing-li], *adv.* in a lisping manner.
LISSE, [lēs], *n.* the warp in tapestry. [Fr. *lisse*].
LISSOM, LISSOME, [lis'-um], *adj.* lithe, agile. [LITHESOME].
LISSOMNESS, [lis'-um-nes], *n.* the quality of being lissom.
LISSOTRICHOUS, [lis-ot'-rik-us], *adj.* (*zool.*) smooth-haired. [Gk. *lissos* smooth and *thrix* hair].
LIST (1), [list], *n.* an edging; the selvedge of cloth; cheap material; (*arch.*) a small rectangular moulding or fillet. [OE. *liste* border].

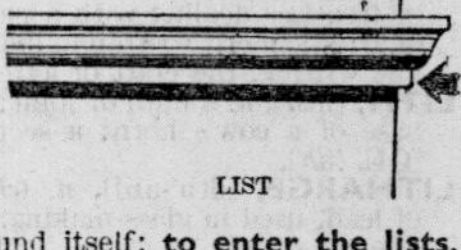
LIST

LIST (2), [list], *n.* (*pl.*) palisades or barriers surrounding a piece of ground set aside for tilting; the tournament ground itself; **to enter the lists,** to defend a cause or enter a quarrel. [Fr. *lisse*].
LIST (3), [list], *n.* a roll or catalogue of entries; an inventory. [LIST (1)].
LIST (4), [list], *n.* a leaning or sloping to one side, *esp.* of a ship. [LIST (7)].
LIST (5), [list], *v.t.* to make a list of; *v.i.* (*coll.*) to enlist in the fighting forces. [LIST (3)].
LIST (6), [list], *v.i.* to incline to one side. [LIST (7)].
LIST (7), [list], *v.i.* (*archaic*) to desire, choose; to please. [OE. *lystan*].
LIST (8), [list], *v.t.* and *i.* (*poet.*) to listen, to listen to. [OE. *hlystan*].
LISTEL, [list-el'], *n.* (*arch.*) a small list or fillet. [AFr. *listel*].
LISTEN, [lis'-en], *v.i.* to pay aural attention, direct the hearing towards something; to pay heed to; **to l. in,** (*wirel.*) to listen to wireless broadcasts; to intercept messages transmitted by wireless or telephone. [OE. *hlysnan*].
LISTENER, [lis'-ner], *n.* one who listens, *esp.* to wireless broadcasts.
LISTER, [list'-er], *n.* one who makes a list; (*U.S.*) an assessor of taxes.
LISTERINE, [list'-er-ēn], *n.* trade name for an antiseptic fluid. [*Next*].
LISTERISM, [list'-er-izm], *n.* antiseptic surgery. [Lord *Lister* (1827-1912), who introduced it].
LISTING, [list'-ing], *n.* salvage; (*naut.*) the narrow strip cut from the edge of a plank. [LIST (1)].

LISTLESS, [list′-les], *adj.* indifferent, apathetic; not attending or interested; languid; spiritless. [ME. *list* desire].

LISTLESSLY, [list′-les-li], *adv.* in listless fashion.

LISTLESSNESS, [list′-les-nes], *n* the condition of being listless.

LIT, [lit], *pret. and p.pt.* of LIGHT; **l. up**, (*coll.*) drunk; hilarious.

LITANY, [lit′-a-ni] *n.* a set form of supplication, being a collection of short prayers recited by clergy with responses from the congregation. [Gk. *litaneia*].

LITAS, [lē′-tas], *n.* the Lithuanian monetary unit. [Lith. *litas*].

LITCHI, LEECHEE, [lē′-chē], *n.* the Chinese tree *Nephelium Litchi*; its edible, aromatic fruit, much prized as a delicacy in the East. [Chin. *lichi*].

LITERACY, [lit′-er-a-si], *n.* the condition or state of being literate.

LITERAL, [lit′-er-al], *adj.* in accordance with the letter; true, accurate, exact; real; strictly following the exact words; relating to an alphabetical letter; (*math.*) expressed in letters. [L. *litteralis*].

LITERALISM, [lit′-er-al-izm], *n.* slavish adherence to the letter; addiction to rigid interpretation of formularies, instructions, etc.

LITERALIST, [lit′-er-al-ist], *n.* one who adheres to literalism.

LITERALITY, [lit′-er-al′-i-ti], *n.* literal meaning; literalness.

LITERALIZE, [lit′-er-al-īz], *v.t.* to make literal; to interpret literally.

LITERALLY, [lit′-er-ali], *adv.* word for word; according to strict grammatical interpretation; (*coll.*) simply, completely.

LITERALNESS, [lit′-er-al-nes], *n.* the quality of being literal or literally exact.

LITERARY, [lit′-er-er-i], *adj.* relating to letters or literature; devoted to or practising literature; of the written rather than the spoken idiom; **l. property**, rights and profits belonging to literary work. [L. *litterarius*].

LITERATE (1), [lit′-er-at], *n.* an educated man, able to read and write.

LITERATE (2), [lit′-er-at], *adj.* acquainted with letters or learning; having learnt to read or write [L. *litteratus*].

LITERATI, [lit-er-ah′-ti, lit-er-ā′-tī], *n.*(*pl.*) men of letters. [It. *literati* from L. *litterati* learned men].

LITERATIM, [lit-er-ā′-tim], *adv.* letter for letter, literally. [L. *litteratim*].

LITERATURE, [lit′-ra-cher], *n.* written works in general, *esp.* non-technical or scientific works; such products of a nation, people, age or culture; the books or treatises dealing with a particular subject; books of artistic merit written in memorable prose or verse; fine writing, the craft of letters. [L. *litteratura*].

LITH, [lith], *n.* a limb or joint; one of the rings at the base of a cow's horn; a section of an orange, etc. [OE. *lith*].

LITHARGE, [lith′-ahj], *n.* (*chem.*) yellow monoxide of lead, used in glass-making. [Gk. *lithos* stone and *arguros* silver].

LITHE (1), see LYTHE.

LITHE (2), [līTH] *adj.* easily bent, nimble, active, supple, willowy. [OE. *lithe*].

LITHENESS, [līTH′-nes], *n.* the quality of being lithe.

LITHER, [līTH′-er], *adj.* supple. [OE. *lythere* lewd].

LITHESOME, [līTH′-sum], *adj.* lithe.

LITHIA, [lith′-i-a], *n.* (*chem.*) oxide of lithium.

LITHIASIS, [lith′-i-ā′-sis], *n.* (*med.*) the disease of stone, *esp.* in the bladder or kidneys. [Gk. *lithiasis*].

LITHIC (1), [lith′-ik], *adj.* pertaining to stone, *esp.* in the bladder.

LITHIC (2), [lith′-ik], *adj.* pertaining to lithium.

LITHIUM, [lith′-i-um], *n.* (*chem.*) a white metallic element, Li, the lightest of metals.

LITHO-, *pref.* stone. [Gk. *lithos*].

LITHOCARP, [lith′-ō-kahp], *n.* a fossil fruit. [LITHO and Gk. *karpos* fruit].

LITHOCHROMATICS, [lith′-ō-krō-mat′-iks], *n.*(*pl.*) the art of colour printing in oils from stone. [LITHO and Gk. *khroma* colour].

LITHODENDRON, [lith′-ō-den′-dron], *n.* a kind of coral, from its resemblance to a branch. [LITHO and Gk. *dendron* tree].

LITHODOME, [lith′-ō-dōm], *n.* a mollusc which bores a hole in a rock and lodges in it; a kind of mussel, date-shell. [LITHO and Gk. *domos* house].

LITHOFRACTEUR, [lith′-ō-frak′-tur′], *n.* a nitro-glycerine explosive largely used in blasting. [LITHO and Fr. *fracteur* breaker].

LITHOGENOUS, [lith-oj′-en-us], *adj.* stone-forming. [LITHO and Gk. *genes* born of].

LITHOGLYPH, [lith′-ō-glif], *n.* an engraving on a gem; the art of making such engravings. [LITHO and Gk. *glupho* I carve].

LITHOGLYPHITE, [lith′-ō-glif′-īt], *n.* a fossil which has the appearance of having been cut by art.

LITHOGRAPH (1), [lith′-ō-graf], *n.* a print from a drawing made on specially prepared stone. [LITHO and GRAPH].

LITHOGRAPH (2), [lith′-ō-graf], *v.t.* to draw on stone and transfer to paper; to make a lithographic print.

LITHOGRAPHER, [lith-og′-raf-er], *n.* one who practises lithography.

LITHOGRAPHIC, [lith′-ō-graf′-ik], *adj.* pertaining to lithography.

LITHOGRAPHICAL, [lith′-ō-graf′-ik-al], *adj.* lithographic.

LITHOGRAPHICALLY, [lith′-ō-graf′-ik-al-i], *adv.* by means of lithography.

LITHOGRAPHY, [lith-og′-ra-fi], *n.* the art or process of making lithographs. [LITHO and Gk. *graphia* writing].

LITHOID, [lith′-oid], *adj.* of the nature of stone; having a stony structure. [LITHO and Gk. *oeides* like].

LITHOIDAL, [lith-oid′-al], *adj.* lithoid.

LITHOLABE, [lith′-ō-lāb], *n.* an instrument for holding fast the stone in lithotomy. [LITHO and Gk. *labo* I take].

LITHOLOGIC, [lith′-ō-loj′-ik], *adj.* relating to lithology.

LITHOLOGICAL, [lith′-ō-loj′-ik-al], *adj.* lithologic.

LITHOLOGIST, [lith-ol′-oj-ist], *n.* one skilled in lithology.

LITHOLOGY, [lith-ol′-o-ji], *n.* (*min.*) the science of the nature and composition of rocks; (*med.*) the study of stones found in the body. [LITHO and Gk. *logos* speech].

LITHOMANCY, [lith′-ō-man′-si], *n.* divination by means of precious stones. [LITHO and Gk. *manteia* divination].

LITHOMARGE, [lith′-ō-mahj], *n.* kaolin, a compact clay of a fine, smooth texture; a kind of marl. [LITHO and L. *marga* marl].

LITHONTRIPTIC (1), [lith′-on-tript′-ik], *n.* a medicine that dissolves or destroys a stone in the bladder.

LITHONTRIPTIC (2), [lith′-on-tript′-ik], *adj.* (*med.*) which acts as a lithontriptic. [LITHO and Gk. *thrupto* I crush].

LITHONTRIPTOR, [lith′-on-tript′-er], *n.* (*med.*) an instrument for crushing stone in the bladder.

LITHONTRIPTY, [lith′-on-tript′-i], *n.* (*surg.*) the operation of crushing a stone in the bladder, using a lithontriptor.

LITHOPHAGOUS, [lith-of′-ag-us], *adj.* addicted to eating or swallowing stones or gravel. [LITHO and Gk. *phago* I eat].

LITHOPHOSPHORIC, [lith′-ō-fos-fo′-rik], *adj.* becoming phosphoric under the influence of heat. [LITHO and PHOSPHORIC].

LITHOPHOTOGRAPHY, [lith′-ō-fō-tog′-ra-fi], *n.* the producing of lithographs from photographs transferred to the stone. [LITHO and PHOTOGRAPHY].

LITHOPHYLL, [lith′-ō-fil], *n.* a fossil leaf or its impression. [LITHO and Gk. *phullon* leaf].

LITHOTINT, [lith′-ō-tint], *n.* the lithographic production of a tinted picture; the picture so produced.

LITHOTOME, [lith′-ō-tōm], *n.* a stone so formed naturally as to seem as if cut artificially; a lithotomic instrument. [LITHO and Gk. *tome* a cutting].

LITHOTOMIC, [lith′-ō-tom′-ik], *adj.* pertaining to, performed by, lithotomy.

LITHOTOMIST, [lith-ot′-om-ist], *n.* a person who performs lithotomy.

LITHOTOMY, [lith-ot′-o-mi], *n.* (*surg.*) the operation of cutting for stone in the bladder. [LITHO and Gk. *tomia* cutting].

LITHOTRIPSY, [lith′-ō-trip′-si], *n.* (*surg.*) the operation of crushing a stone in the bladder. [LITHO and Gk. *tripsis* grinding].

LITHOTRIPTOR, [lith′-ō-tript′-er], *n.* a lithotrite or lithontriptor.

LITHOTRITE, [lith′-ō-trīt], *n.* (*surg.*) an instrument for crushing stone in the bladder.

LITHOTRITIC, [lith′-ō-trit′-ik], *adj.* of, or relating to, lithotrity.

LITHOTRITIST, [lith-ot′-rit-ist], *n.* one skilled in lithotrity.

LITHOTRITY, [lith-ot'-rit-i], *n.* (*surg.*) lithotripsy. [LITHO and L. *tritum*, *p.pt.* of *terere* to crush].

LITHOTYPE, [lith'-ō-tīp], *n.* a kind of stereotype. [LITHO and TYPE].

LITHOXYL, [lith-oks'-il], *n.* petrified wood; wood-opal. [LITHO and Gk. *xulon* wood].

LITHUANIAN (1), [lith-ew-ān'-i-an], *n.* a native of Lithuania; the native language of Lithuania. [Russ. *Letva*].

LITHUANIAN (2), [lith-ew-ān'-i-an], *adj.* of, or pertaining to, Lithuania, its inhabitants, or its language.

LITHY, [lĪTH'-i], *adj.* (*dial.*) easily bent, pliable; unresisting. [OE. *lithig*].

LITIGABLE, [lit'-ig-abl], *adj.* disputable in law.

LITIGANT (1), [lit'-ig-ant], *n.* (*leg.*) a party in a lawsuit. [Fr. *litigant*].

LITIGANT (2), [lit'-ig-ant], *adj.* engaged in a lawsuit. [L. *litigans*].

LITIGATE, [lit'-ig-āt], *v.t.* to contest at law; *v.i.* to carry on a lawsuit. [L. *litigare*].

LITIGATION, [lit'-ig-ā'-shun], *n.* the act of litigating; a judicial contest; legal business in general. [L. *litigatio*].

LITIGIOSITY, [lit-ij'-i-os'-i-ti], *n.* litigiousness.

LITIGIOUS, [lit-ij'-us], *adj.* inclined to engage in lawsuits; fond of disputes, contentious. [Fr. *litigieux*].

LITIGIOUSLY, [lit-ij'-us-li], *adv.* in litigious fashion.

LITIGIOUSNESS, [lit-ij'-us-nes], *n.* the quality of being litigious.

LITMUS, [lit'-mus], *n.* a colouring matter extracted from certain lichens; **l. paper**, unsized paper stained with litmus, used to test acidity or alkalinity by its change of colour. [AFr. *lytemoise*, ~ODu. *leecmos* a blue dye].

LITOTES, [lī'-tot-ēz], *n.* (*rhet.*) understatement, a figure of speech which consists of the toning down of a statement, as when an affirmative is implied by using the negative of the contrary. [Gk. *litotes*].

LITRE, [lē'-ter], *n.* the unit of capacity in the metric system, equivalent to rather more than 1¾ pints. [Fr. *litre*].

LITTER (1), [lit'-er], *n.* a wheel-less vehicle formed with shafts, supporting a couch or carriage between them, in which a person may be carried; a stretcher; straw, hay or other soft material, used as a bed for animals; waste matter, fragments, rubbish, etc., scattered about untidily; the whole number of the young of certain animals, brought forth at one birth. [Fr. *litière*].

LITTER

LITTER (2), [lit'-er], *v.t.* to provide with litter; to pile up with litter; *v.i.* to give birth to a litter.

LITTERATEUR, [lit'-er-ah-tur'], *n.* a man of letters. [Fr. *littérateur*].

LITTERY, [lit'-er-i], *adj.* of the nature of a litter; covered with litter; untidy.

LITTLE (1), [litl], *n.* a small quantity or amount; a short time.

LITTLE (2), [litl], *adj.* small in height, size, quantity, extent; brief; young; of small power and importance; petty, mean, base. [OE. *lytel*].

LITTLE (3), [litl], *adv.* in a small quantity or degree; not much, slightly.

LITTLE-EASE, [litl'-ēz], *n.* (*hist.*) a prison cell so small as to make it impossible for the prisoner to lie down or stand up in it.

LITTLE-ENDIAN, [litl'-end'-i-an], *n.* one who quarrels seriously about trifles. ["Gulliver's Travels," by J. Swift].

LITTLE-ENGLANDER, [litl'-ing'-glan-der), *n.* one who objected to the further expansion of British dominion and influence.

LITTLE-GO, [litl'-gō]. *n.* (*coll.*) the preliminary examination or matriculation at Cambridge University.

LITTLENESS, [litl'-nes], *n.* the quality of being little.

LITTORAL (1), [lit'-er-al], *n.* the seashore, beach; any coastal strip of country.

LITTORAL (2), [lit'-er-al], *adj.* pertaining to the seashore or any littoral. [L. *litoralis*].

LITUATE, [lit'-yōō-āt], *adj.* forked, with the points turned outward. [L. *lituus* clarion].

LITURGIC, [lit-urj'-ik], *adj.* liturgical.

LITURGICAL, [lit-urj'-ik-al], *adj.* connected with a liturgy; in accordance with a religious formulary, calendar, etc.

LITURGICALLY, [lit-urj'-ik-al-i], *adv.* according to the liturgy.

LITURGICS, [lit-urj'-iks], *n.*(*pl.*) the study of liturgical theory and history.

LITURGIOLOGY, [lit-urj'-i-ol'-o-ji], *n.* the study of liturgies and their development. [LITURGY and Gk. *logos* speech].

LITURGIST, [lit'-urj-ist], *n.* one who advocates the use of liturgies; an authority on liturgy.

LITURGY, [lit'-er-ji], *n.* a body of ritual or established formularies for public worship; the Office for the Celebration of the Holy Communion. [Gk. *leitourgia* a public service].

LIVABLE, LIVEABLE, [liv'-abl], *adj.* worth living, endurable; fit to live (in); fit to live (with).

LIVE (1), [līv], *adj.* having life, living; on fire; loaded; covered with animalculae or filth; (*fig.*) lively, spirited; **l. cartridge**, a cartridge containing a bullet; **l. rail**, an electrified rail; **l. wire**, an electrified wire; (*fig.*) a lively, energetic person. [ALIVE].

LIVE (2), [liv], *v.i.* to be alive; to spend one's life; to remain alive; to dwell, reside; to feed, subsist; to gain a livelihood; to lead a vivid life; to feed well; (*fig.*) to be remembered; to spend, pass; to conform to; **to l. down**, to cause to be forgotten; **to l. up to**, to fulfil expectations; **to l. and let l.**, to be tolerant. [OE. *lifian*].

LIVEABLE, see LIVABLE.

LIVED, [livd, līvd], *suff.* possessed of a particular kind or length of life.

LIVELIHOOD, [līv'-li-hŏŏd], *n.* means of subsistence; sustenance. [OE. *lif-gelad* lifetime].

LIVELILY, [līv'-li-li], *adv.* in lively fashion.

LIVELINESS, [līv'-li-nes], *n.* the quality of being lively.

LIVELONG, [liv'-long, līv'-long], *adj.* lasting, enduring; all through. [LIVE (2) and LONG (1)].

LIVELY, [līv'-li], *adj.* brisk, vigorous, full of vitality and animation; gay, sprightly; fresh; keen; vivid; moving quickly.

LIVEN, [līv'-en], *v.t.* to enliven, brighten, cheer up, relieve.

LIVER (1), [liv'-er], *n.* one who lives.

LIVER (2), [liv'-er], *n.* an organ in the abdomen, which secretes the bile; this organ in animals, cooked as food; (*coll.*) an attack of sluggishness of the liver, a depression. [OE. *lifer*].

LIVER (3), [liv'-er], *adj.* dark reddish-brown in colour.

LIVER-FLUKE, [liv'-er-flŏŏk'], *n.* the trematoid worm, *Distomum hepaticum*, infesting the liver of sheep, etc.

LIVERIED, [liv'-er-id], *adj.* wearing livery.

LIVERISH, [liv'-er-ish], *adj.* suffering from a disordered liver; irritable, testy.

LIVERWORT, [liv'-er-wurt], *n.* a member of the *Hepaticæ*, cryptogamic plants related to the mosses.

LIVERY, [liv'-er-i], *n.* a uniform worn by servants and retainers; a body of retainers in the same uniform; *orig.* the provisions and provender delivered to these; any uniform proper to particular persons on particular occasions; (*fig.*) the outward appearance of trees, plants, and animals; garb, dress; (*leg.*) a delivery of property; the writ of such delivery; **at l.**, (of a horse) kept for the owner at a fixed charge. [OFr. *livrée*].

LIVERY COMPANY, [liv'-er-i-kum'-pan-i], *n.* a company of the City of London whose members were formerly entitled to wear a distinctive livery.

LIVERYMAN, [liv'-er-i-man], *n.* a member of a livery company and a freeman of the City of London.

LIVERY-STABLE, [liv'-eri-stābl'], *n.* a jobmaster's stable in which horses are kept at livery or for hire.

LIVESTOCK, [līv'-stok], *n.* cattle, sheep, etc.; (*coll.*) vermin on the person. [LIVE (1) and STOCK (1)].

LIVID, [liv'-id], *adj.* bluish; of a leaden colour; discoloured; very pale. [L. *lividus*].

LIVIDITY, [liv-id'-i-ti], *n.* lividness.

LIVIDNESS, [liv'-id-nes], *n.* the state of being livid.

LIVING (1), [liv'-ing], *n.* wages, salary or income; livelihood; manner and standard of life; trade, craft or profession; the benefice of a parish priest.

LIVING (2), [liv'-ing], *adj.* alive, existing; (of water) running, flowing; full of vitality; life-like; **l. rock**, rock in its natural state.

LIVINGLY, [liv'-ing-li], *adv.* in a living manner.

LIVINGNESS, [liv'-ing-nes], *n.* the state or quality of being alive; vividness.

LIVRAISON, [liv-rā'-zon], *n.* an instalment of a book issued in parts or fascicles. [Fr. *livraison*].

LIVRE, [lēvr], *n.* the old French monetary unit superseded by the franc. [Fr. *livre*].

LIXIVIAL, [liks-iv'-i-al], *adj.* obtained by lixiviation; resembling lye.

LIXIVIATE, [liks-iv'-i-āt], *v.t.* to separate the soluble from the insoluble by soaking in water or other solvent; to form into lye. [L. *lixivius* made into lye].

LIXIVIATED, [liks-iv'-i-āt-id], *adj.* pertaining to lye or lixivium.

LIXIVIATION, [liks'-iv-i-ā'-shun], *n.* the act of lixiviating. [L. *lixiviatio*].

LIXIVIOUS, [liks-iv'-i-us], *adj.* lixivial.

LIXIVIUM, [liks-iv'-i-um], *n.* lye; water impregnated with alkaline salts.

LIZARD, [liz'-erd], *n.* a small reptile of the order *Lacertilia*. [OFr. *lesard*].

LIZARD-STONE, [liz'-erd-stōn'], *n.* the serpentine marble-stone found in Cornwall near Lizard Point.

LLAMA, [lah'-ma], *n.* the South American beast of burden resembling a large sheep, related to the camel. [Span. from Peruvian *llama na*].

LLAMA

LLANERO, [lan-ā-ro], *n.* an inhabitant of a llano. [Span. *llanero*].

LLANO, [lah'-nō], *n.* one of the vast plains of South America. [Span. *llano*].

LLOYD'S, [loidz], *n.(pl.)* the headquarters of the London underwriters and insurance brokers. [*Lloyd's* coffee-house, their original meeting place].

LO, [lō], *int.* see, look, behold. [OE. *la* or *loca* look].

LOACH, LOCHE†, [lōch], *n.* a small freshwater fish, *Cobitis barbatula* or *Nemachilus barbatulus*. [F. *loche*].

LOAD (1), [lōd], *n.* that which is laid on or put in anything for conveyance, a burden, weight; as much as can be, or is, carried at once, *esp.* as a unit of measure; (*fig.*) anything oppressive or depressing; the charge of a gun; (*elect.*) the amount of electricity supplied by a generating station or dynamo at any one time. [OE. *lad*].

LOAD (2), [lōd], *v.t.* to lay a burden on; to place a load on or in; to overburden, encumber; to oppress; to weight at one end or side; to charge a gun; to doctor, adulterate drink.

LOADER, [lōd'-er], *n.* a person employed in loading; an attendant who loads the guns; a machine for loading.

LOADING, [lōd'-ing], *n.* the act of one who loads; a load; **l. gauge**, the hanging bar under which laden goods wagons are run to measure their height.

LOADLINE, [lōd'-līn], *n.* (*naut.*) a line on the side of a ship to indicate the limit to which it may be legally loaded.

LOADSTAR, see LODESTAR.

LOADSTONE, LODESTONE, [lōd'-stōn], *n.* an iron ore which has the power of attracting iron; magnet. [OE. *lad* way and STONE].

LOAF (1), (*pl.* **loaves**), [lōf], *n.* a certain quantity of bread baked in one mass; a conical mould of sugar; a lump of anything. [OE. *hlaf*].

LOAF (2), [lōf], *v.t. and i.* to idle away or about. [Unkn.].

LOAFER, [lōf'-er], *n.* one who loafs; one who allows others to maintain him in idleness.

LOAF-SUGAR, [lōf'-shŏŏg'-er], *n.* sugar refined and formed into a small conical mass or lump.

LOAM (1), [lōm], *n.* a rich soil, mainly clay with an admixture of sandy soil. [OE. *lam*].

LOAM (2), [lōm], *v.t.* to cover with loam.

LOAMY, [lōm'-i], *adj.* consisting of, resembling loam.

LOAN (1), [lōn], *n.* the lending of anything; the thing lent; money lent at interest; an issue of stock by a government. [OIcel. *lan*].

LOAN (2), [lōn], *v.t.* to lend.

LOATHE, [lōTH], *v.t.* to hate, abhor, detest; to feel disgust at. [OE. *lathian*].

LOATHER, [lōTH'-er], *n.* one who loathes.

LOATHFUL, [lōTH'-fŏŏl], *adj.* to be loathed, hateful.

LOATHING, [lōTH'-ing], *n.* extreme dislike or disgust; hatred of.

LOATHINGLY, [lōTH'-ing-li], *adv.* with loathing.

LOATHLINESS, [lōTH'-li-nes], *n.* the quality of arousing loathing.

LOATHLY (1), [lōTH'-li], *adj.* arousing loathing.

LOATHLY (2), [lōTH'-li], *adv.* in a manner to arouse loathing.

LOATHNESS, [lōTH'-nes], *n.* the quality of being loath.

LOATHSOME, [lōTH'-sum], *adj.* exciting loathing; (*coll.*) objectionable.

LOATHSOMELY, [lōTH'-sum-li], *adv.* in a loathsome manner.

LOATHSOMENESS, [lōTH'-sum-nes], *n.* the quality of being loathsome.

LOB (1), [lob], *n.* a dull, sluggish person, a lout; a slow high-pitched ball bowled underhand at cricket; a high-pitched ball at tennis. [Uncert.].

LOB† (2), [lob], *n.* a freshwater fish, the chub. [Unkn.].

LOB (3), (**lobbing, lobbed**), [lob], *v.t.* to toss as a lob at cricket or tennis; *v.i.* to move along heavily and clumsily.

LOBAR, [lōb'-er], *adj.* pertaining to a lobe.

LOBATE, [lōb'-āt], *adj.* (*biol.*) lobed.

LOBBY (1), [lob'-i], *n.* a hall; a passage communicating with rooms; an anteroom or waiting-room; (*parl.*) a large room in the House of Commons for public interviews with members of parliament; a corridor for recording votes on a division. [LL. *lobia* gallery].

LOBBY (2), [lob'-i], *v.t. and i.* (*parl.*) to seek to influence the members of a legislative assembly in order to ensure the passage of a bill.

LOBBY-MEMBER, [lob'-i-mem'-ber], *n.* (*U.S.*) one who frequents the lobby of a house of legislation.

LOBCOCK, [lob'-kok], *n.* (*dial.*) a country bumpkin, a lubber.

LOBE, [lōb], *n.* the lower, soft pendulous part of the ear; any rounded, projecting part, *esp.* of an organ of the body; a division of a leaf; the cotyledon of a seed. [Gk. *lobos*].

LOBED, [lōbd], *adj.* having a lobe or lobes.

LOBELET, [lōb'-let], *n.* a small lobe.

LOBELIA, [lō-bēl'-ya], *n.* (*bot.*) a large genus of brightly flowered plants; a plant of this genus. [M. de *Lobel*, botanist and doctor to James I].

LOBLOLLY, [lob'-lol'-i], *n.* (*naut.*) thick gruel or spoon-meat; **l. bay**, an American ornamental evergreen tree, *Gordonia lasianthus*; **l. boy**, a surgeon's attendant on board ship; **l. tree**, *Varronia alba*. [Uncert.].

LOBSCOUSE, [lob'-skows'], *n.* (*naut.*) a stew of minced salt meat with vegetables and biscuits. [Uncert.].

LOBSPOUND, [lobz'-pownd], *n.* (*dial.*) a prison. [LOB (1)].

LOBSTER, [lob'-ster], *n.* an edible crustacean of the genus *Homarus*, bluish black when alive, red when it has been boiled; **l. pot**, a trap for lobsters. [OE. *lopustre* from L. *locusta*].

LOBULAR, [lob'-yŏŏ-ler], *adj.* having the form or nature of a lobule.

LOBULE, [lob'-yŏŏl], *n.* a small lobe.

LOBWORM, [lob'-wurm], *n.* a worm, *Arenicola piscatorum*, used for bait by anglers.

LOCAL (1), [lō'-kal], *n.* an inhabitant of a particular locality; a train or vehicle which serves the stations of a certain small area; (*coll.*) a public-house.

LOCAL (2), [lō'-kal], *adj.* pertaining to place or space; connected with some particular place, area or district; **l. colour**, background detail and atmosphere in any work of art; **l. option**, regulation of the sale of intoxicants by a local plebiscite. [L. *localis*].

LOCALE, [lō-kahl'], *n.* the location, *esp.* of a story, film, or drama. [Fr. *local*].

LOCALISM, [lō'-kal-izm], *n.* an attachment to a locality; restricted mental outlook; local peculiarity of idiom or behaviour.

LOCALITY, [lō-kal'-i-ti], *n.* a particular district; existence in a place; situation, environment.

LOCALIZATION, [lō'-kal-īz-ā'-shun], *n.* the act of localizing.

LOCALIZE, [lō'-kal-īz], *v.t.* to make local; to restrict to a particular region; to identify with a particular locality.

LOCALLY, [lō'-kal-i], *adv.* in certain localities; in the surrounding district, near at hand; in any particular point.

LOCATE, [lō-kāt'], *v.t.* to set, establish in a particular spot or position; (*U.S.*) to survey and settle the boundary of an area of land; to determine, find where a particular thing is. [L. *locare* to place].

LOCATION, [lō-kā'-shun], *n.* the art of locating; relative situation; that which is located; a place at which parts of a film must be made in order to obtain the correct background. [L. *locatio*].

LOCATIVE (1), [lo'-kat-iv], *n.* (*gram.*) the locative case. [*Next*].

LOCATIVE (2), [lo'-kat-iv], *adj.* (*gram.*) of, or denoting, position. [L. *locus* place].

LOCH, [lok], *n.* a lake or arm of the sea, *esp.* in Scotland. [Gael. *loch* lake].

LOCHABER AXE, [lok-ab'-er-aks'], *n.* a Scottish battle-axe with a long shaft holding a long blade and a hook for catching the bridles of horses. [*Lochaber* in Inverness-shire].

LOCHE†, see LOACH.

LOCHIA, [lok'-i-a], *n.*(*pl.*) the uterine discharge occurring after childbirth. [Gk. *lokhia* from *lokhos* lying-in].

LOCK (1), [lok], *n.* a ringlet of hair, a curl; (*pl.*) hair. [OE. *locc*].

LOCK (2), [lok], *n.* a mechanism for shooting a bar or bolt into a socket so as to hold closed a door, box, etc.; the part of a fire-arm by which it is discharged; a grapple in wrestling; an enclosure on a river or canal with movable watertight gates at each end, through which ships can be moved from one level to another; (*mech.*) any tight coupling; the stoppage of any moving part in a machine; the limits of the turning-circle of a motor-car's steering wheel. [OE. *loc*].

LOCK (3), [lok], *v.t.* to fasten with a lock; to embrace closely; to interlace; to set rigidly; to cause a stoppage of motion in; (*fig.*) to keep fast; *v.i.* to be fastened or be capable of being fastened with a lock; to cease to move or revolve; **to l. out,** to prevent from entering a factory to work; **to l. up,** to imprison.

LOCKAGE, [lok'-ij], *n.* machinery and works which constitute a canal lock; toll dues for passing the locks; amount of ascent and descent by means of the locks.

LOCK-CHAMBER, [lok'-chām'-ber], *n.* the basin of a canal lock.

LOCKER, [lok'-er], *n.* a person who locks; an enclosed space, cupboard, receptacle, etc., that may be closed with a lock; **in Davy Jones's l.,** at the bottom of the sea.

LOCKET, [lok'-it], *n.* a small lock; a catch to fasten a necklace, etc.; a little case usually of gold or silver containing a miniature, etc., and worn as an ornament. [OFr. *locquet*].

LOCK-GATE, [lok'-gāt], *n.* one of the gates enclosing the lock-chamber.

LOCK-HOSPITAL, [lok'-hos'-pit-al], *n.* a hospital for venereal disease.

LOCKIAN, [lok'-i-an], *adj.* of, or connected with, John *Locke* (1632-1704) or his philosophy.

LOCK-JAW, [lok'-jaw], *n.* (*path.*) a violent contraction of the muscles of the jaw, which locks it fast; a form of tetanus.

LOCK-KEEPER, [lok'-kēp'-er], *n.* a man who attends to the lock of a river or canal.

LOCK-KNIT, [lok'-nit], *n.* material woven so as to resemble knitting and having locked stitches.

LOCKLESS, [lok'-les], *adj.* having no lock.

LOCK-OUT, [lok'-owt], *n.* the refusal of an employer to allow workmen to resume work until they accept his terms.

LOCK-PADDLE, [lok'-padl], *n.* a small sluice which serves to fill and empty a lock.

LOCKRAM, [lok'-ram], *n.* a variety of coarse linen. [*Locronan* in France].

LOCK-SILL, [lok'-sil], *n.* the beam at the bottom of a lock, against which the gates shut.

LOCKSMITH, [lok'-smith], *n.* one whose craft is the making and repairing of locks and keys.

LOCK-STITCH, [lok'-stich], *n.* a stitch which fastens two threads firmly together.

LOCK-UP, [lok'-up], *n.* a prison, quarters for the detention of arrested persons; **l. shop,** a shop without living quarters.

LOCK-WEIR, [lok'-wēer], *n.* a weir which has a lock.

LOCO (1), [lō'-kō], *n.* a poisonous American plant of the legume family; **l. disease,** a brain disease affecting animals that have eaten this. [Span. *loco* insane].

LOCO (2), [lō'-kō], *adj.* (*slang*) mad; incapacitated. [*Prec.*].

LOCO- (3), *pref.* by, with, or from, a place. [L. *loco*, ablative of *locus* place].

LOCOMOBILE, [lō'-kō-mō'-bil], *n.* an automobile. [LOCO (3) and MOBILE].

LOCOMOTION, [lō'-kō-mō'-shun], *n.* the act or power of moving from place to place. [LOCO (3) and MOTION].

LOCOMOTIVE (1), [lō'-kō-mō'-tiv], *n.* an engine on wheels moving along by its own power, *esp.* a steam railway engine. [LOCO (3) and MOTIVE].

LOCOMOTIVE (2), [lō'-kō-mō'-tiv], *adj.* moving by its own power from place to place.

LOCOMOTOR, [lō'-kō-mō'-ter], *adj.* pertaining to locomotion.

LOCOMOTORY, [lō'-kō-mō'-ter-i], *adj.* pertaining to, possessing locomotion.

LOCULAMENT, [lok'-yōō-la-ment], *n.* a loculus; (*bot.*) the cell of a pericarp in which the seed is lodged. [L. *loculamentum*].

LOCULAR, [lok'-yōō-ler], *adj.* of, or having, loculi.

LOCULOSE, [lok'-yōō-lōs], *adj.* loculous.

LOCULOUS, [lok'-yōō-lus], *adj.* full of loculi. [L. *loculosus*].

LOCULUS, (*pl.* **loculi**), [lok'-yōō-lus], *n.* a very small cell. [L. *loculus* little place].

LOCUM TENENS, [lō'-kum-tēn'-enz], *n.* a deputy, *esp.* a doctor or clergyman. [L. *locum tenens* holding the place].

LOCUS, (*pl.* **loci**), [lō'-kus, *pl.* lō'-sī], *n.* seat, place in which something is situated; (*math.*) the line generated by a point, or the surface generated by a line, moving according to a fixed law; **l. classicus,** the standard authoritative passage or instance; (*nat. hist.*) the original locality; **l. standi,** official position; (*leg.*) right to intervene in a lawsuit. [L. *locus* place].

LOCUST, [lō'-kust], *n.* an orthopterous insect, allied to the grasshopper, which migrates in vast hordes and is very destructive to vegetation. [L. *locusta*].

LOCUST

LOCUST-TREE, [lō'-kust-trē'], *n.* the false acacia, *Robinia*; the carob tree, *Ceratonia siliqua* or its bean-like fruit.

LOCUTION, [lok-ew'-shun], *n.* speech; mode of expression; phrase, idiom. [L. *locutio*].

LOCUTORY, [lok'-ewt-er-i], *n.* a room in monasteries for speech or conversation; a grille for the same purpose. [MedL. *locutorium*].

LODE, [lōd], *n.* a vein, *esp.* a mineral vein; a reach of water; †course, way. [OE. *lad* load].

LODESTAR, LOADSTAR, [lōd'-stah(r)], *n.* a star that shows the way; the pole-star; (*fig.*) a guiding influence or ideal.

LODESTONE, see LOADSTONE.

LODGE (1), [loj], *n.* a dwelling, *esp.* a temporary habitation; a small house for the use of sportsmen when shooting, etc.; a gatekeeper's cottage; the home of a North American Indian; the den of a beaver, otter, etc.; a secret local association; the place where they meet; a meeting held by them. [Fr. *loge*].

LODGE (2), [loj], *v.t.* to deposit, *esp.* in the official custody of; to harbour; to place, implant; to lay a formal statement before the authorities; *v.i.* to reside for a time; to occupy lodgings; to come to rest securely fixed (in).

LODGEABLE, [loj'-abl], *adj.* that may be lodged.

LODGEMENT, see LODGMENT.

LODGER, [loj'-er], *n.* one who lodges, a paying guest.

LODGING, [loj'-ing], *n.* habitation, *esp.* when temporary; (*pl.*) hired apartments in a house.

LODGING-HOUSE, [loj'-ing-hows'], *n.* a house in which apartments are let out to lodgers.

LODGMENT, LODGEMENT, [loj'-ment], *n.* the act of lodging; the state of being lodged; lodgings; the accumulation of something deposited; (*milit.*) the fortified position taken up by a besieging party.

LOESS, [lō'-es], *n.* (*geol.*) an alluvial tertiary deposit of calcareous loam. [Germ. *löss*].

LOFT (1), [loft], *n.* a room immediately under the roof, *esp.* in a stable; a gallery in a church; (*golf*) the inclination of the head of a club; a stroke which lofts.

LOFT (2), [loft], *v.t.* to place in a loft; (*golf*) to hit a ball high; (of the face of a club) to cause to slope.

LOFTER, [loft'-er], *n.* (*golf*) an iron-headed club for lofting the ball.

LOFTILY, [loft'-i-li], *adv.* in a lofty manner.

LOFTINESS, [loft'-i-nes], *n.* the condition of being lofty.

LOFTY, [loft'-i], *adj.* extending to a great height, tall; (*fig.*) elevated, dignified; haughty, frigid.

LOG (1), [log], *n.* a large piece of undressed timber; an apparatus for measuring speed at sea; a daily record of a voyage or flight; the book in which the record is kept. [ME. *logge*].

LOG (2), [log], *n.* a Hebrew liquid measure variously reckoned at ¾ or ⅚ of a pint. [Heb. *log*].

LOG (3), [log], *n.* a logarithm.

LOG (4), (logging, logged), [log], *v.t.* to cut into logs;

to insert as an entry in a logbook; to record in official or semi-official manner.

LOGANBERRY, [lō'-gan-be'-ri], *n.* a deep red cultivated fruit, resembling the blackberry; the bush on which this grows. [Judge *Logan*, the American who introduced it].

LOGANSTONE, [lō'-gan-stōn'], *n.* a large stone so balanced on another that it will rock when touched, a rocking-stone. [DialE. *log* to rock].

LOGARITHM, [log'-er-ithm], *n.* (of a number) the index of the power to which a base must be raised to give that number. [Gk. *logos* speech and *arithmos* number].

LOGARITHMETIC, [log'-er-ith-met'-ik], *adj.* logarithmic.

LOGARITHMETICAL, [log'-er-ith-met'-ik-al], *adj.* logarithmetic.

LOGARITHMIC, [log'-er-ith'-mik], *adj.* pertaining to, consisting of logarithms.

LOGARITHMICAL, [log'-er-ith'-mik-al], *adj.* logarithmic.

LOGBOARD, [log'-bawd], *n.* (*naut.*) a pair of boards, shutting like a book, on which details of a voyage were chalked, to be written up in the logbook.

LOGBOOK, [log'-book], *n.* the official record of the daily events of a voyage or flight.

LOG-CABIN, [log'-kab'-in], *n.* a hut of undressed timber.

LOGE, [lōzh], *n.* a box in a theatre; a seat in the stalls of a theatre. [Fr. *loge*].

LOGGAN, [log'-an], *n.* a loganstone.

LOGGATS†, [log'-ats], *n.* an old English game resembling ninepins. [LOG].

LOGGE, [log], *n.* (*dial.*) fish, the miller's thumb, *Cottus gobio*.

LOGGER, [log'-er], *n.* one who fells timber; a lumberman.

LOGGERHEAD, [log'-er-hed], *n.* a stupid person or animal; a long handle with a ball at the head, heated and plunged into tar, etc., to melt it; a species of turtle, *Thalassochelys caretta*; **at loggerheads,** at variance. [LOG].

LOGGERHEADED, [log'-er-hed'-id], *adj.* thick-headed, stupid.

LOGGIA, [loj'-i-a], *n.* a gallery, arcade or roofed terrace in front of a building. [It. *loggia*].

LOGGIA

LOG-HUT, [log'-hut], *n.* a log-cabin.

LOGIA, [log'-i-a], *n.(pl.)* of LOGION.

LOGIC, [loj'-ik], *n.* the formal aspect of cogent reasoning; the department of philosophy which determines and evaluates its forms; reasoning; subtlety in thought; (*coll.*) commonsense, cogency; rational nature. [Gk. *logike* (*tekhne*) art of words.]

LOGICAL, [loj'-ik-al], *adj.* belonging to logic; according to logic; skilled in logic; discriminating; consistent.

LOGICALLY, [loj'-ik-al-i], *adv.* in logical fashion.

LOGICIAN, [lo-jish'-an], *n.* one skilled in logic.

LOGICIZE, [loj'-i-sīz], *v.i.* to reason from premises.

LOGION, (*pl.* **logia**), [lo'-gi-on], *n.* any utterance of a religious teacher; (*pl.*) collections of the sayings of Christ. [Gk. *logion*].

LOGISTIC, [lo-jist'-ik], *adj.* logical; skilled in argument; casuistical, over-refined in logic. [Gk. *logistikos*].

LOGISTICAL, [lo-jist'-ik-al], *adj.* logistic.

LOGISTICS, [lo-jist'-iks], *n.(pl.)* subtle argumentation; arithmetical computation; the arithmetic of sexagesimal fractions.

LOGLINE, [log'-līn], *n.* (*naut.*) the long knotted line or cord fastened to the log-ship by means of two legs.

LOGMAN, [log'-man], *n.* a man employed in cutting up and carrying away logs.

LOGO-, *pref.* words, speech, reason. [Gk. *logos*].

LOGOGRAM, [log'-ō-gram], *n.* a sign which stands for a whole word; a puzzle in verse made up of anagrams composed of letters in a term which must be found out. [LOGO and Gk. *gramma* a letter].

LOGOGRIPH, [log'-ō-grif], *n.* an enigma or riddle based on an anagram; a logogram. [LOGO and Gk. *griphos* riddle].

LOGOMACHY, [log-om'-ak-i], *n.* dispute about words. [LOGO and Gk. *makhe* a fight].

LOGOMANIA, [log'-ō-mā'-ni-a], *n.* an impaired faculty of speech often nervous in origin. [LOGO and MANIA].

LOGOMETER, [log-om'-it-er], *n.* (*chem.*) a scale for measuring chemical equivalents. [LOGO and METER].

LOGOMETRIC, [log'-ō-met'-rik], *adj.* serving to measure chemical equivalents graphically.

LOGOS, [log'-os], *n.* (*theol.*) the Divine Word incarnate; the active principle of the universe. [Gk. *logos* speech].

LOGOTYPE, [log'-ō-tīp], *n.* (*print.*) a type having two or more letters cast in one piece, as *ff*. [LOGO and TYPE].

LOG-REEL, [log'-rēl], *n.* (*naut.*) the reel on which the logline is wound.

LOG-ROLL, [log'-rōl], *v.i.* to collect and pile together logs ready for milling; (*fig.*) to indulge in mutual admiration.

LOG-ROLLER, [log'-rōl-er], *n.* one who practises log-rolling; a lumberman.

LOG-ROLLING, [log'-rōl'-ing], *n.* (*fig.*) mutual admiration; the practice whereby writers, etc., praise each other's work on a basis of reciprocity.

LOG-SHIP, [log'-ship], *n.* the piece of wood attached to the end of the logline.

LOG-SLATE, [log'-slāt], *n.* the slate on which the details of a ship's voyage are written down as they occur.

LOGWOOD, [log'-wood], *n.* the American tree *Haemotoxylon campechianum*; shavings of this used to make a rich red dye.

LOHOCK, [lō'-hok], *n.* (*med.*) an opaque oily linctus. [MedL. *lohoc*].

LOIMIC, [loim'-ik], *adj.* of, or pertaining to, plague or pestilence. [Gk. *loimos* plague].

LOIN, [loin], *n.(pl.)* the fleshy part of an animal or human being surrounding the fork, and connecting the abdomen with the legs or hindlegs; meat from this part eaten as food; (*fig.*) male parentage or ancestry; **to gird up one's loins,** to prepare for strenuous effort. [Fr. *loigne*].

LOITER, [loit'-er], *v.i.* to be slow in moving, to linger or delay in a suspicious manner. [Du. *leuteren*].

LOITERER, [loit'-er-er], *n.* one who loiters.

LOITERINGLY, [loit'-er-ing-li], *adv.* in a loitering manner.

LOLL, [lol], *v.t.* to allow to hang out or down; *v.i.* to lounge, sit or stand lazily about; (of the tongue) to hang out.

LOLLARD, [lol'-erd], *n.* a medieval follower of John Wyclif. [Du. *lollard* a mumbler of prayers].

LOLLARDY, [lol'-erd-i], *n.* the teaching, religious doctrine of the Lollards.

LOLLIPOP, [lol'-i-pop], *n.* (*coll.*) a hard-boiled sweet. [Uncert.].

LOLLOP, [lol'-op], *v.i.* to move with an ungainly loping gait. [LOLL].

LOLOS, [lō'-lōs], *n.(pl.)* an aboriginal race of China, quite distinct from the Chinese, the Nersu. [Chin. *lolo*].

LOMBARD, [lom'-bahd], *n.* a native of Lombardy; a moneylender or banker, a profession first practised in London by the Lombards. [*Lombardy* in Italy].

LOMBARDY POPLAR, [lom'-berd-i-pop'-ler], *n.* a tall, conical, black poplar, *Populus nigra* var. *italica*.

LOMENTOSE, [lō-ment'-ōz], *adj.* (*bot.*) resembling a lomentum.

LOMENTUM, [lō-ment'-um], *n.* (*bot.*) a pod which separates into small cells with a seed in each. [L. *lomentum* bean meal].

LOMP, [lomp], *n.* the lump fish, *Cyclopterus lumpus*. [LUMP].

LONDONER, [lun'-dun-er], *n.* an inhabitant of London.

LONDONISM, [lun'-dun-izm], *n.* a London peculiarity of manner or speech.

LONDON PRIDE, [lun'-dun-prīd'], *n.* (*bot.*) a garden saxifrage, St. Patrick's cabbage, *Saxifraga umbrosa*.

LONE, [lōn], *adj.* lonely; solitary, single; unfrequented. [(A)LONE].

LONELINESS, [lōn'-li-nes], *n.* the state of being lonely.

LONELY, [lōn'-li], *adj.* solitary, single; standing by itself; unfrequented, remote; sad in solitude, lacking companionship.

LONENESS, [lōn'-nes], *n.* the quality of being lone.

LONESOME, [lōn'-sum], *adj.* desolate; lonely; lone.

LONESOMELY, [lōn'-sum-li], *adv.* in a lonesome state.

LONESOMENESS, [lōn'-sum-nes], *n.* the condition of being lonesome.

LONG (1), [long], *adj.* of notable extension in length

or in time; tall; lengthy, protracted; lingering, tedious; **l. face,** a dismal face; **l. firm fraud,** a form of fraud in which goods are ordered for remote or non-existent firms, and then appropriated; **l. term policy,** a policy or plan for action envisaging more than the immediate future; **l. wave,** (*wirel.*) the band of longest wave-lengths used for broadcasting; the transmission so broadcast; **in the l. run,** ultimately. [OE. *lang*].

LONG (2), [long], *adv.* to a great extent in space or time; at a point of time far distant before or after. [LONG (1)].

LONG (3), [long], *v.i.* to be filled with longing or desire; to crave (for). [OE. *langian*].

LONG-AGO, [long'-a-gō'], *n.* the distant past.

LONGAN, [long'-gan], *n.* the Indo-Malayan tree, *Nephelium longana*, cultivated for its fruit. [Chin. *longan*].

LONGANIMITY, [long'-gan-im'-i-ti], *n.* patient endurance, long suffering. [LL. *longanimitas*].

LONGBOAT, [long'-bōt], *n.* the largest and strongest boat carried on a sailing ship.

LONGBOW, [long'-bō], *n.* a powerful bow, six feet long, formerly used by English archers; **to draw the l.,** to exaggerate.

LONGBOW

LONG-BREATHED, [long'-brethd], *adj.* able to retain the breath for a long time.

LONGCLOTH, [long'-kloth], *n.* a tough cotton stuff used for sheets and household linen.

LONG-DOZEN, [long'-duz'-en], *n.* thirteen reckoned for each dozen, baker's dozen, devil's dozen.

LONGE, see LUNGE (1).

LONGER (1), [long'-ger], *adj.* greater in time or space.

LONGER (2), [long'-ger], *adv.* after or beyond a specific point in time.

LONGE-REIN, see LUNGE-REIN.

LONGEST, [long'-gest], *adj.* greatest in time or space.

LONGEVAL, [lon-jē'-val], *adj.* long-lived.

LONGEVITY, [lon-jev'-i-ti], *n.* great length of life. [L. *longaevitas*].

LONGEVOUS, [lon-jē'-vus], *adj.* long-lived. [L. *longaevus*].

LONG-FIELD, [long'-fēld], *n.* (*cricket*) the fielder at cricket well behind, and to one side of, the bowler.

LONGHAND, [long'-hand], *n.* ordinary handwriting, as distinguished from shorthand.

LONG-HEADED, [long-hed'-id], *adj.* having a head that is long in proportion; dolichocephalic; (*fig.*) of great discernment.

LONG-HOP, [long-hop'], *n.* (*cricket*) a short-pitched ball which makes a long bounce.

LONG-HUNDRED, [long-hun'-dred], *n.* one hundred and twenty.

LONGI-, *pref.* long. [L. *longus*].

LONGICORN, [lon'-ji-kawn'], *n.* (*zool.*) one of the large beetles so named on account of their long antennae. [LONGI and L. *cornu* horn].

LONGILATERAL, [lon'-ji-lat'-er-al], *adj.* having long sides. [LONGI and LATERAL].

LONGIMANOUS, [lon-jim'-an-us], *adj.* long-handed. [LONGI and L. *manus* hand].

LONGING (1), [long'-ing], *n.* eager desire, yearning.

LONGING (2), [long'-ing], *adj.* desiring earnestly, yearning.

LONGINGLY, [long'-ing-li], *adv.* in a longing manner.

LONGIPENNATE, [lon'-ji-pen'-at], *adj.* having long wings. [LONGI and PENNATE].

LONGIROSTRAL, [lon'-ji-ros'-tral], *adj.* having a long beak. [LONGI and L. *rostrum* beak].

LONGISH, [long'-ish], *adj.* somewhat long.

LONGITUDE, [lon'-ji-tewd], *n.* (*geog.*) distance of a place east or west from a given meridian, usually that of Greenwich, expressed in degrees; (*astron.*) distance from the vernal equinox reckoned eastward on the ecliptic. [L. *longitudo*].

LONGITUDINAL, [lon'-ji-tewd'-in-al], *adj.* lengthwise.

LONGITUDINALLY, [lon'-ji-tewd'-in-al-i], *adv.* in a longitudinal direction; lengthwise.

LONG-MEASURE, [long'-mezh'-ur], *n.* lineal measure.

LONG-MOSS, [long'-mos], *n.* a lichen of the genus *Tillandsia*, Spanish moss.

LONG PRIMER, [long'-prim'-er], *n.* (*print.*) a printing type intermediate in size between small pica and bourgeois.

LONGSHOREMAN, [long-shaw'-er-man], *n.* a man who earns his living in or about boats along the shore.

LONG-SIGHTED, [long-sīt'-id], *adj.* able to see at a great distance; (*fig.*) wise, provident, sagacious; (*med.*) seeing only distant objects distinctly, hyperopic.

LONG-SIGHTEDNESS, [long-sīt'-id-nes], *n.* the quality of being long-sighted.

LONGSOME, [long'-sum], *adj.* tiresome, tedious, lengthy.

LONG-STOP, [long'-stop], *n.* (*cricket*) the player who fields behind the wicket-keeper.

LONG-SUFFERING (1), [long'-suf'-er-ing], *n.* patience in adversity, kindly tolerance.

LONG-SUFFERING (2), [long'-suf'-er-ing], *adj.* patient in adversity, kind.

LONGTAIL, [long'-tāl], *n.* a long-tailed animal, *esp.* a horse or dog; a pheasant; (*naut.*) a Chinaman.

LONG-TAILED, [long'-tāld], *adj.* having a long tail.

LONG-TONGUED, [long'-tungd], *adj.* prating, babbling.

LONGUEUR, [lawng-gur'], *n.* a tedious passage in a book, play, etc.; tedium. [Fr. *longueur*].

LONG-VISAGED, [long-viz'-ijd], *adj.* long-faced.

LONGWAYS, [long'-wāz], *adv.* lengthwise, longitudinally.

LONG-WINDED, [long-wind'-id], *adj.* long-breathed; tediously eloquent.

LONICERA, [lō-nis'-er-a], *n.* the honeysuckle genus of plants. [A. *Lonicer* (1528-1586) a German botanist].

LOO (1), [lōō], *n.* a round card game involving forfeits, the forfeit paid in it. [†*Lanterloo* from Fr. *lanturlu* refrain of a song].

LOO (2), [lōō], *v.t.* to subject to a forfeit at the game of loo.

LOOBY, [lōōb'-i], *n.* (*dial.*) an awkward young man; a lout. [LUBBER].

LOOF, [lōōf], *n.* (*dial.*) the palm of the hand; the rounded part of a ship's bow. [OIcel. *lofi*].

LOOFAH, [lōōf'-a], *n.* the fibrous part of the fruit of the towel-gourd, a species of *Luffa*, used as a washing-sponge. [Arab. *lufah*].

LOOK (1), [lŏŏk], *n.* the act of looking; a consciously directed glance of the eyes; a peep, a brief inspection; appearance; mien; aspect, expression.

LOOK (2), [lŏŏk], *v.t. and i.* to direct the eye at an object; to direct the mind or attention to; to convey an impression with the eyes; to appear, seem; to take care; to search; to expect, hope; **to l. after,** to care for; **to l. down on,** to despise; **to l. at,** to consider; to examine; **to l. for,** to expect; **to l. on,** to remain inactive; **to l. out,** to take care; **to l. up,** (*coll.*) to visit; to improve; to consult in a book or books. [OE. *locian*].

LOOKER, [lŏŏk'-er], *n.* a person who looks; **a good l.,** (*coll.*) a handsome person.

LOOKER-ON, [lŏŏk'-er-on'], *n.* a spectator.

LOOKING, [lŏŏk'-ing], *adj.* having a specified appearance.

LOOKING-GLASS, [lŏŏk'-ing-glahs'], *n.* a mirror.

LOOK-OUT, [lŏŏk'-owt], *n.* a careful watching for someone or something; a person keeping such a watch; a place to look out from.

LOOK-SEE, [lŏŏk'-sē], *n.* (*slang*) a glance, a survey.

LOOM (1), [lōōm], *n.* a weaving machine; the shaft of an oar inboard. [ME. *lome* tool, utensil].

LOOM (2), [lōōm], *v.i.* to appear above the horizon; to appear suddenly, and as though magnified, before the gaze; to appear dimly in the distance. [Unkn.].

LOOM-GALE, [lōōm'-gāl], *n.* (*dial.*) a gentle gale of wind.

LOOMING, [lōōm'-ing], *adj.* that looms up suddenly; menacing.

LOON (1), [lōōn], *n.* a worthless fellow; a boor; (*slang*) a foolish person. [Scots *lown*].

LOON (2), [lōōn], *n.* (*ornith.*) the great northern diver, *Colymbus glacialis*; any species of *Colymbus*. [OIcel. *lomr*].

LOONING, [lōōn'-ing], *n.* the cry of the loon.

LOONY, [lōōn'-i], *adj.* (*slang*) mad, crazy; **l. bin,** (*slang*) an asylum for mentally deficient persons. [LUNATIC].

LOOP (1), [lōōp], *n.* the doubled part of a string, chain, etc.; a noose through which a cord may be run for fastening; a bend; a bight; (*railway*) a loop-line. [ME. *loop*].

LOOP (2), [lōōp], *n.* a loophole.

LOOP (3), [lōōp], *v.t.* to form into a loop; to fasten with a loop; *v.i.* to form a loop or loops; **to l. the l.,** to describe a vertical circle in the air in an aeroplane.

LOOPED, [lōōpt], *adj.* coiled in a loop or loops; furnished with a loop or loops; having loopholes.

LOOPER, [lōōp'-er], *n.* a hook that loops, anything or anyone that loops; the caterpillar of the geometer moth which, in moving along, forms its body into loops.

LOOPHOLE, [lo͞op'-hōl], *n.* a hole in a wall or in the bulkhead of a ship, through which small arms may be discharged; (*fig.*) a way or means of escape. [~MDu. *lupen* to peer].

LOOPHOLED, [lo͞op'-hōld], *adj.* having loopholes.

LOOP-LINE, [lo͞op'-lin], *n.* a railway line which branches from the main line and then rejoins it at another point.

LOOSE (1), [lo͞os], *adj.* unbound, not under restraint, able to move; not compact; not close or tight, having play; not stretched tight, slack; unpacked; inaccurate; (of speech) licentious or merely approximate; (of conduct) lax; not strict; not securely fixed in place; not firm; (*med.*) subject to a flux from the bowels; **at a l. end,** unoccupied, idle. [OScand. *lōuss* free].

LOOSE (2), [lo͞os], *adv.* loosely; **fast and l.,** rashly.

LOOSE (3), [lo͞os], *v.t.* to unfasten; to free from fastenings, restraint or obligation; to liberate; to absolve, remit; to discharge, fire a weapon.

LOOSE-BOX, [lo͞os'-boks], *n.* a stable in which a horse may remain loose.

LOOSE-LEAF, [lo͞os'-lēf'], *adj.* (of a ledger, notebook) with each leaf separate and detachable.

LOOSELY, [lo͞os'-li], *adv.* in a loose manner.

LOOSEN, [lo͞os'-en], *v.t.* and *i.* to make or become loose or looser; **to l. up,** to become more expansive in conversation.

LOOSENESS, [lo͞os'-nes], *n.* the condition of being loose.

LOOSESTRIFE, [lo͞os'-strīf'], *n.* (*bot.*) a plant of the genus *Lysimachia*, or *Lythrum salicaria*.

LOOT (1), [lo͞ot], *n.* plunder, booty; proceeds of war; (*coll.*) any financial return. [Hindi *lut*].

LOOT (2), [lo͞ot], *v.t.* and *i.* to plunder; to take as loot.

LOOTER, [lo͞ot'-er], *n.* one who loots.

LOOTING, [lo͞o'-ting], *n.* plundering.

LOP (1), [lop], *n.* that which is cut from a tree; the action of cutting. [Unkn.].

LOP (2), (lopping, lopped), [lop], *v.t.* to chop; to shorten by cutting off a part, to curtail, *esp.* of trees. [Unkn.].

LOP (3), (lopping, lopped), [lop], *v.t.* to let fall; *v.i.* to hang down, to droop; to move along jerkily. [Echoic].

LOPE, [lōp], *v.i.* to run with a long, leisurely, effortless stride. [OScand. *hloupa* to leap].

LOP-EARED, [lop'-ēerd], *adj.* having pendulous ears.

LOPHOBRANCHIATE, [lō'-fō-brang'-ki-āt], *adj.* with tufted gills like the sea-horses. [Gk. *lophos* a crest and BRANCHIATE].

LOPPER (1), [lop'-er], *n.* a trimmer of trees.

LOPPER (2), [lop'-er], *v.i.* (of milk) to curdle, turn sour. [OIcel. *hloup* coagulated milk].

LOPPING, [lop'-ing], *n.* that which is cut off.

LOPSIDED, LAPSIDED†, [lop-sīd'-id], *adj.* asymmetrical, heavier or larger on one side than the other. [LOP and SIDED].

LOPSIDEDLY, [lop'-sīd'-ed-li], *adv.* so as to appear lopsided, in lopsided fashion.

LOQUACIOUS, [lō-kwā'-shus], *adj.* talkative; eloquent. [L. *loquax*].

LOQUACIOUSLY, [lō-kwā'-shus-li], *adv.* in a loquacious manner.

LOQUACIOUSNESS, [lō-kwā'-shus-nes], *n.* the quality of being loquacious.

LOQUACITY, [lō-kwas'-i-ti], *n.* loquaciousness.

LOQUAT, [lō'-kwat], *n.* an Asiatic tree of the genus *Eriobotrya*, bearing a small fruit. [Chin. *luh kwat* rush orange].

LORATE, [law'-rāt], *adj.* (*bot.*) shaped like a strap. [L. *loratus*].

LORCHA, [law'-cha], *n.* a Chinese vessel of European build, which is rigged like a junk. [Portug. *lorcha*].

LORD (1), [lawd], *n.* one who controls inferiors and is venerated by them; God; a feudal superior; a peer; title of address of certain ranks of the aristocracy and hierarchy, and of certain high officials, as judges, etc.; **the Lords,** the upper chamber of Parliament; **L. Chancellor,** the chief judge of England; **L. Mayor,** the mayor of certain important cities in England; **L. Rector,** the elected head of certain Scottish universities; **Our L.,** the second person of the Trinity; **L. of the Bedchamber,** an official attending on the Sovereign's person; **my L.,** a form of address to bishops and peers below a duke; **the L. of hosts,** God; **good l.,** a common exclamation of surprise. [OE. *hlaford*].

LORD (2), [lawd], *v.i.* to domineer; **to l. it over,** to behave arrogantly to.

LORDLINESS, [lawd'-li-nes], *n.* the quality of being lordly.

LORDLING, [lawd'-ling], *n.* a young or unimportant lord.

LORDLY, [lawd'-li], *adj.* becoming or befitting a lord; haughty, imperious; lavish, sumptuous.

LORDOSIS, [lawd-ō'-sis], *n.* (*anat.*) curvature of the bones, *esp.* forward curvature of the spine. [Gk. *lordosis*].

LORDS-AND-LADIES, [lawdz'-and-lā'-diz], *n.* the wild arum lily, *Arum maculatum*.

LORDSHIP, [lawd'-ship], *n.* the domain, rule, power of a lord; the form used in speaking of a nobleman.

LORE (1), [law(r)], *n.* teaching, instruction; knowledge gained from reading or tradition; abstruse or specialized knowledge. [OE. *lar*].

LORE (2), [law(r)], *n.* the space between a bird's bill and its eye; the space between the nostril and the eye of a snake. [L. *lorum* strap].

LORETTE, [lo-ret'], *n.* a stylish prostitute. [Fr. *lorette*].

LORGNETTE, [lawn-yet'], *n.* a pair of eye-glasses on a long handle. [Fr. *lorgner* to squint].

LORICA, [lo-rī'-ka], *n.* a cuirass or corslet. [L. *lorica*].

LORICATE, [lor'-ik-āt], *v.t.* to plate or coat over, *esp.* for defence, to encrust. [L. *loricare*].

LORICATION, [lor'-ik-ā'-shun], *n.* the act of loricating.

LORIKEET, [lor'-i-kēt], *n.* a small lory, an Australian parrot having an extensile tongue. [LORY and KEET].

LORINER, LORIMER, [lor'-in-er], *n.* a maker of bits and the metal parts of horse furniture. [OFr. *loremier*].

LORGNETTE

LORIOT, [lo'-ri-ot], *n.* the golden oriole, *Oriolus galbula*. [Fr. *loriot*].

LORIS, [lor'-is], *n.* the slow, tailless lemur of Eastern India and the Malay Archipelago, *Nycticebus tardigradus*. [Du. *loeris*].

LORN, [lawn], *adj.* forlorn, lost, undone; forsaken. [ME. *loren*, *p.pt.* of *leesen* to lose].

LORRY, [lo'-ri], *n.* a large strongly-built motor or steam wagon for haulage work. [Unkn.].

LORY, [lo'-ri], *n.* the lorikeet.

LOSABLE, [lo͞oz'-abl], *adj.* that may be lost.

LOSE, (loses, lost), [lo͞oz], *v.t.* to cease to have, to be deprived of possession of; to fail to obtain or win; to destroy; to waste, squander; to cause to perish; to miss; to bewilder; to fail to see or find; *v.i.* to be beaten in a contest; **l. oneself,** to be bewildered, to be deeply absorbed in. [OE. *losian*].

LOSEL†, [loz'-el], *n.* a wasteful or worthless fellow. [ME. *losel*].

LOSER, [lo͞oz'-er], *n.* one who loses; (*billiards*) a losing hazard.

LOSING, [lo͞oz'-ing], *adj.* bringing or causing loss; **l. hazard,** (*billiards*) a stroke in which the cue ball strikes another, and then falls into a pocket.

LOSINGLY, [lo͞oz'-ing-li], *adv.* in a losing fashion.

LOSS, [los], *n.* failure to keep or win; the act or result of losing; damage, waste; that which is lost, or its monetary equivalent; (*milit.*) amount destroyed or killed. [OE. *los*].

LOST, [lost], *adj.* that cannot be found or seen, missing; forfeited, wasted; perplexed, bewildered; ruined; wrecked or drowned at sea; damned, morally abandoned. [LOSE].

LOT, [lot], *n.* chance; destiny, fate; that which falls to one by fortune; a distinct portion or parcel, *esp.* at an auction; a group considered collectively; (*coll.*) a great deal; (*coll.*) a person; **to cast or draw lots,** to decide by throwing dice or drawing one from a number of objects. [OE. *hlot*].

LOTA, [lō'-ta], *n.* a globe-shaped Indian copper or brazen water-vessel. [Hind. *lota*].

LOTH, [lōth], *adj.* unwilling, reluctant. [OE. *loth*].

LOTHARIO, [lō-thah'-ri-ō], *n.* a handsome libertine, a rake. [*Lothario*, a character in "The Fair Penitent," by N. Rowe].

LOTION, [lō'-shun], *n.* (*med.*) a fluid medicinal preparation for outward application. [L. *lotio*].

LOTOS, see LOTUS.

LOTTERY, [lot'-er-i], *n.* a scheme for the distribution of prizes by lot; an outcome which depends largely on chance. [It. *lotteria*].

LOTTO, [lot'-ō], *n.* a table game of chance, in which numbers are drawn from a bag and placed on cards having numbered spaces. [It. *lotto*].

LOTUS, LOTOS, [lō'-tus], *n.* a large genus of

leguminous plants including the bird's-foot trefoil, *Lotus corniculatus*; the sacred Egyptian water-lily, *Nympha Lotus*; a tree or plant, of unspecified identity, frequently referred to by the ancient writers. [Gk. *lotos*].

LOTUS-EATER, [lō'-tus-ēt'-er], *n.* (*Gk. antiq.*) a member of a fabulous race of people who lived a life of dreamy enjoyment; (*fig.*) one who lives in a dreamy, blissful state.

LOUD (1), [lowd], *adj.* characterized by perceptible or considerable noise; hard and pronounced in sound; noisy, clamorous; (*fig.*) in bad taste, vulgarly gaudy. [OE. *hlud*].

LOUD (2), [lowd], *adv.* in a loud manner; aloud.

LOUDLY, [lowd'-li], *adv.* in loud fashion.

LOUDNESS, [lowd'-nes], *n.* the quality of being loud.

LOUD-SPEAKER, [lowd'-spēk'-er], *n.* a vibrant instrument for converting electrical impulses into sound vibrations similar in intensity to those of everyday life; an amplifier.

LOUGH, [lokh], *n.* a lake, a long arm of the sea. [Ir *lough*].

LOUIS-D'OR, [lōō'-i-daw(r)], *n.* a French gold coin, now obsolete, worth twenty francs; (*coll.*) twenty francs. [Fr. *louis d'or*].

LOUKOUM, [lō'-ōō-kōōm], *n.* a sweetmeat of Eastern origin, Turkish delight. [Turk. *loukoum*].

LOUNGE (1), [lownj], *n.* the act of lounging; a comfortably but informally furnished sitting-room, *esp.* in a club or hotel; a couch or sofa; **l. coat**, a lady's jacket for indoor wear; **l. lizard**, a useless, effeminate man; **l. suit**, a suit for informal morning wear.

LOUNGE (2), [lownj], *v.i.* to recline in a lazy manner; to loll comfortably; to walk in a slovenly, lazy manner. [Uncert.].

LOUNGER, [lownj'-er], *n.* one who lounges; an idler.

LOUR, LOWER, [low'-er], *v.i.* to look threatening, frown; (of the sky) to threaten, to be stormy and overcast. [ME. *louren*].

LOUSE, (*pl.* **lice**), [lows], *n.* a small insect, *esp.* of the genus *Pediculus*, parasitic on man, etc. [OE. *lus*].

LOUSEWORT, [lows'-wurt], *n.* a plant of the genus *Pedicularis*.

LOUSILY, [lowz'-i-li], *adv.* (*coll.*) in lousy fashion.

LOUSINESS, [lowz'-i-nes], *n.* the quality of being lousy.

LOUSY, [low'-zi], *adj.* infested with lice; (*coll.*) extremely poor or bad; highly unpleasant.

LOUT, [lowt], *n.* a mean, awkward fellow; a clumsy country bumpkin. [~OE. *lutan* to bow].

LOUTISH, [lowt'-ish], *adj.* like a lout; clumsy, boorish, awkward.

LOUTISHLY, [lowt'ish-li], *adv.* in loutish fashion.

LOUTISHNESS, [lowt'-ish-nes], *n.* the state of being loutish.

LOUVRE, [lōō'-ver], *n.* an open turret or lantern on ancient roofs, originally for the escape of smoke, now often glazed as a skylight; **l. window**, an opening, usually in belfries, crossed by sloping bars of wood, for ventilation or light. [OFr. *lover*].

LOVABLE, [luv'-abl], *adj.* worthy of love; amiable; endearing; attractive.

LOVAGE, [luv'-ij], *n.* a plant of the genus *Ligusticum*; a cordial made from this. [ME. *love-ache*].

LOVE (1), [luv], *n.* intense spiritual attraction towards an object, affection; benevolence, charity, goodwill; self-sacrifice, self-abnegation; the object beloved; a word of endearment; (*tennis, etc.*) no score, nothing. **to give (one's) l. to**, to send affectionate greetings to. [OE. *lufu*].

LOVE (2), [luv], *v.t.* to experience love for; to like very much; to regard with affection; *v.i.* to have the feeling of love. [OE. *lufian*].

LOVE-APPLE, [luv'-apl], *n.* the tomato, *Lycopersicum esculentum*.

LOVEBIRD, [luv'-burd], *n.* a small parrakeet, so named from its affection for its mate, the budgerigar; (*slang*) a lover.

LOVE-CHILD, [luv'-child], *n.* an illegitimate child.

LOVE-FAVOUR, [luv'-fā'-ver], *n.* something given to be worn as a sign of love.

LOVE-FEAST, [luv'-fēst], *n.* (among the early Christians) a meal partaken of in fellowship, the agape; (among Methodists, etc.) a feast in imitation of the agape.

LOVEBIRD

LOVE-IN-A-MIST, [luv'-in-a-mist'], *n.* the fennel flower, a species of *Nigella*.

LOVE-IN-IDLENESS, [luv'-in-īdl'-nes], *n.* heartsease, *Viola tricolor*.

LOVE-KNOT, [luv'-not], *n.* a double knot made up of interlacing bows.

LOVELACE, [luv'-lās], *n.* a well-bred libertine. [*Lovelace*, the hero of "Clarissa" by S. Richardson].

LOVELESS, [luv'-les], *adj.* loving or loved by no one; without love

LOVE-LETTER, [luv'-let'-er], *n.* a tender letter between lovers.

LOVE-LIES-BLEEDING, [luv'-līz-blēd'-ing], *n.* the cultivated plant *Amaranthus caudatus*.

LOVELILY, [luv'-li-li], *adv.* in a lovely way; (*coll.*) very well.

LOVELINESS, [luv'-li-nes], *n.* the condition of being lovely.

LOVE-LOCK, [luv'-lok], *n.* a curl worn by men of fashion in the reign of Elizabeth and James I; any curl trained to lie on the forehead or hang down on the cheek.

LOVE-LORN, [luv'-lawn], *adj.* forsaken by one's lover; jilted; forlorn.

LOVELY, [luv'-li], *adj.* such as to excite love or admiration; beautiful, charming, pretty; (*coll.*) delightful, splendid.

LOVE-MAKING, [luv'-māk-ing], *n.* courtship, amorous intercourse.

LOVEMAN, [luv'-man], *n.* the plant, *Galium Aparine*.

LOVER, [luv'-er], *n.* one who loves; a person carrying on an illicit love-affair.

LOVERLIKE, [luv'-er-līk], *adj.* typical of, befitting, a lover.

LOVE-SHAFT, [luv'-shahft], *n.* the shaft of love, a symbol, the arrow or dart.

LOVESICK, [luv'-sik], *adj.* languishing for love.

LOVE-SONG, [luv'-song], *n.* a song of love.

LOVE STORY, [luv'-staw'-ri], *n.* a story treating of a person or persons in love.

LOVE-TOKEN, [luv'-tōk'-en], *n.* a token of affection.

LOVING, [luv'-ing], *adj.* animated by love, expressing love for; dutiful, affectionate.

LOVING-KINDNESS, [luv'-ing-kīnd'-nes], *n.* a deep and tender regard; mercy.

LOVINGLY, [luv'-ing-li], *adv.* in a loving manner.

LOVINGNESS, [luv'-ing-nes], *n.* the quality of being loving.

LOW (1), [lō], *n.* the cry of the ox or cow [LOW (5)].

LOW† (2), [lō], *n.* a burial mound. [OE. *hlaw*].

LOW (3), [lō], *adj.* not high, not extending far above any surface; below the usual height; (of a sound) soft and deep; depressed in vigour, in poor health; dejected, miserable; poverty-stricken, mean; humble, poor; vulgar, base; immoral; indecent; submissive; weak, feeble; unfavourable; (*biol.*) primitive; (*eccles.*) belonging to the Low Church party; **L. Church**, the Evangelical party in the Church of England; **l. water**, the ebb; (*coll.*) financial straits. [OIcel. *lagr*].

LOW (4), [lō], *adv.* not in a high position, near the ground; in a low voice or pitch; meanly, in a state of poverty, subjection, or disgrace; **to lie l.**, to keep quietly hidden, or inconspicuous. [LOW (3)].

LOW (5), [low], *v.i.* to utter the characteristic sound of an ox or cow. [OE. *hlowan*].

LOW-BELL, [lō'-bel'], *n.* the act of fowling in the night with the aid of light and bells.

LOW-BORN, [lō'-bawn], *adj.* of humble birth.

LOWBROW (1), [lō'-brow], *n.* a non-intellectual person. [LOW (3) and BROW].

LOWBROW (2), [lō-'brow], *adj.* relating to a lowbrow, his interests and tastes.

LOW-DOWN (1), [lō'-down'], *n.* (*slang*) inside information; full details.

LOW-DOWN (2), [lō'-down], *adj.* (*coll.*) mean, dishonourable.

LOWER (1), [lō'-er], *adj.* more low; **l. animals**, all mammals except man; **l. case**, (*print.*) the case which contains the small letters; the small letters; **L. Chamber, L. House**, the House of Commons; **l. classes**, the poor, the working people; **l. regions**, hell; (*coll.*) the basement.

LOWER (2), [lō'-er], *v.t. and i.* to let down; to bring down; to reduce; to diminish in pitch, price, etc.; (*fig.*) to humble.

LOWER (3), see LOUR.

LOWERING, [low'-er-ing], *adj.* cloudy, heavy and threatening.

LOWERINGLY, [low'-er-ing-li], *adv.* in a lowering manner.

LOWERMOST, [lō'-er-mōst], *adj.* the very lowest.

LOWERY, [low'-er-i], *adj.* cloudy, gloomy.

ō (bone), ī (fine), ōō (food), ŏŏ (put), u (up), th (*th*ink), TH (*th*at), zh (a*z*ure), † = obsolete, ~ = related to.

LOWING (1), [lō'-ing], *n.* the sound made by an ox or cow.

LOWING (2), [lō'-ing], *adj.* mooing as a cow, or bellowing as an ox.

LOWLAND (1), [lō'-land], *n.* a flat, low lying country; **the Lowlands,** the southern counties of Scotland.

LOWLAND (2), [lō'-land], *adj.* pertaining to low-lying country; pertaining to the Lowlands of Scotland.

LOWLANDER, [lō'-land-er], *n.* an inhabitant of the lowlands; a native of the Lowlands of Scotland.

LOWLILY, [lō'-li-li], *adv.* in lowly fashion.

LOWLINESS, [lō'-li-nes], *n.* the condition of being lowly.

LOWLY, [lō'-li], *adj.* of humble birth; (*fig.*) meek, humble, modest. [ME. *louly*].

LOW MASS, [lō'-mas'], *n.* (*eccles.*) mass celebrated without music and with the minimum of ceremonial.

LOW-MINDED, [lō'-mīnd'-id], *adj.* base, mean; prurient.

LOW-NECKED, [lō'-nekt], *adj.* (of a garment) cut so as to lay bare the neck, shoulders, and part of the chest.

LOWNESS, [lō'-nes], *n.* the condition of being low.

LOW-PRESSURE, [lō'-presh'-er], *adj.* (*eng.*) (of steam) exerting a pressure on the piston of less than 50 lb. to the square inch; (of a steam engine) employing such a pressure.

LOW-SPIRITED, [lō'-spir'-it-id], *adj.* depressed in spirits; dejected.

LOXODROMIC, [lok'-sō-drom'-ik], *adj.* (*naut.*) relating to oblique sailing by the rhumb line; **l. curve,** a line which always makes an equal angle with every meridian. [Gk. *loxos* crooked and *dromos* course].

LOXODROMICS, [lok'-sō-drom'-iks], *n.(pl.)* the craft of oblique sailing by the rhumb line.

LOY, [loi], *n.* a long narrow spade used in Ireland. [Ir. *laighe*].

LOYAL, [loi'-al], *adj.* faithful in allegiance or in any duty or affection, *esp.* as a subject or soldier of the crown. [OFr. *loial*].

LOYALIST, [loi'-al-ist], *adj.* one who is loyal to the Government in a rebellion.

LOYALLY, [loi'-al-i], *adv.* in a loyal manner.

LOYALTY, [loi'-al-ti], *n.* the quality of being loyal. [OFr. *loialté*].

LOZENGE, [loz'-enj], *n.* a figure with four equal sides and two acute and two obtuse angles, a rhomb; anything similarly shaped; a flat, small, thin pastille or cake that can be dissolved by sucking; (*her.*) a square figure set diagonally. [Fr. *losange*].

LOZENGE

LOZENGE-SHAPED, [loz'-enj-shāpt'], *adj.* having the shape of a lozenge, rhombic.

LOZENGY, [loz'-enj-i], *adj.* (*her.*) divided lozengewise.

LUBBER, [lub'-er], *n.* an awkward clumsy fellow; (*naut.*) a clumsy seaman. [~OFr. *lobeor* swindler].

LUBBERLY, [lub'-er-li], *adv.* in the manner of a lubber.

LUBRA, [lo͝ob'-rah], *n.* an Australian aboriginal woman. [Australian *lubra*].

LUBRICANT (1), [lo͞o'-brik-ant], *n.* an oil or grease used for lubricating purposes.

LUBRICANT (2), [lo͞o'-brik-ant], *adj.* lubricating. [L. *lubricans*].

LUBRICATE, [lo͞o'-brik-āt], *v.t. and i.* to make slippery or smooth; to treat with grease or oil so as to lessen friction; (*slang*) to bribe; to cause to unbend by filling with drink. [L. *lubricare*].

LUBRICATION, [lo͞o'-brik-ā'-shun], *n.* the action of lubricating; lubricating system.

LUBRICATOR, [lo͞o'-brik-āt'-er], *n.* a person who lubricates; a lubricant; an instrument for oiling machinery.

LUBRICITY, [lo͞o-bris'-i-ti], *n.* smoothness, slipperiness; instability; propensity to lewdness, salaciousness. [L. *lubricitas*].

LUBRICOUS, [lo͞o'-brik-us], *adj.* slippery, unstable. [L. *lubricus*].

LUCAN, [lo͞ok'-an], *adj.* pertaining to St. Luke, or the third Gospel and the Acts.

LUCARNE, [lo͞o-kahn'], *n.* a dormer window, a skylight. [Fr. *lucarne*].

LUCCA OIL, [lu'-ka-oil'], *n.* a fine olive oil. [*Lucca*, in Italy, where produced].

LUCE, [lews], *n.* a full-grown pike, *Esox lucius*; a lily. [LL. *lucius*].

LUCENT, [lo͞os'-ent], *adj.* bright, shining; clear, transparent. [L. *lucens*].

LUCERNAL, [lo͞o-sur'-nal], *adj.* pertaining to a lamp. [L. *lucerna* lamp].

LUCERNE, [lo͞o-surn'], *n.* a clover-like plant cultivated for fodder, *Medicago sativa*, alfalfa. [Provenç. *luserno*].

LUCID, [lo͞o'-sid], *adj.* shining, bright; clear, transparent; easily understood; sane, reasonable; clear-thinking. [L. *lucidus*].

LUCIDITY, [lo͞o-sid'-i-ti], *n.* lucidness.

LUCIDLY, [lo͞o'-sid-li], *adv.* in a lucid manner.

LUCIDNESS, [lo͞o'-sid-nes], *n.* the quality of being lucid.

LUCIFER, [lo͞o'-si-fer], *n.* the planet Venus, as morning star; Satan, before his fall; a match tipped with some inflammable substance, and ignited by friction; a Mexican humming-bird, *Trochilus lucifer*. [L. *lucifer* light-bearer].

LUCIFERIAN, [lo͞o'-si-fēer'-i-an], *adj.* pertaining to Lucifer.

LUCIFEROUS, [lo͞o-sif'-er-us], *adj.* bringing light.

LUCK, [luk], *n.* mere chance, unexpected and undeserved fortune; good fortune. [Du. *luk*].

LUCKILY, [luk'-i-li], *adv.* in a lucky manner; fortunately.

LUCKINESS, [luk'-i-nes], *n.* the quality of being lucky.

LUCKLESS, [luk'-les], *adj.* having no luck, unfortunate.

LUCKLESSLY, [luk'-les-li], *adv.* in luckless fashion.

LUCK-PENNY, [luk'-pen'-i], *n.* a small sum returned to the buyer by the seller "for luck."

LUCKY, [luk'-i], *adj.* having good luck, fortunate; productive of good luck; auspicious.

LUCRATIVE, [lo͞o'-krat-iv], *adj.* bringing gain, profitable. [L. *lucrari* to gain].

LUCRATIVELY, [lo͞o'-krat-iv-li], *adv.* in lucrative fashion.

LUCRE, [lo͞o'-ker], *n.* money, gain, *esp.* base gain; **filthy l.,** ill-gotten money; mere money. [L. *lucrum*].

LUCUBRATE, [lo͞o'-kyo͞o-brāt], *v.i.* to do literary or learned work by artificial light, spending great pains on it; to discourse learnedly. [L. *lucubrare* to work by light].

LUCUBRATION, [lo͞o'-ko͞o-brā'-shun], *n.* work produced as the results of laborious study. [L. *lucubratio*].

LUCUBRATORY†, [lo͞o'-ko͞o-brāt'-er-i], *adj.* composed by candle-light or by night; meditative.

LUCULENT, [lo͞o'-kyo͞o-lent], *adj.* full of light, transparent. [L. *luculens*].

LUCULLIAN, [lo͞o-kul'-yan], *adj.* pertaining to, or resembling, *Lucullus* and his sumptuous feasts.

LUCULLITE, [lo͞o-kul'-īt], *n.* a variety of black marble introduced into Rome by *Lucullus*.

LUDDITE, [lud'-īt], *n.* one of those who protested against the introduction of textile machinery into England by rioting and smashing the machines. [King (or Captain) *Ludd*, the nickname of the leader of these riots].

LUDICROUS, [lo͞o'-dik-rus], *adj.* suited to raise laughter; funny, laughable, ridiculous. [L. *ludicrus*].

LUDICROUSLY, [lo͞o'-dik-rus-li], *adv.* in a ludicrous manner.

LUDICROUSNESS, [lo͞o'-dik-rus-nes], *n.* the quality of being ludicrous.

LUDLAMITE, [lud'-lam-īt], *n.* hydrated phosphate of iron. [H. *Ludlam* the mineralogist].

LUDO, [lo͞o'-dō], *n.* a game played with counters which are moved forward along a marked board according to the throw of the dice. [L. *ludo* I play].

LUDWIGITE, [lo͞od'-vig-īt], *n.* borate of iron and magnesium. [Prof. E. *Ludwig* an Austrian scientist].

LUES, [lo͞o'-ēz], *n.* (*med.*) a plague, pestilence; syphilis. [L. *lues*].

LUFF (1), [luf], *n.* the act of luffing; the weather leech of a sail; the loof. [Du. *loef*].

LUFF (2), [luf], *v.i.* to sail near the wind. [Du. *loeven*].

LUFFER, [luf'-er], *n.* a louvre.

LUFF-TACKLE, [luf'-takl], *n.* (*naut.*) a large tackle, consisting of a double and single block.

LUFTWAFFE, [lo͞oft'-vuf-a], *n.* the German Air Force. [Germ. *luftwaffe* from *luft* sky and *waffe* weapon].

LUG (1), [lug], *n.* any projection resembling an ear,

esp. on castings, etc., in machinery, for holding bolts; (*dial.*) the ear.
LUG (2), (lugging, lugged), *v.t. and i.* to draw, pull with difficulty; **to l. in,** (*fig.*) to introduce irrelevantly [~Swed. *lugga* to pull the hair].
LUGE, [lewzh], *n.* a sledge of the simplest type. [Fr. Swiss *luge*].
LUGGAGE, [lug'-ij], *n.* the baggage of a traveller.
LUGGER, [lug'-er], *n.* a small vessel carrying two or three masts and having a running bowsprit and lugsails. [Uncert.].
LUGMARK, [lug'-mahk], *n.* a mark cut in the ear of a dog or sheep to identify it.
LUGSAIL, [lug'-sāl], *n.* (*naut.*) a sail, set fore-and-aft, bent upon a yard which hangs obliquely to the mast.
LUGUBRIOUS, [lo͞o-go͞o'-bri-us], *adj.* mournful, depressed and depressing, dismal. [L. *lugubris*].
LUGUBRIOUSLY, [lo͞o-go͞o'-bri-us-li], *adv.* in lugubrious fashion.
LUGWORM, [lug'-wurm], *n.* a lobworm, a sand worm. [Uncert.].
LUKEWARM, [lo͝ok'-wawm], *adj.* moderately warm, tepid; (*fig.*) half-hearted. [ME. *leuk* pale, tepid and WARM].
LUKEWARMLY, [lo͝ok'-wawm-li], *adv.* in a lukewarm fashion.
LUKEWARMNESS, [lo͝ok'-wawm-nes], *n.* the quality of being lukewarm.
LULL (1), [lul], *n.* a period of relative calm or quiet in the midst of a storm or busy activity, a temporary slackening.
LULL (2), [lul], *v.t.* to quiet, compose; to soothe, allay; *v.i.* to subside, abate. [Swed. *lulla* to sing to sleep].
LULLABY, [lul'-a-bī], *n.* a cradle-song; (*fig.*) a soothing sound. [Echoic].
LUMBAGINOUS, [lum-bā'-jin-us], *adj.* pertaining to lumbago.
LUMBAGO, [lum-bā'-gō], *n.* (*med.*) a rheumatic affection of the loins. [L. *lumbago*].
LUMBAL, [lum'-bal], *adj.* lumbar.
LUMBAR, [lum'-ber], *adj.* pertaining to, or situated near, the loins; **l. region,** the hinder part of the body, from the false ribs down to the haunch-bone. [L *lumbaris*].
LUMBER (1), [lum'-ber], *n.* timber sawn or split for use; anything valueless and cumbersome. [*Lombard*, a pawnbroker's shop, as these were often kept by Lombards].
LUMBER (2), [lum'-ber], *v.t.* to heap together; to fill with lumber; to cut timber for sale; *v.i.* to overcrowd.
LUMBER (3), [lum'-ber]. *v.i.* to move heavily; to make a rumbling noise in moving along. [~Swed. *lomra* to roar].
LUMBERER, [lum'-ber-er], *n.* a lumberman; one engaged in cutting and gathering lumber from the forest.
LUMBERING (1), [lum'-ber-ing], *n.* the felling and sawing up of timber.
LUMBERING (2), [lum'-ber-ing], *adj.* clumsy and heavy of movement.
LUMBERMAN, [lum'-ber-man], *n.* one who cuts down trees and dresses them for the market.
LUMBER-ROOM, [lum'-ber-ro͞om'], *n.* a room in which lumber is stored.
LUMBRICAL (1), [lum'-brik-al], *n.* (*anat.*) one of the small muscles which move the fingers and toes, resembling a worm in shape. [L. *lumbricus* earthworm].
LUMBRICAL (2), [lum'-brik-al], *adj.* pertaining to, resembling, a worm; (*anat.*) pertaining to a lumbrical.
LUMBRICIFORM, [lum-bris'-i-fawm], *adj.* like a worm in shape. [L. *lumbricus* earthworm and FORM].
LUMINANT, [lo͞o'-min-ant], *adj.* luminous. [L. *luminans*].
LUMINARY, [lo͞o'-min-er-i], *n.* a body that gives off light, *esp.* a heavenly body; (*fig.*) a distinguished person, a leading light. [MedL. *luminarium*].
LUMINESCENT, [lo͞o'-min-es'-ent], *adj.* shining, giving out light. [L. *lumen* light].
LUMINIFEROUS, [lo͞o'-min-if'-er-us], *adj.* producing light; transmitting light. [L. *lumen* light and *ferre* to bear].
LUMINOSITY, [lo͞o'-min-os'-i-ti], *n.* the quality of being luminous.
LUMINOUS, [lo͞o'-min-us], *adj.* emitting or diffusing light, bright, glowing; well-lit; (*fig.*) glowing. [L. *luminosus*].
LUMINOUSLY, [lo͞o'-min-us-li], *adv.* in luminous fashion.
LUMINOUSNESS, [lo͞o'-min-us-nes], *n.* the quality of being luminous.
LUMP (1), [lump], *n.* a shapeless mass of matter; a swelling on a surface, *esp.* of the skin; a large piece; (*coll.*) a boorish lout; **l. sum,** a considerable sum of money paid as settlement on the spot; **l. sugar,** loaf sugar formed into small cubes. [ME. *lump*].
LUMP (2), [lump], *v.t.* to put or throw together unsystematically into one mass; (*coll.*) to put up with.
LUMPER, [lump'-er], *n.* a labourer who loads and unloads ships; one who lumps things together indiscriminately.
LUMPFISH, [lump'-fish], *n.* a clumsily shaped sea-fish, *Cyclopterus lumpus.*
LUMPING, [lump'-ing], *adj.* (*coll.*) large, great, heavy.
LUMPISH, [lump'-ish], *adj.* like a lump; heavy, bulky, clumsy, stupid.
LUMPISHLY, [lump'-ish-li], *adv.* in lumpish fashion.
LUMPISHNESS, [lump'-ish-nes], *n.* the quality of being lumpish.
LUMPSUCKER, [lump'-suk-er], *n.* the lumpfish.
LUMPY, [lump'-i], *adj.* full of lumps, heavy, clumsy, shapeless.
LUNACY, [lo͞on'-a-si], *n.* madness, insanity; formerly a species of intermittent madness with lucid intervals, thought to be affected by changes of the moon; extreme foolishness.
LUNAR, [lo͞on'-er], *adj.* pertaining to the moon; measured by the revolutions of the moon; resembling the moon; influenced by the moon; **l. cycle,** the period of time after which the new moons return on the same days of the year; **l. month,** the time in which the moon completes a revolution about the earth, from new moon to new moon; **l. observation,** an observation of the moon's distance from a star to find the longitude of the observer; **l. rainbow,** a rainbow caused by the refraction of the light of the moon; **l. year,** the period of twelve synodic lunar months, 354⅓ days. [L. *lunaris*].
LUNARIAN, [lo͞o-nāer'-i-an], *n.* one who specializes in the study of the moon; a dweller in the moon.
LUNARIUM, [lo͞o-nāer'-i-um], *n.* a model showing the phases of the moon. [L. *lunaris* lunar].
LUNARY (1), [lo͞on'-er-i], *n.* a fern, the moonwort, *Botrychium Lunaria*; the cruciferous plant, honesty, *Lunaria biennis.* [MedL. *lunaria*].
LUNARY (2), [lo͞on'-er-i], *adj.* lunar; monthly.
LUNATE, [lo͞on'-āt], *adj.* shaped like the moon's crescent. [L. *lunatus*].
LUNATIC (1), [lo͞on'-at-ik], *n.* a person suffering from lunacy; (*coll.*) an irresponsible fool.
LUNATIC (2), [lo͞on'-at-ik], *adj.* suffering from lunacy; devoted to the care and treatment of lunatics. [LL. *lunaticus*].
LUNATION, [lo͞on-ā'-shun], *n.* the period of time from one new moon to the next. [MedL. *lunatio*].
LUNCH (1), [lunch], *n.* luncheon. [EarlyE. *lunch* a lump].
LUNCH (2), [lunch], *v.t.* to give luncheon to; *v.i.* to have luncheon.
LUNCHEON, [lunch'-un], *n.* a meal taken at or about mid-day, originally a snack eaten between breakfast and mid-day dinner; **l. set,** a set of table doilies. [LUNCH].
LUNE, [lo͞on], *n.* anything in the shape of a half-moon or crescent. [L. *luna* moon].
LUNETTE, [lo͞on-et'], *n.* (*fort.*) an advanced work of two parallel flanks with two faces which meet to form an angle; (*farriery*) a half-horseshoe shaped like a crescent; a blinker for a horse; (*arch.*) an opening for the admission of light into a concave ceiling; a watch-glass flattened at the centre; the rounded hole in the guillotine in which the neck is laid. [Fr. *lunette* little moon].
LUNG, [lung], *n.* one of the two respiratory organs in an air-breathing animal; (*fig.*) a large open space in a city. [OE. *lungen* lungs].
LUNGE (1), LONGE, [lunj], *n.* a sudden thrust with a weapon; any movement which resembles it. [ALLONGE].
LUNGE (2), [lunj], *n.* a long rope or rein used in training a horse. [Fr. *longe*].
LUNGE (3), [lunj], *v.i.* to make a lunge. [LUNGE (1)].
LUNGE (4), [lunj], *v.t.* to exercise a horse at the end of a lunge. [LUNGE (2)].
LUNGED, [lungd], *adj.* having lungs, or similar organs.

LUNGE-REIN, LONGE-REIN, [lunj-rān], *n.* the long rein used for horsebreaking.
LUNGFISH, [lung'-fish], *n.* any species of fish which have lungs as well as gills.
LUNGI, [lōōn'-gi], *n.* a loin cloth. [Hind. *lungi*].

LUNGFISH

LUNGLESS, [lung'-les], *adj.* without lungs.
LUNGWORT, [lung'-wurt], *n.* (*bot.*) a plant of the genus *Pulmonaria,* having leaves spotted like diseased lungs; a species of lichen, *Lobaria* (*Sticta*) *pulmonaria.* [OE. *lungenwyrt*].
LUNIFORM, [lōōn'-i-fawm], *adj.* like the moon in shape. [L. *luna* moon and FORM].
LUNISOLAR, [lōōn'-i-sōl'-er], *adj.* pertaining to both sun and moon; **l. period,** a cycle of 352 years, the product of the number of years in the cycles of sun and moon. [L. *luna* moon and SOLAR].
LUNISTICE, [lewn'-i-stis], *n.* the extreme north or south point or time at which the moon reaches the limit of her course. [L. *luna* moon and *stitium* a stopping].
LUNKAH, [lungk'-ah], *n.* a cheroot of Indian tobacco. [Hind. *lankah*].
LUNT†, [lunt], *n.* a light; the match-cord used for firing cannon; a slow match. [Dan. *lont* a match].
LUNULAR, [lōōn'-yōō-ler], *adj.* shaped like a crescent.
LUNULATE, [lōōn'-yōō-lāt], *adj.* crescent-shaped, or crescent-marked.
LUNULE, [lōōn'-yōōl], *n.* (*bot., zool.*) a crescent-shaped mark. [L. *lunula* little moon].
LUNULET, [lōōn'-yōō-let], *n.* (*bot., zool.*) a small crescent-shaped mark.
LUPERCAL, [lōō'-per-kal], *n.* an annual feast of the ancient Romans held in February in honour of the god Lupercus; a grotto consecrated to Lupercus. [L. *lupercalis* of Lupercus].
LUPIN, LUPINE, [lōō'-pin], *n.* (*bot.*) a hardy genus of plants of the order *Leguminosae.* [L. *lupinus*].
LUPINE, [lew'-pīn], *adj.* like a wolf. [L. *lupinus*].
LUPINITE, [lōō'-pin-īt], *n.* a bitter substance obtained from the leaves of the white lupin.
LUPULIN, [lōō'-pyōō-lin], *n.* the bitter principle of hops; a fine yellow powder on hops, which contains this. [MdL. *lupulus* hop].
LUPULUS, [lōō'-pyōō-lus], *n.* the hop plant. [MdL. *lupulus*].
LUPUS, [lōō'-pus], *n.* a tuberculous skin disease affecting chiefly the face. [L. *lupus* wolf].
LURCH (**1**), [lurch], *n.* a sudden, unsteady, sideways stagger. [Uncert.].
LURCH (**2**), [lurch], *n.* †a losing position in a game; a game in which such a position regularly occurs; **in the l.,** in difficulties. [Fr. *lourche* backgammon].
LURCH (**3**), [lurch], *v.i.* to stagger sideways with a lurch. [LURCH (1)].
LURCHER, [lurch'-er], *n.* a cross between a collie and a greyhound; one who lurches. [LURK].
LURE (**1**), [lyōōer], *n.* a bait used for recalling hawks from hunting; a decoy for catching animals or fish; (*fig.*) an enticement. [OFr. *leurre, loerre*].
LURE (**2**), [lyōōer], *v.t.* to recall by means of a lure; to attract, entice.

LURCHER

LURID, [lyōōer'-id], *adj.* pale, dismal, wan; gleaming unnaturally; (*fig.*) sensational, highly coloured. [L. *luridus* pale yellow].
LURK, [lurk], *v.i.* to lie furtively in wait; to lie in such a position as to escape observation; (*fig.*) to be implicit or latent. [Uncert.].
LURKER, [lurk'-er], *n.* one who lurks.
LURKING-PLACE, [lurk'-ing-plās'], *n.* a hiding-place, retreat.
LUSCIOUS, [lush'-us], *adj.* ripe almost to over-ripeness; rich in taste and soft in touch; delicious, full-flavoured; (*fig.*) highly sensuous; fulsome. [Uncert.].
LUSCIOUSLY, [lush'-us-li], *adv.* in luscious fashion.
LUSCIOUSNESS, [lush'-us-nes], *n.* the quality of being luscious.
LUSH (**1**), [lush], *n.* liquor, drink; a drinking-bout. [Uncert.].
LUSH (**2**), [lush], *adj.* luxuriant, juicy, rich in growth. [Uncert.].
LUSHINGTON, [lush'-ing-ton], *n.* (*slang*) a drunkard. [Name of a drinking-club styled "The City of *Lushington*"].
LUSHY, [lush'-i], *adj.* intoxicated, drunk; lush.
LUSITANIAN, [lōōs-it-ān'-i-an], *n.* and *adj.* (*poet.*) an inhabitant of Portugal; pertaining to Portugal or its inhabitants. [*Lusitania,* the name of an old Roman province].
LUST (**1**), [lust], *n.* will; intense desire, usually physical; sinful appetite or the resultant sin; (*fig.*) overwhelming passion. [OE. *lust*].
LUST (**2**), [lust], *v.i.* to desire strongly, to have strong carnal desire; to concentrate upon obtaining carnal satisfaction. [OE. *lystan*].
LUSTER, [lust'-er], *n.* one inflamed with lust; a loose liver.
LUSTFUL, [lust'-fōōl], *adj.* wilful; full of carnal desire; in heat; enticing or prompting to lust.
LUSTFULLY, [lust'-fōōl-i], *adv.* in lustful fashion.
LUSTFULNESS, [lust'-fōōl-nes], *n.* the state of being lustful.
LUSTIHOOD, [lust'-i-hōōd], *n.* the quality of being lusty, bodily vigour.
LUSTILY, [lust'-i-li], *adv.* in a lusty way.
LUSTINESS, [lust'-i-nes], *n.* the quality of being lusty, bodily vigour.
LUSTRAL, [lust'-ral], *adj.* pertaining to, used in, ceremonial purification. [L. *lustralis*].
LUSTRATE, [lus'-trāt], *v.t.* to cleanse ritually by lustration. [L. *lustrare*].
LUSTRATION, [lus-trā'-shun], *n.* rites of purification from sin or guilt; ritual cleansing. [L. *lustratio*].
LUSTRATIVE, [lus'-tra-tiv], *adj.* pertaining to lustration.
LUSTRE (**1**), [lust'-er], *n.* smooth sheen, brightness, *esp.* of reflected light; a chandelier made of crystal pendants or drops; (*fig.*) distinction, renown. [Fr. *lustre*].
LUSTRE (**2**), [lust'-er], *n.* a lustrum.
LUSTRELESS, [lust'-er-les], *adj.* lacking lustre.
LUSTRE-WARE, [lust'-er-wāer'], *n.* pottery to which has been imparted a metallic sheen.
LUSTRING, LUTESTRING, [lus'-tring], *n.* a glossy silk fabric. [Fr. *lustrine*].
LUSTROUS, [lus'-trus], *adj.* bright, shining, luminous; scintillating.
LUSTROUSLY, [lus'-trus-li], *adv.* in lustrous fashion.
LUSTRUM, [lus'-trum], *n.* *orig.* a period of five years; a sacrifice of purification amongst the ancient Romans every five years. [L. *lustrum*].
LUSTY, [lust'-i], *adj.* full of youthful vigour and animal health; produced by such vigour; spirited; large and strong.
LUSUS NATURAE, [lew'-sus-nā-tew'-rē], *n.* a freak of nature, a sport. [L. *lusus* freak and *naturae* of nature].
LUTANIST, [lōōt'-an-ist], *n.* a lute player; a composer for the lute. [LL. *lutanista*].
LUTE (**1**), [lōōt], *n.* a stringed musical instrument resembling a guitar, plucked by the fingers. [OFr. *leut*].
LUTE (**2**), [lōōt], *n.* a composition of cement, clay or other tenacious substance used for sealing, making air-tight or fire-proofing. [L. *lutum* mud].
LUTE (**3**), [lōōt], *v.t.* to seal or coat with lute. [LUTE (2)].
LUTEIN, [lōō'-tē-in], *n.* a yellowish substance secreted in the ovaries. [L. *luteus* yellow].
LUTEOLIN, [lōō-tē'-ō-lin], *n.* a yellow colouring principle in dyer's weed, *Reseda Luteola.* [MdL. *luteola*].
LUTEOUS, [lōōt'-i-us], *adj.* of a deep yellow colour. [L. *luteus*].
LUTER, [lōōt'-er], *n.* a lutanist.
LUTESCENT, [lōō-tes'-ent], *adj.* slightly yellow, becoming yellow. [L. *luteus* yellow and *escere* to become].
LUTESTRING, see LUSTRING.
LUTETIAN, [lōō-tē'-shan], *adj.* pertaining to Paris. [L. *Lutetia* an ancient city on the site of Paris].
LUTHERAN (**1**), [lōō'-ther-an], *n.* a disciple or follower of Luther; a member of the Lutheran church.
LUTHERAN (**2**), [lōō'-ther-an], *adj.* pertaining to Luther or to Lutheranism.
LUTHERANISM, [lōō'-ther-an-izm], *n.* Martin Luther's body of Protestant religious principles and practices; the Protestant sect professing them.
LUTHERISM, [lōō'-ther-izm], *n.* Lutheranism.
LUTHERN, [lōō'-thern], *n.* a dormer window. [Uncert.].

LUTING, [lōōt'-ing], *n.* sealing lute or the application of lute.
LUTIST, [lōōt'-ist], *n.* a lutanist.
LUTOSE, [lōōt'-ōs], *adj.* miry, covered with clay or mud. [L. *lutosus*].
LUTRINE, [lōō'-trīn], *adj.* relating to the otter. [L. *lutra* otter].
LUTULENT, [lōō'-tyōō-lent], *adj.* thick, muddy. [~L. *lutum* mud].
LUXATE, [luks'-āt], *v.t.* to put out of joint, to displace, to dislocate. [L. *luxare*].
LUXATION, [luks-ā-shun], *n.* dislocation, putting out of place. [L. *luxatio*].
LUXURIANCE, [luk-zewr'-i-ants], *n.* the quality of being luxuriant; the degree of this.
LUXURIANCY, [luk-zewr'-i-an-si], *n.* luxuriance.
LUXURIANT, [luk-zewr'-i-ant], *adj.* prolific, profuse, abundant; fertile and rich; (*fig.*) florid; extravagant. [L. *luxurians*].
LUXURIANTLY, [luk-zewr'-i-ant-li], *adv.* in luxuriant fashion.
LUXURIATE, [luk-zewr'-i-āt], *v.i.* to grow profusely; (*fig.*) to revel in; to live luxuriously. [L. *luxuriare* grow rank].
LUXURIOUS, [luk-zewr'-i-us], *adj.* indulging freely in, characterized by, luxury; furnished with luxuries; enervated. [L. *luxuriosus*].
LUXURIOUSLY, [luk-zewr'-i-us-li], *adv.* in luxurious fashion.
LUXURIOUSNESS, [luk-zewr'-i-us-nes], *n.* the state or quality of being luxurious; †lustfulness, lechery.
LUXURIST†, [luk'-sher-ist], *n.* one fond of luxury; a lecherous person.
LUXURY, [luk'-sher-i], *n.* costly ease and comfort; profusion of material aids to pleasure; anything acquired for pleasure at noticeable cost. [L. *luxuria* abundance].
LYCANTHROPE, [lī'-kan-thrōp], *n.* one affected with lycanthropy; a were wolf. [Gk. *lukanthropos* wolf-man].
LYCANTHROPY, [lī-kan'-throp-i], *n.* a form of insanity, in which the patient imagines himself to be a wolf, and acts like one; the transformation of a man into a wolf by means of magic. [Gk. *lukanthropia*].
LYCEE, lycée, [lē'-sā], *n.* a state-maintained secondary school in French-speaking countries. [Fr. *lycée* from Gk. *Lukeion* temple of Apollo where Aristotle taught].
LYCEUM, [lī-sē'-um], *n.* a place devoted to study and instruction, *esp.* a literary society and its building. [Gk. *Lukeion*, the place where Aristotle taught, in Athens].
LYCHGATE, see LICHGATE.
LYCODONT, [līk'-ō-dont], *n.* a snake, a member of the *Lycodontidæ*. [Gk. *lukos* wolf and *odous odontos* tooth].
LYCOPERDON, [lī'-kō-per'-don], *n.* the puffball, *Lycoperdon Bovista*. [Gk. *lukos* wolf and *perdomai* I break wind].
LYCOPOD, [lī'-kō-pod], *n.* a plant of the genus *Lycopodium*.
LYCOPODIUM, [lī'-kō-pō'-di-um], *n.* a genus of plants including the club moss, *Lycopodium clavatum*; a yellow powder consisting of the spores of the club-moss, which explodes and burns with a bright flash. [Gk. *lukos* wolf and *pous podos* foot].
LYDDITE, [lid'-īt], *n.* a powerful explosive used in shells and consisting largely of picric acid. [*Lydd*, in Kent, where made].
LYDIAN (1), [lid'-i-an], *n.* an inhabitant of Lydia; the language of Lydia; one of the ancient Greek musical modes.
LYDIAN (2), [lid'-i-an], *adj.* pertaining to Lydia or Lydians; soft, effeminate, *esp.* of the Lydian musical mode. [L. *Lydia*, an ancient country in Asia Minor].
LYDITE, [lid'-īt], *n.* Lydian stone, a hard black variety of jasper, with a flat conchoidal fracture, used for testing gold. [*Lydia*, in Asia Minor].
LYE, LEY, [lī], *n.* a strongly alkaline solution, used *esp.* in the manufacture of soap, etc. [OE. *leah*].
LYING (1), [lī'-ing], *adj.* reclining, prostrate. [LIE (1)].
LYING (2), [lī'-ing], *adj.* false, untrue; telling or given to telling lies. [LIE (2)].
LYING-IN, [lī'-ing-in'], *n.* confinement, childbirth.
LYINGLY, [lī'-ing-li], *adv.* falsely, without truth.
LYME-GRASS, [līm'-grahs], *n.* a coarse grass of the genus *Elymus* serving to bind sand together. [Uncert.].
LYMPH, [limf], *n.* (*poet.*) water; (*physiol.*) one of the fluid principles of an animal body, watery in colour; (*med.*) matter exuded from a sore, and used as a vaccine. [L. *lympha* spring water].
LYMPHADENOMA, [limf'-ad-in-ōm'-a], *n.* (*med.*) a lymphoid tumour. [LYMPH and Gk. *adenoma* inflammation of a gland].
LYMPHATIC (1), [limf-at'-ik], *n.* (usually *pl.*) a small vessel in animal bodies, which contains or conveys lymph.
LYMPHATIC (2), [limf-at-'-ik], *adj.* pertaining to, producing, conveying lymph; sluggish; demented. [L. *lymphaticus* mad].
LYMPHOCYTE, [limf'-ō-sīt], *n.* (*med.*) a leucocyte found in lymph. [LYMPH and Gk. *lukos* container].
LYMPHODUCT, [limf'-ō-dukt], *n.* a lymphatic vessel.
LYMPHOGRAPHY, [limf-og'-ra-fi], *n.* a description of the lymphatic vessels. [LYMPH and Gk. *graphia* writing].
LYMPHOID, [limf'-oid], *adj.* (*med.*) resembling or composed of lymph tissue. [LYMPH and Gk. *œides* like].
LYMPHY, [limf'-i], *adj.* containing or resembling lymph.
LYNCEAN, [lin'-sē-an], *adj.* having eyes like those of a lynx, keen-sighted. [L. *lynceus*].
LYNCH, [linch], *v.t.* to put to death, often barbarously, by mob action, without legal sentence; **l. law,** summary punishment by a mob, barbarism. [C. *Lynch*, a Virginian magistrate, who started this practice].
LYNCHER, [linch'-er], *n.* one who lynches.
LYNCHET, [linch'-et], *n.* a strip of green land separating ploughed pieces; a slope or terrace on the face of a chalk down. [OE. *hlinc* slope].
LYNCHING, [linch'-ing], *n.* summary execution by a mob, without legal sentence; an instance of this.
LYNX, [lingks], *n.* any of several species of feline carnivora with tufted ears, proverbial for their keen-sightedness. [Gk. *lunx*].
LYNX-EYED, [lingks'-īd'], *adj.* sharp-sighted.
LYON, [lī'-on], *n.* the title of the chief Scottish herald, from the royal lion on the shield.

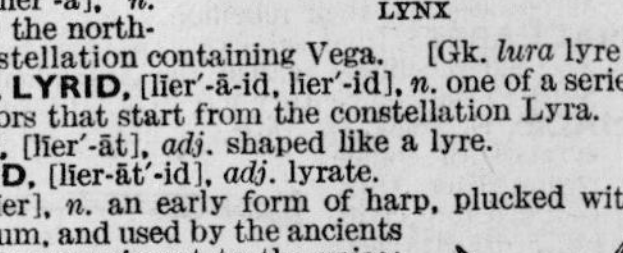
LYNX

LYRA, [līer'-a], *n.* (*astron.*) the northern constellation containing Vega. [Gk. *lura* lyre].
LYRAID, LYRID, [līer'-ā-id, līer'-id], *n.* one of a series of meteors that start from the constellation Lyra.
LYRATE, [līer'-āt], *adj.* shaped like a lyre.
LYRATED, [līer-āt'-id], *adj.* lyrate.
LYRE, [līer], *n.* an early form of harp, plucked with a plectrum, and used by the ancients as an accompaniment to the voice; **l. bird,** an Australian bird of the genus *Menura*, with a lyre-shaped tail; **l. tree,** the tulip tree, *Liriodendron tulipiferum*, from its lyrate leaf. [Gk. *lura*].

LYRE

LYRIC (1), [li'-rik], *n.* the words of a song; a poem in manner or matter resembling a song, subjective, emotional, ejaculatory, and written in a metre originally intended to be sung.
LYRIC (2), [li'-rik], *adj.* singing; apt to sing; pertaining to the lyre as the symbol of song; suitable for singing; (of poetry) having the character of a lyric. [Gk. *lurikos*].
LYRICAL, [li'-rik-al], *adj.* lyric; (*coll.*) copiously eloquent; exuberantly laudatory or excited.
LYRICISM, [li'-ri-sizm], *n.* the quality of being lyrical, lyrical expression; the cult or art of lyric poetry.
LYRID, see LYRAID.
LYRIE, [līer'-i], *n.* a seabird, the Manx shearwater, *Puffinus anglorum*. [Unkn.].
LYRIST, [līer'-ist], *n.* a composer of lyrics; a musician who plays on the lyre.
LYSIMETER, [lī-sim'-it-er], *n.* a rain gauge. [Gk. *lusis* loosening and METER].
LYSIS, [lī'-sis], *n.* the gradual lessening in severity of an acute disease. [Gk. *lusis* loosening].
LYSOL, [lī'-sol], *n.* (*prot.*) (*med.*) a liquid mixture containing creosol and oil, used as an antiseptic and disinfectant.
LYTHE, LITHE, [līTH], *n.* (*Scots*) the pollack, a species of *Gadus*.

M

M, [em], the thirteenth letter of the English alphabet.
MA, [mah], *n.* (*vulg.*) mother. [MAMMA].
MA'AM, [mam], *n.* *contracted form of* MADAM, *used vocatively.*
MAAR, [mah(r)], *n.* a volcanic crater. [Uncert.].
MABOLA, [ma-bōl'-a], *n.* the Philippine tree, *Diospyros discolor.* [Native].
MAC (1), [mak], *n.* (*slang*) a Scotsman. [Gael. *mac* son].
MAC (2), [mak], *n.* (*coll.*) a raincoat. [MACKINTOSH].
MACABRE, [ma-kah'-ber], *adj.* grotesquely terrible, gruesome. [Fr. *macabre*].
MACACO, [ma-kah'-kō], *n.* a monkey of the genus *Macacus* ; the tropical South American tree, *Tococa guianensis.* [Portug. *macaco*].
MACADAM, [ma-kad'-am], *n.* a road-surfacing material made from broken stones. [John *McAdam*, its inventor].
MACADAMIZE, [ma-kad'-am-īz], *v.t.* to surface with macadam.
MACAQUE, MACACO, [ma-kahk'(-o)], *n.* a short-tailed South American monkey of the genus *Macacus.* [Fr. from Portug. *macaco* monkey].
MACARIZE, [mak'-er-īz], *v.t.* to bless. [Gk. *makarizo*].
MACARONI, [mak-er-ō'-ni], *n.* an Italian dish of wheat-paste dried into long tubes; an Italianate dandy. [It. *maccaroni*].
MACARONIC (1), [mak-er-o'-nik], *n.*(*pl.*) macaronic verse.
MACARONIC (2), [mak-er-o'-nik], *adj.* (of verse) composed in a burlesque mixed language using words taken or combined from two languages, *esp.* English words with Latin endings. [MdL. *macaronicus*].
MACAROON, [mak-er-ōōn'], *n.* a sweet cake made from almonds. [It. *maccarone*].
MACASSAR, [ma-kas'-er], *n.* an oil imported from Mangkasara in the Celebes.
MACAW, [ma-kaw'], *n.* a large tropical parrot; the palm, *Acrocomia scelocarpa.* [Portug. *macao*].
MACCABEAN, [mak'-a-bē'-an], *adj.* relating to the Maccabees and their rebellion.
MACCABEES, [mak'-ab-ēz], *n.*(*pl.*) the Jewish family who led rebellions against the Antiochene kings of Syria in the 2nd century B.C. [Gk. *Makkabaios*].
MACE (1), [mās], *n.* (*hist.*) a heavy spiked club; a symbol of office resembling this, borne before civic, etc., dignitaries; a stick used in bagatelle. [OFr. *mace*].

MACE

MACE (2), [mās], *n.* a spice obtained from nutmeg. [OFr. *macis*].
MACE-ALE, [mās'-āl], *n.* ale spiced with mace.
MACEBEARER, [mās'-bāer'-er], *n.* the official who carries the mace in a procession.
MACEDOINE, [mas-i-dwan'], *n.* a jelly containing pieces of diced fruit or vegetables. [Fr. *macédoine*].
MACER, [mās'-er], *n.* a Scottish usher in a court of law. [OFr. *maissier*].
MACERATE, [mas'-er-āt], *v.t.* to soften by soaking; to make suffer, weaken. [L. *macerare*].
MACERATION, [mas'-er-ā'-shun], *n.* the act of macerating, the state of being macerated. [L. *maceratio*].
MACHETE, [ma-chā'-ti], *n.* a heavy chopping knife used in South America. [Span. *machete*].
MACHIAVELLIAN, [mak'-i-a-vel'-i-an], *adj.* following the principles and policy of Machiavelli; subtle, unscrupulous, and ruthless in the pursuit and maintenance of power. [N. *Machiavelli* (1469-1527), the Italian statesman].
MACHIAVELLIANISM, [mak'-i-a-vel'-i-an-izm], *n.* the employment or advocacy of Machiavellian principles and methods.
MACHICOLATED, [ma'-chik-ol-āt-id], *adj.* provided with machicolations. [MedL. *machicolare*].
MACHICOLATION, [mach'-ik-ol-ā'-shun], *n.* an opening between the corbels of overhanging battlements, for dropping missiles, etc., upon attackers. [MedL. *machicolatio*].
MACHINAL, [ma-shēn'-al], *adj.* relating to, by means of, machinery. [L. *machinalis*].
MACHINATE, [mak'-in-āt], *v.i.* to plot, plan, scheme. [L. *machinari*].
MACHINATION, [mak'-in-ā'-shun], *n.* the act or result of machinating; a plot, intrigue. [L. *machinatio*].
MACHINATOR, [mak'-in-āt-er], *n.* one who machinates. [L. *machinator*].
MACHINE (1), [ma-shēn'], *n.* an apparatus consisting of several interconnecting parts, which, by their motion transform or transmit power into work; a person who unfailingly follows a prescribed routine without thought or fatigue; an organization for performing a specified function; †a supernatural intervention, *esp.* in conventional drama or epic; **m. gun,** a small, quick-firing, mechanically operated gun; **m. tool,** a tool designed for the manufacture of machinery. [L. *machina*].
MACHINE (2), [ma-shēn'], *v.t.* to make, treat, or finish by machinery.
MACHINER, [ma-shēn'-er], *n.* a worker operating a machine performing certain mechanical processes.
MACHINERY, [ma-shēn'-er-i], *n.* machines; the parts of a machine; the means by which some process is carried out; a supernatural agency introduced into an epic or drama to help the plot.
MACHINIST, [ma-shēn'-ist], *n.* one who operates a machine; one who understands machinery.
MACIES, [mā'-si-ēz], *n.* (*med.*) emaciation. [L. *macies*].
MACKEREL, [mak'-er-el], *n.* the edible seafish *Scomber vernalis*; **m. (back) sky,** a cloud formation resembling the markings on a mackerel. [OFr. *makerel*].
MACKEREL-GUIDE, [mak'-er-el-gīd], *n.* the garfish, *Belone vulgaris.*
MACKINTOSH, [mak'-in-tosh], *n.* a waterproof fabric lined or coated with rubber; a raincoat of this material. [Charles *Mackintosh* (1766-1843), its inventor].
MACKITE, [mak'-īt], *n.* a compound of asbestos and plaster of Paris used by builders.
MACKLE, [makl], *n.* a blurred impression in printing; a deep colour on a lighter one. [L. *macula* a spot].
MACKLED, [makld], *adj.* mottled with patches of deeper colour.
MACLE, [makl], *n.* a twin crystal. [L. *macula* spot].
MACLED, [makld], *adj.* (*min.*) having a twin crystal, hemitropic.
MACON (1), [mak'-on], *n.* a heavy red wine. [*Macon*, in France, where made].
MACON (2), [māk'-on], *n.* mutton salted and smoked like bacon. [M(UTTON) and (B)ACON].
MACONOCHIE, [ma-kon'-o-ki], *n.* a tinned stew much used in the war of 1914-18. [*Maconochie* Bros., the makers].
MACRAME, macramé, [ma-krah'-mi], *n.* a fringe of twisted thread ; twine made in this way. [Turk. *maqrama* towel].
MACRO-, *pref.* long, large. [Gk. *makros*].
MACROBIOTIC, [mak'-rō-bī-ot'-ik], *adj.* long-lived. [Gk. *makrobiotos*].
MACROCEPHALIC, [mak'-rō-si-fal'-ik], *adj.* macrocephalous.
MACROCEPHALOUS, [mak'-rō-sef'-al-us], *adj.* long-headed. [MACRO and CEPHALOUS].
MACROCOSM, [mak'-rō-kozm'], *n.* the universe. [MACRO and Gk. *kosmos* world].
MACRODACTYLIC, [mak'-rō-dak-til'-ik], *adj.* (of birds) long-toed. [MACRO and Gk. *daktulos* finger].
MACRODIAGONAL, [mak'-rō-dī-ag'-on-al], *n.* the long diagonal of a prism.
MACROGNATHIC, [mak'-rō-gnāth'-ik], *adj.* long-jawed. [MACRO and Gk. *gnathos* jawbone].
MACROLOGY, [ma-krol'-o-ji], *n.* volubility. [Gk. *makrologia*].
MACROMETER, [ma-krom'-it-er], *n.* an instrument for measuring inaccessible objects by means of two reflectors. [MACRO and METER].
MACRON, [mak'-ron], *n.* a long mark (-) over a vowel. [Gk. *makron*].
MACROPTEROUS, [ma-kropt'-er-us], *adj.* long-winged. [MACRO and Gk. *pteron* a wing].
MACROSCOPIC, [mak'-rō-skop'-ik], *adj.* visible to

the naked eye, large enough to be seen. [MACRO and Gk. *skopos* watching].

MACROTHERIUM, [mak'-rō-thēer'-i-um], *n.* a gigantic prehistoric edentate mammal. [MACRO and Gk. *therion* wild beast].

MACROTONE, [mak'-rō-tōn], *n.* a macron.

MACRUROUS, [ma-kro͞oer'-us], *adj.* having a long tail; (of crustaceans) belonging to the *Macrura*, the order which includes lobsters and related animals. [MACRO and Gk. *oura* tail].

MACTATION, [mak-tā'-shun], *n.* sacrificial slaughter. [L. *mactatio*].

MACULA, [mak'-yo͞o-la], *n.* a mark or dark stain; a sun-spot; a flaw in a jewel or mineral; a spot on the skin. [L. *macula*].

MACULATE (1), [mak'-yo͝o-lat], *adj.* stained, spotted. [L. *maculatus*].

MACULATE (2), [mak'-yo͝o-lāt], *v.t.* to stain, mark, spot. [L. *maculare*].

MACULATION, [mak'-yo͝o-lā'-shun], *n.* the act of maculating; the state of being maculated; a spot, blemish. [L. *maculatio*].

MACULE, [mak'-yo͞ol], *n.* a macula, mackle. [L. *macula*].

MAD, [mad], *adj.* insane, out of one's mind; uncontrolled by reason; highly overwrought with some passion or emotion; furiously reckless, behaving as if insane. [OE. *gemæd(e)d* driven mad].

MADAM, [mad'-am], *n.* a formal and respectful mode of address to ladies, *esp.* to married women. [Fr. *madame*].

MADAROSIS, [mad'-er-ō'-sis], *n.* (*med.*) a falling out of the hair. [Gk. *madaros* bald and *osis* denoting condition].

MADCAP, [mad'-kap'], *n.* a harebrained, frolicsome, carefree girl.

MADDEN, [mad'-en], *v.t.* to drive mad, to infuriate.

MADDER, [mad'-er], *n.* a yellow-flowered plant of the genus *Rubia*; the root of this plant used in dyeing. [OE. *mædere*].

MADDING, [mad'-ing], *adj.* mad; that maddens.

MADE, [mād], *pret. and p.pt.* of MAKE; (of the body) built, formed; securely successful; cooked. [OE. *macod*].

MADEIRA, [ma-dēer'-a], *n.* a heavy, sweet wine. [*Madeira*, an island off the west coast of Africa].

MADEIRA-NUT, [ma-dēer'-a-nut'], *n.* a kind of walnut.

MADELEINE, [mad'-el-ēn], *n.* a kind of sweet cake.

MADEMOISELLE, [ma'-dem-waz-el'], *n.* an unmarried woman; (*coll.*) a French governess. [Fr. *mademoiselle*].

MADHOUSE, [mad'-hows], *n.* a lunatic asylum; (*coll.*) a noisy assembly resembling this.

MADIA, [mā'-di-a], *n.* the South American tar-weed, *Madia sativa*. [Chilean *madi*].

MADID, [mad'-id], *adj.* damp, wet. [L. *madidus*].

MADLY, [mad'-li], *adv.* in mad fashion; intensely.

MADMAN, [mad'-man], *n.* a lunatic.

MADNESS, [mad'-nes], *n.* the state of being mad; the behaviour of one who is mad.

MADONNA, [ma-don'-a], *n.* the Virgin Mary; a statue or ikon of the Virgin; **M. lily,** the white lily, *Lilium candidum*. [It. *madonna*].

MADOQUA, [mad'-ok-wa], *n.* a small Somali antelope. [Amharic *madoqua*].

MADREPEARL, [mad'-ri-purl], *n.* mother-of-pearl. [It. *madre* mother and PEARL].

MADREPORE, [mad'-ri-paw(r)], *n.* coral; the coral polyp. [It. *madrepora*].

MADREPORITE, [mad'-ri-pawr'-īt], *n.* fossil madrepore.

MADRIER, [ma-drēer'], *n.* (*fort.*) a beam supporting a wall; a thick, iron-bound plank placed across the mouth of a petard to intensify the force of the charge. [Fr. *madrier*].

MADRIGAL, [mad'-rig-al], *n.* a lyric sung without accompaniment as a part-song; a love lyric. [It. *madrigale*].

MADWORT, [mad'-wurt], *n.* the plant, *Asperugo procumbens*, supposed to be a cure for rabies.

MAECENAS, [mē-sē'-nas], *n.* a wealthy connoisseur and patron of the arts. [*Maecenas*, the patron of Horace].

MAELSTROM, [māl'-strom], *n.* a whirlpool; (*fig.*) a furious tumult of passions or events. [*Maelström*, a famous Norwegian whirlpool].

MAENAD, [mē'-nad'], *n.* a Dionysian nymph, a Bacchante. [Gk. *Mainas Mainados*].

MAESTOSO, [mah'-e-stō'-sō], *adv.* (*mus.*) grandly. [It. *maestoso*].

MAESTRO, [mah-e'-strō], *n.* a master in an art, *esp.* in music. [It. *maestro* master].

MAE WEST, [mā'-west'], *n.* an inflated life-saving jacket worn round the chest by airmen. [*Mae West*, U.S. film-star].

MAFFICK, [maf'-ik], *v.i.* to rejoice, celebrate riotously, vulgarly, and in large crowds. [*Mafeking*, in South Africa, whose relief was celebrated thus in London].

MAGAR, [ma'-gah(r)], *n.* the Indian crocodile. [Native].

MAGAZINE, [mag'-a-zēn'], *n.* a store for weapons, ammunition, etc., and *esp.* for explosives; the chamber in a repeating rifle holding the cartridges in readiness for propulsion into the breech; a periodical publication containing several unconnected compositions. [Arab. *makhazin* storehouses].

MAGDALEN, [mag'-dal-en], *n.* a reformed prostitute; a home for reforming prostitutes. [Mary *Magdalene*, Luke vii, 37].

MAGDALENIAN, [mag'-dal-ēn'-i-an], *adj.* relating to the late Palaeolithic Age. [La *Madeleine*, in France, where first revealed].

MAGE, [māj], *n.* a magician. [L. *magus*].

MAGELLANIC, [maj-el-an'-ik], *adj.* relating to, discovered by, Magellan. [F. de *Magellan* (1480-1521), the Portuguese explorer].

MAGENTA, [ma-jent'-a], *n.* a purplish aniline dye; the colour of this. [*Magenta*, in Italy].

MAGGOT, [mag'-ot], *n.* the larva of a fly; a cheese-mite; (*fig.*) a diseased fancy. [ME. *magot*].

MAGGOTINESS, [mag'-ot-i-nes], *n.* the state of being maggoty.

MAGGOTY, [mag'-ot-i], *adj.* riddled with maggots.

MAGI, [mā'-jī], *n.(pl.)* the wise men of the Nativity. [L. *Magi*].

MAGIAN (1), [mā'-ji-an], *n.* one of the Magi; a magician.

MAGIAN (2), [mā'-ji-an], *adj.* relating to the Magi; wise in magic.

MAGIANISM, [mā'-ji-an-izm], *n.* Persian religious philosophy.

MAGIC (1), [maj'-ik], *n.* the power of supernaturally influencing things and events; the means of exercising such an influence, witchcraft, sorcery; an apparently supernatural power causing wonderful and mysterious happenings; potent and inexplicable attraction; mystifying conjuring. [Gk. (*tekhne*) *magike* magic art].

MAGIC (2), [maj'-ik], *adj.* relating to, caused by, employed in, magic; inexplicable, fascinating; apparently supernatural. [Gk. *magikos*].

MAGICAL, [maj'-ik-al], *adj.* magic.

MAGICALLY, [maj'-ik-al-i], *adv.* in magical fashion.

MAGICIAN, [ma-jish'-an], *n.* one possessing or exercising magic power, a wizard; (*fig.*) one so skilled as apparently to be possessed of magic power. [Fr. *magicien*].

MAGIC LANTERN, [maj'-ik-lan'-tern], *n.* a device for throwing magnified images on to a screen, by shining a powerful light through a transparent picture.

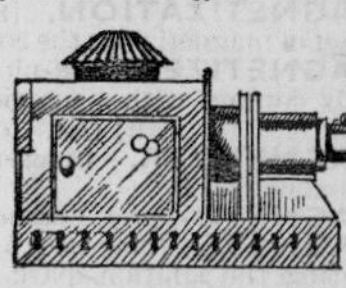

MAGIC LANTERN

MAGIC-TREE, [maj'-ik-trē'], *n.* the Peruvian tree, *Cantua buxifolia*.

MAGILP, see MEGILP.

MAGIRICS, [ma-jīer'-iks], *n.(pl.)* the art of preparing food. [Gk. *mageiros* a cook].

MAGISTERIAL, [maj'-is-tēer'-i-al], *adj.* relating to a master or to a magistrate; dignified, authoritative. [MedL. *magisterialis*].

MAGISTERIALLY, [maj'-is-tēer'-i-al-i], *adv.* in magisterial fashion.

MAGISTERIALNESS, [maj'-is-tēer'-i-al-nes], *n.* the quality of being magisterial.

MAGISTRACY, [maj'-is-tra-si], *n.* the magistrates of a state; the office or status of a magistrate.

MAGISTRAL, [maj'-is-tral], *adj.* relating to a master; (*med.*) specially made up to suit a particular case or patient. [L. *magistralis*].

MAGISTRAND, [maj'-is-trand], *n.* a final-year student of Aberdeen University. [MedL. *magistrandus*].

MAGISTRATE, [maj'-is-trāt], *n.* a civil official with judicial and administrative functions, *esp.* a judicial officer dealing summarily with minor cases, a Justice of the Peace. [L. *magistratus*].

MAGISTRATICAL, [maj'-is-trat'-ik-al], *adj.* pertaining, or proper to, a magistrate.

MAGISTRATURE, [maj'-is-tra-cher], *n.* the magisterial system, the magistracy; the tenure of a magistrate's office.

MAGLEMOSIAN, [mag'-li-mō'-zi-an], *adj.* relating to the early European culture exemplified by the objects discovered at Maglemose, in Denmark.

MAGMA, [mag'-ma], *n.* molten rock in the centre of the earth; a paste-like mass of matter. [Gk. *magma* dough].

MAGNA CARTA, MAGNA CHARTA, [mag'-na-kah'-ta], *n.* the charter of privileges extracted by the feudal lords from King John; also *fig.* [L. *magna carta* great charter].

MAGNALIUM, [mag-nā'-li-um], *n.* a tough alloy of aluminium, with varying proportions of magnesium. [MAGN(ESIUM) and AL(UMIN)IUM].

MAGNANERIE, [man-yan'-er-ē], *n.* a box for rearing silkworms. [Fr. *magnanerie*].

MAGNANIMITY, [mag'-nan-im'-i-ti], *n.* the state or quality of being magnanimous. [L. *magnanimitas*].

MAGNANIMOUS, [mag-nan'-im-us], *adj.* noble-spirited, high-minded, generous. [L. *magnanimus*].

MAGNANIMOUSLY, [mag-nan'-im-us-li], *adv.* in magnanimous fashion.

MAGNATE, [mag'-nāt], *n.* a potentate, *esp.* a great controller and employer of labour. [LL. *magnas*].

MAGNESIA, [mag-nē'-shi-a], *n.* oxide of magnesium; powder of magnesium carbonate used as a mild medical antacid. [Gk. *magnesia* loadstone].

MAGNESIAN, [mag-nē'-shi-an], *adj.* containing magnesia.

MAGNESITE, [mag'-nē-sīt], *n.* magnesium carbonate.

MAGNESIUM, [mag-nē'-zi-um], *n.* (*chem.*) the white, metallic element Mg. [Gk. *magnesia*].

MAGNET, [mag'-nit], *n.* a piece of iron, steel, or nickel with the property of exercising attraction on these same metals; (*fig.*) something exercising strong attraction. [L. *magnetis* (*lapis*) stone from magnesia].

MAGNETIC (1), [mag-net'-ik], *n.* a substance with magnetic properties.

MAGNETIC (2), [mag-net'-ik], *adj.* having the attractive properties of a magnet; (*fig.*) attracting strongly and mysteriously; **m. mine,** a mine exploding by magnetic action; **m. pole,** the location to which the compass-needle points.

MAGNETICAL, [mag-net'-ik-al], *adj.* magnetic.

MAGNETICALLY, [mag-net'-ik-al-i], *adv.* in magnetic fashion.

MAGNETIFEROUS, [mag'-nit-if'-er-us], *adj.* magnetic; that may magnetize. [MAGNET and L. *ferre* to bear].

MAGNETISM, [mag'-nit-izm], *n.* magnetic properties and phenomena; the scientific study of these; (*fig.*) strong personal attraction.

MAGNETIST, [mag'-nit-ist], *n.* one learned in magnetism.

MAGNETITE, [mag'-nit-īt], *n.* magnetic iron oxide.

MAGNETIZATION, [mag'-nit-īz-ā'-shun], *n.* the act of magnetizing; the condition of being magnetized.

MAGNETIZE, [mag'-nit-īz], *v.t.* to make magnetic by contact with a magnet or by passing an electric current through; (*fig.*) to attract intensely.

MAGNETIZER, [mag'-nit-īz-er], *n.* that which magnetizes.

MAGNETO-, *pref.* magnetic. [MAGNET].

MAGNETO, [mag-nē'-tō], *n.* the contrivance generating the ignition-spark in an internal-combustion engine. [Gk. *magnes* magnet].

MAGNETO-ELECTRICITY, [mag-nē'-tō-i-lek-tris'-i-ti], *n.* electricity produced by, or related to, magnetic action.

MAGNETOGRAPH, [mag-nē'-tō-graf], *n.* an instrument for registering magnetic fields.

MAGNETOMETER, [mag'-nit-om'-it-er], *n.* an instrument for measuring magnetism.

MAGNETOMOTOR, [mag'-nit-ō-mō'-ter], *n.* a voltaic series of large plates, producing a quantity of electricity of low tension.

MAGNETOPHONE, [mag-nē'-tō-fōn], *n.* a microphone in which the sound waves strike a flat coil of wire supported in a magnetic field.

MAGNETOSTATICS, [mag-nē'-tō-stat'-iks], *n.*(*pl.*) the study of magnetic fields.

MAGNETOTHERAPY, [mag'-ni-tō-the'-ra-pi], *n.* the use of magnetism in medical treatments. [MAGNETO and Gk. *therapeia* medical attendance].

MAGNIFIABLE, [mag'-ni-fī'-abl], *adj.* that may be magnified.

MAGNIFIC, [mag-nif'-ik]., *adj.* noble, magnificent, splendid. [L. *magnificus*].

MAGNIFICAL, [mag-nif'-ik-al], *adj.* magnific, noble.

MAGNIFICALLY, [mag-nif'-ik-al-i], *adv.* in magnific fashion.

MAGNIFICAT, [mag-nif'-ik-at], *n.* the song of the Virgin Mary, Luke i, 46-55. [L. *magnificat, 3rd pers.sg. pres.ind.* of *magnificare* to magnify].

MAGNIFICATION, [mag'-nif-ik-ā'-shun], *n.* the act of magnifying; the condition or extent of being magnified. [L. *magnificatio*].

MAGNIFICATIVE, [mag-nif'-ik-at-iv], *adj.* tending to magnify.

MAGNIFICENCE, [mag-nif'-is-ents], *n.* splendour, elaborate grandeur, material glory. [L. *magnificentia*].

MAGNIFICENT, [mag-nif'-is-ent], *adj.* splendid, glorious; of outstanding richness, quality, extent, beauty, etc.; (*coll.*) excellent, very good. [OFr. *magnificent*].

MAGNIFICENTLY, [mag-nif'-is-ent-li], *adv.* in magnificent fashion.

MAGNIFICO, [mag-nif'-ik-ō], *n.* a Venetian grandee; a magnificent magnate. [It. *magnifico*].

MAGNIFIER, [mag'-ni-fī-er], *n.* that which, one who, magnifies.

MAGNIFY, [mag'-ni-fī], *v.t.* to extol, exalt; to make great, to enlarge; to increase the apparent size of, *esp.* to make seem larger by means of a lens; (*fig.*) to exaggerate. [OFr. *magnifier*].

MAGNILOQUENCE, [mag-nil'-ō-kwents], *n.* the condition of being magniloquent; that which is magniloquent in style, *esp.* speech.

MAGNILOQUENT, [mag-nil'-ō-kwent], *adj.* pompous, bombastic, grandiose. [~L. *magniloquus*].

MAGNILOQUENTLY, [mag-nil'-ō-kwent-li], *adv.* in magniloquent fashion.

MAGNITUDE, [mag'-ni-tewd], *n.* greatness of size or extent; dimension, size; (*astron.*) degree of brilliance of a fixed star. [L. *magnitudo*].

MAGNOLIA, [mag-nō'-li-a], *n.* a genus of Asiatic and American flowering shrubs. [P. *Magnol* (1638-1715), the botanist].

MAGNUM, [mag'-num], *n.* a winebottle holding two quarts. [L. *magnus* great].

MAGNUM-BONUM, [mag'-num-bōn'-um], *n.* a large pale-skinned plum. [L. *magnum* great and *bonum* good].

MAGPIE, [mag'-pī], *n.* the black and white bird, *Pica caudata*, related to the crow; (*coll.*) a chattering or harmlessly predatory person; a shot hitting the target between the inner and outer positions. [MAG pet form of *Margaret* and PIE (2)].

MAGPIE

MAGUEY, [mag'-wā], *n.* the century plant, *Agave americana*. [Span. *maguey*].

MAGYAR, [mag'-yah(r)], *n.* a member of the Hungarian dominant race; the language of these people. [Hungarian *Magya*(*r*)].

MAHALEB, [mah'-ha-leb], *n.* a dark cherry, used in making dyes and liqueur. [Arab. *mahaleb*].

MAHARAJA, MAHARAJAH, [mah'-hah-rah'-jah], *n.* a major Indian ruling prince. [Hind. *maha* great and RAJAH].

MAHARANEE, [mah'-hah-rah'-nē], *n.* the wife of a maharaja, an Indian female sovereign. [Hind. *maha* and RANEE].

MAHATMA, [mah-hat'-ma], *n.* a Hindu adept. [Skr. *mahatman*].

MAHDI, [mah'-di], *n.* the Moslem saviour who is to appear before the last day; a rebel leader, claiming to be this saviour, in the Sudan towards the end of the nineteenth century. [Arab. *mahdiy*].

MAHJONG, [mah'-jong'], *n.* a Chinese game played with 144 painted blocks. [Chin. *ma* hemp and *tsiang* small birds].

MAHLSTICK, see MAULSTICK.

MAHOGANY, [ma-hog'-a-ni], *n.* a tropical American tree, *Swietenia Mahagoni*, producing a fine wood; the wood itself; the reddish-brown colour of this wood. [Haiti *mahagoni*].

MAHOMETAN, see MOHAMMEDAN.

MAHOUT, [mah'-hōōt], *n.* an elephant-driver. [Hind. *mahout*].

MAHSEER, [mah'-sēr], *n.* a large Indian fish, *Barbus tor*, resembling the barbel. [Hindi *mahasir*].

MAID, [mād], *n.* a maiden, a virgin; an unmarried woman; a female servant; **m. of honour,** an unmarried lady attendant upon a queen or princess;

an almond cheese-cake in a shell of pastry. [MAIDEN].

MAIDEN (1), [mād'-en], *n.* a girl; a virgin, a young unmarried woman; a female attendant; a primitive Scots guillotine; a medieval German instrument of torture; (*cricket*) a maiden over. [OE. *mægden*].

MAIDEN (2), [mād'-en], *adj.* relating to a maiden; unmarried; (*fig.*) virgin, unblemished, unspoiled; experienced or done for the first time; **m. over,** (*cricket*) an over in which no runs are scored; **m. assize,** an assize at which there are no criminal cases; **m. name,** a woman's name before marriage; **m. speech,** the first speech of a new Member of Parliament.

MAIDENHAIR, [mād'-en-hāer], *n.* a species of fern of the genus *Adiantum*; **m. tree,** the tree, *Ginkgo biloba*, with leaves like those of the maidenhair fern.

MAIDENHEAD, [mād'-en-hed], *n.* the hymen; virginity. [~MAIDENHOOD].

MAIDENHOOD, [mād'-en-hŏŏd], *n.* the condition of being a maiden; virginity. [OE. *magdenhad*].

MAIDENLIKE, [mād'-en-līk], *adj.* like a maid; modest.

MAIDENLINESS, [mād'-en-li-nes], *n.* the quality of being maidenly.

MAIDENLY, [mād'-en-li], *adj.* befitting a maiden, modest.

MAIDEN-PINK, [mād'-en-pingk'], *n.* the plant, *Dianthus deltoides*.

MAIDHOOD, [mād'-hŏŏd], *n.* maidenhood.

MAIDSERVANT, [mād'-serv-ant], *n.* a female servant.

MAIEUTIC, [mā-yōōt'-ik], *adj.* relating to delivery in childbirth; (of the Socratic technique) drawing out ideas, information, etc., from a person's mind. [Gk. *maieutikos* obstetric].

MAIGRE (1), MEAGER, [mā'-ger], *n.* the shadow-fish, *Sciæna aquila*. [Fr. *maigre*].

MAIGRE (2), [mā'-ger], *adj.* (of food) not containing or cooked in meat or animal fat. [Fr. *maigre* lean].

MAIL (1), [māl], *n.* armour composed of small overlapping plates, or *esp.* of interlocking rings or links; armour in general. [Fr. *maille*].

MAIL (2), [māl], *n.* a bag, sack for conveying letters, etc., by post; the letters, etc., so conveyed; a postal collection or delivery; the postal system for the collection and delivery of letters, etc. [OFr. *male*].

MAIL (3), [māl], *v.t.* to dispatch by post. [MAIL (2)].

MAILABLE, [māl'-abl], *adj.* that may be mailed.

MAIL-BOAT, [māl'-bōt], *n.* a ship carrying mails.

MAIL-CART, [māl'-kaht], *n.* a cart for transporting mails; a light push-cart for young children.

MAIL-COACH, [māl'-kōch'], *n.* a coach formerly used for carrying mails.

MAILED, [māld], *adj.* protected with mail; **the m. fist,** violence or the threat of it employed as an argument in public affairs.

MAIL-GUARD, [māl'-gahd], *n.* the conductor of a mail-coach.

MAIL-ORDER, [māl'-awd'-er], *adj.* pertaining to the system of buying goods through the post.

MAIL-STEAMER, [māl'-stēm'-er], *n.* a mail-boat.

MAIL-TRAIN, [māl'-trān], *n.* a train carrying mails.

MAIM, [mām], *v.t.* to mutilate, to lame or deprive of a bodily member. [ME. *maime* from OFr. *mahaigner*].

MAIMEDNESS, [māmd'-nes], *n.* the state of being maimed.

MAIN (1), [mān], *n.* the most part; the principal pipe or cable of a gas, water, etc., system; a major number, i.e. a number over 15, in certain games of dice; (*poet.*) the high seas; the Caribbean and its continental coast; physical strength or force. [OE. *mægen*].

MAIN (2), [mān], *n.* a cock-fight. [Uncert.].

MAIN (3), [mān], *adj.* largest, chief, most important, principal; †strong, violent. [OIcel. *meginn* strong].

MAIN-BOOM, [mān'-bōōm], *n.* the large boom at the foot of a fore-and-aft mainsail.

MAIN-BRACE, [mān'-brās], *n.* the mainyard brace; **to splice the m.,** to serve out a double ration of rum.

MAIN-COURSE, [mān'-kaws], *n.* (*naut.*) the mainsail of a square-rigged ship.

MAIN-DECK, [mān'-dek'], *n.* (*naut.*) the principal deck; the deck between poop and forecastle.

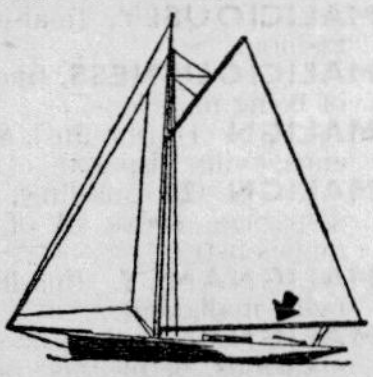

MAIN-BOOM

MAINLAND, [mān'-land], *n.* the continent, the major land-mass, as opposed to an island.

MAINLY, [mān'-li], *adv.* in the main, mostly, chiefly.

MAINMAST, [mān'-mahst], *n.* the principal mast of a ship.

MAINOR, MAINOUR, [mān'-or], *n.* (*leg.*) stolen property taken in the possession of the thief. [OFr. *maneuvre*].

MAINPERNOR, [mān'-per-nor], *n.* a person who is surety for another's appearance before a court on some specific future date. [AFr. *mainpernour*].

MAINPRISE, [mān'-prīz], *n.* (*leg.*) an undertaking to stand surety for the appearance of a prisoner in court. [AFr. *mainprise*].

MAINSAIL, [mānsl], *n.* the principal sail in a ship.

MAINSHEET, [mān'-shēt], *n.* (*naut.*) the rope that extends the mainsail; the rope working the main-boom.

MAINSPRING, [mān'-spring], *n.* the principal spring in a watch, etc.; (*fig.*) the main impulse of an event or activity.

MAINSTAY, [mān'-stā], *n.* (*naut.*) the maintop stay; (*fig.*) the chief and firmest support or prop.

MAINTAIN, [mān-tān'], *v.t.* to support, keep up, sustain; to uphold; to preserve; to keep in good condition; to defend; to affirm, argue strongly. [OFr. *maintenir*].

MAINTAINABLE, [mān-tān'-abl], *adj.* that can be maintained.

MAINTENANCE, [mān'-ten-ants], *n.* the process of maintaining; the state of being maintained; the means of maintaining; (*leg.*) meddlesome interference in a suit in which one has no interest; **cap of m.,** a royal cap of dignity. [OFr. *maintenance*].

MAINTOP, [mān'-top], *n.* (*naut.*) the platform at top of the mainmast.

MAINYARD, [mān'-yahd], *n.* (*naut.*) the mainsail yard.

MAISONNETTE, [māz'-on-et'], *n.* a dwelling consisting of two or three floors only of a building. [Fr. *maisonette*].

MAIZE, [māz], *n.* the edible grain of the plant *Zea Mays*; the plant itself. [Span. *maiz*].

MAIZENA, [māz-ē'-na], *n.* flour made from maize.

MAJESTIC, [ma-jest'-ik], *adj.* displaying, possessing, majesty, nobly dignified.

MAJESTICAL, [ma-jest'-ik-al], *adj.* majestic.

MAJESTICALLY, [ma-jest'-ik-al-i], *adv.* in majestic fashion.

MAJESTICALNESS, [ma-jest'-ik-al-nes], *n.* the quality or manner of being majestic.

MAJESTY, [maj'-es-ti], *n.* impressive and magnificent dignity, grandeur, stateliness; royal power; the title of a sovereign. [L. *majestas*].

MAJOLICA, [ma-jol'-i-ka], *n.* a distinctive kind of enamelled pottery, originally produced in Majorca. [It. *maiolica*].

MAJOR (1), [mā'-jer], *n.* the lowest-ranked field-officer in the British army, the second-in-command of a battalion; a person legally of age.

MAJOR (2), [mā'-jer], *adj.* the more important of two things, groups, issues; elder; larger; (*mus.*) denoting a specific arrangement of semitones in a scale, and also a specific number of semitones in an interval; (*log.*) containing the general rule, or the predicate of the conclusion of a syllogism; **m. suit,** (*cards*) hearts or spades. [L. *major* greater].

MAJORAT, [ma-zhaw-rah'], *n.* primogeniture. [MedL. *majoratus*].

MAJORATE, [mā'-jer-āt], *n.* the office or status of a major.

MAJORDOMO, [mā'-jer-dō'-mō], *n.* the steward of a great household; (*coll.*) the pompous organizer of anything. [MedL. *majordomus* chief of the house].

MAJOR-GENERAL, [mā'-jor-jen'-er-al], *n.* (*milit.*) the military rank next above that of a brigadier-general.

MAJORITY, [ma-jo'-ri-ti], *n.* the most part, the greater number; the number of votes by which a successful candidate exceeds his rival; the rank of a major; the age of full legal responsibility. [MedL. *majoritas*].

MAJORSHIP, [mā'-jer-ship], *n.* the rank of a major.

MAJUSCULE, [ma-jus'-kewl], *n.* a large uncial or capital letter; such lettering in general. [L. *majusculus* rather greater].

MAKE (1), [māk], *n.* the process of making; things made in a certain way; a brand; a method of making; **on the m.,** (*coll.*) in pursuit of personal profit. [*Next*].

MAKE (2), (made), [māk], *v.t.* to construct, compose, build up, put together; to cause to appear, happen, or become; to perform, carry out; to get ready, prepare; to achieve, gain; to result in, act as; to add up to; to reckon to be; to compel, coerce; to lead to do; to create, appoint; to reach; to prepare (a bed) for use; *v.i.* to prepare; to rise; to tend, move; to ripen; **to m. at,** to move to attack; **to m. away with,** to dispose of, kill; **to m. for,** to go towards; **to m. out,** to decipher, understand; to pretend; **to m. up,** to apply paint and cosmetics; to compose a quarrel; to indemnify; to ingratiate oneself; to invent; (*print.*) to set up for the press; **to m. up one's mind,** to decide; **to m. good,** to succeed; to replace or provide compensation for. [OE. *macian*].

MAKE-BELIEVE, [māk'-bi-lēv'], *n.* wish-fulfilment, the deliberate belief in something one knows to be untrue.

MAKE-PEACE, [māk'-pēs], *n.* a peacemaker.

MAKER, [māk'-er], *n.* one who makes; the Creator.

MAKESHIFT (1), [māk'-shift'], *n.* a temporary and approximate substitute.

MAKESHIFT (2), [māk'-shift'], *adj.* prepared or employed as a makeshift.

MAKE-UP, [māk'-up], *n.* the arrangement of a printed page or poster; facial painting and decoration, *esp.* for the stage; materials for this; a person's nature.

MAKEWEIGHT, [māk'-wāt], *n.* something added to bring the weights to a specified level.

MAKIMONO, [ma-kim'-o-nō], *n.* a Japanese hanging picture unrolling horizontally. [Jap. *makimono*].

MAKING, [māk'-ing], *n.* the act of one who makes; (*pl.*) elements promising future realization; profits.

MAL-, *pref.* bad, wrong. [L. *malus*].

MALACCA, [ma-lak'-a], *n.* cane made from the Malaccan palm *Calamus scipionum*; **M. cane,** a walking stick of this. [*Malacca*, in Malaya].

MALACHITE, [mal'-ak-īt], *n.* green native carbonate of copper, polished and used for ornaments. [Gk. *malakhe* mallow].

MALACO-, *pref.* soft; soft-skinned. [Gk. *malakhos*].

MALACOLITE, [mal'-ak-ō-līt], *n.* a kind of augite. [MALACO and Gk. *lithos* stone].

MALACOLOGIST, [mal'-ak-ol'-oj-ist], *n.* one versed in malacology.

MALACOLOGY, [mal'-ak-ol'-o-ji], *n.* the study of molluscs. [MALACO and Gk. *logos* speech].

MALACOPHILOUS, [mal'-ak-of'-il-us], *adj.* pollinated by snails. [MALACO and Gk. *philos* lover].

MALACOPTERYGIAN, [mal'-ak-op-ter-ij'-i-an], *adj.* (*ichth.*) with soft-pointed fins. [MALACO and Gk. *pterux* a fin].

MALACOPTERYGIOUS, [mal'-ak-op-ter-ij'-i-us], *adj.* malacopterygian.

MALACOSTOMOUS, [mal'-ak-os'-tom-us], *adj.* (*ichth.*) toothless and with soft jaws. [MALACO and Gk. *stoma* mouth].

MALACOSTRACA, [mal'-ak-os'-tra-ka], *n.(pl.)* the higher crustaceans. [Gk. *malakostrakas* soft-shelled].

MALADDRESS, [mal'-a-dres'], *n.* clumsy bad manners. [MAL and ADDRESS].

MALADJUSTMENT, [mal'-ad-just'-ment], *n.* wrong adjustment; (*psych.*) inability to cope with the environment.

MALADMINISTRATION, [mal'-ad-min'-is-trā'-shun], *n.* bad administration, mismanagement.

MALADROIT, [mal'-a-droit], *adj.* tactless, clumsy. [Fr. *maladroit*].

MALADROITLY, [mal'-a-droit'-li], *adv.* in maladroit fashion.

MALADROITNESS, [mal'-a-droit'-nes], *n.* the quality of being maladroit.

MALADVENTURE, [mal'-ad-ven'-cher], *n.* an ill chance.

MALADY, [mal'-a-di], *n.* a sickness, an ailment. [Fr. *maladie*].

MALAGA, [mal'-a-ga], *n.* a sweet heavy wine. [*Malaga*, in southern Spain].

MALAGASY (1), [mal'-a-gas'-i], *n.* the language of Madagascar; a native of this country.

MALAGASY (2), [mal'-a-gas'-i], *adj.* relating to Madagascar.

MALAISE, [mal-āz'], *n.* a slight ailment or physical uneasiness. [Fr. *malaise*].

MALANDERS, MALLENDERS†, [mal'-and-erz], *n.(pl.)* chaps or scabs on a horse's legs. [Fr. *malandres*].

MALAPERT, [mal'-a-pert], *adj.* saucy; ill-timed, impudent. [OFr. *malappert*].

MALAPERTLY, [mal'-a-pert-li], *adv.* in malapert fashion.

MALAPERTNESS, [mal'-a-pert-nes], *n.* the quality of being malapert.

MALAPROPISM, [mal'-a-prop-izm], *n.* misuse of words through sound-association, *esp.* of long words. [Mrs. *Malaprop*, a character in "The Rivals" by R. B. Sheridan].

MALAPROPOS (1), [mal'-a-prop-ō'], *adj.* ill-timed; without reference, out of place. [Fr. *mal à propos* little to the purpose].

MALAPROPOS (2), [mal'-a-prop-ō'], *adv.* out of place.

MALAR, [māl'-er], *adj.* relating to the cheek. [L. *mala* the cheek].

MALARIA, [mal-āer'-i-a], *n.* a fever transmitted by mosquito-bite; miasma. [It. *mala aria* bad air].

MALARIAL, [mal-āer'-i-al], *adj.* producing, pertaining to, malaria; marshy and noxious.

MALARIAN, [mal-āer'-i-an], *adj.* malarial.

MALARIOUS, [mal-āer'-i-us], *adj.* malarial.

MALASSIMILATION, [mal'-a-sim'-il-ā'-shun], *n.* imperfect assimilation.

MALATE, [mal'-āt], *n.* a salt of malic acid.

MALAY (1), [ma-lā'], *n.* a native or the language of Malaya. [Native *Malayu*].

MALAY (2), [ma-lā'], *adj.* relating to Malay or to the Malayans. [MALAY (1)].

MALAYAN, [ma-lā'-an], *n.* a native of Malaya; the language of Malaya.

MALCONFORMATION, [mal'-kon-fawm-ā'-shun], *n.* imperfect conformation; disproportion of parts.

MALCONTENT (1), [mal'-kon-tent'], *n.* a discontented person, *esp.* one dissatisfied with the form or administration of government; discontent. [OFr. *malcontent*].

MALCONTENT (2), [mal'-kon-tent'], *adj.* discontented.

MALCONTENTEDLY, [mal'-kon-tent'-id-li], *adv.* like a malcontent.

MALCONTENTEDNESS, [mal'-kon-tent'-id-nes], *n.* the state of being a malcontent.

MALE (1), [māl], *n.* an animal or plant of male sex; a man. [MALE (2)].

MALE (2), [māl], *adj.* having the sexual capability of (depositing seed in, and) impregnating the female ovary; virile; composed of men; (*mech.*) screwing into a threaded hollow counterpart made to receive it. [OFr. *male, masle*].

MALEDICTION, [mal'-i-dik'-shun], *n.* a curse, an imprecation. [L. *maledictio*].

MALEFACTOR, [mal'-i-fakt'-er], *n.* an evil-doer [L. *malefactor*].

MALEFIC, [mal-ef'-ik], *adj.* causing evil, hurtful. [L. *maleficus*].

MALEFICENCE, [mal-ef'-is-ents], *n.* the quality of being maleficent. [L. *maleficentia*].

MALEFICENT, [mal-ef'-is-ent], *adj.* evil, spiteful, hurtful. [L. *maleficus*].

MALEVOLENCE, [mal-ev'-ol-ents], *n.* ill-will, malice. [L. *malevolentia*].

MALEVOLENT, [mal-ev'-ol-ent], *adj.* wishing evil, malicious. [L. *malevolens*].

MALEVOLENTLY, [mal-ev'-ol-ent-li], *adv.* in malevolent fashion.

MAL-EXECUTION, [mal'-ek-si-kew'-shun], *n* faulty execution, incompetent performance.

MALFEASANCE, [mal-fē'-zants], *n.* (*leg.*) wrongdoing in connexion with a legal office. [OFr. *malfaisance*].

MALFORMATION, [mal'-fawm-ā'-shun], *n.* imperfect formation, deformity.

MALFORMED, [mal-fawmd'], *adj.* wrongly formed deformed.

MALIC, [mal'-ik], *adj.* relating to, obtained from, an apple or its juice. [Doric Gk. *malon* apple].

MALICE, [mal'-is], *n.* spite, ill-wishing, desire to injure; (*leg.*) an evil or illegal intention. [Fr. *malice*].

MALICIOUS, [mal-ish'-us], *adj.* feeling or displaying malice, spiteful. [OFr. *malicius*].

MALICIOUSLY, [mal-ish'-us-li], *adv.* in malicious fashion.

MALICIOUSNESS, [mal-ish'-us-nes], *n.* the quality of being malicious.

MALIGN (1), [ma-līn'], *adj.* malevolent, of evil influence, evilly disposed. [L. *malignus*].

MALIGN (2), [ma-līn'], *v.t.* to defame, slander; to disparage, speak ill of. [L. *malignare* to behave maliciously].

MALIGNANCY, [ma-lig'-nan-si], *n.* the state of being malignant.

MALIGNANT, [ma-lig'-nant], *adj.* evilly disposed, malicious, pernicious; (*med.*) dangerous, threatening life. [L. *malignans*].

MALIGNANTLY, [ma-lig'-nant-li], *adv.* in malignant fashion.

MALIGNER, [ma-līn'-er], *n.* one who maligns.

MALIGNITY, [ma-lig'-ni-ti], *n.* the quality of being malignant. [L. *malignitas*].
MALIGNLY, [ma-līn'-li], *adv.* in malign fashion.
MALINGER, [ma-ling'-ger], *v.i.* to pretend illness or incapacity in order to escape a task. [Fr. *malingre* ailing].
MALINGERER, [ma-ling'-ger-er], *n.* one who malingers.
MALINGERY, [ma-ling'-ger-i], *n.* the act of malingering.
MALISM, [ma'-lizm], *n.* the belief that evil is fundamental to matter, and victorious in the universe. [L. *malus* evil].
MALISON†, [mal'-iz-on], *n.* an imprecation. [OFr. *maleison* curse].
MALKIN, [mawl'-kin], *n.* a slut, a scullery maid; a whore. [*Matilda*].
MALL, [mawl], *n.* the game of pall-mall; the mallet used in this; a broad shady walk in a city, originally an alley in London where the game was played. [MAUL (1)].

MALL

MALLARD, [mal'-ahd], *n.* the common wild duck, *Anas boschus*. [OFr. *mallart*].
MALLEABILITY, [mal'-i-a-bil'-i-ti], *n.* the state of being malleable.
MALLEABLE, [mal'-i-abl], *adj.* soft enough to be hammered into shape; (*fig.*) pliable, adaptable; lacking strength of personality. [OFr. *malleable*].
MALLEABLENESS, [mal'-i-abl-nes], *n.* malleability.
MALLEATE, [mal'-i-āt], *v.t.* to hammer out into a sheet. [L. *malleare* to hammer].
MALLEATION, [mal'-i-ā'-shun], *n.* the act of malleating; the state of being malleated. [MedL. *malleatio*].
MALLEE, [mal'-ē], *n.* an Australian dwarf eucalyptus plant. [Native].
MALLEE-BIRD, [mal'-ē-burd], *n.* a mound-bird of the genus *Megapodius*.
MALLEMUCK, [mal'-i-muk], *n.* the fulmar, *Fulmar glacialis*, or any of several related birds. [Du. *mallemok*].
MALLENDERS†, see MALANDERS.
MALLEOLAR, [ma-lē'-ō-ler], *adj.* (*anat.*) belonging to the ankle.
MALLEOLUS, [ma-lē'-ō-lus], *n.* (*anat.*) one of the projecting knobs of bone on either side of the ankle. [L. *malleolus* little hammer].
MALLET, [mal'-et], *n.* a hammer with a large wooden head; a long-handled, wooden-headed striker used in croquet, polo, etc. [Fr. *maillet*].

MALLET

MALLEUS, [mal'-ē-us], *n.* (*anat.*) a bone of the middle ear. [L. *malleus* hammer].
MALLOW, [mal'-ō], *n.* any of the broad-leaved, pink-flowered plants of the genus *Malva*. [OE. *mealuwe*].
MALM, [mahm], *n.* a chalky loam. [OE. *mealm* sand].
MALMAISON, [mal-māz'-on], *n.* the dark pink Bourbon rose; a kind of carnation. [*Malmaison*, a residence of the Empress Josephine].
MALMROCK, [mahm'-rok], *n.* a calcareous sandstone. [OE. *mealm* sand].
MALMSEY, [mahm'-zi], *n.* a heavy, sweet white wine, similar to Madeira. [MedL. *Malmasia*].
MALNUTRITION, [mal'-new-trish'-un], *n.* underfeeding, inadequate nutrition; slow starvation.
MALODOROUS, [mal-ō'-der-us], *adj.* evil-smelling.
MALODOUR, [mal-ō'-der], *n.* an unpleasant smell.
MALPIGHIAN, [mal-pig'-i-an], *n.* (*anat.*) relating to those glands and bodily organs discovered by Malpighi. [M. *Malpighi* (1628-1694), an Italian doctor].
MALPOSITION, [mal'-pōz-ish'-un], *n.* an incorrect or awkward position.
MALPRACTICE, [mal-prak'-tis], *n.* evil practice, *esp.* irregular or criminal acts in an official position; (*leg.*) negligent medical treatment of a patient.
MALT (1), [mawlt], *n.* barley soaked in water, allowed to bud, and dried in a kiln for use in brewing. [OE. *mealt*].
MALT (2), [mawlt], *v.t. and i.* to make into malt; to flavour with malt; to become malt.
MALT-DUST, [mawlt'-dust], *n.* the refuse of malt.
MALTESE (1), [mawlt-ēz'], *n.* the language spoken by the people of Malta; an inhabitant of Malta.
MALTESE (2), [mawlt'-ēz], *adj.* relating to Malta; **M. Cross**, a cross with four equal arms broadening and forking at the extremities.

MALTESE CROSS

MALT-FLOOR, [mawlt'-flaw'-er], *n.* a floor for drying malt.
MALTHA, [mal'-tha], *n.* a compound of wax and pitch. [Gk. *maltha*].
MALT-HORSE, [mawlt'-haws], *n.* a horse employed in grinding malt; (*fig.*) a dull fellow.
MALTHUSIAN, [mal-thew'-zi-an], *adj.* relating to Malthus and his theory of population. [T. R. *Malthus* (1766-1835)].
MALT-LIQUOR, [mawlt'-lik'-er], *n.* alcoholic liquor made from fermented malt.
MALTMAN, [mawlt'-man], *n.* a maltster.
MALTOSE, [mawlt'-ōs], *n.* sugar obtained from starch by the action of malt ferments.
MALTREAT, [mal-trēt'], *v.t.* to ill-treat.
MALTREATMENT, [mal-trēt'-ment], *n.* the act of maltreating.
MALTSTER, [mawlt'-ster], *n.* one who makes malt.
MALT-WORM, [mawlt'-wurm], *n.* (*slang*) a tippler.
MALTY, [mawlt'-i], *adj.* pertaining to, resembling, malt.
MALVACEOUS, [mal-vā'-shus], *adj.* relating to the *Malvaceæ*, the group of plants including the mallows, etc. [MedL. *malvaceus*].
MALVERSATION, [mal'-ver-sā'-shun], *n.* maladministration; corrupt diversion of public funds to private profit. [Fr. *malversation*].
MALVOISIE†, [mal'-vwahz-ē], *n.* malmsey. [Fr. *malvoisie*].
MAMELON, [mam'-el-on], *n.* a rounded mound or protuberance. [Fr. *mamelon* nipple].
MAMELUKE, [mam'-el-ōōk], *n.* one of the bodyguard, and later masters, of the sultans of Egypt, originally recruited from Caucasian slaves; a warlike slave or retainer. [Arab. *mamluk* slave].
MAMEY, see MAMMEE.
MAMILLA, [ma-mil'-a], *n.* the teat or nipple; the leaf-cushion of cactus plants. [L. *mammilla*].
MAMILLARY, [mam'-il-er-i], *adj.* relating to the nipple; with an irregular, nippled surface.
MAMILLATED, [mam'-il-āt'-id], *adj.* having small mamelons or nipple-like projections.
MAMMA (1), [ma-mah', mam'-a], *n.* a childish word for mother. [~L. *mamma*].
MAMMA (2), (*pl.* **mammae**), [mam'-a], *n.* the milk-secreting gland in female mammals; the rudimentary development of this in males; the breast. [L. *mamma*].
MAMMAL, [mam'-al], *n.* one of the mammalia.
MAMMALIA, [ma-mā'-li-a], *n.*(*pl.*) the class of warm-blooded vertebrates that suckle their young. [L. *mammalia*].
MAMMALIAN (1), [ma-mā'-li-an], *n.* a mammal.
MAMMALIAN (2), [ma-mā'-li-an], *adj.* relating to the mammalia.
MAMMALIFEROUS, [mam'-al-if'-er-us], *adj.* (*geol.*) (of strata, etc.) containing traces of mammalian life. [MAMMAL and L. *ferre* to bear].
MAMMALOGIST, [ma-mal'-o-jist], *n.* one learned in mammalogy.
MAMMALOGY, [ma-mal'-o-ji], *n.* the study of the mammalia. [MAMMAL and Gk. *logos* speech].
MAMMARY, [mam'-er-i], *adj.* relating to the breasts.
MAMMATE, [mam'-āt], *adj.* having breasts. [L. *mammatus*].
MAMMEE, MAMEY, [mam-ē'], *n.* the sweet, yellow fruit of the American tree, *Mammea americana*; the tree itself. [Span. *mamey*].
MAMMER†, [mam'-er], *v.i.* to stammer; to waver, dither. [Echoic].
MAMMIFER, [mam'-i-fer], *n.* a mammiferous animal. [MAMMA (2) and L. *ferre* to bear].
MAMMIFEROUS, [mam-if'-er-us], *adj.* having mammae.
MAMMIFORM, [mam'-i-fawm], *adj.* nipple-shaped. [MAMMA (2) and FORM].
MAMMODIS, [mam'-o-dis], *n.* a coarse Indian fabric. [Pers. *mahmudi*].
MAMMON, [mam'-on], *n.* the god of riches; (*fig.*) wealth, cupidity, fatal lust after material things. [Aram. *mamon* riches].

MAMMONISH, [mam'-on-ish], *adj.* mammon-worshipping.

MAMMONISM, [mam'-on-izm], *n.* the worship of wealth.

MAMMONIST, [mam'-on-ist], *n.* a worshipper of material things.

MAMMONITE, [mam'-on-īt], *n.* a mammonist.

MAMMOTH (1), [mam'-oth], *n.* an extinct hairy elephant of great size. [Russ. *mammot*].

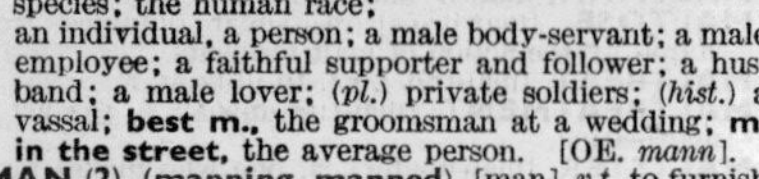
MAMMOTH

MAMMOTH (2), [mam'-oth], *adj.* (*coll.*) enormous, immense.

MAMMULA, [mam'-yŏŏ-la], *n.* a tiny nipple-like lump. [L. *mammula*].

MAMMY, [mam'-i], *n.* mother; (*U.S.*) an American negro nurse or mother.

MAN (1), [man], *n.* the adult male of the human species; the human race; an individual, a person; a male body-servant; a male employee; a faithful supporter and follower; a husband; a male lover; (*pl.*) private soldiers; (*hist.*) a vassal; **best m.**, the groomsman at a wedding; **m. in the street**, the average person. [OE. *mann*].

MAN (2), **(manning, manned)**, [man], *v.t.* to furnish with men, *esp.* for immediate action; to fortify, strengthen.

MANACLE (1), [man'-akl], *n.* a fetter for the wrist, a handcuff. [L. *manicula*].

MANACLE (2), [man'-akl], *v.t.* to fetter or bind with a manacle.

MANAGE, [man'-ij], *v.t.* and *i.* to control, guide with the hands; to control, handle, enforce discipline upon; to deal with; to run, direct (an enterprise, business undertaking, etc.); to look after, see to; to succeed, accomplish; to cope with something. [It. *maneggiare*].

MANAGEABILITY, [man'-ij-a-bil'-i-ti], *n.* manageableness.

MANAGEABLE, [man'-ij-abl], *adj.* that may be managed.

MANAGEABLENESS, [man'-ij-abl-nes], *n.* the quality of being manageable.

MANAGEABLY, [man'-ij-ab-li], *adv.* in manageable fashion.

MANAGELESS, [man'-ij-les], *adj.* unmanaged.

MANAGEMENT, [man'-ij-ment], *n.* the act of managing; the state of being managed; the group of persons managing a business; cunning and tactful methods of managing something or someone.

MANAGER, [man'-ij-er], *n.* one who manages, *esp.* one who manages a business or other undertaking.

MANAGERESS, [man'-ij-er-es], *n.* a female manager.

MANAGERIAL, [man'-ij-ēer'-i-al], *adj.* relating to management or to the office of manager.

MANAGING DIRECTOR, [man'-aj-ing-di-rekt'-er], *n.* the director of a company who is employed to administer its operations.

MANAKIN, [man'-a-kin], *n.* a group of tropical American birds of the genus *Pipra*. [Du. *mannekin*].

MAN-AT-ARMS, [man'-at-ahmz'], *n.* a medieval mounted armed retainer not of knightly rank or birth.

MANATEE, [man'-a-tē], *n.* the Atlantic sea-cow. [Caribbean *manattoui*].

MANCHE, [mahnsh'], *n.* a long, hanging, medieval sleeve, *esp.* (*her.*) used as a charge. [Fr. *manche*].

MANCHESTER (1), [man'-chest-er], *n.* a type of British four-engined bomber. [*Manchester*, a city in Lancashire].

MANCHESTER (2), [man'-chest-er], *adj.* relating to Manchester, the Lancashire cotton-town; **M. school**, a political group, led by Bright and Cobden, advocating an economic doctrine of free-trade and *laissez-faire*.

MANCHET, [man'-chet], *n.* wheaten bread of the finest quality; a loaf of this. [ME. *manchete*].

MAN-CHILD, [man'-chīld], *n.* a male child.

MANCHINEEL, [man'-shin-ēl'], *n.* the tropical American tree, *Hippomane Mancinella*; the poisonous greenish fruit of this tree. [Fr. *mancenille*].

MANCHU, [man-chōō'], *adj.* relating to Manchuria, its people and culture. [Chin. *manchu* pure].

MANCIPLE, [man'-sipl], *n.* the steward of a household, college, etc. [OFr. *manciple*].

MANCUNIAN (1), [man-kew'-ni-an], *n.* a native of Manchester.

MANCUNIAN (2), [man-kew'-ni-an], *adj.* of, or relating to, Manchester. [L. *Mancunium* Manchester].

MANDAMUS, [man-dām'-us], *n.* (*leg.*) a writ from a high to an inferior court. [L. *mandamus* we command].

MANDARIN, [man'-der-in], *n.* an officer of the Imperial Chinese civil service; (*fig.*) an officious and absolute bureaucrat; the form of Chinese spoken by the cultured; a small, originally Chinese, orange; an orange coal-tar dye; an orange liqueur; **m. duck**, a large handsome Chinese duck, *Aix galericulata*. [Portug. *mandarim*].

MANDARINING, [man'-der-ēn-ing], *n.* the process of dyeing yellow with nitric acid.

MANDATARY, [man'-dat-er-i], *n.* a person or power to whom a mandate is entrusted. [L. *mandatarius*].

MANDATE (1), [man'-dāt], *n.* a command, injunction; a commission to exercise power, in a specified way, on behalf of another; the delegation of government by the League of Nations to one of its members, of part of the empire of a defeated enemy state or of a backward people; (*R.C.*) a rescript of the pope; (*Rom. leg.*) a commission to act for another without reward but with indemnification against possible loss; (*E. leg.*) an undertaking, without recompense, to perform some act for another in respect to the thing bailed to one. [L. *mandatum*].

MANDATE (2), [man-dāt'], *v.t.* to delegate to a mandatary.

MANDATORY, [man'-dat-er-i], *adj.* commanding or directing, instructing. [LL. *mandatorius*].

MANDELIC, [man-del'-ik], *adj.* containing, derived from, oil of almonds. [Germ. *mandel* almond].

MANDIBLE, [man'-dibl], *n.* a jaw, *esp.* the lower jaw; either of the halves of a beak or pair of jaws. [LL. *mandibula* jaw].

MANDIBULAR, [man-dib'-yŏŏ-ler], *adj.* relating to the jaw.

MANDIBULATE, [man-dib'-yŏŏ-lāt], *adj.* having mandibles.

MANDIBULATED, [man-dib'-yŏŏ-lāt-id], *adj.* mandibulate.

MANDOLIN(E), [man'-dō-lin], *n.* a pear-shaped, metal-stringed instrument, related to the guitar, and played with a plectrum. [It. *mandolino*].

MANDRAKE, [man'-drāk], *n.* the narcotic and emetic herb, *Mandragora autumnalis*, used in magic, and said to shriek when torn from the ground. [ME. *mandragge*].

MANDREL, **MAUNDRIL**†, [man'-drel], *n.* the shank of a lathe on which the object to be turned is fixed. [Uncert.].

MANDRILL, [man'-dril], *n.* the West African baboon, *Papio maimon*, remarkable for the vivid red-and-blue pigmentation of its face and buttocks. [MAN (1) and DRILL (3)].

MANDUCABLE, [man'-dyōō-kabl], *adj.* able to be chewed.

MANDUCATE, [man'-dyōō-kāt], *v.t.* to chew. [L. *manducare*].

MANDUCATION, [man'-dyōō-kā'-shun], *n.* the act of chewing. [L. *manducatio*].

MANDUCATORY, [man'-dyōō-kāt'-er-i], *adj.* relating to chewing.

MANE, [mān], *n.* the long, thick hair on the neck of an animal. [OE. *manu*].

MANED, [mānd], *adj.* having a mane.

MANEGE, **manège**, [man-āzh'], *n.* horsemanship or the training of horses; a school for teaching this. [Fr. *manège*].

MANES, [mā'-nēz], *n.*(*pl.*) the shades of the family dead, ancestral spirits; the gods of the lower world. [L. *manes*].

MANE-SHEET, [mān'-shēt], *n.* a covering for the upper part of a horse's head.

MANFUL, [man'-fōōl], *adj.* bold, vigorous, manly.

MANFULLY, [man'-fōōl-i], *adv.* in manful fashion.

MANFULNESS, [man'-fōōl-nes], *n.* the quality of being manful.

MANGABEY, [mang'-ga-bi], *n.* a long-tailed African monkey of the genus *Cercocebus*. [*Mangabey*, a district in Madagascar].

MANGANATE, [mang'-gan-āt], *n.* a compound of manganic acid with a base.

MANGANESATE, [mang'-gan-ēz'-āt], *n.* manganate.

MANGANESE, [mang'-gan-ēz], *n.* (*chem.*) the hard, white, brittle metallic element, Mn; the black oxide of this metal. [Fr. *manganèse*].

MANGANESIAN, [mang'-gan-ēz'-i-an], *adj.* manganesic.

MANGANESIC, [mang'-gan-ēz'-ik], *adj.* relating to, containing, obtained from, manganese.
MANGANIC, [mang-gan'-ik], *adj.* manganesic.
MANGANITE, [mang'-gan-īt], *n.* an ore of manganese.
MANGCORN, [mang'-kawn], *n.* (*dial.*) a mixed grain crop.
MANGE, [mānj], *n.* a skin disease in hairy-coated animals, caused by a parasite, and resulting in loss of fur or hair. [OFr. *manjue* itch].
MANGEL-WURZEL, MANGOLD-WURZEL, [mangl'-wurzl'], *n.* a large coarse beet used as food for cattle. [Germ. *mangold* beet and *wurzel* root].
MANGER, [mān'-jer], *n.* an eating trough for cattle. [Fr. *manger* to eat].
MANGINESS, [mānj'-i-nes], *n.* the state of being mangy.
MANGLE (1), [mangl], *n.* a device of wooden rollers used for pressing the water out of washed garments. [Du. *mangel*].
MANGLE (2), [mangl], *v.t.* to wring through a mangle.
MANGLE (3), [mangl], *v.t.* to cut up, lacerate, hack about; (*fig.*) to spoil by incompetent rendering. [AFr. *mahangler* to maim].
MANGLER, [mang'-gler], *n.* one who mangles.
MANGO, [mang'-gō], *n.* the tropical Asiatic tree, *Mangifera indica*; the fruit of this tree. [Tamil *man-kay* fruit of the mango tree].
MANGO-FISH, [mang'-gō-fish'], *n.* a yellow, edible fish found in the Ganges.
MANGOLD-WURZEL, see MANGEL-WURZEL.
MANGONEL, [mang'-gon-el'], *n.* a medieval military machine for catapulting heavy stones. [Gk. *magganon*].

MANGONEL

MANGOSTEEN, [mang'-gō-stēn], *n.* the East Indian tree, *Garcinia mangostana*; the reddish, juicy fruit of this tree. [Malay *mangustan*].
MANGROVE, [mang'-grōv], *n.* a genus of tropical swamp-shrubs. [Malay *manggi-manggi*].
MANGY, [mān'-ji], *adj.* afflicted with mange; moth-eaten, squalidly shabby.
MAN-HANDLE, [man'-handl'], *v.t.* to ill-treat physically, to handle roughly; to move by man-power alone.
MAN-HATER, [man'-hāt'-er], *n.* one who hates mankind; a woman who hates men.
MANHOLE, [man'-hōl], *n.* a circular hole, of sufficient size to admit a man, giving access to sewers, etc.
MANHOOD, [man'-hŏŏd], *n.* the state, age, or status of being a man; men in general; manliness. [MAN and OE. *had* condition].
MANIA, [mā'-ni-a], *n.* a neurotic state of mental disturbance typically characterized by fixation, delusion, and hallucination; (*fig.*) irrational enthusiasm and interest in one subject, obsession. [Gk. *mania* madness].
MANIAC (1), [mā'-ni-ak], *n.* a madman, *esp.* when violent and frenzied.
MANIAC (2), [mā'-ni-ak], *adj.* afflicted with, arising from, characteristic of mania. [L. *maniacus*].
MANIACAL, [mā'-ni-ak-al], *adj.* maniac.
MANICHAEAN (1), [man'-i-kē'-an], *n.* a believer in Manichaeism.
MANICHAEAN (2), [man'-i-kē'-an], *adj.* relating to Manichaeism.
MANICHAEISM, [man'-i-kē'-izm], *n.* the ethico-religious belief in the eternal, universal dualism of good and evil. [Gk. *Manikhaios*, from Mani, a third-century Persian philosopher].
MANICURE (1), [man'-i-kyŏŏer], *n.* the act of manicuring; the state of being manicured.
MANICURE (2), [man'-i-kyŏŏer], *v.t.* to treat the hands and finger-nails, *esp.* to file, polish and trim up the finger-nails. [L. *manus* hand and *cura* care].
MANICURIST, [man'-i-kyŏŏer-ist], *n.* one whose profession is manicuring.
MANIFEST (1), [man'-i-fest], *n.* an inventory of a ship's cargo declared to the customs. [Fr. *manifeste*].
MANIFEST (2), [man'-i-fest], *adj.* clearly evident, obvious. [L. *manifestus*].
MANIFEST (3), [man'-i-fest], *v.t. and i.* to show clearly, to express, display, exhibit; to make evident; (*spiritualism*) to become visible to the senses; (*naut.*) to put down in a manifest. [L. *manifestare*].
MANIFESTABLE [man'-i-fest'-abl], *adj.* that may be manifested.
MANIFESTATION, [man'-i-fest-ā'-shun], *n.* the act of manifesting; the thing manifested; the state of being manifested. [L. *manifestatio*].
MANIFESTLY, [man'-i-fest-li], *adv.* in manifest fashion.
MANIFESTNESS, [man'-i-fest-nes], *n.* the quality of being manifest.
MANIFESTO, [man'-i-fest'-ō], *n.* a public declaration of policy and belief issued by a person or body, *esp.* by a political party. [It. *manifesto*].
MANIFOLD (1), [man'-i-fōld], *n.* (*mech.*) a pipe or chamber with several openings.
MANIFOLD (2), [man'-i-fōld], *adj.* multifarious, many-sided, numerous. [OE. *manigfeald*].
MANIFOLD (3), [man'-i-fōld], *v.t.* to make several copies of a document by carbons or similar devices.
MANIFOLDLY, [man'-i-fōld-li], *adv.* in manifold fashion.
MANIFOLDNESS, [man'-i-fōld-nes], *n.* the quality of being manifold; multiplicity.
MANIGLIONS, [ma-nil'-yunz], *n.(pl.)* the handles over the trunnions of a cannon. [It. *maniglione*].
MANIKIN, MANNIKIN, [man'-i-kin], *n.* an anatomical model of the human body; a dwarf, a small man; a tailor's dummy. [Du. *manneken*].
MANILLA (1), [ma-nil'-a], *n.* a copper leg-ring, etc., used as native currency in West Africa. [Span. *manilla*].
MANILLA (2), [ma-nil'-a], *n.* a cigar made in the Philippines. [*Manila*, capital of the Philippines].
MANILLA (3), [ma-nil'-a], *n.* the second highest card in ombre or quadrille. [Span. *manilla*].
MANILLA (4), [ma-nil'-a], *adj.* relating to Manila; **M. hemp**, a strong fibre from the plantain, *Musa textilis*, used for making ropes and cables; **M. paper**, a strong paper made from Manilla hemp.
MANIOC, [man'-i-ok], *n.* the cassava plant; tapioca, prepared from this. [Braz. *mandioca*].
MANIPLE, [man'-ipl], *n.* a Roman military unit of 200 men, the smallest battle-unit; the embroidered vestment, *orig.* a towel, worn on the left wrist at the Eucharist by the celebrant and his assistants. [L. *manipulus* handful].
MANIPULAR, [man-ip'-yŏŏ-ler], *adj.* pertaining to a maniple. [L. *manipularis*].
MANIPULATE, [man-ip'-yŏŏ-lāt], *v.t.* to work, control, or fashion with the hands; to influence, to handle skilfully; to manage or arrange dishonestly. [MANIPULATION].
MANIPULATION, [man-ip'-yŏŏ-lā'-shun], *n.* the act of manipulating; state of being manipulated. [Fr. *manipulation*].
MANIPULATIVE, [man-ip'-yŏŏ-lat-iv], *adj.* done by manipulation; relating to manipulation.
MANIPULATOR, [man-ip'-yŏŏ-lāt'-er], *n.* one who manipulates.
MANIPULATORY, [man-ip'-yŏŏ-lāt'-er-i], *adj.* manipulative.
MANITOU, [man'-i-tŏŏ], *n.* a Nature spirit or fetish feared and worshipped by North American Indians. [Indian *manito*].
MANITRUNK, [man'-i-trungk], *n.* the anterior segment of the body of an insect. [L. *manus* hand and TRUNK].
MANKIND, [man-kīnd'], *n.* the human race. [OE. *manncynn*].
MANLESS, [man'-les], *adj.* without men.
MANLINESS, [man'-li-nes], *n.* the quality of being manly.
MANLY, [man'-li], *adj.* befitting a man, brave, virile, vigorously determined; like a man.
MAN-MADE, [man'-mād], *adj.* made by man.
MAN-MERCER, [man'-mer'-ser], *n.* a vendor of small articles of men's dress, a hosier.
MANNA, [man'-a], *n.* the food dropped from heaven to feed Israel in the wilderness, supposed to be a sweet gum exuded from tamarisk or a species of *Alhagi*; a sweet juice from two varieties of ash; (*fig.*) providential relief in extremity or want. [Heb. *man*].
MANNEQUIN, [man'-i-kin], *n.* a person trained and employed in wearing new clothes in order to display them for sale; a tailor's dummy. [Fr. *mannequin*].
MANNER, [man'-er], *n.* method, style, or mode of performing an action; bearing, behaviour, way in which a person speaks or behaves; a characteristic style or mode; (*pl.*) observance of the customary

social courtesies and conventions; habits and way of life; (*archaic*) kind, sort. [OFr. *manière*].

MANNERED, [man'-erd], *adj.* having good manners; displaying mannerisms.

MANNERISM, [man'-er-izm], *n.* a peculiarity of manner, a small, distinguishing personal idiosyncrasy; an affectation of manners.

MANNERIST, [man'-er-ist], *n.* one displaying mannerisms.

MANNERLESS, [man'-er-les], *adj.* ill-mannered.

MANNERLINESS, [man'-er-li-nes], *n.* the quality of being mannerly.

MANNERLY, [man'-er-li], *adj.* displaying good manners, well-bred, polite, schooled in urbanity.

MANNIKIN, see MANIKIN.

MANNISH, [man'-ish], *adj.* (of a woman) like a man, masculine in manner and appearance.

MANNISHLY, [man'-ish-li], *adv.* in mannish style.

MANNITE, [man'-īt], *n.* a sweet substance obtained from manna.

MANOEUVRE (1), [man-ōōv'-er], *n.* an adroit move to gain advantage; subtle management, intrigue; (*pl.*) mock warfare carried out by an army as training in strategy and tactics. [Fr. *manœuvre*].

MANOEUVRE (2), [man-ōōv'-er], *v.t. and i.* to intrigue and skilfully manipulate oneself or another into or out of some position; to carry out subtly a tactical scheme for one's own advantage; to move or dispose (troops, etc.) according to stratagem; to carry out manoeuvres. [Fr. *manœuvrer*].

MANOEUVRER, [man-ōōv'-er-er], *n.* one who manoeuvres.

MAN-OF-WAR, [man'-ov-waw(r)'], *n.* a warship.

MANOMETER, [man-om'-it-er], *n.* a pressure gauge measuring the density of gases. [Gk. *manos* diffuse and METER].

MANOMETRIC, [man'-ō-met'-rik], *adj.* of, or pertaining to, a manometer.

MANOR, [man'-er], *n.* a feudal landholding unit consisting of a manor-house and a quantity of land over which the seigneur had rights of service, taxation, and jurisdiction; (*pop.*) a large country house surrounded by lands over which its owner has certain rights. [OFr. *manoir*].

MANOR-HOUSE, [man'-er-hows'], *n.* the dwelling of the lord of the manor.

MANORIAL, [man-aw'-ri-al], *adj.* belonging to a manor.

MANOSCOPE, [man'-ō-skōp], *n.* a manometer. [Gk. *manos* diffuse and SCOPE].

MANPOWER, [man'-pow-er], *n.* the (number of) people available for a particular industrial or military purpose.

MAN-ROPES, [man'-rōps'], *n.(pl.)* (*naut.*) side-ropes to the gangway of a ship.

MANSARD, [man'-sahd], *n.* a form of roof built in two steps, the lower step sloping more acutely than the upper; an attic, garret. [F. *Mansard* (1598-1666), the French architect)].

MANSE, [mants], *n.* the house of a Scots Presbyterian minister. [MedL. *mansus* house].

MAN-SERVANT, [man'-serv'-ant], *n.* a domestic male servant.

MANSION, [man'-shun], *n.* a great residence; (*pl.*) a block of flats. [L. *mansio* halting-place].

MANSLAUGHTER, [man'-slaw'-ter], *n.* (*leg.*) unlawful homicide without malice aforethought.

MAN-SLAYER, [man'-slā'-er], *n.* one who has killed a human being.

MANSUETUDE†, [man'-swi-tewd], *n.* gentleness, meekness. [L. *mansuetudo*].

MANTA, [man'-ta], *n.* a sea-fish, the ox-ray, *Cephaloptera giornæ*. [Span. *manta* blanket].

MANTEL, [man'-tel], *n.* a shelf projecting from, and lying across, the top of a fireplace. [MANTLE (1)].

MANTELET, see MANTLET.

MANTELPIECE, [man'-tel-pēs], *n.* a projecting ledge set over a fireplace.

MANTELSHELF, [man'-tel-shelf'], *n.* a mantel.

MANTIC, [man'-tik], *adj.* relating to divination. [Gk. *mantikos*].

MANTILLA, [man-til'-a], *n.* a Spanish shawl worn round the head and shoulders; a short cloak. [Span. *mantilla* little cloak].

MANTIS, [man'-tis], *n.* a genus of orthopterous insects, including the stick-insect. [Gk. *mantis* prophet].

MANTISSA, [man-tis'-a], *n.* the decimal part of a logarithm. [L. *mantissa* makeweight].

MANTLE (1), [mantl], *n.* a loose outer garment, a cloak; asbestos, thimble-shaped mesh cover placed over a gas flame to increase the light by becoming incandescent; (*her.*) the cloak behind the escutcheon; (*fig.*) anything covering or hiding; (*zool.*) a membranous external fold lining the shell of a mollusc. [L. *mantellum* cloak].

MANTLE (2), [mantl], *v.t. and i.* to cover with a mantle; to conceal; to form a coating, to cover a surface; to suffuse; (of hawks) to hide the legs with the wings.

MANTLET, MANTELET, [mant'-let], *n.* a mail curtain at the back of a helmet; (*milit., fort.*) a screen-work set up to protect guns or advancing troops; a kind of hut to protect miners attacking the foundations of a wall. [OFr. *mantelet*].

MANTLING, [mant'-ling], *n.* cloth for making mantles; (*her.*) a lambrequin; a mantle.

MANTLING

MANTRA, [man'-tra], *n.* a Vedic sacred text used as a subject for meditation. [Skr. *mantra* means of thought].

MAN-TRAP, [man'-trap], *n.* an iron spring trap for catching trespassers by the feet.

MANTUA, [man'-tew-a], *n.* a woman's gown of the eighteenth century. [Fr. *manteau* mantle].

MANTUA-MAKER, [man'-tew-a-māk'-er], *n.* a maker of ladies' dresses.

MANUAL (1), [man'-yōō-al], *n.* a handbook, textbook; a keyboard of an organ; a Roman Catholic service book.

MANUAL (2), [man'-yōō-al], *adj.* performed by hand, relating to the hand. [L. *manualis*].

MANUALLY, [man'-yōō-al-i], *adv.* with the hand.

MANUCODE, [man'-yōō-kōd], *n.* the blue-plumed Papuan bird, *Cicinpurus regius*, the kingbird of paradise. [Malay *manuk dewata*].

MANUFACTORY, [man'-yōō-fakt'-er-i], *n.* a place where goods are manufactured; a factory.

MANUFACTURAL, [man'-yōō-fak'-cher-al], *adj.* relating to manufacture.

MANUFACTURE (1), [man'-yōō-fak'-cher], *n.* the act of manufacturing; the thing manufactured; the way or style in which a thing is manufactured. [L. *manu factura* making by hand].

MANUFACTURE (2), [man'-yōō-fak'-cher], *v.t.* to make finished goods out of raw materials by means of an elaborate and organized system of labour under single control, *esp.* with the aid of machinery; (*fig.*) to falsify, invent what is untrue; to mass-produce.

MANUFACTURER, [man'-yōō-fak'-cher-er], *n.* one who manufactures; the owner of a factory.

MANUFACTURING, [man'-yōō-fak'-cher-ing], *adj.* pertaining to, or employed in, manufacture.

MANUL, [mahn'-ōōl], *n.* a small greyish wild cat found in North Eastern Europe and Tartary. [Native].

MANUMISSION, [man'-yōō-mish'-un], *n.* the act of manumitting; the state of being manumitted; the deed embodying this. [L. *manumissio*].

MANUMIT, (**manumitting, manumitted**), [man'-yōō-mit], *v.t.* to release from slavery. [L. *manumittere*].

MANUMOTOR, [man'-yōō-mō'-ter], *n.* a small wheeled invalid-carriage, propelled by hand. [L. *manus* hand and MOTOR].

MANURE (1), [man-yōōer'], *n.* fertilizer spread on the ground, *esp.* animal excrement.

MANURE (2), [man-yōōer'], *v.t.* to apply manure to. [AFr. *maynoverer* to work by hand].

MANURER, [man-yōōer'-er], *n.* one who, or that which, manures.

MANUSCRIPT (1), [man'-yōō-skript], *n.* a document, book, written by hand; the original draft of a work as prepared by the author for printing. [L. *manu scriptus* written by hand].

MANUSCRIPT (2), [man'-yōō-skript], *adj.* written by hand.

MANUTYPE, [man'-yōō-tīp], *n.* anything written by hand. [L. *manu* by hand and TYPE].

MANX (1), [mangks], *n.* the language of the Isle of Man. [OIcel. *manskr*].

MANX (2), [mangks], *adj.* relating to the Isle of Man and its inhabitants; **M. cat**, a tailless species of cat; **M. shearwater**, the sea bird, *Puffinus anglorum*.

MANY, [men'-i], *adj.* numerous, in considerable number. [OE. *manig*].

MANY-HEADED, [men'-i-hed'-id], *adj.* with many heads.

MANY-SIDED, [men'-i-sīd'-id], *adj.* having many sides; versatile, catholic.

MANY-SIDEDNESS, [men'-i-sīd'-id-nes], *n.* the quality of being many-sided.
MANZANILLA, [man'-zan-ēl'-ya], *n.* a dry brown sherry. [Span. *manzanilla*].
MANZANITA, [man'-zan-ē'-ta], *n.* the North American shrub, *Arctostaphylos glauca.* [Span. *manzanita*].
MAORI, [mah'-er-i], *n.* an autochthonous inhabitant of New Zealand. [Native].
MAP (1), [map], *n.* a plan representing the positions and relations of objects, *esp.* a representation on a plane surface of the earth's surface or the heavens; (*slang*) the face; **on the m.,** important; **off the m.,** out-of-the-way; obsolete. [MedL. *mappa*].
MAP (2), (mapping, mapped), [map], *v.t.* to draw a map of; **m. out,** to draw up (a scheme, plan, etc.).
MAPLE, [māpl], *n.* a tree of the genus *Acer*; the wood of this tree; **m. sugar,** sugar obtained by evaporation from the juice of *Acer saccharinum.* [OE. *mapel*].
MAQUIS, [ma-kē'], *n.* the scrubby undergrowth typical of Corsica. [Fr. dial. *maquis*].
MAR, (marring, marred), [mah(r)], *v.t.* to spoil, damage; to stain, blot, to disfigure; (*dial.*) to pamper, spoil. [OE. *merran* to hinder].
MARABOU, [ma'-ra-bōō], *n.* an adjutant stork of the genus *Leptoptilus*; soft feathers from this. [Arab. *murabit* hermit].
MARABOUT, [ma'-ra-bōōt'], *n.* a Moslem saint or holy hermit; the tomb or shrine of such a person. [Arab. *murabit*].
MARACAN, [ma'-ra-kan'], *n.* a Brazilian parrot. [Tupi *maracana*].
MARACAUBA, [ma'-ra-kow'-ba], *n.* a strong, dark Brazilian wood. [Native].
MARANATHA, [ma'-ran-ath'-a], *n.* intense anathema. [Aram. *maran atha* the Lord comes].
MARASCHINO, [ma'-ra-skē'-nō], *n.* a sweet liqueur made from black cherries. [It. *maraschino*].
MARASMUS, [ma-raz'-mus], *n.* bodily atrophy. [Gk. *marasmos* consumption].
MARATHI, [ma-rah'-thi], *n.* the language of the Mahrattas. [Native].
MARATHON, [ma'-rath-on], *n.* a race of about 26 miles, named after the famous run from Marathon to Athens to bring news of the defeat of the Persians; a prolonged, gruelling, sporting contest.
MARAUD, [ma-rawd'], *v.i.* to wander in quest of plunder and pillage; to go on a looting raid. [OFr. *marauder*].
MARAUDER, [ma-rawd'-er], *n.* one who marauds.
MARAUDING, [ma-rawd'-ing], *adj.* that marauds.
MARAVEDI, [ma'-ra-vā'-di], *n.* a Spanish coin, formerly of gold, now worth about a farthing. [Arab. *murabitin* a Moorish dynasty].
MARBLE (1), [mahbl], *n.* a compact crystalline limestone capable of taking a high polish; an imposing sculpture made of this; a small glass or stone ball used in children's games. [Fr. *marbre*].
MARBLE (2), [mahbl], *adj.* made of, resembling, marble; (*fig.*) callous, unmoved by pity; deathly pale.
MARBLED, [mahbld], *adj.* veined to resemble marble, *esp.* of book boards so treated.
MARBLE-EDGED, [mahbl'-ejd'], *adj.* with marbled edges.
MARBLE-HEARTED, [mahbl'-haht'-id], *adj.* hard-hearted.
MARBLER, [mahb'-ler], *n.* one who veins paper or other material to resemble marble.
MARBLING, [mahb'-ling], *n.* the art or practice of veining like marble; a variegation like that of marble.
MARBLY, [mahb'-li], *adj.* like marble.
MARC, [mahk], *n.* the dry pulp of squeezed fruit. [L. *marcus* hammer].
MARCASITE, [mahk'-a-sīt], *n.* white iron pyrites, orthorhombic sulphide of iron. [MedL. *marcasita*].
MARCASITIC, [mahk'-a-sit'-ik], *adj.* relating to, containing, marcasite.
MARCELINE, [mah'-sel-ēn], *n.* a thin silk tissue. [Fr. *marceline*].
MARCESCENT, [mah-ses'-ent], *adj.* (*bot.*) withering, fading, yet still on the plant. [L. *marcescens*].
MARCESCIBLE, [mah-ses'-ibl], *adj.* capable of withering. [Fr. *marcescible*].
MARCH (1), [mahch], *n.* the third month of the year. [OFr. *marche* from L. (*mensis*) *Martius* month of Mars].
MARCH (2), [mahch], *n.* the border of a country, *esp.* land of disputed ownership along the frontiers. [Fr. *marche*].
MARCH (3), [mahch], *n.* the act of marching; the distance marched; the route marched over; a long, steady, regular advance; the regular measured step of soldiers marching; a musical composition intended to accompany and regulate marching. [Fr. *marche*].
MARCH (4), [mahch], *v.i.* to border on, run contiguous with. [MARCH (2)].
MARCH (5), [mahch], *v.t. and i.* to walk in regular, measured steps, as soldiers in formation; to walk strongly and purposefully; to order troops to march; to make someone walk swiftly and unhesitatingly; to go to war. [Fr. *marcher*].
MARCHER, [mahch'-er], *n.* a border noble.
MARCHIONESS, [mah'-shon-es], *n.* the wife of a marquess. [MedL. *marchionissa*].
MARCHPANE, see MARZIPAN.
MARCID, [mah'-sid], *adj.* wasting, emaciated. [L. *marcidus*].
MARCONIGRAM, [mah-kō'-ni-gram], *n.* a telegram or message sent by wireless. [G. *Marconi*, the Italian inventor (1874-1937)].
MARDI-GRAS, [mah'-di-grah'], *n.* Shrove Tuesday; a carnival held on that day. [Fr. *mardi* Tuesday and *gras* fat].
MARE, [māer], *n.* the female of the horse; **mare's nest,** a discovery that amounts to nothing; **mare's tail,** a long streaky cloud; an aquatic or marshy plant, *Hippuris vulgaris.* [OE. *mere*].
MAREMMA, [ma-rem'-a], *n.* flat, marshy, disease-infested coast-land. [L. *maritima* seaside].
MARGARATE, [mah'-ger-āt], *n.* a salt of margaric acid.
MARGARIC, [mah-ga'-rik], *adj.* pearly; **m. acid,** a fatty animal and vegetable acid of a pearly aspect. [Gk. *margaron* pearl].
MARGARINE, [mah'-ger-ēn', mah'-jer-ēn'], *n.* a butter substitute containing animal and vegetable oils. [Fr. *margarine*].
MARGARITE, [mah'-ger-īt], *n.* pearl mica, a hydrated silicate of aluminium and lime. [L. *margarita*].
MARGARITIFEROUS, [mah'-ger-it-if'-er-us], *adj.* containing, producing, pearls. [L. *margaritifer*].
MARGARODITE, [mah-ga'-rō-dīt], *n.* a hydrated mica with pearly lustre. [Germ. *margarodit*].
MARGARON, [mah'-ger-on], *n.* a fatty substance obtained from margaric acid and quicklime. [Gk. *margaron* pearl].
MARGAY, [mah'-gā], *n.* the South American spotted wildcat. [Fr. *margay* from Tupi *mbaracaia*].
MARGIN, [mah'-jin], *n.* the edge, border, limit; the space round a page of printed or written matter; the additional amount of anything, *esp.* for safety, beyond what is exactly needed; (*comm.*) the difference between the selling and buying price of shares; cover deposited for speculation on market fluctuations. [L. *margo*].
MARGINAL, [mah'-jin-al], *adj.* set in the margin; pertaining to a margin.
MARGINALIA, [mah'-jin-ā'-li-a], *n.(pl.)* marginal notes. [L. *marginalia*].
MARGINALLY, [mah'-jin-al-i], *adv.* in the margin.
MARGINATE, [mah'-jin-āt], *adj.* having a margin. [L. *marginatus*].
MARGINATED, [mah'-jin-āt-id], *adj.* marginate.
MARGODE, [mah'-gōd], *n.* a hard, bluish-grey stone. [Unkn.].
MARGOSA, [mah-gō'-sa], *n.* an East Indian tree, *Melia Azedarach*, the bark of which has medicinal properties. [Portug. *amargoso* bitter].
MARGOT, [mah'-gō], *n.* the Canadian perch. [Fr. *margot*].
MARGRAVATE, [mah'-grav-āt], *n.* the territory of a margrave.
MARGRAVE, [mah'-grāv], *n.* originally a military governor of a march, later the title of certain Princes of the Holy Roman Empire. [Germ. *markgraf*].
MARGRAVINE, [mah'-grav-ēn], *n.* the wife of a margrave. [Du. *markgravin*].
MARGUERITE, [mah'-ger-ēt'], *n.* the ox-eye daisy, *Chrysanthemum leucanthemum.* [Gk. *margarites* pearl].
MARIAN (1), [māer'-i-an], *n.* a supporter of Mary, Queen of Scots.
MARIAN (2), [māer'-i-an], *adj.* connected with the Virgin Mary; connected with Queen Mary I, or Mary, Queen of Scots. [L. *Maria*].
MARIGENOUS, [ma-rij'-in-us], *adj.* born from the sea. [L. *mare* sea and Gk. *genes* born of].
MARIGOLD, [ma'-ri-gōld], *n.* a yellowish composite flower of the genus *Calendula* or *Tagetes.* [*Mary* and GOLD].
MARIGRAPH, [ma'-ri-graf], *n.* a tide-register. [L. *mare* sea and GRAPH].
MARIKIN, [ma'-ri-kin], *n.* a long-tusked marmoset

or tamarin, of the genus *Midas*. [Tupi *miriquina*].
MARINADE (1), [ma'-rin-ād'], *n.* fish or meat pickled in vinegar, wine, and spice; a pickle of vinegar, wine, and spice. [Span. *marinada*].
MARINADE (2), [ma'-rin-ād], *v.t.* to marinate.
MARINATE, [ma'-rin-āt], *v.t.* to pickle in marinade.
MARINE (1), [ma-rēn'], *n.* the ships of a state, considered as a whole; a soldier serving in the navy. [MARINE (2)].
MARINE (2), [ma-rēn'], *adj.* relating to, found in, the sea; relating to shipping; **m. store**, a second-hand junk shop. [L. *marinus*].
MARINER, [ma'-rin-er], *n.* a sailor, *esp.* one in the merchant service. [MedL. *marinarius*].
MARINISM, [ma'-rin-izm], *n.* the affected literary style typical of Marini or his imitators. [G. B. *Marini*, d. 1625].
MARINORAMA, [ma'-rin-ō-rah'-ma], *n.* a seascape. [L. *marinus* of the sea and Gk. *horama* view].
MARIOLATRY, [māer'-i-ol'-a-tri], *n.* the worship of the Virgin Mary. [Gk. *Maria* Mary and *latreia* worship].
MARIONETTE, [ma'-ri-on-et'], *n.* a puppet dangled on strings and so made to dance and act. [Fr. *marionette*].
MARIPUT, [ma'-ri-put], *n.* a species of civet, *Viverra zorilla*. [Native].
MARISH†, [ma'-rish], *n.* a marsh. [OFr. *marais*].
MARITAL, [ma'-ri-tal], *adj.* relating to marriage or to a husband or wife. [L. *maritalis*].
MARITALLY, [ma'-ri-tal-i], *adv.* in marital fashion.
MARITIME, [ma'-ri-tim], *adj.* bordering on the sea; relating to, connected with, the sea, relating to ships and ocean trade. [L. *maritimus*].
MARJORAM, [mah'-jer-am], *n.* an aromatic plant of the genus *Origanum*, used in seasoning and as a stimulant. [MedL. *majorana*].
MARK (1), **MERK**†, [mahk], *n.* a medieval unit of weight for precious metals, of about eight ounces; a medieval coin worth about 14s.; the modern unit of German currency. [Late OE. *marc*].
MARK (2), [mahk], *n.* an impression, distinguishing sign, spot, etc., differentiating something from a similar object, or spoiling the uniformity, design, etc., of its surface; a stain, blemish; a symbol or sign of ownership or identity; an external manifestation of anything; the thing aimed at, vital point; distinction, importance; a standard, level, limit; a symbol or score denoting comparative merit of someone or something, *esp.* in an examination, test or competition; (*hist.*) land held by a tribe in common; a frontier district, a march; the starting point of a race. [OE. *mearc* boundary].
MARK (3), [mahk], *v.t.* to make a mark on, as a distinguishing sign; to stain, blemish; to award marks of merit to; to keep the score in certain games; to pay attention to; to distinguish, make notable; to follow closely an opponent in football; **to m. time**, to move the feet up and down in march rhythm while remaining in the same place; (*fig.*) to cease to progress while remaining potentially active; **to m. out**, to trace the boundaries, etc., of; to destine; **to m. off**, to measure off. [MARK (2)].
MARKED, [mahkt], *adj.* distinguished with a mark; displaying signs of an obvious injury; receiving the closest attention; noticeable.
MARKEDLY, [mahk'-ed-li], *adv.* in marked manner.
MARKER, [mahk'-er], *n.* one marking up the score in a game; a device for this; a bookmark.
MARKET (1), [mah'-ket], *n.* a meeting-place or meeting for the sale, purchase, and exchange of goods; the demand for a commodity; actual or potential trade in a saleable product; the price of a commodity. [ONFr. *market*].
MARKET (2), [mah'-ket], *v.t.* and *i.* to bring goods to market for sale; to offer for sale; to deal at a market.
MARKETABLE, [mah'-ket-abl], *adj.* that can be marketed.
MARKETABLENESS, [mah'-ket-abl-nes], *n.* the quality of being marketable.
MARKET-DAY, [mah'-ket-dā'], *n.* the day on which a public market is held.
MARKET-GARDEN, [mah'-ket-gah'-den], *n.* a garden where fruits and vegetables are grown for market.
MARKET-GARDENER, [mah'-ket-gahd'-ner], *n.* one who grows fruits and vegetables for sale.
MARKETING, [mah'-ket-ing], *n.* the act of bringing goods to market or of offering goods for sale; the buying of goods in a market.
MARKET PLACE, [mah'-ket-plās], *n.* an open space, often in the centre of a town, where a market is held.
MARKET-PRICE, [mah'-ket-pris'], *n.* the price at which goods are offered in open market.
MARKHOR, [mah'-kaw(r)], *n.* the Himalayan wild goat, *Capra falconeri*. [Pers. *markhor* serpent eater].
MARKING, [mahk'-ing], *n.* a distinctive mark on a surface.
MARKING INK, [mah'-king-ingk'], *n.* an indelible ink used to make identifying marks on linen.
MARKSMAN, [mahks'-man], *n.* one skilled in shooting.
MARKSMANSHIP, [mahks'-man-ship], *n.* skill in shooting.

MARKHOR

MARL (1), [mahl], *n.* a rich soil of clay and lime, used for fertilizing. [OFr. *marle*].
MARL (2), [mahl], *v.t.* to treat with marl.
MARLACEOUS, [mahl-ā'-shus], *adj.* marly.
MARLINE (1), [mah'-lin], *n.* thin, two-stranded cord used for binding ropes to prevent galling. [Du. *marlijn*].
MARLINE (2), [mah'-lin] *v.t.* to bind round with marline.
MARLINE-SPIKE, [mah'-lin-spik'], *n.* an iron spike used to open the strands of rope in splicing.

MARLINE-SPIKE

MARLING, [mah'-ling], *n.* the act of twisting a thin cord about a rope to prevent galling. [MARLINE].
MARLITE, [mahl'-it], *n.* a non-pulverizing kind of marl.
MARLITIC, [mahl-it'-ik], *adj.* relating to marlite and its properties.
MARLPIT, [mahl'-pit], *n.* a pit where marl is dug.
MARLSTONE, [mahl'-stōn], *n.* the calcareous and sandy strata separating the upper from the lower lias clays.
MARLY, [mahl'-i], *adj.* containing, consisting of, resembling, marl.
MARMALADE, [mah'-mal-ād], *n.* a jam made from fruits of the citron group, *esp.* jam made from orange pulp boiled with its peel; **m. tree**, the tropical American tree, *Vitellaria mammosa*. [Portug. *marmelada*].
MARMATITE, [mah'-ma-tit], *n.* a black sulphide of zinc. [*Marmato*, in Colombia, where found].
MARMITE, [mah'-mit], *n.* an earthenware casserole. [Fr. *marmite*].
MARMOLITE, [mah'-mō-lit], *n.* green serpentine. [Gk. *marmairo* I shine and *lithos* stone].
MARMORACEOUS, [mah'-mer-ā'-shus], *adj.* like marble. [L. *marmor* marble].
MARMORATED, [mah'-mer-āt'-id], *adj.* marbled. [L. *marmor* marble].
MARMORATUM, [mah'-mer-ā'-tum], *n.* a cement containing powdered marble; an amalgam used in stopping teeth. [L. *marmor* marble].
MARMOREAL, [mah-maw'-ri-al], *adj.* made of, resembling, marble. [L. *marmoreus*].
MARMOREAN, [mah-maw'-ri-an], *adj.* marmoreal.
MARMOSE, [mah'-mōz], *n.* a marsupial mammal resembling the opossum. [Fr. *marmose*].
MARMOSET, [mah'-moz-et'], *n.* the small tropical American monkey of the *Hapalidæ*. [Fr. *marmouset* grotesque statuette].
MARMOT, [mah'-mot], *n.* a burrowing, hibernating rodent of the genus *Arctomys*, related to the squirrel. [Fr. *marmotte*].
MAROCAIN, [ma'-rō-kān'], *n.* a heavy dress material with a grained surface. [Fr. *marocain* Moroccan].
MARONE, [ma-rōn'], *n.* a colour resembling that of claret. [MAROON (1)].
MARONITES, [ma'-ron-its], *n.(pl.)* a body of Eastern Christian heretics formerly centred on Mount Lebanon. [*Maron* their founder].
MAROON (1), [ma-rōōn'], *n.* a deep brownish crimson; a firework exploding with a loud detonation, used formerly as an air-raid warning. [Fr. *marron* chestnut].
MAROON (2), [ma-rōōn'], *n.* a negro, *esp.* a runaway slave living in the mountains and forests of the West Indies; one who is marooned. [Fr. *marron*].

MAROON (3), [ma-rōōn'], *v.t.* to isolate, abandon in a desert island or desolate region. [MAROON (2)].

MAROONING, [ma-rōōn'-ing], *n.* (*U.S. slang*) the act of camping out.

MAROQUIN, [ma'-ro-kin], *n.* morocco leather. [Fr. *maroquin*].

MARPLOT, [mah'-plot], *n.* one whose fussy interference spoils a design.

MARQUE, [mahk], *n.* a pledge; **letters of m.**, a licence to privateer. [Fr. *marque*].

MARQUEE, [mah-kē'], *n.* a large tent, *esp.* one erected for refreshment or entertainment purposes. [MARQUISE].

MARQUESS, MARQUIS, [mah'-kwis], *n.* the title of a peer ranking between earl and duke; the courtesy title of the eldest son of a duke; a title of nobility in certain European countries. [OFr. *marchis* lord of the marches].

MARQUETRY, MARQUETERIE, [mah'-ket-ri], *n.* wood mosaic; a design produced by inlaying one wood with others of different texture and colour. [Fr. *marqueterie*].

MARQUIS, see MARQUESS.

MARQUISATE, [mah'-kwis-āt], *n.* the rank or dignity of a marquess.

MARQUISE, [mah-kēz'], *n.* the wife of a marquess. [Fr. *marquise*].

MARRAM, [ma'-ram], *n.* a coarse grass growing in sand-dunes, the sea matweed *Ammophila arenaria*. [OIcel. *maralmr* sea-straw].

MARRER, [mah'-rer], *n.* one who mars.

MARRIAGE, [ma'-rij], *n.* the legal and religious ceremony and bond sanctioning and involving cohabitation of, and sexual intercourse between, two persons of opposite sex, the union of husband and wife; (*fig.*) indissoluble union. [Fr. *mariage*].

MARRIAGEABLE, [ma'-rij-abl], *adj.* suitable for marriage.

MARRIED, [ma'-rid], *adj.* united in marriage; intimately associated.

MARRON, [ma'-raw(ng)], *n.* a chestnut. [Fr. *marron*].

MARROT, [ma'-rot], *n.* the guillemot. [Uncert.].

MARROW (1), [ma'-rō], *n.* the edible gourd, *Cucurbita ovifera*. [MARROW (2)].

MARROW (2), [ma'-rō], *n.* the soft fatty tissue in the hollow of bones; (*fig.*) the very core, the substantial essence; **m. bone**, a bone containing a generous proportion of marrow, and used in cookery; (*pl.*) the knees. [OE. *mearg*].

MARROWFAT, [ma'-rō-fat'], *n.* a kind of rich pea.

MARROWISH, [ma'-rō-ish], *adj.* like marrow.

MARROWLESS, [ma'-rō-les], *adj.* without marrow; (*fig.*) cowardly.

MARROWY, [ma'-rō-i], *adj.* containing marrow.

MARRY (1), [ma'-ri], *v.t. and i.* to take a person of the opposite sex in marriage; to unite a couple in marriage; (*fig.*) to unite intimately; to enter into marriage; (*naut.*) to splice rope-ends together. [Fr. *marier*].

MARRY† (2), [ma'-ri], *int.* an exclamation of surprise or emphasis. [The Virgin *Mary*].

MARS, [mahz], *n.* the Roman god of war; the fourth planet from the sun; (*fig.*) war. [L. *Mars*].

MARSALA, [mah-sah'-la], *n.* a light white wine resembling sherry. [*Marsala*, in Western Sicily].

MARSEILLAISE, [mah'-el-yāz'], *n.* the French national anthem. [Fr. *marseillaise* of Marseilles].

MARSH, [mahsh], *n.* a tract of soft, very damp land, usually low-lying and partly under water, a swamp. [OE. *mersc*].

MARSHAL (1), [mah'-shal], *n.* a high official in a princely household, regulating rank and precedence on, and supervising in general, ceremonial occasions, a Master of the Horse; (*milit.*) a general officer of the highest rank in certain countries; (*U.S.*) a high-court official with the powers of a sheriff. [OHGerm. *marahscalh* horse servant].

MARSHAL (2), (**marshalling, marshalled**), [mah'-shal], *v.t.* to arrange in suitable or systematic order; (*her.*) to order the quarterings on an escutcheon; (*leg.*) to arrange so as to settle claims in order of precedence.

MARSHALCY, [mah'-shal-si], *n.* marshalship.

MARSHALLER, [mah'-shal-er], *n.* one who marshals.

MARSHALSHIP, [mah'-shal-ship], *n.* the rank or office of a marshal.

MARSH-BEETLE, [mahsh'-bētl'], *n.* the reed-mace, *Typha latifolia*.

MARSH-BETONY, [mahsh'-bet'-o-ni], *n.* the plant *Stachys palustris*.

MARSH-CINQUEFOIL, [mahsh'-singk'-foil], *n.* the plant, *Comarum palustre*.

MARSH-ELDER, [mahsh'-eld'-er], *n.* the guelder rose, *Viburnum Opulus*.

MARSH-GAS, [mahsh'-gas], *n.* an inflammable gas given off from decayed vegetation.

MARSH-HARRIER, [mahsh'-ha'-ri-er], *n.* the moor buzzard, *Circus æruginosus*.

MARSH-HEN, [mahsh'-hen], *n.* the moorhen, *Gallinula chloropus*; the Virginia rail, *Rallus virginianus*.

MARSHINESS, [mahsh'-i-nes], *n.* the state of being marshy.

MARSHLAND, [mahsh'-land], *n.* boggy country.

MARSH-MALLOW, [mahsh'-mal'-ō], *n.* the pink-flowered mallow; a sweet made from the root of this plant.

MARSH-MARIGOLD, [mahsh'-ma'-ri-gōld], *n.* the plant, *Caltha palustris*, with yellow flowers.

MARSH-PARSLEY, [mahsh'-pahs'-li], *n.* celery, *Apium graveolens*.

MARSH-TIT, [mahsh'-tit], *n.* the small black-headed tomtit, *Parus palustris*.

MARSH-TREFOIL, [mahsh'-tref'-oil], *n.* the buck-bean, *Menyanthes trifoliata*.

MARSH-WARBLER, [mahsh'-wawb'-ler], *n.* the verderole, *Acrocephalus palustris*.

MARSHY, [mahsh'-i], *adj.* waterlogged, like a marsh, full of marshes, swampy.

MARSIPOBRANCHIATE, [mah'-si-pō-brangk'-i-āt], *adj.* with purse gills, like the lampreys. [Gk. *marsipos* pouch and BRANCHIATE].

MARSUPIAL (1), [mah-sew'-pi-al], *n.* a marsupial animal, as the kangaroo. [L. *marsupium* pouch].

MARSUPIAL (2), [mah-sew'-pi-al], *adj.* relating to mammals who carry their young in an external pouch.

MARSUPITE, [mah'-sew-pīt], *n.* a pouch-shaped fossil. [L. *marsupium* pouch].

MART, [maht], *n.* a market-place, place for trading, sale-room. [Du. *markt*].

MARTAGON, [maht'-a-gon], *n.* the Turk's-cap lily, *Lilium Martagon*. [Turk. *martagan* a kind of turban].

MARTELLO, [mah-tel'-ō], *n.* a circular, low, stone tower mounting a gun, *esp.* one built along a coast. [*Mortella* in Corsica, where a tower of this sort proved successful].

MARTEN, [mah'-tin], *n.* a carnivorous, fur-bearing mammal of the genus *Mustela*, similar to the weasel. [OFr. *martrine*].

MARTEN

MARTEXT, [mah'-tekst], *n.* a careless preacher.

MARTIAL, [mah'-shal], *adj.* warlike, militant; military, relating to, fitted for war. [L. *martialis* of Mars].

MARTIALLY, [mah'-shal-i], *adv.* in martial fashion.

MARTIN, [mah'-tin], *n.* a species of swallow with feathered toes, *Chelidon urbica*. [*Martin*, the personal name].

MARTINET, [mah'-tin-et'], *n.* a strict and rigid disciplinarian, insisting upon exact observance of regulations. [*Martinet*, a general of Louis XIV].

MARTINETS, [mah'-tin-ets'], *n.*(*pl.*) (*naut.*) the leech-lines of a sail. [Uncert.].

MARTINGALE, [mah'-tin-gāl], *n.* a strap from a horse's girth to hold its head down and prevent rearing; (*naut.*) the jib-boom stay; (*gambling*) the practice of doubling up on losses. [Fr. *martingale*].

MARTINI (1), [mah-tē'-ni], *n.* an early breech-loading rifle. [*Martini* and Henry the inventors].

MARTINI (2), [mah-tē'-ni], *n.* a cocktail made of gin, vermouth, and bitters. [*Martini*, a brand of vermouth].

MARTINMAS, [mah'-tin-mas], *n.* the feast of St. Martin, November 11.

MARTLET, [maht'-let], *n.* (*her.*) a kind of swallow without feet; the house-martin. [Fr. *martelet*].

MARTYR (1), [mah'-ter], *n.* one who undergoes penalty, injury, or death, for refusing to abandon principles or beliefs, *esp.* religious beliefs; (*fig.*) a severe sufferer from anything. [OE. *martyr*].

MARTYR (2), [mah'-ter], *v.t.* to put to death for refusal to abandon principles.

MARTYRDOM, [mah'-ter-dom], *n.* the state of being a martyr; the torture or death of a martyr; severe pain. [OE. *martyrdom*].

MARTYROLOGICAL, [mah'-ter-ol-oj'-ik-al], *adj.* pertaining to martyrology.

MARTYROLOGY, [mah'-ter-ol'-o-ji], *n.* the history,

study of martyrs; a list of the feasts of martyrs. [MARTYR and Gk. *logos* speech].

MARVEL (1), [mah'-vel], *n.* a wonder, a thing to cause amazement; (*coll.*) an astonishingly able person. [OFr. *merveille*].

MARVEL (2), (marvelling, marvelled), [mah'-vel], *v.i.* to wonder, to be amazed, to be filled with astonishment. [OFr. *merveiller*].

MARVELLOUS, [mah'-vel-us], *adj.* arousing wonder, causing to marvel, amazing; (*coll.*) extremely good; remarkable. [OFr. *merveillos*].

MARVELLOUSLY, [mah'-vel-us-li], *adv.* in marvellous fashion.

MARVELLOUSNESS, [mah'-vel-us-nes], *n.* the quality of being marvellous.

MARXIAN (1), [mahk'-si-an], *n.* a Marxist. [Karl *Marx* (1818-1883)].

MARXIAN (2), [mahk'-si-an], *adj.* Marxist.

MARXIST (1), [mahks'-ist], *n.* a believer in the teaching of Marx, that human and political motives are fundamentally economic, and that history is the record of continuous class struggle.

MARXIST (2), [mahks'-ist], *adj.* relating to Marx and his theories.

MARYBUD, [māer'-i-bud], *n.* a marigold.

MARY-SOLE, [māer'-i-sōl'], *n.* the megrim, a flat-fish of the genus *Lepidorhombus*.

MARZIPAN, MARCHPANE, [mah'-zi-pan'], *n.* a sweetmeat made from crushed almonds and sugar. [~Germ. *marzipan*].

MASCARON, [mas'-ker-on], *n.* a face on a door-knocker. [Unkn.].

MASCLE, [maskl], *n.* one of the lozenge-shaped overlapping metal plates sewn on to a jacket in some forms of thirteenth-century armour; (*her.*) a perforated lozenge. [AFr. *mascle*].

MASCLE

MASCOT, [mas'-kot], *n.* a talisman, any thing or person taken with one to bring good luck. [Fr. *mascotte*].

MASCULINE, [mas'-kyŏŏ-lin], *adj.* male in sex; showing male characteristics, manly, virile; mannish; (*gram.*) belonging to the male gender; **m. rhyme**, rhyming of the final stressed syllables of a line. [L. *masculin(us)*].

MASCULINELY, [mas'-kyŏŏ-lin-li], *adv.* in masculine fashion.

MASCULINENESS, [mas'-kyŏŏ-lin-nes], *n.* the quality of being masculine.

MASCULINITY, [mas-kyŏŏ-lin'-i-ti], *n.* masculineness.

MASH (1), MESS†, [mash], *n.* a mixture of bran, grain, or malt and hot water; any pulped-up substance; (*slang*) mashed potatoes. [OE. *masc*].

MASH (2), [mash], *v.t.* to crush or pound into a pulpy mass, *esp.* to prepare potatoes in this way; to mix malt and hot water in brewing.

MASH† (3), [mash], *v.t. and i.* (*slang*) to ogle, flirt with, or attempt to do so. [Uncert.].

MASHER, [mash'-er], *n.* one who mashes a girl; a dandy.

MASHIE, [mash'-i], *n.* a golf-club with a lofted face. [Fr. *massue* club].

MASHIE-NIBLICK, [mash'-i-nib'-lik], *n.* an exceptionally lofted mashie.

MASHING, [mash'-ing], *n.* the process of reducing to a pulp, or of infusing malt with hot water.

MASHTUB, [mash'-tub], *n.* a tub containing mash.

MASHY, [mash'-i], *adj.* in a mashed state.

MASK (1), [mahsk], *n.* a covering or protection for the face; a strip of silk with eye-holes, worn over the eyes; an elaborate religious head and face covering; a wire facial protection in fencing; a representation in clay, etc., of the human face; the head and face of a fox displayed as a hunting trophy; a masker; an apparatus to prevent the breathing of poisonous gas; (*fig.*) a deception, an appearance or open activity to conceal some secret design. [Span. *mascara*].

MASK (2), [mahsk], *v.t. and i.* to conceal with a mask; to disguise; (*milit.*) to conceal and protect from fire; to put on a mask.

MASKED, [mahskd], *adj.* wearing a mask; disguised; concealed; **m. ball**, a ball at which the guests wear masks.

MASKER, [mahsk'-er], *n.* one who wears a mask; one taking part in a masque or masquerade.

MASKINONGE, [mas'-ki-nonj], *n.* a North American species of pike, *Esox estor*. [Native].

MASLIN, MESLIN†, [mŭz'-lin], *n.* bread made of a mixture of different grains; the mixture itself. [OFr. *mesteillon*].

MASOCHISM, [mas'-ō-kizm], *n.* a psycho-pathological state in which the suffering of pain, bullying, and humiliation is essential for sexual satisfaction. [Sacher-*Masoch*, an Austrian novelist who described it].

MASOCHIST, [mas'-ō-kist], *n.* one suffering from masochism.

MASOCHISTIC, [mas'-ō-kist'-ik], *adj.* displaying, tending towards, masochism.

MASON, [mā'-son], *n.* a worker in stone; a Freemason. [OFr. *macon*].

MASONIC, [ma-son'-ik], *adj.* pertaining to Freemasonry.

MASONRY, [mā'-son-ri], *n.* the craft or work of a mason; the stonework of a building; Freemasonry.

MASORA, see MASSORA.

MASORITE, see MASSORITE.

MASQUE, [mahsk], *n.* a spectacular dramatic performance, originally a combination of ballet and tableau, but later containing songs and verse-dialogue; a dramatic composition written for performance in this way. [Fr. *masque*].

MASQUERADE (1), [mahsk'-er-ād], *n.* a dance, party, light-hearted dramatic performance in which the participants are disguised. [Span. *mascarada*].

MASQUERADE (2), [mahsk'-er-ād], *v.i.* to take part in a masquerade; to disguise oneself (as).

MASQUERADER, [mahsk'-er-ād'-er], *n.* one who masquerades.

MASS (1), [mas], *n.* celebration of the Eucharist, *esp.* by Roman Catholics; **High M.**, this ceremony with music and attendant rites; **Low M.**, the simpler ceremony without music. [OE. *mæsse* from L. *Ite, missa est* said at the end of the service].

MASS (2), [mas], *n.* a coherent, formless collection of matter; a large quantity or number of objects or persons, *esp.* close together; the greater part, majority; (*pl.*) the working class, proletariat; (*phys.*) the quantity of matter present in a substance. [L. *massa*].

MASS (3), [mas], *v.t. and i.* to gather together in a mass, *esp.* to concentrate troops.

MASSACRE (1), [mas'-a-ker], *n.* a savage, wholesale slaughter, *esp.* of defenceless persons. [Fr. *massacre*].

MASSACRE (2), [mas'-a-ker], *v.t.* to slaughter indiscriminately in wholesale fashion.

MASSAGE (1), [mas'-ahzh], *n.* medical treatment by manipulating, rubbing, and kneading parts of the body. [Fr. *massage*].

MASSAGE (2), [mas'-ahzh], *v.t.* to apply massage to.

MASSAGIST, [mas'-ahzh-ist], *n.* a masseur.

MASSE, massé, [mas'-i], *n.* (*billiards*) a stroke made with the cue held vertically.

MASSERANDUBA, [mas'-er-an'-dyŏŏ-ba], *n.* the Brazilian milk-tree, *Mimusops elata*.

MASSETER, [mas'-it-er], *n.* a principal masticatory muscle. [Gk. *masseter*].

MASSEUR, [ma-sur'], *n.* one skilled in massage. [Fr. *masseur*].

MASSEUSE, [ma-surz'], *n.* a female masseur. [Fr. *masseuse*].

MASSICOT, [mas'-i-kot], *n.* yellow lead-oxide used as a pigment. [Fr. *massicot*].

MASSIF, [mas-ēf'], *n.* a distinct group of mountains; a mountainous mass splitting into peaks towards its summit. [Fr. *massif*].

MASSINESS, [mas'-i-nes], *n.* the quality of being massy; massiveness.

MASSIVE, [mas'-iv], *adj.* heavy, of great mass and size; ponderous; large and solid; powerful. [MASS (2)].

MASSIVELY, [mas'-iv-li], *adv.* in massive fashion.

MASSIVENESS, [mas'-iv-nes], *n.* the quality of being massive.

MASS MEETING, [mas'-mēt'-ing], *n.* a large public meeting to hear speeches of popular appeal.

MASSORA, MASORA, [mas-aw'-ra], *n.* the traditional critical Hebrew commentary on the Old Testament. [Heb. *masoreth*].

MASSORETIC, [mas'-er-et'-ik], *adj.* relating to the Massora.

MASSORITE, MASORITE, [mas'-er-īt], *n.* one of the compilers of the Massora; one who adheres to its rulings.

MASS-PRODUCE, [mas'-pro-dews'], *v.t.* to produce systematically in large quantities, *esp.* mechanically.

MASS-PRODUCTION, [mas-prod-uk'-shun], *n.* the

production of standardized commodities in large quantities, *esp.* mechanically.

MASSY, [mas'-i], *adj.* of great mass.

MAST (1), [mahst], *n.* the long upright shaft supporting the sails and yards of a ship; an upright pole supporting a wireless aerial. [OE. *mæst*].

MAST (2), [mahst], *n.* the fruit of various forest trees used as food for swine. [OE. *mæst*].

MASTABA, [mast'-a-ba], *n.* a primitive, flat-roofed ancient Egyptian tomb. [Arab. *maçtabah* stone bench].

MASTED, [mahst'-id], *adj.* having a mast or masts.

MASTEL, [mas'-tel], *n.* the maple tree, *Acer campestris.* [Unkn.].

MASTER (1), [mahst'-er], *n.* one exercising control and authority over others; the captain of a merchant ship; a teacher at a school; a teacher or prophet of a religion or philosophy; the head of certain secular and religious orders; a person holding the second degree in various universities; a person pre-eminent in a craft, art, or technique; the ruler of a household; any of various official personages in charge of some specified thing; a courtesy title given to the heirs of certain Scottish baronies; a form of address given to young boys; the head of certain Oxford or Cambridge colleges; (*cards*) a card that will beat all others; **old m.,** a painting by one of the leading artists of the thirteenth to eighteenth centuries; **m. key,** a key that opens many different locks. [OFr. *maistre*].

MASTER (2), [mahst'-er], *v.t.* to make oneself master of, to subdue, overcome; to become proficient at.

MASTER-AT-ARMS, [mahst'-er-at-ahmz'], *n.* the police-officer of a warship.

MASTER-BUILDER, [mahst'-er-bild'-er], *n.* the chief builder; an employer of workmen engaged in the building trade.

MASTERDOM, [mahst'-er-dom], *n.* the state or power of being a master.

MASTERFUL, [mahst'-er-fŏŏl], *adj.* imposing one's will, able to be a master.

MASTERFULLY, [mahst'-er-fŏŏl-i], *adv.* in masterful fashion.

MASTERFULNESS, [mahst'-er-fŏŏl-nes], *n.* the quality of being masterful.

MASTER-HAND, [mahst'-er-hand'], *n.* the skill of an expert.

MASTERHOOD, [mahst'-er-hŏŏd], *n.* the state of being a master.

MASTERLESS, [mahst'-er-les], *adj.* without a master, uncontrolled.

MASTERLINESS, [mahst'-er-li-nes], *n.* the quality of being masterly.

MASTERLY, [mahst'-er-li], *adj.* showing the skill, talent, and assured touch of a master.

MASTER-MIND, [mahst'-er-mind'], *n.* the controlling intelligence of an organization, etc.

MASTERPIECE, [mahst'-er-pēs], *n.* a work of art or craft of the highest excellence and genius.

MASTERSHIP, [mahst'-er-ship], *n.* the state of being a master, mastery.

MASTER-SPRING, [mahst'-er-spring], *n.* the central, controlling spring of a mechanism; the vital centre of an enterprise.

MASTER-STROKE, [mahst'-er-strōk], *n.* a critical and brilliant action in an enterprise.

MASTER-TOUCH, [mahst'-er-tuch'], *n.* a touch or stroke showing in its brilliance the hand of a master.

MASTERWORT, [mahst'-er-wurt], *n.* the umbelliferous plant, *Peucedanum Ostruthium.*

MASTERY, [mahst'-er-i], *n.* authority, dominance; victory, ascendancy; extreme skill, dexterity, or knowledge in a thing. [OFr. *maistrie*].

MASTFUL, [mahst'-fŏŏl], *adj.* abounding with mast.

MASTHEAD, [mahst'-hed], *n.* the highest part of a mast, the topmast.

MASTIC, [mast'-ik], *n.* a resin exuding from trees, *esp. Pistacia Lentiscus,* used in varnish and in mixing a cement; the colour of this; the tree from which it is obtained. [Gk. *mastikhe*].

MASTICABLE, [mast'-ik-abl], *adj.* able to be masticated.

MASTICADOR, [mast'-ik-ād'-er], *n.* the slavering bit. [Span. *masticador*].

MASTICATE, [mast'-ik-āt], *v.t.* and *i.* to chew with the teeth. [L. *masticare*].

MASTICATION, [mast'-ik-ā'-shun], *n.* the act of masticating. [LL. *masticatio*].

MASTICATOR, [mast'-ik-āt'-er], *n.* one who, that which, masticates; a grinding machine.

MASTICATORY, [mast'-ik-āt'-er-i], *adj.* relating to, apt for, mastication.

MASTICINE, [mast'-i-sēn], *n.* that part of mastic which is insoluble in alcohol.

MASTIFF, [mast'-if], *n.* a large, powerful British dog with slavering lips and heavy muzzle. [OFr. *mastin*].

MASTING, [mahst'-ing], *n.* the arrangement of the masts in a ship.

MASTITIS, [mast-it'-is], *n.* inflammation of the breasts, *esp.* during pregnancy. [MAST(O) and Gk. *itis* denoting inflammation].

MASTLESS, [mahst'-les], *adj.* without a mast.

MASTO-, *pref.* breast. [Gk. *mastos*].

MASTODON, [mast'-ō-don], n. a gigantic extinct mammal related to the elephant, having nipple-like protuberances on its teeth. [MASTO and Gk. *odous odontos* tooth].

MASTODON

MASTODYNIA, [mast'-ō-din'-i-a], *n.* neuralgia in the breast. [MASTO and Gk. *odune* pain].

MASTOID, [mast'-oid], *adj* breast-like; relating to, affecting, the mastoid process; **m. process,** a breast-shaped process of the bone behind the ear. [MASTO and Gk. *oeides* like].

MASTOLOGY, [mast-ol'-o-ji], *n.* mammalogy. [MASTO and Gk. *logos* speech].

MASTURBATE, [mast'-er-bāt], *v.i.* to excite one's own genital organs so as to produce an orgasm, *esp.* with the hand. [L. *masturbari*].

MASTURBATION, [mast'-er-bā'-shun], *n.* the act or practice of masturbating. [L. *masturbatio*].

MASTY, [mahst'-i], *adj.* abounding with mast.

MAT (1), [mat], *n.* a coarse fibrous material made from straw, rushes, etc.; a piece of this used for covering part of a floor, or for wiping the feet on; a bolster of this fabric used to break or dull an impact; a small cover on which dishes may be stood when served. [OE. *matt* from LL. *matta*].

MAT (2), MATT, [mat], *adj.* dull, lustreless, not reflecting light. [Fr. *mat*].

MAT (3), (matting, matted), [mat], *v.t.* and *i.* to tangle together; to become tangled like fibre; to cover with mats. [MAT (1)].

MATADOR, [mat'-ad-aw(r)], *n.* the performer in a bull-fight who gives the coup-de-grâce; a chief card in ombre; a kind of dominoes in which seven must be made at each play. [Span. *matador*].

MATAMATA, [mat'-a-mah'-ta], *n.* the South American river-tortoise, *Chelys fimbriata.* [Native].

MATCH (1), [mach], *n.* an object corresponding exactly to another; someone equal in prowess to a rival; someone superior in contest to another; a sporting contest against another person or team; a marriage; a person suitable for marriage with another. [OE. *gemæcca* one of a pair].

MATCH (2), [mach], *n.* a slender piece of wood tipped with inflammable material, ignited by friction to give a flame; a lighted rope for firing artillery, mines, etc. [OFr. *mesche*].

MATCH (3), [mach], *v.t.* and *i.* to bring into contest with another; to find a colour or material similar to; to correspond with, suit; to marry; to equal in contest; to tally or correspond in form, colour, etc. [MATCH (1)].

MATCHABLE, [mach'-abl], *adj.* that may be matched.

MATCH-BOARDING, [mach'-bawd'-ing], *n.* a series of boards fitting into one another by means of a tongue on one edge and a groove on the other.

MATCHBOX, [mach'-boks], *n.* a box for holding matches.

MATCHET, [mach'-et], *n.* a long, heavy knife with a cutlass blade, used in the West Indies and Central America. [Span. *machete*].

MATCHLESS, [mach'-les], *adj.* unequalled, perfect, that cannot be matched.

MATCHLESSLY, [mach'-les-li], *adv.* in matchless fashion.

MATCHLESSNESS, [mach'-les-nes], *n.* the quality of being matchless.

MATCHLOCK, [mach'-lok], *n.* a gun with a lock holding a match for firing it; the lock of such a gun.

MATCHMAKER, [mach'-māk'-er], *n.* one intriguing to bring about marriages; one who makes matches.

MATCHWOOD, [mach'-wŏŏd], *n.* wood from which matches are made; thin or splintered wood.

MATE (**1**), [māt], *n.* a companion, workfellow; a friend; the sexual partner in man or animals; one of a pair; a second in command of anything, *esp.* of a merchant ship. [OLGerm. *gemate*].
MATE (**2**), [māt], *n.* checkmate. [CHECKMATE].
MATE (**3**), **maté**, [mat'-ā], *n.* the South American plant, *Ilex paraguayensis*, from the powdered dried leaves of which is made a kind of tea; an infusion of this; the vessel in which this is made. [Span. *mate*].
MATE (**4**), [māt], *v.t. and i.* to take a sexual partner, to marry; to pair off. [MATE (1)].
MATE (**5**), [māt], *v.t.* to checkmate.
MATELESS, [māt'-les], *adj.* without a mate.
MATELOTE, [mat'-el-ot], *n.* a sauce for fish made of onions, parsley, cloves, claret, and vinegar. [Fr. *matelot* sailor].
MATER, [mā'-ter], *n.* (*anat.*) either of two of the membranes enclosing the brain and spinal cord; (*slang*) mother. [L. *mater* mother].
MATERFAMILIAS, [mā'-ter-fam-il'-i-as], *n.* the mistress of the house. [L. *mater familias*].
MATERIA, [ma-tēer'-i-a], *n.* substances, matter; **m. medica**, substances used in medicine; the study of these. [L. *materia*].
MATERIAL (**1**), [ma-tēer'-i-al], *n.* the substance of which a thing is made, *esp.* cloth, fabric of any kind; information, knowledge necessary for literary work, teaching, etc.; human beings regarded as stuff for a purpose; (*pl.*) implements necessary for doing a thing; that which is material.
MATERIAL (**2**), [ma-tēer'-i-al], *adj.* made of substance, concrete; relating to tangible reality, corporeal; (of persons) not spiritually inclined, preoccupied with substantial profit rather than principle and spirituality; relevant to an issue, important; (*leg.*) affecting judgment. [L. *materialis*].
MATERIALISM, [ma-tēer'-i-al-izm], *n.* the belief accepting only the material as valid and important, and dismissing the spiritual and supernatural as imaginary or of material origin.
MATERIALIST, [ma-tēer'-i-al-ist], *n.* one who professes and practises materialism.
MATERIALISTIC, [ma-tēer'-i-al-ist'-ik], *adj.* relating to, imbued with, materialism.
MATERIALITY, [ma-tēer'-i-al'-i-ti], *n.* the quality of being material.
MATERIALIZATION, [ma-tēer'-i-al-īz-ā'-shun], *n.* the act of materializing; the state of being materialized; a materialized ghost.
MATERIALIZE, [ma-tēer'-i-al-īz], *v.t. and i.* to bring into material form; (of a spirit) to cause to assume bodily shape; to imbue with materialism; to assume tangible or practical form, to be realized.
MATERIALLY, [ma-tēer'-i-al-i], *adv.* in material fashion, from the material aspect.
MATERIALNESS, [ma-tēer'-i-al-nes], *n.* materiality.
MATERIEL, **matériel**, [ma-te'-ri-el'], *n.* the implements or equipment required for some task or operation, *esp.* the equipment of an army. [Fr. *matériel*].
MATERNAL, [ma-turn'-al], *adj.* relating to a mother; on the mother's side; characteristic of a mother. [L. *maternus*].
MATERNALLY, [ma-turn'-al-i], *adv.* in maternal fashion.
MATERNITY [ma-turn'-i-ti], *n.* motherhood; the condition of being a mother; **m. hospital**, a hospital for women about to be confined. [L. *maternitas*].
MATESHIP, [māt'-ship], *n.* companionship.
MATEY, [māt'-i], *adj.* (*coll.*) sociable. [MATE (1)].
MATFELLON, [mat'-fel-on], *n.* knapweed, a variety of *Centaurea*. [OFr. *matefelon*].
MAT-GRASS, [mat'-grahs], *n.* a grass, *Nardus stricta*, growing in tufts.
MATHEMATICAL, [math'-i-mat'-ik-al], *adj.* according to, dealing with, relating to, mathematics; (*fig.*) as exact and calculated as if according to mathematics. [Gk. *mathematikos*].
MATHEMATICALLY, [math'-i-mat'-ik-al-i], *adv.* in mathematical fashion.
MATHEMATICIAN, [math'-i-mat-ish'-an], *n.* one skilled in mathematics. [Fr. *mathématicien*].
MATHEMATICS, [math'-i-mat'-iks], *n.*(*pl.*) the science of numerical or quantitative properties and relations. [L. *mathematicus*].
MATHES, [māTHz], *n.* the mayweed, *Anthemis Cotula*. [OE. *magethe*].
MATHESIS, [ma-thē'-sis], *n.* study, learning. [Gk. *mathesis*].
MATICO, [mat'-ik-ō], *n.* the Peruvian plant, *Artanthe elongata*, used as a powerful styptic. [Span. *matico*].
MATIES, [mā'-tēz], *n.* the goldsinny, *Crenilabrus cornubicus*, related to the wrasse. [Du. *maatjes*].
MATINS, [mat'-inz], *n.*(*pl.*) morning public worship in the Church of England; (*R.C.*) one of the canonical hours. [Fr. *matines*].
MATINAL, [mat'-in-al], *adj.* relating to matins; morning.
MATINEE, **matinée**, [mat'-in-ā], *n.* a dramatic, cinema, etc., performance held in the afternoon; **m. coat**, a woollen jacket for infants. [Fr. *matinée*].
MATLOCKITE, [mat'-lok-īt], *n.* oxychloride of lead. [*Matlock*, in Derbyshire].
MATRASS, [mat'-ras], *n.* a chemical vessel with a round body and tapering, open neck. [Fr. *matras*].
MAT-REED, [mat'-rēd], *n.* the reed-mace, *Typha latifolia*.
MATRIARCH, [mā'-tri-ahk], *n.* the female head of a family; a woman ruling a tribal group. [L. *mater* mother and ~(PATRI)ARCH].
MATRIARCHAL, [mā'-tri-ahk'-al], *adj.* relating to a matriarch or to matriarchy.
MATRIARCHY, [mā'-tri-ahk-i], *n.* a social system in which inheritance and kinship is through the female line, and the mother is head of the family and tribe.
MATRIC., [ma-trik'], *n.* (*coll.*) matriculation.
MATRICES, [mat'-ris-ēz], *n. pl.* of MATRIX.
MATRICIDAL, [mat'-ri-sīd'-al], *adj.* pertaining to matricide.
MATRICIDE, [mat'-ri-sīd], *n.* the killing of one's own mother; one who commits this crime. [L. *matricida*].
MATRICULAR, [ma-trik'-yŏŏ-ler], *adj.* relating to matriculation; relating to the contributions made by federated German States to the Central Government. [MedL. *matricularis*].
MATRICULATE, [ma-trik'-yŏŏ-lāt], *v.t. and i.* to admit to a university; to obtain admittance to a university; to pass the examination formerly intended to qualify for such admittance. [L. *matriculare*].
MATRICULATION, [ma-trik'-yŏŏ-lā'-shun], *n.* the act of matriculating; the examination necessary for this.
MATRIMONIAL, [mat'-ri-mō'-ni-al], *adj.* relating to marriage. [LL. *matrimonialis*].
MATRIMONIALLY, [ma'-tri-mō'-ni-al-i], *adv.* in matrimonial fashion.
MATRIMONY, [mat'-ri-mun-i], *n.* marriage, the state of being married. [L. *matrimonium*].
MATRIX, (*pl.* **matrices**), [ma'-triks], *n.* the womb; the substance in which gems are found; the mould for casting type; the place where a thing is formed. [L. *matrix* womb].
MATRON, [mā'-tron], *n.* a married woman, *esp.* if elderly and a mother; a woman in charge of nursing at a hospital, etc., or of domestic matters at a boarding-school, etc. [L. *matrona*].
MATRONAGE, [mā'-tron-ij], *n.* matronhood; matrons in general.
MATRONAL, [ma-trōn'-al], *adj.* relating to, typical of, suitable for, a matron. [L. *matronalis*].
MATRONHOOD, [mā'-tron-hŏŏd], *n.* the state of being a matron.
MATRONIZE, [mā'-tron-īz], *v.t.* to make into a matron.
MATRON-LIKE, [mā'-tron-līk], *adj.* like a matron.
MATRONLY, [mā'-tron-li], *adj.* like a matron, relating to a matron; elderly and motherly; rather fat.
MATRONYMIC, [mā'-trō-nim'-ik], *n.* a name derived from the female line. [L. *mater* mother and Gk. *onoma* name].
MATT, see MAT (2).
MATTE, [mat], *n.* an impure product of copper; unburnished gilding. [Fr. *matte*].
MATTED, [mat'-id], *adj.* tangled, coarsely twisted together. [MAT (3)].
MATTER (**1**), [mat'-er], *n.* substance, material, stuff of which physical objects are made; the subjects, facts of a book, statement etc.; an affair, business; a thing of consequence; cause; concern; amount, distance, extent, quantity; pus, a discharge from a wound; (*print.*) type set up. [L. *materia*].
MATTER (**2**), [mat'-er], *v.i.* to be of importance; to discharge matter.
MATTERLESS, [mat'-er-les], *adj.* insubstantial.
MATTER-OF-FACT, [mat'-er-ov-fakt'], *adj.* concerned only with facts, unimaginative, casual, commonplace.
MATTERY, [mat'-er-i], *adj.* purulent.
MATTING, [mat'-ing], *n.* coarse woven material; sacking woven from hemp, straw, etc. [MAT (1)].

MATTOCK, [mat′-ok], *n.* a kind of pickaxe with a broad edge to one blade and a point to the other. [OE. *mattuc*].

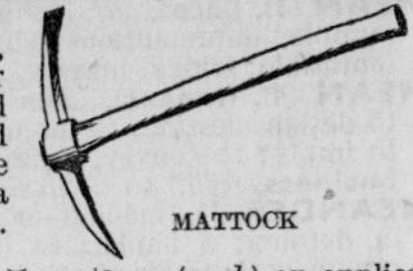
MATTOCK

MATTRESS, [mat′-res], *n.* a sack or container filled with stuffing and used to lie on; a stuffed or sprung contrivance used as a bed or as a support for a bed. [OFr. *materas*].

MATURANT, [mat′-yōō-rant], *n.* (*med.*) an application to an inflamed part to quicken suppuration. [L. *maturans*].

MATURATE, [mat′-yōō-rāt], *v.t. and i.* to cause or accelerate suppuration; to suppurate; to ripen. [L. *maturare*].

MATURATION, [mat′-ew-rā′-shun], *n.* the process of maturating. [L. *maturatio*].

MATURATIVE, [ma-tyōōer′-at-iv], *adj.* causing or promoting maturation. [L. *maturativus*].

MATURE (1), [ma-tyōōer′], *adj.* ripe; fully grown, of maximum development; fully formed; wise, carefully considered; ready; due, payable. [L. *maturus*].

MATURE (2), [ma-tyōōer′], *v.t. and i.* to ripen, make mature; to ponder carefully over, to perfect, to make ready for putting into effect; to become mature; to become payable. [L. *maturare*].

MATURELY, [ma-tyōōer′-li], *adv.* in mature fashion.

MATURENESS, [ma-tyōōer′-ness], *n.* the state of being mature.

MATURESCENT, [mat′-yōō-res′-ent], *adj.* becoming mature. [L. *maturescens*].

MATURITY, [ma-tyōōer-i-ti], *n.* maximum development, the state of being mature. [L. *maturitas*].

MATUTINAL, [mat′-yōō-tin′-al], *adj.* early; relating to, occurring in, the morning. [L. *matutinus*].

MAUD, [mawd], *n.* a Scotch shepherd's woollen plaid. [Unkn.].

MAUDLIN, [mawd′-lin], *adj.* stupidly sentimental, tipsily tearful; displaying embarrassing emotionalism or self-pity. [OFr. *Madelaine* Magdalen].

MAUGRE, [maw′-ger], *prep.* notwithstanding. [OFr. *maugré*].

MAUL (1), [mawl], *n.* a heavy, large-headed wooden mallet. [OFr. *mail*].

MAUL (2), [mawl], *v.t. and i.* to tear savagely, to injure brutally; to mishandle clumsily, paw roughly.

MAULSTICK, MAHLSTICK, MOSTIC, [mawl′-stik], *n.* a rod used by painters to support and steady the wrist for delicate work. [Du. *maalstok*].

MAUND, [mawnd], *n.* a unit of weight, of varying amount, used in many parts of Asia. [Hind. *man*].

MAUNDER, [mawnd′-er], *v.i.* to ramble, mutter vaguely in speech; to saunter pointlessly along. [Unkn.].

MAUNDERER, [mawnd′-er-er], *n.* one who maunders.

MAUNDRIL†, see MANDREL.

MAUNDY, [mawn′-di], *n.* the special distribution of the royal bounty by the Royal Almoner on the Thursday before Easter; the silver pence struck for such distribution; the former ceremony in which the king washed the feet of the poor and gave out alms. [OFr. *mandé*].

MAURESQUE, see MORESQUE.

MAURIST, [maw′-rist], *n.* a monk of the Benedictine congregation of St. Maur.

MAUSER, [maw′-zer], *n.* a magazine firearm. [P. *Mauser*, its inventor].

MAUSOLEAN, [maw′-sō-lē′-an], *adj.* relating to a mausoleum.

MAUSOLEUM, [maw′-sō-lē′-um], *n.* a large, stately, monumental sepulchre. [L. *mausoleum* from *Mausolos*, King of Caria, who was buried in one].

MAUVE (1), [mōv], *n.* a light purple colour. [Fr. *mauve* mallow].

MAUVE (2), [mōv], *adj.* of a light purple colour.

MAVERICK, [mav′-er-ik], *n.* an unbranded calf or yearling; a masterless man. [*Maverick*, a Texan who owned unbranded cattle].

MAVIS, [mā′-vis], *n.* the song thrush, *Turdus musicus*. [OFr. *mauvis*].

MAVOURNEEN, [ma-vōōr′-nēn], *n.* a term of endearment, common in Ireland. [Ir. *mo mhurnin* my darling].

MAW, [maw], *n.* the stomach; the crop of a bird; the fourth stomach of a ruminant; (*fig.*) a gaping chasm. [OE. *maga*].

MAWKISH, [mawk′-ish], *adj.* feeble, sickly, insipid; feebly sentimental, emotionally unreal or exaggerated. [ME. *mathek* maggot].

MAWKISHLY, [mawk′-ish-li], *adv.* in mawkish fashion.

MAWKISHNESS, [mawk′-ish-nes], *n.* the quality of being mawkish.

MAWSEED, [maw′-sēd], *n.* poppy-seed sold for moulting birds. [Germ. *mohn* poppy and SEED].

MAWWORM, [maw′-wurm], *n.* an intestinal worm.

MAXILLA, [maks-il′-a], *n.* the upper jawbone. [L. *maxilla*].

MAXILLAR, [maks-il′-er], *adj.* maxillary.

MAXILLARY, [maks-il′-er-i], *adj.* relating to the jaw or to the jawbone. [L. *maxillaris*].

MAXILLIFORM, [maks-il′-i-fawm], *adj.* in the shape of a jawbone. [MAXILLA and FORM].

MAXILLIPEDE, [maks-il′-i-pēd], *n.* a limb combining the functions of jaw and leg in certain crustaceans. [L. *maxilla* jawbone and *pes pedis* foot].

MAXIM (1), [maks′-im], *n.* a wise saying giving generalized advice on action and conduct; an axiom deduced from experience. [L. *maximus* greatest].

MAXIM (2), [maks′-im], *n.* a type of machine-gun. [Sir H. *Maxim* (1840-1916), its inventor].

MAXIMIZE, [maks′-im-īz], *v.t.* to enlarge, increase to the greatest extent. [L. *maximus* greatest].

MAXIMUM (1), [maks′-im-um], *n.* the greatest extent, quantity, amount, etc., the highest point, the greatest possible. [L. *maximum*].

MAXIMUM (2), [maks′-im-um], *adj.* greatest possible. [L. *maximus*].

MAY (1), [mā], *n.* the fifth month of the year; hawthorn blossom; (*coll.*) the prime of youth. [L. *maius*].

MAY (2), (might), [mā], *v.auxil.* expressing possibility, permissibility and uncertainty, and also wish, hope, or will. [OE. *mæg*].

MAY (3), [mā], *v.i.* to gather flowers in May.

MAY-APPLE, [mā′-apl], *n.* the fruit of the North American plant, *Podophyllum peltatum*.

MAYBE, [mā′-bē], *adv.* possibly, perhaps.

MAYBIRD, [mā′-burd], *n.* the American wood-thrush, *Turdus mustelinus*.

MAY-BLOOM, [mā′-blōōm], *n.* the hawthorn.

MAY-BUG, [mā′-bug], *n.* the cockchafer.

MAY-DAY, [mā′-dā], *n.* the first of May, *esp.* as the Spring festival and as the annual rallying-day of the Socialist workers of the world.

MAY-DUKE, [mā′-dewk], *n.* a variety of the common cherry.

MAYFLOWER, [mā′-flow-er], *n.* the North American plant, *Epigœa repens*; the cuckoo-flower, *Cardamine pratensis*.

MAYFLY, [mā′-flī], *n.* an insect, a species of *Ephemera*; a synthetic imitation of this insect used in fly-fishing.

MAYHAP, [mā-hap′], *adv.* perchance.

MAYHEM, [mā′-hem], *n.* (*leg.*) injury to any important limb or part of the body, *esp.* as ground for legal action and damages. [AFr. *maiheme* injury].

MAYING, [mā′-ing], *n.* the celebration of May-day or of May festivities.

MAY-LADY, [mā′-lā′-di], *n.* Queen of the May.

MAY-LILY, [mā′-lil′-i], *n.* the twin-leaved lily of the valley, *Maianthemum bifolium*.

MAY-MORN, [mā′-mawn′], *n.* the morning of May-day; (*fig.*) the freshness and vigour of youth.

MAYONNAISE, [mā′-on-āz′], *n.* a thick sauce or dressing made from yolk of eggs, oil, vinegar, etc.; a cold dish, usually of fish, eggs, or poultry, served with this dressing. [Fr. *mayonnaise*].

MAYOR, [māer], *n.* the chief officer of a municipal corporation. [Fr. *maire*].

MAYORALTY, [māer′-al′-ti], *n.* the office, status or period of office of a mayor. [OFr. *mairalté*].

MAYORESS, [māer′-es], *n.* the wife of a mayor.

MAYPOLE, [mā′-pōl], *n.* a decorated and garlanded pole, danced round on May-day.

MAY-QUEEN, [mā′-kwēn′], *n.* a young, attractive girl chosen to preside at May-day festivities.

MAYTHE, [māth], *n.* the mayweed. [OE. *mægethe*].

MAYWEED, [mā′-wēd], *n.* the fetid camomile, *Anthemis Cotula*. [MATHES].

MAZAGAN, [maz′-a-gan], *n.* a Moorish broad bean. [*Mazaga*, in Morocco].

MAZARD, [maz′-erd], *n.* the bird-cherry, *Prunus avium*. [OFr. *masere* maple-wood].

MAZARIN (1), [maz′-er-in], *n.* a deep, rich blue colour. [Cardinal *Mazarin* (1602-1661), the French statesman].

MAZARIN (2), [maz′-er-in], *adj.* of a deep rich blue.

MAZE (1), [māz], *n.* a complex mass of enclosed winding paths, designed to puzzle and deceive those attempting to reach the centre or make their way out; (*fig.*) a tangle of puzzling detail; dreamy bewilderment.

MAZE (2), [māz], *v.t.* to puzzle, bewilder, perplex. [ME. *mazen*].

MAZER, [māz'-er], *n.* a large, shallow, wooden drinking-bowl. [ME. *mazer*].

MAZER

MAZILY, [māz'-i-li], *adv.* in mazy fashion.

MAZINESS, [māz'-i-nes], *n.* the condition of being mazy.

MAZOLOGICAL, [māz'-ō-loj'-ik-al], *adj.* relating to mazology.

MAZOLOGY, [maz-ol'-o-ji], *n.* mammalogy. [Gk. *mazos* breast and *logos* speech].

MAZURKA, [ma-zōōer'-ka], *n.* a Polish dance in triple time; music for this. [Polish *mazurka*].

MAZY, [māz'-i], *adj.* labyrinthine, winding; hazy, bewildered.

ME, [mē], *pron. acc. and dat.* of I. [OE. *me*].

MEAD (1), [mēd], *n.* a drink made from fermented honey and spices. [OE. *meodu*].

MEAD (2), [mēd], *n.* (*poet.*) a meadow. [OE. *mæd*].

MEADOW, [med'-ō], *n.* a hayfield, a field of grass; low-lying fertile grassland. [OE. *mædwe*].

MEADOW-CRESS, [med'-ō-kres'], *n.* the ladysmock, *Cardamine pratensis*.

MEADOW-CROCUS, [med'-ō-krō'-kus], *n.* meadow-saffron.

MEADOW-GRASS, [med'-ō-grahs'], *n.* a grass of the genus *Poa* or *Schlerochloa*.

MEADOW-LARK, [med'-ō-lahk'], *n.* the titlark; the North American song-bird, *Sturnella magna*.

MEADOW-ORE, [med'-ō-aw(r)'], *n.* conchoidal bog iron ore.

MEADOW-PINK, [med'-ō-pingk'], *n.* the plant ragged robin, *Lychnis Flos-cuculi*.

MEADOW-RUE, [med'-ō-rōō'], *n.* a plant of the genus *Thalictrum*.

MEADOW-SAFFRON, [med'-ō-saf'-ron], *n.* the bulbous plant, *Colchicum autumnale*, used medicinally.

MEADOWSWEET, [med'-ō-swēt'], *n.* the white-flowered plant, *Spiræa Ulmaria*.

MEADOWY, [med'-ō-i], *adj.* resembling, abounding in, meadows.

MEAGER, see MAIGRE (1).

MEAGRE, MEAGER†, [mē'-ger], *adj.* lean, emaciated; poor, mean, barely sufficient; barren, limited. [OFr. *maigre*].

MEAGRELY, [mē'-ger-li], *adv.* in meagre fashion.

MEAGRENESS, [mē'-ger-nes], *n.* the condition of being meagre.

MEAKER, [mēk'-er], *n.* a minnow. [Unkn.].

MEAL (1), [mēl], *n.* a repast, a taking of food, *esp.* at a customary time; the quantity of food consumed at this. [OE. *mæl* fixed time].

MEADOW-SWEET

MEAL (2), [mēl], *n.* the edible part of grain or pulse, other than wheat, ground to a powder. [OE. *melo*].

MEALIE, [mēl'-i], *n.* an ear of maize; (*pl.*) a quantity of maize. [Afrik. *milje*].

MEALINESS, [mēl'-i-nes], *n.* the quality of being mealy.

MEALMAN, [mēl'-man], *n.* a dealer in meal.

MEALTIME, [mēl'-tīm], *n.* the customary time for a meal.

MEALWORM, [mēl'-wurm], *n.* the larva of the beetle *Tenebrio molitor*.

MEALY, [mēl'-i], *adj.* pertaining to, like, meal; producing, covered with, meal; (of horses) full of small spots; dullish white, pale; **m. bug,** an insect, *Coccus adonidum*, of a mealy appearance, infesting plants; **m. mouth,** the willow wren; **m. tree,** the wayfaring tree, *Viburnum lantana*.

MEALY-MOUTHED, [mēl'-i-mowtht'], *adj.* afraid to use blunt or frank expressions.

MEAN (1), [mēn], *n.* medium, the middle point, course, etc., between extremes or opposites; (*math.*) a mean term or quantity, average; (*pl.*) method by which something is done; resources, income; wealth, money; **by all means,** certainly.

MEAN (2), [mēn], *adj.* middle; average; intervening; (*math.*) intermediate, between the extremes of a series; **m. proportional,** the middle of three quantities, standing in the same proportion to the first as does the third to it. [OFr. *men, moien*].

MEAN (3), [mēn], *adj.* low in rank or birth; inferior; humble, unpretentious; shabby, dingy; base, contemptible; stingy, miserly. [OE. *gemæne* common].

MEAN (4), (meant), [mēn], *v.t.* to intend, purpose; to design, destine; to intend to refer to or indicate; to imply; to convey, signify; *v.i.* to intend; **to m. business,** (*coll.*) to be in earnest. [OE. *mænan*].

MEANDER (1), [mē-and'-er], *n.* a winding course full of detours; a haphazard leisurely progression; an ornamental trellis-work pattern; (*pl.*) twists and bends. [Gk. *Maiandros* a winding river in Phrygia].

MEANDER (2), [mē-and'-er], *v.i.* to flow slowly forming a meander or meanders; (*fig.*) to wander haphazardly and idly.

MEANDERING, [mē-and'-er-ing], *adj.* that meanders.

MEANING (1), [mēn'-ing], *n.* that which is meant, sense; significance; implication; interpretation; reason.

MEANING (2), [mēn'-ing], *adj.* significant, full of meaning.

MEANINGLESS, [mēn'-ing-les], *adj.* having no meaning, expressing nothing.

MEANINGLY, [mēn'-ing-li], *adv.* significantly, expressively.

MEANLY, [mēn'-li], *adv.* in mean fashion.

MEANNESS, [mēn'-nes], *n.* the quality of being mean.

MEANS-TEST, [mēnz'-test], *n.* an official inquiry into the means of subsistence of an insured person seeking further unemployment benefit after a specified time, or seeking any other State grant.

MEANT, [ment], *pret. and p.pt.* of MEAN.

MEANTIME (1), [mēn'-tīm], *n.* the intervening time.

MEANTIME (2), [mēn'-tīm], *adv.* in the intervening time.

MEANWHILE (1), [mēn'-wīl], *n.* the intervening period of time, the interim. [MEAN (2) and OE. *hwil* time].

MEANWHILE (2), [mēn'-wīl], *adv.* during the intervening time.

MEASE, [mēz], *n.* a measure for herrings containing five hundreds (*esp.* long hundreds). [OFr. *meise* a barrel for herrings].

MEASLED, [mēzld], *adj.* infected with or marked by measles.

MEASLES, [mēzls], *n.* an acute infectious disease in which a patchy crimson rash appears on the skin; this rash itself; a disease of swine and certain other beasts. [ME. *maseles*, ~OHGerm. *masala* blood-blister].

MEASLY, [mēz'-li], *adj.* pertaining to, of the nature of, measles; having measles; (*fig.*) paltry, meagre.

MEASURABLE, [mezh'-er-abl], *adj.* able to be measured; moderate. [Fr. *mesurable*].

MEASURABLENESS, [mezh'-er-abl-nes], *n.* the quality of being measurable.

MEASURABLY, [mezh'-er-ab-li], *adv.* so as to be measurable.

MEASURE (1), [mezh'-er], *n.* size, dimensions, quantity, etc.; a system, standard, or unit used in determining these; a graduated rod, standard-sized vessel, etc., for measuring something; a definite quantity or amount, *esp.* a unit of capacity; a limit, a fixed or determinable extent; a Parliamentary Bill; (*fig.*) a criterion, standard; metre, verse or prose rhythm; (*mus.*) a group of notes and/or rests comprised within two consecutive bar lines; the time in which a musical composition is written; rhythm; (*archaic*) a dance; (*pl.*) proceedings, means to an end; (*pl.*) (*geol.*) a group of strata; (*parl.*) a bill or statute; (*arith.*) a number dividing exactly into another; **to have the m. of,** to have summed up; **made to m.,** made to fit by previous measurement; **greatest common m.,** (*arith.*) the greatest quantity dividing exactly into all of a number of given quantities. [Fr. *mesure*].

MEASURE (2), [mezh'-er], *v.t.* to find the dimensions, capacity, quantity, etc., of; to mark off, deal out (a specific quantity); to test by competition with another; to judge by some criterion; *v.i.* to be of certain dimensions; (*poet.*) to go, travel; **to m. swords with,** to fight; **to m. one's length,** to fall full length on the ground; **to m. up to,** to conform to.

MEASURED, [mezh'-erd], *adj.* carefully considered, well chosen; steady, deliberate.

MEASURELESS, [mezh'-er-les], *adj.* without measure, boundless, unlimited.

MEASUREMENT, [mezh'-er-ment], *n.* the act of measuring, the state of being measured; the size, amount, etc., which anything measures.

MEASURER, [mezh′-er-er], *n.* one who, or that which, measures.

MEASURING, [mezh′-er-ing], *adj.* used for measuring; requiring to be measured.

MEAT, [mēt], *n.* the edible flesh of animals; (*archaic*) food, nourishment; a meal; (*fig.*) food for thought. [OE. *mete* food].

MEAT-BISCUIT, [mēt′-bis′-kit], *n.* meat beaten and dried, mixed with meal, and baked.

MEATINESS, [mēt′-i-nes], *n.* the quality of being meaty.

MEATLESS, [mēt′-les], *adj.* containing no meat; **m. day, etc.**, a day, etc., on which either the sale or the consumption of meat may not or does not take place.

MEAT-OFFERING, [mēt′-of′-er-ing], *n.* an offering of flour, oil, and frankincense.

MEAT-SAFE, [mēt′-sāf′], *n.* a cupboard or chamber in which meat may be kept fresh.

MEATUS, [mē-ā′-tus], *n.* (*anat.*) a passage, channel or duct in the body. [L. *meatus* way].

MEATY, [mēt′-i], *adj.* full of meat, fleshy but not fat; of meat, like meat; (*fig.*) providing mental nourishment and stimulus.

MECCA, [mek′-a], *n.* the Arabian capital of the Kingdom of Hejaz, and the city where Mohammed was born; (*fig.*) the place a devotee desires to visit.

MECHANIC, [mi-kan′-ik], *n.* an artisan, a skilled operative, *esp.* one trained in the use or construction of machinery; (*pl.*) that branch of applied mathematics dealing with motion, force, and matter; the science of machinery. [Gk. *mekhanikos* inventive].

MECHANICAL, [mi-kan′-ik-al], *adj.* of or by machines; acting by physical power, *esp.* according to the principles of mechanics; non-creative, performed without thought, according to routine; (*archaic*) relating to, like, a mechanic; **m. drawing**, drawing done with instruments; **m. powers**, certain elementary contrivances of which all machines are primarily composed.

MECHANICALLY, [mi-kan′-ik-al-i], *adv.* in a mechanical way.

MECHANICALNESS, [mi-kan′-ik-al-nes], *n.* the quality of being mechanical.

MECHANICIAN, [mek′-an-ish′-an], *n.* one skilled in the construction and working of machines.

MECHANISM, [mek′-an-izm], *n.* the machinery, the collective parts which by their combined motion operate a piece of machinery; the means by which anything functions; (*art*) technique, mechanical skill; (*philos.*) the doctrine that everything is produced by mechanical action.

MECHANIST, [mek′-an-ist], *n.* (*philos.*) a believer in mechanism.

MECHANISTIC, [mek′-an-ist′-ik], *adj.* (*philos.*) relating to mechanism.

MECHANIZATION, [me′-kan-īz-ā′-shun], *n.* the act or process of mechanizing, *esp.* an army.

MECHANIZE, [mek′-an-īz], *v.t.* to make mechanical; to cause to function by machinery, or like a machine; (*milit.*) to equip with mechanical transport.

MECHLIN, [mek′-lin], *n.* a lace made at *Mechlin*, in Belgium.

MECONATE, [mĕk′-on-āt], *n.* a salt of meconic acid.

MECONIC, [mi-kon′-ik], *adj.* obtained from the poppy; **m. acid**, a crystalline acid obtained from opium. [Gk. *mekon* poppy].

MECONINE, [mĕk′-on-ēn], *n.* a neutral chemical compound present in opium.

MECONIUM, [mi-kō′-ni-um], *n.* †the juice of the poppy; (*med.*) the first excrement voided by a newly born infant. [Gk. *mekonion*].

MEDAL, [med′-al], *n.* a small metal disk containing a device, inscription, etc., issued to commemorate some event, or as a reward, prize, or distinction; **m. play**, (*golf*) stroke play. [Fr. *médaille*].

MEDALET, [med′-al-et], *n.* a small medal.

MEDALLIC, [mi-dal′-ik], *adj.* pertaining to like, occurring on, a medal.

MEDALLION, [mi-dal′-yon], *n.* a large medal; a rounded flat tablet containing devices in relief, a circular bas-relief. [It. *medaglione*].

MEDALLIST, [med′-al-ist], *n.* one skilled in medals; a maker or engraver of medals; one who has gained a medal as a prize, etc.

MEDALLURGY, [med′-al-ur-ji], *n.* the art of striking medals. [MEDAL and Gk. *ergon* work].

MEDDLE, [medl], *v.i.* to interfere unnecessarily and objectionably in other people's affairs; to busy oneself (with something one does not understand). [OFr. *medler*].

MEDDLER, [med′-ler], *n.* a meddlesome creature.

MEDDLESOME, [medl′-sum], *adj.* given to meddling, officiously interfering.

MEDDLESOMENESS, [medl′-sum-nes], *n* the quality of being meddlesome.

MEDDLING, [med′-ling], *adj.* meddlesome.

MEDDLINGLY, [med′-ling-li], *adv.* in a meddlesome way.

MEDIA, [mē′-di-a], *n.* (*anat.*) the middle membrane of an artery or vessel. [L. *media*].

MEDIACY, [mē′-di-a-si], *n.* the state of being intermediate.

MEDIAEVAL, see MEDIEVAL.

MEDIAL, [mē′-di-al], *adj.* middle; pertaining to a mean; average, ordinary. [LL. *medialis*].

MEDIALLY, [mē′-di-al-i], *adv.* in the middle, in a medial position.

MEDIAN (1), [mē′-di-an], *n.* the median vein; (*math.*) each of the lines bisecting the internal angles of a triangle, and meeting at a point within it.

MEDIAN (2), [mē′-di-an], *adj.* situated in, traversing, the middle of something. [LL. *medianus*].

MEDIANT, [mē′-di-ant], *n.* (*mus.*) the third above the tonic in the modern diatonic scale. [LL. *medians*].

MEDIASTINUM, [mē′-di-a-stī′-num], *n.* (*anat.*) the membranous partition dividing two cavities of the body, *esp.* that separating the lungs. [MedL. *mediastinum*].

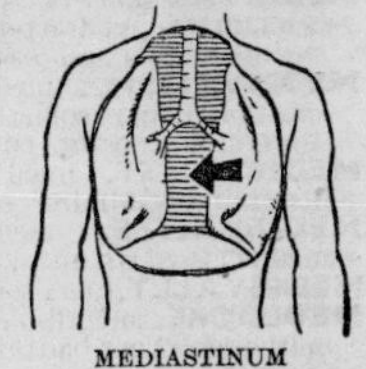
MEDIASTINUM

MEDIATE (1), [mē′-di-āt], *adj.* acting through an intermediary, involving some intervening agent.

MEDIATE (2), [mē′-di-āt], *v.t.* to effect by intervention; to connect; *v.i.* to be situated in an intermediate position; to intervene in order to reconcile disputants. [L. *mediare*].

MEDIATELY, [mē′-di-at-li], *adv.* in a mediate manner.

MEDIATENESS, [mē′-di-at-nes], *n.* the quality of being mediate.

MEDIATION, [mē′-di-ā′-shun], *n.* the act of mediating; the state of being an intermediary. [LL. *mediatio*].

MEDIATIZATION, [mē′-di-at-īz-ā′-shun], *n.* the act of mediatizing; the state of being mediatized.

MEDIATIZE, [mē′-di-at-īz], *v.t.* to annex a small state to a larger one, while permitting its ruler to retain his princely rights and title.

MEDIATOR, [mē′-di-āt′-er], *n.* one who mediates, a peacemaker. [LL. *mediator*].

MEDIATORIAL, [mē′-di-at-aw′-ri-al], *adj.* belonging to a mediator or to mediation.

MEDIATORIALLY, [mē′-di-at-aw′-ri-al-i], *adv.* by mediation, as a mediator.

MEDIATORSHIP, [mē′-di-āt-er-ship], *n.* the office or position of a mediator.

MEDIATORY, [mē′-di-āt′-er-i], *adj.* belonging to mediation.

MEDIATRESS, [mē′-di-āt-res], *n.* a female mediator.

MEDIATRIX, [mē′-di-āt-riks], *n.* a mediatress.

MEDIC, [med′-ik], *n.* (*coll.*) a medical student.

MEDICABLE, [med′-ik-abl], *adj.* that may be cured by medical treatment. [L. *medicabilis*].

MEDICAL (1), [med′-ik-al], *n.* (*coll.*) a student of medicine.

MEDICAL (2), [med′-ik-al], *adj.* pertaining to the healing of disease; relating to medicine and to treatment of disease by medicine; **m. practitioner**, a recognized and qualified doctor. [L. *medicalis* of a doctor].

MEDICALLY, [med′-ik-al-i], *adv.* according to, by means of, medicine.

MEDICAMENT, [med′-ik-am-ent], *n.* a healing application, a medical remedy. [L. *medicamentum*].

MEDICAMENTAL, [med′-ik-am-ent′-al], *adj.* healing, curative, of the nature of a medicament.

MEDICAMENTALLY, [med′-ik-am-ent′-al-i], *adv.* after the fashion of medicaments.

MEDICASTER, [med′-ik-ast-er], *n.* a quack doctor. [L. *medicus* doctor and *aster* denoting partial and inferior resemblance].

MEDICATE, [med′-ik-āt], *v.t.* to tincture with a medicinal substance; to treat with medicine. [L. *medicare*].

MEDICATION, [med′-ik-ā′-shun], *n.* the act of medicating; the state of being medicated.

MEDICATIVE, [med′-ik-at-iv], *adj.* curative, relating to medication.

MEDICEAN, [med′-i-sē′-an], *adj.* relating to the

Medici family of Florence. [MedL. *Mediceus* of the *Medici*].

MEDICINAL, [med-is'-in-al], *adj.* relating to medicine; curative, healing.

MEDICINALLY, [med-is'-in-al-i], *adv.* in a medicinal manner.

MEDICINE, [med'-is-in], *n.* the art of preventing, curing, or alleviating disease, *esp.* by healing compounds, drugs, etc., taken internally; any curative preparation taken internally in the treatment of disease, *esp.* one in liquid form; a magic spell or charm amongst savages; (*fig.*) just punishment for transgression. [L. *medicina*].

MEDICINE-BALL, [med'-is-in-bawl'], *n.* a large stuffed leather ball thrown and caught for exercise.

MEDICINE-MAN, [med'-is-in-man'], *n.* among savages, a witch-doctor professing supernatural powers and practising magic.

MEDICO, [med'-ik-ō], *n.* (*slang*) a medical student; a doctor. [It. *medico*].

MEDICO-LEGAL, [med'-ik-ō-lē'-gal], *adj.* relating to law as concerned with medicine.

MEDIEVAL (1), MEDIAEVAL, [med'-i-ē'-val], *n.* one who lived in the Middle Ages.

MEDIEVAL (2), MEDIAEVAL, [med'-i-ē'-val], *adj.* belonging to, characteristic of, the Middle Ages. [L. *medius* middle and *aevum* age].

MEDIEVALISM, [med'-i-ē'-val-izm], *n.* medieval spirit or quality; something surviving from the Middle Ages; affection for, cult of, that which is medieval.

MEDIEVALIST, [med'-i-ē'-val-ist], *n.* a student, historian, or admirer, of the Middle Ages.

MEDIEVALIZE, [med'-i-ē'-val-īz], *v.t.* to make medieval; *v.i.* to affect the medieval.

MEDIEVALLY, [med'-i-ē'-val-i], *adv.* in a medieval way.

MEDIOCRE, [mē'-di-ō'-ker], *adj.* of moderate quality, neither good nor bad; rather poor, below the average. [L. *mediocris*].

MEDIOCRITY, [mē'-di-ok'-ri-ti], *n.* the quality of being mediocre; a mediocre person. [L. *mediocritas* moderation].

MEDITATE, [med'-it-āt], *v.t.* to plan, contrive; (*poet.*) to dwell on in thought; *v.i.* to be engrossed in deep thought or serious contemplation. [L. *meditari*].

MEDITATION, [med'-it-ā'-shun], *n.* the act of meditating; (*pl.*) a work containing one's thoughts or reflections. [L. *meditatio*].

MEDITATIVE, [med'-it-āt-iv], *adj.* thoughtful, contemplative; resulting from meditation.

MEDITATIVELY, [med'-it-āt'-iv-li], *adv.* in meditative fashion.

MEDITATIVENESS, [med'-it-āt'-iv-nes], *n.* the quality of being meditative.

MEDITERRANEAN, [med'-it-er-ā'-ni-an], *adj.* far from the sea; inland, (of a sea) land-locked; pertaining to, situated on, the Mediterranean Sea; **M. Sea,** the sea which divides Europe from Africa. [L. *mediterraneus*].

MEDIUM (1), (*pl.* **media, mediums**), [mē'-di-um], *n.* that which is medium in quality, size, etc.; means, agency; instrument, vehicle; an intervening substance through which anything may be transmitted; material in which an artist, sculptor, etc., works; a liquid-transmitting substance with which pigments are mixed before painting; (*spiritualism*) an intermediary serving as means of communication between the dead and the living; (*fig.*) conditions of life. [L. *medium*].

MEDIUM (2), [mē'-di-um], *adj.* middling, average, moderate, intermediate; **m. wave,** (*wirel.*) (of wave-lengths) more than 99 metres or less than 801 metres.

MEDIUMISTIC, [mē'-di-um-ist'-ik], *adj.* relating to spiritualistic mediums, their work and powers.

MEDJIDIE, [mej'-i-dē], *n.* an order of knighthood founded by Abdul Medjid, Sultan of Turkey, in 1852; a Turkish silver coin first issued by him.

MEDLAR, [med'-ler], *n.* a tree of the genus *Mespilus* the fruit of which is eaten when half rotten; the small, brown fruit of this tree. [OFr. *medler, mesler*].

MEDLAR

MEDLAR-WOOD, [med'-ler-wood'], *n.* the tree, *Myrtus mespiloides.*

MEDLEY, [med'-li], *n.* a confused mass of dissimilar things; a mixed crowd of people; a literary miscellany; a musical composition made up of short extracts from other works, usually each with some common feature, a musical switch. [OFr. *medlee*].

MEDOC, médoc, [med-ok'], *n.* a claret obtained from *Médoc*, France.

MEDULLA, [mi-dul'-a], *n.* the marrow of bones; the spinal cord, the marrow of this; the innermost part of the hair of mammals; (*bot.*) the pith of plants; (*anat.*) the internal part of certain organs; **m. oblongata,** the upper continuation of the spinal cord to form the back section of the brain. [L. *medulla*].

MEDULLARY, [mi-dul'-er-i], *adj.* pertaining to, consisting of, like, marrow; (*bot.*) filled with pith; **m. rays,** (*bot.*) plates of tissue causing the silver grain in oak, etc.

MEDULLIN, [mi-dul'-in], *n.* a substance derived from the pith of the sunflower and the lilac.

MEDUSA, [med-ew'-sa], *n.* (*Gk. myth.*) the Gorgon whose head was cut off by Perseus; (*zool.*) a jellyfish. [Gk. *Medousa* guardian].

MEED, [mēd], *n.* (*poet.*) reward, recompense; just portion. [OE. *med*].

MEEK, [mēk], *adj.* mild, gentle, submissive, humble, easily coerced. [~OIcel. *mjukr* soft].

MEEKEN, [mēk'-en], *v.t.* to make meek; *v.i.* to become meek.

MEEKLY, [mēk'-li], *adv.* in meek fashion.

MEEKNESS, [mēk'-nes], *n.* the quality of being meek.

MEERKAT, [māer'-kat], *n.* the South African suricate, *Suricata tetradactyla.* [Du. *meerkat* monkey].

MEERSCHAUM, [mēer'-sham], *n.* a fine white clay, a hydrated silicate of magnesium, used in making the bowls of tobacco-pipes; a tobacco-pipe made of it. [Germ. *meerschaum* sea foam].

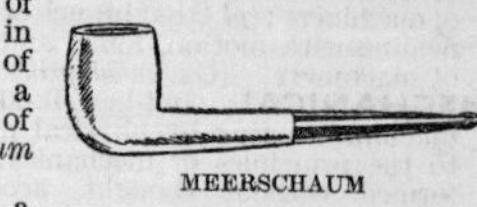
MEERSCHAUM

MEET (1), [mēt], *n.* a meeting of hounds and huntsmen to take part in a foxhunt, etc.; any similar rally.

MEET (2), [mēt], *adj.* fitting, suitable, proper. [OE. *gemæte*].

MEET (3), (met), [mēt], *v.t.* to come face to face with; to encounter or pass when approaching from different directions; to await the arrival of; to come into contact with; to join; to come into or join the company of; to be formally introduced to; to be in opposition against; to come together in negotiation; to deal with; to satisfy; to pay, discharge (debts, etc.); to answer adequately; *v.i.* to come together; to come into contact; to assemble; to become formally acquainted; to see one another; **to m. with,** to experience; to find. [OE. *metan*].

MEETING, [mēt'-ing], *n.* the act of one who, or that which, meets, an encounter; a public gathering of people for a specific purpose; an assembly for public religious worship.

MEETING-HOUSE, [mēt'-ing-hows'], *n.* a Quaker or other dissenting chapel.

MEETLY, [mēt'-li], *adv.* in meet fashion.

MEETNESS, [mēt'-nes], *n.* the quality of being meet.

MEGA-, *pref.* large, great. [Gk. *megas*].

MEGACEPHALOUS, [meg'-a-sef'-al-us], *adj.* large-headed. [MEGA and Gk. *kephale* head].

MEGA-ERG, [meg'-a-erg], *n.* (*elect.*) one million ergs.

MEGAFARAD, [meg'-a-fa'-rad], *n.* (*elect.*) a million farads. [MEGA and FARAD].

MEGALESIAN, [meg'-al-ē'-zi-an], *adj.* relating to Cybele. [Gk. *megas megalos* great].

MEGALITH, [meg'-a-lith], *n.* a large prehistoric stone monument. [MEGA and Gk. *lithos* stone].

MEGALITHIC, [meg'-a-lith'-ik], *adj.* composed of large stones; characterized by the building of megaliths.

MEGALOMANIA, [meg'-al-ō-mā'-ni-a], *n.* a form of insanity in which a person thinks he is a great personage. [Gk. *megas* great and MANIA].

MEGALOMANIAC, [meg'-al-ō-mā'-ni-ak], *n.* a person suffering from megalomania.

MEGALOSAURUS, [meg'-al-ō-saw'-rus], *n.* an extinct genus of gigantic carnivorous reptiles. [Gk. *megas* great and *sauros* lizard].

MEGAPHONE, [meg'-a-fōn], *n.* a cone-shaped speaking-trumpet used to amplify the sound of the voice. [MEGA and Gk. *phone* sound].

MEGAPHONE

MEGAPODE, [meg'-a-pōd], *n.* an Australian game-bird that lays its eggs in a mound it makes for them. [MEGA and Gk. *pous podos* foot].

MEGARON, [meg'-er-on], *n.* (*archae.*) the large principal hall of the ancient Greek palaces. [Gk. *megaron*].
MEGASCOPE, [meg'-a-skōp], *n.* a kind of magic lantern; a form of solar microscope. [MEGA and SCOPE].
MEGASS, [meg'-as], *n.* fibrous refuse cane left after the juice has been removed. [Unkn.].
MEGATHERIUM, [meg'-a-thēer'-i-um], *n.* an extinct gigantic South American edentate resembling a huge sloth. [MEGA and Gk. *therion* wild animal].
MEGGER, [meg'-er], *n.* (*wirel.*) (*prot.*) an instrument for measuring high electrical insulation resistance.
MEGILP, MAGILP, [meg'-ilp], *n.* a mixture of linseed oil and turpentine or mastic varnish, with which oil-paints are prepared. [Unkn.].
MEGOHM, [meg'-ōm], *n.* a million ohms, the unit of electrical resistance. [MEGA and OHM].
MEGRIM (1), [mē'-grim], *n.* the flat-fish, *Lepidorhombus megastoma*. [Unkn.].
MEGRIM (2), [mē'-grim], *n.* a severe neuralgic pain usually attacking one side of the head only; a whim, fad; (*pl.*) depression, melancholy; a nervous disease in cattle and horses causing them to stagger. [MIGRAINE].
MEIONITE, [mī'-on-īt], *n.* (*min.*) a silicate of aluminium and calcium, related to scapolite. [Gk. *meion* less].
MEIOSIS, [mī-ō'-sis], *n.* litotes or understatement in which an opposite qualified by a negative is used; (*med.*) the period when the symptoms of a disease begin to diminish; (*biol.*) reduction of the number of chromosomes in a reproductive cell. [Gk. *meiosis* lessening].
MEKOMETER, [mek-om'-it-er], *n.* a range-finder used on rifles and guns. [Gk. *mekos* length and METER].
MELACONITE, [mel-ak'-on-īt], *n.* a powdery black oxide of copper. [Gk. *melas* black and *konis* dust].
MELAN(O)-, *pref.* black. [Gk. *melas*].
MELANAEMIA, [mel'-an-ē'-mi-a], *n.* a condition of the blood in which it contains blackish particles. [MELAN(O) and Gk. *haima* blood].
MELANCHOLIA, [mel'-an-kō'-li-a], *n.* a form of insanity marked by fits of profound depression. [LL. *melancholia*].
MELANCHOLIC, [mel'-an-kol'-ik], *adj.* affected with, resulting from, melancholy, depressed; mournful, gloomy, sad. [Gk. *melangkholikos* black-biled].
MELANCHOLILY, [mel'-an-kol'-i-li], *adv.* in a melancholy manner.
MELANCHOLINESS, [mel'-an-kol-i-nes], *n.* the condition of melancholy.
MELANCHOLIOUS, [mel'-an-kō'-li-us], *adj.* melancholic.
MELANCHOLY (1), [mel'-an-kol-i], *n.* †melancholia, a disease thought to be due to an excess of black bile; a habitually gloomy state of mind, extremely low spirits. [Gk. *melankolia* black bile].
MELANCHOLY (2), [mel'-an-kol-i], *adj.* gloomy, sad, low-spirited; depressing, dismal.
MELANGE, mélange, [mel-ahnzh'], *n.* a confused mixture, a medley. [Fr. *mélange*].
MELANIN, [mel'-an-in], *n.* the black colouring matter in certain tissues, as in the negro's skin; black pigment of the skin caused by certain diseases.
MELANISM, [mel'-an-izm], *n.* excess of dark colouring matter in the skin, hair, etc.
MELANITE, [mel'-an-īt], *n.* a black kind of garnet.
MELANOCHROI, [mel'-an-ō-krō-ī], *n.*(*pl.*) those members of white races having an unusually swarthy skin. [Gk. *melanokhroos* swarthy].
MELANOSIS, [mel'-an-ō'-sis], *n.* (*path.*) morbid deposit of black pigment in certain bodily tissues resulting in a dark discoloration of the skin, hair, etc. [MELAN(O) and Gk. *osis* expressing condition].
MELANOTIC, [mel'-an-ot'-ik], *adj.* pertaining to, suffering from, melanosis.
MELANTERITE, [mel-an'-ter-īt], *n.* hydrated sulphate of iron, native copperas. [Gk. *melanteria* black dye].
MELANURE, [mel'-an-ewr], *n.* a small sea-bream of the Mediterranean. [Gk. *melanouros* black-tail].
MELAPHYRE, [mel'-a-fīer], *n.* a species of black porphyry. [Gk. *melas* black and (POR)PHYRY].
MELASMA, [mel-az'-ma], *n.* a morbid excess of black colouring matter in the skin; a black spot on the shin-bone of elderly people. [Gk. *melasma* black spot].

MELEE, mêlée, MELLAY†, [mel'-ā], *n.* a confused fight or scuffle, a skirmish. [Fr. *mêlée*].
MELIBOEAN, [mel'-i-bē'-an], *adj.* alternate, interchanging. [*Melibœus*, one of the two speakers in Virgil's first eclogue].
MELIC, [mel'-ik], *adj.* intended for singing. [Gk. *melikos* of a song].
MELICERIS, [mel-is'-er-is], *n.* (*med.*) an encysted tumour containing a honey-like matter. [Gk. *melikeris*].
MELILOT, [mel'-il-ot], *n.* a genus of plants related to the clover, with white or yellow fragrant flowers. [Gk. *meliloton*].
MELINITE, [mel'-in-īt], *n.* a high explosive similar to lyddite. [Fr. *mélinite*].
MELIORATE, [mēl'-yer-āt], *v.t.* to make better, to improve; *v.i.* to grow better. [LL. *meliorare*].
MELIORATER, [mēl'-yer-āt-er], *n.* one who meliorates.
MELIORATION, [mēl'-yer-ā'-shun], *n.* improvement.

MELILOT

MELIORISM, [mēl'-yer-izm], *n.* the doctrine that the world is gradually becoming better and better through human effort. [L. *melior* better].
MELIPHAGOUS, [mel-if'-ag-us], *adj.* (of birds) honey-eating. [Gk. *meli* honey and Gk. *phago* I eat].
MELLAY†, see MELEE.
MELLIFEROUS, [mel-if'-er-us], *adj.* producing honey. [L. *mellifer*].
MELLIFLUENCE, [mel-if'-loo-ents], *n.* the quality of being mellifluent.
MELLIFLUENT, [mel-if'-loo-ent], *adj.* mellifluous. [LL. *mellifluens*].
MELLIFLUOUS, [mel-if'-loo-us], *adj.* (of the voice, etc.) sweetly sounding and smoothly flowing. [L. *mellifluus* flowing with honey].
MELLITE, [mel'-īt], *n.* honey-stone, a yellow compound of alumina present in lignite. [MdL. *mellites*].
MELLIVOROUS, [mel-iv'-or-us], *adj.* eating honey. [L. *mel* honey, and *vorare* to eat].
MELLOW (1), [mel'-ō], *adj.* (of fruit) sweet, ripe, and juicy; (of earth) soft, loamy; (of wine) fully mature and satisfying to the palate; (of sounds, colour, etc.) softened and smooth yet rich and full; possessing a benevolent dignity of character; (*slang*) gay, genial, affably drunk. [ME. *melowe*].
MELLOW (2), [mel'-ō], *v.t.* to make mellow; *v.i.* to become mellow.
MELLOWLY, [mel'-ō-li], *adv.* in mellow fashion.
MELLOWNESS, [mel'-ō-nes], *n.* the quality of being mellow.
MELLOWY, [mel'-ō-i], *adj.* mellow.
MELODEON, [mel-ō'-di-on], *n.* a musical wind instrument similar to a harmonium; a kind of accordion. [MELODY].
MELODIC, [mel-od'-ik], *adj.* relating to or containing melody, tuneful. [Gk. *melodikos*].
MELODIOUS, [mel-ō'-di-us], *adj.* full of melody, tuneful, pleasant to the ear; producing melody. [OFr. *melodieus*].
MELODIOUSLY, [mel-ō'-di-us-li], *adv.* in melodious fashion.
MELODIOUSNESS, [mel-ō'-di-us-nes], *n.* the property of being melodious.
MELODIST, [mel'-od-ist], *n.* a composer or singer of melodies; one especially gifted in writing melodies.
MELODIZE, [mel'-od-īz], *v.t. and i.* to make melodious; to compose melodies.
MELODRAMA, [mel'-ō-drah'-ma], *n.* a type of play highly thrilling in incident, and crude and overdrawn in sentiment and emotional appeal, originally containing songs and incidental music; an incident or series of happenings resembling this. [Gk. *melos* music and DRAMA].
MELODRAMATIC, [mel'-ō-dram-at'-ik], *adj.* of the nature of a melodrama, sensational and touching.
MELODRAMATIST, [mel'-ō-dram'-at-ist], *n.* one skilled in writing melodramas.
MELODY, [mel'-o-di], *n.* a succession of pleasing musical sounds, *esp.* when rhythmically arranged as a tune; a tune; the air of a musical composition; the art of writing this; (*fig.*) musical quality. [Gk. *melodia* song].
MELON, [mel'-on], *n.* any of several varieties of gourd, *esp.* the juicy edible *Itrullus vulgaris* or the

Cucumis melo; **m. cutting,** (slang) a share of profits, etc. [LL. *melo melonis*].
MELON-THISTLE, [mel'-on-thisl'], *n.* a melon-shaped cactus, *Melocactus communis*.
MELOPLASTY, [mel'-ō-plast'-i], *n.* the creation of a new cheek by grafting of tissue. [Gk. *melon* apple and *plastos* moulded].
MELT (1), [melt], *n.* molten metal; the quantity of metal melted at a time.
MELT (2), [melt], *v.t. and i.* to become or make liquid under heat; to dissolve; (*fig.*) to fill with pity or compassion; to blend, merge; to disperse, disappear, vanish; (*coll.*) to be extremely hot and perspiring. [OE. *meltan*].
MELTER, [melt'-er], *n.* one who melts.
MELTING (1), [melt'-ing], *n.* the act of one who, or that which, melts.
MELTING (2), [melt'-ing], *adj.* that melts, full of compassion; deeply affecting; tender, languorous: (of sounds) soothing and liquid.
MELTINGLY, [melt'-ing-li], *adv.* in a melting manner.
MELTINGNESS, [melt'-ing-nes], *n.* the quality of melting or of being melting.
MELTON, [mel'-ton], *n.* a stout woollen cloth for coating; an overcoat of this. [*Melton* Mowbray, in Leicestershire].
MELTON MOWBRAY, [mel'-ton-mō'-brā], *n.* the name of a town in Leicestershire used attributively to denote a kind of meat pie originating there.
MEMBER, [mem'-ber], *n.* a part, limb, or organ of the body; a single component part of a complex whole; an individual belonging to a specific group, organization, etc.; (*math.*) a series of figures or symbols forming part of an expression or formula; (*gram.*) a clause of a sentence; **M. of Parliament,** the elected representative of a constituency in the House of Commons. [L. *membrum*].
MEMBERED, [mem'-berd], *adj.* having limbs.
MEMBERSHIP, [mem'-ber-ship], *n.* the state of being a member of a specific group or organization; the total number of such members.
MEMBRAL, [mem'-bral], *adj.* relating to the limbs.
MEMBRANACEOUS, [mem'-bran-ā'-shus], *adj.* pertaining to, consisting of, like, membrane. [LL. *membranaceus*].
MEMBRANE, [mem'-brān], *n.* (*anat.*) a thin laminar tissue that covers organs, lines cavities, and connects various bodily structures; (*bot.*) a thin white tissue performing similar functions in vegetable bodies; a single piece of parchment of a roll. [L. *membrana*].
MEMBRANEOUS, see MEMBRANOUS.
MEMBRANIFEROUS, [mem'-bran-if'-er-us], *adj.* producing membrane. [MEMBRANE and L. *ferre* to bear].
MEMBRANIFORM, [mem-brān'-i-fawm], *adj.* of the nature of membrane. [MEMBRANE and FORM].
MEMBRANOLOGY, [mem'-bran-ol'-oj-i], *n.* the study of membrane. [MEMBRANE and Gk. *logos* speech].
MEMBRANOUS, MEMBRANEOUS, [mem'-bran-us, mem-brān'-i-us], *adj.* belonging to, consisting of, or resembling, membrane.
MEMENTO, [mi-men'-tō], *n.* something kept to remind one of something or someone, a keepsake; a reminder. [L. *memento* remember!].
MEMO, [mem'-ō], *n.* a memorandum.
MEMOIR, [mem'-wah(r)], *n.* a biography of a person by another; an essay embodying research on a learned subject; (*pl.*) a written account of one's personal recollections and reminiscences; an account of the transactions of a learned society. [Fr. *mémoire*].
MEMOIRIST, [mem'-wahr-ist], *n.* a writer of memoirs.
MEMORABILIA, [mem'-er-a-bil'-i-a], *n.(pl.)* things worthy of remembrance or record. [L. *memorabilia*].
MEMORABILITY, [mem'-er-a-bil'-i-ti], *n.* memorableness.
MEMORABLE, [mem'-er-abl], *adj.* worth remembering, never to be forgotten. [L. *memorabilis*].
MEMORABLENESS, [mem'-er-abl-nes], *n.* the quality of being memorable.
MEMORABLY, [mem'-er-ab-li], *adv.* in a memorable manner.
MEMORANDUM, (*pl.* **memoranda, memorandums**), [mem'-er-and'-um], *n.* a note of certain particulars jotted down for future reference; a brief business note sent to another; (*leg.*) the document stating the terms of a contract, etc.; **m. of association,** the legal articles of registration of a joint-stock company. [L. *memorandum* that must be remembered].
MEMORIAL (1), [mi-maw'-ri-al], *n.* an object, *esp.* a monument or custom which preserves the memory of something; (*pl.*) a chronicle of historical events; (*leg.*) a written statement of the terms of a petition; informal state papers embodying the attitude or suggestions of a State, or containing instructions to an ambassador, in international negotiation.
MEMORIAL (2), [mi-maw'-ri-al], *adj.* pertaining to memory; preserving the memory of, commemorating. [L. *memorialis*].
MEMORIALIST, [mi-maw'-ri-al-ist], *n.* one who writes a memorial; one who presents a legal memorial.
MEMORIALIZE, [mi-maw'-ri-al-īz], *v.t.* to preserve the memory of; to send up a memorial or petition to.
MEMORIA TECHNICA, [mi-maw'-ri-a-tek'-ni-ka], *n.* an artificial aid to memory. [L. *memoria technica* artificial memory].
MEMORIZE, [mem'-er-īz], *v.t.* to commit to memory; to record in writing.
MEMORY, [mem'-er-i], *n.* that aspect of intelligence by which past experience is retained and recollected by the mind; that which is remembered, a recollection; remembrance; fame; time during which one may remember. [L. *memoria*].
MEMPHIAN, [mem'-fi-an], *adj.* pertaining to Memphis, an ancient Egyptian city.
MEMSAHIB, [mem'-sah'-ib], *n.* the Hindu address of respect to a white woman.
MEN, [men], *n.(pl.)* of MAN.
MENACE (1), [men'-as], *n.* a threat. [OFr. *menace*].
MENACE (2), [men'-as], *v.t.* to threaten. [OFr. *menacer*].
MENACER, [men'-as-er], *n.* a person who threatens.
MENACHANITE, [men-ak'-an-īt], *n.* a kind of titanic iron. [*Menachan* in Cornwall].
MENACING, [men'-as-ing], *adj.* threatening.
MENACINGLY, [men'-as-ing-li], *adv.* in threatening fashion.
MENAGE, ménage, [men-ahzh'], *n.* housekeeping; a household. [Fr. *ménage*].
MENAGERIE, [mi-naj'-er-i], *n.* a collection of wild animals kept in cages or special enclosures for public exhibition; the place in which they are housed. [Fr. *ménagerie*].
MENAGOGUE, [men'-a-gog], *n.* a medicine that encourages menstruation. [Gk. *men* month and *agogos* bringing].
MEND (1), [mend], *n.* a darn or patch in a fabric; **on the m.,** improving.
MEND (2), [mend], *v.t.* to repair, put right; to correct, remedy; to improve; to reform; *v.i.* to recover from illness; to become better; to be capable of repair. [AMEND].
MENDABLE, [mend'-abl], *adj.* that may be mended.
MENDACIOUS, [men-dā'-shus], *adj.* lying, false. [L. *mendax*].
MENDACITY, [men-das'-i-ti], *n.* lying, untruthfulness; a falsehood. [L. *mendacitas*].
MENDELIAN (1), [men-dē'-li-an], *n.* a follower or disciple of Mendel. [G. *Mendel*, Abbot of Brunn in Moravia (1822-1884)].
MENDELIAN (2), [men-dē'-li-an], *adj.* pertaining to Mendel or to Mendelism.
MENDELISM, [men'-del-izm], *n.* the theory of heredity propounded by Mendel.
MENDER, [mend'-er], *n.* a person who mends.
MENDICANCY, [men'-di-kan-si], *n.* the state of being a mendicant.
MENDICANT (1), [men'-di-kant], *n.* a beggar; a member of a religious order who lives entirely on alms.
MENDICANT (2), [men'-di-kant], *adj.* begging; (of certain religious orders) living solely on alms. [L. *mendicans*].
MENDICITY, [men-dis'-i-ti], *n.* the life or condition of a beggar; begging. [L. *mendicitas*].
MENDING, [mend'-ing], *n.* the act of repairing.
MENDIPITE, [men'-dip-īt], *n.* an oxychloride of lead. [*Mendip* Hills (Somerset) where found].
MENGITE, [men'-jīt], *n.* a mineral of a hyacinth colour and vitreous lustre, occurring in the Ilmen mountains. [Unkn.].
MENHADEN, [men-hād'-en], *n.* an American sea-fish of the herring family, prized for its oil. [Native].
MENHIR, [men'-hēer], *n.* a single, upright, unhewn stone serving as a prehistoric monument. [Breton *men hir* long stone].
MENIAL (1), [mē'-ni-al], *n.* a domestic servant; a drudge; a base, inferior subordinate.
MENIAL (2), [mē'-ni-al], *adj.* (of work) base, servile; (of servants) domestic. [AFr. *meignal*].
MENILITE, [men'-i-līt], *n.* a brown impure opal. [Fr. *ménilite*].

MENINGEAL, [men'-in-jē'-al], *adj.* relating to the meninges. [MdL. *meningeus*].

MENINGES, [men-in'-jēz], *n.(pl.)* the three membranes that envelop the brain and spinal cord. [L. *meninges* membranes].

MENINGITIS, [men'-in-jī'-tis], *n.* inflammation of the membranes of the brain. [MdL. *meningitis*].

MENISCAL, [men-isk'-al], *adj.* relating to a meniscus.

MENISCUS, (*pl.* **meniscuses**), [men-isk'-us], *n.* a lens, convex on one side and concave on the other; the rounded top of a column of liquid in a tube; (*math.*) a figure shaped like a crescent. [Gk. *meniskos* crescent].

MENISCUS

MENISPERMATE, [men'-i-spurm'-āt], *n.* a compound of menispermic acid and a salifiable base.

MENISPERMIC, [men'-i-spurm'-ik], *adj.* obtained from the seeds of a species of cocculus. [Gk. *mene* moon and *sperma* seed].

MENISPERMINE, [men'-i-spurm'-in], *n.* a tasteless, white, opaque crystalline alkaloid, from the fruit-shells of a species of cocculus.

MENIVER†, see MINIVER.

MENNARD, [men'-erd], *n.* the minnow, *Leuciscus phoxinus.* [Unkn.].

MENNONITE, [men'-on-īt], *n.* a member of a sect of Protestants founded by Menno Simons in the 15th century, who claim to take the New Testament as the sole guide to conduct.

MENOLOGY, [men-ol'-o-ji], *n.* a calendar of saints, *esp.* in the Greek Church, a martyrology. [Gk. *menologion* month account].

MENOPAUSE, [men'-ō-pawz'], *n.* the change of life in women when the menses cease. [Gk. *meno* month and *pausis* cessation].

MENOPOME, [men'-ō-pōm], *n.* the mud-devil, a North American amphibian. [Gk. *meno* I remain and *poma* lid].

MENORRHAGIA, [men'-er-ā'-ji-a], *n.* (*med.*) excessive menstrual discharge. [Gk. *meno* month and *rhagia* bursting].

MENSAL, [men'-sal], *adj.* monthly.

MENSES, [men'-sēz], *n.(pl.)* the monthly discharge of blood-stained mucous membrane from the womb. [L. *menses* months].

MENSHEVIK, [men'-shev-ik], *n.* a Russian socialist of moderate views opposed to and defeated by the extremist Bolsheviks. [Russ. *menshevik* minority].

MENSTRUAL, [men'-strōō-al], *adj.* (*astron.*) monthly; pertaining to the menses. [L. *menstrualis*].

MENSTRUATE, [men'-strōō-āt], *v.i.* to discharge the menses. [L. *menstruare*].

MENSTRUATION, [men'-strōō-ā'-shun], *n.* the act of menstruating.

MENSTRUOUS, [men'-strōō-us], *adj.* having or relating to the menses. [OFr. *menstrueus*].

MENSTRUUM, (*pl.* **menstrua, menstruums**), [men'-strōō-um], *n.* a solvent, so called by the alchemists from some imagined connection of its action with changes of the moon. [L. *menstruum* monthly].

MENSURABILITY, [men'-syŏŏer-a-bil'-i-ti], *n.* the quality of being mensurable.

MENSURABLE, [men'-syŏŏer-abl], *adj.* that may be measured; (*mus.*) written in a set rhythm. [L. *mensurabilis*].

MENSURAL, [men'-syŏŏer-al], *adj.* relating to measure; (*mus.*) mensurable. [MedL. *mensuralis*].

MENSURATION, [men'-syŏŏer-ā-shun], *n.* the act or art of measuring; (*math.*) the branch of mathematics concerned with the determination of lengths, areas, and volumes. [L. *mensuratio*].

MENTAGRA, [men-tag'-ra], *n.* a herpetic eruption on the chin. [L. *mentagra*].

MENTAL (1), [men'-tal], *adj.* pertaining to the mind; performed in the mind; affected with, specializing in, disease of the mind; (*coll.*) mentally defective; **m. arithmetic,** sums worked in the mind and not on paper.

MENTAL (2), [men'-tal], *adj.* pertaining to the chin. [L. *mentum* chin].

MENTALITY, [men-tal'-i-ti], *n.* intelligence, mental capacity; type of mind, mental outlook.

MENTALLY, [men'-tal-i], *adv.* in the mind; as regards the mind.

MENTATION, [men-tā'-shun], *n.* mental activity, cerebration.

MENTHOL, [men'-thol'], *n.* a crystalline substance obtained by cooling oil of peppermint, used medically. [Germ. *menthol* from L. *mentha* mint].

MENTICULTURAL, [men'-ti-kul'-cher-al], *adj.* pertaining to the culture of the mind. [L. *mens mentis* mind and CULTURAL].

MENTION (1), [men'-shun], *n.* a direct reference to; a brief notice of or remarking upon; **honourable m.,** a distinction awarded for specially meritorious work which has failed to secure a prize. [L. *mentio*].

MENTION (2), [men'-shun], *v.t.* to speak of, refer to, name. [MedL. *mentionare*].

MENTIONABLE, [men'-shun-abl], *adj.* fit for mention.

MENTOR, [men'-taw(r)], *n.* a wise and faithful guide and adviser. [*Mentor*, the counsellor of Telemachus].

MENTORIAL, [men-taw'-ri-al], *adj.* giving advice.

MENU, [men'-yōō], *n.* bill of fare, list of dishes; the actual meal. [Fr. *menu* detailed list].

MEPHISTOPHELIAN, [mef'-is-to-fēl'-i-an], *adj.* resembling Mephistopheles, sinister and cynical, sardonic. [*Mephistopheles*, the devil to whom Faust sold his soul].

MEPHITIC, [mi-fit'-ik], *adj.* offensive to the smell, foul. [L. *mephiticus*].

MEPHITIS, [mi-fīt'-is], *n.* an offensive or noxious exhalation from decomposing substances; a foul smell. [L. *mephitis*].

MEPHITISM, [mef'-it-izm], *n.* a foul smell poisoning the atmosphere.

MERCANTILE, [mer'-kan-tīl], *adj.* commercial, pertaining to, employed in, trade or commerce; **m. marine,** the British merchant service engaged in commerce; **m. system,** economic doctrine based on the supposition that money alone is wealth. [It. *mercantile*].

MERCANTILISM, [mer'-kan-til-izm], *n.* trade and commerce; (*econ.*) the mercantile system.

MERCENARILY, [mer'-sen-er-i-li], *adv.* in mercenary fashion.

MERCENARINESS, [mer'-sen-er-i-nes], *n.* the quality of being mercenary.

MERCENARY (1), [mer'-sen-er-i], *n.* a professional soldier hired by a foreign state.

MERCENARY (2), [mer'-sen-er-i], *adj.* hired or procured with money; actuated or moved by love of money; greedy of gain; done for money. [L. *mercenarius*].

MERCER, [mer'-ser], *n.* a dealer in silks, cottons, linens, and woollen cloths. [Fr. *mercier*].

MERCERIZATION, [mer'-ser-iz-ā'-shun], *n.* the process of mercerizing.

MERCERIZE, [mer'-ser-īz], *v.t.* to treat (cotton fabrics) with caustic alkali in order to give them a silky glossy finish. [J. *Mercer* (1791-1866), the inventor of this process].

MERCERSHIP, [mer'-ser-ship], *n.* the business of a mercer.

MERCERY, [mer'-ser-i], *n.* the goods in which a mercer deals; the business of a mercer.

MERCHANDISE, [mur'-chand-īs], *n.* wares, goods, or commodities bought or sold. [OFr. *marchandise*].

MERCHANT (1), [mur'-chant], *n.* one who carries on trade, *esp.* with foreign countries, and on a large scale; (*coll.*) a person, individual. [OFr. *marchand*].

MERCHANT (2), [mur'-chant], *adj.* pertaining to trade or commerce; **m. prince,** a powerful, wealthy trader.

MERCHANTABLE, [mur'-chant-abl], *adj.* fit for market, marketable, that may be sold.

MERCHANT-LIKE, [mur-'-chant-līk'], *adj.* like a merchant.

MERCHANTMAN, [mur'-chant-man], *n.* a ship in the merchant service.

MERCHANTRY, [mur'-chant-ri], *n.* trade or commerce; the whole body of merchants.

MERCHANT SERVICE, [mur'-chant-sur'-vis], *n.* the mercantile marine, consisting of ships engaged solely in commerce or trade.

MERCIFUL, [mur'-si-fŏŏl], *adj.* exhibiting mercy, compassionate; lenient; providential.

MERCIFULLY, [mur'-si-fŏŏl-i], *adv.* in a merciful manner.

MERCIFULNESS, [mur'-si-fŏŏl-nes], *n.* the quality of being merciful.

MERCILESS, [mur'-si-les], *adj.* without mercy, cruel, pitiless.

MERCILESSLY, [mur'-si-les-li], *adv.* in merciless fashion.

MERCILESSNESS, [mur'-si-les-nes], *n.* the quality of being merciless.

MERCURIAL (1), [mer-kewr'-i-al], *n.* a medicinal

drug or preparation containing, or consisting of, mercury.
MERCURIAL (2), [mer-kewr'-i-al], *adj.* pertaining to, consisting of, containing, like, due to, mercury; (*fig.*) nimble, alert, quick; unstable.
MERCURIALISM, [mer-kewr'-i-al-izm], *n.* mercury poisoning.
MERCURIALIST, [mer-kewr'-i-al-ist], *n.* one who advocates the liberal use of mercurial preparations in the treatment of disease.
MERCURIALIZE, [mer-kewr'-i-al-īz], *v.t.* to treat or act upon with mercury; to make mercurial.
MERCURIALLY, [mer-kewr'-i-al-i], *adv.* in a mercurial manner.
MERCURIC, [mer-kewr'-ik], *adj.* of, or containing, mercury; (*chem.*) containing mercury in its higher valency state.
MERCURIFICATION, [mer-kewr'-i-fi-kā'-shun], *n.* the process of mercurifying.
MERCURIFY, [mer-kewr'-i-fī], *v.t.* to obtain pure mercury from its metallic ore.
MERCUROUS, [mer-kew'-rus], *adj.* mercuric; (*chem.*) containing mercury in its lower valency state.
MERCURY, [mer'-kyōō-ri], *n.* the heavy silvery fluid metallic element, Hg; a medical preparation of this; (*myth.*) the messenger of the gods; (*astron.*) the planet nearest the sun; (*bot.*) any of several plants including the all-good; (*coll.*) a messenger; **dog's m.,** the herbaceous plant, *Mercurialis perennis.* [L. *Mercurius*].
MERCY, [mer'-si], *n.* compassion, forbearance, sympathetic leniency; a blessing, a stroke of providence; an act of kindness to someone in one's power; **at the m. of,** helpless in the power of. [OFr. *merci*].
MERCY-SEAT, [mer'-si-sēt'], *n.* the covering of the Ark of the Covenant according to the Jews.
MERE (1), [mēer], *n.* a pool, lake or pond. [OE. *mere*].
MERE (2), [mēer], *n.* (*archaic*) a boundary, a landmark. [OE. *gemære*].
MERE (3), [mēer], *adj.* simple, pure, nothing more than. [L. *merus* unadulterated].
MERELY, [mēer'-li], *adv.* only, simply, purely.
MERETRICIOUS, [me'-ri-trish'-us], *adj.* gaudy, vulgarly ostentatious; deceitfully alluring; (*archaic*) pertaining to, worthy of, a prostitute. [L. *meretricius*].
MERETRICIOUSLY, [me'-ri-trish'-us-li], *adv.* in a meretricious fashion.
MERETRICIOUSNESS, [me'-ri-trish'-us-nes], *n.* the quality of being meretricious.
MERGANSER, [mer-gan'-ser], *n.* (*zool.*) a diving aquatic bird of the genus *Mergus*, allied to the duck. [L. *mergus* diver and *anser* goose].

MERGANSER

MERGE, [murj], *v.t. and i.* to cause to be, or to become, completely absorbed by another; to fade or dissolve imperceptibly into; (*leg.*) to absorb into a greater. [L. *mergere* to immerse].
MERGER, [murj'-er], *n.* (*leg.*) the complete absorption of a smaller property, estate, etc., into a greater; a commercial combine of several business companies under one head. [OFr. *merger*].
MERI, [me'-ri], *n.* a Maori war-club of wood. [Native].
MERICARP, [me'-ri-kahp], *n.* (*bot.*) either of the two single-seeded carpels of the fruit of umbellifers, splitting away as a separate fruit when fully developed. [Gk. *meros* part and *karpos* fruit].
MERIDIAN (1), [mer-id'-i-an], *n.* (*astron., geog.*) a great circle supposed to be drawn so as to pass through the poles of the earth, and the zenith of any place on the surface of the earth, and to intersect the equator at right angles; the highest point reached by the sun or a star; (*fig.*) the full bloom; the height of development, peak of perfection; noon, midday; a brass ring encompassing a model globe; (*geom.*) a great circle of a sphere passing through the poles; **magnetic m.,** a great circle, parallel with the direction of the magnetic needle, and passing through the magnetic poles.
MERIDIAN (2), [me-rid'-i-an], *adj.* pertaining to the sun at its meridian; pertaining to a meridian; (*fig.*) relating to the peak or zenith; pertaining to noon. [L. *meridianus* mid-day].
MERIDIONAL, [mer-id'-i-on-al], *adj.* pertaining to the south or to dwellers in the south (of Europe), southerly; pertaining to a meridian. [L. *meridionalis*].
MERIDIONALITY, [mer-id'-i-on-al'-i-ti], *n.* the quality of being meridional.
MERIDIONALLY, [mer-id'-i-on-al-i], *adv.* towards the meridian.
MERINGUE, [mer-ang'], *n.* white of an egg mixed with pounded sugar; a light cake of this containing thick cream. [Fr. *meringue*].
MERINO (1), [mer-ē'-nō], *n.* a variety of fine-woolled sheep, originally from Spain; a short, fine-stapled, wavy wool from these sheep; a mixture of fine wool and cotton; a fine woollen fabric used in making stockings. [Span. *merino*].
MERINO (2), [mer-ē'-nō], *adj.* made of merino; relating to the merino sheep or to their wool.
MERISMATIC, [me'-riz-mat'-ik], *adj.* (of cells) dividing by means of internal partitions; pertaining to such division. [Gk. *merisma* a separated part].
MERISTEM, [me'-ri-stem], *n.* the formative merismatic tissue of certain cells. [Gk. *meristos* divided].
MERIT (1), [me'-rit], *n.* good quality or excellence entitling to commendation or reward; proved ability or worth; credit; (*pl.*) deserts; (*leg.*) the rights and wrongs of a question at issue; **Order of M.,** a British military and civil order awarded for outstanding eminence. [L. *meritum*].
MERIT (2), [me'-rit], *v.t.* to deserve, earn, to be entitled to.
MERITED, [me'-rit-id], *adj.* earned, deserved.
MERITORIOUS, [me'-rit-aw'-ri-us], *adj.* deserving reward or commendation; praiseworthy. [L. *meritorius* pertaining to earning].
MERITORIOUSLY, [me'-rit-aw'-ri-us-li], *adv.* in a meritorious manner.
MERITORIOUSNESS, [me'-rit-aw'-ri-us-nes], *n.* the quality of being meritorious.
MERK†, see MARK.
MERLE, [merl], *n.* the blackbird. [OFr. *merle*].
MERLIN, [mer'-lin], *n.* the smallest British falcon, *Falco æsalon.* [AFr. *merilun*].
MERLON, [mur'-lon], *n.* (*fort.*) that part of a parapet lying between two embrasures. [Fr. *merlon*].

MERLON

MERMAID, [mur'-mād], *n.* an imaginary marine creature having the head and body of a woman and the tail of a fish; **mermaid's purse,** the egg capsule of a skate or dogfish. [ME. *meremayde*].
MERMAN, [mur'-man], *n.* the male equivalent of a mermaid.
MEROBLAST, [me'-rō-blast'], *n.* an ovum having both germinal and nutritive parts. [Gk. *meros* part and *blastos* bud].
MEROVINGIAN, [me'-rō-ving'-gi-an], *adj.* relating to the Merovingians, the earliest Frankish dynasty ruling in Gaul. [LL. *Merovingi* descendants of Meroveus].
MERRILY, [me'-ri-li], *adv.* in a merry manner.
MERRIMENT, [me'-ri-ment], *n.* mirth, jollity, hilarious gaiety.
MERRINESS, [me'-ri-nes], *n.* the quality of being merry.
MERRY (1), [me'-ri], *n.* the common wild black cherry. [OFr. *merise*].
MERRY (2), [me'-ri], *adj.* gay, cheerful, jolly; fond of fun and laughter; (*archaic*) pleasant; (*slang*) slightly intoxicated. [OE. *myr(i)ge* which gave the ME. form *meri*].
MERRY-ANDREW, [me'-ri-an'-drōō], *n.* a jester, buffoon or clown; a mountebank's assistant.
MERRY-DANCERS, [me'-ri-dahns'-erz], *n.(pl.)* the aurora borealis.
MERRY-GO-ROUND, [me'-ri-gō-rownd'], *n.* a circular rotating structure, mounted with imitation vehicles, horses, etc., and mechanically propelled.
MERRYMAKING, [me'-ri-māk'-ing], *n.* a festival, jovial entertainment; fun and games.
MERRYQUILTS, [me'-ri-kwiltz'], *n.(pl.)* cotton fabrics manufactured in Assam.
MERRYTHOUGHT, [me'-ri-thawt'], *n.* the forked upper bone of the breast of a bird, the wish-bone.
MERSION, [mur'-shun], *n.* immersion. [L. *mersio*].
MESA, [mā'-sa], *n.* a broad, flat, high, rocky tableland. [Span. *mesa* table].
MESALLIANCE, mésalliance, [māz'-al-ē-ahns'], *n.* a marriage in which one of the partners is of inferior social status to the other. [Fr. *mésalliance*].
MESARAIC, [mes'-er-ā'-ik], *adj.* relating to the mesentery. [MedL. *mesaraicus*].
MESCAL, [mes'-kal], *n.* an intoxicant made from the

Mexican agave; **m. plant,** the agave or American aloe. [Mexican *mexcalli*].
MESDAMES, [med'-ahm, mā-dahm'], *n.(pl.)* of MADAME. [Fr. *mesdames*].
MESEEMS, [mi-sēmz'], *v. impers.* (*archaic*) it seems to me.
MESEMBRYANTHEMUM, [mes-em'-bri-an'-thi-mum], *n.* a large genus of plants, including the hottentot fig, *Mesembryanthemum edule*, and the ice plant, *Mesembryanthemum crystallinum*. [Gk. *mesembria* noon and *anthemon* flower].
MESENTERIC, [mes'-en-te'-rik], *adj.* relating to the mesentery.
MESENTERITIS, [mes'-en-ter-īt'-is], *n.* inflammation of the mesentery. [MESENTERY and Gk. *itis* denoting inflammation].
MESENTERY, [mes-en'-ter-i], *n.* (*anat.*) the part of the peritoneum fastening the intestines to the back wall of the abdomen. [Gk. *mesenterion* middle intestine].
MESH (1), [mesh], *n.* one of the small holes enclosed by the threads of a net, a similar hole in a sieve, etc.; a network, an arrangement of threads to form a net; (*fig.*) snare, entanglement. [~OE. *max* net, MDu. *maesche*].
MESH (2), [mesh], *v.t.* to catch in a net; to ensnare; *v.i.* (of gears, etc.) to engage with corresponding parts of machinery. [MESH (1)].
MESHWORK, [mesh'-wurk], *n.* network.
MESHY, [mesh'-i], *adj.* formed like network, reticulated, full of meshes.
MESIAL, [mē'-si-al], *adj.* pertaining to, placed along or towards, a line running down the middle of a body. [Gk. *mesos* middle].
MESITITE, [mes'-it-īt], *n.* carbonate of magnesium and iron. [Gk. *mesitos* intermediary].
MESJID, [mes'-jid], n. a mosque.
MESLIN, see MASLIN.
MESMEREE, [mez'-mer-ē], *n.* a person mesmerized or one to be mesmerized.
MESMERIC, [mez-me'-rik], *adj.* pertaining to, resembling, resulting from, mesmerism.
MESMERISM, [mez'-mer-izm], *n.* hypnotism, the presumed magnetic influence exerted by one person upon another, controlling absolutely his thoughts and actions; the hypnotic state so induced; mesmerization. [*Mesmer*, an Austrian physician (1734-1815)].
MESMERIST, [mez'-mer-ist], *n.* one who practises mesmerism.
MESMERIZATION, [mez'-mer-īz-ā'-shun], *n.* the act of mesmerizing; the state of being mesmerized.
MESMERIZE, [mez'-mer-īz], *v.t.* to hypnotize.
MESNE, [mēn], *adj.* intermediate; **m. process,** a process intervening between the beginning and end of a lawsuit; **m. profits,** intermediate profits of land received by one who is wrongfully in possession, and sued for by the rightful owner when he enters into possession again; **m. lord,** one who holds land from a superior lord, and has tenants holding land from him. [OFr. *mesne*].
MESO-, *pref.* middle. [Gk. *mesos*].
MESOBLAST, [mes'-ō-blast], *n.* the central germinal region of the embryo. [MESO and Gk. *blastos* bud].
MESOCEPHALIC, [mes'-ō-sef-al'-ik], *adj.* pertaining to skulls which are of average size or of indeterminate shape.
MESOCOLON, [mes'-ō-kō'-lon], *n.* that part of the peritoneum supporting the colon.
MESODERM, [mes'-ō-derm], *n.* the mesoblast, the middle layer of bark. [MESO and Gk. *derma* skin].
MESOGASTRIC, [mes'-ō-gas'-trik], *adj.* (*anat.*) situated in the umbilical region, or middle of the belly.
MESOLITE, [mes'-ō-līt], *n.* a hydrated silicate of sodium, aluminium and calcium, needlestone. [MESO and Gk. *lithos* stone].
MESOPHLOEUM, [mes'-ō-flē'-um], *n.* the middle bark. [MESO and Gk. *phloios* bark].
MESOPHYLL, [mes'-ō-fil], *n.* the innermost cellular tissue of a leaf. [MESO and Gk. *phullon* leaf].
MESOPHYTE, [mes'-ō-fīt], *n.* a plant needing an average water supply. [MESO and Gk. *phuton* plant].
MESOSPERM, [mes'-ō-sperm'], *n.* (*bot.*) the middle membranous covering of a seed.
MESOTHORAX, [mes'-ō-thaw'-raks], *n.* (*entom.*) the middle segment of the thorax.
MESOZOIC, [mes'-ō-zō'-ik], *adj.* (*geol.*) pertaining to the period between the Palaeozoic and Cainozoic eras. [MESO and Gk. *zoon* animal].
MESQUIT, [mes'-kēt], *n.* a small North American tree of the acacia family. [Mexican Span. *mezquite*].
MESS (1), [mes], *n.* soft, pulpy food for animals; a hodge-podge, medley; a state of dirty untidiness or disorder; a muddle, awkward situation; (*coll.*) a nuisance; a group of persons in the fighting forces, who regularly dine together; (*archaic*) a quantity of food served at one time, *esp.* a dish of slops. [OFr. *mes*].
MESS (2), [mes], *v.t.* to soil, spoil, dirty; to muddle, bungle; to put into a mess; *v.i.* to take one's meals, *esp.* habitually with the same group of persons; **to m. about,** to waste time doing nothing.
MESS† (3), see MASH (1).
MESSAGE, [mes'-ij], *n.* a communication sent by one person to another by means of an intermediary; a divine revelation. [Fr. *message*].
MESSENGER, [mes'-en-jer], *n.* one who bears a message, *esp.* one employed in delivering dispatches or business communications; (*naut.*) a rope or chain, passing round a capstan, for hauling in a cable; (*archaic*) a harbinger, forerunner. [OFr. *messager*].
MESSERSCHMITT, [me'-ser-shmit], *n.* the name of various types of German (fighter) aircraft. [W. *Messerschmitt* the designer and maker].
MESSIAH, [mi-sī'-a], *n.* Christ, the Saviour of the world; (*fig.*) a deliverer. [Heb. *mashiah* anointed].
MESSIANIC, [mes'-ī-an'-ik], *adj.* pertaining to the Messiah.
MESSIEURS, [mes-yur'], *n.(pl.)* of MONSIEUR. [Fr. *messieurs* sirs].
MESSINESS, [mes'-i-nes], *n.* the state of being messy.
MESSMATE, [mes'-māt], *n.* a companion at meals in a mess; (*coll.*) a friend, colleague, shipmate.
MESSROOM, [mes'-ro͞om], *n.* the room in which a mess assembles.
MESSRS., [mes'-erz], *n.(pl.)* a title placed before the name of a firm, or at the head of a list of men's names. [MESSIEURS].
MESSUAGE, [mes'-wāj], *n.* (*leg.*) a dwelling-house together with the out-buildings and land attached thereto. [OFr. *mesuage*].
MESSY, [mes'-i], *adj.* (*coll.*) in a mess, dirty, untidy, confused.
MESTEE, see MUSTEE.
MESTINO, [mes-tē'-nō], *n.* a mestizo.
MESTIZO, [mes-tē'-zō], *n.* the child of a Spaniard, Portuguese, or creole and a native Indian. [Span. *mestizo*].
META-, *pref.* beyond; after; with; between; among; frequently expressing change. [Gk. *meta*].
METABASIS, [met-ab'-as-is], *n.* (*rhet.*) transition. [Gk. *metabasis*].
METABOLIAN, [met'-a-bōl'-i-an], *n.* an insect which experiences a metamorphosis. [MdL. *metabolia*].
METABOLIC, [met'-a-bol'-ik], *adj.* pertaining to, resulting from, metabolism.
METABOLISM, [met-ab'-ol-izm], *n.* (*biol.*) continual chemical change in living organisms, by which living matter is gradually built up, and complex substances broken down. [Gk. *metabole* change].
METABOLIZE, [met-ab'-ol-īz], *v.t.* to change by metabolism.
METACARPAL, [met'-a-kahp'-al], *adj.* pertaining to the metacarpus; **m. bones,** the bones between the wrist and fingers.
METACARPUS, [met'-a-kahp'-us], *n.* (*anat.*) the part of the hand lying between the wrist and the fingers. [META and Gk. *karpos* wrist].

METACARPAL BONES

METACENTRE, [met'-a-sen'-ter], *n.* the point where the vertical line drawn through the centre of gravity of a floating body in equilibrium cuts that drawn through the centre of buoyancy when the equilibrium is disturbed. [META and CENTRE].
METACETONE, [met-as'-i-tōn], *n.* a liquid produced from the distillation of sugar, or starch, and quicklime. [META and ACETONE].
METACHRONISM, [met-ak'-ron-izm], *n.* an error in chronology by which an event is dated later than its actual date. [MedL. *metachronismus*].
METACHROSIS, [met'-a-krō'-sis], *n.* change of colour in animals so as to blend with their environment. [META and Gk. *khrosis* colour].
METACISM, [met'-as-izm], *n.* (*pros.*) the fault, in

Latin prose composition, of placing a word ending in *m* before a word whose initial letter was a vowel. [L. *metacismus*].

METAGE, [mēt'-ij], *n.* the official weighing of a load of coal, grain, etc.; the fee for this. [METE (2)].

METAGENESIS, [met'-a-jen'-es-is], *n.* (*biol.*) alternation between sexual and asexual reproduction in consecutive generations. [META and GENESIS].

METAL (1), [met'-al], *n.* a malleable, ductile electropositive element, fusible by heat, a good conductor of heat and electricity, and usually solid at ordinary temperatures; glass in a state of fusion; stones broken small for road-making; (*pl.*) rails; (*her.*) either of the heraldic tinctures gold (yellow) or silver (white). [Gk. *metallon* mine].

METAL (2), (**metalling, metalled**), [met'-al], *v.t.* to cover with metal; to repair or make roads with stones broken small.

METALEPSIS, [met'-a-lep'-sis], *n.* (*pros.*) the substitution by metonymy of a word for another word which is itself used figuratively. [Gk. *metalepsis* substitution].

METALEPTIC, [met'-a-lept'-ik], *adj.* relating to metalepsis. [Gk. *metaleptikos*].

METALEPTICALLY, [met'-a-lept'-ik-al-i], *adv.* by metalepsis.

METALLIC, [met-al'-ik], *adj.* pertaining to, like, containing, consisting of, metal; **m. oxide**, a metal combined with oxygen; **m. salts**, salts having a metallic oxide as their base; **m. currency**, currency in which metal coins are used. [Gk. *metallikos*].

METALLIFEROUS, [met'-al-if'-er-us], *adj.* producing metal. [L. *metallifer*].

METALLIFORM, [met-al'-i-fawm], *adj.* having the form of metal.

METALLIFY, [met-al'-i-fī], *v.t.* to obtain the metal from (ore).

METALLINE, [met'-al-īn], *adj.* pertaining to, consisting of, containing, metal, resembling metal.

METALLING, [met'-al-ing], *n.* broken stone used in road construction or repair; the process of repairing or making roads with this.

METALLIST, [met'-al-ist], *n.* a worker or one skilled in metals, one in favour of using a particular metal as currency.

METALLIZATION, [met'-al-īz-ā'-shun], *n.* the act of metallizing; the state of being metallized.

METALLIZE, [met'-al-īz], *v.t.* to form into metal; to give metallic qualities to.

METALLOGRAPHY, [met'-al-og'-ra-fi], *n.* the study of the structure and properties of metals. [Gk. *metallographia*].

METALLOID (1), [met'-al-oid], *n.* an element resembling, but not, a metal.

METALLOID (2), [met'-al-oid], *adj.* resembling a metal. [METAL (1) and Gk. *oeides* like].

METALLOIDAL, [met'-al-oid'-al], *adj.* metalloid.

METALLURGIC, [met'-al-urj'-ik], *adj.* relating to metallurgy.

METALLURGIST, [met'-al-urj-ist], *n.* a worker in metals; one skilled in metallurgy.

METALLURGY, [met'-al-ur-ji], *n.* the art of extracting, smelting, refining and generally preparing metals. [Gk. *metallourgos* a metal worker].

METALMAN, [met'-al-man], *n.* one who works in metals.

METALOGICAL, [met'-a-loj'-ik-al], *adj.* beyond logic.

METAMERE, [met'-a-mēer], *n.* (*zool.*) one of the exactly corresponding segments into which the bodies of certain animals are divided. [META and Gk. *meros* part].

METAMERIC, [met'-a-me'-rik], *adj.* (*chem.*) having the same molecular weight, and the same chemical elements in the same proportion, but exhibiting different properties; (*zool.*) resembling, made up of, metameres.

METAMERISM, [met-am'-er-izm], *n.* (*zool.*) the state of being metameric.

METAMORPHIC, [met'-a-mawf'-ik], *adj.* displaying change of form; (*geol.*) changed in structure or form under external influence. [META and Gk. *morphe* form].

METAMORPHISM, [met'-a-mawf'-izm], *n.* state of being metamorphic, *esp.* of rocks.

METAMORPHOSE, [met'-a-mawf-ōs'], *v.t.* to change into a different form, to transform.

METAMORPHOSIS, [met'-a-mawf'-ō-sis], *n.* change of appearance, character, structure, etc., transformation. [Gk. *metamorphosis*].

METAPHOR, [met'-a-fer], *n.* a figure of speech in which a word or phrase is used to describe or qualify another with which it is not normally associated, so as to imply a comparison. [Gk. *metaphora* transference].

METAPHORIC, [met'-a-fo'-rik], *adj.* metaphorical.

METAPHORICAL, [met'-a-fo'-rik-al], *adj.* pertaining to, of the nature of, a metaphor; containing metaphors, figurative.

METAPHORICALLY, [met'-a-fo'-rik-al-i], *adv.* in metaphorical fashion.

METAPHORICALNESS, [met'-a-fo'-rik-al-nes], *n.* the quality of being metaphorical.

METAPHORIST, [met'-a-for-ist], *n.* one who makes use of metaphors.

METAPHRASE (1), [met'-a-frāz], *n.* a literal translation. [Gk. *metaphrasis*].

METAPHRASE (2), [met'-a-frāz], *v.t.* to translate literally.

METAPHRAST, [met'-a-frast], *n.* one who rewrites a composition in a different literary form. [Gk. *metaphrastes*].

METAPHRASTIC, [met'-a-frast'-ik], *adj.* of the nature of, consisting of, a metaphrase, literal. [Gk. *metaphrastikos*].

METAPHYSIC, [met'-a-fiz'-ik], *adj.* metaphysical.

METAPHYSICAL, [met'-a-fiz'-ik-al], *adj.* relating to, connected with, metaphysics; based on pure reasoning; insubstantial, supernatural; too subtle or nice in making distinctions.

METAPHYSICALLY, [met'-a-fiz'-ik-al-i], *adv.* in a metaphysical manner.

METAPHYSICIAN, [met'-a-fiz-ish'-an], *n.* one skilled in metaphysics.

METAPHYSICS, [met'-a-fiz'-iks], *n.*(*pl.*) the study of the ultimate problems and principles behind all being and knowledge.

METAPLASIA, [met'-a-plā'-zi-a], *n.* the transformation of one form of tissue into another. [MdL. *metaplasia*].

METAPLASM, [met'-a-plazm], *n.* (*biol.*) the protoplasm containing the formative material; (*gram.*) the alteration of a word by changing or removing a letter. [Gk. *metaplasmos*].

METAPOLITICS, [met'-a-pol'-it-iks], *n.*(*pl.*) abstract political theorizing or study.

METAPOPHYSIS, [met'-a-pof'-is-is], *n.* a mammillary process of the vertebrae. [META and APOPHYSIS].

METASOMATISM, [met'-a-sō'-mat-izm], *n.* the changing of one kind of rock into a completely different kind. [META and Gk. *soma* body].

METASTASIS, (*pl.* **metastases**), [met-as'-tas-is], *n.* the removal of a bodily function or of the seat of a disease into another part of the body; (*biol.*) metabolism; (*fig.*) change, transformation. [Gk. *metastasis*].

METATARSAL, [met'-a-tahs'-al], *adj.* pertaining to, involving, the metatarsus.

METATARSUS, [met'-a-tahs'-us], *n.* the group of five bones between the ankle and toes. [META and TARSUS].

METATHESIS, [met-ath'-is-is], *n.* (*phon.*) the transposition of sounds in a word; (*med.*) removal of a morbific substance to another part of the body; (*chem.*) the reaction of two substances to produce two fresh substances. [Gk. *metathesis*].

METATHETICAL, [met'-a-thet'-ik-al], *adj.* relating to metathesis. [Gk. *metathetikos*].

METATHORAX, [met'-a-thaw'-raks], *n.* (*entom.*) the posterior segment of the thorax in insects.

METATOME, [met'-a-tōm], *n.* (*arch.*) the space between two dentils. [META and Gk. *tome* cutting].

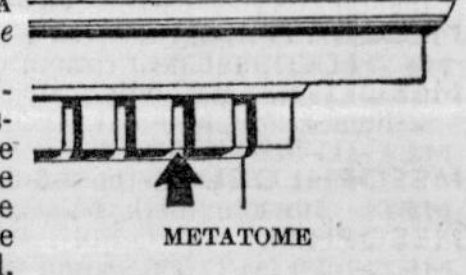
METATOME

METAYAGE, [met'-ā-yahzh'], *n.* a system of land tenure by which the produce is shared between the cultivator and the owner of the land, the latter providing the seed, etc. [Fr. *métayage*].

METAYER, [met'-ā-yā'], *n.* one who rents land for cultivation under metayage. [Fr. *métayer*].

METAZOA, [met'-a-zō'-a], *n.*(*pl.*) animals whose bodies are made up of many cells. [META and Gk. *zoa*, *pl.* of *zoon* animal].

METE (1), [mēt], *n.* boundary, limit; boundary mark. [L. *meta*].

METE (2), [mēt], *v.t.* (*poet.*, *archaic*) to measure; to deal out, distribute. [OE. *metan* to measure].

METEMPIRIC, [met'-em-pir'-ik], *n.* (often *pl.*) the

philosophy of that which lies beyond the experience; a student of this. [META and EMPIRIC].

METEMPIRICISM, [met′-em-pir′-is-izm], *n.* philosophy dealing with that which lies beyond experience.

METEMPSYCHOSIS, [met-em′-sik-ō′-sis], *n.* the passing over of the soul after death from one body to another. [Gk. *metempsukhosis*].

METEMPTOSIS, [met′-em-tō′-sis], *n.* the suppression of the bissextile every 134 years. [META and Gk. *emptosis* falling upon].

METENSOMATOSIS, [met′-en-sō′-mat-ō′-sis], *n.* the transference and incorporation of the elements of one body into that of another. [Gk. *metensomatosis*].

METEOR, [mē′-tē-or], *n.* a transitory luminous body, heated by friction as it shoots through the atmosphere; (*fig.*) anything that dazzles and does not last; †any atmospheric phenomenon. [Gk. *meteoros* high in the sky].

METEORIC, [mē′-tē-o′-rik], *adj.* pertaining to the atmosphere; (*bot.*) affected by the state of the atmosphere; pertaining to, resulting from, meteors; (*fig.*) sudden, swift and dazzling.

METEORITE, [mē′-tē-or-īt], *n.* a meteor, or part of one, that has fallen upon the earth.

METEOROGRAPH, [mē′-tē-or′-ō-graf], *n.* an instrument for taking meteorological readings.

METEOROGRAPHY, [mē′-tē-or-og′-ra-fi], *n.* the registering of meteorological phenomena. [METEOR and Gk. *graphia* writing].

METEOROID, [mē′-tē-or-oid], *n.* a particle of matter which, moving through space, forms a meteor upon encountering the earth's atmosphere. [METEOR and Gk. *oeides* like].

METEOROLITE, [mē′-tē-or-ō-līt], *n.* a meteoric stone, a meteorite. [METEOR and Gk. *lithos* stone].

METEOROLOGICAL, [mē′-tē-or-ol-oj′-ik-al], *adj.* relating to meteorology.

METEOROLOGIST, [mē′-tē-or-ol′-oj-ist], *n.* one versed in meteorology.

METEOROLOGY, [mē′-tē-or-ol′-o-ji], *n.* the scientific study of the atmosphere and its phenomena, *esp.* with regard to its effect upon the weather; the atmospheric conditions of a particular region. [Gk. *meteorologia*].

METEOROUS, [mē′-tē-or-us], *adj.* of the nature of a meteor, meteoric.

METER, [mē′-ter], *n.* a machine for registering the quantity or amount of anything, *esp.* the consumption of gas, water, etc. [Gk. *metron* measure].

METHANE, [meth′-ān], *n.* an inflammable gas, a compound of one atom of carbon and four atoms of hydrogen. [METHYL].

METHEGLIN, [meth-eg′-lin], *n.* a drink of fermented honey and water. [Wel. *meddyglyn* healing juice].

METHINKS, [mi-thingks′], *v. impers.* (*archaic*) it seems to me. [OE. *me thyncth*].

METHOD, [meth′-od], *n.* the manner or way in which anything is done; systematic arrangement or form of procedure, *esp.* in scientific inquiry or exposition, logical orderliness; (*bot., zool.*) classification. [Gk. *methodos* scientific inquiry].

METHODIC, [meth-od′-ik], *adj.* methodical.

METHODICAL, [meth-od′-ik-al], *adj.* displaying method, orderly, systematic.

METHODICALLY, [meth-od′-ik-al-i], *adv.* in methodical fashion.

METHODISM, [meth′-od-izm], *n.* the principles, doctrines, and practices of the Methodists.

METHODIST, [meth′-od-ist], *n.* a member of a nonconformist branch of the Christian church founded by John and Charles Wesley; (*archaic*) a strict observer of method.

METHODISTICAL, [meth′-od-ist′-ik-al], *adj.* resembling the Methodists; strictly and rather narrowly religious.

METHODISTICALLY, [meth′-od-ist′-ik-al-i], *adv.* according to the Methodists.

METHODIZE, [meth′-od-īz], *v.t.* to make methodical, systematize.

METHODOLOGY, [meth′-od-ol′-o-ji], *n.* the study of scientific method.

METHOUGHT, [mi-thawt′], *pret.* of METHINKS. [OE. *me thuhte* it seemed to me].

METHUSELAH, [mi-thew′-zel-a], *n.* a very old person. [*Methuselah*, Gen., v, 27].

METHYL, [meth′-il], *n.* the organic radical CH_3. [Fr. *méthyle* from Gk. *methu* wine].

METHYLATE, [meth′-il-āt], *v.t.* to mix with methyl, *esp.* in order to make unfit for drinking.

METHYLATED, [meth′-il-āt-id], *adj.* mixed with methyl; **m. spirit,** rectified spirit of wine denatured by mixing with wood naphtha or methyl alcohol.

METHYLENE, [meth′-il-ēn], *n.* a radical of the hydrocarbons existing in compounds. [Fr. *méthylène*].

METHYLIC, [meth-il′-ik], *adj.* relating to methyl.

METIC, [met′-ik], *n.* a foreign resident in a Greek city. [Gk. *metoikos*].

METICULOUS, [met-ik′-yōō-lus], *adj.* scrupulously exact. [L. *meticulosus*].

METICULOUSLY, [met-ik′-yōō-lus-li], *adv.* in meticulous fashion.

METIER, métier, [met′-yā], *n.* profession, trade, calling; that for which one has a special aptitude. [Fr. *métier*].

METIS, [met′-is], *n.* a Canadian half-breed of American Indian and white parentage. [Fr. *métis*].

METOCHE, [met′-o-ki], *n.* (*arch.*) the space between one dentil and another. [Gk. *metokhe*].

METOL, [met′-ol], *n.* a substance used as a developer in photography to produce negatives of low contrast. [Germ. trade name *metol*].

METONIC, [met-on′-ik], *adj.* discovered by Meton; **M. cycle,** the period of 19 Julian years, being the time taken by the moon to complete its cycle of movement with respect to the sun. [*Meton*, the Athenian astronomer].

METONYMICAL, [met-on-im′-ik-al], *adj.* pertaining to, using metonymy; used as metonymy.

METONYMY, [met-on′-i-mi], *n.* a figure of speech in which one word is put for another it suggests. [Gk. *metonumia*].

METOPE (1), [met′-ōp], *n.* the face of a crab. [Gk. *metopon* forehead].

METOPE (2), [met′-o-pi, met′-ōp], *n.* (*arch.*) one of the square spaces between the triglyphs of the Doric frieze. [META and Gk. *ope* opening].

METOPOSCOPIST, [met′-ō-pos′-kop-ist], *n.* one versed in metoposcopy.

METOPOSCOPY, [met′-ō-pos′-kop-i], *n.* character reading or fortune telling by a study of the forehead or face. [Gk. *metopon* forehead and *skopos* viewer].

METRE (1), [mē′-ter], *n.* poetical rhythm; a rhythmic arrangement of syllables in verse according to some fixed scheme. [OF. *metre* from Gk. *metron* measure].

METRE (2), [mē′-ter], *n.* the unit of length in the metric system, corresponding to 39·37 inches. [Fr. *mètre* from Gk. *metron* measure].

METRIC, [met′-rik], *adj.* pertaining to the decimal system of measurement based on the metre.

METRICAL, [met′-rikl], *adj.* pertaining to, using measurement; pertaining to, written in metre. [Gk *metrikos*].

METRICALLY, [met′-rik-al-i], *adv.* in metrical fashion.

METRICIAN, [met-rish′-an], *n.* a composer of verses, a metrist.

METRICS, [met′-riks], *n.* the theory and art of verse-composition and metre.

METRIFY, [met′-ri-fī], *v.t. and i.* to versify, to write in metre. [L. *metrificare*].

METRIST, [met′-rist], *n.* one skilled in the use of metre.

METROGRAPH, [met′-rō-graf], *n.* an indicator which shows the hour of arrival and departure of railway trains. [Gk. *metron* measure and GRAPH].

METROLOGICAL, [met′-rō-loj′-ik-al], *adj.* pertaining to metrology.

METROLOGIST, [met-rol′-oj-ist], *n.* one learned in metrology.

METROLOGY, [met-ro′-lo-ji], *n.* the science of weights and measures. [Gk. *metron* measure and *logos* speech].

METROMANIA, [met′-rō-mā′-ni-a], *n.* a passion for composing verses. [Gk. *metron* measure and MANIA].

METRONOME, [met′-rō-nōm], *n.* (*mus.*) an instrument consisting of a weighted pendulum worked by clockwork, which can be adjusted to beat time at any given rate. [Gk. *metron* measure and *nomos* law].

METRONOMIC, [met′-rō-nom′-ik], *adj.* relating to a metronome.

METRONOMY, [met-ron′-o-mi], *n.* (*mus.*) the use of a metronome.

METRONYMIC, [met′-rō-nim′-ik], *n.* a name taken from the mother's family or from a maternal ancestor. [Gk. *metronumikos*].

METROPOLIS, [mi-trop′-o-lis], *n.* the capital, chief city of a country; the see of a metropolitan bishop. [Gk. *metropolis* mother city].

METRONOME

METROPOLITAN (1), [met′-rō-pol′-it-an], *n.* the bishop who presides over the other bishops of a province; a dweller in a metropolis.

METROPOLITAN (2), [met'-rō-pol'-it-an], *adj.* belonging to a metropolis; pertaining to a metropolitan or his see; **m. France,** France as distinct from the French Empire. [Gk. *metropolites*].

METROPOLITANATE, [met'-rō-pol'-it-an-āt], *n.* the see or office of a metropolitan bishop.

METROPOLITICAL, [met'-rō-pol-it'-ik-al], *adj.* relating to a metropolis; metropolitan.

METTLE, [metl], *n.* disposition, character; spirit, courage, fire. [METAL].

METTLED, [metld], *adj.* mettlesome.

METTLESOME, [metl'-sum], *adj.* high-spirited, full of fire.

METTLESOMELY, [metl'-sum-li], *adv.* in mettlesome fashion.

METTLESOMENESS, [metl'-sum-nes], *n.* the quality of being mettlesome.

MEW (1), [mew], *n.* bald-money, the umbelliferous plant *Meum athamanticum.* [Unkn.].

MEW (2), [mew], *n.* a sea-gull. [OE. *mæw*].

MEW (3), [mew], *n.* a cage for hawks, *esp.* during moulting time; the process of moulting; (*pl.*) (*hist.*) the royal stables in London, built upon the site where the king's hawks were mewed; (*pl.*) a series of stables built round an open space or yard. [Fr. *mue*].

MEW (4), [mew], *n.* the cry of a cat. [Echoic].

MEW (5), [mew], *v.t.* to confine in a cage during moulting time; to shut up, imprison. [MEW (3)].

MEW (6), [mew], *v.t.* *and i.* to shed or cast (feathers, etc.), to moult. [OFr. *muer* from L. *mutare* to change].

MEW (7), [mew], *v.i.* to cry as a cat. [MEW (4)].

MEWL, [mewl], *v.i.* to cry as an infant, whimper; to mew like a cat. [Echoic].

MEWLER, [mewl'-er], *n.* a crying child.

MEZEREON, [mez-ēer'-i-on], *n.* the small ornamental flowering shrub, *Daphne Mezereum.* [Arab. *mazaryun*].

MEZQUIT, [mez'-kit], *n.* the Mexican tree, *Prosopis juliflora.* [Mexican Span. *mezquite*].

MEZZANINE, [mez'-an-ēn], *n.* a storey of small height between two higher ones; (*arch.*) a window in this; a floor below the stage of a theatre, used in working traps, etc. [It. *mezzanino* from *mezzano* middle].

MEZZO, [met'-zō], *adj.* middle, mean; (*mus.*) moderately; **m. rilievo,** carving in half relief. [It. *mezzo*].

MEZZO-SOPRANO, [met'-zō-sō-prah'-nō], *n.* a voice in quality between a soprano and a contralto; a singer with such a voice; a part suitable in range for such a singer.

MEZZOTINT (1), [met'-zō-tint'], *n.* a mode of engraving on steel or copper, in which the surface of the plate is first roughened completely, the intended lighter parts being then scraped away; an engraving so produced. [It. *mezzotinto*].

MEZZOTINT (2), [met'-zō-tint'], *v.t* *and i.* to engrave in mezzotint.

MHO, [mō], *n.* the unit of electrical conductance, the reciprocal of the ohm. [Reversed spelling of OHM].

MI, [mē], *n.* (*mus.*) the third note in the tonic sol-fa scale. [L. *mi* (*ra*) wonder, a word from the hymn used in forming the gamut].

MIAOW (1), [mi-ow'], *n.* the cry of a cat. [Echoic].

MIAOW (2), [mi-ow'], *v.i.* to cry as a cat. [Echoic].

MIASMA, (*pl.* **miasmas, miasmata**), [mī'-az'-ma], *n.* infectious matter or pestilential vapours floating in the air. [Gk. *miasma* defilement].

MIASMAL, [mi-az'-mal], *adj.* containing miasma.

MIASMATIC, [mē'-az-mat'-ik], *adj.* pertaining to, containing, caused by, miasma. [Gk. *miasmatos*].

MIASMOLOGY, [mē'-az-mol'-o-ji], *n.* the scientific study of miasmata.

MIAUL, [mi-awl'], *v.i.* to cry as a cat. [Fr. *miauler*].

MICA, [mī'-ka], *n.* a group of mineral silicates, crystallizing in hexagonal transparent plates. [L. *mica* a crumb].

MICACEOUS, [mī-kā'-shus], *adj.* containing or resembling mica.

MICA-SCHIST, [mī'-ka-shist'], *n.* a schistose rock, composed of mica and quartz.

MICAWBERISM, [mi-kaw'-ber-izm], *n.* the habit of unwarranted optimism. [*Micawber*, a character in *David Copperfield* by C. Dickens].

MICE, [mīs], *n.* (*pl.*) of MOUSE. [OE. *mys*].

MICHAELMAS, [mikl'-mas], *n.* the feast of St. Michael, celebrated on September 29; **m. daisy,** the composite plant, *Aster Tripolium,* bearing pinkish-blue flowers; **m. term,** the first university term of the academic year. [The archangel *Michael*].

MICHE, [mich], *v.i.* to lie hid, lurk, skulk; to play truant. [~OFr. *muchier* to hide].

MICHER, [mich'-er], *n.* a truant, a petty thief; a pilferer.

MICKLE, [mikl], *adj.* (*Scots*) small, few. [OIcel. *mykill*].

MICMAC, [mik'-mak], *n.* an American Indian from Nova Scotia and New Brunswick; **m. potato,** the American ground-nut, *Apios tuberosa.* [Native].

MICO, [mī'-kō], *n.* a vegetable butter or solidified oil. [Native].

MICRANTHOUS, [mī-kran'-thus], *adj.* small-flowered. [MICRO and Gk. *anthos* flower].

MICRO-, *pref.* small, minute; (*elect.*) the millionth of. [Gk. *mikros*].

MICROBE, [mī'-krōb], *n.* a micro-organism, *esp.* disease-producing bacteria. [MICRO and Gk. *bios* life].

MICROBIAL, [mī'krōb'-i-al], *adj.* pertaining to or like microbes.

MICRO-BIOLOGIST, [mī'-krō-bī-ol'-oj-ist], *n.* an expert in micro-biology.

MICRO-BIOLOGY, [mī'-krō-bī-ol'-o-ji], *n.* the study of bacteria, schizomycetes and other micro-organisms visible under the microscope.

MICROCEPHALIC, [mī'-krō-se'-fal-ik], *adj.* having an unusually small skull. [MICRO and Gk. *kephale* head].

MICROCEPHALOUS, [mī'-krō-sef'-al-us], *adj.* microcephalic.

MICROCEPHALY, [mī'-krō-sef'-al-i], *n.* the condition of having an unusually small head.

MICROCOCCUS, (*pl.* **micrococci**), [mī'-krō-kok'-us], *n.* any of various bacteria with spherical cells. [MICRO and Gk. *kokkos* berry].

MICROCOSM, [mī'-krō-kozm], *n.* man considered as an epitome of the world; any community, etc., regarded as constituting in itself a world on a small scale. [Gk. *mikros kosmos* little world].

MICROCOSMIC, [mī'-krō-koz'-mik], *adj.* pertaining to or constituting a microcosm; **m. salt,** (*chem.*) sodium and ammonium phosphate.

MICROCOSMICAL, [mī'-krō-koz'-mik-al], *adj.* microcosmic.

MICROCOSMOGRAPHY, [mī'-krō-koz-mog'-raf-i], *n.* description of man as a microcosm. [MICROCOSM and Gk. *graphia* writing].

MICROFARAD, [mī'-krō-fa'-rad], *n.* (*elect.*) the millionth part of a farad, the practical unit of electrical capacity.

MICROGRAPH, [mī'-krō-graf'], *n.* a photograph of an object taken through a microscope.

MICROGRAPHIC, [mī'-krō-graf'-ik], *adj.* pertaining to micrography.

MICROGRAPHOPHONE, [mī'-krō-graf'-o-fōn], *n.* an instrument by which exceptionally delicate sounds are detected and reproduced. [MICRO and Gk. *graphia* writing and *phone* sound].

MICROGRAPHY, [mī-krog'-ra-fi], *n.* the description of objects visible only under the microscope; the art of writing in extremely minute characters. [MICRO and Gk. *graphia* writing].

MICROHM, [mī'-krōm], *n.* the millionth of an ohm.

MICROLINE, [mī'-krō-līn], *n.* an anorthic potash felspar; amazon-stone. [MICRO and LINE].

MICROLOGY, [mī-krol'-o-ji], *n.* the science of objects seen under the microscope; inordinate curiosity about unimportant details or distinctions. [MICRO and Gk. *logos* speech].

MICROMETER, [mī-krom'-it-er], *n.* an instrument for measuring extremely small objects or for taking extremely fine measurements. [MICRO and METER].

MICROMETRICAL, [mī'-krō-met'-rik-al], *adj.* belonging to or obtained by the micrometer.

MICRON, [mī'-kron], *n.* the millionth part of a metre. [Gk. *mikron* small].

MICRO-ORGANISM, [mī'-krō-aw'-gan-izm], *n.* an organism visible (if at all) only under the microscope.

MICROPHONE, [mī'-krō-fōn], *n.* an instrument by which sound is transmitted, the sound waves being converted into electrical energy. [MICRO and Gk. *phone* sound, voice].

MICROPHONICS, [mī'-krō-fon'-iks], *n.* the science of amplifying faint sounds.

MICROPHONY, [mī-krof'-o-ni], *n.* weakness of voice. [MICRO and Gk. *phone*].

MICROPHOTOGRAPH, [mī'-krō-fō'-tō-graf], *n.* †a photograph of a minute object seen under a microscope; a photograph taken on a small negative, and intended to be enlarged. [MICRO and PHOTOGRAPH].

MICROPHONE

MICROPHOTOGRAPHY, [mī′-krō-fot-og′-raf-i], *n.* the making of microphotographs.
MICROPHYTE, [mī′-krō-fīt], *n.* a microscopic organism, *esp.* a bacterium. [MICRO and Gk. *phuton* plant].
MICROPYLE, [mī′-krō-pīl], *n.* (*bot.*) the opening in the covering of an ovule through which the pollen enters; (*zool.*) the opening in a female cell by which the spermatozoon enters. [MICRO and Gk. *pule* gate].
MICRO-RAYS, [mī′-krō-rāz′], *n.*(*pl.*) (*wirel.*) micro-waves.
MICROSCOPE, [mī′-krō-skōp], *n.* an optical instrument for magnifying, and rendering visible, minute objects invisible to the naked eye. [MICRO and SCOPE].
MICROSCOPIC, [mī′-krō-skop′-ik], *adj.* magnifying as a microscope; visible only under the microscope; extremely small, minute.
MICROSCOPICAL, [mī′-krō-skop′-ik-al], *adj.* microscopic.
MICROSCOPICALLY, [mī′-krō-skop′-ik-al-i], *adv.* by or as by the microscope, extremely minutely.
MICROSCOPIST, [mī-kros′-kop-ist], *n.* one skilled in microscopy.
MICROSCOPY, [mī-kros′-kop-i], *n.* the use of the microscope; investigation by means of the microscope.
MICROSOME, [mī′-krō-sōm], *n.* (*biol.*) one of the minute parts of which protoplasm is made up. [MICRO and Gk. *soma* body].
MICROSPORE, [mī′-krō-spaw(r)], *n.* (*bot.*) a minute reproductive spore.
MICROTOME, [mī′-krō-tōm′], *n.* an instrument for cutting thin sections suitable for microscopic slides. [MICRO and Gk. *tomia* cutting].
MICROVOLT, [mī′-krō-volt], *n.* (*elect.*) the millionth of a volt.
MICRO-WAVES, [mī′-krō-wāvz′], *n.*(*pl.*) (*wirel.*) ultra-short wireless waves, *esp.* those having a wave-length under one metre.
MICROZOA, [mī′-krō-zō′-a], *n.*(*pl.*) the microscopic animals. [MICRO and Gk. *zoa* animals].
MICROZYME, [mī′-krō-zīm], *n.* a minute particle forming the germ of certain epizootic and epidemical diseases. [MICRO and Gk. *zume* yeast].
MICTURATE, [mik′-cher-āt], *v.i.* to pass water, urinate. [L. *micturire*].
MICTURITION, [mik′-cher-ish′-un], *n.* a morbid desire to pass urine; the act of micturating. [L. *micturire*].
MID (1), [mid], *adj.* middle, at equal distance from extremes; intervening. [OE. *midd*].
MID (2), [mid], *prep.* (*poet.*) amidst. [AMIDST].
MIDDAY (1), [mid′-dā], *n.* noon. [OE. *middæg*].
MIDDAY (2), [mid′-dā], *adj.* noon.
MIDDEN, [midn], *n.* a pile of kitchen refuse; a dunghill. [ME. *midding*, ~Dan. *mödding*].
MIDDLE (1), [midl], *n.* the middle part or point, the centre; the waist; (*log.*) a median or middle term; (*gram.*) the middle voice; (*cricket*) the guard in which the bat covers the middle stump.
MIDDLE (2), [midl], *adj.* equally distant from the extremes, half-way between the beginning and the end, or between two points, intermediate; (*philol.*) (of a period in the development of a language) between the earliest stage and the modern; **m. voice**, (*gram.*) intermediate voice between active and passive, expressing reflexive action; **m. passage**, the journey by sea between West Africa and the West Indies; **m. term**, (*log.*) a term common to both premises in a syllogism, with which those of the conclusion are successively compared; **m. weight**, (*boxing*) a boxer weighing more than 10 stone 5 lb. and less than 11 stone 6 lb.; **m. watch**, (*naut.*) the watch between midnight and 4 a.m.; **m. ear**, the tympanum. [OE. *middel*].
MIDDLE (3), [midl], *v.t.* to place in the middle; (*cricket*) to hit (the ball) with the full face of the bat; (*football*) to kick (the ball) into the centre of the field from the wings.
MIDDLE AGE, [midl′-āj′], *n.* the period of life between youth and old age; **m.-aged**, having arrived at this period.
MIDDLE AGES, [midl′-āj′-iz], *n.*(*pl.*) that period of history between the fall of the Roman Empire and the Renaissance.
MIDDLE CLASS (1), [midl′-klahs], *n.* the grade of society between the aristocracy and the labouring class, the bourgeoisie.
MIDDLE-CLASS (2), [midl′-klahs′], *adj.* belonging to, characteristic of, the middle class.
MIDDLE DISTANCE, [midl′-dis′-tants], *n.* (*paint.*) the part of a picture between foreground and background.
MIDDLE EAST, [midl-ēst′], *n.* that part of the Orient between Suez and Burma.
MIDDLEMAN, [midl′-man], *n.* an intermediate dealer, *esp.* one who buys from the producer to sell to the retailer; a go-between.
MIDDLEMOST, [midl′-mōst], *adj.* nearest the middle.
MIDDLERAIL, [midl′-rāl], *n.* the crossbar of a door, on which is fixed the handle.
MIDDLING, [midl′-ing], *adj.* of middle rank, size, or quality; fair, moderate; rather mediocre.
MIDDLINGLY, [midl′-ing-li], *adv.* in middling fashion.
MIDDLINGS, [midl′-ingz], *n.*(*pl.*) second-class goods.
MIDDY, [mid′-i], *n.* (*coll.*) a midshipman.
MIDGE, [mij], *n.* a fly of the family *Chironomidæ*; a small singing gnat; (*coll.*) a small person. [OE. *mycg*(*e*)].
MIDGET (1), [mij′-et], *n.* a very small person, a dwarf.
MIDGET (2), [mij′-et], *adj.* tiny, dwarf, miniature.
MIDINETTE, [mid′-in-et′], *n.* a female Parisian shop-assistant. [Fr. *midinette*].
MID-IRON, [mid′-ī-ern], *n.* (*golf*) a metal-headed golf club of medium weight, with the head inclined so as to direct the golf-ball with a moderately low flight.
MIDLAND (1), [mid′-land], *n.*(*pl.*) the middle counties of England.
MIDLAND (2), [mid′-land], *adj.* in the interior of a country; pertaining to the Midlands; surrounded by land.
MID-LEG, [mid′-leg], *n.* the middle of the leg.
MID-LENTING, [mid′-lent′-ing], *n.* the custom of visiting relatives on Mothering Sunday, the fourth in Lent, to take them gifts.
MID-LIFE, [mid′-līf], *n.* the middle of life.
MIDMOST, [mid′-mōst], *adj.* middlemost.
MIDNIGHT (1), [mid′-nīt], *n.* the middle of the night; twelve o'clock at night; complete darkness. [OE. *midniht*].
MIDNIGHT (2), [mid′-nīt], *adj.* in the middle of the night, at midnight; intensely dark; **to burn the m. oil**, to sit up late working.
MID-OFF, [mid′-of′], *n.* (*cricket*) a fieldsman stationed on the off-side of the pitch, near to the bowler.
MID-ON, [mid′-on′], *n.* (*cricket*) a fieldsman stationed on the on-side of the pitch, near to the bowler.
MIDRASH, (*pl.* **midrashim**), [mid′-rash], *n.* an ancient Jewish commentary on the Hebrew scriptures. [Heb. *midrash* commentary].
MIDRIB, [mid′-rib], *n.* (*bot.*) a continuation of the petiole extending as the principal vein down the centre of a leaf.
MIDRIFF, [mid′-rif], *n.* (*anat.*) the diaphragm. [OE. *midhrif*].
MID-SEA, [mid′-sē], *n.* the midst of the sea.
MIDSHIP, [mid′-ship], *adj.* situated in, pertaining to, the middle part of a ship.
MIDSHIPMAN, [mid′-ship-man], *n.* a naval officer ranking below a sub-lieutenant and above a naval cadet.
MIDSHIPMITE, [mid′-ship-mīt], *n.* a midshipman.
MIDSHIPS, [mid′-ships], *adv.* (*naut.*) in the middle of a ship.
MIDST (1), [midst], *n.* the middle; **in the m.**, among; completely involved or occupied in. [ME. *in middes*].
MIDST (2), [midst], *prep.* (*poet.*) amidst.
MID-STREAM, [mid′-strēm], *n.* the middle of the stream.
MIDSUMMER, [mid′-sum-er], *n.* the summer solstice, occurring about June 21; **M. Day**, the feast of the nativity of St. John the Baptist, June 24; **m. madness**, utter folly and recklessness.
MIDWAY, [mid′-wā], *adj. and adv.* (situated) half-way.
MIDWIFE (1), [mid′-wīf], *n.* a woman who assists in childbirth. [ME. *midwif*].
MIDWIFE (2), [mid′-wīf], *v.t. and i.* to act as midwife (to).
MIDWIFERY, [mid-wif′-er-i], *n.* the art or practice of attending women in childbirth; obstetrics.
MIDWINTER, [mid′-win′-ter], *n.* the winter solstice, falling about December 21.
MIEMITE, [mī′-em-īt], *n.* a kind of magnesian limestone. [*Miemo*, in Tuscany].
MIEN, [mēn], *n.* external appearance, look, demeanour, bearing, manner. [Uncert.].
MIFF (1), [mif], *n.* (*slang*) a feeling of slight annoyance or irritation, a huff; a trivial quarrel. [Echoic].
MIFF (2), [mif], *v.i.* to sulk, to get into a huff.
MIGHT (1), [mīt], *n.* power, strength, force. [OE. *miht*].
MIGHT (2), [mīt], *pret.* of MAY.

MIGHTILY, [mīt'-i-li], *adv.* in mighty fashion; (*coll.*) greatly.
MIGHTINESS, [mīt'-i-nes], *n.* the quality of being mighty.
MIGHTY (1), [mīt'-i], *adj.* strong, powerful, having great authority; (*coll.*) great. [OE. *mihtig*].
MIGHTY (2), [mīt'-i], *adv.* (*coll.*) very, greatly.
MIGNON (1), [mēn'-yon], *n.* a pretty little child; a darling. [Fr. *mignon* a dear].
MIGNON (2), [mēn'-yon], *adj.* delicate and pretty, dainty. [Fr. *mignon*].
MIGNONETTE, [min'-yon-et'], *n.* a sort of French lace; a fragrant plant, *Reseda odorata*; a pale green colour. [Fr. *mignonette*].
MIGRAINE, [mig'-rān], *n.* (*med.*) a sick headache, hemicrania, megrims. [Fr. *migraine*].
MIGRANT (1), [mī'-grant], *n.* a creature that migrates.
MIGRANT (2), [mī'-grant], *adj.* migratory. [L. *migrans*].
MIGRATE, [mī'-grāt'], *v.i.* (*zool.*) to make the annual passage from one climate to another to avoid the severities of winter, etc.; (*pop.*) to move to a fresh country or district. [L. *migrare*].
MIGRATION, [mī-grā'-shun], *n.* the act of migrating; a group of persons or birds who migrate. [L. *migratio*].
MIGRATORY, [mī-grāt'-er-i], *adj.* that migrates.
MIKADO, [mi-kah'-dō], *n.* the Emperor of Japan. [Jap. *Mikado* honourable gate].
MIKE (1), [mīk], *n.* (*slang*) a microphone.
MIKE (2), [mīk], *n.* (*slang*) **to be on the m., to have a m.**, to idle. [MIKE (3)].
MIKE (3), [mīk], *v.i.* (*slang*) to idle. [Unkn.].
MILANESE (1), [mil'-an-ēz'], *n.* an inhabitant of Milan; a silk or artificial silk fabric used for women's garments.
MILANESE (2), [mil'-an-ēz'], *adj.* of, or pertaining to, Milan.
MILCH, [milch], *adj.* yielding milk. [ME. *milche*].
MILD, [mīld], *adj.* moderate, not extreme, harsh, or bitter; gentle; kind, even-tempered, not aggressive; temperate, warm. [OE. *milde*].
MILDEW (1), [mil'-dew], *n.* a whitish, small fungus appearing on plants, food, etc., exposed to damp. [OE. *meledeaw* honey-dew].
MILDEW (2), [mil'-dew], *v.i.* to go mildewy.
MILDEWY, [mil'-dew-i], *adj.* affected by mildew.
MILDLY, [mīld'-li], *adv.* in a mild fashion.
MILDNESS, [mīld'-nes], *n.* the quality of being mild.
MILE, [mīl], *n.* a unit of linear measurement, measuring 1760 yards; **nautical, geographical m.**, a distance of 6080 feet. [OE. *mil* from L. *milia* (*passuum*) 1,000 paces].
MILEAGE, [mīl'-ij], *n.* distance travelled, measured in miles; rate of travelling, measured in miles.
MILEPOST, [mīl'-pōst], *n.* a post marking the end of a mile.
MILER, [mīl'-er], *n.* an animal or person specially proficient in races over a mile course.
MILESIAN (1), [mī-lē'-zi-an], *n.* one of the followers of Milesius; an Irishman. [*Milesius*, a legendary Spanish king, supposed to have conquered Ireland in 1300 B.C.].
MILESIAN (2), [mī-lē'-zi-an], *adj.* pertaining to Milesius; Irish.
MILESTONE, [mīl'-stōn], *n.* a stone by the roadside to mark the end of a mile, and giving the distance to the place or places mentioned on it; (*fig.*) an important event in someone's life.
MILFOIL, [mil'-foil], *n.* (*bot.*) the yarrow plant, *Achillea millefolium*. [L. *millefolium* thousand leaf].
MILIARY (1), see MILLIARY.
MILIARY (2), [mil'-i-er-i], *adj.* (*path.*) resembling millet seeds; characterized by an eruption of spots like millet seeds; **m. fever**, (*path.*) a skin disease of this kind. [L. *miliarius* relating to millet].
MILIEU, [mēl-yer'], *n.* surroundings, environment. [Fr. *milieu*].
MILIOLA, (*pl.* **miliolae**), [mil'-i-ō'-la], *n.* (*zool.*) a genus of *Foraminifera*; a member of this genus. [MdL. *miliola*].
MILIOLINE (1), [mil'-i-ō'-līn], *n.* (*zool.*) a member of the genus *Miliola*.
MILIOLINE (2), [mil'-i-ō-līn], *adj.* (*zool.*) pertaining to the genus *Miliola*.
MILIOLITE, [mil'-i-ō'-līt], *n.* (*geol.*) a fossil miliola. [MILIOLA and Gk. *lithos* a stone].

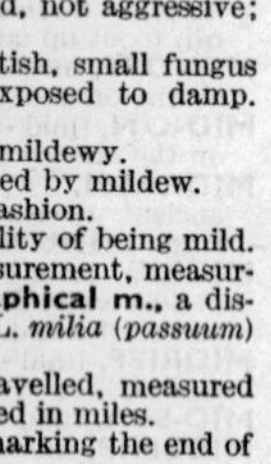

MILFOIL

MILIOLITIC, [mil'-i-ō-lit'-ik], *adj.* (*geol.*) pertaining to miliolites.
MILITANCY, [mil'-it-an-si], *n.* the quality of being militant.
MILITANT, [mil'-it-ant], *adj.* pugnacious, combative; fighting, at war. [L. *militans*].
MILITANTLY, [mil'-it-ant-li], *adv.* in militant fashion.
MILITARILY, [mil'-it-er-i-li], *adv.* in a military fashion; from a military point of view.
MILITARISM, [mil'-it-er-izm], *n.* the spirit or opinions of a soldier or warlike person; the point of view which regards military matters as of first importance; aggressive and warlike patriotism; military government. [Fr. *militarisme*].
MILITARIST, [mil'-it-er-ist], *n.* one versed or concerned in military matters, a soldier; an advocate of militarism.
MILITARISTIC, [mil'-it-er-ist'-ik], *adj.* pertaining to military matters; combative, pugnacious.
MILITARIZATION, [mil'-it-er-īz-ā'-shun], *n.* the act of militarizing; the state of being militarized.
MILITARIZE, [mil'-it-er-īz], *v.t.* to organize on a military basis; to fill with a spirit of militarism.
MILITARY (1), [mil'-it-er-i], *n.* the army authorities, soldiers.
MILITARY (2), [mil'-it-er-i], *adj.* pertaining to warfare and soldiering; connection with the army, martial, warlike; **M. Cross** (Medal), an army decoration awarded to officers (and other ranks) for conspicuous courage under fire. [L. *militaris*].
MILITATE, [mil'-it-āt], *v.i.* to take warlike action; **to m. against**, to oppose, operate against, be unfavourable to. [L. *militare*].
MILITIA, [mil-ish'-a], *n.* an army recruited from the civilian populations, *esp.* a civilian auxiliary force consisting of contingents from each county, available in an emergency. [L. *militia* warfare].
MILITIAMAN, [mil-ish'-a-man], *n.* a member of the militia.
MILK (1), [milk], *n.* the white fluid secreted by the mammary glands of female mammals to nourish their young, *esp.* that secreted by cows; a medical preparation resembling this; the white juice of certain plants. [OE. *meolc*].
MILK (2), [milk], *v.t.* to draw milk from the teats of; (*fig.*) to extort all possible money or benefit from; *v.i.* to supply milk. [OE. *milcian*].
MILK-AND-WATER, [milk'-and-waw'-ter], *adj.* insipid, attenuated.
MILK-BAR, [milk'-bah(r)], *n.* an establishment where attractively flavoured milk drinks may be bought.
MILKER, [milk'-er], *n.* one who, or that which, milks; a cow that yields milk.
MILK-FEVER, [milk'-fē'-ver], *n.* a transitory fever which sometimes accompanies lactation in women.
MILK-FLOAT, [milk'-flōt], *n.* a small flat dray in which milk is carried round to customers.
MILKILY, [milk'-i-li], *adv.* in a milky manner.
MILKINESS, [milk'-i-nes], *n.* the quality of being milky.
MILKING, [milk'-ing], *n.* the act of extracting milk from a milk gland; the quantity of milk drawn.
MILK-LEG, [milk'-leg], *n.* a swelling occasionally occurring in the leg of a parturient woman, white-leg.
MILK-LIVERED, [milk'-liv'-erd], *adj.* timorous, cowardly.
MILKMAID, [milk'-mād], *n.* a woman employed in milking cows and in dairy work.
MILKMAN, [milk'-man], *n.* a man who sells milk; (*rare*) a man employed in milking cows.
MILK-PUDDING, [milk-pŏŏd'-ing], *n.* a pudding made of rice, etc., baked in milk.
MILK-PUNCH, [milk'-punch'], *n.* milk and spirits sweetened and mixed.
MILK-SICKNESS, [milk'-sik'-nes], *n.* a cattle disease peculiar to the western U.S.A.
MILKSOP, [milk'-sop'], *n.* a cowardly effeminate boy.
MILK SUGAR, [milk'-shŏŏg'-ar], *n.* a sugar present in milk; lactose.
MILK-TEETH, [milk'-tēth], *n.*(*pl.*) the first and temporary set of teeth in mammals.
MILK-THISTLE, [milk'-thisl], *n.* the plant, *Silybum marianum*.
MILK-TREE, [milk'-trē], *n.* either of two tropical American trees, *Brosimum galactodendron*, or the *Messaranduba*, *Mimusops elata*, producing a milky juice.
MILK-VETCH, [milk'-vech], *n.* a plant of the genus *Astragalus*.
MILK-WEED, [milk'-wēd], *n.* a plant of the genus *Asclepias*; the sow-thistle, *Sonchus oleraceus*, the

milk parsley, *Peucedanum palustre*, or certain other plants yielding a milky sap.

MILKWORT, [milk'-wurt], *n*. a plant of the genus *Polygala*; **sea m.**, the plant, *Glaux maritima*.

MILKY, [milk'-i], *adj*. resembling milk; white and opaque; full of, yielding, milk; (*fig.*) timorous, lacking spirit; **M. Way**, a broad, luminous path in the heavens formed by millions of stars clustered together.

MILL (1), [mil], *n*. a machine for grinding corn to flour, the building in which this is done; a building equipped with machinery for manufacturing, a factory; a machine for grinding solid material to fine particles; a corn-stamping machine; (*slang*) a fight with the fists; **to go through the m.**, to experience hardship and suffering. [OE. *mylen*, *myln*].

MILL (2), [mil], *n*. (*U.S.*) a money of account, valued at the thousandth part of a dollar. [L. *millesimus* thousandth].

MILL (3), [mil], *v.t.* to grind in a mill; to subject to some manufacturing process; to full (cloth); to roll out (metal); to cut (steel) into shapes; to make a raised and serrated rim round the edge of (a coin) to prevent cutting; to stamp (a coin); to stir (chocolate) up into a froth; (*slang*) to beat severely with the fists; *v.i.* (of cattle) to go round in circles; (*slang*) to fight with the fists.

MILLBOARD, [mil'-bawd], *n*. a strong pasteboard for bookbinding, made of pulp.

MILL-COG, [mil'-kog], *n*. a tooth on the wheel driving a water-mill or windmill.

MILL-DAM, [mil'-dam'], *n*. a dam to obstruct a water-course and divert it.

MILLED, [mild], *adj*. passed through a mill, subjected to the operation of milling.

MILLENARIAN (1), [mil'-en-āer'-i-an], *n*. one who believes in the millennium.

MILLENARIAN (2), [mil'-en-āer'-i-an], *adj*. pertaining to the millennium.

MILLENARIANISM, [mil'-en-āer'-i-an-izm], *n*. belief in the millennium.

MILLENARY (1), [mil-en'-er-i], *n*. a thousand years; a millenarian; a thousandth anniversary.

MILLENARY (2), [mil-en'-er-i], *adj*. consisting of a thousand, *esp*. years; pertaining to the millennium. [L. *millenarius*].

MILLENNIAL, [mil-en'-i-al], *adj*. relating to the millennium.

MILLENNIALIST, [mil-en'-i-al-ist], *n*. a millenarian.

MILLENNIUM, [mil-en'-i-um], *n*. a period of a thousand years, *esp*. that period of a thousand years during which Christ is to reign in person on earth; a golden era of happiness and prosperity. [L. *mille* thousand and *annum* year].

MILLEPEDE, see MILLIPEDE.

MILLEPORE, [mil'-i-paw(r)], *n*. a species of shallow-water reef-corals of the genus *Millepora*, covered with minute pores. [L. *mille* thousand and PORE].

MILLER, [mil'-er], *n*. the owner or manager of a flour mill; the moth, *Acronycta leporina*, with white powdered wings; **miller's dog**, the tope shark, *Galeus vulgaris*; **miller's thumb**, a small freshwater fish, the river bull-head, *Cottus gobio*.

MILLERITE, [mil'-er-īt], *n*. a native nickel sulphide. [W. H. *Miller* (1832-1870), professor of mineralogy].

MILLESIMAL, [mil-es'-im-al], *adj*. thousandth; consisting of, reckoning in, thousandths. [L. *millesimus*].

MILLET, [mil'-et], *n*. any of several cereals producing small seeds, widely cultivated as food or cattle fodder, *esp*. *Panicum miliaceum*, an East Indian plant. [Fr. *millet*].

MILL-HAND, [mil'-hand'], *n*. a subordinate worker in a factory.

MILLIARD, [mil'-yahd], *n*. a thousand millions. [Fr. *milliard*].

MILLIARE, [mil'-i-ah(r)], *n*. the thousandth of an are. [Fr. *milliare*].

MILLIARY (1), MILIARY, [mil'-i-er-i], *n*. a stone marking a Roman mile of a thousand paces; a mile-stone.

MILLIARY (2), MILIARY, [mil'-i-er-i], *adj*. pertaining to a Roman mile of a thousand paces; denoting a mile. [L. *milliarius*].

MILLIBAR, [mil'-i-bah(r)], *n*. (*meteor.*) a thousandth of a bar.

MILLIER, [mil'-i-er], *n*. a weight equal to 1,000 kilogrammes. [Fr. *millier*].

MILLIGRAMME, [mil'-i-gram], *n*. the thousandth part of a gramme, ·0154 of a grain. [Fr. *milligramme*].

MILLILITRE, [mil'-i-lē'-ter], *n*. the thousandth part of a litre, ·06103 cubic inches. [Fr. *millilitre*].

MILLIMETRE, [mil'-i-mē'-ter], *n*. the thousandth part of a metre, ·03937 inches. [Fr. *millimetre*].

MILLINER, [mil'-in-er], *n*. one who makes hats and other apparel for women; †originally one who sold small fancy articles of apparel made in Milan. [*Milaner* a dealer in Milan goods].

MILLINERY, [mil'-in-er-i], *n*. articles sold by milliners; the business or shop of a milliner.

MILLING, [mil'-ing], *n*. the act of one who mills; the serrated rim of a coin.

MILLION, [mil'-yun], *n*. a thousand thousands; (*fig.*) a very great number; **the m.**, the general public, the masses. [Fr. *million*].

MILLIONAIRE, [mil'-yun-āer'], *n*. a man worth a million francs, dollars, or pounds; (*pop.*) a very rich man. [Fr. *millionnaire*].

MILLIONAIRESS, [mil'-yun-āer'-es], *n*. a female millionaire.

MILLIONARY, [mil'-yun-er-i], *adj*. pertaining to, consisting of, worth, millions.

MILLIONFOLD (1), [mil'-yun-fōld], *adj*. a million times the quantity.

MILLIONFOLD (2), [mil'-yun-fōld], *adv*. a million times in quantity.

MILLIONTH (1), [mil'-yunth], *n*. one of a million parts.

MILLIONTH (2), [mil'-yunth], *adj*. a ten hundred thousandth.

MILLIPEDE, MILLEPEDE, [mil'-i-pēd], *n*. a species of myriapod with a large number of legs, and a body divided into segments, of which the wood-louse, *Julus terrestris*, is an example. [L. *millepeda* wood-louse].

MILLPOND, [mil'-pond], *n*. the reservoir used in working a water-mill.

MILLRACE, [mil'-rās], *n*. the current of water that works a mill-wheel.

MILLS BOMB, [milz'-bom'], *n*. a serrated oval-shaped hand-grenade. [*Mills*, its inventor].

MILL-SIXPENCE, [mil'-siks'-pens], *n*. an old English coin, first milled in 1561.

MILLSTONE, [mil'-stōn], *n*. one of a pair of heavy circular flat stones between which corn is milled; (*fig.*) a heavy drag or encumbrance; **m. grit**, a hard, coarse, gritty sandstone.

MILL-STREAM, [mil'-strēm], *n*. a stream used to drive a water-mill.

MILLTAIL, [mil'-tāl], *n*. the rush of water when it has turned the mill-wheel.

MILL-WHEEL, [mil'-wēl], *n*. the water-driven wheel that works the machinery of a mill.

MILLWRIGHT, [mil'-rīt], *n*. one who builds mills or their machinery.

MILREIS, [mil'-rās], *n*. a Portuguese coin worth approximately 4s. 5d., an escudo; a Brazilian coin worth nearly 2s. 3d. [Portug. *milreis* a thousand reis].

MILT (1), [milt], *n*. the spleen; the spawn or roe of the male fish. [OE. *milte*].

MILT (2), [milt], *v.t.* to fecundate (the roe or spawn of the female fish).

MILTER, [milt'-er], *n*. a male fish, *esp*. during the breeding season.

MILTONIC, [mil-ton'-ik], *adj*. like or belonging to Milton or his works; (*fig.*) majestic, lofty. [J. *Milton* (1608-1674)].

MIME (1), [mīm], *n*. (*Gk., Rom. antiq.*) a kind of farce full of mimicry and burlesque; an actor in this; a buffoon, clown, mimic. [Gk. *mimos* actor].

MIME (2), [mīm], *v.i.* to play in a mime; *v.t.* to mimic, *esp*. in dumb-show.

MIMEOGRAPH, [mīm'-ō-graf], *n*. an apparatus for making a stencil copy to be used in a duplicating machine. [MIME and GRAPH].

MIMESIS, [mīm-ē'-sis], *n*. (*bot., zool.*) mimicry; (*rhet.*) a figure of speech intended to imitate the diction of another. [Gk. *mimesis* imitation].

MIMETIC, [mīm-et'-ik], *adj*. imitative; skilful in mimicking; (*bot., zool.*) exhibiting mimicry. [Gk. *mimetikos*].

MIMETICAL, [mīm-et'-ik-al], *adj*. mimetic.

MIMETITE, [mim'-et-īt], *n*. mineral arseniate of lead similar to pyromorphite. [Gk. *mimetes* imitator].

MIMIC (1), [mim'-ik], *n*. one who mimics; a poor imitator.

MIMIC (2), [mim'-ik], *adj*. imitative; that mimics; feigned, counterfeit; mock, copied on a small scale. [L. *mimicus*].

MIMIC (3), [mim'-ik], *v.t.* to imitate in exaggerated manner, burlesque, *esp*. in order to ridicule; to take on the appearance of, resemble; (*bot., zool.*) to resemble its natural surroundings or another animal or plant, *esp.* for protection.

MIMICALLY, [mim'-ik-al-i], *adv.* in a mimicking manner.

MIMICKER, [mim'-ik-er], *n.* a person who mimics.

MIMICRY, [mim'-ik-ri], *n.* the act of, skill in, mimicking; an imitation, copy; (*bot., zool.*) the characteristic by which an animal or plant mimics another or its surroundings.

MIMOSA, [mi-mō'-za], *n.* a large genus of leguminous plants, including the sensitive plant, *Mimosa pudica.* [L. *mimus* mime].

MINA, [mī'-na], *n.* a former Greek and Egyptian unit of weight; a former Attic coin equivalent to 100 drachmas, roughly four pounds. [L. *mina*].

MINACIOUS, [min-ā'-shus], *adj.* threatening, menacing. [L. *minax*].

MINAR, [min'-ah(r)], *n.* a tall tower, or lighthouse. [Arab. *manar*].

MINARET, [min'-er-et], *n.* a tall turret, attached to a mosque, and containing balconies from which the muezzin summons the people to prayer. [Arab. *manaret*].

MINARET

MINATORY, [min'-at-er-i], *adj.* threatening. [LL. *minatorius*].

MINBAR, [min'-bah(r)], *n.* the pulpit in a mosque. [Arab. *minbar*].

MINCE (1), [mints], *n.* meat chopped up into very small pieces, served as a dish when cooked.

MINCE (2), [mints], *v.t. and i.* to chop into very small pieces; to palliate, to express in mild, watered-down terms; to speak, pronounce, or walk in an affectedly genteel manner; **not to m. matters,** to speak plainly and directly. [OFr. *mincier*].

MINCEMEAT, [mints'-mēt], *n.* a mixture of raisins and currants with chopped candied peel, suet, apples, etc.

MINCEPIE, [mints'-pī'], *n.* a pie made with mincemeat.

MINCER, [min'-ser], *n.* one who minces; a mincing-machine.

MINCING, [min'-sing], *adj.* walking or speaking in an affected dainty manner.

MINCINGLY, [mins'-ing-li], *adv.* in mincing fashion.

MINCING-MACHINE, [mins'-ing-ma-shēn'], *n.* a machine for mincing meat, etc.

MIND (1), [mīnd], *n.* memory, remembrance; intellect, reason, intelligence; man, as possessing this; will-power; moral, ethical, or intellectual outlook; the cognitive, emotional, and volitional capacities in man; the cognitive power alone; views, opinions, thoughts; intention, desire; (*philos.*) that aspect of reality other than matter; **to have something on one's m.,** to be worried; **to be in two minds,** to hesitate; **to have a good m. to,** to feel strongly inclined to; **presence of m.,** ability to adapt oneself rapidly to unforeseen situations. [OE. *gemynd*].

MIND (2), [mīnd], *v.t.* to pay attention to, heed; to care about, object to; to be on one's guard against; to take care of, look after; (*archaic*) to remember; to feel strongly about; *v.i.* to take heed, be careful; to object.

MINDED, [mīnd'-id], *adj.* having a particular kind of mind; disposed, inclined.

MINDER, [mīnd'-er], *n.* a worker employed to watch the operation of a piece of machinery.

MINDFUL, [mīnd'-fōōl], *adj.* attentive, heedful.

MINDFULLY, [mīnd'-fōōl-i], *adv.* in mindful fashion.

MINDFULNESS, [mīnd'-fōōl-nes], *n.* the quality of being mindful.

MINDLESS, [mīnd'-les], *adj.* without a mind, unreasoning; heedless, not caring or thinking about.

MIND-READING, [mīnd'-rēd'-ing], *n.* the ability to know what is passing in another person's mind.

MINE (1), [mīn], *n.* a deep excavation in the earth, *esp.* one with subsidiary workings, from which minerals are dug; this together with its attendant machinery and buildings; an underground passage lined with explosives for blowing up fortifications, etc.; a charge of explosive used for this; a metal container filled with explosives, fitted with a detonator, and placed in the sea to blow up a ship; (*fig.*) an abundant store of. [Fr. *mine*].

MINE (2), [mīn], *pron. possessive 1st person sg.* [OE. *min*].

MINE (3), [mīn], *v.t. and i.* to dig a mine in (the earth); to dig (minerals) from the earth in a mine; to blow up with a mine; to lay a mine or mines in or under; (*fig.*) to undermine. [Fr. *miner*].

MINE-CAPTAIN, [mīn'-kap'-tin], *n.* the overseer of a mine.

MINEFIELD, [mīn'-fēld], *n.* (*milit., naut.*) an area on land or sea which has been mined.

MINELAYER, [mīn'-lā'-er], *n.* a vessel for laying mines at sea; a member of the crew of this.

MINER, [mīn'-er], *n.* one who digs in the earth for minerals; (*milit.*) a soldier specially trained in digging mines; any of several insects which burrow. [OFr. *minour*].

MINERAL (1), [min'-er-al], *n.* any substance dug from the earth by mining; (*chem.*) a natural inorganic substance with a definite chemical composition; (*coll. pl.*) aerated drinks. [MedL. *minerale*].

MINERAL (2), [min'-er-al], *adj.* pertaining to, consisting of, of the nature of, a mineral; (*chem.*) inorganic; **m. jelly,** Vaseline; **m. kingdom,** the third great division of natural objects comprising substances other than animal or vegetable; **m. waters,** waters impregnated with mineral matter; (*coll.*) aerated flavoured drinks; **m. wool,** a thin, glossy, fibrous substance obtained from liquid, vitreous slag. [MedL. *mineralis*].

MINERALIZATION, [min'-er-al-īz-ā'-shun], *n.* the process of mineralizing; the state of being mineralized.

MINERALIZE, [min'-er-al-īz], *v.t.* to convert into a mineral; to impregnate with mineral matter; to combine with a metal to form an ore; *v.i.* to go out collecting minerals.

MINERALIZER, [min'-er-al-īz-er], *n.* (*chem.*) a substance which combines with a metal to form an ore.

MINERALOGICAL, [min'-er-al-oj'-ik-al], *adj.* relating to mineralogy.

MINERALOGICALLY, [min'-er-al-oj'-ik-al-i], *adv.* according to mineralogy.

MINERALOGIST, [min'-er-al'-oj-ist], *n.* one learned in mineralogy.

MINERALOGY, [min'-er-al'-o-ji], *n.* the scientific study of minerals. [MINERAL and Gk. *logos* speech].

MINESWEEPER, [mīn'-swēp'-er], *n.* a vessel specially fitted with nets for clearing a minefield; a member of the crew of such a vessel.

MINE-THROWER, [mīn'-thrō'-er], *n.* a trench mortar firing a high-explosive shell. [Translation of Germ. *minenwerfer*].

MINEVER, see MINIVER.

MINGLE, [ming'-gl], *v.t. and i.* to mix, unite, blend, join; to become an indistinguishable part. [ME. *mengel* from OE. *mengan*].

MINGLEDLY, [ming'-gld-li], *adv.* confusedly.

MINGLE-MANGLE, [ming'-gl-mang'-gl], *n.* a hodge-podge, confused jumble.

MINGLEMENT, [ming'-gl-ment], *n.* the state of being mixed; the act of mingling.

MINGLER, [ming'-gler], *n.* a person who mingles.

MINGLINGLY, [ming'-gling-li], *adv.* so as to mingle.

MINIATE, [min'-i-āt], *v.t.* to colour or tinge with vermilion; to illuminate (a manuscript). [L. *miniare*].

MINIATURE (1), [min'-i-ach-er], *n.* an illumination in a manuscript; a small-scale portrait in oil or water-colours on vellum or ivory; a reproduction on a small scale. [It. *miniatura*].

MINIATURE (2), [min'-i-ach-er], *adj.* in the form of a miniature; on a small scale.

MINIATURE (3), [min'-i-ach-er], *v.t.* to illuminate (a manuscript); to paint as a miniature; to represent on a small scale.

MINIATURIST, [min'-i-ach-er-ist], *n.* a painter of miniatures; one who uses miniature cameras.

MINIFY, [min'-if-ī], *v.t.* to make small, minimize. [L. *minor* less].

MINIKIN, [min'-ik-in], *n.* a tiny object; a dwarfish person. [Du. *minneken* a favourite].

MINIM, [min'-im], *n.* (*mus.*) a note equal in time value to half a semibreve; the smallest liquid measure, one-sixtieth of a fluid drachm, a single drop; a single down stroke in writing; a minikin; a jot, trifle; (*R.C.*) one of an order of mendicant friars. [L. *minimus* smallest].

MINIMAL, [min'-im-al], *adj.* least, smallest.

MINIMALIST, [min'-im-al-ist], *n.* a Menshevik; one who is ready to accept temporarily his minimum political demands.

MINIMIZATION, [min'-im-īz-ā'-shun], *n.* the act of minimizing; the state of being minimized.

MINIMIZE, [min'-im-īz], *v.t.* to reduce as far as possible; to under-emphasize, to underestimate, depreciate.

MINIMUM (1), [min'-im-um], *n.* the least possible quantity or amount. [L. *minimum*].

MINIMUM (2), [min'-im-um], *adj.* least or smallest possible required or recorded.
MINIMUS (1), [min'-im-us], *n.* a person or thing of the smallest size.
MINIMUS (2), [min'-im-us], *adj.* (*school slang*) denoting the youngest of three or more boys of the same name. [L. *minimus* least].
MINING, [mīn'-ing], *n.* the act of working a mine or laying mines.
MINION, [min'-yon], *n.* a favourite, darling; a servile hireling, a toady; a variety of pear; a small printing-type. [Fr. *mignon* delicate].
MINISTER (1), [min'-is-ter], *n.* an agent, one who carries out the bidding of another; a person appointed to direct a particular branch of government or state administration; a representative of a government at a foreign court; (*eccles.*) one who conducts the service at public worship, *esp.* a nonconformist clergyman. [L. *minister* servant].
MINISTER (2), [min'-is-ter], *v.t.* (*archaic*) to render; *v.i.* to attend to the wants of another; to tend to promote; to act as a minister of religion. [L. *ministrare* to serve].
MINISTERIAL, [min'-is-tēer'-i-al], *adj.* belonging to a minister or to a ministry; supporting the government ministers; acting or performed at the bidding of a superior. [L. *ministerialis*].
MINISTERIALIST, [min'-is-tēer'-i-al-ist], *n.* a supporter of the ministry in power.
MINISTERIALLY, [min'-is-tēer'-i-al-i], *adv.* in a ministerial manner or capacity.
MINISTERING, [min'-is-ter-ing], *adj.* that ministers to something or someone.
MINISTRANT (1), [min'-is-trant], *n.* a person who ministers.
MINISTRANT (2), [min'-is-trant], *adj.* that ministers, helping. [L. *ministrans*].
MINISTRATION, [min'-is-trā'-shun], *n.* the act of ministering to or performing services for, *esp.* as a minister of religion. [L. *ministratio*].
MINISTRESS, [min'-is-tres], *n.* a woman who ministers.
MINISTRY, [min'-is-tri], *n.* the act of ministering; the office or duties of a minister; the body of ministers; the vocation of a minister of religion; (*pol.*) the Cabinet; a state department; the term of office as a minister. [L. *ministerium*].
MINIUM, [min'-i-um], *n.* red oxide of lead, a bright red colouring matter, vermilion. [L. *minium*].
MINIVER, MINEVER, MENIVER†, [min'-i-ver], *n.* a kind of white fur with occasional black markings, used for ceremonial robes; the white fur of the winter coat of the ermine. [OFr. *menu ver* small spotted fur].
MINK, [mingk], *n.* a carnivore of the weasel family, greatly prized for its fur; the fur of this animal. [~Swed. *menk*].

MINK

MINNESINGERS, [min'-i-sing-erz], *n.(pl.)* a body of lyric poets or singers in medieval Germany who composed songs and poems, chiefly about love. [Germ. *minnesinger* love singer].
MINNIE, [min'-i], *n.* (*slang*) a trench mortar. [Germ. *minenwerfer* a mine-thrower].
MINNOW, [min'-ō], *n.* a small freshwater fish, *Leuciscus phoxinus* or *Phoxinus aphya*, related to the carp; an artificial fish resembling this, used as a bait. [Fr. *menu* (*poisson*) small (fish)].
MINOAN (1), [min-ō'-an], *n.* a native of ancient Crete.
MINOAN (2), [min-ō'-an], *adj.* relating to the prehistoric civilization of Crete. [*Minos*, the fabled king of Crete].
MINOR (1), [mīn'-er], *n.* a person who has not yet come of age; (*mus.*) a minor key or mode; (*log.*) the minor term or minor premise; (*eccles.*) a Franciscan friar.
MINOR (2), [mīn'-er], *adj.* less, inferior; slight, unimportant; (*surg.*) (of operations) with no expected danger to life; (*mus.*) less by a semitone than a major interval; **m. canon,** a clergyman who officiates in the services of a cathedral but is not a member of the chapter; **m. orders,** (*R.C.*) the lesser orders below subdeacon; **m. key,** a key in which the semitones occur between the second and third, and the fifth and sixth notes of the scale; **m. term,** (*log.*) the subject of the conclusion of a syllogism; **m. premise,** (*log.*) the premise containing the minor term; **a m. suit,** (*bridge*) diamonds or clubs. [L. *minor*].
MINORCA, [mi-nawk'-a], *n.* one of a breed of domestic fowls originating in the Spanish island of that name in the Balearic islands group.
MINORITE, [mīn'-er-īt], *n.* a Franciscan friar. [L. (*Fratres*) *Minores* the Lesser Brothers].
MINORITY, [mīn-o'-ri-ti], *n.* the state of being under legal age; the period of life embraced by this state; the smaller number. [MedL. *minoritas*].
MINOTAUR, [mīn'-ō-taw(r)], *n.* a fabled monster, half man and half bull, which dwelt in the Labyrinth at Crete, and was slain by Theseus. [Gk. *Minotauros*].
MINSTER, [min'-ster], *n.* the church of a monastery; a cathedral church. [OE. *mynster*].
MINSTREL, [min'-strel], *n.* (*hist.*) one of a class who earned their living as entertainers, *esp.* one who recited or sang poetry, accompanying himself on the harp, lute, etc.; (*pl.*) a band of singers, banjoists, and entertainers with blackened faces; a poet, musician, or singer. [LL. *ministralis*].
MINSTRELSY, [min'-strel-si], *n.* the art or occupation of minstrels; a group of minstrels; the songs or poetry of minstrels. [OFr. *menestralsie*].
MINT (1), [mint], *n.* an aromatic plant of the genus *Mentha*, producing a pungent essential oil, and used for flavouring. [OE. *minte* from L. *mentha*].
MINT (2), [mint], *n.* the place where money is officially coined and issued; origin, source; (*fig.*) an abundant supply. [OE. *mynet* coin from L. *moneta* money].
MINT (3), [mint], *v.t.* to coin and stamp; (*fig.*) to invent.
MINT (4), [mint], *adj.* (of a stamp, coin, book, etc.) in its unused state. [MINT (2)].
MINTAGE, [mint'-ij], *n.* the process of minting money; that which is minted, *esp.* at a particular mint at a specific time; the duty paid for minting.
MINTER, [mint'-er], *n.* a coiner; (*fig.*) an inventor. [OE. *mynetere*].
MINT-JULEP, [mint'-jōō'-lep], *n.* a drink of brandy, sugar, and pounded ice, flavoured with mint.
MINT-MASTER, [mint'-mahst'-er], *n.* the official in charge of the minting of money.
MINT-SAUCE, [mint-saws'], *n.* mint chopped up, and used with vinegar and sugar as flavouring.
MINUEND, [min'-yŏŏ-end], *n.* (*arith.*) the number from which another is to be subtracted. [L. *minuendus* which must be lessened].
MINUET, [min'-yŏŏ-et'], *n.* a slow graceful dance in triple time; the music for this. [Fr. *menuet*].
MINUS (1), [mīn'-us], *n.* a sign denoting subtraction. [L. *minus* smaller].
MINUS (2), [mīn'-us], *prep.* with the deduction of; **m. quantity,** (*math.*) a quantity preceded by a minus sign; **m. charge,** (*elect.*) a negative charge; **m. mark,** an estimate of worth in an examination.
MINUSCULE, [min'-us-kewl], *n.* a small letter; a small cursive type of handwriting which arose about the seventh century; (*print.*) a lower-case letter. [L. *minusculus*].
MINUTE (1), [min'-it], *n.* the sixtieth part of an hour or a degree; a moment; a brief note or memorandum; (*pl.*) a summarized record of the business at a formal meeting. [L. *minuta*].
MINUTE (2), [mī-newt'], *adj.* very small; trifling, unimportant; precise, exact, detailed. [L. *minutus*].
MINUTE (3), [min'-it], *v.t.* to time exactly; to write the minutes of.
MINUTE-BOOK, [min'-it-bŏŏk'], *n.* the book in which the minutes are recorded.
MINUTE-GLASS, [min'-it-glahs'], *n.* a sand-glass used for timing in minutes.
MINUTE-GUN, [min'-it-gun'], *n.* a gun fired every minute, as a signal of distress or mourning.
MINUTE-HAND, [min'-it-hand'], *n.* the hand that registers the minutes on the dial of a clock or watch.
MINUTELY, [mī-newt'-li], *adv.* in minute fashion, meticulously.
MINUTE-MAN, [min'-it-man], *n.* (*hist.*) a member of the American militia at the time of the revolution.
MINUTENESS, [mī-newt'-nes], *n.* the quality of being minute.
MINUTIAE, [mī-new'-shi-ē], *n.(pl.)* particulars or details of lesser importance. [L. *minutiae*].
MINX, [mingks], *n.* a pert, ill-mannered young woman, a hussy. [Uncert.].
MIOCENE, [mī'-ō-sēn], *adj.* (*geol.*) of the middle division of the tertiary rocks, less recent. [Gk. *meion* less and *kainos* recent].
MIR, [mir], *n.* a former Russian agricultural community. [Russ. *mir*].
MIRABILITE, [mi-rab'-i-līt], *n.* native sodium sulphate found as efflorescence on the soil among salt-springs. [Germ. *mirabilit*].
MIRACLE, [mi'-rakl], *n.* an event which seems contrary

to, or inexplicable by, the laws of nature, and which is thus regarded as the work of a Divine Power; an extremely remarkable happening; an extraordinary example. [L. *miraculum* marvel].

MIRACLE-MONGER, [mi'-rakl-mung'-er], *n.* an impostor who claims to work miracles.

MIRACLE PLAY, [mi'-rakl-plā'], *n.* a form of drama, popular in the Middle Ages, depicting the fall and redemption of man.

MIRACULOUS, [mi-rak'-yōō-lus], *adj.* of the nature of or approaching a miracle, wonderful, extraordinary. [Fr. *miraculeux*].

MIRACULOUSLY, [mi-rak'-yōō-lus-li], *adv.* in a miraculous manner.

MIRACULOUSNESS, [mi-rak'-yōō-lus-nes], *n.* the quality of being miraculous.

MIRADOR, [mi'-ra-daw(r)], *n.* a balcony or turret on the roof of a Spanish house; a watch tower. [Span. *mirador*].

MIRAGE, [mi'-rahzh], *n.* an optical illusion, due to curvature of the light rays in certain atmospheric conditions, by which objects appear out of their true position; (*fig.*) a deceptive hope. [Fr. *mirage*].

MIRBANE, [mir'-bān], *n.* an artificial oil used for scenting soaps and for flavouring; **essence of m.,** nitrobenzol, used in perfumes. [Fr. *mirbane*].

MIRE (1), [mīer], *n.* thick mud, boggy ground; (*fig.*) defilement, dirt. [OIcel. *myrr*].

MIRE (2), [mīer], *v.t.* to immerse or fix in mire; to daub with mud; to defile; *v.i.* to sink in thick mud.

MIRE-CROW, [mīer'-krō'], *n.* the black-headed gull, *Larus ridibundus*.

MIRINESS, [mīer'-i-nes], *n.* the condition of being miry.

MIRK, see MURK.

MIRROR (1), [mi'-rer], *n.* a piece of glass backed with metal, or a highly polished surface, which reflects an image; (*fig.*) a pattern, picture. [OFr. *mireour*].

MIRROR (2), [mi'-rer], *v.t.* to reflect as in a mirror.

MIRTH, [murth], *n.* merriment, gaiety, laughter, hilarity. [OE. *myrigth*].

MIRTHFUL, [murth'-fōōl], *adj.* merry, jovial, jolly.

MIRTHFULLY, [murth'-fōōl-i], *adv.* in mirthful fashion.

MIRTHFULNESS, [murth'-fōōl-nes], *n.* the state of being mirthful.

MIRTHLESS, [murth'-les], *adj.* sad, joyless.

MIRTHLESSLY, [murth'-les-li], *adv.* in mirthless fashion.

MIRTHLESSNESS, [murth'-les-nes], *n.* the state of being mirthless.

MIRY, [mīer'-i], *adj.* abounding in mire, boggy; muddy.

MIRZA, [mur'-za], *n.* a Persian title which, when placed before a name, denotes a scholar, and when placed after, a prince. [Pers. *mirza*].

MIS-, *pref.* wrong, ill, badly, unfavourable. [OE. *mis*, OFr. *mes*].

MISADVENTURE, [mis'-ad-ven'-cher], *n.* mishap, ill-luck, accident, mischance; **by m.,** accidentally.

MISADVENTUROUS, [mis'-ad-ven'-cher-us], *adj.* involving misadventure, disastrous, unlucky.

MISALLIANCE, [mis'-a-lī'-ants], *n.* an improper alliance; an unsuitable marriage.

MISALLIED, [mis'-a-līd'], *adj.* improperly allied.

MISALLOTMENT, [mis'-a-lot'-ment], *n.* a wrong allotment.

MISANTHROPE, [mis'-an-thrōp], *n.* one who hates and shuns mankind. [Gk. *misanthropos* hating mankind].

MISANTHROPIC, [mis'-an-throp'-ik], *adj.* hating mankind.

MISANTHROPIST, [mis-an'-throp-ist], *n.* a misanthrope.

MISANTHROPY, [mis-an'-throp-i], *n.* hatred of mankind.

MISAPPLICATION, [mis'-ap-li-kā'-shun], *n.* a wrong application.

MISAPPLY, [mis'-a-plī'], *v.t.* to apply or use wrongly.

MISAPPRECIATED, [mis'-a-prē'-shi-āt-id], *adj.* not appreciated properly or fully.

MISAPPREHEND, [mis'-a-pri-hend'], *v.t.* to misunderstand.

MISAPPREHENSION, [mis'-a-pri-hen'-shun], *n.* a misunderstanding, a mistaken idea or belief.

MISAPPREHENSIVE, [mis'-a-pri-hen'-siv], *adj.* liable to misapprehend.

MISAPPROPRIATE, [mis'-a-prō'-pri-āt], *v.t.* to apply to a wrong purpose; (*leg.*) to convert wrongfully to one's own use (money, etc., entrusted).

MISAPPROPRIATION, [mis'-a-prō'-pri-ā'-shun], *n.* the act of misappropriating.

MISARRANGE, [mis'-a-rānj'], *v.t.* to arrange wrongly or badly.

MISARRANGEMENT, [mis'-a-rānj'-ment], *n.* wrong or bad arrangement.

MISBECOME, [mis'-bi-kum'], *v.t.* to suit ill.

MISBECOMING, [mis'-bi-kum'-ing], *adj.* unseemly, not becoming.

MISBECOMINGLY, [mis'-bi-kum'-ing-li], *adv.* in unseemly fashion.

MISBECOMINGNESS, [mis'-bi-kum'-ing-nes], *n.* the quality of being misbecoming.

MISBEGOTTEN, [mis'-bi-got'-en], *adj.* unlawfully or irregularly begotten, bastard.

MISBEHAVE, [mis'-bi-hāv'], *v.i.* to behave badly.

MISBEHAVIOUR, [mis'-bi-hāv'-yer], *n.* ill-mannered behaviour; misconduct.

MISBELIEF, [mis'-bi-lēf'], *n.* erroneous belief, *esp.* in religious matters.

MISBELIEVE, [mis'-bi-lēv'], *v.t. and i.* to hold false beliefs (about).

MISBELIEVER, [mis'-bi-lēv'-er], *n.* one who believes wrongly or falsely, a heretic.

MISBORN, [mis-bawn'], *adj.* born to evil or misfortune.

MISCALCULATE, [mis-kal'-kyōō-lāt], *v.t. and i.* to calculate wrongly, to misjudge.

MISCALCULATION, [mis'-kal-kyōō-lā'-shun], *n.* the act of miscalculating; an instance of this.

MISCALL, [mis-kawl'], *v.t.* to misname, to call by a wrong name; (*dial.*) to abuse; (*cards, etc.*) to call incorrectly.

MISCARRIAGE, [mis-ka'-rij], *n.* the act of miscarrying; an instance of this, *esp.* a premature birth.

MISCARRY, [mis-ka'-ri], *v.i.* to go wrong or astray; to fail to be carried out, executed, or administered properly; to give birth prematurely.

MISCAST, [mis-kahst'], *v.t.* to cast unsuitably; to reckon up wrongly.

MISCASTING, [mis-kahst'-ing], *n.* a wrong casting of parts or accounts.

MISCEGENATION, [mis'-i-jen-ā'-shun], *n.* interbreeding and mingling of the races, *esp.* between whites and blacks. [L. *miscere* to mix and *genus* race].

MISCELLANARIAN (1), [mis'-el-an-āer'-i-an], *n.* a compiler of miscellanies.

MISCELLANARIAN (2), [mis'-el-an-āer'-i-an], *adj.* belonging to, of the nature of a miscellany.

MISCELLANEA, [mis'-el-ā'-ni-a], *n.(pl.)* a miscellany; miscellaneous articles. [L. *miscellanea*].

MISCELLANEOUS, [mis'-el-ā'-ni-us], *adj.* mixed, consisting of various kinds. [L. *miscellaneus*].

MISCELLANEOUSLY, [mis'-el-ā'-ni-us-li], *adv.* in a miscellaneous manner.

MISCELLANEOUSNESS, [mis'-el-ā'-ni-us-nes], *n.* the quality of being miscellaneous.

MISCELLANIST, [mis-sel'-an-ist], *n.* a miscellanarian.

MISCELLANY, [mis-sel'-a-ni, mis'-el-a-ni], *n.* a mixture of various kinds; *esp.* a collection of writings or compositions of various kinds, or by various writers. [L. *miscellanea*].

MISCHANCE, [mis-chahnts'], *n.* misfortune, accident, bad luck. [OFr. *meschance*].

MISCHARACTERIZE, [mis-kar'-akt-er-īz], *v.t.* to give a wrong character to.

MISCHARGE (1), [mis-chahj'], *n.* an erroneous entry; a mistake in charging.

MISCHARGE (2), [mis-chahj'], *v.i.* to charge wrongly.

MISCHIEF, [mis'-chif], *n.* harm, injury, damage; wilful wrongdoing or destructive action; disorder, unrest; an irritating feature, annoying part; trouble, vexatious action or conduct; arch playfulness, roguishness; a troublesome child; **to make m.,** to cause ill-feeling. [OFr. *meschef*].

MISCHIEF-MAKER, [mis'-chif-māk'-er], *n.* one who stirs up ill-feeling or strife.

MISCHIEF-MAKING, [mis'-chif-māk'-ing], *adj.* exciting enmity, stirring up strife.

MISCHIEVOUS, [mis'-chiv-us], *adj.* making mischief; naughty, continually getting into mischief; harmful; vexatious, annoying; arch, roguish. [AFr. *meschevous*].

MISCHIEVOUSLY, [mis'-chiv-us-li], *adv.* in a mischievous manner.

MISCHIEVOUSNESS, [mis'-chiv-us-nes], *n.* the quality of being mischievous.

MISCHOOSE, [mis-chōōz'], *v.t.* to make a wrong or improper choice.

MISCIBILITY, [mis'-i-bil'-i-ti], *n.* the quality of being miscible.

MISCIBLE, [mis'-ibl], *adj.* able to be mixed. [L. *miscere* to mix].

MISCITATION, [mis'-sī-tā'-shun], *n.* a false citation.
MISCITE, [mis-sīt'], *v.t.* to quote wrongly.
MISCLAIM (1), [mis'-klām'], *n.* a wrong claim.
MISCLAIM (2), [mis-klām'], *v.t.* to claim wrongly.
MISCOMPUTATION, [mis'-kom-pyōō-tā'-shun], *n.* a wrong calculation.
MISCOMPUTE, [mis'-kom-pewt'], *v.t.* to reckon wrongly.
MISCONCEIVE, [mis'-kon-sēv'], *v.t. and i.* to entertain a false notion, to misapprehend.
MISCONCEPTION, [mis'-kon-sep'-shun], *n.* a false conception, a wrong idea.
MISCONDUCT (1), [mis-kon'-dukt], *n.* improper conduct, misbehaviour; adultery.
MISCONDUCT (2), [mis'-kon-dukt'], *v.t.* to manage badly.
MISCONSTRUCTION, [mis'-kon-struk'-shun], *n.* a false interpretation of words or actions.
MISCONSTRUE, [mis'-kon-strōō'], *v.t.* to interpret or translate inaccurately, misunderstand.
MISCONSTRUER, [mis'-kon-strōō'-er], *n.* one who misconstrues.
MISCOUNSEL, (miscounselling, miscounselled), [mis-kown'-sel], *v.t.* to give wrong advice to.
MISCOUNT (1), [mis'-kownt'], *n.* a wrong counting, *esp.* of votes.
MISCOUNT (2), [mis-kownt'], *v.t. and i.* to count inaccurately.
MISCREANT (1), [mis'-kri-ant], *n.* a scoundrel, base fellow, villain; †a misbeliever, infidel.
MISCREANT (2), [mis'-kri-ant], *adj.* scoundrelly, vile; †infidel, heretical. [OFr. *mescreant* unbelieving].
MISCREATION, [mis'-krē-ā'-shun], *n.* a monstrous creation.
MISCREATIVE, [mis'-krē-āt'-iv], *adj.* forming or creating amiss.
MISCUE (1), [mis-kew'], *n.* (*billiards*) a faulty stroke in which the cue-ball is not struck truly.
MISCUE (2), (miscuing), [mis-kew'], *v.i.* (*billiards*) to make a miscue.
MISDATE (1), [mis-dāt'], *n.* a false date.
MISDATE (2), [mis-dāt'], *v.t.* to date wrongly.
MISDEAL (1), [mis-dēl'], *n.* a wrong deal at cards.
MISDEAL (2), (misdealt), [mis-dēl'], *v.t. and i.* to deal cards wrongly.
MISDEALING, [mis-dēl'-ing], *n.* sharp practice, roguery.
MISDEED, [mis-dēd'], *n.* a wicked deed.
MISDEEM, [mis-dēm'], *v.t.* to misjudge.
MISDEMEAN, [mis'-di-mēn'], *v. reflex.* to misbehave oneself.
MISDEMEANANT, [mis'-di-mēn'-ant], *n.* one guilty of a misdemeanour.
MISDEMEANOUR, [mis'-di-mēn'-er], *n.* (*leg.*) an indictable offence less serious than felony; a petty offence; ill conduct.
MISDESCRIBE, [mis'-di-skrīb'], *v.t.* to describe inaccurately.
MISDIRECT, [mis'-di-rekt'], *v.t.* to direct wrongly, badly, or mistakenly.
MISDIRECTION, [mis'-di-rek'-shun], *n.* a wrong direction; a bad aim; the act of misdirecting.
MISDISTINGUISH, [mis'-dis-ting'-gwish], *v.t.* to distinguish improperly or imperfectly.
MISDO, (misdid, misdone), [mis-dōō'], *v.t. and i.* to do wrongly.
MISDOER, [mis-dōō'-er], *n.* a wrong-doer, a malefactor.
MISDOING, [mis-dōō'-ing], *n.* a wrong action; a fault.
MISDOUBT (1), [mis-dowt'], *n.* †suspicion, misgiving.
MISDOUBT (2), [mis-dowt'], *v.t.* to doubt, suspect.
MISE, [mēz], *n.* a tribute or grant paid for a privilege or immunity; an agreement; a stake; (*leg.*) the issue in a writ of right; †costs or expenses. [OFr. *mise* a setting down].
MISE-EN-SCENE, mise-en-scène, [mēz'-ahn-sān'], *n.* the setting of a play; the external environment. [Fr. *mise-en-scène*].
MISEMPLOY, [mis'-em-ploi'], *v.t.* to put to a wrong use.
MISEMPLOYMENT, [mis'-em-ploi'-ment], *n.* a wrong use; the act of misemploying.
MISENTER, [mis-en'-ter], *v.t.* to enter inaccurately.
MISENTRY, [mis-en'-tri], *n.* a wrong entry.
MISER (1), [mīz'-er], *n.* a very covetous person, a stingy hoarder of wealth; †a miserable wretch. [L. *miser* wretched].
MISER (2), [mīz'-er], *n.* a large auger, a tool for boring. [Unkn.].
MISERABLE, [miz'-er-abl], *adj.* unhappy, sad, dejected; in discomfort; depressing, causing sadness; poor, mediocre; scanty, meagre; squalid, uncomfortable; wretched; depraved; †compassionate. [L. *miserabilis*].
MISERABLENESS, [miz'-er-abl-nes], *n.* the condition of being miserable.
MISERABLY, [miz'-er-ab-li], *adv.* in miserable fashion.
MISERE, misère, [miz-āer'], *n.* a call in solo whist in which the caller undertakes to lose every trick. [Fr. *misère* misery].
MISERERE, [miz'-er-āer'-i], *n.* the fifty-first Psalm, beginning with this word in the Latin version; a musical setting for this; a cry for mercy; a projection on the under surface of a folding seat in a choir stall in a church. [L. *miserere* have mercy].
MISERICORD, [mis-e'-ri-kawd], *n.* a small, slim dagger for piercing the joints of medieval armour, to inflict the death-thrust; a room in a monastery where relaxations of certain rules are allowed; a miserere seat in church. [L. *misericordia* mercy].

MISERICORD

MISERLINESS, [mīz'-er-li-nes], *n.* the state or quality of being miserly.
MISERLY, [mīz'-er-li], *adj.* avaricious; covetous; penurious, like a miser.
MISERY, [miz'-er-i], *n.* wretchedness; distress, unrelieved unhappiness; extreme pain or anguish. [L. *miseria*].
MISESTIMATE, [mis-es'-tim-āt], *v.t.* to estimate wrongly.
MISFALL, (misfell, misfallen), [mis-fawl'], *v.i.* to happen unfortunately, befall ill.
MISFASHION, [mis-fash'-un], *v.t.* to fashion wrongly.
MISFEASANCE, [mis-fēz'-ants], *n.* a trespass, wrongful act; (*leg.*) the doing in a wrongful way of a perfectly legal act. [OFr. *mesfaisance*].
MISFIRE (1), [mis-fīer'], *n.* the failure of a firearm to go off; the failure of an internal-combustion engine to start; (*fig.*) something that misfires badly.
MISFIRE (2), [mis-fīer'], *v.i.* to fail to go off or start; (*fig.*) to fail to produce the desired effect.
MISFIT, [mis'-fit], *n.* a bad fit; anyone or anything not suited to his or its environment or occupation.
MISFORM, [mis-fawm'], *v.t.* to shape badly.
MISFORMATION, [mis'-fawm-ā'-shun], *n.* a flaw in structure, malformation.
MISFORTUNATE, [mis-faw'-tewn-at], *adj.* unlucky.
MISFORTUNE, [mis-faw'-tewn], *n.* bad luck; a mishap, disaster.
MISGIVE, (misgave), [mis-giv'], *v.t.* to cause fear, suspicion, mistrust, doubt.
MISGIVING, [mis-giv'-ing], *n.* a losing of confidence or trust; doubt, scruple.
MISGOVERN, [mis-guv'-ern], *v.t.* to govern ill, mismanage.
MISGOVERNMENT, [mis-guv'-ern-ment], *n.* bad government or administration.
MISGUIDANCE, [mis-gīd'-ants], *n.* wrong guidance, misdirection.
MISGUIDE, [mis-gīd'], *v.t.* to guide into error, mislead.
MISGUIDED, [mis-gīd'-id], *adj. and p.pt.* led astray, ill-advised, mistaken.
MISGUIDEDLY, [mis-gīd'-ed-li], *adv.* in a misguided manner.
MISHANDLE, [mis-handl'], *v.t.* to mismanage; to ill-treat; to handle wrongly.
MISHAP, [mis-hap'], *n.* an accident. [MIS and HAP].
MISHAPPEN, [mis-hap'-en], *v.i.* to happen unluckily.
MISHEAR, (misheard), [mis-hēer'], *v.t.* to hear incorrectly.
MISHIT (1), [mis'-hit], *n.* a faulty, ill-directed stroke.
MISHIT (2), (mishitting), [mis-hit'], *v.t.* to hit by a mishit.
MISHMASH, [mish'-mash], *n.* an ill-assorted medley.
MISHNA, MISHNAH, [mish'-na], *n.* a collection of rabbinical legal traditions and interpretations forming the basis of the Talmud. [Heb. *mishnah* instruction].
MISHNIC, [mish'-nik], *adj.* concerning the Mishna.
MISINFER, (misinferring, misinferred), [mis'-in-fer'], *v.t.* to draw a false inference.
MISINFORM, [mis'-in-fawm'], *v.t.* to give inaccurate information to.
MISINFORMANT, [mis'-in-fawm'-ant], *n.* a misinformer.
MISINFORMATION, [mis-in'-fawm-ā'-shun], *n.* false information.

MISINFORMER, [mis'-in-fawm'-er], *n.* one who misinforms.

MISINSTRUCT, [mis'-in-strukt'], *v.t.* to instruct incorrectly.

MISINSTRUCTION, [mis'-in-struk'-shun], *n* incorrect instruction.

MISINTERPRET, [mis'-in-tur'-prit], *v.t. and i.* to interpret incorrectly.

MISINTERPRETATION, [mis'-in-tur'-prit-ā'-shun], *n.* incorrect interpretation.

MISINTERPRETER, [mis'-in-tur'-prit-er], *n.* one who misinterprets.

MISJOIN, [mis-join'], *v.t.* to join imperfectly.

MISJOINDER, [mis-join'-der], *n.* (*leg.*) improper joining of parties in an action at law

MISJUDGE, [mis-juj'], *v.t.* to judge wrongly; to fail to appreciate or estimate correctly.

MISJUDGMENT, MISJUDGEMENT, [mis-juj'-ment], *n.* the act of misjudging; a wrong judgment.

MISLABEL, [mis-lā'-bel], *v.t.* to label incorrectly.

MISLAY, (**mislaid**), [mis-lā'], *v.t.* to forget where one has put (something), to lose for a time.

MISLAYER, [mis-lā'-er], *n.* a person who mislays.

MISLEAD, (**misled**), [mis-lēd'], *v.t.* to lead astray, to deceive.

MISLIKE (**1**), [mis-līk'], *n.* aversion, dislike.

MISLIKE (**2**), [mis-līk'], *v.t.* dislike.

MISMANAGE, [mis-man'-ij], *v.t.* to manage badly.

MISMANAGEMENT, [mis-man'-ij-ment], *n.* bad management.

MISMATCH, [mis-mach'], *v.t.* to match wrongly

MISMEASURE, [mis-mezh'-er], *v.t. and i.* to measure or judge incorrectly.

MISNAME, [mis-nām'], *v.t.* to name wrongly.

MISNOMER, [mis-nōm'-er], *n.* a wrong or unsuitable name. [OFr. *mesnommer* to misname].

MISO-, *pref.* hatred. [Gk. *misos*].

MISOBSERVE, [mis'-ob-zurv'], *v.t.* to observe wrongly.

MISOGAMIST, [mis-og'-am-ist], *n.* one who hates marriage.

MISOGAMY, [mis-og'-a-mi], *n.* hatred of marriage. [MISO and Gk. *gamos* marriage].

MISOGYNIST, [mis-oj'-in-ist], *n.* one who hates women.

MISOGYNY, [mis-oj'-i-ni], *n.* hatred of women. [MISO and Gk. *gune* woman].

MISOLOGIST, [mis-ol'-oj-ist], *n.* one who hates logic. [MISO and Gk. *logos* speech].

MISPERSUASION, [mis'-per-swā'-zhun], *n.* a wrong persuasion or opinion.

MISPICKEL, [mis'-pikl], *n.* an ore of arsenic; arsenosulphide of iron. [Germ. *mispickel*].

MISPLACE, [mis-plās'], *v.t.* to lay in a wrong place; to mislay; to misdirect.

MISPLACEMENT, [mis-plās'-ment], *n.* the act of placing wrongly; the state of being misplaced.

MISPLEAD, [mis-plēd'], *v.t.* to plead wrongly.

MISPOINT, [mis-point'], *v.t.* to punctuate incorrectly.

MISPRACTICE, [mis-prak'-tis], *n.* improper practice.

MISPRINT (**1**), [mis-print'], *n.* a mistake in printing, a printer's error.

MISPRINT (**2**), [mis-print'], *v.t. and i.* to print incorrectly.

MISPRISE, MISPRIZE, [mis-prīz'], *v.t.* to scorn, undervalue. [OFr. *mespriser*].

MISPRISION (**1**), [mis-prizh'-un], *n.* a mistake; (*leg.*) a failure of duty, misdemeanour, by a public official; **m. of felony, m. of treason,** concealment of a felony or treason. [OFr. *mesprison* a mistake].

MISPRISION (**2**), [mis-prizh'-un], *n.* contempt; disparagement.

MISPRIZE, see MISPRISE.

MISPROCEEDING, [mis'-prō-sēd'-ing], *n.* improper proceeding.

MISPRONOUNCE, [mis'-prō-nownts'], *v.t. and i.* to pronounce wrongly.

MISPRONUNCIATION, [mis'-prō-nun'-si-ā'-shun], *n.* faulty or incorrect pronunciation.

MISPROPORTION, [mis'-prō-paw'-shun], *v.t.* to proportion wrongly or badly.

MISQUOTATION, [mis'-kwō-tā'-shun], *n.* an inaccurate quotation.

MISQUOTE, [mis-kwōt'], *v.t.* to quote inaccurately.

MISREAD, [mis-rēd'], *v.t.* to read something wrongly.

MISRECEIVE, [mis'-ri-sēv'], *v.t.* to receive wrongly.

MISRECITE, [mis'-ri-sīt'], *v.t.* to recite wrongly.

MISRECKON, [mis-rek'-on], *v.t.* to reckon inaccurately.

MISRELATE, [mis'-ri-lāt'], *v.t.* to relate wrongly.

MISRELATION, [mis'-ri-lā'-shun], *n.* wrong relation.

MISREMEMBER, [mis'-ri-mem'-ber], *v.t.* to remember incorrectly; to forget.

MISREPORT (**1**), [mis'-ri-pawt'], *n.* a false report.

MISREPORT (**2**), [mis'-ri-pawt'], *v.t.* to report wrongly.

MISREPRESENT, [mis-rep'-ri-zent'], *v.t.* to represent or describe incorrectly, give a false impression or account of.

MISREPRESENTATION, [mis-rep'-ri-zent-ā'-shun], *n.* an inaccurate representation.

MISREPUTE (**1**), [mis'-ri-pewt'], *n.* doubtful or undesirable reputation.

MISREPUTE (**2**), [mis'-ri-pewt'], *v.t.* to misjudge.

MISRULE (**1**), [mis-rōōl'], *n.* bad government; unruliness, riotous insubordination; **Lord of M.,** the leader of the Christmas revels in former times.

MISRULE (**2**), [mis-rōōl'], *v.t.* to rule badly.

MISS (**1**), (*pl.* **misses**), [mis], *n.* a form of address to an unmarried woman if she does not own any other title; an unmarried woman; a lively young girl. [MISTRESS].

MISS (**2**), [mis], *n.* a failure to hit, attain, or get; escape; (*billiards*) a failure to hit a ball with the cue-ball; **to give a m.,** to stay away from, neglect.

MISS (**3**), [mis], *v.t. and i.* to fail to hit, meet, or find, to pass without touching; to fail to hold, take, or catch; to fail to achieve or attain; to fail to understand, see, or hear; to omit, overlook; to be or do without; to discover or regret the loss of; to avoid, escape; to misfire; **to m. out,** to omit; **to m. stays,** (*naut.*) to fail to go about from one tack to another. [OE. *missan*].

MISSAL, [misl], *n.* the Roman Catholic mass-book; a book of prayers or devotions, *esp.* if illuminated. [EcclesL. *missalis liber* mass book].

MISSAY, (**missaid**), [mis-sā'], *v.t.* to say wrongly.

MISSEL-THRUSH, [misl'-thrush], *n.* the largest European thrush, *Turdus viscivorus*, feeding upon mistletoe. [~MISTLETOE].

MISSEL-THRUSH

MISSEMBLANCE, [mis-sem'-blants], *n.* a wrong resemblance.

MISSEND, (**missent**), [mis-send'], *v.t.* to send to a wrong place.

MISSERVE, [mis-surv'], *v.t.* to serve falsely or unfaithfully.

MISSHAPE, [mis-shāp'], *v.t.* to shape badly, to deform.

MISSHAPEN, [mis-shāp'-en], *adj.* badly shaped, deformed.

MISSILE (**1**), [mis'-īl], *n.* anything thrown or throwable, a projectile.

MISSILE (**2**), [mis'-īl], *adj.* intended to be, or that may be, thrown. [L. *missilis*].

MISSING, [mis'-ing], *adj.* lost; unaccounted for.

MISSION, [mish'-un], *n.* a sending; what one is sent to do; those sent, a delegation sent to a foreign country for a specific purpose; a body of missionaries sent abroad; their outpost, their field of work; a special effort to quicken religious activity in a particular locality; a centre for religious or social work among the poor. [L. *missio*].

MISSIONARY (**1**), [mish'-un-er-i], *n.* one sent to propagate a religion, *esp.* in a heathen country.

MISSIONARY (**2**), [mish'-un-er-i], *adj.* of, or concerning, missions or missionaries.

MISSIONER, [mish'-un-er], *n.* a missionary; a person belonging to or directing a mission.

MISSIS, MISSUS, [mis'-is], *n.* mistress; (*coll.*) wife; form of address to a married woman with no other title. [MISTRESS].

MISSISH, [mis'-ish], *adj.* having a schoolgirlish way.

MISSIVE (**1**), [mis'-iv], *n.* a letter, *esp.* of an official character.

MISSIVE (**2**), [mis'-iv], *adj.* (*archaic*) sent or sendable. [L. *missivus*].

MISSOY-BARK, [mis'-oi-bahk'], *n.* the aromatic bark of *Laurus burmanni*. [Malay *masui*].

MIS-SPELL, (**mis-spelt**), [mis-spel'], *v.t.* to spell incorrectly.

MIS-SPELLING, [mis-spel'-ing], *n.* an incorrect spelling.

MIS-SPEND, (**mis-spent**), [mis-spend'], *v.t.* to spend wrongly, to waste.

MIS-SPENT, [mis'-spent], *adj.* expended to no purpose, wasted.

MIS-STATE, [mis-stāt'], *v.t. and i.* to describe badly or wrongly, misrepresent.

MIS-STATEMENT, [mis-stāt'-ment], *n.* an incorrect statement; the act of mis-stating.

MIS-STAYED, [mis-stād′], *adj.* (*naut.*) having failed to go about from one tack to another.
MISSUS, see MISSIS.
MIST (1), [mist], *n.* a cloud of minute particles of water formed near the surface of the earth; a blurring of the vision; (*fig.*) a state of doubt; that which causes this. [OE. *mist* darkness].
MIST (2), [mist], *v.t. and i.* to obscure, blur; to form a mist.
MISTAKABLE, [mis-tāk′-abl], *adj.* that may be mistaken or misunderstood.
MISTAKE (1), [mis-tāk′], *n.* an error, blunder; a misunderstanding, misconception.
MISTAKE (2), (**mistook, mistaken**), [mis-tāk′], *v.t. and i.* to misunderstand, to make a false judgment of; to identify inaccurately. [OIcel. *mistaka* to take in error].
MISTAKEN, [mis-tāk′-en], *adj.* wrong, erroneous; misdirected.
MISTAKENLY, [mis-tāk′-en-li], *adv.* by mistake.
MISTEACH, (**mistaught**), [mis-tēch′], *v.t.* to teach badly.
MISTER, [mis′-ter], *n.* a form of address to any man not entitled to any other title; also prefixed to certain titles held by virtue of office. [MASTER (1)].
MISTERM, [mis-turm′], *v.t.* to name wrongly.
MISTFUL, [mist′-fŏŏl], *adj.* covered with mist, cloudy.
MISTILY, [mist′-i-li], *adv.* in misty fashion.
MISTIME, [mis-tīm′], *v.t.* to time wrongly.
MISTINESS, [mist′-i-nes], *n.* the condition of being misty.
MISTITLE, [mis-tītl′], *v.t.* to call by the wrong title.
MISTLETOE, [misl′-tō], *n. Viscum album*, a parasitic plant with whitish berries, growing on various trees, *esp.* on the apple and the elm. [OE. *mistel* mistletoe and *tan* twig].
MISTRAIN, [mis-trān′], *v.t.* to train badly.
MISTRAL, [mis′-tral′], *n.* a cold north-west wind in the south of France. [Provenç. *mistral*].
MISTRANSLATE, [mis′-trans-lāt′], *v.t. and i.* to translate incorrectly.
MISTRANSLATION, [mis′-trans-lā′-shun], *n.* an incorrect translation.
MISTRESS, [mis′-tres], *n.* a woman who rules or supervises; the female head of a household or family, *esp.* one employing servants; a woman teacher; a concubine; a woman who has mastered some specified accomplishment; (*fig.*) that which occupies a dominant position; (*archaic*) a polite mode of address to a woman; (*archaic*) a sweetheart. [OFr. *maistresse*].
MISTRESS-SHIP, [mis′-tres-ship], *n.* the status or authority of mistress; the position of woman teacher.
MISTRUST (1), [mis-trust′], *n.* lack of confidence, suspicion.
MISTRUST (2), [mis-trust′], *v.t.* to suspect, doubt, have fears about.
MISTRUSTFUL, [mis-trust′-fŏŏl], *adj.* suspicious.
MISTRUSTFULLY, [mis-trust′-fŏŏl-i], *adv.* in a distrusting way.
MISTRUSTFULNESS, [mis-trust′-fŏŏl-nes], *n.* suspicion.
MISTRUSTINGLY, [mis-trust′-ing-li], *adv.* with mistrust.
MISTRUSTLESS, [mis-trust′-les], *adj.* unsuspecting.
MISTUNE, [mis-tewn′], *v.t.* to tune wrongly.
MISTURN, [mis-turn′], *v.t.* to pervert or invert, to use wrongly; *v.i.* to go wrong.
MISTY, [mist′-i], *adj.* covered with mist; obscure, blurred. [OE. *mistig*].
MISUNDERSTAND, [mis′-un-der-stand′], *v.t.* to take in a wrong sense.
MISUNDERSTANDING, [mis′-un-der-stand′-ing], *n.* a slight dispute, disagreement; misconception, error.
MISUSAGE, [mis-yōōs′-ij], *n.* wrong usage, abuse.
MISUSE (1), [mis-yōōs′], *n.* ill-treatment, wrong use.
MISUSE (2), [mis-yōōz′], *v.t.* to use wrongly; to maltreat.
MISVOUCH, [mis-vowch′], *v.i.* to vouch untruthfully.
MISWORSHIP, [mis-wur′-ship], *n.* false improper worship.
MISWRITE, (**miswrote**), [mis-rīt′], *v.t.* to write incorrectly.
MISWROUGHT, [mis-rawt′], *adj.* ill-made.
MISYOKE, [mis-yōk′], *v.t.* to yoke wrongly.
MITCHELL, [mich′-el], *n.* ready hewn Purbeck stone. [Uncert.].
MITE (1), [mīt], *n.* a small parasitic arachnid sometimes found in food. [OE. *mite* a small insect].
MITE (2), [mīt], *n.* anything very small, *esp.* a small child or a small portion; a small copper coin worth about half a farthing. [MDu. *mijt*].
MITHRAISM, [mith′-rā-izm], *n.* the cult of Mithras the Persian God of Light, and mediator between Man and God.
MITHRIDATE, [mith′-ri-dāt], *n.* an antidote against poison; **M. mustard**, a cruciferous plant, *Thlaspi arvense*. [*Mithridates* VI of Pontus (died 63 B.C.); who was supposed to have immunized himself against poison].
MITHRIDATIC, [mith′-ri-dăt′-ik], *adj.* of, or concerning, a mithridate or Mithridates of Pontus.
MITIGABLE, [mit′-ig-abl], *adj.* able to be mitigated.
MITIGANT (1), [mit′-ig-ant], *n.* that which mitigates.
MITIGANT (2), [mit′-ig-ant], *adj.* soothing, lenitive. [L. *mitigans*].
MITIGATE, [mit′-ig-āt], *v.t.* to soften, moderate, or alleviate. [L. *mitigare* to make mild or soft].
MITIGATING, [mit′-ig-āt-ing], *adj.* tending to mitigate.
MITIGATION, [mit′-ig-ā′-shun], *n.* the act of mitigating; the state of being mitigated; abatement.
MITIGATIVE, [mit′-ig-āt′-iv], *adj.* having the quality of alleviating.
MITIGATOR, [mit′-ig-āt-er], *n.* someone or something that mitigates.
MITIGATORY, [mit′-ig-āt′-er-i], *adj.* mitigative.
MITOSIS, [mit-ō′-sis], *n.* (*biol.*) the process of cell-division. [Gk. *mitos* thread and *osis* condition].
MITRA, [mī′-tra], *n.* (*surg.*) a bandage for the head. [Gk. *mitra* head-band].
MITRAILLEUSE, [mit′-rī-yurz′], *n.* a type of early machine gun, consisting of several barrels discharging in rapid succession. [Fr. from *mitraille* grape-shot].
MITRAL, [mī′-tral], *adj.* of, or resembling, a mitre; **m. valve**, (*anat.*) the left valve of the heart.
MITRE (1), [mī′-ter], *n.* (*eccles.*) the head-dress of a bishop or archbishop and of certain abbots; (*fig.*) episcopal dignity; the head-dress of the Jewish high priest. [Gk. *mitra* head-band].
MITRE (2), [mī′-ter], *n.* (*carp.*) the joining of two pieces of wood at an angle, usually of ninety degrees, by bevelling the adjacent edges at complementary angles. [Uncert.].
MITRE (3), [mī′-ter], *v.t.* to bestow a mitre upon. [MITRE (1)].
MITRE (4), [mī′-ter], *v.t.* (*carp.*) to join with a mitre joint. [MITRE (2)].
MITRED, [mī′-terd], *adj.* wearing a mitre; (*carp.*) joined with a mitre joint.

MITRE

MITRIFORM, [mī′-tri-fawm], *adj.* (*bot.*) resembling a mitre in shape, conical.
MITT, [mit], *n.* a mitten; (*slang*) hand; (*pl.*) (*slang*) boxing-gloves. [MITTEN].
MITTEN, [mit′-en], *n.* a fingerless, open glove covering only the wrist and back and palm of the hand; a glove with a place for the thumb, and one large compartment for the fingers. [OFr. *mitaine*].
MITTIMUS, [mit′-im-us], *n.* (*leg.*) a warrant for committal to prison; (*coll.*) notice of discharge from work. [L. *mittimus* we send].
MITY, [mī′-ti], *adj.* having mites.
MIX, [miks], *v.t.* to blend, mingle together; to unite into a compound; to prepare by combining ingredients; to confuse, muddle; *v.i.* to mingle; (of persons) to enjoy each other's society easily; **to m. up**, to muddle, confuse. [MIXED].
MIXABLE, [miks′-abl], *adj.* that may be mixed.
MIXED, [mikst], *adj.* compounded of several ingredients; confused; of different kinds, things, types, etc.; in which both men and women take part together; **m. up with**, involved in. [L. *mixtum*, *p.pt.* of *miscere*].
MIXEDLY, [miks′-ed-li], *adv.* in mixed fashion.
MIXER, [miks′-er], *n.* someone or something that mixes; an apparatus for blending sounds in broadcasting and talking-films; **a good m.**, a person who easily gets acquainted with others.
MIXTILINEAL, [miks′-ti-lin′-i-al], *adj.* having a mixture of lines.
MIXTILINEAR, [miks′-ti-lin′-i-er], *adj.* mixtilineal.
MIXTURE, [miks′-cher], *n.* the act of mixing; the state of being mixed; something mixed, a combination; (*chem.*) a combination in which each ingredient retains its own properties; (*motoring*) vaporized oil-fuel mixed with air. [L. *mixtura*].
MIX-UP, [miks′-up], *n.* (*coll.*) a muddle.
MIZEN, MIZZEN, [miz′-en], *n.* (*naut.*) the aftermost fore and aft sail of a ship; **m. mast**, the

aftermost mast of a three or more masted ship. [Fr. *misaine* foresail].
MIZZLE (1), [mizl], *n.* fine rain, drizzle.
MIZZLE (2), [mizl], *v.i.* (*slang*) to disappear furtively to decamp. [Uncert.].
MIZZLE (3), [mizl], *v. impers.* to rain in fine drops, to drizzle. [~MDu. *mieselen*].
MIZZLY, [miz'-li], *adj.* drizzling.
MIZZY, [miz'-i], *n.* (*dial.*) a quagmire or bog. [ME. *misy*].
MNEMONIC (1), [ni-mon'-ik], *n.* a device, formula, etc., to aid the memory.
MNEMONIC (2), [ni-mon'-ik], *adj.* aiding the memory. [Gk. *mnemonikos* mindful].
MNEMONICS, [ni-mon'-iks], *n.(pl.)* the science of improving the memory; the use of formulae and other devices to assist the memory. [Gk. *mnemonika*].
MNEMOTECHNY, [nem'-ō-tek'-ni], *n.* mnemonics. [Gk. *mneme* memory and *tekhne* art].
MO, [mō], *n.* (*slang*) moment, short space of time. [MOMENT].
MOA, [mō'-a], *n.* an extinct flightless bird of the genus *Dinornis*, once found in New Zealand. [Maori *moa*].
MOAN (1), [mōn], *n.* a low continued cry of pain or anguish; a lamentation. [ME. *mon*].
MOAN (2), [mōn], *v.i.* to utter a moan; *v.t.* (*poet.*) to bewail, lament.
MOANFUL, [mōn'-fool], *adj.* expressing grief.
MOANFULLY, [mōn'-fool-i], *adv.* in moanful fashion.
MOAT, [mōt], *n.* a water-filled ditch around the outer wall of a fortress, fortified town, castle, etc. [OFr. *mote* rampart, embankment].
MOB (1), [mob], *n.* a tumultuous crowd bent on disorder; a crowd, *esp.* of all types of people and not very select; the disorderly section of the populace, the rabble; an oppressed class; **m. law**, the law or rule imposed by a mob. [L. *mobile vulgus* excitable crowd].

MOA

MOB (2), [mob], *n.* a mob-cap.
MOB (3), **(mobbing, mobbed)**, [mob], *v.t.* to crowd round and maltreat in enthusiastic affection or dislike. [MOB (1)].
MOB† (4), **(mobbing, mobbed)**, [mob], *v.t.* to wrap in a cowl. [~Du. *mop* coif].
MOBBY, [mob'-i], *n.* juice crushed from apples and peaches to make apple or peach brandy. [Uncert.].
MOB-CAP, [mob'-kap], *n.* a loose broad-frilled cap completely covering the hair, worn indoors by women. [~Du. *mop* coif].
MOBILE, [mō'-bīl], *adj.* easily movable, moving readily; changeable and adaptable. [L. *mobilis*].
MOBILE POLICE, [mō'-bīl-po-lēs'], *n.* a section of the police force, equipped with cars, whose special duty is to see that traffic regulations are carried out.
MOBILITY, [mō-bil'-i-ti], *n.* the quality of being mobile.
MOBILIZATION, [mō'-bil-īz-ā'-shun], *n.* the action of mobilizing.
MOBILIZE, [mō'-bil-īz], *v.t.* and *i.* to put armed forces on a war footing; to make available for use. [Fr. *mobiliser* make mobile].
MOBLE†, [mobl], *v.t.* to wrap or muffle the head. [~MOB (4)].
MOBOCRACY, [mob-ok'-ra-si], *n.* mob government; the crowd or mob considered as a ruling class. [MOB (1) and Gk. *kratia* rule].
MOCCASIN, [mok'-a-sin'], *n.* footwear made of soft leather and worn by North American Indians; a soft-soled house-slipper resembling this; **m. snake**, the venomous copper-head, *Ancistrodon contortrix*. [Native].
MOCHA, [mō'-kah], *n.* a fine quality coffee; (*pop.*) coffee. [*Mocha*, in Arabia, where grown].
MOCHA-STONE, [mō'-kah-stōn'], *n.* a kind of chalcedony similar to the moss-agate.
MOCK (1), [mok], *n.* an act or object of contempt or ridicule.
MOCK (2), [mok], *v.t.* to ridicule, scorn, deride; to burlesque; to defeat, render ineffective; to befool. [OFr. *mocquer*].
MOCKER, [mok'-er], *n.* one who mocks.
MOCKERY, [mok'-er-i], *n.* the act of mocking; derision, ridicule; an object of this; travesty, a false show; a thing that deceives.
MOCK-HEROIC, [mok'-hi-rō'-ik], *adj.* burlesquing or mocking the heroic.
MOCKING (1), [mok'-ing], *n.* ridicule, insult.
MOCKING (2), [mok'-ing], *adj.* derisive, scornful.
MOCKING-BIRD, [mok'-ing-burd'], *n.* an American bird of the thrush family, *Mimus polyglottus*.
MOCKINGLY, [mok'-ing-li], *adv.* in a derisive manner.
MOCK-NIGHTINGALE, [mok-nī'-ting-gāl], *n.* the blackcap, *Sylvia atricapilla*.
MOCK-ORANGE, [mok'-o'-rinj], *n.* the shrub, *Philadelphus coronarius*.
MOCK-PRIVET, [mok'-priv'-et], *n.* the evergreen shrub, *Phillyrea angustifolia*.
MOCK-SUN, [mok-sun'], *n.* a parhelion.
MOCK-TURTLE, [mok'-turtl'], *n.* a soup, imitating turtle soup.
MOCK-VELVET, [mok-vel'-vet], *n.* an imitation velvet.
MOCO, [mō'-kō], *n.* the South American rock cavy, *Cavia rupestris*, allied to the guinea-pig. [Native].
MODAL, [mōd'-al], *adj.* pertaining to a mode; (*leg.*) (of a contract, legacy, etc.) containing clauses defining the manner of its effectiveness; (*gram.*) pertaining to, indicating mood; **a m. proposition**, (*log.*) one involving a statement of limitation. [MedL. *modalis*].
MODALISM, [mōd'-al-izm], *n.* the belief that the distinction of Persons in the Trinity is merely a distinction of the mode of manifestation of the Divine nature.
MODALIST, [mōd'-al-ist], *n.* one professing modalism.
MODALITY, [mōd-al'-i-ti], *n.* the quality of being modal.
MODALLY, [mōd'-al-i], *adv.* in a modal fashion.
MODE, [mōd], *n.* method of procedure, manner of doing; fashion, style, custom, convention; the accepted way, current fashion; (*mus.*) a system of sounds, a scale in ancient Greek or medieval church music; an arrangement of tones and semitones in a scale; (*log.*) the manner in which a proposition is qualified or limited. [L. *modus*].
MODEL (1), [mod'-el], *n.* a copy, an exact resemblance, *esp.* a miniature reproduction; a standard, example, that which is to be copied; a three-dimensional plan; someone who poses for an artist; a mannequin; a gown, hat, etc., exhibited for sale. [OFr. *modelle*].
MODEL (2), [mod'-el], *adj.* imitating or reproducing identically or to scale; set up as a model to be imitated.
MODEL (3), **(modelling, modelled)**, [mod'-el], *v.t.* and *i.* to shape, fashion, mould, *esp.* as, or into, a model of something; **to m. on**, to imitate.
MODELLER, [mod'-el-er], *n.* someone who models.
MODELLING, [mod'-el-ing], *n.* the making of a model; the art of working in plastic substances; the way in which anything is modelled.
MODENA, [mo-dē'-nah], *n.* a rich purple colour. [*Modena*, in Italy].
MODER, [mōd'-er], *n.* the matrix of an astrolabe. [OE. *moder* mother].
MODERATE (1), [mod'-er-at], *n.* one who holds moderate views.
MODERATE (2), [mod'-er-at], *adj.* temperate, not excessive or extreme; reasonable, not rash or rigorous; medium, rather small; mediocre, poorish, limited [L. *moderatus*].
MODERATE (3), [mod'-er-āt], *v.t.* and *i.* to keep within bounds; to make less violent; to become less violent; to preside over as moderator. [L. *moderari*].
MODERATELY, [mod'-er-at-li], *adj.* in moderate fashion.
MODERATENESS, [mod'-er-at-nes], *n.* the quality or state of being moderate.
MODERATION, [mod'-er-ā'-shun], *n.* moderateness; the act of moderating; the abatement or avoidance of excess or extremes; (*Scots*) a meeting of a congregation under a moderator to choose a new minister; (*pl.*) a form of first public examination.
MODERATISM, [mod'-er-at-izm], *n.* moderate opinions in religion or politics.
MODERATO, [mod'-er-ah'-tō], *adv.* (*mus.*) at a moderate pace. [It. *moderato*].
MODERATOR, [mod'-er-āt-er], *n.* someone or something that moderates; one who arbitrates; one who presides over an assembly; a Presbyterian minister chosen to preside over a church assembly; an examiner or presiding official in certain degree examinations at Oxford or Cambridge; **m. lamp**, a lamp in which the flow of oil to the wick may be regulated. [L. *moderator*].
MODERATORSHIP, [mod'-er-āt-er-ship], *n.* the office of moderator.

MODERN (1), [mod'-ern], *n.* a modernist; one living in modern times; **m. side,** the division in a school which specializes in science and modern languages.

MODERN (2), [mod'-ern], *adj.* pertaining to, or characteristic of, the present; recent; occurring later than the 15th century; up-to-date, fashionable. [L. *modernus*].

MODERNISM, [mod'-ern-izm], *n.* present-day usage and thought; the methods and principles of certain theologians who attempt to re-interpret the Bible in the light of recent ideas and research; their conclusions.

MODERNIST, [mod'-ern-ist], *n.* an admirer of things modern; a supporter of Modernism in religion.

MODERNITY, [mod-ern'-i-ti], *n.* the quality or condition of being modern.

MODERNIZATION, [mod'-ern-iz-ā'-shun], *n.* the act of modernizing; the state or result of being modernized.

MODERNIZE, [mod'-ern-īz], *v.t.* to make modern or adapt to modern taste.

MODERNLY, [mo'-dern-li], *adv.* in modern fashion, with modern things.

MODEST, [mod'-est], *adj.* having a humble estimate of one's capabilities and merits; unassuming; bashful; decent, chaste, exhibiting a sense of propriety and delicacy; not excessive or exaggerated, moderate. [L. *modestus*].

MODESTLY, [mod'-est-li], *adv.* in a modest way.

MODESTY, [mod'-est-i], *n.* the quality of being modest; chastity; sense of delicacy and propriety. [L. *modestia*].

MODICUM, [mod'-ik-um], *n.* a small quantity. [L. *modicum*].

MODIFIABLE, [mod'-i-fī-abl], *adj.* able to be modified.

MODIFICATION, [mod'-if-ik-ā'-shun], *n.* the act of modifying; the state or result of being modified.

MODIFICATIVE (1), [mod'-if-ik-āt'-iv], *n.* something that modifies.

MODIFICATIVE (2), [mod'-if-ik-āt'-iv], *adj.* modificatory.

MODIFICATORY, [mod'-if-ik-āt'-er-i], *adj.* that modifies.

MODIFIER, [mod'-i-fī-er], *n.* someone or something that modifies.

MODIFY, [mod'-i-fī], *v.t.* to moderate, lessen, qualify; to alter; (*philol.*) to change one vowel by the influence of another that follows. [Fr. *modifier*].

MODILLION, [mod-il'-yon], *n.* (*arch.*) one of a series of projecting brackets set beneath the corona of the cornice in the composite Corinthian and Roman Ionic orders. [It. *modiglione*].

MODIOLAR, [mod'-i-ō'-ler], *adj.* (*anat.*) pertaining to the modiolus.

MODIOLUS, [mod'-i-ō'-lus], *n.* (*anat.*) the conical axis round which winds the cochlea. [L. *modiolus* bucket on a water-wheel].

MODISH, [mōd'-ish], *adj.* stylish; fashionable.

MODISHLY, [mōd'-ish-li], *adv.* in a modish way.

MODISHNESS, [mōd'-ish-nes], *n.* the quality of being modish.

MODIST, [mōd'-ist], *n.* a follower of fashion.

MODISTE, [mōd-ēst'], *n.* a milliner or dressmaker. [Fr. *modiste*].

MODULATE, [mod'-yōō-lāt], *v.t. and i.* to adjust, temper, soften; to inflect; to vary in pitch, tone, etc.; (*mus.*) to pass from one key to another. [L. *modulari*].

MODULATION, [mod-yōō-lā'-shun], *n.* the act of modulating the voice, pitch, key, etc.; an example of this; (*elect.*) variation in the amplitude of continuous waves of frequencies below 14,000 cycles per second. [L. *modulatio* rhythmical measure].

MODULATOR, [mod'-yōō-lāt'-er], *n.* someone or something that modulates; a chart to show the relationship of scales and tones in the tonic sol-fa system. [L. *modulator*].

MODULE, [mod'-yōōl], *n.* a unit of measurement; (*arch.*) a unit of length in the classical orders of architecture for indicating the proportions of the building. [L. *modulus* small measure].

MODULUS, [mod'-yōōl-us], *n.* a constant multiplier, a coefficient. [L. *modulus* a small measure].

MODUS, [mōd'-us], *n.* method or manner; **m. agendi,** way of acting; **m. operandi,** way of operating, manner of procedure; **m. vivendi,** way of living; a working agreement pending settlement. [L. *modus*].

MOESO-GOTHIC (1), [mē'-sō-goth'-ik], *n.* the language of the Moeso-Goths.

MOESO-GOTHIC (2), [mē'-sō-goth'-ik], *adj.* of, or pertaining to, the Moeso-Goths.

MOESO-GOTHS, [mē'-sō-goths'], *n.(pl.)* a Teutonic tribe, once inhabitants of the Roman province of Moesia. [L. *Moesia* (Serbia and Bulgaria)].

MOFETTE, [mof-et'], *n.* a fissure in the surface of the earth emitting a noxious gas; the gas so escaping. [It. *mofeta*].

MOFF, [mof], *n.* an instrument consisting of two compasses, a combination of compass and callipers. [Uncert.].

MOFUSSIL, [mō'-fus-il], *n.* the countryside. [Hind. *mufaççil*].

MOGUL (1), [mō'-gul], *n.* a Mongolian follower of Baber or Genghiz Khan in their invasions of India; **the Great M.,** one of the former Emperors of Delhi. [MONGOL].

MOGUL (2), [mō'-gul], *adj.* pertaining to the Mongolian Empire in India.

MOHAIR, [mō'-hāer], *n.* the hair of the Angora goat; a fine silky cloth made from this; an imitation of such a cloth. [Arab. *mukhayyah* a fine goat's-hair cloth].

MOHAMMEDAN (1), MAHOMETAN, [mō-ham'-id-an], *n.* a follower of Mohammed, a Moslem. [Arab. *Muhammad*].

MOHAMMEDAN (2), MAHOMETAN, [mō-ham'-id-an], *adj.* pertaining to Mohammedanism.

MOHAMMEDANISM, [mō-ham'-id-an-izm], *n.* the religion founded by Mohammed.

MOHAMMEDISM, [mō-ham'-ed-izm], *n.* Mohammedanism.

MOHARRAM, MUHARRAM, [mō-hah'-rahm], *n.* the first month of the Mohammedan year; originally a time of mourning in this month observed by the Shiites to commemorate the deaths of Husein and Ali, now a festival. [Arab. *muharram* sacred].

MOHAWK (1), [mō'-hawk], *n.* a member of the tribe of Mohawk Red Indians; their language; a figure in skating. [Native].

MOHAWK (2), [mō'-hawk], *adj.* pertaining to the Mohawk Indians.

MOHICAN (1), [mō'-ik-an], *n.* a member of the Mohicans; their language.

MOHICAN (2), [mō'-ik-an], *adj.* pertaining to the Mohicans or to their language.

MOHICANS, [mō'-ik-anz], *n.(pl.)* a warlike tribe of North American Indians now extinct.

MOHOCK (1), [mō'-hok], *n.* a fashionable, aristocratic ruffian, belonging to a gang which prowled round London streets in the eighteenth century. [MOHAWK].

MOHOCK (2), [mō'-hok], *v.t.* to attack or ill-use in the manner of a mohock.

MOHOCKISM, [mō'-hok-izm], *n.* the tricks and practices of the mohocks.

MOHR, [maw(r)], *n.* the West African gazelle. [Native].

MOHSITE, [mō'-sīt], *n.* crystallized titanate of iron. [F. *Mohs*, the German mineralogist, its discoverer (1773-1839)].

MOHUR, [mō'-hur], *n.* a former Indian gold coin worth fifteen rupees. [Pers. *muhr* coin].

MOIDER, [moid'-er], *v.i.* to toil; to be overcome with heat; to ramble incoherently; to pester. [Uncert.].

MOIDERT, [moid'-ert], *adj.* (*Scots*) dazed, bewildered.

MOIDORE, [moi'-daw(r)'], *n.* a former Portuguese gold coin, worth about 27s. [Portug. *moeda d'ouro* coin of gold].

MOIETY, [moi'-i-ti], *n.* a half; one of two more or less equal parts, a part; (*leg.*) an exact half-share. [OFr. *moité*].

MOIL, [moil], *v.t. and i.* to make wet and dirty; to drudge and toil. [OFr. *moiller* moisten].

MOINEAU, [mwa'-nō], *n.* (*fort.*) a small flat bastion or fortress. [Fr. *moineau*].

MOIRE (1), moiré, [mwah'-rā], *n.* a watered silk; any other material with a similar appearance; a clouded appearance on metals. [Fr. *moiré*].

MOIRE (2), moiré, [mwah'-rā], *adj.* possessing a watered or clouded appearance, *esp.* of silks.

MOIST, [moist], *adj.* somewhat wet, damp, humid. [OFr. *moiste*].

MOISTEN, [moisn], *v.t.* to make moist, to damp.

MOISTENER, [mois'-ner], *n.* something that moistens.

MOISTFUL, [moist'-fōōl], *adj.* full of moisture, wet.

MOISTNESS, [moist'-nes], *n.* the state of being moist.

MOISTURE, [mois'-cher], *n.* moistness; condensed water vapour. [OFr. *moisteur*].

MOISTURELESS, [mois'-cher-les], *adj.* lacking moisture, dry.

MOKE, [mōk], *n.* (*slang*) a donkey. [Unkn.].

MOLAR (1), [mōl'-er], *n.* a large grinding tooth.

MOLAR (2), [mōl'-er], *adj.* capable of grinding. [L. *molaris* relating to a mill].
MOLAR (3), [mōl'-er], *adj.* (*mech.*) pertaining to mass. [L. *moles* a mass].
MOLASSE, [mō-las'], *n.* a soft, greenish, tertiary sandstone. [Fr. *molasse*].
MOLASSES, [mō-las'-iz], *n.* the thick syrup extracted during the manufacture of sugar; a thickish treacle. [Portug. *melaço*].
MOLE (1), [mōl], *n.* a small dark-brown spot on the human body. [OE. *mal*].
MOLE (2), [mōl], *n.* a stone jetty, or breakwater. [L. *moles* mass].
MOLE (3), [mōl], *n.* a small burrowing mammal of the genus *Talpa*, with a thick, blackish-brown velvety fur. [~MDu. *mol*].

MOLE

MOLECAST, [mōl'-kahst], *n.* a molehill.
MOLE-CRICKET, [mōl'-krik'-it], *n.* a burrowing insect of the genus *Gryllotalpa*.
MOLECULAR, [mol-ek'-yōō-ler], *adj.* pertaining to, or consisting of, molecules.
MOLECULARITY, [mol-ek'-yōō-la'-ri-ti], *n.* the state of being molecular.
MOLECULE, [mol'-i-kewl'], *n.* (*chem.*, *phys.*) the smallest particle of a substance, capable of retaining its distinctive properties; a small particle. [Fr. *molécule*].
MOLE-EYED, [mōl'-īd], *adj.* having very small, feeble eyes.
MOLEHILL, [mōl'-hil], *n.* a little hillock of earth thrown up by a mole as it burrows.
MOLE-RAT, [mōl'-rat], *n.* a burrowing rodent of the genus *Spolax*.
MOLE-SHREW, [mōl'-shrōō], *n.* a burrowing insect-eater of the genus *Urotrichus*.
MOLESKIN (1), [mōl'-skin], *n.* the skin of the mole prepared for use as a fur; a strong cotton fustian the pile of which is shaved; (*pl.*) trousers of this.
MOLESKIN (2), [mōl'-skin], *adj.* made of moleskin.
MOLEST, [mo-lest'], *v.t.* to interfere with, pester, annoy by accosting illegally. [L. *molestare*].
MOLESTATION, [mol'-est-ā'-shun], *n.* act of molesting; state of being molested. [L. *molestatio*].
MOLESTER, [mo-lest'-er], *n.* someone who molests.
MOLESTFUL, [mo-lest'-fōōl], *adj.* annoying, troublesome.
MOLETRACK, [mōl'-trak], *n.* the underground course of a mole.
MOLIMEN, [mol'-i-men], *n.* (*med.*) an effort of the system to perform any natural function. [L. *molimen* effort].
MOLINE, [mo-līn'], *adj.* of, or like the extremities of, the iron supporting the upper millstone; **cross m.**, (*her.*) a cross of which the end of each arm is extended into two curves. [OFr. *molin* mill].

CROSS MOLINE

MOLINISM, [mol'-in-izm], *n.* the doctrine that grace is dependent on its free acceptance by the human will. [L. *Molina*, a Spanish Jesuit and its propounder (1535-1600)].
MOLINIST, [mol'-in-ist], *n.* a follower of Luiz Molina.
MOLLIE, MOLLY, [mol'-i], *n.* Mary.
MOLLIENT, [mol'-i-ent], *adj.* softening, soothing. [L. *molliens*].
MOLLIENTLY, [mo'-li-ent-li], *adv.* in soothing fashion.
MOLLIFIABLE, [mol'-i-fī'-abl], *adj.* capable of being mollified.
MOLLIFICATION, [mol'-i-fi-kā'-shun], *n.* the act of having been mollified. [L. *mollificatio*].
MOLLIFIER, [mol'-i-fī'-er], *n.* one who mollifies.
MOLLIFY, [mol'-i-fī], *v.t.* to soften, pacify, soothe. [L. *mollificare*].
MOLLIPILOSITY, [mol'-i-pil-os'-i-ti], *n.* soft plumage, fluffiness. [L. *mollis* soft and PILOSITY].
MOLLUSC, MOLLUSK, [mol'-usk], *n.* an animal of the groups *Mollusca*.
MOLLUSCA, [mol-usk'-a], *n.*(*pl.*) (*biol.*) invertebrates with soft unsegmented bodies, often enclosed in a hard shell; shell-fish. [L. *molluscus* soft-bodied].
MOLLUSCAN (1), [mol-usk'-an], *n.* a mollusc.
MOLLUSCAN (2), [mol-usk'-an], *adj.* pertaining to mollusca.
MOLLUSCOID, [mol-usk'-oid], *adj.* like a mollusc. [MOLLUSC and Gk. *oeides* like].
MOLLUSCOUS, [mol-usk'-us], *adj.* molluscan.
MOLLUSK, see MOLLUSC.
MOLLY, see MOLLIE.
MOLLY-CODDLE (1), [mol'-i-kodl'], *n.* a pampered, effeminate person.
MOLLY-CODDLE (2), [mol'-i-kodl'], *v.t.* to fuss over, pamper.
MOLOCH, [mō'-lok], *n.* the god of the Ammonites to whom living human sacrifices were made; (*fig.*) anything demanding unnatural sacrifice; the Australian lizard, *Moloch horridus*. [Heb. *molek*].
MOLOTOV, [mo'-lo-tof], *n.* the name of a Russian statesman used to denote certain weapons employed in the Soviet-Finnish War of 1940; **M. bread-basket**, a cluster of incendiary bombs; **M. cocktail**, a fuse-operated, petrol bottle-bomb used to hurl at the vulnerable parts of tanks.
MOLTEN, [mōl'-ten], *adj.* made liquid by heat, melted. [OE. *molten*].
MOLTO, [mol'-tō], *adv.* (*mus.*) very. [It. *molto*].
MOLY, [mō'-li], *n.* a fabulous plant that protected Ulysses against the magic of Circe; a species of garlic. [Gk. *molu*].
MOLYBDATE, [mol'-ib-dāt], *n.* (*chem.*) a salt produced by the action of molybdic acid on a base.
MOLYBDENA, [mol-ib'-den-a], *n.* any of various salts and ores of lead.
MOLYBDENITE, [mol-ib'-den-īt], *n.* molybdenum sulphide.
MOLYBDENOUS, [mol-ib'-den-us], *adj.* relating to molybdena.
MOLYBDENUM, [mol-ib'-dēn-um], *n.* (*chem.*) a metallic element, Mo, used as an alloy in steel manufacture. [Gk. *molubdos* lead].
MOLYBDIC, [mol-ib'-dik], *adj.* of, or pertaining to, molybdenum; **m. acid**, an acid containing molybdenum in its higher valency state.
MOME, [mōm], *n.* (*dial.*) a dolt, dullard. [Uncert.].
MOMENT, [mō'-ment], *n.* a brief space of time; an instant; importance; (*mech.*) the measure of the power of a force in causing rotation. [L. *momentum*].
MOMENTARILY, [mō'-ment-er-i-li], *adv.* for a moment.
MOMENTARY, [mō'-ment-er-i], *adj.* instantaneous; lasting a very short time; short and quick.
MOMENTLY, [mō'-ment-li], *adv.* momentarily, every moment.
MOMENTOUS, [mō-ment'-us], *adj.* important, weighty, of moment.
MOMENTOUSLY, [mō-ment'-us-li], *adv.* in momentous fashion.
MOMENTOUSNESS, [mō-ment'-us-nes], *n.* the quality of being momentous.
MOMENTUM, [mō-ment'-um], *n.* the force given to a moving body by its motion; (*dynamics*) the product of mass and velocity; (*fig.*) progressive increase in effect. [L. *momentum* movement].
MOMUS, [mōm'-us], *n.* the Greek god of ridicule; a fault-finding, finical critic. [Gk. *momos*].
MON-, see MONO-.
MONACHAL, [mon'-ak-al], *adj.* relating to monks; monastic. [EcclesL. *monachalis*].
MONACHISM, [mon'-ak-izm], *n.* monasticism, monastic life.
MONAD, [mon'-ad], *n.* an organic unit; (*zool.*) a hypothetical, elementary organism; (*chem.*) an element having the combining power of one atom of hydrogen; (*philos.*) one of the simple individual entities of which the universe is made up, according to Leibnitz. [L. *monas monadis* unit].
MONADELPHIAN, [mon'-a-delf'-i-an], *adj.* (*bot.*) having the stamens united in a single bundle.
MONADELPHOUS, [mon'-a-delf'-us], *adj.* monadelphian. [MONO and Gk. *adelphos* brother].
MONADIC, [mon-ad'-ik], *adj.* having the nature of a monad.
MONADISM, [mon'-ad-izm], *n.* (*philos.*) the theory of monads expounded by Leibnitz.
MONAL, [mōn'-al], *n.* an Eastern pheasant of gorgeous plumage, of the genus *Lophophorus*. [Hind. *monal*].
MONANDRIAN, [mon-an'-dri-an], *adj.* (*bot.*) having only one stamen.
MONANDROUS, [mon-an'-drus], *adj.* (*bot.*) monandrian; having only one husband.
MONANDRY, [mon-an'-dri], *n.* marriage to only

one husband at a time; (*bot.*) the state of having only one stamen. [MONO and Gk. *aner andros* man].

MONANTHOUS, [mon-an'-thus], *adj.* (*bot.*) productive of only one flower. [MONO and Gk. *anthos* flower].

MONARCH, [mon'-ak], *n.* a supreme hereditary ruler or head of a state; a king, an emperor; someone or something that dominates all others. [L. *monarcha*].

MONARCHAL, [mon-ahk'-al], *adj.* relating to a monarch.

MONARCHIAN (1), [mon-ahk'-i-an], *n.* one who supported the heresy of Monarchianism.

MONARCHIAN (2), [mon-ahk'-i-an], *adj.* pertaining to Monarchianism.

MONARCHIANISM, [mon-ahk'-i-an-izm], *n.* a heresy of the second and third centuries denying the doctrine of the Trinity.

MONARCHIC, [mon-ahk'-ik], *adj.* pertaining to monarchy or a monarch; royal.

MONARCHICAL, [mon-ahk'-ik-al], *adj.* monarchic.

MONARCHISM, [mon'-ak-izm], *n.* the principles of monarchy.

MONARCHIST, [mon'-ak-ist], *n.* an advocate or supporter of monarchy, a royalist.

MONARCHIZE, [mon'-ak-īz], *v.t. and i.* to rule like a king; to make a monarchy of.

MONARCHY, [mon'-ak-i], *n.* a state ruled by a single person, *esp.* a king; the rule of a monarch; the idea of kingly rule. [Gk. *monarkhia*].

MONASTERIAL, [mon'-as-tēer'-i-al], *adj.* relating to a monastery.

MONASTERY, [mon'-as-tri], *n.* the abode of a community of monks. [EcclesL. *monasterium*].

MONASTIC (1), [mon-ast'-ik], *n.* a monk.

MONASTIC (2), [mon-ast'-ik], *adj.* monastical.

MONASTICAL, [mon-ast'-ik-al], *adj.* pertaining to a monastery or to monks and their way of living.

MONASTICALLY, [mon-ast'-ik-al-i], *adv.* in monastic fashion.

MONASTICISM, [mon-ast'-is-izm], *n.* monastic life and thought.

MONASTICIZE, [mon-ast'-is-īz], *v.t.* to convert to monasticism.

MONASTICON, [mon-ast'-ik-on], *n.* a book about monasteries. [Gk. *monastikon*].

MONATOMIC, [mon'-a-tom'-ik], *adj.* consisting of a single atom.

MONAZITE, [mon'-az-īt], *n.* cerium phosphates, red or brown in colour. [Germ. *monazit*].

MONDAINE, [mon-dān'], *n.* a stylish woman. [Fr. *mondaine* worldly].

MONDAY, [mun'-di], *n.* the second day of the week. [OE. *monandæg* Monday, the day of the moon].

MONDAYISH, [mun'-di-ish], *adj.* unsettled; disinclined for work after the week-end.

MONDE, [maw(n)d], *n.* the fashionable world, society. [Fr. *monde* world].

MONDIAL, [mon'-di-al], *adj.* world-wide. [Fr. *mondial*].

MONETARY, [mun'-i-ter-i], *adj.* of, or pertaining to, money or currency. [L. *monetarius*].

MONETIZATION, [mun'-it-iz-ā'-shun], *n.* the act of monetizing.

MONETIZE, [mun'-it-īz], *v.t.* to give a basic value to a currency; to coin into money, authorize as money.

MONEY, [mun'-i], *n.* a piece of metal authoritatively stamped for use as a medium of exchange; any material, *esp.* engraved and watermarked paper notes, authorized for a similar use; wealth, riches; **to make m.**, to become rich. [OFr. *monaie*].

MONEY-BAGS, [mu'-ni-bagz], *n.* (*slang*) a wealthy (*esp.* miserly) person.

MONEY-BOX, [mun'-i-boks], *n.* a receptacle for keeping money or for storing savings.

MONEY-BROKER, [mun'-i-brōk'-er], *n.* a changer of money.

MONEY-CHANGER, [mun'-i-chānj'-er], *n.* one who deals in money, *esp.* one who changes the currency of one country for that of another.

MONEYED, [mun'-id], *adj.* rich.

MONEYER, [mun'-i-er], *n.* one who coins money, a minter.

MONEY-FLOWER, [mun'-i-flow'-er], *n.* (*bot.*) the plant honesty, *Lunaria biennis*.

MONEYGRUBBER, [mun'-i-grub-er], *n.* an avaricious hoarder of wealth.

MONEYLENDER, [mun'-i-lend'-er], *n.* one who lends money at interest.

MONEYLENDING, [mun'-i-lend'-ing], *n.* a moneylender's trade.

MONEYLESS, [mun'-i-les], *adj.* without money.

MONEYMAKING, [mun'-i-māk'-ing], *adj.* highly profitable, lucrative.

MONEY-MARKET, [mun'-i-mahk'-et], *n.* the sphere of commercial and monetary transactions.

MONEY MATTER, [mun'-i-mat'-er], *n.* a financial transaction; (*pl.*) the financial aspect of things.

MONEY ORDER, [mun'-i-aw'-der], *n.* a post-office cash token authorizing the payment of money to the recipient at a particular post-office.

MONEY-SPIDER, [mun'-i-spīd'-er], *n.* the money-spinner.

MONEYSPINNER, [mun'-i-spin'-er], *n.* *Aranca scenica*, a small spider considered to bring luck.

MONEY'S-WORTH, [mun'-iz-wurth'], *n.* full value.

MONEYWORT, [mun'-i-wurt], *n.* (*bot.*) *Lysimachia Nummularia*, the plant creeping-jenny.

MONGER, [mung'-ger], *n.* a dealer, trafficker. [OE. *mangere* merchant].

MONGOL (1), [mon'-gol], *n.* a Mongolian.

MONGOL (2), [mon'-gol], *adj.* Mongolian.

MONGOLIAN (1), [mon-gō'-li-an], *n.* a native of Mongolia; his language. [*Mongolia*, in Central Asia].

MONGOLIAN (2), [mon-gō'-li-an], *adj.* pertaining to Mongolia, its people, culture or language; **M. imbecile**, an imbecile with broadened Mongol-like skull.

MONGOLISM, [mong'-gol-izm], *n.* (*path.*) the occurrence of Mongolian imbecility.

MONGOOSE, MUNGOOSE, (*pl.* **mongooses**), [mung'-gōōs], *n.* (*zool.*) the ichneumon, a small ferret-like Indian animal, related to the civet. [Tamil *mangus*].

MONGREL (1), [mung'-grel], *n.* the result of the crossing of two breeds or kinds of animals or plants; *esp.* a dog of mixed breed. [Uncert.].

MONGREL (2), [mung'-grel], *adj.* of mixed breed.

MONGRELIZE, [mung'-grel-īz], *v.t.* to make mongrel.

MONILIFORM, [mon-il'-i-fawm], *adj.* resembling a necklace. [L. *monile* necklace and FORM (1)].

MONISM, [mon'-izm], *n.* (*philos.*) the belief which regards all phenomena as developed from a single principle. [Gk. *monos* single].

MONISTIC, [mon-ist'-ik], *adj.* relating to monism.

MONITION, [mon-ish'-un], *n.* admonition or warning, *esp.* from an ecclesiastical authority to refrain from some specific conduct. [L. *monitio*].

MONITIVE, [mon'-it-iv], *adj.* warning.

MONITOR (1), [mon'-it-er], *n.* one who admonishes or advises; a senior pupil chosen to perform special duties in school or class-room; a heavily armed warship, with large guns mounted in turrets; a large lizard of the genus *Varanus*; one employed to listen to foreign wireless broadcasts. [L. *monitor*].

MONITOR (2), [mon'-it-er], *v.t.* to listen to (wireless broadcasts) in order to check any deviation from the allotted wavelength; to listen to (foreign broadcasts) for the purpose of using or recording the matter broadcast.

MONITORIAL, [mon'-it-aw'-ri-al], *adj.* pertaining to monitors; warning, admonishing.

MONITORIALLY, [mon'-it-aw'-ri-al-i], *adv.* in the manner of a monitor.

MONITORING, [mon'-it-er-ing], *n.* the act or practice of one who monitors.

MONITORY (1), [mon'-it-er-i], *n.* (*eccles.*) a letter of admonition from an ecclesiastical superior.

MONITORY (2), [mon'-it-er-i], *adj.* giving advice or warning.

MONITRESS, [mon'-it-res], *n.* a female monitor.

MONK, [mungk], *n.* a member of a religious order of men vowed to poverty, chastity, etc., and living a life of contemplation and good works in a community apart from the world; (*hist.*) a religious hermit [OE. *munuc* from L. *monachus*].

MONKERY, [mungk'-er-i], *adv.* pertaining to monasticism, to a monastery or to monks.

MONKEY (1), [mungk'-i], *n.* a mammal of the order Primates, other than man and the lemurs, *esp.* a tailed member of this order; (*fig.*) a mischievous child; the striker of a pile-driver; a bricklayer's hod; (*slang*) a mortgage; (*slang*) £500 or $500; **to get (someone's) m. up**, to anger. [Uncert.].

MONKEY (2), [mungk'-i], *v.t. and i.* to mimic; to play about with.

MONKEY-BARGE, [mungk'-i-bahj'], *n.* a narrow boat for use in canals.

MONKEY-BLOCK, [mungk'-i-blok'], *n.* (*naut.*) a single block strapped to a swivel.

MONKEY-BOAT, [mungk'-i-bōt'], *n.* a half-decked boat for river use.

MONKEY-BREAD, [mungk'-i-bred'], *n.* the fruit of the baobab tree, *Adansonia digitata.*
MONKEY-FACE, [mungk'-i-fās'], *n.* a face like that of a monkey; a person with such a face.
MONKEY-FACED, [mungk'-i-fāst'], *adj.* having a monkey-face.
MONKEY-FLOWER, [mungk'-i-flow'-er], *n.* a plant of the genus *Mimulus*, the flower of which resembles the face of a monkey.
MONKEY-GAFF, [mungk'-i-gaf'], *n.* (*naut.*) a gaff on a top-mast.
MONKEYISH, [mungk'-i-ish], *adj.* mischievous and impudently playful.
MONKEYISM, [mungk'-i-izm], *n.* resemblance to a monkey.
MONKEY-JACKET, [mungk'-i-jak'-it], *n.* a small, close-fitting jacket worn by seamen.
MONKEY-NUT, [mungk'-i-nut'], *n.* a peanut.
MONKEY-POT, [mungk'-i-pot'], *n.* the seed-vessel of the Brazilian tree, *Lecythis ollaria*; the tree itself.
MONKEY-PUZZLE, [mungk'-i-puzl'], *n.* the *Araucaria imbricata* or Chilean pine, so covered with prickles that no monkey can climb it.
MONKEY-RAIL, [mungk'-i-rāl'], *n.* (*naut.*) the small rail over the quarter-rail.
MONKEY-WRENCH, [mungk'-i-rensh'], *n.* a spanner having an adjustable grip.

MONKEY-WRENCH

MONK-FISH, [mungk'-fish], *n.* the *Lophius piscatorus* or angler fish; the *Rhina squatina* or angel fish.
MONKHOOD, [mungk'-hōōd], *n.* the state, status or character of a monk; monks collectively.
MONKISH, [mungk'-ish], *adj.* pertaining to, like, a monk or his way of life.
MONKISM, [mungk'-izm], *n.* monasticism.
MONK-SEAL, [mungk'-sēl], *n.* a variety of seal, *Monachus albiventer.*
MONKSHOOD, [mungks'-hōōd], *n.* the flower, *Aconitum Napellus*, so called from the appearance of its flowers.
MONK'S-SEAM, [mungks'-sēm], *n.* (*naut.*) a seam made by laying the selvedges of sails one above the other.
MONO-, MON-, *pref.* single, alone. [Gk. *monos*].
MONOBASIC, [mon'-ō-bās'-ik], *adj.* (*chem.*) having one base; (of an acid) having one basic radicle equivalent in combination to one hydrogen atom.
MONOCARDIAN, [mon'-ō-kahd'-i-an], *adj.* possessing a single heart. [MONO and Gk. *kardia* heart].
MONOCARP, [mon'-ō-kahp], *n.* (*bot*.) a monocarpic plant, an annual plant. [MONO and Gk. *karpos* fruit].
MONOCARPIC, [mon'-ō-kahp'-ik], *adj.* (*bot.*) bearing fruit once.
MONOCARPOUS, [mon'-ō-kahp'-us], *adj.* (*bot.*) bearing seed in a single ovary; monocarpic.
MONOCEPHALOUS, [mon'-ō-sef'-al-us], *adj.* having only one head. [Gk. *monokephalos*].
MONOCEROS, [mon-os'-er-os], *n.* an animal with one horn. [L. *monoceros*].
MONOCHLAMYDEOUS, [mon'-ō-klam-id'-i-us], *adj.* (*bot.*) having one floral envelope or one perianth. [MONO and Gk. *khlamus* cloak].
MONOCHORD, [mon'-ō-kawd], *n.* an instrument with a single string, used for the scientific measurement of musical intervals. [Gk. *monokhordon*].
MONOCHROMATIC, [mon'-ō-krōm-at'-ik], *adj.* in one colour.
MONOCHROME, [mon'-ō-krōm], *n.* a painting in a single colour. [MedL. *monochroma*].
MONOCLE, [mon'-okl], *n.* an eye-glass for one eye. [Fr. *monocle*].
MONOCLINAL, [mon'-ō-klīn'-al], *adj.* (*geol.*) sloping in the same direction. [MONO and Gk. *klino* I slope].
MONOCLINATE, [mon'-ō-klīn'-āt], *adj.* (*min.*) monoclinic.
MONOCLINIC, [mon'-ō-klin'-ik], *adj.* (of a crystal) having three unequal axes, two of which intersect at right angles, the third intersecting one of these at right angles and the other at some other angle. [Fr. *monoclinique*].
MONOCLINOUS, [mon'-ō-klīn'-us], *adj.* (*bot.*) with pistils and stamens in the same flower, hermaphrodite. [MdL. *monoclinus*].
MONOCOTYLEDON, [mon'-ō-kot'-i-lē'-don], *n.* (*bot.*) a plant with one seed-leaf in the embryo.
MONOCOTYLEDONOUS, [mon'-ō-kot'-i-lē'-don-us], *adj.* with one cotyledon.
MONOCRACY, [mon-ok'-ra-si], *n.* government by one person. [MONO and Gk. *kratia* rule].
MONOCRAT, [mon'-ō-krat], *n.* an absolute ruler.
MONOCULAR, [mon-ok'-yōō-ler], *adj.* with, or for, one eye only.
MONOCULOUS, [mon-ok'-yōō-lus], *adj.* monocular.
MONODACTYLOUS, [mon'-ō-dak'-til-us], *adj.* having only one finger, claw, or toe. [Gk. *monodaktulos*].
MONODIC, [mon-ōd'-ik], *adj.* relating to, of the nature of a monody; (*mus.*) for a single voice. [Gk. *monodikos*].
MONODIST, [mon'-od-ist], *n.* a writer or singer of monodies.
MONODRAMA, [mon'-ō-drah'-ma], *n.* a play requiring only one performer.
MONODRAMATIC, [mon'-ō-dram-at'-ik], *adj.* pertaining to a monodrama.
MONODY, [mon'-o-di], *n.* an ode sung by one actor in a Greek tragedy; a poem of lament, usually for a death; (*mus.*) a composition for a single voice; the art of composing in this way. [Gk. *monoidia*].
MONOECIOUS, [mon-ē'-shus], *adj.* (*bot.*, *zool.*) with both male and female organs of sex in the same individual. [MONO and Gk. *oikos* house].
MONOGAMIST, [mon-og'-am-ist], *n.* a believer in or practiser of monogamy.
MONOGAMOUS, [mon-og'-am-us], *adj.* having a single living husband or wife.
MONOGAMY, [mon-og'-a-mi], *n.* the practice of marriage to only one wife or one husband at one time. [MONO and Gk. *gamos* marriage].
MONOGENESIS, [mon'-ō-jen'-is-is], *n.* derivation from a single cell; the theory that all living organisms are so derived.
MONOGONY, [mon-og'-on-i], *n.* non-sexual propagation; propagation by fission. [MONO and Gk. *gonia* begetting].
MONOGRAM, [mon'-ō-gram'], *n.* a device or cipher composed of two or more letters interwoven. [Gk. *monogramma*].
MONOGRAPH, [mon'-ō-graf], *n.* a piece of writing confined to one subject or to one aspect of a subject.
MONOGRAPHER, [mon-og'-ra-fer], *n.* a writer of a monograph.
MONOGRAPHIC, [mon'-ō-graf'-ik], *adj.* relating to a monograph.
MONOGRAPHIST, [mon-og'-raf-ist], *n.* a monographer.
MONOGYNIAN, [mon'-ō-jin'-i-an], *adj.* monogynous.
MONOGYNOUS, [mon-oj'-in-us], *adj.* (*bot.*) with only one pistil; practising monogyny. [MONO and Gk. *gune* woman].
MONOGYNY, [mon-oj'-i-ni], *n.* marriage to one wife only. [MONO and Gk. *gune* woman].
MONOLITH, [mon'-ō-lith], *n.* a monument consisting of a single stone. [Gk. *monolithos* made of one stone.]
MONOLITHIC, [mon'-ō-lith'-ik], *adj.* of a single stone.
MONOLOGIST, [mon-ol'-oj-ist], *n.* one who soliloquizes; one who monopolizes conversation.
MONOLOGUE, [mon'-ō-log'], *n.* a dramatic composition or recitation for one performer; a long speech by one person, *esp.* in a play or in social conversation. [Gk. *monologos* speaking alone].
MONOLOGUIST, [mon'-ō-log-ist], *n.* one fond of or skilled in, delivering monologues.
MONOLOGY, [mon-ol'-o-ji], *n.* the trick or habit of soliloquizing. [Gk. *monologia*].
MONOMACHY, [mon-om'-a-ki], *n.* a single combat. [L. *monomachia*].
MONOMANIA, [mon'-ō-mā'-ni-a], *n.* mental derangement with regard to one particular subject. [MONO and Gk. *mania* madness].
MONOMANIAC, [mon'-ō-mā'-ni-ak], *n.* a person suffering from monomania.
MONOMARK, [mon'-ō-mahk], *n.* (*prot.*) a registered identification mark.
MONOMEROUS, [mon-om'-er-us], *adj.* (*bot.*) having single joints. [Gk. *monomerus*].
MONOMETALLIC, [mon'-ō-met-al'-ik], *adj.* (of a currency) standardized or based upon one metal.
MONOMETALLISM, [mon'-ō-met'-al-izm], *n.* the use of a monometallic currency system.
MONOMETALLIST, [mon'-ō-met'-al-ist], *n.* one who advocates monometallism.
MONOMETER, [mon-om'-it-er], *n.* (*pros.*) a line in verse consisting of a single metre or measure.

MONOMETRIC, [mon'-ō-met'-rik], *adj.* (*pros.*) written throughout in one metre.

MONOMETRICAL, [mon'-ō-met'-rik-al], *adj.* monometric.

MONOMIAL, [mon-ō'-mi-al], *adj.* (*alg.*) of one term only. [MONO and (BINO)MIAL].

MONOMORPHIC, [mon'-ō-mawf'-ik], *adj.* constant in shape through the different stages of development. [MONO and Gk. *morphe* shape].

MONOMORPHOUS, [mon'-ō-mawf'-us], *adj.* monomorphic. [MONO and Gk. *morphe* shape].

MONOPATHIC, [mon'-ō-path'-ik], *adj.* (*med.*) affected in, or affecting, only one organ.

MONOPATHY, [mon-op'-ath-i], *n.* (*med.*) a disease or derangement affecting a single function or organ only. [MONO and Gk. *patheia* suffering].

MONOPETALOUS, [mon'-ō-pet'-al-us], *adj.* (*bot.*) having the corolla undivided.

MONOPHOBIA, [mon'-ō-fō'-bi-a], *n.* dread of being left alone.

MONOPHTHONG, [mon'-of-thong], *n.* a single vowel. [MONO and Gk. *phthongos* the voice of men].

MONOPHTHONGAL, [mon'-of-thong'-gal], *adj.* having a single vowel sound.

MONOPHYLLOUS, [mon-of'-il-us], *adj.* (*bot.*) consisting of a single leaf. [MONO and Gk. *phullon* leaf].

MONOPHYSITE, [mon-of'-i-sīt], *n.* one who believes that there is only one nature in the person of Jesus Christ. [Gk. *monophusites*].

MONOPLANE, [mon'-ō-plān], *n.* an aeroplane with one plane.

MONOPODIAL, [mon'-ō-pō'-di-al], *adj.* (*bot.*) (of a plant) having a continuous straight main stem that rises above its lateral branches. [MONO and Gk. *pous podos* foot].

MONOPLANE

MONOPOLISM, [mon-op'-ol-izm], *n.* the system of monopoly.

MONOPOLIST, [mon-op'-ol-ist], *n.* one who has a monopoly, or who believes in monopolism.

MONOPOLIZATION, [mon-op'-ol-īz-ā'-shun], *n.* the act of monopolizing; the fact of having been monopolized.

MONOPOLIZE, [mon-op'-ol-īz], *v.t.* to dominate, to gain exclusive possession of, control of, *esp.* for the purposes of trade.

MONOPOLIZER, [mon-op'-ol-īz-er], *n.* a monopolist.

MONOPOLY, [mon-op'-ol-i], *n.* exclusive rights of trade in an article or in certain goods, granted by authority; a licence authorizing this; the persons enjoying this privilege; the goods in question; exclusive possession, enjoyment, or control. [Gk. *monopolion*].

MONOPTERAL, [mon-opt'-er-al], *adj.* (*zool.*) having one wing.

MONOPTERON, [mon-opt'-er-on], *n.* a circular temple or shrine consisting of a dome supported on a ring of columns. [MONO and Gk. *pteron* a wing].

MONORAIL, [mon'-ō-rāl], *n.* a railway in which the carriages run balanced on a single rail. [MONO and RAIL (1)].

MONORGANIC, [mon'-aw-gan'-ik], *adj.* affecting only one organ.

MONORHYME, [mon'-ō-rīm], *n.* a composition in which every line ends with the same rhyme.

MONOSEPALOUS, [mon'-ō-sep'-al-us], *adj.* (*bot.*) having only one lateral sepal.

MONOSPERMOUS, [mon'-ō-spurm'-us], *adj.* (*bot.*) having only one seed. [MONO and Gk. *sperma* seed].

MONOSPHERICAL, [mon'-ō-sfe'-rikl], *adj.* consisting of only one sphere.

MONOSTICH, [mon'-ō-stich], *n.* (*pros.*) a metrical composition of one line only. [MONO and Gk. *stikhos* a row].

MONOSTROPHE, [mon'-ō-strōf'-i], *n.* (*pros.*) a monostrophic metrical composition.

MONOSTROPHIC, [mon'-ō-strof'-ik], *adj.* (*pros.*) consisting of strophes of identical form.

MONOSTYLE, [mon'-ō-stīl], *adj.* (*arch.*) built in one style throughout; having only one shaft, column, or pillar.

MONOSYLLABIC, [mon'-ō-sil-ab'-ik], *adj.* of one syllable.

MONOSYLLABLE, [mon'-ō-sil'-abl], *n.* a word consisting of one syllable only.

MONOTHALAMOUS, [mon'-ō-thal'-am-us], *adj.* having one chamber only. [MONO and Gk. *thalamos* bedchamber].

MONOTHEISM, [mon'-ō-thē'-izm], *n.* the doctrine that there is only one God.

MONOTHEIST, [mon'-ō-thē'-ist], *n.* one who believes in monotheism.

MONOTHEISTIC, [mon'-ō-thē-ist'-ik], *adj.* relating to monotheism.

MONOTINT, [mon'-ō-tint], *n.* a monochrome.

MONOTOME, [mon'-ō-tōm], *adj.* in one volume.

MONOTOMOUS, [mon-ot'-om-us], *adj.* (*min.*) having cleavage distinct in one direction only.

MONOTONE (1), [mon'-ō-tōn], *n.* one pitch or tone; a singing or speaking without variation of pitch; (*fig.*) sameness of manner; steady repetition.

MONOTONE (2), [mon'-ō-tōn], *v.t.* and *i.* to sing or speak without variation of pitch or tone.

MONOTONIC, [mon'-ō-ton'-ik], *adj.* at one pitch, monotonous.

MONOTONOUS, [mon-ot'-on-us], *adj.* persisting on the same unvaried note; (*fig.*) dully repetitive, boring, irksome in its lack of variety. [Gk. *monotonos*].

MONOTONOUSLY, [mon-ot'-on-us-li], *adv.* in monotonous fashion.

MONOTONOUSNESS, [mon-ot'-on-us-nes], *n.* the quality of being monotonous.

MONOTONY, [mon-ot'-o-ni], *n.* absence of variety of pitch or tone; (*fig.*) irksome sameness, dull uniformity. [Gk. *monotonia*].

MONOTREMATA, [mon'-ō-trē'-mat-a], *n.*(*pl.*) mammals with only one external vent for urinary, sexual, and excretory organs. [MONO and Gk. *trema* hole].

MONOTREMATOUS, [mon'-ō-trē'-mat-us], *adj.* like, or pertaining to, monotremata.

MONOTREME, [mon'-ō-trēm], *n.* one of the monotremata.

MONOTRIGLYPH, [mon'-ō-trī'-glif], *n.* (*arch.*) having only one triglyph but two metopes over an intercolumniation. [L. *monotriglyphos*].

MONOTYPE, [mon'-ō-tīp], *n.* (*biol.*) the only type or representative; (*print.*) a type-setting machine in which each letter is cast and set separately as required.

MONOTYPIC, [mon-ō-tip'-ik], *adj.* (*biol.*) consisting of only one type or species.

MONOX, [mon'-oks], *n.* the crowberry plant, *Empetrum nigrum*. [Unkn.].

MONOXIDE, [mon-oks'-īd], *n.* an oxide with only one atom of oxygen.

MONROEISM, [mun-rō'-izm], *n.* the principle enunciated by James Monroe, that his country should not tolerate any further interference on the American mainland by European Powers. [J. *Monroe* (1758-1831), President of the U.S.A. 1817-1825].

MONSEIGNEUR, [mon-sān-yur'], *n.* a French title of address to princes, cardinals and certain other high ecclesiastical dignitaries. [Fr. *monseigneur*].

MONSIEUR, [m(e)s-yur'], *n.* the French form of address to a man; a polite form of address corresponding to "Sir"; (*hist.*) the title of the second brother or second son of the king of France. [Fr. *monsieur*].

MONSIGNOR, [mon-sēn'-yor], *n.* a courtesy title granted by the Pope, *esp.* to officers of the Papal household. [It. *monsignore*].

MONSOON, [mon-sōōn'], *n.* a wind blowing over Southern Asia and the Indian Ocean from October to April from the north-east and from April to October from the south-west; a similar type of seasonal wind; the rainy season. [MdDu. *monssoen*].

MONSTER (1), [mon'-ster], *n.* a monstrosity, a congenitally malformed creature or plant; a legendary beast, either part human or part brute, or part one beast and part another; a strange, huge animal; anything unusually big; a person displaying brutish malice or cruelty. [OFr. *monstre*].

MONSTER (2), [mon'-ster], *adj.* huge, abnormally big, enormous.

MONSTRANCE, [mon'-strants], *n.* a transparent receptacle in which the Host is shown, or in which relics are exhibited. [OFr. *monstrance*].

MONSTROSITY, [mon-stros'-i-ti], *n.* an abnormal growth or product, a freak of nature; the condition or quality of being monstrous; an atrocious object; outrageous conduct. [LL. *monstruositas*].

MONSTROUS, [mon'-strus], *adj.* enormous; horrible; malformed; unnatural; wicked in the extreme. [LL. *monstruosus*].

MONSTROUSLY, [mon'-strus-li], *adv.* in monstrous fashion.

MONSTROUSNESS, [mon'-strus-nes], *n.* the quality of being monstrous.

MONTAGE, [mont'-ahzh], *n.* the final choice of photographs and their arrangement to form a cinematograph film; the art of film cutting; the art or act of combining photographs into one picture. [Fr. *montage*].

MONTANE, [mon'-tān], *adj.* mountainous; associated with or dwelling in mountains. [L. *montanus*].

MONTANISM, [mon'-tan-izm], *n.* a Christian heresy originated by Montanus in the second century.

MONT-DE-PIETE, mont-de-piété, [mawn'-de-pyā'-tā], *n.* a state-supervised French pawnshop operating primarily for the relief of the poor. [Fr. *mont-de-piété*].

MONTE, [mon'-ti], *n.* a South American card game. [Span. *monte* mountain].

MONTEFIASCONE, [mon'-tā-fi-as'-kō-nā], *n.* an Italian wine. [*Montefiascone*, an Italian town].

MONTEITH, [mon-tēth'], *n.* a bowl with a scalloped rim, used in the eighteenth century to cool punch glasses in water. [Uncert.].

MONTEM, [mon'-tem], *n.* an obsolete custom at Eton College in which scholars in fancy dress climbed a hill near Slough on Whit-Tuesday and collected money from passers-by. [L. (*ad*) *montem* (to) the hill].

MONTENEGRIN (1), [mon'-tin-ē'-grin], *n.* a native of Montenegro.

MONTENEGRIN (2), [mon'-tin-ē'-grin], *adj.* pertaining to Montenegro, its people, culture and language.

MONTERO, [mon-tāer'-ō], *n.* a Spanish riding cap. [Span. *montero* a hunter].

MONTESSORIAN, [mon'-ti-saw'-ri-an], *adj.* pertaining to the Montessori system of infant education.

MONTESSORI SYSTEM, [mon'-ti-saw'-ri-sis'-tem], *n.* the system of infant teaching based on self-education, evolved by Madame *Montessori*, the Italian educationalist.

MONTEUR, [mon-tur'], *n.* a person who arranges artificial flowers for trimmings and decorations. [Fr. *monteur*].

MONTH, [munth], *n.* one of the twelve sections which together make up a year; a period of time corresponding to any one of these; the time taken to complete one revolution of the moon; a period of four weeks. [OE. *monath*].

MONTHLING, [munth'-ling], *n.* a child or animal one month old.

MONTHLY (1), [munth'-li], *n.* a publication appearing once a month; a plant which blooms each month; (*pl.*) menses.

MONTHLY (2), [munth'-li], *adj.* occurring, repeated month by month; **m. nurse,** a female attendant on women during childbirth.

MONTHLY (3), [munth'-li], *adv.* every month, once a month, month by month.

MONTICLE, [mont'-ikl], *n.* a hillock. [LL. *monticulus* little hill].

MONTICULATE, [mont-ik'-yōō-lāt], *adj.* bearing small projections.

MONTICULOSE, [mont-ik'-yōō-lōs], *adj.* monticulate. [MedL. *monticulosus*].

MONTON, [mont'-on], *n.* a heap of ore. [Span. *monton* a heap].

MONTURE, [mont'-ewr], *n.* the setting or frame upon which anything is mounted. [Fr. *monture*].

MONUMENT, [mon'-yōō-ment], *n.* a memorial, an erection to commemorate some event or person; a building or other relic of enduring historic interest and value; a great achievement felt to be of permanent value. [L. *monumentum*].

MONUMENTAL, [mon'-yōō-ment'-al], *adj.* relating to, serving as, a monument; of the nature of a monument; vast, impressive; **m. mason,** an engraver of tombstones.

MONUMENTALLY, [mon'-yōō-ment'-al-i], *adv.* in a monumental fashion.

MOO (1), [mōō], *n.* the call of a cow, a low. [Echoic].

MOO (2), [mōō], *v.i.* to low or call like a cow.

MOOCH, MOUCH, [mōōch], *v.i.* to loiter, to idle about; **to m. along,** to saunter leisurely. [OFr. *muchier* to slink].

MOOCHER, MOUCHER, [mōōch'-er], *n.* a skulker, loiterer.

MOO-COW, [mōō'-kow], *n.* name for a cow, used in speaking to children. [MOO (2) and COW (1)].

MOOD (1), [mōōd], *n.* a temporary frame of mind or emotional disposition; **to be in the m. for,** to feel like. [OE. *mod* mind, heart, courage].

MOOD (2), [mōōd], *n.* (*gram.*) a variation in the form of a verb to express the aspect in which the act or fact denoted by the verb is regarded; (*logic*) the nature or form of a syllogism; (*mus.*) mode. [MODE].

MOODILY, [mōōd'-i-li], *adv.* in a moody way.

MOODINESS, [mōōd'-i-nes], *n.* the quality or condition of being moody.

MOODY, [mōōd'-i], *adj.* subject to varying moods, temperamental; disgruntled, bad tempered, sullen. [OE. *modig* brave].

MOOLVIE, [mōōl'-vē], *n.* a learned Mohammedan teacher. [Hind. *mulvi*].

MOON (1), [mōōn], *n.* the satellite of, and which revolves about, the earth; the satellite of another planet; a lunar month, four weeks; (*fig.*) an object or ideal impossible to attain; **the man in the m.,** the markings visible on the surface of the full moon; **once in a blue m.,** very rarely. [OE. *mona*].

MOON (2), [mōōn], *v.i.* to loiter dreamily; **to m. about,** to wander about in an absorbed, aimless or unhappy manner.

MOONBEAM, [mōōn'-bēm], *n.* a ray of light reflected from the moon.

MOON-BLINDNESS, [mōōn'-blīnd'-nes], *n.* moon-eye.

MOONCALF, [mōōn'-kahf], *n.* a misshapen creature or abortion; a dolt.

MOON-DAISY, [mōōn'-dā'-zi], *n.* the ox-eye daisy, *Chrysanthemum leucanthemum*.

MOONET, [mōōn'-et], *n.* a little moon.

MOON-EYE, [mōōn'-ī], *n.* an intermittent affection of the eyes of horses; a North American freshwater fish, *Hyodon tergisus*, the goldeye.

MOON-EYED, [mōōn'-īd], *adj.* having large, open, expressionless eyes; suffering from moon-eye.

MOONFACE, [mōōn'-fās], *n.* a round, full, moon-like face.

MOON-FISH, [mōōn'-fish], *n.* any of several species of fish having the tail-fin shaped like a crescent-moon.

MOONFLOWER, [mōōn'-flow'-er], *n.* the ox-eye daisy; the climbing plant, *Ipomœa bona-nox*.

MOONISH, [mōōn'-ish], *adj.* changeable and fickle, like the moon.

MOONLESS, [mōōn'-les], *adj.* without moonlight or moon.

MOONLIGHT (1), [mōōn'-līt], *n.* the light of the moon.

MOONLIGHT (2), [mōōn'-līt], *adj.* lit by the moon; carried out at night.

MOONLIGHTER, [mōōn'-līt'-er], *n.* a member of the Irish Land League which organized nocturnal agrarian outrages.

MOONLIGHTING, [mōōn'-līt'-ing], *n.* the perpetration of nocturnal agrarian outrages.

MOONLING, [mōōn'-ling], *n.* an oaf, a simpleton.

MOONLIT, [mōōn'-lit], *adj.* lighted by the moon.

MOONRAKER, [mōōn'-rāk'-er], *n.* (*naut.*) a sail over a skysail; a native of Wiltshire.

MOONSEED, [mōōn'-sēd], *n.* a climbing plant of the genus *Menispermum*, with lunate seeds.

MOONSHEE, MUNSHI, [mōōn'-shē], *n.* an Indian linguist or secretary. [Hind. *munshi*].

MOONSHINE, [mōōn'-shīn], *n.* moonlight; (*coll.*) a piece of airy nonsense; (*slang*) smuggled whisky.

MOONSHINER, [mōōn'-shīn-er], *n.* (*slang*) a rum-runner; one who smuggles or distils illicitly whisky or other spirits.

MOONSHINY, [mōōn'-shīn-i], *adj.* moonlit.

MOONSTONE, [mōōn'-stōn], *n.* a variety of potash felspar, of bluish-green colour.

MOONSTRUCK, [mōōn'-struk], *adj.* supposed to be affected by the moon's influence, lunatic, dazed and disordered in the mind.

MOON-TREFOIL, [mōōn'-tre'-foil], *n.* an evergreen shrub of the south of Europe.

MOONWORT, [mōōn'-wurt], *n.* any of several plants such as the fern, *Botrychium Lunaria*; the tree-sorrel, *Rumex Lunaria*; honesty, *Lunaria biennis*.

MOONY, [mōōn'-i], *adj.* crescent-shaped; dreamy; mentally unbalanced; (*slang*) slightly drunk.

MOON-YEAR, [mōōn'-yēer'], *n.* the exact lunar year.

MOOR (1), [mōōer], *n.* a wild, open stretch of waste ground overgrown with heather, often marshy and usually hilly or elevated. [OE. *mor*].

MOOR (2), [mōōer], *n.* a native of Morocco in North Africa. [L. *Maurus* an inhabitant of Mauretania].

MOOR (3), [mōōer], *v.t.* and *i.* to fasten a boat to the shore by a cable; to fasten an airship to the mast at an air-port. [Uncert.].

MOORAGE, [mōōer'-ij], *n.* a place for mooring vessels.

MOORBERRY, [mōōer'-be-ri], *n.* the cranberry.

MOOR-BUZZARD, [mōōer'-buz'-ahd], *n.* the marsh-harrier bird, *Circus æruginosus.*

MOORCOCK, [mōōer'-kok], *n.* *Lagopus scoticus*, the male red grouse.

MOORFOWL, [mōōer'-fowl], *n.* the moorcock.

MOORGAME, [mōōer'-gām], *n.* grouse.

MOOR-GRASS, [mōōer'-grahs], *n.* grass growing on a moor; the bluish grass, *Sesleria cærulea.*

MOORHAWK, [mōōer'-hawk], *n.* the marsh harrier.

MOORHEN, [mōōer'-hen], *n.* the water hen, *Gallinula chloropus.*

MOORING, [mōōer'-ing], *n.* moorage; (*pl.*) tackle used to moor a vessel.

MOORING-MAST, [mōōer'-ing-mahst'], *n.* a mast to which an airship may be moored.

MOORISH, [mōōer'-ish], *adj.* pertaining to the Moors.

MOORLAND, [mōōer'-land], *n.* a moor or heath, country similar to a moor.

MOORHEN

MOORSTONE, [mōōer'-stōn], *n.* (*min.*) a kind of Cornish granite.

MOOR-TETTER, [mōōer'-tet'-er], *n.* the moor-titling.

MOOR-TIT, [mōōer'-tit], *n.* the moor-titling.

MOOR-TITLING, [mōōer'-tit'-ling], *n.* either of two birds, the stone-chat, *Pratincola rubicola*, or the meadow-pipit, *Anthus pratensis.*

MOORUK, [mōōer'-uk], *n.* an Australian bird, Bennett's cassowary, *Casuarius bennetti.* [Echoic].

MOORWHIN, [mōōer'-win], *n.* the petty whin or needle furze, *Genista anglica.*

MOORY, [mōōer'-i], *adj.* of the nature of a moor.

MOOSE, [mōōs], *n.* the North American elk, *Alces machlis.* [Native].

MOOT (1), MOTE, [mōōt], *n.* (*hist.*) an assembly of freemen to discuss matters affecting the community; (*leg.*) a moot-court. [OE. *gemot*].

MOOT (2), [mōōt], *adj.* debatable, open to argument.

MOOT (3), [mōōt], *v.t.* to propose or raise for discussion or debate.

MOOTABLE, [mōōt'-abl], *adj.* open to debate.

MOOT CASE, [mōōt'-kās'], *n.* a moot point.

MOOT-COURT, [mōōt'-kawt], *n.* a meeting of lawyers and law-students for legal debate on points of law.

MOOTER, [mōōt'-er], *n.* one who opens a problem or sets going a discussion; †(*leg.*) one who argues a moot-case.

MOOT-HALL, [mōōt'-hawl], *n.* a moot-court; a place where the moot was held.

MOOT POINT, [mōōt'-point'], *n.* a debatable case, a question or point open to argument.

MOP (1), [mop], *n.* a bundle of rags on the end of a long handle for cleaning floors, etc.; an unkempt head of hair. [Uncert.].

MOP (2), [mop], *n.* a grin or grimace as made by a monkey. [MOP (3)].

MOP (3), (mopping, mopped), [mop], *v.i.* to grimace like a monkey. [~Du. *moppen* to pout].

MOP (4), (mopping, mopped), [mop], *v.t.* to swill or clean with a mop; to wipe; **to m. up**, (*coll.*) to get through quickly; to defeat decisively; to round up the remnants of a defeated force. [MOP (1)].

MOPE (1), [mōp], *n.* sulky, a low-spirited person.

MOPE (2), [mōp], *v.i.* to sulk or mooch in a lifeless, low-spirited manner. [Uncert.].

MOPE-EYED, [mōp'-īd], *adj.* short-sighted.

MOPING, [mōp'-ing], *adj.* depressed, miserable, wandering about in gloomy dejection.

MOPISH, [mōp'-ish], *adj.* moping.

MOPISHLY, [mōp'-ish-li], *adv.* in a mopish way.

MOPISHNESS, [mōp'-ish-nes], *n.* the state of being mopish.

MOPOKE, [mōp'-ōk], *n.* any of several Australasian birds, as the New Zealand owl, *Spiloglaux novæzelandiæ*; the Tasmanian night-jar, *Podargus cuvieri*; and the Australian owl, *Ninox boobook.* [Echoic].

MOPPET, [mop'-et], *n.* a child, a darling; a rag-doll; a mischievous child. [MOP (1)].

MOPSEY, MOPSY†, [mop'-si], *n.* a pretty child; an untidy woman. [MOP (1)].

MOPUS, [mōp'-us], *n.* a mope, a melancholy day-dreamer. [Uncert.].

MOQUETTE, [mō-ket'], *n.* a material used for carpeting and upholstery. [Fr. *moquette*].

MORA (1), [maw'-ra], *n.* a division of the Spartan army. [Gk. *mora*].

MORA (2), [maw'-ra], *n.* the huge tropical American tree, *Mora excelsa*, the bark of which is used for tanning. [Braz. *moira* tree].

MORA (3), [maw'-ra], *n.* (*pros.*) a metrical unit equivalent to the length of a short syllable. [L. *mora* delay].

MORA (4), [mawr'-ah], *n.* a popular Italian game. [It. *mora*].

MORAINAL, [mo-rān'-al], *adj.* pertaining to a moraine.

MORAINE, [mo-rān'], *n.* accumulated debris deposited by a glacier. [Fr. *moraine*].

MORAL (1), [mo'-ral], *n.* the implied meaning, practical significance in a story or event; (*pl.*) principles of conduct, ethics; conduct, habits or outlook considered as right or wrong, *esp.* with regard to matters of sex.

MORAL (2), [mo'-ral], *adj.* concerning conduct or habits considered as right or wrong; observing or teaching a high tone of conduct, virtuous; appealing to or accepting the obligations of what is just and right, however inexpedient; spiritual; chaste; **m. victory**, a defeat that can be regarded as a victory. [L. *moralis*].

MORALE, [mo-rahl'], *n.* disposition, mental state, spirit, *esp.* of troops. [Fr. *morale* moral].

MORALIST, [mo'-ral-ist], *n.* a writer on ethics, one who moralizes.

MORALISTIC, [mo'-ral-ist'-ik], *adj.* teaching ethics.

MORALITY, [mo-ral'-i-ti], *n.* moral quality, ethics; the quality of being moral, virtue; chastity; (*hist.*) a form of early drama in which the characters personify virtues and vices. [L. *moralitas*].

MORALIZATION, [mo'-ral-īz-ā'-shun], *n.* the act of moralizing; that which is moralized; moral reflection.

MORALIZE, [mo'-ral-īz], *v.t. and i.* to draw the moral from, to render moral; to make moral reflections. [Fr. *moraliser*].

MORALIZER, [mo'-ral-īz-er], *n.* one who moralizes, a moralist.

MORALLY, [mo'-ra-li], *adv.* in a moral fashion; according to morality; in effect.

MORASS, [mo-ras'], *n.* a marsh, or bog; (*fig.*) a difficult position. [Du. *moeras*].

MORASSY, [mo-ras'-i], *adj.* marshy.

MORAT, [maw'-rat], *n.* a honey-drink flavoured with mulberry juice. [L. *morus* mulberry].

MORATORIUM, [mo'-ra-taw'-ri-um], *n.* a period of authorized and legal delay in the payment of debts; a decree sanctioning this. [L. *moratorius* delaying].

MORATORY, [mo'-ra-ter-i], *adj.* relating to a moratorium or to delay; that delays.

MORAVIAN (1), [mo-rā'-vi-an], *n.* one who inhabits Moravia; a member of an eighteenth-century Protestant sect holding doctrines derived from Huss.

MORAVIAN (2), [mo-rā'-vi-an], *adj.* pertaining to Moravia or to the Moravian sect.

MORBID, [maw'-bid], *adj.* connected with disease; diseased; unhealthy, unwholesome, gruesome; depressed or depressing.

MORBIDEZZA, [maw'-bid-et'-za], *n.* (*paint.*) a delicate flesh-tint. [It. *morbidezza*].

MORBIDITY, [maw-bid'-i-ti], *n.* morbidness.

MORBIDLY, [maw'-bid-li], *adv.* in morbid fashion.

MORBIDNESS, [maw'-bid-nes], *n.* the condition of being morbid.

MORBIFIC, [maw-bif'-ik], *adj.* tending to cause disease. [L. *morbus* disease and *facere* to make].

MORCEAU, [maw'-sō], *n.* a morsel; a short musical or literary composition. [Fr. *morceau*].

MORCELLEMENT, [maw-sel'-ment], *n.* (*leg.*) a division of an estate. [Fr. *morcellement*].

MORDACIOUS, [maw-dā'-shus], *adj.* biting, pungent, bitter; sarcastic. [L. *mordax*].

MORDACIOUSLY, [maw-dā'-shus-li], *adv* in a mordacious manner.

MORDACITY, [maw-das'-i-ti], *n.* the condition of being mordacious. [L. *mordacitas*].

MORDANT (1), [maw'-dant], *n.* a substance used to fix colours in materials; a glue to make gold-leaf adhere; an acid used in etching to erode the pattern on the copperplate. [OFr. *mordant*].

MORDANT (2), [maw'-dant], *adj.* mordacious; corrosive; bitter, sarcastic; (of pain) burning; fixative. [OFr. *mordant*].

ō (bone), ī (fine), ōō (food), ŏŏ (put), u (up), th (think), TH (that), zh (azure), † = obsolete, ~ = related to.

MORDANTLY, [maw′-dant-li], *adv.* in mordant fashion.
MORDENT, [mawd′-ent], *n.* (*mus.*) a (symbol indicating a) trill on a note and the note below it in the scale. [Germ. *mordent* from It. *mordente* biting].
MORDICANCY, [maw′-dik-an-si], *n.* the quality of being mordicant.
MORDICANT, [maw′-dik-ant], *adj.* biting, pungent, acid; corrosive. [L. *mordicans*].
MORDICATION, [maw′-dik-ā′-shun], *n.* corrosion.
MORE (1), [maw(r)], *n.* a greater quantity, amount, number, etc.; something additional.
MORE (2), [maw(r)], *adj.* greater in quantity, size, quality, degree, etc.; additional, further. [OE. *mara*].
MORE (3), [maw(r)], *adv.* to a greater degree; again, additionally; moreover; **m. or less,** roughly, about.
MOREEN, [mo-rēn′], *n.* a strong woollen cloth, often watered. [Uncert.].
MOREL, MORIL, [mo-rel′], *n.* the edible latticed mushroom, *Morchella esculenta.* [Fr. *morille*].
MORELLO, [mo-rel′-ō], *n.* a bitter, dark-coloured cherry. [LL. *morellus* dark-coloured].
MOREOVER, [mawr-ō′ver], *adv.* besides, in addition.
MORESQUE, MAURESQUE, [mawr-esk′], *adj.* in Moorish style. [It. *Moresco*].
MORGANATIC, [maw′-gan-at-ik], *adj.* **m. marriage,** a legal marriage between a male member of a royal family and a person of lower rank by which neither she nor her children can claim princely status or right of succession. [MedL. (*matrimonium ad*) *morganaticum*].
MORGAY, [maw′-gā], *n.* the lesser spotted dog-fish, *Scyllium canicula.* [Corn. *morgi*].
MORGLAY, [maw′-glā], *n.* a sword, claymore. [Wel. *mawr* great and *cleddyf* sword].
MORGUE, [mawg], *n.* a building where corpses are displayed for identification, a mortuary; frigid aloofness, cool indifference. [Fr. *morgue*].
MORIBUND, [mo′-ri-bund′], *adj.* in a dying state; in the last stages of decay. [L. *moribundus*].
MORICHE, [mo-rēch′-ā], *n.* the South American palm of the genus *Mauritia.* [Carib *moriche*].
MORIGEROUS, [mo-rij′-er-us], *adj.* submissive. [L. *morigerus*].
MORIL, see MOREL.
MORILLON, [mo-ril′-on], *n.* a sort of vine or grape; the golden-eyed duck; a variety of emerald. [Fr. *morillon*].

MORGLAY

MORINGA, [mo-ring′-ga], *n.* the ben-nut tree, *Moringa pterygosperma.* [Native].
MORION, MURRION, [mo′-ri-on], *n.* a 16th-century helmet without neck-guard or visor. [Span. *morrion*].
MORISCO (1), [mo-ris′-kō], *n.* a Spanish Christian Moor; Moorish decoration; a Moorish dance.
MORISCO (2), [mo-ris′-kō], *adj.* Moorish. [Span. *morisco*].

MORION

MORKIN, [maw′-kin], *n.* an animal that has died from illness or accident, not slaughtered. [~L. *mors* death].
MORLING, MORTLING, [maw′-ling], *n.* the wool of a dead sheep. [~MORKIN].
MORMON, [maw′-mon], *n.* a member of an American religious sect founded by Joseph Smith in 1830 originally professing polygamy. ["Book of *Mormon,*" a supposedly ancient book said to have been written for the church of the latter days, and claimed to have been discovered by Smith in 1827].
MORMONISM, [maw′-mon-izm], *n.* the doctrine and practices of the Mormons.
MORN, [mawn], *n.* (*poet.*) the morning; (*Scots*) tomorrow. [OE. *morgen*].
MORNING (1), [mawn′-ing], *n.* the early part of the day from midnight to noon, and *esp.* from dawn to midday; (*fig.*) the beginning. [ME. *morwening*].
MORNING (2), [mawn′-ing], *adj.* pertaining to, suitable for, the morning; done or to be done in the morning; **m. clothes, m. wear,** semi-ceremonial town clothes worn by the professional classes, etc., for business or at functions during the day.
MORNING-GLORY, [mawn′-ing-glaw′-ri], *n.* a climbing plant of the genus *Ipomœa.*
MORNING-GOWN, [mawn′-ing-gown′], *n.* a loose gown to be worn in the morning.
MORNING-ROOM, [mawn′-ing-rōōm′], *n.* a breakfast-room; a sitting-room for use in the morning.
MORNING-STAR, [mawn′-ing-stah(r)′], *n.* a star, *esp.* Venus, when seen before sunrise; (*hist.*) a weapon to pierce armour; (*fig.*) a harbinger.
MOROCCO (1), [mo-rok′-ō], *n.* a fine, supple leather prepared from goatskin; the soft, flexible, grained, sheepskin imitation of this. [*Morocco,* in Africa, from which it first came].
MOROCCO (2), [mo-rok′-ō], *adj.* pertaining to, or coming from, Morocco.
MORON, [maw′-ron], *n.* an adult with an imperfectly developed brain; (*fig.*) a degenerate; (*U.S.*) a half-wit. [Gk. *moros* stupid].
MOROSE, [mo-rōs′], *adj.* sour-tempered, sullen, surly. [L. *morosus*].
MOROSELY, [mo-rōs′-li], *adv.* in morose fashion.
MOROSENESS, [mo-rōs′-nes], *n.* the quality or condition of being morose.
MOROXITE, [mo-roks′-īt], *n.* (*min.*) a bluish-green form of apatite. [Gk. *moroxos* pipeclay].
MORPHIA, [maw′-fi-a], *n.* a narcotic alkaloid extracted from opium, used to alleviate pain. [Gk. *Morpheus* god of sleep].
MORPHINATED, [maw′-fin-āt′-id], *adj.* mingled with or containing morphia.
MORPHINE, [maw′-fēn], *n.* morphia. [Fr. *morphine*].
MORPHINISM, [maw′-fin-izm], *n.* the morbid state brought on by overdoses of morphia; the practice of taking morphia regularly.
MORPHINIST, [maw′-fin-ist], *n.* a morphinomaniac.
MORPHINOMANIA, [maw′-fin-ō-mā′-ni-a], *n.* a craving for morphia.
MORPHINOMANIAC, [maw′-fin-ō-mā′-ni-ak], *n.* a morphia addict.
MORPHOLOGICAL, [maw′-fol-oj′-ik-al], *adj.* pertaining to morphology.
MORPHOLOGIST, [maw-fol′-oj-ist], *n.* one versed in morphology.
MORPHOLOGY, [maw-fol′-o-ji], *n.* the study of the form of plants and animals or of words and languages. [Gk. *morphe* form and *logos* speech].
MORPHONOMY, [maw-fon′-o-mi], *n.* the science of the laws of form in animal and plant life and in crystals. [Gk. *morphe* form and *nomos* law].
MORPHOSIS, [maw-fō′-sis], *n.* (*biol.*) the form of development. [Gk. *morphosis* shaping].
MORRIS (1), [mo′-ris], *n.* a semi-dramatic country dance in which the dancers represent characters of the Robin Hood fable. [MOORISH].
MORRIS (2), [mo′-ris], *n.* an old game played with stones or pegs on a marked-out patch of ground. [Uncert.].
MORRIS-DANCER, [mo′-ris-dahns′-er], *n.* one who dances in a morris.
MORRIS-TUBE, [mo′-ris-tewb′], *n.* a tube inserted into the barrel of a rifle to reduce its bore, for shooting practice on a short range. [R. *Morris,* its inventor, (died 1891)].
MORROW, [mo′-rō], *n.* (*archaic*) the next day; (*archaic*) morning; period of time immediately ensuing after some particular event. [ME. *morwe*].
MORSE (1), [maws], *n.* (*eccles.*) a clasp used to fasten a cope. [L. *morsus*].
MORSE (2), [maws], *n.* the walrus, *Trichechus rosmarus.* [Finnish *mursu*].
MORSE (3), [maws], *n.* the method of signalling by telegraphy or the code employed in it. [S. F. B. *Morse* (1791-1872), its inventor].
MORSE (4), [maws], *adj.* pertaining to telegraphy. [MORSE (3)].
MORSEL, [maws′-el], *n.* a tiny piece, fragment. [OFr. *morsel* a small bite].
MORT, [mawt], *n.* the sounding of the horn at a hunt to signify the death of the quarry. [Fr. *mort* death].
MORTAL (1), [maw′-tal], *n.* a creature liable to die, *esp.* a human being.
MORTAL (2), [maw′-tal], *adj.* liable to death; deadly, causing death; pertaining to death; lasting till death; (*arch.*) long and tedious; (*arch.*) extreme. [L. *mortalis*].
MORTALITY, [maw-tal′-i-ti], *n.* the state of being mortal; the number of deaths, death-rate; the human race, as being mortal. [L. *mortalitas*].
MORTALLY, [maw′-tal-i], *adv.* in mortal fashion, fatally; (*coll.*) extremely.
MORTAR, [maw′-ter], *n.* a mixture of sand, lime, and water used to unite bricks or other building material;

a stout bowl-like vessel in which substances may be crushed under a pestle; a short wide-mouthed cannon for projecting shells, etc., upwards at a high angle. [OE. *mortere* from L. *mortarium*].

MORTAR-BOARD, [maw'-ter-bawd'], *n.* a small board on which bricklayers carry mortar; an academic cap.

MORTGAGE (1), [maw'-gij], *n.* (*leg.*) the temporary making over of property by the owner as security for a loan, the property to be returned to him on the repayment of the loan upon the agreed terms; the deed of such conveyance. [OFr. *mortgage* dead pledge].

MORTGAGE (2), [maw'-gij], *v.t.* to convey property under the terms of a mortgage; (*fig.*) to pledge, lay under a debt or burden.

MORTGAGEE, [maw'-gij-ē'], *n.* the person to whom property is mortgaged.

MORTGAGOR, [maw'-gij-er], *n.* the person who grants property in a mortgage.

MORTICE, see MORTISE.

MORTICIAN, [maw-tish'-an], *n.* (*U.S.*) an undertaker. [L. *mors mortis* death].

MORTIFEROUS, [maw-tif'-er-us], *adj.* bringing death, deadly. [L. *mortiferus*].

MORTIFICATION, [maw'-ti-fi-kā'-shun], *n.* the act of mortifying; the state of being mortified; that which mortifies; humiliation, shame; (*med.*) gangrene. [EcclesL. *mortificatio*].

MORTIFIEDNESS, [maw'-ti-fīd-nes], *n.* the state of being mortified.

MORTIFIER, [maw'-ti-fī-er], *n.* someone or something that mortifies.

MORTIFY, [maw'-ti-fī], *v.t. and i.* to subject the body to spiritual discipline by acts of self-control, penance, etc.; to humiliate, shame and vex; (*med.*) to gangrene. [EcclesL. *mortificare* to put to death].

MORTIFYING, [maw'-ti-fī'-ing], *adj.* humiliating.

MORTIFYINGLY, [maw'-ti-fī'-ing-li], *adv.* in mortifying fashion.

MORTISE (1), MORTICE, [maw'-tis], *n.* (*carp.*) a slot or cavity cut into one piece of material, into which the tenon of another piece fits to form a joint; such a joint. [OFr. *mortaise*].

MORTISE (2), MORTICE, [maw'-tis], *v.t.* (*carp.*) to unite with a tenon and mortise joint; to make a mortise in.

MORTISE-LOCK, [maw'-tis-lok'], *n.* a lock made to fit in a mortise cut in the edge of a door.

MORTLING, see MORLING.

MORTMAIN, [mawt'-mān], *n.* (*leg.*) the possession of property by a body which cannot alienate it. [OFr. *morte main* dead hand].

MORTUARY (1), [maw'-chew-er-i], *n.* a chapel of rest, where bodies may be kept prior to interment; a building in which bodies awaiting identification, an inquest, etc., are placed; (*hist.*) a fee or present received by the parish priest upon the death of a parishioner.

MORTUARY (2), [maw'-chew-er-i], *adj.* pertaining to death or burial. [L. *mortuarius*].

MOSAIC (1), [mō-zā'-ik], *n.* a pattern or design made by cementing together small pieces of coloured stone, glass, or marble; (*fig.*) a compilation of variegated fragments. [LL. *mosaicus*].

MOSAIC (2), [mō-zā'-ik], *adj.* pertaining to mosaic.

MOSAIC (3), [mō-zā'ik], *adj.* relating to Moses. [*Moses*, Hebrew legislator, Exod. ii, 10].

MOSAICIST, [mō-zā'-is-ist], *n.* one who makes mosaics.

MOSAISM, [mō-zā'-izm], *n.* the code ascribed to Moses.

MOSCHATEL, [mos'-kat-el], *n.* a small plant with pale-green blossoms, which emit a musk-like scent. [Fr. *moscatelle*].

MOSCHIFEROUS, [mos-kif'-er-us], *adj.* bearing musk. [L. *moschus* musk and *ferre* to bear].

MOSCHINE (1), [mos'-kīn], *n.* (*zool.*) the musk-deer.

MOSCHINE (2), [mos'-kīn], *adj.* (*zool.*) of, or resembling, the *Moschinæ*, a class of mammals including the musk-deer.

MOSELLE, [mō-zel'], *n.* a light German wine. [The river *Moselle*, a tributary of the Rhine].

MOSLEM (1), MUSLIM, [moz'-lem], *n.* a Mohammedan. [Arab. *muslim*].

MOSLEM (2), MUSLIM, [moz'-lem], *adj.* pertaining to Mohammedans or their faith.

MOSLEYITE, [mōz'-li-īt], *n.* a follower of Sir Oswald *Mosley*; a British Fascist.

MOSQUE, [mosk], *n.* a Mohammedan temple. [Fr. *mosquée* from Arab. *masjid*].

MOSQUITO (1), [mos-kē'-to], *n.* any of several species of gnats of the group *Culicidæ*, the females of which suck the blood of animals. [Span. *mosquito*].

MOSQUITO

MOSQUITO (2), [mos-kē'-tō], *adj.* pertaining to mosquitoes.

MOSQUITO-CRAFT, [mos-kē'-tō-krahft'], *n.* small vessels of war intended for rapid movement; torpedo boats.

MOSQUITO-NET, [mos-kē'-tō-net'], *n.* a net used for protection against mosquitoes.

MOSS, [mos], *n.* (*bot.*) any cryptogamous plant of the group *Musci*, growing on marshy ground, rocks, trees, etc.; a plant resembling these; a bog, fen. [OE. *mos*].

MOSS-BASKET, [mos'-bahs'-kit], *n.* a basket lined with moss.

MOSS-CAMPION, [mos'-kam'-pi-on], *n.* a small moss-like plant, *Silene acaulis*.

MOSS-CHEEPER, [mos'-chēp'-er], *n.* the meadow-pipit.

MOSS-GROWN, [mos'-grōn], *adj.* overgrown with moss.

MOSSINESS, [mos'-i-nes], *n.* the condition of being mossy.

MOSSLAND, [mos'-land], *n.* marshy, peaty ground.

MOSS-PINK, [mos'-pingk'], *n.* a plant, *Phlox subulata*.

MOSS-ROSE, [mos'-rōz], *n.* the cabbage rose, *Rosa centifolia*.

MOSS-TROOPERS, [mos'-trōōp'-erz], *n.*(*pl.*) bands of marauders who harassed the English and Scottish borders until suppressed in the 17th century.

MOSSY, [mos'-i], *adj.* covered with, or like, moss.

MOST (1), [mōst], *n.* the greatest in size, number, quantity or degree; **at m.**, not more than; **to make the m. of**, to extract full advantage from.

MOST (2), [mōst], *adj.* greatest in quantity, size or degree. [OE. *mast*].

MOST (3), [mōst], *adv.* in the greatest measure, to the highest degree.

MOSTAHIBA, see MUSTAIBA.

MOSTIC, see MAULSTICK.

MOSTLY, [mōst'-li], *adv.* for the greatest part; on the whole.

MOT, [mō], *n.* a witticism. [Fr. *mot* word].

MOTE (1), [mōt], *n.* a tiny particle, *esp.* of dust seen in a beam of sunlight, a spot, speck. [OE. *mot*].

MOTE (2), see MOOT (1).

MOTET, [mōt-et'], *n.* a piece of unaccompanied music for several voices. [Fr. *motet*].

MOTH, [moth], *n.* any lepidopterous insect that is not a butterfly; *esp.* the clothes-moth, a nocturnal insect of the genus *Tinea*, the larvae of which feed on cloth, etc.; a light type of aeroplane. [OE. *moththe*].

MOTH-BALLS, [moth'-bawlz'], *n.*(*pl.*) balls of camphor used to keep moths away from clothes.

MOTH-EATEN, [moth'-ēt'-en], *adj.* (of cloth) damaged by the ravages of the clothes-moth; (*fig.*) dilapidated.

MOTHER (1), [muTH'-er], *n.* a female parent; (*fig.*) origin, source, beginning; a person acting as a female parent; **M. Superior**, the head of a convent; **M. Carey's chicken**, the stormy petrel, *Procellaria pelagica*; **M. Carey's goose**, the great black fulmar, *Ossifraga gigantea*; **M. Church**, the church from which all others have arisen; the church of the original parish. [OE. *modor*].

MOTHER (2), [muTH'-er], *n.* a thick sediment produced during the fermentation of liquors. [~MDu. *moeder*].

MOTHER (3), [muTH'-er], *adj.* native; parent; natural; acting as a mother.

MOTHER (4), [muTH'-er], *v.t.* to act as mother towards; to adopt.

MOTHER-COAL, [muTH'-er-kōl'], *n.* coal that has its vegetable structure still visible.

MOTHER-COUNTRY, [muTH'-er-kun'-tri], *n.* the country from which a colony has been founded; one's native land.

MOTHERCRAFT, [muTH'-er-krahft'], *n.* the art and science of rearing children.

MOTHERHOOD, [muTH'-er-hood], *n.* the condition of being a mother; the feelings of a mother.

MOTHERING (1), [muth'-er-ing], *n.* an acting as mother towards.
MOTHERING (2), [muth'-er-ing], *adj.* that mothers; **M. Sunday**, the fourth Sunday in Lent.
MOTHER-IN-LAW, [muth'-er-in-law'], *n.* the mother of one's spouse.
MOTHERLESS, [muth'-er-les], *adj.* lacking a mother.
MOTHERLINESS, [muth'-er-li-nes], *n.* the quality of being motherly.
MOTHER-LODGE, [muth'-er-loj'], *n.* (*freemasonry*) the lodge of a member's initiation.
MOTHERLY, [muth'-er-li], *adj.* affectionate, tender and caring like a mother.
MOTHER-OF-PEARL, [muth'-er-ov-purl'], *n.* the iridescent, hard, inner layer of certain shells.
MOTHER-WATER, [muth'-er-waw'-ter], *n.* a solution from which crystals have been obtained but which still has in it salts and other impurities.
MOTHERWIT, [muth'-er-wit'], *n.* common sense; spontaneous wit.
MOTHERWORT, [muth'-er-wurt], *n.* any of several plants formerly thought to cure diseases of the womb, *esp.* the plants *Leonurus cardiaca* and *Artemisia vulgaris*, the mugwort.
MOTHERY, [muth'-er-i], *adj.* containing mother. [MOTHER (2)].
MOTHY, [moth'-i], *adj.* full of moths.
MOTIF, [mō-tēf'], *n.* a basic conception or feature characterizing an artistic production, *esp.* a recurring theme in a piece of music. [Fr. *motif*].
MOTILE, [mō'-tīl], *adj.* that moves.
MOTION (1), [mō'-shun], *n.* the process of changing position or place; the way in which this is carried out; a change of position, *esp.* of components with regard to a whole; oscillation; gesture; bodily deportment; a working of the bowels; excrement; a proposal made in a deliberative assembly, etc.; (*leg.*) an application to the court or its head to obtain an order or ruling on a matter affecting the action at issue. [L. *motio*].
MOTION (2), [mō'-shun], *v.t. and i.* to beckon, to make a significant gesture to; to propose a motion.
MOTIONER, [mō'-shun-er], *n.* one who proposes a motion; one who motions.
MOTIONIST, [mō'-shun-ist], *n.* a motioner.
MOTIONLESS, [mō'-shun-les], *adj.* without motion, still.
MOTION-PICTURES, [mō'-shun-pik'-cherz], *n.(pl.)* cinema films.
MOTIVATE, [mō'-tiv-āt], *v.t.* to provide a motive, to instigate.
MOTIVATION, [mō'-tiv-ā'-shun], *n.* the act of motivating; that which motivates.
MOTIVE (1), [mō'-tiv], *n.* that which causes and influences an action; the reason for doing something; a motif. [L. *motivum*].
MOTIVE (2), [mō'-tiv], *adj.* causing action or movement; relating to motives. [L. *motivus* moving].
MOTIVE (3), [mō'-tiv], *v.t.* to motivate; to cause to act in a particular way.
MOTIVELESS, [mō'-tiv-les], *adj.* without motive.
MOTIVITY, [mō-tiv'-i-ti], *n.* ability or capacity to produce motion.
MOTLEY (1), [mot'-li], *n.* variegated costume, as worn by a jester.
MOTLEY (2), [mot'-li], *adj.* of different colours; variegated; of diverse kinds; ill-assorted. [ME. *mottelee*].
MOT-MOT, [mot'-mot], *n.* a South and Central American bird of the *Momotidæ*. [Echoic].
MOTOR (1), [mō'-ter], *n.* an internal-combustion engine; any contrivance productive of mechanical motion; a motor-car, automobile; (*anat.*) a muscle that moves some part of the body; a nerve which stimulates such a muscle. [L. *motor* a mover].
MOTOR (2), [mō'-ter], *adj.* (*anat.*) causing movement; (*anat.*) (of a nerve) conveying an impulse which excites movement; driven by a motor.
MOTOR (3), [mō'-ter], *v.t. and i.* to convey in a motor-car; to travel in a motor-car.
MOTOR-BANDIT, [mō'-ter-band'-it], *n.* a thief who uses a motor-car to effect a quick departure.
MOTOR-BICYCLE, [mō'-ter-bī'-sikl], *n.* a motor-cycle.
MOTOR-BOAT, [mō'-ter-bōt'], *n.* a boat driven by an internal-combustion engine.
MOTOR-BUS, [mō'-ter-bus'], *n.* an omnibus driven by an internal-combustion engine.
MOTOR-CAR, [mō'-ter-kah(r)'], *n.* a vehicle propelled by an internal-combustion engine.
MOTOR-CYCLE, [mō'-ter-sīkl], *n.* a two-wheeled vehicle propelled by an internal-combustion engine.
MOTORIAL, [mō-taw'-ri-al], *adj.* pertaining to motion.
MOTORING, [mō'-ter-ing], *n.* the act or habit of riding in a motor-car, *esp.* touring the countryside.
MOTORIST, [mō'-ter-ist], *n.* one who drives a motor-car.
MOTORIZE, [mō'-ter-īz], *v.t.* (*milit.*) to equip with petrol-driven vehicles, *esp.* armoured fighting vehicles. [Fr. *motoriser*, Germ. *motorisieren*].
MOTOR-LORRY, [mō'-ter-lo'-ri], *n.* a lorry propelled by an internal-combustion engine.
MOTORMAN, [mō'-ter-man'], *n.* the driver of a vehicle propelled by an electric motor.
MOTOR SHIP, [mo'-ter-ship'], *n.* a large ship driven by motors.
MOTOR SPIRIT, [mō'-ter-spi'-rit], *n.* petrol, alcohol, or other similar fuel suitable for an internal-combustion engine.
MOTOR VESSEL, [mō'-ter-vesl'], *n.* a motor ship.
MOTORY, [mō'-ter-i], *adj.* producing or pertaining to motion.
MOTTLE (1), [motl], *n.* a spot or blotch; a shading or pattern of such blotches.
MOTTLE (2), [motl], *v.t.* to variegate with spots of different shades and colours [Uncert.].
MOTTLED, [motld], *adj.* marked with spots of different shade or colour.
MOTTO, [mot'-ō], *n.* the phrase associated with a crest or emblem; a short pithy precept supposed to govern conduct, a maxim; a short phrase descriptive of that to which it is attached. [It. *motto*].
MOUCH, see MOOCH.
MOUCHER, see MOOCHER.
MOUFLON, MUFFLON, [mōō'-flon], *n.* the wild mountain sheep of southern Europe, *Ovis musimon*. [Fr. *mouflon*].
MOUJIK, [mōō'-zhik], *n.* a Russian peasant. [Russ. *muzhik*].
MOULD (1), [mōld], *n.* earth, soil, ground, *esp.* fine friable soil. [OE. *molde*].
MOULD (2), [mōld], *n.* the furry, fungoid growth that appears on cloth, vegetable, and animal substances, etc., exposed to damp. [Uncert.].
MOULD† (3), [mōld], *n.* the top of the head. [OE. *molda*].
MOULD (4), [mōld], *n.* a shaped and patterned cavity in which anything may be cast into its intended shape, a matrix; something shaped in such a cavity; (*fig.*) embodiment, pattern; cast, shape, style. [OFr. *modle* from L. *modulus* a small measure].
MOULD (5), [mōld], *v.t.* to cover with mould. [MOULD (1)].
MOULD (6), [mōld], *v.t.* to shape in a mould or with the fingers; to produce (a required shape) out of a particular material; to influence, control; to fashion, base. [MOULD (4)].
MOULDABLE, [mōld'-abl], *adj.* capable of being moulded.
MOULD-BOARD, [mōld'-bawd], *n.* the part of a plough that turns up the furrow.
MOULDER (1), [mōld'-er], *n.* one who moulds or casts. [MOULD (4)].
MOULDER (2), [mōld'-er], *v.i.* to rot, decay, or crumble with age or disuse.
MOULDINESS, [mōld'-i-nes], *n.* the condition of being mouldy.
MOULDING, [mōld'-ing], *n.* the act of one who moulds; that which has been moulded; the way in which a thing is moulded; a patterned or shaped strip of wood to ornament furniture, picture-frames, etc.; (*arch.*) an ornamental projection from a wall, wainscot, column, etc.

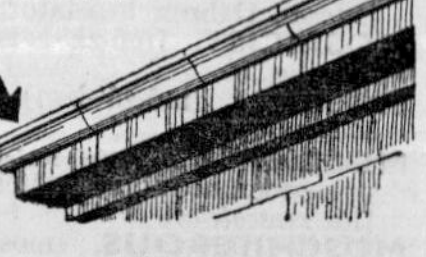
MOULDING

MOULD-LOFT, [mōld'-loft], *n.* a large room where moulds for ships are drawn full-size.
MOULDWARP, [mōld'-wawp], *n.* a mole, from the mounds of earth it casts up. [ME. *moldwarp* earth thrower].
MOULDY, [mōld'-i], *adj.* covered with mould, decaying, musty; (*fig.*) out of date; (*slang*) poor, disappointing; mean. [MOULD (2)].
MOULIN, [mōō'-la(ng)], *n.* a vertical shaft cut in a glacier by surface water pouring through a fissure in it. [Fr. *moulin* mill].

MOULINAGE, [mōō'-lin-ij], *n.* the process of spinning raw silk. [Fr. *moulin* mill].

MOULT (1), [mōlt], *n.* the state, period, or action of moulting.

MOULT (2), [mōlt], *v.t. and i.* to shed, *esp.* feathers or hair, periodically. [OE. (*bi-*)*mutian* to exchange].

MOULTING, [mōlt'-ing], *n.* the periodical shedding of feathers, hair, etc., by birds or other animals.

MOUND (1), [mownd], *n.* a small globe surmounted by a cross, one of the insignia of royal might; an orb. [Fr. *monde*].

MOUND (2), [mownd], *n.* a heap of earth, an earthwork or barrow; a small natural hillock. [Uncert.].

MOUND (3), [mownd], *v.t.* to heap up into a mound.

MOUND-BIRD, [mownd'-burd], *n.* a bird that lays its eggs on a mound, a megapode.

MOUND-BUILDER, [mownd'-bild'-er], *n.* a member of an extinct prehistoric race of North American Indians, builders of huge barrows and mounds.

MOUNT (1), [mownt], *n.* a mountain; hill; (*palmistry*) a fleshy swelling on the palm below a finger. [OE. *munt* from L. *mons montis*].

MOUNT (2), [mownt], *n.* a horse for riding; the cardboard margin added to a picture before framing; a carriage or base for a gun; a setting for a jewel; a glass slide on which objects may be viewed under a microscope. [MOUNT (3)].

MOUNT (3), [mownt], *v.t. and i.* to climb, ascend, go to the top of; to provide with a horse or horses; to set in position in, or on, a mount; to get on the back of a horse; to provide the scenery for (a play); to stuff animal skins, etc.; to rise, increase; **to m. guard**, to watch, guard. [Fr. *monter*].

MOUNTABLE, [mownt'-abl], *adj.* able to be ascended or mounted.

MOUNTAIN (1), [mown'-ten], *n.* a high and natural eminence on the surface of the earth; (*fig.*) anything very large or high; **the M.**, the extremist Jacobin party in the French Revolution. [OFr. *montaigne*].

MOUNTAIN (2), [mown'-ten], *adj.* connected with, resembling, a mountain or mountains; found or used in the mountains.

MOUNTAIN-ASH, [mown'-ten-ash'], *n.* the rowan tree, *Pyrus aucuparia*.

MOUNTAIN-BLUE†, [mown'-ten-blōō'], *n.* a native carbonate of copper.

MOUNTAIN-CORK, [mown'-ten-kawk'], *n.* a light sort of asbestos.

MOUNTAIN-DEW, [mown'-ten-dew'], *n.* Scotch whisky, *esp.* when illicitly distilled in the mountains of Scotland.

MOUNTAIN-ASH

MOUNTAINEER (1), [mown'-ten-ēer'], *n.* one who lives among mountains; one skilled in climbing mountains.

MOUNTAINEER (2), [mown'-ten-ēer'], *v.i.* to climb mountains.

MOUNTAINEERING, [mown'-ten-ēer'-ing], *n.* mountain-climbing.

MOUNTAINET, [mown'-ten-et'], *n.* a little mountain.

MOUNTAIN-FERN, [mown'-ten-fern'], *n.* a fern, *Lastrea Oreopteris*.

MOUNTAIN-FRINGE, [mown'-ten-frinj'], *n.* an American climbing plant, *Adlumia cirrhosa*.

MOUNTAIN-GREEN, [mown'-ten-grēn'], *n.* green earth, glauconite; a West Indian plant, *Spathelia simplex*.

MOUNTAIN-LEATHER, [mown'-ten-leᴛʜ'-er], *n.* mountain-cork.

MOUNTAIN-LIMESTONE, [mown'-ten-lim'-stōn], *n.* (*geol.*) limestone of the carboniferous series.

MOUNTAIN-MILK, [mown'-ten-milk'], *n.* a carbonate of lime, very soft and spongy.

MOUNTAINOUS, [mown'-ten-us], *adj.* with many mountains; rugged; huge, like a mountain in size.

MOUNTAINOUSNESS, [mown'-ten-us-nes], *n.* the quality of being mountainous.

MOUNTAIN-RICE, [mown'-ten-rīs'], *n.* rice grown on the slopes of mountains without irrigation; any grass of the genus *Oryzopsis*.

MOUNTAIN-SOAP, [mown'-ten-sōp'], *n.* a dark-brown mineral used in crayon painting.

MOUNTAIN-SORREL, [mown'-ten-so'-rel], *n.* the plant, *Oxyria reniformis*.

MOUNTAIN-SWEET, [mown'-ten-swēt'], *n.* the plant, *Ceanothus americanus*.

MOUNTAIN-WIDOW, [mown'-ten-wid'-ō], *n.* the plant, *Scabiosa atro-purpurea*.

MOUNTANT (1), [mownt'-ant], *n.* a sticky material for mounting photographs.

MOUNTANT (2), [mownt'-ant], *adj.* rising. [Fr. *montant*].

MOUNTEBANK, [mownt'-i-bangk], *n.* a quack doctor, so called as standing on a bench or trestle; a charlatan, impostor; a clown. [It. *montambanco*].

MOUNTEBANKERY, [mownt'-i-bangk'-er-i], *n.* the quackery or boastful pretences of a mountebank.

MOUNTED, [mownt'-id], *adj.* on horseback; placed in position on, provided with, a mount; (of a horse) provided with a rider.

MOUNTER, [mownt'-er], *n.* one who mounts.

MOUNTING, [mownt'-ing], *n.* the act of one who mounts; that on to which things are, or may be, mounted; the way in which anything is mounted.

MOUNTY, [mownt'-i], *n.* (*falconry*) the ascent of the hawk in pursuit of quarry; (*coll.*) a Canadian mounted policeman, *esp.* in the N.W. Mounted Police.

MOURN, [mawn], *v.t. and i.* to feel or express grief; to sorrow, lament the death of. [OE. *murnan*].

MOURNER, [mawn'-er], *n.* one who mourns; one who goes to a funeral; a paid attendant at a funeral.

MOURNFUL, [mawn'-fōōl], *adj.* causing sorrow; feeling sorrow or grief; expressing sorrow; sad, gloomy.

MOURNFULLY, [mawn'-fōōl-i], *adv.* in mournful fashion.

MOURNFULNESS, [mawn'-fōōl-nes], *n.* the state of mourning, or of being mournful.

MOURNING (1), [mawn'-ing], *n.* lamentation, grief; black clothes worn at a time of bereavement; the period during which these are worn.

MOURNING (2), [mawn'-ing], *adj.* that mourns; expressive of grief.

MOURNING-BROOCH, [mawn'-ing-brōch'], *n.* a jet brooch.

MOURNING-COACH, [mawn'-ing-kōch'], *n.* a coach in which to attend a funeral.

MOURNING-DOVE, [mawn'-ing-duv'], *n.* the American dove, *Zenaidura carolinensis*, so called from its cry.

MOURNINGLY, [mawn'-ing-li], *adv.* in a manner of lamentation.

MOURNING-REGLET, [mawn'-ing-reg'-let], *n.* a metal strip used for printing heavy, black, column-borders in a newspaper to express mourning.

MOUSE (1), (*pl.* **mice**), [mows], *n.* any small rodent of the genus *Mus*; (*fig.*) a quiet, shy person; the leaden weight used in the mechanism of sash-windows; a darkish, browny-grey colour. [OE. *mus*].

MOUSE (2), [mows], *v.i.* to hunt for mice; (*fig.*) to search diligently; to study carefully; (*naut.*) to knot or ring (a hook or stay) with spun yarn to prevent slipping.

MOUSE-COLOUR, [mows'-kul'-er], *n.* a dark brownish-grey colour.

MOUSE-EAR, [mows'-ēer], *n.* any of several plants including the forget-me-not, the hawkweed, *Hieracium Pilosella*, and certain species of chickweed.

MOUSEHOLE, [mows'-hōl'], *n.* a hole through which mice come.

MOUSER, [mows'-er], *n.* a cat that catches mice.

MOUSE-SIGHT, [mows'-sīt'], *n.* myopia.

MOUSE-TAIL, [mows'-tāl], *n.* (*bot.*) the plant, *Myosurus minimus*, so called from the shape of the fruiting stalks.

MOUSETRAP, [mows'-trap], *n.* a trap for catching a mouse.

MOUSMEE, [mōōs'-mē], *n.* an unwedded girl in Japan; a Japanese waitress. [Jap. *musume*].

MOUSQUETAIRE, [mōōs'-ket-āer'], *n.* a member of the French royal bodyguard in the 17th and 18th centuries. [Fr. *mousquetaire*].

MOUSETRAP

MOUSSE, [mōōs], *n.* a sweet dish made with whipped cream, variously flavoured. [Fr. *mousse* foam].

MOUSSELINE, [mōōs-lēn'], *n.* muslin; a very fine glassware ornamented with a decoration resembling lace or muslin. [Fr. *mousseline*].

MOUSTACHE, [mōōs-tahsh'], *n.* hair grown on the upper lip of a man; similar hair on the lip of an animal. [It. *mustaccio*].

MOUSY, [mows'-i], *adj.* overrun with mice; like a mouse in appearance or behaviour.

MOUTAN, [moo'-tan], *n. Pæonia Moutan*, the tree-peony.
MOUTH (1), [mowth], *n.* the opening in the head of animals and humans, bounded and closed by the lips, through which food is taken; the cavity behind the lips, containing the teeth, tongue, etc.; any outlet or aperture as of a river, cave, vessel, etc.; the mouthpiece; a living creature to be fed; **to shut one's m.**, to be silent; **down in the m.**, dejected, depressed; **to make a m.**, to pout, grimace. [OE. *muth*].
MOUTH (2), [mowTH], *v.t. and i.* to speak with affected pomposity and facial movement; to rant; to chew violently; to discipline a horse to the bit.
MOUTHER, [mowTH'-er], *n.* one who mouths.
MOUTHFUL, [mowth'-fōōl], *n.* as much as the mouth contains at once; (*slang*) a great deal.
MOUTHING, [mowTH'-ing], *n.* bombastic utterance.
MOUTHLESS, [mowth'-les], *adj.* lacking a mouth.
MOUTH-ORGAN, [mowth'-aw'-gan], *n.* a small wind instrument containing a series of small rectangular openings from which different notes are produced when played by the lips.
MOUTHPIECE, [mowth'-pēs], *n.* that part of a pipe, tube or musical instrument to be inserted into the mouth; someone or something that expresses the views of others on their behalf.
MOUTHY, [mowTH'-i], *adj.* bombastic, wordy.
MOVABILITY, [mōōv'-a-bil'-i-ti], *n.* the condition of being movable.
MOVABLE, [mōōv'-abl], *adj.* capable of being moved, variable in date, not fixed or stationary; (*Scots leg.*) personal (of estate, property, etc.).
MOVABLES, [mōōv'-ablz], *n.(pl.)* things (*esp.* possessions) that may be moved, chattels, personal property.
MOVABLY, [mōōv'-ab-li], *adv.* in a movable way.
MOVE (1), [mōōv], *n.* the process of moving or of being moved; a change to another residence; a prescribed or tactical movement or act in a game or series of operations, etc.; right or turn to move; **to get a m. on**, to hurry.
MOVE (2), [mōōv], *v.t.* to change the position of; to agitate, stir; to set in motion; to affect emotionally, provoke; to influence; to urge; prevail on; to propose; *v.i.* to be capable of changing its position; to change position, to shift; to vibrate, oscillate, etc.; to be propelled; to change, develop; to change one's place of residence; to live; **to m. in**, to settle in a new residence. [L. *movere*].
MOVEMENT, [mōōv'-ment], *n.* the process of moving; change of place or position; action, activity; the way in which anything or anyone moves; a piece of mechanism, *esp.* that by which a watch works; a prescribed motion or evolution; (*mus.*) a complete section of a long musical composition; the spirit felt to quicken anything; a trend; a widely shared body of opinion, *esp.* in favour of some change or plan; the people sharing this, considered collectively; an organization to further such aims; (*pl.*) all that a person does in a given time.
MOVER, [mōōv'-er], *n.* someone or something that moves; a proposer of a resolution; agent, worker, instigator.
MOVIES, [mōōv'-iz], *n.(pl.)* (*slang*) cinematograph pictures.
MOVING, [mōōv'-ing], *adj.* emotionally affecting, touching; that moves.
MOVINGLY, [mōōv'-ing-li], *adv.* in a moving way
MOVINGNESS, [mōōv'-ing-nes], *n.* the power of moving or affecting, *esp.* the emotions.
MOVING STAIRCASE, [mōōv'-ing-stāer'-kās], *n.* an escalator.
MOW (1), [mō], *n.* a sheaf or stack of corn, hay, or other vegetable produce. [OE. *muga*].
MOW (2), [mō], *n.* a grimace. [Fr. *moue*].
MOW (3), **(mown)**, [mō], *v.t. and i.* to cut down grass, etc., with a scythe or machine; **to m. down**, to kill or fell indiscriminately in large numbers. [OE. *mawan*].
MOW (4), [mō], *v.i.* to grimace. [MOW (2)].
MOWBURN, [mō'-burn], *v.i.* (of a stack of corn, etc.), to ferment.
MOWER, [mō'-er], *n.* someone or something that mows.
MOWING (1), [mō'-ing], *n.* the act of one who mows.
MOWING (2), [mō'-ing], *adj.* grimacing.
MOXA, [mok'-sa], *n.* the plant, *Artemisia Moxa*; the down-like surface on its leaves, dried and applied to the skin as a counter-irritant. [Jap. *mokusa*].
MOXIBUSTION, [moks'-i-bus'-chun], *n.* cauterization by moxa.
MOYA, [moi'-a], *n.* (*geol.*) a volcanic mud. [Native].
MOZARAB, MUZARAB, [mōz-a'-rab], *n.* a Spanish Christian under the Moslem rule. [Span. *mozarabe*].
MOZARABIC, [mōz-a'-rab-ic], *adj.* of, or pertaining to, a type of music or liturgy used by the Spanish Christians under Moorish sovereignty. [Arab. *mustaçrib* desiring to be Arabic].
MOZE, [mōz], *v.t.* to raise the nap of, to gig, teazle. [Uncert.].
MR., [mis'-ter], abbreviation for MISTER.
MRS., [mis'-iz], abbreviation for MISSIS.
MRS. GRUNDY, [mis'-iz-grun'-di], *n.* the personification of respectability and narrow-minded prudery.
MUCATE, [mew'-kāt], *n.* (*chem.*) a salt of mucic acid.
MUCCHERO, [mōōk-āer'-ō], *n.* a sweet-smelling infusion of violets and roses manufactured in Italy. [It. *mucchero*].
MUCEDIN, [mew'-si-din], *n.* a nitrogenous substance contained in gluten. [L. *mucedo mucedinis* mucus].
MUCEDINOUS, [mew-sid'-in-us], *adj.* resembling mould.
MUCH (1), [much], *n.* a large amount, a great deal.
MUCH (2), [much], *adj.* great in quantity or amount. [OE. *mycel*].
MUCH (3), [much], *adv.* greatly, to a large degree or extent; by far; nearly, virtually; often, for long.
MUCHLY, [much'-li], *adv.* (*archaic, coll.*) exceedingly, greatly.
MUCHNESS, [much'-nes], *n.* (*coll.*) greatness in quantity or amount; **much of a m.**, almost alike.
MUCIC, [mew'-sik], *adj.* pertaining to mucus; **m. acid**, an acid obtained by treating various gums with dilute nitric acid.
MUCID, [mew'-sid], *adj.* musty, mouldy, slimy. [L. *mucidus*].
MUCIDNESS, [mew'-sid-nes], *n.* the condition of being mucid.
MUCIFIC, [mew-sif'-ik], *adj.* secreting mucus. [MUCUS and L. *facere* to make].
MUCILAGE, [mew'-sil-ij], *n.* a viscous substance produced by steeping seeds or roots in water; gum; any bodily secretion acting as a lubricant. [L. *mucilago* musty juice].
MUCILAGINOUS, [mew'-sil-aj'-in-us], *adj.* pertaining to, producing, like, mucilage; gummy, slimy.
MUCILAGINOUSNESS, [mew'-sil-aj'-in-us-nes], *n.* the quality of being mucilaginous.
MUCIPAROUS, [mew-sip'-er-us], *adj.* secreting mucus. [MUCUS and L. *parere* to produce].
MUCK (1), [muk], *n.* dung, manure; filth, dirt; (*coll.*) filthy rubbish, trash; **to make a m. of**, (*coll.*) to bungle, mess up; to make dirty and untidy. [ME. *muk*, ~OIcel. *myki*].
MUCK (2), [muk], *v.t.* to manure with muck; (*coll.*) to bungle, do badly or clumsily; **to m. about**, (*coll.*) to loaf about idly; to potter; to play the fool; **to m. up**, (*coll.*) utterly to mismanage; to ruin, upset; to make untidy and dirty.
MUCKER, [muk'-er], *n.* (*coll.*) a bad fall, a cropper.
MUCK-HEAP, [muk'-hēp], *n.* a heap of dung.
MUCK-HILL, [muk'-hil], *n.* a manure-heap.
MUCKINESS, [muk'-i-nes], *n.* the state or quality of being mucky.
MUCKLE, [mukl], *n.* (*Scots*) much, a large quantity. [MICKLE].
MUCKNA, [muk'-na], *n.* a male elephant with undeveloped tusks. [Hind. *makhna*].
MUCK-RAKE, [muk'-rāk], *n.* a rake for collecting muck; (*fig.*) one searching for unsavoury facts or scandal.
MUCK-SWEAT, [muk'-swet], *n.* profuse perspiration.
MUCKWEED, [muk'-wēd], *n.* the plant, white goosefoot, *Chenopodium album*.
MUCK-WORM, [muk'-wurm], *n.* a worm or grub living in muck; (*fig.*) a miser; a dirty child.
MUCKY, [muk'-i], *adj.* dirty, filthy; muddy; nasty; disgusting, obscene.
MUCOSITY, [mew-kos'-i-ti], *n.* the state or quality of being mucous.
MUCOSO-SACCHARINE, [mew-kō'-sō-sak'-er-in], *adj.* having the qualities of mucus and sugar.
MUCOUS, [mew'-kus], *adj.* relating to, secreting, containing, like, mucus; viscous; **m. membrane**, the slimy membranous lining of various canals and cavities of the body. [L. *mucosus*].
MUCOUSNESS, [mew'-kus-nes], *n.* mucosity.
MUCRO, [mew'-krō], *n.* (*bot.*) a stiff, sharp-pointed organ or process. [L. *mucro* point].

MUCRONATE, [mew'-kron-āt], *adj.* (*bot.*) ending in a short sharp point. [L. *mucronatus* pointed].
MUCRONATED, [mew'-kron-āt-id], *adj.* mucronate.
MUCRONATELY, [mew'-kron-āt-li], *adv.* in mucronate fashion.
MUCULENT, [mew'-kyōō-lent], *adj.* slimy, rather viscous. [L. *muculentus*].
MUCUS, [mew'-kus], *n.* the viscid fluid secreted by the mucous membranes; the moist, slimy substance secreted by slugs, etc. [L. *mucus* mucus from the nose].
MUD, [mud], *n.* soft, wet earth or soil; (*fig.*) something vile and contemptible; **m. pack**, a layer of fuller's earth applied to the skin to beautify it; **to sling m. at**, to level insults or accusations at. [ME. *mudde*, ~MLGerm. *mudde*].
MUDAR, [mu'-dah(r)], *n.* the madar, *Calotropis gigantea*, an East Indian shrub the juice of which is used medicinally; the medicinal extract from its root. [Hind. *madar*].
MUDARIN, [mew'-der-in], *n.* the bitter principle from the bark of the roots of the mudar.
MUD-BATH, [mud'-bahth], *n.* a bath of mud taken to cleanse the pores of the skin.
MUD-CART, [mud'-kaht], *n.* a scavenger's cart for carrying away dirt from the streets.
MUDDILY, [mud'-i-li], *adv.* in a muddy manner.
MUDDINESS, [mud'-i-nes], *n.* the quality of being muddy.
MUDDLE (1), [mudl], *n.* a complete mix-up, a misunderstanding; a state of confusion and disorder; a bewildering tangle or perplexity.
MUDDLE (2), [mudl], *v.t. and i.* to confuse, stupefy; to bungle, make a mess of, put into a muddle; to blunder along unmethodically. [~MDu. *moddelen* to make muddy].
MUDDLED, [mudld], *adj.* confused, bewildered.
MUDDLE-HEADED, [mudl'-hed'-id], *adj.* unable to think clearly, stupid.
MUDDY (1), [mud'-i], *adj.* covered with, containing, mud, dirty; resembling mud in colour; drab; turbid, cloudy; muddled, confused.
MUDDY (2), [mud'-i], *v.t.* to make muddy.
MUD-FISH, [mud'-fish], *n.* any of various fishes dwelling in the mud on the bed of streams, etc.
MUDGUARD, [mud'-gahd], *n.* a metal, plastic or wooden shield over the upper part of the wheel of a vehicle, to trap the mud thrown up as it rotates.
MUD-HOLE, [mud'-hōl], *n.* the hole by which the sediment is carried away from a boiler.
MUDIR, [mōōd-ēer'], *n.* an Egyptian or Turkish governor. [Arab. *mudir*].
MUDLARK (1), [mud'-lahk], *n.* one who probes the mud round docks, in sewers, etc., in the hope of finding something; one who plays in the mud; a street urchin; a frolic in the mud.
MUDLARK (2), [mud'-lahk], *v.i.* to frolic in the mud.
MUD PIE, [mud'-pī'], *n.* a moulded cake of mud, *esp.* as made by children.
MUD-PLANTAIN, [mud'-plant'-ān], *n.* a North American aquatic plant of the genus *Heteranthera*.
MUD-PLOVER, [mud'-pluv'-er], *n.* the grey plover, *Squatarola helvetica*.
MUD-SCOW, [mud'-skow], *n.* a flat-bottomed vessel used for carrying mud from a dredger.
MUD-VALVE, [mud'-valv], *n.* the valve by which sediment is emptied from a steam-boiler.
MUD-WALL, [mud'-wawl], *n.* a wall built of earth or clay, or of stones lined with clay.
MUDWORT, [mud'-wurt], *n.* the small plant *Limosella aquatica*.
MUEZZIN, [mōō-ez'-in], *n.* an official attached to a mosque, whose business it is to summon Moslems to prayer. [Arab. *mu'azzin*].
MUFF (1), [muf], *n.* a warm cylindrical covering of fur into which the hands may be placed to keep them warm. [Du. *mof* from Fr. *moufle*].
MUFF (2), [muf], *n.* a clumsy, stupid person, a duffer, *esp.* at games; a blunder, miss, *esp.* in a game. [Uncert.].
MUFF (3), [muf], *n.* the whitethroat, *Sylvia cinerea*. [Unkn.].
MUFF (4), [muf], *v.t.* (*sport*) to bungle, foozle, to miss badly. [MUFF (2)].
MUFFETEE, [muf'-et-ē'], *n.* (*archaic*) a mitten for the wrist.
MUFFIN, [muf'-in], *n.* a flat, circular, spongy cake toasted, buttered, and eaten hot. [Uncert.].
MUFFINEER, [muf'-in-ēer'], *n.* a covered dish for keeping toasted muffins hot; a cruet for sprinkling salt on muffins.
MUFFLE (1), [mufl], *n.* a fire-clay oven or chamber in which substances may be heated without actual contact with the source of heat; a receptacle in which pottery or porcelain is baked after painting; †a boxing glove; †a kind of mitten. [OFr. *moufle* a thick glove].
MUFFLE (2), [mufl], *n.* the thick uncovered end of the upper lip and nose of ruminant animals and rodents. [Fr. *mufle*].
MUFFLE (3), [mufl], *v.t.* to wrap up so as to protect from the weather, or to conceal; to deaden the sound of, render indistinct.
MUFFLER, [muf'-ler], *n.* a scarf worn round the neck for warmth; a silencer for the engine of a motor vehicle; a felt pad interposed between the strings and hammers of a pianoforte by depressing a pedal; (*archaic*) a thick glove.
MUFFLON, see MOUFLON.
MUFTI, [muf'-ti], *n.* an official expounder or doctor of Mohammedan law; plain clothes, civilian attire. [Arab. *mufti*].
MUG (1), [mug], *n.* a drinking vessel which does not taper to its base, fitted with a handle; a large earthenware receptacle for bread; a pot vessel for shaving water. [Unkn.].
MUG (2), [mug], *n.* (*slang*) the face. [*Prec.*].
MUG (3), [mug], *n.* (*slang*) a simpleton who is readily swindled; a fool; a duffer; **general m.**, (*slang*) the person who has to do all the work. [MUG(GINS)].
MUG (4), (**mugging, mugged**), [mug], *v.i.* **to m. up**, (*slang*) to study intensively for examination purposes, to cram. [Unkn.].
MUGGER, [mug'-er], *n.* the magar, the Indian crocodile, *Crocodilus palustris*. [Hind. *magar*].
MUGGINS, [mug'-inz], *n.* a gullible fool, a stupid person; a children's card game; a variety of dominoes.
MUGGISH, [mug'-ish], *adj.* muggy, warm and drizzly.
MUGGLETONIANS, [mugl-tō'-ni-anz], *n.*(*pl.*) a sect of Christians founded in 1651, followers of Muggleton. [L. *Muggleton* (1609-1698), a fanatical tailor who claimed to be the last and greatest of the prophets].
MUGGY, [mug'-i], *adj.* damp and close. [~OIcel. *mugga* soft drizzling mist].
MUGWORT, [mug'-wurt], *n.* the plant, *Artemisia vulgaris*; the wormwood, *Artemisia absinthium*; the crosswort, *Galium cruciata*. [OE. *mycgwyrt*].
MUGWUMP, [mug'-wump], *n.* (*U.S. slang*) one who is above party politics; a superior person; a great man. [NAm. Indian *mugwump* chief, boss].
MUHARRAM, see MOHARRAM.
MULATTO (1), [mew-lat'-ō], *n.* the child of a white and a negro. [Span. *mulato* of mixed breed].
MULATTO (2), [mew-lat'-ō], *adj.* yellowish-brown.
MULBERRY, [mul'-ber-i], *n.* a tree of the genus *Morus*, on whose leaves the silk-worm feeds; the fruit of this tree; the colour of its berries, a deep reddish-purple. [ME. *moolbery* ~MHGerm. *mulbere*].

MULBERRY

MULCH (1), [mulch], *n.* a mixture of decaying damp straw, leaves, manure, etc., used to keep soil moist, and to protect the roots of newly planted shrubs, etc. [~ME. *molsh* soft, decaying].
MULCH (2), [mulch], *v.t.* to spread mulch round or on.
MULCT (1), [mulkt], *n.* a monetary fine imposed for some offence; a penalty, punishment. [L. *mulcta*].
MULCT (2), [mulkt], *v.t.* to fine; to deprive of. [L. *mulctare*].
MULE (1), [mewl], *n.* the offspring of a mare by a male ass; a cross between a canary and some other member of the finch family; a hybrid; a machine for cotton-spinning; (*fig.*) a stubborn, obstinate person. [OE. *mul* from L. *mulus*].
MULE (2), [mewl], *n.* a low heelless slipper. [Fr. *mule*].
MULE-DEER, [mewl'-dēer], *n.* the North American deer, *Cariacus macrotis*, which has mule-like ears.
MULE-SPINNER, [mewl'-spin'-er], *n.* one who spins on a spinning-mule.
MULETEER, [mewl'-tēer], *n.* one who drives mules. [Fr. *muletier*].
MULEWORT, [mewl'-wurt], *n.* a fern of the genus *Hemionitis*. [MULE and OE. *wyrt* plant].
MULGA, [mul'-ga], *n.* an Australian species of acacia, *Acacia aneura*; an aboriginal war implement from the wood of this tree. [Native].

MULIEBRITY, [mewl'-i-e'-brit-i], *n.* womanhood; effeminacy. [L. *muliebritas*].
MULISH, [mewl'-ish], *adj.* like a mule, stubborn, obstinate.
MULISHLY, [mewl'-ish-li], *adv.* in mulish fashion.
MULISHNESS, [mewl'-ish-nes], *n.* the characteristic of being mulish.
MULL (1), [mul], *n.* a snuffbox made of the small end of a ram's horn. [Uncert.].
MULL (2), [mul], *n.* (*Scots*) a headland or promontory. [Gael. *maol*].
MULL (3), [mul], *n.* a thin, soft type of muslin. [Hind. *malmal*].
MULL (4), [mul], *n.* (*coll.*) a mess, muddle, blunder. [Unkn.].
MULL (5), [mul], *v.t.* to heat, sweeten, and season with spices (wine, beer, etc.). [Unkn.].
MULL (6), [mul], *v.t.* (*coll.*) to muddle, bungle, spoil. [MULL (4)].
MULLA, MULLAH, [mul'-a], *n.* a person versed in Mohammedan rites and laws; a Mohammedan religious teacher; a fanatical religious leader. [Pers. and Turk. *mulla*].
MULLED, [muld], *adj.* (of wine, ale, etc.) heated, sweetened and spiced.
MULLEIN, [mul'-in], *n.* a plant of the genus *Verbascum* with rough leaves and yellow, mauve, or white flowers. [AFr. *moleine*].
MULLER, [mul'-er], *n.* a flat-bottomed stone or pestle for grinding painters' colours, medicinal powders, etc.; a grinding or pounding machine. [~OFr. *moloir* grinding].
MULLER-GLASS, [mul'-er-glahs'], *n.* hyalite, a hard glassy mineral.
MULLET (1), [mul'-et], *n.* either of two varieties of sea-fish, the red mullet, genus *Mullus*, of the *Mullidæ*, or the grey mullet, genus *Mugil*, of the *Mugilidæ*. [OFr. *mulet*, *dim.* of L. *mullus* red mullet].
MULLET (2), [mul'-et], *n.* (*her.*) a five-pointed star, often pierced in the centre to represent the rowel of a spur. [OFr. *molette* rowel of a spur].

MULLET

MULLIGATAWNY, [mul'-i-ga-taw'-ni], *n.* a thick, highly seasoned curry soup. [Tamil *milagutannir* pepper water].
MULLIGRUBS, [mul'-i-grubz], *n.* (*coll.*) stomach-ache, colic; a fit of depression. [Invented word].
MULLION (1), MUNNION, [mul'-yun, mun'-yun], *n.* an upright bar dividing the apertures of a window, *esp.* in Gothic windows. [OFr. *moignon* tree-stump].
MULLION (2), MUNNION, [mul'-yun, mun'-yun], *v.t.* to divide by mullions.
MULLIONED, [mul'-yund], *adj.* divided by mullions.
MULLOCK, [mul'-ok], *n.* waste rock from which gold has been extracted, or rock containing no gold. [ME. *mol*, *mul* dirt, rubbish].
MULTANGULAR, [mult-ang'-gyŏŏ-ler], *adj.* with many angles.
MULTANGULARLY, [mult-ang'-gyŏŏ-ler-li], *adv.* with many angles.
MULTARTICULATE, [mult'-ah-tik'-yŏŏ-lat], *adj.* many-jointed.
MULTEITY, [mult-ē'-i-ti], *n.* manifoldness, multiplicity. [L. *multus* many].
MULTI-, *pref.* many. [L. *multus*].
MULTICAPSULAR, [mult'-i-kap'-syŏŏ-ler], *adj.* (*bot.*) with many capsules.
MULTICARINATE, [mult'-i-ka'-rin-āt], *adj.* (of a shell) having many keel-like ridges.
MULTICAVOUS, [mult'-i-kāv'-us], *adj.* full of holes. [L. *multicavus*].
MULTICIPITAL, [mult'-i-sip'-it-al], *adj.* many-headed. [MULTI and L. *caput* head].
MULTICOSTATE, [mult'-i-kost'-āt], *adj.* having several ribs. [MULTI and L. *costatus* ribbed].
MULTICUSPIDATE, [mult'-i-kusp'-id-āt], *adj.* having more than two cusps.
MULTIDENTATE, [mult'-i-dent'-āt], *adj.* having numerous teeth or teeth-like processes.
MULTIDIGITATE, [mult'-i-dij'-it-āt], *adj.* having many fingers or finger-like processes.
MULTIFARIOUS, [mult'-i-fāer'-i-us], *adj.* many and varied; (*bot.*) having branches in many rows. [LL. *multifarius*].
MULTIFARIOUSLY, [mult'-i-fāer'-i-us-li], *adv.* in multifarious fashion.
MULTIFARIOUSNESS, [mult'-i-fāer'-i-us-nes], *n.* the quality of being multifarious.
MULTIFID, [mult'-i-fid], *adj.* having many divisions cleft into many parts. [L. *multifidus*].
MULTIFIDOUS, [mult'-i-fid'-us], *adj.* multifid.
MULTIFLOROUS, [mult'-i-flaw'-rus], *adj.* producing or possessing many flowers. [LL. *multiflorus*].
MULTIFOIL (1), [mult'-i-foil], *n.* (*arch.*) a circular ornament with more than five leaf-like divisions.
MULTIFOIL (2), [mult'-i-foil], *adj.* (*arch.*) with more than five leaf-like divisions.
MULTIFORM, [mult'-i-fawm], *adj.* possessing many forms or shapes. [L. *multiformis*].
MULTIFORMITY, [mult'-i-fawm'-i-ti], *n.* diversity of form. [LL. *multiformitas*].
MULTIFORMOUS, [mult'-i-fawm'-us], *adj.* multiform.
MULTIGENEROUS, [mult'-i-jen'-er-us], *adj.* of many kinds. [L. *multigenerus*].
MULTIGYRATE, [mult'-i-jier'-āt], *adj.* considerably convoluted.
MULTIJUGOUS, [mult'-i-jew'-gus], *adj.* consisting of many pairs of leaflets. [MULTI and L. *jugum* yoke].
MULTILATERAL, [mult'-i-lat'-er-al], *adj.* many-sided.
MULTILINEAL, [mult'-i-lin'-i-al], *adj.* containing many lines.
MULTILOBATE, [mult'-i-lōb'-āt], *adj.* having many lobes.
MULTILOCULAR, [mult'-i-lok'-yŏŏ-ler], *adj.* with many cells or chambers. [MULTI and L. *loculus* little place].
MULTILOQUENCE, [mult-il'-ō-kwents], *n.* loquaciousness, verbosity. [LL. *multiloquentia*].
MULTILOQUOUS, [mult-il'-o-kwus], *adj.* talkative, loquacious. [L. *multiloquus*].
MULTI-MILLIONAIRE, [mult'-i-mil'-yun-āer'], *n.* one who is several times a millionaire.
MULTINODAL, [mult'-i-nōd'-al], *adj.* having many nodes or knots. [MULTI and L. *nodus* knot].
MULTINODATE, [mult'-i-nōd'-āt], *adj.* multinodal.
MULTINOMIAL (1), [mult'-i-nō'-mi-al], *n.* (*alg.*) a multinomial expression.
MULTINOMIAL (2), [mult'-i-nō'-mi-al], *adj.* (*alg.*) containing three or more terms connected by plus or minus signs. [MULTI and (BI)NOMIAL].
MULTIPAROUS, [mult-ip'-er-us], *adj.* producing many at a birth; pertaining to a woman who has borne more than one child. [MdL. *multiparus*].
MULTIPARTITE, [mult'-i-paht'-it], *adj.* split up into many parts. [L. *multipartitus*].
MULTIPED (1), [mult'-i-ped], *n.* an animal with many feet. [L. *multipes*].
MULTIPED (2), [mult'-i-ped], *adj.* having many feet. [L. *multipeda*].
MULTIPINNATE, [mult'-i-pin'-āt], *adj.* pinnated many times.
MULTIPLE (1), [mult'-ipl], *n.* (*math.*) a quantity or number which contains another an exact number of times; **a common m.**, a number that contains two or more different numbers exactly.
MULTIPLE (2), [mult'-ipl], *adj.* having many individual elements or components; containing or involving two or more; (*math.*) repeated; compound; **m. shop**, a retail organization with a chain of shops in different districts; one of such shops; **m. star**, a group of stars appearing as one. [LL. *multiplus*].
MULTIPLEPOINDING, [mult'-ipl-poind'-ing], *n.* (*Scots leg.*) an action raised by a person holding money or property claimed by several, to obtain a settlement of claims in court. [MULTIPLE and Scots *poind* distrain].
MULTIPLEX, [mult'-i-pleks], *adj.* manifold, multiple. [L. *multiplex*].
MULTIPLIABLE, [mult'-i-pli'-abl], *adj.* able to be multiplied.
MULTIPLIABLENESS, [mult'-i-pli'-abl-nes], *n.* capacity of being multiplied.
MULTIPLICABLE, [mult'-i-plik'-abl], *adj.* multipliable. [L. *multiplicabilis*].
MULTIPLICAND, [mult'-i-plik-and'], *n.* (*arith.*) the number to be multiplied by another. [L. *multiplicandus* that must be multiplied].
MULTIPLICATION, [mult'-i-plik-ā'-shun], *n.* the act of multiplying; the state of being multiplied; (*arith.*) the operation whereby any given number is multiplied. [L. *multiplicatio*].
MULTIPLICATIVE, [mult'-i-plik-at-iv], *adj.* able to multiply or be multiplied. [MedL. *multiplicativus*].

MULTIPLICATOR, [mult'-i-plik-āt'-er], *n.* a multiplier. [LL. *multiplicator*].

MULTIPLICITY, [mult'-i-plis'-iti], *n.* the quality of being multiple or numerous; a great number. [L. *multiplicitas*].

MULTIPLIER, [mult'-i-plī-er], *n.* one who, or that which, multiplies; (*arith.*) the number by which another is multiplied; (*elect.*) an instrument for intensifying the sensitiveness of an electric meter.

MULTIPLY, [mult'-i-plī], *v.t.* and *i.* to increase in number; (*math.*) to apply one of two numbers to another in such a way that the second bears the same relation to the first as the first bears to unity; **multiplying glass**, a concave lens with many reflecting facets. [L. *multiplicare*].

MULTIPOLAR, [mult'-i-pōl'-er], *adj.* with many poles.

MULTIPOTENT, [mult-ip'-ot-ent], *adj.* possessing power to do many things. [L. *multipotens*].

MULTIPRESENCE, [mult'-i-prez'-ents], *n.* the quality of being multipresent.

MULTIPRESENT, [mult'-i-prez'-ent], *adj.* having the property or power of being present in many places at the same time.

MULTIRADIATE, [mult'-i-rād'-i-āt], *adj.* many-rayed.

MULTIRAMIFIED, [mult'-i-ram'-i-fīd], *adj.* having many branches. [MULTI and L. *ramus* branch].

MULTI-RANGE, [mult'-i-rānj'], *adj.* (*motoring*) (of a gear-box) having several ratios.

MULTISECT, [mult'-i-sekt], *adj.* divided into many segments or parts. [MdL. *multisectus*].

MULTISILIQUOUS, [mult'-i-sil'-i-kwus], *adj.* having many seed-vessels. [MULTI and L. *siliqua* seed-vessel].

MULTISONOUS, [mult'-i-sōn'-us], *adj.* having many sounds, sounding much, sonorous.

MULTISPIRAL, [mult'-i-spīer'-al], *adj.* (of shells) having many spirals or whorls.

MULTISTAMINATE, [mult'-i-stam'-in-āt], *adj.* having many stamens.

MULTISTRIATE, [mult'-i-strī'-āt], *adj.* adorned with many streaks.

MULTISULCATE, [mult'-i-sulk'-āt], *adj.* containing many furrows, deeply furrowed. [MULTI and L. *sulcatus* furrowed].

MULTISYLLABLE, [mult'-i-sil'-abl], *n.* a word containing many syllables.

MULTITUBERCULATE, [mult'-i-tew-ber'-kyōō-lāt], *adj.* having many tubercles.

MULTITUBULAR, [mult'-i-tewb'-yōō-ler], *adj.* having many tubes.

MULTITUDE, [mult'-i-tewd], *n.* the quality of being numerous; a large number; a great crowd of people; **the m.**, the common people. [L. *multitudo*].

MULTITUDINARY, [mult'-i-tewd'-in-er-i], *adj.* multitudinous.

MULTITUDINOUS, [mult'-i-tewd'-in-us], *adj.* exceedingly numerous, manifold; containing a multitude; having an innumerable variety of forms.

MULTITUDINOUSLY, [mult'-i-tewd'-in-us-li], *adv.* in great numbers.

MULTIVALENT, [mult-iv'-al-ent], *adj.* having more than one valency.

MULTIVALVE (1), [mult'-i-valv'], *n.* a multivalve shell; a mollusc with such a shell.

MULTIVALVE (2), [mult'-i-valv'], *adj.* having many valves.

MULTIVALVULAR, [mult'-i-valv'-yōō-ler], *adj.* having many valves.

MULTIVERSANT, [mult'-i-vers'-ant], *adj.* assuming many shapes. [MULTI and L. *versans* turning].

MULTIVOCAL, [mult'-i-vōk'-al], *adj.* ambiguous, equivocal, capable of different interpretations.

MULTOCA, [mōōl-tō'-ka], *n.* the Turkish code of law. [Turk. *multoca*].

MULTOCULAR, [mult-ok'-yōō-ler], *adj.* many-eyed.

MULTUM, [mult'-um], *n.* any of several compound preparations; **m. in parvo**, much contained in a small compass. [L. *multum* much].

MULTUNGULATE, [mult-ung'-gyōō-lāt], *adj.* (*zool.*) with the hoof divided into more than two parts. [MULTI and L. *ungula* hoof].

MULTURE, [mul'-cher], *n.* a portion of the corn ground given to a miller, for the privilege of grinding corn at his mill; the right to demand this toll. [OFr. *molture*].

MUM (1), [mum], *n.* (*coll.*) mother. [MUMMY (1)].

MUM (2), [mum], *n.* a strong ale originally brewed in Brunswick from wheat. [LGerm. *mumme*]

MUM (3), [mum], *adj.* (*coll.*) silent, dumb. [Echoic].

MUM (4), [mum], *adv.* (*coll.*) silently.

MUM (5), [mum], *int.* hush, be silent; **mum's the word**, do not tell anyone.

MUM (6), **(mumming, mummed)**, [mum], *v.i.* to act in dumb show, usually wearing a mask or other disguise. [~Du. *mommen* to mask].

MUMBLE (1), [mumbl], *n.* an indistinct articulation or sound.

MUMBLE (2), [mumbl], *v.t.* and *i.* to speak or say indistinctly without moving the lips properly, to mutter; to chew or eat slowly and laboriously. [ME. *momelen* from MUM (3)].

MUMBLEMENT, [mumbl'-ment], *n.* mumbled speech or utterance.

MUMBLER, [mum'-bler], *n.* a person who mumbles.

MUMBLINGLY, [mum'-bling-li], *adv.* in a mumbling manner.

MUMBO-JUMBO, [mum'-bō-jum'-bō], *n.* a grotesque negro idol worshipped by certain African tribes; (*fig.*) a foolish fetish. [Unkn.].

MUMCHANCE, [mum'-chahnts], *n.* (*archaic*) a tongue-tied person; †a former game played with dice. [MLGerm. *mummenschanz* dice game].

MUMMER, [mum'-er], *n.* a masked actor in a dumb show; (*coll.*) an actor. [OFr *momeur*].

MUMMERY, [mum'-er-i], *n.* a performance given by mummers; grotesque and empty ceremonial or ritual. [OFr. *momerie*].

MUMMIED, [mum'-id], *adj.* made into a mummy.

MUMMIFICATION, [mum'-i-fik-ā'-shun], *n.* the act of mummifying; the state of being mummified.

MUMMIFORM, [mum'-i-fawm], *adj.* resembling, in the form of, a mummy.

MUMMIFY, [mum'-i-fī], *v.t.* to make into a mummy; *v.i.* to assume the appearance of a mummy. [Fr. *momifier*].

MUMMING, [mum'-ing], *n.* masked acting in dumb show.

MUMMY (1), [mum'-i], *n.* (*coll.*) mother. [MAMMY].

MUMMY (2), [mum'-i], *n.* the dead body of a human being or animal embalmed and dried, *esp.* one preserved in this way by the ancient Egyptians; a bituminous Eastern drug used medicinally; a rich brown tint from a bituminous substance; **m. wheat**, a species of wheat, *Triticum compositum*, reputed to have been grown from seed found in a mummy coffin. [Pers. *mumiya*].

MUMMY

MUMMY (3), [mum'-i], *v.t.* to make into a mummy. [MUMMY (2)].

MUMP, [mump], *v.i.* (*archaic*) to mope, sulk; †to mumble; (*slang*) to beg plaintively. [Echoic].

MUMPER, [mump'-er], *n.* a beggar.

MUMPING, [mump'-ing], *n.* begging.

MUMPISH, [mump'-ish], *adj.* sulky, sullenly angry, morose.

MUMPISHLY, [mump'-ish-li], *adv.* in mumpish fashion.

MUMPS, [mumps], *n.*(*pl.*) epidemic parotitis, an acute contagious disease characterized by swelling and inflammation of the salivary glands, *esp.* of the parotid gland; a sulking bout. [MUMP].

MUMPSIMUS, [mump'-sim-us], *n.* a mistake or opinion adhered to even when proved to be wrong. [~L. *sumpsimus* we have assumed].

MUNCH, [munch], *v.t.* and *i.* to chew in a noisy and conspicuous fashion. [Echoic].

MUNCHAUSEN, [mun'-chow-zen], *n.* a fantastic story. [Baron *Munchausen*, the hero of a series of incredible adventures, written in English by the German writer Raspe (1785)].

MUNDANE, [mun'-dān], *adj.* belonging to this world, worldly. [L. *mundanus*].

MUNDANELY, [mun'-dān'-li], *adv.* in mundane fashion.

MUNDIC, [mund'-ik], *n.* Cornish name for iron pyrites. [Uncert.].

MUNDIFICANT, [mund-if'-ik-ant], *n.* a medicinal preparation that cleanses. [L. *mundificans* cleansing].

MUNDIFICATION, [mund'-i-fi-kā'-shun], *n.* the act of cleansing; the state of being cleansed. [MedL. *mundificatio*].

MUNDIFY, [mund'-i-fī], *v.t.* to cleanse, purify. [L. *mundificare*].

MUNDIL, [mund'-il], *n.* a richly ornamented turban. [Arab. *mandil*].

MUNGEET, see MUNJEET.

MUNGO, [mung'-gō], *n.* a shoddy made by teaselling heavy milled cuttings of woollen cloths. [Unkn.].
MUNGOOSE, see MONGOOSE.
MUNICIPAL, [mewn-is'-ip-al], *adj.* pertaining to the local government of a city, town, or borough; carried on or controlled by the governing body of a city, town, or borough; internal, home, domestic; (*Rom hist.*) relating to a provincial city whose inhabitants enjoyed the rights of Roman citizens. [L. *municipalis* belonging to a *municipium* or free town].
MUNICIPALITY, [mewn-i'-si-pal'-i-ti], *n.* a city, town, borough, etc., governed by a mayor and corporation; its governing body.
MUNICIPALIZATION, [mewn-is'-ip-al-iz-ā'-shun], *n.* the act of municipalizing.
MUNICIPALIZE, [mewn-is'-ip-al-īz], *v.t.* to put under municipal control, to make into a municipality; to decentralize.
MUNICIPALLY, [mewn-is'-ip-al-i], *adv.* from a municipal point of view, by municipal means.
MUNIFICENCE, [mewn-if'-is-ents], *n.* the quality of being munificent. [L. *munificentia*].
MUNIFICENT, [mewn-if'-is-ent], *adj.* liberal, generous, bounteous, unstinted.
MUNIFICENTLY, [mewn-if'-is-ent-li], *adv.* in munificent fashion.
MUNIMENTS, [mewn'-i-ments], *n.(pl.)* title-deeds and other written records by which claims and rights are shown and maintained. [L. *munimentum* defence].
MUNITION (1), [mewn-ish'-un], *n.* (*usually pl.*) materials used for warfare, *esp.* ammunition, shells, bombs, etc. [L. *munitio*].
MUNITION (2), [mewn-ish'-un], *v.t.* to furnish with munitions.
MUNJEET, MUNGEET, [mun'-jēt], *n.* the Indian madder, *Rubia cordifolia*, from the root of which is extracted a red dye. [Bengali *munjith*].
MUNNION, see MULLION.
MUNSHI, see MOONSHEE.
MUNTIN, [munt'-in], *n.* (*arch.*) the central upright bar of a frame between the outside uprights. [MONTANT].
MUNTJAK, [munt'-jak], *n.* the small, Eastern short-horned, barking deer, *Cervulus muntjak*. [Sunda *minchek*].
MUNTZ-METAL, [muntz'-met'-al], *n.* an alloy of 60 parts copper and 40 zinc. [G. F. *Muntz* of Birmingham, its inventor].
MURAENA, [mew-rē'-na], *n.* a soft-finned, eel-like genus of fishes. [Gk. *muraina* sea-eel].
MURAGE, [mewr'-ij], *n.* (*hist.*) a tax formerly imposed upon the residents of a town or city for the building and repair of its walls. [MedL. *muragium*].
MURAL (1), [mewr'-al], *n.* a painting on a wall. [MURAL (2)].
MURAL (2), [mewr'-al], *adj.* pertaining to, resembling, a wall, placed, done, on a wall; **m. circle,** an astronomical instrument used for measuring angular distances in the meridian; **m. crown,** (*Rom. antiq.*) a golden crown formed like the top of a battlemented and masoned circular tower, bestowed on the soldier who was first to scale the walls of a besieged city. [L. *muralis*].

MURAL CROWN

MURCHISONITE, [mur'-chis-on-īt], *n.* a variety of felspar. [Sir R. *Murchison* (1792-1871)].
MURDER (1), [mur'-der], *n.* the unlawful killing of a human being with premeditated malice; an instance of this; wanton and unnecessary destruction of life. [AFr. *moerdre*].
MURDER (2), [mur'-der], *v.t.* to kill unlawfully with deliberate intent and premeditated malice; to slay; (*fig.*) to spoil, mar by an atrocious rendering. [*Prec.*].
MURDERER, [mur'-der-er], *n.* one who commits murder.
MURDERESS, [mur'-dres], *n.* a female murderer.
MURDEROUS, [mur'-der-us], *adj.* guilty of, intent on, murder; attended with, intended to cause, murder; deadly, fatal, highly dangerous; (*fig.*) atrocious.
MURDEROUSLY, [mur'-der-us-li], *adv.* in murderous fashion.
MURE, [mew(r)], *v.t.* to surround with walls; to stop up with bricks, etc.; to imprison. [L. *murare*].
MUREX, [mewr'-eks], *n.* a genus of marine whelk-like molluscs, one species of which produces a purple dye. [L. *murex*].
MUREXAN [mewr'-eks-an], *n.* (*chem.*) purpuric acid.
MUREXIDE, [mewr'-eks-id], *n.* purpurate of ammonia, crystallizing in short four-sided prisms.
MURICATE, [mewr'-ik-āt], *adj.* bristling with sharp points or prickles. [L. *muricatus*].
MURICATED, [mewr'-ik-āt'-id], *adj.* muricate.
MURICULATE, [mew-rik'-yoo-lāt], *adj.* having very short prickles.
MURIFORM [mewr'-i-fawm], *adj.* (*bot.*) resembling the arrangement of bricks in a wall. [L. *murus* wall and FORM].
MURINE, [mew'-rīn], *adj.* relating to a mouse or to mice. [L. *murinus*].
MURK (1), MIRK, [murk], *n.* darkness, gloom.
MURK (2), MIRK, [murk], *adj.* (*archaic*) mirky. [OIcel. *myrkr* dark].
MURKILY, [murk'-i-li], *adv.* in a murky way.
MURKINESS, [murk'-i-nes], *n.* the condition of being murky.
MURKY, [murk'-i], *adj.* dark, obscure, gloomy, dismal; depressingly dirty.
MURMUR (1), [mur'-mer], *n.* a gentle, indistinct, continuous, low-pitched sound; a subdued hum of voices; a muffled grumble or expression of discontent. [L. *murmur*].
MURMUR (2), [mur'-mer], *v.t. and i.* to make or utter a murmur; to grumble, complain in a subdued mutter; to speak in a murmur. [L. *murmurare*].
MURMURER, [mur'-mer-er], *n.* a person who murmurs; a grumbler.
MURMURING (1), [mur'-mer-ing], *n.* a murmur.
MURMURING (2), [mur'-mer-ing], *adj.* that murmurs.
MURMURINGLY, [mur'-mer-ing-li], *adv.* with a low continuous sound.
MURMUROUS, [mur'-mer-us], *adj.* murmuring, filled with murmurs.
MURPHY, [mur'-fi], *n.* (*coll.*) a potato. [*Murphy* the Irish name].
MURRAIN, [mu'-rin], *n.* an infectious disease among cattle. [OFr. *morine*].
MURRE, [mur], *n.* the razorbill; the guillemot. [Unkn.].
MURREY (1), [mu'-ri], *n.* a purplish-red colour, mulberry colour.
MURREY (2), [mu'-ri], *adj.* purplish-red in colour like the mulberry. [OFr. *morée*].
MURRHINE, MYRRHINE, [mu'-rīn], *adj.* made of murrha, a kind of fluorspar; **m. glass,** a delicate ancient Eastern ware, made of fluorspar. [L. *murrhinus*].
MURRION, see MORION.
MURRY, [mu'-ri], *n.* the brightly coloured fish, *Muræna helena*.
MUSCA, (*pl.* **muscae**), [mus'-ka], *n.* a genus of dipterous insects, including the house-flies; **muscae volitantes,** (*med.*) specks floating in the eye. [L. *musca* a fly].
MUSCADEL, see MUSCATEL.
MUSCADINE, [mus'-kad-in], *n.* muscatel wine; any of several musk-flavoured grapes. [Fr. *muscadin* flavoured with musk].
MUSCAL, [mus'-kal], *adj.* of, relating to, the mosses. [L. *muscus* moss].
MUSCARDINE, [musk'-ah-dēn], *n.* a disease which kills silkworms. [Fr. *muscardine*].
MUSCAT, [musk'-at'], *n.* a variety of musk-flavoured grape; the vine from which it comes; muscatel wine. [Provenc. *muscat*].
MUSCATEL, MUSCADEL, [musk'-a-tel'], *n.* a rich, sweet wine; the grapes which produce this; a dessert raisin from these grapes. [OFr. *muscadel*, muscatel].
MUSCHELKALK, [moosh'-el-kalk'], *n.* (*geol.*) shell limestone, a hard greyish German limestone. [Germ. *muschelkalk* mussel-lime].
MUSCITE, [mus'-īt], *n.* a fossil moss found principally in amber. [MedL. *muscites*].
MUSCLE (1), [musl], *n.* a membranous-lined band of elastic fibres, capable of contracting and relaxing to produce bodily movement; a part of the body consisting of these; (*fig.*) strength, physical power. [L. *musculus* little mouse from the supposed resemblance].
MUSCLE (2), [musl], *v.i.* **to m. in on,** (*slang*) to force one's way into.
MUSCLE-BOUND, [musl'-bownd'], *adj.* having the muscles stiff from excessive development or lack of exercise.
MUSCLED, [musld], *adj.* generously equipped with muscle.
MUSCOID (1), [musk'-oid], *n.* a moss-like plant.

MUSCOID (2), [musk'-oid], *adj.* moss-like. [L. *muscus* moss and Gk. *oeides* like].
MUSCOLOGY, [musk-ol'-o-ji], *n.* the science or study of mosses. [L. *muscus* moss and Gk. *logos* speech].
MUSCOVADO, [musk'-o-vah'-dō], *n.* crude sugar obtained by evaporating the juice of the sugar cane and removing the molasses. [Span. *mascabado* unrefined].
MUSCOVITE (1), [musk'-o-vīt], *n.* (*archaic*) a Russian; **m. glass,** common colourless mica. [Russ. *Moskva* Moscow].
MUSCOVITE (2), [musk'-o-vīt], *adj.* Russian.
MUSCOVY-DUCK, [musk'-o-vi-duk'], *n.* the tropical American duck, *Cairina moschata.* [MUSK DUCK].
MUSCULAR, [mus'-kyōō-ler], *adj.* pertaining to a muscle; consisting of, derived from, affecting the muscles; strong, brawny, with well-developed muscles. [L. *musculosus*].
MUSCULARITY, [mus'-kyōō-la'-ri-ti], *n.* the condition of being muscular.
MUSCULARLY, [mus'-kyōō-ler-li], *adv.* in muscular fashion.
MUSCULATION, [mus'-kyōō-lā'-shun], *n.* the arrangement and function of the muscles.
MUSCULATURE, [mus'-kyōō-la-cher], *n.* the muscular system.
MUSCULITE, [mus'-kyōō-līt], *n.* a petrified mussel-shell. [L. *musculus* mussel].
MUSE (1), [mewz], *n.* (*class. myth.*) any of nine sister goddesses, each of whom presided over one of the liberal arts; source of inspiration, *esp.* for poetry; poetry. [Gk. *Mousa*].
MUSE (2), [mewz], *n.* a deep reverie, profound meditation.
MUSE (3), [mewz], *v.i.* to ponder, reflect deeply, to be lost in thought or day-dreams; to contemplate thoughtfully. [OFr. *muser*].
MUSEFUL, [mewz'-fōōl], *adj.* mentally preoccupied, in a state of reverie.
MUSEFULLY, [mewz'-fōōl-i], *adv.* in museful fashion.
MUSENA, [mew-sē'-na], *n.* the bark of the Abyssinian tree, *Albizzia anthelmintica.* [Native].
MUSER, [mewz'-er], *n.* one fond of musing.
MUSETTE, [mew-zet'], *n.* a small bagpipe; a soft simple pastoral tune, fit to be played upon this. [Fr. *musette*].
MUSEUM, [mew-zē'-um], *n.* an institution in which specimens and objects of cultural, historical, or scientific interest are housed and exhibited; the collection so housed; **m. piece,** (*coll.*) an old-fashioned person. [Gk. *Mouseion* shrine of the Muses].
MUSH (1), [mush], *n.* a thick porridge made from the boiled meal of maize; a soft, slushy, spongy mass; (*fig.*) treacly sentiment; (*wirel.*) interference by high-power transmitting stations. [MASH (1)].
MUSH (2), [mush], *n.* (*slang*) an umbrella. [MUSHROOM].
MUSH (3), [mush], *n.* (*U.S.*) a journey on foot with a dog-sleigh. [MUSH (4)].
MUSH (4), [mush], *v.i.* (*U.S.*) to proceed on foot driving a dog-sleigh. [Fr. *marcher* to advance].
MUSHINESS, [mush'-i-nes], *n.* the quality of being mushy.
MUSHROOM (1), [mush'-rōōm], *n.* any variety of edible fungus, *esp.* the species *Agaricus campestris*; (*fig.*) a person or thing that has suddenly shot up into general notice; anything resembling a mushroom in shape or rapid growth. [OFr. *moisseron*].
MUSHROOM (2), [mush'-rōōm], *adj.* like a mushroom in shape or in its sudden growth.
MUSHY, [mush'-i], *adj.* consisting of, like, mush; mawkishly sentimental.
MUSIC, [mew'-zik], *n.* the art of producing a rhythmical sequence or combination of sounds in such a manner as to please the ear and appeal to the aesthetic sensibilities; an example of this art; the printed score of such a composition; (*fig.*) any pleasing sound or sounds; (*archaic*) a body of musicians; **to face the m.,** to answer for one's actions. [Gk. *mousike*].
MUSICAL, [mew'-zik-al], *adj.* belonging to, like, producing, of, music; performed to music; pleasing to the ear; fond of, skilled in performing or appreciating, music. [MedL. *musicalis*].
MUSICAL BOX, [mew'-zik-al-boks'], *n.* a box in which a clockwork mechanism produces a sequence of musical sounds.
MUSICAL CHAIRS, [mew'-zik-al-chāerz'], *n.* an indoor game in which a ring of players moves round a row of chairs to music, each player endeavouring to sit on a chair when the music stops.
MUSICAL CLOCK, [mew'-zik-al-klok'] *n.* a clock containing a mechanism that plays tunes at the hours.
MUSICAL COMEDY, [mew'-zik-al-kom'-i-di], *n.* a light form of musical dramatic entertainment, having a slight, comic plot.
MUSICALE, [mew'-zik-ahl'], *n.* an informal private recital or concert of music. [Fr. *musicale*].
MUSICAL GLASSES, [mew'-zik-al-glahs'-ez], *n.(pl.)* a set of glass vessels emitting musical notes when struck by a small hammer.
MUSICALITY, [mew'-zik-al'-i-ti], *n.* the quality of being musical.
MUSICALLY, [mew'-zik-al-i], *adv.* in a musical manner, from the point of view of music.
MUSICALNESS, [mew'-zik-al-nes], *n.* musicality.
MUSICAL-RIDE, [mew'-zik-al-rīd'], *n.* a military exercise on horseback performed to music.
MUSIC-BOOK, [mew'-zik-bŏŏk'], *n.* a book of tunes or songs.
MUSIC-HALL, [mew'-zik-hawl'], *n.* a theatre in which variety shows are given.
MUSICIAN, [mew-zish'-an], *n.* a person skilled in the art of rendering, composing, or appreciating music. [Fr. *musicien*].
MUSICIANLY, [mew-zi'-shan-li], *adj.* worthy of a musician, musical.
MUSIC MASTER, [mew'-zik-mahst'-er], *n.* a teacher of music.
MUSIC MISTRESS, [mewz'-ik-mis'-tres], *n.* a woman who teaches music.
MUSIC PAPER, [mew'-zik-pā'-per], *n.* specially ruled paper for writing out music.
MUSIC-STAND, [mew'-zik-stand'], *n.* a light frame fitted with a ledge for holding a piece of music.
MUSIC-STOOL, [mew'-zik-stōōl'], *n.* a backless seat, often adjustable, for a player on the pianoforte.
MUSING, [mewz'-ing], *n.* meditation, contemplation, dreamy abstraction of mind.
MUSINGLY, [mewz'-ing-li], *adv.* in musing fashion.
MUSK (1), [musk], *n.* a strong-scented secretion from the musk-deer, used in perfumes; the animal itself; a scent as of musk; any of several plants with a musky odour, *esp. Mimulus moschatus.* [Pers. *musk*].
MUSK (2), [musk], *v.t.* (*rare*) to perfume with musk
MUSK-APPLE, [musk'-apl], *n.* an apple with a musky taste.
MUSK-DEER, [musk'-dēer], *n.* the deer, *Moschus moschiferus*, that secretes musk.
MUSK-DUCK, [musk'-duk], *n.* the Muscovy duck, *Cairina moschata*, of America; the musk-duck, *Bizima lobata*, of Australia.
MUSKET, [musk'-et], *n.* a former muzzle-loading, smooth-bore, hand fire arm. [It. *mosquetto* small sparrow-hawk].
MUSKETEER, [musk'-et-ēer'], *n.* a soldier armed with a musket.
MUSKETOON, [musk'-et-ōōn'], *n.* a short thick musket with a large bore, a blunderbuss; a soldier armed with this. [It. *moschettone*].
MUSKET-REST, [musk'-et-rest'], *n.* the rest on which a musket was laid to be fired.
MUSKETRY, [musk'-et-ri], *n.* the use of small arms or rifles, rifle-shooting; †muskets in general; †troops armed with muskets; †the fire of muskets. [Fr. *mousqueterie*].
MUSKINESS, [musk'-i-nes], *n.* the scent of musk; the quality of being musky.
MUSK-MALLOW, [musk'-mal'-ō], *n.* the plant, *Malva moschata*, emitting a musky odour.
MUSK-MELON, [musk'-mel'-on], *n.* the common melon, *Cucumis melo.*
MUSK-ORCHIS, [musk'-aw'-kis], *n.* the orchid, *Herminium monorchis.*
MUSK-OX, [musk'-oks], *n.* the Arctic American bovine ungulate, *Ovibos moschatus.*
MUSK-PEAR, [musk'-pāer], *n.* a fragrant variety of pear.
MUSK-RAT, [musk'-rat], *n.* the musquash, *Fiber zibethicus*, a North American rodent allied to the beaver, and valued for its fur.

MUSK-RAT

MUSK-ROSE, [musk'-rōz], *n.* a rambling rose with a musky fragrance.
MUSK-SHREW, [musk'-shrew'], *n.* an insect-eating animal of the genus *Crocidura.*
MUSK-THISTLE, [musk'-thisl'], *n.* the plant, *Carduus nutans.*

MUSK-WOOD, [musk'-wŏŏd], *n.* any of several trees whose timber has a musky smell, as the West Indian *Guarea trichilioides*, etc.
MUSKY, [musk'-i], *adj.* having the fragrant odour of musk.
MUSLIM, see MOSLEM.
MUSLIN, [muz'-lin], *n.* a fine, thin cotton fabric used for making dresses, etc. [Fr. *mousseline* from It. *Mussolo* Mosul, where first made].
MUSLIN-DE-LAINE, [muz'-lin-de-lān'], *n.* a light woollen, or cotton and woollen, fabric. [Fr. *mousseline-de-laine*].
MUSLINET, [muz'-lin-et'], *n.* a kind of coarse muslin.
MUSMON, [mus'-mon], *n.* the moufion. [Gk. *mousmon*].
MUSNUD, [mus'-nud], *n.* the cushioned seat forming the state throne of native Indian princes. [Arab. *misnad*].
MUSQUASH, [musk'-wosh'], *n.* the musk-rat; the fur of this animal. [Native *muscassus* the red animal].
MUSS (1), [mus], *n.* a scramble, a mix-up, muddle. [Unkn.].
MUSS (2), [mus], *v.t.* (*U.S.*) to disarrange, mix-up, muddle.
MUSSAL, [mus-ahl'], *n.* a torch of rags. [Urdu *massal*].
MUSSEL, [mus'-el], *n.* a bivalve mollusc of the marine group *Mytilidæ* or of the freshwater group *Unionidæ*. [OE. *muscle* from L. *musculus* little mouse].

MUSSEL

MUSSITATION, [mus'-it-ā'-shun], *n.* a muttering, mumbling or murmuring. [L. *mussitatio*].
MUSSUCK, [mus'-uk], *n.* a leather water-bag. [Hind. *masak*].
MUSSULMAN, (*pl.* **Mussulmans**), [mus'-ul-man], *n.* a Mohammedan. [Pers. *musulman*].
MUST (1), [must], *n.* mould, mustiness. [MUSTY].
MUST (2), [must], *n.* new wine from the fresh unfermented juice of grapes. [OE. *must* from L. *mustum*].
MUST (3), [must], *n.* the state of frenzy to which elephants of a certain age are periodically subject. [MUST (4)].
MUST (4), [must], *adj.* (of elephants, etc.) mad, in a state of frenzy. [Pers. *mast* intoxicated].
MUST (5), [must], *auxiliary v. used to express obligation, necessity, certainty or extreme likelihood and also for emphasis.* [OE. *moste, pret.* of *mot* I may, I must].
MUST (6), [must], *v.t. and i.* to grow or make musty. [MUST (1)].
MUSTACHIO, [mus-tah'-shi-ō], *n.* a moustache. [It. *mustachio*].
MUSTACHIOED, [mus-tah'-shi-ōd], *adj.* wearing a moustache.
MUSTAIBA, MOSTAHIBA, [mus'-ta-ē'-ba], *n.* a hard, close-grained wood from Brazil. [Braz. Portug. *mostahiba*].
MUSTANG, [must'-ang], *n.* a horse, *esp.* of the American prairies. [Span. *mestengo*].
MUSTARD, [must'-erd], *n.* any of several plants of the genus *Sinapis*, *esp. Sinapis alba* and *Sinapis nigra*; a spicy yellow powder from the ground seeds of these two plants, used medically and as a condiment; (*coll.*) something or someone unusually keen; **m. and cress,** a salad of cress and the leaves of white mustard; **oil of m.,** a pungent oil from the seeds of black mustard. [OFr. *moustarde*].
MUSTARD-GAS, [must'-erd-gas'], *n.* a heavy, persistent, irritant poison gas smelling of mustard.
MUSTARD-POT, [must'-erd-pot'], *n.* a small receptacle containing mustard mixed with water, etc.
MUSTEE, MESTEE, [mus-tē'], *n.* the child of a white person and a quadroon, in the West Indies. [Span. *mestizo*].
MUSTELINE, [mus'-tel-īn], *adj.* (*zool.*) belonging to the family of weasels or martens. [L. *mustelinus*].
MUSTER (1), [must'-er], *n.* an assembling of troops for review, numbering, etc.; the number of men present at this; a roll of troops mustered; a gathering, assembly; (of peacocks) a band; **to pass m.,** to be satisfactory. [OFr. *mostre*].
MUSTER (2), [must'-er], *v.t. and i.* to assemble, *esp.* for review, numbering, etc.; to number; **to m. up,** to summon, assemble. [OFr. *mostrer* from L. *monstrare* to show].
MUSTER-BOOK, [must'-er-bŏŏk], *n.* a muster-roll.
MUSTER-MASTER, [must'-er-mahst'-er], *n.* the officer who keeps the muster-roll.
MUSTER-ROLL, [must'-er-rōl'], *n.* a roll or register of troops or a ship's company.
MUSTILY, [must'-i-li], *adv.* in musty fashion.
MUSTINESS, [must'-i-nes], *n.* the property of being musty.
MUSTY, [must'-i], *adj.* mouldy, sour, stale, fusty, antiquated, old-fashioned. [Uncert.].
MUTABILITY, [mewt'-a-bil'-i-ti], *n.* the quality of being mutable. [L. *mutabilitas*].
MUTABLE, [mewt'-abl], *adj.* changeable, unstable, susceptible to alteration. [L. *mutabilis*].
MUTABLENESS, [mewt'-abl-nes], *n.* mutability.
MUTABLY, [mewt'-ab-li], *adv.* in changeable fashion.
MUTAGE, [mewt'-ij], *n.* a process for arresting fermentation in the must of grapes. [Fr. *mutage*].
MUTATE, [mewt'-āt'], *v.t. and i.* to experience or bring about mutation, to change. [L. *mutare*].
MUTATION, [mewt-ā'-shun], *n.* a change, altering; (*biol.*) a sudden change in the characteristics of the offspring, resulting in the formation of a new species; (*philol.*) change in the quality of a vowel due to the presence of a particular vowel in the following syllable. [L. *mutatio*].
MUTATIVE, [mewt-āt'-iv], *adj.* (*biol.*) tending to mutate.
MUTCH, [much], *n.* a woman's linen or muslin cap. [MDu. *mutse*].
MUTCHKIN, [much'-kin], *n.* a Scots liquid measure equivalent to three-quarters of an imperial pint.
MUTE (1), [mewt], *n.* a dumb person; a professional mourner; an actor with a non-speaking part; (*phon.*) a stopped consonant; (*mus.*) a clip placed on the bridge of a stringed instrument to soften the tone; a pad inserted in a wind instrument to deaden the sound. [MUTE (3)].
MUTE (2), [mewt], *n.* the excrement of fowls. [MUTE (5)].
MUTE (3), [mewt], *adj.* dumb; silent; not expressed in speech; (*phon.*) (of a letter) not sounded; (of a consonant) produced with a stoppage of the air-stream; (*leg.*) refusing to plead. [L. *mutus*].
MUTE (4), [mewt], *v.t.* (*mus.*) to soften the sound of by a mute. [MUTE (3)].
MUTE† (5), [mewt], *v.i.* (of birds) to void excrement. [OFr. *muetir*].
MUTELY, [mewt'-li], *adv.* in mute fashion.
MUTENESS, [mewt'-nes], *n.* the condition of being mute.
MUTILATE, [mew'-til-āt], *v.t.* to maim, cut off, or destroy the use of; to render imperfect by removing some part. [L. *mutilare*].
MUTILATION, [mew'-til-ā'-shun], *n.* the act of mutilating; the state of being mutilated; the part mutilated. [L. *mutilatio*].
MUTILATOR, [mew'-til-āt-er], *n.* a person who mutilates.
MUTINEER (1), [mew'-tin-ēer'], *n.* one guilty of mutiny. [Fr. *mutinier*].
MUTINEER (2), [mew'-tin-ēer'], *v.t.* to mutiny.
MUTING, [mewt'-ing], *n.* the dung of birds.
MUTINOUS, [mew'-tin-us], *adj.* inclined to mutiny, guilty of mutiny, rebellious.
MUTINOUSLY, [mew'-tin-us-li], *adv.* in mutinous fashion.
MUTINOUSNESS, [mew'-tin-us-nes], *n.* the quality or state of being mutinous.
MUTINY (1), [mew'-tin-i], *n.* an insurrection against constituted authority, *esp.* the (wholesale) refusal of soldiers, sailors, etc., to obey their commanders. [~Fr. *mutiner*].
MUTINY (2), [mew'-tin-i], *v.i.* to rise in mutiny.
MUTISM, [mewt'-izm], *n.* the state of being dumb; inability to speak or articulate audibly.
MUTT, [mut], *n.* (*U.S. slang*) an incompetent fool. [MUTT(ON-HEAD)].
MUTTER (1), [mut'-er], *n.* a subdued inarticulate utterance.
MUTTER (2), [mut'-er], *v.t. and i.* to speak or utter in a low indistinct voice, barely moving the lips, *esp.* to express resentment or dissatisfaction in this way; to rumble faintly. [ME. *mutteren*].
MUTTERER, [mut'-er-er], *n.* a grumbler, one who mutters.
MUTTERINGLY, [mut'-er-ing-li], *adv.* in a low voice.
MUTTON, [mut'-on], *n.* the edible flesh of sheep. [Fr. *mouton* sheep].
MUTTON-BIRD, [mut'-on-burd'], *n.* the Antarctic petrel.

MUTTON-FIST, [mut′-on-fist′], *n.* a large, brawny hand.
MUTTON-HAM, [mut′-on-ham′], *n.* a leg of mutton salted and cured as a ham.
MUTTON-HEAD, [mut′-on-hed′], *n.* (*coll.*) a thick-headed fool.
MUTTONY, [mut′-on-i], *adj.* like mutton in taste or appearance.
MUTUAL, [mew′-chŏŏal], *adj.* reciprocal, interchanged, entertained by either or each for the other or others; common; joint, combined. [L. *mutuus* exchanged].
MUTUALISM, [mew′-chŏŏal-izm], *n.* (*ethics*) the theory that the members of a well-ordered society should be mutually dependent; (*biol.*) close connexion between two unlike organisms for their mutual benefit.
MUTUALITY, [mew′-chŏŏ-al′-i-ti], *n.* the quality of being mutual.
MUTUALLY, [mew′-chŏŏal-i], *adv.* reciprocally, jointly.
MUTULE, [mew′-tewl], *n.* (*arch.*) a projecting block under the corona of the Doric cornice. [L. *mutulus*].

MUTULE

MUXY, [muk′-si], *adj.* (*dial.*) dirty, gloomy. [~OE. *meox* dung].
MUZARAB, see MOZARAB.
MUZZILY, [muz′-i-li], *adv.* in muzzy fashion.
MUZZINESS, [muz′-i-nes], *n.* the condition of being muzzy.
MUZZLE (1), [muzl], *n.* the projecting nose and mouth of an animal; a guard of straps or wires fastened over this to prevent an animal, *esp.* a dog, from biting; the open end of a fire-arm from which the shot issues. [MedL. *musellus* little snout].
MUZZLE (2), [muzl], *v.t.* to fasten a muzzle over the snout of; to gag, to hinder or restrain from free comment.
MUZZLE-LOADER, [muzl′-lōd′-er], *n.* a fire-arm loaded through the muzzle.
MUZZY, [muz′-i], *adj.* confused, muddle-headed; indistinct; befuddled with drink. [Uncert.].
MY, [mī], *possessive adj.* belonging to me. [OE. *min*].
MYALGIA, [mī-al′-ja], *n.* stiffness and pain in the muscles. [Gk. *mus* muscle and *algos* pain].
MYALISM, [mī′-al-izm], *n.* West Indian native witchcraft. [Native].
MYALL, [mī′-awl], *n.* any of the Australian varieties of acacia, *esp. Acacia homalophylla*; the wood of these trees. [Native].
MYCELIUM, [mī-sē′-li-um], *n.* the vegetative mass of a fungus, mushroom spawn. [MYC(ETO) and Gk. *helos* nail].
MYCETO-, *pref.* fungus. [Gk. *mukes*].
MYCETOMA, [mī′-sē-tō′-ma], *n.* a destructive fungoid disease affecting the foot, and occasionally the hand. [MYCETO and Gk. *oma* denoting diseased state].
MYCETOZOA, [mī′-sē-tō-zō′-a], *n.(pl.)* a group of minute organisms commonly included in the myxomycetes. [MYCETO and Gk. *zoa* animals].
MYCO-, *pref.* fungus. [Gk. *mukes*].
MYCODERMA, [mī′-kō-derm′-a], *n.* a fungous pellicle forming on fermenting liquids; the genus of fungi producing this. [MYCO and Gk. *derma* skin].
MYCOLOGICAL, [mī′-kō-loj′-ikl], *adj.* belonging to mycology.
MYCOLOGIST, [mī-kol′-oj-ist], *n.* one versed in mycology.
MYCOLOGY, [mī-kol′-o-ji], *n.* the study of fungi. [MYCO and Gk. *logos* speech].
MYCOPHAGIST, [mī-kof′-aj-ist], *n.* a fungus-eater. [MYCO and Gk. *phago* I eat].
MYCOSIS, [mī-kō′-sis], *n.* a parasitic fungoid growth on or in the body. [MYCO and Gk. *osis* denoting condition].
MYDRIASIS, [mid′-ri-ā′-sis], *n.* (*path.*) abnormal dilatation of the pupil of the eye. [Gk. *mudriasis*].
MYELITIS, [mī′-el-ī′-tis], *n.* inflammation of the spinal cord. [Gk. *muelos* marrow and *itis* denoting inflammation].
MYELOID, [mī′-el-oid], *adj.* like marrow. [Gk. *muelos* marrow and *oeides* like].
MYLOHYOID, [mī′-lō-hī′-oid], *adj.* relating to the hyoid bone and the molar teeth. [Gk. *mule* molar tooth and HYOID].
MYNA(H), [mī′-na], *n.* the Indian starling, *Eulabes religiosa*, or any variety of the genus *Sturnia*. [Hind. *maina*].
MYNHEER, [mīn-hāer′], *n.* a Dutchman. [Du. *mijnheer* sir].
MYO-, *pref.* muscle. [Gk. *mus muos*].
MYOCARDITIS, [mī′-ō-kahd-ī′-tis], *n.* (*med.*) inflammation of the muscular structure of the heart. [MYO and CARDITIS].
MYODYNAMICS, [mī′-ō-dī-nam′-iks], *n.(pl.)* the science of muscular movement.
MYOGRAPHICAL, [mī′-ō-graf′-ik-al], *adj.* describing the muscles.
MYOLOGICAL, [mī′-ō-loj′-ik-al], *adj.* relating to myology.
MYOLOGIST, [mī-ol′-oj-ist], *n.* one expert in myology.
MYOLOGY, [mī-ol′-o-ji], *n.* the study of the muscles; the description of the muscular system. [MYO and Gk. *logos* speech].
MYOMANCY, [mī′-ō-man′-si], *n.* divination by the movements of mice. [Gk. *mus* mouse and *manteia* divination].
MYONICITY, [mī′-on-is′-i-ti], *n.* the contractility of muscular tissue. [Gk. *mus*].
MYOPATHY, [mī-op′-a-thi], *n.* disease of the muscles. [MYO and Gk. *pathos* suffering].
MYOPE, [mī′-ōp], *n.* a short-sighted person. [Gk. *muops muopos* short-sighted].
MYOPIA, [mī-ō′-pi-a], *n.* short-sightedness.
MYOPIC, [mī-op′-ik], *adj.* short-sighted; pertaining to, characteristic of, myopia.
MYOSIS, [mī-ō′-sis], *n.* a state of the eye characterized by contraction of the pupil. [Gk. *muo* I close the eyes and *osis* denoting condition].
MYOSITIS, [mī′-ō-sī′-tis], *n.* inflammation of the muscles. [MYO and Gk. *itis* denoting inflammation].
MYOSOTIS, [mī′-ō-sō′-tis], *n.* the genus of plants which includes the forget-me-nots. [Gk. *muosotis*].
MYOTOMY, [mī-ot′-o-mi], *n.* dissection of the muscles. [MYO and Gk. *tome* cutting].
MYRIA-, *pref.* countless, innumerable. [Gk. *murias* ten thousand].
MYRIAD (1), [mi′-ri-ad], *n.* ten thousand, a multitude, a countless number. [Gk. *murias muriados*].
MYRIAD (2), [mi′-ri-ad], *adj.* innumerable, countless.
MYRIAMETRE, [mi′-ri-a-mēt′-er], *n.* ten thousand metres.
MYRIAPOD, [mi′-ri-a-pod′], *n.* a centipede or millipede. [MYRIA and Gk. *pous podos* foot].
MYRIAPODA, [mi′-ri-ap′-ō-da], *n.(pl.)* (*zool.*) a class of the arthropoda, including such as have an extremely large number of jointed feet.
MYRIARCH, [mi′-ri-ahk], *n.* a commander of ten thousand men. [MYRIA and Gk. *arkhos* ruler].
MYRICIN, [mi′-ri-sin], *n.* that part of beeswax which does not dissolve when treated with boiling alcohol. [Gk. *murike*].
MYRIOPHYLLOUS, [mi′-ri-of′-il-us], *adj.* (*bot.*) having very many leaves. [MYRIA and Gk. *phullon* leaf].
MYRIORAMA, [mi′-ri-ō-rah′-ma], *n.* a variety of pictures obtained from combinations of sections of views. [MYRIA and Gk. *horama* spectacle].

MYRIAPOD

MYRMIDON, [mur′-mid-on], *n.* a member of a fierce Thessalian race fighting in the Trojan war under Achilles; a ruthless retainer or executor of commands; **myrmidons of the law**, policemen, bailiffs, etc. [Gk. *Murmidones*].
MYRMIDONIAN, [mur′-mid-ō′-ni-an], *adj.* resembling myrmidons.
MYROBALAN, [mier-ob′-al-an], *n.* the dried fruit of several varieties of *Terminalia*, a family of East Indian trees, used in dyeing and tanning. [Gk. *murobalanon* balsam nut].
MYRRH, [mur], *n.* an aromatic gum-resin obtained from several species of *Commiphora*. [OE. *myrra* from Gk. *murra*].
MYRRHIC, [mur′-rik], *adj.* obtained from, or relating to, myrrh.
MYRRHINE, see MURRHINE.
MYRRHOPHORES, [mur′-rō-fawz′], *n.(pl.)* myrrh-bearers. [MYRRH and Gk. *phoros* bearing].
MYRTIFORM, [murt′-i-fawm], *adj.* resembling myrtle-berries in shape.
MYRTLE, [murtl], *n.* any shrub of the genus *Myrtus*,

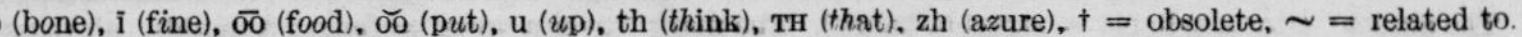

esp. Myrtus communis, which bears white aromatic flowers. [OFr. *myrtille*].

MYRTLE-BERRY, [murtl'-be'-ri], *n.* the fruit of the myrtle.

MYRTLE-WAX, [murtl'-waks], *n.* an oil or vegetable wax obtained from *Myrica cerifera*.

MYSELF, [mī-self'], *pron. used in apposition to "I" for emphasis or as the object of a reflexive verb in the first person.*

MYSTAGOGIC, [mist'-a-goj'-ik], *adj.* pertaining to a mystagogue or to mystagogy.

MYSTAGOGUE, [mist'-a-gog'], *n.* (*Gk. antiq.*) one who initiates into or interprets religious mysteries; one who teaches mysticism. [Gk. *mustagogos*].

MYSTAGOGY, [mist'-a-goj'-i], *n.* initiation into religious mysteries; instruction in preparation for this. [Gk. *mustagogia*].

MYSTERIARCH, [mis-tēer'-i-ahk], *n.* one who presides over mysteries. [Gk. *musteriarkhes*].

MYSTERIOUS, [mis-tēer'-i-us], *adj.* full of mystery, strange, unaccountable extremely puzzling, obscure.

MYSTERIOUSLY, [mis-tēer'-i-us-li], *adv.* in mysterious fashion.

MYSTERIOUSNESS, [mis-tēer'-i-us-nes], *n.* the quality of being mysterious.

MYSTERY (1), [mis'-ter-i], *n.* a baffling secret, something unaccountable or unaccounted for; secrecy, obscurity; (*pl.*) intricacies; a medieval form of drama depicting religious scenes, formerly performed by a particular craft or guild; (*antiq., pl.*) secret religious rites and ceremonies; (*eccles.*) a religious doctrine or truth established by divine revelation; a Christian sacramental rite. [Gk. *musterion*].

MYSTERY (2), [mis'-ter-i], *n.* †a trade or handicraft; the persons engaged in this; a guild. [OFr. *mestier*].

MYSTERY-SHIP†, [mis'-ter-i-ship'], *n.* a warship camouflaged to look like a trading vessel.

MYSTIC (1), [mist'-ik], *n.* one who practises or believes in mysticism.

MYSTIC (2), [mist'-ik], *adj.* pertaining to mysticism; pertaining to the ancient mysteries or to a religious mystery; allegorical, emblematical; occult; mysterious. [Gk. *mustikos* relating to an initiate into the mysteries].

MYSTICAL, [mist'-ik-al], *adj.* mystic.

MYSTICALLY, [mist'-ik-al-i], *adv.* in mystical fashion.

MYSTICALNESS, [mist'-ik-al-nes], *n.* the quality of being mystical.

MYSTICISM, [mist'-is-izm], *n.* an attitude of belief which claims to establish direct communication and union with the Divine Spirit by ecstatic contemplation in which ultimate truths are divinely revealed.

MYSTIFICATION, [mist'-i-fi-kā'-shun], *n.* the act of mystifying, the state of being mystified, a cause of bewilderment.

MYSTIFY, [mist'-i-fī], *v.t.* to bewilder, baffle, puzzle exceedingly; to surround with mystery. [Fr. *mystifier*].

MYTH, [mith], *n.* a legend or traditional tale, often expressing primitive beliefs, and explaining natural and historical phenomena as due to the activities of supernatural beings; a widely believed fiction. [Gk. *muthos* story].

MYTHIC, [mith'-ik], *adj.* mythical.

MYTHICAL, [mith'-ik-al], *adj.* of the nature of pertaining to, a myth; legendary.

MYTHICALLY, [mith'-ik-al-i], *adv.* in mythical fashion.

MYTHICIZE, [mith'-i-sīz], *v.t.* to turn into, explain by, a myth.

MYTHO-, *pref.* myth. [Gk. *muthos*].

MYTHOCLASTIC, [mith'-ō-klast'-ik, mī'-thō-klast'-ik], *adj.* destroying belief in myths. [MYTHO and Gk. *klastes* breaker].

MYTHOGRAPHER, [mith-og'-raf-er, mī-thog'-raf-er], *n.* a writer of myths. [MYTHO and Gk. *graphia* writing].

MYTHOLOGICAL, [mith'-ō-loj'-ik-al, mī'-thō-loj'-ik-al], *adj.* relating to mythology.

MYTHOLOGICALLY, [mith'-ō-loj'-ik-al-i, mī'-thō-loj'-ik-al-i], *adv.* as a myth.

MYTHOLOGIST, [mith-ol'-oj-ist, mī-thol'-oj-ist], *n.* one expert in mythology; a writer of myths.

MYTHOLOGIZE, [mith-ol'-oj-īz, mī-thol'-oj-īz], *v.t.* to mythicize; *v.i.* to relate or make up myths.

MYTHOLOGY, [mith-ol'-o-ji, mī-thol'-o-ji], *n.* a body of myths native to a particular race, country, or people; the study of myths. [Gk. *muthologia*].

MYTHONOMY, [mith-on'-o-mi, mī-thon'-o-mi], *n.* the laws governing the development of myths. [MYTHO and Gk. *nomos* law].

MYTHOPOEIC, [mith'-ō-pē'-ik, mī'-thō-pē'-ik], *adj.* creating, or tending to evolve, myths. [Gk. *muthopoios*].

MYTHOPOESIS, [mith'-ō-pō-ē'-sis, mī'-thō-pō-ē'-sis], *n.* the evolution or production of myths.

MYTHUS, [mith'-us], *n.* a myth. [LL. *mythos*].

MYTILITE, [mit'-il-īt], *n.* (*geol.*) a fossil mussel-shell.

MYTILOID, [mit'-il-oid], *adj.* resembling or relating to mussels. [L. *mytilus* sea-mussel and Gk. *oeides* like].

MYXINE, [miks-ī'-ni], *n.* (*zool.*) the genus of eel-like fishes comprising the hag-fishes. [Gk. *muxinos* slime fish].

MYXINE

MYXOEDEMA, [miks'-ē-dē'-ma], *n.* a disease causing atrophy of the thyroid gland. [Gk. *muxa* slime and *oidema* swelling].

MYXOMYCETES, [miks'-ō-mī-sē'-tēz], *n.*(*pl.*) a group of primitive organisms including the slime fungi. [Gk. *muxa* slime and *mukes* mushroom].

N

N, [en], the fourteenth letter of the English alphabet, and articulated as a voiced naso-dental; (*math.*) an indefinite power or quantity; (*typ.*) a unit of measurement, being half the width of an em.

NAB (1), [nab], *n.* a rocky ledge, a promontory; the top of a ridge or hill, a knoll, a summit. [OIcel. *nabbr*].

NAB (2), **(nabbing, nabbed)**, [nab], *v.t.*(*slang*) to catch or seize suddenly, particularly during an illegal act, to arrest. [~Swed. *nappa* to catch].

NABOB, [nā'-bob], *n.* a deputy lieutenant-governor under the Mogul emperors; †one of the Anglo-Indians who used their position under these emperors to make themselves rich. [Hind. *nawwab* deputy].

NACARAT, [nak'-a-rat], *n.* an iridescent red with a bright orange tinge; any material dyed with this colour. [Span. *nacar* mother-of-pearl].

NACELLE, [nas-el'], *n.* the body of an aeroplane; the car of an airship. [L. *navicella* little ship].

NACODAH, [nak'-od-ah], *n.* an Arab sea-captain. [Arab. *nakhodah*].

NACRE, [nā'-ker], *n.* the iridescent pearly part of shells, mother-of-pearl. [LL. *nacrum*].

NACREOUS, [nā'-kri-us], *adj.* consisting of, relating to, mother-of-pearl; having an iridescent lustre.

NACRITE, [nā'-krīt], *n.* (*min.*) anhydrous silicate of alumina, a mineral consisting of pearly grains or scales.

NADIR, [na'-dēer, na'-der], *n.* (*astron.*) a hypothetical point of the heavens directly under our feet, or directly opposite the zenith; (*fig.*) the lowest point, the most depressed stage. [Arab. *nadir* opposite to].

NAEVE, [nēv], *n.* a congenital mark on the skin caused by excessive size of blood-vessels, a birthmark.

NAEVOSE, [nēv'-ōs], *adj.* (*med.*) characterized by a naeve, spotted, freckled; having a birthmark.

NAEVUS, [nēv'-us], *n.* a naeve. [L. *naevus* mole].

NAG (1), [nag], *n.* a saddle-horse; an inferior kind of horse used for hack work. [ME. *nagge* horse]

NAG (2), [nag], *n.* persistent scolding, continuous complaining.

NAG (3), **(nagging, nagged)**, [nag], *v.t. and i.* to worry by continuous scolding and complaining; to find fault constantly, to scold persistently. [OIcel. *gnaga* to gnaw].

NAGA, [nah'-gah], *n.* a race of Indian people now inhabiting the borders of Burma; (*myth.*) the Hindu symbol of eternity in the form half-man half-serpent. [Hind. *naga*].

NAGANA, [nag-ah´-na], *n.* a disease affecting cattle and caused by the tsetse fly. [Bantu *n'gana*].

NAGELFLUE, [nah´-gel-flōō], *n.* (*min.*) an oligocene rock composed of mutually indented slender pebbles. [Germ. *nagel* nail and *fluh* rock].

NAGGER, [nag´-er], *n.* a person, *esp.* a woman who nags.

NAGGY, [nag´-i], *adj.* given to nagging; contentious.

NAGOR, [nā´-gor], *n.* the Senegal antelope, *Cervicapra redunca.* [Native].

NAGYAGITE, [nag´-yag-īt], *n.* (*min.*) a telluride of gold and lead, black in colour. [*Nagyag*, a place in Hungary, where found].

NAIAD, (*pl.* **naiades**), [nī´-ad], *n.* (*myth.*) a freshwater nymph; the water plant, *Naias flexilis.* [Gk. *naiados*].

NAIANT, [nā´-ant], *adj.* (*her.*) (of fishes) swimming in a horizontal position. [OFr. *najant*, *pres.pt.* of *najier* to swim].

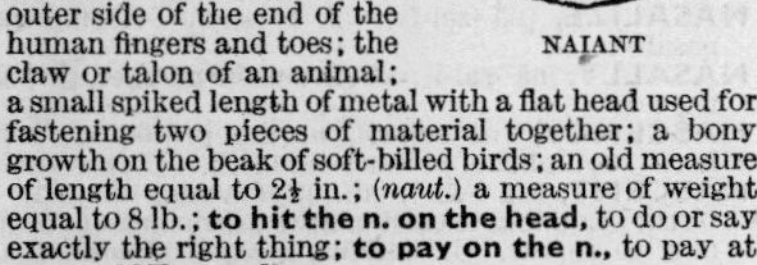
NAIANT

NAIB, [nah´-ib], *n.* a deputy officer in an Indian court of justice. [Arab. *nahib* deputy].

NAIK, [nah´-ik], *n.* a corporal of infantry in the Indian Army. [Hind. *nayak* overseer].

NAIL (1), [nāl], *n.* the horny substance growing on the outer side of the end of the human fingers and toes; the claw or talon of an animal; a small spiked length of metal with a flat head used for fastening two pieces of material together; a bony growth on the beak of soft-billed birds; an old measure of length equal to 2¼ in.; (*naut.*) a measure of weight equal to 8 lb.; **to hit the n. on the head,** to do or say exactly the right thing; **to pay on the n.,** to pay at once. [OE. *nægel*].

NAIL (2), [nāl], *v.t.* to fasten together or fix by means of nails; to provide with nails, as boots; (*slang*) to take into custody, to catch; (*fig.*) to hold to a definite statement or line of action.

NAILBOURNE, [nāl´-bawn], *n.* an intermittent spring; a brook that flows occasionally.

NAILBRUSH, [nāl´-brush], *n.* a toilet brush for cleaning the finger-nails.

NAILER, [nāl´-er], *n.* a maker or user of nails.

NAILERY, [nāl´-er-i], *n.* a place where metal nails are made.

NAILFILE, [nāl´-fīl], *n.* a small file for manicure.

NAIL-HEAD, [nāl´-hed´], *n.* an ornamental carving in the form of the head of a nail.

NAIL-HEADED, [nāl´-hed´-id], *adj.* shaped like a nail; (*arch.*) like the head of a hob-nail.

NAILLESS, [nāl´-les], *adj.* having no nails.

NAIL-SCISSORS, [nāl´-siz´-erz], *n.*(*pl.*) a pair of scissors with short and sometimes curved blades for clipping finger- and toe-nails.

NAINSOOK, [nān´-sŏŏk], *n.* a thick sort of plain cotton fabric formerly made in India. [Hind. *nain* eye and *sukh* delight].

NAISSANT, [nā´-sant], *adj.* (*her.*) issuing from a fesse or ordinary, and showing only the foreparts of its body. [Fr. *naissant*, *pres.pt.* of *naître* to be born].

NAIVE, [nāv, na-ēv´], *adj.* natural, with unaffected simplicity, artless, ingenuous; simple to the point of foolishness, childish, immature. [Fr. *naïve* fem. of *naïf*].

NAIVELY, [nāv´-li, na-ēv´-li], *adv.* in a naive manner, with unaffected simplicity.

NAIVETY, [nāv´-i-ti, na-ēv´-ti], *n.* unaffected manner, simplicity and ingenuousness.

NAKED, [nā´-kid], *adj.* having no clothes on, uncovered, bare, nude; having the parts exposed; without the proper or accustomed covering, open to view; defenceless, unarmed; without ornament or decoration, plain; (*bot.*) having no seed covering; (*fig.*) unconcealed, evident, obvious. [OE. *nacod*].

NAKEDLY, [nā´-kid-li], *adv.* in a naked condition, without covering; simply; evidently.

NAKEDNESS, [nā´-kid-nes], *n.* the state of being naked.

NAMABLE, NAMEABLE, [nām´-abl], *adj.* capable of being named.

NAMBY-PAMBY (1), [nam´-bi-pam´-bi], *n.* a weak, effeminate person; writing of a stupid, babyish, trashy quality.

NAMBY-PAMBY (2), [nam´-bi-pam´-bi], *adj.* lacking ordinary virility feeble, effeminate, sentimental. [Invented to ridicule the poems of *Ambrose* Philips].

NAME (1), [nām], *n.* the word by which a person, place, object, idea, is known, a means of designating an identity, the appellation of an individual, group, or category; renown, reputation, fame; (*gram.*) a noun; **to call someone names,** to insult, abuse; **n. day,** the festival day of a saint from whom a person takes his name. [OE. *nama*].

NAME (2), [nām], *v.t.* to give a name to, to designate, call; to distinguish, separate, classify, mention by name; to nominate, appoint.

NAMELESS, [nām´-les], *adj.* without a name; anonymous; unknown; unnoted; unnamable, undefinable.

NAMELESSLY, [nām´-les-li], *adv.* in a nameless manner.

NAMELY, [nām´-li], *adv.* that is to say.

NAMEPLATE, [nām´-plāt], *n.* a brass or other plate on a door or doorway bearing the name of the occupant of the house or room.

NAMER, [nām´-er], *n.* one who names or who calls by name.

NAMESAKE, [nām´-sāk], *n.* a person having the same name as another. [NAME and SAKE].

NANCY, [nan´-si], *n.* an effeminate male, a homosexual.

NANCY-BOY, [nan´-si-boi], *n.* an effeminate youth; a homosexual.

NANDU, [nan´-dōō], *n.* a species of ostrich, *Rhea americana*, found in South America. [Native].

NANISM, [nān´-izm], *n.* the state of being stunted in growth, dwarfishness. [L. *nanus* dwarf].

NANKEEN, [nan´-kēn´], *n.* a species of cloth, originally made in China, generally brownish-yellow in colour. [*Nanking*, a town in China].

NANNY, [nan´-i], *n.* a female goat; children's term for nurse; (*coll.*) a stupid person. [The female name *Anne*, *Nan*].

NAOS, [nā´-os], *n.* the enclosed apartment of a Greek temple. [Gk. *naos* temple].

NAP (1), [nap], *n.* napoleon, a game of cards; (*fig.*) **to go n. on,** to name as a certainty. [Abbreviation of *Napoleon*].

NAP (2), [nap], *n.* a sort of fitful sleep or slumber, a doze, forty winks [NAP (4)].

NAP (3), [nap], *n.* the woolly or downy substance on the surface of cloth; the downy substance on plants. [ME. *nappe* rough surface of a cloth].

NAP (4), (napping, napped), [nap], *v.i.* to take a nap, to doze; **to be caught napping,** to be taken unawares. [OE. *hnappian*].

NAP (5), (napping, napped), [nap], *v.i.* to raise a nap on cloth.

NAP (6), (napping, napped), [nap], *v.t.* (*racing*) to give a special recommendation that a certain horse will win a race.

NAPE, [nāp], *n.* the back of the neck. [Uncert.].

NAPERY, [nāp´-er-i], *n.* linen for domestic use, *esp.* at table. [LL. *naparia* linen].

NAPHTHA, [naf´-tha], *n.* a fluid, inflammable hydrocarbon drained from bitumen beds. [Pers. *naft* liquid].

NAPHTHALENE, [naf´-thal-ēn], *n.* (*chem.*) a benzene hydrocarbon obtained from the distillation of coal tar used in the manufacture of dyes.

NAPHTHALIC, [naf-thal´-ik], *adj.* (*chem.*) obtained from naphthalene; **n. acid,** a crystalline product obtained from naphthalene.

NAPHTHALIZE, [naf´-thal-īz], *v.t.* to saturate with naphtha.

NAPIFORM, [nāp´-i-fawm], *adj.* having the shape of a turnip. [L. *napus* turnip and FORM].

NAPKIN, [nap´-kin], *n.* a cloth for wiping the hands while eating food; a small cloth used for the toilet of a baby; **n. ring,** a ring to hold a table napkin. [ME. *napekin* from Fr. *nappe* table-cloth].

NAPLESS, [nap´-les], *adj.* without nap, threadbare.

NAPLES-YELLOW, [nāplz´-yel´-ō], *n.* antimoniate of lead, a fine yellow pigment with a hint of ochre in it.

NAPOLEON, [nap-ō´-li-on], *n.* the game of cards generally known as nap; a French gold coin of the value of twenty francs, put into circulation during the First and Second French Empires. [*Napoleon* I, the French Emperor].

NAPOLEONIC, [nap-ō´-li-on´-ik], *adj.* of, resembling, pertaining to, Napoleon; dominating, colossal.

NAPOLEONITE, [nap-ō´-li-on-īt], *n.* orbicular diorite.

NAPOLITE, [na´-pol-īt], *n.* (*min.*) a blue mineral thrown up by Vesuvius. [Ital. *Napoli* Naples].

NAPOO, [nah´-pōō´], *adj.* (*slang*) no good, hopeless.

[Mispronunciation of Fr. *il n'y (en) a plus* there is no more (of it)].

NAPPINESS, [nap'-i-nes], *n.* the condition of having plenty of nap, as on cloth.

NAPPY (1), [nap'-i], *n.* a child's napkin.

NAPPY (2), [nap'-i], *adj.* having a nap; covered with a good deal of nap, shaggy. [MDu. *noppigh*].

NARCEINE, [nah'-sē-in], *n.* (*chem.*) an alkaloid with narcotic properties obtained from opium. [~Gk. *narke* numbness].

NARCISSISM, [nah'-sis-izm], *n.* (*psych.*) a form of neurosis characterized by excessive self-admiration and conceit.

NARCISSUS, [nah-sis'-us], *n.* a genus of plants characterized by bulbous roots and flowers with yellow or white sepals round a corolla, comprising daffodils, jonquils; (*myth.*) a handsome youth who fell in love with his own image reflected in water and was changed into the white flower named after him. [Gk. *narkissos* daffodil].

NARCOLEPSY, [nah'-kō-lep-si], *n.* (*med.*) an epileptic disease characterized by extreme sleepiness. [~Gk. *narke* numbness and (EPI)LEPSY].

NARCOSIS, [nah-kō'-sis], *n.* (*path.*) the state of stupor brought about by a narcotic, stupefaction, deprivation of sense. [Gk. *narkosis* numbness].

NARCOTIC (1), [nah-kot'-ik], *n.* a drug having the effect of inducing drowsiness or allaying pain.

NARCOTIC (2), [nah-kot'-ik], *adj.* having the effect of inducing sleep or drowsiness, soothing.

NARCOTICALLY, [nah-kot'-ik-a-li], *adv.* in the fashion of a narcotic.

NARCOTINE, [nah'-kot-ēn], *n.* (*chem.*) an alkaloid of opium.

NARCOTISM, [nah'-kot-izm], *n.* the effect of a narcotic; the state of stupefaction or drowsiness induced by narcotic poisoning.

NARD, [nahd], *n.* a plant, the spikenard, a species of *Nardostachys*; an odorous unguent prepared from it. [Heb. *nerd*].

NARDINE, [nahd'-in], *adj.* derived from, pertaining to, nard or spikenard.

NARDOO, [nahd'-ōō], *n.* the Australian pillwort, *Marsilea macropus*. [Native].

NARES, [nāer'-ēz], *n.*(*pl.*) (*anat.*) the nostrils. [L. *nares*, *pl.* of *naris* nostril].

NARGHILE, [nah'-gil-i], *n.* a small hookah tobacco pipe from which the smoke is passed through perfumed water. [Pers. *nargil* coconut].

NARGIL, [nah'-gil], *n.* the coconut tree of Southern India. [Native].

NARIAL, [nāer'-i-al], *adj.* (*anat.*) pertaining to the nostrils. [~L. *naris* nostril].

NARIFORM, [nāer'-i-fawm], *adj.* formed like the nostrils. [L. *naris* nostril and FORM].

NARINE, [nāer'-in], *adj.* narial.

NARK (1), [nahk], *n.* (*slang*) an informer, a police spy. [Unkn.].

NARK (2), [nahk], *v.i.* to inform (against).

NARRATE, [na-rāt'], *v.t.* to relate in a connected form past incidents or events; to tell, recite, or write, as a story. [~L. *narrare*].

NARRATION, [na-rā'-shun], *n.* the act of narrating; a statement in words or writing, that which is narrated; the explanatory part of a journal entry. [L. *narratio*].

NARRATIVE (1), [na'-rat-iv], *n.* an account of an event and the incidents it is composed of, a tale, story, narration.

NARRATIVE (2), [na'-rat-iv], *adj.* having the form of a narrative, giving a connected order to a series of recorded events; able to narrate.

NARRATIVELY, [na'-rat-iv-li], *adv.* in the form of a narrative.

NARRATOR, [na-rāt'-or], *n.* a person who narrates, *esp.* one who narrates intervening incidents in a play.

NARROW (1), [na'-rō], *n.* a passage between two seas, lakes, mountains, which is narrow, a strait.

NARROW (2), [na'-rō], *adj.* of small breadth in proportion to length, not wide or broad; limited, restricted at the sides for space; limited in outlook, bigoted; covetous, parsimonious, mean; **a n. escape**, an escape made with minimum safety. [OE. *n(e)aru*].

NARROW (3), [na'-rō], *v.t. and i.* to reduce or lessen the width of, to cause to become narrow; to become narrow; to contract.

NARROWER, [na'-rō-er], *n.* a person or thing which narrows.

NARROWLY, [na'-rō-li], *adv.* in a narrow manner, closely.

NARROW-MINDED, [na'-rō-mind'-id], *adj.* having a narrow mind, prejudiced, bigoted.

NARROW-MINDEDLY, [na'-rō-mind'-id-li], *adv.* in a narrow-minded manner.

NARROW-MINDEDNESS, [na'-rō-mind'-id-nes], *n.* the state of being narrow-minded, illiberality.

NARROWNESS, [na'-rō-nes], *n.* the state of being narrow, smallness of breadth.

NARTHEX, [nah'-theks], *n.* (*arch.*) a long porch built on the west side of a church in the form of an arcade for penitents or catechumens who were forbidden to enter the church; (*bot.*) a genus of plants bearing umbels. [Gk. *narthex* the giant fennel].

NARWHAL, [nah'-wal], *n.* the sea unicorn, the Arctic whale having a long tusk, *Monodon monoceros*. [OIcel. *nar* corpse and *hvalr* whale].

NARWHAL

NASAL (1), [nā'-zal], *n.* (*antiq.*) a piece of metal forming part of a knight's helmet to protect the nose; (*phon.*) a sound modified by closure of the nasal passage.

NASAL (2), [nā'-zal], *adj.* of, belonging to, relating to, the nose; (*phon.*) modified by the nose. [LL. *nasalis* belonging to the nose].

NASALIS, [naz-ā'-lis], *n.* the proboscis monkey which has an enormous nose.

NASALISM, [nā'-zal-izm], *n.* nasal pronunciation.

NASALITY, [nāz-al'-i-ti], *n.* the state or quality of being nasal.

NASALIZATION, [nā'-zal-īz-ā'-shun], *n.* the process of making nasal.

NASALIZE, [nā'-zal-īz], *v.t.* to sound or enunciate nasally.

NASALLY, [nā'-zal-i], *adv.* in a nasal manner, through the nose.

NASCENCY, [nā'-sen-si], *n.* the process of being born; beginning of production, birth. [L. *nascentia*].

NASCENT, [nā'-sent], *adj.* approaching the time of birth; beginning to exist or grow; springing up, beginning to appear. [L. *nascens*, *pres.pt.* of *nasci* to be born].

NASEBERRY, [nāz'-be'-ri], *n.* a tree found in Central America and its fruit, the sapodilla plum, *Achras sapota*. [~Gk. *mespile* medlar].

NASICORN, [nāz'-i-kawn], *adj.* having a horn on the nose. [L. *nasus* nose and *cornu* horn].

NASIFORM, [nāz'-i-fawm], *adj.* in the shape of the nose. [L. *nasus* nose and FORM].

NASTILY, [nahst'-i-li], *adv.* in a nasty manner; obscenely; disagreeably; spitefully.

NASTINESS, [nahst'-i-nes], *n.* the condition of being nasty; filthiness; obscenity.

NASTURTIUM, [nast-ur'-shum], *n.* (*bot.*) the genus of plants that consists of fifty species of watercress; a garden plant of the genus *Tropæolum*. [L. *nasturtium* watercress].

NASTY, [nahst'-i], *adj.* having an offensive effect on the senses; very dirty; defiled; obscene; repellent, nauseous, disagreeable; unpleasant; spiteful, malicious; threatening, dangerous; difficult, awkward. [Uncert.].

NASUTE, [nā'-sewt], *adj.* critically nice; captious. [L. *nasutus* big-nosed].

NATAL, [nā'-tal], *adj.* belonging to birth. [L. *natalis*].

NATALITIAL, [nā'-tal-ish'-al], *adj.* relating to a birthday.

NATALITY, [nā-tal'-i-ti], *n.* birth-rate, opposed to mortality.

NATALS, [nā'-talz], *n.*(*pl.*) the circumstances of one's nativity.

NATANT, [nā'-tant], *adj.* floating, swimming; (*her.*) floating on the surface in a swimming position. [L. *natans*, *pres.pt.* of *natare* to swim].

NATANTLY, [nā'-tant-li], *adv.* in a floating manner.

NATATION, [nat-ā'-shun], *n.* the act or art of swimming. [L. *natatio*].

NATATORIAL, [nā'-tat-aw'-ri-al], *adj.* swimming, adapted to swimming.

NATATORY, [nā'-tat-or-i], *adj.* enabling to swim.

NATCH, [nach], *n.* (*dial.*) the part of an ox between the loins; the rump. [OFr. *nache*].

NATHELESS†, [nā'-THE-les'], *adv.* nevertheless. [ME. *natheles* from OE. *na* no, *a* ever, and LESS].

NATION, [nā'-shun], *n.* people inhabiting the same country, usually coming from the same racial stock and using the same language, subjected to a central government under a common political economy and united in a feeling for their tradition; a group of people having distinguishing characteristics. [L. *natio*].

NATIONAL, [nash'-un-al], *adj.* of, relating to, characteristic of, common to, a nation; having a general application or status throughout a nation; owned and controlled by the government of a people; popular, public, general; **n. anthem,** the song adopted by the state; **n. debt,** money borrowed by the state from the public.

NATIONALISM, [nash'-un-al-izm], *n.* the state of being national; national peculiarity; the sense of national independence; the upholding of the supposed interests of one's country or racial group against competing interests.

NATIONALIST, [nash'-un-al-ist], *n.* a person who places the interests of his own country or racial group before all others; a member of a political party whose principles and programmes are based on fervid patriotism, as opposed to internationalism.

NATIONALITY, [nash'-un-al'-i-ti], *n.* the official status of membership of a particular nation; national character; national attachment; nation.

NATIONALIZATION, [nash'-un-al-īz-ā'-shun], *n.* the act or process of nationalizing.

NATIONALIZE, [nash'-un-al-īz], *v.t.* to make into a nation; to transfer ownership of from private individuals to the nation.

NATIONALIZER, [nash'-un-al-īz-er], *n.* an advocate of nationalization.

NATIONALLY, [nash'-un-a-li], *adv.* from a national viewpoint, as a nation.

NATIONALNESS, [nash'-un-al-nes], *n.* state of being national.

NATIONAL SOCIALISM, [na'-shun-al-sōsh'-al-izm], *n.* the theories, policies, and organization of the German *National Sozialistische Arbeiterpartei* (Nazis).

NATIONAL SOCIALIST (1), [nash'-un-al-sō'-shal-ist], *n.* a Nazi.

NATIONAL SOCIALIST (2), [na'-shun-al-sōsh'-al-ist], *adj.* of, or pertaining to, National Socialism or National Socialists.

NATIVE (1), [nā'-tiv], *n.* a person born in a particular place or country; an indigenous plant or animal; an oyster raised in an artificial bed off the coast of England.

NATIVE (2), [nā'-tiv], *adj.* having a connexion by birth; of, belonging or relating to, one's birthplace; of, belonging or relating to, the people of a particular country; produced by nature, natural; conferred by birth, innate, not acquired, born with; living or growing by nature in a particular place, indigenous; (*chem.*) in an original state, not combined with another element. [L. *nativus* innate].

NATIVELY, [nā'-tiv-li], *adv.* by birth; naturally.

NATIVENESS, [nā'-tiv-nes], *n.* the state of being native.

NATIVITY, [nat-iv'-i-ti], *n.* a birth, a coming into the world; the time, place, or manner of birth, particularly that of Jesus Christ; a representation of the birth of Christ in an aesthetic medium; a festival connected with Christ's birth; (*astrol.*) a representation of the position of the heavenly bodies at the time of a person's birth, a horoscope. [L. *nativitas*].

NATROLITE, [nā'-tro-līt], *n.* a zeolite which is a silicate of aluminium and sodium. [Gk. *natron* soda and *lithos* stone].

NATRON, [nā'-tron], *n.* (*min.*) native carbonate of soda. [Arab. *natrun*, Gk. *nitron*].

NATTERJACK, [nat'-er-jak'], *n.* the yellow-striped running toad, *Bufo calamita.* [OE. *attor* poison and JACK].

NATTIER-BLUE, [nat'-i-ā-bloo'], *n.* a soft shade of blue. [J. M. *Nattier*, a French painter, who used this colour much].

NATTILY, [nat'-i-li], *adv.* in a natty manner, neatly.

NATTY, [nat'-i], *adj.* neat, trim, spruce. [KNACKY].

NATURAL (1), [nach'-er-al], *n.* a person born with an intelligence below normal, one mentally deficient, an idiot; (*cards*) the highest hand dealt to a player in the game of vingt-et-un, being a royalty and an ace; (*mus.*) a white note on a pianoforte keyboard, a note which is neither a sharp nor a flat, expressed thus ♮.

NATURAL (2), [nach'-er-al], *adj.* of, connected with, relating to, or arising from, nature or the external physical world; existing in an uncultivated state, not artificially produced, wild, undomesticated; characterized by or in accordance with the ordinary conditions of nature; ordinary, normal; true to nature, corresponding to the actual nature of an object, real, life-like; possessing from birth, innate; arising out of one's normal behaviour, without pretence or artifice, unaffected, unassumed; habitual, familiar, characteristic of; arising out of human nature, derived from the characteristics of the organism, acting according to governing conditions of existence; born out of wedlock, illegitimate; (*mus.*) without sharps or flats; **n. history,** the science of nature in all its organic aspects; **n. order,** a number of groups of genera having a base of similar characteristics; **n. philosophy,** the science of physics; **n. science,** the science dealing with all branches of the physical world, as distinct from the non-material or psychical; **n. selection,** Darwin's principle that in the process of evolution only those individuals continue to exist and to preserve their favourable differences in characteristics that adapt themselves to their environment. [L. *naturalis*].

NATURALISM, [nach'-er-al-izm], *n.* the state of living and social organization believed to result from the interdependence of nature and human instincts unmodified by reason or any form of conscious control; (*art*) a mode of presentation characterized by close adherence to the forms of nature.

NATURALIST, [nach'-er-al-ist], *n.* a student of the external forms of nature, particularly those of an organic character such as animals and plants, a botanist, geologist, zoologist; a believer in naturalism; an artist who concentrates on naturalism as a means of expression; a dealer in live pets; a taxidermist.

NATURALISTIC, [nach'-er-al-ist'-ik], *adj.* having a close resemblance; pertaining to naturalism or natural history.

NATURALISTICALLY, [nach'-er-al-ist'-ik-al-i], *adv.* in a naturalistic manner.

NATURALIZATION, [nach'-er-al-īz-ā'-shun], *n.* the act or process of naturalizing; the act of investing an alien with the rights and privileges of a citizen.

NATURALIZE, [nach'-er-al-īz], *v.t.* to confer on an alien the rights and privileges of a native; to make native or natural; to adapt to a different climate; to acclimatize, to adopt.

NATURALLY, [nach'-er-a-li], *adv.* in a natural manner, unaffectedly; innately, according to nature; of course.

NATURALNESS, [nach'-er-al-nes], *n.* the state of being natural; conformity to nature.

NATURE, [nā'-cher], *n.* the complete power, composed of innumerable contributory processes, forces, and agencies, which governs the character of all external phenomena and their production in terms of cause and effect; the universe; the material world and its geographical, botanical, and zoological features; a primitive state of social organization, free from any complex system of control, and characterized by purely instinctive reaction; the state of a human being's instinctive, emotional, and intellectual powers, a person's disposition, character; the sum total of properties and qualities of a thing having a recognizable effect; a kind, species, sort. [L. *natura*].

NAUGHT (1), [nawt], *n.* nothing. [OE. *nawiht, naht*].

NAUGHT (2), [nawt], *adj.* useless; having no degree; worthless.

NAUGHTILY, [nawt'-i-li], *adv.* in a naughty manner.

NAUGHTINESS, [nawt'-i-nes], *n.* the state of being naughty; misbehaviour, disobedience.

NAUGHTY, [nawt'-i], *adj.* guilty of improper conduct, disobedient, perverse; mischievous, teasing.

NAUMACHIA, [naw-ma'-ki-a], *n.* in ancient Rome, a sea-fight, or its representation as a spectacle for public entertainment. [Gk. *naumakhia* naval battle].

NAUSEA, [naw'-si-a], *n.* a sensation of sickness; a sickness of the stomach accompanied with a propensity to vomit; (*fig.*) loathing. [Gk. *nautia* sea-sickness].

NAUSEANT, [naw'-si-ant], *n.* (*med.*) a substance which produces nausea.

NAUSEATE, [naw'-si-āt], *v.t.* to cause a feeling of nausea or disgust; to loathe or reject with disgust; to affect with disgust. [L. *nauseare* to feel sick].

NAUSEATING, [naws'-i-āt-ing], *adj.* that nauseates.

NAUSEATION, [naw'-si-ā'-shun], *n.* the act of nauseating.

NAUSEOUS, [naw'-si-us], *adj.* causing feelings of sickness, loathsome, disgusting, revolting.

NAUSEOUSLY, [naw'-si-us-li], *adv.* in a nauseous manner, loathsomely.

NAUSEOUSNESS, [naw'-si-us-nes], *n.* the state of being nauseous, loathsomeness.

NAUTCH, [nawch], *n.* an Indian dance; **n. girl,** an Indian dancing girl. [Skr. *nritya* dancing].

NAUTICAL, [naw'-tikl], *adj.* connected with, pertaining to, sea matters; **n. almanac,** a book of tables and calculations for navigators and astronomers published years in advance; **n. mile**, the sixtieth of a degree of longitude. [~Gk. *nautikos*].

NAUTICALLY, [naw'-tik a-li] *adv.* in a nautical manner.

NAUTILITE, [naw'-til-īt], *n.* a nautilus in a fossil form. [Gk. *nautilos* sailor and *lithos* stone].

NAUTILOID, [naw'-til-oid], *adj.* resembling the nautilus. [Gk. *nautilos* sailor and *oeides* like].

NAUTILUS, [naw'-til-us], *n.* (*zool.*) a cuttle-fish of the genus *Nautilus*, or of the genus *Argonauta*. [Gk. *nautilos* sailor].

NAVAL, [nā'-val], *adj.* consisting of ships; connected with, pertaining to, ships or to a navy; **n. brigade**, a detachment of troops or marines serving on land. [L. *navalis*].

NAVALISM, [nā' val-izm], *n.* the doctrine stipulating the necessity of concentrating on the development of sea power.

NAVE (1), [nāv], *n.* (*arch.*) the middle or body of a church, extending from the chancel or choir to the principal entrance at the west end. [L. *navis* ship].

NAUTILUS

NAVE (2), [nāv], *n.* the centre of a wheel, through which the axle passes, the hub. [OE. *nafu*].

NAVEL, [nā'-vel], *n.* the depression in the abdomen, marking the position where the umbilical cord is attached at birth; the centre. [OE. *nafela*].

NAVEL-ORANGE, [nā'-vel-o'-rinj, *n.* a species of seedless orange with a navel-like base.

NAVEL-STRING, [nā'-vel-string'], *n.* the umbilical cord.

NAVELWORT, [nā'-vel-wurt'], *n.* the plant, *Cotyledon umbilicus*.

NAVETTE, [nav-et'], *n.* the rape plant, cultivated in France for its seed, which produces colza oil; the wild turnip. [Fr. *navette*].

NAVICULAR, [nav-ik'-yōō-ler], *adj.* relating to small ships or boats; shaped like a boat; **n. bone**, (*anat.*) the scaphoid bone in the wrist, or in the foot of animals, shaped like a boat; **n. disease**, (*path.*) inflammation of a horse's navicular bone. [LL. *navicularis*].

NAVIGABILITY, [nav'-ig-ab-il'-i-ti], *n.* the condition of being navigable, navigableness.

NAVIGABLE, [nav'-ig-abl], *adj.* capable of being navigated; able to be steered. [L. *navigabilis*].

NAVIGABLENESS, [nav'-ig-abl-nes], *n.* the state of being navigable.

NAVIGABLY, [nav'-ig-ab-li], *adv.* in a navigable manner.

NAVIGATE, [nav'-ig-āt], *v.t. and i.* to voyage in ships; to conduct a vessel on the sea or in the air according to a set course and making allowances for shifts in tide and wind and weather conditions. [L. *navigare* to sail].

NAVIGATION, [nav'-ig-ā'-shun], *n.* the act or science of navigating; the progress or passage of ships or aircraft; that which is navigated. [L. *navigatio*].

NAVIGATING OFFICER, [nav'-i-gāt-ing-o'-fis-er], *n.* the officer on board ship or on an aircraft responsible for the navigation.

NAVIGATOR, [nav'-ig-āt'-or], *n.* an expert in navigation; one who directs the course of a ship or aircraft; †canal cutter. [L. *navigator* sailor].

NAVVY, [nav'-i], *n.* a person employed at heavy, unskilled labour such as the construction of roads, railways, docks, and other engineering works. [Abbreviation of NAVIGATOR, a person employed in cutting canals].

NAVY, [nā'-vi], *n.* the total number of ships bearing armaments maintained by a state for its defence; a fleet of armed ships; the department run by the state to maintain its sea power. [L. *navis* ship].

NAVY BLUE (1), [nāv-i-blōō'], *n.* navy blue colour.

NAVY BLUE (2), [nāv-i-blōō'], *adj.* of the dark blue typical of naval uniforms.

NAVY-CUT, [nā'-vi-kut'], *n.* cake tobacco cut into fine slices.

NAWAB, [nah'-wahb'], *n.* the hereditary title of a Mohammedan ruler in India corresponding to a rajah among Hindus; a nabob. [Arab. *nawwab*, *pl.* of *na'ib* deputy-governor].

NAY† (1), [nā], *n.* a refusal, denial.

NAY (2), [nā], *adv.* no; not only so, not this alone. [OScand. *nei*].

NAYWORD†, [nā'-wurd], *n.* a by-word, a watch-word.

NAZARENE, [naz-a-rēn'], *n.* Jesus Christ; one of the early converts to Christianity; (*pl.*) an early sect of Christians. [Gk. *nazarenos* an inhabitant of *Nazareth*].

NAZARITE, [naz'-a-rīt], *n.* a Jewish man or woman consecrated to the service of God and bound to austerity of life which forbids him to marry, drink wine, or cut his hair. [Heb. *nazar* to separate oneself].

NAZARITISM, [naz'-ar-īt-izm], *n.* the practices of a Nazarite.

NAZE, [nāz], *n.* a cliff, promontory, a headland. [OE. *næs*].

NAZI, [naht'-si], *n.* a member of the National Socialist party in Germany. [Germ. *Na(tional So)zi(alist)*].

NAZIRITE, [naz'-i-rīt], *n.* a Nazarite.

NEAD-END, [nēd'-end], *n.* the show-end of woollen goods.

NEAP, [nēp], *n.* the tide at the beginning of the moon's second and fourth quarters when the high-water level reaches its lowest point. [OE. *nep*].

NEAPED, [nēpt], *adj.* (*naut.*) left aground between high tides; lacking sufficient depth of water for navigation.

NEAPOLITAN (1), [nē'-ap-ol'-it-an], *n.* an inhabitant of Naples.

NEAPOLITAN (2), [nē'-ap-ol'-it-an], *adj.* connected with, pertaining to, Naples; **N. ice**, an ice of different flavours and layers of colours. [Gk. *Neapolis* Naples].

NEAR (1), [nēer], *adj.* adjacent, neighbouring, close to; closely related, intimate, united in affection; having a close correspondence in condition or quality; mean, miserly; referring to the left side of anything, particularly anything connected with road-travel.

NEAR (2), [nēer], *adv.* within a short distance of, not far from; †almost. [OE. *near*, *comp.* of *neah* nigh].

NEAR (3), [nēer], *v.t. and i.* to draw near to, approach, to come nearer to.

NEAR-BY, [nēer'-bī'], *adj. and adv.* adjacent, close at hand.

NEARCTIC, [nē-ahk'-tik], *adj.* belonging to the American Arctic. [NEO and ARCTIC].

NEAREST, [nēer'-est], *adj.* closest, shortest in distance.

NEARLY, [nēer'-li], *adv.* not quite, almost; intimately, dearly; in a niggardly manner.

NEARNESS, [nēer'-nes], *n.* the state or quality of being near, closeness, propinquity; (*coll.*) parsimony, stinginess.

NEAR-SIGHTED, [nēer'-sīt'-id], *adj.* short-sighted.

NEAR-SIGHTEDNESS, [nēer'-sīt'-id-nes], *n.* the state of being near-sighted, short-sightedness.

NEAT (1), [nēt], *n.* cattle, any bovine animal. [OE. *neat*].

NEAT (2), [nēt], *adj.* of, relating to, bovine cattle; **neat's foot oil**, oil obtained from a neat's foot by melting.

NEAT (3), [nēt], *adj.* simple and tidy in style of dress and appearance, trim; pure, unadulterated, without water; simple, clean and precise in arrangement; skilful, clever; to the point, apt. [OFr. *net* from L. *nitidus* clear].

NEATH, [nēth], *prep.* abbreviated form of BENEATH.

NEAT-HANDED, [nēt'-hand'-id], *adj.* skilful and quick with the hands, dexterous.

NEATHERD, [nēt'-hurd], *n.* a cow-herd.

NEATLY, [nēt'-li], *adv.* in a neat manner, with neatness.

NEATNESS, [nēt'-nes], *n.* the quality of being neat; cleanliness, tidiness.

NEB, [neb], *n.* (*Scots*) the nose; a beak; a nib, tip, point; peak (of a cap). [OE. *nebb* beak].

NEBRIS, [neb'-ris], *n.* (*archae.*) the skin of a fawn as worn by Dionysus. [Gk. *nebris* from *nebros* fawn].

NEBULA, (*pl.* **nebulae**), [neb'-yōō-la], *n.* (*astron.*) a faint luminous mass of misty matter in the sky; a cluster of stars of a luminous misty appearance; (*anat.*) a white cloudy spot on the cornea of the eye. [L. *nebula* mist].

NEBULAR, [neb'-yōō-ler], *adj.* (*astron.*) relating to nebulae; **n. hypothesis**, the theory which derived the orbs of the universe from condensations of nebulous matter.

NEBULARIZATION, [neb'-yōō-ler-īz-ā'-shun], *n.* the act of becoming nebular.

NEBULIUM, [ni-bewl'-i-um], *n.* a hypothetical element detected in certain nebulæ. [NEBULA].

NEBULOSITY, [neb'-yōō-los'-i-ti], *n.* the state of being cloudy or nebulous, cloudiness, vagueness. [Fr. *nebulosité*].

NEBULOUS, [neb'-yōō-lus], *adj.* (*astron.*) having the characteristics of a nebula, like a nebula; obscure; formless; (*fig.*) vague; hazy. [L. *nebulosus* cloudy].

NEBULOUSNESS, [neb'-yōō-lus-nes], *n.* nebulosity.

NEBULY, [neb'-yōō-li], *adj.* (*arch.*) ornamented with waves, having an undulating moulding; (*her.*) representing clouds. [Fr. *nébulé*].

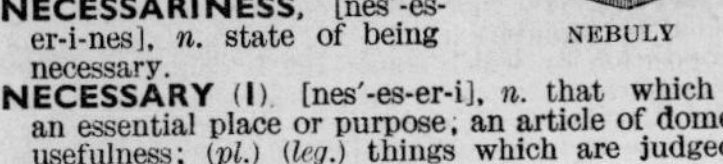
NEBULY

NECESSARIAN, [nes'-es-āer'-i-an], *n.* a necessitarian.

NECESSARIANISM, [nes'-es-āer'-i-an-izm], *n.* necessitarianism.

NECESSARILY, [nes'-es-er'-i-li], *adv.* as an inevitable result of, or by, necessity.

NECESSARINESS, [nes'-es-er-i-nes], *n.* state of being necessary.

NECESSARY (1), [nes'-es-er-i], *n.* that which has an essential place or purpose; an article of domestic usefulness; (*pl.*) (*leg.*) things which are judged as essential accompaniments of living.

NECESSARY (2), [nes'-es-er-i], *adj.* having a natural consequence or essential place, inevitable; fulfilling an essential function, indispensable, requisite; compulsory. [L. *necessarius*].

NECESSITARIAN (1), [nis-es'-it-āer'-i-an], *n.* (*philos.*) an advocate of the doctrine of necessity, by which every event or experience is held to occur because of its being a link in a chain of cause and effect; a determinist, as opposed to a libertarian.

NECESSITARIAN (2), [nis'-es-it-āer'-i-an], *adj.* relating to the doctrine of necessity.

NECESSITARIANISM, [nis-es'-it-āer'-i-an-izm], *n.* (*philos.*) the doctrine of necessity, or that which denies the freedom of the will, determinism.

NECESSITATE, [nis-es'-it-āt], *v.t.* to render necessary or unavoidable, to compel; to occur as a logical consequence.

NECESSITATION, [nis-es'-it-ā'-shun], *n.* the act of making necessary; compulsion.

NECESSITOUS, [nis-es'-it-us], *adj.* poor, needy, indigent.

NECESSITOUSLY, [nis-es'-it-us-li], *adv.* in a necessitous manner.

NECESSITOUSNESS, [nis-es'-it-us-nes], *n.* the condition of being necessitous; poverty or destitution.

NECESSITY, (*pl.* **necessities**), [nis-es'-i-ti], *n.* that which is necessary, particularly an action or decision to act rendered inevitable as a consequence of a particular set of circumstances bearing upon the progress of human life; that which has an inevitable place or consequence; that which is essential or considered essential for the continuance of human life; poverty, want. [L. *necessitas* inevitableness].

NECK (1), [nek], *n.* the part of the body connecting the head and trunk; anything having a similar form or function; a narrow tract of land connecting two larger areas, an isthmus; (*slang*) insolence; **to get it in the n.,** (*slang*) to be severely reprimanded, punished, or attacked; to come off badly; **n. or nothing,** recklessly; **stiff-necked,** obstinate. [OE. *hnecca*].

NECK (2), [nek], *n.* the last sheaf of corn cut at harvest-time. [Uncert.].

NECK (3), [nek], *v.i.* (*U.S. slang*) to flirt, to kiss and cuddle. [Germ. *necken*].

NECKBAND, [nek'-band'], *n.* a band at the top of a shirt fitting round the neck.

NECKBEEF, [nek'-bēf], *n.* coarse flesh of the neck of cattle.

NECKCLOTH, [nek'-kloth'], *n.* a piece of cloth worn on the neck, scarf.

NECKED, [nekt], *adj.* having a neck.

NECKERCHIEF, [nek'-er-chēf], *n.* a kerchief for the neck, a scarf. [NECK and KERCHIEF].

NECKING (1), [nek'-ing], *n.* (*arch.*) the part of a column consisting of a moulding between the capital and shaft; the annulet.

NECKING (2), [nek'-ing], *n.* the action of one who necks. [NECK (3)].

NECKLACE, [nek'-lis], *n.* a string of beads or other ornaments worn round the neck. [NECK (1) and LACE].

NECKLACED, [nek'-last], *adj.* wearing a necklace; marked as with a necklace.

NECKLET, [nek'-let], *n.* a thin necklace holding a locket or other ornament; a fur necktie.

NECK-MOULDING, [nek'-mōld'-ing], *n.* (*arch.*) a moulding where the shaft and capital of a column join.

NECK-PIECE, [nek'-pēs], *n.* a frill worn round the neck; †a piece of armour protecting the neck.

NECKTIE, [nek'-tī], *n.* a tie for the neck.

NECKWEAR, [nek'-wāer], *n.* gentlemen's collars, ties, and scarves.

NECRAEMIA, [nek-rē'-mi-a], *n.* death of the blood from mortification. [NECRO and Gk. *haima* blood].

NECRO-, *pref.* dead. [Gk. *nekros* dead body].

NECROBIOSIS, [nek'-rō-bī-ō'-sis], *n.* morbid rotting of organic tissue. [NECRO and Gk. *biosis* living].

NECROLATRY, [nek-rol'-at-ri], *n.* worship of the dead. [NECRO and Gk. *latreia* worship].

NECROLOGICAL, [nek'-rō-loj'-ikl], *adj.* relating to, or giving an account of, the dead or deaths.

NECROLOGIST [nek-rol'-oj-ist], *n.* a writer of obituary notices.

NECROLOGY, [nek-rol'-o-ji], *n.* a register of deaths; a collection of obituaries. [NECRO and Gk. *logos* speech].

NECROMANCER, [nek'-rō-man-ser], *n.* a person who practises necromancy.

NECROMANCY, [nek'-rō-man-si], *n.* divination by means of pretended communication with the spirits of the dead, black magic, sorcery, witchcraft. [Gk. *nekromanteion*].

NECROMANTIC, [nek'-rō-man'-tik], *adj.* relating to, or performed by, necromancy.

NECROMANTICALLY, [nek'-rō-man'-tik-al-i], *adv.* through necromantic means; by conjuration.

NECRONITE, [nek'-ron-īt], *n.* (*min.*) a variety of orthoclase felspar, which emits a bad smell when broken.

NECROPHAGOUS, [nek-rof'-ag-us], *adj.* eating or feeding on carrion. [NECRO and Gk. *phago* I eat].

NECROPHILISM, [nek-rof'-il-izm], *n.* an unnatural affection for the dead. [NECRO and Gk. *philos* love].

NECROPHILY, [nek-ro'-fil-i], *n.* necrophilism.

NECROPHOBIA, NECROPHOBY, [nek'-rō-fō'-bi-(a)], *n.* a morbid horror of dead bodies or of death. [NECRO and PHOBIA].

NECROPOLIS, [nek-rop'-ol-is], *n.* a city of the dead; a cemetery. [Gk. *nekropolis*].

NECROPSY, [nek-rop'-si], *n.* a post-mortem examination. [NECRO and Gk. *opsis* sight].

NECROSCOPIC, [nek'-rō-skop'-ik], *adj.* relating to post-mortem examinations. [NECRO and Gk. *skopeo* I view].

NECROSED, [nek-rōst], *adj.* (*path.*) affected with necrosis.

NECROSIS, [nek-rō'-sis], *n.* decay of tissue, dry gangrene, mortification in bone; a disease of plants by which they become spotted with black. [Gk. *nekrosis*].

NECROTIC, [nek-rot'-ik], *adj.* affected by, pertaining to, necrosis.

NECROTOMIST, [nek-rot'-om-ist], *n.* a dissector of dead bodies.

NECROTOMY, [nek-rot'-o-mi], *n.* the dissection of dead bodies. [NECRO and Gk. *tome* cutting].

NECTAR, [nek'-ter], *n.* (*myth.*) the drink of the gods of the Greeks; any very sweet beverage; the sweet secretion in flowers which is the source of honey. [Gk. *nektar*].

NECTAREAL, [nek-tāer'-i-al], *adj.* nectarean.

NECTAREAN, [nek-tāer'-i-an], *adj.* having the qualities of, or pertaining to, nectar.

NECTARED, [nek'-terd], *adj.* sweet as nectar, imbued with nectar.

NECTAREOUS, [nek-tāer'-i-us], *adj.* nectarean.

NECTARIAL, [nek-tāer'-i-al], *adj.* (*bot.*) relating to the nectary of a plant.

NECTARIFEROUS, [nek'-ter-if'-er-us], *adj.* (*bot.*) producing nectar. [NECTAR and L. *ferre* to bear].

NECTARINE (1), [nek'-ter-in], *n.* a smooth-skinned variety of the peach, *Prunus persica* var. *lævis*.

NECTARINE (2), [nek'-ter-īn], *adj.* sweet as nectar.

NECTARIUM, [nek-tāer'-i-um], *n.* the nectary.

NECTARIZE, [nek'-ter-īz], *v.t.* to make sweet, to sweeten.

NECTAROTHECA, [nek'-ter-ō-thē'-ka], *n.* (*bot.*) a spur or tube at the base of a petal in which nectar is secreted. [NECTAR and THECA].

NECTAROUS, [nek'-ter-us], *adj.* sweet as nectar.

NECTARY, [nek'-ter-i], *n.* (*bot.*) the honey gland of a flower.

NEDDY, [ned'-i], *n.* hypocoristic form of Edward; a donkey.

NEE, née, [nā], *adj.* the term used to denote a (married) woman's maiden name. [Fr. *née* born].

NEED (1), [nēd], *n.* a state recognized for its serious deficiency in some quality, factor, etc.; want, necessity, state that requires relief, urgent want; want of the means of subsistence, indigence, poverty. [OE. *ned*].

NEED (2), [nēd], *v.t. and i.* to be in need of, to want, to lack, require urgently; to be necessary, to be obliged; to be in want. [OE. *neodian*].

NEEDER, [nēd'-er], *n.* a person who wants.

NEED-FIRE, [nēd'-fīer], *n.* fire obtained by friction, and believed to be potent as a counter-charm in diseases ascribed to sorcery.

NEEDFUL (1), [nēd'-fŏŏl], *n.* (*coll.*) that which is needful, *esp.* money.

NEEDFUL (2), [nēd'-fŏŏl], *adj.* necessary, requisite.

NEEDFULLY, [nēd'-fŏŏl-i], *adv.* in a needful manner, necessarily.

NEEDFULNESS, [nēd'-fŏŏl-nes], *n.* the state of being needful.

NEEDILY, [nēd'-i-li], *adv.* necessitously.

NEEDINESS, [nēd'-i-nes], *n.* the state of being needy; poverty, want, indigence.

NEEDLE (1), [nēdl], *n.* a small tool used for sewing, consisting of a thin, short piece of steel tapered off to a sharp point at one end, and with an eye or hole stamped out of the other, through which thread is drawn; a slim length of rounded metal, bone, wood, etc., used in knitting; a short, thin, pointed piece of steel or wood, etc., for taking the vibrations of a gramophone record; the magnetized strip of steel in a mariner's compass indicating the pole; a hypodermic syringe; an etching tool; a tall sharp-peaked rock; anything in the form of a needle; **n. chervil,** the plant *Scandix Pecten-veneris*; **n. whin,** the shrub, *Genista anglica*. [OE. *nædl*].

NEEDLE (2), [nēdl], *v.t.and i.* to use a needle and thread, to sew, embroider; to pierce with a needle; to form needle-shaped crystals; to distort.

NEEDLE-BAR, [nēdl'-bah(r)], *n.* the bar in a sewing-machine into which the needles are fitted.

NEEDLE-BOOK, [nēdl'-bŏŏk], *n.* a book with leaves or pockets to keep needles in.

NEEDLE-CASE, [nēdl'-kās], *n.* a case for holding needles, a needle-book.

NEEDLE-FISH, [nēdl'-fish], *n.* the garfish; the greater pipefish, *Syngnathus acus*.

NEEDLEFUL, [nēdl'-fŏŏl], *n.* the length of thread inserted into a needle and to be worked to a finish.

NEEDLE-LACE, [nēdl'-lās], *n.* lace made with a needle and not with a bobbin.

NEEDLE-ORE, [nēdl'-aw(r)], *n.* acicular sulphide of bismuth, lead and copper.

NEEDLE-POINT, [nēdl'-point], *n.* point-lace made with a needle.

NEEDLESPAR, [nēdl'-spah(r)], *n.* aragonite.

NEEDLESS, [nēd'-les], *adj.* not wanted, unnecessary, superfluous.

NEEDLESSLY, [nēd'-les-li], *adv.* in a needless manner, without necessity.

NEEDLESSNESS, [nēd'-les-nes], *n.* the state of being needless.

NEEDLE-TAILED, [nēdl'-tāld], *adj.* (*ornith.*) having the tail feathers ending in spines; **n.-tailed swift,** the Indian bird, *Acanthyllis caudacuta*.

NEEDLE-TAILED SWIFT

NEEDLE-WOMAN, [nēdl'-wŏŏm'-an], *n.* a woman who earns a living by sewing, a seamstress.

NEEDLEWORK, [nēdl'-wurk], *n.* work executed with a needle, embroidery.

NEEDMENT†, [nēd'-ment], *n.* anything needed, requisite.

NEEDS, [nēdz], *adv.* necessarily, indispensably. [OE. *nedes*].

NEEDY, [nēd'-i], *adj.* necessitous, indigent, very poor.

NEEM, NIM, [nēm], *n.* margosa oil obtained from the bark of the East Indian tree, *Melia azaderach*. [Hind. *nim*].

NEEP, [nēp], *n.* a turnip. [OE, *næp* from L. *napus*].

NE'ER, [nāer], *adv.* a contraction of NEVER.

NE'ER-DO-WELL, [nāer'-dōō-wel'], *n,* a person who is never likely to do well, a lazy, good-for-nothing fellow.

NEEZE, [nēz], *v.i.* to sneeze. [ME. *nesen*].

NEF, [nef], *n.* a silver model of a ship, often used as a cruet holder or a case for a knife, fork, and spoon. [Fr. *nef*].

NEFANDOUS, [nif-and'-us], *adj.* unmentionable, abominable; very wicked. [L. *nefandus*, *ger.* of *nefari* not to speak].

NEFARIOUS, [nif-āer'-i-us], *adj.* unlawful, impious, wicked in the extreme, abominable. [L. *nefarius* wicked].

NEFARIOUSLY, [nif-āer'-i-us-li], *adv.* in a nefarious manner.

NEFARIOUSNESS, [nif-āer'-i-us-nes], *n.* the quality of being nefarious, iniquity.

NEGATE, [nig-āt'], *v.t.* to nullify; to deny. [L. *negare*].

NEGATION, [nig-ā'-shun], *n.* the act of negating, nullification, denial; declaration that something is not; (*philos.*) the dialectical antithesis of a thesis.

NEGATIONIST, [nig-ā'-shun-ist], *n.* a person who believes in the necessity for the denial of ideas.

NEGATIVE (1), [neg'-at-iv], *n.* a word expressing denial or prohibition, e.g., *no, not*; a statement or proposition by which something is denied, opposite of an affirmative; (*elect.*) the cathode plate or terminal in an electric circuit opposite to the positive; (*phot.*) a chemically prepared glass plate or film bearing an image with the natural light and dark tones in a reversed relationship.

NEGATIVE (2), [neg'-at-iv], *adj.* implying or expressing denial, refusal, prohibition; making no new or valuable contribution, not affirming anything; (*elect.*) derived from, relating to, the cathode or its function; (*math.*) of, or relating to, a minus quantity ; (*phot.*) relating to, of the nature of, a negative. [LL. *negativus*].

NEGATIVE (3), [neg'-at-iv], *v.t.* to expose as logically false, to disprove, to prove the contrary; to reject by vote, to veto; to render ineffective, to neutralize.

NEGATIVELY, [neg'-at-iv-li], *adv.* in a negative manner; with or by a negative; without producing the expected result, making no valuable contribution.

NEGATIVENESS, [neg'-at-iv-nes], *n.* the state of being negative.

NEGLECT (1), [nig-lekt'], *n.* the act of neglecting, lack of care or proper attention, negligence, inattention, slight, indifference; the state of being neglected, the condition resulting from lack of care. [L. *neglectus*].

NEGLECT (2), [nig-lekt'], *v.t.* to give no attention to, not to notice; to leave uncared for, to disregard, slight; to omit to do on account of carelessness. [L. *neglectum*, *p.pt.* of *negligere* to neglect].

NEGLECTABLE, [nig-lekt'-abl], *adj.* able to be neglected.

NEGLECTED, [nig-lekt'-id], *adj.* omitted to be done.

NEGLECTEDNESS, [nig-lekt'-id-nes], *n.* state of being neglected.

NEGLECTER, [nig-lekt'-er], *n.* a person who neglects.

NEGLECTFUL, [nig-lekt'-fŏŏl], *adj.* negligent, accustomed to neglect, inattentive, heedless, indicating neglect.

NEGLECTFULLY, [nig-lekt'-fŏŏl-i], *adv.* in a neglectful manner, with neglect.

NEGLECTINGLY, [nig-lekt'-ing-li], *adv.* with neglect, carelessly.

NEGLIGEE, negligée, [neg'-li-zhā], *n.* a loose, easy dress for informal wear, a dressing-gown, a loose gown; a long necklace, usually of coral. [Fr. *négligé*].

NEGLIGENCE, [neg'-lij-ents], *n.* behaviour due to inattention; condition due to such behaviour; neglect, carelessness. [L. *negligentia*].

NEGLIGENT, [neg'-lij-ent], *adj.* neglectful, careless, heedless, inattentive.

NEGLIGENTLY, [neg'-lij-ent-li], *adv.* in a negligent manner, carelessly.

NEGLIGIBILITY, [neg'-lij-ib-il'-i-ti], *n.* the state of being negligible.

NEGLIGIBLE, [neg'-lij-ibl], *adj.* that need not be noticed; of little value; not worth taking into account. [Fr. *négligeable*].

NEGOCIANT, see NEGOTIANT.

NEGOCIATE, see NEGOTIATE.

NEGOTIABILITY, [nig-ō'-shab-il'-i-ti], *n.* the condition of being negotiable.

NEGOTIABLE, [nig-ō'-shabl], *adj.* able to be negotiated or transferred by assignment; transferable on endorsement by holder; able to provide a foothold or passage.

NEGOTIANT, NEGOCIANT, [nig-ō'-shi-ant], *n.* a person who negotiates.

NEGOTIATE, NEGOCIATE†, [nig-ō'-shi-āt], *v.t. and i.* to arrange terms of business by means of discussion, conference, and meetings, to transact business, to bargain; to exchange a security for cash; to cope with a complex section of a road or passage; to participate in business transactions; to discuss terms of peace. [L. *negotiare* to trade].

NEGOTIATION, [nig-ō'-shi-ā'-shun], *n.* the act of negotiating, the transacting of business; treating

with another in order to come to an agreement over specific terms. [L. *negotiatio*].
NEGOTIATOR, [nig-ō'-shi-āt'-or], *n.* a person who negotiates or treats with others. [L. *negotiator* business agent].
NEGRESS, [nē'-gres], *n.* a female Negro.
NEGRITOS, NEGRILLOS, [neg-rē'-tōz, neg-ril'-ōz], *n.(pl.)* aboriginals of dwarf stature inhabiting the Malay Peninsula and Philippines; pygmies. [Span. *negrito* small negro].
NEGRO (1), [nē'-grō], *n.* member of an African race having as physical characteristics a black skin, woolly tight-curled hair, thick lips, and a flat nose with broad nostrils; a person having some Negro blood. [Span. *negro* from L. *niger* black].
NEGRO (2), [nē'-grō], *adj.* relating to a Negro.
NEGROHEAD, [nē'-grō-hed'], *n.* tobacco mixed with molasses and pressed into cakes.
NEGROID, [nē'-groid], *adj.* resembling a Negro, of Negro type. [NEGRO and Gk. *oeides* like].
NEGROPHILE, [nē'-grō-fil], *n.* a friend of Negroes and a defender of their interests. [NEGRO and Gk. *philos* love].
NEGROPHOBE, [nē'-grō-fōb'], *n.* a hater of Negroes. [NEGRO and Gk. *phobos* fear].
NEGROPHOBIA, [nē'-grō-fō'-bi-a], *n.* a pathological fear of Negroes.
NEGUNDO, [nig-und'-ō], *n.* the American box-elder, *Acer Negundo.* [Native].
NEGUS (1), [nē'-gus], *n.* an Abyssinian title equivalent to king; the Emperor of Abyssinia. [Abyssinian *n'gus* king].
NEGUS (2), [nē'-gus], *n.* a hot drink made of wine, water, sugar, and sometimes nutmeg and lemon-juice. [Col. *Negus* (died 1732), the inventor].
NEHUSHTON, [ni-hoosh'-ton], *n.* a thing of brass. [Heb. *nehushton*].
NEIGH (1), [nā], *n.* the cry of a horse; a whinnying.
NEIGH (2), [nā], *v.i.* to utter a cry, as a horse, to whinny. [OE. *hnægan*].
NEIGHBOUR (1), [nā'-ber], *n.* a person who lives near or next door; a person who is placed near; any member of the community regarded from the human aspects of love and friendship and social matters. [OE. *neahbur* from *neah* near and *bur* peasant].
NEIGHBOUR (2), [nā'-ber], *adj.* nearby, adjoining.
NEIGHBOUR (3), [nā'-ber], *v.t. and i.* to be near to; to act towards like a friendly neighbour; to adjoin, border on.
NEIGHBOURHOOD, [nā'-ber-hood], *n.* a district or area surrounding or near to a specific point or place; a place near, the adjoining district; the state of being near, adjacence, proximity; the inhabitants who live near each other, neighbours considered collectively.
NEIGHBOURING, [nā'-ber-ing], *adj.* living or being near, adjacent.
NEIGHBOURLINESS, [nā'-ber-li-nes], *n.* the quality of being neighbourly, sociability.
NEIGHBOURLY (1), [nā'-ber-li], *adj.* having the good qualities of a neighbour, kind, sociable, friendly.
NEIGHBOURLY (2), [nā'-ber-li], *adv.* in the manner of a neighbour, with social civility.
NEIGHING, [nā'-ing], *n.* the call of a horse.
NEITHER, [nī'-THer], *pron.* and *conj.* not either.
NEK, [nek], *n.* a mountain pass in South Africa. [Du. *nek* neck].
NEKTON, [nek'-ton], *n.* (*biol.*) the different minute forms of organic life swimming at the surface of the ocean. [Gk. *nektos* swimming].
NEMALINE, [nem'-al-īn], *adj.* (*min.*) having the form of threads, fibrous. [Gk. *nema* thread].
NEMALITE, [nem'-al-īt], *n.* (*min.*) a fibrous hydrate of magnesia. [Gk. *nema* thread and *lithos* stone].
NEMATOID, [nem'-at-oid], *adj.* like a thread. [Gk. *nema* thread and *oeides* like].
NEMATODES, [nem'-at-ōdz], *n.(pl.)* (*zool.*) thread-worms, entozoans usually of parasitic habits, with filiform elongated bodies.
NEMERTEA, [nem-ur'-ti-a], *n.(pl.)* a group of marine annelids, remarkable for their length of body and brilliant colours. [Gk. *Nemertes*, a sea nymph].
NEMERTIDS, [nem-er'-tids], *n.(pl.)* the nemertea.
NEMESIS, [nem'-is-is], *n.* (*myth.*) the goddess of vengeance or retributive justice descending on those experiencing undeserved success; (*fig.*) fate bringing retribution. [Gk. *nemesis* righteous anger].
NEMOPHILA, [nem-of'-il-a], *n.* a cultivated variety of garden plant having bright blue petals and a white centre. [Gk. *nemos* wood and *philos* loving].
NEMORAL, [nem'-or-al], *adj.* relating to a wood. [~L. *nemus* grove].
NEMOROSE [nem'-or-ōs], *adj.* growing in groves; full of woods.
NENUPHAR, [nen'-yoo-fah(r)], *n.* (*bot.*) the white waterlily, *Nymphæa alba.* [Pers. *ninufar* waterlily].
NEO-, *pref.* new; later; revived with modifications, based upon. [Gk. *neos* new].
NEOCOMIAN, [nē'-ō-kō'-mi-an], *n.* (*geol.*) the Lower Greensand and Wealden formations combined. [L. *Neocomium*, now Neuchâtel in Switzerland].
NEOCOSMIC, [nē'-ō-koz'-mik], *adj.* relating to the existing condition of the universe. [NEO and COSMIC].
NEODYMIUM, [nē'-ō-dim'-i-um], *n.* (*chem.*) the metallic element denoted by Nd. [NEO and (DI)DYMIUM].
NEOGAMIST, [nē-og'-am-ist], *n.* a person recently married. [NEO and Gk. *gamos* marriage].
NEOGENE, [nē'-ō-jēn], *n.* (*geol.*) the Miocene and Pliocene systems of rocks characteristic of a geological period. [NEO and Gk. *genes* birth].
NEOLITE, [nē'-ō-līt], *n.* (*min.*) a green silicate of aluminium and magnesium. [NEO and Gk. *lithos* stone].
NEOLITHIC, [nē'-ō-lith'-ik], *adj.* relating to a primitive period of civilization characterized by implements of polished stone; the latest of the stone ages. [NEO and Gk. *lithos* stone].
NEOLOGIAN, [nē'-ō-lō'-ji-an], *n.* (*theol.*) a neologist.
NEOLOGICAL, [nē'-ō-loj'-ikl], *adj.* relating to neology; employing new words.
NEOLOGICALLY, [nē'-ō-loj'-ik-a-li], *adv.* in a neological manner.
NEOLOGISM, [nē-ol'-oj-izm], *n.* a word or expression that is new or of new significance; (*theol.*) new doctrine, particularly of a rationalistic nature. [NEO and Gk. *logos* speech].
NEOLOGIST, [nē-ol'-oj-ist], *n.* a person who practises neology, an introducer of new words or doctrines.
NEOLOGISTICAL, [nē-ol'-oj-ist'-ikl], *adj.* neological.
NEOLOGIZE, [nē-ol'-oj-īz], *v.i.* to introduce new terms or doctrines, *esp.* theological.
NEOLOGY, [nē-ol'-o-ji], *n.* aptitude for inventing new words or giving new significance to old words, the introduction of new words or new meanings; rationalistic views in theology.
NEON, [nē'-on], *n.* (*chem.*) the gaseous element denoted by Ne; **n. light,** a type of light obtained by electrically ionizing neon gas in a glass tube. [Gk. *neos* new].
NEONOMIAN, [nē'-ō-nō'-mi-an], *n.* a person who advocates the doctrine that Christianity has introduced a new law which has radically supplanted the Mosaic system. [NEO and Gk. *nomos* law].
NEONOMIANISM, [nē'-ō-nō'-mi-an-izm], *n.* the doctrines of the Neonomians.
NEON SIGN, [nē'on-sīn'], *n.* a display sign for advertising purposes utilizing a neon tube.
NEONTOLOGY, [nē'-on-tol'-o-ji], *n.* the study of existing animals. [NEO and Gk. *on ontos* being and *logos* speech].
NEOPHOBIA, [nē'-ō-fō'-bi-a], *n.* the hatred of anything new. [NEO and Gk. *phobos* fear].
NEOPHRON, [nē'-of-ron], *n.* the white Egyptian vulture, *Neophron percnopterus.*
NEOPHYTE, [nē'-ō-fīt'], *n.* (*eccles.*) a new convert or proselyte; a novice, a tyro. [Gk. *neophutos* newly planted].
NEOPLASM, [nē'-ō-plazm], *n.* (*med.*) new tissue.
NEOPLASTIC, [nē'-ō-plast'-ic], *adj.* characterized by, relating to, neoplasm, freshly formed.
NEOPLASTY, [nē'-ō-plast'-i], *n.* restoration by granulation.
NEOPLATONIC, [nē'-ō-plat-on'-ik], *adj.* pertaining to Neoplatonism.
NEOPLATONISM, [nē'-ō-plā'-ton-izm], *n.* a mixture of Oriental and Platonic philosophy; the philosophy of Plotinus who lived at Alexandria in the third century. [NEO and PLATONISM].

NEOPHRON

NEOPLATONIST, [nē'-ō-plā'-ton-ist], *n.* an advocate of the Neoplatonic philosophy.
NEOTERIC, [nē'-ō-te'-rik], *adj.* new, recent in origin; new-fangled. [Gk. *neoterikos* fresh].
NEOTROPICAL, [nē'-ō-trop'-ikl], *adj.* situated between the tropics in America and its islands.

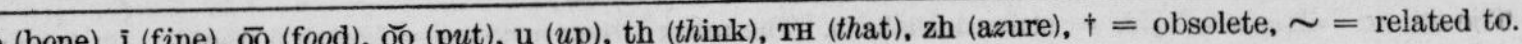

NEOZOIC, [nē'-ō-zō'-ik], *adj.* (*geol.*) denoting the formations from the Trias up to the most recent time. [NEO and Gk. *zoon* animal].

NEPALESE (1), [nep'-awl-ēz], *n.* a native of Nepal.

NEPALESE (2), [nep'-awl-ēz], *adj.* relating to, coming from, Nepal.

NEPAL-PAPER, [nep-awl'-pā'-per], *n.* a strong unsized paper made in Nepal from the pulverized bark of *Daphne papyracea*.

NEPENTHE, [nip-en'-thi], *n.* a drug that relieves pain, originally by inducing forgetfulness. [Gk. *nepenthes* banishing grief].

NEPHELINE, [nef'-el-īn], *n.* (*geol.*) a volcanic mineral composed mainly of the silicate of aluminium, sodium, and potassium, found in lavas and crystal form. [Gk. *nephele* cloud].

NEPHELITE, [nef'-el-īt], *n.* nepheline.

NEPHELOID, [nef'-el-oid], *adj.* (*med.*) cloudy. [Gk. *nephele* cloud and *oeides* like].

NEPHEW, [nev'-yōō], *n.* the son of one's brother or sister. [Fr. *neveu*].

NEPHOSCOPE, [nef'-ō-skōp], *n.* an instrument for observing the motion of the clouds. [Gk. *nephos* cloud and SCOPE].

NEPHRALGIA, [nef-ral'-ji-a], *n.* neuralgia of the kidneys. [Gk. *nephros* kidney and *algos* pain].

NEPHRITE, [nef'-rīt], *n.* (*min.*) jade, a ferrous silicate of magnesium and lime, a mineral formerly worn as a remedy for kidney disease; kidney stone.

NEPHRITIC (1), [nef-rit'-ik], *n.* (*med.*) a medicine for treating kidney diseases.

NEPHRITIC (2), [nef-rit'-ik], *adj.* (*med.*) pertaining to the kidneys, renal; affected with disease of the kidneys. [Gk. *nephritikos* relating to the kidneys].

NEPHRITIS, [nef-rī'-tis], *n.* (*path.*) inflammation of the kidneys. [Gk. *nephros* kidney and *itis* denoting inflammation].

NEPHRO-, *pref.* relating to the kidneys. [Gk. *nephros* kidney].

NEPHROCELE, [nef'-rō-sēl], *n.* (*med.*) hernia of the kidneys. [NEPHRO and Gk. *kele* tumour].

NEPHROGRAPHY, [nef-rog'-raf-i], *n.* a description of the kidneys. [NEPHRO and Gk. *graphia* writing].

NEPHROID, [nef'-roid], *adj.* kidney-shaped. [NEPHRO and Gk. *oeides* like].

NEPHROLOGY, [nef-rol'-o-ji], *n.* a treatise on the kidneys. [NEPHRO and Gk. *logos* speech].

NEPHROTOMY, [nef-rot'-o-mi], *n.* (*surg.*) the extracting of a stone from the kidney by cutting. [NEPHRO and Gk. *tome* cutting].

NEPOTIC, [nep-ot'-ik], *adj.* of the nature of, showing, nepotism.

NEPOTISM, [nep'-ot-izm], *n.* favouritism shown to relatives, particularly in the matter of filling government posts. [L. *nepos nepotis* nephew].

NEPOTIST, [nep'-ot-ist], *n.* a person who practises or advocates nepotism.

NEPTUNE, [nep'-tyōōn], *n.* (*myth.*) the god of the sea; (*astron.*) the large planet beyond Uranus having one moon. [L. *Neptunus*, the sea-god].

NEPTUNIAN (1), [nep-tewn'-i-an], *n.* a Neptunist.

NEPTUNIAN (2), [nep-tewn'-i-an], *adj.* relating to the sea; formed by means of water; **n. theory**, the theory which attempts to relate the formation of rocks and strata to particular activities of water.

NEPTUNIST, [nep'-tewn-ist], *n.* a person who adopted the Neptunian theory.

NEREID, [ne'-ri-id], *n.* (*myth.*) a sea-nymph, any one of the fifty daughters of Nereus, the wise old man of the sea; (*zool.*) a marine annelid or worm. [~Gk. *Nereis*, daughter of Nereus].

NERITE, [ne'-rīt], *n.* (*zool.*) a mollusc of the genus *Nerita*. [L. *nerita* mussel].

NEROLI, [ne'-rol-i], *n.* the essential oil of orange flowers. [Princess *Neroli* who discovered it].

NERVATE, [nurv'-āt], *adj.* (*bot.*) ribbed, veined.

NERVATION, [nerv-ā'-shun], *n.* (*bot.* and *zool.*) the arrangement of nerves or veins; the venation of leaves.

NERVE (1), [nurv], *n.* (*anat.*) any one of a complicated system of sensory and motor fibres, interconnected with nerve trunks and the spinal cord, which respond to stimuli, transmit the sensation to the brain centre, or carry impulses to the muscles; the state of mind under the control of a firm resolve, confidence, courage; (*coll.*) audacity, cheek, impertinence; (*pl.*) a state of apprehension, irritability; (*bot.*) a vein in a leaf; **war of nerves**, a campaign of propaganda, rumour, etc., designed to demoralize an enemy. [L. *nervus* sinew].

NERVE (2), [nurv], *v.t.* to impart strength, vigour, or courage to, embolden.

NERVE-CELL, [nurv'-sel'], *n.* (*anat.*) a cell of organic tissue which is a component part of a nerve.

NERVE-CENTRE, [nurv'-sen'-ter], *n.* (*anat.*) the junction of nerve fibres, a ganglion; (*fig.*) a centre which controls the whole of an organization.

NERVELESS, [nurv'-les], *adj.* having no strength, weak; having no nervous system, dead, unfeeling, numb.

NERVELESSLY, [nurv'-les-li], *adv.* in a nerveless manner.

NERVELESSNESS, [nurv'-les-nes], *n.* the state of being nerveless.

NERVOSE, [nurv'-ōs], *adj.* nerved.

NERVOUS, [nurv'-us], *adj.* (*anat.*) relating to the nervous system; suffering from nerves; strong, vigorous; with nerves in an acutely sensitive condition, jumpy, highly strung; timid, fearful, shyly apprehensive. [L. *nervosus* strong].

NERVOUSLY, [nurv'-us-li], *adv.* in a nervous manner; with strength or vigour; timidly.

NERVOUSNESS, [nurv'-us-nes], *n.* the condition of being nervous; strength, force; weakness of the nerves; timidity.

NERVURE, [nurv'-yer], *n.* (*bot.*) the ramification of veins in leaves; (*entom.*) the corneous divisions in the wings of insects.

NERVY, [nurv'-i], *adj.* having acutely sensitive nerves, nervous, jumpy, on edge.

NESCIENCE, [nes'-i-ents], *n.* want of knowledge; ignorance. [L. *nescientia*].

NESCIENT, [nes'-i-ent], *adj.* not knowing, ignorant, unaware of; agnostic. [L. *nesciens*, *pres.pt.* of *nescire* not to know].

NESH, [nesh], *adj.* (*dial.*) soft, delicate; tender; juicy. [OE. *hnesce*].

NESOGAEAN, [nē'-sō-jē'-an], *adj.* relating to the fauna of Polynesia. [Gk. *nesos* island and *gaia* earth].

NESS, [nes], *n.* a promontory, cape, headland. [OE. *næs*].

NEST (1), [nest], *n.* a structure built by a bird out of such materials as twigs, moss, mud, etc., used as a bed or home in which eggs are laid and hatched; a snug shelter; a breeding ground, haunt, den; a swarm, brood; a number of boxes or tables which are constructed to fit into each other and fit into the largest of the series. [OE. *nest*].

NEST (2), [nest], *v.t. and i.* to put in a nest; to build a nest and use it, as a bird.

NEST-EGG, [nest'-eg'], *n.* a genuine or dummy egg left in the nest to induce the hen to lay or brood; something laid up as a beginning, a small sum of money kept in reserve.

NESTLE, [nesl], *v.t. and i.* to house; to cherish; to move closer; to lie close and snug, as a bird in her nest. [OE. *nestlian* to build a nest].

NESTLING, [nes'-ling], *n.* a young bird from the nest, newly hatched, and unable to fly.

NESTORIAN (1), [nest-aw'-ri-an], *n.* a follower of Nestorius, patriarch of Constantinople in A.D. 428, who maintained the co-existence, but not the union of two natures in the person of Christ.

NESTORIAN (2), [nest-aw'-ri-an], *adj.* relating to Nestorius or his doctrine.

NET (1), [net], *n.* an open-work fabric made of twine, cord, silk, etc., threads, which are knotted together at the points where the parallel horizontal threads cross the parallel vertical threads, the whole piece being used to catch fish, snare birds, protect fruits or a woman's hair, etc.; an oblong strip of such material used to divide a tennis-court or a ping-pong table; the goal in certain games. [OE. *nett*].

NET (2), [net], *adj.* neat, unadulterated; free from, or clear of, discount and all deductions or charges. [Fr. *net* clean].

NET (3), (**netting, netted**), [net], *v.t. and i.* to catch or cover by means of a net; to set with nets; to make a net; to produce a net profit.

NETBALL, [net'-bawl], *n.* an outdoor game played with the hands in which the goals are nets shaped like a bag and hung from an iron loop at the top of a pole.

NETHER, [neTH'-er], *adj.* placed below, lower, opposed to upper; belonging to the regions below. [OE. *neothera*].

NETHERMOST, [neTH'-er-mōst], *adj.* lowest.

NETHINIM, [neth'-in-im], *n.*(*pl.*) tabernacle and temple servants. [Heb. *nethinim*].

NETT, [net], *adj.* free from all charges, without discount, net.

NETTED, [net'-id], *adj.* caught in a net, reticulated; gained as clear.

NETTING, [net'-ing], *n.* a strip, length, or piece of net, network; the making of nets; **n. needle**, a long needle on which twine or thread is wound.

NETTLE (1), [netl], *n.* a plant of the genus *Urtica*, covered with hairlike prickles, which sting severely; **dead n.**, a species of *Lamium*. [OE. *netele*].

NETTLE (2), [netl], *v.t.* to sting into a state of annoyance, to irritate, vex, pique, fret.

NETTLE-CLOTH, [netl'-kloth'], *n.* a material, consisting of a very thick tissued cotton, japanned and prepared as a substitute for leather.

NETTLECREEPER, [netl'-krēp'-er], *n.* a small bird also known as the white-throat, *Sylvia cinerea*.

NETTLECREEPER

NETTLEMONGER, [netl'-mung'-ger], *n.* the blackcap *Sylvia atricapilla*; the reed-bunting.

NETTLER, [net'-ler], *n.* a person who provokes or irritates.

NETTLE-RASH, [netl'-rash'], *n.* an irritable eruption upon the skin, resembling a nettle sting.

NETTLES, [netlz], *n.(pl.)* the lines used to support hammocks when they were slung under the beams.

NETTLE-TREE, [netl'-trē], *n.* a tree allied to the elm, *Celtis australis*.

NET-WINGED, [net'-wingd], *adj.* having net-veined wings.

NETWORK, [net'-wurk], *n.* a complication of reticulated threads, forming interstices between the intersections; anything resembling a net in form or pattern.

NEUM, [newm], *n.* (*mus.*) a group of notes sung to one syllable in plainsong. [Gk. *pneuma* breath].

NEURAL, [newr'-al], *adj.* relating to the nerves. [Gk. *neuron* nerve].

NEURALGIA, [new-ral'-ja], *n.* (*med.*) pain occurring in paroxysms in a nerve situated across the forehead or behind the eyes. [NEURO and Gk. *algos* pain].

NEURALGIC, [new-ral'-jik], *adj.* relating to neuralgia; suffering from neuralgia.

NEURASTHENIA, [newr'-as-thēn'-ya], *n.* a state of nervous exhaustion. [NEURO and Gk. *astheneia* weakness].

NEURASTHENIC, [newr'-as-thēn'-ik], *adj.* relating to neurasthenia.

NEURATION, [newr-ā'-shun], *n.* the arrangement of nerves in a leaf.

NEURECTOMY, [newr-ek'-tom-i], *n.* (*surg.*) the excision of a nerve or part of a nerve. [NEURO and Gk. *ektome* cutting away].

NEURILEMMA, [newr'-il-em'-a], *n.* (*anat.*) the sheath which invests a nerve. [NEURO and Gk. *eilema* covering].

NEURIN, [newr'-in], *n.* (*anat.*) the tissue or the substance which constitutes the matter of the nerves.

NEURITIS, [new-rī'-tis], *n.* inflammation of a nerve. [NEURO and Gk. *itis* denoting inflammation].

NEURO-, *pref.* relating to the nervous system. [Gk. *neuron* nerve].

NEUROGLIA, [new-rog'-li-a], *n.* tissue which encloses or cushions the actual nerve cord. [NEURO and Gk. *glia* glue].

NEUROGRAPHY, [newr-og'-raf-i], *n.* a description of the nerves. [NEURO and Gk. *graphia* writing].

NEUROLOGICAL, [newr-o-loj'-ikl], *adj.* relating to neurology.

NEUROLOGIST, [newr-ol'-oj-ist], *n.* an expert in neurology, a nerve specialist.

NEUROLOGY, [newr-ol'-o-ji], *n.* the study of the nerves, particularly in relation to their states of disturbance. [NEURO and Gk. *logos* speech].

NEUROMA, [newr-ō'-ma], *n.* (*path.*) a tumour formed in or upon a nerve. [NEURO and Gk. *oma* disease].

NEUROPATH, [newr'-ō-path'], *n.* (*med.*) a person liable to nervous disorders; a specialist who devotes himself to the treatment of disease through the medium of the nerves. [NEURO and Gk. *pathos* suffering].

NEUROPATHIC, [newr-ō-path'-ik], *adj.* relating to, affecting the nerves.

NEUROPATHIST [newr-op'-ath-ist] *n.* a nerve specialist.

NEURO-PATHOLOGIST, [newr-ō-path-ol'-o-jist], *n.* an expert in neuro-pathology.

NEURO-PATHOLOGY, [newr-ō-path-ol'-o-ji], *n.* the study of abnormal conditions of the nerves.

NEUROPATHY, [newr-op'-ath-i], *n.* an affection of the nerves, disease of the nerves. [NEURO and Gk. *pathos* suffering].

NEURO-PHYSIOLOGY, [newr'-ō-fiz'-i-ol'-o-ji], *n.* the physiology of the nervous system.

NEURO-PSYCHOLOGY, [newr'-ō-si-kol'-o-ji], *n.* a branch of psychology concerned with the relationship between the nervous system and affected states of emotions and habits.

NEUROPTERA, [newr-op'-ter-a], *n.(pl.)* (*entom.*) an order of insects having four transparent, finely reticulated membranous wings. [NEURO and Gk *pteron* a wing].

NEUROSIS, [new-rō'-sis], *n.* (*med.*) a functional disorder of the nervous system; (*psych.*) a state of nervous disorder attendant upon a type of personality inherently occupied with abnormal self-deceptions, such as obsession, hysteria, etc. [NEURO and Gk. *osis* denoting condition].

NEUROTIC (1), [new-rot'-ik], *n.* a person suffering from neurosis; a drug.

NEUROTIC (2), [new-rot'-ik], *adj.* relating to, affecting, the nerves; suffering from nervous disorder.

NEUROTOMICAL, [new'-rō-tom'-ikl], *adj.* relating to neurotomy.

NEUROTOMIST, [new-rot'-om-ist], *n.* a person practised in neurotomy.

NEUROTOMY, [new-rot'-o-mi], *n.* (*surg.*) dissection of the nerves. [NEURO and Gk. *tome* cutting].

NEUTER (1), [new'-ter], *n.* an animal which is organically deprived of sexual function; a person, group or nation which is recognized as standing apart from a contest or war, a neutral; (*gram.*) a noun, adjective, or pronoun of the neuter gender.

NEUTER (2), [new'-ter], *adj.* having the recognized status of a non-participant in a dispute or war, standing apart from a contest, indifferent, impartial, neutral; (*bot., entom.*) having no sexual function, neither masculine nor feminine; (*gram.*) neither masculine nor feminine in gender. [L. *neuter* neither of two].

NEUTRAL (1), [new'-tral], *n.* an individual, group, or nation which is officially recognized as having the status of non-participant in a dispute or war; a state of having the gears, particularly of a motor-car, disengaged.

NEUTRAL (2), [new'-tral], *adj.* remaining apart from either side engaged in dispute or war, impartial; having no distinguishing marks or qualities; (*bot., entom.*) having no organic sexual function, asexual, of neuter gender; (*chem.*) neither acid nor alkaline. [L. *neutralis*].

NEUTRALITY, [new-tral'-i-ti], *n.* the state of being neutral.

NEUTRALIZATION, [new'-tral-iz-ā'-shun], *n.* the act of neutralizing, or of reducing to a neutral state.

NEUTRALIZE, [new'-tral-īz], *v.t.* to render neutral; to render inert, inactive, or of no effect.

NEUTRALIZER, [new'-tral-īz-er], *n.* one who, or that which, neutralizes.

NEUTRALLY, [new'-tra-li], *adv.* in a neutral manner, impartially.

NEUTRON, [new'-tron], *n.* (*chem.*) a particle consisting of an electron and a proton.

NEVE, névé, [nā'-vā, nev'-ā], *n.* the granular snow that feeds a glacier. [Fr. from L. *nivem, acc.sg.* of *nix* snow].

NEVER, [nev'-er], *adv.* not ever, not at any time; in no degree, not under any condition. [OE. *næfre*].

NEVERMORE, [nev'-er-maw(r)'], *adv.* never any more, never again.

NEVERTHELESS, [nev'-er-THe-les'], *adv.* none the less, in spite of that, notwithstanding.

NEW (1), [new], *adj.* of recent origin, having an existence for the first time, lately produced or invented; recently discovered or known, but of previous existence; recently made, bought, or adopted; different and better, having a superior quality, original; modern, having a fresh application or significance; entering into the next phase of a recurrent cycle; unaccustomed, inexperienced; unfamiliar, strange. [OE. *niwe*].

NEW (2), [new], *adv.* freshly, recently, newly.

NEWCOMER, [new'-kum'-er], *n.* one who has recently arrived and can be considered as inexperienced; a stranger.

NEW DEAL, [new'-dēl'], *n.* the programme of social and economic reform inaugurated by President F. D. Roosevelt in the U.S.A. in 1932.

NEW DEALER, [new-dēl'-er], *n.* an advocate or exponent of the New Deal.

NEWEL, [new'-el] *n.* (*arch.*) the upright post or central shaft supporting a spiral staircase; the post at the foot or head of a staircase acting as a main support for the hand-rail. [OFr. *nuel*].

NEWFANGLED, [new'-fang'-gld], *adj.* believed to be a muddle of modern complexities, formed with the affectation of novelty; fond of novelties. [ME. *newefangel* from *newe* new and *fangel* eager to take].

NEWFANGLEDLY, [new'-fang'-gld-li], *adv.* in a newfangled manner.

NEWFANGLEDNESS, [new-'fang'-gld-nes], *n.* the state of being newfangled.

NEWFOUNDLAND, [new'-fund-land, new-fownd'-land], *n.* a variety of large dog of spaniel breed, originally from Newfoundland.

NEWISH, [new'-ish], *adj.* somewhat new; still retaining some of its freshness.

NEW-LAID, [new'-lād'], *adj.* (of an egg) newly laid, very fresh.

NEWLY, [new'-li], *adv.* recently, lately, freshly, in a new way.

NEWMARKET, [new'-mahk-it], *n.* a card game. [*Newmarket* Races, Cambridgeshire].

NEWNESS, [new'-nes], *n.* the quality of being new.

NEWS, [newz], *n.* information, facts, or a treatment of these, intelligence; a newspaper of this name; a broadcast of news.

NEWSAGENT, [newz'-ā'-jent], *n.* a shopkeeper who sells newspapers and periodicals.

NEWSBOY, [newz'-boi], *n.* a boy who sells or delivers newspapers.

NEWS EDITOR, [newz'-ed'-it-or], *n.* the editor of a newspaper specially engaged to deal with news.

NEWSHAWK, [newz'-hawk'], *n.* (*coll.*) a newspaper reporter.

NEWSLETTER, [newz'-let-er], *n.* a printed sheet or brochure circulating news.

NEWSMAN, [newz'-man'], *n.* a man who sells or delivers newspapers.

NEWSMONGER, [newz'-mung'-ger], *n.* one who deals in newspapers and periodicals; a gossip.

NEWSPAPER, [newz'-pā'-per], *n.* a printed paper issued daily or weekly containing news, editorials, and advertisements, and usually embodying some group of interests or policy.

NEWSPRINT, [newz'-print'], *n.* paper used for printing newspapers.

NEWS-REEL, [newz'-rēl'], *n.* a short film composed of shots of topical events.

NEWS-ROOM, [newz'-rōōm'], *n.* a room in a public or private institution for the reading of newspapers.

NEWS-THEATRE, [newz'-thē'-a-ter], *n.* a cinema showing a continuous programme of short news-reels, documentary films, etc.

NEWSVENDOR, [newz'-vend'-or], *n.* a seller of newspapers, newsagent, newsboy.

NEWSY, [newz'-i], *adj.* (*coll.*) spreading gossip, chatty; full of news.

NEWT, [newt], *n.* a tailed amphibian of the genus *Triton*, an eft. [OE. *efete*].

NEWT

NEWTONIAN (1), [new-tō'-ni-an], *n.* a follower of the physical principles of Sir Isaac *Newton*.

NEWTONIAN (2), [new-tō'-ni-an], *adj.* relating to, or invented, or discovered by Sir Isaac *Newton* (1642-1727).

NEXT (1), [nekst], *adj.* nearest in place, adjoining, neighbouring, having a position immediately before or after a specific point; nearest in time or degree. [OE. *next*].

NEXT (2), [nekst], *adv.* in the most near position, point of time or degree.

NEXT-OF-KIN, [nekst'-ov-kin'], *n.* the nearest blood relative.

NEXUS, [neks'-us], *n.* a connecting link or principle; a group with its units linked together. [L. *nexus* that which binds together].

NIAS, [nī'-as], *n.* a young hawk. [OFr. *niais*].

NIB, [nib], *n.* the bill or beak of a bird; a small pen; the point of anything, particularly of a quill pen split in two; a curved strip of steel or other metal tapering down to a split point and inserted into a pen-holder; (*slang*) a smart person, a "card." [~NEB].

NIBBLE (1), [nibl], *n.* the act of nibbling; a bite of the kind a fish makes, using its mouth on the surface of the food or bait rather than taking the whole piece into its jaws; a small bite made with the edge of the teeth; a piece of food obtained in this way.

NIBBLE (2), [nibl], *v.t. and i.* to eat by nibbles or to take a nibble (at). [Uncert.].

NIBBLER, [nib'-ler], *n.* a person or animal that nibbles.

NIBBLINGLY, [nib'-ling-li], *adv.* in a nibbling manner.

NIBLICK, [nib'-lik], *n.* a club with a broad, flat, round iron head and a face set obliquely, used for getting a ball out of a bunker or other hazard in golf. [Unkn.].

NICCOLITE, [nik'-ol-īt], *n.* (*min.*) a mineral composed of nickel and arsenic, nickeline. [MdL. *niccolum* nickel and Gk. *lithos* stone].

NICE, [nīs], *adj.* dainty, refined, fastidious; too fastidious; precise, exact, requiring precision; discriminating; (*coll.*) agreeable, pleasant, good, attractive, handsome; kind, sociable. [L. *nescius* ignorant].

NICELY, [nīs'-li], *adv.* in a nice manner.

NICENE, [nī'-sēn], *adj.* relating to, or coming from, Nicaea, a city in Asia Minor, the meeting-place for the first important council of the Christian church. [L. *Nicenus*].

NICENESS, [nīs'-nes], *n.* the quality of being nice; delicacy of perception; scrupulousness; precision; (*coll.*) agreeableness.

NICETY, [nīs'-i-ti], *n.* the capacity for delicate, exact perception; delicate handling or treatment; minute accuracy, precision, fastidiousness, squeamishness.

NICHE, [nich], *n.* a recess in a wall for a statue or other ornament; (*fig.*) a position corresponding to the kind of ability a person has. [Fr. *niche*].

NICHED, [nicht], *adj.* placed in a niche.

NICK (1), [nik], *n.* a small, thin, shallow notch, slit or slot, by which a reckoning or point of time is marked; a winning cast in a game of dice. [Uncert.].

NICK (2), [nik], *v.t. and i.* to make a nick in; to steal, pilfer; to nip in.

NICK-EARED, [nik'-ēerd], *adj.* crop-eared.

NICKEL, [nikl], *n.* (*min.*) a metal of a silver-white colour, very hard, ductile, and taking a high polish, used in steel manufacture, the chemical element denoted by Ni; (*U.S.*) a five-cent piece. [Germ. *nickel* demon].

NICKEL-GLANCE, [nikl'-glahnts'], *n.* an ore of nickel, composed of nickel, arsenic, and sulphur.

NICKEL-GREEN, [nikl'-grēn'], *n.* a green arsenate of nickel.

NICKELIC, [nik'-el-ik], *adj.* pertaining to, or containing, nickel.

NICKELINE, [nikl'-in], *n.* niccolite.

NICKELIZE, [nikl'-īz], *v.t.* to plate with nickel.

NICKEL-OCHRE, [nikl'-ō'-ker], *n.* nickel-green.

NICKEL-PLATED, [nikl'-plāt'-id], *adj.* covered with metallic nickel by electrical deposition from a solution of a nickel salt.

NICKEL-SILVER, [nikl'-sil'-ver], *n.* an alloy compounded of copper, nickel, and zinc, German silver.

NICKELURE, [nikl'-ew-er], *n.* the art of nickel-plating.

NICKNAME (1), [nik'-nām], *n.* an additional name given in derision or familiarity, usually of a descriptive nature. [LateME. *a neke name* for *an eke name* an added name].

NICKNAME (2), [nik'-nām], *v.t.* to give a nickname to.

NICOL, [nik'-ol], *n.* a prismatic instrument for polarizing light. [W. *Nicol*, the inventor].

NICOTIAN, [nik-ō'-shan], *adj.* relating to tobacco.

NICOTINE, [nik'-ō-tēn], *n.* a poisonous alkaloid of a very acrid taste, obtained from tobacco. [Jean *Nicot*, introducer of tobacco into France in 1560].

NICOTINISM, [nik'-ō-tēn-izm], *n.* a morbid condition caused by over-indulgence in tobacco.

NICTITATE, [nik'-ti-tāt], *v.i.* to wink. [L. *nictare*].

NICTITATION, [nik'-tit-ā'-shun], *n.* the act of winking. [L. *nictitatio*].

NIDAMENTAL, [nid'-a-ment'-al], *adj.* (*zool.*) relating to nests or their construction, particularly by molluscs. [~L. *nidamentum*].

NIDDERING (1), [nid'-er-ing], *n.* a niddering person.

NIDDERING (2), [nid'-er-ing], *adj.* cowardly, disloyal, infamous. [OE. *nithing* coward].

NIDE, [nīd], *n.* a brood of pheasants. [L. *nidus* nest].

NIDGE, [nij], *v.t.* to trim stones with a pick. [Uncert.].

NIDICOLOUS, [nid-ik'-ol-us], *adj.* remaining in the nest for more than the usual period. [L. *nidus* nest and *colere* to inhabit].

NIDIFICATE, [nid-if'-ik-āt], *v.i.* to build a nest, nidify. [L. *nidificare*].

NIDIFICATION, [nid'-if-ik-ā'-shun], *n.* the building of a nest.
NIDIFY, [nid'-i-fī], *v.i.* to make or build a nest.
NIDULANT, [nid'-yŏŏ-lant], *adj.* nestling as a bird.
NIDULATION, [nid'-yŏŏ-lā'-shun], *n.* the act of building a nest; the time of remaining in the nest, as of a bird.
NIDUS, [nī'-dus], *n.* a nest; (*med.*) the place of incubation of a disease. [L. *nidus* a nest].
NIECE, [nēs], *n.* the daughter of one's brother or sister. [ME. *nece* from L. *neptis* grand-daughter].
NIELLO, [ni-el'-ō], *n.* ornamental engraving in black on silver or gold. [It. *niello* from LL. *nigellum* dark enamel].
NIELLURE, [ni-el'-yōō-er], *n.* the art of working in niello.
NIETZSCHEAN, [nē'-chi-an], *adj.* (*philos.*) based on the philosophy of *Nietzsche* and his doctrine of the superman.
NIFLHEIM, [nifl'-hīm], *n.* (*Norse myth.*) the region of primeval cold and darkness. [Icel. *nifl* cloud and *heim* home].
NIFTINESS, [nift'-i-nes], *n.* smartness, spruceness.
NIFTY, [nift'-i], *adj.* (*U.S. slang*) admirable, smart, stylish; smelly. [Unkn.].
NIGELLA, [nī-jel'-a], *n.* (*bot.*) a genus of annual plants including love-in-a-mist, *Nigella damascena*. [L. *nigellus*].
NIGGARD (1), [nig'-erd], *n.* an avaricious person, a miser. [ME. *nigard*].
NIGGARD (2), [nig'-erd], *adj.* mean, avaricious, stingy, miserly.
NIGGARDLINESS, [nig'-erd-li-nes], *n.* the quality of being niggardly, avarice.
NIGGARDLY (1), [nig'-erd-li], *adj.* avaricious, covetous, mean.
NIGGARDLY (2), [nig'-erd-li], *adv.* in niggard manner.
NIGGER, [nig'-er], *n.* (*coll.*) a Negro; a man of colour; **n.-fish,** edible sea-fish marked with dark specks, found in West Indian waters; **n. minstrel,** an entertainer whose face is made up to resemble a Negro's; **to work like a n.,** (*coll.*) to work as hard as a slave. [~Span. *negro*, L. *niger* black].
NIGGER-BROWN, [nig'-er-brown'], *n.* a dark, chocolate shade of brown.
NIGGER-DRIVER, [nig'-er-drīv'-er], *n.* a brutal, oppressive employer.
NIGGERHEAD, [nig'-er-hed'], *n.* a species of cactus.
NIGGLE, [nigl], *v.i.* to trifle, to waste time in petty details, to worry about trifles, to be finicky. [Uncert.].
NIGGLER, [nig'-ler], *n.* one who niggles.
NIGGLING, [nig'-ling], *adj.* fussy, finicking; petty and over-elaborate, exhibiting a ridiculous care for details.
NIGGLY, [nig'-li], *adj.* niggling, petty, finicky.
NIGH (1), [nī], *adj.* close, near, not distant, not remote; closely allied. [OE. *neah*, *neh*].
NIGH (2), [nī], *adv.* near to, in an adjacent place; nearly, almost.
NIGHNESS, [nī'-nes], *n.* nearness, proximity.
NIGHT, [nīt], *n.* the period of the day between sunset and sunrise, characterized by the absence of sunlight; period of darkness; death; (*fig.*) darkness or obscurity of understanding, adversity. [OE. *niht*].
NIGHT-BLINDNESS, [nīt'-blīnd'-nes], *n.* inability to see except in daylight.
NIGHT-CAP, [nīt'-kap'], *n.* a cap worn in bed; a drink at bed-time.
NIGHT-CLOTHES, [nīt'-klōTHz], *n.*(*pl.*) clothes worn in bed.
NIGHT-COMMODE, [nīt'-kom-ōd'], *n.* a portable convenience used by invalids, etc.
NIGHTDRESS, [nīt'-dres'], *n.* a full-length, slip-over dress for wearing in bed.
NIGHTFALL, [nīt'-fawl], *n.* the close of day, evening.
NIGHT-FIRE, [nīt'-fīer], *n.* fire burning in the night, *Ignis fatuus*, will-o'-the-wisp.
NIGHT-GLASS, [nīt'-glahs], *n.* a binocular telescope which, by concentrating the light, enables one to see objects at night.
NIGHTGOWN, [nīt'-gown], *n.* a nightdress.
NIGHT-HAG, [nīt'-hag'], *n.* a witch; a nightmare.
NIGHT-HAWK, [nīt'-hawk], *n.* the nightjar, the fern-owl; a person who makes a habit of working at night, particularly illegally.
NIGHT-HERON, [nīt'-he'-ron], *n.* the night-raven, *Nycticorax griseus*.
NIGHTINGALE, [nīt'-ing-gāl], *n.* the warbler, *Daulias luscinia*, a migratory bird of Europe being of a brownish colour and outstanding for its sweet singing at night. [OE. *nihtegale* night-singer].
NIGHTJAR, [nīt'-jah(r)], *n.* the goatsucker, *Caprimulgus europæus*.
NIGHTLESS, [nīt'-les], *adj.* having no night.
NIGHTLIGHT, [nīt'-līt'], *n.* a short, thick, slow-burning candle for burning in a bedroom to give light at night.
NIGHTLINE, [nīt'-līn], *n.* a fishing line left baited and set to catch fish during the night.

NIGHTJAR

NIGHTLONG, [nīt'-long], *adj.* lasting all the night, throughout the night.
NIGHTLY (1), [nīt'-li], *adj.* done by night or every night; occurring each night.
NIGHTLY (2), [nīt'-li], *adv.* by night; every night.
NIGHTMAN, [nīt'-man], *n.* a man employed to empty closets or cesspools in the night.
NIGHTMARE, [nīt'-māer], *n.* †a demon, an incubus; a very bad dream of terrifying proportions and frightening reality; a dreadful experience of an extreme state of horror; (*coll.*) a person with an offensive face, habits, or character. [NIGHT and OE. *mara* demon].
NIGHTMARISH, [nīt'-māer-ish], *adj.* like a nightmare, nearly as frightening as a nightmare.
NIGHT-PIECE, [nīt'-pēs], *n.* a painting, so coloured as to be best seen by artificial light; a night scene.
NIGHT-PORTER, [nīt'-pawt'-er], *n.* a servant on duty at night in hotels, hospitals, etc.
NIGHT-RAVEN, [nīt'-rāv'-en], *n.* the night-heron.
NIGHT-SCHOOL, [nīt'-skōōl], *n.* an institution which holds classes in the evening so that those employed in the daytime can further their education.
NIGHTSHADE, [nīt'-shād], *n.* (*bot.*) one of several berry-bearing plants, of the genus *Solanum* or *Atropa Belladonna*. [OE. *nihtscada*].
NIGHTSHIRT, [nīt'-shurt], *n.* a full-length shirt used as sleeping apparel by a man.
NIGHTSINGER, [nīt'-sing'-er], *n.* the hedge warbler, *Acrocephalus phragmitis*.
NIGHT-SOIL, [nīt'-soil], *n.* the sewage contents of closets, removed and used as manure; excrement.
NIGHT-STOOL, [nīt'-stōōl], *n.* a commode.
NIGHTSUIT, [nīt'-sewt], *n.* pyjamas.
NIGHT-WALKER, [nīt'-wawk'-er], *n.* one who walks in his sleep; a somnambulist; prostitute.
NIGHT-WALKING, [nīt'-wawk'-ing], *n.* walking about in one's sleep, somnambulism; street-walking.
NIGHTWARD, [nīt'-werd], *adj.* approaching, towards night.
NIGHTWATCH, [nīt'-woch'], *n.* a guard or watch maintaining a look-out during the night; time of changing the watch or guard at night; period of keeping watch during part of the night.
NIGHT-WATCHMAN, [nīt'-woch-man], *n.* a watchman on duty at night.
NIGRESCENT, [nīg-res'-ent], *adj.* growing black, approaching to blackness. [L. *nigrescens*, *pres.pt.* of *nigrescere* to become black].
NIGRIC, [nīg'-rik], *adj.* black. [~L. *niger* black].
NIGRINE, [nīg'-rīn], *n.* (*min.*) an ore of titanium, a variety of rutile. [~L. *niger* black].
NIGRITUDE, [nīg'-ri-tewd], *n.* blackness. [L. *nigritudo*].
NIHIL, [nī'-hil], *n.* nothing. [L. *nihil*].
NIHILISM, [nī'-hil-izm], *n.* nothingness; (*philos.*) the destruction of existing beliefs or doctrines without making any attempt to establish the reality of phenomena; (*pol.*) system and principles of a Russian revolutionary party who aimed at the overthrow of Tsarism and capitalism by terroristic means in order to establish a state of anarchy. [*Prec.*].
NIHILIST, [nī'-hil-ist], *n.* an advocate of nihilism.
NIHILISTIC, [nī'-hil-ist'-ik], *adj.* relating to nihilism.
NIL, [nil], *n.* nothing. [L. *nil* contraction of *nihil*].
NILGAI, [nil'-gī], *n.* an Indian antelope of bluish colour, a species of *Boselaphus*. [Hind. *nilgai* blue cow].
NILOMETER, [nīl-om'-it-er], *n.* an instrument for showing the rise of water in the Nile during the state of flood. [Gk. *Neilometrion*].
NILOTIC, [nīl-ot'-ik], *adj.* relating to the Nile. [Gk. *Neilotikos*].
NIM, see NEEM.
NIMBIFEROUS, [nim-bif'-er-us], *adj.* storm-bringing. [L. *nimbus* cloud and *ferre* to bring].
NIMBLE, [nimbl], *adj.* light and active in motion, moving with ease and celerity, brisk, agile; alert,

quick-witted. [ME. *nimel*, ~OE. *numol* able to grasp].
NIMBLE-FINGERED, [nimbl'-fing'-gerd], *adj.* dexterous; expert at stealing.
NIMBLE-FOOTED, [nimbl'-fōōt'-id], *adj.* running with speed; light of foot.
NIMBLENESS, [nimbl'-nes], *n.* lightness and celerity.
NIMBLE-WITTED, [nimbl'-wit'-id], *adj.* quick in reply; quick-witted.
NIMBLY, [nim'-bli], *adv.* in a nimble manner, with agility.
NIMBUS, [nim'-bus], *n.* a rain-cloud; (*art*) a disk of light portrayed round the heads of divinities, saints and sovereigns. [L. *nimbus* cloud].
NIMIETY, [nim-ī'-i-ti], *n.* state of excessiveness, redundancy. [LL. *nimietas*].
NIMINY-PIMINY, [nim'-i-ni-pim'-i-ni], *adj.* (*slang*) performed with affectation; prim, effeminate; mincing. [Imitative].
NIMROD, [nim'-rod'], *n* a sportsman; a mighty hunter. [Heb. *Nimrod* the strong one].
NINCOMPOOP, [ning'-kum-pōōp'], *n.* a brainless booby, a blockhead. [Unkn.].
NINE (1), [nīn], *n.* the symbol representing the number nine, 9; **the N.**, the nine Muses; **dressed up to the nines**, wearing ultra-smart clothes.
NINE (2), [nīn], *adj.* one more than eight; **n. days' wonder**, a short-lived piece of sensational scandal; **n. men's morris**, an old English game resembling draughts. [OE. *nigon*].
NINEFOLD, [nīn'-fōld], *adj.* nine times repeated, nine times as many.
NINE-HOLE, [nīn'-hōl], *adj.* (of a golf-course) having nine holes.
NINE-HOLES, [nīn'-hōlz], *n.* a game in which a small ball or marble is played into a series of nine holes.
NINE-PINS, [nīn'-pinz], *n.* a variety of skittles in which nine pieces of wood are set on end, and a ball rolled at them.
NINETEEN (1), [nīn'-tēn], *n.* the number nine and ten united. [OE. *nigontyne*].
NINETEEN (2), [nīn'-tēn], *adj.* being nineteen in number. [*Prec.*].
NINETEENTH, [nīn'-tēnth], *adj.* following the eighteenth; **the n. hole**, (*golf*) the club-house bar.
NINETIETH, [nīn'-ti-eth], *adj.* following the eighty-ninth.
NINETY (1), [nīn'-ti], *n.* the number consisting of nine times ten. [OE. *nigontig*].
NINETY (2), [nīn'-ti], *adj.* being ten times nine in number.
NINEVITE, [nin'-iv-īt], *n.* a native of Nineveh.
NINNY, [nin'-i], *n.* a fool, a booby, a simpleton. [Unkn.].
NINON, [nı'-no(ng)], *n.* a light silk fabric. [Fr. *ninon*].
NINTH (1), [nīnth], *n.* one of nine equal parts; (*mus.*) an interval which is a tone or semitone wider than an octave.
NINTH (2), [nīnth], *adj.* following eight others in a series.
NINTHLY, [nīnth'-li], *adv.* in the ninth place.
NIOBIUM, [nī-ō'-bi-um], *n.* (*chem.*) the metallic element denoted by Nb; columbium. [*Niobe*, a heroine in Gk. mythology whose children were killed because of her too-great pride in them].
NIP (1), [nip], *n.* a sharp bite with the teeth or pinch with the fingers which bruises but does not break the skin; any action which has this effect; an edge of cold or frost to the air or wind.
NIP (2), [nip], *n.* a small drop of liquid, a sip; (*Scots*) a small measure of spirits. [NIP (4)].
NIP (3), **(nipping, nipped)**, [nip], *v.t.* to pinch with the nails, fingers, or teeth without drawing blood; to cut or clip with a tool; to affect the growth of, as by a frost or sharp wind; (*coll.*) to steal, pinch; to catch in the act; (*fig.*) to depress, to put a damper on; *v.i.* to effect by means of nipping, pinching, biting; **to n. along**, to hurry; **to n. in**, to slip into place before another. [ME. *nippen*, ~Du. *nijpen* to pinch].
NIP (4), **(nipping, nipped)**, [nip], *v.t.* to sip, to drink in small quantities. [Du. *nippen* to sip].
NIPPER, [nip'-er], *n.* one who, or that which, nips; a front tooth of a horse; one of the two front claws of a lobster or crab; a small boy, a street arab, urchin.
NIPPERS, [nip'-erz], *n.*(*pl.*) small pincers.
NIPPINESS, [nip'-i-nes], *n.* nimbleness, agility.
NIPPINGLY, [nip'-ing-li], *adv.* in a nipping manner; with bitter sarcasm.
NIPPLE, [nipl], *n.* the teat of a female's breast; anything similar in function or appearance. [Unkn.].
NIPPLEWORT, [nipl'-wurt], *n.* a plant of the genus *Lapsang*, bearing small yellow flowers.
NIPPON, [nip'-on], *n.* Japan. [Jap. *nippon* land of the rising sun].
NIPPY, [nip'-i], *adj.* cold; nimble, active, agile.
NIRVANA, [nur-vah'-na], *n.* (*Buddhist philos.*) a state when all individual reactions are extinguished and the spirit is sublimated by an affinity with the divine. [Skr. *nirvana* a blowing out].
NISAN, [nī'-san], *n.* the first month of the Jewish sacred calendar. [Heb. *nisan*].

NIPPLEWORT

NISI, [nī'-sī], *n.* (*leg.*) a writ which becomes valid unless sufficient cause to the contrary be shown before a certain date. [L. *nisi* unless].
NISSEN HUT, [nis'-en-hut'], *n.* a long portable hut, semi-circular in section. [*Nissen* Buildings Ltd.].
NIT, [nit], *n.* the egg of any small insect, such as a louse. [OE. *hnitu*].
NITRATE, [nī'-trāt], *n.* (*chem.*) a salt of nitric acid; saltpetre in its natural condition. [NITRE].
NITRATED, [nī'-trāt-id], *adj.* treated with nitric acid.
NITRATINE, [nī'-trat-ēn], *n.* the mineral composed of nitrate of soda.
NITRE, [nī'-ter], *n.* (*chem.*) saltpetre; the nitrate of potash; **cubic n.**, nitrate of soda, as crystallizing in cubes, Chile saltpetre. [Gk. *nitron* carbonate of soda].
NITRIC, [nī'-trik], *adj.* (*chem.*) relating to, impregnated with nitre; containing nitrogen in its higher valency; **n. acid**, a compound of hydrogen, oxygen, and nitrogen, HNO_3.
NITRIFEROUS, [nī-trif'-er-us], *adj.* (*chem.*) bearing nitre. [NITRE and L. *ferre* to bear].
NITRIFICATION, [nī'-trif-ik-ā'-shun], *n.* the process of forming nitre.
NITRIFY, [nī'-tri-fī], *v.t.* to form into nitre. [NITRE and L. *ficere* to make].
NITRITE, [nī'-trīt], *n.* (*chem.*) a compound of nitrous acid with a base or an alcohol.
NITRO-, *pref.* made from, or including, nitrogen. [NITRE].
NITRO-BENZENE, [nī'-trō-ben'-zēn], *n.* a combination of benzene and nitric acid with the flavour of the oil of bitter almonds, used in perfumery.
NITRO-CELLULOSE, [nī'-trō-sel'-yōō-lōs], *n.* the explosive product yielded by the action of nitric acid on cellulose, gun-cotton.
NITROGEN, [nī'-trō-jen], *n.* (*chem.*) a gaseous element denoted by N, colourless, tasteless, odourless, composing a large percentage of the atmosphere. [NITRE and Gk. *genes* producing].
NITROGENIZE, [nī-troj'-en-īz], *v.t.* to impregnate with nitrogen.
NITROGENOUS, [nī-troj'-en-us], *adj.* relating to or containing nitrogen.
NITRO-GLYCERIN(E), [nī'-trō-glis'-er-in], *n.* (*chem.*) glycerol trinitrate, a highly explosive liquid prepared by the action of nitric and sulphuric acids on glycerin, used in the manufacture of dynamite.
NITRO-HYDROCHLORIC, [nī'-trō-hī'-drō-klo'-rik], *adj.* (*chem.*) pertaining to the mixture of nitric and hydrochloric acids, formerly called aqua regia.
NITRO-MAGNESITE, [nī'-trō-mag'-nēz-īt], *n.* the nitrate of magnesia, generally found on old walls and in limestone caves.
NITROMETER, [nī-trom'-it-er], *n.* an instrument for ascertaining the quality or value of nitre. [NITRO and METER].
NITRO-NAPHTHALENE, [nī'-trō-naf'-thal-ēn], *n.* a substance prepared by boiling naphthalene in nitric acid.
NITRO-SULPHURIC, [nī'-trō-sul-fewr'-ik], *adj.* denoting a mixture of nitric with sulphuric acid.
NITROUS, [nī'-trus], *adj.* (*chem.*) relating to, containing, nitrogen in its lower valency; **n. oxide**, a gas composed of oxygen and nitrogen, N_2O, laughing-gas. [L. *nitrosus* full of nitre].
NITRY, [nī'-tri], *adj.* nitrous.
NITTY, [nit'-i], *adj.* full of nits.

NITWIT, [nit'-wit], *n.* (*slang*) a person of no sense, a blockhead, a fool. [Ger. *nit* nothing and WIT].
NITWITTED, [nit'-wit'-id], *adj.* (*slang*) having no sense.
NIVEOUS, [niv'-i-us], *adj.* snowy, resembling snow. [L. *niveus*].
NIX (1), [niks], *n.* (*slang*) nil, nothing. [Germ. *nix, nichts* nothing].
NIX (2), NIXIE, [niks], *n.* a water-elf. [Germ. *nixe*].
NIX (3), [niks], *int.* (*slang*) take care, nothing doing as regards. [NIX (1)].
NIZAM, [nēz-ahm'], *n.* the title of the ruler of Hyderabad in the Deccan. [Urdu *nizam*].
NO (1), [nō], *n.* a negative reply. [NO (3)].
NO (2), [nō], *adj.* not any, not one, none; hardly any; **n. go,** (*coll.*) useless; **n. side,** in Rugby football, the conclusion of the match; **n. wonder,** *int.* I do not wonder. [OE. *nan* from *ne an* not one].
NO (3), [nō], *adv.* not at all, in no respect, not in any degree, not any; not; **n. more,** neither. [OE. *na* from *ne* not and *a* ever].
NOACHIAN, [nō-ā'-ki-an], *adj.* relating to Noah, or his time. [Heb. *Noach* Noah].
NOB (1), [nob], *n.* (*slang*) head, cranium; a swell, a nobleman, an upper-class gentleman; (cribbage) the knave. [Uncert.].
NOB (2), (nobbing, nobbed), [nob], *v.t.* (*slang*) to punch on the head. [~KNOB].
NO BALL, [nō'-bawl], *n.* (*cricket*) a ball so declared by the umpire at the time of delivery because its method of delivery infringes the rules.
NOBBLE, [nobl], *v.t.* (*slang*) to render a horse unfit for a race either by injuring it or drugging it; to bribe a jockey for the same ends; to obtain possession of dishonestly; to cheat, swindle. [~*Prec.*].
NOBBLER, [nob'-ler], *n.* a person who nobbles a horse; a glass of spirits; a swindler's confederate.
NOBBY, [nob'-i], *adj.* (*slang*) good enough for a nobleman; grand, smart, stylish.
NOBILIARY, [nō-bil'-i-er-i], *adj.* belonging to the nobility. [Fr. *nobiliaire*].
NOBILITY, [nō-bil'-i-ti], *n.* the quality of being noble, nobleness, dignity of mind; distinction by birth, the rank of being noble; the class of society whose members belong to families possessing an hereditary seat in the House of Lords, the peerage. [L. *nobilitas* nobleness].
NOBLE (1), [nōbl], *n.* a person of high birth born into the class of the nobility, a member of the peerage, a nobleman, a peer; †an old English gold coin worth one-third of a pound.
NOBLE (2), [nōbl], *adj.* famous for high excellence, renowned for chivalry or virtuous deeds; having high ideals, possessing a selfless, courageous nature; expressed by a noble mind; stately, dignified, exalted; having a blood tie with a family of hereditary rank. [L. *nobilis*].
NOBLEMAN, [nōbl'-man], *n.* a member of the nobility, a peer.
NOBLE-MINDED, [nōbl'-mīnd'-ed], *adj.* high-minded.
NOBLENESS, [nōbl'-nes], *n.* the state of being noble; courageous virtue, greatness; dignity, stateliness
NOBLESSE, [nō-bles'], *n.* the nobility, persons of noble rank collectively. [Fr. *noblesse*].
NOBLEWOMAN, [nōbl'-wŏŏm'-an], *n.* a lady of noble rank, a peeress.
NOBLY, [nōb'-li], *adv.* in a noble manner; with noble parentage; bravely, magnificently.
NOBODY, [nō'-bod-i], *n.* not any body, no person, no one; a person of no note. [NO and BODY].
NOCAKE, [nō'-kāk], *n.* a North American Indian paste made of parched maize and water. [Amer. Indian *noohkik* maize].
NOCK, [nok], *n.* a notch, the notch in an arrow; (*naut.*) the weather corner of a gaff sail. [Uncert.].
NOCTAMBULATION, [nokt-am'-bew-lā'-shun], *n.* walking in sleep.
NOCTAMBULISM, [nokt-am'-bew-lizm], *n.* sleep-walking, somnambulism. [NOCTI and L. *ambulare* to walk].
NOCTAMBULIST, [nokt-am'-bew-list], *n.* a sleep-walker, a somnambulist.
NOCTI-, *pref.* of, by, or at night. [L. *nox noctis* night].
NOCTIFLOROUS, [nokt'-i-flaw'-rus], *adj.* (*bot.*) flowering at night, as the tobacco plant. [NOCTI and L. *flos floris* flower].
NOCTILUCOUS, [nok'-til-ew'-kus], *adj.* shining in the night, phosphorescent. [L. *noctiluca* moon].
NOCTIVAGANT, [nok-tiv'-ag-ant], *adj.* wandering in the night. [NOCTI and L. *vagans*, *pres.pt.* of *vagari* to wander].
NOCTOGRAPH, [nokt'-ō-graf], *n.* a writing frame for the blind. [NOCTI and GRAPH].
NOCTULE, [nok'-tewl], *n.* (*zool.*) a European bat of the genus *Vesperugo*. [MedL. *noctula*].
NOCTURN, [nok'-turn], *n.* (*R.C.*) a religious service at night, now part of matins. [L. *nocturnus* nightly].
NOCTURNAL, [nok-turn'-al], *adj.* relating to or happening at night.
NOCTURNALLY, [nok-turn'-al-i], *adv.* during the night, nightly.
NOCTURNE, [nok'-turn], *n.* (*art*) a picture of a night scene; (*mus.*) a piece of music to play at night as reflecting a mood of melancholy. [L. *nocturnus* by night].
NOCUOUS, [nok'-yŏŏ-us], *adj.* harmful, hurtful; poisonous. [L. *nocuus*].
NOCUOUSLY, [nok'-yŏŏ-us-li], *adv.* in a nocuous manner, hurtfully.
NOD (1), [nod], *n.* an intentional quick, sharp inclination of the head expressing assent or a curt form of greeting; an uncontrolled movement of the head as it drops forward through drowsiness; **on the n.,** (*U.S. slang*) on credit, on tick. [NOD (2)].
NOD (2), (nodding, nodded), [nod], *v.t. and i.* to move the head quickly and sharply forward and downward as a curt form of greeting; to make a short, sharp downward movement with the head as a sign of assent or as a curt form of greeting; to be drowsy, to let the head droop forward through drowsiness; (*fig.*) to make a mistake through inattention. [ME. *nodden*].
NODAL, [nōd'-al], *adj.* relating or belonging to a node; **n. lines,** lines which remain at rest while the rest of the body to which they belong vibrates; **n. points,** centres of convergence. [~NODE].
NODDER, [nod'-er], *n.* one who nods; a drowsy person.
NODDLE, [nodl], *n.* (*coll.*) the back of the head; the head. [Uncert.].
NODDY, [nod'-i], *n.* a simpleton, a fool; a sea-fowl allied to the terns, *Anous stolidus*, which is easily caught. [Unkn.].
NODE, [nōd], *n.* a point of intersection; a protuberance or knot caused by a joining; (*bot.*) the point on the stalk of a plant from which the leaf grows; (*astron.*) the point where the orbit of a planet intercepts the ecliptic; (*math.*) the point where a turning curve crosses itself; (*med.*) a swelling of the tendons into a knot; (*phys.*) the point of rest of a vibrating body. [L. *nodus* knot].
NODICAL, [nōd'-ik-al], *adj.* (*astron.*) relating to nodes.
NODIFEROUS, [nōd-if'-er-us], *adj.* (*bot.*) bearing nodes. [L. *nodus* knot and *ferre* to bear].
NODIFORM, [nōd'-i-fawm], *adj.* resembling nodes. [L. *nodus* knot and FORM].
NODOSE, [nōd-ōs'], *adj.* (*bot.*) knotty, having knots or swelling joints.
NODOSITY, [nōd-os'-i-ti], *n.* (*bot.*) the state of being full of knots, knottiness.
NODULAR, [nod'-yŏŏ-ler], *adj.* relating to a nodule or knot; possessing nodes.
NODULATED, [nod'-yŏŏ-lāt-id], *adj.* having nodules.
NODULE, [nod'-yŏŏl], *n.* a small knot; a rounded lump. [L. *nodulus*].
NODULED, [nod'-yŏŏld], *adj.* having little knots or lumps.
NODULOSE, [nod'-yŏŏ-lōs], *adj.* nodulous.
NODULOUS, [nod'-yŏŏ-lus], *adj.* having nodules.
NODUS, [nōd'-us], *n.* a node; (*fig.*) the point of difficulty. [L. *nodus* knot].
NOEL, [nō-el'], *n.* Christmas. [Fr. *noël* from L. *natalis* birthday].
NOEMATIC, [nō'-em-at'-ik], *adj.* noetic.
NOETIC, [nō-et'-ik], *adj.* relating to reason, intellectual; originating in, or performed by, the intellect. [Gk. *noetikos*].

NODUS

NOG (1), [nog], *n.* a little pot; a kind of strong ale; **egg n.,** a kind of drink consisting of a raw egg whipped up in a liquid, either milk or alcohol. [Unkn.].
NOG (2), [nog], *n.* a wooden bolt or peg; a piece of wood shaped like a brick. [Unkn.].
NOGGIN, [nog'-in], *n.* a small mug or wooden cup;

ō (bone), ī (fine), ōō (food), ŏŏ (put), u (up), th (think), TH (that), zh (azure), † = obsolete, ~ = related to.

a measure of liquid, a quartern, a quarter of a pint. [Unkn.].

NOGGING, [nog'-ing], *n.* brickwork or other filling in timber framing.

NOGGLEHEAD, [nogl'-hed'], *n.* (*coll.*) a freshwater fish, the river bullhead or miller's thumb, *Cottus gobio*.

NOHOW, [nō'-how], *adv.* (*U.S. coll.*) in no way, by no means. [NO and HOW].

NOILS, [noilz], *n.(pl.)* the waste ends of wool, the short pieces and knots of wool left after combing out the tops. [Unkn.].

NOISE (1), [noiz], *n.* a sound of any kind having the quality of loudness, sharpness, or composed of a number of discordant tones; a confused, disturbing and unpleasant sound, a turmoil of such sounds, clamour, uproar, din; **big n.**, (*slang*) a person in an influential position; a person who considers himself of great importance. [Fr. *noise* quarrel].

NOISE (2), [noiz], *v.t.* to spread by rumour, to cause to circulate by word of mouth. [*Prec.*].

NOISEFUL, [noiz'-fŏŏl], *adj.* loud, clamorous, noisy.

NOISELESS, [noiz'-les], *adj.* making no noise, silent.

NOISELESSLY, [noiz'-les-li], *adv.* in a noiseless manner, without noise.

NOISELESSNESS, [noiz'-les-nes], *n.* the state of being noiseless, silence.

NOISILY, [noiz'-i-li], *adv.* in a noisy manner, with noise.

NOISINESS, [noiz'-i-nes], *n.* the state of being noisy, clamour.

NOISOME, [noi'-sum], *adj.* noxious to health, hurtful; disgusting, offensive. [(AN)NOY and SOME].

NOISOMELY, [noi'-sum-li], *adv.* in a noisome manner, with a foetid smell.

NOISOMENESS, [noi'-sum-nes], *n.* the quality of being noisome.

NOISY, [noiz'-i], *adj.* making a noise, clamorous, turbulent, rowdy; accompanied by noise.

NOLI-ME-TANGERE, [nō'-li-mē-tan'-jer-i], *n.* (*med.*) an ulcerous disease of the skin; (*bot.*) the name of certain plants, *esp.* of the genus *Impatiens*, characterized by a bursting of the capsules when touched. [L. *noli me tangere* touch me not].

NOLL, [nol], *n.* (*dial.*) the head; the crown of the head. [OE. *cnoll*].

NOMAD (1), [nō'-mad'], *n.* a person who leads a wandering life, generally for pasture, as an inhabitant of a country in a backward state of economic development. [Gk. *nomas*].

NOMAD (2), [nō'-mad'], *adj.* wandering, belonging to a tribe of nomads.

NOMADIC, [nō-mad'-ik], *adj.* wandering, roaming, nomad.

NOMADICALLY, [nō-mad'-ik-al-i], *adv.* in a nomadic manner, as nomads.

NOMADISM, [nō'-mad-izm], *n.* the state of being nomadic; a nomadic life.

NOMADIZE, [nō'-mad-īz], *v.i.* to wander with flocks and herds.

NOMANCY, [nō'-man-si], *n.* telling the fortune and future of persons by the letters which form their names. [Gk. *onoma* name and *manteia* divination].

NO MAN'S LAND, [nō'-manz'-land'], *n.* land having no discoverable owner; the contested area intervening between entrenched hostile forces.

NOMARCH, [nōm'-ahk], *n.* the governor of a nome in ancient Egypt. [Gk. *nomarkhes*].

NOMARCHY, [nōm'-ahk-i], *n.* a province ruled by a nomarch. [Gk. *nomarkhia*].

NOMBLES, [numblz], *n.(pl.)* the edible entrails of a deer. [~NUMBLES].

NOMBRIL, [nom'-bril], *n.* (*her.*) the centre of an escutcheon. [Fr. *nombril* the navel].

NOM-DE-PLUME, [naw(n)'-de-plŏŏm'], *n.* a name adopted by a writer to conceal his identity. [OFr. *nom de plume* pen-name].

NOME, [nōm], *n.* (*hist.*) a division of the country for administrative purposes in Greece and Egypt. [Gk. *nomos* province].

NOMENCLATOR, [nō'-men-klāt-or], *n.* a person who gives names to things, an inventor of new names. [L. *nomenclator* caller of a name].

NOMENCLATORY, [nō'-men-klāt'-er-i], *adj.* naming.

NOMENCLATURAL, [nō'-men-klā'-cher-al], *adj.* pertaining to nomenclature.

NOMENCLATURE, [no-men'-kla-cher], *n.* a system of names allotted to objects or ideas in scientific classification; terminology. [L. *nomenclatura* calling of names].

NOMIC, [nom'-ik], *adj.* ordinary, customary. [Gk. *nomikos*].

NOMINAL, [nom'-in-al], *adj.* concerned with names; existing in name only, titular, verbal, not actual; very light, very low in respect of amount. [L. *nominalis* belonging to a name].

NOMINALISM, [nom'-in-al-izm], *n.* (*philos.*) the doctrine that abstract names or terms are words only, having no existence in nature or any relationship with a corresponding reality.

NOMINALIST, [nom'-in-al-ist], *n.* an upholder of nominalism.

NOMINALLY, [nom'-in-a-li], *adv.* to a nominal degree; by name only.

NOMINATE, [nom'-in-āt], *v.t.* to name or mention by name as a candidate for office or election. [~L. *nominare* to name].

NOMINATELY, [nom'-in-āt-li], *adv.* by name.

NOMINATION, [nom'-in-ā'-shun], *n.* the act or the power of nominating; or the state of being nominated; the entry of a name as a competitor. [L. *nominatio*].

NOMINATIVE (1), [nom'-in-at-iv], *n.* (*gram.*) the case of the subject of a sentence; any word in this case. [L. *nominativus* of a name].

NOMINATIVE (2), [nom'-in-at-iv], *adj.* (*gram.*) belonging to the case of the subject of a sentence.

NOMINATIVELY, [nom'-in-at-iv-li], *adv.* as a nominative.

NOMINATOR, [nom'-in-āt'-or], *n.* a person who nominates.

NOMINEE, [nom'-in-ē'], *n.* a person named or appointed by another for an office; one on whose life an annuity depends. [~L. *nomen* name].

NOMOGRAPHY, [nō-mog'-raf-i], *n.* a treatise on laws. [Gk. *nomos* law and *graphia* writing].

NOMOLOGY, [nō-mol'-o-ji], *n.* the science of law. [Gk. *nomos* law and *logos* speech].

NON-, *pref.* used in compounds to denote negation, lack of, exclusion. [*Prec.*].

NON-ACID, [non'-as'-id], *adj.* without the qualities of an acid.

NONAGE, [nōn'-ij], *n.* the condition of not being of age, minority; the state of being under twenty-one years of age. [OFr. *nonage*].

NONAGENARIAN, [non'-a-jen-āer'-i-an], *n.* a person of from ninety to ninety-nine years old. [~L. *nonagenarius* consisting of ninety].

NONAGESIMAL, [non'-a-jes'-im-al], *n.* (*astron.*) a term applied to the highest point of the ecliptic above the horizon. [L. *nonagesimus* ninetieth].

NONAGON, [non'-ag-on], *n.* (*geom.*) a nine-angled figure. [L. *nonus* ninth and Gk. *gonia* angle].

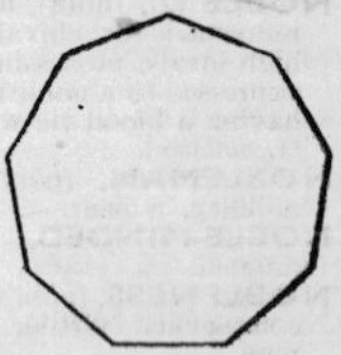

NONAGON

NON-APPEARANCE, [non'-a-pēer'-ants], *n.* (*leg.*) default of appearance in court.

NON-APPOINTMENT, [non'-a-point'-ment], *n.* failure to secure an appointment.

NONARY, [nōn'-er-i], *adj.* (*math.*) based on nine. [L. *nonarius*].

NON-ATTENDANCE, [non'-a-tend'-ants], *n.* a failure to attend.

NON-BELLIGERENT, [non'-bel-ij'-er-ent], *n.* and *adj.* (relating to) a state or party which, while remaining neutral, gives non-military aid to one side in a war.

NONCE, [nonts], *n.* the occasion, the time being. [ME. *for then ones* for the once].

NONCHALANCE, [non'-shal-ants], *n.* the state of being nonchalant, indifference; carelessness, coolness, absence of emotional response.

NONCHALANT, [non'-shal-ant], *adj.* exhibiting no response, indifferent; careless; cool, showing no feeling. [OFr. *nonchalant*, *pres.pt.* of *nonchaloir* to be careless].

NONCHALANTLY, [non'-shal-ant-li], *adv.* in nonchalant fashion.

NON-CLAIM, [non'-klām], *n.* (*leg.*) a failure to make a claim.

NON-COLLEGIATE (1), [non'-kol-ē'-ji-at], *n.* a student at a university who is not a member of a college.

NON-COLLEGIATE (2), [non'-kol-ēj'-i-at], *adj.* of, or pertaining to, non-collegiates.

NON-COMBATANT, [non'-kom'-bat-ant], *n.* a surgeon or chaplain or other person in the navy or army whose duty is not to fight; a civilian.

NON-COMMISSIONED, [non'-kom-ish'-und], *adj.*

not holding a commission in the army, as all soldiers under the rank of second lieutenant.

NON-COMMITTAL, [non'-kom-it'-al], *adj.* remaining neutral, not being committed or pledged.

NON-COMPLIANCE, [non'-kom-plī'-ants], *n.* neglect of compliance.

NONCOMPLYING, [non'-kom-plī-ing], *adj.* refusing or neglecting to comply.

NON-CONCURRENCE, [non'-kon-ku'-rents], *n.* a refusal to concur.

NON-CONDUCTING, [non'-kon-dukt'-ing], *adj.* (*elect.*) not conducting.

NON-CONDUCTOR, [non'-kon-dukt'-or], *n.* (*elect.*) a substance which does not conduct electricity or heat.

NON-CONFORMING, [non'-kon-fawm'-ing], *adj.* not conforming, *esp.* to the established religion.

NONCONFORMIST (1), [non'-kon-fawm'-ist], *n.* a person who does not conform to an established church, a dissenter.

NONCONFORMIST (2), [non'-kon-fawm'-ist], *adj.* of, or pertaining to, nonconformists or nonconformity; **n. conscience**, a conscience governed by nonconformist principles.

NONCONFORMITY, [non'-kon-fawm'-i-ti], *n.* refusal to conform, *esp.* to the principles or practice of an established church; the body of persons who refuse to conform.

NON-CONTAGIOUS, [non'-kon-tāj'-us], *adj.* not contagious.

NON-CONTENT, [non'-kon-tent'], *n.* (*pol.*) in the House of Lords, one who gives a negative vote.

NON-CO-OPERATION, [non'-kō-op-er-ā'-shun], *n.* abstinence from co-operation, *esp.* as an instrument of political policy.

NON-DELIVERY, [non'-dil-iv'-er-i], *n.* failure to deliver.

NONDESCRIPT (1), [non'-dis-kript], *n.* a person or object that is not easily classified according to well-defined characteristics.

NONDESCRIPT (2), [non'-dis-kript], *adj.* having no well-defined character; not easily classified; abnormal, defying description. [NON and L. *descript(um)*, *p.pt* of *describere* to mark off].

NON-DEVELOPMENT, [non'-di-vel'-op-ment], *n.* a lack of, or a failure of, development.

NON-DISCOVERY, [non'-dis-kuv'-er-i], *n.* lack of discovery.

NONE (1), [nun], *pron.* not one, not any, not the least portion. [OE. *nan* from *ne* and *an* one].

NONE (2), [nun], *adv.* none at all, not any, by no account, in no way.

NON-EFFICIENT, [non'-if-ish'-ent], *n.* a recruit who has failed to qualify as an efficient soldier.

NON-EGO, [non'-eg'-ō], *n.* (*psych.*) the external or objective in perception or thought; all that is not the conscious self.

NON-ELECT, [non'-i-lekt'], *n.* (*theol.*) one not elected, *esp.* to salvation.

NON-ELECTION, [non'-i-lek'-shun], *n.* failure to secure election.

NON-EMPHATIC, [non'-em-fat'-ik], *adj.* without emphasis.

NONENTITY, [non'-en'-ti-ti], *n.* the state of being non-existent, non-existence; a thing not existing, or as good as not; a person of no importance, a nobody.

NON-EPISCOPALIAN, [non'-ip-is' kō-pā'-li-an], *n.* a protestant not belonging to the Church of England.

NONES, [nōnz], *n.(pl.)* †the ninth day of the month before the Ides; one of the three divisions of the Roman month; (*eccles.*) a service formerly held at 3 p.m. [L. *nonae* (*dies*) ninth days].

NONE-SO-PRETTY, [nun'-sō-prit'-i], *n.* (*bot.*) the plant London pride, *Saxifraga umbrosa*.

NON-ESSENTIAL (1), [non'-is-en'-shal], *n.* a thing that can be dispensed with, a trifle, a superfluous detail.

NON-ESSENTIAL (2), [non'-is-en'-shal], *adj.* not really necessary, not essential.

NONESUCH, [nun'-such], *n.* a thing that has not its like, nonsuch, nonpareil.

NONET, [nō-net'], *n.* (*mus.*) a musical piece for nine singers or players. [It. *nonetto*].

NON-EXECUTION, [non'-eks-ik-ew'-shun], *n.* non-performance.

NON-EXISTENCE, [non'-egz-ist'-ents], *n.* the state of being non-existent, the negation of being; a thing that has no existence.

NON-EXISTENT, [non'-egz-ist'-ent], *adj.* not having existence.

NON-FEASANCE, [non'-fē'-zants], *n.* (*leg.*) a failure to perform a legal duty.

NON-FERROUS, [non'-fe'-rus], *adj.* (*metal.*) containing no iron or allied metal.

NON-FLAM, [non'-flam'], *adj.* non-inflammable; (*cinema*) applying to films of 16 mm. or under in width. [NON and INFLAMMABLE].

NON-FULFILMENT, [non'-ful-fil'-ment], *n.* neglect to fulfil.

NONILLION, [non-il'-yun], *n.* a million raised to the ninth power, written 1 and fifty-four noughts. [L. *nonus* ninth and (M)ILLION].

NON-INTERVENTION, [non'-in-ter-ven'-shun], *n.* abstention from interfering, particularly as a political policy in connexion with war.

NONJURING†, [non'-jōōer'-ing], *adj.* (*hist.*) refusing or abstaining from taking the oath of allegiance.

NONJUROR, [non'-jōōer'-or], *n.* a person who refused to take the oath of allegiance after the English Revolution of 1688.

NON-METALLIC, [non'-met-al'-ik], *adj.* (*chem.*) having no metallic properties.

NON-MORAL, [non'-mo'-ral], *adj.* neither moral nor immoral, having nothing to do with morality, amoral.

NON-NATURAL, [non'-nach'-er-al], *adj.* having no natural status; unnatural, strained, figurative.

NON-OBEDIENCE, [non'-ō-bē'-di-ents], *n.* neglect of obedience.

NON-OBSERVANCE, [non'-ob-zurv'-ants], *n.* neglect or failure to observe or fulfil.

NONPAREIL (1), [non'-pa-rel'], *n.* a person or object without a superior, that which has no peer; (*typ.*) a type which is six points in size.

NONPAREIL (2), [non'-pa-rel'], *adj.* having no peer or superior, matchless. [Fr. *nonpareil* unequalled].

NON-PERFORMANCE, [non'-per-fawm'-ants], *n.* a failure to perform.

NON-PLACENTAL, [non'-plas-ent'-al], *adj.* without a placenta.

NONPLUS (1), [non'-plus], *n.* a state of perplexity, insuperable difficulty; a quandary.

NONPLUS (2), (**nonplussing, nonplussed**), [non'-plus'], *v.t.* to place in a baffling situation, to puzzle, confound, perplex. [L. *non plus* not more].

NON-PONDEROUS, [non'-pond'-er-us], *adj.* having no weight.

NON-PRODUCTION, [non'-prō-duk'-shun], *n.* the state of suspension of production; a failure to produce or exhibit.

NON-PROFESSIONAL, [non'-prō-fesh'-un-al], *adj.* not acting in a professional capacity; not professional, unskilled.

NON-PROFICIENT, [non'-prō-fish'-ent], *n.* a person who has failed to acquire proficiency.

NON-RESIDENCE, [non'-rez'-id-ents], *n.* the state of being non-resident.

NON-RESIDENT (1), [non'-rez'-id-ent], *n.* one who does not reside permanently in a country; a clergyman non-resident in the district in his charge.

NON-RESIDENT (2), [non'-rez'-id-ent], *adj.* not living in the district claiming official attention.

NON-RESISTANCE, [non'-riz-ist'-ants], *n.* passive obedience to authority.

NON-RESISTANT, [non'-riz-ist'-ant], *adj.* passively obedient to authority.

NONSENSE, [non'-sents], *n.* an illogical or absurd statement, words or language which have no meaning; anything absurd.

NONSENSICAL, [non-sen'sik-al], *adj.* full of nonsense, ridiculous, unmeaning.

NONSENSICALLY, [non-sen'sik-al-i], *adv.* in a nonsensical way.

NONSENSICALNESS, [non-sen'sik-al-nes], *n.* the condition of being nonsensical; jargon; absurdity.

NON-SEQUITUR, [non'-sek'-wit-er], *n.* (*philos.*) a conclusion which does not follow from the premises. [L. *non sequitur* it does not follow].

NON-SEXUAL, [non'-seks'-yōō-al], *adj.* without reference to sex; without union of the sexes.

NON-SKID, [non'-skid'], *adj.* designed to prevent skidding.

NON-SOCIETY, [non'-sō-sī'-i-ti], *adj.* not belonging to a trades union, non-union.

NON-SOLUTION, [non'-sol-ew'-shun], *n.* failure of solution.

NON-STARTER, [non'-staht'-er], *n.* one that does not start; a horse which, though entered for a race, does not appear at the starting-post.

NON-STOP (1), [non'-stop'], *n.* an express, a train not stopping at intermediate stations.
NON-STOP (2), [non-stop'], *adj.* without a break, particularly of a variety show with no pauses between turns.
NON-STOP (3), [non'-stop'], *adv.* without stopping.
NON-SUBMISSIVE, [non'-sub-mis'-iv], *adj.* not submissive.
NONSUCH, [nun'-such], *n.* a person or object without an equal, nonpareil, nonesuch; (*bot.*) the wild plant, *Medicago lupulina*.
NONSUIT (1), [non'-sewt'], *n.* (*leg.*) the judicial quashing of a law case owing to the default, neglect, or non-appearance of the plaintiff.
NONSUIT (2), [non'-sewt'], *v.t.* (*leg.*) to record a nonsuit against.
NONTRONITE, [non'-tron-īt], *n.* (*min.*) hydrated tersilicate of iron. [*Nontron*, a place in France].
NON-UNION, [non'-yōō'-ni-on], *adj.* not belonging to a trade union.
NOODLE (1), [nōōdl], *n.* (*slang*) a simpleton, a blockhead. [Unkn.].
NOODLE (2), [nōōdl], *n.* a baked wheaten strip or ball served with soup, etc. [Uncert.].
NOOK, [nŏŏk], *n.* a corner, a narrow place formed by an angle; a secluded place, a recess. [ME. *nok*].
NOON (1), [nōōn], *n.* the middle of the day; twelve o'clock in the day; the hour between midday and 1 p.m.; meridian height; (*fig.*) the prime of power; height. [OE. *non* from L. *nona* (*hora*) ninth hour].
NOON (2), [nōōn], *adj.* occurring at, relating to, noon. [*Prec.*].
NOONDAY (1), [nōōn'-dā], *n.* noon, midday.
NOONDAY (2), [nōōn'-dā], *adj.* occurring at, relating to, noonday.
NOONTIDE, [nōōn'-tīd], *n.* the time of noon, midday.
NOOSE (1), [nōōs], *n.* a running knot made with a rope which binds the closer the more it is drawn, a slip-knot. [OFr. *nos* knot].
NOOSE (2), [nōōs], *v.t.* to catch in a noose; to ensnare; to lasso.
NOPAL, [nō'-pal], *n.* a Mexican cactus which has no spines and is used in the breeding of cochineal insects. [Mexican *nopalli*].
NOR, [naw(r)], *conj.* a word preceded by NEITHER, used to deny the second of two alternatives; (at beginning of sentence) and . . . not. [ME. *nor* a contraction of *nowther* neither].
NORBERTINE (1), [naw'-bert-īn], *n.* a member of the Premonstratensian order of white canons founded by Norbert.
NORBERTINE (2), [naw'-bert-īn], *adj.* of, pertaining, or relating to, the Norbertines. [Fr. *Norbertin* from *Norbert*, the founder's name].
NORDENFELT, [nawd'-en-felt], *n.* an obsolete kind of machine gun. [K. *Nordenfelt*, the inventor].
NORDIC, [nawd'-ik], *adj.* of, pertaining to, or resembling the blond Germanic type found principally in Northern Europe. [Fr. *nordique* from *nord* north].
NORFOLK JACKET, [naw'-fuk-jak'-it], *n.* a loose-fitting jacket made of tweed, and pleated back and front, with a belt at the back.
NORIA, [naw'-ri-a], *n.* a flush waterwheel consisting of a continuous chain of buckets. [Span. *noria*].
NORLAND (1), [naw'-land], *n.* the north country. [Contracted from NORTH and LAND].
NORLAND (2), [naw'-land], *adj.* northern.
NORM, [nawm], *n.* the acknowledged standard; a rule, a model, typical form, a type. [L. *norma* a carpenter's square].
NORMAL (1), [nawm'-al], *n.* the customary standard; (*math.*) a perpendicular; **n. school**, an institution for training teachers.
NORMAL (2), [nawm'-al], *adj.* according to an accepted standard or type, regular, customary; having the usual value or degree; (*math.*) perpendicular. [L. *normalis*].
NORMALCY, [nawm'-al-si], *n.* normality.
NORMALITY, [nawm-al'-i-ti], *n.* the state of being normal, an average degree or quality.
NORMALIZATION, [nawm'-al-īz-ā'-shun], *n.* the act of normalizing; the state or process of being normalized.
NORMALIZE, [nawm'-al-īz], *v.t.* to render normal.
NORMALLY, [nawm'-al-i], *adv.* in a normal manner, ordinarily.
NORMAN (1), [nawm'-an], *n.* an inhabitant of Normandy; a member of a Scandinavian race which settled in Normandy in the 10th century; a member or descendant of the branch of this race which, after settling in France, conquered England in 1066. [OFr. *Normant* Northman].
NORMAN (2), [nawm'-an], *adj.* pertaining to the Normans; (*arch.*) descriptive of a style of architecture fashionable in England during the 11th century and derived from the French Romanesque.

NORMAN ARCH

NORN, [nawn], *n.* one of the three fates of Norse mythology. [OIcel. *norn*].
NORROY, [no'-roi], *n.* the English king-of-arms whose jurisdiction lies north of the Trent. [NORTH and OFr. *roy* king].
NORSE (1), [naws], *n.* the early language of Scandinavia. [Du. *Noorsch*].
NORSE (2), [naws], *adj.* belonging to Scandinavia, Scandinavian.
NORSEMAN, [naws'-man], *n.* a native of ancient Scandinavia, a northman.
NORTH (1), [nawth], *n.* one of the four cardinal points, directly opposite to the sun in the meridian; the region which lies to the right when the observer is facing due west; the part of a country lying northward of a defined point. [OE. *north*].
NORTH (2), [nawth], *adj.* lying at, or in the direction of, the north, towards the north; coming from the north, opposite the south.
NORTH-EAST (1), [nawth-ēst'], *n.* the point of the compass between the north and east, and equally distant from each; the district or direction lying between the north and the east.
NORTH-EAST (2), [nawth'-ēst], *adj.* belonging to, situated between, coming from the north-east.
NORTH-EASTER, [nawth-ēst'-er], *n.* a north-easterly wind recognized for its coldness and strength.
NORTH-EASTERLY (1), [nawth-ēst'-er-li], *adj.* situated in, or coming from, the north-east.
NORTH-EASTERLY (2), [nawth-ēst'-er-li] *adv.* towards the north-east, in a north-easterly direction.
NORTH-EASTERN, [nawth-ēst'-ern], *adj.* situated in, or relating to, the north-east.
NORTH-EASTWARD (1), [nawth-ēst'-werd], *adj.* situated in, or moving towards, the north-east.
NORTH-EASTWARD (2), [nawth-ēst'-werd], *adv.* in a north-easterly direction.
NORTHERLY (1), [nawTH'-er-li], *adj.* situated in, coming from, or moving towards, the north.
NORTHERLY (2), [nawTH'-er-li], *adv.* towards the north.
NORTHERN, [nawTH'-ern], *adj.* situated in, moving towards, or from, the north. [OE. *northern*].
NORTHERNER, [nawTH'-ern-er], *n.* a person born in, or having the manners of, the north.
NORTHING, [nawth'-ing], *n.* (*naut.*) the distance northward in relation to the last bearings taken.
NORTHMAN, [nawth'-man], *n.* one of the inhabitants of the north of Europe, *esp.* of ancient Norway. [OE. *northman* Norwegian].
NORTH-POLAR, [nawth'-pōl'-er], *adj.* Arctic.
NORTHWARD (1), [nawth'-werd], *adj.* being towards the north.
NORTHWARD (2), [nawth'-werd], *adv.* in a northerly direction. [OE. *northward*].
NORTHWARDLY, [nawth'-werd-li], *adv.* in a northern direction, northerly.
NORTHWARDS, [nawth'-wardz], *adv.* towards the north. [OE. *northweardes*].
NORTH-WEST (1), [nawth'-west'], *n.* the point of the compass exactly between north and west; the region indicated as lying between these two compass points.
NORTH-WEST (2), [nawth'-west'], *adj.* situated in, moving towards, coming from, facing, the north-west.
NORTH-WESTER, [nawth-west'-er], *n.* a north-westerly wind rising to great strength.
NORTH-WESTERLY (1), [nawth'-west'-er-li], *adj.* towards, or coming from, the north-west.
NORTH-WESTERLY (2), [nawth'-west'-er-li] *adv.* in the direction of the north-west.
NORTH-WESTERN, [nawth'-west'-ern], *adj.* situated in, relating to, or coming from, the north-west.

NORWEGIAN (1), [naw-wē'-jan], *n.* a native of Norway; its native language. [OScand. *Norvegr*].

NORWEGIAN (2), [naw-wē'-jan], *adj.* of, relating to, belonging to, Norway or Norwegian.

NOSE (1), [nōz], *n.* the organ, being part of the face and placed between and below the two eyes, by means of which the sense of smell of a human being or animal can function, and through which it is possible to breathe; a keen sense of smell; an ability for detection; the end of anything, a nozzle, spout, a prow, etc.; **to lead by the n.**, to have in one's power; **to turn up one's n.**, to express dislike or contempt. [OE. *nosu*].

NOSE (2), [nōz], *v.t. and i.* to touch with the nose, to nuzzle; to feel the way cautiously; **to n. out**, to detect by smelling, to track; to find out. [*Prec.*].

NOSEAN, [nō'-zi-an], *n.* (*min.*) a silicate of sodium, aluminium, and calcium with sulphate of sodium found in volcanic rocks. [K. W. *Nose*, a German geologist].

NOSEBAG, [nōz'-bag'], *n.* a bag tied to a horse's head containing oats, etc.

NOSEBAND, [nōz'-band'], *n.* the nose-part of a bridle.

NOSED, [nōzd], *adj.* having a nose.

NOSE-DIVE (1), [nōz'-dīv], *n.* a plunge head first towards the ground by an aircraft.

NOSE-DIVE (2), [nōz'-dīv], *v.i.* to make a head-first descent towards the ground in an aircraft.

NOSE-FLUTE, [nōz'-flōōt'], *n.* a flute played by breath from the nostrils.

NOSEGAY, [nōz'-gā], *n.* a bunch of sweet-scented flowers; a small bouquet, usually of wild flowers.

NOSELEAF, [nōz'-lēf], *n.* a membranous appendage on the noses of certain bats.

NOSELESS, [nōz'-les], *adj.* having no nose.

NOSEPIECE, [nōz'-pēs], *n.* a piece at the nose of a horse's bridle; the end of a microscope that carries the objectives; the nozzle of a hose or pipe.

NOSE-RING, [nōz'-ring], *n.* a ring worn by eastern women and savages by way of ornament for the nose; a ring passed through the nose of a bull, etc., by which the animal is led.

NOSEY PARKER, [nōz-i-pahk'-er], *n.* a prying, inquisitive person. [NOSY].

NO-SIDE, [nō'-sīd'], *n.* the announcement by the referee which terminates a game of Rugby football.

NOSING, [nōz'-ing], *n.* projecting rounded part of a moulding, as on the edge of a step.

NOSING

NOSOGRAPHY, [nos-og'-raf-i], *n.* the scientific description and classification of diseases. [Gk. *nosos* disease and *graphia* writing].

NOSOLOGICAL, [nos-ō-loj'-ik-al], *adj.* relating to nosology.

NOSOLOGIST, [nos-ol'-oj-ist], *n.* one expert in nosology.

NOSOLOGY, [nos-ol'-o-ji], *n.* the science of diseases; the defining, naming and grouping of diseases. [Gk. *nosos* disease and *logos* speech].

NOSOPHOBIA, [nos'-ō-fō'-bi-a], *n.* (*psych.*) the fear of disease. [Gk. *nosos* disease and *phobos* fear].

NOSTALGIA, [nos-tal'-ja], *n.* a morbid longing for the place of one's home or birth, home-sickness. [Gk. *nostos* return and *algos* pain].

NOSTALGIC, [nos-tal'-jik], *adj.* of, relating to, nostalgia.

NOSTRIL, [nos'-tril], *n.* an aperture through the nose for the passage of air. [OE. *nosthyrl*].

NOSTRUM, [nos'-trum], *n.* a quack medicine or prescription. [L. *nostrum*, *neut. sg.* of *noster* our].

NOSY, [nō'-zi], *adj.* having a large nose; inquisitive; interfering.

NOT, [not], *adv.* a word expressing negation, denial, or refusal, having various positions in various types of sentences. [ME. *nat*, *not*].

NOTABILIA, [nōt'-a-bil'-i-a], *n.(pl.)* things worthy of note. [L. *notabilia*, *neut. pl.* of *notabilis* notable].

NOTABILITY, [nōt'-ab-il'-i-ti], *n.* the quality of being notable, notableness; a person of note.

NOTABLE (1), [nōt'-abl], *n.* a notable person, notability.

NOTABLE (2), [nōt'-abl], *adj.* worthy of notice, distinguished, remarkable; conspicuous; notorious, known. [L. *notabilis*].

NOTABLENESS, [nōt'-abl-nes], *n.* the quality of being notable, remarkableness.

NOTABLY, [nōt'-ab-li], *adv.* in a notable manner.

NOTALGIA, [not-al'-ji-a], *n.* a pain in the back; backache. [Gk. *notos* the back and *algos* pain].

NOTANDUM, (*pl.* **notanda**), [nōt-and'-um], *n.* thing to be noted. [L. *notandum* ger. of *notare*].

NOTARIAL, [nōt-āer'-i-al], *adj.* relating to a notary; done or taken by a notary.

NOTARY, [nōt'-er-i], *n.* an official whose profession it is to attest and certify contracts of any kind such as deeds, protested bills of exchange, etc., a notary public. [L. *notarius* secretary].

NOTATION, [nōt-ā'-shun], *n.* the act or practice of recording anything by marks; a system of figures and signs. [L. *notatio*].

NOTATIONAL, [nōt-ā'-shun-al], *adj.* of, pertaining, or relating to, (a) notation.

NOTCH (1), [noch], *n.* a slot, slit, cut, or nick made in wood or other material; a nick at the feather end of an arrow to take the bow-string; †a run in cricket. [OFr. *une oche*].

NOTCH (2), [noch], *v.t. and i.* to make a notch, to score.

NOTCH-BOARD, [noch'-bawd], *n.* the notched board which receives the ends of the steps in a staircase.

NOTE (1), [nōt], *n.* a short record, a memorandum; a comment in writing, annotation; a brief, informal letter or communication; a formal diplomatic communication; a paper containing a written promise of payment, *esp.* by a bank, pre-eminence, repute; a mark, sign, or token conveying a specific meaning; (*mus.*) a printed or written character or symbol indicating a particular sound; the sound itself thus indicated; any one of the keys on a pianoforte keyboard; a distinctive tone or tune. [L. *nota* sign].

NOTE (2), [nōt], *v.t.* to make a note of, to set down in writing for future reference, to make a record of; to observe, to attend to, to mark; to annotate; to record the payment or non-payment of a bill of exchange. [L. *notare*].

NOTEBOOK, [nōt'-bŏŏk], *n.* a book in which notes are written.

NOTED, [nōt'-id], *adj.* well known by reputation, distinguished, famous.

NOTEDLY, [nōt'-id-li], *adv.* in a noted manner, to a marked degree.

NOTEDNESS, [nōt'-id-nes], *n.* the quality of being noted.

NOTELESS, [nōt'-les], *adj.* not attracting notice; having no notes; toneless, tuneless.

NOTELET, [nōt'-let], *n.* a short note.

NOTEPAPER, [nōt'-pā-per], *n.* a small-sized writing paper ruled or un-ruled for correspondence purposes.

NOTEWORTHY, [nōt'-wur-THi], *adj.* worthy of note or observation, remarkable, distinctive. [NOTE and WORTHY].

NOTHING (1), [nuth'-ing], *n.* not anything, nought, a cipher; something of superficial importance, that which is negligible; something which comes into a different category, that which has no grounds for comparison. [NO and THING].

NOTHING (2), [nuth'-ing], *adv.* not at all, in no degree.

NOTHINGNESS, [nuth'-ing-nes], *n.* the state of being nothing, non-existence; worthlessness, uselessness.

NOTICE (1), [nōt'-is], *n.* a sensory or mental observation, attention; indication of an intention or action, information, intelligence, warning; a brief formal announcement, particularly one published in a newspaper; a paragraph bearing information; a critical appreciation of a book, play, or film published in a paper or periodical, a review. [L. *notitia* information].

NOTICE (2), [nōt'-is], *v.t.* to observe, to pay attention to, to regard, to heed; to make a remark on, to mention, refer to; to publish a review on. [*Prec.*].

NOTICEABLE, [nōt'-is-abl], *adj.* able to be noticed; worthy of notice, conspicuous, remarkable.

NOTICEABLY, [nōt'-is-ab-li], *adv.* in a noticeable manner, remarkably.

NOTIFIABLE, [nōt'-i-fi-abl], *adj.* (of a disease) required by law to be notified to the authorities.

NOTIFICATION, [nōt'-if-ik-ā'-shun], *n.* the act of notifying; the means of notification; formal notice connected with public services; an announcement, advertisement.

NOTIFY, [nōt'-i-fī], *v.t.* to make known, to give notice to. [L. *notificare* to make known].

NOTION, [nō'-shun], *n.* an experience or number of

experiences reduced to a coherent abstract form by the mind; idea, conception, mental apprehension, sentiment, opinion, inclination. [L. *notio*].

NOTIONAL, [nō-shun-al], *adj.* relating to a notion; speculative, ideal, conveying an idea; fanciful, imaginary.

NOTIONALLY, [nō'-shun-al-i], *adv.* in an abstract or speculative manner.

NOTIONIST, [nō'-shun-ist], *n.* one who does not desire to concretize his opinions, a visionary, a theorist.

NOTOBRANCHIATE, [nō'-tō-brangk'-i-āt], *adj.* (*biol.*) having dorsal gills. [Gk. *notos* back and BRANCHIATE].

NOTOCHORD, [nō'-tō-kawd], *n.* (*zool.*) the rudimentary form of the vertebral column. [Gk. *notos* back and CHORD].

NOTONECTAL, [nō'-tō-nek'-tal], *adj.* (*zool.*) swimming on the back. [Gk. *notos* back and *nektes* swimmer].

NOTORIETY, [nō'-to-rī'-i-ti], *n.* the quality of being notorious.

NOTORIOUS, [nō-taw'-ri-us], *adj.* well-known in an unfavourable capacity, known to disadvantage; manifest to all. [MedL. *notorius* well known].

NOTORIOUSLY, [nō-taw'-ri-us-li], *adv.* to a notorious degree.

NOTORIOUSNESS, [nō-taw'-ri-us-nes], *n.* the state of being notorious.

NO-TRUMPER, [nō'-trump'-er], *n.* (*bridge*) a hand which justifies a no-trump bid.

NO-TRUMPS, [nō'-trumps'], *n.* a bid at bridge in which no suit is trumps.

NOTTURNO, [not-ōōer'-nō], *n.* (*mus.*) a nocturne. [It. *notturno*].

NOTWITHSTANDING, [not'-wiтн-stand-'ing], *adv.* although, nevertheless; (*prep.*) without hindrance or obstruction from, despite, in spite of. [~NOT and WITHSTAND].

NOUGAT, [nōō'-gah], *n.* a confection of sugar, paste, and almonds. [Fr. *nougat* from L. *nux nucis* nut].

NOUGHT, [nawt], *n.* nothing, naught; a cipher, the figure or symbol, 0. [OE. *nawiht*].

NOUMENAL, [now'-men-al], *adj.* (*philos.*) of, relating to, a noumenon, real as opposed to phenomenal.

NOUMENON, [now'-men-on], *n.* (*philos.*) the object of intellectual, as opposed to sensory, perception; a thing, or the conception of a thing, as it is in itself or to pure thought; the real under the phenomenal. [Gk. *nooumenon* what is perceived].

NOUN, [nown], *n.* (*gram.*) the name of anything, whether material or immaterial, abstract or concrete, real or imaginary, a substantive. [ME. *nowne* from L. *nomen* a name].

NOUNAL, [nown'-al], *adj.* having the characteristics of, pertaining to, a noun.

NOURISH, [nu'-rish], *v.t.* to feed, to sustain by providing good food; †to rear, bring up; to encourage, entertain, cherish. [OFr. *nourir* from L. *nutrire* to suckle].

NOURISHABLE, [nu'-rish-abl], *adj.* susceptible of nourishment.

NOURISHER, [nu'-rish-er], *n.* one who, or that which, nourishes.

NOURISHMENT, [nu'-rish-ment], *n.* that which nourishes, food, nutriment.

NOUS, [nows], *n.* intelligent perception, common sense, gumption. [Gk. *nous*].

NOUVEAU-RICHE, [nōō'-vō-rēsh'], *n.* a person of the lower classes whose ability to learn the social conventions of the upper classes does not equal his ability to make money, a parvenu. [Fr. *nouveau riche* new rich].

NOVA, (*pl.* **novae**), [nō'-va], *n.* (*astron.*) a star which appears unexpectedly. [L. *nova* (*stella*) new star].

NOVACULITE, [nō-vak'-yōō-lit], *n.* (*min.*) a variety of clay slate of which hones are made. [L. *novacula* a razor].

NOVATIAN, [nō-vā'-shun], *n.* a member of an early religious sect of extreme strictness who believed in no absolution. [*Novatianus*, the founder].

NOVATION, [nō-vā'-shun], *n.* (*leg.*) the acceptance of a new debt or obligation as a substitute for an old one. [L. *novatio* renewal].

NOVEL (1), [nov'-el], *n.* a narrative in prose dealing with stories of character and incident representing and reflecting the social scene, romance, allegory, fantasy, etc. [It. *novella* new thing].

NOVEL (2), [nov'-el], *adj.* new, unfamiliar, unusual, having an original character. [L. *novellus*].

NOVELETTE, [nov'-el-et'], *n.* a short novel.

NOVELIST, [nov'-el-ist], *n.* a writer of novels; †an innovator.

NOVELIZE, [nov'-el-īz], *v.t.* to relate in the form of a novel; to make new.

NOVELTY, [nov'-el-ti], *n.* the quality of being novel, newness, something new, a product on the market for the first time, a stupid, frippery knick-knack. [OFr. *novelté*].

NOVEMBER, [nō'-vem'-ber], *n.* the eleventh month of the year, being the ninth of the Roman year. [L. *Novembris* (*mensis*) the ninth month].

NOVENA, [nō-vē'-na], *n.* (*eccles.*) a devotion lasting for a period of nine days, a special form of intercession repeated on each of nine successive days. [LL. *novena*].

NOVENNIAL, [nō-ven'-i-al], *adj.* recurring every ninth year. [L. *novennis* from *novem* nine and *annus* year].

NOVERCAL, [nō-vurk'-al], *adj.* pertaining to, or like, a step-mother. [L. *novercalis* from *noverca* step-mother].

NOVICE, [nov'-is], *n.* one who is new in any business, an apprentice, a beginner; one who has entered a religious house but has not yet taken the vows, a probationer, a convert. [L. *novicius*].

NOVITIATE, NOVICIATE, [nō-vish'-i-āt], *n.* the state or time of being a novice; a time of probation before taking full religious vows; a novice. [MedL. *novitiatus*].

NOW (1), [now], *n.* the present time. [OE. *nu*].

NOW (2), [now], *adv.* at the present time, at once, immediately; at that moment; under the circumstances; †very lately.

NOW (3), [now], *conj.* since, seeing that, this being the case, after this, but.

NOWADAYS, [now'-a-dāz'], *adv.* in these days, at the present time.

NOWAYS†, [nō'-wāz], *adv.* in no manner or degree, not at all. [NO and WAY].

NOWED, [nō'-ed], *adj.* (*her.*) tied in a knot, coiled in a knot like a snake. [Fr. *noué*].

NOWED

NOWEL, [now'-el], *n.* (*arch.*) the inner mould of a hollow casting. [OFr. *nouel* stone].

NOWHERE, [nō'-wāer], *adv.* not anywhere, not in any place or state. [OE. *nahwær*].

NOWISE, [nō'-wiz], *adv.* by no means, not in any manner or degree. [NO and WISE].

NOWY, [nō'-i], *adj.* (*her.*) having a projection in the centre. [OFr. *noué* knotted].

NOXIOUS, [nok'-shus], *adj* hurtful, corrupting, injurious. [L. *noxius*].

NOXIOUSLY, [nok'-shus-li], *adv.* in a noxious fashion.

NOXIOUSNESS, [nok'-shus-nes], *n.* the condition or quality of being noxious.

NOYADE, [nwah-yahd'], *n.* an execution by drowning. [Fr. *noyade*].

NOYAU, [nwah-yō'], *n.* a liqueur flavoured with fruit kernels. [Fr. *noyau*].

NOZZLE, [nozl], *n.* a projecting vent or mouthpiece; a snout or nose. [*Dim.* of NOSE (1)].

NUANCE, [new'-ah(n)s], *n.* a subtle, delicate difference or distinction. [Fr. *nuance*].

NUB, [nub], *n.* a small lump. [*Var.* of KNOB].

NUBBIN, [nub'-in], *n.* a small, faulty ear of maize.

NUBBLY, [nub'-li], *adj.* in the form of small lumps.

NUBECULA, [new-bek'-yōō-la], *n.* a cloudy appearance, mistiness; a speck in the eye. [L. *nubecula* a little cloud.

NUBIFEROUS, [new-bif'-er-us], *adj.* bringing or causing clouds. [L. *nubes* cloud and *ferre* to bring].

NUBILE, [new'-bil], *adj.* (of a woman) marriageable, being of an age or condition to marry. [L. *nubilis*].

NUBILITY, [new-bil'-i-ti], *n.* the condition of being marriageable.

NUBILOUS, [new'-bil-us], *adj.* cloudy, cloudlike, misty. [L. *nubilus*].

NUCAMENT, [new'-ka-ment], *n.* a catkin. [L. *nucamentum*].

NUCELLUS, [new-sel'-us], *n.* (*bot.*) the part of the ovule containing the embryo-sac. [MdL. *nucellus*].

NUCHAL, [new'-kal], *adj.* (*zool.*) pertaining to the back of the neck. [LL. *nucha* spinal marrow].

NUCIFORM, [new′-si-fawm], *adj.* having the shape of a nut. [L. *nux nucis* nut and FORM].

NUCIFRAGA, [new-sif′-ra-ga], *n.* a genus of birds which includes the nutcrackers. [L. *nux* nut and *frango* I break].

NUCLEAR, [new′-kli-er], *adj.* of, or pertaining to, a nucleus.

NUCLEATE (1), [new′-kli-āt], *adj.* nucleated.

NUCLEATE (2), [new′-kli-āt], *v.t. and i.* to form or cause to form into or about a nucleus.

NUCLEATED, [new′-kli-āt-id], *adj.* possessing or formed into a nucleus.

NUCLEIFORM, [new′-kli-i-fawm], *adj.* formed or shaped like a nucleus. [NUCLEUS and FORM].

NUCLEOLE, [new′-kli-ōl], *n.* a nucleolus.

NUCLEOLUS, [new′-kli-ōl′-us], *n.* a small nucleus contained within another. [L. *nucleolus* a little nut].

NUCLEUS, (*pl.* **nuclei**), [new′-kli-us], *n.* a central core or kernel about which matter gathers; a beginning, starting-point; centre, the essential, life-giving part of something; (*astron.*) the centre of a sunspot; the head of a comet; (*biol.*) the essential, life-giving part of a cell or organism; (*phys.*) the central unit of an atom. [L. *nucleus* kernel].

NUDATION, [newd-ā′-shun], *n.* the act of stripping bare, the fact of having been stripped bare.

NUDE (1), [newd], *n.* the human figure unclad, undraped; a painting, sculpture, etc., representing the human figure undraped; the state of being unclad.

NUDE (2), [newd], *adj.* naked, bare, without covering or decoration; unclad; (*leg.*) not attested or recorded, void. [L. *nudus*].

NUDELY, [newd′-li], *adv.* in a nude fashion.

NUDENESS, [newd′-nes], *n.* the condition of being nude.

NUDGE (1), [nuj], *n.* a slight, sometimes furtive, push with the elbow.

NUDGE (2), [nuj], *v.t.* to give a slight, furtive push with the elbow so as to attract attention or give point to what one is saying or what is being said. [Unkn.].

NUDIBRANCH (1), [newd′-i-brangk], *n.* (*zool.*) a mollusc of the order *Nudibranchiata* that has no shell and naked gills. [Fr. *nudibranche*].

NUDIBRANCH (2), [newd′-i-brangk], *adj.* nudibranchiate.

NUDIBRANCHIATE, [newd′-i-brangk-i-āt], *adj.* of, or pertaining to, the *Nudibranchiata*, a group of shell-less molluscs having naked gills. [MdL. *nudibranchiatum* from L. *nudus* naked and Gk. *bragkhion* gill].

NUDISM, [newd′-izm], *n.* the cult of the nude.

NUDIST (1), [newd′-ist], *n.* one who practises nudism.

NUDIST (2), [newd′-ist], *adj.* pertaining to nudism.

NUDIST COLONY, [newd′-ist-kol′-on-i], *n.* an open-air camp inhabited by nudists.

NUDITY, [newd′-i-ti], *n.* nudeness, nakedness.

NUGATORY, [new′-gat-or-i], *adj.* ineffectual, invalid, futile. [L. *nugatorius*].

NUGGAR, [nug′-er], *n.* a flat-bottomed boat or barge on the Nile. [Native].

NUGGET, [nug′-it], *n.* a lump of metal, *esp.* of native gold. [Unkn.].

NUISANCE, [new′-sants], *n.* that which causes damage, hindrance, injury, or annoyance, etc. [Fr. *nuisance*].

NULL, [nul], *adj.* void, having no legal validity; ineffectual. [Fr. *nul* from L. *nullus* none].

NULLAH, [nul′-ah], *n.* a watercourse, *esp.* when dry. [Hind. *nala*].

NULLIFICATION, [nul′-if-ik-ā′-shun], *n.* the act of nullifying or rendering void; the fact of having been rendered void. [LL. *nullificatio* contempt].

NULLIFIDIAN, [nul′-i-fid′-i-an], *adj.* having no faith. [L. *nullus* none and *fides* faith].

NULLIFIER, [nul′-i-fī-er], *n.* that which cancels or makes void.

NULLIFY, [nul′-i-fī], *v.t.* to cancel, render void. [L. *nullificare* to despise].

NULLITY, [nul′-i-ti], *n.* the condition of being void, cancelled, or of no validity; a nonentity; (*leg.*) †a procedure to render void. [Fr. *nullité*].

NULLIPARA, [nul-ip′-er-a], *n.* a woman who, though not a virgin, has never borne a child. [L. *nullus* none and *parere* to bring forth].

NUMB (1), [num], *adj.* lacking the sense of touch; deadened, insensible. [OE. *genumen*, *p.pt.* of *niman* to take].

NUMB (2), [num], *v.t.* to render numb.

NUMBER (1), [num′-ber], *n.* total, sum, aggregate; the aggregate of a collection, group, series, etc.; a symbol for an arithmetical total; the name of such a symbol; a total of abstract units; a multitude, a large quantity, a large collection of units; something or somebody distinguished by a numerical symbol; a single issue of a periodical publication; one of a collection of poems, songs, musical pieces; a unit of an opera or oratorio; a song or piece of music; (*gram.*) that quality in a word which is expressive of whether one, two, or more than two are referred to; the form of the word denoting this; **numbers**, lines, verses, poetry; **in n.**, in quantity, considered numerically; **without, out of n.**, uncountable, very many. [Fr. *nombre* from L. *numerus*].

NUMBER (2), [num′-ber], *v.t. and i.* to count, enumerate; to be of a certain numerical quantity; to divide, apportion; to set in a numerical series; to fix the number of, to end; **to n. among**, to include, comprise, contain; **to n. with**, to be equal with numerically, to reckon with. [*Prec.*].

NUMBERER, [num′-ber-er], *n.* one who numbers.

NUMBERLESS, [num′-ber-les], *adj.* too many to be counted.

NUMBER-PLATE, [num′-ber-plāt′], *n.* a metal plate bearing a number; a plate on a motor-car bearing its index mark and number.

NUMBLES, [numblz], *n.*(*pl.*) the entrails of deer. [OFr. *numbles*].

NUMBNESS, [num′-nes], *n.* the condition of being numb.

NUMDAH, [num′-da], *n.* a numnah; **n. rug**, a rug for the house with brightly coloured patterns sewn on it. [Urdu *namda*].

NUMERABLE, [new′-mer-abl], *adj.* able to be numbered, countable. [L. *numerabilis*].

NUMERAL (1), [new′-mer-al], *n.* a symbol representing an arithmetical total ; the name of such a symbol.

NUMERAL (2), [new′-mer-al], *adj.* pertaining to numbers, numbering, or numerical symbols. [LL. *numeralis*].

NUMERALLY, [new′-mer-al-i], *adv.* by number.

NUMERARY, [new′-mer-er-i], *adj.* pertaining to a certain number or numbers. [MedL. *numerarius*].

NUMERATE, [new′-mer-āt], *v.t.* to count, number, reckon. [L. *numeratus* numbered].

NUMERATION, [new′-mer-ā′-shun], *n* the act or art of numbering; counting, calculation. [L. *numeratio*].

NUMERATOR, [new′-mer-āt-or], *n.* (*arith.*) the term in a fraction denoting the number of units in the fraction; the figure or figures following the decimal point. [LL. *numerator*].

NUMERIC, [new-me′-rik], *adj.* numerical.

NUMERICAL, [new-me′-rik-al], *adj.* pertaining to numbers, numeration, etc.; expressed in numbers.

NUMERICALLY, [new-me′-rik-a-li], *adv.* by numbers, with respect to number.

NUMEROUS, [new′-mer-us], *adj.* consisting of a great number, containing many units. [L. *numerosus*].

NUMEROUSLY, [new′-mer-us-li], *adv.* in great numbers.

NUMEROUSNESS, [new′-mer-us-ness], *n.* the quality of being numerous.

NUMISMATIC, [new′-miz-mat′-ik], *adj.* pertaining to coins, medals, or coinage. [Fr. *numismatique*].

NUMISMATICS, [new′-miz-mat′-iks], *n.*(*pl.*) the science and study of coins and medals.

NUMISMATIST, [new-miz′-mat-ist], *n.* one who studies coins or medals, their history, form, etc.

NUMISMATOLOGIST, [new-miz′-mat-ol′-oj-ist], *n.* numismatist.

NUMISMATOLOGY, [new-miz′-mat-ol′-o-ji], *n.* the science and study of coins and medals, their form, history, etc.; numismatics. [L. *numisma* a coin and Gk. *logos* speech].

NUMMARY, [num′-er-i], *adj.* pertaining to coins and money. [~L. *nummus* coin].

NUMMULAR, [num′-yōō-ler], *adj.* pertaining to coins, shaped like a coin. [~*Prec.*].

NUMMULARY, [num′-yōō-ler-i], *adj.* resembling a coin.

NUMMULITE, [num′-yōō-līt], *n.* a fossilized shell of a foraminifer, resembling a coin in shape.

NUMMULITIC, [num′-yōō-lit′-ik], *adj.* composed of nummulites.

NUMNAH, [num′-nah], *n.* a saddle-cloth, a pad placed under a saddle. [Pers. *namda* carpet].

NUMSKULL, [num′-skul′], *n.* a dunce, a dolt [NUMB (2) and SKULL].

NUMSKULLED, [num′-skuld′], *adj.* stupid.

NUN, [nun], *n.* a member of a religious order for women, inhabiting a convent, and living under vows

ō (bone), ī (fine), ōō (food), ŏŏ (put), u (up), th (*th*ink), TH (*th*at), zh (azure). † = obsolete. ~ = related to.

of chastity, etc.; (*zool.*) certain varieties of moths or birds. [OE. *nunne*].

NUNATAK, [nōōn'-at-ak], *n.* a rock that projects above the surface of the ice. [Eskimo *nunatak*].

NUN-BUOY, [nun'-boi], *n.* a buoy made of two circular cones joined at their bases. [ME. *nun* a spinning top and BUOY (1)].

NUNCHEON, [nun'-chun], *n.* light refreshment taken between one meal and the next; a lunch. [ME. *noneshench*].

NUNCIATURE, [nun'-si-ach-er], *n.* the dignity and tenure of the office of Papal Nuncio. [It. *nunciatura*].

NUNCIO, [nun'-si-ō], *n.* a Papal ambassador. [It. *nuncio*].

NUNCLE†, [nungkl], *n.* uncle. [(A)N and UNCLE].

NUNCUPATIVE, [nun'-kew-pāt'-iv], *adj.* conveyed by word of mouth, not by writing. [MedL. *nuncupativus*].

NUNCUPATORY, [nun'-kew-pāt'-er-i], *adj.* nuncupative.

NUNDINAL, [nun'-din-al], *adj.* pertaining to a fair or market day. [L. *nundinalis*].

NUNDINARY, [nun'-din-er-i], *adj.* nundinal.

NUNDINE, [nun'-din], *n.* (*hist.*) a Roman fair or market day held every ninth day. [L. *nundina* from *novem* nine and *dies* day].

NUNG, [nung], *n.* a bale of cloves. [Uncert.].

NUNHOOD, [nun'-hōōd], *n.* the condition of being a nun. [NUN and OE. *had* condition].

NUNNATION, [nun-ā'-shun], *n.* (*gram.*) the adding of the letter "n" to the endings of words. [Arab. *nun* the letter "n"].

NUNNERY, [nun'-er-i], *n.* a house for nuns, a convent. [Fr. *nonnerie*].

NUNNISH, [nun'-ish], *adj.* pertaining to, or characteristic of, a nun.

NUN'S VEILING, [nunz'-vāl'-ing], *n.* a delicate fabric of the sort used for nuns' veils.

NUPHAR, [new'-fah(r)], *n.* the yellow water-lily, *Nuphar luteum.* [~NENUPHAR].

NUPTIAL, [nup'-shal], *adj.* pertaining to a marriage. [L. *nuptialis*].

NUPTIALS, [nup'-shalz], *n.*(*pl.*) the wedding ceremony and all pertaining thereto.

NURL, KNURL, [nurl], *v.t.* to mill the rim of a coin. [Uncert.].

NURLING, KNURLING, [nurl'-ing], *n.* the milled edge of a coin.

NURSE (1), [nurs], *n.* a female attendant upon children; one who suckles children; a person, male or female, skilled to look after the sick under the guidance of a surgeon or physician; (*fig.*) that which fosters and protects. [OFr. *norrice* from L. *nutricia* nurse].

NURSE (2), [nurs], *v.t. and i.* to suckle; to carry (a child, etc.) on the arms or support it in the lap; to give skilled attention to (a sick person); to cherish or foster; to take care of, avoid waste of, etc.; to act as a nurse; **to n. the fire,** (*fig.*) to sit very close to the fire. [*Prec.*].

NURSE-HOUND, [nurs'-hownd], *n.* the shark, *Scyllium catulus.*

NURSEMAID, [nurs'-mād], *n.* a maid who looks after children.

NURSER, [nurs'-er], *n.* someone who cherishes and fosters.

NURSERY, [nurs'-er-i], *n.* a room for children where they can play, have their meals, and keep their toys, etc.; a place for the rearing of young plants prior to their transplantation to the place where it is intended they shall reach maturity; (*fig.*) a place where anything is trained and fostered; **n. school,** a school for children under five.

NURSERYMAN, [nurs'-er-i-man], *n.* a grower of plants for sale, one who keeps a nursery.

NURSING, [nurs'-ing], *adj.* suckling a child; **a n. child,** a suckling.

NURSLING, [nurs'-ling], *n.* a baby under the care of its nurse or mother; also, (*fig.*). [NURSE].

NURTURE (1), [nur'-cher], *n.* food, nourishment; upbringing, training and education. [OFr. *nourture* from LL. *nutritura*].

NURTURE (2), [nur'-cher], *v.t.* to feed or nourish; to rear, educate.

NUSSIERITE, [news'-ēer-īt], *n.* (*geol.*) a sort of rock found at Nussière. [*Nussière*, near Beaujeu, France].

NUT (1), [nut], *n.* the hard-shelled fruit of certain trees and plants the shell of which contains an edible kernel; the kernel of such fruit; a small metal block pierced with a hole which is threaded with a female screw to screw on to a bolt; the contrivance at the lower end of a violin bow by which the hairs may be tightened or relaxed; (*slang*) the head; (*slang*) a young dandy, a wit; (*fig.*) †a thing of little worth; **nuts,** small lumps of coal; **it's nuts to him,** (*slang*) it delights him immensely; **a tough n.,** a very determined person, hard to be persuaded; **a hard n. to crack,** a very difficult problem, a difficulty; **he can't do it for nuts,** (*coll.*) he's very bad at it despite his best endeavour; **to be (dead) nuts on,** (*coll.*) to be very fond of, to be very excited about in a pleased and happy way; **to be off one's n.,** (*coll.*) to be mentally unbalanced, insane; **nuts,** (*slang*) mad, eccentric; (*int.*) rubbish, tosh. [OE. *hnutu*].

NUT (2), (**nutting, nutted**), [nut], *v.i.* to gather nuts; **to go nutting,** to go gathering nuts. [*Prec.*].

NUTANT, [newt'-ant], *adj.* (*bot.*) drooping at the head. [L. *nutans* nodding].

NUTARIAN, [nut-āer'-i-an], *n.* one whose diet consists chiefly of nuts.

NUTATE, [newt-āt'], *v.i.* to incline the head; (*bot.*) of a stem, to make a slight bending movement in growth. [~L. *nutare* to nod].

NUTATION, [newt-ā'-shun], *n.* a drooping of the head; (*astron.*) a slight oscillating movement of the earth's axis; a slight bending of the stem of a plant. [L. *nutatio*].

NUT-BROWN, [nut'-brown], *adj.* brown like a nut.

NUTBUSH, [nut'-bōōsh], *n.* (*bot.*) the hazel, *Corylus Avellana.*

NUT-BUTTER, [nut'-but'-er], *n.* a butter substitute made from the kernels of nuts.

NUTCRACKER (1), [nut'-krak'-er], *n.* a European nut-eating bird, a member of the genus *Nucifraga.*

NUT-CRACKER (2), [nut'-krak'-er], *adj.* (of the nose and chin) tending to meet.

NUT-CRACKERS, [nut'-krak'-erz], *n.*(*pl.*) a pincer-like instrument for cracking nuts.

NUT GALL, [nut'-gawl], *n.* the gall of the oak, *Quercus infectoria,* used in dyeing.

NUTHATCH, [nut'-hach'], *n.* a small bird, the British species of which is *Sitta cæsia,* which feeds upon nuts. [NUT (1) and ~ HACK].

NUTHATCH

NUT-HOOK, [nut'-hōōk], *n.* a rod with a crook on one end, used to pull the branches of trees and bushes into reach, so that nuts may be picked from them.

NUT-JOBBER, [nut'-job'-er], *n.* the nuthatch.

NUTMEG, [nut'-meg'], *n.* the aromatic fruit of the Malay tree, *Myristica fragrans,* used as a spice in cooking. [NUT and OFr. *mugue* musk].

NUTMEGGED, [nut'-megd'], *adj.* flavoured with nutmeg.

NUTMEGGY, [nut'-meg-i], *adj.* nutmegged.

NUT-OIL, [nut'-oil], *n.* the oil crushed from nuts, *esp.* the ground nut.

NUT-PINE, [nut'-pīn], *n.* one of several nut-bearing pines.

NUTRIA, [new'-tri-a], *n.* the fur of the South American water rodent, the coypu. [Span. *nutria* otter].

NUTRIENT (1), [new'-tri-ent], *n.* anything that nourishes.

NUTRIENT (2), [new'-tri-ent], *adj.* nourishing. [L. *nutriens*].

NUTRIMENT, [new'-tri-ment], *n.* that which nourishes; food, nourishment. [L. *nutrimentum*].

NUTRIMENTAL, [new'-tri-ment'-al], *adj.* nutritious.

NUTRITION, [new-trish'-un], *n.* the process by which a living organism feeds itself by assimilating to itself nourishing matter; food, nourishment.

NUTRITIOUS, [new-trish'-us], *adj.* nourishing, promoting growth. [L. *nutritius*].

NUTRITIOUSLY, [new-trish'-us-li], *adv.* in a nutritious way.

NUTRITIOUSNESS, [new-trish'-us-nes], *n.* the quality of being nourishing.

NUTRITIVE, [new'-trit-iv], *adj.* nourishing; pertaining to nutrition.

NUTRITIVELY, [new'-trit-iv-li], *adv.* in a nourishing way, so as to nourish.

NUTRITIVENESS, [new'-trit-iv-nes], *n.* worth as nourishment.

NUT-SCREW, [nut'-skrōō], *n.* a nut-wrench.

NUTSHELL, [nut'-shel], *n.* the hard case about the kernel of a nut; **in a n.,** briefly.

NUTTALLITE, [nut'-awl-īt], *n.* (*min.*) a silicate of

aluminium and calcium occurring in Massachusetts, U.S.A. [*Nuttall* the discoverer].
NUTTINESS, [nut'-i-nes], *n.* the taste of nuts; a flavour resembling this.
NUT-TREE, [nut'-trē], *n.* a nut-bearing tree, *esp.* the hazel.
NUTTY, [nut'-i], *adj.* rich in nuts; having the flavour of nuts; (*slang*) smart, dandy-like; absurd, crazy.
NUT-WRENCH, [nut'-rench'], *n.* a tool with which to fasten or remove nuts on screws.
NUX VOMICA, [nuks'-vom'-ik-a], *n.* the seed of the tree, *Strychnos*, found in the East Indies, containing strychnine; a substance extracted from this and used for medicinal purposes. [L. *nux* nut and MdL. *vomica* from L. *vomere* to vomit].
NUZZER, [nuz'-er], *n.* a present made to someone of higher rank. [Urdu *nazr* gift].
NUZZLE, [nuzl], *v.t. and i.* to push or thrust with the nose. [~NOZZLE].
NYANZA, [nī-an'-za], *n.* an African river that runs through or into a lake. [Native].
NYCTALOPIA, [nik'-tal-ō'-pi-a], *n.* a defect of the vision by which it is easier to see in shadow or twilight than in full light. [Gk. from *nux* night, *alaos* blind, and *ops* eye].
NYCTALOPS, [nik'-tal-ops], *n.* someone affected by nyctalopia. [Gk. *nuktalops*].
NYCTITROPIC, [nik'-ti-trop'-ik], *adj.* (*bot.*) changing position by night or in darkness. [Gk. *nux* night and *tropos* turn].
NYE, [nī], *n.* (*dial.*) a brood of pheasants. [OFr. *ny* from L. *nidus* nest].
NYLGHAU, [nil'-gow], *n.* the nilgai. [Pers. *nil* blue and *gaw* ox or cow].
NYLON, [nī'-on], *n.* (*prot.*) a synthetic silk used to make fabrics and bristles. [From *New York* and *London*].
NYMPH, [nimf], *n.* (*classical myth.*) one of the maiden deities supposed to dwell in and be the spirit of wells, springs, woods, rivers, etc.; (*poet.*) a young woman; (*biol.*) a pupa or chrysalis. [Gk. *numphe*].
NYMPHA, [nim'-fa], *n.* a pupa or chrysalis.
NYMPHEAN, [nim'-fē-an], *adj.* nymphic.
NYMPHIC, [nimf'-ik], *adj.* pertaining to nymphs.
NYMPHISH, [nimf'-ish], *adj.* pertaining to nymphs.
NYMPHLY, [nimf'-li], *adj.* resembling a nymph.
NYMPHOLEPSY, [nim'-fō-lep-si], *n.* the state of frenzy produced by impassioned desire for something unattainable. [Gk. *numpholeptos* caught by the nymphs].
NYMPHOLEPT, [nim'-fō-lept], *n.* a person suffering from nympholepsy; a fanatic.
NYMPHOMANIA, [nim'-fō-mā'-ni-a], *n.* excessive and morbid sexual desire in women. [NYMPH and MANIA].
NYMPHOMANIAC, [nim'-fō-mān'-i-ak'], *n.* one suffering from nymphomania.
NYSTAGMUS, [nis-tag'-mus], *n.* (*med.*) involuntary twitching of the eyelids, *esp.* when one is sleepy. [Gk. *nustagmos* drowsiness].

O (1), [ō], fourth vowel and fifteenth letter of the English alphabet; anything resembling the letter O in shape; the symbol for nought.
O (2), [ō], *int.* an exclamation used in exhortation, invocation, appeal or solemn address (usually poetic or rhetorical).
O' [ō], *prep.* short form of OF; in phrases like *four o'clock, tug-o'-war, man-o'-war*, etc.
OAF, [ōf], *n.* a changeling; a deformed child; a lout; an idiot. [OScand. *alfr* elf].
OAFISH, [ōf'-ish], *adj.* stupid, clumsy, like an oaf.
OAK (1), [ōk], *n.* a tree of the genus *Quercus*; **the Oaks,** a race for three-year-old fillies, run at Epsom on the Friday after the Derby, named after one of the estates of Lord Derby (1779). [OE. *ac*].
OAK (2), [ōk], *adj.* of, made of, or pertaining to, oak.
OAK-APPLE, [ōk'-apl'], *n.* an excrescence produced on oaks by gall-flies; **O. Day,** May 29, the day of the birth and also the restoration of Charles II, when oak-apples and oak leaves were worn in the hat in commemoration of the king's hiding in an oak tree after his defeat at Worcester.
OAK-BARK, [ōk'-bahk], *n.* the bark of an oak tree used in the process of tanning.
OAK-EGGAR, [ōk'-eg-er], *n.* the moth, *Bombyx quercus*. [OAK and EGGAR].
OAKEN, [ōk'-en], *adj.* made of oak. [OE. *acen*].
OAK-FERN, [ōk'-furn], *n.* (*bot.*) the fern, *Polypodium Dryopteris*, which has delicate triangular fronds.
OAK-GALL, [ōk'-gawl], *n.* an oak-apple.
OAK-LEATHER, [ōk'-leTHer], *n.* a fungus resembling white kid-leather, often found growing on old oak trees.
OAKLING, [ōk'-ling], *n.* a young small oak.
OAKUM, [ōk'-um], *n.* fibre obtained by unpicking old ropes and used to caulk the seams of ships. [OE. *acumba* tow].
OAKY, [ōk'-i], *adj.* rich in oaks; hard and strong like an oak.
OAR, [aw(r)], *n.* an instrument for propelling a boat, consisting of a long pole, one end of which is to be grasped by the hands and the other is shaped into a blade; an oarsman; a rowing boat; **pair (four) o.,** a boat for two (four) rowers; (*fig.*) something resembling an oar; **chained to the o.,** tied to a task; **to put one's o. in, to put in one's o.,** to meddle, interfere; **to rest on one's oars,** to slacken effort, content with what has been done; **first oars,** the man rowing stroke in the foremost position; **to pull a good o.,** to row well; **to ship oars,** to take the oars aboard; **to unship oars,** to put them in position for rowing; **to toss oars,** to salute with raised oars. [OE. *ar*].
OARAGE, [aw(r)'-ij], *n.* (*poet.*) rowing; the number of oars in a boat.
OARED, [aw(r)d], *adj.* having oars.
OARFISH, [aw(r)'-fish], *n.* (*zool.*) a genus of large ribbon-fishes, *Regalecus*, inhabiting the deep places of the sea.
OARSMAN, [awz'-man], *n.* a man who rows with an oar.
OARSMANSHIP, [awz'-man-ship], *n.* skill in the use of an oar.
OARSWOMAN, [awz'-wŏom'-an], *n.* a woman who rows.
OASIS, (*pl.* **oases**), [ō-ā'-sis], *n.* a fertile place in a sandy desert; (*fig.*) relief after tedium; a pleasant change amid unpleasant things. [Gk. *oasis*].
OAST, [ōst], *n.* a kiln for drying hops. [OE. *ast*].
OAST-HOUSE, [ōst'-hows], *n.* a building that contains an oast-kiln.
OAT (1), [ōt], *n.* (*poet.*) a pipe, or other simple musical instrument made of an oat stalk. [OE. *at*].
OAT (2), [ōt], *adj.* made of oats; oaten.
OATCAKE, [ōt'-kāk], *n.* a flat cake made of oatmeal.
OATEN†, [ōt'-en], *adj.* made of oats or oat straw.
OATH, [ōth], *n.* a sacred, solemn, and binding promise; the words expressing such a promise; a blasphemous expletive, a vulgar, cursing exclamation, a profanity; **on o., under o.,** (of a testimony) made after taking an official oath on the Bible to tell the truth. [OE. *ath*].
OATH-BREAKING, [ōth'-brāk'-ing], *n.* perjury.
OATMALT, [ōt'-mawlt], *n.* malt made from oats.
OATMEAL, [ōt'-mēl], *n.* meal ground from oats.
OATS, [ōts], *n.* the cereal, *Avena sativa*, or its grains, which are used as food; **wild o.,** *Avena fatua*, the uncultivated species; **to sow one's wild o.,** to indulge in dissipation as a young man; **to feel one's o.,** (*U.S. slang*) to feel important. [OE. *atas*, *pl.* of *at* oat].
OB-, *pref.* against, in the direction of, in the way of, harmful to, hostile to, down, across, over. [L. *ob* towards, against, on account of, etc.].
OBBLIGATO (1), OBLIGATO, [ob'-lig-ah'-tō], *n.* a second instrumental accompaniment to a song in addition to the first accompaniment.
OBBLIGATO (2), OBLIGATO, [ob'-lig-ah'-tō], *adj.* (*mus.*) necessary, intended to be played exactly as written. [It. *obbligato* obliged, bound].
OBCOMPRESSED, [ob'-kom-prest'], *adj.* (*biol.*) flattened both at back and at front.

OBCONIC, [ob-kon′-ik], *adj.* conic-inverted, inversely conical.
OBCORDATE, [ob-kawd′-āt], *adj.* (*bot.*) heart-shaped, but inverted.
OBDIPLOSTEMONOUS, [ob′-di-plō-ste′-mon-us], *adj.* (*bot.*) possessing the stamens of the outer whorl opposite to the petals, but the stamens of the inner whorl alternate with the petals. [OB and DIPLOSTEMONOUS].
OBDUCE, [ob-dews′], *v.t.* to draw over or across. [OB and L. *ducere* to lead].
OBDUCTION, [ob-duk′-shun], *n.* the act of drawing over or covering.

OBCORDATE

OBDURACY, [ob′-dew-ras-i], *n.* stubbornness of character, sentiment, or action.
OBDURATE, [ob′-dew-rat], *adj.* hardened in heart; stubborn; obstinately impenitent, untouched by appeals to tender feeling. [L. *obduratus* hardened].
OBDURATELY, [ob′-dew-rat-li], *adv.* in an obdurate fashion.
OBDURATENESS, [ob′-dew-rat-nes], *n.* the condition of being obdurate.
OBEAH, OBI, [ō-bē′-a], *n.* native West African magic; a magic object, a fetish. [Native].
OBEDIENCE, [ō-bē′-di-ents], *n.* submission to authority, to laws, rules, and orders; the condition of being obedient; (*eccles.*) the fact of being obeyed, dominion, authority, *esp.* such as is possessed by a church over its members; a body of persons belonging to a church over whom it has authority. [L. *obedientia*].
OBEDIENT, [ō-bē′-di-ent], *adj.* submitting to command. [L. *obediens*].
OBEDIENTIAL, [ō-bē′-di-en′-shal], *adj.* rendering obedience.
OBEDIENTIARY, [ō-bē′-di-en′-sher-i], *n.* one submissive to authority; a member of a religious house who gives obedience to the authority of the Superior. [MedL. *obedientiarius*].
OBEDIENTLY, [ō-bē′-di-ent-li], *adv.* in an obedient way.
OBEISANCE, [ō-bā′-sants], *n.* a low bow or curtsey. [OFr. *obeissance*].
OBEISANT, [ō-bā′-sant], *adj.* reverencing.
OBELISCAL, [ob′-il-isk′-al], *adj.* shaped like an obelisk.
OBELISK, [ob′-il-isk], *n.* a four-sided stone pillar, tapering towards the top, and crowned with a small pointed cone or pyramid; a sign used in printed books, thus, †. [Gk. *obeliskos* a pointed implement].
OBELIZE, [ob′-il-īz], *v.t.* to mark with an obelus.
OBELUS, [ob′-il-us], *n.* a mark used in manuscripts to suggest that the text is probably corrupt. [Gk. *obelos* a spit].
OBESE, [ō-bēs′], *adj.* corpulent. [L. *obesus*].
OBESENESS, [ō-bēs′-nes], *n.* obesity.
OBESITY, [ō-bē′-sit-i], *n.* the state of being obese; corpulence. [Fr. *obésité*].
OBEY, [ō-bā′], *v.t. and i.* to execute the commands or wishes of; to render obedience to; to act in accordance with; to be obedient. [L. *obedire*].
OBEYER, [ō-bā′-er], *n.* one who obeys.
OBEYINGLY, [o-bā′-ing-li], *adv.* obediently.

OBELISK

OBFUSCATE, [ob′-fusk-āt], *v.t.* to obscure, render dark; to bewilder. [L. *obfuscare* to darken].
OBFUSCATION, [ob′-fusk-ā′-shun], *n.* the act of obfuscating, the fact of having been obfuscated.
OBI (1), see OBEAH.
OBI (2), [ō′-bi], *n.* a wide sash, worn by women and children in Japan. [Jap. *obi*].
OBIMBRICATE, [ob-im′-brik-āt], *adj.* having the imbrication pointing downwards.
OBIT†, [ō′-bit], *n.* death; an obituary notice; funeral rites; a memorial mass in the Roman Church. [OFr. *obit* from L. *obitus* death].
OBITER, [ob′-it-er, ō′-bit-er], *adv.* incidentally; **o. dictum**, (*pl.* **o. dicta**), (*leg.*) an incidental remark by the judge not to be considered as part of his judgment. [L. *obiter* in passing].
OBITUAL, [ō-bich′-ōō-al], *adj.* pertaining to obits.
OBITUARIST, [ō-bich′-ōō-er-ist], *n.* one who writes obituaries.
OBITUARY (1), [ō-bich′-ōō-er-i], *n.* a notice of a death in a newspaper, usually including a short account of the life and personality of the deceased; (*eccles.*) a list containing the names of members of a religious community who have died.
OBITUARY (2), [ō-bich′-ōō-er-i], *adj.* pertaining or relating to death. [MedL. *obituarius*].
OBJECT (1), [ob′-jekt], *n.* something visible or tangible, a thing seen or touched, that which the senses of sight and touch can ascertain, a material thing; something mentally apprehensible, that may be understood and studied; something that rouses emotion or excites attention; that towards which attention or emotion is directed; that on which desire is set and to which activity is directed, aim, goal, purpose; (*gram.*) a noun, pronoun, phrase or clause governed by a transitive verb; **o. ball**, the ball in billiards at which a player takes aim when striking the cue ball.
OBJECT (2), [ob-jekt′], *v.t. and i.* to state or say as an objection; to protest, oppose. [L. *objectare* to oppose].
OBJECT-FINDER, [ob′-jekt-fīnd′-er], *n.* a device for registering the position of any particular object on a microscopic slide.
OBJECT-GLASS, [ob′-jekt-glahs′], *n.* the glass in a telescope or microscope which is nearest to the object viewed and farthest from the eye of the viewer.
OBJECTIFICATION, [ob-jekt′-i-fik-ā′-shun], *n.* the act or process of making or becoming objective.
OBJECTIFY, [ob-jekt′-i-fī], *v.t.* to regard objectively; to render objective; to present or represent as an object.
OBJECTION, [ob-jek′-shun], *n.* a statement, argument, etc., put forward in disapproval of something; a sense of disapproval and dislike; a defect, drawback or flaw. [L. *objectio*].
OBJECTIONABLE, [ob-jek′-shun-abl], *adj.* liable to objection; offensive; undesirable, unpleasant.
OBJECTIONABLY, [ob-jek′-shun-ab-li], *adv.* in an objectionable manner.
OBJECTIVE (1), [ob-jekt′-iv], *n.* the purpose towards which an action is directed; (*milit.*) a position which is to be reached or attacked; (*gram.*) the objective case; an object-glass; the lens system of a camera.
OBJECTIVE (2), [ob-jekt′-iv], *adj.* relating to objects; existing independently of the mind conceiving it; pertaining to the purpose of an action; (*gram.*) pertaining to a case other than the nominative.
OBJECTIVELY, [ob-jekt′-iv-li], *adv.* in an objective way.
OBJECTIVENESS, [ob-jekt′-iv-nes], *n.* the condition of being objective.
OBJECTIVISM, [ob-jekt′-iv-izm], *n.* (*philos.*) the theory that knowledge derived from sensuous perception possesses objective validity.
OBJECTIVITY, [ob′-jekt-iv′-i-ti], *n.* the quality of being objective.
OBJECTLESS, [ob′-jekt-les], *adj.* lacking object.
OBJECT-LESSON, [ob′-jekt-les′-on], *n.* a lesson in which the teacher has with him the object or a copy of it, with which to point and illustrate his remarks; a piece of teaching by example, usually of a deserved misfortune which is considered as a warning to others.
OBJECTOR, [ob-jekt′-or], *n.* one who objects, *esp.* on grounds of conscience.
OBJECT-STAFF, [ob′-jekt-stahf′], *n.* the surveyor's staff which is the same height as the level.
OBJECT-TEACHING, [ob′-jekt-tēch′-ing], *n.* teaching by object-lessons.
OBJURATION, [ob′-jōōer-ā′-shun], *n.* solemn swearing. [L. *objuratio*].
OBJURE, [ob-jōōer′], *v.t.* to charge under oath. [L. *objurare* to bind by oath].
OBJURGATE, [ob′-jer-gāt], *v.t.* to reprove, to chide. [~L. *objurgare* to blame].
OBJURGATION, [ob′-jer-gā′-shun], *n.* reproof, rebuke.
OBJURGATORY, [ob′-jer-gāt′-er-i], *adj.* conveying censure or reproof.
OBLANCEOLATE, [ob-lants′-i-ō-lāt], *adj.* inversely lanceolate, tapering at the base.
OBLATE (1), [ob-lāt′], *n.* a dedicated person.
OBLATE (2), [ob′-lāt], *adj.* (*eccles.*) dedicated; (*geom.*) used of spheroid bodies that are flattened at the poles. [L. *oblatus*, *p.pt.* of *offerre* to offer].
OBLATENESS, [ob-lāt′-nes], *n.* the condition of being oblate.
OBLATION, [ob-lā′-shun], *n.* an offering, a pious gift; an offering which forms part of an act of worship. [L. *oblatio*].

OBLATIONAL, [ob-lā'-shun-al], *adj.* oblatory.
OBLATORY, [ob-lāt'-er-i], *adj.* pertaining to oblation.
OBLIGATE, [ob'-lig-āt], *v.t.* to place under obligation either legally or morally, to compel. [L. *obligare* to bind].
OBLIGATION, [ob'-lig-ā'-shun], *n.* a legal or moral constraint or compulsion; liability incurred by promise, oath or agreement; the state of being indebted; the moral debt arising from doing or receiving a kindness; necessity. [L. *obligatio* a pledge].
OBLIGATO, see OBBLIGATO.
OBLIGATORY, [ob-lig'-at-ori], *adj.* morally or legally binding; compulsory.
OBLIGE, [ob-līj'], *v.t.* to cause to be indebted by a kindness; to do a service or kindness to; to constrain, compel. [Fr. *obliger* from L. *obligare* to bind].
OBLIGEE, [ob'-lij-ē'], *n.* the person to whom another is under bond, whether legal or moral.
OBLIGEMENT, [ob-līj'-ment], *n.* obligation; a favour, kindness.
OBLIGER, [ob-līj'-er], *n.* one who obliges.
OBLIGING, [ob-līj'-ing], *adj.* kind and courteous.
OBLIGINGLY, [ob-līj'-ing-li], *adv.* in an obliging fashion.
OBLIGINGNESS, [ob-līj'-ing-nes], *n.* the quality of being obliging.
OBLIGOR, [ob'-lig-aw(r)'], *n.* one who gives his bond.
OBLIQUE, [ō-blēk'], *adj.* aslant, neither vertical nor horizontal; indirect, tortuous; allusive; (*gram.*) relating to a case other than the nominative; **o. cone**, a cone the axis of which is not at right angles to the base; **o. angle**, any angle other than a right angle. [L. *obliquus*].

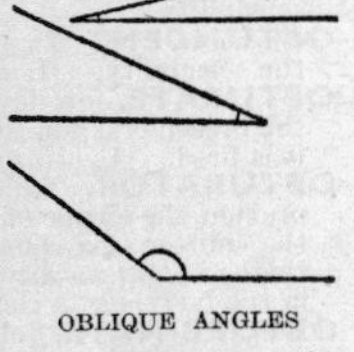
OBLIQUE ANGLES

OBLIQUELY, [ō-blēk'-li], *adv.* in an oblique fashion.
OBLIQUENESS, [ō-blēk'-nes], *n.* the quality of being oblique.
OBLIQUITY, [ō-blik'-wit-i], *n.* obliqueness, indirectness; dishonesty or untruthfulness. [L. *obliquitas*].
OBLITERATE, [ob-lit'-er-āt], *v.t.* to efface, to wear out; to cover up; to render illegible. [L. *obliterare*].
OBLITERATION, [ob-lit'-er-ā'-shun], *n.* the act of obliterating, or the fact of having been obliterated.
OBLIVION, [ob-liv'-i-on], *n.* forgetfulness; the state of being out of mind and unremembered. [L. *oblivio*].
OBLIVIOUS, [ob-liv'-i-us], *adj.* forgetful, unaware. [L. *obliviosus*].
OBLIVIOUSLY, [ob-liv'-i-us-li], *adv.* forgetfully, unconsciously.
OBLIVIOUSNESS, [ob-liv'-i-us-nes], *n.* forgetfulness; the state of being unconscious or unaware.
OBLONG (1), [ob'-long], *n.* a rectangular figure having greater length than breadth, that is with two opposite and equal sides longer than the other two opposite and equal sides.
OBLONG (2), [ob'-long], *adj.* less broad than long. [L. *oblongus* longish].
OBLONGISH, [ob'-long-ish], *adj.* rather oblong.
OBLONGLY, [ob'-long-li], *adv.* in oblong fashion.
OBLONGNESS, [ob'-long-nes], *n.* the quality of being oblong.
OBLOQUY, [ob'-lok-wi], *n.* abusive language; a reproachful, chiding, or accusing utterance. [LL. *obloquium* contradiction].
OBMUTESCENCE, [ob'-mewt-es'-ents], *n.* loss of speech; silence, deliberate silence. [OB and L. *mutescere* to grow mute].
OBNOXIOUS, [ob-nok'-shus], *adj.* odious, giving offence; hurtful; †exposed to harm. [L. *obnoxius*].
OBNOXIOUSLY, [ob-nok'-shus-li], *adv.* in an obnoxious fashion.
OBNOXIOUSNESS, [ob-nok'-shus-nes], *n.* the quality of being obnoxious.
OBNUBILATE, [ob-new'-bil-āt], *v.t.* to cloud over, to render obscure. [L. *obnubilare*].
OBNUBILATION, [ob-new'-bil-ā'-shun], *n.* the act of rendering obscure as by a cloud.
OBOE, [ō'-bō], *n.* a wooden wind-instrument; a hautboy. [It. *oboe*].
OBOIST, [ō'-bō-ist], *n.* an oboe player.
OBOL, [o'-bol], *n.* a small coin of ancient Greece in value the sixth of a drachma; a small weight. [Gk. *obolos*].
OBOVATE, [ob-ō'-vāt], *adj.* shaped like an egg but having the smaller end at the base, inversely ovate.

OBOVATE

OBREPTION, [ob-rep'-shun], *n.* the attempt to obtain something by cunning or deceit; †the act of stealing up to someone quietly and secretly. [L. *obreptio*].
OBREPTITIOUS, [ob'-rept-ish'-us], *adj.* surreptitious; deceitful for the sake of gain.
OBSCENE, [ob-sēn'], *adj.* disgusting, immodest, unchaste, lewd. [L. *obscenus*].
OBSCENELY, [ob-sēn'-li], *adv.* in an obscene way.
OBSCENENESS, [ob-sēn'-nes], *n.* the quality of being obscene; obscenity.
OBSCENITY, [ob-sen'-i-ti], *n.* lewdness; indecent talk, action, etc., immodesty. [L. *obscenitas*].
OBSCURANT (1), [ob'-skew-rant], *n.* a foe to enlightenment.
OBSCURANT (2), [ob-skyōōer'-ant], *adj.* rendering obscure. [L. *obscurans*].
OBSCURANTISM, [ob'-skew-rant'-izm], *n.* the principles of one who opposes enlightenment.
OBSCURANTIST (1), [ob'-skew-rant'-ist], *n.* an obscurant.
OBSCURANTIST (2), [ob'-skew-rant'-ist], *adj.* of, or pertaining to, an obscurantist or obscurantism.
OBSCURATION, [ob'-skew-rā'-shun], *n.* the act of darkening, or fact of having been darkened.
OBSCURE (1), [ob-skyōōer'], *n.* (*poet.*) darkness.
OBSCURE (2), [ob-skyōōer'], *adj.* lacking light, faintly lighted, dim, dark; dismal, gloomy; without clear outline, scarcely perceptible; (of sounds, etc.) confused; indistinct, vaguely conceived; secret, retired, unimportant, humble; puzzling, hard to understand. [L. *obscurus*].
OBSCURE (3), [ob-skyōōer'], *v.t.* to render obscure; to cover, veil, hide, to make only partly visible; to confuse the meaning of, render difficult to understand. [L. *obscurare* to darken].
OBSCURELY, [ob-skyōōer'-li], *adv.* in an obscure fashion.
OBSCUREMENT, [ob-skyōōer'-ment], *n.* obscuration.
OBSCURENESS, [ob-skyōōer'-nes], *n.* the state of being obscure.
OBSCURER, [ob-skyōōer'-er], *n.* someone or something that obscures.
OBSCURITY, [ob-skyōōer'-it-i], *n.* obscureness, darkness; ambiguity; humble state. [L. *obscuritas*].
OBSECRATE, [ob'-sik-rāt], *v.t* to implore, beseech. [L. *obsecrare*].
OBSECRATION, [ob'-sik-rā'-shun], *n.* supplication, entreaty.
OBSEQUIAL, [ob-sē'-kwi-al], *adj.* pertaining to obsequies.
OBSEQUIES, [ob'-sik-wiz], *n.*(*pl.*) funeral ceremonies; a funeral. [OFr. *obsequie*].
OBSEQUIOUS, [ob-sē'-kwi-us], *adj.* complying and obedient; fawning and servile. [L. *obsequiosus*].
OBSEQUIOUSLY, [ob-sē'-kwi-us-li], *adv.* in an obsequious way.
OBSEQUIOUSNESS, [ob-sē'-kwi-us-nes], *n.* the quality of being servile or obsequious.
OBSERVABLE, [ob-zurv'-abl], *adj.* noticeable; noteworthy.
OBSERVABLY, [ob-zurv'-ab-li], *adv.* in an observable fashion; noticeably.
OBSERVANCE, [ob-zurv'-ants], *n.* the act of observing; habit, custom; commemoration rite; †deference. [L. *observantia* attention].
OBSERVANT (1), [ob-zurv'-ant], *n.* one of the branch of the Franciscans called Friars Observant.
OBSERVANT (2), [ob-zurv'-ant], *adj.* strict in the keeping of commands; alert, keenly noticing, vigilant. [L. *observans*].
OBSERVANTLY, [ob-zurv'-ant-li], *adv.* in an observant way; vigilantly, attentively.
OBSERVATION (1), [ob'-zerv-ā'-shun], *n.* the act of observing; the faculty or habit of observing or noticing; the watching and recording of phenomena, etc.; a comment or critical remark, a contribution to conversation; (*pl.*) facts collected as a result of observing; all that has been observed, a collection of critical and deductive comments; **mass o.**, the

systematized observation of the habits, opinions, tendencies, etc., of samples of the population. [L. *observatio* watching].

OBSERVATION (2), [ob'-zerv-ā'-shun], *adj.* pertaining to, or used for, observing.

OBSERVATIONAL, [ob'-zerv-ā'-shun-al], *adj.* pertaining to, or founded on, observation.

OBSERVATORY, [ob-zurv'-at-er-i], *n.* a place equipped for making observations, *esp.* astronomical.

OBSERVE, [ob-zurv'], *v.t. and i.* to obey, keep, be observant of; to watch attentively; to remark, comment; to take notice. [L. *observare*].

OBSERVER, [ob-zurv'-er], *n.* one who watches, observes, or adheres to; **Royal O. Corps,** a body of watchers who report the approach of enemy aircraft.

OBSERVINGLY, [ob-zurv'-ing-li], *adv.* attentively, with observation.

OBSESS, [ob-ses'], *v.t.* to haunt; to monopolize the thoughts of. [L. *obsessum, p.pt.* of *obsidere* to besiege].

OBSESSION, [ob-sesh'-un], *n.* intense mental preoccupation; a fixed unshakable notion, a monomania. [L. *obsessio* a siege].

OBSIDIAN, [ob-sid'-i-an], *n.* a dark, hard, glossy, volcanic rock, volcanic glass. [MdL. *obsidianus lapis* stone of *Obsius*, who discovered it].

OBSIDIONAL, [ob-sid'-i-on-al], *adj.* pertaining to a siege; **o. crown,** the crown of grass accorded to a Roman general who raised a siege. [L. *obsidionalis*].

OBSIGNATION, [ob'-sig-nā'-shun], *n.* the act of sealing or ratifying. [L. *obsignatio* sealing].

OBSOLESCENCE, [ob'-sol-es'-ents], *n.* the process of passing into disuse.

OBSOLESCENT, [ob'-sol-es'-ent], *adj.* going out of use, becoming obsolete. [L. *obsolescens*].

OBSOLETE, [ob'-sol-ēt], *adj.* disused; old-fashioned. [L. *obsoletum, p.pt.* of *obsolescere* to grow old].

OBSOLETENESS, [ob'-sol-ēt-nes], *n.* the condition of being obsolete.

OBSTACLE, [ob'-stakl], *n.* anything which hinders; an impediment or barrier. [L. *obstaculum*].

OBSTACLE-RACE, [ob'-stakl-rās'], *n.* a foot race in which natural or artificial obstacles have to be surmounted.

OBSTETRIC, [ob-stet'-rik], *adj.* obstetrical; **o. toad,** the nurse toad.

OBSTETRICAL, [ob-stet'-rik-al], *adj.* pertaining to, or used in, midwifery. [L. *obstetricus*].

OBSTETRICIAN, [ob'-stet-rish'-an], *n.* one skilled in obstetrics.

OBSTETRICS [ob-stet'-riks], *n.* (*pl.*) the science of midwifery.

OBSTINACY, [ob'-stin-a-si], *n.* dogged resolution; unreasoning persistence in one's projects, opinions, etc.; stubbornness.

OBSTINATE, [ob'-stin-at], *adj.* stubborn and pertinacious; pig-headed, intractable. [L. *obstinatum, p.pt.* of *obstinare* to persist].

OBSTINATELY, [ob'-stin-at-li], *adv.* in an obstinate way.

OBSTINATENESS, [ob'-stin-at-nes], *n.* the quality of being obstinate.

OBSTIPATION, [ob'-stip-ā'-shun], *n.* the act of stopping up; (*med.*) intense constipation. [L. *obstipatio*].

OBSTREPEROUS, [ob-strep'-er-us], *adj.* clamorous, noisy; turbulent and intractable. [LL. *obstreperus*].

OBSTREPEROUSLY, [ob-strep'-er-us-li], *adv.* in an obstreperous fashion.

OBSTREPEROUSNESS, [ob-strep'-er-us-nes], *n.* obstreperous, turbulent behaviour.

OBSTRICTION, [ob-strik'-shun], *n.* the condition of being bound, morally or legally. [MedL. *obstrictio*].

OBSTRUCT, [ob-strukt'], *v.t.* to make impassable; to prevent from moving or passing; to impede, inconvenience, get in the way of; to oppose, thwart; to oppose progress. [L. *obstructum, p.pt.* of *obstruere* to block up].

OBSTRUCTER, [ob-strukt'-er], *n.* one who obstructs.

OBSTRUCTION, [ob-struk'-shun], *n.* the act of obstructing; a hindrance or impediment either material or otherwise; that which is or gets in the way. [L. *obstructio*].

OBSTRUCTIONISM, [ob-struk'-shun-izm], *n.* the act or policy of putting obstacles in the way of progress or reform.

OBSTRUCTIONIST, [ob-struk'-shun-ist], *n.* one who practises obstruction.

OBSTRUCTIVE, [ob-strukt'-iv], *adj.* causing hindrance.

OBSTRUENT (1), [ob'-stro͞o-ent], *n.* something that obstructs.

OBSTRUENT (2), [ob'-stro͞o-ent], *adj.* hindering, obstructive. [L. *obstruens*].

OBTAIN, [ob-tān'], *v.t. and i.* to acquire, get possession of, receive; to be normally done, be prevalent; to hold good, be valid. [Fr. *obtenir* from L. *obtinere* to hold].

OBTAINABLE, [ob-tān'-abl], *adj.* able to be obtained.

OBTAINER, [ob-tān'-er], *n.* one who obtains.

OBTECTED, [ob-tekt'-id], *adj.* (*zool.*) having a hard outer covering or shell. [L. *obtectum, p.pt.* of *obtegere* to cover up].

OBTEMPER, [ob-tem'-per], *v.t.* (*Scots leg.*) to comply with. [L. *obtemperare* to obey].

OBTRUDE, [ob-tro͞od'], *v.t. and i.* to push forward, compel attention to (ideas, etc.); to intrude. [L. *obtrudere*].

OBTRUDER, [ob-tro͞od'-er], *n.* one who obtrudes.

OBTRUNCATE, [ob-trungk'-āt], *v.t.* to truncate; to lop off the top of. [L. *obtruncare*].

OBTRUSION, [ob-tro͞o'-zhun], *n.* the act of thrusting upon or obtruding. [LL. *obtrusio*].

OBTRUSIVE, [ob-tro͞o'-siv], *adj.* disposed to obtrude; pushing and intrusive.

OBTRUSIVELY, [ob-tro͞os'-iv-li], *adv.* in an obtrusive fashion.

OBTRUSIVENESS, [ob-tro͞os'-iv-nes], *n.* the fact or quality of being obtrusive.

OBTUNDENT (1), [ob-tund'-ent], *n.* (*med.*) any substance which can allay irritation by deadening sensibility.

OBTUNDENT (2), [ob-tund'-ent], *adj.* able to dull the sensibility. [L. *obtundens*].

OBTURATE, [ob'-tew-rāt], *v.t.* to stop up; to close the breech of a gun to prevent the escape of gas when it is fired. [L. *obturare* to stop up].

OBTURATOR, [ob'-tew-rāt'-or], *n.* a device to prevent the escape of gas from a gun when it is fired; the shutter of a camera; (*anat.*) a membrane in the thigh; (*surg.*) an artificial plate used to cover a gap in the body, e.g. a cleft palate.

OBTURBINATE, [ob-turb'-in-āt], *adj.* shaped like an inverted top.

OBTUSANGULAR, [ob'-tews-ang'-yo͞o-ler], *adj.* having obtuse angles.

OBTUSE, [ob-tews'], *adj.* blunt, having no sharp point; stupid, heavy-witted, dull; **o. angle,** an angle greater than a right angle and less than 180 degrees. [L. *obtusus* blunted].

OBTUSE-ANGLED, [ob-tews'-ang-gld], *adj.* containing an obtuse angle.

OBTUSELY, [ob-tews'-li], *adv.* in an obtuse way.

OBTUSENESS, [ob-tews'-nes], *n.* the condition of being obtuse; dulness of intellect.

OBTUSION, [ob-tew'-zhun], *n.* act of blunting; state of being blunted.

OBUMBRANT, [ob-um'-brant], *adj.* (*entom.*) overshadowing. [L. *obumbrans*].

OBUS, [ō'-bus], *n.* a small explosive projectile. [Fr. *obus*].

OBVALLATE, [ob-val'-āt], *adj.* (*bot.*) walled up. [L. *obvallatum*].

OBVERSE (1), [ob'-vurs], *n.* (*numis.*) the side of a coin bearing the head; that fact, idea, etc., which is the complement of another.

OBVERSE (2), [ob'-vurs], *adj.* facing, turned towards, the person who is looking; a counterpart or complement; (*bot.*) (of leaves) having the attached end narrower than the tip. [L. *obversum, p.pt.* of *obvertere* to turn towards].

OBVERSE-LUNATE, [ob'-vurs-lo͞on'-āt], *adj.* shaped like an inverted crescent.

OBVERSELY, [ob'-vurs-li], *adv.* in an obverse form or way.

OBVERSION, [ob-vur'-shun], *n.* (*log.*) a process of changing the quality of a proposition so that the opposite is at once inferred. [L. *obversio*].

OBVERT, [ob-vurt'], *v.t.* (*log.*) to infer by obversion. [L. *obvertere* to turn towards].

OBVIATE, [ob'-vē-āt], *v.t.* to clear out of the way, get rid of, render unnecessary, do away with. [L. *obviatum, p.pt.* of *obviare* to meet in the way].

OBVIOUS, [ob'-vi-us], *adj.* plainly apparent, easily perceived, impossible to mistake; too apparent, garish, obtrusive; easily understandable, lacking subtlety, simple; †exposed. [L. *obvius* lying in the way].

OBVIOUSLY, [ob'-vi-us-li], *adv.* evidently, plainly, without doubt.

OBVIOUSNESS, [ob'-vi-us-nes], *n.* the quality of being obvious.
OBVOLUTE, [ob'-vol-ewt], *adj.* (*bot.*) (of leaves) folded over so as to embrace the margin of the other leaf. [L. *obvolutus, p.pt.* of *obvolvere* to wrap round].
OBVOLUTED, [ob'-vol-ewt-id], *adj.* obvolute.
OCA, [ok'-ah], *n.* (*bot.*) either of two South American plants, *Oxalis crenata* and *Oxalis tuberosa*, the tubers of which resemble potatoes. [Span. *oca*].
OCARINA, [ok-a-rē'-na], *n.* a small musical instrument, originally of clay, having mouthpiece and finger-holes, the sound of which resembles that of a flute. [It. *ocarina*].

OCARINA

OCCASION (1), [ok-ā'-zhun], *n.* a point in time marked by a certain action or event; a suitable moment; a chance, opportunity; a cause for action, a reason for acting, an immediate provocation of events actually arising from older and deeper causes; **occasions,** occupation, lawful and necessary business; **on o.,** as and when time or circumstances demand; **to rise to the o.,** to be equal to the demands of the moment; **to take o. to,** to choose, in those circumstances or at that moment, to. [L. *occasio* a happening].
OCCASION (2), [ok-ā'-zhun], *v.t.* to cause; to provide opportunity or occasion for. [OCCASION (1)].
OCCASIONAL, [ok-ā'-zhun-al], *adj.* happening now and then, not frequently or continuously; occurring or appearing at long, and often irregular, intervals; intended for or fitted to a special occasion.
OCCASIONALISM, [ok-ā'-zhun-al-izm], *n.* the Cartesian philosophy of occasional causes.
OCCASIONALITY, [ok-ā'-zhun-al'-i-ti], *n.* the condition of being occasional.
OCCASIONALLY, [ok-ā'-zhun-al-i], *adv.* now and then, at rare intervals, from time to time.
OCCASIONER, [ok-ā'-zhun-er], *n.* one who occasions.
OCCIDENT, [ok'-sid-ent], *n.* the west generally; the western part of the world viewed from a European standpoint but including the west of Europe itself. [L. *occidens*].
OCCIDENTAL, [ok'-sid-ent'-al], *adj.* western; pertaining to the occident.
OCCIDENTALISM, [ok'-sid-ent'-al-izm], *n.* the civilization of the west.
OCCIDENTALIST, [ok'-sid-ent'-al-ist], *n.* a student or admirer of western life and culture.
OCCIDENTALIZE, [ok'-sid-ent'-al-īz], *v.t.* to westernize, give western habits and ideas to.
OCCIPITAL, [ok-sip'-it-al], *adj.* belonging to the occiput.
OCCIPUT, [ok'-sip-ut], *n.* the back section of the head. [OB and L. *caput* head].
OCCLUDE, [ok-lōōd'], *v.t.* to shut in or shut out; (*chem.*) to absorb. [L. *occludere*].
OCCLUSION, [ok-lōō'-zhun], *n.* the act of occluding or fact of having been occluded; (*phon.*) the rapid momentary shutting of the vocal passage in speech; (*chem.*) absorption. [L. *occlusio*].
OCCULT (1), [ok-ult'], *n.* the supernatural; that which lies beyond, or draws its power from beyond the normal; psychic experience. [L. *occultum, p.pt.* of *occulere* to cover up].
OCCULT (2), [ok-ult'], *adj.* hidden, secret; magical, supernatural.
OCCULT (3), [ok-ult'], *v.t. and i.* to become hidden; (*astron.*) to eclipse. [L. *occultare*].
OCCULTATION, [ok'-ult-ā'-shun], *n.* (*astron.*) the eclipse of one body by another. [L. *occultatio*].
OCCULTED, [ok-ult'-id], *adj.* (*astron.*) hidden from view, eclipsed.
OCCULTISM, [ok'-ult-izm], *n.* trust in, and study of, the supernatural; mysticism.
OCCULTIST, [ok'-ult-ist], *n.* a believer in, or of, the supernatural.
OCCULTLY, [ok'-ult-li], *adv.* in an occult way.
OCCULTNESS, [ok-ult'-nes], *n.* the quality of being occult.
OCCUPANCY, [ok'-yŏŏ-pan-si], *n.* the act of taking or retaining possession; (*leg.*) the acquirement of right of possession of that which is owned by no one.
OCCUPANT, [ok'-yŏŏ-pant], *n.* he who occupies; one who inhabits a dwelling.
OCCUPATION, [ok'-yŏŏ-pā'-shun], *n.* the act of obtaining and retaining possession; military possession of the territory of a defeated enemy until all possibility of renewal of hostilities has passed away; period of tenure of a property; tenure, residence; employment, trade. [L. *occupatio* a taking possession].
OCCUPIER, [ok'-yŏŏ-pi-er], *n.* one who occupies or dwells; in a tenant.
OCCUPY, [ok'-yŏŏ-pi], *v.t.* to obtain and retain possession of; to take and hold by military force; to settle troops in the territories of a defeated enemy till peace terms are ratified; to dwell in; to fill with oneself (a chair, etc.); to hold, be regularly in, a particular place; to consume time or attention of; to busy (oneself); **to be occupied with,** to be busy with. [Fr. *occuper* from L. *occupare*].
OCCUR, (**occurring, occurred**), [ok-ur'], *v.i.* to happen; to exist, arise, be met with; **to o. to,** to enter the mind of. [L. *occurrere* to run to meet].
OCCURRENCE, [ok-u'-rents], *n.* an event, that which occurs; the act of occurring. [Fr. *occurrence*].
OCCURRENT (1), [ok-u'-rent], *n.* that which occurs.
OCCURRENT (2), [ok-u'-rent], *adj.* occurring, incidental. [L. *occurrens*].
OCEAN (1), [ō'-shun], *n.* the open sea; (*fig.*) a large quantity, a multitude of; **oceans of,** (*slang*) plenty and to spare of. [Gk. *okeanos*].
OCEAN (2), [ō'-shun], *adj.* belonging to the ocean.
OCEANIC, [ō'-shi-an'-ik], *adj.* pertaining to, or coming from, the ocean.
OCEANID, [ō-sē'-an-id], *n.* an ocean nymph, a daughter of Oceanus; a marine mollusc. [Gk. *Okeanis*].
OCEANOGRAPHER, [ō'-shun-og'-raf-er], *n.* a student of oceanography.
OCEANOGRAPHIC, [ō'-shun-ō-graf'-ik], *adj.* pertaining to oceanography.
OCEANOGRAPHICAL, [ō'-shun-ō-graf'-ik-al], *adj.* oceanographic.
OCEANOGRAPHIST, [ō'-shun-og'-raf-ist], *n.* an oceanographer.
OCEANOGRAPHY, [ō'-shun-og'-raf-i], *n.* the study of the ocean, its movements and its flora and fauna. [OCEAN (1) and Gk. *graphia* writing].
OCELLATED, [ōs'-el-āt-id], *adj.* marked with ocelli. [L. *ocellatus*].
OCELLUS, (*pl.* **ocelli**), [ō-sel'-us], *n.* (*zool.*) a simple eye-like organ in some invertebrates; a spot of colour encircled with bands of another colour and resembling an eye as seen, for example, on the peacock. [L. *ocellus* little eye].
OCELOT, [ō'-sil-ot], *n.* a South American wild cat, *Felis pardalis*; the tiger-cat. [Fr. *ocelot*].
OCHLOCRACY, [ok-lok'-ras-i], *n.* mob-rule, mobocracy. [Gk. *okhlokratia*].
OCHLOCRAT, [ok'-lō-krat'], *n.* one who believes in mob-rule.
OCHLOCRATIC, [ok'-lō-krat'-ik], *adj.* pertaining to mob-rule.
OCHRACEOUS, [ō-krā'-shus], *adj.* containing or coloured like ochre.
OCHRE, [ō'-ker], *n.* a clay-like oxide of iron used for making yellow or brown pigments; colouring made from these. [Gk. *okhra*].
OCHREATE, see OCREATE.
OCHREOUS, [ō'-krē-us], *adj.* resembling or consisting of ochre.
OCHRY, [ō'-kri], *adj.* ochreous.
O'CLOCK, [ō-klok'], *adv.* by or according to the clock. [Shortened from *of the clock*].
OCREA, [ok'-rē], *n.* (*bot.*) the sheath surrounding a stalk; (*zool.*) a similar growth on any stem-like part of an animal or bird. [L. *ocrea* leg-protection for a foot-soldier].
OCREATE, OCHREATE, [ō'-krē-āt], *adj.* (*bot.*) possessing ocreae.
OCT-, OCTA-, OCTO-, *pref.* eight. [Gk. *octo*].
OCTACHORD, [ok'-ta-kawd'], *n.* a musical instrument that has eight strings; diatonic octave. [Gk. *oktakhordos*].
OCTAD, [ok'-tad], *n.* a series of eight; (*chem.*) an element that has the combining power of eight hydrogen atoms. [Gk. *oktas*].

OCREA

OCTAGON, [ok'-tag-on], *n.* (*geom.*) an eight-sided and eight-angled polygon; (*arch.*) an eight-sided building or room. [Gk. *oktagonos*].

OCTAGONAL, [ok-tag′-on-al], *adj.* formed with eight sides and eight angles.
OCTAHEDRAL, [ok′-ta-hē′-dral], *adj.* formed with eight plane faces; resembling an octahedron; consisting of octahedrons.
OCTAHEDRITE, [ok′-ta-hē′-drīt], *n.* (*min.*) anatase.
OCTAHEDRON, (*pl.* **octahedra, octahedrons**), [ok′-ta-hē′-dron], *n.* a solid figure having eight plane faces each of which is, if the figure is regular, an equilateral triangle. [Gk. *oktahedron*].
OCTANE, [ok′-tān], *n.* (*chem.*) a paraffin of the formula C_8H_{18}, obtained from petroleum and used as a fuel for aeroplane engines. [OCT and (METH)ANE].
OCTANGULAR, [okt-ang′-gyo͞o-ler], *adj.* possessing eight angles. [OCT and ANGULAR].
OCTANS, [okt′-anz], *n.* (*astron.*) the constellation of the South Pole.
OCTANT, [okt′-ant], *n.* the eighth part of the area of a circle; the eighth part of the circumference of a circle; (*naut. and astron.*) a device for taking angular measurements. [LL. *octans* half-quadrant].
OCTARCHY, [okt′-ahk-i], *n.* government by eight rulers. [OCT and (HEPT)ARCHY].
OCTASTYLE (1), OCTOSTYLE, [ok′-ta-stīl], *n.* a building with eight columns in front and behind.
OCTASTYLE (2), [ok′-ta-stīl], *adj.* possessing eight columns. [Gk. *oktastulos*].
OCTAVE, [ok′-tiv], *n.* (*eccles.*) the day falling a week after a festival; the period between a festival and its octave; (*mus.*) a note eight diatonic degrees above or below another note (counting both notes); the scale contained by and including those two notes; a chord consisting of two notes eight diatonic degrees apart (counting both notes). [L. *octavus* eighth].
OCTAVO, [ok-tā′-vō], *n.* the size of a book or its pages when each page is one-eighth the size of the sheets from which it has been folded; a book with pages of this size. [L. *octavus*].
OCTENNIAL, [ok-ten′-i-al], *adj.* occurring once in eight years; lasting for eight years. [L. *octennium*].
OCTENNIALLY, [ok-ten′-i-al-i], *adv.* once in every eight years.
OCTET, [ok′-tet, ok-tet′], *n.* (*mus.*) a composition with eight parts or voices; (*pros.*) eight lines of verse; the first eight lines of a sonnet. [OCT and (DU)ET].
OCTILE, [ok′-tīl], *adj.* (*astron.*) (of planets) 45 degrees apart.
OCTILLION, [ok-til′-yun], *n.* a million raised to the eighth power (1 followed by 48 ciphers). [Fr. *octillion*].
OCTINGENTENARY, [ok′-tin-jen-ten′-er-i], *n.* eight hundredth anniversary. [~L. *octingenti* eight hundred].
OCTO-, see OCT-.
OCTOBER, [ok-tō′-ber], *n.* the tenth month of the year. [L. *October* eighth month of the early Roman year].
OCTOCENTENARY, [ok′-tō-sen-tēn′-ar-i], *n.* the eight-hundredth anniversary. [OCTO and CENTENARY].
OCTODECIMO, [ok′-tō-des′-im-ō], *n.* a book the sheets of which are folded into eighteen leaves; the size of a page in such a book (often represented by 18mo). [L. *octodecimus* eighteenth].
OCTODENTATE, [ok′-tō-dent′-āt], *adj.* possessing eight teeth.
OCTOFID, [ok′-tō-fid], *adj.* (*bot.*) divided into eight segments. [OCTO and L. *fid*(*um*), *p.pt.* of *findere* to cleave].
OCTOGENARIAN (1), [ok′-tō-jen-āer′-i-an], *n.* a person over eighty but not yet ninety years of age.
OCTOGENARIAN (2), [ok′-tō-jen-āer′-i-an], *adj.* eighty to ninety years old. [L. *octogenerius* consisting of eighty].
OCTOGENARY, [ok′-tō-jen′-er-i], *adj.* octogenarian.
OCTONAL, [ok′-ton-al], *adj.* divided into groups of eight; (*pros.*) containing eight metrical feet. [L. *octoni* eight each].
OCTONARIAN (1), [ok′-ton-āer′-i-an], *n.* (*pros.*) a verse containing eight metrical feet.
OCTONARIAN (2), [ok′-ton-āer′-i-an], *adj.* (*pros.*) having eight metrical feet. [L. *octonarius*].
OCTONARY (1), [ok′-ton-er-i], *n.* a group containing eight units; a section of Psalm 119.
OCTONARY (2), [ok′-ton-er-i], *adj.* pertaining to, consisting of, or divided into, eight. [L. *octonarius*].
OCTONOCULAR, [ok′-ton-ok′-yo͞o-ler], *adj.* possessing eight eyes.
OCTOPARTITE, [ok′-tō-paht′-īt], *adj.* possessing eight parts.
OCTOPETALOUS, [ok′-tō-pet′-al-us], *adj.* possessing eight petals.
OCTOPOD, [ok′-tō-pod′], *n.* (*zool.*) any of the animals of the sub-order *Octopoda*. [Gk. *oktopodos* having eight feet].
OCTOPUS, (*pl.* **octopodes** or **octopuses**), [ok′-tō-pus], *n.* (*zool.*) a group of cephalopod molluscs, that have eight arms provided with suckers; (*fig.*) a powerful organization with influence and interests in many directions. [Gk. *okto* eight and *pous* foot].
OCTORADIATED, [ok′-tō-rād′-i-āt′-id], *adj.* possessing eight rays.
OCTOROON, [ok′-to-ro͞on′], *n.* a child of a white person and a quadroon, a person having one-eighth Negro blood. [OCTO and (QUAD)ROON].
OCTOSPERMOUS, [ok′-tō-spurm′-us], *adj.* possessing eight seeds. [OCTO and Gk. *sperma* seed].
OCTOSTYLE, see OCTASTYLE.
OCTOSYLLABIC, [ok′-tō-sil-ab′-ik], *adj.* (*pros.*) having eight syllables.
OCTOSYLLABLE, [ok′-tō-sil′-abl], *n.* a word of eight syllables; (*pros.*) a verse having eight syllables.
OCTROI, [ok-trwah′], *n.* a tax levied in France and other European countries upon goods about to enter a town; the barrier at which this tax is gathered; the officials who collect it. [Fr. *octroi*].
OCTUPLE (1), [ok′-tewpl], *adj.* eightfold. [L. *octuplus*].
OCTUPLE (2), [ok′-tewpl], *v.t.* to multiply by eight. [*Prec.*].
OCUBA, [ok′-yo͞o-ba], *n.* a wax produced in South America from the tree, *Myristica Ocuba*.
OCULAR (1), [ok′-yo͞o-ler], *n.* the eyepiece of an optical instrument.
OCULAR (2), [ok′-yo͞o-ler], *adj.* pertaining to eyes or sight; visual; visible. [L. *ocularis*].
OCULARLY, [ok′-yo͞o-ler-li], *adv.* by the eye; by sight.
OCULATE, [ok′-yo͞o-lāt], *adj.* having eyes; ocellated. [L. *oculatus*].
OCULIFORM, [ok-yo͞o′-li-fawm], *adj.* shaped like an eye. [L. *oculus* eye and FORM (1)].
OCULIST, [ok′-yo͞o-list], *n.* a person skilled in the treatment of the eye. [Fr. *oculiste*].
OD (1), [od], *n.* a supposed magnetic force postulated by Baron von Reichenbach (1788-1869) as pervading all living things, etc. [Invented word].
OD† (2), [od], *int.* a minor oath. [Shortened from GOD].
ODALISK, [ō′-dal-isk], *n.* an odalisque.
ODALISQUE, [ō′-dal-isk], *n.* a concubine or female slave in an eastern harem. [Turk. *odaliq* maid-servant].
ODD (1), [od], *n.* the thirteenth, and winning, trick where each side in the game of whist has scored six; (*golf*) the next stroke played after each player has played an equal number of strokes.
ODD (2), [od], *adj.* not yielding a whole number when divided by two; numbered by the series one, three, five, etc.; not a pair; being surplus to the main amount; being left over and to spare; one of a pair left over; strange, peculiar, not normal; occasional, not regular; of small importance. [OScand. *odda* third].
ODDFELLOW, [od′-fel′-ō], *n.* a member of a mutual aid society so named. [ODD and FELLOW (1)].
ODDITY, [od′-i-ti], *n.* a singular person or thing, a misfit or curiosity; the quality of being odd; singularity.
ODD-LOOKING, [od′-lo͝ok′-ing], *adj.* having an odd appearance.
ODDLY, [od′-li], *adv.* in an odd fashion.
ODDMENT, ODDMENTS, [od′-ment], *n.* something left over; odds and ends.
ODDNESS, [od′-nes], *n.* the quality of being odd.
ODDS, [odz], *n.*(*pl.*) things not equal; difference; the balance of probability; that necessary to produce equality; (*betting*) the difference between the amount paid to make the bet and the amount payable if the bet is successful; **it makes no o.,** it does not matter; **against long o.,** against a heavy adverse chance; **to be at o. with,** to disagree with; **o. and ends,** remnants, things left over; **to lay the o.,** (*betting*) to offer to bet at such a price as will be favourable to the other party.
ODE, [ōd], *n.* a song in Greek drama, accompanied by music and dancing; a lyric poem composed for some special occasion, or in honour of some event or person. [Fr. *ode*].
ODEON [ō′-di-on], *n.* an odeum. [Gk. *oideion*].

ODEUM, [ō′-di-um], *n.* a building for dramatic or musical entertainment in the ancient world; a theatre, concert hall. [*Prec.*].

ODIOUS, [ō′-di-us], *adj.* hateful, disgusting, ugly. [L. *odiosus* hateful].

ODIOUSLY, [ō′-di-us-li], *adv.* hatefully, in an odious fashion.

ODIOUSNESS, [ō′-di-us-nes], *n.* the condition of being odious.

ODIUM, [ō′-di-um], *n.* odiousness; hatred or disgust; opprobrium. [L. *odium*].

ODOMETER, [ō-dom′-it-er], *n.* a device for measuring the mileage of a vehicle. [Gk. *hodos* way and METER].

ODONT-, ODONTO-, *pref.* implying connexion with teeth. [Gk. *odous odontos* tooth].

ODONTALGIA, [ō′-dont-al′-ji-a], *n.* toothache. [ODONT and Gk. *algos* pain].

ODONTALGIC (1), [ō′-dont-al′-jik], *n.* a remedy for the toothache.

ODONTALGIC (2), [ō′-dont-al′-jik], *adj.* pertaining to toothache.

ODONTALITE, [ō-dont′-al-īt], *n.* a fossil tooth. [ODONT and Gk. *lithos* stone].

ODONTIC, [ō-dont′-ik], *adj.* pertaining to teeth.

ODONTOBLAST, [ō-dont′-ō-blast′], *n.* a cell on the outside of a tooth secreting the ivory of which the tooth is made. [ODONT and Gk. *blastos* growth].

ODONTOGENY, [ō′-dont-oj′-en-i], *n.* the study of the origin and growth of teeth. [ODONT and Gk. *genes* producing].

ODONTOGLOSSUM, [ō-dont′-ō-glos′-um], *n.* (*bot.*) a group of Central American orchids. [ODONT and Gk. *glossa* tongue].

ODONTOGRAPH, [ō-dont′-ō-graf′], *n.* a device for setting out the teeth of gear-wheels. [ODONT and Gk. *graphia* writing].

ODONTOGRAPHY, [ō′-dont-og′-ra-fi], *n.* the scientific description of teeth. [ODONT and Gk. *graphia* writing].

ODONTOID, [ō-dont′-oid], *adj.* (*anat.*) resembling a tooth. [ODONT and Gk. *oeides* like].

ODONTOLOGY, [ō′-dont-ol′-o-ji], *n.* the study of the teeth. [ODONT and Gk. *logos* speech].

ODORANT, [ō′-der-ant], *adj.* odoriferous.

ODORIFEROUS, [ō′-der-if′-er-us], *adj.* diffusing a pleasant or unpleasant odour. [L. *odorifer*].

ODORIFEROUSLY, [ō′-der-if′-er-us-li], *adv.* fragrantly.

ODORIFEROUSNESS, [ō′-der-if′-er-us-nes], *n.* fragrance, the quality of being odorous.

ODOROUS, [ō′-der-us], *adj.* fragrant, sweet-smelling; (*coll.*) smelly.

ODOROUSLY, [ō′-der-us-li], *adv.* fragrantly.

ODOROUSNESS, [ō′-der-us-nes], *n.* fragrance, the quality of being odorous.

ODOUR, [ō′-der], *n.* smell, perfume, fragrance, scent; reputation; (*fig.*) a suspicion; atmosphere, savour, suggestion (of). [L. *odor*].

ODOURLESS, [ō′-der-les], *adj.* having no smell, free from odour.

ODYSSEY, [od′-i-si], *n.* the second of Homer's epics recounting the return home of Odysseus from the siege of Troy; a long and adventurous journey, a journey. [Gk. *Odussseia*].

OECUMENICAL, see ECUMENICAL.

OECUMENICITY, see ECUMENICITY.

OEDEMA, EDEMA, [ē-dē′-ma], *n.* (*med.*) a localized dropsy. [Gk. *oidema* swelling].

OEDEMATOUS, EDEMATOUS, [ē-dē′-mat-us], *adj.* relating to, in a state of, oedema.

OEDEMIA, [ē-dē′-mi-a], *n.* a genus of sea-ducks.

OEDIPUS, [ē′-dip-us], *n.* (*Gk. myth.*) the Theban king who solved the riddle of the Sphinx and, ignorant of his parentage, killed his father and married his mother; a solver of riddles; **O. complex**, (*psych.*) a state in which a person shows excessive affection for the parent opposite in sex to him- or herself and corresponding distaste for his or her other parent. [Gk. *Oidipos*].

OEIL-DE-BŒUF, [u(r)′-i-de-burf′], *n.* (*arch.*) an oval window.

OENANTHIC, [ē-nan′-thik], *adj.* something like wine. [Gk. *oinanthe* vine blossom].

OENOMEL, [ē′-nō-mel], *n.* a mixture of wine and honey, which was drunk by the Greeks. [Gk. *oinomeli*].

O'ER, [aw(r)], *prep.* (*poet.*) over. [Shortened from OVER].

OESOPHAGEAL, ESOPHAGEAL, [ē′-sof-ā′-ji-al], *adj.* pertaining to the gullet.

OESOPHAGUS, ESOPHAGUS, [ē-sof′-ag-us], *n.* (*anat.*) the gullet. [Gk. *oiso-phagos*].

OESTRIN, (ēs′-trin), *n.* a sex hormone secreted by women. [OESTRUM].

OESTRUM, [ēs′-trum], *n.* an overpowering impulse; (of dogs) the period during which the bitch will copulate; erotic frenzy, desire. [MedL. *oestrum*].

OESTRUS, [ēs′-trus], *n.* a gadfly; oestrum. [Gk. *oistros* a gadfly, sting, frenzy].

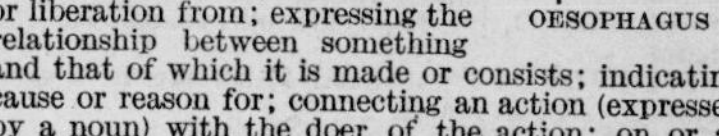

OESOPHAGUS

OF, [ov], *prep.* expressing whence anything comes, its source or origin; indicating real or imaginary point of departure, distance from, measure, separation from or liberation from; expressing the relationship between something and that of which it is made or consists; indicating cause or reason for; connecting an action (expressed by a noun) with the doer of the action; on or at in a temporal sense, during. [OE. *of*].

OFF (1), [of], *n.* (*cricket*) the off side. See OFF (2).

OFF (2), [of], *adj.* not near or to hand; divided or removed from; improbable, unlikely; unlucky, not full of business, dull, uninteresting; not fresh, stale, tainted; disappointing; **o. day**, a dull or disappointing day when things do not go well; **o. side**, the side to the right of the road-user; (*cricket*), the side of the field to the right of the batsman as he faces the bowling. [OFF (3)].

OFF (3), [of], *adv.* not above or on; expressing division, separation, avoidance or postponement, departure, distance between; expressing completion, after certain verbs, e.g. polish off, finish off, etc.; **to knock o.**, to cease work, take a rest; **o. and on**, from time to time, now and then, at irregular intervals of time. [OF].

OFF (4), [of], *prep.* expressing removal from or place whence, reduction, distance away from; near to, at the side of.

OFFAL, [of′-al], *n.* refuse, rubbish, garbage; that which falls off or is cast away as waste; small valueless fish caught in the fishers' nets along with larger and more valuable fish; the edible organs of an animal, liver, kidneys, etc.; carrion. [OFF (3) and FALL (2)].

OFFCAST (1), [of′-kahst], *n.* a person or thing cast off, in annoyance, as useless, etc.

OFFCAST (2), [of′-kahst], *adj.* cast off, thrown away, discarded, disowned.

OFFENCE, [of-ents′], *n.* a breach of law, rule, custom, or tradition, etc.; a wrong-doing, sin or crime; an insult; the sense of rebuff and annoyance felt by an insulted person; (*milit.*) an attack, offensive, act of attacking. [L. *offensus* a striking at].

OFFENCEFUL, [of-ents′-fool], *adj.* giving offence, insulting, displeasing.

OFFENCELESS, [of-ents′-les], *adj.* unoffending, innocent, harmless.

OFFEND, [of-end′], *v.t. and i.* to do wrong, to sin, to commit a breach of law, order, custom or morality, to commit an offence; to disgust or displease; to outrage or violate; to annoy, insult, hurt the feelings of; **to o. against**, to transgress (laws, morality, etc.). [L. *offendere* to strike at].

OFFENDEDLY, [o-fend′-ed-li], *adv.* in offended fashion.

OFFENDER, [of-end′-er], *n.* one who offends; a criminal.

OFFENSIVE (1), [of-en′-siv], *n.* (*milit.*) attack; **to take the o.**, (*milit. and fig.*) to begin to attack before the enemy has a chance to do so.

OFFENSIVE (2), [of-en′-siv], *adj.* giving offence, loathsome, noisome, repulsive; giving moral offence, indecent, obscene; insolent, insulting; suitable to attack with, attacking, provocative. [MedL. *offensivus*].

OFFENSIVELY, [of-ens′-iv-li], *adv.* in an offensive way.

OFFENSIVENESS, [of-ens′-iv-nes], *n.* the state or quality of being offensive.

OFFER (1), [of′-er], *n.* a proposal; a statement of willingness; a bid in a business transaction; the act of offering, presenting, thrusting forward or proposing. [OE. *offrung* sacrifice].

OFFER (2), [of′-er], *v.t. and i.* to bring or thrust forward, to proffer, present, tender; to hold out towards; (of prayers, alms, worship presented to God) to give; to arise, happen; **to o. up**, (*mech.*) to apply one part to another to see if they fit. [OE. *offrian* to offer (to God)].

OFFERABLE, [of′-er-abl], *adj.* able to be offered.

OFFERER, [of′-er-er], *n.* one who offers.

OFFERING, [of′-er-ing], *n.* something offered in worship; (*coll.*) a gift. [OE. *offrung* sacrifice].

OFFERTORY, [of′-er-tor-i], *n.* (*eccles.*) the placing of the bread and wine upon the altar ready for consecration; (*coll.*) the collecting and offering of alms at the Holy Communion service; a piece of music played or sung at this point of the service; alms taken at a religious service; **o.-box,** a box put up in a church for alms.

OFFHAND (1), [of′-hand′], *adj.* extempore, unprepared; curt, rude, aloof, unceremonious. [OFF (3) and HAND (1)].

OFFHAND (2), [of′-hand′], *adv.* in a casual, unprepared, or offhand fashion.

OFFHANDED, [of′-hand′-id], *adj.* casual, curt, offhand.

OFFHANDEDLY, [of′-hand′-id-li], *adv.* in a casual, curt or offhand manner.

OFFHANDEDNESS, [of′-hand′-id-nes], *n.* rudeness, offhand behaviour or manners.

OFFICE, [of′-is], *n.* a function, duty or service; a position carrying with it certain definite and special functions and duties; a state department; a room, house, or set of rooms in which business is transacted, *esp.* business of a clerical or commercial nature; a rite, ceremony or religious service; (*slang*) a hint; **offices,** the rooms in that part of a domestic establishment where the necessary work of the domicile is carried on, e.g., kitchen, scullery, etc., and also lavatories. [OFr. *office* from L. *officium* duty, ceremony, function].

OFFICE-BEARER, [of′-is-bāer′-er], *n.* one who holds a special position or office.

OFFICE BOY, [of′-is-boi], *n.* a boy employed to perform odd jobs in an office.

OFFICER (1), [of′-is-er], *n.* one who holds an office; a person in a recognized position of authority and responsibility and also of service and duty; the holder of a commission in the army, air force, or navy; the master, captain or mate of a merchant-vessel; **police o.,** a police constable; **o. at arms** or **o. of arms,** a herald; **o. of the day,** the officer in charge of the necessary arrangements and routines for a given number of troops on a particular day. [L. *officiarius*].

OFFICER (2), [of′-is-er], *v.t.* to provide with officers; to be in command of, to act as an officer over.

OFFICIAL (1), [of-ish′-al], *n.* a person holding a position of responsibility and authority; a servant of authority; an officer; (*eccles.*) a judge in an ecclesiastical court.

OFFICIAL (2), [of-ish′-al], *adj.* pertaining to an office; serving in a position of responsibility and authority; having authority, emanating from a person or persons in authority; formal, ceremonious; recognized as proper and lawful. [L. *officialis*].

OFFICIALDOM, [of-ish′-al-dum], *n.* officialism, bureaucracy; the typical point of view of officials; the body of state officials, their character, habits, and point of view.

OFFICIALISM, [of-ish′-al-izm], *n.* official routine; over-insistence upon official regulations; red-tape.

OFFICIALITY, [of-ish′-i-al′-i-ti], *n.* the dignity or position of one holding an office; anything official; officialty.

OFFICIALLY, [of-ish′-a-li], *adv.* in an official way; with authority; formally, ceremoniously.

OFFICIALTY, [of-ish′-al-ti], *n.* officiality.

OFFICIANT, [of-ish′-i-ant], *n.* a priest who conducts a religious service, a celebrant.

OFFICIARY, [of-ish′-i-er-i], *adj.* (of titles) held by virtue of office. [LL. *officiarius*].

OFFICIATE, [of-ish′-i-āt], *v.i.* to perform the duties of an office; (of a priest) to perform a rite, to lead a religious service. [MedL. *officiare*].

OFFICINAL, [of-is′-in-al], *adj.* (of drugs, chemicals, etc.) recognized in the pharmacopoeia; of medical utility; sold by chemists. [MedL. *officinalis* pertaining to a workshop].

OFFICIOUS, [of-ish′-us], *adj.* meddlesome, intruding with unwanted advice; presuming too much upon the authority of office; (*diplomacy*) informal, not official; †obliging. [L. *officiosus* obliging].

OFFICIOUSLY, [of-ish′-us-li], *adv.* in an officious way.

OFFICIOUSNESS, [of-ish′-us-nes], *n.* the quality of being officious; officious conduct.

OFFING, [of′-ing], *n.* (*naut.*) the stretch of sea between the shore and the horizon visible from the shore; **in the o.,** (*naut.*) near shore; (*fig.*) to hand, near, likely to happen, likely to take action. [~OFF (3)].

OFFISH, [of′-ish], *adj.* (*coll.*) aloof and unfriendly in a proud, superior way. [OFF (3)].

OFFISHNESS, [of′-ish-nes], *n.* the state or quality of being offish.

OFF-LICENCE, [of′-lī′-sents], *n.* a kind of licence, permitting the sale of intoxicants for consumption away from the premises; a shop or establishment to which one of these licences has been granted.

OFF-PRINT, [of′-print], *n.* a reprint in a self-contained pamphlet of an article from a periodical.

OFF-RECKONING, [of′-rek′-on-ing], *n.* a deduction from military pay to meet expenses.

OFFSADDLE, [of′-sadl′], *v.t.* to unsaddle a horse in order to feed or rest it.

OFFSCOURING, [of′-skow′-er-ing], *n.* refuse and dirt scoured off; rabble.

OFFSCUM, [of′-skum], *n.* scum; rabble.

OFFSET (1), [of′-set′], *n.* that which grows away, springs, or arises, from something else; that which compensates for something else; (*arch.*) a ledge or shoulder produced when the part of a wall below a certain level is thicker than the part above; (*print.*) the smudge or blurred impression of a wet and newly printed sheet that comes off on to the back of the sheet placed immediately above it; a mode of printing by which the impression is taken from a rubber roller which has in turn taken the impression from an inked plate; (*surveying*) a short line measured at right angles to the principal level in calculation of the area of an irregular figure or shape.

OFFSET (2), (offsetting), [of′-set′], *v.t.* to make an offset in building, printing or surveying; to compensate for.

OFF-SHOOT, [of′-shōōt], *n.* a secondary growth or projection away from the main body, a branch; a collateral descendant.

OFFSHORE, [of′-shaw(r)], *adj.* moving from the land; being at some distance away from the shore and out to sea.

OFFSIDE (1), [of′-sīd′], *n.* a position on the off, an offside position.

OFFSIDE (2), [of′-sīd′], *adj.* (*football, etc.*) being in a particular position at which it is illegal by the rules of the game for a participant to receive and play the ball. [OFF (3) and SIDE (1)].

OFFSPRING, [of′-spring], *n.* children, progeny; (*fig.*) result. [OE. *ofspring*].

OFFWARD, [of′-werd], *adj.* (*naut.*) pointing away from the shore. [OFF (3) and (TO)WARD].

OFT, [oft], *adv.* (*poet.*) often. [OE. *oft*].

OFTEN (1), [of′-en], *adj.* (*archaic*) frequent, many.

OFTEN (2), [of′-en], *adv.* frequently, repeatedly. [ME. *often*].

OFTENNESS, [of′-en-nes], *n.* frequency, repetition; the quality of frequent repetition.

OFTENTIMES, [of′-en-tīmz′], *adv.* (*archaic*) often.

OFTTIMES, [oft′-tīmz′], *adv.* (*archaic*) frequently, oftentimes.

OGAM, see OGHAM (1) and (2).

OGEE, [ō-jē′], *n.* an S-shaped moulding, having a double curve; **o. arch,** (*arch.*) an arch each side of which is shaped like an S. [*Var.* of OGIVE].

OGEE MOULDING

OGHAM (1), OGAM, [og′-am], *n.* the ancient Irish alphabet. [OIr. *ogum*].

OGHAM (2), OGAM, [og′-am], *adj.* pertaining to ogham.

OGIVE, [ō′-jīv], *n.* (*arch.*) a pointed arch, a Gothic arch. [Fr. *ogive*].

OGLE (1), [ōgl], *n.* an amorous glance. [OGLE (2)].

OGLE (2), [ōgl], *v.t. and i.* to cast amorous glances (at). [LGerm. *oegeln*].

OGLER, [ōg′-ler], *n.* one who ogles, or is given to ogling.

OGLING, [ōg′-ling], *n.* the act of making amorous glances.

OGPU, [og′-pōō′], *n.* (*coll.*) the G.P.U., the Soviet Russian secret police, particularly devoted to the suppression of political crime and disaffection in Russia. [*O*bedinennoe *G*osudarstvennoe *P*oliticheskoe *U*pravlenie, State Political Control].

OGRE, [ō′-ger], *n.* an ugly giant or monster in fairy tales and folk-lore; (*fig.*) an ugly or cruel person. [Fr. *ogre*].

OGREISH, [ō′-ger-ish], *adj.* resembling an ogre.

OGRESS, [ō′-gres], *n.* a female monster, a female ogre.

OGYGIAN, [o-jij'-i-an], *adj.* pertaining to Ogyges, a legendary king of Attica; very ancient. [Gk. *Ogugios*].

OH, [ō], *int.* an exclamation of surprise or pain.

OHM, [ōm], *n.* a unit of electrical resistance. [G. S. *Ohm*, a German scientist].

OHMIC, [ōm'-ik], *adj.* pertaining to ohms, measured in ohms.

OHMMETER, [ōm'-mē'-ter], *n.* a device for measuring ohms. [OHM and METER].

OHO, [ō-hō'], *int.* an exclamation of interest or surprise.

OIL (1), [oil], *n.* one of many fatty, inflammable substances, animal, vegetable and mineral, which remain fluid at moderate temperatures and are soluble in alcohol and ether but not in water; a painting done with oil colours; **oils**, oil-colours, oilskins; **Holy O.**, consecrated oil used in Extreme Unction, at the coronation of a king, etc.; **to strike o.**, to find a supply of mineral oil; (*fig.*) to have very good luck; to make a profitable discovery or invention; to get rich quickly; **to pour o. on troubled waters**, to soothe a quarrel by sensible, tactful and sympathetic remarks; **to throw o. on the flames**, to heighten the ill-feeling in a dispute by tactless or partisan speech or action; **to burn the midnight o.**, to read or work far into the night. [OFr. *oile* from L. *oleum* from Gk. *elaion*].

OIL (2), [oil], *v.t.* to lubricate or smear with oil; **to o. someone's palm**, (*coll.*) to bribe someone; **to o. one's tongue**, to talk flatteringly; **to o. the wheels**, to help to produce smooth working and happy arrangements by tactful conduct or speech.

OIL-BAG, [oil'-bag'], *n.* (*zool.*) the gland in animals which contains oil.

OIL-BEETLE, [oil'-bētl], *n.* one of the several species of beetles which emit an oil-like substance when alarmed or attacked.

OILBIRD, [oil'-burd], *n.* the guacharo, a South American bird yielding an oily fat.

OIL-BOMB, [oil'-bom'], *n.* an incendiary bomb containing inflammable oil.

OIL-BOX, [oil'-boks'], *n.* a small box-like receptacle attached to the hub of a wheel and containing a supply of lubricating oil.

OILCAKE, [oil'-kāk'], *n.* cattle fodder made by crushing oil-seeds.

OIL-CAN, [oil'-kan'], *n.* a metal can or container for holding oil, usually equipped with a slender funnel so that the oil can be easily poured out to lubricate machinery.

OILCLOTH, [oil'-kloth'], *n.* a covering for a table or a floor made of stout canvas coated with oil-paint; linoleum; American cloth.

OIL-COLOUR, [oil'-kul'-er], *n.* a paint in which the pigments are mixed in oil.

OILED, [oild], *adj.* having been treated with oil, lubricated; smooth-running, smooth-working; silent and efficient; **well o.**, (*slang*) drunk.

OILED-SILK, [oild'-silk'], see OIL-SILK.

OIL-ENGINE, [oil'-en'-jin], *n.* an internal combustion engine using oil for fuel.

OILER, [oil'-er], *n.* an oil-can; a man whose job it is on board ship to keep the ship's engine properly lubricated; a ship engaged in and constructed for carrying oil.

OIL-FIELD, [oil'-fēld], *n.* a tract of country having rich deposits of mineral oil.

OIL-FUEL, [oil'-few'-el], *n.* oil used as fuel to drive an engine.

OIL-GAS, [oil'-gas'], *n.* an inflammable gas produced from oil.

OIL-GAUGE, [oil'-gaj'], *n.* a device for measuring the density of an oil; a device to register the quantity of oil in a container.

OIL-GOLD, [oil'-gōld'], *n.* gold-leaf applied to a surface prepared with linseed oil and a yellow pigment.

OILINESS, [oil'-i-nes], *n.* the condition of being oily; (*fig.*) a servile, obsequious manner.

OIL-MAN, [oil'-man], *n.* a man who sells oil.

OIL-MEAL, [oil'-mēl'], *n.* linseed cake that has been ground.

OIL-MILL, [oil'-mil], *n.* a factory where oil is extracted from oil-bearing seeds, etc.

OIL-NUT, [oil'-nut], *n.* a nut from which oil can be obtained.

OIL-PAINTING, [oil'-pānt'-ing], *n.* the art of making pictures with oil-colours; a picture in oils.

OIL-PALM, [oil'-pahm'], *n.* a species of palm, *Elæis guineensis*, found and cultivated in West Africa, the nuts and fruits of which yield palm-oil.

OIL-PAPER, [oil'-pā'-per], *n.* paper that has been oiled so as to make it semi-transparent and waterproof.

OIL-PRESS, [oil'-pres'], *n.* a press for crushing oil from seeds.

OILSHOP, [oil'-shop'], *n.* a shop where oils may be bought.

OIL-SILK, [oil'-silk'], *n.* silk made waterproof with oil.

OILSKINS, [oil'-skinz], *n.(pl.)* outer garments made waterproof by oil.

OILSTONE, [oil'-stōn], *n.* an oiled whetstone.

OIL-SUMP, [oil'-sump'], *n.* the oil bath in which the crank of an engine moves.

OIL-WELL, [oil'-wel'], *n.* a well containing petroleum.

OILY, [oil'-i], *adj.* greasy, stained or damp with oil; having the consistency of oil; containing oil; (*fig.*) obsequious and flattering.

OINTMENT, [oint'-ment], *n.* a fatty or oily compound for medicinal or cosmetic purposes. [OFr. *oignement*].

OKAPI, [ō-kah'-pi], *n.* a quadruped nearly related to the giraffe and found in West Africa. [Native].

OKAY, [ō-kā'], *int.* (*U.S. slang*) all right, just as you say. [Uncert.].

OKEYDOKE, [ōk'-i-dōk'], *adv. and int.* (*slang*) all right. [OKAY].

OKRA, [ok'-ra, ō'-kra], *n.* an African and American plant, the stem of which provides a fibre suitable for rope-making, and the seeds a vegetable. [African].

OLD (1), [ōld], *n.* the old people as opposed to young people; anything old; old things, habits, times, etc., in general; **of o.**, in times past.

OLD (2), [ōld], *adj.* aged, not young, elderly; of age; worn out with age, exhausted, feeble; belonging to past time, ancient; superseded, old-fashioned, no longer in use; having the wisdom and experience of previous practice, experienced; (*coll.*) dear, familiar, pleasant; **o. woman**, (*coll.*) a fussy, fastidious person, *esp.* a fussy, elderly man; **O. World**, the known world before the discovery of America; **o. masters**, great painters of a previous age, usually the great exponents of Renaissance painting in Italy, Germany, etc.; **o. master**, a work by one of these men, a masterly painting of early date; **o. country**, the homeland or mother country from which colonial settlers have come, *esp.* England; **O. Style calendar**, the Julian calendar, eleven days different from the one at present in general use, given up in England and America in 1752 in favour of the New Style calendar; **O. Testament**, the former of the two great divisions of the Bible, containing Hebrew history, law, philosophy and poetry prior to the coming of Jesus Christ; **O. Nick**, (*coll.*) Satan, the devil; **O. Man of the Mountains**, the leader and founder of the sect of the Assassins; **the O. Man of the Sea**, (from the story of Sindbad in the *Arabian Nights*) (*fig.*) a person or thing from which one cannot get free; **O. Lady of Threadneedle Street**, the Bank of England; **O. Year's Day**, the last day of the year; **O. Age Pension**, a pension granted by Act of Parliament to old persons on account of their age. [OE. *ald*].

OLD-CLOTHESMAN, [ōld'-klōTHz'-man], *n.* one who deals in old clothes.

OLDEN (1), [ōld'-en], *adj.* ancient, old, belonging to the past, antique.

OLDEN (2), [ōld'-en], *v.t. and i.* to render old; to grow old.

OLD-FASHIONED, [ōld'-fash'-und], *adj.* now out of fashion, old, antiquated, not in the latest modern style; (*coll.*) odd.

OLD GLORY, [ōld'-glaw'-ri], *n.* the Stars and Stripes, the U.S. national flag.

OLDISH, [ōld'-ish], *adj.* being a little old.

OLD MAN'S BEARD, [ōld'-manz-bēerd'], *n.* the wild plant, *Clematis Vitalba*, the shaggy fruits of which resemble a white beard.

OLDNESS, [ōld'-nes], *n.* the state of being old.

OLDSTER, [ōld'-ster], *n.* an adult, an elderly person.

OLD-WORLD, [ōld'-wurld'], *adj.* antiquated, quaint, old-fashioned; pertaining to Europe, Africa and Asia.

OLEAGINOUS, [ol'-i-aj'-in-us], *adj.* greasy, unctuous, oily. [L. *oleaginus*].

OLEAGINOUSNESS, [ol'-i-aj'-in-us-nes], *n.* unctuousness, greasiness.

OLEANDER, [ōl'-i-and'-er], *n.* the evergreen rose-bay [Fr. *oléandre*].

OLEASTER, [ō'-li-ast'-er], *n.* (*bot.*) a small tree native to Southern Europe of the genus *Elæagnus*, the shaggy...

OLEATE, [ō'-li-āt], *n.* (*chem.*) a salt of oleic acid.
OLEFIANT, [ō-lē'-fi-ant, o-li-fī'-ant], *adj.* forming or producing oil; **o. gas,** (*chem.*) heavy carburetted hydrogen. [Fr. *oléfiant*].
OLEFINE, [ō-li-fēn], *n.* (*chem.*) any hydrocarbon homologous with ethylene. [OLEF(IANT) and (PARAF-)FIN].
OLEIC, [ō-lē'-ik], *adj.* pertaining to oil; **o. acid,** (*chem.*) a fatty acid. [~L. *oleum* oil].
OLEIFEROUS, [ō'-lē-if'-er-us], *adj.* producing oil. [L. *oleum* oil and *ferre* to bear].
OLEIN, [ō'-lē-in], *n.* the oily liquid in fats. [~L. *oleum*].
OLEO (1), [ō'-li-ō], *n.* an oleograph. [OLEO(GRAPH)].
OLEO- (2), [ō-li-ō], *pref.* pertaining to oil. [L. *oleum* oil].
OLEOGRAPH, [ō'-li-ō-graf], *n.* a lithograph imitating a painting in oils.
OLEOMARGARIN(E), [ō'-li-ō-mah'-ger-ēn'], *n.* a butter-substitute made from animal and vegetable oil and milk.
OLEOMETER, [ō'-li-om'-it-er], *n.* a device for measuring the density of oils.
OLEO-OIL, [ō'-li-ō-oil'], *n.* oil expressed from meat.
OLEOPHOSPHORIC, [ō'-li-ō-fos-for'-ik], *adj.* pertaining to an acidic oil found in the brain.
OLEORESIN, [ō'-li-ō-rez'-in], *n.* a mixture of a volatile oil and a resin.
OLEOSE, [ō'-li-ōs], *adj.* oily.
OLERACEOUS, [ol'-er-ā'-shus], *adj.* pertaining to, or resembling, a pot-herb. [L. *oleraceus*].
OLFACTORY (1), [ol-fakt'-er-i], *n.* (*physiol.*) an organ of smell.
OLFACTORY (2), [ol-fakt'-er-i], *adj.* of, or pertaining to, the sense of smell or the act of smelling. [L. *olefactum*, *p.pt.* of *olefacere* to smell].
OLIBANUM, [ol-ib'-an-um] *n.* frankincense. [MedL. *olibanum*].
OLIFANT, OLIPHANT, [ol'-if-ant], *n.* a horn of ivory. [OFr. *oliphant*].
OLIGAEMIA, [ol'-ig-ē'-mi-a], *n.* (*med.*) an inadequate supply of blood. [OLIGO and Gk. *haima* blood].
OLIGARCH, [ol'-ig-ahk], *n.* a leader or supporter of an oligarchy. [Gk. *oligarkhes*].
OLIGARCHAL, [ol-ig-ahk'-al], *adj.* pertaining to oligarchy.
OLIGARCHY, [ol'-ig-ahk'-i], *n.* government by a few; a state controlled by a few people; a small group of persons conducting the government of a state. [Gk. *oligarhkia*].
OLIGIST, [ol'-ij-ist], *n.* (*min.*) haematite; specular iron. [Gk. *oligistos* least].
OLIGO-, *pref.* few, small. [Gk. *oligos* few, little].
OLIGOCARPOUS, [ol'-ig-ō-kahp'-us], *adj.* (*bot.*) bearing few fruits. [*Prec.* and CARPEL].
OLIGOCENE, [ol'-ig-ō-sēn'], *adj.* (*geol.*) pertaining to the period between the Eocene and Miocene in the Tertiary Era. [OLIGO and Gk. *kainos* recent].
OLIGOCLASE, [ol-ig'-ō-klās], *n.* (*min.*) a triclinic felspar of soda and lime. [OLIGO and Gk. *klasis* fracture].
OLIO, [ō'-li-ō], *n.* a medley or miscellany; a miscellaneous stew. [Span. *olla* stew].
OLIPHANT, see OLIFANT.
OLITORY, [ol'-it-er-i], *adj.* pertaining to a kitchen-garden. [L. *olitorius*].
OLIVACEOUS, [ol'-iv-ā'-shus], *adj.* resembling an olive; olive-coloured, olive-green.
OLIVARY, [ol'-iv-er-i], *adj.* like an olive in shape; oval. [L. *olivarius*].
OLIVE (1), [ol'-iv], *n.* (*bot.*) an evergreen tree of the genus *Olea*, native to the Mediterranean countries; the fruit of the cultivated *Olea europaea*; its wood; its leaves, *esp.* when wreathed into a coronet in token of victory; olive colour; (*cookery*) a dish made of slices of veal or beef rolled and seasoned with onions, olives, etc., and cooked in brown sauce. [L. *oliva*].
OLIVE (2), [ol'-iv], *adj.* having the colour of the fruit of the olive at some stage of its maturing; sallow, pale yellow; olive-green, yellowish-green.
OLIVE-BRANCH, [ol'-iv-brahnch'], *n.* a symbol of peace; a child.
OLIVENITE, [ol'-iv-en-īt], *n.* (*min.*) an arsenate of copper occurring in crystals, so called from its olive-green colour.

OLIVE

OLIVE OIL, [ol'-iv-oil'], *n.* the oil extracted from olives, used for cooking, lubrication, and lighting.
OLIVER (1), [ol'-iv-er], *n.* a small tilt-hammer worked by a treadle. [Uncert.].
OLIVER (2), [ol'-iv-er], *n.* the name of a legendary hero in the Charlemagne stories, used allusively in **to give a Roland for an O.,** to make an equivalent riposte.
OLIVET, [ol'-iv-et], *n.* an imitation pearl, oval in shape. [Fr. *olivette*].
OLIVETANS, [ol'-iv-et'-anz], *n.* a branch of Benedictines founded in Italy in 1313 by St. Bernard Tolomei of Siena. [Mount *Oliveto* Maggiore, where they were founded].
OLIVE-YARD, [ol'-iv-yahd'], *n.* a piece of ground in which olives are grown.
OLIVIL, [ol'-iv-il], *n.* a substance obtained from the gum of the olive tree. [Fr. *olivile*].
OLIVINE, [ol'-iv-ēn], *n.* (*min.*) an olive-green chrysolite.
OLLA, [ol'-a], *n.* a cooking-pot; olio. [Span. *olla*].
OLLA-PODRIDA, [ol'-a-pod-rē'-da], *n.* a Spanish stew of meat and vegetables; a hotchpotch, a miscellany. [Span. *olla podrida*].
OLOGY, [ol'-o-ji], *n.* (*coll.*) a branch of science. [Formed from (BI)OLOGY, (PHIL)OLOGY, etc.].
OLYMPIAD, [ō-limp'-i-ad], *n.* a space of four years, reckoned from one celebration of the Olympic games to the next and used by ancient Greek historians for purposes of chronology, beginning in the year 776 B.C., when the games were first held. [Gk. *olumpias*].
OLYMPIAN (1), [ō-limp'-i-an], *n.* one who lived on Olympus, a Greek god; a stately person, like a Greek god.
OLYMPIAN (2), [ō-limp'-i-an], *adj.* pertaining to Olympus, which, according to Greek mythology, was the mountain on which the gods lived; being fit for a Greek god, magnificent; heavily condescending; Olympic.
OLYMPIC, [ō-limp'-ik], *adj.* pertaining to the plain of Olympia in Greece where, in classical times, the Olympic games were held in honour of Zeus, the chief of the old Greek gods, and revived as an international sport and athletic meeting in modern times. [Gk. *Olumpikos*].
OM, [om], *int.* a sacred word used in Hindu worship. [Skr. *om*].
OMADHAUN, [awm'-ad-awn], *n.* a fool, a simpleton. [Ir. *amadan*].
OMASUM, [ō-mā'-sum], *n.* (*zool.*) the third stomach in a ruminant. [L. *omasum* bullock's tripe].
OMBRE, [om'-ber], *n.* an eighteenth-century card-game for three players. [Span. (*juego*) *del hombre* the man's (game)].
OMBRO-, *pref.* connected with rain. [Gk. *ombros* rain].
OMBROGRAPH, [om'-brō-graf], *n.* a device for automatically recording rainfall.
OMBROLOGY, [om-brol'-o-ji], *n.* the study of rainfall. [OMBRO and Gk. *logos* speech].
OMBROMETER, [om-brom'-it-er], *n.* a rain-gauge.
OMBROPHILE, [om'-brō-fīl], *n.* (*bot.*) a plant that is able to endure continued rain without injury. [OMBRO and Gk. *philos* loving].
OMBROPHOBE, [om'-bro-fōb'], *n.* a plant that is unable to endure continued rain. [OMBRO and Gk. *phobos* fear].
OMEGA, [ō'-meg-a], *n.* the last letter of the Greek alphabet; **alpha and o.,** the beginning and end [Gk. *omega*].
OMELETTE, OMELET, [om'-let], *n.* (*cooking*) a dish of eggs beaten up and fried. [Fr. *omelette*].
OMEN (1), [ō'-men], *n.* a portent of something to happen, either good or bad. [L. *omen*].
OMEN (2), [ō'-men], *v.t.* to portend.
OMENTAL, [ō-ment'-al], *adj.* relating to the omentum.
OMENTUM, (*pl.* **omenta**), [ō-ment'-um], *n.* (*anat.*) a fold in the peritoneum connecting the intestines with the other viscera. [L. *omentum*].
OMER, [ō'-mer], *n.* a Hebrew measure of capacity. [Heb. *omer*].
OMICRON, [ō-mī'-kron], *n.* the short *o* of the Greek alphabet. [Gk. *omikron* small "o"].
OMINOUS, [om'-in-us], *adj.* foreboding evil things; threatening. [L. *ominosus*].
OMINOUSLY, [om'-in-us-li], *adv.* in an ominous fashion.
OMINOUSNESS, [om'-in-us-nes], *n.* the quality of being ominous.
OMISSIBLE, [ō-mis'-ibl], *adj.* capable of being omitted.
OMISSION, [ō-mish'-un], *n.* the act of omitting, the

fact of having been omitted; something omitted. [L. *omissio*].

OMISSIVE, [ō-mis'-iv], *adj.* omitting.

OMIT, (omitting, omitted), [ō-mit'], *v.t.* to leave out; to neglect, fail, to do. [L. *omittere*].

OMNI-, *pref.* all. [L. *omnis* all].

OMNIBUS (1), (*pl.* **omnibuses**), [om'-ni-bus], *n.* a public vehicle for conveying passengers along a particular route or part of it, a bus. [L. *omnibus*, *dat. pl.* of *omnis* all].

OMNIBUS (2), [om'-ni-bus], *adj.* miscellaneous, including a variety of things, including everything; **o. book, o. volume**, a one-volumed miscellany containing all sorts of literary specimens; a single volume containing all the works of an author. [*Prec.*].

OMNICOMPETENT, [om'-ni-kom'-pit-ent], *adj.* (*leg.*) having jurisdiction in everything.

OMNIFARIOUS, [om'-ni-fāer'-i-us], *adj.* of all sorts and varieties. [L. *omnifarius*].

OMNIFEROUS, [om-nif'-er-us], *adj.* producing all kinds of things. [OMNI and L. *ferre* to bear].

OMNIFIC, [om-nif'-ik], *adj.* creating all things. [OMNI and L. *facere* to make].

OMNIFORM, [om'-ni-fawm], *adj.* having all forms.

OMNIFORMITY, [om'-ni-fawm'-i-ti], *n.* the quality of having every form.

OMNIGENOUS, [om-nij'-in-us], *adj.* being of all sorts and kinds. [OMNI and L. *genus* family].

OMNIPARITY, [om'-ni-pa'-rit-i], *n.* general parity; equality in everything.

OMNIPAROUS, [om-nip'-er-us], *adj.* producing all sorts of things, bearing everything. [OMNI and L. *parere* to bear].

OMNIPATIENT, [om'-ni-pā'-shent], *adj.* all-enduring, long-suffering.

OMNIPERCIPIENCE, [om'-ni-per-sip'-i-ents], *n.* perception of all things, all-embracing percipience.

OMNIPERCIPIENT, [om'-ni-per-sip'-i-ent], *adj* perceiving all things.

OMNIPOTENCE, [om-nip'-ot-ents], *n.* all-powerfulness, unfettered, unlimited power. [OMNI and L. *potens* powerful].

OMNIPOTENT (1), [om-nip'-ot-ent], *n.* the Almighty, God.

OMNIPOTENT (2), [om-nip'-ot-ent], *adj.* almighty all-powerful.

OMNIPOTENTLY, [om-nip'-ot-ent-li], *adv.* with unlimited power, in an omnipotent way.

OMNIPRESENCE, [om'-ni-prez'-ents], *n.* presence at every moment in every place.

OMNIPRESENT, [om'-ni-prez'-ent], *adj.* having the quality of omnipresence.

OMNIPRESENTIAL, [om'-ni-priz-en'-shal], *adj.* pertaining to universal presence.

OMNISCIENCE, [om-nis'-i-ents], *n.* unlimited knowledge, knowledge of everything.

OMNISCIENT, [om-nis'-i-ent], *adj.* all-knowing possessing the quality of omniscience. [OMNI and L. *sciens* knowing].

OMNISCIENTLY, [om-nis'-i-ent-li], *adv.* in an omniscient fashion.

OMNIUM, [om'-ni-um], *n.* the sum, the sum total. [L. *omnium*, *gen. pl.* of *omnis* all].

OMNIUM-GATHERUM, [om'-ni-um-gaTH'-er-um], *n.* a very mixed collection. [*Prec.* and a jocular Latinization of GATHERING].

OMNIVOROUS, [om-niv'-er-us], *adj.* able and willing to eat anything; eating both vegetable and animal matter; (*fig.*) eager, all-consuming. [L. *omnivorus*].

OMNIVOROUSLY, [om-niv'-er-us-li], *adv.* in an omnivorous way.

OMOPHAGIA, [ō'-mō-fā'-ji-a], *n.* the habit of feeding on raw flesh. [Gk. *omos* raw and *phago* I eat].

OMOPHAGOUS, [ō-mof'-ag-us], *adj.* feeding on uncooked flesh. [*Prec.*].

OMOPLATE, [ō'-mō-plāt], *n.* (*anat.*) the shoulder-blade. [Gk. *omoplate*].

OMPHACITE, [om'-fas-īt], *n.* (*min.*) a green mineral. [Germ. *omphazit*].

OMPHALIC, [om-fal'-ik], *adj.* pertaining to the navel. [Gk. *omphalos* navel].

OMPHALOCELE, [om-fal'-ō-sēl], *n.* (*med.*) a rupture at or near the navel. [Gk. *omphalos* navel and *kele* tumour].

OMPHALOTOMY, [om'-fal-ot'-o-mi], *n.* an operation severing the navel string. [Gk. *omphalos* the navel and *tomia* cutting].

ON (1), [on], *n.* (*cricket*) the on side. [ON (2)].

ON (2), [on], *adj.* (*cricket*) **the o. side**, that part of the field which is to the left of the batsman as he faces the bowling. [ON (4)].

ON (3), [on], *adv.* not off, so as to rest upon or be in place; onwards, straight ahead, forward, in the same direction as before; without stoppage or interruption, continually; at present in action or in being; **o. and o.**, uninterruptedly; **o. and off**, now and then, from time to time; **to be o.**, to be a member of (a committee, board, etc.). [ON (4)].

ON (4), [on], (*prep.*) upon, above, resting upon, covering, supported by; expressing place where, motion towards; expressing connexion with; concerning, dealing with, about; expressing state or manner; expressing time when. [OE. *on*].

ONAGER, (*pl.* **onagri** or **onagers**), [on'-ag-er], *n.* (*zool.*) the Persian wild ass. [L. *onager*].

ONANISM, [ō'-nan-izm], *n.* self-abuse, masturbation. [*Onan*, a man named in Genesis xxxviii, 9].

ONANIST, [ōn'-an-ist], *n.* one who practises onanism.

ONCE (1), [wunts], *n.* one occasion.

ONCE (2), [wunts], *adv.* on one single occasion; in previous times, formerly; **o. upon a time**, in days gone by; **o. for all**, on one occasion and never again, for the last time, finally; **not o.**, never; **o. in a way**, sometimes but rarely; **all at o.**, suddenly, unexpectedly; **at o.**, forthwith, immediately; **the o. over**, (*slang*) a rapid preliminary inspection or inquiry. [OE. *anes*].

ONCE (3), [wunts], *conj.* as soon as.

ONCOMETER, [on-kom'-it-er], *n.* a device for measuring variations in bulk. [Gk. *ogkos* mass and METER].

ONCOMING (1), [on'-kum'-ing], *n.* approach, drawing near.

ONCOMING (2), [on'-kum-ing], *adj.* approaching, coming on.

ONCOST, [on'-kost], *n.* a miner's bonus.

ON DIT, [aw(ng)'-dē'], *n.* a rumour. [Fr. *on dit* they say].

ONDY, see UNDEE.

ONE (1), [wun], *n.* the first integer; the symbol representing the first integer; a particular, a certain; **o. and all**, everyone; **to be at o.**, to be united, agreed.

ONE (2), [wun], *adj.* single, alone; pertaining to the number representing unity; first; being whole and undivided; having the quality of unity; used to denote something which is contrasted with something else (denoted by *other*); a certain. [OE. *an*].

ONE (3), [wun], *indef. pron* a certain thing or person; anyone; people generally; referring to the speaker.

ONE-EYED, [wun'-īd], *adj.* having one eye only; (*coll.*) poor, inferior, insignificant.

ONEFOLD, [wun'-fōld], *adj* single, not complex, simple.

ONE-HORSE, [wun'-haws], *adj.* drawn by, or constructed to be drawn by, one horse; (*coll.*) poor in quality, inferior.

ONE-IDEA'D, [wun'-ī-dē'-ad], *adj.* possessed by a single idea or purpose.

ONEIRO-, *pref.* dream, pertaining to dreams. [Gk. *oneiros* a dream].

ONEIROCRITIC, [on-īer'-ō-krit'-ik], *n.* one who interprets dreams.

ONEIROCRITICAL, [on-īer'-ō-krit'-ik-al], *adj.* professing to interpret dreams; pertaining to the interpretation of dreams].

ONEIROCRITICS, [on-īer'-ō-krit'-iks], *n.* the art of the interpretation of dreams.

ONEIRODYNIA, [on-īer'-ō-din'-i-a], *n.* mental disturbance producing nightmares, somnambulism, etc. [ONEIRO and Gk. *odune* pain].

ONEIROLOGY, [on-īer-ol'-o-ji], *n.* a treatise on dreams, the study of dreams. [ONEIRO and Gk. *logos* speech].

ONEIROMANCY, [on-īer'-ō-man'-si], *n.* prophecy by dreams and their interpretation. [ONEIRO and Gk. *manteia* divination].

ONEIROMANTIC, [on-īer'-ō-mant'-ik], *adj.* pertaining to oneiromancy.

ONENESS, [wun'-nes], *n.* unity; the condition of being at one and united.

ONER, [wun'-er], *n.* (*slang*) a remarkable person, event or object; a mighty blow; a bold, extravagant lie.

ONERARY, [ōn'-er-re-ri], *adj.* adapted to carry loads; making up a load. [L. *onerarius*].

ONEROUS, [on'-er-us], *adj.* heavy, burdensome; oppressive. [L. *onerosus*].

ONEROUSLY, [on'-er-us-li], *adv.* heavily.

ONESELF, [wun-self′], *reflex. form of indef. pron.* one, the person and ego of an individual.
ONE-SIDED, [wun′-sīd′-id], *adj.* arguing in favour of one side only; (of a game) superior to the other team or side; unbalanced, unequal.
ONE-SIDEDLY, [wun′-sīd′-id-li], *adv.* in a one-sided fashion, unfairly, unequally.
ONE-SIDEDNESS, [wun′-sīd′-id-nes], *n.* the condition of being one-sided.
ONE-TRACK, [wun′-trak′], *adj.* running along only one track; (*fig.*) unimaginative, very restricted in outlook.
ONE-WAY, [wun′-wā], *adj.* (of a street) through which traffic may pass in one direction only.
ONFALL, [on′-fawl], *n.* onset, attack.
ONFLOW, [on′-flō], *n.* a continuous flowing on, a steady stream.
ONGOINGS, [on′-gō-ingz], *n.(pl.)* events, proceedings, actions, actions of an excited or unusual nature; wild behaviour, goings-on.
ONION (1), [un′-yun], *n* (*bot.*) the plant or herb, *Allium Cepa*; its edible bulb, used as a vegetable and to provide flavouring for various savoury dishes; **o. fly**, the insect *Anthomyia ceparum*, whose larvae feed upon onions and destroy them; **flaming o.**, a form of rocket used against hostile aeroplanes; **o. skin**, the outer skin of an onion bulb; **to be off one's o.**, (*slang*) to be slightly mad, off one's head. [Fr. *oignon*].
ONION (2), [un′-yun], *v.t.* to flavour with onions.
ONIONY, [un′-yun-i], *adj.* tasting or smelling like an onion.
ONISCIFORM, [on-is′-i-fawm], *adj.* shaped like a woodlouse. [Gk. *oniskos* woodlouse and FORM].
ONISCOID, [on-is′-koid], *adj.* pertaining to woodlice. [Gk. *oniskos* a woodlouse and *oeides* like].
ONLINESS, [ōn′-li-nes], *n.* uniqueness; †solitude, the condition of being alone.
ONLOOKER, [on′-lo͝ok-er], *n.* a spectator, one who looks on but does not join in.
ONLY (1), [ōn′-li], *adj.* single, being the sole example of its kind; being of a certain, distinct category; outstanding in its kind. [OE. *anlic*].
ONLY (2), [ōn′-li], *adv.* merely, exclusively; under such conditions that nothing else is possible; **o. just**, with no time to spare; a moment ago; **o. too**, very; **if o.**, oh, that only! (expressing a strong desire).
ONLY (3), [ōn′-li], *conj.* except that.
ONOCENTAUR, [on′-ō-sent′-aw(r)], *n.* a fabulous animal, having the body of an ass and the breast, head and arms of a man. [Gk. *onokentauros*].
ONOFRITE, [on′-ō-frīt], *n.* (*min.*) a sulpho-selenide of mercury. [San *Onofre*, in Mexico, where found].
ONOMA-, *pref.* name, names, pertaining to names. [Gk. *onoma* name].
ONOMANCY, [on′-ō-man-si], *n.* the art of divination by the letters of a name. [ONOMA and Gk. *manteia* divination].
ONOMASTIC, [on′-ō-mast′-ik], *adj.* pertaining to a name or names. [Gk. *onomastikos*].
ONOMASTICON, [on′-ō-mast′-ik-on], *n.* a book of names. [Gk. *onomastikon*].
ONOMATOLOGIST, [on′-ō-mat-ol′-oj-ist], *n.* a student of names.
ONOMATOLOGY, [on′-ō-mat-ol′-o-ji], *n.* the study of names, their form, origin, provenance, etc. [ONOMA and Gk. *logos* word].
ONOMATOPE, [on′-ō-ma-tōp′], *n.* a word that both signifies and imitates a sound. [ONOMATOPOEIA].
ONOMATOPOEIA, [on′-om-at′-ō-pē′-a], *n.* the figure of speech by which a word is formed or used to suggest the sound it signifies or a sound associated with its meaning or context. [Gk. *onomatopoiia*].
ONOMATOPOEIC, [on′-om-at′-ō-pē′-ik], *adj.* relating to or displaying onomatopoeia; imitative, echoic. [*Prec.*].
ONOMATOPOETIC, [on′-om-at′-ō-pō-et′-ik], *adj.* formed by or exemplifying onomatopoeia.
ONOMATOPOETICAL, [on′-om-at′-ō-pō-et′-ik-al], *adj.* onomatopoetic.
ONRUSH, [on′-rush], *n.* an onset, an attack; a rapid, rushing approach or advance.
ONSET, [on′-set], *n.* a violent attack, assault, charge.
ONSETTING (1), [on′-set-ing], *n.* vigorous assault, attack.
ONSETTING (2), [on′-set-ing], *adj.* rapidly approaching or advancing; attacking, charging.
ONSLAUGHT, [on′-slawt], *n.* a furious assault, an attack, a charge. [OE. *on* on and *slaeht* blow].
ONTO-, *pref.* being. [Gk. *ontos*].
ONTOGENESIS, [on′-tō-jen′-is-is], *n.* the origin and growth of an individual organism.
ONTOGENETIC, [on′-tō-jen-et′-ik], *adj.* pertaining to ontogenesis.
ONTOGENETICALLY, [on′-tō-jen-et′-ik-al-i], *adv.* by ontogenesis.
ONTOGENY, [on-toj′-en-i], *n.* ontogenesis. [ONTO and Gk. *genes* born of].
ONTOLOGICAL, [on′-tol-oj′-ik-al], *adj.* pertaining to ontology.
ONTOLOGICALLY, [on′-tol-oj′-ik-a-li], *adv.* by ontology.
ONTOLOGISM, [on-tol′-oj-izm], *n.* a mystical or metaphysical system founded on an abstract view of the nature of being.
ONTOLOGY, [on-tol′-o-ji], *n.* (*philos.*) metaphysical contemplation of the nature of being. [ONTO and Gk. *logos* word].
ONUS, [ō′-nus], *n.* a burden, responsibility; **o. probandi**, (*leg.*) the responsibility of producing proof of what has been asserted. [L. *onus* burden].
ONWARD (1), [on′-werd], *adj.* advancing, going straight ahead in the direction already pursued; moving towards the goal. [ON (4) and OE. *weard*].
ONWARD (2), [on′-werd], *adv.* to the front, in front, forwards.
ONWARD (3), [on′-werd], *int.* advance!
ONWARDS, [on′-werdz], *adv. and int.* onward.
ONYCHIA, [ō-nik′-i-a], *n.* (*med.*) inflammation at the base of the toe- or finger-nail. [Gk. *onux onukhos* nail].
ONYCHITIS, [ō′-nik-ī′-tis], *n.* onychia. [*Prec.* and Gk. *itis* denoting inflammation].
ONYCHOMANCY, [ō-nik′-ō-man -si], *n.* divination by finger-nails. [Gk. *onux* and *manteia* divination].
ONYX, [on′-iks, ō′-niks], *n.* a precious stone, a variety of agate. [L. *onux* nail, claw].
OO-, *pref.* egg. [Gk. *oion* egg].
OODLES, [o͞odlz], *n.(pl.)* (*slang*) an abundance, a superabundance. [Uncert.].
OOECIUM, [ō-ē′-si-um], *n.* (*zool.*) a sac which holds the eggs in some polyzoa. [OO and Gk. *oikion* little house].
OOF, [o͞of], *n.* (*slang*) money. [Yiddish *ooftisch* from Germ. *auf dem Tisch* on the table, money down].
OOF-BIRD, [o͞of′-burd], *n.* (*slang*) a rich man.
OOFY, [o͞of′-i], *adj.* (*slang*) rich.
OOGAMOUS, [ō-og′-am-us], *adj.* (*biol.*) heterogamous. [OO and Gk. *gamos* marriage].
OOGENESIS, [ō′-ō-jen′-is-is], *n.* the formation of the ovum before fertilization. [OO and GENESIS].
OOIDAL, [ō-oid′-al], *adj.* of an egg; oval, egg-shaped. [Gk. *ooeides* egg-shaped].
OOLITE, [ō′-ol-īt], *n.* a variety of limestone in small granules like the roe of a fish, roe-stone; (*geol.*) a series of rocks of this kind. [OO and Gk. *lithos* a stone].
OOLITIC, [ō′-ol-it′-ik], *adj.* composed of oolite; (*geol.*) belonging to the oolite formation.
OOLOGICAL, [ō′-ol-oj′-ik-al], *adj.* connected with oology.
OOLOGIST, [ō-ol′-oj-ist], *n.* a collector and student of birds' eggs.
OOLOGY, [ō-ol′-o-ji], *n.* the study of birds' eggs. [OO and Gk. *logos* speech].
OOLONG, OULONG, [o͞o′-long′], *n.* a sort of China tea. [Chin. *wu-lung* black dragon].
OOM, [o͞om], *n.* uncle. [Afrik. *oom*].
OOMIAK, [o͞o′-mi-ak′], *n.* a large Eskimo boat. [Eskimo *oomiak*].
OONT, [o͞ont], *n.* a camel. [Anglo-Indian slang].
OOPAK, [o͞o′-pak], *n.* a sort of black tea. [Chin. *upak*].
OORIAL, see URIAL.
OOSPERM, [ō′-o-sperm′], *n.* (*zool.*) a fertilized ovum. [OO and SPERM].
OOSPHERE, [ō′-os-fēer′], *n.* (*zool.*) an ovum before fertilization.
OOSPORE, [ō′-os-paw(r)′], *n.* (*nat. hist.*) an oosperm.
OOZE (1), [o͞oz], *n.* soft, slimy mud; sediment; liquor employed to tan leather. [OE. *wose*].
OOZE (2), [o͞oz], *v.t. and i.* to trickle slowly forth; to drip; to percolate through; (*fig.*) to diminish, to fade away; to exude, give off; **o. with**, to exude. [*Prec.*].
OOZILY, [o͞oz′-i-li], *adv.* in a sticky, slimy, oozy fashion.
OOZINESS, [o͞oz′-i-nes], *n.* the condition of being oozy.
OOZINGS, [o͞oz′-ingz], *n.(pl.)* that which has oozed out.
OOZY, [o͞oz′-i], *adj.* slimy and muddy.

OPACITY, [ō-pas'-i-ti], *n.* the quality of being opaque; darkness; obscurity of meaning; dulness of intellect. [L. *opacitas*].

OPAH, [ō'-pah], *n.* a brilliantly coloured sea-fish found in the Atlantic, the sun-fish. [W. African *opa*].

OPAL, [ō'-pal], *n.* a precious stone, hydrate of silica, which flashes with rich colours as light plays upon it; opaline. [L. *opalus*].

OPALESCE, [ō'-pal-es'], *v.i.* to gleam with colours like an opal.

OPALESCENCE, [ō'-pal-es'-ents], *n.* the quality of gleaming with many colours like an opal.

OPAH

OPALESCENT, [ō'-pal-es'-ent], *adj.* having the quality of opalescence; iridescent.

OPAL-GLASS, [ō'-pal-glahs'], *n.* opaline.

OPALINE (1), [ō'-pal-in], *n.* a semi-transparent, pearly glass.

OPALINE (2), [ō'-pal-īn], *adj.* resembling an opal.

OPALIZE, [ō'-pal-īz], *v.t.* to render opalescent.

OPAQUE, [ō-pāk'], *adj.* not transmitting light; dark and obscure. [L. *opacus* shady].

OPAQUENESS, [ō-pāk'-nes], *n.* the quality of being opaque.

OPE (1), [ōp], *adj.* (*poet.*) open.

OPE (2), [ōp], *v.t. and i.* (*poet.*) to open.

OPEN (1), [ō'-pen], *n.* the open air, the countryside; **to come into the o.,** (*fig.*) to be frank.

OPEN (2), [ō'-pen], *adj.* not closed or shut, but allowing free passage; not fenced in or hedged about, not enclosed by anything; not barred either legally, morally, or physically; free from restrictions; available for all; accessible; not covered over; (of sores, wounds, etc.) not healed; unfolded, expanded; not defended; (of country) free from trees, bushes and other obstructions; generous; frank; broad-minded, not opinionated; (of an offer) neither accepted nor withdrawn; (of a problem) still to be decided; not disguised, public, well known; (of a business agreement, account at the bank, etc.) still in being; (of a shop) ready for customers; **o. secret,** a so-called secret widely known; **o. order,** (*milit.*) extended formation; **o. syllable,** a syllable ending in a vowel; **o. consonant,** a consonant in the sounding of which the breath passage is never completely blocked; **o. shop,** a business concern employing non-union workers as well as those who belong to a union; **to keep o. house,** to be ever ready to receive and entertain guests; **with o. hand,** generously; **o. mind,** an unprejudiced point of view; **O. Brethren,** a section of the Plymouth Brethren less exclusive than the main body. [OE. *open*].

OPEN (3), [ō'-pen], *v.t.* to unfasten; to fling back (doors, windows, etc.); to remove bars and restrictions from; to render exit and entrance possible; to declare formally open; to unfold, uncover; to start, imitate; *v.i.* to expand, to be opened, to unfold; to commence or recommence; to become visible, to enter on the visible scene; **to o. up,** to explore; to expand, become opened; **to o. out,** to stretch out, to unfold, to drive a car fast; **to o. on to,** to lead into, have a passage-way or door into, give access to. [OE. *openian*].

OPENABLE, [ō'-pen-abl], *adj.* capable of being opened.

OPEN-AIR, [ō'-pen-āer'], *adj.* occurring out of doors; outdoor; habitually delighting in out-of-door activities.

OPEN-ARMED, [ō'-pen-ahmd'], *adj.* cordial, glad, welcoming.

OPEN-EARED, [ō'-pen-ēerd'], *adj.* attentive, eager to hear whatever may be heard.

OPENER, [ō'-pen-er], *n.* someone or something that opens; an implement to open bottles or tins.

OPEN-EYED, [ō'-pen-īd'], *adj.* alert, vigilant; having wide eyes as with amazement, etc.

OPEN-HANDED, [ō'-pen-hand'-id], *adj.* generous.

OPEN-HANDEDLY, [ō'-pen-hand'-id-li], *adv.* in a cordial, generous way.

OPEN-HANDEDNESS, [ō'-pen-hand'-id-nes], *n.* generosity.

OPEN-HEARTED, [ō'-pen-haht'-id], *adj.* frank, magnanimous.

OPEN-HEARTEDLY, [ō'-pen-haht'-id-li], *adv.* in an open-hearted way, frankly.

OPEN-HEARTEDNESS, [ō'-pen-haht'-id-nes], *n.* frankness, magnanimity.

OPEN HEARTH, [ōp'-en-hahth'], *n.* used to denote a process for smelting iron in a kind of reverberatory furnace.

OPENING (1), [ō'-pen-ing], *n.* a gap, hole, breach, aperture; beginning; an opportunity, a vacancy, a chance to set out on a successful career.

OPENING (2), [ō'-pen-ing], *adj.* the first in order; initiatory.

OPENING TIME, [ō'-pen-ing-tīm], *n.* the times when licensed houses open for the sale of alcoholic liquor.

OPENLY, [ō'-pen-li], *adv.* in an open manner, frankly, publicly, without dissimulation.

OPEN-MINDED, [ō'-pen-mīnd'-id], *adj.* being unprejudiced.

OPEN-MINDEDLY, [ō'-pen-mīnd'-id-li], *adv.* in an open-minded fashion.

OPEN-MINDEDNESS, [ō'-pen-mīnd'-id-nes], *n.* the quality of being open-minded.

OPEN-MOUTHED, [ō'-pen-mowTHd'], *adj. and adv.* greedy, greedily; agape with surprise or amazement.

OPENNESS, [ō'-pen-nes], *n.* the condition of being open, unsheltered, undefended; frankness.

OPEN-WORK (1), [ō'-pen-wurk'], *n.* a kind of embroidery in which the material being embroidered is cut and pierced with holes; any tracery or lace-like pattern in wood, stone, or metal.

OPEN-WORK (2), [ō'-pen-wurk], *adj.* characterized or adorned with open-work.

OPEN-WORKED, [ō'-pen-wurkt], *adj.* adorned with open-work.

OPERA, [op'-er-a], *n.* a play set to music in which the main part or all of the words are sung to an orchestral accompaniment; **grand o.,** opera where everything is sung and the story is usually tragic. [Ital. *opera*].

OPERA-BOUFFE, [op'-er-a-bōōf'], *n.* an opera with a farcical plot. [Fr. *opéra-bouffe*].

OPERA-CLOAK, [op'-er-a-klōk'], *n.* a cloak for formal evening wear.

OPERA-DANCER, [op'-er-a-dahns-'er], *n.* a dancer in the ballet of an opera.

OPERA-GLASSES, [op'-er-a-glahs'-iz], *n.*(*pl.*) binocular glasses convenient for use in the threatre.

OPERA-HAT, [op'-er-a-hat'], *n.* a tall, black, collapsible hat for men's evening wear, a gibus.

OPERA-HOUSE, [op'-er-a-hows'], *n.* a theatre where operas are performed.

OPERANT (1), [op'-er-ant], *n.* an operator.

OPERANT (2), [op'-er-ant], *adj.* potent, effective, able to do something. [L. *operans*].

OPERA-SINGER, [op'-er-a-sing'-er], *n.* an actor o. actress who sings a part in an opera.

OPERATE, [op'-er-āt], *v.t. and i.* to perform a certain function or task; to work, manipulate; to have a certain effect. [L. *operari* to work].

OPERATIC, [op'-er-at'-ik], *adj.* pertaining to opera.

OPERATICALLY, [op'-er-at'-ik-a-li], *adv.* in an operatic manner; as in opera.

OPERATING, [op'-er-āt'-ing], *adj.* connected with, used for, performing, an operation.

OPERATION, [op'-er-ā'-shun], *n.* the act of operating; work, task; manipulation; a surgical act; the mode of working; (*milit.*) a series of manoeuvres. [L. *operatio*].

OPERATIVE (1), [op'-er-at-iv], *n.* one who works, a factory worker.

OPERATIVE (2), [op'-er-at-iv], *adj.* working, effective, capable of producing a certain effect; (*leg.*) valid. [L. *operativus*].

OPERATIVELY, [op'-er-at-iv-li], *adv.* effectively.

OPERATIZE, [op'-er-at-īz], *v.t.* to convert (a play, story, etc.) into an opera.

OPERATOR, [op'-er-āt'-or], *n.* one who, or that which, operates a machine; *esp.* one who operates a wireless transmitting set.

OPERCULAR, [op-er'-kyŏŏ-ler], *adj.* (*zool.*) opercu-late; pertaining to the operculum.

OPERCULATE, [op-er'-kyŏŏ-lāt], *adj.* having an operculum.

OPERCULATED, [op-er'-kyŏŏ-lāt'-id], *adj.* opercu-late.

OPERCULIFORM, [op'-ur'-kyŏŏ-li-fawm], *adj.* shaped like a lid or cover. [OPERCULUM and FORM].

OPERCULUM, [op-er'-kyŏŏ-lum], *n.* (*zool.*) the gill-cover of fishes; the lid-like organ that closes down over the opening of the shell of certain varieties of molluscs when they retreat into their shell; (*bot.*) the lid-like structure that closes the fruits of certain plants. [L. *operculum* lid].

OPERETTA, [op'-er-et'-a], *n.* a short light musical play. [It. *operetta*].

OPEROSE, [op′-er-ōs], *adj.* laborious; requiring much labour; very busy and hard-worked. [L. *operosus*].

OPEROSELY, [op′-er-ōs-li], *adv.* laboriously; in a hard-working, operose fashion.

OPEROSENESS, [op′-er-ōs-nes], *n.* the condition of being operose.

OPHICLEIDE, [of′-ik-līd], *n.* a powerful-toned wind instrument, developed from the obsolete serpent. [Gk. *ophis* a serpent and *kleis kleidos* key].

OPHIDIA, [of-id′-i-a], *n.(pl.)* (*zool.*) a group of reptiles, including snakes. [~Gk. *ophis* snake].

OPHIDIAN (1), [of-id′-i-an], *n.* one of the ophidia.

OPHIDIAN (2), [of-id′-i-an], *adj.* belonging or pertaining to the ophidia.

OPHIO-, *pref.* of snakes. [Gk. *ophis*].

OPHIOLATER, [of′-i-ol′-at-er], *n.* a snake worshipper.

OPHIOLATRY, [of′-i-ol′-at-ri], *n.* the worship of serpents. [OPHIO and Gk. *latreia* worship].

OPHIOLITE, [of′-i-ō-līt], *n.* a mineral mixture containing serpentine. [OPHIO and Gk. *lithos* a stone].

OPHIOLOGIC, [of′-i-ō-loj′-ik], *adj.* ophiological.

OPHIOLOGICAL, [of′-i-ō-loj′-ik-al], *adj.* pertaining to ophiology.

OPHIOLOGIST, [of′-i-ol′-oj-ist], *n.* a student of ophiology.

OPHIOLOGY, [of′-i-ol′-o-ji], *n.* the study of snakes. [OPHIO and Gk. *logos* speech].

OPHIOMANCY, [of′-i-ō-man′-si], *n.* divination from snakes. [OPHIO and Gk. *manteia* divination].

OPHIOMORPHOUS, [of′-i-ō-mawf′-us], *adj.* shaped like a snake. [OPHIO and Gk. *morphe* shape].

OPHIOPHAGOUS, [of′-i-of′-ag-us], *adj.* snake-eating. [Gk. *ophiophagos*].

OPHIOPHAGUS, [of′-i-of′-ag-us], *n.* a very venomous sort of snake found in the East Indies. [*Prec.*].

OPHIOSAUR, [of′-i-ō-saw(r)′], *n.* a glass-snake. [OPHIO and Gk. *sauros* lizard].

OPHITE (1), [of′-īt], *n.* (*min.*) a stone resembling serpentine. [Gk. *ophites* resembling a snake].

OPHITE (2), [of′-īt], *n.* a member of the sect of ophites or serpent worshippers, that flourished in the second century. [~OPHIO].

OPHIUCHUS, [of′-i-ōō′-kus], *n.* an ancient constellation supposed to look like a man holding a serpent. [Gk. *ophioukhos* having a snake].

OPHTHALMIA, [of-thal′-mi-a], *n.* inflammation of the eye. [Gk. *ophthalmia*].

OPHTHALMIC, [of-thal′-mik], *adj.* of, or concerning, the eyes. [Gk. *opthalmikos*].

OPHTHALMIOUS, [of-thal′-mi-us], *adj.* suffering from ophthalmia.

OPHTHALMITIS, [of′-thal-mī′-tis], *n.* ophthalmia. [OPHTHALMIA and Gk. *itis* denoting inflammation].

OPHTHALMOLOGIST, [of′-thal-mol′-oj-ist], *n.* one versed in ophthalmology.

OPHTHALMOLOGY, [of′-thal-mol′-o-ji], *n.* the scientific study of the eye. [Gk. *ophthalmos* eye and *logos* speech].

OPHTHALMOPLEGIA, [of-thal′-mō-plē′-ji-a], *n.* (*path.*) paralysis of a muscle or muscles of the eye. [Gk. *ophthalmos* eye and *plege* stroke].

OPHTHALMOSCOPE, [of-thal′-mō-skōp], *n.* an instrument having lenses for examining the interior of the eye. [Gk. *ophthalmos* eye and SCOPE].

OPHTHALMOSCOPIST, [of-thal′-mō-skōp′-ist], *n.* one skilled in the use of the ophthalmoscope.

OPHTHALMOSCOPY, [of′-thal-mos′-kop-i], *n.* the examination of the eye with an ophthalmoscope; skill in using an ophthalmoscope.

OPHTHALMOTOMY, [of′-thal-mot′-o-mi], *n.* an incision of the eye. [Gk. *ophthalmos* eye and *tome* cutting].

OPIATE (1), [ō′-pi-āt], *n.* a medicinal compound containing opium; a soporific or narcotic; (*fig.*) something that causes drowsiness.

OPIATE (2), [ō′-pi-āt], *adj.* containing opium; soporific. [MedL. *opiatus*].

OPIATE (3), [ō′-pi-āt], *v.t.* to mix with opium; to give an opium draught to; (*fig.*) to make drowsy, send to sleep.

OPIATED, [ō′-pi-āt′-id], *adj.* impregnated or drugged with opium.

OPIATIC, [ō′-pi-at′-ik], *adj.* pertaining to opiates.

OPINABLE, [ō-pīn′-abl], *adj.* tenable as an opinion. [L. *opinabilis*].

OPINANT, [ōp′-in-ant], *n.* one who holds an opinion.

OPINE, [ō-pīn′], *v.i.* to think; to be of opinion, to hold an opinion. [L. *opinari*].

OPINER, [ō-pīn′-er], *n.* one who holds an opinion.

OPINIATIVE, [op-in′-yat-iv], *adj.* opinionated.

OPINIATIVENESS, [op-in′-yat-iv-nes], *n.* undue obstinacy of opinion.

OPINING, [ō-pīn′-ing], *n.* an opinion expressed.

OPINION, [op-in′-yun], *n.* what one thinks or believes to be true in circumstances where definite knowledge is impossible; a point of view; judgment, estimation. [L. *opinio*].

OPINIONATED, [op-in′-yun-āt′-id], *adj.* unduly obstinate in one's opinions.

OPINIONATELY, [op-in′-yun-at-li], *adv.* in an opinionated manner.

OPINIONATIVE, [op-in′-yun-at-iv], *adj.* opinionated.

OPINIONATIVENESS, [op-in′-yun-at-iv-nes], *n.* the quality of being opinionated.

OPINIONIST, [op-in′-yun-ist], *n.* a person strongly attached to his or her own opinions.

O-PIP, [ō′-pip′], *n.* (*milit.*) an advanced position for observing the effect of artillery fire upon the enemy. [*O* for observation and *pip* representing *P* for position or post].

OPISOMETER, [ō′-pis-om′-it-er], *n.* an instrument with which curved lines can be measured, a map-measurer. [Gk. *opiso* backwards and METER].

OPISTH-, OPISTHO-, *pref.* in the rear, back behind. [Gk. *opisthen*].

OPISTHOBRANCH, [ō-pis′-thō-brangk′], *n.* a mollusc that is opisthobranchiate.

OPISTHOBRANCHIATE, [ō-pis′-thō-brangk′-i-āt], *adj.* (*zool.*) having the gills behind the heart.

OPISTHOCOELIAN, [ō-pis′-thō-sē′-li-an], *n.* (*zool.*) an animal with opisthocoelous vertebrae.

OPISTHOCOELOUS, [ō-pis′-thō-sē′-lus], *adj.* (*anat.*) with a concave back. [OPISTHO and Gk. *koilos* hollow].

OPISTHOCOMOUS, [ō′-pis-thok′-om-us], *adj.* possessing an occipital crest. [Gk. *opisthokomos* wearing hair long at the back].

OPISTHODONT, [ō-pis′-thō-dont′], *adj.* having back teeth only. [OPISTHO and Gk. *odous odontos* tooth].

OPISTHOGASTRIC, [ō-pis′-thō-gas′-trik], *adj.* lying behind the stomach.

OPISTHOGNATHOUS, [ō′-pis-thog′-nath-us], *adj.* having retreating jaws. [OPISTHO and Gk. *gnathos* jaw].

OPISTHOGRAPH, [ō-pis′-thō-graf′], *n.* a slab of stone or piece of papyrus inscribed on both sides. [OPISTHO and GRAPH].

OPISTHOGRAPHIC, [ō-pis′-thō-graf′-ik], *adj.* having writing on both sides.

OPISTHOTONUS, [ō′-pis-thot′-on-us], *n.* (*med.*) a form of tetanus in which the muscles of the back contract and the body is consequently bent backwards. [Gk. *opisthotonos* drawn backwards].

OPIUM, [ō′-pi-um], *n.* a drug obtained from the immature seed capsules of the *Papaver somniferum*, or white poppy, used medicinally as a sedative and chewed as a narcotic, intoxicant, or stimulant. [L. *opium* from Gk. *opion* poppy juice].

OPIUM DEN, [ō′-pi-um-den′], *n.* a place where opium can be bought and smoked.

OPIUM-EATER, [ō′-pi-um-ēt′-er], *n.* one who habitually indulges in opium.

OPIUM-EATING, [ō′-pi-um-ēt′-ing], *n.* habitual indulgence in opium.

OPIUMISM, [ō′-pi-um-izm], *n.* the habit of taking opium; opium-eating.

OPOBALSAM, OPOBALSAMUM, [ō′-pō-bawl′-sam], *n.* the balsam, balm of Gilead.

OPODELDOC, [ō′-pō-del′-dok], *n.* a kind of soap liniment probably invented by Paracelsus to make various kinds of medical plasters.

OPOPANAX, [ō-pop′-an-aks], *n.* a gum-resin obtained from the plant *Opopanax*, much used in the making of perfumes; a perfume made from this. [Gk. *opopanax*].

OPOSSUM, [ō-pos′-um], *n.* a small, furred, marsupial animal found in America, having a prehensile tail and of nocturnal habits; a similar animal in Australia; [Native].

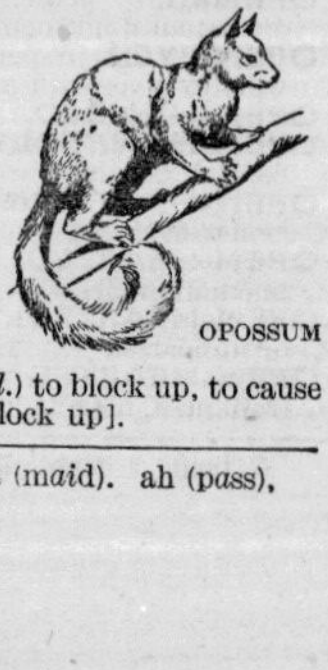

OPOSSUM

OPPIDAN, [op′-id-an], *n.* a member of Eton College who boards outside the school buildings. [L. *oppidanus* living in a town].

OPPILANT, [op′-il-ant], *adj.* (*med.*) obstructing. [L. *oppilans*].

OPPILATE, [op′-il-āt], *v.t.* (*med.*) to block up, to cause a stoppage. [L. *oppilare* to block up].

OPPILATION, [op′-il-ā′-shun], *n.* (*med.*) a stoppage, *esp.* of the bowels. [L. *oppilatio*].
OPPILATIVE, [op′-il-at-iv], *adj.* (*med.*) obstructive, stopping up.
OPPONENCY, [op-ōn′-en-si], *n.* the act of opposing; opposition, antagonism.
OPPONENT (1), [op-ōn′-ent], *n.* one who opposes; an adversary or rival.
OPPONENT (2), [op-ōn′-ent], *adj.* antagonistic, opposed; (*anat.*) used of the muscles which cause the hand and fingers to open and shut; (*poet.*) opposite. [L. *opponens*].
OPPORTUNE, [op′-er-tewn], *adj.* seasonable; occurring at a suitable moment; well-timed. [L. *opportunus*].
OPPORTUNELY, [op′-er-tewn-li], *adv.* at a suitable moment.
OPPORTUNENESS, [op′-er-tewn′-nes], *n.* seasonableness, the condition of being opportune.
OPPORTUNISM, [op′-er-tewn′-izm], *n.* the practice of changing one's intentions and point of view so as to profit by the circumstances of the moment, making the best of passing events.
OPPORTUNIST, [op′-er-tewn′-ist], *n.* one who seizes upon opportunity, who habitually practises opportunism.
OPPORTUNITY, [op′-er-tewn′-i-ti], *n.* a chance to do something; a moment when events and circumstances are favourable to one's ambitions or intentions; a chance to get on in the world. [Fr. *opportunité* from L. *opportunitat(em)*].
OPPOSABILITY, [op-ōz′-ab-il′-i-ti], *n.* the quality of being opposable.
OPPOSABLE, [op-ōz′-abl], *adj.* capable of being opposed.
OPPOSE, [op-ōz′], *v.t. and i.* to resist, fight against, argue against, vote against; to rival with, offer opposition to; to set up as a contrast or rival; to pursue a policy of resistance. [OFr. *opposer*].
OPPOSELESS, [op-ōz′-les], *adj.* (*poet.*) unopposable, irresistible.
OPPOSER, [op-ōz′-er], *n.* one who opposes, an opponent; a rival.
OPPOSING, [op-ōz′-ing], *adj.* acting against, inimical.
OPPOSITE (1), [op′-oz-it], *n.* a thing or person utterly different from another; **two opposites,** two things or persons, the reverse of each other in every way.
OPPOSITE (2), [op′-oz-it], *adj.* facing, being in front of; being on the other side of a real or imaginary division; contrary, utterly different, moving in the reverse direction; inimical, antagonistic; corresponding to. [L. *oppositum*, *p.pt.* of *opponere* to place against].
OPPOSITELY, [op′-oz-it-li], *adv.* in an opposite manner or position.
OPPOSITENESS, [op′-oz-it-nes], *n.* the quality of being opposite.
OPPOSITION (1), [op′-oz-ish′-un], *n.* that which resists and is hostile; antagonism, hostility; those members of a committee who are hostile to a proposal; (*parl.*) those members of parliament who consistently oppose the government; the largest of those parties not in office; (*astron.*) the position of two planets or stars when diametrically opposite. [L. *oppositio*].
OPPOSITION (2), [op′-oz-ish′-un], *adj.* pertaining to the parliamentary opposition.
OPPOSITIONIST (1), [op′-oz-ish′-un-ist], *n.* one who opposes, a member of the opposition.
OPPOSITIONIST (2), [op′-oz-ish′-un-ist], *adj.* befitting an oppositionist, pertaining to the opposition; hostile, opposing.
OPPOSITIVE, [op-oz′-it-iv], *adj.* opposing, tending to oppose.
OPPRESS, [op-res′], *v.t.* to crush down, to treat with injustice and cruelty, to deny freedom to; to govern tyrannically; to depress or dispirit; to render sleepy and languid. [MedL. *oppressare*].
OPPRESSION, [op-resh′-un], *n.* tyranny, harsh rule, denial of liberty; the process of oppressing; physical languor; lassitude of spirit. [L. *oppressio*].
OPPRESSIVE, [op-res′-iv], *adj.* tyrannical, harsh, burdensome; (of the weather and atmosphere) warm, close, stifling; provoking languor of body or spirit.
OPPRESSIVELY, [op-res′-iv-li], *adv.* in an oppressive fashion.
OPPRESSIVENESS, [op-res′-iv-nes], *n.* the quality of being oppressive.
OPPRESSOR, [op-res′-or], *n.* one who oppresses, a tyrant.
OPPROBRIOUS, [op-rō′-bri-us], *adj.* abusive and reproachful; scurrilous; infamous, deserving reproach. [LL. *opprobriosus*].
OPPROBRIOUSLY, [op-rō′-bri-us-li], *adv.* in an opprobrious way.
OPPROBRIOUSNESS, [op-rō′-bri-us-nes], *n* contemptuous or abusive reproach; the quality of deserving reproach.
OPPROBRIUM, [op-rō′-bri-um], *n.* contemptuous reproach; abuse; dishonour, disgrace. [L. *opprobrium*].
OPPUGN, [op-ewn′], *v.t.* to oppose, argue against. [L. *oppugnare* to assault].
OPPUGNANCY, [op-ug′-nan-si], *n.* opposition.
OPPUGNANT, [op-ug′-nant], *adj.* opposing.
OPPUGNATION, [op′-ug-nā′-shun], *n.* opposition, oppugnancy.
OPPUGNER, [op-ewn′-er], *n.* one who oppugns.
OPSIMATH, [op′-sim-ath′], *n.* a person who acquires learning late in life. [Gk. *opsimathes*].
OPSOMANIA, [op′-sō-mā′-ni-a], *n.* an unnatural longing for some particular food or dainty. [Gk. *opsomania*].
OPSOMANIAC, [op′-sō-mā′-ni-ak], *n.* one suffering from opsomania.
OPSONIC, [op-son′-ik], *adj.* pertaining to opsonin.
OPSONIN, [op′-son-in], *n.* (*med.*) a substance obtainable from dead bacteria which, when injected into the blood-stream, strengthens the resistance of a person to that disease. [Gk. *opsono* I buy food].
OPT, [opt], *v.i.* to choose. [L. *optare*].
OPTANT, [opt′-ant], *n.* one who is offered the right of choosing his nationality. [L. *optare* to wish].
OPTATIVE (1), [op′-tat-iv, op-tāt′-iv], *n.* (*gram.*) the optative mood. [L. *optare* to wish].
OPTATIVE (2), [op′-tat-iv, op-tā-tiv], *adj.* (*gram.*) expressing desire in the mood of a verb. [*Prec.*].
OPTIC (1), [op′-tik], *n.* (*coll.*) an organ of sight, an eye.
OPTIC (2), [op′-tik], *adj.* pertaining to the eyes or sight. [Gk. *optikos*].
OPTICAL, [op′-tik-al], *adj.* pertaining to the sight; optic, ocular; **o. glass,** glass used for making lenses; **o. illusion,** an illusion due to faulty interpretation of visual impression; a trick to deceive the eyes.
OPTICALLY, [op′-tik-a-li], *adv.* according to the eye.
OPTICIAN, [op-tish′-an], *n.* one who makes and sells optical instruments, *esp.* spectacles.
OPTICS, [op′-tiks], *n.*(*pl.*) the science and study of light and vision.
OPTIMACY, [op′-tim-a-si], *n.* the nobility, aristocracy; government by the nobility; a state so governed. [L. *optimatia*].
OPTIMATES, [op′-tim-āts], *n.*(*pl.*) the aristocracy; (*hist.*) the nobility of ancient Rome. [L. *optimates*].
OPTIME, [op′-tim-i], *n.* a Cambridge student who gains a second or third class in the mathematical tripos. [L. *optime* excellently].
OPTIMISM, [op′-tim-izm], *n.* the disposition to look on the bright side of things; the doctrine that all things work together for good; (*philos.*) the doctrine of Leibnitz that this world made by a beneficent Creator is the very best possible world. [Fr. *optimisme*].
OPTIMIST, [op′-tim-ist], *n.* one who thinks that everything is for the best; one who believes in optimism.
OPTIMISTIC, [op′-tim-ist′-ik], *adj.* having a cheerful, hopeful outlook; pertaining to optimism.
OPTIMISTICAL, [op′-tim-ist′-ik-al], *adj.* optimistic.
OPTIMISTICALLY, [op′-tim-ist′-ik-a-li], *adj.* in an optimistic way.
OPTIMUM (1), [op′-tim-um], *n.* the best. [L. *optimum*].
OPTIMUM (2), [op′-tim-um], *adj.* best, most favourable. [*Prec.*].
OPTION, [op′-shun], *n.* the right to choose; liberty of choice; a commercial contract made on an initial part payment to sell or purchase something by a fixed date. [L. *optio*].
OPTIONAL, [op′-shun-al], *adj.* at choice; not compulsory.
OPTIONALLY, [op′-shun-al-i], *adv.* by choice, not involuntarily.
OPTO-, *pref.* relating to the eyes or sight. [Gk. *optikos*].
OPTOGRAPHY, [op-tog′-raf-i], *n.* the fixation of an image on the retina. [OPTO and Gk. *graphia* writing].
OPTOMETER, [op-tom′-it-er], *n.* an instrument for measuring range of vision.
OPTOMETRY, [op-tom′-it-ri], *n.* the measurement of the range of vision.
OPTOPHONE, [op′-tō-fōn], *n.* an instrument by

which visual symbols and impressions are converted into sounds. [OPTO and Gk. *phone* sound].
OPULENCE, [op'-yōō-lents], *n.* wealth.
OPULENCY, [op'-yōō-len-si], *n.* opulence, riches.
OPULENT, [op'-yōō-lent], *adj.* wealthy; abundant. [L. *opulentus*].
OPULENTLY, [op'-yōō-lent-li], *adv.* richly, profusely.
OPUNTIA, [op-un'-sha], *n.* (*bot.*) a genus of cactus plants [L. *opuntia*].
OPUNTIOID, [op-un'-ti-oid], *adj.* resembling an opuntia.
OPUS, [ō'-pus], *n.* work, composition, *esp.* a musical composition; **magnum o.,** the principal work of a writer, composer, scholar, etc. [L. *opus* work].
OPUSCULE, [o-pus'-kewl], *n.* a minor work [L. *opusculum, dim.* of *opus* work].
OPUSCULUM, [o-pus'-kyōō-lum], *n.* an opuscule. [*Prec.*].
OR (1), [aw(r)], *n.* (*her.*) gold. [Fr. *or* from L. *aurum* gold].
OR (2), [aw(r)], *conj.* used to express an alternative; used to connect a list of things from which choice is to be made; †moreover. [ME. *owther*, or].
OR (3)†, [aw(r)], *conj.* before (in time); †**o. ever,** before. [ME. *or* from OE. *ar*].
ORACH, ORACHE, ARRACH†, [o'-rich], *n.* red or green mountain spinach. [Fr. *arroche*].
ORACLE, [or'-akl], *n.* a declaration by a Greek priest on behalf of the Gods of what the future holds; the place where such statements were made; the God supposed to inspire them; the answer itself; the priest (or priestess) giving the answer; the sanctuary in the Temple at Jerusalem where the Ark was kept; the breast plate of the Jewish High Priest; divine revelation, the Scriptures; a foretelling of the future; a sure source of knowledge; the wisdom of a person of much knowledge and experience; such a person. [L. *oraculum*].
ORACULAR, [or-ak'-yōō-ler], *adj.* pertaining to an oracle; ambiguous like the replies of the ancient Greek oracles; having the solemn manner or authority of an oracle; prophetic; full of wisdom and knowledge; claiming to possess infallible knowledge like an oracle.
ORACULARITY, [or-ak'-yōō-la'-rit-i], *n.* the quality of being oracular.
ORACULARLY, [or-ak'-yōō-ler-li], *adv.* in an authoritative, oracular manner.
ORACULARNESS, [or-ak'-yōō-ler-nes], *n.* oracularity.
ORAL, [aw'-ral], *adj.* spoken, not written; (*anat.*) pertaining to the mouth. [L. *os oris* mouth].
ORALLY, [aw'-ral-i], *adv.* verbally, by word of mouth.
ORANG, [or-ang'], *n.* abbreviation for ORANG-OUTANG.
ORANGE (1), [or'-inj], *n.* an evergreen tree, *Citrus Aurantium*, grown in Southern Europe and the East, the orange-tree; the fruit of this tree, a large, many-celled berry with a thick yellow rind or skin; the reddish-yellow colour of this rind; **Blenheim o.,** a sort of dessert apple. [OFr. *orange* from Arab. *naranj*].
ORANGE (2), [or'-inj], *n.* the Protestant Unionist party in Ireland originally founded in support of the Protestant succession and William, Prince of Orange-Nassau.
ORANGE (3), [or'-inj], *adj.* having the same colour as orange rind, orange-coloured.
ORANGEADE, [or'-inj-ād'], *n.* a drink made of sweetened and diluted orange juice. [ORANGE and (LEMON)ADE].
ORANGE-BAT, [or'-inj-bat'], *n.* the Australian animal, *Phinonycteris aurantia*, the male species of which has orange-coloured fur.
ORANGE-BLOSSOM, [or'-inj-blos'-um], *n.* the white flower of the orange-tree.
ORANGE-COLOURED, [or'-inj-kul'-erd], *adj.* having the golden-yellow colour of the rind of an orange.
ORANGE-LILY, [or'-inj-lil'-i], *n.* a particular sort of lily which has orange-coloured flowers.
ORANGEMAN, [or'-inj-man], *n.* a member of the Orange party. [ORANGE (2)].
ORANGEMEN, [or'-inj-men], *n.* the Orange party in Ireland.
ORANGE-MUSK, [or'-inj-musk'], *n.* a sort of pear.
ORANGE-PEEL, [or'-ing-pēl'], *n.* the skin of an orange.
ORANGE-ROOT, [or'-inj-rōōt'], *n* a North American plant, the golden-seal.
ORANGERY, [or'-inj-er-i], *n.* an orange garden or hot-house, where orange-trees are grown. [Fr. *orangerie*].
ORANGE-TAWNY, [or'-inj-tawn'-i], *adj.* a rich, reddish-yellow colour.
ORANGE-TIP, [or'-inj-tip'], *n.* a variety of butterfly, the male of which has an orange-coloured patch on the tip of each wing.
ORANGE-TREE, [or'-inj-trē'], *n.* the tree, *Citrus Aurantium*.
ORANGISM, [or'-inj-izm], *n.* the political tenets of the Orange party in Ireland. [ORANGE (2)].
ORANGITE, [or'-inj-īt], *n.* (*min.*) an orange-coloured variety of thorite.
ORANG-OUTANG, ORANG-UTAN, [aw-rang'-ōō-tang'], *n.* the anthropoid ape, *Simia satyrus*. [Malay].
ORANGY, [or'-inj-i], *adj.* resembling an orange in taste, smell, colour, etc.; flavoured with orange juice.
ORANT, [aw'-rant], *n.* a worshipper, a figure in an attitude of prayer or worship. [L. *orans*].
ORARIUM, [aw-räer'-i-um], *n.* (*eccles.*) a stole as worn at one time by deacons. [L. *orarium* napkin].
ORATE, [o-rāt'], *v.i.* (*coll.*) to harangue, to make a speech. [ORATION].
ORATION, [or-ā'-shun], *n.* a formal discourse; †a prayer to a deity; (*gram.*) **direct o.,** direct speech, what the speaker actually said; **indirect o.,** a report of the substance of the words of another speaker, usually prefaced by the conjunction *that*. [L. *oratio*].

ORANG OUTANG

ORATIONING, [or-ā'-shun-ing], *n.* the act of delivering an oration.
ORATOR, [or'-at-or], *n.* one skilled in public speaking; a person who makes speeches; **Public O.,** the official speaker of a university. [L. *orator*].
ORATORIAL, [or'-at-aw'-ri-al], *adj.* pertaining to orators, oratory or oratorios.
ORATORIALLY, [or'-at-aw'-ri-al-i], *adv.* like an orator or oratorio.
ORATORIAN (1), [or'-at-aw'-ri-an], *n.* the priest of an oratory; a member of the Society of the Oratory.
ORATORIAN (2), [or'-at-aw'-ri-an], *adj.* pertaining to an oratory or the Society of the Oratory.
ORATORICAL, [or'-at-or'-ik-al], *adj.* rhetorical; being in the manner of an orator; pertaining to an orator.
ORATORICALLY, [or'-at-or'-ik-a-li], *adv.* in an oratorical way.
ORATORIO, [or'-at-aw'-ri-ō], *n.* a quasi-dramatic and musical arrangement of a religious theme or story in which solo voices represent the characters and are supported by an orchestra and chorus, but which is performed without dramatic movement, scenery, costume, etc. [It. *oratorio*].
ORATORY (1), [or'-at-er-i], *n.* a small chapel for private prayer, often part of a church or private residence; a church of the Society of the Oratory, a R.C. society of secular priests founded in the sixteenth century; **the Fathers of the O.,** members of this society, oratorians. [L. *oratorium*].
ORATORY (2), [or'-at-er-i], *n.* the art of the orator, the art of speaking eloquently; rhetoric. [L. *oratoria*].
ORATRESS, [or'-at-res], *n.* a female orator.
ORB (1), [awb], *n.* a ball, globe, sphere; anything spherical in shape; a small globe surmounted with a cross held in the king's left hand as a symbol of sovereignty. [L. *orbs*].
ORB (2), [awb], *v.t.* (*poet.*) to encircle.
ORBATE, [awb'-āt], *adj.* bereaved; orphaned, widowed. [L. *orbatus*].
ORBED, [awbd], *adj.* round; shaped like an orb; encircled.
ORBICULAR, [awb-ik'-yōō-ler], *adj.* having the form of an orb.
ORBICULARLY, [awb-ik'-yōō-ler-li], *adv.* spherically.
ORBICULARNESS, [awb-ik'-yōō-ler-nes], *n.* the quality of being orbicular.
ORBICULATE, [awb-ik'-yōō-lat], *adj.* shaped in the form of an orb.
ORBICULATED, [awb-ik'-yōō-lāt-id], *adj.* orbiculate.
ORBIT, [awb'-it], *n.* a circular track; (*astron.*) the path of a heavenly body; (*opt.*) the eye-socket; (*fig.*)

a track or path; a way or habit of life. [L. *orbita* path, course].
ORBITAL, [awb'-it-al], *adj.* pertaining to an orbit; (*opt.*) pertaining to the eye-socket.
ORB-LIKE, [awb'-līk], *adj.* shaped like an orb.
ORC, [awk], *n.* a killer-whale; the genus of killer-whales; (*fig.*) an ogre. [L. *orca* a whale].
ORCADIAN (1), [awk-ā'-di-an], *n.* an inhabitant of the Orkney Islands.
ORCADIAN (2), [awk-ā'-di-an], *adj.* pertaining to the Orkney Islands. [L. *Orcades* Orkney Islands].

ORC

ORCHANET, [awk'-an-et], *n.* (*bot.*) a plant, *Alkanna tinctoria*; the dye extracted from it. [OFr. *orcanette*].
ORCHARD, [aw'-cherd], *n.* an enclosure where fruit trees are cultivated. [OE. *ort-geard*].
ORCHARD-HOUSE, [aw'-cherd-hows'], *n.* a greenhouse where fruit trees are grown.
ORCHARDING, [aw'-cherd-ing], *n.* the business and science of cultivating fruit trees in an orchard.
ORCHARDIST, [aw'-cherd-ist], *n.* one who keeps orchards.
ORCHARDMAN, [aw'-cherd-man], *n.* an orchardist.
ORCHESIS, [aw-kē'-sis], *n.* orchestics. [Gk. *orchesis*].
ORCHESOGRAPHY, [aw'-kēz-og'-raf-i], *n.* orchestics; a treatise on dancing. [Gk. *orchesis* dancing and *graphia* writing].
ORCHESTIC, [aw-kest'-ik], *adj.* pertaining to dancing.
ORCHESTICS, [aw-kest'-iks], *n.*(*pl.*) the art of dancing.
ORCHESTRA, [aw'-kes-tra], *n.* the space before the stage in an ancient Greek theatre where the chorus sang and danced; a company of musicians playing various instruments, assembled for the performance of concerted musical works; the place in front of the stage where such musicians sit; the instruments on which they play considered as an entity. [Gk. *orchestra*].
ORCHESTRAL, [aw-kes'-tral], *adj.* pertaining to an orchestra; composed for, or resembling, an orchestra.
ORCHESTRATE, [aw'-kes-trāt], *v.t.* to arrange or edit (a piece of music) for orchestral performance.
ORCHESTRATION, [aw'-kes-trā'-shun], *n.* the art of scoring a piece of music for performance by an orchestra.
ORCHESTRINA, [aw'-kes-trē'-na], *n.* a musical box producing the sounds of several instruments. [ORCHESTRA and INA].
ORCHESTRION, [aw-kes'-tri-on], *n.* a musical instrument similar to an orchestrina.
ORCHIALGIA, [aw'-ki-al'-ji-a], *n.* neuralgia of the testicle. [Gk. *orkhis* testicle *algos* pain].
ORCHID, [aw'-kid], *n.* (*bot.*) a plant of the family *Orchidaceae*, many varieties of which are remarkable for their vivid colouring and curious shapes. [Gk. *orkhis* testicle, tuber].
ORCHIDACEOUS, [aw'-kid-ā'-shus], *adj.* belonging to, relating to, orchids.
ORCHIDEOUS, [aw-kid'-i-us], *adj.* relating to the orchid.
ORCHIDIST, [aw'-kid-ist], *n.* a student or collector of orchids.
ORCHIDOMANIA, [aw'-kid-ō-mā'-ni-a], *n.* excessive interest in orchids.
ORCHIDOMANIAC, [aw'-kid-ō-mā'-ni-ak], *n.* one suffering from orchidomania.
ORCHIL, see ARCHIL.
ORCHIS, [aw'-kis], *n.* an orchid.
ORCHITIS, [aw-kī'-tis], *n.* (*med.*) inflammation of the testicles. [Gk. *orkhis* testicle and *itis* denoting inflammation].
ORCHOTOMY, [aw-kot'-o-mi], *n.* removal of the testicle; castration. [Gk. *orkhis* testicle and *tomia* cutting].
ORCIN, [aw'-sin], *n.* a deep red dye obtained from archil.
ORDAIN, [aw-dān'], *v.t.* to enact, command, resolve, decree; (*eccles.*) to consecrate to holy orders by the laying on of hands. [L. *ordinare* to order].
ORDAINABLE, [aw-dān'-abl], *adj.* able to be ordained.
ORDAINER, [aw-dān'-er], *n.* one who ordains; one of the Lords Ordainers, the commission of nobles appointing themselves to govern the kingdom in the reign of Edward II.
ORDAINMENT, [aw-dān'-ment], *n.* the act of ordaining.
ORDEAL, [aw-dēel'], *n.* (*hist.*) trial by testing in which guilt or innocence was decided by casting lots, or by the ability of the accused to walk through fire, step blindfold over ploughshares, etc.; a severe trial, an exacting and unpleasant testing. [OE. *ordal* judgment].
ORDEAL-BEAN, [aw-dēel'-bēn'], *n.* an African poison used in trial by ordeal, *Physostigma venenosum*.
ORDEAL-TREE, [aw'-dēel'-trē'], *n.* the red-water tree of Sierra Leone, *Erythrophleum guineense*.
ORDER (1), [aw'-der], *n.* arrangement, relative position in place or time; logical sequence, coherence, systematic disposition in any sense, natural succession; (*milit.*) formation, disposition, ordering of ranks; (of dress or equipment) suitable for a specified occasion; discipline, obedience, the state of being quietly obedient to authority, absence of turbulent opposition; (of public meetings) orderly attention; custom and procedure; proper bodily functioning, health; the second broadest botanical and zoological classification; (*arch.*) a specific style; a degree, rank, quality, comparative importance; a social rank, economic status; the collective whole of those performing certain spiritual and ecclesiastical functions; (*pl.*) the office of a priest, deacon, or (*R.C.*) subdeacon; (*eccles.*) the form of a ceremony; a command, instruction; a warrant to a banker instructing him to pay out money, a written permit to go to a place or perform an action; an instruction to a tradesman, etc., to make or supply certain goods; **o. in council,** a command issued direct by the sovereign without the sanction of parliament; **New O.,** a system of government practised in the countries occupied by Germany under the Nazi régime; **in o.,** according to the rules of procedure; **in o. to,** so as to. [OFr. *ordre*].
ORDER (2), [aw'-der], *v.t.* to arrange in regular or proper series, to bring in order; to arrange, ordain, decree; (*milit.*) to bring (the rifle) to a position with the butt on the ground and the barrel well in to the right side; to command, prescribe; to give orders for something to be obtained or prepared. [*Prec.*].
ORDERER, [aw'-der-er], *n.* one who orders.
ORDERING, [aw'-der-ing], *n.* order, disposition.
ORDERLESS, [aw'-der-les], *adj.* without order, disordered.
ORDERLINESS, [aw'-der-li-nes], *n.* the condition of being orderly, of keeping order, of being tidy.
ORDERLY (1), [aw'-der-li], *n.* a soldier in attendance on a superior to carry his orders.
ORDERLY (2), [aw'-der-li], *adj.* arranged in order, systematic, tidy, neatly disposed; quiet, submissive to authority, keeping good order, well controlled, not turbulent; (*milit.*) concerned with carrying out general order on a specific day.
ORDINAL, [aw'-din-al], *n.* a number indicating position in a series; the prescribed form of ceremony of ordination. [L. *ordinalis*].
ORDINANCE, [aw'-din-ants], *n.* a public enactment, a solemn and important order; an ecclesiastical rite. [OFr. *ordinance*].
ORDINAND, [aw'-din-and'], *n.* one who is awaiting ordination. [L. *ordinandus, ger.* of *ordinare* to ordain].
ORDINANT, [aw'-din-ant], *n.* a prelate conferring orders.
ORDINARILY, [aw'-din-er-i-li], *adv.* in ordinary fashion; usually.
ORDINARINESS, [aw'-din-er-i-nes], *n.* the state of being ordinary.
ORDINARY (1), [aw'-din-er-i], *n.* an officer having authority in his own right, a cleric in his own sphere of office; †a set meal at an inn; (*her.*) a simple charge; **Lord O.,** (*Scots leg.*) a judge of the Outer House of the Court of Sessions.
ORDINARY (2), [aw'-din-er-i], *adj.* according to general, regular, customary practice, normal, not remarkable; commonplace, dull, undistinguished. [L. *ordinarius* regular].

ORDINARY

ORDINARYSHIP, [aw'-din-er-i-ship], *n.* an ordinary's office or tenure of office. [ORDINARY (1)].
ORDINATE (1), [aw'-din-at], *n.* a line from a point to one of two co-ordinate axes. [L. *ordinare* arrange].

ORDINATE (2), [aw'-din-āt], *v.t.* to ordain, to appoint to office. [*Prec.*].
ORDINATION, [aw'-din-ā'-shun], *n.* the act of ordaining; the conferring of holy orders. [L. *ordinatio*].
ORDINATIVE, [aw'-din-at-iv], *adj.* relating to ordination.
ORDINATOR, [aw'-din-āt-or], *n.* one who ordains.
ORDINEE, [aw'-din-ē'], *n.* one who is ordained.
ORDNANCE, [awd'-nants], *n.* artillery; military stores; **o. survey**, a detailed geographical survey, originally made by the War Office. [ORDINANCE].
ORDOVICIAN, [aw'-dō-vish'-i-an], *n.* (*geol.*) the series of rocks between the Cambrian and the Silurian. [L. *Ordovices* a Celtic people].
ORDURE, [aw'-dyōōer], *n.* dung, filth, excrement. [Fr. *ordure*].
ORE, [aw(r)], *n.* impure, unrefined metal; rock from which metal may be extracted. [OE. *ora*].
OREAD, [aw'-ri-ad], *n.* (*myth.*) a mountain nymph. [Gk. *oros* mountain].
ORECTIC, [o-rek'-tik], *adj.* of, or pertaining to, orexis or desire. [Gk. *orektikos*].
OREODONTS, [or'-i-ō-donts], *n.*(*pl.*) primitive mammals of the Eocene and Lower Miocene periods thought to be the ancestors of the existing ruminants. [Gk. *oros* mountain and *odous odontos* tooth].
OREXIS, [o-reks'-is], *n.* desire. [Gk. *orexis*].
ORGAN, [aw'-gan], *n.* a part of the body performing a function, an instrument for exercising a function; a means or medium for expressing opinion; a large wind-instrument, consisting of a series of pipes supplied with air by bellows or fans, and having keyed manuals and pedals by means of which the wind is released. [L. *organum* instrument].
ORGAN-BUILDER, [aw'-gan-bild'-er], *n.* one who constructs organs.
ORGANDIE, [aw-gan'-di], *n.* a figured transparent muslin. [Fr. *organdi*].
ORGAN-GRINDER, [aw'-gan-grīnd'-er], *n.* the player of a barrel-organ.
ORGANIC, [aw-gan'-ik], *adj.* relating to, bound up with, affecting, springing from, the bodily organs; having organs specialized for the various functions of life; connected with organisms and their characteristics; fundamental to the nature of a thing; having a complete, organized unity; **o. chemistry**, the chemistry of the carbon compounds. [Gk. *organikos*].
ORGANICAL, [aw-gan'-ik-al], *adj.* organic.
ORGANICALLY, [aw-gan'-ik-a-li], *adj.* in organic fashion; fundamentally; through the bodily organs.
ORGANICALNESS, [aw-gan'-ik-al-nes], *n.* the quality of being organic.
ORGANISM, [aw'-gan-izm], *n.* (*biol.*) anything capable of reproducing its own kind; an independent unity having specialized parts performing the various functions necessary for the life of the whole.
ORGANIST, [aw'-gan-ist], *n.* a player on the organ.
ORGANIZABLE, [aw'-gan-īz'-abl], *adj.* capable of being organized.
ORGANIZATION, [aw'-gan-īz-ā'-shun], *n.* the state of being organized, the act or method of organizing; that which is organized, a systematic relation of specialized parts each performing some function of the whole; an association of persons organized to carry out a common purpose.
ORGANIZE, [aw'-gan-īz], *v.t. and i.* to make organic; to give organization to, to group various parts into a systematic whole where each performs a specialized function; to arrange or rearrange a system or a body of people so as to make an efficient, co-ordinated whole; to become an organization. [MedL. *organizare*].
ORGANIZER, [aw'-gan-īz-er], *n.* one who organizes, one whose sole duty is to organize some undertaking into a systematic and effective working whole.
ORGAN LOFT, [awg'-an-loft'], *n.* the elevated space or gallery where a large organ is situated.
ORGANOGENY, [aw'-gan-oj'-en-i], *n.* the development of organs; the study of this. [ORGAN and Gk. *genes* bearing].
ORGANOGRAPHICAL, [aw'-gan-ō-graf'-ik-al], *adj.* pertaining to organography.
ORGANOGRAPHY, [aw'-gan-og'-raf-i], *n.* a description of the organs of plants or animals. [ORGAN and Gk. *graphia* writing].
ORGANOLOGY, [aw'-gan-ol'-o-ji], *n.* the study of animal organs. [ORGAN and Gk. *logos* speech].
ORGANON, [aw'-gan-on], *n.* a system of philosophical scientific inquiry. [Gk. *organon* implement].
ORGANOPLASTIC, [aw'-gan-ō-plast'-ik], *adj.* formative of organic tissue.
ORGANOTHERAPY, [aw'-gan-ō-the'-rap-i], *n.* medical treatment by organic extracts.
ORGAN-SCREEN, [aw'-gan-skrēn'], *n.* the ornamental wall or framework which supports a church organ.
ORGANZINE, [aw'-gan-zēn], *n.* silk thread with a double twist. [It. *organzino*].
ORGASM, [aw'-gazm], *n.* the culminating excitement, the satisfying crisis in the sexual act; a violent paroxysm of excitement probably sexual in basis. [Gk. *orgasmos* swelling, kneading].
ORGEAT, [aw'-zhah], *n.* a drink made of barley or sweet almonds. [L. *hordeum* barley].
ORGIASTIC, [aw'-ji-ast'-ik], *adj.* relating to an orgy.
ORGUES, [awgz], *n.*(*pl.*) (*milit.*) heavy poles tipped with iron hung loosely together over a gate to be let down as an emergency portcullis; a number of small arms fixed together on the same stock to be fired simultaneously. [Fr. *orgue* machine].
ORGY, [aw'-ji], *n.* †the ceremonial revels in honour of Dionysos; a drunken debauch, a noisy licentious revelry; an excessive and almost disgusting indulgence in any appetite or practice. [Gk. *orgia*].
ORICHALC, [aw'-ri-kalk], *n.* (*min.*) a metallic substance resembling gold. [Gk. *oros* mountain and *khalkos* brass].
ORIEL, [aw'-ri-el], *n.* a projecting or recessed window divided into bays and supported on corbels. [MedL. *oriolum* recess].
ORIENCY, [aw'-ri-en-si], *n.* brightness of colour. [~ORIENT (2)].
ORIENT (1), [aw'-ri-ent], *n.* the East, Asia; a very lustrous pearl.
ORIENT (2), [aw'-ri-ent], *adj.* rising in the East; derived from the East; lustrous. [L. *oriens*].
ORIENT (3), [aw'-ri-ent], *v.t.* to orientate.
ORIENTAL (1), [aw'-ri-ent'-al], *n.* a native of Asia, *esp.* of Further Asia.
ORIENTAL (2), [aw'-ri-ent'-al], *adj.* relating to the Eastern countries, to the Far East. [L. *orientalis*].
ORIENTALISM, [aw'-ri-ent'-al-izm], *n.* the habits, outlook of Asiatics, the affectation of such an outlook.
ORIENTALIST, [aw'-ri-ent'-al-ist], *n.* a student of Asiatic culture.
ORIENTALITY, [aw'-ri-ent-al'-i-ti], *n.* the state of being oriental.
ORIENTALIZE, [aw'-ri-ent'-al-īz], *v.t.* to make oriental in manners, culture and outlook.
ORIENTATE, [aw'-ri-ent-āt], *v.t. and i.* (*arch.*) to plan out a building so that the longest axis runs towards the east, to plan a building to correspond with the points of the compass; to place some object in definite relation to another, to take one's bearings by some object; to align oneself, take up an idea in relation to situation; to insert points of the compass on a map. [ORIENT (2)].
ORIENTATION, [aw'-ri-ent-ā'-shun], *n.* the relation of a body to the points of the compass; tendency, direction.
ORIFICE, [or'-if-is], *n.* the aperture of a tube, the mouth of a thing, a hole. [L. *orificium*].
ORIFLAMME, [or'-i-flam'], *n.* the ancient banner of the kings of France, the standard of St. Denis; a banner as an inspiring symbol. [MedL. *auriflamma* fire of gold].
ORIGAN, [or'-ig-an], *n.* (*bot.*) wild marjoram; a savoury herb of the genus *Origanum*. [Gk. *origanon* marjoram].
ORIGIN, [or'-ij-in], *n.* the source, start, beginning of anything; the initial cause of a thing; ancestry, birth. [L. *origo*].
ORIGINABLE, [or-ij'-in-abl], *adj.* that may be originated.
ORIGINAL (1), [or-ij'-in-al], *n.* the First Cause, the originator, author of a thing; the first pattern from which copies are made; a genuine work of art as opposed to a copy; the original language in which a work was written.
ORIGINAL (2), [or-ij'-in-al], *adj.* relating to an origin, to the beginning of a thing; first-hand, made, written, etc., for the first time, new; (of literature) saying something new, not suggested by anything else; (of persons) having ideas not derived from others, unconventional, inventive. [L. *originalis*].
ORIGINALITY, [or-ij'-in-al'-i-ti], *n.* the state of being original; possession of ideas not derived from others, inventiveness; novel, spontaneous, fresh in conception.

ORIGINALLY, [or-ij'-in-a-li], *adv.* in origin; formerly, at first.
ORIGINATE, [or-ij'-in-āt], *v.t. and i.* to bring about, cause to exist, commence, to initiate, produce for the first time; to have origin (in), arise (from).
ORIGINATION, [or-ij'-in-ā-shun], *n.* the act or process of originating or being originated.
ORIGINATIVE, [or-ij'-in-at-iv], *adj.* having power to originate.
ORIGINATOR, [or-ij'-in-āt'-or], *n.* one who originates.
ORILLION, [or-il'-yun], *n.* a wall covering the flank of a bastion. [Fr. *oreillon*].
ORIOLE, [aw'-ri-ōl], *n.* a passerine bird of the genus *Oriolus*, allied to the shrikes and wagtails. [L. *aureolus* golden].
ORION, [or-ī'-on], *n.* (*myth.*) a hunter slain by Artemis; (*astron.*) a constellation showing a group of seven bright stars. [Gk. *Orion*].
ORISMOLOGY, [or'-iz-mol'-o-ji], *n.* terminology. [Gk. *horismos* definition and *logos* speech].
ORISON, [or'-izn], *n.* a prayer. [OFr. *oraison*].
ORLE, [awl], *n.* (*her.*) a fillet half the width of the bordure, going round the edge of the shield. [MedL. *orla*].
ORLEANS, [aw-lē'-anz], *n.* a cloth of mixed wool and cotton originally made in Orleans.
ORLOP, [aw'-lop], *n.* the lowest deck of a ship. [Du. *overloop*].
ORMER, [awm'-er], *n.* the ear-shell, *Haliotis tuberculata*. [Fr. *oreille* ear and *mer* sea].
ORMOLU, [aw'-mol-ōō], *n.* gilded bronze, lacquered brass; objects decorated with imitation gold; an alloy of copper and zinc. [Fr. *or moulu* milled gold].
ORNAMENT (1), [awn'-a-ment], *n.* a decoration, embellishment, decorative trapping; a small object, piece of bric-à-brac wholly without function beyond that of decorating a room, a trinket; a person, thing or quality bringing credit and lustre to anything by virtue of its presence. [L. *ornamentum*].
ORNAMENT (2), [awn-a-ment'], *v.t. and i.* to decorate, provide with an ornament, serve as an ornament to. [*Prec.*].
ORNAMENTAL, [awn'-a-ment'-al], *adj.* serving only as ornament, decorative.
ORNAMENTALLY, [awn-a-ment'-al-i], *adv.* in ornamental fashion.
ORNAMENTATION, [awn'-a-ment-ā'-shun], *n.* decoration; the act of ornamenting.
ORNATE, [awn-āt'], *adj.* richly adorned, elaborately decorated. [L. *ornatum*, *p.pt.* of *ornare* to adorn].
ORNATELY, [awn-āt'-li], *adv.* in ornate fashion.
ORNATENESS, [awn-āt'-nes], *n.* the state of being adorned.
ORNITHIC, [aw-nith'-ik], *adj.* pertaining to birds. [Gk. *ornis ornithos* bird].
ORNITHICHNITE, [aw-nith'-ik-nīt], *n.* a bird's footprint. [ORNITHO and Gk. *ikhnos* trace].
ORNITHO-, *pref.* relating to birds. [Gk. *ornis ornithos* bird].
ORNITHOLITE, [aw-nith'-ō-līt], *n.* (*geol.*) the fossil remains of a bird. [ORNITHO and Gk. *lithos* stone].
ORNITHOLOGICAL, [aw'-nith-o-loj'-ik-al], *adj.* pertaining to ornithology.
ORNITHOLOGIST, [aw'-nith-ol'-o-jist], *n.* a student of ornithology.
ORNITHOLOGY, [aw'-nith-ol'-o-ji], *n.* the study of birds. [ORNITHO and Gk. *logos* speech].
ORNITHOMANCY, [aw-nith'-ō-man-si], *n.* divination from the flight of birds. [ORNITHO and Gk. *manteia* divination].
ORNITHOPTER, [aw'-nith-opt'-er], *n.* an aeroplane with flapping wings or with revolving vanes; a bird-winged butterfly. [ORNITHO and Gk. *pteron* wing].
ORNITHORHYNCHUS, [aw'-nith-ō-ringk'-us], *n.* an Australian duck-billed mammal that lays eggs, *Ornithorhynchus anatinus*. [ORNITHO and Gk. *rhugkhos* snout].
ORNITHOSCOPY, [aw'-nith-os'-kop-i], *n.* ornithomancy. [ORNITHO and SCOPE].
OROGRAPHIC, [aw'-rō-graf'-ik], *adj.* relating to orography.
OROGRAPHICAL, [aw'-rō-graf'-ik-al], *adj.* orographic.
OROGRAPHY, [aw-rog'-raf-i], *n.* orology. [Gk. *oros* mountain and *graphia* writing].
OROIDE, [aw'-roid], *n.* an alloy of tin, zinc, and other base metals, having the appearance of gold, and used in cheap jewellery. [Fr. *or* gold and Gk. *oeides* like].
OROLOGICAL, [aw'-rō-loj'-ik-al], *adj.* pertaining to orology.
OROLOGIST, [aw-rol'-oj-ist], *n.* a student of orology.
OROLOGY, [aw-rol'-o-ji], *n.* the study of mountains. [Gk. *oros* mountain and *logos* speech].
OROTUND, [o'-rō-tund], *adj.* resonant, clear and loud; pompous. [L. *os oris* mouth and ROTUND].
ORPHAN (1), [aw'-fan], *n.* a child bereft of one or both (usually both) of its parents. [Gk. *orphanos*].
ORPHAN (2), [aw'-fan], *adj.* bereft of parents.
ORPHAN (3), [aw'-fan], *v.t.* to make an orphan.
ORPHANAGE, [aw'-fan-ij], *n.* the state of being an orphan; an institution for bringing up orphans.
ORPHANED, [aw'-fand], *adj.* left an orphan.
ORPHANHOOD, [aw'-fan-hŏŏd], *n.* the state of being an orphan.
ORPHANISM, [aw'-fan-izm], *n.* the state of an orphan.
ORPHEAN, [aw-fē'-an], *adj.* relating to Orpheus or his music. [L. *Orpheus*].
ORPHIC, [aw'-fik], *adj.* relating to religious ceremonies connected with the Orpheus legend.
ORPHREY, [aw'-fri], *n.* an embroidered border on an ecclesiastical vestment. [OFr. *orfreis*].
ORPIMENT, [aw'-pi-ment], *n.* yellow sulphide of arsenic. [OFr. *orpiment*].
ORPIN, [aw'-pin], *n.* a yellow colouring. [*Prec.*].
ORPINE, [aw'-pin], *n.* (*bot.*) the purple-flowered stonecrop, *Sedum Telephium*. [Fr. *orpin*].
ORPINGTON, [awp'-ing-ton], *n.* any of various domestic fowls of a heavy breed originating from *Orpington* in Kent.
ORRERY, [or'-er-i], *n.* a working model of the solar system. [Earl of *Orrery*, who first devised one].
ORRIS (1), [or'-is], *n.* the dried root of the Florentine iris, used in perfumery. [Gk. *iris*].
ORRIS (2), [or'-is], *n.* gold or silver lace. [OFr. *orphreis*].
ORT, [awt], *n.* leavings of a meal. [ME. *ort* refuse].
ORTHITE, [aw'-thīt], *n.* (*min.*) a kind of allanite found in straight crystals. [Gk. *orthos* straight].
ORTHO-, *pref.* right, straight, true, upright. [Gk. *orthos* straight].
ORTHOCHROMATIC, [aw'-thō-krō-mat'-ik], *adj.* (*phot.*) giving true colour values.
ORTHOCLASE, [aw'-thō-klās'], *n.* (*min.*) a monoclinic potash felspar. [ORTHO and Gk. *klasis* breaking].
ORTHOCLASTIC, [awth-ō-klast'-ik], *adj.* (*min.*) of crystals, etc., having the cleavages at right angles to each other. [ORTHO and Gk. *klastos* broken].
ORTHODIAGONAL, [aw'-thō-dī-ag'-on-al], *n.* the inclined lateral axis in the monoclinic system of crystallography.
ORTHODOX, [aw'-thō-doks], *adj.* right, correct in opinion or doctrine; right theologically; holding the opinions laid down by authority, conventional in belief; **O. Church,** the Greek Church, the Church in communion with the Patriarch of Constantinople. [Gk. *orthodoxos* right-opinioned].
ORTHODOXICAL, [aw'-thō-doks'-ik-al], *adj.* orthodox.
ORTHODOXLY, [aw'-thō-doks-li], *adv.* in orthodox fashion.
ORTHODOXNESS, [aw'-thō-doks-nes], *n.* the state or quality of being orthodox.
ORTHODOXY, [aw'-thō-doks-i], *n.* the state of being orthodox; orthodoxness of theological or other opinion. [Gk *orthodoxia*].
ORTHOEPIC, [aw'-thō-ep'-ik], *adj.* pertaining to orthoepy.
ORTHOEPICAL, [aw'-thō-ep'-ik-al], *adj.* orthoepic.
ORTHOEPIST, [aw'-thō'-ep-ist], *n.* one skilled in orthoepy.
ORTHOEPY, [aw'-thō-ep-i], *n.* phonology, the study of correct pronunciation. [Gk. *orthoepeia*].
ORTHOGENY, [aw-thoj'-en-i], *n.* a consistent, determined biological variation. [ORTHO and Gk. *genes* producing].
ORTHOGNATHOUS, [aw-thog'-na-thus], *adj.* having the forehead in a vertical line with the lower jaw. [ORTHO and Gk. *gnathos* jaw].
ORTHOGON, [aw'-thog-on'], *n.* a rectangular figure. [ORTHO and Gk. *gonia* angle].
ORTHOGONAL, [aw-thog'-on-al], *adj.* right-angled.
ORTHOGRAPHER, [aw-thog'-ra-fer], *n.* one skilled in orthography.
ORTHOGRAPHIC, [aw'-thō-graf'-ik], *adj.* pertaining to orthography.
ORTHOGRAPHICAL, [aw'-thō-graf'-ik-al], *adj.* orthographic.

ORTHOGRAPHIST, [aw-thog'-ra-fist], *n.* an orthographer.
ORTHOGRAPHY, [aw-thog'-ra-fi], *n.* correct spelling; the study of the spelling of a certain period; the rules of spelling. [Gk. *orthographia*].
ORTHOMETRY, [aw-thom'-et-ri], *n.* correct versification [ORTHO and Gk. *metria* measurement].
ORTHOPAEDIC, [awth-ō-pēd'-ik], *adj.* (*med.*) of, pertaining to, or practising, orthopaedy.
ORTHOPAEDY, [aw'-thō-pēd'-i], *n.* manipulative surgery for treating deformities of the bone, *esp.* in children. [ORTHO and Gk. *pais paidos* child].
ORTHOPHONY, [aw-thof'-on-i], *n.* correct speaking. [ORTHO and Gk. *phone* voice].
ORTHOPNOEA, [aw-thō-pnē'-a], *n.* form of asthma in which breathing is possible only in an upright position. [Gk. *orthopnoia*].
ORTHOPRAXY, [aw'-thō-prak-si], *n.* rightness of action; manipulative treatment of deformities. [ORTHO and Gk. *praxis* doing].
ORTHOPTERA, [aw-thop'-ter-a], *n.*(*pl.*) the straight-winged insects. [ORTHO and Gk. *pteron* wing].
ORTHOPTEROUS, [aw-thop'-ter-us], *adj.* straight-winged; belonging to the orthoptera.
ORTHOSTYLE, [aw'-thō-stil], *adj.* (*arch.*) having a straight line of columns. [ORTHO and Gk. *stulos* column].
ORTHOTROPAL, [aw-thot'-rop-al], *adj.* orthotropous.
ORTHOTROPOUS, [aw-thot'-rop-us], *adj.* (*bot.*) growing vertically. [ORTHO and Gk. *tropos* turning].
ORTHOTYPOUS, [aw-thot'-ip-us], *adj.* (*min.*) having a perpendicular cleavage. [ORTHO and Gk. *tupto* I strike].
ORTIVE, [awt'-iv], *adj.* eastern. [MedL. *ortivus* rising].
ORTOLAN, [aw'-tō-lan], *n.* (*ornith.*) the garden bunting, *Emberiza hortulanus.* [It. *ortolano* gardener].
ORVAL, [aw'-val], *n.* (*bot.*) the herb, clary, *Salvia Sclarea.* [Fr. *orvale*].
ORYX, [or'-iks], *n.* a straight-horned African antelope. [Gk. *orux*].
OS, [os], *n.* a bone. [L. *os* bone].
OSAGE-ORANGE, [o-sahj'-or'-inj], *n.* the North American bow-wood, *Maclura aurantiaca.*
OSBORNE, [oz'-bern], *n.* a semi-sweet biscuit. [*Osborne*, where formerly made].
OSCAN (1), [os'-kan], *n.* the language of the Osci, a tribe of ancient Italy, closely related to Latin.
OSCAN (2), [os'-kan], *adj.* relating to the Osci, an ancient Campanian people. [~L. *Osci*].
OSCHEOCELE, [os'-ki-ō-sēl], *n.* a tumour of the scrotum. [Gk. *oskhe* scrotum and *kele* tumour].
OSCHITIS, [os-kī'-tis], *n.* inflammation of the scrotum. [Gk. *oskhe* scrotum and *itis* denoting inflammation].
OSCILLATE, [os'-il-āt], *v.t. and i.* to swing, vibrate as a pendulum, to move between two points; to vacillate, to hesitate, to waver between choices; (*elect.*) to cause to swing to and fro; to generate electromagnetic waves.
OSCILLATION, [os'-il-ā'-shun], *n.* the act or state of oscillating; vacillation. [L. *oscillatio* swinging].
OSCILLATOR, [os'-il-āt'-er], *n.* an apparatus generating electro-magnetic waves.
OSCILLATORY, [os'-il-āt'-er-i], *adj.* oscillating, producing oscillation.
OSCILLOGRAPH, [os-il'-ō-graf'], *n.* an apparatus recording electrical oscillations.
OSCINES, [os'-in-ēz], *n.*(*pl.*) the singing birds. [L. *oscen oscinis* singing-bird].
OSCINIAN, [os-in'-i-an], *adj.* relating to the oscines.
OSCITANCY, [os'-it-an-si], *n.* the state of being oscitant.
OSCITANT, [os'-it-ant], *adj.* yawning, drowsy; negligent. [L. *oscitans*, *pres.pt.* of *oscitare* to gape].
OSCITANTLY, [os'-it-ant-li], *adv.* in oscitant fashion.
OSCITATE, [os'-it-āt], *v.i.* to yawn [L. *oscitare*].
OSCITATION, [os'-it-ā'-shun], *n.* yawning, sleepiness; negligence.
OSCULANT, [os'-kyŏŏ-lant], *adj.* kissing; adhering closely together.
OSCULAR, [os'-kyŏŏ-ler], *adj.* relating to kissing; pertaining to an orifice. [L. *osculum* kiss].
OSCULATE, [os'-kyŏŏ-lāt], *v.t. and i.* to kiss; (*math.*) to touch at more than one point. [L. *osculatum*, *p.pt.* of *osculari* to kiss].
OSCULATION, [os'-kyŏŏ-lā'-shun], *n.* a kiss, kissing; (*math.*) contact at more than a single point, as of curves. [L. *osculatio*].
OSCULATORY, [os'-kyŏŏ-lat-er-i], *adj.* kissing; **o. tablet,** a picture of Christ or a saint, kissed by the priest and handed round to be kissed by the congregation.
OSCULE, [os'-kyŏŏl], *n.* one of the openings in a sponge; a rudimentary sucker. [L. *osculum* kiss].
OSHAC, [ō'-shak], *n.* the gum ammoniac plant, *Dorema ammoniacum.* [Pers. *ushak*].
OSIER, [ō'-zi-er], *n.* willow used in basketwork. [Fr. *osier*].
OSIERED, [ō'-zi-erd], *adj.* abounding in osiers.
OSMANLI, [oz'-man-li], *n. and adj.* an Ottoman Turk; pertaining to the language and customs of these. [Sultan *Osman* I].
OSMIC, [oz'-mik], *adj.* relating to osmium in its higher valency.
OSMIOUS, [oz'-mi-us], *adj.* relating to osmium in its lower valency.
OSMIRIDIUM, [oz'-mi-rid'-i-um], *n* (*min.*) a native alloy of osmium and iridium, the heaviest alloy.
OSMIUM, [oz'-mi-um], *n.* (*chem.*) a rare metal, the heaviest element, so called from the peculiar odour of its oxide. [Gk. *osme* smell].
OSMOSIS, [oz-mō'-sis], *n.* the diffusion of fluids through a membrane or porous partition. [Gk. *osmos* pushing].
OSMOTIC, [oz-mot'-ik], *adj.* relating to osmosis.
OSMUNDA, [oz-mund'-a], *n.* a genus of six species of flowering ferns including the royal fern. [Fr. *osmonde*].
OSNABURG, [oz'-na-burg], *n.* a species of coarse linen. [*Orig.* from *Osnabrück* in Germany].
OSPHRESIOLOGY, [os'-frē-zi-ol'-o-ji], *n.* the study of smell. [Gk. *osphresis* smelling and *logos* speech].
OSPREY, [os'-prā], *n.* the sea-eagle, *Pandion haliaetus*; an egret's plume. [L. *ossifraga* bone-breaking].
OSSEIN, [os'-ē-in], *n.* a glue-like substance extracted from bone. [L. *os* bone].
OSSELET, [os'-el-et], *n.* an ossicle; a hard substance in the small bones of a horse's knee. [Fr. *osselet*].
OSSEOUS, [os'-ē-us], *adj.* made of bones; bony, having a skeleton. [L. *osseus*].
OSSIANIC, [os'-i-an'-ik], *adj.* relating to, in the style of, the poet Ossian. [Gael. *Oisin* a legendary poet].

OSPREY

OSSICLE, [os'-ikl], *n.* a small bone, a light bony structure. [L. *ossicu um*].
OSSIFEROUS, [os-if'-er-us], *adj.* having bones. [L. *os* bone and *ferre* to bear].
OSSIFIC, [os-if'-ik], *adj.* tending to ossify.
OSSIFICATION, [os'-i-fik-ā'-shun], *n.* the process of ossifying; the state of becoming ossified.
OSSIFY, [os'-i-fi], *v.t. and i.* to cause to become, turn into, bone; to become changed into bony tissue; (of joints) to become bony and immovable. [L. *os* bone and *facere* to make].
OSSIVOROUS, [os-iv'-er-us], *adj.* feeding on bones. [L. *os* bone and *vorare* to devour].
OSSUARY, [os'-yŏŏ-er-i], *n.* a charnel-house. [LL. *ossuarium*].
OSTEAL, [os'-ti-al], *adj.* (*med.*) of, pertaining to, or resembling, bone. [Gk. *osteon* bone].
OSTEITIS, [os-tē-ī'-tis], *n.* inflammation of the bone-tissue. [OSTEO and Gk. *itis* denoting inflammation].
OSTENSIBILITY, [os-ten'-si-bil'-i-ti], *n.* the quality of being ostensible.
OSTENSIBLE, [os-ten'-sibl], *adj.* apparent, displayed, pretended, professed. [~L. *ostensum* exhibited].
OSTENSIBLY, [os-ten'-sib-li], *adv.* apparently, avowedly, professedly.
OSTENSION, [os-ten'-shun], *n.* (*eccles.*) the exposure and adoration of the Host. [L. *ostensio*].
OSTENSIVE, [os-ten'-siv], *adj.* ostensible.
OSTENSORY, [os-ten'-ser-i], *n.* a transparent pyx. [MedL. *ostensorium*].
OSTENT, [os'-tent'], *n.* a portent. [L. *ostentus*].
OSTENTATION, [os'-tent-ā'-shun], *n.* a deliberate and pretentious show, a vulgar display of some possession, glory, or imagined merit; †a presage, portent, apparition. [L. *ostentatio*].
OSTENTATIOUS, [os'-tent-ā'-shus], *adj.* indulging in, exhibiting, ostentation; intentionally obvious.

OSTENTATIOUSLY, [os'-tent-ā'-shus-li], *adv.* in ostentatious fashion.
OSTENTATIOUSNESS, [os'-tent-ā'-shus-nes], *n.* the quality of being ostentatious.
OSTEO-, *pref.* bone, bony, relating to bone. [Gk. *osteon* bone].
OSTEOCOLLA, [os'-tē-ō-kol'-a], *n.* glue made from bones. [OSTEO and Gk. *kolla* glue].
OSTEOCOPE, [os'-tē-ō-kōp], *n.* syphilitic rheumatism. [Gk. *osteokopos*].
OSTEOGENY, [os'-tē-oj'-en-i], *n.* bone formation. [OSTEO and Gk. *genes* producing].
OSTEOGRAPHY, [os'-tē-og'-ra-fi] *n.* osteology. [OSTEO and Gk. *graphia* writing].
OSTEOLITE, [os'-tē-ō-līt], *n.* calcium phosphate. [OSTEO and Gk. *lithos* stone].
OSTEOLOGER, [os'-tē-ol'-oj-er], *n.* an osteologist; one skilled in osteology.
OSTEOLOGIC, [os'-tē-ol-oj'-ik], *adj.* osteological.
OSTEOLOGICAL, [os'-tē-ol-oj'-ik-al], *adj.* pertaining to osteology.
OSTEOLOGICALLY, [os'-tē-ol-oj'-ik-a-li], *adv.* according to osteology.
OSTEOLOGIST, [os'-tē-ol'-oj-ist], *n.* one skilled in osteology.
OSTEOLOGY, [os'-tē-ol'-o-ji], *n.* the science or study of bones. [OSTEO and Gk. *logos* speech].
OSTEOMALACIA, [os'-tē-ō-mal-ā'-si-a], *n.* a softening in the bone from deficiency of earthy matter; rickets. [OSTEO and Gk. *malakia* softness].
OSTEOMYELITIS, [ost'-ē-ō-mī'-el-īt'-is], *n.* (*path.*) inflammation of the marrow of bone. [OSTEO and MYELITIS].
OSTEOPATH, [os'-tē-ō-path'], *n.* one practising osteopathy.
OSTEOPATHIC, [os'-tē-ō-path'-ik], *adj.* relating to osteopathy.
OSTEOPATHIST, [os'-tē-op'-ath-ist], *n.* an osteopath.
OSTEOPATHY, [os'-tē-op'-ath-i], *n.* the treatment of disease and deformity by manipulation and manipulative surgery. [OSTEO and Gk. *pathos* suffering].
OSTEOSARCOMA, [os'-tē-ō-sah-kō'-ma], *n.* (*med.*) sarcoma of the bone.
OSTEOTOMY, [os'-tē-ot'-o-mi], *n.* dissection of bones. [OSTEO and Gk. *tome* cutting].
OSTEOZOA, [os'-tē-ō-zō'-a], *n.*(*pl.*) (*zool.*) the vertebrata. [OSTEO and Gk. *zoon* living creature].
OSTIOLAR, [os'-ti-ō'-ler], *adj.* relating to an ostiole.
OSTIOLATE, [os'-ti-ō-lāt], *adj.* having an ostiole or ostioles.
OSTIOLE, [os'-ti-ōl], *n.* (*bot.*) a pore in lichens and other plants, the orifice through which spores are discharged in the fungi, etc. [LL. *ostiolum* doorway].
OSTLER, HOSTLER, [os'-ler], *n.* a stableman at a hostel. [ME. *hostiler* inn-keeper].
OSTMEN, [ōst'-men], *n.*(*pl.*) Danish settlers in Ireland. [Dan. *ost* east and MAN (1)].
OSTRACIAN, [os-trā'-shan], *adj.* related to, connected with, the oyster. [Gk. *ostrakon* shell].
OSTRACISM, [os'-tra-sizm], *n.* a method of Athenian democracy for preserving political peace, by which a person might be banished for ten years by the vote of a general plebiscite; social exclusion by one's fellows. [OSTRACIZE].
OSTRACITE, [os'-tra-sīt], *n.* a fossil oyster shell. [~Gk. *ostrakon* shell].
OSTRACIZE, [os'-tra-sīz], *v.t.* to banish by ostracism; to exclude from society by common opinion. [Gk. *ostrakon* shell, potsherd, on which the vote was written].
OSTRACON, [*pl.* **ostraca**), [os'-tra-kon], *n.* an inscribed and baked clay tablet. [Gk. *ostrakon* shell, potsherd].
OSTREICULTURE, [os'-trē-i-kul'-cher], *n.* the artificial breeding of oysters. [Gk. *ostreon* oyster and CULTURE].
OSTRICH, [os'-trich], *n.* a large, flightless long-legged African and Asiatic bird; (*fig.*) a foolish, self-deluded person. [ME. *ostriche* from Gk. *strouthos*].
OSTROGOTH, [os'-trō-goth], *n.* one of the Eastern Goths. [OHGerm. *ostar* eastward].
OTALGIA, [ō-tal'-ji-a], *n.* ear-ache. [Gk. *otalgia* from *ous otos* ear and *algos* pain].
OTHER, [UTH'-er], *adj.* different, distinct from, not the same as, the thing referred to or pointed out; the second of two; additional to, besides this, not the thing here; an alternative, not always specified. [OE. *other*].
OTHERNESS, [UTH'-er-nes], *n.* the quality of being distinct from, other than, the thing known to common experience.
OTHERWHERE†, [UTH'-er-wāer], *adv.* elsewhere.
OTHERWHILE†, [UTH'-er-wīl], *adv.* at another time.
OTHERWISE, [UTH'-er-wīz], *adv.* in another fashion; in different circumstances; unless, if not; in other respects.
OTIC, [ō'-tik], *adj.* relating to the ear. [Gk. *otikos*].
OTIOSE, [ō'-ti-ōs], *adj.* lazy, slothful; futile, useless. [L. *otiosum* idle].
OTITIS, [ō-tī'-tis], *n.* inflammation of the ear. [Gk. *ous otos* ear and *itis* denoting inflammation].
OTO-, *pref.* relating to the ear. [Gk. *ous otos* ear].
OTOCYST, [ō'-tō-sist], *n.* the auditory vesicle. [OTO and CYST].
OTOGRAPHY, [ō-tog'-raf-i], *n.* otology. [OTO and Gk. *graphia* writing].
OTOLITH, [ō'-tō-lith], *n.* an ear-stone, a concretion of lime found in the labyrinth of the ear. [OTO and Gk. *lithos* stone].
OTOLOGY, [ō-tol'-o-ji], *n.* the study of the ear. [OTO and Gk. *logos* speech].
OTORRHOEA, [ō'-tor-ē'-a], *n.* (*med.*) a discharge from the ear. [OTO and Gk. *rhoia* flow].
OTOSCOPE, [ō'-tō-skōp], *n.* an instrument for examining the ear. [OTO and SCOPE].
OTTAR, see ATTAR.
OTTAVA-RIMA, [ot-ah'-va-rē'-ma], *n.* a stanza of eight lines, the first six rhyming alternately and the last two forming a rhymed couplet. [It. *ottava-rima*].
OTTER, [ot'-er], *n.* a furry, aquatic, web-footed mammal of the genus *Lutra*; a fishing device consisting of a heavy plank with bait attached, moored some distance from the shore. [OE. *oter*].

OTTER

OTTO, see ATTAR.
OTTOMAN (1), [ot'-ō-man], *n.* a Turk. [*Osman*, first of the Osmanli Sultans].
OTTOMAN (2), [ot'-ō-man], *n.* a padded settee of various types; a settee whose seat contains a box, or which consists of a circular seat round a pillar serving as a common back. [*Prec.*].
OTTOMAN (3), [ot'-ō-man], *adj.* Turkish.
OUBLIETTE, [ōō'-bli-et'], *n.* a dungeon whose only access is through a trap in the floor of a room above. [Fr. *oubliette* from *oublier* to forget].
OUCH, [owch], *n.* a jewel-socket; a jewelled brooch. [OFr. *nouche*].
OUGHT† (1), [awt], *n.* nought, a cipher; aught. [AUGHT].
OUGHT (2), [awt], *v. auxil.* expressing duty, obligation, necessity; expressing probability. [OE. *ahte*, *pret.* of *agan* to possess].
OUIJA, [wē'-jah], *n.* a planchette, a board lettered with the alphabet and used to receive spiritualist messages. [Fr. *oui* yes and Germ. *ja* yes].
OUISTITI, [wis-tē'-ti], *n.* the common marmoset, *Hapale jacchus*. [WISTITI].
OULONG, see OOLONG.
OUNCE (1), [ownts], *n.* a unit of weight, being one-sixteenth of a pound avoirdupois, 480 grains troy, or one-twentieth of an Imperial pint; (*fig.*) a very little, the smallest noticeable quantity. [ME. *unce* from L. *uncia* twelfth of a pound].
OUNCE (2), [ownts], *n.* the Tibetan snow-leopard; any animal of the leopard family. [Fr. *once*].
OUR, [ow'-er], *possessive adj.* belonging, relating to, connected with, us. [OE. *ure*].
OURANOGRAPHY, see URANOGRAPHY.
OURETIC, [ow-ret'-ik], *adj.* relating to urine. [~Gk. *ouron* urine.]
OUROSCOPY, [ow-ros'-kop-i], *n.* divination by the examination of urine. [Gk. *ouron* urine and *skopos* viewer].
OURS, [ow'-e(r)z], *possessive pron.* belonging to. us.
OURSELF, (ourselves), [ow'-e(r)-self'], *pron.*, *reflex. and emphatic form of* WE.
OUSEL, see OUZEL.
OUST, [owst], *v.t.* to expel, turn out, eject, dispossess from place or position. [OFr. *oster* to remove].
OUSTER, [owst'-er], *n.* illegal dispossession; dismissal.
OUT (1), [owt], *adj.* outer; remote from, unenclosed or uncontained by a position or concept (given or implied); vanished; having reached the final point; mistaken; evident, public; (*cricket*) dismissed by the

decision of the umpire, and so not entitled to bat. [OUT (2)].

OUT (2), [owt], *adv.* not in; with motion away from a point, position, or concept (given or implied); from within such a point, position, etc.; with remoteness from such a point, position, etc.; so as to vanish, to the final stage; so as to be evident to public notice; **o. of**, (of animals) having as female parent; **o. on**, shame on; **o. with**, drive out; **all o., flat o.**, with all possible force or energy; **murder will o.**, (something hidden and discreditable) will always come to light. [OE. *ut(e)*].

OUT (3), [owt], *v.t.* to turn out, expel. [*Prec.*].

OUT- [owt], *pref.* as a prefix denoting almost all its adverbial meanings, out, remote, excessive, superior. [OUT (2)].

OUT-AND-OUT, [owt'-and-owt'], *adj.* thorough, complete.

OUTASKING, [owt'-ahsk'-ing], *n.* the third proclamation of the banns of marriage.

OUTBALANCE, [owt-bal'-ants], *v.t.* to overweigh, be heavier than.

OUTBID, (**outbidding, outbid, outbidden**), [owt-bid'], *v.t.* to bid higher than.

OUTBOARD, [owt'-bawd], *adj.* on the outer side of a ship.

OUTBOUND, [owt'-bownd'], *adj.* outward bound, on the way out.

OUTBRAG, (**outbragging, outbragged**), [owt-brag'], *v.t.* to surpass in boasting.

OUTBRAVE, [owt-brāv'], *v.t.* to defy successfully, bluster out; excel in courage.

OUTBREAK, [owt'-brāk], *n.* a sudden breaking out, a bursting forth of anything (disease, war, etc.).

OUTBREAKING, [owt'-brāk'-ing], *n.* an outbreak.

OUTBUILDING, [owt'-bild-ing], *n.* a subsidiary building detached from the main block.

OUTBURST, [owt'-burst], *n.* an outbreak, *esp.* of passion, etc., into speech.

OUTCAST, [owt'-kahst], *n.* one rejected and cast out by society, etc.; a vagabond.

OUTCASTE, [owt'-kahst], *adj.* in India, belonging to no caste, without caste rights.

OUTCLASS, [owt-klahs'], *v.t.* to excel completely in merit or skill.

OUTCOME, [owt'-kum], *n.* result, upshot of a thing.

OUTCROP, [owt'-krop], *n.* (*geol.*) a formation of rock exposed at the surface.

OUTCROSS, [owt'-kros'], *n.* cross-breeding.

OUTCRY, [owt'-krī], *n.* a cry of indignation, alarm, etc., a noisy uproar of protest at something, a general clamour of disapproval.

OUTDARE, [owt-dāer'], *v.t.* to dare more than.

OUTDISTANCE, [owt-dist'-ants], *v.t.* to get in front of, get ahead of.

OUTDO, (**outdoes, outdid, outdone**), [owt-dōō'], *v.t.* to excel in achievement, do better in performance than.

OUTDOOR, [owt'-daw(r)], *adj.* of the open air, not in a building.

OUTDOORS, [owt-daw(r)z'], *adv.* in the open air.

OUTER (1), [owt'-er], *n.* the ring of a circular target farthest from the bull.

OUTER (2), [owt'-er], *adj.* farther out, farther from the inside or centre; external, outside some intimacy, objective.

OUTERMOST, [owt'-er-mōst], *adj.* farthest out.

OUTFACE, [owt-fās'], *v.t.* to stare out, bluff out, brazen out, successfully defy.

OUTFALL, [owt'-fawl], *n.* the mouth of a flow of water; an outlet, discharge.

OUTFIELD, [owt'-fēld], *n.* (*cricket*) the fieldsmen placed farthest from the batsmen, towards the boundary; a field separate from the main extent of a farm, etc.

OUTFIT, [owt'-fit], *n.* a person's complete clothes, equipment, etc., for a specific task or situation; (*slang*) a party of people and their equipment for some common venture, a group of persons.

OUTFITTER, [owt'-fit-er], *n.* a dealer in outfits, a hosier.

OUTFLANK, [owt-flangk'], *v.t.* to get round the side of an enemy and encompass one of his flanks; (*fig.*) to outwit.

OUTFLOW, [owt'-flō], *n.* an outfall; an outpouring.

OUTFLY, (**outflew, outflown**), [owt-flī'], *v.t.* to fly better or faster than.

OUTGATE, [owt'-gāt], *n.* a passage out.

OUTGENERAL, (**outgeneralling, outgeneralled**), [owt-jen'-er-al], *v.t* to out-manoeuvre, to prove a better general than.

OUTGO, (**outwent, outgone**), [owt-gō'], *v.t.* to excel, go faster than.

OUTGOER, [owt'-gō-er], *n.* one who leaves a place.

OUTGOING (1), [owt'-gō-ing], *n.*(*sg. or pl.*) expenditure, outlay.

OUTGOING (2), [owt'-gō-ing], *adj.* going out, away.

OUTGROW, (**outgrew, outgrown**), [owt-grō'], *v.t.* to grow too large or old for; to grow beyond, to lose (a taste or characteristic) with the passage of time.

OUTGROWTH, [owt'-grōth], *n.* the consequence of something, that which grows from a thing.

OUTGUARD, [owt'-gahd], *n.* a guard at some distance from the thing guarded.

OUTHAUL, [owt'-hawl], *n.* a rope for hauling out the head or foot of a sail.

OUT-HEROD, [owt-he'-rod], *v.t.* to be more savage than (Herod).

OUTHOUSE, [owt'-hows], *n.* an outbuilding, a shed away from the house.

OUTING, [owt'-ing], *n.* an excursion, brief holiday, short trip away from home.

OUTJOCKEY, [owt-jok'-i], *v.t.* to out-manoeuvre.

OUTLANDER, [owt'-land-er], *n.* an alien; a non-Boer in the Transvaal. [Du. *uitlander*].

OUTLANDISH, [owt-land'-ish], *adj.* oddly alien, barbarous.

OUTLAST, [owt-lahst'], *v.t.* to last longer than; to exceed in duration.

OUTLAW (1), [owt'-law], *n.* one placed beyond the protection of the law by legal sentence; a lawless person, a vagabond. [OScand. *utlagi*].

OUTLAW (2), [owt'-law], *v.t.* to sentence to outlawry; to expel from society.

OUTLAWRY, [owt'-law-ri], *n.* a legal declaration making someone an outlaw; the state of being an outlaw.

OUTLAY, [owt'-lā], *n.* expenditure, expenses, *esp.* money spent with the expectation of some definite return.

OUTLEAP, (**outleapt**), [owt-lēp'], *v.t.* to leap farther than.

OUTLET, [owt'-let], *n.* a passage outwards, an orifice; a means or chance of expression.

OUTLIER, [owt'-lī-er], *n.* that which is separate from its main body or proper centre; (*geol.*) an outcrop entirely surrounded by older rocks.

OUTLINE (1), [owt'-līn], *n.* the boundary line of a figure; the apparent edge of an object, defining its shape, *esp.* the outer line of a drawing giving the plane shape of the whole; the general features of a situation, theory, proposal, event, etc., which give an impression of the whole without detail, a short account of a thing giving the main points without particulars.

OUTLINE (2), [owt'-līn], *v.t.* to draw an outline of, to give an outline of, to summarize.

OUTLIVE, [owt-liv'], *v.t.* to live longer than.

OUTLIVER, [owt-liv'-er], *n.* one who outlives.

OUT-LODGER, [owt'-loj'-er], *n.* a non-collegiate student.

OUTLOOK, [owt'-lōōk], *n.* the view seen from a place, a prospect; (*fig.*) a view of the future, a future prospect suggested by present events; an attitude of mind, the way in which things are considered; the place from which a view is seen, a lookout.

OUTLYING, [owt'-lī'-ing], *adj.* lying at a distance, remote.

OUTMAN, (**outmanning, outmanned**), [owt-man'], *v.t.* to outface, overcome by superior courage; to surpass in the number of men.

OUT-MANOEUVRE, [owt-man-ōōv'-er], *v.t.* to defeat by superiority in strategy or tactics, to surpass in generalship.

OUTMARCH, [owt-mahch'], *v.t.* to march more quickly than, to march further than.

OUTMEASURE, [owt-mezh'-er], *v.t.* to exceed in measure.

OUTMOST, [owt'-mōst], *adj.* outermost.

OUTNESS, [owt'-nes], *n.* externality; the state of being outside.

OUTNUMBER, [owt-num'-ber], *v.t.* to exceed in number.

OUT-OF-DOOR, [owt'-ov-daw'-(er)], *adj.* outdoor.

OUT-OF-THE-WAY, [owt'-ov-THe-wā'], *adj.* remote, isolated, difficult of approach; unusual.

OUTPACE, [owt-pās'], *v.t.* to progress or walk faster than.

OUTPARISH, [owt'-pa-rish], *n.* an outlying parish.

OUTPART, [owt'-paht], *n.* a remote part.

OUT-PATIENT, [owt'-pā'-shent], *n.* a non-resident patient coming to hospital for treatment.

OUT-PENSIONER, [owt'-pen'-shun-er], *n.* a person

receiving a pension from an institution without having to reside there.

OUTPLAY, [owt-plā'], *v.t.* to play better than.

OUTPORT, [owt'-pawt], *n.* a port away from a main customs-centre.

OUTPOST, [owt'-pōst], *n.* a detachment of troops holding a post some distance from their main body in order to prevent surprise; (*fig.*) a place where some manner of life or culture exists far from its main home.

OUTPOUR, [owt-paw(r)'], *v.t.* to pour out.

OUTPOURING, [owt'-paw-ring], *n.* an outburst a pouring out, an effusion of words and passionate feelings.

OUTPUT, [owt'-pŏŏt], *n.* the quantity produced by a factory, instrument, or person within a given time.

OUTRAGE (1), [owt'-rāj], *n.* a violent, disgusting and offensive act committed against person, property, or public feeling; rape or sexual violation. [OFr. *outrage*].

OUTRAGE (2), [owt'-rāj], *v.t.* to rape, violate; to commit an outrage against the feelings of.

OUTRAGEOUS, [owt-rāj'-us], *adj.* of the nature of an outrage, excessively and flagrantly offensive, monstrous. [OFr. *outrageus*].

OUTRAGEOUSLY, [owt-rāj'-us-li], *adv.* in outrageous fashion.

OUTRAGEOUSNESS, [owt-rāj'-us-nes], *n.* the quality of being outrageous.

OUTRANCE, [ōō'-trants], *n.* extreme limit. [Fr. *outrance*].

OUTRANGE, [owt-rānj'], *v.t.* (usually of guns) to have a longer range than.

OUTRE, outré, [ōō'-trā], *adj.* excessive, beyond good taste. [Fr. *outré* exaggerated].

OUTREACH, [owt-rēch'], *v.t.* to reach farther than, to overreach.

OUTRIDE, (outrode, outridden), [owt-rīd'], *v.t.* to ride faster than.

OUTRIDER, [owt'-rīd-er], *n.* a mounted attendant riding before, behind, or at the side of, a carriage.

OUTRIGGER, [owt'-rig-er], *n.* a mast and tackle for lifting weights; a rowlock projecting from a boat's side to give extra leverage, a boat having such devices; a projection from a carriage shaft for an extra trace; a counterpoise carried to windward.

OUTRIGHT (1), [owt'-rīt], *adj.* downright, forthright.

OUTRIGHT (2), [owt'-rīt'], *adv.* frankly, brusquely, openly, immediately, all at once.

OUTROOT, [owt-rōōt'], *v.t.* to root out.

OUTRUN, (outrunning, outran, outrun), [owt-run'], *v.t.* to run, or go faster than, to exceed.

OUTSAIL, [owt-sāl'], *v.t.* to sail faster than.

OUTSELL, (outsold), [owt-sel'], *v.t.* to sell more successfully than.

OUTSET, [owt'-set], *n.* the beginning, start of a business, affair, series of events.

OUTSETTLEMENT, [owt'-setl'-ment], *n.* outlying settlement.

OUTSHINE, (outshone), [owt-shīn'], *v.t.* to excel in brilliance, to make a better impression than.

OUTSIDE (1), [owt'-sīd'], *n.* the external parts of a thing, externality, the position of what is not within.

OUTSIDE (2), [owt'-sīd], *adj.* on, related to, the outer part of a thing, external, not within, not connected with a thing; extreme, reaching to the farthest extent; outdoor.

OUTSIDE (3), [owt-sīd'], *adv.* on the exterior, outer side of, beyond, in the open air, not in a particular place.

OUTSIDER, [owt-sīd'-er], *n.* one who is regarded by members of a clique as unworthy of their notice; (*racing*) a horse not considered to have any reasonable chance of a place.

OUTSIZE, [owt'-sīz'], *adj.* larger than normal, *esp.* as applied to ready-made clothes intended for large or fat persons.

OUTSKIRTS, [owt'-skurts], *n.* the borders of a thing, the outer fringes of a town, a distant suburb.

OUTSOAR, [owt-saw(r)'], *v.t.* to soar higher than.

OUTSOLE, [owt'-sōl], *n.* the outer sole.

OUTSPAN, (outspanning, outspanned), [owt-span'], *v.t.* to unyoke (beasts) from a wagon. [Du. *uitspannen*].

OUTSPENT, [owt-spent'], *adj.* tired out.

OUTSPOKEN, [owt'-spōk'-en], *adj.* forthright of speech, frank, devastatingly candid and straightforward in speech.

OUTSPOKENNESS, [owt-spōk'-en-nes], *n.* the quality of being outspoken.

OUTSPREAD, [owt'-spred'], *adj.* spread out; wide.

OUTSPREADING (1), [owt-spred'-ing], *n.* a spreading out.

OUTSPREADING (2), [owt-spred'-ing], *adj.* spreading out.

OUTSTAND, (outstood), [owt-stand'], *v.t. and i.* to withstand; to stand out.

OUTSTANDING, [owt-stand'-ing], *adj.* conspicuous, distinctive, most evident, remarkable; standing over, still owing, unpaid.

OUTSTARE, [owt-stāer'], *v.t.* to stare out of countenance.

OUTSTAY, [owt-stā'], *v.t.* to exceed, stay longer than; **to o. one's welcome**, to stay so long that one is no longer welcome.

OUTSTRETCH, [owt-strech'], *v.t.* to stretch out.

OUTSTRIP, (outstripping, outstripped), [owt-strip'], *v.t.* to leave behind by exceeding in pace, to go faster or do better than.

OUT-TALK, [owt-tawk'], *v.t.* to talk down, surpass in talking.

OUTVALUE, [owt-val'-yōō], *v.t.* to exceed in value.

OUTVIE, [owt-vī'], *v.t.* to surpass.

OUTVOTE, [owt-vōt'], *v.t.* to defeat by polling more votes.

OUT-VOTER, [owt'-vōt-er], *n.* a non-resident voter.

OUTWALK, [owt-wawk'], *v.t.* to walk faster than, to surpass in walking.

OUTWALL, [owt'-wawl], *n.* the exterior wall.

OUTWARD (1), [owt'-werd], *adj.* external, relating to the outside; material, visible; going outwards.

OUTWARD (2), [owt'-werd], *adv.* outwards, towards the outside, away from.

OUTWARDLY, [owt'-werd-li], *adv.* towards the outside; from the outside, externally.

OUTWARDNESS, [owt'-werd-nes], *n.* externality; objectivity.

OUTWARDS, [owt'-werdz], *adv.* towards the outside, from the inside, in a direction away from.

OUTWEAR, (outwore, outworn), [owt-wāer'], *v.t.* to last longer than; to wear out, exhaust.

OUTWEIGH, [owt-wā'], *v.t.* to carry more weight, have more importance, than.

OUTWIND, (outwound), [owt-wīnd'], *v.t.* to wind out.

OUTWING, [owt-wing'], *v.t.* to outflank.

OUTWIT, (outwitting, outwitted), [owt-wit'], *v.t.* to overreach or defeat by superior wit and tactics, to deceive, get the better of by astuteness.

OUTWORK (1), [owt'-wurk], *n.* a fortification in advance of the main defences.

OUTWORK (2), [owt'-wurk], *n.* work done away from the factory, etc.

OUZEL, OUSEL, [ōō'-zel], *n.* one of several kinds of thrush. [OE. *osle*].

OVA, [ō'-va], *n.(pl.)* of OVUM.

OVAL (1), [ō'-val], *n.* a plane figure of oval shape; a piece of ground in this shape.

OVAL (2), [ō'-val], *adj.* elliptical, egg-shaped. [L. *ovum* egg].

OVALBUMEN, [ōv-al'-bew-men], *n.* the albumen or white of an egg. [L. *ov(um)* egg and ALBUMEN].

OUZEL

OVALLY, [ō'-val-i], *adv.* in the figure or shape of an oval.

OVARIAN, [ō-vāer'-i-an], *adj.* relating to the ovary.

OVARIOTOMIST, [ō-vāer'-i-ot'-om-ist], *n.* one skilled in ovariotomy.

OVARIOTOMY, [ō-vāer'-i-ot'-o-mi], *n.* excision of the ovary. [L. *ovarium* and Gk. *tomia* cutting].

OVARIOUS, [ō-vāer'-i-us], *adj.* ovarian.

OVARY, [ō'-ver-i], *n.* (*anat.*) the reproductive organ in female animals producing the eggs for fertilization; (*bot.*) the part of the pistil containing the ovules. [L. *ovarium*].

OVATE, [ō'-vāt], *adj.* oval, egg-shaped, elliptical with one end broader than the other. [L. *ovatus*].

OVATE-OBLONG, [ō'-vāt-ob'-long], *adj.* between ovate and oblong.

OVATION, [o-vā'-shun], *n.* (*hist.*) a lesser Roman triumph granted for important successes that yet did not fulfil the triumphal requirements; an enthusiastic public greeting. [L. *ovatio*].

OVEN, [uvn], *n.* an enclosed receptacle for baking; a small chemical kiln. [OE. *ofen*].

OVEN-BIRD, [uvn'-burd], *n.* a South American bird of the genus, *Furnarius*, which builds nests of mud shaped like ovens on branches or beams.

OVEN-BIRD

OVER (1), [ō'-ver], *n.* (*cricket*) a series of six or eight balls delivered in succession from one end of the pitch before changing over; (*pl.*) excess.

OVER (2), [ō'-ver], *adv.* above, across, towards and across, away and across; from one point, side, station to another; away from the perpendicular, upright, normal position; upwards across and down; finished, gone, past; excessively, too much; everywhere, in every respect; in repetition.

OVER (3), [ō'-ver], *prep.* above, across, spanning, covering, towards and across; more than, superior to, lasting longer than. [OE. *ofer*].

OVER-, *pref.* expressing superiority, situation or passage across or on top of, excess beyond the right or normal.

OVERACT, [ō'-ver-akt'], *v.t. and i.* to act so as to make or be unnatural.

OVERALLS, [ō'-ver-awlz], *n.*(*pl.*) a loose garment worn over others for protection while engaged in manual work; an officer's dress trousers.

OVERARCH, [ō'-ver-ahch'], *v.t. and i.* to arch over.

OVERARM, [ō'-ver-ahm], *adj. and adv.* (*cricket*) (bowled) with the hand and arm raised above the shoulder.

OVERAWE, [ō'-ver-aw'], *v.t.* to browbeat, frighten into respectful submission.

OVERBALANCE, [ō'-ver-bal'-ants], *v.t. and i.* to lose balance so as to fall over; to upset the balance of a thing; to exceed in weight or importance.

OVERBEAR, (**overborne**), [ō'-ver-bāer'], *v.t.* to dominate, gain ascendancy over, to impose one's will upon.

OVERBEARING, [ō'-ver-bāer'-ing], *adj.* tending, endeavouring, to overbear.

OVERBEARINGLY, [ō'-ver-bāer'-ing-li], *adv.* in overbearing fashion.

OVERBID, (**overbidding, overbid**), [ō'-ver-bid'], *v.t.* to outbid.

OVERBLOWN, [ō'-ver-blōn'], *adj.* past full bloom, blowzy.

OVERBOARD, [ō'-ver-bawd], *adv.* over the side of a ship into the sea, (*fig.*) cast aside, out of the way.

OVERBRIDGE, [ō'-ver-brij], *n.* a bridge crossing a road.

OVERBUILD, [ō'-ver-bild'], *v.t. and i.* to build over; to build too much.

OVERBURDEN, [ō'-ver-bur'-den], *v.t.* to burden too heavily.

OVERBUSY, [ō'-ver-biz'-i], *adj.* too officious.

OVERCALL, [ō'-ver-kawl'], *v.t. and i.* (*bridge*) to make a bid higher than; to call more than one's cards justify. [OVER (2) and CALL (2)].

OVER-CAPITALIZE, [ō'-ver-kap'-it-al-iz], *v.t.* to supply (a company) with too much capital.

OVERCAREFUL, [ō'-ver-kāer'-fŏŏl], *adj.* too cautious.

OVERCAST (1), [ō'-ver-kahst], *adj.* cloudy, gloomy.

OVERCAST (2), [ō'-ver-kahst'], *v.t.* to cast a gloom over; to stitch over a seam to prevent unravelling.

OVERCHARGE (1), [ō'-ver-chahj], *n.* an excessive charge. [OVER (2) and CHARGE (2)].

OVERCHARGE (2), [ō'-ver-chahj'], *v.t. and i.* to charge (a person) too high a price; to charge too heavily with electricity, to overload.

OVERCOAT, [ō'-ver-kōt], *n.* a coat worn over the rest of the garments, a top-coat.

OVERCOMABLE, [ō'-ver-kum'-abl], *adj.* able to be overcome.

OVERCOME, (**overcame**), [ō'-ver-kum'], *v.t.* to subdue, defeat, master, surmount.

OVERCOSTLY, [ō'-ver-kost'-li], *adj.* too costly.

OVERCROWD, [ō'-ver-krowd'], *v.t.* to crowd to excess, to pack too close, to force to live in insufficient space.

OVERCROWDING, [ō'-ver-krowd'-ing], *n.* the act or fact of having or placing too many persons or things in a given space.

OVERDO, (**overdoes, overdid, overdone**), [ō'-ver-dōō'], *v.t.* to overact, over-emphasize, to go too far, to cook too long; **to o. things**, to tire oneself out by attempting too much.

OVERDONE, [ō'-ver-dun'], *adj.* cooked too much.

OVERDOSE (1), [ō'-ver-dōs], *n.* too great a dose.

OVERDOSE (2), [ō'-ver-dōs'], *v.t.* to administer too great a dose to.

OVERDRAFT, [ō'-ver-drahft], *n.* a loan from a bank; such a debt incurred by withdrawing more than is at one's credit.

OVERDRAW, (**overdrew, overdrawn**), [ō'-ver-draw'], *v.t.* to run up an overdraft on one's account.

OVERDRIVE, (**overdrove, overdriven**), [ō'-ver-drīv'], *v.t.* to drive or work too hard.

OVERDUE, [ō'-ver-dew'], *adj.* behind its due time.

OVERESTIMATE (1), [ō'-ver-es'-tim-at], *n.* an exaggerated estimate, too great an expectation.

OVERESTIMATE (2), [ō'-ver-es'-tim-āt], *v.t. and i.* to make an overestimate (of).

OVERFEED, (**overfed**), [ō'-ver-fēd'], *v.t. and i.* to feed immoderately.

OVERFLOW (1), [ō'-ver-flō], *n.* that which overflows; an outlet for overflowing; amount in excess of space, etc.; **o. meeting**, a secondary meeting held when the number of people exceeds the capacity of the original place of meeting.

OVERFLOW (2), [ō'-ver-flō'], *v.t. and i.* to flow over the edge of something by reason of being too much for the space within; to flood something by flowing over into it; to be too much or too many for the available space; to be abundant (with)].

OVERFREIGHT, [ō'-ver-frāt'], *v.t.* to load too heavily.

OVERGROW, (**overgrew, overgrown**), [ō'-ver-grō'], *v.t.* to grow over; to outgrow.

OVERGROWTH, [ō'-ver-grōth], *n.* that which grows over, an excessive growth.

OVERHAND (1), [ō'-ver-hand'], *adj.* done with the hand above the shoulder.

OVERHAND (2), [ō'-ver-hand'], *adv.* with the hand above the shoulder.

OVERHANG (1), [ō'-ver-hang'], *n.* that which overhangs, a part projecting over.

OVERHANG (2), (**overhung**), [ō'-ver-hang'], *v.t. and i.* to hang out over, project over; (*fig.*) to hang over threateningly, to impend.

OVERHARDY, [ō'-ver-hahd'-i], *adj.* foolhardy; unduly daring.

OVERHASTY, [ō'-ver-hās'-ti], *adj.* precipitate; unduly hasty.

OVERHAUL (1), [ō'-ver-hawl], *n.* a thorough examination and repairing.

OVERHAUL (2), [ō'-ver-hawl'], *v.t.* thoroughly to inspect and examine for faults (*esp.* machinery); to overtake and pass, *esp.* at sea.

OVERHEAD (1), [ō'-ver-hed'], *adj.* above the head, above; (of expenses) permanent, not related to price and wage fluctuations or to marketing.

OVERHEAD (2), [ō'-ver-hed'], *adv.* above, above the head.

OVERHEADS, [ō'-ver-hedz'], *n.*(*pl.*) overhead expenses.

OVERHEAR, (**overheard**), [ō'-ver-hēer'], *v.t.* to hear what is meant for another, to listen to by stealth.

OVERHEAT, [ō'-ver-hēt'], *v.t.* to heat to excess.

OVERINDULGENCE, [ō'-ver-in-dulj'-ents], *n.* excessive indulgence.

OVERISSUE, [ō'-ver-is'-yōō], *v.t.* to issue too great a quantity of.

OVERJOYED, [ō'-ver-joid'], *adj.* extremely pleased and happy at a thing.

OVERLADE, [ō'-ver-lād'], *v.t.* to overload (a ship).

OVERLAND (1), [ō'-ver-land], *adj.* lying across country or overland, travelling by land.

OVERLAND (2), [ō'-ver-land'], *adv.* by land, across land. [OVERLAND (1)].

OVERLAP, (**overlapping, overlapped**), [ō'-ver-lap'], *v.t. and i.* to lap over, to project beyond the edge of something so as partly to cover it; (*fig.*) partly to correspond in subject or coincide in time.

OVERLAVISH, [ō'-ver-lav'-ish], *adj.* lavish to excess.

OVERLAY (1), [ō'-ver-lā], *n.* that which overlays, a covering.

OVERLAY (2), (**overlaid**), [ō'-ver-lā'], *v.t.* to coat, cover over heavily.

OVERLEAF, [ō'-ver-lēf], *adv.* on the next page.

OVERLEAP, [ō'-ver-lēp'], *v.t.* to leap over.

OVERLEATHER, [ō'-ver-leTH-er], *n.* the upper leather of a shoe or boot.

OVERLIE, (**overlay, overlain**), [ō'-ver-lī'], *v.t.* to lie upon, to smother by lying upon.

OVERLOAD (1), [ō'-ver-lōd], *n.* an excessive load or electric charge.

OVERLOAD (2), [ō'-ver-lōd'], *v.t.* to load too heavily.

OVERLOOK, [ō'-ver-lŏŏk'], *v.t.* to look down on from a higher position; to supervise, superintend;

to ignore through oversight, to forget, neglect; to condone, to excuse; to pay no account to.

OVERLOOKER, [ō'-ver-lŏŏk-er], *n.* an overseer.

OVERLORD, [ō'-ver-lawd], *n.* a feudal superior.

OVERMAN, [ō'-ver-man], *n.* (*philos.*) a superman, Nietzsche's dominant hero.

OVERMANTEL, [ō'-ver-mantl'], *n.* a mantelshelf.

OVERMASTER, [ō'-ver-mahst'-er], *v.t.* to master, overcome.

OVERMATCH, [ō'-ver-mach'], *v.t.* to be too much for, to overcome.

OVERMEASURE, [ō'-ver-mezh'-er], *n.* a surplus.

OVERMODEST, [ō'-ver-mod'-ist], *adj.* excessively modest.

OVERMOST, [ō'-ver-mōst], *adj.* most superior.

OVERMUCH, [ō'-ver-much'], *adv.* too much.

OVERNICE, [ō'-ver-nīs'], *adj.* too refined or fastidious.

OVERNIGHT, [ō'-ver-nīt'], *adv.* on the previous night; through the night; in the coming night; suddenly, with great swiftness and unexpectedness.

OVERNIGHTER, [ō'-ver-nīt'-er], *n.* an article written overnight; writing bearing traces of hurried work.

OVERPAY, (**overpaid**), [ō'-ver-pā'], *v.t.* to pay more than is due.

OVERPLUS, [ō'-ver-plus'], *n.* a surplus, excess.

OVERPOWER, [ō'-ver-pow'-er], *v.t.* to overcome, subdue, overmaster, reduce to helplessness, vanquish.

OVERPOWERING, [ō'-ver-pow'-er-ing], *adj.* that overpowers.

OVERPRAISE, [ō'-ver-prāz'], *v.t.* to praise too highly.

OVERPRINT (**1**), [ō'-ver-print], *n.* something printed on printed material such as postage stamps.

OVERPRINT (**2**), [ō'-ver-print'], *v.t.* to print too many copies of; to provide with an overprint.

OVERPRODUCE, [ō'-ver-pro-dews'], *v.t. and i.* to produce in excess of demand.

OVERPRODUCTION, [ō'-ver-pro-duk'-shun], *n.* production too great for demand.

OVERPROOF, [ō'-ver-prŏŏf'], *adj.* above alcoholic proof.

OVERRAKE, [ō'-ver-rāk'], *v.t.* to break in upon, as a heavy sea.

OVERRATE, [ō'-ver-rāt'], *v.t.* to rate too highly.

OVERREACH, [ō'-ver-rēch'], *v.t. and i.* to outwit, get the best of; (*reflex.*) to defeat oneself by attempting too much subtlety; (of a horse) to cut the hind leg against the front hoof in jumping.

OVERRIDE, (**overrode, overridden**), [ō'-ver-rīd'], *v.t.* to ride down, ride over (as cavalry over infantry); to ride to excess, so as to strain, fatigue; to overrule, brush aside, disregard.

OVERRIPE, [ō'-ver-rīp'], *adj.* excessively ripe.

OVERRULE, [ō'-ver-rŏŏl'], *v.t.* to set aside (a ruling), to decide against; to master, overcome the will of another.

OVERRULING, [ō'-ver-rŏŏl'-ing], *adj.* tending to overrule, dominating.

OVERRUN, (**overrunning, overran**), [ō'-ver-run'], *v.t.* to spread over, infest, occupy, conquer by spreading far and wide in great numbers, to exceed (a limit); (*typ.*) to shift lines of type in making an adjustment.

OVERRUNNER, [ō'-ver-run'-er], *n.* one who overruns.

OVERSEAS (**1**), [ō'-ver-sēz], *adj.* beyond the sea, across the sea, foreign.

OVERSEAS (**2**), [ō'-ver-sēz'], *adv.* beyond, across the sea, abroad.

OVERSEE, (**oversees, oversaw, overseen**), [ō'-ver-sē'], *v.t.* to superintend.

OVERSEER, [ō'-ver-sēer], *n.* a superintendent; a parish officer.

OVERSELL, (**oversold**), [ō'-ver-sel'], *v.t. and i.* to sell more of a thing than one possesses.

OVERSET, (**oversetting, overset**), [ō'-ver-set'], *v.t. and i.* to overthrow, to upset; to tip over.

OVERSEW, (**oversewn**), [ō'-ver-sō], *v.t.* to sew two edges together, passing the needle through from the same side in every stitch.

OVERSHADOW, [ō'-ver-shad'-ō], *v.t.* to cover with shade or shadow; to put into the shade, make dim by contrast; to cast gloom on, make depressed.

OVERSHOE, [ō'-ver-shŏŏ], *n.* an outer shoe worn for additional protection over bad going, a golosh.

OVERSHOOT, (**overshot**), [ō'-ver-shŏŏt'], *v.t.* to shoot above or beyond; **to o. the mark,** to exaggerate, overdo, go too far.

OVERSHOT, [ō'-ver-shot], *adj.* (of a water-wheel) turned by water falling from above.

OVERSIGHT, [ō'-ver-sīt], *n.* supervision, overseeing; lapse through carelessness, careless failure to observe something, error made through such a mistake.

OVERSLAUGH (**1**), [ō'-ver-slaw], *n.* (*milit.*) the omission of one duty in favour of another more pressing. [Du. *overslag* omission].

OVERSLAUGH (**2**), [ō'-ver-slaw'], *v.t.* to remit from a duty because of another more pressing; (*U.S.*) to hinder, obstruct (legislation). [*Prec.*].

OVERSLEEP, (**overslept**), [ō'-ver-slēp'], *v.i.* to sleep beyond the proper time for waking.

OVERSMAN, [ō'-verz-man], *n.* an overseer, foreman.

OVERSTAND, (**overstood**), [ō'-ver-stand'], *v.i.* to be outstanding; (of bills, etc.) to stand over.

OVERSTATE, [ō'-ver-stāt'], *v.t.* to state (a case) too strongly, to exaggerate.

OVERSTATEMENT, [ō'-ver-stāt'-ment], *n.* an exaggeration.

OVERSTAY, [ō'-ver-stā'], *v.i.* to stay too long.

OVERSTEP, (**overstepping, overstepped**), [ō'-ver-step'], *v.t.* to step over, exceed, go beyond (proper bounds of behaviour).

OVERSTOCK, [ō'-ver-stok'], *v.t.* to stock with too many goods, to furnish too great a supply of.

OVERSTOREY, OVERSTORY, [ō'-ver-staw'-ri], *n.* an upper storey.

OVERSTRAIN (**1**), [ō'-ver-strān'], *n.* weakness, nervous disturbance, due to excessive mental or physical effort.

OVERSTRAIN (**2**), [ō'-ver-strān'], *v.t.* to put too great a strain on.

OVERSTRUNG, [ō'-ver-strung'], *adj.* too highly strung, overstrained, having too sensitive nerves, neurotic; (of a piano) having diagonally crossing strings.

OVERSUBSCRIBED, [ō'-ver-sub-skrībd'], *adj.* (of a loan or issue of shares) producing applications for more than the amount available.

OVERSUBSCRIPTION, [ō'-ver-sub-skrip'-shun], *n.* the act of oversubscribing.

OVERT, [ō'-vert], *adj.* obvious, done openly, apparent. [OFr. *overt*].

OVERTAKE, (**overtook, overtaken**), [ō'-ver-tāk'], *v.t.* to catch up with, come upon suddenly, overcome.

OVERTASK, [ō'-ver-tahsk'], *v.t.* to overtax.

OVERTAX, [ō'-ver-taks'], *v.t.* to tax (one's strength, etc.) excessively.

OVERTHROW (**1**), [ō'-ver-thrō], *n.* a defeat, destruction, the state of being overthrown; (*cricket*) a fielded ball thrown past the wicket so that extra runs can be scored, a run so made.

OVERTHROW (**2**), (**overthrew, overthrown**), [ō'-ver-thrō'], *v.t.* to throw down, overcome, defeat, destroy.

OVERTHWART, [ō'-ver-thwawt], *adv.* athwart.

OVERTIME, [ō'-ver-tīm], *n.* time spent in work beyond the hours for which wages are paid; extra wages received for such work.

OVERTLY, [ō'-vert-li], *adv.* in overt fashion.

OVERTONE (**1**), [ō'-ver-tōn], *n.* a harmonic.

OVERTONE (**2**), [ō'-ver-tōn'], *v.t.* to give too deep a tone to.

OVERTOP, (**overtopping, overtopped**), [ō'-ver-top'], *v.t.* to exceed in height, to rise over the top of.

OVERTRADE, [ō'-ver-trād'], *v.t. and i.* to oversell.

OVERTURE, [ō'-ver-tyŏŏ-er], *n.* (*mus.*) an orchestral prelude to a work, a preliminary piece of music played before a performance; (*fig.*) the preliminaries of a great event; (*pl.*) friendly approaches, formal tentative advances. [OFr. *overture*].

OVERTURN, [ō'-ver-turn'], *v.t. and i.* to upset, throw over; to fall, tip over.

OVERVALUE, [ō'-ver-val'-yŏŏ], *v.t.* to value too highly.

OVERWASH, [ō'-ver-wosh], *n.* (*geol.*) the detritus carried by water over frontal moraines.

OVERWEENING, [ō'-ver-wēn'-ing], *adj.* presumptuously proud, arrogant, full of insolent conceit. [OVER and OE. *wenan* to think].

OVERWEENINGLY, [ō'-ver-wēn'-ing-li], *adv.* in overweening fashion.

OVERWEIGH, [ō'-ver-wā'], *v.t. and i.* to bear more weight than, to overbalance, to outbalance.

OVERWEIGHT, [ō'-ver-wāt], *adj.* more in weight than the required or permissible amount.

OVERWHELM, [ō'-ver-welm'], *v.t.* to pour down over, utterly to overpower by pouring upon, to sweep over, completely to master by extreme force or weight of numbers, to astound, abash, overcome.

OVERWHELMING, [ō'-ver-welm'-ing], *adj.* so as to overwhelm, tending to overwhelm.

OVERWHELMINGLY, [ō'-ver-welm'-ing-li], *adv.* in overwhelming fashion.
OVERWIND, (overwound), [ō'-ver-wīnd'], *v.t.* to wind to excess.
OVERWORK (1), [ō'-ver-wurk], *n.* excessive work, work too great for the system to endure.
OVERWORK (2), [ō'-ver-wurk'], *v.t.* and *i.* to work a person or machine too hard; to perform more work than one can stand.
OVERWROUGHT, [ō'-ver-rawt'], *adj.* overstrained, too much excited.
OVI- (1), *pref.* relating to an egg. [L. *ovum* egg].
OVI- (2), *pref.* relating to sheep. [L. *ovis* sheep].
OVIBOS, [ō'-vi-bos], *n.* the musk-ox. [OVI (2) and L. *bos* ox].
OVICULAR, [ō-vik'-yŏŏ-ler], *adj.* pertaining to an egg. [OVI (1)].
OVIDIAN, [ov-id'-i-an], *adj.* relating to the poet Ovid. [L. *Ovidius*].
OVIDUCT, [ō'-vi-dukt], *n.* the passage through which the egg passes from the ovary. [OVI (1) and DUCT].

OVIBOS

OVIFEROUS, [ō-vif'-er-us], *adj.* having eggs. [OVI (1) and L. *ferre* to bear].
OVIFORM, [ō'-vi-fawm], *adj.* egg-shaped. [OVI (1) and FORM].
OVINE, [ō'-vīn], *adj.* relating to sheep. [~OVI (2)].
OVIPAROUS, [ō-vip'-er-us], *adj.* bringing forth young in eggs. [OVI (1) and L. *parere* to beget].
OVIPOSIT, [ō'-vi-poz'-it], *v.t.* and *i.* to lay eggs. [OVI (1) and L. *positum*, *p.pt.* of *ponere* to place].
OVIPOSITION, [ō'-vi-poz-ish'-un], *n.* the act of laying eggs.
OVIPOSITOR, [ō'-vi-poz'-it-er], *n.* the egg-laying organ in fish and insects.
OVISAC, [ō'-vi-sak'], *n.* the cavity containing the egg in the ovary. [OVI (1) and SAC].
OVO-, *pref.* egg. [L. *ovum* egg].
OVOID, [ō'-void], *adj.* egg-shaped, egg-like. [OVO and Gk. *oeides* like].
OVOIDAL, [ō-void'-al], *adj.* ovoid.
OVOLO, [ō'-vol-ō], *n.* (*arch.*) a convex, elliptical, downward sloping moulding, having a section one-quarter of a circle. [OVO].
OVOLOGY, [ō-vol'-o-ji], *n.* the study of the ovum. [OVO and Gk. *logos* speech].
OVOVIVIPAROUS, [ō'-vō-vī-vip'-er-us], *adj.* producing eggs which hatch inside the parent. [OVO and VIVIPAROUS].
OVULARY, [ō'-vew-ler-i], *adj.* relating to the ovule.
OVULE, [ō'-vewl], *n.* (*bot.*) the unfertilized seed. [OVUM].
OVULIFEROUS, [ō'-vewl-if'-er-us], *adj.* producing ovules. [OVULE and L. *ferre* to bear].
OVULITE, [ō'-vew-līt], *n.* a fossil egg. [L. *ovum* egg and Gk. *lithos* stone].
OVUM, [ō'-vum], *n.* the female germ-cell in the ovary before fertilization. [L. *ovum* egg].
OWE, [ō], *v.t.* and *i.* to be indebted (to someone for something); to be under some obligation to a person, to have as a result of; to be in debt. [OE. *agan* to possess].
OWING, [ō'-ing], *adj.* in the state of being a debt, not paid; **o. to,** as a result of, on account of. [*Prec.*].
OWL, [owl], *n.* a large-headed, hook-beaked, carnivorous, nocturnal bird of the family *Strigidae*, having very many species; (*fig.*) a solemn, stupid, sleepy person. [OE. *ule*].
OWLET, HOWLET, [owl'-et], *n.* a young owl.
OWLING, [owl'-ing], *n.* illegal export, *esp.* the illegal export of wool from medieval England. [OWL, because of its furtive and nocturnal character].
OWLISH, [owl'-ish], *adj.* foolish, sleepy as an owl.
OWL-LIGHT, [owl'-lit], *n.* faint, glimmering light.
OWL-LIKE, [owl'-līk], *adj.* like an owl.
OWN (1), [ōn], *adj.* possessed by, related to, someone in the closest, completest, most intimate degree; performed by a person for himself by his own skill and effort; **to hold one's o.,** to maintain one's position, hold one's ground against attack. [OE. *agen* possessed by].
OWN (2), [ōn], *v.t.* to possess, have legal title to, to acknowledge, admit as belonging to oneself, to admit; confess to something. [OE. *agnian*].
OWNER [ōn'-er], *n.* one who owns, one with legal title.
OWNERLESS, [ōn'-er-les], *adj.* that lacks an owner.
OWNERSHIP, [ōn'-er-ship], *n.* the condition or title of an owner, the period of being an owner, the régime of an owner.
OWSE, [owz], *n.* the liquor in a tan vat. [OOZE].
OWSER, [owz'-er], *n.* owse.
OX, (*pl.* **oxen**), [oks], *n.* the castrated male of the species *Bos taurus*; (*fig.*) a lumpish, senseless, patient, extremely strong person. [OE. *oxa*].
OXALATE, [oks'-al-āt], *n.* (*chem.*) a salt of oxalic acid.
OXALIC, [oks-al'-ik], *adj.* relating to, derived from, oxalis; **o. acid,** a poisonous acid used in dyeing and bleaching.
OXALIS, [oks'-al-is], *n.* (*bot.*) the wood-sorrel, a plant with white or pink flowers, and bright green leaves containing potassium oxalate. [Gk. *oxalis* sorrel].
OXBIRD, [oks'-burd], *n.* the dunlin, *Tringa alpina*.
OXBOW, [oks'-bō], *n.* the U-shaped yoke of a draught ox; a horseshoe bend in a river.
OXEN, [oksn], *n.*(*pl.*) of ox.
OXER, [oks'-er], *n.* a fence against oxen.
OX-EYE, [oks'-ī], *n.* the marguerite daisy, *Chrysanthemum leucanthemum*.
OX-EYED, [oks'-īd], *adj.* having ox-like eyes.
OXFORD, [oks'-ferd], *n.* a university town in England; a kind of monocle; a kind of shoe lacing up over the instep; **O. accent,** an affected drawling form of speech; **O. bags,** wide legged trousers formerly fashionable; **O. Group,** a religious movement, publicized by Dr. Buchman; **O. Movement,** the High Church Anglo-Catholicism of Pusey and Newman.
OXFORDIAN, [oks-fawd'-i-an], *n.* a division of the Jurassic rocks.
OX-GALL, [oks'-gawl], *n.* the gall of the ox.

OX-EYE

OXGANG, [oks'-gang'], *n.* as much land as an ox can plough in a day, about twelve acres. [OE. *oxgang*].
OXGATE, [oks'-gāt], *n.* an oxgang.
OXIDABILITY, [oks'-id-ab-il'-i-ti], *n.* the state of being oxidable.
OXIDABLE, [oks'-id-abl], *adj.* able to be oxidized.
OXIDATE, [oks'-id-āt], *v.t.* and *i.* to make into, become, an oxide.
OXIDATION, [oks'-id-ā'-shun], *n.* the process of oxidizing, the state of being oxidized, the process occurring when oxygen is combined with another element.
OXIDE, [oks'-īd], *n.* a compound of oxygen with a radical or another element. [Fr. *oxide* from *ox*(*ygène*) and (*ac*)*ide* acid].
OXIDIZABLE, [oks'-i-dīz-abl], *adj.* capable of being oxidized.
OXIDIZATION, [oks'-id-īz-ā'-shun], *n.* the process of combining oxygen with a radical or element; the state or process of being oxidized.
OXIDIZE, [oks'-id-īz], *v.t.* and *i.* to make into an oxide, to combine with oxygen or subject to an equivalent process; to cover with oxide; to become an oxide, to become rusty through oxidization.
OXIDIZEMENT, [oks'-id-īz-ment], *n.* oxidation.
OXIDIZING, [oks'-i-dīz-ing], *adj.* that tends to oxidize.
OX-LIKE, [oks'-līk], *adj.* resembling an ox.
OXLIP, [oks'-lip], *n.* the plant, *Primula elatior*. [OE. *oxanslyppe*].
OXONIAN (1), [oks-ō'-ni-an], *n.* a native of Oxford, a student at Oxford University.
OXONIAN (2), [oks-ō'-ni-an], *adj.* of, or pertaining to, Oxford, Oxonians, or the adherents of the theory that Shakespeare's works were written by the Earl of Oxford.
OXPECKER, [oks'-pek'-er], *n.* an African bird of the genus *Buphaga*.
OXSTALL, [oks'-stawl], *n.* a stall or stand for oxen.
OXTAIL, [oks'-tāl], *n.* the tail of the ox as used for making soup, etc.
OX-TONGUE, [oks'-tung'], *n.* the tongue of the ox used as food; the plant bugloss, *Helminthia echioides*.
OXY-, *pref.* relating to oxygen or an oxide. [Gk. *oxus* sharp].
OXYACETYLENE, [oks'-i-a-set'-i-lēn], *adj.* of, or pertaining to, the welding process employing acetylene gas burnt in a stream of oxygen. [OXY(GEN) and ACETYLENE].
OXYCHLORIDE, [oks'-i-klaw'-rīd], *n.* a combination including oxygen and chlorine.

OXYGEN, [oks′-i-jen], *n.* (*chem.*) the gaseous element denoted by O, a common colourless gas, essential to life, existing free in the atmosphere, and forming 87.5 per cent of water. [Gk. *oxus* sharp and *genes* producing].
OXYGENATE, [oks′-ij-en-āt], *v.t.* to impregnate with oxygen
OXYGENATION, [oks′-ij-en-ā′-shun], *n.* the act of oxygenating, the state of being oxygenated.
OXYGENIZABLE, [oks′-ij-en-īz′-abl], *adj.* capable of being oxygenized.
OXYGENIZE, [oks′-ij-en-īz], *v.t.* to oxygenate.
OXYGON, [oks′-i-gon], *n.* a triangle with two acute angles. [Gk. *oxus* sharp and *gonia* angle].
OXYGONAL, [oks-ig′-on-al], *adj.* having acute angles.
OXYHYDROGEN, [oks′-i-hī′-drō-jen], *adj.* containing a mixture of oxygen and hydrogen.
OXYMEL, [oks′-im-el′], *n.* a mixture of vinegar and honey. [Gk. *oxus* sharp and *meli* honey].
OXYMORON, [oks′-im-aw′-ron], *n.* a rhetorical figure in which diametrically opposite words and ideas are associated, e.g., bitter-sweet. [Gk. *oxumoros* sharply foolish].
OXYTONE, [oks′-i-tōn], *adj.* uttered in a high tone. [OXY and TONE].
OYER, [oi′-er], *n.* (*leg.*) a Royal commission to Judges to try cases at Assize. [AFr. *oyer et terminer* to hear and determine].
OYEZ, [ō-yez′], *int.* a call for silence by an usher or town-crier. [OFr. *oyez* hear ye!].
OYSTER, [ois′-ter], *n.* an edible bivalve marine mollusc of the genus *Ostrea*; **as dumb as an o.**, completely uncommunicative; **the world is mine o.**, all is mine for the taking. [ME. *oystre* from Gk. *ostreon*].
OYSTER-BAR, [oist′-er-bah(r)′], *n.* a bar where oysters and other shell-fish are served.
OYSTER-BED, [ois′-ter-bed′], *n.* a breeding ground for oysters.
OYSTER-CATCHER, [ois′-ter-kach′-er], *n.* the wading-bird, the sea-pie.
OYSTER-PATTY, [ois′-ter-pat′-i], *n.* a patty containing baked oysters.
OYSTER-PLANT, [ois′-ter-plahnt′], *n.* a plant, the salsify, *Tragopogon porrifolius*, whose leaves taste like an oyster.
OYSTERSHELL, [ois′-ter-shel′], *n.* the shell of an oyster.
OZAENA, [ō-zē′-na], *n.* a foetid discharge from the nose. [Gk. *ozaina*].
OZOCERITE, OZOKERIT(E), [ō-zō′-ser-īt, ō-zō′-ker-īt], *n.* a wax-like mineral found in shale and used for making candles. [Gk. *ozo* I smell and *keros* wax].
OZONE, [ō′-zōn′], *n.* a triatomic form of oxygen obtained by electric discharges in oxygen, so called from its smell; (*coll.*) the bracing smell of the seaside. [Gk. *ozo* I smell].
OZONIC, [ō-zon′-ik], *adj.* pertaining to ozone.
OZONIZE, [ō′-zōn-īz], *v.t.* to impregnate with ozone.
OZONIZED, [ō′-zōn-īzd], *adj.* charged with ozone.
OZONOMETER, [ō′-zōn-om′-it-er], *n.* an instrument used for measuring the quantity of ozone in a gas.

P

P, [pē], the sixteenth letter of the English alphabet.
PA, [pah], *n.* (*slang*) father. [Shortened from PAPA].
PABULAR, [pab′-yōō-ler], *adj.* relating to, providing, food. [L. *pabularius*].
PABULOUS, [pab′-yōō-lus], *adj.* providing food, fodder. [L. *pabulosus*].
PABULUM, [pab′-yōō-lum], *n.* food, fodder. [L. *pabulum*].
PACA, [pah′-ka], *n.* the South American spotted rodent, *Cœlogenus paca*. [Braz. *pak*].

PACA

PACATION, [pak-ā′-shun], *n.* the act of pacifying, the state of being pacified. [L. *pacatio*].
PACE (1), [pās], *n.* a single step in walking or running, the space covered in such a single step; speed of walking, progression, the speed of any (progressive) motion; a mode of walking; running; the manner of a horse's stepping, *esp.* in ambling and sometimes that in which both legs on the same side move together (rack). [L. *passus* step].
PACE (2), [pās], *v.t. and i.* to take paces, to walk with regular step; to help a runner by running beside him and setting a suitable speed, to try out someone's (something's) speed; **to p. out**, to measure out (a length by counting regular steps. [*Prec.*].
PACE (3), [pā′-si], *prep.* notwithstanding, with deferential contradiction of. [L. *pace*, ablative of *pax* peace].
PACED, [pāsd], *adj.* having a certain pace.
PACEMAKER, [pās′-māk-er], *n.* one who sets a runner's pace.
PACER, [pās′-er], *n.* a pacemaker; a horse that paces.
PACHISI, [pach-ē′-zi], *n.* an Indian game played with dice and pieces on a board. [Hind. *pachisi* twenty-five].
PACHYDACTYL, [pak′-i-dak′-til], *n.* a thick-toed animal. [Gk. *pakhus* thick and *daktulos* finger].
PACHYDERM, [pak′-i-durm], *n.* a thick-skinned animal, a hooved non-ruminant. [Gk. *pakhus* thick and *derma* skin].
PACHYDERMATOUS, [pak′-i-durm′-at-us], *adj.* thick-skinned, stolid, like a pachyderm.
PACHYMETER, [pak-im′-it-er], *n.* an instrument for measuring thickness. [Gk. *pakhus* thick and METER].
PACIFIABLE, [pas′-i-fī′-abl], *adj.* able to be pacified.
PACIFIC (1), [pas-if′-ik], *n.* the great ocean lying between the Americas and Asia. [PACIFIC (2)].
PACIFIC (2), [pas-if′-ik], *adj.* peaceful, mild, desiring, promoting peace; pertaining to the Pacific. [L. *pacificus*].
PACIFICATION, [pas′-if-ik-ā′-shun], *n.* the act of pacifying, subduing resistance. [L. *pacificatio*].
PACIFICATOR, [pas′-if-ik-āt′-or], *n.* one who, or that which, pacifies. [L. *pacificator*].
PACIFICATORY, [pas-if′-ik-āt′-e-ri], *adj.* tending to pacify. [L. *pacificatorius*].
PACIFIER, [pas′-i-fī′-er], *n.* one who pacifies.
PACIFISM, [pas′-if-izm], *n.* the belief that violence, *esp.* military action as an instrument of policy, is evil; the doctrine and policy of disarmament and non-resistance.
PACIFIST (1), [pas′-if-ist], *n.* an upholder of pacifism.
PACIFIST (2), [pas′-if-ist], *adj.* relating to, advocating, in accordance with, pacifism.
PACIFY, [pas′-i-fī], *v.t.* to make peaceful, assuage (danger or hostility), appease; ruthlessly to suppress hostility and opposition in a conquered country. [L. *pacificare*].
PACK (1), [pak], *n.* a bundle of goods tied together for carriage on the back or by a beast of burden, a haversack carried on the back; a complete set of playing cards, a deck; (*Rugby football*) that part of the team forming the scrum, the forwards; a herd of animals hunting together; a group, mob of persons; a group of grouse; a cold compress to reduce inflammation. [ME. *pakke*].
PACK (2), [pak], *v.t.* to bundle together, to fit, crowd together in a box, etc., for storage or travel; to get together (personal belongings) for travel; to crowd, cram together, fill tightly; (*med.*) to wrap in a wet cloth to reduce inflammation; to fill (an assembly, jury) with one's own supporters; *v.i.* to crowd together, to gather one's goods together ready for travel; to come together in a pack; **to p. off**, to send (a person) away. [*Prec.*].
PACKAGE, [pak′-ij], *n.* a packed bundle, a parcel.
PACKER, [pak′-er], *n.* one who, or that which, packs.
PACKET, [pak′-it], *n.* a small package, parcel, a package sent through the post, a packet-boat; a publication containing news; (*slang*) a large sum of money made or lost in business or gambling; **to catch a p.**, (*slang*) to receive a heavy blow. [Fr. *paquet*].

PACKET-BOAT, [pak'-it-bōt'], *n.* a vessel conveying mails under a government contract.

PACKHORSE, [pak'-haws], *n.* a horse employed in carrying packs.

PACK-ICE, [pak'-is'], *n.* broken ice crushed together into heaps.

PACKING, [pak'-ing], *n.* the act of making packages or storing goods for travel; stuff used to pack round a delicate object for transport, or packed round pipes or machinery to prevent jarring or freezing; **to send a person p.**, to hurry someone unceremoniously away.

PACKING-CASE, [pak'-ing-kās'], *n.* a wooden case in which goods are packed.

PACKING-NEEDLE, [pak'-ing-nēdl'], *n.* a needle for sewing up packages.

PACKING-SHEET, [pak'-ing-shēt'], *n.* coarse canvas for packing goods.

PACKMAN, [pak'-man], *n.* a pedlar.

PACK-SADDLE, [pak'-sadl'], *n.* a saddle on which packs are laid.

PACKSTAFF, [pak'-stahf], *n.* a stick on which a package is slung over the shoulder.

PACKTHREAD, [pak'-thred'], *n.* coarse, strong thread for sewing up packages.

PACKWAX, see PAXWAX.

PACKWAY, [pak'-wā], *n.* a bridle-path for pack-horses.

PACO, [pah'-kō], *n.* the alpaca. [Peruvian *paco*].

PACT, [pakt], *n.* an agreement made between two or more parties, a covenant. [L. *pactum*, *p.pt.* of *pacisci* to make an agreement].

PACTION, [pak'-shun], *n.* a pact. [L. *pactio*].

PACTIONAL, [pak'-shun-al], *adj.* relating to a pact.

PAD (1), [pad], *n.* a road; an easy-paced horse; a footpad. [Du. *pad* path].

PAD (2), [pad], *n.* something stuffed with soft material used to fill out, protect, prevent friction; a stuffed leg-guard worn in cricket and other games; the soft parts of an animal's paw, the fleshy undersurface of a foot; a number of pieces of writing, blotting or drawing paper fastened one above the other in a block. [Uncert.].

PAD (3), (**padding, padded**), [pad], *v.i.* to trudge along on foot; (of an animal) to move with a soft padding sound. [PAD (1)].

PAD (4), (**padding, padded**), [pad], *v.t.* to stuff out, cover with soft material, to fill, protect with a pad; (*fig.*) to fill out a literary work with unnecessary verbiage so as to take more space. [PAD (2)].

PADAR, [pad'-ah(r)], *n.* coarse flour or meal. [Unkn.].

PADCLOTH, [pad'-kloth'], *n.* a cover for a horse's loins.

PADDING, [pad'-ing], *n.* stuffing material, stuff used to pad; literary verbiage to fill up space.

PADDLE (1), [padl], *n.* a short oar with broad, rounded blade, wielded with both hands without a rowlock, used in canoes; one of the boards of a paddlewheel. [Unkn.].

PADDLE (2), [padl], *n.* slush. [PUDDLE].

PADDLE (3), [padl], *v.t.* *and i.* to propel (a boat), move along by means of a paddle. [PADDLE (1)].

PADDLE (4), [padl], *v.i.* to walk in shallow water, to dabble the feet or hands in water. [PADDLE (2)].

PADDLE-BOARD, [padl'-bawd], *n.* one of the boards of a paddle-wheel.

PADDLE-BOX, [padl'-boks'], *n.* a wooden projection on each side of a steamboat to contain a paddle-wheel

PADDLER, [pad'-ler], *n.* one who paddles.

PADDLE-WHEEL, [padl'-wēl], *n.* a great wheel propelling a ship by means of boards fixed at right angles to its circumference, which push against the water when the wheel is revolved.

PADDLING, [pad'-ling], *n.* a flock of ducks when swimming.

PADDOCK (1), [pad'-ok], *n.* a toad. [ME. *paddok*].

PADDOCK (2), [pad'-ok], *n.* a small field for exercising horses; the enclosure on a racecourse where the horses are assembled. [OE. *pearroc*].

PADDOCK-STOOL, [pad'-ok-stōōl], *n.* a toad-stool; a mushroom.

PADDY (1), [pad'-i], *n.* (*coll.*) an Irishman; a fit of violent, childish temper. [Ir. *Padraig* Patrick].

PADDY (2), [pad'-i], *n.* growing rice. [Malay *padi*].

PADDY-BIRD, [pad'-i-burd], *n.* the Java sparrow, *Munia oryzivora*.

PADDY-MELON, [pad'-i-mel'-on], *n.* a wallaby. [Australian].

PADELLA, [pad-el'-a], *n.* a flat dish in which grease is burnt through a wick to give illumination. [It. *padella* flat pan].

PADISHA, [pad'-ish-ah'], *n.* great king, *esp.* the Shah of Persia, and the King of England as Emperor of India. [Pers. *padi* master and SHAH].

PADLOCK (1), [pad'-lok], *n.* a detachable lock with hinged link to be fixed through a staple. [Uncert.].

PADLOCK

PADLOCK (2), [pad'-lok'], *v.t.* to fasten with a padlock.

PADNAG, [pad'-nag'], *n.* an easy-going horse. [PAD (1) and NAG (1)].

PADOUK, [pa-dōōk'], *n.* a Burmese timber-tree. [Native].

PADRA, [pah'-dra], *n.* a kind of black tea. [Chin. *padra*].

PADRE, [pah'-drā], *n.* a military chaplain; (*coll.*) a clergyman. [Portug. *padre* father].

PADRONE, [pad-rō'-ni], *n.* the master of a Mediterranean coaster; inn-keeper; †an employer of beggars and street-musicians. [It. *padrone* patron].

PADUASOY, [pad'-yōō-as-oi], *n.* a corded silk stuff. [Fr. *pou-de-soie*].

PAEAN, PEAN, [pē'-an], *n.* a hymn of thanksgiving sung to Apollo; a song of joy and triumph. [Gk. *Paian* the Healer, an epithet of Apollo].

PAEDO-, PEDO-, *pref.* relating to education. [Gk. *pais paidos* boy].

PAEONY, see PEONY.

PAGAN (1), [pā'-gan], *n.* a heathen; (*fig.*) one without religion, morals or taste. [L. *paganus* countryman].

PAGAN (2), [pā'-gan], *adj.* relating to a pagan, his beliefs and his barbarism; non-Christian. [*Prec.*].

PAGANISM, [pā'-gan-izm], *n.* the state of being pagan, the beliefs of a pagan.

PAGANIZE, [pā'-gan-iz], *v.t.* to make pagan.

PAGE (1), [pāj], *n.* a youthful retainer of a prince or noble, a youth of noble birth in attendance upon a lord; a liveried boy servant, employed as footman or messenger. [OFr. *page* boy].

PAGE (2), [pāj], *n.* one side of a leaf or sheet of writing paper or leaf of a book. [*Fr. page*].

PAGE (3), [pāj], *v.t.* to call out for a person through the rooms of a hotel, etc. [PAGE (1)].

PAGE (4), [pāj], *v.t.* to paginate. [PAGE (2)].

PAGEANT, [paj'-ent], *n.* a splendid, colourful display of pomp and beauty; an easy and spectacular form of dramatics in which historical incidents are reconstructed by costumed players. [OFr. *pageant* mystery play].

PAGEANTRY, [paj'-ent-ri], *n.* the display, pomp, colour of a pageant.

PAGEHOOD, [pāj'-hōōd], *n.* the status or service of a page. [PAGE (1) and OE. *had* condition].

PAGINAL, [paj'-in-al], *adj.* relating to pages, in pages. [L. *paginalis*].

PAGINATE, [paj'-in-āt], *v.t.* to number the pages of a book in sequence. [L. *pagina* page].

PAGINATION, [paj'-in-ā'-shun], *n.* the act of paginating; the numerical order of the pages of a book.

PAGODA, [pag-ō'-da], *n.* a Far-Eastern sacred tower, built in a series of tapering storeys culminating in a slender pinnacle; a pointed booth where papers and tobacco are sold in a public park; an Indian gold coin. [Portug. *pagode*].

PAGODA-STONE, [pag-ō'-da-stōn'], *n.* (*min.*) a limestone containing orthoceratites which in section somewhat resemble pagodas; pagodite.

PAGODITE, [pag'-od-it], *n.* a kind of soft serpentine, used in China for carving into figures. [PAGODA].

PAGURIAN (1), [pag-yōōer'-i-an], *n.* a hermit crab, one of the *Paguridæ*. [Gk. *pagouros* a species of crab].

PAGURIAN

PAGURIAN (2), [pag-yōōer'-i-an], *adj.* relating to the *Paguridæ*.

PAH (1), [pah], *n.* a Maori fortified place, stockaded village. [Maori *pa*].

PAH (2), [pah], *int.* an expression of disgust, contempt, impatient anger.

PAID, [pād], *adj.* receiving pay for services. [*P.pt.* of PAY].

PAIDEUTICS, [pī-dewt'-iks], *n.* the science of education. [Gk. *paideutikos* relating to teaching].

PAIGLE, [pāgl], *n.* (*dial.*) the cowslip, *Primula veris*. [Uncert.].

PAIL, [pāl], *n.* a bucket, a conical open vessel for carrying liquid; the quantity of liquid contained in this. [OE. *pægel* wine-vessel].
PAILFUL, [pāl'-fŏŏl], *n.* the quantity of liquid a pail will contain.
PAILLASSE, see PALLIASSE.
PAILLETTE, [pal-yet'], *n.* a spangle. [Fr. *paillette*].
PAIN (1), [pān], *n.* physical suffering, an unpleasant nervous sensation in a part of the body, a smart, pang, ache, etc.; (*fig.*) distress, grief; care, trouble; punishment, penalty. [L. *poena* penalty].
PAIN (2), [pān], *v.t.* to cause pain to, inflict suffering upon, distress. [OFr. *pener*].
PAINFUL, [pān'-fŏŏl], *adj.* causing, inflicting pain; painstaking, laboriously careful and conscientious; distressing, deplorably bad.
PAINFULLY, [pān'-fŏŏl-i], *adv.* in painful fashion.
PAINFULNESS, [pān'-fŏŏl-nes], *n.* the state of being painful.
PAINIM†, see PAYNIM.
PAINLESS, [pān'-les], *adj.* causing no pain, free from pain.
PAINLESSLY, [pān'-les-li], *adv.* without pain.
PAINLESSNESS, [pān'-les-nes], *n.* the state of being painless, the quality of not producing pain.
PAINS, [pānz], *n.(pl.)* trouble, conscientious care, careful and laborious effort.
PAINSTAKER, [pānz'-tāk-er], *n.* one who takes pains.
PAINSTAKING, [pānz'-tāk-ing], *adj.* taking pain, taking laborious care to accomplish a thing.
PAINT (1), [pānt], *n.* a colouring substance, a pigment mixed with water or other liquid to colour a surface; rouge, cosmetics; (*fig.*) superficial colouring, appearance.
PAINT (2), [pānt], *v.t. and i.* to colour (a surface) by covering with paint; to cover, smear a surface with liquid; to make designs on a surface with coloured paint; to colour the face with cosmetics; to create a pictorial work of art with pigmented liquid; to describe, delineate vividly in speech or writing; to apply paint, to practise the art of painting; to use facial cosmetics; **to p. the town red,** to indulge in a drunken, riotous orgy of stupid horseplay and dissipation in public places. [OFr. *peint* from L. *pinctus*, *p.pt.* of *pingere* to paint].
PAINT-BOX, [pānt'-boks'], *n.* a box or tin made to contain artists' paints.
PAINT-BRUSH, [pānt'-brush'], *n.* a brush suitable for painting.
PAINTED LADY, [pānt'-ed-lād'-i], *n.* a handsome orange, black and white butterfly, *Vanessa cardui*; a variety of runner bean with parti-coloured flowers.
PAINTER (1), [pānt'-er], *n.* one whose trade is painting, a house-painter; a painter of pictures.
PAINTER (2), [pānt'-er], *n.* the rope mooring the bow of a boat; **to cast the p.,** to set oneself adrift. [ME. *pantere* noose].
PAINTER (3), [pānt'-er], *n.* (*U.S.*) a panther. [Fr. *panthère*].
PAINTER-STAINER, [pānt'-er-stān'-er], *n.* a painter of coats of arms.
PAINTING, [pānt'-ing], *n.* a painted picture, the act of painting such a picture; the act of painting generally; the occupation of painting pictures.
PAINTY, [pānt'-i], *adj.* covered with paint.
PAIR (1), [pāer], *n.* two of a kind; two similar, corresponding, or matching things; a group of two objects or animals, a mated couple of persons or animals; a couple in close association, two horses harnessed together; applied to an object consisting of two corresponding parts working in conjunction. [ME. *paire* from L. *par* equal].
PAIR (2), [pāer], *v.t. and i.* to put, bring together, in pairs; to come together in a pair, to mate; to be absent from a parliamentary division together with a member of the hostile party, both agreeing to refrain from voting; **to p. off,** to mate, separate into couples. [*Prec.*].
PAIRING-TIME, [pāer'-ing-tīm'], *n.* mating-time.
PAIR-WISE, [pāer'-wīz], *adv.* in pairs.
PAKEHA, [pak-ā'-ah], *n.* a white man. [Maori *pakeha*].
PAL (1), [pal], *n.* (*slang*) a friend. [Romany *pal* brother].
PAL (2), (palling, palled), [pal], *v.i.* to become pals, become friends.
PALA, [pah'-la], *n.* a South African antelope of the genus *Æpyceros*. [Native].
PALACE, [pal'-is], *n.* the residence of a prince, bishop, or potentate; a great and splendid mansion; (*slang*) a music hall, a dance hall. [OFr. *palais* from L. *Palatium* Palatine Hill].
PALADIN, [pal'-ad-in], *n.* one of Charlemagne's twelve peers; a noble knight, a chivalrous hero. [L. *palatinus* of the Palatine household].
PALAEARCTIC, [pal-i-ahk'-tik], *adj.* belonging to the northern region of the eastern hemisphere.
PALAEO-, *pref.* ancient, primitive. [Gk. *palaios* ancient].
PALAEOBOTANY, [pal'-ē-ō-bot'-an-i], *n.* the study of fossil plants. [PALAEO and BOTANY].
PALAEOCRYSTIC, [pā'-li-ō-krist'-ik], *adj.* pertaining to ancient ice. [PALAEO and Gk. *krustallos* ice].
PALAEOGEOGRAPHY, [pal'-ē-ō-jē-og'-raf-i], *n.* the study of prehistoric geography. [PALAEO and GEOGRAPHY].
PALAEOGRAPHY, [pa'-li-og'-raf-i], *n.* the study of ancient writing and inscriptions. [PALAEO and Gk. *graphia* writing].
PALAEOLITHIC, [pa'-li-ō-lith'-ik], *adj.* (*geol.*) relating to the Old Stone Age. [PALAEO and Gk. *lithos* stone].
PALAEOLOGY, [pa'-li-ol'-o-ji], *n.* the study of the ancient. [PALAEO and Gk. *logos* speech].
PALAEONTOGRAPHICAL, [pa'-li-ont'-ō-graf'-ik-al], *adj.* relating to palaeontography.
PALAEONTOGRAPHY, [pa'-li-ont-og'-raf-i], *n.* the description of extinct life. [PALAEO, Gk. *onta* beings and *graphia* writing].
PALAEONTOLOGICAL, [pa'-li-ont'-o-loj'-ik-al], *adj.* pertaining to palaeontology.
PALAEONTOLOGY, [pā'-li-ont-ol'-o-ji], *n.* the study of fossils; the science of extinct organisms. [PALAEO, Gk. *onta* beings and *logos* speech].
PALAEOZOIC, [pa'-li-ō-zō'-ik], *adj.* (*geol.*) of the second earliest geological era; containing the earliest forms of life. [PALAEO and Gk. *zoe* life].
PALAGONITE, [pal-ag'-on-īt], *n.* (*geol.*) a volcanic rock related to basalt. [*Palagonia* a place in Sicily].
PALANQUIN, [pal'-an-kēn'], *n.* a covered Oriental litter. [Portug. *palanquim*].
PALATABLE, [pal'-at-abl], *adj.* pleasing to the taste, agreeable.
PALATABLENESS, [pal'-at-abl-nes], *n.* the condition of being palatable.
PALATABLY, [pal'-at-ab-li], *adv.* so as to be palatable.
PALATAL (1), [pal'-at-al], *n.* (*phon.*) a front consonant, sounded by the palate and tongue. [*Next*].
PALATAL (2), [pal'-at-al], *adj.* pertaining to the palate; (*phon.*) produced by contact of the tongue with the palate. [Fr. *palatal*].
PALATE (1), [pal'-at], *n.* the roof of the mouth; a sense of taste, judgment of wines. [L. *palatum*].
PALATE (2), [pal'-at], *v.t.* to put up with, to stomach.
PALATIAL, [pal-ā'-shal], *adj.* like a palace; (of buildings, rooms) great and splendid, large and sumptuous. [PALACE].
PALATINATE (1), [pal-at'-in-at], *n.* the province of a Count Palatine; the dominion of the Count Palatine of the Rhine. [PALATINE (1)].
PALATINATE (2), [pal-at'-in-at], *n.* pale purple, lavender. [(County) *Palatine* (of Durham) whose University colours include this colour].
PALATINE (1), [pal'-at-īn], *adj.* pertaining to a lord who does homage to an overlord but is free within his own territory. [L. *palatinus* of the Imperial palace].
PALATINE (2), [pal'-at-īn], *adj.* relating to the palate.
PALAVER (1), [pal-ah'-ver], *n.* a conference between African natives and Europeans; idle talk. [Portug. *palavra* talk from L. *parabola* discourse].
PALAVER (2), [pal-ah'-ver], *v.i.* to hold a palaver, to chatter idly or fussily.
PALAVERER, [pal-ah'-ver-er], *n.* one who palavers.
PALE (1), [pāl], *n.* a pointed stake used for a fence or boundary; (*hist.*) the district round Dublin in English control after the 12th century; (*her.*) a vertical stripe about one-third the width of the shield; **beyond the p.,** outside the limits of proper behaviour. [L. *palus* stake].

PALE

PALE (2), [pāl], *adj.* whitish, pallid, without much colour, wan; dim, faint. [OFr. *pâle* from L. *pallidus*].
PALE (3), [pāl], *v.i.* to become pale (through fear), to fade, become dim by comparison.
PALEA, [pāl'-i-a], *n.* the inner husk of a grass. [L. *palea* chaff].
PALEACEOUS, [pāl'-i-ā'-shus], *adj.* (*bot.*) resembling chaff; covered with chaff-like scales. [*Prec.*].

PALE-EYED, [pāl'-īd'], *adj.* having dim or light eyes.
PALE-FACE, [pāl'-fās], *n.* a white man as named by American Indians.
PALE-FACED, [pāl'-fāst], *adj.* having a wan face.
PALELY, [pāl'-li], *adv.* dimly, wanly.
PALENESS, [pāl'-nes], *n.* the condition of being pale.
PALEOUS, [pāl'-i-us], *adj.* paleaceous.
PALESTRA, [pal-es'-tra], *n.* a wrestling-ground. [Gk. *palaistra*].
PALESTRIC, [pal-es'-trik], *adj.* pertaining to wrestling or the palestra.
PALETTE, [pal'-et], *n.* the small board on which an artist mixes his colours; the range of colours in a painting. [Fr. *palette*].
PALFREY, [pawl'-fri], *n.* a saddle-horse. [OFr. *palefrei*].
PALI (1), [pah'-li], *n.* the sacred Buddhist language. [Skr. *pali* canon].
PALI (2), [pah'-li], *adj.* of, in, or pertaining to, Pali.
PALIFICATION, [pal'-if-ik-ā'-shun], *n.* the setting up of a fence. [PALE (1)].
PALILOGY, [pal-il'-o-ji], *n.* verbal repetition for emphasis. [Gk. *palillogia*].
PALIMPSEST, [pal'-imp-sest], *n.* a parchment, etc., on which two or more writings are found superimposed, the earlier having been imperfectly erased. [Gk. *palimpsestos*].
PALINDROME, [pal'-in-drōm], *n.* a word or series of words reading the same in either direction. [Gk. *palindromos* running back].
PALING, [pāl'-ing], *n.* a fence formed of a line of stakes planted close together. [PALE (1)].
PALINGENESIS, [pal'-in-jen'-is-is], *n.* reincarnation; (*biol.*) the reproduction of parental characteristics. [Gk. *palin* again and GENESIS].
PALINODE, [pal'-in-ōd], *n.* a poem retracting a previous one, a recantation. [Gk. *palinoidia*].
PALISADE (1), [pal'-is-ād'], *n.* a defensive barrier of stakes set close together, an enclosure surrounded by such a fence; a pointed stake. [Fr. *palissade*].
PALISADE (2), [pal'-is-ād'], *v.t.* to surround with a palisade.
PALISANDER, [pal'-is-and'-er], *n.* rose-wood. [Fr. *palissandre*].
PALISH, [pāl'-ish], *adj.* rather pale.
PALKI, [pawl'-ki], *n.* an East Indian palanquin. [Native].
PALL (1), [pawl], *n.* a dark velvet cloth draped over a coffin, any dark, heavy covering, real or metaphorical; a pallium; (*her.*) a Y-shaped bearing on an escutcheon. [OE. *pæll* from L. *pallium* cloak].
PALL (2), [pawl], *v.i.* to become tedious or wearisome. [ME. *pallen* to lose spirit].
PALLADIAN, [pal-ā'-di-an], *adj.* (*arch.*) in the style of Andrea *Palladio*.
PALLADIUM (1), [pal-ā'-di-um], *n.* a safeguard, a protecting mascot. [L. *palladium* of Pallas, goddess of wisdom, whose statue defended Troy].
PALLADIUM (2), [pal-ā'-di-um], *n.* a heavy, white metal resembling platinum; the chemical element Pd. [*Pallas* the name of an asteroid].
PALLBEARER, [pawl'-bāer-er], *n.* one of the attendants of the coffin at a funeral.
PALLET (1), [pal'-et], *n.* a narrow straw mattress. [OFr. *paillet*].
PALLET (2), [pal'-et], *n.* a palette; a potter's implement. [PALETTE].
PALLET (3), [pal'-et], *n.* (*her.*) a half-pale. [PALE (1)]
PALLIAL, [pal'-i-al], *adj.* relating to a pallium.
PALLIASSE, PAILLASSE, [pal'-i-as'], *n.* a straw mattress. [Fr. *paillasse*].
PALLIATE, [pal'-i-āt], *v.t.* to mitigate, alleviate, extenuate, soften. [L. *palliare* to cloak].
PALLIATION, [pal'-i-ā'-shun], *n.* the act of palliating, an extenuating circumstance, mitigation.
PALLIATIVE (1), [pal'-i-at-iv], *n.* that which palliates.
PALLIATIVE (2), [pal'-i-at-iv] *adj.* tending to palliate. [Fr. *palliatif*].
PALLID, [pal'-id], *adj.* wan, colourless, pale of complexion. [L. *pallidus*].
PALLIDLY, [pal'-id-li], *adv.* wanly, palely.
PALLIDNESS, [pal'-id-nes], *n.* the condition of being pallid.
PALLIUM, [pal'-i-um], *n.* a rectangular cloak; a white Y-shaped vestment with four purple crosses worn by the Pope. [L. *pallium*].
PALL-MALL, [pel'-mel'], *n.* an obsolete game in which a ball was driven through a hoop by a mallet, as in croquet; the court in which the game was played. [It. *palla* ball and *maglio* mallet].
PALLOMETRY, [pal-om'-et-ri], *n.* the measurement of artificial vibrations in the earth. [Gk. *pallo* I shake and METRE].
PALLONE, [pal-ō'-ni], *n.* an Italian game resembling fives. [It. *pallone* large ball].
PALLOR, [pal'-or], *n.* the state of being pale, paleness of complexion. [L. *pallor*].
PALM (1), [pahm], *n.* the soft inner surface of the hand between wrist and fingers; the breadth of a palm; **to oil a person's p.,** (*coll.*) to bribe a person. [L. *palma*].
PALM (2), [pahm], *n.* (*bot.*) one of the family *Palmaceæ*) whose many species have in common a branchless trunk surmounted by a tuft of foliage; the branch of a palm as symbolizing victory and triumph; (*fig.*) victory, success. [OE. *palm* from L. *palma*].
PALM (3), [pahm], *v.t. and i.* to conceal in the palm of the hand, to deceive, to make disappear, to substitute one thing for another by sleight of hand; **p off,** to pass off, foist on, by dexterous fraud or plausibility. [PALM (1)].
PALMACEOUS, [pal-māsh'-us], *adj.* of, pertaining, or relating to, the palm family. [MdL. *palmaceus* resembling a palm].
PALMA-CHRISTI, [pal'-ma-krist'-i], *n.* the castor-oil plant, with a palm-shaped leaf. [L. *palma Christi* Christ's palm].
PALMAR, [pahl'-mer], *adj.* relating to, connected with, the palm of the hand.
PALMARY, [pahl'-mer-i], *adj.* relating to the palm of the hand or to the palm of triumph.
PALMATE, [pahl'-māt], *adj.* shaped like the palm of the hand; (*bot.*) (of leaves) having segments radiating from a centre. [L. *palmatus*].
PALMATIFID, [pahl-mat'-i-fid], *adj.* (*bot.*) divided like a palm and fingers. [PALMATE and L. *fidus* split].
PALMATIN, [pahl'-mat-in], *n.* a kind of castor oil.
PALMER, [pahm'-er], *n.* a professional pilgrim who carried a palm leaf as a symbol of having been to the Holy Land.
PALMER-WORM, [pahm'-er-wurm'], *n.* a hairy caterpillar.
PALMETTO, [pal-met'-ō], *n.* (*bot.*) a kind of small palm, *Sabal Palmetto*. [Span. *palmito*].
PALM-HOUSE, [pahm'-hows], *n.* a house for tropical plants.
PALMIFEROUS, [pahm-if'-er-us], *adj.* bearing palms. [PALM and L. *ferre* to bear].
PALMIGRADE, [pahl'-mi-grād], *adj.* walking on the soles of the feet. [PALM and L. *gradus* step].
PALMIPED (1), [pahl'-mi-ped]', *n.* a web-footed creature. [L. *palmipes*].
PALMIPED (2), [pahl'-mi-ped'], *adj.* web-footed.
PALMIST, [pahm'-ist], *n.* one who practises palmistry.
PALMISTRY, [pahm'-is-tri], *n.* the science or art of telling a person's past, future, and character from lines on the hands.
PALMITATE, [pahl'-mit-āt], *n.* (*chem.*) a salt of palmitic acid.
PALMITIC ACID, [pahl-mit'-ik-as'-id], *n.* (*chem.*) an acid extracted from palm-oil and other fats, used in the manufacture of soap. [Fr. *acide palmitique*].
PALM-OIL, [pahm'-oil], *n.* a vegetable fat obtained from the fruit of several species of palms; (*slang*) bribery.
PALM-SUNDAY, [pahm'-sun'-di], *n.* the last Sunday before Easter, kept in commemoration of Christ's triumphal entry into Jerusalem.
PALMY, [pahm'-i], *adj.* abounding in palm trees; (*fig.*) (of times and periods) flourishing, affluent, easily prosperous.
PALOLO, [pal-ō'-lō], *n.* a Polynesian nereid worm annually spawning on the reefs and used as food [Native].
PALP, [palp], *n.* a jointed feeler in insects. [L. *palpus* from L. *palpare* to touch].
PALPABILITY, [palp'-ab-il'-i-ti], *n.* palpableness.
PALPABLE, [palp'-abl], *adj.* perceptible to the touch; (*fig.*) very evident, obvious, easily perceived. [L. *palpabilis*].
PALPABLENESS, [palp'-abl-nes], *n.* the state of being palpable.
PALPABLY, [palp'-ab-li], *adv.* in palpable fashion.
PALPATE, [palp'-āt], *v.t.* to examine by touch. [L. *palpare* to touch].
PALPATION, [palp-ā'-shun], *n.* the act of palpating. [L. *palpatio*].
PALPEBRAL, [palp'-eb-ral], *adj.* pertaining to the eyebrow or eyelid. [L. *palpebra* eyelid].
PALPEBRATE, [palp'-eb-rāt], *adj.* having eyelids.
PALPEBROUS, [palp'-eb-rus], *adj.* palpebrate.

PALPI, [pal'-pī], *n.(pl.)* palps. [L. *palpi*, *pl.* of *palpus*].
PALPIFORM, [pal'-pi-fawm], *adj.* having the form of palpi. [PALPI and FORM].
PALPIGEROUS, [pal-pij'-er-us], *adj.* having palpi. [PALPI and L. *gerere* to bear].
PALPITATE, [pal'-pit-āt], *v.i.* to pulsate; (of the heart) to beat irregularly. [L. *palpitare*].
PALPITATION, [pal'-pit-ā'-shun], *n.* the act, state, or condition of palpitating; irregular action of the heart. [L. *palpitatio*].
PALSGRAVE, [pawlz'-grāv], *n.* (*hist.*) the County Palatine of the Rhine. [Du. *paltsgrave*].
PALSIED, [pawl'-zid], *adj.* afflicted with palsy, surprised or terrified almost to palsy.
PALSTAVE, [pawl'-stāv], *n.* a prehistoric implement consisting of a stone or bronze head fitted into a cleft wooden handle. [OIcel. *palstafr*].
PALSY (1), [pawl'-zi], *n.* paralysis, an uncontrollable trembling of the limbs. [ME. *palesie* from Gk. *paralusis*].
PALSY (2), [pawl'-zi], *v.t.* to make palsied, to paralyse.
PALT, [pawlt], *n.* rubbish. [Du. *palt*].
PALTER, [pawlt'-er], *v.i.* to potter about, to trifle, shuffle, haggle, dither. [Swed. *pallta* to hobble].
PALTERER, [pawlt'-er-er], *n.* one who palters.
PALTRILY, [pawl'-tri-li], *adv.* in paltry fashion.
PALTRINESS, [pawl'-tri-nes], *n.* the state of being paltry.
PALTRY, [pawl'-tri], *adj.* petty, trifling, worthless. [LGerm. *paltrig*].
PALUDAL, [pal-ewdl'], *adj.* marshy, relating to marshes, malarial. [L. *palus* marsh].
PALUDINOUS, [pal-ewd'-in-us], *adj.* paludal.
PALY, [pāl'-i], *adj.* (*her.*) divided into equal parts by pales.

PALY

PAM, [pam], *n.* the knave of clubs at loo. [Fr. *pamphile*].
PAMPAS, [pam'-pas], *n.* (*pl.*) the grassy plains of South America south of the Amazon; **p. grass**, the tall showy grass, *Cortaderia argentea*. [Peruvian *pampa* plain].
PAMPER, [pam'-per], *v.t.* to cosset, treat with too much indulgence, feed too richly and plentifully. [Uncert.].
PAMPERO, [pam-pāer'-ō], *n.* the cold wind from the Andes that sweeps the pampas. [Sp. *pampero*].
PAMPHLET, [pamf'-let], *n.* small, unbound, printed tract or treatise, *esp.* one dealing with current controversy. [OFr. *pamflet*].
PAMPHLETEER, [pamf'-let-ēer'], *n.* a writer of pamphlets.
PAN- *pref.* embracing all, the whole of a thing. [Gk. *pas, pan* all].
PAN (1), [pan], *n.* the Greek satyr deity of the countryside, usually symbolic of Arcadian goatishness.
PAN (2), [pan], *n.* a broad, flat vessel used in cooking, anything of similar shape, the quantity it contains; a shallow depression in the ground; a small ice-floe; the part of a matchlock holding the priming. [OE. *panne* from L. *patina* dish].
PAN (3), [pahn], *n.* betel leaf. [Hindi *pan*].
PAN (4), [pan], *adj.* (*cinema*) **pan-shot**, a panoramic shot, a continuous shot in which the camera moves to take a panorama of a scene. [Shortened from PANORAMIC].
PAN (5), [pan], *n.* (*phot.*) panchromatic film. [PAN-(CHROMATIC)].
PAN (6), (**panning, panned**), [pan], *v.t.* to wash auriferous earth to extract the gold; **to p. out**, to produce money; *v.i.* **to p. out**, to yield gold; (*fig.*) to turn out well. [PAN (2)].
PANACEA, [pan'-as-ē'-a], *n.* a universal cure, remedy for every ill. [Gk. *panakeia* all-healing herb].
PANACHE, [pan-ash'], *n.* the plume of a helmet; pretentious display. [It. *pennachio*].
PANADA, [pan-ah'-da], *n.* boiled bread-pulp. [Span. *panada*].
PANAMA, [pan'-am-ah], *n.* a hat made from fibre of the plant, *Carludovica palmata*. [*Panama*, where the fibre is grown].
PANARY, [pan'-er-i], *adj.* pertaining to bread. [L. *panarius*].
PANATROPE, [pan'-a-trōp], *n.* (*prot.*) an electrical device for magnifying the sound of a gramophone record.
PANCAKE (1), [pan'-kāk], *n.* a thin cake of fried batter; (*aeron.*) a flattened-out landing; **p. ice**, a thin piece of floating ice.
PANCAKE (2), [pan'-kāk], *v.i.* (*aeron.*) to make a pancake landing.
PANCARTE, [pan'-kaht], *n.* a royal charter granted to a subject, confirmatory of his possessions. [PAN (4) and L. *carta* charter].
PANCH, [panch], *n.* (*naut.*) a thick mat to prevent friction. [PAUNCH].
PANCHAYAT, [pan-chī'-at], *n.* an Indian village council. [Skr. *pancha* five].
PANCHROMATIC, [pan'-krō-mat'-ik], *adj.* (*phot.*) equally sensitive to all visible colours. [PAN (4) and CHROMATIC].
PANCRATIC, [pan-krat'-ik], *adj.* relating to a pancratium. [Gk. *pankratikos*].
PANCRATIST, [pan'-krat-ist], *n.* one competing in the pancratium.
PANCRATIUM, [pan-krat'-i-um], *n.* a Greek and Roman athletic contest, combining boxing and wrestling in a violent and brutal spectacle. [Gk. *pankration*].
PANCREAS, [pang'-kri-as], *n.* (*anat.*) the intestinal gland discharging digestive fluid into the duodenum; the sweetbread. [Gk. *pankreas*].
PANCREATIC, [pan(g)'-kri-at'-ik], *adj.* pertaining to the pancreas; **p. juice**, the fluid secreted by the pancreas.
PANCREATITIS, [pan(g)'-kri-at-ī'-tis], *n.* inflammation of the pancreas. [PANCREAS and Gk. *itis* denoting inflammation].
PANDA, [pan'-da], *n.* the Himalayan bear-cat, *Ailurus fulgens*; **giant p.**, a large white bear with black markings. [Native].
PANDEAN, [pan-dē'-an], *adj.* relating, belonging to, the god Pan.
PANDECT, [pan'-dekt], *n.* Justinian's digest and codification of the whole of Roman law; a digest of the whole of a body of knowledge. [Gk. *pandektes* receiver of all].
PANDEMIC, [pan-dem'-ik], *adj.* (of disease) prevalent over a whole area or amongst a whole population. [Gk. *pandemos* of the whole people].
PANDEMONIUM, [pan'-di-mō'-ni-um], *n.* an immense, demonic uproar, tumult and confusion. [Coined by Milton as capital of Hell, from PAN- and DEMON].
PANDER (1), [pan'-der], *n.* one who procures sexual gratification for another, a pimp; one who provides the satisfaction of another's passions. [Chaucer's *Pandare* in *Troilus and Criseyde*].
PANDER (2), [pan'-der], *v.i.* to act as pander to someone, to play the pander; to toady (to someone).
PANDERAGE, [pan'-der-ij], *n.* the dealings of a pander.
PANDERESS, [pan'-der-es'], *n.* a female pander.
PANDERISM, [pan'-der-izm], *n.* the business of a pander.
PANDICULATION, [pan'-dik'-yŏŏ-lā'-shun], *n.* the act of stretching one's body, yawning. [L. *pandiculari* to stretch].
PANDIT, see PUNDIT.
PANDORE, [pan'-daw(r)], *n.* a stringed instrument related to the lute. [Gk. *pandoura*].
PANDUR, [pan'-dŏoer], *n.* a Croatian irregular recruited against the Turks in the 17th century; a brutal and undisciplined soldier. [MedL. *banderius* follower of a banner].
PANDURIFORM, [pan-dyŏoer-i-fawm], *adj.* fiddle-shaped. [PANDORE and FORM].
PANDY, [pan'-di], *n.* a slap on the open hand. [L. *pande* (*palmam*) put out (the hand)].
PANE, [pān], *n.* a single piece of glass in a division of a window; a rectangular panel in a design. [ME. *pane* piece (of glass) from L. *pannus* piece of cloth].
PANED, [pānd], *adj.* made up of panels or panes, strips of different materials or designs.
PANEGYRIC, [pan-i-ji'-rik], *n.* a formal eulogy of a thing or person, a laudatory oration, flowery and extravagant praise. [Gk. *panegurikos*].
PANEGYRICAL, [pan'-i-ji'-rik-al], *adj.* eulogistic, laudatory, of the nature of a panegyric.
PANEGYRIST, [pan'-ij-i-rist], *n.* the writer or speaker of a panegyric.
PANEGYRIZE, [pan'-i-ji-rīz], *v.t.* and *i.* to praise with a panegyric; to write or speak a panegyric.
PANEL (1), [pan'-el], *n.* a rectangular piece of wood or other material, forming part of a surface, but slightly raised or depressed, and surrounded by a frame; a piece of parchment, a list, people on such a list, those

liable for jury service or those receiving medical treatment under the Health Insurance Act; a strip of material inserted into a body of different kind, colour or design. [ME. and OF. *panel* from L. *pannus* piece of cloth].

PANEL (2), (panelling, panelled), [pan'-el], *v.t.* to divide into panels, to decorate, provide with panels.

PANELESS, [pān'-les], *adj.* without panes.

PANELLING, [pan'-el-ing], *n.* panels.

PANG, [pang], *n.* a sudden strong spasm of physical or mental pain. [Uncert.].

PANGENESIS, [pan-jen'-is-is], *n.* the Darwinian hypothesis that heredity functions by every bodily cell throwing off germs of itself to be reproduced in the offspring. [PAN- and GENESIS].

PANGOLIN, [pang'-gol-in], *n.* a scaly, long-tongued Asiatic mammal notable for its practice of rolling itself into a ball when alarmed. [Malay *peng-guling* the roller].

PANHANDLE, [pan'-handl'], *n.* a straight projecting handle; a narrow promontory; (*U.S.*) a division between two political districts. [PAN (2) and HANDLE].

PANHELLENIC, [pan'-hel-ēn'-ik], *adj.* pertaining to all Greeks. [PAN- and HELLENIC].

PANIC (1), [pan'-ik], *n.* a sudden violent, senseless terror, *esp.* such terror spreading infectiously through a crowd, a sudden general alarm and collapse of reason for no adequate motive. [Gk. *panikos* under the influence of Pan].

PANIC (2), [pan'-ik], *n.* the grass, *Panicum.*

PANIC (3), [pan'-ik], *adj.* impelled by panic.

PANIC (4), [pan'-ik], *v.t. and i.* to throw into a panic, to lose one's head, be seized with panic.

PANICKY, [pan'-ik-i], *adj.* tending, or ready, to panic.

PANICLE, [pan'-ikl], *n.* (*bot.*) an irregular flower-cluster. [L. *panicula*].

PANICLED, [pan'-ikld], *adj.* having panicles.

PANIC-STRICKEN, [pan'-ik-strikn'], *adj.* struck with panic.

PANICULATE, [pan-ik'-yōō-lāt], *adj.* having the flowers in panicles.

PANICUM, [pan'-ik-um], *n.* panic grass, a genus of 300 species of grasses of which *Panicum miliaceum* is the Indian millet.

PANIDIOMORPHIC, [pan-id'-i-ō-mawf'-ik], *adj.* idiomorphic; pertaining to the rock structure in which each of the component crystals has assumed its usual form. [PAN- and IDIOMORPHIC].

PANISLAMIC, [pan-iz-lam'-ik], *adj.* pertaining to all Mohammedans. [PAN- and ISLAMIC].

PANIVOROUS, [pan-iv'-er-us], *adj.* living on, eating, bread. [L. *panis* bread and *vorare* to devour].

PANJANDRUM, [pan-jan'-drum], *n.* an important and absurdly pompous official personage [Word invented by Samuel Foote].

PANMUG, [pan'-mug], *n.* a crock pan to hold half a hundredweight of butter.

PANNADE, [pan-ād'], *n.* the curvetting of a horse. [Fr. *pannade*].

PANNAGE, [pan'-ij], *n.* the right to pasture swine in a wood; the food the swine so obtain, fruit of forest trees. [OFr. *pasnage*].

PANNEL, [pan'-el], *n.* a primitive saddle; a hawk's crop. [PANEL].

PANNIER, [pan'-i-er], *n.* one of a pair of wicker baskets, primarily a bread-basket, carried by a beast of burden; a framework of whalebone or bunched drapery for making a woman's dress appear very full on the hips. [Fr. *panier* from L. *panarium* bread-basket].

PANNIKIN, [pan'-ik-in], *n.* a small tin mug or basin. [*Dim.* of PAN (2)].

PANNOSE, [pan'-ōs], *adj.* felt-like. [L. *pannosus* rag-like].

PANNUS, [pan'-us], *n.* (*path.*) vascularity of the cornea of the eye manifested in opacity and swelling. [L. *pannus* cloth].

PANOPLIED, [pan'-ō-plid], *adj.* fully armed, accoutred.

PANOPLY, [pan'-ō-pli], *n.* complete armour; any kind of imposing array, *esp.* on important state occasions; armour for spiritual contest. [Gk. *panoplia*].

PANOPTICON, [pan-opt'-ik-on], *n.* a circular prison so constructed that a warder may observe all the prisoners from one central point. [PAN- and Gk. *optikon* relating to sight].

PANORAMA, [pan'-or-ah-ma], *n.* a realistic picture or series of pictures produced during the unrolling of a cylinder on the interior surface of which are represented all the objects of nature that are visible from any one point in all directions; an extensive view; a series of scenes passing rapidly across the vision; (*fig.*) a general survey of a subject. [PAN- and Gk. *horama* a view].

PANORAMIC, [pan'-or-ahm'-ik, pan'-or-am-ik], *adj.* pertaining to a panorama.

PANPIPE, [pan'-pīp], *n.* (*mus.*) a primitive wind instrument made of reeds; a mouth-organ. [*Pan,* the Greek god who was supposed to have invented this pipe].

PANSCLEROSIS, [pan'-skler-ō'-sis], *n.* (*path.*) the thickening and hardening of the interstitial tissue. [PAN- and Gk. *sklerosis* hardening].

PANSIED, [pan'-zid], *adj.* covered with pansies.

PANSLAVIC, [pan-slahv'-ik], *adj.* pertaining to, including, all the Slavic nations. [PAN- and SLAVIC].

PANSLAVISM, [pan-slahv'-izm], *n.* a movement aiming at unity among all the Slavic nations.

PANSOPHICAL, [pan-sof'-ikl], *adj.* claiming universal knowledge. [PAN- and Gk. *sophia* wisdom].

PANSY (1), [pan'-zi], *n.* a common wild and garden flower, *Viola tricolor*; heartsease; (*slang*) an effeminate young man, a sissy, a male homosexual. [AFr. *pensée* thought].

PANSY (2), [pan'-zi], *adj.* (*slang*) smart; effeminate. [*Prec.*].

PANSY (3), [pan'-zi], *v. reflex.* (*slang*) to put on one's best clothes and smarten up one's appearance.

PANT (1), [pant], *n.* a palpitation of the heart; a gasping for want of breath; a gasp. [PANT (2)].

PANT (2), [pant], *v.i.* to palpitate or throb; to gasp for want of breath; (*fig.*) to desire ardently, to yearn. [OFr. *panteisier*].

PANT-, PANTA-, see PANTO-.

PANTAGRAPH, see PANTOGRAPH.

PANTAGRUELISM, [pant'-a-grōō-el'-izm], *n.* coarse satirical humour. [*Pantagruel,* one of Rabelais's characters, who indulged in this].

PANTALETS, [pant'-al-ets], *n.(pl.)* frilled drawers coming below the skirts, as worn in the mid-19th century. [PANTAL(OON)].

PANTALOON, [pant'-al-ōōn], *n.* (in Italian comedy and pantomime) the foolish old man who is the butt of the clown's jokes; (*pl.*) long, tight-fitting trousers fastened well above the ankle with ribbons; (*coll.*) trousers. [It. *pantalone*].

PANTASCOPIC, see PANTOSCOPIC.

PANTATROPHY, [pant-at'-rof-i], *n.* a state of general atrophy. [PANT(O) and ATROPHY].

PANTECHNICON, [pan-tek'-ni-kon], *n.* a large warehouse for storing furniture; a furniture van. [PAN- and Gk. *tekhnikon* pertaining to art].

PANTER, [pant'-er], *n.* one who, or that which, pants.

PANTHEISM, [pan'-thi-izm], *n.* the religious belief that identifies the universe with God. [PAN- and THEISM].

PANTHEIST, [pan'-thi-ist], *n.* a believer in pantheism.

PANTALOONS

PANTHEISTIC(AL), [pan'-thi-ist'-ik(al)], *adj.* of the nature of pantheism.

PANTHEON, [pan'-thi-on], *n.* a temple dedicated to the worship of all the gods; a system of deities; a building dedicated to the great men of a nation. [PAN- and Gk. *theos* god].

PANTHER, [pan'-ther], *n.* a leopard; **American p.,** a puma. [Gk. *panther*].

PANTILE, PENTILE, [pan'-tīl], *n.* a roofing tile with two curves, one shallow and one deep. [PAN (2) and TILE].

PANTISOCRACY, [pan'-tis-ok'-ras-i], *n.* an ideal republic, in which all the inhabitants were to be equal in rank and power. [PANT-, Gk. *isos* equal and *kratia* rule].

PANTLER, [pant'-ler], *n.* an officer in charge of the bread and other provisions in large establishments; a butler. [AFr. *paneter*].

PANTO- PANT-, PANTA-, *pref.* all, universal. [Gk. *pantos*, *gen.* of *pas* all].

PANTO [pant'-ō], *n.* (*coll.*) a pantomime. [PANTO-(MIME)].

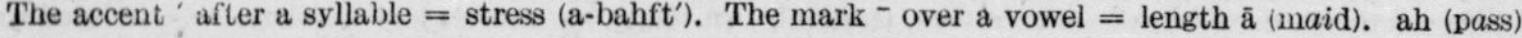

PANTOFLE, [pant-ōōfl′], *n.* a slipper. [Fr. *pantoufle*].

PANTOGRAPH, PANTAGRAPH, [pan′-tō-graf], *n.* an instrument that consists of a jointed parallelogram for copying, reducing, or enlarging plans and other drawings. [PANTO- and GRAPH].

PANTOFLE

PANTOGRAPHIC, [pan′-tō-graf′-ik], *adj.* pertaining to a pantograph.

PANTOGRAPHY, [pan-tog′-raf-i], *n.* general comprehensive description. [PANTO- and Gk. *graphia* writing].

PANTOLOGICAL, [pan′-to-loj′-ik-al], *adj.* pertaining to universal knowledge.

PANTOLOGY, [pan-tol′-o-ji], *n.* universal knowledge; a compendium of useful information. [PANTO- and Gk. *logos* speech].

PANTOMETER, [pan-tom′-it-er], *n.* an instrument that measures elevations and angles.

PANTOMIME, [pan′-to-mīm], *n.* a person who expresses his meaning by mute action; a representation in dumb show, in which the characters are Harlequin and Columbine, pantaloon and clown; a Christmas theatrical entertainment, generally a travesty of a fairy-tale; a representation in mute action. [Gk. *pantomimos* imitator of all].

PANTOMIMIC, [pan′-tō-mim′-ik], *adj.* of, or pertaining to, pantomime.

PANTOMIMIST, [pan′-tō-mīm-ist], *n.* one who acts in pantomime.

PANTOMORPHIC, [pan′-tō-mawf′-ik], *adj.* having or taking all shapes.

PANTOPHAGIST, [pan-tof′-a-jist], *n.* a person or an animal that can eat any kind of food. [PANTO- and Gk. *phago* I eat].

PANTOSCOPIC, PANTASCOPIC, [pan′-to-skop′-ik], *adj.* (*opt.*) with a wide field of vision; (of a lens) wide-angled. [PANTO- and Gk. *skopos* viewer].

PANTRY, [pan′-tri], *n.* a small room for plate, glass and china; a room or cupboard in which provisions are kept. [MedL. *panetaria* bread-shop].

PANTS, [pants], *n.(pl.)* men's drawers; (*U.S.*) trousers; **to be caught with one's p. down**, to be taken at a disadvantage. [Abbreviation of PANTALOONS].

PANZER, [pant′-ser], *n.* a German armoured fighting vehicle; **p. division**, an armoured division. [Germ. *panzer* armour].

PAP (1), [pap], *n.* the nipple of the breast; a rounded, conical hill. [Echoic of infant's feeding].

PAP (2), [pap], *n.* soft, starchy food suitable for infants. [*Prec.*].

PAPA, [pap-ah′], *n.* father; a Greek parish priest; the Pope. [Gr. *papa* from L. *papa* father].

PAPACY, [pāp′-a-si], *n.* the office of the Pope; papal authority; the papal organization of the Roman Catholic Church. [MedL. *papatia*].

PAPAL, [pāp′-al], *adj.* proceeding from the Pope; pertaining to the papacy. [MedL. *papalis*].

PAPALIST, [pāp′-al-ist] *n.* one who favours the papacy.

PAPALIZE, [pāp′-al-īz], *v.t.* to render papal; to spread papal doctrines; *v.i.* to conform to popery.

PAPALLY, [pāp′-al-i], *adv.* in a papal manner; by the Pope.

PAPAPHOBIA, [pāp′-a-fō′-bi-a], *n.* fear of the papacy, and its teachings and power. [L. *papa* pope and Gk. *phobos* terror].

PAPAVERACEOUS, [pap-av′-er-ā′-shus], *adj.* belonging to the poppy family; pertaining to poppies. [L. *papaver* the poppy].

PAPAVEROUS, [pap-av′-er-us], *adj.* pertaining to, or like, the poppy; soporific.

PAPAW, [pap-aw′], *n.* a tropical tree of the genus *Carica*; its orange-coloured fruit, used for pickles. [Carib. *papai*].

PAPER (1), [pā′-per], *n.* a substance manufactured from pulped vegetable fibre or linen rags rolled into thin sheets and used as writing, printing, wrapping or cleaning material; a newspaper; a literary or scientific essay or lecture; a set of questions to be answered by candidates in an examination; (*pl.*) documents, *esp.* legal documents; **to commit to p.**, to write down; **on p.**, judging by written accounts; **to send in one's papers**, to resign; **p. money**, specially printed pieces of paper used officially as currency. [OFr. *papier* from L. *papyrus*].

PAPER (2), [pā′-per], *v.t.* to line or cover with paper; to hang paper on walls as a covering; **p. up**, to fasten up any aperture by pasting paper over it.

PAPERCHASE, [pā′-per-chās′], *n.* a cross-country run following a trail of paper; hare and hounds.

PAPER-CREDIT, [pā′-per-kred′-it], *n.* notes or bills that promise payment of money.

PAPERHANGER, [pā′-per-hang′-er], *n.* a workman who hangs wall-paper.

PAPERHANGING, [pā′-per-hang′-ing], *n.* the craft of covering interior walls with paper; (*pl.*) wall-paper.

PAPERKNIFE, [pā′-per-nīf], *n.* a knife or sharp instrument for cutting open the leaves of books or opening envelopes; a thin blade for folding paper.

PAPER-MILL, [pā′-per-mil], *n.* a mill where paper is made.

PAPERSTAINER, [pā′-per-stān′-er], *n.* a person who stains, stamps, or colours wall-paper.

PAPERWEIGHT, [pā′-per-wāt], *n.* a weight that keeps papers from being blown about.

PAPERY, [pā′-per-i], *adj.* of a paper-like texture; resembling paper; (*fig.*) unsubstantial.

PAPETERIE, [pap′-et-rē], *n.* a case containing stationery and other writing materials. [Fr. *papeterie*].

PAPHIAN, [pā′-fi-an], *adj.* pertaining to the rites or worship of Venus or to prostitution. [*Paphos* an island famed for the worship of Venus].

PAPIER-MACHE, papier-mâché, [pap′-yā-mash′-ā], *n.* the pulp of paper shaped by pressure whilst moist and dried hard. [Fr. from *papier* paper and *mâché* chewed].

PAPILIO, [pap-il′-i-ō], *n.* the typical genus of butterflies. [L. *papilio*].

PAPILIONACEOUS, [pap-il′-yon-ā′-shus], *adj.* resembling the butterfly; having flowers like the wings of a butterfly.

PAPILLA, (*pl.* **papillae**), [pap-il′-a], *n.* the nipple of the breast; a nipple-like projection in any part of the body or on a plant. [L. *papilla*].

PAPILLARY, [pap-il′-er-i], *adj.* of, pertaining to, or resembling, the nipple; covered with papillae.

PAPILLATE, [pap′-il-āt], *adj.* papillary.

PAPILLOSE, [pap′-il-ōs], *adj.* papillous; warty, pimply.

PAPISM, [pāp′-izm], *n.* popery; Roman Catholicism. [Fr. *papisme*].

PAPIST, [pāp′-ist], *n.* a Roman Catholic.

PAPISTIC, [pāp-ist′-ik], *adj.* pertaining to popery or the Roman Catholic Church.

PAPISTICAL, [pāp-ist′-ik-al], *adj.* papistic.

PAPOOSE, [pap-ōōs′], *n.* an American Indian baby or small child. [Native].

PAPPESCENT, [pap-es′-ent], *adj.* (*bot*) growing a pappus.

PAPPOSE, [pap′-ōs], *adj.* (*bot.*) having a pappus, downy.

PAPPOUS, [pap′-us], *adj.* pappose.

PAPPUS, [pap′-us], *n.* (*bot.*) the tuft of down or soft hairs on the seeds of composite plants. [Gk. *pappos* old man].

PAPPY, [pap′-i], *adj.* resembling pap; succulent; (*slang*) foolishly simple.

PAPRIKA, [pap′-rik-a], *n.* red pepper. [Hungarian *paprika*].

PAPULA, [pap′-yōō-la], *n.* a pimple. [L. *papula*].

PAPULAR, [pap′-yōō-ler], *adj.* like a papula.

PAPULE, [pap′-yōōl], *n.* a pimple.

PAPULOSE, [pap′-yōō-lōs], *adj.* having many papillae.

PAPULOUS, [pap′-yōō-lus], *adj.* pimply.

PAPYRACEOUS, [pap′-i-rā′-shus], *adj.* pertaining to papyrus; of the consistency of paper.

PAPYROLOGIST, [pa′-pi-rol′-o-jist], *n.* a student of papyrology.

PAPYROLOGY, [pa′-pi-rol′-o-ji], *n.* the study of ancient texts written on papyrus. [PAPYRUS and Gk. *logos* speech].

PAPYRUS, [pap-ier′-us], *n.* an Egyptian sedge, *Papyrus antiquorum*, from which the ancients made paper; a scroll, document, written on papyrus. [L. *papyrus* from Gk. *papuros*].

PAR (1), [pah(r)], *n.* equality of value or standing; (*comm.*) the standard value of the currency of one country for purposes of exchange with that of another; (*golf*) the number of strokes a scratch player should require for the course; **at p.**, at the face value, *esp.* of stocks and shares; **below p.**, below face value; (*fig.*) not up to a normal state of mental or physical vigour; **above p.**, above face value. [L. *par* equal].

PAR (2), [pah(r)], *n.* the young of salmon. [PARR].

PARA- (1), *pref.* beside, beyond; contrary to. [Gk. *para*].

PARA- (2), *pref.* defence, protection from. [It. *para*].

PARA (3), [pa-rah'], *n.* a Turkish or Bulgarian coin worth a fraction of a farthing. [Pers. *parah*].

PARABASIS, [pa-rab'-as-is], *n.* in a Greek comedy the " coming forward " of the chorus to address the audience in the name of the poet and for a purpose not concerned with the plot of the play. [Gk. *parabasis*].

PARABLE, [pa'-rabl], *n.* a fable or short story containing some moral; a short allegory. [Gk. *parabole* comparison].

PARABLEPSIS, [pa'-ra-blep'-sis], *n.* faulty vision; an oversight, *esp.* in reading. [PARA (1) and Gk. *blepsis* vision].

PARABOLA, [pa-rab'-ol-a], *n.* (*math.*) a conic section obtained when cutting a cone by a plane parallel to its side. [Gk. *parabole* juxtaposition].

PARABOLE, [pa-rab'-ol-i], *n.* (*rhet.*) a metaphor; a similitude, comparison. [Gk. *parabole*].

PARABOLIC, [pa'-rab-ol'-ik], *adj.* expressed by parable; metaphorical; pertaining to, shaped like, a parabola.

PARABOLICAL, [pa'-rab-ol'-ik-al], *adj.* expressed in parable form.

PARABOLICALLY, [pa'-rab-ol'-ik-a-li], *adv.* in the form of a parable or a parabola.

PARABOLOID, [pa-rab'-ol-oid], *n.* a solid generated by the revolution of a parabola about its axis. [PARABOLA and Gk. *oeides* like].

PARACELSIAN, [pa'-ras-el'-si-an], *adj.* pertaining to Paracelsus, a Swiss physician and natural philosopher (1490-1541).

PARACENTRIC, [pa'-ra-sen'-trik], *adj.* deviating from circularity; not circular.

PARACHRONISM, [pa-rak'-ron-izm], *n.* a mistake arising from the post-dating of an event. [PARA (1) and Gk. *khronos* time].

PARACHUTE, [pa'-ra-shōōt], *n.* an apparatus of an umbrella-like shape fastened to, or held by, a person leaping from an aeroplane, the density of the air causing the contrivance to open wide, so checking the speed of descent; a natural contrivance on plant or animal for a similar purpose; **p. troops,** parachutists. [Fr. *parachute* from PARA (2) and *chute* fall].

PARACHUTIST, [pa'-ra-shōōt-ist], *n.* one who makes descents by parachute; a soldier trained to land by parachute in order to attack an objective.

PARACLETE, [pa'-ra-klēt], *n.* a comforter, advocate; the Holy Spirit. [Gk. *parakletos*].

PARACME, [pa-rak'-mi], *n.* decadence after attaining the prime. [Gk. *parakme*].

PARACROSTIC, [pa'-ra-krost'-ik], *n.* a poetical composition in which the first verse contains in order all the letters with which the others begin. [PARA (1) and ACROSTIC].

PARACUSIS, [pa'-ra-kew'-sis], *n.* (*path.*) disordered hearing. [PARA (1) and Gk. *akousia*].

PARACYANOGEN, [pa'-ra-sī-an'-ō-jen], *n.* (*chem.*) a polymer of cyanogen obtained from cyanide of mercury.

PARADE (1), [pa-rād'], *n.* show, ostentation; military display, mustering and review of any organized body of people; the ground on which a display is held; thoroughfare, promenade, esplanade. [Fr. *parade*].

PARADE (2), [pa-rād'], *v.t.* to make a display of; to array in military order; *v.i.* to move in military array; to walk about for show.

PARADIGM, [pa'-ra-dīm'], *n.* an example; a model; (*gram.*) a scheme of the inflexions of a verb or noun. [Gk. *paradeiknumi* I represent].

PARADIGMATIC, [pa'-ra-dig-mat'-ik], *adj.* formed like a paradigm.

PARADIGMATICALLY, [pa'-ra-dig-mat'-ik-a-li], *adv.* in the manner of a paradigm.

PARADISAIC, PARADISIAC, [pa'-ra-dis-ā'-ik, pa'-ra-diz'-ē-ak], *adj.* pertaining to Paradise; heavenly.

PARADISAICAL, PARADISIACAL, [pa'-ra-dis-ā'-ik-al, pa'-ra-diz-ī'-ak-al], *adj.* heavenly.

PARADISE, [pa'-ra-dīs], *n.* the Garden of Eden, home of Adam and Eve before the Fall; heaven; any delightful place or state of perfect happiness; **bird of p.,** one member of a family of about fifty species of passerine birds native to New Guinea and remarkable for their beautiful plumage; **p. fish,** a brightly coloured Chinese species of *Polycanthus* with a large broad tail and many soft rays in its dorsal and ventral fins. [Gk. *paradeisos* pleasure garden].

PARADOS, [pa'-rad-os], *n.* (*milit.*) an artificial elevation, usually of earth, behind a fortified place to secure it from attack from the rear; a defensive rampart behind a trench. [Fr. *parados*].

PARADOX, [pa'-rad-oks], *n.* a proposition contrary to received opinion; a proposition seemingly absurd, yet really true; anything that appears to contradict the seemingly sensible or possible; a person whose characteristics seem to contradict each other. [Gk. *paradoxos*].

PARADOXICAL, [pa'-rad-oks'-ik-al], *adj.* having the nature of a paradox; not according to that which might reasonably be expected.

PARADOXICALLY, [pa'-rad-oks'-ik-a-li], *adv.* in a paradoxical fashion.

PARADOXICALNESS, [pa'-rad-oks'-ik-al-nes], *n.* the quality of being paradoxical.

PARADOXURE, [pa'-rad-oks'-yōōer], *n.* (*zool.*) a palm-civet or palm-cat, any of the eleven species of *Paradoxurus* found from India to Formosa, and so called from their long curving tails. [PARADOX and Gk. *oura* tail].

PARAFFIN, [pa'-raf-in], *n.* a tasteless, inodorous fatty matter, derived from the distillation of wood or shale, or from petroleum, and so called from its resistance to chemical union; **p. oil,** refined petroleum; **p. wax,** solid paraffin. [L. *parum* little and *affinis* related].

PARAGENIC, [pa'-ra-jen'-ik], *adj.* developed by paragenesis.

PARAGENESIS, [pa'-ra-jen'-is-is], *n.* hybridism; (*min.*) the formation of single crystals into masses of granite or marble.

PARAGOGE, [pa'-ra-gō'-ji], *n.* the adding of a letter or syllable to the end of a word. [Gk. *para agoge* leading past].

PARAGOGIC, [pa'-ra-go'-jik], *adj.* pertaining to paragoge.

PARAGON (1), [pa'-ra-gon], *n.* a model or pattern of perfection; a nonpareil. [OFr. *paragon*].

PARAGON (2), [pa'-ra-gon], *v.t.* to compare, equal, parallel.

PARAGRAMMATIST, [pa'-ra-gram'-at-ist], *n.* one who makes paragrams.

PARAGRAPH (1), [pa'-ra-grahf], *n.* a short passage in any writing consisting of one or several sentences relating to a particular point or aspect of a subject, generally distinguished by having the first line indented; a short item of news or commentary in a newspaper; a symbol ¶ used to distinguish a new paragraph. [Gk. *paragraphe* marginal note].

PARAGRAPH (2), [pa'-ra-grahf], *v.t.* to divide into paragraphs.

PARAGRAPHIC, [pa'-ra-graf'-ik], *adj.* consisting of, forming, paragraphs.

PARAGRAPHIST, [pa'-ra-graf'-ist], *n.* one who writes paragraphs; a journalist.

PARAGUAY-TEA, [pa'-ra-gwī-tē'], *n.* the shrub maté, *Ilex paraguayensis*, the dried leaves of which are used for a kind of tea. [*Paraguay* in South America and TEA].

PARAHELIOTROPISM, [pa'-ra-hē'-li-ō-trŏp'-izm], *n.* the tendency of leaves to protect themselves from the intense heat of the sun by turning parallel to the rays of light. [PARA (2) and HELIOTROPISM].

PARAKEET, PARAQUET, PAROQUET, PARRAKEET, [pa'-ra-kēt, pa'-ra-ket], *n.* a small variety of long-tailed parrot. [OFr. *paroquet*].

PARALDEHYDE, [pa-ral'-di-hīd], *n.* a strong sedative drug, a polymer of aldehyde. [PARA (1) and ALDEHYDE].

PARALEIPSIS, PARALIPSIS, [pa'-ra-līp'-sis], *n.* (*rhet.*) a figure of speech in which a speaker affects to pass over what he is really calling attention to. [Gk. *paraleipsis* omission].

PARAKEET

PARALLACTIC, [pa'-ral-ak'-tik], *adj.* pertaining to a parallax.

PARALLAX, [pa'-ral-aks], *n.* apparent displacement of distant objects caused by shifting the point of view; (*astron.*) the difference in the position of a heavenly body as seen from the earth's surface and from the centre of the earth or of the sun. [Gk. *parallaxis* change].

PARALLEL (1), [pa'-ra-lel], *n.* a line which throughout its whole extent is equidistant from another line; a person, thing or event closely resembling another; likeness, close comparison, counterpart; (*milit.*) trench in front of a fortified place parallel to the defences; **p. of latitude,** one of the lines on a map

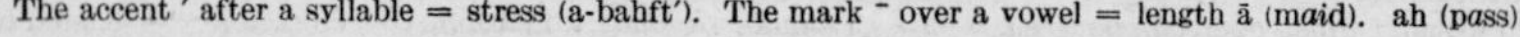

or globe, parallel to the equator and indicating degree of latitude as measured from the equator.

PARALLEL (2), [pa'-ra-lell *adj.* equidistant for any distance; in the same plane but never meeting; (*fig.*) resembling in essential particulars, similar, corresponding; **p. bars**, a gymnastic apparatus consisting of two horizontal bars of equal height and length; **p. ruler**, a mathematical instrument formed of two equal rulers connected by a pair of links; **in p.** (*elect.*) with like poles connected together. [Gk. *parallelos*].

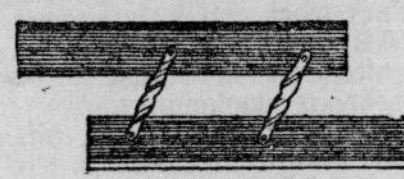
PARALLEL RULER

PARALLEL (3), **(parallelling, parallelled)**, [pa'-ra-lel], *v.t.* to place parallel; to compare, liken to; to correspond, be equivalent; to equal. [*Prec.*].

PARALLELEPIPED, PARALLELOPIPED, [pa'-ra-lel-ep'-i-ped], *n.* (*geom.*) an oblong solid bounded by six parallelograms, of which the opposite pairs are equal and parallel. [Gk. *parallelepipedon*].

PARALLELISM [pa'-ral-el-izm], *n.* the condition of being parallel; resemblance; comparison.

PARALLELOGRAM, [pa'-ra-lel'-ō-gram], *n.* (*geom.*) a four-sided rectilinear figure with its opposite sides parallel. [Fr. *parallélogramme*].

PARALLELOPIPED, see PARALLELEPIPED.

PARALOGISM, [pa-ral'-ō-jizm], *n.* a fallacious argument or syllogism. [Fr. *paralogisme*].

PARALOGIZE, [pa-ral'-ō-jīz], *v.i.* to reason beside the point. [Gk. *paralogia* fallacy].

PARALYSE, PARALYZE, [pa'-ral-īz], *v.t.* to affect with paralysis; (*fig.*) to destroy or weaken the power of mental or physical action; to render impotent. [Fr. *paralyser*].

PARALYSIS, [pa-ral'-is-is], *n.* (*anat.*) inability to contract a voluntary muscle; total or partial loss of sensation or motion in one or more parts of the body; palsy; (*fig.*) mental powerlessness; suspension of activity; impotence. [L. *paralusis*].

PARALYTIC (1), [pa'-ral-it'-ik], *n.* one affected with paralysis.

PARALYTIC (2), [pa'-ral-it'-ik], *adj.* pertaining to, affected with, paralysis. [Gk. *paralutikos*].

PARALYZE, see PARALYSE.

PARAMAGNETIC, [pa'-ra-mag-net'-ik], *adj.* attracted towards that part of the magnetic field which is stronger.

PARAMETER, [pa-ram'-it-er], *n.* (*geom.*) the focal chord which is at right angles to the axis in each of the three conic sections; the constant quantity which enters into the equation of a curve. [PARA and METER].

PARA-MILITARY, [pa'-ra-mil'-it-er-i], *adj.* semi-military, subsidiary to the army. [PARA (1) and MILITARY (2)].

PARAMNESIA, [pa'-ram-nē'-zi-a], *n.* false memory. [PARA (1) and (A)MNESIA].

PARAMO, [pa-rah'-mō], *n.* a high-lying desert tract on the Andes; any species of *Espeletia*, a genus of plants found on the Paramo. [Span. *paramo*].

PARAMOUNT, [pa'-ra-mownt], *adj.* of the highest rank or authority; supreme; pre-eminent. [AFr. *paramont*].

PARAMOUR, [pa'-ra-mo͝oer], *n.* a lover (of either sex); a mistress. [OFr. *par amour* through love]

PARANAPHTHALINE, [pa'-ra-naf'-thal-ēn], *n.* anthracine.

PARANOIA, [pa'-ran-oi'-a], *n.* (*path.*) a chronic mental derangement characterized by delusions of grandeur or persecution. [Gk. *paranoia*].

PARANOIAC (1), [pa'-ra-noi'-ak], *n.* one suffering from paranoia.

PARANOIAC (2), [pa'-ra-noi'-ak], *adj.* of, pertaining to, or resembling, paranoia or a paranoiac.

PARANYMPH, [pa'-ra-nimf], *n.* (*Gk. antiq.*) a groomsman or bridesmaid; one who woos on behalf of another. [Gk. *paranumphos*].

PARANZELLO, [pa'-ran-tsel'-ō], *n.* a small Mediterranean ship with lateen mainsail and mizen and a large jib. [It. *paranzello*].

PARAPET, [pa'-ra-pet], *n.* a wall breast-high; a rampart in front of a trench; a wall or elevation for protecting soldiers from an enemy's shot. [It. *parapetto*].

PARAPH, [pa'-raf], *n.* a flourish completing a signature. [Fr. *paraphe*].

PARAPHERNALIA, [pa'-raf-er-nā'-li-a], *n.* the goods which a bride on her marriage brings with her and which are her own; the gifts from a husband to his wife which she cannot but he can dispose of during his lifetime; appendages; ornaments; trappings; baggage. [L. *parapherna* personal property of a married woman].

PARAPHIMOSIS, [pa'-ra-fim-ō'-sis], *n.* (*path.*) strangulation of the prepuce. [PARA (1) and PHIMOSIS].

PARAPHRASE (1), [pa'-ra-frāz], *n.* a rendering of a text or passage in fuller and clearer terms; a free translation. [Gk. *paraphrasis*].

PARAPHRASE (2), [pa'-ra-frāz], *v.t.* to make a paraphrase of, to render in other words.

PARAPHRAST, [pa'-ra-frast'], *n.* one who paraphrases; a paraphraser.

PARAPHRASTIC, [pa'-ra-frast'-ik], *adj.* of the nature of a paraphrase.

PARAPLEGIA, [pa'-ra-plē'-ji-a], *n.* (*path.*) paralysis which is confined to the lower parts of the body. [PARA (1) and Gk. *plege* a blow].

PARAPLEURITIS, [pa'-ra-plo͞o-rī'-tis], *n.* (*path.*) a slight form of pleuritis.

PARAPODIUM, [pa'-ra-pō'-di-um], *n.* (*zool.*) a foot tubercle or rudimentary lateral process of annelids. [PARA (1) and Gk. *pous podos* foot].

PARAPOPHYSIS, [pa'-ra-pof'-is-is], *n.* (*anat.*) the inferior or anterior transverse process on the side of a vertebra. [PAR(A) (1) and APOPHYSIS].

PARAQUET, see PARAKEET.

PARASANG, [pa'-ra-sang], *n.* a Persian measure equal to about four English miles. [Pers. *parasang*].

PARASCENE, [pa'-ra-sēn], *n.* the side rooms of an ancient Greek theatre used as retiring and dressing rooms. [Gk. *paraskene*].

PARASCEVE, [pa'-ra-sēv], *n.* the evening before the Jewish sabbath or Passover. [L. *parasceve*].

PARASELENE, [pa'-ra-sel-ē'-ni], *n.* a mock moon or a lunar halo. [PARA (1) and Gk. *selene* the moon].

PARASITE, [pa'-ra-sīt], *n.* a person who frequents the tables of the rich, and earns his welcome by flattery; a hanger-on; a sycophant; a plant or animal which attaches itself to, and lives entirely upon, another. [Gk. *parasitos*].

PARASITIC, [pa'-ra-sit'-ik], *adj.* in the nature of a parasite; fawning to obtain favours; living on another.

PARASITICAL, [pa'-ra-sit'-ik-al], *adj.* parasitic.

PARASITISM, [pa'-ra-sit-izm], *n.* the practice of a parasite.

PARASITOLOGY, [pa'-ra-sit-ol'-o-ji], *n.* (*biol.*) the study of the habits of parasites. [PARASITE and Gk. *logos* speech].

PARASOL, [pa'-ra-sol'], *n.* an umbrella used as a shade from the sun. [PARA (2) and L. *sol* sun].

PARASOL

PARASYNTHESIS, [pa'-ra-sin'-thes-is], *n.* the formation of a word by a double process of combination and derivation.

PARASYNTHETIC, [pa'-ra-sin-thet'-ik], *adj.* formed by parasynthesis.

PARATAXIS, [pa'ra-taks'-is], *n.* (*gram.*) the joining of successive clauses without grammatical links between them. [Gk. *parataxis* juxtaposition].

PARATHESIS, [pa'-ra-thē'-sis], *n.* (*gram.*) apposition; (*rhet.*) a parenthetical remark; (*print.*) parenthesis, matter enclosed within a bracket. [PARA (1) and THESIS].

PARATHYROID, [pa'-ra-thī'-roid], *adj.* (*med.*) pertaining to the four ductless glands close to the thyroid gland. [PARA (1) and THYROID].

PARATROOPS, [pa'-ra-troops'], *n.*(*pl.*) troops trained to descend by parachute. [PARA(CHUTE) and TROOP (1)].

PARATYPHOID, [pa'-ra-tī'-foid], *n.* (*path.*) an infectious disease which, though resembling typhoid fever, is a distinct malady.

PARAVANE, [pa'-ra-vān], *n.* a device for removing mines from the path of a ship. [PARA (2) and VANE].

PARBOIL, [pah'-boil], *v.t.* to half-boil; (*fig.*) to cause to become unpleasantly warm. [OFr. *parboillir*].

PARBUCKLE (1), [pah'-bukl], *n.* (*naut.*) a rope for rolling bales and casks up a slope by looping it round them. [Fr. *par* by and †*bunkle*].

PARBUCKLE (2), [pah'-bukl], *v.t.* to roll a spar or package by looping it round with a rope that has one end fastened and hauling in the free end. [*Prec.*].

PARCAE, [pah'-sē], *n.*(*pl.*) the three Fates of classical mythology. [L. *parcae*].

PARCEL (1), [pah'-sel], *n.* part, portion, *esp.* of land; piece, section; a small package. [Fr. *parcelle*].
PARCEL (2), [pah'-sel], *adv.* partly; **p. gilt**, partly gilded.
PARCEL (3), (**parcelling, parcelled**), [pah'-sel], *v.t.*; **to p. out**, to share, divide into parts; (*naut.*) to cover a rope with strips of canvas; **to p. up**, (*coll.*) to wrap up, make into a parcel. [PARCEL (1)].
PARCELLING, [pah'-sel-ing], *n.* (*naut.*) long narrow slips of canvas wound round a rope daubed with tar.
PARCENARY, [pah'-sen-er-i], *n.* (*leg.*) co-heirship. [AFr. *parcenarie*].
PARCENER, [pah'-sen-er], *n.* a joint heir. [AFr. *parcener*].
PARCH, [pahch], *v.t.* to make very dry; to shrivel with heat; to dry to excess; *v.i.* to become excessively dry, to be very thirsty. [Uncert.].
PARCHEDNESS, [pahcht'-nes], *n.* the state of being parched.
PARCHMENT, [pahch'-ment], *n.* the skin of a sheep, goat or calf, dressed and rendered fit for writing on; any document written on parchment; a substance resembling parchment. [Fr. *parchemin* from L. *pergamena* (*charta*) paper of Pergamum].
PARD (1), [pahd], *n.* a leopard; a panther. [Gk. *pardos*].
PARD (2), [pahd], *n.* (*U.S. slang*) a partner, mate. [Abbreviation from PARTNER].
PARDON (1), [pah'-don], *n.* forgiveness, the act of pardoning; the excusing of a fault or breach of manners; (*eccles.*) forgiveness of sins; (*leg.*) remission of the legal consequences of a crime. [Fr. *pardon*].
PARDON (2), [pah'-don], *v.t.* to forgive; to excuse a lapse in manners or a small fault; (*leg.*) to grant a pardon. [LL. *perdonare* to remit].
PARDONABLE, [pah'-don-abl], *adj.* excusable.
PARDONABLY, [pahd'-on-ab-li], *adv.* excusably.
PARDONER, [pahd'-ner], *n.* one who pardons; (*eccles.*) †a cleric licensed to sell or grant papal indulgences.
PARE, [pāer], *v.t.* to cut or shave off; to trim; to diminish little by little. [Fr. *parer*].
PAREGORIC, [pa'-ri-go'-rik], *n.* a medicine that deadens pain; a tincture of opium. [Gk. *paregorikos* soothing].
PAREIRA, [pa-rāer'-a], *n.* a South American plant, *Abuta rufescens*, the root of which is valuable in medicine, also its substitute, the roots and stems of the velvet plant, *Cissampelos pareira*. [Portug. *parreira* vine].
PARELLA, [pa-rel'-a], *n.* (*bot.*) the lichen, *Lecanora parella*, which produces litmus. [Fr. *parelle*].
PAREMBOLE, [pa-rem'-bol-i], *n.* (*rhet.*) an explanation inserted in a sentence as a parenthesis. [PARA (1) and Gk. *embole* insertion].
PARENCHYMA, [pa-reng'-kim-a], *n.* (*anat.*) the tissue peculiar to the glandular organs of the body; soft, pulpy, cellular tissue; (*bot.*) the pith of plants. [PARA (1) and Gk. *egkhuma* infusion].
PARENCHYMAL, [pa-reng'-kim-al], *adj.* pertaining to parenchyma.
PARENCHYMATOUS, [pa'-reng-kim'-at-us], *adj.* parenchymal.
PARENETIC, [pa'-ren-et'-ik], *adj.* hortatory, persuasive. [Gk. *parainetikos*].
PARENT, [pāer'-ent], *n.* a father or mother; an ancestor, forefather; a protector, guardian; (*fig.*) origin, root. [OFr. *parent* from L. *parens* begetting].
PARENTAGE, [pāer'-ent-ij], *n.* extraction, birth, lineage. [Fr. *parentage*].
PARENTAL, [pa-rent'-al], *adj.* pertaining to a parent.
PARENTALLY, [pa-rent'-a-li], *adv.* in a parental manner.
PARENTHESIS, (*pl.* **parentheses**), [pa-ren'-this-is], *n.* (*gram.*) a clause inserted in a sentence, which is grammatically complete without it, for explanation, confirmation or enlargement, and usually indicated thus ( ). [Gk. *parenthesis*].
PARENTHETIC, [pa'-ren-thet'-ik], *adj.* pertaining to a parenthesis; introduced as a parenthesis.
PARENTHETICAL, [pa'-ren-thet'-ik-al], *adj.* parenthetic.
PARENTHETICALLY, [pa'-ren-thet'-ik-a-li], *adv.* in a parenthetical manner.
PARENTHOOD, [pāer'-ent-hŏŏd], *n.* the condition of being a parent; fatherhood, motherhood. [PARENT and OE. *had* condition].
PARENTICIDE, [pa-rent'-i-sīd], *n.* one who murders his parent. [PARENT and L. *cidium* murder].
PARENTLESS, [pāer'-ent-les], *adj.* without parents.
PARER, [pāer'-er], *n.* an instrument for paring or peeling.
PARERGON, [pa-rur'-gon], *n.* subordinate or secondary work. [Gk. *parergon*].
PARESIS, [pa'-res-is], *n.* (*path.*) partial paralysis affecting the muscles but not the nerves. [Gk. *paresis* slackening].
PARETIC, [pa-rĕt'-ik], *adj.* (*path.*) of, arising from, or resembling, paresis. [Gk. *paretos* paralysed].
PARGASITE, [pah'-ga-sīt], *n.* (*min.*) a kind of hornblende. [*Pargas*, a town in Finland, where found].
PARGET (1), [pah'-jet], *n.* rough plaster laid upon walls and ceilings; work in plaster bearing a decorative impress.
PARGET (2), [pah'-jet], *v.t.* to cover with plaster or parget, to roughcast; to cover with decorative plasterwork. [OFr. *parjeter* to throw or cast over the surface].
PARGETER, [pah'-jet-er], *n.* one who pargets; a plasterer.
PARGETING, [pah'-jet-ing], *n.* plaster-work; the decorative pattern on plaster-work.
PARHELION, (*pl.* **parhelia**), [pah-hē'-li-on], *n.* a spot of intensely bright light on the solar halo; a mock sun [PARA (1) and Gk. *helios* sun].
PARIAH, [pa-rī'-a, pa'-ri-a], *n.* a member of one of the lowest Indian castes; one without caste; (*fig.*) an outcast, a person (or animal) of a low or outcast class. [Tamil *paraiyar*].
PARIAN (1), [pāer'-i-an], *n.* a fine white clay used for porcelain and statuettes.
PARIAN (2), [pāer'-i-an], *adj.* pertaining to the island of Paros, famed for its marble; resembling marble. [L. *Parius* of the island of Paros].
PARIETAL, [pa-rī'-et-al], *adj.* pertaining to the wall of a cavity of the body; pertaining to the sides and upper part of the skull; (*bot.*) growing from the sides of hollow organs, *esp.* the ovary. [Fr. *pariétal*].
PARI-MUTUEL, (*pl.* **paris-mutuels**), [pa'-ri-mew'-chŏŏ-el'], *n.* a betting-machine, totalisator, by means of which the winners share the money staked by the losers. [Fr. *pari mutuel* mutual wager].
PARING, [pāer'-ing], *n.* that which is pared off; the rind; a shaving.
PARISH, [pa'-rish], *n.* a civil or ecclesiastical subdivision of a county; a district assigned to a particular church; those living in such a district; **p. council**, a body administering local affairs; **to be on the p.**, to be in receipt of Poor Law relief. [ME. *paresche* from Gk. *paroikia* land round a church].
PARISHIONER, [pa-rish'-on-er], *n.* a resident in a parish.
PARISH-REGISTER, [pa'-rish-rej'-ist-er], *n.* a register in which the christenings, marriages, and deaths in a parish are recorded.
PARISIAN (1), [pa-riz'-i-an], *n.* an inhabitant of Paris.
PARISIAN (2), [pa-riz'-i-an], *adj.* pertaining to Paris.
PARISITE, [pa'-ris-īt], *n.* (*min.*) a mineral containing salts of cerium, lanthanum, neodymium and praseodymium. [J. *Paris*, its discoverer (1845)].
PARISYLLABIC, [pa'-ri-sil-ab'-ik], *adj.* having an equal number of syllables. [PAR and SYLLABLE].
PARITY, [pa'-rit-i], *n.* equality; equivalence; similarity, parallelism; (*comm.*) equivalence in another currency; the standard rate of exchange. [L. *paritas*].
PARK (1), [pahk], *n.* (*hist.*) an enclosed tract of land preserved for hunting; an ornamental piece of ground enclosed for public or private recreation; an enclosure round a mansion; a place in which motor-cars may be left for a stated period of time; (*milit.*) an artillery encampment. [OE. *pearroc*].
PARK (2), [pahk], *v.t.* to enclose, bring together in a park; to put vehicles in a space reserved for their special use; (*coll.*) to put, place, leave. [*Prec.*].
PARKA, [pahk'-ah], *n.* a fur jacket with a hood worn by Eskimos. [Eskimo *parka*].
PARKER, [pahk'-er], *n.* †a park-keeper; a rabbit.
PARKIN, [pahk'-in], *n.* a kind of cake made with oatmeal, treacle and ginger. [Unkn.].
PARKY, [pahk'-i], *adj.* (*coll.*) chilly. [PARK (1)].
PARLANCE, [pah'-lants], *n.* speech, conversation; idiom. [AFr. *parlance*].
PARLEY (1), [pah'-li], *n.* a conference between opponents; a discussion on a disputed point. [Fr. *parler* to speak].
PARLEY (2), [pah'-li], *v.t.* (*coll.*) to talk fluently in a foreign language; *v.i.* to confer, or treat with, as an enemy. [*Prec.*].
PARLEYVOO (1), [pah'-li-vōō], *n.* (*slang*) the French

language; a Frenchman. [Fr. *parlez-vous (français)?* do you speak (French)?].

PARLEYVOO (2), [pah'-li-vōō], *v.i.* to speak French. [*Prec.*].

PARLIAMENT, [pah'-li-ment], *n.* a deliberative assembly; a national assembly, or senate; the supreme legislature of the British nation, consisting of the Lords and the Commons acting with the Sovereign. [OFr. *parlement* speaking].

PARLIAMENTARIAN, [pah'-li-ment-āer'-i-an], *n.* a person skilled in the procedure of the English Parliament or other similar legislative bodies; an adherent of Parliament and in opposition to the King in the time of Charles I, a Roundhead.

PARLIAMENTARY, [pah'-li-ment'-er-i], *adj.* pertaining to, enacted by, Parliament; **p. language,** language such as is allowable in Parliament, civil, courteous, concealing censure under a polite exterior.

PARLOUR, [pah'-ler], *n.* a family sitting-room; a large formally furnished room for public receptions as those of a mayor; **p. tricks,** elegant amusements and accomplishments. [OFr. *parleor*].

PARLOUR-MAID, [pah'-ler-mād], *n.* a woman servant who attends to the dining-room and answers the door-bell.

PARLOUS, [pah'-lus], *adj.* perilous; difficult; critical. [*Var.* of PERILOUS].

PARMESAN, [pahm'-iz-an], *n.* a strong-tasting cheese much used for cooking. [Fr. *parmesan* from *Parma*, in Italy, where first made].

PARNASSIAN (1), [pahn-as'-i-an], *n.* a member or follower of the Parnassian school.

PARNASSIAN (2), [pah-nas'-i-an], *adj.* pertaining to Parnassus, a mountain in Greece, considered sacred to the Muses; devoted to poetry; pertaining to a school of French poetry in the second half of the nineteenth century. [Gk. *Parnassos*].

PAROCHIAL, [pa-rō'-ki-al], *adj.* pertaining to a parish; (*fig.*) narrow in range or interests; provincial. [LL. *parochialis*].

PAROCHIALISM, [pa-rō'-ki-al-izm], *n.* approval of the parish as the unit of local government; narrowness of opinion; narrow provincialism.

PARODIC, [pa-rod'-ik], *adj.* in the manner of a parody.

PARODIST, [pa'-rod-ist], *n.* one who writes a parody.

PARODY (1), [pa'-rod-i], *n.* a burlesque imitation of a literary work or style; (*fig.*) a feeble imitation, a travesty. [Gk. *parodia* burlesque song].

PARODY (2), [pa'-rod-i], *v.t.* to compose a parody on; ridicule; (*fig.*) to imitate feebly, to travesty.

PAROLE, [pa-rōl'], *n.* word of mouth; word of honour; a promise given by a prisoner when he has leave to depart from custody that he will report at the times agreed upon; a military password. [AFr. *parole* from L. *parabola* word].

PARONOMASIA, [pa'-rō-no-mā'-zi-a], *n.* a word-play, a pun. [Gk. *paronomasia*].

PARONYCHIA, [pa'-ron-ik'-i-a], *n.* a whitlow; inflammation at the edge of the finger-nail. [PARA (1) and Gk. *onux* nail].

PAROQUET, see PARAKEET.

PAROTID, [pa-ro'-tid], *adj.* pertaining to the parotis.

PAROTIS, [pa-ro'-tis], *n.* (*anat.*) a salivary gland near the ear. [PARA (1) and Gk. *ous otos* ear].

PAROTITIS, [pa'-rō-tī'-tis], *n.* (*path.*) inflammation of the parotis; common mumps. [*Prec.* and Gk. *itis* denoting inflammation].

PAROXYSM, [pa'-roks-izm], *n.* a fit or exacerbation of any disease; any sudden violent spasm or action; an outburst of emotion. [Gk. *paroxusmos* exasperation].

PAROXYSMAL, [pa'-roks-iz'-mal], *adj.* pertaining to, occurring in, or occasioned by, a paroxysm.

PAROXYTONE, [pa-roks'-i-tōn], *n.* a word bearing an accent on the last syllable but one. [PAR(A) (1) and OXYTONE].

PARPEN, [pah'-pen], *n.* a binding-stone which passes through a wall from side to side; **p. wall,** a thin partition wall. [OFr. *parpain*].

PARQUET, [pah'-ki, pah'-ket], *n.* a wooden floor made of small rectangular pieces of wood laid on a base. [Fr. *parquet*].

PARQUETRY, [pah'-ket-ri], *n.* inlaid woodwork flooring; parquet flooring.

PARR, [pah(r)], *n.* a young salmon in its striped stage. [Unkn.].

PARRAKEET, see PARAKEET.

PARRAL, PARREL, [pa'-rel], *n.* (*naut.*) a rope or chain for preventing yards and gaffs from slipping from the mast. [OFr. *parail*].

PARRHESIA, [pa-rē'-zi-a], *n.* frankness freedom of speech. [Gk. *parrhesia* frankness].

PARRICIDAL, [pa'-ri-sīd'-al], *adj.* pertaining to parricide.

PARRICIDE (1), [pa'-ri-sīd], *n.* a murderer of a father or near relative; a traitor to one's native land. [L. *parricida*].

PARRICIDE (2), [pa'-ris-īd], *n.* the act of murdering a father or near relative. [L. *parricidium*].

PARROCK, PURROCK, [pa'-rok, pu'-rok], *n.* a small enclosed field; a paddock. [OE. *pedrroc*].

PARROT, [pa'-rot], *n.* one of an order of tropical birds with two toes in front and two behind and a hooked beak, remarkable for their beautiful colours, their apparent intelligence, and, in some cases, their power of imitating the human voice; (*fig.*) a talkative person; **p. fish,** any of various tropical fish having a superficial resemblance to a parrot. [Fr. *perrot*].

PARROTRY, [pa'-rot-ri], *n.* servile imitation, mechanical repetition.

PARRY (1), [pa'-ri], *n.* the action of parrying; in boxing, wrestling, fencing, the warding off of a blow or thrust.

PARRY (2), [pa'-ri], *v.t.* to ward off, turn aside. [Fr. *parer*].

PARSE, [pahz], *v.t.* (*gram.*) to describe the form, etc., of parts of speech (in a sentence), and their relations to each other. [L. *pars* part].

PARSEE, [pah'-sē'], *n.* a person of Persian descent and of the religion of Zoroaster, living in India. [Pers. *Parsi*].

PARSEEISM, [pah'-sē-izm], *n.* the religion of the Parsees.

PARSIMONIOUS, [pah'-si-mō'-ni-us], *adj.* very sparing in spending money, greedy, grudging, niggardly.

PARSIMONIOUSLY, [pah'-si-mō'-ni-us-li], *adv.* meanly, sparingly.

PARSIMONIOUSNESS, [pah'-si-mō'-ni-us-nes], *n.* the quality of being parsimonious.

PARSIMONY, [pah'-si-mon-i], *n.* extreme carefulness in expenditure; frugality; niggardliness; stinginess. [L. *parsimonia*].

PARSLEY, [pahs'-li], *n.* a green herb of the genus *Petroselinum* with crinkled leaves of a slight fragrance used in cookery; **cow p.,** wild chervil. [Gk. *petroselinon* rock-parsley].

PARSNIP, [pahs'-nip], *n.* a biennial umbelliferous plant with a succulent light yellow root used as a vegetable. [ME. *passenep*].

PARSON, [pah'-son], *n.* the rector of a parish; a clergyman, pastor; **p. bird,** the New Zealand honey-eater, of the genus *Prosthemadera*; **p. gull,** the great black-backed gull, *Larus marinus*; **parson's nose,** the rump of a bird cooked for the table. [ME. *persone*].

PARSONAGE, [pah'-son-ij], *n.* the residence of a parson; the vicarage.

PARSONIC, [pah-son'-ik], *adj.* pertaining to a parson; having the manner of a parson.

PARSONICAL, [pah-son'-ik-al] *adj.* parsonic.

PART (1), [paht], *n.* a portion, piece, fragment; a portion considered apart, slice; a division, part contributing to the whole; a certain number but not all; ingredient; share; proportional quantity; essential constituent, duty, concern; party, side; rôle, character; (*mus.*) one of the melodies in a harmony; (*pl.*) the genitals; **p. of speech,** (*gram.*) a unit of speech; **to take in good p.,** not to be annoyed by; **to play a p.,** to be insincere, conceal the real self; **a man of parts,** a man of power or talent; **in good p.** favourably, good-naturedly. [L. *pars partis*].

PART (2), [paht], *v.t.* to sever into two or more pieces; to separate; to divide into parts or sections; to break friendships, to cause to break asunder; *v.i.*, to be separated; to pursue a different path; to fork; to open up; **to p. with,** to give up, surrender. [OFr. *partir* from L. *partire* to divide].

PARTAKABLE, [pah-tāk'-abl], *adj.* able to be partaken of.

PARTAKE, (partook, partaken), [pah-tāk'], *v.t.* to have a part in, to share; *v.i.* to take a part or share along with others. [PART and TAKE].

PARTAKER, [pah-tāk'-er], *n.* one who partakes; a participator sharer.

PARTED, [paht'-id], *adj.* separated, severed, divided.

PARTER, [paht'-er], *n.* one who parts.

PARTERRE, [pah-tāer'], *n.* a system of flower-beds with intervening spaces to walk on; the ground floor seating of a theatre immediately behind the orchestra, part of the pit. [Fr. *parterre* from *par terre* on the ground].

PARTHENOGENESIS, [pah'-then-ō-jen'-is-is], *n.*

(*biol.*) reproduction through the agency of unimpregnated ova or germs. [Gk. *parthenos* virgin and GENESIS].

PARTHIAN (1), [pah'-thi-an], *n.* a native or inhabitant of Parthia, a former kingdom in northern Persia.

PARTHIAN (2), [pah'-thi-an], *adj.* pertaining to Parthia; **p. shot,** a piercing remark spoken at parting.

PARTIAL, [pah'-shal], *adj.* biased in favour of one party or side; inclined to favour without reason; affecting a part only; subordinate; **p. to,** having a liking for, prejudiced in favour of. [LL. *partialis*].

PARTIALITY, [pah'-shi-al'-i-ti], *n.* inclination to favour one party more than another; an undue bias of mind; particular fondness.

PARTIALLY, [pah'-shal-i], *adv.* in a partial manner, not entirely.

PARTIBILITY, [paht'-ib-il'-i-ti], *n.* divisibility, separability.

PARTIBLE, [paht'-ibl], *adj.* capable of being separated; divisible. [L. *partibilis*].

PARTICIPANT, [pah-tis'-i-pant], *n.* one who participates; a partaker. [L. *participans*].

PARTICIPATE, [pah-tis'-ip-āt], *v.t.* to partake, share in, enjoy in common with; *v.i.* to partake, to have a part or share; to share. [L. *participare*].

PARTICIPATION, [pah'-tis-ip-ā'-shun], *n.* the action of participating; the sharing in common with others. [L. *participatio*].

PARTICIPATIVE, [pah-tis'-ip-at-iv], *adj.* capable of participating.

PARTICIPATOR, [pah-tis'-ip-āt-or], *n.* one who participates; a partaker.

PARTICIPIAL, [pah'-tis-ip'-i-al], *adj.* having the nature and function of a participle; formed from a participle.

PARTICIPIALLY, [pah'-tis-ip'-i-a-li], *adv.* in a participial manner.

PARTICIPLE, [pah'-tis-ipl], *n.* (*gram.*) a word that has the nature partly of an adjective and partly of a verb; a derivative of a verb with the function of an adjective; a verbal adjective. [OFr. *participle*].

PARTICLE, [paht'-ikl], *n.* a minute part or portion; the very smallest conceivable amount of anything; (*gram.*) a minor part of speech that is not inflected or used alone; (*phys.*) the smallest component part of matter. [L. *particula*].

PARTI-COLOURED, [paht'-i-kul'-erd], *adj.* of two or more colours; variegated; (*fig.*) diversified, chequered. [PARTY and COLOURED].

PARTICULAR (1), [per-tik'-yōō-ler], *n.* a single instance; a distinct part, a special detail.

PARTICULAR (2), [per-tik'-yōō-ler], *adj.* pertaining to a single person or thing; single, individual, special; detailed, exact; fastidious, difficult to please, exclusive. [L. *particula* small part].

PARTICULARISM, [per-tik'-yōō-ler-izm], *n.* exclusive regard for oneself or one's party; (*theol.*) the doctrine that redemption is the lot of a selected part, not the whole of the human race; (*pol.*) a policy permitting each state in an empire or federation to act independently in certain matters of government.

PARTICULARIST, [per-tik'-yōō-ler-ist], *n.* an advocate of particularism.

PARTICULARITY, [per-tik'-yōō-la'-rit-i], *n.* the quality of being particular; the fact of appearing in some way out of the ordinary; specification of particulars; a special detail; minuteness of detail. [Fr. *particularité*].

PARTICULARIZATION, [per-tik'-yōō-ler-iz-ā'-shun], *n.* the act of particularizing.

PARTICULARIZE, [per-tik'-yōō-ler-iz], *v.t.* to state or enumerate in detail; to give particulars of, specify; *v.i.* to be attentive to details.

PARTICULARLY [per-tik'-yōō-ler-li], *adv.* in a particular manner, especially, notably; minutely, in detail.

PARTING (1), [paht'-ing], *n.* the act of dividing· division, separation, rupture; leave-taking; the division made in combing the hair from the forehead in two directions.

PARTING (2), [paht'-ing], *adj.* given, or happening, at the time of departure or separation.

PARTISAN (1), **PARTIZAN,** [paht-iz-an'], *n.* an adherent to a party or faction; a prejudiced adherent; a guerrilla fighter outside the regular army organization. [Fr. *partisan*].

PARTISAN (2), **PARTIZAN,** [paht'-iz-an'], *n.* a military weapon formerly used by foot soldiers and resembling the halberd; a soldier armed with such a weapon. [It. *partisana*].

PARTISANSHIP, [paht'-iz-an-ship], *n.* adherence to a party; zealous support of a party.

PARTITE, [paht'-īt], *adj.* (*bot.*) divided almost to the base. [L. *partitum*].

PARTITION (1), [pah-tish'-un], *n.* the act of dividing; division, separation; a part separated from another; a dividing wall. [L. *partitio*].

PARTITION (2), [pah-tish'-un], *v.t.* to divide into parts or shares.

PARTITIVE (1), [paht'-it-iv], *n.* (*gram.*) a word denoting a part of a whole.

PARTITIVE (2), [paht'-it-iv], *adj.* having the quality of denoting a part. [L. *partitivus*].

PARTIZAN, see PARTISAN.

PARTLET, [paht'-let], *n.* a hen. [OFr. *Pertelote*].

PARTLY, [paht'-li], *adv.* in part; not wholly; to some extent.

PARTNER (1), [paht'-ner], *n.* one who shares with another; a joint owner of stock or capital used in a business undertaking; one who dances with another; a player on the same side; a husband or wife. [*Var.* of PARCENER].

PARTNER (2), [paht'-ner], *v.t.* to become a partner with; to be partner of. [*Prec.*].

PARTNERS, [paht'-nerz], *n.*(*pl.*) (*naut.*) the frame between the deck beams which holds and supports the mast. [PARTNER (1)].

PARTNERSHIP, [paht'-ner-ship], *n.* the association of persons for the purpose of business or ownership; the sharing of interests in any undertaking. [PARTNER (1) and OE. *scipe* state, quality].

PARTRIDGE, [pah'-trij], *n.* a game bird of the genus *Perdrix*, preserved in England for purposes of sport. [ME. *pertriche*].

PARTRIDGE

PARTRIDGE-WOOD, [pah'-trij-wŏŏd'], *n.* a hard variegated wood from South America much used in cabinet-work.

PART-SINGING, [paht'-sing'-ing], *n.* singing where parts are taken by different voices to make harmony.

PART-SONG, [paht'-song'], *n.* a song in which the parts are sung in harmony.

PART-TIME (1), [paht'-tīm'], *adj.* giving or requiring only part of the time during which work may be done.

PART-TIME (2), [paht'-tīm'], *adv.* for only part of the time during which work may be done.

PARTURIENT, [pah-tyōōer-i-ent], *adj.* about to bring forth young, travailing; (*fig.*) struggling to evolve ideas or forms. [L. *parturiens*].

PARTURITION, [pah'-tew-rish'-un], *n.* the act of giving birth, labour, travail. [L. *parturitio*].

PARTY, [pah'-ti], *n.* a number of persons united in opinion or design; one of two litigants; one concerned in an affair; a side; a distinct person; a select company; a social gathering; a political faction; (*milit.*) a small company of troops; (*coll.*) a person. [Fr. *partie*].

PARTYISM, [pah'-ti-izm], *n.* devotion to party.

PARTY-SPIRIT, [pah'-ti-spi'-rit], *n.* the convictions animating a party or group of persons.

PARTY-WALL, [pah'-ti-wawl'], *n.* common wall dividing two tenements or other properties.

PARVANIMITY, [pah'-van-im'-i-ti], *n.* pettiness, lack of magnanimity. [L. *parvus* small and *animus* mind].

PARVENU, [pah'-ven-ew], *n.* a person who has risen quickly from humble origin to a position of wealth or importance; an upstart. [Fr. *parvenu*].

PARVIS, [pah'-vis], *n.* the enclosed space in front of a church; a church porch. [OFr. *parevis* from L. *paradisus*].

PAS, [pah], *n.* a step in dancing; a kind of dance; right of precedence. [Fr. *pas* step].

PASCH, [pask], *n.* the Jewish festival of the Passover; Easter. [L. *pascha* from Heb. *pesakh*].

PASCHAL, [pask'-al], *adj.* pertaining to the Jewish Passover; of, or pertaining to, Easter or Easter celebrations.

PASCUAL, [pas'-kew-al], *adj.* growing in pastures; pertaining to, abounding in, pastures. [MedL. *pascualis*].

PASHA, [pash'-a, pash-ah'], *n.* a Turkish title bestowed on officers of high rank. [Turk. *pasha*].

PASHALIK, [pash'-ah-lik], *n.* the jurisdiction of a pasha. [Turk. *pashalik*].

PASHM, [pashm] *n.* under-fur; the under-fur of the

Cashmere goat from which woollen shawls are made. [Pers. *pashm*].

PASIGRAPHY, [pas-ig′-raf-i], *n.* a system of universal writing or language where the characters represent ideas not words. [Gk. *pasi* for all and *graphia* writing].

PASQUE-FLOWER, [pahsk′-flow-er], *n.* a species of anemone, that flowers about Easter. [OFr. *pasque* Easter and FLOWER].

PASQUIL, PASQUIN, [pask′-wil, pask′-win], *n.* a lampoon displayed or circulated publicly; a pasquinade. [It. *pasquino*, a statue set up in Rome in 1501, on which lampoons were hung].

PASQUILLANT, [pask′-wil-ant], *n.* a lampoonist.

PASQUILLER, [pask′-wil-er], *n.* the writer of a pasquil or lampoon.

PASQUIN, see PASQUIL.

PASQUINADE, [pask-win-ād′], *n.* a lampoon affixed to some public place; a pasquil. [It. *pasquinata*].

PASS (1), [pahs], *n.* the act of passing; the satisfying of examiners in an examination; a critical state of affairs; a permission to pass; a passport; a ticket authorizing the holder to travel on the railway; a free ticket on the railway or to a theatre or concert; a threatening gesture; (*sport*) the transferring of the ball by a player to another on his own side; (*fencing*) lunge, thrust. [PASS (3)].

PASS (2), [pahs], *n.* a passage; a narrow gap or pathway through mountains; a track or path through difficult or dangerous ground; a passage across a river, a ford; a navigable channel at a river's mouth; (*milit.*) a narrow pathway, usually in the mountains, commanding the entrance to a country. [L. *passus* step, track].

PASS (3), [pahs], *v.t.* to move past, to leave behind; to leave unmentioned, omit; to go from side to side, to cross; to approve; to come up to the required standard; surpass; overshoot (a mark); outstrip; to transcend; to send, transport, convey; to make (a thing) go in a certain direction; to strain; to utter, pronounce; to emit; **to p. away,** to go, die; **to p. in review,** to contemplate, consider; **to p. by,** to go by, ignore; **to p. for,** to be thought of as; **to p. off,** to go away, decrease; (*fig.*) to put in a false light; **to p. out,** to become unconscious; **to p. over,** to overlook, forgive; **to p. through,** to travel across; (*fig.*) to endure, experience; **to p. a dividend,** not to declare a dividend; *v.i.* to move from one place to another or from one state to another; move onward, proceed; to be impelled onwards; to go from one place to another, be transferred; to be interchanged or transacted between two or more persons; to depart from this life, die; to elapse, glide by; to go unchecked or uncensured; to be allowed or approved by a deliberative body; to get through an examination successfully; to take place, occur; to make a pass in fencing or football, etc. [Fr. *passer*].

PASSABLE, [pahs′-abl], *adj.* able to be traversed or navigated; receivable; tolerable.

PASSABLY, [pahs′-ab-li], *adv.* in a passable manner, tolerably.

PASSADO, [pas-ahd′-ō], *n.* a thrust, lunge; a turn or course of a horse backward or forward. [It. *passata*].

PASSAGE (1), [pas′-ij], *n.* the act of passing; transition; the migratory flight of birds; the passing or lapse of time; a journey, a voyage across the sea; accommodation booked for a journey; sum paid for journey; the passing into law of a bill, a way, route, channel, pass; a narrow corridor or hall; an interchange of blows; (*fig.*) an argument, heated discussion; a certain specified part of a speech, book or musical composition. [Fr. *passage*].

PASSAGE (2), [pas′-ij], *v.i.* to move sideways in riding; *v.t.* to cause a horse to passage. [Fr. *passager*].

PASSAGEWAY, [pas′-ij-wā], *n.* a passage.

PASSANT, [pas′-ant], *n.* (*her.*) walking. [Fr. *passant*].

PASS-BOOK, [pahs′-bŏŏk], *n.* the book in which a bank customer's transactions are recorded, that is, sums deposited and cheques paid out.

PASSE, passé, [pas′-ā], *adj.* out of date, stale, "on the shelf." [Fr. *passé* passed].

PASSENGER, [pas′-in-jer], *n.* one who travels in some conveyance; **p. pigeon,** a North American pigeon notable for its migratory habits. [OFr. *passager*].

PASSE-PARTOUT, [pas′-pah-tōō′], *n.* a master-key; gummed paper strip for framing pictures; a picture so framed. [Fr. *passe partout* pass everywhere].

PASSER-BY, [pahs′-er-bī′], *n.* one who passes by or near; a casual observer; a foot-passenger.

PASSERINE, [pas′-er-in], *adj.* (*ornith.*) pertaining to perching birds or to the sparrow; of about the size of a sparrow. [L. *passer* sparrow].

PASSIBILITY, [pahs′-ib-il′-i-ti], *n.* passibleness.

PASSIBLE, [pahs′-ibl], *adj.* (*theol.*) capable of suffering; susceptible of feeling, or of impressions from external agents. [L. *passibilis* capable of suffering].

PASSIBLENESS, [pahs′-ibl-nes], *n.* the state of being passible.

PASSIM, [pas′-im], *adv.* here and there; everywhere; in all parts (in reference to an author or book). [L. *passim*].

PASSIMETER, [pas′-i-mē-ter], *n.* a machine for printing railway tickets as each one is required. [PASSENGER and METER].

PASSING (1), [pahs′-ing], *n.* the action of one who, or that which, passes; death.

PASSING (2), [pahs′-ing], *adj.* that passes; ephemeral; incidental.

PASSING (3), [pahs′-ing], *adv.* (*archaic*) surpassingly exceedingly.

PASSING-BELL, [pahs′-ing-bel′], *n.* a bell tolled at the hour of a person's death, to remind people to pray for the passing soul.

PASSING-NOTE, [pahs′-ing-nōt′], *n.* (*mus.*) a note introduced between two harmonies to soften the interval.

PASSION (1), [pash′-un], *n.* an effect produced by external agency; the condition of being acted upon; extreme suffering, *esp.* that of Christ; any strong, deep feeling or excitement, such as desire, fear, joy, grief, love, hatred; a temper; ardour, eager desire; deep enthusiasm. [L. *passio* suffering].

PASSION (2), [pash′-un], *v.i.* (*poet.*) to be affected by passion.

PASSIONAL, [pash′-un-al], *adj.* pertaining to passion, or to Christ's passion.

PASSIONATE, [pash′-un-at], *adj.* easily moved to anger; moved, prompted or inspired by passion or strong emotion; intense, fervent. [MedL. *passionatus*].

PASSIONATELY, [pash′-un-at-li], *adv.* in a passionate manner.

PASSIONATENESS, [pash′-un-at-nes], *n.* the quality of being passionate.

PASSIONED, [pash′-und], *adj.* violently affected, inspired by passion; impassioned.

PASSION-FLOWER, [pash′-un-flow′-er], *n.* a flower of the genus *Passiflora*, adopted as the symbol of Christ's passion.

PASSION-FLOWER

PASSIONISTS, [pash′-un-ists], *n.(pl.)* a religious order founded to bear witness to the significance of Christ's passion.

PASSIONLESS, [pash′-un-les], *adj.* without passion; not easily excited, calm; unimpassioned.

PASSION-PLAY, [pash′-un-plā′], *n.* a drama, medieval in origin, representing Christ's passion.

PASSION-SUNDAY, [pash′-un-sun′-di], *n.* the fifth Sunday in Lent.

PASSION-WEEK, [pash′-un-wēk′], *n.* (*eccles.*) the week before Palm Sunday; (*coll.*) Holy Week, the week in which Good Friday occurs.

PASSIVE (1), [pas′-iv], *n.* (*gram.*) the passive voice.

PASSIVE (2), [pas′-iv], *adj.* acted upon but not acting; offering no active resistance; inert, inactive; suffering without protest; quiescent; (*gram.*) that changes a verbal function so that the logical object of the action becomes the grammatical subject and suffers the action expressed by the verb; **p. resistance,** resistance to force by denial of its powers but not by any physical measures, submission to punishment rather than complying with laws considered unjust. [L. *passivus*].

PASSIVELY, [pas′-iv-li], *adv.* in a passive manner.

PASSIVENESS, [pas′-iv-nes], *n.* the condition of being passive; passibility; capacity for suffering; patience.

PASSIVITY, [pas-iv′-i-ti], *n.* passiveness; inertia; submissiveness.

PASS-KEY, [pahs′-kē], *n.* a key that will open any of a number of locks; a master key.

PASSLESS, [pahs′-les], *adj.* having no passage; (*poet.*) impassable.

PASSMAN, [pahs′-man], *n.* one who takes a pass degree at a university.

PASSOVER, [pahs'-ō-ver], *n.* a feast of the Jews to commemorate the night in Egypt when the destroying angel passed over their homes

PASSPORT, [pahs'-pawt], *n.* a document issued to a national by his government stating his identity and granting him the right to receive international protection when travelling; (*naut.*) a sea-letter or document issued to neutral vessels in time of war granting them rights in certain waters; (*fig.*) those qualities of purse or person whereby an individual gains entry and acceptance into a certain social, business or political circle. [Fr. *passeport*].

PASSWORD, [pahs'-wurd], *n.* a watchword; (*fig.*) a secret of admission.

PAST (1), [pahst], *n.* time that has elapsed; things that happened in a time that has gone by; a person's early life or life that has now gone by; a doubtful or disreputable past life. [PASS (3)].

PAST (2), [pahst, past], *adj.* gone by, ended, finished, spent, accomplished; (*gram.*) expressing actions that have gone by. [PASS (3)].

PAST (3), [pahst], *prep. and adv.* beyond in time or space; without power of. [*Prec.*].

PASTE (1), [pāst], *n.* a composition of a doughy consistency, whether of flour in baking or of clay in the arts; a cement, as of flour and water boiled; a fine glass compounded for artificial gems; a soft edible compound made by beating various ingredients together as in meat or almond paste. [OFr. *paste*].

PASTE (2), [pāst], *v.t.* to fasten, stick, with paste; (*coll.*) to beat or pound.

PASTEBOARD, [pāst'-bawd], *n.* thick, stiff paper board made by pasting sheets of paper together; a wooden board on which dough is rolled in making pastry.

PASTE-GRAIN, [pāst'-grān], *n.* imitation morocco leather.

PASTEL (1), [past'-el], *n.* the plant woad; the blue dye obtained from this. [Fr. *pastel*].

PASTEL (2), [past'-el], *n.* (*paint.*) a dry flaky crayon made of pigments and gum-water; a drawing made with such pigments; a soft colour. [Fr. *pastel*].

PASTERN, [past'-ern], *n.* that part of a horse's leg between the fetlock and the hoof; **p. joint**, the joint in a horse's leg next to the hoof. [OFr. *pasturon*].

PASTERN

PASTEURISM, [past'-er-izm], *n.* the cure or prevention of disease by inoculation. [Louis *Pasteur*, the great French bacteriologist].

PASTEURIZATION, [past'-er-īz-ā'-shun], *n.* the act of pasteurizing.

PASTEURIZE, [pas'-ter-īz], *v.t.* to kill germs (*esp.* in milk) by sterilizing with heat.

PASTICCIO, [past-ich'-i-ō], *n.* a pastiche. [It. *pasticcio* a pie].

PASTICHE, [past-ēsh'], *n.* a literary, musical or pictorial composition made up of a number of parts from other works loosely connected together; a work in another's style and manner. [Fr. *pastiche*].

PASTILLE, [pas-tēl', past'-il], *n.* an aromatic cone which is burnt for fumigating purposes; a medicated lozenge; a unit of measurement for X-ray dosage. [Fr. *pastille*].

PASTIME, [pahs'-tīm], *n.* recreation, amusement, diversion; a game. [PASS (3) and TIME (1)].

PASTING, [pāst'-ing], *n.* (*coll.*) a violent beating, a drubbing.

PASTMASTER, [pahst'-mahst'-er], *n.* one who has long been an expert.

PASTOR, [pahst'-or], *n.* a shepherd; a clergyman in charge of a congregation; (*ornith.*) the rose-coloured starling. [L. *pastor* shepherd].

PASTORAL (1), [pahst'-er-al], *n.* a poem on rural or shepherd life; a bucolic; a letter addressed from a bishop to his diocese or from a minister to his congregation.

PASTORAL (2), [pahst'-er-al], *adj.* pertaining to shepherds or shepherd life; describing the loves of shepherds and shepherdesses in a conventionalized manner; relating to the pastor of a church; **p. staff**, a crosier; **p. theology**, the study of the duties of spiritual pastors; **p. epistles**, the epistles of Paul to Timothy and Titus. [L. *pastoralis*].

PASTORALE, [pahst-or-ahl'], *n.* a simple melody in a rustic style or on a rustic theme; a dance in the manner of shepherds and shepherdesses. [It. *pastorale*].

PASTORALISM, [pahst'-er-al-izm], *n.* a pastoral quality or character.

PASTORATE, [pahst'-er-at], *n.* the office or position of a pastor; the body of spiritual pastors collectively. [MedL. *pastoratus*].

PASTORLESS, [pahst'-er-les], *adj.* having no pastor.

PASTRY, [pās'-tri], *n.* a food made of flour and fat kneaded to a dough, rolled and baked; pies, tarts, etc., made of pastry. [~PASTE].

PASTRYCOOK, [pās'-tri-ko͝ok], *n.* one whose occupation is to make pastry.

PASTURABLE, [pahs'-cher-abl], *adj.* fit for pasture; affording pasture.

PASTURAGE, [pahs'-cher-ij], *n.* the action of pasturing; grazing; pasture-land.

PASTURE (1), [pahs'-cher], *n.* grass for grazing; land on which cattle feed. [L. *pastura* pasture].

PASTURE (2), [pahs'-cher], *v.t.* to feed on grass; *v.i.* to graze.

PASTURELESS, [pahs'-cher-les], *adj.* having no pasture.

PASTY (1), [pas'-ti], *n.* a pie of meat or fruit enclosed in pastry and baked without a dish. [OFr. *pastée*].

PASTY (2), [pāst'-i], *adj.* of a colour or consistency resembling paste; pale.

PAT (1), [pat], *n.* a light quick slap of the hand; a small sound made by striking lightly with something flat; a small lump of butter shaped by patting. [Echoic].

PAT (2), [pat], *adv.* oppositely, at the right moment, with precision. [*Prec.*].

PAT (3), (**patting, patted**), [pat], *v.t.* to touch or hit lightly with the hand or some flat surface; to make a small sound when striking lightly; *v.i.* to carry out the action of patting; **to p. on the back**, to congratulate, express satisfaction with. [PAT (1)].

PATAGIUM, [pat-ā'-ji-um], *n.* (*zool.*) a wing membrane, as in bats and flying squirrels. [L. *patagium* a gold edging or border].

PATAMAR, [pat'-a-mah(r)], *n.* a Bombay coasting vessel having a prow as long as the keel and two masts with lateen sails. [Malay. *pattamari*].

PATAVINITY, [pat'-a-vin'-i-ti], *n.* the provincialism of Livy, the historian; use of local words. [*Patavium*, Livy's birthplace].

PATCH (1), [pach], *n.* a piece of material sewn on a garment to repair a hole or strengthen a weak place; a small piece of brown plaster formerly worn by women on the face to show up the beauty of the complexion; a shield for an injured eye; a small piece of land; a part of an area different in colour or appearance from the whole extent; **not a p. on**, not to be compared with, much inferior to; **bad p.**, a spell of bad luck, a difficult situation. [ME. *pacche*].

PATCH (2), [pach], *v.t.* to mend by sewing or fixing on pieces of material; to repair clumsily; to make up of pieces; **p. up**, (*fig.*) to bring to an end, settle (a quarrel). [*Prec.*].

PATCHER, [pach'-er], *n.* one who patches.

PATCHERY, [pach'-eri], *n.* foolish work, bungling.

PATCHILY, [pa'-chi-li], *adv.* in patches.

PATCHOULI, [pach-o͞o'-li], *n.* the odoriferous dried branches of an eastern plant, *Pogostemon patchouly*; a perfume produced from this. [Tamil *pachai* green and *ilai* leaf].

PATCHWORK, [pach'-wurk], *n.* work composed of pieces sewn together; a jumble; a surface divided into many small areas of various sizes.

PATE, [pāt], *n.* the head, crown of the head. [ME. *pate*].

PATE, pâté, [pat'-i], *n.* a small pie; patty; **p. de foie gras**, goose-liver paste. [Fr. *pâté*].

PATEE, patée, [pat'-ē], *adj.* (*her.*) (of a cross) expanding towards the ends. [Fr. *patée*].

PATEE

PATEFACTION†, [pat'-if-ak'-shun], *n.* the act of manifesting, making open, visible, known. [L. *patefactio*].

PATELLA, [pat-el'-a], *n.* the knee-pan or knee-cap; (*arch.*) a small dish-like vessel or vase; (*zool.*) a genus of mollusca including the limpet. [L. *patella*].

PATELLAR, [pat-el'-er] *adj.* pertaining to the knee-cap.

PATELLIFORM, [pat-el'-i-fawm], *adj.* of the shape of a patella; shaped like a shallow dish or saucer.

PATEN, PATIN, PATINE, [pat'-en], *n.* a plate; the plate or vessel on which the consecrated bread in the Eucharist is put. [L. *patena* shallow dish].

PATENT (1), [pā'-tent, pat'-ent], *n.* a royal or official grant of privilege, as a title of nobility, or the exclusive rights to property in a process or an invention; the document giving such rights; **p. office,** a government office for the granting of patents; **p. rolls,** the records of patents. [PATENT (2)].

PATENT (2), [pā'-tent], *adj.* open, obvious, manifest; protected by a patent; (*coll.*) ingenious, well contrived; **letters p.,** a royal patent. [L. *patens*].

PATENT (3), [pat'-ent, pā'-tent], *v.t.* to secure by patent, to take out a patent for. [*Prec.*].

PATENTABLE, [pat'-ent-abl, pā'-tent-abl], *adj.* able to be patented.

PATENTEE, [pat'-ent-ē], *n.* one who has obtained a patent.

PATER, [pā'-ter], *n.* (*coll.*) father. [L. *pater*].

PATERA, [pat'-er-a], *n.* (*arch.*) a shallow, circular dish. [L. *patera*].

PATERFAMILIAS, [pat'-er-fam-il'-i-as], *n.* the father of a family. [L. *paterfamilias*].

PATERNAL, [pat-urn'-al], *adj.* of a father; fatherly; descended or derived from a father. [LL. *paternalis*].

PATERNALISM, [pa-turn'-al-izm], *n.* the quality or policy of being paternal; benevolent despotism.

PATERNALLY, [pat-urn'-al-i], *adv.* in a paternal manner.

PATERNITY, [pat-urn'-i-ti], *n.* the quality or condition of being a father; fatherhood; (*fig.*) source, origin. [L. *paternitas*].

PATERNOSTER, [pat'-er-nos'-ter], *n.* the Lord's Prayer; the eleventh bead in a rosary; a fishing-line having a bullet at the end and pairs of hooks at equal intervals. [L. *Pater noster* Our Father].

PATH, [pahth], *n.* a way trodden by the foot of man or beast; a track for foot-passengers only at the side of the road, pavement; the course along which anything proceeds, line of action; (*fig.*) the way, development. [OE. *pæth*].

PATHAN, [pā'-than, pa-tahn'], *n.* a member of the Afghan race of N.W. India. [Pushtu *Patan*].

PATHETIC, [path-et'-ik], *adj.* affecting the tender passions; causing pity, sympathy or sadness; full of pathos; **p. fallacy,** the fallacy that Nature has human feelings. [Gk. *pathetikos*].

PATHETICAL, [path-et'-ik-al], *adj.* pathetic.

PATHETICALLY, [path-et'-ik-a-li], *adv.* in a pathetic manner.

PATHETICALNESS, [path-et'-ikl-nes], *n.* pathetic quality or character.

PATHLESS, [pahth'-les], *adj.* having no path; untrodden, trackless.

PATHO-, *pref.* concerning suffering or disease. [Gk. *pathos*].

PATHOGENETIC, [path'-ō-jen-et'-ik], *adj.* relating to the production or development of disease.

PATHOGENY, [path-oj'-en-i], *n.* the origin and development of disease. [PATHO and Gk. *genes* producing].

PATHOGNOMONIC, [path-ŏg-nō-mon'-ik], *adj.* (*med.*) characteristic and indicative of a disease.

PATHOGNOMY, [path-og'-nom-i], *n.* expression of the passions; the study of their several manifestations. [PATHO and Gk. *gnome* sign].

PATHOLOGICAL, [path'-o-loj'-ik-al], *adj.* pertaining to pathology.

PATHOLOGIST, [path-ol'-oj-ist], *n.* one skilled in pathology.

PATHOLOGY, [path-ol'-o-ji], *n.* the study of disease. [PATHO and Gk. *logos* speech].

PATHOPHOBIA, [path'-ō-fō'-bi-a], *n.* fear of disease. [PATHO and Gk. *phobia* fear].

PATHOS, [pā'-thos], *n.* deep emotion such as moves one to sympathy; the literary quality which induces such feelings. [Gk. *pathos*].

PATHWAY, [pahth'-wā], *n.* a path, a way or course; a path for foot-passengers.

PATIBULARY, [pat-ib'-yŏŏ-ler-i], *adj.* resembling the gallows. [L. *patibulum* gallows].

PATIENCE, [pā'-shents], *n.* calm endurance, fortitude, resignation; perseverance in pursuit of an end; capacity for quietly waiting an event or issue; a game of cards played by one person. [L. *patientia*].

PATIENT (1), [pā'-shent], *n.* a person under medical treatment.

PATIENT (2), [pā'-shent], *adj.* showing patience; sustaining pain, affliction or annoyance with calmness and fortitude; slow to anger; long-suffering; persistent, diligent in following out a long course of action. [L. *patiens* enduring].

PATIENTLY, [pā'-shent-li], *adv.* in a patient manner; with patience.

PATIN, see PATEN.

PATINA, [pat'-in-a], *n.* the green incrustation on bronze coins, works of art, and on the face of ancient stone instruments; the high polish acquired by old furniture and woodwork from long and constant polishing. [L. *patina* dish].

PATINE, see PATEN.

PATIO, [pah'-ti-ō], *n.* a Spanish courtyard; the open quadrangle enclosed by a large house. [Span. *patio*].

PATLY, [pat'-li], *adv.* aptly, conveniently, fitly.

PATNESS, [pat'-nes], *n.* fitness; suitableness; (*slang*) slickness.

PATOIS, [pat'-wah], *n.* a provincial form of speech; a local dialect. [Fr. *patois*].

PATRIARCH, [pā'-tri-ahk], *n.* the father or ruler of a family or tribe; one of the early fathers of the Hebrew race; a bishop or metropolitan dignitary in the Eastern Church; a venerable old man or chief; a veteran of a class or profession. [Gk. *patriarkhes*].

PATRIARCHAL, [pā'-tri-ahk-al], *adj.* belonging to, subject to, a patriarch.

PATRIARCHATE, [pā'-tri-ahk-āt], *n.* the office, jurisdiction, or place of residence of, a patriarch.

PATRIARCHISM, [pā'-tri-ahk-izm], *n.* government by patriarchs.

PATRIARCHY, [pā'-tri-ahk-i], *n.* a primitive form of government in which the oldest man of the family or tribe is ruler; the jurisdiction of a patriarch.

PATRICIAN (1), [pat-rish'-an], *n.* in ancient Rome, a nobleman of senatorial descent; a nobleman, an aristocrat. [L. *patricius*].

PATRICIAN (2), [pat-rish'-an], *adj.* pertaining to the old Roman nobility; noble, aristocratic.

PATRICIDE, [pat'-ri-sīd], *n.* the murderer of his or her father; parricide. [L. *pater* and *cida* killer].

PATRICO, [pat'-rik-ō], *n.* (*gipsy slang*) a gipsy priest; a hedge priest. [PATTER (1) and COVE (2)].

PATRIMONIAL, [pat'-ri-mōn'-i-al], *adj.* pertaining to a patrimony; inherited from ancestors.

PATRIMONY, [pat'-ri-mon-i], *n.* property inherited from a father or forebears; (*fig.*) hereditary qualities of mind or body; (*eccles.*) church estate or revenue. [L. *patrimonium*].

PATRIOT, [pā'-tri-ot, pat'-ri-ot], *n.* one who is devoted to his country. [Gk. *patriotes* fellow-countryman].

PATRIOTIC, [pā'-tri-ot'-ik, pat'-ri-ot'-ik], *adj.* having the feelings of a patriot; actuated by patriotism.

PATRIOTICALLY, [pā'-tri-ot'-ik-a-li, pat'-ri-ot'-ik-a-li], *adv.* in a patriotic spirit.

PATRIOTISM, [pā'-tri-ot-izm, pat'-ri-ot-izm], *n.* love for, loyalty to, one's own country.

PATRISTIC, [pat-rist'-ik], *adj.* pertaining to the fathers of the Christian Church; relating to the study of their writings. [Fr. *patristique*].

PATROL (1), [pa-trōl'], *n.* the act of going the rounds of a certain area by police, soldiers, etc., for the purposes of guard; a detachment of men appointed to perform this duty; a small group of people. [Fr. *patrouille*].

PATROL (2), (**patrolling, patrolled**), [pa-trōl'], *v.t. and i.* to go the rounds in a camp or garrison town; to reconnoitre; to march backwards and forwards in.

PATRON, [pā'-tron, pat'-ron], *n.* a protector, one who stands to another in a paternal capacity; one who supports or protects a person or cause; a regular customer or client; (*eccles.*) the holder of an advowson; **p. saint,** a saint constantly invoked as the particular protector of a person, place or cause. [L. *patronus*].

PATRONAGE, [pat'-ron-ij], *n.* support given by a patron; power to appoint to offices; condescension of manner in relations with another; (*coll.*) regular custom to a shopkeeper; (*eccles.*) the right of appointing to a church benefice.

PATRONAL, [pat'-ron-al], *adj.* performing the office of patron.

PATRONESS, [pā'-tron-es'], *n.* a female patron.

PATRONIZE, [pat'-ron-iz], *v.t.* to perform the functions of a patron to; to give one's custom to; to condescend to, assume airs of superiority over.

PATRONIZER, [pat'-ron-iz-er], *n.* a person who patronizes.

PATRONIZING, [pat'-ron-iz-ing], *adj.* that patronizes, condescending.

PATRONLESS, [pā'-tron-les], *adj.* having no patron.

PATRONYMIC, [pat'-ron-im'-ik], *n.* a name derived from a father's or ancestor's name; a family name. [Gk. *pater* father and *onoma* name].

PATTEN, [patn], *n.* a clog shod with an iron ring; (*arch.*) the base of a column. [MedL. *patinus*]

PATTENED, [patnd], *adj.* wearing pattens.

PATTER (1), [pat'-er], *n.* the professional talk of an entertainer; a succession of words spoken or sung at a very rapid rate; jargon. [PATTER (3)].

PATTER (2), [pat'-er], *n.* a quick light sound as of rain falling. [~PAT (4)].

PATTER (3), [pat'-er], *v.t.* to utter hurriedly and rapidly; *v.i.* to talk glibly, chatter. [PATER(NOSTER)].

PATTER (4), [pat'-er], *v.t.* to strike with a succession of quick light sounds; *v.i.* to move lightly and swiftly along with a patter of feet. [PAT (1)].

PATTERN (1), [pat'-ern], *n.* a model to be copied; a specimen or sample; anything cut or formed into a shape to be copied, *esp.* a shaped piece of wood from which a mould is made for casting metal in the same shape; small pieces of various materials from which the customer in a shop chooses the kind he requires. [OFr. *patron* patron, person to be imitated].

PATTERN (2), [pat'-ern], *v.t.* to make in imitation of a model; to draw a pattern on.

PATTERNED, [pat'-ernd], *adj.* having a pattern.

PATTERNMAKER, [pat'-ern-māk'-er], *n.* one who makes patterns for foundry moulds.

PATTY, [pat'-i], *n.* a little pie; **p. tin**, see PATTY-PAN. [Fr. *pâté*].

PATTY-PAN, [pat'-i-pan'], *n.* a pan to bake patties in. [*Prec.* and PAN].

PATULOUS, [pat'-yōō-lus], *adj.* spreading, extending. [L. *patulus*].

PATULOUSNESS, [pat'-yōō-lus-nes], *n.* the quality of being patulous.

PAUCITY, [paw'-si-ti], *n.* fewness; smallness of number. [L. *paucitas*].

PAULINE, [paw'-līn], *adj.* pertaining to the Apostle *Paul*.

PAUL PRY, [pawl'-prī'], *n.* an interfering, meddling person. [*Paul Pry*, a character in J. Poole's comedy (1825)].

PAUNCH, [pawnch], *n.* the belly, abdomen; in ruminants, the first and largest stomach; (*coll.*) a protruding stomach in a man. [AFr. *panche*].

PAUNCHY, [pawnch'-i], *adj.* displaying or possessing a paunch.

PAUPER, [paw'-per], *n.* a person who, on account of his poverty, is dependent on public funds; one in very poor circumstances; (*leg.*) a poor person, allowed to plead or defend a case without paying costs. [L. *pauper* poor].

PAUPERISM, [paw'-per-izm], *n.* the state of being a pauper.

PAUPERIZATION, [paw'-per-īz-a'-shun], *n.* the process of reducing to a pauper; the act of pauperizing.

PAUPERIZE, [paw'-per-īz], *v.t.* to reduce to pauperism; to make dependent on public relief.

PAUSE (1), [pawz], *n.* a cessation or intermission in speaking or action; suspense; a break in writing; (*mus.*) a mark of cessation, a rest, denoted 𝄐. [L. *pausa*].

PAUSE (2), [pawz], *v.i.* to make a pause; to stop; to hesitate; to linger, dwell upon.

PAUSINGLY, [pawz'-ing-li], *adv.* with pausing.

PAVAGE, [pāv'-ij], *n.* a toll paid for paving streets, the laying of a pavement. [MdL. *pavagium*].

PAVANE, [pav-ahn'], *n.* a stately sixteenth-century costume dance in two-four time; music for this dance. [Fr. *pavane*].

PAVE, [pāv], *v.t.* to lay with stone or brick, so as to make a level surface for walking on; to put a surface layer on a path or road; **to p. a way**, to prepare a way; (*fig.*) to render easy the introduction of. [Fr. *paver* from L. *pavire* to tramp, beat down].

PAVEMENT, [pāv'-ment], *n.* a paved footpath by the side of a road; **p. artist**, one who draws on the pavements to obtain alms. [OFr. *pavement*].

PAVID, [pav'-id], *adj.* timid, fearful. [L. *pavidus*].

PAVIER, see PAVIOR.

PAVILION (1), [pav-il'-yun], *n.* a large tent; a temporary movable habitation; a building or annex with a tent-shaped roof; a club-house in a field devoted to outdoor games. [Fr. *pavillon*].

PAVILION (2), [pav-il'-yun], *v.t.* to cover or shelter with, or as with, a pavilion or tent. [*Prec.*].

PAVING, [pāv'-ing], *n.* the upper surface of a road or path, usually of stone or brick.

PAVIOR, PAVIER, [pāv'-i-er], *n.* one who paves.

PAVISADE, [pav'-is-ād'], *n.* (*milit.*) a defence or screen made by a line of shields; a screen of canvas erected round the sides of a ship in time of war to protect the crew. [It. *pavesade*].

PAVON, [pav'-on], *n.* a lance, pennon. [OFr. *pavon*].

PAVONINE, [pav'-on-īn], *adj.* like a peacock; resembling the tail of a peacock; iridescent, many-hued. [L. *pavoninus*].

PAW (1), [paw], *n.* the foot of an animal having claws or nails; (*coll.*) the hand. [OFr. *powe*].

PAW (2), [paw], *v.t.* to scrape with the forefoot; to touch, feel, with the paw; (*coll.*) to handle unnecessarily; *v.i.* (of a horse) to strike the ground repeatedly and restively with the fore-hoofs. [*Prec.*].

PAWED, [pawd], *adj.* having paws.

PAVON

PAWKILY, [pawk'-i-li], *adv.* in pawky fashion.

PAWKY, [paw'-ki], *adj.* shrewd, drolly artful. [Unkn.].

PAWL, [pawl], *n.* a catch which prevents recoil or lifting as it engages; a short bar attached as a catch to a capstan. [PALE (1)].

PAWN (1), [pawn], *n.* a piece or chessman of the lowest rank; an agent used by another in effecting his own ends. [AFr. *poun*].

PAWN (2), [pawn], *n.* a pledge; **in p.**, pledged; in the hands of the pawnbroker. [OFr. *pan*].

PAWN (3), [pawn], *v.t.* to give or deposit in pledge to a pawnbroker; to stake, risk. [*Prec.*].

PAWNBROKER, [pawn'-brōk-er], *n.* one who lends money on interest on the security of personal property given over into his charge. [PAWN (2) and BROKER].

PAWNBROKING, [pawn'-brōk-ing], *n.* the business of a pawnbroker.

PAWNEE (1), [paw-nē'], *n.* one who takes anything in pawn.

PAWNEE (2), [paw'-nē'], *n.* a member of a tribe of American Indians.

PAWNER, [pawn'-er], *n.* a person who pledges anything as security for the payment of borrowed money.

PAWNSHOP, [pawn'-shop], *n.* a shop where pawnbroking is carried on.

PAWNTICKET, [pawn'-tik'-it], *n.* a voucher or ticket for anything pledged at a pawnshop.

PAX, [paks], *n.* a small plate of metal bearing the image of Christ upon the cross, which is kissed during Mass. [L. *pax* peace].

PAXIUBA, [paks'-i-ōō'-bah], *n.* (*bot.*) the South American palm, *Irartea ventricosa*, characterized by a stem with a large oval expansion midway from the ground. [Amer.Indian *paxiuba*].

PAXWAX, PACKWAX, [pak(s)'-waks'], *n.* (*anat.*) a strong tendon in the neck of an animal; faxwax. [OE. *feax* hair and **weax* growth].

PAY (1), [pā], *n.* money or remuneration for services rendered; wages, salary.

PAY (2), (**pays, paid**), [pā], *v.t.* to give to a person money or remuneration for services rendered; to discharge a debt; to give an adequate or agreed sum of money for goods received; to fulfil; to render what is due, make payment of; to make profit for, recompense; to give, render as a duty; *v.i.* to make payment, meet a debt; to recompense for work; to be profitable; **to p. away**, to spend; (*naut.*) to let out (a line) gradually; **to p. back**, to give back, to return tit for tat; **to p. off**, to settle a debt; to discharge with wages paid; **to p. out**, to get one's own back on; (*naut.*) to let out. [OFr. *payer*].

PAY (3), [pā], *v.t.* to coat with pitch or any watertight composition; to render waterproof. [AFr. *peier* from L. *picare* coat with pitch].

PAYABLE, [pā'-abl], *adj.* able to be paid; due.

PAY-BILL, [pā'-bil], *n.* a written statement of money to be paid to soldiers or workmen.

PAY-DAY, [pā'-dā], *n.* the day on which payment of wages is to be made or debts discharged.

PAY-DIRT, [pā'-durt], *n.* alluvial deposit worth working for the gold it contains.

PAYEE, [pā'-ē], *n.* the person to whom a sum of money is or will be paid.

PAYER, [pā'-er], *n.* the person who pays or must pay.

PAY-LIST, [pā'-list], *n.* pay-roll.

PAYMASTER, [pā'-mahst'-er], *n.* a man who regularly pays wages; an officer in the navy or army whose duty it is to pay the officers and men; **p. general**, the officer responsible for payments by the Treasury.

PAYMENT, [pā'-ment], *n.* the act of paying; amount paid; (*fig.*) reward, recompense.

PAYNIM, PAINIM†, [pā'-nim], *n.* a pagan, *esp.* a Moslem or Saracen. [OFr. *paienime*].
PAY-ROLL, [pā'-rōl], *n.* pay-sheet.
PAY-SHEET, [pā'-shēt], *n.* a list of names and wages of employees.
PEA, [pē], *n.* a leguminous climbing plant cultivated for its flowers or for its fruit-pods containing edible seeds. [OE. *pise* PEASE].
PEACE, [pēs], *n.* freedom from disturbance or agitation; freedom from war, hostility or quarrel; a treaty of peace between two nations; a state of quiet or tranquillity; freedom from interference or disturbance; mental calm; concord; rest; **to be at p.**, to be amicable, become reconciled; **to hold one's p.**, to be silent. [AFr. *pes* from L. *pax*].
PEACEABLE, [pēs'-abl], *adj.* disposed for peace, tranquil; at peace.
PEACEABLENESS, [pēs'-abl-nes], *n.* the condition of being peaceable.
PEACEABLY, [pēs'-ab-li], *adv.* in a peaceable manner.
PEACEBREAKER, [pēs'-brāk'-er], *n.* one who disturbs the public peace; an agitator.
PEACEFUL, [pēs'-fōōl], *adj.* disposed to peace, pacific; characterized by peace, undisturbed, tranquil, calm.
PEACEFULLY, [pēs'-fōōl-i], *adv.* in a peaceful manner.
PEACEFULNESS, [pēs'-fōōl-nes], *n.* the condition of being peaceful.
PEACELESS, [pēs'-les], *adj.* without peace; restless, disturbed.
PEACEMAKER, [pēs'-māk'-er], *n.* one who brings about peace or reconciliation where there was formerly war or disagreement.
PEACE-OFFERING, [pēs'-of'-er-ing], *n.* an offering that is designed to effect peace or bring about a reconciliation.
PEACE-OFFICER, [pēs'-of'-is-er], *n.* a civil officer whose duty it is to preserve the public peace; a policeman.
PEACH (1), [pēch], *n.* a rosaceous tree or its fruit; a large edible fruit of a yellow colour flushed with pink with a downy skin and sweet pulpy flesh; (*coll.*) a pretty young girl; **p. brandy**, a kind of brandy flavoured with peaches. [ME. *peche* from L. *Persicum* (*malum*) Persian apple].
PEACH (2), [pēch], *v.i.* (*slang*) to turn informer; tell tales. [OFr. *empechier* to appeal against].
PEACH-COLOURED, [pēch'-kul'-erd], *adj.* a deep soft pinky-cream like the blossom of the peach.
PEACHERY, [pēch'-er-i], *n.* a glasshouse where peaches are grown.
PEACHICK, [pē'-chik'], *n.* a young peacock or peahen.
PEACH MELBA, [pēch'-mel'-ba], *n.* a sweet consisting of ice-cream, peaches and raspberries. [Mme *Melba*, the Australian prima donna, to whom it was first served].
PEACHY, [pēch'-i], *adj.* resembling a peach.
PEACOCK (1), [pē'-kok], *n.* the male bird of the genus *Pavo*, which has beautifully coloured plumage and a fine fan-shaped tail; a proud, strutting, vainglorious person. [OE. *pea* from L. *pavo* and COCK].
PEACOCK (2), [pē'-kok], *v.i.* to strut vaingloriously about; to give oneself airs; to make a great display in dress. [*Prec.*].
PEACOCK-BLUE, [pē'-kok-blōō'], *n.* a rich blue colour like that of the plumage of a peacock's neck.
PEACOCK BUTTERFLY, [pē'-kok-but'-er-flī], *n.* a butterfly, *Vanessa io*, with a pattern on each wing resembling that on a peacock's feathers.
PEACOCK-FISH, [pē'-kok-fish'], *n.* the blue-striped wrasse.
PEA-FLOUR, [pē'-flow-(r)'], *n.* flour made from ground dried peas.
PEAFOWL, [pē'-fowl], *n.* a peacock or peahen; any species of bird of the genus *Pavo*.
PEA-GREEN, [pē'-grēn'], *n.* a light soft green colour as of fresh pea-pods.
PEAHEN, [pē'-hen'], *n.* the female of the peacock.
PEA-JACKET, [pē'-jak'-it], *n.* a pilot coat or sailor's short overcoat. [Du. *pij-jakket*].
PEAK (1), [pēk], *n.* the top of anything terminating in a point, *esp.* the top of a hill or mountain; the projecting shade in front of a cap; (*naut.*) the narrow end of a hull at the bow; a ship's hold in the bow; **p. load, period, etc.**, the load, period, etc., when maximum effect is present. [*Var.* of PIKE].
PEAK (2), [pēk], *v.t.* to tilt upwards; (*naut.*) to raise a yard obliquely to the mast. [*Prec.*].
PEAK (3), [pēk], *v.i.* to pine away, to grow thin and pale. [Uncert.].
PEAKED, [pēkt], *adj.* with a peak, pointed.
PEAKISH†, [pēk'-ish], *adj.* looking thin and sickly from illness. [PEAK (3)].
PEAKY, [pēk'-i], *adj.* having peaks; peaked, peak-like.
PEAL (1), [pēl], *n.* a set of bells or the changes rung on them; a chime of bells; a loud, reverberating sound. [~APPEAL].
PEAL (2), [pēl], *v.i.* to ring out loudly and clearly; *v.t.* to cause to peal. [*Prec.*].
PEAN (1), see PAEAN.
PEAN (2), [pēn], *n.* (*her.*) heraldic ermine fur when the field is black and the spots gold. [Uncert.].
PEANISM, [pē'-an-izm], *n.* a song of praise, shout of triumph.
PEANUT, [pē'-nut], *n.* the plant, *Arachis hypogaea*; the oily nutritious seed of this plant much valued for food.
PEA-ORE, [pē'-aw(r)], *n.* (*min.*) an argillaceous oxide of iron, made up of round, smooth grains.
PEAR, [pāer], *n.* the tree, *Pyrus communis*; the fleshy fruit of this tree. [OE. *pere* from L. *pirum* pear].
PEARL (1), [purl], *n.* a silvery-white, smooth and iridescent product of many bivalved molluscs, *esp.* the pearl-oyster; mother-of-pearl; something round and clear, like a dew-drop; anything very precious; (*typ.*) a small size of type; **p. button**, a button made of mother-of-pearl. [Fr. *perle*].
PEARL (2), [purl], *v.t.* to set or adorn with pearls; to decorate with pearl-like drops; *v.i.* to fish or dive for pearls; to form into pearl-like drops. [*Prec.*].
PEARLACEOUS, [purl-ā'-shus], *adj.* resembling mother-of-pearl; shaped like pearls.
PEARL-ASH, [purl'-ash'], *n.* an impure carbonate of potash, of a white, pearly appearance.
PEARL-BARLEY, [purl'-bah'-li], *n.* barley reduced to small, round grains.
PEARL-DIVER, [purl'-dīv'-er], *n.* a man who dives for pearl-oysters.
PEARLED, [purld], *adj.* decorated with pearls; bespangled with pearl-like drops.
PEARL-EYE, [purl'-ī], *n.* cataract.
PEARL-FISHER, [purl'-fish'-er], *n.* a pearl-diver.
PEARLIES, [purl'-iz], *n.(pl.)* (*coll.*) pearl buttons as worn for ornament on a costermonger's jacket; clothes bearing these adornments. [PEARL (1)].
PEARLINESS, [purl'-i-nes], *n.* a pearl-like quality.
PEARL-OYSTER, [purl'-ois'-ter], *n.* the oyster yielding pearls, a species of *Meleagrina*.
PEARL-SINTER, [purl'-sin'-ter], *n.* florite; a kind of siliceous sinter.
PEARL-SPAR, [purl'-spah(r)], *n.* (*min.*) bitter spar.
PEARLSTONE, [purl'-stōn], *n.* (*min.*) a pitchstone that contains small spherical nodules.
PEARL-WHITE, [purl'-wīt], *n.* (*chem.*) a white powder taken from nitrate of bismuth.
PEARLWORT, [purl'-wurt], *n.* (*bot.*) a plant of the genus *Sagina*.
PEARLY, [purl'-i], *adj.* resembling a pearl in shape or texture; abounding in pearls; made of, adorned with pearls; **p. king**, a costermonger dressed in pearlies.
PEARMAIN, [pāer'-mān'], *n.* a smallish fairly soft apple ripening in August. [OFr. *permain* of Parma].
PEAR-TREE, [pāer'-trē'], *n.* the tree, *Pyrus communis*, or one of its cultivated varieties, bearing a soft edible fruit of distinctive flavour.
PEASANT, [pez'-ant], *n.* a countryman, a rustic labourer; a countryman who owns and cultivates a small piece of land. [AFr. *paisant*].
PEASANT-LIKE, [pez'-ant-līk], *adj.* having the manners and opinions of a peasant; rustic; illiterate, boorish.
PEASANTRY, [pez'-ant-ri], *n.(pl.)* peasants as a class.
PEASCOD†, [pēs'-kod], *n.* the legume or pericarp of the pea; pea-pod. [PEASE and OE. *codd* husk].
PEASE, [pēs], *n.(pl.)* peas; **p. pudding**, split peas boiled and mashed. [OE. *pise* pea].
PEA-SHOOTER, [pē'-shōōt'-er], *n.* a narrow tube used by children to blow peas through as missiles; (*fig.*) an inadequate weapon.
PEA SOUP, [pē'-sōōp'], *n.* a thick nourishing soup made from dried peas.
PEA-SOUPER, [pē'-sōōp'-er], *n.* (*coll.*) a thick yellow fog, *esp.* a London fog.
PEASTONE, [pē'-stōn], *n.* (*min.*) a kind of limestone; pisolite.
PEAT, [pēt], *n.* a fibrous brown substance formed in bogs or moors by partial carbonization of vegetable matter, and used as fuel. [ME. *pete*].
PEAT-BOG, [pēt'-bog'], *n.* moorland covered with peat.
PEAT-HAG, [pēt'-hag'], *n.* a hole in the earth from which peat has been removed.

PEAT-MOSS, [pēt′-mos′], *n.* a peat-bog; any species of *Sphagnum* moss whose habitat is the peat-bog.

PEATY, [pēt′-i], *adj.* composed of, resembling, peat.

PEBA, [pē′-ba], *n.* the black tatou, a variety of armadillo, *Tatusia novemcincta*, ranging from Texas to Paraguay. [SAmerInd *peba*].

PEBA

PEBBLE, [pebl], *n.* a small rounded fragment of rock of any variety; a transparent rock crystal; an agate. [OE. *papol (stan)*, ME. *pibbel*].

PEBBLED, [pebld], *adj.* covered or heaped with pebbles; pebbly.

PEBBLY, [peb′-li], *adj.* covered with, full of, pebbles.

PEBRINE, [peb′-rin], *n.* (*path.*) a fatal disease among silkworms caused by internal parasites. [Fr. *pébrine* from Provenc. *pebre* pepper, referring to the black spots on the victim].

PECAN, [pē′-an′], *n.* a species of hickory common in U.S.A.; the nut or fruit of this tree. [Span. *pacana*].

PECCABILITY, [pek′-ab-il′-i-ti], *n.* tendency to sin.

PECCABLE, [pek′-abl], *adj.* capable of, with a tendency to, sin. [MedL. *peccabilis*].

PECCADILLO, [pek′-ad-il′-ō], *n.* a petty crime or fault; a venial offence; an indiscretion. [Span. *pecadillo* from L. *peccare* to sin].

PECCANCY, [pek′-an-si], *n.* a sin, offence; (*med.*) morbid condition. [L. *peccantia* sin].

PECCANT, [pek′-ant], *adj.* wrong, erroneous, sinful; (*med.*) morbid.

PECCARY, [pek′-er-i], *n.* (*zool.*) a South American ungulate related to the swine. [SAmerInd *pakira*].

PECCAVI, [pek-ā′-vi], *n.* a confession of sin or error. [L. *peccavi* I have sinned].

PECK (1), [pek], *n.* the fourth part of a bushel or two gallons; (*coll.*) a great deal, a heap. [OFr. *pek*].

PECK (2), [pek], *n.* a poke or bite made with the beak; a hasty and perfunctory kiss.

PECK (3), [pek], *v.t.* to strike with the beak; to make a hole in by striking with the beak; to pick up with the beak, pluck out by pecking; to give a hasty and perfunctory kiss to; **to p. at,** to aim at with the beak, to eat indifferently and without appetite. [*Var.* of PICK].

PECKER, [pek′-er], *n.* one who, or that which, pecks; the woodpecker; **to keep one's p. up,** (*coll.*) to keep up one's courage.

PECKISH, [pek′-ish], *adj.* (*coll.*) hungry.

PECKSNIFF, [pek′-snif], *n.* a pompous hypocrite, a humbug. [*Pecksniff*, a character in Dickens' *Martin Chuzzlewit*].

PECTATE, [pek′-tāt], *n.* (*chem.*) a salt of pectic acid.

PECTEN, [pek′-ten], *n.* (*biol.*) a vascular membrane on the eyes of birds and reptiles resembling the teeth of a comb in shape; a genus of marine bivalves including the scallops. [L. *pecten* comb].

PECTIC, [pek′-tik], *adj.* (*chem.*) of the nature of an acid and having the property of forming a jelly; **p. acid,** an acid obtained from the action of an alkali on pectin. [Gk. *pektikos* congealing].

PECTIN, [pek′-tin], *n.* the gelatinizing principle of certain fruits, such as apples and plums. [Gk. *pektos* congealed].

PECTINAL, [pek′-tinl], *adj.* resembling a comb; (*anat.*) belonging to the pubic or sharebone.

PECTINATE, [pek′-tin-āt], *adj.* shaped like, having teeth like, a comb. [L. *pectinatus*].

PECTINATION, [pek′-tin-ā′-shun], *n.* the condition of being pectinated. [L. *pectinatio*].

PECTINIBRANCHIATE, [pek′-tin-i-brangk′-i-āt], *adj.* with pectinated gills. [PECTEN and Gk. *bragkhia* gills].

PECTORAL (1), [pek′-ter-al], *n.* a breastplate; a sacerdotal habit worn by the Jewish high priest; a medicine to relieve chest complaints; a pectoral fin. [OFr. *pectoral* breastplate from L. *pectorale*].

PECTORAL ARCH

PECTORAL (2), [pek′-ter-al], *adj.* of, pertaining to, the breast, worn on the breast; (*med.*) good for diseases of the chest; **p. arch,** (*anat.*) the shoulder girdle. [L. *pectoralis*].

PECTORILOQUISM, [pek′-ter-il′-ok-wizm], *n.* pectoriloquy.

PECTORILOQUY, [pek′-ter-il′-ok-wi], *n.* (*med.*) the sound of the voice coming from the chest, when the stethoscope is applied there. [Fr. *pectoriloquie*].

PECULATE, [pek′-yōō-lāt], *v.i.* to appropriate to one's own use money or goods entrusted to one's care. [L. *peculare*].

PECULATION, [pek′-yōō-lā′-shun], *n.* embezzlement of public money to one's own use; embezzlement.

PECULATOR, [pek′-yōō-lāt-or], *n.* a person who peculates; an embezzler.

PECULIAR (1), [pik-ew′-li-er], *n.* exclusive property; (*eccles.*) a church or parish exempt from the ordinary ecclesiastical authority; (*typ.*) a form of type employed only for certain languages, etc.

PECULIAR (2), [pik-ew′-li-er], *adj.* characteristic of one person, individual; solely or specially belonging (to); singular, uncommon, marked, queer; **in p.,** in particular. [L. *peculiaris*].

PECULIARITY, [pik-ew′-li-a′-rit-i], *n.* the quality of being peculiar; a characteristic, distinguishing quality; eccentricity.

PECULIARIZE, [pik-ew′-li-er-īz], *v.t.* to make peculiar; to appropriate.

PECULIARLY, [pik-ew′-li-er-li], *adv.* in a peculiar manner; especially, unusually.

PECUNIARILY, [pik-ew′-ni-er-i-li], *adv.* in a pecuniary manner; from a monetary point of view.

PECUNIARY, [pik-ew′-ni-er-i], *adj.* relating to, consisting of, money; (*leg.*) having a money penalty. [L. *pecuniarius*].

PEDAGOGIC, [ped′-a-goj′-ik], *adj.* belonging to a pedagogue.

PEDAGOGICAL, [ped′-a-goj′-ik-al], *adj.* pedagogic.

PEDAGOGICS, [ped′-a-goj′-iks], *n.(pl.)* the science of pedagogy.

PEDAGOGISM, [ped′-a-goj′-izm], *n.* the business, character or manners of a pedagogue; the system of pedagogy.

PEDAGOGUE, [ped′-a-gog′], *n.* a teacher of children or young people; a schoolmaster; a pedantic teacher. [Gk. *paidagogos* slave who escorted children to school].

PEDAGOGY, [ped′-a-goj-i], *n.* the art or practice of teaching. [Gk. *paidagogia* education].

PEDAL (1), [ped′-al], *n.* part of a machine or instrument worked by the foot; (*mus.*) one of the wooden keys of the organ keyboard worked by the feet; of one, two or three levers on a piano or harp, which are worked by the foot, *esp.* the loud pedal of a piano. [Fr. *pédal*].

PEDAL (2), [ped′-al], *adj.* pertaining to a foot or feet. [L. *pedalis* of a foot].

PEDAL (3), (**pedalling, pedalled**), [ped′-al], *v.t. and i.* to work with a pedal.

PEDANT, [ped′-ant], *n.* a person who makes a display of his learning; one who prides himself on his book-learning and meticulous observation of the letter, but is devoid of real taste or discrimination; one slavishly devoted to a system of rules. [Fr. *pédant*].

PEDANTIC, [pid-ant′-ik], *adj.* given to, or characterized by, pedantry.

PEDANTICALLY, [pid-ant′-ik-al-i], *adv.* in pedantic fashion.

PEDANTRY, [ped′-an-tri], *n.* vain ostentation of learning; slavish insistence on rules and forms.

PEDATE, [ped′-āt], *adj.* (*biol.*) having feet or some arrangement resembling the formation of the foot or toes. [L. *pedatus*].

PEDDLE, [pedl], *v.t.* to sell small wares usually by travelling about the country; *v.i.* to trade as a pedlar. [~PEDLAR].

PEDDLER†, see PEDLAR.

PEDDLERY, [ped′-ler-i], *n.* small wares sold by pedlars; the business of a pedlar.

PEDDLING, [ped′-ling], *adj.* (*fig.*) small-minded; trifling. [PEDDLE and PIDDLING].

PEDESTAL, [ped′-es-tal], *n.* the base of a column or statue; either of the two tiers of drawers supporting a knee-hole writing-desk; **to put on a p.,** (*fig.*) to look up to, venerate. [Fr. *piédestal* from L. *pes pedis* foot].

PEDESTRIAN (1), [pid-es′-tri-an], *n.* one who journeys on foot.

PEDESTRIAN (2), [pid-es′-tri-an], *adj.* on foot; walking; representing a person on foot; (*fig.*) prosaic, commonplace. [L. *pedester* going on foot].

PEDESTRIAN CROSSING, [pid-es′-tri-an-kros′-ing], *n.* a marked crossing in the streets over which pedestrians have the prior right of way.

PEDESTRIANISM, [pid-es′-tri-an-izm], *n.* walking; the art of walking as a sport.

PEDI-, *pref.* relating to a foot or feet. [L. *pes pedis* foot].

PEDICEL, [ped′-is-el], *n.* (*bot.*) the stalk of each individual flower; (*zool.*) a footstalk or stem by which certain invertebrate animals attach themselves to any object. [MdL. *pedicellus*].

PEDICELLATE, [ped′-is-el-āt], *adj.* having a pedicel.

PEDICLE, [ped′-ikl], *n.* a pedicel.

PEDICULAR, [ped-ik′-yōō-ler], *adj.* lousy. [L. *pedicularis*].

PEDICULATION, [ped-ik′-yōō-lā′-shun], *n.* (*path.*) a disease bred by infestation with lice. [LL. *pediculatio*].

PEDICULOUS, [ped-ik′-yōō-lus], *adj.* pedicular.

PEDICURE, [ped′-i-kyōōe(r)], *n.* treatment of the feet; a chiropodist. [Fr. *pédicure*].

PEDIGEROUS, [ped-ij′-er-us], *adj.* bearing feet. [PEDI and L. *gerere* to bear].

PEDIGREE (1), [ped′-i-grē], *n.* a genealogical table or family tree; genealogy, ancestry, descent. [Fr. *pied de grue* crane's foot].

PEDIGREE (2), [ped′-i-grē], *adj.* (of an animal) having a known pedigree.

PEDIMANOUS, [ped-im′-an-us], *adj.* (*zool.*) having feet resembling hands. [PEDI and L. *manus* a hand].

PEDIMENT, [ped′-i-ment], *n.* (*arch.*) a triangular structure, often sculptured, over the portico of a Greek building; any structure resembling this in form. [Corruption of PYRAMID].

PEDIMENT

PEDIMENTAL, [ped′-i-ment′-al], *adj.* pertaining to a pediment.

PEDIPALP, [ped′-i-palp], *n.* (*zool.*) one of a group of spiders having large pincer-like feelers. [PEDI and L. *palpus* feeler].

PEDIREME, [ped′-i-rēm], *n.* (*zool.*) a crustacean, with feet which are used in the manner of oars. [PEDI and L. *remus* oar].

PEDLAR, PEDDLER†, [ped′-ler], *n.* a travelling salesman who carries his pack from door to door. [ME. *pedlere*].

PEDLARY, [ped′-ler-i], *n.* the occupation of a pedlar; small wares.

PEDO-, see PAEDO-.

PEDOBAPTISM, PÆDOBAPTISM, [pēd′-ō-bap′-tizm], *n.* the baptism of infants. [PAEDO and BAPTISM].

PEDOBAPTIST, PÆDOBAPTIST, [pēd′-ō-bap′-tist], *n.* one who believes in the baptism of infants.

PEDOMETER, [ped-om′-it-er], *n.* an instrument which measures distances in walking. [PEDI and METER].

PEDOMOTOR, [ped′-ō-mō′-tor], *n.* a machine which is worked by the foot; a treadle. [PEDI and MOTOR].

PEDRERO, [ped′-räer′-ō], *n.* a small swivel gun. [Span. *pedrero*].

PEDUNCLE, [ped′-ungkl], *n.* (*bot.*) the stalk either of the flower or the cluster; (*zool.*) a stalk-like joining. [MdL. *pedunculus*].

PEDUNCULAR, [ped-ungk′-yōō-ler], *adj.* pertaining to a peduncle.

PEDUNCULATE, [ped-ungk′-yōō-lāt], *adj.* furnished with a peduncle; stalked.

PEDUNCULATED, [ped-ungk′-yōō-lāt-id], *adj.* having a stalk or peduncle.

PEEK, [pēk], *v.i.* to peep. [ME. *piken*].

PEEL (1), [pēl], *n.* a small square fortress tower on the Scottish border. [OFr. *pel*].

PEEL (2), [pēl], *n.* the long-handled wooden shovel used by bakers for removing bread from the oven. [OFr. *pele* from L. *pala* spade].

PEEL (3), [pēl], *n.* the skin or rind of fruit; **candied p.,** the rind of lemon, orange, or citron preserved in sugar.

PEEL (4), [pēl], *v.t.* to strip off, remove, the skin, rind, peel or outer coating of; *v.i.* to shed (its) peel, rind or covering; **to p. off,** to come off in strips or patches. [OE. *pilian* from L. *pilare* take the hair off].

PEELER (1), [pēl′-er], *n.* one who peels.

PEELER (2), [pēl′-er], *n.* a member of the 19th-century constabulary; a policeman. [Sir Robert *Peel*, the founder].

PEELING, [pēl′-ing], *n.* that which is peeled off.

PEEN, [pēn], *n.* the blunt wedge-shaped end of a hammer head. [Uncert.].

PEEP (1), [pēp], *n.* the small, shrill cry of a young bird; a cheep, chirp. [Echoic].

PEEP (2), [pēp], *n.* a glimpse or hasty view; the first tentative appearance. [PEEP (4)].

PEEP (3), [pēp], *v.i.* to chirp or cry as young birds; to cheep, squeak. [PEEP (1)].

PEEP (4), [pēp], *v.i.* to look through a restricted space, to catch a glimpse; to peer cautiously; to take a hasty look; to make a first tentative appearance; (*fig.*) to be revealed unexpectedly through some small sign. [PEEP (2)].

PEEPER, [pēp′-er], *n.* a bird, animal that peeps; a young bird; (*coll.*) an eye.

PEEP-HOLE, [pēp′-hōl], *n.* a small aperture in a wall or door for peeping through.

PEEP-O'-DAY, [pēp′-ō-dā′], *n.* daybreak, dawn. [PEEP OF DAY].

PEEP-SHOW, [pēp′-shō], *n.* a well-lighted box in the side of which a magnifying glass is fixed through which are viewed the pictures arranged within a small diorama; (*fig.*) a spectacle for the curious.

PEEPUL, PIPAL, [pēpl], *n.* the Indian bo-tree, *Ficus religiosa.* [Hind. *peepul, pipal*].

PEER (1), [pēer], *n.* a person of equal rank or importance with another; one entitled to sit in the House of Lords by hereditary right or as a bishop or under rights granted for life and not hereditary; **temporal p.,** a peer who is not a bishop; **spiritual p.,** a bishop who has a seat in the House of Lords. [OFr. *per* from L. *par* equal].

PEER (2), [pēer], *v.i.* to look carefully, narrowly, intently. [LGerm. *piren*].

PEERAGE, [pēer′-ij], *n.* peers collectively; the rank of a peer; a book with names and details of the families of peers.

PEERESS, [pēer′-es], *n.* the consort of a peer; a woman who holds a peerage.

PEERLESS, [pēer′-les], *adj.* having no equal; without peers.

PEERLESSLY, [pēer′-les-li], *adv.* in a peerless manner.

PEERLESSNESS, [pēer′-les-nes], *n.* the condition of having no peers or equals.

PEEVE, [pēv], *v.t.* (*coll.*) to annoy. [PEEVISH].

PEEVISH, [pēv′-ish], *adj.* fretful; querulous; hard to please; petulant, irritable; (of a wind) piercing cold. [ME. *peyveche*].

PEEVISHLY, [pēv′-ish-li], *adv.* in a peevish manner, querulously.

PEEVISHNESS, [pēv′-ish-nes], *n.* the condition of being peevish.

PEEWIT, PEWIT, [pē′-wit′], *n.* the lapwing, the green plover, *Vanellus cristatus*; the cry of this bird. [Imitative].

PEG (1), [peg], *n.* a small wooden or metal pin used to fasten pieces of wood or metal together; a split stick used to affix clothes to a line to dry; a short projecting pin used as a support; a drink (from the small measuring pegs inside tankards); **to take a person down a p.,** to drink more than he does, to humiliate him. [Du. *pegge*].

PEG (2), (pegging, pegged), [peg], *v.t.* to fasten, score, with pegs; (*econ.*) to maintain a steady price for stock, etc., by regulation or manipulation of the market; **to p. away,** to work doggedly; **to p. down,** to secure by pegging to the ground; **to p. out,** to stake, mark out, with pegs; (*coll.*) to die. [*Prec.*].

PEGAMOID, [peg′-am-oid], *n.* an artificial or imitation leather. [Invented trade name].

PEGASUS, [peg′-as-us], *n.* the winged horse, sprung from the blood of Medusa that with a stroke opened a spring in the ground whence the poets were fabled afterwards to have drawn their inspiration; the poetic muse; (*astron.*) a northern constellation; (*zool.*) a genus of fishes with large pectoral fins. [Gk. *Pegasos* from *pege* fountain].

PEGMATITE, [peg′-mat-īt], *n.* (*min.*) binary granite made up of quartz and felspar.

PEG-TOP, [peg′-top′], *n.* a pear-shaped spinning-top; **p. trousers,** trousers wide at the hips and narrow at the ankles.

PEIGNOIR, [pān′-wah(r)], *n.* a woman's dressing jacket, a dressing wrap. [Fr. *peignoir*].

PEIRASTIC, [pī-rast′-ik], *adj.* making trial, tentative. [Gk. *peirastikos*].

PEISHWA, [pāsh′-wa], *n.* the chief minister or ruler of the Mahrattas. [Hind. *peishwa*].

PEJORATIVE, [pē′-jer-at-iv], *adj.* disparaging; with a depreciatory meaning. [L. *pejorare* to make worse].

PEKAN [pe'-kan], *n.* (*ornith.*) the fisher-marten, *Mustela pennanti*. [Amer.Indian *pekané*].
PEKINESE, PEKINGESE, [pē'-kin-ēz], *n.* a breed of Chinese pug-dogs, with large pendent ears [*Pekin* the Chinese city].
PEKOE, [pek'-ō, pēk-ō], *n.* a variety of black tea made of young leaves with the down still on them. [Chin. *pekoe* from *pek* white and *hao* down].
PELAGE, [pel-ahzh'], *n.* the covering fur or skin of a mammal. [Fr. *pelage*].
PELAGIAN (1), [pel-ā'-ji-an], *n.* a follower of Pelagius, a British monk of the fourth century who denied the doctrine of original sin and asserted man's innate capacity for working out his own salvation; a disciple of Pelagius.
PELAGIAN (2), [pel-ā'-ji-an], *adj.* of, or pertaining to, Pelagius or his belief.
PELAGIAN (3), [pel-ā'-ji-an], *n.* an inhabitant of the deep-sea.
PELAGIAN (4), [pel-ā'-ji-an], *adj.* pertaining to, or inhabiting, the deep-sea; oceanic. [Gk. *pelagos* open sea].
PELAGIANISM, [pel-ā'-ji-an-izm], *n.* the doctrines of Pelagius and his followers.
PELAGIC, [pel-aj'-ik], *adj.* belonging to the deep-sea. [PELAGIAN (4)].
PELARGIC, [pel-ahj'-ik], *adj.* pertaining to storks. [Gk. *pelargikos*].
PELARGONIUM, [pel'-ah-gō'-ni-um], *n.* (*bot.*) a genus of ornamental plants allied to the geranium, but differing from it in having its flowers irregular instead of regular and having five or fewer stamens instead of ten. [Gk. *pelargos* stork].
PELASGIC, [pel-as'-jik], *adj.* of, pertaining to, the Pelasgi, a prehistoric people of South-Eastern Europe and Asia Minor. [Gk. *Pelasgoi*].
PELERINE, [pel'-er-ēn], *n.* a woman's mantle or cape; a tippet. [Fr. *pèlerine* from *pèlerin* pilgrim].
PELF, [pelf], *n.* money, wealth; money doubtfully acquired. [OFr. *pelfre*].
PELICAN, [pel'-ik-an], *n.* a genus of birds, *Pelecanus*, allied to the storks, with all four toes pointing forwards and a great bill with a large pouch; a dentist's instrument. [Gk. *pelekan*].
PELISSE, [pel-ēs'], *n.* a woman's long, sleeved cloak; a child's loose coat; a cape or coat worn as part of a military uniform. [Fr. *pelisse*].
PELL, [pel], *n.* (*hist.*) skin or hide; a roll of parchment or vellum. [L. *pellis*].
PELLAGRA, [pel-ā'-gra], *n.* an eruptive skin disease caused by vitamin B1 deficiency. [It. *pelle* skin and *agra* rough].
PELLET, [pel'-it], *n.* a small ball of some soft substance as of medicine or food; a pill; small shot. [Fr. *pelote*].
PELLICLE, [pel'-ikl], *n.* a thin skin or crust; a membrane; a film. [L. *pellicula*].
PELLITORY (1), [pel'-it-er-i], *n.* (*bot.*) a plant of the genus *Parietaria* growing on old walls. [L. *parietaria*].
PELLITORY (2), [pel'-it-er-i], *n.* (*bot.*) a herb of the aster family formerly used to alleviate toothache. [Gk. *purethron*].
PELL-MELL, [pel'-mel'], *adv.* in disorder, confusedly. [Fr. *pêle-mêle*].
PELLUCID, [pel-ōō'-sid], *adj.* allowing the passage of light; translucent; (*fig.*) clear, lucid. [L. *perlucidus*].
PELLUCIDNESS, [pel-ōō'-sid-nes], *n.* the quality of being pellucid; (*fig.*) lucidity.
PELMET, [pel'-met], *n.* a narrow strip of material usually matching the curtains, fixed over the tops of doors and windows for decoration and to hide curtain fixtures. [Fr. *palmette*].
PELOTA, [pel-ō'-ta], *n.* a Spanish ball game resembling tennis in which the ball is struck from a wickerwork shield strapped to the arm. [Span. *pelota*].
PELT (1), [pelt], *n.* the skin or coat of an animal. [OFr. *pel*].
PELT (2), [pelt], *n.* the action of pelting; a blow from something thrown; **at full p.**, rapidly. [PELT (3)].
PELT (3), [pelt], *v.t.* to strike with something thrown; to throw something at; *v.i.* (of rain, hail) to pour down heavily, in full force. [ME. *pelten* to push, thrust].
PELTATE, [pelt'-āt], *adj.* (*bot.*) shaped like a shield and bearing a stalk in the centre. [Gk. *pelte* small shield].
PELTER, [pelt'-er], *n.* a person who pelts; (*coll.*) a pelting shower.
PELTRY, [pel'-tri], *n.* skins with the fur on, undressed skins. [AFr. *pelterie*].
PELT-WOOL, [pelt'-wōōl], *n.* wool plucked from the pelts of sheep.
PELVIC, [pel'-vik], *adj.* pertaining to the pelvis.
PELVIMETER, [pel-vim'-it-er], *n.* an instrument for measuring the pelvis.
PELVIS, [pel'-vis], *n.* (*anat.*) the hip-girdle at which the legs are joined to the body, the bones forming it, being the sacrum and coccyx with a haunch bone on each side. [L. *pelvis* basin].
PEMMICAN, [pem'-ik-an], *n.* lean meat dried, pounded and pressed with fat into cakes, for long voyages; (*U.S.*) a summary, a literary digest. [Amer. Indian *pimecan* fat meat].
PEMPHIGUS, [pem'-fig-us], *n.* (*path.*) a skin disease, characterized by round or oval blisters two or three inches in diameter. [Gk. *pemphix* blister].
PEN (1), [pen], *n.* a small enclosure for animals. [OE. *penn*].
PEN (2), [pen], *n.* the female swan. [Unkn.].
PEN (3), [pen], *n.* a feather, quill; a writing tool made formerly of a feather with the end of the shaft pointed, but now a metal nib fitted into a wooden or vulcanite handle; (*fig.*) writing, the profession of letters, literary style; **fountain p.**, a pen with a storage tube for ink which runs on to the nib as required. [L. *penna* feather].
PEN (4), (**penning, penned**), [pen], *v.t.* to shut in a pen, coop up; confine. [PEN (1)].
PEN (5), [pen], *v.t.* to write with a pen; to compose. [PEN (3)].
PENAL, [pē'-nal], *adj.* pertaining to legal punishment; making one liable to legal punishment; inflicted as legal punishment; **p. servitude**, imprisonment for three years or more with hard labour; **p. settlement**, one for convicts. [Fr. *pénal* from L. *poenalis*].
PENALIZE, [pē'-nal-īz], *v.t.* to lay under a penalty, to punish; to handicap, put a penalty on.
PENALLY, [pē'-nal-i], *adv.* in a penal manner; meriting punishment.
PENALTY, [pen'-al-ti], *n.* a legal punishment; a fine; loss or injury which results from wrongdoing; (*sport*) handicap, disadvantage imposed on one player or a side for breaking a rule of the game.
PENANCE, [pen'-ants], *n.* a sacrament of the Roman and Greek Churches involving contrition, confession and absolution; a religious discipline undertaken as an earnest of repentance; (*fig.*) discomfort, misery, vexation. [OFr. *peneance* from L. *penitentia*].
PEN-AND-INK, [pen'-and-ingk'], *adj.* written, or drawn, with pen and ink.
PENANNULAR, [pen-an'-yōō-ler], *adj.* almost annular or circular. [L. *paene* almost and ANNULAR].
PENATES, [pen-ā'-tēz], *n.*(*pl.*) (*Rom. myth.*) the guardian deities of the household, household gods; household possessions. [L. *penates*].
PENCE, [pents], *n.*(*pl.*) pennies. [PENNY].
PENCHANT, [pah(n)-shahn(g)'], *n.* inclination, liking, partiality. [Fr. *penchant*].
PENCIL (1), [pen'-sil], *n.* a small brush used by painters for laying on colours; a bar of blacklead or coloured chalk in a wooden or metal sheath; (*opt.*) a collection of rays of light, rays of light meeting in a point; **p. cedar**, the red wood used for lead pencils, *Juniperus virginiana*; **p. compass**, a drawing compass with a pencil on one of its legs. [OFr. *pincel* from L. *penicillum*].
PENCIL (2), (**pencilling, pencilled**), [pen'-sil], *v.t.* to write, draw, mark with a pencil.
PENCIL-CASE, [pen'-sil-kās'], *n.* a case or small holder in which pencils are stored.
PENCILLED, [pen'-sild], *adj.* painted, marked, drawn, written with or as with a pencil; (*fig.*) finely marked.
PENCILLIFORM, [pen-sil'-i-fawm], *adj.* shaped like a pencil.
PENCILLING, [pen'-sil-ing], *n.* painting, sketching; marked with fine, delicate lines.
PENCRAFT, [pen'-krahft], *n.* penmanship.
PEND, [pend], *v.i.* to hang, depend.
PENDANT (1), PENDENT, [pend'-ant], *n.* anything hanging as an ornament, particularly on a chain or ribbon from the neck; a hanging fitment for a lamp; (*arch.*) a stone ornament depending from ceiling or roof; (*naut.*) a pennant flown from the masthead. [Fr. *pendant*].
PENDANT (2), PENDENT, [pend'-ant], *adj.* hanging; overhanging, projecting. [PEND].
PENDENCY, [pend'-en-si], *n.* the state of being undecided.
PENDENTIVE, [pend'-ent-iv], *n.* (*arch.*) a portion of a vault resting on a single pier and extending from the springing to the apex. [Fr. *pendentif*].
PENDENTLY, [pend'-ent-li], *adv.* in a pendent way.

PENDING, [pend'-ing], *adj.* not decided, awaiting decision; awaiting the occurrence of.

PENDRAGON, [pen'-drag'-on], *n.* an elected chief among the Ancient Britons and Welsh. [Wel. *penn* chief and DRAGON].

PENDULINE, [pend'-yōō-lin], *adj.* hanging (*esp.* of birds' nests which hang suspended). [Fr. *penduline*].

PENDULOUS, [pend'-yōō-lus], *adj.* hanging down loosely so as to swing; drooping. [L. *pendulus*].

PENDULOUSNESS, [pend'-yōō-lus-nes], *n.* the condition of being pendulous.

PENDULUM, [pend'-yōō-lum], *n.* a weight suspended from a fixed point and free to swing rhythmically; **swing of the p.,** (*fig.*) the movement of popular feeling or opinion away from its former loyalties to opposite ones. [L. *pendulum*].

PENECONTEMPORANEOUS, [pē'-ni-kon-tem'-per-ā'-ni-us], *adj.* almost contemporary. [L. *paene* nearly and CONTEMPORANEOUS].

PENELOPE, [pen-el'-op-i], *n.* the name of the wife of Odysseus in ancient Greek legend; a faithful wife. [Gk. *Penelope*].

PENEPLAIN, [pē'-ni-plān'], *n.* a stretch of land almost a plain. [L. *paene* almost and PLAIN (1)].

PENETRABILITY, [pen'-it-rab-il'-i-ti], *n.* the quality of being penetrable by another body.

PENETRABLE, [pen'-it-rabl], *adj.* able to be penetrated; (*fig.*) capable of being affected, susceptible. [L. *penetrabilis*].

PENETRALIA, [pen'-it-rā'-li-a], *n.*(*pl.*) the innermost parts of a temple or shrine; (*fig.*) mysteries. [L. *penetralia, pl.* of *penetral*].

PENETRANT, [pen'-it-rant], *adj.* having the property of penetrating; (*fig.*) acute, subtle. [L. *penetrans*].

PENETRATE, [pen'-it-rāt], *v.t.* to pass into the interior of; to pierce; to permeate; (*fig.*) to see into, discern, reach by the intellect; *v.i.* to go through the action of penetrating. [L. *penetrare*].

PENETRATING, [pen'-it-rāt-ing], *adj.* sharp, piercing, permeating; searching; piercing, shrill; (*fig.*) discerning, subtle, acute.

PENETRATION, [pen-it-rā'-shun], *n.* the action of penetrating; the state of being penetrated; intellectual acumen, comprehension, discernment; **peaceful p.,** method of spreading a doctrine by steady persistent dissemination of ideas rather than by force. [L. *penetratio*].

PENETRATIVE, [pen'-it-rat-iv], *adj.* having the power of penetrating.

PENETRATIVELY, [pen'-it-rat-iv-li], *adv.* in a penetrative manner.

PENETRATIVENESS, [pen'-it-rat-iv-nes], *n.* the quality of being penetrative.

PENGUIN, [peng'-gwin], *n.* any species of the *Impennes*, an order of sea-birds of the southern hemisphere having the wings developed into paddles; (*aeron.*) an instructional aeroplane of low power not intended for flight. [Uncert.].

PENGUINERY, [peng'-gwin-er-i], *n.* a place frequented by penguins for breeding purposes.

PENHOLDER, [pen'-hōld'-er], *n.* a holder or handle, usually of wood, for holding the pen-nib.

PENIAL, [pē'-ni-al], *adj.* relating to the penis.

PENICIL, [pen'-is-il], *n.* (*zool.*) a small brush of fine hairs; (*med.*) a pledget for wounds. [L. *penicillus*].

PENICILLATE, [pen-is'-il-āt], *adj.* furnished with small tufts of fine hairs; having fine markings like those of a pencil.

PENICILLIN, [pen-is'-il-in], *n.* a germ-killing substance derived from the bacterial mould *Penicillium notatum*.

PENINSULA, [pen-ins'-yōō-la], *n.* a tract of land nearly surrounded by water; **the P.,** Spain and Portugal. [L. *paeninsula* from *paene* almost and *insula* island].

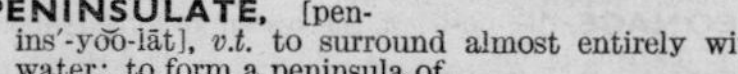

PENINSULA

PENINSULAR, [pen-ins'-yōō-ler], *adj.* like, in the form of, a peninsula; pertaining to a peninsula, *esp.* Spain and Portugal.

PENINSULARITY, [pen-ins'-yōō-la'-rit-i], *n.* the state of being peninsular.

PENINSULATE, [pen-ins'-yōō-lāt], *v.t.* to surround almost entirely with water; to form a peninsula of.

PENIS, [pē'-nis], *n.* the male organ of copulation. [L. *penis*].

PENITENCE, [pen'-it-ents], *n.* the state of being penitent; a feeling of contrition for wrong-doing; repentance. [L. *paenitentia*].

PENITENCY, [pen'-it-en-si], *n.* the state of being penitent.

PENITENT (1), [pen'-it-ent], *n.* a repentant sinner; one who has made his confession to a priest and been admitted to penance.

PENITENT (2), [pen'-it-ent], *adj.* contrite; repentant. [L. *paenitens*].

PENITENTIAL (1), [pen'-it-en'-shal], *n.* a book prescribing penitences.

PENITENTIAL (2), [pen'-it-en'-shal], *adj.* pertaining to penitence; expressing penitence. [*Prec.*].

PENITENTIARY (1), [pen'-it-en'-sher-i], *n.* the Roman Catholic organ which deals with the punishment of serious ecclesiastical offences; a house of correction; (*U.S.*) a State prison.

PENITENTIARY (2), [pen'-it-en'-sher-i], *adj.* pertaining to penance; penitential.

PENITENTLY, [pen'-it-ent-li], *adv.* in a penitent manner.

PENKNIFE, [pen'-nif'], *n.* a small folding pocket knife, originally used for making and mending quill pens.

PENMAN, [pen'-man], *n.* a man who teaches the art of handwriting, or who writes a good hand; an author; a forger.

PENMANSHIP, [pen'-man-ship], *n.* the art of, or skill in, handwriting.

PEN-NAME, [pen'-nām], *n.* a name assumed by a writer; a pseudonym, a nom-de-plume.

PENNANT, [pen'-ant], *n.* a small flag, pointed or swallow-tailed; a long strip of bunting flown at the mast-head of warships to show that they are in commission; a streamer. [~PENNON and PENDANT].

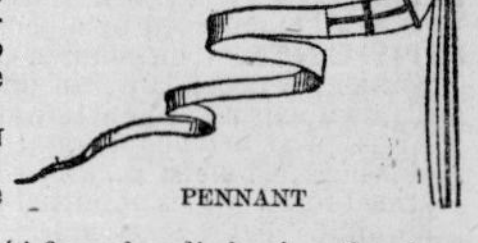

PENNANT

PENNATE, see PINNATE.

PENNIFORM, [pen'-i-fawm], *adj.* having the form or appearance of a feather. [L. *penna* feather and FORM].

PENNIGEROUS, [pen-ij'-er-us], *adj.* feather-bearing. [L. *penna* feather and *gerere* to bear].

PENNILESS, [pen'-i-les], *adj.* not having a penny; poor, destitute.

PENNILESSNESS, [pen'-i-les-nes], *n.* the state of having no money; destitution.

PENNINITE, [pen'-in-it], *n.* (*min.*) a silicate of alumina and magnesia containing some oxide of iron. [*Pennine* Chain, in the north of England].

PENNON, [pen'-on], *n.* a small narrow flag, forked or swallow-tailed, attached to the lance so that, when the lance was held horizontally for the charge, the arms emblazoned on it appeared in their proper position. [OFr. *penon*].

PENN'ORTH, [pen'-erth], *n.* abbreviation of pennyworth.

PENNY, (*pl.* **pence, pennies**), [pen'-i], *n.* a British bronze coin worth one-twelfth of a shilling; **not to have a p.,** to be destitute; **a pretty p.,** a large sum of money; **to turn an honest p.,** to make a little honest money. [OE. *penig*].

PENNY-A-LINER, [pen'-i-a-līn'-er], *n.* one who writes for a journal for a small sum per line; a reporter; a journalist, particularly one who pads out his material so as to earn more for his work.

PENNY-CRESS, [pen'-i-kres'], *n.* (*bot.*) a small plant of the genus, *Thlaspi*.

PENNY-FARTHING, [pen'-i-fah'-THing], *n.* an old-fashioned high bicycle with one large and one small wheel.

PENNY-IN-THE-SLOT, [pen'-i-in-THe-slot'], *adj. phr.* denoting an automatic machine, etc., operated by the insertion of a penny in a slot provided for the purpose.

PENNY-POST, [pen'-i-pōst'], *n.* an organization for the conveyance of letters at the charge of one penny introduced in 1840 by Rowland Hill.

PENNYROYAL, [pen'-i-roi'-al], *n.* (*bot.*) an aromatic plant, *Mentha pulegium*, yielding a medicinal oil. [ME. *pulyol ryal* from OFr. *puliol* thyme and *ryal* royal].

PENNYWEIGHT, [pen'-i-wāt], *n.* a troy weight of twenty-four grains, originally the weight of a silver penny.

PENNYWISE, [pen'-i-wīz], *adj.* saving small sums;

foolishly niggardly; **p. and pound-foolish,** economical in small matters, extravagant in large ones.

PENNYWORT, [pen'-i-wurt], *n.* (*bot.*) a small herb, *Cotyledon umbilicus*, growing in the crevices of rocks and walls; a small herb, *Hydrocotyle vulgaris*, growing in damp places. [PENNY and WORT].

PENNYWORTH, [pen'-i-wurth], *n.* the amount that may be bought for a penny; (*coll.*) a small quantity.

PENOLOGY, [pēn-ol'-o-ji], *n.* the study of prison discipline and its bearing on the prevention of crime. [L. *poena* punishment and Gk. *logos* speech].

PENSILE, [pen'-sīl], *adj.* hanging down, pendent; penduline. [L. *pensilis*].

PENSILENESS, [pen'-sīl-nes], *n.* the state of being pensile.

PENSION (1), [pen'-shun], *n.* a periodical allowance in consideration of past services; a periodic payment made to public servants or members of the fighting services, or servants of certain business companies or individuals who have completed their term of service or who have resigned office at the convenience of the State or business; **old age p.,** a weekly pension paid by the state to old people. [L. *pensio* payment].

PENSION (2), [pah(ng)s'-yaw(ng)'], *n.* a foreign boarding-house; **en p.,** paying a fixed inclusive rate for board and lodging. [Fr. *pension*].

PENSION (3), [pen'-shun], *v.t.* to pay a pension to; **p. off,** to cause to retire from service with a pension.

PENSIONABLE, [pen'-shun-abl], *adj.* entitling one to a pension; entitled to a pension.

PENSIONARY (1), [pen'-shun-er-i], *n.* a person receiving a pension; a pensioner; one who is attached by a pension to the interests of another, a tool.

PENSIONARY (2), [pen'-shun-er-i], *adj.* relating to a pension; maintained by a pension.

PENSIONER, [pen'-shun-er], *n.* the holder of a pension; a dependant; an undergraduate, living at his own expense; **Gentleman P.,** a Gentleman-at-Arms, who attends upon the sovereign on state occasions; **Chelsea p.,** a pensioner from the regular armed forces who is admitted to residence at Chelsea hospital. [OFr. *pensionnier*].

PENSIVE, [pen'-siv], *adj.* thoughtful; thoughtful with sadness; wistful. [Fr. *pensif*].

PENSIVELY, [pen'-siv-li], *adv.* in a pensive manner.

PENSIVENESS, [pen'-siv-nes], *n.* the state or quality of being pensive.

PENSTEMON, see PENTSTEMON.

PENSTOCK, [pen'-stok], *n.* a trough leading the water on to the waterwheel; a sluice, flood-gate. [PEN (1) and STOCK].

PENT, [pent], *adj.* shut up, imprisoned; cooped up. [*P.pt.* of PEN (4)].

PENTA-, PENT-, *pref.* five. [Gk. *pente* five].

PENTACAPSULAR, [pen'-ta-kap'-syōō-ler], *adj.* (*bot.*) with five capsules.

PENTACHORD, [pen'-ta-kawd], *n.* (*mus.*) a five-stringed musical instrument; a musical scale of five notes.

PENTACLE, [pen'-takl], *n.* the pentagram, formerly a five-pointed star, an early symbol of the five virtues. [MedL. *pentaculum*].

PENTACOCCOUS, [pen'-ta-kok'-us], *adj.* (*bot.*) possessing five grains, or five cells with a grain in each. [PENTA and Gk. *kokkos* a seed].

PENTACRINITE, [pen-tak'-rin-īt], *n.* a stone-lily or fossil crinoid of the genus *Pentacrinus*. [PENTA and Gk. *krinos* lily].

PENTACROSTIC, [pen'-ta-kros'-tik], *adj.* having five acrostics of the same word.

PENTAD, [pen'-tad'], *n.* the number five; a group of five things. [Gk. *pentas*].

PENTADACTYLOUS, [pen'-ta-dak'-til-us], *adj.* (*biol.*) having five fingers or toes or five processes resembling these. [PENTA and DACTYLOUS].

PENTADELPHOUS, [pen'-ta-del'-fus], *adj.* (*bot.*) having the stamens in five bundles joined by the filaments. [PENTA and Gk. *adelphos* brother].

PENTAFID, [pen'-ta-fid'], *adj.* (*bot.*) separated into five. [PENTA and L. *-fidus* split].

PENTAGON, [pen'-ta-gon], *n.* (*geom.*) a plane figure with five sides and angles; (*fort.*) a fort with five bastions. [PENTA and Gk. *gonia* angle].

PENTAGONAL, [pen-tag'-on-al], *adj.* having the form of a pentagon.

PENTAGRAM, [pen'-ta-gram'], *n.* a pentacle. [Gk. *pentagramma*].

PENTAHEDRAL, [pen'-ta-hē'-dral], *adj.* having five faces, five equal sides.

PENTAHEDRON, [pen'-ta-hē'-dron], *n.* a solid figure with five equal sides. [PENTA and Gk. *hedra* base].

PENTAHEXAHEDRAL [pen'-ta-heks'-a-hē'-dral], *adj.* (*crystal.*) consisting of five six-faced ranges of facets one above another.

PENTAMEROUS, [pent-am'-er-us], *adj.* having its parts arranged in fives. [PENTA and Gk. *meros* part].

PENTAMETER, [pen-tam'-it-er], *n.* (*pros.*) a verse or line of poetry of five feet.

PENTANE, [pent'-ān], *n.* (*chem.*) a paraffin hydrocarbon. [PENTA].

PENTANGULAR, [pent-ang'-gew-ler], *adj.* having five angles or angular points.

PENTAPETALOUS, [pent'-a-pet'-al-us], *adj.* (*bot.*) possessing five petals.

PENTAPHYLLOUS, [pen'-ta-fil'-us], *adj.* (*bot*). possessing five leaves. [PENTA and Gk. *phullon* leaf].

PENTARCHY, [pent'-ahk-i], *n.* a government by five rulers; a group of five districts each under its own ruler. [PENT(A) and Gk. *arkhia* rule].

PENTASEPALOUS, [pent'-a-sep'-al-us], *adj.* (*bot.*) having five sepals.

PENTASPERMOUS, [pen'-ta-sperm'-us], *adj.* (*bot.*) having five seeds. [PENTA and Gk. *sperma* seed].

PENTASTYLE, [pen'-ta-stīl], *n.* (*arch.*) a building or portico having five columns.

PENTATEUCH, [pen'-ta-tewk], *n.* the first five books in the Old Testament. [Gk. *pentateukhos* consisting of five books].

PENTATHLON, [pent-ath'-lon], *n.* an athletic contest at the ancient Olympic Games now revived, in which each competitor takes part in five exercises. [PENTA and Gk. *athlon* contest].

PENTECOST, [pen'-ti-kost], *n.* a solemn festival of the Jews held fifty days after the second day of the Passover; Whitsuntide, a solemn feast of the Church in commemoration of the descent of the Holy Spirit. [Gk. *pentekostos* fiftieth].

PENTECOSTAL, [pen'-ti-kostl'], *adj.* relating to, occurring at, Pentecost.

PENTHOUSE, [pent'-hows], *n.* a subsidiary structure such as a shed, porch, outhouse attached to the wall of a main building; a roof sloping away from the main wall of a building and forming a shelter; an awning, canopy, a covering formed of soldiers' shields held over their heads; (*U.S.*) a dwelling-house on the roof of a skyscraper. [PENTICE].

PENTICE†, [pen'-tis], *n.* a penthouse. [ME. *pentis* from L. *appendix* appendage].

PENTILE, see PANTILE.

PENTLANDITE, [pent'-land-īt], *n.* (*min.*) a mineral consisting of iron, nickel and sulphur. [J. B. *Pentland* (1856), its discoverer].

PENT-ROOF, [pent'-rōōf], *n.* a roof which slopes on one side only.

PENTSTEMON, PENSTEMON, [pent-ste'-mon], *n.* (*bot.*) a genus of perennial herbaceous plants of the family, *Scrophulariaceae* with bright flower-spikes. [PENT(A) and Gk. *stemon* spike].

PENULTIMATE (1), [pen-ult'-im-at], *n.* the last but one. [L. *paene* almost and ULTIMATE].

PENULTIMATE (2), [pen-ult'-i-mat], *adj.* last but one, next to the last.

PENUMBRA, [pen-um'-bra], *n.* the partly shaded region around the complete shadow of an opaque body; (*astron.*) the shadow surrounding the deep shadow of the moon or the earth during an eclipse; the lighter border round the dark centre of a sun spot; (*paint.*) the point of a picture or drawing where the light and the shade are blended. [L. *paene* almost and *umbra* shadow].

PENURIOUS, [pen-yōōer'-i-us], *adj.* poor, yielding little, scanty; slight, mean; niggardly.

PENURIOUSLY, [pen-yōōer'-i-us-li], *adv.* in a penurious manner; scantily, meanly.

PENURIOUSNESS, [pen-yōōer'-i-us-nes], *n.* the state of being penurious.

PENURY, [pen'-yōō-ri] *n.* extreme poverty, indigence, want; destitution. [L. *penuria* want].

PENWIPER, [pen'-wip-er], *n.* a small pile of pieces of cloth, etc., fastened together, and suitable for cleaning the nib of a pen.

PEON, [pē'-on], *n.* (in India) a foot-soldier, a policeman; (in Spanish America) a day labourer; a bondman for debt. [Span. *peon* labourer].

PEONAGE, [pē'-on-ij], *n.* the system of forced labour employing peons.

PEONY, PAEONY, [pē'-on-i], *n.* a plant of the genus *Paeonia* with large red, pink or white flowers. [OFr. *peonie* from Gk. *paionia*].

PEOPLE (1), [pēpl], *n.* the body of persons forming a race, community, nation; the populace; the vulgar; the democracy; a body of persons of a certain class, place, occupation; persons generally; kindred, relations, forebears; attendants, servants. [AFr. *people* from L. *populus*].
PEOPLE (2), [pēpl], *v.t.* to stock with inhabitants; to populate. [*Prec.*].
PEP (1), [pep], *n.* (*slang*) vim, vigour, life, vivacity, go. [PEPPER (1)].
PEP (2), [pep], *v.i.* (*slang*) **to p. up,** to put new life into, brighten, liven up. [*Prec.*].
PEPERINO, [pep'-er-ē'-nō], *n.* a dark brown granular tufa, found mainly near Rome. [It. *peperino*].
PEPO, [pē'-pō], *n.* (*bot.*) a fleshy fruit with numerous seeds, as the gourd and cucumber. [L. *pepo* pumpkin].
PEPPER (1), [pep'-er], *n.* a hot pungent condiment, the berry of *Piper nigrum*, used whole or ground to a powder; (*fig.*) fiery action, vigour, enthusiasm. [OE. *pipor* from Gk. *peperi*].
PEPPER (2), [pep'-er], *v.t.* to sprinkle with pepper; (*fig.*) to beat; to pelt with shot. [*Prec.*].
PEPPERBOX, [pep'-er-boks'], *n.* a small box with a perforated lid, for sprinkling ground pepper on food; a projecting wall of a fives court.
PEPPER-CAKE, [pep'-er-kāk'], *n.* a form of spiced cake or gingerbread.
PEPPERCASTER, [pep'-er-kahst'-er], *n.* a pepperbox.
PEPPERCORN, [pep'-er-kawn], *n.* the berry of the pepper plant; **p. rent,** a nominal rent for land or premises held on a long lease.
PEPPERING, [pep'-er-ing], *n.* a sprinkling with pepper; a pelting with missiles or blows.
PEPPERMINT, [pep'-er-mint], *n.* the pungent aromatic mint plant, *Mentha piperita*; a liqueur distilled from peppermint; a sweet flavoured with essence of peppermint. [PEPPER and MINT (1)].
PEPPER-TREE, [pep'-er-trē'], *n.* the tropical South American tree, *Schinus molle*, which yields mastic; *Melia Azedarach*, growing on the Mediterranean coast.
PEPPER-WATER, [pep'-er-waw'-ter], *n.* a liquor prepared from powdered black pepper, and used in microscopic observations.
PEPPERWORT, [pep'-er-wurt], *n.* (*bot.*) a species of cress, *Lepidium latifolium*. [PEPPER and WORT].
PEPPERY, [pep'-er-i], *adj.* like, having the qualities of, pepper; (*fig.*) testy, hasty, hot-tempered.
PEPSIN, [pep'-sin], *n.* an enzyme in the gastric juice of the stomach necessary in the digestive process for converting proteids into peptones; an extract of this from the mucous membrane of certain ungulates used medically to assist imperfect digestion. [Gk. *pepsis* cooking].
PEPTIC (1), [pep'-tik], *n.* a substance that promotes digestion.
PEPTIC (2), [pep'-tik], *adj.* promoting digestion; able to digest; **p. glands,** glands secreting pepsin.
PEPTICITY, [pep-tis'-i-ti], *n.* a good peptic condition.
PEPTONE, [pep'-tōn], *n.* the substances formed in the stomach from proteids. [Gk. *pepton* cooked, digested].
PEPTONIZE, [pep'-ton-īz], *v.t.* to turn (proteids) into peptones.
PER, *prep.* by means of, by, through; for each. [*Next*].
PER- *pref.* through, all over; thoroughly, completely; (*chem.*) containing the maximum amount of a substance. [L. *per* through, across, by means of].
PERADVENTURE†, [per'-ad-ven'-cher], *n.* chance; *adv.* perhaps, perchance; by any chance.
PERAMBULATE, [per-am'-byōō-lāt], *v.t.* to walk through or round, *esp.* in order to survey; to walk round the boundaries of.
PERAMBULATION, [per-am'-byōō-lā'-shun], *n.* the action of passing through; a travelling survey or inspection; jurisdiction; a survey or settling of boundaries.
PERAMBULATOR, [per-am'-byōō-lāt-or], *n.* one who perambulates; a light carriage for babies pushed along by hand.
PER ANNUM, [per'-an'-um], *adv.* by the year, yearly; annually. [L. *per annum*].
PERBEND, see PERPEND (1).
PERCEIVABLE, [per-sēv'-abl], *adj.* perceptible, intelligible, appreciable.
PERCEIVE, [per-sēv'], *v.t.* to apprehend by the senses; to observe, discover, discern. [OFr. *percever* from L. *percipere*].
PERCEIVER, [per-sēv'-er], *n.* one who perceives.
PER CENT, [per-sent'], *adv.* by the hundred; for or in every hundred. [L. *per centum*].
PERCENTAGE, [per-sent'-ij], *n.* the rate per hundred; the interest paid on money per cent; a proportion, part.
PERCEPT, [per'-sept], *n.* (*philos.*) the thing perceived. [L. *perceptum*, *p.pt.* of *percipere* to perceive].
PERCEPTIBILITY, [per-sept'-ib-il'-i-ti], *n.* the quality of being perceptible.
PERCEPTIBLE, [per-sept'-ibl], *adj.* able to be perceived by the mind or the senses. [L. *perceptibilis*].
PERCEPTIBLY, [per-sept'-ib-li], *adv.* in a perceptible manner; to a perceptible degree or extent.
PERCEPTION, [per-sep'-shun], *n.* the act or faculty of perceiving through the intellect or the senses; consciousness; intuition, insight. [L. *perceptio*].
PERCEPTIONAL, [per-sep'-shun-al], *adj.* pertaining to, capable of, perceiving.
PERCEPTIVE, [per-sept'-iv], *adj.* capable of perceiving; pertaining to perception.
PERCEPTIVELY, [per-sept'-iv-li], *adv.* in a perceptive manner.
PERCEPTIVENESS, [per-sept'-iv-nes], *n.* the condition of being perceptive.
PERCEPTIVITY, [per-sept-iv'-i-ti], *n.* the state of being perceptive; perceptiveness.
PERCH (1), [purch], *n.* an edible freshwater fish of the genus *Perca*. [Fr. *perche* from Gk. *perke*].

PERCH

PERCH (2), [purch], *n.* a pole; a roost pole for fowls; a measure of $5\frac{1}{2}$ yds.; a measure of $30\frac{1}{4}$ sq. yds.; anything serving for a person, bird or animal to rest on, *esp.* if high up; (*fig.*) an elevated, secure, comfortable position. [Fr. *perche* from L. *pertica* pole].
PERCH (3), [purch], *v.t.* to place on a perch; to put down, fix, set in an inaccessible or insecure place; *v.i.* (of a bird) to alight or settle after flight, to sit or balance oneself on. [*Prec.*].
PERCHANCE, [per-chahnts'], *adv.* by chance.
PERCHER, [purch'-er], *n.* one who perches.
PERCHERON, [pursh'-er-on], *n.* a breed of draught-horses. [*La Perche*, a district in Northern France where bred].
PERCIFORM, [pur'-si-fawm], *adj.* of the form of, resembling, a perch. [L. *perca* perch and FORM].
PERCINE, [pur'-sīn], *adj.* belonging to the perch family. [L. *perca* perch].
PERCIPIENCE, [per-sip'-i-ents], *n.* the action of perceiving; the state of being percipient.
PERCIPIENT (1), [per-sip'-i-ent], *n.* a percipient person; one capable of receiving communications telepathically.
PERCIPIENT (2), [per-sip'-i-ent], *adj.* having the faculty of perceiving; having the power of perception. [L. *percipiens*].
PERCLOSE, [per'-klōz], *n.* an enclosure; a screen; a railing enclosing a tomb. [ME. *perclose*].
PERCOID, [purk'-oid], *adj.* resembling, or akin to, a perch. [L. *perca* perch and Gk. *oeides* like].
PERCOLATE, [pur'-kol-āt], *v.t.* to cause to percolate; *v.i.* to ooze, drip, pass, filter through. [L. *percolare* to strain].
PERCOLATION, [pur'-kol-ā'-shun], *n.* the action or process of percolating; filtration. [L. *percolatio*].
PERCOLATOR, [pur'-kol-āt'-or], *n.* a filtering machine; a coffee-pot where the water percolates through the coffee.
PERCURSORY, [per-kur'-ser-i], *adj.* running rapidly or hastily through something, cursory. [L. *percursor* one who runs through].
PERCUSS, [per-kus'], *v.t.* to strike forcibly; (*med.*) to tap or strike firmly some part of the body for purposes of diagnosis. [L. *percussum*, *p.pt.* of *percutere* to shake].
PERCUSSION, [per-kush'-un], *n.* collision; the shock produced by collision of bodies; impression of sound on the ear; **p. bullet,** an explosive bullet; **p. cap,** a small copper cap, containing fulminating powder; **p. lock,** a gun-lock in which the percussion cap is struck by a hammer; **p. instruments,** instruments played by striking, as drums. [L. *percussio*].
PERCUSSIVE, [per-kus'-iv], *adj.* pertaining to percussion, liable to detonate.

PERCUTANEOUS, [per'-kew-tā'-ni-us], *adj.* acting, effected, through the skin. [PER- and CUTANEOUS].
PERCUTIENT, [per-kew'-shi-ent], *adj.* striking, percussive. [L. *percutiens*].
PERDITION, [per-dish'-un], *n.* utter destruction; ruin; the utter loss of the soul or of happiness in a future state; damnation. [L. *perditio*].
PERDU, PERDUE, [per-dyōō'], *adj.* concealed, hidden; **to lie p.**, to conceal one's whereabouts, to disappear. [Fr. *perdu*, *p.pt.* of *perdre* to lose].
PERDURABLE, [per-dyōōer'-abl], *adj.* very durable; everlasting.
PERDURATION, [per'-dew-rā'-shun], *n.* continuous duration, continuance.
PERDURE, [per-dyōōer'], *v.i.* to endure, continue. [Fr. *perdurer* from PER- and L. *durare* to harden].
PEREGRINATE, [pe'-rig-rin-āt], *v.i.* to travel; to wander from place to place; to travel abroad. [L. *peregrinari*].
PEREGRINATION, [pe'-rig-rin-ā'-shun], *n.* the act of peregrinating; a travelling, journeying from one place to another. [L. *peregrinatio*].
PEREGRINATOR, [pe'-rig-rin-āt'-or], *n.* one who peregrinates; a traveller. [L. *peregrinator*].
PEREGRINE, [pe'-rig-rin], *adj.* foreign, imported from abroad; strange; **p. falcon**, the blue falcon, *Falco peregrinus*, employed in hawking, and so called because the young birds migrate in the autumn. [L. *peregrinus* foreign].

PEREGRINE FALCON

PEREMPTORILY, [per'-emp-ter-i-li], *adv.* in a peremptory manner.
PEREMPTORINESS, [per'-emp-ter-i-nes], *n.* the quality or character of being peremptory.
PEREMPTORY [per'-emp-ter-i], *adj.* excluding debate or expostulation; dictatorial; positive; dogmatic; (*leg.*) absolute, decisive. [L. *peremptorius*].
PERENNIAL, [per-en'-i-al], *adj.* lasting, existing or continuing for a succession of years, permanent, continual; (*fig.*) remaining fresh through a succession of years; (of a topic or idea) recurring afresh regularly year by year; (*bot.*) remaining alive through a number of years. [L. *perennis*].
PERENNIALLY, [per-en'-i-a-li], *adv.* throughout the year or a succession of years; constantly, permanently.
PERFECT (1), [pur'-fekt], *adj.* complete in all its parts; faultless, excellent; completely accurate, skilled, precise; of supreme moral excellence, righteous; sheer, thorough, utter; (*gram.*) of that tense which expresses completed action. [L. *perfectum*, *p.pt.* of *perficere* to accomplish].
PERFECT (2), [per-fekt'], *v.t.* to finish, complete, bring to a state of perfection; to instruct fully in some specific direction; (*print.*) to print the second side of (a sheet of paper). [*Prec.*].
PERFECTER, [per-fekt'-er], *n.* one who, or that which, perfects.
PERFECTIBILITY, [per-fekt'-ib-il'-i-ti], *n.* the capacity of becoming or being made perfect; the doctrine that believes in the attainability of perfection.
PERFECTIBLE, [per-fekt'-ibl], *adj.* capable of becoming perfect.
PERFECTION, [per-fek'-shun], *n.* the state or quality of being perfect; the act of making perfect; completeness, maturity, flawlessness, faultlessness; great proficiency in some accomplishment; **to p.** completely, perfectly. [L. *perfectio*].
PERFECTIONAL, [per-fek'-shun-al], *adj.* of the nature of perfection.
PERFECTIONISM, [per-fek'-shun-izm], *n.* a system or doctrine of religious, moral, or political perfection; the theory that man can attain moral perfection.
PERFECTIONIST, [per-fek'-shun-ist], *n.* one who holds the doctrine of perfectionism.
PERFECTIVE, [per-fekt'-iv], *adj.* tending to make perfect.
PERFECTLY, [pur'-fekt-li], *adv.* in a perfect manner; completely, thoroughly.
PERFECTNESS, [pur'-fekt-nes], *n.* the quality of being perfect, perfection.
PERFERVID, [per-furv'-id], *adj.* extremely fervid.
PERFICIENT, [per-fish'-ent], *adj.* that does something, effectual. [L. *perficiens*].
PERFIDIOUS, [per-fid'-i-us], *adj.* faithless, false to a vow or a trust, unfaithful, treacherous, traitorous. [L. *perfidiosus*].
PERFIDIOUSLY, [per-fid'-i-us-li], *adv.* in a perfidious way.
PERFIDIOUSNESS, [per-fid'-i-us-nes], *n.* the quality of being perfidious, treachery.
PERFIDY, [pur'-fid-i], *n.* breach of faith or allegiance, violation of trust reposed, treachery, faithlessness. [L. *perfidia*].
PERFOLIATE, [per-fō'-li-āt], *adj.* (*bot.*) with the stem seeming to pass through the leaves.
PERFORATE (1), [pur'-fer-āt], *adj.* of a postage stamp, having perforations at the edges. [~(IM)PERFORATE].
PERFORATE (2), [pur'-fer-āt], *v.t.* to bore through, pierce, make a hole or holes in; to make a series of holes round the edge of, or a line of holes in, in order to assist tearing off or detachment; *v.i.* to penetrate. [L. *perforare*].
PERFORATION, [pur'-fer-ā'-shun], *n.* the act of perforating, the state of being perforated; a hole, a line or border of small holes pierced close together to assist tearing or separation (as in a stamp).
PERFORATIVE, [pur'-fer-āt-iv], *adj.* having power to pierce, tending to perforate.
PERFORATOR, [pur'-fer-āt'-er], *n.* a perforating machine or tool.
PERFORCE, [per-faws'], *adv.* of necessity [OFr. *par force*].
PERFORM, [per-fawm'], *v.t.* to accomplish, do, carry out, fulfil, discharge; to render, enact, execute; *v.i.* to act, play, exhibit one's prowess, skill or talent before an audience; (of animals) to give a display of tricks acquired after special training. [OFr. *parformer*].
PERFORMABLE, [per-fawm'-abl], *adj.* able to be performed.
PERFORMANCE, [per-fawm'-ants], *n.* the act of performing, the carrying of anything into effect, the execution or doing of anything; the action performed, thing done, feat, display of skill or ability, achievement; public exhibition or rendering of a play or other form of entertainment, a show.
PERFORMER, [per-fawm'-er], *n.* one who performs, *esp.* one who displays considerable skill in some branch of the arts, athletics, or sport; one who takes part in a play or other form of public entertainment.
PERFORMING, [per-fawm'-ing], *adj.* (of animals) trained to perform tricks.
PERFUME (1), [pur'-fewm], *n.* smell, odour, aroma; sweet smell, fragrance, pleasant odour or aroma; scent, a pleasant-smelling liquid preparation sprinkled upon the clothes or person. [OFr. *parfum*].
PERFUME (2), [per-fewm'], *v.t.* to scent, to fill or impregnate with fragrant odours or with manufactured perfume. [OFr. *parfumer* from PER (2) and L. *fumare* to smoke].
PERFUMER, [per-fewm'-er], *n.* a maker or seller of perfumes.
PERFUMERY, [per-fewm'-er-i], *n.* perfumes in general; an establishment at which perfumes are made or sold; the occupation or business of a perfumer.
PERFUNCTORILY, [per-fungk'-ter-i-li], *adv.* carelessly, in a perfunctory manner.
PERFUNCTORINESS, [per-fungk'-ter-i-nes], *n.* the quality of being perfunctory.
PERFUNCTORY, [per-fungk'-ter-i], *adj.* done merely as a matter of form or as a duty which must be got through somehow; careless, negligent, superficial, slight. [L. *perfunctorius*].
PERFUSE, [per-fewz'], *v.t.* to sprinkle, pour or spread over, to suffuse, flood, cover. [L. *perfusum*, *p.pt.* of *perfundere* to besprinkle].
PERFUSION, [per-few'-zhun], *n.* the act of perfusing, the state of being perfused.
PERFUSIVE, [per-fews'-iv], *adj.* that perfuses, apt to perfuse.
PERGAMENEOUS, [pur'-gam-ē'-ni-us], *adj.* like, consisting of, parchment. [L. *pergamena* parchment].
PERGOLA, [pur'-gol-a], *n.* a long covered arbour, a garden walk built over with a light wooden structure of intersecting laths, along the sides and top of which climbing plants are trained to intertwine. [L. *pergula*].
PERGUNNAH, [per-gun'-ah], *n.* a collection of Indian villages grouped together as a subdivision of a district. [Hind. *pargunah*].
PERHAPS, [per-haps'], *adv.* possibly. [PER (2) and HAP].
PERI, [pe'-ri], *n.* (*Pers. myth.*) a fairy being, a descendant of a fallen spirit, originally considered as evil and wicked, but later as good and beautiful; (*fig.*) a beauteous creature. [Pers. *peri*].

PERI- *pref.* around, near, about. [Gk. *peri*].
PERIAGUA, see PIRAGUA.
PERIANTH, [pe′-ri-anth], *n.* (*bot.*) the floral envelope, the calyx and corolla. [PERI- and Gk. *anthos* flower].
PERIAPT, [pe′-ri-apt′], *n.* a charm, amulet. [Gk. *periapton* something hung].
PERIBOLOS, [pe-rib′-ol-os], *n.* (*Gk. antiq.*) a court surrounding a temple. [Gk. *peribolos* enclosure].
PERICARDIAC, [pe′-ri-kahd′-i-ak], *adj.* pertaining to the pericardium.
PERICARDIAL, [pe′-ri-kahd′-i-al], *adj.* relating to, involving, connected with, the pericardium.
PERICARDIAN, [pe′-ri-kahd′-i-an], *adj.* pericardiac.
PERICARDITIS, [pe′-ri-kahd-ī′-tis], *n.* inflammation of the pericardium. [PERICARDIUM and Gk. *itis* denoting inflammation].
PERICARDIUM, [pe′-ri-kahd′-i-um], *n.* (*anat.*) a membrane that surrounds the heart. [Gk. *perikardion* around the heart].
PERICARP, [pe′-ri-kahp], *n.* (*bot.*) the seed-vessel of a plant, the envelope in which the seed is enclosed. [Gk. *perikarpion*].
PERICARPAL, [pe′-ri-kahp′-al], *adj.* pertaining to the pericarp.
PERICHAETIAL, [pe′-ri-kēt′-i-al], *adj.* (*bot.*) of, or belonging to, the perichaetium.
PERICHAETIUM, [pe′-ri-kē′-ti-um], *n.* (*bot.*) a cluster of leaflets at the base of the fruit stalk or reproductive organs of certain liverworts and mosses. [PERI- and Gk. *khaite* bristle].
PERICHONDRIUM, [pe′-ri-kon′-dri-um], *n.* the membrane that covers a cartilage except at the joints. [PERI- and Gk. *khondros* cartilage].
PERICLASE, [pe′-ri-klās], *n.* (*min.*) a mineral consisting of magnesia and a slight amount of ferrous oxide, and crystallizing in greenish octahedrons. [PERI- and Gk. *klasis* breaking].
PERICLINAL, [pe′-ri-klīn-al], *adj.* (*geol.*) sloping down on all sides from a central point. [Gk. *periklines* dipping on all sides].
PERICLINE, [pe′-ri-klīn], *n.* (*min.*) a variety of albite; a soda-felspar.
PERICOPE, [pe-rik′-o-pi], *n.* an extract or short passage from something written; a selected passage of Scripture read as a lesson in church. [Gk. *perikope* section].
PERICRANIUM, [pe′-ri-krā′-ni-um], *n.* the membrane surrounding the skull. [Gk. *perikranion* around the skull].
PERICYSTITIS, [pe′-ri-sist-ī′-tis], *n.* inflammation round the bladder. [PERI- and CYSTITIS].
PERIDOT, [pe′-ri-dot], *n.* (*min.*) a green transparent variety of olivine. [Fr. *péridot*].
PERIDROME, [pe′-ri-drōm], *n.* (*arch.*) the open space of a temple between the columns and the walls of the cell. [Gk. *peridromos* surrounding].
PERIECI, see PERIOECI.
PERIGANGLIONIC, [pe′-ri-gang′-gli-on′-ik], *adj.* around a ganglion.
PERIGEAN, [pe′-ri-jē′-an], *adj.* pertaining to the perigee.
PERIGEE, [pe′-ri-jē], *n.* that point in the orbit of the moon, or a planet, which is nearest the earth. [Gk. *perigeon*].
PERIGYNOUS, [pe-rij′-in-us], *adj.* (*bot.*) with the stamens growing round the ovary. [PERI- and Gk. *gune* female].
PERIHELION, [pe′-ri-hē′-li-on], *n.* the point in a planet's orbit when it is nearest the sun. [PERI- and Gk. *helios* sun].
PERIHEXAHEDRAL, [pe′-ri-heks′-a-hē′-dral], *n.* a crystal whose primitive form is a four-sided prism and whose secondary form has six sides.
PERIKON, [pe′-ri-kon], *n.* (*wirel.*) zincite and bornite in contact; **p. detector**, a crystal detector made from this.
PERIL (1), [pe′-ril], *n.* danger, risk, exposure to injury, harm or destruction. [L. *periculum*].
PERIL (2), (perilling, perilled), [pe′-ril], *v.t.* to expose to danger, to imperil, endanger.
PERILOUS, [pe′-ril-us], *adj.* dangerous, hazardous, fraught with peril.
PERILOUSLY, [pe′-ril-us-li], *adv.* dangerously, so as to imperil.
PERILOUSNESS, [pe′-ril-us-nes], *n.* the quality of being perilous, danger.
PERIMETER, [per-im′-it-er], *n.* (*geom.*) the line enclosing an area, or marking the limit of a closed figure, the outline; the length of this line; a sight-testing instrument. [Gk. *perimetros*].
PERIMETRICAL, [pe′-ri-met′-rik-al], *adj.* relating to the perimeter.
PERIMORPH, [pe′-ri-mawf], *n.* a mineral surrounding another. [PERI- and Gk. *morphe* shape].
PERINEUM, PERINAEUM, [pe′-rin-ē′-um], *n.* the part of the body extending from the anus to the genitals. [Gk. *perinaion*].
PERIOCTAHEDRAL, [pe′-ri-ok′-ta-hē′-dral], *adj.* of a crystal whose primitive form is a four-sided prism, and its secondary form one of eight sides.
PERIOD (1), [pēer′-i-od], *n.* a portion of time marked by the recurrence of certain astronomical happenings, and used as a unit in reckoning time; any indefinite portion of time; a specified portion of time; the time which a disease lasts, a particular stage of a disease; a cycle, a space of time in which a complete revolution of a recurring phenomenon is accomplished; the interval of time elapsing between two consecutive occurrences of a recurring phenomenon; the time during a woman's menstrual cycle at which bleeding occurs; a portion of time constituting, or regarded as, a separate unit, phase or stage of history or individual development, and possessing distinct individual characteristics; †the end or conclusion; (*gram.*) a sentence, *esp.* one containing a number of clauses or phrases; (*pl.*) flowery passages in writing; a pause at the end of a sentence, a full stop marking this; (*phys.*) the interval between repetition of vibrations or oscillations. [Gk. *periodos* circuit].
PERIOD (2), [pēer′-i-od], *adj.* characteristic of, dealing with, a particular period in history.
PERIODATE, [pēer′-ī-ō-dāt], *n.* (*chem.*) a salt of periodic acid.
PERIODIC, [pur′-ī-od′-ik], *adj.* recurring at intervals, usually at regular intervals; pertaining to, written in, rhetorical periods; relating to the cycle or revolution of a heavenly body; **p. table**, (*chem.*) the arrangement of the elements in groups according to their atomic number, valency, etc.
PERIODIC ACID, [pur′-ī-od′-ik-as′-id], *n.* (*chem.*) an acid of iodine containing the maximum proportion of oxgyen.
PERIODICAL (1), [pēer′-i-od′-ik-al], *n.* a magazine or journal published periodically.
PERIODICAL (2), [pēer′-i-od′-ik-al], *adj.* recurring at intervals, usually at regular intervals; published at regular intervals of more than a day.
PERIODICALIST, [pēer′-i-od′-ik-al-ist], *n.* a writer in a periodical.
PERIODICALLY, [pēer′-i-od′-ik-al-i], *adv.* in a periodical manner, at more or less regular intervals; from time to time.
PERIODICITY, [pēer′-i-od-is′-i-ti], *n.* the quality of being periodic.
PERIOECI, PERIECI, [pe′-ri-ē′-sī], *n.*(*pl.*) people dwelling on opposite sides of the globe, but in the same latitude; (*Gk. antiq.*) dwellers in the neighbouring villages, country towns, or districts surrounding a city. [Gk. *perioikoi*, *pl.* of *perioikos* neighbouring].
PERIOSTEAL, [pe′-ri-os′-ti-al], *adj.* pertaining to the periosteum, enveloping a bone.
PERIOSTEUM, [pe′-ri-os′-ti-um], *n.* a nervous vascular membrane which surrounds the bones of animals. [Gk. *periosteos* round the bones].
PERIOSTITIS, [pe′-ri-os-tī′-tis], *n.* inflammation of the periosteum. [PERIOSTEUM and Gk. *itis* denoting inflammation].
PERIOTIC, [pe′-ri-ot′-ik], *adj.* around the inner ear. [PERI- and Gk. *otikos* of the ear].
PERIPATETIC (1), [pe′-ri-pa-tet′-ik], *n.* a follower of Aristotle; a travelling hawker.
PERIPATETIC (2), [pe′-ri-pa-tet′-ik], *adj.* pertaining to Aristotle or to his philosophy (from his custom of walking up and down when he taught); itinerant, walking about, travelling round from place to place. [Gk. *peripatetikos* walking about].
PERIPATETICISM, [pe′-ri-pa-tet′-is-izm], *n.* the system of Aristotle and his disciples; the custom or practice of travelling round from place to place.
PERIPETEIA, [pe′-ri-pet-ī′-a], *n.* abrupt change of fortune, sudden and dramatic change in the situation in a play, story, etc. [Gk. *peripeteia*].
PERIPHERAL, [per-if′-er-al], *adj.* relating to, or constituting, a periphery; relating to the outskirts of a town, borders of a country.
PERIPHERIC, [per-if′-er-ik], *adj.* peripheral.
PERIPHERY, [per-if′-er-i], *n.* the circumference of a curvilinear figure, the perimeter; the external surface. [Gk. *periphereia*].
PERIPHRASE, [pe′-ri-frāz], *v.t.* to express in periphrasis: *v.i.* to use circumlocution.

PERIPHRASIS, [per-if′-ras-is], *n.* (*rhet.*) circumlocution, roundabout indirect method of expressing oneself; an instance of this. [Gk. *periphrasis*].

PERIPHRASTIC, [pe′-ri-frast′-ik], *adj.* using, speaking in, expressed by means of, periphrasis, circumlocutory.

PERIPHRASTICALLY, [pe′-ri-frast′-ik-a-li], *adv.* with circumlocution, by means of periphrasis.

PERIQUE, [per-ēk′], *n.* a strong, curly tobacco used in mixtures. [Fr. *perique*].

PERIRHINAL, [pe′-ri-rīn′-al], *adj.* around the nose. [PERI- and Gk. *rhis rhinos* nose].

PERISCOPE, [pe′-ri-skōp], *n.* an optical instrument fitted with mirrors and lenses, and providing a reflected image of objects otherwise hidden from sight by an obstruction in the direct line of vision, an elaborate variety of this being used in submarines when submerged, to observe the position of objects on the surface of the water. [PERI- and SCOPE].

PERISCOPE

PERISCOPIC, [pe′-ri-skop′-ik], *adj.* pertaining to, seen through, a periscope; increasing the width of the field of vision.

PERISH, [pe′-rish], *v.i.* to die, to come to an end of existence, to be destroyed; to decay, to become rotten; to pass away. [ME. *perischen* from OFr. *perissant*, *pres.pt.* of *perir*].

PERISHABILITY, [pe′-rish-ab-il′-i-ti], *n.* the quality of being perishable.

PERISHABLE (1), [pe′-rish-abl], *n.* a perishable object or article.

PERISHABLE (2), [pe′-rish-abl], *adj.* liable to perish or decay, easily destroyed.

PERISHABLENESS, [pe′-rish-abl-nes], *n.* the quality of being perishable.

PERISHABLY, [pe′-rish-ab-li], *adv.* in a perishable manner.

PERISHED, [pe′-risht], *adj.* (*coll.*) completely exhausted, almost dead, suffering physical distress, because of cold, starvation, hunger, etc.

PERISHER, [pe′-rish-er], *n.* (*slang*) a blighter, an annoying individual.

PERISHING, [pe′-rish-ing], *adj.* deadly, intense, extreme; that perishes; (*coll.*) infernal, confounded.

PERISHINGLY, [pe′-rish-ing-li], *adv.* (*coll.*) extremely, to such an extent as to kill one.

PERISPERM, [pe′-ri-spurm′], *n.* (*bot.*) the thick farinaceous part of the seed of plants; the albumen outside the embryo sac. [PERI- and SPERM].

PERISSODACTYL(E), [pe′-ris-ō-dak′-til], *adj.* of hoofed mammals, having an odd number of toes on each foot; pertaining to that division of the ungulates consisting of odd-toed mammals, and comprising the horse, tapir and rhinoceros. [Gk. *perissos* uneven and DACTYL].

PERISTALITH, [per-is′-ta-lith], *n.* a series of stones around a burial mound. [Gk. *peristatos* standing round and *lithos* stone].

PERISTALSIS, [pe-ri-stal′-sis], *n.* (*physiol.*) the wave-like motion of the intestines that carries food along the bowel. [Gk. *peristello* I send round].

PERISTALTIC, [pe′-ri-stalt′-ik], *adj.* contracting in successive circles, as the wave-like motion set up by the involuntary muscular movement of the intestines. [Gk. *peristaltikos* sending round].

PERISTERONIC, [per-is′-ter-on′-ik], *adj.* relating to pigeons. [Gk. *peristeron*].

PERISTEROPOD, [per-is′-ter-ō-pod′], *adj.* having toes like a pigeon, arranged on a level. [Gk. *peristera* pigeon and *pous podos* foot].

PERISTREPHIC, [pe′-ri-stref′-ik], *adj.* turning round, revolving. [Gk. *peristrepho* I turn round].

PERISTYLE, [pe′-ri-stīl], *n.* (*arch.*) a series of columns round a building or square; an enclosure with columns on three sides. [Gk. *peristulon*].

PERISYSTOLE, [pe-ri-sis′-tōl-i], *n.* the interval between the contraction and dilatation of the heart. [PERI- and Gk. *sustole* contraction].

PERITOMOUS, [pe-rit′-om-us], *adj.* (*min.*) splitting in more directions than the one parallel to the axis. [PERI- and Gk. *tomos* cutting].

PERITONEAL, [pe′-rit-on-ē′-al], *adj.* relating to the peritoneum.

PERITONEUM, [pe′-ri-tō-nē′-um], *n.* the serous membrane lining the internal surface of the abdomen, and more or less completely covering all the viscera contained in it. [Gk. *peritonaion*].

PERITONITIS, [pe′-ri-ton-ī′-tis], *n.* inflammation of the peritoneum. [*Prec.* and Gk. *itis* indicating inflammation].

PERITROPAL, [pe′-ri-trōp′-al], *adj.* (*biol.*) directed from the axis towards the sides of the pericarp. [PERI- and Gk. *tropos* a turning].

PERITYPHLITIS, [pe′-ri-tif-lī′-tis], *n.* inflammation in the region of the caecum. [PERI- and Gk. *tuphlon* caecum].

PERIVISCERAL, [pe′-ri-vis′-ser-al], *adj.* around the viscera.

PERIWIG, [pe′-ri-wig], *n.* a wig, peruke. [Fr. *perruque*].

PERIWINKLE (1), [pe′-ri-wingkl], *n.* a genus of creeping evergreen plants with blue flowers. [OE. *pervince* from L. *pervinca*].

PERIWINKLE (2), [pe′-ri-wingkl], *n.* a small univalve mollusc of the genus *Littorina*, having a snail-like shell, and eaten as food. [~OE. *pinewincle*].

PERIWINKLE

PERJURE, [pur′-jer], *v.refl.* to swear falsely, to give false witness. [L. *perjurare*].

PERJURED, [pur′-jerd], *adj.* guilty of perjury.

PERJURER, [pur′-jer-rer], *n.* one guilty of perjury, a false swearer.

PERJURIOUS, [per-jōōer′-i-us], *adj.* guilty of perjury; exhibiting, full of, involving, perjury.

PERJURY, [pur′-jer-i], *n.* the crime of wilfully giving false evidence on oath, the violation of a solemn promise or oath; false testimony. [L. *perjurium*].

PERK (1), [purk], *adj.* smart, spruce; lively, brisk, self-confident.

PERK (2), [purk], *v.i.* to hold up the head in a jaunty, self-confident manner; to assume a lively smart bearing; to make one's presence felt in an offensively assertive manner, to be saucy or impudent; to cheer up, recover spirits, to become perky.

PERKILY, [purk′-i-li], *adv.* in a perky manner.

PERKIN, [pur′-kin], *n.* a kind of weak perry or cider. [Unkn.].

PERKY, [pur′-ki], *adj.* smart, brisk, lively, jaunty; self-confident, presumptuous.

PERLITE, [pur′-līt], *n.* (*min.*) a variety of obsidian consisting of a mass of pearl-like globules. [PEARL].

PERLUSTRATION, per′-lus-trā′-shun], *n.* the act of viewing all over or examining thoroughly. [L. *perlustrare* to wander through].

PERM, [purm], *n.* (*coll.*) a permanent hair-wave. [PERMANENT].

PERMALLOY, [purm′-al-oi], *n.* an alloy of 78 per cent of nickel and 22 per cent of soft iron used for wrapping the inner copper conductor of an electric cable. [PERM(EABLE) and ALLOY].

PERMANENCE, [purm′-an-ents], *n.* the quality or state of being permanent; continuance in the same state or activity.

PERMANENCY, [purm′-an-en-si], *n.* the quality of being permanent; something that is permanent; (*coll.*) security of tenure in employment.

PERMANENT, [purm′-an-ent], *adj.* lasting, continuing without change, remaining or enduring indefinitely; **p. way**, the railway lines and the bed on which they rest; **p. wave**, an artificial wave produced in the hair by a special apparatus, and intended to last for a considerable time. [L. *permanens*].

PERMANENTLY, [purm′-an-ent-li], *adv.* in a permanent fashion, for an indefinite period of time.

PERMANGANATE, [per-mang′-gan-āt], *n.* (*chem.*) a salt of permanganic acid; **p. of potash**, purplish needle-shaped crystals which, when dissolved in water, form a strong disinfectant solution.

PERMANGANIC, [per-mang′-gan-ik], *adj.* (*chem.*) denoting an acid derived from manganese.

PERMEABILITY, [pur′-mi-ab-il′-i-ti], *n.* the state of being permeable; the magnetic conductivity of a substance.

PERMEABLE, [pur′-mi-abl], *adj.* penetrable, able to be passed or diffused through; porous. [L. *permeabilis*].

PERMEABLY, [pur′-mi-ab-li], *adv.* in a permeable way.

PERMEATE, [pur′-mi-āt], *v.t.* to pass through the pores and interstices, to penetrate, soak into, pervade, be diffused through; *v.i.* to diffuse itself. [L. *permeare*].

PERMEATION, [pur′-mi-ā′-shun], *n.* the act of permeating; the state of being permeated, diffusion.

PERMIAN, [pur'-mi-an], *adj.* belonging to the series of rocks overlying the carboniferous and underlying the trias, and consisting largely of red sandstone and limestone. [*Perm*, a province in northern Russia].

PERMISSIBLE, [per-mis'-ibl], *adj.* that may be permitted, allowable. [MedL. *permissibilis*].

PERMISSIBLY, [per-mis'-ib-li], *adv.* in a permissible manner, allowably.

PERMISSION, [per-mish'-un], *n.* leave, consent, liberty formally granted to do something, licence. [L. *permissio*].

PERMISSIVE, [per-mis'-iv], *adj.* allowing, granting permission, permitting; allowed, permitted. [L. *permissum*, *p.pt.* of *permittere* to allow].

PERMISSIVELY, [per-mis'-iv-li], *adv.* by permission.

PERMIT (1), [pur'-mit], *n.* an official document giving formal written permission to do something, a warrant, a licence.

PERMIT (2), (permitting, permitted), [per-mit'], *v.t.* to allow, to give leave or liberty to; to suffer, tolerate, assent to; to provide the means of, make possible; *v.i.* to allow, to provide opportunity or means. [L. *permittere*].

PERMITTEE, [pur'-mit-ē'], *n.* one who is permitted.

PERMITTER, [per-mit'-er], *n.* one who permits.

PERMUTABLE, [per-mewt'-abl], *adj.* that may be changed one for another, interchangeable. [L. *permutabilis*].

PERMUTABLENESS, [per-mewt'-abl-nes], *n.* the quality of being permutable.

PERMUTABLY, [per-mewt'-ab-li], *adv.* by exchange or interchange.

PERMUTATION, [pur'-mewt-ā'-shun], *n.* change, alteration; (*math.*) the act of finding the different combinations or ways of arrangement of a given number of quantities; (*pl.*) all the different possible combinations or orders in which a given number of things may be arranged. [L. *permutatio* changing].

PERMUTE, [per-mewt'], *v.t.* (*math.*) to arrange in different ways, to change the order of. [L. *permutare* to interchange].

PERN, [purn], *n.* the honey-buzzard, *Pernis apivorus*. [MedL. *pernis*].

PERNANCY, [purn'-an-si], *n.* (*leg.*) the receiving or taking of anything. [AFr. *pernance*].

PERNICIOUS, [per-nish'-us], *adj.* destructive, extremely harmful, tending to injure or destroy; **p. anaemia,** a severe progressive form of anaemia. [L. *perniciosus*].

PERNICIOUSLY, [per-nish'-us-li], *adv.* in a pernicious manner, harmfully.

PERNICIOUSNESS, [per-nish'-us-nes], *n.* the property of being pernicious.

PERNICKETY, [per-nik'-et-i], *adj.* fastidious, touchy, cantankerous about small matters, fussy. [Unkn.].

PERNOCTATION, [pur'-nokt-ā'-shun], *n.* a remaining all night; (*eccles.*) an all-night vigil. [LL. *pernoctatio* spending the night].

PERONE, [pe'-rō-ni], *n.* (*anat.*) the fibula. [Gk. *perone* buckle].

PERONEAL, [pe'-rō-nē'-al], *adj.* relating to the perone.

PERORATE, [per'-or-āt], *v.i.* to declaim at length, to deliver an elaborate speech or formal discourse; to sum up and bring to an end a speech. [L. *perorare*].

PERORATION, [per'-or-ā'-shun], *n.* the concluding part of a speech in which a general summing up is made; an oration, formal discourse. [L. *peroratio*].

PEROXIDE, [per-oks'-īd], *n.* (*chem.*) an oxide which contains more oxygen than a normal oxide; **p. of hydrogen,** a colourless fluid used for bleaching hair and as an antiseptic. [PER- and OXIDE].

PERPEND (1), PERBEND, [pur'-pend], *n.* originally any perpendicular joint in brickwork; a stone extending through the thickness of a wall, and serving as a bond-stone.

PERPEND (2), [per-pend'], *v.t.* and *i.* to weigh in the mind, to ponder (over), deliberate (about), reflect (upon), to consider. [L. *perpendere*].

PERPENDER, [per-pend'-er], *n.* a coping stone.

PERPENDER

PERPENDICULAR (1), [pur'-pend-ik'-yŏŏ-ler], *n.* a vertical or upright position; an instrument for finding the perpendicular line from a certain point or level surface; a plumb-line; (*geom.*) a line at right angles to a given line or plane.

PERPENDICULAR (2), [pur'-pend-ik'-yŏŏ-ler], *adj.* upright, vertical, at right angles to the plane of the horizon; (*fig.*) extremely steep, (of a slope) sheer; (*geom.*) at right angles to a given line or surface; (*arch.*) applied to the late pointed Gothic style of English architecture from the end of the 14th to the early part of the 16th century, characterized by long upright lines, *esp.* in its tracery. [L. *perpendicularis*].

PERPENDICULARITY, [pur'-pend-ik'-yŏŏ-la'-rit-i], *n.* the state of being perpendicular.

PERPENDICULARLY, [pur'-pend-ik'-yŏŏ-ler-li], *adv.* in a perpendicular manner, upright.

PERPETRATE, [pur'-pit-rāt], *v.t.* to perform, to commit (something bad or wicked). [L. *perpetrare* to accomplish].

PERPETRATION, [pur'-pit-rā'-shun], *n.* the act of committing, *esp.* a crime or outrage. [L. *perpetratio*].

PERPETRATOR, [pur'-pit-rāt'-or], *n.* one who commits, *esp.* a crime. [L. *perpetrator*].

PERPETUAL, [per-pet'-ŏŏ-al], *adj.* continuing for ever, never ceasing, continual, everlasting; throughout the whole or remainder of one's life; acting or applicable for all time; continuing unbroken. [L. *perpetualis*].

PERPETUALLY, [per-pet'-ŏŏ-al-i], *adv.* continually, for ever and ever; unceasingly.

PERPETUATE, [per-pet'-ŏŏ-āt], *v.t.* to make perpetual; to preserve from extinction or oblivion. [L. *perpetuare*].

PERPETUATION, [per-pet'-ŏŏ-ā'-shun], *n.* the act of perpetuating. [L. *perpetuatio*].

PERPETUATOR, [per-pet'-ŏŏ-āt-or], *n.* one who makes perpetual or preserves from oblivion or extinction.

PERPETUITY, [pur'-pit-ew'-i-ti], *n.* the quality of being perpetual, endless duration; that which is perpetual; a perpetual annuity; (*leg.*) the quality of being inalienable for an indefinite period, or beyond the period permitted by law; an estate limited in this way. [L. *perpetuitas*].

PERPHOSPHATE, [per-fos'-fāt], *n.* a highly oxidized phosphate.

PERPLEX, [per-pleks'], *v.t.* to puzzle, baffle, bewilder, confuse, to harass with doubt or uncertainty; to complicate, make intricate or obscure, to confuse, muddle. [L. *perplexus* complicated].

PERPLEXED, [per-plekst'], *adj.* puzzled, bewildered, confused; involved, complicated.

PERPLEXEDLY, [per-pleks'-id-li], *adv.* in a perplexed fashion.

PERPLEXEDNESS, [per-pleks'-id-nes], *n.* the state of being perplexed or confused.

PERPLEXING, [per-pleks'-ing], *adj.* bewildering, confusing, involved.

PERPLEXINGLY, [per-pleks'-ing-li], *adv.* so as to perplex.

PERPLEXITY, [per-pleks'-i-ti], *n.* the quality of being perplexed, bewilderment, confusion; doubt; that which perplexes or is perplexing. [LL. *perplexitas*].

PERQUISITE, [pur'-kwiz-it], *n.* anything obtained by one in employment beyond his or her ordinary salary, or occasionally in lieu of a salary; (*leg.*) casual profits accruing to the lord of the manor in addition to revenue; a gratuity; anything claimed as a sole personal right or province. [L. *perquisitum*, *p.pt.* of *perquirere* to search carefully for].

PERQUISITION, [pur'-kwiz-ish'-un], *n.* close inquiry or search, diligent investigation. [MedL. *perquisitio*].

PERRIER†, [pe'-ri-er], *n.* a military machine for throwing large stones; a catapult. [OFr. *perrier*].

PERRON, [pe'-ron], *n.* (*arch.*) a flight of stairs leading up to a kind of platform forming the entrance to the outside door of a large building. [Fr. *perron*].

PERRUQUE, see PERUKE.

PERRUQUIER, [pe-rŏŏk'-i-ā], *n.* a maker of wigs. [Fr. *perruquier*].

PERRIER

PERRY, [pe'-ri], *n.* a drink made from the fermented juice of pears. [OFr. *peré*].

PERSCRUTATION, [pur'-skrōō-tā'-shun], *n.* minute inquiry, thorough examination or investigation. [L. *perscrutatio*].

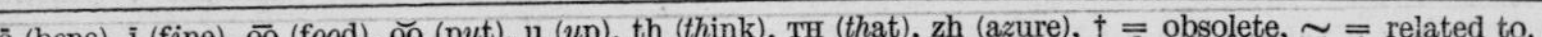

PERSECUTE, [pur'-sik-ewt], *v.t.* to harass with unjust and cruel treatment, *esp.* on account of religious opinions; to oppress continually with injurious attacks; to worry, importune, weary. [L. *persecutum*, *p.pt.* of *persequi* to follow].

PERSECUTING, [pur'-si-kewt-ing], *adj.* tending to persecute.

PERSECUTION, [pur'-sik-ew'-shun], *n.* the act of persecuting; the state of being persecuted; continual oppression because of religious beliefs. [L. *persecutio*].

PERSECUTIVE, [pur'-sik-ewt-iv], *adj.* tending to persecute.

PERSECUTOR, [pur'-sik-ewt-or], *n.* one who persecutes. [L. *persecutor*].

PERSECUTRIX, [pur'-si-kewt-riks], *n.* a female persecutor. [L. *persecutrix*].

PERSEVERANCE, [pur'-si-vēer'-ants], *n.* persistence in anything undertaken, steadfast endeavour, ability to persevere; (*theol.*) continuance in the state of grace. [L. *perseverantia* constancy].

PERSEVERE, [pur'-si-vēer'], *v.i.* to persist in any business or enterprise undertaken, in spite of difficulties, rebuffs, failures, hardships, etc. [L. *perseverare*].

PERSEVERING, [pur'-si-vēer'-ing], *adj.* steady in the pursuit of any object, persistent in endeavour, full of perseverance.

PERSEVERINGLY, [pur'-si-vēer'-ing-li], *adv.* in a persevering fashion.

PERSIAN (1), [pur'-shan], *n.* a native of Persia; the language of Persia; a Persian cat; (*arch.*) a male figure in Persian attire supporting an entablature.

PERSIAN (2), [per'-shan], *adj.* pertaining to, obtained from, Persia; **P. berry**, the unripe fruit of the plant *Rhamus infectorius*, yielding a yellow dye; **P. blinds**, outside shutters operating like Venetian blinds; **P. powder**, a preparation from the flowers of a Caucasian composite plant, used as an insecticide; **P. wheel**, a large wheel, with buckets on the rim, for raising water. [*Persia*, the country].

PERSIFLAGE, [pur'-si-flahzh], *n.* light banter, mockingly frivolous treatment of a subject. [Fr. *persiflage*].

PERSIFLEUR, [pur'-si-flur'], *n.* one given to persiflage. [Fr. *persifleur*].

PERSIMMON, [per-sim'-on], *n.* the date-plum, the fruit of the North American tree *Diospyros virginiana*, a variety of ebony; the tree itself, from which a fine hard timber is obtained. [Native].

PERSIMMON

PERSIST, [per-sist'], *v.i.* to continue steadfastly and obstinately in any course, belief, etc., in spite of opposition; to last, survive, remain, continue to be present. [L. *persistere*].

PERSISTENCE, [per-sist'-ents], *n.* the act or state of persisting; the quality of being persistent; continuous survival.

PERSISTENCY, [per-sist'-en-si], *n.* the quality of being persistent; obstinacy in adhering to some opinion, purpose or action; pertinacity, stubborn continuance and insistency.

PERSISTENT, [per-sist'-ent], *adj.* persisting stubbornly in some action, purpose or belief in spite of rebuff or discouragement; enduring, surviving unchanged, remaining, not easily shaken off or got rid of; continual. [L. *persistens*].

PERSISTENTLY, [per-sist'-ent-li], *adv.* steadfastly, in a persistent manner.

PERSISTIVE, [per-sist'-iv], *adj.* tending to persist.

PERSON, [pur'-son], *n.* a human being in a general sense, as distinct from an animal or inanimate object; a particular human being; a distinct personality; the bodily form, appearance or figure of a human being; the actual physical body itself; a human being of importance; a creature, a contemptuous term for a human being; (*theol.*) one of the three states of existence of the Godhead; (*leg.*) a human being or corporation regarded as having certain legal rights and duties; (*gram.*) one of three classes of pronouns considered in relation to a verb, namely oneself, the one spoken to, or the one spoken about; **in p.**, personally; **in the p. of**, in the character of. [L. *persona* an actor's mask, character played by an actor].

PERSONABLE, [pur'-son-abl], *adj.* of good appearance, comely.

PERSONAGE, [pur'-son-ij], *n.* a person, *esp.* one of distinction, eminence, or importance; one of the characters in a play; external appearance, bodily form. [OFr. *personage*].

PERSONAL, [pur'-son-al], *adj.* pertaining to, characteristic of, peculiar to, a particular person; individual, private; carried on, performed, done, in person, affecting or involving an actual person himself and not a representative; aimed at insulting, offensively directed against a particular person; referring offensively to a particular person; belonging to a person as distinct from an animal or thing; pertaining to the external appearance or human bodily form or figure; (*gram.*) denoting, referring to, one of the three persons; **p. property**, (*leg.*) movables, chattels, goods, things belonging to the person as distinct from real estate in land and houses; **p. column**, part of a newspaper containing short advertisements or messages of a confidential or private nature. [L. *personalis*].

PERSONALISM, [pur'-son-al-izm], *n.* (*psych.*) the conception of personality as an organic whole.

PERSONALITY, [pur'-son-al'-i-ti], *n.* the quality of being a person as distinct from a thing or animal, personal identity, existence as an individual person; a personage, an individual distinguished or well known because of some particular idiosyncrasy, a local character, an eminent, famous, or celebrated person; qualities of mind and temperament constituting a particular person's character; the quality of being personal or being aimed at a particular person; (*pl.*) offensive personal remarks directed against particular persons; **multiple p.**, (*psych.*) the existence of more than one contrasting personality in an individual which leads him to behave with abnormal inconsistency. [MedL. *personalitas*].

PERSONALIZE, [pur'-son-al-iz], *v.t.* to make personal, to personify.

PERSONALLY, [pur'-son-al-i], *adv.* as a person; in person; oneself, individually; for my part, as for myself.

PERSONALTY, [pur'-son-al-ti], *n.* personal estate, personal goods, chattels and movables. [AFr. *personalte*].

PERSONATE (1), [pur'-son-āt], *adj.* (*bot.*) having a two-lipped corolla in which the lower lip projects to close the opening. [L. *personatus* masked].

PERSONATE (2), [pur'-son-āt], *v.t.* to act the part of, to represent the character of, in a play; to impersonate, to represent oneself as being, to pretend to be. [LL. *personare* to play the role of].

PERSONATION, [pur'-son-ā'-shun], *n.* the counterfeiting of the person and character of another impersonation.

PERSONATOR, [pur'-son-āt-or], *n.* one who personates.

PERSONIFICATION, [per-son'-i-fik-ā'-shun], *n.* representation as a person, embodiment in personal form; a person regarded as embodying in himself an abstract quality, the very pattern or exemplification of a quality.

PERSONIFY, [per-son'-i-fī], *v.t.* to represent as a person or human being; to exemplify or represent in one's own person. [Fr. *personnifier*].

PERSONNEL, [pur'-son-el'], *n.* the staff of persons employed, *esp.* in a public institution; the body of men constituting an army, navy or air force. [Fr. *personnel*].

PERSPECTIVE (1), [per-spekt'-iv], *n.* the art of representing objects in drawing on a plane surface so as to produce a realistic effect of relative position, distance, size, etc.; a view, vista, distant scene; the apparent relative position, distance and size of objects seen by the eye; (*math.*) the science of the visual relations of objects; **in p.**, (*fig.*) in (its) true relation and significance. [MedL. (*ars*) *perspectiva*].

PERSPECTIVE (2), [per-spekt'-iv], *adj.* pertaining to the art of perspective, in perspective. [MedL. *perspectivus*].

PERSPECTIVELY, [per-spekt'-iv-li], *adv.* according to the laws of perspective.

PERSPICACIOUS, [pur'-spik-ā'-shus], *adj.* shrewd, keen-witted, quick and acute in discernment, wise, clear-minded, possessing a penetrating insight. [L. *perspicax* quick-sighted].

PERSPICACIOUSLY, [pur'-spik-ā'-shus-li], *adv.* in a perspicacious way.

PERSPICACIOUSNESS, [pur'-spik-ā'-shus-nes], *n.* the quality of being perspicacious.

PERSPICACITY, [pur'-spik-as'-i-ti], *n.* the quality of being perspicacious, shrewdness, penetrating insight, mental acuteness and discernment. [L. *perspicacitas*].

PERSPICUITY, [pur'-spik-ew'-i-ti], *n.* perspicuousness, clearness, freedom from obscurity or ambiguity, lucidity. [L. *perspicuitas*].

PERSPICUOUS, [per-spik'-yōō-us], *adj.* clear, not obscure or ambiguous, lucid, easily followed and understood, plainly expressed. [L. *perspicuus*].

PERSPICUOUSLY, [per-spik'-yōō-us-li], *adv.* in a perspicuous fashion.

PERSPICUOUSNESS, [per-spik'-yōō-us nes], *n.* the quality of being perspicuous.

PERSPIRABILITY, [per-spīer'-ab il'-i-ti], *n.* the state of being perspirable.

PERSPIRABLE, [per-spīer'-abl], *adj.* able, or liable, to perspire.

PERSPIRATION, [pur'-spi-rā'-shun], *n.* the act of perspiring; the moisture perspired, sweat.

PERSPIRATIVE, [per-spīer'-at-iv], *adj.* perspiratory.

PERSPIRATORY, [per-spīer'-at-er-i], *adj.* causing or concerned in the process of perspiration.

PERSPIRE, [per-spīer'], *v.t. and i.* to discharge moisture through the pores of the skin, to sweat. [L. *perspirare* to breathe].

PERSTRINGE, [per-strinj'], *v.t.* to censure, criticize. [L. *perstringere* to bind tightly].

PERSUADABLE, [per-swād'-abl], *adj.* able to be persuaded.

PERSUADE, [per-swād'], *v.t.* to induce to believe something, to convince by argument; to cause or prevail upon (a person) to do a particular thing by appealing to his judgment, reason or feelings. [L. *persuadere*].

PERSUADER, [per-swād'-er], *n.* one who, or that which, persuades.

PERSUASIBILITY, [per-swāz'-ib-il'-i-ti], *n.* the degree to which one is open to persuasion.

PERSUASIBLE, [per-swāz'-ibl], *adj.* open to persuasion. [L. *persuasibilis*].

PERSUASIBLENESS, [per-swāz'-ibl-nes], *n.* the state of being persuasible.

PERSUASION, [per-swā'-zhun], *n.* the act of persuading; the state of being persuaded; power of persuading; conviction, firm opinion, belief; religious denomination or sect. [L. *persuasio*].

PERSUASIVE (1), [per-swāz'-iv], *n.* that which persuades or tends to persuade, an inducement, incentive.

PERSUASIVE (2), [per-swāz'-iv], *adj.* having the power of persuading, tending to persuade. [MedL. *persuasivus*].

PERSUASIVENESS, [per-swāz'-iv-nes], *n.* the quality of being persuasive.

PERSULPHATE, [per-sulf'-āt], *n.* (*chem.*) a sulphate containing a larger proportion of oxygen than an ordinary sulphate.

PERSULTATION, [per'-sult-ā'-shun], *n.* (*path.*) a spouting of blood from an artery. [L. *persultatio*].

PERT, [purt], *adj.* brisk, smart, forward, saucy, impertinent, impudent. [ME. *pert* bold from OFr. *apert* open].

PERTAIN, [per-tān'], *v.i.* to belong to, be connected with; to relate to, be concerned with; to be appropriate to, suitable for. [OFr. *partenir* from L. *pertinere* belong].

PERTAINING, [per-tān'-ing], *adj.* belonging; **p. to,** connected or associated with, having to do with, relating to. [*Prec.*].

PERTINACIOUS, [pur'-tin-ā'-shus], *adj.* obstinate, perversely persistent, resolute, stubborn. [L. *pertinax* steadfast].

PERTINACIOUSLY, [pur'-tin-ā'-shus-li], *adv.* in a pertinacious fashion.

PERTINACIOUSNESS, [pur'-tin-ā'-shus-nes], *n.* the quality of being pertinacious.

PERTINACITY, [pur'-tin-as'-i-ti], *n.* the quality of being pertinacious, obstinate persistency, stubborn tenacity or resoluteness. [OFr. *pertinacité*].

PERTINENCE, [pur'-tin-ents], *n.* relevancy, appositeness, the quality of being pertinent.

PERTINENCY, [pur'-tin-en-si], *n.* pertinence.

PERTINENT (1), [pur'-tin-ent], *n.* (*Scots leg.*) that which belongs to another, appurtenance.

PERTINENT (2), [pur'-tin-ent], *adj.* relevant, apposite, appropriate, to the point. [L. *pertinens*].

PERTINENTLY, [pur'-tin-ent-li], *adv.* in a pertinent manner.

PERTINENTNESS, [pur'-tin-ent-nes], *n.* the quality of being pertinent.

PERTLY, [purt'-li], *adv.* in a pert fashion.

PERTNESS, [purt'-nes], *n.* sauciness, impudence, offensive smartness.

PERTURB, [per-turb'], *v.t.* to upset, disturb, to agitate, alarm, discompose, ruffle. [L. *perturbare*].

PERTURBATION, [per'-turb-ā'-shun], *n.* agitation of mind, disturbance, upset, anxiety; a cause of disturbance; (*astron.*) an irregularity or deviation in the motion of a heavenly body in its orbit. [L. *perturbatio*].

PERTURBATOR, [pur'-terb-āt'-or], *n.* a perturber.

PERTURBED, [per-turbd'], *adj.* upset, alarmed, agitated, apprehensive, restless.

PERTURBER, [per-turb'-er], *n.* one who disturbs, causes upset or arouses agitation.

PERTUSED, [per-tewzd'], *adj.* punched; pierced with holes; perforated. [L. *pertusum*, *p.pt.* of *pertundere*].

PERTUSSAL, [per-tus'-al], *adj.* relating to whooping-cough.

PERTUSSIS, [per-tus'-is], *n.* whooping-cough. [PER (2) and L. *tussis* cough].

PERUKE, PERRUQUE, [pe-rōōk'], *n.* an artificial cap or head of hair, a wig. [Fr. *perruque*].

PERUSAL, [per-ōōz'-al], *n.* the act of perusing or reading through.

PERUSE, [per-ōōz'], *v.t.* to read through, *esp.* to read through closely or carefully. [PER- and USE].

PERUSER, [per-ōōz'-er], *n.* one who peruses.

PERUVIAN, [per-ōō'-vi-an], *adj.* pertaining to Peru; **P. balsam,** the fragrant, pungent, bitter balsam of *Toluifera Pereirae*; **P. bark,** the bark of several species of *Cinchona* used as a medicine. [MdL. *Peruvia* Peru].

PERUVIN, [pe'-rōō-vin], *n.* a substance distilled from Peruvian balsam.

PERVADE, [per-vād'], *v.t.* to permeate, to fill, to spread or be diffused completely in, to penetrate into every part of. [L. *pervadere* to pass through].

PERVASION, [per-vā'-zhun], *n.* the act of pervading; thorough diffusion. [L. *pervasio*].

PERVASIVE, [per-vās'-iv], *adj.* tending to pervade.

PERVASIVELY, [per-vās'-iv-li], *adv.* in pervasive fashion; so as to pervade.

PERVERSE, [per-vurs'], *adj.* deliberately persisting in what is wrong or wicked; wilfully and stupidly obstinate, intractable; contrary, cantankerous, awkward, delighting in thwarting and vexing others; perverted, misguided; (*leg.*) contrary to the evidence or judge's direction. [L. *perversum*, *p.pt.* of *pervertere* to turn about].

PERVERSELY, [per-vurs'-li], *adv.* in perverse fashion.

PERVERSENESS, [per-vurs'-nes], *n.* the state of being perverse.

PERVERSION, [per-vur'-shun], *n.* the act of perverting; the state of being perverted, *esp.* sexually perverted; distortion, misapplication. [L. *perversio*].

PERVERSITY, [per-vurs'-i-ti], *n.* perverseness, a tendency to thwart or annoy, contrariness. [L. *perversitas*].

PERVERSIVE, [per-vurs'-iv], *adj.* tending to pervert.

PERVERT (1), [pur'-vurt'], *n.* one who has been perverted from truth to error, *esp.* in religious matters, an apostate; one in whom natural desires and instincts are perverted.

PERVERT (2), [per-vurt'], *v.t.* to turn from its proper purpose, use or meaning, to misapply, misconstrue; to corrupt, lead astray, distort, turn from the right, to cause to be depraved; to convert to a false religious belief. [L. *pervertere* to turn about].

PERVERTER, [per-vurt'-er], *n.* one who, or that which, perverts.

PERVERTIBLE, [per-vurt'-ibl], *adj.* able to be perverted.

PERVICACIOUS, [pur'-vik-ā'-shus], *adj.* very obstinate, wilfully contrary, stubborn, intractable. [L. *pervicax*].

PERVICACIOUSNESS, [pur'-vik-ā'-shus-nes], *n.* wilful obstinacy, stubbornness.

PERVICACITY, [pur'-vik-as'-i-ti], *n.* pervicaciousness. [LL. *pervicacitas*].

PERVIOUS, [pur'-vi-us], *adj.* allowing passage through, able to be penetrated and passed through, permeable; open to suggestion, persuasion or reason, capable of being influenced by argument; (*biol.*) open. [L. *pervius*].

PERVIOUSNESS, [pur'-vi-us-nes], *n.* the state of being pervious.

PERVITIN, [pur'-vit-in], *n.* a concentrated stimulating drug. [Germ. *pervitin*].

PESADE, [pes-ād'], *n.* the motion of a horse when he raises his fore-quarters without moving his hind legs. [Fr. *pesade*].

PESETA, [pes-ā'-ta], *n.* a Spanish silver coin corresponding to the franc or lira. [Span. *peseta*, *dim.* of *pesa* weight].

PESHITO, [pesh-ē'-tō], *n.* the principal Syriac version of the Old and New Testaments. [Syriac *p'shito* simple].

PESHWA, [pesh'-wah], *n.* the hereditary king of the Mahratta State, originally the Prime Minister of the Mahratta princes. [Pers. *peshwa* chief].

PESKY, [pes'-ki], *adj.* (*U.S. slang*) troublesome, annoying, vexatious. [Uncert.].

PESO, [pā'-sō], *n.* a former Spanish gold or silver coin worth about 4s. [Span. *peso* weight].

PESSARY, [pes'-er-i], *n.* a surgical instrument or appliance for supporting a prolapse of the uterus; a vaginal suppository. [MedL. *pessarium*].

PESSIMISM, [pes'-im-izm], *n.* a tendency to look on the gloomy side of things, and to expect that everything will be for the worst; the philosophical doctrine that the universe is radically bad and evil. [L. *pessimus* worst].

PESSIMIST, [pes'-im-ist], *n.* one who expects that everything will turn out for the worst; one who believes in the philosophical doctrine of pessimism.

PESSIMISTIC, [pes'-im-ist'-ik], *adj.* pertaining to, characterized by, pessimism; taking it for granted that everything will turn out for the worst.

PEST, [pest], *n.* (*rare*) a plague or widespread epidemic disease; an insect very injurious to crops, etc.; (*coll.*) a troublesome, harmful, destructive thing or person, a nuisance. [L. *pestis* pestilence].

PESTALOZZIAN, [pest'-al-ots'-i-an], *adj.* relating to the educational system of Pestalozzi. [J. H. *Pestalozzi* (1746-1827), the educationist].

PESTER, [pest'-er], *v.t.* to trouble, annoy, plague, to worry to death. [Fr. *empestrer*].

PESTERER, [pest'-er-er], *n.* one who pesters.

PESTIFEROUS, [pest-if'-er-us], *adj.* pestilential, producing plague, noxious or destructive to life or health; harmful to morals or to society, pernicious. [PEST and L. *ferre* to bring].

PESTIFEROUSLY, [pest-if'-er-us-li], *adv.* in a pestiferous way.

PESTILENCE, [pest'-il-ents], *n.* any widespread infectious or contagious disease, the bubonic plague; (*fig.*) something that is morally injurious or noxious. [L. *pestilentia*].

PESTILENT, [pest'-il-ent], *adj.* injurious or destructive to health or life, deadly; noxious or harmful to morals or society, morally pernicious; (*coll.*) troublesome, annoying. [L. *pestilens*].

PESTILENTIAL, [pest'-il-en'-shal], *adj.* of the nature of, or producing, a pestilence; morally harmful or injurious; (*coll.*) extremely troublesome.

PESTILENTLY, [pest'-il-ent-li], *adv.* in a pestilent fashion.

PESTLE (1), [pesl], *n.* a club-shaped implement with a heavy rounded head, used for pounding substances in a mortar. [OFr. *pestel*].

PESTLE (2), [pesl], *v.t.* and *i.* to pound with a pestle. [OFr. *pesteler*].

PESTLE

PESTOLOGY, [pest-ol'-o-ji], *n.* the study of pests. [PEST and Gk. *logos* speech].

PET (1), [pet], *n.* a fit of peevishness, an ill temper. [Uncert.].

PET (2), [pet], *n.* a tame animal reared and kept as a companion or object to be pampered, fussed over and indulged; a favourite, darling, a pampered and spoiled child. [Uncert.].

PET (3), [pet], *adj.* favourite; kept and cherished as a pet, frequently ironical.

PET (4), (petting, petted), [pet], *v.t.* to fondle, caress; to treat as a pet, to spoil, pamper; *v.i.* (*coll.*) to kiss and cuddle.

PETAL, [pet'-al], *n.* (*bot.*) a single distinct part of the corolla of a flower. [Gk. *petalon* leaf].

PETALINE, [pet'-al-in], *adj.* pertaining to a petal; attached to a petal; like a petal.

PETALISM, [pet'-al-izm], *n.* temporary banishment in Syracuse by writing the name on an olive leaf. [PETAL].

PETALITE, [pet'-al-īt], *n.* (*min.*) a translucent silicate of alumina with its structure lamellar in one direction.

PETALOID, [pet'-al-oid], *adj.* like, in the form of, a petal. [PETAL and Gk. *oeides* like].

PETALON, [pet'-al-on'], *n.* the ornamental thin gold plate adorning the mitre of a Jewish high priest. [Gk. *petalon*].

PETALOUS, [pet'-al-us], *adj.* having petals.

PETAL-SHAPED, [pet'-al-shāpt'], *adj.* petaloid.

PETARD, [pet-ahd'], *n.* an explosive device, formerly used in war for breaking in gates or making breaches; a firework cracker; **hoist with his own p.,** caught in his own trap. [Fr. *pétard*].

PETASUS, [pet'-as-us], *n.* (*antiq.*) the winged cap of Mercury; a low-crowned broad-brimmed hat worn by the ancient Greeks. [Gk. *petasos*].

PETECHIAE, [pet-ē'-ki-ē], *n.*(*pl.*) purple spots which appear on the skin in certain malignant fevers. [It. *petecchia* speckle].

PETECHIAL, [pet-ē'-ki-al], *adj.* spotted, speckled, pertaining to petechiae.

PETER, [pē'-ter], *v.i.* **to p. out,** to give out gradually, to become exhausted. [Uncert.].

PETER-BOAT, [pē'-ter-bōt'], *n.* a small fishing-boat without a proper stem, and shaped the same both fore and aft.

PETERMAN, [pē'-ter-man], *n.* a fisherman. [Simon *Peter* who was a fisherman].

PETERPENCE, PETER'S PENCE, [pē'-ter(z)-pents'], *n.*(*pl.*) an annual tribute formerly paid to the pope of a penny per family by landowners; voluntary donations given by Roman Catholics to the papal treasury. [St. *Peter*, the first pope].

PETERSHAM, [pē'-ter-sham], *n.* a heavy cloth used for overcoats; an overcoat or breeches made from this; a strong kind of ribbed silk. [Lord *Petersham*].

PETIOLAR, [pet'-i-ō'-ler], *adj.* like, pertaining to, a petiole.

PETIOLATE, [pet'-i-ō-lāt], *adj.* having, growing upon, a leaf-stalk.

PETIOLE, [pet'-i-ōl], *n.* a leaf-stalk. [L. *petiolus*].

PETIOLULE, [pet'-i-ōl-ewl], *n.* a small petiole, a stalklet. [~*Prec.*].

PETIT, [pet-ē'], *adj.* small. [Fr. *petit*].

PETITE, [pet-ēt'], *adj.* (of a woman) small, trim and dainty. [Fr. *petite*].

PETITION (1), [pet-ish'-un], *n.* the act of begging or humbly entreating; a humble request, prayer, entreaty, or supplication; a formal written request to a superior, official body or person in authority to put right some wrong or grievance or grant a favour; (*leg.*) formal written application made to a court of law; **P. of Right,** (*hist.*) a declaration by parliament in the time of Charles I of the rights and liberties of the people; (*leg.*) the mode of procedure to recover personal property or land which has come into the possession of the Crown. [L. *petitio*].

PETITION (2), [pet-ish'-un], *v.t.* to make a formal written request or application (to), to deliver a petition (to); to entreat, solicit. [*Prec.*].

PETITIONARY, [pet-ish'-un-er-i], *adj.* containing or making a petition; supplicatory.

PETITIONER, [pet-ish'-un-er], *n.* one who petitions.

PETIT-MAITRE, petit-maître, [pet'-ē-mātr'], *n.* a spruce fellow that dangles about women, a fop, a lady's man. [Fr. *petit-maître* little master].

PETITORY, [pet'-it-er-i], *adj.* petitionary. [L. *petitorius*].

PETREL, [pet'-rel], *n.* a small sea-bird with long wings and black and greyish-white feathers; **stormy p.,** the smallest web-footed bird, *Procellaria pelagica*, known as Mother Carey's chicken; (*fig.*) a person who brings disturbance and excitement wherever he goes. [Uncert.].

PETREL

PETRESCENCE, [pet-res'-ents], *n.* the changing into stone.

PETRESCENT, [pet-res'-ent], *adj.* becoming stony or petrified.

PETRIFACTION, [pet'-ri-fak'-shun], *n.* the process of petrifying; the state of being petrified; anything petrified, an incrustation; (*fig.*) amazement. [L. *petra* stone and *facere* to make].

PETRIFACTIVE, [pet'-ri-fakt'-iv], *adj.* producing petrifaction.

PETRIFIC, [pet-rif'-ik], *adj.* causing petrifaction.

PETRIFICATION, [pet'-rif-ik-ā'-shun], *n.* the process of petrifying; a petrifaction; (*fig.*) obduracy, callousness.

PETRIFY, [pet'-ri-fī], *v.t.* to convert into stone or into a stony substance, to encrust with a mineral deposit; (*fig.*) to deaden, to deprive of life or feeling, to make callous or obdurate; to stupefy, dumbfound; *v.i.*

to become changed into stone or a stony substance. [Fr. *pétrifier*].
PETRO-, *pref.* rock, stone. [Gk. *petra* rock].
PETROGLYPHY, [pet-rog′-lif-i], *n.* the practice of carving in stone. [PETRO and Gk. *gluphe* carving].
PETROGRAPHY, [pet-rog′-ra-fi], *n.* the description and classification of rocks. [PETRO and Gk. *graphia* writing].
PETROL, [pet′-rol], *n.* a liquid hydrocarbon obtained by distillation from petroleum and forming an explosive gas when mixed with air, used in internal combustion engines. [PETROLEUM].
PETROLEUM, [pet-rō′-li-um], *n.* a mineral oil consisting almost entirely of liquid hydrocarbons. [PETRO and L. *oleum* oil].
PETROLOGICAL, [pet′-ro-loj′-ik-al], *adj.* relating to petrology.
PETROLOGIST, [pet-rol′-oj-ist], *n.* a student of petrology.
PETROLOGY, [pet-rol′-o-ji], *n.* the study of rocks and their structure. [PETRO and Gk. *logos* speech].
PETROL-PUMP, [pet′-rol-pump′], *n.* a pumping machine for the convenient supply of measured quantities of petrol to motor-vehicles.
PETRONEL, [pet′-ron-el′], *n.* a kind of large sixteenth-century carbine used by cavalry. [Fr. dial. *pétrinal*].
PETROSILEX, [pet′-rō-sī′-leks], *n.* rock flint, a hard variety of felspar. [PETRO and L. *silex* flint].
PETROSILICEOUS, [pet′-rō-sil-ish′-us], *adj.* consisting of petrosilex.
PETROUS, [pet′-rus], *adj.* consisting of, like, stone or rock, extremely hard. [L. *petrosus*].
PETTED, [pet′-id], *adj.* pampered, spoiled.
PETTICOAT, [pet′-i-kōt], *n.* a kind of underskirt worn by females; (*coll.*) a woman. [PETTY and COAT (1)].
PETTIFOG, [pet′-i-fog′], *v.i.* to act as a pettifogger, to indulge in disreputable trickery.
PETTIFOGGER, [pet′-i-fog′-er], *n.* an inferior lawyer, one who indulges in disreputable trickery and other sharp practices. [PETTY and *Fugger*, a notorious financier of Augsburg].
PETTIFOGGERY, [pet′-i-fog′-er-i], *n.* disreputable legal trickery, quibbling.
PETTIFOGGING, [pet′-i-fog′-ing], *adj.* resorting to pettifoggery; paltry, contemptible.
PETTILY, [pet′-i-li], *adv.* in a petty fashion.
PETTINESS, [pet′-i-nes], *n.* the condition of being petty.
PETTISH, [pet′-ish], *adj.* fretful, peevish, spoiled.
PETTISHLY, [pet′-ish-li], *adv.* in a pet; irritably.
PETTISHNESS, [pet′-ish-nes], *n.* the state of being pettish.
PETTITOES, [pet′-i-tōz], *n.* the feet of a pig, eaten as food, pig's trotters. [Uncert.].
PETTO, [pet′-ō], *n.* the breast; **in p.**, in secrecy, not made public. [It. *petto* from L. *pectus* breast].
PETTY, [pet′-i], *adj.* trivial, small in amount or importance; mean, contemptible, paltry; minor, inferior, on a small scale; **p. cash**, miscellaneous small payments received or made; **p. jury**, a common jury; **p. larceny**, theft of articles or goods of comparatively small value; **p. sessions**, a court of law presided over by justices of the peace; **p. officer**, an officer in the navy of similar rank to a non-commissioned officer in the army. [Fr. *petit* small].
PETULANCE, [pet′-yŏŏ-lants], *n.* peevishness, waywardness, fretful irritability. [L. *petulantia* insolence].
PETULANCY, [pet′-yŏŏ-lan-si], *n.* petulance.
PETULANT, [pet′-yŏŏ-lant], *adj.* peevish, irritable, manifesting or proceeding from petulance, cross-grained. [L. *petulans*].
PETULANTLY, [pet′-yŏŏ-lant-li], *adv.* with petulance.
PETUNIA, [pet-ewn′-i-a], *n.* a genus of herbaceous plants allied to the nightshade, of the order *Solanaceae*, bearing attractive white or purple flowers; a purple colour. [Fr. *petun* from Brazilian *pety* tobacco plant].
PETUNTSE, [pet-unt′-si], *n.* a kind of fine clay used in the manufacture of porcelain. [Chin. *pai-tun-tze* white stone].
PEUCYL, [pew′-sil], *n.* an oily substance obtained from turpentine; terebilene.
PEULVAN, PEULVEN, [pu(r)l′-ven′], *n.* a prehistoric rough, stone pillar, set upright, *esp.* in Brittany; an artificially balanced rocking-stone. [Fr. *peulven*].
PEW, [pew], *n.* a long, fixed and partially enclosed bench with a back, on which the congregation sit in a place of worship; (*coll.*) a seat, a chair. [OFr. *puie* raised seat].
PEW-FELLOW, [pew′-fel′-ō], *n.* a fellow worshipper.
PEWIT, see PEEWIT.
PEW-OPENER, [pew′-ōp′-ner], *n.* a person who is employed to open privately owned pews for worshippers at a church service.
PEWTER (1), [pew′-ter], *n.* an alloy containing about 95 per cent tin and 5 per cent copper, with an occasional trace of lead or antimony; a utensil made of this, a collection of pewter vessels or objects. [ME. *peutre* from It. *peltro*].
PEWTER (2), [pew′-ter], *adj.* made of pewter.
PEWTERER, [pew′-ter-er], *n.* one who makes utensils of pewter.
PEWTERY, [pew′-ter-i], *adj.* belonging to, or like, pewter.
PFAHLBAUTEN, [pfahl′-bow-ten], *n.(pl.)* lake dwellings. [Germ. *pfahlbauten* stake buildings].
PFENNIG, [pfen′-ig], *n.* a German copper coin, a hundredth of a mark. [Ger. *pfennig*].
PHACITIS, [fas-ī′-tis], *n.* inflammation of the crystalline lens of the eye. [Gk. *phakos* lentil and *itis* denoting inflammation].
PHACOID, [fak′-oid], *adj.* (of the crystalline lens of the eye) shaped like a lentil. [Gk. *phakos* lentil and *oeides* like].
PHAENOGAM, [fē′-nō-gam′], *n.* a phanerogam. [Gk. *phainomai* I appear and *gamos* marriage].
PHAENOGAMOUS, [fēn-og′-am-us], *adj.* (*bot.*) phanerogamous. [Gk. *phainomai* I appear and *gamos* marriage].
PHAENOLOGY, see PHENOLOGY.
PHAETON, [fā′-ton], *n.* a light, open, four-wheeled carriage, usually drawn by two horses. [Gk. *Phaeton* who obtained the chariot of the sun and nearly set the world on fire by his driving].
PHAGEDENA, [faj′-i-dē′-na], *n.* (*med.*) a spreading sore or ulcer. [Gk. *phagedaina*].
PHAGEDENIC, [faj′-i-dē′-nik], *adj.* of the nature of a phagedena.
PHAGOCYTE, [fag′-ō-sīt], *n.* a white blood corpuscle that destroys harmful bacteria in the system. [Gk. *phago* I eat and *kutos* cell].
PHALANGE, [fal′-anj], *n.* (*anat.*) one of the small bones forming the finger and toe; (*entom.*) a joint of the tarsus in insects; (*bot.*) a group of stamens fastened together by their filaments. [*Phalanges pl.* of PHALANX].
PHALANGEAL, [fal-anj′-i-al], *adj.* like, pertaining to, the phalanges.
PHALANGER, [fal′-anj-er], *n.* a genus of tree-living web-footed marsupials, inhabiting Australasia, of nocturnal habits. [Gk. *phalangion* spider's web].
PHALANGIAN, [fal-anj′-i-an], *adj.* phalangeal.
PHALANGIOUS, [fal-anj′-i-us], *adj.* pertaining to *Phalangium*, a genus of spiders having long thin legs.
PHALANSTERIAN (1), [fal′-an-stēer′-i-an], *n.* a member of, or supporter of the idea of, a phalanstery.
PHALANSTERIAN (2), [fal′-an-stēer′-i-an], *adj.* pertaining to a phalanstery.
PHALANSTERY, [fal-an′-ster-i], *n.* a small compact community living together on a communal basis; the group of buildings inhabited by such a community. [Fr. *phalanstère*].

PHALANGER

PHALANX, (*pl.* **phalanges, phalanxes**), [fal′-angks], *n.* (*Gk. antiq.*) a compact body of heavily armed infantry drawn up so closely as to form a solid wall or block; any body of troops or men in such close formation or massing; a band of people solidly united in a common purpose or cause; (*anat.*) a phalange. [Gk. *phalanx* battle line].
PHALAROPE, [fal′-er-ōp′], *n.* a genus of plover-like wading birds with lobed feet. [Gk. *phalaris* white-headed coot].
PHALLIC, [fal′-ik], *adj.* pertaining to the phallus or its worship. [Gk. *phallikos*].
PHALLUS, [fal′-us], *n.* a representation of the erected penis as a symbol of the procreative power of nature. [Gk. *phallos* penis].
PHANEROGAM, [fan′-er-ō-gam′], *n.* a plant that is propagated by plainly visible flowers. [Gk. *phaneros* visible and *gamos* marriage].
PHANEROGAMOUS, [fan′-er-og′-am-us], *adj.* (*bot.*) having visible flowers.
PHANTASM, [fan′-tazm], *n.* fancy, illusion; an

image created by the fancy, a figment of the imagination; a spectre, apparition. [Gk. *phantasma*].

PHANTASMAGORIA, [fan'-taz-mag-aw'-ri-a], *n.* a series of optical illusions arranged for public display; an array and procession of shadowy, rapidly moving figures, real or illusory. [PHANTASM and Gk. *agora* crowd].

PHANTASMAGORIAL, [fan'-taz-mag-aw'-ri-al], *adj.* relating to a phantasmagoria.

PHANTASMAGORIC, [fan-taz'-ma-go'-rik], *adj.* of or like a phantasmagoria.

PHANTASMAL, [fan-taz'-mal], *adj.* like a phantasm.

PHANTASY, see FANTASY.

PHANTOM, [fan'-tom], *n.* an apparition, spectre; a vision; an optical illusion, delusion of the mind, hallucination. [OFr. *fantome* phantasm].

PHARAOH, [fāer'-ō], *n.* the title borne by the kings of Ancient Egypt; **P. chicken,** the Egyptian vulture, *Neophron percnopterus*; **Pharaoh's rat,** the Egyptian ichneumon; **Pharaoh's serpent,** a kind of firework melting in the form of a serpent.

PHARISAIC, [fa'-ris-ā'-ik], *adj.* resembling the Pharisees; making a show of religion; formal, hypocritical.

PHARISAICAL, [fa'-ris-ā'-ik-al], *adj.* pharisaic.

PHARISAICALLY, [fa'-ris-ā'-ik-a-li], *adv.* in a pharisaical manner, hypocritically.

PHARISAICALNESS, [fa'-ris-ā'-ikl-nes], *n.* the quality of being pharisaical.

PHARISAISM, [fa'-ris-ā'-izm], *n.* the principles, doctrines and conduct of the Pharisees; hypocrisy.

PHARISEE, [fa'-ris-ē], *n.* a member of a Jewish sect particularly noted for their strict observance of traditional rites and ceremonies and their professed sanctity; one who attaches more importance to outward forms and ceremonies than to the inner meaning; hypocrite. [Gk. *Pharisaios* from Heb. *Perushim* the separated].

PHARMACEUTICAL, [fahm'-a-sew'-tik-al], *adj.* pertaining to, occupied in, the preparation and dispensing of medicines; involving the use of medicines. [Gk. *pharmakeutikos*].

PHARMACEUTICS, [fahm'-a-sewt'-iks], *n.(pl.)* the science of the preparation and mixing of drugs to be taken as medicine.

PHARMACEUTIST, [fahm'-a-sewt'-ist], *n.* a person skilled or occupied in the art of preparing medicinal drugs.

PHARMACIST, [fahm'-as-ist], *n.* a person skilled or engaged in pharmacy.

PHARMACOLITE, [fahm'-ak-o-līt'], *n.* (*min.*) lime mixed with arsenic acid, and occurring as a coating of silky fibres. [Gk. *pharmakon* poison and *lithos* stone].

PHARMACOLOGY, [fahm'-ak-ol'-o-ji], *n.* the study of the preparation and use of drugs as medicines. [Gk. *pharmakon* drug and *logos* speech].

PHARMACOPOEIA, [fahm'-ak-ō-pē'-a], *n.* a book of directions, published by authority, for the preparation, mixture and use of drugs as medicines; a stock of drugs for medicinal use. [Gk. *pharmakopoiia* drug-making].

PHARMACOSIDERITE, [fahm'-ak-ō-sid'-er-īt], *n.* arsenate of iron. [Gk. *pharmakon* poison and *sideros* iron].

PHARMACY, [fahm'-a-si], *n.* the study or practice of preparing and dispensing medicinal drugs; dispensary. [Gk. *pharmakeia*].

PHAROLOGY, [fa-rol'-o-ji], *n.* the science of signalling by light from the shore, and by lighthouses. [PHAROS and Gk. *logos* speech].

PHAROS, [fāer'-os], *n.* a lighthouse; a beacon. [Named from a lighthouse on the island of *Pharos* near Alexandria].

PHARYNGEAL, [fa-rinj'-i-al], *adj.* relating to the pharynx.

PHARYNGITIS, [fa'-rinj-ī'-tis], *n.* inflammation of the membrane of the pharynx. [PHARYNX and Gk. *itis* denoting inflammation].

PHARYNGOSCOPE, [fa-ring'-go-skōp'], *n.* an instrument for examining the pharynx.

PHARYNGOTOMY, [fa'-rin-got'-o-mi], *n.* the operation of making an incision into the pharynx. [PHARYNX and Gk. *tome* cutting].

PHARYNX, (*pl.* **pharynges**), [fa'-ringks], *n.* the muscular cavity at the back of the throat, lying between the mouth and the gullet. [Gk. *pharugx*].

PHASE, [fāz], *n.* the amount of illuminated surface, of the moon or a planet, visible to the eye at a given time; the aspect of a heavenly body at a given time; a particular aspect, side, stage or state of a phenomenon which undergoes periodic change. [Gk. *phasis* appearance].

PHEASANT, [fez'-ant], *n.* a game-bird of the genus *Phasianus*, highly esteemed for the beauty of its plumage and the delicacy of its flesh; **pheasant's eye,** the plants, *Adonis autumnalis* and *Narcissus poeticus*. [ME. *fesant*].

PHEASANTRY, [fez'-ant-ri], *n.* a place devoted to the rearing of pheasants.

PHELLOPLASTIC, [fel'-ō-plast'-ik], *n.* a figure modelled in cork. [Gk. *phellos* cork and PLASTIC].

PHENACETIN, [fen-as'-et-in], *n.* a product of phenol used medicinally as an antipyretic. [PHENOL and ACETYL].

PHENAKITE, [fē'-nak-īt], *n.* silicate of beryllium, resembling quartz in appearance. [Gk. *phenax* cheat].

PHENATE, [fē'-nāt], *n.* a salt of phenol. [Gk. *phainos* shining].

PHENGITE, FENGITE, [fen'-jīt], *n.* a species of mica, muscovite. [Gk. *phengites*].

PHENICINE, [fen'-is-in], *n.* the purple powder precipitated when a sulphurated solution of indigo is diluted with water. [Gk. *phoinix* purplish red].

PHENOCRYST, [fē'-nō-krist], *n.* a large crystal in porphyritic rocks. [Gk. *phainomai* I appear and *krustallos* crystal].

PHENOIC, [fē-nō'-ik], *adj.* relating to phenol.

PHENOL, [fē'-nol], *n.* carbolic acid, a hydroxyl derivative of benzene, used as an antiseptic and disinfectant. [Gk. *phainos* shining].

PHENOLOGY, PHAENOLOGY, [fē-nol'-o-ji], *n.* the study of the influence of climate on life and vegetation. [Gk. *phainomai* I appear and *logos* speech].

PHENOMENAL, [fin-om'-in-al], *adj.* pertaining to phenomena, of the nature of a phenomenon, perceptible to the senses, apparent; extraordinary, exceptional.

PHENOMENALISM, [fin-om'-in-al-izm], *n.* that system of philosophy which maintains that knowledge is limited to phenomena perceptible to the senses.

PHENOMENALLY, [fin-om'-in-a-li], *adv.* in a phenomenal manner.

PHENOMENIST, [fin-om'-in-ist], *n.* one who holds the philosophical doctrine of phenomenalism.

PHENOMENOLOGY, [fin-om'-in-ol'-o-ji], *n.* the science dealing with phenomena; scientific investigation and classification of phenomena. [PHENOMENON and Gk. *logos* speech].

PHENOMENON, (*pl.* **phenomena**), [fin-om'-in-on], *n.* anything that appears or is observed, a thing that is perceptible by the senses; an extraordinary thing, something extremely remarkable, a marvel, wonder; (*coll.*) a wizard, prodigy; (*philos.*) that which is directly perceived by the senses. [Gk. *phainomenon* apparent].

PHENOTYPE, [fē'-nō-tīp], *n.* (*biol.*) a type of organism classified by its appearance as distinct from its inherited constitution. [Gk. *phainomai* I appear and TYPE].

PHENYL, [fē'-nil], *n.* the organic radical present in carbolic acid, etc.

PHEON, [fē'-on], *n.* (*her.*) a representation of a broad barbed arrow or head of a dart. [Unkn.].

PHEON

PHIAL, (fī'-al], *n.* a small glass vessel or bottle in which liquids are kept. [Gk. *phiale*].

PHILANDER, [fil-and'-er], *v.i.* to flirt, to play at making love, to indulge in light-hearted love affairs without serious intentions. [Gk. *philandros* lover of men].

PHILANDERER, [fil-and'-er-er], *n.* one who philanders.

PHILANTHROPE, [fil'-an-thrōp], *n.* a philanthropist.

PHILANTHROPIC, PHILANTHROPICAL, [fil'-an-throp'-ik], *adj.* pertaining to, practising, philanthropy.

PHILANTHROPISM, [fil-an'-throp-izm], *n.* philanthropy.

PHILANTHROPIST, [fil-an'-throp-ist], *n.* one filled with a love of mankind, who spends time, energy and money in helping others, a person who makes large and frequent gifts to charity.

PHILANTHROPY, [fil-an'-throp-i], *n.* love of

mankind, marked generosity in making charitable gifts. [Gk. *philanthropos*].
PHILATELIC, [fil-at'-el-ik], *adj.* relating to philately.
PHILATELIST, [fil-at'-el-ist], *n.* one who collects postage stamps.
PHILATELY, [fil-at'-el-i], *n.* the study and collection of postage stamps. [PHILO and Gk. *ateleia* exemption from payment of tax].
PHILHARMONIC, [fil'-ah-mon'-ik], *adj.* loving music. [PHILO and HARMONIC].
PHILHELLENIST, [fil-hel-ēn'-ist], *n.* one who was in favour of Greece's efforts to secure independence from the Ottoman empire; an admirer of Greece and the Greek spirit. [Gk. *phileilen*].
PHILIBEG, see FILIBEG.
PHILIPPIC, [fil-ip'-ik], *n.* one of three orations of Demosthenes against Philip of Macedon; Cicero's orations against Antony; any discourse full of acrimonious invective. [Gk. *philippikos* pertaining to Philip].
PHILIPPINE, [fil'-ip-ēn], *n.* a nut having a double kernel; the custom of sharing such a nut with another person, the one who first greets the other as *philippine* at their next meeting, receiving a present from the other; such a present given. [Germ. *viel-liebchen* darling].
PHILIPPIZE, [fil'-ip-īz], *v.i.* to write or utter invective.
PHILISTINE (1), [fil'-is-tīn, fil'-is-tin], *n.* a member of a hostile warlike tribe of southern Palestine, who engaged in struggles with the Israelites for the possession of the country; an inveterate enemy; a prosperous, uncultured middle-class person completely oblivious of the arts, and solely concerned with his material welfare. [Gk. *Philistinos*].
PHILISTINE (2), [fil'-is-tīn], *adj.* uncultured, boorish.
PHILISTINISM, [fil'-is-tin-izm], *n.* the outlook, tastes and modes of thinking of the uncultured Philistine.
PHILLIPSITE, [fil'-ip-sīt], *n.* a silicate of alumina resembling harmotome. [*Phillips*, a chemist].
PHILO-, *pref.* loving, fond of. [Gk. *philos* loving].
PHILOGYNY, [fil-oj'-i-ni], *n.* uxoriousness, love of women. [PHILO and Gk. *gune* woman].
PHILOLOGER, [fil-ol'-oj-er], *n.* a philologist.
PHILOLOGICAL, [fil'-ō-loj'-ik-al], *adj.* pertaining to, concerned with, in accordance with, philology.
PHILOLOGICALLY, [fil'-ol-oj'-ik-a-li], *adv.* according to philology.
PHILOLOGIST, [fil-ol'-oj-ist], *n.* a student of philology.
PHILOLOGY, [fil-ol'-o-ji], *n.* the study of linguistic principles, the study of languages, *esp.* their origin, structure and development; (*archaic*) love of learning and literature. [Gk. *philologia* love of learning].
PHILOMATH, [fil'-ō-math], *n.* a lover of learning, and *esp.* of mathematics. [Gk. *philomathes*].
PHILOMATHIC, [fil'-ō-math'-ik], *adj.* relating to or having a love of learning.
PHILOMATHY, [fil'-ō-math-i], *n.* the love of learning. [Gk. *philomathia*].
PHILOMEL, [fil'-ō-mel'], *n.* the nightingale. [Gk. *philomela*].
PHILOMUSICAL, [fil'-ō-mewz'-ik-al], *adj.* loving music.
PHILOPOLEMIC, [fil'-ō-pol-em'-ik], *adj.* fond of dissension.
PHILOPROGENITIVENESS, [fil'-ō-prō-jen'-it-iv-nes], *n.* the love of producing offspring, fertility, tendency to produce many offspring. [PHILO and L. *progenitum*, *p.pt.* of *progignere*].
PHILOSOPHASTER, [fil-os'-of-ast-er], *n.* a pretender to philosophy, a quack philosopher. [L. *philosophaster*].
PHILOSOPHER, [fil-os'-of-er], *n.* one who studies or is versed in philosophy; one who adopts a philosophic attitude to life, attempting to model his behaviour and conduct on reason and wisdom; **philosopher's stone**, an imaginary substance formerly sought by alchemists as a means of converting baser metals into gold. [Gk. *philosophos* lover of wisdom, philosopher].
PHILOSOPHIC, [fil'-os-of'-ik], *adj.* philosophical; pertaining to philosophy.
PHILOSOPHICAL, [fil'-os-of'-ik-al], *adj.* pertaining to philosophy; of the nature of, based on, like, philosophy; like a philosopher, wise; learned or versed in philosophy; behaving in a wise, reasonable manner; bearing misfortune resignedly.
PHILOSOPHICALLY, [fil'-os-of'-ik-a-li], *adv.* in a philosophical manner, from the point of view of philosophy.
PHILOSOPHISM, [fil-os'-of-izm], *n.* sham or shallow philosophy.
PHILOSOPHIST, [fil-os'-of-ist], *n.* a sham philosopher.
PHILOSOPHIZE, [fil-os'-of-īz], *v.t.* to deal with in a philosophical manner; *v.i.* to reason, speculate or theorize as a philosopher.
PHILOSOPHIZER, [fil-os'-of-īz-er], *n.* one who philosophizes.
PHILOSOPHY, [fil-os'-o-fi], *n.* the study of ultimate reality, an attempt to understand or explain the nature of phenomena or matter, of human action and conduct, or of consciousness, the mind and its reasoning; the science dealing with the causes and principles of things; a particular philosophical system; a rationalized outlook on life, a mental attitude influencing and shaping one's behaviour. [Gk. *philosophia* love of wisdom].
PHILOTECHNIC, [fil'-ō-tek'-nik], *adj.* fond of the arts. [Gk. *philotekhnikos*].
PHILOZOIC, [fil'-ō-zō'-ik], *adj.* loving animals. [PHILO and Gk. *zoon* animal].
PHILTRE, PHILTER, [fil'-ter], *n.* a love potion or charm. [Gk. *philtron*].
PHINOC, see FINNOC.
PHIZ, [fiz], *n.* (*coll.*) the face or visage. [Short for PHYSIOGNOMY].
PHLEBITIS, [fleb-ī'-tis], *n.* inflammation of the lining or walls of a vein. [Gk. *phleps* vein and *itis* denoting inflammation].
PHLEBOLITES, [fleb'-ō-līts], *n.(pl.)* (*med.*) small calculi, sometimes found in the veins. [Gk. *phleps* vein and *lithos* stone].
PHLEBOLOGY, [fleb-ol'-o-ji], *n.* the anatomy of the veins; a treatise on the veins. [Gk. *phleps* vein and *logos* speech].
PHLEBOTOMIST, [fleb-ot'-om-ist], *n.* one who opens a vein to let blood.
PHLEBOTOMIZE, [fleb-ot'-om-īz], *v.t.* to bleed by opening a vein; *v.i.* to let blood from a vein.
PHLEBOTOMY, [fleb-ot'-o-mi], *n.* the practice of blood-letting as a remedy for certain diseases. [Gk. *phlebotomia*].
PHLEGM, [flem], *n.* thick viscous fluid secreted by the mucous membrane of the throat and chest; (*fig.*) coolness, apathy, indifference, sluggishness. [Gk. *phlegma* inflammation].
PHLEGMASIA, [fleg-mā'-zi-a], *n.* (*med.*) inflammation; **p. dolens**, inflammation of the veins of the leg, sometimes present in women after childbirth, white leg. [Gk. *phlegmasia*].
PHLEGMATIC, [fleg-mat'-ik], *adj.* sluggish, not easily stirred or excited, stolid.
PHLEGMATICALLY, [fleg-mat'-ik-al-i], *adv.* in phlegmatic fashion.
PHLEGMON, [fleg'-mon], *n.* an inflammatory tumour in the cellular tissue, a boil or other inflamed swelling on the skin, discharging matter. [Gk. *phlegmone* inflammation].
PHLEGMY, [flem'-i], *adj.* pertaining to, resembling, phlegm.
PHLEME†, see FLEAM.
PHLOEM, [flō'-em], *n.* (*bot.*) the soft vascular tissue in plants. [Gk. *phloos* bark].
PHLOGISTIC, [flō-jist'-ik], *adj.* (*chem.*) pertaining to, consisting of, resembling, phlogiston; (*med.*) inflammatory.
PHLOGISTON†, [flō-jist'-on], *n.* the supposed principle of inflammability present in all combustible substances, and separated by combustion. [Gk. *phlogiston*].
PHLOGOPITE, [flō'-gō-pīt], *n.* a uniaxial magnesian mica, resembling chocolate in colour, and having a metallic sheen. [Gk. *phlogopos* fiery].
PHLOX, [floks], *n.* a North American genus of the *Polemoniaceae*, cultivated for their clusters of variously coloured flowers. [Gk. *phlox* flame].
PHOBIA, [fō'-bi-a], *n.* (*psych.*) a morbid fear, dislike or aversion. [Gk. *phobos* fear].
PHOBOS, [fō'-bos], *n.* (*astron.*) a satellite of the planet Mars. [Gk. *phobos* fear].
PHOCA, [fō'-ka], *n.* the seal; any member of the seal or walrus family. [Gk. *phoke* seal].
PHOCAL, [fō'-kal] *adj.* relating to a seal or to the seal tribe.
PHOCENIC, [fō-sen'-ik], *adj.* pertaining to the dolphin; **p. acid**, an acid derived from dolphin oil. [Gk. *phokaina* porpoise].
PHOCID, see PHOCINE.
PHOCINE, PHOCID, [fō'-sīn, fō'-sid], *adj.* relating to the true seals. [Gk. *phoke* seal].

PHOEBUS, [fē'-bus], *n.* (*myth.*) the god Apollo; the sun. [Gk. *phoibos* shining].

PHOENIX (1), [fē'-niks], *n.* (*myth.*) a fabulous Egyptian bird, supposed to be the only one of its kind, which was fabled to live for 500 years, at the end of which it sacrificed itself by cremation on a funeral pile, and rose again in the renewal of youth from the ashes; a person of singular distinction. [Gk. *phoinix*].

PHOENIX

PHOENIX (2), [fē'-niks], *n.* a genus of tropical palms including the date palm, *Phoenix dactylifera.* [*Prec.*].

PHONATE, [fōn-āt'], *v.i.* to utter vocal sounds. [Gk. *phone* voice].

PHONAUTOGRAPH†, [fōn-awt'-ō-graf], *n.* an apparatus for registering sound waves in graphic form on a revolving cylinder, by means of a vibrating membrane. [Gk. *phone* voice, *autos* self and GRAPH].

PHONE (1), [fōn], *n.* a single vowel or consonant sound. [Gk. *phone* voice].

PHONE (2), [fōn], *n.* (*coll.*) a telephone. [(TELE)-PHONE].

PHONE (3), [fōn], *v.t. and i.* to telephone.

PHONEME, [fōn'-ēm], *n.* (*phon.*) a speech sound whose possible variations do not affect the significance of a word in which it occurs. [Gk. *phone* voice].

PHONETIC, [fō-net'-ik], *adj.* pertaining to, representing, involving, dealing with, the sounds of speech and their pronunciation; **p. symbols**, a system of symbols used to represent the sounds of speech; **p. spelling**, a method of spelling in which words would be spelt as they are pronounced, each letter or combination of letters always being used to represent the same sound. [Gk. *phonetikos*].

PHONETICALLY, [fō-net'-ik-a-li], *adv.* according to the principles of phonetics.

PHONETICIAN, [fōn'-it-ish'-an], *n.* one who studies, or is versed in, phonetics.

PHONETICIZE, [fon-et'-is-īz], *v.t.* to represent in phonetic symbols or spelling.

PHONETICS, [fō-net'-iks], *n.*(*pl.*) that part of linguistic study dealing with the sounds of speech, their production, pronunciation, and graphical representation by written characters.

PHONEY, [fōn'-i], *adj.* (*slang*) false, spurious, faked; suspicious, underhand. [Unkn.].

PHONIC, [fon'-ik], *adj.* pertaining to sound, acoustic; pertaining to sounds of speech.

PHONO-, *pref.* voice, speech, vocal sound. [Gk. *phone* voice].

PHONOCAMPTIC, [fō'-nō-kamp'-tik], *adj.* reflecting sound, causing an echo. [PHONO and Gk. *kamptikos* bending].

PHONOGRAM, [fōn'-ō-gram], *n.* a written sign or character representing a particular sound of speech; a record, in the form of a cylinder, made by a phonograph. [PHONO and Gk. *gramma* something written].

PHONOGRAPH, [fō'-nō-graf], *n.* an instrument which records and repeats sounds, in which a record was made upon a revolving cylinder coated with hard wax.

PHONOGRAPHER†, [fōn-og'-raf-er], *n.* a shorthand writer.

PHONOGRAPHIC, [fōn'-ō-graf'-ik], *adj.* pertaining to, made by, a phonograph; (*archaic*) pertaining to shorthand writing.

PHONOGRAPHY, [fōn-og'-raf-i], *n.* Pitman's system of shorthand; the recording and reproduction of sounds by means of the phonograph. [PHONO and Gk. *graphia* writing].

PHONOLITE, [fōn'-ō-līt], *n.* clinkstone, a volcanic rock consisting mainly of nepheline and sanidine, and which emits a metallic ringing sound when struck. [PHONO and Gk. *lithos* stone].

PHONOLOGICAL, [fōn'-o-loj'-ik-al], *adj.* relating to phonology.

PHONOLOGY, [fōn-ol'-o-ji], *n.* the study of the history and development of the sounds of speech; the system of speech sounds existing in a particular language. [PHONO and Gk. *logos* speech].

PHONOTYPE, [fōn'-ō-tīp], *n.* a symbol or letter of a phonetic alphabet in type; a phonetic type.

PHONOTYPY, [fōn-ot'-i-pi] *n.* a proposed mode of printing in which each sound of speech shall be represented by a distinct letter or phonetic character.

PHORMIUM, [faw'-mi-um], *n.* New Zealand flax, *Phormium tenax.* [Gk. *phormion*].

PHOSGENE, [foz'-jēn], *n.* a poisonous, non-persistent, lung-irritant, chemical gas used in warfare, carbon oxychloride. [Gk. *phos* light and *genes* born of].

PHOSGENITE, [fos'-jēn-īt], *n.* (*chem.*) a compound of carbonate and chloride of lead.

PHOSPHAM, [fos'-fam], *n.* a compound of ammonia and phosphoric acid, in the form of a white or reddish powder. [PHOSPH(ORUS) and AM(MONIA)].

PHOSPHATE, [fos'-fāt], *n.* a salt of phosphoric acid, used largely as manure in agriculture.

PHOSPHATIC, [fos-fat'-ik], *adj.* pertaining to, containing, phosphates.

PHOSPHATIZE, [fos'-fat-īz], *v.t.* to make phosphatic.

PHOSPHENE, [fos'-fēn], *n.* a luminous impression of a spectrum produced on the eye by pressing in the eyeball. [Gk. *phos* light and *phainomai* I appear].

PHOSPHIDE, [fos'-fīd], *n.* a combination of phosphorus and another element.

PHOSPHINE, [fos'-fēn], *n.* phosphuretted hydrogen gas.

PHOSPHITE, [fos'-fīt], *n.* a salt of phosphorous acid.

PHOSPHOCERATE, [fos-fō-sēer'-āt], *n.* phosphate of cerium, lanthanum and didymium. [PHOSPHO(RUS) and CER(IUM)].

PHOSPHOCHALCITE, [fos'-fō-kal'-sīt], *n.* phosphate of copper. [PHOSPHO(RUS) and Gk. *khalkos* copper].

PHOSPHOLITE, [fos'-fol-īt], *n.* an earth mixed with phosphoric acid. [PHOSPHO(RUS) and Gk. *lithos* stone].

PHOSPHONIUM, [fos-fōn'-i-um], *n.* (*chem.*) the metallic radical, PH_4, containing phosphorus and hydrogen, analogous to ammonium. [PHOSPH(ORUS) and (AMM)ONIUM].

PHOSPHOR, [fos'-fer], *n.* the morning star. [L. *phosphorus*].

PHOSPHORATE, [fos'-fer-āt], *v.t.* to combine with phosphorus, to make phosphorescent.

PHOSPHOR-BRONZE, [fos'-fer-bronz'], *n.* an alloy of copper, tin and phosphorus.

PHOSPHOR-COPPER, [fos'-fer-kop'-er], *n.* copper containing about ten per cent of phosphorus.

PHOSPHORESCE, [fos'-fer-es'], *v.i.* to give out light without apparent combustion or heat, to shine in the dark.

PHOSPHORESCENCE, [fos'-fer-es'-ents], *n.* the quality of being phosphorescent, emission of light without apparent combustion or heat; the act or power of shining in the dark.

PHOSPHORESCENT, [fos'-fer-es'-ent], *adj.* emitting a faint light or glow without apparent heat or combustion; shining in the dark.

PHOSPHORIC, [fos-for'-ik], *adj.* pertaining to, containing, phosphorus in its higher valency state; phosphorescent.

PHOSPHORITE, [fos'-fer-īt], *n.* (*min.*) a massive variety of apatite, or native phosphate of lime.

PHOSPHORIZE, [fos'-fer-īz], *v.t.* to combine or impregnate with phosphorus.

PHOSPHOROUS, [fos'-fer-us], *adj.* containing phosphorus in its lower valency state.

PHOSPHORUS, [fos'-fer-us], *n.* (*chem.*) the non-metallic element denoted by P, a yellowish wax-like inflammable substance, appearing luminous in the dark. [Gk. *phosphorikos* light-bringing].

PHOSPHURETTED, [fos'-few-ret'-id], *adj.* combined with phosphorus.

PHOSSY-JAW, [fos'-i-jaw'], *n.* (*med.*) necrosis of the jaw due to poisoning by yellow phosphorus.

PHOTIZITE, [fō'-tiz-īt], *n.* silicate of manganese. [Gk. *photizo* I shine].

PHOTO-, *pref.* light. [Gk. *phos photos* light].

PHOTO, [fō'-tō], *n.* abbreviation of PHOTO(GRAPH).

PHOTOCHEMISTRY, [fō'-tō-kem'-ist-ri], *n.* the study of chemical changes caused by the action of light.

PHOTOCHROMOTYPE, [fō'-tō-krōm'-ō-tīp], *n.* printing in colours from photographic process blocks.

PHOTOCHROMY, [fō'-tō-krōm'-i], *n.* colour-photography; the art of colouring photographs. [PHOTO and Gk. *khroma* colour].

PHOTO-ELECTRIC CELL, [fō'-tō-il-ek'-trik-sel'], *n.* a cell whose electrical resistance varies according to the intensity of light to which it is exposed, used as a means of measuring small amounts of light, and recording slight changes in its intensity.

PHOTO-ENGRAVING, [fō'-tō-en-grāv'-ing], *n.* any

photographic process for producing printing blocks.

PHOTO-ETCHER, [fō'-tō-ech'-er], *n.* a maker of printing blocks by photographic processes.

PHOTOGENIC, [fō'-tō-jen'-ik], *adj.* producing light; applied to a subject which photographs well. [PHOTO and Gk. *genes* producing].

PHOTOGLYPH, [fō'-tō-glif'], *n.* an engraved plate produced by the chemical action of light. [PHOTO and Gk. *gluphe* carving].

PHOTOGLYPHY, [fō'-tō-glif'-i], *n.* the process of making engraving blocks by the action of light.

PHOTOGRAPH (1), [fō'-to-grahf], *n.* a negative picture produced by the action of light on a film or glass plate sensitized with a chemically prepared emulsion, and developed and fixed thereon by chemical means; a positive print on an emulsified paper made from this. [PHOTO and GRAPH].

PHOTOGRAPH (2), [fō'-to-grahf], *v.t.* to take a photograph or photographs of; *v.i.* to take photographs, to be a suitable subject for photography.

PHOTOGRAPHER, [fōt-og'-raf-er], *n.* one who photographs.

PHOTOGRAPHIC, [fō'-tō-graf'-ik], *adj.* pertaining to photography; resembling a photograph, faithfully recording or reproducing everything in the manner of a photograph.

PHOTOGRAPHICALLY, [fō'-tō-graf'-ik-al-i], *adv.* in a photographic manner, from the point of view of photography.

PHOTOGRAPHY, [fot-og'-raf-i], *n.* the process of taking photographs. [PHOTO and Gk. *graphia* writing].

PHOTOGRAVURE, [fō'-tō-grav-yōōer'], *n.* a photographic process by which printing plates are obtained, from which prints or engravings can be taken by intaglio printing. [PHOTO and Fr. *gravure* engraving].

PHOTO-LITHOGRAPHY, [fō'-tō-lith-og'-raf-i], *n.* the art of printing from photographs produced upon lithographic stone.

PHOTOLOGICAL, [fō'-to-loj'-ik-al], *adj.* relating to photology.

PHOTOLOGY, [fō-tol'-o-ji], *n.* (*archaic*) the science of light, optics. [PHOTO and Gk. *logos* speech].

PHOTOLYSIS, [fō-tol'-is-is], *n.* the action of light upon the movements of protoplasm. [PHOTO and Gk. *lusis* loosening].

PHOTOMATON, [fō-tom'-a-ton], *n.* (*prot.*) a machine which takes a series of portraits of a person's face in rapid succession.

PHOTOMECHANISM, [fō'-tō-mek'-an-izm], *n.* reproduction by means of process blocks.

PHOTOMETER, [fō-tom'-it-er], *n.* an instrument for measuring the intensity of light.

PHOTOMETRICAL, [fō'-tō-met'-rik-al], *adj.* relating to a photometer or to photometry.

PHOTOMETRY, [fot-om'-et-ri], *n.* the measurement of light and its intensity. [PHOTO and Gk. *metria* measurement].

PHOTO-MICROGRAPH, [fō'-tō-mī'-krō-grahf], *n.* a photograph of a microscopic object enlarged through a microscope.

PHOTO-MICROGRAPHY, [fō'-tō-mi-krog'-raf-i], *n.* the art of making photo-micrographs.

PHOTON, [fō'-ton], *n.* the smallest particle of light.

PHOTOPHOBIA, [fō'-tō-fō'-bi-a], *n.* morbid hatred of light.

PHOTOPHONE, [fō'-tō-fōn], *n.* an apparatus for transmitting sound vibrations by a beam of light, the sound vibrations causing variations in the intensity of the beam of light, and these variations being received upon a selenium cell, and changed back into sound vibrations. [PHOTO and Gk. *phonos* sounding].

PHOTOPHORE, [fō'-tō-faw(r)], *n.* a luminous organ producing phosphorescence in certain animals and fishes. [Gk. *photophoros* light-bearing].

PHOTOSCULPTURE, [fō'-tō-skulp'-cher], *n.* a photographic process for the production of statuettes, in which a subject is simultaneously photographed from all angles, and outlines in clay are modelled from these photographs.

PHOTOSPHERE, [fō'-tō-sfēer], *n.* the luminous envelope of the sun or a star.

PHOTOSTAT (1), [fō'-tō-stat], *n.* (*prot.*) an apparatus for obtaining direct, facsimile, photographic reproductions of a manuscript, drawing or other document without the necessity of printing from a negative, a reproduction or photographic copy obtained in this way.

PHOTOSTAT (2), [fō'-tō-stat], *v.t.* to take photostatic copies of.

PHOTOSTATIC, [fō'-tō-stat'-ik], *adj.* taken by means of a photostat, in the form of a photostat.

PHOTOTELEGRAPHY, [fō'-tō-tel-eg'-raf-i], *n.* the telegraphic transmission of photographs and drawings.

PHOTOTYPE (1), [fō'-tō-tīp], *n.* a photographic impression of an engraving from which copies can be printed, a process block.

PHOTOTYPE (2), [fō'-tō-tīp'], *v.t.* to make a phototype of.

PHOTOXYLOGRAPHY, [fō'-tō-zī-log'-raf-i], *n.* a photographic process for preparing wood blocks for printing or engraving from.

PHRAGMACONE, [frag'-mak-ōn], *n.* the chambered portion of the internal shell of a belemnite. [Gk. *phragmos* fence and CONE].

PHRASE (1), [frāz], *n.* a group of words used to express something and forming part of a sentence; a group of words corresponding in function to a single part of speech; (*archaic*) style or method of expression; a short idiomatic expression; a short telling expression or catchword; (*mus.*) a short passage considered as a unity in itself, yet forming part of a longer passage or complete division of a work; **p. book,** a book giving examples of the idioms and peculiar phrases of a language. [Gk. *phrasis* speech].

PHRASE (2), [frāz], *v.t.* to express in words or by a particular phrase, to use a particular idiom or combination of words to express. [*Prec.*].

PHRASEMONGER, [frāz'-mung'-ger], *n.* a coiner or repeater of phrases and catchwords.

PHRASEOGRAM, [frāz'-i-ō-gram'], *n.* a symbol representing a phrase, *esp.* in shorthand. [PHRASE and Gk. *gramma* writing].

PHRASEOLOGICAL, [frāz'-i-o-loj'-ik-al], *adj.* relating to phraseology; composed of phrases.

PHRASEOLOGY, [frāz-i-ol'-o-ji], *n.* manner of expression, diction, choice of words and phrases, *esp.* those characteristic of a period, person, people, etc. [PHRASE and Gk. *logos* speech].

PHRATRY, [frat'-ri], *n.* (*Gk. antiq.*) a clan or subdivision of the people; a tribal division amongst primitive peoples. [Gk. *phratria*].

PHRENETIC, [fren-et'-ik], *adj.* crazy, frantic, delirious. [Gk. *phrenetikos*].

PHRENIC, [fren'-ik], *adj.* (*anat.*) relating to the diaphragm. [Gk. *phren* diaphragm].

PHRENITIS, [fren-ī'-tis], *n.* an inflammation of the brain, attended with fever and delirium, brain-fever. [Gk. *phren* mind and *itis* denoting inflammation].

PHRENOLOGICAL, [fren'-o-loj'-ik-al], *adj.* relating to phrenology.

PHRENOLOGICALLY, [fren'-o-loj'-ik-a-li], *adv.* in accordance with phrenology.

PHRENOLOGIST, [fren-ol'-oj-ist], *n.* one who practises or believes in phrenology.

PHRENOLOGY, [fren-ol'-o-ji], *n.* the theory that the mental faculties and powers are connected with particular areas of action in the brain, and their development shown by the external undulations of the cranium; the art of reading the bumps on a person's skull. [Gk. *phren* mind and *logos* speech].

PHRENSY†, see FRENZY.

PHRYGIAN, [frij'-i-an], *adj.* pertaining, belonging, to Phrygia; **P. bonnet,** the cap worn by the French Revolutionaries as a symbol of liberty; **P. mode,** (*mus.*) one of the ancient Greek modes. [L. *Phrygianus*].

PHTHANITE, [tan'-īt], *n.* (*min.*) chert, an impure calcareous variety of flint. [Fr. *phthanite*].

PHTHIRIASIS, [thi-rī'-as-is], *n.* (*med.*) disease of the skin, characterized by great itching, and caused by the presence of large numbers of lice on the body, the louse disease. [Gk. *phtheiriasis* lousiness].

PHTHISICAL, [tī'-sikl], *adj.* of the nature of phthisis; suffering from phthisis, consumptive. [Gk. *phthisikos*].

PHTHISIOLOGY, [tī'-si-ol'-o-ji], *n.* a treatise on phthisis; the scientific study of consumption. [PHTHISIS and Gk. *logos* speech].

PHTHISIS, [tī'-sis], *n.* pulmonary consumption, tuberculosis of the lungs. [Gk. *phthisis* wasting].

PHUT, [fut], *adv.* **to go p.,** (*coll.*) to collapse, break down, cease to function, fail. [Hind. *phatna* to burst].

PHYCOGRAPHY, [fī-kog'-raf-i], *n.* a treatise on seaweeds. [Gk. *phukos* seaweed and *graphia* writing].

PHYCOLOGY, [fī-kol'-o-ji], *n.* the study of the algae, or seaweeds. [Gk *phukos* seaweed and *logos* speech].

PHYLACTERIC, [fil-ak′-ter-ik], *adj.* pertaining to phylacteries.

PHYLACTERY, [fil-ak′-ter-i], *n.* strips of parchment inscribed with certain texts of Scripture, enclosed in small leather cases, attached to the forehead or the left arm, and worn by the Jews at prayer as a reminder to observe the law; a charm or amulet worn as a safeguard against danger or disease, a talisman; (*fig.*) ostentatious profession of the outward forms of religion and righteousness; a case or chest in which is enclosed a holy relic. [Gk. *phulakterion* amulet].

PHYLARCHY, [fī′-lahk-i], *n.* government of a tribe. [Gk. *phularkhos*].

PHYLETIC, [fī-let′-ik], *adj.* pertaining to a tribe, phylum or race. [Gk. *phuletikos*].

PHYLLITE, [fil′-īt], *n.* a variety of magnesia-mica. [Gk. *phullon* leaf].

PHYLLO-, *pref.* leaf. [Gk. *phullon* leaf].

PHYLLODE, [fil′-ōd], *n.* a dilated and flattened leaf-stalk resembling, and taking the place of, a true leaf-blade. [Gk. *phullodes* like a leaf].

PHYLLOID, [fil′-oid], *n.* a leaf-like appendage or organ. [PHYLLO and Gk. *oeides* like].

PHYLLOPHAGANS, [fil-of′-ag-anz], *n.*(*pl.*) animals and insects that feed on leaves. [PHYLLO and Gk. *phagos* eating].

PHYLLOPHAGOUS, [fil-of′-ag-us], *adj.* leaf-eating.

PHYLLOPODS, [fil-ō-podz′], *n.*(*pl.*) a tribe of crustaceans with leaf-like feet. [PHYLLO and Gk. *pous podos* foot].

PHYLLOSTOM, [fil′-ō-stom], *n.* a leaf-nosed bat. [PHYLLO and Gk. *stoma* mouth].

PHYLLOSTOM

PHYLLOTAXIS, **PHYLLOTAXY**, [fil′-ō-taks′-i(s)], *n.* (*bot.*) the arrangement of leaves on the stem. [PHYLLO and Gk. *taxis* arrangement].

PHYLLOXERA, [fil′-oks-ēer′-a], *n.* a genus of plant lice destroying the roots and leaves of the grape-vine. [PHYLLO and Gk. *xeros* dry].

PHYLOGENESIS, [fī′-lō-jen′-is-is], *n.* evolution or development of a type, species or tribe. [Gk. *phulon* race and GENESIS].

PHYLOGENETIC, [fī′-lō-jen-et′-ik], *adj.* relating to phylogeny.

PHYLOGENY, [fī-loj′-en-i], *n.* the evolution or development of a type, species or race; history of the development of a tribe, race or species. [Gk. *phulon* tribe and *genea* birth].

PHYLUM, [fī′-lum], *n.* (*biol.*) a division or group of related animals or plants. [Gk. *phulon* race, tribe].

PHYMA, [fī′-ma], *n.* an inflamed swelling or tumour. [Gk. *phuma*].

PHYSALITE, [fis′-al-īt], *n.* a mineral of a yellowish-white colour; a variety of prismatic topaz. [Germ. *physalith*].

PHYSIC (1), [fiz′-ik], *n.* the science or art of healing diseases, the medical profession; a purgative medicine. [Gk. *phusike* natural science].

PHYSIC (2), [fiz′-ik], *v.t.* to treat with medicine, to dose.

PHYSICAL, [fiz′-ik-al], *adj.* pertaining to, connected with, material things or phenomena perceived by the senses; pertaining to physics or the forces of nature, dealing with the natural features of the world; in accordance with the laws of nature, from the point of view of physics; bodily, connected with the body as opposed to the mind or soul. [MedL. *physicalis*].

PHYSICALIST, [fiz′-ik-al-ist], *n.* one who believes that everything is to be explained in terms of physics and physical phenomena.

PHYSICALLY, [fiz′-ik-al-i], *adv.* according to the laws of nature or physics; bodily, with regard to the body.

PHYSICIAN, [fiz-ish′-an], *n.* a doctor of medicine, a member of the medical profession, one whose profession is to prescribe remedies in the form of medicines for the treatment of disease. [OFr. *fisicien*].

PHYSICISM, [fiz′-is-izm], *n.* a doctrine which assumes that everything is to be explained in terms of physics or physical forces, materialism.

PHYSICIST, [fiz′-is-ist], *n.* a student of physics, one who attempts to explain everything on physical principles.

PHYSICOLOGIC, [fiz′-i-kol-oj′-ik], *n.* logic illustrated by natural philosophy. [Gk. *phusikos* of nature and LOGIC].

PHYSICS, [fiz′-iks], *n.* the science dealing with the properties of matter and the effects of forces upon matter; (*archaic*) natural science, natural philosophy.

PHYSIO-, *pref.* nature. [Gk. *phusis* nature].

PHYSIOCRACY, [fiz′-i-ok′-ras-i], *n.* a system of political economy in which government should be based upon nature and natural laws, with a minimum of interference by the state. [PHYSIO and Gk. *kratia* rule].

PHYSIOCRAT, [fiz′-i-ō-krat′], *n.* one of a school of political economists who advocated physiocracy.

PHYSIOGENY, [fiz′-i-oj′-en-i], *n.* the evolution or development of the vital functions. [PHYSIO and Gk. *genea* birth].

PHYSIOGNOMIC, [fiz′-i-ō-nom′-ik], *adj.* pertaining to, skilled in, physiognomy; pertaining to the face as a guide to character.

PHYSIOGNOMIST, [fiz′-i-on′-om-ist], *n.* one who is skilled in physiognomy; one who is able to read a person's character from his face.

PHYSIOGNOMY, [fiz′-i-on′-o-mi], *n.* the art of judging character from the features or general appearance of a person; the countenance, *esp.* the type of face, or habitual expression of the face; (*vulg.*) the face; the general external appearance of a region, etc. [Gk. *phusiognomia*].

PHYSIOGRAPHER, [fiz′-i-og′-raf-er], *n.* a student of physiography.

PHYSIOGRAPHY, [fiz′-i-og′-raf-i], *n.* the branch of geography dealing with the natural features of the surface of the earth, physical geography. [PHYSIO and Gk. *graphia* writing].

PHYSIOLATRY, [fiz′-i-ol′-at-ri], *n.* nature worship. [PHYSIO and Gk. *latreia* worship].

PHYSIOLOGICAL, [fiz′-i-o-loj′-ik-al], *adj.* relating to physiology.

PHYSIOLOGICALLY, [fiz′-i-ō-loj′-ik-al-i], *adv.* according to physiology.

PHYSIOLOGIST, [fiz′-i-ol′-oj-ist], *n.* an authority upon physiology.

PHYSIOLOGY, [fiz′-i-ol′-o-ji], *n.* the science dealing with the constituent parts of living organisms, whether animal or vegetable, and their functions. [Gk. *phusiologia* knowledge of nature].

PHYSIQUE, [fiz-ēk′], *n.* bodily structure or appearance, physical development, build. [Fr. *physique*].

PHYSOGRADE (1), [fiz′-ō-grād], *n.* a member of the *Physograda*, a group of oceanic hydrozoa, moving by means of a hollow float or air-bladder. [Gk. *phusa* bladder and L. *gradus* moving].

PHYSOGRADE (2), [fiz′-ō-grād], *adj.* moving by means of a hollow air-bladder.

PHYTO-, *pref.* plant. [Gk. *phuton* plant].

PHYTOGENESIS, [fī′-tō-jen′-is-is], *n.* the study of the evolution or generation of plants.

PHYTOGENY, [fī-toj′-en-i], *n.* phytogenesis. [PHYTO and Gk. *geneia* birth].

PHYTOGEOGRAPHY, [fī′-tō-jē-og′-raf-i], *n.* the study of the distribution of plants over the surface of the earth.

PHYTOGRAPHY, [fī-tog′-raf-i], *n.* descriptive systematic botany. [PHYTO and Gk. *graphia* writing].

PHYTOID, [fī′-toid], *adj.* plant-like. [PHYTO and Gk. *oeides* like].

PHYTOLOGIST, [fī-tol′-oj-ist], *n.* a botanist.

PHYTOLOGY, [fī-tol′-o-ji], *n.* botany. [PHYTO and Gk. *logos* speech].

PHYTONOMY, [fī-ton′-o-mi], *n.* the science of the laws of vegetable growth. [PHYTO and Gk. *nomos* law].

PHYTOPHAGOUS, [fī-tof′-ag-us], *adj.* eating plants. [PHYTO and Gk. *phagos* eating].

PI (1), [pī], *n.* (*math.*) the symbol π (the Greek P) of the ratio of the circumference to the diameter of a circle.

PI (2), see PIE (3).

PIACULAR, [pī-ak′-yŏŏ-ler], *adj.* expiatory, requiring expiation, atrociously bad, utterly wicked. [L. *piacularis*].

PIAFFE, [pē-af′], *v.i.* (of a horse) to amble along at an easy trot. [Fr. *piaffer* to paw the ground].

PIAFFER, [pē-af′-er], *n.* a slow trot. [Fr. *piaffer*].

PIA MATER, [pī′-a-mā′-ter], *n.* the innermost of the three membranes in which the brain and spinal cord are enveloped. [MedL. *pia mater* a translation of Arab. *umm raqiqah* tender mother].

PIANETTE, [pē-an-et'], *n.* a small upright piano.

PIANINO, [pē-an-ē'-no], *n.* a pianette. [It. *pianino*, *dim.* of *piano* soft].

PIANISSIMO, [pē'-an-is'-im-ō], *adj. and adv.* (*mus.*) very softly. [It. *pianissimo*].

PIANIST, [pē'-an-ist], *n.* one who plays the piano.

PIANO (1), [pi-an'-o], *n.* a keyed musical instrument in which the notes are produced by the action of hammers, operated by the keyboard, striking against wires tuned to a certain pitch; **grand p.,** a large piano in which the strings are placed horizontally, and struck by hammers placed below them; **upright p.,** a piano in which the strings are placed vertically; **p. accordion,** an accordion in which the keys are arranged similarly to those of a piano. [Abbrev. of PIANOFORTE].

PIANO (2), [pi-ahn'-ō], *adv.* (*mus.*) softly. [It. *piano*].

PIANOFORTE, [pi-an'-ō-faw'-ti], *n.* a piano. [It. *piano e forte* soft and loud].

PIANOLA, [pē'-an-ō'-la], *n.* (*prot.*) an automatic piano operated by pedals.

PIANO-TUNER, [pi-an'-ō-tewn'-er], *n.* one who tunes a piano.

PIASSABA, [pi-as-ah'-ba], *n.* a vegetable fibre from Brazil, obtained from *Leopoldinia Piassaba* or *Attalea funifera*, used in making brushes. [Tupi *piasaba*].

PIASTRE, [pē-as'-ter], *n.* a small silver coin varying in value from twopence to sixpence, used in Turkey, Egypt, etc.; the Spanish dollar or piece-of-eight. [It. *piastra* metal plate].

PIAZZA, [pē-at'-sa], *n.* an open square or market-place surrounded by buildings; (*U.S.*) the verandah of a house. [It. *piazza*].

PIBROCH, [pib'-rok], *n.* a special kind of music played on the Highland bagpipe, usually a march or a dirge. [Gael. *piobaireachd*].

PICA, [pī'-ka], *n.* (*eccles.*) †a collection of rules for dealing with the possible clashing of religious devotional services as a result of the movable feasts; (*typ.*) a standard large size of type averaging six lines to the inch; (*path.*) a morbid craving for substances unfit for food as chalk, clay, coal, etc., caused by certain diseases. [L. *pica* magpie].

PICADOR, [pik'-ad-aw(r)], *n.* a mounted rider in a bull-fight, armed with a lance, who rouses and infuriates the bull by pricking him. [Span. *picador* from *picar* to prick].

PICAMAR, [pik'-am-ah(r)], *n.* thick bitter oil obtained by distilling wood-tar. [L. *pix picis* pitch and *amarus* bitter].

PICARESQUE, [pik'-a-resk'], *adj.* (of literature) concerned with the exploits of rogues and adventurers. [Span. *picaresco* from *picaro* rogue].

PICARIAN, [pik-āer'-i-an], *adj.* of, relating to, the *Picariae*, an order of non-passerine birds. [L. *picus* woodpecker].

PICAROON (1), [pik'-a-rōōn'], *n.* a rogue, a plunderer, a pirate; a pirate ship. [Span. *picaron*].

PICAROON (2), [pik'-a-rōōn'], *v.i.* to engage in piracy; to live as an adventurer or trickster.

PICAYUNE, [pik'-ā-yōōn'], *n.* a small silver coin of the Southern States, U.S.A., worth 6¼ cents, now obsolete; (*U.S. slang*) anything mean or of slight worth. [Provenc. *picaioun* copper coin].

PICAYUNISH, [pik'-a-yewn'-ish], *adj.* (*U.S.*) niggling over trivial details.

PICCALILLI, [pik'-a-lil'-i], *n.* a kind of mixed pickle made with chopped vegetables, mustard and boiling vinegar. [Unkn.].

PICCANINNY, PICKANINNY, [pik'-a-nin'-i], *n.* (*coll.*) a negro baby; a small child. [Span. *pequeño* child].

PICCOLO, [pik'-ol-ō], *n.* a small flute, with the notes an octave higher in pitch than the ordinary flute. [It. *piccolo* small].

PICE, [pis], *n.* an Indian coin, the fourth of an anna. [Hind. *paisa*].

PICHURIM-BEAN, [pich'-er-im-bēn'], *n.* the seed-lobe of the South American plant *Nectandra Puchury*, used to flavour chocolate. [Native].

PICK (1), [pik], *n.* a tool consisting of a slightly curved narrow bar of iron, one end of which is pointed and the other shaped like a chisel, through the centre of which is fastened a wooden handle set at right angles to it, used for breaking up ground, etc.; any sharp pointed instrument used for picking. [PIKE (1)].

PICK (2), [pik], *n.* the act of picking, the right of selection; that which is picked, choice; the best, the choicest; (*print.*) dirt, caked ink or other foul matter collecting in the hollows of printing types.

PICK (3), [pik], *v.t.* to break up with a pick; to make or dig with a pick; to pluck with the fingers so as to remove or detach, to gather; to choose, select; to separate so as to loosen or pull apart; to strike with or take up into the beak; (of a lock) to open by a pointed instrument other than a key; to steal from, to remove the contents of feloniously; *v.i.* to steal; to eat slowly and without appetite, to nibble; **to p. on,** to select as an object of questioning, censure, reproach, etc.; **to p. out,** to select; to distinguish, recognize, make out; to make colourful or conspicuous, to set in relief or contrast; to play (a tune); **to p. up,** to take hold of in the hand or arms, to gather; to take in, to receive more (passengers); to meet with; to obtain (a living); to become acquainted with; to acquire; to regain; (*wirel.*) to succeed in receiving signals from; to make out, see by means of a searchlight, etc.; *v.i.* (*motoring*) to accelerate; (*elect*). to reach full voltage; (*coll.*) to be better in health, to become more lively and cheerful; **to p. a quarrel with,** to engage in dispute with; **to p. holes in,** to criticize minutely, to point out the flaws in; **to have a bone to p. with,** to have a cause of quarrel against. [~OE. *pican*].

PICKABACK, [pik'-a-bak'], *adv.* on the back of another in the manner of a pack carried on the shoulders. [PACK].

PICKAGE, [pik'-ij], *n.* (*leg.*) money paid at fairs for breaking the ground in order to erect stalls, etc.

PICKANINNY, see PICCANINNY.

PICKAXE (1), [pik'-aks'], *n.* a pick for breaking up ground, etc. [OFr. *picois*].

PICKAXE (2), [pik'-aks'], *v.t.* to strike or break with a pickaxe; *v.i.* to use a pickaxe.

PICKAXE

PICKED†, [pikt], *adj.* pointed.

PICKER, [pik'-er], *n.* one who picks or gathers; an instrument for picking or separating.

PICKEREL (1), [pik'-er-el], *n.* a young pike; (*U.S.*) a freshwater fish of the genus *Esox*; **p. weed,** one of various species of pondweed.

PICKEREL (2), [pik'-er-el], *n.* the dunlin, *Tringa alpina*.

PICKERINGITE, [pik'-er-ing-īt], *n.* a variety of magnesian alum. [J. *Pickering*, a former president of the American Academy].

PICKET (1), [pik'-et], *n.* a small sharp pointed stake or peg used in making a palisade, etc.; (*milit.*) a small body of men selected as an outpost or for special duty or service, formerly the military punishment of being made to stand on a pointed stake; a striker posted on guard outside a place of employment during a strike, to dissuade blacklegs or non-unionists from continuing at work. [Fr. *piquet* stake].

PICKET (2), [pik'-et], *v.t.* to enclose, secure, fortify or fasten with pickets; to post as a picket; to patrol with pickets; *v.i.* to endeavour to dissuade persons from remaining at work by the use of pickets; to act as picket.

PICKING, [pik'-ing], *n.* the act of one who picks; (*pl.*) gleanings, scraps left behind; petty objects obtained by theft.

PICKLE (1), [pikl], *n.* a solution of salt and water or vinegar, etc., in which foodstuffs are seasoned and preserved; (*pl.*) vegetables preserved in pickle and used as a condiment; a weak acid solution used for scouring metals, etc.; an awkward situation, a fix, an unfavourable condition; (*coll.*) a mischievous child, a scamp; **to have a rod in p. for,** to have trouble or punishment coming to. [MDu. *pekel*].

PICKLE (2), [pikl], *v.t.* to preserve in pickle; to scour or clean with pickle; (*naut.*) to rub salt or vinegar into after flogging.

PICKLED, [pikld], *adj.* (*slang*) drunk, intoxicated.

PICKLE-HERRING, [pikl'-he'-ring], *n.* (*slang*) a merry-andrew, a clown, jester.

PICKLOCK, [pik'-lok'], *n.* a tool for opening locks without the key; a person who picks locks.

PICK-ME-UP, [pik'-mi-up'], *n.* a stimulant, tonic.

PICKPOCKET, [pik'-pok'-it], *n.* one who steals from the pocket of another.

PICKTHANK, [pik'-thangk'], *n.* †an informer; a flatterer, one who continually curries favour.

PICKTOOTH, [pik'-tōōth], *n.* a tooth-pick; (*bot.*) the plant *Ammi Visnaga*.

PICK-UP, [pik'-up], *n.* (*wirel.*) a broadcast received by a wireless station from another, and in turn transmitted by this station to its listeners; a point in the route covered by a motor bus or motor coach service at which passengers may be picked up; an electrical device fitted to a gramophone, by means of which a record may be heard through the loudspeaker of a wireless set.

PICNIC (1), [pik'-nik], *n.* a pleasurable outing into the country or to the seaside in which an outdoor meal is eaten, the members of the party usually taking with them the food for this; (*coll.*) an easy matter, that which presents no difficulty at all; an uncommonly good or lively time. [Fr. *pique-nique*].

PICNIC (2), [picnicking, picnicked), [pik'-nik], *v.i.* to go on, take part in, a picnic.

PICOT, [pēk'-ō], *n.* a small loop of thread used as edging. [Fr. *picot*].

PICOTEE, [pik-ot-ē'], *n.* (*hort.*) a variety of the pink in which the edges of the petals are often a darker colour than the flowers. [Fr. *picoté*].

PICOTITE, [pik'-ot-īt], *n.* one of the spinel group of minerals containing chromium. [*Picot*, Baron de la Peyrouse, a French mineralogist].

PICQUET†, see PIQUET.

PICRATE, [pik'-rāt], *n.* a salt of picric acid.

PICRIC, [pik'-rik], *n.* (*chem.*) pertaining to picrin; **p. acid,** trinitro-phenol, a bitter yellow crystalline substance used in dyeing, making explosives, and treating burns. [Gk. *pikros* bitter].

PICRIN, [pik'-rin], *n.* a bitter substance procured from the foxglove. [Gk. *pikros* bitter].

PICRITE, [pik'-rīt], *n.* a blackish-green crystalline rock containing traces of olivine. [Gk. *pikros* bitter].

PICROLITE, [pik'-rol-īt], *n.* a fibrous variety of serpentine. [Gk. *pikros* bitter and *lithos* stone].

PICROMEL, [pik'-rō-mel'], *n.* a sharp sweet substance obtained from bile. [Gk. *pikros* bitter and *meli* honey].

PICROSMINE, [pik'-roz-min], *n.* a mineral which, when moistened, has an argillaceous smell. [Germ. *picrosmin* from Gk. *pikros* bitter and *osme* odour].

PICROTOXIN, [pik'-rō-toks'-in], *n.* a bitter principle obtained from the seeds of *Cocculus indicus*. [Gk. *pikros* bitter and TOXIN].

PICT, [pikt], *n.* one of a race of people formerly dwelling in the north-east of Scotland; **Picts' houses,** ancient stone dwellings in Scotland in which no mortar was used. [LL. *Picti* painted (people)].

PICTORIAL (1), [pik-taw'-ri-al], *n.* an illustrated journal.

PICTORIAL (2), [pik-taw'-ri-al], *adj.* pertaining to, consisting of, containing, illustrated by, pictures; picturesque, like or suitable for a picture. [L. *pictorius* pertaining to painters].

PICTORIALLY, [pik-taw'-ri-a-li], *adv.* in a pictorial manner, by means of pictures.

PICTURE (1), [pik'-cher], *n.* a painting, a drawing, or photograph; likeness, image; a mental image or concept; a graphic description; a cinematograph film; the representation, embodiment or example (of an abstract quality or thing); (*pl.*) the cinema; (*coll.*) a strikingly beautiful or picturesque person, object or scene; **p. book,** a book for children, consisting chiefly of pictures; **p. card,** a court-card or face-card; **p. gallery,** an apartment or building for the exhibition of pictures; **p. hat,** a wide-brimmed hat worn by women; **p. house, p. palace,** a cinema; **p. writing,** the use of pictures instead of written characters to express ideas, words, etc. [L. *pictura*].

PICTURE (2), [pik'-cher], *v.t.* to draw, paint, represent in a picture; to describe vividly; to imagine, form a picture of in the mind, to conceive.

PICTURESQUE, [pik'-cher-esk'], *adj.* like, suitable for, forming, a pleasing or pretty picture; vivid, forceful, graphic; strikingly original and interesting, colourful. [It. *pittoresco*].

PICTURESQUELY, [pik-cher-esk'-li], *adv.* in picturesque fashion.

PICTURESQUENESS, [pik'-cher-esk'-nes], *n.* the quality of being picturesque.

PICUL, [pik'-ul], *n.* Chinese weight of 133⅓ pounds. [Malay *pikul*].

PIDDLE, [pidl], *v.i.* to toy with one's food, to eat slowly and in small quantities without relish or appetite; to trifle, dabble, dally, to play (at or with); (*coll.*) to make water. [PUDDLE].

PIDDLING, [pid'-ling], *adj.* paltry, insignificant. [*Prec.*].

PIDDOCK, [pid'-ok], *n.* a bivalve mollusc of the genus *Pholas*. [Unkn.].

PIDGIN-, PIGEON-ENGLISH, [pij'-un-ing'-glish], *n.* jargon or a bastard form of English used as a medium of communication between the Chinese natives and the English traders in Chinese ports. [Chin. corruption of BUSINESS ENGLISH].

PIE (1), [pī], *n.* a crust baked with meat or fruit in it or under it; (*coll.*) that which presents no difficulty at all; **to have a finger in the p.,** to be concerned or directly interested in a transaction or other activity. [ME. *pie*].

PIE (2), [pī], *n.* the magpie; a variety of woodpecker; (*eccles.*) a collection of rules for dealing with movable feasts in arranging devotional services. [OFr. *pie* from L. *pica* magpie].

PIE (3), PI, [pī], *n.* (*print.*) a confused mixture of printing type; (*fig.*) a medley, jumble, mix-up, chaos. [Unkn.].

PIE (4), [pī], *n.* a small Anglo-Indian copper coin. [Hind. *pa'i*].

PIE (5), [pī], *v.t.* (*print.*) to make into pie.

PIEBALD, [pī'-bawld], *adj.* marked with large irregular patches of two different colours, one light and one dark; (*fig.*) motley, of mixed constituents or character. [PIE (2) and BALD].

PIECE (1), [pēs], *n.* a separate part, bit or fragment; a portion or fraction; some, a quantity, an amount; a definite limited area of land; a single object, *esp.* when forming part of a set; a firearm; a coin; one of a set of draughts or chessmen; an individual example or specimen; a literary, musical or artistic composition; a definite or specific quantity; a sheet of paper; a length of cloth or wallpaper; (*coll.*) a girl or woman; **a p. of work,** a creation, production; **by the p.,** according to the quantity or amount; **a p.,** (*coll.*) each; **of a p.,** of the same kind; **a p. of eight,** a Spanish dollar; **to give a p. of one's mind,** to say exactly what one thinks about something or someone. [LL. *pecia*].

PIECE (2), [pēs], *v.t.* to join, mend, patch, unite, *esp.* to fasten together the threads in spinning; **to p. out,** to extend by the addition of a piece or pieces; **to p. together,** to fit together into a whole; **to p. up,** to patch.

PIECE DE RESISTANCE, pièce de résistance, [pyes'-de-rāz-ēs-tah(ng)s'], *n.* the chief item, principal feature, *esp.* of a meal. [Fr. *pièce de résistance*].

PIECE GOODS, [pēs'-gŏŏdz], *n.*(*pl.*) fabrics woven in definite, standardized lengths.

PIECEMEAL (1), [pēs'-mēl], *adj.* made, done, piece by piece.

PIECEMEAL (2), [pēs'-mēl'], *adv.* by pieces, bit by bit, a little at a time. [PIECE (1) and OE. *mæl* measure].

PIECER, [pēs'-er], *n.* one who pieces, *esp.* one employed in joining the threads in spinning.

PIECE-WORK, [pēs'-wurk], *n.* work paid according to the amount done, and not according to the time spent in doing it.

PIED, [pīd], *adj.* marked or coloured with two contrasting colours, variegated, parti-coloured; (*print.*) disarranged (type). [PIE (2) and (3)].

PIEDNESS, [pīd'-nes], *n.* the quality of being pied.

PIEMAN, [pī'-man], *n.* a maker or seller of pies.

PIENO, [pē-ā'-nō], *adj.* (*mus.*) in full; with all performing. [It. *pieno*].

PIER, [pēer], *n.* a solid column or mass of stone or brick for taking the thrust of an arch, the span of a bridge, or for supporting the roof of a building; the supporting wall between windows and doors; a mole or breakwater; a jetty or wharf projecting into the sea, and used as a landing-stage, sometimes equipped with seats, and providing entertainments for seaside visitors. [LL. *pera*].

PIERAGE, [pēer'-ij], *n.* toll for using a pier.

PIERCE, [pēers], *v.t.* to penetrate, to break through the surface and enter; to thrust a pointed instrument into, to cause to be penetrated by (a point), to make a hole in; to make itself perceptible through, to be seen, heard or felt through; to affect deeply, to afflict sorely, stab; *v.i.* to penetrate, enter, make a hole. [OFr. *percer*].

PIERCEABLE, [pēers'-abl], *adj.* able to be pierced.

PIERCER, [pēers'-er], *n.* one who, or that which, pierces.

PIERCING, [pēers'-ing], *adj.* keen, sharp, penetrating with force.

PIERCINGLY, [pēers'-ing-li], *adv.* in a piercing way.

PIERCINGNESS, [pēers'-ing-nes], *n.* the quality of being piercing.

PIER-GLASS, [pēer'-glahs], *n.* a long narrow mirror, formerly set between windows.

PIERIAN, [pī-ēer'-i-an], *adj.* pertaining to Pieria or to the Muses. [L. *Pierius* pertaining to Pieria, the mountain in Thrace, where the Muses were worshipped].

PIERRETTE, [pēer-et'], *n.* a female pierrot. [Fr. *pierrette*].

PIERROT, [pēer'-ō], *n.* a clownish character in French pantomime; one of a group of entertainers or minstrel troupe dressed in loose-fitting clown's clothes. [Fr. *pierrot, dim.* of *Pierre* Peter].

PIER-TABLE, [pēer'-tābl], *n.* a table between windows.

PIET, [pī'-et], *n.* (*dial.*) the magpie, the dipper or water-ouzel, *Cinclus aquaticus*. [ME. *piot*].

PIETA, [pē-ā'-ta], *n.* a representation of the Virgin Mary lamenting over the dead body of Jesus resting in her lap. [It. *pietà*].

PIETISM, [pī'-et-izm], *n.* the principles and practices of the Pietists; religious devotion, piety, godliness; affected hypocritical pious cant, uncontrolled hysterical religious fervour.

PIETIST, [pī'-et-ist], *n.* one of a group of seventeenth century Lutheran reformers who began a religious revival; one who attaches supreme importance to piety and to emotional religious fervour.

PIETISTIC, [pī'-et-ist'-ik], *adj.* pertaining to, affecting, pietism.

PIETRA-DURA, [pē-e'-tra-dōō'-ra], *n.* the finest kind of Florentine mosaic work. [It. *pietra dura* hard stone].

PIETY, [pī'-et-i], *n.* godliness, sincere devotion to, and reverence for, God, and faithful observance of religious principles and practices; respect for filial bonds, duties, and obligations; natural affection between parents and offspring. [L. *pietas* loyalty].

PIEWIFE, [pī'-wīf], *n.* the lapwing.

PIEZO-ELECTRIC, [pī'-ez-ō-i-lek'-trik], *adj.* of, pertaining to, operating by, electric currents generated in certain crystals by physical pressure. [Gk. *piezo* I press and ELECTRIC].

PIEZOMETER, [pī'-ez-om'-it-er], *n.* an instrument for measuring the compressibility of fluids; an instrument for measuring the pressure of gas or water in a confined space; an instrument for measuring the sensitiveness to pressure of different areas of the body. [Gk. *piezo* I press and METER].

PIFFERO, [pif'-er-ō], *n.* a primitive form of oboe; the Italian bagpipe. [It. *piffero*].

PIFFLE (1), [pifl], *n.* nonsense, rubbish.

PIFFLE (2), [pifl], *v.t. and i.* (*rare*) to talk or act in a stupid, meaningless manner. [Uncert.].

PIG (1), [pig], *n.* a swine or hog, originally a young swine; any member of the family *Suidæ*, a class of hoofed mammals with snouts; the flesh of the hog, eaten as food; (*fig.*) a selfish, greedy, ill-mannered, highly objectionable individual; an oblong mass of unforged metal; **to buy a p. in a poke**, to buy something without knowing how much it is really worth. [ME. *pigge*].

PIG (2), [pig], *n.* an earthenware vessel. [Unkn.].

PIG (3), (**pigging, pigged**), [pig], *v.t. and i.* to bring forth pigs, to lie together or herd like pigs; to crowd together like pigs; **to p. it**, to live like a pig.

PIGEON (1), [pij'-un], *n.* a wild or tame bird of the dove family; (*slang*) a person easily imposed on and swindled; **clay p.**, a clay disk thrown up into the air from a trap, to be shot at; **p. post**, a system of letter-carrying using homing pigeons; **pigeon's foot**, the long-stalked geranium, *Geranium columbinum*. [OFr. *pijon*].

PIGEON

PIGEON (2), [pij'-un], *v.t.* to fleece, cheat, swindle. [*Prec.*].

PIGEON-BREASTED, [pij'-un-brest'-id], *adj.* having a breast shaped like that of a pigeon.

PIGEON-ENGLISH, see PIDGIN-ENGLISH.

PIGEON-HEARTED, [pij'-un-haht'-id], *adj.* timid.

PIGEON-HOLE (1), [pij'-un-hōl], *n.* an entrance in a dovecot; a small recess or open compartment in a desk, etc., for keeping documents, etc., in order.

PIGEON-HOLE (2), [pij'-un-hōl'], *v.t.* to file or put in a pigeon-hole; to put aside for future reference; to classify, arrange in the proper order, and under the proper headings or divisions; to build a series of pigeon-holes for the reception of letters or documents.

PIGEON-HOUSE, [pij'-un-hows'], *n.* a dovecot.

PIGEON-LIVERED, [pij'-un-liv'-erd], *adj.* timid, easily frightened.

PIGEON-PEA, [pij'-un-pē'], *n.* a kind of pulse, the seed of the leguminous shrub, *Cajanus indicus*.

PIGEONRY, [pij'-un-ri], *n.* a building in which pigeons are housed.

PIGEON-TOED, [pij'-un-tōd'], *adj.* with turned-in toes.

PIG-EYED, [pig'-īd], *adj.* having small eyes set deep in the head.

PIGGERY, [pig'-er-i], *n.* an enclosure or establishment where pigs are kept, a pigsty; (*fig.*) an untidy dwelling.

PIGGIN, [pig'-in], *n.* a small wooden drinking vessel, a wooden pail. [Uncert.].

PIGGISH, [pig'-ish], *adj.* like a pig, pigheaded.

PIGGY, [pig'-i], *n.* (*child's talk*) a pig.

PIGHEADED, [pig'-hed'-id], *adj.* stupidly obstinate.

PIGHEADEDLY, [pig'-hed'-id-li], *adv.* obstinately.

PIGHEADEDNESS, [pig'-hed'-id-nes], *n.* the quality of being pigheaded.

PIG-IRON, [pig'-īern], *n.* iron from a blast-furnace cast in oblong moulds.

PIGLET, [pig'-let], *n.* a young pig.

PIGMEAN, see PYGMEAN.

PIGMENT, [pig'-ment], *n.* a dry colour powder for paint; paint; colouring matter, *esp.* the natural colouring matter of a plant or animal. [L. *pigmentum*].

PIGMENTAL, [pig'-ment'-al], *adj.* pertaining to, consisting of, producing, pigment.

PIGMENTARY, [pig'-ment'-er-i], *adj.* pigmental. [L. *pigmentarius*].

PIGMENTATION, [pig'-ment-ā'-shun], *n.* coloration due to the presence of pigment in the tissue.

PIGMY, see PYGMY.

PIGNORATE, [pig'-ner-āt], *v.t.* to pledge, mortgage, give as security. [L. *pignorare*].

PIGNORATION, [pig'-ner-ā'-shun], *n.* the act of pledging. [*Prec.*].

PIGNUT, [pig'-nut], *n.* the earthnut, *Bunium flexuosum*.

PIGSKIN, [pig'-skin], *n.* leather made from the skin of the pig; (*slang*) the saddle.

PIGSTICKING, [pig'-stik-ing], *n.* hunting the wild boar with a spear on horseback.

PIGSTY, [pig'-sti], *n.* a sty or pen in which pigs are kept; an untidy room or dwelling.

PIGTAIL, [pig'-tāl], *n.* a plait of hair worn hanging down the back; a small roll of twisted tobacco.

PIKE (1), [pīk], *n.* a weapon consisting of a long wooden shaft with a pointed flat steel head. [Fr. *pique*].

PIKE (2), [pīk], *n.* the large voracious freshwater fish, *Esox lucius*. [ME. *pik*].

PIKE (3), [pīk], *n.* (*dial.*) a hill with a pointed summit or peak. [Norse *pik*].

PIKE (4), [pīk], *n.* a toll-bar or toll-gate; the toll paid at such a gate; a turnpike road. [(TURN)PIKE].

PIKED, [pīkt], *adj.* ending in a point, equipped with a sharp point.

PIKELET, [pīk'-let], *n.* a crumpet, muffin. [Wel. (*bara*)-*pyglyd* bread of pitch].

PIKEMAN, [pīk'-man], *n.* a soldier armed with a pike; a miner who uses a pick; the keeper of a toll-bar.

PIKER, [pīk'-er], *n.* (*U.S. slang*) one who gambles timidly and on a very modest scale, one afraid to risk his money or take a chance. [PIKE (4)].

PIKESTAFF, [pīk'-stahf], *n.* the shaft of a pike; **plain as a p.**, perfectly clear.

PILASTER, [pil-ast'-er], *n.* a square pillar, with a capital and base, projecting from the face of a wall. [MedL. *pilastrum*].

PILAU, PILAW, [pil-aw'], *n.* an Oriental dish consisting of rice boiled with fowl, meat or fish and flavoured with spices. [Pers. *pilaw*].

PILCH, [pilch], *n.* an infant's wrapper or drawers over the napkin; a light children's saddle; †an outer cloak made of animal's skin trimmed with hair. [OE. *pylece* from L. *pellicea* a fur coat].

PILCHARD, [pil'-cherd], *n.* a small edible sea-fish of the herring family, *Clupea pilchardus*. [Unkn.].

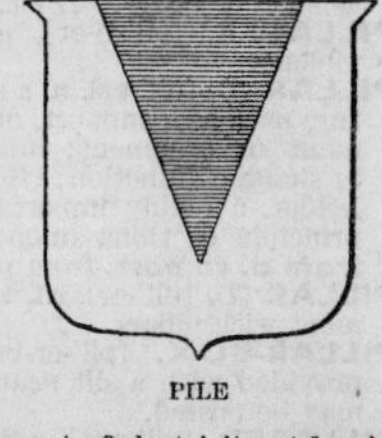

PILE

PILE (1), [pīl], *n.* a heap, a mass or collection of objects stacked up, one upon another, in more or less orderly fashion; a heaped-up mass of combustibles on which a corpse is burnt; a large imposing building or group of buildings; (*elect.*) a series of plates so arranged as to produce a current of electricity; (*slang*) a large amount of money, a fortune. [L. *pila* pillar].

PILE (2), [pīl], *n.* a pointed stake, a large stake driven into the bed of a river or soft, marshy ground as support for the foundations of a building, etc.; an iron or concrete pillar used for the same purpose; (*her.*) a charge in the form of two lines meeting in an acute angle like an arrow-head, issuing from the chief and pointing downwards. [OE. *pil* from L. *pilum* javelin].

PILE (3), [pīl], *n.* the nap or fine, soft, hairy substance on the surface of woven fabrics such as velvet, plush, carpet, etc. [L. *pilus* hair].

PILE (4), [pīl], *n.* (*archaic*) the reverse side of a coin. [OFr. *pile*].

PILE (5), [pīl], *v.t.* to form or arrange in a heap or pile, to stack up, to load; **to p. up,** to accumulate, amass, collect; **to p. on,** to intensify, add to. [PILE (1)].

PILE (6), [pīl], *v.t.* to drive piles into; to support with piles. [PILE (2)].

PILEATE, [pil'-i-āt], *adj.* (*bot., zool.*) having a cap-like structure. [L. *pileatus*].

PILEATED, [pil'-i-āt-id], *adj.* pileate.

PILEDRIVER, [pil'-drīv'-er], *n.* a machine for driving down piles; (*coll.*) a powerful blow.

PILER, [pīl'-er], *n.* one who piles.

PILES, [pīlz], *n.*(*pl.*) haemorrhoids, tumours formed by the dilatation of the veins of the lower rectum. [L. *pila* ball].

PILEUS, [pil'-ē-us], *n.* (*class. antiq.*) the brimless felt hat of the Greeks and Romans; (*bot.*) the cap or umbrella-shaped top of a mushroom. [L. *pileus*].

PILEWORM, [pīl'-wurm], *n.* the shipworm, a boring mollusc of the genus *Teredo.*

PILEWORT, [pīl'-wurt], *n.* the lesser celandine, *Ranunculus Ficaria,* a perennial plant related to the buttercup, and whose roots were used in treating piles.

PILFER, [pil'-fer], *v.t. and i.* to steal on a small scale, to practise petty theft. [OFr. *pelfrer*].

PILFERER, [pil'-fer-er], *n.* one who pilfers.

PILFERING, [pil'-fer-ing], *n.* petty theft or larceny.

PILFERINGLY, [pil'-fer-ing-li], *adv.* in a pilfering fashion.

PILGARLIC, [pil-gahl'-ik], *n.* a poor, forsaken wretch. [PILL (2) and GARLIC].

PILGRIM, [pil'-grim], *n.* (*poet., archaic*) a traveller, wayfarer; one who makes a journey to a holy place or shrine from religious motives; **P. Fathers,** a band of Puritans who set sail from Plymouth and landed in North America, where they founded the colony of New Plymouth in 1620; **pilgrim's shell,** a scallop shell worn as a sign of having visited certain well-known shrines. [ME. *pelegrim* from L. *peregrinus* foreigner].

PILGRIMAGE, [pil'-grim-ij], *n.* a journey to some holy place or shrine; a visit to some place revered because of its associations; (*fig.*) the journey of human life. [*Prec.*].

PILIFEROUS, [pī-lif'-er-us], *adj.* bearing hair, covered with hair, hairy. [L. *pilus* hair and *ferre* to bear].

PILIGEROUS, [pī-lij'-er-us], *adj.* piliferous, hairy, coarse. [L. *pilus* hair and *gerere* to bear].

PILL (1), [pil], *n.* a medicinal substance in the form of a small ball or pellet to be swallowed whole; (*slang*) a ball used for games; **the bitter p.,** an unpleasant thing that must be suffered; **to gild the p.,** to make the unpleasant more palatable. [L. *pilula, dim.* of *pila* ball].

PILL (2), [pil], *v.t.* (*archaic*) to rob, plunder, pillage, spoil; to peel, to remove the rind, outer skin, bark, etc.; *v.i.* to become peeled. [ME. *pillen* probably from OFr. *piller*].

PILLAGE (1), [pil'-ij], *n.* the act of plundering or robbing; spoil, plunder taken from an enemy in war. [Fr. *pillage*].

PILLAGE (2), [pil'-ij], *v.t.* to plunder, to loot; to take as spoil or booty. [*Prec.*].

PILLAGER, [pil'-ij-er], *n.* one who plunders with violence.

PILLAR (1), [pil'-er], *n.* a single slender upright structure used as a support, or standing alone as a monument or ornament; anything resembling a pillar in shape or function; (*fig.*) a prop, supporter or upholder, a highly important member; foundation, a principle or thing upon which anything is based; **from p. to post,** from place to place. [ME. *piler*].

PILLAR (2), [pil'-er], *v.t.* to provide, support or ornament with pillars.

PILLAR-BOX, [pil'-er-boks'], *n.* a hollow pillar provided with a slit near the top into which letters may be posted.

PILLARED, [pil'-erd], *adj.* supported by pillars; like a pillar; decorated with pillars.

PILL-BOX, [pil'-boks'], *n.* a small round box in which pills are kept; (*milit.*) a small concrete blockhouse or shelter resembling a pill-box in shape.

PILLION, [pil'-yun], *n.* a pad, seat, or cushion behind the saddle for a second rider to ride on a horse; a similar seat behind the driver on a motor-bicycle. [Ir. *pillean*].

PILLORY (1), [pil'-er-i], *n.* a wooden frame on posts, with movable boards and holes in them, through which the head and hands of a criminal were put by way of punishment; (*fig.*) general ridicule, derisive contempt. [OFr. *pellori*].

PILLORY (2), [pil'-er-i], *v.t.* to punish with the pillory; (*fig.*) to expose to general abuse and public ridicule.

PILLOW (1), [pil'-ō], *n.* a cushion filled with feathers, down, or other soft material, used as a support for the head when sleeping or lying in bed; any object used for a similar purpose; a block resembling a pillow in shape and used as a support in machinery; a pad. [OE. *pylu* from L. *pulvinar*].

PILLOW (2), [pil'-ō], *v.t.* to rest or lie on for support; to serve as a pillow; to bolster up with pillows; *v.i.* to rest as on a pillow.

PILLOWCASE, [pil'-ō-kās], *n.* the removable linen or cotton covering slipped over a pillow.

PILLOW-SLIP, [pil'-ō-slip'], *n.* a pillowcase.

PILLOWY, [pil'-ō-wi], *adj.* like a pillow; soft and downy.

PILLWORT, [pil'-wurt], *n.* a plant of the genus *Pilularia.* [PILL (1) and WORT].

PILOCARPINE, [pī'-lō-kahp'-ēn], *n.* a medicinal alkaloid preparation obtained from a Brazilian shrub of the genus *Pilocarpus.* [Gk. *pilos* wool and *karpos* fruit].

PILOSE, [pī-lōs'], *adj.* hairy, covered with hair. [L. *pilosus*].

PILOSELY, [pī-lōs'-li], *adv.* in a pilose fashion.

PILOSITY, [pī-los'-i-ti], *n.* hairiness.

PILOT (1), [pī'-lot], *n.* a person who steers a ship, *esp.* one licensed to take charge of a vessel where navigation is difficult; (*aeron.*) a person who navigates aircraft; a guide, a director of one's course. [It. *pilota*].

PILOT (2), [pī'-lot], *v.t.* to act as pilot, to direct the course of, to guide, steer, navigate; also (*fig.*).

PILOTAGE, [pī'-lot-ij], *n.* the act of piloting; a pilot's fee.

PILOT-BALLOON, [pī'-lot-bal-ōōn'], *n.* a balloon sent up to reveal the direction of the wind.

PILOT-BOAT, [pī'-lot-bōt'], *n.* a boat used to take a pilot to meet a vessel he has to navigate.

PILOT-CLOTH, [pī'-lot-kloth'], *n.* a stout blue cloth used for greatcoats, as worn by pilots.

PILOT-ENGINE, [pī'-lot-en'-jin], *n.* the leading engine when two are used to draw a train; an engine sent on ahead of a train to ensure that the road is clear.

PILOT-FISH, [pī'-lot-fish'], *n.* a small fish, *Naucrates ductor,* allied to the horse-mackerel.

PILOT-JACKET, [pī'-lot-jak'-it], *n.* a jacket made of pilot-cloth, a pea-jacket.

PILOT LIGHT, [pī'-lot-līt'], *n.* a small gas jet kept burning to ignite a geyser, etc.; a light used to illuminate the dial of a wireless set, etc., and to show that the current has been switched on.

PILOT OFFICER, [pī'-lot-of'-is-er], *n.* an officer of the Royal Air Force of equivalent rank to a second lieutenant in the Army.

PILOT TUBE, [pī'-lot-tewb'], *n.* (*aeron.*) the airspeed indicator, in the form of a tube, on an aircraft.

PILOUS, [pī'-lus], *adj.* hairy, covered with or consisting of hair, like hair. [L. *pilosus*].

PILSENER, [pils'-ner], *n.* a kind of lager beer. [*Pilsen,* a place in Czechoslovakia, where made].

PILTDOWN, [pilt'-down], *n.* a place in Sussex in which a famous skull of a prehistoric man was found.

PILULAR, [pil'-yōō-ler], *adj.* pertaining to, resembling, a pill.

PILULE, [pil'-yōōl], *n.* a small pill. [L. *pilula*].

PIMELITE, [pim'-el-īt], *n.* a green clay or earth, greasy to the touch, and consisting of aluminium, iron, nickel and magnesium silicates. [Gk. *pimele* fat].

PIMELODE, [pim'-el-ōd], *n.* the cat-fish. [Gk. *pimelodes* fatty].

PIMENTO, [pim-en'-tō], *n.* Jamaica pepper, allspice, the berry of *Pimenta officinalis*; the tree from which this is obtained. [Span. *pimienta* from L. *pigmentum* paint, spice].

PIMP (1), [pimp], *n.* a procurer. [Uncert.].

PIMP (2), [pimp], *v.i.* to pander, to act as procurer.

PIMPERNEL, [pim'-per-nel'], *n.* an annual plant of

the genus *Anagallis*, bearing scarlet, blue or white flowers. [OFr. *pimprenelle*].

PIMPLE, [pimpl], *n.* a small rounded inflamed pustule on the skin. [Unkn.].

PIMPLED, [pimpld], *adj.* pimply.

PIMPLY, [pimp'-li], *adj.* having, covered with, pimples.

PIN (1), [pin], *n.* a short, thin, rigid, pointed piece of wire with a projecting, slightly curved head used for fastening or securing parts of garments, papers, etc.; a small round piece of metal or wood usually sharpened to a point and used for fastening things together, as a peg or handle, etc., a peg, bolt; anything shaped like a pin, or having the function of a pin; (*pl.*) (*coll.*) legs; the tuning peg of a stringed musical instrument; a cask holding half a firkin or four and a half gallons; **pins and needles**, a prickly tingling sensation in the limbs when coming to life again after numbness; **not to care two pins**, not to care at all. [OE. *pinn* probably from L. *pinna*].

PIN (2), (**pinning, pinned**), [pin], *v.t.* to fasten, attach, support with a pin; to pierce with a pin; to bolt, peg; to hold fast so that one cannot move, to restrict the movement of; to enclose, impound, shut up in a confined space; (*fig.*) to place or stake wholeheartedly or entirely (of faith, hope, etc.); **to p. down**, to bind to. [*Prec.*].

PINA-CLOTH, [pē'-na-kloth'], *n.* a fine fabric, made in Manila, from the fibres of the leaf of the pineapple. [Span. *pina* pineapple].

PINACOID, [pin'-ak-oid], *n.* one of two faces in a crystal intersecting one axis and parallel to the others. [Gk. *pinax pinakos* slab and *oeides* resembling].

PINAFORE, [pin'-a-faw(r)], *n.* a loose sleeveless kind of overall or long apron worn over the dress. [PIN (2) and AFORE].

PINANG, [pin-ang'], *n.* the areca palm, or the nut it produces. [Malay *pinang* betel nut].

PINASTER, [pī'-nast-er], *n.* the cluster pine of the south of Europe, *Pinus Pinaster*. [L. *pinaster* wild pine].

PIN-CASE, [pin'-kās], *n.* a case for holding pins.

PINCE-NEZ, [pans'-nā', pins'-nā'], *n.* a pair of eyeglasses that clip on the nose with springs. [Fr. *pince-nez* from *pincer* to pinch and *nez* nose].

PINCERS, [pins'-erz], *n.* a tool consisting of a pair of pivoted jaws, which can be pressed together to grip objects tightly, by means of two handles working as levers; an organ in certain animals similar in appearance and function to pincers. [ME. *pinsours*].

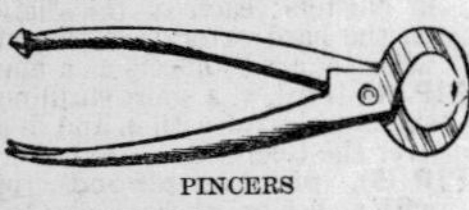
PINCERS

PINCETTE, [pins-et'], *n.* a small pair of pincers. [Fr. *pincette*].

PINCH (1), [pinch], *n.* a nip, squeeze, a painful compression of a portion of the skin by means of the tip of the thumb and finger; as much as can be taken between thumb and finger, a small amount; (*fig.*) distress, straits, pressure, grip, restricting discomforting influence; **at a p.**, as a last resort, if needs be.

PINCH (2), [pinch], *v.t.* to squeeze, nip, grip forcibly and painfully between the thumb and finger or between two hard objects, to press painfully upon; to distress, oppress, cause hardship and suffering, to afflict painfully so as to cause a drawn, shrunken appearance; (*slang*) to steal; to arrest; *v.i.* to press painfully upon some part of the skin; to live frugally; **to p. back**, to nip off part of (a shoot). [ONFr. **pinchier* from OFr. *pincier*].

PINCHBECK (1), [pinch'-bek'], *n.* an alloy containing about 80 parts of copper and 20 parts of zinc, used for cheap jewellery. [C. *Pinchbeck*, the supposed inventor].

PINCHBECK (2), [pinch'-bek'], *adj.* spurious, sham, counterfeit, imitation. [*Prec.*].

PINCHER (1), [pinch'-er], *n.* he who, or that which, pinches; (*pl.*) an instrument for pinching or gripping some object tightly.

PINCHER (2), [pinch'-er], *n.* a sea fish, the argentine, *Argentina sphyræna*.

PINCHINGLY, [pinch'-ing-li], *adv.* in a pinching fashion.

PIN-COP, [pin'-kop], *n.* a roll of yarn used for the weft in a power loom.

PINCUSHION, [pin'-kŏŏsh-un], *n.* a small firm cushion in which to stick pins ready for use.

PINDARIC (1), [pin-da'-rik], *n.* an ode in the style of those by Pindar, the Greek lyric poet.

PINDARIC (2), [pin-da'-rik], *adj.* pertaining to, composed by, in the style of, Pindar. [Gk. *Pindarikos*].

PINDARISM, [pin'-der-izm], *n.* style or expression in the manner of Pindar.

PINDER, [pin'-der], *n.* an official whose duty it was to impound straying animals. [OE. *gepyndan* to enclose].

PINE (1), [pīn], *n.* a genus of cone-bearing evergreen trees having clusters of thin needle-shaped leaves, and valued for their timber; the timber of this tree; a pineapple. [OE. *pin* from L. *pinus*].

PINE (2), [pīn], *v.i.* to waste away through anxiety, longing or illness, to languish; to long for eagerly. [OE. *pinian* to torture].

PINEAL, [pin'-ē-al], *adj.* shaped like a pine-cone; **p. gland**, a small cone-shaped body situated behind the third ventricle of the brain. [L. *pinea* pine-cone].

PINEAPPLE, [pīn'-apl], *n.* a tropical plant of the genus *Ananas*, yielding a fruit covered with a hard prickly rind, and resembling in shape a pine-cone; the brownish-yellow juicy fruit of this plant; (*slang*) a bomb.

PINE-BARREN, [pīn'-ba-ren], *n.* a level sandy stretch of land sprinkled with pine-trees.

PINE BEAUTY, [pīn'-bewt'-i], *n.* a moth whose larvae feed on pine-trees.

PINECHAFER, [pīn'-chāf'-er], *n.* an American beetle, *Aromala pinicola*, destructive to the leaves of the pine.

PINE-CLAD, [pīn'-klad], *adj.* abounding in pine trees.

PINE-CONE, [pīn'-kōn'], *n.* the woody cone-shaped structure in which the seeds of the pine tree are found.

PINE-MARTEN, [pīn'-maht'-en], *n.* the wild animal, *Mustela martes*, related to the weasel.

PINERY, [pīn'-er-i], *n.* a hothouse where pineapples are grown; a plantation of pine trees.

PINETUM, [pīn-ē'-tum], *n.* a plantation of different kinds of pine trees. [L. *pinetum*].

PIN-FEATHER, [pin'-feTH'-er], *n.* a small feather not fully formed.

PIN-FEATHERED, [pin'-feTH'-erd], *adj.* not completely fledged.

PINFOLD, [pin'-fōld], *n.* a pound, the place in which stray cattle are confined. [OE. *pundfald*].

PING (1), [ping], *n.* a sharp sudden ringing sound as of a bullet striking a hard surface. [Echoic].

PING (2), [ping], *v.i.* to emit a ping.

PING-PONG, [ping'-pong'], *n.* table-tennis. [Echoic].

PINGUID, [ping'-gwid], *adj.* greasy, oily, fatty; (of soil) luxurious, rich. [L. *pinguis* fat].

PIN-HEAD, [pin'-hed'], *n.* the small, protruding, slightly curved head of a pin; anything resembling this.

PINHOLE, [pin'-hōl], *n.* a very small aperture, a hole made by a pin.

PINIC, [pīn'-ik], *adj.* obtained from, or relating to, pine.

PINICOLINE, [pīn-ik'-ol-īn], *adj.* dwelling in pine woods. [PINE (1) and L. *cola* inhabitant].

PININGLY, [pīn'-ing-li], *adv.* in a languishing fashion.

PINION (1), [pin'-yun], *n.* the joint of a bird's wing farthest away from the body; one of the outer wing-feathers; (*poet.*) a wing. [OFr. *pignon*].

PINION (2), [pin'-yun], *n.* a small cog-wheel or cogged axle whose teeth work in the teeth of a larger one. [*Prec.*].

PINION (3), [pin'-yun], *v.t.* to cut off the outermost joint of one wing of, to prevent from flying, to confine by binding the wings of; to bind the arms of closely to the sides, to shackle.

PINITE, [pīn'-īt], *n.* a soft crystallized mineral, formed from iolite. [Germ. *pinit*].

PINK (1), [pingk], *n.* a plant of the genus *Dianthus*, of which there are many species, yielding fragrant white, pink and crimson flowers; the highest degree of excellence, the height; a pale red colour; a fox-hunter's coat; **in the p.**, feeling perfectly fit and healthy. [Uncert.].

PINK (2), [pingk], *n.* a vessel having a narrow stern. [MDu. *pincke*].

PINK (3), [pingk], *n.* a young undeveloped salmon. [Uncert.].

PINK (4), [pingk], *adj.* pale red in colour.

PINK (5), [pingk], *v.t.* (of cloth, leather, etc.) to pierce the edge of with small holes, figures, etc., so as to form a decorative pattern, to cut the edge in a zigzag to prevent fraying; to stab, pierce, wound; *v.i.* (*archaic*) to make holes; (*motoring*) to work unevenly causing a metallic knocking sound to be heard. [LGerm. *pinken* to strike].

PINK-EYE, [pingk'-ī'], *n.* a variety of potato; a contagious disease in horses in which the eyes become very red and swollen; a form of conjunctivitis.

PINK-EYED, [pingk'-īd], *adj.* having small, half-shut, blinking eyes.

PINKISH, [pingk'-ish], *adj.* rather pink.

PINKNESS, [pingk'-nes], *n.* the quality of being pink.

PINK-ROOT, [pingk'-rōōt], *n.* the root of the Indian pink, *Dianthus chinensis.*

PINKSTER, [pingk'-ster], *n.* (*U.S.*) Whitsuntide; **p. flower**, the pink azalea. [Du. *pinkster*].

PINK-STERNED, [pingk'-sturnd'], *adj.* having a narrow stern.

PINMAKER, [pin'-māk-er], *n.* one who makes pins.

PIN-MONEY, [pin'-mun'-i], *n.* money received as gifts or wages by one who is not economically compelled to work for a living, and used to provide personal luxuries, etc.

PINNA, [pin'-a], *n.* (*zool.*) a fin-like appendage or organ; (*anat.*) the upper portion of the external ear; (*bot.*) a single section of a pinnate leaf. [L. *pinna* fin].

PINNACE, [pin'-as], *n.* a warship's boat or small boat belonging to a larger vessel, and used for taking people to and from the shore; (*hist.*) a small vessel rigged with two fore-and-aft sails. [Fr. *pinasse*].

PINNACLE (1), [pin'-akl], *n.* a slender turret, an ornamental pointed top surmounting a roof, parapet, or buttress; a small peak; (*fig.*) the highest point, the culmination. [LL. *pinnaculum*].

PINNACLE (2), [pin'-akl], *v.t.* to ornament with pinnacles; to set upon a pinnacle; to act as pinnacle to.

PINNATE, PENNATE, [pin'-āt], *adj.* (*bot.*) branching like a feather; (*zool.*) arranged on each side of an axis in the manner of a feather. [L. *pinnatus* feathered].

PINNATED, [pin'-āt-id], *adj.* pinnate.

PINNATELY, [pin'-āt-li], *adv.* (*bot.*) in pinnate fashion.

PINNATIFID, [pin-at'-if-id], *adj.* (of leaves) cleft like a feather.

PINNATIPED, [pin-at'-ip-ed], *adj.* (*zool.*) fin-footed; having the toes joined with membranes, web-footed.

PINNER, [pin'-er], *n.* †a woman's cap with two long hanging side-flaps; one who pins; a pinafore.

PINNIPEDIA, [pin'-i-pē'-di-a], *n.* a branch of the carnivorous animals having fin-like limbs, and including the seals, walruses and sea-lions. [L. *pinnipes* fin-footed].

PINNOCK, [pin'-ok], *n.* the hedge-sparrow, the tomtit. [Echoic].

PINNOTHERE, [pin'-o-thēer], *n.* one of a genus of small crab-like animals living as a kind of parasite in the shells of oysters, mussels, etc. [Gk. *pinnotheres*].

PINNULATE, [pin'-yōō-lāt], *adj.* furnished with pinnules.

PINNULE, [pin'-yōōl], *n.* (*bot.*) a branchlet or division of a pinnate leaf; (*zool.*) a small wing-like or fin-like organ. [L. *pinnula*].

PINNY, [pin'-i], *n.* a pinafore.

PINOCHLE, [pin'-okl], *n.* a card game similar to bezique. [Unkn.].

PINOLE, [pin-ōl'-i], *n.* dried grain of maize, corn, etc., mixed with sugar, flavoured with spice, and eaten with milk in Mexico and the Southern States of the U.S.A. [Span. *pinole*].

PINPATCH, [pin'-pach'], *n.* the periwinkle, *Littorina littorea.*

PINPOINT, [pin'-point'], *v.t.* (*aeron.*) to locate with the greatest precision.

PIN-PRICK, [pin'-prik'], *n.* a tiny hole made by a pin; (*fig.*) a small thing causing irritation.

PIN-STRIPED, [pin'-stript'], *adj.* bearing a series of exceedingly narrow stripes no thicker than a pin.

PINT, [pīnt], *n.* a measure of capacity equal to an eighth of a gallon. [Fr. *pinte*].

PIN-TABLE, [pin'-tābl'], *n.* a game of skill or chance in the form of a penny-in-the-slot machine, in which balls must pass pins stuck in a flat surface.

PINTADO, [pin-tah'-dō], *n.* the guinea-fowl, a variety of petrel, *Daption capensis.* [Portug. *pintado* painted].

PIN-TAIL, [pin'-tāl], *n.* the sea-duck *Dafila acuta*, the male of which has a pointed tail; a pointed-tailed variety of grouse.

PINTLE, [pintl], *n.* †the penis; a vertical projecting pin, *esp.* one used as a pivot; (*milit.*) a long iron bolt on which the carriage axle of a gun turns; (*naut.*) the hook or pin by which the rudder is attached to the gudgeons. [OE. *pintel*].

PINTO, [pin'-tō], *n.* (*U.S.*) a pied horse. [Span. *pinto*].

PIN-TUCK, [pin'-tuk], *n.* a small ornamental tuck.

PIN-VICE, [pin'-vīs], *n.* a small hand-vice in which pins and similar objects are held for filing.

PIN-VICE

PIN-WHEEL, [pin'-wēl], *n.* a small firework similar to a Catherine-wheel.

PIOLET, [pē'-ō-lā'], *n.* the spiked stick used by skiers. [Fr. dial. *piolet*].

PIONEER (1), [pī-on-ēer'], *n.* (*milit.*) *orig.* a foot-soldier who cleared obstructions and made a road ahead of an army; now, a second-line soldier, usually unfit for front-line service, whose main duty is clearing and elementary construction behind the lines; one who takes the lead in anything, and prepares the way for others, one who explores new avenues or fields of activity or unknown lands, the earliest investigator or exponent of anything. [Fr. *pionnier* foot-soldier, pioneer].

PIONEER (2), [pī-on-ēer'], *v.t.* to lead the way in, initiate, to be the earliest exponent or investigator of; *v.i.* to act as pioneer, to undertake pioneer work.

PIONEER CORPS, [pī'-o-nēer'-kaw(r)], *n.* a corps of the British Army employed to carry out road repairs, building, etc.

PIOUS, [pī'-us], *adj.* devout, godly, sincere in and observant of one's religious duties, reverent; (*archaic*) having due respect and affection for one's parents and relatives; **p. fraud**, a fraud practised under pretence of religion or some laudable object; **p. hope**, a prediction based more on wish than on probability. [L. *pius* dutiful].

PIOUSLY, [pī'-us-li], *adv.* in a pious manner, devoutly.

PIOUSNESS, [pī'-us-nes], *n.* the quality of being pious.

PIP (1), [pip], *n.* a disease in poultry in which thick mucus gathers in the mouth and throat, and a white horny pellicle forms on the edge of the tongue; (*coll.*) a fit of depression, a sense of boredom mingled with annoyance. [MDu. *pippe* from LL. *pipita*].

PIP (2), [pip], *n.* the seed of an apple, orange or other similar fruit. [OFr. *pepin* seed].

PIP (3), [pip], *n.* one of the spots on playing cards, dice or dominoes; a single blossom of a flower growing in clusters; each of the diamond-shaped segments on the hard exterior of the pineapple; (*coll.*) a star worn by army officers as a mark of rank. [Uncert.].

PIP (4), [pip], *n.* a short shrill note repeated as a time-signal in broadcasting, and in giving the precise time over the telephone. [Echoic].

PIP (5), (**pipping, pipped**), [pip], *v.t.* (*slang*) to hit with a shot or other missile; to defeat, baffle, thwart; to blackball; to fail; *v.i.* (*slang*) to fail in an examination; **to p. out**, (*coll.*) to die. [Uncert.].

PIPAL, see PEEPUL.

PIPE (1), [pīp], *n.* a musical wind-instrument in the form of a tube pierced with holes which are stopped by the fingers to produce different notes; a boatswain's whistle; (*pl.*) bagpipes; the sound made by a pipe, the shrill call of a bird, a thin squeaky voice of a child; a short thin tube or stem with a bowl at one end into which tobacco is packed; the quantity contained in the bowl of a pipe; a long cylindrical tube for conveying water, gas, steam, etc.; each of the cylindrical tubes with tapering bases in which the sound is produced in an organ; a tubular channel in an animal body, *esp.* that by which air passes from the mouth to the lungs; a measure of wine, being a cask containing about 105 imperial gallons; a roll of the Exchequer or record of the annual accounts of the state, first kept in 1131 and discontinued in 1832. [OE. *pipe*].

PIPE (2), [pīp], *v.t.* to play (a tune) on a pipe, to sing or chirp in a shrill treble voice; to call by means of a boatswain's whistle; (of pinks) to propagate by taking cuttings from a stem-joint; to ornament with piping; to provide with pipes, to lay pipes in; **to p. up**, to begin to speak or pipe; **to p. down**, (*slang*) to remain quiet, make less noise, to make oneself heard less; *v.i.* to play on a pipe; to speak in a thin shrill treble voice, to whistle; (of a bird) to utter shrill notes. [OE. *pipian*].

PIPECLAY (1), [pīp'-klā], *n.* a fine, white, plastic clay used in making tobacco pipes and for whitening leather and military outfit; (*fig.*) inordinate attention to details of dress in a regiment.

PIPECLAY (2), [pīp'-klā], *v.t.* to whiten with pipeclay.

PIPEFISH, [pīp'-fish], *n.* a fish of the genus *Nerophis*, having a long and very slender body, and jaws in the form of a tube, with the mouth at the end.

PIPEFUL, [pīp'-fōōl], *n.* the amount of tobacco that will fill a pipe.
PIPELIGHTER, [pīp'-līt-er], *n.* a thin narrow shaving of wood or strip of twisted paper used for lighting a pipe.
PIPE-LINE, [pīp'-līn], *n.* a line of pipes for conveying oil or water.
PIPE-OFFICE, [pīp'-of'-is], *n.* an ancient office in the court of exchequer, the duties of which are now merged with those of the remembrancer.
PIPER, [pīp'-er], *n.* one who plays upon the pipes, *esp.* the bagpipes; name given to several varieties of fish, *esp.* the gurnard, *Trigla lyra*; a dog trained to act as decoy for catching birds; a broken-winded horse; **to pay the p.**, to bear the cost of anything.
PIPE-RACK, [pīp'-rak'], *n.* a rack in which tobacco pipes may be hung.
PIPERIC, [pip-ē'-rik], *adj.* relating to, obtained from, pepper. [L. *piper* pepper].
PIPERIN, [pip'-er-in], *n.* a peculiar crystalline substance extracted from black pepper, solidifying into rhomboidal prisms.
PIPE ROLL, [pīp'-rōl], *n.* (*hist.*) one of the Great Rolls of the Exchequer. [PIPE (1)].
PIPESTONE, [pīp'-stōn], *n.* a variety of clay slate used by the American Indians for making pipe-bowls.
PIPE-TREE, [pīp'-trē], *n.* the lilac, *Syringa vulgaris*; the orange-blossom tree, *Philadelphus coronarius*.
PIPETTE, [pip-et'], *n.* a glass tube, swollen in the middle, and used for transferring liquids in small quantities. [Fr. *pipette*].
PIPEWORT, [pīp'-wurt], *n.* a plant of the genus *Eriocaulon*, water-pepper.
PIPING (1), [pīp'-ing], *n.* the act of one who pipes; the sound produced when playing a pipe; thin, shrill, treble voice, utterance, or song of a bird; a group or arrangement of pipes for conveying water, steam, gas, etc.; ornamental trimming resembling a pipe.
PIPING (2), [pīp'-ing], *adj.* shrill and thin, as of a pipe; **p. hot**, extremely hot.
PIPING-CROW, [pīp'-ing-krō'], *n.* the flute-player, an Australian bird of the genus *Gymnorrhina*, of which the white-backed species forms the badge of South Australia.
PIPISTREL(LE), [pip-is-trel'], *n.* the small bat, *Vesperugo pipistrellus*, having the membrane extending to the toe. [It. *pipistrello*].
PIPIT, [pip'-it], *n.* a passerine bird of the genus *Anthus*, related to the wagtails. [Echoic].
PIPKIN, [pip'-kin], *n.* a small earthenware pot or pan, used as a cooking utensil. [Unkn.].
PIPPIN, [pip'-in], *n.* †an apple grown from seed and not from a graft; one of various kinds of dessert apples. [OFr. *pepin* seed].
PIP-SQUEAK, [pip'-skwēk], *n.* (*slang*) a small high velocity shell; a mean or paltry thing or person.
PIQUANCY, [pēk'-an-si], *n.* the quality of being piquant, sharpness, pungency.
PIQUANT, [pēk'-ant], *adj.* sharp, pungent, pleasantly biting to the taste; agreeably stimulating, charmingly disturbing, whetting the appetite or curiosity. [Fr. *piquant*].
PIQUANTLY, [pēk'-ant-li], *adv.* in a piquant manner, pungently.
PIQUE (1), [pēk], *n.* petulant anger or resentful irritation arising from wounded feelings, huff. [Fr. *pique*].
PIQUE (2), [pēk], *n.* (*piquet*) the scoring of thirty points before the opponent has opened his score. [Fr. *pic*].
PIQUE (3), [pēk], *v.t.* to offend, irritate, to wound the pride of; to stimulate, whet (curiosity, etc.); *v.reflex.* to have a good opinion about one's ability or skill. [Fr. *piquer* to prick].
PIQUE (4), [pēk], *v.t. and i.* (*piquet*) to score a pique (against).
PIQUE, piqué, [pēk-ā'], *n.* a stout ridged or ribbed cotton material patterned in the weaving. [Fr. *piqué*].
PIQUET, PICQUET†, [pik-et'], *n.* a card game for two players played with thirty-two cards. [Fr. *piquet*].
PIRACY, [pīer'-as-i], *n.* the occupation, act, or crime of robbing on the high seas; an act of a similar kind. [Gk. *peirateia*].
PIRAGUA, PERIAGUA, PIROGUE, [pi-rag'-wa], *n.* a canoe formed out of the hollowed-out trunk of a tree, a dug-out; a two-masted flat-bottomed boat. [Span. *piragua*].
PIRATE (1), [pīer'-at], *n.* a person engaged in robbery upon the high seas; a ship used by sea robbers or marauders; one who infringes the law of copyright; a private omnibus running for hire along the recognized licensed routes covered by a motor-bus company, *esp.* one in which higher fares than normal are charged; (*wirel.*) a person who operates a wireless receiving or transmitting set without a licence. [Gk. *peirates*].
PIRATE (2), [pīer'-at], *v.t.* to plunder, rob (a ship); to publish or print (a book, etc.) for profit without leave from the author or owner of the copyright.
PIRATICAL, [pī-rat'-ik-al], *adj.* pertaining to a pirate, addicted to piracy.
PIRATICALLY, [pī-rat'-ik-a-li], *adv.* in a piratical manner.
PIRATING, [pīer'-at-ing], *adj.* practising piracy.
PIRN, [purn], *n.* a weaver's spool, a bobbin; the length of thread on a reel. [Uncert.].
PIROGUE, see PIRAGUA.
PIROUETTE (1), [pi'-rōō-et'], *n.* a dancing step performed by spinning round on the tips of the toes; the circling of a horse in its own length. [Fr. *pirouette* spinning-top].
PIROUETTE (2), [pi'-rōō-et'], *v.i.* to perform a pirouette.
PISANG, [pē-sang'], *n.* the banana; the plantain. [Malay *pisang*].
PISCARY, [pis'-ka-ri], *n.* (*leg.*) the right of fishing in another man's waters. [L. *piscarius*].
PISCATOR, [pis-kā'-tor], *n.* an angler. [L. *piscator*].
PISCATORIAL, [pis'-kat-aw'-ri-al], *adj.* relating to fishing.
PISCATORY, [pis'-kat-er-i], *adj.* piscatorial.
PISCES, [pis'-ēz], *n.(pl.)* (*astrol.*) the twelfth sign of the Zodiac, the Fishes. [L. *pisces*, *pl.* of *piscis* fish].
PISCICULTURAL, [pis'-i-kul'-cher-al], *adj.* relating to pisciculture.
PISCICULTURE, [pis'-i-kul'-cher], *n.* the artificial culture and rearing of fish. [L. *piscis* fish and CULTURE].
PISCICULTURIST, [pis'-i-kul'-cher-ist], *n.* an expert in pisciculture.
PISCIFORM, [pis'-i-fawm], *adj.* having the shape of a fish. [L. *piscis* fish and FORM].
PISCINA, [pis-ī'-na], *n.* a fish-pond; (*eccles.*) a basin near the altar into which the priest empties the water used in the service. [L. *piscina*].
PISCINE, [pis'-in], *adj.* relating to fishes.
PISCIVOROUS, [pis-iv'-or-us], *adj.* living by, feeding on, fishes. [L. *piscis* fish and *vorare* to devour].
PISE, pisé, [pē'-zā], *n.* stiff earth or clay hardened between boards and left standing to form walls. [Fr. *pisé*].
PISH, [pish], *int.* a word expressing contempt and disgust. [Imitative].
PISIFORM, [pīz'-i-fawm], *adj.* (*bot.*) having the form of a pea. [L. *pisum* pea and FORM].
PISMIRE†, [pis'-mīer], *n.* an ant. [ME. *pissemyre*].
PISOLITE, [pis'-ol-īt], *n.* (*min.*) pea-stone, a calcareous stone made up of pea-like globular concretions. [Gk. *pisos* pea and *lithos* stone].
PISOLITIC, [pis'-o-lit'-ik], *adj.* of the nature of pisolite.
PISS (1), [pis], *n.* (*vulg.*) urine.
PISS (2), [pis], *v.t. and i.* (*vulg.*) to saturate with urine; to discharge urine, to make water. [OFr. *pissier*].
PISTACHIO, [pis-tah'-chi-ō], *n.* the nut of *Pistacia vera*; the pale-green colour of this nut. [Gk. *pistakion*].
PISTACIA, [pist-ā'-sha], *n.* (*bot.*) the pistachio-tree, *Pistacia vera*. [Gk. *pistake*].
PISTACITE, [pis'-tas-īt], *n.* (*min.*) epidote.
PISTAREEN, [pis'-ta-rēn], *n.* a Spanish silver coin worth about 9d. [Corruption of PESETA].
PISTE, [pēst], *n.* the foot-track of a horse. [L. *pista*].
PISTIL, [pis'-til], *n.* (*bot.*) the female seed-bearing part of the flower. [L. *pistillum*].
PISTILLARY, [pis-til'-er-i], *adj.* relating to, growing on, the pistil.
PISTILLATE, [pis'-til-āt], *adj.* (*bot.*) having a pistil.
PISTILLIFEROUS, [pis'-til-if'-er-us], *adj.* (*bot.*) having pistils without stamens. [L. *pistillum* and *ferre* to bear].
PISTOL (1), [pis'-tol], *n.* a small fire-arm adapted for holding in one hand, a hand-gun. [It. *pistola* dagger].
PISTOL (2), (**pistolling, pistolled**), [pis'-tol], *v.t.* to shoot with a pistol.
PISTOLE†, [pis-tōl'], *n.* a gold coin in Spain formerly worth about 16s. [Uncert.].
PISTOLET, [pis'-tol-et], *n.* a miniature pistol. [Fr. *pistolet*].

PISTON, [pis'-ton], *n.* (*mech.*) in a machine, a sliding circular plate fitted into a cylinder and which by moving causes pressure or which pressure causes to move; **p.-rod,** the rod connecting the piston with other parts of the machine; (*mus.*) a valve of a wind-instrument. [L. *pistum*, *p.pt.* of *pinsere* to pound].

PISTON

PIT (1), [pit], *n.* a hole in the earth left bare; a hole in the ground made for a purpose by artificial means, an excavation; an abyss; a grave; an arena for cock-fighting contests; the middle and rear section of an auditorium as distinct from the stalls; a natural depression in the human or animal body, a hollow; a hole from which the underside of a motor-car can be inspected or overhauled. [OE. *pytt*].

PIT (2), [pit], *n.* a card game.

PIT (3), (pitting, pitted), [pit], *v.t.* to mark with hollows or small depressions; to place, store, or press into hollows; **to p. against,** to oppose to.

PITAPAT (1), [pit'-a-pat'], *n.* a series of light, quick steps or taps. [Imitative].

PITAPAT (2), [pit'-a-pat'], *adv.* with a series of light taps or beats quickly following one another, in a flutter, with palpitation.

PITCH (1), [pich], *n.* a thick black substance obtained by boiling down tar, used in the manufacture of varnish and for preserving wood exposed to the weather. [OE. *pic* from L. *pix* pitch].

PITCH (2), [pich], *n.* the act of pitching or tossing; the distance covered by an object that has been pitched; the habitual station, place or area of a person or object; the point of elevation or degree of height, particularly that of a preying falcon; degree, height, size, limit, stature; the angle or degree of inclination, the measured rise of a slope; in cricket, the prepared turf and levelled ground situated between the wickets; the point where the ball delivered by the bowler hits the ground, particularly an imaginary point falling just short of a batsman's stretch from the popping crease; (*mech.*) the distance between the apices of two cogs on a wheel or saw; the longitudinal distance travelled in one revolution of a screw, worm, or propeller; (*mus.*) the frequency of a note.

PITCH (3), [pich], *v.t.* to cover or smear with pitch.

PITCH (4), [pich], *v.t.* to throw, hurl, toss, cast, particularly with a fork; to throw headlong; to throw at an objective; to fix, set up in a marked-out position, as a tent or stall; (in cricket) to set up the two wickets in readiness for a game; to deliver a ball so that it falls at a particular point between the wickets; (*mus.*) to arrange the tune in a specific key; *v.i.* to encamp, to settle down; to fall headlong, to plunge downward heavily; to plunge and rock from head to stern, as a ship; **to p. into,** (*coll.*) to attack fast and furiously, particularly with the fists. [ME. *pichen*].

PITCH-AND-TOSS, [pich'-and-tos'], *n.* a game in which the person who pitches his coin nearest a mark is the first entitled to spin for the coins so thrown.

PITCH-BLACK, [pich'-blak'], *adj.* black as pitch.

PITCHBLENDE, [pich'-blend'], *n.* uraninite; a black ore, an oxide of uranium yielding radium. [Germ. *pech-blende*].

PITCH-DARK, [pich'-dahk'], *adj.* completely dark, as dark as pitch.

PITCHER (1), [pich'-er], *n.* a large earthen jug for holding liquid having two handles like ears; a ewer. [MedL. *picarium* vessel].

PITCHER (2), [pich'-er], *n.* an instrument for piercing the ground.

PITCHER (3), [pich'-er], *n.* a person who pitches, particularly a player who delivers the ball, a bowler; a feeder at baseball.

PITCHERFUL, [pich'-er-fŏŏl], *n.* the amount a pitcher can hold.

PITCHER-PLANT, [pich'-er-plahnt'], *n.* an American insectivorous plant with pitcher-shaped leaves.

PITCHFORK, [pich'-fawk], *n.* a long-handled fork having two curved prongs used in lifting and pitching hay or sheaves of grain.

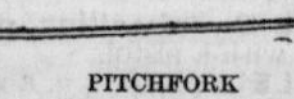

PITCHFORK

PITCHINESS, [pich'-i-nes], *n.* the quality of pitch, stickiness; blackness, darkness.

PITCHOMETER, [pich-om'-it-er], *n.* an instrument for measuring the pitch of the blades of a screw propeller or tractor.

PITCH-PINE, [pich'-pīn], *n.* the Norwegian or red pine, *Pinus resinosa*; the American tree, *Pinus palustris*.

PITCHPIPE, [pich'-pīp], *n.* a tuning pipe sounding the pitch for wind instruments or for unaccompanied singers.

PITCHSTONE, [pich'-stōn], *n.* (*min.*) an obsidian having a resinous lustre, a volcanic rock resembling indurated pitch.

PITCH-WHEEL, [pich'-wēl], *n.* a gear-wheel.

PITCHY, [pich'-i], *adj.* resembling, or mixed with, pitch, black, dark.

PIT-COAL, [pit'-kōl], *n.* mineral coal as distinct from charcoal.

PITEOUS, [pit'-i-us], *adj.* that may excite pity, deserving compassion; lamentable, wretched, pitiful; paltry. [OFr. *pitous*].

PITEOUSLY, [pit'-i-us-li], *adv.* in a piteous manner; sorrowfully.

PITEOUSNESS, [pit'-i-us-nes], *n.* the quality of being piteous.

PITFALL, [pit'-fawl], *n.* a pit slightly covered so that an animal may fall into it, a concealed trap; (*fig.*) an unseen danger.

PITH (1), [pith], *n.* the soft, spongy, organic tissue at the centre of plant stems; the stringy parts and white under-skin of an orange; the marrow in the bones of an animal; (*fig.*) the essential part, the concentrated strength vigour; the importance, weight; the spinal cord. [OE. *pitha*].

PITH (2), [pith], *v.t.* to cut the spinal cord.

PITHEAD, [pit'-hed'], *n.* the entrance to a coal pit; **p. price,** the price of coal at the pithead.

PITHECOID, [pith'-i-koid], *adj.* ape-like. [Gk. *pithekos* ape and *oeides* like].

PITHECUS, [pith-ē'-kus], *n.* an ape. [Gk. *pithekos*].

PITHILY, [pith'-i-li], *adv.* in a pithy manner.

PITHINESS, [pith'-i-nes], *n.* the quality of being pithy; concentrated force.

PITHLESS, [pith'-les], *adj.* having no pith; (*fig.*) wanting strength.

PITHY, [pith'-i], *adj.* relating to, containing, or abounding with, pith; (*fig.*) concise, pointed, forcible.

PITIABLE, [pit'-i-abl], *adj.* deserving pity, miserable, rueful; worthy of contempt.

PITIABLENESS, [pit'-i-abl-nes], *n.* the quality of being pitiable.

PITIABLY, [pit'-i-ab-li], *adv.* in a pitiable manner.

PITIFUL, [pit'-i-fŏŏl], *adj.* full of pity, compassionate; miserable; contemptible.

PITIFULLY, [pit'-i-fŏŏl-i], *adv.* in a pitiful manner.

PITIFULNESS, [pit'-i-fŏŏl-nes], *n.* the quality of being pitiful.

PITILESS, [pit'-i-les], *adj.* feeling no pity, merciless, hard-hearted, ruthless.

PITILESSLY, [pit'-i-les-li], *adv.* in a pitiless manner.

PITILESSNESS, [pit'-i-les-nes], *n.* the quality of being pitiless.

PITMAN, [pit'-man], *n.* one who works in a pit.

PIT-PROP, [pit'-prop'], *n.* (*mining*) a prop of wood used as a temporary support for coal seams when undercut.

PITSAW, [pit'-saw], *n.* a long double-handed saw for dividing timber worked by the top-sawyer on the log and the pit-sawyer in the pit below.

PITSAWYER, [pit'-saw'-yer], *n.* one who stands in the pit to work the lower handle of a pitsaw.

PITTANCE, [pit'-ants], *n.* a small inadequate allowance; a small portion. [ME. *pitance* charity dole].

PITTED, [pit'-id], *adj.* marked with little hollows.

PITTITE, [pit'-īt], *n.* a frequenter of the pit in theatres.

PITTIZITE, [pit'-iz-īt], *n.* arsenio-sulphate of iron. [Gk. *pitta* pitch].

PITUITARY, [pit-yŏŏ'-it-er-i], *adj.* secreting mucus; **p. gland,** an endocrine gland at the base of the brain having a metabolic function. [L. *pituita* phlegm].

PITUITE, [pit-yŏŏ'-īt], *n.* mucus or phlegm. [*Prec.*].

PITUITOUS, [pit-yŏŏ'-it-us], *adj.* composed of mucus.

PITY (1), [pit'-i], *n.* a human emotion arising out of a capacity to feel with another, sympathizing, experiencing another's grief or misery, and promoting desire to provide help; compassion, a matter of regret. [OFr. *piété* compassion].

PITY (2), [pit'-i], *v.t.* to feel pity for, to commiserate with; (*fig.*) to despise.

PITYINGLY, [pit'-i-ing-li], *adv.* in a pitying manner, compassionately.

PITYRIASIS, [pit'-i-ri'-as-is], *n.* (*med.*) a chronic inflammation of the skin characterized by flaking. [Gk. *pituron* bran and *iasis* condition].

PIU, [pew], *adv.* (*mus.*) more. [It. *più*].

PIVOT (1), [piv'-ot], *n.* a point on which anything turns; (*milit.*) the soldier at the flank round whom a company wheels. [Fr. *pivot*].

PIVOT (2), [piv'-ot], *v.i.* to turn as though on a pivot; to hinge, to turn on a pivot.

PIVOTAL, [piv'-otl], *adj.* relating to a pivot; (*fig.*) of prime importance.

PIX, see PYX.

PIXY, [pik'-si], *n.* a fairy, an elf. [Swed. *pyske*].

PIXYLLATED, [piks'-i-lāt-ed], *adj.* bewitched by the pixies. [PIXY].

PIZZICATO, [pits'-ik-ah'-tō], *adv.* (*mus.*) with the finger-tips instead of the bow. [It. *pizzicato*].

PIZZLE, [pizl], *n.* the penis of a bull, etc. (used as an instrument of flagellation). [Germ. *pesel*].

PLACABILITY, [plak'-ab-il'-it-i], *n.* the quality of being placable, placableness.

PLACABLE, [plak'-abl], *adj.* able to be appeased, willing to forgive. [L. *placabilis* easily appeased].

PLACABLENESS, [plak'-abl-nes], *n.* the quality of being appeasable.

PLACARD (1), [plak'-ahd], *n.* a large-sized sheet of paper on which is written, printed or painted a public notice for display. [OFr. *placard*].

PLACARD (2), [plak-ahd'], *v.t.* to affix a placard to, to provide with a placard; to advertise by medium of a placard.

PLACATE, [plak-āt'], *v.t.* to soothe out of anger or irritation, to appease, to pacify. [L. *placare*].

PLACE (1), [plās], *n.* any part or specific area in space; a particular locality, a definite social unit of habitation, a village, town, etc.; the space occupied by one person, particularly at a table or in a vehicle, a seat; a residence, a house; station in life, rank, social class, position, in relation to one's associates; a passage in a book; (in racing) a position in the first three. [ME. *place* from Gk. *plateia* (*hodos*) broad road].

PLACE (2), [plās], *v.t.* to put or set in a particular place; to arrange for a commercial matter to be dealt with; to fix; to invest; to put out at interest, to lend; to recognize; (in racing) to judge a horse to finish in the first three. [*Prec.*].

PLACEBO, [plas-e'-bō], *n.* (*eccles.*) the introductory antiphon of the vespers for the dead; (*med.*) a medicine having no real curative power other than psychological. [L. *placebo* I shall please].

PLACEHUNTER, [plās'-hunt'-er], *n.* a person who lays himself out to obtain a government situation.

PLACE-KICK, [plās'-kik], *n.* (*Rugby football*) a kick at the ball taken after a try has been scored, the ball being held over a mark by one player, another taking a running kick in an attempt to score a goal.

PLACEMAN, [plās'-man], *n.* a holder of any office under government whose position was obtained by influence rather than merit.

PLACENTA, [plas-ent'-a], *n.* (*anat.*) the protective tissue discarded after birth surrounding the foetus in the womb; (*bot.*) the part of a plant feeding the ovules. [Gk. *plakous plakontos* flat cake].

PLACENTAL, [plas-entl'], *adj.* of, relating to, the placenta.

PLACENTALIA, [plas-ent-ā'-li-a], *n.*(*pl.*) (*zool.*) the mammalia which have a placenta connecting the foetus with the uterus. [L. *placentalia*, *neut. pl.* of *placentalis* of a placenta].

PLACENTATION, [plas'-ent-ā'-shun], (*bot. and zool.*) the formation and arrangement of the placenta in plants and animals.

PLACENTITIS, [plas-en-ti'-tis], *n.* (*path.*) inflammation of the placenta. [PLACENTA and Gk. *itis* denoting inflammation].

PLACER, [plās'-er], *n.* a person who places or locates; an auriferous gravel. [L. *platea* broad road].

PLACET, [plas'-et], *n.* an affirmative vote given on a motion; **non p.**, a negative vote. [L. *placet*, *3rd pers. sg. pres.indic.* of *placere* to please].

PLACID, [plas'-id], *adj.* having an unruffled disposition, gentle, quiet, serene. [L. *placidus* smooth].

PLACIDITY, [plas-id'-it-i], *n.* the quality or state of being placid, calmness.

PLACIDLY, [plas'-id-li], *adv.* in a placid manner.

PLACIDNESS, [plas'-id-nes], *n.* the state of being placid.

PLACKET, [plak'-et], *n.* the slit where a skirt or petticoat is fastened; a woman's pocket. [Uncert.].

PLACODERMS, [plak'-ō-dermz], *n.*(*pl.*) (*zool.*) the placoid fishes. [Gk. *plax* plate and *derma* skin].

PLACOID, [plak'-oid], *adj.* (*zool.*) having the skin covered with plate-like scales. [Gk. *plax* plate and *oeides* like].

PLAFOND, [plaf-ond'], *n.* (*arch.*) the ceiling of a room; any soffit. [Fr. *plafond* ceiling].

PLAGAL, [plāgl], *adj.* (*mus.*) ranging between the dominant and the octave. [Gk. *plagios* oblique].

PLAGATE, [plā'-gāt], *adj.* (*zool.*) striped, marked with one or more streaks. [L. *plaga* stripe].

PLAGE, [plahzh], *n.* a promenade beach at a fashionable seaside resort. [Fr. *plage*].

PLAGIARISM, [plā'-ja-rizm], *n.* the act of plagiarizing; matter plagiarized; the attempt to establish as one's own another person's literary work, literary theft.

PLAGIARIST, [plā'-ja-rist], *n.* a person who has plagiarized; a copyist without acknowledgment.

PLAGIARIZE, [plā'-ja-riz], *v.t.* to adopt and attempt to pass off as one's own the writings of another.

PLAGIARY, [plā'-ja-ri], *n.* a person who wrongly appropriates what another writes; the act of plagiarizing. [L. *plagiare* to kidnap].

PLAGIOCLASE, [plā'-ji-ō-klās], *n.* (*min.*) a felspar with oblique cleavage, that is, a triclinic felspar mainly composed of albite or anorthite. [Gk. *plagios* oblique and *klasis* cleavage].

PLAGIONITE, [plā'-ji-o-nit], *n.* (*min.*) sulphantimonite of lead forming thick crystals grey-black in colour.

PLAGIOSTOMOUS, [plā'-ji-ost'-om-us], *adj.* of, relating to, that order of fishes which includes the sharks and rays. [Gk. *plagios* oblique and *stoma* mouth].

PLAGUE (1), [plāg], *n.* a dreadful pestilence, a fatal disease; any terrible affliction suddenly descending on the whole population, calamity; (*coll.*) any troublesome and persistent person or recurring situation; (*fig.*) a superabundance. [ME. *plague* from L. *plaga* pestilence].

PLAGUE (2), [plāg], *v.t.* to afflict with a plague, to infest with any sudden and widespread calamity; to harass, be persistently troublesome to. [PLAGUE (1)].

PLAGUESOME, [plāg'-sum], *adj.* pestering, annoying.

PLAGUE-SPOT, [plāg'-spot], *n.* a place or district harbouring disease; a spot on the flesh left by the plague; (*fig.*) a haunt of evil-doers.

PLAGUILY, [plāg'-ili], *adv.* in a plaguy manner.

PLAGUY, [plāg'-i], *adj.* troublesome, vexatious.

PLAICE, [plās], *n.* the edible flat-fish, *Pleuronectes platessa*. [ME. *plais* from Gk. *platus* flat].

PLAID, [plad, plād], *n.* a woollen garment of Scottish origin generally of a checked fabric, to wrap round the body; a tartan. [Uncert.].

PLAIDED, [plad'-id, plā'-did], *adj.* wearing a plaid.

PLAICE

PLAIN (1), [plān], *n.* a wide area of level land or open field. [L. *planum*].

PLAIN (2), [plān], *adj.* flat, smooth, level; having no elaborate ornament or pattern, simple; easy to perceive by the senses, distinctly visible, clearly heard; easy to understand; straightforward, unaffected, sincere, frank; blunt, ordinary-looking, possessing a somewhat ugly face. [L. *planus* flat, simple].

PLAIN (3), [plān], *adv.* clearly, distinctly.

PLAIN-CHANT, [plān'-chahnt], *n.* plain-song.

PLAIN-DEALING (1), [plān'-dēl'-ing], *n.* frankness in word and deed, particularly in commercial association.

PLAIN-DEALING (2), [plān'-dēl'-ing], *adj.* behaving with frankness and sincerity, honest, straightforward.

PLAIN-HEARTED, [plān'-haht'-id], *adj.* having a sincere heart; of a frank disposition.

PLAINLY, [plān'-li], *adv.* in a plain manner.

PLAINNESS, [plān'-nes], *n.* the state or quality of being plain.

PLAINSMAN, [plānz'-man], *n.* a man who works and lives on a plain, particularly in the U.S.A.

PLAIN-SONG, [plān'-song], *n.* a form of modal music consisting of a chant sung in unison, generally within the range of an octave, with the accents placed according to verbal emphasis, a Gregorian chant.

PLAINSPOKEN, [plān'-spōk'-en], *adj.* direct in speech, speaking with plain, frank sincerity, outspoken. [PLAIN (3) and SPOKEN].

PLAINT, [plānt], *n.* lamentation, complaint, a sad song; (*leg.*) a complaint setting forth the cause of the action in a formal accusation. [L. *planctus* lamentation].

PLAINTIFF, [plānt'-if], *n.* (*leg.*) the person who sues another called the defendant. [OFr. *plaintif* complaining].

PLAINTIVE, [plānt'-iv], *adj.* expressive of sorrow or sadness, mournful; continually harping on miseries. [OFr. *plaintive*, *fem.* of *plaintif* complaining].

PLAINTIVELY, [plānt'-iv-li], *adv.* in a plaintive manner.

PLAINTIVENESS, [plānt'-iv-nes], *n.* the quality of being plaintive.

PLAISTER†, see PLASTER.

PLAIT (1), [plat], *n.* a combination of three or more interlaced strands forming a single length, particularly of a woman's hair, a braid; a fold of material creased at the bend, a pleat. [ME. *plait* from L. *plicitum* *p.pt.* of *plicare* to fold together].

PLAIT (2), [plat], *v.t.* to interlace in the form of a plait, to braid; to pleat. [PLAIT (1)].

PLAITER, [plat'-er], *n.* person who, or that which, plaits.

PLAITLESS, [plat'-les], *adj.* having no plaits.

PLAKODINE, [plak'-ō-dīn], *n.* (*min.*) sub-arsenide of nickel.

PLAN (1), [plan], *n.* a drawing on a plane surface, a proportionate design of a projected or completed structure or building; a scheme; a project set out on paper, the proposed method of carrying it out. [L. *planus* flat].

PLAN (2), (**planning**, **planned**), [plan], *v.t.* to make a plan, to draw up plans of a projected scheme, showing all its aspects, details and the method of approach; to work out a project of in the head, to scheme. [PLAN (1)].

PLANCH, [plahnch], *v.t.* to cover with planks, to support by means of a strong plate of material. [L. *planca* plank].

PLANCHET, [plahnch'-et], *n.* a flat piece of metal from which is stamped a coin.

PLANCHETTE, [plahn-shet'], *n.* a small, thin piece of board cut in the shape of a heart and mounted on two wheels, with a pencil acting as a third support, which is supposed to respond without deliberate guidance to hands placed upon it writing spiritualistic messages. [Fr. *planchette*, *dim.* of *planche* plank].

PLANE (1), [plān], *n.* a tool used in smoothing wood, consisting of a flat blade inserted or adjusted to project slightly beyond the bottom surface of a wooden or metal block or frame. [LL. *plana* a plane].

PLANE

PLANE (2), [plān], *n.* any tree of the genus *Platanus* characterized by the periodical patchy appearance of the trunk due to the bark peeling. [Fr. *plane* from Gk. *platanos* plane-tree].

PLANE (3), [plān], *n.* an aeroplane; a wing of an aeroplane. [Abbreviated form of AEROPLANE].

PLANE (4), [plān], *n.* an accurately flattened surface; stage, level, degree; **p. geometry**, the manipulation of figures on a plane surface; **p. table**, a surveying instrument consisting of a drawing-board marked off in degrees from the centre. [L. *planum* plain].

PLANE (5), [plān], *adj.* having a perfectly flat surface. [L. *planus* level].

PLANE (6), [plān], *v.t.* to smooth, to make level by means of a plane. [PLANE (1)].

PLANE (7), [plān], *v.i.* to glide through the air in an aeroplane with the engine switched off. [PLANE (3)].

PLANE-IRON, [plān'-iern], *n.* the cutter blade of a plane.

PLANER, [plān'-er], *n.* a person who planes.

PLANET, [plan'-et], *n.* a celestial body which revolves in an orbit around the sun. [ME. *planete* from Gk. *planetes* (*asteres*) wandering (stars)].

PLANETARIUM, [plan'-et-āer'-i-um], *n.* a model astronomical machine which represents the motions of the planets, an orrery. [LL. *planetarium*, *neut. sg.* of *planetarius* of planets].

PLANETARY, [plan'-et-er-i], *adj.* of, relating to, consisting of, or produced by, planets; having the characteristics of a planet, erratic or revolving. [L. *planetarius* of planets].

PLANETESIMAL, [plan'-et-es'-iml], *n.* one of an infinite number of minute bodies which are believed to form the planets. [PLANET and (INFINIT)ESIMAL].

PLANETOID, [plan'-et-oid], *n.* a minor planet, one of the small planets revolving between the orbits of Mars and Jupiter. [PLANET and Gk. *oeides* like].

PLANGENCY, [plan'-jen-si], *n.* the fact or quality of being plangent.

PLANGENT, [plan'-jent], *adj.* beating with noise, as of a wave, noisy, resounding in great splashes of sound. [L. *plangens*, *pres.pt.* of *plangere* to beat].

PLANI-, *pref.* level, flat. [L. *planus*].

PLANIMETER, [plan-im'-it-er], *n.* an instrument to measure the area of an irregular plane figure. [PLANI and METER].

PLANIMETRICAL, [plan'-im-et'-rikl], *adj.* relating to planimetry.

PLANIMETRY, [plan-im'-et-ri], *n.* the mensuration of plane surfaces. [PLANI and Gk. *metria* measuring].

PLANIPETALOUS, [plan'-i-pet'-al-us], *adj.* (*bot.*) having flat petals.

PLANISH, [plan'-ish], *v.t.* to polish, to smooth by hammering. [OFr. *planir* to smooth].

PLANISHER, [plan'-ish-er], *n.* a person who planishes; a tool to planish brass, etc.

PLANISPHERE, [plan'-is-fēer], *n.* a sphere projected on a plane. [PLANI and SPHERE].

PLANK (1), [plangk], *n.* a long strip of sawn timber usually not smaller than an inch and a half thick by six inches wide. [ME. *planke* from LL. *planca*].

PLANK (2), [plangk], *v.t.* to cover, to build a floor, with planks closely fitted in rows; (*slang*) **to p. down**, to put down in concrete form, particularly cash. [PLANK (1)].

PLANKTON, [plangk'-ton], *n.*(*pl.*) (*biol.*) a general word for the minute organisms drifting on or near the surface of seas and rivers. [Gk. *plagkton*, *neut.* of *plagktos* wandering].

PLANLESS, [plan'-les], *adj.* having no plan.

PLANNER, [plan'-er], *n.* person who forms a plan.

PLANO-, [plān'-ō], *pref.* flat, level; **p.-concave**, flat on one side and concave on the other; **p.-conical**, flat on one side and conical on the other; **p.-convex**, level on one side and convex on the other; **p.-horizontal**, having a flat, horizontal surface or position.

PLANT (1), [plahnt], *n.* (*slang*) hoax, a swindle, a put-up job. [PLANT (3)].

PLANT (2), [plahnt], *n.* any vegetable organism which can feed on substances collected from the soil and air; a small green vegetable organism, as distinguished from a tree; a sapling; the total equipment of a factory; a complete system of machinery. [OE. *plante* from L. *planta* shoot].

PLANT (3), [plahnt], *v.t.* to set in the soil as a necessary condition of intended growth; to set out seeds, to provide with plants; to place in the ground to a depth which prevents toppling; to place in position firmly; to settle, particularly as colonizers; **to p. on**, (*slang*) to conceal on another's person stolen or incriminating property. [OE. *plantian* from L. *plantare* to plant].

PLANTABLE, [plahnt'-abl], *adj.* capable of being planted.

PLANTAIN (1), [plant'-in], *n.* a genus of wild plants with long broad leaves growing close to the ground. [ME. *plantein* from L. *plantago*].

PLANTAIN (2), [plant'-in], *n.* a tropical plant yielding a fruit extensively serviceable for food, *Musa paradisiaca*; **p. lily**, a plant of the genus *Funkia*. [L. *platanus* plane-tree].

PLANTAR, [plan'-tah(r)], *adj.* (*anat.*) of, belonging to, the sole of the foot. [L. *plantaris*].

PLANTATION, [plant-ā'-shun], *n.* the place planted; a group of planted trees; a large cultivated estate; an estate cultivated by slave labour for specific crops; †a new settlement, a colony.

PLANT-CANE, [plahnt'-kān], *n.* the first year's growth of the sugar cane.

PLANTER, [plahnt'-er], *n.* a person who plants; one who owns a plantation; a settler.

PLANTERSHIP, [plahnt'-er-ship], *n.* the business of a planter, or the management of a plantation.

PLANTIGRADE (1), [plan'-ti-grād'], *n.* a plantigrade animal.

PLANTIGRADE (2), [plan'-ti-grād'], *adj.* (*zool.*) walking on the sole of the foot, distinguished from digitigrade. [L. *planta* sole of the foot and GRADE].

PLANTING, [plahnt'-ing], *n.* the act of setting in the ground for propagation; the forming of plantations.

PLANTLET, [plahnt'-let], *n.* a little plant.

PLANT-LIKE, [plahnt'-līk], *adj.* having some of the characteristics of a plant.

PLANT-LOUSE, [plahnt'-lows], *n.* (*entom.*) an aphis that feeds on plants.
PLANT-NAME, [plahnt'-nām], *n.* the popular name given to a plant as distinct from its botanical name.
PLANXTY, [plangks'-ti], *n.* a lively tune or jig, Irish or Welsh, played on the harp. [Uncert.].
PLAQUE, [plak], *n.* a disk or piece of metal, china, wood, stone, etc., ornamented in relief; such a disk enamelled; the enamel itself. [Flem. *placke* little coin].
PLAQUETTE, [plak-et'], *n.* a small plaque. [Fr. *plaquette*].
PLASH (1), [plash], *n.* a shallow puddle; a splash; the sound of water when broken at the surface. [OE. *plæsc*, ME. *plasch* puddle].
PLASH (2), [plash], *n.* a branch partly lopped and bound to others. [PLASH (4)].
PLASH (3), [plash], *v.t.* to dabble in water; to sprinkle with water or colour, to splash. [PLASH (1)].
PLASH (4), [plash], *v.t.* to bend (a branch) by half cutting through and interweaving it with others. [OFr. *plaissier* from L. *plectere* to plait].
PLASHING, [plash'-ing], *n.* the act of cutting branches half through and interweaving them with others, so as to form an effective hedge; hedge; the dashing of colouring matter on walls, in imitation of granite.
PLASHY, [plash'-i], *adj.* abounding with puddles.
PLASM, [plazm], *n.* a mould or matrix in which anything is cast or formed; plasma; (*biol.*) the living matter forming a cell. [Gk. *plasma* that which is moulded].
PLASMA, [plaz'-ma], *n.* a variety of green, transparent quartz; the colourless fluid from which is formed the organic lymph and the red corpuscles of the blood stream. [Gk. *plasma* that which is moulded].
PLASMATICAL, [plaz-mat'-ikl], *adj.* giving form; of, relating to, plasma.
PLASMIC, [plaz'-mik], *adj.* of, relating to protoplasm or plasma.
PLASMODIUM, [plaz-mō'-di-um], *n.* a mass of protoplasm. [Gk. *plasma* that which is moulded].
PLASMOGEN, [plaz'-mō-jen], *n.* protoplasm. [Gk. *plasma* that which is moulded and *genes* producing].
PLASTER (1), **PLAISTER**†, [plahst'-er], *n.* a mixture of lime, sand and water used for applying in coats to walls of houses; a wad of fabric, cotton, etc., treated with medicated liquids and applied externally to affected parts; an adhesive tape for protecting wounds or broken skin. [OE. *plaster* from Gk. *emplastron*].
PLASTER (2), [plahst'-er], *v.t.* to smear or coat with plaster; to cover and protect (a wound) with strips of adhesive tape; to cover all over with a generous amount. [PLASTER (1)].
PLASTERER, [plahst'-er-er], *n.* a person who overlays with plaster; a person who makes figures in plaster.
PLASTERING, [plahst'-er-ing], *n.* the act of overlaying with plaster; a covering of plaster.
PLASTER-OF-PARIS, [plahst'-er-ov-pa'-ris], *n.* a malleable substance consisting of finely ground roasted gypsum mixed with water, used in building and for surgical dressing to set broken bones.
PLASTIC, [plast'-ik], *adj.* having a consistency which allows manipulation by pressing, rolling, etc.; capable of being shaped; capable of shaping or creating; (*art*) of, relating to, formed by, the art of modelling into solid form, as distinct from graphic form, connected with the media of clay, wood, metal, etc.; (*biol.*) capable of metabolic change; (*fig.*) capable of radical response, impressionable; (*med.*) relating to, formed by, the art of grafting fresh organic tissue by surgical operation. [Gk. *plastikos* of moulding].
PLASTICS, [plast-iks] *n.* the science or craft of connecting various resins by rolling or moulding into durable materials for use in industry or commerce; the articles, materials, etc. so made.
PLASTICALLY, [plast'-ik-ali], *adv.* in a plastic manner.
PLASTICINE, [plast'-is-ēn], *n.* (*prot.*) a proprietary brand of plastic material which does not harden, a substitute for modelling clay.
PLASTICITY, [plast-is'-i-ti], *n.* the quality of being plastic.
PLASTICIZE, [plast'-is-īz], *v.t.* to render plastic.
PLASTID, [plast'-id], *n.* (*biol.*) a living cell, a unit of protoplasm.
PLASTOGRAPHY, [plast-og'-raf-i], *n.* the art of making figures in plaster; counterfeit writing. [Gk. *plastos* moulded and *graphia* writing].
PLASTRON, [plast'-ron], *n.* a breastplate of steel worn as a piece of armour; a leather guard used in fencing to protect the chest; a decorative ornamental piece of a woman's dress; the ventral part of the shells of chelonians. [Fr. *plastron*].
PLAT (1), [plat], *n.* work done by platting or weaving [PLAIT].
PLAT (2), [plat], *n.* a small plot of ground. [PLOT].
PLAT (3), [plat], *n.* a hole at the end of a level in a metal mine where the ore is put ready for hoisting. [Fr. *plat*].
PLAT (4), **(platting, platted)**, [plat], *v.t.* to weave, plait.
PLATANE, [plat'-ān], *n.* the eastern plane-tree, *Platanus orientalis*. [L. *platanus*].
PLAT-BAND, [plat'-band], *n.* a border of flowers; (*arch.*) a flat square moulding; the lintel of a door or window; a fillet between the flutings of a column.

PLAT-BAND

PLATE (1), [plāt], *n.* a flat shallow domestic utensil of various forms, usually circular, made of tin, enamelled tin, porcelain or earthenware, glass, silver or gold, for holding food at table; the amount of food on a plate, a helping; a shallow vessel similar to these, but not used at mealtimes; articles, such as candlesticks, forks and spoons, etc., of domestic use, plated with gold or silver; a flat sheet of metal used as a support; a thin plate of copper or steel engraved with designs from which impressions are printed; an impression from such a plate; an oblong of brass or metal engraved with the name of a person; a thin piece of moulded vulcanite or other material into which a set of artificial teeth are fitted; (in horseracing) a light shoe worn by racehorses; the prize consisting of a piece of silver or gold plate set up for the winner of a race; a race the winner of which must be sold for a minimum sum; (*baseball*) the home base for the batting side; (*phot.*) a sheet of sensitized glass acting as a negative; (*wirel.*) the metal cylinder of a thermionic valve. [ME. *plate* from Gk. *platus* flat].
PLATE (2), [plāt], *v.t.* to cover or overlay with metal or precious metal plates; to beat into thin plates, to laminate. [PLATE (1)].
PLATE-ARMOUR, [plāt'-ahm'-er], *n.* armour consisting of overlaid metal plates; very thick plates of metal used for protecting warships.
PLATEAU, [plat-ō'], *n.* a broad plain of elevated land; a large ornamental dish for the centre of a table. [Fr. *plateau*].
PLATEFUL, [plāt'-fool], *n.* as much as a plate will hold, a helping of food.
PLATE-GLASS, [plāt'-glahs], *n.* a high-class kind of glass cast on a table so as to form thick plates, used for mirrors and shop-fronts.
PLATELAYER, [plāt'-lā'-er], *n.* a workman employed on a railroad to lay the rails and keep them in order. [PLATE (1) and LAYER].
PLATEMARK, [plāt'-mahk], *n.* a legal mark indicative of various makes of plated ware and of the quality of a metal; the mark on postage stamps that distinguishes the plate from which they are printed.
PLATEN, [plat'-en], *n.* the part of a printing-press upon which the impression is made; the roller of a typewriter. [OFr. *platine*].
PLATER, [plāt'-er], *n.* a horse, usually of inferior quality, competing in selling races for a cup or plate.
PLATE-RACK, [plāt'-rak], *n.* a kitchen apparatus for holding plates and dishes when drying.
PLATEY, [plāt'-i], *adj.* like a plate, flat.
PLATFORM, [plat'-fawm], *n.* a level place raised above the general level, as in an assembly-hall or at a railway station; a declared party scheme of action or policy, an immediate political programme; important people seated on the platform at a meeting. [OFr. *plateforme* ground-plan].
PLATINA, [plat'-in-a], *n.* platinum. [Span. *platina*].
PLATING, [plāt'-ing], *n.* the art or process of covering anything with a coating of metal; such a coating of metal.
PLATINIC, [plat-in'-ik], *adj.* relating to, made from, platinum.
PLATINIFEROUS, [plat'-in-if'-er-us], *adj.* bearing, yielding, platinum. [PLATINUM and L. *ferre* to bear].
PLATINIZE, [plat'-in-īz], *v.t.* to coat with platinum.
PLATINOIDS, [plat'-in-oidz], *n.*(*pl.*) metals like, and found associated with, platinum.
PLATINOTYPE, [plat'-in-ō-tīp], *n.* a photographic printing process using platinum-black. [PLATINUM and TYPE].

PLATINOUS, [plat'-in-us], *adj.* of, relating to, containing, platinum.
PLATINUM (1), [plat'-in-um], *n.* the rare metallic element Pt, grey-white in colour, very heavy, and malleable. [Span. *platina*, *dim.* of *plata* silver].
PLATINUM (2), [plat'-in-um], *adj.* relating to, made of, resembling, platinum; **p. blonde**, a woman with hair of a natural or artificially dyed grey-gold colour.
PLATINUM-BLACK, [plat'-in-um-blak'], *n.* a modified form of platinum, consisting of a black powder.
PLATITUDE, [plat'-it-ewd], *n.* vapidness, flatness, dulness; a futile remark, an obvious and over-used observation. [Fr. *platitude* from *plat* flat].
PLATITUDINARIAN, [plat'-it-ewd-in-āer'-i-an], *n.* a person who has a reputation for uttering platitudes.
PLATITUDINIZE, [plat'-it-ewd'-in-iz], *v.i.* to talk in platitudes.
PLATITUDINOUS, [plat'-it-ewd'-in-us], *adj.* of, resembling, a platitude.
PLATITUDINOUSLY, [plat'-it-ewd'-in-us-li], *adv.* in a platitudinous manner.
PLATONIC, [plat-on'-ik], *adj.* of, relating to, derived from, Plato or his teachings; descriptive of a relationship or love believed to be based on pure friendship and sympathy without any tendency to partake of or experience physical passion or communion. [Gk. *Platonikos* of Plato, the Greek philosopher].
PLATONICALLY, [plat-on'-ik-al-i], *adv.* in the Platonic manner.
PLATONISM, [plā'-ton-izm], *n.* the philosophy or doctrines of Plato and his followers; a principle established by Plato.
PLATONIST, [plā'-ton-ist], *n.* a follower of Plato.
PLATONIZE, [plā'-ton-īz], *v.t.* to convert to Platonism; to explain platonically; *v.i.* to adopt the principles of the Platonic school.
PLATOON, [plat-ōōn'], *n.* a subdivision of a company in a modern infantry battalion. [Fr. *peloton*].
PLATTER, [plat'-er], *n.* a large shallow dish; a wooden plate for bread. [ME. *plater* from OFr. *plat* dish].
PLATTING, [plat'-ing], *n.* the process of working in plats; work done by plaiting; slips of cane or straw braided for making into hats.
PLATYPUS, [plat'-ip-us], *n.* the duckbill *Ornithorhynchus anatinus*. [Gk. *platus* broad and *pous* foot].
PLATYRRHINE, [plat'-i-rīn], *adj.* (*zool.*) having a broad nose. [Gk. *platus* broad and *rhis rhinos* nose].
PLAUDIT, [plaw'-dit], *n.* praise bestowed; a public expression of applause, particularly by clapping the hands. [L. *plaudite*, *imper. pl.* of *plaudere* to applaud].
PLAUSIBILITY, [plauz'-ib-il'-iti], *n.* the quality of being plausible, speciousness.
PLAUSIBLE, [plauz'-ibl], *adj.* superficially worthy of approval, apparently reasonable, specious; having a persuasive but unsound quality of argument. [L. *plausibilis* praiseworthy].
PLAUSIBLENESS, [plauz'-ibl-nes], *n.* the quality of being plausible, speciousness, plausibility.
PLAUSIBLY, [plauz'-ib-li], *adv.* in a plausible manner.
PLAUSIVE, [plauz'-iv], *adj.* expressive of approval, applauding; plausible.
PLAY (1), [plā], *n.* an action or activity, physical, mental or emotional, undertaken or experienced for the sake of the anticipated or consequent pleasure and relaxation, diversion, amusement; the style or manner of playing; gambling; rapid movement; room, space for movement; the amount or limit of space for or between connected or mechanical parts, give; (*fig.*) unrestricted scope; a literary composition designed for the stage, a drama; a stage performance, a performance on a musical instrument. [OE. *plega*, ME. *plei*].
PLAY (2), [plā], *v.t.* to cause to move in a more or less defined direction; to take part in a game; to perform, to carry out; to introduce into a game, as a card; to compete against; to strike (a ball); to act the part of on the stage; to perform on a musical instrument; in angling, to tire a fish out; *v.i.* to undertake or experience any kind of activity for the sake of amusement, to sport; to gambol; to participate in a game; to strike a ball as part of a game; to gamble; to deal with or use superficially, to trifle or toy (with); to move about lightly and freely; to move in accordance with a limited scope; **to p. off**, to use as a foil or contrast, to display; **to p. on**, to continue to play; (*cricket*) to permit the ball to hit the stumps after it has touched bat or body; **to p. upon**, to deceive, to endeavour to affect. [OE. *plegian*, ME. *pleien* to play].
PLAYABLE, [plā'-abl], *adj.* capable of being played.
PLAY-ACT, [plā'-akt'], *v.i.* to pretend. [PLAY (1) and ACT].
PLAY-ACTOR, [plā'-akt'-or], *n.* a theatrical performer, particularly an actor who plays to the gallery.
PLAYBILL, [plā'-bil], *n.* the programme of a theatrical performance, distributed by hand; a printed advertisement of a play in the form of a handbill or poster.
PLAYBOOK, [plā'-bōōk], *n.* a book of dramatic compositions.
PLAY-BOX, [plā'-boks], *n.* a wooden box in which children keep their toys or tuck.
PLAY-BOY, [plā'-boi], *n.* a man with no serious purpose in life who spends his whole time seeking amusement; an entertaining fellow full of life and energy.
PLAY-DAY, [plā'-dā], *n.* a day given to play, a holiday.
PLAY-DEBT, [plā'-det], *n.* a debt contracted in gambling at cards.
PLAYER, [plā'-er], *n.* a person who plays; a stage actor; a musician; a professional athlete, particularly a footballer or cricketer.
PLAYER-PIANO, [plā'-er-pi-an'-ō], *n.* a piano fitted with a mechanical apparatus which plays music from specially prepared rolls.
PLAYFELLOW, [plā'-fel'-ō], *n.* a companion of one's childhood amusements.
PLAYFUL, [plā'-fōōl], *adj.* sportive, given to play, indulging a sportive fancy, full of playfulness; expressive of a happy mood.
PLAYFULLY, [plā'-fōōl-i], *adv.* in a playful manner.
PLAYFULNESS, [plā'-fōōl-nes], *n.* the quality or the state of being playful, sportiveness.
PLAYGOER, [plā'-gō-er], *n.* a person who habitually goes to the theatre.
PLAYGOING, [plā'-gō-ing], *n.* the habit of frequenting the theatre.
PLAYGROUND, [plā'-grownd], *n.* a piece of ground near to a school on which games are played; a part of a public park fitted out for children.
PLAYHOUSE, [plā'-hows], *n.* a theatre.
PLAYING, [plā'-ing], *n.* the act of one who plays; **p. cards**, cards used for games.
PLAYING-FIELD, [plā'-ing-fēld], *n.* a field prepared and marked out for the playing of games.
PLAYLET, [plā'-let], *n.* a short play, usually of one scene or act.
PLAYMATE, [plā'-māt], *n.* a playfellow.
PLAY-OFF, [plā'-of], *n.* a second game played between two teams playing for a cup after they have drawn a match.
PLAYPEN, [plā'-pen'], *n.* a portable framework of wood with railings, usually collapsible, inside which a young child can be safely left to play.
PLAY-ROOM, [plā'-rōōm], *n.* a room set aside for children to play in.
PLAYSOME, [plā'-sum], *adj.* playful; wanton.
PLAYSOMENESS, [plā'-sum-nes], *n.* the quality of being playsome, playfulness; wantonness.
PLAYTHING, [plā'-thing], *n.* that designed to be played with, a toy.
PLAYTIME, [plā'-tīm], *n.* time given up to recreation.
PLAYWRIGHT, [plā'-rīt], *n.* a writer of plays, a dramatist. [PLAY and WRIGHT].
PLAZA, [plah'-za], *n.* a market-place. [Span. *plaza* place].
PLEA, [plē], *n.* an excuse, pretext; entreaty, urgent request; (*leg.*) a defendant's allegation in answer to the plaintiff's case. [ME. *plei*, *ple* from L. *placitum* that which pleases].
PLEACH, [plēch], *v.t.* to interweave branches of trees or shrubs, to plash. [ME. *plechen*].
PLEAD, [plēd], *v.t. and i.* to help or support by arguing on behalf of, e.g., another person's cause; to allege in defence, to put forward as an apology; to supplicate, to entreat; (*leg.*) to present an answer in a formal capacity to the declared accusation of a plaintiff, to make a plea. [ME. *plaiden* from OFr. *plaid* plea].
PLEADABLE, [plēd'-abl], *adj.* capable of being pleaded, that may be alleged in proof or vindication.
PLEADER, [plēd'-er], *n.* (*leg.*) a person who argues in a court of justice, one who forms pleas or pleadings, an advocate, a barrister.
PLEADING, [plēd'-ing], *n.* the act of supporting by arguments; (*leg.*) (*pl.*) the case of both plaintiff and defendant in documentary form.
PLEADINGLY, [plēd'-ing-li], *adv.* in a pleading manner, by pleading.
PLEASABLE†, [plēz'-abl], *adj.* able to be pleased.
PLEASANCE†, [plez'-ans], *n.* pleasure, pleasantry; a secluded pleasure garden. [OFr. *plaisance*].
PLEASANT, [plez'-ant], *adj.* having a pleasing quality, agreeable to the mind and senses, satisfying as an

experience of enjoyment; having an easy-going and amiable nature, affable; gay, lively, enlivening. [OFr. *plaisant, pres.pt.* of *plaisir* to please].

PLEASANTLY, [plez'-ant-li], *adv.* in a pleasant manner.

PLEASANTNESS, [plez'-ant-nes], *n.* the state or the quality of being pleasant.

PLEASANTRY, [plez'-ant-ri], *n.* an instance of happy association, merriment; a sprightly saying, lively talk; a joke or humorous remark. [Fr. *plaisanterie*].

PLEASE, [plēz], *v.t. and i.* to give or bring pleasure to, to render satisfied, to behave or bring about a set of circumstances so as to produce a sense of happy satisfaction; to give happy satisfaction, to be a source of delight; to choose, prefer, like, think fit. [ME. *plaisen*, OFr. *plaisir* from L. *placere* to please].

PLEASED, [plēzd], *adj.* experiencing or having experienced happy satisfaction, gratified.

PLEASEDNESS, [plēzd'-nes], *n.* the state of being pleased.

PLEASER, [plēz'-er], *n.* a person who pleases or gratifies.

PLEASING, [plēz'-ing], *adj.* gratifying to the senses or the mind; agreeable, giving satisfaction or pleasure.

PLEASINGLY, [plēz'-ing-li], *adv.* in a pleasing manner.

PLEASINGNESS, [plēz'-ing-nes], *n.* the quality of giving pleasure.

PLEASURABLE, [plezh'-er-abl], *adj.* capable of affording pleasure, pleasing, affording gratification, enjoyable.

PLEASURABLENESS, [plezh'-er-abl-nes], *n.* the quality of being pleasurable.

PLEASURABLY, [plezh'-er-ab-li], *adv.* in a pleasurable manner.

PLEASURE (1), [plezh'-er], *n.* a state of emotional or mental satisfaction with a basis of well-being and happiness due to the absence of pain or fear; an experience, or series of contributory experiences, producing an agreeable effect on the senses, enjoyment, delight; temporary sensual satisfaction, the gratification of the desires; a favour; arbitrary choice; a source of satisfaction. [OFr. *plaisir, plesir*].

PLEASURE (2), [plezh'-er], *v.t.* to give or bring pleasure to, to gratify, please. [PLEASURE (1)].

PLEASURE-BOAT, [plezh'-er-bōt'], *n.* a boat owned or hired for pleasure.

PLEASURE-GROUND, [plezh'-er-grownd'], *n.* a ground laid out for public amusement, a recreation ground.

PLEASURE-STEAMER, [plezh'-er-stēm'-er], *n.* a steamer which takes passengers for short excursion trips.

PLEASURE-TRIP, [plezh'-er-trip'], *n.* an excursion for pleasure.

PLEAT (1), [plēt], *n.* a fold made in material and ironed flat. [*Var.* of PLAIT].

PLEAT (2), [plēt], *v.t.* to make a pleat in, to fold flat, to double over and iron out flat. [PLEAT (1)].

PLEBE, [plēb], *n.* (*U.S. slang*) a junior member of a military academy.

PLEBEIAN (1), [plib-ē'-an], *n.* a member of the lower classes. [PLEBEIAN (2)].

PLEBEIAN (2), [plib-ē'-an], *adj.* belonging to, originating in, the lower classes; bad-mannered, common, having a strong accent. [L. *plebeius* of the common people].

PLEBEIANISM, [plib-ē'-an-izm], *n.* plebeian quality or manners.

PLEBEIANIZE, [plib-ē'-an-īz], *v.t.* to make plebeian or common.

PLEBISCITARY, [pleb'-is-īt'-eri], *adj.* of, relating to, derived from, a plebiscite.

PLEBISCITE, [pleb'-is-īt, pleb'-is-it], *n.* the vote of a whole community expressed in a national ballot, or a decree founded on it. [L. *plebiscitum*].

PLEBS, [plebz], *n.* the working classes of ancient Rome; the proletariat. [L. *plebs*].

PLECTRUM, [plek'-trum], *n.* a small stick or quill with which the ancients plucked the lyre; a small flat thin piece of bone or flexible material held between the thumb and first finger used in playing a modern stringed instrument such as the banjo. [Gk. *plektron* a striking instrument].

PLEDGE (1), [plej], *n.* something handed over as a security for the fulfilment of an obligation, contract or engagement, a surety, a token, earnest, sign, something put in pawn in return for a money loan; a promise, a verbal bond of contract; a drinking to the health of another as an expression of friendship, a toast. [ME. *pledge* from OFr. *plege, pleige* security].

PLEDGE (2), [plej], *v.t.* to deposit or hand over as a security, to put in pledge; to make a promise, to place oneself under a binding engagement, particularly to abstain from drinking alcoholic liquor; to drink a person's health, to toast. [PLEDGE (1)].

PLEDGEABLE, [plej'-abl], *adj.* able to be pledged; worth being pledged, acceptable as a pledge.

PLEDGEE, [plej-ē'], *n.* the person to whom anything is pledged.

PLEDGER, [plej'-er], *n.* a person who pledges or pawns anything; one who drinks to the health of another.

PLEDGET, [plej'-et], *n.* (*surg.*) a compress or wad of lint laid over a wound. [Unkn.].

PLEIAD, (*pl.* **pleiades, pleiads**), [plī'-ad, plī'-ad-ēz, plī'-adz], *n.* (*astron.*) one of a group of stars in the constellation Taurus; (*myth.*) originally, one of the seven daughters of Atlas transformed into stars. [Gk. *Pleiades* the name by which the seven daughters of Atlas are known].

PLEISTOCENE, [plīs'-to-sēn], *adj.* (*geol.*) pertaining to the series of rocks above the Pliocene, the glacial series. [Gk. *pleistos* most and *kainos* new].

PLENARILY, [plēn'-er-il-i], *adv.* in a plenary manner, fully, completely.

PLENARINESS, [plēn'-er-i-nes], *n.* fulness, completeness.

PLENARTY, [plēn'-er-ti], *n.* the state of a benefice when occupied, as distinct from *vacancy*. [ME. *plenerte* from OFr. *plenierete* abundance].

PLENARY, [plēn'-er-i], *adj.* full, entire, complete; fully representative of all sections. [LL. *plenarius* full].

PLENILUNAR, [plen'-i-lo͞on'-er], *adj.* of, relating to, the full moon. [L. *plenus* full and LUNAR].

PLENILUNARY, [plen'-i-lo͞on'-eri], *adj.* plenilunar.

PLENIPOTENTIARY (1), [plen'-i-pot-en'-sher-i], *n.* an envoy or ambassador to a foreign court furnished with full diplomatic powers to make decisions on behalf of his State on his own authority. [PLENIPOTENTIARY (2)].

PLENIPOTENTIARY (2), [plen'-i-pot-en'-sher-i], *adj.* possessing full powers of authority. [MedL. *plenipotentiarius*].

PLENIST, [plēn'-ist], *n.* a person who maintains that all space is full of matter. [L. *plenus* full].

PLENITUDE, [plen'-it-ewd], *n.* the state of being full, fulness, repletion, abundance, completeness. [L. *plenitudo*].

PLENTEOUS, [plen'-ti-us], *adj.* plentiful, copious, sufficient for every purpose, having abundance. [ME. *plentevous, plentivous* from OFr. *plentivous*].

PLENTEOUSLY, [plen'-ti-us-li], *adv.* in a plenteous manner.

PLENTEOUSNESS, [plen'-ti-us-nes], *n.* the state of being plenteous.

PLENTIFUL, [plen'-ti-fo͝ol], *adj.* abundant, copious; fruitful; available in large quantities. [PLENTY and FULL].

PLENTIFULLY, [plen'-ti-fo͝ol-i], *adv.* in a plentiful manner; to a plentiful degree.

PLENTIFULNESS, [plen'-ti-fo͝ol-nes], *n.* the state of being plentiful.

PLENTY (1), [plen'-ti], *n.* full supply, a large quantity or supply, abundance; fruitfulness. [L. *plenitas* fulness].

PLENTY (2), [plen'-ti], *adv.* to an abundant degree, quite sufficient, to a more than satisfactory extent. [PLENTY (1)].

PLENUM, [plēn'-um], *n.* fulness of matter in space, space as filled with matter, as opposed to *vacuum*; a fully attended conference. [L. *plenum, neut.sg.* of *plenus* full].

PLEOCHROISM, [plē'-ō-krō'-izm], *n.* variation in colour of crystals as apparent from different directions or by transmitted light. [Gk. *pleon* more and *khroos* complexion].

PLEONASM, [plē'-on-azm'], *n.* redundancy of words, a repetitive style of expression. [Gk. *pleonasmos*].

PLEONASTE, [plē'-on-ast], *n.* (*min.*) a variety of spinel. [Gk. *pleonastos* abundant].

PLEONASTIC, [plē'-on-ast'-ik], *adj.* having the characteristic of a pleonasm, redundant in words. [Gk. **pleonastikos*].

PLEONASTICALLY, [plē'-on-ast'-ik-al-i], *adv.* in a pleonastic manner, with redundancy of words.

PLESIOSAURUS, [plē'-si-ō-saw'-rus], *n.* a genus of extinct reptiles with very long necks who lived from the days of the Lias to those of the White Chalk. [Gk. *plesios* near to and *sauros* lizard].

PLETHORA, [pleth'-or-a], *n.* a superabundant quantity; (*med.*) excessive fulness of blood. [Gk. *plethore* fulness].

PLETHORETIC, [pleth'-or-et'-ik], *adj.* plethoric.

PLETHORIC, [pleth-or'-ik], *adj.* of, characterized by, plethora; having a full habit of body, full-blooded.
PLEURA, (*pl.* **pleurae**), [plōōer'-a], *n.* (*anat.*) a thin membrane which covers the interior of the thorax, and encloses the lungs. [Gk. *pleura* rib].
PLEURAL, [plōōer'-al], *adj.* of, relating to, connected with, the pleura.
PLEURISY, [plōōer'-is-i], *n.* (*path.*) an inflammation of the pleura. [Gk. *pleura* rib and *itis* denoting inflammation].
PLEURITIC, [plōō-rit'-ik], *adj.* of, relating to, or affected with, pleurisy. [*Prec.*].
PLEURITICAL, [plōō-rit'-ikl], *adj.* pleuritic.
PLEUROCARPOUS, [plōōer'-ō-kahp'-us], *adj.* (*bot.*) of a moss, bearing its fructification at the sides of the stem. [Gk. *pleura* side and *karpos* fruit].
PLEURODYNIA, [plōōer'-rō-din'-i-a], *n.* (*med.*) a painful affection in the walls or muscles of the chest. [Gk. *pleura* side and *odyne* pain].
PLEURON, [plōōer'-on], *n.* (*zool.*) a lateral extension of a crustacean shell.
PLEURO-PNEUMONIA, [plōōer'-ō-new-mō'-ni-a], *n.* a disease appearing as an inflammation of the pleura and the lungs at the same time.
PLEXIFORM, [pleks'-i-fawm], *adj.* having the structure of a plexus, in the form of a network; complicated. [PLEXUS and FORM].
PLEXIMETER, [pleks-im'-it-er], *n.* (*med.*) a plate of ivory or other substance, used in the testing of the chest or abdomen by percussion. [Gk. *plexis* striking and METER].
PLEXOR, [pleks'-or], *n.* (*med.*) the hammer used with the pleximeter. [Gk. *plexis* a striking].
PLEXUS, [pleks'-us], *n.* (*anat.*) a complicated junction of blood-vessels, nerves or fibres; (*fig.*) any involved structure of assembled units. [L. *plexus* network].
PLIABILITY, [plī'-ab-il'-it-i], *n.* the quality or state of being pliable, pliableness, flexibility.
PLIABLE, [plī'-abl], *adj.* capable of being manipulated, easy to be bent, flexible; (*fig.*) flexible in disposition, easily persuaded or influenced, too easily controlled by another person, owing to lack of purpose or will-power. [Fr. *pliable* from L. *plicare* to bend].
PLIABLENESS, [plī'-abl-nes], *n.* the quality of being pliable.
PLIABLY, [plī'-ab-li], *adv.* in a pliable manner.
PLIANCY, [plī'-an-si], *n.* the quality or state of being pliant, easiness to be bent; (*fig.*) readiness to be influenced.
PLIANT, [plī'-ant], *adj.* of a nature which permits of bending, flexible, easily moulded; easily influenced, tractable. [Fr. *pliant*, *pres.pt.* of *plier* to bend].
PLIANTLY, [plī'-ant-li], *adv.* in a pliant manner.
PLIANTNESS, [plī'-ant-nes], *n.* the quality of being pliant.
PLICA, [plī'-ka], *n.* (*med.*) a disease of the hair, by which it becomes matted and the scalp tender; (*bot.*) a disease in plants in which the branches collect into a tangled mass; a fold. [L. *plica* fold].
PLICATE, [plī-kāt'], *adj.* plicated.
PLICATED, [plī-kāt'-id], *adj.* (*bot.*) having ridges; plaited; folded like a fan. [L. *plicatum*, *p.pt.* of *plicare* to fold].
PLICATELY, [plī-kāt'-li], *adv.* in a folded manner.
PLICATION, [plī-kā'-shun], *n.* the act of folding, a fold.
PLICATURE, [plik'-ach-er], *n.* a fold, a doubling over.
PLIERS, [plī'-erz], *n.*(*pl.*) small pincers made of metal for seizing, bending, or extracting nails and similar objects. [ME. *plien* from OFr. *plier* to bend].

PLIERS

PLIFORM, [plī'-fawm], *adj.* in the form of a fold. [Fr. *plier* to bend and FORM].
PLIGHT (1), [plīt], *n.* a pledge; a taking of a binding oath. [PLIGHT (3)].
PLIGHT (2), [plīt], *n.* condition, state; sorry circumstances, predicament. [ME. *plit*, *pliht* from AFr. *plit* and OE. *pliht*].
PLIGHT (3), [plīt], *v.t.* to promise to marry submitting to the conventions of a formal engagement, to engage, to pledge under formal conditions. [OE. *plihtan* to pledge].
PLIMSOLL-MARK, [plim'-sol-mahk'], *n.* the line painted on the sides of a vessel to indicate the loading capacity. [S. *Plimsoll*, sponsor of the system].
PLINTH, [plinth], *n.* (*arch.*) a square-shaped, projecting part or base of a column, a pedestal or a wall; a base for statuettes, etc. [Gk. *plinthos* brick].
PLINTHITE, [plinth'-īt], *n.* a brick-red variety of clay containing iron and alumina.
PLIOCENE, [plī'-ō-sēn], *adj.* (*geol.*) pertaining to the uppermost of the Tertiary rocks lying above the Miocene and below the Pleistocene. [Gk. *pleion* more and *kainos* new].
PLIOSAURUS, [plī'-ō-saw'-rus], *n.* an extinct reptile allied to the plesiosaurus, but having a short neck, and found only in the Jurassic rocks. [Gk. *pleion* more and *sauros* a lizard].
PLOD, (plodding, plodded), [plod], *v.i.* to walk or to travel slowly and steadily but laboriously; (*fig.*) to work slowly but conscientiously. [Uncert.].
PLODDER, [plod'-er], *n.* a person who plods, a steady slow worker.
PLODDING, [plod'-ing], *adj.* steadily laborious, but slow; conscientious but not brilliant.
PLODDINGLY, [plod'-ing-li], *adv.* in a plodding manner.
PLONK, [plongk], *n.* a hollow report or sound. [Echoic].
PLOP (1), [plop], *n.* a slightly resonant sound made by a solid body, such as a frog, as it enters the water. [Probably echoic].
PLOP (2), (plopping, plopped), [plop], *v.i.* to fall into water with a plop. [PLOP (1)].
PLOT (1), [plot], *n.* a small extent of ground, a plat, particularly one used for growing vegetables or crops; a plan drafted out. [OE. *plott*].
PLOT (2), [plot], *n.* a scheme worked out in elaborate secrecy to gain a specific end, usually of an illegal nature, a conspiracy, intrigue; a scheme, stratagem of a more harmless character; the story of a book, film or play as embodied in the actions of the characters. [Fr. *complot* conspiracy].
PLOT (3), (plotting, plotted), [plot], *v.t.* to divide into plots. [PLOT (1)].
PLOT (4), (plotting, plotted), [plot], *v.t. and i.* to work out a complicated scheme in secrecy with some specific end in view, usually of an illegal nature, to plan surreptitiously, to intrigue; to set down as a record in mathematical terms; to participate in a plot, to conspire. [PLOT (2)].
PLOTLESS, [plot'-les], *adj.* without a plot.
PLOTTER, [plot'-er], *n.* a person who plots or contrives, a conspirator.
PLOTTING, [plot'-ing], *n.* the recording on paper of the lines of a survey.
PLOUGH (1), PLOW, [plow], *n.* an implement used in agricultural work consisting of a blade or series of blades firmly fitted into a framework which is worked by hand, horses or machines in order to drive furrows through the soil, cutting the sod up in slices in preparation for sowing; (*astron.*) a constellation in the form of a plough; (*slang*) an examination failure. [OE. *ploh*, ME. *plouh*].
PLOUGH (2), [plow], *v.t. and i.* to turn up the soil with a plough; to form by ploughing; to work at ploughing; (*fig.*) to drive a way (through); (*slang*) to refuse to pass an examination candidate; **to p. through**, (*fig.*) to work one's way through heavy or difficult reading matter. [PLOUGH (1)].
PLOUGHABLE, [plow'-abl], *adj.* able to be ploughed; arable.
PLOUGHBOY, [plow'-boi], *n.* a boy who drives the plough; a rustic, a yokel.
PLOUGHER, [plow'-er], *n.* a person who ploughs land, a ploughman.
PLOUGHING, [plow'-ing], *n.* the act or process of turning up ground with a plough.
PLOUGH-IRON, [plow'-iern], *n.* the coulter that cuts the soil at the top of the furrow.
PLOUGHLAND, [plow'-land], *n.* †a hide or carucate of land; land that is suitable for tilling.
PLOUGHMAN, [plow'-man], *n.* a man who ploughs or holds a plough.
PLOUGH-MONDAY, [plow'-mun'-di], *n.* the Monday after Twelfth-day.
PLOUGHSHARE, [plow'-shāer], *n.* the pointed shoe of a plough which cuts the soil at the bottom of the furrow, as distinct from the coulter. [PLOUGH and SHARE].
PLOUGH-STAFF, [plow'-stahf], *n.* a long pole topped with a head resembling a spade and used by a ploughman for freeing the ploughshare of mud and muck.
PLOUGHTAIL, [plow'-tāl], *n.* the part of a plough which the ploughman holds. [PLOUGH and TAIL].
PLOUGH-TREE, [plow'-trē], *n.* the plough handle.

PLOUGHWRIGHT, [plow'-rīt], *n.* a maker or repairer of ploughs. [PLOUGH and WRIGHT].
PLOVER, [pluv'-er], *n.* the popular name for several species of *Charadrius* and other birds frequenting low, moist ground; the lapwing. [OFr. *plovier*].
PLOW, see PLOUGH.
PLUCK (1), [pluk], *n.* the act, or a single instance, of plucking, a tug; that which is plucked out, *esp.* the heart, liver and lungs of an animal; (*fig.*) courage, spirit. [PLUCK (2)].
PLUCK (2), [pluk], *v.t. and i.* to break, extract, gather with a quick jerk, to pull with sudden force, or with a twitch; to pull, twitch or tug using the thumb and first finger; to strip feathers from; (*fig.*) to dispossess by fraud, to swindle. [OE. *pluccian*, ME. *plukken*].
PLUCKED, [plukt], *adj.* (*slang*) rejected in an examination.
PLUCKILY, [pluk'-ili], *adv.* in a plucky manner, bravely.
PLUCKINESS, [pluk'-i-nes], *n.* the state or quality of being plucky.
PLUG (1), [plug], *n.* anything used to stop a hole, a stopper, a bung, a large peg; a cake of tobacco; a piece of this; the handle of a water-closet which causes the bowl to be flushed with water. [Uncert.].
PLUG (2), (**plugging, plugged**), [plug], *v.t. and i.* to stop up by means of a plug, to put a plug or stopper in; (*slang*) to plod, to work continuously under difficulties; (*slang*) to shoot with a bullet; (*slang*) to bring well to the fore by means of publicity, to repeat or perform constantly (a song, etc.) so as to catch the attention of the public. [PLUG (1)].
PLUGGING, [plug'-ing], *n.* a stopping with a plug; the material employed.
PLUG-IN, [plug'-in], *adj.* (*elect.*) having a connexion made by an electric plug.
PLUM, [plum], *n.* a tree of the genus *Prunus*, or its fruit, which is round and has a juicy flesh sweet in flavour when ripe; a raisin; (*slang*) the sum of £100,000, a fortune; (*fig.*) anything good or choice, the best, the pick of its kind; **p. duff**, a boiled suet pudding made of flour and raisins. [OE. *plume* from Gk. *proumnon*].
PLUMAGE, [plōōm'-ij], *n.* the feathers of a bird considered collectively. [OFr. *plumage*].
PLUMB (1), [plum], *n.* a lump of lead or a weight of any matter attached to a line and used for taking soundings or measuring perpendiculars. [L. *plumbum* lead].
PLUMB (2), [plum], *adj.* perpendicular, vertical, true. [PLUMB (1)].
PLUMB (3), [plum], *adv.* perpendicularly, absolutely, exactly. [PLUMB (1)].
PLUMB (4), [plum], *v.t.* to adjust or measure by means of a plumb-line; to test the perpendicular of; to take the soundings of; (*fig.*) to see or reach the bottom of, to understand. [PLUMB (1)].
PLUMBAGINOUS, [plum-bā'-jin-us], *adj.* resembling, consisting of, or of the nature of, plumbago. [L. *plumbago* lead ore].
PLUMBAGO, [plum-bā'-gō], *n.* (*min.*) graphite, nearly pure carbon, used for pencils, crucibles and lubrication, and popularly called blacklead; (*bot.*) leadwort, a plant with pale-blue-coloured flowers. [L. *plumbago* lead ore].
PLUMBEOUS, [plum'-bē-us], *adj.* consisting of, or resembling, lead. [L. *plumbeus* of lead].
PLUMBER, [plum'-er], *n.* a person who works in lead; a person whose trade it is to repair plumbing systems. [L. *plumbarius* lead-worker].
PLUMBERY, [plum'-er-i], *n.* works or articles in lead; the place where lead is wrought; the business of a plumber.
PLUMBIC, [plum'-bik], *adj.* (*chem.*) of, relating to, or containing, lead; (*path.*) symptomatic of the presence of lead.
PLUMBIFEROUS, [plum-bif'-er-us], *adj.* yielding, producing, or containing, lead. [L. *plumbum* lead and *ferre* to bear].
PLUMBING, [plum'-ing], *n.* the art of working in lead; the work studied or accomplished by a plumber, involving an understanding of plumbing and draining systems and devices.
PLUMBISM, [plum'-bizm], *n.* (*path.*) lead poisoning.
PLUMBLESS, [plum'-les], *adj.* that cannot be plumbed.
PLUMBLINE, [plum'-līn], *n.* a device used by a mason for testing perpendiculars, consisting of a cord with a plumb attached to it; a perpendicular line. [PLUMB and LINE].
PLUMB-RULE, [plum'-rōōl], *n.* a bricklayer's or carpenter's straight-edge fitted with a plumb-line.
PLUM-CAKE, [plum'-kāk], *n.* a large cake containing raisins.
PLUME (1), [plōōm], *n.* a bird's feather, particularly a large or distinctive one; a feather or group of feathers worn as an ornament; a crest; a tuft of hair. [L. *pluma*].
PLUME (2), [plōōm], *v.t.* to provide with plumes; to clean or preen the feathers; to adorn with feathers; to strip of feathers; *v. reflex.* (*fig.*) to pride oneself on. [PLUME (1)].
PLUME-ALUM, [plōōm-al'-um], *n.* feathery or fibrous alum.
PLUME-BIRD, [plōōm'-burd], *n.* a long-tailed bird of paradise of the genus *Epimachus*.
PLUMELESS, [plōōm'-les], *adj.* without feathers or plumes.
PLUMELET, [plōōm'-let], *n.* a down feather; a small plume.

PLUMB-RULE

PLUMELIKE, [plōōm'-līk], *adj.* resembling a plume.
PLUMIGEROUS, [plōōm-ij'-er-us], *adj.* having feathers. [L. *plumiger* feather-bearing].
PLUMILIFORM, [plōōm-il'-i-fawm], *adj.* shaped like a plume. [L. *pluma* and FORM].
PLUMIPED, [plōōm'-i-ped], *n.* a bird with feathered feet. [L. *pluma* feather and *pes pedis* foot].
PLUMIST, [plōōm'-ist], *n.* a feather-dresser.
PLUMMER-BLOCK, [plum'-er-blok'], *n.* the bearing on which a shaft revolves.
PLUMMET, [plum'-et], *n.* a weight of lead or other heavy matter attached to a line for the purpose of testing depths and perpendiculars, a plumbline; a small weight attached to a fishing-line to keep the float upright in the water. [ME. *plummet* from OFr. *plommet*].
PLUMMING, [plum'-ing], *n.* (*mining*) the operation of sounding the place where to sink a shaft.
PLUMMY, [plum'-i], *adj.* of, or resembling, a plum or plums; (of a singer's voice) sounding as if the singer had a plum in the mouth.
PLUMOSE, [plōōm'-ōs], *adj.* feathery.
PLUMOUS, [plōōm'-us], *adj.* resembling feathers; having feathers, feathery. [L. *plumósus*].
PLUMP† (1), [plump], *n.* a bunch, a cluster, a clump. [Uncert.].
PLUMP (2), [plump], *n.* the act of plumping; the fall or plunge of a solid body into water making a resounding noise, a plop, a heavy fall. [PLUMP (3)].
PLUMP (3), [plump], *adj.* outright, flat, downright. [PLUMP (7)].
PLUMP (4), [plump], *adj.* having a well filled out form, having the flesh rounded and on the fat side. [ME. *plump*].
PLUMP (5), [plump], *adv.* suddenly, with a quick, heavy and resounding fall or plunge. [PLUMP (3)].
PLUMP (6), [plump], *v.t. and i.* to make plump, to fatten up; to become plump. [PLUMP (4)].
PLUMP (7), [plump], *v.t. and i.* to cause to fall suddenly and heavily; to fall abruptly so as to produce a resounding hollow sound; **to p. for**, to restrict one's vote (to one candidate), to express a decided preference for. [ME. *plumpen*].
PLUMPER, [plump'-er], *n.* anything intended to swell out; a person who gives several votes to a single candidate; (*slang*) a full unqualified lie.
PLUMPLY, [plump'-li], *adv.* in a plump manner, fully, roundly.
PLUMPNESS, [plump'-nes], *n.* the quality or the state of being plump.
PLUM-PUDDING, [plum'-pŏŏd'-ing] *n.* pudding containing raisins and currants and cooked by boiling or steaming; a pudding containing plums.
PLUMPY, [plump'-i], *adj.* plump, fat.
PLUMULA, see PLUMULE.
PLUMULACEOUS, [plōōm'-yōō-lā'-shus], *adj.* having the characteristics of a plumule.
PLUMULAR, [plōōm'-yōō-ler], *adj.* (*bot.*) of, relating to, a plumule.
PLUMULE, PLUMULA, [plōōm'-yōōl], *n.* (*bot.*) the first growth of stem from a germinating seed. [L. *plumula* little feather].
PLUMY, [plōōm'-i], *adj.* covered with feathers; adorned with plumes.
PLUNDER (1), [plun'-der], *n.* the act of plundering; that which is seized, booty, loot, profit. [PLUNDER (2)].
PLUNDER (2), [plun'-der], *v.t.* to seize property, possessions or money by violence, to pillage, to spoil;

to take by pillage or open force; to rob, steal, embezzle. [Germ. *plundern*].

PLUNDERAGE, [plun'-der-ij], *n.* embezzlement of goods on board a ship.

PLUNDERER, [plun'-der-er], *n.* a person who plunders, a hostile pillager; a robber.

PLUNDEROUS, [plun'-der-us], *adj.* given to plundering.

PLUNGE (1), [plunj], *n.* the act of plunging, a sudden propulsion of a body downwards; a sudden act of complete immersion; a sudden entry into a risky field of activity. [PLUNGE (2)].

PLUNGE (2), [plunj], *v.t. and i.* to thrust suddenly and forcibly downwards into water or any liquid, to immerse; to cause to enter into new and dangerous circumstances; to dive with a rush into water or any liquid; to move violently and dangerously downwards or forwards; (of a horse) to throw all its weight suddenly and violently on to its forefeet; to gamble recklessly. [ME. *plungen*, *plonge* from LL. **plumbicare* to throw out the lead].

PLUNGER, [plunj'-er], *n.* a person or animal that plunges; one who bets heavily; a diver; a cylinder used as a forcer in pumps.

PLUNK (1), [plungk], *n.* a heavy fall; a plucking sound, as that made by a banjo. [Imitative].

PLUNK (2), [plungk], *v.t.* to throw so as to make fall heavily; to strum.

PLUPERFECT, [plōō-pur'-fekt], *adj.* (*gram.*) denoting an event that took place previous to another specified action that took place in the past. [L. *plus quam perfectum* more than perfect].

PLURAL (1), [plooer'-al], *n.* (*gram.*) the form which expresses more than one. [PLURAL (2)].

PLURAL (2), [plooer'-al], *adj.* (*gram.*) denoting more than one, or more than two. [L. *pluralis* of more than one].

PLURALISM, [plooer'-al-izm], *n.* the state of being plural; the system, particularly of ecclesiastical application, of holding more offices than one; (*philos.*) the theory that there are more first causes than one.

PLURALIST, [plooer'-al-ist], *n.* (*eccles.*) a clergyman who holds more than one benefice; (*philos.*) a follower of pluralism.

PLURALITY, [plooer-al'-it-i], *n.* the state of being plural; a number of more than one; a greater number; pluralism. [L. *pluralitas*].

PLURALIZE, [plooer'-al-īz], *v.t.* to make plural.

PLURALLY, [plooer'-al-i], *adv.* in a plural manner or sense.

PLURILITERAL, [plooer-i-lit'-er-al], *adj.* having more than three letters. [L. *pluris*, *gen. sg.* of *plus* more and LITERAL].

PLURIPAROUS, [plooer-ip'-er-us], *adj.* (*zool.*) bringing forth more than one at a time. [L. *pluris*, *gen. sg.* of *plus* more and *parere* to bring forth].

PLUS (1), [plus], *n.* the symbol +, used as the sign of addition; extra quantity. [PLUS (2)].

PLUS (2), [plus], *adj.* having or including more, additional, extra. [L. *plus* more].

PLUS-FOURS, [plus-faw(r)z'], *n.(pl.)* roomy knickerbockers having an extra few inches allowed to drop in a fold below the knee.

PLUSH, [plush], *n.* a species of shaggy cloth, generally with a velvety nap. [Fr. *pluche*].

PLUTARCHY, [ploot'-ah'-ki], *n.* plutocracy.

PLUTO, [plōō'-tō], *n.* (*myth.*) the god of the nether world; (*astron.*) a planet discovered in 1930. [Gk. *Plouton*].

PLUTOCRACY, [ploot-ok'-ras-i], *n.* government by the wealthy. [Gk. *ploutokratia*].

PLUTOCRAT, [ploot'-ōk-rat], *n.* a person who is influential merely on account of his wealth. [*Prec.*].

PLUTOCRATIC, [ploot'-ō-krat'-ik], *adj.* of, pertaining to, resembling, a plutocrat or plutocracy.

PLUTONIAN, [plōō-tō'-ni-an], *n.* a plutonist.

PLUTONIC, [plōō-ton'-ik], *adj.* of, relating to, the kingdom of Pluto, infernal; dark; igneous; **P. rocks,** unstratified rocks such as granite, consolidated from a melted state at a great depth beneath the surface of the earth; **P. theory,** a theory holding that the heat of the earth is responsible for geological phenomena.

PLUTONISM, [plōō'-ton-izm], *n.* the Plutonic theory.

PLUTONIST, [plōō'-ton-ist], *n.* an advocate of the Plutonic theory in regard to the igneous rocks.

PLUVIAL, [plōō'-vi-al], *adj.* of, relating to, caused by, rain; rainy, humid; (*geol.*) due to rain. [L. *pluvialis* rainy].

PLUVIAMETER, PLUVIOMETER, [plōō'-vi-am'-it-er], *n.* a rain gauge. [L. *pluvia* rain and METER].

PLUVIAMETRICAL, [plōō'-vi-am-et'-rikl], *adj.* of, relating to, made by a pluviameter.

PLUVIOGRAPH, [plōō'-vi-ō-graf], *n.* a recording rain gauge. [L. *pluvia* rain and GRAPH].

PLUVIOMETER, see PLUVIAMETER.

PLY (1), [plī], *n.* a fold, a layer, a thickness; a strand, thread, twist, plait. [Fr. *pli* a fold from L. *plicare* to fold].

PLY (2), [plī], *v.t. and i.* to work with diligently, to wield or use energetically; to work at; to urge, solicit persistently; to offer repeatedly; to bend, fold; to wait in a particular place or follow a particular route regularly, day in day out, for business purposes; (*naut.*) to make way against the wind. [ME. *plye*].

PLYER, [plī'-er], *n.* he who or that which plies.

PLYMOUTH BRETHREN, [plim'-uth-breTH'-ren], *n.* name used to denote a Christian sect of strict evangelical principles, founded at *Plymouth* about 1830.

PLYMOUTHISM, [plim'-uth-izm], *n.* the principles of the Plymouth Brethren.

PLYWOOD, [plī'-wŏŏd'], *n.* wood made of three or more layers glued together under pressure with the grain of each layer set at right angles to that of the adjoining layer.

PNEUMATIC, [new-mat'-ik], *adj.* of, relating to, consisting of, air or gases; inflated by air; moved by compressed air; **p. dispatch,** a system of conveying messages or bills through tubes by means of compressed air; **p. trough,** (*chem.*) apparatus for collecting gases over a surface of water or mercury. [Gk. *pneumatikos*].

PNEUMATICALLY, [new-mat'-ik-al-i], *adv.* in a pneumatic way or form; by means of pneumatics.

PNEUMATICITY, [new'-mat-is'-it-i], *n.* (*anat.*) the condition of having hollow bones containing air.

PNEUMATICS, [new-mat'-iks], *n.(pl.)* the study of gases, *esp.* of the air.

PNEUMATO-, *pref.* of, relating to, driven by, air. [Gk. *pneuma* wind].

PNEUMATOLOGICAL, [new'-mat-o-loj'-ikl], *adj.* pertaining to pneumatology.

PNEUMATOLOGIST, [new'-mat-ol'-oj-ist], *n.* an expert in pneumatology.

PNEUMATOLOGY, [new'-mat-ol'-oj-i], *n.* the science of, or a treatise on, the properties of elastic fluids; (*theol.*) the doctrine of spiritual essences or existences. [PNEUMATO and Gk. *logos* speech].

PNEUMATOMETER, [new'-mat-om'-it-er], *n.* an instrument for testing respiratory power by recording the quantity of air which the lungs can inhale at a time. [PNEUMATO and METER].

PNEUMOCOCCUS, [newm'-ō-kok'-us], *n.* (*path.*) the micro-organism causing pneumonia. [Gk. *pneumon* lung and *kokkos* berry].

PNEUMOGASTRIC, [new'-mō-gas'-trik], *adj.* of, relating to, the lungs and stomach. [Gk. *pneumon* lung and GASTRIC].

PNEUMONIA, [new-mō'-ni-a], *n.* (*path.*) a condition of acute inflammation of the lungs. [Gk. *pneumonia* disease of the lungs].

PNEUMONIC (1), [new-mon'-ik], *n.* one suffering from congestion of the lungs; a medicine for diseased lungs.

PNEUMONIC (2), [new-mon'-ik], *adj.* of, relating to, the lungs or to pneumonia, pulmonic.

PNEUMOTHORAX, [new'-mō-thaw'-raks], *n.* the presence of air in the pleura, its artificial introduction in the treatment of disease. [Gk. *pneumon* lung and THORAX].

POACH (1), [pōch], *v.t.* to cook eggs by breaking them into boiling water. [OFr. *pochier*, *pocher*].

POACH (2), [pōch], *v.t. and i.* to trespass on private property and to steal game; *v.i.* to trespass on land in pursuit of game; (*tennis slang*) to take one's partner's shots. [OFr. *pochier*, *poucher* to finger].

POACH (3), [pōch], *v.t.* to stab or pierce, particularly by trampling, as cattle. [OFr. *pocher*].

POACHER, [pōch'-er], *n.* a person who poaches.

POACHINESS, [pōch'-i-nes], *n.* the state of being poachy.

POACHING, [pōch'-ing], *n.* the act or practice of one who poaches.

POACHY, [pōch'-i], *adj.* wet and soft, so as to be easily churned up by the feet of cattle.

POCHARD, [pōch'-erd], *n.* a sea-duck of the genus *Nyroca*. [Unkn.].

POCK, [pok], *n.* a pustule of the small-pox. [OE. *pocc*, ME. *pokke*].

POCKET (1), [pok'-it], *n.* a small bag unobtrusively tacked into one's clothing and used for carrying handkerchiefs, money, etc.; any small bag, pouch, cavity or receptacle; one of six net bags forming part of a billiard table; a section of air in which a partial vacuum has been created eliminating the necessary lift for an aeroplane; a measure, particularly of hops, in the form of a sack. [ME. *poket* from OFr. *poquette*, *dim.* of *poche* pouch].

POCKET (2), [pok'-it], *v.t.* to pick up and place in one's pocket, particularly with a view to keeping for good; to conceal in the pocket; to keep as profit. [POCKET (1)].

POCKET-BATTLESHIP, [pok'-it-batl'-ship], *n.* a small battleship.

POCKET-BOOK, [pok'-it-bo͝ok], *n.* a small book for carrying papers in the pocket; a small notebook.

POCKET-BOROUGH, [pok'-it-bu'-ro], *n.* a parliamentary constituency before 1832 providing a candidate with an absolutely safe seat in the House of Commons.

POCKETFUL, [pok'-it-fo͝ol], *n.* the amount a pocket can hold.

POCKET-GLASS, [pok'-it-glahs], *n.* a portable looking-glass.

POCKET-HANDKERCHIEF, [pok'-it-hang'-ker-chif], *n.* a handkerchief for the trousers or coat pockets.

POCKET-KNIFE, [pok'-it-nīf'], *n.* a small clasp-knife for carrying in the pocket.

POCKET-MONEY, [pok'-it-mun'-i], *n.* money for occasional expenses; a small weekly allowance given by a parent to his child.

POCKMARK, [pok'-mahk], *n.* a mark or scar made by the small-pox.

POCKMARKED, [pok'-mahkt'], *adj.* having pockmarks.

POCKWOOD, [pok'-wo͝od], *n.* a very hard wood.

POCKY, [pok'-i], *adj.* infected with the small-pox; covered with pockmarks, full of pocks; vile or contemptible.

POCO, [pō'-kō], *adv.* (*mus.*) a little, rather. [It. *poco* slightly].

POCOCURANTISM, [pō'-kō-ko͞o-rant'-izm], *n.* indifferentism; carelessness. [It. from *poco* little and L. *curante*, *pres.pt.* of *curare* to care].

POD (1), [pod], *n.* the shell of a pea and other such leguminous plants which contains the seeds. [Unkn.].

POD (2), [pod], *n.* a shoal or small group of whales or seals. [Unkn.].

POD (3), [pod], *n.* the socket of a brace-and-bit; a pad. [Unkn.].

POD (4), (**podding, podded**), [pod], *v.i.* to produce pods, to swell and grow because of the seeds ripening. [POD (1)].

PODAGRA, [pod-ag'-ra], *n.* gout in the feet. [Gk. *podagra* an attack in the feet].

PODAGRAL, [pod-ag'-ral], *adj.* afflicted with the gout.

PODAGRIC, [pod-ag'-rik], *adj.* gouty.

PODAGRICAL, [pod-ag'-rikl], *adj.* podagric.

PODALGIA, [pod-al'-ji-a], *n.* neuralgia in the foot. [Gk. *pous podos* foot and *algos* pain].

PODDED, [pod'-id], *adj.* furnished with pods.

PODESTA, [pod-es'-ta], *n.* the title of a magistrate in certain Italian towns. [It. *podestà* governor].

PODGE, [poj], *n.* a puddle, a plash; a person of short, fat figure. [Unkn.].

PODGY, [poj'-i], *adj.* short and fat, dumpy.

PODISMUS, [pod-iz'-mus], *n.* a spasm in the muscles of the foot. [Gk. *podismos* a binding of the feet].

PODIUM, [pō'-di-um], *n.* a pedestal, with plinth and cornice continued horizontally to support pillars; (*arch.*) the part of an amphitheatre projecting over the arena; a balcony. [Gk. *podion*].

PODIUM

PODO-, *pref.* foot. [Gk. *pous podos* foot].

PODOCARP, [pod'-ō-kahp], *n.* (*bot.*) a fruit-stalk. [PODO and Gk. *karpos* fruit].

PODOCARPOUS, [pod'-ō-kahp'-us], *adj.* (*bot.*) belonging to the genus *Podocarpus*.

PODOPHYLLIN, [pod-of'-il-in, pod'-ō-fil'-in], *n.* a drug obtained from the may-apple, *Podophyllum peltatum*, which is an active purgative. [PODO and Gk. *phullon* leaf].

PODOPHYLLOUS, [pod-of'-il-us], *adj.* (*entom.*) having leaf-shaped feet.

PODOPHYLLUM, [pod-of'-il-um], *n.* the genus of the may-apple. [PODO and Gk. *phullon* leaf].

PODOSCAPH, [pod'-ō-skaf], *n.* a boat propelled by the feet. [PODO and Gk. *scaphos* boat].

PODOSPERM, [pod'-ō-sperm], *n.* a filament connecting the ovule with the placenta. [PODO and SPERM].

PODRIDA, [pod-rē'-da], *n.* a miscellaneous dish eaten in Spain of meats cooked as a stew; (*fig.*) a hotch-potch. [Span. *podrida*].

POE-BIRD, [pō'-i-burd], *n.* the tui or parson bird of New Zealand, *Prosthemadera novæ-zealandiæ*. [Native *poe* pearl].

POEM, [pō'-im], *n.* a composition created in the literary medium, expressing an imaginative or intensely felt experience or series of related experiences, using language in a particularly heightened form which may, or may not, require rhyme, rhythm or metre in order to arrive at a perceptible unity of matter and manner, content and style; a piece of poetry; anything which appears to possess some of the qualities of a poem. [Gk. *poiema* that which is made].

POESY, [pō'-iz-i], *n.* the art of composing poems; poetry; metrical composition. [Fr. *poésie* from Gk. *poiesis* a creating].

POET, [pō'-it], *n.* a man who consistently practises the art of poetry; a person whose creative powers of expressing his experiences find their natural outlet in language raised to a fine pitch of quality and concentration of related thought and imagery; any person who has written a poem. [Gk. *poietes*].

POETASTER, [pō'-it-ast-er], *n.* a writer of poor poems, a petty poet, a pitiful rhymer. [POET and L. *aster* expressing poor quality].

POETESS, [pō'-it-es'], *n.* a female poet.

POETIC, [pō-et'-ik], *adj.* poetical; **p. justice**, the triumph of good over evil; **p. licence**, permissible departure from exact regard for objective reality or from strict maintenance of the conventions of poetry. [Gk. *poietikos*].

POETICAL, [pō-et'-ikl], *adj.* of, relating to, poetry; suitable to poetry; expressed in poetry; possessing the qualities peculiar to poetry; characterized by a fine imaginative and emotional power.

POETICALLY, [pō-et'-ik-al-i], *adv.* in a poetical manner.

POETICS, [pō-et'-iks], *n.*(*pl.*) the study of the nature of poetry, particularly the treatise of Aristotle.

POETIZE, [pō'-et-īz], *v.t.* and *i.* to render poetical; to write as a poet, to compose poetry.

POET-MUSICIAN, [pō'-it-mewz-ish'-an], *n.* an appellation given to the bard and lyrist of former ages.

POETRY, [pō'-it-ri], *n.* the art or work of poets; the art of raising all the capacities of language, rhythm, assonance and accent to a high degree of concentration in order to recreate for an audience an intense emotional, imaginative and mental experience; any composition adopting the classical poetic conventions; any quality which has a recognizable emotional effect. [L. *poietria*].

POGGE, [pog], *n.* (*ichth.*) the armed bull-head, *Agonus cataphractus*. [Unkn.].

POGO-STICK, [pō'-gō-stik'], *n.* a sturdy stick used as a child's toy fitted with two supports for the feet and with springs by which jumps are made.

POGROM, [po'-grom], *n.* an act of systematic plunder and slaughter of a certain section or class of the population, particularly of the Jews. [Russ. *pogrom* devastation].

POIGNANCY, [poin'-an-si], *n.* the quality or the state of being poignant.

POIGNANT, [poin'-ant], *adj.* sharply evoking the emotions of misery; keen, sharp, satirical; acutely painful. [OFr. *poignant*, *pres.pt.* of *poindre* to sting from L. *pungere* to prick].

POIGNANTLY, [poin'-ant-li], *adv.* to a poignant degree.

POIGNARD, see PONIARD.

POILU, [pwah'-lew], *n.* a French private soldier. [Fr. from *poilu* hairy].

POIND, [poind], *v.t.* (*Scots leg.*) to put in the pound; to distrain. [OE. *pyndan* to impound].

POINDING, [poind'-ing], *n.* (*leg.*) in Scotland, a seizing and selling of a debtor's goods, under legal warrant, to pay his debts.

POINSETTIA, [poin-set'-i-a], *n.* (*bot.*) a genus of Mexican plants with large red bracts. [J. R. *Poinsett*].

POINT (1), [point], *n.* the sharp tip of a tapering end, that which pricks; the mark, dot or full-stop made by the sharp end of a piercing instrument, particularly a period of punctuation, a full-stop or decimal dot; a real or imaginary means of indicating position, a spot or place without specific definition of characteristics, a verge; an exact place or moment; a particular division, issue, heading, item, entry, detail; a distinctive characteristic, a peculiarity, capacity; a degree; a unit of play, a single stake; the gist of an argument or remark; a remark with a sharp edge, the sting of an epigram; a small promontory or sea-cape; a needle used by lace-makers; lace made by a needle; the switch rail by which a train is transferred from one track to another; (*astron.*) an imaginary spot, usually an effect of intersection; (*cricket*) a position on the off-side of the field practically at right angles with the batsman and some four to six yards from him; (*her.*) one of the divisions of an escutcheon designed to bear a charge; (*mach.*) specific position relative to the functioning of various parts; (*math.*) that which has position but no length, breadth or thickness; (*naut.*) one of the thirty-two dividing lines of the compass; (*typ.*) a unit of measurement, a seventy-second of an inch; (*cross-country racing*) a landmark serving as the finish; **p. of view,** the mental basis or principle of an attitude; **at all points,** completely, in full detail; **to stretch a p.,** to modify or waive a demand; **what's the p.,** what's the use; **p. steak,** a corner cut from a rump steak; **dry p.,** an engraving tool; a print taken from an engraved-plate. [Fr. *point* a piercing from L. *punctum*, *p.pt.* of *pungere* to prick].

POINT (2), [point], *v.t.* to give a point to by cutting or shaping, to sharpen; to add force to; to direct by showing the way with the first finger or the hand, to indicate by word or gesture; to mark with points, stops or dots; to fill in the joints with mortar using the point of the trowel; (*mus.*) to indicate pauses by points; *v.i.* (of dogs), to stand stock-still with the nose directed towards game and the tail in a straight line with the back; **to p. at,** to direct a finger at as a means of indication; **to p. out, to p. to,** to call attention to, indicate. [OFr. *pointer*].

POINT-BLANK, [point'-blangk'], *adj.* aimed horizontally, direct, at close range; (*fig.*) outright.

POINT D'APPUI, [pwa(ng)'-dap-wē'], *n.* (*milit.*) a strategic base offering support to advancing troops. [Fr. *point d'appui* point of support].

POINT-DUTY, [point'-dew'-ti], *n.* a policeman's tour of duty at a certain (traffic) point.

POINTED, [point'-id], *adj.* sharpened, having a point; aimed at someone or something; epigrammatic, incisive.

POINTEDLY, [point'-id-li], *adv.* in a pointed manner, suggestively.

POINTEDNESS, [point'-id-nes], *n.* the quality or the state of being pointed.

POINTER, [point'-er], *n.* anything that points; a hint, a cue, a breed of sporting dog, so called from its habit of indicating the position of game with its nose while standing stock-still; a small advertisement directing the reader's attention to a larger one.

POINTILLISTE, [pwan'-ti-yēst], *n.* an artist, influenced by the theories of light developed by the impressionists, who has based his style of applying paint to canvas on a series of dots of different colours. [Fr. *pointilliste*].

POINTING, [point'-ing], *n.* the act of punctuating; the act of trimming mortar placed between joints by means of the trowel point; **flat p.,** method of trimming flush with the brickwork; **tuck p.,** method of raising a thin edge to the pointing for ornamental purposes; **weather p.,** pointing sloping from the lower brick to the upper, and affording a means of draining the rain away from the joint.

POINTLESS, [point'-les], *adj.* having no point; having no significance; ineffective, meaningless.

POINTLESSLY, [point'-les-li], *adv.* without point, without relevance.

POINTLESSNESS, [point'-les-nes], *n.* the quality of being pointless.

POINTSMAN, [pointz'-man], *n.* a man who works or cares for the switches or points on a railway.

POINTS RATIONING, [points'-rash'-un-ing], *n.* a system of rationing by means of which specified foods, etc., bearing stated values measured in units or points may be obtained according to the individual's free choice of allocation of the aggregate points issued to him.

POISE (1), [poiz], *n.* the balanced distribution and support of the body's weight, equilibrium; that which affords a means of balancing, a regulating power; style of carrying oneself; a central balanced dignity of mind or body. [OFr. *pois* weight].

POISE (2), [poiz], *v.t.* and *i.* to maintain in a balanced state, to carry, to maintain in a particular position; to remain balanced; to hover, as a bird. [ME. *peisen*, *poisen* from L. *pensum*, *p.pt.* of *pendere* to hang].

POISON (1), [poizn], *n.* any substance or liquid which when absorbed into the system destroys or injures the power of life; (*fig.*) any social activity or expression of opinion by word or deed which exercises a corrupting influence upon accepted standards of morality or undermines the power of existing institutions. [ME. *puison*, *poyson* from L. *potio* drink, poison].

POISON (2), [poizn], *v.t.* to kill or injure by poison; to add poison to, to cover with poison, to infect with poison; (*fig.*) to introduce an influence designed to corrupt, to pervert. [POISON (1)].

POISONER, [poizn'-er], *n.* a person who poisons or corrupts.

POISON-GAS, [poizn'-gas'], *n.* any injurious chemical used for purposes of warfare.

POISONING, [poizn'-ing], *n.* the act or process of poisoning.

POISONOUS, [poizn'-us], *adj.* having the qualities or effect of poison; (*fig.*) having the power to pervert, corrupting; highly disagreeable.

POISONOUSLY, [poizn'-us-li], *adv.* in a poisonous manner.

POISONOUSNESS, [poizn'-us-nes], *n.* the quality of being poisonous.

POKE (1), [pōk], *n.* a pocket; a small bag. [Uncert.].

POKE (2), [pōk], *n.* a poking, a thrust, a push, a dig, a nudge. [POKE (3)].

POKE (3), [pōk], *v.t.* and *i.* to push or thrust against as though to force a way through; to thrust into with an instrument which is moved about, to stir; to force a way moving from side to side without seeing far in front, to grope about; **p. bonnet,** a bonnet which has a rim projecting high over the forehead; **to p. fun at,** to make fun of, ridicule; **to p. about,** (*slang*) to meddle, to be inquisitive. [ME. *poken*].

POKER, [pōk'-er], *n.* an iron bar used in stirring a fire; the pochard duck; a game at cards for three to seven people, each player being dealt a hand of five cards which is compared to a specified order of value and betted on, the element of bluff being an important factor in the game. [Uncert.].

POKER-FACE, [pōk'-er-fās], *n.* a person whose face is inscrutable (during a game of poker); (*fig.*) a countenance giving no signs of emotion.

POKERWORK, [pōk'-er-wurk'], *n.* the decoration of wood or leather by burning patterns into it with a heated point, pyrography.

POKY, [pōk'-i], *adj.* cramped, confined, small in size.

POLACCA (1), [pol-ak'-a], *n.* a vessel with three masts, used in the Mediterranean. [Unkn.].

POLACCA (2), [pol-ak'-a], *n.* a polonaise. [It. (*danza*) *polacca* Polish (dance)].

POLAR, [pōl'-er], *adj.* of, relating to, belonging to, the North or South Pole; relating to a magnetic pole; possessing two opposed properties in a functioning relationship; diametrically opposed; **p. angle,** the angle formed by two meridians at the pole; **p. bear,** a large white bear, *Ursus maritimus*. [Gk. *polos* pivot].

POLARIMETER, [pōl'-er-im'-it-er], *n.* (*opt.*) an instrument for testing the polarization of light. [POLARIZE and METER].

POLARIMETRIC, [pōl'-er-i-met'-rik], *adj.* of, relating to, the polarimeter.

POLARIMETRY, [pōl'-er-im-et-ri], *n.* the art or science of making proper use of the polarimeter. [POLARIZE and Gk. *metria* measurement].

POLARIS, [pōl-āer'-ris], *n.* (*astron.*) the pole-star.

POLARISCOPE, [pōl-a'-ris-kōp], *n.* (*opt.*) an instrument for testing the phenomena of polarized light. [POLARIZE and SCOPE].

POLARITY, [pōl-a'-rit-i], *n.* the power of reacting and pointing to the poles of the earth, which is peculiar to the magnetic needle; action by, or susceptibility to, magnetic influences; a state of possessing two powers or properties in functional opposition.

POLARIZABLE, [pōl'-er-īz-abl], *adj.* susceptible of polarization.

POLARIZATION, [pōl'-er-īz-ā'-shun], *n.* the act or process of polarizing, the state of being polarized; **p. of light,** (*opt.*) the modification of light waves by the action of certain media by which the waves are compressed laterally.

POLARIZE, [pōl'-er-īz], *v.t.* to change light or heat waves by means of certain media, to communicate polarity.

POLARIZED, [pōl'-er-īzd], *adj.* having polarity.

POLARIZER, [pōl'-er-īz-er], *n.* that which polarizes light, particularly a special type of prism.

POLATOUCHE, [pol'-at-ōōsh], *n.* a Siberian flying-squirrel. [Russ. *poletucha* flying animal].

POLDER, [pol'-der], *n.* reclaimed lowland below the level of the sea or a river that has been drained and cultivated and is protected by dykes. [Du. *polder*].

POLE (1), [pōl], *n.* a long, relatively thin, and rounded piece of wood made out of the stem of a young tree whittled of its bark; any such piece of wood having a domestic or commercial use, such a piece used for propelling a punt, or for supporting a tent, or coloured and placed as a sign outside a barber's shop, a flag-staff; a single shaft of a carriage; a measure of length being 5½ yards, a rod or perch; a square measure of 30¼ square yards; **up the p,** silly, mad. [OE. *pal* from L. *palus* stake].

POLE (2), [pōl], *n.* (*astron.*) one of the two extremities of the earth's axis or of the celestial sphere; the area round either the North or South Pole; the pole-star which is vertical to the pole of the earth; one of the two points in a magnetic body embodying the positive or negative power; (*elect.*) the positive or negative terminal of a battery or accumulator, an electrode; **magnetic p.,** one of the two points in a magnet corresponding to the poles of the earth. [ME. *pol* from Gk. *polos* pivot].

POLE (3), [pōl], *n.* a native of Poland. [Pol. *pole* a plain].

POLE (4), [pōl], *v.t. and i.* to propel by means of a pole, to punt; to convey on poles; to provide with poles. [POLE (1)].

POLE-AXE, [pōl'-aks'], *n.* a slaughterer's axe having a hammer edge on the opposite side of the axe edge; a poll-axe. [ME. *pollax*].

POLECAT, [pōl'-kat'], *n.* a small carnivore allied to the weasel, the fitchet, *Putorius fœtidus*, which has glands secreting a fetid liquor. [ME. *polcat*].

POLECAT

POLE-JUMP, [pōl'-jump'], *n.* a high jump in which the jumper uses a pole which he drops as he clears the bar.

POLEMAST, [pōl'-mahst'], *n.* (*naut.*) a mast without a topmast and extending some distance above the shrouds. [POLE and MAST].

POLEMIC (1), [pol-em'-ik], *n.* a disputant, a person who participates in a controversy; a controversy, a dispute; (*pl.*) controversies on religious subjects; the history of these in the Christian Church. [POLEMIC (2)].

POLEMIC (2), [pol-em'-ik], *adj.* polemical. [Gk. *polemikos* of war].

POLEMICAL, [pol-em'-ik-al], *adj.* relating to, arising out of, a controversy, controversial, disputative.

POLEMICALLY, [pol-em'-ik-al-i], *adv.* in a polemic manner.

POLEMIZE, [pol'-em-īz], *v.i.* to argue according to the rules or methods of polemics.

POLENTA, [pol-en'-ta], *n.* a food dish, being a preparation of semolina or maize; cornflour; a porridge of various ingredients. [It. *polenta* pearl-barley].

POLE-STAR, [pōl'-stah(r)] *n.* the star Polaris, which is nearly vertical to the pole of the earth; a lodestar, a guide, particularly to sailors; (*fig.*) a fixed principle.

POLE-VAULT, [pōl'-vawlt], *n.* a pole-jump.

POLIANITE, [pol'-i-an-īt], *n.* (*min.*) a variety of pyrolusite. [Gk. *poliaino* I make grey].

POLICE (1), [pol-ēs'], *n.* a civil force for the preservation of law and order. [LL. *politia* community].

POLICE (2), [pol-ēs'], *v.t.* to maintain law and order by means of the police; to patrol by police; (*fig.*) to regulate. [POLICE (1)].

POLICE-CAR, [pol-ēs'-kah(r)], *n.* a special car used by policemen for chasing motor-bandits and operating a speed control.

POLICE-CONSTABLE, [pol-ēs'-kun'-stabl], *n.* a member of the police force, a policeman.

POLICE COURT, [po-lēs'-kawt'], *n.* a court of summary jurisdiction presided over by a stipendiary magistrate.

POLICEMAN, [pol-ēs'-man], *n.* a member of a police force.

POLICE-STATION, [pol-ēs'-stā'-shun], *n.* the building which a local branch of the police force uses as headquarters.

POLICLINIC, [pol'-i-klin'-ik], *n.* the out-patient department of a hospital. [Gk. *polis* city and CLINIC].

POLICY (1), [pol'-is-i], *n.* a writing or instrument by which a contract or indemnity is effected, *esp.* a document setting out an insurance contract. [Fr. *police* insurance contract].

POLICY (2), [pol'-isi], *n.* the art or science of governing a nation; a set of accepted principles and plans constituting a programme of political action; any single plan, scheme or measure adopted by a government or party in its management of public affairs; a line of action laid down in theoretical form and directed towards personal ends; prudence, sagacity in the management of affairs; (*pl.*) (*Scots*) embellished land, improvements, etc., in an estate. [Gk. *politeia* constitution].

POLING, [pōl'-ing], *n.* a structure of poles erected for scaffolding or to support the walls of buildings or other works.

POLIOMYELITIS, [pol'-i-ō-mī'-el-īt'-is], *n.* (*med.*) inflammation in the spinal cord, infantile paralysis. [Gk. *polios* grey and MYELITIS].

POLISH (1), [pol'-ish], *n.* glossiness, smoothness of surface effected by rubbing; a substance which aids the process of polishing; (*fig.*) elegance, correctness of social manners; refinement of literary style, finish. [POLISH (4)].

POLISH (2), [pōl'-ish], *n.* the language of Poland. [POLISH (3)].

POLISH (3), [pōl'-ish], *adj.* of, relating to, coming from, Poland, or made by the Poles. [POLE (3)].

POLISH (4), [pol'-ish], *v.t. and i.* to make smooth and glossy by rubbing; (*fig.*) to make refined in manners, to alter in style and form till considered in a state of perfection; to become smooth, to receive a gloss; **to p. off,** (*slang*) to finish summarily; to murder. [ME. *polischen* from L. *polire* to polish].

POLISHABLE, [pol'-ish-abl], *adj.* capable of being polished.

POLISHER, [pol'-ish-er], *n.* the person or instrument that polishes.

POLISHING, [pol'-ish-ing], *adj.* making smooth or glossy, either with rubbing, varnish or powder.

POLITARCH, [pol'-i-tahk], *n.* an oriental magistrate in the Roman Empire. [Gk. *politikos* of a citizen, *arkhos* leader].

POLITE, [pol-īt'], *adj.* courteous and considerate in society, refined, well-mannered, well-bred. [L. *politum*, *p.pt.* of *polire* to polish].

POLITELY, [pol-īt'-li], *adv.* in a polite manner.

POLITENESS, [pol-īt'-nes], *n.* the quality of being polite, polish of manners, refinement, courtesy.

POLITESSE, [pol-ē-tes'], *n.* tactful politeness; over-acted politeness. [Fr. *politesse*].

POLITIC, [pol'-it-ik], *adj.* of, relating to, the polity; constituting the state; astute, prudent; scheming, crafty; nicely adapted to a specific purpose; expedient, opportune; **body p.,** the people as a collective political body. [Gk. *politikos* of a citizen].

POLITICAL, [pol-it'-ikl], *adj.* of, relating to, derived from, politics or the government of a state, its institutions, forms of administration, and international relationships; concerned with politics; **p. economy,** the study of the laws of national wealth as utilized by society in terms of raw materials, means of production and methods of distribution; **p. geography,** the study of the earth according to its political division.

POLITICALLY, [pol-it'-ik-al-i], *adv.* in a political or politic manner; with reference to politics.

POLITICIAN, [pol'-it-ish'-an], *n.* a person who assumes the status of an expert in the art of governing, a person engaged in politics. [Fr. *politicien*].

POLITICIZE, [pol-it'-is-īz], *v.t.* to talk politics; to make political.

POLITICS, [pol'-it-iks], *n.(pl.)* the science or the art of governing; the whole system of principles and forms of administration concerned with the theoretical and practical aspects of social organization; political affairs, the management of party affairs.

POLITY, [pol'-it-i], *n.* the form or constitution of civil government; the constitution of a state. [Gk. *politeia*].

POLKA, [pol'-ka], *n.* a lively dance in four-four time with a half-step in it, which originated in Central Europe; its appropriate music. [Uncert.].

POLL (1), [pol], *n.* a parrot; abbreviated form of Polly, a girl's name. [*Var.* of Molly].

POLL (2), [pōl], *n.* †the head, particularly the crown and back part above the nape of the neck; a register of voters; the voting at an election; the place of voting; the number of votes. [ME. *pol*, *polle* from LGerm. *polle* head].

POLL (3), [pōl], *v.t. and i.* to cut, trim, lop the branches of a tree; to remove the horns of cattle; to enter names on a register of votes; to vote. [POLL (2)].

POLLACK, POLLOCK, [pol'-ak], *n.* a sea-fish allied to the whiting, of the species *Gadus pollachius*, which has food value. [Unkn.]

POLLACK

POLLAN, [pol'-an], *n.* a freshwater fish, *Coregonus pollan*, of the salmon family, found in Ireland. [Uncert.].

POLLARD† **(1),** [pol'-ahd], *n.* a freshwater fish, the chub, *Leuciscus cephalus*.

POLLARD (2), [pol'-erd], *n.* a tree that has been polled; a stag that has cast his horns; a mixture of bran and meal as cattle feed.

POLLARD (3), [pol'-erd], *v.t.* to lop the tops of (trees) so as to allow for a new bushy growth, as in willows.

POLL-AXE, [pōl'-aks], *n.* a pole-axe.

POLL-BOOK, [pōl'-bŏŏk], *n.* the register of voters.

POLLED, [pōld], *adj.* lopped, cropped; without horns.

POLLEN, [pol'-en], *n.* (*bot.*) the fertilizing granules shed by the anther of a flower, the male element of flowering plants. [L. *pollen*].

POLLER, [pol'-er], *n.* a person who polls trees; a person who registers voters; a voter.

POLLEX, [pol'-eks], *n.* (*anat.*) the thumb. [L. *pollex*].

POLLICITATION, [pol'-is-it-ā'-shun], *n.* (*leg.*) a voluntary engagement or a document containing it. [L. *pollicitationem*].

POLLINATE, [pol'-in-āt], *v.t.* (*bot.*) to fertilize with pollen.

POLLINATION, [pol'-in-ā'-shun], *n.* (*bot.*) fertilization by conveyance of pollen from anther to stigma.

POLLINIFEROUS, [pol'-in-if'-er-us], *adj.* of, relating to, producing, pollen. [POLLEN and L. *ferre* to bear].

POLLINOSE, [pol'-in-ōs], *adj.* covered with fine pollen-like dust.

POLLIWIG, [pol'-i-wig], *n.* a tadpole, as if all head. [ME. *polwygle*].

POLL-MAN, [pōl'-man], *n.* (*slang*) a person who passes his Cambridge degree without taking honours, a pass-man.

POLLOCK, see POLLACK.

POLL-TAX, [pōl'-taks'], *n.* a capitation tax, a tax levied on every person.

POLLUCITE, [pol-yōōs'-īt], *n.* (*min.*) a hydrated silicate of aluminium and caesium. [POLLUX].

POLLUTE, [pol-ōōt'], *v.t.* to defile or to make unclean; (*fig.*) to taint with guilt, to profane, to corrupt; to violate. [L. *pollutum*, *p.pt.* of *polluere*].

POLLUTEDLY, [pol-ōōt'-id-li], *adv.* to a polluted degree, with pollution.

POLLUTEDNESS, [pol-ōōt'-id-nes], *n.* the state of being polluted.

POLLUTER, [pol-ōōt'-er], *n.* a defiler, a corrupter.

POLLUTION, [pol-ōō'-shun], *n.* the act of polluting; the state of being polluted; defilement, corruption; (*med.*) involuntary discharge of semen. [L. *pollutionem*].

POLLUX, [pol'-uks], *n.* (*myth.*) the twin brother of Castor; (*astron.*) a fixed star in the constellation Gemini. [L. *Pollux*].

POLO, [pō'-lō], *n.* a game like hockey, played on ponies; **water p.,** a game played in the water between two teams of swimmers. [Indian *polo*].

POLO-COLLAR, [pō'-lō-kol'-er], *n.* a type of high collar which rolls down all round the neck, usually as part of a jersey.

POLONAISE, [pol-on-āz'], *n.* a full bodice in Polish fashion worn by women; a Polish air and dance in a dignified measure. [Fr. *polonaise* Polish (dance)].

POLONIUM, [pol-ō'-ni-um], *n.* a radio-active element discovered by Pierre and Marie Curie. [MedL. *Polonia* Poland].

POLONY, [pol-ō'-ni], *n.* a dry sausage of partly-cooked meat. [*Bologna* in Italy].

POLTERGEIST, [polt'-er-gīst'], *n.* a spirit reputed to be responsible for certain otherwise inexplicable violent movements of furniture and the like. [Germ. *poltergeist* from *polter* uproar and *geist* spirit].

POLTROON, [pol-trōōn'], *n.* an arrant coward, a dastard. [It. *poltrone* coward].

POLTROONERY, [pol-trōōn'-er-i], *n.* cowardice, baseness of mind, want of spirit. [Fr. *poltronnerie*].

POLY-, *pref.* many, much. [Gk. *polus*].

POLYADELPHOUS, [pol'-i-ad-elf'-us], *adj.* (*bot.*) having stamens grouped in three or more bundles. [POLY and ADELPHOUS].

POLYANDRIAN, [pol'-i-an'-dri-an], *adj.* having many husbands; (*bot.*) having many stamens.

POLYANDROUS, [pol'-i-an'-drus], *adj.* polyandrian.

POLYANDRY, [pol'-i-an'-dri], *n.* the practice of having more than one husband at a time. [POLY and Gk. *aner andros* husband].

POLYANTHOUS, pol'-i-an'-thus], *adj.* (*bot.*) having a cluster of flowers springing from the same peduncle. [POLY and Gk. *anthos* flower].

POLYANTHUS, [pol'-i-an'-thus], *n.* (*bot.*) a garden plant resembling the cowslip, but with larger flowers. [POLY and Gk. *anthos* flower].

POLYARCHY, [pol'-i-ahk-i], *n.* a government by the multitude, as opposed to monarchy.

POLYBASIC, [pol'-i-bās'-ik], *adj.* (*chem.*) having two or more equivalents to a base. [POLY and BASIC].

POLYBASITE, [pol'-i-bās-īt], *n.* (*min.*) sulphantimonite of silver.

POLYCARPIC, [pol'-i-kahp'-ik], *adj.* (*bot.*) bearing fruit several times; bearing many seeds in each receptacle. [POLY and Gk. *karpos* fruit].

POLYCHORD, [pol'-i-kawd], *adj.* having many chords. [POLY and CHORD].

POLYCHROITE, [pol'-i-krō'-īt], *n.* the colouring matter of saffron. [POLY and Gk. *khroa* complexion].

POLYCHROMATIC, [pol'-i-krōm-at'-ik], *adj.* (*min.*) exhibiting a play of colours. [POLY and CHROMATIC].

POLYCHROME (1), [pol'-i-krōm], *n.* a substance extracted from chestnut bark; a vase painted in many colours. [POLY and Gk. *khroma* colour].

POLYCHROME (2), [pol'-i-krōm], *adj.* having many colours; in the manner of polychromy. [POLYCHROME (1)].

POLYCHROMY, [pol'-i-krōm-i], *n.* the ancient art of colouring statuary or buildings.

POLYCLADOUS, [pol'-i-klā'-dus], *adj.* with many branches.

POLYCOTYLEDON, [pol'-i-kot-il-ē'-don], *n.* (*bot.*) a plant that has more than two cotyledons. [POLY and COTYLEDON].

POLYCOTYLEDONOUS, [pol'-i-kot-il-ē'-don-us], *adj.* (*bot.*) having more than two cotyledons.

POLYCRACY, [pol-ik'-ras-i], *n.* government by many. [POLY and Gk. *krateia* rule].

POLYERGIC, [pol'-i-er'-jik], *adj.* acting in many ways. [POLY and Gk. *ergon* work].

POLYFOIL, [pol'-i-foil], *n.* (*arch.*) a circle with many arches on the inner side of its circumference. [POLY and FOIL].

POLYGAMIST, [pol-ig'-am-ist], *n.* a person who practises or advocates polygamy.

POLYGAMOUS, [pol-ig'-am-us], *adj.* inclined to, or practising, polygamy; (*bot.*) having some perfect and some separated flowers on the same or different plants. [Gk. *polugamous*].

POLYGAMY, [pol-ig'-ami], *n.* the practice of having more than one wife at a time. [Gk. *polugamia*].

POLYGASTRIC, [pol'-i-gast'-rik], *adj.* having many stomachs. [POLY and GASTRIC].

POLYGENESIS, [pol'-i-jen'-is-is], *n.* the theory that the various races of man are not from one pair, but many, and that organisms are not from one cell but several. [POLY and GENESIS].

POLYGENOUS, [pol-ij'-en-us], *adj.* (*geol.*) consisting of many kinds. [POLY and Gk. *genos* kind].

POLYGLOT (1), [pol'-i-glot'], *n.* a Bible in several languages; one who speaks many languages. [Gk. *poluglottos* many-tongued].

POLYGLOT (2), [pol'-i-glot'], *adj.* containing, written in, many languages. [POLYGLOT (1)].

POLYGON, [pol'-ig-on], *n.* (*geom.*) a closed figure of many angles. [Gk. *polugonos* many-angled].

POLYGONAL, [pol-ig'-on-al], *adj.* (*geom.*) having many angles.

POLYGONOUS, [pol-ig'-on-us], *adj.* polygonal.

POLYGRAM, [pol'-i-gram'], *n.* a figure consisting of many lines. [Gk. *polugrammos* many-lined].

POLYGRAPH, [pol'-i-graf'], *n.* an instrument for multiplying copies of a writing; a brass disk so perforated as to be of use in the drawing of polygons and curves; an author of different works. [Gk. *polugraphos* writing much].

POLYGRAPHIC, [pol'-i-graf'-ik], *adj.* of, relating to, polygraphy; printed by a polygraph.

POLYGRAPHY, [pol-ig'-raf-i], *n.* the art of writing in and deciphering various ciphers; a method of reproducing paintings. [Gk. *polugraphia* a writing of much].

POLYGYNIAN, [pol'-ij-in'-i-an], *adj.* (*bot.*) having many styles.

POLYHEDRAL, [pol′-i-hē′-dral], *adj.* (*geom.*) having many sides.
POLYHEDRON, [pol′-i-hē′-dron], *n.* (*geom.*) a solid containing many sides or planes; (*opt.*) a multiplying glass or lens, consisting of several plane surfaces arranged convexly. [Gk. *poluhedron*].
POLYMATH, [pol′-i-math′], *n.* one versed in many (unrelated) learned subjects. [Gk. *polumathes* that has learned much].
POLYMATHY†, [pol-im′-athi], *n.* knowledge of many arts and sciences. [Gk. *polumathia*].
POLYMER, [pol′-i-mer], *n.* (*chem.*) a substance having the same ingredients in the same proportion as another but with the number of atoms in each molecule a multiple of those in the substance compared. [POLY and Gk. *meros* part].
POLYMERISM, [pol′-im-er-izm], *n.* (*chem.*) the composition of substances by which the atoms of one are in a multiple relationship with those of another and the molecular weights of the two are in a corresponding relationship. [Gk. *polumeres* having many parts].
POLYMIGNITE, [pol′-i-mig′-nīt], *n.* (*min.*) a titanate of zirconium and other metals which occurs as black crystals.
POLYMORPH, [pol′-i-mawf], *n.* an animal or plant organism having many forms. [Gk. *polumorphos*].
POLYMORPHIC, [pol′-i-mawf′-ik], *adj.* polymorphous.
POLYMORPHISM, [pol′-i-mawf′-izm], *n.* the power of assuming different forms.
POLYMORPHOUS, [pol′-i-mawf′-us], *adj.* having, or occurring in, many shapes.
POLYNESIAN (1), [pol′-in-ē′-zi-an], *n.* a native of Polynesia. [POLY and Gk. *nesos* island].
POLYNESIAN (2), [pol′-in-ē′-zi-an], *adj.* of, relating to, coming from, Polynesia, a group of archipelagoes in the Pacific Ocean. [POLYNESIAN (1)].
POLYNOMIAL, [pol′-i-nōm′-i-al], *adj.* (*math.*) containing many terms or names.
POLYOPIA, [pol′-i-ōp′-i-a], *n.* (*path.*) a disease of the eye characterized by multiple vision. [POLY and Gk. *ops* eye].
POLYOPTRON, [pol′-i-op′-tron], *n.* (*opt.*) a glass through which objects appear multiplied, but diminished. [POLY and Gk. *optron* eye-instrument].
POLYORAMA, [pol′-i-ō-rah′-ma], *n.* a view of many objects, a panorama. [POLY and Gk. *horama* view].
POLYP, [pol′-ip], *n.* (*zool.*) a sea-anemone or any animal of the same class; (*med.*) a polypus. [Gk. *polupous* cuttle-fish].
POLYPARY, [pol′-ip-er-i], *n.* (*zool.*) the hard chitinous covering secreted by many of the hydrozoa, often acting as a breeding ground for polyps.

POLYP

POLYPETALOUS, [pol′-i-pet′-al-us], *adj.* (*bot.*) having many petals. [POLY and PETAL].
POLYPHAGOUS, [pol-if′-ag-us], *adj.* (*zool.*) living on many kinds of food. [POLY and Gk. *phago* I eat].
POLYPHARMACY, [pol′-i-fahm′-asi], *n.* medicine of many ingredients; prescription of many drugs and medicines in curative treatment. [POLY and PHARMACY].
POLYPHASE, [pol′-i-fāz], *adj.* (*elect.*) having three or more phases.
POLYPHONIC, [pol′-i-fon′-ik], *adj.* consisting of many voices; (*mus.*) consisting of two or more parts, each of which has an independent melody of its own, contrapuntal. [POLY and Gk. *phone* sound].
POLYPHONISM, [pol-if′-on-izm], *n.* the study of the multiplication of sounds.
POLYPHONIST, [pol-if′-on-ist], *n.* an expert in polyphony; a ventriloquist.
POLYPHONY, [pol′-i-fo′-ni], *n.* polyphonic music.
POLYPHYLLOUS, [pol′-i-fil′-us], *adj.* (*bot.*) having many leaves. [POLY and Gk. *phullon* leaf].
POLYPLASTIC, [pol′-i-plast′-ik], *adj.* assuming many forms. [POLY and PLASTIC].
POLYPODE, [pol′-i-pōd], *n.* an animal with many feet, as the millipede or wood-louse. [Gk. *polupous* many-footed].
POLYPODY, [pol′-i-pō-di], *n.* (*bot.*) a fern of the genus, *Polypodium* of which there are over five hundred species. [Gk. *polupodion*, *dim.* of *polupous* many-footed].
POLYPOID, [pol′-ip-oid], *adj.* (*zool.*) having the characteristics of, resembling, polyps. [POLYP and Gk. *oeides* like].
POLYPOUS, [pol′-i-pus], *adj.* of the nature of a polyp.
POLYPRISMATIC, [pol′-i-priz-mat′-ik], *adj.* (*min.*) having crystals presenting many prisms in a single form. [POLY and PRISMATIC].
POLYPUS, [pol′-i-pus], *n.* (*zool.*) a polyp; (*path.*) a tumour, so named because it was supposed to have numerous attachments, feet, or roots. [Gk. *polupous* cuttle-fish].
POLYRHIZOUS, [pol′-i-rīz′-us], *adj.* having many small roots. [POLY and Gk. *rhiza* root].
POLYSCOPE, [pol′-i-skōp], *n.* a multiplying glass. [POLY and SCOPE].
POLYSEPALOUS, [pol′-i-sep′-al-us], *adj.* (*bot.*) having separate sepals. [POLY and SEPAL].
POLYSPERM, [pol′-i-sperm], *n.* a tree whose fruit contains many seeds. [POLY and SPERM].
POLYSPERMOUS, [pol′-i-spurm′-us], *adj.* containing many seeds.
POLYSPOROUS, [pol′-i-spaw′-rus], *adj.* (*bot. and zool.*) producing many spores. [Gk. *polusporos*].
POLYSTOME, [pol′-i-stōm], *n.* an animal with many mouths. [POLY and Gk. *stoma* a mouth].
POLYSTYLE, [pol′-i-stīl], *n.* (*arch.*) an edifice with numerous columns. [Gk. *polustulos*].
POLYSYLLABIC, [pol′-i-sil-ab′-ik], *adj.* consisting of many syllables, usually of three or more. [POLY and SYLLABIC].
POLYSYLLABICALLY, [pol′-i-sil-ab′-ik-al-i], *adv.* in a polysyllabic manner or form.
POLYSYLLABLE, [pol′-i-sil′-abl], *n.* a word of many syllables, usually of three or more. [POLY and SYLLABLE].
POLYSYNDETON, [pol′-i-sin′-dit-on], (*rhet.*) a figure of speech in which a conjunction is often repeated. [POLY and Gk. *sundetos* bound together].
POLYSYNTHETIC, [pol′-i-sin-thet′-ik], *adj.* composed of several distinct words fused to form a whole, each retaining its signification. [POLY and SYNTHETIC].
POLYTECHNIC (1), [pol′-i-tek′-nik], *n.* a school for technical instruction in many sciences and practical arts. [POLYTECHNIC (2)].
POLYTECHNIC (2), [pol′-i-tek′-nik], *adj.* of, relating to, teaching, the technique of many arts and sciences. [POLY and Gk. *tekhnikos* of the arts].
POLYTHALAMOUS, [pol′-i-thal′-am-us], *adj.* many-chambered. [POLY and Gk. *thalamos* bedroom].
POLYTHEISM, [pol′-i-thē′-izm], *n.* the worship of many gods. [POLY and THEISM].
POLYTHEIST, [pol′-i-thē′-ist], *n.* a person who believes in a plurality of gods.
POLYTHEISTIC, [pol′-i-thē-ist′-ik], *adj.* of, relating to, or embracing, polytheism.
POLYZOA, [pol′-i-zō′-a], *n.*(*pl.*) (*zool.*) a group of invertebrate animals living in colonies, leaf-like or tree-like in form, often resembling seaweeds or forming incrustations on stones and plants, the bryozoa. [POLY and Gk. *zoa*, *pl.* of *zoon* animal].
POLYZOAN, [pol′-i-zō′-an], *n.* one of the polyzoa growing together, produced by germination.
POLYZONAL, [pol′-i-zōn′-al], *adj.* (*opt.*) descriptive of a lens composed of many zones or segments. [POLY and ZONAL].
POM, [pom], *n.* a Pomeranian dog. [*Pomerania* a Prussian province].
POMACEOUS, [pom-ā′-shus], *adj.* of, relating to, apples. [L. *pomum* apple].
POMADE, [pom-ahd′], *n.* perfumed ointment for the hair. [It. *pomata* scented with apples].
POMANDER, [pom-and′-er], *n.* a perfumed ball of herbs and powder used as preventive of infection. [OFr. *pomme d'ambre* apple of amber].
POMATUM, [pom-ā′-tum], *n.* perfumed unguent used for the hair, pomade.
POME, [pōm], *n.* (*bot.*) a pulpy pericarp without valves, like the apple, pear, etc. [L. *pomum* apple].
POME-CITRON, [pōm′-sit-ron], *n.* a citron apple.
POMEGRANATE, [pom′-gran-it], *n.* the tree that produces a fruit with a thick rind and full of seeds, *Punica Granatum*; the fruit itself which resembles an orange. [ME. *pomegrenat* from L. *pomum* apple and *granatum* many-seeded].
POMELOE, [pom′-el-ō], *n.* a variety of the shaddock, *Citrus decumana*, the grape-fruit. [Uncert.].

POMERANIAN (1), [pom'-er-ā'-ni-an], *n.* a spitz dog; a breed derived from the Eskimo dog, but characterized by long soft hair and a thick ring of hair round the neck.

POMERANIAN

POMERANIAN (2), [pom'-er-ā'-ni-an], *adj.* of, relating to, coming from, Pomerania in Prussia.

POMFRET (1), [pom'-fret], *n.* an edible fish of the genus *Stromateus*, found in the Pacific Ocean. [Uncert.].

POMFRET (2), [pom'-fret], *n.* a sweet, round or flat in shape, made of liquorice. [*Pontefract* in Yorkshire].

POMICULTURE, [pōm'-i-kul'-cher], *n.* the cultivation of fruit trees. [L. *pomum* apple and CULTURE].

POMIFEROUS, [pom-if'-er-us], *adj.* apple-bearing, pome-bearing. [L. *pomum* apple and *ferre* to bear].

POMIFORM, [pōm'-i-fawm], *adj.* apple-like. [L. *pomum* apple and FORM].

POMMARD, [pom'-ahd'], *n.* a superior red wine from a district of that name in Burgundy.

POMMEL (1), **PUMMEL**, [pum'-el], *n.* the raised front part of a saddle; the hilt of a sword; (*pl.*) the handles which can be fixed on to a vaulting-horse to facilitate certain gymnastics. [ME. *pomel* from OFr. *pomel*].

POMMEL (2), **PUMMEL**, (**pommelling, pommelled**), [pum'-el], *v.t.* to give a beating to by punching; †to beat with the pommel of a sword. [POMMEL (1)].

POMMELLING, [pum'-el-ing], *n.* a beating or bruising.

POMOLOGY, [pom-ol'-oj-i], *n.* the science or art of growing fruits, particularly apples. [L. *pomum* apple and Gk. *logos* speech].

POMP, [pomp], *n.* display of grandeur and splendour, pageantry; a boastful parade; ostentation. [Gk. *pompe* a solemn parade].

POMPADOUR, [pom'-pad-ōōer], *n.* a style of hair-dressing in which the hair is brushed back and upwards from the forehead. [Madame de *Pompadour*].

POMPHOLYX†, [pom'-fōl-iks], *n.* (*chem.*) flowers of zinc; (*path.*) an eruptive disease attacking the hands and feet. [Gk. *pompholux* blister].

POMPION, PUMPION, [pump'-i-on], *n.* a pumpkin, *Cucurbita pepo*. [Fr. *pompon* melon].

POMPIRE, [pom'-pīer], *n.* a variety of apple.

POMPOM, [pom'-pom], *n.* a quick-firing automatic gun using one-pound shells. [Imitative].

POMPON, [pom'-pon], *n.* (*milit.*) a tuft ornament, a round tuft on a soldier's headgear; a coloured ball of wool, *esp.* on a clown's costume. [Fr. *pompon*].

POMPOSITY, [pomp-os'-it-i], *n.* the quality of being pompous, pompousness; ostentation, boasting.

POMPOSO, [pomp-ō'-sō], *adv.* (*mus.*) majestically. [It. *pomposo*].

POMPOUS, [pomp'-us], *adj.* excessively dignified, arrogant and heavy in speech or bearing, displaying pomp or grandeur; ostentatious, self-important. [LL. *pomposus* dignified].

POMPOUSLY, [pomp'-us-li], *adv.* in a pompous manner.

POMPOUSNESS, [pomp'-us-nes], *n.* the quality or the state of being pompous.

PONCHO, [pon'-chō], *n.* a woollen cloak formed out of a blanket, worn in South America, with a slit in the middle for the head to pass through, and hanging down before and behind. [Native *poncho*].

POND, [pond], *n.* a small body of stagnant water forming in a natural hollow and fed by the rains or dew and not by a running stream; a small lake. [ME. *ponde*].

PONDER, [pond'-er], *v.t. and i.* to formulate in thought and consider all the aspects in the mind, to weigh in the mind; to examine; to think, cogitate. [ME. *pondere* from L. *ponderare* to weigh].

PONDERABILITY, [pond'-er-ab-il'-it-i], *n.* ponderableness.

PONDERABLE, [pond'-er-abl], *adj.* capable of being pondered; able to be weighed.

PONDERABLENESS, [pond'-er-abl-nes], *n.* the state of being ponderable; heaviness.

PONDERAL, [pond'-er-al], *adj.* of, relating to, estimated by, weight.

PONDERER, [pond'-er-er], *n.* person who ponders.

PONDERINGLY, [pond'-er-ing-li], *adv.* in a pondering manner, with consideration.

PONDEROSITY, [pond'-er-os'-it-i], *n.* ponderousness. [Fr. *ponderosité*].

PONDEROUS, [pond'-er-us], *adj.* very heavy, weighty; forcible; clumsy. [L. *ponderosus* weighty].

PONDEROUSLY, [pond'-er-us-li], *adv.* in a ponderous manner, with great weight.

PONDEROUSNESS, [pond'-er-us-nes], *n.* the state of being ponderous.

PONDWEED, [pond'-wēd'], *n.* a plant of the genus *Potamogeton*.

PONDWORT, [pond'-wurt], *n.* a plant also known as the water-soldier, *Stratiotes aloides*. [POND and WORT].

PONE (1), [pō'-ni], *n.* the cardplayer to the right of the dealer whose duty it is to cut the cards. [L. *pone*, *imper.* of *ponere* to place].

PONE (2), [pōn], *n.* Indian bread made of maize flour, Johnny cake. [Uncert.].

PONENT, [pōn'-ent], *adj.* western. [L. *ponens*, *pres.pt.* of *ponere* to place].

PONGEE, [pon'-jē], *n.* a soft kind of fabric made from the silk of wild silkworms. [Uncert.].

PONIARD, POIGNARD (1), [pon'-yahd], *n.* a small dagger. [Fr. *poignard*].

PONIARD, POIGNARD (2), [pon'-yahd], *v.t.* to stab. [PONIARD (1)].

PONTAC, [pon'-tak], *n.* a kind of claret from Pontac, a district in the south of France.

PONIARD

PONTIC, [pont'-ik], *adj.* of, relating to, found in, the region around the Black Sea. [L. *Pontus* the Black Sea].

PONTIFEX, [pon'-tif-eks], *n.* (*eccles.*) a Roman pontiff, a member of the college of priests; **p. maximus**, the chief of the pontiffs, the pope. [L. *pontifex* high priest].

PONTIFF, [pon'-tif], *n.* a high priest; the pope. [Fr. *pontife*].

PONTIFIC, [pon-tif'-ik], *adj.* pontifical.

PONTIFICAL (1), [pon-tif'-ikl], *n.* a book of rites and ceremonies for bishops; (*pl.*) episcopal vestments.

PONTIFICAL (2), **PONTIFICIAL**, [pon-tif'-ikl], *adj.* of, relating to, issued by, a pontiff or bishop, *esp.* the pope, as the bishop of Rome; pompous. [L. *pontificalis*].

PONTIFICALLY, [pon-tif'-ik-ali], *adv.* in a pontifical manner; with excessive ritual.

PONTIFICATE, [pon-tif'-ik-āt], *n.* the dignity or the office of a pontiff; the reign of a pope. [L. *pontificatus*].

PONTIFICIAL, see PONTIFICAL.

PONTINE, [pont'-īn], *adj.* of, relating to, the large marsh between Rome and Naples. [L. *pons pontis* bridge].

PONTLEVIS, [pont'-lev'-is], *n.* a drawbridge; the disobedient rearing of a horse on his hind legs. [Fr. *pont-levis*].

PONTONIER, [pon-ton-ēer'], *n.* (*milit.*) the constructor or authority in charge of a bridge. [Fr. *pontonnier*].

PONTOON (1), [pon-tōōn'], *n.* a flat-bottomed boat or structure used for constructing temporary bridges; a large lighter fitted with cranes; a game of cards, vingt-et-un. [Fr. *ponton*].

PONTOON (2), [pon-tōōn'], *v.t. and i.* to form a bridge by means of pontoons; to cross by means of a pontoon-bridge. [PONTOON (1)].

PONTOON-BRIDGE, [pon-tōōn'-brij'], *n.* a bridge constructed on pontoons.

PONY, (*pl.* **ponies**), [pō'-ni], *n.* a small horse of thirteen to fourteen hands high; (*slang*) a bet of £25. [Scots *powney* from OFr. *poulenet*, *dim.* of *poulain* colt].

POOD, [pōōd], *n.* a Russian weight, equal to thirty-six English pounds avoirdupois. [Russ. *pud*].

POODLE, [pōōdl], *n.* a breed of dog with long curly hair often clipped to form affected designs, remarkable for its sagacity and affection. [LGerm. *pudel* to splash].

POODLE-FAKER, [pōōdl'-fāk'-er], *n.* (*slang*) a young man who frequents ladies' society. [Of Anglo-Indian origin].

POOGYE, [pōō'-ji], *n.* a nose-flute used in India. [Hind. *pungi*].

POOH, [pōō], *int.* an exclamation of dislike or contempt.

POOH-POOH, [pōō'-pōō'], *v.t.* (*coll.*) to pour scorn on, to say "pooh" about. [POOH].
POOJA, see PUJA.
POOL (1), [pōōl], *n.* a small sheet of water or liquid, a puddle; a specific area of a river or running stream which is deeper and sometimes wider than the main stream. [OE. *pol*].
POOL (2), [pōōl], *n.* the stakes played for in a number of card and gambling games; the receptacle to hold these stakes; a form of gambling on the results of football matches, the winners taking a percentage of the fund created by the entrance fees; a form of billiards in which each player takes a different coloured ball; a general fund contributed to by various participants for gambling on the Stock Exchange; (*comm.*) an economic form of organization, amalgamating various firms and interests in order to eliminate competition and constitute a central, monopolistic control of the market. [Fr. *poule* chicken].
POOL (3), [pōōl], *v.t.* to form into a pool; to establish a common fund. [POOL (2)].
POOLER, [pōōl'-er], *n.* an implement for stirring a tan vat.
POOL-SNIPE, [pōōl'-snīp], *n.* the redshank, *Totanus calidris*.
POONAC, [pōōn'-ak], *n.* the pulpy mass of coconut after the oil has been extracted. [Singhalese *punakku*].
POONSPAR, [pōōn'-spah(r)], *n.* the Indian tree, *Calophyllum elatum*, used for masts and spars. [Singhalese *puna* and SPAR].
POOP (1), [pōōp], *n.* the raised deck in the stern of a ship. [L. *puppis* stern].
POOP (2), [pōōp], *n.* (*U.S. slang*) a fool, a booby. [Unkn.].
POOP (3), [pōōp], *v.t.* to strike or break over the stern of a vessel, as a wave. [POOP (1)].
POOPED, [pōōpt], *adj.* having a poop; struck on the poop.
POOPING, [pōōp'-ing], *n.* the shock of a heavy sea on the stern of a ship.
POOP-ROYAL, [pōōp'-roi'-al], *n.* a deck on the aftermost part of the poop, the top-gallant poop or round-house.
POOR (1), [pōōer], *n.* a collective name for the class of people who have little money or possessions, who own no property or means of production by which they could enrich themselves, and who are dependent on employment or charity given them by the rich; the working class, proletariat. [POOR (2)].
POOR (2), [pōōer], *adj.* having no wealth, having no means of support, not rich, necessitous, needy; pitiably mean and contemptible in character and strength; barren, unproductive, lacking in fertility; worth very little, empty of importance; worthy of pity, unlucky, dejected; lacking in good qualities, inferior, unhealthy, weak. [ME. *poure*, *povre* from L. *pauper* poor].
POOR-BOX, [pōōer'-boks'], *n.* a box set aside in a church for charity contributions for a parish's poor; a fund established to assist poor persons who appear in police courts.
POOR-HOUSE, [pōōer'-hows], *n.* a public institution maintained for the support of the poor, a workhouse.
POOR-LAWS, [pōōer'-lawz'], *n.*(*pl.*) regulations for the state care and local support of the poor.
POORLY (1), [pōōer'-li], *adj.* somewhat ill, indisposed, not fit and healthy.
POORLY (2), [pōōer'-li], *adv.* without wealth, in indigence; with little or no success, ineffectively; in a poor manner.
POORNESS, [pōōer'-nes], *n.* the quality or state of being poor.
POOR-RATE, [pōōer'-rāt'], *n.* a rate established for the support of the poor.
POOR-SPIRITED, [pōōer'-spir'-it-id], *adj.* having little courage, of a mean spirit; cowardly; base.
POOR-SPIRITEDNESS, [pōōer'-spir'-it-id-nes], *n.* the quality of being poor-spirited.
POP (1), [pop], *n.* a popular concert. [Contraction of POPULAR].
POP (2), [pop], *n.* a sudden sharp sound which is not loud and is very brief; (*coll.*) ginger-beer; a shot. [Imitative].
POP (3), [pop], *adv.* with the sound of a pop; suddenly so as to startle. [POP (2)].
POP (4), (**popping, popped**), [pop], *v.t. and i.* to cause to pop, usually because of the release of air under pressure; to put in or take out with a quick, sudden movement; to enter or exit in person quickly and unexpectedly, remaining for a very brief time; (*slang*) to pawn; to explode with a pop; **to p. the question**, to make a proposal of marriage; **to p. in**, to pay an unexpected and brief visit; **to p. off**, to leave quickly and unexpectedly, particularly without being noticed; (*slang*) to die. [POP (2)].
POPCORN, [pop'-kawn], *n.* parched maize eaten as confectionery when sugar-coated.
POPE (1), [pōp], *n.* the ruff, a freshwater fish of the genus *Acerina*. [POPE (2)].
POPE (2), [pōp], *n.* the Bishop of Rome, head of the Roman Catholic Church; (*fig.*) a person who believes his judgments to be infallible; **pope's eye**, a gland in a sheep's thigh; **pope's head**, a feather brush with a long handle. [OE. *papa*, ME. *pape* from Gk. *pappas* father].
POPE (3), [pōp], *n.* a Russian parish priest. [Russ. *pop*].
POPEDOM, [pōp'-dom], *n.* the office or dignity of the Pope; the jurisdiction of the Pope.
POPE-JOAN, [pōp'-jōn'], *n.* a game of cards without the eight of diamonds, and named after the legendary female Pope Joan.
POPELING, [pōp'-ling], *n.* a little pope; an adherent of the pope; a person who would claim the powers of a pope.
POPERY, [pōp'-er-i], *n.* a term describing the principles and power of Roman Catholicism and used by its enemies.
POP-EYED, [pop'-īd], *adj.* (*U.S. slang*) having bulging eyes; daft, soppy.
POPGUN, [pop'-gun'], *n.* a small toy gun worked by compressed air which fires a cork fixed by a string to the barrel.
POPINJAY, [pop'-in-jā], *n.* a parrot; the green woodpecker; a mark for shooting at; an effeminate over-dressed youth, a dandy, a fop or coxcomb. [ME. *popingay*, *papegay* from OFr. *papegai*].
POPISH, [pōp'-ish], *adj.* of, relating or belonging to, having some of the characteristics of, the Pope or popery.
POPISHLY, [pōp'-ish-li], *adv.* in a popish manner.
POPLAR, [pop'-ler], *n.* a tree of the genus *Populus*, with a relatively slender trunk of a white, soft wood. [ME. *popler*, *poplere* from L. *populus*].
POPLARISM, [pop'-ler-izm], *n.* a term applied to the policy of the Board of Guardians in *Poplar* when granting out-relief in 1920, and implying extravagance in poor-relief.
POPLIN, [pop'-lin], *n.* a stuff made of silk and worsted wool. [Uncert.].
POPLITEAL, [pop'-lit-ē'-al], *adj.* poplitic.
POPLITIC, [pop-lit'-ik], *adj.* situated near, relating to, the knee-joint or ham. [L. *poples poplitis* ham].
POPOVER, [pop'-ōv-er], *n.* (*U.S.*) a small light cake which rises and falls over to one side when baked.
POPPET, [pop'-et], *n.* a timber used to support a ship in launching; the head of a lathe; a term of endearment for a child. [*Var.* of PUPPET].
POPPING-CREASE, [pop'-ing-krēs'], *n.* in cricket, the crease marked in white chalk four feet from the stumps which is the batsman's ground and in which his bat or person must be grounded to invalidate any appeal for stumped or run-out.
POPPLE, [popl], *v.t.* to bubble; to ripple; to bob up and down. [ME. *poplen*].
POPPY, [pop'-i], *n.* a plant of the genus *Papaver*; **p. oil**, oil from the seeds of the white, or opium poppy, *Papaver somniferum*; **Welsh p.**, a species of *Meconopsis*. [OE. *popæg*, ME. *popy*].
POPPYCOCK, [pop'-i-kok'], *n.* (*U.S. slang*) dreams, nonsense. [POPPY and COCK, shortened form of COCAINE].
POPPY-HEAD, [pop'-i-hed'], *n.* (*arch.*) a finial of foliage or other ornaments in woodwork; the seed-case of the poppy.
POP-SHOP, [pop'-shop], *n.* (*coll.*) a pawnshop. [POP (4) and SHOP (1)].
POPULACE, [pop'-yōō-las], *n.* the common people considered collectively as a class without hereditary or acquired rank; the inhabitants of a city. [It. *popolaccio* from L. *populus* people].
POPULAR, [pop'-yōō-ler], *adj.* of, relating to, appealing to, the populace; easily comprehensible, plain; obvious, superficial, low-brow; **p. government**, government according to a majority vote; **p. front**, a movement advocating a coalition (government) of progressive political parties. [L. *popularis* of the people].
POPULARITY, [pop'-yōō-la'-rit-i], *n.* the state of being popular or in favour with the people.
POPULARIZE, [pop'-yōō-ler-īz], *v.t.* to render popular

or common; to spread among the people by using simple and attractive means.

POPULARLY, [pop'-yŏŏ-ler-li], *adv.* in a popular manner.

POPULATE, [pop'-yŏŏ-lāt'], *v.t.* to furnish with inhabitants, to provide with people. [LL. *populatum*, *p.pt.* of *populare*].

POPULATION, [pop'-yŏŏ-lā'-shun], *n.* the act of populating; the number of people or inhabitants in a country; state of a country as regards population. [LL. *populatio*].

POPULIN, [pop'-yŏŏ-lin], *n.* (*chem.*) a crystallizable substance separated from the bark of the aspen. [L. *populus* poplar].

POPULOUS, [pop'-yŏŏ-lus], *adj.* full of inhabitants, abounding with people, thickly peopled. [L. *populosus*].

POPULOUSLY, [pop'-yŏŏ-lus-li], *adv.* to a populous degree, with many inhabitants.

POPULOUSNESS, [pop'-yŏŏ-lus-nes], *n.* the state of being populous.

PORBEAGLE, [paw-bēgl'], *n.* the shark, *Lamna cornubica*, found in the North Atlantic. [Uncert.].

PORCATE, [paw'-kāt], *adj.* (*zool.*) formed in ridges. [L. *porca* ridge].

PORCELAIN (1), [paw'-sel-in], *n.* a fine white semi-transparent earthenware; chinaware. [PORCELAIN (2)].

PORCELAIN (2), [paw'-sel-in], *adj.* made of porcelain. [It. *porcellana* glazed].

PORCELAINIZE, [paw'-sel-in-īz], *v.t.* to turn into porcelain.

PORCELAINIZED, [paw'-sel-in-īzd], *adj.* (*geol.*) baked like porcelain.

PORCELLANEOUS, see PORCELLANOUS.

PORCELLANITE, [paw'-sel-an-īt], *n.* (*min.*) argillite; baked shale; porcelain-jasper.

PORCELLANOUS, PORCELLANEOUS, [paw-sel'-an-us, paw'-sel-ā'-ni-us], *adj.* having the characteristics of, or resembling, porcelain or its texture.

PORCH, [pawch], *n.* a covered structure built round an entrance to a building; **The P.,** the public portico in Athens used as a school by the Stoics. [L. *porticus*].

PORCINE, [paw'-sīn], *adj.* of, relating to, resembling, swine. [L. *porcinus*].

PORCUPINE, [pawk'-yŏŏ-pīn], *n.* a rodent of the genus *Hystrix* which is covered with protective quills; **Canadian p.,** a rodent of the genus *Erethiyon*; **tree p.,** a rodent of the genus *Syntheres*; **p. grass,** a coarse grass growing in Australia. [ME. *porcepyn* from OFr. *porcespin* prickly pig].

PORCUPINE

PORCUPINE-FISH, [pawk'-yŏŏ-pīn-fish'], *n.* a fish of the tropical seas covered with spines, *Diodon hystrix*.

PORCUPINE-WOOD, [pawk'-yŏŏ-pīn-wŏŏd'], *n.* the outer wood of the coconut palm.

PORE (1), [paw(r)], *n.* a minute opening in the membranous surfaces of plants or animals by which fluids are exhaled or absorbed; a small interstice between the molecules or particles of bodies. [Gk. *poros* passage].

PORE (2), [paw(r)], *v.i.* **to p. over,** to study steadily and persistently with attention. [ME. *puren*, *pouren*].

POREBLIND, see PURBLIND.

PORER, [pawr'-er], *n.* person who pores or studies diligently.

PORGY, [paw'-ji], *n.* a salt-water fish valued as food. [Uncert.].

PORIFERA, [paw-rif'-era], *n.*(*pl.*) (*zool.*) the sponges. [L. *porifera*, *neut. pl.* of *porifer* bearing pores].

PORIFORM, [paw'-ri-fawm], *adj.* resembling a pore in form. [L. *porus* pore and FORM].

PORINESS, [paw'-ri-nes], *n.* the state of being pory.

PORITE, [paw'-rīt], *n.* (*zool.*) a species of coral of the genus *Porites*, the surface of which is covered with minute pores. [Gk. *poros* pore].

PORK, [pawk], *n.* the flesh of a pig, fresh or salted for eating. [L. *porcus* pig].

PORK BUTCHER, [pawk'-bŏŏch'-er], *n.* a butcher who sells only pork and sausages, etc., made from pork.

PORKER, [pawk'-er], *n.* a young pig; a pig fattened up for the table.

PORKET, [pawk'-et], *n.* a piglet.

PORKLING, [pawk'-ling], *n.* a young pig, a porker.

PORK PIE, [pawk'-pī'], *n.* a pie containing minced or chopped pork, usually sold cold.

PORK-PIE HAT, [pawk'-pī-hat'], *n.* a soft felt hat with a round flat crown.

PORKY, [pawk'-i], *adj.* resembling, containing, or tasting of, pork.

PORNOGRAPHER, [pawn-og'-raf-er], *n.* a writer or seller of pornographic literature.

PORNOGRAPHIC, [pawn'-o-graf'-ik], *adj.* of, relating to, pornography; obscene.

PORNOGRAPHICALLY, [pawn'-o-graf'-ik-al-i], *adv.* in a pornographical manner, obscenely.

PORNOGRAPHY, [pawn-og'-raf-i], *n.* licentious painting or writing; literature which is deliberately obscene. [Gk. *porne* whore and *graphia* writing].

POROSCOPE, [paw'-ros-kōp], *n.* an instrument for testing the porosity of a body. [Gk. *poros* pore and SCOPE].

POROSCOPIC, [paw'-ros-kop'-ik], *adj.* of, relating to, by means of, a poroscope.

POROSE, [po'-rōs], *adj.* having pores. [L. *porosus*].

POROSITY, [paw-ros'-it-i], *n.* porousness.

POROTIC, [paw-rot'-ik], *adj.* capable of forming into hard matter or callus. [Gk. *poros* callus].

POROUS, [paw'-rus], *adj.* having pores, or full of pores or interstices; capable of absorbing water.

POROUSNESS, [paw'-rus-nes], *n.* the state of having pores or interstices.

PORPEZITE, [paw'-pez-īt], *n.* (*min.*) a mineral containing gold and palladium. [*Porpez* in Brazil].

PORPHYRITE, [paw'-fer-īt], *n.* (*min.*) a porphyritic rock. [L. *porphyrites* a purple precious stone].

PORPHYRITIC, [paw'-fer-it'-ik], *adj.* (*geol.*) of, relating to, resembling or containing, porphyry.

PORPHYRIZE, [paw'-fer-īz], *v.t.* to cause to resemble porphyry.

PORPHYROID, [paw'-fer-oid], *adj.* resembling porphyry. [PORPHYRY and Gk. *oeides* like].

PORPHYRY, [paw'-fer-i], *n.* a rock, having a compact felspathic base, through which crystals of a different colour are disseminated. [Gk. *porphura* purple].

PORPHYRY-SHELL, [paw'-fer-i-shel'], *n.* a univalve shell of the genus *Murex*.

PORPOISE, [paw'-pus], *n.* the hog-fish or sea-hog with a stubby snout; a mammal of the dolphin family of the genus *Phocæna*. [OFr. *porpeis*].

PORPOISE

PORPORINO, [paw'-paw-rē'-nō], *n.* a composition of mercury, tin and sulphur used by medieval artists instead of gold. [It. *porporino*].

PORRACEOUS, [po-rā'-shus], *adj.* leek-green. [L. *porraceus*].

PORRECT, [po'-rekt], *adj.* extending horizontally. [L. *porrectum*, *p.pt.* of *porrigere* to extend].

PORRECTION, [po-rek'-shun], *n.* (*eccles.*) the ritual of delivering by outstretched hands. [L. *porrectio*].

PORRIDGE, [po'-rij], *n.* oatmeal or other meal boiled in water or milk as food. [POTTAGE].

PORRIDGE-POT, [po'-rij-pot'], *n.* the pot in which porridge is boiled.

PORRIGO, [po-rī'-gō], *n.* scurf; dandruff. [L. *porrigo*].

PORRINGER, [po'-rinj-er], *n.* a small dish for holding porridge; a small shallow cooking utensil. [POTAGER].

PORT (1), [pawt], *n.* a heavy red wine, originally from Oporto. [*Oporto* in Portugal].

PORT (2), [pawt], *n.* †a gate; a port-hole; a hole in the hull of a man-of-war for a gun to shoot through; in machinery, a hole for light and air or for steam, fuel and exhaust gases. [L. *porta* gate].

PORT (3), [pawt], *n.* a harbour for the protection and loading and unloading of ships; a town provided with such; (*fig.*) a place of refuge, a shelter; **p. admiral,** the officer in charge of a port; **p. of entry,** a port providing customs facilities. [OE. *port* from L. *portus*].

PORT (4), [pawt], *n.* style of gait or bearing, mien. [L. *portare* to carry].

PORT (5), [pawt], *n.* the left side of a ship viewed from the stern, larboard. [Unkn.].

PORT (6), [pawt], *v.t.* to turn the helm so that a ship moves to the left; (*obs.*) to move the helm to the left so that the ship moves to the right.
PORT (7), [pawt], *v.t.* (*milit.*) to present (a rifle) for inspection.
PORTABILITY, [pawt'-ab-il'i-ti] *n.* portableness.
PORTABLE, [pawt'-abl], *adj.* able to be carried about easily, movable; not bulky. [L. *portabilis*].
PORTABLENESS, [pawt'-abl-nes], *n.* the quality of being portable.
PORTAGE, [pawt'-ij], *n.* the act of carrying; the price of carrying; a stretch of land between watercourses, over which a boat or canoe is carried. [Fr. *portage*].
PORTAL, [pawtl], *n.* a gate, entrance or doorway, particularly one architecturally designed, an arched gateway; (*anat.*) a passage leading to the liver. [L. *porta* gate].
PORTAMENTO, [pawt-a-ment'-ō], *n.* a slurring or glide in moving from one note to another in singing. [It. *portamento* from *portare* to carry].
PORTATIVE, [pawt'-at-iv], *adj.* serving to carry. [Fr. *portatif*].
PORT-BAR, [pawt'-bah(r)], *n.* a boom barring the entrance to a harbour.
PORT-CHARGES, [pawt'-chahj'-iz], *n.*(*pl.*) charges to which a ship or its cargo is subjected for use of a port.
PORTCRAYON, PORTECRAYON, [pawt'-krā'-on], *n.* a small metallic handle for holding a crayon. [Fr. *portcrayon*].
PORTCULLIS, [pawt-kul'-is], *n.* (*fort.*) a powerful grating held in position over a gateway and let down as a means of defence; (*her.*) a charge of this form; title of one of the pursuivants of the English College of Arms. [Fr. *porte-coulisse*].
PORTE†, [pawt], *n.* the former government of Turkey, so called from the high gate of the imperial palace. [Fr. *porte* gate].

PORTCULLIS

PORTECRAYON, see PORTCRAYON.
PORTEND, [paw-tend'], *v.t.* to indicate some future event or incident by signs, to foreshow, to presage. [L. *portendere*].
PORTENT, [paw'-tent], *n.* an omen of evil, a significant sign. [L. *portentum* omen].
PORTENTOUS, [paw-tent'-us], *adj.* having the power of a portent, ominous, foreshadowing ill; monstrous; imposing; pompous. [*Prec.*].
PORTENTOUSLY, [paw-tent'-us-li], *adv.* in a portentous manner.
PORTER (1), [pawt'-er], *n.* a doorkeeper or gatekeeper, particularly of a hotel or public institution. [LL. *portarius*].
PORTER (2), [pawt'-er], *n.* a carrier of burdens or parcels; a man employed at a railway station or elsewhere to handle passengers' luggage and to shift heavy loads; a dark brown beer once a favourite drink of London porters. [OFr. *porteour*].
PORTERAGE, [pawt'-er-ij], *n.* the work of a porter; money paid to a porter.
PORTERESS, [pawt'-er-es], *n.* a female gatekeeper.
PORTERHOUSE, [pawt'-er-hows], *n.* a restaurant; a chop-house; **p. steak,** a steak cut from between the sirloin and tenderloin.
PORTFIRE, [pawt'-fier], *n.* a firework device used for igniting purposes, *esp.* in mining operations. [Fr. *porte-feu*].
PORTFOLIO, [pawt-fō'-li-ō], *n.* a portable case for keeping papers, maps and drawings in; a collection of papers connected with a state department; the minister of the department. [It. *portafogli*].
PORT-HOLE, [pawt'-hōl], *n.* a hole for ventilation purposes in the side of a ship; a passage for steam.
PORTICO, [pawt'-i-kō], *n.* a covered walk or entrance enclosed by columns. [It. *portico*].
PORTIERE, portière, [pawt-i-āer'], *n.* a curtain hung over a doorway. [Fr. *portière*].
PORTION (1), [paw'-shun], *n.* a part, small share or division; part of an estate; a helping (of food, etc.). [L. *portio*].
PORTION (2), [paw'-shun], *v.t.* to divide into shares; to allot a certain amount, to endow. [OFr. *portionner*].
PORTIONED, [paw'-shund], *adj.* having a portion.
PORTIONER, [paw'-shun-er] *n.* one who divides into shares; portionist.
PORTIONIST, [paw'-shun-ist], *n.* (*eccles.*) the joint incumbent of a benefice.
PORTIONLESS, [paw'-shun-les], *adj.* having no portion.
PORTLAND, [pawt'-land], *adj.* relating to the Isle of Portland; **P. cement,** a yellowish cement; **P. stone,** a variety of oolite, yellowish-white in colour, found in Portland. [*Portland* in Dorset].
PORTLANDIAN, [pawt-land'-i-an], *adj.* relating to the middle series of Portland oolites, comprising the Portland stone and sands.
PORTLINESS, [pawt'-li-nes], *n.* the quality of being portly.
PORTLY, [pawt'-li], *adj.* dignified in mien; corpulent.
PORTMANTEAU, [pawt-man'-tō], *n.* a framed leather bag hinged at the middle for carrying clothes in. [Fr. *portmanteau*].
PORTMANTEAU-WORD, [pawt-man'-tō-wurd'], *n.* a word which is a novel combination in form and meaning of two words or parts of two words.
PORTOLAN, [pawt'-ō-lan], *n.* (*hist.*) a book of charts and sailing directions formerly used by sailors. [It. *portolano* from *porto* port].
PORTRAIT, [pawt'-rit], *n.* a representation of a person in paint or writing with emphasis on the facial characteristics and appearance; a picture of an individual; **p. painter,** an artist who paints such. [Fr. *portrait*].
PORTRAITIST, [pawt'-rāt-ist], *n.* a maker of portraits.
PORTRAITURE, [pawt'-ri-cher], *n.* the art of portrait-painting; vivid delineation.
PORTRAY, POURTRAY†, [paw-trā'], *v.t.* to paint or draw a likeness of; to describe in words. [OFr. *pourtraire*].
PORTRAYAL, [paw-trā'-al], *n.* the act of portraying; a representation, delineation.
PORTRAYER, [paw-trā'-er], *n.* one who paints or describes vividly.
PORTREEVE, [pawt'-rēv], *n.* the chief magistrate of a port town. [OE. *portgerefa*].
PORTRESS, [pawt'-res], *n.* a female gatekeeper; a porteress.
PORTUGUESE (1), (*pl.* **Portuguese**), [pawt'-yōō-gēz'], *n.* a native of Portugal; the native language of Portugal.
PORTUGUESE (2), [pawt'-yōō-gēz'], *adj.* of, or pertaining to, Portugal, the Portuguese, or their language. [Portug. *Portuguez*].
PORY, [paw'-ri], *adj.* full of pores.
POSE (1), [pōz], *n.* a position, posture adopted by the body; an attitude of mind which is unnatural, a pretence.
POSE (2), **posé,** [pō-zā'], *adj.* (*her.*) (of a beast) standing still with all four feet on the ground. [Fr. *posé*].
POSE (3), [pōz], *v.t.* and *i.* to place in a pose, to arrange (the body) in a particular position, *esp.* to form a composition for a picture; to set out as a problem; to assume an unnatural attitude based on insincere belief; to take up a deliberately conceived position. [Fr. *poser* from L. *pausare* to pause].

POSÉ

POSE (4), [pōz], *v.t.* to confuse by asking difficult questions, to puzzle; to bring to a stand. [Abbreviated from OPPOSE].
POSER, [pōz'-er], *n.* one who poses; a puzzle.
POSEUR, [pōz-ur'], *n.* one who parades affected attitudes, an exhibitionist. [Fr. *poseur*].
POSH (1), [posh], *adj.* (*slang*) good, smart. [Unkn.].
POSH (2), [posh], *v.t.* and *i.* **to p. up,** to smarten up. [POSH (1)].
POSING, [pōz'-ing], *adj.* puzzling, questioning closely.
POSINGLY, [pōz'-ing-li], *adv.* so as to puzzle.
POSIT, [pos'-it], *v.t.* to postulate; to lay down, affirm, or assume as a fact. [L. *positum*, *p.pt.* of *ponere* to place].
POSITION (1), [poz-ish'-un], *n.* the state of being placed; the place or situation occupied by anything; a state reached in the development of affairs; rank, social standing; a situation providing employment, a job; a pose. [L. *positio*].
POSITION (2), [poz-ish'-un], *v.t.* to place in a particular position, to assign a position to; *v. reflex.* to take up a position (chiefly in sport).
POSITIONAL, [poz-ish'-un-al], *adj.* relating to position.
POSITIVE (1), [poz'-it-iv], *n.* that which is positive;

(*elect.*) the positive pole, the anode; a print or film which is the reverse in tones to the negative.

POSITIVE (2), [poz'-it-iv], *adj.* expressed explicitly, affirmed without qualification, definite, specific, direct, stated as a fact; unconditional; being absolutely convinced, without any mental reservation; over-confident, dogmatic; existing in fact, actual, real; having definite characteristics; having power to act directly; (*elect.*) a state of electrical potential due to a deficiency in electrons; denoting a conventional current imagined to flow contrary to the movement of electrons; (*gram.*) expressing the simple state or degree; (*math.*) more than nought, plus; (*philos.*) of, related to, positivism. [L. *positivus*].

POSITIVELY, [poz'-it-iv-li], *adv.* in a positive manner.

POSITIVENESS, [poz'-it-iv-nes], *n.* the state of being positive.

POSITIVISM, [poz'-it-iv-izm], *n.* (*philos.*) philosophy based on empirical investigation; dogmatism. [Fr. *positivisme*].

POSITIVIST, [poz'-it-iv-ist], *n.* (*philos.*) an advocate of positivism.

POSITIVISTIC, [poz'-it-iv-ist'-ik], *adj.* relating to positivism.

POSNET, [poz'-net], *n.* a little basin fitted with a handle and three supports. [OFr. *pocenet*].

POSOLOGICAL, [pos'-o-loj'-ik-al], *adj.* relating to posology.

POSOLOGY, [pos-ol'-o-ji], *n.* (*med.*) the branch of medicine which treats of doses. [Gk. *posos* how much and *logos* speech].

POSSE, [pos'-i, pos], *n.* a number of men; **p. comitatus**, (*leg.*) the body of men liable to be called out by the sheriff to enforce the law or resist invasion. [Uncert.].

POSSESS, [poz-es'], *v.t.* to hold, to own, to occupy; to seize; to have the power over, to have sole control of, to dominate. [L. *possidere* to occupy].

POSSESSED, [pō-zest'], *adj.* suffering from possession (by the devil); in a frenzy.

POSSESSION, [poz-esh'-un], *n.* the act of possessing; the state of being possessed; ownership; that which is possessed, goods, property, estate owned and in one's keeping, territory controlled by a country outside of its own boundaries. [L. *possessio*].

POSSESSIVE, [poz-es'-iv], *adj.* relating to possession; **p. case**, (*gram.*) the genitive case indicating possession. [L. *possessivus*].

POSSESSIVELY, [poz-es'-iv-li], *adv.* in a possessive manner, in a way showing possession.

POSSESSOR, [poz-es'-er], *n.* one who possesses.

POSSESSORY, [poz-es'-er-i], *adj.* relating to possession; having possession. [L. *possessorius*].

POSSET, (**possetting, possetted**), [pos'-it], *n.* milk curdled with wine or stout and spiced. [ME. *possot*].

POSSIBILITY, [pos'-ib-il'-i-ti], *n.* the quality of being possible, the power of existing or of happening; state of being possible; a possible thing, an event not likely to occur, a chance; (*pl.*) potentialities. [L. *possibilitas*].

POSSIBLE, [pos'-ibl], *adj.* likely to occur, able to come about, that can be; that can be done; practicable, that may happen; able to be considered, tolerable. [L. *possibilis*].

POSSIBLY, [pos'-ib-li], *adv.* according to events which may occur, perhaps, may be.

POSSUM, [pos'-um], *n.* (*coll.*) an opossum; **to play p.**, to sham death; to sham disinterest or ignorance; to hide. [OPOSSUM].

POST (1), [pōst], *n.* an upright stake set in the ground to serve as a support; a pillar of rock left unhewed to support the roof of a mine-gallery; **driven from pillar to p.**, driven from one place, extremity, to another. [OE. *post* from L. *postis* door-post].

POST (2), [pōst], *n.* a position occupied by troops, air-raid wardens, etc. ; an isolated position, outlying settlement occupied as part of a general plan; a position, duty to which someone is assigned; an employment, job; a group of men stationed at intervals for the transmission of messages; the state-managed transmission and delivery of messages, letters, and parcels; an office, box where letters are left for transmission; the delivery of such letters; the time of clearing a post-box; the time taken in delivering letters by post; a postman's round; a standard size for notepaper; **last p.**, a military bugle-call sounded at tattoo and at funerals; **general-p.**, a parlour game. [Fr. *poste* from L. *positum* placed].

POST (3), [pōst], *v.t.* to affix (a notice) to a post, *hence* to put up (a notice) for public reading; to appoint, place a soldier in his post, allot a duty to; (*book-keeping*) to transfer to a ledger, to bring a ledger up to date; to keep a person well informed. [POST (1) and (2)].

POST (4), [pōst], *v.t. and i.* to dispatch a letter, entrust to the postal authorities for delivery; to travel by stages (posts), to travel in great haste; **p.-haste**, as fast as possible. [POST (2)].

POST- (5), *pref.* after, later than; behind. [L. *post*].

POSTABLE, [pōst'-abl], *adj.* small enough to be delivered by post.

POSTAGE, [pōst'-ij], *n.* the rate charged for postal conveyance; **p. stamp**, an adhesive piece of paper used to prepay postage on letters, etc.

POSTAL, [pōst'-al], *adj.* relating to transmission by post; **p. order**, a money order cashable at a post office.

POST-BAG, [pōst'-bag], *n.* a mail bag. [POST (2) and BAG].

POST-BILL, [pōst'-bil], *n.* a way-bill of letters sent through the post. [POST (2) and BILL].

POSTBOY, [pōst'-boi], *n.* a postilion. [POST (2) and BOY].

POST-CAPTAIN†, [pōst'-kap'-tin], *n.* (*naut.*) commander of a ship of more than twenty guns. [POST (2) and CAPTAIN].

POSTCARD, [pōst'-kahd], *n.* a card capable of bearing a message to be sent through the post. [POST (2) and CARD].

POST-CHAISE, [pōst'-shāz'], *n.* a four-wheeled, covered travelling-carriage, changing its horses at each post. [POST (2) and CHAISE].

POST-DATE, [pōst'-dāt'], *v.t.* to date a document, *esp.* a cheque, later than the time of writing. [POST (5) and DATE (3)].

POST-DAY, [pōst'-dā], *n.* mail day, a day on which the post arrives or departs. [POST (2) and DAY].

POSTEA, [pōst'-ē-a], *n.* (*leg.*) the record of a cause subsequent to the joining of issue. [L. *postea* afterwards].

POST-ENTRY, [pōst'-en-tri], *n.* an entry inserted in a ledger after the proper time. [POST (5) and ENTRY].

POSTER, [pōst'-er], *n.* one who posts notices; a bill, usually coloured, posted on walls, etc., for advertisement and propaganda. [POST (3)].

POSTE-RESTANTE, [pōst'-rest'-ahnt], *n.* the department of a post office at which letters are kept till called for. [Fr. *poste-restante*].

POSTERIOR (1), [pos-tēer'-i-or], *n.* the buttocks, the rear of a thing. [POSTERIOR (2)].

POSTERIOR (2), [pos-tēer'-i-or], *adj.* subsequent, succeeding; behind. [L. *posterior* coming after].

POSTERIORITY, [pos-tēer'-i-or'-it-i], *n.* the state of being posterior.

POSTERIORLY, [pos-tēer'-i-er-li], *adv.* subsequently; towards the behind.

POSTERITY, [pos-te'-rit-i], *n.* descendants, children of a common forebear; the future generations. [ME. *posterite* from Fr. *postérité*].

POSTERN, [pos'-tern], *n.* a small door in the walls of a castle; a back door. [OFr. *posterne* from LL. *posterula*].

POST-EXILIC, [pōst'-ek-zil'-ik], *adj.* after the Babylonian captivity of the Jews. [POST (5) and EXILIC].

POST-FACT, [pōst'-fakt], *n.* a fact occurring after another. [POST (5) and FACT].

POSTFIX, [pōst'-fiks], *n.* a suffix.

POST-FREE, [pōst'-frē'], *adj.* delivered without any charge for postage. [POST (2) and FREE].

POST-GLACIAL, [pōst'-glā'-si-al], *adj.* after the glacial epoch. [POST (5) and GLACIAL].

POST-HORN, [pōst'-hawn], *n.* the horn blown by the guard of a mail-coach. [POST (2) and HORN].

POST-HORN

POST-HORSE, [pōst'-haws'], *n.* a horse kept at mail-stages for coaches and post-chaises. [POST (2) and HORSES].

POSTHUMOUS, [post'-ew-mus], *adj.* happening after death; born after the father's death, received, awarded, after death. [L. *postumus*].

POSTHUMOUSLY, [post'-ew-mus-li], *adv.* after death.

POSTICAL, [pos'-tik-al], *adj.* (*bot.*) lying behind, on the hinder side. [L. *posticus* hinder].

POSTICHE, [pos-tēsh'], *n.* an artificial or superfluous decoration; a wig, false hair. [It. *posticcio* from L. *posticus* after].

POSTIL, [pos'-til], *n.* a marginal note, a short gloss on a text, *esp.* on the Bible; a homily on the Gospel. [MedL. *postilla*].

POSTILION, POSTILLION, [pos-til'-i-un], *n.* one riding on the foremost near horse of a carriage-team; (*wrongly*) the driver of a carriage. [Fr. *postillon* from It. *postiglione*].

POSTILLATE, [pos'-til-āt], *v.t.* to make postils on a text; to expound the Scripture. [MedL. *postillatum* *p.pt.* of *postillare*].

POSTILLATION, [pos'-til-ā'-shun], *n.* the act of postillating, the exposition itself. [MedL. *postillatio*].

POSTILLER, [pos'-til-er], *n.* one who postillates.

POSTILLION, see POSTILION.

POST-IMPRESSIONISM, [pōst'-im-presh'-un-izm], *n.* an advanced form of impressionism. [POST (5) and IMPRESSIONISM].

POST-IMPRESSIONIST (1), [pōst'-im-presh'-un-ist], *n.* a disciple or admirer of post-impressionism.

POST-IMPRESSIONIST (2), [pōst'-im-presh'-un-ist], *adj.* of, or pertaining to, post-impressionism or post-impressionists.

POSTING, [pōst'-ing], *n.* transference to a ledger.

POSTIQUE, [pos-tēk'], *adj.* (*arch. and sculp.*) inappropriately added to a finished work. [It. *posticcio* counterfeit].

POSTLIMINY, POSTLIMINIUM, [pōst-lim'-i-ni, post'-lim-in'-i-um], *n.* the right of an exile or prisoner of war to regain his previous citizenship and national status. [L. *postliminium*].

POSTMAN, [pōst'-man], *n.* a person who collects and delivers postal packages. [POST (2) and MAN].

POSTMARK (1), [pōst'-mahk], *n.* the place, time, and cancellation mark stamped on a letter, etc., sent through the post. [POST (2) and MARK].

POSTMARK (2), [pōst'-mahk'], *v.t.* to put a postmark on.

POSTMASTER, [pōst'-mahst-er], *n.* the head of a post office; a foundation scholar at Merton College, Oxford; **p.-general,** the chief officer of the postal system. [POST (2) and MASTER].

POSTMERIDIAN, [pōst'-mer-id'-i-an], *adj.* afternoon, after the sun has passed the meridian. [POST (5) and MERIDIAN].

POST-MORTEM (1), [pōst'-mawt'-em], *n.* an official examination, autopsy of a dead body to ascertain the cause of death; also *fig.* [POST (5) and L. *mortem*, *acc. sg.* of *mors* death].

POST-MORTEM (2), [pōst'-mawt'-em], *adj.* done, happening to, the body after death.

POST-NOTE, [pōst'-nōt], *n.* a post-dated promissory note. [POST (5) and NOTE].

POSTNUPTIAL, [pōst-nup'-shal], *adj.* occurring after marriage. [POST (5) and NUPTIAL].

POST-OBIT (1), [pōst'-ō'-bit], *n.* a loan repayable only after the death of the borrower and secured by a reversion. [POST-OBIT (2)].

POST-OBIT (2), [pōst'-ō'-bit], *adj.* (*leg.*) effective, payable after the death of a person. [POST (5) and L. *obitum* death].

POST OFFICE, [pōst'-of-is], *n.* an office for handling the dispatch and delivery of postal packages and communications; the department of state concerned with postal, telephone, and telegraphic services. [POST (2) and OFFICE].

POST-PAID, [pōst'-pād'], *adj.* with postage prepaid. [POST (2) and PAID].

POSTPONE, [pōst-pōn'], *v.t.* to delay, defer to a later time. [L. *postponere* to place after].

POSTPONEMENT, [pōst-pōn'-ment], *n.* the act of postponing, the length of time postponed.

POSTPONER, [pōst-pōn'-er], *n.* one who postpones.

POSTPOSITION, [pōst'-poz-ish'-un], *n.* a word placed after another; the state of being placed behind or after. [POST (5) and POSITION].

POSTPOSITIVE, [pōst'-poz'-it-iv], *adj.* placed after something, after another word.

POSTPRANDIAL, [pōst-pran'-di-al], *adj.* after dinner. [POST (5) and L. *prandium* midday meal].

POSTRORSE, [pōst-raws'], *adj.* doubled back. [L. *postrorsus*].

POSTSCENIUM, [pōst-sē'-ni-um], *n.* the back part of a theatre. [L. *postscaenium*].

POSTSCRIPT, [pōst'-skript], *n.* note added to a completed letter, a written afterthought; a talk at the end of a news broadcast. [L. *postscriptum*, *p.pt.* of *postscribere* to write afterwards].

POSTULANT, [pos'-chōō-lant], *n.* one who postulates; a candidate for Holy Orders, one who argues the case for canonization. [L. *postulantem*, *pres.pt.* of *postulare*].

POSTULATE (1), [pos'-chōō-lat], *n.* a demand, request; an assumption made as a basis, without proof. [POSTULATE (2)].

POSTULATE (2), [pos'-chōō-lāt], *v.t.* to request, demand; to assume as basis of argument; (*eccles.*) to nominate for a benefice. [L. *postulatum*, *p.pt.* of *postulare* to demand].

POSTULATION, [pos'-chōō-lā'-shun], *n.* the act of postulating, a postulate. [L. *postulatio*].

POSTULATORY, [pos'-chōō-lāt'-er-i], *adj.* by, relating to, postulation.

POSTURAL, [pos'-cher-al], *adj.* pertaining to posture.

POSTURE (1), [pos'-cher], *n.* position, bearing of the body, *esp.* an attitude, pose consciously assumed; attitude of mind, affected outlook. [L. *positura* position].

POSTURE (2), [pos'-cher], *v.i.* to assume a posture, to adopt an affected attitude of mind or body, to assume an unnatural character. [POSTURE (1)].

POST-WAR, [pōst'-waw(r)], *adj.* after the war; **p. credit,** a sum deducted in income-tax and repayable after the war. [POST (5) and WAR].

POSY, [pō'-zi], *n.* a sentiment or motto in verse, accompanying a gift; a small bouquet of flowers. [POESY].

POT (1), [pot], *n.* a rounded vessel for holding liquids; the contents of a pot, *hence* (*pl.*) a large amount; the contents of the pool in certain card games; a silver cup won as a trophy in athletic or other contests; a deep hole containing water; a casual, rapid shot from a short distance; a vessel containing earth for growing flowers; **big p.,** (*slang*) an important person; **chamber-p.,** (*coll.*) a bedroom utensil; **jack-p.,** a form of poker in which play cannot be opened unless one of the players holds a pair of jacks or better. [OE. *pott*].

POT (2), (potting, potted), [pot], *v.t. and i.* to place in a pot, *esp.* in order to keep or preserve, to plant in a pot; (*billiards*) to drive the red or the white into the pocket by striking with the cue-ball; to shoot casually, take a pot-shot. [POT (1)].

POTABILITY, [pōt-a-bil'-i-ti], *n.* fitness for drinking.

POTABLE, [pō'-tabl], *adj.* drinkable. [L. *potabilis*].

POTABLENESS, [pō'-tabl-nes], *n.* the quality of being drinkable.

POTAGE, see POTTAGE.

POTAGER, [pot'-ij-er], *n.* a porringer.

POTALE, [pot'-āl], *n.* the refuse from a grain distillery, used to fatten swine.

POTAMOLOGY, [pot'-am-ol'-o-ji], *n.* the study of rivers. [Gk. *potamos* a river and *logos* speech].

POTANCE, [pō'-tants], *n.* (*watchmaking*) the stud in which is placed the lower pivot of the verge. [Fr. *potance*].

POTASH, [pot'-ash], *n.* potassium carbonate obtained from vegetable ashes, *hence* any compound of potassium; **caustic p.,** potassium hydroxide. [Du. *potasschen* pot-ashes].

POTASSA, [pot-as'-a], *n.* potash. [MdL. *potassa*].

POTASSIUM, [pot-as'-i-um], *n.* the metallic alkaline element symbolized by K. [MdL. *potassa*].

POTATION, [pō-tā'-shun], *n.* a deep draught, the act of taking such a draught. [L. *potatio*].

POTATO, [pot-ā'-tō], *n.* the edible tuber of the American plant, *Solanum tuberosum*; the plant itself. [Native *batata* sweet potato].

POTATORY, [pō-tāt'-er-i], *adj.* pertaining to drinking. [L. *potatorius*].

POTATO-STONE, [pot-ā'-tō-stōn'], *n.* a geode of quartz in the shape of a potato which when broken is found to be hollow and lined with crystals.

POT-BELLIED, [pot'-bel'-id], *adj.* having a round, prominent belly.

POTBOILER, [pot'-boil-er], *n.* an inferior literary or artistic work produced solely to obtain money.

POT-BOUND, [pot'-bownd], *adj.* (*hort.*) (of a plant) growing in a flowerpot too small for its roots.

POT-BOY, [pot'-boi], *n.* a boy employed in a public-house.

POT-COMPANION, [pot'-kum-pan'-yun], *n.* a drinking companion.

POT-EAR, [pot'-eer'], *n.* the handle, rim or lip of a pot. [POT and EAR].

POTEEN, POTHEEN, [pot-ēn'], *n.* whisky made in an illicit still. [Ir. *poitin* a little pot].

POTENCE (1), [pō'-tents], *n.* (*her.*) a T-shaped cross. [Fr. *potence* a crutch].

POTENCE (2), [pō'-tents], *n.* power, potency. [OFr. *potence*].

POTENCY, [pō'-ten-si], *n.* power, strength, *esp.* sexual vigour. [L. *potentia*].

POTENT (1), [pō'-tent], *adj.* strong, effective, (of a man) sexually capable. [L. *potens*].

POTENT (2), [pō'-tent], *adj.* (*her.*) (of a cross) with the limbs ending in the form of crutches. [Fr. *potence*].

POTENTATE, [pō'-tent-āt], *n.* one exercising power, a powerful ruler, a prince. [L. *potentatus* rule, dominion].

POTENTIAL (1), [pot-en'-shal], *n.* that which is potential (2), potentiality; (*elect.*) electrical pressure, force compelling the flow of current from higher to lower. [POTENTIAL (2)].

POTENTIAL (2), [pot-en'-shal], *adj.* having latent power, possessing inherent powers, capable of exerting power, energy; (*gram.*) expressing possibility. [LL. *potentialis*].

POTENTIALITY, [pot-en'-shi-al'-it-i], *n.* inherent capacity, possibility of development.

POTENTIALIZE, [pot-en'-shal-iz], *v.t.* (*phys.*) to make potential.

POTENTIALLY, [pot-en'-shal-i], *adv.* in potential respects, in possibility.

POTENTILLA, [pot-ent-il'-a], *n.* a genus of rosaceous flowering plants and shrubs. [MedL. *potentilla* from L. *potens* powerful].

POTENTIOMETER, [pō-ten'-shi-o'-mit-er], *n.* (*elect.*) a variable resistance used to adjust the current in a circuit. [POTENTIAL and METER].

POTENTLY, [pō'-tent-li], *adv.* in potent fashion.

POTENTNESS, [pō'-tent-nes], *n.* the quality of being potent.

POT-HANGER, [pot'-hang'-er], *n.* a pothook.

POTHEEN, see POTEEN.

POTHER, PUDDER, [poTH'-er], *n.* noisy bother, fussy to-do. [Unkn.].

POT-HERB, [pot'-herb], *n.* a herb used in cooking.

POT-HOLE, [pot'-hōl], *n.* a deep hole in a river bed, eroded by an eddy; a hole in a road surface.

POTHOOK, [pot'-ho͝ok], *n.* an S-shaped hook on which pots are hung; an S-shaped figure used in learning to write.

POTHOUSE, [pot'-hows], *n.* a small, disreputable public-house.

POT-HUNTING, [pot'-hunt'-ing], *n.* (*coll.*) the practice of entering sporting contests for the sake of the cups and trophies offered.

POTIN, [po-ta(ng)'], *n.* an alloy of varying metals used for making base coins in late Roman times. [Fr. *potin*].

POTION, [pō'-shun], *n.* a draught of poison, drug, or highly intoxicating liquid; a mixed drink. [L. *potio* a draught].

POT-LID, [pot'-lid'], *n.* the cover of a pot.

POTLUCK, [pot'-luk'], *n.* anything got haphazard on the spur of the moment, the result of entirely casual choice; any food that happens to be going.

POTMAN, [pot'-man], *n.* an employee in public-houses who collects and cleans the glasses, etc.

POT-METAL, [pot'-metl], *n.* an alloy of scrap-metal; stained glass coloured in the melting-pot.

POT-POURRI, [pō'-po͞o'-rē], *n.* dried herbs mixed together and kept as a perfume; a musical medley. [Fr. *pot pourri*].

POTSHERD, [pot'-sherd'], *n.* a fragment of broken pottery.

POT-SHOT, [pot'-shot'], *n.* a chance shot taken without proper aim.

POTSTONE, [pot'-stōn], *n.* a kind of soapstone used in the Stone Age for making vessels.

POTTAGE, POTAGE, [pot'-ij], *n.* thick meat soup boiled with vegetables; **mess of p.** something worthless. [Fr. *potage*].

POTTED, [pot'-id], *adj.* preserved in a pot; (*fig.*) applied to any condensed or synthetic abstract of a whole subject.

POTTER (1), [pot'-er], *n.* a maker of earthenware vessels. [OE. *potere*].

POTTER (2), [pot'-er], *v.i.* to dawdle about, to fuss weakly and incompetently, to lounge. [ME. *poten* to poke].

POTTERY, [pot'-er-i], *n.* earthenware; the art of making earthenware; the place where earthenware is made.

POTTING, [pot'-ing], *n.* the art or act of making pots; the act of placing in a pot; the act of taking pot-shots.

POTTINGER, [pot'-in-jer], *n.* (*Scots*) a cook.

POTTLE, [potl], *n.* a liquid measure of two quarts; a small fruit-basket. [ME. *potel*].

POTTO, [pot'-ō], *n.* the West African lemur. [Native].

POTTOROO, [pot'-er-o͞o], *n.* the rat kangaroo, *Potorous tridactylus*, an Australian marsupial. [Native].

POTTY, [pot'-i], *adj.* (*coll.*) mad, crazy. [Unkn.].

POTWALLOPER, [pot'-wol'-op-er], *n.* (*hist.*) the holder of a household franchise. [POT (1) and ME. *walloppen* to boil, i.e. one who boils his own pot].

POUCH (1), [powch], *n.* a purse, a small bag or pocket, one of the small pockets in military equipment for carrying cartridges; a protuberant sac (e.g. under the eye); the pocket in which a marsupial carries its young. [ME. *pouche*].

POUCH (2), [powch], *v.t.* to put in a pouch, to hold in the cavity of the cheek, to pocket. [POUCH (1)].

POUCHED, [powcht], *adj.* having, in the form of, a pouch.

POUFFE, [po͞of], *n.* a circular stuffed satin cushion. [Fr. *pouffe*].

POULP, [po͞olp], *n.* the octopus. [Fr. *poulpe*].

POULT, [pōlt], *n.* a young pheasant or chicken. [ME. *pulte*].

POULTERER, [pōlt'-er-er], *n.* a dealer in poultry.

POULTICE (1), [pōlt'-is], *n.* a mass of hot, damp meal applied to sores or inflammation. [L. *puls pultem* porridge].

POULTICE (2), [pōlt'-is], *v.t.* to apply a poultice to. [POULTICE (1)].

POULTRY, [pōl'-tri], *n.* domestic fowls used for food. [OFr. *pouleterie*].

POULTRY-HOUSE, [pōl'-tri-hows'], *n.* a shed for keeping and rearing poultry.

POULTRY-YARD, [pōl'-tri-yahd'], *n.* a place where poultry are fed and let run.

POUNCE (1), [pownts], *n.* the front toe of a bird of prey's claws; a sudden downward swoop with intent to seize. [Uncert.].

POUNCE (2), [pownts], *n.* a fine bone powder used to prepare vellum for writing or sprinkled on paper to prevent ink from spreading. [Fr. *ponce* from L. *pumicem* pumice].

POUNCE (3), [pownts], *v.i.* to leap (upon) swoop (on) suddenly in order to seize; to intervene suddenly and fiercely; (*fig.*) to seize (on), detect rapidly and suddenly. [POUNCE (1)].

POUNCE (4), [pownts], *v.t.* to make a pattern, design, by punching holes in a surface. [Uncert.].

POUNCE (5), [pownts], *v.i.* to prepare paper with pounce. [POUNCE (2)].

POUNCE-BOX, [pownts-boks], *n.* a box from which pounce is sprinkled, a box with pounced lid, used for holding perfumes.

POUNCED, [pownst], *adj.* having claws.

POUNCET-BOX, [pown'-set-boks'], *n.* a pounce-box.

POUND (1), [pownd], *n.* a unit of weight containing 16 ounces, 7,000 grains; a monetary unit (£) containing, in England, 20 shillings or 240 pence, used in numerous phrases and proverbs with the sense of high value; **p. troy,** the standard for weighing precious metals and stones (12 ounces, 5,760 grains). [OE. *pund*, L. *pondere* by weight].

POUND (2), [pownd], *n.* a walled enclosure for keeping strayed or distrained cattle; a place for confiscated or impounded objects. [OE. **pund*].

POUND (3), [pownd], *n.* a heavy thump. [POUND (6)].

POUND (4), [pownd], *v.i.* to test coins by weighing the number that go to a pound weight. [POUND (1)].

POUND (5), [pownd], *v.t.* to place in a pound, to impound. [POUND (2)].

POUND (6), [pownd], *v.t. and i.* to hammer to powder, to break up into small pieces, to beat in a mortar; to thump heavily, to pummel, to bombard heavily; to walk, run, heavily and thumpingly. [OE. *punian* to grind in a mortar].

POUNDAGE, [pownd'-ij], *n.* (*hist.*) a 5 per cent tax levied on all imported and exported goods; a commission charged on the sale of distrained goods; the commission charged on postal orders, etc.

POUNDAL, [pownd'-al], *n.* a foot-pound, the force required to impart to a pound of matter in one second, a velocity of one foot per second. [Coined word].

POUND-CAKE, [pownd'-kāk], *n.* a plum-cake containing a pound of each ingredient.

POUNDER, [pownd'-er], *n.* a pestle, that which pounds; (of a gun) firing shells of so many pounds weight.

POUND-KEEPER [pownd'-kēp'-er], *n.* one who has the care of a cattle-pound.

POUPETON, [po͞o'-pet-on], *n.* a puppet; a bacon and pigeon pie. [Uncert.].

POUR (1), [paw(r)], *n.* the amount of molten metal poured into a mould; a spout for pouring; the process of pouring out or through. [POUR (2)].

POUR (2), [paw(r)], *v.t. and i.* to cause to flow out in a stream, to discharge copiously; to dispense lavishly, to shower upon, to flow tumultuously in great numbers; (*coll.*) to rain heavily. [ME. *pouren*].

POURBOIRE, [pōōer'-bwah(r)], *n.* a tip, gratuity. [Fr. *pour boire* (*lit.*) for drinking].

POURER, [paw'-rer], *n.* that which pours.

POURPARLER, [pōōer'-pah-lā], *n.* a preliminary diplomatic conversation. [Fr. *pour* for and *parler* to speak].

POURPOINT, [pōōer'-point], *n.* a quilted doublet. [OFr. *pour* for and *point* pricked through].

POURTRAY†, see PORTRAY.

POUSSETTE (1), [pōō-set'], *n.* a figure in a country dance, in which couples circle with clasped hands. [Fr. *poussette*, *dim.* of *pousse* push].

POUSSETTE (2), [pōō-set'], *v.i.* to dance the poussette. [POUSSETTE (1)].

POUSSIN, [pōō'-sa(ng)], *n.* a young chicken for the table. [Fr. *poussin* chick].

POUT (1), [powt], *n.* the sea-fish whiting pout, *Gadus luscus*. [OE. *puta*].

POUT (2), [powt], *n.* the act of pouting; sulkiness, state of being sulky. [POUT (3)].

POUT (3), [powt], *v.t.* and *i.* to thrust the lips forward, assume a sulky expression. [Unkn.].

POUTASSOU, [pōōt'-as-ōō], *n.* Couch's whiting, *Gadus poutassou*. [Provenc. place-name].

POUTER, POWTER†, [powt'-er], *n.* one who pouts; a pigeon with an excessively dilated crop.

POUTER

POVERTY, [pov'-er-ti], *n.* the state of being poor, of being deficient in any quality, indigence. [ME. *poverte* from L. *paupertas*].

POVERTY-STRICKEN, [pov'-er-ti-strik'-en], *adj.* afflicted with, displaying, poverty.

POWAN, [pō'-an], *n.* the gwiniad, the freshwater fish, *Coregonus clupeoides*. [Scots form of POLLAN].

POWDER (1), [pow'-der], *n.* fine particles produced by pulverizing a substance, *esp.* gunpowder; cosmetic powder applied to the skin; a medicine in the form of powder. [ME. *powder*, Fr. *poudre* from L. *pulvis*].

POWDER (2), [pow'-der], *v.t.* and *i.* to sprinkle, cover with powder; to grind to powder; to use powder on the hair or face. [POWDER (1)].

POWDER-BOX, [pow'-der-boks'], *n.* a box for cosmetic powder.

POWDER-CART, [pow'-der-kaht'], *n.* an ammunition cart.

POWDER-CHEST, [pow'-der-chest'], *n.* a box containing ammunition on board ship.

POWDER-FLASK, [pow'-der-flahsk'], *n.* a flask in which gunpowder was carried.

POWDER-HORN, [pow'-der-hawn'], *n.* a powder-flask.

POWDER-HOSE, [pow'-der-hōz'], *n.* a linen tube filled with powder for firing mines.

POWDER-MAGAZINE, [pow'-der-mag'-az-ēn], *n.* a magazine for storing explosives.

POWDER-MILL, [pow'-der-mil'], *n.* a gunpowder factory.

POWDER-MINE, [pow'-der-mīn'], *n.* a mine exploded by gunpowder.

POWDER-MONKEY, [pow'-der-mungk'-i], *n.* a boy who carried charges of powder from the ship's magazine to the guns.

POWDER-PUFF, [pow'-der-puf'], *n.* a pad or bunch of down for applying powder to the face.

POWDER-ROOM, [pow'-der-rōōm'], *n.* the powder-magazine of a ship; a ladies' dressing room.

POWDERY, [pow'-der-i], *adj.* friable, resembling powder; covered with powder.

POWER, [pow'-er], *n.* the capacity for action, the capacity for exerting force, influence, the capacity for using the bodily organs; (*pl.*) the organs themselves, physical vitality, bodily vigour; force exerted, capacity in action, the exercise of strength; the capacity for, or exercise of, control, authority, rule, influence (over), government (over); a person having influence or authority; a nation-state and its government in respect of its effective military strength, *esp.* one of the great imperialist nations; (*pl.*) supernatural influences, deities, one of the Orders of Angels; (*leg.*) authority of action granted to another; (*math.*) the product obtained by multiplying a quantity by itself; (*mech.*) energy doing work; (*opt.*) the magnifying capacity of a lens; (*dial.*) **a p. of**, a great number of. [ME. *poer*, *pouer* from AFr. *pouair*].

POWERFUL, [pow'-er-fōōl], *adj.* having power, capable of exerting great strength, having great authority, producing great energy, cogent.

POWERFULLY, [pow'-er-fōōl-i], *adv.* with great power.

POWERFULNESS, [pow'-er-fōōl-nes], *n.* the quality of being powerful.

POWER-HOUSE, [pow'-er-hows], *n.* a building or section of a building where electric power is produced.

POWERLESS, [pow'-er-les], *adj.* without power, helpless.

POWERLESSLY, [pow'-er-les-li], *adv.* in powerless fashion.

POWERLESSNESS, [pow'-er-les-nes], *n.* the quality of being powerless.

POWER-LOOM, [pow'-er-lōōm'], *n.* a loom operated by mechanical power.

POWTER†, see POUTER.

POW-WOW (1), [pow'-wow], *n.* a conference among North American Indians, usually connected with magic rites; a friendly discussion. [NAmerInd. *pow-wow* medicine-man].

POW-WOW (2), [pow'-wow], *v.i.* to hold a pow-wow; to hold a friendly and informal discussion. [POW-WOW (1)].

POX (1), [poks], *n.* one of several diseases marked by pustular eruptions on the skin, *esp.* syphilis. [*Pl.* of POCK.]

POX (2), [poks], *v.t.* to infect with the pox. [POX (1)].

POY, [poi], *n.* a long pole, a barge pole. [Uncert.].

POYOU, [poi'-ōō], *n.* the weasel-headed armadillo, *Dasypus sexcinctus*. [Guarani *poyou*].

POZZUOLANA, [pot'-zōō-ō-lah'-na], *n.* volcanic ashes used to make mortar. [*Pozzuoli*, near Naples].

PRAAM, [prahm], *n.* a flat-bottomed Baltic lighter. [Du. *praam*].

PRACTICABILITY, [prak'-tik-ab-il'-it-i], *n.* the quality of being practicable, possibility.

PRACTICABLE, [prak'-tik-abl], *adj.* feasible, possible of use or operation.

PRACTICABLENESS, [prak'-tik-abl-nes], *n.* practicability.

PRACTICABLY, [prak'-tik-ab-li], *adv.* in practicable fashion.

PRACTICAL, [prak'-tikl], *adj.* concerned with, related to, action, practice, active possibility; workable; effective, virtual; soundly functional; (of persons) capable, sound, efficient, good at affairs, competent, common-sense, unimaginative, trained and experienced in a thing. [Gk. *praktikos* fit for action].

PRACTICALLY, [prak'-tik-al-i], *adv.* in practical fashion; almost, virtually, in effect.

PRACTICALNESS, [prak'-tikl-nes], *n.* the state of being practicable.

PRACTICE, [prak'-tis], *n.* the performance of a thing, action in accordance with a theory; habitual, customary action, regular or usual performance, customary observance or ritual; repeated exercise of some kind in order to become skilled in its performance, time devoted to such training, the training itself; the exercise of a doctor's profession, his patients, the field of his activity (also, though less usually, applied to barristers, architects, etc.); (*arith.*) a concise method of calculating; (*leg.*) the procedure of a Court of Law. [PRACTISE].

PRACTICIAN, [prak-tish'-an], *n.* a practitioner. [OFr. *practicien*].

PRACTISE, [prak'-tis], *v.t.* to carry out (a theory) in action; to perform, do as a custom or regular performance; constantly to perform some action, carry out (some activity) in order to become skilled in its exercise; to follow a profession; *v.i.* to make a habitual practice, to carry out an activity repeatedly in order to become skilled; to follow the profession of medicine outside a hospital; to play upon. [ME. *practisen*, OFr. *practiser* from MedL. *practicare*].

PRACTISED, [prak'-tist], *adj.* skilled by practice.

PRACTISER, [prak'-tis-er], *n.* one who practises. [ME. *practisour*].

PRACTISING, [prak'-tis-ing], *adj.* actively engaged in.

PRACTITIONER, [prak-tish'-un-er], *n.* one who practises an art or profession, *esp.* a doctor. [PRACTICIAN].

PRAE-, *pref.* before, prior to. [L. *prae*].

PRAECIPE, [prē'-sip-i], *n.* (*leg.*) a writ commanding appearance, or the performance of, something. [L. *praecipe*, *imper.* of *praecipere* to order].

PRAECOGNITA, [prē-kog'-nit-a], *n.* necessary basic knowledge for making an assumption or arriving at further knowledge. [L. *praecognitus* known before].

PRAECORDIA, [prē-kawd'-i-a], *n.* (*anat.*) *n.* the diaphragm, the thoracic viscera. [L. *praecordia*].

PRAEMORSE, [prē'-maws], *adj.* with the end or root truncate. [L. *praemorsus* bitten off].

PRAEMUNIRE, PREMUNIRE, [prē'-mewn-ier'-i], *n.* a writ against a person who asserts papal jurisdiction in England; the offence of asserting this. [L. *praemunire* to warn].

PRAENOMEN, [prē-nō'-men], *n.* (*Roman hist.*) the first, personal, name. [L. *praenomen*].

PRAETEXTA, [prē-tekst'-a], *n.* (*Roman hist.*) the purple-edged robe worn by children of senatorial class. [L. (*toga*) *praetexta* fringed robe].

PRAETOR, PRETOR, [prē'-tor], *n.* (*Roman hist.*) a magistrate next in rank to the consul, having military and judicial functions. [L. *praetor*].

PRAETORIAL, PRETORIAL, [prē-taw'-ri-al], *adj.* relating to a praetor or to his office.

PRAETORIAN, PRETORIAN (1), [prē-tawr'-i-an], *n.* a member of the Praetorian Guard. [PRAETORIAN (2)].

PRAETORIAN, PRETORIAN (2), [prē-tawr'-i-an], *adj.* relating to a praetor; **P. Guard**, the Roman Imperial Bodyguard. [L. *praetorianus*].

PRAETORIUM, PRETORIUM, [prē-taw'-ri-um], *n.* the tent of a Roman general; the residence of a Roman provincial governor. [L. *praetorium*].

PRAETORSHIP, PRETORSHIP, [prē'-ter-ship], *n.* the office, rank, or tenure of a praetor.

PRAGMATIC, [prag-mat'-ik], *adj.* (*hist.*) relating to affairs of state; pragmatical; relating to pragmatism. [Gk. *pragmatikos* business-like].

PRAGMATICAL, [prag-mat'-ikl], *adj.* officious, meddlesome, dogmatic; pragmatic.

PRAGMATICALLY, [prag-mat'-ik-al-i], *adv.* in pragmatical fashion.

PRAGMATICALNESS, [prag-mat'-ikl-nes], *n.* the quality of being pragmatical.

PRAGMATISM, [prag'-mat-izm], *n.* (*philos.*) the system that judges the truth of a conception by its concrete effects. [Gk. *pragma* the act done].

PRAGMATIST, [prag'-mat-ist], *n.* a believer in pragmatism.

PRAGMATIZE, [prag'-mat-iz], *v.t.* to treat as real and true what seems most expedient.

PRAIRIE, [prāer'-i], *n.* a grassy plain, a great tract of level grassland. [Fr. *prairie* from L. *pratum* meadow].

PRAIRIE-CHICKEN, [prāer'-i-chik'-en], *n.* the sharp-tailed grouse, *Pediœcetes phasianellus*.

PRAIRIE-DOG, [prāer'-i-dog'], *n.* a rodent of the genus *Cynomys*, allied to the marmots, inhabiting western North America.

PRAIRIE-HEN, [prāer'-i-hen'], *n.* the pinnated grouse, *Tympanuchus americanus*.

PRAIRIE-OYSTER, [prāer'-i-ois'-ter], *n.* a pick-me-up, usually containing raw egg and Worcester sauce.

PRAIRIE-SQUIRREL, [prāer'-i-skwir'-el], *n.* the gopher.

PRAIRIE-TURNIP, [prāer'-i-turn'-ip], *n.* the edible tuberous root of *Psoralea esculenta*.

PRAIRIE-DOG

PRAIRIE-WOLF, [prāer'-i-wulf'], *n.* the coyote.

PRAISABLE, [prāz'-abl], *adj.* worthy of praise.

PRAISE (1), [prāz], *n.* the act of praising, the expression of commendation or approval; veneration of the Deity, glorification. [PRAISE (2)].

PRAISE (2), [prāz], *v.t.* to express approval, approbation of, to commend highly, to eulogize, to glorify, to magnify. [ME. *preisen*, OFr. *preisier* from L. *pretium* price].

PRAISER, [prāz'-er], *n.* one who praises.

PRAISELESS, [prāz'-les], *adj.* unpraised, without praise.

PRAISEWORTHILY, [prāz'-wur-THi-li], *adv.* in praiseworthy fashion.

PRAISEWORTHINESS, [prāz'-wur-THi-nes], *n.* the state of being praiseworthy.

PRAISEWORTHY, [prāz'-wur-THi], *adj.* worthy of praise.

PRAKRIT, [prah'-krit], *n.* the Aryan vernacular, as distinct from Sanskrit, the literary language. [Skr. *prakrta* natural, vulgar].

PRALINE, [prah'-lēn], *n.* a sweetmeat of nut kernels roasted in boiling sugar. [Fr. *praline*].

PRAM, [pram], *n.* (*coll.*) a perambulator. [Abbreviation of PERAMBULATOR].

PRANCE, [prahnts], *v.i.* (of a four-footed animal) to spring up on the hind legs, to rear up; (of persons) to strut, swagger about. [ME. *prauncen*].

PRANCING, [prahns'-ing], *n.* the act of prancing; swagger.

PRANCINGLY, [prahns'-ing-li], *adv.* in prancing fashion.

PRANDIAL, [pran'-di-al], *adj.* relating to luncheon. [L. *prandium* midday meal].

PRANK (1), [prangk], *n.* an irresponsible frolic, a jolly joking action. [Uncert.].

PRANK (2), [prangk], *v.t. and i.* to deck out; to dress oneself up. [ME. *pranken*].

PRANKER, [prangk'-er], *n.* one who dresses ostentatiously.

PRANKING, [prangk'-ing], *adj.* ostentatious display.

PRANKINGLY, [prangk'-ing-li], *adv.* in pranking fashion.

PRANKISH, [prangk'-ish], *adj.* full of pranks.

PRASE, [prāz], *n.* translucent green quartz. [Gk. *prasios* leek-green].

PRASEODYMIUM, [prāz'-i-ō-dim'-i-um], *n.* the metallic element Pr. [Gk. *prasios* leek-green and *didumos* twin].

PRASINOUS, [praz'-in-us], *adj.* grass-green. [L. *prasinus*].

PRASITES, [pra-sī'-tēz], *n.* wine containing an infusion of the leaves of horehound. [Gk. *prasites*].

PRATE, [prāt], *v.i.* to talk emptily, pretentiously and volubly, to chatter sententiously. [ME. *praten* from OIcel. *prata* to talk].

PRATER, [prāt'-er], *n.* one who prates.

PRATINCOLE, [prat'-in-kōl], *n.* a kind of sandpiper with a plover-like gait. [MdL. *pratincola* from *pratum* meadow and *incola* inhabitant].

PRATING (1), [prāt'-ing], *n.* stupid, idle, sententious talk.

PRATING (2), [prāt'-ing], *adj.* talking idly and dully sententiously gossiping.

PRATINGLY, [prāt'-ing-li], *adv.* in prating fashion.

PRATIQUE, [prat'-ēk], *n.* permission to communicate with the shore granted to a vessel showing a clean bill of health. [Fr. *pratique*].

PRATTLE (1), [pratl], *n.* childish chatter, aimless baby-talk.

PRATTLE (2), [pratl], *v.i.* to chatter childishly, to babble inconsequently. [PRATE].

PRATTLER, [prat'-ler], *n.* one who prattles.

PRATY, [prāt'-i], *n.* (*dial.*) a potato. [Anglo-Ir. *praty*].

PRAVITY, [prav'-it-i], *n.* depravity, weak viciousness. [L. *pravuitas* from *pravus* crooked].

PRAWN (1), [prawn], *n.* the edible marine crustacean, *Palsemon serratus*. [ME. *prayne*].

PRAWN (2), [prawn], *v.i.* to fish for prawns. [PRAWN (1)].

PRAXIS, [praks'-is], *n.* the exercise or actual practice of a thing, as distinct from the theory; a set of grammatical exercises. [Gk. *praxis* action, performance].

PRAY, [prā], *v.t. and i.* to beg for, entreat for; to utter prayers (for a thing), to beg earnestly, to address oneself to God. [ME. *preien* from L. *precari*].

PRAYER, [prāer], *n.* the act of praying; a supplication made to superior powers, earthly or supernatural, a petition to God; words, form in which such petition or worship is made; a fervent request or desire; **p. rug**, a rug used by a Mohammedan for his devotions; **p. wheel**, a wheel or disk in which prayers are enclosed and rotated by Buddhists. [ME. *preiere*, OFr. *preiere* from L. *precarius* obtained by prayer].

PRAYER-BOOK, [prāer'-bōōk], *n.* a book containing set forms of prayer for various occasions.

PRAYERFUL, [prāer'-fōōl], *adj.* devout, fervent in prayer.

PRAYERFULLY, [prāer'-fōōl-i], *adv.* in prayerful fashion.

PRAYERFULNESS, [prāer'-fōōl-nes], *n.* the state of being prayerful.

PRAYERLESS, [prāer'-les], *adj.* not given to prayer; not prayed for.

PRAYING, [prā'-ing], *n.* the act of making prayers.

PRAYINGLY, [prā'-ing-li], *adv.* in prayer.

PRE-, *pref.* before, in front of, prior to. [L. *prae*].

PREACCUSATION, [prē'-ak-ewz-ā'-shun], *n.* previous accusation.

PREACH, [prēch], *v.t. and i.* to proclaim the Gospel, teach the lessons of the Scriptures, utter moral exhortations, deliver a sermon; to proclaim, announce, deliver (a discourse); (*slang*) to give uncalled-for moral advice or instruction. [ME. *prechen*, OFr. *prechier* from L. *praedicare* to proclaim].

PREACHER, [prēch'-er], *n.* one who preaches, a minister of religion. [PREACH].
PREACHERSHIP, [prēch'-er-ship], *n.* the office or post of preacher.
PREACHIFY, [prēch'-i-fī], *v.i.* to preach pratingly.
PREACHING (**1**), [prēch'-ing], *n.* the act of preaching; a sermon; mode of speaking a sermon.
PREACHING (**2**), [prēch'-ing], *adj.* relating to preaching or to a preacher.
PREACHMENT, [prēch'-ment], *n.* a tedious sermon.
PREACHY, [prēch'-i], *adj.* over-fond of moral admonishment.
PREACQUAINTANCE, [prē'-ak-wānt'-ants], *n.* previous acquaintance. [PRE and ACQUAINTANCE].
PREACQUAINTED, [prē'-ak-wānt'-id], *adj.* previously acquainted.
PRE-ADAMITE, [prē-ad'-am-it], *adj.* existing previous to Adam.
PREADMINISTRATION, [prē'-ad-min-is-tra'-shun], *n.* the act of administering beforehand. [PRE and ADMINISTRATION].
PREADMONISH, [prē'-ad-mon'-ish], *v.t.* to admonish beforehand. [PRE and ADMONISH].
PREADMONITION, [prē'-ad-mon-ish'-un], *n.* previous admonition. [PRE and ADMONITION].
PREAMBLE (**1**), [prē'-ambl], *n.* a preface, an introductory statement, the opening remarks of a speech. [MedL. *preambulum* from L. *preambulare* to precede].
PREAMBLE (**2**), [prē'-ambl], *v.i.* to make a preamble. [PREAMBLE (1)].
PREAMBULATE, [prē-am'-byōō-lāt], *v.i.* to walk in front; to stroll casually about. [L. *preambulatum*, *p.pt.* of *preambulare* to precede].
PREAMBULATION, [prē'-am-byōō-lā'-shun], *n.* the act of preambulating. [L. *preambulationem*].
PREAMBULATORY, [prē'-am-byōō-lāt'-eri], *adj.* preceding; preambulating.
PREAPPOINT, [prē'-ap-oint'], *v.t.* to appoint in advance. [PRE and APPOINT].
PREAPPOINTMENT, [prē'-ap-oint'-ment], *n.* previous appointment. [PRE and APPOINTMENT].
PREAPPREHENSION, [prē'-ap-ri-hen'-shun], *n.* an opinion formed in advance of evidence. [PRE and APPREHENSION].
PREARRANGED, [prē'-a-rānjd'], *adj.* arranged beforehand.
PREASSURANCE, [prē'-ash-ōōer'-ants], *n.* assurance in advance. [PRE and ASSURANCE].
PREAUDIENCE, [prē-awd'-i-ents], *n.* right of audience before others; legal precedence. [PRE and AUDIENCE].
PREBEND, [preb'-end], *n.* an endowment given to a church for the maintenance of one of the chapter; a benefice in the gift of a chapter. [OFr. *prebende* from MedL. *prebenda* stipend].
PREBENDAL, [preb-end'-al], *adj.* relating to a prebend.
PREBENDARY, [preb'-end-er-i], *n.* the holder of a prebend. [MedL. *prebendarius*].
PREBENDARYSHIP, [preb'-end-er-i-ship], *n.* the office of prebendary.
PRECARIOUS, [prik-āer'-i-us], *adj.* insecure, dependent on chance, resting on uncertain premises; held during the pleasure, life, or office of another. [L. *precarius* gained by prayer].
PRECARIOUSLY, [prik-āer'-i-us-li], *adv.* in precarious fashion.
PRECARIOUSNESS, [prik-āer'-i-us-nes], *n.* the condition of being precarious.
PRECATORY, [prek'-at-er-i], *adj.* requesting, expressing, a wish; (*gram.*) expressing wish; (*leg.*) recommending without directing. [LL. *precatorius* petitioning from L. *precari* to pray].
PRECAUTION, [prik-aw'-shun], *n.* cautious foresight; a provision made in advance, measures taken against a coming danger. [LL. *precautio*].
PRECAUTIONARY, [prik-aw'-shun-er-i], *adj.* relating to, by way of, precaution.
PRECAUTIOUS, [prik-aw'-shus], *adj.* precautionary. [PRE and CAUTIOUS].
PRECAUTIOUSLY, [prik-aw'-shus-li], *adv.* in precautious fashion.
PRECEDE, [prē-sēd'], *v.t. and i.* to go, come, be before; to be superior in rank to, to take precedence over, to be more important than. [L. *praecedere*].
PRECEDENCE, [prē-sēd'-ents], *n.* the act of preceding; the right to a certain specific position (at functions, etc.) by virtue of birth or office; the position to which one is so entitled. [PRECEDENT (2)].
PRECEDENT (**1**), [pres'-id-ent], *n.* a previous occurrence from which guidance and example may be drawn and related to an analogous present circumstance; (*leg.*) a previous decision or ruling that may be cited in subsequent cases. [PRECEDENT (2)].
PRECEDENT (**2**), [prē-sēd'-ent], *adj.* preceding, previous to. [L. *praecedentem*, *pres.pt.* of *praecedere*].
PRECEDENTED, [pres'-id-ent'-id], *adj.* having precedents, based upon precedent.
PRECEDENTIAL, [pres'-id-en'-shal], *adj.* acting as a precedent.
PRECEDENTLY, [pre-sēd'-ent-li], *adv.* beforehand.
PRECEDING, [prē-sēd'-ing], *adj.* antecedent.
PRECENTOR, [prē-sen'-tor], *n.* the director of music and choir in a cathedral; the hymn-leader of a congregation. [LL. *praecentor*].
PRECENTORSHIP, [prē-sen'-tor-ship], *n.* the position or tenure of a precentor.
PRECEPT, [prē'-sept'], *n.* a moral maxim, a rule of conduct; (*leg.*) an order for payment issued by local authority; an election writ. [L. *praeceptum* maxim].
PRECEPTIVE, [prē-sept'-iv], *adj.* relating to a precept, morally didactic.
PRECEPTOR, [prē-sept'-or], *n.* a teacher, tutor. [L. *praeceptor*].
PRECEPTORIAL, [prē'-sept-aw'-ri-al], *adj.* relating to a preceptor.
PRECEPTORY, [prē-sept'-er-i], *n.* a community of knights templar. [MedL. *preceptoria*].
PRECEPTRESS, [prē-sept'-res], *n.* a female teacher.
PRECESSION, [pri-sesh'-un], *n.* an outward movement; **p. of the equinoxes**, (*astron.*) a slow continuous shifting of the equinoctial points from east to west. [L. *praecessio*].
PRECESSIONAL, [pri-sesh'-unl], *adj.* relating to precession.
PRECESSOR, [pri-ses'-er], *n.* a predecessor. [OFr. *precesseur*].
PRE-CHRISTIAN, [prē-kris'-chan], *adj.* before the Christian era. [PRE and CHRISTIAN].
PRECINCT, [prē'-singkt], *n.* an enclosure within the boundaries of a group of buildings (*esp.* ecclesiastical); (*pl.*) the environs of a town or building; an American electoral division. [LL. *precinctum* boundary from L. *praecingere* to encircle].
PRECIOUS, [presh'-us], *adj.* of great value or price; held to be very valuable, highly esteemed; affected and refined to an irritating degree, over-sensitive and fastidious; (*coll.*) utter, complete (in jeering contempt or hostile emphasis); (used elliptically as a noun), **p. metals**, gold, silver, platinum; **p. stones**, ruby, diamond, sapphire, emerald, etc. [ME. *precious*, OFr. *precios* from L. *pretiosus* highly priced].
PRECIOUSLY, [presh'-us-li], *adv.* in precious fashion.
PRECIOUSNESS, [presh'-us-nes], *n.* the quality of being precious.
PRECIPICE, [pres'-ip-is], *n.* a sudden, sharp, deep declivity; a perpendicular face of rock; (*fig.*) a dangerous situation, a crisis. [Fr. *précipice* from L. *praecipitium*].
PRECIPIENT, [prē-sip'-i-ent], *adj.* admonishing, directing. [L. *praecipientem*, *pres.pt.* of *praecipere* to command].
PRECIPITABILITY, [pri-sip'-it-ab-il'-iti], *n.* condition of being precipitable.
PRECIPITABLE, [pri-sip'-it-abl], *adj.* capable of being precipitated.
PRECIPITANCE, [pri-sip'-it-ants], *n.* precipitancy.
PRECIPITANCY, [pri-sip'-it-an-si], *n.* the state of being precipitate, rashness; swiftness.
PRECIPITANT, [pri-sip'-it-ant], *n.* (*chem.*) a substance causing precipitation in a liquid. [L. *praecipitans*, *pres.pt.* of *praecipitare*].
PRECIPITANTLY, [pri-sip'-it-ant-li], *adv.* hastily, rashly, headlong.
PRECIPITATE (**1**), [pri-sip'-it-at], *n.* (*chem.* or *meteor.*) something precipitated. [PRECIPITATE (3)].
PRECIPITATE (**2**), [pri-sip'-it-at], *adj.* violent, hasty. [L. *praecipitatus*].
PRECIPITATE (**3**), [pri-sip'-it-āt], *v.t. and i.* to hurl down from a height; to hurry on, accentuate (a development), bring on faster than would naturally have developed; (*chem.*) to cause matter held in solution in liquid to fall as a deposit; to condense vapour to snow or water; to be precipitated. [L. *praecipitatum*, *p.pt.* of *praecipitare* to cast down].
PRECIPITATELY, [pri-sip'-it-at-li], *adv.* in precipitate fashion.

PRECIPITATION, [pri-sip′-it-ā′-shun], *n.* impetuosity, hasty action; (*chem.*) the process of precipitating or being precipitated; that which has been precipitated. [L. *praecipitatio*].

PRECIPITATOR, [pri-sip′-it-āt′-or], *n.* that which precipitates; a vessel for precipitation. [LL. *praecipitator*].

PRECIPITOUS, [pri-sip′-it-us], *adj.* very steep, of the nature of a precipice. [OFr. *precipiteux*].

PRECIPITOUSLY, [pri-sip′-it-us-li], *adv.* in precipitous fashion.

PRECIPITOUSNESS, [pri-sip′-it-us-nes], *n.* the condition of being precipitous, hasty rashness.

PRECIS, précis (1), [prā′-sē], *n.* an abstract, a short summary of the main features of a document. [Fr. *précis*].

PRECIS, précis (2), [prā′-sē], *v.t.* to make a précis of. [PRÉCIS (1)].

PRECISE, [pri-sis′], *adj.* exact, clearly defined; punctilious, pedantically exact, nicely conventional; carefully articulated. [Fr. *précis* from L. *praecisum* cut off short].

PRECISELY, [pri-sis′-li], *adv.* in precise fashion, exactly, unambiguously.

PRECISENESS, [pri-sis′-nes], *n.* the state of being precise.

PRECISIAN, [pri-sizh′-an], *n.* a formalist, a precise observer of custom.

PRECISIANISM, [pri-sizh′-an-izm], *n.* the attitude or behaviour of a precisian.

PRECISION, [pri-sizh′-un], *n.* exactness, preciseness, accuracy; **p. tools, etc.,** tools capable of very accurate work. [L. *praecisio*].

PRECISIVE, [pri-sis′-iv], *adj.* exactly limiting.

PRECLUDE, [pri-klōōd′], *v.t.* to exclude, make impossible, rule out, be totally incompatible with. [L. *praecludere* to shut off].

PRECLUSION, [pri-klōō′-zhun], *n.* prevention in advance, the act of precluding, state of being precluded. [L. *praeclusio*].

PRECLUSIVE, [pri-klōō′-siv], *adj.* tending to preclude.

PRECLUSIVELY, [pri-klōō′-siv-li], *adv.* in preclusive fashion.

PRECOCIOUS, [pri-kō′-shus], *adj.* prematurely developed, either physically, mentally, or morally. [L. *praecox* premature].

PRECOCIOUSLY, [pri-kō′-shus-li], *adv.* in precocious fashion.

PRECOCIOUSNESS, [pri-kō′-shus-nes], *n.* the condition of being precocious.

PRECOCITY, [pri-kos′-it-i], *n.* precociousness. [Fr. *précocité*].

PRECOGITATE, [prē-koj′-it-āt], *v.t. and i.* to consider beforehand. [PRE and COGITATE].

PRECOGITATION, [prē′-koj-it-ā′-shun], *n.* previous thought. [PRE and COGITATION].

PRECOGNITION, [prē′-kog-nish′-un], *n.* foreknowledge, previous cognition; (*Scots leg.*) a preliminary examination to find whether there is a case for trial; written proof of evidence used for examination at the trial. [L. *praecognitio*].

PRECOLLECTION, [prē′-kol-ek′-shun], *n.* previous collection; forethought. [PRE and COLLECTION].

PRECOMPOSE, [prē′-kom-pōz′], *v.t.* to compose beforehand. [PRE and COMPOSE].

PRECONCEIT, [prē′-kon-sēt′], *n.* a notion formed in advance. [PRE and CONCEIT].

PRECONCEIVE, [prē′-kon-sēv′], *v.t.* to form an opinion of beforehand. [PRE and CONCEIVE].

PRECONCEPTION, [prē′-kon-sep′-shun], *n.* a judgment formed beforehand, a prejudice. [PRE and CONCEPTION].

PRECONCERT (1), [prē-kon′-sert], *n.* a previous agreement. [PRECONCERT (2)].

PRECONCERT (2), [prē′-kon-sert′], *v.t.* to prearrange. [PRE and CONCERT (2)].

PRECONCERTED, [prē′-kon-sert′-id], *adj.* previously planned and agreed.

PRECONCERTEDLY, [prē′-kon-sert′-id-li], *adv.* by preconcert.

PRECONDEMN, [prē′-kon-dem′], *v.t.* to condemn in advance. [PRE and CONDEMN].

PRECONDEMNATION, [prē′-kon′-dem-nā′-shun], *n.* condemnation beforehand. [PRE and CONDEMNATION].

PRECONIZATION, [prē′-kon-iz-ā′-shun], *n.* the papal proclamation to the cardinals, announcing the names and sees of newly appointed bishops. [MedL. *preconizatio*].

PRECONSIGN, [prē′-kon-sīn′], *v.t.* to consign beforehand. [PRE and CONSIGN].

PRECONSIGNMENT, [prē′-kon-sīn′-ment], *n.* consignment beforehand. [PRE and CONSIGNMENT].

PRECONSOLIDATED, [prē′-kon-sol′-id-āt′-id], *adj.* consolidated beforehand.

PRECONSTITUTE, [prē-kon′-stit-ewt], *v.t.* to constitute beforehand. [PRE and CONSTITUTE].

PRECONSUME, [prē′-kon-sewm′], *v.t.* to consume beforehand. [PRE and CONSUME].

PRECONTRACT (1), [prē′-kon′-trakt], *n.* a contract made previously to another; (*leg.*) an agreement to marry, inhibiting any subsequent marriage to another. [PRE and CONTRACT (1)].

PRECONTRACT (2), [prē′-kon-trakt′], *v.t.* to make a previous contract for; to contract beforehand. [PRE and CONTRACT (2)].

PRECORDIA, see PRAECORDIA.

PRECURSOR, [pri-kurs′-or], *n.* a harbinger, a predecessor. [L. *praecursor*].

PRECURSORY, [pri-kurs′-er-i], *adj.* introductory, preceding, announcing in advance.

PREDACEAN, [pri-dā′-shan], *adj.* predacious.

PREDACIOUS, [pri-dā′-shus], *adj.* predatory, living by preying on others. [L. **praedax*].

PREDATE, [prē-dāt′], *v.t.* to antedate. [PRE and DATE].

PREDATORY, [pred′-at-er-i], *adj.* living by plunder and pillage, wandering in search of prey. [L. *praedatorius* from *praedari* to plunder].

PREDAZZITE, [pre-dats′-īt], *n.* a variety of bitter spar found in Southern Tyrol. [*Predazzo* in the Tyrol].

PREDECEASE (1), [prē′-dis-ēs′], *n.* a death previous to another's. [PRE and DECEASE].

PREDECEASE (2), [prē′-dis-ēs′], *v.t.* to die before (another). [PRE and DECEASE].

PREDECESSOR, [prē′-dis-es-or], *n.* one who precedes another temporally, in some rank, place or tenure; an ancestor. [ME. *predecessour* from LL. *predecessor*].

PREDECLARED, [prē′-dik-lāerd′], *adj.* declared beforehand.

PREDELINEATION, [prē′-dil-in-ē-ā′-shun], *n.* previous delineation. [PRE and DELINEATION].

PREDELLA, [prid-el′-a], *n.* the platform supporting the altar; the raised ledge behind the altar; a painting or design on the face of the altar-step. [It. *predella* kneeling-stool].

PREDESIGN, [prē′-diz-īn′], *v.t.* to design, plan, beforehand.

PREDESTINARIAN (1), [prē′-des-tin-āer′-i-an], *n.* a believer in predestination.

PREDESTINARIAN (2), [prē′-des-tin-āer′-i-an], *adj.* relating to predestination.

PREDESTINATE, [prē-des′-tin-āt], *v.t.* to predestine; (*theol.*) to foreordain. [L. *praedestinatum*, *p.pt.* of *praedestinare* to determine beforehand].

PREDESTINATION, [prē′-des-tin-ā′-shun], *n.* (*theol.*) the belief (*esp.* as held by the Calvinists) that God has foreordained every action, and predestined every soul to hell or salvation. [MedL. *praedestinationem*].

PREDESTINATOR, [prē′-des-tin-āt′-or], *n.* one who predestinates.

PREDESTINE, [prē-des′-tin], *v.t.* to destine or decree beforehand. [L. *praedestinare*].

PREDETERMINABLE, [prē′-dit-erm′-in-abl], *adj.* possible of predetermination.

PREDETERMINATE, [prē′-dit-erm′-in-at], *adj.* predetermined. [PRE and DETERMINATE].

PREDETERMINATION, [prē′-dit-erm-in-ā′-shun], *n.* determination made, decreed beforehand; predestination. [PRE and DETERMINATION].

PREDETERMINE, [prē′-dit-erm′-in], *v.t.* to predestine, to decide, decree, settle in advance; to prejudice another. [L. *praedeterminare*].

PREDIAL, [prē′-di-al], *adj.* (*leg.*) relating to landed property; pertaining to material objects. [MedL. *predialis* from L. *praedium* farm].

PREDICABILITY, [pred′-ik-ab-il′-it-i], *n.* the quality of being predicable.

PREDICABLE (1), [pred′-ik-abl], *n.* (*philos.*) a general attribute. [PREDICABLE (2)].

PREDICABLE (2), [pred′-ik-abl], *adj.* that may be predicated or affirmed. [Fr. *prédicable* or L. *praedicabilis*].

PREDICAMENT, [prid-ik′-am-ent], *n.* a predicable; a difficult and puzzling situation. [LL. *praedicamentum* a predicable].

PREDICAMENTAL, [pred′-ik-am-entl′], *adj.* relating to a predicament.

PREDICANT (1), [pred′-ik-ant], *n.* a preaching friar. [PREDICANT (2)].

PREDICANT (2), [pred′-ik-ant], *adj.* relating to,

devoted to, preaching. [L. *praedicantem*, *pres.pt.* of *praedicare* to preach].

PREDICATE (1), [pred'-ik-at], *n.* that which is affirmed of a thing; (*gram.*) the words affirming things about the subject of a sentence. [PREDICATE (2)].

PREDICATE (2), [pred'-ik-āt], *v.t.* to assert; to declare something (about a thing). [L. *praedicatum*, *p.pt.* of *praedicare* to proclaim].

PREDICATION, [pred'-ik-ā'-shun], *n.* the act of predicating; the thing predicated; a predicate. [L. *praedicatio*].

PREDICATIVE, [prid-ik'-at-iv, pred'-ik-āt-iv], *adj.* expressing predication. [L. *praedicativus*].

PREDICATIVELY, [pri-dik'-at-iv-li], *adv.* (*gram.*) as a predicate.

PREDICATORY, [pred'-ik-āt'-er-i], *adj.* relating to preaching. [LL. *predicatorius*].

PREDICT, [pri-dikt'], *v.t.* to foretell, prophesy. [L. *praedictum*, *p.pt.* of *praedicere*, to speak beforehand].

PREDICTION, [pri-dik'-shun], *n.* the act of predicting; that which is predicted. [L. *praedictio*].

PREDICTIVE, [pri-dikt'-iv], *adj.* prophetic, predicting. [L. *praedictivus*].

PREDICTOR, [pri-dikt'-or], *n.* one who predicts; an instrument enabling a gunner to predict the course or position of a moving aeroplane. [L. *praedictor*].

PREDICTORY, [pri-dikt'-er-i], *adj.* prophetic.

PREDIGESTION, [prē'-di-jes'-chun], *n.* artificial digestion of a food before consumption. [PRE and DIGESTION].

PREDILECTION, [prē'-dil-ek'-shun], *n.* prepossession, partiality for. [PRE and L. *dilectio* liking].

PREDISCOVERY, [prē'-dis-kuv'-eri], *n.* prior discovery. [PRE and DISCOVERY].

PREDISPOSE, [prē'-dis-pōz'], *v.t.* to incline beforehand (towards an attitude), to make susceptible beforehand. [PRE and DISPOSE].

PREDISPOSITION, [prē'-dis-poz-ish'-un], *n.* the state of being predisposed, an attitude formed beforehand. [PRE and DISPOSITION].

PREDOMINANCE, [pri-dom'-in-ants], *n.* the state of being predominant; supremacy, ascendancy. [PRE and DOMINANCE].

PREDOMINANT, [pri-dom'-in-ant], *adj.* most noticeable, superior, ascendant. [Fr. *prédominant*].

PREDOMINANTLY, [pri-dom'-in-ant-li], *adv.* in predominant fashion.

PREDOMINATE, [pri-dom'-in-āt], *v.i.* to be predominant, ascendant over; to preponderate. [PRE and DOMINATE].

PREDOMINATINGLY, [pri-dom'-in-āt'-ing-li], *adv.* so as to predominate.

PREDOMINATION, [pri-dom'-in-ā'-shun], *n.* the state or power of predominating; superiority, ascendancy. [PRE and DOMINATION].

PREDORSAL, [prē-daws'-al], *adj.* before the back. [PRE and DORSAL].

PRE-ELECT, [prē'-il-ekt'], *v.t.* to elect beforehand. [PRE and ELECT (2)].

PRE-ELECTION, [prē'-il-ek'-shun], *n.* election in advance. [PRE and ELECTION].

PRE-EMINENCE, [prē-em'-in-ents], *n.* the state of being pre-eminent, superiority, outstanding distinction. [PRE and EMINENCE].

PRE-EMINENT, [prē-em'-in-ent], *adj.* supremely eminent, surpassingly excellent. [PRE and EMINENT].

PRE-EMINENTLY, [prē-em'-in-ent-li], *adv.* in pre-eminent degree.

PRE-EMPT, [prē-empt'], *v.t.* to buy or obtain by pre-emption. [PRE-EMPT(ION)].

PRE-EMPTION, [prē-emp'-shun], *n.* (*leg.*) the prior right to purchase goods. [MedL. *preemptum*, *p.pt.* of *preimere* to buy in advance].

PRE-EMPTIVE, [prē-emp'-tiv], *adj.* by, relating to, pre-emption; **p. bid**, (*bridge*) a high bid intended to prevent further calling.

PREEN, [prēn], *v.t.* (of birds) to clean (the feathers) with the beak; (of persons) to strut, to show conceit and self-satisfaction. [ME. *prunen*].

PRE-ENGAGE, [prē'-en-gāj'], *v.t.* to engage, contract, or interest beforehand. [PRE and ENGAGE].

PRE-ENGAGEMENT, [prē'-en-gāj'-ment], *n.* previous engagement. [PRE and ENGAGEMENT].

PRE-ESTABLISH, [prē'-es-tab'-lish], *v.i.* to establish beforehand. [PRE and ESTABLISH].

PRE-ESTABLISHED, [prē'-es-tab'-lisht], *adj.* established beforehand.

PRE-ESTABLISHMENT, [prē'-es-tab'-lish-ment], *n.* previous establishment, settlement. [PRE and ESTABLISHMENT].

PRE-EXAMINE, [prē'-egz-am'-in], *v.t.* to examine beforehand. [PRE and EXAMINE].

PRE-EXILIC, [prē'-egz-il'-ik], *adj.* before the Babylonian captivity of the Jews.

PRE-EXIST, [prē'-egz-ist'], *v.i.* to exist in a previous life. [PRE and EXIST].

PRE-EXISTENCE, [prē'-egz-ist'-ents], *n.* existence in a previous state, on a previous plane. [PRE and EXISTENCE].

PRE-EXISTENT, [prē'-egz-ist'-ent], *adj.* existing previously. [PRE and EXISTENT].

PREFABRICATE, [prē'-fab'-rik-āt], *v.t.* to construct (buildings, etc.) in shaped sections ready to be assembled on the site. [PRE and FABRICATE].

PREFACE (1), [pref'-as], *n.* an introductory and explanatory statement at the beginning of a book, etc., the initial part of a speech. [Fr. *préface* from L. *praefari* to say beforehand].

PREFACE (2), [pref'-as], *v.t.* to introduce by a preface; to precede, introduce. [PREFACE (1)].

PREFATORILY, [pref'-at-o-ril-i], *adv.* in prefatory fashion.

PREFATORY, [pref'-at-o-ri], *adj.* as, by way of, a preface. [L. **praefatorius*].

PREFECT, [prē'-fekt'], *n.* (*hist.*) a Roman magistrate of high rank; a public school monitor. [L. *praefectus*].

PREFECTORIAL, [prē'-fekt-aw'-ri-al], *adj.* of, or pertaining to, a prefect or to his status or powers. [LL. *praefectorius*].

PREFECTSHIP, [prē'-fekt-ship], *n.* the office and authority of a prefect; a prefecture.

PREFECTURE, [prē'-fek'-cher], *n.* the jurisdiction, residence, office, or tenure of a prefect. [Fr. *préfecture*].

PREFER, [pri-fur'], *v.t.* to like better than, wish rather than; to bring forward, submit, to promote. [L. *praeferre* to bear in front].

PREFERABILITY, [pref'-er-ab-il'-it-i], *n.* preferableness.

PREFERABLE, [pref'-er-abl], *adj.* more to be desired, fit to be preferred.

PREFERABLENESS, [pref'-er-abl-nes], *n.* the state of being preferable.

PREFERABLY, [pref'-er-ab-li], *adv.* in preference.

PREFERENCE, [pref'-er-ents], *n.* the act of preferring, the feeling that inspires such action, the thing so preferred, the power of preferring; (*econ.*) special tariff discrimination in favour of a country; **p. share**, a share entitled to first call on profits for its dividend payment. [MedL. *preferentia*].

PREFERENTIAL, [pref'-er-en'-shal], *adj.* enjoying or giving a preference.

PREFERMENT, [pri-fur'-ment], *n.* the act of preferring; promotion to a higher office, *esp.* in the Church.

PREFERRER, [pri-fur'-er], *n.* one who prefers.

PREFIGURATE, [prē-fig'-yōō-rāt], *v.t.* to represent what is to come. [L. *praefiguratum*, *p.pt.* of *praefigurare*].

PREFIGURATION, [prē'-fig-yōō-rā'-shun], *n.* a prototype, a representation of what is to come. [LL. *prefiguratio*].

PREFIGURATIVE, [prē-fig'-yōō-rat-iv], *adj.* being a prototype, prefigurating. [MedL. *praefigurativus*].

PREFIGURE, [prē-fig'-er], *v.t.* to prefigurate. [MedL. *prefigurare*].

PREFIGUREMENT, [prē-fig'-er-ment], *n.* prefiguration.

PREFINE, [prē-fīn'], *v.t.* to limit beforehand. [On the analogy of DEFINE].

PREFIX (1), [prē'-fiks], *n.* a word coming before other words; (*gram.*) a preceding particle forming part of a compounded word. [Fr. *préfixe*].

PREFIX (2), [prē-fiks'], *v.t.* to place before; to put before as a prefix. [OFr. *prefixer*].

PREFLORATION, [prē'-flaw-rā'-shun], *n.* (*bot.*) the arrangement of the floral envelopes before they expand. [Fr. *préfloraison*].

PREFORM, [prē-fawm'], *v.t.* to form beforehand. [L. *praeformare*].

PREFORMATIVE (1), [prē-fawm'-at-iv], *n.* a prefix, a formative preceding syllable.

PREFORMATIVE (2), [prē-fawm'-at-iv], *adj.* forming beforehand; (*philol.*) added as a formative prefix. [PRE and FORMATIVE].

PREGLACIAL, [prē'-glāsh'-i-al], *adj.* before the Pleistocene period. [PRE and GLACIAL].

PREGNABLE, [preg'-nabl], *adj.* capable of being captured. [ME. *prenable* from L. *prehendere* to take hold of].

PREGNANCY, [preg'-nan-si], *n.* the state of being pregnant.

ō (bone), ī (fine), ōō (food), ŏŏ (put), u (up), th (think), TH (that), zh (azure), † = obsolete, ~ = related to.

PREGNANT, [preg'-nant], *adj.* with child in the womb, having conceived; prolific; full of importance, matter, or implication; (*gram.*) implying more than is directly expressed. [L. *praegnans*].

PREGNANTLY, [preg'-nant-li], *adv.* in pregnant fashion.

PREGUSTATION, [prē'-gust-ā'-shun], *n.* foretaste. [L. *praegustare* to taste beforehand].

PREHALLUX, [prē-hal'-uks], *n.* a rudimentary digit on the inner side of the foot in certain creatures. [MdL. *praehallux*].

PREHENSIBLE, [pri-hens'-ibl], *adj.* possible to be grasped.

PREHENSILE, [pri-hens'-il], *adj.* capable of prehension. [L. *prehensum*, *p.pt.* of *prehendere* to grasp].

PREHENSILITY, [prē'-hens-il'-it-i], *n.* the quality of being prehensile.

PREHENSION, [pri-hen'-shun], *n.* the act of, capacity for, grasping, taking hold of, seizing; simple apprehension. [L. *prehensio*].

PREHENSORY, [pri-hens'-e-ri], *adj.* prehensile.

PREHISTORIC, [prē'-his-tor'-ik], *adj.* related to the periods before written records; (*coll.*) old, outmoded. [PRE and HISTORIC].

PREHISTORY, [prē-his'-tri], *n.* the history of the ages before written records; prehistoric archaeology. [PRE and HISTORY].

PREHNITE, [prān'-īt], *n.* a hydrous silicate of calcium and aluminium. [From von *Prehn*, its discoverer].

PREINSTRUCT, [prē'-in-strukt'], *v.t.* to instruct beforehand. [PRE and INSTRUCT].

PREINTIMATION, [prē'-in-tim'-ā'-shun], *n.* previous intimation. [PRE and INTIMATION].

PREJUDGE, [prē-juj'], *v.t.* to judge before examination, to decide in advance of evidence. [PRE and JUDGE].

PREJUDGMENT, [prē-juj'-ment], *n.* act of prejudging. [PRE and JUDGMENT].

PRE-JUDICAL, [prē'-jew-dik'-al], *adj.* relating to prejudgment. [PRE and JUDICAL].

PREJUDICATE, [prē-jōō'-dik-āt], *v.t.* and *i.* to form a judgment beforehand; to prejudice. [L. *praejudicatum*, *p.pt.* of *praejudicare*].

PREJUDICATION, [prē-jōō'-dik-ā'-shun], *n.* the act of prejudicating, prejudgment; (*Rom. leg.*) a preliminary inquiry related to the case in hand.

PREJUDICATIVE, [prē-jōō'-dik-at-iv], *adj.* relating to, through, prejudication.

PREJUDICE (1), [prej'-ōōd-is], *n.* a partial opinion, a view formed without consideration, a bias, a prepossession; (*leg.*) harm, injury; **without p.,** without detraction from, or abrogation of, any right or claim. [L. *praejudicium* precedent, prejudice].

PREJUDICE (2), [prej'-ōōd-is], *v.t.* to inspire with a prejudice; to injure, detract from. [PREJUDICE (1)].

PREJUDICED, [prej'-ōōd-ist], *adj.* having a prejudice, biased.

PREJUDICIAL, [prej'-ōōd-ish'-al], *adj.* tending to prejudice; injurious to.

PREJUDICIALLY, [prej'-ōōd-ish'-al-i], *adv.* in prejudicial fashion.

PREJUDICIALNESS, [prej'-ōōd-ish'-al-nes], *n.* the quality of being prejudicial.

PREKNOWLEDGE, [prē-nol'-ij], *n.* previous knowledge. [PRE and KNOWLEDGE].

PRELACY, [prel'-as-i], *n.* the office of a prelate; the collective body of prelates; episcopacy. [MedL. *prelatia*].

PRELATE, [prel'-at], *n.* an ecclesiastical dignitary, *esp.* a bishop or archbishop. [ME. *prelat* from LL. *prelatus* set in authority].

PRELATESS, [prel'-at-es'], *n.* an abbess or prioress.

PRELATICAL, [prel-at'-ikl], *adj.* relating to prelates, usually in a hostile sense.

PRELATISM, [prel'-at-izm], *n.* episcopacy; government by prelates.

PRELATIST, [prel'-at-ist], *n.* supporter of prelatism.

PRELATIZE, [prel'-at-īz], *v.t.* to bring under prelates.

PRELATURE, [prel'-ach-ōōer], *n.* prelacy. [MedL. *praelatura*].

PRELECT, [prē-lekt'], *v.i.* to lecture, to be a prelector. [L. *praelectum*, *p.pt.* of *praelegere* to lecture].

PRELECTION, [prē-lek'-shun], *n.* a public lecture. [L. *praelectio*].

PRELECTOR, [prē-lek'-tor], *n.* a university lecturer. [L. *praelector*].

PRELIBATION, [prē'-lib-ā'-shun], *n.* a foretaste, an offering of first-fruits. [LL. *praelibatio*].

PRELIMINARILY, [pril-im'-in-er-i-li], *adv.* as preliminary.

PRELIMINARY (1), [pril-im'-in-er-i], *n.* an introductory measure, a preliminary action, examination. [PRELIMINARY (2)].

PRELIMINARY (2), [pril-im'-in-er-i], *adj.* prefatory, preceding the main action or business. [PRE and L. *liminaris* bounding].

PRELUDE (1), [prel'-yōōd], *n.* a preliminary, an introduction, that which precedes the main event; (*mus.*) the opening movement introducing the principal theme; a piece of music resembling this. [MedL. *preludium*].

PRELUDE (2), [prel'-yōōd], *v.t.* and *i.* to introduce, foreshadow; to serve as a prelude. [L. *praeludere*].

PRELUDER, [prel'-yōōd-er], *n.* one who preludes.

PRELUDIAL, [prel-yōōd'-i-al], *adj.* introductory.

PRELUDIOUS, [prel-yōōd'-i-us], *adj.* preludial.

PRELUMBAR, [prē-lumb'-er], *adj.* before the lumbar region. [PRE and LUMBAR].

PRELUSIVE, [pril-yōōs'-iv], *adj.* preluding. [L. *praelusum*, *p.pt.* of *praeludere*].

PRELUSIVELY, [pril-yōōs'-iv-li], *adv.* as a prelude.

PRELUSORILY, [pril-yōōs'-er-i-li], *adv.* prelusively.

PRELUSORY, [pril-yōōs'-e-ri], *adj.* prelusive.

PREMANDIBULAR, [prē-man-dib'-yōō-ler], *adj.* in front of the lower jaw. [PRE and MANDIBULAR].

PREMATURE, [prem'-at-ew-er], *adj.* before its time, earlier than is fitting, or usual; untimely; **p. birth,** a birth occurring before gestation is complete. [L. *praematurus*].

PREMATURELY, [prem'-at-ew-er-li], *adv.* before the proper time.

PREMATURENESS, [prem'-at-ew-er-nes], *n.* the condition of being premature.

PREMATURITY, [prem-a-tyōōer-it-i], *n.* prematureness, precocity, too early development.

PREMAXILLARY, [prē-maks-il'-er-i], *adj.* in front of the upper jaw.

PREMEDITATE, [prē-med'-it-āt], *v.t.* to contrive in advance. [L. *praemeditari*].

PREMEDITATION, [prē-med-it-ā'-shun], *n.* act of premeditating, contrivance beforehand. [L. *praemeditatio*].

PREMIER (1), [prem'-i-er, prē'-mi-er], *n.* the Prime Minister. [PREMIER (2)].

PREMIER (2), [prem'-i-er, prē'-mi-er], *adj.* principal, foremost, first in importance or rank. [L. *primarius*].

PREMIERE, première, [prem'-i-āer], *n.* the first public performance of a dramatic entertainment, or of a film. [Fr. *première*].

PREMIERSHIP, [prem'-i-er-ship, prē'-mi-er-ship], *n.* the office of Prime Minister.

PREMISE (1), [prem'-is], *n.* the assumption on which an argument is based; (*log.*) one of the two propositions of a syllogism; (*leg.*) the introductory part of a lease describing the property in question; (*pl.*) a building or part of a building, and any land going with it, occupied under a lease. [OFr. *premisse* from LL. *premissa*].

PREMISE (2), [prim-īz'], *v.t.* to take as a premise, to assume.

PREMIUM, [prēm'-i-um], *n.* something paid over and above what is normally due, as recompense for some special service or advantage; a fee paid to join a business or be taught a profession; the yearly payment on an insurance policy; the amount by which the market value of shares exceeds their par value; (*fig., coll.*) a high value, price, or advantage. [L. *praemium* reward].

PREMOLAR, [prē-mōl'-er], *n.* a biscupid tooth. [PRE and MOLAR].

PREMONISH, [prē-mon'-ish], *v.t.* to forewarn. [L. *praemonere*].

PREMONITION, [prē'-mon-ish'-un], *n.* a forewarning; a presentiment, irrational foreboding. [L. *praemonitio*].

PREMONITOR, [prē-mon'-it-or], *n.* a forewarner. [L. *praemonitor*].

PREMOLAR

PREMONITORY, [prē-mon'-it-er-i], *adj.* forewarning. [L. *praemonitorius*].

PREMONSTRANT, [prē-mons'-trant], *n.* a member of the monastic order of St. Norbert. [MedL. *Premonstratus*, L. form of *Prémontré*, near Laon, where the order had its headquarters].

PREMONSTRATENSIAN, [prē'-mons-trat-en'-si-an], *adj.* relating to the premonstrants, Norbertine. [L. *Praemonstratensis*].

PREMORSE, [prē-maws'], *adj.* (*bot., zool.*) abruptly truncated, with the end cut off short. [L. *praemorsum*, *p.pt.* of *praemordere* to bite off in front].

PREMOTION, [prē-mō'-shun], *n.* previous motion. [PRE and MOTION].

PREMUNIRE, see PRAEMUNIRE.

PRENASAL, [prē-nāz'-al], *adj.* in front of the nose. [PRE and NASAL].

PRENATAL, [prē-nā'-tal], *adj.* before birth. [PRE and NATAL].

PRENDER, [pren'-der], *n.* the right of taking something without its being offered. [Fr. *prendre* to take].

PRENOMINATE, [prē-nom'-in-āt'], *v.t.* to name beforehand. [LL. *prenominatum, p.pt.* of *prenominare*].

PRENOMINATION, [prē-nom-in-ā'-shun], *n.* the act of prenominating, state of being prenominated. [MedL. *prenominatio*].

PRENOTION, [prē-nō'-shun], *n.* perception in advance, prescience. [L. *praenotio*].

PRENTICE, [pren'-tis], *n. and adj.* an apprentice, relating to an apprentice. [APPRENTICE].

PREOBTAIN, [prē'-ob-tān'], *v.t.* to obtain beforehand.

PREOCCUPANCY, [prē-ok'-yōō-pan-si], *n.* previous occupancy. [PRE and OCCUPANCY].

PREOCCUPATION, [prē-ok'-yōō-pā'-shun], *n.* the act of preoccupying, a previous occupation; the state of being mentally occupied with some matter other than the one in hand, deeply thoughtful, oblivious of immediate events and surroundings. [L. *praeoccupatio*].

PREOCCUPIED, [prē-ok'-yōō-pīd], *adj.* in a state of mental preoccupation.

PREOCCUPY, [prē-ok'-yōō-pī], *v.t.* to occupy, take possession of, in advance; to engross, obsess, occupy the mind of to the neglect or ignoring of immediate surroundings or considerations. [L. *praeoccupare*].

PREOPINION, [prē'-op-in'-yun], *n.* an opinion formed in advance. [PRE and OPINION].

PREOPTION, [prē-op'-shun], *n.* first option. [PRE and OPTION].

PREORAL, [prē-aw'-ral], *adj.* before the mouth. [PRE and ORAL].

PREORDAIN, [prē'-awd-ān'], *v.t.* to determine in advance. [LL. *preordinare*].

PREORDINANCE, [prē-awd'-in-ants], *n.* previous ordinance.

PREORDINATE, [prē-awd'-in-at], *adj.* foreordained. [LL. *preordinatum, p.pt.* of *preordinare*].

PREORDINATION, [prē'-awd-in-ā'-shun], *n.* previous ordination, the act of preordaining, predetermination. [LL. *preordinatio*].

PREP, [prep], *n.* (*schoolboy slang*) preparation; **p. school,** a preparatory school.

PREPAID, [prē'-pād'], *adj.* paid in advance. [PRE and PAID].

PREPARABLE, [pri-pāer'-abl], *adj.* possible to prepare.

PREPARATION, [prep'-a-rā'-shun], *n.* the act of preparing, state of being prepared; the act of, time spent in, preparing school work; a medicine, lotion, etc., specially prepared for a specific purpose. [L. *praeparatio*].

PREPARATIVE, [pri-pa'-rat-iv], *adj.* preparing, preparatory.

PREPARATIVELY, [pri-pa'-rat-iv-li], *adv.* in preparative fashion.

PREPARATOR, [pri-pa'-rat-or], *n.* a preparer of anatomical specimens. [LL. *preparator*].

PREPARATORY, [pri-pa'-rat-er-i], *adj.* preparing, introductory; (of schools) preparing for a public or high school. [MedL. *preparatorius*].

PREPARE, [pri-pāer'], *v.t. and i.* to make ready or suitable, arrange for some specific purpose; to construct, put together, blend, mix, cook, etc., so as to be suitable for some use; to equip; to plan out; to teach, train; to learn; to become ready, (of states) to lay up armaments and make other military preparations. [L. *praeparare*].

PREPAREDLY, [pri-pāer'-ed-li], *adv.* in a state of preparedness, in a prepared manner.

PREPAREDNESS, [pri-pāer'-ed-nes], *n.* the state of being prepared, *esp.* in a military sense.

PREPARER, [pri-pāer'-er], *n.* he who prepares.

PREPAY, [prē'-pā'], *v.t.* to pay in advance. [PRE and PAY].

PREPAYABLE, [prē-pā'-abl], *adj.* payable in advance.

PREPAYMENT, [prē-pā'-ment], *n.* payment in advance. [PRE and PAYMENT].

PREPENSE, [prē-pents'], *adj.* deliberate, previously planned. [Fr. *prepenser* from OFr. *purpenser.*]

PREPENSELY, [prē-pents'-li], *adv.* with premeditation.

PREPOLLENCY, [prē-pol'-en-si], *n.* the state of being prepollent. [L. *praepollentia*].

PREPOLLENT, [prē-pol'-ent], *adj.* predominating, having superior power. [L. *praepollens, pres.pt.* of *praepollere* to prevail].

PREPONDERANCE, [pri-pond'-er-ants], *n.* the state of being preponderant, the preponderant force. [PRE and PONDERANCE].

PREPONDERANT, [pri-pond'-er-ant], *adj.* outweighing, more important. [L. *praeponderare* to outweigh].

PREPONDERANTLY, [pri-pond'-er-ant-li], *adv.* to a preponderant extent.

PREPONDERATE, [pri-pond'-er-āt], *v.i.* to outweigh outnumber, predominate. [L. *praeponderare*].

PREPONDERATION, [pri-pond'-er-ā'-shun], *n.* the act of preponderating. [L. *praeponderatio*].

PREPOSITION (1), [prep'-oz-ish'-un], *n.* (*gram.*) a word placed before a noun or pronoun to express temporal, causal, or other abstract relations. [L. *praepositio*].

PRE-POSITION (2), [prē'-poz-i'-shun], *n.* the act or fact of setting or being set before.

PREPOSITIONAL, [prep'-oz-ish'-unl], *adj.* relating to, in the place of, a preposition.

PREPOSITIONALLY, [prep'-oz-ish'-un-al-i], *adv.* in the fashion of a preposition.

PREPOSITIVE, [prē-poz'-it-iv], *adj.* (*gram.*) prefixed, capable of being prefixed. [L. *praepositivus*].

PREPOSITOR, [prē-poz'-it-or], *n.* a monitor, prefect. [LL. *praepositor*].

PREPOSITURE, [prē-poz'-ich-er], *n.* a provostship.

PREPOSSESS, [prē'-poz-es'], *v.t.* to influence, prejudice (usually favourably), to make a good impression upon.

PREPOSSESSING, [prē'-poz-es'-ing], *adj.* tending to prepossess, attractive.

PREPOSSESSION, [prē'-poz-esh'-un], *n.* the state of being prepossessed; strong inclination; obsession.

PREPOSTEROUS, [pri-post'-er-us], *adj.* ridiculous, contrary to reason, absurd. [L. *praeposterus* inverted, reversed].

PREPOSTEROUSLY, [pri-post'-er-us-li], *adv.* in preposterous fashion.

PREPOSTEROUSNESS, [pri-post'-er-us-nes], *n.* the state of being preposterous.

PREPOTENCY, [prē-pō'-ten-si], *n.* the state of being prepotent; (*biol.*) the power of one parent to transmit its characteristics to offspring. [L. *praepotentia*].

PREPOTENT, [prē-pō'-tent], *adj.* having superior power; (*biol.*) having prepotency. [L. *praepotens, pres.pt.* of *praeposse* to be more powerful].

PRE-PREFERENCE, [prē-pref'-er-ents], *n.* a share ranking above a preference share. [PRE and PREFERENCE].

PREPUCE, [prē'-pews], *n.* the foreskin. [L. *praeputium*].

PREPUNCTUAL, [prē-pungk'-chōō-al], *adj.* too punctual, early. [PRE and PUNCTUAL].

PREPUTIAL, [prē-pew'-shal], *adj.* relating to the foreskin. [L. *praeputialis*].

PRE-RAPHAELITE (1), [prē-raf'-el-īt], *n.* a member of the group of artists, centred round Holman Hunt and Rossetti, who admired and imitated Italian painting before Raphael.

PRE-RAPHAELITE (2), [prē-raf'-el-īt], *adj.* belonging to, in the style of, the pre-Raphaelites.

PRE-RAPHAELITISM, [prē-raf'-el-īt-izm], *n.* the pre-Raphaelite movement and theory.

PREREGNANT, [prē-reg'-nant], *adj.* previously reigning.

PREREMOTE, [prē'-ri-mōt'], *adj.* more remote. [PRE and REMOTE].

PREREQUIRE, [prē'-ri-kwīer'], *v.t.* to require beforehand. [PRE and REQUIRE].

PREREQUISITE (1), [prē-rek'-wiz-it], *n.* that which is prerequisite (2).

PREREQUISITE (2), [prē-rek'-wiz-it], *adj.* necessary beforehand.

PRERESOLVE, [prē'-riz-olv'], *v.i.* to resolve beforehand. [PRE and RESOLVE].

PREROGATIVE, [pri-rog'-at-iv], *n.* a special, unlimited right, a peculiar privilege attaching to some person, office, or condition; the right of exercising such privilege; the exercise itself; **the Royal P.,** the theoretical royal right to act without Parliament. [L. *praerogativa*, right of prior voting].

PRESAGE (1), [pres'-ij], *n.* a portent, omen, foreboding. [Fr. *présage* from L. *praesagium* foreknowledge, omen].

PRESAGE (2), [pri-sāj'], *v.t.* to foretell, forebode. [Fr. *présager*].

PRESAGEFUL, [pri-sāj'-fŏŏl], *adj.* warning, foreboding.

PRESAGEMENT, [pri-sāj'-ment], *n.* a presage, foreboding.

PRESAGER, [pri-sāj'-er], *n.* one who, that which, presages.

PRESANCTIFY, [prē-sangk'-ti-fī], *v.t.* to sanctify beforehand. [PRE and SANCTIFY].

PRESARTORIAL, [prē'-sah-taw'-ri-al], *adj.* previous to tailoring. [PRE and SARTORIAL].

PRESBYOPE, [prez'-bi-ōp], *n.* a sufferer from presbyopia.

PRESBYOPIA, [prez'-bi-ōp'-i-a], *n.* defective vision of old age, due to inability to focus near objects. [Gk. *presbus* old and *ops* eye].

PRESBYTER, [prez'-bit-er], *n.* a church elder, in either the Early Christian, the Episcopal, or the Presbyterian Churches. [Gk. *presbuteros* elder].

PRESBYTERAL, [prez-bit'-er-al], *adj.* relating to a presbyter or a presbytery.

PRESBYTERIAL, [prez'-bit-ēer'-i-al], *adj.* Presbyterian.

PRESBYTERIAN (1), [prez'-bit-ēer'-i-an], *n.* a member of the Presbyterian Church.

PRESBYTERIAN (2), [prez'-bit-ēer'-i-an], *adj.* relating to church government by presbyters; **P. Church,** a Christian sect which does not recognize an order of bishops, and is governed by presbyters.

PRESBYTERIANISM, [prez-bit-ēer'-i-an-izm], *n.* the order, system, and government of the Presbyterian Church.

PRESBYTERY, [prez'-bit-ri], *n.* a body of Church elders; the house of a parish priest; the district court of the Presbyterian Church. [OFr. *presbiterie* from LL. *presbyterium*].

PRESCIENCE, [prē'-shi-ents], *n.* foreknowledge, foresight. [L. *praescientia*].

PRESCIENT, [prē'-shi-ent], *adj.* foreseeing, having foreknowledge. [L. *praesciens, pres.pt.* of *praescire*].

PRESCIENTIFIC, [prē'-sī-ent-if'-ik], *adj.* previous to science. [PRE and SCIENTIFIC].

PRESCIND, [prē-sind'], *v.t. and i.* to separate, abstract from; to withdraw from. [L. *praescindere* to cut off short].

PRESCRIBE, [pri-skrīb'], *v.t. and i.* to direct, ordain; (*med.*) to recommend (a specific medicine or treatment); (*leg.*) to claim by prescription; to lay down rules. [L. *praescribere* to appoint].

PRESCRIBER, [pri-skrīb'-er], *n.* one who prescribes.

PRESCRIPT, [prē'-skript], *n.* a decree. [L. *praescriptus, p.pt.* of *praescribere*].

PRESCRIPTIBLE, [pri-skript'-ibl], *adj.* (*leg.*) subject to prescription.

PRESCRIPTION, [pri-skrip'-shun], *n.* the act of prescribing; that which is prescribed; (*leg.*) uninterrupted possession for sufficient time to give legal title; right or title gained in this way; a written recipe for the preparation of a medicine, the medicine itself. [L. *praescriptio*].

PRESCRIPTIVE, [pri-skript'-iv], *adj.* owned, claimed, by prescription. [LL. *prescriptivus*].

PRE-SELECTOR, [prē'-si-lekt'-er], *n.* an apparatus enabling the driver of a motor-car to select a fresh gear before changing; **p. gear,** a gear embodying this principle.

PRESENCE, [prez'-ents], *n.* the state of being present, of being in a specified place at a certain time; the state of being in the neighbourhood or sight of another; *esp.* of a sovereign or potentate; the closeness, immanence, of anything; the bearing of a person, the impression given at close quarters; a feeling that something other than oneself is present, the mysterious something itself; **p. of mind,** steadiness, mental quickness and control in novel or disturbing circumstances; **p. chamber,** a royal audience chamber. [ME. *presens*, L. *praesentia*].

PRESENSATION, [prē'-sen-sā'-shun], *n.* previous sensation. [PRE and SENSATION].

PRESENSION, [prē-sen'-shun], *n.* previous perception, foreknowledge. [L. *praesensio*].

PRESENT (1), [prez'-ent], *n.* the present time; the present tense; (*leg.*) (*pl.*) the document itself. [PRESENT (4)].

PRESENT (2), [prez'-ent], *n.* a gift. [OFr. *present* from *en present* in the presence of].

PRESENT (3), [priz-ent'], *n.* (*milit.*) the act of raising the weapon (firearm, pike, etc.), and pointing it towards someone; the position of the weapon so held, the vertical position of the rifle in the ceremonial salute. [PRESENT (5)].

PRESENT (4), [prez'-ent], *adj.* being here, by, near, in one's presence, being in a specified place at a specified time; occurring now, existing now (not in past or future); (*gram.*) belonging to the tense expressing action at this time; immediate and effective. [ME. *present* from OFr. *present*].

PRESENT (5), [priz-ent'], *v.t.* to bring to the presence of, to introduce to, to give directly (to), to introduce formally at court; to exhibit publicly, to bring (some performance, or player in a performance) before the public; to offer, display; to nominate for a benefice; to point (a weapon) at; to bring (a rifle) to the ceremonial salute. [L. *praesentare* to set before].

PRESENTABILITY, [priz-ent'-ab-il'-i-ti], *n.* the state of being presentable.

PRESENTABLE, [priz-ent'-abl], *adj.* fit for presentation; of pleasing immediate, external appearance; well-mannered.

PRESENTANEOUS, [prez'-ent-ān'-i-us], *adj.* quick acting. [L. *praesentaneus*].

PRESENTATION, [prez'-ent-ā'-shun], *n.* the act of presenting, mode of exposition, publishing for display; right of presenting to a benefice; the position in which a child is born; the performance of a show or fashion in which it is produced. [L. *praesentatio*].

PRESENTATIVE, [priz-ent'-a-tiv], *adj.* possible of direct apprehension; subject to the right of presentation.

PRESENTEE, [prez'-ent-ē'], *n.* one who is presented to a benefice.

PRESENTER, [priz-ent'-er], *n.* one who presents.

PRESENTIENT, [prē-sen'-shi-ent], *adj.* perceiving beforehand. [L. *praesentire* to perceive beforehand].

PRESENTIMENT, [priz-ent'-i-ment], *n.* a foreboding, a feeling of a future event (generally in unpleasant sense). [PRE and SENTIMENT].

PRESENTIVE, [priz-ent'-iv], *adj.* presenting an idea directly to the mind (opposite of symbolic).

PRESENTIVENESS, [priz-ent'-iv-nes], *n.* the state of being presentive.

PRESENTLY, [prez'-ent-li], *adv.* †immediately; after a short time, soon, not immediately.

PRESENTMENT, [priz-ent'-ment], *n.* the act or manner of presenting; (*eccles.*) a formal statement or complaint before a court or a visiting bishop; representation.

PRESERVABLE, [priz-erv'-abl], *adj.* possible to preserve.

PRESERVATION, [prez'-erv-ā'-shun], *n.* the act of preserving, state of being preserved. [MedL. *praeservatio*].

PRESERVATIVE (1), [priz-urv'-at-iv], *n.* a substance that preserves, *esp.* food. [PRESERVATIVE (2)].

PRESERVATIVE (2), [priz-urv'-at-iv], *adj.* having the property of preserving. [MedL. *praeservativus*].

PRESERVATORY, [priz-urv'-at-er-i], *adj.* tending to preserve.

PRESERVE (1), [priz-urv'], *n.* that which is preserved, *esp.* jam, tinned fruit; a game covert, a river reserved for fishing. [PRESERVE (2)].

PRESERVE (2), [priz-urv'], *v.t.* to maintain, keep safe from harm, damage, or decay, to treat so as to prevent decay; to rear and protect (game) for hunting, etc. [LL. *preservare*].

PRESERVER, [priz-urv'-er], *n.* one who, that which, preserves.

PRESES, [prē'-sēz], *n.* in Scotland, the chairman of a meeting. [L. *praeses* president].

PRESIDE, [priz-īd'], *v.i.* to hold the place of authority at a meeting, to be in the chair. [L. *praesidere* to protect].

PRESIDENCY, [prez'-id-en-si], *n.* the office of president; the tenure of such office; an Indian administrative province. [MedL. *praesidentia*].

PRESIDENT, [prez'-id-ent], *n.* a supreme officer of various kinds, *esp.* the elected head of a republic; the chief of a great business concern; the official head and chairman of a society; the head of certain colleges, etc. [L. *praesidens, pres.pt.* of *praesidere* to protect].

PRESIDENTIAL, [prez'-id-en'-shal], *adj.* relating to a president or his office. [MedL. *presidentialis*].

PRESIDENTSHIP, [prez'-id-ent-ship], *n.* the office and tenure of a president.

PRESIDIAL, [pri-sid'-i-al], *adj.* relating to a province; or garrison. [LL. *presidialis*].

PRESIDIARY, [pri-sid'-i-er-i], *adj.* defended; relating to a garrison. [L. *praesidiarius*].

PRESIDIUM, [pri-sid'-i-um], *n.* the permanent central

committee of various political groups and organizations. [L. *praesidium*].

PRESIGNIFY, [prē-sig'-ni-fī], *v.t. and i.* to signify beforehand. [PRE and SIGNIFY].

PRESS (1), [pres], *n.* the act of pressing; that which is to be pressed; that which presses, any machine or device for exerting pressure, *esp.* a machine for squeezing juice from fruit, a device for pressing and creasing clothes; a great, closely compact crowd; a cupboard, a set of shelves; a printing-press, the process of printing, a publishing and printing establishment; newspapers, periodicals. [ME. *presse* from Fr. *presse*].

PRESS (2), [pres], *n.* impressment. [IMPRESS].

PRESS (3), [pres], *v.t. and i.* to exert strong, steady force upon so as to crush or compress; to squeeze; to thrust (an object) against resistance; to crowd in upon, to assail hotly so as to drive back, to harry; to urge strongly, to urge acceptance of (a thing); to oppress, afflict, to exert pressure; **to p. on,** to hasten onwards. [ME. *pressen* from L. *pressare*].

PRESS (4), [pres], *v.t.* to enlist forcibly for military or naval service; to force (someone or something) into one's service. [PRESS (3)].

PRESS-AGENT, [pres'-āj'-ent], *n.* one professionally employed in obtaining press publicity for a person or organization, or in maintaining contact between the press and an organization.

PRESS-BED, [pres'-bed], *n.* a bed that can be folded into a case.

PRESS-BOX, [pres'-boks], *n.* the place reserved for reporters at a show or ceremony.

PRESS-CUTTING, [pres'-kut-ing], *n.* an extract cut out from a newspaper or periodical.

PRESSER, [pres'-er], *n.* one who, that which, presses.

PRESS-GALLERY, [pres'-gal'-eri], *n.* the place reserved for journalists in the House of Commons.

PRESSGANG, [pres'-gang'], *n.* a party of men entitled to kidnap and press into military or naval service.

PRESSING, [pres'-ing], *adj.* insistent, importunate; urgent, demanding immediate attention.

PRESSINGLY, [pres'-ing-li], *adv.* in pressing fashion.

PRESSION, [presh'-un], *n.* the act of pressing; pressure. [L. *pressio*].

PRESSIROSTRAL, [pres'-i-ros'-tral], *adj.* having a compressed or flattened beak. [L. *pressum*, *p.pt.* of *premere* to press and *rostrum* beak].

PRESSMAN, [pres'-man'], *n.* a printing machine-minder; a journalist.

PRESSMARK, [pres'-mahk'], *n.* the marking on a library book showing its place on the shelves.

PRESS-ROOM, [pres'-rōōm'], *n.* the room in a printing works where the printing is carried out.

PRESS-STUD, [pres'-stud'], *n.* a form of fastener for clothing, etc., consisting of a nipple which is gripped in position by a W-shaped spring. [PRESS (3) and STUD (1)].

PRESSURE, [presh'-er], *n.* the act of pressing, force exerted by pressing; (*fig.*) the force and compulsion of business and circumstance; (*mech.*) the force exerted by one body against another; (*phys.*) the force exerted on its surroundings by a liquid, solid, or gas; **p. point,** (*med.*) a point at which the blood flows near enough to the skin to be temporarily stopped by pressure. [L. *pressura*].

PRESSURE-GAUGE, [presh'-er-gāj'], *n.* an instrument for registering the pressure of steam in a boiler.

PRESSURE-GAUGE

PRESSWORK, [pres'-wurk], *n.* the work of a printing press, printing technique.

PRESTATION, [prest-ā'-shun], *n.* the customary payment of money or service to a superior. [L. *praestatio*].

PRESTER†, [pres'-ter], *n.* a priest. [OFr. *prestre*].

PRESTIDIGITATION, [pres'-tid-ij-it-ā'-shun], *n.* conjuring, legerdemain. [Fr. *prestidigitation*].

PRESTIDIGITATOR, [pres'-tid-ij'-it-ā-ter], *n.* a conjurer. [Fr. *prestidigitateur*].

PRESTIGE, [pres-tēzh'], *n.* repute for power and importance, good opinion, influence due to a glorious or powerful reputation. [Fr. *prestige*].

PRESTIMONY, [pres'-ti-mun-i], *n.* a fund to support a priest. [MedL. *prestimonium*].

PRESTISSIMO, [pres-tis'-im-ō], *adv.* (*mus.*) very quickly. [It. *prestissimo*, *superl.* of *presto*].

PRESTO, [pres'-tō], *adv.* (*mus.*) quickly (also used as an exclamation by conjurers). [It. *presto*].

PRESTRICTION, [prē-strik'-shun], *n.* blindfolding, blinding. [LL. *prestrictio*].

PRE-STUDY, [prē-stud'-i], *v.t. and i.* to study beforehand. [PRE and STUDY].

PRESUMABLE, [priz-ewm'-abl], *adj.* that may be presumed.

PRESUMABLY, [priz-ewm'-ab-li], *adv.* as one may suppose; probably.

PRESUME, [priz-ewm'], *v.t. and i.* to assume, to accept as true without evidence; to assume for oneself more latitude than one possesses; to be arrogant, presumptuous, to take too much for granted. [L. *praesumere* to presuppose].

PRESUMER, [priz-ewm'-er], *n.* one who presumes.

PRESUMING, [priz-ewm'-ing], *adj.* presumptuous.

PRESUMINGLY, [priz-ewm'-ing-li], *adv.* in presuming fashion.

PRESUMPTION, [priz-ump'-shun], *n.* the act or process of presuming, the thing presumed; probability, reason for presuming; arrogance, effrontery. [L. *praesumptio*].

PRESUMPTIVE, [priz-ump'-tiv], *adj.* based on presumption, probable, likely. [LL. *presumptivus*].

PRESUMPTIVELY, [priz-ump'-tiv-li], *adv.* in presumptive fashion.

PRESUMPTUOUS, [priz-ump'-chŏŏ-us], *adj.* showing presumption and arrogance, insolently assuming. [LL. *presumptiosus*].

PRESUMPTUOUSLY, [priz-ump'-chŏŏ-us-li], *adv.* in presumptuous fashion.

PRESUMPTUOUSNESS, [priz-ump'-chŏŏ-us-nes], *n.* the quality of being presumptuous.

PRESUPPOSAL, [prē'-sup-ōz'-al], *n.* presupposition.

PRESUPPOSE, [prē-sup-ōz'], *v.t.* to assume in advance, to assume, require, as a necessary preliminary. [Fr. *présupposer*].

PRESUPPOSITION, [prē'-sup-oz-ish'-un], *n.* the act of presupposing; that which is presupposed. [MedL. *presuppositio*].

PRESURMISE, [prē'-sur-mīz'], *v.t.* to surmise in advance. [PRE and SURMISE].

PRETENCE, [prit-ents'], *n.* the act of pretending; the thing pretended, a pretension, a false assumption of some attitude, a fraud, a misrepresentation with intent to deceive. [AFr. *pretensse*].

PRETEND, [prit-end'], *v.t. and i.* to feign, to assume in order to deceive, to simulate; to put forward false claims; to play at being, imagine oneself as, someone one is not. [ME. *pretenden* from L. *praetendere*].

PRETENDED, [prit-end'-id], *adj.* false, feigned.

PRETENDEDLY, [prit-end'-id-li], *adv.* in pretence, falsely.

PRETENDER, [prit-end'-er], *n.* one who pretends, *esp.* one who makes false claim to rank or position; the claimant to a throne, etc.

PRETENDERSHIP, [prit-end'-er-ship], *n.* the claims of a pretender.

PRETENDINGLY, [prit-end'-ing-li], *adv.* pretentiously.

PRETENSION, [prit-en'-shun], *n.* an assertion, claim (*esp.* an arrogant one). [MedL. *pretensio*].

PRETENTIOUS, [prit-en'-shus], *adj.* showing pretentions, presuming, ostentatious, attempting more than can be fulfilled. [Fr. *prétentieux*].

PRETENTIOUSLY, [prit-en'-shus-li], *adv.* in pretentious fashion.

PRETENTIOUSNESS, [prit-en'-shus-nes], *n.* the state or quality of being pretentious.

PRETER-, *pref.* beyond, above, before, more than, etc. [L. *praeter*].

PRETERHUMAN, [prē'-ter-hew'-man], *adj.* superhuman.

PRETERIST, [pret'-er-ist], *n.* (*theol.*) one believing that the prophecies of Revelation have already been fulfilled; one obsessed with the past.

PRETERITE (1), PRETERIT, [pret'-er-it], *n.* (*gram.*) the past definite tense. [PRETERITE (2)].

PRETERITE (2), [pret'-er-it], *adj.* (*gram.*) relating to the past definite tense. [ML. *preteritus* past].

PRETERITION, [pret'-er-ish'-un], *n.* (*theol.*) God's disregard of those who are not included among the elect; (*rhet.*) the mention of a thing by professing to omit it. [L. *praeteritio* a passing over].

PRETERLAPSED, [prē'-ter-lapst'], *adj.* passed over [L. *praeterlapsum*, *p.pt.* of *praeterlabi* to glide by].

PRETERMISSION, [prē'-ter-mish'-un], *n.* omission, passing over. [L. *praetermissio*].

PRETERMIT, (**pretermitting, pretermitted**),

[prē′-ter-mit′], *v.t.* to neglect, omit, break off. [L. *praetermittere*].

PRETERNATURAL, [prē′-ter-nach′-er-al], *adj.* supernatural. [PRETER and NATURAL].

PRETERNATURALLY, [prē′-ter-nach′-er-al-i], *adv* in preternatural fashion.

PRETERNATURALNESS, [prē′-ter-nach′-er-al-nes], *n.* the quality of being preternatural.

PRETERNUPTIAL, [prē′-ter-nup′-shal], *adj.* adulterous. [PRETER and NUPTIAL].

PRETEXT (1), [prē′-tekst], *n.* a false reason, an excuse for doing something different, a pretended motive. [Fr. *prétexte*].

PRETEXT (2), [pri-tekst′], *v.t.* to use as a pretext. [Fr. *prétexter*].

PRETIBIAL, [prē-tib′-i-al], *adj.* (*anat.*) in front of the tibia. [PRE and L. *tibia* shin].

PRETONE, [prē′-tōn], *n.* the sound immediately preceding the stressed syllable. [PRE and TONE].

PRETONIC, [prē-ton′-ik], *adj.* of, or pertaining to, a syllable immediately preceding the stress or accent in a word. [PRE and TONIC (2)].

PRETOR, see PRAETOR.

PRETORIAL, see PRAETORIAL.

PRETORIAN, see PRAETORIAN.

PRETORIUM, see PRAETORIUM.

PRETORSHIP, see PRAETORSHIP.

PRETTIFY, [prit′-i-fī], *v.t.* to make pretty (usually in contemptuous sense).

PRETTILY, [prit′-i-li], *adv.* in pretty fashion.

PRETTINESS, [prit′-i-nes], *n.* the state or quality of being pretty.

PRETTY (1), [prit′-i], *n.* (*golf*) the fairway. [PRETTY (2)].

PRETTY (2), [prit′-i], *adj.* superficially but pleasantly attractive, pleasing without arousing any strong emotion, nice, neat, clever in a minor fashion, stylish; (*in irony*) fine, grand, pleasant, foppish; (*coll.*) of considerable quantity, of fair extent; dear. [OE. *prætig* from *prætt* trick].

PRETTY (3), [prit′-i], *adv.* fairly, to a small extent; excessively, very. [PRETTY (1)].

PRETTYISH, [prit′-i-ish], *adj.* fairly pretty.

PRETTY-PRETTY, [prit′-i-prit′-i], *adj.* superficially and affectedly pretty, feebly charming.

PRETTY-SPOKEN, [prit′-i-spōk′-en], *adj.* having a pleasing manner of speech.

PRETYPIFY, [prē-tip′-i-fī], *v.t.* to prefigure. [PRE and TYPIFY].

PREVAIL, [pri-vāl′], *v.i.* to have advantage or victory over, to be current, to be habitual (with an understood triumph over something else); **to p. on,** to persuade, induce (someone) against his inclinations. [ME. *prevaylle* from L. *praevalere*].

PREVAILING, [pri-vāl′-ing], *adj.* ruling, current, habitual.

PREVAILINGLY, [pri-vāl′-ing-li], *adv.* so as to prevail, predominantly, chiefly.

PREVALENCE, [prev′-al-ents], *n.* the state of being prevalent, the extent to which (a thing, belief, etc., is) prevalent. [MedL. *prevalentia*].

PREVALENCY, [prev′-al-en-si], *n.* prevalence.

PREVALENT, [prev′-al-ent], *adj.* prevailing, widely received, practised, etc., current, general. [L. *praevalens, pres.pt.* of *praevalere*].

PREVALENTLY, [prev′-al-ent-li], *adv.* in prevalent fashion, to a prevalent extent.

PREVARICATE, [pri-va′-rik-āt], *v.i.* to lie, to avoid telling the truth, to make an evasive answer, to quibble. [L. *praevaricatum, p.pt.* of *praevaricari* to walk crookedly].

PREVARICATION, [pri-va′-rik-ā′-shun], *n.* the act of prevaricating; an equivocation, a verbal deception. [L. *praevaricatio*].

PREVARICATOR, [pri-va′-rik-āt-er], *n.* one who prevaricates. [L. *praevaricator*].

PREVENANCY, [prev′-en-an-si], *n.* courteous complaisance. [Fr. *prévenir* to anticipate].

PREVENIENT, [pri-vēn′-i-ent], *adj.* preceding; preventive; **p. grace,** (*theol.*) grace inspiring repentance. [L. *praeveniens, pres.pt.* of *praevenire*].

PREVENT, [pri-vent′], *v.t.* †to precede; stop, safeguard from, hamper, check, thwart. [L. *praeventum, p.pt.* of *praevenire* to go before].

PREVENTABLE, [pri-vent′-abl], *adj.* possible to prevent.

PREVENTATIVE (1), [pri-vent′-at-iv], *n.* that which prevents; a medicine for preventing some disease.

PREVENTATIVE (2), [pri-vent′-at-iv′], *adj.* preventing, guarding against.

PREVENTER, [pri-vent′-er], *n.* one who prevents; a rope or stay taking the strain off another.

PREVENTION, [pri-ven′-shun], *n.* the act or process of preventing; that which prevents. [LL. *preventio*].

PREVENTIONAL, [pri-ven′-shun-al], *adj.* preventive.

PREVENTIVE, [pri-vent′-iv], *adj.* preventing, antidotal, checking in advance, prophylactic.

PREVENTIVELY, [pri-vent′-iv-li], *adv.* so as to prevent.

PREVERTEBRAL, [prē-vurt′-ib-ral], *adj.* before the backbone. [PRE and VERTEBRAL].

PREVIOUS (1), [prē-vi-us], *adj.* preceding, prior, earlier; hasty, anticipating, too early. [L. *praevius* going before].

PREVIOUS (2), [prē′-vi-us], *adv.* before (with *to*). [PREVIOUS (1)].

PREVIOUSLY, [prē′-vi-us-li], *adv.* before.

PREVIOUSNESS, [prē′-vi-us-nes], *n.* the quality, condition, of being previous.

PREVISE, [prē-vīz′], *v.t.* to foresee. [L. *praevisum, p.pt.* of *praevidere*].

PREVISION, [prē-vizh′-un], *n.* foresight, prescience. [PRE and VISION].

PRE-WAR, [prē′-waw(r)′], *adj.* before the war. [PRE and WAR].

PREWARN, [prē-wawn′], *v.t.* to warn beforehand. [PRE and WARN].

PREY (1), [prā], *n.* an animal hunted and devoured by another; (*fig.*) a person, thing, that becomes an easy victim of another person, or of circumstances; booty. [ME. *preie*, OFr. *preie* from L. *praeda* booty].

PREY (2), [prā], *v.i.* to seize for prey, devour; rob, swindle, despoil, devour, wear down, eat away. [ME. *preien*, OFr. *preier* from LL. *predare*].

PREYER, [prā-yer], *n.* one who preys (upon).

PRIAPEAN, [prī-a-pē′-an], *adj.* relating to Priapus, pertaining to sexuality or fertility; grossly lustful and obscene. [L. *Priapeius*].

PRIAPISM, [prī′-ap-izm], *n.* (*path.*) persistent morbid erection of the penis. [Gk. *priapismos*].

PRIAPUS, [prī-āp′-us], *n.* the Greek and Roman phallic god, the deity of procreation, sensuality, and fertility. [Gk. *Priapos*].

PRICE (1), [prīs], *n.* the exchange value of anything, the value received as recompense for any goods, service, or expenditure; the marked value of goods offered for sale; recompense, value, worth; (*betting*) odds; **starting p.,** the odds offered on a horse, etc., at the last moment before the race begins. [ME. *price*, OFr. *pris* from L. *pretium*].

PRICE (2), [prīs], *v.t.* to set a price on, value at. [PRICE (1)].

PRICELESS, [prīs′-les], *adj.* beyond price, irreplaceable, enormously valuable; (*slang*) remarkably witty or amusing, utterly absurd.

PRICER, [prīs′-er], *n.* one who prices goods.

PRICK (1), [prik], *n.* a sharp, pointed, slender, piercing object, a goad, a thorn, a discomfort, misfortune; a slight wound inflicted by a needle, sword-point, thorn, etc., the feeling of such a wound; a qualm; a small mark or dot; **to kick against the pricks,** to rebel against the inevitable. [OE. *prica*].

PRICK (2), [prik], *v.t. and i.* to pierce, stab with a sharp, pointed object, to wound with a prick; to make holes (in) by pricking, to spur (a horse); to point; to wound by pricking; to feel such a wound or pain, to spur on, ride (a horse) vigorously; (of animal ears) to stiffen in attention. [OE. *prician*].

PRICKEARED, [prik′-ēerd], *adj.* with erect, pricked-up ears.

PRICKER, [prik′-er], *n.* that which pricks; an instrument for pricking.

PRICKET, [prik′-et], *n.* a two-year-old buck; a primitive spiked candlestick. [MedL. *prikettus*].

PRICKING, [prik′-ing], *n.* the act of pricking; a feeling as of being pricked.

PRICKLE (1), [prikl], *n.* a growth, process of pricks or spines on the surface of a tree or plant, the spines of the hedgehog, etc.; a pricking sensation in the skin; a basket of twigs. [OE. *pricel*].

PRICKLE (2), [prikl], *v.t. and i.* to prick; to feel prickly, to have a pricking in the skin. [PRICKLE (1)].

PRICKLE-BACK, [prikl′-bak], *n.* a small fish; a stickleback; any species of *Gasterosteus*.

PRICKLE-BACK

PRICKLETANG, [prikl′-tang], *n.* the seaweed *Fucus serratus*.

PRICKLINESS, [prik′-li-nes], *n.* the state of being prickly, of having prickles.

PRICKLY, [prik′-li], *adj.* pricking, covered with

prickles; causing a tingling in the skin as if being pricked.

PRICKLY-ASH, [prik'-li-ash], *n.* the toothache tree, *Zanthoxylum fraxineum.*

PRICKLY-HEAT, [prik'-li-hēt'], *n.* a skin eruption caused by inflammation of the sweat glands.

PRICKLY-PEAR, [prik'-li-pāer'], *n.* the cactus *Opuntia*, or its fruit.

PRICKPUNCH, [prik'-punch'], *n.* a piece of tempered steel with a round point.

PRICKSONG, [prik'-song], *n.* music written in dots; counterpoint noted above the plain-song.

PRICKWOOD, [prik'-wŏod], *n.* the dogwood, *Cornus sanguinea*, or the spindle-tree, *Euonymus europæus.*

PRIDE (1), [prīd], *n.* a feeling of self-esteem, merit, and self-satisfaction; a proper awareness of one's own superiority; arrogance; conceit; the display of this self-satisfaction as a motive of action and conduct; pleasure, satisfaction felt in the merits or achievements of something with which one has identified oneself; flamboyant pomp; radiant beauty; a troop (of lions), a flock (of peacocks); **in his p.,** (of a peacock) with wings and tail extended. [OE. *pryto, pryde* from L. *prodesse* to be profitable].

PRIDE (2), [prīd], *v.reflex.* **to p. oneself on,** to take pride in, claim credit for. [ME. *pruden, priden*].

PRIDELESS, [prīd'-les], *adj.* without pride or self-respect.

PRIDIAN, [prid'-i-an], *adj.* relating to the previous day. [L. *pridianus*].

PRIER, [prī-er], *n.* one who pries.

PRIEST (1), prēst], *n.* one whose office it is to perform sacred rites and act as intermediary between the people and God; a Roman Catholic cleric; (*eccles.*) a cleric below the rank of bishop and above that of deacon; a mallet used to kill fish. [OE. *preost* from Gk. *presbuteros*].

PRIEST (2), [prēst], *v.t.* to ordain a priest. [PRIEST (1)].

PRIESTCRAFT, [prēst-krahft], *n.* the exercise of the priestly office; clerical policy directed towards political control.

PRIESTESS, [prēst'-es], *n.* a female priest.

PRIESTHOOD, [prēst'-hŏod], *n.* the office of a priest; priests or the priestly order.

PRIEST-LIKE, [prēst'-līk], *adj.* like a priest in character or behaviour.

PRIESTLINESS, [prēst'-li-nes], *n.* the state or quality of being priestly.

PRIESTLY, [prēst'-li], *adj.* like, relating to, a priest or the priesthood.

PRIEST-RIDDEN, [prēst'-ridn], *adj.* governed by, overrun by, priests.

PRIG (1), [prig], *n.* a prim, precise, conventional, conceited person, sure of his own morality and shocked by, or disdainful of, everyone else's. [Uncert.].

PRIG (2), (prigging, prigged), [prig], *v.t.* to steal, pick pockets. [Uncert.].

PRIGGERY, [prig'-er-i], *n.* the fact or quality of being priggish.

PRIGGISH, [prig'-ish], *adj.* having the characteristics and ideas of a prig.

PRIGGISHLY, [prig'-ish-li], *adv.* in priggish fashion.

PRIGGISHNESS, [prig'-ish-nes], *n.* the quality of being priggish.

PRIGGISM, [prig'izm], *n.* priggishness.

PRILL, [pril], *n.* a fish like the turbot without the tubercles, the brill, *Rhombus lævis*; a solid piece of pure ore. [Uncert.].

PRIM, [prim], *adj.* neatly conventional, proper, easily shocked, restrained to the point of repression in the less respectable physical enjoyments. [Uncert.].

PRIMACY, [prī'-mas-i], *n.* the state of being first, predominating, pre-eminent; the office of a primate. [MedL. *primatia*].

PRIMA DONNA, [prē'-ma don'-a], *n.* the principal female singer in an opera. [It. *prima donna* first lady].

PRIMAEVAL, see PRIMEVAL.

PRIMAEVALLY, see PRIMEVALLY.

PRIMAGE, [prī'-mij], *n.* a charge (additional to the freight charge) for loading cargo. [LL. *primagium*].

PRIMAL, [prīm'-al], *adj.* primary. [MedL. *primalis*].

PRIMALITY, [prīm-al'-it-i], *n.* the state of being primal.

PRIMARILY, [prīm'-er-il-i], *adv.* originally, chiefly, mainly.

PRIMARINESS, [prīm'-er-i-nes], *n.* the state of being primary.

PRIMARY, [prīm'-eri], *adj.* first in time or importance, principal; original, elementary, preparatory, rudimentary; (*geol.*) of the lowest, Palaeozoic, strata; (*elect.*) producing current; **p. colours,** fundamental colours from whose mixture others are derived. [L. *primarius* of the first rank].

PRIMATE, [prīm'-at], *n.* the chief ecclesiastic in a prelatic national church; an archbishop; **P. of all England,** the Archbishop of Canterbury; **P. of England,** the Archbishop of York. [LL. *primas* principal].

PRIMATES, [prīm-āt'-ēz], *n.(pl.)* the order of mammals which includes man, the anthropoid apes, the monkeys and the lemurs. [L. *primates, pl.* of *primas* principal].

PRIMATESHIP, [prīm'-at-ship], *n.* the office or dignity of a primate.

PRIMATIAL, [prīm-ā'-shal], *adj.* pertaining to a primate.

PRIME (1), [prīm], *n.* the best or earliest period of a thing, the most vigorous period of a person's life; the first of the day canonical hours; a guard in fencing; that which is prime. [OE. *prim* from L. (*hora*) *prima* the first canonical hour].

PRIME (2), [prīm], *adj.* first in time, rank or importance; of the highest quality; vigorous, initial, essential, fundamental; **P. Minister,** the chief minister of the Cabinet; **p. mover,** (*mech.*) the initial source of motive power; **p. number,** (*math.*) a number divisible only by one or itself. [L. *primus* first].

PRIME (3), [prīm], *v.t.* and *i.* to charge, fill up (with), *esp.* a firearm, with explosive, or a person with food or information; to lay on a first coat of paint; to impregnate; to act as priming for a firearm. [PRIME (2)].

PRIMELY, [prīm'-li], *adv.* excellently, healthily.

PRIMENESS, [prīm'-nes], *n.* fine condition.

PRIMER (1), [prīm'-er], *n.* a book of hours for the use of laymen; an elementary text-book; a kind of type. [L. *primarius*].

PRIMER (2), [prīm'-er], *n.* a small explosive device for firing a gun, bomb, or charge.

PRIMERO, [prim-āer'-ō], *n.* a 16th-century card game. [Span. *primero*].

PRIMEVAL, PRIMAEVAL, [prīm-ēv'-al], *adj.* belonging to the earliest times, prehistoric, ancient. [L. *primaevus*].

PRIMEVALLY, PRIMAEVALLY, [prīm-ēv'-al-i], *adv.* in primaeval fashion.

PRIMIGENIAL, [prīm'-i-jē'-ni-al], *adj.* primigenous.

PRIMIGENOUS, [prīm-ij'-in-us], *adj.* original, first created. [L. *primigenus*].

PRIMINE, [prīm'-in], *n.* (*bot.*) the outer integument of an ovule. [Fr. *primine*].

PRIMING, [prīm'-ing], *n.* the act of priming; the powder, etc., exploding a charge; the first coat of paint.

PRIMIPAROUS, [prīm-ip'-er-us], *adj.* bearing young for the first time. [L. *primipara* an animal that has given birth for the first time].

PRIMITIAE, [prīm-ish'-i-ī], *n.(pl.)* first fruits; (*eccles.*) first year's profits of a living. [L. *primitiae*].

PRIMITIVE, [prim'-it-iv], *adj.* related to the earliest stage of development; prehistoric; rude, original; uncivilized; unelaborated; (*art*) antecedent to the Renaissance. [L. *primitivus*].

PRIMITIVELY, [prim'-it-iv-li], *adv.* in the beginning; in primitive fashion.

PRIMITIVENESS, [prim'-it-iv-nes], *n.* the state of being primitive.

PRIMLY, [prim'-li], *adv.* in prim fashion.

PRIMNESS, [prim'-nes], *n.* the state or quality of being prim.

PRIMO, [prē'-mō], *n.* (*mus.*) the leading part. [It. *primo* first].

PRIMOGENITAL, [prīm'-ō-je'-nit-al], *adj.* first-born, primary, original.

PRIMOGENITARY, [prīm'-ō-jen'-it-e-ri], *adj.* primogenitive. [L. *primogenitus* first-born].

PRIMOGENITIVE, [prīm'-ō-jen'-it-iv], *adj.* relating to primogeniture or a primogenitor.

PRIMOGENITOR, [prīm'-ō-jen'-it-or], *n.* the first begetter. [MedL. *primogenitor*].

PRIMOGENITURE, [prīm'-ō-jen'-i-chŏoer], *n.* (*leg.*) the system by which the eldest son inherits the whole of his father's property. [MedL. *primogenitura*].

PRIMOGENITURESHIP, [prīm'-ō-jen'-i-chŏoer-ship], *n.* the rights of the eldest son under primogeniture.

PRIMORDIAL, [prīm-awd'-i-al], *adj.* primary, existing from the beginning, first-created. [MedL. *primordialis*].

PRIMORDIALLY, [prīm-awd'-i-al-i], *adv.* from the beginning, originally.

PRIMORDIATE, [prīm-awd'-i-āt], *adj.* first-created, existing from the beginning.

PRIMP, [primp], *v.t. and reflex.* (*U.S.*) to prink. [PRINK].
PRIMROSE, [prim'-rōz], *n.* the yellow spring flower, *Primula veris*; the yellow colour of this flower. [MedL. *prima rosa* the first rose].

PRIMROSE

PRIMULA, [prim'-yŏŏ-la], *n.* the genus including the primrose. [L. *primula*].
PRIMUM MOBILE, [prīm'-um-mōb'-il-i], *n.* (*hist. astron.*) the first cause of motion in the universe; the outer revolving sphere of the heavens. [L. *primum mobile* first movable thing].
PRIMUS, [prīm'-us], *n.* the eldest of several brothers; the presiding bishop of the Scottish Episcopal Church. [L. *primus* first].
PRINCE, [prins], *n.* a ruler, a potentate; a male relation of the ruling monarch. [Fr. *prince* from L. *princeps*].
PRINCEDOM, [prins'-dum], *n.* the territory or dignity of a prince.
PRINCELIKE, [prins'-lik], *adj.* like a prince, fitting for a prince.
PRINCELINESS, [prins'-li-nes], *n.* the state of being princely.
PRINCELING, [prins'-ling], *n.* a young prince; an unimportant ruler.
PRINCELY, [prins'-li], *adj.* like, befitting, a prince; splendidly lavish.
PRINCE'S-METAL, [prins'-iz-met'-al], *n.* a false gold, made of zinc and copper.
PRINCESS, [prin-ses'], *n.* a female relation of a ruling monarch. [ME. *princesse* from OFr. *princesse*].
PRINCESSE, [prin-ses'], *n.* a woman's close-fitting, one-piece gown, called after Queen Alexandra, when Princess of Wales.
PRINCIPAL (1), [prin'-sip-al], *n.* the head of an institution, the principal person; the capital sum on which interest is paid; one of the chief parties in a transaction. [PRINCIPAL (2)].
PRINCIPAL (2), [prin'-sip-al], *adj.* most important, first, highest in rank. [L. *principalis*].
PRINCIPALITY, [prin'-sip-al'-it-i], *n.* the territory of a reigning prince, the power, authority, reign of a prince; an independent territorial unit less than a kingdom; †a ruler, power, potentate, an order of angels. [MedL. *principalitas*].
PRINCIPALLY, [prin'-sip-al-i], *adv.* chiefly, mainly, in the principal respect.
PRINCIPALNESS, [prin'-sip-al-nes], *n.* the condition of being principal.
PRINCIPATE, [prin'-si-pāt'], *n.* the office or tenure of a prince or ruler; (*Rom. hist.*) the rule of the earliest Roman emperors when some of the forms of the Republic were still retained. [L. *principatus*].
PRINCIPIA, [prin-sip'-i-a], *n.(pl.)* the first, fundamental principles of a science or study. [L. *principium* beginning].
PRINCIPIANT, [prin-sip'-i-ant], *adj.* relating to principle or principles. [OFr. *principiant*].
PRINCIPLE, [prin'-sipl], *n.* the fundamental essence, first origin of a thing; a basic truth from which other deductions can be made; a fundamental moral conviction, moral tenet, from which rules of conduct can be derived; a constituent substance from which particular qualities can be derived. (L. *principium* beginning).
PRINK, [pringk], *v.i.* to dress showily, to have a fine conceit for clothes and appearance. [PRANK].
PRINKER, [pringk'-er], *n.* one who prinks.
PRINT (1), [print], *n.* a mark or impression on anything made by the pressure of another body; a die designed for making such impressions, an impression produced by a die, *esp.* lettering, printed matter; a picture or representation reproduced from an engraved metal plate; (*phot.*) a positive picture made from a negative; (*textiles*) fabric stamped with a pattern by means of dies; **in p.**, printed, published; still for sale as freshly printed; **out of p.**, (of books, etc.) no longer obtainable except at second hand. [ME. *printe* stamp, impression from OFr. *priente, preinte*].
PRINT (2), [print], *v.t. and i.* to mark by pressure, to stamp with a mark, to imprint, (*fig*) to leave a strong impression (on the mind, face, etc.), to reproduce words by stamping paper with inked type, to cause to be so reproduced, to publish in printed form, to write so that each letter is separate, like a printed character; (*phot.*) to obtain a positive of by exposing the negative to light; to practise the art of a printer. [ME. *prenten*].
PRINTABLE, [print'-abl], *adj.* able or fit to be printed.
PRINTER, [print'-er], *n.* one who prints, *esp.* one who prints (books, etc.) for publication.
PRINTING, [print'-ing], *n.* the art of the printer, the style, mode, in which a thing is printed; the whole amount of books, pamphlets, etc., printed at one time; handwriting in which every letter is written separately in capitals; typography.
PRINTING-INK, [print'-ing-ingk'], *n.* ink used for printing.
PRINTING-MACHINE, [print'-ing-mash-ēn'], *n.* a mechanical printing-press.
PRINTING-OFFICE, [print'-ing-of'-is], *n.* a place where printing is carried out.
PRINTING-PAPER, [print'-ing-pā'-per], *n.* paper used in printing.
PRINTING-PRESS, [print'-ing-pres'], *n.* a machine for printing.
PRINTLESS, [print'-les], *adj.* without print, making no impression.
PRINTSELLER, [print'-sel-er], *n.* a dealer in engravings and pictorial prints.
PRINTSHOP, [print'-shop], *n.* the shop of a printseller.
PRINT-WORKS, [print'-wurks], *n.* a factory for the mechanical printing of fabrics.
PRIOR (1), [prī'-or], *n.* the superior of a monastery, the next in rank to an abbot. [ME. *priour* from L. *prior*].
PRIOR (2), [prī'-er], *adj.* previous, antecedent; first, demanding first attention. [L. *prior* former].
PRIORATE, [prī'-or-āt], *n.* the office, tenure of a prior. [MedL. *prioratus*].
PRIORESS, [prī'-or-es], *n.* the superioress of a convent.
PRIORITY, [pri-o'-rit-i], *n.* the state of being prior, the right to first consideration. [Fr. *priorité*].
PRIORSHIP, [prī'-or-ship], *n.* the office of prior.
PRIORY, [prī'-er-i], *n.* a monastic community governed by a prior. [ME. *priorie* from MedL. *prioria*].
PRISE, [prīz], *v.i.* to force (open) with a lever; (*fig.*) to open, force out, by indirect pressure. [Fr. *prise, p.pt.* of *prendre* to take].
PRISM, [prizm], *n.* (*geom.*) any solid figure with similar, equal, and parallel bases, and whose sides are parallelograms; (*opt.*) a transparent body with parallel bases and rectangular sides used for refracting light; any refracting body resembling this. [Gk. *prisma* something sawn off].

PRISMS

PRISMATIC, [priz-mat'-ik], *adj.* of, employing, shaped like, a prism, refractive, capable of being refracted, iridescent; **p. colours**, colours in sunlight that may be separated by a prism.
PRISMATICALLY, [priz-mat'-ik-al-i], *adv.* in the manner of, or by means of, a prism.
PRISMATOIDAL, [priz'-mat-oid'-al], *adj.* in the shape of a prism. [PRISMATIC and Gk. *oeides* like].
PRISMOID, [priz'-moid], *n.* a body shaped like a prism, but without equal bases. [PRISM and Gk. *oeides* like].
PRISMOIDAL, [priz-moid'-al], *adj.* like a prismoid.
PRISMY, [priz'-mi], *adj.* resembling a prism.
PRISON (1), [priz'-on], *n.* a place of confinement, that which confines, *esp.* a building devoted to the confinement of those obnoxious to the government or to society. [OFr. *prisun*].
PRISON (2), [priz'-on], *v.t.* to imprison, confine. [PRISON (1)].
PRISON-BREAKING, [priz'-on-brāk'-ing], *n.* escape from prison, *esp.* on a mass scale.
PRISONER, [priz'-on-er], *n.* one imprisoned, held in confinement or captivity, one detained or restricted by any person or situation, a person sentenced to imprisonment or detained and charged with a criminal offence. [OFr. *prisonier*].
PRISON-HOUSE, [priz'-on-hows'], *n.* a prison.
PRISTINE, [pris'-tēn], *adj.* primitive, belonging to an early age; former; fresh, undiminished. [L. *pristinus*].
PRITHEE, [prith'-i], *int.* †pray. [*I pray thee*].
PRITTLE-PRATTLE, [pritl'-pratl'], *n.* tittle-tattle.
PRIVACY, [prīv'-as-i, pri'-va-si], *n.* the state of being private; secrecy, freedom from observation. [PRIVATE].
PRIVATE (1), [prīv'-it], *n.* (*milit.*) a common soldier,

a soldier without command over others; (*pl.*) the sexual organs. [PRIVATE (2)].
PRIVATE (2), [prīv'-it], *adj.* peculiar to an individual, not public, concerning only a particular thing; secluded, undisturbed; **p. parts,** the sexual organs. [L. *privatum, p.pt.* of *privare* to set apart].
PRIVATEER, [prīv'-at-ēer], *n.* a privately owned ship licensed to make war on behalf of its government; a sailor in such a vessel.
PRIVATEERING, [prīv'-at-ēer'-ing], *n.* the activities of a privateer.
PRIVATEERSMAN, [prīv'-at-ēerz'-man], *n.* a privateer.
PRIVATELY, [prīv'-at-li], *adv.* in private fashion.
PRIVATENESS, [prīv'-at-nes], *n.* the state of being private.
PRIVATION, [prīv-ā'-shun], *n.* hardship, destitution, absence of comfort. [L. *privatio*].
PRIVATIVE, [priv'-at-iv], *adj.* causing privation; (*gram.*) implying deprivation. [L. *privativus*].
PRIVATIVELY, [priv'-at-iv-li], *adv.* in privative fashion.
PRIVET, [priv'-it], *n.* the shrub, *Ligustrum vulgare,* used for making garden hedges. [Uncert.].
PRIVILEGE (1), [priv'-il-ij], *n.* an advantage or benefit peculiar to a particular person or body, and not shared in by others; prerogative; that which confers a peculiar advantage. [L. *privilegium* a private law].
PRIVILEGE (2), [priv'-il-ij], *v.t.* to allow special advantages or immunities to. [PRIVILEGE (1)].
PRIVILEGED, [priv'-il-ijd], *adj.* having a privilege, enjoying special immunity.
PRIVILY, [priv'-i-li], *adv.* in privy fashion.
PRIVITY, [priv'-it-i], *n.* private agreement with, or knowledge of, a thing; the state of being private. [OFr. *privité*].
PRIVY (1), [priv'-i], *n.* a water-closet; (*leg.*) one having an interest in a lawsuit. [PRIVY (2)].
PRIVY (2), [priv'-i], *adj.* knowing what is secret, private; **p. council,** an advisory council appointed directly by the king; **p. purse,** the sovereign's private money. [ME. *privy* from OFr. *privé*].
PRIZAGE, [prīz'-ij], *n.* the part of a lawful prize taken by the Crown.
PRIZE (1), [prīz], *n.* that which is captured in war, *esp.* a ship captured from the enemy; a reward for merit, a reward won by chance; a very valuable or envied acquisition. [ME. *prise* from L. *pretium* price].
PRIZE (2), [prīz], *adj.* won, awarded as a prize; (*coll.*) excellent, extreme, excessive; **p. money,** money given to the crew of a ship that has taken an enemy vessel. [PRIZE (1)].
PRIZE (3), [prīz], *v.t.* to esteem highly, hold valuable. [ME. *prisen* from OFr. *prisier*].
PRIZE-FIGHT, [prīz'-fīt], *n.* a boxing-match for money.
PRIZEMAN, [prīz'-man], *n.* the winner of a university prize.
PRIZE-MASTER, [prīz'-mahst'-er], *n.* the officer who takes charge of a prize in port.
PRIZE-RING, [prīz'-ring], *n.* the ring where a prize-fight takes place, a boxing-ring.
PRO- (1), *pref.* for, in favour of, on behalf of, before (in place). [L. *pro*].
PRO (2), [prō], *n.* (*coll.*) a professional sportsman. [Abbreviation of PROFESSIONAL].
PROA, [prō'-a], *n.* a Malay canoe with outrigger and lateen sails. [Malay *prau*].
PROBABILISM, [prob'-ab-il-izm], *n.* the doctrine that, in the absence of certain knowledge, the probable may be taken as the true.
PROBABILIST, [prob'-ab-il-ist], *n.* a believer in probabilism.
PROBABILITY, [prob-ab-il'-it-i], *n.* the state of being probable, likelihood; the more probable of several alternatives. [L. *probabilitas*].

PROA

PROBABLE, [prob'-abl], *adj.* likely, having more of the apparent evidence on its side. [L. *probabilis*].
PROBABLY, [prob'-ab-li], *adv.* more likely than not.
PROBANG, [prō'-bang], *n.* (*med.*) a piece of bone tipped with sponge, used for removing obstructions from the throat. [Uncert.].
PROBATE, [prōb'-et], *n.* the official proof of wills, a certified copy of a will so proved; **Court of P.,** a court having jurisdiction over wills, etc. [L. *probatum, p.pt.* of *probare* to prove].
PROBATION, [prōb-ā'-shun], *n.* the act of proving; the state of being under trial; (*leg.*) a system by which a sentence is suspended on the condition that the offender report every so often. [L. *probatio*].
PROBATIONAL, [prob-ā'-shunl], *adj.* relating to, under, probation.
PROBATIONARY, [prob-ā'-shun-eri], *adj.* probational.
PROBATIONER, [prob-ā'-shun-er], *n.* a novice in certain religious orders; a nurse, teacher, etc., in the early stages of training; an offender dismissed under probation.
PROBATIVE, [prōb'-at-iv], *adj.* serving as proof. [L. *probativus*].
PROBATOR, [prōb-āt'-er], *n.* an examiner. [L. *probator*].
PROBATORY, [prōb-āt'-eri], *adj.* relating to probation; serving for proof. [MedL. *probatorius*].
PROBE (1), [prōb], *n.* (*med.*) an instrument for probing into a wound; (*U.S.*) a thorough investigation or enquiry. [L. *proba* proof].
PROBE (2), [prōb], *v.t.* to examine (a wound) by inserting an instrument into (it), to examine by poking; (*fig.*) to investigate thoroughly. [PROBE (1)].
PROBE-SCISSORS, [prōb'-siz'-ors], *n.*(*pl.*) scissors used in exploring wounds.
PROBITY, [prōb'-it-i], *n.* proved integrity. [L. *probitas*].
PROBLEM (1), [prob'-lem], *n.* something to be solved, a question involving uncertainty and difficulty; (*geom.*) a proposition to be solved, *esp.* by introducing new factors. [ME. *probleme* from Gk. *problema*].
PROBLEM (2), [prob'-lem], *adj.* relating to, or containing, a problem; **p. child,** a child whose behaviour is so unbalanced as to call for special treatment; **p. play,** a play whose theme is a moral or social problem; **p. picture,** a picture whose subject is obscure.
PROBLEMATICAL, [prob'-lem-at'-ikl], *adj.* questionable, relating to a problem.
PROBLEMATICALLY, [prob'-lem-at'-ik-al-i], *adv.* in problematical fashion.
PROBLEMATIZE, [prob'-lem-at-īz], *v.i.* to propose problems.
PROBLEMIST, [prob'-lem-ist], *n.* a deviser of problems, a student of mathematical problems.
PROBOSCIDEAN, PROBOSCIDIAN (1), [prob'-os-id'-i-an], *n.* an animal with a trunk; (*zool.*) a member of the mammalian order, *Proboscidea.*
PROBOSCIDEAN, PROBOSCIDIAN (2), [prob'-os-id'-i-an], *adj.* relating to a proboscis or a proboscidean.
PROBOSCIS, [prob-os'-is], *n.* a prolongation of the nose, as in the elephant; (*slang*) a large nose. [Gk. *proboskis* an elephant's trunk].
PROCATARCTIC, [prō'-kat-ahk'-tik], *adj.* antecedent. [Gk. *prokatarktikos*].
PROCATARXIS, [prō'-kat-ahk'-sis], *n.* the increasing of disease by a prior cause. [Gk. *prokatarxis*].
PRO-CATHEDRAL, [prō'-kath-ē'-dral], *n.* a church used temporarily for a cathedral.
PROCEDURE, [pro-sē'-jer], *n.* technique, proper fashion in which to perform or proceed. [Fr. *procédure*].
PROCEED, [pro-sēd'], *v.i.* to move (from or towards a place); to make progress; to begin to do or perform; to behave in some fashion. [L. *procedere*].
PROCEEDER, [pro-sēd'-er], *n.* one who proceeds.
PROCEEDING, [pro-sēd'-ing], *n.* the act of performing something, a transaction, a mode of doing; (*pl.*) the mode, act of doing some action, of carrying out an action.
PROCEEDS, [prō'-sēdz], *n.*(*pl.*) the money gained by an action or performance.
PROCEPHALIC, [prō-sef'-al'-ik], *adj.* relating to the front of the head. [PRO (1) and CEPHALIC].
PROCERITY, [prō-se'-rit-i], *n.* height. [L. *proceritas*].
PROCESS (1), [prō'-ses], *n.* a method of doing a thing, a mode of doing in which each step proceeds out of that which precedes it, all the stages of a development regarded as a whole; (*leg.*) the whole course of court proceedings; (*anat.*) a bony protuberance; (*bot.*) a structure; (*print.*) the making of printing blocks by photography. [L. *processus* advance].
PROCESS (2), [prō'-ses], *v.t.* to make a printing block of by photography; to subject to a process. [*Prec.*].
PROCESSION, [prō-sesh'-un], *n.* the act of proceeding, that which proceeds; a number of persons or things proceeding past a point, *esp.* if formally arranged. [L. *processio*].
PROCESSIONAL, [prō-sesh'-un-al], *adj.* relating

to a procession, *esp.* to those in the Roman Catholic Church.

PROCESSIONARY, [prō-sesh'-un-er-i], *adj.* moving in procession.

PROCHRONISM, [prō'-kron-izm], *n.* an error in chronology in assigning an event to too early a date, ante-dating. [Gk. *prokhronos*].

PROCIDENCE, [prō'-sid-ents], *n.* (*med.*) a prolapsus. [L. *procidentia*].

PROCIDUOUS, [prō-sid'-yōō-us], *adj.* falling from its place. [L. *prociduus*].

PROCLAIM, [pro-klām'], *v.t.* to announce publicly, promulgate. [ME. *proclamen* from L. *proclamare*].

PROCLAIMER, [pro-klām'-er], *n.* one who proclaims.

PROCLAMATION, [prok'-lam-ā'-shun], *n.* an official public announcement; the act of proclaiming. [L. *proclamatio*].

PROCLITIC (1), [prō-klit'-ik], *n.* (*gram.*) a word prefixed to another word and thereby losing its own accent. [PRO and (EN)CLITIC].

PROCLITIC (2), [prō-klit'-ik], *adj.* (*gram.*) of, pertaining to, or resembling, a proclitic or its functions.

PROCLIVITY, [prō-kliv'-it-i], *n.* inclination. [L. *proclivitas*].

PROCOELOUS, [prō-sēl'-us], *adj.* concave in front. [PRO and Gk. *koilos* hollow].

PROCONSUL, [prō-kon'-sul], *n.* (*Rom. hist.*) the governor of a senatorial province. [L. *proconsul*].

PROCONSULAR, [prō-kon'-syōōl-er], *adj.* pertaining to a proconsul. [L. *proconsulatus*].

PROCONSULATE, [prō-kon'-syōōl-at], *n.* the office of a proconsul. [L. *proconsularis*].

PROCONSULSHIP, [prō-kon'-sul-ship], *n.* the tenure of a proconsul.

PROCRASTINATE, [prō-kras'-tin-āt], *v.t.* and *i.* to postpone continually; to delay. [L. *procrastinatum*, *p.pt.* of *procrastinare*].

PROCRASTINATION, [prō-kras'-tin-ā'-shun], *n.* the act of procrastinating. [L. *procrastinatio*].

PROCRASTINATOR, [prō-kras'-tin-āt-er], *n.* one who procrastinates.

PROCRASTINATORY, [prō-kras'-tin-āt'-er-i], *adj.* dilatory.

PROCREANT, [prō'-kri-ant], *adj.* generating, begetting. [L. *procreans*, *pres.pt.* of *procreare*].

PROCREATE, [prō'-kri-āt], *v.t.* and *i.* to beget. [L. *procreatus*, *p.pt.* of *procreare*].

PROCREATION, [prō'-kri-ā'-shun], *n.* the act of procreating. [L. *procreatio*].

PROCREATIVE, [prō'-kri-āt'-iv], *adj.* able to, tending to, procreate.

PROCREATIVENESS, [prō'-kri-āt'-iv-nes], *n.* the condition of being procreative.

PROCREATOR, [prō'-kri-āt'-er], *n.* one who begets; a male parent. [L. *procreator*].

PROCRUSTEAN, [prō-krust'-i-an], *adj.* seeking to produce uniformity by violence. [*Procrustes*, the name of a legendary highway robber in Greek legend who enticed travellers into his dwelling, and then either stretched them or cut off their extremities to make them fit his bed].

PROCTALGIA, [prok-tal'-ja], *n.* a pain in the anus. [Gk. *proktos* anus and *algos* pain].

PROCTOR (1), [prok'-tor], *n.* an agent who manages the affairs of, and represents, his employer; (*eccles.*) the representative of a cathedral chapter or the clergy of a diocese at convocation; one of two disciplinary officials at Oxford and Cambridge, who in theory represent the Masters of Arts of the university; **King's P.,** the representative of the Crown in probate and matrimonial causes with power to intervene to prevent collusion. [ME. *proketour* from L. *procurator*].

PROCTOR (2), [prok'-tor], *v.i.* to act as a proctor. [PROCTOR (1)].

PROCTORAGE, [prok'-tor-ij], *n.* management by proctor.

PROCTORIAL, [prok-taw'-ri-al], *adj.* of, or pertaining to, a proctor.

PROCTORIZE, [prok'-tor-īz], *v.t.* and *i.* to exercise proctorial authority, to perform the duties of a proctor ; to bring before the proctors.

PROCTORSHIP, [prok'-tor-ship], *n.* the office of proctor.

PROCUMBENT, [prō-kum'-bent], *adj.* lying with the face downwards, prone; (*bot.*) (of the stem of certain plants) trailing along the ground without making roots. [L. *procumbens*, *pres.pt.* of *procumbere* to fall forwards].

PROCURABLE, [pro-kyōōer'-abl], *adj.* able to be procured or obtained.

PROCURATION, [prok'-yōō-rā'-shun], *n.* the function of a procurator or agent acting on another's behalf; the empowering or appointment of a procurator or proxy. [L. *procuratio* management].

PROCURATOR, [prok'-yōō-rāt-or], *n.* the official agent or proxy of another; (*eccles.*) an agent in an ecclesiastical law-court; (*Rom. hist.*) a treasury official in ancient Rome whose duty was to collect taxes, pay soldiers, etc., in whatever province he was appointed. [L. *procurator*].

PROCURATORIAL, [prok'-yōō-rat-aw'-ri-al], *adj.* pertaining to the office of a procurator.

PROCURATORSHIP, [prok'-yōō-rāt'-or-ship], *n.* the office and duties of procurator.

PROCURATORY, [prok'-yōō-rāt'-er-i], *n.* **letters of p.,** (in civil and Scots law) authorization to act as an agent or proxy. [LL. *procuratorius* pertaining to an agent or procurator].

PROCURATRIX, [prok'-yōō-rat-riks], *n.* the inmate of a nunnery who attends to its business affairs. [L. *procuratrix* a female agent].

PROCURE, [pro-kyōōer'], *v.t.* to obtain, acquire, purchase; to cause, bring about; to obtain (objects of sexual satisfaction) for another. [Fr. *procurer* from L. *procurare* to take care of, manage].

PROCUREMENT, [pro-kyōōer'-ment], *n.* the action of procuring.

PROCURER, [pro-kyōōer'-er], *n.* one who procures; a pimp or pander. [OFr. *procureour*].

PROCURESS, [prok'-yōō-res], *n.* a bawd.

PROCYON, [prō'-si-on], *n.* the lesser dog-star, the chief star in the constellation *Canis minor.* [L. *Procyon*].

PROD, (**prodding, prodded**), [prod], *v.t.* to poke with a stick or similar instrument; (*fig.*) to urge or incite. [Uncert.].

PRODIGAL (1), [prod'-igl], *n.* a spendthrift; one who wastes his means. [PRODIGAL (2)].

PRODIGAL (2), [prod'-igl], *adj.* lavish, extravagant, and wasteful; given to lavish and unnecessary expenditure. [OFr. *prodigal* from L. *prodigus* lavish].

PRODIGALITY, [prod'-ig-al'-it-i], *n.* extravagance; wasteful expenditure. [Fr. *prodigalité*].

PRODIGALLY, [prod'-ig-al-i], *adv.* in a prodigal fashion.

PRODIGIOUS, [prod-ij'-us], *adj.* monstrous, abnormal; amazing; of large dimensions. [L. *prodigiosus*].

PRODIGIOUSLY, [prod-ij'-us-li], *adv.* in a prodigious way.

PRODIGIOUSNESS, [prod-ij'-us-nes], *n.* the condition or quality of being prodigious.

PRODIGY, [prod'-ij-i], *n.* an amazing phenomenon, a marvel; an amazing example; a person of abnormal powers. [L. *prodigium*].

PRODITION, [prod-ish'-un], *n.* treachery, betrayal. [L. *proditio*].

PRODITOR, [prōd'-it-or], *n.* a traitor or betrayer. [L. *proditor*].

PRODROMUS, (*pl.* **prodromi**), [prō'-drom-us], *n.* an introductory treatise. [MdL. *prodromus* from Gk. *prodromos* a precursor].

PRODUCE (1), [prod'-ews], *n.* that which is produced either by the labour of man or the action of nature; product. [PRODUCE (2)].

PRODUCE (2), [pro-dews'], *v.t.* and *i.* to bring forth, yield; to give rise to; to make; to present for inspection; (*geom.*) to extend (a line); **to p. a play,** to arrange the stage presentation, controlling and co-ordinating the work of the actors and all others concerned. [L. *producere* to lead forward].

PRODUCER, [pro-dews'-er], *n.* someone or something that produces; one who produces a play; (*films*) the person who directs or initiates the production of a film; **p. gas,** a gas made by passing air and steam through glowing coke.

PRODUCIBILITY, [pro-dews'-ib-il'-it-i], *n.* the quality of being producible.

PRODUCIBLE, [pro-dews'-ibl], *adj.* able to be produced.

PRODUCIBLENESS, [pro-dews'-ibl-nes], *n.* producibility.

PRODUCT, [prod'-ukt], *n.* that which is produced, produce; the result of labour or of natural growth or action; outcome, result; (*math.*) the result of multiplying one number by another; (*chem.*) a substance produced by chemical change or chemical action. [L. *productum*, *p.pt.* of *producere* to lead forward].

PRODUCTILE, [pro-dukt'-il], *adj.* capable of being extended.

PRODUCTION, [pro-duk'-shun], *n.* the act of producing; manufacture, creation; the act of producing a play; that which is produced, produce, product; a play produced, thought of as a play actually on the stage and not as a play written in a book; extension. [L. *productio* extension].

PRODUCTIONAL, [pro-duk'-shun-al], *adj.* of, or pertaining to, production.

PRODUCTIVE, [pro-dukt'-iv], *adj.* fertile, having the power to produce; yielding produce; giving results; causing; yielding wealth.

PRODUCTIVELY, [pro-dukt'-iv-li], *adv.* in a productive fashion.

PRODUCTIVENESS, [pro-dukt'-iv-nes], *n.* the condition or quality of being productive.

PRODUCTIVITY, [prod'-ukt-iv'-i-ti], *n.* productiveness.

PROEM, [prō'-im], *n.* a preface or prelude. [OFr. *proeme*, L. *proemium* from Gk. *prooimion* prelude].

PROEMIAL, [prō-ē'-mi-al], *adj.* prefatory.

PROEMPTOSIS, [prō'-emp-tō'-sis], *n.* the occurring of a natural event before its expected time. [MedL. *proemptosis*].

PROFANATION, [prof'-an-ā'-shun], *n.* the act of desecrating, the treating of sacred things with disrespect and irreverence. [EcclesL. *profanatio*].

PROFANE (1), [pro-fān'], *adj.* not holy; secular, pertaining to the world, to ordinary things and not to religion; not concerned with or connected with religious things, common, commonplace; heathen; blasphemous. [L. *profanus* unholy].

PROFANE (2), [pro-fān'], *v.t.* to desecrate, to commit profanation in; to vulgarize, to treat with disrespect; to use wrongly and dishonourably. [L. *profanare* to desecrate].

PROFANELY, [pro-fān'-li], *adv.* in a profane way; irreverently.

PROFANENESS, [pro-fān'-nes], *n.* the condition or quality of being profane.

PROFANER, [pro-fān'-er], *n.* one who profanes.

PROFANITY, [pro-fan'-i-ti], *n.* profaneness; blasphemy, profane talk. [EcclesL. *profanitas*].

PROFESS, [pro-fes'], *v.t.* and *i.* to declare, confess, affirm; to accept and practise as a religion; to follow as a calling; to teach in a professorial capacity; to pretend or feign; **to p. oneself,** to declare oneself to be. [L. *professus*, *p.pt.* of *profiteri* to profess].

PROFESSED, [pro-fest'], *adj.* openly declared and acknowledged; untruthfully declared.

PROFESSEDLY, [pro-fes'-id-li], *adj.* by open declaration, ostensibly, in accordance with, or according to, one's profession or statement.

PROFESSION, [pro-fesh'-un], *n.* a confession or statement, either true or untrue; a learned calling as distinct from a trade; the members and practitioners of such a calling; the act of taking religious vows before entering a religious order or community. [L. *professio* declaration].

PROFESSIONAL (1), [pro-fesh'-unl], *n.* one engaged in a profession or calling so as to earn his or her livelihood by it; one who plays a game for profit. [PROFESSIONAL (2)].

PROFESSIONAL (2), [pro-fesh'-unl], *adj.* belonging or pertaining to one of the learned callings; earning one's living as; trained in, so as to earn one's living by; characteristic of a profession; skilled.

PROFESSIONALISM, [prō-fesh'-un-al-izm], *n.* the practice of giving or receiving payment for participating in activities originally indulged in solely as recreation.

PROFESSIONALLY, [pro-fesh'-un-al-i], *adv.* in a professional way, from a professional point of view.

PROFESSOR, [pro-fes'-or], *n.* one who professes or believes in (a religious creed or doctrine); a teacher holding a chair of a subject at a university; a teacher. [L. *professor* a public teacher].

PROFESSORIAL, [prof'-es-aw'-ri-al], *adj.* pertaining to, or characteristic of, a professor.

PROFESSORSHIP, [pro-fes'-or-ship], *n.* the position of a professor.

PROFFER (1), [prof'-er], *n.* the act of proffering; that which is proffered; an offer or suggestion. [PROFFER (2)].

PROFFER (2), [prof'-er], *v.t.* to present, bring forward, for inspection or consideration, to propose or suggest; to offer as a present. [ME. *profren*, OFr. *profrir* from L. *proferre*].

PROFFERER, [prof'-er-er], *n.* one who proffers.

PROFICIENCY, [pro-fish'-en-si], *n.* the quality or state of being proficient.

PROFICIENT (1), [pro-fish'-ent], *n.* one who is proficient, an expert. [PROFICIENT].

PROFICIENT (2), [pro-fish'-ent], *adj.* competent, skilled, trained. [L. *proficiens*, *pres.pt.* of *proficere* to go forward].

PROFICIENTLY, [pro-fish'-ent-li], *adv.* in a proficient way.

PROFILE (1), [prō'-fīl', prō'-fēl], *n.* the side-view of a face; an outline drawing, *esp.* of a side-view, of a face; (*arch.*) the outline drawing of a vertical section. [It. *proffilo* (earlier *profilo*) an outline drawing].

PROFILE

PROFILE (2), [prō'-fīl', prō'-fēl], *v.t.* to draw in profile. [PROFILE (1)].

PROFILIST, [prō'-fil-ist], *n.* one who draws profiles or silhouettes.

PROFIT (1), [prof'-it], *n.* advantage or gain produced by labour or endeavour; pecuniary gain produced by commercial activity; (*pl.*) pecuniary gain; **gross p.**, the total pecuniary gain from any transaction or period of transaction, before the deduction of incidental and consequent costs; **net p.**, the pecuniary gain from a commercial transaction when all costs arising from the transaction have been deducted; **office of p.**, an office under the Crown which yields financial profit to the holder and which if accepted by a member of parliament formerly necessitated resignation from his seat. [L. *profectum* progress].

PROFIT (2), [prof'-it], *v.t.* and *i.* to benefit, yield profit to; to be useful to or of profit to; to gain profits or advantage; to make financial gains. [ME. *profiten*].

PROFITABLE, [prof'-it-abl], *adj.* being of use or benefit; yielding profit.

PROFITABLENESS, [prof'-it-abl-nes], *n.* the condition or quality of being profitable.

PROFITABLY, [prof'-it-ab-li], *adv.* in a profitable way, with advantage.

PROFITEER (1), [prof'-it-ēer'], *n.* a commercial opportunist who uses other people's necessity to make large and unjustifiable profits.

PROFITEER (2), [prof'-it-ēer'], *v.i.* to make large and unjustifiable profits by taking advantage of the hardship or necessity of other people. [PROFITEER (1)].

PROFITLESS, [prof'-it-les], *adj.* yielding no profit or benefit.

PROFITLESSLY, [prof'-it-les-li], *adv.* in a profitless way.

PROFLIGACY, [prof'-lig-a-si], *n.* profligate living; the condition or quality of being profligate.

PROFLIGATE (1), [prof'-lig-at], *n.* a dissipated and depraved person. [PROFLIGATE (2)].

PROFLIGATE (2), [prof'-lig-at], *adj.* dissolute and immoral; having no regard to morality and decency. [L. *profligatus* wretched, depraved].

PROFLIGATELY, [prot'-lig-at-li], *adv.* in a profligate way.

PROFLIGATENESS, [prof'-lig-at-nes], *n.* profligacy.

PROFLUENT, [prof'-lōō-ent], *adj.* flowing outward. [L. *profluens*, *pres.pt.* of *profluere* to flow out].

PROFOUND (1), [pro-fownd'], *n.* (*poet.*) the ocean; the vast reaches of space; a great abyss. [PROFOUND (2)].

PROFOUND (2), [pro-fownd'], *adj.* having great depth, very deep; showing rich intellectual powers or great intellectual thoroughness; subtle, not easily comprehended, but nevertheless felt to be true and justified; touching one's deepest feelings, moving one's heart to the full; (of a bow or curtsey) very low [OFr. *profund* from L. *profundus* deep].

PROFOUNDLY, [pro-fownd'-li], *adv.* in a profound fashion.

PROFOUNDNESS, [pro-fownd'-nes], *n.* profundity.

PROFUNDITY, [pro-fund'-iti], *n.* the state or quality of being profound; a deep, abstruse thought; a great abyss. [L. *profunditas* depth].

PROFUSE, [pro-fews'], *adj.* liberal to the point of prodigality; abundant. above necessity, copious. [L. *profusus* extended, lavish].

PROFUSELY, [pro-fews'-li], *adv.* in a profuse way.

PROFUSENESS, [pro-fews'-nes], *n.* profusion.

PROFUSION, [pro-few'-zhun], *n.* lavishness; extravagance; copious supply. [L. *profusio* copiousness].

PROG (1), [prog], *n.* (*slang*) food. [Unkn.].

PROG (2), [prog], *n.* a university proctor. [*Coll.* form of PROCTOR (1)].

PROG (3), (progging, progged), [prog], *v.t.* (*coll.*) to summon before a university proctor. [PROG (2)].

PROGENITIVE, [prō-jen′-it-iv], *adj.* able to beget offspring.

PROGENITOR, [prō-jen′-it-or], *n.* a forefather or ancestor. [ME. *progenitour* from L. *progenitor* ancestor].

PROGENITORIAL, [prō-jen′-it-aw′-ri-al], *adj.* of, or pertaining to, a progenitor.

PROGENITRESS, [prō-jen′-it-res], *n.* a female ancestor.

PROGENITRIX, [prō-jen′-it-riks], *n.* a progenitress.

PROGENITURE, [prō-jen′-ich-er], *n.* the act of begetting; ancestry.

PROGENY, [proj′-en-i], *n.* children, offspring or descendants. [L. *progenies* lineage, offspring].

PROGLOTTIS, [prō-glot′-is], *n.* a section of a tapeworm containing both male and female organs of reproduction, and so in itself capable of reproduction. [PRO (1) and Gk. *glottis* a mouthpiece].

PROGNATHIC, [prog-nath′-ik], *adj.* having jaws which project. [PRO (1) and GNATHIC].

PROGNATHISM, [prog′-nath-izm], *n.* the condition of being prognathic.

PROGNATHOUS, [prog′-nath-us], *adj.* prognathic.

PROGNOSIS, [prog-nō′-sis], *n.* the act of pronosticating; an omen; (*med.*) the outlook, the probable course, of a disease or malady; a symptom upon which such an opinion may be based. [Gk. *prognosis* foreknowledge].

PROGNOSTIC (1), [prog-nost′-ik], *n.* an omen, sign, or symptom; an indication of the future, a prognostication. [PROGNOSTIC (2)].

PROGNOSTIC (2), [prog-nost′-ik], *adj.* foretelling. [MedL. *prognosticus* from Gk. *prognostikos* foretelling].

PROGNOSTICABLE, [prog-nost′-ik-abl], *adj.* able to be foretold, predictable.

PROGNOSTICATE, [prog-nost′-ik-āt], *v.t.* to foretell or foreshadow. [MedL. *prognosticatum*, *p.pt.* of *prognosticare* to foretell].

PROGNOSTICATION, [prog-nost′-ik-ā′-shun], *n.* the science of prognosticating; that which prognosticates, a sign of the future, an omen. [MedL. *prognosticatio*].

PROGNOSTICATIVE, [prog-nost′-ik-at-iv], *adj.* predictive.

PROGNOSTICATOR, [prog-nost′-ik-āt′-or], *n.* one who predicts the future by prognostics.

PROGRAMME (1), PROGRAM, [prō′-gram′], *n.* a sheet or pamphlet on which the necessary details (e.g., order of events, those taking part, etc.) of a concert, theatrical entertainment, sports meeting, etc., are printed; a card printed with a list of dances at a ball or dance on which the name of one's intended partner for each dance may be entered; the actual entertainment provided at a theatre or concert, etc.; a statement of what is to be done, the course of one's intended actions, *esp.* when directed to a particular end; a statement of the policy a political party intends to pursue when it reaches office. [Fr. *programme* from L. *programma* from Gk. *programma* an edict].

PROGRAMME (2), [prō′-gram], *v.t.* to draw up a plan of, to design. [PROGRAMME (1)].

PROGRESS (1), [prō′-gres], *n.* movement onward; movement from a starting point and towards a chosen goal; forward movement, improvement, betterment, increase and expansion; an official or state journey. [OFr. *progres* from L. *progressus* an advance].

PROGRESS (2), [prō-gres′], *v.i.* to move in a forward direction, to move towards the intended goal; to draw nearer to completion; to improve, grow better, get on. [PROGRESS (1)].

PROGRESSION, [pro-gresh′-un], *n.* the act of passing from one thing to the next, the act of moving forwards, *esp.* in due order, stage by stage; progress, advance, improvement, a series, *esp.* one of significant arrangement; (*math.*) a series of numbers each of which differs from the next by a constant law; (*mus.*) a passing from one chord to the next, a succession of chords. [L. *progressio* advance].

PROGRESSIONAL, [pro-gresh′-unl], *adj.* (*poet.*) relating to progress or progression.

PROGRESSIONIST, [pro-gresh′-un-ist], *n.* one who believes in the steady natural improvement of the world and mankind towards an ultimate perfection.

PROGRESSIVE (1), [pro-gres′-iv], *n.* a member of a political party advocating reform, to be obtained by lawful and constitutional means and not by revolution. [PROGRESSIVE (2)].

PROGRESSIVE (2), [pro-gres′-iv], *adj.* moving forward by gradual and proper stages; growing better, developing, extending, improving by stages; advocating political change and development and reforms, *esp.* of a social nature; (*med.*) (of a disease, etc.) increasing in severity; (**p. taxation,** taxation graded in proportion to the means of the taxpayers; **p. whist,** whist in which partners and opponents are changed after every game, according to some regular arrangement based on the numbering of the tables. [Fr. *progressif*].

PROGRESSIVELY, [pro-gres′-iv-li], *adv.* in a progressive way.

PROGRESSIVENESS, [pro-gres′-iv-nes], *n.* the condition or quality of being progressive.

PROHIBIT, [pro-hib′-it], *v.t.* to forbid, to oppose by law and authority; to render impossible, to debar; **prohibited area,** an area controlled by the army in wartime, the entry into which of civilians is restricted. [L. *prohibitum*, *p.pt.* of *prohibere* to restrain, prevent].

PROHIBITER, [pro-hib′-it-er], *n.* one who prohibits.

PROHIBITION, [prō′-hib-ish′-un], *n.* the act of prohibiting, a forbidding, *esp.* by lawful authority; the prohibiting by law of the manufacture, sale and consumption of alcohol; (*leg.*) a writ from a higher court to a lower forbidding the latter to deal with some matter considered outside its jurisdiction by the former. [L. *prohibitio*].

PROHIBITIONIST (1), [prō′-hib-ish′-un-ist], *n.* one who opposes the sale, consumption, and manufacture of alcoholic liquors.

PROHIBITIONIST (2), [prō′-hib-ish′-un-ist], *adj.* governed by a law forbidding the sale, consumption, or manufacture of alcoholic liquors; advocating prohibition.

PROHIBITIVE, [pro-hib′-it-iv], *adj.* forbidding; preventing or tending to prevent; **p. price** or **cost,** price or cost so high as to render purchase impossible. [Fr. *prohibitif*].

PROHIBITIVELY, [prō-hib′-it-iv-li], *adv.* so as to prohibit; excessively.

PROHIBITORY, [pro-hib′-it-er-i], *adj.* prohibitive.

PROJECT (1), [pro′-jekt], *n.* a plan or scheme. [OFr. *project*].

PROJECT (2), [pro-jekt′], *v.t.* and *i.* to throw, cast forth, hurl; to cast with deliberate aim, *esp.* of a beam of light; (of the mind) to imagine, *esp.* what has not yet happened; to form a mental picture of; to cast (a picture) on a screen by means of a magic lantern or cinematograph; to stick out or protrude; (*geom.*) to represent a three-dimensional figure in a two-dimensional diagram. [L. *projectum*, *p.pt.* of *projicere* to throw forward].

PROJECTILE (1), [pro′-jekt-il], *n.* something intended to be thrown, a missile; a shell or bullet. [PROJECTILE (2)].

PROJECTILE (2), [pro-jekt′-il], *adj.* hurling, projecting; intended to be hurled. [Fr. *projectile*].

PROJECTING, [pro-jekt′-ing], *adj.* jutting out.

PROJECTION, [pro-jek′-shun], *n.* the act of casting, hurling, or projecting; the act of casting the mind forward; the act of planning; the act of jutting out; something that juts out; an image or shadow that is projected; a two-dimensional diagram of a three dimensional figure; a vivid mental image; (*psychol.*) the attribution to others of one's own motives and characteristics. [L. *projectio* a throwing forth].

PROJECTIVE, [pro-jekt′-iv], *adj.* characterized by projection.

PROJECTIVELY, [pro-jekt′-iv-li], *adv.* in a projective manner, by projection.

PROJECTOR, [pro-jekt′-or], *n.* someone or something that projects; someone who raises projects; a device for projecting and focusing films, etc., on to a screen.

PROJECTURE, [pro-jek′-cher], *n.* a jutting out, something that juts out. [Fr. *projecture*].

PROJET, [prozh′-ā], *n.* a preliminary draft of a treaty [Fr. *projet* proposal].

PROLABIUM, [prō-lā′-bi-um], *n.* (*anat.*) the outer and projecting part of a lip. [PRO and L. *labium* lip].

PROLAPSE (1), [prō-laps′], *n.* (*med.*) the act of falling out of position, *esp.* of the womb or rectum; condition of having so fallen. [L. *prolapsus* a sliding forward].

PROJECTOR

PROLAPSE (2), [prō-laps′], *v.i.* (*med.*) to fall from position. [PROLAPSE (1)].
PROLAPSUS, [prō-laps′-us], *n.* prolapse; **p. uteri,** prolapse of the womb.
PROLATE, [prō′-lāt], *adj.* (*geom.*) having the polar axis lengthened; (*fig.*) extended. [L. *prolatus, p.pt.* of *proferre* to extend, carry forward].
PROLATIVE, [prō-lat′-iv], *adj.* (*gram.*) used of a verbal form that completes the predicate.
PROLEGOMENA, (*rare sg.* **prolegomenon**), [prō′-leg-om′-en-a], *n.* a preface, a prefatory treatise. [Gk. *prolegomenon* prefacing].
PROLEGOMENARY, [prō′-leg-om′-en-er-i], *adj.* prefatory.
PROLEGS, [prō′-legz′], *n.*(*pl.*) (*entom.*) fleshy abdominal limbs resembling legs placed behind the true legs of certain larvae. [PRO (1) and LEG (1)].
PROLEPSIS, [prō-lep′-sis], *n.* a figure of speech by which that which will occur is referred to as though it already has occurred. [Gk. *prolepsis* anticipation].
PROLEPTIC, [prō-lep′-tik], *adj.* of, or pertaining to, prolepsis.
PROLEPTICALLY, [prō-lep′-tik-al-i], *adv.* in a proleptic fashion.
PROLETARIAN (1), [prō′-lit-āer′-i-an], *n.* one of the proletariat. [PROLETARIAN (2)].
PROLETARIAN (2), [prō′-lit-āer′-i-an], *adj.* belonging to the lower classes, *orig.* the lower classes in ancient Rome; belonging to, characteristic of, the proletariat. [L. *proletarius*].
PROLETARIAT, PROLETARIATE, [prō′-lit-āer′-i-at], *n.* the lower classes, the masses, the workers. [Fr. *prolétariat*].
PROLICIDE, [prōl′-is-īd], *n.* the slaying of one's offspring. [L. *proles* offspring and *cida* a murderer].
PROLIFERATE, [prol-if′-er-at], *v.t.* and *i.* to reproduce by proliferation.
PROLIFERATION, [prol′-if-er-ā′-shun], *n.* the state of being proliferous; reproduction by division; the development of new elementary parts. [Fr. *prolifération*].
PROLIFEROUS, [prol-if′-er-us], *adj.* pertaining to proliferation; reproducing or growing by proliferation. [MedL. *prolifer* bearing offspring].
PROLIFEROUSLY, [prol-if′-er-us-li], *adv.* in a proliferous way.
PROLIFIC, [prol-if′-ik], *adj.* producing numerous offspring; fertile, fruitful; abundant; rich in, abounding in.
PROLIFICACY, [prol-if′-ik-a-si], *n.* fruitfulness; the condition or quality of being prolific.
PROLIFICALLY, [prol-if′-ik-al-i], *adv.* in a prolific way.
PROLIFICATION, [prol′-if-ik-ā′-shun], *n.* prolificness. [MedL. *prolificatio* fertilization].
PROLIFICNESS, [prol-if′-ik-nes], *n.* the quality or condition of being prolific.
PROLIGEROUS, [prol-ij′-er-us], *adj.* producing offspring. [Fr. *proligère*].
PROLIX, [prō-liks′], *adj.* lengthy, verbose. [L. *prolixus* stretched out].
PROLIXITY, [prō-liks′-i-ti], *n.* the condition or quality of being prolix; verbosity.
PROLIXLY, [prō-liks′-li], *adv.* in a prolix style.
PROLIXNESS, [prō-liks′-nes], *n.* prolixity.
PROLOCUTOR, [prō-lok′-yŏŏ-ter], *n.* the chairman of the lower house of convocation and spokesman of that house in the upper house. [L. *prolocutor* one who speaks for another].
PROLOCUTORSHIP, [prō-lok′-yŏŏ-ter-ship], *n.* the office of prolocutor.
PROLOGIZE, PROLOGUIZE, [prō′-log-iz], *v.i.* to make or deliver a prologue.
PROLOGUE, [prō′-log], *n.* an introduction; a prefatory section of a literary composition; a short passage, usually in verse, at one time frequently spoken before the first scene of a play to beg the goodwill of the audience, make any necessary explanations, and introduce the play; (*fig.*) an event which occurs before another, and leads up to it. [Gk. *prologos*].
PROLOGUIZE, see PROLOGIZE.
PROLONG, [prō-long′], *v.t.* to make longer, to extend; to lengthen in time, to protract, spin out. [OFr. *prolonguer* from LL. *prolongare* to prolong].
PROLONGABLE, [prō-long′-abl], *adj.* able to be prolonged.
PROLONGATE, [prō′-long′-gāt], *v.t.* to prolong.
PROLONGATION, [prō′-long-gā′-shun], *n.* the act of prolonging or state of having been prolonged.
PROLONGER, [pro-long′-er], *n.* someone or something that lengthens.
PROLUSION, [pro-lew′-zhun], *n.* a preface, a prelude; a rehearsal. [L. *prolusio* prelude].
PROLUSORY, [pro-lew′-zer-i], *adj.* prefatory.
PROM, [prom], *n.* (*coll.*) a promenade concert; a promenade. [Abbreviation of PROMENADE].
PROMENADE (1), [prom′-en-ahd′], *n.* a short leisurely excursion, usually on foot, taken for pleasure and exercise; any place designed for walking or promenading. [Fr. *promenade, promener* to take out for a walk from L. *prominare* to drive (cattle) to pasture].
PROMENADE (2), [prom′-en-ahd′], *v.t.* and *i.* to make a short excursion, usually on foot, for pleasure and exercise; to walk along with a jaunty, leisurely air. [PROMENADE (1)].
PROMENADE CONCERT, [prom′-en-ahd′-kon′-sert], *n.* a musical entertainment at which all the audience are not provided with seats but may stand or walk about the floor of the hall.
PROMENADER, [prom′-en-ahd′-er], *n.* one who promenades.
PROMETHEAN, [prom-ē′-thi-an], *adj.* of, or pertaining to, *Prometheus*, a Titan who, according to Greek legend, stole fire from heaven for mankind, and was therefore condemned to be chained to a crag and be at the mercy of a vulture that daily fed on his liver, which each night was renewed.
PROMINENCE, [prom′-in-ents], *n.* the condition or quality of being prominent, protruding, important or notable; a projecting point of land or rock, a great crag.
PROMINENCY, [prom′-in-en-si], *n.* the condition or quality of being prominent.
PROMINENT, [prom′-in-ent], *adj.* jutting out, projecting; distinguished, conspicuous; eminent, famous, noted and notable. [L. *prominens, pres.pt.* of *prominere* to jut out].
PROMINENTLY, [prom′-in-ent-li], *adv.* in a prominent fashion.
PROMISCUITY, [prom′-is-kew′-it-i], *n.* the quality or condition of being promiscuous, indiscriminate, intermingling.
PROMISCUOUS, [prom-is′-kew-us], *adj.* composed of elements of various sorts; mingled indiscriminately; indiscriminate, *esp.* sexually. [L. *promiscuus* mixed].
PROMISCUOUSLY, [prom-is′-kew-us-li], *adv.* in a promiscuous fashion.
PROMISCUOUSNESS, [prom-is′-kew-us-nes], *n.* promiscuity.
PROMISE (1), [prom′-is], *n.* an informal undertaking or guarantee about future conduct; the probability of success or fulfilment; **to make a p.,** to give such an undertaking; **to break a p.,** to fail to keep a promise; **breach of p.,** failure to fulfil an engagement to marry. [Fr. *promesse* from L. *promissum, p.pt.* of *promittere* to promise, send forward].
PROMISE (2), [prom′-is], *v.t.* and *i.* to give an informal guarantee of one's future conduct; to give an undertaking concerning; to give pledge or promise to; to foreshadow, point to; to provide reasons for hope, give indications of success or fulfilment. [PROMISE (1)].
PROMISEE, [prom′-is-ē′], *n.* (*leg.*) someone to whom a promise is made, or in whose favour a promissory note is made out.
PROMISER, [prom′-is-er], *n.* one who promises.
PROMISING, [prom′-is-ing], *adj.* likely to get on, succeed, improve.
PROMISINGLY, [prom′-is-ing-li], *adv.* in a promising way.
PROMISSIVE, [prō-mis′-iv], *adj.* promissory.
PROMISSOR, [prom′-is-or], *n.* (*leg.*) one who makes a promise.
PROMISSORILY, [prom′-is-er-il-i], *adv.* in a promissory fashion.
PROMISSORY, [prom′-is-er-i], *adj.* of, or pertaining to, a promise; containing a promise; **p. note,** a note promising over the promissor's signature to pay a sum of money, on demand, to a specified person. [MedL. *promissorius*].
PROMONTORY, [prom′-on-ter-i], *n.* a crag or cliff jutting out into the sea; the spur of a hill projecting into a plain or valley; (*anat.*) a protuberance on the body. [LL. *promontorium* headland].
PROMOTE, [prom-ōt′], *v.t.* to forward, set going, originate; to propose, suggest and make the preliminary arrangements for; to assist the growth or spread of; to raise the rank of; to evoke or incite; (*leg.*) to start (a legal action). [L. *promotum, p.pt.* of *promovere* to promote].
PROMOTER, [prom-ōt′-er], *n.* one who promotes;

one who originates or suggests or helps to organize; one who encourages, lends his or her support or patronage; one who evokes or incites.

PROMOTION, [prom-ō'-shun], *n.* the act of promoting; the act of founding and fostering; the act of advancing (someone) in rank; the fact of having been advanced in rank, preferment; **to obtain p.**, to be raised to higher rank. [ME. *promocion* from L. *promotio* promotion, moving forward].

PROMOTIVE, [prom-ōt'-iv], *adj.* causing promotion, tending to promote.

PROMPT (1), [prompt], *n.* a word or line supplied by a prompter. [PROMPT (5)].

PROMPT (2), [prompt], *n.* (*comm.*) a time limit for payment. [PROMPT (3)].

PROMPT (3), [prompt], *adj.* ready, quick to act; quickly done; being to time, not late; **p. cash**, cash paid forthwith; **p. goods**, goods delivered forthwith. [L. *promptus* ready, quick].

PROMPT (4), [prompt], *adv.* promptly.

PROMPT (5), [prompt], *v.t.* to urge, incite, suggest; to aid the memory of (*esp.* the memory of a speaker which has temporarily failed, by supplying the word, name, or phrase he has forgotten); (*stage*) to aid an actor's memory by whispering the line he has forgotten, from the wings; to act as a prompter. [PROMPT (3)].

PROMPT-BOOK, [prompt'-boo͝k], *n.* the copy of the text of a play as prepared with notes and directions for the prompter's use.

PROMPT-BOX, [prompt'-boks], *n.* (*stage*) the place where the prompter sits plainly visible to the actors but hardly so to the audience.

PROMPTER, [prompt'-er], *n.* someone who prompts; (*stage*) one whose job it is to follow the action of the play from the text and be ready to remedy any lapse of memory on the part of the actors.

PROMPTITUDE, [prompt'-it-ewd], *n.* readiness, quickness, alertness; the quality or condition of being to time; promptness. [Fr. *promptitude* from LL. *promptitudo*].

PROMPTLY, [prompt'-li], *adv.* readily, quickly, in a prompt manner; immediately; sharp to time.

PROMPTNESS, [prompt'-nes], *n.* promptitude.

PROMPT NOTE, [prompt'-nōt'], *n.* (*comm.*) a note fixing a time limit for payment.

PROMPT SIDE, [prompt'-sīd'], *n.* (*stage*) the side of the stage to the right of an actor facing the audience, i.e., the side of the stage on which the prompter always used to be.

PROMPTUARY, [promp'-choo͝-er-i], *n.* a store-house; a place where stocks and supplies are kept in readiness for use. [LL. *promptuarium* storehouse].

PROMPTURE, [promp'-cher], *n.* suggestion, prompting.

PROMULGATE, [prom'-ulg-āt], *v.t.* to make public, proclaim, give publicity to (facts, decrees, etc.); to make, or endeavour to make, widely known. [L. *promulgatum*, *p.pt.* of *promulgare* to publish].

PROMULGATION, [prom'-ulg-ā'-shun], *n.* the act of promulgating; publication; a declaration, a public and official announcement, a proclamation. [L. *promulgatio*].

PROMULGATOR, [prom'-ulg-āt-or], *n.* one who promulgates.

PROMULGE, [prō-mulj'], *v.t.* to promulgate officially. [L. *promulgare* to publish].

PROMULGER, [prō-mulj'-er], *n.* one who promulges.

PRONAOS, [prō-nā'-os], *n.* a vestibule, usually columned, in front of and leading to the main body of a Greek temple. [Gk. *pronaos*].

PRONATE (1), [prōn'-āt], *adj.* (*anat.*) turned so that the palm or underside is facing downwards. [PRONATE (2)].

PRONATE (2), [prōn-āt'], *v.t.* (*anat.*) to cause the hand to turn so that the palm is underneath; to turn any limb so that the underside faces downwards. [LL. *pronatus*, *p.pt.* of *pronare* to bow].

PRONATION, [prōn-ā'-shun], *n.* (*anat.*) the act of pronating.

PRONATOR, [prōn-āt'-or], *n.* (*anat.*) any muscle which causes pronation.

PRONE, [prōn], *adj.* lying prostrate with the face to the ground; steeply sloping; liable, disposed. [L. *pronus* leaning forward, sloping].

PRONELY, [prōn'-li], *adv.* in a prone position.

PRONENESS, [prōn'-nes], *n.* the condition of being prone; tendency, disposition, inclination.

PRONG (1), [prong], *n.* a forked tool used to move hay, etc.; one of the projecting divisions of a fork; any spur-like projection on a larger body; any slim spur-like thing or instrument that may be used for prodding. [Uncert.].

PRONG (2), [prong], *v.t.* to prod with a prong; to shift with a prong (hay, etc.). [PRONG (1)].

PRONGBUCK, [prong'-buk], *n.* the *Antilocapra americana*, a horned ruminant found in America, the pronghorn. [PRONG (1)].

PRONGED, [prongd], *adj.* possessing, or divided into, prongs.

PRONG-HOE, [prong'-hō], *n.* a hoe with prongs used for breaking the soil.

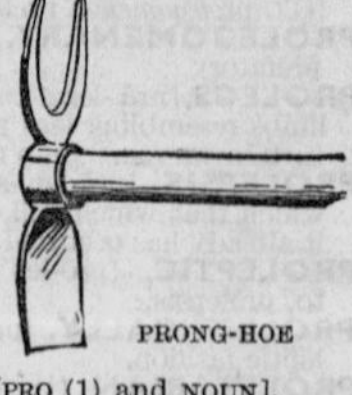
PRONG-HOE

PRONGHORN, [prong'-hawn], *n.* the prongbuck.

PRONOMINAL, [prō-nom'-in-al], *adj.* (*gram.*) of, or pertaining to, pronouns, resembling a pronoun in function.

PRONOMINALLY, [prō-nom'-in-al-i], *adv.* (*gram.*) like a pronoun in function, etc.

PRONOUN, [prō'-nown], *n.* (*gram.*) a word used in place of a noun or name. [PRO (1) and NOUN].

PRONOUNCE, [prō-nownts'], *v.t.* and *i.* to give solemn utterance to, to say solemnly and with emphasis; to state; to utter with the vocal organs, say, articulate; to deliver one's opinion; **to p. against**, to give judgment against, condemn, declare to be contrary to one's opinion or wishes, to oppose with argument, vote against; **to p. for**, to give verbal support to, argue in favour of, support, vote for; **to p. on**, to give one's considered opinion about, *esp.* by an expert. [OFr. *pronuncier* from L. *pronuntiare* to announce, proclaim].

PRONOUNCEABLE, [prō-nowns'-abl], *adj.* capable of being pronounced.

PRONOUNCED, [prō-nownst'], *adj.* decided, emphatic, well defined.

PRONOUNCEDLY, [prō-nowns'-ed-li], *adv.* in a pronounced way, with emphasis, emphatically.

PRONOUNCEMENT, [prō-nowns'-ment], *n.* the act of pronouncing; a solemn or formal declaration; a considered statement of opinion.

PRONOUNCER, [prō-nowns'-er], *n.* one who pronounces.

PRONOUNCING, [prō-nowns'-ing], *adj.* **p. dictionary**,, a dictionary which sets out to give pronunciations.

PRONTO, [pron'-tō], *adv.* (*U.S. slang*) quickly, at once. [Sp.].

PRONUNCIAMENTO, [pro-nuns'-i-am-en'-tō], *n.* a manifesto, *esp.* a Spanish political manifesto. [Sp. *pronunciamiento*].

PRONUNCIATION, [prō-nuns'-i-ā'-shun], *n.* the act of pronouncing; the way of pronouncing, *esp.* the generally received way of saying a word, phrase, etc. [L. *pronuntiatio* a proclaiming, announcement].

PROOF (1), [proo͞f], *n.* the act or process of proving a fact or showing it to be true; evidence demonstrating the truth of a fact, statement, belief, etc.; examination, test, trial, probation; (*leg.*) attested evidence, *esp.* a written statement of what a witness is prepared to swear to in court, or a written record of evidence given in court; (*engraving*) an impression taken for the artist to correct; (*print.*) a preliminary impression taken for the proof-reader or author to correct; (*bookbinding*) the rough edges of the narrower leaves of a book, left untrimmed to show the pages have not been cut; (*milit.*) a place where explosives are tested. [ME. *profe*, OFr. *preuve* from L. *proba* proof].

PROOF (2), [proo͞f], *adj.* capable of resisting penetration by any specified thing, hard, impenetrable; (*fig.*) undefeated by, invulnerable to; (*of liquors*) containing a standard quantity of alcohol. [PROOF (1)].

PROOF (3), [proo͞f], *v.t.* to render proof against; to render waterproof, *esp.* of cloths. [PROOF (2)].

PROOF-COPY, [proo͞f'-kop'-i], *n.* (*print.*) an impression taken before the final printing, for correction by the author or proof-reader, a proof.

PROOF-HOUSE, [proo͞f'-hows], *n.* (*milit.*) a building where gun-barrels and explosives are tested.

PROOFLESS, [proo͞f'-les], *adj.* not proved or established by evidence as true.

PROOF-READER, [proo͞f'-rēd-er], *n.* one who corrects printer's proofs.

PROOF-READING, [proo͞f'-rēd-ing], *n.* (*print.*) the business of correcting printer's proofs.

PROP (1), [prop], *n.* a stick or stake used as a support or partial support for a weight or body leaning upon it; anything which acts as a support; (*fig.*) backing, moral support, a source of financial aid or material aid, a source of spiritual comfort, etc., anything which helps one through life or gives one courage to face its difficulties. [ME. *proppe*].

PROP (2), [prop], *n.* (*school slang*) a proposition in geometry. [Short for PROPOSITION].

PROP (3), [prop], *n.* (*thieves' slang*) a tie-pin or scarf-pin. [Unkn.].

PROP (4), [prop], *n.* (*stage*) a necessary accessory to the performance of a stage play usually within the categories of costume and furniture, a property. [Short for PROPERTY (1)].

PROP (5), [prop], *n.* (*aeron.*) a propeller. [PROP-(ELLER)].

PROP (6), (**propping, propped**), [prop], *v.t.* to act as a prop to, to support morally or physically; to provide props for; **to p. up**, to support as a prop. [PROP (1)].

PROPAEDEUTIC, [pro-pid-ewt'-ik], *adj.* pertaining to propaedeutics; giving a preliminary course of instruction. [Gk. *propaideuo* I give a preliminary course of instruction to].

PROPAEDEUTICAL, [prō-pid-ewt'-ik], *adj.* relating to propaedeutics.

PROPAEDEUTICS, [pro-pid-ewt'-iks], *n.*(*pl.*) preliminary training.

PROPAGABLE, [prop'-ag-abl], *adj.* capable of being propagated.

PROPAGANDA, [prop'-ag-an'-da], *n.* (*R.C.*) the committee of cardinals in charge of foreign missions; any organization to propagate a set of ideas, facts or ideals; the facts, ideals, ideas, etc., propagated; books, talks, broadcasts and pamphlets used to propagate a set of ideas, ideals, facts, etc. [L. *propaganda* from *propagare* to put forth].

PROPAGANDISM, [prop'-ag-an'-dizm], *n.* a system or practice of disseminating propaganda.

PROPAGANDIST, [prop'-ag-an'-dist], *n.* one who spreads propaganda; a member of Propaganda in the Roman Catholic Church.

PROPAGANDIZE, [prop'-ag-an'-diz], *v.t. and i.* to disseminate propaganda to or among; to spread propaganda.

PROPAGATE, [prop'-ag-āt], *v.t. and i.* to breed, multiply by taking cuttings, etc., to disseminate, spread, to transmit; to have offspring. [L. *propagatum*, *p.pt.* of *propagare* to breed, propagate].

PROPAGATION, [prop'-ag-ā'-shun], *n.* the act of propagating, of producing offspring, or spreading propaganda; the act of spreading or transmitting. [L. *propagatio*].

PROPAGATIVE, [prop'-ag-at-iv], *adj.* of, or pertaining to, propagation; able to propagate.

PROPAGATOR, [prop'-ag-āt'-or], *n.* a propagandist, one who propagates.

PROPAROXYTONE (1), [prō'-par-oks'-it-ōn], *n.* (*Gk. gram.*) a word having the accent on the third syllable from the end. [PROPAROXYTONE (2)].

PROPAROXYTONE (2), [prō'-par-oks'-it-ōn], *adj.* (*Gk. gram.*) having the accent on the third syllable before the end of the word. [Gk. *proparoxutonos*].

PROPED, [prō'-ped'], *n.* (*entom.*) a proleg. [MdL. *propes propedis*].

PROPEL, (**propelling, propelled**), [prō-pel'], *v.t.* to cause to move forward; to drive forward. [L. *propellere* to drive forward].

PROPELLENT (1), [prō-pel'-ent], *n.* something that propels. [PROPELLENT (2)].

PROPELLENT (2), [prō-pel'-ent], *adj.* driving forward. [L. *propellens*, *pres.pt.* of *propellere* to propel].

PROPELLER, [prō-pel'-er], *n.* that which propels; the screw of a ship, launch, aeroplane, etc.

PROPELLER

PROPEND†, [prō-pend'], *v.i.* to lean forward or in a certain direction; (*fig.*) to be disposed to. [L. *propendere* to hang forward].

PROPENSE, [pro-pents'], *adj.* inclined to, biased towards, disposed to. [L. *propensus*, *p.pt.* of *propendere* to hang forward].

PROPENSELY, [pro-pens'-li], *adv.* in a propense fashion.

PROPENSENESS, [pro-pens'-nes], *n.* the condition or quality of being propense.

PROPENSION, [pro-pen'-shun], *n.* inclination, propensity.

PROPENSITY, [pro-pens'-i-ti], *n.* bent of mind; disposition, inclination, liability, natural tendency, addiction.

PROPER (1), [prop'-er], *n.* (*eccles.*) an office or part of an office appointed for use on some special occasion or during a particular season. [PROPER (2)].

PROPER (2), [prop'-er], *adj.* belonging to, pertaining to, or fitting for, oneself, one's own; special, distinctive, individual; apt, suitable, appropriate, right; pertaining or belonging to, according to rule or custom, regular, normal; decent, chaste, modest; polite; prim; complete; out-and-out, thorough, thoroughgoing;†handsome; (*her.*) depicted in natural colours; **p. noun**, (*gram.*) the name denoting a particular place, person, etc.; **p. fraction**, (*arith.*) a fraction the numerator of which is less than the denominator, i.e., whose value is less than unity. [Fr. *propre* from L. *proprius*].

PROPERLY, [prop'-er-li], *adv.* in a proper way; correctly, according to rule or custom; decently.

PROPERTIED, [prop'-er-tid], *adj.* possessed of property, *esp.* landed property.

PROPERTY, [prop'-er-ti], *n.* a characteristic, an attribute or quality proper to or inherent in anything; a thing or things possessed, possessions, belongings; an estate, land owned; (*pl.*) (*stage*) the accessories of a stage-play, the costume and furniture and other articles necessary to the action of the play; **personal p.**, movable property, goods, chattels; **real p.**, land owned; **p. owner**, one who owns property, *esp.* land, houses, etc.; **p. man**, the man who provides and looks after the properties in a stage production. [ME. *proprete*, OFr. *proprieté* from L. *proprietas* ownership, property].

PROPHASIS, [prof'-as-is], *n.* (*med.*) prognosis, foreknowledge. [Gk. *prophasis*].

PROPHECY, [prof'-i-si], *n.* the power of prophesying; something prophesied, a prediction. [OFr. *profecie*, LL. *prophetia* from Gk. *propheteia*].

PROPHESIER, [prof'-is-i'-er], *n.* one who prophesies, a prophet.

PROPHESY, [prof'-is-i], *v.t. and i.* to make prophesies, to foretell the future; to give forewarning of.

PROPHESYING, [prof'-is-i-ing], *n.* a prophecy or foretelling.

PROPHET, [prof'-it], *n.* the human spokesman of a deity, *esp.* a teacher or leader inspired by God to declare His will and judgments; one of the great non-Christian and non-Judaic religious teachers; a religious teacher, a preacher, claiming or credited with special inspiration; a leader or pioneer in any human venture; a soothsayer, one who foretells the future; an omen; one of an order of ministers in the Catholic Apostolic Church; **Prophets**, the prophetical books of the Old Testament; **Major Prophets**, Isaiah, Jeremiah, Ezekiel and Daniel and their books in the Old Testament; **Minor Prophets**, the twelve prophetical books of the Old Testament from Hosea to Malachi inclusive; **racing p.**, a tipster. [LL. *propheta* from Gk. *prophetes* an interpreter].

PROPHETESS, [prof'-it-es'], *n.* a female prophet.

PROPHETHOOD, [prof'-it-hood], *n.* the condition of being a prophet.

PROPHETIC, [pro-fet'-ik], *adj.* of, or pertaining to, a prophet or prophecy; containing prophecy; foretelling. [LL. *propheticus* from Gk. *prophetikos*].

PROPHETICAL, [pro-fet'-ik], *adj.* prophetic.

PROPHETICALLY, [pro-fet'-ik-al-i], *adv.* in a prophetic way.

PROPHETISM, [prof'-et-izm], *n.* skill in prophecy.

PROPHYLACTIC (1), [prof'-il-ak'-tik], *n.* (*med.*) a preventive medicine or medical treatment. [PROPHYLACTIC (2)].

PROPHYLACTIC (2), [prof'-il-ak'-tik], *adj.* (*med.*) preventive. [Gk. *prophulaktikos*].

PROPHYLAXIS, [prof'-il-ak'-sis], *n.* (*med.*) a preventive medicine or treatment. [Gk. *prophulax* an outpost].

PROPINQUITY, [prop-in'-kwit-i], *n.* nearness in place, time, relationship, etc. [OFr. *propinquité* from L. *propinquitas* nearness].

PROPITIABLE, [prō-pish'-i-abl], *adj.* capable of being propitiated.

PROPITIATE, [prō-pish'-i-āt], *v.t.* to conciliate, appease, win the favour of. [L. *propitiatus*, *p.pt.* of *propitiare* to render favourable].

PROPITIATION, [prō-pish'-i-ā'-shun], *n.* the act of propitiating; the fact of having been propitiated; that with which reconcilement is purchased. [LL. *propitiatio*].

PROPITIATOR, [prō-pish'-i-āt-or], *n.* one who propitiates.
PROPITIATORILY, [prō-pish'-i-āt-er-i-li], *adv.* by means of propitiation.
PROPITIATORY, [prō-pish'-i-āt-er-i], *adj.* able, intended or serving, to propitiate. [EcclesL. *propitiatorius*].
PROPITIOUS, [prō-pish'-us], *adj.* favourable, auspicious. [L. *propitius* favourable].
PROPITIOUSLY, [prō-pish'-us-li], *adv.* in a propitious way.
PROPITIOUSNESS, [prō-pish'-us-nes], *n.* the condition or quality of being propitious.
PROPODIUM, [prō-pō'-di-um], *n.* (*zool.*) the anterior part of the foot of some molluscs. [PRO and Gk. *pous podos* foot].
PROPOLIS, [prop'-ol-is], *n.* a resinous substance which bees gather from the buds of trees and use to fill the crevices of their hives. [Gk. *propolis* bee-glue, a suburb].
PROPONENT (1), [pro-pōn'-ent], *n.* someone who brings forward a proposal or argument. [PROPONENT (2)].
PROPONENT (2), [pro-pōn'-ent], *adj.* proposing, bringing forward. [L. *proponens*, *pres.pt.* of *proponere* to set forward, declare].
PROPORTION (1), [prop-aw'-shun], *n.* a part or portion; ratio, comparative relation (in size, quantity, quality, etc.); symmetry, balance; (*math.*) a relation of quantities in which, when the first number is divided by the second, the quotient is equal to that produced when the third is divided by the fourth; the rule of three; (*pl.*) dimensions; **out of all p.,** (*fig.*) unreasonable, outrageous; **in due p.,** with proper balance; (*fig.*) sensible, reasonable, modest. [OFr. *proporcion* from L. *proportio* proportion].
PROPORTION (2), [prop-aw'-shun], *v.t.* to render duly proportionate; to share out, share out in due proportion. [PROPORTION (1)].
PROPORTIONABLE, [prop-aw'-shun-abl], *adj.* able to be proportioned; being in proportion.
PROPORTIONABLENESS, [prop-aw'-shun-abl-nes], *n.* the state or quality of being proportionable.
PROPORTIONABLY, [prop-aw'-shun-ab-li], *adv.* in a proportionable way, proportionally.
PROPORTIONAL (1), [prop-aw'-shunl], *n.* (*math.*) a term in a proportion. [PROPORTIONAL (2)].
PROPORTIONAL (2), [prop-aw'-shunl], *adj.* being in proportion; **p. representation,** an electoral system by which strength of representation is in ratio with the strength of political parties; **p. compasses,** a two-legged geometrical instrument both legs of which join at a common pivot, which can be adjusted so as to obtain any desired ratio between the lengths of the legs measuring from the tips to the pivot. [LL. *proportionalis*].

PROPORTIONAL COMPASSES

PROPORTIONALITY, [prop-aw'-shun-al'-i-ti], *n.* the condition or quality of being proportional.
PROPORTIONALLY, [prop-aw'-shun-al-i], *adv.* in proportion, proportionately.
PROPORTIONATE (1), [prop-aw'-shun-at], *adj.* proportional, being in proportion. [LL. *proportionatus* proportioned].
PROPORTIONATE (2), [prop-aw'-shun-āt], *v.t.* to render proportional. [PROPORTIONATE (1)].
PROPORTIONATELY, [prop-aw'-shun-at-li], *adv.* in a proportionate manner, proportionally.
PROPORTIONATENESS, [prop-aw'-shun-at-nes], *n.* the condition or quality of being proportionate.
PROPORTIONED, [prop-aw'-shund], *adj.* symmetrical, balanced, being to scale; evenly divided out.
PROPORTIONLESS, [prop-aw'-shun-les], *adj.* without proportion.
PROPORTIONMENT, [prop-aw'-shun-ment], *n.* the manner or act of proportioning; the condition of having been proportioned.
PROPOSAL, [prop-ōz'-al], *n.* the act of proposing; that which is proposed, a suggestion, plan, scheme; an offer, an offer of marriage.
PROPOSE, [prop-ōz'], *v.t. and i.* to bring forward, proffer (a suggestion, scheme, plan, etc.) for consideration; to make a suggestion; to present as a resolution (to a meeting, committee, etc.); to make an offer of marriage; to plan, scheme, intend. [Fr. *proposer*].
PROPOSER, [prop-ōz'-er], *n.* someone who proposes, *esp.* someone who moves a resolution at a committee, meeting, assembly, etc.
PROPOSITION, [prop'-ō-zish'-un], *n.* a statement; a plan, scheme or project; (*log.*) a statement in which something is denied or affirmed of something; (*math.*) a formal statement of a theorem or problem; (*coll.*) an affair, problem, person; **tough p.,** (*coll.*) a difficult job, a difficult person to have dealings with. [L. *propositio*].
PROPOSITIONAL, [prop'-ō-zish'-un-al], *adj.* of, or pertaining to, a proposition, founded on a proposition.
PROPOUND, [pro-pownd'], *v.t.* to set forth, explain. [~†*propone* from L. *proponere* to set forth].
PROPOUNDER, [pro-pownd'-er], *n.* a person who propounds.
PROPRAETOR, [prō'-prē'-tor], *n.* a magistrate of the Roman republic who at the end of the usual year's office as praetor was set in charge for one year of the administration of a province. [L. *propraetor*].
PROPRIETARY, [prop-ri'-et-er-i], *adj.* pertaining to a proprietor or proprietorship; (of goods) bearing a branded trade-mark. [L. *proprietarius*].
PROPRIETOR, [prop-ri'-et-er], *n.* an owner.
PROPRIETORIAL, [prop'-ri-et-aw'-ri-al], *adj.* of, or pertaining to, ownership.
PROPRIETORSHIP, [prop-ri'-et-er-ship], *n.* the condition of being proprietor.
PROPRIETRESS, [prop-rī'-et-res], *n.* a female proprietor.
PROPRIETRIX, [prop-rī'-et-riks], *n.* a proprietress.
PROPRIETY, [prop-rī'-e-ti], *n.* appropriateness, suitability; accordance with standards of decency and respectability; decorum. [ME. *proprietee* from L. *proprietas* the quality of being characteristic].
PROPSTER, [prop'-ster], *n.* the property man in a theatre.
PROPTOSIS, [prop-tō'-sis], *n.* (*med.*) prolapse or protuberance. [Gk. *proptosis* a falling forward].
PROPULSION, [prō-pul'-shun], *n.* the act of driving forward, or fact of being driven forward. [Fr *propulsion*].
PROPULSIVE, [prō-pul'-siv], *adj.* driving forward.
PROPULSORY, [pro-pul'-ser-i], *adj.* propulsive.
PROPYLAEUM, [prop-il-ē'-um], *n.* the entrance of a temple or shrine in classical times; a vestibule. [L. *propylaeum*].
PROPYLITE, [prop'-il-īt], *n.* a tertiary volcanic rock, common in regions where silver is mined.
PROPYLON, [prō-pī'-lon], *n.* the gateway of an ancient Egyptian temple. [Gk. *propulon*].
PRO RATA, [prō'-rāt'-a], *adj. and adv. phrase* in proportion, proportionate(ly). [L. *pro rata* for the rate].
PRORATE, [prō-rāt'], *v.t.* to distribute or assess according to proportion. [L. *pro rata*].
PRORE†, [praw(r)], *n.* a prow. [L. *prora* prow].
PRORECTOR, [prō-rek'-tor], *n.* a deputy rector in a college or university.
PROREPTION, [prō-rep'-shun], *n.* a slow, creeping advance.
PROROGATION, [prō-ro-gā'-shun], *n.* the act of proroguing or fact of being prorogued. [L. *prorogatio* extension, prolongation].
PROROGUE, [prō-rōg'], *v.t.* to adjourn the meetings of an assembly (*esp.* of Parliament) for an indefinite period, without actually dissolving it. [L. *prorogare* to prolong].
PRORUPTION, [prō-rup'-shun], *n.* the action of bursting forth. [LL. *proruptio*].
PROSAIC, [prō-zā'-ik], *adj.* dull, unimaginative commonplace; †pertaining to prose. [MedL. *prosaicus*].
PROSAICAL†, [prō-zā'-ikl], *adj.* prosaic.
PROSAICALLY, [prō-zā'-ik-al-i], *adv.* in a prosaic fashion.
PROSAISM, [prō'-zā-izm], *n.* a dull phrase; dull unimaginative style. [Fr. *prosaïsme*].
PROSAIST, [prō'-zā-ist], *n.* one who writes prose; (*fig.*) a dull unimaginative person.
PROSCENIUM, [prō-sē'-ni-um], *n.* the platform or stage of the classical theatre; in the modern theatre, the space between the curtain and the orchestra, *esp.* the arch framing the stage. [L. *proscenium*].
PROSCRIBE, [prō-skrīb'], *v.t.* to banish, outlaw; to condemn or prohibit. [L. *proscribere*].
PROSCRIBER, [prō-skrīb'-er], *n.* a person who proscribes.
PROSCRIPTION, [prō-skrip'-shun], *n.* the act of

proscribing or fact of being proscribed. [L. *proscriptio*].

PROSCRIPTIVE, [prō-skript'-iv], *adj.* pertaining to, or concerned with, proscription; causing or demanding proscription.

PROSCRIPTIVELY, [prō-skript'-iv-li], *adv.* in a proscriptive way.

PROSE (1), [prōz], *n.* the unmetrical language of ordinary speech and writing; literature not written in verse; a dull mode of expression, a commonplace phrase; dull, tedious writing; a passage set in examinations for unmetrical translation into another language. [L. *prosa* unadorned].

PROSE (2), [prōz], *adj.* written as prose; prosaic, in prose. [PROSE (1)].

PROSE (3), [prōz], *v.i.* to talk or write in a dull, tedious fashion. [PROSE (1)]

PROSECTOR, [prō-sek'-tor], *n.* a person who prepares bodies for use in anatomical demonstrations or lectures. [LL. *prosector*].

PROSECUTABLE, [pros'-ik-ewt'-abl], *adj.* liable to be prosecuted.

PROSECUTE, [pros'-ik-ewt], *v.t and i.* to follow out, pursue, carry through to an end; to take legal proceedings against; to institute or conduct a prosecution. [L. *prosecutus*, *p.pt.* of *prosequi* to pursue].

PROSECUTION, [pros'-ik-ew'-shun], *n.* the following out (of a plan or ambition); (*leg.*) the indictment or laying of information in court in order to put a person on trial; the taking of legal action against a person; the person or persons (together with their legal advisers) taking action against another person or persons. [L. *prosecutio* pursuit].

PROSECUTOR, [pros'-ik-ewt'-or], *n.* one who prosecutes; one who institutes legal proceedings (against another person or persons); **public p.,** a law officer of the state who conducts legal proceedings on behalf of the Crown. [L. *prosecutor* a pursuer].

PROSECUTRIX, [pros'-ik-ewt-riks], *n.* a female prosecutor. [MdL. *prosecutrix*].

PROSELYTE (1), [pros'-il-īt], *n.* a Gentile convert to Judaism; any kind of convert. [LL. *proselytus* from Gk. *proselutos* a convert to Judaism].

PROSELYTE (2), [pros'-il-īt], *v.t.* to convert. [PROSELYTE (1)].

PROSELYTISM, [pros'-il-it-izm], *n.* the condition of being or becoming a proselyte; the act of proselytizing.

PROSELYTIZE, [pros'-il-it-īz], *v.t. and i.* to convert, to make proselytes.

PROSELYTIZER, [pros'-il-it-īz'-er], *n.* one who proselytizes.

PROSENCHYMA, [pros-engk'-im-a], *n.* (*bot.*) a fibrous tissue containing long open cells of which one end of one enters one end of the next, so that a series of these cells forms a tube-like duct or vein. [Gk. *pros* forward, *en* in and *khumos* juice].

PROSENCHYMATOUS, [pros-engk-im'-at-us], *adj.* consisting of, or resembling, prosenchyma.

PROSER, [prōz'-er], *n.* a writer of prose; a dull talker or writer.

PROSEUCHA, [pros-ew'-ka], *n.* a place of prayer, *esp.* an open place used for prayer by Jews. [LL. *proseucha* from Gk. *proseukhe*].

PROSIFY, [prōz'-i-fī], *v.t. and i.* to write in prose; to turn into prose. [PROS(E) (1) and (VERS)IFY].

PROSILY, [prōz'-il-i], *adv.* in a prosy style.

PROSINESS, [prōz'-i-nes], *n.* the condition or quality of being prosy.

PROSING, [prōz'-ing], *n.* tedious talk or writing.

PROSIT, [prō'-sit], *int.* good luck! [A German drinking toast from L. *prosit*, *3rd person sg. pres.subj.* of *prodesse* to profit, prosper].

PRO-SLAVERY, [prō-slāv'-eri], *adj.* in favour of slavery. [PRO (1) and SLAVERY].

PROSODIAL, [pros-ō'-di-al], *adj.* of, or pertaining to, the rules of prosody.

PROSODIAN, [pros-ō'-di-an], *n.* a person skilled in prosody.

PROSODIC, [pros-o'-dik], *adj.* pertaining to prosody.

PROSODICAL, [pros-o'-dik-al], *adj.* prosodic.

PROSODIST, [pros'-od-ist], *n.* one skilled in prosody, a prosodian.

PROSODY, [pros'-od-i], *n.* the art and theory of versification. [L. from Gk. *prosodia* a song sung to music, the accent on a syllable].

PROSOMA, [prō-sō'-ma], *n.* the front part of the body of such creatures as oysters, mussels, barnacles and cuttlefishes. [MdL. *prosoma* from PRO (1) and Gk. *soma* body].

PROSOPOPOEIA, [pros'-ō-pop-ē'-a], *n.* a rhetorical figure of speech in which absent persons are represented as speaking; personification. [L. *prosopopoeia* from Gk. *prosopopoiia* personification].

PROSPECT (1), [pros'-pekt], *n.* the action of looking forth; the condition of facing or being turned in a certain direction; a view, a wide expanse or range of sight; a landscape or vista; a view presented to the mental eye, a scheme, plan, ambition, outlook; the probable trend of events; (*pl.*) the expectation or probability of advances in a career; (*mining*) a plot or area giving good promise of mineral deposit; the examination of a plot or region to see if it might be considered to have mineral deposits; (*coll.*) a likely customer. [L. *prospectus* a view].

PROSPECT (2), [pros-pekt'], *v.t. and i.* (*mining*) to survey an area for signs of mineral deposits; to survey for mineral deposits; (*fig.*) to search (for something); (*fig.*) to make a survey of the probable trend of future events, to examine evidence as to what may be expected to happen, to take stock of the prospects or outlook (of any venture or enterprise). [PROSPECT (1)].

PROSPECTION, [pros-pek'-shun], *n.* the action of prospecting.

PROSPECTIVE, [pros-pekt'-iv], *adj.* having an eye on the future; pertaining to the probable trend of future events; looking forward, expected. [MedL. *prospectivus*].

PROSPECTIVELY, [pros-pekt'-iv-li], *adv.* with reference to the future, in a prospective fashion.

PROSPECTIVENESS, [pros-pekt'-iv-nes], *n.* regard for the future, the quality or condition of being prospective.

PROSPECTOR, [pros-pekt'-er], *n.* one who prospects, *esp.* for minerals. [L. *prospector* one who surveys and provides for the future].

PROSPECTUS, ((*pl.* **prospectuses**), [pros-pekt'-us], *n.* a description of a forthcoming production or intended enterprise issued with a view to advertisement; a pamphlet describing an educational establishment, its advantages, usages, etc.

PROSPER, [pros'-per], *v.t. and i.* to thrive, succeed, turn out well; to cause to thrive. [L. *prosperare* to cause to be fortunate].

PROSPERITY, [pros-pe'-rit-i], *n.* the condition or quality of being prosperous.

PROSPEROUS, [pros'-per-us], *adj.* successful, fortunate, thriving; doing well, getting on; rich, flourishing, profitable. [Fr. †*prospereus*].

PROSPEROUSLY, [pros'-per-us-li], *adv.* successfully, in a prosperous fashion.

PROSPEROUSNESS, [pros'-per-us-nes], *n.* the state or quality of being prosperous.

PROSTATE, [pros'-tāt], *n.* (*anat.*) a gland accessory to the male generative organs in mammals. [MedL. *prostata*].

PROSTATECTOMY, [pro'-stāt-ek'-tom-i], *n.* (*med.*) excision of the prostate gland. [PROSTATE and Gk. *ektome* excision].

PROSTATIC, [pros-tat'-ik], *adj.* of, or pertaining to, the prostate. [Gk. *prostatikos*].

PROSTATITIS, [pros'-tat-ī'-tis], *n.* inflammation of the prostate. [PROSTATE and Gk. *itis* denoting inflammation].

PROSTHESIS, [pros'-this-is], *n.* the placing of a prefix before a word to make a compound; (*surg.*) any surgical operation concerned with supplying an artificial part, limb, or organ where the natural one is lost or lacking. [Gk. *prosthesis* addition].

PROSTHETIC, [pros-thet'-ik], *adj.* of, or pertaining to, prosthesis; prefixed.

PROSTITUTE (1), [pros'-tit-ewt], *n.* a woman who hires out her body for promiscuous sexual intercourse, a harlot. [*Next*].

PROSTITUTE (2), [pros'-tit-ewt], *adj.* put to infamous or unworthy use, employed merely for gain. [L. *prostitutus*, *p.pt.* of *prostituere* to expose in public, prostitute].

PROSTITUTE (3), [pros'-tit-ewt], *v.t.* (of a woman) to sell (herself); to employ for base and unworthy purpose, to defile or corrupt. [L. *prostituere*].

PROSTITUTION, [pros'-tit-ew'-shun], *n.* the act of debasing or prostituting; the fact of being or having been prostituted; the practice of a woman who sells her body to promiscuous sexual intercourse; the use of skill or talent for vile or unworthy ends. [L. *prostitutio*].

PROSTITUTOR, [pros'-tit-ew-tor], *n.* one who prostitutes. [LL. *prostitutor*].

PROSTRATE (1), [pros'-trāt], *adj.* lying face down flat on the ground; (*fig.*) utterly vanquished, unable to resist further; at the mercy of another without power or spirit to resist; physically exhausted;

morally exhausted, spiritless, dejected, utterly overcome. [L. *prostratus*, *p.pt.* of *prosternere* to prostrate].
PROSTRATE (2), [pros-trāt'], *v.t.* to cast down flat on the ground; (*fig.*) to exhaust; to render weak and powerless; (*reflex.*) to make a low and submissive bow; to fall flat in worship and adoration. [*Prec.*].
PROSTRATION, [pros-trā'-shun], *n.* the act of prostrating or fact of being prostrated; humiliation, abasement, exhaustion. [LL. *prostratio*].
PROSTYLE (1), [prō'-stīl], *n.* a columned portico in front of a Greek temple. [PROSTYLE (2)].

PROSTYLE

PROSTYLE (2), [prō'-stīl], *adj.* having a prostyle. [L. *prostylos* from Gk. *prostulos*].
PROSY, [prōz'-i], *adj.* written in a dull, wearisome, long-winded style; habitually talking in a dull roundabout fashion.
PROSYLLOGISM, [prō-sil'-o-jizm], *n.* (*log.*) a syllogism the conclusion of which forms a premise of another syllogism. [MedL. *prosyllogismus*].
PROTAGONIST, [prō-tag'-on-ist], *n.* the first actor in a Greek drama; a principal character in a play, story, novel, etc.; the chief champion of a cause. [Gk. *protagonistes*].
PROTANDROUS, [prō-tan'-drus], *adj.* (*bot.*) see PROTERANDROUS.
PROTASIS, [prot'-as-is], *n.* the first part of a play introducing the characters and stating the theme; (*gram.*) the first clause of a sentence, *esp.* when it states a condition upon which the main clause depends. [Gk. *protasis*].
PROTATIC, [prō-tat'-ik], *adj.* of, or pertaining to, the protasis; introductory. [Gk. *protatikos*].
PROTEA, [prō'-tē-a], *n.* one of a numerous genus of South African shrubs distinguished for their large cone-like heads of blossom. [MdL. *protea*].
PROTEAN, [prō-tē'-an], *adj.* readily appearing under different shapes; (*fig.*) versatile. [PROTEUS].
PROTECT, [prō-tekt'], *v.t.* to defend from physical injury or assault; to guard, shield, cover, keep safe and unhurt; to tend the welfare of; (*political economy*) to attempt to promote (a native industry) by laying a duty upon similar foreign products imported; (*comm.*) to set aside a sum of money against the future payment of a bill. [L. *protectus*, *p.pt.* of *protegere* to cover, protect].
PROTECTINGLY, [prō-tekt'-ing-li], *adv.* so as to give protection.
PROTECTION, [prō-tek'-shun], *n.* the act of protecting; the state of being protected; defence, guardianship, shelter, covering; guarantee; (*political economy*) the policy which seeks to foster native industry by laying a duty on similar products from abroad. [ME. *protection* from LL. *protectio*].
PROTECTIONISM, [prō-tek'-shun-izm], *n.* the economic theory or policy of protection.
PROTECTIONIST, [prō-tek'-shun-ist], *n.* an advocate of the economic policy of protection.
PROTECTIVE, [prō-tekt'-iv], *adj.* affording protection; of, or pertaining to, the economic theory of protection; **p. custody,** imprisonment of political opponents without trial on the pretext of providing for their safety; **p. foods,** foods containing (large quantities of) vitamins and similar substances necessary to health.
PROTECTIVELY, [prō-tekt'-iv-li], *adv.* in protective fashion; so as to protect.
PROTECTOR, [prō-tekt'-er], *n.* someone or something that protects; a guardian; **Lord P.,** the head of the state during the Cromwellian interregnum. [ME. *protector*, OFr. *protecteur* from L. *protector*].
PROTECTORATE, [prō-tekt'-er-at], *n.* the dignity and office of, or period of rule by, a regent or protector; the government of an uncivilized state by a greater power, a state so governed.
PROTECTORIAL, [prō'-tekt-aw'-ri-al], *adj.* of, or pertaining to, a protector or protectorate.
PROTECTORLESS, [prō-tekt'-er-les], *adj.* lacking a protector.
PROTECTORSHIP, [prō-tekt'-er-ship], *n.* the dignity and office of protector.
PROTEGE(E), protégé(e), [prot'-ezh-ā], *n.* a male (female) person under guardianship or patronage. [Fr. *protégé(e)*].
PROTEID, [prō'-tēd], *n.* a protein.
PROTEIFORM, [prō-tē'-i-fawm], *adj.* variable in form, protean.
PROTEIN, [prō'-tēn], *n.* (*chem.*) a member of a class of highly complex compounds which are fundamental constituents of animal and vegetable matter, of primary importance in foods, and are composed of carbon, hydrogen, nitrogen, oxygen and sulphur; an albuminoid. [Fr. *protéine* from Gk. *proteios* primary].
PROTEINACEOUS, [prō'-tēn-ā'-shi-us], *adj.* proteinic.
PROTEINIC, [prō-tēn'-ik], *adj.* of, or pertaining to, protein.
PROTEINOUS, [prō-tēn'-us], *adj.* proteinic.
PROTEND, [prō-tend'], *v.t.* to stretch forth, hold forward. [L. *protendere*].
PROTENSIVE, [prō-ten'-siv], *adj.* continuous, extended in length or duration.
PROTEOLYSIS, [prō'-tē-ol'-is-is], *n.* the extraction of a protein from a mixture in which it is contained. [MdL. *proteolysis*].
PROTERANDROUS, [prō'-ter-and'-rus], *adj.* (*bot.*) developing male generative organs first, protandrous. [PROTERO and Gk. *aner andros* man].
PROTERO-, *pref.* placed before, preceding. [Gk. *proteros* anterior, former, preceding].
PROTEROGYNOUS, [prō-ter-oj'-in-us], *adj.* (*bot.*) developing the female organs of generation first. [PROTERO and Gk. *gune* woman].
PROTEROZOIC (1), [prō'-ter-ō-zō'-ik], *n.* (*geol.*) the geological period which preceded the Cambrian period. [PROTEROZOIC (2)].
PROTEROZOIC (2), [prō'-ter-ō-zō'-ik], *adj.* (*geol.*) pertaining to the geological era which preceded the Cambrian period. [PROTERO and Gk. *zoe* life].
PROTERVITY, [prō-tur'-vit-i], *n.* petulance, sauciness. [L. *protervitas*].
PROTEST (1), [prō'-test], *n.* a solemn assertion or avowal, a protestation, an expression of disapproval or dissent; the raising of an objection; (*leg.*) the written statement by a notary public that payment or acceptance of a bill duly presented has been refused; **to lodge (or make) a p.,** to give expression to an objection, to protest formally; **under p.,** against one's will. [OFr. *protest* from MedL. *protestum*].
PROTEST (2), [prō-test'], *v.t. and i.* to make a solemn avowal; to raise an objection; (*leg.*) to declare formally in writing the non-acceptance or non-payment of (a bill of exchange duly presented); **to p. against,** to raise objections to. [L. *protestari* to give public testimony].
PROTESTANT (1), [prot'-est-ant], *n.* a member of a Christian church which by adherence to the principles of the Reformation holds itself distinct from the Roman Catholic Church. [Germ. and Fr. *Protestant* from L. *protestans*, *pres.pt.* of *protestari* to testify publicly].
PROTESTANT (2), [pro-test'-ant], *n.* one who protests strongly against a rule or decision. [*Prec.*].
PROTESTANT (3), [prot'-est-ant], *adj.* pertaining to, or supporting, the principles of Protestantism. [PROTESTANT (1)].
PROTESTANT (4), [pro-test'-ant], *adj.* assuming an attitude of protest. [PROTESTANT (1)].
PROTESTANTISM, [prot'-est-ant-izm], *n.* the principles of the Reformation and in particular, severance from the Church of Rome.
PROTESTANTIZE, [prot'-est-ant-īz], *v.t.* to convert to Protestantism.
PROTESTATION, [pro'-test-ā'-shun], *n.* an affirmation or avowal. [LL. *protestatio*].
PROTESTER, [prō-test'-er], *n.* one who protests.
PROTESTINGLY, [prō'-test'-ing-li], *adv.* with protests.
PROTEUS, [prō'-tews], *n.* (*class. myth.*) a sea-god who, if caught and held, could be compelled to foretell the future but who would assume all shapes of beasts and birds in attempting to escape; (*biol.*) a bacillus found in decomposing animal matter; a genus of eel-like amphibians with four short, weak legs, inhabiting cave pools; (*fig.*) a person who easily changes his opinion, a turncoat. [Gk. *Proteus*].
PROTHALAMIUM, [prō'-thal-ā'-mi-um], *n.* a bridal song. [PRO (1) and Gk. *thalamos* bridal chamber].
PROTHALLIUM, [prō-thal'-i-um], *n.* the prothallus.
PROTHALLUS, [prō-thal'-us], *n.* (*bot.*) the thallus bearing the male and female organs, from which ferns and their allies are developed. [PRO (1) and Gk. *thallos* a shoot].
PROTHESIS, [proth'-is-is], *n.* the setting forth of the

elements before the eucharist on the credence table. [Gk. *prothesis* a setting forth in public].
PROTHONOTARY, see PROTONOTARY.
PROTHORAX, [prō-thaw'-raks], *n.* (*biol.*) the first segment of an insect's thorax. [PRO (1) and THORAX].
PROTISTA, [prō-tist'-a], *n.*(*pl.*) (*biol.*) a class of creatures which seem to be neither plants nor animals. [Gk. *protista*, *neut.pl. superl.* of *protos* first].
PROTO-, *pref.* first. [Gk. *protos* first].
PROTOCHORDATES, [prō'-tō-kawd'-āts], *n.*(*pl.*) the lowest order of vertebrates, the semi-vertebrates.
PROTOCOCCUS, (*pl.* **protococci**), [prō'-tō-kok'-us], *n.* a genus of green algae commonly seen forming green patches on trees, fences, etc., in which each organism consists of one cell. [PROTO and Gk. *kokkos* a seed].
PROTOCOL (1), [prō'-tō-kol'], *n.* a preliminary agreement in negotiations for a major treaty; a small tab affixed to an official document giving the name of the writer of the document and the date of writing; a formula opening or concluding a papal bull. [OFr. *prothocole*, MedL. *protocollum* from LateGk. *protokollon*].
PROTOCOL (2), [prō'-tō-kol'], *v.t. and i.* to make a protocol; to draw up in the form of a protocol. [PROTOCOL (1)].
PROTOGENIC, [prō'-tō-jen'-ik], *adj.* primitive, primary, original. [Gk. *protogenes* first-formed].
PROTOGINE, [prō'-tō-jīn], *n.* a variety of granite found in the Alps. [Fr. *protogine*].
PROTOGYNOUS, [prō-toj'-in-us], *adj.* (*bot.*) proterogynous. [PROTO and Gk. *gune* woman].
PROTOMARTYR, [prō'-tō-mah'-ter], *n.* the first martyr in any cause, *esp.* St. Stephen, the first Christian martyr. [MedL. *protomartyr* from EcclesGk. *protomartur*].
PROTON, [prō'-ton], *n.* a unit of measurement of positive charges of electricity. [Gk. *proton*, *neut.sg.* of *protos* first].
PROTONEMA, [prō-tō-nēm'-a], *n.* (*bot.*) the green filamentous process from which the new moss plant grows. [PROTO and Gk. *nema* thread].
PROTONOTARY, PROTHONOTARY, [prō'-tō-nō'-ter-i], *n.* ((*leg.*) the chief clerk in a court of law; (*Gk. Orthodox Church*) the chief secretary of the Patriarch of Constantinople; (*R.C.*) a member of the College of Apostolic Protonotaries constituted to register papal acts. [LL. *protonotarius* from Gk. *protonotarios*].
PROTOPHYTE, [prō'-tō-fīt], *n.* (*bot.*) a member of the lowest order of plant life consisting of a single cell. [MdL. *protophytum* from PROTO and Gk. *phuton* a plant].
PROTOPLASM, [prō'-tō-plazm], *n.* a complex semi-fluid, colourless substance which is essential in the composition of every living cell. [Germ. *protoplasma* from Gk. *protos* first and *plasma* something moulded].
PROTOPLASMIC, [prō'-tō-plaz'-mik], *adj.* of, or pertaining to, protoplasm.
PROTOPLASTIC, [prō'-tō-plas'-tik], *adj.* having the first or original shape. [PROTO and PLASTIC].
PROTOTHERIA, [prō'-tō-thēer'-i-a], *n.*(*pl.*) (*biol.*) the name given to the lowest subclass and order of mammals. [PROTO and Gk. *theron* beast].
PROTOTYPAL, [prō'-tō-tīp'-al], *adj.* serving as a pattern or prototype.
PROTOTYPE, [prō'-tō-tīp], *n.* the primary type of a series; a pattern. [Gk. *prototupos* original].
PROTOZOA, [prō-tō-zō'-a], *n.*(*pl.*) (*zool.*) a term used for all the simplest, unicellular forms of animal life. [PROTO and Gk. *zoa*, *pl.* of *zoon* animal].
PROTOZOAN (1), [prō-tō-zō'-an], *n.* any one of the protozoa.
PROTOZOAN (2), [prō-tō-zō'-an], *adj.* of, or pertaining to, the protozoa.
PROTOZOIC, [prō-tō-zō'-ic], *adj.* (*geol.*) pertaining to those strata containing evidence of the earliest forms of life; pertaining to that period when the earliest and simplest forms of life existed.
PROTRACT, [prō-trakt'], *v.t.* to lengthen, *esp.* to cause to last longer, to delay; (*surveying*) to draw to scale; (*zool.*) to thrust out, extend. [L. *protractum*, *p.pt.* of *protrahere* to draw forth].
PROTRACTED, [prō-trakt'-id], *adj.* prolonged, delayed, made to last a long while.
PROTRACTEDLY, [prō-trakt'-id-li], *adv.* in a protracted fashion.
PROTRACTER, [prō-trakt'-er], *n.* someone or something that draws out.
PROTRACTION, [prō-trak'-shun], *n.* the act of protracting, delaying, lengthening in duration; the fact of being protracted; (*zool.*) the act of thrusting out (an organ or limb); (*surveying*) the act of making a scale plan of. [L. *protractio*].
PROTRACTOR, [prō-trakt'-or], *n.* a draughtsman's instrument for measuring angles; **p. muscle**, (*anat.*) a muscle that causes a limb or organ to protract. [MedL. *protractor*].

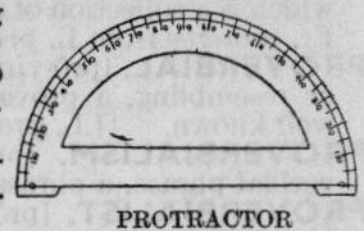
PROTRACTOR

PROTREPTIC, [prō-trept'-ik], *adj.* protreptical. [Gk. *protreptikos*].
PROTREPTICAL, [prō-trept'-ikl], *adj.* exhortatory, didactic.
PROTRUDE, [prō-trōōd'], *v.t. and i.* to project, jut out; to cause to project, thrust out, extend. [L. *protrudere*].
PROTRUSILE, [prō-trōō'-sīl], *adj.* able to be protruded.
PROTRUSION, [prō-trōō'-zhun], *n.* the act of protruding or fact of being protruded.
PROTRUSIVE, [prō-trōō'-siv], *adj.* thrusting forward, causing to protrude; able to be protruded; obtrusive.
PROTRUSIVELY, [prō-trōō'-siv-li], *adv.* in a protrusive fashion.
PROTUBERANCE, [prō-tew'-ber-ants], *n.* the state of being protuberant; anything that is protuberant, a lump, knob, or projection.
PROTUBERANT, [prō-tewb'-er-ant], *adj.* swelling or jutting out, bulging, prominent. [L. *protuberans*, *pres.pt.* of *protuberare* to bulge out, swell].
PROTUBERANTLY, [prō-tew'-ber-ant-li], *adv.* in a protuberant way.
PROTUBERATE, [prō-tew'-ber-āt], *v.i.* to bulge out, swell. [L. *protuberatus*, *p.pt.* of *protuberare* to bulge out].
PROTUBERATION, [prō-tew'-ber-ā'-shun], *n.* the condition of swelling beyond the surrounding surface; a protuberance.
PROUD (1), [prowd], *adj.* having a sense of just and proper pride; indulging in a feeling of undue or unwarranted satisfaction with oneself, arrogant; unwilling to lower one's dignity; arising from arrogance; haughty, intolerant; giving cause for proper pride; splendid, gorgeous; heroic; eminent, outstanding; **p. flesh**, a granulated over-growth of flesh round a healing wound. [OE. *prut* or *prud*].
PROUD (2), [prowd], *adv.* (in *coll.* phrase) **to do (someone) proud**, to entertain (someone) splendidly; to give great satisfaction. [PROUD (1)].
PROUDLY, [prowd'-li], *adv.* in a proud way.
PROUDNESS, [prowd'-nes], *n.* the condition or quality of being proud.
PROUSTITE, [prōō'-stit], *n.* (*min.*) light-red silver ore, sulpharsenide of silver. [Fr. *proustite* from J. L. *Proust*, who discovered it].
PROVABLE, [prōōv'-abl], *adj.* able to be proved, demonstrable.
PROVABLENESS, [prōōv'-abl-nes], *n.* the condition of being provable.
PROVABLY, [prōōv'-ab-li], *adv.* in a manner that can be proved, demonstrably.
PROVE, [prōōv], *v.t.* to test or try; to test the worth or genuineness of, to test the quality of; to put to the test; to demonstrate to be true, to establish as true; to demonstrate the reality of, to show to exist; (*refl.*) to give proof that (one) is, to show (oneself) as; to experience, undergo, suffer, to get to know by experience; (*leg.*) to establish the validity of; (*arith.*) to test the accuracy of (a calculation); *v.i.* to turn out to be, to be shown to be. [OFr. *prover* from L. *probare*].
PROVEDORE, [prov-id-aw'-ri], *n.* a commander or governor in the state of the old republic of Venice; a steward or caterer. [It. *provedore*].
PROVEN, [prōv'-en, prōōv'-en], (*archaic*) *p.pt.* of PROVE.
PROVENANCE, [prov'-in-ants], *n.* origin or source. [Fr. *provenance*].
PROVENCAL, Provençal (1), [prov-ah(ng)-sahl'], *n.* an inhabitant of Provence; the language spoken there. [Fr. *provençal*].
PROVENCAL, Provençal (2), [prov-ah(ng)-sahl'], *adj.* pertaining to Provence or the people who live there. [Fr. *provençal*].
PROVENDER, [prov'-en-der], *n.* food, *esp.* a supply of food for horses. [OFr. *provendre*].
PROVENIENCE, [prō-vēn'-i-ents], *n.* source, provenance. [L. *proveniens*, *pres.pt.* of *provenire* to arise].
PROVER, [prōōv'-er], *n.* a person who proves.
PROVERB, [prov'-erb], *n.* a short traditional phrase

or sentence, often in a laconic style, expressing some maxim of worldly wisdom or some view that experience bears out; (*fig.*) a familiar or notorious example; **B. of Proverbs,** a book of the *O.T.* attributed to Solomon which is a collection of such maxims. [ME. *proverbe*, Fr. *proverbe* from L. *proverbium*].

PROVERBIAL, [prō-vurb'-i-al], *adj.* of, pertaining to, or resembling, a proverb; (*fig.*) notorious, familiar, well known. [LL. *proverbialis*].

PROVERBIALISM, [prō-vurb'-i-al-izm], *n.* a proverbial phrase, a phrase resembling a proverb.

PROVERBIALIST, [prō-vurb'-i-al-ist], *n.* one given to using or collecting proverbs.

PROVERBIALIZE, [prō-vurb'-i-al-īz], *v.i.* to speak in proverbs, to quote a proverb.

PROVERBIALLY, [prō-vurb'-i-al-i], *adv.* in a proverbial fashion, commonly, notoriously.

PROVIANT, [prov'-i-ant], *n.* the food supply of an army. [Germ. *proviant*].

PROVIDE, [prō-vīd'], *v.t. and i.* to make provision; to render available, supply; **to p. against,** to take steps to prevent, to make provision in anticipation of; to prohibit by law; **to p. for,** to supply at least the necessaries of life for; to make provision against the future on behalf of, to make allowance for, to anticipate in one's preparations; to render legally permissible; **to p. that,** to stipulate that; **to p. with,** to furnish with, equip with. [L. *providere* to foresee, to attend to].

PROVIDED, [prō-vīd'-id], *conj.* **p. that,** on condition that. [*p.pt.* of PROVIDE].

PROVIDENCE, [prov'-id-ents], *n.* the quality of being provident; thrift; foresight; the benevolent personality of God. [L. *providentia* foresight].

PROVIDENT, [prov'-id-ent], *adj.* having foresight, careful about the future, thrifty. [L. *providens*, *pres.pt.* of *providere* to foresee].

PROVIDENTIAL, [prov'-id-en'-shal], *adj.* as of the benevolence of God; fortuitous.

PROVIDENTIALLY, [prov'-id-en'-shal-i], *adv.* in a providential fashion.

PROVIDENTLY, [prov'-id-ent-li], *adv.* with foresight, with frugality, with careful attention to the future.

PROVIDENTNESS, [prov'-id-ent-nes], *n.* prudence, foresight, the quality of being provident.

PROVIDER, [prō-vīd'-er], *n.* one who provides or supplies, one who makes provision.

PROVIDING, [prō-vīd'-ing], *conj.* on condition that.

PROVINCE, [prov'-ints], *n.* a large tract of territory forming one unit in the administration of a great government; a large piece of territory united by tradition dialect, trade, etc., though possibly now no longer an administrative unit; the territory under the ecclesiastical jurisdiction of an archbishop; (*fig.*) a sphere of activity, learning, experience, etc.; (*pl.*) those parts of any country that lie outside and away from the capital. [OFr. *province* from L. *provincia*].

PROVINCIAL (1), [prō-vin'-shal], *n.* one who inhabits a province or the provinces. [PROVINCIAL (2)].

PROVINCIAL (2), [prō-vin'-shal], *adj.* of, or pertaining to, a province or the provinces; lacking in urban or metropolitan polish, countrified. [L. *provincialis*].

PROVINCIALISM, [prō-vin'-shal-izm], *n.* that outlook which puts the needs and considerations of a province before the needs of the whole country; the outlook of a provincial; a dialectal trick of speech; a provincial habit or custom.

PROVINCIALITY, [prō-vin'-shi-al'-i-ti], *n.* provincialism.

PROVINCIALLY, [prō-vin'-shi-al-i], *adv.* in a provincial fashion.

PROVINE, [prō-vīn'], *v.i.* to plant out a slip or cutting from a vine. [Fr. *provignier* to provine, OFr. *provain* from L. *propago* a shoot].

PROVISION, [prō-vizh'-un], *n.* the action of providing, the act of making arrangements for future events and circumstances; the act of making available necessary supplies; anything, *esp.* a necessary thing, provided against the future; a demand or condition formally laid down against stated conditions, a stipulation, a proviso; (*eccles.*) the act of making an appointment to a benefice not yet vacant, *esp.* by the Pope, who thereby in that instance abrogates the normal right of patronage to that particular benefice; (*pl.*) a supply of necessary things, a stock or store, *esp.* of food; necessary foodstuffs; **to make p. for,** to make arrangements for, prepare for, provide for. [L. *provisio*].

PROVISIONAL, [prō-vizh'-un-al], *adj.* having the nature of a temporary arrangement made to meet special circumstances, and intended to last only as long as these circumstances last.

PROVISIONALLY, [prō-vizh'-un-al-i], *adv.* in a provisional manner.

PROVISIONARY, [prō-vizh'-un-er-i], *adj.* provisional, temporary; (*eccles.*) pertaining to a provision or appointment to a not-yet-vacant benefice.

PROVISO, [prō-vī'-zō], *n.* a clause in a legal document or agreement controlling the validity of that document or agreement by stating those conditions under which it is operative; a condition, provision, stipulation. [MedL. *proviso* (*quod*) it being provided that].

PROVISOR, [prō-vīz'-er], *n.* (*hist.* and *eccles.*) one appointed by provision to a living not yet vacant. [ME. *provisour* provisor from L. *provisor* one who provides].

PROVISORILY, [prō-vīz'-er-i-li], *adv.* provisionally.

PROVISORY, [prō-vīz'-er-i], *adj.* provisional, temporary; controlled by a proviso.

PROVOCATION, [prov'-ok-ā'-shun], *n.* the act of provoking or being provoked; anything that provokes, instigates, annoys, etc. [L. *provocatio* the act of calling forth].

PROVOCATIVE, [prov-ok'-at-iv], *adj.* causing provocation, annoying, challenging. [LL. *provocativus*].

PROVOCATIVENESS, [prov-ok'-at-iv-nes], *n.* the condition or quality of being provocative.

PROVOKABLE, [prō-vōk'-abl], *adj.* able to be provoked.

PROVOKE, [prō-vōk'], *v.t.* to call forth, bring about, induce, produce, give rise to; to stir up, cause by agitation; to annoy, exasperate; to challenge; **to p. (someone) to,** to incite or urge (someone) to, to spur or prick (someone) on to. [L. *provocare* to call forth].

PROVOKER, [prō-vōk'-er], *n.* someone or something that provokes.

PROVOKING, [prō-vōk'-ing], *adj.* annoying, irritating, exasperating, vexing.

PROVOKINGLY, [prō-vōk'-ing'-li], *adv.* in a provoking fashion.

PROVOST, [prov'-ost], *n.* the head of certain university colleges; the officer of a Scottish burgh, corresponding to a mayor in an English borough. [OE. *profost* from LL. *propositus* from L. *praepositus* an officer, one set in authority].

PROVOST-MARSHAL, [prov'-ō-mah'-shal], *n.* (in the army) the head of the military police in a given place or with a given force; (in the navy) the master-at-arms on a ship where a court-martial is in progress.

PROVOSTSHIP, [prov'-ost-ship], *n.* the office, dignity and function of provost.

PROW, [prow], *n.* the foremost part of a ship or boat; anything resembling this. [Fr. *proue* from L. *proa*].

PROW

PROWESS, [prow'-es], *n.* valour, courage, skill. [ME. *proewsse* from OFr. *prouesse* courage].

PROWL (1), [prowl], *n.* the act of prowling; **to go on the p.,** to prowl. [PROWL (2)].

PROWL (2), [prowl], *v.i.* (of animals) to move about, usually warily and stealthily, in search of prey; (of persons) to walk about in a way resembling this; (*coll.*) to walk or wander about. [ME. *prollen*].

PROWLER, [prowl'-er], *n.* an animal prowling about for prey; a person given to wandering about, *esp.* in a furtive manner.

PROWLING, [prowl'-ing], *adj.* wandering about in search of prey.

PROWLINGLY, [prowl'-ing-li], *adv.* a prowling fashion.

PROXIMAL, [proks'-im-al], *adj.* (*anat.*) situated near to the centre of the body or to the point of attachment of a limb, distal.

PROXIMATE, [proks'-im-at], *adj.* close, adjacent, next, in time or space; **p. cause,** the immediate cause. [LL. *proximatus*, *p.pt.* of *proximare* to approach].

PROXIMATELY, [proks'-im-at-li], *adv.* in a proximate way.

PROXIME, [proks'-im-ē], *adv.* next nearest; **p. accessit,** (used of) the runner-up in a contest. [L. *proxime*].

PROXIMITY, [proks-im'-i-ti], *n.* the condition or quality of being close, in space or time; affinity, close relationship by blood. [L. *proximitas* nearness].

PROXIMO, [proks'-im-ō], *adv.* in the next month. [L. *proximo* (*mense*) in the next (month)].

PROXY, [proks'-i], *n.* a person acting as agent for another; the authority, function or capacity of a person so acting; a document authorizing a person to act thus. [ME. *prouksie*, OFr. *procuracie* from MedL. *procuratia*].

PROXYSHIP, [proks'-i-ship], *n.* the office or function of a proxy.

PRUDE, [prōōd], *n.* a person (usually a woman) of affected or exaggerated modesty. [OFr. *prude* modest].

PRUDENCE, [prōōd'-ents], *n.* the quality of being prudent; the practice of discreet and politic conduct; wise, circumspect outlook or actions, care, foresight, sagacity. [L. *prudentia*].

PRUDENT, [prōōd'-ent], *adj.* characterized by, or acting according to, discreet and politic principles; not given to taking risks; wise, cautious, circumspect, worldly wise, discerning. [L. *prudens* from *providens*, *pres.pt.* of *providere* to foresee].

PRUDENTIAL, [prōōd-en'-shal], *adj.* of, or pertaining to, prudence, to prudent actions or character; characterized by prudence. [MedL. *prudentialis*].

PRUDENTIALLY, [prōōd-en'-shal-i], *adv.* in a prudential way.

PRUDENTLY, [prōōd'-ent-li], *adv.* in a prudent fashion.

PRUDERY, [prōōd'-er-i], *n.* affected or exaggerated modesty, the point of view of a prude.

PRUDISH, [prōōd'-ish], *adj.* affectedly modest, characterized by prudery.

PRUDISHLY, [prōōd'-ish-li], *adv.* in a prudish fashion.

PRUDISHNESS, [prōōd'-ish-nes], *n.* the state or quality of being prudish.

PRUINOSE, [prōō'-in-ōs], *adj.* (*bot.*) covered with a white dust or powder resembling frost. [L. *pruinosus* frosty].

PRUNE (1), [prōōn], *n.* a kind of dried plum; the rich purple colour of a dried plum. [Fr. *prune*, MedL. *pruna*, L. *prunum* from Gk. *prounon* plum].

PRUNE (2), [prōōn], *v.t.* (*hort.*) to cut off unnecessary growths on (trees or bushes); (*fig.*) to cut down, curtail, lop off excrescences on. [OFr. *proigner* to trim, cut].

PRUNELLA (1), **PRUNELLO**, [prōō-nel'-a, prōō-nel'-ō], *n.* a strong worsted cloth having a dark plum colour, at one time used for legal, clerical or academic robes.

PRUNELLA (2), [prōō-nel'-a], *n.* a disease of the throat, *esp.* quinsy; (*bot.*) a genus of plants including the herb, *Prunella vulgaris*, used to cure quinsy. [Unkn.].

PRUNELLO (1), see PRUNELLA (1).

PRUNELLO (2), [prōōn-el'-ō], *n.* a fine variety of prune.

PRUNER, [prōōn'-er], *n.* one who, or that which, prunes.

PRUNIFEROUS, [prōōn-if'-er-us], *adj.* (of a tree) yielding plums. [L. *prunum* plum and *ferre* to bear].

PRUNING, [prōōn'-ing], *n.* (*hort.*) the act of cutting unnecessary growth from trees and bushes.

PRUNING-HOOK, [prōōn'-ing-hŏŏk'], *n.* a knife with a curved blade used in pruning.

PRUNING-KNIFE, [prōōn'-ing-nīf'], *n.* a knife used for pruning.

PRUNING-KNIFE

PRURIENCE, [prŏŏer'-i-ents], *n.* the state or quality of being prurient; a morbid preoccupation with sex or obscenity.

PRURIENCY, [prŏŏer'-ri-en-si], *n.* prurience.

PRURIENT, [prŏŏer'-i-ent], *adj.* preoccupied with thoughts of sex or obscenity; itching. [L. *pruriens*, *pres.pt.* of *prurire* to itch].

PRURIENTLY, [prŏŏer'-i-ent-li], *adv.* in a prurient fashion.

PRURIGINOUS, [prŏŏer-ij'-in-us], *adj.* suffering from prurigo. [LL. *pruriginosus*].

PRURIGO, [prŏŏer'-ī'-gō], *n.* (*med.*) a disease of the skin characterized by chronic itching and the appearance of reddish papules. [L. *prurigo* itching].

PRUSSIAN (1), [prush'-an], *n.* an inhabitant or native of Prussia; **Old P.**, the ancient Baltic language of Prussia. [PRUSSIAN (2)].

PRUSSIAN (2), [prush'-an], *adj.* of, or pertaining to, Prussia or the Prussians; **p. blue**, a deep greeny-blue colour. [MdL. *Prussianus*].

PRUSSIANISM, [pru'-shan-izm], *n.* the policy or attitude proverbially characteristic of the Prussians, *esp.* one of brutality and militarism.

PRUSSIATE, [prus'-i-āt], *n.* any salt of prussic acid. [Fr. *prussiate*].

PRUSSIC ACID, [pru'-sik-as'-id], *n.* hydrocyanic acid, HCN, in an aqueous solution. [~PRUSSIAN BLUE].

PRY (1), [prī], *v.i.* to peer into, spy on; **to p. into**, to be curious about, search into, *esp.* impertinently. [ME. *pryen*].

PRY (2), [prī], *v.t.* to raise or burst with a lever. [*Var.* of PRISE].

PRYAN, [prī'-an], *n.* a soft white clay found in Cornish mines. [Corn. *pryan*].

PRYING, [prī'-ing], *adj.* spying, peering; impertinently curious.

PRYINGLY, [prī'-ing-li], *adv.* with impertinent curiosity, in a prying manner.

PRYTANEUM, [prit'-an-ē'-um], *n.* the public banqueting hall in an ancient Greek city where the sacred fire was kept always burning. [L. *prytaneum* from Gk. *prutaneion*].

PRYTHEE†, [priTH'-ē], *int.* I pray thee! used to introduce a question or request.

PSALM, [sahm], *n.* a sacred song, a hymn; one of the songs in the Book of Psalms (*O.T.*); (*pl.*) the songs in the Book of Psalms as used in Christian worship. [L. *psalmus* from Gk. *psalmos* the act of plucking the strings of a harp].

PSALMIST, [sahm'-ist], *n.* a writer of psalms; **the P.**, King David, traditionally considered the author of the Book of Psalms. [L. *psalmista*].

PSALMODIC, [sahm-od'-ik], *adj.* of, or relating to, psalmody.

PSALMODIST, [sahm'-od-ist], *n.* a singer of psalms.

PSALMODY, [sahm'-o-di], *n.* the art of singing psalms; a collection of psalms and music for these. [L. *psalmodia* from Gk. *psalmoidia*].

PSALTER, [sawl'-ter], *n.* the Book of Psalms, *esp.* the version in the Book of Common Prayer; a collection of psalms; a special version of the Book of Psalms. [ME. *sauter*, OFr. *sautier*, from L. *psalterium*].

PSALTERY, [sawl'-ter-i], *n.* an ancient stringed instrument resembling a dulcimer, but played by plucking, not striking, the strings. [OFr. *sauterie*].

PSAMMITE, [sam'-īt], *n.* (*min.*) a sort of fine sandstone. [Fr. *psammite* from Gk. *psammos* sand].

PSAMMITIC, [sam-it'-ik], *adj.* of, or pertaining to, psammite.

PSATUROSE, [sat'-ew-rōs], *n.* stephanite.

PSCHENT, [pshent], *n.* the ancient Egyptian double crown consisting of the red crown of Lower Egypt and the white crown of Upper Egypt. [Egyptian Demotic *pskhent*].

PSELLISM, [sel'-izm], *n.* defective enunciation. [Gk. *psellismos* stammering].

PSEUDAESTHESIA, [sewd'-es-thē'-zia], *n.* the sensation of being able to feel in an organ that is defunct or has been removed. [PSEUDO and Gk. *aisthesis* feeling].

PSEUDEPIGRAPHY, [sew'-dep-ig'-raf-i], *n.* mistaken ascription of authorship. [Gk. *pseudepigraphos* having a false title].

PSEUDO-, [sew'-dō], *pref.* false, sham. [Gk. from *pseudos* a lie].

PSEUDOBLEPSIS, [sew'-dō-blep'-sis], *n.* (*opt.*) false vision. [PSEUDO and Gk. *blepsis* sight].

PSEUDOBULB, [sew'-dō-bulb'], *n.* (*bot.*) a swelling at the bottom of the stem (*esp.* in orchids) resembling a bulb. [PSEUDO and BULB].

PSEUDOGRAPH, [sew'-dō-graf'], *n.* a literary work purporting to be written by someone other than the actual author. [PSEUDO and Gk. *graphia* writing].

PSEUDOLOGY, [sew-dol'-oj-i], *n.* the art or practice of telling lies. [PSEUDO and Gk. *logos* speech].

PSEUDOMORPH, [sew'-dō-mawf'], *n.* a false, unnatural form. [PSEUDO and Gk. *morphe* form].

PSEUDOMORPHOUS, [sew'-dō-mawf'-us], *adj.* having a false form.

PSEUDONYM, [sew'-dō-nim], *n.* an assumed name; *esp.* a name assumed for the publication of literary works. [PSEUDO and Gk. *onoma* name].

PSEUDONYMITY, [sew'-dō-nim'-it-i], *n.* the act of using a false name, the fact of being known under a false name.

PSEUDONYMOUS, [sew-don'-im-us], *adj.* known under a false name, bearing a false name.

PSEUDOPODIA, [sew'-dō-pō'-dia], *n.*(*pl.*) the protrusive extension made by protozoa to move about or take in food; (*bot.*) false setae or pedicels in mosses. [PSEUDO and Gk. *podion* a little foot].

PSEUDOSCOPE, [sew'-dō-skōp], *n.* (*opt.*) an optical instrument which makes any object viewed through it appear concave where it is convex and convex where it is concave. [PSEUDO and SCOPE].

PSHAW, [pshaw], *int.* expressing disdain.

PSILANTHROPISM, [sīl-an′-throp-izm], *n.* the teaching of the psilanthropists. [Gk. *psilanthropos* merely human].

PSILANTHROPIST, [sīl-an′-throp-ist], *n.* a believer in the doctrine that Jesus Christ was only human.

PSILANTHROPY, [sīl-an′-throp-i], *n.* psilanthropism.

PSILOMELANE, [sī-lom′-el-ān], *n.* (*min.*) a black amorphous ore of manganese. [Gk. *psilos* bare, mere and *melas* black].

PSITTACEOUS, [sit-ā′-shus], *adj.* belonging to the parrot group of birds, the *Psittacidæ*. [Gk. *psittakos* parrot].

PSITTACINE (1), [sit′-as-īn], *n.* a bird of the parrot family. [*Next*].

PSITTACINE (2), [sit′-as-īn], *adj.* of, or pertaining to, parrots; resembling a parrot. [L. *psittacinus*].

PSITTACOSIS, [sit-ak-ō′-sis], *n.* (*path.*) a disease among parrots communicable to human beings. [Gk. *psittakos* parrot and *osis* denoting condition].

PSOAS, [sō′-as], *n.* the name of the two hip muscles. [Gk. *psoa* muscle of the loins].

PSORIASIS, [so-rī′-as-is], *n.* a severe but non-contagious skin disease which makes itself apparent in red scaly patches. [Gk. *psoriasis* itch].

PSYCHE, [sī′-ki], *n.* (*class. myth.*) the name of a young girl, represented as having butterfly wings, beloved of Eros the god of love and representing immortality; the soul, the principle of life in man; (*entom.*) a genus of moths. [L. *psyche* from Gk. *psukhe* breath].

PSYCHIATRIST, [sī-kī′-at-rist], *n.* a doctor skilled in treating mental diseases.

PSYCHIATRY, [sī-kī′-at-ri], *n.* the cure of mental diseases. [Fr. *psychiatrie* from Gk. *psukhe* breath and *iatria* healing].

PSYCHIC (1), [sī′-kik], *n.* a medium in spiritualist investigation. [PSYCHIC (2)].

PSYCHIC (2), [sī′-kik] *adj.* of, or pertaining to, the soul or mind; pertaining to the spirit world; susceptible to spirit influence; **p. bid,** a bid at bridge having no justification beyond intuition. [Gk. *psukikos*].

PSYCHICAL, [sī′-kikl], *adj.* psychic, spiritualistic, supernatural.

PSYCHICALLY, [sī′-kik-al-i], *adv.* in a psychic fashion.

PSYCHICS, [sī′-kiks], *n.(pl.)* psychical study and research.

PSYCHIST, [sī′-kist], *n.* a student of the supernatural, a medium.

PSYCHO-, [sī′-kō], *pref.* pertaining to the mind. [Gk. *psukhe* breath].

PSYCHO-ANALYSIS, [sī′-kō-an-al′-is-is], *n.* investigation into mental processes based on the researches of Freud and Jung. [PSYCHO and ANALYSIS].

PSYCHO-ANALYST, [sī′-kō-an′-al-ist], *n.* one who practises psycho-analysis.

PSYCHO-ANALYTIC, [sī′-kō-an-al-it′-ik], *adj.* of, or pertaining to, psycho-analysis.

PSYCHOGENESIS, [sī′-kō-jen′-is-is], *n.* the origin and development of the mind or soul. [PSYCHO and GENESIS].

PSYCHOGONY, [sī-kog′-o-ni], *n.* psychogenesis. [Gk. *psukhogonia*].

PSYCHOLOGICAL, [sī-kol-oj′-ikl], *adj.* of, or pertaining to, psychology; pertaining to the mind, mental; **p. moment,** the momentum of a fact, idea, event or sensation upon the mind; (*coll.*) the precise moment when the greatest effect can be gained.

PSYCHOLOGICALLY, [sī-kol-oj′-ik-al-i], *adv.* mentally, from a psychological point of view.

PSYCHOLOGIST, [sī-kol′-oj-ist], *n.* one who practises psychology.

PSYCHOLOGY, [sī-kol′-o-ji], *n.* the study of the mind, its nature, processes, habits, etc. [MdL. *psychologia* from PSYCHO and Gk. *logos* speech].

PSYCHOMANCY, [sī′-kom-an-si], *n.* necromancy, spiritualistic communication. [PSYCHO and Gk. *manteia* divination].

PSYCHOMETRICAL, [sī′-kom-et′-rikl], *adj.* pertaining to psychometry.

PSYCHOMETRY, [sī-kōm′-et-ri], *n.* the measurement of mental processes in relation to time; the psychic power of divining information about dead or absent persons when in physical contact with objects they have possessed or persons they have known. [PSYCHO and Gk. *metria* measuring].

PSYCHOMOTOR, [sī′-kō-mō′-tor], *adj.* relating to physical action produced as a result of mental condition. [PSYCHO and MOTOR].

PSYCHOPATH, [sī′-kō-path′], *n.* a sufferer from a mental disease. [PSYCHO and Gk. *pathos* emotion, suffering].

PSYCHOPATHIC, [sī′-kō-path′-ik], *adj.* suffering from a mental disease or disorder; highly emotional; hysterical.

PSYCHOPATHIST, [sī-kop′-ath-ist], *n.* a student of mental disorders.

PSYCHOPATHOLOGY, [sī′-kō-path-ol′-o-ji], *n.* the science and study of mental disorders. [PSYCHO and PATHOLOGY].

PSYCHOPATHY, [sī-kop′-ath-i], *n.* mental disorder; medical treatment by hypnotism. [PSYCHO and Gk. *pathos* emotion, suffering].

PSYCHOPHYSICAL, [sī′-kō-fiz′-ikl], *adj.* of, or pertaining to, psychophysics. [PSYCHO and PHYSICAL].

PSYCHOPHYSICIST, [sī′-kō-fiz′-is-ist], *n.* one who studies psychophysics. [PSYCHO and PHYSICIST].

PSYCHOPHYSICS, [sī′-kō-fiz′-iks], *n.(pl.)* the study of the relations between mind and body. [PSYCHO and PHYSICS].

PSYCHOPHYSIOLOGY, [sī′-kō-fiz′-i-ol′-oj-i], *n.* that science which is concerned with the inter-relations of psychology and physiology. [PSYCHO and PHYSIOLOGY].

PSYCHOPLASM, [sī′-kō-plazm′], *n.* the name given to the basis of consciousness conceived materially, *esp.* protoplasm. [PSYCHO and Gk. *plasma* something formed].

PSYCHOSIS, [sī-kō′-sis], *n.* mental disease that is not represented by any disorder or disease of the actual physical structure of the brain. [PSYCHO and Gk. *osis* denoting condition].

PSYCHOTHERAPEUTICS, [sī′-kō-the′-rap-ew′-tiks], *n.(pl.)* the treatment of illness or disease by non-physical methods, i.e., by hypnotism or psycho-analysis. [PSYCHO and THERAPEUTICS].

PSYCHOTHERAPY, [sī′-kō-the′-ra-pi], *n.* psychotherapeutics.

PSYCHROMETER, [sī-krom′-it-er], *n.* a device for measuring the humidity of the atmosphere. [Gk. *psukhros* cold and METER].

PTARMIC (1), [tah′-mik], *n.* a substance that causes one to sneeze. [PTARMIC (2)].

PTARMIC (2), [tah′-mik], *adj.* causing sneezing. [L. *ptarmicus* from Gk. *ptarmikos*].

PTARMIGAN, [tah′-mig-an], *n.* the white grouse of Northern Europe, *Lagopus mutus*, of a grey plumage which turns white in winter; the willow grouse, *Lagopus lagopus*, found in America and Europe. [Gael. *tarmachan*].

PTERIDOLOGIST, [te′-rid-ol′-o-jist], *n.* a student of pteridology.

PTERIDOLOGY, [te′-rid-ol′-o-ji], *n.* the study of ferns. [Gk. *pteris* a fern and *logos* speech].

PTERIDOPHYTE, [te′-rid-ō-fit], *n.* one of a group of plants, *Pteridophyta*, of which the ferns are the principal members.

PTERO-, [te′-rō], *pref.* winged, connected with wings or feathers. [Gk. *pteron* wing, feather].

PTERODACTYL, [te′-rō-dak′-til], *n.* an extinct winged reptile whose membranous wings extended on either side from the body to the last digit, but no farther, the other digits being unconnected with the wings. [MdL. *pterodactylus* from Gk. *pteron* a wing and *daktulos* a finger].

PTERODACTYL

PTEROGRAPHY, [te-rog′-raf-i], *n.* a branch of ornithology dealing with the plumage of birds. [PTERO and Gk. *graphia* writing].

PTEROLOGY, [te-rol′-o-ji], *n.* the branch of entomology concerned with the study of insects' wings. [PTERO and Gk. *logos* speech].

PTEROPODS, [te′-rōp-odz′], *n.(pl.)* a class of molluscs in which the middle section of the creature's foot is formed into a pair of lobes or flappers by means of which the animal can swim. [PTERO and Gk. *pous podos* foot].

PTERYGOID, [te′-rig-oid], *adj.* shaped like a wing. [PTERO and Gk. *oeides* like].

PTERYLOGRAPHY, [te′-ril-og′-rafi], *n.* pterography. [PTERO, Gk. *hule* wood and *graphia* writing].

PTERYLOSIS, [te'-ril-ō'-sis], *n.* the arrangement of feathers on a bird's body. [PTERO, Gk. *hule* wood and *osis* denoting condition].

PTILOSIS†(1), [til-ō'-sis], *n.* a disease of the eyelids involving loss of the eyelashes. [Gk. *ptilosis*].

PTILOSIS (2), [til-ō'-sis], *n.* pterylosis. [Gk. *ptilon* soft feathers and *osis* denoting condition].

PTOLEMAIC (1), [tol'-em-ā'-ik], *n.* a supporter of the theories of Ptolemy of Alexandria.

PTOLEMAIC (2), [tol'-em-ā'-ik], *adj.* of, or pertaining to, *Ptolemy* (2nd century A.D.), an astronomer of Alexandria; of, or pertaining to, the Ptolemies, a Greek dynasty ruling in Egypt from the death of Alexander the Great to Cleopatra.

PTOMAINE, [tō'-mān], *n.* poisonous alkaloid matter formed by the putrefaction of animal and vegetable matter; **p. poisoning,** poisoning caused by eating such matter, usually by eating tainted food. [It. *ptomaina* from Gk. *ptoma* corpse].

PTOSIS, [tō'-sis], *n.* (*med.*) a drooping of the eyelid due to paralysis of the muscle controlling it. [Gk. *ptosis* a falling].

PTYALIN, [tī'-al-in], *n.* (*med.*) a chemical substance found in human saliva. [Gk. *ptualon* spittle].

PTYALISM, [tī'-al-izm], *n.* (*med.*) excessive salivation.

PTYALOGOGUE, [tī'-al-ō-gog'], *n.* (*med.*) a medicine promoting salivation.

PUB, [pub], *n.* (*coll.*) a public-house.

PUBERAL, [pew'-ber-al], *adj.* of, or pertaining to, puberty. [LL. *puberalis*].

PUBERTY, [pew'-ber-ti], *n.* the age at which a member of either sex becomes capable of parenthood. [L. *pubertas* marriageable age].

PUBES, [pew'-bēz], *n.* the hair around the groin which makes its appearance at puberty; the part of the body where this grows. [L. *pubes*].

PUBESCENCE, [pew-bes'-ents], *n.* the state of reaching puberty; (*nat. hist.*) a down on the bodies of insects and on the leaves and stems of certain plants. [Fr. *pubescence* from MedL. *pubescentia*].

PUBESCENT, [pew-bes'-ent], *adj.* attaining puberty; (of plants and insects) covered with pubescence. [L. *pubescens*, *pres.pt.* of *pubescere* to grow up].

PUBIC, [pew'-bik], *adj.* of, or pertaining to, the pubes.

PUBIS, [pew'-bis], *n.* (*anat.*) one of the bones of the pelvic arch. [L. (*os*) *pubis* the bone in the groin].

PUBLIC (1), [pub'-lik], *n.* the mass of persons making up a community or nation; that part of the general community interested or likely to be interested in any particular idea, article or activity; (*coll.*) a public-house, a tavern. [PUBLIC (2)].

PUBLIC (2), [pub'-lik], *adj.* of, or pertaining to, the people as a whole, to the community generally; national, general, not private or personal; being in the name of, done on behalf of, the people generally, concerning or involving the people at large; generally known, open or available to all and sundry, well known, notorious, manifest, not secret or concealed; concerning, known to or serving the whole nation; concerning humanity at large, international; (in a university) concerning, or open to, the whole university as contrasted with one college in it; **P. Prosecutor,** (*leg.*) the legal officer of the Crown who undertakes the prosecution of persons charged with grave offences; **p. nuisance,** (*leg.*) an act, punishable by law, that is contrary to the interest of the community at large rather than of a private individual; (*coll.*) a generally annoying or disturbing person; **p. notary** (*or* **notary p.**), an official appointed to draw up and attest formal documents, such as deeds, bills of exchange, etc.; **p. act, bill** or **statute,** an Act of Parliament of general application; **p. enemy,** an enemy to the community at large; **p. debt,** a debt at the charge of the nation, the national debt; **p. health,** the health of the nation at large; **p. holiday,** a statutory holiday enjoyed by everybody except the most essential trades and services; **p. ownership,** ownership by the nation or government; **p. orator,** (in a university) the orator appointed to deliver addresses on behalf of the whole university; **p. good,** the welfare and interest of the people generally; **p. opinion,** the opinion or point of view of the people at large, the attitude of the community generally; **p. scandal,** a scandal known to, interesting, or affecting the nation at large; **p. benefactor,** a person who, by generosity, wise action or doctrine, benefits the community generally; **p. utility company,** a privately owned firm operating public services under Government supervision. [ME. *publike* from L. *publicus*].

PUBLICAN, [pub'-lik-an], *n.* (*Rom. hist.*) one who farmed the taxes of the state, a tax-gatherer; one who runs a public-house, an innkeeper.

PUBLICATION, [pub-lik-ā'-shun], *n.* the act of publishing or making public, the act of proclaiming; the act of issuing printed matter for sale to the general public; anything published, a book, pamphlet, magazine, music, etc., issued for sale to the general public; a proclamation or announcement; (*leg.*) the act of publishing or making known to a third person or group of persons, *esp.* any libellous matter so communicated. [ME. *publicacion* from L. *publicatio*].

PUBLIC-HOUSE, [pub'-lik-hows'], *n.* an inn or tavern, a house where by licence alcoholic liquors may be sold and consumed.

PUBLICIST, [pub'-lis-ist], *n.* an authority on international law, the art of government, etc.; a journalist who concerns himself with current political topics and events.

PUBLICITY, [pub-lis'-i-ti], *n.* the quality or condition of being public; the act or practice of advertising; advertisements. [Fr. *publicité* from MedL. *publicitas*].

PUBLICLY, [pub'-lik-li], *adv.* in a public fashion.

PUBLICNESS, [pub'-lik-nes], *n.* the condition of being public.

PUBLIC SCHOOL, [pub'-lik-skōōl'], *n.* one of a certain type of school, *esp.* in England, whose chief object is to prepare its scholars, usually boarders, for the universities, the professions and higher government service; a school, the headmaster of which is entitled to attend the Headmasters' Conference; a state-controlled primary school in Scotland; (*U.S.*) a state-controlled elementary or secondary school.

PUBLIC-SPIRITED, [pub'-lik-spi'-rit-id], *adj.* actuated by zeal for public welfare.

PUBLIC-SPIRITEDLY, [pub'-lik-spi'-rit-id-li], *adv.* in a public-spirited manner.

PUBLIC-SPIRITEDNESS, [pub'-lik-spi'-rit-id-nes], *n.* the condition or quality of being public-spirited.

PUBLISH, [pub'-lish], *v.t.* to make public, to make known to the public, to announce, proclaim, promulgate; to issue (printed matter, music, etc.) for sale to the general public; **to p. the banns of marriage,** to announce in the church of the parish where each is resident the names of couples intending to marry; **to p. a will,** to execute a will before witnesses; **to p. a libel,** to communicate a libel to more than one person. [ME. *publishen*, OFr. *publier* from L. *publicare*].

PUBLISHABLE, [pub'-lish-abl], *adj.* able, fit, worthy to be published.

PUBLISHER, [pub'-lish-er], *n.* one who publishes, *esp.* a person or company engaged in the trade of issuing books, music and printed matter generally for sale to the general public.

PUBLISHMENT, [pub-lish-ment], *n.* the act of publishing, publication.

PUCCOON, [puk-ōōn'], *n.* the blood-root, a plant found in North America, and yielding a red dye. [Native].

PUCE, [pews], *n.* a rich purple-brown colour. [Fr. *puce* from L. *pulex* flea].

PUCK (1), [puk], *n.* a mischievous goblin, *esp.* Robin Goodfellow, a mischievous sprite of rural legend, used by Shakespeare as a character in *A Midsummer Night's Dream*; (*fig.*) a mischievous child. [OE *puca*].

PUCK (2), [puk], *n.* an English bird also called the puck-bird, the nightjar or the goatsucker; a cattle disease supposed to be caused by this bird. [Unkn.].

PUCK (3), [puk], *n.* a flat rubber disk used in place of a ball in ice hockey. [Unkn.].

PUCKA, see PUKKA.

PUCKBALL, [puk'-bawl], *n.* an erroneous variant for PUFF-BALL.

PUCK-BIRD, [puk'-burd'], *n.* the goatsucker or nightjar.

PUCKER (1), [puk'-er], *n.* a wrinkle or crease. [PUCKER (2)].

PUCKER (2), [puk'-er], *v.t.* and *i.* to knit into wrinkles, to crease up; to shrivel into wrinkles and creases. [Uncert.].

PUCKERIDGE, [puk'-er-ij], *n.* the English bird, the nightjar or goatsucker.

PUCKISH, [puk'-ish], *adj.* impish, suggestive of Puck. [PUCK (1)].

PUDDENING, [pōōd'-en-ing], *n.* (*naut.*) a fender of rope to prevent chafing. [Dial. *pudden* pudding].

PUDDER, see POTHER.

PUDDING, [pōōd'-ing], *n.* the intestine of a pig or

sheep stuffed, seasoned and boiled, and eaten cold like a sausage; a boiled or baked preparation of flour, suet, eggs or milk, etc., to which either meat or dried fruit may be added; a batter; a milk dish made with rice, sago, tapioca, etc.; (*naut.*) a puddening, a fender; (*fig.*) anything resembling a pudding. [ME. *poding*].

PUDDING-FACED, [pŏŏd'-ing-fāsd'], *adj.* having a large, flat, unintelligent face.

PUDDING-SLEEVE, [pŏŏd'-ing-slēv'], *n.* a very full sleeve gathered closely at the wrist, common in clerical habits.

PUDDINGSTONE, [pŏŏd'-ing-stōn'], *n.* a conglomerate having pebbles embedded in it which resemble the fruit in a suet pudding.

PUDDLE (1), [pudl], *n.* a small, shallow, dirty pool of water left after a fall of rain; any small shallow pool of water or any other liquid; a mixture of sand and clay with water to form a watertight base for a pool or a lining for a canal. [ME. *pudel*, possibly a *dim.* of OE. *pudd* a ditch].

PUDDLE (2), [pudl], *v.t. and i.* to dabble or paddle, *esp.* in dirty water; to make a mixture of clay, water and sand for lining ponds or canals; to stir molten iron so that what would otherwise have cooled into cast-iron becomes wrought-iron. [PUDDLE (1)].

PUDDLER, [pud'-ler], *n.* one who puddles.

PUDDLING, [pud'-ling], *n.* the process of kneading clay, sand and water into a mixture for lining pools and canals, etc.; the process of stirring molten iron so that it will cool into wrought-iron instead of into cast-iron.

PUDDLY, [pud'-li], *adj.* foul and muddy like a puddle; abounding in puddles.

PUDDOCK, [pud'-ok], *n.* a small enclosure, a paddock.

PUDENCY, [pew'-den-si], *n.* a sense of shame, modesty, bashfulness. [LL. *pudentia*].

PUDENDA, (*sg.* **pudendum**), [pewd-en'-da], *n.(pl.)* the external genital organs, *esp.* of the female. [L. *pudendum* something of which one should be ashamed].

PUDGE, [puj], *n.* a short, thick-set, plump person. [Unkn.].

PUDGY, [puj'-i], *adj.* short and plump. [Unkn.].

PUDIC, [pew'-dik], *adj.* of, or pertaining to, the external genital organs; †chaste; modest. [L. *pudicus* modest].

PUDICAL, [pew'-dikl], *adj.* pudic.

PUDICITY, [pew-dis'-iti], *n.* pudency.

PUDU, [pŏŏ'-dŏŏ], *n.* the small deer, *Pudua humilis*, found in the Andes. [Chilean].

PUERILE, [pew'-er-il], *adj.* childish; trifling, of small account. [L. *puerilis* boyish, pertaining to boyhood].

PUERILELY, [pew'-er-il-li], *adv.* in a puerile fashion.

PUERILENESS, [pew'-er-il-nes], *n.* the quality or condition of being puerile.

PUERILITY, [pew'-er-il'-i-ti], *n.* puerileness; something that is puerile. [L. *puerilitas*].

PUERPERAL, [pew-er'-per-al], *adj.* of, or pertaining to, childbirth; **p. fever**, a fever arising from septic infection after confinement. [L. *puerperus* bearing children].

PUFF (1), [puf], *n.* the action of puffing; a short, quick blast of air, smoke, vapour, gas, etc.; the sound accompanying puffing; a swelling, a puffing; (in clothes) a puffed-up piece of cloth made by gathering in the ends and leaving the middle full and loose; a fluffy ball of ribbons, hair or feathers; **powder p.**, a small ball or pad of swans' down or similar material for applying cosmetic powder. [PUFF (2)].

PUFF (2), [puf], *v.t. and i.* to emit a short, sharp blast, to blow with abrupt blasts; to send forth puffs; to breathe heavily and jerkily, to pant; to cause to be out of breath; to blow at in puffs so as to propel or agitate; to emit in puffs, to escape in puffs; **to p. out**, to emit in puffs; to render breathless and exhausted; to utter with breathlessness; to inflate, distend; to extinguish by puffing; to swell; to come forth in puffs; **to p. away**, to drive off by puffing; to emit a steady series of puffs; to move away while puffing; **to p. up**, to distend, inflate; (*fig.*) to make arrogant and elated; to rise up in puffs. [OE. *pyffan* to blow from the mouth].

PUFF-ADDER, [puf'-ad'-er], *n.* a great venomous African viper that distends its body when annoyed.

PUFF-BALL, [puf'-bawl], *n.* a fungus of the genus, *Lycoperdon*, the rounded head of which when ripe will burst at a touch emitting spores in a cloud; the feathery head on a dandelion when the blossom has died; (*rare*) a powder-puff.

PUFF-BIRDS, [puf'-burdz], *n.(pl.)* the birds of a South American group, *Bucconidæ*, whose feathers are puffed out and not sleek on the body.

PUFFER, [puf'-er], *n.* someone or something that puffs; a flatterer; a name given to various sorts of fish that can distend their bodies; (in childish talk) a steam train or steam locomotive.

PUFFIN, [puf'-in], *n.* a North Atlantic flightless seabird of the genus, *Fratercula*, *esp.* the *Fratercula arctica*, the common puffin, that has black and white feathers and an orange bill. [Uncert.].

PUFFIN

PUFFINESS, [puf'-i-nes], *n.* the quality or condition of being puffy.

PUFFING (1), [puf'-ing], *n.* extravagant praise, flattery.

PUFFING (2), [puf'-ing], *adj.* emitting puffs; praising extravagantly.

PUFFINGLY, [puf'-ing-li], *adv.* in a puffing way.

PUFF-PASTE, [puf'-pāst], *n.* a light, flaky pastry.

PUFFY, [puf'-i], *adj.* moving in puffs; exhausted, panting; swollen.

PUG (1), [pug], *n.* one of a breed of small, short-nosed dogs; a short, snub nose; (*prov.*) a monkey; a fox; (*rare*) an affectionate name for a pet, *esp.* a dog or monkey; †an imp, puck. [Unkn.].

PUG (2), [pug], *n.* clay kneaded for brick-making or pottery; sawdust and other material used for sound-proofing. [PUG (4)].

PUG (3), [pug], *n.* the footprint of a wild animal. [Hind. *pag* foot].

PUG (4), (**pugging, pugged**), [pug], *v.t.* to knead clay for bricks and pottery; to pad (a wall, floor, etc.) with refuse, sawdust, etc., to make partially sound-proof. [Uncert.].

PUG (5), (**pugging, pugged**), [pug], *v.t.* to track down by following pugs or footprints. [PUG (3)].

PUG-DOG, [pug'-dog], *n.* a pug, a small pet bulldog.

PUG-FACE, [pug'-fās], *n.* a broad flat face like a monkey's. [PUG (1) and FACE (1)].

PUG-FACED, [pug'-fāst], *adj.* monkey-faced, having a broad, flat face with a snub nose.

PUGGAREE, PUGGREE, [pug'-a-rē', pug'-rē], *n.* a high veil over the back of the neck suspended from a hat or turban. [Hind. *pagri* turban].

PUGGING (1), [pug'-ing], *n.* the act of kneading clay for bricks or pottery; stuffing of sawdust and other material used for sound-proofing.

PUGGING† (2), [pug-ing], *adj.* (of a tooth) aching, throbbing.

PUGGREE, see PUGGAREE.

PUGH, [pew], *int.* expressing contempt.

PUGILISM, [pew'-jil-izm], *n.* the art of boxing. [L. *pugil* a boxer].

PUGILIST, [pew'-jil-ist], *n.* a boxer, a prize-fighter; (*fig.*) a relentless opponent. [L. *pugil* a boxer].

PUGILISTIC, [pew'-jil-ist'-ik], *adj.* of, or pertaining to, pugilism.

PUG-MILL, [pug'-mil], *n.* a mill where clay is kneaded and mixed for brick-making, pottery, etc. [PUG (4) and MILL (1)].

PUGNACIOUS, [pug-nā'-shus], *adj.* quarrelsome, combative. [L. *pugnax* pugnacious].

PUGNACIOUSLY, [pug-nā'-shus-li], *adv.* in a pugnacious fashion.

PUGNACIOUSNESS, [pug-nā'-shus-nes], *n.* pugnacity.

PUGNACITY, [pug-nas'-i-ti], *n.* the quality of being pugnacious; quarrelsomeness. [L. *pugnacitas*].

PUG-NOSE, [pug'-nōz], *n.* a snub nose. [PUG (1) and NOSE (1)].

PUG-NOSED, [pug'-nōzd], *adj.* having a pug-nose.

PUISNE (1), [pew'-ni], *n.* a puisne judge. [PUISNE (2)].

PUISNE (2), [pew'-ni], *adj.* (*leg.*) subordinate, junior, of lower rank. [OFr. *puisné* junior].

PUISSANCE, [pwē-sants], *n.* power, might, strength. [Fr. *puissance*].

PUISSANT, [pwē'-sant], *adj.* mighty. [Fr. *puissant*].

PUISSANTLY, [pwē'-sant-li], *adv.* in a puissant way, with might.

PUISSANTNESS, [pwē'-sant-nes], *n.* the condition or quality of being puissant.

PUJA, POOJA, [pŏŏ'-ja], *n.* a Hindu religious ceremony; the act of worshipping a Hindu idol. [Hind. *puja* worship].

PUKE (1), [pewk], *n.* the act of puking; an emetic. [PUKE (2)].

PUKE (2), [pewk], *v.i.* to vomit. [Echoic].

PUKEKO, [pŏŏ'-kek-ō], *n.* an Australian swamp-hen. [Maori].
PUKER, [pewk'-er], *n.* one who pukes; an emetic.
PUKING (1), [pewk'-ing], *n.* the action of vomiting.
PUKING (2), [pewk'-ing], *adj.* vomiting, causing to vomit.
PUKKA, PUCKA, [puk'-a], *adj.* (*coll.*) excellent, first-class, the best of its kind; **p. sahib,** a true gentleman (often ironically). [Hind. *pakka* ripe].
PUKU, [pōō'-kōō], *n.* the African waterbuck, a small reddish-brown antelope found in Central Africa. [Zulu *m'puku*].
PULAS, [pul'-as], *n.* the Indian dhak tree. [Hind. *palas*].
PULCHRITUDE, [pul'-krit-ewd], *n.* beauty. [L. *pulcritudo*].
PULE, [pewl], *v.i.* to whimper like a fretful baby. [Echoic].
PULEX, [pew'-leks], *n.* (*zool.*) the genus including the common flea. [L. *pulex* flea].
PULING, [pewl'-ing], *adj.* whining, fretful.
PULINGLY, [pewl'-ing-li], *adv.* in a puling fashion.
PULKA, [pŏŏl'-ka], *n.* a travelling sledge used in Lapland. [Finnish *pulkka*].
PULL (1), [pŏŏl], *n.* the act of pulling; a short tug, a sustained pulling action; the force exerted when pulling, the strain or tension caused by the action of pulling; the act of drawing, dragging or heaving; the act of moving forward and causing an object to follow after by dragging on it; influence, attraction other than physical; backstairs or secret influence; (*coll.*) advantage; the act of rowing; the act of taking a draught of liquor; the act of sucking at a pipe, cigar or cigarette, etc.; that which is pulled, that part of a mechanism which is grasped and pulled, a handle or lever, *esp.* the handle of a beer-engine; the amount of beer emitted at one movement of the handle of a beer-engine; (*print.*) a rough proof or impression; (*cricket*) a stroke which drives a ball that has pitched on the off-side, over to the leg field; (*riding, racing*) a tug of the bridle to check a horse, *esp.* when deliberately given to prevent a horse from winning a race; (*golf*) a shot which drives the ball widely to the left of the striker; **long p.,** an excess amount of liquor due to too long or slow a movement of the handle of a beer-engine; **p. at an oar,** a short spell of rowing. [PULL (2)].
PULL (2), [pŏŏl], *v.t.* to exert such a force upon something as to cause it to move towards the point from which the force is exerted; to cause to move towards oneself; to draw, drag, tug, haul, heave; to cause (an object) to shift, change position, advance, proceed by exerting a force which is always moving away from that object; to extract, take out by exerting a force away from the position occupied by the object of the action; to exert a force upon (an object) such as might make it move towards the point from which the force is exerted, to tug at, strain at, make tense or tight by tugging or dragging; to pluck, twitch or tug; to cause to operate by tugging or straining at; to proceed or advance and by so doing cause (an object) to follow after; to row, to propel by rowing; (*fig.*) to attract, draw by means not physical; to pluck or gather (fruit or flowers); to uproot (weeds, root-crops, etc.); to remove the feathers and entrails from (a bird) for culinary purposes; (*tanning*) to remove hair from a hide; (*hat-making*) to remove unwanted hair from a skin; (of a horse) to tug or strain constantly at the bit; (*thieves' slang*) to arrest, to raid (a low haunt, gambling den, etc.); to steal; (*cricket*) to strike a ball, that has pitched on the off-side, so as to propel it into the leg field; (*golf*) to strike a ball hard over to the left; (*print.*) to take a pull or impression of; (*racing*) to hold (a horse) back deliberately so as to prevent it from winning; (of a punch in boxing) to strike with less force than is possible or expected; *v.i.* to tug, drag, draw, heave, haul; to exert a dragging or drawing force towards the point from which the force is exerted; to advance or proceed by rowing; (of a pipe, cigarette, cigar, etc.,) to draw, admit of suction when sucked; to smoke, draw, suck at a pipe, cigar, cigarette, etc.; **to p. about,** to treat roughly and with scant ceremony; **to p. at,** to suck at (a pipe, etc.); to drink liquor from (a glass tankard, etc.); **to p. down,** to lower, abase, humble in reputation, pride, standing, etc.; to weaken, in health, etc.; to render more likely to fail in an examination or test of any sort; **to p. in,** to retract, withdraw, contract; to reduce, cut down, curtail; (of a belt) to tighten, contract; to gain the help, support, co-operation of; (*thieves' slang*) to arrest; (*motoring, etc.*) to draw to the side of the road and stop; **to p. in at,** to make a short stop or stay at; **to p. off,** to be successful in, achieve, attain; to depart, move away; to row away; **to p. out,** *v.t.* to bring forth, extract, produce, to extend, protract, prolong; (*coll.*) to produce, utter, relate; **to p. round,** *v.t.* to render successful when failure appeared imminent; to make well again; *v.i.* to recover from illness, danger or imminent defeat; **to p. through,** *v.t.* to help over danger or difficulty; *v.i.* to be successful despite difficulties, to win through; **to p. together,** to co-operate; **to p. oneself together,** to recover one's energies, wits, resources, to regain one's self-control, to rally oneself; **to p. up,** to stop, check, interrupt; to rein in (a horse); to cause someone to stop and think; *v.i.* to stop, pause, make a halt; **to p. up with** (or **to**), to overtake, get level with; **to p. to pieces,** to tear in shreds, unravel; (*fig.*) to expend strong and destructive criticism upon; **to p. a face** (or **faces**), to grimace; **to p. a foot,** to run, run away; **to p. someone's leg,** to make someone the butt of a playful deception; **to p. (so many) oars,** (of a boat) to be equipped for (so many) rowers; **to p. a good oar,** to row well; **to p. one's weight,** to do all that could be expected of one; **to p. it,** to run, run away; **to p. in one's belt,** to curtail one's diet; **to p. strings** (or **wires**), to exert secret or backstairs influence; **to p. wool over someone's eyes,** to dupe someone; **to p. one out of the bag,** to perform a sudden unexpected and successful action; **to p. it over someone,** to trick or dupe someone; **to p. (something) out of the fire,** (*esp.* of a game or adventurous or risky enterprise) to save the situation with regard to. [OE. *pullian*].
PULLBACK, [pŏŏl'-bak'], *n.* anything which keeps back.
PULLER, [pŏŏl'-er], *n.* one who, or that which, pulls.
PULLET, [pŏŏl'-et], *n.* a young hen. [Fr. *poulet*].
PULLEY (1), [pŏŏl'-i], *n.* a hoisting mechanism, consisting of a rope passed over a grooved wheel held in a block; any more complicated variant of this, i.e., with more wheels and therefore giving greater mechanical advantage. [ME. *polie* from OFr. *polie*].
PULLEY (2), [pŏŏl'-i], *v.t.* to hoist with a pulley. [PULLEY (1)].
PULLMAN, [pŏŏl'-man), *n.* a restaurant car or sleeping coach on a railway train. [*Pullman* the designer].
PULLOVER, [pŏŏl'-ō-ver], *n.* a woollen jersey, without buttons, pulled on or off over the head.
PULL-THROUGH, [pŏŏl'-thrōō], *n.* (*milit.*) a looped and weighted cord used for cleaning the bore of a rifle barrel.

PULLEY

PULLULATE, [pŏŏl'-yŏŏ-lāt], *v.i.* to sprout, spring up, multiply rapidly. [L. *pullulatus*, *p.pt.* of *pullulare* to sprout].
PULL-UP, [pŏŏl'-up], *n.* (*coll.*) an eating-house or coffee-stall by the road.
PULMO-, *pref.* pertaining to the lungs. [L. *pulmo* lung].
PULMOBRANCHIATE, [pul'-mō-brangk'-i-āt], *n.* (*zool.*) equipped with gills that can breathe in air as well as water. [PULMO and BRANCHIATE].
PULMONARY, [pul'-mon-er-i], *adj.* of, pertaining to, or affecting, the lungs. [L. *pulmonarius*].
PULMONATE, [pul'-mon-āt], *adj.* equipped with lungs. [L. *pulmonatus*].
PULMONIC (1), [pul-mon'-ik], *n.* a medicine for diseased lungs; a person suffering from a lung disease.
PULMONIC (2), [pul-mon'-ik], *adj.* pertaining to, or affecting, the lungs. [Fr. *pulmonique*].
PULMONIFEROUS, [pul'-mon-if'-er-us], *adj.* having lungs. [PULMO and L. *ferre* to bear].
PULP (1), [pulp], *n.* any soft fleshy matter like the soft interior of a gourd or fruit; a soft formless mass of matter reduced from fibrous matter by rubbing, crushing and boiling, as in the manufacture of paper from cloth or wood; anything of similar substance to this, marrow, etc.; (*mining*) ore that has been wetted and crushed; the soft nerve tissue in a tooth. [L. *pulpa* flesh].
PULP (2), [pulp], *v.t.* to reduce to pulp, to make pulpy. [PULP (1)].
PULPINESS, [pulp'-i-nes], *n.* the quality or state of being pulpy.
PULPIT, [pŏŏl'-pit], *n.* a raised box-like structure from which an oration or sermon may be delivered;

religious teaching such as is delivered from a pulpit; a body of preachers expounding the same doctrine or doctrines. [OFr. *pulpite* from L. *pulpitum* a scaffold or stage].

PULPITEER (1), [pōōl'-pit-ēer], *n.* a preacher (disapprovingly or disparagingly referred to); a fanatical preacher.

PULPITEER (2), [pōōl-pit-ēer'], *v.i.* to preach from a pulpit with political intent; to preach or hold forth in and out of season. [PULPITEER (1)].

PULPLESS, [pulp'-les], *adj.* dry, having no pulp.

PULPOUS, [pulp'-us], *adj.* consisting of pulp; soft and pulpy. [L. *pulposus*].

PULPOUSNESS, [pulp'-us-nes], *n.* the condition or quality of being pulpous.

PULPY, [pulp'-i], *adj.* like pulp, consisting of pulp, soft and succulent.

PULQUE, [pōōl'-kā], *n.* an intoxicating beverage made in Mexico from the juice of the agave. [Span. Amer. *pulque*].

PULSATE, [puls'-āt, puls-āt'], *v.i.* to throb, to beat or move with a regular pulse. [L. *pulsatus*, *p.pt.* of *pulsare* to beat].

PULSATILE, [puls'-at-il], *adj.* pulsating, able to pulsate; (*mus.*) (of an instrument) played by striking.

PULSATION, [puls-ā'-shun], *n.* a steady rhythmic beating or throbbing movement; a steadily repeated pulse-like sound; one sound or movement in such a series of steady sounds or movements, *esp.* the variation of a pulsating electric current. [L. *pulsatio*].

PULSATIVE, [puls'-at-iv], *adj.* throbbing, pulsating; of, or pertaining to, pulsation.

PULSATOR, [puls-ā'-tor], *n.* something that throbs.

PULSATORY, [puls-ā'-ter-i], *adj.* throbbing, pulsative.

PULSE (1), [puls], *n.* a rhythmic beating, throbbing, vibration or palpitation; one beat, throb, vibration or palpitation of a series rhythmically repeated; any movement regularly and frequently repeated; one of a series of even and flowing undulations, a wave; (*anat.*) the rhythmic beating or throbbing of the heart and blood stream, *esp.* the throbbing of this as felt at the wrist, the rate of this pulsation; the rhythmic stress of verse, music, stylized prose, etc.; rhythm; (*fig.*) a thrill, a sensation of excitement, energy or vitality; **to feel** (or **take**) **someone's p.**, to feel or time the pulsations of the artery at the wrist; **to stir the p.**, to quicken to vitality and excitement. [OFr. *pous*, *pouls*, L. *pulsus* beating or throbbing].

PULSE (2), [puls], *n.* the seeds of leguminous plants grown for food as beans, lentils, peas, etc. [ME. *puls*, L. *puls* from Gk. *pultos* porridge].

PULSE (3), [puls], *v.t.* and *i.* to beat or throb rhythmically, to vibrate or pulsate, to perform a series of rhythmic regular and exactly similar movements; to sound or be uttered with regular stress or pulsation; to be driven or moved by pulses. [L. *pulsare* to push, drive].

PULSELESS, [puls'-les], *adj.* not marked by pulsation, lifeless.

PULSELESSNESS, [puls'-les-nes], *n.* lack of pulsation.

PULSIMETER, [puls-im'-it-er], *n.* (*med.*) an instrument for measuring the throb of the blood stream, a sphygmograph. [PULSE (1) and METER].

PULSION, [pul'-shun], *n.* (*rare*) the act of pushing or driving forward. [L. *pulsio*].

PULSOMETER, [puls-om'-it-er], *n.* a steam-condensing vacuum pump. [PULSE and METER].

PULTACEOUS, [pult-ā'-shus], *n.* soft and pulpy, like porridge. [PULSE (2)].

PULU, [pōō-lōō'], *n.* a yellow, silky wool, made from the fibres of various Hawaiian tree-ferns. [Native].

PULVERABLE, [pul'-ver-abl], *adj.* able to be pulverized.

PULVERIZABLE, [pul'-ver-iz-abl], *adj.* able to be pulverized.

PULVERIZATION, [pul'-ver-iz-ā'-shun], *n.* the act of pulverizing.

PULVERIZE, [pul'-ver-iz], *v.t.* and *i.* to reduce to fine powder, or dust; to crumble away to dust; to divide a liquid into tiny particles as in spray; (*fig.*) to destroy, crush, overwhelm, criticize most adversely. [LL. *pulverizare*].

PULVERIZER, [pul'-ver-iz-er], *n.* someone or something that pulverizes.

PULVEROUS, [pul'-ver-us], *adj.* powdery.

PULVERULENCE, [pul-ver'-ōōl-ents], *n.* the condition or quality of being pulverulent.

PULVERULENT, [pul-ve'-ryōōl-ent], *adj.* consisting of powder, like powder; dusty; (of birds) given to rolling in dust. [L. *pulverulentus* dusty].

PULVINAR, [pul'-vin-ah(r)], *n.* (*class. myth.*) a couch of the gods; (*Rom. antiq.*) a cushioned seat at the circus. [L. *pulvinar* couch].

PULVINATE, [pul'-vin-āt], *adj.* (*bot.*) having a swelling where the leaf joins the stem; (*entom.*) having a pad on the foot; (*arch.*) bulging like a cushion, *esp.* of a moulding. [L. *pulvinatus* resembling a cushion].

PULVINATED, [pul'-vin-āt-id], *adj.* pulvinate.

PUMA, [pew'-ma], *n.* a large feline quadruped, *Felis concolor*, the cougar, found in South America. [Peruvian].

PUMICE (1), [pum'-is], *n.* a light, porous, grey lava used to remove stains and dirt from the skin by scrubbing, pumice-stone. [ME. *pomice* (or *pomys*)].

PUMA

PUMICE (2), [pum'-is], *v.t.* to scrub with pumice. [PUMICE (1)].

PUMICEOUS, [pew-mish'-us], *adj.* consisting of, or resembling, pumice. [L. *pumiceus*].

PUMICE-STONE, [pum'-is-stōn'], *n.* pumice in lump form. [PUMICE (1) and STONE (1)].

PUMICIFORM, [pew-mis'-i-fawm], *adj.* like pumice in form or texture. [PUMICE (1) and FORM (1)].

PUMMEL, see POMMEL.

PUMP (1), [pump], *n.* a mechanical device for moving gases and liquids, consisting in its simplest form of a piston moving in a cylinder; anything resembling this either in form, principle or function; (*slang*) a dull, prosy person. [ME. *pumpe*].

PUMP (2), [pump], *n.* a light, low (buckled) shoe worn by men for dancing or evening wear. [Unkn.].

PUMP (3), [pump], *v.t.* and *i.* to work a pump; to move by means of a pump; to move in a way resembling a pump or a person working a pump; (*fig.*) to exhaust; to extract information from by repeated questioning; to teach, instil laboriously; **to p. out**, to empty by using a pump; to exhaust, fatigue; **to p. up**, to raise by means of a pump; to inflate with a pump; **to p. ship**, (*coll.*) to make water. [PUMP (1)].

PUMPAGE, [pump'-ij], *n.* the amount of water raised by a pump.

PUMP-BARREL, [pump'-ba-rel], *n.* the tube of a pump.

PUMP-BRAKE, [pump'-brāk], *n.* the handle of a pump.

PUMP-DALE, [pump'-dāl], *n.* a wooden cylinder used to convey water across a ship from a chain pump.

PUMPER, [pump'-er], *n.* one who, or that which, pumps.

PUMPERNICKEL, [pōōmp'-er-nikl], *n.* a sweet, sticky, dark-coloured bread containing malt. [Germ. *pumpernickel*].

PUMP-GEAR, [pump'-gēer], *n.* the gear and tackle pertaining to a pump.

PUMP-HANDLE, [pump'-handl], *n.* the lever or handle of a pump.

PUMP-HOOD, [pump'-hŏŏd], *n.* a wooden covering for the upper wheel of a chain pump.

PUMPION†, see POMPION.

PUMPKIN, [pump'-kin], *n.* the large tough-rinded fruit of the plant *Cucurbita pepo*, a pompion; the plant *Cucurbita pepo*. [PUMPION or POMPION, Fr. *pompon* from L. *pepo* melon].

PUMP-SPEAR, [pump'-spēer], *n.* the piston-rod in a pump.

PUMP-STOCK, [pump'-stok], *n.* the main body of a pump.

PUN (1), [pun], *n.* a humorous use of words that have like sounds but different meanings. [Unkn.].

PUN (2), (**punning, punned**), [pun], *v.i.* to make a pun or puns. [PUN (1)].

PUNA, [pōō'-na], *n.* a high plateau in Peru; a dry cold wind that blows over this plateau; the difficulty in breathing commonly experienced in a high, dry atmosphere, mountain sickness. [Peruvian *puna*].

PUNCH (1), [punch], *n.* the crook-backed, harlequin-like hero of the puppet show *Punch and Judy*. [It. *Punchinello*].

PUNCH (2), [punch], *n.* a short, thick person or animal; **Suffolk p.**, one of a sturdy breed of draught horses. [Uncert.].

PUNCH (3), [punch], *n.* a drink consisting of a spirit diluted in milk or water, flavoured with lemon and spice and sweetened. [Uncert.].
PUNCH (4), [punch], *n.* an instrument consisting of a short piece of steel with one flat end for hitting with a hammer and the other prepared so as to fit it for its various uses, e.g., for piercing leather, cardboard, wood, etc., for driving a nail right in so that its head is lower than the surface of the wood; a small device containing such an instrument and used to pierce tickets on buses, trams, trains, etc. [Short for PUNCHEON].
PUNCH (5), [punch], *n.* a sharp hard blow delivered with the clenched fist; (*coll.*) energy, wit, pointedness, vivid personality, etc. [PUNCH (7)].
PUNCH (6), [punch], *v.t.* to pierce with a punch. [PUNCH (4)].
PUNCH (7), [punch], *v.t. and i.* to strike with a sharp hard blow using the clenched fist; to deliver such a blow. [ME. *punchen*].
PUNCHBOWL, [punch'-bōl'], *n.* a bowl for brewing or serving punch; (*fig.*) a deep hollow in a hill-side; a wide river boat.
PUNCH-DRUNK, [punch'-drungk'], *adj.* of a boxer, suffering from some sort of concussion as the result of continual punches, and giving the impression of being drunk.
PUNCHEON (1), [pun'-chun], *n.* (*metal work*) a steel punch or die; (*carp.*) a short upright support used in framings. [ME. *punchon*, OFr. *ponchon* or *poinçon* an awl].
PUNCHEON (2), [pun'-chun], *n.* a large cask, usually of 120 gallons capacity if containing rum, 84 if containing wine, and 72 if containing beer. [Uncert.].
PUNCHER, [pun'-cher], *n.* one who, or that which, punches.
PUNCHINELLO, [punch'-in-el'-ō], *n.* the chief character in an Italian puppet-show; a buffoon, a comic character.
PUNCH-LADLE, [punch'-lādl], *n.* a long-handled spoon used to fill glasses with punch from a punch-bowl.
PUNCHY, [punch'-i], *n.* short and stocky. [PUNCH (2)].
PUNCTATE, [pungk'-tāt], *adj.* (*bot., zool.*) dotted or pitted. [MdL. *punctatus*].
PUNCTATED, [pungk-tā'-tid], *adj.* punctate.
PUNCTIFORM, [pungk'-ti-fawm], *adj.* (*path., zool.*) looking like a dot or mass of dots.
PUNCTILIO, [pungk-til'-i-ō], *n.* a delicate point of conduct; precise and ceremonious behaviour; scrupulous attention to niceties of conduct. [Span. *puntillo*]
PUNCTILIOUS, [pungk-til'-i-us], *adj.* scrupulous over even the smallest points of behaviour; scrupulous, very careful and precise.
PUNCTILIOUSLY, [pungk-til'-i-us-li], *adv.* in a punctilious fashion.
PUNCTILIOUSNESS, [pungk-til'-i-us-nes], *n.* the quality of being punctilious.
PUNCTO, see PUNTO.
PUNCTUAL, [pungk'-choo-al], *adj.* arriving exactly to time, not late, prompt; †punctilious. [Fr. *ponctual*].
PUNCTUALITY, [pungk'-choo-al'-i-ti], *n.* the condition or quality of being punctual. [MedL. *punctualitas*].
PUNCTUALLY, [pungk'-choo-al-i], *adv.* in a punctual manner, promptly to time, not late.
PUNCTUALNESS, [pungk'-choo-al-nes], *n.* punctuality.
PUNCTUATE, [pungk'-choo-āt], *v.t.* to mark (a passage of writing) with commas, stops, etc.; **to p. with,** to interrupt with, mark with, diversify with. [MedL. *punctuatus*, *p.pt.* of *punctuare* to prick].
PUNCTUATION, [pungk'-choo-ā'-shun], *n.* the act of punctuating, the fact of being punctuated; the systematic use of stops, commas, colons, etc., in writing; the inserting of points in a Semitic script. [MedL. *punctuatio*].
PUNCTUATOR, [pungk'-choo-āt'-or], *n.* one who punctuates, or inserts punctuation. [MedL. *punctuator*].
PUNCTUIST [pungk'-choo-ist], *n.* (*rare*) a punctuator.
PUNCTUM, [pungk'-tum], *n.* (*anat., bot., zool.*) a dot or spot, a tiny hollow. [L. *punctum* a point].
PUNCTURE (1), [pungk'-cher], *n.* a prick, a perforation, *esp.* a cut or prick in a pneumatic tyre. [L. *punctura* a prick].
PUNCTURE (2), [pungk'-cher], *v.t. and i.* to prick; to receive a prick or perforation (*esp.* in a pneumatic tyre). [PUNCTURE (1)].
PUNDIT, PANDIT, [pun'-dit], *n.* a Hindu learned in the law, philosophy and religion of his race; an authority on any subject, a learned person, *esp.* when referred to humorously or derogatively; one who pretends to more learning and wisdom than he has. [Hind. *pandit*].
PUNGENCY, [pun'-jen-si], *n.* the condition or quality of being pungent.
PUNGENT, [pun'-jent], *adj.* (*bot., zool.*) pricking, used for pricking, having prickles; affecting the senses of taste and smell strongly; rich tasting or rich smelling; sharp, acrid, bitter; (*fig.*) biting, sarcastic, caustic, acute (of intellect, wit, conversation, etc.). [L. *pungens*. *pres.pt.* of *pungere* to pierce, prick].
PUNGENTLY, [pun'-jent-li], *adv.* in a pungent fashion.
PUNIC, [pew'-nik], *adj.* of, or pertaining to, Carthage and the Carthaginians; **P. faith,** bad faith, treachery such as the Romans attributed to the Carthaginians; **P. apple,** a pomegranate. [L. *Punicus*].
PUNICEOUS, [pew-nish'-us], *adj.* having a purple or a reddish-yellow colour. [L. *puniceus* purple or red].
PUNILY, [pew'-nil-i], *odv.* in a puny fashion.
PUNINESS, [pew'-ni-nes], *n.* the condition or quality of being puny.
PUNISH, [pun'-ish], *v.t.* to penalize for wrong-doing, to chastise, to inflict a penalty on; to inflict a penalty for; (*coll.*) to treat roughly. [ME. *punissen*, Fr. *punir* from L. *punire* to punish].
PUNISHABILITY, [pun'-ish-ab-il'-i-ti], *n.* punishableness.
PUNISHABLE, [pun'-ish-abl], *adj.* deserving punishment.
PUNISHABLENESS, [pun'-ish-abl-nes], *n.* the condition or quality of being punishable.
PUNISHER, [pun'-ish-er], *n.* a person who punishes.
PUNISHING, [pun'-ish-ing], *n.* punishment.
PUNISHMENT, [pun'-ish-ment], *n.* the act of punishing; the fact of being punished; a penalty inflicted for wrong-doing; (*coll.*) rough treatment. [OFr. *punissement*].
PUNITIVE, [pew'-nit-iv], *adj.* inflicting punishment. [Fr. *punitif* from MedL. *punitivus*].
PUNITORY, [pew'-nit-er-i], *adj.* punitive; pertaining to punishment.
PUNK (1), [pungk], *n.* a harlot. [Unkn.].
PUNK (2), [pungk], *n.* dry fungus that can be used for tinder, decayed wood; (*U.S. slang*) any worthless thing. [~SPUNK].
PUNKAH, PUNKA, [pungk'-a], *n.* a large curtain which is swayed to and fro to keep a room cool in tropical countries. [Hind. *pankha* fan].
PUNNER, [pun'-er], *n.* a heavy ramming tool, a beetle. [Unkn.].
PUNNET, [pun'-et], *n.* a small shallow chip basket used to hold fruit (*esp.* strawberries) in small quantities. [Unkn.].
PUNSTER, [pun'-ster], *n.* one who is given to making puns.
PUNT (1), [punt], *n.* a rectangular, flat-bottomed boat used on rivers and propelled with a pole. [OE. *punt* from L. *ponto* a flat boat used by the natives of Gaul].
PUNT (2), [punt], *n.* the concave base of a glass bottle. [~PUNTY].
PUNT (3), [punt], *n.* a bet. [PUNT (7)].
PUNT 4), [punt], *n.* (*football*) a volleying kick. [PUNT (6)].
PUNT (5), [punt], *v.t. and i.* to propel a punt; to carry in a punt. [PUNT (1)].
PUNT (6), [punt], *v.i.* (*football*) to drop the ball from the hands and kick it before it touches the ground. [Unkn.].
PUNT (7), [punt], *v.i.* (*cards*) to lay a stake against the bank; (*racing*) to back a horse heavily, to bet. [Uncert.].
PUNTER, [punt'-er], *n.* one who bets recklessly; one who uses a punt on a river.
PUNTO, PUNCTO, [punt'-ō], *n.* a delicate point of conduct or ceremony; †a thrust in fencing. [It. *punto* from L. *punctum* point].
PUNTY, [punt'-i], *n.* a glassblower's rod. [Uncert.].
PUNY, [pew'-ni], *adj.* small, weak, feeble; †junior. [Fr. *puis* after and *né* born].
PUP (1), [pup], *n.* a very young dog, a puppy; a young seal; a young otter; a conceited young fellow;

in p., (of a bitch) pregnant; **to sell (someone) a p.,** to swindle. [Short form of PUPPY].

PUP (2), (pupping, pupped), [pup], *v.i.* (of a bitch) to be delivered of pups.

PUPA, (*pl.* **pupae**), [pew′-pa], *n.* (*entom.*) an insect at the chrysalis stage. [L. *pupa* a doll].

PUPAL, [pewpl], *adj.* of, pertaining to, a pupa.

PUPATE, [pew-pāt′], *v.i.* (*entom.*) to become a pupa.

PUPAE

PUPIL, [pew′-pil], *n.* a person, *esp.* a young person, undergoing instruction by a teacher; (*opt.*) the opening in the iris through which light reaches the retina; (*leg.*) a ward under the age of puberty. [L. *pupillus*].

PUPILAGE, PUPILLAGE, [pew′-pil-aj], *n.* the condition of being a pupil; (*leg.*) wardship, minority.

PUPILARITY, [pew′-pil-ar′-i-ti], *n.* (*Scots leg.*) pupilage. [Fr. *pupillarité*].

PUPILARY, PUPILLARY, [pew′-pil-er-i], *adj.* having the status of a pupil (in a university) until after taking the Master's degree; (*opt.*) pertaining to the pupil. [L. *pupillarius*].

PUPILATE, [pew′-pil-āt], *adj.* marked with a central spot like a pupil. [MdL. *pupillatus*].

PUPILLAGE, see PUPILAGE.

PUPILLARY, see PUPILARY.

PUPIL-TEACHER, [pew′-pil-tēch′-er], *n.* a young person who intends to become a teacher, and while completing his academic training spends part of his time gaining practical experience of teaching in a school.

PUPIPARA, [pew-pip′-e-ra], *n.*(*pl.*) (*entom.*) insects that develop as far as the pupa stage in the matrix. [PUPA and L. *parere* to beget].

PUPIPAROUS, [pew-pip′-er-us], *adj.* (*entom.*) used of certain insects that develop their young to the pupal stage in the matrix.

PUPIVOROUS, [pew-piv′-er-us], *adj.* living on pupae. [PUPA and L. *vorare* to eat].

PUPOID, [pew′-poid], *adj.* like a pupa. [PUPA and Gk. *oeides* like].

PUPPET, [pup′-et], *n.* a doll, *esp.* a small jointed figure worked by wires attached to the limbs and body in a toy theatre or marionette show, a marionette; (*fig.*) a person of feeble will and character easily controlled by others and used for their ends; (*carp.*) part of a lathe. [ME. *popet*, OFr. *poupette*, *dim.* from L. *puppa* a doll].

PUPPET-PLAYER, [pup′-et-plā′-er], *n.* one who manages the puppets in a toy theatre or marionette show.

PUPPETRY, [pup′-et-ri], *n.* a performance by puppets; a false appearance, affectation.

PUPPET-SHOW, [pup′-et-shō′], *n.* a play, etc., performed by puppets.

PUPPET-STATE, [pup′-et-stāt], *n.* a territory controlled by a government set up by a greater power and claiming to be independent but actually controlled by its originators, usually in their own interest.

PUPPY, [pup′-i], *n.* a pup, a young dog; (*fig.*) a conceited insolent youngster. [Fr. *poupée* a doll].

PUPPYDOM, [pup′-i-dom], *n.* the world of puppies.

PUPPYHOOD, [pup′-i-hŏŏd], *n.* the condition of being a puppy.

PUPPYISH, [pup′-i-ish], *adj.* like a puppy or a puppy's ways.

PUPPYISM, [pup′-i-izm], *n.* the ill-bred conceited talk and habits of an insolent youngster.

PURANA, [pŏŏ-rah′-na], *n.* a sacred book of the Hindu religion. [Skr. *purana* ancient].

PURANIC, [pŏŏ-ran′-ik], *adj.* of, or pertaining to, the puranas.

PURBECKIAN, [per-bek′-ian], *adj.* (*geol.*) of, or pertaining to, the *Purbeck* beds.

PURBLIND, POREBLIND, [pur′-blīnd], *adj.* partly blind; (*fig.*) obtuse. [PURE (2) and BLIND (2)].

PURBLINDLY, [pur′-blīnd-li], *adv.* in a purblind fashion.

PURBLINDNESS, [pur′-blīnd-nes], *n.* the condition of being purblind; dulness of perception.

PURCHASABLE, [pur′-chas-abl], *adj.* able to be purchased.

PURCHASE (1), [pur′-chis], *n.* the act of purchasing; something purchased; value reckoned in annual returns or profits; leverage, grip, pull; (*leg.*) the acquisition of property other than by inheritance. [ME. *purchas* from OFr. *porchas*].

PURCHASE (2), [pur′-chis], *v.t.* to buy, acquire in exchange for money; to obtain in exchange for something else (often in *fig.* senses); (*naut.*) to hoist with leverage or by pulleys, etc.; (*leg.*) to acquire other than by inheritance. [ME. *purchasen* from OFr. *porchacier* to purchase].

PURCHASER, [pur′-chis-er], *n.* one who purchases; (*leg.*) one who has acquired property other than by inheritance.

PURDAH, [pur′-dah], *n.* the curtain shutting the women's apartments in India; the custom of secluding women in India; an Indian cloth with blue and white stripes. [Hind. *purdah* curtain].

PURE, [pyŏŏer], *adj.* clean, uncontaminated; unmixed, unadulterated; chaste; upright, honourable, disinterested; (*coll.*) unmitigated. [ME. *pur*, Fr. *pur* from L. *purus*].

PUREE, purée, [pew′-rā], *n.* any soft pulpy material, *esp.* a mashed foodstuff; a soup made from such a foodstuff. [Fr. *purée*].

PURELY, [pyŏŏer-li], *adv.* in a pure manner; innocently, chastely; merely, solely, absolutely.

PURENESS, [pyŏŏer′-nes], *n.* the condition or quality of being pure.

PURFLE (1), [purfl], *n.* embroidery at the edge of a cloth or garment; (*arch.*) a parapet, etc., with crockets; a purfled shield. [PURFLE (2)].

PURFLE (2), [purfl], *v.t.* (*arch.*) to ornament with crockets; (*her.*) to edge a shield with vair or fur; †to embroider with a flowered border. [ME. *purfilen* from OFr. *pourfiler*].

PURFLING, [pur′-fling], *n.* embroidery at the edge of a cloth or garment.

PURGATION, [pur-gā′-shun], *n.* cleansing, purifying, *esp.* the purification of the soul from worldly sin while in purgatory; the evacuation of the bowels by means of a purgative. [OFr. *purgacion* from L. *purgatio*].

PURGATIVE (1), [pur′-gat-iv], *n.* (*med.*) a medicine promoting the evacuation of the bowels. [Fr. *purgatif* from LL. *purgativus*].

PURGATIVE (2), [pur′-gat-iv], *adj.* cleansing, purifying; (*med.*) having the effect of clearing the bowels. [*Prec.*].

PURGATIVELY, [pur′-gat-iv-li], *adv.* in a purgative way.

PURGATORIAL, [pur′-gat-aw′-ri-al], *adj.* expiatory of, or pertaining to, purgatory.

PURGATORIAN (1), [pur′-gat-aw′-ri-an], *n.* a person who believes in purgatory.

PURGATORIAN (2), [pur′-gat-aw′-ri-an], *adj.* purgatorial.

PURGATORY, [pur′-gat-er-i], *n.* (*theol.*) the condition of the souls of the departed who have died in the faith and in grace but still have to be cleansed from venial sins; the place of this cleansing; (*loosely*) a place or condition of torment or punishment. [MedL. *purgatorium*].

PURGE (1), [purj], *n.* the act or process of purging; a purgative; an evacuation of the bowels; (*pol.*) wholesale and drastic removal of undesirable elements, often by forcible methods. [PURGE (2)].

PURGE (2), [purj], *v.t.* to cleanse or purify; (*med.*) to provoke an evacuation of the bowels; (*leg.*) to clear (oneself) of a charge; (*pol.*) to rid of undesirable elements by a purge. [ME. *purgen*, OFr. *purger* from L. *purgare*].

PURGER, [purj′-er], *n.* someone or something that purges.

PURGING (1), [purj′-ing], *n.* diarrhoea or dysentery; **p. cassia,** the plant *Cassia fistula*.

PURGING (2), [pur′-jing], *adj.* that purges.

PURIFICATION, [pyŏŏer′-if-ik-ā′-shun], *n.* the act of purifying, the condition of being purified; **the P. of the Blessed Virgin Mary,** a feast of the Church kept on February 2. [L. *purificatio*].

PURIFICATIVE, [pyŏŏer′-if-ik-āt′-iv], *adj.* having the power to purify, tending to cleanse or purify. [Fr. *purificatif*]

PURIFICATORY, [pyŏŏer′-if-ik-āt′-or-i], *adj.* purificative. [LL. *purificatorius*].

PURIFIER, [pyŏŏer′-if-ī-er], *n.* someone or something that purifies.

PURIFORM, [pyŏŏer′-i-fawm], *adj.* (*med.*) resembling pus.

PURIFY, [pyŏŏer′-i-fī], *v.t.* to render pure, cleanse. [ME. *purifien*, Fr. *purifier* from L. *purificare*].

PURIM, [pew′-rim], *n.* a Jewish feast held in commemoration of the defeat of Haman's plot to massacre their nation. [Heb. *purim* lots, Esther ix, 26].

PURINE, PURIN, [pew′-rēn], *n.* (*chem.*) a white

crystalline compound occurring in urine. [Germ. *purin*].

PURISM, [pyŏŏer'-izm], *n.* the practice of laboured correctness in speech and writing.

PURIST, [pyŏŏer'-ist], *n.* one who insists on and practises correctness in writing.

PURISTIC, [pyŏŏer'-ist'-ik], *adj.* of, or pertaining to, purism.

PURITAN (1), [pyŏŏer'-it-an], *n.* a member of the Church of England in the reign of Queen Elizabeth opposed to liturgical prayer and ceremonial; an opponent of the Crown in the English Civil War; a severe, austere person who attaches great importance to moral rectitude, condemning even minor pleasures; an extreme purist. [~L. *puritas* purity].

PURITAN (2), [pyŏŏer'-it-an], *adj.* pertaining to, characteristic of, a puritan or Puritans.

PURITANIC, [pyŏŏer'-it-an'-ik], *adj.* of, or pertaining to, Puritans or puritanism; observing or insisting upon strict purity in any matter or practice.

PURITANICAL, [pyŏŏer'-it-an'-ikl], *adj.* puritanic.

PURITANICALLY, [pyŏŏer'-it-an'-ik-al-i], *adv.* in a puritanical manner.

PURITANISM, [pyŏŏer'-it-an-izm], *n.* the ideals, ideas and practices of the Puritans.

PURITANIZE, [pyŏŏer'-it-an-īz'], *v.t.* to make puritanical, to convert to puritanism.

PURITY, [pyŏŏer'-it-i], *n.* the condition or quality of being pure; cleanliness, decency; freedom from obscenity; chastity, continence; innocence, high-mindedness; freedom from mixture, contamination or adulteration. [ME. *puretee*, OFr. *pureté* from L. *puritas*].

PURL (1), [purl], *n.* a loop at the edge of lace or ribbon; (*knitting*) an inverted stitch the use of which gives a ribbed appearance to the work; (*embroidery*) †a twisted cord of gold or silver strands. [Uncert.].

PURL (2), [purl], *n.* the quiet murmur of a brook. [PURL (6)].

PURL (3), [purl], *n.* a beverage of beer or ale warmed and flavoured with wormwood; a warm mixture of ale and gin. [Uncert.].

PURL (4), [purl], *n.* a fall from a horse. [PURL (7)].

PURL (5), [purl], *v.i.* to put a looped edging to ribbon or lace; to knit with a purl stitch. [PURL (1)].

PURL (6), [purl], *v.i.* (of a brook) to flow with a gentle murmuring. [Echoic].

PURL (7), [purl], *v.t. and i.* (*dial.*) (of a horse) to throw (its rider).

PURLER, [purl'-er], *n.* (*dial.*) a fall from a horse; (*slang*) a cropper. [*Prec.*].

PURLIEU, [pur'-lew], *n.* (*leg. hist.*) a part of a forest marked off by perambulation, within which forest laws were not considered as applying; (*pl.*) outskirts, outlying or surrounding districts, *esp.* the unimportant, poor and dingy parts of a town. [Anglo-Fr. (*leg.*) *puralée* from OFr. *puraler* to mark (the boundary of) by perambulation and ~Fr. *lieu* place].

PURLIN, [pur'-lin], *n.* (*arch.*) a beam in a roof running at right angles to the principal beams and common rafters, resting on the former but carrying the latter. [Unkn.].

PURLOIN, [pur-loin'], *v.t.* to steal. [ME. *perloynen*, OFr. *porloigner* to put away].

PURLOINER, [pur-loin'-er], *n.* one who filches.

PURPLE (1), [purpl], *n.* a secondary colour obtained by combining red and blue; purple clothing, *esp.* considered as the clothing of kings, emperors, etc., hence, royal birth, imperial rank; **born in the p.**, born to royal, imperial or very exalted rank; **raised to the p.**, made an emperor; made a cardinal. [ME. *purpel* from OFr. *pourpre* from L. *purpura* crimson].

PURPLE (2), [purpl], *adj.* coloured with purple or sometimes (*esp. poet.*) crimson, blood-red; **to go p. with rage**, to be furiously angry. [PURPLE (1)].

PURPLE (3), [purpl], *v.t. and i.* to colour or dye with purple; to turn purple. [PURPLE (1)].

PURPLE EMPEROR, [purpl'-emp'-er-er], *n.* a butterfly noted for its large size and its large strong wings, which are of a shot-purple colour in the male.

PURPLE FISH, [purpl'-fish], *n.* a gastropod marine mollusc from which a purple dye was obtained in classical times, the murex.

PURPLE-HEART, [purpl'-haht], *n.* purple-wood.

PURPLES, [purplz], *n.*(*pl.*) (*path.*) the purple spots that accompany some malignant diseases; purpura.

PURPLE-WOOD, [purpl'-wŏŏd], *n.* the hard purple wood of the tree, *Copaifera*, which grows in Brazil, often called purple-heart, and used in cabinet-making, *esp.* for inlays.

PURPLEWORT, [purpl'-wurt], *n.* the plant, *Potentilla Comarum*, the marsh cinquefoil.

PURPLISH, [purp'-lish], *adj.* rather purple.

PURPORT (1), [pur'-pawt], *n.* purpose, intention; meaning, significance, import. [PURPORT (2)].

PURPORT (2), [pur'-pawt, pur-pawt'], *v.i.* to mean or signify, to seem to mean or signify; to imply, hint at, indicate. [OFr. *pourporter* to intend, import, contain, from L. *pro* and *portare* to carry].

PURPORTLESS, [pur'-pawt-les], *adj.* being without purport.

PURPOSE (1), [pur'-pus], *n.* aim, intention, design. [ME. *purpos*, OFr. *pourpos* from L. *propositum* something expounded or placed before].

PURPOSE (2), [pur'-pus], *v.t. and i.* to intend, aim, design. [OFr. *pourposer*].

PURPOSED, [pur'-pust], *adj.* determined, intending.

PURPOSEFUL, [pur'-pus-fŏŏl], *adj.* resolute, firm of purpose; meaningful, full of import, rich in significance.

PURPOSEFULLY, [pur'-pus-fŏŏl-i], *adv.* intentionally, in a purposeful way.

PURPOSEFULNESS, [pur'-pus-fŏŏl-nes], *n.* the condition or quality of being purposeful.

PURPOSELESS, [pur'-pus-les], *adj.* having no purpose, irresolute; without point, aimless, lacking significance, futile.

PURPOSELESSLY, [pur'-pus-les-li], *adv.* in a purposeless fashion.

PURPOSELESSNESS, [pur'-pus-les-nes], *n.* the condition or quality of being purposeless.

PURPOSELY, [pur'-pus-li], *adv.* by design, intentionally, on purpose.

PURPOSIVE, [pur'-pus-iv], *adj.* done for a purpose; signifying a purpose.

PURPRESTURE, [pur-pres'-cher], *n.* (*leg.*) an illegal enclosure of common land or (formerly) an illegal encroachment on the land or property of another. [OFr. *pourpresture*].

PURPUR, PURPURE, [pur'-pyŏŏer], *n.* (*her.*) the colour purple. [ME. *purpre*, OFr. *pourpre* from L. *purpura* purple].

PURPURA, [pur'-pew-ra], *n.* (*path.*) a disease due to ill-condition of the blood, characterized by extreme debility and an eruption of purple spots on the skin; (*zool.*) a genus of gastropods, including those molluscs such as the murex from which, in classical times, a purple dye was extracted. [L. *purpura* from Gk. *porphura* purple].

PURPURE, see PURPUR.

PURPUREAL, [pur-pyŏŏer'-al], *adj.* (*poet.*) purple-coloured. [L. *purpureus*].

PURPURIC, [pur-pyŏŏer'-ik], *adj.* (*path.*) pertaining to purpura; (*chem.*) of, or pertaining to, an unisolated nitrogenous acid found only in certain salts, all of which are purple in colour.

PURPURIN, [pur'-pew-rin], *n.* (*chem.*) a red dye found in madder.

PURR (1), [pur], *n.* the sound a cat makes when it is pleased or contented; any similar low humming sound, *esp.* that of the engine of a motor-car travelling smoothly and rapidly. [PURR (2)].

PURR (2), [pur], *v.i.* to utter the low vibratory humming sound by which cats express content or satisfaction; (*fig.*) to talk in a manner that suggests the contented purring of a cat; (of a motor-car) to move rapidly and smoothly along with a low humming sound coming from the engine. [Echoic].

PURRE, [pur], *n.* (*dial.*) the bird, *Tringa variabilis*, the dunlin. [Uncert.; probably echoic].

PURREE, [pu'-rē], *n.* a yellow colouring matter used in China and India to colour the walls of houses and, in the west, in the preparation of the pigment known as Indian yellow. [Hind. *poori*].

PURROCK, see PARROCK.

PURSE (1), [purs], *n.* a small pouch (usually of leather) for carrying money; cash; wealth, money; a sum of money collected as a prize for a competition or contest; anything resembling a purse or pouch. [OE. *purs* from LL. *bursa* a pouch].

PURSE (2), [purs], *v.t.* †to put in a purse; **to p. one's lips** or **to p. up one's lips** or **mouth**, to thrust out and wrinkle together one's lips (expressing hesitancy, consideration, doubt).

PURSE-BEARER, [purs'-bāer'-er], *n.* one who bears a purse *esp.* on behalf of another, *esp.* the officer who carries the Great Seal on behalf of the Lord Chancellor in a procession.

PURSE-CRAB, [purs'-krab], *n.* a large tropical crab with a pouch-like abdomen.

PURSEFUL, [purs'-fŏŏl], *n.* the quantity that may

be contained in a purse; (*fig.*) (of money) a good round sum.

PURSE-NET, [purs'-net], *n.* a net shaped like a bag, with a mouth that can be closed by tightening a string, used to catch rabbits.

PURSE-PROUD, [purs'-prowd'], *adj.* proud of one's wealth.

PURSER, [purs'-er], *n.* (*naut.*) the ship's officer who keeps the accounts, *esp.* on a passenger vessel; †a paymaster in the navy.

PURSERSHIP, [purs'-er-ship], *n.* (*naut.*) the office of purser.

PURSE-SEINE, [purs'-sēn'], *n.* a bag-like fishing net with a closeable mouth, a purse-net.

PURSE-STRINGS, [purs'-stringz'], *n.*(*pl.*) the ends of a cord that closes the mouth of a pouch or purse; (*fig.*) control of the funds; **to hold the p.,** to control expenditure.

PURSINESS, [purs'-i-nes], *n.* the condition of being pursy.

PURSLANE, [purs'-lān], *n.* the salad herb, *Portulaca oleracea.* [OFr. *porcelaine* from L. *porcillaca* or *portulaca*].

PURSUABLE, [pur-sew'-abl], *adj.* able to be pursued.

PURSUANCE, [pur-sew'-ants], *n.* the act of pursuing or carrying out; performance, obedience, following out.

PURSUANT, [pur-sew'-ant], *adj.* done in consequence (of), conforming, conformable, being in accordance (with).

PURSUANTLY, [pur-sew'-ant-li], *adv.* in accordance with, conformably.

PURSUE, [pur-sew'], *v.t.* and *i.* to follow in order to overtake and capture or kill, to chase, hunt; to accompany closely, dog; to aim at, have as one's ambition; to follow, practise, undertake and perform; to continue, follow out, go on with; (*Scots leg.*) to prosecute. [ME. *pursuen*, OFr. *porsuivre* from L. *prosequi* to follow].

PURSUER, [pur-sew'-er], *n.* someone who pursues; (*Scots leg.*) the prosecutor.

PURSUIT, [pur-sewt'], *n.* the act of pursuing; a chase or hunt; the act of seeking or searching; the act of following up, continuing to act in accordance with; the doing or performance; that which one does or is engaged upon, an activity, profession, hobby, etc. [AFr. *purseute* from OFr. *poursuite*].

PURSUIVANT, [pur'-swiv-ant], *n.* a junior officer of the College of Heralds; an attendant, a follower. [OFr. *porsivant* or *pursivant* from L. *prosequi* to follow].

PURSY (1), [pur'-si], *adj.* short and stout· short-breathed. [ME. *purseyf*, OFr. *polsif* from *polser* to push].

PURSY (2), [pur'-si], *adj.* puckered.

PURTENANCE, [pur'-ten-ants], *n.* an appurtenance.

PURULENCE, [pew'-rōō-lents], *n.* the formation of pus; the condition or quality of being purulent. [LL. *purulentia*].

PURULENCY, [pew'-rōō-len-si], *n.* purulence.

PURULENT, [pew'-rōō-lent], *adj.* containing or discharging pus; putrid, septic. [L. *purulentus*].

PURVEY, [pur-vā'], *v.t.* and *i.* to provide, supply, procure; to supply with, obtain supplies (food, equipment, necessaries, etc.) for.

PURVEYANCE, [pur-vā'-ants], *n.* the act of purveying or providing. [ME. *purveaunce*, OFr. *purveaunce* from L. *providentia*].

PURVEYOR, [pur-vā'-or], *n.* one who provides or purveys (*esp.* food, necessaries, etc.), a caterer. [ME. *purveour*].

PURVIEW, [pur'-vew], *n.* a proviso or stipulation; a clause limiting the scope or application of a statement, agreement, etc.; range, scope, sphere. [OFr. *porveu*, provided].

PUS, [pus], *n.* purulent matter of a yellowish-white colour produced in a wound, sore, etc., by suppuration. [L. *pus*].

PUSEYISM, [pew'-zi-izm], *n.* the Oxford Movement in the Church of England, *esp.* when unsympathetically referred to. [Dr. *Pusey*, one of the leaders of the movement].

PUSEYITE, [pew'-zi-īt], *n.* a supporter of the Oxford Movement, a follower of Dr. Pusey.

PUSH (1), [pŏŏsh], *n.* the action of pushing; a thrust, jostle or shove; (*milit.*) a vigorous attack; a vigorous attempt or endeavour, a determined effort to get something done; vigorous pursuit of one's ambitions, self-assertion; **to make a p.,** to make a vigorous and determined effort; **at a p.,** if necessary, in an emergency, by special effort; **to get the p.,** (*slang*) to lose one's job, be dismissed. [PUSH (2)].

PUSH (2), [pŏŏsh], *v.t.* and *i.* to exert pressure against (an object) so as to cause it to move or tend to move away from the point from which the pressure is exerted; to thrust, shove, drive forward; to jostle, shove; to urge on (*esp. fig.*), to press, prosecute with vigour; to present or advocate urgently for sale, use, promotion, etc.; to oppress or harass; (*pass.*) to be hard pressed; to thrust oneself forward, make oneself conspicuous in order to achieve one's ambitions; **to p. by,** to thrust oneself past; **to p. in,** (of a boat) to move to the shore; **to p. off,** (of a boat) to move from the shore; (*coll.*) to depart; **to p. on,** to advance eagerly and urgently, *esp.* against difficulties; **to p. out,** (of a boat) to move away from shore; **to p. through,** to cause to be done by exerting force or influence. [ME. *pussen* from L. *pulsare* to beat].

PUSHABLE, [pŏŏsh'-abl], *adj.* able to be pushed.

PUSHBALL, [pŏŏsh'-bawl], *n.* a game for two teams of eleven players, played with a very large ball which is pushed to the goals, not thrown or kicked.

PUSH-BICYCLE, [pŏŏsh'-bī'-sikl], *n.* a pedal cycle.

PUSHBIKE, [pŏŏsh'-bīk'], *n.* (*coll.*) a push-bicycle. [PUSH-BICYCLE].

PUSH-CART, [pŏŏsh'-kaht], *n.* a cart or barrow small enough to be pushed by hand; a small cart in which a baby can be pushed along.

PUSHER, [pŏŏsh'-er], *n.* someone or something that pushes; an ambitious self-assertive person; a piece of cutlery used by babies to push pieces of food into a spoon.

PUSHFUL, [pŏŏsh'-fōōl], *adj.* enterprising, self-assertive, pushing.

PUSH-HALFPENNY, [pŏŏsh'-hāp-ni], *n.* shove-halfpenny.

PUSHING, [pŏŏsh'-ing], *adj.* pressing forward in one's affairs, energetic, enterprising, self-assertive, *esp.* in a presumptuous fashion.

PUSHINGLY, [pŏŏsh'-ing-li], *adv.* in a pushing way.

PUSHPIN, [pŏŏsh'-pin], *n.* a childish game played with pins.

PUSHTU, PUSHTOO, [push'-tōō'], *n.* the Afghan language. [Pers. *pashto*].

PUSILLANIMITY, [pew'-sil-an-im'-it-i], *n.* the quality of being pusillanimous, cowardice; timidity. [EcclesL. *pusillanimitas*].

PUSILLANIMOUS, [pew'-sil-an'-im-us], *adj.* cowardly, timid, feeble, mean-spirited. [EcclesL. *pusillanimis*].

PUSILLANIMOUSLY, [pew'-sil-an'-im-us-li], *adv.* in a pusillanimous manner or spirit.

PUSILLANIMOUSNESS, [pew'-sil-an'-im-us-nes], *n.* pusillanimity.

PUSS, [pŏŏs], *n.* (*coll.*) a cat; a hare; a mischievous girl. [Uncert.].

PUSS-IN-THE-CORNER, [pŏŏs'-in-THE-kaw'-ner], *n.* a nursery game.

PUSS-MOTH, [pŏŏs'-moth], *n.* the large woolly-bodied moth, *Cerura vinula*, light grey in colour.

PUSS-MOTH

PUSS-TAIL, [pŏŏs'-tāl], *n.* a name given in the U.S. to *setaria* or bristle-grass.

PUSSY, [pŏŏs'-i], *n.* a pet-name for a cat; a willow or hazel catkin.

PUSSYFOOT (1), [pŏŏs'-i-foot], *n.* a prohibitionist; a stealthy schemer. [PUSSY and FOOT (1)].

PUSSYFOOT (2), [pŏŏs'-i-fōōt], *v.i.* to pursue a plan warily or stealthily. [PUSSYFOOT (1)].

PUSSY-WILLOW, [pŏŏs'-i-wil'-ō], *n.* a willow-tree bearing woolly catkins.

PUSTULAR, [pus'-chōō-ler], *adj.* resembling or displaying pustules. [MdL. *pustularis*].

PUSTULATE (1), [pus'-chōō-lāt], *adj.* pustular. [LL. *pustulatus*, *p.pt.* of *pustulare* to form pustules].

PUSTULATE (2), [pus'-chōō-lāt], *v.t.* and *i.* to shape into, or take the shape of, pustules. [*Prec.*].

PUSTULATION, [pus'-chōō-lā'-shun], *n.* the formation of blisters or pustules. [LL. *pustulatio*].

PUSTULE, [pus'-tewl], *n.* a pimple containing pus. [L. *pustula* a blister or pimple].

PUSTULOUS, [pus'-chōō-lus], *adj.* full of pustules, pustular.

PUT (1), [pŏŏt], *n.* the act of "putting the weight." [see PUT (4)].

PUT† (2), [put], *n.* a fool. [Uncert.].

PUT (3), see PUTT.

PUT (4), [pŏŏt], *v.t.* and *i.* to set, place, lay; (*fig.*) to assign a particular rank or value to in one's estimation; to move (towards); (*fig.*) to cause to be in or come into (a certain mental or physical condition or set of circumstances); to arrange, lay out, set down; to affix, join; to turn (in a particular direction); (*fig.*) to apply (the mind to); (of a point of view, idea, proposition, etc.) to lay before, explain; to suggest or propose; to state or set out; **to p. about,** *v.i.* (*naut.*) to steer in a different course; *v.t.* to spread (a rumour) abroad; (*pass.*) to worry, trouble; to be worried or harassed; **to p. away,** (*fig.*) to store or save; †to divorce; (*coll.*) to eat or drink; **to p. back,** (*naut.*) to return; **to p. by,** to save or store; **to p. down,** (*fig.*) to repress, check, end; to write; to value or estimate; **to p. in,** to insert, interpose; to speak; **to p. in for,** to apply for; **to p. in at,** to make a short stay at; **to p. off,** (*fig.*) to delay, postpone, to fob off, evade; to dissuade from; **to p. on,** to simulate, affect; to bring into action, (of a play) to stage; to add or increase; to bet; **to p. out,** (*fig.*) to dislocate; to extinguish; to disturb, disconcert; **to p. over,** (*slang*) to be successful with (a plan, scheme, etc.); **to p. through,** (*coll.*) to do or cause to be done; to subject or submit to; **to p. to,** to cause to follow (a certain career, training, occupation, way of life, etc.; **to p. up,** to propose; to offer, *esp.* for sale; to restore to a former position; to provide food and lodging for; **to p. up at,** to lodge at; **to p. up to,** to tell to (do), to incite; **to p. up with,** to tolerate, suffer; **to p. the weight,** (*athletics*) to raise a weight to the shoulder on the hand and fling it by suddenly straightening the arm.

PUTAMEN, [pew-tā'-men], *n.* (*bot.*) the stone in a fruit with soft flesh like a plum or peach; (*zool.*) the grey, outer layer within the brain; the membrane or skin that lines the shell of a bird's egg. [L. *putamen* that which is cut off or clipped].

PUTATIVE, [pewt-at'-iv], *adj.* reputed, supposed. [Fr. *putatif* from LL. *putativus*].

PUTATIVELY, [pewt'-at-iv-li], *adv.* reputedly, supposedly.

PUTCHOCK, PUTCHUK, [pu'-chuk], *n.* the root of the plant *Haplotaxis auriculata*, a plant grown in Kashmir, imported and used by the Chinese to make joss-sticks. [Hind. *pachak*].

PUTEAL, [pew'-ti-al], *n.* the low stone wall round the mouth of a well. [L. *puteal*].

PUTID, [pew'-tid], *adj.* mean, base, worthless. [L. *putidus* stinking].

PUTIDITY, [pew-tid'-it-i], *n.* putidness. [MedL. *putiditatem*].

PUTIDNESS, [pew'-tid-nes], *n.* the quality of being putid, vileness.

PUTLOG, PUTLOCK, [put'-log, put'-lok], *n.* in scaffolding, one of a series of small pieces of wood, one end of which is inserted in a hole in the wall, and the other, which juts out, used to rest the main scaffolding boards on. [Uncert.].

PUTREFACIENT (1), [pew'-trif-āsh'-i-ent], *n.* putrefactive matter. [PUTREFACIENT (2)].

PUTREFACIENT (2), [pew'-trif-āsh'-i-ent], *adj.* causing putrefaction. [L. *putrefaciens*, *pres.pt.* of *putrefacere* to make rotten].

PUTREFACTION, [pew'-trif-ak'-shun], *n.* the process of becoming putrid; putrid matter. [L. *putrefactio*].

PUTREFACTIVE, [pew'-trif-ak'-tiv], *adj.* of, pertaining to, or causing putrefaction. [Fr. *putréfactif*].

PUTREFY, [pew'-tri-fī], *v.t.* and *i.* to make putrid; to become putrid. [L. *putrefacere* to make putrid].

PUTRESCENCE, [pew-tres'-ents], *n.* the condition of being putrescent; putrescent matter.

PUTRESCENT, [pew-tres'-ent], *adj.* in the process of becoming putrid. [L. *putrescens*, *pres.pt.* of *putrescere* to become putrid].

PUTRESCIBLE, [pew-tres'-ibl], *adj.* liable to become putrid.

PUTRID, [pew'-trid], *adj.* decayed and rotten (of organic bodies, *esp.* animal flesh); (*coll.*) unpleasant, disappointing, very bad. [L. *putridus* rotten, stinking].

PUTRIDITY, [pew-trid'-i-ti], *n.* the state of being putrid; something putrid. [MedL. *putriditas*].

PUTRIDNESS, [pew'-trid-nes], *n.* the condition of being putrid.

PUTSCH, [pōōch], *n.* an attempt at revolution or coup d'état by a reactionary minority. [Germ. *putsch*].

PUTT (1), PUT, [put], *n.* the act of putting, a stroke intended to hole the ball at golf. [PUTT (2)].

PUTT (2), PUT, [put], *v.t.* and *i.* to strike the ball with the putter; to use a putter at golf. [*Var.* of PUT].

PUTTEE, [put-ee', put'-i], *n.* a cloth legging which is wound round the leg in spiral fashion from the ankle to the knee. [Hindi *patti* bandage].

PUTTING GREEN, [put'-ing-grēn], *n.* (*golf*) the closely mown green surrounding the hole on a golf course, where putting is done; a small green with several holes for practising short strokes.

PUTTER, [put'-er], *n.* a short club with a flat face used in golf for holing the ball when playing on a green.

PUTTY (1), [put'-i], *n.* fine lime and cement mixed with water, used by builders; a kind of plastic cement made of whiting mixed with linseed oil, and used in fixing window-panes; a polishing powder made of calcined tin and used by jewellers; (*fig.*) a feeble filling to cover faults. [Fr. *potée* a potful].

PUTTY (2), [put'-i], *v.t.* to fix by means of putty.

PUZZLE (1), [puzl], *n.* something that puzzles, that which appears to have no solution; the state of being puzzled, perplexity; a problem, conundrum; a contrivance which permits of an ingenious solution.

PUZZLE (2), [puzl], *v.t.* and *i.* to offer conditions, circumstances which are so complex or difficult that they confuse and bewilder, to baffle, to keep the solution or significance hidden from; **to p. out,** to solve after hard thinking. [Unkn.].

PUZZLEDOM, [puzl'-dom], *n.* the state of being puzzled, bewilderment.

PUZZLE-HEADED, [puzl'-hed'-id], *adj.* full of confused notions.

PUZZLE-HEADEDNESS, [puzl-hed'-id-nes], *n.* the condition of being puzzle-headed.

PUZZLEMENT, [puzl'-ment], *n.* puzzled state, perplexity.

PUZZLER, [puz'-ler], *n.* one who, or that which, perplexes.

PUZZLING, [puz'-ling], *adj.* perplexing, bewildering.

PUZZOLANA, [pōōt'-zō-lah'-na], *n.* a substance formed of volcanic ashes compacted together. [*Pozzuoli*, near Naples].

PYAEMIA, [pī-ē'-mi-a], *n.* blood-poisoning, due to the absorption into the system of putrid matter and characterized by abscesses. [Gk. *puon* pus and *haima* blood].

PYAEMIC, [pī'-ē'-mik], *adj.* of, or like, pyaemia.

PYCNITE, [pik'-nīt], *n.* (*min.*) a massive variety of topaz. [Gk. *puknos* thick].

PYCNODONTS, [pik'-nō-donts], *n.*(*pl.*) (*geol.*) an extinct family of fishes occurring throughout the Oolite rocks. [Gk. *puknos* thick and *odous odontos* tooth].

PYCNOGONIDS, [pik'-nō-gon'-idz], *n.*(*pl.*) (*zool.*) the sea-spiders. [Gk. *puknos* thick and *gonu* knee].

PYCNOSTYLE, [pik'-nō-stīl], *n.* (*arch.*) a colonnade in which the columns stand very close to one another, at intervals equal to one and a half times the diameter of the columns. [Gk. *puknostulos*].

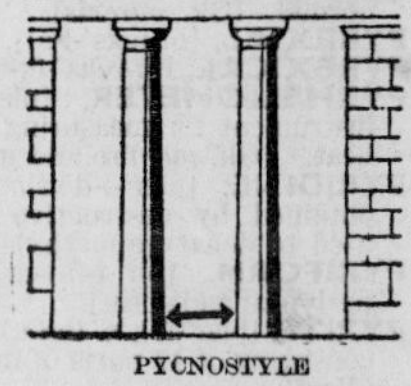
PYCNOSTYLE

PYEDOG, [pī'-dog], *n.* a stray mongrel. [Hind. *pahi* outsider and DOG].

PYELITIS, [pī-el-īt'-is], *n.* (*path.*) inflammation of the mucous membranes of the cavities of the kidneys. [Gk. *puelon* cavity and *itis* denoting inflammation].

PYGAL, [pī'-gal], *adj.* (*zool.*) relating to the posterior region. [Gk. *puge* buttock].

PYGMEAN, PIGMEAN, [pig'-mē-an], *adj.* relating to a pygmy or dwarf; very small, dwarfish.

PYGMY (1), PIGMY, *n.* a person of stunted growth, a dwarf, originally one of a fabled race of dwarfs who waged war with the cranes. [Gk. *pugmaios* having the length of a forearm].

PYGMY (2), PIGMY, *adj.* very small, dwarfish.

PYJAMAS, [pi-jah'-maz], *n.*(*pl.*) a sleeping suit of jacket and trousers; a loose pair of trousers as worn by Moslems. [Hind. *pajama* drawers].

PYLON, [pī'-lon], *n.* a gateway; a tower erected as a landmark for aircraft; a tower structure for overhead suspension of electric cables. [Gk. *pulon* temple gateway].

PYLORIC, [pī-lo'-rik], *adj.* (*anat.*) of, or relating to, the pylorus.

PYLORUS, [pī-law'-rus], *n.* (*anat.*) the lower opening of the stomach, leading into the intestines. [Gk. *puloros* gatekeeper].

PYOGENESIS, [pī′-ō-jen′-is-is], *n.* the formation of pus. [Gk. *puon* pus and GENESIS].
PYOGENIC, [pī-ō-jen′-ik], *adj.* relating to, affected by, the formation of pus.
PYOID, [pī′-oid], *adj.* of the nature of pus. [Gk. *puon* pus and *oeides* like].
PYORRHOEA, [pī′-o-rē′-a], *n.* (*path.*) a disease of the gums characterized by bad breath, inflammation, and bleeding. [Gk. *puon* pus and *rhoia* a flowing].
PYRACANTH, [pīer′-a-kanth], *n.* an evergreen species of thorn with bright orange berries. [Gk. *puracantha* firethorn].
PYRALLOLITE, [pi-ral′-ō-līt], *n.* (*min.*) an altered form of augite, a greenish mineral found in Finland. [Gk. *pur* fire and *lithos* stone].
PYRAMID, [pi′-ra-mid], *n.* (*arch.*) an Egyptian building with a square foundation, four sides each in the form of a triangle and rising to terminate in a point; anything in the shape of a pyramid; (*pl.*) a form of billiards played with fifteen red balls. [Gk. *puramidos*].
PYRAMIDAL, [pi-ram′-id-al], *adj.* relating to the pyramids, pyramidical.
PYRAMIDALLY, [pi-ram′-id-a-li], *adv.* in the form of a pyramid.
PYRAMIDICAL, [pi′-ra-mid′-ik-al], *adj.* having the form of a pyramid.
PYRAMIDICALLY, [pi′-ra-mid′-ik-a-li], *adv.* in a pyramidical manner.
PYRAMIDICALNESS, [pi′-ra-mid′-ik-al-nes], *n.* the state of being pyramidical.
PYRAMIDOID, [pi-ram′-id-oid], *n.* a pyramoid. [PYRAMID and Gk. *oeides* like].
PYRAMOID, [pi′-ram-oid], *n.* a solid resembling a pyramid. [PYRAMID and Gk. *oeides* like].
PYRARGILLITE, [pi-rah′-jil-īt], *n.* a silicate of alumina which emits an argillaceous odour. [Gk. *pur* fire and ARGILLITE].
PYRARGYRITE, [pi-rah-jier′-it], *n.* a sulphide of silver and antimony forming a valuable ore of silver. [Gk. *pur* fire and *arguros* silver].
PYRE, [pīer], *n.* a funeral pile of wood for burning a corpse. [Gk. *pur* fire].
PYRENE (1), [pīer′-ēn], *n.* (*bot.*) the stone of a drupe. [Gk. *puren*].
PYRENE (2), [pīer′-ēn], *n.* (*chem.*) a crystalline substance obtained from coal-tar. [Gk. *pur* fire].
PYRENEITE, [pīer-en-ē′-īt], *n.* (*min.*) a variety of garnet. [Fr. *Pyrénées* where found].
PYRETIC, [pī-ret′-ik], *n.* a medicine for curing fever. [Gk. *puretos* fever].
PYRETOLOGY, [pīer′-et-ol′-o-ji], *n.* that branch of medicine which treats of fevers. [Gk. *puretos* fever and *logos* speech].
PYREXIA, [pī-rek′-si-a], *n.* (*med.*) the febrile state, or an attack of fever; a body temperature above normal. [Gk. *purexis*].
PYREXIAL, [pī-reks′-i-al], *adj.* feverish.
PYREXICAL, [pī-reks′-ik-al], *adj.* feverish.
PYRHELIOMETER, [pīer′-hē′-li-om′-it-er], *n.* an instrument for measuring the intensity of the sun's heat. [Gk. *pur* fire and HELIOMETER].
PYRIDINE, [pīer′-i-dēn], *n.* a poisonous alkaloid, obtained by destructive distillation of coal, etc., used to denature methylated spirit. [Gk. *pur* fire].
PYRIFORM, [pir′-i-fawm], *adj.* pear-shaped. [L. *pyris* pear and FORM].
PYRITE, [pīer′-īt], *n.* (*min.*) lustrous disulphide of iron consisting of 47 parts of iron and 53 parts of sulphur. [*Next*].
PYRITES, [pīer-ī′-tēz], *n.* a combination of sulphur with iron, copper, cobalt or nickel, so called because it strikes fire with steel. [Gk. *purites* fiery].
PYRITIC, [pīer-it′-ik], *adj.* pyritous.
PYRITIFEROUS, [pīer′-it-if′-er-us], *adj.* producing pyrites. [PYRITES and L. *ferre* to bear].
PYRITIZE, [pīer′-it-īz], *v.t.* to convert into pyrites.
PYRITOLOGY, [pīer′-it-ol′-o-ji], *n.* the study of pyrites. [PYRITES and Gk. *logos* speech].
PYRITOUS, [pīer′-it-us], *adj.* relating to, or resembling, pyrites.
PYRO-, *pref.* produced or treated by fire or heat. [Gk. *pur* fire].
PYROCHLORE, [pīer′-ō-klaw(r)], *n.* (*min.*) a mineral consisting mainly of niobate of lime, occurring in brownish octahedrans. [PYRO and Gk. *khloros* green].
PYRO-ELECTRIC, [pīer′-ō-il-ek′-trik], *adj.* becoming electric under heat.
PYROGALLIC, [pīer′-ō-gal′-ik], *adj.* obtained from gallic acid by heating it.
PYROGENIC, [pīer′-ō-jen′-ik], *adj.* producing feverishness.
PYROGENOUS, [pīer-oj′-en-us], *adj.* (*geol.*) produced by fire, igneous.
PYROGRAPHY, [pīer-og′-raf-i], *n.* the art of drawing on wood with a red-hot point of a poker or needle. [PYRO and Gk. *graphia* writing].
PYROLATRY, [pīer-ol′-at-ri], *n.* worship of fire. [PYRO and Gk. *latreia* worship].
PYROLIGNEOUS, [pīer′-ō-lig′-ni-us], *adj.* (*chem.*) generated by the distillation of wood; **p. acid**, impure acetic acid.
PYROLIGNIC, [pīer-ō-lig′-nik], *adj.* pyroligneous.
PYROLIGNITE, [pīer-ō-lig′-nīt], *n.* (*chem.*) a salt of pyroligneous acid.
PYROLOGIST, [pīer-ol′-oj-ist], *n.* an expert in the science of heat; one who uses the blowpipe.
PYROLOGY, [pīer-ol′-o-ji], *n.* the science of heat; blowpipe analysis; a treatise on the blowpipe. [PYRO and Gk. *logos* speech].
PYROLUSITE, [pīer-ō-lew′-sīt], *n.* (*min.*) a black ore of manganese. [PYRO and Gk. *luo* I wash].
PYROMAGNETIC, [pīer′-ō-mag-net′-ik], *adj.* relating or reacting to magnetism as affected by heat.
PYROMANCY, [pīer′-ō-man-si], *n.* divination by fire. [PYRO and Gk. *manteia* divination].
PYROMANIA, [pīer′-ō-mā′-ni-a], *n.* an insane desire to destroy by fire.
PYROMETER, [pīer-om′-it-er], *n.* an instrument for measuring the expansion of bodies by heat; a thermometer for measuring high degrees of temperature.

PYROMETER

PYROMETRICAL, [pīer-ō-met′-rik-al], *adj.* relating to the pyrometer or pyrometry.
PYROMETRY, [pīer-om′-it-ri], *n.* the measurement of heat by expansion; the measurement of high degrees of heat.
PYROMORPHITE, [pīer′-ō-mawf′-īt], *n.* (*min.*) native phosphate of lead. [PYRO and Gk. *morphe* shape].
PYROMORPHOSIS, [pīer-ō′-mawf-ō′-sis], *n.* (*geol.*) the change in rocks due to contact with lavas.
PYROMORPHOUS, [pīer-ō-mawf′-us], *adj.* (*min.*) having the property of crystallization by fire. [*Prec.*].
PYROPE, [pīer′-ōp], *n.* (*min.*) a brilliant red garnet, Bohemian garnet. [Gk. *puropos* eye of fire].
PYROPHANE, [pīer′-ō-fān], *n.* a mineral that becomes transparent by heat. [PYRO and Gk. *phainomai* I appear].
PYROPHANOUS, [pī-rof′-an-us], *adj.* rendered transparent by heat.
PYROPHOROUS, [pī-rof′-er-us], *adj.* consisting of or like a pyrophorus. [Gk. *purophoros* fire-bearing].
PYROPHORUS, [pī-rof′-er-us], *n.* a substance which takes fire on exposure to air. [Gk. *purophoros* fire-bearing].
PYROSCOPE, [pīer′-ō-skōp] *n.* an instrument for measuring the intensity of radiant heat or cold.
PYROSIS, [pīer-ō′-sis], *n.* (*path.*) a form of indigestion characterized by frequent eructation of a tasteless fluid and by a burning sensation in the stomach. [Gk. *purosis* burning].
PYROSMALITE, [pīer-oz′-mal-īt], *n.* (*min.*) chlorosilicate of iron and manganese which emits an odour resembling chlorine when submitted to heat. [PYRO and Gk. *osmalkos* stinking].
PYROTECHNIC, [pīer′-ō-tek′-nik], *adj.* relating to fireworks or the art of forming them. [PYRO and Gk. *tekhne* art].
PYROTECHNICS, [pīer′-ō-tek′-niks], *n.* the art of making fireworks.
PYROTECHNIST, [pīer′-ō-tek′-nist], *n.* a maker of fireworks.
PYROTECHNY, [pīer′-ō-tek′-ni], *n.* pyrotechnics.
PYROXENE, [pīer-ok′sēn], *n.* (*min.*) common augite and similar minerals. [PYRO and Gk. *xenos* stranger].
PYROXENIC, [pīer-ok-sen′-ik], *adj.* relating to, or composed of, pyroxene.
PYROXYLE, [pīer-ok′-sīl], *n.* (*chem.*) gun cotton. [PYRO and Gk. *xulon* wood].
PYROXYLIC, [pīer-ok-sil′-ik], *adj.* relating to, obtained by, the destructive distillation of wood.
PYROXYLIN, [pīer-ok′-sil-in], *n.* collodion cotton;

gun cotton obtained by the action of nitric acid on cellulose.

PYRRHIC (1), [pi′-rik], *n.* a war-dance of the ancient Greeks; (*pros.*) a foot consisting of two short syllables. [*Purrhikhos* of Pyrrhus (the composer of the dance)].

PYRRHIC (2), [pi′-rik], *adj.* typical of King *Pyrrhus*, who won a victory but only at an enormous cost of life. [Gk. *purrhikos*].

PYRRHONISM, [pi′-ron-izm], *n.* a philosophic system based on scepticism or universal doubt. [*Pyrrho* (300 B.C.), the founder].

PYRRHONIST, [pi′-ron-ist], *n.* a sceptic, a universal doubter, a philosopher adopting the principles of pyrrhonism.

PYRRHOTITE, [pi′-rō-tīt], *n.* (*min.*) magnetic pyrites, copper-red in colour. [Gk. *purrhos* ruddy].

PYTHAGOREAN (1), [pī-thag-ō-rē′-an], *n.* a follower of Pythagoras and his principles.

PYTHAGOREAN (2), [pī-thag-ō-rē′-an], *adj.* relating to Pythagoras and his philosophic principles of a metaphysical nature. [Gk. *Puthagoras*].

PYTHAGORISM, [pī-thag′-or-izm], *n.* the doctrines of Pythagoras.

PYTHIAD, [pith′-i-ad′], *n.* the interval between two celebrations of the Pythian games. [Gk. *puthias*].

PYTHIAN (1), [pith′-i-an], *n.* the priestess of Apollo who possessed oracular powers.

PYTHIAN (2), [pith′-i-an], *adj.* relating to Apollo's shrine at Delphi. [Gk. *Puthios*].

PYTHON, [pī′-thon], *n.* (*zool.*) a genus of large non-venomous serpents; (*myth.*) the serpent slain by Apollo. [Gk. *puthon*].

PYTHONESS, [pī′-thon-es], *n.* the priestess who gave oracular answers at Delphi, in Greece; a witch, sorceress. [LL. *pythonissa*].

PYTHONIC, [pī-thon′-ik], *adj.* relating to prophecy, oracular.

PYTHONISM, [pī′-thon-izm], *n.* divination after the manner of the Delphic oracle.

PYX (1), PIX, [piks], *n.* a richly wrought vessel used in the Roman Catholic Church for holding the consecrated host; a case for sample coins at the Royal Mint. [Gk. *puxis* box].

PYX

PYX (2), [piks], *v.t.* to test coins according to a standard of fineness and weight. [*Prec.*].

PYXIDIUM, [piks-id′-i-um], *n.* (*bot.*) a capsule which divides into an upper and lower half. [Gk. *puxidion*].

PYXIS (1), [piks′-is], *n.* a box; (*astron.*) the Mariner's Compass, a southern constellation. [Gk. *puxis* box].

PYXIS (2), [piks′-is], *n.* (*bot.*) a pyxidium as in the pimpernels, *Anagallis*, etc.

Q

Q, [kew], the seventeenth letter of the English alphabet.

Q-BOAT, [kew′-bōt′], *n.* a type of warship used in the First World War (1914-18) and disguised as a merchantman; a mystery ship. [*Query-boat*].

QUA, [kwā], *adv.* as being, in the capacity of. [L. *qua*].

QUA-BIRD, [kwā′-burd], *n.* the American night-heron, *Nycticorax nœvius*.

QUACK (1), [kwak], *n.* an ignorant person pretending to specialized knowledge, *esp.* in surgery and medical science, a charlatan; an itinerant pedlar in bogus medicines and drugs. [QUACKSALVER].

QUACK (2), [kwak], *n.* the cry, sound, or noise natural to a duck. [Imitative].

QUACK (3) [kwak], *adj.* made or prescribed by a quack doctor, bogus. [QUACK (1)].

QUACK (4), [kwak], *v.i.* to make the noise or cry natural to a duck; (*fig.*) to chatter. [QUACK (2)].

QUACKERY, [kwak′-er-i], *n.* the arts, tricks, treatment and practice of a quack, particularly in medicine; imposture.

QUACKISH, [kwak′-ish], *adj.* resorting to the methods of a quack; boasting of skill not possessed.

QUACKISM, [kwak′-izm], *n.* quack practice or pretence, quackery.

QUACKSALVER, [kwak′-sal-ver], *n.* an ignorant person who claims great skill in medicines and salves, a travelling pedlar in ointments, plasters, medicines, etc., for which the most fantastic claims are made. [Du. *kwakzalver*].

QUAD (1), [kwod], *n.* an abbreviation of quadrangle.

QUAD (2), [kwod], *n.* abbreviation of quadrat.

QUAD (3), see QUOD.

QUADRA, [kwod′-ra], *n.* (*arch.*) a square border or frame enclosing a panel. [L. *quadra* a square].

QUADRAGENARIAN (1), [kwod′-raj-en-āer′-i-an], *n.* a person in the forties. [QUADRAGENARIAN (2)].

QUADRAGENARIAN (2), [kwod′-raj-en-āer′-i-an], *adj.* aged forty to fifty. [L. *quadragenarius* of forty each].

QUADRAGENE, [kwod′-raj-ēn], *n.* (*eccles.*) a papal indulgence of forty days. [L. *quadrageni* forty each].

QUADRAGESIMA, [kwod′-raj-es′-i-ma], *n.* Lent, so called because it consists of forty days; **Q. Sunday**, first Sunday in Lent. [L. *quadragesima* forty].

QUADRAGESIMAL, [kwod′-raj-es′-iml], *adj.* of, relating to, belonging to, or used in, Lent. [LL. *quadragesimalis*].

QUADRAGESIMALS, [kwod′-raj-es′-im-alz], *n.*(*pl.*) (*eccles.*) offerings formerly made to the mother church on Mid-Lent Sunday.

QUADRANGLE, [kwod′-rang-gl], *n.* (*geom.*) a plane figure with four angles and four sides; (*arch.*) a rectangular court surrounded by buildings. [LL. *quadrangulum*].

QUADRANGULAR, [kwod-rang′-gyŏŏ-ler], *adj.* (*geom.*) having four angles and four sides. [LL. *quadrangularis*].

QUADRANGULARLY, [kwod-rang′-gyŏŏ-ler-li], *adv.* in a quadrangular form.

QUADRANT, [kwod′-rant], *n.* (*astron.*, *naut.*) an instrument used in measuring angles and heights; (*geom.*) the quarter of a circle or sphere. [L. *quadrans* a quarter].

QUADRANT

QUADRANTAL, [kwod-ran′-tal], *adj.* of, relating to, having the form or dimensions of, a quadrant.

QUADRAT, [kwod′-rat], *n.* an instrument used for measuring altitudes; (*typ.*) one of the pieces of metal used to space out short lines, usually called a quad; (*nat. hist.*) an area of ground set aside for geological investigation. [QUADRATE (3)].

QUADRATE (1), [kwod′-rat], *n.* a square; (*astron.*) a measured position of the heavenly bodies. [QUADRATE (3)].

QUADRATE (2), [kwod′-rāt], *adj.* square, particularly in bone formation. [QUADRATE (3)].

QUADRATE (3), [kwod′-rāt], *v.t. and i.* to square up, to make square; to make correspond, conform. [L. *quadratus*, *p.pt.* of *quadrare* to make square].

QUADRATIC (1), [kwod-rat′-ik], *n.* a quadratic equation; (*pl.*) the branch of algebra dealing with quadratic equations. [QUADRATIC (2)].

QUADRATIC (2), [kwod-rat′-ik], *adj.* of, resembling, relating to, a square; **q. equation**, (*alg.*) an equation in which the unknown quantity is of the power of a square. [L. **quadraticus* squared].

QUADRATRIX, (*pl.* **quadratrices**), [kwod′-rat-riks], *n.* (*geom.*) a curve by means of which other curves are squared. [L. *quadratrix*].

QUADRATURE, [kwod′-rach-er], *n.* (*astron.*) the position of a heavenly body when measured as ninety degrees distant from another; (*math.*) the expression

of an area, *esp.* of a circle, in terms of an equivalent square. [L. *quadratura* a squaring].
QUADRENNIAL, [kwod-ren'-i-al], *adj.* lasting, comprising, four years; occurring once in four years. [L. *quadrennium*].
QUADRENNIALLY, [kwod-ren'-i-al-i], *adv.* once in four years.
QUADRI-, *pref.* four. [L. *quattuor*].
QUADRICAPSULAR, [kwod'-ri-kap'-syōō-ler], *adj.* (*bot.*) having four capsules. [QUADRI and CAPSULAR].
QUADRICORN, [kwod'-ri-kawn], *n.* (*zool.*) an animal with four horns. [QUADRI and L. *cornu* horn].
QUADRICORNOUS, [kwod'-ri-kawn'-us], *adj.* (*zool.*) having four horns.
QUADRICOSTATE, [kwod'-ri-kost'-āt], *adj.* (*zool.*) having four ribs. [QUADRI and COSTATE].
QUADRIDENTATE, [kwod'-ri-dent'-āt], *adj.* (*bot.*) having four teeth. [QUADRI and DENTATE].
QUADRIDIGITATE, [kwod'-ri-dij'-it-āt], *adj.* with four digits. [QUADRI and DIGITATE].
QUADRIFID, [kwod'-ri-fid], *adj.* (*bot.*) four-cleft, split in four parts. [L. *quadrifidus*].
QUADRIFOLIATE, [kwod'-ri-fōl'-i-āt], *adj.* (*bot.*) four-leaved. [QUADRI and FOLIATE].
QUADRIGA, [kwod-rī'-ga], *n.* a chariot drawn by four horses abreast. [QUADRI and L. *jugum* yoke].
QUADRIGENARIOUS, [kwod'-rij-en-āer'-i-us], *adj.* consisting of four hundred.
QUADRIJUGATE, [kwod'-ri-jew'-gāt], *adj.* (*bot.*) pinnate and with four pairs of leaflets. [QUADRI and JUGATE].
QUADRILATERAL (1), [kwod'-ri-lat'-er-al], *n.* a plane figure with four sides and angles; a district in N. Italy defended by four fortresses. [QUADRILATERAL (2)].
QUADRILATERAL (2), [kwod'-ri-lat'-er-al], *adj.* having four sides. [QUADRI and LATERAL].
QUADRILATERALNESS, [kwod'-ri-lat'-er-al-nes], *n.* the state or quality of being quadrilateral.
QUADRILITERAL, [kwod'-ri-lit'-er-al], *adj.* consisting of four letters. [QUADRI and LITERAL].
QUADRILLE, [kwod-ril', kad-ril'], *n.* a game played by four persons with forty cards; a square dance for four or more couples; the music for such a dance. [It. *quadriglia* a cavalry squadron].
QUADRILLION, [kwod-ril'-i-on], *n.* the number produced by raising a million to the fourth power.
QUADRILOBATE, [kwod'-ri-lōb'-āt], *adj.* (*bot.*) having four lobes. [QUADRI and LOBATE].
QUADRILOCULAR, [kwod'-ri-lok'-yōō-ler], *adj.* (*bot.*) four-celled. [QUADRI and L. *loculus* a little place].
QUADRINOMIAL, [kwod'-ri-nō'-mi-al], *adj.* (*alg.*) consisting of four terms. [QUADRI and NOMINAL].
QUADRIPARTITE, [kwod'-ri-paht'-īt], *adj.* (*bot., zool.*) divided into four parts. [QUADRI and PARTITE].
QUADRIPARTITION, [kwod'-ri-pah-tish'-un], *n.* the act of dividing into four.
QUADRIPENNATE, [kwod'-ri-pen'-āt], *adj.* (*zool.*) having four wings. [QUADRI and PENNATE].
QUADRIPHYLLOUS, [kwod'-ri-fil'-us], *adj.* (*bot.*) having four leaves. [QUADRI and Gk. *phullon* leaf].

QUADRIPHYLLOUS

QUADRIREME, [kwod'-ri-rēm], *n.* a galley with four benches of oars. [L. *quadriremis*].
QUADRISYLLABIC, [kwod'-ri-sil-ab'-ik], *adj.* consisting of four syllables.
QUADRISYLLABLE, [kwod'-ri-sil'-abl], *n.* a word consisting of four syllables. [QUADRI and SYLLABLE].
QUADRIVALVULAR, [kwod'-ri-valv'-yōō-ler], *adj.* (*bot.*) four-valved. [QUADRI and VALVULAR].
QUADRIVIAL, [kwod-riv'-i-al], *adj.* having four ways or roads meeting in a point. [L. *quadrivialis*].
QUADRIVIUM†, [kwod-riv'-i-um], *n.* the course of higher studies for medieval scholars, consisting of astronomy, arithmetic, music, and geometry. [QUADRI and L. *via* road].
QUADROON, [kwod-rōōn'], *n.* the offspring of a mulatto and a white. [Span. *cuarteron*].
QUADRUMANOUS, [kwod-rōō'-man-us], *adj.* (*zool.*) four-handed. [QUADRI and L. *manus* hand].
QUADRUNE, [kwod'-rōōn], *n.* a gritstone with a calcareous cement.
QUADRUPED (1), [kwod'-rōō-ped'], *n.* (*zool.*) a term for a mammal, a four-footed animal. [QUADRUPED (2)].
QUADRUPED (2), [kwod'-rōō-ped'], *adj.* (*zool.*) having four feet. [L. *quadrupes*].
QUADRUPEDAL, [kwod-rōō'-ped-al], *adj.* relating to a quadruped.
QUADRUPLE (1), [kwod'-rōōpl'], *adj.* fourfold. [L. *quadruplus*].
QUADRUPLE (2), [kwod-rōōpl'], *v.t.* to multiply by four. [QUADRUPLE (1)].
QUADRUPLET, [kwod'-rōō'-plet], *n.* one of four children born at one birth. [QUADRU(PLE) and (TRI)-PLET].
QUADRUPLEX, [kwod'-rōō-pleks], *adj.* fourfold. [L. *quadruplex*].
QUADRUPLICATE (1), [kwod-rōō'-plik-at], *adj.* multiplied by four, reproduced in four copies. [L. *quadruplicatus*, *p.pt.* of *quadruplicare* to multiply four times].
QUADRUPLICATE (2), [kwod-rōō'-plik-āt], *v.t.* to make fourfold, to multiply by four. [QUADRUPLICATE (1)].
QUADRUPLICATION, [kwod-rōō'-plik-ā'-shun], *n.* the act of making fourfold.
QUAERE, [kwēer'-i], *v.t. imper. sg.* question, seek, enquire. [L. *quaere* ask].
QUAESTOR, [kwēs'-tor], *n.* an official in ancient Rome whose duties were of a financial or magisterial nature. [L. *quaestor*].
QUAESTORSHIP, [kwēs'-tor-ship], *n.* the office of quaestor.
QUAFF (1), [kwof], *n.* a quick large drink. [QUAFF (2)].
QUAFF (2), [kwof], *v.t. and i.* to drink, to swallow in large draughts. [Unkn.].
QUAFFER, [kwof'-er], *n.* a person who quaffs or drinks in large draughts.
QUAG, [kwag], *n.* a quagmire, a bog.
QUAGGA, [kwag'-a], *n.* a South African species of the genus *Equus*, allied to the wild asses and zebras, striped only on the fore-parts. [Native *quagga*].

QUAGGA

QUAGGY, [kwag'-i], *adj.* of the nature of, resembling, a quag; of soft, wet earth, boggy.
QUAGMIRE, [kwag'-mīer], *n.* soft, wet ground that shakes or yields under the foot. [QUAG and MIRE].
QUAHOG, [kwa'-hawg], *n.* an edible clam found off the east coast of North America. [AmerInd. *poquauhock*].
QUAIGH, QUAICH, [kwākh], *n.* a shallow drinking-cup. [Gael. *cuach* cup].
QUAIL (1), [kwāl], *n.* a small game-bird of the genus *Coturnix*, allied to the partridge; **painted q.,** a bird of the genus *Excalphatoria*, found in Asia; **swamp q.,** a bird of the genus *Synœcus*, found in Australia. [OFr. *quaille* from MedL. *quacula*].

QUAIL

QUAIL (2), [kwāl], *v.t. and i.* to lose heart, to be afraid, to cower; †to cause to quail. [OE. *cwelan* to die].
QUAIL-CALL, [kwāl'-kawl], *n.* a quail-pipe.
QUAIL-PIPE, [kwāl'-pīp], *n.* a pipe or call for alluring quails into a net; a kind of leathern purse.
QUAINT, [kwānt], *adj.* unusual but not displeasing in form, fanciful; old-fashioned, antique; eccentric, odd in character. [ME. *cointe*, *queint* neat].
QUAINTLY, [kwānt'-li], *adv.* in a quaint manner.
QUAINTNESS, [kwānt'-nes], *n.* the quality of being quaint.
QUAKE (1), [kwāk], *n.* a trembling, tremor, a shake, a quag. [QUAKE (2)].
QUAKE (2), [kwāk], *v.i.* to rock perceptibly but not violently from side to side, to shiver, to quiver, shudder, tremble, particularly as a symptom of fear. [OE. *cwacian*, ME. *quaken* to tremble].
QUAKER, [kwāk'-er], *n.* a person who quakes; a member of the Society of Friends. [Used of George Fox and his followers by a judge who was trying them].
QUAKER-BIRD, [kwāk'-er-burd'], *n.* the sooty albatross, *Diomedea fuliginosa*.
QUAKERESS, [kwāk'-er-es], *n.* a female Quaker.

QUAKER-GRASS, [kwāk'-er-grahs'], *n.* quaking-grass.
QUAKERISH, [kwāk'-er-ish], *adj.* of, or like, a Quaker.
QUAKERISM, [kwāk'-er-izm], *n.* the principles and manners of the Quakers.
QUAKERLY, [kwāk'-er-li], *adv.* to a degree resembling Quakers.
QUAKERY, [kwāk'-eri], *n.* quakerism.
QUAKETAIL, [kwāk'-tāl], *n.* the pied wagtail, *Motacilla melanope.* [QUAKE (2) and TAIL].
QUAKINESS, [kwāk'-i-nes], *n.* the state of being quaky, shakiness.
QUAKING, [kwāk'-ing], *adj.* shaking.
QUAKING-GRASS, [kwāk'-ing-grahs'], *n.* a ray grass of the genus *Briza,* whose spikelets have a tremulous motion.
QUAKY, [kwāk'-i], *adj.* shaky.
QUALIFIABLE, [kwol'-i-fī'-abl], *adj.* able to be qualified or modified.
QUALIFICATION, [kwol'-if-ik-ā'-shun], *n.* the act of qualifying, modification; suitable acquirement and ability; the fact of being qualified; legal or requisite power, restriction. [L. *qualificatio*].
QUALIFICATORY, [kwol'-if-ik-āt'-er-i], *adj.* relating to qualification, modifying, restricting.
QUALIFIED, [kwol'-if-īd], *adj.* possessing the requisite qualifications, competent; modified.
QUALIFIEDLY, [kwol'-if-īd-li], *adv.* with qualification.
QUALIFIEDNESS, [kwol'-if-īd-nes], *n.* the state of being qualified.
QUALIFIER, [kwol'-i-fī'-er], *n.* one who, or that which, qualifies or modifies.
QUALIFY, [kwol'-i-fī], *v.t.* to give the requisite qualifications to, to train for any employment or professional practice; to limit or restrict by qualifications, to make conditional; to moderate, lessen, ease; dilute; to modify, alter, regulate; *v.i.* to carry out a course of study and thus obtain the requisite professional qualifications; to become competent. [L. *qualificare* to impart a certain quality to].
QUALITATIVE, [kwol'-it-at-iv], *adj.* of, relating to, quality. [L. *qualitativus*].
QUALITY, [kwol'-it-i], *n.* the fundamental characteristic or sum of characteristics by which anything can be identified when compared with other things of a similar nature; an attribute, property, characteristic; the distinguishing degree of a particular power or property inherent in anything; disposition, nature, temper; virtue, vice; accomplishment, acquirement; rank in the social scale; high rank; people of high rank born into the upper classes or aristocracy. [ME. *quality* from L. *qualitas*].
QUALM, [kwahm], *n.* faintness, a fit or a sensation of nausea; (*fig.*) a doubt concerning the morality of one's conduct, a scruple of conscience. [OE. *cwealm,* ME. *qualm* evil, ~OE. *cwellan* to kill].
QUALMLESS, [kwahm'-les], *adj.* feeling no qualms.
QUAMASH, [kwah'-mash'], *n.* the bulb of *Camassia esculenta.* [NAmerInd. *quamash*].
QUAMOCLIT, [kwam'-ok-lit], *n.* the climbing plant, *Ipomœa Quamoclit,* found in tropical America. [Mexican *quamo-chitl*].
QUANDARY, [kwon'-der-i], *n.* a baffling situation capable of more than one solution each of which might prove the best or worst, a dilemma. [Uncert.].
QUANNET, [kwon'-et], *n.* a flat file. [Uncert.].
QUANT, [kwont], *n.* a long pole with a flanged end for use in punting on a muddy river or for propelling barges. [ME. *quante*].
QUANTIC, [kwont'-ik], *n.* (*alg.*) a rational function of variables. [L. *quantus* how much].
QUANTIFICATION, [kwont'-if-ik-ā'-shun], *n.* the act of quantifying.
QUANTIFY, [kwont'-i-fī], *v.t.* (*log.*) to indicate the quantity or extent of. [MedL. *quantificare*].
QUANTIMETER, [kwont-im'-it-er], *n.* an instrument for recording the emission of X-rays. [L. *quantus* how much and METER].
QUANTITATIVE, [kwont'-it-at-iv], *adj.* of, concerned with, relating to, quantity; estimable according to quantity. [LL. *quantitativus*].
QUANTITIVE, [kwont'-it-iv], *adj.* quantitative.
QUANTITIVELY, [kwont'-it-iv-li], *adv.* in a quantitive manner.
QUANTITY, [kwont'-it-i], *n.* the property of anything which is measurable in terms of weight, size, bulk, extent, and which can be added to or subtracted from; any specified amount or number; (*log.*) the extent of an assertion or term according to the universal or particular; (*math.*) the means of measurement; (*mus.*) the relative duration of a tone; (*pros.*) the length of a syllable; **bill of quantities,** working estimate of building job. [ME. *quantite* from LL. *quantitas* amount].
QUANTITY SURVEYOR, [kwont'-it-i-surv-ā'-or], *n.* an expert in estimating costs of erecting a building.
QUANTIVALENCE, [kwont-iv'-al-ents], *n.* (*chem.*) the power of an atom to hold other atoms in combination. [L. *quantus* how much and VALENCE].
QUANTUM, [kwont'-um], *n.* the quantity, the amount, a sufficiency; (*phys.*) one of the units of uniform value (quanta) of which radiant energy is constituted; **q. sufficit,** a sufficient amount. [L. *quantum, neut. sg.* of *quantus* how much].
QUANTUM THEORY, [kwont'-um-thē'-er-i], *n.* (*phys.*) the theory that radiant energy is emitted from bodies through space in the form of discrete quanta.
QUAQUAVERSAL, [kwā'-kwav-urs'-al], *adj.* (*geol.*) sloping downward in every direction from a central point. [L. *quaquaversus*].
QUAQUAVERSALLY, [kwā'-kwav-urs'-al-i], *adv.* in a quaquaversal manner.
QUARANTINE (1), [kwo-rant-ēn'], *n.* the period, formerly forty days, during which a ship, passengers, crew, and goods suspected of, or known to be, carrying infectious diseases are kept in isolation and under medical observation as preventive measures; a state of medical isolation. [OFr. *quarantaine*].
QUARANTINE (2), [kwo-rant-ēn'], *v.t.* to put into quarantine. [QUARANTINE (1)].
QUARENDON, [kwo'-ren-don], *n.* a type of small early red apple. [*Quarendon,* a village in Somerset].
QUARREL (1), [kwo'-rel], *n.* an angry dispute or heated argument perhaps developing into a brawl or fight; a reason for quarrelling; a breach of friendship or love. [ME. *querele* from L. *querella* complaint].
QUARREL (2), [kwo'-rel], *n.* an arrow with a square head; a diamond-shaped pane of glass or a square pane placed diagonally in a lead frame. [L. *quadrellus, dim.* of *quadrus* a square].
QUARREL (3), (quarrelling, quarrelled), [kwo'-rel], *v.i.* to be a participant in a quarrel, to argue heatedly, to squabble; to find fault; to fall out, to disagree temporarily. [QUARREL (1)].
QUARRELLER, [kwo'-rel-er], *n.* a person who wrangles or fights.
QUARRELLING, [kwo'-rel-ing], *n.* disputing with angry words; cavilling or finding fault; a break in a friendship.
QUARRELSOME, [kwo'-rel-sum], *adj.* inclined by temperament to quarrel; easily irritated, or provoked to contest, irascible.
QUARRELSOMELY, [kwo'-rel-sum-li], *adv.* in a quarrelsome manner.
QUARRELSOMENESS, [kwo'-rel-sum-nes], *n.* the state of being quarrelsome.
QUARRIED, [kwo'-rid], *adj.* dug out of a quarry.
QUARRIER, [kwo'-ri-er], *n.* a quarryman.
QUARRY (1), [kwo'-ri], *n.* an animal hunted by man, hawk or hound; those entrails of game given to the hounds; a heap of game; the object of one's revenge. [ME. *querré* from OFr. *cuirée* the spoil].
QUARRY (2), [kwo'-ri], *n.* a diamond-shaped pane of glass; an arrow with a square head. [~QUARREL (2)].
QUARRY (3), [kwo'-ri], *n.* a pit from which stone is cut, an excavation worked above ground. [ME. *quarey* from LL. *quadraria*].
QUARRY (4), [kwo'-ri], *v.i.* to prey upon. [QUARRY (1)].
QUARRY (5), [kwo'-ri], *v.t.* to dig out of a quarry, to excavate; *v.i.* to form a quarry by digging; (*fig.*) to seek out information at the source. [QUARRY (3)].
QUARRYING, [kwo'-ri-ing], *n.* the act or process of digging stones from a quarry; (*pl.*) small pieces chipped off from the different materials found in quarries.
QUARRYMAN, [kwo'-ri-man], *n.* a worker at a quarry.
QUART (1), [kwawt], *n.* a measure of liquid amounting to a quarter of a gallon; two pints; a vessel of this content. [OF. *quarte*].
QUART (2), [kwawt], *n.* four successive cards of the same suit in a game of piquet. [Fr. *quarte*].
QUART (3), QUARTE, [kwawt], *n.* a position in fencing, a carte. [QUART (2)].
QUARTAN (1), [kwawt'-an], *n.* a measure containing the fourth part of some other; a fever recurring every fourth day. [*Next*].
QUARTAN (2), [kwawt'-an], *adj.* occurring on every fourth day. [L. *quartanus*].

QUARTATION, [kwawt-ā'-shun], *n.* the alloying of one part of gold with three parts of silver.

QUARTER (1), [kwawt'-er], *n.* a fourth part; the fourth part of a cwt., measuring 28 lb.; a unit of wheat measurement, 8 bushels, totalling 480 lb.; the first or third of the moon's phases; any one of the four cardinal points of the compass, north, south, east, west; one of the four regions of the globe; a district of a town with particular characteristics; mercy to an enemy who has surrendered; legal division of the year when rent, rates, and taxes fall due; (*pl.*) lodgings for troops, temporary barracks; post or station allotted to troops; (*her.*) one of the four quarters of a shield which has been divided crosswise; (*naut.*) (*pl.*) posts in battle formation; (*shoemaking*) the part of a boot behind the ankle seams; a section of an orange. [L. *quartus* fourth].

QUARTER (2), [kwawt'-er], *v.t. and i.* to divide or cut into quarters; to provide troops with lodgings, billets; to be stationed in temporary lodgings. [*Prec.*].

QUARTERAGE, [kwawt'-er-ij], *n.* a quarterly allowance.

QUARTER-BACK, [kwawt'-er-bak'], *n.* (*U.S.*) in football, the back whose position is behind the forwards, and in front of the half-backs.

QUARTER-BINDING, [kwawt'-er-bīnd'-ing], *n.* a style of bookbinding which covers the back only and not the corners of the covers.

QUARTER-BRED, [kwawt'-er-bred'], *adj.* having only one fourth good blood.

QUARTER-DAY, [kwawt'-er-dā'], *n.* a day when quarterly payments are made (in England, March 25, June 24, September 29, and December 25).

QUARTER-DECK, [kwawt'-er-dek'], *n.* (*naut.*) formerly that part of the upper deck abaft the mainmast; the after part of the promenade deck restricted to the use of officers.

QUARTERED, [kwawt'-erd], *adj.* divided into quarters or distinct parts; lodged or stationed for lodging.

QUARTERING, [kwawt'-er-ing], *n.* the act of dividing into quarters; the provision of billets for troops; the upright posts in a partition which carry the laths and plaster; (*her.*) the division of a shield so as to include allied coats-of-arms; (*naut.*) the method of sailing with the wind on the quarter.

QUARTERING

QUARTERLY (1), [kwawt'-er-li], *n.* a periodical published once every three months.

QUARTERLY (2), [kwawt'-er-li], *adj.* recurring each quarter of the year; consisting of a fourth part.

QUARTERLY (3), [kwawt'-er-li], *adv.* once every quarter of the year.

QUARTERMASTER, [kwawt'-er-mahst'-er], *n.* (*milit.*) a commissioned officer whose primary duty it is to attend to the supply of provisions and equipment; (*naut.*) a petty officer in charge of signals and ships' instruments; **q. general**, the officer in charge of the stores and equipment of an army; **q. sergeant**, a warrant officer assisting a quartermaster.

QUARTER-MILER, [kwawt'-er-mīl'-er], *n.* an athlete who specializes in quarter-mile races.

QUARTERN, [kwawt'-ern], *n.* a measure of liquid capacity being the fourth part of a pint or other measure, a gill; a 4-lb. loaf of bread. [ME. *quarteroun* from OFr. *quarteron* quarter].

QUARTER-PLATE, [kwawt'-er-plāt'], *n.* a photographic plate, film or print measuring 4¼ in. by 3¼ in.

QUARTER-ROUND, [kwawt'-er-rownd'], *n.* (*arch.*) a moulding, an echinus or ovolo.

QUARTER-SESSIONS, [kwawt'-er-sesh'-unz], *n.* (*leg.*) a court held every three months in each county or borough for the trial of criminal cases and general administrative purposes, and presided over by Justices of the Peace or local magistrates.

QUARTERSTAFF, [kwawt'-er-stahf'], *n.* (*sport*) a stout pole used for purposes of defence, being an iron-shod pole 6½ feet long, and wielded at the middle and a quarter from the end by both hands. [QUARTER and STAFF].

QUARTET, QUARTETTE, [kwawt-et'], *n.* a group of four; a composition for four performers; a stanza in four lines. [It. *quartetto, dim.* of *quarto* fourth].

QUARTILE, [kwawt'-īl], *n.* (*astrol.*) an aspect of the planets when distant from each other a quarter of a circle. [MedL. *quartilis*].

QUARTINE, [kwawt'-īn], *n.* (*bot.*) the fourth envelope of the nucleus of a seed. [L. *quartus* fourth].

QUARTO, [kwawt'-ō], *n.* a book with four leaves to each sheet; (*comm.*) a special size of paper about 9 by 12 inches produced when a sheet is folded into four leaves. [L. (*in*) *quarto* in a fourth part].

QUARTZ, [kwawts], *n.* (*min.*) a mineral made of silica; silica in the insoluble state or that cannot be taken up by a potash solution. [Germ. *quarz*].

QUARTZIFEROUS, [kwawts-if'-er-us], *adj.* consisting of quartz. [QUARTZ and L. *ferre* to bear].

QUARTZITE, [kwawts'-īt], *n.* quartz rock.

QUARTZITIC, [kwawts-it'-ik], *adj.* of the nature of, containing, quartz.

QUARTZOID, [kwawts'-oid], *n.* a crystal in the form of a double six-sided pyramid. [QUARTZ and Gk. *oeides* like].

QUARTZOSE, [kwawts'-ōs], *adj.* containing, or resembling, quartz.

QUARTZY, [kwawts'-i], *adj.* relating to, containing, or resembling, quartz.

QUASH (1), [kwosh], *n.* the red gourd or pumpkin, *Cucurbita pepo*; squash. [Unkn.].

QUASH (2), [kwosh], *v.t.* to crush, to subdue; to annul or make void. [ME. *quaschen* from L. *quassare* to shake].

QUASI, [kwā'-sī], *adv.* apparently, as if, as it were, in a sort. [L. *quasi*].

QUASIMODO, [kwā'-sī-mōd'-ō], *n.* Low Sunday, the first Sunday after Easter; the introit (1 Peter ii, 2) of the mass for the day beginning with this word. [L. *quasimodo*].

QUASS, [kvahs], *n.* a weak Russian beer, produced by pouring warm water on rye-meal, kvass. [ML Germ. *quassi*].

QUASSIA, [kwos'-i-a], *n.* the bitter ash, an American tropical tree, *Picræna excelsa*, the wood of which yields a bitter principle used as a tonic and a garden insecticide. [From *Quassi*, the negro who discovered it].

QUASSINE, [kwas'-in], *n.* the bitter principle of quassia.

QUATERCENTENARY, [kwot'-er-sen-tēn'-ar-i], *n.* the four-hundredth anniversary.

QUATERNARY (1), [kwot-urn'-e-ri], *n.* the number four; a group of four. [QUATERNARY (2)].

QUATERNARY (2), [kwot-urn'-e-ri], *adj.* consisting of four, by fours; (*geol.*) the rocks above the Pliocene. [L. *quaternarius*].

QUATERNATE, [kwot-urn'-āt], *adj.* (*bot.*) consisting of four parts.

QUATERNION, [kwot-urn'-i-on], *n.* a set of four; a file of four soldiers; (*pl.*) a method in mathematics. [LL. *quarternio* a sum of four].

QUATERNITY, [kwot-urn'-iti], *n.* combination of fours; four fused in one. [LL. *quaternitas*].

QUATORZAIN, [kat-awz'-ān], *n.* a sonnet containing fourteen lines keeping to a strict rhyming scheme as in Shakespeare's sonnets. [Fr. *quatorzaine* a group of fourteen].

QUATORZE, [kat-awz'], *n.* the four aces, kings, queens, and jacks, or tens in the game of piquet. [Fr. *quatorze* fourteen].

QUATRAIN, [kwot'-rān], *n.* a stanza of four lines, sometimes rhyming alternately. [Fr. *quatrain*].

QUATREFOIL, [kat'-re-foil'], *n.* (*arch.*) an ornamental figure, being an opening in tracery divided by cusps into four leaves or petals; (*her.*) a device in the same design on a shield. [OFr. *quatrefoil* four leaves].

QUATREFOIL

QUATTROCENTIST, [kwat'-rō-chent'-ist], *n.* a practitioner of the art of the quattrocento.

QUATTROCENTO, [kwat'-rō-chent'-ō], *n.* the fifteenth century in Italian art, a period of revival, the early stage of the Renaissance. [It. *quattrocento* four hundred].

QUAVER (1), [kwā'-ver], *n.* a sound or note, *esp.* one made by the voice, which is governed by a tremolo;

(*mus.*) a note held half the length of a crotchet. [QUAVER (2)].

QUAVER (2), [kwā′-ver], *v.i.* to talk, sing, or play a musical instrument so that the sound or tone produced is affected by vibration or tremolo. [ME. *quaven* to shake].

QUAVERY, [kwā′-ver-i], *adj.* tremulous, shaky, as a quavery voice.

QUAY, KEY, [kē], *n.* a pier, mole, or wharf for loading and unloading vessels, a landing-place. [ME. *kay*, *key* from OFr. *kai*].

QUAYAGE, KEYAGE, [kē′-ij], *n.* quay dues.

QUAY-WALL, [kē′-wawl], *n.* the wall of a harbour.

QUEAN, [kwēn], *n.* a worthless woman; a saucy girl, a hussy; (*Scots*) a woman, usually young. [OE. *cwene*, ME. *quene*].

QUEASILY, [kwēz′-i-li], *adv.* in a queasy manner.

QUEASINESS, [kwēz′-i-nes], *n.* the quality or state of being queasy, nausea, qualmishness.

QUEASY, [kwēz′-i], *adj.* affected with nausea, inclined to vomit; fastidious, squeamish; causing nausea. [Uncert.].

QUEBRACHO, [kwib-rah′-chō], *n.* a substitute for quinine; **red q.**, the Mexican tree, *Loxopterygium lorentzii*; **white q.**, the Argentine redwood, *Aspidosperma quebracho*. [Span. *quebracho*].

QUEBRADA, [kwib-rah′-da], *n.* a ravine. [Span. *quebrada*].

QUEEN (1), [kwēn], *n.* a woman who is sovereign in her own right, the consort of a king; a large, fertile female among certain kinds of insects; the most revered or admired woman of a group or class; a goddess of a realm of fancy; a court card or honour in value ranking between king and knave; a piece in chess; **q. dowager**, the widow of a king; **q. mother**, the mother of a reigning monarch; **q. of the meadow**, a plant of the genus *Spiraea*; **q. of the prairie**, the plant *Spiraea lobata*. [OE. *cwen*].

QUEEN (2), [kwēn], *v.t. and i.* to make a queen of; to rule over in the capacity of a queen; **to q. it**, to play the queen; (*chess*) to convert a pawn which has been moved up to the opponent's back-line into a queen. [QUEEN (1)].

QUEENHOOD, [kwēn′-hŏŏd], *n.* the office of a queen; her period of office; queenly character.

QUEENING, [kwēn′-ing], *n.* a winter apple. [Unkn.].

QUEENLESS, [kwēn′-les], *adj.* having no queen.

QUEENLIKE, [kwēn′-līk], *adj.* having the style and dignity expected from a queen.

QUEENLINESS, [kwēn′-li-nes], *n.* conduct or appearance worthy of a queen.

QUEENLY (1), [kwēn′-li], *adj.* of, like, or befitting a queen. [OE. *cwenlic*].

QUEENLY (2), [kwēn′-li], *adv.* in the manner of a queen; worthy of a queen, with dignity.

QUEEN-POST, [kwēn′-pōst], *n.* (*arch.*) one of two upright posts in a roof.

QUEEN'S-METAL, [kwēnz′-met′-al], *n.* (*min.*) an alloy composed of tin, bismuth, antimony, and lead.

QUEEN'S-WARE, [kwēnz′-wāer], *n.* glazed earthenware of a cream colour.

QUEER (1), [kweer], *adj.* out of the ordinary, odd, singular; unwell, poorly, indisposed; shady, questionable; a little mad. [Uncert.].

QUEER (2), [kweer], *v.t.* (*slang*) **to q. someone's pitch**, to spoil, upset or disarrange someone's plans, etc. [QUEER (1)].

QUEERISH, [kweer′-ish], *adj.* somewhat queer or singular.

QUEERLY, [kweer′-li], *adv.* in a queer manner.

QUEERNESS, [kweer′-nes], *n.* the quality of being queer, oddity, singularity.

QUEEST, [kwēst], *n.* (*dial.*) the wood-pigeon or the ringdove, *Columba palumbus*. [ME. *quisht*].

QUELL, [kwel], *v.t.* to crush, to subdue by force; to allay. [OE. *cwellan*, ME. *quellen* to kill].

QUELLER, [kwel′-er], *n.* a person who crushes or subdues.

QUELLERZ, [kwel′-āerts], *n.* (*min.*) a variety of limonite. [Germ. *quellerz*].

QUENCH, [kwench], *v.t.* to put out, to extinguish, to still or repress; to allay; to destroy. [OE. *cwencan*, ME. *quenchen*].

QUENCHABLE, [kwench′-abl], *adj.* able to be extinguished.

QUENCHER, [kwench′-er], *n.* he who, or that which, extinguishes; a drink, a thirst-quencher.

QUENCHLESS, [kwench′-les], *adj.* not able to be quenched; inextinguishable, unquenchable; irrepressible.

QUENCHLESSLY, [kwench′-les-li], *adv.* in a quenchless manner.

QUENCHLESSNESS, [kwench′-les-nes], *n.* the quality or the state of being quenchless.

QUENELLE, [ken-el′], *n.* a forcemeat ball for seasoning. [Fr. *quenelle*].

QUERCETIN, [kwer′-sit-in], *n.* a product obtained from quercitrin.

QUERCITRIN, [kwer′-sit-rin], *n.* the colouring principle of quercitron bark, a valuable article for dyeing yellow. [L. *quercus* oak and CITRON].

QUERCITRON, [kwer′-sit-ron], *n.* the American oak, *Quercus tinctoria*, the bark of which is used as a dyestuff as well as for tanning. [L. *quercus* oak and CITRON].

QUERENT, [kweer′-ent], *n.* an inquirer, a complainant, a plaintiff. [L. *quaerens*, *pres.pt.* of *quaerere* to complain].

QUERIMONIOUS, [kwer′-i-mō′-ni-us], *adj.* querulous. [L. *querimonia* complaint].

QUERIMONIOUSLY, [kwer′-i-mō′-ni-us-li], *adv.* in querimonious fashion.

QUERIMONIOUSNESS, [kwer′-i-mō′-ni-us-nes], *n.* state, disposition, of being querimonious; querulousness.

QUERIST, [kweer′-ist], *n.* an inquirer, questioner.

QUERL, [kwurl], *n.* a curl, twirl. [Germ. *querl*].

QUERN, [kwurn], *n.* a hand-mill for grinding corn. [OE. *cweorn*].

QUERULOUS, [kwe′-ryōō-lus], *adj.* complaining, peevish, fretfully nagging. [L. *querulus*].

QUERULOUSLY, [kwe′-ryōō-lus-li], *adv.* in querulous fashion.

QUERULOUSNESS, [kwe′-ryōō-lus-nes], *n.* the state of being querulous.

QUERY (1), [kweer′-i], *n.* a question, an inquiry, a doubt put in the form of a question; a question-mark. [QUAERE].

QUERY (2), [kweer′-i], *v.t.* to question or doubt something, to mark (a written statement) as doubtful, to require confirmation; to put a question-mark after. [QUERY (1)].

QUEST (1), [kwest], *n.* a search, a journey in search of; an inquest. [OFr. *queste* from L. *quaesita*, *fem. p.pt.* of *quaerere* to seek].

QUEST (2), [kwest], *v.i.* to search, follow in search and pursuit. [OFr. *quester*].

QUESTION (1), [kwes′-chun], *n.* a request for information, a remark demanding a reply, an interrogation, an expression of doubt; a problem, a doubt, a point of discussion, subject of debate; torture to extract information; a matter, situation, etc., with a general sense of doubt, problem, or interrogation; **out of the q.**, totally impossible; **to put to the q.**, to put to the vote; to torture to extract information. [L. *questio* a seeking].

QUESTION (2), [kwes′-chun], *v.t. and i.* to interrogate, inquire of; to doubt, call in doubt, dispute; to ask questions. [OFr. *questionner*].

QUESTIONABILITY, [kwes′-chun-ab-il′-i-ti], *n.* questionableness.

QUESTIONABLE, [kwes′-chun-abl], *adj.* dubious, open to question, disputable; underhand, of doubtful honesty, shady.

QUESTIONABLENESS, [kwes′-chun-abl-nes], *n.* the quality or state of being questionable.

QUESTIONABLY, [kwes′-chun-ab-li], *adv.* in questionable fashion.

QUESTIONARY, [kwes′-chun-er-i], *adj.* interrogative.

QUESTIONER, [kwes′-chun-er], *n.* one who questions.

QUESTIONIST, [kwes′-chun-ist], *n.* a questioner.

QUESTIONLESS, [kwes′-chun-les], *adj.* unquestionable.

QUESTIONNAIRE, [kes′-chun-āer′], *n.* a series (usually written) of questions on a specific subject. [Fr. *questionnaire*].

QUESTMAN, [kwest′-man], *n.* a member of a committee of inquiry; a parish official.

QUESTUARY, [kwes′-chōō-e-ri], *adj.* profit-making; connected with profits. [L. *quaestuarius*].

QUETZAL

QUETZAL, [kwet′-zal], *n.* a large, brilliant Central American bird, *Paromacrus mocinno*; the badge and coinage of Guatemala. [Mexican *quetzalli*].

QUEUE (1), [kew], *n.* a twisted pigtail tied with

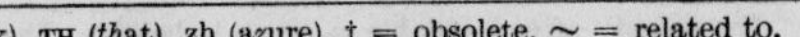

ribbon worn hanging down from the back of the head; a long narrow line of people waiting for admission to something or to perform some action. [Fr. *queue* tail].
QUEUE (2), [kew], *v.i.* to line up in, wait in, a queue. [QUEUE (1)].
QUEY, [kwā], *n.* a young cow or heifer. [OIcel. *kviga*].
QUIB, [kwib], *n.* a gibe; a quibble. [Perhaps from L. *quibus, dat.* and *abl. pl.* of *qui* who].
QUIBBLE (1), [kwibl], *n.* a trivial objection, distinction, or equivocation, an evasive, niggling objection raised to avoid defeat in argument or the fulfilment of an obligation. [~QUIB].
QUIBBLE (2), [kwibl], *v.i.* to use quibbles. [*Prec.*].
QUIBBLER, [kwib'-ler], *n.* one who quibbles.
QUIBBLING, [kwib'-ling], *adj.* using, marked by, quibbles.
QUIBBLINGLY, [kwib'-ling-li], *adv.* in quibbling fashion.
QUICK (1), [kwik], *n.* sensitive flesh, *esp.* that below the nails; sensitivity in general, the centre of feeling and emotion; (*pl.*) living creatures in general; **to cut to the q.,** to hurt deeply, to pain the feelings greatly. [QUICK (2)].
QUICK (2), [kwik], *adj.* living; pregnant; swift, sudden; (*fig.*) swift of mind, lively of intellect, responsive to feeling or idea, having presence of mind; happening in a short space of time, brief; (*coll.*) jumping to conclusions. [OE. *cwicu* living].
QUICK (3), [kwik], *adv.* quickly, swiftly, briefly. [OE. *cwice* quickly].
QUICKEN, [kwik'-en], *v.t. and i.* to make live, give life to; to stir to action; to hasten; to become alive, to become stimulated; (of a pregnant woman) to have the foetus showing signs of life; to move more rapidly. [ME. *quicken*].
QUICKENER, [kwik'-en-er], *n.* that which quickens, invigorates, revives.
QUICKENING, [kwik'-en-ing], *adj.* reviving, invigorating.
QUICK-EYED, [kwik'-īd], *adj.* keen-sighted.
QUICKFIRER, [kwik-fīer'-er], *n.* an automatic, rapid-firing gun.
QUICKFIRING, [kwik-fīer'-ing], *adj.* firing bullets in rapid succession.
QUICK-HEDGE, [kwik'-hej], *n.* a hedge of growing plants.
QUICKLIME, [kwik'-līm], *n.* unslaked lime.
QUICKLY, [kwik'-li], *adv.* rapidly, with speed, in a short time.
QUICK MARCH, [kwik'-mahch'], *n.* a march in quick time; (*imper.*) the command to march in quick time.
QUICKMATCH†, [kwik'-mach], *n.* a rapid-burning fuse made of cotton steeped in gunpowder and vinegar.
QUICKNESS, [kwik'-nes], *n.* the state or quality of being quick; activity of mind, rapidity of apprehension.
QUICKSAND, [kwik'-sand'], *n.* wet, loose, unstable sand, tending to hold and engulf those walking on it; (also *fig.*).
QUICK-SCENTED, [kwik'-sent'-id], *adj.* having an acute sense of smell.
QUICKSET, [kwik'-set'], *adj.* formed of living, growing plants, *esp.* of hawthorn.
QUICKSIGHTED, [kwik'-sīt'-id], *adj.* having acute sight.
QUICK-SIGHTEDNESS, [kwik'-sīt'-id-nes], *n.* the quality, state of being quick-sighted.
QUICKSILVER, [kwik'-sil-ver], *n.* mercury; (*fig.*) a mercurial, unstable temperament.
QUICKSILVERED, [kwik'-sil-verd], *adj.* like, covered with, quicksilver.
QUICKSTEP, [kwik'-step], *n.* the pace of the military quick march; a dance in quick-time.
QUICK-TIME, [kwik'-tīm], *n.* 120 to 140 steps or yards per minute, the speed of the military quick march; this speed of step used as a base for dance music.
QUICK-WITTED, [kwik-wit'-id], *adj.* having quick wits.
QUICK-WITTEDNESS, [kwik-wit'-id-nes], *n.* the state or quality of being quick-witted.
QUICKWORK, [kwik'-wurk], *n.* the hull of a ship below the water-line.
QUID (1), [kwid], *n.* a piece of chewing tobacco. [*Var.* of CUD].
QUID (2), [kwid], *n.* (*slang*) a pound (of money), *esp.* a pound note or sovereign; **to be quids in,** (*slang*) to be very favourably situated. [Unkn.].
QUIDAM, [kwī'-dam], *n.* somebody. [L. *quidam*].
QUIDDATIVE, [kwid'-at-iv], *adj.* relating to the quiddity of a thing; equivocative.
QUIDDITY, [kwid'-iti], *n.* the fundamental essence of a thing; a quibble, an unnecessary subtlety. [MedL. *quidditas* from *quid* what].
QUIDDLE, [kwidl], *v.i.* to trifle, waste time. [Unkn.].
QUIDDLER, [kwid'-ler], *n.* a trifler.
QUIDNUNC, [kwid'-nungk], *n.* a gossip, a trivial idler. [L. *quid* what? and *nunc* now].
QUIESCE, [kwī-es'], *v.i.* to become still. [L. *quiescere*].
QUIESCENCE, [kwī-es'-ents], *n.* the state of being quiescent. [LL. *quiescentia*].
QUIESCENCY, [kwī-es'-en-si], *n.* quiescence.
QUIESCENT, [kwī-es'-ent], *adj.* quiet, still, passive, silent. [L. *quiescens, pres.pt.* of *quiescere*].
QUIESCENTLY, [kwī-es'-ent-li], *adv.* in quiescent fashion.
QUIET (1), [kwī'-et], *n.* absence of noise, silence, almost silence, rest, freedom from trouble, disturbance, activity; serenity, repose; absence of discord, tumult, or conflict. [L. *quies*].
QUIET (2), [kwī'-et], *adj.* free from noise, movement, or disturbance; still, calm, undisturbed; unnoticed, unobvious, undiscussed; peaceful, monotonous; informal; unostentatious, restrained; silent. [L. *quietus* calm, resting].
QUIET (3), [kwī'-et], *v.t. and i.* to cause to be quiet, to pacify; to become quiet, calm, restrained, to die away, to become abated. [MedL. *quietare*].
QUIETEN, [kwī'-etn], *v.t. and i.* to make quiet, to quiet; to become quiet.
QUIETER, [kwī'-et-er], *n.* one who, that which, quiets. [QUIET (3)].
QUIETISM, [kwī'-et-izm], *n.* a doctrine of passive mysticism and subordination of will; tranquillity of mind or spirit. [Fr. *quiétisme*].
QUIETIST, [kwī'-et-ist], *n.* an advocate, practiser, of quietism.
QUIETISTIC, [kwī'-et-ist'-ik], *adj.* pertaining to quietism.
QUIETLY, [kwī'-et-li], *adv.* in quiet fashion.
QUIETNESS, [kwī'-et-nes], *n.* the state or quality of being quiet.
QUIETUDE, [kwī'-it-ewd], *n.* quietness, tranquillity. [LL. *quietudo*].
QUIETUS, [kwī-ē'-tus], *n.* quittance, final discharge, a getting rid of once and for all, *esp.* release from life. [L. *quietus, p.pt.* of *quiescere*].
QUIFF, [kwif], *n.* a curl or forelock over the forehead. [COIF].
QUILL (1), [kwil], *n.* a large feather, the hollow stem of such a feather; a pen made from a feather; the spine of a porcupine; the reed of a wooden wind-instrument; a bobbin. [Unkn.].

QUILL

QUILL (2), [kwil], *v.t.* to pleat; to wind (thread) round a bobbin. [QUILL (1)].
QUILLDRIVER, [kwil'-drīv-er], *n.* (*slang*) an overworked clerk; one who writes continually.
QUILLET†, [kwil'-et], *n.* quibble. [Unkn.].
QUILLING, [kwil'-ing], *n.* lace ruffles. [QUILL (2)].
QUILLWORK, [kwil'-wurk], *n.* porcupine embroidery.
QUILLWORT, [kwil'-wurt], *n.* a water plant of the genus *Isoëtes*.
QUILT (1), [kwilt], *n.* a coverlet made by stuffing some thick, woolly stuff between two layers of material, an eiderdown. [OFr. *cuilt* from L. *culcita* mattress].
QUILT (2), [kwilt], *v.t.* to make into a quilt. [QUILT (1)].
QUILTED, [kwilt'-id], *adj.* padded like a quilt.
QUILTING, [kwilt'-ing], *n.* quilted stuff.
QUIN, [kwin], *n.* (*coll.*) a quintuplet. [QUIN(TUPLET)].
QUINA, [kē'-na, kwī'-na], *n.* quinine. [Span. *quina*].
QUINARY, [kwīn'-e-ri], *adj.* arranged in fives. [L. *quinarius*].
QUINATE (1), [kwin'-āt], *n.* a salt of quinic acid.
QUINATE (2), [kwīn'-āt], *adj.* (*bot.*) made of five leaflets. [L. *quini* five at a time].
QUINCE, [kwints], *n.* the pear-shaped fruit of *Pyrus cydonia*, notable for its deep yellow colour and extreme sharpness of flavour. [OFr. *coin* from Gk. *kudonia*].
QUINCENTENARY, [kwin'-sent-ē'-ner-i], *n.* the five-hundredth anniversary. [L. *quin(que)* five and CENTENARY].

QUINCUNCIAL, [kwin-kun'-shal], *adj.* shaped like a quincunx. [L. *quincuncialis*].

QUINCUNX, [kwin'-kungks], *n.* a group of five objects, four forming the corners of a square, the fifth as a centre, *esp.* shrubs, trees so arranged. [L. *quincunx*].

QUINDECAGON, [kwin-dek'-ag-on], *n.* (*geom.*) a plane figure with fifteen angles. [L. *quinque* five, Gk. *deka* ten and *gonia* an angle].

QUINDECEMVIR, [kwin'-dis-em'-vir], *n.* one of the fifteen custodians of the Sibylline Books. [L. *quindecemviri*].

QUINIC, [kwin'-ik], *adj.* denoting an acid obtained from quinine bark.

QUINICINE, [kwin'-is-in], *n.* an alkaloid produced from quinine.

QUININE, [kwin-ēn'], *n.* a bitter-tasting alkaloid, obtained from the bark of the cinchona; a preparation of this used medicinally. [Span. *quinquina* from Peruvian *kina*].

QUINK, [kwingk], *n.* the brent goose, *Bernicla brenta.* [Uncert.].

QUINOA, [kin-ō'-a], *n.* a South American plant whose seeds are baked into cake. [Peruvian *kinoa*].

QUINOLOGY, [kwin-ol'-o-ji], *n.* the study of quinine. [QUINA and Gk. *logos* speech].

QUINQUAGENARY (1), [kwin'-kwaj-en'-e-ri], *n.* a fiftieth anniversary. [L. *quinquagenarius*].

QUINQUAGENARY (2), [kwin'-kwaj-en'-e-ri], *adj.* occurring every fifty years. [QUINQUAGENARY (1)].

QUINQUAGESIMA, [kwin'-kwaj-es'-i-ma], *n.* the Sunday before Lent, as the fiftieth day before Easter. [MedL. *quinquagesima* (*dies*)].

QUINQUANGULAR, [kwin-kwang'-gyōō-ler], *adj.* having five angles. [QUINQUE and ANGULAR].

QUINQUARTICULAR, [kwin'-kwaht-ik'-yōō-ler], *adj.* composed of five articles. [QUINQUE and ARTICULAR].

QUINQUE-, *pref.* denoting five. [L. *quinque* five].

QUINQUECAPSULAR, [kwin'-kwi-kap'-sew-ler], *adj.* (*bot.*) having five capsules. [QUINQUE and CAPSULAR].

QUINQUECOSTATE, [kwin'-kwi-kost'-āt], *adj.* having five ribs. [QUINQUE and L. *costa* rib].

QUINQUEDENTATE, [kwin'-kwi-dent'-āt], *adj.* five-toothed. [QUINQUE and DENTATE].

QUINQUEFARIOUS, [kwin'-kwi-fāer'-i-us], *adj.* having the leaves or branches arranged in five rows.

QUINQUEFID, [kwin'-kwi-fid], *adj.* divided into five parts. [QUINQUE and L. *fidum*, *p.pt.* of *findere* to cleave].

QUINQUEFOLIATE, [kwin'-kwi-fōl'-i-āt], *adj.* (*bot.*) having five leaves. [QUINQUE and FOLIATE].

QUINQUELITERAL, [kwin'-kwi-lit'-er-al], *adj.* consisting of five letters. [QUINQUE and LITERAL].

QUINQUELOBATE, [kwin'-kwi-lōb'-āt], *adj.* (*bot.*) five-lobed. [QUINQUE and LOBATE].

QUINQUELOCULAR, [kwin'-kwi-lok'-yōō-ler], *adj.* (*bot.*) having five loculi. [QUINQUE and LOCULAR].

QUINQUENNIAD, [kwin-kwen'-i-ad'], *n.* a period of five years.

QUINQUENNIAL, [kwin-kwen'-i-al], *adj.* occurring every five years; lasting for five years. [L. *quinquennalis*].

QUINQUENNIALLY, [kwin-kwen'-i-al-i], *adv.* every five years.

QUINQUENNIUM, [kwin-kwen'-i-um], *n.* a period of five years. [L. *quinquennium*].

QUINQUEPARTITE, [kwin'-kwi-paht'-it], *adj.* divided into five parts. [QUINQUE and PARTITE].

QUINQUEREME, [kwin'-kwi'-rēm], *n.* (*hist.*) a Greek or Roman warship with oars arranged in fives. [QUINQUE and L. *remus* oar].

QUINQUESEPTATE, [kwin'-kwi-sept'-āt], *adj.* (*bot.*) with five septa. [QUINQUE and SEPTATE].

QUINQUEVALVULAR, [kwin'-kwi-valv'-yōō-ler], *adj.* having five valves. [QUINQUE and VALVULAR].

QUINQUINA, [kin-kē'-na], *n.* cinchona, quinine; an aperitif made from this; a tree of the genus *Myroxylon.* [Peruvian *kin-kina*].

QUINSY, [kwin'-zi], *n.* inflammation and suppuration of the tonsils. [ME. *quinacy*, MedL. *quinancia* from Gk. *kunagkhe*].

QUINT, [kwint], *n.* (*mus.*) an interval of a fifth; the E string of a violin; (*piquet*) a sequence of five in the same suit. [L. *quintus* fifth].

QUINTAIN, [kwint'-ān], *n.* a tilting post with the target fixed to a revolving bar that swung round and struck the tilter in the back unless he was away quickly. [MedL. *quintana*].

QUINTAIN

QUINTAL, KENTLE, [kwintl], *n.* a measure of weight used in several parts of Europe, the French quintal being 100 kilogrammes. [OFr. *quintal* from Arab. *qinta*].

QUINTAN, [kwint'-an], *adj.* occurring every five days, *esp.* of fevers. [L. *quintanus*].

QUINTESSENCE, [kwint-es'-ents], *n.* (*hist., philosophy*) the fifth, insubstantial, permeating element; *hence*, the fundamental essence of a thing, the highest, most concentrated, embodiment of a quality. [MedL. *quinta essentia*].

QUINTESSENTIAL, [kwint'-is-en'-shal], *adj.* of the nature of, relating to, quintessence.

QUINTET, [kwint-et'], *n.* a musical composition for five performers; the five performers themselves. [Fr. *quintette*].

QUINTILE, [kwint'-il], *n.* the aspect of planets when distant from each other by one-fifth of the zodiac. [L. *quintus* fifth].

QUINTILLION, [kwint-il'-yon], *n.* the fifth power of a million.

QUINTUPLE, [kwin'-tyōō'-pl], *adj.* fivefold. [Fr. *quintuple*].

QUINTUPLET, [kwin'-tyōō'-plet], *n.* one of five children born at a single birth. [QUINTUPLE].

QUINZAINE, [kwinz'-ān], *n.* a stanza of fifteen lines. [Fr. *quinzaine*].

QUINZE, [kanz], *n.* a variety of vingt-et-un, in which fifteen is the required number. [Fr. *quinze* fifteen].

QUIP, [kwip], *n.* a jesting retort, a witty remark, *esp.* if directed against anyone. [Uncert.].

QUIPU, [kip'-ōō], *n.* an Inca method of recording or sending messages by means of coloured and knotted cords. [Quichuan *quipu* knot].

QUIRE† **(1),** [kwier], *n.* a choir.

QUIRE (2), [kwier], *n.* the twentieth of a ream of paper, twenty-four sheets. [OFr. *quaier*].

QUIRINAL, [kwi'-rin-al], *n.* the royal court of Italy. [L. *Quirinalis*, one of the Seven Hills of Rome].

QUIRK, [kwurk], *n.* a quibbling subterfuge. [Uncert.].

QUIRKISH, [kwurk'-ish], *adj.* relating to, by means of, a quirk.

QUIRKY, [kwurk'-i], *adj.* full of quirks.

QUIRT, [kwurt], *n.* a riding-whip. [Span. *corto* short].

QUISLING, [kwiz'-ling], *n.* one who accepts an administrative post under a foreign conqueror; (*pop.*) a fifth columnist. [V. *Quisling*, Norwegian Hitlerite].

QUIT (1), [kwit], *adj.* free (of), discharged (from). [ME. *quite* from OFr. *quite*].

QUIT (2), (quitting, quitted), [kwit], *v.t. and i.* to leave, depart from; to release, discharge; get rid of; to throw in one's hand, give up a task. [ME. *quiten* from OFr. *quiter*].

QUITCH, [kwich], *n.* a troublesome grass, couch-grass, *Agropyrum repens.* [OE. *cwice* quick, from its rapid growth].

QUIT-CLAIM, [kwit'-klām], *n.* a deed of release. [AFr. *quiteclame*].

QUITE; (*as int.*) certainly; [kwit], *adv.* utterly, wholly, fairly, largely, reasonably. [QUIT].

QUIT-RENT, [kwit'-rent], *n.* a rent in lieu of all other service.

QUITS, [kwitz], *n.* the condition of being even with a person; **double or q.,** an undertaking to repeat a wager so that the previous loser will lose double or be even.

QUITTABLE, [kwit'-abl], *adj.* that may be vacated.

QUITTAL, [kwit'-al], *n.* quittance.

QUITTANCE, [kwit'-ants], *n.* discharge from an obligation, final recompense. [OFr. *quitance*].

QUITTER, [kwit'-er], *n.* one who quits, *esp.* one who shows cowardice in difficulties.

QUIVER (1), [kwiv'-er], *n.* a case for carrying arrows; **to have one's q. full,** to have a very large family. [AFr. *quiveir*].

QUIVER (2), [kwiv'-er], *n.* the act of quivering. [QUIVER (3)].

QUIVER (3), [kwiv'-er], *v.i.* to quake and tremble. [Imitative].

QUIVERED, [kwiv'-erd], *adj.* having a quiver.

QUIVERINGLY, [kwiv'-er-ing-li], *adv.* in a quivering manner.
QUIVERISH, [kwiv'-er-ish], *adj.* inclined to quiver.
QUIXOTIC, [kwiks-ot'-ik], *adj.* showing absurd chivalrousness. [Don *Quixote*, hero of a novel by Cervantes].
QUIXOTICALLY, [kwiks-ot'-ik-a-li], *adv.* in a quixotic manner.
QUIXOTISM, [kwiks'-ot-izm], *n.* quixotry.
QUIXOTRY, [kwiks'-ot-ri], *n.* quixotic behaviour.
QUIZ (1), [kwiz], *n.* a puzzle; an enquiry, investigation by means of questions; one who quizzes. [Uncert.].
QUIZ (2), [kwiz], *v.t.* to banter, to mock at jestingly [QUIZ (1)].
QUIZZICAL, [kwiz'-ik-al], *adj.* fond of quizzing, faintly mocking, bantering.
QUIZZING, [kwiz'-ing], *adj.* relating to a quiz; quizzical.
QUOAD, [kwō'-ad'], *prep.* with respect to. [L. *quoad*].
QUOD, QUAD, [kwod], *n.* (*slang*) a prison. [Uncert.].
QUODLIBET, [kwod'-lib-et], *n.* a subtle or delicate point. [L. *quodlibet* what you please].
QUODLIBETICAL, [kwod'-lib-et'-ik-al], *adj.* not confined to a single subject.
QUOIN, [koin], *n.* a wedge-shaped brick used as a corner-stone; (*print.*) a wedge used for locking type. [COIGN].
QUOIT, [koit], *n.* a ring to be pitched over a pin set in the ground; (*pl.*) the game in which this is the object. [Uncert.].

QUOIT

QUONDAM, [kwon'-dam], *adj.* former. [L. *quondam*].
QUORUM, [kwaw'-rum], *n.* the number of members sufficient to transact the business of a body [L. *quorum* of whom].
QUOTA, [kwōt'-a], *n.* a proportionate share, *esp.* one allotted in advance; **the q.,** the legally determined proportion in which cinema renters must use British films. [MedL. *quota* (*pars*) how great a part].
QUOTABILITY, [kwōt'-ab-il'-it-i], *n.* capacity for being quoted.
QUOTABLE, [kwōt'-abl], *adj.* that may be quoted.
QUOTATION, [kwōt-ā'-shun], *n.* the act of quoting; that which is quoted, a previously written passage reproduced in a later work; the price demanded for a proposed service; a quotation mark (') or ('); (*print.*) a large, hollow quadrat used to fill blanks. [MedL. *quotatio*].
QUOTE (1), [kwōt], *n.* a quotation mark; (*vulg.*) a quotation. [QUOTE (2)].
QUOTE (2), [kwōt], *v.t. and i.* to repeat a passage that has already been written or uttered, to cite; to make a quotation, to offer; to perform the action of quoting. [MedL. *quotare* to mark by numbers].
QUOTELESS, [kwōt'-les], *adj.* without quotation.
QUOTER, [kwōt'-er], *n.* one who quotes.
QUOTH, [kwōth], *v.i.* (*poet.* or *sham archaic*), said.
QUOTHA†, [kwōth'-a], *int.* said he. [QUOTH and HE].
QUOTIDIAN, [kwōt-id'-i-an], *adj.* occurring daily. [L. *quotidies*].
QUOTIENT, [kwō'-shent], *n.* the number of times a greater quantity contains a less. [L. *quotiens* how many times?].
QUOTIETY, [kwō-ti'-et-i], *n.* the relation of an object to a number. [L. *quotiens* how many times?].

R

R, [ah(r)], the eighteenth letter of the alphabet; **the three R's,** reading, writing, and arithmetic.
RABBET (1), [rab'-it], **REBATE,** [rē-bāt'], *n.* a groove cut lengthwise in the edge of a piece of wood to receive the edge of a plank, etc. [OFr. *rabat* recess].
RABBET (2), [rab'-it], *v.t.* to join by a rabbet.
RABBI, [rab'-ī], *n.* a teacher of the Judaic Law; a Jewish minister of religion. [Heb. *rabbi* my master].
RABBIN, [rab'-in], *n.* a rabbi. [MedL. *rabbinus*].
RABBINATE, [rab'-in-āt], *n.* the office of rabbi.
RABBINIC, [rab-in'-ik], *adj.* relating to the rabbis or to Jewish law and ritual; pertaining to, written in, the later Hebrew language. [Fr. *rabbinique*].
RABBINICAL, [rab-in'-ik-al], *adj.* rabbinic.
RABBINISM, [rab'-in-izm], *n.* the teaching of the rabbis; a rabbinic idiom.
RABBINIST, [rab'-in-ist], *n.* one who adheres to or studies the Talmud and the traditions of the rabbis.
RABBINITE, [rab'-in-īt], *n.* a rabbinist.
RABBIT (1), [rab'-it], *n.* the gregarious burrowing rodent, *Lepus cuniculus*; (*coll.*) cheap fur; (*fig.*) a feeble, cowardly person; a bad performer at some game. [ME. *rabet*].
RABBIT (2), [rab'-it], *v.i.* to hunt rabbits.
RABBITING, [rab'-it-ing], *n.* rabbit-catching.
RABBITRY, [rab'-it-ri], *n.* an enclosure for rabbits.
RABBIT-WARREN, [rab'-it-wo'-ren], *n.* a mass of rabbit burrows; (*fig.*) a place with a complicated system of rooms and passages, an overcrowded warren-like slum.
RABBLE (1), [rabl], *n.* a ragged, unorganized, tumultuous mob, *esp.* when consisting of the poorest and dirtiest sections of the population. [ME. *rabel*].
RABBLE (2), [rabl], *n.* an iron for stirring molten metal, a puddling-iron. [Fr. *râble*].
RABBLEMENT, [rabl'-ment], *n.* a tumultuous crowd of low people; a rabble.
RABELAISIAN, [rab'-el-ā'-zi-an], *adj.* resembling, or supposed to resemble, the style and humour of Rabelais; (*coll.*) broadly obscene.
RABID, [rab'-id], *adj.* afflicted with rabies, mad; (*fig.*) dangerously furious in some conviction, fanatically vehement. [L. *rabidus*].
RABIDITY, [rab-id'-i-ti], *n.* the state or quality of being rabid.
RABIDLY, [rab'-id-li], *adv.* in rabid fashion.
RABIDNESS, [rab'-id-nes], *n.* rabidity.
RABIES, [rāb'-ēz], *n.* hydrophobia, canine madness. [L. *rabies*].
RACCOON, see RACOON.
RACE (1), [rās], *n.* a division of mankind whose members share certain obvious physical characteristics distinguishing them from the other divisions; (*bot.*) a variety that reproduces its own peculiarities; a stock or breed of people; a group of persons having a common peculiarity. [Fr. *race*].
RACE (2), [rās], *n.* a contest, competition in progression, in covering distance in the shortest possible time; (*pl.*) horse-races; a swiftly-moving stream of water; the groove of a shuttle. [OScand. *ras* running].
RACE (3), [rās], *v.t. and i.* to oppose in a race, to enter (a horse, etc.) for a race; to compete in a race; to move, progress rapidly in order to outspeed and outdistance another; to overtake; (*mech.*) to move at too great a speed owing to insufficient resistance; (*coll.*) to attend race-meetings, to gamble on horse-races. [*Prec.*].
RACE-CARD, [rās'-kahd], *n.* the card on which is printed the day's programme at a race-meeting.
RACECOURSE, [rās'-kaws], *n.* the track on which a horse-race is run.
RACE-GINGER, [rās'-jin'-jer], *n.* ginger in the root, or not pulverized. [OFr. *rais* root].
RACEGROUND, [rās'-grownd], *n.* a race-track.
RACEHORSE, [rās'-haws], *n.* a horse bred and trained for racing.
RACEME, [ras-ēm'], *n.* (*bot.*) a spike of regular stalked flowers springing from a common central stalk. [L. *racemus* a cluster of grapes].
RACE-MEETING, [rās'-mēt'-ing], *n.* a series of horse-races held at a special course and time.
RACEMIC, [ras-ēm'-ik], *adj.* obtained from grapes; **r. acid,** an acid, isomeric with tartaric, obtained from certain vineyards on the Rhine.
RACEMOSE, [ras'-em-ōs], *adj.* growing in, resembling, a raceme. [L. *racemosus*].
RACER, [rās'-er], *n.* one who races; a vehicle designed for racing; a rail along which the platform of a heavy gun recoils.
RACH, [rach], *n.* a hunting dog pursuing by scent; a setter. [OE. *ræcc*].
RACHIDIAN, [rak-id'-i-an], *adj.* relating to the rachis.

RACHILLA, [rak-il′-a], *n.* a species of inflorescence, as in the spikelets of grasses. [Gk. *rakhis*].
RACHIS, [rā′-kis], *n.* (*anat.*) the spine; the shaft of a feather; (*bot.*) the stalk in compound leaves from which spring the leaflets. [Gk. *rhakhis* the spine].
RACHITIC, [rak-it′-ik], *adj.* relating to, suffering from, rachitis.
RACHITIS, [rak-ī′-tis], *n.* rickets. [MdL. *rachitis*].
RACIAL, [rā′-shal], *adj.* pertaining to race.
RACIALISM, [rā′-shal-izm], *n.* race sentiments, prejudices, and loyalties; the view that race is of primary importance.
RACILY, [rās′-i-li], *adv.* in racy fashion.
RACINESS, [rās′-i-nes], *n.* the quality of being racy.
RACING, [rās′-ing], *n.* the act of promoting, attending or gambling on horse-racing.
RACK (1), [rak], *n.* a framework of bars for holding and containing something, *esp.* a receptacle for hay in a manger from which the animal pulls its food; small structures for holding, supporting or containing garments, vessels, etc.; (*mech.*) a toothed bar fitting into the cogs of a wheel; the rigging-sheaves of a sailing ship; an instrument of torture consisting of a horizontal frame on which the victim was stretched until his limbs were dislocated. [ME. *rakke*].
RACK (2), [rak], *n.* arrack. [ARRACK].
RACK (3), [rak], *n.* drifting mist or cloud vapour; wreckage, the state of being wrecked. [~Norw. *rak* refuse].
RACK (4), [rak], *n.* a horse's gait, between a trot and a canter, in which both feet on the same side are off the ground simultaneously. [Uncert.].
RACK (5), [rak], *v.t.* to place in a rack; to torture upon the rack, to torment with pains in the joints, etc., as on the rack; (*fig.*) to torment, urge (one's brain) to think of something or solve some problem; to extort, oppress with demands.
RACK (6), [rak], *v.t.* to drain off wine from the dregs. [Provenc. *arracar*].
RACKAROCK, [rak′-a-rok], *n.* a mining explosive. [RACK (5) and ROCK].
RACKER, [rak′-er], *n.* one who racks. [RACK (1)].
RACKET (1), RACQUET, [rak′-it], *n.* an oval bat used in tennis and related games, *esp.* such a bat made with catgut stretched taut across a frame; (*pl.*) a game related to tennis and fives, played in a four-walled court. [ME. *rakket* from Arab. *rahat* palm of the hand].
RACKET (2), [rak′-it], *n.* a confused, rowdy, clamorous noise; a business organization for making illegal or immoral profits; the act of operating such a business; **to stand, face the r.,** to meet the expense (of), face the consequences (of). [Uncert.].
RACKET (3), [rak′-it], *v.i.* to behave rowdily; to lead a life of stupid, noisy dissipation. [*Prec.*].
RACKETEER (1), [rak′-it-ēer′], *n.* (*U.S. slang*) one who operates a racket. [RACKET (2)].
RACKETEER (2), [rak′-it-ēer′], *v.i.* to operate a racket.
RACKETEERING, [rak′-et-ēer′-ing], *n.* the act or practices of a racketeer.
RACKETING, [rak′-it-ing], *n.* the act of making a racket.
RACKET-TAILED, [rak′-it-tāld′], *adj.* with a tail in which the two middle feathers are shaped like rackets.
RACKETY, [rak′-i-ti], *adj.* making a racket.
RACKING, [rak′-ing], *n.* the act of drawing off wine or liquor from the sediment.
RACKRAIL, [rak′-rāl], *n.* a toothed rail used on inclined railways, placed between or alongside the bearing rails.
RACK-RENT, [rak′-rent′], *n.* an extortionate rent, a rent nearly equal to the maximum value of the land.
RACKWORK, [rak′-wurk], *n.* a mechanical device in which motion is communicated by means of a toothed wheel and a toothed bar; rack and pinion.
RACONTEUR, [rak′-awn-tur′], *n.* one skilled in relating amusing anecdotes. [Fr. *raconteur*].
RACOON, RACCOON, [rak-ōōn′], *n.* the bushy-tailed arboreal carnivorous mammal *Procyon*. [Amer. Indian *rakoon*].
RACQUET, see RACKET (1).
RACY, [rās′-i], *adj.* vigorously piquant, swift, daring and entertaining (now with a slightly salacious implication); **r. of the soil,** conveying the true local atmosphere of a district.
RADAR, [rā′-dah(r)], *n.* radiolocation. [RA(DIO) D(ETECTION) A(ND) R(ANGING)].
RADDLE (1), [radl], *n.* a lath fastened between upright posts to form a fence; a piece of wattled work. [OFr. *reddalle* pole].
RADDLE (2), [radl], *v.t.* to twist, twine together.
RADIAL, [rā′-di-al], *adj.* relating to a radius or to a ray; radiating, having radiations; relating to the radius bone of the forearm. [LL. *radialis*].
RADIALITY, [rā′-di-al′-i-ti], *n.* the state of being radial.
RADIALIZATION, [rā′-di-al-īz-ā′-shun], *n.* the act of radializing, the state of being radialized.
RADIALIZE, [rā′-di-al-īz], *v.t.* to arrange in radial fashion.
RADIALLY, [rā′-di-a-li], *adv.* in radial fashion.
RADIAN, [rā′-di-an], *n.* an angle at the centre of a circle subtending an arc equal in length to the radius of the circle.
RADIANCE, [rā′-di-ants], *n.* the condition of being radiant; brightness.
RADIANCY, [rā′-di-an-si], *n.* radiance.
RADIANT (1), [rād′-i-ant], *n.* a piece of refractory material which may be heated to radiate heat from an electric or gas fire.
RADIANT (2), [rā′-di-ant], *adj.* emitting rays of light, shining brightly; (*fig.*) bright with pleasure, joy, health; intellectually brilliant, enlightening; (*astron.*) radiating from a focus; (*phys.*) related to, transmitted by, radiation. [L. *radians*].
RADIANTLY, [rā′-di-ant-li], *adv.* in radiant fashion.
RADIATE (1), [rā′-di-āt], *adj.* radial, radiating, having rays. [L. *radiatus*].
RADIATE (2), [rā′-di-āt], *v.t. and i.* to emit rays; to issue in rays, to spread in all directions equally; to branch out; (*fig.*) to penetrate, have effect all around; to emit in, or as if in, rays; (*fig.*) to spread all around. [L. *radiare* to shine].
RADIATION, [rā′-di-ā′-shun], *n.* the act of radiating, the emission, transmission of heat, etc., by rays; that which is radiated, diffusion from a centre. [L. *radiatio*].
RADIATIVE, [rā′-di-at-iv], *adj.* capable of, tending to, radiate.
RADIATOR, [rā′-di-āt′-or], *n.* that which radiates; a device for heating by means of hot water or air in pipes; a device for cooling the water heated in the cylinder jacket of a petrol engine.
RADICAL (1), [rad′-ik-al], *n.* (*chem.*) an element or group passing unchanged from compound to compound; (*math.*) the root symbol; (*pol.*) one advocating complete change, holding radical views or belonging to the Radical Party. [*Next*].
RADICAL (2), [rad′-ik-al], *adj.* relating to, reaching to, springing from, the root of a thing, original, complete; (*pol.*) advocating complete reform; (*math.*) relating to the root of a number; (*bot.*) relating to the root of a plant. [LL. *radicalis*].
RADICALISM, [rad′-ik-al-izm], *n.* radical political theory.
RADICALITY, [rad′-ik-al′-i-ti], *n.* radicalness.
RADICALIZE, [rad′-ik-al-īz], *v.t.* to make radical, convert to radical ideas.
RADICALLY, [rad′-ik-a-li], *adv.* in radical fashion; completely.
RADICALNESS, [rad′-ik-al-nes], *n.* the quality of being radical.
RADICANT, [rad′-ik-ant], *adj.* taking root. [L. *radicans*].
RADICATE (1), [rad′-ik-āt], *adj.* rooted.
RADICATE (2), [rad′-ik-āt], *v.t.* to plant, cause to take root. [~L. *radicare*].
RADICATED, [rad′-ik-āt-id], *adj.* radicate.
RADICATION, [rad′-ik-ā′-shun], *n.* the process of taking root. [L. *radicatio*].
RADICEL, [rad′-is-el′], *n.* a small root.
RADICIFORM, [rad-is′-i-fawm], *adj.* in the form of a root. [L. *radix* root and FORM].
RADICIVOROUS, [rad′-is-iv′-er-us], *adj.* devouring roots. [L. *radix* root and *vorare* to devour].
RADICLE, [rad′-ikl], *n.* (*bot.*) an embryonic root; (*anat.*) the beginning of a vein. [L. *radicula*].
RADICULOSE, [rad-ik′-yŏŏ-lōs], *adj.* having many small roots.
RADIO- (1), *pref.* ray, radiation; connected with wireless telegraphy; radius. [L. *radius* staff, spoke, ray].
RADIO (2), [rā′-di-ō], *n.* wireless telegraphy or telephony; an apparatus for receiving these; (*coll.*) the programmes transmitted by wireless. [*Prec.*].
RADIO (3), [rā′-di-ō], *v.t.* to send by wireless telegraphy.
RADIO-ACTIVE, [rā′-di-ō-akt′-iv], *adj.* having the quality of spontaneously and continuously emitting electronic energy, as radium, thorium, etc.
RADIO-ACTIVITY, [rā′-di-ō-ak-tiv′-i-ti], *n.* the properties and qualities of radio-active substances.
RADIOGONIOMETER, [rād′-i-ō-gon′-i-o′-met-er], *n.* (*wirel.*) an apparatus employed to determine the

direction from which a wireless transmission is radiated. [RADIO, Gk. *gone* angle and METER].

RADIOGRAM (1), [răd'-i-ō-gram'], *n.* a radio-telegram. [RADIO and (TELE)GRAM].

RADIOGRAM (2), [răd'-i-ō-gram'], *n.* a radio-gramophone. [RADIO and GRAM(OPHONE)].

RADIO-GRAMOPHONE, [rā'-di-ō-gram'-o-fōn], *n.* an apparatus combining a wireless receiving set and a gramophone.

RADIOGRAPH, [rā'-di-ō-graf], *n.* an X-ray photograph; an actinograph. [RADIO (1) and GRAPH].

RADIOGRAPHER, [răd'-i-og'-raf-er], *n.* one who practises radiography.

RADIOGRAPHY, [rā'-di-og'-raf-i], *n.* the science of taking a radiograph, of measuring or examining by means of a radiograph. [RADIO (1) and Gk. *graphia* writing].

RADIOLARIAN (1), [rā'-di-ō-lāer'-i-an], *n.* (*biol.*) a protozoon with a membrane round the nucleus. [L. *radiolus* little ray].

RADIOLARIAN (2), [rā'-di-ō-lāer'-i-an], *adj.* relating to, resembling, consisting of, radiolarians.

RADIOLOCATION, [răd-i-ō-lōk-ā'-shun], *n.* a system by which the presence of aircraft, etc., may be detected by means of electro-magnetic waves of very high frequency. [RADIO and LOCATION].

RADIOLOGIST, [răd'-i-ol'-oj-ist], *n.* one expert in radiology; a person in charge of an X-ray machine.

RADIOLOGY, [rā'-di-ol'-ō-ji], *n.* the science of radio-activity and X-rays. [RADIO (1) and Gk. *logos* speech].

RADIOMETER, [rā'-di-om'-it-er], *n.* an instrument for measuring radiation. [RADIO (1) and METER].

RADIOMETRY, [rā'-di-om'-et-ri], *n.* measurement by radiometer. [RADIO (1) and Gk. *metria* measurement].

RADIO-PLAY, [rā'-di-ō-plā'], *n.* a play written or adapted to be broadcast by radio.

RADIOSCOPE, [rā'-di-ō-skōp], *n.* an instrument for detecting radio-activity or for examining the interior of opaque objects. [RADIO (1) and SCOPE].

RADIOSCOPY, [rā'-di-os'-kop-i], *n.* the use of the radioscope.

RADIO-TELEGRAM, [rā'-di-ō-tel'-i-gram'], *n.* a telegram transmitted by wireless.

RADIO-TELEGRAPHY, [rā'-di-ō-tel-eg'-raf'-i], *n.* wireless telegraphy.

RADIOMETER

RADIO-THERAPY, [rā'-di-ō-the'-rap-i], *n.* the treatment of disease by radiations.

RADISH, [rad'-ish], *n.* a pungent, coarse-leaved plant of the genus, *Raphanus*. [OFr. *radis*].

RADIUM, [rā'-di-um], *n.* the metallic element denoted by Ra, notable for its intense radio-activity. [RADIO (1)].

RADIUS, [rā'-di-us], *n.* (*geom.*) the distance of a circle's circumference from its centre, *hence*, anything resembling a circle's radius, the spoke of a wheel; a circular area centred on a specified point, a distance in any direction from a centre; (*anat.*) the shorter of the bones in the forearm. [L. *radius*].

RADIX, [rā'-diks], *n.* (*math.*) a number used as the basis of a system of numeration; a number taken as a basis for calculations of percentage. [L. *radix* root].

RADON, [rā'-don], *n.* an inert gaseous element produced by the disintegration of radium. [RADIUM].

RADULA, [rad'-yoo-la], *n.* the lingual ribbon of a mollusc. [L. *radula* rasp].

RADULIFORM, [rad-yōō'-li-fawm], *adj.* shaped like a rasp. [*Prec.* and FORM].

RAFF, [raf], *n.* a worthless, common rabble. [RIFF-RAFF].

RAFFE, [raf], *n.* the sail set flying over a schooner's foretopsail. [Unkn.].

RAFFIA, RAPHIA, [raf'-i-a], *n.* the cuticle of the leaf of the long-leaved Madagascar palm, *Raphia ruffia*, or of the Brazilian species, *R. tædigera*, both being used for tying up plants and for making mats, hats, etc. [Malagasy *rofia*].

RAFFISH, [raf'-ish], *adj.* rakish, vulgarly dissipated. [RAFF].

RAFFLE (1), [rafl], *n.* a sale by lottery in which each ticket is sold for an equal part of the object's value, and tickets equal the whole value. [ME. *rafle* game of dice].

RAFFLE (2), [rafl], *v.t.* to sell by a raffle.

RAFFLESIA, [raf-lē'-zi-a], *n.* (*bot.*) a genus of five species of parasitic plants, having no stem but bearing a flower a yard or more across. [Sir S. *Raffles* its discoverer].

RAFT (1), [rahft], *n.* a flat structure of planks, logs, etc., used as a conveyance over water; a flat floating structure used as a mooring or landing-place. [OScand. *raftr* a rafter].

RAFT (2), [rahft], *v.t.* to convey by means of a raft.

RAFTER (1), [rahft'-er], *n.* a man working a raft.

RAFTER (2), [rahft'-er], *n.* a sloping beam supporting the frame of a roof. [OE. *ræfter*].

RAFTING, [rahft'-ing], *n.* the act of working a raft.

RAFTSMAN, [rahfts'-man], *n.* a man who manages a raft.

RAFTY, [rahft'-i], *adj.* damp, musty; stale. [Uncert.].

RAG (1), [rag], *n.* a torn, dirty, useless piece of cloth; (*pl.*) tattered, old, dirty garments; anything resembling a rag; a hard, rough limestone, a rough slate. [ME. *ragge* from Swed. *ragg* shaggy hair].

RAG (2), [rag], *n.* a rough, boisterous, good-humoured prank indulged in by a group of young people, a rowdy, practical joke, a drunken frolic among undergraduates. [Uncert.].

RAG (3), (ragging, ragged), [rag], *v.t. and i.* to persecute, taunt, and ridicule, often with rowdy horse-play and rough physical jokes. [*Prec.*].

RAGAMUFFIN, [rag'-a-muf'-in], *n.* a ragged, disreputable child, a street urchin. [RAG (1) and MUFF (2)].

RAG-BAG, [rag'-bag'], *n.* a bag in which rags or odd pieces of dress materials are kept.

RAG-BOLT, [rag'-bōlt], *n.* an iron pin with barbs on its shank to retain it in its place.

RAGE (1), [rāj], *n.* furious anger, fury of temper or of the elements, emotional frenzy; (*coll.*) a temporary, unreasoned, fashionable craze. [Fr. *rage*].

RAGE (2), [rāj], *v.i.* to be in a rage, to inveigh furiously (against); to display furious passion and violence; of elements or disease, to be violently agitated, to be at a height of destructiveness. [*Prec.*].

RAGEFUL, [rāj'-fōōl], *adj.* full of rage; violent.

RAG-FAIR, [rag'-fāer], *n.* a sale of second-hand wearing apparel.

RAGG, [rag], *n.* ragstone. [ME. *ragge*].

RAGGED, [rag'-id], *adj.* irregular in outline, (of cloth). torn into rags; unkempt, rough, jagged; irregular, not in regular form or time; **r. school,** formerly, a school for very poor children.

RAGGEDLY, [rag'-id-li], *adv.* in ragged fashion.

RAGGEDNESS, [rag'-id-nes], *n.* the state of being ragged.

RAGI, RAGGEE, [rag'-ē], *n.* an Indian millet, *Eleusine coracana*. [Hind. *ragi*].

RAGING, [rāj'-ing], *adj.* displaying rage and furious violence; violently tempestuous.

RAGINGLY, [rāj'-ing-li], *adv.* in a raging manner, furiously.

RAGLAN, [rag'-lan], *n.* an informal type or style of overcoat with no shoulder seams. [Lord *Raglan*].

RAGMAN (1), [rag'-man], *n.* a rag-collector.

RAGMAN (2), [rag'-man], *n.* a list or catalogue; a piece of writing bearing many signatures or seals. [Uncert.].

RAGOUT, [rag-ōō'], *n.* a highly seasoned dish of chopped meat and vegetables. [Fr. *ragoût*].

RAG-PAPER, [rag'-pā'-per], *n.* paper made from linen rags.

RAG-PICKER, [rag'-pik'-er], *n.* one who collects and sorts rags for remanufacture.

RAGSTONE, [rag'-stōn], *n.* (*min.*) a dark-grey siliceous sandstone so named from its rough fracture.

RAG-TAG, [rag'-tag], *n.* (usually) **r. and bobtail,** the lowest orders of society, riff-raff.

RAGTIME, [rag'-tīm], *n.* a form of syncopated music as in negro dances and songs; jazz. [RAGGED TIME].

RAGULED, [rag'-yōōld], *adj.* (*her.*) notched, jagged. [Uncert.].

RAG-WHEEL, [rag'-wēl], *n.* a wheel with a notched or toothed edge.

RAGWORT, [rag'-wurt], *n.* one of several common weeds with deeply indented leaves and clusters of bright yellow flowers, of the genus *Senecio*. [RAG(1) and WORT].

RAHAT-LAKOUM, [rah'-hat-lah-kōōm'], *n.* an Oriental sweetmeat, *esp.* Turkish delight. [Turk. *rahat-lakoum*].

RAGULED

RAHU, [rah'-hōō], *n.* an alleged dark planet which the ancient Hindus believed caused eclipses. [Skr. *rahu*].

RAI, [rah'-i], *n.* a Siamese land measure equivalent to half an acre. [Siamese *rai*].

RAID (1), [rād], *n.* a sudden invasion, usually for purposes of destruction or plunder; a sudden descent on certain premises by the civil authorities; an aerial bombardment. [OE. *rad*].

RAID (2), [rād], *v.t.* to make a raid into or upon; to plunder, attack.

RAIDER, [rād'-er], *n.* one who, or that which, raids; a raiding aircraft.

RAIL (1), [rāl], *n.* any of various kinds of small birds of the *Rallidæ*, including the corn-crake and moor-hen. [OFr. *raale*].

RAIL (2), [rāl], *n.* a wooden or metal bar; a wooden or iron fence formed of such bars; a bar supported by brackets and used for hanging clothes on; a balustrade on a staircase; one of the parallel steel lines forming the permanent way for railway vehicles or trams; railway; (*pl.*) a fence; railway stocks and shares; **r. motor,** a petrol-driven vehicle running over the track of a steam-operated railway; **off the rails,** derailed; (*fig.*) gone astray in conduct or ideas, unhinged. [OFr. *reille* from L. *regula* straight piece of wood].

RAIL (3), [rāl], *v.t.* to furnish with rails; to send by rail; **to r. in,** to fence in; **to r. off,** to shut off, separate by rails or a fence. [*Prec.*].

RAIL (4), [rāl], *v.i.* **r. at, against,** to utter reproaches against, revile bitterly. [Fr. *railler*].

RAIL-CAR, [rāl'-kah(r)], *n.* (*U.S.*) a railway coach.

RAILER (1), [rāl'-er], *n.* one who makes rails.

RAILER (2), [rāl'-er], *n.* one who rails against.

RAIL-FENCE, [rāl'-fents], *n.* a fence made of wooden or iron rails.

RAILHEAD, [rāl'-hed'], *n.* the farthest point to which a railway penetrates.

RAILING (1), [rāl'-ing], *n.* a fence of wooden or iron rails; rails in general; materials for rails.

RAILING (2), [rāl'-ing], *n.* bitter reproaches, expression of contempt and anger; banter.

RAILING (3), [rāl'-ing], *adj.* uttering reproaches, insulting; jesting, bantering.

RAILINGLY, [rāl'-ing-li], *adv.* in a railing manner; banteringly.

RAILLERY, [rāl'-er-i], *n.* banter, jesting, light scoffing, persiflage. [Fr. *raillerie*].

RAILLESS, [rāl'-les], *adj.* devoid of rails; functioning without rails.

RAILROAD, [rāl'-rōd], *n.* (*U.S.*) a railway.

RAILWAY, [rāl'-wā], *n.* a permanent way of steel rails on which trains are run; the whole system of lines, stations, etc., used for this purpose. [RAIL (2) and WAY].

RAIMENT, [rā'-ment], *n.* clothing; garments for wear. [~OFr. *arraiement*].

RAIN (1), [rān], *n.* the moisture of the atmosphere condensed and falling as small drops of water; a shower or storm of such drops; (*fig.*) a fall or stream of small drops or particles; a rapid succession or repetition (of blows, bullets, etc.). [OE. *regn*].

RAIN (2), [rān], *v.i.* to fall as rain, to fall in rapid drops; to send down rain; to come in rapid succession like drops of rain; to pour down (upon), to shower; to give in great profusion, shower (upon); **to r. cats and dogs,** to rain heavily; **it never rains but it pours,** troubles never come singly but always in profusion. [OE. *regnan*].

RAINBAND, [rān'-band'], *n.* a dark band of the solar spectrum caused by the absorption of the aqueous vapour in the atmosphere.

RAINBERRY, [rān'-be'-ri], *n.* (*bot.*) the common buckthorn, *Rhamnus catharticus*.

RAINBIRD, [rān'-burd], *n.* the green woodpecker whose cry is supposed to predict rain; the Jamaican cuckoo.

RAINBOW, [rān'-bō], *n.* an arched bow showing the colours of the spectrum, formed in the sky opposite to the sun or moon by the refraction and reflection of light from the raindrops; **secondary r.,** a second rainbow with reversed order of colours formed by double refraction and reflection. [OE. *regnboga*].

RAINBOW-TINTED, [rān'-bō-tint'-id], *adj.* having colours like the rainbow; many-coloured.

RAINCOAT, [rān'-kōt], *n.* a waterproof coat worn as a protection against the rain.

RAINDROP, [rān'-drop], *n.* a drop of rain.

RAINFALL, [rān'-fawl], *n.* a fall of rain; the amount of rain that falls in any particular place during a certain time.

RAIN-GAUGE, [rān'-gāj], *n.* an instrument for measuring the rainfall.

RAININESS, [rān'-i-nes], *n.* the condition of being rainy.

RAINLESS, [rān'-les], *n.* without rain; very dry.

RAINPROOF, [rān'-proof], *adj.* proof against rain, resisting rain.

RAIN-TIGHT, [rān'-tīt], *adj.* able to resist rain, rain-proof.

RAINTREE, [rān'-trē], *n.* either of the two South American trees *Andira inermis* or *Pithecolobium saman*, so called because the exudation caused by insects gives an effect as if it is always raining underneath the tree. [RAIN (1) and TREE].

RAIN-WATER, [rān'-waw'-ter], *n.* water trapped from rainfall.

RAINY, [rān'-i], *adj.* characterized by rain; showery; **r. day,** (*fig.*) a time of need.

RAISE (1), [rāz], *n.* (*U.S.*) a rise (in wages).

RAISE (2), [rāz], *v.t.* to cause to rise; to lift; to set upright; to build; to exalt, promote; to bring to a higher rank or social position; to increase the amount, value of; to enhance; to excite, inspire, conjure up in the mind; to stir up, cause to fly up; to bring into being, to produce, rear; to collect together, recruit; to collect; to levy; to obtain possession of (money); **to r. Cain,** to create a violent disturbance; **to r. one's head,** to give evidence of one's independent existence; **to r. from the dead,** to bring to life again; **to r. a laugh,** to cause a laugh; **to r. a point,** to mention, bring up a point for consideration; **to r. a siege, blockade, ban,** to withdraw from, remove; **to r. the wind,** (*slang*) to obtain a loan, gain possession of a sum of money. [OScand. *reisa*].

RAISER, [rāz'-er], *n.* one who, or that which, raises.

RAISIN, [rāz'-in], *n.* a special kind of dried grape that will keep for a long time. [OFr. *raizin* grape].

RAISINEE, raisinée, [rāz-ēn-ā'], *n.* a confection made from grapes and apples. [Fr. *raisinée*].

RAISING, [rāz'-ing], *n.* the action of lifting, elevating, restoring to life.

RAISON D'ETRE, raison d'être, [rāz-aw(ng)-detr'], *n.* reason for the existence of, justification for, explanation of. [Fr. *raison d'être*].

RAISONNE, raisonné, [rā-zon-ā'], *adj.* logical; systematic and descriptive. [Fr. *raisonné*].

RAJ, [rahj], *n.* sovereignty, rule, dominion. [Hind. *raj*].

RAJAH, RAJA, [rah'-jah], *n.* in India, the title of a native king or prince, a chief. [Hind. *raja* king].

RAJAHSHIP, [rah'-jah-ship], *n.* the rank or territory of a rajah.

RAJPUT, [rahj'-poot], *n.* a member of the Hindu military caste; a substantial landowner. [Hind. *raj* king and *putra* son].

RAKE (1), [rāk], *n.* an agricultural or garden implement of wood or metal with a long handle attached to a horizontal bar of teeth or prongs for gathering together loose hay, leaves, etc., or for smoothing the soil; a similar implement of metal for drawing out the ashes from underneath a fireplace or a furnace; a small wooden instrument used by the croupier for drawing towards him the stakes won by the bank at a gaming table. [OE. *raca*].

RAKE (2), [rāk], *n.* (*naut.*) the projection of the upper parts of a ship at the stern and stem beyond the keel; the inclination of a mast from the perpendicular; the inclination of the stage of a theatre, etc., from the perpendicular. [RAKE (5)].

RAKE (3), [rāk], *n.* a dissolute, loose-living man; a dissipated person. [RAKEHELL].

RAKE (4), [rāk], *v.t.* to use a rake upon; to scrape, gather together with a rake; to clear or smooth with a rake; to collect, scrape together from every source; to enfilade, to sweep with fire lengthways; to allow the eyes to travel along, scan carefully; *v.i.* to work with a rake; (*fig.*) to search minutely, ferret out; **to r. out,** to draw ashes from; (*fig.*) to ferret out, etc.; **to r. up,** to bring to light, revive. [RAKE (1)].

RAKE (5), [rāk], *v.i.* to incline, lean from the perpendicular; to incline as the upper parts of a ship's stem or stern beyond the line of the keel. [Uncert.].

RAKEHELL†, [rāk'-hel'], *n.* a dissipated man; a rake; a debauchee. [RAKE (3) and HELL].

RAKE-OFF, [rāk'-of'], *n.* (*slang*) a percentage or profit taken or abstracted by an intermediary in a transaction.

RAKER, [rāk'-er], *n.* one who, or that which, rakes.

RAKING (1), [rāk'-ing], *n.* that which is collected with a rake; the collecting with a rake.

RAKING (2), [rāk'-ing], *adj.* sloping; inclining; enfilading.

RAKISH (1), [rāk'-ish], *adj.* sloping backwards, set at an angle; (*naut.*) having the appearance of fast-sailing and smartness; jaunty. [RAKE (2)].

RAKISH (2), [rāk'-ish], *adj.* having the manners of a rake; given to a dissolute life. [RAKE (3)].

RAKISHLY, [rāk'-ish-li], *adv.* in a rakish manner.

RAKISHNESS, [rāk'-ish-nes], *n.* the quality of being rakish.

RAKSHASA, [rak'-shas-ah], *n.* an evil spirit, an ogre. [Hind. *rakshasa*].

RALE, râle, [rahl], *n.* (*med.*) a rattling sound heard in the lungs when these are not in a healthy condition. [Fr. *râle* death rattle].

RALLENTANDO, [ral'-en-tan'-dō], *adv.* (*mus.*) in increasingly slower time. [It. *rallentando*].

RALLY (1), [ral'-i], *n.* the act of reassembling, for a further attack, disordered troops or parties of adherents after a repulse; recovery of strength; an assembly, a reunion†; (*sport*) a rapid interchange of strokes between opposing players in a game played with rackets. [RALLY (2)].

RALLY (2), [ral'-i], *v.t.* to gather, collect together again; to reassemble (disordered forces) for a further attack after a repulse; to rouse, revive for further effort; *v.i.* to come back to order after a repulse; to recover strength; (*comm.*) (of shares, goods) to rise again, command higher prices. [Fr. *rallier*].

RALLY (3), [ral'-i], *v.t.* to attack with raillery; to banter, tease. [Fr. *railler*].

RAM (1), [ram], *n.* a full-grown male sheep, a tup; (*astron.*) the sign of the zodiac and constellation, Aries; (*milit.*) an engine formerly used for demolishing walls and known as a battering-ram; (*nav.*) a steel beak at the bow of a warship; (*eng.*) a hydraulic engine for raising weights; any of the various devices for applying energy by pushing, thrusting, forcing. [OE. *ram*].

RAM

RAM (2), (ramming, rammed), [ram], *v.t.* to drive with violence; to crash into forcibly; to butt like a ram; to force in; to beat, batter; to crush, cram; (*fig.*) to assert something violently, to convince by repeated forceful assertion; **to r. down a person's throat,** to force into a reluctant mind. [*Prec.*].

RAMADAN, [ram'-ad-an], *n.* the ninth month of the Mohammedan year observed as a thirty days' fast between the hours of sunrise and sunset. [Arab. *ramadan* the hot month].

RAMAL, [rām'-al], *adj.* (*bot.*) belonging to a branch. [L. *ramus* a branch].

RAMBLE (1), [rambl], *n.* an irregular excursion; a stroll; (*fig.*) a discursive talk, essay, or book.

RAMBLE (2), [rambl], *v.i.* to wander about, to roam; to saunter about for pleasure; (*fig.*) to read discursively; to wander about in talk or writing; to be delirious and babble inconsequentially; (*bot.*) to grow in long slender shoots, to trail. [Uncert.].

RAMBLER, [ramb'-ler], *n.* one who, or that which, rambles; a rover; a climbing rose-tree.

RAMBLING, [ramb'-ling], *adj.* inclined to ramble; straggling, irregular; (*fig.*) desultory, disconnected, discursive.

RAMBLINGLY, [ramb'-ling-li], *adv.* in a rambling manner.

RAMBUTAN, [ram-bo͞ot'-an], *n.* the fruit of the Malayan tree, *Nephelium lappaceum*, with a pulpy centre and a reddish, hairy skin. [Malay *rambutan*].

RAMEKIN, [ram'-ek-in], *n.* a dish made of cheese, eggs and breadcrumbs baked and served in a mould. [Fr. *ramequin*].

RAMENTACEOUS, [ram'-ent-ā'-shus], *adj.* covered with scales.

RAMENTUM, (*pl.* **ramenta**), [ra-ment'-um], *n.* a fragment scraped off; (*bot.*) a thin, brown scale formed on the surface of leaves and stalks. [L. *ramentum*].

RAMEOUS, [rā'-mi-us], *adj.* (*bot.*) belonging to a branch or branches. [L. *ramus* branch].

RAMICORN, [ram'-i-kawn], *n.* (*ornith.*) the horny sheath of the barbs of the lower mandible. [L. *ramus* branch and *cornu* horn].

RAMIE, [ram'-ē], *n.* fibre obtained from the stingless nettle of China; the nettle itself. [Malay *rami*].

RAMIFICATION, [ram'-if-ik-ā'-shun], *n.* division into branches; a branch; a subdivision or single part of a complex structure; (*fig.*) a penetration in many directions.

RAMIFY, [ram'-i-fī'], *v.t.* to divide into branches; to form into ramifications; *v.i.* to produce ramifications; to be divided or subdivided. [L. *ramificare*].

RAM-LINE, [ram'-līn], *n.* the rope stretched from stem to stern by which the frames were adjusted in shipbuilding.

RAMMER, [ram'-er], *n.* one who, or that which, rams or drives in; a tool for ramming; a wooden instrument with a flat, heavy end for beating down earth; a machine for driving piles into place; a rod for forcing down the charge of a muzzle-loading gun.

RAMMISH, [ram'-ish], *adj.* rank, strong-smelling; †lustful. [RAM (1)].

RAMMISHNESS, [ram'-ish-nes], *n.* the quality of being rammish; rankness; a strong and disagreeable smell.

RAMMY, [ram'-i], *adj.* like a ram; rank.

RAMOLLISSEMENT, [ram' - ol - ēs' - mah(ng)], *n.* (*path.*) a morbid softening of an organ or tissue. [Fr. *ramollissement*].

RAMOSE, [ram-ōs'], *adj.* branching; consisting of, full of, branches. [L. *ramosus*].

RAMOUS, [rām'-us], *adj.* branching. [*Prec.*].

RAMP (1), [ramp], *n.* a slope; an inclined plane connecting two different levels; the slope of, or change of, level in a stair-rail or coping; (*fort.*) a slope on the interior face of a wall or rampart serving as a connecting passage way; the slope connecting two different levels of a road; (*coll.*) commotion, rampage; (*slang*) swindle, fraud. [Fr. *rampe* slope].

RAMP (2), [ramp], *v.t.* to build, make a ramp; *v.i.* to climb and spread luxuriantly as a plant; to rage, storm violently; (*fort.*) †to slope upwards or downwards from one level to another. [OFr. *ramper*].

RAMPAGE (1), [ramp-āj'], *n.* violent behaviour, riot, frolic; **on the r.,** inclined to, indulging in riotous behaviour. [RAMP (1)].

RAMPAGE (2), [ramp-āj'], *v.i.* to be on the rampage.

RAMPAGEOUS, [ramp-āj'-us], *adj.* rowdy, noisy.

RAMPAGEOUSLY, [ramp-āj'-us-li], *adv.* in a rowdy manner.

RAMPANCY, [ramp'-an-si], *n.* the condition of being rampant.

RAMPANT, [ramp'-ant], *adj.* rearing, standing with the forepaws in the air; (*her.*) of an animal, thus rearing, the right forepaw being held above the left and the head in profile; angry, impatient; luxurious in growth, abundant, spreading; rife, prevalent. [Fr. *rampant*].

RAMPANTLY, [ramp'-ant-li], *adv.* in a rampant manner; vigorously, flourishingly, freely, prevalently.

RAMPART, [ramp'-aht], *n.* a mound of earth raised for the defence of a place, usually broad enough to carry guns and protected by a stone wall or parapet; that which defends and fortifies from assault; (*fig.*) protection, defence. [Fr. *rempart*].

RAMPION, [ram'-pi-on], *n.* (*bot.*) a kind of campanula, *Campanula Rapunculus*, with an angled stem and a panicle of pale blue bell-shaped flowers; a plant of the genus *Phyteuma*. [Fr. *rampion*].

RAMROD, [ram'-rod'], *n.* the metal rod used for ramming home the charge in a muzzle-loaded gun; (*fig.*) a person of stiff, uncompromising appearance.

RAMSHACKLE, [ram'-shakl'], *adj.* loose and rickety as if liable to fall to pieces; makeshift; badly built. [†*ransackle* to destroy by plundering].

RAMSONS, [ram'-suns], *n.* (*bot.*) the broad-leaved hedgerow garlic, *Allium ursinum*; the root of this used in salads. [OE. *hramsa*].

RAMULOSE, [ram'-yo͞o-lōs], *adj.* bearing many small branches. [L. *ramulosus*].

RAMULOUS, [ram'-yo͞o-lus], *adj.* ramulose.

RAN, [ran], *pret.* of RUN.

RANCE, [rans], *n.* a kind of variegated marble with a dark-red ground and blue and white veining. [Fr. *rance*].

RANCH, [rahnch], *n.* a cattle farm, usually in America; a large farm or estate. [SpanAmer. *rancho*].

RANCHER, [rahnch'-er], *n.* a ranchman; one who owns or works on a ranch.

RANCHERO, [ranch-āer'-ō], *n.* one employed on, or owning, a ranch; a herdsman. [Span. *ranchero*].

RANCHMAN, [rahnch'-man], *n.* one who owns or works on a ranch.

RANCHO, [ranch'-ō], *n.* in Spanish America, a rudely built hut or collection of huts, a village; in Western U.S. a cattle-farm, a ranch. [Span. *rancho*].

RANCID, [ran'-sid], *adj.* having a sour, stale smell of fats that have gone bad. [L. *rancidus*].

RANCIDITY, [ran-sid'-i-ti], *n.* a rancid smell or taste.

RANCIDLY, [ran'-sid-li], *adv.* in a rancid manner.

RANCIDNESS, [ran′-sid-nes], *n.* the quality of being rancid.
RANCIERITE, [ran′-sēer-īt], *n.* an oxide of manganese.
RANCOROUS, [rangk′-er-us], *adj.* bitter, spiteful.
RANCOROUSLY, [rangk′-er-us-li], *adv.* in a rancorous manner.
RANCOUR, [rangk′-er], *n.* deep-seated bitterness; a smarting sense of injury; malignity; spite. [OFr. *rancour*].
RAND, [rand], *n.* border, edge; the unploughed edge of an arable field; a strip of leather in the heel-piece of a boot or shoe inserted to level up the heel. [OE. *rand*].
RANDAN, [ran-dan′], *n.* a rowing boat for three persons, one using a pair of sculls, stroke and bow using each an oar. [Unkn.].
RANDEM, [ran′-dem], *n.* a team of three horses driven one in front of another. [~TANDEM].
RANDOM (1), [ran′-dom], *n.* **at r.**, aimlessly, without direction or thought. [OFr. *randon*].
RANDOM (2), [ran′-dom], *adj.* done at hazard, aimlessly, without direction, without previous calculation or thought.
RANDY, [ran′-di], *adj.* (*coll.*) lustful; rowdy. [~RAND].
RANEDEER†, see REINDEER.
RANEE, RANI, [rah′-nē], *n.* a Hindu queen or princess; the wife of a rajah. [Hind. *rani*].
RANG, [rang], *pret.* of RING.
RANGE (1), [rānj], *n.* a row, group, collection, series; the space through which anything in motion carries, as the distance to which the projectile of a gun reaches, the distance at which one can see or hear or be seen or heard; extent, area; a kitchen grate or cooking stove; (*fig.*) intellectual reach, scope of knowledge, capacity, power.
RANGE (2), [rānj], *v.t.* to set, place in a row, ranks, or series; to classify; to get the range of (with a gun, etc.); to rove over, traverse; *v.i.* to lie in a particular direction, to extend; to move at large; to vary between two specified limits; (of guns) to have a certain range; (*fig.*) to include in its intellectual grasp; **to r. oneself**, to put oneself in a certain group, take a certain side; **to r. in**, to be found in, to inhabit. [OFr. *ranger*].
RANGE-FINDER, [rānj′-fīnd′-er], *n.* an optical instrument for ascertaining the distance of an object at one observation.
RANGER, [rānj′-er], *n.* a rover; an officer appointed to patrol a royal park or forest; (*pl.*) a body of troops used for scouting purposes, *esp.* those used to patrol the frontiers or as commando troops.
RANGERSHIP, [rānj′-er-ship], *n.* the office of ranger of a royal park or forest.
RANI, see RANEE.
RANINE, [ran′-īn], *adj.* pertaining to a frog; (*anat.*) belonging to the underside of the tip of the tongue. [L. *rana* a frog].
RANK (1), [rangk], *n.* a row, line of things or people; a social class, division, order; eminence, high station; degree of worth; **to fall into r.**, to fall into an orderly arrangement; **to break ranks**, to be thrown into confusion; **to take r.**, to enjoy precedence; **the r. and file**, the whole body of common soldiers, ordinary people. [OFr. *ranc*.]
RANK (2), [rangk], *adj.* luxuriant in growth; high-grown; coarse, strong; rampant; strong smelling, rancid; corrupt, loathsome. [OE. *ranc* strong, proud].
RANK (3), [rangk], *v.t.* to place abreast or in line; to dispose methodically; to assign a rank, class, position to; *v.i.* to take rank, belong to a certain rank, class, position to have validity. [RANK (1)].
RANKER, [rangk′-er], *n.* one who disposes in ranks; a commissioned officer who has risen from the ranks.
RANKLE, [rangkl], *v.i.* to grow strong, to fester; to be the cause of soreness or irritation; (*fig.*) to be the cause of pain or ill-feeling. [OFr. *rancler*].
RANKLING, [rangk′-ling], *n.* a deep and active irritation, soreness.
RANKNESS, [rangk′-nes], *n.* the condition of being rank. [RANK (2)].
RANSACK, [ran′-sak′], *v.t.* to search thoroughly; to examine thoroughly; to turn everything upside down in searching; to plunder; (*fig.*) to search (the mind) thoroughly. [OScand. *rannsaka* to search a house as for plunder].
RANSOM (1), [ran′-sum], *n.* the price paid for the redemption of a prisoner or slave or for goods captured by an enemy; release of a prisoner or deliverance of goods from the possession of an enemy; the price paid to procure the pardon of sins and the redemption of the sinner; (*theol.*) the sacrifice of Christ regarded as the price paid for the redemption of man. [OFr. *ranson*].
RANSOM (2), [ran′-sum], *v.t.* to redeem from captivity or bondage; to exact ransom from; (*theol.*) to redeem from sin by sacrifice. [OFr. *ransonner*].
RANSOMER, [ran′-sum-er], *n.* one who ransoms.
RANSOMLESS, [ran′-sum-les], *adj.* free from a ransom; without a ransom.
RANT (1), [rant], *n.* a boisterous and idle declamation; a noisy, extravagant speech.
RANT (2), [rant], *v.i.* to rave in violent, empty declamation; to talk on religious matters in a dramatic and extravagant manner. [MDu. *ranten* to rave].
RANTER, [rant′-er], *n.* one who rants; a boisterous, extravagant preacher; (*pl.*) a fanatical religious sect in England during the Commonwealth; (*coll.*) a 19th-century nonconformist preacher.
RANTINGLY, [rant′-ing-li], *adv.* in a ranting manner.
RANTIPOLE, [ran′-ti-pōl], *n.* a romp; a wild rakish person. [Uncert.].
RANULA, [ran′-yŏŏ-la], *n.* (*path.*) a glandular swelling under the tongue caused by the obstruction of a salivary gland. [L. *ranula* little frog].
RANUNCULUS, [ran-ungk′-yŏŏ-lus], *n.* (*bot.*) a numerous genus of plants including the common buttercup and crowfoot. [L. *ranunculus* a little frog, the crowfoot].
RANZ-DES-VACHES, [rah(ng)-dā-vahsh′], *n.* a melody sung or played on the horn by the Alpine herdsmen as they drive their cattle to and from the pastures. [Fr Swiss *ranz-des-vaches* the calling of the cows].
RAP (1), [rap], *n.* a quick, smart blow or tap; a knock at a door, table, etc. [Echoic].
RAP (2), [rap], *n.* a counterfeit Irish halfpenny; something worthless, of no consequence; **not worth a r.**, worthless. [Uncert.].
RAP (3), [rap], *n.* a skein of yarn 120 yards long. [Unkn.].
RAP (4), **(rapping, rapped)**, [rap], *v.t. and i.* to strike with a quick, sharp blow; to knock; **to r. out**, to express by rapping, to strum; to utter sharply.
RAP (5), **(rapping, rapped)**, [rap], *v.t.* to snatch or hurry away; to seize by violence; to affect with rapture. [~RAPT].
RAPACIOUS, [rap-ā′-shus], *adj.* greedy, hungry; given to plunder; extortionate. [L. *rapax*].
RAPACIOUSLY, [rap-ā′-shus-li], *adv.* in a rapacious manner.
RAPACIOUSNESS, [rap-ā′-shus-nes], *n.* the condition of being rapacious.
RAPACITY, [rap-as′-it-i], *n.* the quality of being rapacious; ravenousness; greediness of gain; avarice. [Fr. *rapacité*].
RAPE (1), [rāp], *n.* a seizing and carrying off by force; the violation of a woman against her will.
RAPE (2), [rāp], *n.* a land division of the county of Sussex. [OE. *rap*].
RAPE (3), [rāp], *n.* a plant of the genus *Brassica*, grown as food for sheep. [L. *rapa*].
RAPE (4), [rāp], *n.* what is left of the grapes after the juice has been extracted for wine; **r. wine**, a thin wine made from the rape of grapes. [Fr. *râpe*].
RAPE (5), [rāp], *v.t.* to seize and carry off by force; to ravish. [L. *rapere* to seize].
RAPE-CAKE, [rāp′-kāk], *n.* a cake made from the remains of the rape-seed after the extraction of the oil.
RAPE-SEED, [rāp′-sēd], *n.* the seed of the rape from which colza oil is extracted.
RAPHAELESQUE, [raf′-ā-el-esk′], *adj.* in the manner of the Italian painter *Raphael*, 1483-1520.
RAPHAELISM, [raf′-ā-el-izm], *n.* the principles of art introduced by the Italian painter *Raphael*; his method of painting.
RAPHAELITE, [raf′-ā-el-īt], *n.* one who adopts the style, follows the principles of *Raphael*.
RAPHANIA, [raf-ā′-ni-a], *n.* a form of ergotism, so called by Linnaeus, because he believed it due to the use of grain containing seeds of *Raphanus*.
RAPHE, [rā′-fi], *n.* (*anat., bot.*) a juncture between the two halves of an organ; a seam, suture. [Gk. *rhaphe*].
RAPHIA, see RAFFIA.
RAPHILITE, [raf′-il-īt], *n.* a variety of tremolite composed of needle-forming crystals. [Gk. *raphis* needle and *lithos* stone].
RAPHIS, (*pl.* **raphides**), [rāf′-is, rāf′-i-dēz], *n.* one of the minute transparent crystals found in the tissues of plants. [Gk. *raphis* needle].
RAPID (1), [rap′-id], *n.* (usually in *pl.*) that part of a river where the current flows very rapidly owing to a steep descent of the bed.

RAPID (2), [rap'-id], *adj.* very quick, swift, abrupt, steep. [L. *rapidus*].

RAPIDITY, [rap-id'-it-i], *n.* the state of being rapid; swiftness. [L. *rapiditas*].

RAPIDLY, [rap'-id-li], *adv.* in a rapid manner; swiftly, quickly.

RAPIDNESS, [rap'-id-nes], *n.* rapidity; the quality of being rapid.

RAPIER, [rā'-pi-er], *n.* a light sword with long narrow blade used only for thrusting; **r. glance,** keen, piercing glance. [Fr. *rapière*].

RAPIER

RAPIER-FISH, [rā'-pi-er-fish'], *n.* the sword-fish, *Xiphias gladius.*

RAPIER-THRUST, [rā'-pi-er-thrust'], *n.* the thrust of a rapier; (*fig.*) a penetrating glance or riposte.

RAPINE, [rap'-in], *n.* the act of plundering; pillage; violent robbery. [Fr. *rapine*].

RAPPAREE, [rap'-a-rē'], *n.* an Irish pike-man employed in the Revolution of 1688-1691; a freebooter, armed robber. [Ir. *rapaire* robber].

RAPPEE, [rap-ē'], *n.* a strong coarse variety of snuff. [Fr. (*tabac*) *râpé*].

RAPPEL, [rap-el'], *n.* the roll of drums summoning to arms. [Fr. from *rappeler* to recall].

RAPPER, [rap'-er], *n.* one who raps; a device for rapping; a door-knocker; (*dial.*) a downright falsehood.

RAPPORT, [rap-aw(r)'], *n.* intimate relation; harmony; **to be in r. with,** to have close intimate relations with; to be in communication with (a spirit) through a medium. [Fr. *en rapport*].

RAPPROCHEMENT, [rap-rosh'-mah(ng)], *n.* the act of reconciling, bringing together; the re-establishing of cordial relations between individuals or nations. [Fr. *rapprochement*].

RAPSCALLION, [rap'-skal'-i-on], *n.* a rascally vagabond, a scamp. [RASCAL].

RAPT, [rapt], *adj.* in an ecstasy; carried away, engrossed. [L. *raptus, p.pt.* of *rapere* to seize].

RAPTORES, [rap-taw'-rez], *n.(pl.)* birds of prey of the order *Raptores*, including the eagle, hawk, vulture. [L. *raptores* robbers].

RAPTORIAL, [rap-taw'-ri-al], *adj.* predatory; belonging to the order *Raptores.* [*Prec.*].

RAPTORIOUS, [rap-tawr'-i-us], *adj.* raptorial.

RAPTURE, [rap'-cher], *n.* ecstasy; extreme delight; a powerful pleasurable emotion; **to go into raptures over,** to express extreme pleasure in. [RAPT].

RAPTUROUS, [rap'-cher-us], *adj.* feeling, expressing rapture; ecstatic.

RAPTUROUSLY, [rap'-cher-us-li], *adv.* with rapture, ecstatically.

RARA AVIS, [rāer'-a-āv'-is], *n.* an unusual person or thing. [L. *rara avis* rare bird].

RARE (1), [rāer], *adj.* nearly raw, underdone. [OE. *hrer*].

RARE (2), [rāer], *adj.* thinly scattered, not dense, of loose texture; rarefied, thin; widely distributed and infrequent, unusual, precious, excellent. [Fr. *rare*].

RARE (3), [rāer], *adv.* very, extremely.

RAREBIT, [rāer'-bit], *n.* **Welsh r.,** a preparation of cooked cheese on toast. [~WELSH-RABBIT].

RARE EARTH, [rāer'-urth'], *n.* (*chem.*) one of various rare, closely allied metallic elements or their oxides found in Scandinavia.

RAREE-SHOW, [rāer'-ē-shō], *n.* a peep-show carried in a box. [RARE and SHOW].

RAREFACTION, [rāer'-i-fak'-shun], *n.* the act of rarefying; the state of being rarefied. [Fr. *rarefaction*].

RAREFIABLE, [rāer'-i-fī-abl], *adj.* capable of being rarefied.

RAREFY, [rāer'-i-fī], *v.t.* to make rare; to make thin and porous or less dense; to refine, render spiritual; *v.i.* to become rarefied. [Fr. *raréfier*].

RARELY, [rāer'-li], *adv.* seldom; exceptionally.

RARENESS, [rāer'-nes], *n.* the quality of being rare.

RARERIPE, [rāer'-rīp], *n.* an early fruit or vegetable, particularly a kind of early peach. [†*rare* early and RIPE].

RARITY, [rāer'-it-i], *n.* the state of being rare; lack of density; infrequency, uncommonness. [L. *raritas*].

RASCAL, [rahs'-kal], *n.* a mean fellow, a scoundrel, a rogue; (*coll.*) fellow. [OFr. *rascaille* the rabble].

RASCALDOM, [rahs'-kal-dum], *n.* rascals, rogues collectively. [RASCAL and OE. *dom* state].

RASCALITY, [rahs-kal'-it-i], *n.* rascally action or conduct; base fraud.

RASCALLY, [rahs'-kal-i], *adj.* dishonest, mean, scoundrelly.

RASE, see RAZE.

RASH (1), [rash], *n.* an eruption of the skin. [OFr. *rasche* scurf].

RASH (2), [rash], *adj.* hasty in action or judgment; headstrong; imprudent. [ME. *rasch*].

RASH (3), [rash], *v.t.* to cut, slash; to slice. [Uncert.].

RASHER, [rash'-er], *n.* a thin slice of bacon or ham. [*Prec.*].

RASHLY, [rash'-li], *adv.* in a rash manner; hastily, imprudently.

RASHNESS, [rash'-nes], *n.* the quality of being rash; imprudence; precipitancy.

RASKOLNIK, [ras-kol'-nik], *n.* a sect in Russia dissenting from the Eastern Orthodox Church. [Russ. *raskolnik* separatist].

RASORIAL, [raz-aw'-ri-al], *adj.* (of birds) scratching, scraping for food; gallinaceous. [L. *rasor* scraper].

RASP (1), [rahsp], *n.* a coarse file; a rough, grating sound. [OFr. *raspe*].

RASP (2), [rahsp], *v.t. and i.* to file with a rasp; to produce a harsh, grating sound; (*fig.*) to irritate, exacerbate. [OFr. *rasper*].

RASPATORY, [rahs'-pat-er-i], *n.* a surgeon's rasp for scraping diseased bone. [MedL. *raspatorium*].

RASPBERRY (1), [rahz'-be-ri], *n.* the plant, *Rubus Idæus*; the fruit of this plant. [Uncert.].

RASPBERRY (2), [rahz'-ber-i], *n.* (*slang*) a rasping sound made with the tongue and lower lip as a sign of contempt. [Uncert.].

RASPBERRY-CANES, [rahz'-be-ri-kānz'], *n.(pl.)* the new annual shoots of the raspberry plant which bear the fruit.

RASPBERRY-JAM, [rahz'-be-ri-jam'], *n.* a jam made of this fruit; the Australian tree, *Acacia acuminata,* so called because of the scent from its wood.

RASPBERRY-VINEGAR, [rahz'-be-ri-vin'-ig-er], *n.* a syrup made from raspberry-juice and vinegar.

RASPER, [rahsp'-er], *n.* a large rasp or file; (*hunting*) a high fence, difficult to jump; (*coll.*) something very difficult.

RASPING, [rahsp'-ing], *adj.* scraping, grating, harsh.

RASSE, [ras], *n.* a small, tree-climbing civet-cat, *Viverra malaccensis,* native to Indo-China and Malaya. [Javanese *rase*].

RASURE, [rā'-zher], *n.* the act of scraping out something written; effacement. [Fr. *rasure*].

RAT (1), [rat], *n.* a small rodent; (*fig.*) a cowardly, treacherous person, one who deserts a place or cause when danger threatens; **water r.,** the water vole, *Microtus amphibius*; **to smell a r.,** to be suspicious; **like a drowned r.,** wet to the skin; **to have the rats,** (*coll.*) to be disagreeable. [OE. *ræt*].

RAT (2), (ratting, ratted), [rat], *v.i.* to hunt rats; to desert one's party or cause, to behave in a cowardly and treacherous manner. [*Prec.*].

RATA, [rah'-ta], *n.* a New Zealand tree, *Meirosideros robusta,* with dark-red wood and crimson flowers. [Maori *rata*].

RATABLE, [rāt'-abl], *adj.* that which may be set at a certain value or rate; liable to taxation; **r. value,** the yearly sum at which a house or land is assessed for rates and taxes.

RATABLY, [rāt'-ab-li], *adv.* by rate, proportionally.

RATAFIA, [ra-taf-ē'-a], *n.* a liqueur distilled from fruits and flavoured with crushed kernels; a biscuit similarly flavoured. [Fr. *ratafia*].

RATAL, [rāt'-al], *n.* the rateable value of property.

RATANY see RHATANY.

RATAPLAN, [rat-a-plan'], *n.* the beat of the drum. [Fr. *rataplan*].

RAT-CATCHER, [rat'-kach'-er], *n.* a person employed in catching rats.

RATCH, [rach], *n.* a ratchet-wheel. [RATCHET].

RATCHEL, RATCHIL, [rach'-el], *n.* fragments of loose stone. [Unkn.].

RATCHET, [rach'-it], *n.* a set of teeth on a bar or wheel, connected with a pawl, and so allowing the wheel to turn in only one direction. [Fr *rochet* bobbin, spindle].

RATCHET-WHEEL, [rach'-it-wēl], *n.* a wheel equipped with a ratchet.

RATCHIL, see RATCHEL.

RATE (1), [rāt], *n.* the proportion or ratio by which an unvarying relation between two things different in kind is measured, as 30 miles an hour or 2d. per £; price fixed or stated; class based on estimated worth; a municipal tax; (*nav.*) the order or class of a ship. [OFr. *rate* price].

RATE (2), [rāt], *v.t.* to value, fix the rate or the grade of;

to assess for rating; (*nav.*) to class (a vessel) according to its grade; *v.i.* to be classed in a certain grade or at a certain rate. [*Prec.*].

RATE (3), [rāt], *v.t.* to scold, chide. [ME. *raten*].

RATEABLE, [rāt'-abl], *adj.* ratable; capable of being rated.

RATEEN, see RATTEEN.

RATEL, [rā'-tel], *n.* a carnivorous mammal resembling a badger; the honey-badger. [Afrik. *ratelmius*].

RATEL

RATEPAYER, [rāt'-pā'-er], *n.* a person who pays municipal rates on house or land.

RATER, [rāt'-er], *n.* an assessor; one of a certain rate or class.

RATH (1), [rahth], *n.* a prehistoric Irish hill fort; a mound. [Ir. *raith*].

RATH (2), RATHE, [rāTH], *adj.* coming early into flower; early ripening. [OE. *hræth* early].

RATHER, [rah'-THer], *adv.* sooner, preferably; willingly; more properly, truly, accurately; slightly, somewhat; (*coll.*) certainly. [OE. *hrathor*].

RATIFICATION, [rat'-if-ik-ā'-shun], *n.* the act of ratifying, confirming; sanction. [MedL. *ratificatio*].

RATIFIER, [rat'-i-fī-er], *n.* one who, or that which, ratifies.

RATIFY, [rat'-i-fī], *v.t.* to confirm, make valid; to approve, sanction. [Fr. *ratifier*].

RATING, [rāt'-ing], *n.* the act of valuing, assessing, fixing a rate; the tonnage class or type of a vessel; the status in a ship's crew of an individual sailor; rank, grade. [RATE (1)].

RATIO, [rā'-shi-ō], *n.* the fixed relation of one thing to another; proportion; (*math.*) the relation of one quantity or magnitude to another expressed by their quotient. [L. *ratio* reckoning].

RATIOCINATE, [rat'-i-os'-in-āt], *v.i.* to reason; to carry on a process of formal reasoning. [L. *ratiocinari*].

RATIOCINATION, [rat'-i-os'-in-ā'-shun], *n.* the process of reasoning; the act of deducing consequences from given premises. [L. *ratiocinatio*].

RATIOCINATIVE, [rat'-i-os'-in-at-iv], *adj.* characterized by ratiocination.

RATION, [rash'-un], *n.* a fixed allowance of anything, *esp.* of provisions; (*pl.*) provisions; **r. book,** a booklet containing coupons by which the permitted ration can be obtained; **short rations,** short commons, restricted provisions. [L. *ratio*].

RATIONAL, [rash'-un-al], *adj.* endowed with reason; pertaining to, having the faculty of, reason; intelligent; judicious; **r. quantity,** (*math.*) one expressed without a radical sign or by a whole number.

RATIONALE, [rash'-on-ā'-li], *n.* a rational explanation; the principle of a matter. [L. *rationale* the rational thing].

RATIONALISM, [rash'-un-al-izm], *n.* (*theol.*) the doctrine which claims to explain the universe by reason alone, and rejects revelation; (*philos.*) the doctrine that reason is the sole source of knowledge; reliance on reason.

RATIONALIST (1), [rash'-un-al-ist], *n.* a believer in rationalism in philosophy or theology; one who is guided by reason.

RATIONALIST (2), [rash'-un-al-ist], *adj.* pertaining to rationalists or rationalism.

RATIONALISTIC, [rash'-un-al-ist'-ik], *adj.* relating to, or in accordance with, rationalism.

RATIONALISTICALLY, [rash'-un-al-ist'-ik-al-i], *adv.* in a rationalist manner; reasonably.

RATIONALITY, [rash'-un-al'-it-i], *n.* the condition of being rational; reasonableness. [Fr. *rationalité*].

RATIONALIZATION, [rash'-un-al-iz-ā'-shun], *n.* the act of rationalizing; the policy of reforming industry on a rational basis so as to avoid useless effort or cost.

RATIONALIZE, [rash'-un-al-īz], *v.t.* to explain entirely by reason; to apprehend rationally; to explain away by means of reasoning; (*math.*) to clear from radical or irrational quantities; *v.i.* to rely solely or unduly on reason.

RATIONALLY, [rash'-un-al-i], *adv.* in a rational manner; with reason; sensibly.

RATIONALNESS, [rash'-un-al-nes], *n.* the condition of being rational; reasonableness.

RATITE, [rā'-tīt], *adj.* (*ornith.*) belonging to the *Ratitæ*, a group of flightless birds having a keelless breastbone, as the ostrich, emu. [L. *ratis* raft].

RATLINS, RATLINGS, [rat'-linz, rat'-lingz], *n.* ropes stretched horizontally across the shrouds of a ship and forming the steps up the rigging. [Uncert.].

RATOON, [rat-ōōn'], *n.* a second year's shoot from a sugar-cane after it has been cut down. [Span. *retoño* sprout].

RAT'S-BANE, [rats'-bān], *n.* rat poison; one of various poisonous plants.

RATSNAKE, [rat'-snāk], *n.* a snake domesticated in Ceylon for the purpose of killing rats.

RAT-TAIL(ED), [rat'-tāl(d)], *adj.* narrow and tapering; (of a horse) having a thin hairless tail resembling that of a rat; (of a spoon) having a narrow tapering extension of the handle under the bowl.

RATTAN, [rat-an'], *n.* a species of climbing plant, *Calamus Rotang*, found in the East Indies; the stem of this plant when peeled; used for walking-sticks, etc.; a walking stick made of rattan. [Malay *rotan*].

RAT-TAT, [rat'-tat'], *n.* the sound of a loud knocking at the door. [Echoic].

RATTEEN, RATEEN, [rat-ēn'], *n.* a thick twilled woollen material used for lining. [Fr. *ratine*].

RATTEN, [rat'-en], *v.t.* to destroy or take away the tools or property of non-unionists during a labour dispute. [~RAT (2)].

RATTER, [rat'-er], *n.* one who hunts rats; a dog or ferret that hunts rats; a man deserting his political party or trade union in a crisis.

RATTINET, [rat'-in-et'], *n.* a woollen material thinner and lighter than ratteen. [Fr. *ratine*].

RATTING, [rat'-ing], *n.* the catching and killing of rats; desertion of one's party in a crisis.

RATTLE (1), [ratl], *n.* a rapid succession of sharp, clattering sounds; the name of certain plants in which the ripe seeds rattle in their capsules; the sound produced by loose objects shaking against each other; intermittent sound produced by a loose door, window, etc.; an instrument by which a clattering sound is made; a noisy, empty talker.

RATTLE (2), [ratl], *v.t.* to cause to make a rattling sound; to cause to move briskly or with much clattering; **to r. off,** to complete briskly; (*coll.*) to disturb, put off; *v.i.* to make a rattle; to make a series of quick, clattering sounds; to move quickly or with a rattling sound; to speak briskly. [Echoic].

RATTLEBOX, [ratl-'boks'], *n.* a baby's toy; (*bot.*) the plant, *Rhinanthus Christagalli*.

RATTLE-HEADED, [ratl'-hed'-ed], *adj.* noisy, giddy shallow-pated.

RATTLE-PATED, [ratl'-pāt'-id], *adj.* shallow, empty-headed.

RATTLER, [rat'-ler], *n.* one who, or that which, rattles; a noisy person; a rattlesnake; (*coll.*) a first-rate person or thing.

RATTLEROOT, [ratl'-rōōt], *n.* the North American black snakeroot, *Cimicifuga racemosa*.

RATTLESNAKE, [ratl'-snāk], *n.* a venomous snake of the genus *Crotalus*, so called because of the noise that the loosely interlocking joints at the end of the tail make when shaken.

RATTLETRAP (1), [ratl'-trap'], *n.* a shaky vehicle; a rickety old motor-car. [RATTLE (2) and TRAP (1)].

RATTLETRAP (2), [ratl'-trap'], *adj.* rickety, shaky.

RATTLEWING, [ratl'-wing], *n.* the golden-eye duck. *Clangula glaucion*.

RATTLING, [rat'-ling], *adj.* making the sound of a rattle; quick, brisk; excellent; **a r. good fellow** a fine fellow.

RAT-TRAP, [rat'-trap'], *n.* a trap for catching rats; a toothed pedal on a bicycle.

RATTY, [rat'-i], *adj.* infested with rats; (*slang*) angry, bad-tempered.

RAUCITY, [raw'-sit-i], *n.* roughness, hoarseness. [L. *raucitas*].

RAUCOUS, [raw'-kus], *adj.* rough, harsh, loud and coarse. [L. *raucus*].

RAVAGE (1), [rav'-ij], *n.* destruction by violence or decay; waste; (*pl.*) the effects of these. [Fr. *ravage*].

RAVAGE (2), [rav'-ij], *v.t.* to lay waste, plunder; to ruin, destroy; *v.i.* to commit ravages. [Fr. *ravager*].

RAVAGER, [rav'-ij-er], *n.* one who ravages; a plunderer, a spoiler.

RAVE, [rāv], *v.i.* to wander in mind or intellect; to speak incoherently or irrationally like a madman; (of a storm) to howl, roar; **to r. about,** to speak very enthusiastically about. [OFr. *raver*].

RAVEL (1), [ravl], *n.* a tangled mass; (*fig.*) confusion.

RAVEL (2), (ravelling, ravelled), [ravl], *v.t.* to unweave, untwist; to twist together, make into a tangled mass; *v.i.* to fray out, become untwisted; **to r. out,** to disentangle. [MDu. *ravelen*].

RAVELIN, [rav′-lin], *n.* (*fort.*) a triangular detached outwork making a salient angle which protects a curtain wall. [It. *ravellino*].

RAVELLING, [rav′-el-ing], *n.* thread or threads of material or rope which have come untwisted.

RAVELMENT, [rav′-el-ment], *n.* entanglement, confusion, perplexity.

RAVEN (1), [rā′-ven], *n.* the largest of the crow family, *Corvus corax*. [OScand. *hrafn*].

RAVEN (2), [rā′-ven], *adj.* black in colour like the raven.

RAVEN (3), [rav′-en], *v.t.* to devour with eager greed; *v.i.* to plunder with rapacity; to be ravenous. [OFr. *raviner*].

RAVENER, [rav′-en-er], *n.* one who ravens, plunders, preys.

RAVENING, [rav′-en-ing], *adj.* voracious, eager for plunder.

RAVENOUS, [rav′-en-us], *adj.* furiously voracious, eager for gratification; famished; (*coll.*) very hungry. [~RAVEN (3)].

RAVENOUSLY, [rav′-en-us-li], *adv.* in a ravenous manner; hungrily, greedily.

RAVENOUSNESS, [rav′-en-us-nes], *n.* the condition of being ravenous; extreme voraciousness.

RAVER, [rāv′-er], *n.* one who raves.

RAVINE (1), **RAVIN**, [rav′-in], *n.* plunder, pillage, prey. [OFr. *ravine*].

RAVINE (2), [rav-ēn′], *n.* a long deep gully; a narrow valley or gorge, usually one worn by water. [AFr. *ravine* violent rush of water].

RAVINGLY, [rāv′-ing-li], *adv.* incoherently, with furious wildness.

RAVISH, [rav′-ish], *v.t.* to carry away by violence; to commit a rape upon; to delight, transport, fill with ecstasy. [~OFr. *ravir*].

RAVISHER, [rav′-ish-er], *n.* one who ravishes.

RAVISHING, [rav′-ish-ing], *adj.* delightful, entrancing, bewitching.

RAVISHINGLY, [rav′-ish-ing-li], *adv.* in a ravishing manner.

RAVISHMENT, [rav′-ish-ment], *n.* the act of ravishing; abduction; rapture, extreme delight.

RAW (1), [raw], *n.* a sore place; **on the r.**, in the most tender, sensitive place.

RAW (2), [raw], *adj.* in the natural state, not cooked, prepared or treated; (of leather) untanned; (of silks, cottons, wools) not spun or twisted; (of spirits) undiluted; unripe; untrained, inexperienced; sore, having the skin badly rubbed off; cold, damp and piercing; (of manners or literature) crude. [OE. *hreaw*].

RAW-BONED, [raw′-bōnd], *adj.* having little flesh on the bones; gaunt.

RAW-HEAD, [raw′-hed′], *n.* a nursery bugbear, a spectre to frighten children, a skull.

RAWISH, [raw′-ish], *adj.* somewhat raw.

RAWLY, [raw′-li], *adv.* in a raw manner; immaturely; crudely.

RAWNESS, [raw′-nes], *n.* the quality of being raw; immaturity; unskilfulness.

RAY (1), [rā], *n.* any species of cartilaginous fishes of the genus *Raia*, such as the skates. [AFr. *raye*].

RAY (2), [rā], *n.* a beam, shaft of light; a glimmering; a beam of intellectual light; (*geom.*) a radius; (*phys.*) a line of radiant energy; (*bot.*) (*pl.*) the outer whorl of a compound radiate flower; (*zool.*) any part of a radial arrangement as a spine in a fin. [OFr. *raye*].

RAY

RAY (3), [rā], *v.t. and i.* to shine forth, to issue in rays.

RAYAH, [rah′-ya], *n.* a non-Mohammedan Turkish subject of the Sultan. [Arab. *roçiah*].

RAYED, [rād], *adj.* having rays or radiations.

RAYLESS, [rā′-les], *adj.* having no rays; destitute of light.

RAYON, [rā′-on], *n.* artificial silk. [Fr. *rayon*].

RAZE, **RASE**, [rāz], *v.t.* to erase, efface; to lay level with the ground, destroy. [Fr. *raser*].

RAZEE (1), [raz′-ē], *n.* a ship, usually a warship, with one deck cut away so as to have less freeboard. [Fr. *rasée*, *p.pt.* of *raser*].

RAZEE (2), [raz′-ē], *v.t.* to convert a ship into a lower rating by cutting down one deck.

RAZOR, [rāz′-or], *n.* a sharp instrument for shaving off the hair; **to be on the razor's edge**, to be in great difficulties, at a crisis. [OFr. *rasour*].

RAZOR-BACK, [rāz′-or-bak′], *n.* the fin-backed whale; the rorqual.

RAZOR-BILL, [rāz′-or-bil′], *n.* one of various birds with bills shaped like a razor, *esp.* the auk.

RAZOR-EDGE, [rāz′-or-ej′], *n.* the sharp edge of a razor; a very keen edge; a sharp ridge on mountains.

RAZOR-FISH, [rāz′-or-fish′], *n.* any shellfish of the genus *Solen*, having a long narrow shell like the handle of a razor.

RAZOR-SHELL, [rāz′-or-shel′], *n.* the shell of the razor-fish.

RAZOR-STROP, [rāz′-or-strop′], *n.* the strop on which a razor is sharpened.

RAZZIA, [raz′-i-a], *n.* a hostile raid for pillage, *esp.* of the Mohammedan peoples of Africa. [Fr. *razzia* from Arab. *razzia*].

RAZZLE, [razl], *n.* (*slang*) razzle-dazzle.

RAZZLE-DAZZLE, [razl′-dazl′], *n.* (*coll.*) a drunken jollification, spree.

RE- *pref.* back; again; against. [L. *re*].

RE (1), [rā], *n.* the second note of the diatonic scale. [L. *re*(*sonare*)].

RE (2), [rē], *prep.* in the matter of, as regards, referring to. [L. *re*, *abl. sg.* of *res* thing, matter].

REABSORB, [rē′-ab-sawb′], *v.t.* to absorb again.

REABSORPTION, [rē-ab-sawp′-shun], *n.* the act of reabsorbing; the state of being reabsorbed.

REACCESS, [rē-ak′-ses], *n.* fresh access or approach.

REACH (1), [rēch], *n.* the act of reaching; the power of reaching, touching, or grasping by extending the arm or other limb; the range of the arm; power of understanding; power of attaining, scope; possibility of being reached, *esp.* of being easily accessible; range of influence or power; range of carrying, distance over which something is perceptible; a stretch of water on a river, etc.

REACH (2), [rēch], *v.t.* to stretch out, extend (usually with *out*); to take hold of, grasp, or touch with outstretched arm; to take (down or from) by extending the arm; to pass, obtain for, hand to; to realize, achieve; to attain to, arrive at; to influence, affect; to come into possession of or contact with; to extend to, to penetrate to, carry as far as; *v.i.* to stretch out an arm or leg; to be extended so as to touch; to extend, carry; **to r. after, for,** to aspire to, strive after. [OE. *ræcan*].

REACH (3), [rēch], *v.i.* (*prov.*) to retch, to strive to vomit. [OE. *hræcan*].

REACHABLE, [rēch′-abl], *adj.* within reach.

REACH-ME-DOWN, [rēch′-mē-down′], *n.* a garment that is ready made; (*pl.*) trousers.

REACT, [rē-akt′], *v.t.* to act over again; *v.i.* to act in response to a mental or physical stimulus; to act or move in the opposite way, to resist by an opposite force or tendency (with *against*); to act reciprocally on.

REACTANCE, [rē-akt′-ants], *n.* (*elect.*) the ratio of the oscillating electro-motive force to the oscillating current in an alternating circuit, the resistance to a current in an alternating circuit.

REACTION, [rē-ak′-shun], *n.* action in response or opposition to a mental or physical stimulus; reciprocal action; (*chem.*) the action of one agent upon another or the effects of such action; action in the contrary direction, opposite feeling or state induced as a result of a strong influence or continued force exerted on the mind or body, as collapse after prolonged strain; suppression of reform or progress; (*wirel.*) energy produced by currents in an output circuit of a valve passed back to its grid.

REACTIONARY (1), [rē-ak′-shun-er-i], *n.* one in favour of reaction, one who adopts a policy of reaction in politics, etc.

REACTIONARY (2), [rē-ak′-shun-er-i], *adj.* involving or favouring reaction, opposed to reform or progress.

REACTIONIST, [rē-ak′-shun-ist], *n.* a reactionary.

REACTIVE, [rē-akt′-iv], *adj.* having power to react, caused by reaction; reactionary.

REACTIVELY [rē-akt′-iv-li], *adv.* in a reactive manner.

REACTIVENESS, [rē-akt′-iv-nes], *n.* the property of being reactive.

REACTIVITY, [rē-ak-tiv′-i-ti], *n.* the state of being reactive, power or property of reacting.

READ (1), [rēd], *n.* a perusal, a reading, the act of reading.

READ (2), [red], *adj.* learned, versed in a subject by reading. [*p.pt.* of READ (3)].

READ (3), **(reading, read)**, [rēd], *v.t.* to look at and make out the words and characters written, printed, or engraved in a book, document, etc.; to be able to understand (works written in a foreign language); to learn, acquire knowledge of by perusing; to find recorded in writing; to solve or discover the answer to; to interpret or discover by contemplating or studying; (of an instrument) to register; to give as a reading, variant, emendation or correction; to understand, interpret, take; to utter aloud (anything written), to translate (the written word) into the spoken word; to study (for a degree); (*parl.*) to offer (a bill) for discussion and voting upon by a legislative assembly; to correct (proofs of a MS.); *v.i.* to perform the act of reading; to be able to read; to utter aloud anything written; to study or learn by reading; to stand written; to produce a certain impression when read; **to r. for,** to study in order to be officially admitted to; **to r. into,** to assume that a particular sense or meaning is included or implied in; **to r. of,** to learn by reading; **to r. up,** to increase one's knowledge of or become better acquainted with by reading and study; **to r. oneself in,** to enter into formal possession of a benefice in the Church of England by reading aloud in public the Thirty-nine Articles and the Declaration of Assent; **to r. between the lines,** to discover the real meaning or implication as distinct from what is expressed. [OE. *rædan*].

READABILITY, [rēd′-ab-il′-i-ti], *n.* the quality of being readable.

READABLE, [rēd′-abl], *adj.* able to be read; (of handwriting) legible; pleasant and interesting to read.

READABLENESS, [rēd′-abl-nes], *n.* the quality of being readable.

READABLY, [rēd′-ab-li], *adv.* in a readable way.

READDRESS, [rē-ad-res′], *v.t.* to redirect a letter or parcel to another address than that it already bears.

READER, [rēd′-er], *n.* one who reads, *esp.* one fond of reading; one who reads lessons and other parts of the service in church; one employed in reading and correcting proofs for the press; a university teacher usually ranking in status between professor and lecturer; a person employed by publishers to read and give his opinion upon manuscripts submitted to them; a reading-book.

READERSHIP, [rēd′-er-ship], *n.* the office or tenure of office of a reader.

READILY, [red′-i-li], *adv.* in a ready manner, promptly, easily, willingly.

READINESS, [red′-i-nes], *n.* the quality of being ready, preparedness; willingness; quickness.

READING (1), [rēd′-ing], *n.* the act of one who reads; erudition and knowledge acquired from books; readable matter; public recital of selected passages of literature; the form of a word, the words used, or the way in which a passage reads in different copies or editions of a text; interpretation, rendering; record or figure registered by a barometer, etc., when read; (*parl.*) the formal presentation of a bill to the legislative body, and the succeeding stages it has to pass through before it can become an act.

READING (2), [rēd′-ing], *adj.* addicted or devoted to reading.

READING-BOOK, [rēd′-ing-bo͝ok], *n.* a book with selected passages for practice in reading.

READING-DESK, [rēd′-ing-desk], *n.* a desk with a sloping top for supporting a book while being read, a lectern.

READING-LAMP, [rēd′-ing-lamp′], *n.* a portable lamp with a shade, which directs the light on to the book when reading.

READING-ROOM, [rēd′-ing-ro͞om], *n.* a room at a public institution set apart for reading or writing in quietness.

READJOURN, [rē-a-jurn′], *v.t.* to adjourn again.

READJUST, [rē′-a-just′], *v.t.* to adjust or put in order afresh.

READJUSTMENT, [rē′-a-just′-ment], *n.* a fresh adjustment.

READMISSION, [rē′-ad-mish′-un], *n.* the act of admitting again; the state of being readmitted, re-entry.

READMIT, (**readmitting, readmitted**), [rē′-ad-mit′], *v.t.* to admit anew.

READMITTANCE, [rē′-ad-mit′-ants], *n.* readmission.

READOPT, [rē-ad-opt′], *v.t.* to adopt afresh.

READORN, [rē-ad-awn′], *v.t.* to adorn afresh.

READY (1), [red′-i], *n.* (*slang*) ready cash; **at the r.,** (of a fire-arm) held in readiness for immediate aiming and firing.

READY (2), [red′-i], *adj.* prepared, able to do something immediately, fit for immediate use; willing; inclined; liable to, on the point of; quick, dexterous, easy; near at hand; **to make, get r.,** to prepare. [~OE. *geræde*].

READY (3), [red′-i], *v.t.* to make ready; (*racing slang*) to hold in or check (a horse) preventing it from winning, and thus bettering its handicap for a future race.

READY-MADE, [red′-i-mād], *adj.* made ready for immediate use, *esp.* of clothes as opposed to those made to measure or to order; not original; (of ideas, opinions, etc.) set, fixed and produced on every available occasion.

READY MONEY (1), [red′-i-mun′-i], *n.* hard cash, actual coin.

READY-MONEY (2), [red′-i-mun′-i], *adj.* done or conducted by immediate payment in money.

READY RECKONER, [red′-i-rek′-on-er], *n.* a book of tables for rapid arithmetical calculations in business, etc.

READY-WITTED, [red′-i-wit′-id], *adj.* quick in understanding and reply, having a sharp mind.

REAFFIRM, [rē′-a-furm′], *v.t.* to affirm again, to reiterate.

REAFFOREST, [rē′-a-fo′-rest], *v.t.* to plant with new trees in place of those cut down or destroyed.

REAFFORESTATION, [rē′-a-fo′-rest-ā′-shun], *n.* the scientific replanting of trees in former forest areas now laid bare.

REAGENT, [rē-āj′-ent], *n.* that which reacts or sets up reaction; (*chem.*) a substance employed in chemical analysis to detect the presence of another substance by setting up a reaction or chemical change with this substance.

REAGGRAVATION, [rē′-ag′-rav-ā′-shun], *n.* (*R.C.*) the last monitory issued after three admonitions and before the last excommunication.

REAL (1), [rē′-al], *n.* that which is real.

REAL (2), [rā-ahl′], *n.* a small silver Spanish coin (2½d.), the fourth of a peseta, also applied to a former Spanish coin (6¼d.), one-eighth of a dollar. [Span. *real* royal].

REAL (3), [rē′-al], *adj.* actually being or existing; not imaginary, founded on fact; natural, authentic, genuine (as opposed to artificial); sincere, undoubted, proper; true; (of fictional characters) giving the impression of living or existing; (*philos.*) existing in fact; (*leg.*) relating to or connected with things or property, *esp.* pertaining to property or things that are fixed and permanent, such as lands and houses (as opposed to personal); **r. action,** an action which concerns real property, or in which a real thing is sued for and not a compensatory sum of money; **r. estate,** freehold landed property, lands and houses, etc.; **r. property,** lands and houses; **r. presence,** the body and blood of Jesus Christ as believed to be actually present in the consecrated bread and wine of the Eucharist. [LL. *realis*].

REALGAR, [rē-al′-gah], *n.* native disulphide of arsenic, known as red arsenic, used as a pigment and in making certain kinds of fireworks. [MedL. *realgar* from Arab. *rahj-alghar* powder of the cave].

REALISM, [rē′-al-izm], *n.* concentration upon actual fact or what is real, mental outlook that sees things as they actually are; the principle in art and literature of representing life as it actually is with a faithful recording of actual details; (*philos.*) the doctrine that general terms are not abstractions but have a real existence; the doctrine that external physical objects have a separate, real existence independent of the mind's perception and sensation of them.

REALIST, [rē′-al-ist], *n.* one who supports or believes in the philosophical doctrine of realism; a man who claims to see life as it actually is; a follower or disciple of realism in art and literature.

REALISTIC, [rē′-al-ist′-ik], *adj.* pertaining to, characteristic of, the realists or realism; actual; practical.

REALISTICALLY, [rē′-al-ist′-ik-al-i], *adv.* in realistic fashion.

REALITY, [rē-al′-i-ti], *n.* the state or quality of being real, actual existence; fact; the real nature of anything, the real thing; realistic quality. [MedL. *realitas*].

REALIZABLE, [rē′-al-īz-abl], *adj.* able to be realized.

REALIZATION, [rē′-al-īz-ā′-shun], *n.* the act of forming a clear and full conception of or becoming fully aware in the mind of; the bringing into being or achievement; the act of converting into cash.

REALIZE, [rē′-al-īz], *v.t.* to comprehend clearly, to bring home to oneself, to become fully conscious or aware of, to make real, to achieve, bring into existence as an accomplished fact; to acquire, build up, to obtain, fetch by sale; to convert into money or cash.

ō (bōne), ī (fīne), o͞o (fo͞od), o͝o (pu͝t), u (up), th (think), TH (that), zh (azure), † = obsolete, ~ = related to.

REALLIANCE, [re′-al-ī′-ants], *n.* a renewed alliance.

REALLY, [rē′-a-li], *adv.* actually, truly, in point of fact; a mild exclamation of surprise or protest and for emphasis.

REALM, [relm], *n.* a kingdom, country, or territory ruled over by a king or queen; sphere, domain, province; (*bot., zool.*) a primary division of the earth's surface from the point of view of distribution of plants and animals. [OFr. *reaume, realme*].

REALNESS, [rē′-al-nes], *n.* the state or property of being real; actuality.

REALPOLITIK, [rā-ahl′-pol-i-tēk′], *n.* the theory and practice of material self-interest in international politics. [Germ. *real* actual and *politik* politics].

REALTOR, [rē-al′-ter], *n.* (*U.S.*) one who deals in real estate.

REALTY, [rē′-al-ti], *n.* (*leg.*) real property; real estate.

REAM (1), [rēm], *n.* a quantity of paper consisting usually of 20 quires or 480 sheets, but often consisting of 500 or 516 sheets to allow for wastage; (*fig.*) (*pl.*) a great mass of writing or paper; **printer's r.,** a ream of 21½ quires or 516 sheets. [OFr. *rayme*].

REAM (2), [rēm], *v.t.* to bevel out; to enlarge (a hole or gunbore) by using a special tool. [OE. **reman* to make room].

REAMER, [rēm′-er], *n.* a tool for enlarging or shaping holes; a rimer.

REANIMATE, [rē-an′-im-āt], *v.t.* to revive, resuscitate, to liven up, hearten.

REAMER

REANIMATION, [rē-an-im-ā′-shun], *n.* the act or process of reanimating; the state of being reanimated.

REANNEX, [rē-an-eks′], *v.t.* to annex anew; to reunite.

REAP, [rēp], *v.t. and i.* to cut down (corn) with a sickle or reaping machine; to cut down the grain from; to obtain by reaping; (*fig.*) to gather, to receive as a reward or the fruits of some action or behaviour; (*fig.*) to receive. [OE. *ripan*].

REAPER, [rēp′-er], *n.* one who reaps; a machine for reaping.

REAPING-HOOK, [rēp′-ing-hŏŏk′], *n.* a sickle, a tool used in reaping.

REAPING-MACHINE, [rēp′-ing-mash-ēn′], *n.* a machine for reaping corn.

REAPPEAR, [rē′-a-pēer′], *v.i.* to appear again, after having disappeared for a time.

REAPPEARANCE, [rē′-a-pēer′-ants], *n.* a fresh appearance.

REAPPLY, [rē′-a-plī′], *v.t. and i.* to apply afresh.

REAPPOINT, [rē′-a-point′], *v.t.* to appoint again to the post previously held.

REAPPOINTMENT, [rē′-a-point′-ment], *n.* a renewed appointment.

REAPPORTION, [rē′-a-paw′-shun], *v.t.* to apportion again.

REAR (1), [rēer], *n.* that which is behind; that part of an army, navy, procession, etc., which comes last in order, or which follows behind the rest; the back part of anything; the place or position behind; **in the r.,** behind the rest; from behind. [~ARREAR].

REAR (2), [rēer], *v.t.* to raise, lift; to breed, grow; to nourish; (*archaic*) to set up; *v.i.* to rise up on the hind legs. [OE. *ræran* to raise].

REAR-ADMIRAL, [rēer′-ad′-mi-ral], *n.* a rank in the British Navy between those of captain and vice-admiral.

REAR-ARCH, [rēer′-ahch], *n.* (*arch.*) the inner arch of a window, doorway, etc., *esp.* when of a different size or shape from the outer arch.

REAR-COMMODORE, [rēer′-kom′-o-daw(r)], *n.* the lowest grade of commodore.

REAR-GUARD, [rēer′-gahd], *n.* a special body of troops marching in the rear of an army, and protecting it from attacks from behind, *esp.* when retreating; **r. action,** an engagement fought by the rear-guard to assist and protect the retreat of the main body of troops.

REARISE, (rearose, rearisen), [rē′-a-rīz′], *v.i.* to arise again.

REAR-LINE, [rēer′-līn], *n.* the line at the rear of an army.

REARM, [rē-ahm′], *v.t.* to furnish with fresh arms and fighting equipment; *v.i.* to arm again, to increase and strengthen one's fighting forces and resources.

REARMAMENT, [rē-ahm′-a-ment], *n.* the act or process of rearming, the piling up of war materials.

REARMOST, [rēer′-mōst], *adj.* last in position, coming at the end, hindmost.

REARMOUSE†, REREMOUSE†, [rēer′-mows], *n.* a bat. [OE. *hreremus*].

REARRANGE, [rē′-a-rānj′], *v.t.* to arrange or put in a new order.

REARRANGEMENT, [rē′-a-rānj′-ment], *n.* the act of putting into fresh order.

REAR-RANK, [rēer′-rangk′], *n.* the line of men on parade behind the front rank.

REARWARD (1), REREWARD†, [rēer′-werd], *n.* the rear part or position.

REARWARD (2), [rēer′-werd], *adj. and adv.* in or towards the rear.

REASCEND, [rē′-a-send′], *v.t. and i.* to mount again, to ascend afresh.

REASCENSION, [rē′-a-sen′-shun], *n.* the act of reascending; a remounting. [RE (1) and ASCENSION].

REASON (1), [rē′-zon], *n.* that power of the mind by which we think, deduce conclusions, or draw valid inferences from facts, and make judgments from observation; the mind in its normal state, sanity; the logical motive, ground, or justification for saying or doing a particular thing; the cause or series of connected events, circumstances, etc., producing a particular result or happening; that which is according to reason or logic, commonsense, logical argument, sensible thought or behaviour; (*log.*) the premise, *esp.* the minor premise, of an argument; **it stands to r.,** it is obvious or only to be expected; **to have neither rhyme nor r.,** to be sheer nonsense. [OFr. *raisun* from L. *ratio*].

REASON (2), [rē′-zon], *v.t.* to base on reason; to persuade by reasoning (with *into* or *out of*); to examine or discuss in a logical or sensible manner; *v.i.* to exercise the faculty of reason, to think logically, deduce observations, make (sound) judgments; to argue, debate, think. [*Prec.*].

REASONABLE, [rē′-zon-abl], *adj.* fair, just, moderate; in accordance with, or conforming to, reason; governed by, or exercising, reason, sensible, open to reason; endowed with reason, able to reason. [OFr. *raisonable*].

REASONABLENESS, [rē′-zon-abl-nes], *n.* the quality of being reasonable.

REASONABLY, [rē′-zon-ab-li], *adv.* in a reasonable manner, within reason.

REASONER, [rē′-zon-er], *n.* one who reasons or argues.

REASONING (1), [rē′-zon-ing], *n.* the exercise of the power of reason; reasons or arguments given or used, method of argumentation.

REASONING (2), [rē′-zon-ing], *adj.* able to reason, endowed with, and exercising, reason; used in reasoning, that reasons.

REASONLESS, [rē′-zon-les], *adj.* void of reason, irrational, illogical, senseless.

REASSEMBLE, [rē′-as-embl′], *v.t.* to put together again, to gather together again; *v.i.* to come or collect together again.

REASSERT, [rē′-a-surt′], *v.t.* to assert again, reiterate.

REASSESS, [rē′-a-ses′], *v.t.* to assess afresh.

REASSESSMENT, [rē′-a-ses′-ment], *n.* the act of assessing afresh.

REASSIGN, [rē′-a-sīn′], *v.t.* to assign again or back.

REASSUME, [rē′-a-sewm′], *v.t.* to assume once more.

REASSURANCE, [rē′-a-shŏŏer′-ants], *n.* repeated or renewed assurance, restored confidence; a second insurance against loss or damage.

REASSURE, [rē′-a-shŏŏer′], *v.t.* to dispel the doubts, fears, anxieties of, etc., to give fresh confidence to, to restore courage to; to insure a second time against loss or damage.

REASSURING, [rē′-a-shŏŏer′-ing], *adj.* comforting, restoring courage and hope, renewing confidence.

REASTY, [rēs′-ti], *adj.* (*dial.*) rancid. [RESTY].

REATTACH, [rē′-a-tach′], *v.t.* to attach again.

REAUMUR, Réaumur, [rā′-ō-myŏŏer], *adj.* relating to Réaumur or the thermometric scale he invented, in which the freezing point is zero degrees and the boiling point eighty degrees. [R. A. F. de *Réaumur*, a French physicist].

REAVE†, REIVE, (reft), [rēv], *v.t. and i.* to plunder, ravage, seize unlawfully. [OE. *reafian*].

REAVER, [rēv′-er], *n.* a robber, plunderer. [OE. *reafere*].

REBAPTIZE, [rē′-bap-tīz′], *v.t.* to baptize a second time, to give a fresh name to.

REBATE (1), [rē′-bāt], *n.* a deduction, discount from the full price; a repayment. [Fr. *rabat*].

REBATE (2), see RABBET (1).

REBATE† (3), [rē-bāt′], *n.* a kind of hard freestone. [Unkn.].

REBATE (4), [rē'-bāt], *v.t.* (*her.*) to cut off (a point or projection) from a charge; to diminish (a charge) by cutting off an end portion; (*rare*) to blunt; to diminish. [OFr. *rabattre*].
REBEC, [re'-bek], *n.* an ancient Moorish three-stringed fiddle. [OFr. *rebec* from Arab. *rebab*].
REBEL (1), [reb'-el], *n.* one who defies legally established authority, *esp.* one who revolts against a lawful government; a person who resists control or discipline or convention, an insubordinate, untractable person. [Fr. *rebelle*].
REBEL (2), [reb'-el], *adj.* in revolt, rebellious; of, pertaining to, rebels.
REBEL (3), (**rebelling, rebelled**), [ri-bel'], *v.i.* to revolt, to rise up in arms and seek to overthrow the lawful government or ruler; to feel an overpowering distaste or repugnance, to resist, oppose, react against, from a strong feeling of aversion to. [Fr. *rebeller* from L. *rebellare* to make war again].
REBELLION, [ri-bel'-yun], *n.* armed insurrection against, or open resistance to, lawfully established government or authority, a state of revolt; deliberate unconcealed resistance to any form of control. [L. *rebellio* renewal of war].
REBELLIOUS, [ri-bel'-yus], *adj.* engaged in rebellion; insubordinate; characterized by rebellion; belonging to, connected with, rebels or rebellion; (*med.*) difficult to treat, hard to cure.
REBELLIOUSLY, [ri-bel'-yus-li], *adv.* in a rebellious spirit or manner.
REBELLIOUSNESS, [ri-bel'-yus-nes], *n.* the quality or condition of being rebellious.
REBIND, (**rebound**), [rē'-bīnd'], *v.t.* to bind anew, to put a fresh binding on.
REBINDING, [rē'-bīnd'-ing], *n.* the process of binding anew; a fresh binding.
REBIRTH, [rē'-burth'], *n.* (*fig.*) a fresh birth.
REBITE, [rē'-bīt'], *v.t.* to sharpen the lines of an engraved plate by biting in again with acid.
REBOANT, [ri-bō'-ant], *adj.* rebellowing, re-echoing loudly. [L. *reboans*].
REBOIL, [rē'-boil'], *v.t. and i.* to boil again.
REBORE (1), [rē'-baw(r)'], *n.* the act of reboring; the process of being rebored.
REBORE (2), [rē'-baw(r)'], *v.t.* to bore again; to provide (the cylinder of an internal combustion engine) with a fresh bore.
REBOUND (1), [rē'-bownd], *n.* the act or process of rebounding, power of rebounding, resilience, bounce.
REBOUND (2), [rē'-bownd'], *adj.* that has been bound again, provided with a new binding. [*P.pt.* of REBIND].
REBOUND (3), [ri-bownd'], *v.i.* to bound back after striking some hard resisting surface; to come back (upon); to recoil. [OFr. *rebonder*].
REBUFF (1), [ri-buf'], *n.* a sudden sharp check, a snub, a point-blank refusal to an offer or to advances; a set-back to hopes or progress. [OFr. *rebuffe*].
REBUFF (2), [ri-buf'], *v.t.* to check, snub, to repel coldly and severely. [OFr. *rebuffer*].
REBUILD, [rē'-bild'], *v.t.* to build up again, *esp.* what has been demolished or fallen into decay, to restore.
REBUKE (1), [ri-bewk'], *n.* a reproof, reprimand, reprehension, merited censure.
REBUKE (2), [ri-bewk'], *v.t.* to reprove, censure, express merited disapproval of. [AFr. *rebuker* to beat].
REBUKINGLY, [ri-bewk'-ing-li], *adv.* by way of rebuke.
REBURY, [rē'-be'-ri], *v.t.* to inter again.
REBUS, [rē'-bus], *n.* a kind of puzzle in which combinations of figures, pictures, objects, letters, etc., represent a word or phrase; (*her.*) a coat of arms which bears an allusion to the name of the person bearing it. [L. *rebus* by things].
REBUT, (**rebutting, rebutted**), [ri-but'], *v.t.* to repel, check, refute, disprove; (*leg.*) to oppose, answer, meet, show to be false, by argument, plea, or other counteracting proof. [AFr. *reboter*].
REBUTTABLE, [ri-but'-abl], *adj.* capable of being rebutted.
REBUTTAL, [ri-but'-al], *n.* the act of refuting; the production of evidence in refutation of a previous statement made in a legal trial.
REBUTTER, [ri-but'-er], *n.* (*leg.*) the reply of a defendant to a plaintiff's surrejoinder.
RECALCITRANCE, [ri-kal'-sit-rants], *n.* the condition of being recalcitrant, recalcitrant nature or conduct.
RECALCITRANT, [ri-kal'-sit-rant], *adj.* unsubmissive, refractory, wayward, refusing to submit to control or discipline. [L. *recalcitrans*].
RECALL (1), [ri-kawl'], *n.* a calling back, an order, message, or invitation to return; (*milit.*) a signal to return to camp or to a certain place; power of remembering, calling back or revoking, reversal or annulment.
RECALL (2), [ri-kawl'], *v.t.* to call back, to summon or order to return; to remember; to bring to mind, cause to remember; to revive, restore; to bring back, to revoke, annul, cancel, rescind.
RECALLABLE, [ri-kawl'-abl], *adj.* able to be recalled, revocable.
RECANT, [ri-kant'], *v.t. and i.* to retract, take back, renounce as being wrong, *esp.* applied to religious doctrines when formally repudiated in public. [L. *recantare* to sing again, recant].
RECANTATION, [rē'-kant-ā'-shun], *n.* the act of recanting, formal repudiation.
RECAPACITATE, [rē'-kap-as'-it-āt], *v.t.* to make legally eligible or competent again.
RECAPITULATE, [rē'-kap-it'-yōō-lāt], *v.t.* to go over again briefly, by way of summary or conclusion, the principal facts, points, or arguments of. [L. *recapitulare*].
RECAPITULATION, [rē'-kap-it-yōō-lā'-shun], *n.* the act of recapitulating; a summary of the principal points; (*biol.*) repetition of the principal stages a species has passed through in the course of its evolution, during the growth of an animal of that species. [L. *recapitulatio*].
RECAPITULATORY, [rē'-kap-it-yōō-lāt'-er-i], *adj.* repeating in a condensed form, summarizing, that recapitulates.
RECAPTION, [rē-kap'-shun], *n.* (*leg.*) a second distress before a suit, arising after the first distress has been settled; peaceful recovery, without the aid of the law, of property and possessions wrongfully stolen or seized from one.
RECAPTOR, [rē-kapt'-or], *n.* one who recaptures; (*leg.*) one who takes property or possession by means of a recaption. [RE (1) and CAPTOR].
RECAPTURE (1), [rē-kap'-cher], *n.* a retaking or capture again; that which is recaptured.
RECAPTURE (2), [rē'-kap'-cher], *v.t.* to capture again.
RECAST (1), [rē'-kahst'], *n.* the act of recasting; the state of being recast; that which is recast.
RECAST (2), [rē'-kahst'], *v.t.* to cast again, to mould in a new form; to compute again (accounts, etc.); to plan again, reconstruct; (of a play) to provide with a fresh cast; to cause to play a different part or character.
RECEDE, [ri-sēd'], *v.i.* to move backwards or to a more distant position; to slope backwards; to fade away into the background; to retreat, depart, to suffer a decline, to slump slightly. [L. *recedere*].
RE-CEDE, [rē-sēd'], *v.t.* to cede back, to grant or yield to a former possessor.
RECEIPT (1), [ri-sēt'], *n.* the act of receiving; the fact of being received; (*hist.*) the place where anything is received; the amount received (usually in *pl.*); a written acknowledgment of anything received, *esp.* of money received in payment, or of goods received; a recipe, prescription. [AFr. *receite*].
RECEIPT (2), [ri-sēt'], *v.t.* to give a receipt for, affix a receipt to. [*Prec.*].
RECEIVABLE, [ri-sēv'-abl], *adj.* capable of being received.
RECEIVABLENESS, [ri-sēv'-abl-nes], *n.* capability of being received.
RECEIVE, [ri-sēv'], *v.t.* to obtain, acquire, take as being offered, sent, gained, due or dealt; to accept; to contain, harbour; to meet with; to bear, support, take; to admit to one's presence; to welcome formally and individually as a guest or visitor; to treat, hear, welcome; to recognize as valid, acknowledge as true; *v.i.* to accept, obtain, acquire; (*eccles.*) to consume part of the consecrated elements; to entertain guests or visitors; (*tennis, fives, etc.*) to (stand ready to) return the service; **to r. the sacrament**, to partake of the consecrated elements in the communion service. [AFr. *receivre* from L. *recipere*].
RECEIVED, [ri-sēvd], *adj.* generally recognized or admitted as true; standard, correct, generally accepted as proper.
RECEIVER, [ri-sēv'-er], *n.* one who receives; (*leg.*) a person appointed by law to receive money due, to administer the property of a bankrupt, infant, etc., or property or estate of which the ownership is in dispute; a fence; that which receives, a vessel for receiving and condensing the products of distillation; a

vessel for receiving and containing gases; a vessel on the plate of an air pump for producing a vacuum; the earpiece of a telephone; the apparatus which detects and rectifies electro-magnetic waves in a wireless set; **Official R.**, an officer of the bankruptcy court who takes possession of the debtor's assets when the receiving order is made.

RECEIVERSHIP, [ri-sēv'-er-ship], *n.* the office of an Official Receiver, the term of office of an Official Receiver.

RECEIVING (1), [ri-sēv'-ing], *n.* the act of one who receives; the crime of receiving goods known to have been stolen.

RECEIVING (2), [ri-sēv'-ing], *adj.* that receives, intended to receive; **r. order**, an official order to appoint a person to administer an estate in bankruptcy.

RECENCY, [rē'-sen-si], *n.* the quality of being recent.

RECENSION, [ri-sen'-shun], *n.* the critical revision of a text; a text so revised. [L. *recensio* reviewing].

RECENT, [rē'-sent], *adj.* of late origin or occurrence, new, fresh. [L. *recens*].

RECENTLY, [rē'-sent-li], *adv.* at a recent date, lately, not long ago.

RECENTNESS, [rē'-sent-nes], *n.* the quality of being recent.

RECEPTACLE, [ri-sept'-akl], *n.* that which holds, contains or receives anything, a vessel, container, repository, store place; (*bot.*) the apex of the peduncle, forming the support of a head of flowers; the axis in certain forms of inflorescence; the axis bearing the reproductive organs in ferns, mosses, fungi, etc. [L. *receptaculum* reservoir].

RECEPTACLE

RECEPTACULAR, [rē'-sept-ak'-yōō-ler], *adj.* (*bot.*) relating to the receptacle, or growing on it.

RECEPTIBILITY, [re-sept'-ib-il'-i-ti], *n.* the possibility of receiving or of being received.

RECEPTIBLE, [ri-sept'-ibl], *adj.* able to receive or be received. [LL. *receptibilis*].

RECEPTION, [ri-sep'-shun], *n.* the act of receiving, the state of being received; formal and official welcoming of persons as guests or visitors; an occasion or gathering for such a welcoming; the manner of welcoming, receiving or greeting anyone or anything; admission, acceptance; the process of absorption by the mind; **r. area**, a district considered to be safe from bombing and suitable for reception of evacuees in wartime; **r. order**, an order for the detention of a lunatic in an asylum or similar public institution; **r.-room**, a living-room as distinct from other rooms. [L. *receptio*].

RECEPTIONIST, [ri-sep'-shun-ist], *n.* one employed to receive people, *esp.* one employed to receive guests, visitors or clients and to book appointments.

RECEPTIVE, [ri-sept'-iv], *adj.* able to receive, susceptible to ideas or impressions. [MedL. *receptivus*].

RECEPTIVELY, [ri-sept'-iv-li], *adv.* in receptive fashion.

RECEPTIVITY, [rē'-sept-iv'-i-ti], *n.* the state or quality of being receptive.

RECESS (1), [ri-ses'], *n.* withdrawing or retirement; cessation from work or employment, suspension of business, *esp.* of Parliament or of a court of law; (*U.S.*) vacation, holiday; place of retirement; a retired, secluded spot; a hollowed space, alcove or part set back in a wall; an indentation or creek in a coastline; (*bot. and anat.*) a cleft. [L. *recessus* a going back].

RECESS (2), [ri-ses'], *v.t.* to make a recess in; to set in a recess. [L. *recessus*, *p.pt.* of *recedere* to go back].

RECESSION, [ri-sesh'-un], *n.* the act of withdrawing or retiring from a place; the act of receding; (*econ.*) a slackening of trade and industry. [L. *recessio*].

RE-CESSION, [rē'-sesh'-un], *n.* the act of ceding back again, restoration to a former possessor.

RECESSIONAL (1), [ri-sesh'-un-al], *n.* a hymn sung during the recession of choir and clergy from the church after the service.

RECESSIONAL (2), [ri-sesh'-un-al], *adj.* pertaining to a recession of choir and clergy after the service; pertaining to a recess of Parliament.

RECESSIVE, [ri-ses'-iv], *adj.* receding, tending to recede; (*biol.*) (of a characteristic) tending to be replaced in the offspring by a dominant trait of the other parent.

RECHABITES, [rek'-a-bīts], *n.(pl.)* among the Jews, the descendants of Jonadab, the son of Rechab, who bound themselves, among other things, to abstain from wine; a society of abstainers from alcoholic indulgence.

RECHARGE (1), [rē'-chahj'], *n.* a second charge.

RECHARGE (2), [rē'-chahj'], *v.t. and i.* to charge again, to reload; to accuse again; to attack anew.

RECHARTER, [rē'-chaht'-er], *v.t.* to charter again.

RECHAUFFE, réchauffé, [rā-shōf'-ā], *n.* a rehash. [Fr. *réchauffé* warmed up again].

RECHERCHE, recherché, [re-shāer'-shā], *adj.* choice, rare, much sought after, carefully chosen. [Fr. *recherché*].

RECHRISTEN, [rē'-kris'-en], *v.t.* to give a fresh name to.

RECIDIVISM, [ri-sid'-iv-izm], *n.* habitual indulgence in, or relapse into, crime. [Fr. *récidivisme*].

RECIDIVIST, [ri-sid'-iv-ist], *n.* a habitual and incorrigible criminal, one who continually relapses into crime after punishment. [Fr. *récidiviste*].

RECIPE, [res'-ip-ē], *n.* a list of ingredients and quantities to be used, together with instructions for their mixing and preparation into a food or drink; (*med.*) †a prescription; a remedy, a means of acquiring and maintaining. [L. *recipe* take].

RECIPIENCY, [ri-sip'-i-en-si], *n.* the fact of receiving.

RECIPIENT (1), [ri-sip'-i-ent], *n.* one who receives.

RECIPIENT (2), [ri-sip'-i-ent], *adj.* receiving, receptive. [L. *recipiens*].

RECIPROCAL (1), [ri-sip'-rok-al], *n.* that which is complementary, a counterpart, corresponding thing; (*math.*) the result of dividing unity by a given number or quantity, the reciprocal of 8 being ⅛.

RECIPROCAL (2), [ri-sip'-rōk-al], *adj.* shared or experienced equally by each of two parties for the other, mutual, felt or done in return for some similar thing received; complementary, inversely equivalent or corresponding; (*gram.*) expressing mutual relationship; (*gram.*) reflexive; (*log.*) mutually convertible or interchangeable; **r. ratio**, (*math.*) the ratio between the reciprocals of two quantities; **r. terms**, (*log.*) terms that have the same signification, and are mutually convertible. [L. *reciprocus*].

RECIPROCALITY, [ri-sip'-rōk-al'-i-ti], *n.* the state or property of being reciprocal.

RECIPROCALLY, [ri-sip'-rōk-a-li], *adv.* mutually, in return, conversely; (*math.*) inversely.

RECIPROCALNESS, [ri-sip'-rōk-al-nes], *n.* the quality of being reciprocal.

RECIPROCATE, [ri-sip'-rōk-āt], *v.t.* to give and take, to return in like manner, to exchange mutually; to cause to move backwards and forwards in a straight line; (*math.*) to determine the reciprocal to; *v.i.* (of a piston or machinery) to alternate, to move backwards and forwards in a straight line; to do likewise in return, to give and take, to make a similar gesture, to act reciprocally; (*math.*) to change by reciprocation. [~L. *reciprocare*].

RECIPROCATING, [ri-sip'-rōk-āt-ing], *adj.* moving alternately backwards and forwards along a straight line.

RECIPROCATION, [ri-sip'-rōk-ā'-shun], *n.* the act of reciprocating, reciprocal interchange of acts, giving and returning, mutual exchange; motion backwards and forwards along a straight line. [L. *reciprocatio*].

RECIPROCITY, [res'-ip-ros'-i-ti], *n.* the state of being reciprocal; mutual giving and taking between two parties, equal rights or benefits that are mutually granted, *esp.* in trading and commercial relations.

RECISION, [ri-sizh'-un], *n.* the act of cutting off or back. [L. *recisio*].

RECITAL, [ri-sīt'-al], *n.* the act of reciting; that which is recited, a detailed account, rehearsal, list or enumeration of a number of things, happenings, etc., a narrative, tale, story; a musical performance by a single vocal or instrumental artist, a musical performance devoted to the works of a single composer, or single period in musical history; an entertainment at which selections from the works of a single author or literary "school" are read aloud; (*leg.*) a formal statement of facts in a legal or official document, the part of the document devoted to this.

RECITATION, [res'-it-ā'-shun], *n.* the act of reciting; the speaking in public of a composition or extract, in prose or verse, previously learnt off by heart; the passage or composition recited or chosen to be recited. [L. *recitatio* a reading aloud].

RECITATIVE (1), [res'-it-at-ēv'], *n.* a kind of declamatory singing in opera or oratorio, to the accompaniment of occasional chords or with full accompaniment, as a means of expressing narrative and dialogue musically; passages sung in this way. [It. *recitativo*].

RECITATIVE (2), [res'-it-at-iv'], *adj.* of the nature of, in the form of, recitative.

RECITE, [ri-sīt'], *v.t.* to repeat aloud from memory; to relate, narrate, enumerate, give a verbal account of; (*leg.*) to state in a deed or document; *v.i.* to repeat aloud in public pieces of poetry or prose previously learnt by heart. [L. *recitare* to read aloud].

RECITER, [ri-sīt'-er], *n.* one who recites; a narrator; a book containing selections for recitation.

RECK, [rek], *v.t.* *and i.* (*poet.*) †to care for or about, to mind, to be concerned about; to know, be aware of; *impers.* to concern, trouble, bother. [OE. *reccan*].

RECKLESS, [rek'-les], *adj.* rash, not caring at all, without consideration. [OE. *recceleas*].

RECKLESSLY, [rek'-les-li], *adv.* in a reckless manner.

RECKLESSNESS, [rek'-les-nes], *n.* extreme heedlessness or carelessness, the quality of being reckless.

RECKON, [rek'-on], *v.t.* to count up, calculate; to include, class, set in the number of; to account, regard, judge; to think; *v.i.* to calculate, count; to guess, conclude, think, suppose; **to r. on**, to rely on, count on, depend on; **to r. with**, to have to deal with, to take into account; to deal with, settle accounts with. [OE. *gerecenian*].

RECKONER, [rek'-on-er], *n.* one who reckons; that which assists in reckoning; a book of calculations; a ready-reckoner.

RECKONING, [rek'-on-ing], *n.* the act of one who reckons; the act of counting or calculating; a statement of accounts or charges, a bill of charges incurred; manner of counting; (*naut.*) calculation of a ship's position from the account of the ship's course and progress in a log-book, or observation of the sun or stars; **day of r.**, a day on which all accounts must be paid, settling day; Judgment Day.

RECLAIM (1), [ri-klām'], *n.* recovery, restoration, reclamation.

RECLAIM (2), [ri-klām'], *v.t.* to claim back; to call back from error into the right way, to reform; to tame and train (a hawk); to recover from the sea or from being waste land; *v.i.* †to cry out in protest; (*Scots leg.*) to appeal to the Inner House of the Court of Session against judgments by the Lord Ordinary. [OFr. *reclamer*].

RECLAIMABLE, [ri-klām'-abl], *adj.* capable of being reclaimed.

RECLAIMING, [ri-klām'-ing], *adj.* tending to reclaim; (*Scots leg.*) appealing.

RECLAMATION, [rē'-klam-ā'-shun], *n.* the act of bringing back from error, barbarism, or wrong-doing; the act of bringing under cultivation waste land; the act of protesting or remonstrating. [L. *reclamatio*].

RECLAME, réclame, [rā-klahm'], *n.* notoriety and the art of achieving it, self-publicity. [Fr. *réclame* advertisement].

RECLINATION, [rek'-lin-ā'-shun], *n.* the act of leaning or reclining. [L. *reclinatio*].

RECLINE, [ri-klīn'], *v.i.* to lie down, to rest leaning back upon something. [L. *reclinare* to bend back].

RECLINER, [ri-klīn'-er], *n.* one who, or that which, reclines.

RECLOSE, [rē'-klōz'], *v.t.* to close or shut anew.

RECLOTHE, [rē'-klōTH'], *v.t.* to dress in fresh garments; to put garments on again.

RECLUSE, [ri-klōōs'], *n.* one who lives in seclusion; a hermit, anchorite or monk who confines himself to a cell. [Fr. *reclus*].

RECLUSORY, [ri-klōōs'-er-i], *n.* a hermitage, the cell to which a recluse confines himself.

RECOAL, [rē'-kōl'], *v.t.* to refill (the bunkers of a ship) with coal.

RECOCTION, [rē-kok'-shun], *n.* boiling or cooking a second time, a second preparation, a serving up a second time. [L. *recoquere* to recook].

RECOGNITION, [rek'-og-nish'-un], *n.* the act of recognizing; the state of being recognized; acknowledgment as being lawful, valid or authentic; notice, appreciation, acknowledgment; the fact of identifying a person or thing as being a particular person or thing, or as being the same as someone or something previously known, by perception or by the senses; formal acknowledgment of a sovereign or ruler by his people; formal admission of the new status of a country or state, *esp.* by one to whom it was formerly subject. [L. *recognitio*].

RECOGNITOR, [ri-kog'-nit-or], *n.* (*hist.*) a member of a jury. [MedL. *recognitor*].

RECOGNITORY, [ri-kog'-nit-er-i], *adj.* relating to, or connected with, recognition.

RECOGNIZABLE, [rek'-og-nīz'-abl], *adj.* able to be recognized, capable of recognition.

RECOGNIZABLY, [res'-og-nīz-ab-li], *adv.* so as to be recognized.

RECOGNIZANCE, [ri-kog'-niz-ants, ri-kon'-iz-ants], *n.* (*leg.*) an obligation, entered into before a court of record, to keep some guarantee, as to appear before a court on a certain date, keep the peace, pay a debt, etc., in default of which a sum of money is to be forfeited; the sum of money to be thus forfeited. [OFr. *reconaissance*].

RECOGNIZANT, [ri-kog'-nīz-ant], *adj.* that recognizes or acknowledges, displaying recognition.

RECOGNIZE, [rek'-og-nīz], *v.t.* to perceive by the senses as being a particular person or thing previously known or known about; to give tangible sign of recognition of by greeting, salutation, etc.; to admit as lawful, valid, or authentic; to realize, to accept as being true or as a fact; to appreciate or acknowledge in some tangible way; to acknowledge formally as possessing a certain status, position, or rank. [L. *recognoscere* to know again].

RECOIL (1), [ri-koil'], *n.* the act of rebounding or springing back, *esp.* the rebound of a gun when fired; a shrinking away from, feeling of repugnance.

RECOIL (2), [ri-koil'], *v.i.* to fall or draw back, retreat; to stagger back; to rebound, spring back; (of a gun) to kick; to shrink; **to r. from**, to feel disgust and loathing at; **to r. on**, to affect the one responsible, return to its source of origin. [OFr. *reculer*].

RECOILER, [ri-koil'-er], *n.* one who falls back or recoils.

RECOILING, [ri-koil'-ing], *adj.* that recoils, starting back.

RECOILINGLY, [ri-koil'-ing-li], *adv.* in a recoiling manner.

RECOIN, [rē'-koin'], *v.t.* to coin again, to mint anew.

RECOINAGE, [rē'-koin'-ij], *n.* the act of coining anew; new coinage.

RECOLLECT (1), [rek'-o-lekt'], *v.t.* to remember, recall, call to mind again.

RECOLLECT (2), see RECOLLET.

RE-COLLECT, [rē'-ko-lekt'], *v.t.* to collect again, to gather together again, to muster, rally. [L. *recollectus*, *p.pt.* of *recolligere*].

RECOLLECTION, [rek'-o-lek'-shun], *n.* the act of recollecting; the power of remembering, memory; that which is recollected.

RECOLLECTIVE, [rek'-o-lekt'-iv], *adj.* having the power of recollecting, that recollects.

RECOLLET, RECOLLECT, [rek'-ol-ā'], *n.* a member of a reformed branch of the Franciscan Order. [Fr. *récollet*].

RECOLONIZATION, [rē'-kol'-on-īz-ā'-shun], *n.* a fresh colonization.

RECOLONIZE, [rē'-kol'-on-īz], *v.t.* to colonize afresh.

RECOLOUR, [rē-kul'-er], *v.t.* to colour afresh.

RECOMBINATION, [rē'-kom'-bin-ā'-shun], *n.* a fresh combination.

RECOMBINE, [rē'-kom-bīn'], *v.t.* to combine afresh.

RECOMFORT, [rē-kum'-fert], *v.t.* to comfort afresh; to give new strength to. [Fr. *reconforter*].

RECOMMENCE, [rē'-kom-ents'], *v.t.* *and i.* to begin again, to start afresh.

RECOMMENCEMENT, [rē'-kom-ents'-ment], *n.* a new beginning, a starting again.

RECOMMEND, [rek'-o-mend'], *v.t.* to commend to favour, speak favourably of, as suitable for a certain use or for a particular position; to make acceptable; to commit, entrust to the care or keeping of another, to counsel, advise. [MedL. *recommendare*].

RECOMMENDABLE, [rek'-o-mend'-abl], *adj.* to be recommended; worthy of commendation.

RECOMMENDABLENESS, [rek'-o-mend'-abl-nes], *n.* the quality of being worthy of recommendation.

RECOMMENDABLY, [rek'-o-mend'-ab-li], *adv.* in a recommendable fashion.

RECOMMENDATION, [rek'-o-mend-ā'-shun], *n.* the act of recommending; that which recommends; qualities, qualifications serving to recommend a person to the favour of another; a letter, statement, or document requesting a favourable or kind reception for a person.

RECOMMENDATORY, [rek'-o-mend'-at-eri], *adj.* that recommends, serving to recommend.

RECOMMENDER, [rek'-o-mend'-er], *n.* one who recommends.

RECOMMISSION, [rē'-kom-ish'-un], *v.t.* to commission again.

RECOMMIT, (**recommitting, recommitted**),

[rē′-kom-it′], *v.t.* to commit again; (*parl.*) to refer (a Bill) again to committee.

RECOMMITTAL, [rē′-kom-it′-al], *n.* a second commitment; (*parl.*) a referring back of a bill to a committee.

RECOMMUNICATE, [rē′-kom-ewn′-ik-āt], *v.t. and i.* to communicate anew.

RECOMPACT, [rē′-kom-pakt′], *v.t.* to join afresh.

RECOMPENSE (1), [rek′-om-pents], *n.* that which is given or done in return for acts performed or things received, reward, compensation, reparation for wrong, loss, or injury undergone. [OFr. *recompense*].

RECOMPENSE (2), [rek′-om-pents], *v.t.* to requite, repay; to compensate, make amends to for some wrong, loss, or injury undergone. [LL. *recompensare*].

RECOMPENSER, [rek′-om-pen-ser], *n.* one who recompenses.

RECOMPILE, [rē′-kom-pīl′], *v.t.* to compile afresh.

RECOMPOSE, [rē′-kom-pōz′], *v.t.* to compose anew, to form or put together again in a different way, to adjust afresh; to cause to regain composure, to quiet anew.

RECOMPOSITION, [rē′-kom′-pōz-ish′-un], *n.* the act of recomposing, composition afresh.

RECOMPOUND, [rē′-kom-pownd′], *v.t.* to compound again, to remix.

RECONCILABLE, [rek′-on-sīl′-abl], *adj.* able to be reconciled.

RECONCILABLENESS, [rek′-on-sīl′-abl-nes], *n.* the quality of being reconcilable; consistency.

RECONCILABLY, [rek′-on-sīl′-ab-li], *adv.* in a reconcilable fashion.

RECONCILE, [rek′-on-sīl], *v.t.* (often followed by *to* or *with*) to restore to friendship, cause to be friends (of former enemies or persons temporarily at variance); to make consistent or compatible with; to settle, adjust; (*v. reflex.*) to acquiesce in; (*eccles.*) to consecrate afresh after profanation; (*shipbuilding*) to make flush with. [L. *reconciliare*].

RECONCILEMENT, [rek′-on-sīl′-ment], *n.* the act of reconciling, the state of being reconciled.

RECONCILER, [rek′-on-sīl-er], *n.* one who, or that which, reconciles.

RECONCILIATION, [rek′-on-sil′-i-ā′-shun], *n.* the act of reconciling persons at variance or things which seem to be opposed; the state of being reconciled.

RECONCILIATORY, [rek′-on-sil′-i-at-er-i], *adj.* intended or tending to reconcile.

RECONDENSATION, [rē′-kon′-dens-ā′-shun], *n.* the act or fact of recondensing.

RECONDENSE, [rē′-kon-dents′], *v.t. and i.* to condense afresh.

RECONDITE, [rek′-ond-īt], *adj.* obscure, hidden from view; abstruse; profound; dealing in abstruse matters. [L. *reconditus* hidden].

RECONDITION, [rē′-kon-dish′-un], *v.t.* to put into fresh condition, renovate, refit, repair.

RECONDUCT, [rē′-kon-dukt′], *v.t.* to lead back again.

RECONFIRM, [rē′-kon-furm′], *v.t.* to confirm afresh.

RECONJOIN, [rē′-kon-join′], *v.t.* to join together afresh.

RECONNAISSANCE, [ri-kon′-is-ants], *n.* the act of reconnoitring; (*milit.*) a detailed investigation of a region or district in order to find out its general characteristics and resources, the strength, arrangement, position, and movements of the enemy occupying it, etc.; an examination or survey preliminary to practical or scientific operations; a body of troops engaged in reconnoitring. [Fr. *reconnaissance*].

RECONNOITRE (1), [rek′-on-oit′-er], *n.* a reconnaissance.

RECONNOITRE (2), [rek′-on-oit′-er], *v.t.* to examine, explore, survey by way of reconnaissance; to view, inspect; *v.i.* to make a reconnaissance, to be engaged in the work of reconnaissance. [OFr. *reconnoître*].

RECONQUER, [rē′-kong′-ker], *v.t.* to conquer afresh, to recover by conquest.

RECONQUEST, [rē′-kong′-kwest], *n.* conquest back or again, a fresh conquest.

RECONSECRATE, [rē′-kon′-sik-rāt], *v.t.* to consecrate afresh.

RECONSECRATION, [rē′-kon-sik-rā′-shun], *n.* a fresh consecration.

RECONSIDER, [rē′-kon-sid′-er], *v.t.* to consider again or afresh with a view to changing or modifying.

RECONSIDERATION, [rē′-kon-sid′-er-ā′-shun], *n.* a fresh or renewed consideration.

RECONSTITUTE, [rē-kon′-sti-tewt], *v.t.* to constitute afresh; to reconstruct, reform.

RECONSTITUTION, [rē-kon′-sti-tew′-shun], *n.* the act of constituting afresh.

RECONSTRUCT, [rē′-kon-strukt′], *v.t.* to construct again; to rebuild, *esp.* to build up into what one supposes is the original form, from extant fragmentary remains or details.

RECONSTRUCTION, [rē′-kon-struk′-shun], *n.* the act of constructing again; that which is reconstructed.

RECONSTRUCTIVE, [rē′-kon-strukt′-iv], *adj.* that reconstructs, tending to reconstruct.

RECONVENE, [rē′-kon-vēn′], *v.t.* to summon again; *v.i.* to assemble again. [~MedL. *reconvenire*].

RECONVERSION, [rē′-kon-vur′-shun], *n.* a fresh conversion.

RECONVERT (1), [rē-kon′-vert], *n.* one who is reconverted.

RECONVERT (2), [rē′-kon-vurt′], *v.t.* to convert back again into the original form, state, or faith.

RECONVEY, [rē′-kon-vā′], *v.t.* (*leg.*) to transfer back to a former owner; (*rare*) to convey back again.

RECORD (1), [rek′-awd], *n.* a register, an official note of any fact, copy of any writing, or authentic account of any proceeding or event, preserved in writing; an authentic memorial or representation of something past; a thin, flat, hard circular disk containing a series of grooves made by a recording apparatus, which, when played on a gramophone or similar instrument, reproduces musical and other sounds; a unique phenomenon or feat, the best performance of the kind hitherto accomplished; (*leg.*) the formal written statements or pleadings of parties in a litigation, a written copy of the evidence and judgment of a lawsuit preserved for possible future reference; (*fig.*) the known facts of a person's ability or character as determined by previous actions; **on r.,** known, *esp.* from documentary evidence; **off the r.,** in confidence, not to be put on the record. [OFr. *record*].

RECORD (2), [ri-kawd′], *v.t.* to register, note, keep a record of, set down in writing; to preserve in a permanent fashion; to make a gramophone record of; to give (a vote, record); *v.i.* to make gramophone records. [OFr. *recorder* to repeat].

RECORDER, [ri-kawd′-er], *n.* one who records in writing, the judge presiding at the court of Quarter Sessions of a borough or city; that which records, an apparatus or instrument for recording sounds or signals; †an ancient form of flute.

RECORDER

RECORDERSHIP, [ri-kawd′-er-ship], *n.* the office or period of office of a recorder.

RECORDING (1), [ri-kawd′-ing], *n.* a record.

RECORDING (2), [ri-kawd′-ing], *adj.* registering, that records.

RECOUNT (1), [rē′-kownt], *n.* a second count.

RECOUNT (2), [rē-kownt′], *v.t.* to count a second time or over again.

RECOUNT (3), [ri-kownt′], *v.t.* to narrate, recite, to relate in detail. [AFr. *reconter*].

RECOUNTAL, [ri-kownt′-al], *n.* a narration or recital.

RECOUP, [rē-ko͞op′], *v.t.* to compensate, make good, indemnify; (*leg.*) to diminish by keeping back a part. [Fr. *recouper* to cut back].

RECOUPMENT, [rē-ko͞op′-ment], *n.* the act of recouping, that which is recouped.

RECOURSE, [ri-kaws′], *n.* resorting to a person, thing, or action for help or assistance. [Fr. *recours*].

RE-COVER, [rē′-kuv′-er], *v.t.* to provide with a new cover.

RECOVER, [ri-kuv′-er], *v.t.* to get back or obtain again, to regain; to make good, retrieve; to reclaim; (*leg.*) to get possession of again by judgment, to obtain by way of compensation; (*archaic*) to restore to health; *v.i.* to regain health after sickness or injury; to win back a former condition, position, or state, to improve one's position after a decline; (*comm.*) (of shares, etc.) to improve after a drop; (*leg.*) to succeed in a lawsuit involving a claim; (*fencing*) to resume a defensive position after attacking. [OFr. *recovrer*].

RECOVERABLE, [ri-kuv′-er-abl], *adj.* capable of being recovered or restored.

RECOVERABLENESS, [ri-kuv′-er-abl-nes], *n.* the quality of being recoverable.

RECOVERER, [ri-kuv′-er-er], *n.* one who recovers.

RECOVERY, [ri-kuv′-er-ɪ], *n.* the act of recovering;

the regaining of what has been lost or taken away; restoration to health from sickness; restoration to a former position; (*leg.*) the obtaining of anything by a judgment in one's favour in a court of law, the process to enable entailed estate to be transferred from one ownership to another. [AFr. *recoverie*].

RECREANCY, [rek'-ri-an-si], *n.* a cowardly yielding.

RECREANT (1), [rek'-ri-ant], *n.* a coward; an apostate, one who is false to his duty or principles.

RECREANT (2), [rek'-ri-ant], *adj.* crying for mercy, cowardly, craven; apostate, false to one's faith or duty. [OFr. *recreant*].

RECREANTLY, [rek'-ri-ant-li], *adv.* in a recreant manner, like a coward.

RECREATE, [rek'-ri-āt], *v.t. and i.* to refresh. [L. *recreare*].

RE-CREATE, [rē'-kri-āt'], *v.t.* to create or form afresh.

RECREATION, [rek'-ri-ā'-shun], *n.* refreshment of the body and mind after toil by taking part in some form of pleasurable voluntary activity, mental or physical; the act of reviving or refreshing the mind and body in this way; that which refreshes the mind and body after toil; amusement, diversion, entertainment, sport, etc.; **r. ground,** a playground, an enclosed space set apart for outdoor games. [L. *recreatio* refreshment].

RE-CREATION, [rē'-kri-ā'-shun], *n.* a forming anew; a fresh creation.

RECREATIVE, [rek'-ri-āt-iv], *adj.* providing recreation, tending to divert and refresh, giving new vigour and animation.

RECREATIVELY, [rek'-ri-āt-iv-li], *adv.* so as to provide recreation.

RECREATIVENESS, [rek'-ri-āt-iv-nes], *n.* the quality of being recreative.

RECREMENT, [rek'-ri-ment], *n.* superfluous matter separated from what is useful, dross, refuse, scum; (*physiol.*) waste products of the body, excretion; a fluid given out from the blood and later absorbed into it again. [L. *recrementum* refuse].

RECREMENTAL, [rek'-ri-mental], *adj.* pertaining to, consisting of, recrement.

RECREMENTITIAL, [rek'-ri-ment-ish'-al], *adj.* of the nature of dross, worthless, rubbishy.

RECRIMINATION, [ri-krim'-in-ā'-shun], *n.* the replying to one accusation with another, a countercharge to an accusation. [~MedL. *recriminare*].

RECRIMINATIVE, [ri-krim'-in-āt-iv], *adj.* retorting with counter-accusation.

RECRIMINATOR, [ri-krim'-in-āt-or], *n.* one who replies to a charge with a counter-accusation.

RECRIMINATORY, [ri-krim'-in-āt-er-i], *adj.* employing, of the nature of, consisting of, recrimination.

RECROSS, [rē'-kros'], *v.t. and i.* to cross again.

RECRUDESCE, [rē'-kroō-des'], *v.i.* to recur.

RECRUDESCENCE, [rē'-kroōd-es'-ents], *n.* a fresh outbreak, renewed activity, the act or state of breaking out again (of a sore, disease, epidemic, etc.).

RECRUDESCENT, [rē'-kroōd-es'-ent], *adj.* breaking out afresh with renewed activity. [L. *recrudescens*].

RECRUIT (1), [ri-kroōt'], *n.* a newly enlisted person in the army, navy, air force, police force, etc.; (*fig.*) a new member of any body, party, etc., one who has recently joined a movement, organization, etc. [Fr. *recrute* reinforcement].

RECRUIT (2), [ri-kroōt'], *v.t.* to seek or enlist reinforcements of (persons) for the army, navy, air force, police force, etc.; to supply (a regiment) with new men; (*rare*) to repair, restore, revive, build up (health, strength, etc.); to increase or maintain by the addition of recruits; *v.i.* to seek or enlist recruits or new members; (*rare*) to recuperate, gain new stores of strength, recover health. [Fr. *recruter* to levy troops].

RECRUITER, [ri-kroōt'-er], *n.* one who recruits, a recruiting officer.

RECRUITING, [ri-kroōt'-ing], *n.* the act of enlisting new members or fresh recruits.

RECRUITMENT, [ri-kroōt'-ment], *n.* the business of raising new supplies of men for an army, navy, air force, etc.; the act of recruiting new members.

RECRYSTALLIZE, [rē'-krist'-al-īz], *v.t. and i.* to subject to, undergo, recrystallization.

RECRYSTALLIZATION, [rē-krist'-al-iz-ā'-shun], *n.* a repeated crystallization from solution as a means of purifying chemicals.

RECTAL, [rek'-tal], *adj.* of, or pertaining to, the rectum.

RECTANGLE, [rekt'-ang'-gl], *n.* a plane, four-sided figure whose interior angles are right angles. [LL. *rectangulum* a right-angled triangle].

RECTANGLED, [rekt'-ang'-gld], *adj.* having one or more angles of ninety degrees.

RECTANGULAR, [rekt-ang'-gyoō-ler], *adj.* right-angled; having the shape of a rectangle.

RECTANGULARITY, [rekt-ang'-gyoō-la'-rit-i], *n.* the quality of being rectangular.

RECTANGULARLY, [rekt-ang'-gyoō-ler-li], *adv.* in a rectangular manner, at right angles.

RECTIFIABLE, [rek'-ti-fī-abl], *adj.* that may be put right or rectified.

RECTIFICATION, [rek'-ti-fik-ā'-shun], *n.* the act of rectifying, correcting, or putting right; (*geom.*) reduction of a curve to a straight line; (*chem.*) refinement or purification by repeated distillation; (*elect.*) conversion of an alternating current into a direct current. [L. *rectificatio*].

RECTIFIED, [rek'-ti-fīd], *adj.* put right; re-distilled, refined, purified (of spirit).

RECTIFIER, [rek'-ti-fī-er], *n.* one who, or that which, rectifies; one who refines spirits by repeated distillation, an apparatus used in this process; (*naut.*) †an instrument that shows the variations of the compass and rectifies a ship's course; (*elect.*) an apparatus or valve for transforming an alternating current into a direct current.

RECTIFY, [rek'-ti-fī], *v.t.* to put right, correct, amend; to remedy, reform; to refine by repeated distillation; to adjust, set right (an instrument, apparatus); (*geom.*) to reduce (a curve) to a straight line; (*elect.*) to transform (an alternating current) into a direct current. [LL. *rectificare* to correct].

RECTIGRADE, [rek'-ti-grād], *adj.* walking straight forwards. [L. *rectus* straight and GRADE].

RECTILINEAL, [rek'-ti-lin'-i-al], *adj.* rectilinear.

RECTILINEALLY, [rek'-ti-lin'-i-al-i], *adv.* in a straight line.

RECTILINEAR, [rek'-ti-lin'-i-er], *adj.* in a straight line, bounded by straight lines; (*arch.*) composed mainly of, exhibiting many, straight lines. [LL. *rectilineus* from *rectus* straight and *linea* line].

RECTILINEARLY, [rek'-ti-lin'-i-er-li], *adv.* rectilineally.

RECTIROSTRAL, [rek'-ti-ros'-tral], *adj.* possessing a straight beak. [L. *rectus* straight and *rostrum* beak].

RECTITIS, [rek-tī'-tis], *n.* inflammation of the rectum. [RECTUM and Gk. *itis* denoting inflammation].

RECTITUDE, [rek'-ti-tewd], *n.* rightness of principle or conduct, uprightness, integrity. [L. *rectitudo*].

RECTO, [rek'-tō], *n.* the right-hand page of an open book; the front, as opposed to the back, of a page. [L. *recto (folio)* on the right-hand page].

RECTOR, [rek'-ter], *n.* (*eccles.*) the priest holding a parish benefice who has the right to its great tithes; the head of a continental university; the head of various English and Scottish colleges and similar institutions. [L. *rector* ruler, leader].

RECTORATE, [rek'-ter-at], *n.* the office or position of rector.

RECTORIAL, [rek-taw'-ri-al], *adj.* relating to a rector.

RECTORSHIP, [rek'-ter-ship], *n.* the office or rank of rector; the period of office as a rector.

RECTORY, [rek'-ter-i], *n.* a benefice of which the holder is a rector; the house in which the rector of a parish lives. [MedL. *rectoria*].

RECTRICES, [rek-trī'-sēz], *n.(pl.)* the tail feathers of a bird, acting as a rudder. [L. *rectrices*, *pl.* of *rectrix* a female ruler or leader].

RECTUM, [rek'-tum], *n.* the final bottom section of the large intestine. [L. *rectum (intestinum)* straight (intestine)].

RECTUS, [rek'-tus], *n.* (*anat.*) one of several muscles in various parts of the human body, having straight fibres. [L. *rectus* straight].

RECUMBENCE, [ri-kumb'-ents], *n.* recumbency.

RECUMBENCY, [ri-kumb'-en-si], *n.* the state of being recumbent, a reclining position.

RECUMBENT, [ri-kumb'-ent], *adj.* leaning, reclining, reposing, lying down. [L. *recumbere*].

RECUMBENTLY, [ri-kumb'-ent-li], *adv.* in a recumbent fashion.

RECUPERABLE, [ri-kewp'-er-abl], *adj.* capable of recuperating. [OFr. *recuperable*].

RECUPERATE, [ri-kewp'-er-āt], *v.t.* to restore to health; *v.i.* to recover health and strength; to recover from monetary losses. [L. *recuperare* to recover].

RECUPERATION, [ri-kewp'-er-ā'-shun], *n.* recovery, *esp.* of health. [L. *recuperatio*].

RECUPERATIVE, [ri-kewp'-er-at-iv], *adj.* that recuperates or tends to recuperate, having the power to recuperate. [L. *recuperativus*].

RECUR, (**recurring, recurred**), [ri-kur'], *v.i.* to repeat itself; to return to the mind; to refer back, to

return; (*math.*) to be repeated indefinitely. [L. *recurrere* run back].
RECURRENCE, [ri-ku'-rents], *n.* the act of recurring, return, repeated occurrence; resort, recourse.
RECURRENT, [ri-ku'-rent], *adj.* returning, *esp.* from time to time, occurring again or repeatedly; (*anat.*) turned back so as to face the opposite direction.
RECURRING, [ri-kur'-ing], *adj.* returning, *esp.* periodically, occurring again repeatedly; (*math.*) repeated indefinitely.
RECURVE, [rē'-kurv'], *v.t.* to bend back; *v.i.* to be bent back, in the form of a curve, in the opposite direction. [L. *recurvare*].
RECURVIROSTER, [rē-kurv'-i-ros'-ter], *n.* the avocet, a bird whose beak bends upwards. [L. *recurvare* to bend back and *rostrum* beak].
RECUSANCY, [rek'-yōō-zan-si], *n.* the state of being recusant; nonconformity, refusal to attend the Church of England for public religious worship (*esp.* applied to Roman Catholics); refusal to obey authority.
RECUSANT (1), [rek'-yōō-zant], *n.* one who refuses to attend the Established Church for public religious worship, applied *esp.* to Roman Catholics in the 17th century; one who refuses to obey authority.
RECUSANT (2), [rek'-yōō-zant], *adj.* refusing to conform to state authority, *esp.* in religious matters. [L. *recusans, pres.pt.* of *recusare* to object].
RECUSATION, [rek'-yōō-zā'-shun], *n.* (*leg.*) the act of objecting to or challenging the judge appointed to hear the suit. [L. *recusatio* objection].
RED (1), [red], *n.* a primary colour of long wave-length forming one of the extremes of the visible spectrum; various objects of this colour, the red ball at billiards; the red colour in roulette; (*pl.*) red cattle; North American Indians; members of the Communist Party.
RED (2), [red], *adj.* being of the primary colour red; inflamed, bloodshot; ruddy; (*pol.*) pertaining or belonging to the Communist Party or extreme Left Wing Movement; **to paint the town r.,** to indulge in drunken riotous behaviour; **to see r.,** to become violently angry. [OE. *read*].
REDACT, [ri-dakt'], *v.t.* to arrange or reduce to a form suitable for publication, to edit. [L. *redactum, p.pt.* of *redigere* to gather together].
REDACTION, [ri-dak'-shun], *n.* the act of editing or arranging in a form suitable for publication; an edition.
REDACTOR, [ri-dakt'-er], *n.* an editor.
RED ADMIRAL, [red'-ad'-mi-ral], *n.* the brightly coloured butterfly, *Vanessa atalanta.*
REDAN, [ri-dan'], *n.* (*fort.*) a field-work with a salient angle formed by two projecting faces. [Fr. *redan*].
REDARGUE, [red-ah'-gew], *v.t.* (*Scots*) to refute, prove (an argument) wrong; to prove to be wrong by argument. [L. *redarguere*].
RED BOOK, [red'-bōōk], *n.* one of various official books, documents, or records bound in red, as a court directory, list of civil servants, etc.
REDBREAST, [red'-brest'], *n.* the European robin, *Erithacus rubecula,* so called from the colour of its breast.
REDBUD, [red'-bud], *n.* (*U.S.*) the Judas tree, a species of *Cercis.*
RED-BUTTON, [red'-but'-on], *n.* the official button worn on the cap to denote mandarins of the first and second rank.
REDCAP, [red'-kap'], *n.* the goldfinch; a goblin, sprite; (*coll.*) a military policeman.
RED-CEDAR, [red'-sē'-der], *n.* the tree, *Juniperus virginiana,* whose wood is widely used in the manufacture of pencils; the Moulmein cedar or toon-tree, *Cedrela toona;* the Australian tree, *Flindersia australis.*
RED CENT, [red'-sent'], *n.* a copper cent; **not a r.,** nothing at all.
RED-COAT†, [red'-kōt], *n.* a British soldier, from the colour of the tunic formerly worn.
RED CROSS, [red'-kros'], *n.* a red cross on a white background, used as the national emblem of England; the emblem borne by Christian soldiers fighting in the Crusades; the Geneva cross, the badge of the ambulance and hospital service organized under the Geneva Convention, a society organized in accordance with the Geneva Convention, 1864, to provide an ambulance and hospital service for those wounded in war.
RED CURRANT, [red'-ku'-rant], *n.* the currant, *Ribes rubrum,* the fruit of which is used in making jam, flavouring jelly, etc.; the fruit of this plant.
REDD, [red], *v.t.* to make tidy, arrange; to clear or make (a passage); to unravel; to separate (persons fighting). [Du. *reden*].
RED DEER, [red'-dēer'], *n.* a species of brown-coloured deer, *Cervus elaphus,* which is the largest native British deer.

RED DEER

REDDEN, [red'-en], *v.t.* to make red; *v.i.* to grow or become red; to blush.
REDDISH, [red'-ish], *adj.* rather red.
REDDISHNESS, [red'-ish-nes], *n.* the quality of being reddish.
REDDITION†, [red-ish'-un], *n.* restoration, restitution; surrender; moral application of a parable or comparison; a translation. [L. *redditio*].
REDDLE†, see RUDDLE.
REDE† (1), [rēd], *n.* counsel, advice; plot, scheme, plan; a tale, story, proverb. [OE. *ræd*].
REDE† (2), [rēd], *v.t.* to counsel, advise; to explain, guess. [OE. *rædan*].
REDEEM, [ri-dēm'], *v.t.* to purchase back, rebuy; to free (a mortgaged thing), obtain again by paying the stipulated sum; to rid oneself of (debt), to clear off by payment; to regain or recover by diligence and effort; to fulfil, make good; to make atonement for; to compensate for; to ransom, set free, rescue from restraining bonds; (*theol.*) to deliver from the bondage of sin and its penalties. [L. *redimere* to buy back].
REDEEMABLE, [ri-dēm'-abl], *adj.* that may be redeemed.
REDEEMABLENESS, [ri-dēm'-abl-nes], *n.* the quality of being redeemable.
REDEEMER, [ri-dēm'-er], *n.* one who redeems or ransoms; the Saviour, Jesus Christ.
REDELESS†, [rēd'-les], *adj.* without advice; unwise, foolish. [OE. *rædleas*].
REDELIVER, [rē'-di-liv'-er], *v.t.* to deliver back; to deliver again; to liberate again.
REDELIVERANCE, [rē'-di-liv'-er-ants], *n.* a fresh or new deliverance.
REDELIVERY, [rē'-di-liv'-er-i], *n.* a delivering back, restoration; a new liberation; a fresh delivery.
REDEMAND, [rē'-di-mahnd'], *v.t.* to demand back; to demand again.
REDEMISE, [rē'-dem-iz'], *n.* (*leg.*) reconveyance of land to one who has previously granted it by lease, deed, etc., to another.
REDEMPTION, [ri-demp'-shun], *n.* a buying back, release, or restoration of mortgaged or pledged property; the clearing off of a debt by payment of a lump sum; ransom, release, deliverance of slaves by making a payment; the act of delivering from evil ways; (*theol.*) the deliverance of sinners from the penalty and bondage of sin; the act of freeing, releasing, or recovery of anything; atonement for wrong done; that which redeems; **beyond r.,** without hope of recovery, restoration, or reformation. [L. *redemptio*].
REDEMPTIONER, [ri-demp'-shun-er], *n.* one who redeems himself from an obligation; (*U.S.*) an emigrant to U.S.A. who had to repay his passage money to the owners of the vessel out of his earnings upon arrival.
REDEMPTIONISTS, [ri-demp'-shun-ists], *n.(pl.)* an order of monks devoted to freeing Christian slaves or captives from slavery.
REDEMPTIVE, [ri-demp'-tiv], *adj.* pertaining to redemption, that redeems or tends to redeem.
REDEMPTORIST, [ri-demp'-ter-ist], *n.* a member of a Roman Catholic order of priests, founded in 1732 by St. Alphonsus Liguori for the religious instruction of the poor and the education of youth. [L. *redemptor*].
REDEMPTORISTINE, [ri-demp'-ter-ist'-ēn], *n.* one of an order of nuns connected with the Redemptorists.
REDEMPTORY, [ri-demp'-ter-i], *adj.* redeeming, serving to redeem.
RED ENSIGN, [red'-en'-sīn], *n.* the flag of the British merchant service.
RED-EYE, [red'-i], *n.* the rudd, a fish of the carp family, so called from its red iris; the American

rock-bass; the American green or blue-spotted sunfish.

RED-FISH, [red'-fish], *n.* a male salmon at spawning time; the salmon in general as distinct from fish with white flesh; the red gurnard; the Pacific blue-backed salmon, a species of *Oncorrhynchus*; the American red perch.

RED FLAG, [red'-flag'], *n.* the signal of danger; the symbol of revolution and of Communism; name of a song sung by political parties of the Left.

RED-GUM, [red'-gum], *n.* an eruption of red pimples in early infancy, connected with teething; one of several species of the Australian *Eucalyptus*, a medicinal drug obtained from the bark of the tree; a red-coloured resin obtained from the bark of the Australian eucalyptus tree.

RED-HANDED, [red'-hand'-id], *adj.* in the very act of doing something wrong, *orig.* with the hands stained from recent bloodshed.

RED-HEAD, [red'-hed'], *n.* the American woodpecker; a person with red hair.

RED HEAT, [red'-hēt'], *n.* the state or temperature at which a thing is red-hot.

RED-HERRING, [red'-he'-ring], *n.* a herring cured and made red by smoking; (*fig.*) a point, topic or thing introduced to divert attention from the real matter at issue, and set people on a false trail.

RED-HOT, [red'-hot'], *adj.* heated to redness; (*slang*) fresh and of a sensational nature; (of dance music) highly syncopated, and full of elaborate rhythm and ornate solo passages for various instruments; **r. poker**, a garden plant, *Tritoma*, whose flowers resemble this.

REDIF, [rid-if'], *n.* a soldier or reservist in the Turkish army. [Turk. *redif*].

REDIFFERENTIATION, [rē-dif'-er-en-shi-ā'-shun], *n.* (*math.*) the differentiation of a differential coefficient.

RED INDIAN, [red'-ind'-i-an], *n.* one of, a descendant of, the aboriginal inhabitants of America.

REDINGOTE, [red'-ang-got'], *n.* a long, double-breasted coat. [Fr. *redingote* from E. *riding coat*].

REDINTEGRATE (1), [red-in'-tig-rāt], *adj.* renewed, restored to wholeness or to a perfect state. [L. *redintegratus* made whole].

REDINTEGRATE (2), [red-in'-tig-rāt], *v.t.* to make whole again, to restore to a unified or a perfect state. [L. *redintegrare*].

REDINTEGRATION, [red-in'-tig-rā'-shun], *n.* renovation, restoration to a whole or sound state, renewal. [L. *redintegratio*].

REDINTEGRATOR, [red-in'-tig-rāt-or], *n.* one who renews or redintegrates.

REDIRECT, [rē'-dī-rekt'], *v.t.* to readdress, to send on to a new address; to direct afresh.

REDIRECTION, [rē'-dī-rek'-shun], *n.* a fresh direction; the act of redirecting or readdressing.

REDISCOVER, [rē'-dis-kuv'-er], *v.t.* to discover anew.

REDISSEIZIN, [rē'-dis-ēz'-in], *n.* a repeated disseizin by a person against another. [AFr. *redisseisine*].

REDISSEIZOR, [rē'-dis-ēz'-or], *n.* a person who disseizes lands or tenements a second time. [AFr. *redisseisour*].

REDISTRIBUTE, [rē'-dis-trib'-yōōt], *v.t.* to distribute again or in a fresh way.

REDISTRIBUTION, [rē'-dis'-trib-ew'-shun], *n.* a fresh or different distribution; (*parl.*) rearrangement of the size and limits of parliamentary constituencies.

REDIVIDE, [rē'-di-vīd'], *v.t.* to divide anew.

REDIVIVUS, [red'-iv-ī'-vus], *adj.* revived, come to life again. [L. *redivivus*].

RED LAMP, [red'-lamp'], *n.* a brothel.

RED LANE, [red'-lān'], *n.* a childish word for the gullet.

RED-LEAD, [red'-led'], *n.* a red oxide of lead, used as a pigment and as a cement for jointing pipes.

RED-LEG(S), [red'-leg(z)'], *n.* one of various birds with red legs including the purple sandpiper, *Tringa maritima*.

RED-LETTER, [red'-let'-er], *adj.* marked by a red letter, as a principal saint's day or church festival in a calendar; **a r. day**, a principal saint's day or church festival; (*fig.*) an auspicious, memorable day.

RED LIGHT, [red'-līt'], *n.* a light shining through red glass; a danger signal.

REDLY, [red'-li], *adv.* with redness.

RED MULLET, [red'-mul'-et], *n.* the edible fish, *Mullus barbatus*, whose flesh has a reddish tinge.

REDNESS, [red'-nes], *n.* the state of being red; the shade of red; red colour.

RE-DO, (**re-did, re-done**), [rē-dōō'], *v.t.* to do over again.

RED OCHRE, [red'-ō'-ker], *n.* ruddle, a substance used as a colouring pigment.

REDOLENCE, [red'-ō-lents], *n.* a sweetness of scent, fragrance, perfume. [OFr. *redolence*].

REDOLENT, [red'-ō-lent], *adj.* diffusing a pleasant scent, sweet-smelling, fragrant, aromatic; (*fig.*) **r. of**, suggesting the presence of, reminiscent of, smacking of. [L. *redolens*, *pres.pt.* of *redolere* to smell].

REDONDILLA, [red'-on-dēl'-ya], *n.* (*pros.*) a Spanish form of stanza in which the rhymes were between the first and fourth and second and third lines, but which has been variously modified. [Span. *redondilla*].

REDOUBLE, [rē-dubl'], *v.t.* to double again, to increase to approximately twice as much (penalties at cards) as a double; to increase, renew; *v.i.* to become twice as much; to become greater; (*bridge*) to double a bid already doubled.

REDOUBT, [ri-dowt'], *n.* (*fort.*) a small temporary fort or field-work, usually in the form of an enclosed polygonal work. [Fr. *redoute*].

REDOUBTABLE, [ri-dowt'-abl], *adj.* formidable, dread, to be feared. [Fr. *redoutable*].

REDOUBTED, [ri-dowt'-id], *adj.* formidable, celebrated for feats of valour, dread.

REDOUND, [ri-downd'], *v.i.* to conduce, contribute as a result, to add; to fall or come (to); to recoil, react (upon). [L. *redundare* flow over].

REDPOLL, [red'-pōl], *n.* one of three species of linnets with red heads.

REDRAFT (1), [rē'-drahft'], *n.* a fresh draft; (*comm.*) a fresh bill of exchange to cover an earlier one.

REDRAFT (2), [rē'-drahft'], *v.t.* to draft again or in a fresh form.

RED RAG, [red'-rag'], *n.* anything that arouses anger or provokes to fury.

RED RATTLE, [red'-ratl'], *n.* the plant, *Pedicularis sylvatica*, with pink blossoms.

REDRAW, (**redrew, redrawn**), [rē-draw'], *v.t.* to draw out again; to make out a fresh draft or copy; (*comm.*) to draw (a new bill of exchange) to cover an earlier one; to draw afresh.

REDRESS (1), [ri-dres'], *n.* the act of redressing; reparation, compensation, indemnification for a loss or injury inflicted. [AFr. *redresse*].

REDRESS (2), [ri-dres'], *v.t.* to set right, remedy, repair, relieve, rectify; to adjust (balance of); to correct, amend; to indemnify, compensate, obtain reparation for (a person). [Fr. *redresser*].

RE-DRESS, [rē-dres'], *v.t.* to dress again or in different clothes; to put fresh dressings on.

REDRESSER, [ri-dres'-er], *n.* one who provides redress.

REDRESSIBLE, [ri-dres'-ibl], *adj.* able to be redressed.

REDRESSIVE, [ri-dres'-iv], *adj.* giving redress.

RED RIBBON, [red'-rib'-on], *n.* the emblem or ribbon that denotes membership of the Order of the Bath or the Legion of Honour.

REDRIVE, (**redrove, redriven**), [rē-drīv'], *v.t.* to drive back again.

REDRUTHITE, [red'-rōōth-īt], *n.* copper glance, sulphide of copper. [*Redruth*, a place in Cornwall].

REDSHANK, [red'-shangk'], *n.* a bird allied to the plover, the sandpiper, *Totanus calidris*, so called from its red legs; one who has red legs, *esp.* (*hist.*) one of the Celtic dwellers in Ireland and the Scottish Highlands.

RED-SHORT, [red'-shawt], *adj.* brittle, or breaking short when red-hot, as a metal.

REDSKIN, [red'-skin], *n.* a North American Indian, so called from the coppery hue of his skin.

RED SPIDER, [red'-spīd'-er], *n.* the harvest mite, *Tetranychus telarius*, resembling a red spider in appearance, and destructive to vines.

REDSTART, [red'-staht], *n.* the migratory warbler, *Ruticilla phoenicurus*, allied to the thrush, having a certain resemblance to the redbreast, but of a more slender form, and having a red tail. [RED and OE. *steort* rump].

REDSTREAK, [red'-strēk], *n.* a cider-producing apple having a streaky red skin.

RED TAPE, [red'-tāp'], *n.* †the pink tape used in tying up official documents; (*fig.*) excessive attention to the formality of official routine, often resulting in unnecessary delay in getting things done; official rules, regulations, and methods of procedure which must be complied with.

RED-TAPISM, [red'-tāp'-izm], *n.* strict adherence

to official routine often involving unnecessary delay and protraction before anything can be done.

RED-TAPIST, [red'-tāp'-ist], *n.* one who adheres excessively to official routine and the formalities of procedure.

REDUCE, [ri-dews'], *v.t.* to diminish, lessen, make smaller or fewer; to lower in rank or position; to bring into some unpleasant condition, to force (to indulge in some degrading or disagreeable activity), to constrain; to weaken, impair; to bring into a different or simpler form, to break down or convert into a different form; to bring into any specific state or condition; to bring into classes or under rules; to subdue, bring into subjection or submission, to bring under complete control or obedience by force, influence or compulsion; (*surg.*) to restore or adjust to its original position (a dislocation, fracture, rupture, etc.); (*arith.*) to change from one denominator into a lower; (*chem.*) to decompose, take away oxygen from, increase the metal in; (*metal.*) to smelt; *v.i.* to get rid of superfluous fat, to slim; **reduced circumstances,** comparative poverty; **to r. to the ranks,** (*milit.*) to degrade a non-commissioned officer for misconduct to the rank of private soldier. [L. *reducere* to bring back].

REDUCER, [ri-dews'-er], *n.* one who, or that which, reduces; (*phot.*) a substance used to reduce the contrast or density of negatives.

REDUCIBILITY, [ri-dews'-ib-il'-i-ti], *n.* the quality of being reducible.

REDUCIBLE, [ri-dews'-ibl], *adj.* capable of being reduced.

REDUCIBLENESS, [ri-dews'-ibl-nes], *n.* the quality of being reducible.

REDUCTION, [ri-duk'-shun], *n.* the act of reducing; the state of being reduced; diminution, shortening, lessening; subjugation; conversion or changing into a different or simpler form; (*arith.*) changing numbers from one denominator into a lower or from a different denominator into a common denominator; (*surg.*) replacement of a displaced part. [L. *reductio*].

REDUNDANCE, [ri-dun'-dants], *n.* the state or quality of being redundant; that which is redundant, an excess or superfluity. [L. *redundantia*].

REDUNDANCY, [ri-dun'-dan-si], *n.* redundance.

REDUNDANT, [ri-dun'-dant], *adj.* superfluous, excessive, unnecessary, tautological; needlessly prolix or verbose; copious, abundant to excess; exceedingly plentiful. [L. *redundans, pres.pt.* of *redundare* to overflow].

REDUNDANTLY, [ri-dun'-dant-li], *adv.* in a redundant fashion.

REDUPLICATE, [ri-dew'-plik-āt], *v.t.* to redouble, repeat; (*gram.*) to form (a tense) by repeating the initial syllable or letter; *v.i.* to undergo reduplication. [L. *reduplicare*].

REDUPLICATION, [ri-dew'-plik-ā'-shun], *n.* the act of reduplicating; that which is produced by reduplicating; (*gram.*) repetition of the first syllable to form a new tense, etc.; an example of this.

REDUPLICATIVE, [ri-dew'-plik-at-iv], *adj.* that reduplicates or tends to reduplicate; (*gram.*) formed by reduplication.

RED-WATER, [red'-waw'-ter], *n.* a disease in cattle, due to a parasite infecting the blood, and appearing in the reddening colour of the urine, Texas fever.

REDWING, [red'-wing], *n.* the fieldfare, *Turdus iliacus*, a bird of the thrush family, which has a bright scarlet patch on its wings.

REDWOOD, [red'-wood], *n.* name given to trees producing red timber, *esp.* to trees of the genus *Sequoia*, that grow to a great height; red coloured timber.

RE-DYE, [rē-dī'], *v.t.* to dye afresh.

REE, [rē], *n.* the female of the ruff. [*Var.* of REEVE].

RE-ECHO (1), [rē-ek'-ō], *n.* the echo of an echo.

RE-ECHO (2), [rē-ek'-ō], *v.i.* to echo back, reverberate.

REECHY, [rēch'-i], *adj.* (*dial.*) dirty, smoky. [~REEK (1)].

REED (1), [rēd], *n.* an aquatic grass with a long jointed stem, growing along banks of streams, lakes, rivers, etc., and comprising plants of the genera *Arundo*, *Phragmites*, and *Psamma*; a single straight stem of one of these plants; an arrow made from this; a musical pipe made from the stem of a reed; (*mus.*) a thin slip of reed cane or metal in the mouthpiece of certain musical wind-instruments and vibrated by a column of air from the mouth of the player, a similar device producing the sound in an organ pipe or bagpipe; a musical wind-instrument of this type; (*weaving*) that part of a loom by which the threads of the warp are separated in weaving; (*arch.*) one of a series of mouldings like a group of reeds laid side by side and parallel to each other; (*fig.*) pastoral poetry; **a broken r.,** a person without moral fibre or strength. [OE. *hreod*].

REED (2), [rēd], *v.t.* to thatch with reed; to ornament with reed-moulding; (*mus.*) to fit reeds to.

REED-BUNTING, [rēd'-bunt'-ing], *n.* the waterside bird, *Emberiza schœniclus*.

REEDED, [rēd'-id], *adj.* covered with reeds; full of channels and ridges like reeds.

RE-EDIFICATION, [rē-ed'-if-ik-ā'-shun], *n.* the operation of rebuilding, restoring or reviving.

RE-EDIFY, [rē-ed'-i-fī], *v.t.* to rebuild; (*fig.*) to restore, revive, establish again. [L. *reaedificare*].

REEDING, [rēd'-ing], *n.* moulding like parallel reeds placed side by side.

RE-EDIT, [rē-ed'-it], *v.t.* to edit afresh.

RE-EDITION, [rē'-id-ish'-un], *n.* a fresh edition.

REEDLESS, [rēd'-les], *adj.* lacking reeds.

REEDLING, [rēd'-ling], *n.* the bearded tit, *Panurus biarmicus*.

REED-MACE, [rēd'-mās], *n.* the cat's tail, *Typha latifolia*, frequently, and erroneously, called the bulrush, and having long sword-shaped leaves, with a club-shaped cluster of small brownish flowers.

REED-PIPE, [rēd'-pīp], *n.* an organ-pipe fitted with a reed; a musical pipe made of a reed.

REED-WARBLER, [rēd'-wawb'-ler], *n.* the reed-wren, *Acrocephalus streperus*.

REED-WREN, [rēd'-ren'], *n.* the reed-warbler.

REEDY, [rēd'-i], *adj.* abounding in reeds; (of a pipe) made of reeds; long, thin and slender; thin and rough in tone like a reed.

REEF (1), [rēf], *n.* (*naut.*) one of the horizontal portions of a sail that may be rolled or folded up to lessen the amount of sail when the wind is violent. [~OScand. *rif*].

REEF (2), [rēf], *n.* a ridge, shelf, or range of rocks, shingle or sand lying at or near the surface of the water; a mineral lode or vein. [Du. *rif*].

REEF (3), [rēf], *v.t.* to reduce the area of (a sail) by folding or rolling up a part; to lower (a topmast) in order to shorten; to slide inboard (a bowsprit) in order to shorten; (*fig.*) to shorten or draw up. [REEF (1)].

REEF-BAND, [rēf'-band'], *n.* the strong strip of canvas stitched across a sail, in which are made the holes for the reef points.

REEFER, [rēf'-er], *n.* a short, thick, double-breasted coat as worn by sailors; one who reefs; a midshipman.

REEF-KNOT, [rēf'-not'], *n.* the knot used for tying reefs, and made by passing the end of the cord through a simple loop, bringing it back over the loop and passing it out under the loop on the same face of the loop as that by which it entered.

REEF-KNOT

REEF-POINTS, [rēf'-points], *n.(pl.)* the short lengths of cord used in tying up reefs.

REEFY, [rēf'-i], *adj.* full of reefs or rocks.

REEK (1), [rēk], *n.* smoke, steam, vapour; a strong unpleasant odour or smell, a stench, stink. [OE. *rec*].

REEK (2), [rēk], *v.i.* to emit smoke or vapour, to steam, to smoke with heat or perspiration; to emit a strong disagreeable odour or smell, to stink; (*fig.*) to be blatantly and offensively filled (with). [OE. *reocan*].

REEKING, [rēk'-ing], *adj.* smoking, steaming, emitting vapour; giving off strong and unpleasant odours.

REEKY, [rēk'-i], *adj.* smoky, steamy, emitting vapours.

REEL (1), [rēl], *n.* a rotatory framework on which thread or silk is wound after being spun; a bobbin on which thread or silk is wound, ready for use; the amount wound on a reel; a spool or flattened cylinder on which a length of cinema film is wound; the length of film wound on a reel; a large cylindrical drum on which cable, wire, rope, etc., is wound; a small cylindrical winch attached to a fishing-rod, for winding in or out the line; **off the r.,** without stopping, in uninterrupted succession; **news r.,** a short topical cinema film showing pictures of recent happenings of interest, accompanied by an explanatory commentary. [OE. *hreol*].

REEL (2), [rēl], *n.* a lively Scottish dance in which the couples pass and repass each other and swing round, describing a number of figure eights; the music to which this is danced. [Gael. *righil*].

REEL (3), [rēl], *v.t.* to wind upon a reel; *v.i.* (of insects)

to make a noise like that of a reel being wound or unwound; **to r. off,** to rattle off, to utter quickly and without stopping; to unwind from a reel.
REEL (4), [rēl], *v.i.* to stagger and lurch from one side to another; to sway and totter under the effects of a blow; to be shaken, tremble, wilt under some powerful force or shock; to whirl round, to be in a giddy whirl; (of the mind, brain) to lose its poise or equilibrium under some powerful shock or feeling of dizziness.
RE-ELECT, [rē-il-ekt'], *v.t.* to elect again.
RE-ELECTION, [rē'-il-ek'-shun], *n.* a fresh election; election again.
REELER, [rēl'-er], *n.* the grasshopper warbler, *Locustella nævia*; one who reels; something that consists of reels.
RE-ELIGIBILITY, [rē-el'-ij-ib-il'-i-ti], *n.* the fact or quality of being re-eligible.
RE-ELIGIBLE, [rē-el'-ij-ibl], *adj.* eligible for re-election.
RE-EMBARK, [rē'-em-bahk'], *v.t.* to put on board again; *v.i.* to go on board again.
RE-EMBARKATION, [rē'-em'-bahk-ā'-shun], *n.* the act of embarking afresh.
RE-EMBODY, [rē'-em-bod'-i], *v.t.* to embody afresh.
RE-EMERGE, [rē'-im-urj'], *v.i.* to emerge again, reappear.
REEMING, [rēm'-ing], *n.* the opening of the seams between the planks of a vessel with a caulking-iron before caulking. [OE. * *eman* to make room].
RE-ENABLE, [rē'-en-ā'-bl], *v.t.* to enable again.
RE-ENACT, [rē-en-akt'], *v.t.* to enact over again.
RE-ENFORCE, see REINFORCE (2).
RE-ENFORCEMENT, see REINFORCEMENT.
RE-ENGINE, [rē-en'-jin], *v.t.* to provide with a fresh engine or engines.
RE-ENLIST, [rē'-en-list'], *v.t. and i.* to enlist again.
RE-ENLISTMENT, [rē'-en-list'-ment], *n.* the act of re-enlisting.
RE-ENTER, [rē-en'-ter], *v.t.* to enter again, to come into again; (*leg.*) to regain or resume possession of (leased property) upon the failure of the lessee to observe the conditions of tenure; to cut more deeply and sharply (engraved lines); *v.i.* to enter again; (*leg.*) to regain or resume possession; (*fort.*) to point inwards away from the enemy (of an angle).
RE-ENTERING, [rē-en'-ter-ing], *adj.* (*fort.*) pointing inwards away from the enemy's lines.
RE-ENTRANCE, [re-en'-trants], *n.* the act of entering again, a fresh entrance.
RE-ENTRANT (1), [rē-en'-trant], *n.* a re-entrant angle.
RE-ENTRANT (2), [rē-en'-trant], *adj.* (*fort.*) (of an angle) repointing inwards towards the home lines; (of a gramophone horn) having a flare in which the sound re-enters and crosses its path at a wider stage.
RE-ENTRY, [rē-en'-tri], *n.* the act of entering again, re-entrance; (*leg.*) the act of entering into, or resuming possession of, leased property upon the lessee failing to observe the conditions of tenure.
REE-RAW (1), [rē'-raw'], *n.* a rowdy party; rough noisy celebration. [AIr. *prob.* echoic].
REE-RAW (2), [rē'-raw'], *adj.* riotous. [*Prec.*].
RE-ESTABLISH, [rē'-es-tab'-lish], *v.t.* to establish anew, restore, bring about again.
RE-ESTABLISHMENT, [rē'-es-tab'-lish-ment], *n.* the act of re-establishing; the condition of being re-established.
REEVE (1), [rēv], *n.* a steward or bailiff; (*hist.*) the chief magistrate of a district; (*mining*) a foreman. [OE. *gerefa*].
REEVE (2), [rēv], *n.* the female ruff, *Machetes pugnax*. [Uncert.].
REEVE (3), **(rove, reeved, roven)**, [rēv], *v.t.* (*naut.*) to pass the end of (a rope) through a hole in a bolt, block, etc.; to pass the end of a rope through (a hole); to secure (a rope) in this way. [Du. *reven* to reef].
RE-EXAMINATION, [rē-egz-am'-in-ā'-shun], *n.* a fresh examination.
RE-EXAMINE, [rē'-egz-am'-in], *v.t.* to examine afresh.
RE-EXCHANGE, [rē'-eks-chānj'], *n.* a renewed exchange; (*comm.*) the exchange chargeable on the redraft of a bill of exchange.
RE-EXPORT (1), [rē-eks'-pawt], *n.* a commodity or goods re-exported.
RE-EXPORT (2), [rē'-eks-pawt'], *v.t.* to export again; to export what has been imported.
RE-EXPORTATION, [rē'-eks-pawt-ā'-shun], *n.* the act of re-exporting, a fresh exportation.
REFACE, [rē'-fās'], *v.t.* to provide (masonry, stonework, etc.) with a fresh surface or face.
REFASHION, [rē'-fash'-un], *v.t.* to change the form of, to fashion anew.
REFECTION, [ri-fek'-shun], *n.* refreshment after hunger or fatigue; a slight meal, snack. [L. *refectio*].
REFECTORY, [ri-fekt'-er-i], *n.* a room where meals are taken, *esp.* the dining-room of a monastery, college, etc. [MedL. *refectorium*].
REFER, **(referring, referred)**, [ri-fur'], *v.t.* to attribute, assign; to pass on, send on, to instruct, to seek for information or further consideration, to submit to for decision or settlement; **to r. to,** to have recourse to, appeal to; to allude to, mention, indicate; to apply to, relate to, be concerned with; **to r. back,** to defer a decision on at a meeting until after consultation with the bodies from which delegates receive their mandates. [L. *referre* to bring back].
REFERABLE, [ref'-er-abl], *adj.* that may be referred to.
REFEREE (1), [ref'-er-ē'], *n.* one to whom anything is referred, *esp.* an arbitrator, a person appointed by a body or court to hear a cause of dispute between two parties and to adjudicate on it; (*games*) an umpire or person in charge of a football match, boxing contest, billiards match, etc.
REFEREE (2), [ref'-er-ē'], *v.t. and i.* to act as referee for (a sporting contest).
REFERENCE, [ref'-er-ents], *n.* the act of referring to, or submission to, another person for further consideration or decision; the act of referring to for information; a note or indication as to the source of some particular information mentioned or allusion made, usually giving the title and page of the work and the author's name; an allusion; connexion, relation, respect; a person who may be referred to, and who will furnish information as to one's ability, qualifications, and personal character if required; a testimonial, a signed statement as to a person's qualifications, abilities, and personal character written usually by someone holding some official position, or by a former employer; **book of r.,** a book to be referred to for some specific information, and not intended to be read straight through; **r. Bible,** a Bible annotated with references to corresponding passages; **r. library,** a library in which specialized books may be consulted for information, but from which books may not be borrowed; **with r. to,** concerning, in regard to; **cross-r.,** a reference in a work to another page or section in that work.
REFERENDARY, [ref'-er-end'-er-i], *n.* (*hist.*) a high court official who had to investigate and answer petitions, requests, etc., and who was also the Keeper of the King's Seal; a referee. [MedL. *referendarius*].
REFERENDUM, [ref'-er-end'-um], *n.* the referring of parliamentary or constitutional issues to the general vote of the electorate, the holding of a plebiscite. [L. *referendum* that which must be referred].
REFERENTIAL, [ref'-er-en'-shal], *adj.* that has a reference to something; as a reference.
RE-FERMENT, [rē'-fer-ment'], *v.t.* to ferment again.
REFERRIBLE†, [ri-fur'-ibl], *adj.* referable.
REFILL (1), [rē'-fil], *n.* a fresh fill, that which fills again, or is used to replenish something that has been exhausted or emptied.
REFILL (2), [rē-fil'], *v.t. and i.* to fill afresh.
RE-FIND, [rē'-fīnd'], *v.t.* to find again, rediscover.
REFINE, [ri-fīn'], *v.t.* to purify, free from impurities or dross, to make finer in quality; to free from imperfections; to make polished, cultured, and elegant, to remove traces of coarseness, roughness, or rudeness; *v.i.* to become purified, finer in quality, or more polished and cultured in manner, to be freed from coarseness, impurity, or imperfection; to affect nicety or subtlety in speech or argument; **to r. on,** to improve by refinement.
REFINED, [ri-fīnd'], *adj.* made finer in quality, purified, freed from impurities, dross or imperfections; polished, elegant, cultured, with all traces of coarseness, rudeness, or roughness in speech or manner excluded; (*vulg.*) fastidious, affectedly elegant, snobbish.
REFINEDLY, [ri-fīnd'-li], *adv.* in a refined way.
REFINEDNESS, [ri-fīnd'-nes], *n.* the quality of being refined.
REFINEMENT, [ri-fīn'-ment], *n.* the act of refining; the state or quality of being refined; polish and elegance in manner and speech, culture; an example of this; a subtlety, nicety, something brought to a more perfect or elaborate form; snobbish affectation of nicety and elegance.

REFINER, [ri-fīn'-er], *n.* one who refines, *esp.* one whose occupation is refining; an apparatus used in refining.

REFINERY, [ri-fīn'-er-i], *n.* a place or apparatus for refining substances.

REFIT (1), [rē'-fit], *n.* a refitment.

REFIT (2), **(refitting, refitted)**, [rē'-fit'], *v.t.* to fit out or prepare again, to furnish with fresh equipment and supplies, to repair; to fit on again; *v.i.* to undergo refitment; to take on fresh supplies or equipment.

REFITMENT, [rē'-fit'-ment], *n.* a fitting out afresh, *esp.* of a ship.

REFLATION, [rē'-flāsh'-un], *n.* the act or process of correcting deflation or inflation. [RE (1) and (IN)FLATION].

REFLECT, [ri-flekt'], *v.t.* to throw back after striking against (a hard surface); to give back an image or picture of, on its polished surface, to mirror; to cast upon, shed, bring upon; (*fig.*) to record, express faithfully, give a true indication of; (*archaic*) to bend back, turn aside; *v.i.* to throw back light, heat or sound waves; to give back an image or picture, in its polished surface, of an object facing it; **to r. on, upon**, to meditate, ponder over, consider carefully and thoughtfully; to bring into descredit or reproach, cast censure on; to disparage, to run down, cast doubt on. [L. *reflectere* to bend back].

REFLECTED, [ri-flekt'-id], *adj.* thrown back from what it strikes on; (*fig.*) indirect.

REFLECTIBLE, [ri-flekt'-ibl], *adj.* capable of being reflected.

REFLECTING, [ri-flekt'-ing], *adj.* that reflects; **r. telescope**, a telescope in which the image is seen from a concave reflector instead of through a lens, used especially in astronomical observation.

REFLECTINGLY, [ri-flekt'-ing-li], *adv.* by or with reflection, so as to reflect.

REFLECTION, REFLEXION, [ri -flek'-shun], *n.* the act or process of reflecting; that which is reflected, *esp.* an image or picture reflected in a polished surface or mirror; meditation, thoughtful consideration, profound and usually introspective thought; (*pl.*) thoughts arising after thinking something over; remarks or observations made after thinking something over; reproach, censure; aspersion, intended or implied disparagement; that which casts discredit or reproach upon someone; (*anat.*) a bending back. [L. *reflexion*].

REFLECTIVE, [ri-flekt'-iv], *adj.* that reflects; thoughtful, meditative, given to introspective consideration of things past, indulging in reflection; exercising, capable of reflection; (*gram.*) reflexive; reflected.

REFLECTIVELY, [ri-flekt'-iv-li], *adv.* in a reflective manner, by way of reflection.

REFLECTIVENESS, [ri-flekt'-iv-nes], *n.* the power of reflection.

REFLECTOR, [ri-flekt'-or], *n.* that which reflects, a hard polished surface reflecting light, heat, or sound, *esp.* in a particular direction; a mirror, a reflecting telescope or other similar optical instrument; one who reflects.

REFLEX (1), [rē'-fleks], *n.* that which is reflected or brought about by reflection, a reflection in a polished surface; (*fig.*) an outward reproduction or visible expression of some essential feature or fact; (*physiol.*) a reflex action, an involuntary movement caused by this. [L. *reflexus* a bending back].

REFLEX (2), [rē'-fleks], *adj.* directed back; (*bot.*) bent or turned back; (*paint.*) reflected, illuminated by light reflected from another part of the picture; produced in reaction; **r. action**, an involuntary action of a muscle or other organ caused by an impulse or stimulus; **r. camera**, a camera in which the object photographed is visible through the lens up to the moment of exposure. [L. *reflexus*, *p.pt.* of *reflectere* to bend back].

REFLEXED, [ri'-flekst'], *adj.* (*bot.*) curved back; bent back abruptly.

REFLEXIBILITY, [ri-fleks'-ib-il'-i-ti], *n.* the property of being reflexible.

REFLEXIBLE, [ri-fleks'-ibl], *adj.* that may be reflected.

REFLEXION, see REFLECTION.

REFLEXITY, [ri-fleks'-i-ti], *n.* the capacity for being reflected.

REFLEXIVE (1), [ri-fleks'-iv], *n.* a reflexive verb or pronoun.

REFLEXIVE (2), [ri-fleks'-iv], *adj.* of the nature of a reflex; (*gram.*) referring back to the subject of a sentence; in which the object of an action is the same as the subject (of a verb).

REFLEXIVELY, [ri-fleks'-iv-li], *adv.* in a reflexive manner, by means of a reflexive pronoun or verb.

REFLEXLY, [ri-fleks'-li], *adv.* in a reflex fashion.

REFLOAT, [rē'-flōt'], *v.t.* *and* *i.* (of a boat) to float again after it has been sunk or has gone aground.

REFLOW, [rē-flō'], *v.i.* to flow back, to ebb.

REFLUENT, [ref'-lōō-ent], *adj.* flowing back, ebbing. [L. *refluens*].

REFLUX, [rē'-fluks'], *n.* a flowing back; backward course, ebbing.

REFOLD, [rē'-fōld'], *v.t.* to fold anew.

REFOOT, [rē'-fōōt'], *v.t.* to provide (a stocking) with a new foot.

REFORGE, [rē'-fawj'], *v.t.* to forge afresh.

REFORM (1), [ri-fawm'], *n.* a changing for the better, amendment, improvement of something faulty, removal of an abuse, wrong, or injustice, *esp.* social or political; abandonment of evil ways or vices and amendment of conduct and character; **R. Acts**, political measures passed to extend, and obtain a more equable distribution of, the franchise.

REFORM (2), [ri-fawm'], *v.t.* to change for the better, to improve by removing abuses or wrongs in, to amend; to cause to abandon evil ways and lead a better life; *v.i.* to give up one's vices and evil ways and lead a better life, to improve one's conduct, character, and habits. [L. *reformare* shape again].

RE-FORM, [rē'-fawm'], *v.t.* to form or arrange again; *v.i.* to assume a new formation; to resume a formation that had been temporarily destroyed or abandoned, to come into formation again.

REFORMATION, [ref'-awm-ā'-shun], *n.* the act of reforming; the state of being reformed; change for the better, amendment, removal or correction of abuses and faults, abandonment of evil ways and improvement in behaviour and character; **The R.**, the great religious revolt in the 16th century against the Roman Catholic Church and Papacy. [L. *reformatio*].

RE-FORMATION, [rē'-fawm-ā'-shun], *n.* the forming or arranging again, a fresh formation.

REFORMATIVE, [ri-fawm'-at-iv], *adj.* that reforms or is intended to reform.

REFORMATORY (1), [ri-fawm'-at-er-i], *n.* an institution to which juvenile criminals are sent to be reformed.

REFORMATORY (2), [ri-fawm'-at-er-i], *adj.* tending to, intended to, reform; **r. school**, a reformatory.

REFORMED, [ri-fawmd'], *adj.* that has undergone reform, amended, made better, improved; **R. Church**, the Protestant Church; the Calvinist Church as opposed to the Lutheran.

REFORMER, [ri-fawm'-er], *n.* one who reforms; an advocate of social or political reform; a supporter of the Reform Bill of 1832; one who took a prominent part in the Reformation.

REFORMIST, [ri-fawm'-ist], *n.* one who supports or works for reform in political or religious matters.

REFORTIFY, [rē'-fawt'-i-fī], *v.t.* to fortify afresh.

RE-FOUND, [rē'-fownd'], *v.t.* to establish afresh. [RE (1) and FOUND (2)].

REFRACT, [ri-frakt'], *v.t.* to bend (light, heat or sound rays) at an angle as in refraction. [L. *refractus*, *p.pt.* of *refringere* to break].

REFRACTED, [ri-frakt'-id], *adj.* (of rays of light, heat, or sound) deflected from a direct course.

REFRACTING, [ri-frakt'-ing], *adj.* turning rays from a direct course, causing refraction; provided or fitted with a device to refract rays; **r. angle**, the angle made by two faces of a prism; **r. telescope**, a telescope in which an object glass bends the rays of light to bring them to a focus.

REFRACTION, [ri-frak'-shun], *n.* the act of refracting, the bending at an angle, or change of direction, which light, heat, or sound waves undergo as they pass from one medium into another of a different density; **angle of r.**, the angle made by a ray of light and a line perpendicular to the surface of the medium through which it is passing; **astronomical r.**, the apparent increase in angular elevation of the celestial bodies above their true places due to the refracting power of the air through which their rays of light pass; **double r.**, the refracting of a ray of light in two successive directions. [L. *refractio*].

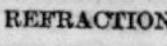
REFRACTION

REFRACTIONAL, [ri-frak'-shun-al], *adj.* (*opt.*) of, or pertaining to, or caused by, refraction; refractive.

REFRACTIONIST, [ri-frak′-shun-ist], *n.* one expert in measuring refractive defects in the eye.

REFRACTIVE, [ri-frakt′-iv], *adj.* that refracts, refracting; pertaining to, caused by, refraction; **r. index**, the ratio of the refracting power of a medium compared with that of water.

REFRACTIVENESS, [ri-frakt′-iv-nes], *n.* the property of refracting, the quality of being refractive.

REFRACTIVITY, [rē′-frak-tiv′-i-ti], *n.* refractiveness.

REFRACTOMETER, [rē′-frak-tom′-it-er], *n.* an apparatus for measuring refraction.

REFRACTOR, [ri-frakt′-er], *n.* that which refracts; a refracting telescope.

REFRACTORILY, [ri-frakt′-er-i-li], *adv.* in a refractory fashion.

REFRACTORINESS, [ri-frakt′-er-i-nes], *n.* the quality of being refractory.

REFRACTORY (1), [ri-frakt′-er-i], *n.* a refractory substance.

REFRACTORY (2), [ri-frakt′-er-i], *adj.* sullen, perverse in opposition or disobedience, stubborn, obstinate, mulish; (of a disease) difficult to deal with, not responding to treatment, hard to cure; heat-resisting, hard to fuse. [L. *refractarius*].

REFRAIN (1), [ri-frān′], *n.* a line or verse regularly repeated at intervals, *esp.* at the end of each fresh stanza of a poem or song, the chorus. [OFr. *refrein*].

REFRAIN (2), [ri-frān′], *v.t.* (*archaic*) to restrain, check, repress; *v.i.* to forbear, abstain, do without (usually with *from*). [L. *refrenare* to bridle].

REFRAME, [rē′-frām′], *v.t.* to frame again, to draft anew.

REFRANGIBILITY, [ri-franj′-ib-il′-i-ti], *n.* refrangibleness.

REFRANGIBLE, [ri-franj′-ibl], *adj.* that may be refracted.

REFRANGIBLENESS, [ri-franj′-ibl-nes], *n.* the quality of being refrangible.

REFRESH, [ri-fresh′], *v.t.* to make fresh again; to give new strength and energy to; to cool and revive; (*fig.*) to stimulate, stir up, jog (the memory); *v. reflex.* to recover one's strength, vigour and freshness by taking food, drink, sleep, etc.; *v.i.* to take in refreshment, obtain fresh supplies or stores; (*coll.*) to eat and drink. [OFr. *refrescher*].

REFRESHER, [ri-fresh′-er], *n.* he who, or that which, refreshes; (*coll.*) a cooling, refreshing drink; (*leg.*) an additional daily fee paid to a barrister; **r. course**, a course of instruction to revise or bring up to date the knowledge of people already qualified in a particular subject.

REFRESHING, [ri-fresh′-ing], *adj.* cooling and reviving, making fresh again, giving new strength and vigour when one is tired; stimulating; attractive in its unexpectedness.

REFRESHINGLY, [ri-fresh′-ing-li], *adv.* so as to refresh.

REFRESHINGNESS, [ri-fresh′-ing-nes], *n.* the quality of being refreshing.

REFRESHMENT, [ri-fresh′-ment], *n.* the act of refreshing; the state of being refreshed, new life, strength and vigour; that which refreshes; (*pl.*) food and drink, *esp.* a light and informal meal; (*coll.*) drink. [OFr. *refreschement*].

REFRIGERANT (1), [ri-frij′-er-ant], *n.* a medicine that reduces fever or excessive heat in inflammation; a cooling and refreshing drink; a substance used in freezing anything.

REFRIGERANT (2), [ri-frij′-er-ant], *adj.* cooling, reducing fever or excessive heat in inflammation.

REFRIGERATE, [ri-frij′-er-āt], *v.t.* to make cool, to freeze; to chill or reduce to a very low temperature by putting into a refrigerator, in order to preserve and keep fresh; to make into ice; *v.i.* to become cold, freeze. [L. *refrigerare*].

REFRIGERATING, [ri-frij′-er-āt′-ing], *adj.* that refrigerates, used for refrigeration.

REFRIGERATION, [ri-frij′-er-ā′-shun], *n.* the act of refrigerating; the state of being cooled or frozen; preservation of food by keeping in cold storage.

REFRIGERATIVE, [ri-frij′-er-at-iv], *adj.* cooling, reducing fever, refrigerant; pertaining to, of, refrigeration.

REFRIGERATOR, [ri-frij′-er-āt-or], *n.* an ice-chest or chamber into which food may be put into cold storage to be preserved; that which refrigerates, a refrigerating machine.

REFRIGERATORY (1), [ri-frij′-er-āt-er-i], *n.* a vessel filled with cold water and containing a spiral metallic pipe through which the vapour passes in distillation, and in which it is cooled and condensed; a refrigerator, an ice-chest or chamber for keeping things at a low temperature. [*Prec.*].

REFRIGERATORY (2), [ri-frij′-er-āt-er-i], *adj.* cooling, freezing; pertaining to, of, refrigeration.

REFRINGENT, [ri-frinj′-ent], *adj.* refractive. [L. *refringens*].

REFT, [reft], *p.pt.* of REAVE; bereft, deprived.

REFUGE (1), [ref′-yōōj], *n.* shelter, protection from danger or distress; any place affording such protection, an asylum, retreat, a place of safety for hiding; a raised narrow portion of pavement in the middle of a broad and busy road for the convenience of pedestrians; an expedient adopted as a means of escaping trouble or retribution. [L. *refugium*].

REFUGE (2), [ref′-yōōj], *v.t.* (*archaic*) to shelter; *v.i.* (*archaic*) to seek or take refuge. [*Prec.*].

REFUGEE, [ref′-yōō-jē′], *n.* one who flees for shelter to a place of refuge, *esp.* to a foreign country, for political reasons or in times of persecution. [Fr. *réfugié*].

REFUGEEISM, [ref′-yōō-jē′-izm], *n.* the condition of being a refugee.

REFULGENCE, [ri-ful′-jents], *n.* a flood of light, splendour, brightness. [L. *refulgentia*].

REFULGENCY, [ri-ful′-jen-si], *n.* refulgence.

REFULGENT, [ri-ful′-jent], *adj.* gleaming, shining brightly, brilliant, radiant, dazzling.

REFULGENTLY, [ri-ful′-jent-li], *adv.* in a refulgent manner; dazzlingly.

REFUND (1), [rē′-fund′], *n.* money paid back, repayment.

REFUND (2), [ri-fund′], *v.t.* to repay, to give back, return (money paid); *v.i.* to make repayment. [L. *refundere*].

REFUNDER, [ri-fund′-er], *n.* one who pays back or refunds.

REFUNDMENT, [ri-fund′-ment], *n.* the act of refunding, a repayment.

REFURBISH, [rē′-fur′-bish], *v.t.* to furbish or to do up again, to restore to its former new condition.

REFURNISH, [rē′-fur′-nish], *v.t.* to furnish again, to provide with fresh furniture.

REFUSABLE, [ri-fewz′-abl], *adj.* capable of being refused.

REFUSAL, [ri-fewz′-al], *n.* the act of refusing, denial or rejection of anything demanded or offered; the choice of taking or refusing.

REFUSE (1), [ref′-yōōs], *n.* that which is rejected or discarded as useless or worthless, waste products or matter, garbage, rubbish; the scum, dregs, lowest and most degraded elements of (society, a class); **r. destructor**, an incinerator in which the refuse of a town or city is burnt.

REFUSE (2), [ref′-yōōs], *adj.* discarded or thrown out as useless or worthless. [OFr. *refus*].

REFUSE (3), [ri-fewz′], *v.t. and i.* to deny or decline (a request, command, or what is sought); to reject, decline to accept (an offer); (*cards*) to be unable to follow suit in; (of a horse) to jib at, to make no attempt to clear. [Fr. *refuser* from L. *refusus*, *p.pt.* of *refundere*].

RE-FUSE, [rē′-fewz′], *v.t.* to fuse again.

REFUTABILITY, [ri-fewt′-ab-il′-i-ti], *n.* the possibility of being refuted.

REFUTABLE, [ri-fewt′-abl], *adj.* able to be refuted.

REFUTAL, [ri-fewt′-al], *n.* the act of refuting; that which refutes.

REFUTATION, [ref′-yōō-tā′-shun], *n.* the act of refuting; that which refutes or disproves. [L. *refutatio*].

REFUTATORY, [ri-few′-tat-er-i], *adj.* tending to refute, by way of refutation.

REFUTE, [ri-fewt′], *v.t.* to prove (a person) to be wrong; to prove (an argument) to be false. [L. *refutare*].

REFUTER, [ri-fewt′-er], *n.* one who refutes.

REGAIN, [ri-gān′], *v.t.* to recover possession of, get back again; to win again; to reach again. [OFr. *regaigner*].

REGAL (1), [rē′-gal], *n.* a small portable organ in use in the sixteenth century, played by the right hand and blown by the left. [Fr. *régale*].

REGAL (2), [rē′-gal], *adj.* of, or belonging to, a king, royal, kingly; as befits a king, worthy of a king, splendidly magnificent. [L. *regalis*].

REGALE, [ri-gāl′], *v.t.* to entertain, feast sumptuously; to delight, charm, give pleasure to; *v.i.* to feast. [Fr. *régaler*].

REGALEMENT, [ri-gāl′-ment], *n.* the act of regaling; a lavish entertainment or feast.

REGALIA (1), [ri-gāl′-i-a], *n.* (*hist.*) the rights and prerogatives of a king; the emblems, tokens, or insignia of royalty; the symbols, badges, or ornaments of office of certain societies and orders of knighthood. [L. *regalia* royal things].

REGALIA (2), [ri-gāl'-i-a], *n.* a cigar of large size and of the highest quality. [Span. *regalia* royal privilege].

REGALISM, [rē'-gal-izm], *n.* the doctrine of royal supremacy in church matters.

REGALIST, [rē'-gal-ist], *n.* a supporter of regalism.

REGALITY, [rē-gal'-i-ti], *n.* royalty, sovereignty, kingly rule or power; (*Scots leg.*) power or jurisdiction over a territory, corresponding to that enjoyed by the king; a particular territory under such jurisdiction; (*archaic*) a kingdom; (*pl.*) a royal right or privilege.

REGALLY, [rē'-gal-i], *adv.* in a royal fashion.

REGARD (1), [ri-gahd'], *n.* a look, gaze, *esp.* of a particular meaning or significance; esteem, consideration, respect; heed, attention, concern; (*pl.*) expressions of kindly feeling and well-being towards a particular person; **with r. to,** in respect of, with reference to. [OFr. *regard*].

REGARD (2), [ri-gahd'], *v.t.* to look, gaze at, stare at; contemplate, view in the mind; to value, esteem; to consider, think; to pay attention to, heed, care about, observe; to concern; **as regards,** with reference to. [Fr. *regarder*].

REGARDANT, [ri-gahd'-ant], *adj.* (*her.*) looking behind or backwards.

REGARDFUL, [ri-gahd'-fŏŏl], *adj.* taking notice, heedful, respectful, attentive, mindful.

REGARDFULLY, [ri-gahd'-fŏŏl-i], *adv.* with regard, attentively, mindfully.

REGARDFULNESS, [ri-gahd'-fŏŏl-nes], *n.* the quality of being regardful.

REGARDING, [ri-gahd'-ing], *prep.* respecting, concerning, about, with reference to.

REGARDLESS, [ri-gahd'-les], *adj.* heedless, unobservant, without regard, unmindful.

REGARDLESSLY, [ri-gahd'-les-li], *adv.* heedlessly, without regard.

REGARDLESSNESS, [ri-gahd'-les-nes], *n.* heedlessness, the quality of being regardless.

REGATHER, [rē-gaTH'-er], *v.t.* *and* *i.* to gather again.

REGATTA, [ri-gat'-a], *n.* a race-meeting for yachts, rowing boats and other water craft; a gondola race on the Grand Canal at Venice. [It. *regatta*].

REGELATION, [re-jel-ā'-shun], *n.* joining together by re-freezing.

REGENCY (1), [rē'-jen-si], *n.* government by a regent, or by a body of men having similar powers; the office, position, or jurisdiction of a regent; the period during which a kingdom, or country is governed by a regent, *esp.* in the Regency of George IV in England.

REGENCY (2), [rē'-jen-si], *adj.* of, pertaining to, the styles of architecture, dress, etc., current during the Regency of George IV.

REGENERACY, [ri-jen'-er-a-si], *n.* the state of being regenerated.

REGENERATE (1), [rē-jen'-er-at], *adj.* having experienced spiritual rebirth; reformed, improved, made better. [L. *regeneratus*].

REGENERATE (2), [rē-jen'-er-āt], *v.t.* to generate or produce again, reproduce, re-create; to cause to experience spiritual rebirth, to bring about a moral change for the better in, to reform spiritually; to establish on a higher level, to revive and raise to greater heights; (*path.*) to form again; *v.i.* to be born again spiritually; to reform. [L. *regenerare*].

REGENERATENESS, [rē-jen'-er-at-nes], *n.* the quality of being regenerate.

REGENERATION, [rē'-jen-er-ā'-shun], *n.* the act or process of regenerating; the state of being regenerated; revival and raising to new heights; spiritual rebirth; (*path.*) formation of fresh tissue; (*wirel.*) reaction.

REGENERATIVE, [rē-jen'-er-at-iv], *adj.* reproducing, renewing, tending or having the power to regenerate; using the device of a regenerator.

REGENERATOR, [rē-jen'-er-āt-or], *n.* one who, or that which, regenerates; a device fitted to a furnace by which the hot air or gas from the furnace heats layers of firebricks, which in turn heat the incoming cool air or gas.

REGENERATORY, [rē-jen'-er-āt-er-i], *adj.* having the power to renew; tending to reproduce or reform, regenerative.

REGENESIS, [rē-jen'-is-is], *n.* rebirth; reproduction.

REGENT (1), [rē'-jent], *n.* one who rules or governs for another, one who governs or rules over a kingdom in the minority, absence, or disability, of a monarch.

REGENT (2), [rē'-jent], *adj.* acting as regent, ruling on behalf of another. [Fr. *regent*].

REGENT-BIRD, [rē'-jent-burd'], *n.* an Australian bower-bird, *Sericulus chrysocephalus*, named after the Prince Regent, later George IV.

REGENTSHIP, [rē'-jent-ship], *n.* the office of a regent, regency.

REGICIDAL, [rēj'-is-id'-al], *adj.* pertaining to, disposed to, in favour of, regicide.

REGICIDE, [rēj'-is-id], *n.* one who kills a king; the crime of killing a king; **The Regicides,** the persons who tried and ordered the execution of Charles I. [L. *rex regis* king and *cida* murderer].

REGIE, régie, [rā-zhē'], *n.* a monopoly by which revenue comes to a government. [Fr. *régie*].

REGILD, (regilt), [rē-gild'], *v.t.* to gild afresh.

REGIME, régime, [rā-zhēm'], *n.* a mode or system of government, rule, order, social and political administration; mode of living, a regulated course of treatment to ensure sound health. [Fr. *régime*].

REGIMEN, [rej'-im-en], *n.* (*archaic*) rule, method or system of government, social and political administration; (*gram.*) the governing of one word by another, the relation of a word to the word it governs; (*med.*) beneficial regulation of diet, habits, exercise, etc., to ensure better health. [L. *regimen* rule].

REGIMENT (1), [rej'-im-ent], *n.* a body of troops or an infantry unit, on a territorial basis, consisting of a varying number of battalions; a cavalry unit; a general term for artillery as a whole; (*coll.*) a vast number, swarm; (*archaic*) rule, government. [L. *regimentum* rule].

REGIMENT (2), [rej'-im-ent], *v.t.* to form into a regiment or regiments; to organize into a trained and disciplined body or ordered system.

REGIMENTAL, [rej'-im-ent'-al], *adj.* relating to a regiment.

REGIMENTALS, [rej'-im-ent'-alz], *n.*(*pl.*) the distinguishing uniform worn by the soldiers of particular regiments.

REGIMENTATION, [rej'-im-ent-ā'-shun], *n.* division into regiments; arrangement by regiments; organization into an ordered system or trained and disciplined body.

REGINA, [ri-ji'-na], *n.* queen; an official designation of a reigning female monarch [L. *regina*].

REGION, [rē'-jun], *n.* a tract, area of land, sea or space of indefinite, but usually considerable, extent; a part of the body; (*fig.*) sphere, realm; (*pl.*) the provinces. [L. *regio*].

REGIONAL, [rē'-jun-al], *adj.* pertaining to a region or particular part or district, occurring in a particular part or parts.

REGIONALLY, [rē'-jun-a-li], *adv.* from a regional point of view.

REGISTER (1), [rej'-is-ter], *n.* an official written record of events, names and addresses, etc., *esp.* a record of births, marriages, and deaths kept by a registrar; the book in which such a record is kept; (*archaic*) one who keeps a register; an apparatus for regulating the admission of air or heat; a mechanical device for recording something; (*mus.*) range, compass; range of notes that can be sung without change of voice; a slider in an organ; an organ stop; (*print.*) corresponding alignment of a page of printed matter with that of the reverse side; adjusting of the impression in printing from blocks or plates; (*shipping*) a record of the seamen in the mercantile marine; **parliamentary** or **municipal r.,** a list of persons eligible to vote at elections. [MedL. *registrum*].

REGISTER (2), [rej'-is-ter], *v.t.* to record or enter in a register; to indicate, record automatically; to insure against loss or damage in postal transit or non-delivery, by payment of an extra fee; (*print.*) to cause to correspond in alignment; to adjust; to record and fix indelibly (in the mind, memory); (*cinema*) to express (some particular emotion) on the countenance; *v.i.* to sign one's name in a register; to report for registration, *esp.* for the forces or national service; (*print.*) to correspond in alignment. [MedL. *registrare*].

REGISTER-OFFICE, [rej'-is-ter-of'-is], *n.* an office for purposes of registration, or in which a public register is kept; a registry-office.

REGISTERSHIP, [rej'-is-ter-ship], *n.* the office of register or registrar.

REGISTRABLE, [rej'-is-trabl], *adj.* able or requiring to be registered.

REGISTRAR, [rej'-is-trah(r)'], *n.* an official keeper of records or a register, one who registers; **R. General,** the official appointed to superintend registration of any kind, *esp.* of births, marriages and deaths in England and Wales. [MedL. *registrarius*].

REGISTRARSHIP, [rej'-is-trah-ship], *n.* the office of registrar.

REGISTRATION, [rej'-is-trā'-shun], *n.* the act of registering or entering in a register; an entry in a register; (*print.*) adjustment to secure correspondence of alignment on each side of a printed page or correct imposition of colours; (*mus.*) combination of tonal colouring in organ playing.

REGISTRY, [rej'-is-tri], *n.* the act of recording in a register; the place where a register is kept; an entry in a register; a register; **r.-office,** the office at which a registrar performs civil marriages, the office at which the registrar keeps a register of the births, marriages, and deaths within his district; an office for supplying domestic servants.

REGIUS, [re'-ji-us], *adj.* royal; **R. Professor,** the holder of a professorship founded by Henry VIII or one having the same status. [L. *regius* royal].

REGLET, [reg'-let], *n.* (*arch.*) a flat, narrow moulding; (*print.*) a slip of wood used for separating lines or filling up blank spaces. [Fr. *réglet*, *dim.* of *règle* rule].

REGNAL, [reg'-nal], *adj.* relating to a reign of a sovereign; **r. year,** a year counted from the date of accession of a king; **r. day,** the day or its anniversary on which the accession of a king took place.

REGNANT, [reg'-nant], *adj.* reigning, exercising regal power and authority, ruling; predominant, prevalent. [L. *regnans*].

REGORGE, [rē-gawj'], *v.t.* to vomit; to swallow again; to swallow eagerly; *v.i.* to flow back again. [OFr. *regorger*].

REGRANT (1), [rē'-grahnt'], *n.* a renewed grant.

REGRANT (2), [rē'-grahnt'], *v.t.* to grant again.

REGRATE, [rē-grāt'], *v.t.* (*hist.*) to buy provisions and sell them again in the same market or fair, a practice which, by raising the price, was at one time a public offence and punishable. [OFr. *regrater*].

RE-GRATE, [rē'-grāt'], *v.t.* to scrape and freshen (the dirty or blackened walls of a building) in order to provide a clean new surface.

REGRATER, [rē-grāt'-er], *n.* (*hist.*) one who buys provisions and sells them in the same market.

REGRATING, [rē-grāt'-ing], *n.* the process of scraping off the surface of old hewn stone, to give it a fresh appearance.

REGREET, [rē'-grēt'], *v.t.* to greet afresh, to return the greeting or salutation of.

REGRESS (1), [rē'-gres], *n.* a going back, return, passage back; backward movement or tendency, retrogression; (*leg.*) the right of entering upon a benefice again upon the death of the incumbent. [L. *regressus*].

REGRESS (2), [ri-gres'], *v.i.* to move or go backwards. [L. *regressus, p.pt.* of *regredi* to move backward].

REGRESSION, [ri-gresh'-un], *n.* the act of going or moving back, return; retrogression, relapse to a former worse state; (*math.*) the turning or bending back of a curve. [L. *regressio*].

REGRESSIVE, [ri-gres'-iv], *adj.* returning; moving backward, retrogressive, relapsing to a former inferior condition.

REGRESSIVELY, [ri-gres'-iv-li], *adv.* in a regressive fashion.

REGRET (1), [ri-gret'], *n.* sorrow, grief at some external unpleasant event, usually involving loss or deprivation of some kind; remorse, mortification, discomfort of mind upon reflecting on something which has been done or has happened. [Fr. *regret*].

REGRET (2), (regretting, regretted), [ri-gret'], *v.t.* to feel sorrow at, grieve at, to be sorry (at, for), lament, deplore; to remember or think of with regret. [OFr. *regreter*].

REGRETFUL, [ri-gret'-fŏŏl], *adj.* full of regret.

REGRETFULLY, [ri-gret'-fŏŏl-i], *adv.* with regret.

REGRETTABLE, [ri-gret'-abl], *adj.* to be regretted or deprecated; deplorable, lamentable, unfortunate.

REGRETTABLY, [ri-gret'-ab-li], *adv.* in a regrettable fashion.

REGROUP, [rē'-grōōp'], *v.t. and i.* to form anew into a group or groups, to re-form.

REGULAR (1), [reg'-yōō-ler], *n.* (*eccles.*) a member of a religious order bound by a rule; a soldier who is a member of the standing or permanent army.

REGULAR (2), [reg'-yōō-ler], *adj.* following some rule, plan, or arrangement, symmetrical, even, orderly; habitual, constant, not varying, continued without interruption or deviation, pursued with uniformity, or as if in accordance with a rule, never failing to do some action, and (often with the implication of) at a set time, recurring at set times; conforming to rule, custom, or established precedent, in accordance with what is deemed normal or correct; ordered, steady, normal; proper, fully qualified; (of an army) permanent, standing; (*eccles.*) belonging to a monastic order, bound by the rule of a religious order; (*gram.*) formed in accordance with a uniform pattern; (*geom.*) with the sides and angles equal; (of a solid) having exactly corresponding faces; (*bot.*) with its parts of the same size and shape; (*coll.*) utter, complete, typical, thorough; **r. troops,** the troops of the standing or permanent army. [L. *regularis* of a rule].

REGULARITY, [reg'-yōō-la'-rit-i], *n.* the quality of being regular; uniformity, symmetry; recurrence at fixed intervals; orderliness; conformity to principle, rule or precedent; steadiness in pursuing a course.

REGULARIZATION, [reg'-yōō-ler-iz-ā'-shun], *n.* the act of making regular; the state of being made regular.

REGULARIZE, [reg'-yōō-ler-iz], *v.t.* to make regular.

REGULARLY, [reg'-yōō-ler-li], *adv.* in a regular manner; at regular periods, without fail; with regularity, constantly, much more often than not; (*coll.*) completely.

REGULATE, [reg'-yōō-lāt], *v.t.* to base upon and govern by rule, to subject to rule; to put in order, to adjust so that it functions accurately; to adjust to a particular standard or rate, to control. [~L. *regulare*].

REGULATION (1), [reg'-yōō-lā'-shun], *n.* the act of regulating; the state of being regulated; a prescribed rule or order to be complied with.

REGULATION (2), [reg'-yōō-lā'-shun], *adj.* in accordance with, prescribed or fixed by, regulation.

REGULATIVE, [reg'-yōō-lat-iv], *adj.* tending to regulate, that regulates.

REGULATOR, [reg'-yōō-lāt-er], *n.* one who regulates; a mechanical device for regulating or controlling the movement or working of a machine, or the flow, pressure, or force of air, steam, gas, etc.; a lever for regulating the movement of a watch or clock.

REGULUS, [reg'-yōō-lus], *n.* (*astron.*) a star of the first magnitude in the constellation Leo; †(*chem.*) the metallic part of a mineral separated from its compound by means of a reducing agent; a still impure product of smelting; a minor king or ruler; the golden-crested wren; †the alchemists' name for metallic antimony. [L. *regulus*].

REGURGITATE, [rē-gurj'-it-āt], *v.t.* to throw or pour back, to vomit out or eject from (the stomach or other receptacle); *v.i.* to be thrown or poured back or ejected, as from the stomach.

REGURGITATION, [rē-gurj'-it-ā'-shun], *n.* the act of pouring or flowing back, or of being cast out again; a backward flow of blood to the heart or food to the mouth. [L. *regurgitatio*].

REHABILITATE, [rē'-hab-il'-it-āt], *v.t.* to restore to a former capacity, position, or estate, to reinstate; to re-establish in favour again, to restore to esteem or good repute, to clear from stain or suspicion. [L. *rehabilitare*].

REHABILITATION, [rē'-hab-il-it-ā'-shun], *n.* an act of reinstating in a former rank or capacity; restoration to former rights or estate; restoration to favour or good repute again.

REHANDLE, [rē'-handl'], *v.t.* to handle afresh.

REHANG, (rehung), [rē'-hang'], *v.t.* to hang afresh.

REHASH (1), [rē'-hash'], *n.* a serving up anew in a different form or way.

REHASH (2), [rē'-hash'], *v.t.* to hash up again, to dish up anew or offer again in a slightly modified form or new guise.

REHEAR, (reheard), [rē'-hēer'], *v.t.* to hear or try over again.

REHEARING, [rē'-hēer'-ing], *n.* a fresh hearing.

REHEARSAL, [ri-hurs'-al], *n.* the act of rehearsing; practice, performance or recital in private in preparation for future public performance.

REHEARSE, [ri-hurs'], *v.t.* to repeat, narrate, recount, relate, enumerate; to go through repeatedly or practise in private in preparation for future public performance; *v.i.* to have a rehearsal. [OFr. *rehercer* to harrow again].

REHEARSER, [ri-hurs'-er], *n.* one who rehearses.

RE-HEAT, [rē'-hēt'], *v.t.* to heat up again.

REHOUSE, [rē'-howz'], *v.t.* to provide new dwellings for.

REICH, [rīkh], *n.* the German State; **Third R.,** the name given to Germany while under National-Socialist rule. [Germ. *reich*].

REICHSRAT, [rīkhs'-raht], *n.* the parliament of the former Austrian Empire. [*Prec.* and Germ. *rat* counsel].

REICHSTAG, [rīkhs'-tahk], *n.* one of the houses of the supreme legislature of Germany. [Germ. *reich* empire and *tag* day].

REIFY, [rē'-i-fī], *v.t.* to materialize, to put into a real or concrete form. [L. *res* thing and *facere* to make].

REIGN (1), [rān], *n.* rule, supreme power of a king or sovereign, royal authority, sovereignty; the period during which a monarch reigns; sway, dominion, prevailing influence; predominance. [OFr. *regne* from L. *regnum*].

REIGN (2), [rān], *v.i.* to rule as a monarch; to be the temporary supreme example of something, to hold sway; to prevail, be predominant. [OFr. *regner* from L. *regnare*].

REIGNING, [rān'-ing], *adj.* ruling, exercising supreme power; predominating; prevailing.

RE-IGNITE, [rē-ig-nīt'], *v.t. and i.* to rekindle.

REILLUMINATION, [rē'-il-ōōm-in-ā'-shun], *n.* the act of reillumining; the state of being reillumined; fresh illumination.

REILLUMINE, [rē'-il-ōōm'-in], *v.t.* to enlighten again; to illumine afresh.

REIM, [rēm], *n.* a strip of ox-hide rendered pliable. [Du. *riem*].

REIMBURSABLE, [rē'-im-burs'-abl], *adj.* repayable.

REIMBURSE, [rē-im-burs'], *v.t.* to refund; to pay back to.

REIMBURSEMENT, [rē'-im-burs'-ment], *n.* repayment, refunding of money expended.

REIMBURSER, [rē-im-burs'-er], *n.* one who reimburses.

REIMPORT, [rē'-im-pawt'], *v.t.* to import back again (what has been exported), *esp.* in a manufactured form.

REIMPORTATION, [rē'-im-pawt-ā'-shun], *n.* the act of reimporting.

REIMPOSE, [rē'-im-pōz'], *v.t.* to impose again; (*print.*) to rearrange pages for printing.

RE-IMPRESSION, [rē'-im-presh'-un], *n.* a reprint or second impression.

REIN (1), [rān], *n.* a long leather strap fastened to each side of the bit or bridle of a horse, by which the horse is controlled (often in *pl.*); (*fig.*) anything that curbs, restrains, controls, governs or guides; **to give r. to,** to indulge without restraint, give free play to; **to keep a tight r. on,** to keep under rigid control. [OFr. *rene*].

REIN (2), [rān], *v.t.* to provide with a rein, to fit a rein to; to hold in or check with a rein (often with *in*); (*fig.*) to restrain, curb, keep under rigid control. [*Prec.*].

REINCARNATE (1), [rē'-in-kahn'-at], *adj.* re-embodied, born again in another body.

REINCARNATE (2), [rē'-in-kahn-āt'], *v.t. and i.* to re-embody, to appear again in bodily form.

REINCARNATION, [rē'-in-kahn-ā'-shun], *n.* re-embodiment; the return of the soul to earth after death, in a fresh bodily form.

REINCORPORATE, [rē'-in-kawp'-er-āt], *v.t.* to incorporate afresh.

REINDEER, RANEDEER†, [rān'-dēēr], *n.* a species of deer, *Rangifer tarandus*, found in N. Europe and Asia, having large, curved branching antlers, and used for drawing sledges and milking purposes; **r. moss,** a lichen, *Cladonia rangiferina*, on which the reindeer feeds during winter. [OScand. *hreinn* reindeer and DEER].

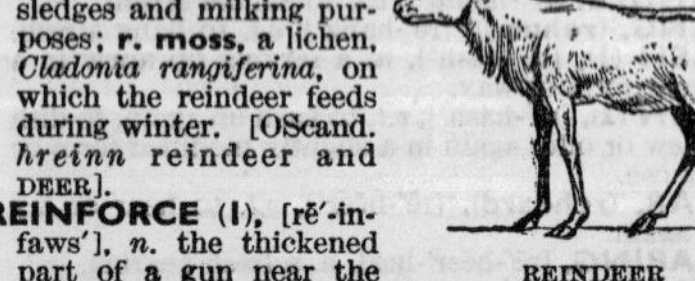

REINDEER

REINFORCE (1), [rē'-in-faws'], *n.* the thickened part of a gun near the breech.

REINFORCE (2), RE-ENFORCE, [rē'-in-faws'], *v.t.* to strengthen by additional men, material or supplies; to increase the numbers of in order to strengthen; to strengthen by additional support, thickness, etc.; to make stronger, add to the strength of, back up; **reinforced concrete,** concrete strengthened by having steel bars or netting embedded in it.

REINFORCEMENT, RE-ENFORCEMENT, [rē'-in-faws'-ment], *n.* the act of reinforcing; that which reinforces; (*pl.*) (*milit.*) fresh troops or supplies to reinforce an army, etc.

REINLESS, [rān'-les], *adj.* without a rein; (*fig.*) without restraint, unchecked.

REINS (1), see REIN (1).

REINS (2), [rānz], *n.(pl.)* the kidneys; the loins; the lower part of the back. [OFr. *reins* from L. *renes*].

REINSERT, [rē'-in-surt'], *v.t.* to insert again.

REINSTALL, [rē'-in-stawl'], *v.t.* to install afresh.

REINSTATE, [rē'-in-stāt'], *v.t.* to restore to a former state or position.

REINSTATEMENT, [rē'-in-stāt'-ment], *n.* re-establishment; the act of reinstating, the state of being reinstated.

REINSURANCE, [rē'-in-shōōer'-ants], *n.* a transfer of the risks of insurance to others by an insurer to insure himself against possible loss on a policy of insurance he has issued.

REINSURE, [rē'-in-shōōer'], *v.i.* (of an insurance company or agent) to safeguard oneself against possible loss of a policy of insurance issued by insuring again with a different insurer.

REINSURER, [rē'-in-shōōer'-er], *n.* one who reinsures.

REINTEGRATE, [rē'-in'-tig-rāt], *v.t.* to integrate afresh, make whole again, restore, re-establish in complete form.

REINTEGRATION, [rē'-in-tig-rā'-shun], *n.* a renewing; restoration, re-establishment in perfect form, making whole again.

REINVEST, [rē'-in-vest'], *v.t.* to restore to, endow again (with); to invest (money) again.

REINVESTITURE, [rē'-in-ves'-tich-er], *n.* the act of investing again (with), a fresh investiture.

REINVESTMENT, [rē'-in-vest'-ment], *n.* the act of investing money anew.

REINVIGORATE, [rē'-in-vig'-er-āt], *v.t.* to reanimate, give fresh vigour to, brace up.

REIS, [rās], *n.* a Portuguese money of account. [Portug. *reis*, *pl.* of REAL (2)].

REISSUE (1), [rē'-ish'-yōō], *n.* a fresh issue.

REISSUE (2), [rē'-ish'-yōō], *v.t.* to issue afresh; to reprint (a book, etc.).

REITERANT, [rē-it'-er-ant], *adj.* repeating.

REITERATE, [rē'-it'-er-āt], *v.t.* to repeat again and again. [L. *reiterare* to go over again].

REITERATEDLY, [rē'-it'-er-āt'-id-li], *adv.* repeatedly.

REITERATION, [rē'-it-er-ā'-shun], *n.* repetition.

REITERATIVE (1), [rē'-it'-er-at-iv], *n.* (*gram.*) a word formed by repetition or reduplication.

REITERATIVE (2), [rē'-it'-er-at-iv], *adj.* exhibiting or characterized by repetition or reiteration.

REIVE, see REAVE.

REJECT (1), [rē'-jekt], *n.* that which has been rejected.

REJECT (2), [ri-jekt'], *v.t.* to throw away, discard, as being worthless or unsatisfactory; to refuse or decline to accept; to refuse to grant or recognize; (of the stomach) to refuse to digest and assimilate. [L. *rejectus*, *p.pt.* of *rejicere* to throw back].

REJECTABLE, [ri-jekt'-abl], *adj.* capable of being rejected.

REJECTAMENTA, [ri-jekt'-am-en'-ta], *n.(pl.)* refuse; matter thrown away as useless or rubbish. [MdL. *rejectamentum*].

REJECTER, [ri-jekt'-er], *n.* one who rejects or refuses.

REJECTION, [ri-jek'-shun], *n.* the act of rejecting; refusal to accept or grant. [L. *rejectio*].

REJECTIVE, [ri-jekt'-iv], *adj.* tending to reject or refuse.

REJECTMENT, [ri-jekt'-ment], *n.* matter thrown away as rubbish, refuse.

REJECTOR, [ri-jekt'-or], *n.* a rejecter.

REJOICE, [ri-jois'], *v.t.* to gladden, make joyful; *v.i.* to be joyful, make merry; to experience great pleasure, to be delighted. [ME. *rejoysen* from OFr. *réjoir*].

REJOICER, [ri-jois'-er], *n.* one who rejoices.

REJOICING, [ri-jois'-ing], *n.* a feeling of joy, manifestation or expression of gladness or exultation, an occasion or subject for joy (often *pl.*).

REJOICINGLY, [ri-jois'-ing-li], *adv.* with joy or exultation.

REJOIN (1), [rē'-join'], *v.t.* to join together again; to meet or join again, become reunited with; *v.i.* to come together again.

REJOIN (2), [ri-join'], *v.i.* to reply to an answer; (*leg.*) (of a defendant) to answer to the plaintiff's replication. [Fr. *rejoindre*].

REJOINDER, [ri-join'-der], *n.* a reply to an answer; an answer; (*leg.*) the defendant's answer to the plaintiff's replication. [Fr. *rejoindre* to rejoin].

REJOINT, [rē'-joint'], *v.t.* to reunite joints; to fill up old joints of walls with new mortar.

REJOINTING, [rē'-joint'-ing], *n.* the filling up of the joints of stones in buildings with fresh mortar.

REJUDGE, [rē'-juj'], *v.t.* to judge afresh; to re-examine; to call to a new trial and decision.

REJUVENATE, [rē-jōō'-ven-āt], *v.t.* to make young and active again; *v.i.* to become young and fresh again. [RE (1) and L. *juvenis* young].

REJUVENATION, [rē-jōō'-ven-ā'-shun], *n.* the act of rejuvenating; the state of being rejuvenated.

REJUVENESCE, [rē-jōō'-ven-es'], *v.t.* (*biol.*) to cause to acquire fresh vitality; *v.i.* to become young again; (*biol.*) to acquire fresh vitality and activity (of cells).

REJUVENESCENCE, [rē-jōō'-ven-es'-ents], *n.* renewal of youth; the state of being made or of becoming young again; (*biol.*) the formation of new cells to replace older ones.

REJUVENESCENT, [rē-jōō'-ven-es'-ent], *adj.* growing young once again.

REJUVENIZE, [rē-jōō'-ven-iz], *v.t.* to make young again.

REKINDLE, [rē-kindl'], *v.t.* to kindle again; to inflame or rouse anew; *v.i.* to be rekindled, to blaze up again.

RELABEL, [rē'-lā'-bel], *v.t.* to put a fresh label on, to rechristen.

RELAIS, [ri-lā'], *n.* (*fort.*) a narrow walk outside the rampart to prevent the soil from being washed down into the ditch. [Fr. *relais*].

RELAND, [rē'-land'], *v.t. and i.* to land again.

RELAPSE (1), [ri-laps'], *n.* a sliding or falling back to a former bad state or worse condition.

RELAPSE (2), [ri-laps'], *v.i.* to fall or slip back to a former worse state, to fall back into error, to resume one's former evil ways or practices; (of a sick person) to fall back into a worse state of bodily health, to become worse; (of shares and stocks) to depreciate. [L. *relapsum*, *p.pt.* of *relabi* to slip back].

RELAPSER, [ri-laps'-er], *n.* one who relapses into vice or error.

RELATE, [ri-lāt'], *v.t.* to tell, narrate, recount; to bring into connexion with, show the connexion between; *v.i.* to refer, to have reference; **to r. to,** to be in relation, accord, to show connexion with; (*pass.*) to belong to the same family as, to be allied to, to be connected by blood, marriage, or distinct fundamental traits (to). [L. *relatus*, *p.pt.* of *referre* to bring back].

RELATED, [ri-lāt'-id], *adj.* belonging to the same family, connected by birth or marriage; allied, standing in some relation to each other.

RELATEDNESS, [ri-lāt'-id-nes], *n.* the state of being related.

RELATER, [ri-lāt'-er], *n.* one who relates or narrates; an informant; a relator.

RELATION, [ri-lā'-shun], *n.* that which, or one who, is related; blood connexion, kinship, connexion by birth, family, or marriage; a person related to another by birth or marriage, one belonging to the same family as another, a kinsman or kinswoman, relative; the way in which things or persons are related, the connexion, the way in which things correspond or differ; (*pl.*) mutual intercourse and dealings whether personal or otherwise, *esp.* the manner in which these are carried out; the act of telling or relating, a narrative, account. [L. *relatio* a bringing back].

RELATIONAL, [ri-lā'-shun-al], *adj.* having, expressing, or belonging to, relation.

RELATIONSHIP, [ri-lā'-shun-ship], *n.* the state of being related by kindred, affinity, or other alliance; the way in which things are related; the way in which things correspond or differ, connexion.

RELATIVE (1), [rel'-at-iv], *n.* a person related to another by blood or marriage, a kinsman or kinswoman; that which has relation to something else; (*gram.*) a word which relates to, or stands in place of, another word, clause or sentence, called its antecedent.

RELATIVE (2), [rel'-at-iv], *adj.* considered in relation to, or with respect to, something else, comparative, not absolute, taken in connexion with something else, having or implying a relation to something else; referring, belonging, pertinent, respecting; possessing mutual relationship, respective, of each in relation to each; (*gram.*) relating to a previous word, sentence, or clause. [L. *relativus* having relation].

RELATIVELY, [rel'-at-iv-li], *adv.* in a relative manner, not absolutely, comparatively.

RELATIVENESS, [rel'-at-iv-nes], *n.* the state of being relative.

RELATIVITY, [rel'-at-iv'-i-ti], *n.* the state or quality of being relative; (*philos.*) the doctrine that all knowledge is merely relative, there being a distinction between things as they actually are and as they are perceived by us; (*phys.*) a mathematical theory of the universe, first put forward by Einstein, that all measurements made in the ordinary way are relative, since nothing in the universe is at rest, and therefore there is no absolute standard to which all measurements of velocity may be referred.

RELATOR, [ri-lāt'-or], *n.* (*leg.*) an informer, one who gives information leading to the instituting of legal proceedings by the state. [L. *relator*].

RELAX, [ri-laks'], *v.t.* to loosen, slacken, make less tense or rigid; to slacken the strain of, to make less strict or severe, to lessen the force of, abate in intensity, ease; to relieve from constipation; to enervate, make languid; *v.i.* to slacken, loosen, to become less tense, excited, strained, or firm, to let oneself go, become limp and at rest; to become less severe or strict; to slacken or abate in zeal and intensity; **relaxed throat,** a form of sore throat. [L. *relaxare*].

RELAXABLE, [ri-laks'-abl], *adj.* capable of being relaxed.

RELAXANT, [ri-laks'-ant], *n.* a medicine that relaxes.

RELAXATION, [re'-laks-ā'-shun], *n.* the act of relaxing; the state of being relaxed; abatement of tension, rigour, attention, or application; that which relaxes, recreation, amusement, rest or diversion from work or toil; (*leg.*) the remission of a portion of a sentence, penalty, etc.

RELAXING, [ri-laks'-ing], *adj.* that relaxes; enervating.

RELAY (1), [rē'-lā], *n.* a fresh shift of workers to relieve those who have worked a certain length of time; a fresh supply of hounds for hunting, or horses in travelling, kept in readiness at various points along a route, to take the place of those tired; (*elect.*) a device for making and breaking a local circuit when current is put through the coils of an electro-magnet; a device by which a circuit of relatively weak current is able to control a circuit of high current; (*wirel.*) a broadcast in which the programme is sent to a broadcasting station from which it is re-diffused to listeners in the ordinary way; a relay-race; **r. system,** (*wirel.*) a system of wireless reception in which the broadcast programme is received by a central receiving set, and thence transmitted along telephone lines to subscribers who pay a weekly or monthly rental; **r. station,** (*wirel.*) a broadcasting station transmitting programmes received by telephone line from another station. [OFr. *relais*].

RELAY (2), [rē-lā'], *v.t.* (*teleg. or wirel.*) to receive from a transmitting apparatus or broadcasting station, and then re-broadcast to listeners; to replace by relays. [*Prec.*].

RE-LAY, [rē'-lā'], *v.t.* to lay again.

RELAY-RACE, [rē'-lā-rās'], *n.* a race in which two or more teams take part, each member running a portion of the total distance to be covered, and handing over a baton, as he completes his lap, to another member of the team, who may not start until he has received it, the winner being the team whose member comes in first over the final lap.

RELEASABLE, [ri-lēs'-abl], *adj.* capable of being, or that may be, released.

RELEASE (1), [ri-lēs'], *n.* discharge from an obligation; liberation from pain, suffering, trouble, etc.; setting at liberty from captivity or confinement; the act of releasing or discharging; the act of allowing a thing to be exhibited, published, or offered for sale on a particular date; that which is exhibited, published, or offered for sale in this way; the catch by which some part of machinery is released; (*leg.*) formal written discharge of a debt or obligation; a conveyance, transfer of ownership, or alteration in the conditions, of an estate, right, title, action, etc.; the document in which this is set forth. [OFr. *reles*].

RELEASE (2), [ri-lēs'], *v.t.* to set at liberty, set free from restraint, confinement or captivity; to free from pain, trouble, anxiety, etc.; to discharge; (*leg.*) to give up, surrender, convey, transfer; to permit to be exhibited, published, or offered for sale on a certain date. [OFr. *relesser* from L. *relaxare*].

RE-LEASE, [rē'-lēs'], *v.t.* to give a new lease to, to lease again. [RE (1) and LEASE].

RELEASEE, [ri-lēs'-ē'], *n.* (*leg.*) one to whom something is released.

RELEASEMENT, [ri-lēs'-ment], *n.* the act of releasing.

RELEASER, [ri-lēs'-er], *n.* one who releases.

RELEASOR, [ri-lēs'-or], *n.* (*leg.*) one who releases a right, claim, debt, estate, etc.

RELEGATE, [rel'-ig-āt], *v.t.* †to banish, send into exile; to consign to an inferior rank, status, or less important place; to transfer, hand over for carrying out, to submit or refer for decision; (*sport,* chiefly Association football) to cause to play in a lower division for the next season at least, as a penalty for finishing the season at the foot of the division. [L. *relegare* to banish].

RELEGATION, [rel′-ig-ā′-shun], *n.* the act of relegating; the state of being relegated; (*Rom. antiq.*) temporary banishment without loss of civil rights. [L. *relegatio*].

RELENT, [ri-lent′], *v.i.* to soften in temper, to become less severe in intention, to yield to entreaty, etc. [OFr. *ralentir* to slacken].

RELENTING, [ri-lent′-ing], *n.* the act of becoming more mild or compassionate.

RELENTINGLY, [ri-lent′-ing-li], *adv.* in a relenting manner.

RELENTLESS, [ri-lent′-les], *adj.* unmoved by pity; unrelenting, merciless, stern, inflexible, obdurate, unyielding, inexorable.

RELENTLESSLY, [ri-lent′-les-li], *adv.* in a relentless fashion.

RELENTLESSNESS, [ri-lent′-les-nes], *n.* the quality of being relentless.

RELET, (**reletting, relet**), [rē′-let′], *v.t.* to let (a house, etc.) anew.

RELEVANCE, [rel′-iv-ants], *n.* relevancy.

RELEVANCY, [rel′-iv-an-si], *n.* the state or quality of being relevant, pertinence, appositeness.

RELEVANT, [rel′-iv-ant], *adj.* pertinent, applicable, apposite, concerned with or bearing on the matter in hand, having to do with what is being considered. [MedL. *relevans*].

RELEVANTLY, [rel′-iv-ant-li], *adv.* pertinently, appositely.

RELIABILITY, [ri-lī′-ab-il′-i-ti], *n.* the quality of being reliable; **r. trials**, long-distance trials for motor vehicles to test their reliability rather than their speed.

RELIABLE, [ri-lī′-abl], *adj.* that may be relied on or trusted, trustworthy, dependable.

RELIABLENESS, [ri-lī′-abl-nes], *n.* the quality of being reliable.

RELIABLY, [ri-lī′-ab-li], *adv.* in a reliable manner; on good authority.

RELIANCE, [ri-lī′-ants], *n.* the act of relying, confidence, trust, dependence; (*archaic*) something upon which one relies.

RELIANT, [ri-lī′-ant], *adj.* confident, trusting.

RELIC, RELIQUE, [rel′-ik], *n.* a memorial of some holy person, usually a part of the body, a personal possession or the like, kept and regarded with reverence; any fragment left over from the past, an object, custom, belief, etc., surviving in a period when it is outmoded; any valued token of the past, of past emotions or events; (*poet.* usually in *pl.*) the remains of a dead person. [L. *reliquiae* remains].

RELICT, [rel′-ikt], *n.* a widow. [L. *relicta*].

RELIEF (**1**), [ri-lēf′], *n.* the condition of being relieved; alleviation of pain, distress, etc.; that which affords such alleviation; help, aid, assistance; the raising of a siege of a besieged town, castle, etc.; an official grant of money to relieve poverty, distress, etc.; anything providing a change from that which has become tedious or monotonous; release from a duty or office, or from a spell of duty; the person or persons who so relieve one; (*leg.*) exemption, remission. [OFr. *relef*].

RELIEF (**2**), [ri-lēf′], *n.* a mode of carving in which the figures stand out from the background; the amount by which the figures stand out; an example of such relief; (*fig.*) sharpness or distinctness provided by contrast, contrast. [It. *rilievo*].

RELIEF MAP, [ril-ēf′-map′], *n.* a map in which the contour of the country is suggested by shading or hachuring on the surface of the map. [*Prec.* and MAP].

RELIER, [ri-lī′-er], *n.* a person who relies on another or on some external aid.

RELIEVABLE, [ri-lēv′-abl], *adj.* able to be relieved.

RELIEVE, [ri-lēv′], *v.t.* to lessen, alleviate, lighten, assuage, mitigate; to free, help, assist, succour, release; to deprive; to break the monotony or tedium of; **to r. one's feelings**, to give expression to one's feelings; **to r. oneself**, to evacuate the bowels. [L. *relevare* to raise, lighten].

RELIEVER, [ri-lēv′-er], *n.* one who relieves.

RELIEVING-ARCH, [ri-lēv′-ing-ahch′], *n.* (*arch.*) an arch built into a wall to help carry the weight above.

RELIEVING OFFICER, [ri-lēv′-ing-of′-is-er], *n.* an officer who administers poor-relief in a given district.

RELIEVO, [ril-ē′-vō], *n.* relief; **alto r.**, high relief; **basso r.**, low relief. [It. *rilievo*].

RELIGHT, [rē′-līt′], *v.t. and i.* to light anew; to catch fire again.

RELIGIEUSE, [ril-ij′-i-urz′], *n.* a nun. [Fr. *religieuse*].

RELIGIEUX, [ril-ij′-i-u(r)′], *n.* a monk, or friar. [Fr. *religieux*].

RELIGION, [ri-lij′-on], *n.* the belief in a supernatural power or powers, belief in a god or gods, *esp.* such belief as entails acts of worship on the part of the believer; a developed system of philosophical, theological, and ethical opinions, tenets and theories depending ultimately and essentially upon a belief in a deity or deities, and the necessity of worshipping that deity or those deities; the Christian religion; monastic life, a rule of monastic life; (*fig.*) an object of great devotion, an obsession. [L. *religio*].

RELIGIONARY (**1**), [ril-ij′-on-er-i], *n.* a member of a religious order.

RELIGIONARY (**2**), [ril-ij′-on-er-i], *adj.* pertaining to religion.

RELIGIONER, [ri-lij′-on-er], *n.* a religionary; an enthusiast for religion.

RELIGIONISM, [ri-lij′-on-izm], *n.* an enthusiastic profession of religion, *esp.* an unreal or exaggerated enthusiasm.

RELIGIONIST, [ri-lij′-on-ist], *n.* a religionary.

RELIGIONIZE, [ri-lij′-on-īz], *v.t. and i.* to convert to a religion; to make a display of religion.

RELIGIONLESS, [ri-lij′-on-les], *adj.* having no religion.

RELIGIOSE, [ri-lij′-i-ōs′], *adj.* excessively or morbidly religious. [L. *religiosus*].

RELIGIOSITY, [ri-lij′-i-os′-i-ti], *n.* the state of being religiose.

RELIGIOUS, [ri-lij′-us], *adj.* pertaining to religion; believing in a religion, controlled by a religion, pious, godly; connected with a monastery or convent; (*fig.*) exact, scrupulous, regular, conscientious; unquestioning. [L. *religiosus*].

RELIGIOUSLY, [ri-lij′-us-li], *adv.* in a religious way, piously; scrupulously.

RELIGIOUSNESS, [ri-lij′-us-nes], *n.* the condition of being religious.

RELINE, [rē′-līn′], *v.t.* to provide with new lining.

RELINQUISH, [ri-ling′-kwish], *v.t.* to resign, let go one's hold on; to leave, surrender; to desist or cease from. [Fr. *relinquir* from L. *relinquere* to leave].

RELINQUISHER, [ri-ling′-kwish-er], *n.* one who relinquishes.

RELINQUISHMENT, [ri-ling′-kwish-ment], *n.* the act of relinquishing or surrendering.

RELIQUARY, [rel′-ik-wer-i], *n.* a casket or shrine where a sacred relic is kept. [MedL. *reliquarium*].

RELIQUE, see RELIC.

RELIQUIAE, [ri-lik′-wi-ē], *n.*(*pl.*) relics; literary remains; (*bot.*) leaves that do not fall from the stem when withered; (*geol.*) fossilized remains of plants or animals. [L. *reliquiae* remains].

RELISH (**1**), [rel′-ish], *n.* a taste or smell, a flavour or aroma, *esp.* an appetizing flavour of any kind; a spice or condiment added to food to make it richer and more appetizing; a stimulating, spicy quality; keenness or zest for anything. [OFr. *reles* an after-taste].

RELISH (**2**), [rel′-ish], *v.t. and i.* to make appetizing, impart a special flavour or relish to; to eat with pleasure, enjoy in the eating; (*fig.*) to enjoy, be eager for; to taste of; to contain a hint or suspicion of; to affect the taste. [*Prec.*].

RELISHABLE, [rel′-ish-abl], *adj.* able to be relished.

RELIVE, [rē′-liv′], *v.t. and i.* to live through again, revive; to live again.

RELOAD, [rē-lōd′], *v.t. and i.* to load again

RELUCENT, [rē-lōō′-sent], *adj.* (*poet.*) shining, bright. [L. *relucens*].

RELUCTANCE, [ri-luk′-tants], *n.* the quality or state of being reluctant.

RELUCTANCY, [ri-luk′-tan-si], *n.* the condition of being reluctant.

RELUCTANT, [ri-luk′-tant], *adj.* unwilling, showing distaste, expressing disinclination, loth; unmanageable. [L. *reluctari* to struggle against].

RELUCTANTLY, [ri-luk′-tant-li], *adv.* with reluctance, in a reluctant manner.

RELUME, [rē-lōōm′], *v.t.* (*poet.*) to rekindle; to make bright. [RE (1) and (IL)LUME].

RELUMINE, [rel-ōō′-min], *v.t.* to rekindle, to relume. [L. *reluminare*].

RELY, [ril-ī′], *v.i.* to trust (in), depend (on, upon). [OFr. *relier*].

REMAIN, [ri-mān′], *v.i.* to be left over; to survive, persist; to stay behind in the same place; to be unchanged in condition, to continue to be. [OFr. *remaindre* from L. *remanere*].

REMAINDER, (1), [ri-mān'-der], *n.* that which is left over; that which is left behind, a residue, remnant. [OFr. *remaindre*].

REMAINDER (2), [ri-mān'-der], *v.t.* to offer (a book) for sale as a remainder at a reduced price.

REMAINS, [ri-mānz], *n.(pl.)* persons or things left over, survivors; relics; those works of an author not yet published at his death; a corpse. [~REMAIN].

REMAKE, [rē-māk'], *v.t.* to make again, to reshape.

REMAN, [rē'-man'], *v.t.* to supply with fresh men.

REMAND (1), [ri-mahnd'], *n.* the act of remanding.

REMAND (2), [ri-mahnd'], *v.t.* to order a charged person to be recommitted to prison pending the discovery or examination of further evidence. [OFr. *remander*].

REMANET, [rem'-an-et], *n.* something left over; (*leg.*) a case postponed to another sitting; (*parl.*) a bill left over till another session. [L. *remanet* it remains].

REMARGIN, [rē'-mahj'-in], *v.t.* to provide (a print, etc.) with a fresh margin or margins.

REMARK (1), [ri-mahk'], *n.* the act of observing or remarking; a comment spoken or written, a reflection. [Fr. *remarque*].

REMARK (2), [ri-mahk'], *v.t. and i.* to observe or notice; to feel; to perceive; to say or write by way of comment. [Fr. *remarquer*].

RE-MARK, [rē'-mahk'], *v.t.* to mark once more.

REMARKABLE, [ri-mahk'-abl], *adj.* worthy of notice; conspicuous, extraordinary, striking.

REMARKABLENESS, [ri-mahk'-abl-nes], *n.* the condition of being remarkable.

REMARKABLY, [ri-mahk'-ab-li], *adv.* in a remarkable manner, to a remarkable extent or degree.

REMARKER, [ri-mahk'-er], *n.* one who makes remarks.

REMARQUE, [ri-mahk'], *n.* a small sketch at the edge of an engraved plate frequently omitted in later impressions. [Fr. *remarque*].

REMARRIAGE, [rē'-ma'-rij], *n.* the act of marrying again after divorce or loss by death of a former spouse.

REMARRY, [rē'-ma'-ri], *v.t. and i.* to join together again in wedlock; to marry again (a partner to whom one has previously been married); to enter wedlock again. [RE (1) and MARRY].

REMAST, [rē'-mahst'], *v.t.* to provide with a new mast.

REMBLAI, [rom'-blā'], *n.* (*fort.*) earth and other material used to make a rampart. [Fr. *remblai*].

REMBRANDTESQUE, [rem'-brant-esk'], *adj.* resembling the manner of Rembrandt. [*Rembrandt*, a Dutch painter].

REMEDIABLE, [ri-mē'-di-abl], *adj.* able to be remedied.

REMEDIABLENESS, [ri-mēd'-i-abl-nes], *n.* the quality of being remediable.

REMEDIABLY, [ri-mē'-di-ab-li], *adv.* in a way that can be remedied.

REMEDIAL, [ri-mē'-di-al], *adj.* providing a remedy; intended for a remedy. [L. *remedialis*].

REMEDIALLY, [ri-mē'-di-a-li], *adv.* by way of remedy, so as to cure.

REMEDILESS, [rem'-id-i-les], *adj.* without remedy; incurable; hopeless.

REMEDILESSLY, [rem'-id-i-les-li], *adv.* in a remediless state.

REMEDILESSNESS, [rem'-id-i-les-nes], *n.* the quality of being remediless.

REMEDY (1), [rem'-id-i], *n.* that which heals or cures, a treatment or medicine; that which counteracts or corrects an evil, trouble, etc.; reparation for wrong endured; the margin of variation in weight or quality permitted in coinage; (*leg.*) damages for injury or loss of rights, etc. [L. *remedium* remedy].

REMEDY (2), [rem'-id-i], *v.t.* to put right, improve, provide a remedy for. [Fr. *remédier*].

REMELT, [rē'-melt'], *v.t. and i.* to melt again. [RE (1) and MELT].

REMEMBER, [ri-mem'-ber], *v.t. and i.* to call to mind, bear in mind (something learned or experienced in the past); to recall; to have the faculty of memory; to present with a gift either on some special occasion or in recognition of some service received; **to r. someone to somebody else,** to convey the regards of one to the other. [OFr. *remembrer*].

REMEMBERABLE, [ri-mem'-ber-abl], *adj.* worthy of remembrance, memorable.

REMEMBERER, [ri-mem'-ber-er], *n.* one who remembers.

REMEMBRANCE, [ri-mem'-brants], *n.* the act of remembering; the state of being remembered; the faculty of memory; a souvenir, a token serving to remind; (*pl.*) kindly greetings. [OFr. *remembrance*].

REMEMBRANCER, [ri-mem'-bran-ser], *n.* a person or thing that serves to remind; a token, a remembrance; **the King's R.,** an officer of the Supreme Court representing the Exchequer, who collects debts and dues on behalf of the Crown; **the City R.,** the legal officer of the City of London Corporation who represents its interests on Parliamentary committees, etc. [AFr. *remembrancer*].

REMIFORM, [rem'-i-fawm], *adj.* shaped like an oar. [L. *remus* oar and FORM (1)].

REMIGES, [rem'-ij-ēz], *n.(pl.)* a bird's flight-feathers. [L. *remus* oar].

REMIGES

REMIGRATE, [rē'-mī-grāt'], *v.i.* to migrate back.

REMIGRATION, [rē'-mī-grā'-shun], *n.* the act of remigrating.

REMIND, [ri-mīnd'], *v.t.* to cause to remember. [RE (1) and MIND (1)].

REMINDER, [ri-mīnd'-er], *n.* anything which reminds.

REMINDFUL, [ri-mīnd'-fŏol], *adj.* serving to remind.

REMINISCE, [rem'-in-is'], *v.i.* (*coll.*) to indulge in reminiscence. [REMINISCENCE].

REMINISCENCE, [rem'-in-is'-ents], *n.* the act and faculty of remembering; recollection, memory; something remembered, an anecdote of some remembered event; something that causes one to remember something else, usually by similarity or echo; (*philos.*) the Platonic doctrine that the acquisition of knowledge is really the recollection of what the spirit has known from before birth. [Fr. *reminiscence*].

REMINISCENT, [rem'-in-is'-ent], *adj.* serving to recall; dwelling on and telling reminiscences.

REMINISCENTIAL, [rem'-in-is-en'-shal], *adj.* (*philos.*) pertaining to reminiscence.

REMINISCENTLY, [rem'-in-is'-ent-li], *adv.* in a reminiscent way.

REMINT, [rē'-mint'], *v.t.* to mint (new coinage) from old.

REMIPED (1), [rem'-i-ped], *n.* (*zool.*) a crustacean of the genus, *Remipes*, having oar-shaped feet. [L. *remus* oar and *pes pedis* foot].

REMIPED (2), [rem'-i-ped], *adj.* having oar-shaped feet or feet used like oars.

REMISE (1), [rē-mīz'], *n.* (*leg.*) the legal surrender of any right or claim. [Fr. *remis*].

REMISE (2), [rem-ēz'], *n.* (*fencing*) a second thrust in a lunge, made without recovery from the first. [Fr. *remise*].

REMISE (3), [rē-mīz'], *v.t.* (*leg.*) to surrender (a right or claim).

REMISS, [ri-mis'], *adj.* careless, negligent. [L. *remissus*, *p.pt.* of *remittere* to relax].

REMISSIBILITY, [ri-mis'-ib-il'-i-ti], *n.* the state of being remissible.

REMISSIBLE, [ri-mis'-ibl], *adj.* able to be remitted or forgiven.

REMISSION, [ri-mish'-un], *n.* the act of remitting; pardon, forgiveness; the condition of being pardoned; the act of yielding, giving up, or surrendering (something); abatement. [OFr. *remission*].

REMISSIVE, [ri-mis'-iv], *adj.* remitting, causing or permitting remission.

REMISSLY, [ri-mis'-li], *adv.* in a remiss way.

REMISSNESS, [ri-mis'-nes], *n.* negligence, laxness, the quality of being remiss.

REMIT, [ri-mit'], *v.t. and i.* to abstain from exacting; to give up, surrender; to pardon; to moderate, cause to diminish, abate; to send back, return; to put off, postpone; to send (money), pay; (*leg.*) to direct (a case) to a lower court; to refer a case for authoritative decision. [L. *remittere* to send back].

REMITMENT, [ri-mit'-ment], *n.* the act of remitting; forgiveness; remittance.

REMITTAL, [ri-mit'-al], *n.* the act of remitting.

REMITTANCE, [ri-mit'-ants], *n.* the act of sending money; money sent as a payment or allowance, etc.

REMITTANCE-MAN, [ri-mit'-ants-man'], *n.* one living abroad on an allowance from home.

REMITTEE, [ri'-mit-ē'], *n.* one who receives a remittance.

REMITTENT (1), [ri-mit'-ent], *n.* (*path.*) a remittent fever.

REMITTENT (2), [ri-mit'-ent], *adj.* abating from time to time; **r. fever,** a fever which while getting much better at recurring periods never entirely leaves the patient.

REMITTER, [ri-mit'-er], *n.* one who remits or pardons; one who remits money to another; (*leg.*) the remitting of a case to another court.

REMNANT, [rem'-nant], *n.* a thing or collection of things or persons left over, a relic; (*pl.*) short pieces of fabric left over after the main pieces have been used or sold. [OFr. *remanant*].

REMODEL, [rē-mod'-el], *v.t.* to model or cast anew.

REMONETIZATION, [rē-mun'-it-ī-zā'-shun], *n.* the act of remonetizing.

REMONETIZE, [rē-mun'-it-īz], *v.t.* to restore (a currency) to its previous validity as legal tender.

REMONSTRANCE, [ri-mon'-strants], *n.* the act of remonstrating; a protest; a statement of grievances. [OFr. *remonstrance*].

REMONSTRANT (1), [ri-monst'-rant], *n.* one who remonstrates.

REMONSTRANT (2), [ri-monst'-rant], *adj.* expostulating.

REMONSTRATE, [ri-monst'-rāt], *v.i.* to expostulate, make formal protestation. [~MedL. *remonstrare* to point out].

REMONSTRATINGLY, [rem'-on-strāt-ing-li], *adv.* with remonstration.

REMONSTRATION, [rem'-on-strā'-shun], *n.* the act of protesting or remonstrating.

REMONSTRATIVE, [ri-mon'-strat-iv], *adj.* characterized by remonstrance, protesting, remonstrating.

REMONSTRATOR, [rim-on'-strāt-or], *n.* one who remonstrates.

REMONTANT (1), [ri-mont'-ant], *n.* (*bot.*) a remontant plant.

REMONTANT (2), [ri-mont'-ant], *adj.* (*bot.*) flowering twice in a season. [Fr. *remontant*].

REMONTOIR, [re'-mon-twah(r)'], *n.* a device in a clock that gives an exactly uniform impulse to the pendulum. [Fr. *remontoir*].

REMORSE, [ri-maws'], *n.* a strong sense of sorrow and regret for a sin or wrong committed or for a duty left undone, repentance, scruple, compunction; **without r.**, unscrupulously, callously. [OFr. *remors*].

REMORSEFUL, [ri-maws'-fool], *adj.* full of remorse, repentant.

REMORSEFULLY, [ri-maws'-fool-i], *adv.* in a remorseful way.

REMORSEFULNESS, [ri-maws'-fool-nes], *n.* the condition of being remorseful.

REMORSELESS, [ri-maws'-les], *adj.* having no pity, relentless, showing no remorse or compunction.

REMORSELESSLY, [ri-maws'-les-li], *adv.* in a remorseless way, pitilessly, relentlessly.

REMORSELESSNESS, [ri-maws'-les-nes], *n.* the quality of being without remorse.

REMOTE, [ri-mōt'], *adj.* distant, far removed; sequestered, far off (either in terms of geographical distance, time, spirit, etc.); having only a slight connexion (with), improbable, unlikely; (of ideas, etc.) vague, not clearly formulated. [L. *remotus, p.pt.* of *removere* to move away].

REMOTE CONTROL, [ri-mōt'-kon-trōl'], *n.* manipulation of electrical apparatus from a point some distance away.

REMOTELY, [ri-mōt'-li], *adv.* in a remote manner or degree.

REMOTENESS, [ri-mōt'-nes], *n.* the condition of being remote.

REMOULD, [rē'-mōld'], *v.t.* to shape anew, recast.

REMOUNT, [rē'-mownt'], *v.t.* to ascend, climb again; to provide with fresh horses; to provide (a picture) with another mount; to mount (a horse) again.

REMOVABILITY, [ri-mōōv'-a-bil'-i-ti], *n.* the quality of being removable.

REMOVABLE, [ri-mōōv'-abl], *adj.* able to be removed.

REMOVAL, [ri-mōōv'-al], *n.* the act of removing; the act of transferring effects from one house to another; the act of abolishing, getting rid of.

REMOVE (1), [ri-mōōv'], *n.* the distance that one thing is from another, a natural step or degree of that separation or distance; a degree of relationship; (in schools) a form between the upper fourth and lower fifth.

REMOVE (2), [ri-mōōv'], *v.t.* to take, carry, move away; to draw back; to get rid of, abolish; to clean off; to relieve (a person) of his office, post, function; to dismiss; *v.i.* to change one's residence. [L. *removere*].

REMOVED, [ri-mōōvd'], *adj.* separated.

REMOVEDNESS, [ri-mōōvd'-nes], *n.* the state of being removed.

REMOVER, [ri-mōō'-ver], *n.* one who removes, *esp.* a person who employs vans and men to remove furniture from one house to another.

REMPLISSAGE, [rahm'-plis-ahj'], *n.* padding, irrelevant matter in a book. [Fr. *remplissage*].

REMUGIENT, [ri-mew'-ji-ent], *adj.* resounding. [L. *remugiens*].

REMUNERABILITY, [ri-mew'-ner-ab-il'-i-ti], *n.* the quality of being remunerable.

REMUNERABLE, [ri-mew'-ner-abl], *adj.* able to be remunerated.

REMUNERATE, [ri-mew'-ner-āt], *v.t.* to pay, give reward to; to recompense, reward. [L. *remunerari* to repay].

REMUNERATION, [ri-mew'-ner-ā'-shun], *n.* the act of remunerating; that by which remuneration is made, payment, wages.

REMUNERATIVE, [ri-mew'-ner-at-iv], *adj.* yielding remuneration, profitable.

REMUNERATIVELY, [ri-mew'-ner-at-iv-li], *adv.* profitably.

REMUNERATIVENESS, [ri-mew'-ner-at-iv-nes], *n.* the quality of being profitable.

RENAISSANCE, [re-nā'-sants], *n.* a rebirth; a revival; **the R.**, the great fifteenth-century European revival of interest in classical (*esp.* ancient Greek) culture. [Fr. *renaissance*].

RENAL, [rēn'-al], *adj.* pertaining or adjacent to the kidneys. [L. *renalis*].

RENAME, [rē'-nām'], *v.t.* to name anew.

RENARD, [ren'-ahd], *n.* a fox. [Fr. *renard*].

RENASCENCE, [re-nas'-ents, re-nā'-sents], *n.* the state of being renascent; a rebirth, a revival; the Renaissance.

RENASCENCY, [re-nas'-en-si], *n.* renascence, rebirth.

RENASCENT, [re-nas'-ent], *adj.* renewing reviving, rejuvenating. [L. *renascens*].

RENCONTRE, [rahn'-kontr'], *n.* an encounter, duel, scuffle, clash; an unexpected meeting. [Fr. *rencontre*].

REND, (rent), [rend], *v.t. and i.* to tear in pieces; to split, to shatter; to be torn. [OE. *rendan*].

RENDER (1), [rend'-er], *n.* one who tears asunder with violence; a coat of plaster; †a payment.

RENDER (2), [rend'-er], *v.t.* to give in return, to pay back, to return; to inflict; to give, submit, tender; to perform, to do a service to, act on behalf of; to cause to be, to make; to extract; to boil down; to depict, reproduce, represent; to translate, interpret; to apply a coat of plaster; to ease, slacken. [LL. *rendere* to restore].

RENDERABLE, [rend'-er-abl], *adj.* able to be rendered.

RENDERER, [rend'-er-er], *n.* one who renders.

RENDERING, [rend'-er-ing], *n.* the act of one who renders; that which is rendered; version, translation; representation, delineation; the laying on of a first coat of plaster.

RENDEZVOUS (1), [rahnd'-ā-vōō], *n.* a place appointed for a meeting. [Fr. *rendez-vous*].

RENDEZVOUS (2), [rahnd'-ā-vōō], *v.i.* to meet by appointment at a rendezvous.

RENDIBLE, [rend'-ibl], *adj.* able to be yielded; that may be torn.

RENDITION, [rend-ish'-un], *n.* †the act of surrendering; version, translation; rendering. [LL. *renditio*].

RENEGADE (1), [ren'-i-gād], *n.* one who abjures his faith, an apostate, a deserter. [MedL. *renegatus, p.pt.* of *renegare* to forswear].

RENEGADE (2), [ren'-i-gād], *adj.* pertaining to a renegade; deserting.

RENEGADO, [ren'-ig-ahd'-ō], *n.* a renegade, a traitor, deserter. [Span. *renegado*].

RENEGUE, RENEGE, [rē-nēg', ri-nēg'], *v.i.* to fail to follow suit in a card game. [MedL. *renegare* to deny].

RENEW, [ri-new'], *v.t.* to make as good as new again, to restore to its original state, renovate; to give fresh energy to, revitalize, regenerate; to recommence, to begin again, resume; to repeat, reiterate; to call into existence again, to revive; to grant again, to prolong.

RENEWABILITY, [ri-new'-ab-il'-i-ti], *n.* the quality of being renewable.

RENEWABLE, [ri-new'-abl], *adj.* able to be renewed.

RENEWAL, [ri-new'-al], *n.* the act of renewing; the state of being renewed; restoration, revival; regeneration, revitalization; **r. shoot,** (*bot.*) a shoot in the leaf-axis which lasts over the winter.

RENEWED, [ri-newd'], *adj.* made new again; restored, revived; continued.

RENEWEDNESS, [ri-newd'-nes], *n.* the quality of being renewed.

RENEWER, [ri-new′-er], *n.* one who, that which, renews.
RENIDIFICATION, [rē-nid′-i-fik-ā′-shun], *n.* the act of building another nest.
RENIDIFY, [rē-nid′-i-fī], *v.i.* to build another nest.
RENIFORM, [ren′-i-fawm], *adj.* (*bot.*) having the shape of a kidney. [L. *ren* kidney and FORM].
RENITENT, [ren′-it-ent], *adj.* offering resistance, resisting pressure or the effect of it; acting against a movement of force. [L. *renitens*].
RENNET (1), [ren′-it], *n.* a substance prepared from the inner membrane of a calf's stomach, and used for curdling milk. [ME. *rennet*].
RENNET (2), [ren′-it], *n.* a variety of apple. [Fr. *reinette* little queen].
RENOMINATE, [rē-nom′-in-āt], *v.t.* to nominate again.
RENOMINATION, [rē′-nom-in-ā′-shun], *n.* the act of renominating.
RENOUNCE, [ri-nowns′], *v.t.* and *i.* to announce by means of a formal statement the giving up of a right or claim, to disclaim, disown, reject; to resign; to forsake, cast off, to give up participating in. [OFr. *renouncer* from L. *renuntiare* to refuse].
RENOUNCEMENT, [ri-nowns′-ment], *n.* the act of renouncing, renunciation.
RENOUNCER, [ri-nowns′-er], *n.* one who renounces.
RENOVATE, [ren′-ōv-āt], *v.t.* to make as good as new by repairing dilapidations, to restore to its former state, to renew, to do up. [L. *renovare* to restore].
RENOVATION, [ren′-ōv-ā′-shun], *n.* the act of renewing, state of being renewed.
RENOVATIONIST, [ren′-ōv-ā′-shun-ist], *n.* a believer in spiritual rather than material agencies as governing the progress of human life.
RENOVATOR, [ren′-ōv-āter], *n.* one who, or that which, renews or restores.
RENOWN, [ri-nown′], *n.* the fact or condition of being widely celebrated for achievement; celebrity, fame. [OFr. *renown*].
RENOWNED, [ri-nownd′], *adj.* having renown, famous, celebrated.
RENOWNEDLY, [ri-nown′-ed-li], *adv.* to a renowned degree, with renown.
RENOWNLESS, [ri-nown′-les], *adj.* not possessing renown.
RENT (1), [rent], *n.* a payment made by a tenant to a landlord whose house or lands he occupies over a stipulated period; payment made for temporary use, hire money. [OFr. *rente*].
RENT (2), [rent], *n.* a slit or hole formed in thin material due to a tear, an opening produced by rending or violent separation; (*fig.*) a difference of opinion; a division of forces due to this; a schism, a separation.
RENT (3), [rent], *v.t.* and *i.* to occupy as a tenant certain rooms, lands or tenements for an agreed payment paid more or less regularly; to lease, let, hire out on specified terms; to be leased or rented. [RENT (1)].
RENT (4), [rent], *pret.* and *p.pt.* of REND.
RENTABLE, [rent′-abl], *adj.* able to be rented.
RENTAL, [rent′-al], *n.* a schedule or account of rents, rent-roll; the amount of the rent. [L. *rentale* rent-roll].
RENT-CHARGE, [rent′-chahj′], *n.* a rent from land payable by settlement to a nominee other than the landlord.
RENT-DAY, [rent′-dā], *n.* the day on which the rent falls due.
RENTE, [rah(ng)t], *n.* an annuity derivable from the state funds of France. [OFr. *rente*].
RENTER (1), [rent′-er], *n.* one who pays or receives rent; a person who leases an estate or holds premises on the payment of rent; a wholesale dealer in cinematograph films.
RENTER (2), [rent′-er], *n.* one who, or that which, rends or tears.
RENTER-WARDEN, [rent′-er-wawd′-en], *n.* an overseer of rents in respect of leased property, a rent collector.
RENT-FREE, [rent′-frē′], *adj.* (of a room, house or lands) occupied without payment of rent.
RENTIER, [rah(ng)′-ti-ā, ren′-ti-er], *n.* a person whose income is derived from interest on investments. [Fr. *rentier*].
RENT-ROLL, [rent′-rōl], *n.* an account of rents or income drawn up by a landlord or his agents.
RENUENT, [ren′-yōō-ent], *adj.* (*anat.*) descriptive of a pair of muscles in the neck which throw the head back. [L. *renuens*].
RENULE, [ren′-yōōl], *n.* (*anat.*) a small kidney peculiar to some animals.
RENUMBER, [rē′-num′-ber], *v.t.* to recount, to number again; to place a new number upon.
RENUMERATE, [re-new′-mer-āt], *v.t.* to enumerate again, to recount.
RENUNCIATION, [ri-nun′-si-ā′-shun], *n.* the act of renouncing; disownment, repudiation. [L. *renunciatio*].
RENUNCIATIVE, [ri-nun′-si-at-iv], *adj.* characterized by renunciation, pertaining to a renunciation.
RENUNCIATORY, [ri-nun′-si-at-er-i], *adj.* having the nature of a renunciation.
RENVERSE, **renversé**, [ren′-vurs′-i], *adj.* (*her.*) inverted, having the head downward. [Fr. *renversé*].
REOBTAIN, [rē-ob-tān′], *v.t.* to get again, recover.
REOCCUPY, [rē-ok′-yōō-pī], *v.t.* to occupy again, to take possession of (a town) again.
REOPEN, [rē-ō′-pen], *v.t.* and *i.* to open again, resume, renew. [RE (1) and OPEN (3)].
REORGANIZATION, [rē-awg′-an-īz-ā′-shun], *n.* the act of reorganizing.
REORGANIZE, [rē-awg′-an-īz], *v.t.* to organize anew, to change the system of organization of; to reform.
REORDER, [rē-awd′-er], *v.t.* to order anew, to repeat an order.
REORIENT, [rē-awr′-i-ent], *adj.* rising again. [RE (1) and ORIENT].
REORIENTATE, [rē-awr′-i-ent-āt], *v.t.* to orientate afresh, give new direction to. [RE (1) and ORIENTATE].
REORIENTATION, [rē′-awr-i-ent-ā′-shun], *n.* the act of reorientating.
REP (1), [rep], *n.* a fabric with a ribbed or corded texture, repp. [REPP].
REP (2), [rep], *n.* (*slang*) a debauchee, a rip. [Abbreviation of REPROBATE (1)].
REP (3), [rep], *n.* (*school slang*) recitation, repetition. [Abbreviation of REPETITION].
REP (4), [rep], *adj.* made of rep material. [REP (1)].
REPACIFY, [rē′-pas′-i-fī], *v.t.* to pacify again; to subject to further pacification.
REPACK, [rē-pak′], *v.t.* and *i.* to pack a second time, to pack once more.
REPAID, [rē-pād′], *pret.* and *p.pt.* of REPAY.
REPAINT (1), [rē-pānt′], *n.* a golf-ball that has been furbished and painted again for further use.
REPAINT (2), [rē′-pānt], *v.t.* to paint again, to give a fresh coat of paint to.
REPAIR (1), [ri-pāer′], *n.* the act of restoring to a sound condition or state; adjustment made to, or work performed on, any object in order to restore it to a sound or satisfactory state once more; relative degree to which a thing requires repairing, state of soundness; **under r.**, being repaired; **in good r.**, in a sound or satisfactory state. [*Next*].
REPAIR (2), [ri-pāer′], *v.t.* to restore to a sound or proper state once more, to mend; to make good, put right, make amends for, remedy; to revive. [OFr. *reparer* from L. *reparare*].
REPAIR (3), [ri-pāer′], *v.i.* to go, to betake oneself, resort. [OFr. *repairier*].
REPAIRABLE, [ri-pāer′-abl], *adj.* capable of being repaired; mendable.
REPAIRER, [ri-pāer′-er], *n.* one who, or that which, repairs or makes amends.
REPAND, [ri-pand′], *adj.* having a regular wavy margin, sinuated. [L. *repandus* turned up].
RE-PAPER, [rē-pā′-per], *v.t.* to put fresh wallpaper on.
REPARABLE, [rep′-er-abl], *adj.* able to be remedied or recovered. [L. *reparabilis*].
REPARABLY, [rep′-er-ab-li], *adv.* in a reparable fashion.
REPARATION, [rep′-er-ā′-shun], *n.* the act of putting right or repairing; amends, indemnification, compensation for injury, damage, or loss inflicted; atonement, restitution. [L. *reparatio*].
REPARATORY, [ri-par′-at-er-i], *adj.* repairing; indemnifying, compensating, making reparation.
REPARTEE, [rep′-ah-tē], *n.* a ready and witty reply, a smart retort; lively, clever retorts. [Fr. *repartie*].
REPARTITION (1), [rē′-paht-ish′-un], *n.* a second dividing up, a redistribution, fresh apportionment or allotment.
REPARTITION (2), [rē′-paht-ish′-un], *v.t.* to divide up, partition afresh.
REPASS, [rē′-pahs′], *v.t.* to pass again; to travel back across or over; *v.i.* to go or move back, to return. [Fr. *repasser*].
REPASSAGE, [rē-pas′-ij], *n.* a laying of another coat of size over an unpolished surface.

REPASSANT, [ri-pas'-ant], *adj.* (*her.*) passing each other in contrary directions. [Fr. *repassant*].

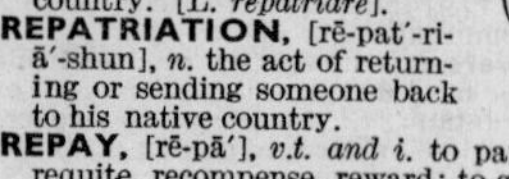
REPASSANT

REPAST, [ri-pahst'], *n.* a meal, feast, a quantity of food and drink taken on one occasion. [OFr. *repast*].

REPASTURE†, [ri-pahs'-cher], *n.* food and drink; a meal.

REPATRIATE, [rē-pat'-ri-āt, rē-pā'-tri-āt], *v.t.* to send (someone) back to his native country. [L. *repatriare*].

REPATRIATION, [rē-pat'-ri-ā'-shun], *n.* the act of returning or sending someone back to his native country.

REPAY, [rē-pā'], *v.t.* and *i.* to pay back, refund; to requite, recompense, reward; to give back in return; to make repayment. [OFr. *repaier*].

REPAYABLE, [rē-pā'-abl], *adj.* that may or must be repaid.

REPAYMENT, [rē'-pā'-ment], *n.* the act of paying back, requital, reimbursement; the money repaid.

REPEAL (1), [ri-pēl'], *n.* the act of repealing, revoking, or permanently cancelling, abrogation. [AFr. *repel*].

REPEAL (2), [ri-pēl'], *v.t.* to revoke, abrogate, annul, cancel, to declare to be no longer enforceable or in force (law, judicial sentence, etc.). [AFr. *repeller*].

REPEALABILITY, [ri-pēl'-ab-il'-i-ti], *n.* repealableness.

REPEALABLE, [ri-pēl'-abl], *adj.* capable of being repealed or rescinded; revocable.

REPEALABLENESS, [ri-pēl'-abl-nes], *n.* the quality or condition of being repealable.

REPEALER, [ri-pēl'-er], *n.* one who seeks a repeal; †an advocate of Home Rule for Ireland.

REPEALMENT, [ri-pēl'-ment], *n.* the act of repealing.

REPEAT (1), [ri-pēt'], *n.* the act of repeating, repetition; a pattern that repeats itself; (*mus.*) a passage that is to be repeated; a sign on a score indicating that a particular passage is to be repeated.

REPEAT (2), [ri-pēt'], *v.t.* to say again; to recite by heart; to spread abroad, circulate; to do again, cause to recur or happen again; *v.i.* to strike the last hour or part of the hour again (of a clock, etc.); to recur; to rise and leave an unpleasant after-taste in the mouth. [L. *repetere* to seek again].

REPEATABLE, [ri-pēt'-abl], *adj.* fit for repetition.

REPEATED, [ri-pēt'-id], *adj.* done again, recurring, continual.

REPEATEDLY, [ri-pēt'-id-li], *adv.* with repetition; again and again; several times, continually.

REPEATER, [ri-pēt'-er], *n.* one who, or that which, repeats; a watch that strikes again the hours and parts of hours, on the compression of a spring; a firearm that may be discharged a number of times without being reloaded; (*arith.*) a decimal in which the same figures constantly recur; (*teleg.*) an automatic retransmitting instrument.

REPEATING, [ri-pēt'-ing], *adj.* regurgitating; reproducing; saying or doing anything again; able to be fired several times without reloading; **r. circle,** a mathematical instrument for diminishing the effects of errors of graduation in measuring angles.

REPEL, (repelling, repelled), [ri-pel'], *v.t.* to drive back, repulse; to reject, spurn, refuse; to repress, resist, put down; to inspire or fill with abhorrence or distaste, to cause to shrink back from; (*phys.*) to act in opposition to, force back, refuse to mix with. [L. *repellere*].

REPELLENCY, [ri-pel'-en-si], *n.* the principle of repulsion; repulsive quality, the power that repels.

REPELLENT (1), [ri-pel'-ent], *n.* (*med.*) a medicine that drives back morbid humours into the blood; a medicine to prevent an afflux of blood to a part of the body.

REPELLENT (2), [ri-pel'-ent], *adj.* that repels or drives back; loathsome, highly distasteful, provoking disgust or aversion.

REPELLENTLY, [ri-pel'-ent-li], *adv.* in repellent fashion; so as to repel.

REPENT (1), [rē'-pent], *adj.* (*bot., zool.*) creeping. [L. *repens*].

REPENT (2), [ri-pent'], *v.t.* to feel sorrow or regret at, and resolve to make amends for, to remember with sorrow, feel contrite about; *v.i.* to be sorry, feel regret for something done and resolve to make amends and change one's ways. [Fr. *repentir*].

REPENTANCE, [ri-pent'-ants], *n.* penitence, contrition; sorrow, regret, or grief at what has been wrongfully done or said mingled with a resolve to make amends or change one's ways.

REPENTANT, [ri-pent'-ant], *adj.* inclined to repent; sorry or regretful for past remiss conduct, penitent; expressing repentance.

REPENTANTLY, [ri-pent'-ant-li], *adv.* in a penitent fashion.

REPENTINGLY, [ri-pent'-ing-li], *adv.* with repentance.

REPEOPLE, [rē'-pēpl'], *v.t.* to people afresh.

REPERCUSSION, [rē'-per-kush'-un], *n.* recoil, rebound; reverberation, echo; (*fig.*) (usually *pl.*) events arising as a result of some action, often widespread and remotely connected with their causes.

REPERCUSSIVE, [rē'-per-kus'-iv], *adj.* driving back; causing to reverberate; producing repercussions, of the nature of a repercussion.

REPERTOIRE, [rep'-er-twah(r)], *n.* a repertory; stock of pieces or tricks readily at command. [Fr. *repertoire*].

REPERTORY, [rep'-er-ter-i], *n.* a place in which things are so arranged that they may easily be found when wanted, a storehouse, treasury; a repertoire, a list of pieces, tricks, etc., with which a performer is familiar; **r. theatre,** a theatre in which a succession of plays are performed, usually by a permanent company, for short runs, rather than a single play for a long run. [L. *repertorium* catalogue].

REPERUSAL, [rē'-per-ōōz'-al], *n.* a fresh perusal.

REPERUSE, [rē'-per-ōōz'], *v.t.* to peruse once more.

REPETEND, [rep'-it-end'], *n.* (*arith.*) that part of a repeating decimal which recurs; a recurring decimal. [L. *repetendus*].

REPETITION, [rep'-et-ish'-un], *n.* the act of doing or uttering again; that which is done or said again; a copy or reproduction in a slightly varying form; the art of reciting that which has been learnt by heart; (*mus.*) the rapid repeating of a note, harmony, or interval. [L. *repetitio*].

REPETITIONAL, [rep'-et-ish'-un-al], *adj.* repetitionary.

REPETITIONARY, [rep'-et-ish'-un-er-i], *adj.* containing, of the nature of, repetition.

REPETITIVE, [ri-pet'-it-iv], *adj.* repeating, containing repetition.

REPINE, [ri-pīn'], *v.i.* to fret, be discontented, to complain, grumble.

REPINER, [ri-pīn'-er], *n.* one who repines or frets.

REPININGLY, [ri-pīn'-ing-li], *adv.* with repining, discontentedly.

REPIQUE (1), [ri-pēk'], *n.* (*cards*) the winning of an extra sixty points at piquet by scoring thirty points in one's hand before actual play has begun. [Fr. *repic*].

REPIQUE (2), [ri-pēk'], *v.t.* to score a repique against; *v.i.* to make a repique.

REPLACE, [rē-plās'], *v.t.* to put back into its proper or original position; to restore to a former position; to take the place of, supersede; to fill the place of; to find an effective substitute for.

REPLACEABLE, [rē-plās'-abl], *adj.* capable of replacement, that may be replaced.

REPLACEMENT, [rē-plās'-ment], *n.* the act of replacing; the state of being replaced; an article that replaces another; (*min.*) the removal of an angle or an edge.

REPLACER, [rē-plās'-er], *n.* one who, or that which, replaces, a substitute for anything.

REPLACING-SWITCH, [rē-plās'-ing-swich'], *n.* a device enabling a derailed locomotive to be placed again upon the rails.

REPLAIT, [rē'-plat'], *v.t.* to plait again; to fold up.

REPLANT, [rē'-plahnt'], *v.t.* to plant anew, to provide with fresh plants.

REPLAY (1), [rē'-plā], *n.* (*sport*) a match replayed after a previous draw.

REPLAY (2), [rē'-plā'], *v.t.* (*sport*) to play a match over again as the previous game has ended in a draw.

REPLEADER, [rē-plēd'-er], *n.* (*leg.*) a second pleading; the right of pleading again.

REPLEDGE, [rē'-plej'], *v.t.* to pledge once more. [OFr. *repleger*].

REPLENISH, [ri-plen'-ish], *v.t.* to fill up again, obtain a fresh supply of, restock; †to stock with abundance of living beings. [~OFr. *replenir*].

REPLENISHER, [ri-plen'-ish-er], *n.* one who, or that which, replenishes; a device used in electrical engineering for keeping up the charge of a quadrant electrometer.

REPLENISHMENT, [ri-plen'-ish-ment], *n.* the act of filling up again; the state of being replenished.

REPLETE, [ri-plēt′], *adj.* completely filled, crammed full; thoroughly equipped, abundantly provided. [L. *repletus, p.pt.* of *replere* to fill again].

REPLETENESS, [ri-plēt′-nes], *n.* the state of being replete.

REPLETION, [ri-plē′-shun], *n.* the act of eating and drinking to capacity; the state of being completely full; (*med.*) fulness of blood, plethora.

REPLEVIABLE, [ri-plev′-i-abl], *adj.* (*leg.*) capable of being replevied.

REPLEVIN, [ri-plev′-in], *n.* (*leg.*) recovery by a person of what has been distrained or taken from him, upon his guarantee to test the legality of the seizure, and to return the goods if the seizure is held to be valid; the action which decides the legality or illegality of the seizure; the writ by which a person obtains temporary recovery of goods in this way. [AFr. *replevine*].

REPLEVISABLE, [ri-plev′-is-abl], *adj.* that may be replevied.

REPLEVISOR, [ri-plev′-is-or], *n.* the person seeking recovery of goods in an action for replevin.

REPLEVY, [ri-plev′-i], *v.t.* (*leg.*) to recover (goods) upon giving security to test the validity of the seizure at law; to bail. [OFr. *replevir*].

REPLICA, [rep′-lik-a], *n.* a copy of a work of art, *esp.* one by the author of the original. [It. *replica*].

REPLICATE (1), [rep′-lik-āt], *n.* (*mus.*) a note one or more octaves in pitch below or above a given note.

REPLICATE (2), [rep′-lik-āt], *adj.* (*bot.*) doubled back or down upon itself. [L. *replicare* to fold over].

REPLICATION, [rep′-lik-ā′-shun], *n.* (*leg.*) a reply; the plaintiff's reply to the defendant's plea; a copy. [L. *replicatio*].

REPLIER, [ri-plī′-er], *n.* one who replies.

REPLUM, [rē′-plum], *n.* the frame of a pod or legume, remaining when the valves fall off. [L. *replum* a bolt].

REPLY (1), [ri-plī′], *n.* that which is said, written, or done in answer to something, a response, rejoinder.

REPLY (2), [ri-plī′], *v.t.* to return by way of answer; *v.i.* to answer, to say, write, or do something in response to something said, written, or done; (*leg.*) to answer a defendant's plea. [OFr. *replier* to fold back].

REPLY-PAID, [ri-plī′-pād′], *adj.* (of a telegram) requiring a telegraphic answer for which previous payment has been made.

REPOINT, [rē′-point′], *v.t.* to renew the edges of mortar in (brickwork and masonry), to point afresh.

REPOLISH, [rē′-pol′-ish], *v.t.* to polish afresh.

REPONE, [ri-pōn′], *v.t.* (*Scots leg.*) to restore to an office formerly held, rehabilitate. [L. *reponere*].

REPOPULATE, [rē′-pop′-yōō-lāt], *v.t.* to populate afresh.

REPORT (1), [ri-pawt′], *n.* rumour, gossip; a rumour, tale; a statement of facts obtained as a result of some investigation or in reply to some enquiry, *esp.* the official statement issued by a person or commission appointed to investigate some particular matter; periodical account of a pupil's progress and conduct at school, issued by his teachers; a written account of some ceremony, event, or proceedings, *esp.* of speeches made upon such an occasion; a loud sudden noise, a bang, the noise of an explosion; (*archaic*) reputation, fame; (*leg.*) a formal account of a case together with the legal arguments used, and the decisions made, for use in establishing precedents or for possible future reference; **r. stage,** (*parl.*) the end of the Committee stage of a Bill, after the second and before the third reading. [OFr. *report, raport*].

REPORT (2), [ri-pawt′], *v.t.* to give an account of, relate; to communicate, tell, to convey as a message; to write an account of for publication in a newspaper or journal; to write down word for word or in condensed form (a speech) for future publication in the Press; to announce officially, to issue a formal statement of after making an investigation; to give a periodical account of to some authority; to complain about to a higher authority; (*parl.*) to announce the end of the Committee stage of (a Bill); *v.i.* to make a report; to present oneself for duty or questioning, or in order to comply with some regulation or order; to act as a press reporter. [OFr. *reporter* from L. *reportare* to carry back].

REPORTABLE, [ri-pawt′-abl], *adj.* suitable for publication, fit or requiring to be reported.

REPORTAGE, [re′-pawt-ahzh], *n.* a running commentary in literary form on current events as seen by the writer. [Fr. *reportage*].

REPORTER, [ri-pawt′-er], *n.* one who reports, *esp.* one employed to write the official legal reports of law cases; one whose occupation is to write accounts of events, proceedings, ceremonies, speeches, etc., and to gather news in general, for publication in newspapers.

REPORTERISM, [ri-pawt′-er-izm], *n.* the occupation of a reporter; his manner of working.

REPORTING, [ri-pawt′-ing], *n.* the act of making a report, the occupation or art of a reporter.

REPORTORIAL, [rē′-pawt-aw′-ri-al], *adj.* connected with newspaper reporting or reporters.

REPOSAL, [ri-pōz′-al], *n.* the act of reposing.

REPOSE (1), [ri-pōz′], *n.* rest, pause from or cessation of activity; state of rest, complete relaxation; stillness, peace, undisturbed condition, serene tranquillity; composure; restful harmony of colour and treatment in a work of art. [Fr. *repos*].

REPOSE (2), [ri-pōz′], *v.t. and i.* to rest, to lay at rest; *v.i.* to lie at rest; to dwell, remain; to rely; to rest in confidence. [LL. *repausare*].

REPOSE (3), [ri-pōz′], *v.t.* to set or place in. [L. *repositus, p.pt.* of *reponere* to place again].

REPOSEDLY, [ri-pōz′-id-li], *adv.* in a reposeful manner, at rest.

REPOSEFUL, [ri-pōz′-fōōl], *adj.* inducing repose, restful.

REPOSIT, [ri-poz′-it], *v.t.* to lay up, to lodge, as for safety or preservation, to store, deposit. [L. *repositus, p.pt.* of *reponere* to place again].

REPOSITION, [rē′-pōz-ish′-un], *n.* the act of repositing or replacing; (*surg.*) the act of putting back into its normal position; storing.

REPOSITORY, [ri-poz′-it-er-i], *n.* a place or receptacle where things are deposited for preservation or safety, a store, warehouse, depository; a copious source, a mine, storehouse; one to whom secrets, confidences, etc., are entrusted. [L. *repositorium*].

REPOSSESS, [rē′-pōz-es′], *v.t.* to possess anew.

REPOSSESSION, [rē′-pōz-esh′-un], *n.* the act of repossessing, recovery.

REPOSURE, [ri-pō′-zher], *n.* peace, rest, repose.

REPOT, (**repotting, repotted**), [rē′-pot′], *v.t.* to transfer (a plant) from one pot to another, usually larger.

REPOUSSAGE, [re-pōōs-ahzh′], *n.* the act of embossing by hammering on the back. [Fr. *repoussage*].

REPOUSSE, repoussé, [ri-pōōs′-ā], *adj.* set in relief or embossed by hammering, or punching from behind, and afterwards by chasing. [Fr. *repoussé*].

REPP, [rep], *n.* rep. [Fr. *reppe*].

REPPED, [rept], *adj.* corded or ribbed transversely. [REP (1)].

REPREHEND, [rep′-ri-hend′] *v.t.* to censure, to reprove, reprimand, rebuke. [L. *reprehendere* to hold back].

REPREHENSIBLE, [rep′-ri-hens′-ibl], *adj.* deserving reproof, blamable, censurable, meriting rebuke.

REPREHENSIBLENESS, [rep′-ri-hens′-ibl-nes], *n.* the quality of being reprehensible.

REPREHENSIBLY, [rep′-ri-hens′-ib-li], *adv.* in a reprehensible fashion.

REPREHENSION, [rep′-ri-hen′-shun], *n.* the act of reprehending; censure, blame, reproof.

REPREHENSIVE, [rep′-ri-hens′-iv], *adj.* containing reproof, rebuking.

REPRESENT, [rep′-riz-ent], *v.t.* to depict, portray, delineate, show by resemblance; to describe as, make out to be, give a picture of as; to state, show clearly, point out; to signify, mean, convey; to give the impression; to typify, be an image of, symbolize, stand for; to embody, exhibit, exemplify; to be similar to, correspond to; to act on behalf of, or as agent for, to take the place of; to be Member of Parliament for, or be the elected deputy for, on a legislative council; to play the part of in a play; (*rare*) to present before the mind, to give a clear mental picture of; (*reflex.*) to claim (to be) [L. *repraesentare*].

RE-PRESENT, [rē′-priz-ent′], *v.t.* to present anew.

REPRESENTABILITY, [rep′-riz-ent-ab-il′-i-ti], *n.* capability of being represented.

REPRESENTABLE, [rep′-riz-ent′-abl], *adj.* able to be represented.

REPRESENTAMEN, [rep′-riz-ent-ā′-men], *n.* the idea resulting from the representation of some thing to the mind.

REPRESENTATION, [rep′-riz-ent-ā′-shun], *n.* the act of representing; that which represents; a delineation, depicting; likeness, picture, or pictorial account; reproduction in visible or concrete form (of abstract conceptions); reproduction by acting on the stage; a statement or account intended to convey a point of view; an expression of remonstration together with a statement of attitude to a particular event.

a protest; the act of representing a body of voters on an assembly appointed by election; the state of being represented in this way. [L. *repraesentatio*].

REPRESENTATIONAL, [rep'-ri-zen-tā'-shun-al], *adj.* of, involving, or implying representation.

REPRESENTATIONISM, [rep'-riz-en-tā'-shun-izm], *n.* the theory that the object immediately perceived by the human intelligence is not the external entity itself but simply a representation of it.

REPRESENTATIVE (1), [rep'-riz-ent'-at-iv], *n.* one who, or that which, represents someone or something else; an agent, delegate, deputy, or substitute acting on behalf of another; one who represents a body of electors in a legislative assembly; embodiment, type, specimen, example; (*leg.*) one who stands in the place of another; **real, natural r.,** heir.

REPRESENTATIVE (2), [rep'-riz-ent'-at-iv], *adj.* describing, characteristic or symbolizing; typical, stock; representing, or acting on behalf of, others, *esp.* in a governing or legislative capacity; conducted by elected delegates or deputies; (*philos.*) conveying or bringing ideas before the mind; (*bot.*) typical in character; **r. peers,** those Scottish and Irish peers elected to sit in the House of Lords.

REPRESENTATIVELY, [rep'-riz-ent'-at-iv-li], *adv.* in a representative manner.

REPRESENTATIVENESS, [rep'-riz-ent'-at-iv-nes], *n.* the quality of being representative.

REPRESENTER, [rep'-riz-ent'-er], *n.* one who exhibits; a representative.

REPRESENTMENT, [rep'-riz-ent'-ment], *n.* the act of representing; the state of being represented.

REPRESS (1), [ri-pres'], *v.t.* to put down, crush, suppress; to check, restrain forcibly, keep under strict control, curb; (*psych.*) to shut out from the conscious mind and force into the unconscious (instinctive tendencies, fears, etc.). [L. *repressus*, *p.pt.* of *reprimere* press back].

REPRESS (2), [rē-pres'], *v.t.* to press once more.

REPRESSER, [ri-pres'-er], *n.* one who represses.

REPRESSIBLE, [ri-pres'-ibl], *adj.* capable of repression.

REPRESSION, [ri-presh'-un], *n.* the act of repressing; the state of being repressed; suppression, check, restraint; (*psych.*) a shutting out of fears, instinctive tendencies, etc., from the conscious mind, from which they are driven down into the unconscious.

REPRESSIVE, [ri-pres'-iv], *adj.* tending to subdue or restrain; reactionary.

REPRESSIVELY, [ri-pres'-iv-li], *adv.* in a repressive manner.

REPRIEVAL, [ri-prēv'-al], *n.* respite; reprieve.

REPRIEVE (1), [ri-prēv'], *n.* the act of reprieving; the suspension or postponement of the execution of a criminal's sentence, *esp.* by remission of a death sentence; the official document authorizing this; respite, temporary relief or release.

REPRIEVE (2), [ri-prēv'], *v.t.* to suspend or delay the execution of a sentence, *esp.* the death sentence, upon; to grant a respite to. [~ME. *repreven*].

REPRIMAND (1), [rep'-ri-mahnd], *n.* severe reproof, rebuke or censure, *esp.* when administered officially. [Fr. *réprimande*].

REPRIMAND (2), [rep'-ri-mahnd], *v.t.* to reprove, rebuke, censure severely, *esp.* to rebuke publicly and officially. [Fr. *réprimander*].

REPRINT (1), [rē'-print], *n.* a new impression of a printed work, without alterations, from a previous edition.

REPRINT (2), [rē'-print'], *v.t.* to print again, to publish a fresh impression or new edition of.

REPRISAL, [ri-prīz'-al], *n.* (usually *pl.*) counteraction taken by a person attacked against the attacker, as revenge for injury or wrong suffered; retaliatory measures taken by one state against another. [OFr. *reprisaille*].

REPRISE, [ri-prīz', re-prēz], *n.* yearly deductions or payments from an estate; the resumption of an action; a fresh attempt to accomplish something; (*mus.*) resumption of the first subject of a movement after the development section; †a reprisal. [Fr. *reprise*].

REPROACH (1), [ri-prōch'], *n.* rebuke, strong disapproval, censure tinged with sorrow and disgust; shame or disgrace; anything bringing shame and discredit on one; (*archaic*) an object of censure, scorn or contempt; (*pl. R.C.*) a set of antiphons and responses of a reproachful nature sung on Good Friday. [OFr. *reproche*].

REPROACH (2), [ri-prōch'], *v.t.* to rebuke, censure, upbraid. [OFr. *reprochier*].

REPROACHABLE, [ri-prōch'-abl], *adj.* deserving reproach.

REPROACHABLENESS, [ri-prōch'-abl-nes], *n.* the state or quality of being reproachable.

REPROACHFUL, [ri-prōch'-fōōl], *adj.* expressing or containing reproach, upbraiding; bringing reproach, shameful, worthy of reproach.

REPROACHFULLY, [ri-prōch'-fōōl-i], *adv.* in a reproaching manner.

REPROACHFULNESS, [ri-prōch'-fōōl-nes], *n.* the quality of being reproachful.

REPROBATE (1), [rep'-rō-bāt], *n.* a depraved, worthless person, utterly abandoned to sin, and completely lacking in honourable principles; (*coll.*) a rascal.

REPROBATE (2), [rep'-rō-bāt], *adj.* damned by God, lost to salvation; depraved, unprincipled, abandoned, sinful, wicked. [L. *reprobatus*].

REPROBATE (3), [rep'-rō-bāt], *v.t.* to condemn, disapprove of wholeheartedly; (*theol.*) to reject or exclude from salvation, to condemn to everlasting damnation; (*Scots leg.*) to reject, disallow. [L. *reprobare*].

REPROBATENESS, [rep'-rō-bāt-nes], *n.* the state of being reprobate.

REPROBATION, [rep'-rō-bā'-shun], *n.* the act of reprobating; the state of being reprobated; the state of being abandoned to eternal destruction, *esp.* by divine decree; wholehearted condemnation and disapproval, severe censure. [L. *reprobatio*].

REPROBATIONER, [rep'-rō-bā'-shun-er], *n.* one who believes that sinners are abandoned by God to eternal damnation.

REPROBATOR, [rep'-rō-bāt'-or], *n.* (*Scots leg.*) an action which seeks to prove that a witness was prejudiced or perjured.

REPRODUCE, [rē'-prōd-ews'], *v.t.* to propagate, generate, procreate; to produce again, cause to grow afresh; to make a copy of; to imitate; to revive, bring back again, to repeat exactly; to publish, present; *v.i.* to propagate one's species.

REPRODUCER, [rē'-prōd-ews'-er], *n.* one who, or that which, reproduces; a device for reproducing sounds.

REPRODUCIBLE, [rē'-prōd-ews'-ibl], *adj.* that can be reproduced; capable of reproduction.

REPRODUCTION, [rē'-prōd-uk'-shun], *n.* the act or process of reproducing, *esp.* the process by which fresh members of the same species are generated, or fresh organisms produced by parent organisms; something reproduced, a copy.

REPRODUCTIVE, [rē'-prōd-ukt'-iv], *adj.* concerned with, relating to, employed in, reproduction; that reproduces or tends to reproduce.

REPRODUCTIVELY, [rē'-prōd-ukt'-iv-li], *adv.* by reproduction.

REPRODUCTIVENESS, [rē'-prōd-ukt'-iv-nes], *n.* the quality of being reproductive.

REPRODUCTIVITY, [rē'-prōd-ukt-iv'-i-ti], *n.* the state or quality of being reproductive.

REPROOF (1), [ri-prōōf'], *n.* censure, rebuke, scolding, chiding, reprehension; an expression of this. [OFr. *reprove*].

REPROOF (2), [rē-prōōf'], *v.t.* to make waterproof once more.

REPROVABLE, [ri-prōōv'-abl], *adj.* worthy of reproof; deserving censure; blamable.

REPROVABLENESS, [ri-prōōv'-abl-nes], *n.* the state of being reprovable.

REPROVABLY, [ri-prōōv'-ab-li], *adv.* in a reprovable manner.

REPROVAL, [ri-prōōv'-al], *n.* the act of reproving, reproof, reprimand.

REPROVE (1), [ri-prōōv'], *v.t.* to blame, censure, scold, rebuke, reprimand, charge with a fault. [OFr. *reprover*].

REPROVE (2), [rē-prōōv'], *v.t.* to prove again.

REPROVER, [ri-prōōv'-er], *n.* one who reproves.

REPROVINGLY, [ri-prōōv'-ing-li], *adv.* by way of reproof.

REPRUNE, [rē'-prōōn'], *v.t.* to prune afresh.

REPTANT, [rep'-tant], *adj.* (*zool.*) creeping; (*bot.*) creeping and rooting. [L. *reptans*].

REPTATION, [rep-tā'-shun], *n.* the act of creeping.

REPTATORIAL, [rep'-tat-aw'-ri-al], *adj.* crawling.

REPTILE (1), [rep'-tīl], *n.* a creeping animal moving on its belly or on very short legs, *esp.* (*zool.*) a class of cold-blooded, lung-breathing, crawling vertebrates covered with plates or scales; (*fig.*) an insignificant, base, sly creature. [LL. *reptile*, *neut.* of *reptilis* creeping].

REPTILE (2), [rep'-tīl], *adj.* creeping, crawling, like a reptile; (*fig.*) grovelling, base, mean. [*Prec.*].

REPTILIA, [rep-til'-i-a], *n.(pl.)* a class of vertebrates, embracing the tortoises and turtles, dinosaurs, crocodiles, lizards, and serpents. [L. *reptilia*, *pl.* of *reptile* creeping].

REPTILIAN (1), [rep-til'-i-an], *n.* a reptile.

REPTILIAN (2), [rep-til'-i-an], *adj.* pertaining to, or resembling, reptiles.

REPTILIFEROUS, [rep'-til-if'-er-us], *adj.* (*geol.*) (of rocks) in which are found fossil reptiles. [REPTILE and L. *ferre* to bear].

REPTILIFORM, [rep-til'-i-fawm], *adj.* allied to or resembling reptiles.

REPTILIOUS, [rep-til'-i-us], *adj.* resembling a reptile.

REPTILIUM, [rep-til'-i-um], *n.* a reptile-house.

REPTILIVOROUS, [rep'-til-iv'-er-us], *adj.* reptile-eating.

REPUBLIC, [ri-pub'-lik], *n.* a form of government in which the supreme ruling power is vested in representatives elected by the people; a state or country in which this form of government is found, the head of the state being elected by popular vote, and being usually known as President; **r. of letters**, the collective body of literary men and women. [L. *respublica* the state].

REPUBLICAN (1), [ri-pub'-lik-an], *n.* one who favours or prefers a republican form of government; a member of the Republican Party in the United States.

REPUBLICAN (2), [ri-pub'-lik-an], *adj.* relating to, by means of, according to, a republic; in the spirit or manner of, in favour of, a republic; of, or pertaining to, the Republicans; (*ornith.*) living and nesting in communities.

REPUBLICANISM, [ri-pub'-lik-an-izm], *n.* a republican form or system of government; attachment to a republican form of government; the principles of a republican government.

REPUBLICANIZE, [ri-pub'-lik-an-iz], *v.t.* to convert to republican principles; to make into a republic.

REPUBLICATION, [rē'-pub-lik-ā'-shun], *n.* the act of republishing; a fresh publication or edition of something previously published.

REPUBLISH, [rē'-pub'-lish], *v.t.* to issue a fresh edition of (a book, etc.); to publish again.

REPUBLISHER, [rē'-pub'-lish-er], *n.* one who republishes.

REPUDIABLE, [ri-pew'-di-abl], *adj.* that may be repudiated; fit or proper to be repudiated.

REPUDIATE, [ri-pew'-di-āt], *v.t.* to disown, deny responsibility for or connexion with; to refuse to recognize, accept, or admit, to disavow, reject; to refuse to acknowledge, to refuse to pay, to disclaim (a debt or liability)· to put away, divorce, get rid of (a wife). [L. *repudiare*].

REPUDIATION, [ri-pewd'-i-ā'-shun], *n.* divorce of a wife; disclaiming of a responsibility or obligation; refusal to acknowledge and discharge a debt. [L. *repudiatio*].

REPUDIATIONIST, [ri-pewd'-i-ā'-shun-ist], *n.* one who advocates the disclaiming of a public debt, liability, or obligation.

REPUDIATOR, [ri-pewd'-i-āt'-or], *n.* one who repudiates.

REPUGN, [ri-pewn'], *v.t.* to oppose, resist, reject scornfully; *v.i.* to offer resistance. [L. *repugnare*].

REPUGNANCE, [ri-pug'-nants], *n.* aversion, scornful distaste, violent dislike; incompatibility. [L. *repugnans*].

REPUGNANCY, [ri-pug'-nan-si], *n.* repugnance.

REPUGNANT, [ri-pug'-nant], *adj.* distasteful, highly unpleasant, offensive; adverse, opposing, hostile; contrary. [L. *repugnans*].

REPUGNANTLY, [ri-pug'-nant-li], *adv.* in a repugnant manner.

REPULSE (1), [ri-puls'], *n.* the act of repelling or driving back; the state of being checked or repelled; a check, set-back; a rebuff, refusal, vigorous rejection of advances. [L. *repulsus*].

REPULSE (2), [ri-puls'], *v.t.* to repel, drive back, beat off; to rebuff, discourage, reject. [L. *repulsus*, *p.pt.* of *repellere*].

REPULSER, [ri-puls'-er], *n.* one who drives back or repulses.

REPULSION, [ri-pul'-shun], *n.* the act of repelling; dislike, aversion; (*phys.*) the tendency of bodies to be driven farther apart from one onother. [LL. *repulsio*].

REPULSIVE, [ri-puls'-iv], *adj.* arousing abhorrence or repulsion, loathsome, disgusting, objectionable; cold, forbidding, repellent, unattractive; (*phys.*) exhibiting repulsion. [Fr. *repulsif*].

REPULSIVELY, [ri-puls'-iv-li], *adv.* in a repulsive manner.

REPULSIVENESS, [ri-puls'-iv-nes], *n.* the quality of being repulsive.

REPURCHASE (1), [rē-pur'-chas], *n.* the act of buying back again.

REPURCHASE (2), [rē-pur'-chas], *v.t.* to buy back again.

REPUTABLE, [rep'-yōōt-abl], *adj.* being in good repute; held in esteem; honourable.

REPUTABLENESS, [rep'-yōōt-abl-nes], *n.* the quality of being reputable.

REPUTABLY, [rep'-yōōt-ab-li], *adv.* in a reputable manner.

REPUTATION, [rep'-yōō-tā'-shun], *n.* the esteem or regard in which a person or thing is commonly held, character according to public report; established popular opinion of a person or thing, *esp.* as having some particular attribute or quality; good name, credit or regard resulting from established favourable public opinion; honour, celebrity, fame, renown. [L. *reputatio*].

REPUTE (1), [ri-pewt'], *n.* esteem, regard, reputation, general public opinion of a person or thing; good reputation, high esteem, honour, good character.

REPUTE (2), [ri-pewt'], *v.t.* (*archaic*) to consider, reckon, account, esteem; (*pass.*) to be generally considered as being, to be commonly regarded as (being). [L. *reputare* to reckon again].

REPUTED, [ri-pewt'-id], *adj.* generally regarded or accepted (though often implying uncertainty or lack of conviction), supposed, ostensible; famous, renowned, celebrated; **r. pint, quart, etc.**, a measure which, while not officially stamped as imperial, is generally accepted as being accurate.

REPUTEDLY, [ri-pewt'-id-li], *adv.* by repute.

REQUEST (1), [ri-kwest'], *n.* the expression of a desire or need for something, entreaty, petition; that which is asked for or requested; demand; **in r.**, eagerly sought after, generally called for; **letter of r.**, (*eccles.*) a document expressing a formal request that a case be transferred to another (usually a superior) court. [OFr. *requeste*].

REQUEST (2), [ri kwest'], *v.t.* to beg, ask for, to express a strong desire or need for, seek; to ask. [OFr. *requester*].

REQUESTER, [ri-kwest'-er], *n.* a petitioner; one who requests.

RE-QUICKEN, [rē'-kwik'-en], *v.t.* to reanimate; *v.i.* to come to life again, revive.

REQUIEM, [rek'-wi-em], *n.* (*R.C.*) a mass for the dead, beginning with this word; a musical setting of the words of this mass; a dirge, a funeral chant or poem recited or sung upon the death of a person. [L. *requiem*, *acc. sg.* of *requies* repose].

REQUIRABLE, [ri-kwier'-abl], *adj.* that may be required; fit or proper to be demanded.

REQUIRE, [ri-kwier'], *v.t.* to need, want; to order, wish, command; to ask or demand as by right or authority, to claim; to request, make necessary, call for; *v.i.* to be necessary. [L. *requirere* to seek once more].

REQUIREMENT, [ri-kwier'-ment], *n.* (usually *pl.*) that which is required, need, demand, want; that which must be conformed to, condition, stipulation.

REQUIRER, [ri-kwier'-er], *n.* one who requires.

REQUISITE (1), [rek'-wiz-it], *n.* that which is necessary for something, something required or indispensable for a particular purpose or occasion.

REQUISITE (2), [rek'-wiz-it], *adj.* needed, necessary, required, essential for some purpose or occasion. [L. *requisitus*, *p.pt.* of *requirere* to seek again].

REQUISITELY, [rek'-wiz-it-li], *adv.* necessarily.

REQUISITENESS, [rek'-wiz-it-nes], *n.* the state of being requisite; necessity.

REQUISITION (1), [rek'-wiz-ish'-un], *n.* a formal demand or request for something, made as of right, *esp.* an official application or request, made by authority, that something shall be done or provided for military purposes; the state of being put into service or active use; requirement, stipulation, condition. [L. *requisitio* inquiry].

REQUISITION (2), [rek'-wiz-ish'-un], *v.t.* to commandeer, require to be done or provided for military purposes; to make a requisition upon; to call into service, to acquire for use or as supplies.

REQUISITORY, [ri-kwiz'-it-er-i], *adj.* of the nature of, making, a requisition; able to make a requisition.

REQUITABLE, [ri-kwit'-abl], *adj.* that may be requited.

REQUITAL, [ri-kwit'-al], *n.* the act of requiting, an action repaying or in return for a previous action; retaliation, punishment; recompense, reward.

REQUITE, [ri-kwīt'], *v.t.* to repay, to do or give back in return; to avenge, retaliate for; to reward; to punish (a person); to recompense (a person). [RE (1) and~QUIT].

REQUITER, [ri-kwīt'-er], *n.* one who requites.

RE-RAIL, [rē'-rāl'], *v.t.* to provide with a fresh set of rails; to place on the rails again.

RE-READ, [rē'-rēd'], *v.t.* to read through once more.

REREBRACE, [rēer'-brās], *n.* armour on the upper part of the arm between the shoulder-plate and the vambrace. [AFr.*rerebras behind the arm].

REREBRACE

REREDOS, [rēer'-dos], *n.* a screen, usually decorated with ornamental carving, at the back of the altar in a church; a screen in front of the choir. [AFr. *arere-dos* from OFr. *arere* behind and *dos* the back].

REREMOUSE†, see REARMOUSE†.

REREWARD†, see REARWARD (1).

RES, [rēz], *n.* (*leg.*) property; the subject of an action; thing; cause; **r. gestae,** things done (and, as such, forming evidence). [L. *res*].

RESAIL, [rē'-sāl'], *v.t. and i.* to sail over again.

RESALE, [rē'-sāl'], *n.* the act of selling afresh what has been bought.

RESALUTE, [rē'-sal-ōōt'], *v.t.* to salute afresh or back again.

RESCIND, [ri-sind'], *v.t.* to annul; to revoke; to abrogate, repeal, reverse. [L. *rescindere* to tear].

RESCISSION, [ri-sish'-un], *n.* the act of rescinding, annulment, revocation. [L. *rescissio*].

RESCISSORY, [ri-sis'-er-i], *adj.* having power to rescind or annul. [L. *rescissorius*].

RE-SCORE, [rē'-skaw(r)'], *v.t.* to rearrange the score of, so as to make suitable for different voices, instruments, or groups of instruments.

RESCRIBE, [rē'-skrīb'], *v.t.* to write afresh, rewrite. [L. *rescribere*].

RESCRIPT, [rē'-skript], *n.* a written official answer, having the force of law, made by the Pope or Emperor in reply to some question in jurisprudence submitted to him for decision; an official edict or decree issued by a ruler. [L. *rescriptus*, *p.pt.* of *rescribere* to answer in writing].

RESCRIPTION, [rē-skrip'-shun], *n.* a writing over again, rewriting; a writing back in reply, a written answer; a written order authorizing payment of a sum of money. [L. *rescriptio*].

RESCRIPTIVELY, [rē-skript'-iv-li], *adv.* by rescript.

RESCUABLE, [res'-kew-abl], *adj.* capable of being rescued.

RESCUE (1), [res'-kew], *n.* deliverance or liberation from danger, captivity, destruction, or other harmful plight; (*leg.*) forcible release or removal from the custody of the law; **to come to the r.,** to provide necessary assistance; **r. squad,** a squad of people organized to rescue persons trapped in débris after an air-raid. [*Next*].

RESCUE (2), [res'-kew], *v.t.* to set free from confinement, danger, harmful influences, or any hazardous plight; to extricate from a difficulty; to liberate from a state of siege; to recover by force (that which has been unlawfully seized); (*leg.*) to liberate violently from the custody of the law. [AFr. *reskeure*].

RESCUER, [res'-kew-er], *n.* one who rescues.

RESEARCH, [ri-surch'], *n.* diligent investigation in order to discover some particular fact or facts about something or someone, *esp.* methodical and original inquiry into, or study of, some subject by trained investigators, in order to add materially to existing knowledge of, or to furnish new ideas upon, that subject. [OFr. *recerche*].

RESEARCHER, [ri-surch'-er], *n.* a person engaged in research work.

RESEARCHFUL, [ri-surch'-fōōl], *adj.* making a fetish of research; containing the results of research work.

RESEAT, [rē'-sēt'], *v.t.* to seat or set up again; to put fresh seats into; to provide with a new seat.

RESEAU, [re'-zō], *n.* net ground for lace; (*print., phot.*) a fine screen, a crosswork of fine lines. [Fr. *réseau*].

RESECT, [rē-sekt'], *v.t.* to cut down, pare off, cut away. [L. *resectus*, *p.pt.* of *resecare*].

RESECTION, [rē-sek'-shun], *n.* the act of cutting or paring off; (*surg.*) the operation of cutting out, or the excision of, the diseased bone of a joint. [L. *resectio*].

RESEDA, [res-ē'-da], *n.* a genus of over fifty species of plants, including the mignonette, *Reseda odorata*; a light greenish colour. [L. *reseda*].

RESEIZE, [rē-sēz'], *v.t.* to seize again; (*leg.*) to take possession of disseized lands and tenements.

RESEIZER, [rē-sēz'-er], *n.* (*leg.*) one who recovers possession of disseized lands and tenements.

RESEIZURE, [rē-sē'-zher], *n.* (*leg.*) the act of reseizing.

RESELL, [rē-sel'], *v.t.* to sell again.

RESEMBLABLE, [ri-zem'-blabl], *adj.* comparable.

RESEMBLANCE, [ri-zem'-blants], *n.* the state of being like or resembling, likeness, similitude, similarity of appearance or any other aspect; †likeness, reproduction. [AFr. *resemblance*].

RESEMBLE, [ri-zembl'], *v.t.* to be like, to possess certain attributes in common with, to be similar to. [OFr. *resembler*].

RESEMINATE, [rē-sem'-in-āt], *v.t.* to seminate anew. [L. *reseminare*].

RESEND, (**resent**), [rē'-send'], *v.t.* to send again, return.

RESENT, [ri-zent'], *v.t.* to object to strongly as a personal offence or source of annoyance, to feel angry and aggrieved at; to consider as a personal affront or injury. [Fr. *ressentir*].

RESENTFUL, [ri-zent'-fōōl], *adj.* filled with resentment; inclined to harbour grievances, quick to take offence.

RESENTFULLY, [ri-zent'-fōōl-i], *adv.* in a resentful manner.

RESENTMENT, [ri-zent'-ment], *n.* feeling of soreness or aggrievedness, anger and indignation aroused by a strong sense of personal injury or affront; grievance, ill-will, animosity. [~Fr. *ressentiment*].

RESERVATION, [rez'-er-vā'-shun], *n.* the act of reserving or keeping back something; that which is reserved; a qualification, exception or limitation expressed or mentally resolved; the act of reserving some privilege or right for oneself; the reserving to the Pope of the right to appoint a candidate to a vacant benefice; (*eccles.*) the act of holding back or keeping some part of the consecrated elements after the celebration of the eucharist, for subsequent use or some particular purpose; a tract of land set apart for the sole use of certain native tribes or for any other special purpose; (*leg.*) the retention of a right or interest in property conveyed or leased to another; the right or interest retained in this way; the clause in the deed expressing this retention; **mental r.,** the withholding in the mind of something which, if expressed, would alter a statement. [LL. *reservatio*].

RESERVE (1), [ri-zurv'], *n.* that which is reserved for some special reason; a limitation, qualification, restriction, or exception; the withholding of wholehearted approval or acceptance; the lowest price at which a thing may be sold at an auction; restraint, aloofness, avoidance of undue familiarity, enthusiasm, or exuberance, refusal to unburden oneself, accept a situation wholeheartedly; deliberate withholding of truth where unpleasant or inconvenient; a stretch of country enclosed for some particular use or persons; that which is kept back for future use, a spare supply, an extra stock which may be drawn upon; (*milit.*) (*pl.*) troops or armed forces kept back from action to give later support when needed; (*milit.*) that branch of the fighting forces consisting of men who have been trained and have served for a period of time, and whose services are now only required in the event of war or special emergency; (*sport*) a player or athlete selected to take the place of a member of a team if required; (*pl., sport*) the second best team of a club; (*comm.*) funds or capital held in readiness to meet ordinary or likely demands; **gold r.,** sufficient quantity of gold kept to meet the issue of paper money; **without r.,** unrestrictedly; **in r.,** in readiness for possible future use. [Fr. *réserve*].

RESERVE (2), [ri-zurv'], *v.t.* to keep back for future use, to keep as a spare supply; to set aside or keep for the use of a particular person or number of persons; to set apart, to keep in store (for); to defer, put off, postpone; (*leg.*) to retain (rights or interest) in property which is conveyed; (*eccles.*) to withhold for consideration by a superior authority; (*eccles.*) to set aside (part of the consecrated elements) for use in some particular purpose; to declare exempt from military service on grounds of national expediency. [L. *reservare*].

RESERVED, [ri-zurvd'], *adj.* aloof, reticent, shy, diffident, avoiding undue familiarity, keeping apart or to oneself; kept apart for the use of some particular person or persons, booked in advance; **R. list,** a list of naval officers no longer in active service, but who could be called upon in the event of war or emergency; **r. occupation,** an occupation in which workers are exempt from national service.

RESERVEDLY, [ri-zurv'-ed-li], *adv.* in a reserved manner.

RESERVEDNESS, [ri-zurv'-ed-nes], *n.* the quality of being reserved.

RESERVER, [ri-zurv'-er], *n.* one who reserves.

RESERVIST, [ri-zurv'-ist], *n.* a member of the reserve forces.

RESERVOIR, [rez'-er-vwah(r)], *n.* a large receptacle or hollow place built or adapted to collect and store water for the use of the inhabitants of a town, city, etc.; that part of an apparatus or implement in which liquid is stored; a sac or receptacle in an animal or plant organism in which fluid is contained; a store, supply. [Fr. *réservoir*].

RESET (1), [ri-set'], *n.* (*Scots leg.*) the receiving of stolen goods; †the receiving and harbouring of a criminal or outlaw. [OFr. *recet*].

RESET (2), (**resetting, reset**), [ri-set'], *v.t. and i.* to receive stolen goods. [OFr. *receter*].

RE-SET, (**re-setting, re-set**), [rē'-set'], *v.t.* to set again; to put a fresh edge upon; to replant; (*typ.*) to set up again.

RESETTER, [ri-set'-er], *n.* a receiver of stolen goods. [OFr. *recetour*].

RESETTLE, [rē'-setl'], *v.t.* to settle, decide again; to cause to take up a fresh settlement, to install again; to establish with settlers again.

RESETTLEMENT, [rē'-setl'-ment], *n.* a fresh settlement.

RESHAPE, [rē'-shāp'], *v.t.* to shape again; *v.i.* to assume a new shape or aspect, to take a fresh turn.

RESHIP, (**reshipping, reshipped**), [rē'-ship'], *v.t.* to ship again; to put on a fresh ship.

RESHIPMENT, [rē'-ship'-ment], *n.* the act of reshipping; that which is reshipped.

RESHUFFLE (1), [rē'-shufl'], *n.* a fresh shuffle; a rearrangement of positions.

RESHUFFLE (2), [rē'-shufl'], *v.t.* to shuffle afresh; to rearrange.

RESIDE, [ri-zīd'], *v.i.* to live (in or at) permanently or for a considerable length of time, to inhabit, dwell (in or at); to lie (in), rest (in); to be present, inhere; to live at some official residence in order to discharge some office or stipulation. [L. *residere* to rest, sit behind].

RESIDENCE, [rez'-id-ents], *n.* the act of residing or dwelling in a place; the act of residing in a specified place in order to satisfy some condition or discharge some duty; the place where one resides, dwelling-place, abode; time during which one resides in a place; an imposing style of house. [LL. *residentia*].

RESIDENCY, [rez'-id-en-si], *n.* residence; the official residence of the representative of the British government at the court of an Indian prince.

RESIDENT (1), [rez'-id-ent], *n.* one who resides or lives more or less permanently in a place; a political agent or representative of the Viceroy and British government at the court of an Indian prince; the governor of an administrative division in the Dutch East Indies.

RESIDENT (2), [rez'-id-ent], *adj.* residing, dwelling in a place for a considerable length of time; living at a particular place in order to satisfy some condition or discharge some duty; (of birds) non-migratory; present, inherent, settled, found. [L. *residens*].

RESIDENTIAL, [rez'-id-en'-shal], *adj.* suitable for, in which are found, residences; containing few or no industrial buildings; pertaining to residence.

RESIDENTIARY (1), [rez'-id-en'-sher-i], *n.* a resident; (*eccles.*) an ecclesiastic, *esp.* a canon who has to live in an official residence for a certain period of time.

RESIDENTIARY (2), [rez'-id-en'-sher-i], *adj.* necessitating official residence; having to live at an official residence; resident.

RESIDENTIARYSHIP, [rez'-id-en'-sher-i-ship], *n.* the position of a residentiary canon.

RESIDENTSHIP, [rez'-id-ent-ship], *n.* the office, or tenure of office, of a resident.

RESIDUAL, [riz-id'-yōō-al], *adj.* outstanding, remaining, left over after a part has been taken away, left as a residue; (*math.*) left after subtraction; (*phys.*) unable to be accounted for or explained; **r. air,** the air still remaining in the lungs after one has breathed out as far as possible; **r. quantity,** (*math.*) a binomial expression containing the minus sign. [L. *residuum*].

RESIDUARY, [riz-id'-yōō-er-i], *adj.* remaining, outstanding, left over; in the form of a residue; (*leg.*) relating to the residue of an estate; **r. clause,** that clause in a will which disposes of the residue of the estate; **r. legatee,** the person to whom is bequeathed that part of the estate which remains after all debts, expenses, and special legacies have been deducted.

RESIDUE, [rez'-i-dew], *n.* the remainder, rest, that which is left over after something has been subtracted or taken away; (*chem.*) residuum; (*leg.*) that which remains of an estate after all debts, charges upon it, and special legacies have been deducted. [Fr. *résidue*].

RESIDUENT, [riz-id'-yōō-ent], *n.* a by-product of a process of manufacture; a waste product left after the chief constituent has been removed.

RESIDUOUS, [riz-id'-yōō-us], *adj.* remaining, left over, residual. [L. *residuus*].

RESIDUUM, (*pl.* **residua**), [riz-id'-yōō-um], *n.* remainder; (*chem.*) that which is left after a process of separation, combustion, evaporation, purification, etc., a waste product or deposit; (*leg.*) residue. [L. *residuum*].

RESIGN, [ri-zīn'], *v.t.* to give up, relinquish; to withdraw, abandon; *v.i.* to give up an office, post, or position; *v. reflex.* to surrender, yield, submit, hand oneself over (to), to become reconciled with, accept patiently, passively and with equanimity. [L. *resignare* to unseal].

RE-SIGN, [rē'-sīn'], *v.t.* to sign again.

RESIGNATION, [rez'-ig-nā'-shun], *n.* the act of resigning; the expression of one's desire or intention to resign; the state of being resigned, submission with equanimity to the will of Providence, patient and passive acceptance of what must be, reconcilement to one's fate. [MedL. *resignatio*].

RESIGNED, [ri-zīnd'], *adj.* submissive, patiently and passively accepting, reconciled.

RESIGNEDLY, [ri-zīn'-ed-li], *adv.* with resignation.

RESILE, [ri-zīl'], *v.i.* to seek to withdraw (from an engagement, agreement, obligation, etc.), to draw back; to change one's view upon, react or recoil (from); to return to its original shape after being distorted, to spring back to its original position after displacement, to rebound. [L. *resilire* to jump back].

RESILIENCE, [ri-zil'-i-ents], *n.* elasticity, power of rebounding, quality of returning to its original shape and position after stretching or compression; the act of springing back or rebounding; a shrinking back or recoil from anything; power of recovering from a shock, etc.

RESILIENCY, [ri-zil'-i-en-si], *n.* resilience.

RESILIENT, [ri-zil'-i-ent], *adj.* elastic, springing back to its original position or shape; rebounding; (*fig.*) readily recovering from depression.

RESIN (1), [rez'-in], *n.* a gum-like secretion, insoluble in water, and commonly found in the form of a vitreous solid. [L. *resina*].

RESIN (2), [rez'-in], *v.t.* to treat with resin, rub resin upon.

RESINACEOUS, [rez'-in-ā'-shus], *adj.* resinous.

RESINATE, [rez'-in-āt], *n.* (*chem.*) a salt of the resinic acids.

RESINIC, [rez-in'-ik], *adj.* (*chem.*) produced from resin.

RESINIFEROUS, [rez'-in-if'-er-us], *adj.* producing or containing resin.

RESINIFICATION, [rez'-in-if-ik-ā'-shun], *n.* treatment with resin; conversion into resin.

RESINIFORM, [rez-in'-i-fawm], *adj.* in the form of resin.

RESINIFY, [rez-in'-i-fī], *v.i.* to become resinous.

RESINOUS, [rez'-in-us], *adj.* like resin; obtained from resin; containing resin; having the properties of resin.

RESINOUSLY, [rez'-in-us-li], *adv.* like or by resin.

RESINOUSNESS, [rez'-in-us-nes], *n.* the quality of being resinous.

RESINY, [rez'-in-i], *adj.* like resin; resinous.

RESIPISCENCE, [res'-ip-is'-ents], *n.* wisdom derived from bitter experience, repentance for misbehaviour, adoption of a sensible attitude, progression from folly to wisdom, a coming to one's senses. [L. *resipiscentia*].

RESIPISCENT, [res'-ip-is'-ent], *adj.* becoming wiser through experience, return to a sensible state of mind, seeing reason.

RESIST (1), [riz-ist′], *n.* a preparation used to preserve certain parts from the effect of the dye in calico-printing, thus keeping them uncoloured; (*print.*) a substance similarly used to prevent certain parts of a process plate being etched by acid.

RESIST (2), [riz-ist′], *v.t.* to obstruct, act in opposition to, impede, strive against, hamper; to withstand, endure the force of without giving way; to be proof against, to be unaffected by; to oppose, repel, stand firm against; to refuse to succumb to; to frustrate, thwart; *v.i.* to offer opposition or resistance. [L. *resistere* to stand back].

RESISTANCE, [riz-ist′-ants], *n.* the act of resisting; opposition, hindrance; power of resisting; endeavour to resist, antagonism; ability to withstand or be unaffected by a specified influence; (*phys.*) tendency or ability of any form of matter to oppose force exerted by, or pressure of, another body upon it; (*phys.*) non-conductivity; (*elect.*) degree of opposition offered by an electric circuit to the passage of an electric current; an apparatus designed to resist the passage of an electric current; **passive r.,** any form of protest in which no active opposition is offered; **line of least r.,** the easiest though not always the best course to follow. [Fr. *résistance*].

RESISTANCE-BOX, [riz-ist′-ants-boks′], *n.* (*elect.*) a box fitted with resistances.

RESISTANCE-COIL, [riz-ist′-ants-koil′], *n.* (*elect.*) a coil of wire, offering a resistance of known value to the passage of an electric current, placed in an electric circuit to increase its resistance.

RESISTANT (1), [riz-ist′-ant], *n.* one who, or that which, resists.

RESISTANT (2), [riz-ist′-ant], *adj.* resisting, offering opposition. [Fr. *résistant*].

RESISTER, [riz-ist′-er], *n.* one who resists.

RESISTIBILITY, [riz-ist′-ib-il′-i-ti], *n.* capacity to resist.

RESISTIBLE, [riz-ist′-ibl], *adj.* that may be resisted.

RESISTIBLENESS, [riz-ist′-ibl-nes], *n.* the quality of being resistible, capacity for resistance.

RESISTIBLY, [riz-ist′-ib-li], *adv.* in a resistible manner.

RESISTIVE, [riz-ist′-iv], *adj.* having the power to resist; tending to resist.

RESISTLESS, [riz-ist′-les], *adj.* irresistible; that cannot be opposed.

RESISTLESSLY, [riz-ist′-les-li], *adv.* in a resistless manner; irresistibly.

RESISTLESSNESS, [riz-ist′-les-nes], *n.* the quality of being resistless.

RESISTOR, [riz-ist′-or], *n.* a resistance.

RESMOOTH, [rē′-smōōTH′], *v.t.* to smooth anew.

RESOLDER, [rē′-sol′-der], *v.t.* to solder anew.

RESOLE, [rē′-sōl′], *v.t.* to provide with a fresh sole.

RESOLUBLE, [rez′-ol-yōōbl], *adj.* able to be resolved. [LL. *resolubilis*].

RE-SOLUBLE, [rē-sol′-yōōbl], *adj.* able to be melted or dissolved again.

RESOLUTE, [rez′-ol-ōōt], *adj.* firm, determined, unwavering, grimly steadfast, boldly fixed in purpose. [L. *resolutus*].

RESOLUTELY, [rez′-ol-ōōt-li], *adv.* in a resolute manner.

RESOLUTENESS, [rez′-ol-ōōt-nes], *n.* the quality of being resolute.

RESOLUTION, [rez′-ol-ōō′-shun], *n.* the act of resolving or splitting up into its component parts, analysis; the state of being so resolved; solution, unravelling; formal statement of opinion passed by, or decision made at, a meeting or public assembly; a proposal offered to such a meeting for consideration and its decision; the act of determining to perform some specific course of action, a fixed intention or determination intended to be strictly adhered to; resoluteness, conversion or change to something else; (*pros.*) the using of two short syllables for one long one; (*med.*) the disappearance of inflammation without discharge of matter; (*mus.*) the moving from a discord to a concord to complete the harmony; **r. (of an equation),** (*math.*) reduction in order to find the value of the unknown quantity; **r. of forces,** (*mech.*) division of a single force into two or more forces which together are mechanically equivalent to it. [L. *resolutio*].

RESOLUTIONER, [rez′-ol-ōō′-shun-er], *n.* one who concurs in, or helps to make, a resolution.

RESOLUTIVE (1), [rez′-ol-ōōt′-iv], *n.* (*med.*) a medicine or application which disperses an inflammation or tumour.

RESOLUTIVE (2), [rez′-ol-ōōt′-iv], *adj.* (*med.*) dissolving, dispersing; **r. condition,** (*leg.*) a condition which, when fulfilled, terminates a contract, obligation, or agreement.

RESOLVABILITY, [ri-zolv′-ab-il′-i-ti], *n.* resolvableness.

RESOLVABLE, [ri-zolv′-abl], *adj.* able to be resolved.

RESOLVABLENESS, [ri-zolv′-abl-nes], *n.* the state or quality of being resolvable.

RESOLVE (1), [ri-zolv′], *n.* determination, resolution, firm intention; resoluteness, grim steadfastness of purpose, bold firmness.

RESOLVE (2), [ri-zolv′], *v.t.* to analyse, split up into its constituent elements; to break up or separate (a complex idea or problem) into simple parts or aspects; to put an end to, clear up, settle; to explain; (*pass.*) to be determined; (*med.*) to remove without suppuration; *v.i.* to determine, decide, make up one's mind (to); (*mus.*) to pass from a discord to a concord to complete the harmony; (*leg.*) to lapse; *v. reflex.* to amount, reduce; to melt. [L. *resolvere* to loosen].

RESOLVED, [ri-zolvd′] *adj.* determined in purpose, resolute.

RESOLVEDLY, [ri-zolv′-ed-li], *adv.* in a resolved manner, resolutely.

RESOLVEDNESS, [ri-zolv′-ed-nes], *n.* fixedness of purpose, resoluteness.

RESOLVENT (1), [ri-zolv′-ent], *n.* (*med.*) that which has the power of resolving or dispersing (an inflammation or tumour), a solvent.

RESOLVENT (2), [ri-zolv′-ent], *adj.* having the power of resolving, dissolving, or dispersing.

RESOLVER, [ri-zolv′-er], *n.* one who, or that which, resolves, one who makes resolutions.

RESONANCE, [rez′-on-ants], *n.* vibration set up in a body in sympathy with another body already vibrating; the sound set up by such sympathetic vibration; continuation or strengthening of vibration by periodic absorption of wave-energy by a vibrating body, at a frequency which synchronizes with that at which it vibrates; sonority; (*elect.*) the state of an alternating current in which the frequency of the circuit coincides with that of a current of particular frequency, so that a large current of this frequency is built up in the circuit. [L. *resonantia* echo].

RESONANT, [rez′-on-ant], *adj.* sonorous, resounding, echoing back, ringing; setting up resonance, producing sympathetic vibrations.

RESONATE, [rez′-on-āt], *v.t.* to produce or possess resonance. [~L. *resonare* to sound again].

RESONATOR, [rez′-on-āt-or], *n.* an instrument which vibrates in response to a certain single note, and is used to detect this note amidst a number of sounds sounding together; a device to increase resonance, or to cause amplification of sound by resonance.

RESORB, [ri-sawb′], *v.t.* to absorb afresh. [L. *resorbere* to drink in again].

RESORBENT, [ri-sawb′-ent], *adj.* absorbing again, taking in once more.

RESORCIN, [ri-saw′-sin], *n.* a fusion of resins with caustic potash used in the preparation of dyes, and in medicine and photography. [RES(IN) and ORCIN].

RESORPTION, [ri-sawp′-shun], *n.* re-absorption.

RESORPTIVE, [ri-sawp′-tiv], *adj.* relating to resorption.

RESORT (1), [ri-zawt′], *n.* the act of resorting to, recourse; the act of betaking oneself to or visiting frequently; an expedient, means to accomplish something, a thing or person to which one has recourse; a place which one regularly visits, a place frequented, *esp.* for a specific purpose or by a particular type of people. [OFr. *resort*].

RESORT (2), [ri-zawt′], *v.i.* to have recourse, to use as a means of accomplishing some purpose; to proceed, betake oneself, repair, go regularly. [OFr. *resortir* to rebound].

RE-SORT, [rē′-sawt′], *v.t.* to sort afresh.

RE-SORTED, [rē′-sawt′-id], *adj.* sorted again.

RESORTER, [ri-zawt′-er], *n.* one who resorts or frequents.

RESOUND, [ri-zownd′], *v.t.* to re-echo, return, send back; (*fig.*) to proclaim, extol, to spread abroad, celebrate; *v.i.* to reverberate, re-echo, ring with a particular sound; to echo, be sent back (of sound), to sound loudly and continually; (*fig.*) to be celebrated, to be proclaimed far and wide, be extolled.

RE-SOUND (2), [rē′-sownd′], *v.t.* to sound again.

RESOUNDING, [ri-zownd′-ing], *adj.* that resounds, re-echoing, sounding loudly.

RESOUNDINGLY, [ri-zownd′-ing-li], *adv.* so as to resound or sound loudly.

RESOURCE, [ri-saws′], *n.* expedient, shift, resort,

thing to which one may have recourse, any source of aid or support; source of distraction, recreation or entertainment; ingenuity, skill in devising ways and means of dealing with a problem or accomplishing something; (*pl.*) stock, means of supplying requirements; money or property, source of wealth, means of support. [Fr. *ressource*].

RESOURCEFUL, [ri-saws'-fōōl], *adj.* clever at devising ways and means of dealing with or accomplishing anything.

RESOURCEFULLY, [ri-saws'-fōōl-i], *adv.* in a resourceful manner.

RESOURCEFULNESS, [ri-saws'-fōōl-nes], *n.* the state of being resourceful.

RESOURCELESS, [ri-saws'-les], *adj.* lacking resource; destitute of resources.

RESOW, [rē'-sō'], *v.t.* to sow again.

RESP, [resp], *n.* a disease or disorder attacking sheep. [Uncert.].

RESPEAK, [rē'-spēk'], *v.t.* to repeat, speak again.

RESPECT (1), [ri-spekt'], *n.* esteem or appreciation; suitable deference; proper heed, attention, consideration; due regard; a particular aspect or detail; regard, reference, relation; favour, partiality, discrimination; (*archaic*) end, consideration influencing action; (*pl.*) greetings, good wishes, kind regards; **to pay one's respects to**, to visit or go to see in order to express one's goodwill towards; **in r. of**, concerning. [L. *respectus* looking about].

RESPECT (2), [ri-spekt'], *v.t.* to pay due heed to, to appreciate fully, to be mindful of and not belittle or treat with contempt; to regard with fitting deference, to honour, esteem; to show consideration for, observe, keep; (*archaic*) to relate or refer to, be concerned with. [L. *respectus*, *p.pt.* of *respicere*].

RESPECTABILITY, [ris-pekt'-ab-il'-i-ti], *n.* the quality of being respectable; a person who is accounted respectable; conduct considered proper by those who claim to be respectable; slavish and snobbish adherence to a conventional social creed of conduct.

RESPECTABLE, [ris-pekt'-abl], *adj.* worthy of, held in, respect; decent, possessing qualities commanding respect, honest, well-behaved; snobbishly and blindly adhering to the conventional creed of conduct in accordance with accepted rules or standards of propriety; suitable, proper, appropriate, presentable; fair, reasonably good, above the average.

RESPECTABLENESS, [ris-pekt'-abl-nes], *n.* the quality of being respectable.

RESPECTABLY, [ris-pekt'-ab-li], *adv.* in a respectable manner.

RESPECTANT, [ris-pekt'-ant], *adj.* (*her.*) regarding each other, face to face.

RESPECTER, [ris-pekt'-er], *n.* one who respects.

RESPECTANT

RESPECTFUL, [ris-pekt'-fōōl], *adj.* showing respect, deferential, expressive of respect.

RESPECTFULLY, [ris-pekt'-fōōl-i], *adv.* in a respectful manner.

RESPECTFULNESS, [ris-pekt'-fōōl-nes], *n.* the quality of being respectful.

RESPECTING, [ris-pekt'-ing], *prep.* concerning, in regard to, about, with reference to.

RESPECTIVE, [ris-pekt'-iv], *adj.* of each one compared with each of the others mentioned, relative; several, individual, separate, particular.

RESPECTIVELY, [ris-pekt'-iv-li], *adv.* as relating to each, referring to each individually.

RESPECTIVENESS, [ris-pekt'-iv-nes], *n.* the act of being respective.

RESPECTLESS, [ris-pekt'-les], *adj.* having no respect; without regard, not respecting.

RE-SPELL, [rē-spel'], *v.t.* to spell over again.

RESPIRABILITY, [ris-pīer'-ab-il'-i-ti, res'-pi-ra-bil'-i-ti], *n.* respirableness.

RESPIRABLE, [ris-pīer'-abl, res'-pi-rabl], *adj.* fit to be breathed. [LL. *respirabilis*].

RESPIRABLENESS, [ris-pīer'-abl-nes, res'-pi-rabl-nes], *n.* the quality of being respirable.

RESPIRATION, [res'-pir-ā'-shun], *n.* the act of breathing; a single breath; (*bot.*) the process by which a plant takes in oxygen from the air, and gives out carbon dioxide. [L. *respiratio*].

RESPIRATIONAL, [res'-pi-rā'-shun-al], *adj.* relating to respiration.

RESPIRATIVE, [res'-pi-rat-iv], *adj.* respiratory.

RESPIRATOR, [res'-pi-rāt-er], *n.* an apparatus for protecting the lungs from the inspiration of smoke, fumes, gases, or cold air; a gas-mask.

RESPIRATORIUM, [res'-pi-rat-aw'-ri-um], *n.* the respiratory chamber in which the gills are concealed in some insects.

RESPIRATORY, [res-pi'-rat-er-i], *adj.* of, or pertaining to, respiration.

RESPIRE, [ris-pīer'], *v.t.* to exhale; to breathe out; *v.i.* to breathe; to inhale air into the lungs and exhale it; to take a respite. [L. *respirare*].

RESPIROMETER, [res'-pi-rom'-it-er], *n.* an apparatus for measuring respirations. [RESPIRE and METER].

RESPITE (1), [res'-pit, res'-pīt], *n.* temporary intermission of labour, pain, or danger, interval of rest; pause; suspension of the execution of a criminal; the prolongation of time for the payment of a debt. [OFr. *respit*].

RESPITE (2), [res-pīt'], *v.t.* to relieve by an interval of rest; to suspend temporarily the execution of; to postpone; to reprieve.

RESPLENDENCE, [ris-plend'-ents], *n.* brilliant lustre; vivid brightness; splendour. [LL. *resplendentia*].

RESPLENDENCY, [ris-plend'-en-si], *n.* resplendence.

RESPLENDENT, [ris-plend'-ent], *adj.* very bright; shining with brilliant lustre; (*coll.*) very fine. [~L. *resplendere*].

RESPLENDENTLY, [ris-plend'-ent-li], *adv.* in a resplendent fashion.

RESPLIT, [rē'-split'], *v.t.* *and i.* to split again.

RESPOND (1), [res'-pond], *n.* (*eccles.*) response.

RESPOND (2), [ris-pond'], *v.t.* *and i.* to reply; to answer; to reply to a letter; to be responsive. [L. *respondere*].

RESPONDENCE, [ris-pond'-ents], *n.* the act of responding; the condition of being respondent.

RESPONDENT (1), [ris-pond'-ent], *n.* (*leg.*) a person who answers to a suit at law, *esp.* one for divorce; a defendant.

RESPONDENT (2), [ris-pond'-ent], *adj.* that responds to a demand or expectation.

RESPONDENTIA, [ris'-pond-en'-shi-a], *n.* (*comm.*) a loan upon the security of a ship's cargo.

RESPONSE, [ris-pons'], *n.* reply; reaction to stimulus, mental or physical; (*eccles.*) (in the litany) the answer of the congregation to the priest; (*R.C. church*) a kind of anthem sung after a lesson at matins. [L. *responsum*].

RESPONSIBILITY, [ris-pon'-sib-il'-it-i], *n.* the act of being responsible; what one is responsible for; obligation; trust; duty.

RESPONSIBLE, [ris-pon'-sibl], *adj.* answerable; liable to account; able to discharge an obligation; trustworthy; involving responsibility. [OFr. *responsible*].

RESPONSIBLENESS, [ris-pon'-sibl-nes], *n.* the quality of being responsible; responsibility.

RESPONSIBLY, [ris-pon'-sib-li], *adv.* in a responsible fashion.

RESPONSIONS, [ris-pon'-shunz], *n.(pl.)* the first of three examinations at Oxford for the degree of B.A.

RESPONSIVE, [ris-pon'-siv], *adj.* responding; answering, replying; reacting easily to mental or physical stimulus; sensitive.

RESPONSIVELY, [ris-pon'-siv-li], *adv.* in a responsive fashion.

RESPONSIVENESS, [ris-pon'-siv-nes], *n.* the state of being responsive.

RESPONSORY, [ris-pon'-ser-i], *n.* an anthem sung during the church service after the lesson. [LL. *responsorium*].

REST† (1), [rest], *n.* the holder for the butt of a lance which was welded on to the body-armour of a knight. [~ARREST].

REST (2), [rest], *n.* cessation from motion or action of any kind; repose; quiet, sleep; peace; a place of quiet or repose; death, the grave; that on or in which anything rests; a short pause; a pause or interval of time, during which there is an intermission of the voice or sound. [OE. *rest*].

REST (3), [rest], *n.* the remainder; what is left. [Fr. *reste*].

REST (4), [rest], *v.t.* to place; to quiet; to allow to rest; to lay in rest; *v.i.* to cease from action or motion of any kind; to be quiet; to repose; to sleep; to be dead; to lean; to stand (on); to acquiesce; to rely; to abide. [OE. *restan*].

REST (5), [rest], *v.i.* to remain. [Fr. *rester*].

RESTAMP, [rē'-stamp'], *v.t.* to stamp again. [STAMP (2)].
RESTANT, [rest'-ant], *adj.* remaining; (*bot.*) persistent. [L. *restans*].
RESTATE, [rē'-stāt'], *v.t.* to state a second or subsequent time.
RESTATEMENT, [rē'-stāt'-ment], *n.* the act of stating a thing for a second time.
RESTAUR, [ris-taw(r)'], *n.* (*leg.*) a justified claim for indemnity as against a guarantor.
RESTAURANT, [rest'-er-ant, rest'-er-o(ng)], *n.* an establishment for the provision of food and drink; a superior eating-house. [Fr. *restaurant*].
RESTAURATEUR, [rest'-awr-at-ur'], *n.* one who keeps a restaurant.
RESTAURATION, [rest'-awr-ā'-shun], *n.* restoration.
REST-CURE, [rest'-kyōōer], *n.* a treatment for nervous illnesses, in which the patient is kept quiet, without visitors, newspapers, or private correspondence, and helped to eat, sleep and rest well.
REST-DAY, [rest'-dā], *n.* a day of rest; Sunday.
RESTFUL, [rest'-fōōl], *adj.* affording rest, quiet; reposeful; soothing.
RESTFULLY, [rest'-fōōl-i], *adv.* in a restful fashion.
RESTFULNESS, [rest'-fōōl-nes], *n.* the quality of being restful.
RESTHARROW, [rest'-ha'-rō], *n.* (*bot.*) the cammock or any one of the various species of the genus *Ononis*. [ARREST and HARROW (1)].
REST-HOUSE, [rest'-hows], *n.* a hostel for travellers in India, equipped and maintained by the Government; a quiet guest-house in the country.
RESTIFORM, [rest'-i-fawm], *adj.* twisted; resembling a cord. [L. *restis* cord and FORM (1)].
RESTINCTION†, [ri-stingk'-shun], *n.* the act of extinguishing.
RESTING-PLACE, [rest'-ing-plās'], *n.* a place where a person or thing may rest or remain; the grave.
RESTINGUISH†, [ri-sting'-wish], *v.t.* to quench or extinguish; subdue. [L. *restinguere*].

RESTHARROW

RESTITUTION, [rest'-it-ew'-shun], *n.* the act of restoring some right of which a person has been unjustly deprived; indemnification; compensation; state of restoration; (*phys.*) a resuming of original shape. [L. *restitutio*].
RESTITUTIVE, [rest'-it-ewt'-iv], *adj.* relating to restitution.
RESTITUTOR, [rest'-it-ewt'-or], *n.* a person who makes restitution.
RESTIVE, [rest'-iv], *adj.* unwilling to be driven; obstinate; stubborn; restless or impatient under restraint; inclined to jib. [OFr. *restif*].
RESTIVELY, [rest'-iv-li], *adv.* in a restive fashion.
RESTIVENESS, [rest'-iv-nes], *n.* the state or quality of being restive.
RESTLESS, [rest'-les], *adj.* continually moving; sleepless; uneasy; not satisfied to remain at rest; turbulent; unsettled; without tranquillity.
RESTLESSLY, [rest'-les-li], *adv.* in a restless fashion.
RESTLESSNESS, [rest'-les-nes], *n.* the condition of being restless.
RESTOCK, [rē'-stok'], *v.t.* to stock afresh.
RESTORABLE, [ri-stawr'-abl], *adj.* capable of being restored.
RESTORABLENESS, [ri-stawr'-abl-nes], *n.* the condition of being restorable.
RESTORATION, [rest'-or-ā'-shun], *n.* the act of restoring; renewal; recovery; the final recovery of all men from sin to a state of salvation; (*hist.*) the return to the English throne of Charles II in 1660; (*geol.*) a model or drawing of an extinct animal according to the knowledge obtained by studying the fossil bones. [RESTAURATION].
RESTORATIONIST, [rest'-or-ā'-shun-ist], *n.* a person who believes in the final restoration of all men.
RESTORATIVE (1), [ri-stawr'-at-iv], *n.* a medicine or food for restoring strength. [OFr. *restoratif*].
RESTORATIVE (2), [ri-stawr'-at-iv], *adj.* capable of giving fresh strength to. [OFr. *restoratif*].
RESTORATIVELY, [ri-stawr'-at-iv-li], *adv.* in the manner of, as, a restorative.
RESTORE, [ri-staw(r')], *v.t.* to bring back to a former condition; to repair; to heal; to rebuild; to revive; to recover; to give back; to return; to replace. [L. *restaurare*].
RE-STORE, [rē'-staw(r)'], *v.t.* to (put in) store again.
RESTORER, [ri-stawr'-er], *n.* a person or thing that restores.
RESTRAIN, [ris-trān'], *v.t.* to hold back or check; to repress; to hinder; to restrict; to withhold; to hold under restraint. [OFr. *restreigner*].
RESTRAINABLE, [ris-trān'-abl], *adj.* able to be restrained.
RESTRAINEDLY, [ris-trān'-ed-li], *adv.* in a restrained fashion.
RESTRAINER, [ri-strān'-er], *n.* a person or thing that restrains.
RESTRAINING, [ris-trān'-ing], *adj.* curbing; restricting; limiting; checking or hindering from sin.
RESTRAINMENT, [ris-trān'-ment], *n.* the action of restraining.
RESTRAINT, [ris-trānt'], *n.* the act of restraining, abridgment of liberty; that which restrains; a check; a curb. [OFr. *restrainte*].
RESTRAINT-CHAIR, [ris-trānt'-chāer'], *n.* a chair in which a violently insane person may be held down.
RESTRICT, [ris-trikt'], *v.t.* to limit; to confine; to restrain within bounds; to impose legal limitations upon. [L. *restrictus* from *restringere* to bind back].
RESTRICTED, [ri-strikt'-id], *adj.* under a legal limitation; confined, restrained; **r. area**, an area in which the speed limit for motor vehicles is restricted to thirty miles per hour.
RESTRICTEDLY, [ris-trikt'-ed-li], *adv.* in a restricted fashion.
RESTRICTION, [ris-trik'-shun], *n.* the action of restricting; limitation, restraint. [L. *restrictio*].
RESTRICTIVE, [ris-trikt'-iv], *adj.* having the quality of limiting; imposing restrictions.
RESTRICTIVELY, [ris-trikt'-iv-li], *adv.* in a restrictive fashion.
RESTY, [rest'-i], *adj.* indolent, restive.
RESUBLIMATION, [rē'-sub'-lim-ā'-shun], *n.* the second subliming.
RESULT (1), [ri-zult'], *n.* consequence; conclusion; effect; decision; outcome; (*math.*) the answer following a process of calculation.
RESULT (2), [ri-zult'], *v.i.* to follow as a consequence; to issue. [L. *resultare* to leap back].
RESULTANT (1), [ri-zult'-ant], *n.* the outcome (of something); (*phys.*) the force which is the combined effect of two or more forces acting in various directions; **r. tones**, secondary sounds that make their action heard when two differently pitched tones are sounded simultaneously and sustained.
RESULTANT (2), [ri-zult'-ant], *adj.* resulting; following as a result.
RESULTING, [ri-zult'-ing], *adj.* following as a result; resultant.
RESULTLESS, [ri-zult'-les], *adj.* without result.
RESUMABLE, [riz-yōōm'-abl], *adj.* capable of being resumed.
RESUME, résumé, [rez'-yōōm-ā], *n.* a summing up; a condensed statement; a précis. [Fr. *résumé*].
RESUME, [riz-yōōm'], *v.t.* to take back; to take again what has been given; to begin again; to take up again; to continue once more. [L. *resumere*].
RESUMMON, [rē'-sum'-on], *v.t.* to summon or call for a second or subsequent time.
RESUMPTION, [ri-zump'-shun], *n.* the action of resuming. [L. *resumptio*].
RESUMPTIVE, [ri-zumpt'-iv], *adj.* resuming; taking back or again.
RESUPINATE, [rē-sōōp'-in-āt], *adj.* (*bot.*) twisted upward. [L. *resupinare* to bend back].
RESUPINATION, [rē-sōōp'-in-ā'-shun], *n.* (*bot.*) the condition of being resupinate.
RESURGENT, [ri-surj'-ent], *adj.* renewed; rising; reviving.
RESURRECT, [rez'-er-ekt'], *v.t.* to restore to life; to raise again from the dead; to bring into use again something previously discarded or hidden away.
RESURRECTION, [rez'-er-ek'-shun], *n.* a rising again; a resuscitation; **the R.**, Christ's rising from the grave; the rising of man from death on the Day of Judgment. [L. *resurrectio*].
RESURRECTIONAL, [rez'-ur-ek'-shun-al], *adj.* of, or pertaining to, resurrection.
RESURRECTIONIST†, [rez'-er-ek'-shun-ist], *n.* a man who stealthily exhumes dead bodies for dissection; a body-snatcher.
RESURVEY (1), [rē'-sur'-vā], *n.* a second survey.
RESURVEY (2), [rē'-ser-vā'], *v.t.* to survey once again.
RESUSCITABLE, [ri-sus'-it-abl], *adj.* capable of being resuscitated.

RESUSCITANT, [ri-sus'-it-ant], *n.* a person or thing that resuscitates.

RESUSCITATE, [ri-sus'-it-āt], *v.t.* to revivify; to revive; to recover from apparent death; to resurrect; *v.i.* to revive. [L. *resuscitare*].

RESUSCITATION, [ri-sus'-it-ā'-shun], *n.* the action of reviving from a state of apparent death; the state of being resuscitated.

RESUSCITATIVE, [ri-sus'-it-at-iv], *adj.* revivifying; raising from apparent death; reviving.

RESUSCITATOR, [ri-sus'-it-āt'-or], *n.* a person who resuscitates.

RET, [ret], *v.t.* to destroy cohesion among the fibres of flax by steeping it; *v.i.* to rot from undue exposure to moisture. [ME. *reten* to soak].

RETABLE, [rē-tābl'], *n.* a ledge above the back of an altar on which candelabra and other objects may be set; a decoration or painted panel or carving, forming the rear piece of an altar. [Fr. *rétable*].

RETABLE

RETAIL (1), [rē'-tāl], *n.* the sale of commodities in small quantities to the consumer. [OFr. *retail*].

RETAIL (2), [rē'-tāl], *adj.* pertaining to the sale of goods by retail or to the goods thus sold.

RETAIL (3), [rē-tāl'], *v.t.* to sell in small quantities; to sell direct to the consumer goods bought wholesale; (*fig.*) to tell to many, to repeat.

RETAIL (4), [rē'-tāl], *adv.* by retail.

RETAILER, [rē'-tāl-er], *n.* a person who retails; one who sells goods by retail.

RETAILMENT, [rē-tāl'-ment], *n.* the act of retailing.

RE-TAILOR, [rē'-tāl'-er], *v.t.* to tailor anew, remake.

RETAIN, [ri-tān'], *v.t.* to hold or keep in possession; to remember; to detain; to keep back; to keep in pay; to engage by prepayment. [OFr. *retenir* from L. *retinere* to hold back].

RETAINABLE, [ri-tān'-abl], *adj.* able to be retained.

RETAINER, [ri-tān'-er], *n.* one who, or that which, retains; an attendant, servant; a dependant; (*leg.*) a fee paid to engage a barrister, usually termed a retaining fee; retention by legal right.

RETAINING, [ri-tān'-ing], *adj.* keeping in possession; engaging by a fee; **r. fee,** a fee paid in advance to a barrister to accept a brief; a fee paid to an adviser for an option on his services; **r. wall,** a wall to prevent a bank of earth from collapsing.

RETAKE, [rē'-tāk'], *v.t.* to take again; recapture.

RETAKER, [rē-tāk'-er], *n.* one who retakes.

RETALIATE, [ri-tal'-i-āt], *v.t.* to return like for like; to requite; *v.i.* to practise reprisals; to pay back injury for injury. [LL. *retaliare*].

RETALIATION, [ri-tal'-i-ā'-shun], *n.* the act of returning like for like; requital of evil, reprisals.

RETALIATIVE, [ri-tal'-i-at-iv], *adj.* practising retaliation; retaliatory.

RETALIATOR, [ri-tal'-i-āt'-or], *n.* one who retaliates.

RETALIATORY, [ri-tal'-i-at-er-i], *adj.* pertaining to retaliation; returning like for like.

RETARD (1), [ri-tahd'], *n.* retardation.

RETARD (2), [ri-tahd'], *v.t.* to diminish the speed of; to hinder; to hamper; to delay. [L. *retardare*].

RETARDANT, [ri-tahd'-ant], *adj.* that which retards.

RETARDATION, [ri-tahd-ā'-shun], *n.* the action of retarding; hindrance; delay; (*phys.*) the rate of loss of velocity.

RETARDATIVE, [ri-tahd'-a-tiv], *adj.* that may retard; retarding.

RETARDER, [ri-tahd'-er], *n.* a person or thing that retards.

RETARDMENT, [ri-tahd'-ment], *n.* the act of retarding.

RETCH, [rēch], *v.i.* to try hard to vomit; to strain, as in vomiting. [OE. *hræcan* to spit].

RETE, [rē'-tē], *n.* (*anat.*) a network of blood-vessels. [L. *rete* net].

RE-TELL, [rē'-tel'], *v.t.* to tell again; to repeat.

RETENTION, [ri-ten'-shun], *n.* the action of retaining; the power of retaining, *esp.* ideas in the mind; restraint. [OFr. *retencion*].

RETENTIVE, [ri-tent'-iv], *adj.* having the power to retain in the memory; not forgetful. [OFr. *retentif*].

RETENTIVELY, [ri-tent'-iv-li], *adv.* in a retentive fashion.

RETENTIVENESS, [ri-tent'-iv-nes], *n.* the state of being retentive.

RETENTOR, [ri-tent'-or], *n.* (*anat.*) a retaining muscle.

RETEXTURE, [rē-teks'-cher], *n.* a weaving again.

RETIARY, [rē'-shi-er-i], *n.* a spider that weaves a net; a gladiator whose weapons were a net and trident. [L. *retiarius*].

RETICENCE, [ret'-is-ents], *n.* reserve in speech, *esp.* about one's own affairs; uncommunicativeness. [L. *reticentia*].

RETICENCY, [ret'-is-en-si], *n.* reticence.

RETICENT, [ret'-is-ent], *adj.* reserved in speech; taciturn; uncommunicative.

RETICENTLY, [ret'-i-sent-li], *adv.* in reticent fashion.

RETICLE, [ret'-ikl], *n.* †a small net; interlacing lines drawn on glass and used with the lens of a telescope to facilitate the location of objects. [L. *rete* net].

RETICULAR, [re-tik'-yōōl-er], *adj.* having the form of, resembling, network; formed with interstices.

RETICULARLY, [re-tik'-yōōl-er-li], *adv.* in a reticular fashion.

RETICULATE, [re-tik'-yōōl-āt], *adj.* reticulated.

RETICULATED, [re-tik'-yōōl-āt-id], *adj.* netted; resembling network; **r. work,** a kind of masonry formed of small square stones or bricks placed lozenge-wise.

RETICULATION, [re-tik'-yōō-lā'-shun], *n.* the condition of being reticulated; network.

RETICULE, [ret'-ik-ewl], *n.* a small handbag formerly of network. [L. *reticulum*].

RETICULOSE, [re-tik'-yōōl-ōs], *adj.* forming an irregular network.

RETICULUM, [re-tik'-yōōl-um], *n.* a network; the second stomach of ruminants, so called because of the honeycombed structure of the membrane. [L. *reticulum*].

RETIERCE, retiercé, [ret'-ēer'-sā], *adj.* (*her.*) horizontally partitioned into three bands, each being itself divided into three strips and each having three similar colours. [Fr. *retiercé*].

RETIFORM, [rēt'-i-fawm], *adj.* like a network.

RETINA, [ret'-in-a], *n.* a retiform expansion of the optic nerve in the eye, which receives the impressions of light that give rise to vision. [L. *retina*].

RETINACULUM, [ret'-in-ak'-yōōl-um], *n.* (*entom.*) a set of hooks, etc., locking together the upper and lower wings of insects when in flight. [L. *retinaculum*].

RETINAL, [ret'-in-al], *adj.* pertaining to the retina.

RETINALITE, [ret-in'-al-īt], *n.* (*min.*) a massive variety of serpentine, with a resinous content. [Gk. *rhetine* resin and *lithos* stone].

RETINERVED, [rēt'-in-urvd], *adj.* (*bot.*) retiform, cross-veined.

RETINITE, [ret'-in-īt], *n.* (*min.*) pitchstone, a form of obsidian. [Gk. *retine* resin].

RETINITIS, [ret'-in-īt'-is], *n.* severe inflammation of the retina. [RETINA and Gk. *itis* denoting inflammation].

RETINOSCOPE, [ret'-in-ō-skōp'], *n.* (*opt.*) a mirror with a perforation in the centre, employed to project light on to the retina for purposes of clinical examination. [RETINA and SCOPE].

RETINOSCOPY, [ret'-in-os'-kop-i], *n.* the technique of employing the retinoscope.

RETINUE, [ret'-in-ew], *n.* the train of attendants of a distinguished personage; the suite, the staff of a flag-officer. [OFr. *retenue*].

RETIRACY, [ri-tīer'-a-si], *n.* (*U.S.*) retirement; retirement from business; the income retired on.

RETIRAL, [ri-tīer'-al], *n.* the act of retiring; the withdrawing from circulation of banknotes, or bills before they become due.

RETIRE, [ri-tīer'], *v.i.* to go from company or from a public place into privacy; to give up one's occupation or office; to withdraw; to go to bed; to retreat, fall back; to recede; *v.t.* to cause to withdraw, resign; to withdraw from publicity; (*comm.*) to take up and pay a bill when due. [Fr. *retirer* to withdraw].

RETIRED, [ri-tīerd'], *adj.* secluded from society; quiet; private, gone into retirement; **r. list,** a list of officers who have retired from service; **to put on the r. list,** to send into retirement from active life.

RETIREDLY, [ri-tīerd'-li], *adv.* in a retired fashion.

RETIREDNESS, [ri'-tīerd'-nes], *n.* the condition of being retired.

RETIREMENT, [ri-tīer'-ment], *n.* the act of retiring; the withdrawing from society or public life; the state of being retired; retired abode; privacy; the act of going to bed.

RETIRING, [ri-tīer'-ing], *adj.* reserved; not forward or obtrusive; given on retirement from work.

RE-TOLD, [rē'-told'], *pret. and p.pt.* of RE-TELL.

RETORT (1), [ri-tawt'], *n.* a ready reply; an answer; a sharp contradictory statement.

RETORT (2), [ri-tawt'], *n.* a glass or earthenware vessel with a long curved neck, for the purpose of distillation. [L. *retortus*].

RETORT

RETORT (3), [ri-tawt'], *v.t. and i.* to reply in answer to a question or argument; to answer sharply. [L. *retortus* from *retorquere* to twist back].

RETORTER, [ri-tawt'-er], *n.* a person who retorts.

RETORTION, [ri-taw'-shun], *n.* the action of retorting; reflection. [MedL. *retortio*].

RETORTIVE, [ri-tawt'-iv], *adj.* in the nature of a retort.

RETOUCH (1), [rē-tuch'], *n.* the action of retouching.

RETOUCH (2), [rē-tuch'], *v.t.* to touch again; to improve by touching up here and there.

RETRACE, [rē-trās'], *v.t.* to go over once more; to trace back; to renew the outline of, as a drawing; to return by the same way.

RETRACEABLE, [ri-trās'-abl], *adj.* able to be retraced.

RETRACT (1), [ri-trakt'], *v.t.* to draw back; to withdraw. [L. *retractus* from *retrahere*].

RETRACT (2), [ri-trakt'], *v.t.* to withdraw, recall; to recant; *v.i.* to withdraw (one's words). [L. *retractare*].

RETRACTABILITY, [ri-trakt'-ab-il'-it-i], *n.* the state or quality of being retractable.

RETRACTABLE, [ri-trakt'-abl], *adj.* able to be retracted.

RETRACTED, [ri-trakt'-id], *adj.* drawn or pulled back; (*her.*) bounded by a diagonal line.

RETRACTILE, [ri-trakt'-il], *adj.* retractable.

RETRACTION, [ri-trak'-shun], *n.* the act of drawing back; act of retracting, withdrawing; recantation; disavowal. [L. *retractio*].

RETRACTIVE, [ri-trakt'-iv], *adj.* causing to retract; retracting. [OF. *retractif*].

RETRACTOR, [ri-trakt'-or], *n.* an appliance used for holding back something; (*anat.*) a muscle serving to retract a part of the body.

RETRAL, [rēt'-ral], *adj.* situated at the rear; retrorse. [L. *retro* backwards].

RETRANSFER (1), [rē-trans'-fer], *n.* something retransferred; the act of retransferring.

RETRANSFER (2), [rē'-trans-fur'], *v.t.* to transfer back or back again.

RETRANSFORM, [rē'-trans-fawm'], *v.t.* to transform again.

RETRANSLATE, [rē'-trans-lāt'], *v.t.* to translate afresh; to translate back into the original language.

RETRANSMISSION, [rē'-tranz-mish'-on], *n.* the act of transmitting again or back to the original source.

RETRAVERSE, [rē'-tra-vurs'], *v.t.* to traverse again or frequently.

RETRAXIT, [ri-traks'-it], *n.* (*leg.*) the withdrawal of a suit and consequent loss of the action. [L. *retraxit* he has withdrawn].

RETREAD, [rē'-tred'], *v.t.* to tread a second time; retrace; to put a new tread on (a worn-out rubber tyre).

RETREAT (1), [ri-trēt'], *n.* the act of retiring; retirement or seclusion; place of retirement; place of safety or security; short retirement for quiet meditation into a religious institution; the retiring of an army from the face of an enemy or an advanced position; a signal for retiring to quarters or from an engagement. [OFr. *retrait*].

RETREAT (2), [ri-trēt'], *v.i.* to retire from any position or place; to withdraw to seclusion or safety; to retire from an enemy; to abandon one's position in an argument. [OFr. *retraiter*].

RETREATMENT, [rē'-trēt'-ment], *n.* further treatment.

RETREE, [re-trē'], *n.* paper damaged or left unfinished in the course of manufacture. [Fr. *retrait* wastage].

RETRENCH, [ri-trench'], *v.t.* to cut off; to pare away; to lessen; to curtail; (*milit.*) to furnish with an entrenchment; *v.i.* to cut down expenses, to economize. [OFr. *retrencher*].

RETRENCHMENT, [ri-trench'-ment], *n.* the act of lopping off or removing what is superfluous; curtailment; reduction of expenditure; (*milit.*) a work constructed within another to prolong the defence.

RETRIAL, [rē'-trī'-al], *n.* a renewed attempt, test; (*leg.*) the act of trying a case over again; a second trial.

RETRIBUTE, [rē-trib'-yōōt], *v.t.* to pay back; to compensate, to repay. [L. *retribuere*].

RETRIBUTION, [ret'-ri-bew'-shun], *n.* suitable requital for good or evil; reward or punishment; just requital; distribution of rewards and punishments at the Judgment Day. [L. *retributio*].

RETRIBUTIVE, [ri-trib'-yōōt-iv], *adj.* retributory.

RETRIBUTORY, [ri-trib'-yōōt-er-i], *adj.* rewarding for good deeds and punishing for offences; pertaining to retribution.

RETRIEVABLE, [ri-trēv'-abl], *adj.* capable of being retrieved.

RETRIEVABLENESS, [ri-trēv'-abl-nes], *n.* the condition of being retrievable.

RETRIEVABLY, [ri-trēv'-ab-li], *adv.* in a retrievable fashion.

RETRIEVAL, [ri-trēv'-al], *n.* the act of retrieving.

RETRIEVE, [ri-trēv'], *v.t.* to find again; to restore; to rescue. [OFr. *retrouver*].

RETRIEVEMENT, [ri-trēv'-ment], *n.* the act of retrieving.

RETRIEVER, [ri-trēv'-er], *n.* one who, or that which, retrieves; a dog trained to fetch game that has been shot.

RETRIM, [rē'-trim'], *v.t.* to trim again; to clean and put a lamp into good working order.

RETRO-, *pref.* back, backwards; in return. [L. *retro*].

RETROACT, [ret'-rō-akt'], *v.i.* to act in opposition, in an opposite direction; to act relevantly to past action.

RETROACTION, [ret'-rō-ak'-shun], *n.* action in a backward direction; retrospective action.

RETROACTIVE, [ret'-rō-ak'-tiv], *adj.* working backwards; affecting what is past; retrospective.

RETROACTIVELY, [ret'-rō-ak'-tiv-li], *adv.* in a retroactive fashion.

RETROBULBAR, [ret'-rō-bul'-ber], *adj.* located on the reverse side of the eyeball.

RETROCEDE, [ret'-rō-sēd], *v.t.* to cede back again; *v.i.* to go back.

RETROCEDENT, [ret'-rō-sēd'-ent], *adj.* inclined to retrocede; (*med.*) moving from an outer part of the body to an inner. [L. *retrocedens*].

RETROCESSION, [ret'-rō-sesh'-un], *n.* a ceding or granting back; the act of giving back.

RETROCHOIR, [ret'-rō-kwier'], *n.* a small chapel or other space behind the high altar; a lady-chapel.

RETROCOLLIC, [ret'-rō-kol'-ik], *adj.* of, or pertaining to, the back of the neck.

RETRODATE, [ret'-rō-dāt'], *v.t.* to assign a book or manuscript to an earlier period than it belongs to.

RETRODUCTION, [ret'-rō-duk'-shun], *n.* a bringing back, withdrawing.

RETROFLEX, [ret'-rō-fleks'], *adj.* (*bot.*) bent backwards towards the trunk. [RETRO and L. *flexus* bent].

RETROFLEXION, [ret'-rō-flek'-shun], *n.* the act of bending back; the state of being bent back.

RETROFRACT, [ret'-rō-frakt'], *adj.* retrofracted.

RETROFRACTED, [ret'rō-frakt'-ed], *adj.* (*bot.*) bent back to appear as though broken. [RETRO and L. *fractus* broken].

RETROGRADATION, [ret'-rō-grad-ā'-shun], *n.* the act of moving backwards; decline in excellence. [L. *retrogradatio*].

RETROGRADE (1), [ret'-rō-grād], *adj.* going or moving backwards; going from a civilized to a less civilized condition; (*astron.*) apparently moving backwards, and contrary to the succession of the signs of the zodiac; declining from a better to a worse state; deteriorating. [L. *retrogradus*].

RETROGRADE (2), [ret'-rō-grād], *v.i.* to go or move backwards; to deteriorate. [*Prec.*].

RETROGRESS, [ret'-rō-gres'], *v.i.* to deteriorate; move backwards. [L. *retrogressum*, *p.pt.* of *retrogradi*].

RETROGRESSION, [ret'-rō-gresh'-un], *n.* the act of going backwards; retrogradation; deterioration.

RETROGRESSIVE, [ret'-rō-gres'-iv], *adj.* going or moving backwards; declining in excellence; having a tendency to retrogress.

RETROGRESSIVELY, [ret'-rō-gres'-iv-li], *adv.* in a retrogressive fashion.

RETROGRESSIVENESS, [ret'-rō-gres'-iv-nes], *n.* the condition of being retrogressive.

RETROJECT, [ret'-rō-jekt'], *v.t.* to throw or cast backwards. [RETRO and L. *jacere* to throw].

RETROMINGENT, [ret'-rō-minj'-ent], *adj.* urinating backwards. [RETRO and L. *mingere* to urinate].

RETROPOSITION, [ret'-rō-pōz-i'-shun], *n.* displacement backwards or to the rear.

RETROPULSION, [ret'-rō-pul'-shun], *n.* a driving

rearwards; (*path.*) the tendency shown in certain palsy cases to walk backwards. [RETRO and L. *pulsus* from *pellere* to drive].

RETROPULSIVE, [ret'-rō-pul'-siv], *adj.* driving backwards; repelling.

RETRORSE, [ri-traws'], *adj.* (*biol.*) bent backwards or downwards. [L. *retrorsus*].

RETRORSELY, [re-traws'-li], *adv.* in a retrorse manner or direction.

RETRORSION, [re-traw'-shun], *n.* the state of being retrorse.

RETROSERRATE, [ret'-rō-se'-rāt], *adj.* having serrations pointing backwards.

RETROSPECT, [ret'-rō-spekt'], *n.* a looking back on things past; review in the memory. [L. *retrospectum*].

RETROSPECTION, [ret'-rō-spek'-shun], *n.* the act of looking back on things past; the faculty of doing so.

RETROSPECTIVE, [ret'-rō-spek'-tiv], *adj.* pertaining to the past; looking back to the past; applying to, based on, the past.

RETROSPECTIVELY, [ret'-rō-spek'-tiv-li], *adv.* in a retrospective fashion.

RETROUSSAGE, [re-trōōs-ahzh'], *n.* a process by which a soft tone can be given to etchings through wiping off the ink from portions of the plates. [Fr. *retroussage*].

RETROUSSE, **retroussé**, [re-trōōs'-ā], *adj.* (of the nose) turned up, tip-tilted. [Fr. *retroussé*].

RETROVACCINATE, [ret'-rō-vak'-sin-āt], *v.t.* to vaccinate (a cow) with lymph taken from the human body.

RETROVACCINE, [ret'-rō-vak'-sēn], *n.* the lymph taken from a retrovaccinated animal.

RETROVENE, [ret'-rō-vēn'], *adj.* sloping backwards.

RETROVERSION, [ret'-rō-vur'-shun], *n.* the act of retroverting; a turning or falling backwards. [~L. *retroversum*].

RETROUSSÉ

RETROVERT (1), [ret'-rō-vurt'], *n.* a person or thing that retroverts.

RETROVERT (2), [ret'-rō-vurt'], *v.t.* to turn or bend back. [RETRO and L. *vertere* to turn].

RETROVISION, [ret'-rō-vizh'-un], *n.* the capacity for visualizing the past in the mind.

RETRUDE, [ri-trōōd'], *v.t.* to thrust back. [L. *retrudere*].

RETRY, [rē'-trī'], *v.t.* to try a second time; (*leg.*) to try again.

RETTERY, [ret'-er-i], *n.* a place where the retting of flax is done.

RETTING, [ret'-ing], *n.* the process of steeping flax to separate the fibre. [RET].

RETURF, [rē'-turf'], *v.t.* to cover again with turf.

RETURN (1), [ri-turn'], *n.* the act of going back; the act of giving back; a periodical coming back; periodical renewal; an official report; profit of business; dividends on capital invested; repayment; restitution; (*leg.*) the rendering back or delivery of a writ, precept, or execution; a ticket on a public conveyance entitling the holder to a journey to the destination and back again. [RETURN (2)].

RETURN (2), [ri-turn'], *v.i.* to come back, go back to same place, condition, state; to answer; to revert; to recur; *v.t.* to bring or send back; to repay; to give back in recompense; to yield; to give back in reply; to retort; to retaliate; to give in an official account; to transmit; to elect. [OFr. *returner*].

RE-TURN, [rē'-turn'], *v.t. and i.* to turn again; to turn back.

RETURNABLE, [ri-turn'-abl], *adj.* capable of being returned; required to be returned or restored; that is legally to be returned or rendered.

RETURN-DAY, [ri-turn'-dā'], *n.* (*leg.*) the day when the defendant must appear in court, and the sheriff has to make his return.

RETURNER, [ri-turn'-er], *n.* a person or thing that returns; one who repays or remits money.

RETURNING-OFFICER, [ri-turn'-ing-of'-is-er], *n.* the official whose duty it is to make returns of writs, precepts or juries; the presiding officer at a municipal or parliamentary election.

RETURNLESS, [ri-turn'-les], *adj.* admitting no return.

RETUSE, [ri-tews'], *adj.* (*zool.*) blunt; rounded; (*bot.*) terminating in a blunt end the centre of which is depressed. [L. *retusus*].

REUNIFY, [rē-yōōn'-i-fī], *v.t.* to unify again; to reunite.

REUNION, [rē-yōōn'-i-on], *n.* the act of reuniting; union formed anew after separation; a meeting or an assembly of friends or associates.

REUNITE, [rē'-yōōn-īt'], *v.t.* to unite again; to join after a separation; to reconcile after variance; *v.i.* to be united again.

REUS, [rē'-us], *n.* (*leg.*) †a litigant; a defendant in an action at civil law; a debtor. [L. *reus*].

RE-USE, [rē'-yōōz'], *v.t.* to use again.

REUSSITE, [rois'-īt], *n.* (*min.*) a native anhydrous sulphate of soda and magnesium. [*Reuss*, a German mineralogist].

REV, [rev], *v.t. and i.* (usually with *up*) (of an engine), to increase the number of revolutions per minute (of). [REV(OLUTION)].

REVACCINATE, [rē'-vak'-sin-āt], *v.t.* to vaccinate again.

REVALORIZATION, [rē-val'-er-īz-ā'-shun], *n.* the re-establishment of a country's currency.

REVALUATION, [rē-val'-yōō-ā'-shun], *n.* the act of revaluing.

REVALUE, [rē'-val'-yōō], *v.t.* to value afresh.

REVAMP, [rē-vamp'], *v.t.* to patch up once more.

REVEAL (1), [ri-vēl'], *n.* (*arch.*) the vertical space or opening between the side of a door or window and the frame.

REVEAL (2), [ri-vēl'], *v.t.* to disclose to view (what previously was hidden or covered); to make known, divulge; to explain, impart knowledge concerning; (of God) to make known (by divine power or agency). [L. *revelare* to uncover].

REVEALABLE, [ri-vēl'-abl], *adj.* able to be revealed.

REVEALABLENESS, [ri-vēl'-abl-nes], *n.* the condition of being revealable.

REVEALED, [ri-vēld'], *adj.* made known, declared, divulged; **r. religion**, a religion taught by divine revelation or supernatural agency.

REVEALER, [ri-vēl'-er], *n.* a person who makes known.

REVEALMENT, [ri-vēl'-ment], *n.* the act of revealing.

REVEILLE, [ri-val'-i], *n.* (*milit.*) a bugle-call sounded to rouse sleeping men. [Fr. *réveillez* awake!].

REVEL (1), [rev'-el], *n.* a carousal, a noisy merrymaking; (*pl.*) a prearranged entertainment, including mumming, pageantry, singing, dancing, etc.; **Master of the Revels**, official responsible for court entertainments. [OFr. *revel*].

REVEL (2), [rev'-el], *v.t. and i.* to carouse, to make merry riotously; **to r. in**, to take delight or enjoyment in, to indulge in without restraint. [OFr. *reveler*].

REVELATION, [rev'-el-ā'-shun], *n.* the act of revealing; that which is revealed; the condition of being revealed; a disclosure (of something hitherto secret); (*coll.*) an event, fact, or experience which opens a wider field of knowledge or understanding; (*religion*) a declaration of the mystery of God to man by divine power; **R. of St. John the Divine**, the Apocalypse, the last book of the Bible. [L. *revelatio*].

REVELATIONAL, [rev'-el-ā'-shun-al], *adj.* pertaining to revelation.

REVELATIONIST, [rev'-el-ā'-shun-ist], *n.* one who accepts divine revelation; **the R.**, St. John the Divine, the traditional author of the Apocalypse.

REVELLER, [rev'-el-er], *n.* one who revels; a habitual and riotous merrymaker.

REVELMENT, [rev'-el-ment], *n.* the act of revelling, revelry.

REVEL-ROUT, [rev'-el-rowt'], *n.* revelry; a crowd of revellers.

REVELRY, [rev'-el-ri], *n.* noisy festivity, revels, carousal.

REVENANT, [rev'-en-ant], *n.* a person returned after a very long absence; one risen from the dead, a ghost. [Fr. *revenant*].

REVENDICATION, [ri-vend'-ik-ā'-shun], *n.* (*leg.*) the act of recovering property by a formal claim. [Fr. *revendication*].

REVENGE (1), [ri-venj'], *n.* the act of taking vengeance on; the malicious desire to do this; a return game.

REVENGE (2), [ri-venj'], *v.t. and i.* to avenge, requite for (an injury), take or exact vengeance for; **to be revenged**, to take vengeance; **to r. oneself (up)on**, to inflict vengeance on, repay with evil for evil. [OFr. *revenger*].

REVENGEFUL, [ri-venj'-fŏŏl], *adj.* full of revenge, vindictive, expressing vindictiveness.

REVENGEFULLY, [ri-venj'-fŏŏl-i], *adv.* in a revengeful way.

REVENGEFULNESS, [ri-venj'-fōōl-nes], *n.* the condition of being revengeful.
REVENGEMENT, [ri-venj'-ment], *n.* the act of revenging, revenge.
REVENGER, [ri-venj'-er], *n.* one who seeks revenge.
REVENGINGLY, [ri-venj'-ing-li], *adv.* with revenge, in the manner of a revenger.
REVENUE, [rev'-en-ew], *n.* income, profits, total income, *esp.* the total income of the state; **Inland R.,** the revenue to the state from taxes, duties, etc.; **the R.,** the government department concerned with the collecting of taxes and duties; **r. officer,** a customs official. [OFr. *revenue*].
REVER, see REVERS.
REVERBERANT, [ri-vur'-ber-ant], *adj.* reverberating; resounding. [L. *reverberans*].
REVERBERATE, [ri-vur'-ber-āt], *v.t.* *and i.* to cause to re-echo or resound; (*fig.*) to reflect; to resound; to be reflected. [L. *reverberare* to cause to rebound].
REVERBERATION, [ri-vur'-ber-ā'-shun], *n.* the act of reverberating; a re-echoing sound.
REVERBERATIVE, [ri-vurb'-er-at-iv], *adj.* reverberating, pertaining to reverberation.
REVERBERATORY, [ri-vur'-ber-at-er-i], *adj.* reverberative; **r. furnace,** a furnace so constructed that the heat is reflected on to the object.
REVERE, [ri-vēēr'], *v.t.* to regard with profound veneration, to respect greatly, to venerate. [L. *revereri* to respect].
REVERENCE (1), [rev'-er-ents], *n.* a feeling of profound admiration or respect, veneration; a deep bow or other action expressive of great respect; a person to whom such respect is or should be paid, *esp.* used formerly in England and still in Ireland as a title of address to a cleric. [L. *reverentia*].
REVERENCE (2), [rev'-er-ents], *v.t.* to regard with loving respect and veneration, to venerate, revere. [*Prec.*].
REVERENCER, [rev'-er-en-ser], *n.* a person who reverences.
REVEREND, [rev'-er-end], *adj.* worthy of reverence; as a title of address to a clergyman (in writing shortened to *Rev.*); †reverent.
REVERENT, [rev'-er-ent], *adj.* moved by a feeling of pious and religious reverence; exhibiting such a manner as befits nearness or reference to sacred things. [L. *reverens*].
REVERENTIAL, [rev'-er-en'-shal], *adj.* pertaining to, or proceeding from, reverence.
REVERENTIALLY, [rev'-er-en'-shal-i], *adv.* in a reverential fashion.
REVERENTLY, [rev'-er-ent-li], *adv.* in a reverent fashion.
REVERER, [ri-vēēr'-er], *n.* one who reveres.
REVERIE, REVERY, [rev'-er-i], *n.* a daydream, a trance-like mood of pensive abstraction and reflection, a dreamy musing in which one becomes temporarily oblivious of one's surroundings; a piece of music supposed to express or be a result of such a mood. [Fr. *rêverie*].
REVERS, REVER, [ri-vēer'], *n.* a lapel or any similar part of the edge of a garment that turns back so as to show the inner surface. [Fr. *revers*].
REVERSAL, [ri-vurs'-al], *n.* the act of reversing; a change or overthrowing, a defeat, check.
REVERSE (1), [ri-vurs'], *n.* a complete change round in the course of events, a contrary turn of affairs; a misfortune, check, set-back; the opposite, the contrary; the surface opposite the one facing a person, the back surface, the underside; the back of a leaf of paper, etc.; the design on the face of a coin, medal, etc., opposite the head, the tail of a coin; a reversing gear; (*milit.*) a defeat; (*sport*) a set-back, defeat. [OFr. *revers* from L. *reversus* turned back].

REVERSE (of a coin)

REVERSE (2), [ri-vurs'], *adj.* turned completely round or backward, contrary, having an opposite direction, coming from the opposite side.
REVERSE (3), [ri-vurs'], *v.t.* to turn upside down or completely round, to turn over or backwards, to turn in a contrary direction, to cause what was formerly the back or bottom to be the front or top and vice versa; to cause to move backwards, to cause to work in a backward direction; to cause to be contrary to the normal or present state; to cancel, revoke, make void; *v.i.* to proceed in a direction opposite to that usually followed, to move backwards; **to r. arms,** to hold a rifle, etc., with the barrel pointing to the ground. [LL. *reversare* to turn round].
REVERSED, [ri-vurst'], *adj.* turned round, backwards or upside down, placed in an opposite direction, often implying to the normal; changed to the contrary; annulled, cancelled; (*bot.*) resupinate; with volutions like a left-handed screw.
REVERSEDLY, [ri-vurs'-id-li], *adv.* in a reversed fashion.
REVERSELESS, [ri-vurs'-les], *adj.* unable to be reversed.
REVERSELY, [ri-vurs'-li], *adv.* in a reverse manner or direction.
REVERSI, [ri-vur'-si], *n.* a parlour game played with a chequered board and circular counters of a different colour on their upper and under surfaces, which are turned over as they are won from one player by another. [Fr. *reversi* from *reverser* to turn round].
REVERSIBILITY, [ri-vurs'-ib-il'-i-ti], *n.* ability to be reversed.
REVERSIBLE, [ri-vurs'-ibl], *adj.* capable of being reversed.
REVERSING-GEAR, [ri-vurs'-ing-gēēr'], *n.* the gear by which the direction of the motion of an engine is reversed.
REVERSION, [ri-vur'-shun], *n.* (*leg.*) the return of an estate to the grantor, lessor, or to his heirs upon the termination of the grant or lease; an estate granted in this way, *esp.* one to be transferred to a specified person on the death of the person to whom it was granted; right of succession to an estate or thing; a sum of money due upon the death of an insured person; the act of reverting or turning back to a former thing or state; the act of turning round or upside down; (*biol.*) atavism, the reproduction of remote ancestral traits or characteristics in a descendant, which may have been absent in the intervening generations. [L. *reversio*].
REVERSIONARY, [ri-vur'-shun-er-i], *adj.* (*leg.*) pertaining to, issuing from, a reversion; by way of reversion.
REVERSIONER, [ri-vur'-shun-er], *n.* (*leg.*) one to whom property or estate goes by reversion.
REVERSO, [ri-vur'-sō], *n.* the left-hand page in a book. [It. *reverso*].
REVERT (1), [ri-vurt'], *n.* one who returns to a former state or religious belief.
REVERT (2), [ri-vurt'], *v.t.* (*rare*) to turn back, reverse; *v.i.* to return again to a former state or time, to go back (to), to return; (*leg.*) to return to the original possessor, lessor or grantor or his heirs upon the expiry of the lease or grant; to return to the original topic or subject under discussion. [L. *revertere* turn back].
REVERTIBLE, [ri-vurt'-ibl], *adj.* able to be reverted, returning by reversion.
REVERTIVE, [ri-vurt'-iv], *adj.* reverting, tending to revert.
REVERTIVELY, [ri-vurt'-iv-li], *adv.* by reversion.
REVERY, see REVERIE.
REVEST, [rē'-vest'], *v.t.* to reinvest with something; to vest afresh; *v.i.* to be reinvested.
REVESTIARY, [rē-vest'-i-er-i], *n.* the vestry of a church or temple. [MedL. *revestiarium*].
REVET, (**revetting, revetted**), [rē-vet'], *v.t.* to furnish with a revetment, to face (a wall, sloping surface, etc.) with a covering of harder material. [Fr. *revêtir*].
REVETMENT, [rē-vet'-ment], *n.* (*fort.*) a strong retaining wall on the outside of an entrenchment or earthwork, to support the earth at a steeper slope than that which it would naturally tend to form, a facing of steel, stone, or other material to support and strengthen a mound. [Fr. *revêtement*].
REVICTUAL, [rē'-vit'-al], *v.t.* *and i.* to provision again, to provide with a fresh supply of victuals; to take on a fresh supply of victuals.
REVIEW (1), [ri-vew'], *n.* a retrospect, reflective contemplation of something past, a summary in retrospect, a detailed résumé of a situation, etc.; critical examination, notice, or consideration, revision with a view to correction and amendment; a written notice or article containing a critical examination of a new literary composition, a written consideration of the merits and demerits of a recent publication or performance; a periodical containing articles and essays on various topics, and usually including a critical examination or estimation of recent literary or artistic work; (*leg.*) consideration by a higher court of the decisions of an inferior court; formal official inspection

by an eminent person, *esp.* of troops, certain state employees, etc. [OFr. *reveue*, *p.pt.* of *revoir*].

REVIEW (2), [ri-vew'], *v.t.* to consider in retrospect, look back on; to examine critically, weigh in one's mind, consider carefully; to revise, go through carefully again to correct or amend; to write a press review of; to inspect formally and in an official capacity; (*leg.*) to examine (findings of an inferior court) for acceptance or modification; *v.i.* to write reviews. [*Prec.*].

REVIEWABLE, [ri-vew'-abl], *adj.* capable of being reviewed.

REVIEWAL, [ri-vew'-al], *n.* the act of reviewing; a review.

REVIEWER, [ri-vew'-er], *n.* one who reviews, *esp.* a writer of reviews of books, plays, films, concerts, artistic exhibitions, or performances.

REVIGORATE, [rē-vig'-er-āt], *v.t.* to give fresh vigour to. [MedL. *revigorare*].

REVILE, [ri-vīl'], *v.t.* to curse, to shower abuse and reproaches upon, to treat with opprobrium; *v.i.* to indulge in abuse and reproach, to curse and swear. [OFr. *reviler*].

REVILEMENT, [ri-vīl'-ment], *n.* abuse and reproach.

REVILER, [ri-vīl'-er], *n.* one who reviles.

REVILING (1), [ri-vīl'-ing], *n.* the act of one who reviles.

REVILING (2), [ri-vīl'-ing], *adj.* that reviles.

REVILINGLY, [ri-vīl'-ing-li], *adv.* in a reviling manner.

REVINDICATE, [rē-vind'-ik-āt], *v.t.* to vindicate afresh; to reclaim; to recover possession of. [MedL. *revindicare*].

REVISAL, [ri-vīz'-al], *n.* the act of revising, that which has been revised, revision.

REVISE (1), [ri-vīz'], *n.* review; (*print.*) a proof-sheet taken after the first correction; (*rare*) revision.

REVISE (2), [ri-vīz'], *v.t.* to go through or examine again in detail for purposes of correction or amendment; to read up again, study afresh in order to become better acquainted with for examination purposes; *v.i.* to be engaged in revision. [L. *revisere*].

REVISER, [ri-vīz'-er], *n.* one who revises.

REVISING BARRISTER, [ri-vīz'-ing-ba'-rist-er], *n.* a barrister appointed to revise the list of persons in a district entitled to vote in parliamentary elections.

REVISION, [ri-vizh'-un], *n.* the act of revising, detailed examination again for purposes of correction or revision, re-reading or study of something again for purposes of examination; that which is revised. [L. *revisio* a seeing again].

REVISIONAL, [ri-vizh'-un-al], *adj.* revisionary.

REVISIONARY, [ri-vizh'-un-er-i], *adj.* relating to revision, by way of revision.

REVISIONIST, [ri-vizh'-un-ist], *n.* one of the group advocating revision of the Bible.

REVISIT, [rē-viz'-it], *v.t.* to visit again.

REVISITATION, [rē-viz'-it-ā'-shun], *n.* act of revisiting; a fresh or new visitation.

REVISORY, [ri-vīz'-er-i], *adj.* pertaining to, by way of, revision, revising, having power to revise.

REVITALIZE, [rē-vī'-tal-īz], *v.t.* to bring back vitality to, to put fresh life into.

REVIVABLE, [ri-vīv'-abl], *adj.* capable of being revived.

REVIVAL, [ri-vīv'-al], *n.* the act of reviving, the state of being revived, recall or return to activity, re-awakening or increase of attention and interest in something formerly neglected, a flourishing again; the process of bringing back or returning into use or fashion again (something formerly current) after a period of disuse; an evangelical campaign seeking to bring about a recall to religion; **the r. of learning**, the Renaissance.

REVIVALISM, [ri-vīv'-al-izm], *n.* recall to religion by means of evangelical campaigns.

REVIVALIST (1), [ri-vīv'-al-ist], *n.* one who promotes and takes part in revivals of religion.

REVIVALIST (2), [ri-vīv'-al-ist], *adj.* pertaining to, of the nature of, a religious revival.

REVIVE, [ri-vīv], *v.t.* to bring to life again, to bring round; to restore or rouse from depression, exhaustion, etc., to refresh, renew, raise again, quicken; to bring into fashion or use again after a period of disuse, to recall, to cause to flourish again after a period of neglect or inactivity, to cause to be active again, re-awaken; to produce again (a play that has not been produced for a long time); (*chem.*) to restore to its natural state; *v.i.* to recover life or consciousness, to come round; to recover, quicken, rise, be renewed, be roused again; to flourish again after a period of inactivity, to become active or current once more, to return to use or favour; (*chem.*) to recover its natural state. [L. *revivere* to live again].

REVIVER, [ri-vīv'-er], *n.* one who, or that which, revives, restores, renews.

REVIVIFICATION, [rē-viv'-if-ik-ā'-shun], *n.* restoration of life and vigour.

REVIVIFY, [rē-viv'-i-fī], *v.t.* to recall to life, to reanimate; to give new life or vigour to; (*chem.*) to restore to its natural state. [L. *revivificare*].

REVIVINGLY, [ri-vīv'-ing-li], *adv.* in a reviving manner, so as to revive.

REVIVOR, [ri-vīv'-or], *n.* (*leg.*) the reviving of a suit which has been abated by death.

REVOCABLE, [rev'-ok-abl], *adj.* capable of being revoked.

REVOCABLENESS, [rev'-ok-abl-nes], *n.* the quality of being revocable.

REVOCABLY, [rev'-ok-ab-li], *adv.* in a revocable fashion.

REVOCATION, [rev'-ōk-ā'-shun], *n.* the act of revoking; the state of being revoked; (*leg.*) repeal, reversal, annulment or making void of a decree, edict, deed, etc. [L. *revocatio* a calling back].

REVOCATORY, [rev'-ok-at-er-i], *adj.* revoking, tending to revoke, having the power of revoking. [L. *revocatorius*].

REVOKE (1), [ri-vōk'], *n.* (*cards*) a failure to follow suit when able to do so.

REVOKE (2), [ri-vōk'], *v.t.* to rescind, repeal, annul, reverse, declare void; *v.i.* (*cards*) to fail to play a card of the suit led, when able to do so. [L. *revocare* to call back].

REVOKEMENT, [ri-vōk'-ment], *n.* revocation; reversal.

REVOLT (1), [ri-vōlt'], *n.* widespread rebellion or insurrection, wholesale rising against authority and renunciation of allegiance to the governing body, open and active resistance to authority; a feeling of disgust and strong aversion.

REVOLT (2), [ri-vōlt'], *v.i.* to rise against and seek to overthrow established authority, to rebel, to refuse to obey, renounce allegiance to, the governing body; to fill with disgust and repugnance, to shock, nauseate, repel. [Fr. *revolter* from RE (1) and L. *volutare* to turn about].

REVOLTER, [ri-vōlt'-er], *n.* one who rises in revolt against someone or something.

REVOLTING, [ri-vōlt'-ing], *adj.* disgusting, exciting abhorrence, nauseating, filling with repugnance and loathing.

REVOLTINGLY, [ri-vōlt'-ing-li], *adv.* in a revolting manner.

REVOLUTE, [rev'-ol-ōōt], *adj.* (*bot.*, *zool.*) rolled or curled back at the edge towards the underside. [L. *revolutus*, *p.pt.* of *revolvere*].

REVOLUTION, [rev'-ol-ōō'-shun], *n.* rotation, circular motion of a body on its axis so that each part periodically returns to the same point or position; movement of a body round a centre, or movement of a series of bodies round a central body, to form a closed curve; a single complete turning or rotation round an axis, centre, or central body; the period of time taken to complete such a movement; a regular recurring succession of events, a regular periodic return of some phenomenon, a cycle; violent overthrow of an existing political system or established authority, and its replacement by a new, and often radically different, form of government; complete and violent change in attitude, belief, theories, and methods of working. [L. *revolutio*].

REVOLUTIONARY (1), [rev'-ol-ōō'-shun-er-i], *n.* one in favour of, or engaged in, revolution.

REVOLUTIONARY (2), [rev'-ol-ōō'-shun-er-i], *adj.* pertaining to, tending towards, in favour of, of the nature of, producing, or engaged in, political revolution; causing, tending to produce, of the nature of, a revolution in theory, belief, or practice; (*rare*) revolving.

REVOLUTIONIST, [rev'-ol-ōō'-shun-ist], *n.* a revolutionary.

REVOLUTIONIZE, [rev'-ol-ōō'-shun-īz], *v.t.* to effect radical changes in, to alter drastically, to produce a revolution in existing theory, method, and practice.

REVOLVE, [ri-volv'], *v.t.* to cause to revolve, rotate; to turn over and over in the mind; *v.i.* to rotate about an axis; to go round, to move in a circular course round a centre or central object; to return or recur in regular periodic succession. [L. *revolvere*].

REVOLVER, [ri-volv'-er], *n.* a pistol fitted with a revolving cylinder containing several chambers for cartridges, and thus able to be fired several times without reloading.

REVOLVING, [ri-volv'-ing], *adj.* turning round with a circular motion, that revolves.

REVUE, [ri-vew'], *n.* a spectacular musical variety entertainment, consisting of a number of disconnected scenes, in the form of sketches, songs and dances, designed *esp.* to feature solo performers or a chorus, and usually sprinkled with topical references. [Fr. *revue*].

REVULSION, [ri-vul'-shun], *n.* an abrupt and complete change or swing round in the opposite direction, a violent recoil or reaction against something; (*rare*) a withdrawal, a holding or drawing back; (*med.*) the diversion of a pain, etc., from one part of the body by treating another. [L. *revulsio* a tearing off].

REVULSIVE (1), [ri-vuls'-iv], *n.* that which has the power of withdrawing; (*med.*) a medicine having the power of revulsion.

REVULSIVE (2), [ri-vuls'-iv], *adj.* (*med.*) having the power of revulsion.

REWARD (1), [ri-wawd'], *n.* something received in return for something done, recompense, requital for good or evil; a money payment offered to the finder of lost articles, to a person giving information leading to the arrest of a criminal, etc. [AFr. *reward*].

REWARD (2), [ri-wawd'], *v.t.* to recompense, requite, to give something in return for; to result as a recompense for, or in return for; to give a reward to, to pay or pay back for merit or services specially rendered. [AFr. *rewarder*].

REWARDABLE, [ri-wawd'-abl], *adj.* worthy of reward.

REWARDLESS, [ri-wawd'-les], *adj.* without reward.

REWIN, [rē'-win'], *v.t.* to win back, to win again.

REWORD, [rē'-wurd'], *v.t.* to express in different words. [RE (1) and WORD (2)].

REWRITE, [rē'-rit'], *v.t.* to write out again or afresh; to write over again in a different way making various alterations.

REXINE, [reks'-ēn], *n.* a kind of artificial leather used in upholstery. [Invented].

REXIST, [reks'-ist], *n.* a member of the Belgian Fascist Party. [Fr. *rexiste*].

RHABDOIDAL, [rab-doid'-al], *adj.* like a rod. [Gk. *rhabdos* rod and *oeides* like].

RHABDOLOGY, [rab-dol'-o-ji], *n.* the art of reckoning by means of Napier's rods. [Gk. *rhabdos* rod and *logos* speech].

RHABDOMANCY, [rab'-dō-man-si], *n.* divination by means of rods, *esp.* to find out the locality of minerals and springs underground, by means of a hazel twig, water-divining. [Gk. *rhabdomanteia*].

RHABDOPHANE, [rab'-dō-fān], *n.* scovillite, a hydrated phosphate of cerium, lanthanum, neodymium, praseodymium and yttrium. [Gk. *rhabdos* rod and *phainomai* I appear].

RHADAMANTHINE, [rad'-am-an'-thīn], *adj.* rigorous, inflexible and scrupulously just. [*Rhadamanthus*, one of the three judges of the dead in the lower world].

RHAETIC, [rē'-tik], *adj.* of the uppermost group of the Triassic rocks. [L. *Rhaeticus* pertaining to *Rhaetia*, the Roman province between the valleys of the Danube, Po, and Rhine].

RHAETO-ROMANIC, [rē'-tō-rō-man'-ik], *adj.* in, of, or pertaining to, the distinctive Romance languages spoken in the Grisons and *esp.* in the Engadine Valley in Switzerland. [RHAETIC and L. *Romanicus* Roman].

RHAPSODE, [rap'-sōd], *n.* a wandering minstrel reciting the poems of Homer and other epic poets, amongst the ancient Greeks. [Gk. *rhapsoidos*].

RHAPSODIC, [rap-sod'-ik], *adj.* pertaining to, in the style of, a rhapsody.

RHAPSODICAL, [rap-sod'-ik-al], *adj.* pertaining to, of the nature of, a rhapsody; rambling, disconnected, unrestrained and emotionally effusive.

RHAPSODIST, [rap'-sod-ist], *n.* amongst the ancient Greeks, a wandering minstrel whose profession was to recite the poems of Homer and other epic poets; one who writes, or indulges in, rhapsodies.

RHAPSODIZE, [rap'-sod-iz], *v.i.* to utter rhapsodies; *v.t.* to express in the form of a rhapsody.

RHAPSODY, [rap'-sod-i], *n.* an ancient Greek epic poem; a recitation or chanting of an epic poem by a rhapsodist; the part of the epic recited in this way; a rambling, disconnected, literary or musical composition expressing an unrestrained, lyrical, passionate outburst of feeling; (*pl.*) wild transports of joy and delight. [Gk. *rhapsoidia*].

RHATANY, RATANY, [rat'-a-ni], *n.* the root of a Peruvian shrub, *Krameria triandra*, with astringent and tonic properties; the shrub itself. [Portug. *ratanhia*].

RHEA (1), [rē'-a], *n.* a genus of flightless birds, the three-toed South American ostrich, of which there are several species. [Gk. *Rhea*, the mother of the gods].

RHEA (2), [rē'-a], *n.* the fibre of *Boehmeria nivea*. [Native Assam].

RHEIN, [rē'-in], *n.* an acid obtained from rhubarb; chrysophanic acid. [~RHEUM (2)].

RHEMISH, [rēm'-ish], *adj.* pertaining to Rheims. [*Rhemes*, the early name for Rheims].

RHEA

RHENISH (1), [ren'-ish], *n.* wine from the Rhine or Rhine valley.

RHENISH (2), [ren'-ish], *adj.* pertaining to, obtained from, the Rhine, or the Rhine valley. [MHGerm. *rhinisch*, AFr. *reneis* of the Rhine].

RHENIUM, [rēn'-i-um], *n.* (*chem.*) a rare metallic element, related to manganese, found in the Rhineland. [L. *Rhenus* the Rhine].

RHEO-, *pref.* current, *esp.* electric current. [Gk. *rheos* flow].

RHEOSTAT, [rē'-ō-stat'], *n.* a resistance, whose value can be varied so as to regulate the strength of an electric current. [RHEO and Gk. *statos* placed, standing].

RHESUS, [rē'-zus], *n.* an Indian monkey belonging to the macaques, *Macacus rhesus*. [Gk. *Rhesos* king of Thebes].

RHETORIC, [ret'-er-ik], *n.* the art of oratory, the art of speaking with elegance, eloquence, and persuasiveness; the art of prose composition and style; florid, artificial oratory; a highly ornate manner of writing or speaking in which the elegance of the style cannot hide the barrenness of the meaning. [Gk. *rhetorike* (*tekhne*) art of rhetoric].

RHETORICAL, [ri-to'-rik-al], *adj.* pertaining to rhetoric, oratorical; given to empty rhetoric; bombastic, highly ornate, florid (of style); **r. question**, a question put merely for the sake of emphasis or effect, to which no answer is expected or needed.

RHETORICALLY, [ri-to'-rik-al-i], *adv.* in a rhetorical fashion.

RHETORICIAN, [ret'-er-ish'-an], *n.* one skilled in, an expert in, the art of rhetoric, a consummate orator; one who indulges in florid, empty rhetoric or oratory.

RHETORIZE, [ret'-er-iz], *v.t.* to represent by a figure of oratory; *v.i.* to indulge in rhetoric, to play the orator.

RHEUM (1), [rōōm], *n.* (*archaic*) an increased discharge from the mucous glands of the mouth, nose, etc., a running cold; a thin serous fluid secreted excessively by the mucous membrane, as in catarrh. [Gk. *rheuma* flow, discharge].

RHEUM (2), [rē'-um], *n.* a genus of plants including rhubarb. [Gk. *rheon*].

RHEUMATIC (1), [rōōm-at'-ik], *n.* a person afflicted with rheumatism; (*coll.*) (*pl.*) rheumatic pains, rheumatism.

RHEUMATIC (2), [rōōm-at'-ik], *adj.* pertaining to, due to, afflicted with, rheumatism. [Gk. *rheuma* flow].

RHEUMATICALLY, [rōōm-at'-ik-al-i], *adv.* in a rheumatic fashion.

RHEUMATICKY, [rōōm-at'-ik-i], *adj.* (*coll.*) suffering from rheumatism; resembling rheumatism.

RHEUMATISM, [rōōm'-at-izm], *n.* the name given to a group of diseases or ailments characterized by a painful affliction of the muscles and joints of the body, which become swollen, stiff, and inflamed. [Gk. *rheumatismos*].

RHEUMATOID, [rōōm'-at-oid], *adj.* simulating or resembling rheumatism; **r. arthritis**, a disease indicated by the wasting of the joint-surfaces, the thickening of the parts around the joint, and distortion due to muscular contraction. [Gk. *rheumatos* of rheum and *oeides* like].

RHEUMY, [rōōm'-i], *adj.* (*archaic*) full of rheum or watery matter, consisting of rheum; causing catarrh.

RHINAL, [rī'-nal], *adj.* relating to the nose.

RHINE, [rīn], *n.* a ditch, a large open drain. [Uncert.].

RHINENCEPHALIC, [rī'-nen-sef-al'-ik], *adj.* pertaining to the olfactory lobe of the brain. [RHINO and Gk. *enkephalos* the brain].

RHINO- (1), *pref.* nose. [Gk. *rhis rhinos* nose].

RHINO (2), [rī'-nō], *n.* a rhinoceros. [RHINOCEROS].
RHINO (3), [rī'-nō], *n.* (*slang*) money. [Unkn.].
RHINOCERIAL, [rī'-nō-sēer'-i-al], *adj.* relating to, or resembling, a rhinoceros.
RHINOCEROS, [rī-nos'-er-us], *n.* a large, heavy-hoofed mammal with a thick hide creased into folds, and with one or two horns rising from the nose. [Gk. *rhinokeros*].
RHINOCEROTIC, [rī'-nō-se-rot'-ik], *adj.* like, or belonging to, a rhinoceros.
RHINOLITH, [rī'-nō-lith'], *n.* (*med.*) a calculous formation in the nose. [RHINO and Gk. *lithos* stone].
RHINOLOGY, [rī-nol'-o-ji], *n.* the study of the nose. [RHINO and Gk. *logos* speech].
RHINOPLASTIC, [rī'-nō-plast'-ik], *adj.* pertaining to, involving, rhinoplasty.
RHINOPLASTY, [rī'-nō-plast'-i], *n.* the operation of remoulding or reshaping the nose, or grafting on an artificial nose. [RHINO and Gk. *plasso* I mould].
RHINOSCOPE, [rī'-no-skōp], *n.* an instrument by which the nasal passages can be seen reflected in a mirror.
RHINOSCOPY, [rī-nos'-kop-i], *n.* examination of the nose and nasal passages by means of the rhinoscope. [RHINO and Gk. *skopos* viewing].
RHIZIC, [rī'-zik], *adj.* relating to the root.
RHIZO-, *pref.* root. [Gk. *rhiza* root].
RHIZOCARP, [rī'-zō-kahp], *n.* (*bot.*) a plant having a perennial root but an annual stem. [RHIZO and Gk. *karpos* fruit].
RHIZOGEN, [rī'-zō-jen], *n.* (*bot.*) a parasitic plant organism living on the roots of another plant. [RHIZO and Gk. *genes* producing].
RHIZOID (1), [rī'-zoid], *n.* (*bot.*) a thin hair-like structure taking the place of a root in certain plants which do not possess real roots.
RHIZOID (2), [rī'-zoid], *adj.* like a root. [RHIZO and Gk. *oeides* like].
RHIZOMATOUS, [rī-zōm'-at-us], *adj.* consisting of, resembling, rhizomes.
RHIZOME, [rī'-zōm], *n.* (*bot.*) a creeping stem which grows underground, sending out shoots above and roots below. [Gk. *rhizoma* root].
RHIZOPHAGOUS, [rī-zof'-ag-us], *adj.* living on roots. [RHIZO and Gk. *phago* I eat].
RHIZOPHOROUS, [rī-zof'-er-us], *adj.* bearing roots. [RHIZO and Gk. *phoros* bearing].
RHIZOPOD, [rī'-zō-pod], *n.* a simple microscopic animal organism forming the lowest class of the protozoa. [RHIZO and Gk. *pous podos* foot].
RHIZOTAXIS, [rī'-zō-taks'-is], *n.* (*bot.*) the way in which the roots of a plant are arranged. [RHIZO and Gk. *taxis* arrangement].
RHODE ISLAND RED, [rōd'-ī-land-red'], *n.* one of a breed of reddish-brown poultry originating in the U.S.A. [*Rhode Island*, a state of the U.S.A.].
RHODIAN (1), [rō'-di-an], *n.* a native of Rhodes.
RHODIAN (2), [rō'-di-an], *adj.* pertaining to, coming from, belonging to, Rhodes. [L. *Rhodius* of Rhodes].
RHODIUM, [rō'-di-um], *n.* a silvery white metallic element resembling platinum, producing rose-coloured solutions of its salts, and possessing heat-resisting properties. [Gk. *rhodon* rose].
RHODOCHROME, [rō'-dō-krōm], *n.* a rose-coloured silicate of magnesium and aluminium. [Gk. *rhodon* rose and *khroma* colour].
RHODODENDRON, [rō'-dō-den'-dron], *n.* a numerous ericaceous genus of ornamental evergreen shrubs and trees, with beautiful flowers. [Gk. *rhododendron* from *rhodon* rose and *dendron* tree].
RHODOMONTADE, see RODOMONTADE.
RHODONITE, [rō'-don-īt], *n.* a rose-coloured variety of manganese, manganese spar. [Gk. *rhodon* rose].
RHODOUS, [rō'-dus], *adj.* obtained from rhodium.
RHOMB, [romb], *n.* a rhombus. [Gk. *rhombos* a spinning top].
RHOMBIC, [romb'-ik], *adj.* in the shape of, resembling, a rhombus.
RHOMBOHEDRAL, [romb'-ō-hē'-dral], *adj.* pertaining to, consisting of, in the form of, a rhombohedron.
RHOMBOHEDRON, [romb'-ō-hē'-dron], *n.* a solid bounded by six equal rhombic planes. [RHOMB and Gk. *hedra* side].
RHOMBOID (1), [romb'-oid], *n.* a parallelogram with only its opposite sides equal. [*Next*].
RHOMBOID (2), [romb'-oid], *adj.* resembling a rhombus in shape; in the form of a rhomboid. [RHOMB and Gk. *oeides* like].
RHOMBOIDAL, [romb-oid'-al], *adj.* in the shape of a rhomboid; having facets in the shape of a rhomboid.
RHOMBUS, [romb'-us], *n.* an oblique-angled equilateral parallelogram. [RHOMB].
RHOMBSPAR, [romb'-spah(r)], *n.* bitterspar, a crystallized variety of dolomite. [RHOMB and SPAR].
RHONCHUS, [rong'-kus], *n.* a sound heard by means of auscultation in cases of bronchitis and asthma. [L. *rhonchus* from Gk. *rhogkhos* snoring].
RHOPALIC, [rō-pal'-ik], *adj.* formed like a club and thickening towards the end. [Gk. *rhopalos* a club].
RHOPALOCERA, [rō'-pal-os'-er-a], *n.(pl.)* lepidoptera having clubbed antennae; the butterflies. [Gk. *rhopalos* club and *keras* horn].
RHOTACISM, [rō'-tas-izm], *n.* mispronunciation of the sound *r*; substitution of the sound *r* for another sound and vice versa.
RHOTACIZE, [rō'-tas-īz], *v.i.* to mispronounce the sound *r*; to sound *r* in place of another sound or vice versa. [Gk. *rhotakizo* from Gk. *rho* the letter *r*].
RHUBARB, [rōō'-bahb], *n.* a genus of large-leaved plants with thick fleshy stems or leaf-stalks; the thick acid-bearing leaf-stalks of certain varieties of this plant, cooked and eaten as food; the roots of several varieties of this plant used medicinally as a purgative and astringent; **garden r.**, *Rheum rhaponticum*, whose roots are medicinal, and whose leaf-stalks are cooked and eaten. [MedL. *rhabarbarum* from L. *rha barbarum* foreign rhubarb].
RHUBARBY, [rōō'-bahb-i], *adj.* resembling rhubarb.
RHUMB, [rum], *n.* one of the points of the compass; the angle of eleven degrees fifteen minutes opposite the arc joining two consecutive points of the compass. [~RHOMB.]
RHUMBA, RUMBA, [rŏom'-ba], *n.* a ballroom dance based on Caribbean folk-dances.
RHUMB-LINE, [rum'-līn], *n.* a line making the same angle with all meridians.
RHYME (1), **RIME** (2), [rīm], *n.* correspondence of sound in the terminating words or syllables of two or more lines of poetry; a word or syllable which corresponds in sound to another; verse in which the terminating words or syllables of the lines correspond in sound; poetry; a poem; **feminine r.**, rhyme in which the two final syllables of the line rhyme, the accent usually being on the first of these; **masculine r.**, rhyme in which only the final syllables rhyme; **without r. or reason**, without sense. [OFr. *rime* from Gk. *rhuthmos* rhythm].
RHYME (2), [rīm], *v.t.* to put into rhyme; to use as a rhyme; *v.i.* to form a rhyme, to correspond in sound; to compose verses in rhyme. [*Prec.*].
RHYMED, [rīmd], *adj.* that makes a rhyme.
RHYMELESS, [rīm'-les], *adj.* not rhyming, unrhymed.
RHYMER, [rīm'-er], *n.* one who makes rhymes, a versifier.
RHYMESTER, [rīm'-ster], *n.* a rhymer, an inferior poet.
RHYMING, [rīm'-ing], *adj.* that rhyme(s), exhibiting rhyme; **r. dictionary**, a dictionary containing lists of words that rhyme.
RHYMIST, [rīm'-ist], *n.* one who uses rhyme.
RHYNCHOLITE, [rin'-kōl-īt], *n.* the fossilized beak of a bird. [Gk. *rhugkhos* beak and *lithos* stone].
RHYOLITE, [rī'-ō-līt], *n.* quartz-trachyte, an acidic rock of volcanic origin, occurring in dykes or as lava. [Gk. *rhuax* lava and *lithos* stone].
RHYTHM, [riTHm], *n.* periodic variation or regular alternation of strong and weak or weaker stress, regular recurrence of emphasis or accent according to a particular scheme or pattern; an example of this, a particular scheme in which the emphasis or stress occurs according to a set pattern; a regular periodic recurrence or cycle of events, phenomena, etc., in anything; symmetry in some form of activity or operation; **r. section**, a unit of a dance band concerned with emphasizing the rhythm of a piece, containing piano, drums, guitars, etc. [Gk. *rhuthmos*].
RHYTHMIC, [riTH'-mik], *adj.* rhythmical.
RHYTHMICAL, [riTH'-mik-al], *adj.* characterized by, exhibiting, rhythm; according to, in, a rhythm.
RHYTHMICALLY, [riTH'-mik-al-i], *adv.* in a rhythmical fashion, with rhythm.
RIANCY, [rī'-an-si], *n.* the quality of being riant, cheerfulness, gaiety.
RIANT, [rī-ant], *adj.* gay, smiling, genial, cheerful. [Fr. *riant*].
RIB (1), [rib], *n.* one of the curved side bones of vertebrate animals, extending from the spine and serving to enclose the thorax; a long, narrow strip slightly raised to form a ridge-like protuberance in anything; (*arch.*)

a piece of timber which is part of the framework of a roof; a supporting arch of a vault; a projecting moulding on the interior of a vaulted roof, a groin; one of the curved vertical side pieces forming part of the framework of a ship; one of the curved members supporting a bridge, usually arranged in parallel formation; one of the stiff wire strips supporting the cover of an umbrella when open; one of the curved pieces of wood forming the belly of a lute or the sides of a violin; (*bot.*) the main vein of a leaf continuing from the petiole along the middle of the leaf; (*entom.*) a vein of an insect's wing; (*geol.*) a vein of ore; the shaft of a feather; (*coll.*) a wife; **floating r.,** a rib which is not fastened to the breast-bone. [OE. *rib*].

RIB (2), (ribbing, ribbed), [rib], *v.t.* to furnish with ribs, to form into rib-like projections.

RIBALD (1), [rib'-awld], *n.* a low, vulgar, foul-mouthed creature.

RIBALD (2), [rib'-awld], *adj.* scurrilous, base, obscene, lewd, coarse. [OFr. *ribauld*].

RIBALDISH, [rib'-awld-ish], *adj.* disposed to ribaldry.

RIBALDROUS, [rib'-awld-rus], *adj.* ribald in nature, scurrilous.

RIBALDRY, [rib'-ald-ri], *n.* low, vulgar, or obscene language; irreverent jesting.

RIBAND, [rib'-and], *n.* a ribbon. [OFr. *riban*].

RIBBAND, [rib'-band'], *n.* one of the flexible, long, thin timbers temporarily binding the ribs of a ship in place. [RIB (1) and BAND (1)].

RIBBED, [ribd], *adj.* furnished with ribs; narrowly ridged; marked with rising lines and channels.

RIBBING, [rib'-ing], *n.* a series or assemblage of ribs; the act of marking or furnishing with ribs.

RIBBON (1), [rib'-on], *n.* a long narrowish strip of silk, satin, or material of similar texture; a length of this worn as a head band or ornament; a short coloured strip of ribbon by which a cross or medal is suspended, or which forms a badge of knighthood or mark of other high honour; a narrow strip of anything, anything like a ribbon in shape; (*pl.*) (*coll.*) driving reins; **r. building, etc.,** building, etc. (*esp.* of houses), in long strips at the side of main roads. [OFr. *riban*].

RIBBON (2), [rib'-on], *v.t.* to adorn with ribbons.

RIBBONFISH, [rib'-on-fish], *n.* a fish having a long, narrow flattened body, *esp.* the oar-fish, *Regalecus banksii.*

RIBBONFISH

RIBBON-GRASS, [rib'-on-grahs], *n.* a variously coloured grass with ribbon-like leaves.

RIBBONISM, [rib'-on-izm], *n.* the principles of a Roman Catholic secret organization formed in Ireland to oppose the Orange confederation.

RIBBONMAN, [rib'-on-man'], *n.* a member of a secret society in Ireland formed to oppose Protestantism and the Orange confederation.

RIBBON-SAW, [rib'-on-saw'], *n.* a long bandsaw.

RIBES, [rī'-bēz], *n.* a genus of the saxifrage family containing about fifty species including *Ribes rubrum*, the red currant, *Ribes nigrum*, the black currant, and *Ribes Grossularia*, the gooseberry. [MedL. *ribes*].

RIBGRASS, [rib'-grahs], *n.* ribwort, *Plantago lanceolata*; an Australian variety of plantain.

RIBLESS, [rib'-less], *adj.* having no ribs.

RIBSTON PIPPIN, [rib'-ston-pip'-in], *n.* a variety of eating apple. [*Ribston* Park in the W. Riding of Yorkshire].

RIBWORT, [rib'-wurt'], *n.* the common plantain with lanceolate leaves, *Plantago lanceolata.* [MLGerm. *rib(be)wort*].

RICE, [rīs], *n.* a cereal plant, *Oryza sativa*, the seeds of which are extensively used as food. [OFr. *ris*].

RICEBIRD, [rīs'-burd], *n.* the bobolink, the reedbird, *Dolichonyx oryzivorus*; the Java sparrow, *Munia oryzivora.*

RICEFLOWER, [rīs'-flow'-er], *n.* the Victorian bird-cherry, *Pimelea elegans.*

RICE-MILK, [rīs'-milk], *n.* boiled milk thickened with rice.

RICE-PAPER, [rīs'-pā-per], *n.* a fine paper prepared in China from the pith of a tree, *Fatsia papyrifera.*

RICE-WEEVIL, [rīs'-wē'-vil], *n.* the beetle, *Sitophilus oryzæ*, allied to the common wheat-weevil.

RICH (1), [rich], *n.* the wealthy.

RICH (2), [rich], *adj.* abounding in money and possessions; wealthy; blessed (with); abundant, fertile; abundant in valuable materials or qualities; splendid; costly; full of beauty; vivid; sumptuous; abounding in a variety of delicious or nourishing foods; (of colour and sound) deep, strong, intense; (*coll.*) funny, affording grounds for laughter. [OFr. *riche*].

RICHES, [rich'-iz], *n.(pl.)* possession of land, goods, money in abundance; wealth; abundance; plenty; (*fig.*) spiritual grace, richness. [OFr. *richesse*].

RICHLY, [rich'-li], *adv.* in a rich fashion; abundantly, fully.

RICHNESS, [rich'-nes], *n.* the condition or quality of being rich; opulence, wealth; splendour, abundance.

RICK (1), [rik], *n.* a stack of grain, hay, or peas. [OE. *hreac*].

RICK (2), [rik], *n.* a strain or wrench, usually in the back. [WRICK].

RICKETS, [rik'-its], *n.* (*path.*) a disease of young children resulting from malnutrition, and characterized by softening of the bones which causes deformity, particularly in the legs. [Unkn.].

RICKETY, [rik'-it-i], *adj.* having rickets; weak, unhealthy; shaky, unstable.

RICKSHAW, [rik'-shaw], *n.* a jinricksha.

RICKSTAND, [rik'-stand'], *n.* the stage or set of wooden or stone pillars on which a rick is built.

RICOCHET (1), [rik'-ōsh-ā, rik'-ōsh-et], *n.* the rebounding of a projectile when it strikes the ground or other solid object; a glancing blow. [Fr. *richochet*].

RICKSHAW

RICOCHET (2), [rik'-ōsh-ā, rik'-ōsh-et], *v.t.* to induce to rebound, glance off; *v.i.* to glance off, rebound; to skim.

RICTUS, [rik'-tus], *n.* the vertical width of an open mouth; the extent of opening of a bird's beak; (*bot.*) the gap at the mouth of a labiate corolla [*L. rictus*].

RID (1), [rid], *adj.* cleared.

RID (2), [rid], *v.t.* to free; drive away; to clear from, disencumber; **to get r. of,** free oneself from.

RIDDANCE, [rid'-ants], *n.* the act of getting rid; condition of being rid; **a good r.,** a welcome freedom from some nuisance.

RIDDEL, [rid'-el], *n.* a curtain, *esp.* one hung beside an altar. [OE. *ridel*].

RIDDEN, [rid'-en], *p.pt.* of RIDE.

RIDDLE (1), [ridl], *n.* an enigmatic proposition or puzzle; anything ambiguous or puzzling; any person or thing difficult to understand. [OE. *rædels*].

RIDDLE (2), [ridl], *n.* a large sieve with meshes for separating grosser materials from finer. [OE. *hriddel*].

RIDDLE (3), [ridl], *v.t.* to sift with a riddle; to make many holes in, perforate with (bullets). [*Prec.*].

RIDDLER, [ridl-er], *n.* a person who speaks in riddles; one who riddles, perforates.

RIDDLING, [rid'-ling], *n.* that which is riddled; siftings, screenings; the action of sifting with a riddle.

RIDDLINGLY, [rid'-ling-li], *adv.* in the manner of a riddle; enigmatically.

RIDE (1), [rīd], *n.* the act of riding; a journey on horseback or in a vehicle; a track for riding.

RIDE (2), [rīd], *v.t.* to sit on, be carried by; to be held up by; **to r. down,** to overtake on horseback, knock down and trample underfoot; (*fig.*) to override ruthlessly; **to r. to death,** to kill by riding too hard; (*fig.*) to bore with, make tiresome by constant repetition; **to r. the storm,** to weather the storm; *v.i.* to be borne along on a horse, bicycle or in a vehicle; to practise riding habitually; to sit upon someone's back as on a vehicle and be carried; to float; to move, be supported; **to r. easy,** (of a ship) to be at anchor without a great strain on her cables; **to r. hard,** to ride at full speed; (*naut.*) to pitch violently; **to r. for a fall,** to ride or behave recklessly; **to r. up,** to work out of position, climb upward. [OE. *ridan*].

RIDEAU, [rē'-dō], *n.* (*fort.*) a small mound of earth to cover an approach. [Fr. *rideau* curtain].

RIDER, [rid-er], *n.* one who rides; an addition made to a verdict; an additional clause; (*geom.*) a further development of a geometrical proposition; (*mech.*) part of a machine placed above and working upon another part.

RIDERLESS, [rī'-der-les], *adj.* without a rider, having lost the rider.

RIDGE (1), [rij] *n.* the top, crest, rim of any long narrow elevation; a long, narrow range of hills or mountains; a long crest; the edge of the coping where the two sloping sides of a roof meet; a raised rim or edge between two grooves; a raised hot-bed for cucumbers, etc. [OE. *hrycg*].
RIDGE (2), [rij], *v.t.* to form a ridge; to wrinkle; *v.i.* to form into ridges, to extend in ridges.
RIDGED, [rijd], *adj.* rising in, characterized by, a ridge or ridges.
RIDGEL, [rij'-el], *n.* an animal with an undescended testicle. [~RIDGE (1)].
RIDGE-POLE, [rij'-pōl'], *n.* an upright piece of timber supporting the ridge of the roof or the top of a rectangular tent.
RIDGEWAY, [rij'-wā], *n.* a path or road along the ridge of a hill or downs.
RIDGY, [rij'-i], *adj.* having a ridge or ridges.
RIDICULE (1), [rid'-i-kewl], *n.* contemptuous laughter; mockery, derision. [L. *ridiculum*].
RIDICULE (2), [rid'-i-kewl], *v.t.* to treat with derision; to expose to contempt; to make fun of.
RIDICULER, [rid'-ik-ewl-er], *n.* one who ridicules.
RIDICULOUS, [rid-ik'-yŏŏl-us], *adj.* arousing ridicule; absurd, comical, laughable. [L. *ridiculus*].
RIDICULOUSLY, [rid-ik'-yŏŏl-us-li], *adv.* in a ridiculous fashion; absurdly.
RIDICULOUSNESS, [rid-ik'-yŏŏl-us-nes], *n.* the condition of being ridiculous.
RIDING (1), [rid'-ing], *n.* one of the three administrative divisions of Yorkshire; a district. [OScand. *thrithjungr* third part].
RIDING (2), [rīd'-ing], *n.* the action of one who rides, *esp.* one travelling on horseback; a track for riding.
RIDING-BOOT, [rīd'-ing-bōōt'], *n.* a boot worn for horse-riding.
RIDING-GLOVE, [rīd'-ing-gluv'], *n.* a glove worn for horse-riding, usually a gauntlet.
RIDING-HABIT, [rīd'-ing-hab'-it], *n.* a costume worn by women for horse-riding consisting of a tight-fitting coat with a long full skirt or breeches.
RIDING-HOOD, [rīd'-ing-hŏŏd], *n.* a large hood worn when riding; this as an outdoor costume in bad weather.
RIDING-LIGHT, [rīd'-ing-līt], *n.* a light carried in a ship's rigging while she is anchored.
RIDING-MASTER, [rīd'-ing-mah'-ster], *n.* a teacher of the art of horse-riding; (*milit.*) an officer who instructs soldiers in horsemanship.

RIDING-BOOT

RIDING-RHYME, [rīd'-ing-rīm'], *n.* a rhyme in a decasyllabic couplet.
RIDING-SCHOOL, [rīd'-ing-skōōl], *n.* a school where horsemanship is taught.
RIDING-WHIP, [rīd'-ing-wip], *n.* a whip used when on horseback.
RIDOTTO, [rid-ot'-ō], *n.* a social gathering for the pleasures of music and dancing. [It. *ridotto*].
RIEM, [rēm], *n.* a strip of oxhide rendered pliable for making into ropes. [Du. *riem*].
RIEMANITE, [rē'-man-īt], *n.* an allophane. [*Riemann*, who first observed it].
RIFACIMENTO, [ri-fah'-chi-men'-tō], *n.* a recasting of a literary work or musical composition. [It. *rifacimento*].
RIFE, [rif], *adj.* prevalent; everywhere flourishing; abundant; luxurious to excess. [OE. *rif*].
RIFFLE, [rifl], *n.* (*mining*) a channel formed by placing a crossbar in the bed of a trough or cradle to catch the gold particles. [~RIFLE (2)].
RIFFLER, [rif'-ler], *n.* a file with a convex side used by sculptors and metal-workers. [Fr. *rifloir*].
RIFF-RAFF, [rif'-raf'], *n.* the sweepings, refuse; the rabble, scum of society; worthless or disreputable people. [OFr. *rif et raf*].
RIFLE (1), [rifl], *n.* a gun with its barrel spirally grooved; (*pl.*) infantry armed with rifles.
RIFLE (2), [rifl], *v.t.* to seize and bear away by force; to ransack in search of loot; to rob; to cut spiral grooves in (*esp.*) the barrel of a rifle or gun. [OFr. *rifler* to scratch].

RIFLE

RIFLE-BIRD, [rifl'-burd], *n.* a bird of paradise, *Ptilornis paradisea*, with beautiful plumage. [Uncert.].
RIFLEMAN, [rifl'-man], *n.* a man, usually a soldier, armed with a rifle; a member of a rifle brigade.
RIFLE-PIT, [rifl'-pit'], *n.* a trench for riflemen in warfare.
RIFLER, [rifl-er], *n.* one who rifles, a robber.
RIFLE-RANGE, [rifl'-rānj], *n.* a place used for the practice of shooting with the rifle; the distance which a rifle-shot carries.
RIFLE-SHOT, [rifl'-shot'], *n.* a shot fired with a rifle; the distance which the shot covers; one who is a good shot with a rifle.
RIFLING, [rif-ling], *n.* the process of making the spiral grooves in the barrel of a gun; the grooves themselves.
RIFT (1), [rift], *n.* an opening, cleft, break, fissure; **a r. in the lute,** an unfavourable circumstance which disturbs harmonious relations. [OScand. *rift*].
RIFT (2), [rift], *v.t.* to cleave, rive; *v.i.* to burst open [*Prec.*].
RIG (1), [rig], *n.* the style and number of the masts of a ship; a dress, outfit; a curious and absurd style of dress. (*Scot* and *dial.*) ridge.
RIG (2), [rig], *v.t. and i.* to dress, put on; to furnish with apparatus; (*naut.*) to fit with tackle, rigging; **to r. out,** to fit completely, provide with clothes; **to r. up,** to construct; improvise, contrive. [OScand. *rigga*].
RIG (3), [rig], *v.t.* manipulate, influence dishonestly or secretly. [Unkn.].
RIGADOON, [rig'-a-dōōn'], *n.* a brisk, lively dance for two people. [Fr. *rigaudon*].
RIGEL, [rī'-gel], *n.* the star of the first magnitude in the constellation, Orion. [Arab. *rigel*].
RIGGED, [rigd], *adj.* carrying a certain type of rigging.
RIGGER, [rig'-er], *n.* a man who rigs ships; (*mech.*) a cylindrical pulley or drum.
RIGGING, [rig'-ing], *n.* (*naut.*) the tackle; the ropes which support the masts, and set and work the sails of a ship.
RIGGING-LOFT, [rig'-ing-loft'], *n.* (*naut.*) the place where rigging is attended to; in a theatre, a place above stage from which scenery is raised or lowered into position.
RIGGISH, [rig'-ish], *adj.* (*dial.*) wanton, skittish, lewd.
RIGHT (1), [rīt], *n.* that which is true, in keeping with the facts, correct, accurate; that which is in conformity with truth and justice; rectitude, justice; propriety; just claim; legal title; prerogative; privilege; authority; property; the side (of the body or any object) opposed to the left; **the R.,** formerly the ministerial side in Parliament, but now mainly a conservative party or that section of a party most conservative in its principles; **by r. of,** held, enjoyed, as a consequence of; **in one's own r.,** independently, without reference to others. [OE. *riht*].
RIGHT (2), [rīt], *adj.* straight; most convenient, most suitable in view of existing circumstances, most likely to achieve a desired end; correct; well performed; dexterous; most direct; opposite to the left side, towards the east when facing north; just, fit, proper, equitable, lawful; sound, healthy; **r. side,** the side made to be seen; **r. as rain,** perfectly right, absolutely sound and healthy. [OE. *riht*].
RIGHT (3), [rīt], *adv.* in a right or straight line; rightly, justly, correctly; thoroughly, very; quite; precisely, absolutely; towards, on to, the right; **r. and left,** everywhere, on every side; **to put r.,** to repair (a machine), smooth over, settle (a disagreement or difficulty), cure (an illness); (*U.S.*) **r. here,** in this very place, absolutely here; (*geom.*) **r. angle,** an angle of ninety degrees. [OE. *rihte*].
RIGHT (4), [rīt], *v.t.* to put in its original position, to set upright; to do justice, to relieve from wrong, correct, redress, reform, improve; **r. oneself,** recover one's balance; (*fig.*) to explain one's conduct satisfactorily. [OE. *rihtan*].
RIGHTABOUT (1), [rīt'-a-bowt], *n.* the opposite direction, **to the r.,** facing the other way; **to send to the r.,** to dismiss peremptorily.
RIGHTABOUT (2), [rīt'-a-bowt], *adj.* reverse, having a reverse movement.
RIGHTABOUT (3), [rīt'-a-bowt], *adv.* to the right-about. [RIGHTABOUT (1)].
RIGHT-ANGLED, [rīt'-ang-gld], *adj.* having, forming, a right angle.
RIGHTEOUS, [rī'-chus], *adj.* characterized by justice, equity, virtue; virtuous, upright, just; justifiable. [OE. *rihtwis*].
RIGHTEOUSLY, [rī'-chus-li], *adv.* in a righteous fashion, justly, uprightly.
RIGHTEOUSNESS, [rī'-chus-nes], *n.* the quality of being righteous; justice, rectitude, integrity.
RIGHTER, [rī'-ter], *n.* one who settles or sets right, a vindicator.
RIGHTFUL, [rīt'-fŏŏl], *adj.* disposed to do right; in conformity with what is right; having a lawful claim.

RIGHTFULLY, [rīt′-fool-i], *adv.* in a rightful fashion; justly, fairly, rightly.
RIGHTFULNESS, [rīt′-fool-nes], *n.* the state of being rightful; righteousness; justice; moral rectitude.
RIGHT-HAND, [rīt′-hand′], *adj.* on or to the right hand; clockwise; (*fig.*) indispensable.
RIGHT-HANDED, [rīt′-hand′-ed], *adj.* using the right hand more easily than the left; constructed for the use of the right hand; clockwise.
RIGHT-HANDEDNESS, [rīt-hand′-ed-nes], *n.* the quality of being right-handed.
RIGHT-HEARTED, [rīt′-hah′-ted], *adj.* having a good disposition.
RIGHTLY, [rīt′-li], *adv.* in accordance with right, justly, uprightly.
RIGHT-MINDED, [rīt-mīnd′-ed], *adj.* just, moral, well-disposed.
RIGHT-MINDEDNESS, [rīt-mīnd′-ed-nes], *n.* the condition of being right-minded.
RIGHTNESS, [rīt′-nes], *n.* the quality or condition of being right; uprightness, integrity, appositeness.
RIGHTWARD, [rīt′-wurd], *adj.* towards the right, on the right hand.
RIGHT-WHALE, [rīt′-wāl], *n.* the large whalebone whale, *Balæna mysticetus*.
RIGID, [rij′-id], *adj.* stiff, not pliant, not easily bent; immobile; (*fig.*) unyielding, stern, severe; fixed, inflexible, stiff. [L. *rigidus*].
RIGIDITY, [rij-id′-i-ti], *n.* the quality of being rigid; stiffness, want of pliability; unadaptability.
RIGIDLY, [rij′-id-li], *adv.* in a rigid fashion, severely, strictly.
RIGIDNESS, [rij′-id-nes], *n.* the condition of being rigid; rigidity.
RIGLET, [rig′-let], *n.* reglet; a flat thin piece of wood used for picture frames and also in printing.
RIGMAROLE, [rig′-mer-ōl], *n.* a rambling, incoherent discourse; a confused story. [ME. *ragman roll* register of names].
RIGOL, [rig′-ol], *n.* †a circle, diadem; (*dial.*) a little gutter or ditch. [Fr. *rigole* watercourse].
RIGOR, [rig′-or], *n.* a sudden chill, *esp.* when accompanied by fits of shivering as in some fevers; **r. mortis**, stiffness of the muscles that sets in a few hours after death. [L. *rigor*].
RIGOROUS, [rig′-er-us], *adj.* stern, inflexible, uncompromising, thorough, inclement, harsh.
RIGOROUSLY, [rig′-er-us-li], *adv.* in a rigorous fashion.
RIGOROUSNESS, [rig′-er-us-nes], *n.* the quality of being rigorous.
RIGOUR, [rig′-er], *n.* severity, austerity, stiffness; relentlessness, strictness, thoroughness; inclemency.
RIGSDAG, [rigz′-dahg′], *n.* the Danish Parliament. [Dan. *rigsdag*].
RIG-VEDA, [rig′-vā′-da], *n.* the principal of the four Vedas, a collection of the sacred hymns of the Hindus. [Skr. *ric* hymn of praise and *veda* knowledge].
RIKSDAG, [rēks′-dahg′], *n.* the Swedish Parliament. [Swed. *riksdag*].
RILE, [rīl], *v.t.* (*U.S.* and *dial.*) to stir up, make muddy; (*fig.*) stir up, make angry, exacerbate. [ME. *roilen*].
RILL (1), [ril], *n.* a small brook, a little stream, rivulet. [Germ. *rille* furrow].
RILL (2), [ril], *v.i.* to run in a small rill.
RIM (1), [rim], *n.* a border or margin, a brim; a raised margin or edge; the verge of the horizon; the outer part of a wheel on which the tyre fits. [OE. *rima*].
RIM (2), **(rimming, rimmed)**, [rim], *v.t.* to put a rim on, to form a rim round.
RIME (1), [rīm], *n.* hoar-frost. [OE. *hrim*].
RIME (2), see RHYME (1).
RIME (3), [rīm], *v.t.* to cover with rime.
RIME (4), [rīm], *v.t.* to rhyme.
RIMER, [rī′-mer], *n.* a tool used in metal-working for enlarging holes; a reamer. [OE. *ryman* to widen].
RIMLESS, [rim′-les], *adj.* without a rim or rims.
RIMLET, [rim′-let], *n.* a thin or small rim.
RIMMER, [rim′-er], *n.* an implement for marking the edges of pastry.
RIMMON, [rim′-on], *n.* a heathen god of the Syrians whose temple stood in Damascus; **to bow down in the house of R.**, to conform to principles one does not really accept. [2 Kings, v. 18].
RIMOSE, [rim-ōs′, rī-mōs′], *adj.* abounding in clefts, fissures. [L. *rimosus* from *rima* fissure].
RIMOSITY, [rim-os′-it-i], *n.* the state of being rimous.
RIMOUS, [rīm′-us], *adj.* rimose.
RIMPLE (1), [rimpl], *n.* a fold or wrinkle. [OE. *hrympel*].
RIMPLE (2), [rimpl], *v.t.* to fold, wrinkle, to ripple.
RIMY, [rī′-mi], *adj.* covered with hoar-frost, frosty.
RIND, [rīnd], *n.* the outer coating of a fruit that may be peeled off; peel, bark; the hard, outer coating of cheese or bacon. [ME. *rind*].
RINDERPEST, [rin′-der-pest′], *n.* a malignant and contagious cattle plague. [Germ. *rinderpest* from *rinder* oxen and *pest* plague].
RINDLE, [rindl], *n.* a small watercourse or gutter; a ditch, a runnel. [OE. *rynel*].
RING (1), [ring], *n.* a circle or anything in the form of a circular line or hoop; a circular course or area; a circular object with hollow centre; a hoop of gold, silver, or other metal, sometimes ornamented with jewels and worn on the finger or some other part of the body; a group standing together or around; an enclosed space for boxing or prize-fighting; a betting enclosure; (*collect.*) bookmakers generally; (*comm.*) a group of firms in a particular industry combining for private gain. [OE. *hring*].
RING (2), [ring], *n.* the sound produced when anything metallic is struck; any clear, ringing sound; a reverberation; the sound made by a bell; a peal of bells harmonically tuned; (*fig.*) a convincing sound, character. [RING (4)].
RING (3), [ring], *v.t.* to encircle; to fit with a ring or rings; to make circular grooves in the bark of a tree trunk; *v.i.* to rise in rings or a spiral.
RING (4), **(rang, rung)**, [ring], *v.t.* to cause to sound with a clear resonant note, particularly by striking a metallic body; to sound by means of bells; *v.i.* to sound, produce a clear, resonant note; to resound, echo; to reverberate; to practise the art of ringing bells; **to r. true (false)**, to produce sound characteristic of a genuine (false) article; (*fig.*) to be sincere, genuine (untruthful); **to r. the changes**, to pass from one theme to another and back again; **to r. the knell of**, to signify the ruin or downfall of; **to r. down the curtain**, to give the sign for lowering the curtain at the end of a play; **to r. in**, to celebrate by ringing bells; **to r. off**, to conclude a telephone call; **to r. up**, to give the signal for raising; to get into telephone communication with. [OE. *hringan*].
RING-BOLT, [ring′-bōlt], *n.* an iron bolt with a ring in one end of it.
RING-BONE, [ring′-bōn], *n.* a callus formed in the hollow circle of the little pastern of the horse.
RING-DIAL†, [ring′-dī′-al], *n.* a pocket sundial in the shape of a ring.
RING-DOVE, [ring′-duv], *n.* the wood-pigeon, *Columba palumbus*, so named from the white ring round the neck.
RINGENT, [rinj′-ent], *adj.* (*bot.*, *zool.*) gaping, wide open. [L. *ringens*].
RINGER (1), [ring′-er], *n.* one who rings; a bell-ringer; an arrangement for making bells ring.
RINGER (2), [ring′-er], *n.* a quoit thrown on to the peg.
RING-FENCE, [ring′-fents′], *n.* a fence enclosing a large tract or an estate in one enclosure.
RING-FINGER, [ring′-fing′-ger], *n.* the third finger of the left hand, where the engagement and marriage rings are placed.
RING-GOAL, [ring′-gōl], *n.* a game where a wooden ring is propelled towards a goal by two sticks.
RINGING (1), [ring′-ing], *n.* the act of one who rings; a ringing sound; (*path.*) tinnitus.
RINGING (2), [ring′-ing], *adj.* clear, reverberating, resonant.
RINGLEADER, [ring′-lē-der], *n.* the leader of an association, *esp.* when it is engaged in some mischievous or illegal enterprise.
RINGLESTONE, [ringl′-stōn], *n.* the ring-plover.
RINGLET, [ring′-let], *n.* a little ring; a little curl; a circle; a dancing ring formed by the feet of fairies; any of several species of butterflies of the wall brown family, such as *Hipparchia hyperanthus*.
RINGLETED, [ring′-let-ed], *adj.* having ringlets; arranged in ringlets.
RINGLETY, [ring′-let-i], *adj.* adorned with, wearing, ringlets.
RING-LOCK, [ring′-lok′], *n.* a lock in which a series of grooved rings must be adjusted before the latch can be moved.
RING-MAIL, [ring′-māl], *n.* armour of small rings sewn on leather; chain-mail.
RING-MASTER, [ring′-mah-ster], *n.* one directing the performance in a circus arena.

RING-NECKED, [ring'-nekt'], *adj.* characterized by a distinctive ring of colour round the neck.

RING-OUZEL, [ring'-o͞ozl], *n.* a British bird of the thrush genus, with a white band round the throat, *Turdus torquatus*.

RING-OUZEL

RING-PLOVER, [ring'-pluv'-er], *n.* any of various plovers with a distinctive ring of feathers round the neck.

RING-STAND, [ring'-stand'], *n.* a small branched stand, usually of china, glass, or silver, for hanging finger-rings upon.

RING-STREAKED, [ring'-strēkt], *adj.* characterized by circular streaks or lines on the body.

RING-TAIL, [ring'-tāl], *n.* the female hen-harrier, *Circus cyaneus*.

RINGTAIL, [ring'-tāl], *n.* (*naut.*) a narrow sail fixed on the gaff abaft the spanker as a fore-and-aft studding sail.

RING-TAILED, [ring'-tāld], *adj.* having the tail marked with rings.

RING-WALL, [ring'-wawl], *n.* a ring-fence entirely enclosing an estate or piece of ground.

RINGWORM, [ring'-wurm], *n.* tinea, a contagious fungus, usually affecting the scalp, giving rise to a circular eruption in small vesicles with a reddish base.

RINK (1), [ringk'], *n.* a space on the ice measured off for curling; a sheet of artificial ice for skating on; a place in which people skate on roller-skates; a smooth, flat, hard surface, *esp.* prepared for roller-skating; the building in which skating takes place; (*sport*) a team of players, *esp.* in bowls. [ME. *rink* jousting-ground].

RINK (2), [ringk], *v.i.* to skate on a rink.

RINSE (1), [rints], *n.* the act of rinsing; liquid used for rinsing purposes; the liquid after rinsing has taken place; dregs.

RINSE (2), [rints], *v.t.* to cleanse with clean water; to cleanse with repeated applications of water after the first washing; **to r. out**, to cleanse (a utensil, clothes, the mouth) by the repeated application of clean water or other cleansing liquid. [Fr. *rincer*].

RINSER, [rin'-ser], *n.* a person or thing that rinses.

RIOT (1), [rī'-ot], *n.* a violent disturbance of the public peace by three or more than three persons; tumultuous uprising; uproar; noisy festivity; (*fig.*) an abundance, profusion; **to read the R. Act**, to read during a riot a proclamation ordering the dispersal of riotous gatherings ; (*coll.*) to utter a warning against people behaving in an unruly way; **to run r.**, to behave or move about without restraint; to grow luxuriantly. [OFr. *riote*].

RIOT (2), [rī-ot], *v.i.* to take part in a riot; to raise an uproar, disturbance; to run to excess in indulgence; to revel. [OFr. *rioter*].

RIOTER, [rī'-ot-er], *n.* a person who riots; one guilty of disturbing the peace.

RIOTING, [rī'-ot-ing], *n.* the act of taking part in a riot.

RIOTOUS, [rī'-ot-us], *adj.* characterized by rioting; marked by excessive revelry; dissolute; extravagant, unrestrained; luxurious, abundant. [OFr. *riotous*].

RIOTOUSLY, [rī'-ot-us-li], *adv.* in a riotous fashion.

RIOTOUSNESS, [rī'-ot-us-nes], *n.* the condition of being riotous.

RIP (1), [rip], *n.* (*dial.*) a wicker basket to carry fish in. [OScand. *hrip*].

RIP (2), [rip], *n.* a worn-out horse, a dissolute woman; a worthless fellow, a rake. [~REP (2)].

RIP (3), [rip], *n.* a tear, long slash.

RIP (4), [rip], *v.t.* to cut or tear open or asunder; to unstitch; *v.i.* to slash vigorously; to tear asunder; to move with great speed; to rush in a headlong course; **to r. asunder, open, up**, to cut or tear apart, or in pieces, in a violent manner; **to r. off**, to tear off with a violent movement. [OScand. *ripa*].

RIPARIAN, [rīp-āer'-i-an], *adj.* pertaining to the bank of a river; (*bot., zool.*) growing on, living in or near, the banks of a river; **r. rights**, rights of the owner of the banks of a river. [L. *riparius*].

RIPE (1), [rīp], *adj.* brought to perfection in growth; mature; having fully developed, matured; ready, prepared, finished. [OE. *ripe*].

RIPE† (2), [rīp], *v.t. and i.* to mature, ripen; to grow ripe.

RIPELY, [rī'-pli], *adv.* in a ripe, mature fashion, with mature consideration.

RIPEN, [rī'-pen], *v.t.* to make ripe, mature; to bring to maturity or perfection; *v.i.* to grow ripe, attain maturity.

RIPENESS, [rīp'-nes], *n.* the condition of being ripe.

RIPIDOLITE, [rip-id'-ō-līt], *n.* a silicate consisting of aluminium, magnesium, and iron monoxide. [Gk. *rhipidos* fan and Gk. *lithos* stone].

RIPOSTE, [rip-ost'], *n.* (*fencing*) a lightning-like return lunge; a counter-stroke; (*fig.*) a quick repartee. [Fr. *riposte*].

RIPPER, [rip'-er], *n.* a person or thing that rips; a rip-saw; (*slang*) a splendid person or thing.

RIPPING, [rip'-ing], *adj.* that rips or tears; (*slang*) splendid, admirable; most enjoyable.

RIPPLE (1), [ripl], *n.* the slight fretting of the surface of water, a little undulation or wave; a slight movement or mark suggestive of a ripple or little wave on water; the light swish as of rippling water. [Uncert.].

RIPPLE (2), [ripl], *n.* a large, long-toothed, metal comb for cleaning flax. [Du. *repel*].

RIPPLE (3), [ripl], *v.t.* to cause to ripple, undulate lightly; to fret slightly; to curl, undulate as with ripples; *v.i.* to move in wavelets, to be gently ruffled; to sound like ripples in water.

RIPPLE (4), [ripl], *v.t.* to clean away seed from flax.

RIPPLE-CLOTH, [ripl'-kloth'], *n.* a woollen or cotton material with a ripple-like surface.

RIPPLE-MARK, [ripl'-mahk], *n.* a slight undulation on the surface of a sea-beach, left by the receding waves; (*geol.*) a similar undulation on the surface of rocks.

RIPPLE-MARKED, [ripl'-mahkt], *adj.* marked as with ripples.

RIPPLET, [rip'-let], *n.* a small ripple.

RIPPLING, [rip'-ling], *n.* the forming of ripples; the sound of ripples.

RIPPLINGLY, [rip'-ling-li], *adv.* in a rippling manner; with ripples.

RIPPLY, [rip'-li], *adj.* having ripples, rippling.

RIPRAP, [rip'-rap'], *n.* (*U.S.*) a loose foundation of stones thrown down in deep water on a soft bottom to form a foundation for constructional work. [Uncert.].

RIPSAW, [rip'-saw], *n.* a saw with large teeth used for sawing wood in the direction of the grain. [RIP (1) and SAW (1)].

RIPTOWEL, [rip'-tow-el], *n.* a gratuity given to tenants when they had reaped their lord's corn. [Uncert.].

RIPUARIAN, [rip-yo͞o-āer'-i-an], *adj.* pertaining to the ancient Franks settled on the banks of the Rhine between the Moselle and the Meuse. [MedL. *ripuarius*].

RIP VAN WINKLE, [rip'-van-winkgl'], *n.* a very old man or a person very much behind the times, old-fashioned. [A character in Washington Irving's *Sleepy Hollow* who sleeps for twenty years].

RISE (1), [rīz], *n.* upward motion, ascent, elevation; the appearing of the sun or moon above the horizon; advance in rank, honour, fame; upward slope; origin, source, process of developing; increase in amount, value, degree; **to take its r. in**, to originate in; (*coll.*) **to take a r. out of**, to make fun of, get the better of, tease.

RISE (2), (**rose, risen**), [rīz], *v.i.* to get up from a recumbent position; to come to a standing position; to get up from sleep, to get out of bed; to ascend, to go from a lower to a higher level; to end a session; to stand up to make a speech; to increase in power and volume, to swell; to grow louder; to be raised; to appear above the horizon; to increase in force, speed; to get on in the world; to appear, to spring, stir; to originate; to be roused; to be raised above; (*fig.*) **the curtain rises**, the play begins, the situation develops; **to r. to a bait**, to be gulled into action by a false hope of reward; **to r. to it**, to respond to a certain stimulus, allow (oneself) to be teased. [OE. (*a*)*risan*].

RISER, [rī'-zer], *n.* a person or thing that rises; the vertical part of a step in a stairway; escape vent in a casting mould.

RISHI, [rish'-i], *n.* a poet or inspired singer of the Vedic hymns; a person inspired; a seer; **Seven Rishis**, the stars of the Great Bear. [Skr. *rishi*].

RISIBILITY, [riz'-ib-il'-it-i], *n.* a tendency to laugh.

RISIBLE, [riz'-ibl], *adj.* concerned with the faculty of laughing; capable of exhibiting laughter; laughable.

RISIBLENESS, [riz'-ibl-nes], *n.* the faculty of being able to laugh; risibility.

RISIBLY, [riz'-ib-li], *adv.* in a risible fashion; laughably.

RISING (1), [rī'-zing], *n.* the action of that which rises; a getting up, ascension; resurrection; a rebellion, revolt, riot; the act of closing a session; the coming above the horizon; a swelling; (*fig.*) a strong surge of emotion often accompanied by physical effects; advance in importance, power.

RISING (2), [rī'-zing], *adj.* ascending, having an upward slope; mounting; growing in strength, intensity, volume; increasing in wealth, power, or distinction; approaching any given age, amount, or size; **R. Sun**, the Japanese national emblem, hence, Japan.

RISK (1), [risk], *n.* hazard of danger; chance of injury, loss; exposure to danger; (*comm.*) the chances of financial loss. [Fr. *risque*].

RISK (2), [risk], *v.t.* to expose to the possibility of injury, loss; to venture, dare, face the possibility of. [Fr. *risquer*].

RISKY, [ris'-ki], *adj.* dangerous, full of risk; risqué.

RISORIAL, [riz-aw'-ri-al], *adj.* pertaining to laughter; risible.

RISOTTO, [riz-ot'-ō], *n.* an Italian dish, made with (meat,) rice, cheese and onions. [It. *risotto*].

RISQUE, risqué, [rē'-skā, ris'-kā], *adj.* bordering on indecency or immorality. [Fr. *risqué*].

RISSOLE, [ris'-ōl], *n.* meat or fish minced, mixed with potatoes or breadcrumbs and egg, moulded into cakes, and fried. [Fr. *rissole*].

RITE, [rit], *n.* a ceremonial usage in religious worship or in other observances; (*fig.*) a formal observance, a rigid and solemnly performed habit. [L. *ritus*].

RITORNELLO, [ri-taw-nel'-ō], *n.* (*mus.*) a repetition; the burden of a song; a brief introduction. [It. *ritornello*].

RITUAL (1), [rit'-yōō-al], *n.* the body of religious rites and observances; the manner of performing religious or other services; a book of rites. [L. *ritualis*].

RITUAL (2), [rit'-yōō-al], *adj.* pertaining to, consisting of, rites.

RITUALISM, [rit'-yōō-al-izm], *n.* the system of ritual or prescribed forms and ceremonies of religious worship; the observance of these; a more than usual respect for, and observance of, ritual or religious forms.

RITUALIST, [rit'-yōō-al-ist], *n.* a man skilled in ritual; one who attaches great importance to ritual in the church.

RITUALISTIC, [rit'-yōō-al-is'-tik], *adj.* pertaining to, devoted to, ritual.

RITUALLY, [rit'-yōō-al-i], *adv.* in accordance with ritual.

RIVAGE, [rīv'-ij], *n.* a bank, shore, coast, margin of the sea or a river. [Fr. *rivage*].

RIVAL (1), [rī'-val], *n.* one who competes with another in any pursuit; an antagonist or opponent; an equal. [L. *rivalis*].

RIVAL (2), [rī'-val], *adj.* rivalling; competing; having the same claims.

RIVAL (3), [rī'-val], *v.t.* to stand in competition with; to strive to equal or excel; to emulate; to equal.

RIVALRY, [rī'-val-ri], *n.* the act of being a rival; competition; emulation; similarity or equality in status.

RIVALSHIP, [rī'-val-ship], *n.* a state of rivalry; competition; contention for superiority.

RIVE, (rove or rived, riven), [rīv], *v.t.* to rend, to tear, to split; *v.i.* to be rent. [OScand. *rifa* to break].

RIVEL†, [riv'-el], *v.t.* to cause to wrinkle; to shrink as with heat; *v.i.* to wrinkle, shrivel up. [ME. *rivelen*].

RIVELLED, [riv'-eld], *adj.* wrinkled, shrunken, by heat.

RIVEN, [riv'-en], *adj.* rent, torn, split. [OScand. *rifinn*].

RIVER (1), [rī'-ver], *n.* one who rives, splits, tears.

RIVER (2), [riv'-er], *n.* a big stream of water following a natural course into the sea, a lake, or another river; an abundant flow or flood. [OFr. *rivere*].

RIVERAIN (1), [riv'-er-ān], *n.* one who lives on the bank of a river. [Fr. *riverain*].

RIVERAIN (2), [riv'-er-ān], *adj.* of, pertaining to, or dwelling by, the bank of a river.

RIVER-BASIN, [riv'-er-bā'-sin], *n.* the land drained by a river.

RIVER-BED, [riv'-er-bed'], *n.* the trough in which a river runs.

RIVER-CRAB, [riv'-er-krab'], *n.* a freshwater crab.

RIVER-CRAFT, [riv'-er-krahft'], *n.* any small boats used on rivers.

RIVER-GOD, [riv'-er-god'], *n.* the deity who presides over a river, and personifies its character and forces.

RIVER-HORSE, [riv'-er-haws'], *n.* the hippopotamus.

RIVERINE, [riv'-er-īn], *adj.* riparian; pertaining to a river.

RIVERSIDE, [riv'-er-sīd'], *n.* the ground on either bank of a river.

RIVET (1), [riv'-it], *n.* a headed metal pin or bolt on which a second head is formed when it is in position. [OFr. *rivet*].

RIVET (2), [riv'-it], *v.t.* to fasten with rivets; make firm; (*fig.*) to attract, fix (the attention).

RIVETER, [riv'-it-er], *n.* one who, or a machine which, rivets.

RIVIERE, rivière, [riv'-i-āer'], *n.* a necklace of diamonds or other precious stones, usually made up of particular strings fastened together. [Fr. *rivière*].

RIVOSE, [riv-ōs'], *adj.* (*zool.*) indented with sinuate furrows. [LL. *rivosus*].

RIVULET, [riv'-yōō-let], *n.* a little river.

RIX-DOLLAR, [riks'-dol-er], *n.* a silver dollar formerly current in Germany, Holland, and Scandinavia. [Du. *rijksdaler* state dollar].

ROACH (1), [rōch], *n.* a small, silvery, freshwater fish, *Leuciscus rutilus*. [OFr. *roche*].

ROACH

ROACH (2), [rōch], *n.* (*naut.*) a curve cut in the foot of a sail. [Uncert.].

ROACH (3), [rōch], *n.* (*coll.*) a cockroach.

ROAD, [rōd], *n.* the highway; a public, metalled way for travelling; a way; a place where ships may ride at anchor; **r. sense**, skill in driving vehicles on the road. [OE. *rad*].

ROAD-BOOK, [rōd'-bōōk], *n.* a book with maps of roads, distances, and other information for travellers.

ROAD-HOG, [rōd'-hog'], *n.* (*coll.*) a reckless and inconsiderate driver.

ROAD-HOUSE, [rōd'-hows], *n.* a large restaurant or hotel situated in the country on one of the main roads.

ROADLESS, [rōd'-les], *adj.* without roads.

ROAD-MAN, [rōd'-man], *n.* a man who works on the roads, building or keeping them in repair.

ROAD-MAP, [rōd'-map'], *n.* a map in which the roads are shown and usually graded according to condition.

ROAD-METAL, [rōd'-met'-al], *n.* broken stones used in constructing or repairing roads.

ROADSIDE, [rōd'-sīd], *n.* the strip of free ground which commonly borders a road on either hand.

ROADSTEAD, [rōd'-sted], *n.* a place near, but outside, the harbour, where ships may ride at anchor.

ROADSTER, [rōd'-ster], *n.* a horse, vehicle, or motorcar for use on long journeys by road; (*naut.*) a vessel riding at anchor in a roadstead.

ROAD-USER, [rōd'-yōōz'-er], *n.* one who uses or drives along the public roads.

ROADWAY, [rōd'-wā], *n.* the highway; that part of a road used by vehicles.

ROAM, [rōm], *v.t.* to wander over; *v.i.* to wander, to travel haphazardly. [ME. *romen*].

ROAMER, [rō'-mer], *n.* one who roams.

ROAMING, [rō'-ming], *n.* the act of roaming.

ROAN (1), [rōn], *n.* a soft sheepskin leather, often used for binding books. [*Rouen*, a town in France].

ROAN (2), [rōn], *n.* a roan horse.

ROAN (3), [rōn], *adj.* of a ground colour with white or grey intermixed. [OFr. *rouen*].

ROAR (1), [raw(r)], *n.* the loud, deep cry of an animal; a cry of pain; any sudden cry; any loud, deep sound resembling this.

ROAR (2), [raw(r)], *v.i.* to cry with a loud, deep sound; to bellow. [OE. *rarian*].

ROARER, [raw'-rer], *n.* one who, or that which, roars; a broken-winded horse.

ROARING (1), [raw'-ring], *n.* a sound made by anything that roars; a disease of a horse's windpipe, which causes it to make a grating sound.

ROARING (2), [raw'-ring], *adj.* noisy, boisterous, disorderly; brisk, active.

ROARINGLY, [raw'-ring-li], *adv.* in a roaring fashion; briskly.

ROAST (1), [rōst], *n.* something roasted, *esp.* a joint of beef.

ROAST (2), [rōst], *v.t.* to cook by simple exposure to heat in an oven or before a fire; to heat thus; to parch by exposure to heat; (*coll.*) reprimand severely; *v.i.* to become exceedingly hot; (*metal.*) to dissipate the volatile parts of ore by heat. [OFr. *roster*].

ROASTER, [rō'-ster], *n.* one who roasts meat; a device for roasting on a gridiron; a fowl suitable for roasting.

ROASTING-JACK, [rō'-sting-jak'], *n.* a contrivance for turning a spit.

ROB (1), [rob], *n.* the juice of ripe fruit, reduced by boiling with sugar to a syrup, and used as jam. [Fr. *rob* from Arab. *robb* syrup].

ROB (2), [rob], *v.t.* to steal from someone, often with violence; to plunder; to withhold forcibly what is due. [OFr. *rober*].

ROBBER, [rob′-er], *n.* one who robs.

ROBBERY, [rob′-er-i], *n.* the act of robbing; an unlawful taking of another person's goods by force; unfair exaction.

ROBE (1), [rōb], *n.* a long, loose, outer garment; a ceremonial garment; an elegant frock; any covering serving to drape the figure; a drapery. [OFr *robe* dress].

ROBE (2), [rōb], *v.t.* to put a robe on (someone), dress with a robe; to array; to cover; *v.i.* to dress oneself in robes.

ROBERT, [rob′-ert], *n.* (*slang*) a policeman. [Sir *Robert* Peel, who instituted the police force].

ROBIN, [rob′-in], *n.* a small, brown singing-bird with a red breast, *Erithacus rubecula*. [OFr. *Robin*].

ROBIN-GOODFELLOW, [rob′-in-gŏŏd′-fel′-ō], *n.* a roguish, merry elf or sprite.

ROBINIA, [rob-in′-i-a], *n.* the false acacia or locust-tree. [J. and V. *Robin*, the seventeenth-century French botanists].

ROBIN-REDBREAST, [rob′-in-red′-brest′], *n.* (*coll.*) the robin.

ROBORANT, [rō′-bor-ant], *n.* a medicine that strengthens; a tonic. [L. *roborans*].

ROBOT, [rō′-bot′], *n.* an automaton with some of the powers of man. [The mechanical man in Karel Capek's play, *R.U.R.* (Rossum's Universal Robots.)].

ROB-ROY, [rob′-roi′], *n.* a light canoe paddled by a double-bladed paddle. [*Rob Roy*, the pseudonym of its inventor, John MacGregor].

ROBURITE, [rō′-ber-it], *n.* a powerful explosive used for blasting, composed of dinitrobenzine and ammonium nitrate. [L. *robur* strength].

ROBUST, [rō-bust′], *adj.* possessing great strength and vigour; sound, healthy. [L. *robustus* oaken, strong].

ROBUSTIOUS†, [rō-bus′-ti-us], *adj.* robust, boisterous, full of animal spirits; big and strong, massive.

ROBUSTLY, [rō-bust′-li], *adv.* in a robust fashion.

ROBUSTNESS, [rō-bust′-nes], *n.* the character or quality of being robust.

ROC, [rok], *n.* a fabulous eastern bird of immense size and strength. [Arab. *rokh*].

ROCAMBOLE, [rok′-am-bōl], *n.* a form of wild garlic, *Allium Scorodoprasum*. [Fr. *rocambole*].

ROCCELLA, [rok-sel′-a], *n.* the lichen, archil. [MdL. from Portug. *roccha* rock].

ROCHELLE-SALT, [rosh-el′-sawlt′], *n.* salt exported from Rochelle, with medicinal and electrical properties. [La *Rochelle*, in France].

ROCHET (1), [roch′-et], *n.* a long, white, linen vestment with wide sleeves gathered to the wrist worn by bishops. [OFr. *rochet*].

ROCHET (2), [roch′-et], *n.* the red gurnard. [OFr. *rouget*].

ROCK (1), [rok], *n.* the hard mineral matter of the earth's crust; a cliff, crag, boulder, or stone; a projecting crag or stone above or close to the surface of the sea; a hard kind of boiled sugar sweetmeat; (*fig.*) a source of danger; something which affords a firm foundation; **on the rocks**, wrecked on rocks; (*fig.*) in financial straits. [OFr. *roke*].

ROCK (2), [rok], *n.* the act of rocking.

ROCK (3), [rok], *v.t.* to make to swing backwards and forwards; to shake; to lull a child to sleep by moving it backwards and forwards in a cradle; *v.i.* to sway, move suddenly and violently. [OE. *roccian*].

ROCK-ALUM, [rok′-al′-um], *n.* crystallized alum.

ROCKAWAY, [rok′-a-wā], *n.* an open-sided, four-wheeled, two-seater carriage once common in the United States.

ROCK-BASIN, [rok′-bā′-sin], *n.* a rocky-sided hollow.

ROCK-BOTTOM (1), [rok′-bot′-um], *n.* the solid rocky bed of the ocean; the lowest level to which prices and the like descend.

ROCK-BOTTOM (2), [rok′-bot′-om], *adj.* down to the living rock, to the very bottom; the very lowest.

ROCK-BOUND, [rok′-bownd], *adj.* surrounded by rocks.

ROCK-BUN, [rok′-bun′], *n.* a small currant bun with a rough, hard outside.

ROCK-CAKE, [rok′-kāk], *n.* a rock-bun.

ROCK-COD, [rok′-kod], *n.* a North American cod found on a rocky sea floor.

ROCK-CORK, [rok′-kawk], *n.* a kind of asbestos resembling cork.

ROCK-CRESS, [rok′-kres′], *n.* a plant of the genus, *Arabis*.

ROCK-CRYSTAL, [rok′-krist′-al], *n.* the finest transparent quartz, often carved into ornaments, and much valued.

ROCK-DOVE, [rok′-duv], *n.* the wild pigeon, *Columba livia*.

ROCKER, [rok′-er], *n.* one who, or that which, rocks or causes to rock; the curved piece of wood on which a cradle or chair rocks; a skate with a curved blade; (*slang*) **off his r.**, crazy.

ROCKERY, [rok′-er-i], *n.* an artificial, rock-strewn bank on which, in a garden, rock plants grow.

ROCKET (1), [rok′-it], *n.* a firework which, when lighted, shoots through the air, and serves for display purposes; to give a signal, or to carry a life-line; such a projectile used as a lethal weapon. [It. *rocchetta*].

ROCKET (2), [rok′-it], *n.* a popular name for some species of *Sisymbrium*, *Cakile*, and other cruciferous plants. [Fr. *roquette*].

ROCKET (3), [rok′-it], *v.t.* to fire rockets at something; *v.i.* to fly straight upwards; to rush swiftly and noisily like a rocket.

ROCKETER, [rok′-it-er], *n.* a rocketing bird.

ROCKETING, [rok′-it-ing], *adj.* flying swiftly upwards.

ROCK-FISH, [rok′-fish], *n.* a fish frequenting a rocky sea floor, *esp.* the wrasse and the sea-gudgeon.

ROCK-GARDEN, [rok′-gah′-den], *n.* a large rockery or garden where Alpine and rock plants grow.

ROCK-HEWN, [rok′-hewn], *adj.* cut out of the rock.

ROCKILY, [rok′-i-li], *adv.* in a rocky manner; shakily.

ROCKINESS, [rok′-i-nes], *n.* the condition of being rocky.

ROCKING, [rok′-ing], *adj.* moving backwards and forwards or from side to side; unsteady, shaky.

ROCKING-CHAIR, [rok′-ing-chāer′], *n.* a chair mounted on rockers.

ROCKING-HORSE, [rok′-ing-haws′], *n.* a toy wooden horse mounted on rockers.

ROCKING-STONE, [rok′-ing-stōn], *n.* a great boulder which can be made to rock to and fro.

ROCKLESS, [rok′-les], *adj.* destitute of rocks.

ROCKLING, [rok′-ling], *n.* a small fish allied to the cod, *esp.* the whistle-fish.

ROCKLING

ROCK-OIL, [rok′-oil], *n.* natural naphtha; petroleum.

ROCK-PIGEON, [rok′-pij′-on], *n.* a species of pigeon inhabiting rocks and caves; the rock-dove.

ROCK RABBIT, [rok′-rab′-it], *n.* a tailless rodent of the genus *Hyrax*, resembling a rabbit, and found in Syria and South Africa.

ROCK-ROSE, [rok′-rōz], *n.* a plant of the genus *Cistus* or *Helianthemum* with (single) yellow, white or pink flowers somewhat like those of the wild rose.

ROCK-RUBY†, [rok′-rōō′-bi], *n.* a species of garnet or amethyst of a fine bluish-red.

ROCK-SALT, [rok′-sawlt], *n.* mineral salt or chloride of sodium.

ROCK-SOAP, [rok′-sōp], *n.* a soft, greasy mineral composed of silica, alumina, and peroxide of iron, used for crayons.

ROCK-TEMPLE, [rok′-templ′], *n.* a temple hollowed out of the solid rock.

ROCK-WOOD, [rok′-wŏŏd], *n.* a kind of ligniform asbestos.

ROCK-WORK, [rok′-wurk], *n.* stones fixed in mortar in imitation of rough rock; a rockery; a natural wall of rock.

ROCKY (1), [rok′-i], *adj.* full of rocks; rock-like; very hard; stony; unfeeling. [ROCK (1)].

ROCKY (2), [rok′-i], *adj.* (*slang*) shaky. [ROCK (3)].

ROCOCO, [rok-ō′-kō], *n.* a florid form of architectural ornamentation; the style in furniture and decoration fashionable in the reigns of Louis XIV and Louis XV; out of date. [Fr. *rococo* perhaps from *rocaille* rock-work].

ROD, [rod], *n.* a long twig; a wand; an instrument of correction or punishment; a slender, tapering cane or stick, used by anglers to carry the line, and generally jointed; a slender metal bar; a measure of 5¼ yards; a pole; a perch. [OE. *rod*].

RODE, [rōd], *pret.* of RIDE.

RODENT (1), [rō′-dent], *n.* a rodent animal.

RODENT (2), [rō′-dent], *adj.* of the order of those vertebrates which have chisel-edged incisor teeth; gnawing. [L. *rodens*].

RODENTIAL, [rō-densh′-al], *adj.* pertaining to a rodent.
RODEO, [rō-dā′-o], *n.* a round-up of cattle on an American ranch; a display of skill in such rounding-up, often made for entertainment. [Span. *rodeo*].
RODGE, [roj], *n.* the gadwall, *Anas streperus.* [Uncert.].
RODLIKE, [rod′-līk], *adj.* shaped like a rod.
RODOMONTADE (1), RHODOMONTADE, [rod′-ō-mon-tād′], *n.* bluster, vain boasting, bombast. [*Rodomonte*, a personage in Ariosto's *Orlando Furioso*].
RODOMONTADE (2), RHODOMONTADE, [rod′-ō-mon-tād′], *adj.* boastful, bombastic.
RODSTER, [rod′-ster], *n.* an angler.
ROE (1), [rō], *n.* a small kind of deer, *Capreolus capræa*; the female of the hart. [OE. *rah*].
ROE (2), [rō], *n.* a mass of fish eggs. [OIcel. *ra*].
ROEBUCK, [rō′-buk], *n.* the male of the roe-deer.
ROE-STONE, [rō′-stōn], *n.* (*geol.*) oolite, so called as being formed of small globules like the roe of fishes.
ROGATION, [rō-gā′-shun], *n.* (*hist.*) submission of a Roman law to the people for formal approval, or the law so approved; (*eccles.*) (*pl.*) a litany; **R. Days,** the three days before Ascension Day; **R. Week,** the week in which the three Rogation Days fall. [L. *rogatio*].
ROGATIONAL, [rō-gā′-shun-al], *adj.* pertaining to rogation.
ROGATORY, [rō-gā′-ter-i], *adj.* relating to an investigation, interrogatory. [L. *rogatorius*].
ROGER, [roj′-er], *n.* a man's name; **Jolly R.,** the pirates' flag; **Sir R. de Coverley,** an English country dance. [Fr. *Roger*].

JOLLY ROGER

ROGUE, [rōg], *n.* a wandering beggar; a dishonest person; **r. elephant,** an elephant living and wandering apart from the herd and usually savage. [Uncert.].
ROGUERY, [rōg′-er-i], *n.* knavish tricks; cheating; fraud; mischievousness.
ROGUESHIP, [rōg′-ship], *n.* the state of being a rogue.
ROGUISH, [rōg′-ish], *adj.* like a rogue; waggish.
ROGUISHLY, [rōg′-ish-li], *adv.* in a roguish fashion; waggishly.
ROGUISHNESS, [rōg′-ish-nes], *n.* the state of being roguish.
ROISTER, [rois′-ter], *v.i.* to act boisterously; to swagger. [OFr. *rustre* clown, boor].
ROISTERER, [roi′-ster-er], *n.* one who roisters; a bold, boisterous person.
ROISTERING, [roi′-ster-ing], *adj.* boisterous, blustering.
ROKELAY†, [rok′-lā], *n.* a short cloak worn in the eighteenth century. [Fr. *roquelaire*].
ROKER, [rōk′-er], *n.* any fish of the ray family. [Dan. *rokke*].
ROLAND, [rō′-land], *n.* a courageous person who is a match for another; **a R. for an Oliver,** an apt repartee. [*Roland*, the nephew of Charlemagne, who, with his comrade Oliver, accomplished many brave deeds].
ROLE, rôle, [rōl], *n.* the part played by an actor; the part a person plays in life or in any set of events. [Fr. *rôle*].
ROLL (1), [rōl], *n.* the action of rolling; the thing that is rolled; any instrument for rolling; a swaying movement; a rapid series of beats on a drum; any reverberating sound.
ROLL (2), [rōl], *n.* a quantity of material wrapped so as to form a cylinder; a long strip of papyrus, parchment, or paper written upon and rolled up instead of being bound in leaves; an official document; an official register; a small loaf; (*arch.*) a scroll in an Ionian capital; **Master of the Rolls,** one of the four ex-officio judges of the Court of Appeal. [OFr. *rolle*].
ROLL (3), [rōl], *v.t.* to revolve along; to cause something to move forward by rotating it; to wrap round and round; to spread out or level something with a roller; *v.i.* to move on by revolving; to move, as waves; to form into a ball; to spread under a roller; to move from side to side; to waddle along; to beat a drum with rapid strokes; **to r. off,** to print or duplicate on a rotary machine; **to r. up,** (*slang*) to put in an appearance; to overwhelm.
ROLL-CALL, [rōl′-kawl], *n.* the calling over of a list of names to ascertain who is present.
ROLLED, [rōld], *adj.* plated by rolling; **r. gold,** a thin film of gold rolled over another metal so as to cover it.
ROLLER (1), [rōl′-er], *n.* the picarian bird, *Coracias garrulus*, so called from its strange flight; a breed of canary with a rolling or trilling song.
ROLLER (2), [rōl′-er], *n.* that which turns on its own axis; any cylinder for rolling; (*pl.*) heavy waves that set in after a storm; **r. bandage,** a long surgical bandage; **r. towel,** an endless towel suspended round a roller; **r. skate,** a skate to which four wheels have been fitted in place of a runner; **r. skating,** the amusement of skating on roller skates.

ROLLER SKATE

ROLLICK, [rol′-ik], *v.i.* to behave in a sportive manner. [Uncert.].
ROLLICKING, [rol′-ik-ing], *adj.* careless and gay.
ROLLING, [rōl′-ing], *adj.* used for rolling; moving along by turning round and round; running on wheels; undulating.
ROLLING-MILL, [rōl′-ing-mil′], *n.* a mill or machine for rolling out metal.
ROLLING-PIN, [rōl′-ing-pin], *n.* a short, round bar of wood or glass with which dough is flattened for baking.
ROLLING-PRESS, [rōl′-ing-pres′], *n.* a press for calendering; a press for copperplate printing.
ROLLING-STOCK, [rōl′-ing-stok′], *n.* the locomotives, carriages, wagons, etc., used on a railway.
ROLLING STONE, [rōl′-ing-stōn′], *n.* (*fig.*) a wanderer, good for nothing.
ROLY-POLY, [rōl′-i-pōl′-i], *n.* a game in which a ball wins by rolling into a certain place; a suet pudding spread out, covered with jam, rolled up and boiled; a short, plump person. [ROLL (1) and POLL (1)].
ROM, [rom], *n.* a gipsy man. [Romany *rom* man].
ROMAIC (1), [rō-mā′-ik], *n.* the language spoken in modern Greece. [Gk. *Rhomaikos* Roman].
ROMAIC (2), [rō-mā′-ik], *adj.* pertaining to Romaic.
ROMAL, [rō′-mal], *n.* an East Indian silk handkerchief; a whip of plaited rawhide. [Pers. *rumal*].
ROMAN (1), [rōm′-an], *n.* a citizen of the ancient Roman Empire or of Rome; a Roman Catholic; (*print.*) roman type.
ROMAN (2), [rōm′-an], *adj.* pertaining to, derived from, Rome or the ancient Roman Empire; of, pertaining to, the Latin Church whose centre is Rome; **R. alphabet,** the form of alphabet used by the Romans, and still used over all Western Europe and America; **R. Catholic,** a member of the Catholic Church which regards the Pope as its head; **r. numerals,** capital letters (I, IV) used as numerals; **r. type,** (*print.*) ordinary upright type (like this) as distinct from black letter or italic types; **r. candle,** a kind of firework. [*Rome* in Italy].
ROMANCE (1), [rō-mants′], *n.* the group of languages developed from Latin; a tale of chivalry, often in verse; a fictitious story or novel; an extravagant story; imaginative character or quality. [OFr. *romans*].
ROMANCE (2), [rō-mants′], *adj.* in, of, or pertaining to, Romance languages.
ROMANCE (3), [rō-mants′], *v.i.* to tell fictitious stories; to exaggerate, give a highly coloured account of events.
ROMANCER, [rō-mans′-er], *n.* a person who romances; a writer of romances; one who tells far-fetched stories, a liar.
ROMANCIST, [rō-mans′-ist], *n.* a romancer.
ROMANESE, [rō-man-ēz′], *n.* the Romany language.
ROMANESQUE (1), [rō′-man-esk′], *n.* a sub-Roman round-arched style of architecture of which the Norman style is a particular school.
ROMANESQUE (2), [rō′-man-esk′], *adj.* pertaining to Romanesque; resembling Romanesque architecture.
ROMANIC, [rō-man′-ik], *adj.* pertaining to the Romance languages; derived from Latin; †pertaining to Rome or its civilization. [L. *romanicus* Roman].
ROMANISM, [rō′-man-izm], *n.* the doctrine and organization of the Roman Catholic Church.

ROMANIST, [rō'-man-ist], *n.* a member of the Church of Rome.

ROMANISTIC, [rō'-man-is'-tik], *adj.* Roman Catholic.

ROMANISTICALLY, [rō'-man-is'-tik-al-i], *adv.* in a Romanistic manner.

ROMANIZATION, [rō'-man-iz-ā'-shun], *n.* the action of making Roman.

ROMANIZE, [rō'-man-īz], *v.t.* to Latinize; to convert to the Roman Catholic faith; *v.i.* to conform to Roman Catholic opinions.

ROMANIZER, [rō'-man-īz-er], *n.* a person who romanizes.

ROMANSCH, [rō-mahnsh'], *n.* a Rhaeto-Romanic dialect spoken in the Engadine. [LL. *romanice*].

ROMANTIC (1), [rō-man'-tik], *n.* a romantic writer, painter, sculptor, etc.; one of a school or tradition of romantic poets.

ROMANTIC (2), [rō-man'-tik], *adj.* pertaining to romance; based on romances; remote from everyday life, heroic, extravagant, wild, unreal, sentimental; (*art*) strange or picturesque in episode or style; allowing form to be dominated by atmosphere and mood; emotional and unregulated as distinct from classical. [Fr. *romantique*].

ROMANTICALLY, [rō-man'-tik-al-i], *adv.* in a romantic manner.

ROMANTICISM, [rō-man'-tis-izm], *n.* the quality of being romantic; (*art*) the anti-classical movement in late eighteenth- and early nineteenth-century art and literature towards a more subjective and emotional treatment.

ROMANTICIST, [rō-man'-tis-ist], *n.* an adherent of romanticism; an artist of the romantic school.

ROMANTICIZE, [rō-man'-tis-īz], *v.t.* to treat romantically; *v.i.* to adopt a romantic treatment or manner.

ROMANTICNESS, [rō-man'-tik-nes], *n.* the quality of being romantic.

ROMANY, [rom'-an-i], *n.* a gipsy; the gipsy language. [Gipsy *romani* from *rom* man].

ROMAUNT†, [rō-mawnt'], *n.* a romance. [OFr. *romant*].

ROME, [rōm], *n.* the city of Rome, the Roman Empire; the Roman Church. [L. *Roma*].

ROMEINE, [rō'-mā-in], *n.* (*min.*) a mineral consisting of antimony and lime. [*Romé* de Lisle, a mineralogist].

ROMEWARDS, [rōm'-werdz], *adv.* towards Rome or the Roman Catholic Church.

ROMISH, [rō'-mish], *adj.* Roman Catholic, Papistical.

ROMP (1), [romp], *n.* a person, *esp.* a girl who plays roughly or noisily; a noisy game.

ROMP (2), [romp], *v.i.* to play boisterously, noisily and energetically; **to r. home,** to win a race with ease. [~RAMP (2)].

ROMPERS, [rom'-perz], *n.(pl.)* an overall with leg openings for a child just beginning to crawl or walk.

ROMPISHLY, [rom'-pish-li], *adv.* in a romping manner.

ROMPISHNESS, [rom'-pish-nes], *n.* the quality of being rompy.

ROMPU, [rom'-pew], *n.* (*her.*) an ordinary that is broken, or a chevron or bend whose upper points are truncated. [Fr. *rompu*].

ROMPU

ROMPY, [rom'-pi], *adj.* inclined to romp.

RONDEAU, [ron'-dō], *n.* a type of verse consisting of ten or thirteen lines with only two rhymes and a refrain repeated from the first line in the eighth and last but not rhyming; a kind of jig which ends with the first strain repeated. [Fr. *rondeau*].

RONDEL, [ron'-del], *n.* a verse form similar to, but earlier than, the rondeau, having fourteen lines with two rhymes and a refrain. [Fr. *rondel*].

RONDO, [ron'-dō], *n.(mus.)* a musical piece, a jig, in which return is repeatedly made to the first theme; a rondeau. [It. *rondo*].

RONEO (1), [rō'-ni-ō], *n.* (*prot.*) an instrument for duplicating typescript.

RONEO (2), [rō'-ni-ō], *v.t.* to duplicate on a roneo; *v.i.* to use a roneo. [*Prec.*].

RONTGENOGRAM, röntgenogram, [rurnt'-gen-ō-gram'], *n.* a photograph taken by Röntgen-rays. [RÖNTGEN(-RAYS) and Gk. *gramma* letter].

RONTGEN-RAYS, röntgen-rays, [rurnt'-gen-rāz'], *n.(pl.)* rays which are invisible but capable of penetrating many opaque substances, and revealing their internal structure on a screen or sensitive plate. [Professor *Röntgen*, the discoverer].

ROOD, [rōōd], *n.* a crucifix, *esp.* one placed above the entrance to the chancel with supporting figures of St. Mary and St. John; the cross; a measure of one-fourth of an acre in extent. [OE. *rod* cross].

ROOD-LOFT, [rōōd'-loft'], *n.* a gallery in a church on which the rood stands.

ROOD-SCREEN, [rōōd'-skrēn], *n.* a carved stone or wooden screen separating the nave from the choir in a church.

ROOD-TREE†, [rōōd'-trē], *n.* the cross on which Christ died.

ROOF (1), [rōōf], *n.* the covering of the top of a building; anything resembling the roof of a building, e.g., the top of a car, coach or other vehicle; **the r. of the mouth,** the palate. [OE. *hrof*].

ROOF (2), [rōōf], *v.t.* to cover with a roof; to shelter.

ROOFAGE, [rōōf'-ij], *n.* roofing material; roofing of any kind. [ROOF (1)].

ROOFER, [rōōf'-er], *n.* a man who builds a roof.

ROOFING, [rōōf'-ing], *n.* covering with a roof; materials used for this purpose.

ROOFLESS, [rōōf'-les], *adj.* without a roof; homeless; destitute.

ROOF-SPOTTER, [rōōf'-spot-er], *n.* one who keeps watch on the roof of a building for the approach of hostile aircraft. [ROOF and SPOTTER].

ROOF-TREE, [rōōf'-trē], *n.* the main horizontal beam of the roof, the ridge; (*fig.*) the house or family.

ROOFY, [rōōf'-i], *adj.* having a roof; with many roofs.

ROOK (1), [rŏŏk], *n.* one of the chess pieces, a castle. [OFr. *roc* from Pers. *rukh*].

ROOK (2), [rŏŏk], *n.* a large, black bird, *Corvus frugilegus*, having a raucous cry and building its nest high in the trees in colonies; the crow; (*fig.*) a cheat. [OE. *hroc*].

ROOK (3), [rŏŏk], *v.t.* to cheat; to charge an excessive price to. [*Prec.*].

ROOKERY, [rŏŏk'-er-i], *n.* the nests of a colony of rooks.

ROOKY, [rŏŏk'-i], *adj.* having many rooks.

ROOM (1), [rōōm], *n.* space, area; an enclosed portion of a house or building, an apartment; opportunity, scope. [OE. *rum*].

ROOM (2), [rōōm], *v.i.* to share a room, lodge (with).

ROOMAGE, [rōōm'-ij], *n.* space for stowage; accommodation.

ROOMFUL, [rōōm'-ful], *n.* the number or quantity that fills any room.

ROOMILY, [rōōm'-i-li], *adv.* with ample room; capaciously.

ROOMINESS, [rōōm'-i-nes], *n.* the condition of being roomy.

ROOMY, [rōōm'-i], *adj.* having ample room or space; capacious.

ROOP, [rōōp], *n.* hoarseness; a hoarse sound. [Echoic].

ROOPY, [rōōp'-i], *adj.* hoarse.

ROOST (1), [rōōst], *n.* the pole where fowls perch at night; a group of roosting fowls. [OE. *hrost*].

ROOST (2), [rōōst], *v.i.* to perch on a pole, to sleep as fowls; (*fig.*) to rest, lodge.

ROOSTER, [rōōst'-er], *n.* a cock.

ROOT (1), [rōōt], *n.* that part of a plant which grows downwards and draws nourishment from the soil; that which resembles a root in position or function; the fundamental cause or source of anything; (*math.*) the quantity which, multiplied by itself, produces a given quantity or a particular series; (*philol.*) the basic element of a word; **to take r.,** to become fixed or established. [OE. *rot*].

ROOT (2), [rōōt], *v.t.* to fix by the root, to plant deeply; (*fig.*) to impress deeply, ineradicably on the mind; *v.i.* to fix its root, be firmly established; to put out roots; **to r. up** or **out,** to tear up, eradicate, destroy completely.

ROOT (3), [rōōt], *v.t. and i.* to dig (up), *esp.* with the snout. [OE. *wrotan*].

ROOTAGE, [rōōt'-ij], *n.* root system; (*fig.*) firm basis.

ROOT-CROP, [rōōt'-krop'], *n.* a crop of edible roots.

ROOT-EATER, [rōōt'-ē'-ter], *n.* an animal that eats roots.

ROOTED, [rōōt'-id], *adj.* having roots; firmly fixed; (*fig.*) deep, well-grounded; deep-seated.

ROOTEDLY, [rōōt'-id-li], *adv.* deeply, firmly, determinedly.

ROOTEDNESS, [rōōt'-id-nes], *n.* the quality of being rooted, firmly established.

ROOTER, [rōōt'-er], *n.* one who pulls up by the roots; one who destroys completely.
ROOTERY, [rōōt'-er-i], *n.* a pile of tree roots or stumps interspersed with earth where plants are grown as in a rockery. [~ROOT (1) on the analogy of ROCKERY].
ROOT-LEAF, [rōōt'-lēf], *n.* a leaf that grows from the root, a radical leaf.
ROOTLESS, [rōōt'-les], *adj.* having no root.
ROOTLET, [rōōt'-let], *n.* a small branch of a root; a radicle.
ROOT-STOCK, [rōōt'-stok'], *n.* (*bot.*) a prostrate rooting stem which produces shoots.
ROOTY, [rōōt'-i], *adj.* having many roots.
ROPE, [rōp], *n.* a cord of some thickness formed of twisted strands often made of hemp; a row or number of things strung together; **to give a person r.**, to give him wide freedom in the hope that he will make a mistake; **to know the ropes**, to be among the initiated. [OE. *rap*].
ROPE-DANCER, [rōp'-dahn'-ser], *n.* one who performs difficult feats while standing or walking on a rope stretched at some height above the ground.
ROPE-LADDER, [rōp'-lad'-er], *n.* a ladder made of rope.
ROPEMAKER, [rōp'-māk'-er], *n.* one who makes ropes.
ROPEMAKING, [rōp'-māk'-ing], *n.* the business of making rope.
ROPERY, [rō'-per-i], *n.* a place where ropes are made.
ROPEWALK, [rōp'-wawk], *n.* a long, narrow, covered alley where ropes are made.
ROPEWAY, [rōp'-wā], *n.* an overhead rope used as a means of transport.
ROPEYARN, [rōp'-yahn], *n.* yarn used in ropemaking.
ROPINESS, [rōp'-i-nes], *n.* stringiness; viscosity; fibrousness.
ROPY, [rōp'-i], *adj.* like a rope; stringy; viscous; adhesive.
ROQUE, [rōk'], *n.* a form of croquet. [Fr. *roque*].
ROQUEFORT, [rok'-faw(r)], *n.* a kind of cheese of the milk of goats and sheep. [*Roquefort*, in France, where made].
ROQUELAURE, [rok'-el-aw(r)], *n.* a cloak, buttoning from top to bottom and worn mainly in the eighteenth century. [Fr. *roquelaure* from the name of the Duke of *Roquelaure*].
ROQUET, [rōk'-i], *v.t.* in croquet, to strike another player's ball in playing one's own. [~CROQUET (1)].
RORAL, [rōer'-al], *adj.* pertaining to dew; dewy. [~L. *ros* dew].
RORIFEROUS, [rōer-if'-er-us], *adj.* producing or bearing dew. [L. *rorifer*].
RORQUAL, [rawk'-wal], *n.* a whale with a dorsal fin, of the genus *Balænoptera*. [Fr. *rorqual* from OScand. *reythar-hvalr*].
RORTY, [raw'-ti], *adj.* (*slang*) in good spirits; quarrelsome; obstreperous. [Uncert.].
ROSACEOUS, [rōz-ā'-shus], *adj.* rose-like; (*bot.*) belonging to the natural order *Rosaceæ*. [L. *rosaceus*].
ROSANILINE, [rōz-an'-i-lin], *n.* (*chem.*) an aniline dye of a bright red colour. [ROSE and ANILINE].
ROSARIAN, [rōz-āer'-i-an], *n.* one who specializes in the cultivation of roses. [L. *rosarium* rose garden].
ROSARY, [rōz'-er-i], *n.* a rose garden; a string of beads for counting prayers; an anthology. [L. *rosarium* rose garden].
ROSCID, [ro'-sid], *adj.* dewy; resembling dew. [L. *roscidus*].
ROSE (1), [rōz], *pret.* of RISE.
ROSE (2), [rōz], *n.* any of various wild or cultivated plants or their flowers of the genus *Rosa*, of many species and varieties; a pink colour resembling that of certain roses; a knot of ribbons; a perforated nozzle; a card of the compass; (*fig.*) a beautiful person; (*arch.*) a rosette carved in stone; **under the r.**, secretly; (*hist.*) **Wars of the Roses**, the Civil War between the Houses of York and Lancaster, whose emblems were the white and red rose respectively. [OE. *rose* from L. *rosa*].
ROSE-ACACIA, [rōz'-a-kā'-sha], *n.* the flowering tree, *Robinia hispida*.
ROSEAL, [rōz'-i-al], *adj.* like a rose, roseate.
ROSE-APPLE, [rōz'-apl'], *n.* the Malay apple, one of the numerous species of *Eugenia*, with edible fruit.
ROSEATE, [rōz'-i-at], *adj.* rosy; like a rose in colour or form; full of roses; (*fig.*) hopeful. [L. *roseus*].
ROSE-BAY, [rōz'-bā], *n.* a species of willowherb, *Epilobium angustifolium*; also *Nerium Oleander*; the rhododendron.
ROSE-BOX, [rōz'-boks'], *n.* (*bot.*) the plant *Cotoneaster microphylla*.
ROSE-BUD, [rōz'-bud'], *n.* the bud of the rose; (*fig.*) an attractive girl.
ROSE-BUG, [rōz'-bug'], *n.* a diurnal beetle which feeds on roses; the rose-chafer.
ROSE-BUSH, [rōz'-bŏŏsh'], *n.* the bush of the rose.
ROSE-CHAFER, [rōz'-chāf'-er], *n.* a beetle, *Cetonia aurata*, destructive to rose-trees.
ROSE-COLOUR, [rōz'-kul'-er], *n.* a deep rich pink colour, as of certain roses; (*fig.*) optimism.
ROSE-COLOURED, [rōz'-kul'-erd], *adj.* of the colour deep rich pink; (*fig.*) unwarrantedly hopeful.
ROSE-DIAMOND, [rōz'-dī'-a-mond], *n.* a diamond cut into twenty-four triangular surfaces.
ROSE-DROP, [rōz'-drop'], *n.* an ear-ring; a lozenge flavoured with rose essence; a pimple due to excessive drinking of alcholic liquors.
ROSE-FACED, [rōz'-fāst], *adj.* with a rosy face.
ROSE-GALL, [rōz'-gawl], *n.* an excrescence on rose leaves, caused by the insect *Rhodites rosea*.
ROSE-HUED, [rōz'-hewd], *adj.* having the colour deep rich pink as of certain roses.
ROSE-KNOT, [rōz'-not'], *n.* a rosette.
ROSELITE, [rōz'-el-īt], *n.* (*min.*) a native arseniate of cobalt. [Gustav *Rose*, the mineralogist].
ROSELLA, [rōz-el'-a], *n.* the Australian Rose-hill parakeet, *Platycercus eximius* or *Platycercus icterotis*. [*Rose Hill* in Australia, where found].
ROSELLANE, [rōz'-el-ān], *n.* (*min.*) an altered form of the mineral anorthite.
ROSE-MALLOW, [rōz'-mal'-ō], *n.* (*dial.*) the hollyhock.
ROSEMARY, [rōz'-mer-i], *n.* an evergreen shrub *Rosmarinus officinalis*, with a fragrant smell, yielding an aromatic oil. [L. *ros marinus*].
ROSE-NOBLE, [rōz'-nōbl'], *n.* an old English gold coin, so called as having a rose stamped on it.
ROSEOLA, [rōz-ē'-ōl-a], *n.* (*path.*) a rash occurring in measles, German measles, and similar diseases, and characterized by red spots on the skin. [MdL. *roseola*].
ROSE-QUARTZ, [rōz'-kwawts'], *n.* (*min.*) a variety of quartz, rose-red in colour.
ROSE-RASH, [rōz'-rash'], *n.* (*path.*) roseola.
ROSE-TREE, [rōz'-trē'], *n.* a rose plant, *esp.* one grafted on to a standard.
ROSETTA-WOOD, [rōz-et'-a-wŏŏd'], *n.* an Indian wood of a bright orange-red colour with dark markings.
ROSETTE, [rōz-et'], *n.* an imitation of a rose made of ribbons; (*arch.*) a stone ornament in the form of a rose. [Fr. *rosette*].

ROSETTE

ROSE-WATER, [rōz'-waw'-ter], *n.* water tinctured with roses and used as a perfume.
ROSE-WINDOW, [rōz'-win'-dō], *n.* a round window in the form of a fully opened rose.
ROSEWOOD, [rōz'-wŏŏd'], *n.* the fragrant wood of a species of *Dalbergia* and of other genera, growing in tropical countries, and used largely for furniture.
ROSICRUCIAN (1), [roz'-i-krōō'-shan], *n.* one of a fraternity who in the beginning of the fifteenth century affected an intimate acquaintance with the secrets of nature, and pretended, by the study of alchemy and other occult sciences, to possess extraordinary powers. [Christian *Rosenkreuz*, its supposed founder].
ROSICRUCIAN (2), [roz'-i-krōō'-shan], *adj.* of, pertaining, or relating to, Rosicrucians or Rosicrucianism.
ROSICRUCIANISM, [rōz'-i-kroo'-shan-izm], *n.* the doctrines and practices of the Rosicrucians.
ROSILY, [rōz'-i-li], *adv.* in a rosy manner, with a rosy flush.
ROSIN (1), [roz'-in], *n.* the residue after oil of turpentine has been distilled from crude turpentine; resin. [~RESIN].
ROSIN (2), [roz'-in], *v.t.* to rub or smear with rosin, as a violin bow.
ROSINANTE, [roz'-in-ant'-i], *n.* a broken-down nag. [*Rosinante*, Don Quixote's steed].
ROSINESS, [rōz'-i-nes], *n.* the quality of being rosy.
ROSINWEED, [ro'-zin-wēd'], *n.* (*bot.*) the plant *Silphium laciniatum*.
ROSINY, [ro'-zi-ni], *adj.* containing rosin; resinous.
ROSLAND, [ros'-land], *n.* (*dial.*) heathy moorland. [Wel. *rhos* moor and LAND (1)].
ROSOLIO, [rōz-ōl'-i-ō], *n.* an Italian and south European drink made from raisins. [It. *rosolio*].

ROSSIGNOL, [ros'-ēn-yol'], *n.* †the nightingale; the Canadian song-sparrow. [Fr. *rossignol*].
ROSTEL, [ros'-tel], *n.* (*bot.*) the first radicle which develops from the seed and forms the root of the plant. [L. *rostellum* small beak].
ROSTELLATE, [ros'-tel-āt], *adj.* (*bot.*) having a small beak.
ROSTER, [ro'-ster], *n.* a prescribed order regulating the rotation in which individuals, companies, and regiments are to be called on duty. [Du. *rooster* table, list].
ROSTRAL, [ro'-stral], *adj.* furnished with, or pertaining to, a rostrum or beak. [L. *rostralis*].
ROSTRATE, [ro'-strāt], *adj.* rostral; beak-like. [L. *rostratus*].
ROSTRIFORM, [ro'-stri-fawm], *adj.* having the shape of a beak.
ROSTROID, [rost'-roid], *adj.* formed like a beak. [L. *rostrum* beak and Gk. *oeides* like].
ROSTRUM, [rost'-rum], *n.* the beak or bill of a bird; the beak or head of a ship; in ancient Rome, a stage in the Forum for orators to speak from, so called as being adorned with the beaks of ships captured in a naval engagement; a platform from which a speaker addresses his audience; a pulpit; (*chem.*) a pipe for conveying distilled liquor into its receiver; (*surg.*) a crooked pair of scissors for dilating wounds. [L. *rostrum* beak].
ROSULATE, [roz'-yŏŏl-āt], *adj.* (*bot.*) having the leaves arranged tightly over each other as the petals of a double rose. [LL. *rosula* little rose].
ROSY, [rōz'-i], *adj.* resembling a rose; of a deep pink colour; of a bright healthy colour in complexion; flushing; (*fig.*) bright, promising, favourable.
ROT (1), [rot], *n.* putrefaction; rubbish; a fatal distemper incident to sheep; a disease of the potato; (*fig.*) deterioration; (*slang*) nonsense. [OScand. *rot*].
ROT (2), [rot], *v.t. and i.* to (cause to) decay, to decompose; to develop the rot; to grow ill and wasted, deteriorate with confinement or inactivity; (*slang*) to joke, make fun of. [*Prec.*].
ROTA, [rōt'-a], *n.* an ecclesiastical court in Rome composed of twelve prelates; a club of politicians in the time of Charles I, in favour of a system of government by which the ministers and a number of members of Parliament should retire in rotation; a list determining the order of service; a roster. [L. *rota* wheel].
ROTARIAN, [rōt-āer'-i-an], *n.* a man who is a member of the Rotary Club. [*Next*].
ROTARY, [rōt'-er-i], *adj.* moving round on an axis like a wheel; acting in rotation; **R. Club**, an international business men's organization for the promotion of good relations locally and internationally. [LL. *rotarius*].
ROTATABLE, [rō'-tāt'-abl], *adj.* capable of rotation.
ROTATE (1), [rōt-āt'], *adj.* wheel-shaped; (*bot.*) (of a corolla) spreading flat without any tube.
ROTATE (2), [rōt-āt'], *v.t. and i.* to revolve round a centre; to go by rotation. [L. *rotare* to revolve].
ROTATION, [rōt-ā'-shun], *n.* the act of turning round about an axis; regular succession. [L. *rotatio*].
ROTATIONAL, [rōt-ā'-shun-al], *adj.* pertaining to rotation.
ROTATIONALLY, [rōt-ā'-shun-al-i], *adv.* in a rotative fashion.
ROTATIVE, [rōt-āt'-iv], *adj.* rotating, turning as a wheel; of, or pertaining to, rotation.
ROTATOR, [rōt-āt'-er], *n.* that which produces rotatory action; (*anat.*) a muscle which has this function. [L. *rotator*].
ROTATORY, [rōt-āt'-er-i], *adj.* pertaining to rotation; turning about an axis like a wheel; following in succession.
ROTCHE, [roch'-i], *n.* (*ornith.*) the little auk, *Mergulus alce*. [~ROTGE].
ROTE, [rōt], *n.* †repetition; **by r.**, by a mere mechanical repetition without attending to the underlying meaning or principles; by heart. [Uncert.].
ROTGE, [rot'-ji], *n.* (*ornith.*) the little auk, the rotche. [Fris. *rotgies* brentgoose].
ROTHERNAILS, [ro'-THer-nālz], *n.*(*pl.*) nails with full heads, used for fastening the rudder irons of ships. [~RUDDER NAILS].
ROTHOFFITE, [rōt'-of-īt], *n.* (*min.*) a kind of garnet. [*Rothoff*, a mineralogist].
ROTIFER, [rōt'-i-fer], *n.* a minute animalcule of the class *Rotifera*. [L. *rota* wheel and *ferre* to bear].
ROTIFERA, [rōt-if'-er-a], *n.*(*pl.*), a class of animalculae, so called from the apparently rotary movement of their cilia.
ROTOGRAPH, [rōt'-ō-graf'], *n.* a photostat. [Uncert.].
ROTOR, [rōt'-or], *n.* a machine driven by the wind acting on fans working in lofty funnels; any revolving part, *esp.* an electric coil capable of rotation. [ROTATOR].
ROTTEN, [rot'-en], *adj.* decayed, putrid, decomposed; unsound; (*fig.*) corrupt, unsound, treacherous; (*slang*) unpleasant, beastly. [ROT].
ROTTENLY, [rot'-en-li], *adv.* in a rotten fashion.
ROTTENNESS, [rot'-en-nes], *n.* the condition of being rotten.
ROTTEN-STONE, [rot'-en-stōn], *n.* a soft stone, resulting from the decomposition of shale or siliceous limestone, used in polishing metal.
ROTTER, [rot'-er], *n.* one who, or that which, rots; (*coll.*) a person of bad moral character.
ROTUND, [rō-tund'], *adj.* round in form; (of a person) short and plump. [L. *rotundus*].
ROTUNDA, [rō-tund'-a], *n.* a building circular both within and without, roofed with a dome. [L. *rotundus*].
ROTUNDIFOLIOUS, [rō-tund'-i-fōl'-i-us], *adj.* (*bot.*) with rounded leaves. [L. *rotundus* round and *folium* leaf].
ROTUNDITY, [rō-tund'-i-ti], *n.* roundness; plumpness.
ROUBLE, [rōōbl], *n.* a (silver) coin, the Russian monetary unit. [Russ. *ruble*].
ROUCOU, [rōōk-ōō'], *n.* a substance used in dyeing. [Fr. *roucou* from Brazilian *urucu*].
ROUE, roué, [rōō'-ā], *n.* a dissipated man; a rake; a debauchee; a profligate. [Fr. *roué* broken on the wheel].
ROUGE (1), [rōōzh], *n.* a red cosmetic for reddening the lips and cheeks; a red powder used for polishing plate. [Fr. *rouge* red].
ROUGE (2), [rōōzh], *v.t.* to apply rouge to.
ROUGE-ET-NOIR, [rōōzh'-ān-wah(r)'], *n.* a game of chance played with cards, so-called because of certain red and black markings on the table where the players place their cards according to choice. [Fr. *rouge et noir* red and black].
ROUGH (1), [ruf], *n.* ground which has an uneven surface, and is broken up with undergrowth; the unpleasant, difficult side of anything; hardship; a rowdy, turbulent person; (*golf*) the uneven ground off the greens and fairway; **in the r.**, in an unfinished state; **r. diamond**, an uncut diamond; (*fig.*) an uncouth but worthy fellow.
ROUGH (2), [ruf], *adj.* not smooth or even; not polished; abounding with stones or stumps; rugged; stormy; harsh; grating to the ear; shaggy; rugged in temper or manners; uncouth; difficult; **r. house**, a free fight; **r. neck**, a hooligan. [OE. *ruh*].
ROUGH (3), [ruf], *v.t.* to make rough, ruffle; **to r. it**, to live hardly and without the usual comforts of life.
ROUGHAGE, [ruf'-ij], *n.* that which is discarded as rough; food that stimulates the excretive processes by its bulk.
ROUGH-CAST, [ruf'-kahst], *n.* plaster mixed with small pebbles for coating the outsides of brick houses; (*fig.*) a crude, exterior coating, something imperfectly contrived.
ROUGH-DRAFT, [ruf'-drahft], *v.t.* to make a sketch, a preliminary draft.
ROUGH-DRAWN, [ruf'-drawn], *adj.* roughly drawn.
ROUGH-DRY, [ruf'-drī], *adj.* (of clothes) dry but not ironed or pressed.
ROUGHEN, [ruf'-en], *v.t.* to make rough; *v.i.* to grow rough.
ROUGH-HEW, [ruf'-hew'], *v.t.* to hew roughly; to give a preliminary rough shape to.
ROUGH-HEWN, [ruf'-hewn'], *adj.* coarsely hewn into shape; (*fig.*) rugged, unpolished.
ROUGH-HOUND, [ruf'-hownd], *n.* the small shark, *Scyllium canicula*; the dog-fish.
ROUGHISH, [ruf'-ish], *adj.* rather rough.
ROUGHLY, [ruf'-li], *adv.* in a rough manner; brusquely; approximately, in a general way.
ROUGHNESS, [ruf'-nes], *n.* the quality of being rough.
ROUGH-RIDER, [ruf'-rīd'-er], *n.* one who breaks in horses; one who rides unbroken horses.
ROUGH-SHOD, [ruf'-shod'], *adj.* shod with shoes of which the nail-heads project; **to ride r. over**, to flout.
ROUGH-WROUGHT, [ruf'-rawt], *adj.* coarsely executed.

ROULADE, [rōōl-ahd′], *n.* (*mus.*) in singing, a run of short notes. [Fr. *roulade*].
ROULEAU, [rōōl-ō′], *n.* a little roll of coins neatly wrapped in paper; a roll; a piping or trimming in the form of a tight roll. [Fr. *rouleau* roll].
ROULETTE, [rōōl-et′], *n.* a game of chance employing a revolving disk and ball; a wheeled instrument for making a dotted line or series of punctures. [Fr. *roulette* little wheel].
ROULETTED, [rōō-let′-id], *adj.* of postage stamps, etc., prepared for separation by means of a roulette (as distinct from being "perforated" by means of a punch).
ROUMANIAN, see RUMANIAN.
ROUNCE, [rownts], *n.* (*typ.*) the handle in a hand printing press by which the bed is moved under the platen. [Du. *ronds*].
ROUND (1), [rownd], *n.* that which is round, e.g., a circle or sphere; that which goes or passes round, a passage round; a series of events or duties coming back to the beginning again; a walk of surveillance, a beat; a daily series of visits; a dance in a ring; a turn in a boxing match; (*milit.*) a general discharge of firearms in which each soldier fires once; ammunition for firing once; (*mus.*) a short composition in three or more parts, each starting at the beginning.
ROUND (2), [rownd], *adj.* having every part of the surface at an equal distance from the centre; having the form of a circle, sphere, ball or cylinder; plump, well-rounded; having a curved form; approximately calculated; positive; candid, free or plain in speech; **r. dance**, a dance in which the dancers are ranged in a circle; **r. game**, a game, particularly at cards, in which an indefinite number of players can take part each on his own account; **r. number**, a number that ends with a cipher. [OFr. *rond* from L. *rotundus*].
ROUND (3), [rownd], *adv.* on all sides, circularly, not in a direct line; from one side or party to another.
ROUND (4), [rownd], *prep.* with circular movement or encirclement about.
ROUND (5), [rownd], *v.t.* to make round; to make circular, spherical, cylindrical; to encircle; to move round or about; to make full, smooth, flowing; *v.i.* to grow or become round; to become complete, full; to develop into the full type; **to r. off**, to finish, to put the final touch to; **to r. up**, to collect together.
ROUNDABOUT (1), [rownd′-a-bowt], *n.* a merry-go-round; a circular enclosure at crossroads round which all traffic must pass in one direction.
ROUNDABOUT (2), [rownd′-a-bowt], *adj.* indirect; not straightforward.
ROUNDABOUT (3), [rownd′-a-bowt], *prep.* around and about.
ROUNDARM, [rownd′-ahm], *n.* (*cricket*) a style of bowling in which the arm turns at shoulder level.
ROUND-BACKED, [rownd′-bakt′], *adj.* having a round back; round-shouldered.
ROUNDEL, [rown′-del], *n.* a round figure, a circle; a round Norman shield; (*fort.*) a semicircular bastion; (*poet.*) a roundelay. [OF. *rondel*].
ROUNDELAY, [rown′-del-ā], *n.* a simple song with refrain. [OFr. *rondelet*].
ROUNDERS, [rownd′-erz], *n.*(*pl.*) a ball-game played with a ball and a short stick in which the players try to make a round of a number of bases after striking the ball; an early type of baseball.
ROUND-HAND, [rownd′-hand], *n.* a bold, well-rounded style of penmanship.
ROUNDHEAD, [rownd′-hed], *n.* a nickname given to the Puritans by the Cavaliers in the Civil War from their close-cropped hair.
ROUNDHOUSE, [rownd′-hows], *n.* the circular building, usually of wood, round the post of a windmill; †a constable's prison; (*in a ship*) lavatory and water-closet for the use of officers; †a cabin under the poop; the cabins on deck.
ROUNDING (1), [rownd′-ing], *n.* anything that is rounded; (*naut.*) spun-yarn wound round a rope to prevent its chafing; the act of one who rounds.
ROUNDING (2), [rownd′-ing], *adj.* †surrounding; circular; roundish.
ROUNDISH, [rownd′-ish], *adj.* somewhat round.
ROUNDISHNESS, [rownd′-ish-nes], *n.* the condition of being nearly round or roundish.
ROUNDLET, [rownd′-let], *n.* a small, circular clump or group. [OFr. *rondelet*].
ROUNDLY, [rownd′-li], *adv.* in a round manner; in a downright, outspoken fashion.
ROUNDNESS, [rownd′-nes], *n.* the condition or quality of being round.
ROUND-ROBIN, [rownd′-rob′-in], *n.* a petition with signatures arranged in a ring. [ROUND (2) and ~RIBBON].
ROUND-SHOT, [rownd′-shot′], *n.* spherical cannon balls.
ROUND-SHOULDERED, [rownd′-shōld′-erd], *adj.* having round shoulders or a rounded back.
ROUNDSMAN, [rowndz′-man], *n.* one who goes the rounds from house to house.
ROUND-TOWER, [rownd′-tow′-er], *n.* a kind of ancient tower; *n.*(*pl.*) ancient towers, found chiefly in Ireland, of a tall, tapering structure, and with a conical top, erected near a church or monastery, and presumably of Christian origin.
ROUND TRIP, [rownd′-trip′], *n.* a journey to one's destination and back; **r. ticket**, a return ticket.
ROUND-UP (1), [rownd′-up], *n.* the herding of cattle or other animals into large groups to brand them, pick out the young, etc.; any forcible collecting together of a group of people.
ROUND-UP (2), [rownd′-up′], *v.t.* to drive together for capture and confinement.
ROUP (1), [rōōp], *n.* a disease found among poultry. [Unkn.].
ROUP (2), [rowp], *n.* (*Scots*) an auction sale, *esp.* one held under warrant of the court. [~OIcel. *raupa*].
ROUPY, [rōōp′-i], *adj.* (of poultry) having the roup.
ROUSE (1), [rowz], *n.* a carouse. [~CAROUSE].
ROUSE (2), [rowz], *v.t.* to startle (game) and cause it to rise; to wake up, stir up, to agitate, to startle; *v.i.* to awake. [Uncert.].
ROUSEABOUT, [rowz′-a-bowt], *n.* (*Australian slang*) a station-hand; an odd man on a sheep farm.
ROUSER, [rowz′-er], *n.* a person or thing that rouses.
ROUSING, [rowz′-ing], *adj.* stirring, exciting, stimulating; great; violent.
ROUSINGLY, [rowz′-ing-li], *adv.* in a rousing fashion.
ROUST, [rowst], *v.t.* (*dial.* and *U.S.*) to drive out, rout. [ROUSE (2)].
ROUSTABOUT, [rowst′-a-bowt], *n.* (*U.S. coll.*) a hand on a barge or other river boat, a deck-hand.
ROUT (1), [rowt], *n.* a clamorous multitude, a tumultuous crowd, uproar; †a large evening party; (*leg.*) the assembly and attempt of three or more people to avenge some common wrong; the defeat and flight of an army in confusion. [OFr. *route*].
ROUT (2), [rowt], *v.t. and i.* to dig up with the snout (of swine); to root up; to drive (a person out of bed, the house, etc.). [~ROOT (3)].
ROUT (3), [rowt], *v.t.* to defeat heavily, to put to flight in confusion.
ROUTE (1), [root, rowt], *n.* a way, course travelled; an itinerary; (*milit.*) the order to change quarters; **en r.**, during the journey, on the way; **r.-march**, a long military march in column. [Fr. *route*].
ROUTE (2), (**routeing, routed**), [rōōt, rowt], *v.t.* to plan, map, the course to be travelled. [*Prec.*].
ROUTER, (rowt′-er], *n.* (*carp.*) a grooving plane.
ROUTINE, [rōōt-ēn′], *n.* a round or course of duties regularly or frequently returning; fixed habit of proceeding; organization. [Fr. *routine*].

ROUTER

ROUTINIST, [rōōt-ēn′-ist], *n.* one who follows a routine.
ROUX, [rōō], *n.* a preparation of butter and flour used to thicken soups and gravies. [Fr. *roux*].
ROVE, [rōv], *v.i.* to wander about at large; to ramble, roam; (*fig.*) of the attention, the eye, etc.; to move restlessly. [ROVER].
ROVE-BEETLE, [rōv′-bētl], *n.* one of the cocktail beetles of the *Staphylinidæ*.
ROVER, [rōv′-er], *n.* one who roves; a senior grade of boy scout; one who leads a roving life, *esp.* at sea; a pirate, a privateer. [MDu. *rover*].
ROVING (1), [rōv′-ing], *n. and adj.* wandering or rambling; in archery, shooting at a random target; giving the first twist to cotton thread in spinning.
ROVING (2), [rōv′-ing], *adj.* that roves; **r. commission**, a commission that leaves the person to whom it is entrusted full liberty to travel or do what seems best fitted to execute the commission.
ROVINGLY, [rōv′-ing-li], *adv.* in a roving fashion.
ROW (1), [rō], *n.* a series of persons or things arranged in line; a line, rank, file. [OE. *raw*].
ROW (2), [rō], *n.* a trip in a rowing boat. [ROW (4)].
ROW (3), [row], *n.* a noisy disturbance; a riot; a quarrel. [~ROWDY].

ROW (4), [rō], *v.t.* *and* *i.* to propel or move along the surface of water by oars or sculls; to transport by rowing; **to r. out**, to exhaust by rowing. [OE. *rowan*].

ROW (5), [row], *v.t.* to quarrel with, upbraid noisily.

ROWAN, [rō'-an], *n.* the mountain ash tree, *Pyrus Aucuparia*; the berry of this tree. [Norw. *roun*].

ROWDILY, [row'-di-li], *adv.* in a rowdy manner.

ROWDINESS, [row'-di-nes], *n.* the state or quality of being rowdy; noisy behaviour.

ROWDY (1), [row'-di], *n.* a noisy turbulent fellow. [Uncert.].

ROWDY (2), [row'-di], *adj.* noisy, causing a noisy disturbance; unruly.

ROWDYISM, [row'-di-izm], *n.* rude, turbulent conduct.

ROWEL (1), [row'-el], *n.* the sharply spiked wheel of a spur; a flat ring on horses' bits; a seton made of hair or silk to pass through the flesh of horses. [OFr. *rouel*].

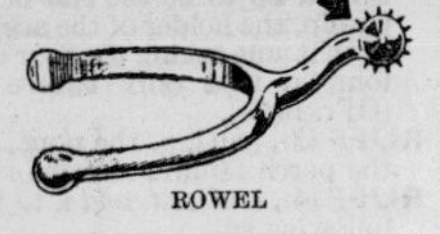

ROWEL

ROWEL (2), (**rowelling, rowelled**), [row'-el], *v.t.* to insert a rowel in the skin of (a horse).

ROWEN, [row'-en], *n.* a second crop of grass; a field kept until after Michaelmas for its grass. [Uncert.].

ROWER, [rō'-er], *n.* a person who rows a boat.

ROWING, [rō'-ing], *n.* the act of propelling a boat with oars or sculls.

ROWLOCK, [rul'-ok], *n.* that part of a boat's gunwale, or the crutch, which provides a fulcrum for an oar. [OE. *arloc* oar lock, influenced by ROW (4)].

ROWPORT, [rō'-pawt], *n.* (*naut.*) a port-hole on a small vessel used for working an oar.

ROXBURGHE, [roks'-brur], *n.* a cloth or paper binding for books with a leather back and rough edges. [The third Duke of *Roxburghe* who used this style].

ROYAL (1), [roi'-al], *n.* a gold coin formerly current in England; a large size of paper; a stag with twelve or more tines; (*naut.*) the sail immediately above the topgallant; (in vingt-et-un) an ace with a court-card of the same suit.

ROYAL (2), [roi'-al], *adj.* pertaining to a king or the crown, regal; noble; generous. [OFr. *roial* from L. *regalis*].

ROYALISM, [roi'-al-izm], *n.* attachment to a system of kingly government.

ROYALIST, [roi'-al-ist], *n.* a supporter of a king, line of kings, or kingly government *esp.* in the reigns of Charles I and II; an adherent of their house.

ROYALIZE, [roi'-al-īz], *v.t.* to make royal; *v.i.* to assume the rôle of king.

ROYALLY, [roi'-al-i], *adv.* in a royal manner; magnificently and with dignity.

ROYAL-MAST, [roi-al-mahst'], *n.* (*naut.*) the mast immediately above the topgallant.

ROYALTY, [roi'-al-ti], *n.* the character, state, office, or person of a king; royal domains; one of a royal family; proprietary right of part profit; payment to an author of a part of the price of each copy sold, or to a writer of plays for each performance, or to a proprietor of a patent for each specified number of articles sold under it; (*pl.*) †the rights or prerogatives of a king or superior; emblems of royalty. [OFr. *roialté*].

RUB (1), [rub], *n.* the act of rubbing; friction; something that makes motion or progress difficult or painful; difficulty; obstruction; sarcasm, gibe.

RUB (2), (**rubbing, rubbed**), [rub], *v.t.* to apply friction to the surface of; to wipe, clean, polish, scour; to massage; *v.i.* to move (along) with pressure; to chafe; to get along with difficulty; **to r. down**, to clean by rubbing; **to r. off**, to clean off by rubbing; **to r. out**, to erase; **to r. up**, to cause to shine by rubbing; **to r. up the wrong way**, to irritate; **to r. along**, to get along fairly well. [ME. *rubben*].

RUB-A-DUB, [rub'-a-dub'], *n.* the beats of a drum. [Echoic].

RUBASSE, [rōō-bas'], *n.* rock-crystal filled with bright red spangles.

RUBATO, [rōōb-ah'-to], *n.* (*mus.*) lengthening and proportionally curtailing adjacent notes in order to make the rhythm more flexible. [It. (*tempo*) *rubato*, robbed time].

RUBBER, [rub'-er], *n.* one who, or that which, rubs; the instrument or thing used in rubbing or cleaning; a whetstone; a coarse file; at cards, a series of games or hands, ended when one side has won most of them; an elastic material, sometimes called india-rubber, made from the coagulated latex of certain trees; (*pl.*) overshoes made of rubber. [RUB (2)].

RUBBERNECK, [rub'-er-nek'], *n.* (*U.S. slang*) a gaping, prying person, a sightseer.

RUBBING, [rub'-ing], *n.* the reproduction of a raised or incised design by means of rubbing superimposed paper with chalk, heel-ball, etc.; friction; the act of one who rubs.

RUBBISH, [rub'-ish], *n.* fragments of buildings or any structure, ruins; waste matter; anything useless. [Uncert.].

RUBBISHING, [rub'-ish-ing], *adj.* rubbishy, worthless.

RUBBISHY, [rub'-ish-i], *adj.* pertaining to rubbish; worthless.

RUBBLE, [rubl], *n.* rough undressed stones; old building materials used again; débris left by the destruction of a building, etc.; (*geol.*) a mass of rock fragments often found beneath alluvium. [Uncert.].

RUBBLE-STONE, [rubl'-stōn], *n.* the upper fragmentary and decomposed parts of a mass of stone.

RUBBLE-WORK, [rubl'-wurk], *n.* coarse walling constructed of rough stones; rubble mixed with mortar and used for filling in cracks.

RUBBLY, [rub'-li], *adj.* containing rubble.

RUBE, [rōōb], *n.* (*U.S.*) a country bumpkin. [*Reuben* a Christian name].

RUBEFACIENT (1), [rōōb-i-fā'-shi-ent], *n.* a rubefacient substance.

RUBEFACIENT (2), [rōōb-i-fā'-shi-ent], *adj.* (*med.*) of the nature of a counter-irritant, producing redness or inflammation of the skin. [L. *rubefacere* to make red].

RUBEFACTION, [rōōb-i-fak'-shun], *n.* (*med.*) the reddening of the skin caused by rubefacients.

RUBELLA, [rōōb-el'-a], *n.* (*path.*) German measles, so called from the redness of the spots. [L. *rubellus* red].

RUBELLAN, [rōōb-el'-an], *n.* (*min.*) an altered form of biotite. [*Prec.*].

RUBELLITE, [rōōb-el'-īt], *n.* (*min.*) a form of pink tourmaline.

RUBEOLA, [rōōb-i-ōl'-a], *n.* (*path.*) †measles; German measles.

RUBEROID, [rōōb'-er-oid], *n.* (*prot.*) a bituminized felt for roofing, etc. [RUBBER and Gk. *oeides* like].

RUBESCENT, [rōōb-es'-ent], *adj.* turning red; blushing. [~L. *rubescens*].

RUBEZAHL, [rōōb'-et-zahl], *n.* a mischievous mountain sprite appearing in German fairylore. [Germ. *Rubezahl*].

RUBIA, [rōōb'-i-a], *n.* (*bot.*) the genus of plants including *Rubia tinctorum*, madder. [L. *rubia* madder].

RUBIAN, [rōōb'-i-an], *n.* the colouring principle of madder-root.

RUBICELLE, [rōōb'-is-el'], *n.* a stone like a ruby of an orange-red colour. [Fr. *rubicelle*].

RUBICON, [rōōb'-ik-on], *n.* a river in Italy, the crossing of which by Caesar, on a certain occasion, was tantamount to a declaration of war against the Republic; **crossing the R.**, the taking of any decisive or momentous step.

RUBICUND, [rōōb'-ik-und], *adj.* inclined to redness; ruddy, highly coloured; red-faced. [L. *rubicundus*].

RUBICUNDITY, [rōōb'-ik-und'-it-i], *n.* the condition of being rubicund.

RUBICUNDNESS, [rōōb'-ik-und-nes], *n.* rubicundity.

RUBIDIUM, [rōōb-id'-i-um], *n.* a soft metal of the potassium group, so named from the two red lines in its spectrum. [L. *rubidus* red].

RUBIED, [rōōb'-id], *adj.* ruby-coloured.

RUBIFIC, [rōōb-if'-ik], *adj.* making red. [~L. *rubificus*].

RUBIFICATION, [rōōb'-if-ik-ā'-shun], *n.* the action of making red.

RUBIFY, [rōōb'-i-fī], *v.t.* to make red.

RUBIGINOUS, [rōōb-ij'-in-us], *adj.* rust-coloured; †mildewed. [L. *rubigo* rust].

RUBRIC, [rōōb'-rik], *n.* writing in red ink, pencil, etc.; a heading to a paragraph in a prayer-book, legal code, etc., *esp.* when printed or written in red; an instruction contained in such a heading. [Fr. *rubrique* from L. *rubrica* red ochre].

RUBRICAL, [rōōb'-rik-al], *adj.* marked with red; pertaining to a rubric or rubrics.

RUBRICATE, [rōōb'-rik-āt], *v.t.* to write, decorate, or print in red letters. [L. *rubricare*].

RUBRICIAN, [rōōb-rish'-an], *n.* a student of ecclesiastical rubrics; one who advocates or observes the strict interpretation of these rubrics.

ō (bone), ī (fine), ōō (food), ŏŏ (put), u (up), th (think), TH (that), zh (azure), † = obsolete, ~ = related to.

RUBSTONE, [rub'-stōn], *n.* a kind of whetstone used for sharpening instruments.
RUBY (1), [rōōb'-i], *n.* a precious stone, a kind of corundum of a carmine-red colour; anything red; redness; a carbuncle; (*print.*) a small-sized type. [OFr. *rubi*].
RUBY (2), [rōōb'-i], *adj.* red like the ruby.
RUCHE, [rōōsh], *n.* a pleated frilling, usually of lace material; a ruffle. [Fr. *ruche* beehive, frill].
RUCK (1), [ruk], *n.* a wrinkle, ridge, *esp.* in material. [OIcel. *hrukka*].
RUCK (2), [ruk], *n.* a heap; a crowd, throng; the losing horses that come in a group behind the winners of a race. [ME. *ruke*].
RUCK (3), [ruk], *v.t. and i.* to wrinkle, crease; to pucker or gather into small folds.
RUCKLE, [rukl], *v.t.* to ruck, wrinkle, crease. [Norw. *rukle* wrinkle].
RUCKSACK, [rook'-sak], *n.* a kind of knapsack carried on the back by straps round the shoulders. [Germ. *rucksack*].
RUCTATION, [ruk-tāsh'-un], *n.* belching. [L. *ructatio*].
RUCTION, [ruk'-shun], *n.* (*dial.*) an uproar, disturbance, row. [Uncert.].
RUDD, [rud], *n.* a freshwater fish with red fins, called also the red-eye, a species of *Leuciscus*. [OE. *rudu* red].
RUDDER, [rud'-er], *n.* the vertical plate at the stern of a ship or aeroplane by which it is steered; that which guides or governs the course of anything; the tail-feathers of a bird with which it steers its flight. [OE. *rother* rudder].
RUDDERFISH, [rud'-er-fish], *n.* the popular name of several species of fish, so called because they follow ships.
RUDDERLESS, [rud'-er-les], *adj.* without a rudder; (*fig.*) directionless.
RUDDIED, [ru'-did], *adj.* made ruddy.
RUDDLE, REDDLE†(1), [rudl], *n.* red ochre used for marking sheep. [OE. *reod* red].
RUDDLE, REDDLE† (2), [rudl], *v.t.* to mark or dye with ruddle.
RUDDLE-MAN, REDDLE-MAN†, [rudl'-man], *n.* a man who digs or hawks ruddle.
RUDDINESS, [rud'-i-nes], *n.* the condition of being ruddy.
RUDDOCK, [rud'-ok], *n.* (*dial.*) the robin. [OE. *rudduc*].
RUDDY, [ru'-di], *adj.* of a bright red colour; fresh complexioned; (*slang*) great, offensive, unmitigated. [OE. *rudig*].
RUDE, [rōōd], *adj.* rough, rustic, uncouth; unlettered; untaught; boorish, ill-mannered, discourteous. [OFr. *rude* from L. *rudis* unformed].
RUDELY, [rōōd'-li], *adv.* in a rude manner, discourteously.
RUDENESS, [rōōd'nes], *n.* the quality of being rude; discourteousness.
RUDENTURE, [rōōd-en'-cher], *n.* (*arch.*) the figure of a rope or staff, with which the flutings of columns are sometimes filled to strengthen the sides. [Fr. *rudenture*].
RUDIMENT, [rōōd'i-ment], *n.* a thing in its first stages, a preliminary step; an unformed, embryonic thing; (*pl.*) the preliminary stages of a subject, the foundations or elementary first principles. [L. *rudimentum* beginning].
RUDIMENTAL, [rōōd'-i-ment'-al], *adj.* rudimentary.
RUDIMENTARY, [rōōd'-i-ment'-er-i], *adj.* pertaining to the rudiments; primitive, undeveloped.
RUDOLPHINE, [rōōd-ol'-fin], *adj.* describing the astronomical tables published by Kepler in 1627. [*Rudolf* II of Austria, Kepler's patron].
RUE (1), [rōō], *n.* a strong-smelling evergreen plant, *Ruta graveolens*. [Fr. *rue*].
RUE (2), [rōō], *n.* sorrow, remorse, pity. [OE. *hreow*].
RUE (3), [rōō], *v.t.* to lament, to repent, feel penitence for; to fill with remorse, cause to repent; *v.i.* to repent, regret. [OE. *hreowan*].
RUEFUL, [rōō'-fōōl], *adj.* remorseful, regretful, doleful.
RUEFULLY, [rōō'-fōōl-i], *adv.* in a rueful fashion.
RUEFULNESS, [rōō'-fōōl-nes], *n.* the condition of being rueful.
RUELLE, [rōō-el'], *n.* the narrow space between the wall and the bed; a bedroom where in the eighteenth century fashionable ladies held morning receptions; a reception; a côterie. [Fr. *ruelle* little street].
RUFESCENT, [rōōf-es'-ent], *adj.* somewhat reddish-brown, tinged with reddish-brown. [L. *rufescens*].
RUFF (1), [ruf], *n.* a pleated linen collar worn round the neck; something puckered or pleated; a bird allied to the sandpipers, a species of *Machetes*, having a ruff of feathers round its neck; a species of pigeon with a ruff of feathers.

RUFF

RUFF (2), [ruf], *n.* the act of trumping; the old game of cards from which whist is derived, in which twelve cards were dealt to each player and the top card of the remaining four was turned up to be the ruff or trump, the holder of the ace of that suit taking the four cards, and throwing down four so that only twelve tricks were obtainable. [OFr. *roffe*].
RUFF (3), [ruf], *n.* the pope, a small freshwater fish of the perch family, *Acerina vulgaris*. [ROUGH (2)].
RUFF (4), [ruf], *v.t. and i.* to trump at cards in place of following suit.
RUFF (5), [ruf], *v.t.* to make into ruffs; to disorder, ruffle.
RUFFED, [ruft], *adj.* having a ruff; ruffled.
RUFFIAN, [ruf'-i-an], *n.* a low and violent fellow; a desperate character. [OFr. *rufien*].
RUFFIANISH, [ruf'-i-an-ish], *adj.* ruffianly.
RUFFIANISM, [ruf'-i-an-izm], *n.* ruffianly behaviour.
RUFFIANLY, [ruf'-i-an-li], *adj.* of, or like, a ruffian.
RUFFLE (1), [rufl], *n.* a strip of fine cloth pleated and attached to some border of a garment; small ruffs worn round the wrist or neck; disturbance; agitation.
RUFFLE (2), [rufl], *n.* a subdued roll on the drums. [Echoic].
RUFFLE (3), [rufl], *v.t.* to disorder, disturb something smooth, even; to agitate, disturb; to furnish with ruffles; *v.i.* to stir, flutter, to grow rough. [Uncert.].
RUFFLEMENT, [rufl'-ment], *n.* the action of ruffling.
RUFFLER, [rufl'-er], *n.* a low swaggering bully.
RUFFLING, [rufl'-ing], *n.* the action of disturbing; commotion.
RUFOUS, [rōōf'-us], *adj.* of a red-brown colour. [L. *rufus* red].
RUG, [rug], *n.* a large piece of thick woollen cloth, used as a wrap or coverlet for the feet or on a bed; a mat of wool, fur, etc., for the floor; a rough, woolly or shaggy dog. [Scand. *rug*].
RUGATE, [rōōg'-āt], *adj.* wrinkled. [L. *ruga* wrinkle].
RUGBEIAN, [rug'-bē'-an], *n.* a past or present pupil of Rugby School.
RUGBY, [rug'-bi], *n.* a type of football. [*Rugby* School, where this game was first played].
RUGGED, [rug'-id], *adj.* rough, rocky, craggy; strong and rough; (of features) strongly marked; (of character) strong and without superficial refinement. [RUG].
RUGGEDLY, [rug'-id-li], *adv.* in a rugged fashion.
RUGGEDNESS, [rug'-id-nes], *n.* the state of being rugged.
RUGGER, [rug'-er], *n.* (*coll.*) Rugby football.
RUGOSE, [rōōg'-ōs], *adj.* (*biol.*) wrinkled, ridgy. [L. *rugosus*].
RUGOSITY, [rōōg-os'-i-ti], *n.* (*biol.*) the state or quality of being rugose.
RUIN (1), [rōō'-in], *n.* destruction, overthrow; that which is destroyed or overthrown; physical or moral deterioration or destruction; (*pl.*) the remains of anything decayed or partly demolished, *esp.* a building. [OFr. *ruine* from L. *ruina*].
RUIN (2), [rōō-in], *v.t.* to demolish, destroy, overthrow, spoil; to impoverish; to destroy morally.
RUINATE, [rōō'-in-āt], *v.t.* to bring to ruin. [L. *ruinare*].
RUINATION, [rōō-in-ā'-shun], *n.* the act or means of ruining; that which is ruined.
RUINED, [rōō'-ind], *adj.* destroyed; in ruins.
RUINER, [rōō'-in-er], *n.* one who, or that which, ruins.
RUINIFORM, [rōō-in'-i-fawm], *adj.* (*min.*) looking like ruins.
RUINOUS, [rōō'-in-us], *adj.* fallen into ruins; bringing to ruin; disastrous; (*coll.*) exorbitant. [L. *ruinosus*].
RUINOUSLY, [rōō'-in-us-li], *adv.* in a ruinous fashion.
RUINOUSNESS, [rōō'-in-us-nes], *n.* the condition or quality of being ruinous, of bringing to ruin.

RULE (**1**), [rōōl], *n.* an established principle regulating conduct or the running of institutions, etc.; government, regulation; custom, habit; routine; an accepted regulation in a game; an instrument for drawing and measuring lines; (*gram.*) an established form of construction in a particular class of words or in syntax; (*math.*) a determinate method for performing any operation and producing certain results; (*leg.*) an order made by a court of justice for regulating a certain case in question; **r. of the road,** the rules prescribed in the Highway Code; **r. of thumb,** a system worked out by practical experience; **slide r.,** a ruler divided into scales and having slides for facilitating calculation. [L. *regula*].

RULE (**2**), [rōōl], *v.t.* to govern, sway, manage, regulate; to settle as by rule; to determine; to mark lines with a rule; *v.i.* to have power or command; (*comm.*) to stand or maintain a certain level; **to r. the roost,** (*coll.*) to be master of the situation, to be top dog. [L. *regulare*].

RULER, [rōōl'-er], *n.* one who rules; an instrument of wood, metal, etc., for ruling lines and for measuring, a rule.

RULING (**1**), [rōōl'-ing], *n.* a regulation, an authoritative decision.

RULING (**2**), [rōōl'-ing], *adj.* that rules; dominating.

RULINGLY, [rōōl'-ing-li], *adv.* by way of rule.

RULLEY, [rul'-i], *n.* a four-wheeled dray. [Uncert.].

RUM (**1**), [rum], *n.* a spirituous liquor distilled from sugar cane. [Uncert.].

RUM (**2**), [rum], *adj.* (*slang*) odd, strange, queer. [Uncert.].

RUMAL, [rum'-al], *n.* a veil or kerchief. [Hind. *rumal*].

RUMANIAN, ROUMANIAN (**1**), [rōōm-ā'-ni-an], *n.* the language, or a native inhabitant, of Rumania.

RUMANIAN, ROUMANIAN (**2**), [rōōm-ā'-ni-an], *adj.* of, or pertaining to, Rumania, its language or inhabitants.

RUMBA, see RHUMBA.

RUMBLE (**1**), [rumbl], *n.* a low, dull, continuous sound; the back part of a carriage used for an extra seat or for luggage; a dickey.

RUMBLE (**2**), [rumbl], *v.i.* to make a low, dull, continuous sound by rolling along heavily; *v.t.* (*slang*) to understand, see through. [ME. *romblen*].

RUMBLER, [rumbl'-er], *n.* that which rumbles.

RUMBLE-TUMBLE, [rumbl'-tumbl'], *n.* a vehicle that rumbles; a rumbling motion.

RUMBLING (**1**), [rumb'-ling], *n.* a rumbling sound.

RUMBLING (**2**), [rumb'-ling], *adj.* that rumbles, causing vehicles to rumble.

RUMBLINGLY, [rumb'-ling-li], *adv.* in a rumbling manner.

RUM-BUD, [rum'-bud], *n.* (*coll.*) a redness of the nose or face arising from excessive drinking of alcoholic liquors.

RUMBUSTIOUS, [rum-bus'-chus], *adj.* (*coll.*) boisterous, hilarious. [~ROBUST].

RUMEN, [rōō'-men'], *n.* the first and biggest stomach of a ruminant. [L. *rumen* throat].

RUMINANT (**1**), [rōō'-min-ant], *n.* an animal of the *Ruminantia,* like the cow, that chews the cud.

RUMINANT (**2**), [rōō'-min-ant], *adj.* chewing the cud; (*fig.*) thoughtful. [~L. *ruminari*].

RUMINANTLY, [rōō'-min-ant-li], *adv.* in a ruminant manner.

RUMINATE, [rōō'-min-āt], *v.i.* to chew the cud; (*fig.*) to consider deeply, turn thoughts over repeatedly in the mind. [L. *ruminari*].

RUMINATINGLY, [rōō'-min-āt'-ing-li], *adv.* in ruminating fashion.

RUMINATION, [rōō'-min-ā'-shun], *n.* the action of ruminating.

RUMINATOR, [rōō'-min-āt-or], *n.* one who ruminates.

RUMMAGE (**1**), [rum'-ij], *n.* the action of rummaging; things brought to light by rummaging; lumber. [OFr. *arromage* stowing goods in a hold].

RUMMAGE (**2**), [rum'-ij], *v.t.* to ransack; to find in rummaging; *v.i.* to tumble things about indiscriminately in searching.

RUMMAGER, [rum'-ij-er], *n.* a person who rummages.

RUMMER, [rum'-er], *n.* a kind of deep glass or cup; a glass spoon or stirrer. [Du. *romer*].

RUMMILY, [rum'-i-li], *adv.* (*slang*) in a peculiar manner; oddly.

RUMMY (**1**), [rum'-i], *n.* an American card game for two or more players. [Unkn.].

RUMMY (**2**), [rum'-i], *adj.* (*slang*) queer, odd. [RUM (2)].

RUMNESS, [rum'-nes], *n.* (*slang*) the quality of being rum or peculiar.

RUMOUR, [rōōm'-er], *n.* hearsay, gossip; popular report; a current story not based on definite facts. [L. *rumor* noise].

RUMOURER, [rōōm'-er-er], *n.* a person who circulates rumours.

RUMP, [rump], *n.* the hindquarters; the buttocks. [ME. *rumpe*].

RUMPLE, [rumpl], *v.t.* to crease up, tousle, crumple. [MDu. *rompelen*].

RUMPLESS, [rump'-les], *adj.* without a rump.

RUMPSTEAK, [rump'-stāk'], *n.* a cut of beefsteak from near the animal's rump.

RUMPUS, [rump'-us], *n.* (*slang*) a row, quarrel. [Unkn.].

RUM-SHRUB, [rum'-shrub], *n.* a drink, the basis of which is rum.

RUM-TUM, [rum'-tum'], *n.* a one-man sculling boat used on the lower Thames. [Uncert.].

RUN (**1**), [run], *n.* the action of running on foot or in a vehicle; the swift movement of a vehicle; a voyage, trip, journey; a slope for a vehicle to run down; successful course; a continuous flow (of); a period of some length; rush, eager call on; a continuous stretch of land used for animals or fowls; a hole caused by a dropped stitch in knitted materials; the ordinary type, average; (*cricket*) a point scored by, the act of, running successfully from one wicket to the other; (*comm.*) an uncommon pressure on a bank for payment; (*mus.*) a rapid series of notes for the voice or instrument; (*aeron.*) the sweep of a bomber on its target; **in the long r.,** in the end, as a whole; **to have a r. for one's money,** to get fun or benefit out of one's efforts or expenditure.

RUN (**2**), (**running, ran**), [run], *v.t.* to drive, force; to cause to run; to fuse, to cast; to incur; to take on, venture; to thrust; to draw; to discharge; to smuggle; *v.i.* to pass swiftly over the ground on the legs, or in a vehicle; to sail; to rush violently; to spread, extend; to slide; to move quickly; to work, to turn round (of machinery); to contend in a role or competition; to flee; to discharge matter; to press with numerous demands; to continue in operation; (*fig.*) to pursue in thought; **to r. after,** to pursue, pester; **to r. at,** to attack; **to r. up against,** to collide with; to meet by chance; **to r. down,** to run over, cause to sink; (*fig.*) to depreciate; **to r. on,** to go on endlessly, babble incessantly; **to r. out of,** to come to an end of, exhaust; **to r. over,** to overflow; to knock down and move over in a vehicle; (*fig.*) to cast the eye rapidly over; **to r. riot,** to behave in a completely disorderly manner; (of flowers) grow in riotous profusion; **to r. through,** to look quickly over; to waste, spend up; **to r. up,** to go for a brief visit; incur; **also ran,** was in the contest but not successful, also of a person only moderately successful; **to r. in,** (*mech.*) to put into gentle motion prior to using; (*slang*) to arrest.

RUNABOUT, [run'-a-bowt], *n.* a person who runs about from place to place; a light unreliable person; a light inexpensive motor-car.

RUNAGATE†, [run'-a-gāt], *n.* a deserter, fugitive; apostate. [~RENEGADE].

RUNAWAY (**1**), [run'-a-wā], *n.* one who, or that which, has run away; a fugitive; a horse that has bolted.

RUNAWAY (**2**), [run'-a-wā], *adj.* having run away, bolted; **r. marriage,** an elopement; **r. victory,** (*sport*) a win by overwhelming odds.

RUNCINATE, [run'-sin-āt], *adj.* (*biol.*) having serrations curving backwards or downwards. [L. *runcina* a plane].

RUNDLE, [rundl], *n.* a rung of a ladder, a wooden cylinder. [~ROUNDEL].

RUNDLET, [rund'-let], *n.* a little barrel holding about eighteen gallons. [~ROUNDEL].

RUNE, [rōōn], *n.* one of the characters of the early alphabet in use among the ancient Germanic peoples; a character or symbol supposed to have magical powers; a poem, song or verse, *esp.* Finnish. [OE. *run* secret].

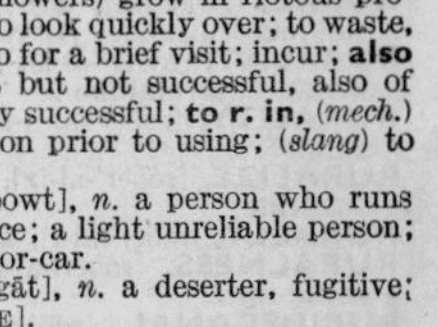

RUNES

RUNER†, [rōōn'-er], *n.* one who writes runes.

RUNG (**1**), [rung], *p.pt.* of RING.

RUNG (**2**), [rung], *n.* a step of a ladder; the cross rail on chair legs; the spoke of a wheel. [OE. *hrung*].

RUNIC (1), [rōōn'-ik], *n.* (*typ.*) a thick lettering used for display work.
RUNIC (2), [rōōn'-ik], *adj.* of, or pertaining to, runes.
RUNLET, [run'-let], *n.* a little stream, runnel.
RUNNEL, [run'-el], *n.* a small stream; a gutter. [OE. *rynel*].
RUNNER, [run'-er], *n.* one who, that which, runs; a racer; a messenger; a shoot from which roots grow; the name for certain climbing plants; the blade of a skate or sledge; the moving stone of a mill; a horse which runs in a race; **rum r.,** a smuggler of dutiable drink.
RUNNER-UP, [run'-er-up'], *n.* the second in a race, competition, or application for a post.
RUNNET, [run'-et], *n.* (*dial.*) rennet. [~RENNET].
RUNNING (1), [run'-ing], *n.* the act of passing with speed; racing; that which runs or flows; a discharge; **in the r.,** having a fair chance of success; **to make the r.,** to set the standard or pace.
RUNNING (2), [run'-ing], *adj.* that runs; flowing; continuous; discharging; **r. commentary,** a succession of comments accompanying any event; **r. fire,** a continuous rain of shots; **r. title,** the title in a book that reappears at the top of every (other) page.
RUNNING BOARD, [run'-ing-bawd], *n.* (*U.S.*) a foot-board on a locomotive; a foot-board for use as a step on either side of a motor-car.
RUNT, [runt], *n.* a variety of pigeon; a small thick-set ox; a person or animal stunted in growth, a dwarf. [Unkn.].
RUNWAY, [run'-wā'], *n.* a path or track; a (sloping) track prepared for the transfer of vehicles from their parking place, *esp.* of aircraft from their hangars.
RUPEE, [rōō'-pē], *n.* a silver coin, the Indian monetary unit. [Hind. *rupuja*].
RUPESTRAL, [rōōp-est'-ral], *adj.* living or growing on rocks.
RUPIA, [rōōp'-i-a], *n.* (*path.*) a severe skin disease. [Gk. *rupos* filth].
RUPTION, [rup'-shun], *n.* disturbance, breaking or bursting open. [Fr. *ruption*].
RUPTURE (1), [rup'-cher], *n.* the action of breaking or bursting; the state of being broken or violently parted; a quarrel, breach of friendship or amity; (*med.*) hernia. [L. *ruptura*].
RUPTURE (2), [rup'-cher], *v.t.* to burst; *v.i.* to suffer a breach or disruption; (*path.*) to produce a rupture, hernia.
RUPTUREWORT, [rup'-cher-wurt], *n.* the plant, *Herniaria glabra*, thought formerly to be a cure for rupture.
RURAL, [rōōer'-al], *adj.* pertaining to the country-side; agricultural. [L. *ruralis*].
RURALIST, [rōōer'-al-ist], *n.* a countryman; one in favour of a rural life.
RURALITY, [rōōer'-al'-i-ti], *n.* the quality of being rural.
RURALIZE, [rōōer'-al-īz], *v.t.* to make rural; *v.i.* to rusticate.
RURALLY, [rōōer'-al-i], *adv.* in a rural manner.
RURALNESS, [rōōer'-al-nes], *n.* the condition of being rural.
RURIDECANAL, [rōō'-ri-dek-ān'-al], *adj.* pertaining to a rural dean or his office.
RURITANIAN, [rōōer'-it-ān'-i-an], *adj.* of, pertaining to, or resembling, Ruritania, a fictitious Balkan kingdom used as the setting for modern romances of royal intrigue. [*Ruritania* in A. Hope's *The Prisoner of Zenda*].
RUSA, [rōōz-ah], *n.* a species of large-sized Indian deer. [Malay *rusa*].
RUSE, [rōōz], *n.* a trick, stratagem. [Fr. *ruse*].
RUSH (1), [rush], *n.* an aquatic plant of the genus *Juncus*, with a very pliant stem, used when dry for basket making, etc.; (*fig.*) any person or thing that is pliant, of little worth, unreliable. [OE. *rysc*].
RUSH (2), [rush], *n.* a moving forward in a burst of speed and energy; a run; a sudden outburst, a gush; great bustle and activity; **gold r.,** a sudden drive forward to reach the gold-fields.
RUSH (3), [rush], *v.t.* to cause to travel or act rapidly; to get over by going at high speed; to take by storm; to perform with very great haste; *v.i.* to press forward with vigour; to flow rapidly; to blow strongly; to enter impetuously; to come rapidly into the mind or on to the lips. [OFr. *rehusser*].
RUSH-BOTTOMED, [rush'-bot'-omd], *adj.* (of chairs) having a seat made of rush.
RUSH-CANDLE, [rush'-kandl'], *n.* a narrow taper made from the pith of a rush dipped in tallow.
RUSHEN, [rush'-en], *adj.* made of (woven) rushes.
RUSHER, [rush'-er], *n.* a person or thing that rushes; (*coll.*) an enterprising person.
RUSHINESS, [rush'-i-nes], *n.* the condition or quality of being rushy.
RUSHLIGHT, [rush'-līt], *n.* the light of a rush candle; (*fig.*) a mere glimmer of light.
RUSH-LIKE, [rush'-līk], *adj.* resembling a rush; pliant, weak.
RUSH-MAT, [rush'-mat'], *n.* a mat made of rushes woven together.
RUSHY, [rush'-i], *adj.* abounding in, made of, strewn with, rushes.
RUSK, [rusk], *n.* a kind of light, crusty biscuit or sweetened bread crisply baked throughout. [Sp. *rosca* roll].
RUSSET (1), [rus'-it], *n.* a red-brown colour; a coarse home-spun cloth; a kind of apple with a coarse reddish-brown skin. [L. *russus* red].
RUSSET (2), [rus'-it], *adj.* reddish-brown; of russet material.
RUSSETY, [rus'-it-i], *adj.* russet coloured.
RUSSIA LEATHER, [rush'-a-leTH'-er], *n.* a fine aromatic dyed leather impregnated with oil distilled from birch bark.
RUSSIAN (1), [rush'-an], *n.* a native of, the language of, Russia.
RUSSIAN (2), [rush'-an], *adj.* of, or pertaining to, Russia, its language or inhabitants.
RUSSIANIZATION, [rush'-an-īz-ā'-shun], *n.* the action or process of making Russian.
RUSSIANIZE, [rush'-an-īz], *v.t.* to make Russian, give Russian characteristics to.
RUSSIFICATION, [rus'-if-ik-ā'shun], *n.* the action of impregnating with Russian ideals or qualities.
RUSSIFY, [rus'-i-fī], *v.t.* to Russianize.
RUSSO-, *pref.* pertaining to Russia or the Russians. [~RUSSIA].
RUSSOPHIL(E), [rus'-ō-fil], *n.* a lover of Russia and Russian institutions. [RUSSO and Gk. *philos* love].
RUSSOPHILISM, [rus'-ō-fil-izm'] *n.* whole-hearted admiration for Russia and its institutions.
RUSSOPHOBE, [rus'-ō-fōb'], *n.* one who detests Russia and its institutions.
RUSSOPHOBIA, [rus'-ō-fōb'-i-a], *n.* hatred of Russia and its institutions. [RUSSO and Gk. *phobos* fear].
RUST (1), [rust], *n.* the red incrustation on iron, caused by its oxygenation under exposure to air and moisture; anything like rust; a disease of plants, due to fungi, and resembling rust in its manifestation; (*fig.*) mental dulness. [OE. *rust*].
RUST (2), [rust], *v.t.* to cause to contract rust; (*fig.*) to cause to degenerate, lose skill or dexterity; *v.i.* to contract rust; to grow rusty; (*fig.*) to degenerate mentally, grow stale; to lose one's skill.
RUSTIC (1), [rus'-tik], *n.* a countryman; an uneducated boor.
RUSTIC (2), [rus'-tik], *adj.* of, or pertaining to, the country; living in the country; rural; unpolished, uncouth; plain, simple, artless; (of woodwork) made of rough branches fastened together. [L. *rusticus*].
RUSTICALLY, [rus'-tik-al-i], *adv.* in a rustic manner.
RUSTICALNESS, [rus'-tik-al-nes], *n.* the condition of being rustic.
RUSTICATE, [rus'-tik-āt], *v.t.* to compel to live in the country; to banish for a time from a university as a punishment; *v.i.* to dwell in the country. [L. *rusticari*].
RUSTICATION, [rus'-tik-ā'-shun], *n.* the action of rusticating; the condition of being rusticated.
RUSTICITY, [rus-tis'-i-ti], *n.* the quality of being rustic.
RUSTILY, [rust'-i-li], *adv.* in a rusty fashion.
RUSTINESS, [rust'-i-nes], *n.* the condition of being rusty.
RUSTLE (1), [rusl], *n.* a soft crisp sound caused by the surfaces of dry yet pliable things rubbing together.
RUSTLE (2), [rusl], *v.t.* to make to rustle; (*U.S. slang*) to steal; *v.i.* to make a rustle; to move with the sound of rustling clothes. [Echoic].
RUSTLER, [rus'-ler], *n.* a person or thing that rustles; (*U.S. slang*) a cattle- or horse-thief.
RUSTLESS, [rust'-les], *adj.* without rust; that will not rust.
RUSTPROOF, [rust'-prōōf], *adj.* proof against rust.
RUSTY, [rust'-i], *adj.* covered with rust; affected by rust; (*fig.*) out of practice; brownish-red; **to cut up r.,** (*slang*) to become difficult, cross, menacing.

RUT (1), [rut], *n.* sexual heat of a male animal, particularly the deer. [OFr. *ruit* from L. *rugitus* rearing].
RUT (2), [rut], *n.* groove or depression made by wheels; a well-worn groove; (*fig.*) settled habits. [Uncert.].
RUTH†, [rōōth], *n.* mercy, pity, compassion. [OE. *hreowth*].
RUTHENIUM, [rōōth-ēn'-i-um], *n.* a metallic element of the platinum group originally mined in Russia. [MedL. *Ruthenia* Russia].
RUTHERFORDITE, [ruᴛʜ'-er-ferd-īt], *n.* titanate of calcium. [Lord *Rutherford*, the chemist].
RUTHFUL†, [rōōth'-fōōl], *adj.* full of ruth, compassionate.
RUTHFULLY†, [rōōth'-fōōl-i], *adv.* compassionately.
RUTHLESS, [rōōth'-less], *adj.* without pity, cruel.
RUTHLESSLY, [rōōth'-les-li], *adv.* in a ruthless fashion.
RUTHLESSNESS, [rōōth'-les-nes], *n.* the quality of being ruthless, without concern as to consequences.
RUTILANT, [rōō'-til-ant], *adj.* shining, glowing. [L. *rutilans*].
RUTILE, [rōō'-tīl], *n.* (*min.*) dioxide of titanium, of a dull red colour. [L. *rutilus* red].
RUTTISH†, [rut'-ish], *adj.* lustful. [RUT (1)].
RUTTISHNESS†, [rut'-ish-nes], *n.* the condition of being ruttish.
RUTTY, [rut'-i], *adj.* full of ruts.
RYE (1), [rī], *n.* a young man. [Romany *rye*].
RYE (2), [rī], *n.* the grain obtained from the *Secale cereale*; the flour obtained from this grain. [OE. *ryge*].
RYE-GRASS, [rī'-grahs], *n.* a grass of the genus *Lolium*, *esp.* that largely cultivated for fodder for cattle.
RYEPECK, [rī'-pek], *n.* an iron-shod mooring pole for a punt; a quant. [Unkn.].
RYOT, [rī'-ot], *n.* a Hindu cultivator or peasant. [Urdu *raiyat*].
RYOTWARY, [rī'-ot-wah'-ri], *n.* in Indian land tenure, the system of direct holding of land by the ryots from the government. [Urdu *raiyatwari*].

S

S, [es], the nineteenth letter in the English alphabet, generally sounded as in *sand*; but it has often the sound of *z* as in *rose* and sometimes of *sh* as in *sugar*; as a final it denotes the possessive case, the plural of nouns, and the present singular third person of verbs.
SABADILLA, [sab-ad-il'-a], *n.* the Mexican plant, *Schœnocaulon officinale*, from whose seeds veratrin is made. [Sp. *cebadilla* from *cebada* barley].
SABAEAN (1), SABEAN, [sab-ē'-an], *n.* a native of Saba or Yemen in South Arabia, the biblical Sheba. [L. *sabaeus* from Arab. *saba* trader].
SABAEAN (2), SABEAN, [sab-ē'-an], *adj.* of, or pertaining to, the Sabaeans.
SABAISM, [sā'-a-izm], *n.* star-worship. [Heb. *çaba* a host].
SABAOTH, [sab-ā'-oth], *n.* armies, hosts. [Heb. *sabaoth* hosts].
SABBATARIAN (1), [sab'-at-āer'-i-an], *n.* one who observes the seventh day of the week as the sabbath; a rigid observer of the sabbath; one who considers that Sunday should be observed as strictly as the Jewish sabbath. [L. *sabbatarius*].
SABBATARIAN (2), [sab'-at-āer'-i-an], *adj.* of, or pertaining to, sabbatarians or sabbatarianism.
SABBATARIANISM, [sab'-at-āer'-i-an-izm], *n.* the tenets of the sabbatarians.
SABBATH, [sab'-ath], *n.* a day of the week set apart for rest and divine worship; a time of rest, a sabbatical year; Sunday. [Heb. *shabbath* day of rest].
SABBATH-BREAKER, [sab'-ath-brāk'-er], *n.* a person who profanes the sabbath.
SABBATH-BREAKING, [sab'-ath-brāk'-ing], *n.* the act of profaning the sabbath.
SABBATHLESS, [sab'-ath-les], *adj.* having no sabbath.
SABBATICAL, SABBATIC, [sab-at'-ik-(al)], *adj.* pertaining to, or resembling, the sabbath; **s. year**, in the Jewish economy, every seventh year, during which the lands were to rest or lie fallow; hence, the name given to the one year's vacation in every seven awarded to teachers in certain universities.
SABBATISM, [sab'-at-izm], *n.* observation of the sabbath; intermission of labour.
SABEAN, see SABAEAN.
SABELLIAN, [sab-el'-i-an], *n.* a disciple of Sabellius, who maintained that there was but one person in the Godhead, and that the Trinity was only a trinity of function and manifestation.
SABELLIANISM, [sab-el'-i-an-izm], *n.* the tenets of Sabellius.
SABELLINE, [sab'-el'-īn], *adj.* like, pertaining to, sable.
SABIAN, [sā'-i-an], *n.* a member of a religious group mentioned in the Koran. [Arab. *as-sabiun*].
SABIANISM, [sāb'-i-an-izm], *n.* the theories and beliefs of the Sabians.
SABINE, [sab'-īn], *n.* a member of an ancient Italian race which inhabited the Apennines and later merged into the Roman people. [L. *Sabinus*].
SABLE (1), [sābl], *n.* a small carnivore of the weasel family, *Mustela zibellina*, whose fur is highly valued; the fur of this animal. [Russ. *sabol*].
SABLE (2), [sābl], *n.* a black colour; black clothes, *esp.* those worn in mourning; blackness, darkness; a paint brush of sable hairs used for very fine work.
SABLE (3), [sābl], *adj.* black, dark; made of the dark brown fur of the sable; (*her.*) black.
SABOT, [sab'-ō], *n.* a wooden shoe worn by the French and Belgian peasantry. [Fr. *sabot*].
SABOTAGE, [sab'-ot-ahzh], *n.* deliberate damage to machinery, tools, plant, or property; other forms of deliberate injury to business by enemies or malcontents. [Fr. *saboter* to wreck].
SABOTEUR, [sab'-ot-ur'], *n.* one who performs an act or acts of sabotage. [Fr. *saboteur*].
SABRE, [sā-er], *n.* a heavy cavalry sword sometimes curved. [Fr. *sabre*].
SABRETACHE, [sāb'-er-tahsh'], *n.* a leather case hung from the sword-belt of a cavalry officer. [Germ. *säbel* sabre and *tasche* pocket].

SABRE

SABRE-TOOTHED, [sāb'-er-tōōtht], *adj.* with long, curved, canine teeth.
SABULOUS, [sab'-yōō-lus], *adj.* sandy. [L. *sabulosus*].
SABURRA, [sab-u'-ra], *n.* (*path.*) a gritty deposit in the stomach. [L. *saburra* sand].
SABURRATION, [sab'-er-ā'-shun], *n.* (*med.*) bathing in hot sand.
SAC (1), [sak], *n.* (*biol.*) a small bag or receptacle. [L. *saccus*].
SAC (2), [sak], *n.* (*leg.*) certain judicial privileges held by the Lord of the Manor by right of his tenure. [OE. *sacu* jurisdiction].
SACBUT, see SACKBUT.
SACCADE, [sak-ād'], *n.* a violent check of a horse with the reins. [Fr. *saccade*].
SACCATE, [sak'-āt], *adj.* (*biol.*) having the form of a sac. [L. *saccus* a bag].
SACCHAR-, SACCHARO-, *pref.* containing, with other things, sugar; sweet like sugar. [L. *saccharum*].
SACCHARIC, [sak-a'-rik], *adj.* pertaining to sugar; saccharine.
SACCHARIFEROUS, [sak'-a-rif'-er-us], *adj.* sugar-bearing. [SACCHAR and L. *ferre* to bear].
SACCHARIFY, [sak-a'-ri-fī], *v.t.* to turn starch into sugar.
SACCHARIMETER, [sak'-a-rim'-i-ter], *n.* an instrument used for estimating sugar by polarized light.
SACCHARINE (1), SACCHARIN, [sak'-a-rin], *n.* a chemical compound of extreme sweetness obtained from coal-tar.
SACCHARINE (2), [sak'-a-rēn], *adj.* pertaining to sugar; sweet; (*fig.*) over-sweet, sugary.
SACCHARITE, [sak'-a-rīt], *n.* (*min.*) a granular felspar resembling sugar in appearance.

SACCHARIZE, [sak'-a-rīz], *v.t.* to turn starch into sugar.
SACCHARO-, see SACCHAR-.
SACCHAROID, [sak'-a-roid], *adj.* resembling loaf-sugar in its granular texture. [SACCHAR and Gk. *oeides* like].
SACCHAROMETER, [sak'-a-rom'-it-er], *n.* a form of hydrometer for estimating the quality of saccharine matter in liquids.
SACCHAROMETRY, [sak'-a-rom'-it-ri], *n.* the process of measuring the amount of sugar in a mixture.
SACCHAROSE, [sak'-a-rōs], *n.* cane sugar as contrasted with glucose.
SACCHARUM, [sak'-a-rum], *n.* a form of cane sugar used mainly in brewing; a tropical genus of twelve species of grasses including the sugar cane. [MedL. *saccharum*].
SACCHOLACTIC, [sak'-ō-lak'-tik], *adj.* made from the sugar of milk. [SACCH(AR) and LACTIC].
SACCIFORM, [sak'-si-fawm], *adj.* having the shape of a sac. [SAC (1) and FORM].
SACCULAR, [sak'-yōō-ler], *adj.* resembling a sac.
SACCULATE, [sak'-yōō-lāt], *adj.* encysted. [SACCULE].
SACCULE, [sak'-yōōl], *n.* a small sac. [L. *sacculus*].
SACELLUM, [sas-el'-um], *n.* (*eccles., arch.*) a small monumental chapel often within a larger church; (*antiq.*) an unroofed temple dedicated to some god; an unroofed enclosure with an altar; a canopied tomb used as an altar. [L. *sacellum* from *sacrum* shrine].
SACERDOTAL, [sas'-er-dōt'-al], *adj.* pertaining to priests; given to undue regard for priests or the priesthood. [L. *sacerdotalis*].
SACERDOTALISM, [sas'-er-dōt'-al-izm], *n.* a priestly system; undue regard for the priesthood or the power of priests.
SACERDOTALIST, [sas'-er-dōt'-al-ist], *n.* a supporter of sacerdotalism.
SACERDOTALLY, [sas'-er-dōt'-al-i], *adv.* in a sacerdotal fashion.
SACHEM, [sa'-chem], *n.* a sagamore, any hereditary chief among the North American Indians. [Native].
SACHEMSHIP, [sā'-chem-ship], *n.* the office of a sachem.
SACHET, [sash'-ā], *n.* a small bag of soft material for holding handkerchiefs or lavender. [Fr. *sachet*].
SACK (1), [sak], *n.* a large oblong bag of coarse material used mainly for holding flour, potatoes, coal, etc.; the quantity of goods contained in a sack; a loose rather shapeless dress or coat; (*coll.*) (notice of) dismissal from employment. [OE. *sacc*].
SACK (2), [sak], *n.* the plunder or pillage of a captured town or village by troops; looting, pillage. [Fr. *sac* plunder].
SACK (3), [sak], *n.* a dry white Spanish wine much drunk during the sixteenth century. [Fr. (*vin*) *sec* dry wine].
SACK (4), [sak], *v.t.* to put in a sack; (*coll.*) to give notice of dismissal from employment.
SACK (5), [sak], *v.t.* to plunder (a captured town, etc.); to loot.
SACKAGE, [sak'-ij], *n.* the act of pillaging a town. [Fr. *saccage*].
SACKBUT, SACBUT, [sak'-but], *n.* an obsolete wind instrument resembling the trombone; a Babylonian harp. [Uncert.].

SACKBUT

SACKCLOTH, [sak'-kloth'], *n.* cloth of which sacks are made; coarse cloth formerly worn in expression of mourning, distress, or penitence.
SACKER, [sak'-er], *n.* one who pillages a town.
SACKFUL, [sak'-ful], *n.* as much as a sack will contain; a full sack.
SACKING, [sak'-ing], *n.* a coarse cloth used for making sacks and as wrapping material for heavy packages.
SACKLESS†, [sak'-les], *adj.* innocent, without blame; peaceable, quiet. [OE. *sæ cleas* innocent].
SACRAL, [sak'-ral], *adj.* (*anat.*) of, or pertaining to, the sacrum.
SACRAMENT, [sak'-ra-ment], *n.* a ceremonial observance in the Christian Church, *esp.* one instituted as an external and visible sign of an inward and spiritual grace; the Lord's Supper; baptism. [Fr. *sacrement*].
SACRAMENTAL, [sak'-ra-ment'-al], *adj.* pertaining to a sacrament; very sacred.
SACRAMENTALISM, [sak'-ra-ment'-al-izm], *n.* excessive observance of sacraments.
SACRAMENTALLY, [sak'-ra-ment'-al-i], *adv.* in a sacramental way.
SACRAMENTARIAN, [sak'-ra-ment-āer'-i-an], *n.* (*hist.*) a person who rejects the doctrine of the Real Presence as taught in the Roman and Lutheran Churches.
SACRAMENTARY (1), [sak'-ra-ment'-er-i], *n.* an ancient book of the Roman Church used during the celebration of the sacraments; a sacramentarian.
SACRAMENTARY (2), [sak'-ra-ment'-er-i], *adj.* of, or pertaining to, the sacraments.
SACRARIUM, [sak-rāer'-i-um], *n.* (*antiq.*) a place where sacred objects were stored; (*eccles.*) that part of the chancel inside the altar rails.
SACRED, [sā'-red], *adj.* holy, consecrated, inviolable; consecrated to a religious purpose; hallowed by association; held in very dear regard. [L. *sacer* dedicated to a divinity].
SACREDLY, [sā'-red-li], *adv.* with religious care; reverently.
SACREDNESS, [sā'-red-nes], *n.* the condition of being sacred.
SACRIFICANT, [sak-rif'-ik-ant], *n.* a person who offers a sacrifice.
SACRIFICE (1), [sak'-ri-fīs], *n.* the making of an offering to a god, primarily of a slaughtered animal, later of any possession, valuable in itself or symbolical; the thing sacrificed; a victim; one who destroys himself or sinks his own desires for the benefit of another; a sale at a loss; (*theol.*) the offering by Christ of His life to expiate the sins of men; the Eucharistic celebration. [OFr. *sacrifice*].
SACRIFICE (2), (**sacrificing, sacrificed**), [sak'-ri-fīs], *v.t.* to offer to a divinity upon an altar; to surrender.
SACRIFICIAL, [sak'-ri-fish'-al], *adj.* of, or pertaining to, sacrifice.
SACRIFICIALLY, [sak'-ri-fi'-shal-i], *adv.* as a sacrifice; in sacrificial fashion.
SACRILEGE, [sak'-ri-lij], *n.* the sin of profaning sacred things; alienation to a common purpose of what has been consecrated; breaking into a church and stealing from it. [L. *sacrilegium* robbing of a temple].
SACRILEGIOUS, [sak'-ri-lij'-us], *adj.* violating sacred things; polluted with sacrilege; profane; irreverent.
SACRILEGIOUSLY, [sak'-ri-lij'-us-li], *adv.* in a sacrilegious fashion; profanely.
SACRILEGIOUSNESS, [sak'-ri-lij'-us-nes], *n.* the state of being sacrilegious.
SACRILEGIST, [sak'-ri-lij'-ist], *n.* a person guilty of sacrilege.
SACRING, [sā'-ring], *n.* (*R.C.*) the consecration of the Eucharistic elements at mass; **s. bell**, a bell rung at the elevation of the Host in the Eucharist. [ME. *sacring*].
SACRIST, [sak'-rist], *n.* a keeper of the sacristy; a church official who has charge of the sacred vessels and vestments; one who used to copy out the music and keep the books for the choir. [OFr. *sacriste*].
SACRISTAN, [sak'-rist-an], *n.* a keeper of the sacristy, a sexton. [MedL. *sacristanus*].
SACRISTY, [sak'-rist-i], *n.* the room in a church where the sacred utensils and vestments are kept; the vestry. [MedL. *sacristia*].
SACRO-ILIAC, [sak'-rō-il'-i-ak], *adj.* (*anat.*) pertaining both to the sacrum and ilium. [SACRUM and ILIUM].
SACROSANCT, [sak'-rō-sangkt'], *adj.* sacred, inviolable. [L. *sacrosanctus*].
SACRUM, [sak'-rum], *n.* (*anat.*) a triangular bone at the base of the vertebral column joining with the haunch bones to form the pelvis. [L. (*os*) *sacrum* sacred bone].
SAD, [sad], *adj.* sorrowful, grieved; melancholy; heavy-hearted; deplorable; heavy, solid; improperly risen (of bread); sober coloured. [OE. *sæd* satiated].
SADDEN, [sad'-en], *v.t.* to make sad, sorrowful; to make solid, heavy; *v.i.* to become sad.
SADDLE (1), [sadl], *n.* a seat on a horse's back or on a cycle or similar machine for the rider to sit on; something like a saddle; a ridge on a high hill resembling a saddle; **in the s.**, on horseback; (*fig.*) in the middle of active work. [OE. *sadol*].

SADDLE

SADDLE (2), [sadl], *v.t.* to place a saddle on; (*fig*). to load, to place a burden or responsibility upon.

SADDLEBACK, [sadl'-bak'], *n.* the great black-backed gull, *Larus marinus*; the harp-seal, *Phoca grœnlandica*; the saddle of a hill.

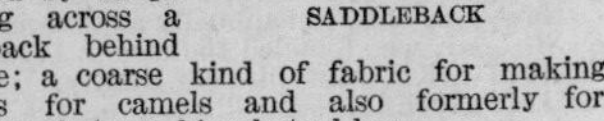

SADDLEBACK

SADDLEBACKED, [sadl'-bakt'], *adj.* shaped like a saddle.
SADDLEBAG, [sadl'-bag'], *n.* one of a pair of bags joined by straps and slung across a horse's back behind the saddle; a coarse kind of fabric for making saddlebags for camels and also formerly for upholstering chairs; a bicycle tool-bag.
SADDLEBAR, [sadl'-bah(r)], *n.* the bar joining the pommel with the cantle of a saddle; the stay in a stained-glass window.
SADDLEBOW, [sadl'-bō], *n.* the bows of a saddle or the pieces which form the front of the framework.
SADDLECLOTH, [sadl'-kloth], *n.* the cloth placed under a horse's saddle.
SADDLEGIRTH, [sadl'-gurth], *n.* the band passing under a horse's body to keep the saddle in place.
SADDLE-HORSE, [sadl'-haws], *n.* a horse used for riding.
SADDLER, [sad'-ler], *n.* one who makes or sells saddles and horse furniture.
SADDLE-ROOF, [sadl'-rōōf], *n.* a roof having two gables.
SADDLERY, [sad'-ler-i], *n.* the trade of a saddler; goods made or sold by a saddler; a saddler's shop.
SADDLE-TREE, [sadl'-trē], *n.* the framework of a saddle; the tulip-tree.
SADDUCEAN, [sad'-yōō-sē'-an], *adj.* pertaining to a Sadducee.
SADDUCEE, [sad'-yōō-sē], *n.* a member of a moderate rationalistic party of the old school among the Jews, who held by the written word to the exclusion of tradition, and denied the doctrine of immortality or the separate existence of the spirit; (*fig.*) a self-righteous materialist. [LL. *sadducaeus*].
SADDUCEEISM, [sad'-yōō-sē'-izm], *n.* the doctrine, spirit of the Sadducees.
SADIRON, [sad'-ī-on], *n.* a solid flat-iron.
SADISM, [sād'-izm], a form of sexual perversion in which cruelty is a characteristic feature; pleasure arising from inflicting or watching cruelty. [The Marquis *de Sade* (1740-1814) whose writings and conduct were thus characterized].
SADIST, [sād'-ist], *n.* one addicted to sadism.
SADISTIC, [sad-ist'-ik], *adj.* of, pertaining to, or resembling sadism or sadists.
SADLY, [sad'-li], *adv.* with sadness; seriously, very much; (*coll.*) unwell, poorly.
SADNESS, [sad'-nes], *n.* the quality of being sad.
SAFE (1), [sāf], *n.* a strong cupboard, usually of steel, and fitted with locks, for storing valuables; a cupboard for storing food, *esp.* meat and milk; **s. deposit**, an institution which contains strong rooms and safes to be let separately.
SAFE (2), [sāf], *adj.* secure; free from danger, hurt, injury or damage; (*fig.*) reliable; predictable, presumed to be safe from enemy bombing. [Fr. *sauf* from L. *salvus* whole, safe].
SAFE-CONDUCT, [sāf'-kon'-dukt], *n.* a convoy, guard, or passport ensuring a safe passage.
SAFEGUARD (1), [sāf'-gahd], *n.* one who or that which guards safely; defence; a protection; a protective convoy; a tax imposed on certain foreign goods entering a country with a view to protecting home products.
SAFEGUARD (2), [sāf'-gahd], *v.t.* to guard; to protect, look after; (*comm.*) to impose tariffs on (goods entering the country) so as to protect home industry.
SAFE-KEEPING, [sāf-kēp'-ing], *n.* the action of preserving in safety from injury or escape.
SAFELY, [sāf'-li], *adv.* in safety.
SAFENESS, [sāf'-nes], *n.* the condition of being safe.
SAFETY, [sāf'-ti], *n.* freedom from danger, hurt, injury or loss; close custody; security; **s. curtain**, a fireproof curtain which can be lowered to cut off the stage premises from the auditorium; **s. glass**, glass which is made up of a number of layers fastened together, and which does not splinter dangerously when broken. [Fr. *sauveté*].
SAFETY-BICYCLE, [sāf'-ti-bī'-sikl], *n.* the modern bicycle with two wheels of equal size.
SAFETY-LAMP, [sāf'-ti-lamp'], *n.* a miner's lamp, so constructed as to give light without danger of firing explosive gases.
SAFETY-MATCH, [sāf'-ti-mach], *n.* a match that ignites by being rubbed on a specially prepared surface only.
SAFETY-PIN, [sāf'-ti-pin], *n.* a pin shaped like a brooch and with a guarded point.
SAFETY-RAZOR, [sāf'-ti-rāz'-or], *n.* a razor with a detachable blade, fitted with a guard to minimize risk of accidental laceration during shaving.
SAFETY-VALVE, [sāf'-ti-valv'], *n.* a valve fitted to the boiler of a steam-engine, which opens and lets out the surplus steam so as to avert the risk of explosion; a valve fitted to any container or system of pipes holding liquids or gases under pressure, which opens automatically when the pressure is excessive; (*fig.*) any outlet for suppressed feelings that prevents an outburst.

SAFETY-VALVE

SAFFLORITE, [saf'-lor-it], *n.* (*min.*) a kind of smaltine. [~SAFFLOWER].
SAFFLOWER, [sa'-flow-er], *n.* a composite plant, *Carthamus tinctorius*, allied to the thistle, yelding a red dye used in the making of rouge. [Du. *saffloer*].
SAFFRON, [saf'-ron], *n.* the bulbous plant, *Crocus sativus*; the bright orange colouring and flavouring matter obtained from this plant; a bright orange-yellow colour. [Arab. *zafaran*].
SAFFRONY, [saf'-ron-i], *adj.* almost saffron coloured.
SAFRANIN, [saf'-ran-in], *n.* (*chem.*) the colouring matter in saffron; a saffron-coloured dye obtained from coal-tar.
SAG (1), [sag], *n.* the fact of sagging.
SAG (2), [sag], *v.i.* to yield; to incline from an upright position for want of support; to sink down; to go limp, flaccid; (*fig.*) to droop, become depressed; (*comm.*) to drop in price. [~Norw. *sakka*].

SAFFRON

SAGA, [sah'-ga], *n.* an old heroic Scandinavian story; an ancient composition dealing with the history and mythology of the northern European races. [OIcel. *saga* story].
SAGACIOUS, [sag-ā'-shus], *adj.* wise, discerning, acute; having shrewd practical insight. [L. *sagax*].
SAGACIOUSLY, [sag-ā'-shus-li], *adv.* in a sagacious fashion.
SAGACIOUSNESS, [sag-ā'-shus-nes], *n.* the state of being sagacious.
SAGACITY, [sag-as'-i-ti], *n.* the quality of being sagacious.
SAGAMORE, [sag'-a-maw(r)], *n.* a North American Indian chief. [NAmerIndian *sagamo*].
SAGAN, [sāg'-an], *n.* the suffragan or deputy of the Jewish high priest. [Heb. *sagan*].
SAGE (1), [sāj], *n.* a savoury herb, *Salvia officinalis*, much used in cooking, *esp.* as a stuffing. [OFr. *sauge* from L. *salvus* safe].
SAGE (2), [sāj], *n.* a wise man; a venerable old man of tried wisdom.
SAGE (3), [sāj], *adj.* wise, venerable, sagacious. [OFr. *sage*].
SAGE-BRUSH, [sāj'-brush], *n.* a North American species of *Artemisia*.
SAGE-GROUSE, [sāj'-grows], *n.* an American grouse of the genus *Centrocerus* which feeds on the aromatic leaves of the sage-brush.
SAGELY, [sāj'-li], *adv.* wisely, with sagacity.
SAGENE (1), [sazh'-ēn], *n.* see SAJENE.
SAGENE (2), [saj-ēn'], *n.* a network. [Gk. *sagene* a fishing-net].

SAGE

SAGENESS, [sāj'-nes], *n.* the quality of being sage; sagacity; deep wisdom.
SAGGAR, see SEGGAR.
SAGGING, [sag'-ing], *adj.* that sags.
SAGITTAL, [saj'-it-al], *adj.* pertaining to or resembling an arrow.
SAGITTARIUS, [saj'-it-āer'-i-us], *n.* (*astron.*) the ninth sign of the zodiac, the Archer. [L. *Sagittarius* archer].
SAGITTARY (1), [saj'-it-er-i], *n.* a centaur; a legendary animal, half man, half horse, armed with a bow and quiver; bow and arrows. [*Prec.*].
SAGITTARY (2), [saj'-it-er-i], *adj.* sagittal.

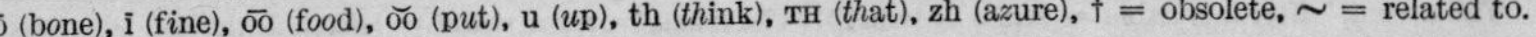

SAGITTATE, [saj'-it-āt], *adj.* (*bot.*) in shape like the head of an arrow. [L. *sagitta* arrow].

SAGO, [sā'-gō], *n.* a starch food obtained from the pith of several palms native to Malaya. [Malay *sagu*].

SAGOIN, [sa-goin'], *n.* any species of *Cebus*, the genus of the sapajou or capuchin monkeys of South America. [Fr. *sagouin*].

SAGUM, [sāg'-um], *n.* a Roman military cloak. [L. *sagum*].

SAHARA, [sa-hah'-ra], *n.* the great North African desert; (*fig.*) any dry and barren place. [Arab. *çahra* desert].

SAHIB, [sahb, sah'-ib], *n.* a courtesy title given to any gentleman of rank in India by the Indians; an English gentleman in India; **pukka s.,** a European gentleman of the ruling classes in India, an Englishman with all the ostensible marks and manners of his class, usually a member of one of the Services. [Arab. *sahib* companion, lord].

SAHLITE, [sah'-līt], *n.* (*min.*) a variety of green augite found in Swedish lead mines. [*Sahla*, a town in Sweden].

SAIC, [sā'-ik], *n.* a kind of ketch, common in the Levant. [Turk. *shaiqa*].

SAID, [sed], *pret. and p.pt.* of SAY.

SAIGA, [sī'-ga], *n.* the puff-nosed antelope found on the steppes of Eastern Europe and Western Asia. [Russ. *saiga*].

SAIL (1), [sāl], *n.* a spread of canvas for receiving the impulse of the wind by which a ship is driven; a ship or other vessel; an excursion in some vessel; one of various objects which are spread out like a sail to catch the wind as the revolving arms on a windmill; **to take the wind out of the sails of,** to destroy the confidence of; **under s.,** under way; **to set s.,** to begin the journey; **to shorten s.,** to reduce the extent of sail; **to strike s.,** to lower the sails suddenly. [OE. *segel*].

SAIL (2), [sāl], *v.t.* to pass over in a ship; to navigate; *v.i.* to be driven along by the action of wind upon sails; to go by water; to glide through the air; to move smoothly along; to walk along with smooth dignity; **to s. near the wind,** to steer a sailing ship as near into the wind as possible to maintain way on her; (*fig.*) to carry on any undertaking approaching as nearly as possible the border-line of safety or honesty. [OE. *seglian*].

SAILABLE, [sāl'-abl], *adj.* navigable.

SAILCLOTH, [sāl'-kloth'], *n.* strong canvas used for making sails.

SAILER, [sāl'-er], *n.* one who sails; a sailing ship with reference to her speed or manner of sailing.

SAILING, [sāl'-ing], *n.* the act of sailing; the act or art of navigating; the act of moving by means of sails; the departure of a ship on its journey; the act of moving smoothly along through the air or on the ground.

SAILING-MASTER, [sāl'-ing-mahst'-er], *n.* an officer in a warship who superintends the details of navigating the ship.

SAILLESS, [sāl'-les], *adj.* without sails.

SAIL-LOFT, [sāl'-loft'], *n.* a loft or apartment in which sails are cut and made.

SAIL-MAKER, [sāl'-māk'-er], *n.* a man who makes or repairs sails.

SAIL-NEEDLE, [sāl'-nēdl], *n.* a large needle having a triangular tapering point.

SAILOR, [sāl'-or], *n.* a seaman, mariner; one of the crew of a ship; **bad (good) s.,** one who travels with (without) discomfort on board ship.

SAILOR-LIKE, [sāl'-or-līk], *adj.* in the manner of a sailor.

SAILPLAN, [sāl'-plan'], *n.* the plan of the sails of a ship.

SAILPLANE, [sāl'-plān'], *n.* an aeroplane without an engine; a glider.

SAIL-ROOM, [sāl-rōōm'], *n.* a room in a ship where the sails are stored and kept in order.

SAIL-YARD, [sāl'-yahd], *n.* the yard or spar on which sails are stretched.

SAINFOIN, [sān'-foin], *n.* the leguminous plant, *Onobrychis sativa*, largely cultivated for fodder. [Fr. *sain* wholesome and *foin* hay].

SAINT (1), [sānt], *n.* a holy man or woman; one of the blessed dead in Paradise; a person eminent for piety and virtue; (*R.C.*) one canonized by the Church; **saint's day,** a church festival in commemoration of some particular saint. [OFr. *seint* from L. *sanctus* holy].

SAINT (2), [sānt], *v.t.* to canonize; give the name of saint to.

ST. BERNARD, [sent-burn'-erd], *n.* a breed of mastiffs kept by the monks of the hospice of St. Bernard in Switzerland to help in the rescue of travellers exposed to danger on the mountains.

ST. DOMINGO FEVER, [san'-do-ming'-gō-fēv'-er], *n.* yellow fever.

SAINTED, [sānt'-ed], *adj.* canonized; holy.

SAINTHOOD, [sānt'-hood], *n.* the condition of being a canonized saint, saintly life.

ST. JOHN'S WORT, [sn-jonz'-wurt], *n.* a low-growing plant, with yellow flowers, of the genus *Hypericum*.

ST. LEGER, [sint-lej'-er], *n.* famous horserace for three-year-olds, run annually at Doncaster. [Colonel *St. Leger*, who founded the race in 1776].

SAINT-LIKE, [sānt'-līk], *adj.* saintly.

SAINTLINESS, [sānt'-li-nes], *n.* the condition or quality of being saintly.

SAINTLY, [sānt-li], *adj.* sainted; pertaining to, resembling, a saint.

SAINTSHIP, [sānt'-ship'], *n.* sainthood.

SAINT-SIMONIAN, [sānt'-sim-ōn'-i-an], *adj.* a system of socialism, whereby the State would own and control all the means of production, paying the workers according to the work they do. [*Saint-Simon*, the French economist].

ST. VITUS'S DANCE, [sint-vīt'-us-dahnts'], *n.* chorea.

SAJENE, SAGENE (1), [sazh'-ēn], *n.* a Russian measure of length of approximately seven feet. [Russ. *sozhene*].

SAJOU, [sah-jōō'], *n.* one of the small weeping monkeys of Brazil, *esp. Cebus capucinus*. [Fr. *sajou*].

SAKE (1), [sāk], *n.* account; end; purpose; regard; **for the s. of,** on account of, because of, out of regard for, in the interests of. [OE. *sacu*].

SAKE, saké (2), [sah-ki], *n.* a Japanese drink made from fermented rice. [Jap. *saké*].

SAKER, [sā'-ker], *n.* the hawk, *Falco sacer*; a small piece of seventeenth-century artillery. [Arab. *çaqr* hawk].

SAKI, [sah'-ki], *n.* an American monkey of the genus *Pithecia* having a hairy tail which is not prehensile. [Tupi *çahij*].

SAL (1), [sahl], *n.* an Indian tree, *Shorea robusta*, valuable for timber. [Hind. *sal*].

SAL (2), [sal], *n.* (*chem.*) salt or salts; **s. alembroth,** a compound of the corrosive sublimate of mercury and sal-ammoniac; **s.-ammoniac,** the hydrochloride of ammonia; **s. prunella,** nitrate of potash fused, cast into cakes or balls; **s. seignette,** Rochelle salt; **s. volatile,** an aromatic solution of carbonate of ammonia. [L. *sal* salt].

SALAAM (1), [sal-ahm'], *n.* a ceremonious Oriental salutation; an obeisance. [Arab. *salam*].

SALAAM (2), [sal-ahm'], *v.i.* to make a salaam.

SALABLE, see SALEABLE.

SALACIOUS, [sal-ā'-shus], *adj.* lewd, lustful; dealing with lewd matters; (*coll.*) spicy, hot. [L. *salax* leaping].

SALACIOUSLY, [sal-ā'-shus-li], *adv.* in a salacious fashion.

SALACIOUSNESS, [sal-ā'-shus-nes], *n.* the quality of being salacious; salacity.

SALACITY, [sal-as'-i-ti], *n.* the condition of being salacious. [L. *salacitas*].

SALAD, [sal'-ad], *n.* a dish consisting of various mixtures of prepared vegetables, raw or cooked, and flavoured to taste with a dressing of mixed oil, vinegar and mustard; lettuce as the main ingredient of a salad. [Portug. *salada*].

SALADING, [sal'-ad-ing], *n.* vegetables, greenstuff, herbs used for salad.

SALAD-PLATE, [sal'-ad-plāt], *n.* a crescent-shaped plate for salad placed by the dinner-plate on the table.

SALAMANDER, [sal'-a-mand'-er], *n.* (*zool.*) a tailed amphibian allied to the newts, of the genus *Salamandra*, one species of which, *Salamandra maculosa*, was fabled to be able to live in fire; **salamander's hair,** a species of asbestos. [Gk. *salamandra*].

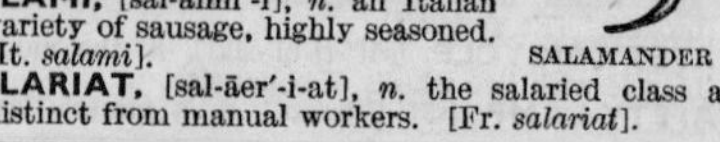

SALAMANDER

SALAMANDRINE, [sal'-a-man'-drīn], *adj.* having the characteristics of a salamander; enduring fire.

SALAMANDROID, [sal'-a-man'-droid], *adj.* (*zool.*) having the characteristics of a salamander. [SALAMANDER and Gk. *oeides* like].

SALAMI, [sal-ahm'-i], *n.* an Italian variety of sausage, highly seasoned. [It. *salami*].

SALARIAT, [sal-āer'-i-at], *n.* the salaried class as distinct from manual workers. [Fr. *salariat*].

SALARIED, [sal'-a-rid], *adj.* paid by, receiving, salary.
SALARY, [sal'-er-i], *n.* a fixed payment paid at regular intervals, as per year, quarter or month, to a person in a clerical or administrative position in business, etc., as distinct from a wage paid for manual labour; a stipend. [L. *salarium* soldier's pay].
SALE, [sāl], *n.* the act of selling; the transfer of goods, produce, or possession from the owner, manufacturer or retailer to the consumer or purchaser at a price, held to be mutually advantageous to both parties; a period during which the goods of a retail shop are offered to the public at reduced prices; an auction; **sales resistance,** apathy of buyers to be overcome by salesmanship. [OE. *sala*].
SALEABLE, SALABLE, [sāl'-abl], *adj.* able to be sold; marketable.
SALEABLENESS, [sāl'-abl-nes], *n.* the quality of being saleable.
SALEABLY, [sāl'-ab-li], *adv.* in a saleable manner.
SALEBROSITY, [sa'-li-bros'-i-ti], *n.* ruggedness.
SALEBROUS, [sal'-i-brus], *adj.* uneven, rough, rugged. [L. *salebrosus*].
SALE OF WORK, [sāl'-oy-wurk'], *n.* a charitable function at which goods made or presented by helpers are sold.
SALEP, [sal'-ep], *n.* the dried tubers of different species of *Orchis*, used as a drug. [Arab. *tha'leb* fox orchid].
SALE-PRICE, [sāl'-prīs'], *n.* the specially reduced price of an article at a general sale.
SALERATUS, [sal'-er-ā'-tus], *n.* (*U.S.*) impure bicarbonate of potash; bicarbonate of sodium used in cake-baking. [L. *sal aeratus* aerated salt].
SALE-ROOM, [sāl'-rōōm], *n.* a room in which goods are sold by auction or tender.
SALESMAN, [sālz-man], *n.* one who sells merchandise, *esp.* wholesale.
SALESMANSHIP, [sālz'-man-ship'], *n.* the technique of inducing people to buy goods.
SALESWOMAN, [sālz'-wŏŏ-man], *n.* a woman who sells goods.
SALE-WORK, [sāl'-wurk], *n.* things made for sale.
SALIAN (1), [sā'-li-an], *adj.* salic. [L. *Salii* the Franks].
SALIAN (2), [sā'-li-an], *adj.* relating to the priests who performed rituals in honour of Mars. [L. *salire* to leap].
SALIC, [sā'-lik], *adj.* relating to the Salian Franks; **s. law,** an alleged constitutional law of the French, supposed to have been adopted from the Franks, excluding women from succeeding to the crown. [LL. *salicus*].
SALICET, [sal'-is-et], *n.* a stop in an organ emitting a sound like a flute. [L. *salix* willow].
SALICIN, [sā'-lis-in], *n.* (*chem.*) the bitter principle obtained from certain species of willow. [L. *salix* willow].
SALICIONAL, [sal-ish'-onl], *n.* an organ stop with a tone like a willow pipe. [~SALIX].
SALICYL, [sal'-is-il], *n.* (*chem.*) the base of salicylic acid. [L. *salix* willow].
SALICYLATE, [sal-is'-il-āt], *n.* (*chem.*) a salt of salicylic acid.
SALICYLIC, [sal'-is-il'-ik], *adj.* relating to, obtained from, salicin; **s. acid,** a medicinal acid originally derived from salicin.
SALIENCE, [sā'-li-ents], *n.* the state of being salient.
SALIENCY, [sā'-li-en-si], *n.* salience; (*pl.*) prominent features.
SALIENT (1), [sā'-li-ent], *n.* a prominent or projecting angle in a line, particularly a line of troops in advance of the main line.
SALIENT (2), [sā'-li-ent], *adj.* projecting, jutting, outward; (*fig.*) †leaping; conspicuous; (*her.*) of the position of an animal about to spring but keeping both hind feet on the ground. [L. *saliens* leaping].
SALIENTLY, [sā'-i-ent-li], *adv.* in a salient manner.
SALIFEROUS, [sal-if'-er-us], *adj.* (*geol.*) producing salt; containing rock-salt. [SAL and L. *ferre* to bear].
SALIFIABLE, [sal'-i-fī'-abl], *adj.* capable of combining with an acid to form a salt.
SALIFICATION, [sal'-if-ik-ā'-shun], *n.* the process or act of salifying; changing into salt.
SALIFY, (salified, salifies, salifying), [sal'-i-fī], *v.t.* to make salty; (*chem.*) to convert into a salt; to form into a salt by combining an acid with a base.
SALIGOT†, [sal'-i-got], *n.* the water chestnut, *Trapa natans*. [OFr. *saligot*].
SALIMETER, [sal-im'-it-er], *n.* an instrument for measuring saltness. [SAL and METER].
SALINA, [sal-ī'-na], *n.* a salt marsh, spring, pond, lake; a salt-works, salt-pan, salt-mine. [L. *salina*].
SALINATION, [sal'-in-ā'-shun], *n.* the act of washing with a solution of salt.
SALINE (1), [sā'-līn], *n.* a deposit of salt; a salt-spring; an effervescing aperient. [~SAL].
SALINE (2,) [sā'-līn], *adj.* containing salt; tasting of salt; of the nature of a salt.
SALINENESS, [sā'-līn-nes], *n.* the quality of being saline.
SALINIFEROUS, [sal'-in-if'-er-us], *adj.* producing salt. [SALINE and L. *ferre* to bear].
SALINITY, [sal-in'-i-ti], *n.* saltness.
SALINOMETER, [sal'-in-om'-it-er], *n.* an apparatus for testing the density of sea-water in marine steam-boilers. [SALINE and METER].
SALINO-TERRENE, [sal-īn'-ō-te-rēn'], *adj.* consisting of salt and earth.
SALIVA, [sal-ī'-va], *n.* the fluid secreted by the salivary glands, which serves to moisten the mouth and promote the digestion of food, spittle. [L. *saliva*].
SALIVAL†, [sal-ī'-val], *adj.* salivary. [L. *salivalis*].
SALIVANT, [sal'-iv-ant], *adj.* stimulating saliva.
SALIVARY, [sal'-iv-er-i], *adj.* relating to saliva; secreting saliva. [L. *salivarius*].
SALIVATE, [sal'-iv-āt], *v.t. and i.* to cause to produce an excessive secretion and discharge of saliva; to secrete saliva to an abnormal extent. [L. *salivare*].
SALIVATION, [sal'-iv-ā'-shun], *n.* the act of producing an increased secretion of saliva; an abnormally abundant flow of saliva.
SALIX, [sā'-liks], *n.* (*bot.*) the numerous genus of willows and osiers. [L. *salix* willow].
SALLAL, [sal'-al'], *n.* the edible fruit of *Gaultheria shallon*; a cottonwood found in Canada.
SALLE, [sal], *n.* a large room with a high ceiling; a hall. [Fr. *salle*].
SALLET, [sal'-et], *n.* (*milit.*) a bowl-shaped helmet used in ancient warfare. [Uncert.].
SALLOW (1), [sal'-ō], *n.* a willow identified by its broad leaves, particularly the goat willow, *Salix caprea*; **s. thorn,** the sea-buckthorn, *Hippophaë rhamnoides*. [OE. *sealh*, ~L. *salix* willow].

SALIX

SALLOW (2), [sal'-ō], *adj.* having a complexion of a pale, sickly, yellow colour. [OE. *salu*].
SALLOWISH, [sal'-ō-ish], *adj.* somewhat sallow.
SALLOWNESS, [sal'-ō-nes], *n.* the quality of being sallow.
SALLY (1), [sal'-i], *n.* (*fig.*) a sudden flash of wit, a witty piece of bantering; (*milit.*) a sudden attack by troops from a besieged position for the purpose of harrying the enemy. [Fr. *saillie*].
SALLY (2), (sallied, sallies, sallying), [sal'-i], *v.i.* to set out on an excursion; (*milit.*) to make a sally; **s. forth,** to emerge hopefully. [*Prec.*].
SALLY LUNN, [sal'-i-lun'], *n.* a kind of light tea-cake. [*Sally Lunn*, of Bath].
SALLYPORT, [sal'-i-pawt], *n.* (*fort.*) a postern gate or other passage from which troops can make a sally.
SALMAGUNDI, [sal'-mag-un'-di], *n.* a mixture of chopped meat and pickled herring and various other ingredients with seasoning. [Fr. *salmigondis*].
SALMI, [sal'-mē], *n.* partly roasted game cooked in wine and condiments as a highly seasoned stew. [Fr. *salmi*].
SALMON, [sam'-on], *n.* a species of large fish with firm, pink flesh, *Salmo salar*, found in the North Atlantic and round the northern shores, which it quits to make a considerable journey up difficult rivers and streams to its spawning ground; the light pink colour resembling that of a salmon; **rock s.,** name in the fish trade for the large blenny fish; **s. cobble,** a rowing boat used in sea salmon fishing; **s. leap,** a small waterfall up which salmon leap in their journey upstream; **s. peal,** a small grilse; **s. pool,** a deep part of a river where salmon abound. [L. *salmo* leaping fish].

SALMON

SALMONOID, [sam'-on-oid], *adj.* like a salmon. [SALMON and Gk. *oeides* like].
SALMON-TROUT, [sam'-on-trowt'], *n.* the sea-trout, *Salmo trutta*, sometimes sold as salmon.
SALON, [sal'-o(ng)'], *n.* a drawing-room used for receptions in a private house; a circle of friends, *esp.* artistic; an exhibition of pictures. [Fr. *salon*].

SALOON, [sal-ōōn'], *n.* a large reception-room; any large room used for various forms of public entertainment; the largest cabin in a passenger steamer; a large room in a liner; a luxurious railway carriage not divided into compartments; a large automobile without a special compartment for a chauffeur; a motor-car with a closed-in body; a more comfortable and expensive bar in a public-house. [*Prec.*].

SALOOP, [sal-ōōp'], *n.* a hot drink made from salep.

SALPICON, [sal'-pik-on], *n.* a Spanish dish of minced meat and bread; a stuffing made with minced meat and savoury herbs. [Span. *salpicon*].

SALSE, [sals], *n.* (*geol.*) a mud volcano. [It. *salsa*].

SALSIFY, [sal'-sif-i], *n.* the composite plant *Tragopogon porrifolius*, or purple goat's beard, cultivated for its root which is eaten as a vegetable. [Uncert.].

SALT (1), [sawlt], *n.* a substance found in crystalline form and in solution which is prepared for various domestic and industrial uses, known by chemists as chloride of sodium; a sailor; a salt-cellar; (*chem.*) a substance composed of an acid and a base; (*fig.*) a piquancy, a characteristic flavour, wit, keenness of humour; (*med.*) (*pl.*) various popular brands of purgatives, as Epsom, Glauber's, etc.; **with a grain of s.**, with reserve; **not worth his s.**, (*coll.*) worthless. [OE. *sealt* salt].

SALT (2), [sawlt], *adj.* having the flavour of salt; impregnated with salt; growing among salt; salacious; (*fig.*) witty.

SALT (3), [sawlt], *v.t.* to sprinkle or season with salt; to preserve by means of impregnating with salt; (*coll.*) to create a false deposit of precious metal in; to falsify credits or profits in.

SALTANT, [sal'-tant], *adj.* (*her.*) leaping, dancing. [L. *saltans*].

SALTARELLO, [sal'-ta-rel'-ō], *n.* an Italian dance or jig; the music for such a dance. [It. *saltarello*].

SALTATION, [salt-ā'-shun], *n.* a leaping or jumping; a beating or palpitation. [L. *saltatio*].

SALTATORIAL, [sal'-tat-aw'-ri-al], *adj.* governed by, relating to, jumping; saltatory.

SALTATORIOUS, [salt'-at-aw'-ri-us], *adj.* saltatory.

SALTATORY, [salt'-at-er-i], *adj.* leaping or dancing; (*biol.*) not regular in development. [L. *saltatorius*].

SALT-BOX, [sawlt'-boks], *n.* a small box with a lid, used for holding salt.

SALT-BUSH, [sawlt'-bōōsh], *n.* an Australian species of plant, *Atriplex*.

SALT-CAKE, [sawlt'-kāk], *n.* crude sulphate of soda.

SALT-CAT, [sawlt'-kat'], *n.* a mixture of gravel, seed and salt given to pigeons.

SALT-CELLAR, [sawlt'-sel'-er], *n.* a small domestic utensil of various forms and materials used for holding the table salt; (*coll.*) a deep hollow at the base of the neck above the collar-bones.

SALTER, [sawlt'-er], *n.* a person who salts; a dealer in salt.

SALTERN, [sawlt'-ern], *n.* a place where salt is extracted from sea-water by a process of evaporation. [OE. *sealtærn*].

SALTIGRADA, (*pl.* **saltigradae**), [sal'-ti-grā'-da], *n.* (*zool.*) one of a family of spiders that leap to seize their prey. [L. *saltus* a jump and *gradus* step].

SALTIGRADE (1), [sal'-ti-grād], *n.* one of the saltigradae.

SALTIGRADE (2), [sal'-ti-grād], *adj.* (*zool.*) having the characteristics of the saltigradae.

SALTINESS, [sawlt'-i-nes], *n.* the condition of being salty.

SALTING, [sawlt'-ing], *n.* a salt-water marsh; the process of applying salt to the preservation of animal and vegetable substances for food.

SALTIRE, [sal'-tēer], *n.* (*her.*) a diagonal cross; a St. Andrew's cross; an ordinary, representing a bend sinister conjoined with a bend dexter, in the form of an X. [LL. *saltatorium* stirrup].

SALTIRE

SALTISH, [sawlt'-ish], *adj.* somewhat salt.

SALTISHLY, [sawlt'-ish-li], *adv.* with a moderate degree of saltness.

SALTISHNESS, [sawlt'-ish-nes], *n.* a moderate degree of saltness.

SALT JUNK, [sawlt'-junk], *n.* dry salt beef.

SALTLESS, [sawlt'-les], *adj.* not flavoured with salt; not containing salt; (*fig.*) insipid, pointless, weak.

SALT-LICK, [sawlt'-lik], *n.* a place where the ground is impregnated with salt to which wild animals come for the salt; an artificial preparation of salt placed ready for cattle.

SALTLY, [sawlt'-li], *adv.* with taste of salt.

SALT-MARSH, [sawlt'-mahsh], *n.* land sometimes covered with grass, which is invaded by the overflow of salt-water.

SALT-MINE, [sawlt'-mīn], *n.* a mine where rock-salt is worked.

SALTNESS, [sawlt'-nes], *n.* the quality of being salt; the taste of salt.

SALT-PAN, [sawlt'-pan'], *n.* a pan, basin, or pit where salt is obtained from brine by evaporation.

SALTPETRE, [sawlt-pē'-ter], *n.* nitre; nitrate of potash. [LL. *salpetra* salt of stone].

SALTPETROUS, [sawlt-pē'-trus], *adj.* relating to saltpetre; of the nature of saltpetre; impregnated with saltpetre.

SALT-PIT, [sawlt'-pit], *n.* a pit where salt is obtained.

SALT-RHEUM, [sawlt'-rōōm], *n.* (*U.S.*) a cutaneous eruption; herpes.

SALT-SPOON, [sawlt'-spōōn], *n.* a small spoon kept in the salt-cellar with which to take helpings of salt.

SALT-SPRING, [sawlt'-spring], *n.* a spring of salt-water.

SALT-WATER, [sawlt'-waw'-ter], *n.* sea water; water impregnated with salts.

SALTWORK, [sawlt'-wurk], *n.* a place where salt is made.

SALTWORT, [sawlt'-wurt], *n.* (*bot.*) one of several species of plants growing in salt marshes and on seashores.

SALTY, [sawl'-ti], *adj.* salt in flavour; containing salt.

SALUBRIOUS, [sal-ōō'-bri-us], *adj.* favourable to health; healthful. [L. *salubris* healthy].

SALUBRIOUSLY, [sal-ōō'-bri-us-li], *adv.* in a salubrious manner, so as to promote health.

SALUBRIOUSNESS, [sal-ōō'-bri-us-nes], *n.* the condition or quality of being salubrious.

SALUBRITY, [sal-ōō'-bri-ti], *n.* salubriousness. [L. *salubritas*].

SALUKI, [sal-ōō'-ki], *n.* a handsome breed of dog, very fast, with long legs, a sharp nose, a fine silky coat of hair, and a flowing tail, used in Persia for hunting gazelles. (Arab. *seluqi* of *Seluq*, a Greek town.)

SALUTARILY, [sal'-yōō-ter-i-li], *adv.* in a salutary manner.

SALUTARINESS, [sal'-yōō-ter-i-nes], *n.* the state or quality of being salutary.

SALUTARY, [sal'-yōō-ter-i], *adj.* wholesome, promoting health; contributing to some beneficial purpose, having a moral effect for good. [L. *salutaris*].

SALUTATION, [sal'-yōō-tā'-shun], *n.* the act or style of saluting or paying respect; words or gestures expressive of a greeting. [L. *salutatio* greeting].

SALUTATIONAL, [sal'-yōō-tā'-shun-al], *adj.* relating to, resembling, a salutation.

SALUTATORILY, [sal-yōō'-ta-ter-i-li], *adv.* by way of salutation.

SALUTATORY, [sal-yōō'-ta-ter-i], *adj.* greeting. [L. *salutatorius*].

SALUTE (1), [sal-ōōt'], *n.* the act of saluting; a greeting in one of various forms, a kiss, a firing of a number of guns as a ritual of honour, act of dipping flags; (*fencing*) formal crossing of swords or foils; (*milit.*) a disciplinary gesture of respect made by a soldier to a superior officer. [Fr. *salut*].

SALUTE (2), [sal-ōōt'], *v.t.* to greet or welcome in a conventional mode of address, to make a salutation to; to make a conventional gesture to as an act of respect, to bow to, kiss the hand of, touch the hat to, dip the colours, fire guns in honour of. [L. *salutare*].

SALUTER, [sal-ōōt'-er], *n.* one who salutes.

SALUTIFEROUS, [sal'-yōō-tif'-er-us], *adj.* bringing health; healthy. [L. *salutifer*].

SALVABILITY, [salv'-a-bil'-i-ti], *n.* the state or quality of being salvable.

SALVABLE, [salv'-abl], *adj.* able to be salved or soothed; admitting of being salved.

SALVABLENESS, [salv'-abl-nes], *n.* the state of being salvable.

SALVAGE (1), [salv'-ij], *n.* the saving of a derelict ship by another vessel, *esp.* by means of diving apparatus in accordance with specific contract; compensation allowed by law for the saving of a ship or goods from loss at sea; the cargo or ship which is so saved; the act of saving; waste specially collected to be re-used for manufacture.

SALVAGE (2), [salv'-ij], *v.t.* to save from total loss; to recover (property, etc.) from effects of fire, flood, etc.

SALVARSAN, [salv'-ahs'-an], *n.* an arsenical compound used as a cure for syphilis. [L. *salvus* whole, AR(SENIC) and L. *san(itas)* health].

SALVATION, [salv-ā'-shun], *n.* the act of saving, particularly from sin or from habitual immorality; deliverance, redemption; the person who, or that which, saves; preservation from entire destruction, rescue from danger which might have proved mortal; **S. Army,** an organization acting on Christian principles and engaged in missionary and rescue work among native tribes and poverty-stricken classes. [LL. *salvatio*].

SALVATIONIST, [salv-ā'-shun-ist], *n.* a member of the Salvation Army; one who believes in salvation.

SALVE (1), [salv, sahv], *n.* a kind of adhesive composition; an ointment with curative powers applied to wounds or sores; help; remedy. [OE. *sealf* ointment].

SALVE (2), [salv, sahv], *v.t.* to save, to rescue, to salvage. [SALVAGE].

SALVE (3), [salv, sahv], *v.t.* to soothe, to heal by means of a salve. [OE. *sealfian*].

SALVER, [salv'-er], *n.* a tray or waiter on which anything is presented. [Span. *salvar* to taste as a precaution].

SALVER

SALVIA, [sal'-vi-a], *n.* (*bot.*) a genus of herbs allied to sage. [L. *salvus* safe].

SALVO (1), [salv'-ō], *n.* an exception, a reservation; (*leg.*) a conditional clause. [L. *salvo jure* with a reserved right].

SALVO (2), [salv'-ō], *n.* a volley of guns discharged in salute; a double broadside. [L. *salve* hail!].

SALVOR, [salv'-or], *n.* one who saves a ship or goods from destruction at sea or by fire.

SAMARA, [sam-ah'-ra], *n.* (*bot.*) a fruit dispersed by means of two wing-like growths such as the fruit of the maple or sycamore. [L. *samara* elm seed].

SAMARITAN (1), [sam-a'-rit-an], *n.* the language or an inhabitant of Samaria; a charitable person like the man in the parable, Luke x, 33. [*Next*].

SAMARITAN (2), [sam-a'-rit-an], *adj.* relating to the people or language of Samaria. [L. *Samaritanus*].

SAMARIUM, [sam-āer'-i-um], *n.* (*chem.*) the metallic element denoted by Sm. [~SAMARSKITE].

SAMARSKITE, [sam-ahsk'-īt], *n.* (*min.*) niobate of uranium. [*Samarski*, the discoverer].

SAMBAR, SAMBUR, [sam'-bar], *n.* (*zool.*) the large woodland deer of south-eastern Asia, *Cervus unicolor*. [Hind. *sambar*].

SAM BROWNE, [sam'-brown'], *n.* a leather belt worn as part of the uniform of officers in the British Army. [General Sir *Sam(uel) Browne*].

SAMBUCA, [sam'-bōō-ka], *n.* an ancient instrument of music resembling a large triangular harp. [Gk. *zambuke*].

SAMBUR, see SAMBAR.

SAME, [sām], *adj.* identical; having reciprocal possession of points of comparison, not different; of the identical kind, sort, or degree, exactly similar, corresponding in every respect; mentioned before; unchanged, being no different in condition, particularly of health. [OE. *same*].

SAMENESS, [sām'-nes], *n.* the state of being the same; identity, resemblance, similarity; uniformity, monotony.

SAMBUCA

SAMIAN (1), [sā'-mi-an], *n.* an inhabitant of Samos.

SAMIAN (2), [sā'-mi-an], *adj.* relating to, coming from, possessing the artistic or functional characteristics native to, the people of the Grecian isle of Samos. [Gk. *Samios*].

SAMIEL, [sā'-mi-el], *n.* the simoom. [Turk. *samyel* wind].

SAMISEN, [sam'-is-en], *n.* a Japanese three-stringed guitar. [Chin. *san-hsien*].

SAMITE†, [sā'-mīt], *n.* a fabric of silk woven with gold thread. [L. *samitum* from Gk. *hexamiton* fabric woven with six threads].

SAMLET, [sam'-let], *n.* a little salmon, a parr. [SALMON].

SAMOVAR, [sam'-ō-vahr], *n.* a Russian copper tea-urn kept hot by heated air. [Russ. *samovar* self-boiler].

SAMOYED, [sam-ō'-yed], *n.* a member of a Mongol race in the extreme north of Asia; their breed of dog.

SAMOYED DOG

SAMP, [samp], *n.* boiled crushed maize and milk. [NAmerInd *samp*].

SAMPAN, [sam'-pan], *n.* a Chinese river boat propelled by a single oar from the stern and often used for habitation. [Chin. *sampan* three boards].

SAMPHIRE, [sam'-fīer], *n.* (*bot.*) a fleshy umbelliferous plant of the genus, *Crithmum*, usually found on cliffs by the sea. [ME. *sampire*, *sainpere* from OFr. (*l'herbe de*) *Saint Pierre* St. Peter's (herb)].

SAMPLE (1), [sahmpl], *n.* a single part, portion, or specimen representing the characteristics and qualities of the whole, particularly a single example of a quantity of mass-produced products. [ME. *sample* from OFr. *ensaumple*].

SAMPLE (2), [sahmpl], *v.t.* to take a sample of a group or series, to test the quality of by means of a specimen; to try, to examine the standard of by testing or sipping.

SAMPLER, [sahmp'-ler], *n.* a pattern of work; a specimen of embroidery or needlework; one who samples.

SAMSHU, [sam'-shōō], *n.* a Chinese spirit distilled from rice. [Chin. *samshu*].

SAMSON-POST, [sam'-son-pōst'], *n.* a strong post resting on the keelson and supporting a beam of the deck over the hold; the post to which the harpoon rope is fastened.

SAMURAI, [sam'-ōō-rī], *n.(pl.)* the military class in Japan under the feudal system; a Japanese gentleman who has hereditary class privileges. [Jap. *samurai* guard].

SANAD, [san'-ad], *n.* a warrant. [Hind. *sanad* signature].

SANATIVE, [san'-at-iv], *adj.* sanatory, having the power to heal, tending to heal. [LL. *sanativus*].

SANATIVENESS, [san'-at-iv-nes], *n.* the power of healing.

SANATORIUM, SANITARIUM, [san'-at-aw'-ri-um, san'-it-aer'-i-um], *n.* an establishment for the treatment of tuberculosis or other diseases; a health station; a resort for invalids; the hospital of a school. [L. *sanatorium*].

SANATORY, [san'-a-ter-i], *adj.* curative, conducive to health.

SANBENITO, [san'-ben-ē'-tō], *n.* a robe painted with nightmarish figures, worn on their way to execution by impenitents condemned to death by the Inquisition. [Span. *sambenito* from *San Benito* Saint Benedict].

SANCHO, [sang'-kō], *n.* a primitive negro guitar. [Ashanti *osanku*].

SANCTIFICATION, [sangk'-tif-ik-ā'-shun], *n.* the act or process of sanctifying; sanctified state; consecration. [L. *sanctificatio*].

SANCTIFIED, [sangk'-tif-īd], *adj.* made holy, consecrated; affectedly pious, pretentiously holy.

SANCTIFIER, [sangk'-tif-i-er], *n.* one who sanctifies; the Holy Spirit.

SANCTIFY, [sangk'-ti-fī], *v.t.* to make holy, hallow, to consecrate; to purify from sin prior to divine service; to sanction as a recipient of reverence; to justify, sanction, vindicate as holy. [L. *sanctificare*].

SANCTIFYING, [sangk'-ti-fī-ing], *adj.* tending to sanctify; intended to increase holiness.

SANCTIMONIOUS, [sangk'-tim-ō'-ni-us], *adj.* assuming the outward appearance of sanctity, hypocritically pious.

SANCTIMONIOUSLY, [sangk'-tim-ō'-ni-us-li], *adv.* in a sanctimonious manner, with sanctimony.

SANCTIMONIOUSNESS, [sangk'-tim-ō'-ni-us-nes], *n.* the state of being sanctimonious; sanctity, the appearance of sanctity.

SANCTIMONY, [sangk'-tim-on-i], *n.* devoutness; the affectation of devoutness. [L. *sanctimonia*].

SANCTION (1), [sangk'-shun], *n.* ratification of a subordinate's act by a superior authority, consent to a specific action; acknowledged acceptance of general conduct; justification; (*leg.*) the penalty which gives weight to the power of a law and its observance. [L. *sanctio* ordinance].

SANCTION (2), [sangk'-shun], *v.t.* to ratify, allow; to give sanction to.

SANCTIONARY, [sangk'-shun-er-i], *adj.* relating to or implying a sanction; having penal force.

SANCTITUDE, [sangk'-ti-tewd], *n.* holiness, devoutness. [L. *sanctitudo*].
SANCTITY, [sangk'-ti-ti], *n.* the state of being sacred or holy, godliness, saintliness, purity, sacredness; solemnity; a saint, that which is held holy. [L. *sanctitas*].
SANCTUARIZE†, [sangk'-choo-er-iz], *v.t.* to shelter by means of a sanctuary or sacred privileges.
SANCTUARY, [sangk'-choo-er-i], *n.* a sacred place, a holy shrine; a consecrated building; the most holy part of a church or temple; the altar place in a church; an asylum for fugitives, a place of refuge, formerly sanctioned by ecclesiastical authority; territory set apart for the protection and preservation of wild animals or birds; (*fig.*) a place of private holiness. [L. *sanctuarium* shrine].
SANCTUM, [sangk'-tum], *n.* a sacred place; a private study; **s. sanctorum,** the holy of holies in a tabernacle. [L. *sanctum*].
SANCTUS, [sangk'-tus], *n.* a hymn sung in the communion service beginning "Holy, holy, holy"; **S. bell,** a bell rung when the Sanctus is sung. [L. *sanctus*].
SAND (1), [sand], *n.* a mass of minute grains of disintegrated rock accumulating on seashores or river beds; (*pl.*) a stretch of sand; (*fig.*) the moments of time; (*slang*) grit, courage. [OE. *sand*].
SAND (2), [sand], *v.t.* to sprinkle or cover with sand; to mix with sand.
SANDAL, [sandl], *n.* a kind of open-worked shoe consisting of a sole fastened to the foot by straps. [Gk. *sandalion*].
SANDALLED, [sand'-ald], *adj.* wearing sandals; like sandals.
SANDALWOOD, [sand'-al-wood], *n.* the close-grained wood of an East Indian tree, *Santalum album*, remarkable for its fragrance, and much used for cabinet work. [SANDAL].
SANDARAC, [sand'-a-rak'], *n.* a resinous substance which exudes from the North-West African tree, *Callitris quadrivalvis*; realgar. [Gk. *sandarake*].
SAND-BADGER, [sand'-baj'-er], *n.* the hog-badger, an Indian species of *Arctonyx*.
SANDBAG (1), [sand'-bag'], *n.* a canvas bag filled with sand, used in fortification, etc.
SANDBAG (2), (**sandbagging, sandbagged**), [sand'-bag'], *v.t.* to hit over the head with a sandbag, so as to render unconscious; to protect with sandbags.
SANDBAGGER, [sand'-bag'-er], *n.* a thief who stuns his victim from behind with a sandbag.
SANDBANK, [sand'-bank'], *n.* a sandy shoal.
SAND-BAR, [sand'-bah(r)], *n.* a bank of sand formed across the mouth of a river.
SANDBATH, [sand'-bahth], *n.* a bath made by warm sand, to envelop something; a vessel containing sand for the even heating of chemical retorts.
SANDBLAST, [sand'-blahst], *n.* a jet of sand forcibly driven against glass or hard metal by means of steam pressure for cutting or engraving purposes.
SAND-BLIND, [sand'-blind'], *adj.* having a defect of sight due to specks floating before the eye. [OE. *sam* half and *blind* blind].
SAND-BLINDNESS, [sand'-blind'-nes], *n.* the state of being sand-blind.
SAND-BOX (1), [sand'-boks'], *n.* a box for containing sand for sprinkling roads or making golf tees, etc.
SANDBOX (2), [sand'-boks'], *n.* the tropical West Indian tree *Hura crepitans*, the seeds of which, when the pericarp bursts, are scattered about with a loud report.
SANDBOY, [sand'-boi'], *n.* **as happy as a s.,** as happy as a carefree boy.
SAND-CRACK, [sand'-krak'], *n.* a crack in the horny fibres of a horse's hoof, extending mostly from above downwards.
SAND-DUNE, [sand'-dewn'], *n.* a ridge of drifted sand.
SANDED, [sand'-id], *adj.* sprinkled or covered with sand; of a sandy colour.
SAND-EEL, [sand'-ēl], *n.* a small elongated fish of the genus *Ammodytes*, which buries itself in the sand between the tide-marks, the sand-launce.
SANDEMANIAN, [san'-dim-ā'-ni-an], *n.* a follower of Robert *Sandeman*, leader of a religious sect.
SANDERLING, [sand'-er-ling], *n.* a small wading bird allied to the sandpipers, *Calidris arenaria*. [Uncert.].
SANDERS, [sand'-erz], *n.* the red sandal-wood, *Pterocarpus santalina*. [OFr. *sandre*].
SANDEVER, see SANDIVER.
SANDFLOOD, [sand'-flud], *n.* a vast body of sand carried by winds through the deserts of Arabia.
SANDFLY, [sand'-flī'], *n.* a stinging fly of the genus *Simulium*, occurring in hot, sandy countries.
SANDGLASS, [sand'-glahs], *n.* a glass apparatus pinched in at the middle to form a bottle-neck through which sand from the upper chamber trickles into the lower, emptying itself after exactly one hour, an hour-glass; a glass on the same principle used for measuring the time required to cook a "boiled" egg.
SAND-GROUSE, [sand'-grows], *n.* a genus of birds allied to the pigeons, inhabiting the deserts of Asia and Africa, one species of which, *Syrrhaptes paradoxus*, has been an occasional visitor to Britain since 1863.
SAND-HEAT, [sand'-hēt], *n.* the heat applied by means of warm sand, in chemical operations.
SANDHILL, [sand'-hil], *n.* a hill of sand.
SAND-HOPPER, [sand'-hop-er], *n.* (*zool.*) the small leaping amphipod crustacean, *Talitrus saltator*.
SANDINESS, [sand'-i-nes], *n.* the quality or state of being sandy.
SAND-IRON, [sand'-iern], *n.* a golf club with a special face for lifting a ball from sand.
SANDIVER, SANDEVER, [sand'-iv-er], *n.* a whitish salt scum cast up from glass in a state of fusion, glass-gall. [Fr. *suin de verre* sweat of glass].
SANDIX, [sand'-iks], *n.* (*min.*) a kind of minium, red-lead. [L. *sandix*].
SAND-LAUNCE, [sand'-lahnts], *n.* a sand-eel.
SAND-MARTIN, [sand'-mah'-tin], *n.* a species of martin, nesting in sand pits and sandbanks, *Cotile riparia*.
SANDPAPER (1), [sand'-pā-per], *n.* paper covered with a gritty substance for smoothing and polishing wood.
SANDPAPER (2), [sand'-pā-per], *v.t.* to smooth or polish by means of sandpaper.
SANDPIPER, [sand'-pī-per], *n.* one of several species of small plovers allied to the ruff and dunlin.
SANDPIPES, [sand'-pīpz], *n.* (*pl.*) cylindrical hollows tapering down into the chalk and filled with sand, clay or gravel.
SANDSHOE, [sand'-shoo'], *n.* a light shoe of canvas with straw or rubber soles suitable for wear on a sandy beach.

SANDPIPER

SANDSTONE, [sand'-stōn], *n.* (*geol.*) a stone or rock composed chiefly of grains of quartz, felspar and mica.
SANDSTORM, [sand'-stawm'], *n.* a storm in which clouds of fine sand are blown about, *esp.* in the desert.
SANDWICH (1), [sand'-wij], *n.* two pieces of bread and butter with a thin slice of ham, meat, or jam, etc., between them; a sponge cake in this form with jam spread in the middle. [John, fourth Earl of *Sandwich*].
SANDWICH (2), [sand'-wij], *v.t.* to insert, to interpose, to squeeze.
SANDWICH BOARD, [sand'-wij-bawd'], *n.* one of a pair of boards on which advertisements are displayed, carried on the back and chest by perambulating sandwichmen.
SANDWICHMAN, [sand'-wij-man], *n.* a man employed to parade in the streets with two advertisement-boards hanging over his shoulders, one in front and one at the back.
SANDWORT, [sand'-wurt], *n.* a plant of the genus *Arenaria*.
SANDY (1), [sand'-i], *n.* (*Scots coll.*) a Christian name. [Abbreviation for *Alexander*].
SANDY (2), [sand'-i], *adj.* abounding with or full of sand; covered or sprinkled with sand; having some or all of the characteristics of sand, like sand, gritty; loose, not firm or solid; of the colour of sand, yellowish-brown.
SANDYHEAD, [sand'-i-hed'], *n.* a sea-duck, the pochard, *Nyroca ferina*.
SANDYISH, [san'-di-ish], *adj.* somewhat sandy; a little gritty; rather pale in colour.
SANE, [sān], *adj.* of a balanced emotional and rational nature, sound in mind; sound in opinion; reasonable, sober in judgment, sensible. [L. *sanus* sound].
SANELY, [sān'-li], *adv.* in a sane manner.
SANENESS, [sān'-nes], *n.* the quality or state of being sane.
SANG, [sang], *pret.* of SING. [OE. *sang*].
SANGAREE, [sang'-ga-rē'], *n.* a cold West Indian

drink consisting of wine and water, sweetened and spiced. [Span. *sangria* bleeding].

SANGFROID, [sah(ng)'-frwah'], *n.* freedom from excitement or nervousness, presence of mind, natural capacity for keeping calm in awkward or dangerous circumstances. [Fr. *sang-froid* cool blood].

SANGHA, [sang'-ha], *n.* the Buddhist community or order of monks.

SANGRAAL, [san'-grāl'], *n.* the Holy Grail. [OFr. *sangraal*].

SANGUIFEROUS, [sang-gwif'-er-us], *adj.* conveying blood. [L. *sanguis* blood and *ferre* to bear].

SANGUIFICATION, [sang'-gwi-fik-ā'-shun], *n.* the conversion of food into blood.

SANGUINARILY, [sang'-gwin-a-ri-li], *adv.* in a sanguinary manner.

SANGUINARINESS, [sang'-gwin-a-ri-nes], *n.* the quality of being sanguinary.

SANGUINARY, [sang'-gwin-er-i], *adj.* attended with much bloodshed; bloodthirsty in nature; bloody. [L. *sanguinarius*].

SANGUINE, [sang'-gwin], *adj.* having the colour of blood, deep ruby in colour; courageous, confident, cheerful, optimistic. [L. *sanguineus* blood-red].

SANGUINELY, [sang'-gwin-li], *adv.* in a sanguine manner.

SANGUINENESS, [sang'-gwin-nes], *n.* the state of being sanguine; the colour of blood; fulness of blood; ardour, confidence, optimism.

SANGUINEOUS, [sang-gwin'-i-us], *adj.* abounding with blood; sanguine; blood-red. [L. *sanguineus*].

SANGUINIVOROUS, [sang'-gwin-iv'-er-us], *adj.* subsisting on blood. [SANGUINE and L. *vorare* to devour].

SANHEDRIM, [san'-id-rim], *n.* the great council of justice of the ancient Jews, consisting of an equal number of priests, scribes and elders, presided over by the high priest. [Heb. *sanhedrin*].

SANICLE, [san'-ikl], *n.* (*bot.*) the umbelliferous plant, *Sanicula europæa*. [MedL. *sanicula*].

SANIDINE, [san'-id-ēn], *n.* (*min.*) a glassy-fissured orthoclase felspar. [Gk. *sanis* board].

SANIES, [sā'-ni-ēz], *n.* (*med.*) serous matter, or blood-infested discharge from wounds or sores, less thick and white than pus. [L. *sanies*].

SANIFY, [san'-i-fī], *v.t.* to make healthy and hygienic.

SANIOUS, [sā'-ni-us], *adj.* relating to, consisting of, sanies, or partaking of its nature; thin and serous; running with sanies. [L. *saniosus*].

SANITARIAN, [san'-it-āer'-i-an], *n.* an advocate of sanitary reforms or reforms in sanitation.

SANITARILY, [san'-it-er-i-li], *adv.* in a sanitary manner.

SANITARINESS, [san'-it-er-i-nes], *n.* the condition of being sanitary.

SANITARIUM, see SANATORIUM.

SANITARY, [san'-it-er-i], *adj.* relating to health or hygienic principles and conditions, designed to promote health, healthy, hygienic; clean, disinfected, free from dirt; having proper drainage; **s. inspector**, an official employed to make regular inspections of local drainage and plumbing systems.

SANITARY-TOWEL, [san'-it-er-i-tow'-el], *n.* an absorbent pad used by women for personal hygiene during menstruation.

SANITATION, [san'-it-ā'-shun], *n.* sanitary science and its application.

SANITY, [san'-i-ti], *n.* the state of being sane, saneness. [L. *sanitas* health].

SANJAK, [san'-jak'], *n.* an administrative subdivision of a Turkish province. [Turk. *sanjak* flag].

SANK, [sangk], *pret.* of SINK. [OE. *sanc*].

SANKHYA, [sang'-kya], *n.* one of the systems of Hindu philosophy. [Hind. *sankhya*].

SANNYASIN, [san-yas'-in], *n.* a Hindu anchorite. [Native].

SANS†, [sanz], *prep.* without. [Fr. *sans*].

SANSCULOTTE, [sah(ng)'-kyōōl-ot'], *n.* (*French hist.*) a contemptuous term for the mob or working classes; the revolutionaries who did not wear the aristocratic knee-breeches but loose trousers. [Fr. *sans culotte* without breeches].

SANSCULOTTIC, [sah(ng)'-kyōōl-ot'-ik], *adj.* connected with, proceeding from, sansculottism.

SANSCULOTTISM, [sah(ng)'-kyōōl-ot'-izm], *n.* a term of abuse for the doctrine of universal equality.

SANSERIF, [sanz'-se'-rif], *n.* a type fount designed without serifs, as that in which the headwords of this dictionary are set up. [Fr. *sans* without and SERIF].

SANSKRIT (1), [san'-skrit], *n.* the ancient language of the Hindus. [Skr. *samskrta*].

SANSKRIT (2), [san'-skrit], *adj.* relating to, written in, Sanskrit.

SANSKRITIST, [san'-skrit-ist], *n.* a Sanskrit scholar.

SANTA CLAUS, [san'-ta-klawz'], *n.* Father Christmas. [Du. *Sante Klaus* Saint Nicholas].

SANTAL, [sant'-al], *n.* sandalwood. [L. *santalum*].

SANTALIN, [sant'-al-in], *n.* (*chem.*) the colouring matter of red sandalwood. [MedL. *santalum* sandalwood].

SANTALWOOD, [san'-tal-wŏŏd'], *n.* sandalwood.

SANTON, [san'-ton], *n.* an Eastern dervish. [~L. *sanctus* holy].

SANTONIN, [sant'-on-in], *n.* (*chem.*) a crystalline vegetable principle, obtained from *Artemisia maritima*, used for purging worms from the bowels. [L. *santonica* wormwood].

SAP (1), [sap], *n.* the circulating juice of plants; vital fluid; (*fig.*) vitality, vigour, life-blood. [OE. *sæp*].

SAP (2), [sap], *n.* (*milit.*) a trench providing head protection; (*slang*) a fool, a dupe. [OFr. *sappe* trench-tool].

SAP (3), **(sapping, sapped)**, [sap], *v.t. and i.* (*milit.*) to attack by means of a sap, to undermine, to dig a sap; to weaken by draining away vital energy or by tapping the source of strength, to devitalize.

SAPAJOU, [sap'-a-zhōō], *n.* a South American monkey of the genus *Cebus*. [Fr. *sapajou*].

SAPAJOU

SAPAN, [sap'-an], *n.* an Asiatic dye-wood, *Caasalpinia Sappan*, yielding a red colour. [Malay *sapang*].

SAP-COLOUR, [sap'-kul'-er], *n.* vegetable juice used as paint.

SAP-GREEN, [sap'-grēn], *n.* a light green pigment from the juice of buckthorn berries.

SAPID, [sap'-id], *adj.* having a savour; affecting the taste, savoury; affected. [L. *sapidus* savoury].

SAPIDITY, [sap-id'-i-ti], *n.* the quality of being sapid, sapidness.

SAPIDNESS, [sap'-id-nes], *n.* sapidity.

SAPIENCE, [sā'-pi-ents], *n.* wisdom; (*esp.* when used ironically) stupidity. [L. *sapientia*].

SAPIENT, [sā'-pi-ent], *adj.* sagacious, wise; would-be wise. [L. *sapiens*].

SAPIENTIAL, [sā'-pi-en'-shal], *adj.* relating to wisdom; **s. books**, certain scriptural books ("Proverbs," "Ecclesiastes," etc.). [L. *sapientialis*].

SAPIENTLY, [sā'-pi-ent-li], *adv.* in a sapient manner.

SAPLESS, [sap'-les], *adj.* destitute of sap; dry.

SAPLING, [sap'-ling], *n.* a young tree; a young greyhound; (*fig.*) an adolescent youth not fully developed physically.

SAPODILLA, [sap'-od-il'-a], *n.* a large West Indian tree, *Achras Sapota*, of which the seeds are diuretic. [Mexican *tzapotl*].

SAPONACEOUS, [sap'-on-ā'-shus], *adj.* resembling or having the qualities of soap, soapy; (*fig.*) oily. [L. *sapo saponis* soap].

SAPONIFICATION, [sap-on'-if-ik-ā'-shun], *n.* conversion into soap by a chemical process.

SAPONIFY, [sap-on'-i-fī], *v.t.* to convert into soap.

SAPONINE, [sap'-on-in], *n.* a vegetable principle from the root of soapwort.

SAPORIFIC, [sap'-or-if'-ik], *adj.* producing taste.

SAPOROUS, [sap'-or-us], *adj.* having taste; yielding some kind of taste; savoury. [L. *saporosus*].

SAPPER, [sap'-er], *n.* one who saps, undermines; (*milit.*) a non-commissioned rank in the Royal Engineers; (*milit. coll.*) an officer in the Royal Engineers.

SAPPHIC (1), [saf'-ik], *n.* a poetic stanza or poem in the sapphic form.

SAPPHIC (2), [saf'-ik], *adj.* derived from, relating to, Sappho, who used a form of verse consisting of three five-beat lines followed by a short fourth line. [Gk. *Sappho*, a poetess].

SAPPHIRE (1), [saf'-ier], *n.* a precious stone of an intense translucent blue, being a brightly coloured variety of corundum, pure crystallized alumina; a deep, bright blue. [Gk. *sappheiros*].

SAPPHIRE (2), [saf'-ier], *adj.* relating to, made of, sapphire or sapphires; having the colour of a sapphire.

SAPPHIRINE (1), [saf'-i-rin], *n.* a pale-blue mineral resembling sapphire.

SAPPHIRINE (2), [saf'-i-rin], *adj.* consisting of, having the qualities of, resembling or relating to, sapphire; **s. gurnard**, the tub-fish, *Trigla hirundo*.

SAPPINESS, [sap'-i-nes], *n.* the quality of being sappy; succulence, juiciness.
SAPPING, [sap'-ing], *n.* the art of making trenches.
SAPPY, [sap'-i], *adj.* full of sap, juicy; (*slang*) weak. [OE. *sæpig*].
SAPRAEMIA, [sap-rē'-mi-a], *n.* (*med.*) septicaemia. [Gk. *sapros* decayed and *haima* blood].
SAPRO-, *pref.* decaying, rotten, putrid. [Gk. *sapros*].
SAPROGENIC, [sap'-rō-jen'-ik], *adj.* producing decay.
SAPROPHAGANS, [sap-rof'-ag-anz], *n.*(*pl.*) (*entom.*) a tribe of coleopterous insects feeding on putrid animal and vegetable substances. [SAPRO and Gk. *phago* I eat].
SAPROPHYTE, [sap'-rō-fīt], *n.* (*bot.*) a plant that lives on decaying vegetable matter. [SAPRO and Gk. *phuton* a plant].
SAP-ROT, [sap'-rot'], *n.* dry rot.
SAPSAGO, [sap'-sā-gō], *n.* a kind of sweet hard cheese made in Switzerland, flavoured with the flowers of *Melilotus cærulea*, which contain much honey. [Germ. *schabziger*].
SAPUCAIA, [sap'-yōōk-ī'-a], *n.* a South American tropical tree of the genus *Lecythis*, famous for its nuts. [Braz. *sapucaia*].
SAPWOOD, [sap'-wŏŏd], *n.* the external part of wood, newly formed under the bark, the alburnum.
SARABAND, [sa'-ra-band'], *n.* a Spanish slow dance; a short piece of music composed for this in three-four time having the second beat accented. [Span. *zarabanda*].
SARACEN, [sa'-ra-sen], *n.* a Mohammedan, *esp.* in the Middle Ages, an enemy of the Crusaders. [Gk. *Sarakenos*].
SARACENIC, [sa'-ra-sen'-ik], *adj.* connected with, pertaining to, the Saracens.
SARCASM, [sah'-kazm'], *n.* a bitter jibe, taunt; a remark uttered with scorn or contempt. [Gk. *sarkasmos*].
SARCAST, [sah'-kast], *n.* a sarcastic speaker or writer. [*Prec.*].
SARCASTIC, [sah-kast'-ik], *adj.* embodying sarcasm, bitterly satirical or ironical; having a nature which delights in sarcasm. [Gk. *sarkastikos*].
SARCASTICALLY, [sah-kast'-ik-a-li], *adv.* in a sarcastic vein or manner.
SARCEL†, [sah'-sel], *n.* the pinion of a falcon's wing. [OFr. *cercel*].
SARCENET, see SARSENET.
SARCIN, [sah'-sin], *n.* (*chem.*) a nitrogenous substance obtained from certain muscular and glandular tissues. [Gk. *sarkinos* fleshy].
SARCINA, [sah'-sin-a], *n.* (*bot.*) a plant of a fungoid nature found in animal secretions. [L. *sarcina* bundle].
SARCO-, *pref.* flesh. [Gk. *sarx sarkos*].
SARCOCARP, [sah'-kō-kahp], *n.* (*bot.*) the fleshy part of some fruit. [SARCO and Gk. *karpos* fruit].
SARCOCELE, [sah'-kō-sēl], *n.* (*path.*) a fleshy tumour of the testicle. [SARCO and Gk. *kele* tumour].
SARCODE, [sah'-kōd], *n.* (*biol.*) animal protoplasm. [Fr. *sarcode*].
SARCODIC, [sah-kō'-dik], *adj.* consisting of, pertaining to, sarcode.
SARCOID, [sah'-koid], *adj.* flesh-like. [SARCO and Gk. *oeides* like].
SARCOLEMMA, [sah'-kō-lem'-a], *n.* (*anat.*) a membrane coating muscular tissue. [SARCO and Gk. *lemma* that which is taken].
SARCOLINE, [sah'-kō-lin], *adj.* (*min.*) flesh-coloured.
SARCOLITE, [sah'-kō-līt], *n.* (*min.*) a mineral of a flesh-colour, a silicate of calcium and aluminium with iron, magnesium and sodium. [SARCO and Gk. *lithos* stone].
SARCOLOGICAL, [sah'-kō-loj'-ik-al], *adj.* relating to sarcology.
SARCOLOGY, [sah-kol'-o-ji], *n.* that branch of anatomy which treats of the fleshy parts of the body. [SARCO and Gk. *logos* speech].
SARCOMA, [sah-kō'-ma], *n.* a cancerous tumour of the connective cells. [Gk. *sarkoma*].
SARCOPHAGOUS, [sah-kof'-ag-us], *adj.* feeding on flesh. [SARCO and Gk. *phago* I eat].
SARCOPHAGUS, (*pl.* **sarcophagi**), [sah-kof'-ag-us], *n.* a variety of stone, credited with the power of disintegrating flesh within a few weeks, of which the ancient Greeks made coffins; (*archæ.*) a large, carved coffin found in Egypt, etc. [Gk. *sarkophagos* flesh-eating].
SARD, [sahd], *n.* (*min.*) a variety of semi-precious hard quartz of a blood-red colour. [Gk. *sardion* Sardian].
SARDINE, [sah-dēn'], *n.* the young of the pilchard, *Clupea pilchardus*, abundant in the Mediterranean and Bay of Biscay, and exported preserved in oil. [Fr. *sardine* pertaining to *Sardinia*].

SARDINE

SARDIUS, [sah'-di-us], *n.* a sard. [Gk. *sardios*].
SARDONIC, [sah-don'-ik], *adj.* expressive of irony or of cynicism; having a nature governed by a cynical frame of mind; malicious, bitter; unfriendly. [Late Gk. *sardonios* indicating a herb which made the eater pull a wry face].
SARDONICALLY, [sah-don'-ik-al-i], *adv.* in a sardonic manner.
SARDONYX, [sah-don'-iks], *n.* (*min.*) a semi-precious stone, being a banded variety of sard. [Gk. *sardonux*].
SARGASSO, [sah-gas'-ō], *n.* the floating gulfweed, *Sargassum bacciferum*, characterized by pods like air-bubbles or grapes. [Portug. *sargaço*].
SARI, [sah'-rē], *n.* a Hindu woman's chief article of dress, which is a cloth or robe wound round the body. [Hind. *sari*].
SARK, [sahk], *n.* a shirt or chemise. [OE. *serc* tunic].
SARKING, [sahk-ing], *n.* the sheathing of a roof above the rafters.
SARLAC, [sah'-lak], *n.* the yak. [Mongolian *sarlac*].
SARMATIAN, [sah-mā'-shun], *adj.* coming from, pertaining to, Sarmatia or Poland.
SARMENTOSE, [sah-ment'-ōs], *adj.* (*bot.*) having runners. [L. *sarmentosus*].
SARMENTUM, [sah-ment'-um], *n.* a runner. [L. *sarmentum*].
SARONG, [sa-rongh'], *n.* a knee-length garment worn wrapper-wise by natives of the East Indies. [Malay *sarung*].
SARPLIER, SARPLAR, [sah'-plēer, sah'-pler], *n.* canvas, packing cloth; a sack of wool containing eighty tods. [AFr. *sarplier*].
SARRACENIA, [sa'-ra-sē'-ni-a], *n.* (*bot.*) a genus of North American pitcher-plants. [Dr. *Sarrazin*, its discoverer].
SARRUSOPHONE, [sa-rōōz'-ō-fōn], *n.* one of a series of brass instruments played with a double reed. [M. *Sarrus*, the designer, and PHONE].
SARSAPARILLA, [sahs'-a-pa-ril'-a], *n.* a species of *Smilax*, with a medicinal root, found in tropical America. [Span. *zarzaparrilla*].
SARSE, [sahs], *n.* a fine sieve.
SARSEN, [sah'-sen], *n.* a large block of indurated sandstone such as is found scattered over chalk downs and from which some of the prehistoric stones of Stonehenge were cut. [~SARACEN].
SARSENET, SARCENET, [sahs'-en-et], *n.* a fine, thin woven silk. [OFr. *sarcenet* from LL. *saracenicus* Saracen].
SARTORIAL, [sah-taw'-ri-al], *adj.* of, relating to, a tailor or tailoring. [L. *sartor* tailor].
SARTORIUS, [sah-taw'-ri-us], *n.* (*anat.*) the muscle on the inner side of the thigh used when crossing the legs, called the tailor's muscle.
SASH (1), [sash], *n.* a scarf worn for ornament or military decoration round the waist or over the shoulder. [Arab. *shash* muslin].
SASH (2), [sash], *n.* the frame of a window into which the panes of glass are fitted; **s. cord (line)**, the rope by which a vertically moving sash is hung in a window-frame. [Fr. *chassis* frame].
SASH (3), [sash], *v.t.* to provide with a sash or sashes.
SASH-FASTENER, [sash'-fahst'-ner], *n.* a metal fitment for keeping a window firmly closed.
SASIN, [sa'-sin], *n.* the Indian antelope, known as the blackbuck, *Antilope cervicapra*. [Native].
SASSAFRAS, [sa'-sa-fras], *n.* the North American tree, *Sassafras officinale*, from the wood and bark of which a medicinal tonic oil is obtained. [Span. *sasafras*].
SASSENACH, [sas'-en-ak'], *n.* a Scots name for an Englishman; a lowlander. [Gael. *sassunach* Saxon].
SASSOLITE, [sas'-ō-līt], *n.* native boracic acid. [*Sasso*, the name of a lake in Italy].
SASTRA, [sas'-tra], *n.* the Shastra.
SAT, [sat], *pret. and p.pt.* of SIT. [OE. *sæt*].
SATAN, [sā'-tan], *n.* the devil or prince of darkness, *esp.* as regarded as the spiritual enemy of mankind. [Heb. *Satan* the enemy].
SATANIC, [sat-an'-ik], *adj.* relating to Satan; having the qualities of Satan; fiendish, devilish, infernal; extremely malicious, wicked or self-centred.

SATANICALLY, [sat-an'-ik-al-i], *adv.* in a Satanic manner.
SATANISM, [sā'-tan-izm], *n.* devil worship as a travesty of Christianity by inversion; deliberate wickedness; the evil and malicious disposition of Satan.
SATANIST, [sāt'-an-ist], *n.* one who believes in Satanism.
SATANOLOGY, [sā'-tan-ol'-o-ji], *n.* the study of the origin and meaning of Satan; literature about the devil. [SATAN and Gk. *logos* speech].
SATANOPHOBIA, [sā'-tan-ō-fō'-bi-a], *n.* a morbid fear of the devil. [SATAN and PHOBIA].
SATCHEL, [sach'-el], *n.* a little sack or bag, slung from the shoulder, for books, papers, or money, particularly used by schoolchildren. [OFr. *sachel* little sack].
SATE (1), [sāt], *v.t.* to satisfy the appetite of; to glut, surfeit. [L. *satis* enough].
SATE (2)†, [sāt], *pret.* of SIT.
SATEEN, [sat-ēn'], *n.* a cotton imitation of satin. [~SATIN].
SATELLITE, [sat'-el-īt], *n.* (*astron.*) a moon; a small body attendant on a planet; (*fig.*) an obsequious attendant, hanger-on; **s. town,** a smaller town at a short distance from, and depending upon, a larger one. [L. *satelles* attendant].
SATIABLE, [sā'-shi-abl], *adj.* able to be satiated.
SATIATE (1), [sā'-shi-āt], *adj.* having experienced more than enough, glutted, filled to satiety; surfeited.
SATIATE (2), [sā'-shi-āt], *v.t.* to satisfy fully; to satisfy beyond the natural capacity, surfeit. [~L. *satiare*].
SATIATION, [sā'-shi-ā'-shun], *n.* the state of being filled to satiety.
SATIETY, [sat-ī'-i-ti], *n.* the state of full satisfaction or of gratification beyond desire. [L. *satietas*].
SATIN (1), [sat'-in], *n.* a species of glossy silk fabric of a thick close texture with a smooth shining surface. [Fr. *satin*].
SATIN (2), [sat'-in], *adj.* made of satin; having some or all of the characteristics of satin.
SATIN-BIRD, [sat'-in-burd], *n.* the satin bower-bird, *Ptilonorrhynchus violaceus.*
SATINET, SATINETTE, [sat'-in-et'], *n.* a thin kind of satin; a glossy cloth woven with cotton and silk in imitation of satin.
SATINITY, [sat-in'-it-i], *n.* smoothness like that of satin. [SATIN (1)].
SATIN-PAPER, [sat'-in-pā'-per], *n.* a glossy writing-paper.
SATIN-SILVER, [sat'-in-sil'-ver], *adj.* having a silver gloss imitative of satin.
SATIN-SPAR, [sat'-in-spahr'], *n.* a fine fibrous variety of gypsum, having a satiny lustre.
SATIN WALNUT, [sat'-in-wawl'-nut], *n.* the wood of the sweet-gum tree, *Liquidambar styraciflua*, much prized for furniture.
SATINWOOD, [sat'-in-wŏŏd], *n.* the hard, lemon-coloured wood of the East Indian tree, *Chloroxylon swietenia*, or the tropical American tree, *Ferolaguianensis*, of a mottled grain, used in cabinet work.
SATINY, [sat'-in-i], *adj.* like satin in gloss or softness.
SATIRE, [sat'-īer], *n.* the denunciation of vices, folly or abuses of any kind, generally presented with a greater or lesser degree of distortion, by means of sarcasm, irony, derision, etc.; any literary composition of this kind, *esp.* when in verse; a lampoon; (*fig.*) a circumstance or thing which has the effect of making some person or thing ridiculous.
SATIRICAL, [sat-i'-rik-al], *adj.* having the nature of satire; derived from satire; characterized by satire; having a nature addicted to satire, of a satirical frame of mind.
SATIRICALLY, [sa-ti'-rik-al-i], *adv.* in a satirical manner or style.
SATIRIST, [sat'-i-rist], *n.* a person who satirizes or writes satire; a writer of satire.
SATIRIZE, [sat'-i-rīz], *v.t.* to represent satirically; to censure or ridicule with severity.
SATISFACTION, [sa'-tis-fak'-shun], *n.* the state of being satisfied; the act of satisfying; that which satisfies; content; gratification; atonement, reparation, amends; payment. [L. *satisfactio* apology].
SATISFACTORILY, [sa'-tis-fak'-ter-i-li], *adv.* in a satisfactory manner.
SATISFACTORINESS, [sa'-tis-fak'-ter-i-nes], *n.* the condition of being satisfactory or giving content.
SATISFACTORY, [sa'-tis-fak'-ter-i], *adj.* meeting one's requirements or desires, satisfying one's sense of fitness, producing a feeling of satisfaction; giving satisfaction, supplying one's demands, pleasing, suitable, good; (*theol.*) making amends, atoning.
SATISFIABLE, [sa'-tis-fī-abl], *adj.* that may be satisfied.
SATISFIER, [sa'-tis-fī-er], *n.* one who gives satisfaction.
SATISFY, [sa'-tis-fī], *v.t.* to provide with means which render the mind, the emotions or the body contented; to gratify; to provide enough for, to supply fully; to meet one's requirements, to pay so as to make complete amends to, indemnify; to discharge a debt; to free from doubt, to convince, persuade; *v.i.* to come up to standard; to give satisfaction. [L. *satisfacere* to make content].
SATISFYINGLY, [sat'-is-fī'-ing-li], *adv.* to a satisfying degree.
SATRANGI, [sat-ranj'-i], *n.* a cheap Indian carpet made of cotton. [Bengali *satrangi*].
SATRAP, [sa'-trap], *n.* in ancient history, the governor of a Persian province, ruling it with the power of an absolute monarch; a lesser tyrant. [Pers. *khsatrapavan* protector of a province].
SATRAPY, [sā'-tra-pi], *n.* the government or province of a satrap. [Gk. *satrapeia*].
SATSUMA, [sat'-sōō-ma], *n.* hard, glazed, pale yellow Japanese pottery; the most powerful of the Japanese great clans. [Jap. *Satsuma*, a group of islands near Japan].
SATTARA, [sat-ah'-ra], *n.* a ribbed, lustred, woollen material. [*Satara*, in India].
SATURABLE, [sach'-yŏŏer-abl], *adj.* able to be saturated. [L. *saturabilis*].
SATURANT (1), [sach'-yŏŏer-ant], *n.* a substance which neutralizes the acid in the stomach.
SATURANT (2), [sach'-yŏŏer-ant], *adj.* saturating.
SATURATE, [sach'-yŏŏ-rāt], *v.t.* to soak, to add as much to as can be absorbed, to drench, to cause to absorb so much moisture that it can contain no more; (*chem.*) to dissolve in or combine with to the maximum; (*fig.*) to steep (in facts, etc.). [L. *saturare* to satiate].
SATURATION, [sach'-yŏŏ-ra-shun], *n.* the act of saturating; the state of being saturated; impregnation of one body with another till the receiving body can contain no more. [L. *saturatio*].
SATURDAY, [sat'-er-dā], *n.* the seventh day of the week. [OE. *sæternesdæg* from L. *Saturni dies* Saturn's day].
SATURN, [sat'-urn], *n.* (*astron.*) one of the major planets, being the second largest and the sixth farthest from the sun, distinguished by its nine major satellites and its three rings of densely packed satellite fragments; (*myth.*) the ancient Italian god of agriculture and husbandry, later identified mistakenly with the Greek god Kronos. [L. *Saturnus* the sower].

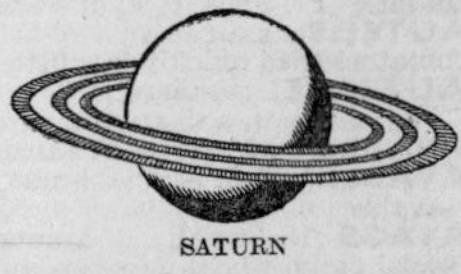
SATURN

SATURNALIA, [sat'-ern-ā'-li-a], *n.(pl.)* the annual feast of Saturn during which all distinctions of class were forgotten. [L. *saturnalia*].
SATURNALIAN, [sat'-ern-ā'-li-an], *adj.* relating to the saturnalia; loose, dissolute, sportive.
SATURNIAN, [sat-urn'-i-an], *adj.* relating to Saturn whose reign is called the golden age; golden, happy, distinguished for purity, integrity and simplicity; of an old metre used by the working classes of ancient Rome and Italy in their folksongs.
SATURNINE, [sat'-ern-īn], *adj.* supposed to be under the influence of Saturn; dull, heavy, phlegmatic, not easily susceptible of excitement; dark in visage, glowering.
SATURNIST, [sat'-ern-ist], *n.* a person of a grave, gloomy temperament.
SATYAGRAHA, [sut-yah'-gra-hah], *n.* the Indian policy of civil disobedience. [Hind. *satyagraha*].
SATYR, [sat'-er], *n.* (*myth.*) a sylvan deity, represented as part man and part goat, with a snub nose and pointed ears, believed to be addicted to promiscuous loving; a lecher. [Gk. *saturos*].
SATYRIASIS, [sat'-i-rī'-a-sis], *n.* sexual mania in males, immoderate sexual appetite, promiscuity. [Gk. *saturiasis*].
SATYRIC, [sat-i'-rik], *adj.* relating to satyrs.
SAUCE (1), [saws], *n.* a preparation taken with meat, fish, sweets, etc., to enhance the flavour; (*coll.*) cheek, impudence, impertinence. [L. *salsus* salted].
SAUCE (2), [saws], *v.t.* to season with sauce; (*coll.*) to be impudent or impertinent to.

SAUCEBOAT, [saws'-bōt], *n.* a small deep dish to hold sauce for use at table.
SAUCEBOX, [saws'-boks'], *n.* a saucy, impudent fellow.
SAUCEPAN, [saws'-pan], *n.* a cooking pot, with a handle, used for boiling, a stew-pan.
SAUCER, [saw'-ser], *n.* a shallow circular dish of china or other ware, in which a cup is set; †a saucepan for the table. [OFr. *saussier*].
SAUCILY, [saws'-i-li], *adv.* in a saucy manner, impudently, petulantly.
SAUCINESS, [saw'-si-nes], *n.* the quality of being saucy; impertinent boldness; contempt for superiors.
SAUCY, [saw'-si], *adj.* of a cheeky nature, impudent, rude; expressive of impudence. [SAUCE].
SAUERKRAUT, [sow'-er-krowt'], *n.* chopped cabbage pressed in layers with salt between till it ferments. [Germ. from *sauer* sour and *kraut* cabbage].
SAULT, [soo, sō], *n.* a rapid in a Canadian river. [OFr. *sault* leap].
SAUMUR, [sō-myooer'], *n.* a sparkling white wine. [*Saumur*, a French district].
SAUNTER (1), [sawn'-ter], *n.* a sauntering, a stroll; place for sauntering.
SAUNTER (2), [sawn'-ter], *v.i.* to walk in a leisurely aimless way, to stroll, to wander idly having no fixed destination or time limit; to loiter, linger. [Unkn.].
SAUNTERER, [sawn'-ter-er], *n.* one who saunters.
SAURIAN (1), [saw'-ri-an], *n.* a reptile of the lizard group.
SAURIAN (2), [saw'-ri-an], *adj.* belonging to, resembling, a reptile. [Gk. *sauros* lizard].
SAUROID, [saw'-roid], *n.* a fish resembling a saurian in structure. [Gk. *sauros* lizard and *oeides* like].
SAURY, [saw'-ri], *n.* the skipper, *Scombresox saurus*, a sea-fish allied to the garpike. [Gk. *sauros* lizard].
SAUSAGE, [sos'-ij], *n.* a roll of seasoned, finely chopped meat, etc., packed in a skin. [OFr. *saussiche* from L. *salsus* salted].
SAUSAGE-MEAT, [sos'-ij-mēt'], *n.* meat and bread, etc., minced up together and seasoned.
SAUSAGE-ROLL, [sos'-ij-rōl], *n.* a small oblong pasty filled with sausage-meat and lightly baked.
SAUSSURITE, [sōs'-yooer-īt], *n.* (*min.*) a mineral of a greenish-grey colour formed by the decomposition of felspar. [H. B. de *Saussure*, a Swiss naturalist].
SAUTE, sauté, [sō'-tā], *adj.* fried quickly and lightly in fat. [Fr. *sauté*, *p.pt.* of *sauter* to jump].
SAUTEE(S), sautée(s), [sō'-tā], *n.* a dish of boiled potatoes fried quickly in a little fat.
SAUTERNE, [sō-tāern'], *n.* a sweet, white claret. [Fr. *Sauternes*, a district in Gironde].
SAVABLE, [sāv'-abl], *adj.* capable of being saved.
SAVABLENESS, [sāv'-abl-nes], *n.* the state of being savable.
SAVAGE (1), [sav'-ij], *n.* a human being born into a social group whose members are at a primitive stage of development and who is conditioned by crude or repetitive patterns of emotional behaviour; any person whose nature is predominantly fierce, cruel, and instinctive; a bad-mannered person.
SAVAGE (2), [sav'-ij], *adj.* having the nature of a savage, primitive, uncivilized, cruel, wild; of, relating to, inhabited by, a savage; fierce, untamed; barbarous, merciless, brutal; (*coll.*) furiously angry, in a raging temper. [OFr. *salvage* from L. *silva* wood].
SAVAGE (3), [sav'-ij], *v.t.* to handle savagely; (of horses) to harm viciously by suddenly turning wild.
SAVAGEDOM, [sav'-ij-dum], *n.* the world of savages; the level of life or civilization characteristic of savages.
SAVAGELY, [sav'-ij-li], *adv.* in a savage manner.
SAVAGENESS, [sav'-ij-nes], *n.* the state of being savage, wildness, cruelty.
SAVAGERY, [sav'-ij-er-i], *n.* the savage or wild state; a cruel disposition; cruelty, barbarity, mercilessness.
SAVAGISM, [sav'-ij-izm], *n.* savagery.
SAVANNA, [sav-an'-a], *n.* a grass-covered treeless plain, a prairie. [Span. *zavana*].
SAVANT, [sav'-ant], *n.* an expert in one or more branches of learning; a scientist. [Fr. *savant*].
SAVATE, [sav-aht'], *n.* boxing in the French way with hands, feet and head. [Fr. *savate* shoe].
SAVE (1), [sāv], *n.* (*sport*) an act of saving a goal, run, ball, point, or otherwise preventing an opponent from scoring an advantage.
SAVE (2), [sāv], *v.t.* to extricate from a dangerous situation, to lead to safety, to rescue from any form of menace or injury; to preserve or store for future use, to put aside for the sake of economy, to hoard; to eliminate (inconvenience), to act so as to dispense with, to avoid (a disadvantage), to set free from the influence of evil or sin, to redeem; *v.i.* to hoard, economize. [OFr. *sauver* from L. *salvus* safe].
SAVE-ALL, [sāv'-awl], *n.* a small spike inserted for the sake of economy in a candlestick to save the ends of candles; (*naut.*) a strip of canvas along the roach of a sail.
SAVELOY, [sav'-el-oi], *n.* a highly seasoned sausage of salted young pork, originally of brains, kept in a comparatively dry condition. [It. *cervello* brain].
SAVER, [sā'-ver], *n.* one who saves, one who is thrifty; an economist.
SAVIN, [sav'-in], *n.* the small evergreen conifer, *Juniperus sabina*, which yields a volatile medicinal oil. [OE. *safine*].
SAVING (1), [sā'-ving], *n.* the act of saving; that which is saved, an economy.
SAVING (2), [sā'-ving], *adj.* of a thrifty disposition, frugal, incurring no loss, though yielding no gain; exempting from censure; excepting, involving a condition or reservation.
SAVING (3), [sā-ving], *prep.* excepting, with the exception of.
SAVINGLY, [sā'-ving-li], *adv.* in a saving manner.
SAVINGNESS, [sā'-ving-nes], *n.* the quality of being saving.
SAVINGS-BANK, [sāv'-ingz-bangk'], *n.* a bank in which small sums are deposited at low interest.
SAVIOUR, [sāv'-yer], *n.* a person who saves or delivers from danger; **The S.**, Jesus Christ, as the Redeemer of mankind. [OFr. *saviour* from LL. *salvator*].
SAVONETTE, [sav'-on-et'], *n.* a ball of perfumed soap; a washball. [Fr. *savonette* small piece of soap].
SAVORY, [sā'-ver-i], *n.* an aromatic pot-herb of the genus *Satureia*. [Fr. *savorie*].
SAVOUR (1), [sā'-ver], *n.* taste or flavour discerned by the palate; sweet scent or fragrance; (*fig.*) distinctive quality; spice, sharpness, zest; hint, smack. [OFr. *savour*].
SAVOUR (2), [sā'-ver], *v.t. and i.* to appreciate a flavour by deliberately giving oneself up to the experience, to relish; to possess a distinctive characteristic affecting one of the senses, particularly the sense of taste; (*fig.*) to appreciate; to embody a slight suggestion, to hint, to smack (of). [OFr. *savourer*].
SAVOURILY, [sā'-ver-i-li], *adv.* in a savoury manner.
SAVOURINESS, [sā'-ver-i-nes], *n.* the quality of being savoury.
SAVOURLESS, [sā'-ver-les], *adj.* destitute of smell or taste.
SAVOURY (1), [sā'-ver-i], *n.* a light dish, usually seasoned or salted.
SAVOURY (2), [sā'-ver-i], *adj.* pleasing to the smell or taste, seasoned and salted; pleasant, (*fig.*) clean, attractive, reputable.
SAVOY, [sa-voi'], *n.* a curly-leafed cabbage cultivated for winter use. [*Savoie*, a French province].
SAVOYARD, [sa-voi'-ahd], *n.* a member of the original casts of the Gilbert and Sullivan operas at the *Savoy* Theatre.
SAVVY (1), [sav'-i], *n.* (*coll.*) acumen, shrewdness, a high degree of common sense. [*Next*].
SAVVY (2), [sav'-i], *v.i.* (*slang*) to comprehend, understand. [Fr. (*vous*) *savez* (you) know].
SAW (1), [saw], *n.* a tool made in various forms, consisting of a steel blade with a serrated edge, used for cutting purposes. [OE. *sage*].
SAW (2), [saw], *n.* a traditional saying or maxim. [OE. *sagu*, ME. *sawe*].
SAW (3), **(sawn)**, [saw], *v.t. and i.* to cut by means of a saw; to form by means of a saw; to use a saw, to work with a saw. [SAW (1)].
SAW (4), [saw], *pret.* of SEE. [OE. *sæh*].
SAWBILL, [saw'-bil], *n.* the goosander, *Mergus merganser*.
SAWBONES, [saw'-bōnz], *n.* (*slang*) a surgeon.
SAWDER†, [saw'-der], *n.* solder; **soft s.**, flattery.
SAWDUST, [saw'-dust], *n.* the dust or small fragments of wood caused by the sawing of wood.
SAWFISH, [saw'-fish], *n.* a fish of the genus *Pristis*, whose upper jaw is prolonged into a flattened snout set with horizontal spines or teeth resembling a thin, tapering saw.

SAWFISH

SAWFLIES, [saw'-fliz], *n.*(*pl.*) a group of about 2,000 species of flies distinguished by the pair of saws with

which the female bores holes into which she deposits her eggs. [SAW and FLY].
SAW-MILL, [saw'-mil], *n.* a mill or works for sawing timber.
SAWNEB, [saw'-neb], *n.* the sawbill; the red-breasted merganser, *Mergus serrator*.
SAWNEY, [saw'-ni], *n.* (*dial.*) a simpleton, fool.
SAWPIT, [saw'-pit], *n.* a pit over which timber is sawn by two men, one standing below the timber, and the other above.
SAWSET, [saw'-set'], *n.* a tool used to set the teeth of saws.
SAW-WORT, [saw'-wurt], *n.* (*bot.*) a plant of the genus *Serratula*, having flowers resembling thistles, and its leaves edged with cutting teeth.
SAW-WRACK, [saw'-rak], *n.* a seaweed having leaves with serrated edges.
SAW-WREST, [saw'-rest], *n.* a sawset.
SAWYER, [saw'-yer], *n.* a person who saws timber into planks; a tree in a river, whose branches sway up and down with the current; a variety of beetle which cuts through twigs.
SAX (1), [saks], *n.* a slater's chopper or hammer with a point for making holes for the nails. [OE. *sæx* knife].

SAX

SAX (2), [saks], *n.* (*coll.*) a saxophone. [SAX(OPHONE)].
SAXATILE, [saks'-a-til], *adj.* living among rocks. [L. *saxatilis*].
SAXE, [saks], *adj.* made in Saxony; of a light bright blue in colour. [Germ. *Sachsen*].
SAXHORN, [saks'-hawn], *n.* a brass musical instrument with valves, resembling the trumpet. [Joseph Adolphe *Sax*, the inventor].
SAXICAVOUS, [saks'-i-kā'-vus], *adj.* (*zool.*) rock-boring. [L. *saxum* rock and *cavus* hollow].
SAXICOLOUS, [saks'-i'-kol-us], *adj.* inhabiting or growing on rocks. [L. *saxum* rock and *colere* to inhabit].
SAXIFRAGE, [saks'-i-frāj], *n.* (*bot.*) a plant growing among rocks, any of the 200 species of *Saxifraga* such as London Pride. [L. *saxifragus* rock-breaking].
SAXIFRAGOUS, [saks-if'-rag-us], *adj.* lithotritic.
SAXIN, [saks'-in], *n.* a concentrated preparation of saccharin.
SAXON (1), [saks'-on], *n.* a member of a race of people that inhabited part of the northern coast of Germany and conquered Britain during the fifth and sixth centuries with the aid of the Angles and Jutes; the language of these tribes. [LL. *Saxo Saxonis*].
SAXON (2), [saks'-on], *adj.* relating to the Saxons or their country and language.
SAXONDOM, [saks'-on-dom], *n.* territory ruled by the Saxons; nations of Saxon origin.
SAXONISM, [saks'-on-izm], *n.* a Saxon idiom still surviving in the English language.
SAXONIST, [saks'-on-ist], *n.* one expert in the Anglo-Saxon language.
SAXOPHONE, [saks'-ō-fōn], *n.* a brass musical instrument with plated keys and a reed and clarinet mouthpiece. [*Sax*, the inventor, and Gk. *phonos* sound].

SAXOPHONE

SAY (1), [sā], *n.* a kind of thin woollen serge, one of the earliest woollen cloths made in England. [L. *sagum* cloak].
SAY (2), [sā], *n.* that which is said, one's opinion, a speech.
SAY (3), (**said**), [sā], *v.t.* to utter in the form of words, to express by means of words, to speak, declare; to repeat by heart, to recite; to allege, report, pronounce; *v.i.* to assert, to state by speaking, to express an opinion in words; **Says you!** an ironic retort implying disbelief. [OE. *secgan*, ME. *seyen*].
SAYING, [sā'-ing], *n.* something said; an expression; a proverb, a maxim, saw, a folk aphorism.
SBIRRO, (*pl.* **sbirri**), [sbi'-rō], *n.* a kind of Italian policeman. [It. *sbirro*].
SCAB (1), [skab], *n.* a dry crust formed over a healed-up sore or wound; a rough incrustation formed by congealed pus; a disease of potatoes, etc.; a worker who persists in working when a strike has been declared by his comrades; **s. labour**, work done by scabs; non-union workers; **s. shop**, a firm employing exclusively non-union labour. [OScand. *skabbr*].
SCAB (2), (**scabbing, scabbed**), [skab], *v.i.* to form a scab; to follow the line of action taken by a scab.
SCABBARD, [skab'-ard], *n.* the sheath of a sword, dagger, or bayonet. [OFr. *escauberc*].

SCABBARD

SCABBARD-FISH, [skab'-ard-fish], *n.* the sea-fish like a sword-sheath, *Lepidopus caudatus*, allied to the hairtail.
SCABBED, [skabd], *adj.* covered with a scab or with scabs; mean, worthless.
SCABBEDNESS, [skabd'-nes], *n.* the state of being scabbed.
SCABBINESS, [skab'-i-nes], *n.* the state of being scabby.
SCABBLE, [skabl], *v.t.* to dress a stone to a rough surface. [Uncert.].
SCABBY, [skab'-i], *adj.* covered, affected, with scabs; mangy, itchy.
SCABIES, [skā'-bēz], *n.* the itch, a troublesome contagious skin disease. [L. *scabies* the mange].
SCABIOUS, [skā'-bi-us], *n.* (*bot.*) any of the species of *Scabiosa*, plants having blue or purple flowers like small pom-poms, formerly believed to be efficacious in scaly eruptions.
SCABRID, [skab'-rid], *adj.* somewhat scabrous.
SCABROUS, [ska'-brus], *adj.* (*bot.*, *zool.*) bristly; rough, rugged; having sharp points; (*fig.*) indecent. [LL. *scabrosus* rough].
SCABROUSLY, [ska'-brus-li], *adv.* in a scabrous manner, indecently.
SCABROUSNESS, [ska'-brus-nes], *n.* the quality of being scabrous.
SCAD, [skad], *n.* the horse-mackerel, *Caranx trachurus*. [Uncert.].
SCAFFOLD (1), [skaf'-old], *n.* a temporary structure of poles and boards roped together, or of jointed metal struts, providing support to workmen erecting or renovating a building; a raised platform on which a display takes place before spectators, *esp.* one upon which criminals are executed; the place of execution; gallows. [OFr. *eschafault*].
SCAFFOLD (2), [skaf'-old], *v.t.* to furnish or surround with a scaffold.
SCAFFOLDER, [skaf'-old-er], *n.* a workman who erects and attends to scaffolds in the building trade.
SCAFFOLDING, [skaf'-old-ing], *n.* a temporary structure for support in an elevated place; a frame; materials such as poles, boards, planks, etc., for scaffolds.
SCAGLIA, [skahl'-ya], *n.* a whitish or reddish limestone of the Southern Alps. [It. *scaglia* scale].
SCAGLIOLA, [skah'-li-ō'-la], *n.* imitation marble made of irregular portions of white and coloured plasters. [It. *scagliola* a small sliver].
SCALABLE, [skāl'-abl], *adj.* able to be scaled.
SCALADE, SCALADO, [skal-ād'(-ō)], *n.* (*milit.*) a storm or assault on a fortified place by means of ladders; an escalade. [L. *scala* a ladder].
SCALAR, [skā'-lar], *n.* (*math.*) a quantity having magnitude but not direction. [L. *scalaris*].
SCALARIFORM, [skā-la'-ri-fawm], *adj.* (*bot.*) ladder-shaped.
SCALAWAG, see SCALLYWAG.
SCALD (1), [skawld], *n.* the dodder, a parasitic plant of the genus *Cuscuta*.
SCALD (2), [skawld], *n.* scurf on the head. [SCALL].
SCALD (3), [skawld], *n.* a poet in ancient Scandinavia whose art was honoured. [OScand. *skaldr*].
SCALD (4), [skawld], *n.* an injury to the tissues caused by the heat of boiling liquid or steam.
SCALD† (5), [skawld], *adj.* scurvy; mean, poor. [SCALL].
SCALD (6), [skawld], *v.t.* to injure (the skin or flesh) by contact with boiling water or steam; to heat (milk, etc.) till it nearly reaches boiling point; to sterilize by means of boiling water. [LL. *excaldare* to soak in hot water].
SCALDER, [skawld'-er], *n.* a person who scalds.
SCALDFISH, [skawld'-fish], *n.* the flatfish, *Arnoglossus laterna*, with deciduous scales.
SCALDHEAD, [skawld'-hed'], *n.* a fungous parasitic disease of the scalp such as ringworm. [SCALD (1)].
SCALDIC, [skawld'-ik], *adj.* relating to, or composed by, a scald.
SCALE (1), [skāl], *n.* one of the two plates, pans, or bowls of a balance; (*pl.*) Libra, a sign of the Zodiac; a weighing-machine for checking the weight of jockey and saddle before and after a race. [OFr. *escale*].
SCALE (2), [skāl], *n.* one of the many thin plates of horny substance grown by fishes and reptiles as a protective device; anything resembling in flaky thinness

the scales of a fish, particularly flakes of crust, rust, or skin; any of the minute feather-like particles which cover the wings of butterflies and moths, giving them their colour; a film which forms over the pupil of the eye; (*fig.*) any blinding covering.

SCALE (3), [skāl], *n.* a ladder, a series of steps; the act of storming a fortification by means of ladders; a system of classification consisting of a graded range of specified standards; system of proportional reproduction of an original, a representation in terms of a mathematical ratio; a set of marks graded at equal distances as on a ruler; (*math.*) a system of numerical rotation based on a specified constant; (*mus.*) sounds graded in succession so as to form a gamut of regular notes. [L. *scala* ladder].

SCALE (4), [skāl], *v.t. and i.* to pare off a surface, to scrape protuberances, roughnesses, or scales from; to cause scales to form; to peel or flake off, to come off in scales.

SCALE (5), [skāl], *v.t.* to climb up by means of a ladder; to climb over, or clamber over the top of (some obstruction or height); to set in proportion, to design or regulate according to a ratio.

SCALE-ARMOUR, [skāl'-ahm'-er], *n.* armour consisting of steel plates overlapping each other like the scales of a fish.

SCALED, [skāld], *adj.* having scales like a fish; squamous; conforming to a scale.

SCALELESS, [skāl'-les], *adj.* having no scales.

SCALENE (1), [skā'-lēn], *n.* a triangle having its sides and angles unequal.

SCALENE (2), [skā'-lēn], *adj.* (*geom.*) having unequal sides; set obliquely. [Gk. *skalenos* odd].

SCALENOHEDRON, [skā-lē'-nō-hē'-dron], *n.* a solid having twelve faces, each of which is a scalene triangle. [*Prec.* and Gk. *hedra* base].

SCALENOHEDRON

SCALER, [skāl'-er], *n.* one who, or that which, scales.

SCALINESS, [skā'-li-nes], *n.* the state or quality of being scaly.

SCALING-HAMMER, [skāl'-ing-ham'-er], *n.* a hammer with a spike for chipping scale off boilers.

SCALING-LADDER, [skāl'-ing-lad'-er], *n.* a ladder for enabling troops to scale a wall.

SCALL†, [skawl], *n.* scab; leprosy. [OIcel. *skalle* bald head].

SCALLION, [skal'-yun], *n.* a kind of onion. [ONFr. *escalun* from L. (*caepa*) *Ascalonia* (onion) of Ascalon].

SCALLOP (1), SCOLLOP, [skol'-up], *n.* a bivalvular marine mollusc of the genus *Pecten* having a fan-shaped shell with a corrugated surface; a scallop shell as the badge of a pilgrim in the Middle Ages; (*pl.*) pleats giving an undulating edge to a dress. [OFr. *escalope*].

SCALLOP (2), [skol'-up], *v.t.* to cook in a scallop shell; to edge a piece of material, etc., in the wavy line of a scallop shell.

SCALLYWAG, SCALAWAG, [ska'-li-wag'], *n.* a scapegrace, a scamp; *orig.* (*U.S.*) a Southern collaborator with the Northern conquerors after the Civil War.

SCALP (1), [skalp], *n.* the hairy skin of the head; this skin, or part of it, with the hair on, torn off as a trophy by Red Indians. [OIcel. *skalpr*].

SCALP (2), [skalp], *v.t.* to remove the scalp of with a knife.

SCALPEL, [skalp'-el], *n.* a dissecting knife used in anatomical and surgical operations. [L. *scalpellum*].

SCALPER, [skalp'-er], *n.* a surgical instrument used in scraping foul and carious bones.

SCALY, [skāl'-i], *adj.* covered or abounding with scales; resembling scales; composed of scales lying over each other.

SCALY-WINGED, [skāl'-i-wingd], *adj.* having wings with scales.

SCAMBLE†, [skambl], *v.t.* to mangle; to maul; *v.i.* to be busy; to scramble, *esp.* for money. [*Var.* of SCRAMBLE].

SCAMILLUS, [skam'-il-us], *n.* (*arch.*) a small plinth at the base of a column. [L. *scamillus* small bench].

SCAMMONY, [skam'-on-i], *n.* (*bot.*) the plant, *Convolvulus Scammonia*; an inspissated gum run from the plant, used in medicine as a cathartic. [Gk. *skammonia* bindweed].

SCAMP (1), [skamp], *n.* a lazy rogue, one who lives on his wits; a lovable rascal; a mischievous boy. [Uncert.].

SCAMP (2), [skamp], *v.t.* to do a job of work leaving it in an unfinished state, to work on so as to leave a poor, ragged slip-shod finish, to skimp. [Uncert.].

SCAMPER (1), [skamp'-er], *n.* a rapid, ragged run or canter, a hasty departure, a scurry.

SCAMPER (2), [skamp'-er], *v.i.* to run off in flight with a ragged action due to haste; to run about aimlessly, gaily as children, to romp. [OFr. *escamper* to decamp].

SCAMPISH, [skamp'-ish], *adj.* befitting a scamp.

SCAN, [skan], *v.t. and i.* to examine critically, to scrutinize; to speak (verse) accenting the correct beats and giving them their full rhythmic value; to analyse verse into its metrical elements, determining the type of its basic metre, and placing the beats properly; to be written according to the rules of scansion; (*television*) to resolve the image of (an object) into its components of light and shade. [L. *scandere* to climb].

SCANDAL, [skand'-al], *n.* outrageous gossip; allegations of disgraceful or immoral conduct on the part of others calculated to injure their reputations or to shock the feelings of their acquaintances; the outraged feeling caused by such talk or conduct; malicious rumour usually with an immoral flavour; (*leg.*) defamation of character. [Gk. *skandalon* offence].

SCANDAL-BEARER, [skand'-al-bāer'-er], *n.* a spreader of scandal.

SCANDALIZE, [skand'-al-iz], *v.t.* to offend or shock by some immoral or unconventional action; to reproach; to disgrace; to defame; (*naut.*) to haul up the tack of a gaff-sail. [Gk. *skandalizo*].

SCANDALMONGER, [skand'-al-mung'-ger], *n.* a scandal-bearer; a person who delights in talking or inventing scandal.

SCANDALOUS, [skand'-al-us], *adj.* having the effect of scandal, giving offence; disgraceful to reputation, defamatory; giving cause for scandal.

SCANDALOUSLY, [skand'-al-us-li], *adv.* in a scandalous manner.

SCANDALOUSNESS, [skand'-al-us-nes], *n.* the quality of being scandalous.

SCANDENT, [skand'-ent], *adj.* climbing. [L. *scandens*].

SCANDINAVIAN (1), [skand'-in-ā'-vi-an], *n.* a native, or the language, of Scandinavia.

SCANDINAVIAN (2), [skand'-in-ā'-vi-an], *adj.* relating to Scandinavia; relating to the ancient language and literature of Scandinavia and Iceland.

SCANDIUM, [skan'-di-um], *n.* (*chem.*) the chemical element denoted by Sc. [L. *Scandia* Scandinavia].

SCANSION, [skan'-shun], *n.* the process of scanning; the metrical base of verse. [L. *scansio*].

SCANSORES, [skan-saw'-rēz], *n.*(*pl.*) climbers; the zygodactylic birds such as the woodpeckers and parrots. [~L. *scansus* climbed].

SCANSORIAL, [skan-saw'-ri-al], *adj.* fitted for climbing. [L. *scansorius*].

SCANT (1), [skant], *adj.* few in numbers; small, not large or plentiful; insufficient, deficient; grudging, unsatisfying. [OIcel. *skamt*, *neut.* of *skammr* brief].

SCANT (2), [skant], *v.t. and i.* to stint, skimp; to fall short of.

SCANTIES, [skant'-iz], *n.*(*pl.*) (*coll.*) women's underwear.

SCANTILY, [skant'-i-li], *adv.* in a scanty measure, barely, meagrely.

SCANTINESS, [skant'-i-nes], *n.* the state of being scanty; want of sufficiency.

SCANTLING, [skant'-ling], *n.* a small amount or portion; a specific proportion or dimension in building; a timber frame. [OFr. *escantillon* sample].

SCANTLY, [skant'-li], *adv.* not fully or sufficiently.

SCANTNESS, [skant'-nes], *n.* the state of being scant; narrowness; smallness.

SCANTY, [skant'-i], *adj.* scarcely sufficient in amount or extent; narrow; small; not ample, sparing.

SCAPE, [skāp], *n.* (*bot.*) a leafless flower-stalk rising from the root; the shaft of a feather; (*arch.*) the spring of a column. [Gk. *skapos*].

SCAPE

SCAPEGOAT, [skāp'-gōt], *n.* in Hebraic ritual, a goat let loose in the wilderness symbolically bearing all the sins of the people; a person who is made to suffer for another's mistakes or offences. [ESCAPE and GOAT].

SCAPEGRACE, [skāp'-grās], *n.* a graceless, good-for-nothing fellow, a rogue, a rascal. [ESCAPE and GRACE].

SCAPELESS, [skāp'-les], *adj.* (*bot.*) without a scape.

SCAPHISM, [skaf'-izm], *n.* a form of capital punishment formerly practised by the Persians, in which the miscreant was imprisoned in a hollow tree, smeared with honey, and exposed to the stings of bees and insects. [Gk. *skaphe* a hollowed-out place].

SCAPHITE, [skaf'-īt], *n.* a boat-shaped ammonite. [L. *scapha* boat].

SCAPHOID, [skaf'-oid], *adj.* (*anat.*) resembling a boat in form, *esp.* applied to certain bones in the wrist and ankle. [Gk. *skaphe* dug-out and *oeides* like].

SCAPHOPOD, [skaf'-ō-pod'], *n.* a tooth-shell; any species of *Dentalium.* [Gk. *skaphe* dug-out and *pous podos* foot].

SCAPOLITE, [skap'-o-līt], *n.* (*min.*) a silicate of lime and aluminium in rod-like crystals. [SCAPE and Gk. *lithos* stone].

SCAPPLE, [skapl], *v.t.* to reduce a stone to a straight surface. [*Var.* of SCABBLE].

SCAPULA, [skap'-yŏŏ-la], *n.* (*anat.*) the shoulder-blade. [LL. *scapula*].

SCAPULAR (1), SCAPULARY, [skap'-yŏŏ-ler(-i)], *n.* (*eccles.*) a vestment worn by members of various religious orders consisting of two narrow pieces of stuff hung over the shoulders by means of straps. [L. *scapularium*].

SCAPULAR (2), [skap'-yŏŏ-la(r)], *n. and adj.* relating to the scapula; (*anat.*) the name of two pairs of veins running close to the shoulder-blades; (*zool.*) a feather springing from the shoulder joint of the wing and lying flat along the back. [LL. *scapularis*].

SCAPULARY, see SCAPULAR (1).

SCAPULATED, [skap'-yŏŏ-lāt-ed], *adj.* (*zool.*) possessing conspicuous shoulder-feathers. [L. *scapulatus*].

SCAR (1), [skah(r)], *n.* a mark left on the body by a wound or sore; a blemish; a bare patch on a rock, a groove or chip along the surface of a piece of inorganic matter. [Gk. *eskhara* hearth].

SCAR (2), [skah(r)], *n.* (*ichth.*) a species of *Scarus*, the genus of the parrot-wrasses. [L. *scarus*].

SCAR (3), [skah(r)], *n.* a steep rock; an isolated crag. [OIcel. *sker* reef].

SCAR (4), (scarred, scarring), [skah(r)], *v.t.* to mark with a scar.

SCARAB, [ska'-rab], *n.* a black-winged beetle of the genus *Scarabaeus*; a gem with the scarabaeus engraved upon it, originally worn by the Egyptians as a charm or symbol of fertility. [L. *scarabaeus*].

SCARABAEUS, [ska-rab-ē'-us], *n.* a genus of beetles living on dung, revered by the ancient Egyptians as a symbol of long life and creation; an amulet bearing a representation of this beetle. [L. *scarabaeus*].

SCARAMOUCH, [ska'-ra-mōōsh], *n.* a clown in the old comedy, representing one who is a cowardly braggart; a rascal and braggart. [It. *scaramuccia* skirmish].

SCARCE (1), [skāers], *adj.* not plentiful, deficient, insufficient; rarely come across, rare. [OFr. *eschars*].

SCARCE (2), [skāers], *adv.* scarcely.

SCARCELY, [skāers'-li], *adv.* barely, only just, hardly; with difficulty.

SCARCENESS, [skāers'-nes], *n.* the condition of being scarce, scarcity.

SCARCITY, [skāers'-i-ti], *n.* the quality of being scarce, deficiency, dearth. [AFr. *escarseté*].

SCARE (1), [skāer], *n.* a state of being scared, particularly one experienced collectively, a panic; a state of alarm caused by unfounded rumour.

SCARE (2), [skāer], *v.t.* to strike with sudden and uncontrollable terror, to terrify; to keep in a state of apprehension by threatening danger; **to s. away, etc.,** to frighten away, etc. [ME. *skeren*].

SCARECROW, [skāer'-krō], *n.* a dummy device set up to frighten crows or other birds from crops; a needless terror; a guy, an object of ridicule.

SCARED, [skāerd], *adj.* frightened. [SCARE (2)].

SCAREMONGER, [skāer'-mung-ger], *n.* a person who spreads news calculated to cause the listeners to panic. [SCARE and MONGER].

SCARF (1), (*pl.* scarfs or scarves), [skahf], *n.* a covering worn about the shoulders; a light neckerchief or necktie; a length of warm material or knitted wool to be wound round the throat. [ONFr. *escarpe* arm-sling].

SCARF (2), [skahf], *n.* (*carp.*) a special form of joint keeping two ends of timber firmly clamped together.

SCARF JOINT

SCARF (3), [skahf], *v.t.* (*carp.*) to fasten by means of a scarf. [Swed. *skarfva* to fasten together].

SCARFING, [skahf'-ing], *n.* (*carp.*) the process of uniting into a beam two pieces of timber, *esp.* by means of a scarf joint; the product of such process.

SCARF-PIN, [skahf'-pin], *n.* a decorative pin worn in a scarf to secure it.

SCARF-RING, [skahf'-ring], *n.* an ornamental ring used to secure a scarf.

SCARFSKIN, [skahf'-skin], *n.* the outer layer of the skin coming off in scales, the cuticle. [SCARF (1)].

SCARIFICATION, [ska'-ri-fik-ā'-shun], *n.* the act of scarifying. [LL. *scarificatio*].

SCARIFICATOR, [ska'-ri-fik-ā'-tor], *n.* (*surg.*) an instrument used in scarifying.

SCARIFIER, [ska'-ri-fī'-er], *n.* a person who scarifies; an instrument so used; (*agric.*) an implement for breaking up the soil.

SCARIFY, [ska'-ri-fī], *v.t.* (*surg.*) to scratch or cut the skin so as to draw blood; to break up the soil.

SCARIOUS, [skāer'-i-us], *adj.* (*bot.*) tough, shrivelled and semi-transparent. [L. *scariosus*].

SCARLATINA, [skah'-lat-ē'-na], *n.* scarlet fever. [It. *scarlattina*].

SCARLET (1), [skah'-let], *n.* a brilliant, bright red colour with a hint of yellow in it; cloth of this colour worn by the military and clergy. [Turk. *iskerlet*].

SCARLET (2), [skah'-let], *adj.* having a scarlet colour; (*fig.*) sinful; **s. fever,** an infectious disease characterized by the presence of red pimples or flushing of the skin, inflammation of the tonsils, and a peeling off of the skin in the later stages.

SCARLET RUNNER, [skah'-let-run'-er], *n.* an edible variety of climbing bean with a scarlet flower, *Phaseolus multiflorus.*

SCARP (1), [skahp], *n.* the steep face of a mountain side, a nearly perpendicular slope, an escarpment; (*milit.*) the interior slope of the ditch beneath a rampart. [It. *scarpa*].

SCARP (2), [skahp], *n.* (*her.*) a diminutive bend sinister, the representation of a military scarf. [ONFr. *escarpe* a sash].

SCARP (3), [skahp], *v.t.* to cut so as to leave a steep slope; (*fort.*) to provide with a scarp.

SCARPED, [skahpt], *adj.* steeply cut down, like the scarp of a fortification.

SCARRED, [skahd], *adj.* marked with scars.

SCART, [skaht], *n.* the cormorant or shag. [*Var.* of SCARF].

SCAT, [skat], *n.* a tax paid for land to the Crown by a feudal tenant. [OIcel. *skattr*].

SCATHE (1), SCATH, [skāᴛʜ], *n.* damage, injury, particularly one for which legal compensation is claimed. [OIcel. *skathi* harm].

SCATHE (2), [skāᴛʜ], *v.t.* to injure.

SCATHELESS, [skāᴛʜ'-les], *adj.* unharmed, without scathe or damage.

SCATHING, [skāᴛʜ'-ing], *adj.* withering in its effect, bitterly severe in censure.

SCATHINGLY, [skāᴛʜ'-ing-li], *adv.* in a scathing manner, witheringly.

SCATOLOGICAL, [skat'-ō-loj'-ik-al], *adj.* of, or relating to, scatology.

SCATOLOGY, [skat-ol'-o-ji], *n.* the study of (fossilized) excrements; (*fig.*) (*rare*) pornography. [Gk. *skatos* of dung and *logos* speech].

SCATTER, [skat'-er], *v.t. and i.* to throw loosely about in various directions, to fling indiscriminately around; to disperse, to cause to disintegrate; to be dispersed or dissipated. [OE. *scaterian*].

SCATTER-BRAIN, [skat'-er-brān], *n.* a person who is temperamentally unable to concentrate, a careless, unreliable person.

SCATTER-BRAINED, [skat'-er-brānd], *adj.* having no ability to concentrate, thoughtless; flighty.

SCATTERED, [skat'-erd], *adj.* (*bot.*) placed in irregular position.

SCATTERING, [skat'-er-ing], *n.* the action of one who scatters; a sparse amount or quantity; (*phys.*) the dispersal of rays or fine particles.

SCATTERINGLY, [skat'-er-ing-li], *adv.* in a scattered fashion.

SCATTERINGS, [skat'-er-ingz], *n.*(*pl.*) things scattered.

SCATTERLING, [skat'-er-ling], *n.* a tramp, a vagabond.

SCAUP, [skawp], *n.* the sea duck, *Fuligula marila,* which frequents mussel beds. [*Var.* of SCALP].

SCAUPER, [skawp'-er], *n.* an engraver's tool resembling a gouge. [*Var.* of SCALPER].

SCAUR, [skaw(r)], *n.* a steep bank of clays and sands; a precipitous crag or cliff; a bluff precipice of rock. [OIcel. *sker* reef].

SCAVAGE, [skav'-ij], *n.* (*hist.*) the right or duty in the Middle Ages of exacting toll on imported goods offered for sale; the toll so exacted. [OFr. *escavage*].

SCAVENGE, [skav'-enj], *v.t. and i.* to scour the streets for refuse; to act as a scavenger.

SCAVENGER, [skav'-in-jer], *n.* a person employed as a street cleaner, *orig.* one who took scavage; a device for exhausting gases from a combustion-engine cylinder. [~SCAVAGE].

SCAZON, [skā'-zun], *n.* an irregular iambic metre used in Greek and Latin verse, ending in a spondee. [Gk. *skazo* I limp].

SCENARIO, [sē-nah'-ri-ō, si-nāer'-i-ō], *n.* the plan of a play, giving the order of the scenes and a synopsis of the story; a detailed exposition of the theme of a film in terms of the practical conventions of the medium. [It. *scenario*].

SCEND, [send], *n.* the upward lift of a ship before she pitches. [~ASCEND].

SCENE, [sēn], *n.* the place where any event occurs; a picture, real or imaginary, of a locality; any remarkable sight viewed as a whole; a stage fitted up with a backcloth or background depicting suitable scenery and containing the necessary "props" (properties) for the production of a play; any locality representing the background of a literary work of art; one of the short divisions of a play, a subdivision of an act, usually brought to an end by the lowering of the curtain; an incident, episode, particularly one marked by an emotional outburst. [Gk. *skene* booth].

SCENE-DOCK, [sēn'-dok'], *n.* the scenery store behind the stage at a theatre.

SCENE-PAINTER, [sēn'-pānt-er], *n.* a person who paints scenes for theatres.

SCENE-PAINTING, [sēn'-pānt-ing], *n.* the art or act of painting stage scenery.

SCENERY, [sēn'-er-i], *n.* the general appearance of a natural view in terms of the related disposition of its larger features, landscape; the painted representation of a scene for the stage, as made up of the various backcloths, flies, flats, etc. [L. *scenarius* of the stage].

SCENE-SHIFTER, [sēn'-shift-er], *n.* a man who changes the scenery at a theatre between the acts and scenes.

SCENIC, [sēn'-ik, sen'-ik], *adj.* of, relating to, the stage, dramatic, theatrical; having qualities suitable for scenery; **s. railway,** a miniature railway running on a small-gauge track, carrying passengers for amusement through artificial scenery, a switchback. [Gk. *skenikos*].

SCENICAL, [sēn'-ik-al, sen'-ik-al], *adj.* scenic, overdramatic in effect.

SCENICALLY, [sēn'-ik-al-i, sen'-ik-al-i], *adv.* by means of scenery, theatrically.

SCENOGRAPH, [sēn'-ō-grahf], *n.* a drawing in accurate perspective.

SCENOGRAPHER, [sēn-og'-raf-er], *n.* an expert in scenography.

SCENOGRAPHIC, [sē'-nō-graf'-ik], *adj.* relating to scenography; drawn in perspective.

SCENOGRAPHICALLY, [sē'-nō-graf'-ik-al-i], *adv.* in perspective.

SCENOGRAPHY, [sēn-og'-ra-fi], *n.* the science of drawing an object on a perspective plane. [Gk. *skenographia*].

SCENT (1), [sent], *n.* that which stimulates the sense of smell, odour; a manufactured distillation of essence having an agreeable fragrance; perfume; the odour which lingers in an animal's tracks and is perceptible to other animals; a flair for a particular activity; sense of smell; **on the s.,** (of animals) on the track as perceived by the sense of smell; (*fig.*) proceeding in the right direction when on a quest.

SCENT (2), [sent], *v.t.* to become aware of by means of the sense of smell, to smell; to sense; to sprinkle or spray with perfume. [L. *sentire* to sense].

SCENT-BOTTLE, [sent'-botl'], *n.* a bottle, usually of a decorative nature, to contain perfume.

SCENTLESS, [sent'-les], *adj.* having or leaving no scent, inodorous, destitute of smell.

SCEPTIC (1), [skep'-tik], *n.* a person whose attitude of mind causes him to doubt any dogmatic or given statement of fact; a person with a critical temperament who refuses to acknowledge or yield to any emotional dominion; a person who doubts the validity or the divine origins of religious principles; (*philos.*) a thinker who believes the evidence of the senses to be an untrustworthy guide to absolute truth.

SCEPTIC (2), [skep'-tik], *adj.* sceptical. [Gk. *skeptikos* doubting].

SCEPTICAL, [skep'-tik-al], *adj.* being temperamentally inclined to doubt; suspicious; (*philos.*) adopting an attitude of mind which refuses to admit without absolute proof the certainty of doctrines or principles; denying the truth of revelation.

SCEPTICALLY, [skep'-tik-al-i], *adv.* from a sceptical point of view, with doubt.

SCEPTICALNESS, [skep'-tik-al-nes], *n.* the condition of being sceptical.

SCEPTICISM, [skep'-tis-izm], *n.* an attitude of mind characterized by a natural inclination to doubt the truth of statements of fact, or by being on the defensive against submitting to belief or faith in any person or principle; (*philos.*) the principles of the sceptics; the observance of the principle of guarding against belief; the doctrine which expresses doubt in the reliability of the senses as guides to the transcendental.

SCEPTICIZE, [skep'-tis-īz], *v.i.* to act the part of a sceptic.

SCEPTRE, [sept'-er], *n.* a royal mace of ornamental gold carried by a monarch as an emblem of authority; (*fig.*) royal power or authority. [Gk. *skeptron*].

SCEPTRED, [sept'-erd], *adj.* invested with a sceptre.

SCEPTRELESS, [sept'-er-les], *adj.* without a sceptre.

SCHADENFREUDE, [shahd'-en-froid'-a], *n.* (*psych.*) malicious pleasure at another's discomfort. [Germ. *schade* damage and *freude* joy].

SCHAPPE, [shap], *n.* fabric woven out of waste silk. [Germ. *schappe* waste silk].

SCHEDULE (1), [shed'-yōōl], *n.* a piece of paper on which is written or printed an inventory, list, or catalogue, particularly giving details under heads of a programme of work to be carried out to time; a time-table. [L. *scedula*].

SCHEDULE (2), [shed'-yōōl], *v.t.* to draw up in the form of a schedule; to enter in a schedule; to settle the time for an event to take place.

SCHEELITE, [shāl'-īt], *n.* (*min.*) tungstate of lime which forms crystals of bright colours. [*Scheele* a Swedish scientist and Gk. *lithos* stone].

SCHEMA, (*pl.* **schemata**), [skē'-ma], *n.* a synopsis, an outline; (*logic*) a figure of the syllogism. [Gk. *skhema* appearance].

SCHEMATIC, [skēm-at'-ik], *adj.* relating to, in the form of, a scheme, arranged in the order of a synopsis. [Gk. *skhema* appearance].

SCHEMATICALLY, [skēm-at'-ik-a-li], *adv.* in a schematic order.

SCHEMATIST, [skē'-mat-ist], *n.* a person who delights in forming schemes.

SCHEME (1), [skēm], *n.* an arrangement of activities or data drawn up in accordance with a definite plan, a systematic order for future steps or events; any project laid out in broad outline; a suspicious plan, a plot. [Gk. *skhema*].

SCHEME (2), [skēm], *v.t. and i.* to work on a plan, to formulate a scheme; to work out a scheme in secret, to intrigue; to form a plan, design.

SCHEMER, [skē'-mer], *n.* a person who schemes, a contriver; an intriguer.

SCHEMING, [skēm-ing], *adj.* of a designing nature, given to forming schemes, intriguing.

SCHEMINGLY, [skēm'-ing-li], *adv.* in a scheming manner, by scheming.

SCHEMIST, [skēm'-ist], *n.* a person who plans, a schemer, a projector of schemes.

SCHENE, [skēn], *n.* an Egyptian lineal measure of 7½ miles. [L. *schaenus*].

SCHERZO, [skāert'-sō], *n.* a playful movement in a musical composition; a section of a sonata or symphony scored and played in such a style. [It. *scherzo* sport].

SCHIEDAM, [skē-dam'], *n.* Hollands gin, schnapps.

SCHIEFER-SPAR, SHIVER-SPAR, [shēf'-er-spah(r)'], *n.* a carbonate of lime crystallized in tabular crystals. [Ger. *schiefer* slate and SPAR].

SCHIPPERKE, [skip'-er-ki, ship'-er-ki], *n.* a Belgian breed of dog allied to the Pomeranian, smooth-haired but without a tail. [Du. *schipperke*].

SCHISM, [sizm], *n.* division or separation, *esp.* in religion; a deliberate split in the ranks of an organized society; (*eccles.*) the sin of causing schism. [OF. *scisme* from Gk. *skhisma* a split].

SCHISMATIC (1), [siz-mat'-ik], *n.* a person who separates from an established church or religious faith on the ground of disagreement on principles. [Gk. *skhismatikos*].

SCHISMATIC (2), [siz-mat'-ik], *adj.* tending to schism, schismatical.

SCHISMATICAL, [siz-mat'-ik-al], *adj.* relating to, connected with, tending to, or implying, schism; disruptive.

SCHISMATICALLY, [siz-mat'-ik-al-i], *adv.* so as to effect a schism; in a schismatic manner.

SCHISMATICALNESS, [siz-mat'-ik-al-nes], *n.* the condition or quality of being schismatic.
SCHISMATIZE, [siz'-mat-iz], *v.i.* to commit or practise schism.
SCHIST, [shist], *n.* (*geol.*) an igneous rock having a foliated structure and tending to split easily into layers. [Gk. *skhistos* split].
SCHISTOSE, SCHISTOUS, [shist'-ōs, shist'-us], *adj.* (*geol.*) relating to, resembling a schist, having the constituent minerals crystallized in parallel, lenticular and wavy layers or folia; foliated.
SCHIZANTHUS, [skiz-anth'-us], *n.* (*bot.*) a genus of annual plants with bright flowers found growing in Chile. [Gk. *skhizo* I split and *anthos* flower].
SCHIZOCARP, [skiz'-ō-kahp], *n.* (*bot.*) a dry fruit splitting into single-seeded mericarps or portions. [Gk. *skhizo* I split and *karpos* fruit].
SCHIZOGENESIS, [skiz'-ō-jen'-es-is], *n.* (*biol.*) reproduction by fission. [Gk. *skhizo* I split and GENESIS].
SCHIZOMYCETES, [skī-zō-mi-sēt'-ēz], *n.*(*pl.*) (*biol.*) the lowest forms of life which multiply by division; the bacteria. [Gk. *skhizo* I split and *muketes* fungi].
SCHIZOPHRENIA, [skī'-zō-frēn'-i-a], *n.* (*psych.*) a form of hallucinatory insanity characterized by dis-association of different aspects of the personality. [Gk. *skhizo* I split and *phren* brain].
SCHNAPPER, [shnap'-er], *n.* an edible sea-fish found in Australian waters. [Germ. *schnapper*].
SCHNAPPS, [shnaps], *n.* schiedam, a raw variety of Hollands gin. [Germ. *schnapps*].
SCHNAUZER, [shnowt'-ser], *n.* a breed of German house-dog resembling a short-haired terrier.
SCHNORRER, [shnawr'-er], *n.* a beggar. [Yiddish from Germ. *schnorren* to beg].
SCHOLAR, [skol'-er], *n.* a man of learning; an expert in a branch of knowledge, an undergraduate who belongs to the foundation of a college, receiving an annual grant so that he can pursue his studies; a pupil; a disciple. [LL. *scholaris*].
SCHOLARLIKE, [skol'-er-līk], *adj.* like a scholar; characteristic of a scholar.
SCHOLARLY, [skol'-er-li], *adj.* erudite, wise, learned, scholarlike.
SCHOLARSHIP, [skol'-er-ship], *n.* the capacity for, or acknowledged status attained in, detailed, thorough and accurate knowledge; erudition, a high standard of specialized learning; a study of problems, as distinct from research; a foundation granted to a scholar in the form of an annual allowance to permit a continued pursuit of studies, an annual grant of money to a scholar.
SCHOLASTIC (1), [skol-ast'-ik], *n.* a teacher in a medieval university; an over-subtle and pedantic philosopher.
SCHOLASTIC (2), [skol-ast'-ik], *adj.* relating to a scholar; relating to the schoolmen, connected with a scholastic; characterized or produced by erudition; scholarly; too subtle, pedantic; **s. profession,** teaching profession. [Gk. *skholastikos* studious].
SCHOLASTICALLY, [skol-ast'-ik-al-i], *adv.* in a scholastic fashion.
SCHOLASTICISM, [skol-ast'-is-izm], *n.* scholastic philosophy or learning which kept strictly to the principles of Aristotle; adherence to the subtleties of the schools.
SCHOLIAST, [skōl'-i-ast], *n.* an ancient commentator on Greek or Latin classics; a writer of explanatory notes in texts. [Gk. *skholiastes*].
SCHOLIASTIC, [skōl-i-ast'-ik], *adj.* relating to a scholiast or to commentaries.
SCHOLIUM, (*pl.* **scholia**), [skōl'-i-um], *n.* an explanatory note, annotation, *esp.* on a passage in a Greek or Latin classic. [Gk. *skhole* leisure to learn].
SCHOOL (1), [skōōl], *n.* a shoal of whales, porpoises, etc. [Du. *school*].
SCHOOL (2), [skōōl], *n.* an institution which specializes in providing a systematic method of teaching the young, an educational establishment; the pupils of a school considered as a whole or as belonging to one of various grades; the school buildings and grounds; the time devoted to attendance in the class rooms; an institution for research by adults; a group of disciples acknowledging the authority and principles of a master; the body of learning, principles, and style established by a master or leader; a university faculty offering a degree to a successful student; **grammar s.,** *orig.* a school at which Latin was taught, now, a secondary school; **high s.,** a secondary school. [OE. *scol* from Gk. *skhole* leisure to learn].
SCHOOL (3), [skōōl], *v.t.* to educate, to apply the methods of a school to, to instruct; to train a horse in jumping; (*reflex.*) to submit to discipline.
SCHOOLABLE, [skōōl'-abl], *adj.* capable of being schooled.
SCHOOL AGE, [skōōl'-aj'], *n.* the ages between which a child attends or is fit to attend school.
SCHOOL BOARD, [skōōl'-bawd], *n.* a committee (now superseded) elected by local ratepayers to provide and administer public elementary (and, in Scotland, secondary) education in the district.
SCHOOLBOOK, [skōōl'-bŏŏk], *n.* a book used at schools for instruction, a text-book.
SCHOOLBOY, [skōōl'-boi], *n.* a boy attending a school or of school age.
SCHOOL CERTIFICATE, [skōōl'-sert-if'-ik-at], *n.* a certificate granted, after an examination, by a University Board, affirming the successful candidate's proficiency in certain groups of subjects up to the standard expected at the conclusion of a normal four-years' course of study at a secondary or public school.
SCHOOLCRAFT, [skōōl'-krahft'], *n.* learning acquired at school.
SCHOOL-DIVINE, [skōōl'-div-īn'], *n.* a person who believes in the scholastic theology.
SCHOOL-DIVINITY, [skōōl'-div-in'-i-ti], *n.* divinity as advocated by the schoolmen, argumentative theology.
SCHOOLFELLOW, [skōōl'-fel-ō], *n.* one of a number of boys or girls educated at the same school at the same time.
SCHOOLGIRL, [skōōl'-gurl], *n.* a girl attending a school or of school age.
SCHOOL-HOUSE, [skōōl'-hows], *n.* a house containing class-rooms for the use of a school; the residence of the principal of a school adjoining it.
SCHOOLING, [skōōl'-ing], *n.* instruction in school education, tuition; reproof, reprimand.
SCHOOLMAN, [skōōl'-man], *n.* a man of the Middle Ages expert in the niceties of academical disputation, or of school philosophy or divinity.
SCHOOLMARM, [skōōl'-mahm], *n.* (*coll.*) a school-mistress, particularly of a priggish, prudish type.
SCHOOLMASTER, [skōōl'-mahst-er], *n.* a man who presides over, or teaches in, a school; one who acts like a schoolmaster.
SCHOOLMATE, [skōōl'-māt], *n.* a schoolfellow, a friend at school.
SCHOOLMISTRESS, [skōōl'-mis-tres], *n.* a woman following the teaching profession.
SCHOOLTEACHER, [skōōl'-tēch-er], *n.* one who teaches at a school.
SCHOOL-TEACHING, [skōōl'-tēch-ing], *n.* the profession of a schoolteacher.
SCHOONER, SCOONER, [skŏŏ'-ner], *n.* a fore-and-aft sailing vessel fitted with two or more masts, the rig consisting of two gaff sails and a head, set on a bowsprit; a measure of beer, reputed to contain 14 fluid ounces. [Uncert.].

SCHOONER

SCHORL, SHORL, [shawl], *n.* (*min.*) a variety of black tourmaline. [Germ. *schurl*].
SCHOTTISCHE, [shot-ēsh'], *n.* a German round dance resembling a polka; the music for this dance in two-four time. [Germ. *schottisch* Scottish].
SCIAGRAPH, SKIAGRAPH, [sī'-a-graf, skī'-a-graf], *n.* a section of a building exhibiting its interior; an X-ray photograph. [Gk. *skiagraphia* a drawing].
SCIAGRAPHER, [sī'-a-graf-er], *n.* a specialist in sciagraphy.
SCIAGRAPHIC, [sī'-a-graf-ik], *adj.* relating to sciagraphy.
SCIAGRAPHICAL, [sī'-a-graf'-ik-al], *adj.* sciagraphic.
SCIAGRAPHY, [sī'-a'-gra-fi], *n.* (*arch.*) the art of delineating shadows; the profile or vertical section of a building, exhibiting its interior; (*astron.*) the art of finding the hour by the shadows of the sun or moon; the art of dialling.
SCIAMACHY, SCIOMACHY, [sī-am'-a-ki, sī-om'-a-ki], *n.* fighting with shadows, shadow boxing. [Gk. *skiamakhia* sham fighting].
SCIAMANCY, SCIOMANCY, [sī'-a-man-si, sī'-ō-man-si], *n.* divination by communication with the dead. [Gk. *skia* a shadow and *manteia* divination].

SCIATHERIC, [sī'-a-the'-rik], *adj.* relating to sundials. [Gk. *skiatherikos*].

SCIATIC, [sī-at'-ik], *adj.* relating to or affecting the hip. [Gk. *iskhiadikos* ill with lumbago].

SCIATICA, [sī-at'-ik-a], *n.* neuralgia in the sciatic nerve. [MedL. *sciatica*].

SCIENCE, [sī'-ents], *n.* the accumulation and organization of knowledge acquired by means of tested methods of observation and systematized with a view to the formulation of general laws or hypotheses to account for natural phenomena or their behaviour; any branch of knowledge so organized; **applied s.,** knowledge adapted for material or functional use, as in industry. [L. *scientia*].

SCIENTER, [sī-ent'-er], *adv.* (*leg.*) out of full knowledge, deliberately. [L. *scienter*].

SCIENTIAL, [sī-en'-shal], *adj.* relating to, producing, science. [MedL. *scientialis*].

SCIENTIFIC, [sī'-en-tif'-ik], *adj.* pertaining, relating to, science; employed in science; according to science, arranged or performed in a systematic manner with regard to the greatest degree of accuracy; precise, exact; expert, highly trained, skilled in applying principles. [MedL. *scientificus*].

SCIENTIFICALLY, [sī'-en-tif'-ik-a-li], *adv.* in a scientific manner, in accordance with scientific principles or methods.

SCIENTISM, [sī'-ent-izm], *n.* the views of scientists; scientific methods.

SCIENTIST, [sī'-ent-ist], *n.* a person trained in science; an authority on scientific matters; a man of science; (*sport*) an expert exponent.

SCILICET, [sī'-li-set], *adv.* to wit, namely, viz. [L. *sci(re) licet* you may know].

SCILLA, [sil'-a], *n.* (*bot.*) a genus of bulbous plants including the squills and the English wild bluebell. [Gk. *skilla*].

SCILLITIN, [sil'-et-in], *n.* (*chem.*) the active bitter principle of the squill.

SCIMITAR, CIMETER†, [sim'-it-ar], *n.* a short curved sword with a single cutting edge and used by Orientals. [It. *scimitarra*].

SCIMITAR

SCINCOID, [sing'-koid], *adj.* resembling a skink. [Gk. *skinkoeides*].

SCINTILLA, [sin-til'-a], *n.* a gleam, a spark; (*fig.*) a trace. [L. *scintilla*].

SCINTILLANT, [sint'-il-ant], *adj.* sparkling, emitting sparks, glittering. [L. *scintillans*].

SCINTILLATE, [sin'-til-āt], *v.i.* to emit sparks, to sparkle; to gleam, glitter; (*fig.*) to shine in company, particularly by wit or brilliance of conversation. [L. *scintillare* to sparkle].

SCINTILLATION, [sin'-til-ā'-shun], *n.* the act of sparkling or twinkling; the twinkling of the stars owing to atmospheric disturbances. [L. *scintillatio*].

SCIOLISM, [sī'-ō-lizm], *n.* pretentious wisdom, superficial knowledge. [*Next*].

SCIOLIST, [sī'-ol-ist], *n.* a pretentiously wise person, one who knows little or who knows many things superficially. [L. *sciolus* a smatterer].

SCIOLUS, [sī'-ō-lus], *adj.* being superficially or imperfectly wise.

SCIOMACHY, see SCIAMACHY.

SCIOMANCY, see SCIAMANCY.

SCION, [sī'-un], *n.* a slip, young shoot or twig for grafting; a young branch or offshoot of the family, a descendant. [OFr. *sion*].

SCIRRHOSITY, [si-ros'-i-ti], *n.* (*med.*) a hardening of the glands. [L. *scirrhositas*].

SCIRRHOUS, [si'-rus], *adj.* having the characteristics of a scirrhus; proceeding from scirrhus, hardened, knotty.

SCIRRHUS, [si'-rus], *n.* (*path.*) a hardened tumour, proceeding from the induration of a gland; a variety of cancer. [Gk. *skirhos* hard].

SCISSEL, [sis'-el], *n.* the clippings of metals; the remainder of a metal plate after the blanks for coins are minted out of it. [OFr. *cisaille* clipping].

SCISSILE, [sis'-il], *adj.* able to be cut or divided by a sharp instrument. [L. *scissilis* quickly split].

SCISSION, [sizh'-un], *n.* the act of cutting or dividing by an edged instrument; the state of being split. [L. *scissio*].

SCISSOR, [siz'-or], *v.t.* to cut or clip with scissors.

SCISSOR-BILL, [siz'-or-bil], *n.* a skimmer, a sea-bird of the genus, *Rhyncops*, the shearwater.

SCISSORS, [siz'-erz], *n.*(*pl.*) a small cutting tool, resembling shears, consisting of two blades each having a looped handle crossing the other and fixed at a pivot, the cutting being performed by two blades being worked against each other. [OFr. *cissoire*].

SCISSOR-TAIL, [siz'-er-tāl], *n.* the fork-tailed fly-catcher, a species of *Milvulus* found in tropical America.

SCISSURE, [sish'-ōōer], *n.* a slit or opening in a body made by cutting. [L. *scissura*].

SCIURINE, [sī-ōōer'-in], *adj.* belonging or pertaining to squirrels. [Gk. *skiouros* shadow-tail].

SCIURUS, [sī-ōōer'-us], *n.* a family of rodents including the squirrel. [Gk. *skiouros* shadow-tail].

SCLERENCHYMA, [sklēer-eng'-ki-ma], *n.* (*bot.*) woody cell tissue found in plants. [SCLERO and Gk. *egkhuma* infusion].

SCLERIASIS, [skle-rī'-as-is], *n.* (*path.*) morbid hardening of tissues. [SCLERO and Gk. *iasis* condition].

SCLERO-, *pref.* hard, dry. [Gk. *skleros*].

SCLERODERM, [sklēer'-ō-durm], *n.* the exoskeleton or hardened integument, particularly of corals; skeletal tissue. [SCLERO and Gk. *derma* skin].

SCLEROGEN, [sklēer'-ō-jen], *n.* (*bot.*) the woody substance, lignin, which deposits itself in the cells of plants. [SCLERO and Gk. *gennao* I produce].

SCLEROID, [sklēer'-oid], *adj.* (*bot.*) being hard in texture. [SCLERO and Gk. *oeides* like].

SCLEROSIS, [skler-ō'-sis], *n.* (*path.*) a hardening of the tissues. [Gk. *sklerosis* induration].

SCLEROTIC (1), [skler-ot'-ik], *n.* the firm white outer coat of the eye formed of a hard substance; a medicine which hardens the parts to which it is applied.

SCLEROTIC (2), [skler-ot'-ik], *adj.* hard and dry, indurated; affected by sclerosis.

SCLEROTITIS, [skler'-o-tī'-tis], *n.* inflammation affecting the sclerotic coat of the eye. [SCLERO and Gk. *itis* characterized by inflammation].

SCLEROUS, [sklēer'-us], *adj.* bony, indurated, hardened.

SCOBBY, [skob'-i], *n.* (*dial.*) the chaffinch.

SCOBIFORM, [skōb'-i-fawm], *adj.* resembling sawdust or raspings. [L. *scobs* sawdust and FORM].

SCOBS, [skobz], *n.*(*pl.*) filings or raspings of ivory, hartshorn, or other hard substance. [L. *scobs* sawdust].

SCOFF (1), [skof], *n.* (*slang*) anything to eat. [Du. *schoft* one of the four daily meals].

SCOFF (2), [skof], *n.* an expression of scorn or derision, a gibe; an object of contempt, a butt for ridicule. [~OIcel. *skop* scoff].

SCOFF (3), [skof], *v.* **to s. at,** to deride, ridicule, scorn; to show scorn or contempt for; to exhibit a lack of respect for.

SCOFF (4), [skof], *v.t.* (*slang*) to eat greedily or quickly. [SCOFF (1)].

SCOFFER, [skof'-er], *n.* one who scoffs.

SCOFFING, [skof'-ing], *n.* the act of treating with scorn, mockery.

SCOFFINGLY, [skof'-ing-li], *adv.* in a scoffing fashion; by way of derision.

SCOLD (1), [skōld], *n.* a nagging woman who uses abusive language; a display of scolding by such a person. [OIcel. *skald* a poet, a libeller].

SCOLD (2), [skōld], *v.t. and i.* to reprimand, to rate, chide with a stream of blame; to reprove loudly; to find fault and make a commotion about, to rail loudly. [*Prec.*].

SCOLDER, [skōld-er], *n.* a person who scolds or rails.

SCOLDING, [skōld-ing], *n.* a rating, an angry reprimand; railing language.

SCOLECITE, [skol'-is-īt], *n.* (*min.*) a substance resembling natrolite, hydrated silicate of lime and aluminium. [Gk. *skolex* worm].

SCOLEX, (*pl.* **scolices**), [skōl'-eks], *n.* the embryo form of a tape-worm. [Gk. *skolex* worm].

SCOLIOSIS, [skol'-i-ō'-sis], *n.* curvature of the spine to one side. [Gk. *skolios* crooked].

SCOLLOP, see SCALLOP.

SCOLOPACEOUS, [skol'-op-ā'-shus], *adj.* belonging to or resembling a woodcock. [Gk. *skolopax* woodcock].

SCOMBER, [skom'-ber], *n.* (*zool.*) a genus of fishes including the mackerel. [Gk. *skombros* mackerel].

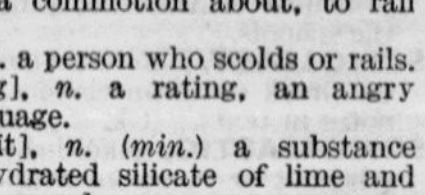

SCOMBER

SCONCE, [skonts], *n.* a cover, a fort or bulwark; a head-piece, the head; the tube of a candlestick for holding the candle; a hanging or projecting candlestick fitted with a reflector. [OFr. *esconse* hiding-place].

SCONE, [skōn, skon], *n.* a plain cake, usually triangular, of wheat or barley flour, baked on a girdle. [~LGerm. *schonbrod*].

SCOONER, see SCHOONER.

SCOOP (1), [skōōp], *n.* a ladle with a shallow bowl used for baling up liquid or shovelling loose-grained substances like wheat or sugar, a gouge; the act of using a scoop; (*slang*) a profitable piece of good luck; an exclusive item of news for newspaper publication; a profitable transaction made suddenly at the expense of one's competitors. [LGerm. *schope* ladle, Du. *schoppe* shovel].

SCOOP (2), [skōōp], *v.t.* to ladle, lift, shovel, bale out by means of a scoop; to make hollow, to dig out, to excavate; (*slang*) to get away with, to clear, to win; to obtain suddenly at the expense of competitors; (*esp. journalism*) to score over.

SCOOPER, [skōōp'-er], *n.* one who, or that which, scoops; a water-fowl, the avocet.

SCOOP-NET, [skōōp'-net'], *n.* a net manipulated by hand, so formed as to sweep the bottom of a river.

SCOOP-WHEEL, [skōōp'-wēl'], *n.* a wheel fitted with buckets, used in dredging.

SCOOT, [skōōt], *v.i.* (*slang*) to hurry off, to run away hurriedly. [Uncert.].

SCOOTER, [skōōt'-er], *n.* a kind of low bicycle consisting of a narrow short board used as a foot-rest, and a steering rod; (*U.S.*) a coastal motor-boat; a small motor-truck on a railway.

SCOOP-WHEEL

SCOPE, [skōp], *n.* range, area, field for mental or physical activity; aim, intention; room; (*naut.*) cable-length. [Gk. *skopos* shooting mark].

SCORBUTIC, [skaw-bew'-tik], *adj.* pertaining to, affected by, scurvy. [Fr. *scorbutique*].

SCORCH (1), [skawch], *n.* a burn made by scorching; (*slang*) a ride at high speed; **scorched earth,** territory abandoned by a combatant after being rendered useless to the attacking force.

SCORCH (2), [skawch], *v.t.* to burn superficially; to affect painfully with heat so as to injure and discolour the skin or surface; (*slang*) to ride at top speed; *v.i.* to be parched, to become scorched. [OFr. *escorchier* from L. *excorticare* to flay].

SCORCHER, [skawch'-er], *n.* one who, or that which, scorches; (*slang*) a very hot day.

SCORCHINGLY, [skawch'-ing-li], *adv.* in a scorching manner; to a scorching degree.

SCORE (1), [skaw(r)], *n.* a notch, cut, or mark leaving an indelible groove; such a mark used on a tally; a reckoning, an account, a bill of expenses; a number of runs in cricket made by a single batsman or by a side; an advantage over another; a point made at a rival's expense; twenty, particularly as a unit of reckoning; (*mus.*) a copy of a composition giving the parts on separate staves. [OE. *scoru* from OIcel. *skor* notch, twenty].

SCORE (2), [skaw(r)], *v.t.* to mark or record by means of scores or notches; to mark with pen lines, to hatch; to make a score in games; to enter as an item in an account; (*mus.*) to arrange in separate staves, to orchestrate; *v.i.* to reap an advantage; **to s. off,** to make runs from, to triumph at the expense of.

SCORE-BOARD, [skaw(r)'-bawd], *n.* a board, tablet or slate on which a record of the score is kept in games.

SCORER, [skawr'-er], *n.* one who scores; the person who keeps the score in a game; a tablet on which the score is kept, particularly one for bridge.

SCORIA, (*pl.* **scoriae**), [skaw'-ri-a], *n.* the slag of smelted ore, dross; metals in fusion; (*pl.*) volcanic ashes. [Gk. *skoria* refuse].

SCORIACEOUS, [sko'-ri-āsh'-us], *adj.* relating to, or like, scoria, of the nature of scoria.

SCORIFICATION, [skaw'-rif-ik-ā'-shun], *n.* the process of reducing all or part of a body into scoria.

SCORIFIER, [skaw'-ri-fī-er], *n.* a receptacle of fireclay used in the process of scorifying.

SCORIFORM, [skaw'-ri-fawm], *adj.* resembling scoria; in the form of dross.

SCORIFY, [skaw'-ri-fī], *v.t* to reduce to scoria by a process of fusion.

SCORN (1), [skawn], *n.* a state of mental superiority taking satisfaction in refusing to see value in other's acts or opinions, a contemptuous attitude of mind; a disdainful expression or utterance, derision; an object of contempt. [OFr. *escarn* mockery].

SCORN (2), [skawn], *v.t.* to feel or express scorn for, to hold in contempt, to hold up to mockery, to treat disdainfully.

SCORNER, [skawn'-er], *n.* one who scorns; a derider, *esp.* of sacred things.

SCORNFUL, [skawn'-fōōl], *adj.* expressing, or full of, scorn; disdainful, contemptuous.

SCORNFULLY, [skawn'-fōōl-i], *adv.* in a scornful fashion.

SCORNFULNESS, [skawn'-fōōl-nes], *n.* the state or quality of being scornful.

SCORODITE, [sko'-rō-dīt], *n.* (*min.*) hydrated arseniate of iron which when heated gives off a smell like garlic. [Gk. *skorodon* garlic].

SCORPIO, [skaw'-pi-ō], *n.* a scorpion; any species of *Scorpio* or *Buthus*; the Scorpion, the eighth sign of the zodiac. [L. *scorpio*].

SCORPIOID, [skaw'-pi-oid], *adj.* (*bot.*) curled up at the end. [Gk. *skorpioeides*].

SCORPION, [skaw'-pi-on], *n.* an arachnid having sharp mandibles and four pairs of legs with two claws like a lobster and a six-jointed tail ending in a sting; a whip armed with points like a scorpion's tail; the eighth sign of the zodiac; (*fig.*) a painful scourge. [SCORPIO].

SCORPION-FLY, [skaw'-pi-on-flī'], *n.* the black flatwinged fly, *Panopus communis*, with the body-segments curving like a scorpion's tail.

SCORPION-GRASS, [skaw'-pi-on-grahs], *n.* (*bot.*) the myosotis or wild forget-me-not.

SCORPION-PLANT, [skaw'-pi-on-plahnt], *n.* (*bot.*) a large yellow or white orchid resembling a spider, growing in Java.

SCORPION-SHELL, [skaw'-pi-on-shel], *n.* a shell resembling the form of a scorpion.

SCORZONERA, [skawz'-on-ēer'-a], *n.* a plant, the viper's grass, *Scorzonera hispanica*, grown for its edible root. [It. *scorzonera*].

SCOT (1), [skot], *n.* (*leg.*) a tax; **s. and lot,** parish payments assessed according to means. [OIcel. *skot*].

SCOT (2), [skot], *n.* a native of Scotland, a Scotsman. [OE. *Scot*].

SCOTCH (1), [skoch], *n.* a variety of whisky distilled in Scotland; (E. *coll.*) the natives of Scotland considered collectively.

SCOTCH (2), [skoch], *n.* a slight cut or shallow incision, a notch, particularly one in the ground; a sprag or strut; a brake.

SCOTCH (3), [skoch], *v.t.* to make a scotch, to score, to cut a mark; †to cut slightly, to give a superficial wound to; to kill, or maim mortally; to bring to a cruel end, to suppress brutally; to stop. [Uncert.].

SCOTCH BARLEY, [skoch'-bah-li], *n.* barley with its husk removed.

SCOTCH BROTH, [skoch'-broth'], *n.* mutton broth containing pearl barley.

SCOTCH FIR, [skoch'-fur'], *n.* the Scots pine.

SCOTCH-HOPPER, [skoch'-hop'-er], *n.* a game in which children compete in hopping over scotches or lines on the ground; hop-scotch. [SCOTCH (3) and HOP (2)].

SCOTCHMAN, [skoch'-man], *n.* a tall crane for lifting girders, used in the building trade.

SCOTCH MIST, [skoch'-mist], *n.* a fine drizzle mixed with mist.

SCOTCH PINE, [skoch'-pīn'], *n.* the Scots pine.

SCOTCH TERRIER, [skoch'-te'-ri-er], *n.* a breed of terrier with short stubby legs, rough coat, and short tail.

SCOTCH WOODCOCK, [skoch'-wōōd'-kok], *n.* scrambled egg on toast with anchovies on top.

SCOTER, [skōt'-er], *n.* a sea-duck with black feathers, of the genus *Oedemia*, found in Arctic waters. [Uncert.].

SCOT-FREE, [skot'-frē], *adj.* free from payment, untaxed; unhurt, safe; let off punishment. [SCOT (1) and FREE (1)].

SCOTIA (1), [skō'-sha], *n.* Scotland personified.

SCOTIA (2), [skō'-sha], *n.* (*arch.*) a hollow moulding in the base of a column in which a dark shadow is formed. [Gk. *skotia*].

SCOTISM, [skōt'-izm], *n.* the philosophy of Duns Scotus. [Duns *Scotus*, the scholar].

SCOTOMA, [skot'-ō'-ma], *n.* (*path.*) a blind spot due to disease of the retina or the optic nerve, usually causing giddiness. [Gk. *skotoma* giddiness].

SCOTOSCOPE, [skot'-ō-skōp], *n.* an instrument facilitating sight in the dark, a night-glass. [Gk. *skotos* darkness and SCOPE].

SCOTS (1), [skots], *n.(pl.)* the Gaelic race who emigrated from Ireland and invaded the west of Scotland; the dialect of the Lowland Scots.

SCOTS (2), [skots], *adj.* relating to, connected with, Scotland, its people or language; Scottish. [ME. *Scottis*].

SCOTSMAN, [skots'-man], *n.* a native of Scotland.

SCOTS PINE, [skots'-pīn'], *n.* the common pine tree, *Pinus sylvestris*, found in North Europe.

SCOTTICE, [skot'-is-ē], *adv.* in the Scottish manner of pronunciation. [L. *Scotticus* Scottish].

SCOTTICISM, [skot'-is-izm], *n.* a Scots idiom, word, or phrase.

SCOTTISH, [skot'-ish], *adj.* connected with, belonging to, Scotland or its people.

SCOUNDREL, [skown'-drel], *n.* a vicious and dangerous member of society, a hypocritical blackguard, a rascal, a villain. [Uncert.].

SCOUNDRELISM, [skown'-drel-izm], *n.* the practice and conduct of a scoundrel, rascality.

SCOUNDRELLY, [skown'-drel-i], *adj.* fit for a scoundrel; like a scoundrel.

SCOUR (1), [skow(e)r], *n.* a cleaning or clearing; a swift deep current which washes away anything in its path.

SCOUR (2), [skow(e)r], *v.t. and i.* to clean by continual hard rubbing; to cleanse by rubbing with something rough of surface such as sand; to clean by flushing with water; to purge violently, as the intestines of cattle; to get rid of dirt by scouring. [L. *excurare*].

SCOUR (3), [skow(e)r], *v.t. and i.* to range over; to search through thoroughly; to run about, searching here and there for food. [Uncert.].

SCOURER, [skow(e)r'-er], *n.* one who scours; a strong cathartic; one who runs with speed; a rover.

SCOURGE (1), [skurj], *n.* an instrument for flogging, a whip; a drastic, thorough punishment; an evil pest or plague of drastic persistence.

SCOURGE (2), [skurj], *v.t.* to flog thoroughly, to whip; to afflict persistently and drastically. [ME. *scourgen* from L. *excoriare* to take the skin off].

SCOURGER, [skurj'-er], *n.* one who scourges or afflicts severely.

SCOUT (1), [skowt], *n.* a person or service unit dispatched ahead of the main body to spy on enemy movements and make reports of these to the general staff; a male servant in service at Oxford University; a fieldsman; a dart thrown outside the board when aiming for a final double; **boy s.,** a member of an organization for boys encouraging open-air life and social responsibility, founded in 1908 by Lord Baden-Powell; **A.A.** or **R.A.C. s.,** a man employed by the Automobile Association or Royal Automobile Club to patrol the roads and render assistance to members. [OFr. *escoute*].

SCOUT (2), [skowt], *v.i.* to act as a scout, to reconnoitre.

SCOUT (3), [skowt], *v.t.* to sneer at, to treat with scorn. [OIcel. *skuta*].

SCOUT (4), [skowt], *n.* a flat-bottomed river boat, a kind of Dutch barge. [Du. *schuit*].

SCOUTMASTER, [skowt'-mahst-er], *n.* a leader of a troop of scouts; an officer in charge of boy scouts.

SCOVAN, [skov'-an], *n.* (*mining*) in Cornwall, a tin lode below the surface. [Corn. *scovan*].

SCOVILLITE, [skōv'-il-īt], *n.* (*min.*) a hydrous phosphate of cerium, lanthanum, didymium and yttrium, rhabdophane. [*Scoville*, an ore-bed in Connecticut, U.S.A.].

SCOW, [skow], *n.* a large flat-bottomed boat used for ferry or transport purposes. [Du. *schouw*].

SCOWL (1), [skowl], *n.* a facial expression as a sign of anger or displeasure, characterized by the eyebrows drawn together and a puckered forehead; an angry frown.

SCOWL (2), [skowl], *v.i.* to assume a scowl, to look angry or sullen. [ME. *scoulen*].

SCRABBLE, [skrabl], *v.i.* to make irregular unmeaning marks, to scribble; to scrape haphazardly so as to cover a surface with irregular marks. [Du. *schrabbelen* to scrawl].

SCRAG (1), [skrag], *n.* any thin or lean object or person; a crooked branch; the bony part of a sheep's neck. [Norw. *skragg* lean person].

SCRAG (2), (scragging, scragged), [skrag], *v.t.* (*slang*) to screw or twist the neck of; to make a pretence of throttling; (in Rugby football) to tackle round the neck.

SCRAGGED, [skragd], *adj.* scraggy.

SCRAGGEDNESS, [skrag'-ed-nes], *n.* scragginess.

SCRAGGILY, [skrag'-i-li], *adv.* in a scraggy fashion.

SCRAGGINESS, [skrag'-i-nes], *n.* the condition of being scraggy.

SCRAGGY, [skrag'-i], *adj.* lean and bony in appearance, skinny; rugged. [SCRAG (1)].

SCRAM, (scramming, scrammed), [skram], *v.i.* (*U.S. slang*) to clear off, to depart hurriedly (when unwanted). [SCRAMBLE (2)].

SCRAMBLE (1), [skrambl], *n.* the act of scrambling; a means of movement, particularly climbing over rough ground using both arms and legs, a clamber; a friendly struggle for something.

SCRAMBLE (2), [skrambl], *v.t. and i.* to mix together; (*cookery*) to beat up egg with butter, etc., and cook; to proceed or climb by means of a scramble; to hurry across rough ground affording a poor foothold. [Uncert.].

SCRAMBLER, [skramb'-ler], *n.* one who scrambles.

SCRAMBLING, [skramb'-ling], *adj.* scuffling, straggling.

SCRAMBLINGLY, [skramb'-ling-li], *adv.* in a scrambling fashion.

SCRAN, [skran], *n.* (*coll.*) food, *esp.* of a makeshift kind. [Unkn.].

SCRANNEL, [skran'-el], *adj.* thin, slight, slender. [~Norw. *skran* lean].

SCRAP (1), [skrap], *n.* a small piece, a broken or torn oddment; a very small portion of food; refuse, a piece of waste metal; a fight, a scuffle, a scrimmage; **not to care a s.,** to be quite indifferent. [OIcel. *skrap*].

SCRAP (2), (scrapping, scrapped), [skrap], *v.t. and i.* to throw away or clear out as useless, to discard, to destroy; to fight without doing much damage.

SCRAPBOOK, [skrap'-book], *n.* a book of blank sheets on which press-cuttings or pictures are pasted.

SCRAPE (1), [skrāp], *n.* the act of scraping; a scoring mark, scratch; a smearing, a rubbing, a thin layer; the sound of the foot drawn over the floor; a clumsy bow; an awkward situation due to one's bad behaviour, a difficulty, perplexity.

SCRAPE (2), [skrāp], *v.t. and i.* to clean or make smooth a surface by rubbing it up and down with a sharp-edged instrument; to injure, scratch, or abrade by sliding along a hard or rough surface; to gather together slowly and laboriously in the form of bits and pieces, odds and ends; to produce a sharp, harsh sound by drawing one surface across another; to play (a string instrument) badly; to save money laboriously; **to s. acquaintance with,** to get to know (someone) slightly; to get to know (someone) by dubious methods; **to s. a living by,** to manage to live by means of; **to s. through,** to manage to escape from a difficult situation; to pass by a narrow margin, particularly an examination; **to bow and s.,** to behave obsequiously. [~OE. *screpen*].

SCRAPER, [skrāp'-er], *n.* a person who scrapes; a tool for scraping with; a contrivance for scraping the mud off boots; a clumsy fiddler.

SCRAPER

SCRAP-HEAP, [skrap'-hēp], *n.* a pile of refuse; a rubbish heap; (*fig.*) anonymity; oblivion.

SCRAPING, [skrāp'-ing], *n.* the act of scraping; anything scraped off.

SCRAP-IRON, [skrap'-īern], *n.* any old discarded iron in any form.

SCRAPPILY, [skrap'-i-li], *adv.* in a scrappy manner.

SCRAPPINESS, [skrap'-i-nes], *n.* the condition of being scrappy.

SCRAPPY, [skrap'-i], *adj.* consisting of bits and pieces; fragmentary, covered with tags; having no logical sequence.

SCRATCH (1), [skrach], *n.* the act of scratching; a mark made by scratching, a tear, a superficial wound, a slit in the skin, particularly one made by the fingernails; a scraping, fidgety sound made by scratching; official mark from which a race is started; a mark which divides two boxers before the match; the top of the handicap, par, zero; a wig; **to play (start) from s.,** to play (start) without handicap; **to come up to s.,** (*fig.*) to meet requirements, to be on form.

SCRATCH (2), [skrach], *adj.* composed of members drawn from sources of different standards; hastily formed into a group or team; receiving no handicap.

SCRATCH (3), [skrach], *v.t. and i.* to break into a surface, particularly the skin, leaving a slight mark, to tear with a sharp point or with the fingernails; to rub slightly to and fro as a remedy for itching; to fondle with the fingertips; to excavate with the claws or fingernails; to use the fingernails or claws to fight with, to rub with or to scrape with; to withdraw an entry in a race or contest; **s. my back and I'll**

s. yours, let's indulge in mutual admiration; **to s. out,** to delete, erase. [Uncert.].

SCRATCHER, [skrach'-er], *n.* one who, or that which, scratches; (*zool.*) a rasorial bird that scratches for food.

SCRATCHES, [skrach'-iz], *n.*(*pl.*) cracked ulcers forming on a horse's foot.

SCRATCHILY, [skrach'-i-li], *adv.* in a scratchy manner.

SCRATCHINESS, [skrach'-i-nes], *n.* the condition of being scratchy.

SCRATCHMAN, [skrach'-man], *n.* a man who plays or races from scratch.

SCRATCH-RACE, [skrach'-rās], *n.* a race in which all competitors start from the scratch mark.

SCRATCH-WIG, [skrach'-wig], *n.* a wig only partially covering the head.

SCRATCHY, [skrach'-i], *adj.* that is scratched on the surface; making a noise resembling scratching; itchy, irritating; mixed (of a collection of players).

SCRAW, [skraw], *n.* turf or short strips of grass used as roof covering or fuel. [Gael. *sgrath*].

SCRAWL (1), [skrawl], *n.* a piece of hasty bad handwriting; a poor piece of literature.

SCRAWL (2), [skrawl], *v.t. and i.* to write hastily and in poor handwriting; to write badly; to move a pencil or pen haphazardly and meaninglessly on a surface or paper, etc. [Uncert.].

SCRAWLER, [skrawl'-er], *n.* one who scrawls; a hasty or clumsy writer.

SCRAWNY, [skrawn'-i], *adj.* gaunt and lean, rawboned. [Norw. *skran* lean].

SCRAY, [skrā], *n.* the common tern, *Sterna fluviatilis*. [Wel. *yscraen* tern].

SCREAK (1), [skrēk], *n.* (*dial.*) a harsh cry, a screech.

SCREAK (2), [skrēk], *v.t.* to utter suddenly a short piercing sound, to scream, to screech. [OScand. *skrækja*].

SCREAM (1), [skrēm], *n.* a sudden, loud, shrill cry as an expression of intense pain or terror, a shriek; (*slang*) a comedian; an object of mirth.

SCREAM (2), [skrēm], *v.i.* to utter a scream as the result of experiencing terror or pain; to utter a sudden harsh, piercing cry. [OIcel. *skræma* to scare].

SCREAMER, [skrēm'-er], *n.* a person who screams; a bird found in tropical America, allied to the geese and as large as a turkey, having two spurs on each wing; **crested s.,** a species of *Chauna* with a crest on the head; **horned s.,** a species of *Palamedea* with a horn on the head.

SCREAMER

SCREE, [skrē], *n.* a steep slope covered with small loose stones; a collection of insecure stones at the foot of a cliff. [OIcel. *skritha* landslide].

SCREECH (1), [skrēch], *n.* a short, loud scream, a shrill, piercing cry.

SCREECH (2), [skrēch], *v.i.* to utter harsh piercing sounds disagreeable to the ear, to shriek. [*Var.* of SHRIEK].

SCREECH-OWL, [skrēch'-owl], *n.* an owl that when hunting at night utters a harsh, disagreeable cry, and is regarded as a bird of evil omen; a popular name for the barn-owl, *Strix flammea*, or the tawny owl, *Strix aluco*.

SCREED, [skrēd], *n.* a long reprimand or list of misdoings; a hysterical appeal or scolding; a lengthy, somewhat boring epistle; (*arch.*) a level piece of plastering used as a guide in running a cornice. [*Var.* of SHRED].

SCREEN (1), [skrēn], *n.* a structure or device to provide shelter or protection, particularly a piece of furniture consisting of a light covered framework of two or more sections, used to shut off draughts; a device fitted to a motor-car for protecting driver and passengers from the wind; an elaborate partition in a church separating the choir from the nave; a large sheet or other smooth surface upon which cinematograph or magic-lantern pictures are projected; a large framework of white wooden boards placed in the cricket field on the boundary behind the bowler's arm; a person who acts for a higher authority; a coarse sieve; (*fig.*) the motion-picture industry; (*elect.*) a device in the form of a sheet of metal to protect a circuit from being affected by stray magnetic fields; (*phot.*) a mesh device for breaking up a photograph into small dots for reproduction by means of a half-tone block. [~OFr. *escren* curtain].

SCREEN (2), [skrēn], *v.t.* to give protection and shelter to by means of a screen; to act as a shield between a person and moral or physical danger; to pass through a sieve, to sift; to project on to a screen; to convert into a film; **to s. off,** to shut off. [*Prec.*].

SCREENED-GRID, [skrēnd'-grid], *adj.* (*wirel.*) descriptive of a four-electrode thermionic valve built with one grid screening another.

SCREENING, [skrēn'-ing], *n.* the act of one who, that which, screens; material used for making screens; (*elect.*) a device consisting of a metal screen for preventing one electric circuit carrying an alternating current from affecting another adjacent to it.

SCREEVER, [skrēv'-er], *n.* (*slang*) a person who writes a begging letter; a pavement artist. [~L. *scribere* to write].

SCREW (1), [skrōō], *n.* a mechanical device of various sizes for joining two pieces of wood or metal together, consisting of a cylindrical shaft of metal with a spiral groove cut round its surface and a flat or round head at the end opposite the point provided with a straight groove by means of which the shaft can be turned or undone; one of several principles of mechanical power, being a more complex development of the inclined plane; the action of screwing; a screw-propeller; that which is screwed up or is in the form of a twisted length, particularly a half-ounce of tobacco; a person who economizes to the utmost, a miser; (*slang*) salary, wages; a prison-warder; a worn-out horse; **to have a s. loose,** to be slightly mentally deficient. [ME. *screu* from OFr. *escroe*].

SCREW (2), [skrōō], *v.t. and i.* to fasten by means of a screw, to join tightly together; to twist round and round as far as possible in one direction; to twist, distort, contort; to press, squeeze, extract, wring out; in billiards, to make the ball spin by putting side on it; to function as a screw; to give side or spin to a billiard ball; **to have one's head screwed on the right way,** to have plenty of common sense. [*Prec.*].

SCREWBOLT, [skrōō'-bōlt], *n.* a bolt in the form of a screw fitted with a nut.

SCREWDRIVER, [skrōō'-driv-er], *n.* a tool with a blunt-edged shaft for turning screws, a turn-screw.

SCREWED, [skrōōd], *adj.* fastened with screws; (*slang*) drunk, intoxicated.

SCREWER, [skrōō'-er], *n.* one who, or that which, screws.

SCREWJACK, [skrōō'-jak'], *n.* a tool wound up on a spiral screw for raising heavy weights.

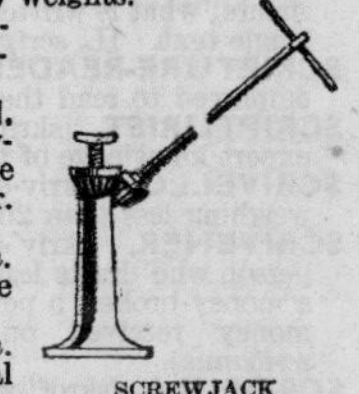

SCREWJACK

SCREWMATICS, [scrōō-mat'-iks], *n.*(*pl.*) (*coll.*) rheumatism. [~RHEUMATIC].

SCREW NAIL, [skrōō'-nāl'], *n.* a screw with a shallow, low-pitched thread, intended to be driven in with a hammer. [SCREW (1) and NAIL (1)].

SCREWPILE, [skrōō'-pil], *n.* a pile fitted with a screw at the end.

SCREW-PINE, [skrōō'-pīn], *n.* any one of a group of tropical palms found in the Malay States of the genus *Pandanus* or *Freycinetia*, in which the stem is twisted so that the leaves are formed into spirals.

SCREW-PROPELLER, [skrōō'-pro-pel'-er], *n.* a modification of the screw, consisting of two or more vanes set obliquely in a boss, and used for propelling ships and aircraft.

SCREW-THREAD, [skrōō'-thred'], *n.* the ridge formed by the groove on a screw.

SCRIBBLE (1), [skribl], *n.* handwriting written hastily and indistinctly; writing composed too carelessly or hastily to be of value.

SCRIBBLE (2), [skribl], *v.t. and i.* to write hastily so that the letters are badly formed; to compose too hastily for any concern with style; to form a series of inconsequential marks; to write or compose carelessly; to work as a hack author. [Med.L *scribillare*].

SCRIBBLER, [skrib'-ler], *n.* one who scribbles; a careless writer; an author of inferior compositions; a carding machine.

SCRIBBLING, [skrib'-ling], *n.* that which is scribbled.

SCRIBBLINGLY, [skrib'-ling-li], *adv.* in a scribbling fashion.

SCRIBBLY, [skrib'-li], *adj.* characterized by, resembling, scribbles; untidily written. [SCRIBBLE (2)].

SCRIBE (1), [skrīb], *n.* an author who earns his living by his pen; formerly, a writer who lived by copying manuscripts; (*hist.*) a Jewish lawyer expert in ecclesiastical law. [L. *scriba* clerk].

SCRIBE (2), [skrīb], *v.t. and i.* in carpentry, to score a line by means of a sharp metal point; to act as a scribe.

SCRIBER, [skrīb'-er], *n.* an inferior writer, a journalist, a scribe; a pointed metal tool for marking metals with guide-lines.

SCRIBER

SCRIMMAGE, SCRUMMAGE, [skrim'-ij], *n.* a close, confused struggle; (in Rugby football) the formation of two opposing sets of forwards when packed tightly head to head; a scrummage. [*Var.* of SKIRMISH].

SCRIMP (1), [skrimp], *adj.* reduced, stinted.

SCRIMP (2), [skrimp], *v.t.* to reduce, shorten, or stint, particularly in regard to food or cloth. [~OE. *scrimman*].

SCRIMPNESS, [skrimp'-nes], *n.* the condition of being scrimp, scantiness.

SCRIMSHANKER, [skrim'-shangk-er], *n.* (*slang*) a person, particularly a soldier, who shirks duty. [Unkn.].

SCRIMSHAW, [skrim'-shaw], *n.* an engraved shell, piece of ivory or tooth. [Unkn.].

SCRIP (1), [skrip], *n.* a small bag or leather wallet, widely used in the Middle Ages. [LL. *scrippum*].

SCRIP (2), [skrip], *n.* a brief piece of writing, certificate or schedule; (*comm.*) a provisional certificate of stock or of shares in a joint-stock company. [SCRIPT].

SCRIPT, [skript], *n.* characters or letters written in the style of a sanserif type fount; handwriting as distinct from print or typewriting; manuscript; typescript; the text of a play, etc. [OFr. *escript*].

SCRIPTORIUM, [skript-aw'-ri-um], *n.* the room set aside for writing manuscripts in a monastery. [LL. *scriptorium*].

SCRIPTURAL, [skrip'-cher-al], *adj.* relating to, according to, Scripture.

SCRIPTURALISM, [skrip'-cher-al-izm], *n.* strict adherence to the letter of Scripture.

SCRIPTURALIST, [skrip'-cher-al-ist], *n.* one who adheres literally to the Scriptures.

SCRIPTURALLY, [skrip'-cher-al-i], *adv.* in the Scriptures.

SCRIPTURALNESS, [skrip'-cher-al-nes], *n.* the quality of being scriptural.

SCRIPTURE, [skrip'-cher], *n.* any manuscript of holy writings; the Bible, the Old and New Testaments; what is written in Scripture, particularly any single text. [L. *scriptura* writing].

SCRIPTURE-READER, [skrip'-cher-rēd'-er], *n.* one employed to read the Scriptures to the poor.

SCRIPTURIST, [skrip'-cher-ist], *n.* a person with expert knowledge of the Scriptures.

SCRIVELLO, [skriv-el'-ō], *n.* an elephant's tusk weighing less than 20 lb. [Portug. *escrevelho*].

SCRIVENER, [skriv'-en-er], *n.* a law-stationer; a person who drafts legal contracts or other writings; a money-broker; a person whose business is to place money received on deposit at interest. [LL. *scribanus*].

SCROFULA, [skrof'-yo͝o-la], *n.* (*path.*) the formation and deposition of tubercle in the lymphatic glands; king's evil. [L. *scrofula* little pig].

SCROFULOUS, [skrof'-yo͝o-lus], *adj.* of, relating to, affected by, scrofula.

SCROFULOUSLY, [skrof'-yo͝o-lus-li], *adv.* in a scrofulous style.

SCROFULOUSNESS, [skrof'-yo͝o-lus-nes], *n.* the condition of being scrofulous.

SCROG, [skrog], *n.* (*dial.*) a stunted shrub or bush; (*her.*) a branch of a tree. [Unkn.].

SCROLL, [skrōl], *n.* a roll of paper or parchment; a writing in the form of a roll; a ribbon carrying a motto in armorial bearings; (*arch.*) a spiral ornament of the Ionic period. [ME. *scrowl* from OFr. *escroue* screw].

SCROTAL, [skrō'-tal], *adj.* of, or relating to, the scrotum.

SCROTIFORM, [skrō'-ti-fawm], *adj.* (*bot.*) pouch-shaped. [SCROTUM and FORM].

SCROTOCELE, [skrōt'-ō-sēl], *n.* (*med.*) a hernia into the scrotum. [SCROTUM and Gk. *kele* a tumour].

SCROTUM, [skrō'-tum], *n.* (*anat.*) the bag of skin which contains the testicles. [L. *scrotum*].

SCROUNGE, [skrownj], *v.t. and i.* (*slang*) to help oneself to things with possible intent to keep them.

SCROUNGER, [skrownj'-er], *n.* a person who indulges in scrounging.

SCRUB (1), [skrub], *n.* underwood, stunted dwarf trees and bushes; (*U.S. slang*) an athlete not a member of the first team. [*Var.* of SHRUB].

SCRUB (2), [skrub], *n.* the act of scrubbing; a person who labours hard and lives meanly; a worn-out brush.

SCRUB (3), (scrubbing, scrubbed), [skrub], *v.t. and i.* to clean by rubbing hard with a brush, to scour out with a brush; to clean by vigorous rubbing with something rough. [ODan. *skrubbe*].

SCRUBBER, [skrub'-er], *n.* one who or that which scrubs; a charwoman; an apparatus for cleaning gas by a process of spraying.

SCRUBBINESS, [skrub'-i-nes], *n.* the condition of being scrubby.

SCRUBBING-BRUSH, [skrub'-ing-brush'], *n.* a brush, fitted with tough bristles, used for scrubbing floors.

SCRUBBY, [skrub'-i], *adj.* small and mean; stunted in growth, dwarf; dirty and untidy in appearance.

SCRUFF, [skruf], *n.* the skin on the back of the neck. [OE. *scruf*].

SCRUFFY, [skruf'-i], *adj.* scurfy; having a disreputable appearance.

SCRUM (1), [skrum], *n.* a scrimmage. [Abbreviated from SCRUMMAGE].

SCRUM (2), (scrumming, scrummed), [skrum], *v.i.* to form a scrum; **to s. down,** to form a scrimmage.

SCRUMMAGE, see SCRIMMAGE.

SCRUMPTIOUS, [skrump'-shus], *adj.* (*slang*) pleasant, delightful. [Uncert.].

SCRUPLE (1), [skro͞opl], *n.* a measurement of weight, twenty grains, the third part of a drachm; a very small quantity; hesitation, *esp.* from conscientious motives, doubt arising from difficulty in judging the ethics of one's action, a nice point in morale. [L. *scrupulus* small stone].

SCRUPLE (2), [skro͞opl], *v.t. and i.* †to doubt, to question; to have scruples, to hesitate for ethical reasons.

SCRUPULOSITY, [skro͞op'-yo͝o-los'-i-ti], *n.* the quality of being scrupulous, scrupulousness, preciseness. [L. *scrupulositas*].

SCRUPULOUS, [skro͞op'-yo͝o-lus], *adj.* being by nature careful over the ethics of one's conduct, having scruples; cautious, careful; taking strict care over details and accuracy, exact, strict. [L. *scrupulosus* stony].

SCRUPULOUSLY, [skro͞op'-yo͝o-lus-li], *adv.* in a scrupulous fashion.

SCRUPULOUSNESS, [skro͞op'-yo͝o-lus-nes], *n.* the condition of being scrupulous.

SCRUTABLE, [skro͞ot'-abl], *adj.* able to be subjected to inquiry or critical examination. [LL. *scrutabilis*].

SCRUTATOR, [skro͞ot-ā'-tor], *n.* one who scrutinizes; an examiner. [L. *scrutator* investigator].

SCRUTINEER, [skro͞ot'-in-ēer'], *n.* one who scrutinizes or examines, *esp.* ballot papers.

SCRUTINIZE, [skro͞ot'-in-īz], *v.t.* to search closely; to examine minutely or critically.

SCRUTINIZER, [skro͞ot'-in-īz-er], *n.* one who scrutinizes.

SCRUTINOUSLY, [skro͞ot'-in-us-li], *adv.* in a scrutinous manner, with scrutiny.

SCRUTINY, [skro͞ot'-in-i], *n.* close search; minute critical examination; an examination of the votes given at an election after the demand for a recount. [L. *scrutinium*].

SCRYING, [skrī'-ing], *n.* a perceiving, *esp.* by crystal-gazing; descrying. [*Var.* of DESCRY].

SCUD (1), [skud], *n.* the act of scudding; a swift running, gliding movement given impetus by a strong wind; a mass of loose, rain-laden clouds driven along by the winds.

SCUD (2), (scudding, scudded), [skud], *v.i.* to move rapidly along on a level driven by the wind, to glide swiftly and smoothly propelled by the wind. [Uncert.].

SCUDO, (*pl.* scudi), [sko͞o'-dō], *n.* an old Italian silver coin, corresponding to the crown or the dollar; a modern coin worth approximately four or five shillings, 5 liras. [It. *scudo* shield].

SCUFFLE (1), [skufl], *n.* a garden hoe. [~Du. *schoffelen*].

SCUFFLE (2), [skufl], *n.* a struggle for mastery with close grappling; a confused fight; a brief hand-to-hand tussle.

SCUFFLE (3), [skufl], *v.i.* to struggle, to wrestle in catch-as-catch-can form; to engage in a short bout of grappling and tussling. [~Swed. *skuffa* to push].

SCUFFLER, [skuf'-ler], *n.* one who scuffles.
SCULL (1), [skul], *n.* (*dial.*) name for the great skua; the pirate gull. [Uncert.].
SCULL (2), [skul], *n.* a light one-handed oar; a light boat for sculling in; the action of sculling. [Unkn.].
SCULL (3), [skul], *v.t.* and *i.* to row (a boat) by means of a scull; to use a scull in rowing.
SCULLER, [skul'-er], *n.* one who sculls; a boat for sculling.
SCULLERY, [skul'-er-i], *n.* the room adjoining the kitchen in which dishes are washed and other rough household work is carried out. [MedL. *scutellarius* from *scutella* tray].
SCULLION, [skul'-i-on], *n.* †a boy employed in washing up, a washer-up of kitchen utensils. [OFr. *escouillon* a swab].
SCULLIONLY, [skul'-i-on-li], *adj.* like a scullion; low, dirty.
SCULPIN, [skul'-pin], *n.* a fish of the North Atlantic, the dragonet, a sea-fish of the genus *Callionymus*. [Uncert.].
SCULPTOR, [skulp'-tor], *n.* a person who practises the art of sculpture, a carver of wood, stone, or other material, a modeller in plastic material. [L. *sculptor*].
SCULPTRESS, [skulpt'-res], *n.* a female sculptor.
SCULPTURAL, [skulp'-cher-al], *adj.* relating to sculpture; having the characteristics of sculpture.
SCULPTURALLY, [skulp'-cher-al-i], *adv.* in a sculptural fashion, by sculpture.
SCULPTURE (1), [skulp'-cher], *n.* the art of using three-dimensional material by cutting, chiselling or carving it into masses with compositional value so as to reproduce a natural object or an emotional experience about such an object; the art of modelling in plastic material such as clay; any work of art created in wood, stone, metal, clay, etc. [L. *sculptura*].
SCULPTURE (2), [skulp'-cher], *v.t.* and *i.* to work at, or produce a sculpture of, in stone, wood, or any other manipulable material; to decorate with pieces of sculpture; to practise the art of representation by means of pieces of sculpture. [*Prec.*].
SCULPTURESQUE, [skulp'-cher-esk'], *adj.* in the style of, resembling, sculpture, as in sculpture; statuesque.
SCUM (1), [skum], *n.* the froth bearing the impurities which rise to the surface of liquors in boiling or fermentation; the refuse; the throw-outs, leavings; that which is vile or worthless. [~Dan. *skum* foam].
SCUM (2), (scumming, scummed), [skum], *v.t.* to skim off the scum.
SCUMBLE, [skumbl], *v.t.* to rub over with a semi-opaque colour; to diffuse an outline in a painting.
SCUMBLING, [skum'-bling], *n.* in oil painting, the process of thinly rubbing semi-opaque colours over others, to soften the effect, *esp.* of sharp outlines.
SCUMMINGS, [skum'-ingz], *n.*(*pl.*) impure matter skimmed from boiling liquors.
SCUMMY, [skum'-i], *adj.* full of, covered with, scum.
SCUNCHEON, [skun'-shun], *n.* (*arch.*) a small buttress set in the angle of a square tower to support one of the alternate sides of the spire; bevelled splays inside a window-frame. [OFr. *escoinson*].
SCUPPER (1), [skup'-er], *n.* (*naut.*) the channel, lined with lead, cut through the sides of a ship, for draining the sea water or swab water from off the deck. [~OFr. *escope* a scoop].
SCUPPER (2), [skup'-er], *v.t.* (*naut.*) to cut holes for emergency draining in a ship's side; to throw a ship on to its side.
SCUPPER-HOSE, [skup'-er-hōz], *n.* (*naut.*) a pipe of leather or canvas, attached to the mouth of the scuppers on the outside of a vessel, which is used to prevent sea water washing in on to the deck.
SCUPPER-PLUG, [skup'-er-plug], *n.* an emergency plug to stop a scupper.
SCURF, [skurf], *n.* small dry bits of skin which flake off a scalp in bad condition, dandruff; a dry miliary scab formed on the skin; an exfoliation; anything adhering to the surface. [OIcel. *skurfr*].
SCURFF, [skurf], *n.* the sea-trout, *Salmo eriox*, characterized by an unforked tail.
SCURFINESS, [skurf'-i-nes], *n.* the condition of being scurfy.
SCURFY, [skurf'-i], *adj.* suffering from, covered with, scurf; resembling scurf.
SCURRILITY, [sku-ril'-i-ti], *n.* the quality of being scurrilous; that which is scurrilous; low vulgar abuse. [L. *scurrilitas*].
SCURRILOUS, [sku'-ril-us], *adj.* characterized by coarse invective, using the low and indecent language of the vulgar; containing low indecency or abuse; foul, abusive; coarsely opprobrious or jocular.
SCURRILOUSLY, [sku'-ril-us-li], *adv.* in a scurrilous fashion.
SCURRILOUSNESS, [sku'-ril-us-nes], *n.* the state or quality of being scurrilous.
SCURRY (1), [sku'-ri], *n.* a hasty running movement, a scamper; a short race between horses or boats. [Uncert.].
SCURRY (2), [sku'-ri], *v.i.* to run with rapid scampering steps, to scuttle.
SCURVILY, [skurv'-i-li], *adv.* in a scurvy manner; meanly, contemptibly.
SCURVINESS, [skurv'-i-nes], *n.* the condition of being scurvy.
SCURVY (1), [skurv'-i], *n.* a disease due to the lack of fresh fruit and vegetables.
SCURVY (2), [skurv'-i], *adj.* suffering from scurvy; mean, contemptible, shabby, low. [~SCURF].
SCURVY-GRASS, [skurv'-i-grahs], *n.* (*bot.*) a plant of the genus *Cochlearia*, formerly used in the treatment of scurvy.
SCUT, [skut], *n.* the short tail of a hare or rabbit. [Uncert.].
SCUTAGE, [skew'-tij], *n.* in feudal times, a tax levied upon those who held lands by knight service, as a substitute for the personal military services of the vassal. [MedL. *scutagium*].
SCUTATE, [skew'-tāt], *adj.* (*bot.*) having the form of a shield; (*zool.*) protected by large scales. [L. *scutatus* armed with a shield].
SCUTCH, [skuch], *v.t.* to beat or whip slightly so as to eliminate dust; to comb; to loosen fibres of flax by beating. [OFr. **escoucher*].
SCUTCHEON, [skuch'-un], *n.* an escutcheon; a plate for an inscription; the ornamental plate protecting a keyhole. [ESCUTCHEON].
SCUTE, [skewt], *n.* (*zool.*) a scale, as of a reptile. [L. *scutum* a shield].
SCUTELLATE, SCUTELLATED, [skewt'-i-lāt(-id)], *adj.* (*bot.*, *zool.*) divided into surfaces like little plates; covered with small scales. [SCUTELLUM].
SCUTELLUM, [skewt-el'-um], *n.* (*biol.*) a small process resembling a shield in shape or function. [L. *scutella* a dish].
SCUTIFORM, [skewt'-i-fawm], *adj.* (*bot.*, *zool.*) having the shape of a shield. [SCUTUM and FORM].
SCUTTLE (1), [skutl], *n.* a broad shallow basket; a receptacle made of metal for holding coals. [OE. *scutel* bowl from L. *scutella* tray].
SCUTTLE (2), [skutl], *n.* a small opening with a hinged cover in a wall or roof, a trap-door; a motor-car fitment connecting bonnet with chassis; (*naut.*) an opening in a deck protected by a cover, a small hatchway. [Span. *escotilla* hatchway].
SCUTTLE (3), [skutl], *n.* a quick pace with short steps; a hasty flight with a scurrying movement.
SCUTTLE (4), [skutl], *v.t.* to sink a ship by making holes in its hull. [SCUTTLE (2)].
SCUTTLE (5), [skutl], *v.i.* to run off in a hasty scurrying manner, to bolt. [~SCUD].
SCUTTLE-CASK, [skutl'-kahsk], *n.* (*naut.*) a butt or cask kept on deck to hold water for daily use.
SCUTUM, [skewt'-um], *n.* ancient Roman shield used by heavy infantry; (*zool.*) the large scutiform scales of certain reptiles; (*entom.*) the second segment of each of the three divisions of the upper part of the thorax; (*bot.*) the broad dilated stigma of certain plants. [L. *scutum* a shield].
SCYPHUS, [sīf'-us], *n.* (*bot.*) a cup-shaped structure bearing the fruit in certain lichens. [Gk. *skuphos* drinking horn].
SCYTHE (1), [sīTH], *n.* an agricultural implement with a long, curving blade, sharp on the inner edge, for mowing grass and cutting grain. [OE. *sigthe*].
SCYTHE (2), [sīTH], *v.t.* and *i.* to cut with a scythe; to handle a scythe for mowing purposes.
SCYTHIAN (1), [siTH'-i-an], *n.* a native, or the language, of Scythia. [Gk. *Skuthia*].
SCYTHIAN (2), [siTH'-i-an], *adj.* relating to, made or born in, Scythia, an ancient country on the north-east of the Black Sea.
SEA, [sē], *n.* the body of salt water covering the major part of the earth's surface, the ocean; any particular part of this water, *esp.* if partly enclosed or defined by land; a large expanse of salt water, even if completely land-locked; a wave, billow of water; (*fig.*) a great expanse of anything, a mass of objects so closely compacted that they seem a continuous surface, a vast, overwhelming mass of anything. [OE. *sæ*].
SEA-ACORN, [sē'-āk'-awn], *n.* an acorn-shaped barnacle, *esp.* the acorn-barnacle *Balanus*.

SEA-ANCHOR, [sē'-ang'-ker], *n.* a floating anchor to check drifting.
SEA-ANEMONE, [sē'-an-em'-on-i], *n.* a marine polyp of the order *Actinaria*.
SEA-APE, [sē'-āp], *n.* the thresher shark; the sea-otter.
SEA-BANK, [sē'-bangk'], *n.* a mole to prevent encroachment; the seashore.
SEA-BAT, [sē'-bat'], *n.* a flying fish.
SEA-BEAR, [sē'-bāer], *n.* the Pacific fur-bearing seal.
SEA-BEATEN, [sē'-bēt'-en], *adj.* battered by waves.
SEA-BEET, [sē'-bēt], *n.* the plant *Beta maritima*.
SEA-BIRD, [sē'-bird], *n.* a bird living on the sea-coast, a maritime bird.

SEA-ANEMONE

SEABOARD, [sē'-bawd], *n.* the sea-coast, the land adjoining the sea.
SEA-BOAT, [sē'-bōt], *n.* a seagoing ship, a ship judged by its seaworthiness.
SEA-BORN, [sē'-bawn], *adj.* born from the sea, *esp.* applied to Aphrodite.
SEABORNE, [sē'-bawn], *adj.* transported over sea, borne by the sea.
SEA-BREACH, [sē'-brēch], *n.* a breach in a mole, etc., made by the sea.
SEA-BREAM, [sē'-brēm], *n.* a fish of the genus *Pagellus*.
SEA-BREEZE, [sē'-brēz], *n.* a breeze blowing from the sea.
SEA-BUCKTHORN, [sē'-buk'-thawn], *n.* the sallow-thorn *Hippophaë rhamnoides*.
SEA-CALF, [sē'-kahf], *n.* the common seal, a species of *Phoca*.
SEA-CAPTAIN, [sē'-kap'-tin], *n.* the captain of a seagoing vessel.
SEA-CARD, [sē'-kahd], *n.* the compass-card.
SEA-COAL, [sē'-kōl], *n.* (*hist.*) coal transported by sea.
SEA-COAST, [sē'-kōst], *n.* the land bordering on the sea.
SEA-COB, [sē'-kob'], *n.* a seagull.
SEA-COW, [sē'-kow], *n.* the dugong.
SEACRAFT, [sē'-krahft], *n.* knowledge of seamanship.
SEA-CROW, [sē'-krō], *n.* the cormorant.
SEA-CUCUMBER, [sē-kew'-kum-ber], *n.* a large slug of the genus *Holothuria* living in the sea.
SEA-DACE, [sē'-dās], *n.* the bass, *Labrax lupus*.
SEA-DEVIL, [sē'-dev-il], *n.* a species of great ray, the devil-fish.
SEA-DOG, [sē'-dog'], *n.* a hardened sailor; the dog-fish; the seal.
SEA-DOTTEREL, [sē'-dot'-er-el], *n.* the turnstone, *Strepsilas interpres*.
SEA-DRAGON, [sē'-drag'-on], *n.* the Australian pipefish; the sea-serpent.
SEA-EAGLE, [sē'-ēgl], *n.* the fishing eagle *Haliaetus*; the osprey.
SEA-EAR, [sē'-ēer], *n.* an ear-shaped mollusc of the genus *Haliotis*.
SEA-EGG, [sē'-eg'], *n.* a sea-urchin.
SEA-ELEPHANT, [sē-el'-i-fant], *n.* the great Atlantic seal, *Macrorhinus proboscideus*, remarkable for its trunk-like proboscis.
SEAFARER, [sē'-fāer-er], *n.* one who travels by sea, a seaman, mariner.
SEAFARING, [sē'-fāer'-ing], *n.* the act of travelling by sea; the occupation of a sailor.
SEA-FENNEL, [sē'-fen'-el], *n.* samphire.
SEA-FIGHT, [sē'-fīt], *n.* a naval battle.
SEA-FISH, [sē'-fish], *n.* a fish living in the sea.
SEA-FOWL, [sē'-fowl], *n.* a sea-bird, sea-birds collectively.
SEA-FOX, [sē'-foks'], *n.* the thresher shark.
SEA-FRONT, [sē'-frunt], *n.* the marine parade of a seaside town.
SEA-GAUGE, [sē'-gāj], *n.* a ship's draught; a device for sounding depth.
SEA-GIRT, [sē'-gurt], *adj.* surrounded and protected by the sea.
SEA-GOD, [sē'-god'], *n.* Poseidon, Neptune, an ocean deity.
SEA-GODDESS, [sē'-god'-es], *n.* a goddess of the sea.
SEAGOING, [sē'-gō-ing], *adj.* travelling across the open sea.
SEA-GREEN, [sē'-grēn], *n. and adj.* the bluish-green colour of shallow water; of this colour.

SEAGULL, [sē'-gul], *n.* a sea-bird of the *Laridæ*.
SEA-HARE, [sē'-hāer], *n.* a nudibranch mollusc of the genus *Aplysia*.
SEA-HEATH, [sē'-hēth], *n.* the plant *Frankenia lævis*.
SEA-HOG, [sē'-hog'], *n.* the porpoise.
SEA-HOLLY, [sē'-hol'-i], *n.* the plant *Eryngium maritimum*.
SEA-HORSE, [sē'-haws], *n.* the warm-water fish, *Hippocampus*, remarkable for its horse-like head.

SEA-HORSE

SEA ISLAND, [sē'-il'-and], *adj.* denoting a type of fine cotton from the islands off Georgia and South Carolina in the U.S.A.
SEAKALE, [sē'-kāl], *n.* edible colewort.
SEA-KING, [sē'-king], *n.* the leader of a seagoing people; a Norse viking.
SEA-KITTIE, [sē'-kit-i], *n.* the kittiwake.
SEAL (1), [sēl], *n.* an amphibious marine mammal with flippers or webbed feet. [OE. *seole*].
SEAL (2), [sēl], *n.* a device stamped on wax or similar material by an engraved die, and attached to documents, etc., to prove their authenticity; the die itself, or anything used as a die; (*fig.*) a token, sure sign of genuineness; something securing secrecy, an undertaking of inviolable silence or discretion; that which closes. [AFr. *seal*].
SEAL (3), [sēl], *v.i.* to hunt seals.
SEAL (4), [sēl], *v.t.* to stamp, mark, validate with a seal; to secure, close with a seal, to utterly shut up and secure from any access; to mark as determined, to set aside as certain, or already performed; to confirm, ratify.
SEA-LARK, [sē'-lahk], *n.* the dunlin.
SEA-LAVENDER, [sē-lav'-en-der], *n.* the plant *Statice Limonium* with mauve flowers.
SEA-LAWYER, [sē-law'-yer], *n.* an argumentative amateur lawyer, one who is forever standing out for the rights of himself and others.
SEA-LEGS, [sē'-legz'], *n.* ability to keep steady on a moving ship.
SEA-LEMON, [sē-lem'-on], *n.* a mollusc of the genus *Doris*.
SEA-LEOPARD, [sē'-lep'-erd], *n.* a spotted seal.
SEALER, [sēl'-er], *n.* a vessel or person engaged in seal hunting.
SEALERY, [sēl'-er-i], *n.* a seal-fishing station.
SEA-LETTER, [sē'-let'-er], *n.* a passport issued to a neutral ship in time of war, stating the nature of its cargo.
SEA-LEVEL, [sē'-lev'-el], *n.* the mean tidal level.
SEA-LILY, [sē'-lil'-i], *n.* a crinoid.
SEA-LINE, [sē'-lin], *n.* the horizon at sea.
SEALING, [sēl'-ing] *n.* the occupation of hunting seals. [SEAL (3)].
SEALING-WAX, [sēl'-ing-waks'], *n.* a substance of resin and shellac that becomes plastic when heated, used in sealing documents, etc. [SEAL (4) and WAX (1)].
SEA-LINTIE, [sē'-lin-ti], *n.* the rock pipit.
SEA-LION, [sē'-lī'-un], *n.* a species of large seal, distinguished by mane and ears.
SEA-LORD, [sē'-lawd], *n.* a naval member of the Board of Admiralty.
SEALSKIN, [sēl'-skin], *n.* the fur of the seal.
SEALYHAM, [sēl'-i-am], *n.* a breed of white terrier with short legs. [*Sealyham* in Pembrokeshire].

SEA-LION

SEAM (1), [sēm], *n.* a join where two pieces of material are sewn together; a junction where two boards are caulked together; a suture; the line of a scar; (*geol.*) a vein, thin layer, between two thicker strata. [OE. *seam*].
SEAM (2), [sēm], *n.* (*hist.*) a varying measure of weight, based upon the amount a horse could draw. [OE. *seam*].
SEAM (3), [sēm] *v.t.*, to join with a seam, mark as if with a seam.
SEAMAN, [sē'-man], *n.* a sailor; (*nav.*) a sailor below the rank of officer. [OE. *sæman*].
SEAMANLIKE, [se'-man-līk], *adj.* like a seaman, showing the skill of a seaman.
SEAMANLY, [sē'-man-li], *adj.* seamanlike.
SEAMANSHIP, [sē'-man-ship], *n.* the skill or craft of a seaman, the quality of being a good seaman.

SEAMARK, [sē´-mahk], *n.* a beacon or mark to guide a ship approaching land.

SEA-MEW, [sē´-mew], *n.* the common gull, *Larus canus.*

SEA-MILE, [sē´-mil´], *n.* the geographical mile of 6,080 feet used at sea.

SEA-MILKWORT, [sē´-milk´-wurt], *n.* a plant of the genus *Glaux.*

SEAMLESS, [sēm´-les], *adj.* without seam, unseamed.

SEA-MEW

SEA-MOSS, [sē´-mos´], *n.* a bryozoan, a kind of *Corallina*; a marine alga.

SEA-MOUSE, [sē´-mows], *n.* a marine, annelid worm of the genus *Aphrodite.*

SEAMSTRESS, [sem´-stres], *n.* a woman who sews, a professional needlewoman. [OE. *seamestre*].

SEAMY, [sē´-mi], *adj.* showing the rough underside of a seam; relating to the unattractive underworld of a thing; **the s. side,** the sordid aspect.

SEANCE, séance, [sā´-ahnts], *n.* a meeting of a society, *esp.* a gathering of spiritualists in order to communicate with the spirits of the dead. [Fr. *séance*].

SEA-NEEDLE, [sē´-nēdl], *n.* the garfish.

SEA-NETTLE, [sē´-netl´], *n.* a stinging jellyfish.

SEA-ONION, [sē´-un´-yon], *n.* the squill, *Urginea scilla.*

SEA-OOZE, [sē´-ōōz], *n.* the soft mud on the sea-bottom.

SEA-OTTER, [sē´-ot´-er], *n.* the furry carnivorous marine mammal *Latrax lutris.*

SEA-OWL, [sē´-owl], *n.* the lump-fish.

SEA-PAD, [sē´-pad´], *n.* the starfish.

SEA-PARROT, [sē´-pa-rot], *n.* the puffin.

SEA-PECK, [sē´-pĕk], *n.* the dunlin, *Tringa alpina.*

SEA-PEN, [sē´-pen´], *n.* a feathery species of polyp.

SEA-PHEASANT, [sē´-fez´-ant], *n.* the pintail duck, *Dafila acuta.*

SEA-PIE (1), [sē´-pī´], *n.* the oyster-catcher, *Hæmatopus ostralegus.*

SEA-PIE (2), [sē´-pī´], *n.* a stodgy boiled meat pie commonly eaten by seamen.

SEA-PIECE, [sē´-pēs], *n.* a seascape.

SEA-PIG, [sē´-pig], *n.* the dugong.

SEA-PIGEON, [sē´-pij´-on], *n.* the rock-dove.

SEA-PIKE, [sē´-pīk], *n.* the fish *Centropomus undecimalis.*

SEA-PINK, [sē´-pingk], *n.* the pink-and-white flowered sea plant, *Statice Armeria,* thrift.

SEAPLANE, [sē´-plān´], *n.* an aeroplane designed to alight on or take off from the sea.

SEA-PLOVER, [sē´-pluv´-er], *n.* the grey plover.

SEA-PORCUPINE, [sē´-pawk´-yōō-pīn], *n.* the globe-fish.

SEAPORT, [sē´-pawt], *n.* a town with a harbour for seagoing ships.

SEAPURSE, [sē´-purs], *n.* the egg-case of the skate.

SEAR (1), [sēer], *n.* a catch in the lock of a gun that holds the hammer at cock. [L. *sera* bar of a door].

SEAR (2), SERE, [sēer], *adj.* withered, shrivelled, dry. [OE. *sear*].

SEAR (3), [sēer], *v.t.* to dry up, cause to wither, shrivel up; to parch, cauterize; to make faded; to scorch; to make hard or calloused. [OE. *searian*].

SEA-RAT, [sē´-rat´], *n.* the rabbit-fish, *Chimaera monstrosa.*

SEARCH (1), [surch], *n.* the act of searching, seeking, hunting out; the actual inquiry, going about in which the seeking is carried out; pursuit, quest of a thing.

SEARCH (2), [surch], *v.t. and i.* to examine thoroughly in order to find or discover, to overhaul, go through, ransack a thing for this purpose; to examine carefully the garments and body of a person in order to find something; to scrutinize carefully, read through thoroughly, in order to find something; to penetrate searchingly, to probe; to seek, look for, inquire, pursue; **s. me,** (*coll.*) I am at a loss. [OFr. *cerchier*].

SEARCHABLE, [surch´-abl], *adj.* able to be searched for.

SEARCHABLENESS, [surch´-abl-nes], *n.* the condition of being searchable.

SEARCHER, [surch´-er], *n.* one who, or that which, searches, *esp.* a person employed to search passengers and baggage at a Customs; a surgical instrument for probing a wound.

SEARCHING, [surch´-ing], *adj.* thorough, penetrating, such as searches keenly; illuminating weaknesses.

SEARCHINGLY, [surch´-ing-li], *adv.* in searching fashion.

SEARCHINGNESS, [surch´-ing-nes], *n.* the condition of being searching.

SEARCHLESS, [surch´-les], *adj.* unsearched, unsearchable.

SEARCHLIGHT, [surch´-līt], *n.* a lamp producing a powerful beam of light directed upon distant objects, *esp.* used at sea and against aircraft; the beam so produced.

SEARCH-WARRANT, [surch´-wo´-rant], *n.* a magistrate's warrant giving authority to enter and search private premises.

SEARED, [sēerd], *adj.* withered, shrivelled, cauterized, hardened.

SEAREDNESS, [sēerd´-nes], *n.* the state of being seared, hardened.

SEA-RISK, [sē´-risk], *n.* risk of injury or loss at sea.

SEA-ROBBER, [sē´-rob´-er], *n.* a pirate.

SEA-ROBIN, [sē´-rob´-in], *n.* the American red gurnard, *Prionotus.*

SEA-ROCKET, [sē´-rok´-it], *n.* the plant *Cakile maritima.*

SEA-ROOM, [sē´-rōōm], *n.* space enough for a ship to sail without danger of collision or grounding.

SEA-ROVER, [sē´-rō-ver], *n.* a pirate, a pirate vessel.

SEASCAPE, [sē´-skāp], *n.* a picture giving a view of the sea. [SEA and (LAND)SCAPE].

SEA-SCORPION, [sē´-skawp´-i-on], *n.* the fish *Cottus scorpius.*

SEA-SERPENT, [sē´-sur´-pent], *n.* a fabulous sea-monster of enormous size and fantastic but varying shape, reported to have been observed at a distance on numerous occasions.

SEA-SERVICE, [se´-sur-vis], *n.* a regular transport service by sea; service in the Navy.

SEASHELL, [sē´-shell], *n.* the shell of a marine mollusc.

SEASHORE, [sē´-shaw(r)], *n.* the sea-coast, land bordering the sea between high and low water.

SEA-SICK, [sē´-sik´], *adj.* nauseated by or vomiting from the motion of a ship.

SEA-SICKNESS, [sē´-sik-nes], *n.* the state of being sea-sick.

SEASIDE, [sē´-sīd´], *n.* the land by the sea; the sea-coast as a holiday resort.

SEA-SNIPE, [sē´-snīp], *n.* the dunlin.

SEASON (1), [sēz´-on], *n.* a division of the year distinguished by the altitude of the noon-day sun above the horizon, temperature, weather, and the growth of plants; part of the year dedicated to certain processes or human activities, the time of the year when certain animals are hunted, or fit to be eaten; the suitable time for anything; early summer, when London's upper-class social life is at its most active; †a space of time. [OFr. *seson* from L. *satio* a sowing].

SEASON (2), [sēz´-on], *v.t.* to render mature or fit for some use by exposure to some process or climate; to acclimatize, to accustom; to spice food; to add zest to something; †to temper, moderate. [*Prec.*].

SEASONABLE, [sēz´-on-abl], *adj.* appropriate, suitable to a particular season.

SEASONABLENESS, [sēz´-on-abl-nes], *n.* the condition of being seasonable.

SEASONABLY, [sēz´-on-ab-li], *adv.* in seasonable fashion.

SEASONAL, [sēz´-on-al], *adj.* occurring only at certain seasons.

SEASONALLY, [sēz´-on-al-i], *adv.* in seasonal fashion.

SEASONED, [sēz´-ond], *adj.* accustomed or hardened to certain conditions; spiced.

SEASONER, [sēz´-on-er], *n.* that which seasons.

SEASONING, [sēz´-on-ing], *n.* spice, condiments, that which is used to season food.

SEASONLESS, [sēz´-on-les], *adj.* without seasons; having no seasoning.

SEA-SPIDER, [sē´-spī-der], *n.* a marine arthropod resembling a spider.

SEA-SQUIRT, [sē´-skwurt], *n.* an ascidian.

SEA-SWALLOW, [sē´-swol´-ō], *n.* a tern; the stormy petrel.

SEAT (1), [sēt], *n.* that which is sat upon; that which is made to be sat upon; a space in which one may sit down; the part of a chair, etc., that directly supports the body; the part of the body that sits, the buttocks, the part of the trousers, etc., covering the buttocks, sitting accommodation for a specific time, place, and occasion; membership of a body, symbolized by the right to sit in a certain place, *esp.* membership of Parliament, of the Bench; the location of a thing, the permanent situation of a central authority, the principal residence of a dignitary, family, *esp.* a great country house; the fashion in which one sits on a horse. [OScand. *sæti*].

SEAT (2), [sēt], *v.t.* to place on or in a seat; to accommodate in seats, to be able to afford seats for; to put a seat in a chair or garment.

SEATING, [sēt'-ing], *n.* provision of seats, accommodation in seats.

SEA-TROUT, [sē'-trowt], *n.* a species of salmon trout, *Salmo trutta*.

SEA-UNICORN, [sē'-yōōn'-i-kawn], *n.* the narwhal.

SEA-URCHIN, [sē'-ur-chin], *n.* the echinus.

SEAVE, [sēv], *n.* a kind of rush. [OScand. *sef*].

SEA-WALL, [sē'-wawl], *n.* a wall against the encroachment of the sea.

SEAWARD, [sē'-werd], *adv.* towards the sea.

SEA-WAY, [sē'-wā], *n.* the forward progress of a ship.

SEAWEED, [sē'-wēd], *n.* any of the larger marine algae.

SEA-WOLF, [sē'-wōōlf], *n.* the wolf-fish *Anarrhicas lupus*.

SEA-URCHIN

SEA-WOODCOCK, [sē'-wōōd'-kok], *n.* the bar-tailed godwit.

SEAWORTHINESS, [sē'-wurTH-i-nes], *n.* the condition of being seaworthy.

SEAWORTHY, [sē'-wurTH-i], *adj.* (of ships) fit to go to sea, without structural defect.

SEBACEOUS, [seb-ā'-shus], *adj.* fatty, containing fat. [L. *sebaceus* tallow-candle].

SEBIFEROUS, [seb-if'-er-us], *adj.* containing, producing fat. [L. *sebum* fat and *ferre* to bear].

SECANCY, [sēk'-an-si], *n.* the property of being secant.

SECANT (1), [sēk'-ant], *n.* (*geom.*) a cutting, intersecting line; (*trigonometry*) the ratio of the hypotenuse of a right-angled triangle to an adjacent side, viewed as a function of the angle (or its supplement) that these subtend.

SECANT (2), [sēk'-ant], *adj.* (*geom.*) cutting, intersecting. [L. *secans*].

SECATEURS, [sek'-at-erz'], *n.*(*pl.*) a pair of clippers operated with one hand, employed to prune shrubs, etc. [Fr. *sécateur*].

SECCO, [sek'-ō], *n.* tempera painting, painting on dry plaster. [It. *secco* dry].

SECEDE, [si-sēd'], *v.i.* to withdraw voluntarily from membership of a group, *esp.* in a political or religious sense. [L. *secedere*].

SECEDER, [si-sēd'-er], *n.* one who secedes; (*pl.*) a sect seceding from the Church of Scotland in 1733.

SECESSION, [si-sesh'-un], *n.* the act of seceding. [L. *secessio*].

SECESSIONIST, [si-sesh'-un-ist], *n.* an advocate of secession.

SECLUDE, [si-klōōd'], *v.t.* to shut up apart, to keep away from others. [L. *secludere*].

SECLUDED, [si-klōōd'-ed], *adj.* separated from others, solitary, quiet and undisturbed.

SECLUDEDLY, [si-klōōd'-ed-li], *adv.* in secluded fashion.

SECLUDEDNESS, [si-klōōd'-ed-nes], *n.* the state of being secluded.

SECLUSION, [si-klōō'-zhun], *n.* the state of being secluded, the act of secluding, retired privacy. [MedL. *seclusio*].

SECLUSIVE, [si-klōō'-ziv], *adj.* tending to seclude, seeking seclusion.

SECOND (1), [sek'-ond], *n.* the sixtieth part of a minute (of time or of an angle); (*coll.*) a very short period of time; (*motoring*) the second gear of a motor engine. [MedL. (*minuta*) *secunda*].

SECOND (2), [sek'-ond], *n.* a supporter in a duel, who manages the preliminary arrangements on behalf of his principal; a second-class degree; the competitor in a contest who comes nearest to the winner; (*mus.*) interval between two tones of the diatonic scale.

SECOND (3), [sek'-ond], *adj.* ordinal of two; next to, following closest after, the first in space, time, position, value, dignity, or importance; exactly resembling another, being a counterpart. [L. *secundus*].

SECOND (4), [sek'-ond], *v.t.* to support someone, act as his second in a duel; (*parl.*) to support a motion immediately after the proposer.

SECOND (5), [sik-ond'], *v.t.* (*milit.*) to withdraw (an officer) from the active list of a regiment in order to employ (him) specially on other service.

SECOND (6), [sek'-ond], *adv.* in the second place.

SECONDARILY, [sek'-ond-er-i-li], *adv.* in secondary fashion, in secondary degree.

SECONDARINESS, [sek'-ond-er-i-nes], *n.* the condition of being secondary.

SECONDARY, [sek'-ond-er-i], *adj.* second in order, importance, dignity, urgency, etc., second in time or order of development; inferior; (*astron.*) revolving round a primary planet; (*biol.*) applied to differences between the sexes not directly connected with generation; (*geol.*) pertaining to the strata between the palaeozoic and tertiary, mesozoic; **s. school,** a school giving instruction to pupils who have completed the primary stage of their education. [L. *secundarius*].

SECONDER, [sek'-ond-er], *n.* one supporting the proposer of a motion ; one seconding another's effort.

SECOND-HAND (1), [sek'-ond-hand'], *n.* the hand of a clock or watch marking the seconds.

SECOND-HAND (2), [sek'-ond-hand'], *adj.* already used, not new; (of ideas, etc.) derived, not original.

SECONDLY, [sek'-ond-li], *adv.* in the second place.

SECOND-RATE, [sek'-ond-rāt], *adj.* not first-class, of inferior quality, mediocre.

SECRECY, [sē'-kres-i], *n.* the state of being secret, state of being concealed, condition of concealment or occurrence without general knowledge of awareness; secretiveness.

SECRET (1), [sē'-kret], *n.* that which is secret, something known to a very small number of people who have undertaken not to reveal it; the truth of something mysterious and obscure, the hidden meaning of a thing, the unknown means by which something wonderful was performed; a mystery.

SECRET (2), [sē'-kret], *adj.* hidden from sight and knowledge, designed for concealment; done in secret, carried on without being generally known; clandestine; remote and hidden; secretive; mysterious, inscrutable. [L. *secretus*, *p.pt.* of *secernere* to set apart].

SECRETAIRE, [sek'-rit-āer'], *n.* a bureau, a writing-desk. [Fr. *secrétaire*].

SECRETARIAL, [sek'-rit-āer'-i-al], *adj.* relating to a secretary or to the functions of a secretary.

SECRETARIAT, [sek'-rit-āer'-i-at], *n.* a body of officials carrying out the secretarial functions of a great organization. [Fr. *secrétariat*].

SECRETARY, [sek'-rit-er-i], *n.* a person employed to manage the correspondence, written records, etc., of an organization or person; one employed to assist a person in the organizational and routine part of his business or intellectual work; the principal assistant to a minister or ambassador, the head of a department of state (nominally responsible to the king); the second responsible official of a department; a secretaire; (*typ.*) a type resembling longhand. [MedL. *secretarius* confidential].

SECRETARY BIRD, [sek'-rit-er-i-burd], *n.* an African bird preying on snakes.

SECRETARYSHIP, [sek'-rit-er-i-ship], *n.* the office of a secretary.

SECRETE, [si-krēt'], *v.t.* to conceal in a secret place; (*physiol.*) to extract from the system and give out as a secretion; †to separate. [L. *secretus*, *p.pt.* of *secernere* to set apart].

SECRETION, [si-krē'-shun], *n.* the act of secreting; (*physiol.*) the biological process whereby extractions from the blood or sap are either discharged as waste or elaborated into functional substances. [L. *secretio*].

SECRETARY BIRD

SECRETIONAL, [si-krē'-shun-al], *adj.* relating to secretion.

SECRETIONARY, [si-krē'-shun-er-i], *adj.* secretional.

SECRETITIOUS, [sik'-rē-tish'-us], *adj.* produced by secretion.

SECRETIVE, [si-krē'-tiv], *adj.* tending to conceal one's thoughts and actions, over-reticent; causing secretion.

SECRETIVENESS, [si-krē'-tiv-nes], *n.* the condition of being secretive.

SECRETLY, [sē'-kret-li], *adv.* in secret.

SECRETNESS, [sē'-kret-nes], *n.* secrecy.

SECRETORY, [si-krēt'-er-i], *adj.* relating to, causing, secretion.

SECT, [sekt], *n.* a body of persons with certain religious or philosophical views, *esp.* such a group that has seceded from one of the great Churches. [OFr. *secte* from L. *secta* path].

SECTARIAL, [sek-tāer'-i-al], *adj.* peculiar to a sect.

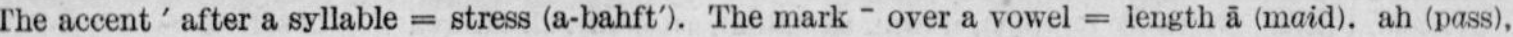

SECTARIAN, [sek-tāer'-i-an], *n. and adj.* (one who or that which is) characteristic of, peculiar to, a sect, narrowly exclusive; supporting a sect (usually in disparagement), tending to destroy the unity of some broad body of opinion; a member of a sect.

SECTARIANISM, [sek-tāer'-i-an-izm], *n.* devotion to a sect, the habit of mind that seeks sect and schism, narrow intolerance on petty points of doctrine.

SECTARY, [sek'-ter-i], *n.* a sectarian; (*hist.*) a Protestant dissenter. [MedL. *sectarius*].

SECTILE, [sek'-til], *adj.* capable of being cut cleanly. [L. *sectilis*].

SECTION (1), [sek'-shun], *n.* the act or process of cutting or dividing; the thing cut off, the severed portion; a slice cut off across the whole of an object, a representative cutting of an object; a separate part of a thing, a separate part made to be joined to other parts; a subdivision of something written; (*zool.*) a natural subdivision of a genus; (*milit.*) one of the subdivisions of a platoon, troop, or battery; (*geom.*) the intersection of a solid by a plane; a representation of an object as if cut through by a plane, thus showing its internal structure, etc., the subdivision mark §. [L. *sectio* a cutting].

SECTION (2), [sek'-shun], *v.t.* to divide into sections; to represent by a section.

SECTIONAL, [sek'-shun-al], *adj.* related to, divided into, sections or a section; pertaining to local divisions.

SECTIONALISM, [sek'-shun-al-izm], *n.* preoccupation with the interests of a section as distinct from those of the whole community.

SECTIONALLY, [sek'-shun-al-i], *adv.* in sectional fashion.

SECTOR, [sek'-tor], *n.* an astronomical or mathematical measuring instrument; (*geom.*) part of a circle contained between two of its radii; (*milit.*) part of a front or position, *esp.* as a scene of military operations. [L. *sector* cutter].

SECTOR

SECULAR, [sek'-yŏŏl-er], *adj.* (*Rom. hist.*) occurring once in a century or generation; continuing over a very long period; relating to this world, temporal, material, not ecclesiastical; (*R.C.*) not bound by monastic vows. [L. *saecularis* belonging to an age].

SECULARISM, [sek'-yŏŏl-er-izm], *n.* a theory of the separation of church from state; a theory of morality divorced from religion; temporalism.

SECULARIST, [sek'-yŏŏl-ler-ist], *n.* a believer in secularism.

SECULARITY, [sek'-yŏŏl-la'-rit-i], *n.* the state of being secular.

SECULARIZATION, [sek'-yŏŏl-er-riz-ā'-shun], *n.* the act of secularizing; state of being secularized.

SECULARIZE, [sek'-yŏŏl-er-riz], *v.t.* to make secular, to transfer from church to state, to make temporal; (*R.C.*) to absolve from monastic vows.

SECULARLY, [sek'-yŏŏl-er-li], *adv.* in secular fashion.

SECULARNESS, [sek'-yŏŏl-er-nes], *n.* the condition of being secular.

SECUND, [sē'-kund], *adj.* (*bot.*) growing on or inclined to only one side of the stem. [L. *secundus* following].

SECUNDINE, [sek-und'-īn], *n.* (*bot.*) the second membrane of an ovule; (*med.*) the placenta. [~SECOND].

SECURE (1), [si-kyŏŏer'], *adj.* safe, free from danger, care or anxiety, undisturbed; firm, stable, fast, firmly held and retained; certain, firmly fixed. [L. *securus* free from care].

SECURE (2), [si-kyŏŏer'], *v.t.* to make secure, to make safe against danger or loss; to fix firmly, to make fast, to hold firmly, safely; (*milit.*) to hold (a rifle) muzzle down with breech under the armpit; to make certain; (*leg.*) to confirm possession of by deed or will; to get hold of, obtain sure possession of; to guarantee by security. [*Prec.*].

SECURELY, [si-kyŏŏer'-li], *adv.* in secure fashion.

SECURENESS, [si-kyŏŏer'-ness], *n.* the state of being secure.

SECURER, [si-kyŏŏer'-er], *n.* one who, or that which, secures.

SECURIFORM, [si-kyŏŏer'-i-fawm], *adj.* axe-shaped. [L. *securis* axe].

SECURITE, [sek'-yŏŏer-it], *n.* (*chem.*) ammonium nitrate and oxalate with nitro-benzene, an explosive used in mining because it does not ignite fire-damp. [~SECURE].

SECURITY, [si-kyŏŏer'-it-i], *n.* the state of being secure; safety; feeling of being secure; a defence, protection; something of value deposited as pledge for the repayment of a loan, etc., a person who guarantees a loan; (*pl.*) bonds, shares, etc.; **s. police**, the military police. [L. *securitas*].

SEDAN, [si-dan'], *n.* a portable covered chair carried by means of poles projecting before and behind. [*Sedan*, in France, where invented].

SEDAN

SEDATE, [si-dāt'], *adj.* calmly staid, tranquil, composedly quiet and self-possessed. [L. *sedatus*].

SEDATELY, [si-dāt'-li], *adv.* in sedate fashion.

SEDATENESS, [si-dāt'-nes], *n.* the state of being sedate.

SEDATIVE (1), [sed'-at-iv], *n.* a drug or medicine producing a sedative effect.

SEDATIVE (2), [sed'-at-iv], *adj.* calming, soothing, having the effect of reducing mental and bodily excitement or agitation. [Fr. *sédatif*].

SEDENTARILY, [sed'-ent-er-i-li], *adv.* in sedentary fashion.

SEDENTARINESS, [sed'-ent-er-i-nes], *n.* the state of being sedentary.

SEDENTARY, [sed'-ent-er-i], *adj.* sitting still; tending to keep or be inactive, immobile; (of occupations) involving no bodily activity; (of animals) remaining in one district, not migratory. [L. *sedentarius*].

SEDERUNT, [sed-ēer'-unt], *n.* the session of a court or assembly. [L. *sederunt* they sat].

SEDGE, [sej], *n.* a coarse, perennial, tufted grass-like plant of the genus *Carex*. [OE. *secg*].

SEDGE-WARBLER, [sej'-wawb-ler], *n.* a brown and white bird, *Acrocephalus schœnobænus*.

SEDGE-WARBLER

SEDGY, [sej'-i], *adj.* covered with sedge.

SEDILIA, [sed-il'-i-a], *n.* the three seats for the clergy recessed in the wall of a church behind the altar rail. [L. *sedilia* seats].

SEDIMENT, [sed'-i-ment], *n.* the solid matter that settles to the bottom of a liquid, the dregs of wine. [L. *sedimentum* a settling down].

SEDIMENTARY, [sed'-i-ment'-er-i], *adj.* formed of, relating to, containing, sediment; (*geol.*) formed or deposited by the action of water.

SEDIMENTATION, [sed'-i-ment-ā'-shun], *n.* the precipitation or formation of sediment.

SEDITION, [sid-i'-shun], *n.* unlawful action or propaganda directed against the state or its authority; an offence against the government not amounting to treason; a seditious tumult. [L. *seditio*].

SEDITIONARY, [sid-i'-shun-er-i], *n.* one practising or encouraging sedition.

SEDITIOUS, [sid-i'-shus], *adj.* relating to, of the nature of, inciting to, guilty of, tending to produce, sedition. [L. *seditiosus*].

SEDITIOUSLY, [sid-i'-shus-li], *adv.* in seditious fashion.

SEDITIOUSNESS, [sid-i'-shus-nes], *n.* the condition of being seditious.

SEDUCE, [si-dews'], *v.t.* to lead away, entice away or persuade (almost invariably in sense of leading away from good to evil), to debauch, to sexual surrender. [L. *seducere* to lead away].

SEDUCEMENT, [si-dews'-ment], *n.* that which seduces; seduction.

SEDUCER, [si-dews'-er], *n.* one who, or that which, seduces, *esp.* sexually.

SEDUCIBLE, [si-dews'-ibl], *adj.* able to be seduced.

SEDUCINGLY, [si-dews'-ing-li], *adv.* so as to seduce.

SEDUCTION, [si-duk'-shun], *n.* the act of seducing, *esp.* sexually; that which seduces, means of seducing. [L. *seductio*].

SEDUCTIVE, [si-duk'-tiv], *adj.* tending to seduce, attractive, enticing, offering seductions.

SEDUCTIVELY, [si-duk'-tiv-li], *adv.* in seductive fashion.

SEDUCTIVENESS, [si-dukt'-iv-nes], *n.* the fact or quality of being seductive.

SEDULITY, [si-dyŏŏl'-i-ti], *n.* the state of being sedulous; diligence, application. [L. *sedulitas*].

SEDULOUS, [sed′-yo͝ol-us], *adj.* assiduous, carefully eager, persistently attentive. [L. *sedulus*].

SEDULOUSLY, [sed′-yo͝ol-us-li], *adv.* in sedulous fashion.

SEDULOUSNESS, [sed′-yo͝ol-us-nes], *n.* the state or quality of being sedulous.

SEE (1), [sē], *n.* the diocese of a bishop or an archbishop. [OFr. *sée* from L. *sedes* seat].

SEE (2), **(sees, saw, seen)**, [sē], *v.t.* to perceive visually, obtain an impression of through the eyes; to understand, perceive intellectually, grasp mentally; to experience, observe, encounter; to perceive emotionally or mystically; to witness, examine, be spectator at, attend (some visual spectacle), witness (a play); to meet, encounter, to interview (a person) officially; *v.i.* to have sight, to have the capacity of apprehending visually; to possess intellectual perception, to understand; to enquire, investigate; to take care that, take consideration to ensure; to consider, deliberate; **to s. about**, to attend to, inquire into; **to s. after**, to look after; **to s. off**, to attend the departure of; **to s. out**, to see the end of; **to s. through**, to perceive the deception of; **to s. (something) through**, to go through with something. [OE. *seon*].

SEEABLE, [sē′-abl], *adj.* able to be seen.

SEED (1), [sēd], *n.* the fertilized germ of a plant that can develop into a new plant of the same kind; (*coll.*) seeds used in sowing; semen in men or animals, posterity, descendants; the source of a thing, the germ of an idea; **to run to s.**, to form seed, (*fig.*) to lose one's energy and initiative. [OE. *sæd*].

SEED (2), [sēd], *v.t.* to plant with seed, to sort out.

SEEDBED, [sēd′-bed′], *n.* earth prepared to receive seed.

SEED-CAKE, [sēd′-kāk], *n.* a cake flavoured with caraway seeds.

SEEDCOAT, [sēd′-kōt], *n.* the outer covering of a seed.

SEED-CORN, [sēd′-kawn], *n.* corn used for sowing.

SEED-FIELD, [sēd′-fēld], *n.* a place for sowing seed.

SEED-GRAIN, [sēd′-grān], *n.* grain used for sowing.

SEEDILY, [sēd′-i-li], *adv.* in seedy fashion.

SEEDINESS, [sēd′-i-nes], *n.* the quality of being seedy.

SEED-LAC, [sēd′-lak′], *n.* dried resin lac.

SEEDLEAF, [sēd′-lēf], *n.* (*bot.*) a cotyledon.

SEEDLESS, [sēd′-les], *adj.* having no seed; (of man) sterile.

SEEDLING, [sēd′-ling], *n.* a young plant grown from seed.

SEEDLOBE, [sēd′-lōb], *n.* the lobe of a seed.

SEED-LOP, [sēd′-lop′], *n.* a basket for carrying seed to be sown. [OE. *sædleap*].

SEED-PEARL, [sēd′-purl], *n.* a diminutive pearl.

SEEDPLOT, [sēd′-plot], *n.* ground devoted to raising plants from seed.

SEEDSMAN, [sēdz′-man], *n.* a dealer in garden seeds and requisites.

SEEDTIME, [sēd′-tīm′], *n.* the season for sowing.

SEED-VESSEL, [sēd′-ves′-el], *n.* the pericarp containing the seeds.

SEEDY, [sēd′-i], *adj.* full of seeds; (*coll.*) slightly unwell; shabby.

SEEING, [sē′-ing], *conj.* since; in view of the fact (that).

SEEK, [sēk], *v.t.* *and i.* to look for, search out, go in search of, search to obtain, strive to achieve, pursue; inquire after; **to s. to**, to attempt to. [OE. *secan*].

SEEKER, [sēk′-er], *n.* one who seeks.

SEEL†, [sēl], *v.t.* to close the eyes of a hawk by sewing the lids; to blindfold; to dupe. [OFr. *siller*].

SEEM, [sēm], *v.t.* to appear to be, to be apparently. [OScand. *sōma*].

SEEMER, [sēm′-er], *n.* one who seems.

SEEMING (1), [sēm′-ing], *n.* external appearance; the immediate impression given.

SEEMING (2), [sēm′-ing], *adj.* apparent, outward, ostensible.

SEEMINGLY, [sēm′-ing-li], *adv.* in appearance.

SEEMINGNESS, [sēm′-ing-nes], *n.* appearance; plausibility.

SEEMLINESS, [sēm′-li-nes], *n.* the quality or appearance of being seemly.

SEEMLY, [sēm′-li], *adj.* proper, suitable; decent, fitting, comely, decorous, pleasing of appearance. [OScand. *sæmiligr*].

SEEN (1), [sēn], *p.pt.* of SEE (2). [OE. *gesegen*].

SEEN† **(2)**, [sēn], *adj.* equipped or provided. [~SEE (2)].

SEEP, [sēp], *v.i.* to ooze (through), percolate. [OE. *sipian* to soak].

SEEPAGE, [sēp′-ij], *n.* liquid that has seeped through.

SEER (1), [sēer], *n.* one who sees; a prophet, one who foresees by magic.

SEER (2), [sēer], *n.* an Indian weight of about two pounds. [Hind. *ser*].

SEERSHIP, [sēer′-ship], *n.* the office of a seer.

SEE-SAW (1), [sē′-saw], *n.* a plank balanced on a central fulcrum, so that the minimum of downward pressure on one side elevates the other; a children's game where a child sits at each end alternately raising and depressing the plank; (*fig.*) an almost equal balance of power, so that now one side, now the other is predominant. [Imitative].

SEE-SAW (2), [sē′-saw], *adj.* moving like a see-saw.

SEE-SAW (3), [sē′-saw], *v.i.* to ride on, move like, a see-saw.

SEETHE, [sēᴛʜ], *v.t.* *and i.* to cook by boiling; to soften by steeping; to boil up, to swirl and bubble; to be violently stirred and agitated. [OE. *seothan* to boil].

SEETHER, [sēᴛʜ′-er], *n.* a vessel for boiling.

SEG, [seg], *n.* an animal castrated when fully grown. [Uncert.].

SEGGAR, SAGGAR, [seg′-er], *n.* a case of fireclay in which potters enclose finer ware for baking. [~SAFEGUARD].

SEGMENT (1), [seg′-ment], *n.* a part into which a body may be divided, a separable section; (*geom.*) a portion cut from a figure by a line or plane. [L. *segmentum*].

SEGMENT (2), [seg′-ment], *v.t.* *and i.* to divide into segments; to split up into segments.

SEGMENTAL, [seg-ment′-al], *adj.* relating to, containing, divided into, segments.

SEGMENTARY, [seg′-ment-er-i], *adj.* segmental.

SEGMENTATION, [seg′-ment-ā′-shun], *n.* division into segments; (*biol.*) cellular formation by cleavage.

SEGNO, [se′-nyō], *n.* (*mus.*) a mark denoting repetition. [It. *segno*].

SEGREGATE, [seg′-rig-āt], *v.t.* *and i.* to separate, to put apart from the main body, to isolate; to become separated, to separate oneself from the main body; (of crystals) to separate and collect round a nucleus. [L. *segregare* to set apart].

SEGREGATION, [seg′-rig-ā′-shun], *n.* the act or process of segregating; the state, condition, position of being segregated. [L. *segregatio*].

SEICHE, [sāsh], *n.* variation of the level of the surface of a lake through changes in barometric pressure. [Germ. *seiche* sinking].

SEIDLITZ, [sed′-lits], *n.* a seidlitz powder, a saline aperient. [*Seidlitz*, in Bohemia].

SEIGNEUR, [sān′-yer], *n.* (*hist.*) a feudal lord; the **Grand S.**, the Sultan of Turkey. [OFr. *seigneur*].

SEIGNEURIAL, [sān-yur′-i-al], *adj.* held by feudal tenure; relating to a seigneur.

SEIGNIORAGE, [sān′-yer-ij], *n.* the authority, territory of a seigneur; the profit derived from issuing coins at more than their intrinsic value. [OFr. *seignorage*].

SEIGNIORY, [sān′-yer-i], *n.* the territory and jurisdiction of a seigneur. [OF. *seignorie*].

SEINE, [sān], *n.* a large fishing-net suspended vertically in the water by means of floats on one edge and weights on the other. [Fr. *seine*].

SEINER, [sān′-er], *n.* a fisherman or fishing-boat using a seine.

SEISE, [sēz], *v.t.* (*leg.*) to seize.

SEISED, [sēzd], *adj.* (*leg.*) taken in fee-simple, possessed.

SEISIN, see SEIZIN.

SEISMAL, [sīz′-mal], *adj.* seismic.

SEISMIC, [sīz′-mik], *adj.* relating to, caused by, an earthquake. [Gk. *seismos* earthquake].

SEISMO-, *pref.* relating to earthquake. [*Prec.*].

SEISMOGRAPH, [sīz′-mō-graf], *n.* an instrument for measuring and recording earthquakes. [SEISMO and GRAPH].

SEISMOGRAPHIC, [sīz′-mō-graf′-ik], *adj.* of, or relating to, seismography.

SEISMOGRAPHY, [sīz-mog′-raf-i], *n.* the science of measuring earthquakes.

SEISMOLOGIST, [sīz-mol′-oj-ist], *n.* one skilled in seismology.

SEISMOLOGY, [sīz-mol′-oj-i], *n.* the science treating of earthquakes. [SEISMO and Gk. *logos* speech].

SEISMOMETER, [sīz-mom′-it-er], *n.* an instrument for measuring the direction and intensity of earthquakes. [SEISMO and METER].

SEISMOSCOPE, [sīz′-mō-skōp], *n.* a simple seismometer. [SEISMO and SCOPE].

SEIZABLE, [sēz′-abl], *adj.* capable of being seized.

SEIZE, [sēz], *v.t. and i.* (*leg.*) to put in possession of, take possession of; to grasp, take hold of suddenly and forcibly; to grasp, grab, clutch with the hand; (*fig.*) to take, grasp, take advantage of, immediately understand; (*naut.*) to bind, lash together with pieces of cord; to adhere, become stuck. [OFr. *saisir*].

SEIZER, [sēz'-er], *n.* one who seizes.

SEIZIN, SEISIN, [sēz'-in], *n.* (*leg.*) the act of taking possession of land; the land so taken. [OFr. *seisine*].

SEIZOR, [sēz'-er], *n.* (*leg.*) one who takes possession of freehold land.

SEIZURE, [sēz'-yer], *n.* the act of seizing; (*med.*) a fit, stroke, sudden paroxysm of illness.

SEJANT, [sē'-jant], *adj.* (*her.*) sitting. [~AFr. *seier* to sit].

SEJANT

SEJUNCTION, [si-jungk'-shun], *n.* the act of separating, the state of being divided. [L. *sejunctio*].

SELACHIAN, [sel-āk'-yan], *adj.* (*zool.*) belonging to the class of fishes including the shark and dog-fish, the *Selachii*. [Gk. *selakhos* shark].

SELADANG, [sel-ah'-dang], *n.* the Malayan tapir. [Native].

SELAH, [sē'-lah], *n.* a Hebrew word of uncertain meaning found at the end of verses in the Psalms.

SELAMLIK, [sel-ahm'-lik], *n.* the male quarters of a Moslem household. [Turk. *selamlik*].

SELDOM, [sel'-dum], *adv.* not often, rarely. [OE. *seldan*].

SELDOMNESS, [sel'-dum-nes], *n.* the condition of occurring seldom.

SELECT (1), [sil-ekt'], *adj.* picked out from a number, chosen from others, *esp.* on account of merit or for a specific purpose; fastidiously chosen, carefully selected. [L. *selectum*, *p.pt.* of *seligere* to choose out].

SELECT (2), [sil-ekt'], *v.t.* to pick out, choose out of a number of others, choose for a specific purpose.

SELECTED, [sil-ek'-ted], *adj.* chosen, carefully picked out (with the implication of being the best).

SELECTEDLY, [sil-ekt'-ed-li], *adv.* by selection.

SELECTION, [sil-ek'-shun], *n.* the act of selecting, the thing selected; a number of things from which choice can be made, representative specimens extracted from a large number; a number of isolated passages selected from an author's works; **natural s.,** the Darwinian biological theory of the survival of the fittest. [L. *selectio*].

SELECTIVE, [sil-ekt'-iv], *adj.* tending to select; (*wirel.*) of, or pertaining to, a set or system of tuning that will separate transmissions on neighbouring wave-lengths.

SELECTIVITY, [sē-lek'-tiv'-i-ti], *n.* (*wirel.*) the ability of a tuning system to separate transmissions on adjoining wave-bands.

SELECTNESS, [sil-ekt'-nes], *n.* the condition of being select.

SELECTOR, [sil-ekt'-er], *n.* one who selects or chooses; (*wirel.*) a device for eliminating certain wave-lengths; (in Australia) a squatter on Crown land.

SELENATE, [sel'-en-āt], *n.* (*chem.*) a salt of selenic acid.

SELENIC, [sel-ēn'-ik], *adj.* (*chem.*) relating to, containing, the element selenium in its higher valency.

SELENIDE, [sel'-en-īd], *n.* a compound of selenium with another element.

SELENIFEROUS, [sel'-en-if'-er-us], *adj.* (*chem.*) containing selenium. [SELENIUM and L. *ferre* to bear].

SELENIOUS, [se-lēn'-i-us], *adj.* (*chem.*) of, pertaining to, containing, selenium in its lower valency.

SELENITE, [sel'-en-īt], *n.* a salt of selenious acid; a kind of gypsum.

SELENITIC, [sel'-en-it'-ik], *adj.* relating to selenite or gypsum.

SELENIUM, [sel-ēn'-i-um], *n.* the non-metallic element denoted by Se, resembling sulphur. [Gk. *selene* the moon].

SELENODONT, [sel-ēn'-ō-dont], *adj.* having teeth with crescent-like ridges. [Gk. *selene* the moon and *odous odontus* tooth].

SELENOGRAPHIC, [sel'-en-ō-graf'-ik], *adj.* relating to selenography.

SELENOGRAPHY, [sel'-en-og'-raf-i], *n.* the scientific description of the moon. [Gk. *selene* moon and *graphia* writing].

SELENOLOGY, [sel'-en-ol'-oj-i], *n.* the study of the moon. [Gk. *selene* moon and *logos* speech].

SELENOTROPIC, [sel-ēn'-ō-trop'-ik], *adj.* (*bot.*) turning to face the moon. [Gk. *selene* moon and *tropos* turn].

SELF, [self], *n.* the individual being, identity, personality, interests; the fundamental, essential character of a person; one's own person, myself. [OE. *self*].

SELF-, *pref.* indicating the agent or the objective of an action or condition; **s.-abandoned,** given up to one's desires, without restraint, reckless; **s.-abandonment,** surrender of oneself (to a cause, situation, etc.); **s.-abasement,** abasement of self; **s.-absorbed,** absorbed in oneself; **s.-abuse,** masturbation, ill-treatment of one's own body, misuse of one's faculties or talents; **s.-acting,** automatic; **s.-adjusting,** automatically adjusting itself; **s.-advertisement,** conceited display of oneself; **s.-assertion,** insistence on one's claims, pushing oneself forward; **s.-assurance,** self-confidence; **s.-binder,** a reaping machine which automatically binds the sheaves, a device for automatically clipping papers together; **s.-centred,** egoistic; **s.-centring,** automatically maintaining (something) on a given centre; **s.-collected,** unperturbed; **s.-coloured,** of only one colour, undyed, of the natural colour; **s.-command,** self-control; **s.-complacent,** pleased with oneself; **s.-conceit,** a good opinion of oneself; **s.-confidence,** confidence in oneself; **s.-conscious,** acutely aware of one's own personality, shy; **s.-consciousness,** the state of being self-conscious; **s.-contained,** reticent, self-sufficient; (of flats, etc.) having all offices, etc., within its own boundaries; **s.-control,** control of oneself or of one's desires; **s.-deceit,** self-deception; **s.-deception,** the process of deceiving oneself, the state of being so deceived, an instance of this; **s.-defence,** defence of one's own interests or safety; boxing; **s.-denial,** asceticism, denial of the body; **s.-denying,** characterized by, involving, self-denial; **s.-determination,** the act of deciding for oneself; **s.-educated,** educated by one's own efforts, without external assistance; **s.-educator,** a form of publication designed for home study without a teacher; **s.-esteem,** favourable opinion of oneself; **s.-evident,** obvious, evident on (a thing's) own merits; **s.-exciting,** (*elect.*) (of a dynamo) that excites its own field; **s.-existent,** existing independently; selfish, self-sufficient; **s.-explanatory,** explaining itself without external assistance; **s.-feeding,** automatically supplying itself (with fuel, etc.); **s.-fertile,** hermaphrodite, (*bot.*) fertilizing itself by its own pollen; **s.-help,** unassisted efforts, improvement of oneself; **s.-importance,** full of a sense of one's own importance; **s.-imposed,** imposed on one by oneself; **s.-improvement,** improvement of oneself by one's own efforts; **s.-indulgence,** indulgence of one's desires; **s.-interest,** one's personal interest or profit; **s.-love,** high regard for oneself and one's interests; **s.-made,** owing one's position entirely to one's own efforts; **s.-opinionated,** aggressively convinced of one's own rightness; **s.-pity,** pity for oneself; **s.-possessed,** self-collected, with confidence in one's own abilities; **s.-preservation,** the preservation of one's own life; **s.-raising,** containing substances such as bicarbonate of soda which, when heated, evolve gas; containing a substitute for yeast; **s.-registering,** registering automatically; **s.-regulating,** automatically regulating itself; **s.-reliant,** self-sufficient, self-possessed; **s.-repression,** repression of one's own desires, opinions; **s.-reproach,** reproach of oneself; **s.-respect,** proper regard for one's person or position; **s.-restraint,** restraint imposed by oneself on one's actions or desires; **s.-righteous,** convinced of one's own virtue; **s.-righting,** automatically righting (itself) after being upset; **s.-sacrifice,** sacrifice of oneself or one's own interests; **s.-satisfied,** satisfied with oneself, self-complacent; **s.-seeking,** seeking one's own advantage; **s.-sown,** (*bot.*) sown by itself without external assistance; **s.-styled,** called by oneself, but without authorization; **s.-sufficient,** requiring no aid or companionship from others; economically self-supporting; **s.-sufficing,** self-sufficient; **s.-support,** supporting oneself, itself, without external assistance; **s.-taught,** taught by oneself, self-educated; **s.-testing,** (of questions) intended to be put to oneself to test one's own comprehension, knowledge, or intelligence; **s.-willed,** self-opinionated, obstinate; **s.-winding,** (of clocks, etc.) winding automatically.

SELF-GOVERNING, [self'-guv'-ern-ing], *adj.* governed by its own representatives and without external assistance or supervision.

SELF-GOVERNMENT, [self'-guv'-ern-ment], *n.* the

government of a people by its own representatives.

SELF-HEAL, [self′-hēl′], *n.* (*bot.*) the labiate plant, *Prunella vulgaris.*

SELFHOOD, [self′-hŏŏd], *n.* one's personality or identity.

SELFISH, [self′-ish], *adj.* solely influenced by one's own interests, not altruistic, preoccupied by considerations of personal benefit.

SELFISHLY, [self′-ish-li], *adv.* in selfish fashion.

SELFISHNESS, [self′-ish-nes], *n.* the condition or quality of being selfish.

SELFLESS, [self′-les], *adj.* unselfish.

SELFLESSNESS, [self′-les-nes], *n.* the quality of being selfless.

SELF-PORTRAIT, [self′-pawt′-rāt], *n.* a portrait by an artist of himself.

SELFSAME, [self′-sām], *adj.* the very same.

SELF-STARTER, [self′-staht′-er], *n.* the electrical starter of a car, etc.

SELL (1), [sel], *n.* (*coll.*) that which deceives expectation, a swindle.

SELL (2), (**sold**), [sel], *v.t.* to barter, to transfer to another in return for a valuable consideration, to obtain a price in exchange for; to deal in, to have for sale, be prepared to sell; to help to sell, to be in charge of the actual transaction, although neither owning the goods nor retaining the price; to betray, give up, for material gain; (*pass.*) to be tricked, swindled; to be prepared to sell goods, to live by selling; (of commodities) to attract purchasers; **to s. off,** to sell cheaply for quick disposal; **to s. out,** to sell so as to exhaust the supply; to betray cause or companions and retire with a profit; **to s. up,** to sell the goods of (a debtor) to pay (his) creditors. [OE. *sellan*].

SELLABLE, [sel′-abl], *adj.* able to be sold.

SELLANDER, [sel′-and-er], *n.* a pathological dry eruption on a horse's hock. [Unkn.].

SELLER, [sel′-er], *n.* one who sells.

SELTZER, [selt′-ser], *n.* an aerated mineral water. [*Selters*, near Wiesbaden, in Germany].

SELVAGE, see SELVEDGE.

SELVAGEE, [sel′-vaj-ē], *n.* (*naut.*) rope-yarn lashed tightly together and used for heavy loads. [SELVAGE].

SELVEDGE, SELVAGE, [selv′-ij], *n.* the edge of a cloth woven to prevent ravelling; the edge of a lock into which the bolt is driven. [~MDu. *selfegghe*].

SELVEDGED, [selv′-ijd], *adj.* having a selvedge.

SELVES, [selvz], *pron., pl.* of SELF.

SEMANTIC, [se-mant′-ik], *adj.* of, or relating to, meaning. [Gk. *semantikos*].

SEMANTICS, [se-mant′-iks], *n.* semasiology.

SEMAPHORE (1), [sem′-a-faw(r)], *n.* a signalling device consisting of two movable arms worked by levers; the alphabet used in such signalling; the act of sending messages by such or similar means. [Gk. *sema* sign and *phora* a carrying].

SEMAPHORE (2), [sem′-a-faw(r)], *v.t. and i.* to send messages by semaphore.

SEMAPHORIC, [sem′-a-fo′-rik], *adj.* relating to, transmitted by, semaphore.

SEMASIOLOGY, [sē-māz′-i-ol′-o-ji], *n.* the scientific study of the meanings of words and the development of these. [Gk. *semasia* meaning and *logos* speech].

SEMATIC, [sēm-at′-ik], *adj.* (*biol.*) acting as a sign, having significance. [Gk. *sema* sign].

SEMBLANCE, [sem′-blants], *n.* seeming, likeness, appearance. [Fr. *semblance*].

SEMBLANT, [sem′-blant], *adj.* seeming. [*Prec.*].

SEME, semé, [sem′-ā], *adj.* (*her.*) speckled (with), having the field strewn (with). [Fr. *semer* to sow].

SEMÉ

SEMEIOGRAPHY, [sēm-i-og′-raf-i], *n.* the scientific description of symptoms. [Gk. *semeion* sign and *graphia* writing].

SEMEIOLOGICAL, [sēm′-i-ō-loj′-ik-al], *adj.* relating to semeiology.

SEMEIOLOGY, [sēm′-i-ol′-oj-i], *n.* the study of symbols; (*med.*) the scientific study of symptoms. [Gk. *semeion* sign and *logos* speech].

SEMEIOTIC, [sēm′-i-ot′-ik], *adj.* relating to signs, symbols or symptoms. [Gk. *semeiotikos*].

SEMEN, [sē′-men], *n.* the sperm-bearing fluid of male mammals. [L. *semen* seed].

SEMESTER, [sem-es′-ter], *n.* a period, university term, of six months. [Germ. from L. *semestris* every six months].

SEMI-, *pref.* half; partly, to some (small) extent. [L. *semi* half].

SEMI-ANGLICIZED, [sem′-i-ang′-glis-īzd], *adj.* partly anglicized.

SEMI-ANNUAL, [sem′-i-an′-yŏŏ-al], *adj.* half-yearly.

SEMI-ARTICULATE, [sem′-i-aht-ik′-yŏŏl-āt], *adj.* not wholly articulate.

SEMI-ATTACHED, [sem′-i-a-tacht′], *adj.* partly attached.

SEMI-BARBARIAN, [sem′-i-bah-bāer′-i-an], *n. and adj.* (one) half-civilized.

SEMI-BARBAROUS, [sem′-i-bahb′-a-rus], *adj.* partly barbarous.

SEMIBREVE, [sem′-i-brēv], *n.* (*mus.*) a note of half a breve, a note equal in length to four crotchets.

SEMI-BULL, [sem′-i-bul′], *n.* a Papal Bull issued after election but before enthronement, so called from having the seal blank on one face.

SEMICIRCLE, [sem′-i-surkl′], *n.* a half circle; a group of persons, things, arranged in a half circle.

SEMICIRCULAR, [sem′-i-surk′-yŏŏl-ar], *adj.* having the form of a semicircle.

SEMICOLON, [sem′-i-kōl′-on], *n.* the punctuation mark (;) intermediate in force between a comma and a colon.

SEMI-CONSCIOUS, [sem′-i-kon′-shus], *adj.* partially conscious.

SEMI-CRYSTALLINE, [sem′-i-krist′-a-līn], *adj.* partially crystalline.

SEMI-CYLINDER, [sem′-i-sil′-in-der], *n.* half a cylinder, divided vertically.

SEMI-CYLINDRICAL, [sem′-i-sil-in′-drik-al], *adj.* shaped like a half-cylinder.

SEMI-DEMISEMIQUAVER, [sem′-i-dem′-i-sem′-i-kwā′-ver], *n.* (*mus.*) half a demisemiquaver.

SEMI-DETACHED, [sem′-i-di-tacht′], *adj.* (of houses) pertaining to either of two houses which together form a single detached building.

SEMI-DIAMETER, [sem′-i-dī-am′-it-er], *n.* half a diameter, a radius.

SEMI-DIURNAL, [sem′-i-dī-urn′-al], *adj.* lasting half a day; occurring at half-daily intervals.

SEMI-FINAL (1), [sem′-i-fīn′-al], *n.* the last match but one in a competition.

SEMI-FINAL (2), [sem′-i-fīn′-al], *adj.* the last but one, the penultimate.

SEMI-FLUID, [sem′-i-flŏŏ′-id], *adj.* half-liquid.

SEMI-GLOBOSE, [sem′-i-glōb-ōs′], *adj.* half-spherical.

SEMI-INDEPENDENT, [sem′-i-ind-i-pend′-ent], *adj.* partly independent.

SEMILUNAR, [sem′-i-lŏŏn′-er], *adj.* shaped like a half-moon.

SEMI-METAL†, [sem′-i-met′-al], *n.* (*chem.*) a substance possessing some of the properties of metals and some of non-metals; a metalloid.

SEMI-METALLIC, [sem′-i-met-al′-ik], *adj.* having the properties of a semi-metal.

SEMINAL, [sem′-in-al], *adj.* relating to, or containing, semen; relating to seed or sowing; primary; fruitful. [L. *seminalis*].

SEMINALITY, [sem′-in-al′-it-i], *n.* the quality of being seminal.

SEMINAR, [sem′-in-ah(r)], *n.* a discussion class for senior students of a subject. [Germ. from L. *seminarium* seed-plot].

SEMINARIST, [sem′-in-a-rist], *n.* a student of a seminary.

SEMINARY, [sem′-in-er-i], *n.* a school, college, place of education, a training college for Roman Catholic priests. [L. *seminarium* seed-plot].

SEMINATE, [sem′-in-āt], *v.t.* to plant with seed, to sow, to impregnate. [L. *seminare* to procreate].

SEMINATION, [sem′-in-ā′-shun], *n.* the act of seminating; dissemination; (*bot.*) process of seeding. [L. *seminatio*].

SEMINIFEROUS, [sem′-in-if′-er-us], *adj.* bearing seed or semen. [L. *semen* seed and *ferre* to bear].

SEMINIFIC, [sem′-in-if′-ik], *adj.* producing seed.

SEMI-NUDE, [sem′-i-newd′], *adj.* partially naked.

SEMI-OPAL, [sem′-i-ō′-pal], *n.* a non-opalescent opal.

SEMI-OPAQUE, [sem′-i-ō-pāk′], *adj.* only partly opaque.

SEMI-ORBICULAR, [sem′-i-awb-ik′-yŏŏl-er], *adj.* half-spherical.

SEMI-OSSEOUS, [sem′-i-os′-i-us], *adj.* partly osseous; cartilaginous, of gristly structure.

SEMI-PALMATE, [sem'-i-pah'-māt], *adj.* having feet only partially webbed.
SEMI-PELAGIANISM, [sem'-i-pel-ā-ji'-an-izm], *n.* the belief that man's will and God's grace are together necessary for salvation.
SEMI-PELLUCID, [sem'-i-pel-ōōs'-id], *adj.* partly pellucid.
SEMI-PLANTIGRADE, [sem'-i-plant'-i-grād], *adj.* partly plantigrade.
SEMIQUAVER, [sem'-i-kwāv'-er], *n.* (*mus.*) a note of the length of half a quaver.
SEMI-SAVAGE, [sem'-i-sav'-ij], *adj.* half-savage.
SEMI-SPHERIC, [sem'-i-sfe'-rik], *adj.* in the shape of a half-sphere.
SEMITE, [sēm'-īt], *n.* one belonging to an Asiatic racial group that includes Jews, Arabs, Babylonians, Assyrians, etc. [~Heb. *shem*].
SEMITIC, [sem-it'-ik], *adj.* of or relating to the Semites and their culture.
SEMITONE, [sem'-i-tōn], *n.* (*mus.*) a half-tone.
SEMITONIC, [sem'-i-ton'-ik], *adj.* (*mus.*) consisting of a semitone.
SEMI-TRANSPARENT, [sem'-i-trans-pa'-rent], *adj.* partly transparent.
SEMI-VITREOUS, [sem'-i-vit'-ri-us], *adj.* partly glassy.
SEMIVOCAL, [sem'-i-vōk'-al], *adj.* partly vocal; relating to a semivowel. [L. *semivocalis*].
SEMIVOWEL, [sem'-i-vow'-el], *n.* a sound having the characteristics of both vowel and consonant.
SEMI-WEEKLY, [sem'-i-wēk'-li], *adj.* occurring half-weekly.
SEMNOPITHECUS, [sem'-nō-pith-ēk'-us], *n.* a genus of monkeys including the langurs. [Gk. *semnos* holy and *pithekos* ape].
SEMOLINA, [sem'-ō-lēn'-a], *n.* a coarsely ground meal of wheat, used in making macaroni. [It. *semolina*].

SEMNOPITHECUS

SEMPERVIVUM, [sem'-per-vīv'-um], *n.* (*bot.*) a genus of plants including the houseleek. [L. *semper* always and *vivus* living].
SEMPITERNAL, [semp'-it-urn'-al], *adj.* everlasting.
SEMPITERNITY, [semp'-it-urn'-it-i], *n.* endurance forever. [L. *sempiternitas*].
SEMPLICE, [sem'-plich-i], *adv.* (*mus.*) with simplicity. [It. *semplice*].
SEMPSTER, [semp'-ster], *n.* one who sews.
SEMPSTRESS, [semp'-stres], *n.* a seamstress.
SEN, [sen], *n.* a Japanese coin, the hundredth part of a yen. [~Chinese *ch'ien* coin].
SENARMONTITE, [sen'-ah-mont'-īt], *n.* an isomorphous antimonious oxide. [H. de *Senarmont*, the French mineralogist].
SENARY, [sēn'-er-i], *adj.* containing, consisting of, six. [L. *senarius*].
SENATE, [sen'-at], *n.* a deliberative assembly of elders; the administrative and legislative council of ancient Rome, the Upper House in the parliamentary system of many countries; the academic governing body of various universities. [L. *senatus*].
SENATOR, [sen'-at-or], *n.* a member of a senate. [L. *senator*].
SENATORIAL, [sen'-at-aw'-ri-al], *adj.* of, or relating to, a senate or a senator.
SENATORIALLY, [sen'-at-aw'-ri-al-i], *adv.* in senatorial fashion.
SENATORSHIP, [sen'-at-er-ship], *n.* the office, dignity, or term of office of a senator.
SEND, (**sent**), [send], *v.t.* to cause to go, be carried, be dispatched to some other place; to have conveyed, compel to go away from the place where the speaker is, to discharge, thrust; to launch upon (schooling); to elect, appoint; to propel (something) in some direction, towards some other place; to bestow on, afflict with; to cause to become, drive, compel to be; *v.i.* to send, dispatch a message to someone; **to s. after,** to send a message after one who has gone; **to s. away,** to dismiss, command to go; **to s. to Coventry,** to ostracize; **to s. down,** to expel from the university; to remit; **to s. for,** to summon to come to a place; **to s. forth,** emit, discharge; bear fruit; **to s. home,** to expel; to deliver (a blow) effectively; to cause to retire from service; **to s. in,** to send for consideration to a particular person; **to s. on,** to dispatch in advance; **to s. out,** to dispatch, send on some mission; **to s. packing, about (one's) business,** to dismiss. [OE. *sendan*].
SENDAL, [send'-al], *n.* a fine medieval textile. [OFr. *sendal*].
SENDER, [send'-er], *n.* one who, or that which, sends.
SEND-OFF, [send'-of'], *n.* a demonstration in honour of a departing traveller.
SENEGA, [sen'-eg-a], *n.* the dried root of *Polygala Senega*, used as an antidote to snake bite. [AmerInd. *seneca*].
SENESCENCE, [sen-es'-ents], *n.* the state of being senescent.
SENESCENT, [sen-es'-ent], *adj.* growing old or grey. [L. *senescens*].
SENESCHAL, [sen'-esh-al], *n.* the steward of a great medieval household. [OFr. *seneschal*].
SENGREEN, [sen'-grēn], *n.* the houseleek. [OE. *singrene*].
SENILE, [sēn'-īl], *adj.* characteristic of old age; mentally and physically decayed with age. [L. *senilis*].
SENILITY, [sen-il'-it-i], *n.* the weakness of old age.
SENIOR, [sēn'-i-er], *adj.* older than another; more advanced in rank than another, of a higher educational standard; **s. service,** the navy. [L. *senior*].
SENIORITY, [sēn'-i-o'-rit-i], *n.* the state of being senior in any respect.
SENNA, [sen'-a], *n.* an aperient made from cassia pods. [Arab. *sena*].
SENNIGHT†, [sen'-īt], *n.* a week. [SEVEN and NIGHT].
SENNIT, [sen'-it], *n.* (*naut.*) braided cordage of rope-yarn. [Uncert.].
SENOCULAR, [sen-ok'-yōōl-ar], *adj.* with six eyes. [L. *seni* six each and *oculus* eye].

SENNA

SENOR (-A), (-ITA), **señor (-a), (-ita),** [sen'-yaw-r (-a) (-ēta)], *n.* a Spanish form of address corresponding to Mr. (Mrs.), (Miss).
SENSATION, [sen-sā'-shun], *n.* sensual perception, nervous impression produced by the stimulus of a sense organ; feeling; profound emotional excitement produced by some event, the event or news itself. [L. *sensatus* intelligent].
SENSATIONAL, [sen-sā'-shun-al], *adj.* tending to produce a sensation, astonishing and exciting in the highest degree.
SENSATIONALISM, [sen-sā'-shun-al-izm], *n.* a theory that physical sensation is the only source of knowledge; that style of writing or journalism intended to provoke a violent and exciting emotional effect of a crude, and often undesirable, sort.
SENSATIONALIST, [sen-sā'-shun-al-ist], *n.* a believer in the theory of sensationalism; one who propagates sensations.
SENSATIONALLY, [sen-sāsh'-un-al-i], *adv.* in a sensational manner.
SENSE (1), [sens], *n.* the faculty of perceiving through the stimulation of bodily organs; any one of these bodily means of perception; perception by the bodily organs; the reason, the intellectual, cognitive faculty, judgment, the lowest form of understanding, the capacity for comprehending simple relationships; (*coll.*) that attitude of mind which is at home with simple concretes, and is able to carry on material transactions; the intellectual meaning of a thing, the direct message conveyed to the intelligence by a verbal or pictorial stimulus, the general meaning of a thing as perceived by the intelligence. [L. *sensus*].
SENSE (2), [sens], *v.t.* to perceive intuitively but not directly through the senses or intelligence. [*Prec.*].
SENSELESS, [sens'-les], *adj.* without sensation, unconscious, deprived of the senses; stupid, not dictated or guided by reason or intelligence.
SENSELESSLY, [sens'-les-li], *adv.* in senseless fashion.
SENSELESSNESS, [sens'-les-nes], *n.* the state or quality of being senseless.
SENSIBILITY, [sen'-sib-il'-it-i], *n.* the capacity of sensation, power of responding to stimuli; sensual refinement, delicacy of aesthetic or emotional response, sensitiveness of perception; that part of a person that feels moral, emotional, and spiritual refinements. [LL. *sensibilitas*].
SENSIBLE, [sen'-sibl], *adj.* capable of stimulating the senses, or being perceived by them; having command of the senses, having the capacity of comprehending realities and causal relations, controlled by the

reason, reasonable, undisturbed by emotions, according to common sense, judicious. [L. *sensibilis*].

SENSIBLENESS, [sen'-sibl-nes], *n.* the condition of being sensible.

SENSIBLY, [sen'-sib-li], *adv.* in sensible fashion, to an extent sufficient to be perceived by the senses.

SENSITIVE, [sen'-sit-iv], *adj.* highly perceptive of sensations, very sensible of sensory stimulation, tender, easily pained or hurt, delicate of sensory perception; easily stirred emotionally, easily hurt or distressed; refined, highly perceptive of emotional atmosphere; delicately adjusted, very easily disturbed by outside factors; responding very easily to physical stimuli. [Fr. *sensitif*].

SENSITIVELY, [sen'-sit-iv-li], *adv.* in sensitive fashion.

SENSITIVENESS, [sen'-sit-iv-nes], *n.* the condition of being sensitive.

SENSITIVE-PLANT, [sen'-sit-iv-plahnt], *n.* (*bot.*) a plant of the genus *Mimosa*, so called from the drooping of its leaves when touched.

SENSITIVITY, [sen'-sit-iv'-it-i], *n.* the state of being sensitive, *esp.* chemically or emotionally, or in connexion with delicate instruments.

SENSITIZE, [sen'-sit-iz], *v.t.* (*phot.*) to render sensitive to light.

SENSITIZER, [sen'-sit-iz-er], *n.* (*phot.*) a substance that makes photographic material sensitive to light.

SENSITOMETER, [sen'-sit-om'-eter], *n.* (*phot.*) a device for measuring photographic sensitivity.

SENSORIAL, [sen-saw'-ri-al], *adj.* sensory.

SENSORIUM, [sen-saw'-ri-um], *n.* the grey matter of the brain; the nervous system as a whole.

SENSORY, [sen'-ser-i], *adj.* of, or relating to, the senses or sensation, or sensation-bearing ganglia.

SENSUAL, [sensh'-ōō-al], *adj.* relating to, perceived by, the senses; relating to the sexual passions and their gratification, or the carnal pleasures generally; licentious, sexually inclined. [LL. *sensualis*].

SENSUALISM, [sen'-shōō-al-izm], *n.* sensuality, sensual pleasure; sensationalism.

SENSUALIST, [sen'-shōō-al-ist], *n.* one preoccupied with sensual pleasures, a licentious person.

SENSUALISTIC, [sen'-shōō-al-ist'-ik], *adj.* relating to sensualism.

SENSUALITY, [sen'-shōō-al'-it-i], *n.* the quality of being sensual; sensual indulgence, preoccupation with sexual pleasure.

SENSUALIZATION, [sen'-shōō-al-iz-ā'-shun], *n.* the process of sensualizing, state of being sensualized.

SENSUALIZE, [sen'-shōō-al-iz], *v.t.* to make sensual, to teach the love of sexual pleasure.

SENSUALLY, [sen'-shōō-al-i], *adv.* in sensual fashion.

SENSUALNESS, [sen'-shōō-al-nes], *n.* the condition of being sensual.

SENSUOUS, [sen'-shōō-us], *adj.* relating to, appealing to, the semi-aesthetic senses.

SENSUOUSLY, [sen'-shōō-us-li], *adv.* in sensuous fashion.

SENSUOUSNESS, [sen'-shōō-us-nes], *n.* the condition or quality of being sensuous.

SENTENCE (1), [sent'-ents], *n.* (*gram.*) a conventionally grammatical arrangement of words coherently expressing a single identifiable thought; (*leg.*) the statement of the penalty imposed by a criminal court; a period of imprisonment; the penalty itself; a judgment; †an opinion, a maxim. [L. *sententia* opinion].

SENTENCE (2), [sent'-ents], *v.t.* (*leg.*) to pass sentence upon.

SENTENTIAL, [sen-ten'-shal], *adj.* relating to a judicial or grammatical sentence. [L. *sententialis*].

SENTENTIALLY, [sen-ten'-shal-i], *adv.* by sentence, in the manner of a sentence.

SENTENTIOUS, [sen-ten'-shus], *adj.* prone to expressing worthless opinions in a pompous fashion; (of statements) ponderously trite. [L. *sententiosus* full of meaning].

SENTENTIOUSLY, [sen-ten'-shus-li], *adv.* in sententious fashion.

SENTENTIOUSNESS, [sen-ten'-shus-nes], *n.* the state of being sententious.

SENTIENCY, [sen'-shi-en-si], *n.* the quality of being sentient.

SENTIENT, [sen'-shi-ent], *adj.* perceiving by the senses, having the capacity of feeling, living and thinking. [L. *sentiens*].

SENTIENTLY, [sen'-shi-ent-li], *adv.* in sentient fashion.

SENTIMENT, [sent'-i-ment], *n.* feeling expressed intellectually; view; expressed opinion; a banal aphorism; that which is intended to appeal to the weaker emotions, sentimentality. [LL. *sentimentum*].

SENTIMENTAL, [sent'-i-ment'-al], *adj.* relating to, arising from, feeling rather than reason; mawkish, weakly emotional over some foolish object.

SENTIMENTALISM, [sent'-i-ment'-al-izm], *n.* sentimentality.

SENTIMENTALIST, [sent'-i-ment'-al-ist], *n.* one prone to sentimentality.

SENTIMENTALITY, [sent'-i-ment-al'-it-i], *n.* the state of being sentimental.

SENTIMENTALIZE, [sent'-i-ment'-al-iz], *v.t.* to make sentimental, regard in a sentimental light.

SENTIMENTALLY, [sent'-i-ment'-al-i], *adv.* in sentimental fashion.

SENTINEL, [sent'-in-el], *n.* one who stands guard, a sentry. [OFr. *sentinelle*].

SENTRY, [sent'-ri], *n.* an armed guard posted to give warning of hostile approach. [OFr. *senterel*].

SENTRY-BOARD, [sen'-tri-bawd'], *n.* a platform for sentries outside the gangway of a ship.

SENTRY-BOX, [sen'-tri-boks'], *n.* a sentry's shelter.

SENTRY-GO, [sen'-tri-gō], *n.* the duty of a sentry, his march up and down his beat.

SENZA, [sent'-sa], *prep.* (*mus.*) without. [It. *senza*].

SEPAL, [sep'-al], *n.* (*bot.*) a leaf of a flower's calyx. [Fr. *sépale*].

SEPALINE, [sep'-al-in], *adj.* pertaining to a sepal.

SEPALODY, [sep-al'-od-i], *n.* the reversion of petals to sepals.

SEPALOID, [sep'-al-oid], *adj.* like a sepal. [SEPAL and Gk. *oeides* like].

SEPARABILITY, [sep'-er-ab-il'-it-i], *n.* the quality of being separable.

SEPARABLE, [sep'-er-abl], *adj.* able to be separated.

SEPARABLENESS, [sep'-er-abl-nes], *n.* the state of being separable.

SEPARABLY, [sep'-er-ab-li], *adv.* in separable fashion.

SEPARATE (1), [sep'-er-at], *adj.* not joined, divided, disunited, disconnected, distinct, not the same, isolated, having distinctive functions, individual, not related.

SEPARATE (2), [sep'-er-āt], *v.t.* and *i.* to disunite, make separate, remove from each other's proximity; to estrange, cause disagreement; to divide, come between, keep separate from; to discriminate, sift; to become separate, to go apart, to leave each other's company, to cease to cohabit, to secede. [L. *separare*].

SEPARATELY, [sep'-er-at-li], *adv.* in separate fashion, individually.

SEPARATENESS, [sep'-er-at-nes], *n.* the condition of being separate or separable.

SEPARATION, [sep'-er-ā'-shun], *n.* the act of separating, the state of being separate; a formal or informal arrangement by which a married couple cease to cohabit; **s. allowance**, the allowance received by the wife or other dependant of someone on active service. [L. *separatio*].

SEPARATISM, [sep'-ar-at-izm], *n.* a policy based upon the desire of certain groups to obtain independence from larger organizations to which they belong.

SEPARATIST (1), [sep'-er-at-ist], *n.* one who wishes to secede from the main body of a church or policy.

SEPARATIST (2), [sep'-er-at-ist], *adj.* of or pertaining to separatism or separatists.

SEPARATIVE, [sep'-er-at-iv], *adj.* tending to separate; with the purpose of separating.

SEPARATOR, [sep'-er-āt'-er], *n.* one who separates; a machine for separating substances.

SEPARATORY, [sep'-er-at-er-i], *adj.* separative.

SEPARATRIX, [sep'-er-at-riks], *n.* the mark formerly used to separate the integer from the decimal fraction, now superseded by the decimal point; (*typ.*) the diagonal stroke separating alterations in proof-correcting.

SEPAWN, [sep-awn'], *n.* maize-meal boiled in water. [Uncert.].

SEPHARDIM, [sef-ahd'-im], *n.*(*pl.*) Iberian Jews. [Heb. *sephardim*].

SEPIA, [sēp'-i-a], *n.* a coloured secretion of the cuttle-fish; a pigment made from this; the dark brown colour of this pigment. [Gk. *sepia* cuttle-fish].

SEPOY, [sēp'-oi], *n.* a European-trained Indian soldier. [Hind. *sipahi* soldier].

SEPSIS, [sep'-sis], *n.* putrefaction, infection of the blood. [Gk. *sepsis* decay].

SEPT, [sept], *n.* an Irish clan; a branch of a Highland clan or family. [OFr. *septe*].

SEPT-, *pref.* seven, containing, relating to, connected with, seven.

SEPTAN, [sept'-an], *adj.* (of fever) with paroxysms recurring at intervals of seven days. [L. *septem* seven].

SEPTANGLE, [sept'-angl'], *n.* (*geom.*) a figure having seven angles. [SEPT- and ANGLE (1)].
SEPTANGULAR, [sept-ang'-gewl-er], *adj.* with seven angles.
SEPTARIA, [sept-āer'-i-a], *n.* (*bot.*) a genus of fungi; (*geol.*) a limestone concretion; (*zool.*) a genus of molluscs. [L. *septum* division].
SEPTATE, [sept'-āt], *adj.* divided by a septum. [L. *saeptatus*].
SEPTEMBER, [sept-emb'-er], *n.* the ninth (in the Roman calendar the seventh) month of the year. [L. *September*].
SEPTEMBRIST, [sept-emb'-rist], *n.* a participant in the September massacres, during the French Revolution. [Fr. *septembriste*].
SEPTEMPARTITE, [sept'-em-paht'-it], *adj.* having seven parts.
SEPTEMVIR, [sept-em'-ver], *n.* one of an oligarchy of seven. [L. *septem viri* seven men].
SEPTENARY, [sep-tĕn'-er-i], *adj.* consisting of seven. [L. *septenarius*].
SEPTENATE, [sep'-tĕn-āt], *adj.* (*bot.*) with seven parts.
SEPTENNATE, [sep-ten'-āt], *n.* tenure for seven years. [Fr. *septennat*].
SEPTENNIAL, [sep-ten'-i-al], *adj.* happening every seven years, lasting seven years. [L. *septennium* seven-year period].
SEPTENNIALLY, [sep-ten'-i-al-i], *adv.* every seven years.
SEPTENTRION, [sep-ten'-tri-on], *n.* and *adj.* northern; the north. [L. *septentrio* the Great Bear].
SEPTENTRIONAL, [sep-ten'-tri-on-al], *adj.* northern.
SEPTENTRIONALLY, [sep-ten'-tri-on-al-i], *adv.* towards the north.
SEPTET, [sep'-tet'], *n.* (*mus.*) a composition for seven performers; a group of seven performers.
SEPTFOIL, [sept'-foil], *n.* a symbolic figure made of seven equal segments; (*bot.*) the plant *Potentilla Tormentilla*. [LL. *septifolium*].
SEPTIC, [sep'-tik], *adj.* relating to sepsis; poisoned, putrefied. [Gk. *septikos*].
SEPTICAEMIA, [sept'-i-sēm'-i-a], *n.* blood-poisoning. [Gk. *septikos* putrid and *haima* blood].
SEPTICIDAL, [sep'-ti-sid'-al], *adj.* (*bot.*) (of pods) splitting the dissepiments. [SEPTUM and L. *cidere* to cut].
SEPTICITY, [sep-tis'-it-i], *n.* the state of being septic, tendency to become septic.
SEPTIFEROUS, [sep-tif'-er-us], *adj.* having a septum.
SEPTIFLUOUS, [sep-tif'-lōō-us], *adj.* running in seven streams. [L. *septem* seven and *fluere* to flow].
SEPTIFOLIOUS, [sep'-ti-fōl'-i-us], *adj.* like a septfoil, having seven leaves. [LL. *septifolium*].
SEPTIFORM, [sep'-ti-fawm], *adj.* like a septum.
SEPTILATERAL, [sep'-ti-lat'-er-al], *adj.* seven-sided.
SEPTILLION, [sep-til'-yon], *n.* (*math.*) the seventh power of a million. [Fr. *septillion*].
SEPTINSULAR, [sept-ins'-yool-er], *adj.* consisting of seven islands; **S. Republic**, the Ionian islands.
SEPTUAGENARIAN, [sept'-yōō-a-jen-āer'-i-an], *n.* a person aged between seventy and eighty years. [L. *septuagenarius*].
SEPTUAGENARY, [sept'-yōō-a-jĕn'-er-i], *adj.* consisting of seventy, seventy years old. [L. *septuagenarius*].
SEPTUAGESIMA, [sept'-yōō-a-jes'-im-a], *n.* the third Sunday before Lent. [L. *septuagesima* (*dies*) seventieth (day before Easter)].
SEPTUAGESIMAL, [sept'-yōō-a-jes'-im-al], *adj.* relating to Septuagesima.
SEPTUAGINT, [sept'-yōō-a-jint], *n.* the Hellenistic version of the Old Testament, supposed to have been made by seventy writers. [L. *septuaginta* seventy].
SEPTUM, (*pl.* **septa**), [sep'-tum], *n.* a membrane dividing two bodily cavities; (*bot.*) the membrane dividing the chambers of a seed-vessel; (*zool.*) the dividing wall between the chambers of a coral skeleton, ammonite shell, nautilus, etc.; (*min.*) a thin mineral lode partitioning a small rock specimen. [L. *septum* partition].

SEPTUM

SEPTUPLE, [sep'-tyōōpl], *adj.* sevenfold. [L. *septuplus*].
SEPULCHRAL, [sep-ul'-kral], *adj.* like, relating to, a sepulchre, dismal, funereal. [L. *sepulchralis*].
SEPULCHRE (1), [sep'-ŏŏl-ker], *n.* a tomb cut out of rock, a vault, building, etc., for the interment of the dead; **whited s.**, a hypocrite. [L. *sepulcrum*].
SEPULCHRE (2), [sep'-ŏŏl-ker], *v.t.* to bury in a tomb.
SEPULTURE, [sep'-ŏŏl-cher], *n.* the act, process, or mode of burying the dead. [L. *sepultura*].
SEQUACIOUS, [si-kwā'-shus], *adj.* following, attendant; docile; consistent, logically following.
SEQUACIOUSNESS, [si-kwā'-shus-nes], *n.* the quality of being sequacious.
SEQUACITY, [si-kwas'-it-i], *n.* the tendency to be sequacious. [LL. *sequasitas*].
SEQUEL, [sēk'-wel], *n.* that which follows and is related to something preceding it, the outcome, continuation of a thing after it is apparently completed; a literary work carrying on and continuing one that preceded it; a result, consequence. [L. *sequela*].
SEQUELA, [sik-wēl'-a], *n.* the morbid, abnormal state succeeding a disease. [*Prec.*].
SEQUENCE, [sēk'-wents], *n.* the order of a series of events, a series of events leading out of each other, or occurring in succession; a series of cards in uninterrupted order of value; (*mus.*) a succession of graduate tones; (*films*) a continuous action ended by a dissolve, the equivalent of a theatrical scene. [LL. *sequentia*].
SEQUENT, [sēk'-went], *adj.* following, consequent. [L. *sequens*].
SEQUENTIAL, [si-kwen'-shal], *adj.* following, succeeding, consequential. [LL. *sequentia*].
SEQUENTIALLY, [si-kwen'-shal-i], *adv.* in sequential fashion.
SEQUESTER, [si-kwes'-ter], *v.t.* and *reflex.* (*leg.*) to take possession of for a definite purpose and time, to confiscate; to withdraw from society; to sequestrate. [LL. *sequestrare* to surrender].
SEQUESTERED, [si-kwes'-terd], *adj.* retired, in seclusion.
SEQUESTRABLE, [si-kwes'-trabl], *adj.* able to be sequestered.
SEQUESTRATE, [si-kwes'-trāt], *v.t.* and *i.* (*leg.*) to take (a person's property) and hold it against the satisfaction of claims; to confiscate. [L. *sequestrare*].
SEQUESTRATION, [sē'-kwes-trā'-shun], *n.* the act or process of sequestrating. [LL. *sequestratio*].
SEQUESTRATOR, [sē'-kwes-trā'-tor], *n.* one who sequesters property, one holding sequestered property. [LL. *sequestrator*].
SEQUIN, ZECCHIN, ZECHIN, [sē'-kwin, zek'-in] *n.* a medieval Italian gold coin; an ornamental circular spangle. [Arab. *sikkah* die stamp].
SEQUOIA, [sē-kwoi'-a], *n.* (*bot.*) a genus of American coniferous evergreen trees. [Amer. Ind. *sequoia*].
SERAC, sérac, [sā'-rak], *n.* a pinnacle of glacial ice. [Fr. *sérac*].
SERAFILE, [se'-ra-fīl], *n.* (*milit.*) the end soldier in a file. [Portug. *serrafila*].
SERAGLIO, [ser-ahl'-i-o], *n.* the old palace of the Sultans of Turkey; a harem; the concubines of an Oriental ruler. [It. *seraglio* enclosure].
SERAI, [ser-ī'], *n.* an Eastern inn. [Pers. *serai* palace].
SERALBUMEN, [sē-ral'-bew-men], *n.* albumen in the body-fluids. [SERUM and ALBUMEN].

SEQUOIA

SERANG, [se-rang'], *n.* a Malay boatswain. [Pers. *sarhang* commander].
SERAPH, (*pl.* **seraphim**), [se'-raf], *n.* an angel of the highest order, having six wings. [Heb. *seraphim*].
SERAPHIC, [ser-af'-ik], *adj.* relating to a seraph; angelic, holy.
SERAPHICALLY, [ser-af'-ik-al-i], *adv.* in seraphic fashion.
SERAPHIM, [se'-raf-im], *pl.* of SERAPH.
SERAPHINE, [se'-ra-fēn], *n.* a primitive harmonium. [~SERAPH].
SERASKIER, [ser-as'-kēer], *n.* the Imperial Turkish Commander-in-Chief. [Pers. *sir* chief and Arab. *asker* army].
SERBIAN, [surb'-i-an], *n.* the South Slavonic language spoken in Old Serbia. [Serbian *Srb* a Serb].
SERBO-CROAT, [surb'-ō-krō'-at], *n.* the closely related dialects of Old Serbia and Croatia regarded as a linguistic unit. [Germ. *Serbo-Kroatisch* from Serbian *Srb* a Serb and *Hrvat* a Croat].
SERBONIAN, [ser-bōn'-i-an], *adj.* presenting a treacherous and quaking surface in which one may

be imminently engulfed. [Lake *Serbonis*, in the Nile delta, where whole armies are said to have been swallowed up].

SERE, see SEAR (2).

SERENADE (1), [se'-ren-ād'], *n.* music played at night in the open air, *esp.* under a lover's window; (*mus.*) a piece composed to be performed in the open air. [Fr. *sérénade*].

SERENADE (2), [se'-ren-ād'], *v.t. and i.* to play, sing a serenade to; to perform a serenade.

SERENADER, [se'-ren-ād'-er], *n.* one who serenades.

SERENATA, [se'-ren-aht'-a], *n.* (*mus.*) a piece played as a serenade. [It. *serenata*].

SERENE (1), [si-rēn'], *n.* a placid expanse, a clear sky.

SERENE (2), [si-rēn'], *adj.* calm, peaceful, smooth, placid, tranquil, undisturbed, unclouded; (*coll.*) safe; also used as a royal title. [L. *serenus*].

SERENELY, [si-rēn'-li], *adv.* in serene fashion.

SERENENESS, [si-rēn'-nes], *n.* the condition of being serene.

SERENITY, [se-ren'-it-i], *n.* sereneness, undisturbed tranquillity. [L. *serenitas*].

SERF, [surf], *n.* (*hist.*) a peasant who, while personally free, is bound to his lord's land; (*coll.*) an oppressed wage-slave, a person degraded by virtual servitude. [L. *servus* slave].

SERFDOM, [surf'-dom], *n.* the condition of being a serf, the institution of serf tenantry.

SERGE, [surj], *n.* a twilled woollen stuff used in making heavy garments. [L. *serica* silken stuff].

SERGEANT, SERJEANT, [sah'-jant], *n.* (*milit.*) a non-commissioned officer next above a corporal; the police officer next above a constable; (*hist.*) a mounted soldier not of the knightly class; any one of various court officials. [OFr. *serjant*].

SERGEANT-MAJOR, [sah'-jant-mā'-jer], *n.* (*milit.*) a warrant officer of various functions and positions.

SERGEANTSHIP, [sah'-jant-ship], *n.* the rank or duty of a sergeant.

SERIAL (1), [sēer'-i-al], *n.* a work, film, etc., published or exhibited in a succession of instalments.

SERIAL (2), [sēer'-i-al], *adj.* relating to, arranged in, a series; (of literary works) appearing at intervals in instalments; **s. rights,** rights of publishing instalments of a work in a journal. [~SERIES].

SERIALIZE, [sēer'-i-al-īz], *v.t.* to dispose of the serial rights of a literary work, to prepare a work for publication in instalments.

SERIALLY, [sēer'-i-al-i], *adv.* in a series or serial.

SERIATE, [sēer'-i-āt], *adj.* arranged in, pertaining to, a series.

SERIATELY, [sēer'-i-āt-li], *adv.* in seriate fashion.

SERIATIM, [sēer'-i-āt'-im], *adv.* in regular series, point by point. [MedL. *seriatim*].

SERICEOUS, [se-ris'-i-us], *adj.* resembling, relating to silk. [Gk. *serikos*].

SERICITE, [se'-ris-īt], *n.* (*min.*) a talc-like kind of muscovite. [L. *sericus* silken].

SERICULTURE, [sēer'-i-kul'-cher], *n.* the cultivation of silkworms. [L. *sericum* silk and CULTURE].

SERIES, (*pl.* **series**), [sēer'-ēz], *n.* a number of things arranged in some graded order, a number of things standing in some successive relation; a number of books published successively having a common format; (*math.*) a succession of terms in accordance with a common law; sequence, progressive gradation. [L. *series* row, sequence].

SERIF, [se'-rif], *n.* the flourishes and decorative lines on letters in most printing types. [Uncert.].

SERIN, [se'-rin], *n.* the European yellow finch. [Fr. *serin*].

SERIO-COMIC, [sēer'-i-ō-kom'-ik], *adj.* partly serious and partly comic.

SERIOUS, [sēer'-i-us], *adj.* sober, thoughtful, occupied with, interested in, grave or important matters; not marked by or subject to levity; said, done, or intended in earnest, and not as a jest; dangerous, critical, requiring earnest attention; thorough, not superficial, careful. [LL. *serius*].

SERIOUSLY, [sēer'-i-us-li], *adv.* in serious fashion.

SERIOUSNESS, [sēer'-i-us-nes], *n.* the condition of being serious.

SERJEANT, see SERGEANT.

SERJEANT-AT-ARMS, [sah'-jant-at-ahmz'], *n.* the officer in charge of the mace in the House of Commons.

SERJEANT-AT-LAW, [sah'-jant-at-law'], *n.* a member of a now abolished order of barristers.

SERJEANTY, [sah'-jant-i], *n.* (*feudal leg.*) land tenure by services other than military. [OFr. *sergantie*].

SERMON, [sur'-mon], *n.* a moral, doctrinal, and religious address delivered during a Church service; (*coll.*) a moralizing lecture of reproach for some evil behaviour. [OFr. *sermon*].

SERMONIZE, [sur'-mon-īz], *v.i.* to harangue, moralize, affect a sermonic tone.

SERMONIZER, [sur'-mon-īz-er], *n.* one who sermonizes.

SEROON, CEROON, [ser-ōōn'], *n.* a bale (of Oriental stuffs) wrapped in an animal's skin. [Span. *seron* hamper].

SEROSITY, [se-ros'-it-i], *n.* the condition of being serous; a serous fluid.

SEROTINE, [se'-rot-ēn], *n.* a small, brownish bat, *Vespertilio serotinus*. [L. *serotinus* happening in the evening].

SEROTINOUS, [se-rot'-in-us], *adj.* (*bot.*) developing or flowering late in the season. [L. *serotinus*].

SEROUS, [sēer'-us], *adj.* resembling, secreting, serum.

SEROW, [se-rō'], *n.* a species of Asiatic antelope. [Native].

SERPENS, [sur'-pens], *n.* (*astron.*) one of the northern constellations. [L. *serpens*].

SERPENT, [sur'-pent], *n.* a snake; (*fig.*) a treacherous, smooth-tongued tempter, the Devil; (*mus.*) †a wood-wind instrument with a long curved tube. [*Prec.*].

SERPENTIFORM, [ser-pent'-i-fawm], *adj.* having the shape of a serpent.

SERPENTINE (1), [sur'-pen-tīn], *n.* (*geol.*) a highly polishable rock consisting of hydrous magnesium silicate; an ancient cannon with a thin barrel, largely used on ships.

SERPENTINE (2), [sur'-pent-īn], *adj.* sinuous like a serpent, meandering; (*fig.*) treacherously subtle.

SERPENTINELY, [sur'-pen-tīn-li], *adv.* in serpentine fashion.

SERPENTRY, [sur'-pen-tri], *n.* a place where serpents breed.

SERPIGINOUS, [ser-pij'-in-us], *adj.* relating to serpigo.

SERPIGO, [ser-pīg'-ō], *n.* (*med.*) ringworm; shingles. [MedL. *serpigo*].

SERRATE, SERRATED, [ser-āt'-(id)], *adj.* with a notched edge. [L. *serratus*].

SERRATION, [se-rā'-shun], *n.* the state of being serrated; a notched edge like that of a saw.

SERRATIROSTRAL, [ser-āt'-i-ros'-tral], *adj.* having a serrated bill. [SERRATE and L. *rostrum* beak].

SERRATURE, [se'-ra-cher], *n.* a notching, a serration. [L. *serratura*].

SERRIED, [se'-rid], *adj.* packed compactly together, *esp.* of troops in close formation. [Fr. *serré*].

SERRULATE, [se'-rewl-āt], *adj.* finely serrated. [L. *serrula* a little saw].

SERULA, [se'-rew-la], *n.* the red-breasted merganser *Mergus serrator*. [L. *serrula* small saw].

SERUM, [sēer'-um], *n.* a watery fluid remaining after the coagulation of the blood; such a fluid as prepared for use in inoculation. [L. *serum* whey].

SERVAL, [sur'-val], *n.* a brownish, ring-tailed African wild-cat. [Native].

SERVANT, [surv'-ant], *n.* one who serves, a person in the service of another, one employed to wait upon another's bodily or domestic requirements, one employed by any person or organization, a devoted adherent of anything, that which aids any purpose or person. [OFr. *servant*].

SERVE (1), [surv], *n.* the act of serving, a turn to serve at a game.

SERVE (2), [surv], *v.t.* to aid, help, assist, tend, work for, be servant to (any person or thing), to wait upon, supply the needs of, attend the wants of (any one), to present food to (a person); to fulfil (a purpose); do what is required; (*eccles.*) to assist a priest at Mass; to undergo (a prison sentence) (usually **to s. time**); to operate (a machine), load and work a gun; (of male animals) to mate with; (*tennis, etc.*) to strike the ball to begin a rally; (*leg.*) to deliver (a summons or notice of a legal process to a person); (*naut.*) to protect a rope by twining it with cords, etc.; **to s. a person right,** to give a person what he deserves; *v.i.* to be, or to perform the duties of, a servant or a slave, to perform duties in the armed forces, to perform an office; to suffice, to be adequate, to be suitable for a specific purpose; **to s. as,** to perform the functions of. [L. *servire* to serve].

SERVER, [surv'-er], *n.* one who serves; one serving at Mass; an implement for serving food.

SERVICE (1), [surv'-is], *n.* the act, process or occupation of serving, by which a person is served; employment, *esp.* as a domestic servant; a feudal due; a period of employment in one of the services; an official administrative department, a department for providing a public utility; (*pl.*) the armed forces of a government; (*eccles.*) the formal performance of religious worship or ritual; attention given to a customer; the way in which, means by which, food is served, a set of implements and dishes for eating food; (*leg.*) the serving of a process or summons; (*tennis*) the striking of the ball that begins play; **active s.,** military service involving actual fighting; **senior s.,** the Royal Navy. [OFr. *servise* from L. *servitium* servitude].

SERVICE (2), [surv'-is], *adj.* pertaining or belonging to one of the armed forces; **ex-s.,** discharged from one of the armed forces. [*Prec.*].

SERVICE (3), [surv'-is], *v.t.* to provide service for (machinery, etc.).

SERVICEABLE, [surv'-is-abl], *adj.* fit for use, useful rather than decorative.

SERVICEABLENESS, [surv'-is-abl-nes], *n.* the state or fact of being serviceable.

SERVICEABLY, [surv'-is-ab-li], *adv.* in serviceable fashion.

SERVICE-BOOK, [surv'-is-bŏŏk], *n.* a book containing an order of religious service.

SERVICE-FLAT, [surv'-is-flat'], *n.* a flat where the rent covers domestic service.

SERVICE-LINE, [surv'-is-lin], *n.* a line across a tennis court, twenty-one feet from the net, between which and the net the ball must fall in service.

SERVICE-PIPE, [surv'-is-pīp], *n.* a pipe leading from a main into a house.

SERVICE-TREE, [surv'-is-trē], *n.* a rosaceous tree allied to the mountain-ash. [~OE. *syrfe* and TREE].

SERVIETTE, [surv'-i-et'], *n.* a table napkin. [Fr. *serviette*].

SERVILE, [surv'-il], *adj.* relating to slaves or slavery, in the condition of a slave; fawning, cringing slavishly; (of labour) bodily. [L. *servilis*].

SERVILELY, [surv'-īl-li], *adv.* in servile fashion.

SERVILENESS, [surv'-il-nes], *n.* servility.

SERVILITY, [serv-il'-it-i], *n.* the state or quality of being servile; servitude.

SERVING-MAID, [surv'-ing-mād], *n.* a female domestic servant.

SERVING-MAN, [surv'-ing-man], *n.* a male domestic servant.

SERVITOR, [surv'-it-or], *n.* one who serves another, *esp.* in a personal capacity; (*hist.*) a sizar at Oxford University. [L. *servitor*].

SERVITORSHIP, [surv'-it-or-ship], *n.* the rank or place of a servitor.

SERVITUDE, [surv'-i-tewd], *n.* slavery, complete subjection; (*Scots leg.*) a right over (another's) property, easement; **penal s.,** imprisonment with hard labour for three years or more. [L. *servitudo*].

SESAME, [ses'-am-i], *n.* an East Indian herb, yielding an oil similar to olive oil; **open s.!** a magic invocation by which Ali Baba opened the robbers' cave; (*fig.*) that which assists in making a difficult entry or approach. [OFr. *sésame* from Gk. *sesame*].

SESAMOID, [ses'-am-oid], *adj.* (*anat.*) (of a knee-bone) shaped like a sesame seed.

SESBAN, [ses'-ban], *n.* (*bot.*) a leguminous marsh plant, *Sesbania aculeata*, having floating roots. [Pers. *sisaban*].

SESQUI-, *pref.* one and one-half more. [L. *sesqui*].

SESQUIALTERA, [ses'-kwi-al'-ter-a], *n.* a compound organ stop.

SESQUIALTERAL, [ses'-kwi-al'-ter-al], *adj.* in the ratio of 3 to 2. [L. *sesquialter*].

SESQUICENTENNIAL, [ses'-kwi-sen-ten'-i-al], *adj.* of, or relating to, the one-hundred-and-fiftieth anniversary of a happening.

SESQUIDUPLICATE, [ses'-kwi-dew'-plik-at], *adj.* in the ratio of 5 to 2.

SESQUIOXIDE, [ses-kwi-oks'-īd], *n.* (*chem.*) an oxide containing two atoms of the combining element and three atoms of oxygen. [SESQUI and OXIDE].

SESQUIPEDALIAN, [ses'-kwi-ped-āl'-i-an], *adj.* containing a foot and a half; (of speech) many-syllabled, long-worded. [L. *sesquipedalis*].

SESQUIPLICATE, [ses-kwip'-li-kat], *adj.* in the ratio of the square roots to the cube roots of the terms of a ratio. [L. *sesquiplicatus*].

SESQUITERTIAN, [ses'-kwi-tur'-shan], *adj.* in the ratio of 4 to 3. [L. *sesquitertius*].

SESQUITONE, [ses'-kwi-tōn], *n.* (*mus.*) an interval of three semitones. [SESQUI and TONE (1)].

SESSILE, [ses'-il], *adj.* (*bot.*) attached directly to the main stem. [L. *sessilis* sitting].

SESSION, [sesh'-un], *n.* a formal sitting, meeting, of a body or assembly, the time occupied by such a sitting, the period for which an assembly remains sitting without dissolution; the university year; (*pl.*) the meetings of certain judicial courts; (*coll.*) a period, usually protracted, continuously occupied by some business or discussion. [L. *sessio*].

SESSIONAL, [sesh'-un-al], *adj.* relating to a session.

SESTERTIUS, [ses-tur'-shi-us], *n.* a Roman coin, one quarter of a denarius. [L. *sestertius*].

SESTET, [ses-tet'], *n.* a sextet; the last six lines of the Italian sonnet. [L. *sextus* sixth].

SET (1), [set], *n.* a group of individual objects bearing a natural relationship to each other, and together making up a complete series or whole; the way in which a thing is placed in relation to something else, the angle at which a thing rests; a general, undetailed but definite, inclination in a certain direction, mental or physical; a drift, a determined inclination; a group of persons having some interest in common (generally used colloquially); the number of eggs hatched at one time; (*tennis*) the game's principal scoring unit, gained by the first side to win six or more games with a clear lead of two; a riveting instrument, a sort of punch; (*films, theatre*) the complete scenery and setting for a part of the action; (*films*) the part of the studio in which acting is taking place; the act of setting; an adjustment of the hair. [SET (3)].

SET (2), [set], *adj.* rigid, fixed (*esp.* of facial expression), determined in some course; established, ordered, prescribed.

SET (3), [set], *v.t.* to take and put in a certain position in relation to something else, to put facing, direct towards, a certain direction, to fix (a jewel, etc.) in a metal holder, to put, adjust (machinery) to a certain purpose, to prepare (a device) for some future action, to get (a thing) absolutely ready, prepare for something to follow, to prepare (circumstances) for a future situation; (*typ.*) to arrange (type) for printing; to put (eggs) under a bird to be hatched; to make become stiff, rigid, *esp.* to solidify (a liquid); to cause (the thoughts, opinions) to take a certain direction, to have a definite influence on (the mind); to appoint some duty for, to direct to some action or task, to incite; to compose music for (words); to fix the hair in waves; *v.i.* (of liquids) to become solidified, to form a jelly; to become rigid and determined; **to s. about a person,** to attack a person; **to s. aside,** to disregard; **to s. back,** to hinder the progress of; **to s. down,** to record, write down; **to s. in,** to become noticeably and increasingly present; **to s. off,** to explode, cause to begin; to begin a journey; to enhance the appearance of; **to s. on,** to urge on; **to s. out,** to give an exposition of; to begin a journey; **to s. to,** to eat vigorously, to begin vigorous effort; **to s. up,** to establish in good style, to establish oneself as in some profession, to found. [OE. *settan*].

SETA, [sēt'-a], *n.* (*bot.*) the stalk on which the capsule of a moss is borne. [L. *seta* bristle].

SETACEOUS, [sit-ā'-shus], *adj.* having bristles, bristly. [L. *seta* a bristle].

SET-BACK, [set'-bak], *n.* a rebuff; a discouraging encounter or experience.

SET-DOWN, [set'-down], *n.* a humiliating set-back.

SETIFEROUS, [sēt-if'-er-us], *adj.* bristly. [L. *seta* a bristle and *ferre* to bear].

SETIFORM, [sēt'-i-fawm], *adj.* bristle-shaped.

SETIGEROUS, [sēt-ij'-er-us], *adj.* bristly. [L. *setiger*].

SET-OFF, [set'-of'], *n.* that which enhances a thing; the compensation of a gain against a loss; (*leg.*) settlement of a debt by a counter-claim by the debtor.

SETON, [sē'-ton], *n.* (*med.*) a twist of thread drawn under the skin to provoke an issue, a counter-irritant. [Fr. *séton*].

SETOSE, [sē'-tōs], *adj.* bristly. [L. *setosus*].

SET-PIECE, [set'-pēs'], *n.* some performance elaborately prepared in advance, a large and elaborate pictorial firework display on a framework.

SET-SPEECH, [set'-spēch'], *n.* a speech carefully rehearsed beforehand.

SET-SQUARE, [set'-skwāer'], *n.* a flat, right-angled, triangular drawing instrument.

SET-SQUARE

SETT, [set], *n.* a block of wood or stone used in street-paving; a screw used in jointing masts. [SET (3)].

SETTEE (1), [set-ē'], *n.* an upholstered sofa with back and arms, capable of holding two or more persons.

SETTEE (2), [set-ē'], *n.* a swift, sharp-prowed

Mediterranean vessel with lateen sails. [It. *saetta* from L. *sagitta* arrow].

SETTER, [set'-er], *n.* one who, or that which, sets; one of several kinds of game-dog.

SETTERWORT, [set'-er-wurt], *n.* (*bot.*) the stinking hellebore, *Helleborus fœtidus.*

SETTING, [set'-ing], *n.* the act of setting, the manner or material in which a thing is set; the process of solidifying or jellying; the surroundings or environment of a thing.

SETTLE (1), [setl], *n.* a long, high-backed seat. [OE. *setl* seat].

SETTLE (2), [setl], *v.t.* to set and place securely in, to establish (people) as inhabitants, to provide (a place) with inhabitants, to install, establish (a person) in a place or situation; to make calm or peaceful, to decide, resolve; to determine, to make up one's mind about, to bring to a conclusion, to fix, finally to dispose of; to pay (a debt); (*coll.*) to deal firmly with; *v.i* to go to a place as an inhabitant, to establish oneself in a place or occupation, to become used to a new abode or situation; to become staple, decided; to come to rest, to subside, sink down so as to level out by its own weight; (of sediment) to sink to the bottom; **to s. down,** to adapt oneself to a new mode of life; **to s. on,** (*leg.*) to endow with; **to s. up,** to pay all one's outstanding debts; **to s. with,** to make a settlement with; deal with finally. [ME. *settlen*].

SETTLEMENT, [setl'-ment], *n.* the act of settling, state of being settled; a group of settlers, the place in which they have settled, *esp.* a township of settlers; (*leg.*) a formal conveyance of property, the property so conveyed.

SETTLER, [set'-ler], *n.* one who settles, *esp.* one settling in an undeveloped country, a colonist.

SETTLING, [set'-ling], *n.* the act of making settled, the result of such action.

SET-TO, [set'-tōō'], *n.* a fracas, a fight or violent dispute.

SEVEN, [sev'-en], *n.* the number between six and eight, the numeral representing this; a playing card with seven pips. [OE. *seofon*].

SEVENFOLD, [sev'-en-fōld], *adj.* repeated seven times; with seven folds.

SEVENTEEN, [sev'-en-tēn'], *n.* the number equalling seven plus ten. [OE. *seofontene*].

SEVENTEENTH, [sev'-en-tēnth'], *n. and adj.* the ordinal of seventeen.

SEVENTH, [sev'-enth], *n. and adj.* the ordinal of seven; **s. heaven,** the ultimate height of bliss.

SEVENTHLY, [sev'-enth-li], *adv.* in the seventh place.

SEVENTIETH, [sev'-en-ti-eth], *n. and adj.* the ordinal of seventy.

SEVENTY, [sev'-en-ti], *n.* the number equalling seven times ten. [OE. *seofontig*].

SEVEN-WHISTLER, [sev'-en-wis'-ler], *n.* the whimbrel, *Numenius phæopus.*

SEVER, [sev'-er], *v.t.* to divide by cutting, to separate from, cut in two; (*fig.*) to estrange, divide (from). [OF. *sever* from L. *separare*].

SEVERABLE, [sev'-er-abl], *adj.* able to be severed.

SEVERAL, [sev'-er-al], *adj.* separate, distinct, various, not together; a few, more than two but not a great many; (*leg.*) able to be treated separately. [AFr. *several*].

SEVERALITY, [sev'-er-al'-it-i], *n.* the state of being separate and distinct, or held individually.

SEVERALLY, [sev'-ral-i], *adv.* separately, individually.

SEVERANCE, [sev'-er-ants], *n.* the act of severing, the state of being severed. [OF. *sevrance*].

SEVERE, [si-vēer'], *adj.* strict, stern, rigorous, harsh, exacting; grave, sober, austere; violent, strong, excessive, intense. [L. *severus*].

SEVERELY, [si-vēer'-li], *adv.* in severe fashion.

SEVERENESS, [si-vēer'-nes], *n.* severity.

SEVERITY, [si-ve'-ri-ti], *n.* the act or state of being severe. [L. *severitas*].

SEVILLE, [sev-il'], *n.* the name of a city in Spain used to denote a type of bitter orange.

SEW, [sō], *v.t. and i.* to fasten together by drawing thread, to stitch together, to make by stitching; to stitch, to work with needle and thread. [OE. *seowian*].

SEWAGE, [sew'-ij], *n.* waste matter carried through sewers; **s. farm,** a place outside a town where sewage is rendered innocuous.

SEWELLEL, [si-wel'-el], *n.* a North American rodent of the genus *Haplodon.* [AmerInd].

SEWER (1), [sō'-er], *n.* one who sews.

SEWER (2), [sew'-er], *n.* a main drain, an underground conduit for removing excreta and waste from a town; †a stream, ditch, drainage channel. [OFr. *seuwiere*].

SEWER† (3), [sew'-er], *n.* a medieval servant waiting at meals. [OFr. *asseour*].

SEWERAGE, [sew'-er-ij], *n.* the system of drains and sewers in a town, disposal of waste by means of sewage.

SEWING, [sō'-ing], *n.* the craft of stitching; needlework.

SEWING-COTTON, [sō'-ing-kot'-on], *n.* cotton thread used in sewing.

SEWING-MACHINE, [sō'-ing-ma-shēn'], *n.* a machine for sewing.

SEWING-PRESS, [sō'-ing-pres'], *n.* the frame used in bookbinding for stitching books.

SEX, [seks], *n.* the distinguishing physiological characteristics of male and female, one of these two groups as a whole; everything relating to these organic differences and the various emotions and ideas associated with them. [L. *sexus*].

SEXAGENARIAN, [seks'-a-jen-āer'-i-an], *n. and adj.* sixty years old; a person between sixty and seventy years of age. [L. *sexagenarius*].

SEXAGENARY, [seks'-a-jēn'-er-i], *adj.* relating to sixty, having sixty parts. [*Prec.*].

SEXAGESIMA, [seks'-a-jes'-im-a], *n.* the second Sunday before Lent, about sixty days before Easter. [L. *sexagesima* (*dies*) sixtieth (day)].

SEXAGESIMAL, [seks'-a-jes'-im-al], *adj.* relating to sixty.

SEXANGLE, [seks'-angl'], *n.* a figure with six angles.

SEXANGULAR, [seks-ang'-gyōō-ler], *adj.* with six angles, hexagonal.

SEXANGULARLY, [seks-ang'-gyōō-ler-li], *adv.* hexagonally.

SEX-APPEAL, [seks'-a-pēl'], *n.* the attribute or power which excites sexual desire in the opposite sex.

SEXCENTENARY, [seks'-sen-tēn'-er-i], *n.* a six-hundredth anniversary.

SEXENNIAL, [seks-en'-i-al], *adj.* lasting six years, occurring once in six years. [L. *sexennium*].

SEXENNIALLY, [seks-en'-i-al-i], *adv.* every six years.

SEXFID, [seks'-fid], *adj.* (*bot.*) cleft into six. [L. *sex* six and *findere* cleave].

SEXLESS, [seks'-les], *adj.* lacking sexual passions or characteristics.

SEXTAIN, [seks'-tān], *n.* a six-line stanza. [L. *sextus* sixth].

SEXTAN, [seks'-tan], *adj.* happening every sixth day.

SEXTANT, [seks'-tant], *n.* an instrument for determining position by finding latitude and longitude; (*math.*) the sixth part of a circle. [L. *sextans* sixth part].

SEXTANT

SEXTET, [seks-tet'], *n.* (*mus.*) a composition for six performers, a group of six performers. [L. *sextus* sixth].

SEXTILE, [seks'-tīl], *adj.* relating to sixty degrees; **s. aspect,** the aspect of two planets when they are separated by sixty degrees. [L. *sextilis*].

SEXTILLION, [seks-til'-i-on], *n.* (*math.*) (in England) the sixth power of a million.

SEXTO, [seks'-tō], *n.* (*typ.*) a book made up of sheets folded into six. [L. *sextus*].

SEXTON, [seks'-ton], *n.* a man employed to dig graves and tend church and churchyard. [~SACRISTAN].

SEXTONSHIP, [seks'-ton-ship], *n.* the office of sexton.

SEXTUPLE, [seks'-tewpl], *adj.* sixfold.

SEXUAL, [sek'-shōō-al], *adj.* relating to, connected with, arising from, preoccupied by, or tending to sex, its characteristics, or the emotions it arouses. [L. *sexualis*].

SEXUALITY, [sek-shōō-al'-it-i], *n.* the quality or fact of being sexual.

SEXUALLY, [sek'-shōō-al-i], *adv.* in sexual fashion.

SEXY, [seks'-i], *adj.* exploiting or flaunting sex.

SEYM, [sām], *n.* the Polish Diet or Parliament. [Pol. *seym*].

SFORZANDO, [sfawts-and'-ō], *adv.* (*mus.*) emphatically, with force. [It. *sforzando*].

SGRAFFITO, [sgraf-ē'-tō], *n.* a design made by cutting away a coloured surface to reveal a different colour beneath. [It. *sgraffito*].

SHABBILY, [shab'-i-li], *adv.* in shabby fashion.

SHABBINESS, [shab'-i-nes], *n.* the state of being shabby.
SHABBY, [shab'-i], *adj.* ragged, wearing threadbare, outworn (clothes); squalid, drab; mean, despicable, sordidly selfish. [~OE. *sceabb* scab].
SHABRACQUE, [shab'-rak], *n.* a cavalry officer's saddle-cloth, often covered with animal skin. [Turk. *chabraq*].
SHACK, [shak], *n.* a roughly built hut, a cabin, a shanty.
SHACKLE (1), [shakl], *n.* a horseshoe-shaped link closed by a bolt or pin across the ends; a chain joined to the wrist- or ankle-rings of a prisoner, and serving to restrict his movement, a fetter; (*fig.*) a restraint, bond, that which binds. [OE. *sceacul*].
SHACKLE (2), [shakl], *v.t.* to bind with a shackle, to restrict, fetter. [*Prec.*].
SHAD, [shad], *n.* an edible marine fish related to the herring. [OE. *sceadd*].
SHADDOCK, [shad'-ok], *n.* the grapefruit; the tree bearing this fruit. [Captain *Shaddock*, who first introduced it to the West Indies].

SHAD

SHADE (1), [shād], *n.* darkness caused by the intervention of something before a source of light, an area shielded from the direct rays of the sun, that which provides such protection from direct light, a shield attached to a lamp to soften its light; darkening in a pictorial representation to represent a suppression of light; a very slight difference in colour or brightness, a slight difference in any quantity or quality, the faintest tinge or degree of some feeling, an almost imperceptible change in intensity; a ghost, the spirit of a dead person, the memory of one dead; **in the s.,** overshadowed, outdone, by another. [OE. *sceadu*].
SHADE (2), [shād], *v.t. and i.* to cast shade on, shield from the light, to cut off light from, to indicate gradations of light on a drawing, etc.; **to s. away,** to fade slowly into difference; **to s. into,** to change gradually into.
SHADILY, [shād'-i-li], *adv.* in shady fashion.
SHADINESS, [shād'-i-nes], *n.* the condition or quality of being shady.
SHADING, [shād'-ing], *n.* darkening in a drawing to indicate difference of light; the act of giving shade.
SHADOOF, [sha-dōōf'], *n.* a method of raising water by lowering a bucket on a long lever pivoted on an upright post by a river bank. [Arab. *shaduf*].
SHADOW (1), [shad'-ō], *n.* the patch of shade produced on a surface by the intervention of an object between it and a source of light, *esp.* such a shade as falls in the shape of the object that produces it; the space from which light is cut off by the presence of an object; (*fig.*) that which casts a shade, gloom, depression; an imperfect, insubstantial copy of a thing, a feeble reflection of someone or something; the slightest degree, a shade; a person following another as closely and continually as his shadow, *esp.* someone following and spying on another; an overhanging threat, a warning of coming ill. [OE. *sceadwe* (*dat.* of *sceadu*)].
SHADOW (2), [shad'-ō], *v.t.* to throw a shadow upon, throw into the shade, quite outdo; to shade (a drawing); to outline, foretell, adumbrate; to follow and spy upon.
SHADOW BOXING, [shad'-ō-boks'-ing], *n.* practice boxing against an imaginary opponent.
SHADOW CABINET, [shad'-ō-kab'-in-et], *n.* (*pol.*) a potential cabinet, the draft list of members of a cabinet made before the party concerned is in office.
SHADOW FACTORY, [shad'-ō-fak'-tor-i], *n.* a factory prepared for use only in the event of the destruction by war, etc., of another.
SHADOWGRAPH, [shad'-ō-graf], *n.* a picture formed by a shadow; an X-ray photograph.
SHADOWINESS, [shad'-ō-i-nes], *n.* the condition of being shadowy.
SHADOWLESS, [shad'-ō-les], *adj.* without shadow.
SHADOWY, [shad'-ō-i], *adj.* shady; full of shadows; mysterious; insubstantial.
SHADY, [shād'-i], *adj.* shaded, giving shade, in the shade; (*coll.*) underhand, of dubious reputation, not open, probably dishonest.
SHAFT, [shahft], *n.* the stem, stock of an arrow or spear, the haft of various implements; anything resembling such a haft, anything long, straight, and slim in proportion to its length, a bar, the part of a column between base and capital, an upright stalk, a narrow beam of light, a narrow, vertical opening leading down to a mine; (*pl.*) the two parallel poles between which a horse is harnessed to pull a vehicle. [OE. *sceaft* spear, shaft].
SHAFTED, [shahft'-ed], *adj.* having a shaft.
SHAG, [shag], *n.* a rough, untidy mass of hair; a coarse tobacco; a coarse cloth; a small crested cormorant. [OE. *sceacga* rough hair].
SHAGBARK, [shag'-bahk], *n.* the white hickory tree. [Uncert.].
SHAGGED, [shag'-id], *adj.* shaggy; (*coll.*) tired out, exhausted; debauched.
SHAGGEDNESS, [shag'-ed-nes], *n.* shagginess.
SHAGGINESS, [shag'-i-nes], *n.* the state of being shaggy.
SHAGGY, [shag'-i], *adj.* rough, unkempt, with long, thick, untidy hair.
SHAGREEN, [sha-grēn'], *n.* rough, untanned leather made from horse-hide, with an artificially granulated surface; the skin of various sharks which resembles this. [Pers. *saghri* rump of a horse].
SHAH, [shah], *n.* the king of Persia. [Pers. *shah* king].
SHAKE (1), [shāk], *n.* the act of shaking, a single movement of shaking, a negative gesture of the head; a drink made by shaking two or more ingredients together; (*mus.*) a trill; (*coll.*) a very short time.
SHAKE (2), [shāk], *v.t.* to move a thing violently backwards and forwards, to hold in the hand and move (suddenly); to cause to vibrate rapidly, to cause to tremble; to weaken the stability of, to render less firm or solid; (*fig.*) to disturb, upset, weaken; **to s. hands,** to grasp another's hand in greeting or farewell; *v.i.* to vibrate, to move rapidly back and forth, to tremble, to quiver, to shiver with fear or excitement, to quake; **to s. down,** to settle down on an impromptu bed; to accustom oneself to new surroundings; **to s. off,** to get rid of for good; **to s. up,** to mix by shaking; to shock and disturb severely. [OE. *scacan*].
SHAKEDOWN, [shāk'-down], *n.* a makeshift bed.
SHAKEN, [shāk'-en], *adj.* disturbed, perturbed, upset by some experience.
SHAKER, [shāk'-er], *n.* one who, or that which, shakes; a member of the religious sect whose devotions were characterized by tremblings; a container for mixing drinks by shaking.
SHAKESPEAREAN, [shāk-spēer'-i-an], *adj.* like, relating to, derived from, Shakespeare.
SHAKILY, [shāk'-i-li], *adv.* in shaky fashion.
SHAKINESS, [shāk'-i-nes], *n.* the state of being shaky.
SHAKO, [shak-ō'], *n.* a peaked, plumed, flat-topped military headgear. [Hungarian *csakos* peaked].
SHAKY, [shāk'-i], *adj.* easily shaken, unstable, flimsy; tottering, feeble in bodily movements; (*fig.*) uncertain, vague, unreliable.
SHALE, [shāl], *n.* laminated clay-rock. [Germ. *schale*].
SHALL, [shal], *v. auxil.* expressing future intention, obligation, or compulsion. [OE. *sceal*].
SHALLOON, [shal-ōōn'], *n.* a light worsted material. [*Chalons* a French town].
SHALLOP, [shal'-op], *n.* a light boat without decks. [Du. *sloep*].
SHALLOT, [shal-ot'], *n.* the small species of onion, *Allium ascalonicum.* [OFr. *eschalote*].
SHALLOW (1), [shal'-ō], *n.* the freshwater fish, the rudd. [OE. *scealga*].
SHALLOW (2), [shal'-ō], *n.* a shallow place; a shallow basket or cart used by costermongers.
SHALLOW (3), [shal'-ō], *adj.* not deep; (*fig.*) lacking depth, intensity, profundity; having few original ideas, superficial. [ME. *schadowe*].
SHALLOW (4), [shal'-ō], *v.i.* (of water) gradually to become shallow.
SHALLOW-BRAINED, [shal'-ō-brānd], *adj.* empty-headed, with no depth of thought.
SHALLOWLY, [shal'-ō-li], *adv.* in shallow fashion.
SHALLOWNESS, [shal'-ō-nes], *n.* the quality of being shallow; superficiality of intellect.
SHALLOWS, [shal'-oz], *n.*(*pl.*) a tract of shallow water, shoals.
SHALM, [shahm], *n.* a shawm.
SHALY, [shāl'-i], *adj.* abounding in, resembling shale.
SHAM (1), [sham], *n.* that which is sham, a counterfeit, a fake; an assumption of some quality or attribute not really possessed, a deception, a fraud.
SHAM (2), [sham], *adj.* bogus, not genuine, spurious, counterfeit.
SHAM (3), [sham], *v.t. and i.* to feign, simulate; to pretend, act, affect (to be). [~SHAME].
SHAMA, [shah'-ma], *n.* a song-bird of the genus *Cittocincla.*
SHAMAN, [sham'-an], *n.* a medicine-man among the North Asiatic peoples. [Pers. *shaman* heathen].

SHAMANISM, [sham'-an-izm], *n.* primitive religious practices of Northern Asiatic peoples, based on the belief that good and evil spirits can be controlled by magic.

SHAMBLE (1), [shambl], *n.* a shambling walk, a clumsy, shuffling gait.

SHAMBLE (2), [shambl], *v.i.* to shuffle, to walk in clumsy and ungainly fashion. [ODu. *schampelen* to stumble].

SHAMBLES, [shamblz], *n.* a butcher's stall, a slaughter-house, a place of blood and slaughter, a bloody massacre. [OE. *scamel* stool from L. *scamellum* bench].

SHAMBLING, [shamb'-ling], *n. and adj.* walking with a shamble; a shambling gait.

SHAME (1), [shām], *n.* a strong emotion of regret, self-disgust, or embarrassment, a feeling of guilt, a feeling of offended modesty; a disgrace, dishonour, ignominy; a cause of ignominy, disgrace, embarrassment, or disgust; (*coll.*) unfairness, disgraceful bad luck. [OE. *sceamu*].

SHAME (2), [shām], *v.t.* to bring shame upon, to make feel ashamed, to disgrace; to coerce by making feel ashamed. [OE. *sceamian*].

SHAMEFACED, [shām'-fāst], *adj.* bashful, shy; showing shame at some ill-conduct, ashamed of oneself, sheepish. [OE. *scamfæst*].

SHAMEFACEDLY, [shām'-fāst-li], *adv.* in shamefaced fashion.

SHAMEFACEDNESS, [shām'-fāst-nes], *n.* the state of being shamefaced.

SHAMEFUL, [shām'-fŏŏl], *adj.* that which shames, disgraceful, outrageous, disgusting.

SHAMEFULLY, [shām'-fŏŏl-i], *adv.* in shameful fashion.

SHAMEFULNESS, [shām'-fŏŏl-nes], *n.* the quality of being shameful.

SHAMELESS, [shām'-les], *adj.* without shame, immodest, indecent, brazen, impudent.

SHAMELESSLY, [shām'-les-li], *adv.* in shameless fashion.

SHAMELESSNESS, [shām'-les-nes], *n.* the quality of being shameless.

SHAMMER, [sham'-er], *n.* one who shams; an impostor.

SHAMMOY, [sham'-oi], *v.t.* to prepare (leather) by rubbing in oil or grease. [~CHAMOIS].

SHAMMY, [sham'-i], *n.* chamois leather. [~CHAMOIS].

SHAMPOO (1), [sham-pōō'], *n.* the act of shampooing; soap, etc., used for shampooing the hair; **dry s.,** absorbent powder brushed into the hair to remove dirt and grease; a shampoo prepared with spirit or other volatile liquid in place of water.

SHAMPOO (2), [sham-pōō'], *v.t.* to wash the hair with a shampoo, or under a spray of water; to knead and massage the limbs. [Hind. *champna* to knead].

SHAMROCK, [sham'-rok'], *n.* the white clover, *Trifolium repens*; this or similar plants used as an Irish national emblem. [Ir. *seamrog* trefoil].

SHAMROCK

SHANDRYDAN, [shan'-dri-dan], *n.* a light, two-wheeled Irish cart; an old-fashioned carriage. [Uncert.].

SHANDYGAFF, [shand'-i-gaf'], *n.* a drink consisting of beer and lemonade or gingerbeer, mixed in equal quantities. [Unkn.].

SHANGHAI, [shang-hī'], *v.t.* to drug or slug (a man) insensible and put him aboard an outgoing ship as a sailor. [*Shanghai*, the Asiatic port].

SHANK (1), [shangk], *n.* the shin of a man or certain animals; (*coll.*) the legs; the shaft, haft of an instrument; the part of a tool between handle and working end. [OE. *sceanca* leg].

SHANK (2), [shangk], *v.i.* to decay away, (of flowers) to wither and fall off the stem.

SHANKED, [shangkt], *adj.* having a shank.

SHANK-PAINTER, [shangk'-pānt-er], *n.* (*naut.*) a short rope and chain which sustains the anchor against the ship's side.

SHANNY, [shan'-i], *n.* a small sea-fish of the genus, *Blennius pholis*, a blenny. [Unkn.].

SHANTUNG, [shan'-tung'], *n.* silk from the Chinese province of *Shantung*, usually of a creamy-brown colour.

SHANTY (1), [shant'-i], *n.* a sailor's chanty. [~CHANTY].

SHANTY (2), [shant'-i], *n.* a lean-to shed, a shack, a small hut; (in Australia) a public-house. [Uncert.].

SHAPABLE, [shāp'-abl], *adj.* able to be shaped.

SHAPE (1), [shāp], *n.* the external form, two- or three-dimensional outline of a thing; something having a shape, something of which only the outlines can be distinguished; (*fig.*) a definite, orderly plan or conception; practical expression of some conception; pattern from which to copy something; mould for shaping something; that which is shaped in a mould; **to be in good s.** to be in good spirits and physical condition. [OE. *gesceap* creation].

SHAPE (2), [shah'-pē], *n.* a Tibetan minister of state. [Native].

SHAPE (3), [shāp] *v.t. and i.* to give shape to, mould, form; to assume a shape, become formed, ordered; to develop; **to s. up to,** to approach in a boxing attitude; (*fig.*) to assert (oneself).

SHAPELESS, [shāp'-les], *adj.* without shape, with an undistinguishable outline, unsymmetrical.

SHAPELESSNESS, [shāp'-les-nes], *n.* the quality of being shapeless.

SHAPELINESS, [shāp'-li-nes], *n.* the quality of being shapely; beauty or proportion of form.

SHAPELY, [shāp'-li], *adj.* well shaped, well proportioned (*esp.* of the female body).

SHARD, SHERD, [shahd, shurd], *n.* a fragment of pottery; the hard wing-case of a beetle. [OE. *sceard* broken thing].

SHARE (1), [shāer], *n.* a portion of something held in common allocated to one of the possessors, a portion of a thing obtained by any one party by division, part obtained from, borne in anything in which others also participate; a part ownership of a business undertaking, entitling the owner to a proportionate part of the profits, one of the equal parts into which is divided the invested capital of a joint-stock company; (*pl.*) stock. [OE. *scearu* a cutting].

SHARE (2), [shāer], *n.* a ploughshare. [OE. *scear*]

SHARE (3), [shāer], *v.t. and i.* to give out shares in a thing, to divide a thing with others, to participate with in the possession of a thing; to have a share, to take part in.

SHARE-BONE, [shāer'-bōn'], *n.* the pubic bone. [OE. *scearu* groin and BONE (1)].

SHAREBROKER, [shāer'-brō-ker], *n.* a stockbroker.

SHAREHOLDER, [shāer'-hōld-er], *n.* one holding shares in a joint-stock company.

SHARE-LIST, [shāer'-list], *n.* a list showing the current prices of joint-stock shares.

SHARE-PUSHER, [shāer'-pŏŏsh'-er], *n.* one who peddles shares in dubious joint-stock companies.

SHARER, [shāer'-er] *n.* one who shares with another.

SHARK (1), [shahk], *n.* one of a group of voracious sea-fishes, characterized by a rounded tapering body, a mouth on the under side, and a skin covered with hard tubercles; (*fig.*) a predatory rogue. [Uncert.].

SHARK

SHARK (2), [shahk], *v.t.* to cheat, swindle, rob by trickery. [*Prec.*].

SHARP (1), [shahp], *n.* (*mus.*) a sharp note, the symbol for this note, one of the black keys on a piano; a sharper, swindler.

SHARP (2), [shahp], *adj.* keen, having a cutting edge, piercing, able to divide or penetrate substances; pointed, acute, abrupt, steep; shrill; distinctly outlined; sour, bitter, astringent; swift, sudden, decisive; quick, clever, swift in apprehension, alert; (*mus.*) raised a semitone in pitch, too high in pitch; brusque, quick-tempered. [OE. *scearp*].

SHARP (3), [shahp], *adv.* punctually, exactly.

SHARP (4), [shahp], *v.t.* (*coll.*) to sharpen; (*coll.*) to swindle, cheat.

SHARP-CUT, [shahp'-kut'], *adj.* clear-cut.

SHARPEN, [shahp'-en], *v.t. and i.* to make sharp, to whet, to make quick or ready; to become sharp.

SHARPENER, [shahp'-en-er], *n.* one who, or that which, sharpens, *esp.* a contrivance for sharpening pencils.

SHARPER, [shahp'-er], *n.* a swindler, trickster, one who sharps, *esp.* at cards.

SHARPIE, [shahp'-i], *n.* a sharp-pointed, flat-bottomed sailing-boat. [SHARP (2)].

SHARPLY, [shahp'-li], *adv.* in sharp fashion.

SHARPNESS, [shahp'-nes], *n.* the quality of being sharp; acuity; intensity.

SHARP-SET, [shahp'-set'], *adj.* hungry, eager.

SHARPSHOOTER, [shahp'-shōōt'-er], *n.* (*milit.*) a

sniper, a skilled marksman, a lightly equipped skirmisher.

SHARPSHOOTING, [shahp'-shōōt'-ing], *n.* sniping, rapid accurate shooting at the enemy by a carefully located marksman.

SHARP-SIGHTED, [shahp'-sīt'-id], *adj.* quick, keen-sighted.

SHARP-WITTED, [shahp'-wit'-id], *adj.* quick-witted, acute.

SHASTRA, [shahs'-tra], *n.* a sacred book of the Hindus. [Skr. *çastra*].

SHATTER, [shat'-er], *v.t. and i.* to break to fragments, smash to pieces; (*fig.*) to destroy quickly and utterly, cripple; to jar upon. [ODu. *schetteren* to scatter].

SHATTERY, [shat'-er-i], *adj.* brittle.

SHAVE (1), [shāv], *n.* the act of shaving, the state of the face after having been shaved; a shaving; a very narrow escape, the barest contact with something; a tool for paring wood. [OE. *sceafa* plane].

SHAVE (2), [shāv], *v.t. and i.* to cut, scrape hair from the body with a razor, *esp.* so to remove hair from the face; to cut, pare, thin slices from a surface; to graze very slightly; to perform the action of shaving the face. [OE. *sceafan* to scrape].

SHAVE-HOOK, [shāv'-hōōk], *n.* a workman's tool in the form of a triangular blade set across a handle, used for scraping metal clean for soldering, for removing paint, etc.

SHAVE-HOOK

SHAVER, [shāv'-er], *n.* one who, that which, shaves; (*coll.*) a young boy.

SHAVIAN, [shā'-vi-an], *adj.* relating to the literary style or philosophy of George Bernard *Shaw*.

SHAVING, [shāv'-ing], *n.* the act of removing hair from the body with a razor; a paring, thin slice of wood or metal.

SHAW, [shaw], *n.* a small wood. [OE. *sceaga*].

SHAW-FOWL, [shaw'-fowl], *n.* a dummy fowl for shooting practice.

SHAWL, [shawl], *n.* a piece of material for loosely covering the head and (usually) shoulders, as a protection from cold. [Pers. *shal*].

SHAWM, [shawm], *n.* a double-reed instrument, forerunner of the oboe. [OFr. *chalenie* from Gk. *kalamos* reed].

SHAY, [shā], *n.* a chaise. [~CHAISE].

SHE, [shē], *pron.3rd person sg.fem. personal pron., nom. case.* [ME. *scæ, sche*].

SHEA, [shē'-a], *n.* a tropical African tree yielding a sort of butter, *Butyrospermum Parkii.* [Native].

SHEADING, [shēd'-ing], *n.* one of the six administrative divisions of the Isle of Man. [~OE. *sceadan* divide].

SHEAF, (*pl.* **sheaves**), [shēf], *n.* a bundle of reaped grain tied together in a stack; the number of arrows sufficient to fill the quiver; a bundle of papers or banknotes. [OE. *sceaf*].

SHEALING, SHIELING, [shēl'-ing], *n.* a small shepherd's or fisherman's hut or croft. [~ONorw. *skali* hut].

SHEAR (1), [shēer], *n.* a rupture or distortion in any material caused by forces acting in opposite directions but not in the same straight line.

SHEAR (2), [shēer], *v.t. and i.* to cut with shears, to cut off at a stroke, to cut off (the hair); to remove (fleece) with the shears; to be altered in shape under stress. [OE. *scearan*].

SHEARBILL, [shēer'-bil], *n.* a water-fowl, the black skimmer, *Rhyncops nigra.*

SHEARER, [shēer'-er], *n.* one who shears sheep.

SHEARHOG, [shēer'-hog'], *n.* a sheep when it has been shorn for the first time, a shearling.

SHEARING, [shēer'-ing], *n.* the act of clipping wool from sheep with shears; (*pl.*) the wool so cut off.

SHEAR-LEGS, SHEER-LEGS, [shēer'-legz'], *n.(pl.)* a crane-like device consisting of three poles lashed together at the top and splayed out trianglewise at the bottom, and fitted at the top with pulley and tackle to raise heavy weights.

SHEARLING, [shēer'-ling], *n.* a sheep that has only been shorn once.

SHEARMAN, [shēer'-man], *n.* one who shears metal; †one who shears cloth.

SHEARS, [shēerz], *n.(pl.)* a large scissor-like cutting tool consisting of two blades which are provided with handles and bolted together at a point on each between the blade and the handle and pivoting about that point so that the action of bringing the handles together closes the blades and causes them to cut.

SHEAR-STEEL, [shēer'-stēl'], *n.* a sort of steel made by welding small bars or pieces together, used to make cutting implements.

SHEAR-TAIL, [shēer'-tāl], *n.* a humming bird with a forked tail.

SHEARWATER, [shēer'-wawt'-er], *n.* a sea-bird of the genus *Puffinus.*

SHEARWATER

SHEAT-FISH, [shēt'-fish], *n.* a large edible freshwater fish of Central Europe belonging to the cat-fish family. [Uncert.].

SHEATH, [shēth], *n.* a close-fitting case or covering used to encase a sharp tool or weapon when it is not being used, or so that it may be easily and safely carried about the person; the scabbard of a sword; any similar covering or envelope, *esp.* in the anatomy of animals, birds, fish, etc., or in the structure of plants; a form of contraceptive. [OE. *scæth*].

SHEATHE, [shēTH], *v.t.* to place or replace in a sheath; to cover or overcast with a protecting case or envelope.

SHEATHED, [shēTHd], *adj.* fitted in a sheath, protected by a close outer covering.

SHEATHING, [shēTH'-ing] *n.* the act of placing in a sheath; anything which sheathes or envelopes closely.

SHEATHLESS, [shēth'-les], *adj.* lacking a sheath, uncovered, unsheathed.

SHEAVE (1), [shēv], *n.* a grooved pulley-wheel over which a rope moves. [Uncert.].

SHEAVE (2), [shēv], *v.t.* to gather into sheaves. [~SHEAF].

SHEAVE-HOLE, [shēv'-hōl], *n.* a groove in which a sheave may be fixed.

SHEBANG, [shi-bang'], *n.* (*U.S. slang*) a gambling house; business in hand. [Unkn.].

SHEBEEN (1), [shi-bēn'], *n.* a place in which alcoholic liquor is secretly and illegally manufactured and sold. [~Ir. *siopa* shop].

SHEBEEN (2), [shi-bēn'], *v.i.* to pursue an illicit commerce in drink.

SHECHINAH, see SHEKINAH.

SHED (1), [shed], *n.* a small temporary or permanent structure; a hut or outhouse used for storage or as a temporary shelter; a lean-to. [~SHADE].

SHED (2), [shed], *n.* a parting in the wool of a sheep made so that the animal's skin may be reached and treated medicinally; (in weaving) the parting of the threads of the warp on the loom so that the shuttle may pass between; hair-parting. [OE. *gescead* division].

SHED (3), [shed], *n.* something shed or poured out.

SHED (4), [shed], *n.* a salmon not yet two years old.

SHED (5), [shed], *v.t.* to let fall, cast off, abandon, divest oneself of; to let flow, pour forth, diffuse; to cause to flow; **to s. the blood of,** to slay. [OE. *sceadan* divide].

SHEDDER, [shed'-er], *n.* one who sheds.

SHEDDING (1), [shed'-ing], *n.* the act of casting off, pouring forth, or causing to pour forth; that which is shed; a division or parting.

SHEDDING (2), [shed'-ing], *n.* a group of sheds; material out of which sheds may be made.

SHEEN, [shēn], *n.* gloss, lustre. [OE. *scene* beautiful].

SHEENY (1), [shēn'-i], *n.* (*coll.*) a Jew. [Uncert.].

SHEENY (2), [shēn'-i], *adj.* lustrous, bright and glossy.

SHEEP, (*pl.* **sheep**), [shēp], *n.* one of the ungulate ruminant mammals of the genus *Ovis* frequently having small curved horns, and valuable for their woolly coats and edible flesh; sheepskin, leather or parchment prepared from the skin of sheep; (*fig.*) a member or members of a religious congregation; (*coll.*) a timid person lacking in initiative; **a black s.,** a rogue; **sheep's eyes,** amorous glances; **a lost s.,** a person who has strayed from previous upright habits or who has left a community or group to which he previously belonged; **the s. and the goats,** the good and the bad. [OE. *sceap*].

SHEEPCOTE, [shēp'-kōt], *n.* a sheepfold; a shelter for sheep.

SHEEPDOG, [shēp'-dog'], *n.* a dog trained to help a shepherd in looking after sheep.

SHEEP-FACED, [shēp'-fāst], *adj.* bashful, shy.

SHEEPFOLD, [shēp'-fōld], *n.* an enclosure for sheep; (*fig.*) a church, religious organization.

SHEEP-HOOK, [shēp'-hōōk], *n.* a crooked staff used by shepherds.

SHEEPISH, [shēp'-ish], *adj.* shy, bashful; silly.

SHEEPISHLY, [shēp'-ish-li], *adv.* bashfully, shyly.

SHEEPISHNESS, [shēp'-ish-nes], *n.* the condition of being sheepish; timorousness.
SHEEP-LOUSE, [shēp'-lows], *n.* the insect, *Malophagus ovinus*, infesting sheep.
SHEEP-MARKET, [shēp'-mah'-kit], *n.* a market where sheep are bought and sold.
SHEEPMASTER, [shēp'-mah'-ster], *n.* a sheep-owner, one who rears sheep.
SHEEP-RUN, [shēp'-run], *n.* a stretch of sheep-pasture.
SHEEP'S-BANE, [shēps'-bān], *n.* the plant, *Hydrocotyle vulgaris*, the marsh pennywort.
SHEEP'S-BIT, [shēps'-bit], *n.* the scabious, *Jasione montana*.
SHEEPSHANK, [shēp'-shangk'], *n.* the leg of a sheep; (*naut.*) a knot made in a rope so as to shorten it without cutting it.
SHEEP'S-HEAD, [shēps'-hed'], *n.* the head of a sheep; a large edible fish, *Sargus ovis*, found off the north-east coast of America; a silly, dull-witted person.
SHEEP-SHEARING, [shēp'-shēer-ing], *n.* the process of shearing sheep; the time of year when sheep are sheared; a rural feast held at this time.
SHEEPSKIN, [shēp'-skin], *n.* the skin of sheep; parchment or leather made from it; a rug or coat made from the skin of a sheep with the wool still on.
SHEEP-SORREL, [shēp'-so'-rel], *n.* the plant, *Rumex acetosella*.
SHEEP-TICK, [shēp'-tik], *n.* the bont tick, *Amblyomma hebræum*, troublesome to sheep.
SHEEPWALK, [shēp'-wawk], *n.* a tract of sheep pasture.
SHEEP-WASH, [shēp'-wosh'], *n.* a lotion used to clean sheep of vermin.
SHEER (1), [shēer], *n.* (*naut.*) a deviation in the course of a ship.
SHEER (2), [shēer], *adj.* unmixed; absolute, mere, downright; precipitous; (of fabric) transparent, very thin, diaphanous; †bright. [~OScand. *skeerr*].
SHEER (3), [shēer], *adv.* absolutely, utterly; precipitously, straight down without a break.
SHEER (4), [shēer], *v.i.* (*naut.*) to turn aside; **to s. off**, (*coll.*) to depart, leave. [Du. *scheren*].
SHEER-HULK, [shēer'-hulk], *n.* the hulk of a dismantled ship equipped with cranes and shear-legs for removing heavy cargoes from other ships in port.
SHEER-LEGS, see SHEAR-LEGS.
SHEERS, [shēerz], *n.*(*pl.*) shear-legs.
SHEET (1), [shēt], *n.* a rectangular piece of cloth, usually of linen or some cotton mixture, used as bed-clothing; (*naut.*) a sail; a piece of paper; a thin expanse of any material; an expanse resembling a sheet in appearance; **a clean s.**, an unbroken record of good conduct; **a blank s.**, an unbiased mind ready to receive impressions; **a winding s.**, a shroud; **a news s.**, a small newspaper. [OE. *sceete*].
SHEET (2), [shēt], *n.* (*naut.*) a chain or cable fixed to the lower part of a sail to control its tension; **three sheets in the wind**, (*coll.*) very inebriated.
SHEET (3), [shēt], *v.t.* to provide a sheet or sheets for; to cover with a sheet.
SHEET-ANCHOR, [shēt-ang'-ker], *n.* (*naut.*) a large anchor for use in emergency; (*fig.*) a last hope, a mainstay in difficulty.
SHEET-COPPER, [shēt'-kop'-er], *n.* copper in sheet form.
SHEETING, [shēt'-ing], *n.* cloth suitable for use as sheets on a bed; any material in sheet form; a lining or surface covering of timber; the act of making into sheets; the act of covering with sheets.
SHEET-IRON, [shēt'-īern], *n.* iron in sheet form.
SHEET-LEAD, [shēt'-led'], *n.* lead in sheet form.
SHEET-METAL, [shēt'-metl'], *n.* metal in sheet form, *esp.* tinplate.
SHEET-MUSIC, [shēt'-myōō'-zik], *n.* music published on unbound sheets.
SHEET-SAW, [shēt'-saw], *n.* a saw with a tapering blade, used for cutting sheet-metal.
SHEET-ZINC, [shēt'-zingk], *n.* zinc in the form of sheets.

SHEET-SAW

SHEIK, SHEIKH, [shēk, shāk], *n.* the head of a tribe or family in Arab and Moslem lands; the head of an Arab village. [Arab. *sheikh* an elder].
SHEKAREE, SHEKARY, see SHIKARI.
SHEKEL, [shek'-el], *n.* an old Hebrew measure of weight of about half an ounce; an old Hebrew coin of this weight, their principal silver coin; (*pl.*) (*slang*) cash, money. [Heb. *shekel*].
SHEKINAH, SHECHINAH, [shek-kēn'-ah], *n.* a symbolical radiancy or similar manifestation of the presence of God (*esp.* in the temple of Solomon). [Heb. *shekinah* dwelling].
SHELDRAKE, SHIELDRAKE, [shel'-drāk'], *n.* a wild sea-duck of the genus, *Tadorna*. [ME. *schelledrake*].
SHELDUCK [shel'-duk], *n.* the female of the sheldrake.

SHELDRAKE

SHELF, (*pl.* **shelves**), [shelf], *n.* a narrow flat projection in a cupboard or case or on a wall, usually made of wood, where articles may be stood for storing or ornament; a ledge on the face of a cliff; a flat bank or reef beneath the surface of a river or of the sea; **continental s.**, the higher level of the sea-bottom around the shores of a continent. [OE. *scelf*].
SHELFFUL, [shelf'-fōōl], *n.* that which fills a shelf.
SHELFY, [shelf'-i], *adj.* having shelves; (of a sea or river) dangerous to shipping by reason of reefs and banks below the surface of the water.
SHELL (1), [shel], *n.* a hard outer covering, a husk; the stiff, hard, protective outer coat of many fish, crustaceans, molluscs, reptiles, animals, insects, and vegetable growths; the outer part or outer casing of anything, *esp.* when emptied of its contents; tortoise-shell; the outer ear; a rough coffin; a framework, *esp.* of a building; outer appearance; (*milit.*) a heavy explosive, metal projectile, often filled with shrapnel, gases, etc., fitted with a time-fuse and fired from guns; (*fig.*) **to retire into one's s.**, to become extremely reserved of manner in company; **to come out of one's s.**, to cease to be reserved. [OE. *scele*].
SHELL (2), [shel], *v.t.* *and i.* to remove the shell, pod, husk, etc., from, to peel; to cover with shells, to adorn with shells; (*milit.*) to bombard with shells; to cast off one's shell; **to s. out**, to make a due or demanded payment. [*Prec.*].
SHELLAC (1), [shel-ak'], *n.* lac melted, strained and made into thin layers and used to make varnishes, etc. [SHELL (1) and LAC (1)].
SHELLAC (2), [shel-ak'], *v.t.* to cover with a coating of shellac.
SHELLBACK, [shel'-bak'], *n.* (*slang*) an old mariner.
SHELL-BARK, [shel'-bahk], *n.* a sort of hickory the bark of which is loose and peels easily.
SHELLED, [sheld], *adj.* provided with a shell; deprived of its shell; (*milit.*) bombarded with shells.
SHELL-FISH, [shel'-fish], *n.* an edible crustacean or mollusc having a hard external shell.
SHELL-JACKET, [shel'-jak'-it], *n.* a close-fitting military jacket, for undress use.
SHELL-LIME, [shel'-līm], *n.* lime obtained by burning shells.
SHELL-MARL, [shel'-mahl], *n.* a deposit of shells crushed into a mass.
SHELL-PROOF, [shel'-prōōf], *adj.* proof against explosive projectiles.
SHELLSHOCK, [shel'-shok'], *n.* a nervous derangement reputedly caused by the patient's having suffered the near-by explosion of a shell.
SHELL-WORK, [shel'-wurk], *n.* ornamentation made of shells.
SHELLY, [shel'-i], *adj.* abounding in shells.
SHELTA, [shel'-ta], *n.* a slang language used by Irish and Welsh vagabonds. [Uncert.].
SHELTER (1), [shel'-ter], *n.* a state of protection and safety from hurt or danger either physical or moral; that which provides such protection; a place of refuge; anything which protects; a small erection built as a refuge from danger, cold, etc.; an air-raid shelter. [OE. *sceldtruma* a shield-troop].
SHELTER (2), [shel'-ter], *v.t.* *and i.* to give shelter to, protect morally or physically, to screen; to take under one's care; to give lodging and entertainment to, *esp.* a benighted or distressed stranger; to seek or take shelter.
SHELTERER, [shelt'-er-er], *n.* one who gives or takes shelter.
SHELTERLESS, [shel'-ter-les], *adj.* lacking a shelter.
SHELTER MARSHAL, [shelt'-er-mahsh'-al], *n.* a person appointed to supervise a public air-raid shelter.
SHELTIE, SHELTY, [shel'-ti], *n.* (*Scots*) any small pony, *esp.* a Shetland pony; (*coll.*) any sort of light horse. [~ONorw. *hjalti* Shetlander].

SHELVE (1), [shelv], *v.t.* to put on a shelf; to cease to use; to put out of the way or on one side; to get rid of.
SHELVE (2), [shelv], *v.t.* to slope gently; to fit with shelves. [OE. *scelf*].
SHELVING (1), [shelv'-ing], *n.* strips of wood suitable to be employed as shelves.
SHELVING (2), [shelv'-ing], *adj.* gently sloping.
SHELVINGLY, [shelv'-ing-li], *adv.* in a gently sloping position.
SHELVY, [shel'-vi], *adj.* (of the sea or rivers) shallow, dangerous by reason of banks and reefs not far beneath the surface.
SHEMOZZLE, [shi-mozl'], *n.* (*slang*) a quarrel, a brawl. [Yiddish *schlimm mazzal* bad luck].
SHEOL, [shē'-ōl], *n.* the place of departed spirits according to Hebrew theology, hell. [Heb. *sheol*].
SHEPHERD (1), [shep'-erd], *n.* a man who tends sheep; a pastor, minister or priest; **the good S.,** Jesus Christ. [OE. *sceapherde*].
SHEPHERD (2), [shep'-erd], *v.t.* to care for, look after, protect; guide, conduct.
SHEPHERDESS, [shep'-erd-es], *n.* a female shepherd.
SHEPHERD'S-CRESS, [shep'-erdz-kres'], *n.* the plant, *Teesdalia nudicaulis*.
SHEPHERD'S-CROOK, [shep'-erdz-krŏŏk'], *n.* a shepherd's crooked staff; a sheep-hook.
SHEPHERD'S-NEEDLE, [shep'-erdz-nēdl'], *n.* a plant of the genus *Scandix*, sometimes called Venus's comb.
SHEPHERD'S-PLAID, [shep'-erdz-plad'], *n.* a woollen fabric with a black and white check pattern; any cloth with a similar pattern.
SHEPHERD'S-PURSE, [shep'-erdz-purs'], *n.* the weed, *Capsella bursa-pastoris*.
SHEPHERD'S-ROD, [shep'-erdz-rod'], *n.* a plant of the genus, *Dipsacus*, a small variety of teasel.
SHEPPEY, [shep'-i], *n.* a sheep-fold or sheepcote.
SHERATON (1), [she'-rat-on], *n.* a piece of furniture in the mode of Sheraton; that mode itself. [*Sheraton*, an 18th-century cabinet-maker].
SHERATON (2), [she'-rat-on], *adj.* in the style of furniture popularized in England by Sheraton. [*Prec.*].
SHERBET, [shur'-bet], *n.* an Oriental drink of sweetened fruit juices, cooled with snow; an effervescent beverage made by adding water to a powder containing bicarbonate of soda and tartaric acid, sweetened and flavoured in various ways. [Pers. *sharbat*].

SHEPHERD'S-PURSE

SHERD, see SHARD.
SHEREEF, SHERIF, [sher-ēf'], *n.* a descendant of Fatima, a daughter of Mohammed; **the Grand S.,** the governor of Mecca who is also guardian of the Holy Places there. [Arab. *sharif* noble].
SHEREEFIAN, SHERIFIAN, [sher-ēf'-i-an], *adj.* pertaining to a shereef.
SHERIFF, [she'-rif], *n.* the representative of the English crown in the counties of Great Britain and Ireland, now an honorary official in counties and some cities of the United Kingdom performing certain mainly judicial functions; (*Scots leg.*) a judge who presides over the Sheriff Court, sometimes referred to as Sheriff Principal to distinguish him from Sheriffs-substitute; an elected county official in the U.S.A. responsible for keeping the peace and performing certain judicial functions. [OE. *scir-gerefa*].
SHERIFF-CLERK, [she'-rif-klahk'], *n.* the clerk of the court of a Scottish sheriff.
SHERIFF COURT, [she'-rif-cawt'], *n.* an inferior court of law in Scotland which has certain limited jurisdiction in civil and criminal cases, and is presided over by a sheriff or one of his sheriffs-substitute.
SHERIFFDOM, [she'-rif-dom], *n.* the area comprising the jurisdiction of a sheriff; the office of sheriff.
SHERIFF-SUBSTITUTE, [she'-rif-sub'-sti-tewt], *n.* a deputy for a sheriff in Scotland.
SHERIFIAN, see SHEREEFIAN.
SHERRY, [she'-ri], *n.* a dry brown wine from southern Spain. [*Xeres*, now called *Jerez de la Frontera*, a Spanish town].
SHERRY-COBBLER, [she'-ri-kob'-ler], *n.* a drink made of iced sherry, lemon and sugar.
SHETH, [sheth], *n.* a strip of wood forming part of a framework. [Uncert.].
SHETLAND, [shet'-land], *n.* the name of a group of islands off the north-east of Scotland used to designate the products of these islands; **S. pony,** a dwarf pony from the Shetland islands.
SHEW, see SHOW (3).
SHEWBREAD, see SHOWBREAD.
SHIA, [shē'-ah], *n.* an adherent of that sect of the Mohammedans who believe that Ali was the prophet's true successor. [Arab. *shiça* sect].
SHIBBOLETH, [shib'-ol-eth], *n.* (*O.T.*) a word used as a means of distinguishing between Gileadites and Ephraimites, the latter being unable to pronounce the *sh* sound; any single tenet, article of faith, or formula of doctrine; an arbitrary test of conformity to any given creed. [Heb. *shibboleth* river].
SHIELD, [shēld], *n.* a piece of protective armour, varying in length and design, formerly carried on the left arm in battle; (*fig.*) any source of protection or defence; a defensive covering; any protective covering or screen; a sports trophy, often of silver or gold, usually in the shape of a shield; the base for a crest and (*pop.*) the crest itself. [~OE. *sceld*].
SHIELD-BEARER, [shēld'-bāer'-er], *n.* one who carried a knight's shield before him.
SHIELD-FERN, [shēld'-furn], *n.* the fern *Dryopteris*.
SHIELD-HAND, [shēld'-hand'], *n.* the left hand.
SHIELDLESS, [shēld'-les], *adj.* lacking any protection.
SHIELDLESSLY, [shēld'-les-li], *adv.* in a shieldless fashion.
SHIELDLESSNESS, [shēld'-les-nes], *n.* the condition of being shieldless.
SHIELDRAKE, see SHELDRAKE.
SHIELING, see SHEALING.
SHIER, [shī'-er], *n.* a horse that has a habit of shying.
SHIFT (1), [shift], *n.* a change in position, a re-arrangement; a variation in direction of advance; any change of habit, mood, work, ambition, faith, rank, etc.; a trick or expediency, a revised plan or method; work introduced to overcome hitherto unanticipated circumstances; a group of labourers working in relays with other similar groups at the same piece of work; the number of hours or period of time spent at the job by any one such group; a method of bricklaying in which the joins of one row do not come immediately above or beneath the joins of the next; a change of clothes; †an undergarment for women; (*agr.*) a rotation of crops; (*mus.*) a change in the position of the left hand when playing the violin; (*min.*) a fault; **to make a s.,** to adopt an expedient; (*coll.*) to depart, set off for somewhere else; **to get a s. on,** (*coll.*) to make a start; to begin to speed things up; **to make s. with,** to make do with, manage with, to make as good use of (something) as possible; **to make s. to,** to set about to (do something) despite difficulties; **a last s.,** a final resource. [ME. *shifte*].
SHIFT (2), [shift], *v.t. and i.* to remove, rearrange, to cause to move; to get rid of, part with, transfer; to make a move or change of position; to depart; to be unstable; to manage with, make the best of; **to let s.,** to exert no guidance over, leave to get on alone; **to s. for oneself,** to manage one's affairs and face one's difficulties without the assistance of others; **to s. in the world,** to face the problems and chances of life for oneself; **to s. along somehow,** to make the best of things, to struggle against life's difficulties not utterly without success, to succeed in just making ends meet financially. [OE. *sciftan* to divide].
SHIFTER, [shift'-er], *n.* a shifty, unreliable person; one who shifts the scenery in a theatre.
SHIFTILY, [shift'-il-i], *adv.* in a shifty fashion.
SHIFTINESS, [shift'-i-nes], *n.* the condition of being shifty; low cunning, slyness.
SHIFTING, [shift'-ing], *adj.* moving, uncertain, unstable, variable, varying.
SHIFTINGLY, [shift'-ing-li], *adv.* in a shifting or unreliable way.
SHIFTLESS, [shift'-les], *adj.* displaying no resource.
SHIFTLESSLY, [shift'-les-li], *adv.* in a shiftless way.
SHIFTLESSNESS, [shift'-les-nes], *n.* the condition or quality of being shiftless.
SHIFTY, [shift'-i], *adj.* cunning and resourceful, full of sly tricks, unreliable, deceitful, changeable.
SHIKAR, [shik-ah(r)'], *n.* big-game hunting, *esp.* in India. [Hind.].
SHIKARI, SHEKAREE, SHEKARY, [shik-ah'-ri], *n.* a native Indian hunter; a native who acts as a guide to a hunting party. [Hind.].
SHILLELAGH, [shil-ā'-la], *n.* a tough oaken cudgel. [*Shillelagh*, an Irish village in Co. Wicklow, famous for its oak trees].
SHILLING, [shil'-ing], *n.* a silver coin, worth twelve pence, one-twentieth of a pound. [OE. *scilling*].

SHILLY-SHALLY (1), [shil′-i-shal′-i], *n.* unnecessary delay; irritating, pettifogging hesitation and lack of decision. [~*Shall I? shall I?*].
SHILLY-SHALLY (2), [shil′-i-shal′-i], *v.i.* to vacillate, to fail to make up one's mind. [*Prec.*].
SHIM (1), [shim], *n.* (*agr.*) a metal implement with a wooden handle, used for scratching or turning the surface of the earth; (*eng.*) a thin piece of metal foil used for wedging up. [Unkn.].
SHIM (2), [shim], *v.t.* to wedge up; to use a shim on.
SHIMMER (1), [shim′-er], *n.* a trembling, glinting light; a gleam; glossiness.
SHIMMER (2), [shim′-er], *v.i.* to emit or reflect a quivering light; to glitter or gleam in an uncertain way. [OE. *scimrian*].
SHIMMY, [shim′-i], *n.* a kind of jazz dance. [Unkn.].
SHIN (1), [shin], *n.* the front of the leg-bone from knee to ankle; (*coll.*) a leg. [OE. *scinu*].
SHIN (2), [shin], *v.t.* and *i.* to hit on the shin; **to s. up,** to climb.
SHINDY, [shind′-i], *n.* (*slang*) disturbance, row, quarrel. [Unkn.].
SHINE (1), [shīn], *n.* glossiness, polish; **to take the s. out of,** to take the excellence from.
SHINE (2), [shīn], *n.* (*coll.*) quarrel, tumult. [Uncert.].
SHINE (3), [shīn], *v.t.* and *i.* to glow with light either by creating and emitting it or by reflecting it; to be bright and full of lustre; to have a fresh appearance of vigour and alertness both mental and physical; to be intellectually brilliant, to be eminent; to excel; to polish, rub, render glossy; **to s. at,** to excel at; **to s. out,** to become suddenly bright; to be conspicuous. [OE. *scinan*].

SHIN

SHINER, [shīn′-er], *n.* (*coll.*) a new coin.
SHINGLE (1), CHINGLE†, [shing′-gl], *n.* large loose pebbles often found in banks on the seashore. [Uncert.].
SHINGLE (2), [shing′-gl], *n.* a small rectangular piece of wood having a greater thickness at one of its edges than at the edge opposite and the surface sloping evenly between, used for roofing; a mode of hairdressing for women. [ME. *shingle* from L. *scindula*].
SHINGLE (3), [shing′-gl], *v.t.* to roof over with shingles; to cut and dress (a woman's hair) short and close to the neck and wave the hair so that the effect of the waves resembles the appearance of a roof made of shingles.
SHINGLES, (shing′-glz], *n.*(*pl.*) a painful virus disease causing an eruption on the skin above the affected nerve, often encircling the middle of the body. [~L. *cingulum* girdle].
SHINGLY, [shing′-gli], *adj.* abounding in shingles, very pebbly.
SHINING (1), [shīn′-ing], *n.* the act of glowing with light; a radiance.
SHINING (2), [shīn′-ing], *adj.* glowing with light, brilliant, gleaming; outstanding.
SHINNY, see SHINTY.
SHINTO (1), [shin′-tō], *n.* a religious faith of Japan, Shintoism; an adherent of Shintoism. [Jap. *shin to* way of the gods].
SHINTO (2), [shin′-tō], *adj.* pertaining to Shintoism, Shintoistic.
SHINTOISM, SINTOOISM, [shin′-tō-izm], *n.* the primitive and original religion of Japan, which teaches that the emperor is the descendant of the Sun and inculcates ancestor- and hero-worship.
SHINTOIST, [shin′-tō-ist], *n.* an adherent of Shintoism, a Shinto.
SHINTOISTIC, [shin′-tō-ist′-ik], *adj.* pertaining to Shintoism.
SHINTOIZE, [shin-tō′-īz], *v.t.* to convert to Shinto.
SHINTY, SHINNY, [shint′-i, shin′-i], *n.* a Scottish game similar to hockey. [Uncert.].
SHINY, [shīn′-i], *adj.* bright, glossy.
SHIP (1), [ship], *n.* a large ocean-going vessel; (*astron.*) the southern constellation, *Argo Navis*; the crew of a ship; any vessel of transport not necessarily seagoing, as an airship, aeroplane, etc.; **s. of the desert,** a camel; **when my s. comes home,** when my fortune turns, and wealth comes my way; **to take s.,** to go on board ship; **old s.,** a mariner, old salt. [OE. *scip*].
SHIP (2), [ship], *v.t.* and *i.* to transport by ship; to put on board a ship for transport; to go aboard ready for a voyage; to accept (sailors) as crew; (of seamen) to enter into an engagement to work aboard ship; **to s. off,** to send away, to transport.
SHIPBOY, [ship′-boi], *n.* a boy serving in a ship.
SHIP-BREAKER, [ship′-brāk′-er], *n.* one who purchases old and useless ships and breaks them up for materials.
SHIPBROKER, [ship′-brōk′-er], *n.* a broker who obtains cargoes for or insurance on ships.
SHIPBUILDER, [ship′-bild′-er], *n.* one who builds ships.
SHIPBUILDING, [ship′-bild′-ing], *n.* the art or practice of building ships.
SHIP-CANAL, [ship′-kan-al′], *n.* a canal big enough for sea-going vessels.
SHIP-CHANDLER, [ship′-chahnd-ler], *n.* one who supplies small necessary stores for a ship.
SHIP-CHANDLERY, [ship′-chahnd-ler-i], *n.* the business of a ship-chandler.
SHIPHOLDER, [ship′-hold-er], *n.* a shipowner.
SHIPLESS, [ship′-les], *adj.* lacking a ship.
SHIPLOAD, [ship′-lōd], *n.* the amount that one ship can carry.
SHIPMASTER, [ship′-mah-ster], *n.* the captain of a merchant vessel.
SHIPMATE, [ship′-māt], *n.* a sailor who serves with another in the same ship.
SHIPMENT, [ship′-ment], *n.* the act of taking or placing aboard ship for overseas transport; a shipload, a consignment, the quantity of goods carried in one ship on one journey.
SHIPMONEY†, [ship′-mun-i], *n.* a tax formerly levied on seaside towns and cities to provide ships for national defence.
SHIPOWNER, [ship′-ōn-er], *n.* an owner of ships.
SHIPPEN, SHIPPON, [ship′-en], *n.* a cowhouse. [OE. *scypen*].
SHIPPER, [ship′-er], *n.* one who sends goods by ship.
SHIPPING, [ship′-ing], *n.* the trade or business of overseas commerce by ship; a collection or group of ships; ships in general.
SHIPPING-MASTER, [ship′-ing-mah-ster], *n.* the official witness of the agreement between captain and crew.
SHIPPON, see SHIPPEN.
SHIPPY, [ship′-i], *adj.* pertaining to ships; seamanlike, shipshape.
SHIP-RIGGED, [ship′-rigd], *adj.* square-rigged.
SHIP'S-CARPENTER, [ships′-kah′-pent-er], *n.* a carpenter carried on board a ship as a member of the ship's complement.
SHIPSHAPE, [ship′-shāp], *adj.* being in good trim, as tidy as on board a ship.
SHIP'S-HUSBAND, [shipz′-huz′-band], *n.* the official of a company responsible for the provision of the necessary equipment, for seeing that lawful regulations are satisfied, and that all incidental financial transactions are satisfactory for and with regard to that company's ship or shipping.
SHIPWORM, [ship′-wurm], *n.* a wood-boring mollusc of the genus *Teredo*.
SHIPWRECK, [ship′-rek], *n.* the loss or damage of a ship at sea, *esp.* by collision, etc.; the broken hulk of a ship so damaged, *esp.* when left stranded upon a shoal or reef; (*fig.*) any disaster ruinous to an ambition or enterprise.
SHIPWRIGHT, [ship′-rīt], *n.* a skilled person or company engaged in the building of ships.
SHIPYARD, [ship′-yahd], *n.* a yard where ships are built.
SHIRE (1), [shīer], *n.* the former name for an English, Welsh, or Scottish county; the second element in the names of most of these counties; (*pl.*) a name given to the rest of England by the people of East Anglia, Surrey, Kent and Sussex; the fox-hunting counties of the Midlands. [OE. *scir*].
SHIRE (2), [shīer], *n.* a shire-horse.
SHIRE-HORSE, [shīer′-haws′], *n.* one of a heavily built English breed of draught horses notable for their pulling power and remarkable for a shaggy growth of hair at each fetlock.
SHIREMOTE, SHIREMOOT, [shīer′-mōt], *n.* (*hist.*) an Anglo-Saxon judicial court held shire by shire. [OE. *scirgemot*].
SHIRK (1), [shurk], *n.* a shirker.
SHIRK (2), [shurk], *v.t.* and *i.* to evade, avoid, refuse to face, *esp.* duty, danger, difficulty, etc. [*Var.* of SHARK (2)].
SHIRKER, [shurk′-er], *n.* one who will not work, one who evades responsibilities.
SHIRKING, [shurk′-ing], *n.* the act of evading or refusing to face responsibilities, etc.; idling.

SHIRKY, [shurk'-i], *adj.* liable to shirk or given to shirking.
SHIRLEY POPPY, [shurl'-i-pop'-i], *n.* a cultivated variety of the common wild poppy. [*Shirley*, Surrey, where the variety originated].
SHIRR, [shur], *n.* a pucker or gathering. [Uncert.].
SHIRT, [shurt], *n.* a loose long-sleeved undergarment worn by men; any loose garment resembling a shirt; a plain blouse for women; **stripped to the s.,** without jacket or waistcoat; (*fig.*) existing on bare necessities; **to put one's s. on,** (*fig.*) to back with everything one possesses, to give one's fullest possible support to; **to have one's s. out,** (*slang*) to be in a bad temper; **to get someone's s. up,** to annoy to the point of ill-temper; **not to have a s. to one's back,** (*fig.*) to lack even the necessities of life. [OE. *scyrte*].
SHIRTFRONT, [shurt'-frunt], *n.* the stiffened front of a shirt.
SHIRTING, [shurt'-ing], *n.* material for making shirts.
SHIRTLESS, [shurt'-les], *adj.* lacking a shirt.
SHIRT-WAIST, [shurt'-wāst], *n.* (*U.S.*) a blouse for women.
SHIRTY, [shurt'-i], *adj.* (*coll.*) angry, peevish.
SHITTAH, (*pl.* **shittim**), [shit'-ah], *n.* (*O.T.*) a sort of acacia tree from the wood of which the Ark of the Covenant was made. [Heb.].
SHITTIM, [shit'-im], *n. and adj.* (pertaining to) the wood of the shittah or acacia.
SHIVE, [shīv], *n.* (*dial.*) a slice, a splinter or fragment; a slice of bread; a bung for a cask. [ME. *shive*].
SHIVER (1), [shiv'-er], *n.* a fragment, splinter, or flake. [ME. *schivere*].
SHIVER (2), [shiv'-er], *n.* a tremor; a trembling of one's body when cold or excited, etc.; **the shivers,** repeated attacks of shivering; nervous revulsion, terror, horrified fear.
SHIVER (3), [shiv'-er], *v.t. and i.* to break into fragments or shivers; **s. my timbers,** an expression of surprise or protest.
SHIVER (4), [shiv'-er], *v.i.* to quiver and shake, as with cold, excitement, fear, etc.; *v.t.* (*naut.*) to bring (a sail) edge-on to the wind, causing it to flutter; to luff, gybe. [ME. *chiveren*].
SHIVERING (1), [shiv'-er-ing], *n.* the act of smashing to pieces.
SHIVERING (2), [shiv'-er-ing], *n.* a quivering or trembling.
SHIVERINGLY, [shiv'-er-ing-li], *adv.* with trembling and shivers.
SHIVER-SPAR, see SCHIEFER-SPAR.
SHIVERY, [shiv'-er-i], *adj.* shivering, shaking; cold enough to make one shiver.
SHOAD, SHODE, [shōd], *n.* loose pieces of the ores of tin, lead, or copper lying at or near the surface of the earth, and indicating a neighbouring lode. [~OE. *scaden* to divide].
SHOAL (1), [shōl], *n.* a large massed group of individuals, a school or bank of fish (e.g., herrings); **shoals of,** (*coll.*) plenty of. [OE. *scolu* crowd].
SHOAL (2), [shōl], *n.* a shallow place in a river or the sea, such as is caused by a deposit of sand; (*fig.*) a trap, pitfall, danger. [*Var.* of SHALLOW (2)].
SHOAL (3), [shōl], *adj.* shallow. [*Prec.*].
SHOAL (4), [shōl], *v.i.* to move or swim in a shoal or shoals; (of a river or the sea) to become shallow.
SHOALINESS, [shōl'-i-nes], *n.* the quality of being shoaly.
SHOALY, [shōl'-i], *adj.* full of shoals or shallows.
SHOAT, [shōt], *n.* (*dial.*) a young hog. [~Flem. *schote*].
SHOCK (1), [shok], *n.* a sudden violent impact or jolting producing a disturbance or overthrow of stability; a sharp and violent impact of opposing forces, a violent onset between two opposing bodies of troops; an earthquake; any event which shakes civilization; a strong emotional excitement or reaction due to some unexpected or violent circumstance; a collapse of the nervous system due to some violent or sudden experience; such an experience itself; the physical and nervous disturbance due to the passage of an electric current through an animal body. [Fr. *choc*].
SHOCK (2), [shok], *n.* a heap of twelve corn sheaves. [ME. *schokke*].
SHOCK (3), [shok], *n.* a mass of unkempt hair.
SHOCK (4), [shok], *adj.* employing, employed for, or associated with, violent physical action; **s. tactics,** tactics of violent onslaught by overwhelming numbers; **s. troops,** troops used for such tactics.
SHOCK (5), [shok], *adj.* having the nature of an unkempt mop of hair; **s.-head,** a head of shaggy, luxuriant hair.
SHOCK (6), [shok], *v.t. and i.* to cause to suffer a shock; to stagger or cause to oscillate by a violent impact; to produce a sudden instability; to overwhelm with a sudden and violent emotion, to cause great surprise to; to give grave offence to the moral opinion of; to collide with violence.
SHOCK (7), [shok], *v.t.* to arrange in shocks. [SHOCK (2)].
SHOCK-ABSORBER, [shok'-ab-sawb'-er], *n.* a device attached to the springs of a vehicle to even out the jolts and vibrations set up while the vehicle is in motion, *esp.* over uneven roads.
SHOCKER, [shock'-er], *n.* a sensational novelette with a strong story, usually of crime, horror, and detection; a melodrama.
SHOCK-HEADED, [shok'-hed'-id], *adj.* having a bushy, luxuriant head of hair.
SHOCKING, [shok'-ing], *adj.* causing repugnance, scandalous, revolting; of poor quality.
SHOCKINGLY, [shok'-ing-li], *adv.* in a shocking way; (*coll.*) outrageously.
SHOCKINGNESS, [shok'-ing-nes], *n.* the quality of being shocking.
SHOCK-PROOF, [shok'-proof], *adj.* proof against electric shocks or violent impact; (*fig.*) innured to emotional disturbance.
SHOD, [shod], *pret. and p.pt.* of SHOE (2).
SHODDY (1), [shod'-i], *n.* a coarse fabric made of worn out woollen cloth unwoven and combed out and rewoven; the fibre from which this cloth is made; (*fig.*) any cheap article made in imitation of something more valuable. [Unkn.].
SHODDY (2), [shod'-i], *adj.* made of shoddy; (of material objects) cheap, inferior in quality, not as good as appearance suggests; (of conduct) mean.
SHODE, see SHOAD.
SHOE (1), [shōō], *n.* a covering for the foot, usually of leather, distinguished from a boot in that it does not cover the ankle; a crescent-shaped strip of metal nailed to the under-side of a horse's hoof; anything resembling a shoe in shape; a holder for a brake block or lining, a brake block; **to wait for a dead man's shoes,** to wait for someone to die in the hope of obtaining his position; **to die in one's shoes,** to die in harness, at work; **to put the s. on the right foot,** to make a just accusation; **another pair of shoes,** a different set of circumstances, an entirely different position; **to stand in another man's shoes,** to enjoy the same fortune, good or bad, as someone else; to usurp or succeed to another man's honours, wealth, authority, position, problems, difficulties, etc.; **to step into someone's shoes,** to succeed to his position, favourable or unfavourable; **to shake in one's shoes,** (*fig.*) to be apprehensive, nervous, afraid; **to feel where the s. pinches,** to have experienced grief, sorrow, etc., and so be in a position to sympathize with others. [OE. *sceoh*].
SHOE (2), [shōō], *v.t.* to furnish (a horse) with shoes; to furnish (a stick, etc.) with a ferrule; to fit a wheel with an iron tyre.
SHOEBLACK, [shōō'-blak'], *n.* one who cleans boots or shoes; a black preparation used for cleaning shoes.
SHOEBRUSH, [shōō'-brush], *n.* a brush for cleaning shoes.
SHOEBUCKLE, [shōō'-bukl'], *n.* a buckle with which a shoe is fastened.
SHOEFLOWER, [shōō'-flow(er)], *n.* the plant, *Hibiscus rosa-sinensis.*
SHOEHORN, [shōō'-hawn], *n.* a horn or metal curved blade which, when placed in the back of the shoe, enables the foot to slip into it more easily.
SHOELACE, [shōō'-lās], *n.* a cord or ribbon used to lace up a shoe.
SHOELEATHER, [shōō'-leTH'-er], *n.* leather for making shoes.
SHOELESS, [shōō'-les], *adj.* lacking shoes.
SHOEMAKER, [shōō'-māk'-er], *n.* one who makes shoes, a cobbler.
SHOER, [shōō'-er], *n.* a farrier.
SHOESTRING, [shōō'-string], *n.* a shoelace.
SHOE-TIE, [shōō'-tī], *n.* a shoelace.
SHOFAR, [shōf'-ah(r)], *n.* a ram's horn trumpet. [Heb.].
SHOG (1), [shog], *n.* (*dial.*) a shock, jerk.
SHOG (2), [shog], *v.t. and i.* to shake; **to s. off,** (*dial.*) to depart. [ME. *shogge*].
SHOGUN, [shōg'-ōōn], *n.* a Japanese military chief of great power. [Jap.].
SHOLE, [shōl], *n.* a horizontal plate or plank placed beneath a vertical stake or timber to prevent it sinking into the earth and minimize gathering water. [Uncert.].

SHONE, [shon], *pret. and p.pt.* of SHINE (3).

SHOO (1), [shōō], *n.* a cry intended to frighten intruders, *esp.* animals or birds. [Imitative].

SHOO (2), [shōō], *int.* begone!

SHOO (3), [shōō], *v.i.* to make a shoo; **to s. away,** to scare, frighten off.

SHOOK (1), [shōōk], *n.* a set of staves suitable to make a barrel with; a shock of corn. [~MLGerm. *schok*].

SHOOK (2), [shōōk], *v.t.* to arrange (staves) in a shook.

SHOOK (3), [shōōk], *pret.* of SHAKE (2).

SHOON†, [shōōn], *pl.* of SHOE (1).

SHOOT (1), [shōōt], *n.* a sprout just appearing above the ground, a new growth on a plant; a jet of water; a chute; a shooting party; land over which game may be shot.

SHOOT (2), (shot), [shōōt], *v.t.* to hurl, throw or propel swiftly and suddenly forward; to dart out, send forth in flashes; to project (a missile); to discharge (a gun, rifle, etc.); to fasten (a bolt); to wound or kill with an arrow or bullet; (*naut.*) to lower into the sea; to traverse rapidly by sliding down, to pass over (rapids, etc.) in a boat; (*carp.*) to plane smoothly; *v.i.* to move rapidly, flash forth, dart about; (of a pain) to stab; to discharge a firearm; to practise the sport of shooting at game; (*football, etc.*) to aim a shot at the goal; (*cricket*) (of the ball) to leave the ground with increased speed at the first bounce; to travel along the ground after first touching it; **to s. up,** to rise sharply or suddenly up; (of children, buildings, etc.) to grow very rapidly; to fire at persons with the intent to kill them; **to s. about,** to dart hither and thither; **to s. ahead,** to outdistance competitors; **to s. down,** to kill with firearms, to massacre; **to s. off,** to depart suddenly; to deflect suddenly from a previous line of advance; **to s. home,** to hit the mark; to make a penetrating observation; **to s. beside the mark,** (*fig.*) to miss the point; (*coll.*) **to s. out one's neck,** to air one's views volubly and unasked; **to s. the moon,** to remove by night from a rented dwelling to avoid paying the rent; **to s. the gulf,** (*fig.*) to pass successfully through a difficulty; **to s. one's (last) bolt,** to exhaust one's capabilities; **to s. a scene,** to film a scene. [OE. *sceotan*].

SHOOTABLE, [shōōt'-abl], *adj.* able to be shot.

SHOOTER, [shōōt'-er], *n.* one who shoots; a ball at cricket that keeps low and does not bounce.

SHOOTING, [shōōt'-ing], *n.* the action of one who shoots; the pursuit of game with firearms; land over which game may be shot; the pursuit of this sport.

SHOOTING-BOOTS, [shōōt'-ing-bōōts'], *n.(pl.)* strong boots worn on a shooting expedition.

SHOOTING-BOX, [shōōt'-ing-boks'], *n.* a small house with good shooting land round it.

SHOOTING-GALLERY, [shōōt'-ing-gal'-er-i], *n.* a miniature shooting-range.

SHOOTING-RANGE, [shōōt'-ing-rānj'], *n.* a place for practice at shooting.

SHOOTING-STAR, [shōōt'-ing-stah(r)'], *n.* a star-like meteor that flashes across the sky.

SHOOTING-STICK, [shōōt'-ing-stik'], *n.* (*print.*) the stick with which quoins are driven into place; a walking-stick convertible into a seat used during a shoot.

SHOP (1), [shop], *n.* the room or building where retail trade is conducted; a workshop; (*slang*) any building; **to talk s.,** to converse on or discuss one's business; **all over the s.,** in great disorder; **to set up s.,** to commence a retail business; **to shut (up) s.,** to close (one's business) either permanently or temporarily; (*fig.*) to desist from any given activity. [OE. *sceoppa* booth].

SHOP (2), [shop], *v.t.* to cause to be put in prison; *v.i.* to visit shops or stores to make purchases.

SHOP-ASSISTANT, [shop'-as-is'-tant], *n.* a salesman (or woman) in a retail shop.

SHOP-BELL, [shop'-bel'], *n.* a bell that rings whenever the shop door is opened.

SHOP-BOARD, [shop'-bawd], *n.* a counter in a shop.

SHOP-BOY, [shop'-boi], *n.* a boy working in a shop.

SHOP-GIRL, [shop'-gurl], *n.* a girl working in a shop.

SHOPKEEPER, [shop'-kēp'-er], *n.* the proprietor of a retail shop.

SHOPLIFTER, [shop'-lift'-er], *n.* one who steals goods from a shop when it is open.

SHOPLIFTING, [shop'-lift'-ing], *n.* the act of stealing from a shop when it is open.

SHOPMAN, [shop'-man], *n.* a man who keeps a shop or works in a shop.

SHOPPING, [shop'-ing], *n.* the act of making purchases in a shop; goods purchased at a shop.

SHOPSOILED, [shop'-soild], *adj.* faded, soiled or damaged as a result of being displayed or handled.

SHOPWALKER, [shop'-wawk'-er], *n.* one who walks about a large shop or store to guide customers and see that the assistants attend to them properly.

SHOPWOMAN, [shop'-wōōm'-an], *n.* a woman working in or owning a shop.

SHORE (1), [shaw(r)], *n.* that part of the land immediately adjacent to the sea or to a lake or estuary; **on s.,** ashore, on the land; moving towards the land; **in s.,** (*naut.*) near to the shore. [ME. *schore*].

SHORE (2), [shaw(r)], *n.* a large, heavy supporting prop. [ME. *schore*].

SHORE (3), [shaw(r)], *v.t.* to support with shores.

SHORE† (4), [shaw(r)], *pret.* of SHEAR.

SHORE-LARK, [shaw(r)'-lahk], *n.* the bird, *Otocorus alpestris*.

SHORELESS, [shaw(r)'-les], *adj.* having no shore or coast; boundless.

SHORELING, SHORLING, [shaw(r)'-ling], *n.* a newly shorn sheep.

SHORE-PIPIT, [shaw(r)'-pip-it], *n.* the pipit, *Anthus obscurus*.

SHOREWARD, [shaw(r)'-werd], *adv.* in the direction of the shore.

SHOREWEED, [shaw(r)'-wēd], *n.* the plant, *Littorella lacustris*.

SHORING, [shawr'-ing], *n.* beams suitable for use as shores.

SHORE-PIPIT

SHORL, see SCHORL.

SHORLING, see SHORELING.

SHORN, [shawn], *p.pt.* of SHEAR (2).

SHORT (1), [shawt], *n.* anything that is short, short things or persons in general; a short film; **the long and the s. of it,** the essential point, the net result; **for s.,** by way of abbreviation.

SHORT (2), [shawt], *adj.* of no great length or extension; not tall, of no great height; brief in duration; concise, curt; of reduced or inadequate amount, not up to standard; inadequately supplied; (*coll.*) inadequately supplied with money; on the verge of exhaustion, almost gone; (*comm.*) (of a bill, etc.) maturing at an early date; (of pastry) crumbly; (*pros.*) not long, unstressed; **s. commons,** low rations; **s. weight,** inadequate weight, or less than the stated amount according to weight; **s. measure,** less than the stated quantity; **s. story,** a piece of fiction dealing with one phase or incident, or at least with a small and compact theme, longer than an anecdote but much shorter than a novel; **s. cut,** a quick route, a route taking less time than a more orthodox one; **s. temper,** a testy irritable disposition; **s. term,** (of a policy) giving quick results at the possible expense of later ones; (of a loan) repayable within a short time; **s. sight,** myopia, inability to see distant objects; **s. ball,** (*cricket*) a ball bowled so as not to pitch close enough to the wicket; **to make s. work of,** to dispense with quickly, to consume, perform, etc., rapidly; **nothing s. of,** quite, truly; **s. sea,** a choppy sea; **s. shrift,** brusque attention. [OE. *sceort*].

SHORT (3), [shawt], *adv.* in a short manner, shortly; abruptly; **s. of,** except; **to fall s.,** to be inadequate; **to fall s. of,** not to come up to the standard of; **to cut (someone) s.,** to interrupt in speech; **to run s.,** to approach exhaustion; **to stop s.,** to come to a sudden cessation; to cause to come to a sudden cessation; **to stop s. of (something),** to do everything else except . . . .

SHORT (4), [shawt], *v.t.* (*elect.*) to cause a short-circuit; *v.i.* to become short-circuited.

SHORTAGE, [shawt'-ij], *n.* lack, deficiency.

SHORTBREAD, [shawt'-bred], *n.* shortcake.

SHORTCAKE, [shawt'-kāk], *n.* a brittle kind of cake made of flour, sugar, and butter; shortbread.

SHORT-CIRCUIT (1), [shawt'-sur'-kit], *n.* a path, other than that intended, taken by an electric current; a closed electric circuit offering negligible resistance to the passage of a current.

SHORT-CIRCUIT (2), [shawt'-sur'-kit], *v.t. and i.* to cause (an electric current) to take a short-circuit; (*fig.*) to adopt briefer methods for in place of orthodox procedure.

SHORTCOMING, [shawt'-kum-ing], *n.* deficiency, failure to meet a required standard; a foible; an imperfection.

SHORT-DATED, [shawt'-dāt'-id], *adj.* (*comm.*) maturing early, payable soon.

SHORTEN, [shawt'-en], *v.t. and i.* to reduce in extent

in length or time, to abbreviate, cut down; to become shorter; to dress (a child) in shorter clothes.

SHORTHAND, [shawt'-hand'], *n.* a system of rapid writing based on the substitution of symbols or contractions for sounds, words or phrases; stenography.

SHORT-HANDED, [shawt'-hand'-id], *adj.* under-staffed.

SHORT HEAD, [shawt'-hed'], *n.* the amount, less than the length of its head, by which a racehorse, or greyhound, reaches the winning-post ahead of the next horse or greyhound; also (*fig.*) (*coll.*) a bare margin.

SHORTHORN, [shawt'-hawn], *n.* a breed of short-horned cattle.

SHORT-HORNED, [shawt'-hawnd'], *adj.* with short horns.

SHORT-HOSE, [shawt'-hōz'], *n.* stockings reaching to only just below the knee.

SHORT-LEG, [shawt'-leg'], *n.* (*cricket*) a position close in on the leg-side; the man fielding there.

SHORTLIVED, [shawt'-livd'], *adj.* being of brief duration, not surviving for long.

SHORTLY, [shawt'-li], *adv.* soon; briefly; curtly.

SHORTNESS, [shawt'-nes], *n.* the quality of being short.

SHORT-RIB, [shawt'-rib'], *n.* a false rib.

SHORTS (1), [shawts], *n.*(*pl.*) short trousers ending just above the knee.

SHORTS (2), [shawts], *n.*(*pl.*) a less coarse sort of bran.

SHORT SIGHT, [shawt'-sīt'], *n.* a defect of vision by which distant objects are seen less clearly, and near objects more clearly, than is normal.

SHORT-SIGHTED, [shawt'-sīt'-id], *adj.* suffering from short sight, myopic; (*fig.*) lacking in imagination, unable to anticipate future circumstances.

SHORT-SIGHTEDLY, [shawt'-sīt'-ed-li], *adv.* in short-sighted fashion.

SHORT-SIGHTEDNESS, [shawt'-sīt'-id-nes], *n.* the condition of being short-sighted; myopia.

SHORT-SLIP, [shawt'-slip'], *n.* (*cricket*) a position in the slips close in to the wicket; the man fielding there.

SHORT-SPOKEN, [shawt'-spōk'-en], *adj.* curt, brusque.

SHORT-SUITED, [shawt'-sōōt'-ed], *adj.* (*cards*) having a relatively small number of cards of a particular suit.

SHORT-TEMPERED, [shawt'-temp'-erd], *adj.* irritable, peevish, easily annoyed and made cross.

SHORT-WAISTED, [shawt'-wāst'-id], *adj.* (of persons) not long in the waist; (of clothes) cut so as to give the impression of a short waist.

SHORT-WINDED, [shawt'-wind'-id], *adj.* subject to shortness of breath.

SHOT (1), [shot], *n.* a missile suitable to be projected from a gun, rifle, pistol, etc.; one of the small leaden pellets fired from a sporting gun, a quantity of these; the sound or act of shooting a firearm; an attempt to hit with some sort of missile; a stroke at a game, *esp.* billiards, cricket, tennis, or football; an injected dose of a drug; (*mining*) a charge of explosive for blasting; an explosion of this; one who shoots; (*cinema*) the photographing of a scene in a film; the scene so photographed; **dead s.,** a man who never misses; **in s.,** in range of fire; **out of s.,** out of range of fire; **pot-s.,** an easy shot that could not possibly miss; a bird in flight; **s. in the dark,** a random attempt; **to have a s. at,** make an attempt, guess; **to put the s.,** to throw a weight or shot; **s. in the locker,** a reserve of ability, ready cash; **like a s.,** very rapidly; **not by a long s.,** (*coll.*) by no means, not at all; **big s.,** (*coll.*) an important person. [OE. *gesceot*].

SHOT (2), (shot), *n.* contribution, share of payment; **to pay one's s.,** to pay one's share of the expenses. [~SCOT].

SHOT (3), [shot], *adj.* fashioned so that the colour changes according to the angle from which viewed; (*fig.*) commingled. [SHOOT (4)].

SHOT (4), [shot], *pret. and p.pt.* of SHOOT (2).

SHOTBELT, [shot'-belt'], *n.* a belt across the shoulder for holding shot.

SHOTFREE, [shot'-frē], *adj.* scot-free.

SHOTGAUGE, [shot'-gāj], *n.* a device for gauging the diameter of shot.

SHOTGUN, [shot'-gun], *n.* a sporting gun which discharges shot, a fowling-piece.

SHOT-HOLE, [shot'-hōl], *n.* a hole made by a bullet, a bullet hole.

SHOTPROOF, [shot'-prōōf], *adj.* impenetrable by shot.

SHOTTEN†, [shot'-en], *adj.* (of fish) having ejected or shot its spawn; (*fig.*) emaciated, sour.

SHOT-TOWER, [shot'-tow'-er], *n.* a high round tower in which molten lead is dropped from the top to the bottom through a sieve so that the lead falls in round pellets at the bottom.

SHOUGH†, [shuf], *n.* a sort of lap-dog.

SHOULD, [shŏŏd], *pret.* of SHALL, expressing probability, intention and obligation, and used in forming the conditional mood.

SHOULDER (1), [shōld'-er], *n.* either of the two projections on the body of an animal below or behind the neck and from which depend the arms or forelegs; (butchering) the upper part of an animal's foreleg; anything resembling a shoulder; **to put one's s. to the wheel,** to make a vigorous effort; **s. to s.,** united, together; **to give the cold s. to,** to act unsociably towards, avoid. [OE. *sculdor*].

SHOULDER (2), [shōld'-er], *v.t.* to place on the shoulders ready to carry; (*fig.*) to undertake; to push with the shoulder, to make a path for oneself by pushing with one's shoulder; **to s. arms,** (*milit.*) to place one's rifle muzzle upward on the right shoulder, the stock being held by the right hand.

SHOULDER-BELT, [shōld'-er-belt'], *n.* a belt that passes over one shoulder, a baldrick.

SHOULDER-BLADE, [shōld'-er-blād], *n.* one of the two large flat triangular bones of the shoulder.

SHOULDER-BONE, [shōld'-er-bōn], *n.* the shoulder-blade.

SHOULDER-KNOT, [shōld'-er-not], *n.* a knot of ribbon or lace worn on the shoulder in certain uniforms.

SHOULDER-SHOTTEN, [shōld'-er-shot'-en], *adj.* (of a horse, etc.) having strained its shoulder.

SHOULDER-STRAP, [shōld'-er-strap'], *n.* a length of leather or other material attached to a bag, etc. for carrying it over the shoulder(s); (*milit.*) a small strap extending from the base of the collar to the point of the shoulder in officers' uniforms and bearing the officer's badge of rank; a tape or ribbon to support neckless garments from the shoulders.

SHOULDER-WASHER, [shōld'-er-wosh'-er], *n.* a washer set between wheel and axle-tree.

SHOUT (1), [showt], *n.* a loud vocal utterance, an outcry or bawling; a sudden cry.

SHOUT (2), [showt], *v.t. and i.* to emit a loud cry, to call; to speak in a very loud voice, to bawl; to utter very loudly; **to s. down,** to drown someone else's words by bawling or speaking more loudly; **s. at,** to demand attention, insist on being noticed. [ME. *shouten*].

SHOUTER, [showt'-er], *n.* one who shouts.

SHOVE (1), [shuv], *n.* the action of shoving.

SHOVE (2), [shuv], *v.t. and i.* to inflict a rough push or thrust on; to push or jostle roughly; (*coll.*) to put or place; **to s. off,** to push away from the shore in a boat; (*coll.*) to depart. [OE. *scufan*].

SHOVE-HALFPENNY, [shuv'-hāp'-en-i], *n.* the game of shovel-board. [SHOVE (2) and HALFPENNY].

SHOVEL (1), [shuv'-el], *n.* a spade-like implement used to move loose hard material; any similar implement, a scoop. [OE. *scofl*].

SHOVEL (2), [shuv'-el], *adj.* resembling, pertaining to, a shovel; **s. hat,** a flat clerical hat.

SHOVEL (3), [shuv'-el], *v.t. and i.* to use a shovel, to move with a shovel; **to s. in,** to collect quickly, gain rapid possession of.

SHOVEL-BOARD, SHUFFLE-BOARD, [shuv'-el-bawd'], *n.* a game played by sliding coins along a marked board; the board on which this is played; a similar game played on the deck of a ship with disks moved by cues across chalk-marked divisions.

SHOVELFUL, [shuv'-el-fŏŏl], *n.* as much as may be held on a shovel.

SHOVELLER, [shuv'-el-er], *n.* one who shovels; a freshwater broad-billed duck of the genus *Spatula.*

SHOVELLER

SHOW (1), [shō], *n.* a display or exhibition; something displayed or exhibited; something which attracts attention, a spectacle, an object of interest; anything presenting itself to the view; (*slang*) any institution or organization; a theatrical performance; pomp, worthless ceremony; a false appearance, a pretence; sign, vestige, trace, appearance; **a s. of hands,** a vote taken by raising hands.

SHOW (2), [shō], *adj.* (*coll.*) fit for display, surpassingly excellent; **a s. piece,** a piece of work fit for exhibition.

SHOW (3), SHEW, [shō], *v.t. and i.* to present to view, allow to be seen; to offer proof of, explain; to guide to; to be or become visible; **to s. off,** to display, *esp.* in an extravagant manner; **to s. out,** to guide to the exit; **to s. up,** to reveal, *esp.* that which has been wrongly hidden; to expose the character of; **to s. (someone) the door,** to give a broad hint to leave; **to s. one's mind,** to reveal one's opinion; **to s. one's hand,** to declare one's intentions; **to s. fight,** to display an inclination to fight, to resist. [OE. *sceawian* to examine].

SHOWBILL, [shō'-bil], *n.* a broad-sheet advertisement, *esp.* of a theatrical entertainment, a playbill.

SHOW-BOAT, [shō'-bōt'], *n.* (*U.S. slang*) a large river boat in which theatrical performances, *esp.* of a light kind, are given.

SHOW-BOX, [shō'-boks'], *n.* a case containing exhibits on display.

SHOWBREAD, SHEWBREAD, [shō'-bred'], *n.* twelve loaves placed by a Jewish priest on the golden table in the sanctuary as an offering to God.

SHOWCARD, [show'-kahd'], *n.* a large card used for advertisement.

SHOW-CASE, [shō'-kās'], *n.* a case containing articles for exhibition.

SHOWDOWN, [shō'-down], *n.* (*cards*) the laying down of everybody's cards on the table; a deliberate disclosure of their intentions by the conflicting parties in a dispute; open conflict; exposure.

SHOWER (1), [show(e)r], *n.* a light or brief fall of rain, snow, hail, etc.; a sprinkling; a massed and copious flood or discharge of missiles, liquids, dust or falling or projected objects of any kind; a rapid succession of things arriving. [OE. *scur*].

SHOWER (2), [show(e)r], *v.t. and i.* to discharge in a shower; to arrive in a shower; to give or bestow copiously and constantly.

SHOWER-BATH, [show(e)r'-bahth'], *n.* a bath in which water is showered from above.

SHOWERINESS, [show'-er-i-nes], *n.* the quality of being showery.

SHOWERLESS, [show'-er-les], *adj.* lacking showers.

SHOWERY, [show'-er-i], *adj.* tending to rain in showers.

SHOW-GIRL, [shō'-gurl'], *n.* an actress engaged rather for her beauty than her histrionic ability.

SHOWILY, [shō'-i-li], *adv.* in a showy fashion.

SHOWING, [shō'-ing], *n.* the act of presenting to the view; one in a series of identical cinema programmes.

SHOWMAN, [shō'-man], *n.* the exhibitor of a show, one who arranges an exhibition; one skilled in making an impression on his audience.

SHOWMANSHIP, [shō'-man-ship], *n.* skill as a showman.

SHOWN, [shōn], *p.pt.* of SHOW (3).

SHOW-PLACE, [shō'-plās], *n.* a place much resorted to by tourists because of its sights.

SHOW-ROOM, [shō'-rōōm], *n.* a room where wares are exhibited for sale.

SHOWY, [shō'-i], *adj.* pretentious, ostentatious, gaudy.

SHOWYARD, [shō'-yahd], *n.* an enclosure where cattle or horses are exhibited.

SHRANK, [shrangk], *pret.* of SHRINK.

SHRAPNEL, [shrap'-nel], *n.* a shell that explodes and scatters pieces of metal and bullets in all directions; the pieces so scattered. [General *Shrapnel*, the inventor].

SHRED (1), [shred], *n.* a small fragment, a strip torn or cut off; (*fig.*) a particle, fragment. [OE. *scread*].

SHRED (2), [shred], *v.t. and i.* to tear or cut into shreds; to flake, break up into shreds.

SHREDDING, [shred'-ing], *n.* that which is torn or cut off in shreds, fragments, shredded pieces.

SHREDDY, [shred'-i], *adj.* consisting of shreds.

SHREDLESS, [shred'-les], *adj.* without shreds.

SHREW, [shrōō], *n.* a nagging, ill-tempered woman, a scold; a shrew-mouse. [OE. *screawa* shrew-mouse].

SHREWD, [shrōōd], *adj.* sharp-witted, cunning, sagacious; piercing; †malicious, ill-tempered, shrewish. [ME. *shrewed* cursed].

SHREWDLY, [shrōōd'-li], *adv.* in a shrewd fashion.

SHREWDNESS, [shrōōd'-nes], *n.* the quality of being shrewd; sagacity.

SHREWISH, [shrōō'-ish], *adj.* of, or like, a shrew; cross-tempered.

SHREW-MOLE, [shrōō'-mōl], *n.* a small, mole-like animal of the genus *Urotrichus*, the mole shrew.

SHREW-MOUSE, [shrōō'-mows], *n.* a small brownish insectivore of the genus *Sorex*, resembling a mouse in appearance.

SHRIEK (1), [shrēk], *n.* a sudden shrill and piercing cry of alarm, pain or laughter; a shrill sound.

SHRIEK (2), [shrēk], *v.t. and i.* to utter a sudden, loud, shrill, piercing cry, to scream; to utter in shrieking tones; **to s. with laughter,** to laugh with loud and uncontrolled mirth; to laugh hysterically. [ME. *schriken*].

SHRIEKER, [shrēk'-er], *n.* one who shrieks.

SHRIEVALTY, [shrēv'-al-ti], *n.* the office, dignity or jurisdiction of a sheriff.

SHRIFT, [shrift], *n.* confession and absolution; **short s.,** (*fig.*) brief and inadequate attention, curt treatment. [OE. *scrift*].

SHRIKE, [shrīk], *n.* any one of the butcher-birds of the genus *Lanius*. [OScand. *skrikja*].

SHRIKE

SHRILL (1), [shril], *adj.* (of a sound) high-pitched, sharp and penetrating; (*fig.*) complaining and insistent. [ME. *schrill*].

SHRILL (2), [shril], *v.t. and i.* to utter a shrill cry; to make a shrill sound. [ME. *schrillrn*].

SHRILLNESS, [shril'-nes], *n.* acuteness of sound, the condition of being shrill.

SHRILL-TONGUED, [shril'-tungd'], *adj.* having a shrill voice, angry, quarrelsome.

SHRILLY, [shril'-i], *adv.* in a shrill fashion.

SHRIMP (1), [shrimp], *n.* a small, slender, long-legged crustacean with a long tail, of the genus *Crangon*, the common shrimp, found about the English coast and commonly used for food; (*fig.*) a little man, a little person, any little thing; a pale pink colour like that of a boiled shrimp. [ME. *schrimpe*].

SHRIMP (2), [shrimp], *v.i.* to go fishing for shrimps.

SHRIMPER, [shrimp'-er], *n.* one who fishes for shrimps; a boat used for shrimp-fishing.

SHRIMP-NET, [shrimp'-net'], *n.* a net used for shrimp-fishing.

SHRINE (1), [shrīn], *n.* an ornamental casket containing holy objects, relics, etc.; the tomb of a martyr or saint; a holy place; an object of pilgrimage; any place or object rendered precious by its associations. [OE. *scrin* from L. *scrinium*].

SHRINE (2), [shrīn], *v.t.* to enshrine.

SHRINK, [shringk], *v.t. and i.* to become less in size; to cause to become smaller; to cower; **to s. away,** to diminish gradually; **to s. away from, to s. from, to s. back from,** to draw back from, withdraw from. [OE. *scrincan*].

SHRINKAGE, [shringk'-ij], *n.* contraction in bulk or area; the act of shrinking.

SHRINKER, [shringk'-er], *n.* one who shrinks, a nervous person.

SHRINKINGLY, [shringk'-ing-li], *adv.* with contraction; nervously.

SHRIVE, [shrīv], *v.t.* to hear the confession of and give absolution to. [OE. *scrifan*].

SHRIVEL, [shrivl], *v.t. and i.* to wrinkle up, shrink; to cause to contract and wrinkle. [Unkn.].

SHROFF, [shrof], *n.* an Oriental money-changer, *esp.* a man skilled in testing good and bad coinage. [Arab. *çarraf*].

SHROFFAGE, [shrof'-ij], *n.* the art of testing good or bad coins.

SHROUD (1), [shrowd], *n.* a burial cloth, a winding-sheet; (*fig.*) anything that envelops, covers, or conceals; (*pl.*) (*naut.*) a set of stays connecting the mast-head with the bulwarks of a ship, a ship's rigging. [OE. *scrud* garment].

SHROUD (2), [shrowd], *v.t.* to wrap in a shroud; (*fig.*) to cover up, conceal.

SHROUD-LAID, [shrowd'-lād], *adj.* consisting of four strands twisted about a core.

SHROUDLESS, [shrowd'-les], *adj.* without shrouds.

SHROVE-TIDE, [shrōv'-tīd], *n.* the four days before Ash Wednesday (the first day of Lent) ending with Shrove Tuesday, a time for making confessions in preparation for Lent. [~SHRIVE].

SHROVE TUESDAY, [shrōv'-tews'-di], *n.* the last day of Shrove-tide, the day before Ash Wednesday.

SHROVING, [shrōv'-ing], *n.* the celebrations and festivities of Shrove-tide, as the last period for merry-making before the long fast of Lent.

SHRUB (1), [shrub], *n.* a low, tree-like plant or bush. [ME. *schrub*].

SHRUB (2), [shrub], *n.* a drink of fruit-juice, usually lemon juice, mixed with sugar and rum. [Arab. *sharab* a drink].

SHRUBBERY, [shrub'-er-i], *n.* a plantation of shrubs.

SHRUBBINESS, [shrub'-i-nes], *n.* the condition of being shrubby.

SHRUBBY, [shrub'-i], *adj.* full of shrubs; resembling a shrub.

SHRUBLESS, [shrub'-les], *adj.* without any shrubs.

SHRUG (1), [shrug], *n.* the act of shrugging the shoulders.

SHRUG (2), [shrug], *v.t.* (of the shoulders) to raise or hunch up a little to express doubt, indifference, or disapproval. [Unkn.].

SHRUNK, [shrungk], *p.pt.* of SHRINK.

SHRUNKEN, [shrung'-ken], *adj.* shrivelled, contracted, withered. [SHRINK].

SHUCK, [shuk], *n.* a husk, pod, or covering; (*pl.*) (*U.S.*) nonsense! [Unkn.].

SHUDDER (1), [shud'-er], *n.* an intense trembling expressing disgust or terror or excessive chill; a spasmodic vibration.

SHUDDER (2), [shud'-er], *v.i.* to tremble violently; to shake with disgust, terror or excessive chill, etc.; (*fig.*) to shake or vibrate spasmodically. [ME. *schuderen*].

SHUDDERING, [shud'-er-ing], *adj.* quaking with fear or horror.

SHUDDERINGLY, [shud'-er-ing-li], *adv.* with shudders.

SHUFFLE (1), [shufl], *n.* the action of shuffling; the act of mixing playing cards, etc.; the act of shuffling the feet; the act of fidgeting in one's chair, a step in dancing consisting of a quick backward and forward drag first on one foot and then on the other; a trick, lie, swindle.

SHUFFLE (2), [shufl], *v.t. and i.* to walk scraping the feet on the ground without lifting them; to fidget in one's seat; to move (something) about in a purposeless fashion; to mix playing cards before a game; to mix promiscuously and incongruously; to act or speak evasively, to boggle; **to s. off,** to depart with a shuffling, ungainly walk, to wriggle out of; **to s. out of,** to avoid by devious means. [LGerm. *schuffeln*].

SHUFFLE-BOARD, see SHOVEL-BOARD.

SHUFFLE-CAP, [shufl'-cap'], *n.* a game played by shaking up money in a cap.

SHUFFLER, [shuf'-ler], *n.* one who shuffles; a trickster.

SHUFFLE-WING, [shufl'-wing], *n.* the hedge-sparrow.

SHUFFLING, [shuf'-ling], *adj.* evasive, sly.

SHUFFLINGLY, [shuf'-ling-li], *adv.* evasively, slyly.

SHUN, [shun], *v.t.* to avoid, turn away from, have nothing to do with. [OE. *scunian*].

'SHUN, [shun], *imper.* attention! a word of command in drill. [Short form of ATTENTION].

SHUNT (1), [shunt], *n.* the act of shunting or being shunted; an alternative circuit for an electric current; a switch by which an electric current may be diverted over such a circuit.

SHUNT (2), [shunt], *v.t. and i.* to divert, switch off on to another track, to turn (rolling-stock) on a railway from one track to another; to provide an alternative track for (an electric current); (*coll.*) to push aside, shelve, get rid of; **to s. off,** (*coll.*) to depart or cause to depart. [Unkn.].

SHUNTER, [shunt'-er], *n.* a person employed in shunting on a railway.

SHUT (1), (shutting, shut), [shut], *v.t.* (of a door, gate, window, lid, etc.) to close; to place in such a position that it blocks the aperture or passage which it commands; to cover with a lid; (of a drawer) to thrust home so that the interior is not accessible unless the drawer be reopened; (of an aperture, etc.) to block with something; to fold up; to encase with an outer covering; to lock up; to bring to an end; *v.i.* to close of its own accord or by some concealed mechanism; to be capable of being closed; **to s. off,** to cut off, sever from things beyond, to prevent egress by or from, or contact with, to separate from; **to s. down,** to close by a downward movement; to bring to an end, to close down (a factory, etc.); **to s. out,** to keep outside by shutting, to exclude from entrance; to hide from view; **to s. up,** to shut completely, lock up (a building) so that no one can get in or out, to fold up into a shut or closed position; to store or place for storage in a closed receptacle; to confine in close quarters; to seal, close permanently; (*coll.*) to cease speaking; **to s. one's eyes to,** to ignore, refuse to consider; **to s. one's mouth,** to refuse to speak, keep silent; **to s. someone else's mouth,** to induce or compel silence. [OE. *scyttan* to shoot a bolt].

SHUT (2), [shut], *adj.* closed; **to be s. of,** to be no longer troubled with, to be rid of.

SHUTTER (1), [shut'-er], *n.* something that shuts; a hinged outer covering of wood for a window; (*phot.*) a small movable screen in a camera that makes the exposure.

SHUTTER (2), [shut'-er], *v.t.* to fit or close with a shutter.

SHUTTERLESS, [shut'-er-les], *adj.* having no shutter.

SHUTTLE, [shutl], *n.* (*weaving*) a small instrument, usually of metal or wood, which carries the weft thread and is shot to and fro between the warp in a loom; a sliding thread-holder that carries the under-thread in a sewing-machine; **s. train,** a train running up and down a short branch line; **s. service,** a service operating to and fro on one line. [OE. *scytel* a bolt].

SHUTTLE-COCK, [shutl'-kok'], *n.* a ball of cork fitted with evenly spaced feathers, the points of which are stuck into the ball and splayed outwards and upwards.

SHWANPAN, see SWANPAN.

SHY (1), [shī], *n.* (of a horse) the act of shying.

SHY (2), [shī], *n.* (*coll.*) a throw; (*coll.*) an attempt.

SHY (3), [shī], *adj.* timid, nervous, self-conscious, bashful; expressing or suggesting shyness. [OE. *sceoh*].

SHY (4), [shī], *v.i.* (of a horse) to swerve nervously aside; **to s. at,** (of a horse) to swerve nervously away from; (of persons) to be unwilling to face or do (something), to have scruples about.

SHY (5), [shī], *v.t. and i.* (*coll.*) to throw. [Unkn.].

SHYER, [shī'-er], *n.* a horse given to shying.

SHYLY, [shī'-li], *adv.* in a shy way.

SHYNESS, [shī'-nes], *n.* the condition or quality of being shy.

SHYSTER, [shī'-ster], *n.* (*U.S. slang*) a lawyer; a rogue. [Germ. *schiesce*].

SI, [sē], *n.* (*mus.*) in the sol-fa system the seventh note of the diatonic scale. [Invented].

SIAMANG, [sē'-am-ang], *n.* a species of black-haired ape found in Malay and Sumatra. [Malay *siamang*].

SIAMESE (1), [sī'-am-ēz], *n.* an inhabitant of Siam; the language of Siam.

SIAMESE (2), [sī'-am-ēz], *adj.* pertaining to Siam; **S. cat,** a breed of cat from Siam; **S. twins,** twins born imperfectly separated.

SIB, [sib], *n. and adj.* a close blood-relation or relationship; closely related by blood. [OE. *sib*].

SIBERIAN, [si-bēer'-i-an], *adj.* of, pertaining or relating to, originating from, Siberia.

SIBERITE, [sib'-er-īt], *n.* rubellite, a red variety of tourmaline. [*Siberia*, where found].

SIBILANCE, [sib'-il-ants], *n.* the condition or quality of being sibilant.

SIBILANCY, [sib'-il-an-si], *n.* sibilance.

SIBILANT (1), [sib'-il-ant], *n.* a hissing sound; (*phon.*) a sound produced by the rapid passage of air between the raised tip of the tongue and the upper teeth or the alveolar ridge.

SIBILANT (2), [sib'-il-ant], *adj.* hissing; uttered with a hissing sound. [L. *sibilans*].

SIBILATE, [sib'-il-āt], *v.t.* to utter with a hiss, to make a hissing sound. [L. *sibilare* to hiss].

SIBILATION, [sib'-il-ā'-shun], *n.* the act of sibilating.

SIBLING, (sib'-ling), *n.* a sib.

SIBYL, [sib'-il], *n.* one of certain women in classical times reputed to possess gifts of prophecy and divination; a prophetess, a witch. [Gk. *sibulla*].

SIBYLLINE, [sib-il'-īn], *adj.* pertaining to sibyls; **the S. Books,** a collection of prophecies of the fate of Rome which, according to legend, were sold by the Sibyl of Cumae to Tarquin the Proud.

SIC, [sik], *adv.* thus (usually printed in brackets after a word or phrase quoted which is, or looks as if it is, a mistake). [L. *sic* so, thus].

SICCA, [sik'-ah], *n.* a coin that is new and not much worn and therefore of greater value than those that have been a long while in circulation. [Arab. *sikkah* die for coining].

SICE (1), SYCE, SAYCE, etc., [sīs], *n.* an Indian groom. [Hind. *sayis*].

SICE (2), SISE, SIZE, [sīz], *n.* six on a dice. [OFr. *sis* six].

SICELIOT (1), SIKELIOT, [sis-el'-i-ot], *n.* one of the settlers in the first Greek settlement of Sicily in classical times. [Gk. *sikeliotes*].

SICELIOT (2), SIKELIOT, [sis-el'-i-ot], *adj.* pertaining to the Siceliots.

SICILIAN (1), [sis-il'-i-an], *n.* an inhabitant of Sicily.

SICILIAN (2), [sis-il'-i-an], *adj.* pertaining to Sicily.

SICILIANA, [sich-il'-i-ahn'-a], *n.* a peasant dance of Sicily; a piece of music composed for, or as if for, this dance. [It. *(danza) siciliana*].
SICK (1), [sik], *n.(pl.)* sick persons.
SICK (2), [sik], *adj.* in bad health, suffering from a disease or illness, ill; vomiting, tending to vomit; *(coll.)* disgusted, exasperated, put out, disappointed; weary, bored; **s. at heart,** dejected; **s. for,** longing for, dejected with desire for; **to be s.,** to vomit; to be ill; **to look s.,** *(coll.)* to have a look of disgust, annoyance, disappointment etc.; **s. benefit,** allowance made to a worker or member of a benefit club when sick; **s. leave,** leave granted for medical reasons. [OE. *seoc*].
SICK-BAY, [sik'-bā], *n.* *(naut.)* that part of a ship reserved for sick persons.
SICK-BED, [sik'-bed'], *n.* a bed on which a sick person is lying.
SICK-BRAINED, [sik'-brānd'], *adj.* mentally disordered.
SICKEN, [sik'-en], *v.t. and i.* to become ill; to show signs that one has an illness coming on; to nauseate, to cause to vomit; to cause a sense of disgust or nausea; **to s. of,** to grow weary of.
SICKENER, [sik'-en-er], *n.* something causing disgust.
SICKENING, [sik'-en-ing], *adj.* disgusting, nauseating; *(coll.)* annoying.
SICKENINGLY, [sik'-ning-li], *adv.* in sickening fashion; *(coll.)* disgustingly.
SICKISH, [sik'-ish], *adj.* inclined to be sick or sickened.
SICKISHLY, [sik'-ish-li], *adv.* in a sickish way.
SICKISHNESS, [sik'-ish-nes], *n.* a feeling of sickness or disgust.
SICKLE, [sikl], *n.* a small reaping-hook. [OE. *sicol*].
SICKLED, [sikld], *adj.* furnished with a sickle.
SICKLIED, [sik'-lid], *adj.* pale, sickly.

SICKLE

SICKLINESS, [sik'-li-nes], *n.* the state of being sickly.
SICK-LIST, [sik'-list'], *n.* a list of sick persons' names.
SICKLY, [sik'-li], *adj.* inclined to be ill, inclined to vomit; constantly ailing; noted for, marked by, sickness, having the appearance of being unwell, pale; *(fig.)* feeble; provoking a sense of nausea; stupid, mawkish.
SICKNESS, [sik'-nes], *n.* the condition of being unwell; a disease or illness; the act of vomiting.
SICK-PARADE, [sik'-par-ād], *n.* formal attendance of service personnel for medical attention.
SICK-ROOM, [sik'-rōōm], *n.* a room where a person is lying ill.
SIDE (1), [sīd], *n.* a lateral surface or boundary; the lateral part or substance of anything; the material forming the external surface of an object; either surface of a leaf or sheet of anything; that part of an object near to its lateral surface or boundary; either of two parts of an object, space, etc., divided or considered to be divided in half; space or volume, etc., lying to the right or left of a division; (of the human body) that part of the body between either hip and the ribs above it; a line of descent by one parent; one of two opposing parties; one of two opposing points of view; the slope of a hill or mountain; the bank of a river, lake or sea; *(fig.)* a way of approach, point of view, aspect; *(coll.)* an arrogant, over-self-confident, or patronizing manner; *(billiards)* a sideways rotation of the cue ball in addition to its forward rotation; **to put (something) on one s.,** to lay something aside, to shelve it, to ignore it, refuse to deal with it; **to put on s.,** to behave in a pretentious manner; **to take sides,** to go into dispute, to divide into parties or factions; **to take sides with,** to join the party of (in a dispute); **on all sides, on every s.,** everywhere; **from every s.,** from every direction; **s. by s.,** together, unitedly; **on s.** *(football)* in such a position in relation to opposing players on the field as not to transgress the laws of the game, not offside; **on the s.,** as a sideline (often involving the idea of secrecy or dishonesty). [OE. *side*].
SIDE (2), [sīd], *adj.* pertaining to, belonging to, fitting, a side; **a s. line,** a subsidiary activity or interest.
SIDE (3), [sīd], *v.t.* **to s. with,** to take the part of in a dispute.
SIDE-ARM, [sīd'-ahm], *n.* *(milit.)* a weapon carried on the left side.
SIDEBOARD, [sīd'-bawd], *n.* a piece of dining-room furniture consisting essentially of a shelf and cupboard where cutlery and crockery, etc., may be kept; a board exhibiting the destination, advertisements, etc., on the side of a vehicle; *(pl.)* short sidewhiskers. Spanish whiskers.
SIDEBOX, [sīd'-boks'], *n.* a box set to one side in a theatre.
SIDECAR, [sīd'-kah(r)], *n.* a small carriage for one person attached at the side to a motor-cycle; a kind of cocktail.
SIDECOMB, [sīd'-kōm'], *n.* a comb worn by women on the side of the head.
SIDECUT, [sīd'-kut], *n.* a lesser road or canal branching off from a main road or canal.
SIDE-DISH, [sīd'-dish], *n.* an extra course in a meal.
SIDE-DRUM, [sīd'-drum], *n.* a small drum.
SIDE-LIGHT, [sīd'-līt], *n.* a light from the side, a small light on the side of a vehicle; *(fig.)* information, usually of an accessory nature, obtained by approaching a subject from an unusual or special angle.
SIDELING (1), [sīd'-ling], *adj.* moving sideways; sloping.
SIDELING (2), [sīd'-ling], *adv.* sideways, obliquely.
SIDELONG, [sīd'-long'], *adj.* aimed or moving in a sideways direction.
SIDE-NOTE, [sīd'-nōt], *n.* a note at the side of a page.
SIDER, [sīd'-er], *n.* one who takes sides.
SIDEREAL, [sīd-ēer'-i-al], *adj.* pertaining to, or concerned with, the stars; measured by the stars.
SIDERITE, [sīd'-er-īt], *n.* a blue quartz; a variety of carbonate of iron. [Fr. *siderite*].
SIDE-ROD, [sīd'-rod'], *n.* the coupling shaft of a locomotive.
SIDEROGRAPHIC, [sīd'-er-ō-graf'-ik], *adj.* pertaining to siderography.
SIDEROGRAPHIST, [sīd'-er-og'-raf-ist], *n.* one engaged in engraving on steel. [*Next*].
SIDEROGRAPHY, [sīd'-er-og'-ra-fi], *n.* the art of engraving on steel. [Gk. *sideros* iron and *graphia* writing].
SIDEROLITE, [sīd'-er-ō-līt'], *n.* a meteor containing iron. [Gk. *sideros* iron and *lithos* stone].
SIDEROSCOPE, [sīd'-er-ō-skōp'], *n.* an instrument used for detecting iron in a substance.
SIDEROSTAT, [sīd'-er-ō-stat'], *n.* *(astron.)* an instrument which enables an observer to keep a given star in a part of the field of his telescope.
SIDE-SADDLE (1), [sīd'-sadl'], *n.* a saddle for women on which they sit with both feet on the same side of the horse.
SIDE-SADDLE (2), [sīd'-sadl'], *n.* a pitcher-plant of the genus, *Sarracenia*, growing in swamps.
SIDE-SADDLE (3), [sīd'-sadl'], *adv.* on a side-saddle.
SIDE-SCREW, [sīd'-skrōō], *n.* a wooden screw at the side of a carpenter's bench.
SIDESEAT, [sīd'-sēt], *n.* a seat that faces sideways; a seat at the side.
SIDE-SHOW, [sīd'-shō], *n.* a subordinate exhibition or display; *(coll.)* any subsidiary or merely subordinate matter.
SIDESLIP, [sīd'-slip], *n.* a skid to one side.
SIDESMAN, [sīdz'-man], *n.* an assistant to a churchwarden.
SIDE-SPLITTING, [sīd'-split'-ing], *adj.* so funny as to make the sides ache with laughter.
SIDESTEP (1), [sīd'-step'], *n.* a step to the side.
SIDESTEP (2), [sīd'-step'], *v.t. and i.* to make a sidestep; to avoid by making a sidestep.
SIDESTROKE, [sīd'-strōk], *n.* a stroke in swimming made when swimming on the side.
SIDE-TABLE, [sīd'-tābl], *n.* a table placed at the side.
SIDE-TRACK (1), [sīd'-trak'], *n.* a track at the side.
SIDE-TRACK (2), [sīd'-trak'], *v.t.* to divert; to cause to converse about something other than intended.
SIDE-VIEW, [sīd'-vew], *n.* a view from one side.
SIDE-WALK, [sīd'-wawk], *n.* a path at the side; *(U.S.)* a pavement.
SIDEWAYS, [sīd'-wāz], *adv.* towards one side and neither forwards nor backwards, laterally.
SIDEWHEEL, [sīd'-wēl], *n.* a wheel at the side, a paddle-wheel.
SIDEWHISKERS, [sīd'-wisk'-erz], *n.(pl.)* whiskers on the face between the temples and the jaws.
SIDEWISE, [sīd'-wīz], *adv.* to the side, sideways.
SIDI, [sē'-di], *n.* a negro. [Urdu *sidi*].
SIDING, [sīd'-ing], *n.* a track at the side of the main line of a railway where rolling-stock may be shunted and kept till wanted.
SIDLE, [sīdl], *v.i.* to walk sideways, to walk in a shy, nervous manner. [~SIDE].
SIEGE, [sēj], *n.* *(milit.)* the surrounding of a town, castle, or fortified place by a hostile force with a view to its capture; the condition of besieging or being

besieged; a hewer's block-bench; **to lay s. to**, to besiege; **to raise a s.**, to cease in an attempt to take a city, castle, etc., by siege; **to stand s.**, to be besieged. [OFr. *sege* chair].

SIEGE-GUN, [sēj'-gun], *n.* a piece of artillery used in a siege.

SIEGE-PIECE, [sēj'-pēs], *n.* a piece of money issued in a town or city during a siege.

SIEGE-TRAIN, [sēj'-trān], *n.* the equipment necessary to conduct a siege.

SIEGE-WORKS, [sēj'-wurks], *n.(pl.)* trenches, temporary forts, etc., built during a siege.

SIENNA, [si-en'-a], *n.* a ferruginous earth pigment; the colour produced by it, a rich brown. [Ital. *Siena* where found].

SIERRA, [sē-e'-ra], *n.* a jagged mountain range. [Span. *sierra*].

SIESTA, [sē-es'-ta], *n.* a sleep taken in warm countries during the hot early afternoon. [Span. *siesta*].

SIEVE (1), [siv], *n.* a wire mesh stretched over a frame through which a broken substance may be shaken to separate the large from the smaller pieces; any similar device; (*fig.*) someone incapable of keeping a secret; **a head like a s.**, a bad memory; **to put water in a s.**, to attempt a hopeless job. [OE. *sife*].

SIEVE (2), [siv], *v.t.* to sift in a sieve.

SIFAKA, [sif'-ak-a], *n.* the lemur of Madagascar. [Native].

SIFFLATION, [sif-lā'-shun], *n.* the act of whistling.

SIFFLEUR, [sif'-lur'], *n.* one who entertains by whistling. [Fr. *siffleur*].

SIFAKA

SIFT, [sift], *v.t. and i.* to shake through a sieve or sprinkler; to filter through a sieve, to pass through anything as if through a sieve; to examine very critically. [OE. *siftan*].

SIFTER, [sift'-er], *n.* one who sifts; a small sieve.

SIGH (1), [sī], *n.* a long, slow intaking and exhaling of breath, expressive of great weariness or sorrow; the sound accompanying this; any similar sound.

SIGH (2), [sī], *v.t. and i.* to make a sigh; to utter with a sigh; to utter a sound like a sigh; **to s. for**, to long for, desire; to grieve over. [ME. *sighen* from OE. *sican*].

SIGHER, [sī'-er], *n.* one who sighs.

SIGHINGLY, [sī'-ing-li], *adv.* with a sigh.

SIGHT (1), [sit], *n.* the faculty of the eye to see, the act or power of seeing; vision; (*fig.*) spiritual vision; a glimpse, a view; the presentation of something to the view; range of vision, field of view; (*fig.*) point of view, opinion, judgment; something seen, something worth seeing, a spectacle or display, something unusually conspicuous; any device helping to direct the vision, a small projection on the barrel of a gun to aid the user to get the weapon in line with the target; (*dial.*) a great amount, a comic figure; **long s.**, power of long-ranged vision; **short** or **near s.**, myopia; **second s.**, the faculty of psychic or supernatural vision; **in one's s.**, in one's opinion; **the sights**, places of note which every visitor should see; **a s. draft**, a money order to be honoured at sight; **at s., on s., at first s.**, as soon as seen; according to first impressions; **love at first s.**, love felt at a first encounter; **out of all s. and knowledge**, beyond ken or comprehension; **out of s. out of mind**, unthought of, unconsidered; **get out of my s.!**, go away!; **to keep s. of**, to keep in view; (*fig.*) to keep in mind; **to keep in s.**, to remain visible; to have constantly in mind or view; **to lose s. of**, to be no longer able to see; to forget. [OE. *gesihth*].

SIGHT (2), [sit], *v.t.* to see; to approach near to (so as to see); to look at through a telescope, etc.; to equip (a gun, rifle, etc.) with sights; to aim a gun or rifle by means of the sight on it; to aim a gun or rifle at, very carefully using the sight on it.

SIGHT-BILL, [sīt'-bil], *n.* a money order payable at sight.

SIGHTED, [sīt'-id], *adj.* equipped with a sight; trained on a target, aimed; enjoying the faculty of sight.

SIGHTLESS, [sīt'-les], *adj.* blind; †dark, invisible.

SIGHTLESSLY, [sīt'-les-li], *adv.* (as if) without sight.

SIGHTLESSNESS, [sīt'-les-nes], *n.* the condition of being sightless, blindness.

SIGHTLINESS, [sit'-li-nes], *n.* comeliness.

SIGHTLY, [sīt'-li], *adj.* pleasing to the view, handsome.

SIGHT-READER, [sīt'-rēd'-er], *n.* one who can read (music) at sight.

SIGHT-READING, [sīt'-rēd'-ing], *n.* the faculty or skill to read music, shorthand, etc., at sight.

SIGHT-SEEING, [sīt'-sē'-ing], *n.* the act of travelling about to see sights.

SIGHTSEER, [sīt'-sēer], *n.* a person engaged in sight-seeing, a tourist.

SIGIL, [sij'-il], *n.* a seal, signet. [LL. *sigillum*].

SIGILLARY, [sij'-il-er-i], *adj.* pertaining to a seal or signet.

SIGILLATE, [sij'-il-āt], *adj.* (*bot.*) marked, decorated, as if with a seal. [L. *sigillatus*].

SIGMA, [sig'-ma], *n.* the name for the Greek letter, Σ σ, ς, that is, *s.* [Gk. *sigma*].

SIGMATION, [sig-mā'-shun], *n.* the adding of an *s* to a word.

SIGMATISM, [sig'-mat-izm], *n.* the repeated use or addition of a sigma.

SIGMOID, [sig'-moid], *adj.* curved like an uncial sigma (C or S.) [SIGMA and Gk. *oeides* like].

SIGMOIDAL, [sig-moid'-al], *adj.* sigmoid.

SIGN (1), [sin], *n.* that by which anything is shown, indicated, or represented; a token; a nod or gesture indicative of a wish or command; a wonder; a miracle; evidence or proof; something hung out for notice; a memorial; a visible representation; a mark of distinction; a signature; a sign-post; a symptom, indication; a symbol; a constellation occupying one of the twelve divisions of the zodiac; (*math.*) a mark indicative of operation; (*mus.*) a character. [Fr. *signe* from L. *signum* mark].

SIGN (2), [sin], *v.t.* to mark by means of a sign; to put one's signature to; to signify; to indicate by a sign; *v.i.* to make a signal; **to s. on**, to write one's signature, to register, *esp.* at an employment exchange. [Fr. *signer* from L. *signare*].

SIGNABLE, [sīn'-abl], *adj.* able to be signed.

SIGNAL (1), [sig'-nal], *n.* a sign; a sign agreed upon as denoting some special thing; a device for distant communication; a notice or sign for giving information or warning, a semaphore as used on railways to show that the track is free or not; a message; a transmission that is received. [Fr. *signal*].

SIGNAL (2), [sig'-nal], *adj.* singular, remarkable, outstanding; pertaining to signals.

SIGNAL (3), [sig'-nal], *v.t.* to announce by signal; to make signals; *v.i.* to communicate by signalling.

SIGNAL-BOOK, [sig'-nal-book], *n.* a book which gives a list of signals.

SIGNAL-BOX, [sig'-nal-boks'], *n.* a room or hut from which railway signals are worked.

SIGNAL-CABIN, [sig'-nal-kab'-in], *n.* a small signal-box.

SIGNAL-CODE, [sig'-nal-kōd], *n.* an agreed system of signals.

SIGNAL-FIRE, [sig'-nal-fīer], *n.* a beacon fire, fire lighted as a signal.

SIGNAL-FLAG, [sig'-nal-flag'], *n.* a flag used for signalling.

SIGNAL-GUN, [sig'-nal-gun], *n.* a gun firing a signal.

SIGNALIZE, [sig'-nal-īz], *v.t.* to mark out as signal, noteworthy, or eminent.

SIGNALLER, [sig'-nal-er], *n.* one who signals.

SIGNALLY, [sig'-nal-i], *adv.* in a remarkable way, extraordinarily.

SIGNALMAN, [sig'-nal-man], *n.* a man who works signals, usually on a railway.

SIGNAL-POST, [sig'-nal-pōst'], *n.* a post on which signals are shown.

SIGNAL-SERVICE, [sig'-nal-sur'-vis], *n.* the service of the railway signalling system or of the maintenance of military communications.

SIGNATORY (1), [sig'-nat-er-i], *n.* one who signs a document, *esp.* as representing a state. [L. *signatorius*].

SIGNATORY (2), [sig'-nat-or-i], *adj.* that is a signatory.

SIGNATURE, [sig'-na-cher], *n.* a sign, stamp, or mark impressed; sign-manual; the name of a person written by himself; the sign that shows the key in music; (*print.*) a letter or figure by which the sheets are distinguished and their order designated, as a direction to the binder; the sheet so distinguished; **doctrine of signatures**, the old belief that plants and animals indicate by their external characters the diseases for which Nature intends them as remedies; **s. tune**, a tune introducing certain regularly appearing stage artists, turns, shows, etc., or certain series in broadcasting for identification purposes. [Fr. *signature*].

SIGN-BOARD, [sīn'-bawd], *n.* a board on which a man announces his name, or that of his house or his trade.
SIGNER, [sīn'-er], *n.* one who signs his name.
SIGNET, [sig'-net], *n.* a small seal; (in England) a seal for the authentication of royal grants; the privy seal; **writer to the s.**, a Scottish law officer acting as attorney in the Court of Session. [Fr. *signet*].
SIGNET-RING, [sig'-net-ring'], *n.* a finger-ring bearing an embossed seal.
SIGNIFICANCE, [sig-nif'-ik-ants], *n.* meaning, import, implication; the action of signifying. [OFr. *significance*].
SIGNIFICANCY, [sig-nif'-ik-an-si], *n.* the quality of being significant.
SIGNIFICANT, [sig-nif'-ik-ant], *adj.* full of meaning; important; expressive of something; indicative of some important reality. [L. *significans*].
SIGNIFICANTLY, [sig-nif'-ik-ant-li], *adv.* in a significant fashion.
SIGNIFICATION, [sig'-nif-ik-ā'-shun], *n.* the action of signifying; that which is signified; particular and specific meaning.
SIGNIFICATIVE, [sig-nif'-ik-a-tiv], *adj.* betokening or representing by an external sign; having a signification; serving to indicate something. [LL. *significativus*].
SIGNIFICATIVELY, [sig-nif'-ik-at-iv-li], *adv.* in a significative manner.
SIGNIFICATIVENESS, [sig-nif'-ik-at-iv-nes], *n.* the quality of being significative.
SIGNIFICATOR, [sig'-nif-ik-āt'-or], *n.* that which signifies; (*astrol.*) the planet which indicates the querent. [LL. *significator*].
SIGNIFICATORY, [sig-nif'-ik-at-er-i], *adj.* having significance or special meaning.
SIGNIFY, [sig'-ni-fī], *v.t.* to represent by sign or symbol; to make known by words or signs; to declare; to mean, to import; to matter; *v.i.* to be of significance. [Fr. *signifier*].
SIGN-MANUAL, [sīn'-man'-yōō-al], *n.* a signature appended to a document, *esp.* by a sovereign or important state official.
SIGNOR, [sēn'-yawr], *n.* an Italian title of address to a gentleman, equal to Mr. [It. *signor*].
SIGNORA, [sēn-yaw'-ra], *n.* an Italian title of address corresponding to Mrs.; an Italian lady. [It. *signora*].
SIGNORINA, [sēn'-yaw-rēn'-a], *n.* the Italian courtesy title for an unmarried lady, corresponding to Miss. [It. *signorina*].
SIGNORY, [sēn-yer-i], *n.* a seigniory.
SIGNPAINTER, [sīn'-pānt'-er], *n.* a man who paints signs and sign-boards.
SIGN-POST, [sīn'-pōst], *n.* a post to which a sign is fastened, *esp.* one at cross-roads giving directions; (*fig.*) mark, indication.
SIKELIOT, [sik-el'-i-ot], see SICELIOT.
SIKH, [sēk], *n.* a member of a race embracing a monotheistic and casteless adaptation of Hinduism. [Hind. *sikh* disciple].
SILAGE, [sīl'-ij], *n.* ensilage; fodder dried in a silo. [~ENSILAGE].
SILENCE (1), [sīl'-ents], *n.* complete absence of sound; absolute quiet; abstinence from speaking or making a noise; secrecy; absence of mention; oblivion; **s.!** a demand for silence. [OFr. *silence* from L. *silentium*].
SILENCE (2), [sīl'-ents], *v.t.* to induce or enforce silence on; to suppress the noise of; to cause to stop speaking; to overcome in argument; to repress; (*milit.*) to cause to cease firing; to affix a silencer to (a gun).
SILENCER, [sīl'-ens-er], *n.* an appliance for reducing the sound of the escaping gases in motor engines or for silencing the report of a gun.
SILENT, [sīl'-ent], *adj.* absolutely quiet; speechless; still, calm; (*phon.*) (of a letter) not sounded; **s. film**, a film having no sounds recorded with it. [L. *sileus*].
SILENTIARY, [sīl-en'-sher-i], *n.* a man appointed to keep silence in court; one sworn not to divulge state secrets.
SILENTLY, [sīl'-ent-li], *adv.* in a silent manner; noiselessly.
SILENTNESS, [sīl'-ent-nes], *n.* the condition of being silent.
SILENUS, [sīl-ēn'-us], *n.* (*myth.*) the foster-father and teacher of Bacchus; a satyr; a lewd old man. [L. *Silenus*].
SILESIA, [sīl-ēz'-i-a], *n.* a kind of linen cloth, originally from *Silesia*; a light fabric of twilled cotton.
SILEX, [sī'-leks], *n.* flint, chert, etc.; silica. [L. *silex*].
SILHOUETTE (1), [sil'-ōō-et'], *n.* a portrait made by drawing the outline only of a face or figure and filling in the rest with black; a profile; a shadowgraph; the aspect of any opaque object when seen outlined against a strong light; (*fig.*) an outline portrait in literature; **in s.**, in outline. [M. de *Silhouette*, a French politician].
SILHOUETTE (2), [sil'-ōō-et'], *v.t.* to make a silhouette; to throw up in relief against a light background.

SILHOUETTE

SILICA, [sil'-ik-a], *n.* silicon dioxide, a substance which enters into the composition of most earthy minerals, being the chief constituent of the earth's surface. [~L. *silex*].
SILICATE, [sil'-ik-āt], *n.* a combination of silicic acid and a base.
SILICATED, [sil'-ik-āt-ed], *adj.* fully impregnated with silica.
SILICEOUS, [sil-is'-i-us], *adj.* flinty; pertaining to silica or partaking of its nature and properties. [L. *siliceus*].
SILICIC, [sil-is'-ik], *adj.* pertaining to silica; **s. acid**, the acid, H_2SiO_4.
SILICICALCAREOUS, [sil-is'-i-kal-kāer'-i-us], *adj.* having both siliceous and calcareous matter.
SILICIFEROUS, [sil'-is-if'-er-us], *adj.* yielding silica. [SILICA and L. *ferre* to bear].
SILICIFICATION, [sil-is'-if-ik-ā'-shun], *n.* the process of changing into silica.
SILICIFY, [sil-is'-i-fī], *v.t.* to turn into silica; *v.i.* to become silica. [SILICA and L. *facere* to make].
SILICITE, [sil'-is-īt], *n.* a variety of white labradorite.
SILICO-, *pref.* containing, in combination with, silica or silicon. [SILICA].
SILICON, [sil'-ik-on], *n.* the non-metallic chemical element denoted by Si, found always in combination and very abundant in nature. [L. *silex*].
SILICOSIS, [sil-i-kōs'-is], *n.* (*path.*) an affection of the lungs, miners' phthisis, caused by inhalation of gritty particles. [SILICA and Gk. *osis* denoting condition].
SILICULA, [sil-ik'-yōōl-a], *n.* (*bot.*) a short broad pod. [L. *silicula*].
SILICULOSE, [sil-ik'-yōōl-ōs], *adj.* (*bot.*) having short broad pods.
SILIQUA, (*pl.* **siliquae**), [sil'-ik-wa], *n.* the long, narrow seed vessel or pod of a cruciferous plant; a carat, of which six make a scruple. [L. *siliqua* pod].
SILIQUIFORM, [sil-ik'-wi-fawm], *adj.* in the form of a siliqua.
SILIQUOSE, SILIQUOUS, [sil'-ik-wōs, sil'-ik-wus], *adj.* having pods or siliquae.
SILK (1), [silk], *n.* the fine lustrous thread produced by the pupa of a moth of the genus *Bombyx*; cloth made of silk; a dress or gown of silk; **artificial s.**, a silky material made chemically from cellulose; **to take s.**, to become a King's Counsel. [OE. *seolc* from Gk. *seres* the fabric of the Chinese].
SILK (2), [silk], *adj.* silken, made of silk.
SILK-COTTON, [silk'-kot'-on], *n.* a silky fibre of several varieties produced by tropical trees of the genus *Bombax* and others.
SILK-COTTON-TREE, [silk'-kot'-on-trē'], *n.* a tropical tree of the genus *Bombax*, yielding silk-cotton.
SILKEN, [silk'-en], *adj.* like silk; made of silk; of a silky texture or feel; smooth and soft.
SILKINESS, [silk'-i-nes], *n.* the quality of being silky.
SILKMAN, [silk'-man], *n.* a man who manufactures or deals in silk.
SILK-MERCER, [silk'-mur'-ser], *n.* a dealer in silks.
SILKMILL, [silk'-mil], *n.* a mill for spinning and weaving silk.
SILK-THROWER, SILK-THROWSTER, [silk'-thrō-er (thrōst-er)], *n.* a worker who spins and prepares silk for weaving.
SILKWEAVER, [silk'-wēv'-er], *n.* one engaged in weaving silk fabrics.
SILKWORM, [silk'-wurm], *n.* the caterpillar of the moth *Bombyx mori*, which produces silk.
SILKWORM-GUT, [silk'-wurm-gut'], *n.* a material prepared from the entrails of silkworms.

SILKWORM

SILKY, [silk'-i], *adj.* made of silk; like silk; silken; smooth and soft; (of wine) smooth and pleasing in taste; (*bot.*) having a covering of soft hairs.

SILL, [sil], *n.* the wood, metal, or stone which forms the lower horizontal part of a window or door frame; the horizontal bar of timber against which the base of the gate of a river lock closes. [OE. *syll* foundation].
SILLABUB, SYLLABUB, [sil'-ab-ub], *n.* a liquor made by mixing wine or cider with milk and sugar to form a soft curd. [Uncert.].
SILLILY, [sil'-i-li], *adv.* in a silly fashion.
SILLIMANITE, [sil'-i-man-īt], *n.* fibrolite, a fibrous silicate of aluminium. [Professor *Silliman*].
SILLINESS, [sil'-i-nes], *n.* the state of being silly.
SILLY, [sil'-i], *adj.* †innocent, helpless, useless; foolish, weak in intellect, dull, unintelligent; unwise, injudicious; frivolous, trivial, tiresome; **s. symphony,** a cartoon film in which the movements are synchronized with a piece of music. [OE. *sælig* innocent, happy].
SILO, [sī'-ō], *n.* a pit or kind of tall barn from which air is excluded and in which grain, green fodder, etc., is stored. [Span. *silo*].
SILPHOLOGY, [sil-fol'-oj-i], *n.* the study of larval forms. [Gk. *silphe* beetle and *logos* speech].
SILT (1), [silt], *n.* a deposit in water of mud or sand. [ME. *silte*].
SILT (2), [silt], *v.t.* to obstruct, choke up with silt; **to s. up,** to become blocked up with silt; **to s. through,** to trickle through an obstruction of silt. [*Prec.*].
SILURIAN, [sil-yōōer'-i-an], *adj.* of a tribe of Britons inhabiting the south-eastern part of Wales; (*geol.*) of the Palaeozoic rocks lying below the Devonian. [L. *Silures*].
SILVAN, SYLVAN, [silv'-an], *adj.* wooded, rural, pertaining to woods, trees. [L. *silvanus*].
SILVER (1), [silv'-er], *n.* the metallic element denoted by Ag; a precious metal of a brilliant white colour; coin made of silver; money; articles made of or plated with silver; anything resembling silver in colour or lustre. [OE. *seolfor*].
SILVER (2), [silv'-er], *adj.* made of silver; looking like silver in colour or lustre; bright; of a soft grey colour; melodious, dulcet; eloquent; **s. age,** (in cultural history) the period which follows after the finest, the golden age; **s. thaw,** slippery surface of roads, etc., when moisture freezes there.
SILVER (3), [silv'-er], *v.t.* to cover with silver; to give the appearance of silver to; to cover with hoar frost.
SILVER-BATH, [silv'-er-bahth], *n.* (*phot.*) a solution of, or the vessel used to contain, silver salts for sensitizing.
SILVER-FISH, [silv'-er-fish'], *n.* a silvery-coloured insect of the genus *Lepisma* which resembles a fish in its shape and darting motion.
SILVER-FOX, [silv'-er-foks'], *n.* the black fox, distinguished by its rich fur and white tips to its hairs.
SILVER-GILT, [silv'-er-gilt'], *n.* silver or silver-plate with a coating of gold.
SILVER-GRAIN, [silv'-er-grān'], *n.* and *adj.* a flecked grain in wood, *esp.* oak and elm, which appears superimposed on the ordinary grain when it is cut longitudinally.
SILVER-GREY, [silv'-er-grā], *adj.* of a silvery grey colour.
SILVER-HAIRED, [silv'-er-hāerd], *adj.* having silvery grey or white hair.
SILVERINESS, [silv'-er-i-nes], *n.* the quality of being silvery.
SILVERING, [silv'-er-ing], *n.* a plating of silver; anything used for making like silver.
SILVERIZE, [silv'-er-īz], *v.t.* to coat thinly with silver.
SILVER-LEAF, [silv'-er-lēf'], *n.* silver beaten into thin leaves; a fungus disease of plum-trees, etc.
SILVERLY, [silv'-er-li], *adv.* with a silvery colour or sound.
SILVER-PAPER, [silv'-er-pāp'-er], *n.* very thin sheets of tin-foil, etc., used for wrapping purposes.
SILVER-PLATE, [silv'-er-plāt], *n.* an article or articles coated with silver; electroplate.
SILVER-POINT, [silv'-er-point], *n.* a process of drawing with a pencil tipped with silver; the pencil itself; the drawing produced.
SILVER SAND, [sil'-ver-sand'], *n.* fine white sand.
SILVERSIDE, [silv'-er-sīd], *n.* topside of beef suitable for salting.
SILVERSMITH, [silv'-er-smith'], *n.* a workman or dealer in silver.
SILVER-TONGUED, [silv'-er-tungd], *adj.* sweet-voiced, eloquent, persuasive.
SILVER-TREE, [silv'-er-trē], *n.* the South African tree, *Leucadendron argenteum*, with silvery leaves.
SILVER-WEED, [silv'-er-wēd], *n.* the British wayside perennial plant, *Potentilla anserina*.
SILVERY, [silv'-er-i], *adj.* like silver; besprinkled or covered with silver; covered with hoar frost.
SILVICULTURE, [sil'-vi-kul'-cher], *n.* forestry. [L. *silva* a wood and CULTURE].
SIMEONITE, [sim'-i-on-īt], *n.* a low churchman. [Charles *Simeon*, a Cambridge clergyman who propagated evangelical principles].
SIMIAL, [sim'-i-al], *adj.* simian.
SIMIAN (1), [sim'-i-an], *n.* a simian ape.
SIMIAN (2), [sim'-i-an], *adj.* pertaining to the anthropoid apes; ape-like in appearance. [L. *simia* ape].
SIMILAR, [sim'-il-ar], *adj.* like, resembling; having the same form, appearance or nature; (*math.*) having all corresponding angles equal. [L. *similis* like].
SIMILARITY, [sim'-il-a'-ri-ti], *n.* the condition of being similar.
SIMILARLY, [sim'-il-er-li], *adv.* in a like manner.
SIMILE, [sim'-il-i], *n.* a similitude; (*rhet.*) a figure of speech in which, for the sake of illustration, emphasis, or beauty of effect, one thing is compared with another. [L. *simile*].
SIMILITIVE, [sim-il'-it-iv], *adj.* expressing similitude.
SIMILITUDE, [sim-il'-it-ewd], *n.* likeness, resemblance, similar appearance. [L. *similitudo*].
SIMILOR, [sim'-il-aw(r)], *n.* an alloy of copper and zinc of a bright yellow colour used to imitate gold in cheap jewellery. [L. *similis* like and Fr. *or* gold].
SIMIOUS, [sim'-i-us], *adj.* resembling an anthropoid ape; simian. [L. *simia*].
SIMMER (1), [sim'-er], *n.* a gentle boil.
SIMMER (2), [sim'-er], *v.t.* and *i.* to boil gently; (*coll.*) to be in a state of suppressed excitement. [Echoic].
SIMMERING, [sim'-er-ing], *adj.* that simmers.
SIMNEL, [sim'-nel], *n.* a rich cake coloured with saffron and made of the same ingredients as a Christmas cake, eaten on Mothering Sunday, the fourth in Lent. [OFr. *simenel*].
SIMONIAC, [sim-ōn'-i-ak], *n.* one who is guilty of simony.
SIMONIACAL, [sim'-ōn-ī'-ak-al], *adj.* involving simony.
SIMONIACALLY, [sim'-ōn-ī'-ak-al-i], *adv.* in a simoniacal fashion.
SIMONY, [sī'-mon-i], *n.* the crime of buying or selling holy orders or church preferment. [*Simon* Magus, who sought to purchase the power of conferring spiritual benefit, Acts viii. 18].
SIMOOM, [si-mōōm'], *n.* a hot, arid, suffocating wind, which blows in Africa, Arabia, etc., from the interior deserts. [Arab. *semum*].
SIMOUS, [sīm'-us], *adj.* snub-nosed. [Gk. *simos* concave].
SIMP, [simp], *n.* (*slang*) a simpleton. [SIMP(LETON)].
SIMPAI, [sim'-pī], *n.* the red-crested lutong of Sumatra, *Semnopithecus cristatus*. [Malay *simpai*].
SIMPER (1), [simp'-er], *n.* a silly affected smile; a smirk.
SIMPER (2), [simp'-er], *v.i.* to smile in an insincere and affected manner; to smirk. [Uncert.].
SIMPERER, [simp'-er-er], *n.* one who simpers.
SIMPERINGLY, [simp'-er-ing-li], *adv.* in a simpering way.
SIMPLE (1), [simpl], *n.* a herbal medicine, originally with one constituent.
SIMPLE (2), [simpl], *adj.* consisting of one thing; uncompounded; pure; not complex; artless; unaffected; unadorned; straightforward; unlearned; unsophisticated; silly, weak in intellect; (*bot.*) undivided; **pure and s.,** absolute. [Fr. *simple* from L. *simplex*].
SIMPLE-HEARTED, [simpl'-haht'-ed], *adj.* sincere, without duplicity; unsophisticated.
SIMPLE-MINDED, [simpl'-mīnd'-ed], *adj.* artless, undesigning; ingenuous; feeble-minded.
SIMPLENESS, [simpl'-nes], *n.* the quality of being simple; artlessness; unassuming manners.
SIMPLETON, [simpl'-ton], *n.* a foolish person.
SIMPLICITER, [sim-plis'-it-er], *adv.* (*leg.*) unconditionally, simply. [L. *simpliciter*].
SIMPLICITY, [sim-plis'-i-ti], *n.* the state or quality of being simple.
SIMPLIFICATION, [sim'-plif-ik-ā'-shun], *n.* the act of simplifying; the thing simplified.
SIMPLIFY, (simplifying, simplifies, simplified), [sim'-pli-fī], *v.t.* to make simple; (*math.*) to reduce to its simplest terms. [Fr. *simplifier*].
SIMPLY, [simp'-li], *adv.* in a simple manner; without ostentation or affectation; without adornment; unequivocally; absolutely; by itself, merely.
SIMULACRUM, [sim'-yōōl-ak'-rum], *n.* something made to represent something else; a representation;

a mere form or shadow of a reality; a sham. [L. *simulacrum*].

SIMULANT, [sim'-yōōl-ant], *adj.* simulating.

SIMULATE, [sim'-yōōl-āt], *v.t.* to feign; to counterfeit; to assume the mere appearance of without the reality; *v.i.* to pretend. [L. *simulare*].

SIMULATION, [sim'-yōōl-ā'-shun], *n.* the act of simulating; the assumption of a false appearance or character. [L. *simulatio*].

SIMULTANEITY, [sim'-ōōl-tan-ē'-i-ti], *n.* simultaneousness.

SIMULTANEOUS, [sim'-ōōl-tā'-ni-us], *adj.* existing or taking place at the same time. [LL. *simultaneus*].

SIMULTANEOUSLY, [sim'-ōōl-tā'-ni-us-li], *adv.* at the same time.

SIMULTANEOUSNESS, [sim'-ōōl-tā'-ni-us-nes], *n.* the fact or condition of being simultaneous.

SIN (1), [sin], *n.* an offence against the divine law; iniquity; a violation of the moral code; depravity, immorality; wrong-doing; an offence; an offence against good manners; (*coll.*) a shame, a pity; **original s.,** sin inherited from Adam after the Fall; inherited tendency to evil; **like s.,** (*coll.*) excessively, intensely. [OE. *synn*].

SIN (2), [sin], *v.i.* to commit sin; to offend against. [OE. *syngian*].

SINAITIC, [sīn'-ā-it'-ik], *adj.* pertaining to, or originating from, Mount Sinai.

SINANTHROPUS, [sīn-an'-throp-us], *n.* an extinct species of sub-human mammal discovered in China. [Gk. *Sinai* the Chinese and *anthropos* man].

SINAPIN, [sin'-ap-in], *n.* (*chem.*) an organic base from the white mustard seed. [L. *sinapis* mustard].

SINAPISINE, [sin-ap'-iz-in], *n.* (*chem.*) an organic base extracted from the black mustard seed.

SINAPISM, [sin-ap'-izm], *n.* (*med.*) a mustard plaster. [Fr. *sinapisme*].

SINCE (1), [sints], *adv.* from that time, after that time; from then till now, in the interval; ago. [OE. *siththan*].

SINCE (2), [sints], *prep.* after, from that time.

SINCE (3), [sints], *conj.* because that; inasmuch as; from the time when.

SINCERE, [sin-sēer'], *adj.* genuine; unmixed; pure; not simulated; true, heartfelt. [L. *sincerus* pure].

SINCERELY, [sin-sēer'-li], *adv.* in a sincere fashion; unfeignedly; **yours s.,** the common formula used to close a personal letter.

SINCERENESS, [sin-sēer'-nes], *n.* the quality of sincerity; the condition of being sincere.

SINCERITY, [sin-se'-ri-ti], *n.* the quality of being sincere; honesty of mind and intention; genuineness. [L. *sinceritas*].

SINCIPITAL, [sin-sip'-it-al], *adj.* (*anat.*) pertaining to the sinciput.

SINCIPUT, [sin'-si-put], *n.* (*anat.*) the front part of the head from the forehead to the coronal suture. [L. *sinciput*].

SINDON, [sind'-on], *n.* a wrapper; a shroud. [OFr. *syndone*].

SINE, [sīn], *n.* (*math.*) the ratio of the line opposite a given angle to the hypotenuse of a right-angled triangle containing that angle. [L. *sinus*].

SINE- [si-ni], *pref.* without. [L. *sine* without].

SIN-EATING, [sin'-ēt'-ing], *n.* the assuming of the sins of a dead person by eating food laid on his corpse.

SINECURE, [sīn'-i-kyōōer], *n.* an ecclesiastical benefice entailing no cure of souls; an office with a salary but no work. [L. *sinecura* without a cure (of souls)].

SINECURISM, [sīn'-i-kyōōer-izm], *n.* the possession of a sinecure; the toleration of sinecures.

SINECURIST, [sin'-i-kyōōer-ist], *n.* one who holds or is trying to obtain a sinecure.

SINEW, [sin'-yōō], *n.* that which unites a muscle to a bone; a tendon; (*pl.*) muscles; (*fig.*) strength, essential motive power, necessary material. [OE. *seonu*].

SINEWED, [sin'-yōōd], *adj.* having sinews; strong; vigorous.

SINEWLESS, [sin'-yōō-les], *adj.* without sinews.

SINEWY, [sin'-yōō-i], *adj.* consisting of sinews; strong; well-braced with sinews; (*fig.*) vigorous, without flabbiness, terse.

SINFONIA, [sin-fōn'-i-a], *n.* (*mus.*) harmony; an overture. [It. *sinfonia*].

SINFUL, [sin'-fōōl], *adj.* wicked; involving sin.

SINFULLY, [sin'-fōōl-i], *adv.* in a sinful fashion.

SINFULNESS, [sin'-fōōl-nes], *n.* the condition or quality of being sinful.

SING, (sang, sung), [sing], *v.t.* to articulate with musical inflections of voice; to give praises to, tell of, in verse; **to s. to sleep,** to put to sleep by singing; **to s. out,** (*coll.*) to call out; (*fig.*) **to s. another (a different) tune,** to speak or act in a quite different manner; *v.i.* to utter sweet or melodious sounds; to make a small shrill or humming sound; to relate in poetry; to produce a ringing, murmuring sound; to reverberate. [OE. *singan*].

SINGABLE, [sing'-abl], *adj.* able to be sung.

SINGE (1), [sinj], *n.* a burning of the surface; a scorch.

SINGE (2), [sinj], *v.t.* to burn the surface of slightly; to burn superficially. [OE. *sencgan*].

SINGEING, [sinj'-ing], *n.* a superficial burning; a burning of the surface or ends.

SINGER, [sing'-er], *n.* one who, or that which, sings; a professional vocal artist.

SINGH, [sing], *n.* a Sikh who has been initiated as full member of the community. [Skr. *simha* lion].

SINGHALESE, CINGALESE, [sing'-al-ēz'], *n.* a native of Ceylon; the language of Ceylon. [Skr. *Simhala* Ceylon].

SINGING, [sing'-ing], *n.* vocal music.

SINGING-BIRD, [sing'-ing-burd], *n.* a song-bird.

SINGING-BOOK, [sing'-ing-bōōk], *n.* a music-book; a book containing songs and music.

SINGINGLY, [sing'-ing-li], *adv.* in a singing fashion.

SINGING-MASTER, [sing'-ing-mah'-ster], *n.* a man who teaches singing professionally.

SINGLE (1), [sing'-gl], *n.* (*tennis*) a game in which only two players take part.

SINGLE (2), [sing'-gl], *adj.* separate; consisting of one only; not complex; sole; individual; solitary; alone; not married; not double; sincere; direct and honest. [OFr. *sengle* from L. *singulus*].

SINGLE (3), [sing'-gl], *v.t.* to separate; select; choose; to cause to stand (out).

SINGLE-ENTRY, [sing'-gl-ent'-ri], *n.* (*comm.*) entry of a transaction into one account only of the ledger.

SINGLE-HANDED, [sing'-gl-hand'-ed], *adj.* having no one to help; working alone and unassisted.

SINGLE-HEARTED, [sing'-gl-haht'-ed], *adj.* devoted to one thing; sincere, without duplicity.

SINGLE-MINDED, [sing'-gl-mīnd'-ed], *adj.* having one purpose; single-hearted.

SINGLE-MINDEDNESS, [sing'-gl-mīnd'-ed-nes], *n.* the fact or quality of being single-minded.

SINGLENESS, [sing'-gl-nes], *n.* the quality or fact of being single.

SINGLES, [sing'-glz], *n.*(*pl.*) reeled filaments of silk.

SINGLE-STICK, [sing'-gl-stik], *n.* a stick about the length of a sword used for sword exercise.

SINGLET, [sing'-glet], *n.* an undervest not buttoning in front; a vest.

SINGLETON, [sing'-gl-ton], *n.* the only one of a suit in a hand at cards; a solitary entry in a competition.

SINGLY, [sing'-gli], *adv.* individually; alone; by one's self; in a single-minded manner.

SINGSONG (1), [sing'-song], *n.* a jolly, informal concert; a monotonous tone of voice.

SINGSONG (2), [sing'-song'], *adj.* having a monotonous droning sound; having no modulations; drawling.

SINGULAR, [sing'-gyōō-ler], *adj.* relating to one person or thing; not common; peculiar, unusual; unique; outstanding; **s. number,** (*gram.*) the number denoting one person or thing. [L. *singularis*].

SINGULARIST, [sing'-gyōō-la-rist], *n.* †one who is different from others, assumes certain eccentricities; the holder of one ecclesiastical benefice only.

SINGULARITY, [sing'-gyōō-la'-ri-ti], *n.* the quality of being singular; peculiarity; uncommon character or form; peculiar privilege; oddity. [L. *singularitas*].

SINGULARIZE, [sing'-gyōō-la-rīz], *v.t.* to make singular; to make into the singular number.

SINGULARLY, [sing'-gyōō-ler-li], *adv.* in a singular manner; peculiarly; strangely; specially.

SINGULTOUS, [sin-gult'-us], *adj.* affected with hiccough.

SINGULTUS, [sin-gult'-us], *n.* (*path.*) hiccough. [L. *singultus*].

SINICAL, [sin'-ik-al], *adj.* pertaining to a sine.

SINISM, [sīn'-izm], *n.* a Chinese custom or expression.

SINISTER, [sin'-is-ter], *adj.* on the left hand; having a secret meaning; of evil import; mysteriously evil, threatening; ominous; base or underhand. [L. *sinister*].

SINISTERLY, [sin'-ist-er-li], *adv.* in a sinister manner.

SINISTRAL, [sin'-ist-ral], *adj.* on the left-hand side.

SINISTRALLY, [sin'-ist-ral-i], *adv.* in a sinistral manner; on the left.

SINISTRATION, [sin'-ist-rā'-shun], *n.* a turning towards the left.

SINISTRORSE, [sin'-ist-raws], *adj.* (*bot.*), growing upward spirally from right to left; like a spiral turning in a counter-clockwise direction. [L. *sinistrorsus*].

SINISTROUS, [sin'-ist-rus], *adj.* on the left side; inclined leftwards; wrong; absurd; perverse. [~L. *sinister*].

SINISTROUSLY, [sin'-ist-rus-li], *adv.* in a sinister manner.

SINK (1), [singk], *n.* a drain to carry off filthy water; a basin of stone or wood to receive filthy water; a place of filth; a depression due to the removal of rock-salt by underground waters; a depression due to mining; (*fig.*) an evil place.

SINK (2), [singk], *v.t.* to cause to sink; to immerse in a fluid; to make by digging, excavation, boring; to depress; to degrade; to reduce, diminish; to suppress, conceal; *v.i.* to fall towards the bottom; to subside; to fall gradually; to become lower; to settle to a level; to decline; (*fig.*) to fall lower in social position or standard of behaviour. [OE. *sincan*].

SINKER, [singk'-er], *n.* a plummet; a weight fixed on anything to sink it; **hook, line and s.,** completely, in a credulous manner.

SINK-HOLE, [singk'-hōl], *n.* a hole for foul water to run through.

SINKING (1), [singk'-ing], *n.* the excavation of shafts and wells.

SINKING (2), [singk'-ing], *adj.* falling, subsiding; **s. feeling,** (*coll.*) heavy sensation in the pit of the stomach caused by hunger or fear; **s. fund,** a fund set aside by a government or company for the reduction of debts or other liabilities.

SINLESS, [sin'-les], *adj.* without sin; innocent; pure.

SINLESSLY, [sin'-les-li], *adv.* in sinless fashion.

SINLESSNESS, [sin'-les-nes], *n.* the condition of being sinless.

SINNER, [sin'-er], *n.* one who sins; an offender, criminal; a morally guilty person.

SINNET, [sin'-et], *n.* (*naut.*) sennit; yarn bound round ropes to prevent them from galling.

SINN FEIN, [shin'-fān'], *n.* the political party in Ireland which worked for national unity and the complete political and economic independence of Ireland. [Ir. *sinn fein* we ourselves].

SIN-OFFERING, [sin'-of'-er-ing], *n.* a sacrifice for sin; an offering made in expiation for sin.

SINOLOGICAL, [sīn'-ō-loj'-ik-al], *adj.* pertaining to sinology.

SINOLOGIST, [sīn-ol'-oj-ist], *n.* a sinologue.

SINOLOGUE, [sīn'-ol-og], *n.* one versed in Chinese culture.

SINOLOGY, [sīn-ol'-oj-i], *n.* the study of Chinese culture, history, religion and art. [Gk. *Sinai* the Chinese people and *logos* speech].

SINTER, [sint'-er], *n.* a siliceous or calcareous deposit of mineral springs. [Germ. *sinter* dross].

SINTOOISM, see SHINTOISM.

SINUATE, [sin'-yōō-āt], *adj.* sinuous; (*bot.*) having wavy indentations. [L. *sinuatus*].

SINUATELY, [sin'-yōō-at-li], *adv.* in sinuate fashion.

SINUATION, [sin'-yōō-ā'-shun], *n.* a curving in and out, following a sinuous course. [L. *sinuatio*].

SINUOSE, [sin'-yōō-ōs], *adj.* sinuous.

SINUOSITY, [sin'-yōō-os'-i-ti], *n.* the quality of curving in and out; a series of bends, turns, or windings. [Fr. *sinuosité*].

SINUOUS, [sin'-yōō-us], *adj.* bending in and out; winding; undulating; supple. [L. *sinuosus*].

SINUOUSLY, [sin'-yōō-us-li], *adv.* in a sinuous fashion.

SINUPALLIATE, [sin'-yōō-pal'-i-āt], *adj.* having a sinuous pallial margin on the shell. [SINUS and PALLIAL].

SINUS, [sīn'-us], *n.* a curve, bend; a cavity usually in a bone or other tissue of the body; (*path.*) an abscess or suppurating place, usually in the passages of the nose or ear; (*zool.*) (of shells, fossils, etc.) a line indicating some structural characteristic. [L. *sinus* a curve].

SINUSITIS, [sīn'-us-īt'-is], *n.* (*path.*) inflammation of the nasal sinus. [SINUS and Gk. *itis* denoting inflammation].

SINUSOID, [sīn'-yōō-soid'], *n.* (*math.*) the curve of sines.

SINUSOIDAL, [sīn'-yōō-soidl'], *adj.* wave-like, undulating; (*math.*) relating to, consisting of, a sinusoid.

SIOUX, [sōō], *n.* (one of) a nation of American Indians of the Dakotan group so styled; the language of this people. [Fr. *Sioux*].

SIP (1), [sip], *n.* the taking of liquid with the lips; a small drink of liquid; a small taste of anything.

SIP (2), [sip], *v.t.* to take into the mouth by the lips in very small quantities; to take very small drinks of; to drink out of in the above way; (*fig.*) to taste; *v.i.* to take in small tastes. [OE. *sypian* to absorb moisture].

SIPAGE, [sīp'-ij], *n.* leakage or oozing of water; dripping, trickling; water which has oozed or percolated.

SIPE, see SYPE.

SIPHON (1), SYPHON, [sīf'-on], *n.* a bent tube or pipe, having one end lower than the other, used for drawing off fluids by atmospheric pressure; a bottle which uses this principle to deliver its contents, usually soda-water; a tube by which the chambers of a shell communicate. [Gk. *siphon* small tube].

SIPHON

SIPHON (2), SYPHON, [sīf'-on], *v.t.* to draw (off) by the action of a siphon.

SIPHONAGE, SYPHONAGE, [sī'-fon-ij], *n.* the action of a siphon.

SIPHONAL, SYPHONAL, [sīf'-on-al], *adj.* siphonic.

SIPHONIC, SYPHONIC, [sīf-on'-ik], *adj.* pertaining to a siphon.

SIPHONIFER, [sīf-on'-if-er], *n.* (*zool.*) a nautiloid mollusc with a siphuncle by which the chambers of the shell communicate with one another. [SIPHON and L. *ferre* to bear].

SIPHUNCLE, [sī'-fung'-kl], *n.* the tube running through the partitions of nautiloid shells. [L. *siphunculus* little siphon].

SIPHUNCULAR, [sī-fungk'-yōōl-er], *adj.* pertaining to a siphuncle.

SIPHUNCULATED, [sī-fungk'-yōōl-āt-ed], *adj.* having a small siphon or spout, as in a cephalopod.

SIPPER, [sip'-er], *n.* one who sips.

SIPPET, [sip'-it], *n.* a small piece of bread, fried or toasted, served as a garnish for hashes. [~SOP].

SIR, [sur], *n.* the title of honour used of a knight or baronet; a word of respect used formerly in addressing a man of superior station, and now generally; sirrah. [OFr. *sire*].

SIRCAR, [sur'-kar], *n.* a Hindoo clerk or scribe. [Hind. *sircar*].

SIRDAR, [surd'-ar], *n.* the commander-in-chief of the Egyptian Army; a leader, chieftain. [Pers. *sardar*].

SIRE, [sīer], *n.* a father; a title used in addressing the sovereign; the male parent; a progenitor; an ancestor. [OFr. *sire* from L. *senior*].

SIREN (1), SYREN, [sīer'-en], *n.* a mermaid; one of a class of sea-nymphs who, according to Greek mythology, used to lure passing sailors to ruin by the fascination of their music; a woman dangerous from her enticing arts; a steam-whistle; a hooter used to sound an air-raid warning; (*zool.*) a genus of tailed amphibians including the mud-eel. [L. *siren* from Gk. *seiren*].

SIREN (2), SYREN, [sīer'-en], *adj.* of, or like a siren.

SIRENIAN, [sī-rēn'-i-an], *n.* a member of the aquatic order of fish-like mammals, *Sirenia*. [~SIREN].

SIREN SUIT, [sīer'-en-sōōt'], *n.* a suit made in one piece, with trousers, for wear during air-raids.

SIRIUS, [si'-ri-us], *n.* (*astron.*) a bright star of the first magnitude, in the constellation, *Canis Major*, also called the Dog Star. [L. *Sirius*].

SIRLOIN, [sur'-loin], *n.* the upper part of the loin of beef. [OFr. *surlonge*].

SIROCCO, [si-rok'-ō], *n.* a hot, southerly wind from the Libyan deserts, blowing chiefly in Italy, Malta, and Sicily. [It. *sirocco*].

SIRRAH, [si'-ra], *n.* a mode of address used to a man or boy, and implying reproach or contempt. [~SIR].

SIRUP, see SYRUP.

SISAL, [sīz'-al], *n.* the fibre plant, *Agave rigida*, largely cultivated in Malaya and the Bahamas, and used for making rope. [*Sisal*, a seaport in Yucatan].

SISE, see SICE (2).

SISKIN, [sis'-kin], *n.* a small song-bird of the finch family, *Carduelis spinus*. [Flem. *sijsken*].

SISSOO, [sis-ōō'], *n.* a valuable dark timber obtained from the tree, *Dalbergia Sissoo*. [Hind. *sisu*].

SISSY (1), [sis'-i], *n.* (*slang*) a foolish, ineffective, effeminate male. [Uncert.].

SISSY (2), [sis'-i], *adj.* like, or typical of, a sissy.

SIST, [sist], *v.t.* (*leg.*) to stop proceedings; to summon. [L. *sistere* to cause to stop].

SISTER, [sist'-er], *n.* a female of the same parentage; one who acts like a sister; a female of the same society, a nun; one of the same kind; a nurse in charge of a hospital ward; (*U.S.*) a term of familiar address to a woman. [OScand. *systir*].

SISTERHOOD, [sist'-er-hōōd], *n.* a community of sisters; a society of sisters; a society of women joined in one faith or order; the relationship of a sister.

SISTER-HOOK, [sist′-er-hŏŏk], *n*. a clasp-hook, a steel hook in two parts moving upon the same pivot with one overlapping the other.
SISTER-IN-LAW, [sist′-er-in-law′], *n*. the sister of a husband or wife; the wife of a brother.
SISTERLY, [sist′-er-li], *adj*. of a sister.
SISTINE, [sist′-ēn], *adj*. pertaining to one of the popes called Sixtus or to any work done under their rule. [It. *sistino* from L. *sextus* sixth].
SISTRUM, [sis′-trum], *n*. a form of rattle used in the worship of Isis. [L. *sistrum*].
SISYPHEAN, [sis′-if-ē′-an], *adj*. pertaining to Sisyphus, an ancient king of Corinth, who for his sins was condemned in the underworld endlessly to roll up a hill a great stone which always rolled down again at once; **s. labour, task**, an endless and ineffective labour. [Gk. *sisupheios*].
SIT (1), [sit], *n*. the way in which anything sits, is fixed, or hangs; a certain time taken up in sitting.
SIT (2), (**sitting, sat**), [sit], *v.i.* to rest upon the haunches, to rest upon a seat; to rest; to lie; to remain, abide; to have a seat or position; to be placed; to cover eggs for hatching; to hold a session, be convened; to hold a seat in Parliament; to weigh heavily (upon); to remain seated upon; **to s. down**, to place oneself on a seat; to settle down; **to s. on**, (*coll.*) to snub; **to s. out**, to remain seated and endure; **to s. out a dance**, to refrain from joining in; **to s. under**, to sit underneath, receive instruction from; **to s. up**, to refrain from going to bed; (*coll.*) to pay attention, to be on the alert. [OE. *sittan*].
SITAR, [sēt′-ahr], *n*. an Indian musical instrument similar to the guitar. [Hind. *sitar*].
SITE (1), [sīt], *n*. situation; local position; ground plot for building. [AFr. *site*].
SITE (2), [sīt], *v.t.* to locate; find the position of.
SITFAST, [sit′-fahst], *n*. an ulcer or sore on a horse's back.
SITOLOGY, SITIOLOGY, [sit-ol′-oj-i], *n*. a treatise on food values or the regulation of diet; dietetics. [Gk. *sitos* food and *logos* speech].
SITOPHOBIA, [sit′-ō-fōb′-i-a], *n*. repugnance to food or to certain forms of food. [Gk. *sitos* food and *phobia* fear].
SITTER, [sit′-er], *n*. a person who sits, *esp*. to an artist; a bird that incubates; an easy target.
SITTING (1), [sit′-ing], *n*. the action of one who sits; a session; a business meeting; the time during which one sits; the time during which one sits for a portrait; a seat in the pew of a church; a clutch of eggs for incubation.
SITTING (2), [sit′-ing], *adj*. being in the position of one who, or that which, sits.
SITTING-ROOM, [sit′-ing-rŏŏm], *n*. a room for sitting in; a reception-room; a drawing-room.
SITUATE (1), [sit′-yŏŏ-āt], *adj*. situated.
SITUATE (2), [sit′-yŏŏ-āt], *v.t.* to place, locate; to provide a site for; to place in a particular situation or set of circumstances; *v.i.* †to have, acquire, a certain situation. [MedL. *situatus*].
SITUATION, [sit′-yŏŏ-ā′-shun], *n*. position; state; condition; place; office; employment; job. [Fr. *situation*].
SITZ-BATH, [sits′-bahth], *n*. a bath for bathing in a sitting position; a hip-bath. [Germ. *sitzbad*].
SIX (1), [siks], *n*. the cardinal number next after five; twice three; **at sixes and sevens**, confused. [OE. *sex*].
SIX (2), [siks], *adj*. of the number six.
SIXFOLD, [siks′-fōld], *adj*. six times or things together; six times as much or many.
SIX-FOOTER, [siks′-fŏŏt′-er], *n*. any person or thing six feet in length or height.
SIXPENCE, [siks′-pents], *n*. a silver coin of the value of six pennies; the value of sixpence.
SIXPENNY, [siks′-pen-i], *adj*. worth sixpence; (*fig.*) cheap, paltry.
SIXPENNYWORTH, [siks′-pen′-i-wurth], *n*. what is worth or may be had for sixpence.
SIX-SHOOTER, [siks′-shŏŏt′-er], *n*. a revolver that can fire six shots with one loading.
SIXTEEN (1), [siks-tēn′], *n*. the cardinal number after fifteen and before seventeen; six and ten. [OE. *sextyne*].
SIXTEEN (2), [siks′-tēn], *adj*. of the number sixteen.
SIXTEENTH (1), [siks-tēnth′], *n*. one of sixteen identical parts; (*mus.*) a semiquaver; an interval of two octaves and a second.
SIXTEENTH (2), [siks′-tēnth′], *adj*. the ordinal of sixteen. [~OE. *sexteotha*].
SIXTH (1), [siksth], *n*. the sixth part; (*mus.*) an interval of six notes; a chord of two notes so separated.
SIXTH (2), [siksth], *adj*. the ordinal of six. [OE. *sexta*].
SIXTHLY, [siksth′-li], *adv*. in the sixth place.
SIXTIETH (1), [siks′-ti-eth], *n*. one of sixty equal parts.
SIXTIETH (2), [siks′-ti-eth], *adj*. the ordinal of sixty.
SIXTY (1), [siks′-ti], *n*. the number equal to six times ten; the figure representing this.
SIXTY (2), [siks′-ti], *adj*. six times ten. [OE. *sixtig*].
SIZABLE, [sīz′-abl], *adj*. of some size; of a certain size; of considerable size.
SIZAR, [sīz′-ar], *n*. an undergraduate student at Cambridge and Dublin of a corresponding grade with the servitor at Oxford. [SIZE (1)].
SIZARSHIP, [sīz′-ar-ship], *n*. the status or emoluments of a sizar.
SIZE (1), see SICE.
SIZE (2), [sīz], *n*. bulk; magnitude; dimensions; settled quantity or allowance, *esp*. of food and drink, made to sizars at Cambridge; a standard measure of goods, formerly fixed at assizes, from which derive present standard dimensions of gloves, shoes, hats, etc. [OFr. *size*].
SIZE (3), [sīz], *n*. liquid glue. [Uncert.].
SIZE (4), [sīz], *v.t.* to put in order according to size; to make of a certain dimension; *v.i.* to order food or drink from the buttery (at Cambridge University); **to s. up**, to form an estimate of.
SIZE (5), [sīz], *v.t.* to prepare or cover with size. [SIZE (3)].
SIZED, [sīzd], *adj*. covered or prepared with size.
SIZEL, [sizl], *n*. scissel.
SIZER, [sīz′-er], *n*. one who, or a machine which, applies size.
SIZZLE, [sizl], *v.i.* to emit a sizzling, spluttering noise in process of frying. [Echoic].
SJAMBOK, [syam′-bok′], *n*. a whip made of rhinoceros hide. [Afrik. *sjambok*].
SKALD†, [skald], *n*. a poet in ancient Scandinavia.
SKAT, [skat], *n*. a German game of cards for three persons. [Germ. *skat*].
SKATE (1), [skāt], *n*. a large flat fish of the genus *Raia*. [OIcel. *skata*].
SKATE (2), [skāt], *n*. a kind of frame strapped on to the foot and furnished with steel runners for gliding over the ice; **roller s.**, a skate with wheels instead of runners used for gliding on any smooth surface. [Du. *schaatzen*].
SKATE (3), [skāt], *v.i.* to slide along on skates; **to s. on thin ice**, (*fig.*) to venture into a dangerous or awkward situation.
SKATER, [skāt′-er], *n*. a person who skates.
SKEAN, SKENE, [skēn], *n*. a Gaelic dagger; a short sword or knife. [Gael. *sgian*].

SKATE

SKEAN-DHU, SKENE-DHU, [skē′-an-d(y)ōō, skēn′-dōō′], *n*. a Highlander's dirk or knife, usually carried stuck into the top of the stocking. [Gael. *sgian dubh* black knife].
SKEDADDLE, [ski-dadl′], *v.i.* (*slang*) to rush off, disappear in a panic; to bolt. [Unkn.].
SKEEL, [skēl], *n*. (*dial.*) a wooden vessel with handles, used for holding milk or water; a kind of cage for lifting coal during its mining. [Icel. *skjola*].
SKEET (1), [skēt], *n*. the pollack, a fish of the same family as the cod. [Unkn.].
SKEET (2), [skēt], *n*. (*naut.*) a long scoop used to wet the sides of ships to keep them cool, or the sails of small vessels for making them hold the wind better. [Unkn.].
SKEG, [skeg], *n*. a kind of bearded oats. [OIcel. *skegg* beard].
SKEIN, [skān], *n*. a measure of thread, yarn, or silk; **a tangled s.**, (*fig.*) a sadly confused affair. [OFr. *escaigne*].
SKELETAL, [skel′-it-al], *adj*. (*biol.*) of, pertaining to, of the nature of, a skeleton.
SKELETOLOGY, [skel′-it-ol′-oj-i], *n*. the anatomy of the solid or bony structure of the body. [Gk. *skeletos* dried up and *logos* speech].
SKELETON, [skel′-it-on], *n*. the bones of an animal body in their natural arrangement, separated from the flesh; the supporting parts of an animal whether vertebrate or invertebrate; the general supporting framework of anything; outline; a very thin, emaciated person. [Gk. *skeletos* dried up].

SKELETONIZE, [skel'-it-on-iz], *v.t.* to make a skeleton of; *v.i.* to become a skeleton.
SKELETON-KEY, [skel'-it-on-kē'], *n.* a thin light key, with the side-webs filed away, capable of opening many locks; a master-key.
SKENE, SKENE-DHU, see SKEAN, SKEAN-DHU.
SKEP, [skep], *n.* a light wicker basket; the amount of goods that may be carried in such a basket; a straw beehive. [OIcel. *skeppa* basket, bushel].

SKEP

SKERRY, [ske'-ri], *n.* a small rocky island; a reef. [OIcel. *sker*].
SKETCH (1), [skech], *n.* an outline or general delineation of anything; a first rough draft; a descriptive essay or newspaper article; a slight character play in one act; (*coll.*) an absurdly dressed person. [Du. *schets* from Gk. *skhedios* extempore].
SKETCH (2), [skech], *v.t.* to delineate the outline or general figure of; to make a first draft of; to plan by outlining the principal ideas of; to write out the preliminary basic details of; *v.i.* to make sketches.
SKETCHABLE, [skech'-abl], *adj.* able to be sketched.
SKETCHBOOK, [skech'-bo͝ok], *n.* a book for sketching in.
SKETCHER, [skech'-er], *n.* a person who sketches.
SKETCHILY, [skech'-i-li], *adv.* in a sketchy fashion.
SKETCHINESS, [skech'-i-nes], *n.* the state of being sketchy.
SKETCHING, [skech'-ing], *n.* the act of sketching; a sketch.
SKETCHY, [skech'-i], *adj.* drawn in outline; rough, unfinished; inadequate.
SKEW (1), [skew], *n.* (*arch.*) the sloping line of stones forming the coping of a gable; one of the slates which forms part of the gutter of a roof. [OFr. *escu*].
SKEW (2), [skew], *adj.* slanting, oblique; **s. chisel,** a chisel designed to give an oblique stroke; **s. gearing,** (*eng.*) an obliquely toothed gear; **on the s.,** aslant. [~AFr. *eskuer* to slip away].
SKEWBACK, [skew'-bak'], *n.* (*arch.*) a sloping course of stone or brick from which an arch springs.

SKEW GEARING

SKEWBALD, [skew'-bawld], *adj.* (of a horse) marked with patches of white, brown or red.
SKEW-BRIDGE, [skew'-brij], *n.* a bridge which crosses a road or river at an angle.
SKEWER (1), [skew'-er], *n.* a pin of wood or metal for keeping a joint of meat in shape; a creel or pin for taking the bobbins in cotton spinning.
SKEWER (2), [skew'-er], *v.t.* to fasten with skewers.
SKEW-WHIFF, [skew'-wif'], *adj.* (*coll.*) slanting, awry.
SKI (1), [skē, shē], *n.* a long, flat, wooden runner with a curved front used for moving quickly over snow. [Norw. *ski* from OScand. *skith*].
SKI (2), [skē, shē], *v.i.* to go on skis.
SKID (1), [skid], *n.* a curving timber to preserve a ship's side from injury; a drag to check the wheel of a wagon when descending a hill; a brake; a piece of timber to keep one object from resting on another; a sideslip in motor-car or bicycle on a road. [OScand. *skith*].
SKID (2), [skid], *v.i.* to sideslip with a car or bicycle.
SKIED, [skid], *adj.* hung high up in the air; hit high into the air.
SKIER, [skē'-er, shē'-er], *n.* one who skis.
SKIFF, [skif], *n.* a light sculling boat; any light, small boat. [OFr. *esquif*].
SKI-JORING, [skē-yur'-ing], *n.* the sport or practice of being towed on skis by a horse.
SKILFUL, [skil'-fo͝ol], *adj.* showing skill; well versed in any occupation; dexterous; expert.
SKILFULLY, [skil'-fo͝ol-i], *adv.* in a skilful way.
SKILFULNESS, [skil'-fo͝ol-nes], *n.* the quality of being skilful.
SKILL, [skil], *n.* familiar knowledge of any art, united with dexterity in the practice of it; expertness in execution; proficiency. [OIcel. *skil* reason].
SKILLED, [skild], *adj.* having or demanding skill.
SKILLET, [skil'-it], *n.* a small, long-handled vessel, of iron or other metal, used for boiling or heating. [OFr. *escuellette*].
SKILLING (1), [skil'-ing], *n.* a bay of a barn; a small addition to a cottage. [Uncert.].
SKILLING (2), [skil'-ing], *n.* a copper coin of a small value formerly in circulation in Scandinavia. [Scand. *skilling*].
SKILL-LESS, SKILLESS, [skil'-les], *adj.* without skill.
SKILLY (1), [skil'-i], *n.* a watery oatmeal gruel formerly used as food for paupers and convicts. [Uncert.].
SKILLY (2), [skil'-i], *adj.* skilful. [SKILL].
SKIM, [skim], *v.t.* to take the scum off; to take off (matter) floating on the surface; to brush the surface of lightly; to scan superficially; *v.i.* to pass over lightly; to glide over the surface; to hurry over superficially. [~OIcel. *skum*].
SKIMBLE-SKAMBLE, [skimbl'-skambl'], *adj.* confused, incoherent, wandering. [~SCAMBLE].
SKIM-COULTER, [skim'-kōlt'-er], *n.* a coulter fitted with an iron plate for paring off the surface of land.
SKIMMER, [skim'-er], *n.* one who, or that which, skims; a scoop used for skimming milk; the scissor-bill bird, a species of *Rhynchops*.
SKIM-MILK, [skim'-milk'], *n.* milk from which the cream has been skimmed; (*fig.*) weak stuff.
SKIMMINGLY, [skim'-ing-li], *adv.* in a skimming fashion; lightly, touching the surface only.
SKIMMINGS, [skim'-ingz], *n.* matter skimmed from the surface of liquids.
SKIMP, [skimp], *v.t.* to stint; to use insufficient material; to give poor amount of; *v.i.* to be mean, parsimonious. [Uncert.].
SKIMPILY, [skimp'-i-li], *adv.* in skimpy fashion, inadequately.
SKIMPING, [skimp'-ing], *adj.* skimpy, mean.
SKIMPY, [skimp'-i], *adj.* scanty; meagre; having insufficient material; practising petty economies.
SKIN (1), [skin], *n.* the natural outer covering of an animal; a hide; the bark of a plant; the outer covering; the rind of a fruit; a skin receptacle for wine or water; **to have a thick (thin) s.,** to be insensitive (sensitive); **by the s. of the teeth,** narrowly. [OScand. *skinn*].
SKIN (2), [skin], *v.t.* to strip off the skin or hide of; to flay; to graze the skin of; to peel; to cover with, or as with, skin; (*coll.*) to punish severely; swindle; *v.i.* to be covered with skin; **to s. over,** to have a skin growing over; (*coll.*) **to keep one's eyes skinned,** to be on the look-out.
SKIN-DEEP, [skin'-dēp'], *adj.* on the surface, superficial.
SKIN EFFECT, [skin'-i-fekt'], *n.* the localization of an electric current of very high frequency on the surface of a conductor.
SKINFLINT, [skin'-flint], *n.* a greedy, grasping person; miser.
SKINFUL, [skin'-fo͝ol], *n.* as much as a skin will hold; (*coll.*) the quantity that a person can drink.
SKINK, [skingk], *n.* a small lizard of the genus, *Scincus*, having four short legs, five serrated toes, and a short conical tail. [Gk. *skigkos*].
SKINLESS, [skin'-les], *adj.* having no skin; thin-skinned.
SKINNER, [skin'-er], *n.* one who sells skins, a furrier.
SKINNINESS, [skin'-i-nes], *n.* the condition of being skinny.
SKINNY, [skin'-i], *adj.* having much skin; very thin; tough and fibrous; (*coll.*) mean, parsimonious.
SKIN-WOOL, [skin'-wo͝ol], *n.* wool taken from the dead sheep.
SKIP (1), [skip], *n.* a small leap, bound, spring.
SKIP (2), [skip], *n.* a basket used in textile factories; a basket or bucket used in mines for hoisting coal. [~SKEP].
SKIP (3), [skip], *v.t.* to leave out, omit, pass hastily over; *v.i.* to leap; to jump over a rope repeatedly in play; to frisk, frolic; to read quickly leaving out passages; (*coll.*) to run away hastily; to visit quickly and for a short time. [ME. *skippen*].
SKIP-JACK, [skip'-jak'], *n.* an upstart; a click-beetle of the *Elateridæ*; the blue-fish, *Temnodon saltator*.
SKIPPER (1), [skip'-er], *n.* the captain of a ship; (*coll.*) the captain of a side. [MDu. *schipper*].
SKIPPER (2), [skip'-er], *n.* one who, or that which, skips.
SKIPPET, [skip'-et], *n.* the box in which deeds or the seal attached to legal documents may be housed. [ME. *skipet*].
SKIPPINGLY, [skip'-ing-li], *adv.* in a skipping way.

SKIPPING-ROPE, [skip'-ing-rōp], *n.* a rope for skipping with.

SKIRL (1), [skurl], *n.* a shrill sound; the sound of the bagpipes.

SKIRL (2), [skurl], *v.i.* to emit a shrill sound like the note of the bagpipes. [~Norw. *skrylla*].

SKIRMISH (1), [skurm'-ish], *n.* an irregular engagement in which small numbers are engaged; a contest; (*fig.*) an argument, a brief contest of wits.

SKIRMISH (2), [skurm'-ish], *v.i.* to fight irregularly, in small scattered parties; to fight in extended order; to have a skirmish. [OFr. *eskermir*].

SKIRMISHER, [skurm'-ish-er], *n.* a man who skirmishes.

SKIRMISHING, [skurm'-ish-ing], *n.* the act of skirmishing; fighting in open order.

SKIRRET, [ski'-rit], *n.* a water parsnip, *Sium sisarum*; the edible tubers of this. [OFr. *escherirs*].

SKIRT (1), [skurt], *n.* the lower and loose part of a coat or other garment; border; margin; a woman's garment fitted in at the waist and falling over the legs; the diaphragm or midriff in animals; a skirting-board; (*slang*) a woman. [OIcel. *skyrt*].

SKIRT (2), [skurt], *v.t.* to run, pass along the edge, margin of; to border; *v.i.* to be on the border; to live near the extremity.

SKIRTING, [skurt'-ing], *n.* a border; the lower edge of a dado; material for women's skirts.

SKIRTING-BOARD, [skurt'-ing-bawd], *n.* the board that runs along a wall where it joins the floor.

SKIT (1), [skit], *n.* a lampoon, caricature, light humorous sketch.

SKIT (2), [skit], *v.t.* to ridicule; to write a skit upon; *v.i.* to make satirical fun of. [Uncert.].

SKITTER, [skit'-er], *v.i.* to move quickly, scamper off; to skim along the surface of water; (in angling) to cause the hook to skim rapidly over the surface of the water. [SKIT (2)].

SKITTISH, [skit'-ish], *adj.* easily frightened, nervous; volatile; unsuitably frolicsome or gay.

SKITTISHLY, [skit'-ish-li], *adv.* in a skittish way.

SKITTISHNESS, [skit'-ish-nes], *n.* the state of being skittish.

SKITTLE, [skitl], *v.t.* (*cricket*) **to s. out,** to bowl out as easily as if the bails were skittle-pins.

SKITTLEDOG, [skitl'-dog'], *n.* the spur dogfish, *Acanthias vulgaris.*

SKITTLES, [skitlz], *n.*(*pl.*) a set of nine-pins; a game played with these. [Dan. *skyttel* an earthen ball].

SKIVE, [skiv], *v.t.* to pare off, to shave (leather) into thin pieces. [Norw. *skive*].

SKIVER, [skīv'-er], *n.* part of a sheepskin split or divided for bookbinding; inferior leather; the knife used in skiving. [*Prec.*].

SKIVVY, [skiv'-i], *n.* (*slang*) a domestic servant in a house, usually a "general." [Uncert.].

SKOAL, [skōl], *n.* a toast in drinking. [Norw. *skaal* from OScand. *skal* bowl].

SKUA, [skew'-a], *n.* a pirate gull belonging to the genus *Megalestris.* [~OIcel *skufr*].

SKULK, [skulk], *v.i.* to lurk in corners; to hide furtively; to sneak about; to malinger. [~Norw. *skulka* to lurk].

SKULKER, [skulk'-er], *n.* one who skulks.

SKULKINGLY, [skulk'-ing-li], *adv.* in a skulking fashion.

SKULL, [skul], *n.* the bony structure that encloses the brain in man and certain animals; the human skull as a symbol of mortality; **the s. and crossbones,** the pirate's symbol. [ME. *skulle*].

SKULL-CAP, [skul'-kap'], *n.* a cap fitting closely to the head; a headpiece; a plant of the genus *Scutellaria.*

SKULPIN, [skulp'-in], *n.* a sea-fish belonging to the genus *Callionymus.* [Uncert.].

SKUNK, [skungk], *n.* a species of American carnivore of the genus *Mephitis,* which defends itself when pursued, by the ejection of offensively foetid matter, and whose fur when dressed is known as Alaska-sable; (*fig.*) a mean, low type of person. [NAmerInd. *seganku*].

SKUNK

SKUNK-BIRD, [skungk'-burd], *n.* the common marsh blackbird, *Dolichonix oryzivorus.*

SKUNKISH, [skungk'-ish], *adj.* resembling a skunk.

SKUPSHTINA, [skōōpsh'-tēn-a], *n.* the legislative assembly of Yugoslavia. [Serb. *skupshtina*].

SKUTTERUDITE, [skut'-ter-ōōd-īt], *n.* (*min.*) a compound of cobalt and arsenic. [*Skutterud,* Norway, where mined].

SKY (1), [skī], *n.* the aerial region which surrounds the earth; the apparent vault of heaven; the heavens; (*fig.*) the prospect, situation. [OIcel. *sky*].

SKY (2), (skying, skied), [skī], *v.t.* to hit or throw high into the air; to place anything in a high position, *esp.* to hang a picture in an unflatteringly high place at an exhibition.

SKY-BLUE, [skī'-blōō'], *adj.* of a blue colour like that of a clear summer sky.

SKY-BORN, [skī'-bawn], *adj.* born in heaven; heavenly.

SKY-COLOUR, [skī'-kul'-er], *adj.* sky-blue; azure.

SKYE TERRIER, [skī'-te'-ri-er], *n.* a breed of small terrier with short legs. [*Skye* in the Inner Hebrides].

SKYEY, [skī'-i], *adj.* pertaining to the sky.

SKY-HIGH, [skī'-hī'], *adj.* very high.

SKYISH, [skī'-ish], *adj.* like the sky; lofty; sky-blue.

SKYLARK, [skī'-lahk], *n.* the common lark, *Alauda arvensis,* that mounts and sings as it flies.

SKYLARKING, [skī'-lahk'-ing], *n.* frolicking about a ship's rigging; boisterous merrymaking.

SKYLIGHT, [skī'-līt], *n.* a window built in the roof of a building or room.

SKYLINE, [skī'-līn], *n.* the horizon; the outline of anything against the sky.

SKY-PILOT, [skī'-pīl'-ot], *n.* (*coll.*) a clergyman.

SKYROCKET, [skī'-rok'-it], *n.* a rocket that rises high into the air and then burns spectacularly or explodes.

SKYSAIL, [skī'-sāl, skisl], *n.* (*naut.*) a square-sail set immediately above a royal.

SKYSCRAPER, [skī'-skrāp'-er], *n.* a skysail; a many-storied, very high building.

SKYWARD, SKYWARDS, [skī'-werd(z)], *adv.* heavenwards; upwards.

SLAB (1), [slab], *n.* a thin, flat piece of marble or other stone; an outside piece taken from timber in sawing it into planks; (*coll.*) a large thick slice of bread or cake. [OFr. *esclape*].

SLAB (2), [slab], *v.t.* to cut into slabs; to cut into thick slices.

SLABBER (1), [slab'-er], *n.* a saw for cutting slabs from logs.

SLABBER (2), see SLOBBER.

SLABBERER, see SLOBBERER.

SLABBERY, see SLOBBERY.

SLABBINESS, [slab'-i-nes], *n.* the quality of being slabby.

SLABBY, [slab'-i], *adj.* thick; viscous; wet; miry; sloppy. [~Dan. *slab* mud].

SLABLINE, [slab'-līn], *n.* (*naut.*) a line with which seamen haul up the foot of the mainsail or foresail.

SLABSTONE, [slab'-stōn], *n.* a flagstone.

SLACK (1), [slak], *n.* the part of a rope that hangs loose; a loose part; low tide; a dull season in trade; small coal. [*Next*].

SLACK (2), [slak], *adj.* not tense, tight, taut; loose, sagging; careless, indifferent; inefficient, slipshod; not prosperous; having little work. [OE. *slæc*].

SLACK (3), [slak], *v.t.* to slacken; *v.i.* to become slack; (*coll.*) to be remiss, idle, indifferent, careless; **to s. off,** to stop working hard.

SLACK-BAKED, [slak'-bākt], *adj.* imperfectly baked.

SLACKEN (1), [slak'-en], *n.* a spongy semi-vitrified substance, used by miners to mix with the ores of metals, to prevent their fusion. [Germ. *schlacken*].

SLACKEN (2), [slak'-en], *v.t.* to lessen the tension of; to relax; to mitigate; to cause to become slower; to abate; to withhold; to deprive of cohesion; to repress; *v.i.* to become less tense; to be remiss; to lose cohesion; to abate; to become slower, less energetic. [~SLACK].

SLACKER, [slak'-er], *n.* a lazy person, one who slacks.

SLACKLY, [slak'-li], *adv.* in a slack manner; not tightly; negligently.

SLACKNESS, [slak'-nes], *n.* looseness; remissness; slowness; weakness; absence of diligence; laxity.

SLACKS, [slaks], *n.*(*pl.*) loose trousers worn by persons of either sex for leisure or work.

SLADE, [slād], *n.* a little dell or vale; a flat piece of low moist ground. [OE. *slæd*].

SLAG, [slag], *n.* vitrified cinders; the scoria or refuse left after the smelting of a metal; the scoria of a volcano. [~Swed. *slagg* dross].

SLAGGY, [slag'-i], *adj.* like slag.

SLAIN, [slān], *p.pt.* of SLAY. [OE. *geslægen*].

SLAKE, [slāk], *v.t.* to quench; to extinguish; to mix with water; *v.i.* to become mixed with water; to go out; to become extinct; to abate; (*fig.*) to moderate, assuage. [OE. *slacian*].

SLAM (1), [slam], *n.* a violent shutting of a door; the noise so produced; (at whist or bridge), the winning of all the tricks; the refuse of alum-works; **grand s.,** the winning of thirteen tricks (at bridge); **small s.,** the winning of twelve tricks.

SLAM (2), [slam], *v.t. and i.* to shut with violence; to bang; to throw noisily down; (*bridge*) to win all or all but one of the tricks. [~Swed. *slemma* to bang].

SLAMKIN, SLAMMERKIN, [slam'-(er-)kin], *n.* an untidy slovenly woman; a slattern. [Uncert.].

SLANDER (1), [slahnd'-er], *n.* a malicious report uttered to damage a person's character; a defamation. [AFr. *esclaundre*].

SLANDER (2), [slahnd'-er], *v.t.* to defame; to injure by maliciously uttering a false report; to traduce. [OFr. *esclandrer*].

SLANDERER, [slahnd'-er-er], *n.* one who slanders.

SLANDEROUS, [slahnd'-er-us], *adj.* containing, uttering, implying, slander; calumnious. [OFr. *esclandreux*].

SLANDEROUSLY, [slahnd'-er-us-li], *adv.* in a slanderous way.

SLANDEROUSNESS, [slahnd'-er-us-nes], *n.* the state, or fact, of being slanderous.

SLANG (1), [slang], *n.* colloquial language; a conversational expression of an irregular but not necessarily vulgar type, familiar to and in vogue among a class, and often vivid and expressive; **back s.,** a thieves' slang in which words are pronounced approximately as if spelt backwards; **rhyming s.,** a Cockney slang in which a word is represented by a word or phrase which rhymes with it. [Uncert.].

SLANG (2), [slang], *v.i.* to abuse; to scold in a violent and abusive fashion.

SLANGILY, [slang'-i-li], *adv.* in a slangy way.

SLANGINESS, [slang'-i-nes], *n.* slangy quality.

SLANGY, [slang'-i], *adj.* pertaining to slang; using slang.

SLANT (1), [slahnt], *n.* a slope; an inclined plane; an oblique reflection or gibe; **s. on,** (*coll.*) an angle of approach to, useful information concerning. [ME. *slante*].

SLANT (2), [slahnt], *adj.* slanting.

SLANT (3), [slahnt], *v.t.* to turn from a direct line, to give an oblique direction to; *v.i.* to slope; to incline away from the straight. [ME. *slenten*].

SLANTING, [slahnt'-ing], *adj.* sloping, oblique.

SLANTINGLY, [slahnt'-ing-li], *adv.* in a slanting direction.

SLANTLY, [slahnt'-li], *adv.* slantingly.

SLANTWISE, [slahnt'-wiz], *adv.* obliquely, in a slanting direction.

SLAP (1), [slap], *n.* a blow with the open hand or with something flat; (*fig.*) a nasty snub.

SLAP (2), [slap], *v.t.* to give a slap to; to strike with the open hand; **to s. down,** (*coll.*) to throw rudely or carelessly down. [Echoic].

SLAP-BANG, [slap'-bang'], *adv.* (*coll.*) violently, noisily.

SLAPDASH, [slap'-dash], *adj.* rash, careless, slipshod.

SLAPJACK, [slap'-jak'], *n.* a kind of pancake baked on a grid.

SLAPPING, [slap'-ing], *adj.* large; well built; strong; strapping.

SLAPSTICK (1), [slap'-stik], *n.* a wooden wand of two flat boards fastened together at the handle so as to make a noisy slap when shaken; knockabout comedy, farce.

SLAPSTICK (2), [slap'-stik], *adj.* relating to, consisting of, rough knockabout farce.

SLAP-UP, [slap'-up], *adj.* (*coll.*) first-rate; sumptuous.

SLASH (1), [slash], *n.* a long cut; a cut made at random; a large slit formerly made in garments in order to show a bright-coloured lining.

SLASH (2), [slash], *v.t.* to cut by striking violently; to cut gashes in; to lash; (*fig.*) to criticize savagely; *v.i.* to strike violently with an edged weapon; to lay about one with blows. [OFr. *esclachier* to split up].

SLASHING, [slash'-ing], *adj.* cutting, severe, violent.

SLAT, SLATT, [slat], *n.* a thin wooden strip such as a blind-lath or a bed-lath; a hoop of a covered wagon; a narrow piece or slip of timber, used to fasten together larger pieces; a thin slab of stone used for roofing instead of a slate. [OFr. *esclat* splinter].

SLATCH, [slach], *n.* (*naut.*) a short period of fair weather; an interval. [OE. *slæc* slack].

SLATE (1), [slāt], *n.* a hard, blue-black or purple shaly rock which splits easily into thin plates; a piece of this rock squared up and used as a section of roof tiling; an oblong piece of this rock set in a wooden frame and used for chalking words or diagrams on; the colour of slate, dark blue-grey. [ME. *sclat*].

SLATE (2), [slāt], *adj.* made of, consisting of, slate; having the colour of slate; **s. club,** a voluntary society, usually of working-class members, who subscribe a small sum each week, with a view to a share-out.

SLATE (3), [slāt], *v.t.* to cover with a slate roofing; to criticize harshly; to reprimand severely.

SLATE-AXE, [slāt'-aks'], *n.* a slater's mattock for shaping rough slate into tiles.

SLATE-COLOURED, [slāt'-kul'-erd], *adj.* having the colour of slate, dark blue-grey.

SLATE-GREY, [slāt'-grā], *adj.* bluish-grey, like slate.

SLATE-PENCIL, [slāt'-pen'-sil], *n.* a pencil made of slate powder moistened and compressed into a thin stick, used for writing on slate.

SLATER, [slāt'-er], *n.* one who shapes or fixes slates; a wood-louse.

SLATINESS, [slāt'-i-nes], *n.* the quality of being slaty.

SLATING, [slāt'-ing], *n.* the act of covering with slates; a covering of slates; materials for slating, slates; a harsh criticism.

SLATT, see SLAT.

SLATTER, [slat'er], *v.t. and i.* to slit, split, particularly clothes; to be careless of dress and dirty; to be wasteful, to spill carelessly.

SLATTERN, [slat'-ern], *n.* a woman who is careless over her dress, or untidy, a slut. [*Prec.*].

SLATTERNLY, [slat'-ern-li], *adj.* sluttish, like a slattern, untidy.

SLATY, [slā'-ti], *adj.* resembling slate; having the nature or properties of slate; full of slate; somewhat like slate in colour.

SLAUGHTER (1), [slaw'-ter], *n.* the act of slaughtering; the condition or fact of having been slaughtered, the indiscriminate dealing out of death on a large scale as in battle, senseless killing; the butchering of animals. [ME. *slauhter*, ~OIcel. *slatr* slain flesh].

SLAUGHTER (2), [slaw'-ter], *v.t.* to kill indiscriminately and savagely; to kill in large numbers, to massacre; to butcher animals for their meat.

SLAUGHTERER, [slaw'-ter-er], *n.* one employed to slaughter cattle; a slayer.

SLAUGHTER-HOUSE, [slaw'-ter-hows], *n.* a shed where beasts are killed for the market; a scene of slaughter or massacre.

SLAUGHTERMAN, [slaw'-ter-man], *n.* a man employed to slaughter cattle, a slaughterer.

SLAUGHTEROUS, [slaw'-ter-us], *adj.* feeling roused, to be destructive, murderous.

SLAUGHTEROUSLY, [slaw'-ter-us-li], *adv.* in a slaughterous fashion.

SLAV (1), [slahv], *n.* a member of a race inhabiting Eastern Europe, including among others the Russians, Poles, and Czechs, and speaking closely related languages. [~OSlav. *sloviti* to speak].

SLAV (2), [slahv], *adj.* of, relating to, made by, the Slavs or their languages.

SLAVE (1), [slāv], *n.* a person whose conditions of living are imposed by the will of another, one who has no power to choose his mode of life or work, one who is legally recognized as being under the absolute control of an owner; a serf, a thrall, one who is compelled to spend his life working hard for the profit of an employer, a drudge; one who is dominated in his actions by psychological weaknesses. [~SLAV (1)].

SLAVE (2), [slāv], *adj.* of, relating to, dealing with, a slave or slaves; composed of slaves.

SLAVE (3), [slāv], *v.i.* to work under conditions resembling a slave's, to drudge.

SLAVE-BORN, [slāv'-bawn], *adj.* born into slavery.

SLAVEDRIVER, [slāv'-drīv'-er], *n.* a person who is in charge of slaves, and keeps them at their work; a person who overworks subordinates.

SLAVE-DRIVING, [slāv'-drīv'-ing], *n.* the bullying methods of a slavedriver.

SLAVE-GROWN, [slāv'-grōn], *adj.* produced by slave labour.

SLAVEHOLDER, [slāv'-hold'-er], *n.* a slave owner.

SLAVEHOLDING, [slāv'-hold'-ing], *adj.* maintaining others in slavery.

SLAVE-HUNTER, [slāv'-hunt'-er], *n.* one who hunts for slaves.

SLAVE-LIKE, [slāv'-līk], *adj.* like a slave, resembling the activities of a slave.

SLAVER (1), [slāv'-er], *n.* a ship employed in slave traffic; a person who trades in slaves.

SLAVER (2), [slav'-er], *n.* the act of salivating; saliva dribbling from the mouth; (*coll.*) mawkish drivel.

SLAVER (3), [slav'-er], *v.t. and i.* to smear or cover with saliva; to dribble at the mouth, to salivate, slobber; (*coll.*) to address mawkishly. [OIcel. *slafra*].
SLAVERER, [slav'-er-er], *n.* a person who dribbles at the mouth, a driveller; an idiot.
SLAVERY, [slāv'-er-i], *n.* the condition of life of a slave; the system of society which permits of slave ownership; excessive hard work, drudgery. [~MDu. *slaveria*].
SLAVEY, [slāv'-i], *n.* (*slang*) a servant girl who does the dirtiest jobs of work in the house.
SLAVIC, [slav'-ik], *adj.* relating to the Slavs, Slavonic.
SLAVISH, [slāv'-ish], *adj.* relating to or like slaves; servile, mean; laborious, consisting of drudgery; mechanical.
SLAVISHLY, [slāv'-ish-li], *adv.* to a slavish degree, in a slavish manner.
SLAVISHNESS, [slāv'-ish-nes], *n.* the quality of being slavish; slavish character; the state of being slavish.
SLAVONIC, [slav-on'-ik], *adj.* of, or relating to, the Slavs or their languages.
SLAVOPHILE, [slav'-ō-fil], *n.* an admirer of the Slavs and their customs. [SLAV and Gk. *philos* loving].
SLAVOPHOBE, [slav'-ō-fōb], *n.* a person who hates the Slavs. [SLAV and Gk. *phobos* hate].
SLAW, [slaw], *n.* (*U.S.*) a vegetable salad made out of lightly boiled, cold cabbage sliced up. [Du. *sla* salad].
SLAY (1), [slā], *n.* a weaver's reed for beating the weft. [OE. *slege* strike].
SLAY (2), (slew, slain), [slā], *v.t.* to put to death with a weapon or by violence, to kill, to destroy. [OE. *slean*].
SLAYER, [slā'-er], *n.* one who slays, a murderer, a destroyer of life.
SLEAVE† **(1),** [slēv], *n.* soft floss or unwrought silk, a thin filament of silk.
SLEAVE (2), [slēv], *v.t.* to separate (a silk strand) into threads. [OE. *slæfan*].
SLEAVED, [slēvd], *adj.* separated into threads.
SLED (1), [sled], *n.* a carriage or vehicle consisting of a low framework of wood and metal moved on runners for transporting loads over snow, a sledge.
SLED (2), (sledding, sledded), [sled], *v.t.* to travel or transport by means of a sled. [MDu. *sledde* to slide].
SLEDDED†, [sled'-ed], *adj.* transported or mounted on sleds.
SLEDDING, [sled'-ing], *n.* the act of transporting on a sled; the means of conveying on sleds; snow in a fit state of firmness and smoothness for the running of sleds.
SLEDGE (1), [slej], *n.* a large heavy type of hammer, used chiefly by smiths and ironworkers, and wielded with both hands. [OE. *slecg*].
SLEDGE (2), [slej], *n.* a means of transport over ice or snow, consisting of a low framework of wood fitted with metal runners, a sled, a sleigh. [MDu. *sleedse*].

SLEDGE

SLEDGE (3), [slej], *v.t. and i.* to transport by means of a sledge; to travel on a sledge.
SLEDGE HAMMER, [slej'-ham'-er], *n.* a large heavy hammer, a sledge; **s. blows,** violent, heavy blows. [SLEDGE (1) and HAMMER (1)].
SLEEK (1), [slēk], *adj.* having a smooth, glossy surface or appearance, not rough; smooth in manners, oily, smug. [OIcel. *slikr* smooth].
SLEEK (2), [slēk], *v.t.* to smooth, to make sleek.
SLEEKLY, [slēk'-li], *adv.* to a sleek degree, in a sleek manner.
SLEEKNESS, [slēk'-nes], *n.* the condition of being sleek; smoothness of surface.
SLEEKY, [slēk'-i], *adj.* characterized by sleekness, of a sleek or smooth appearance.
SLEEP (1), [slēp], *n.* the state of temporary unconsciousness, recurring naturally in human beings every twenty-four hours; the time such a state lasts; (*fig.*) mental apathy or lethargy; **last s.,** death. [OE. *slæp*].
SLEEP (2), (slept), [slēp], *v.i.* to experience sleep; to be in a state of inactivity, to be lethargic; to become numb or unfeeling; to spin round at high speed, as a top, the movement being imperceptible; to be dead. [OE. *slæpan*].
SLEEPER, [slēp'-er], *n.* a person who sleeps; a hibernating animal; one of the stout oblong pieces of timber used on a permanent way to support railway lines; a railway coach designed to accommodate passengers who wish to sleep during a night journey; a single compartment in such a carriage.
SLEEPILY, [slēp'-i-li], *adv.* in a sleepy manner, drowsily.
SLEEPINESS, [slēp'-i-nes], *n.* the state of being sleepy, inclination to sleep.
SLEEPING (1), [slēp'-ing], *n.* the state of being asleep, sleepiness.
SLEEPING (2), [slēp'-ing], *adj.* taking rest; inducing sleep; set aside for sleep.
SLEEPING-BAG, [slēp'-ing-bag'], *n.* a thick, warm, waterproofed bag in the form of a sack, used by officers on active service, and by people sleeping out in tents.
SLEEPING-CAR, [slēp'-ing-kah(r)], *n.* a railway coach fitted with sleeping accommodation.
SLEEPING-DRAUGHT, [slēp'-ing-drahft], *n.* a medicine which induces sleep, a soporific, an opiate.
SLEEPING-PARTNER, [slēp'-ing-paht'-ner], *n.* a director of a firm who draws a salary but does no work.
SLEEPING-SICKNESS, [slēp'-ing-sik'-nes], *n.* a disease, *Trypanosomiasis*, spread by a species of tsetse-fly, the characteristic symptom being a deep sleep which usually terminates in death.
SLEEPLESS, [slēp'-les], *adj.* marked by the absence of sleep, wakeful, having no rest; alert, ever watchful; restless, perpetually agitated.
SLEEPLESSLY, [slēp'-les-li], *adv.* in a sleepless fashion.
SLEEPLESSNESS, [slēp'-les-nes], *n.* the state of being sleepless; absence or lack of sleep.
SLEEPWALKER, [slēp'-wawk-er], *n.* one who walks while asleep, a somnambulist.
SLEEPWALKING, [slēp'-wawk-ing], *n.* the habit of walking in one's sleep, somnambulism.
SLEEPY, [slēp'-i], *adj.* requiring, overcome by, sleep; drowsy, inclined to sleep; tending to induce sleep, having no stimulating qualities; characterized by relative inactivity; dull; lazy; over-ripe; **s. sickness,** a disease, *Encephalitis lethargica*, caused by a virus, and resulting in lethargy and mental deterioration.
SLEET (1), [slēt], *n.* fine snow mingled with rain, rain frozen to smaller grains of softer consistency than hail. [ME. *slete*].
SLEET (2), [slēt], *v.i.* (*impers.*) to shower down sleet.
SLEETINESS, [slēt'-i-nes], *n.* the condition of being sleety.
SLEETS, [slētz], *n.(pl.)* the parts of a mortar from the chamber to the trunnions.
SLEETY, [slēt'-i], *adj.* having the characteristics of sleet; bringing or consisting of sleet.
SLEEVE (1), [slēv], *n.* that part of a garment or coat which covers the arm; a mechanism consisting of a tube enclosing a smaller tube; **to have up one's s.,** to keep in secret reserve; **to laugh up one's s.,** to laugh at another unobserved, to gloat slyly over another's discomfiture. [OE. *slefe*].
SLEEVE (2), [slēv], *v.t.* to provide with sleeves.
SLEEVE-BUTTON, [slēv'-but'-on], *n.* a button sewn on to a sleeve as a fastening or ornament.
SLEEVED, [slēvd], *adj.* designed or provided with sleeves.
SLEEVE-FISH, [slēv'-fish], *n.* the cuttle-fish or squid.
SLEEVELESS, [slēv'-les], *adj.* having no sleeves; †futile, uncalled for, fruitless.
SLEEVE-LINK, [slēv'-lingk], *n.* two studs joined by a link, a cuff-link.
SLEEVE-VALVE, [slēv'-valv'], *n.* (*eng.*) a valve consisting of a shaped cylindrical tube sliding inside a cylindrical chamber and outside the piston.
SLEEVE-WAISTCOAT, [slēv'-wāst'-kōt], *n.* an old-fashioned waistcoat with sleeves of full length.
SLEIGH (1), [slā], *n.* a vehicle for one or more passengers in the form of a carriage on runners for use on snow; a sledge or sled. [Du. *slee*].
SLEIGH (2), [slā], *v.t. and i.* to travel by means of a sleigh; to use a sleigh as a vehicle.
SLEIGH-BELL, [slā'-bel'], *n.* a small, jingling bell hanging on a sleigh or its harness.
SLEIGHING, [slā'-ing], *n.* the state of the snow when fit for sledging; the act of travelling on a sleigh.
SLEIGHT, [slīt], *n.* a dexterous trick, a deceptive device; an illusion created by manipulation; **s. of hand,** tricks performed by a skilful conjuror. [ME. *sleighte* from OIcel. *slægr* cunning].
SLENDER, [slend'-er], *adj.* small in width compared with length, narrow in circumference, thin, slim; small in the waist; slight, inconsiderable; feeble, weak; inadequate, scarcely sufficient, scanty. [ME. *slendre*].
SLENDERLY, [slend'-er-li], *adv.* to a slender degree; slightly.
SLENDERNESS, [slend'-er-nes], *n.* the state of being

slender, thinness, slimness; feebleness, weakness; spareness.
SLEPT, [slept], *pret. and p.pt.* of SLEEP. [OE. *slæpte*].
SLEUTH (1), [slōōth], *n.* the track of an animal; the animal or person who follows a track; a bloodhound; (*coll.*) a detective. [OIcel. *sloth* trail].
SLEUTH (2), [slōōth], *v.t.* to follow, to track; (*coll.*) to act as a detective.
SLEUTH-HOUND, [slōōth'-hownd], *n.* a hound trained to track a man by scent; (*coll.*) a man who is expert in detection.
SLEW (1), [slōō], *pret.* of SLAY. [ME. *slew*].
SLEW (2), SLUE, [slōō], *v.t.* to swing round or askew. [Uncert.].
SLEY (1), [slā], *n.* a reed used by a weaver for combing, a guiding comb. [OE. *slege*].
SLEY (2), [slā], *v.t.* to comb out (the threads of the warp) by means of a sley.
SLICE (1), [slīs], *n.* a thin, broad piece cut off something, a piece cut out of a whole; a share, a portion; an implement for cutting; an implement used in cooking; a broad, flat knife with which fish is served; a spatula; (*sport*) a stroke in which the ball veers to the right of the line of flight; **s. of life,** a typical specimen of life, in a play or story. [OFr. *esclice*].
SLICE (2), [slīs], *v.t. and i.* to cut up in slices, to divide into thin portions by cutting; to cause to slide off sharply; (*sport*) to make a slice. [*Prec.*].
SLICER, [slīs'-er], *n.* one who, or that which, slices.
SLICK† (1), [slik], *n.* (*mining*) the ore of a metal, particularly of gold, pounded into fine powder for further working. [Germ. *schlich*].
SLICK (2), [slik], *adj.* smooth, sleek; clever, smart, deft. [ME. *slike* smooth].
SLICK (3), [slik], *adv.* at once; effectually, cleverly, easily done; head-on.
SLICKENSIDES, [slik'-en-sīdz], *n.(pl.)* (*geol.*) scratches and grooves on the polished surfaces of fissures or faults in rocks. [SLICK (2) and SIDE].
SLID, [slid], *pret. and p.pt.* of SLIDE. [OE. *gesliden*].
SLIDABLE, [slīd'-abl], *adj.* designed for sliding.
SLIDE (1), [slīd], *n.* the act of sliding; a stretch of smooth, slippery surface, particularly of ice or snow; a highly polished incline providing a means of transport, a chute; a small piece of glass used as a base for objects put under a microscope; a piece of glass on which scenes or designs are drawn or printed, and which is slid into a magic lantern or cinema projector; a landslip; a hair grip in the form of a clip, used by women; (*mus.*) a grace of two semitones; a rapid chromatic run on an instrument; a slider; **s.-valve,** (*eng.*) a valve controlling, by means of a sliding motion, the admission and expulsion of steam or gases to or from a cylinder.
SLIDE (2), (slid), [slīd], *v.t. and i.* to cause to slide, to thrust along a slippery surface, to make glide; to put into position with an oblique movement; to move smoothly along a polished surface, to glide, to slip along; to work easily in a specific groove; to move into a position obliquely or unobserved; to pass silently; (*fig.*) to undergo imperceptible change from one state to another; to treat superficially, to pass (over) lightly or too facilely. [OE. *slidan*].
SLIDER, [slīd'-er], *n.* one who slides; the part of an instrument or machine that slides.
SLIDE-REST, [slīd'-rest], *n.* (*eng.*) a tool holder on a lathe which traverses the bed both laterally and at an angle to the centres.
SLIDE-RULE, SLIDING-RULE, [slīd'-rōōl], *n.* a ruler fitted with a sliding attachment by means of which certain mathematical calculations are simplified.

SLIDE-REST

SLIDING (1), [slīd'-ing], *n.* the act of sliding; the distance slid; a lapse.
SLIDING (2), [slīd'-ing], *adj.* adapted for slides, worked by means of a slide.
SLIDING-KEEL, [slīd'-ing-kēl], *n.* (*naut.*) an adjustable keel let down through the bottom of a yacht to take the wind tilt.
SLIDING-RULE, see SLIDE-RULE.
SLIDING-SCALE, [slīd'-ing-skāl], *n.* a scale of duties, wages, or charges which is modified in terms of current market prices or similar factors.
SLIDING-SEAT, [slīd'-ing-sēt], *n.* a seat on a rowing-boat that slides on runners with the swing of the body so as to enable the stroke to be lengthened.
SLIGHT (1), [slīt], *n.* a gesture with a social significance of disrespect, a breach of convention, an insult.
SLIGHT (2), [slīt], *adj.* having a physical constitution or frame of body which is not strong; slender of limb, slim, inclined to thinness; delicate, fragile, particularly in health; having little effect, making little difference, mild, not severe; inconsiderable, of no consequence, not deep; insignificant, superficial, trivial. [ME. *sliht*].
SLIGHT (3), [slīt], *v.t.* to subject to a slight, to treat with contempt, to insult.
SLIGHTINGLY, [slīt'-ing-li], *adv.* in a contemptuous manner, insultingly, with disrespect.
SLIGHTLY, [slīt'-li], *adv.* to a slight extent, only a little, in a slight manner.
SLIGHTNESS, [slīt'-nes], *n.* the condition of being slight, slenderness, weakness.
SLILY, see SLYLY.
SLIM (1), [slim], *adj.* having a natural constitutional tendency not to put on flesh; being small-boned; slender; of small diameter; weak, slight; astute, cunning, crafty. [~Du. *slim*].
SLIM (2), (slimming, slimmed), [slim], *v.t. and i.* to make slim; to reduce one's weight.
SLIME (1), [slīm], *n.* liquid mud in a greasy or sticky condition, viscous mud; bitumen; viscous secretion, as of snails; any viscous substance. [OE. *slim*].
SLIME (2), [slīm], *v.t.* to cover or smear with slime.
SLIME-PIT, [slīm'-pit], *n.* a pit full of slime.
SLIMILY, [slīm'-i-li], *adv.* in a slimy manner.
SLIMINESS, [slīm'-i-nes], *n.* the condition of being slimy.
SLIMLY, [slim'-li], *adv.* to a slim degree, slenderly.
SLIMNESS, [slim'-nes], *n.* the quality of being slim, slenderness; cunning.
SLIMY, [slīm'-i], *adj.* resembling, consisting of, smeared with, slime; having the characteristics of slime; sticky, filthy, viscous; (*fig.*) offensively ingratiating.
SLING (1), [sling], *n.* a primitive weapon consisting of a strip of looped leather with a pad in the centre from which a pebble is hurled; a throw made by means of a sling; a loop used as a support, particularly one placed round the neck to hold up an injured arm.
SLING (2), [sling], *n.* (*U.S.*) an iced drink consisting of equal parts of rum, gin, or other spirit, and water sweetened. [Uncert.].
SLING (3), (slung), [sling], *v.t.* to throw by means of a sling; to hurl from the hand by swinging the arm; to lift by means of a loop; to suspend in a sling; **to s. out,** to throw out bodily; **s. your hook!** (*slang*) go away! [OE. *slingan* to creep].
SLINGER, [sling'-er], *n.* one who slings.
SLINGSTONE, [sling'-stōn], *n.* a pebble fit to be thrown with a sling.
SLINK (1), [slingk], *n.* a calf born before its time. [~SLINK (2)].
SLINK (2), (slank†, slunk), [slingk], *v.t. and i.* (of animals) to give birth to prematurely; to miscarry. [OE. *slincan* to creep].
SLIP (1), [slip], *n.* a fish, a young sole, *Solea vulgaris*.
SLIP (2), [slip], *n.* the act of slipping; an accidental movement of the foot caused by a slippery or uneven surface, a stumble, a false step; an accidental movement out of an accustomed position; an error, a slight mistake; a slope from which a vessel is launched, a slipway; deficiency in transmission; (in cricket) an offside fielder whose position is behind the popping-crease; (*aeron.*) a sideslip; **propeller s.,** the difference between the actual and theoretical headway made by a propeller; **s. of the tongue,** something said which was not intended; **to give someone the s.,** to escape from someone. [SLIP (4)].
SLIP (3), [slip], *n.* a shoot or twig cut from a stock or plant for grafting or transplanting; a young boy or girl, an adolescent needing adult protection; a blank microscope slide; a leash securing a dog, particularly a greyhound; an escape by subterfuge; a loose undergarment; the modern equivalent of a petticoat; an outer covering for a pillow or bolster; a narrow strip of material, particularly a small piece of paper; a galley proof in the form of a long piece of paper with the type printed in a column on one side of the paper; (*pl.*) short bathing drawers or trunks worn by men round the loins. [MDu. *slippe*].
SLIP (4), (slipping, slipped), [slip], *v.t.* to cause to move into a specific position quietly and easily; to slide; to place in position quietly and furtively; to cause to make a slip, to omit; to cut a slip from a parent branch or stem; to escape from, evade, unseen or by subterfuge; to let loose, release, to let go; to give

premature birth to, to miscarry; *v.i.* to move along a smooth surface, to slide, glide; to progress swiftly and easily; to move accidentally out of an accustomed position; to make a false step owing to an uneven or slippery surface, to stumble, to trip up, to trip over; to fall unexpectedly out of one's hand; to escape unseen, to slink away; to make a mistake, to do the wrong thing by accident, to err; to pass rapidly. [MDu. *slippe*].

SLIP-BOARD, [slip′-bawd], *n.* a board fitted for sliding in grooves.

SLIP-COACH, [slip′-kōch], *n.* a railway carriage at the rear of the train which can be detached from a train while in motion.

SLIP-COUPLING, [slip′-kup′-ling], *n.* the coupling by which a slip-coach can be detached.

SLIPE, [slīp], *n.* a mining skip provided with runners instead of wheels. [Uncert.].

SLIP-KNOT, [slip′-not′], *n.* a knot which slips along the rope on which it is made, making a loop which can be tightened or loosened by a pull.

SLIP-OVER, [slip′-ō-ver], *n.* an article of men's wear in the form of a light sleeveless sweater.

SLIPPER, [slip′-er], *n.* a loose shoe easily slipped on, designed for comfort rather than smartness; a light, smart shoe worn by ladies with evening wear, particularly for dancing; a man who releases coursing greyhounds; a child's apron easily slipped on over the clothes to keep them clean.

SLIPPERED, [slip′-erd], *adj.* wearing slippers; **s. ease**, comfort of the sort accompanying the wearing of slippers.

SLIPPERILY, [slip′-er-i-li], *adv.* in a slippery fashion.

SLIPPERINESS, [slip′-er-i-nes], *n.* the condition of being slippery.

SLIPPERWORT, [slip′-er-wurt], *n.* (*bot.*) any plant of the genus *Calceolaria*, *esp.* the lady's slipper.

SLIPPERY, [slip′-er-i], *adj.* not affording a firm footing, causing the foot to slip, skid or slide by reason of smoothness of surface; unreliable, uncertain, changeable; (*fig.*) crafty in conduct. [OE. *slipor*].

SLIPPY, [slip′-i], *adj.* (*coll.*) slippery, lively, quick.

SLIPSHOD, [slip′-shod′], *adj.* originally descriptive of a person wearing shoes down at heel; careless, slovenly and inaccurate.

SLIPSLOP (1), [slip′-slop′], *n.* poor quality liquor; a feeble composition; anything weak or trivial or lacking drive. [SLIP (4) and SLOP (2)].

SLIPSLOP (2), [slip′-slop′], *adj.* weak, feeble; lacking quality or substance; trivial, trashy.

SLIPSTREAM, [slip′-strēm′], *n.* (*aeron.*) the backwash from a propeller.

SLIPWAY, [slip′-wā], *n.* a slope for launching a vessel from a dock or shipyard; a launching way; a slope for transferring seaplanes to the water.

SLIT (1), [slit], *n.* a long, narrow incision, a clean cut; an opening of small width.

SLIT (2), (**slitting, slit**), [slit], *v.t.* and *i.* to cut into two strips, to split, to make a clean cut lengthwise; to make an incision; to be slit. [OE. *slitan*].

SLITHER (1), [sliTH′-er], *n.* the act of slithering.

SLITHER (2), [sliTH′-er], *v.i.* to slip or slide along a slippery surface; to slide about, particularly on wet ground. [OE. *slidrian*].

SLITHERING, [sliTH′-er-ing], *adj.* involved in a slither, slithery.

SLITHERY, [sliTH′-er-i], *adj.* slippery; deceitful.

SLITTER, [slit′-er], *n.* one who, or that which, slits.

SLITTING-MILL, [slit′-ing-mil′], *n.* a machine in which iron plates are slit into strips; a machine for slitting gems; a sawing-machine for making laths.

SLIVER (1), [slī′-ver], *n.* a long, thin, narrow piece split, cut or chipped off a mass. [ME. *sliver*].

SLIVER (2), [slī′-ver], *v.t.* and *i.* to split or cut a sliver off a mass, to reduce to slivers; to cut into slivers. [~OE. *slifan* to slice].

SLOAT, [slōt], *n.* a wooden crossbar which holds together larger pieces forming the bottom of a wagon. [*Var.* of SLOT].

SLOB, [slob], *n.* a stretch of mud or ooze, muddy ground. [Ir. *slab* mud].

SLOBBER (1), SLABBER, [slob′-er], *n.* the act of slobbering; that which is slobbered, saliva.

SLOBBER (2), SLABBER, [slob′-er], *v.t.* and *i.* to smear with saliva; to run at the mouth with saliva, to dribble; to bungle; (*fig.*) to fuss sentimentally. [ME. *sloberen*].

SLOBBERER, SLABBERER, [slob′-er-er] *n.* one who slobbers, gushes sentimentally.

SLOBBERY, SLABBERY, [slob′-er-i], *adj.* covered with slobber; gushingly sentimental, nauseating.

SLOB-ICE, [slob′-īs], *n.* a mixture of ice and snow.

SLOE, [slō], *n.* a small wild plum of bluish-black colour and bitter flavour, the fruit of the blackthorn, *Prunus spinosa*. [OE. *sla*].

SLOE-GIN, [slō′-jin′], *n.* gin in which sloes have been steeped.

SLOG (1), [slog], *n.* the act of slogging; a rather wild, violent hit at a ball, a swipe. [Uncert.].

SLOG (2), (**slogging, slogged**), [slog], *v.t.* and *i.* to hit hard, to make a powerful but rather wild stroke at (a ball), to swipe; to work hard by a series of strong laborious efforts, to plod. [Uncert.].

SLOGAN, [slō′-gan], *n.* the battle-cry or gathering cry of a Highland clan; a phrase giving pithy expression to a principle, and used to stimulate public response; a catch-phrase for advertising purposes. [Gael. *sluagh* army and *gairm* shout].

SLOGGER, [slog′-er], *n.* a person who slogs; a hard reckless hitter; a hard worker.

SLOID, SLOYD, [sloid], *n.* a simple method of manual training by means of carpentry. [Swed. *slöjd* skill].

SLOOP, [slōōp], *n.* (*naut.*) a small single-masted vessel, rigged fore-and-aft. [Du. *sloep*].

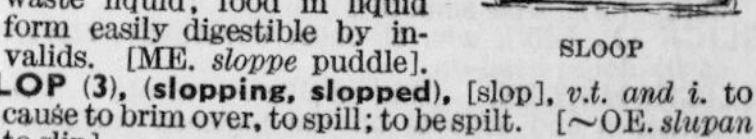

SLOOP

SLOP (1), [slop], *n.*(*pl.*) loose-fitting clothes, an overall; sailor's equipment. [OIcel. *sloppr* loose robe].

SLOP (2), [slop], *n.* an act of slopping; that which is slopped over, a pool of spilt water or liquid; (*pl.*) washing-up water, waste liquid; food in liquid form easily digestible by invalids. [ME. *sloppe* puddle].

SLOP (3), (**slopping, slopped**), [slop], *v.t.* and *i.* to cause to brim over, to spill; to be spilt. [~OE. *slupan* to slip].

SLOP-BASIN, [slop′-bā-sin], *n.* a bowl for containing the dregs of tea-cups.

SLOPE (1), [slōp], *n.* a direction or position inclined away from a flat or upright plane, real or imaginary; a plane inclining downwards, a decline or declivity; a measurement of ascent or descent using ground level as a base; (*milit.*) the position of a rifle when held sloping across the shoulder. [ME. *aslope*].

SLOPE (2), [slōp], *v.t.* and *i.* to make take up a sloping position, to place obliquely, to cause to slant; to take or lie in an oblique direction or position, to possess a surface slanting upwards.

SLOPEWISE, [slōp′-wīz], *adv.* in a sloping direction, aslant, obliquely.

SLOPING, [slōp′-ing], *adj.* slanting, oblique, declivous, inclining or inclined from a horizontal or upright plane, real or imaginary.

SLOPINGLY, [slōp′-ing-li], *adv.* in a sloping position or direction, in a sloping manner.

SLOP-PAIL, [slop′-pāl], *n.* a bucket for collecting household slops.

SLOPPILY, [slop′-i-li], *adv.* in sloppy fashion.

SLOPPINESS, [slop′-i-nes], *n.* the quality of being sloppy.

SLOPPY, [slop′-i], *adj.* lying saturated and immersed in liquid or water, wet; muddy, covered with rain water, as the surface of a road; careless, untidy, floppy; weak, flabby; (*fig.*) having no depth of feeling, sentimental.

SLOPSELLER, [slop′-sel′-er], *n.* a shopkeeper who sells ready-made clothes; a sailor's outfitter.

SLOPSHOP, [slop′-shop′], *n.* a shop where ready-made clothes are sold.

SLOSH (1), [slosh], *n.* (*slang*) slush, foolish sentimentality. [*Var.* of SLUSH].

SLOSH (2), [slosh], *n.* a punch, a hit. [*Var.* of SLASH].

SLOSH (3), [slosh], *v.t.* to hit in an uncontrolled manner, to punch wildly; to beat, to thrash.

SLOT (1), [slot], *n.* the track of a deer, the trail of an animal, a spoor. [OFr. *esclot*].

SLOT (2), [slot], *n.* a slit, a narrow opening designed to contain a smaller object, a groove; a slat or broad, flat wooden bar, to hold larger pieces together, a sloat. [Uncert.].

SLOT (3), (**slotting, slotted**), [slot], *v.t.* to make a slot in.

SLOTH (1), [slōth], *n.* absence of desire for exertion, mental and physical apathy, lethargy, indolence; an American mammal of arboreal habits and characterized by a slow, lumbering gait; **three-toed s.**, a species of *Bradypus*; **two-toed s.**, a species of *Choloepus*; **giant s.**, the *Megatherium*. [OE *slæwth*].

SLOTH-BEAR, [slōth'-bāer], *n.* a long-clawed bear found in India, *Melursus ursinus*.

SLOTH-BEAR

SLOTHFUL, [slōth'-fŏŏl], *adj.* indolent by nature, lazy, inactive, sluggish.
SLOTHFULLY, [slōth'-fŏŏl-i], *adv.* in a slothful fashion.
SLOTHFULNESS, [slōth'-fŏŏl-nes], *n.* the condition of being slothful; laziness.
SLOT-MACHINE, [slot'-ma-shēn'], *n.* a machine which automatically delivers goods after its mechanism has been set in motion by a coin inserted in a slot.
SLOTTERY, [slot'-er-i], *adj.* (*dial.*) sluggish, idle; squalid; dirty, wet. [~ME. *slotteren* to soil].
SLOUCH (1), [slowch], *n.* a shuffling gait, an ungainly bearing; a clumsy person; a felt hat with a turned-down brim. [Uncert.].
SLOUCH (2), [slowch], *v.t. and i.* to cause to hang down, to make stoop; to allow one's body to move or rest in a slouch, to carry oneself with a slouch.
SLOUCH-HAT, [slowch'-hat'], *n.* a soft felt hat with a slouching brim.
SLOUCHING, [slowch'-ing], *adj.* characterized by a slouch; hanging down; walking with a slouch.
SLOUGH (1), [slow], *n.* a muddy swamp, a bog, a quagmire. [OE. *sloh*].
SLOUGH (2), [sluf], *n.* the skin, particularly that of a snake, which has been cast off; the dead tissue shed by a healed-up wound. [ME. *slouh*].
SLOUGH (3), [sluf], *v.t. and i.* to cast off, to shed; to discard a dead skin, as a snake.
SLOUGHY (1), [slow'-i], *adj.* full of sloughs, marshy, boggy, miry.
SLOUGHY (2), [sluf'-i], *adj.* of the nature of slough; resembling dead tissue.
SLOVAK (1), [slō'-vak'], *n.* a member of a western branch of the Slavs living to the north of Hungary. [Czech *Slowak* Slavic].
SLOVAK (2), [slō'-vak'], *adj.* of, pertaining or relating to, the Slovak language or people.
SLOVAN, [slōv'-an], *n.* (*geol.*) the end of a lode. [Unkn.].
SLOVEN, [sluv'-en], *n.* a person careless of dress or cleanliness; a dirty, lazy person; a slattern. [ME. *sloveyn*].
SLOVENE, [slō'-vēn], *n.* a member of a southern branch of the Slavs living to the east of the Julian Alps.
SLOVENIAN (1), [slo-vēn'-i-an], *n.* the native language of the Slovenes. [OSlav. *Slovene*].
SLOVENIAN (2), [slo-vēn'-i-an], *adj.* in Slovenian; of, or pertaining to, Slovenian or the Slovenes.
SLOVENLINESS, [sluv'-en-li-nes], *n.* the condition or the habit of being slovenly; neglect of personal appearance.
SLOVENLY (1), [sluv'-en-li], *adj.* habitually untidy, negligent of dress or neatness; disorderly.
SLOVENLY (2), [sluv'-en-li], *adv.* in the manner of a sloven, carelessly, untidily.
SLOW (1), [slō], *adj.* taking a long time to travel a relatively short distance, characterized by a relatively low rate of progress, not rapid, not quick in motion; taking a long time to come to an end or to take effect; sluggish, not alert, inactive, reluctant to move; hard to rouse; behind time, not punctual, late; being in a condition which necessitates a lower rate of progress than normal; having qualities which do not stimulate, tedious, boring; **s.-motion**, (*cinema*), having the action slowed below normal rate by increasing the number of exposures per second on the film. [OE. *slaw*].
SLOW (2), [slō], *adv.* slowly.
SLOW (3), [slō], *v.t. and i.* to cause to move more slowly, to retard, to reduce speed; to become slow.
SLOWCOACH, [slō'-kōch], *n.* a dull person, a laggard.
SLOWLY, [slō'-li], *adv.* in a slow manner, not rapidly.
SLOW-MATCH, [slō'-mach'], *n.* a fuse designed to burn slowly.
SLOWNESS, [slō'-nes], *n.* the quality or fact of being slow.
SLOW-SIGHTED, [slō'-sīt'-ed], *adj.* slow to perceive or discern.
SLOW-WINGED, [slō'-wingd], *adj.* flying with slow beating of the wings.
SLOW-WORM, [slō'-wurm], *n.* the limbless lizard, *Anguis fragilis*, the blindworm. [OE. *slawyrm*].
SLOYD, see SLOID.
SLUB (1), [slub], *n.* a twisted strand of cotton or wool fibres ready for spinning; a lump in a yarn. [Unkn.].
SLUB (2), (**slubbing, slubbed**), [slub], *v.t.* to draw out and twist ready for the process of spinning. [Unkn.].
SLUBBER (1), [slub'-er], *n.* an operative working a slubbing machine; the machine itself.
SLUBBER (2), [slub'-er], *v.t.* (*dial.*) to stain, soil, or daub; **to s. up**, to perform carelessly, to botch. [~MDu. (*over*)*slubberen* to wade in mud].
SLUBBERDEGULLION, [slub'-er-di-gul'-yon], *n.* (*slang*) a botcher; a mean, dirty fellow, a sloven. [SLUBBER and *gullion*, an onomatopoeic word].
SLUD, [slud], *n.* a soft, muddy rock made by washing ore. [ME. *slowde*].
SLUDGE, [sluj], *n.* a layer of slushy snow; thick, soft mud; wet refuse. [ME. *sluche*].
SLUDGER, [sluj'-er], *n.* a boat for transporting sewage out to sea and dropping it there; a mechanical apparatus for boring through sand; a boat fitted for lifting up mud or sewage and transporting it, a dredger.
SLUDGY, [sluj'-i], *adj.* composed of sludge, slushy, muddy.
SLUE, see SLEW (2).
SLUG (1), [slug], *n.* a slow, lazy fellow, a sluggard; an air-breathing mollusc in which the shell is rudimentary or absent. [ME. *slugge*].
SLUG (2), [slug], *n.* a piece of metal used as crudely formed shot to fire from a rifle; (*coll.*) a bullet, *esp.* of an air-gun; (*typ.*) a metal casting of a line of type; a prefix to a cabled message; (*pl.*) (*mining*) heavy pieces of crude, half-roasted ore. [Uncert.].
SLUG (3), (**slugging, slugged**), [slug], *v.t.* (*slang*) to hit so as to knock unconscious; to prefix with a slug. [*Var.* of SLOG].
SLUGABED, [slug'-a-bed'], *n.* one who lies abed, a sluggard. [SLUG (1) and ABED].
SLUGGARD (1), [slug'-erd], *n.* a person habitually lazy, an idler by repute and desire. [~ME. *sluggen* to be lazy].
SLUGGARD (2), [slug'-erd], *adj.* lazy, slothful, idle.
SLUGGARDIZE, [slug'-erd-īz], *v.t.* to make lazy, to convert to idle ways.
SLUGGISH, [slug'-ish], *adj.* reluctant to move, indolent or lazy, slothful; slow; inert, inactive; slightly unhealthy, not toned up.
SLUGGISHLY, [slug'-ish-li], *adv.* in a sluggish way.
SLUGGISHNESS, [slug'-ish-nes], *n.* the condition of being sluggish, indolence; slowness; inertness.
SLUICE (1), [slōōs], *n.* an artificial vent for stream or river water, fitted with an adjustable gate for the control of the volume of water, a flood-gate; the water which flows through a flood-gate; a trough used in gold-mining in which earth is washed away from gold dust by a stream of water; a quick wash. [OFr. *escluse*].
SLUICE (2), [slōōs], *v.t. and i.* to provide with sluices; to flood with water for washing purposes; to wash quickly; to flow freely.
SLUICE-GATE, [slōōs'-gāt], *n.* a gate sliding in grooves, permitting of an adjustable aperture controlling the volume of water allowed to flow through.
SLUIT, [slōōt], *n.* a narrow passage or channel to convey water drained off higher levels. [Du. *sloot* ditch].
SLUM (1), [slum], *n.* a squalid quarter of a town or city, or a street in such a quarter, characterized by insanitary, dilapidated and overcrowded houses; also (*pl.*). [Uncert.].
SLUM (2), (**slumming, slummed**), [slum], *v.i.* to visit a slum for the purpose of sight-seeing, or to give charity.
SLUMBER (1), [slum'-ber], *n.* sleep, rest, repose.
SLUMBER (2), [slum'-ber], *v.i.* to sleep lightly, to doze; to sleep; to be in a dormant or inactive state. [ME. *slumeren*].
SLUMBERER, [slum'-ber-er], *n.* one who slumbers.
SLUMBERING, [slum'-ber-ing], *adj.* asleep, indulging in slumber, dozing.
SLUMBERINGLY, [slum'-ber-ing-li], *adv.* in a slumbering manner, sleepily.
SLUMBERLESS, [slum'-ber-les], *adj.* characterized by absence of slumber, sleepless.
SLUMBEROUS, [slum'-ber-us], *adj.* tending to induce sleep, soporiferous; drowsy, sleepy; not waking.
SLUMBERSOME, [slum'-ber-sum], *adj.* slumberous.
SLUMBERY, [slum'-ber-i], *adj.* slumberous.
SLUM-CLEARANCE, [slum'-klēer'-ants], *n.* (a scheme for) demolishing slum areas and building new, sanitary houses in their place.
SLUMMOCK, [slum'-ok], *v.t. and i.* to eat greedily; to stumble. [Unkn.].
SLUMMY, [slum'-i], *adj.* of, pertaining to, or resembling, a slum.
SLUMP (1), [slump], *n.* a sudden decline in value or

reputation, particularly a sudden fall in price level or demand; a financial depression, national or international in effect; †a fall into a bog or ice-covered water. [Uncert.].

SLUMP (2), [slump], *v.i.* to fall suddenly in value or esteem; to collapse in confidence; †to fall suddenly into a bog or into water covered by ice.

SLUNG, [slung], *pret. and p.pt.* of SLING. [OE. *geslungen*].

SLUNG-SHOT, [slung'-shot'], *n.* a missile consisting of a heavy lead ball attached to a thong or strap.

SLUNK, [slungk], *pret. and p.pt.* of SLINK. [OE. *geslunćen*].

SLUR (1), [slur], *n.* the act of slurring; an insult, a stain on a reputation, or a suggestion, hint, of such an insult; (*mus.*) a carelessly or deliberately played passage in which the notes are made to slide one into the other; the symbol ⌒, or ‿.

SLUR (2), (**slurring, slurred**), [slur], *v.t. and i.* †to insult, disparage; to run syllables together in pronunciation so as to be indistinct; (*mus.*) to play or sing a passage, by accident or design, so that the notes slide by degrees one into another. [ME. *slore* mud].

SLURRED, [slurd], *adj.* played or uttered with a slur.

SLURRY (1), [slur'-i], *n.* a mixture, in a semi-liquid state, of fireclay and ganister for repairing joining in foundries. [~SLUR (2)].

SLURRY (2), [slur'-i], *v.t.* (*dial.*) to soil, to dirty; to smear.

SLUSH, [slush], *n.* sludge, soft watery mud; melted snow and mud; a soft greasy mixture; (*fig.*) sentimental trash, particularly in the form of literature. [*Var.* of SLUDGE].

SLUSHY, [slush'-i], *adj.* covered with, consisting of, slush.

SLUT, [slut], *n.* a slovenly woman; a name of contempt for a disreputable woman. [ME. *slutte*, ~OIcel. *slota* to slouch].

SLUTTERY, [slut'-er-i], *n.* neglect of cleanliness and order; disorder; dirtiness, sluttishness.

SLUTTISH, [slut'-ish], *adj.* characteristic of a sloven, careless of dress or cleanliness, untidy and dirty.

SLUTTISHLY, [slut'-ish-li], *adv.* in a sluttish way.

SLUTTISHNESS, [slut'-ish-nes], *n.* the condition of being sluttish.

SLY, [slī], *adj.* artful, meanly cunning, crafty; artful in doing illegal acts for one's own advantage and escaping observation; quietly humorous, playful. [ME. *sleigh* from OIcel. *slōgr* cunning].

SLY-BOOTS, [slī'-bōōts], *n.* (*coll.*) a sly, cunning person, a rogue, a rascal.

SLY-GOOSE, [slī'-gōōs], *n.* the shelduck, *Tadorna cornuta*, which builds its nest in disused rabbit holes.

SLYLY, SLILY, [slī'-li], *adv.* in a sly manner.

SLYNE, [slīn], *n.* (*coal-mining*) the natural divisions in the face or board of a seam. [Unkn.].

SLYNESS, [slī'-nes], *n.* the quality of being sly, artful secrecy or cunning.

SLYPE, [slīp], *n.* a covered passage between two walls, *esp.* the covered passage from a cathedral or monastery to any adjoining building. [Uncert.].

SMACK (1), [smak], *n.* a small fishing boat with a single mast rigged fore-and-aft; a small coaster, a yawl. [Du. *smacke* boat].

SMACK (2), [smak], *n.* a distinctive flavour, a characteristic taste; a trace of a substance imparting such a flavour; a hint, a trace. [OE. *smæc*].

SMACK (3), [smak], *n.* a sharp, loud sound like the crack of a whip or the clap of a hand against flesh; a slap, a blow with the open hand held flat; a loud kiss; **s. in the eye**, (*coll.*) a distinct rebuff; **to have a s. at**, to make an attempt at.

SMACK (4), [smak], *v.t. and i.* to press (the lips) together and then part them sharply so as to produce a quick, slapping sound; to strike with the flat palm of the hand, to slap; to make a sharp loud noise as of hands clapped together, to crack, as a whip. (Du. *smakken* to throw down].

SMACK (5), [smack], *v.i.* to have a characteristic taste, to experience a distinct flavour, to savour; to possess a suggestion (of), to hold a hint (of).

SMACKER, [smak'-er], *n.* one who, or that which, smacks; (*coll.*) a loud kiss.

SMACKSMAN, [smaks'-man], *n.* the master of a fishing smack.

SMALL (1), [smawl], *n.* the slim or small part of anything, *esp.* the middle of the back just above the buttocks and beneath the shoulder-blades.

SMALL (2), [smawl], *adj.* comparatively little in size, height, bulk, or stature, of slight extent, not large, less than normal size; being few in number; slender, slim, delicate; of little importance, insignificant petty, trivial; mean, narrow-minded; of inferior quality, below average standard. [OE. *smæl* narrow]

SMALLAGE, [smawl'-ij], *n.* (*bot.*) wild celery, *Apium graveolens*. [ME. *smalache*].

SMALL ARMS, [smawl'-ahmz'], *n.(pl.)* small hand fire-arms such as rifles and revolvers as distinguished from artillery.

SMALL-BEER, [smawl'-bēer'], *n.* weak, thin beer made without hops; (*fig.*) anything insignificant.

SMALL-CLOTHES, [smawl'-klōTHz], *n.(pl.)* †knee-breeches; underpants.

SMALL-COAL, [smawl'-kōl], *n.* coals broken up into small pieces.

SMALL-CRAFT, [smawl'-krahft], *n.* boats of a small size.

SMALL-DEBTS, [smawl'-dets'], *n.(pl.)* (*leg.*) debts so small that a legal claim can be made for them only through the county courts.

SMALL-FRY, [smawl'-frī], *n.* tiny young fish; people or objects of little value or importance.

SMALLHOLDER, [smawl'-hōld'-er], *n.* the tenant of a small-holding.

SMALLHOLDING, [smawl'-hōld'-ing], *n.* a small strip of land leased by a county council to a local tenant for the cultivation of vegetable produce.

SMALL HOURS, [smawl'-ow(er)z'], *n.(pl.)* the hours after midnight and before dawn.

SMALLISH, [smawl'-ish], *adj.* rather small.

SMALL-MINDED, [smawl'-mīnd'-id], *adj.* having a mind occupied with insignificant details, trivialities, having a petty mind; narrow-minded.

SMALL-MINDEDNESS, [smawl'-mīnd'-id-nes], *n.* the quality of being small-minded.

SMALLNESS, [smawl'-nes], *n.* the condition of being small.

SMALLPOX, [smawl'-poks'], *n.* a contagious and infectious fever, attended by eruptions which leave small round scars pitted in the skin, *variola*.

SMALL-REED, [smawl'-rēd], *n.* (*bot.*) one of several species of *Calamagrostis*.

SMALLS, [smawlz], *n.(pl.)* the first examination following matriculation in the University of Oxford, responsions; (*coll.*) ladies' underwear.

SMALLSWORD, [smawl'-sawd], *n.* a light duelling sword, a rapier.

SMALL-WARES, [smawl'-wāerz], *n.(pl.)* various small articles sold as haberdashery.

SMALT, [smalt], *n.* a dark blue pigment, composed of the silicates of cobalt and potassium; glass made out of this substance, and of a fine deep blue. [It. *smalto* enamel].

SMALTINE, SMALTITE, [smal'-tīn, smal'-tīt], *n.* (*min.*) a compound of cobalt, nickel, iron and arsenic. [SMALT].

SMARAGD†, [sma'-ragd], *n.* an emerald. [OFr. *esmaragde*].

SMARAGDINE†, [sma-rag'-dīn], *adj.* relating to, mounted with, an emerald; resembling emerald; of the colour of an emerald, green. [Gk. *smaragdinos*].

SMARAGDITE, [sma-rag'-dīt], *n.* (*min.*) a grass-green variety of augite or hornblende. [Gk. *smaragdites* like emerald].

SMARMY, [smah'-mi], *adj.* (*coll.*) marked by smooth, ingratiating manners. [Dial. *smalm* to smear].

SMART (1), [smaht], *n.* sharp pain that is diffused superficially, such as the sensation of salt or acid on open flesh; emotional suffering, real but superficial, resentment, the after-effects of distress. [SMART (3)].

SMART (2), [smaht], *adj.* causing a sharp but superficial pain, mental or physical; severe, energetic; rapid, alert; capable, efficient; quick to seize an opportunity of personal advancement; quick-witted, witty, vivacious; neat in appearance, tastefully and expensively dressed, wearing well-cut clothes; fashionable.

SMART (3), [smaht], *v.t.* to experience a sensation of sharp pain superficially diffused over an area, to feel a hurt as though on raw flesh; to suffer from emotional distress real but not deep, to feel the effects of emotional hurt, to be resentful. [OE. *smeortan*].

SMART-ALEC(K), [smaht'-al'-ik], *n.* a person who fancies himself as clever. [SMART (2) and the Christian name *Alec*].

SMARTEN, [smaht'-en], *v.t.* to make smart, to impart a neat, spruce appearance to.

SMARTISH, [smaht'-ish], *adj.* quite smart.

SMARTLY, [smaht'-li], *adv.* in a smart manner; keenly; rapidly, briskly; efficiently, capably; vigorously; sprucely, neatly.

SMART-MONEY, [smaht'-mun'-i], *n.* compensation; payment for exemption from an unwanted or awkward set of circumstances, particularly from military service; (*milit.*) money paid as compensation for wounds received on active service.

SMARTNESS, [smaht'-nes], *n.* the condition of being smart.

SMART-TICKET, [smaht'-tik-it], *n.* (*milit.*) a certificate entitling a sailor or soldier to smart-money.

SMASH (1), [smash], *n.* the act of smashing, a violent breaking beyond repair; the sound of such an act; the result of being involved in such a situation; **a s.-up,** a catastrophic collision; **a s. and grab raid,** a raid by a thief who smashes a shop-window and grabs the valuables displayed.

SMASH (2), [smash], *n.* (*U.S. dial.*) an iced drink of flavoured brandy.

SMASH (3), [smash], *v.t. and i.* to break beyond repair, to dash to pieces, to shatter with violence, to crush into little pieces; to hit hard; to bring destruction to, to cause to fall into ruin, *esp.* to make bankrupt; to come into violent collision with; to be destroyed; (*slang*) to mint counterfeit coins. [Uncert.].

SMASHER, [smash'-er], *n.* one who smashes; something having a decisive effect; (*slang*) a coiner of bad money, a counterfeiter; a remarkable person or thing.

SMASHING, [smash'-ing], *adj.* (*slang*) splendid, admirable.

SMATTERER, [smat'-er-er], *n.* one who has only a smattering, a sciolist. [ME. *smatteren* to chatter].

SMATTERING, [smat'-er-ing], *n.* a slight superficial knowledge (of a subject).

SMEAR (1), [smēer], *n.* the act of smearing; a rough layer of greasy, dirty substance, a mark, blotch, stain; (*U.S.*) scandalous rumour. [OE. *smeoru* grease].

SMEAR (2), [smēer], *v.t. and i.* to mark with a smear, to put a mark or layer of grease or dirt upon, to make blotchy, to daub, soil, stain; to spread a crude layer of grease on; to blur by rubbing; to produce a smear; (*U.S.*) to circulate a smear about. [OE. *smerwan*].

SMEARINESS, [smēer'-i-nes], *n.* the condition of being smeary; stickiness.

SMEARY, [smēer'-i], *adj.* covered with smears; adhesive, sticky, greasy.

SMECTITE, [smek'-tīt], *n.* (*min.*) a variety of fuller's earth. [Gk. *smektis*].

SMEGMA, [smeg'-ma], *n.* a soapy secretion forming in the folds of the skin. [Gk. *smegma* soap].

SMEGMATIC, [smeg-mat'-ik], *adj.* soapy, detergent, cleansing.

SMELL (1), [smel], *n.* the faculty of smelling, the sense dependent for sensations on the stimulation of the olfactory nerve in the nasal organ; that which is experienced by means of this sense, a scent; a stench, stink. [ME. *smel*].

SMELL (2), (smelt), [smell], *v.t. and i.* to experience through the sense faculty provided by the nose, to make sensory contact with a smell; to emit an odour; to exercise the sense of smell, to perceive the odour of by means of the nasal organ; **to s. of,** to be permeated with; **to s. a rat,** to be suspicious; **to s. out,** to track, discover. [ME. *smellen*].

SMELLABLE, [smel'-abl], *adj.* able to be smelt.

SMELLER, [smel'-er], *n.* one who smells; (*slang*) the nose.

SMELLING, [smel'-ing], *n.* the sense or act by which odours are experienced.

SMELLING-BOTTLE, [smel'-ing-botl'], *n.* a bottle containing smelling-salts to stimulate the olfactory nerves.

SMELLING-SALTS, [smel'-ing-sawlts'], *n.*(*pl.*) perfumed ammonium carbonate, etc., used to revive a person feeling faint or giddy.

SMELLY, [smel'-i], *adj.* having an odour, *esp.* an unpleasant one.

SMELT (1), [smelt], *n.* a small edible fish of the salmon family with a transparent skin and a silver stripe, *Osmerus eperlanus.* [OE. *smelt*].

SMELT (2), [smelt], *pret. and p.pt.* of SMELL (2).

SMELT (3), [smelt], *v.t.* to heat (ore) so as to extract metal. [~Norw. *smelta*].

SMELTER, [smelt'-er], *n.* one who smelts ore.

SMELTERY, [smelt'-er-i], *n.* a house or factory for smelting.

SMELTING, [smelt'-ing], *n.* the process of heating ores to extract the metal.

SMELTING-FURNACE, [smelt'-ing-furn'-is], *n.* a furnace in which ores are smelted.

SMEW, [smew], *n.* a small migratory sea duck, allied to the goosander, *Mergus albellus.* [Uncert.].

SMICKER, [smik'-er], *v.i.* (*Scots*) to look amorously or lecherously; to ogle, to smirk. [OE. *smicer* handsome].

SMIFT, [smift], *n.* a fuse used in blasting. [Unkn.].

SMILACIN, [smī'-las-in], *n.* (*chem.*) a white crystallizable powder compound, found in certain species of smilax, parillin. [~Gk. *smilax* bindweed].

SMILAX, [smī'-laks], *n.* (*bot.*) a numerous liliaceous genus of plants, the roots of several containing sarsaparilla. [Gk. *smilax* bindweed].

SMILE (1), [smīl], *n.* the act of smiling; a facial expression as a response to a pleasurable experience, usually marked by a slight lifting of the corners of the mouth and a brightening of the eyes, a look indicating pleasure or mild happiness.

SMILE (2), [smīl], *v.t. and i.* to indicate by means of a smile; to express pleasure, approval, or mild happiness by a smile; to allow the face to break slowly into a mild expression of joy; **to s. at,** to consider almost with contempt. [ME. *smilen*, ~Dan. *smile*].

SMILAX

SMILELESS, [smīl'-les], *adj.* without a smile.

SMILER, [smīl'-er], *n.* one who smiles.

SMILING, [smīl'-ing], *adj.* wearing a smile, expressed with a smile; favourable.

SMILINGLY, [smīl'-ing-li], *adv.* in a smiling manner, with a smile of pleasure.

SMIRCH (1), [smurch], *n.* the act of smirching; the mark such an act leaves, a blot, stain, blur, smear.

SMIRCH (2), [smurch], *v.t.* to blur or stain, to cloud, to soil, to smear; to depreciate, to disparage. [Uncert.].

SMIRK (1), [smurk], *n.* an unpleasant expression of the face, half smile, half sneer, the obvious outcome of self-satisfaction, a silly smile, a simper.

SMIRK (2), [smurk], *v.i.* to wear an unpleasant expression on the face, parading one's pride or superiority in a self-satisfied smile. [OE. *smearcian*].

SMIT, [smit], *n.* a coloured clay made into balls for marking sheep. [OE. *smitta* spot].

SMITE, (smote, smitten), [smīt], *v.t. and i.* to strike hard; to give a blow calculated to kill; to descend on with a tremendous impact, to affect the senses violently, to afflict; to strike or affect with passion. [OE. *smitan*].

SMITER, [smīt'-er], *n.* one who smites; a hard hitter.

SMITH, [smith], *n.* one who forges with the hammer; a worker in molten or heated metals. [OE. *smith*].

SMITHEREENS, [smiTH-er-ēnz'], *n.*(*pl.*) (*coll.*) little pieces, small fragments. [Ir. *smidirin*, fragments].

SMITHERY, [smith'-er-i], *n.* the workshop of a smith; the business of a smith; smithing.

SMITHING, [smith'-ing], *n.* the art or process of working iron into shape.

SMITHSONITE, [smith'-son-īt], *n.* (*min.*) silicate of zinc. [James *Smithson*, an English chemist].

SMITHY, [smiTH'-i], *n.* the workshop of a smith, the forge of a blacksmith. [SMITH influenced by OE. *stithig* smithy].

SMITTEN, [smitn], *p.pt.* of SMITE.

SMOCK (1), [smok], *n.* †a woman's undergarment, a petticoat, a chemise; a loose-fitting overall of linen, a smock-frock; a child's romping frock. [OE. *smocc*].

SMOCK (2), [smok], *v.t.* to clothe with a smock.

SMOCK-FACED, [smok'-fāst], *adj.* having an effeminate countenance or complexion.

SMOCK-FROCK, [smok'-frok'], *n.* a coarse linen frock, reaching to the knees, formerly worn by farm-labourers over the other clothes.

SMOCKING, [smok'-ing], *n.* pleating closely in the form of a honeycomb.

SMOCKLESS, [smok'-les], *adj.* without a smock.

SMOKABLE, [smōk'-abl], *adj.* able to be smoked.

SMOKE (1), [smōk], *n.* the finely divided particles given off by burning matter and held in suspension in the air, a cloud of vapour, steam or fumes; the act of smoking a cigarette or cigar; that which is smoked, a cigarette, cigar; **s. gas,** one of various kinds of heavy fumes used as poison gas. [OE. *smoca*].

SMOKE (2), [smōk], *v.t. and i.* to subject to smoke, to apply smoke to, to cure, as meat or fish; to make taste of smoke; to fumigate, to expel by means of smoke; to emit, eject smoke, to give off fumes; to indulge in the practice of inhaling and exhaling tobacco smoke from a cigarette, cigar, or pipe. [*Prec.*].

SMOKE-BLACK, [smōk'-blak'], *n.* a sooty substance obtained from the smoke of burning oil; lampblack.

SMOKEBOARD, [smōk'-bawd], *n.* a board placed across the upper part of a fireplace to increase the draught, and prevent the fumes from the chimney entering the room.

SMOKE-BOMB, [smōk'-bom'], *n.* (*milit.*) a bomb used in warfare to throw out dense clouds of smoke which afford a protective screen for manoeuvres.

SMOKE-BOX, [smōk'-boks'], *n.* a chamber in a railway engine in which the smoke from the firebox collects before it passes up the funnel.

SMOKE-CLOUD, [smōk'-klowd], *n.* a cloud composed of smoke.

SMOKE-CONSUMING, [smōk'-kon-sewm'-ing], *adj.* designed to consume smoke.

SMOKE-DRIED, [smōk'-drīd], *adj.* dried in smoke, cured.

SMOKELESS, [smōk'-les], *adj.* unattended by smoke, having no smoke, producing no smoke.

SMOKER, [smōk'-er], *n.* a worker at a process of drying by smoke; one who smokes tobacco; a concert at which smoking is permitted, an informal show; a railway carriage where smoking is permitted.

SMOKESAIL, [smōk'-sāl], *n.* (*naut.*) a small sail placed in front of the funnel of a vessel's galley as a screen.

SMOKE-SCREEN, [smōk'-skrēn], *n.* (*milit.*) a dense cloud of smoke raised for concealing movements from the enemy; *fig.* a barrage of words intended to confuse or to conceal motive.

SMOKESTACK, [smōk'-stak'], *n.* a tall chimney of a factory, a funnel.

SMOKILY, [smōk'-i-li], *adv.* with smoke.

SMOKINESS, [smōk'-i-nes], *n.* the quality of being smoky.

SMOKING (1), [smōk-ing], *n.* the act of emitting smoke; the process of curing by smoke; the practice of inhaling and emitting tobacco fumes.

SMOKING (2), [smōk'-ing], *adj.* emitting or discharging smoke; where smoking is allowed.

SMOKY, [smōk'-i], *adj.* giving off smoke, emitting smoke in an uncontrolled manner; filled with smoke, full of fumes, permeated with smoke; having the appearance of smoke, cloudy; tarnished by smoke.

SMOLT, [smōlt], *n.* a two-year-old salmon, characterized by developed scales. [Uncert.].

SMOOTH (1), [smōōth], *n.* anything smooth, *esp.* a pleasant experience unaccompanied by discomfort; the act of making smooth.

SMOOTH (2), [smōōth], *adj.* having an even, regular surface, free from roughness, polished, level; not broken up, calm, unruffled; flowing gently and easily, not syncopated, having an even movement of rhythm; having a fine texture; having suave manners, bland, flattering. [OE. *smoth*].

SMOOTH (3), SMOOTHE, [smōōth], *v.t. and i.* to make smooth, to clear away ruffles, lumps, or rucks; to remove obstructions, to make easy in progress; to calm, to soothe; to become smooth; **to s. down,** to become (make) less disordered.

SMOOTHBORE, [smōōth'-baw(r)], *n.* a gun with a barrel that has not been rifled.

SMOOTHE, see SMOOTH (3).

SMOOTH-FACED, [smōōth'-fāst], *adj.* clean-shaven; having a mild, soft look; (*fig.*) bare-faced, brazen.

SMOOTH-HOUND, [smōōth'-hownd], *n.* the small shark, *Mustelus vulgaris*.

SMOOTHING, [smōōth'-ing], *adj.* designed for making smooth; having the power to smooth.

SMOOTHING-IRON, [smōōth'-ing-iern], *n.* a polished iron for smoothing clothes, used by dressmakers and tailors.

SMOOTHING-PLANE, [smōōth'-ing-plān], *n.* a small carpenter's plane used for smoothing and finishing work.

SMOOTHING-PLANE

SMOOTHLY, [smōōth'-li], *adv.* so as to smooth; in a smooth manner.

SMOOTHNESS, [smōōth'-nes], *n.* the condition of being smooth.

SMOOTHSPOKEN, [smōōth'-spōk'-en], *adj.* bland, hypocritical in speech.

SMOOTH-TONGUED, [smōōth'-tungd'], *adj.* conciliatory in speech, plausible; flattering.

SMOTE, [smōt], *pret.* of SMITE. [OE. *smat*].

SMOTHER (1), [smuth'-er], *n.* the act of smothering; a suffocating cloud of smoke or dust. [ME. *smother*].

SMOTHER (2), [smuth'-er], *v.t. and i.* to envelop so as to stifle or suffocate, to block up the passage of air so as to cause choking; to kill by suffocation; to suppress, conceal; to be suffocated, to feel stifled, to find it difficult to breathe. [ME. *smotheren*].

SMOTHERED, [smuth'-erd], *adj.* subjected to smothering, suffocated, stifled.

SMOTHERY, [smuth'-er-i], *adj.* tending to smother, stifling.

SMOULDER (1), [smōld'-er], *n.* the act of smouldering; that which smoulders.

SMOULDER (2), [smōld'-er], *v.i.* to burn away slowly, the fire being barely sustained; to burn or exist in a stifled state; to exist in a powerful latent but suppressed condition. [ME. *smolderen*].

SMUDGE (1), [smuj], *n.* a smeared smut, a black stain, a smear, a dirty mark of a blurred character.

SMUDGE (2), [smuj], *n.* (*U.S.*) a smouldering fire; **s. pot,** a container that emits a smoke-screen. [Uncert.].

SMUDGE (3), [smuj], *v.t. and i.* to smear a smut across, to make a dirty mark on, to make dirty with marks of a blurred character. [ME. *smogen*].

SMUDGY, [smuj'-i], *adj.* smudged; grubby.

SMUG, [smug], *adj.* maintaining an attitude of prudish self-satisfaction, complacent in appearance; †neat, affectedly nice in dress; prim. [~Du. *smuk* spruce].

SMUG-BOAT, [smug'-bōt], *n.* a boat carrying contraband off the coast of China, a vessel trafficking in opium.

SMUG-FACED, [smug'-fāst], *adj.* wearing a smug expression on the face, prim-looking.

SMUGGLE, [smugl], *v.t. and i.* to take (goods) in or out of a country with deliberate intent to evade customs duties; to give illegal transport over a frontier. [LGerm. *smuggeln*].

SMUGGLER, [smug'-ler], *n.* one who smuggles; a vessel employed in carrying contraband.

SMUGGLING, [smug'-ling], *n.* the act of a smuggler; the practice of importing or exporting prohibited goods or other goods with the deliberate intent of evading customs duties or other official control.

SMUGLY, [smug'-li], *adv.* to a smug degree, in a smug manner; †neatly.

SMUGNESS, [smug'-nes], *n.* the condition of being smug; †neatness, spruceness.

SMUT (1), [smut], *n.* a particle of coal dust or soot, a spot of dirt; a mark or stain made by such a particle; a parasitic fungus on grass cereals characterized by a mass of black spots; obscenity. [~Swed. *smuts*].

SMUT (2), (smutting, smutted), [smut], *v.t. and i.* to make or be made dirty with smut, to stain with grains of soot or coal dust, to cover with particles of dirt.

SMUTBALL, [smut'-bawl], *n.* a grain of cereal affected by the fungus, *Tilletia caries*; the fungus, *Lycoperdon Bovista*.

SMUTCH (1), [smuch], *n.* a smut, a smudge. [*Var.* of SMUDGE].

SMUTCH (2), [smuch], *v.t.* to blacken with smoke, soot, or coal, to smut or smudge.

SMUTTILY, [smut'-i-li], *adv.* in a smutty fashion.

SMUTTINESS, [smut'-i-nes], *n.* the quality of being smutty.

SMUTTY, [smut'-i], *adj.* marked, soiled with smut; tainted with mildew; obscene.

SNACK, [snak], *n.* a share; a light meal eaten to save time. [Uncert.].

SNACK-BAR, [snak'-bah(r)], *n.* a small shop or counter *esp.* in the bar of a public-house, where light refreshments are on sale.

SNAFFLE (1), [snafl], *n.* a bit to place in a horse's mouth by means of which a severe pressure can be brought to bear on the animal's mouth as a curb. [Du. *snavel* muzzle of a horse].

SNAFFLE (2), [snafl], *v.t.* to place a snaffle on (a horse); (*slang*) to steal, to pilfer.

SNAG (1), [snag], *n.* a projecting piece of broken branch, root, or tree-stump, *esp.* one sticking up from a river bed and forming a danger to boats; (*fig.*) an unexpected difficulty, a source of trouble or obstruction. [OIcel. *snagi* peg].

SNAG (2), (snagging, snagged), [snag], *v.t. and i.* to collide with a snag; to lop off the projecting parts of trees, to remove snags.

SNAGGY, SNAGGED, [snag'-i], [snagd], *adj.* having the characteristics of a snag; full of snags; abounding with knots.

SNAIL, [snāl], *n.* one of a number of species of slimy, slow-creeping, air-breathing univalve molluscs; a slow-moving person; a spiral cam. [OE. *snægl*].

SNAILERY, [snāl'-er-i], *n.* a small farm where edible snails, *Helix pomatia*, are commercially propagated.

SNAIL-LIKE (1), [snāl'-līk], *adj.* resembling a snail in motion.
SNAIL-LIKE (2), [snāl'-līk], *adv.* in the manner of a snail.
SNAKE (1), [snāk], *n.* (*zool.*) any member of the order *Ophidia*, having the characteristics of a reptile, limbless, long, tubular form, compact of muscle, and covered with small scales, which drags its length by muscular convulsion along the ground; (*fig.*) a cunning, malevolent person; **a s. in the grass**, a hidden danger, a concealed trap; a deceitful enemy. [OE. *snaca*].
SNAKE (2), [snāk], *v.t.* (*naut.*) to bind (a rope) spirally with another rope; *v.i.* to move in the manner of a snake, to wend one's way smoothly and quickly.
SNAKE-BIRD, [snāk'-burd], *n.* the darter, a fish-eating species of *Plotus*, so called from the length of its neck; the wryneck, *Iynx torquilla*.
SNAKE-CHARMER, [snāk'-chahm'-er], *n.* one who gives a performance with snakes which he charms into obedience by various means.
SNAKE-EATER, [snāk'-ēt'-er], *n.* the secretary-bird.
SNAKE-EEL, [snāk'-ēl'], *n.* a species of eel having a tail without any fin.
SNAKELIKE, [snāk'-līk], *adj.* resembling a snake; crafty; sinuous; elongated.
SNAKE-ROOT, [snāk'-rōōt], *n.* (*bot.*) one of several genera of plants found in America, and believed efficacious against snake bites.
SNAKE'S-HEAD, [snāks'-hed'], *n.* (*bot.*) a bulbous plant of Arabia with markings on the petals resembling those of a snake, *Iris tuberosa*; the British plant, *Fritillaria Meleagris*, the fritillary.
SNAKESTONE, [snāk'-stōn], *n.* an ammonite, a small piece of rounded stone or other hard substance, alleged to be an antidote for snake bites.
SNAKEWEED, [snāk'-wēd], *n.* (*bot.*) the plant, *Polygonum Bistorta*, allied to buckwheat.
SNAKEWISE, [snāk'-wīz], *adv.* moving like a snake; in the manner of a snake.
SNAKE-WOOD, [snāk'-wŏŏd], *n.* the wood of a Brazilian tree believed to be a remedy for snake bite.
SNAKILY, [snāk'-i-li], *adv.* in a snaky manner.
SNAKINESS, [snāk'-i-nes], *n.* the condition of being snaky.
SNAKISH, [snāk'-ish], *adj.* having the qualities of, resembling, a snake, snaky.
SNAKY, [snāk'-i], *adj.* relating to, or resembling, a snake; serpentine, winding; sly, insinuating, crafty, deceitful; having snakes.
SNAP (1), [snap], *n.* the act of snapping; the sound that snapping teeth make; a quick, sudden bite; a sudden breaking; the cracking sound made by such an act; a clasp that snaps to when used as a fastening, a small catch, a sudden spell of cold weather, the bite in a frost; conciseness, swiftness of expression; a small cake or biscuit of gingerbread; a simple game of cards in which the word "snap" is used; (*phot.*) an instantaneous photograph taken by an amateur.
SNAP (2), [snap], *adj.* unexpected, done by surprise, quickly accomplished.
SNAP (3), (**snapping, snapped**), [snap], *v.t.* to break suddenly and sharply; to cause to make a cracking sound, to crack; to strike suddenly so as to make a sharp report; to catch at suddenly bringing the teeth together sharply, to bite; to bring together, make fall into place suddenly so as to make a sharp noise, to fasten with a click; to take a snapshot of; in cricket, to catch smartly a ball coming quickly off the bat; *v.i.* to break sharply in two; to come apart suddenly making a sharp sound; to bring the teeth together sharply, particularly so as to make a sharp noise; to bring together with a click, particularly to fasten, close or shut suddenly so as to make a sharp report; to have one's photograph taken in a snapshot; **to s. a person's head off**, to interrupt rudely with the purpose of reprimanding; **to s. one's fingers at**, to show one's contempt for. [MLGerm. *snappen*].
SNAPDRAGON, [snap'-drag'-on], *n.* (*bot.*) the herbaceous plant, *Antirrhinum*, with bright flowers fashioned like the mouth of a dragon; a game played at Christmas of snatching hot raisins out of burning brandy.
SNAPE, [snāp], *v.t.* (*dial.*) to make taper, to bevel. [Uncert.].
SNAPHANCE, [snap'-hants'], *n.* an old-fashioned gun or pistol with a spring lock. [Du. *snap* snapping and *haan* hen].
SNAPPER, [snap'-er], *n.* one who snaps; the alligator-terrapin, *Chelydra serpentina*.
SNAPPILY, [snap'-i-li], *adv.* in a snappy manner.
SNAPPISH, [snap'-ish], *adj.* inclined to snap, eager to bite; curt in reply; inclined to speak angrily or sharply.
SNAPPISHLY, [snap'-ish-li], *adv.* in a snappish way.
SNAPPISHNESS, [snap'-ish-nes], *n.* the quality of being snappish.
SNAPPY, [snap'-i], *adj.* abrupt, curt, irritable, in manner or speech; full of snap, efficient, lively; neat in appearance, smart; **to make it s.**, to be quick about it.
SNAPSHOT, [snap'-shot'], *n.* a shot without a deliberate aim; (*phot.*) a snap as taken by an amateur. [SNAP (2) and SHOT].
SNAP-VOTE, [snap'-vōt'], *n.* a vote called for suddenly.
SNARE (1), [snāer], *n.* a contrivance, based on various principles, such as a noose, pit, or trap for catching birds or animals; that which has power to entangle; a bunch of wired gut strings laid along the surface of the vellum of a side drum to increase the rattling timbre. [OIcel. *snara*].
SNARE (2), [snāer], *v.t.* to catch by means of a snare; to entangle, entrap.
SNARER, [snāer'-er], *n.* one who lays snares.
SNARKY, [snah'-ki], *adj.* (*coll.*) short of temper, irritable; unpleasant.
SNARL (1), [snahl], *n.* the act of snarling; the vicious growling sound made when snarling.
SNARL (2), [snahl], *n.* an entanglement, a complication difficult to unravel.
SNARL (3), [snahl], *v.i.* to show the teeth and growl as an emotional reaction when roused to vicious anger; to speak savagely or surlily; †to emboss. [~MDu. *snarren* quarrel].
SNARLER, [snahl'-er], *n.* one who snarls; a savage, surly, growling animal; a grumbling, quarrelsome fellow.
SNARLING, [snahl'-ing], *adj.* given to vicious growling; grumbling angrily; snappish; †**s. iron**, a tool for embossing on metal.
SNATCH (1), [snach], *n.* the act of snatching, a hasty vigorous effort to seize, a sudden catching, a grab; a short spell of exertion; a fragment, a bit or small portion; a snack.
SNATCH (2), [snach], *v.t. and i.* to seize hastily and vigorously; to catch up in the hand firmly and swiftly, to grasp, to grab; to take without permission, to get hold of so as to keep; to remove by sudden force; to seize suddenly with the hand; to attempt to seize vigorously. [ME. *snacchen*].
SNATCH-BLOCK, [snach'-blok'], *n.* (*naut.*) a kind of block with a hole in one side to receive the bight of a rope.
SNATCHER, [snach'-er], *n.* one who snatches or takes abruptly.
SNATCHILY, [snach'-i-li], *adv.* in a snatchy manner.
SNATCHINGLY, [snach'-ing-li], *adv.* in a snatching manner, by snatching; hastily, abruptly.
SNATCHY, [snach'-i], *adj.* bitty, scrappy.
SNATHE, [snāTH], *n.* the shaft of a scythe. [OScand. *sneith*].
SNEAK (1), [snēk], *n.* a mean fellow; (*slang*) a person who tells tales, an informer; (*cricket*) a ball that keeps low to the ground.
SNEAK (2), [snēk], *v.t.* to steal, pinch, pilfer; *v.i.* to move quickly and furtively as though hoping not to be seen, to keep close to cover while stealing away, to creep, to crouch while slinking away so as to escape observation; (*slang*) to tell of another's punishable activities. [Uncert.].
SNEAKER, [snēk'-er], *n.* one who sneaks; †a small vessel, *esp.* one for holding punch.
SNEAKING, [snēk'-ing], *adj.* acting like a sneak; mean; furtive; servile; engaged in telling tales; crouching; niggardly, small, private.
SNEAKINGLY, [snēk'-ing-li], *adv.* as a sneak, in a sneaking manner.
SNEAKINGNESS, [snēk'-ing-nes], *n.* the characteristic of being sneaking; meanness; niggardliness.
SNEER (1), [snēer], *n.* the act of sneering; a facial expression characterized by a superior smile indicating contempt, a look of disdain; a verbal expression of contempt, a gibe, a remark obviously arising out of the speaker's false pride in his own superiority.
SNEER (2), [snēer], *v.t. and i.* to express by means of a sneer; to assume a facial expression consisting of a mocking contemptuous smile indicating a boastful belief in one's own personal superiority; to make contemptuous mocking remarks, to disparage by means of a sneer. [ME. *sneren* to scorn].

SNEERER, [snēer'-er], *n.* one who sneers.
SNEERINGLY, [snēer'-ing-li], *adv.* in a sneering manner; by means of a scornful look.
SNEEZE (1), [snēz], *n.* the act of sneezing; the sound made by such an act.
SNEEZE (2), [snēz], *v.i.* to make an involuntary response to an irritant affecting the inner mucous membrane of the nose by blowing air loudly and violently through the nose in an effort to be rid of the irritant; **not to be sneezed at,** having values or advantages worth considering. [OE. *snesan*].
SNEEZEWOOD, [snēz'-wo͝od], *n.* an African tree, *Ptaeroxylon utile*; a timber of a valuable quality obtained from this tree and so-called from the sternutatory properties of its sawdust.
SNEEZEWORT, [snēz'-wurt], *n.* (*bot.*) the wild plant, *Achillea Starmica*, with numerous white flowers.
SNEEZING, [snēz'-ing], *n.* the act of one who sneezes.
SNELL (1), [snel], *n.* a short length of catgut or horse-hair joining a fish-hook to a fishing line. [Unkn.].
SNELL (2), [snel], *adj.* (*Scots*) sharp, keen.
SNICK (1), [snik], *n.* the act of snicking; a nick cut in a piece of wood, a notch; (*cricket*) a slight touch of the ball with the edge of the bat.
SNICK (2), [snik], *v.t.* to mark with a small notch, to nick; (*cricket*) to touch slightly with the edge of the bat so that the ball is scarcely deflected from its course. [Unkn.].
SNICKER, [snik'-er], *v.i.* to snigger.
SNIFF (1), [snif], *n.* the act of sniffing; the sound made by such an act; that which is sniffed.
SNIFF (2), [snif], *v.t. and i.* to breathe in through the nose, to inhale, to draw in with the breath, particularly so as to experience a scent; to obtain a sensation of a scent or smell by means of a sniff, to smell; to draw in air swiftly and shortly through the nose so as to make a brief, thin noise; to act in this way as an expression of disapproval. [~Dan. *snive*].
SNIFFY, [snif'-i], *adj.* (*coll.*) off-hand, contemptuous, expressing a sense of superiority in a slightly insulting fashion.
SNIFTING-VALVE, [snift'-ing-valv'], *n.* a valve in the cylinder of a steam-engine permitting the escape of steam or air when starting.
SNIG, [snig], *n.* a young eel. [Unkn.].
SNIGGER (1), [snig'-er], *n.* the act of sniggering.
SNIGGER (2), [snig'-er], *v.i.* to laugh with half-suppressed catches of voice, to keep up a continual nervous, high-pitched laugh unsuccessfully suppressed, to giggle. [Uncert.].
SNIGGLE, [snigl], *v.t.* to fish for eels by dropping the bait into their holes, to snare fish. [SNIG].
SNIP (1), [snip], *n.* a patch of white hair on a horse's muzzle. [Uncert.].
SNIP (2), [snip], *n.* the act of snipping; a single, quick cut made by means of scissors or shears; (*coll.*) a tailor; a small piece snipped off; a certainty; a bargain.
SNIP (3), (snipped, snipping), [snip], *v.t.* to cut by means of a short, quick clip, or series of such, to clip by means of scissors or shears. [~LGerm. *snippeln*].
SNIPE (1), [snīp], *n.* a marshland bird of the genus *Gallinago*, with brown mottled plumage and a long straight bill; the trumpeter fish, *Centriscus scolopax*. [OIcel. *snipa*].

SNIPE

SNIPE (2), [snīp], *v.t. and i.* to shoot from an ambush; to kill by such means; to shoot at enemy troops one by one as an expert marksman from a concealed position.
SNIPER, [snīp'-er], *n.* one who snipes, a sharpshooter.
SNIPPER, [snip'-er], *n.* one who snips or clips; (*slang*) a tailor.
SNIPPET, [snip'-it], *n.* a small part or share, a clipping, a small snip.
SNIPPETY, [snip'-i-ti], *adj.* consisting of snippets, fragmentary.
SNIPPY, [snip'-i], *adj.* mean, stingy. [Du. *snippig* snappish].
SNIPS, [snips], *n.*(*pl.*) a pair of hand shears for cutting thin metal, etc.
SNIP-SNAP, [snip'-snap'], *n.* a passage of smart dialogue.

SNIPS

SNITCH (1), [snich], *n.* (*coll.*) the nose; (*slang*) an informer. [Unkn.].
SNITCH (2), [snich], *v.i.* (*slang*) to inform, to turn informer; to catch (salmon, etc.) by means of a noose.
SNITCHER, [snich'-er], *n.* (*slang*) an informer, a police-spy; (*pl.*) handcuffs.
SNIVEL (1), [sniv'-el], *n.* the act of snivelling; a whining, whimpering expression of misery or sorrow.
SNIVEL (2), (snivelling, snivelled), [sniv'-el], *v.i.* to run at the nose with mucus so as to sniff continually, to snuffle; to complain of misery in a whimpering way. [OE. *snyflung* mucus].
SNIVELLER, [sniv'-el-er], *n.* one who snivels; one who whines for slight causes.
SNIVELLY, [sniv'-el-i], *adj.* characterized by running at the nose; whining, wretched.
SNOB, [snob], *n.* one who pretentiously assumes a superior social status, a social climber who attempts to hide vulgarity beneath affected manners and continual boasting of important connexions. [Unkn.].
SNOBBERY, [snob'-er-i], *n.* the condition of being a snob, snobbishness.
SNOBBISH, [snob'-ish], *adj.* affected by snobbery, belonging to, or resembling, a snob.
SNOBBISHLY, [snob'-ish-li], *adv.* in the manner of a snob.
SNOBBISHNESS, [snob'-ish'-nes], *n.* the condition or fact of being a snob.
SNOBBISM, [snob'-izm], *n.* snobbishness. [Fr. *snobisme*].
SNOBBY, [snob'-i], *adj.* inclined to be snobbish.
SNOOD (1), [sno͞od], *n.* a band or net with which the hair is tied up; a short length of gut to which a fish-hook is bound; a head-dress. [OE. *snod* head-dress].
SNOOD (2), [sno͞od], *v.t.* to dress with a snood.
SNOOK, [sno͞ok], *n.* a derisive gesture made by opening out the fingers and placing the thumb at the tip of the nose. [Unkn.].
SNOOKER, [sno͞ok'-er], *n.* a variety of billiards played with six variously coloured balls, a triangle of ten red balls and one white ball. [Unkn.].
SNOOKER-POOL, [sno͞ok'-er-po͞ol'], *n.* snooker.
SNOOP, [sno͞op], *v.i.* (*coll.*) to investigate stealthily affairs with which one has no concern. [Du. *snoepen* to enjoy secretly].
SNOOZE (1), [sno͞oz], *n.* a short sleep or nap, a doze.
SNOOZE (2), [sno͞oz], *v.i.* to indulge in a short sleep, to doze. [Uncert.].
SNOOZER, [sno͞oz'-er], *n.* one who snoozes.
SNORE (1), [snaw(r)], *n.* the act of snoring, a hoarse, nasal breathing in sleep, the sound made by such an act.
SNORE (2), [snaw(r)], *v.i.* to breathe noisily, as though snorting, while asleep. [ME. *snoren*].
SNORER, [snawr'-er], *n.* one who snores.
SNORT (1), [snawt], *n.* the act of snorting; the sound made by such an act.
SNORT (2), [snawt], *v.i.* to force air violently through the nostrils. [ME. *snorten*].
SNORTER, [snawt'-er], *n.* a person or animal that snorts; the wheatear, *Saxicola œnanthe*; (*coll.*) a rude, abusive letter, etc.; a strong wind; a difficult problem.
SNORTING, [snawt'-ing], *n.* the act of one who snorts, the act of forcing air violently through the nose.
SNORTY, [snaw'-ti], *adj.* (*coll.*) angry, annoyed.
SNOT, [snot], *n.* (*slang*) mucus discharged from the nose. [ME. *snotte*].
SNOTTER, [snot'-er], *n.* (*naut.*) a collar of rope forming a joint to hold the butt end of a sprit. [Unkn.].
SNOTTY (1), [snot'-i], *n.* (*slang*) a midshipman.
SNOTTY (2), [snot'-i], *adj.* dribbling with mucus; mean, dirty; (*coll.*) angry, short-tempered.
SNOUT, [snowt], *n.* the projecting nose or muzzle of a beast; the nozzle of a pipe; anything that projects from a mass, as a cliff; (*coll.*) the nose of a human being. [ME. *snoute*].
SNOUTED, [snowt'-ed], *adj.* having a snout.
SNOUTY, [snowt'-i], *adj.* resembling a beast's snout, having a shape like a snout.
SNOW (1), [snō], *n.* a small sailing-vessel, similar to a brig, equipped with two masts. [Du. *snaauw*].
SNOW (2), [snō], *n.* the moisture in the atmosphere frozen into delicate, light, fluffy crystals or flakes which float to the earth, a fall of snow; (*slang*) cocaine in powder form; silver money. [OE. *snaw*].
SNOW (3), [snō], *v.t. and i.* to cause to shower down like snow; to fall from the sky as snow, to descend in the form of snow; **snowed under,** overwhelmed; **snowed up,** prevented from moving by a heavy fall of snow. [OE. *sniwan*].
SNOWBALL (1), [snō'-bawl], *n.* a round ball of snow, pressed or rolled together by the hands into a compact mass; (*coll.*) a white-haired negro; a scheme, petition, etc., which increases in size as it progresses.

SNOWBALL (2), [snō'-bawl], *v.t.* and *i.* to pelt with snowballs; to hurl snowballs.
SNOWBALL-TREE, [snō'-bawl-trē], *n.* the guelder rose, having ball-shaped clusters of white flowers.
SNOWBERRY, [snō'-be'-ri], *n.* an ornamental garden shrub of the genus *Symphoricarpus*, having snow-white berries.
SNOWBIRD, [snō'-burd], *n.* the American finch, *Fringilla hiemalis*; the snow-bunting.
SNOW-BLIND, [snō'-blīnd'], *adj.* incapable of seeing owing to prolonged exposure to the dazzle of snow.
SNOW-BLINDNESS, [snō'-blīnd-nes], *n.* amblyopia due to continual exposure of the eyes to the glare from snow.
SNOWBLINK, [snō'-blink], *n.* the reflections from snow appearing on the horizon.
SNOWBOOTS, [snō'-bōōts], *n.(pl.)* boots designed to protect the feet from snow.
SNOWBOUND, [snō'-bownd], *adj.* snowed up, unable to move because of a heavy fall of snow.
SNOW-BROTH, [snō'-broth'], *n.* snow mixed with water from melted snow; very cold liquor.
SNOW-BUNTING, [snō'-bunt'-ing], *n.* an Arctic bird of the genus *Plectrophanes* with brown and white plumage.
SNOWCAPT, SNOW-CAPPED, [snō'-kapt'], *adj.* capped, crowned with snow.
SNOWDRIFT, [snō'-drift], *n.* snow driven by the wind into a bank, heap, or pile.
SNOWDROP, [snō'-drop'], *n.* (*bot.*) a bulbous plant of the genus *Galanthus*, bearing a white flower of a delicate cup form which appears in early spring.

SNOWDROP

SNOWFALL, [snō'-fawl], *n.* the amount of snow fallen in a given time; a fall of snow spread over a specific area.
SNOWFIELD, [snō'-fēld], *n.* a permanent expanse of snow common to cold regions.
SNOWFLAKE, [snō'-flāk], *n.* a flake of snow in the form of a frozen crystal; the snow-bunting; (*bot.*) a plant of the genus *Leucojum* resembling a large snowdrop.
SNOW-GLORY, [snō'-glaw-ri], *n.* (*bot.*) a plant of the genus *Chionodoxa*.
SNOW-GOOSE, [snō'-gōōs], *n.* the North American wild goose, *Anser hyperboreus*, with white plumage and wings with black tips.

SNOW-GOOSE

SNOW-GROUSE, [snō'-grows], *n.* the ptarmigan, *Tetrao mutus*.
SNOW-ICE, [snō'-īs'], *n.* ice formed from the freezing of half-melted snow.
SNOWILY, [snō'-i-li], *adv.* in a snowy way.
SNOW-LEOPARD, [snō'-lep'-ard], *n.* the ounce.
SNOWLESS, [snō'-les], *adj.* characterized by the absence of snow.
SNOWLIKE, [snō'-līk], *adj.* resembling snow.
SNOWLINE, [snō'-līn], *n.* the lower limit of perpetual snow, the line farthest south marking the end of snowfields.
SNOW-PLOUGH, [snō'-plow], *n.* an implement for clearing away snow from roadways and railways.
SNOW-PLUME, [snō'-plōōm], *n.* a scarf of snow blown by the wind into the air off the top of a high ridge.
SNOWSHED, [snō'-shed'], *n.* a rough roof built across a railway cutting for protecting a railroad against snowdrifts.
SNOWSHOE, [snō'-shōō], *n.* a shoe in the form of a racket to prevent the feet from sinking into the snow; one of a pair of skis.
SNOWSLIP, [snō'-slip], *n.* an avalanche, a large mass of snow which is dislodged by melting and slips down the side of a mountain.
SNOW-SPECTACLES, [snō'-spek'-taklz], *n.(pl.)* spectacles fitted with tinted lenses to take away the dazzle of snow.
SNOWSTORM, [snō'-stawm], *n.* a storm of falling snow; a very heavy fall of snow driven by a strong wind.
SNOW-WREATH, [snō'-rēth], *n.* a heap of snow blown together by the wind, a snowdrift.
SNOWY, [snō'-i], *adj.* covered with snow; white like snow; having the characteristics of snow; pure white, pure, unblemished.
SNUB (1), [snub], *n.* the act of snubbing, a rebuke; a snub nose; †a projecting piece of timber, a snag.
SNUB (2), [snub], *adj.* short and turned up at the end (*esp.* of a nose).
SNUB (3), (**snubbing, snubbed**), [snub], *v.t.* †to nip, cut short, clip off; to check by means of a contemptuous cutting remark, to reprove by a pose of indifference; **to s. a cable**, (*naut.*) to check a rope being paid out by means of a snubbing post. [OIcel. *snubba* to reprimand].
SNUBBY, [snub'-i], *adj.* having a snub form, snub.
SNUB-NOSE, [snub'-nōz], *n.* a short or flat nose with a turned-up end.
SNUB-NOSED, [snub'-nōzd], *adj.* having a snub nose.
SNUFF (1), [snuf], *n.* a pinch of powdered tobacco or drug to be sniffed up the nose, a sniff.
SNUFF (2), [snuff], *n.* the charred wick of a candle left by the flame as it burns its way downwards.
SNUFF (3), (**snuffing, snuffed**), [snuf], *v.t.* and *i.* to take in through the nose, to inhale snuff; to sniff, to snort. [MDu. *snuffen* to blow the nose].
SNUFF (4), (**snuffing, snuffed**), [snuf], *v.t.* and *i.* to clip off (the wick or snuff of a candle). [ME. *snuffen*].
SNUFFBOX, [snuf'-boks'], *n.* a small ornamental box or tin for carrying snuff about the person.
SNUFFER, [snuf'-er], *n.* one who takes snuff.
SNUFFERS, [snuf'-erz], *n.(pl.)* an instrument in the form of a pair of scissors for trimming the wick of a candle.
SNUFFINESS, [snuf'-i-nes], *n.* the condition of being snuffy.
SNUFFLE (1), [snufl], *n.* the act of snuffling; the sound of a snuffle.
SNUFFLE (2), [snufl], *v.i.* to sniff weakly through a dribbling nose; to breathe or speak through the nose when obstructed.
SNUFFLER, [snuf'-ler], *n.* one who snuffles.
SNUFFLES, [snuflz], *n.(pl.)* the condition or effect resulting from obstruction of the nose by mucus causing persistent sniffing, cold in the nose.
SNUFFLING, [snuf'-ling], *n.* the act of one who snuffles, a speaking through the nose.
SNUFFTAKER, [snuf'-tāk'-er], *n.* one who habitually takes snuff by inhaling it into the nose.
SNUFFY, [snuf'-i], *adj.* resembling snuff; soiled with tobacco snuff, covered with snuff.
SNUG (1), [snug], *n.* a small and comfortable place, *esp.* a small private bar in a public-house.
SNUG (2), [snug], *adj.* neatly pressed, well-trimmed, that is made to fit or lie close together and tidily; so designed or arranged as to be small, compact and cosy, warm, sheltered. [Unkn.].
SNUG (3), [snug], *v.t.* and *i.* to make snug; to make oneself comfortable and cosy, to snuggle.
SNUGGERY, [snug'-er-i], *n.* a small cosy room, a snug.
SNUGGLE, [snugl], *v.t.* and *i.* to enfold so as to warm, to cuddle; to lie close for comfort and warmth.
SNUGLY, [snug'-li], *adv.* to a snug degree, in a snug manner.
SNUGNESS, [snug'-nes], *n.* the quality of being snug.
SO (1), [sō], *adv.* in such a manner, in this way, in that way; to that extent, to such a degree; in the same way, in like manner; for that reason, therefore; too, as well; more or less, approximately; in such a way; **s. much for,** that dismisses; **and s. on,** etcetera; **s. s.,** in a not particularly noteworthy manner or condition. [OE. *swa*].
SO (2), [sō], *pron.* **s. and s.,** a person whose name is understood; (*slang*) a person to whom an abusive name is given by implication.
SO (3), [sō], *conj.* therefore; in order that; in such a way; **s. long as,** providing that, on condition that.
SOAK (1), [sōk], *n.* the act of soaking; the condition of being soaked; a water-hole; (*coll.*) a drenching shower of rain, a period of such weather; a habitual drinker.
SOAK (2), [sōk], *v.t.* and *i.* to immerse in water or liquid so as to be thoroughly impregnated, to steep till saturated; to wet thoroughly, to drench; to lie immersed in water or liquid, to steep; **to s. through,** to percolate through; (*coll.*) to drink (alcohol) immoderately and habitually. [OE. *socian*].
SOAKAGE, [sōk'-ij], *n.* liquid which has soaked in; (*elect.*) the residual charge in a cable or condenser.

SOAKER, [sōk'-er], *n.* one who, or that which, soaks in a liquid; (*coll.*) a hard drinker.

SOAKING, [sōk'-ing], *adj.* having the power to wet thoroughly.

SOAP (**1**), [sōp], *n.* a substance made of animal or vegetable fats mixed with an alkaline base, moulded into cakes or bars, and used for cleansing and washing when dissolved in water. [OE. *sape*].

SOAP (**2**), [sōp] *v.t. and i.* to clean or wash by means of soap and water; to cause to lather by rubbing; to use soap and water for washing purposes.

SOAPBALL, [sōp'-bawl'], *n.* a cake of soap in the form of a ball.

SOAPBERRY-TREE, [sōp'-be'-ri-trē], *n* an evergreen tropical tree, *Sapindus saponaria*, bearing red saponaceous berries which, producing a lather when immersed in water, are used as a substitute for soap.

SOAPBERRY-TREE

SOAPBOILER, [sōp'-boil'-er], *n.* a soap manufacturer; a soap-pan.

SOAP-BUBBLE, [sōp'-bubl], *n.* a bubble of air formed by a film of soapy water.

SOAPILY, [sōp'-i-li], *adv.* in a soapy manner.

SOAPINESS, [sōp'-i-nes], *n.* the quality of being soapy.

SOAP-PAN, [sōp'-pan'], *n.* a boiling pan used in the manufacture of soap.

SOAPSTONE, [sōp'-stōn], *n.* a soft, cloudy stone, talc or steatite, used in cheap jewellery.

SOAPSUDS, [sōp'-sudz], *n.(pl.)* water impregnated with soap so as to form a mass of lather.

SOAP-TREE, [sōp'-trē], *n.* a tree, *Quillaja saponaria*, found in Chile, the bark of which gives a lather.

SOAPWORKS, [sōp'-wurks], *n.(pl.)* a soap factory.

SOAPWORT, [sōp'-wurt], *n.* (*bot.*) a plant of the genus *Saponaria*, the leaves of which can be crushed in water to produce a froth.

SOAPY, [sōp'-i], *adj.* resembling soap; having the qualities of soap; soft and smooth; covered with soap, containing soap; (*coll.*) unctuous.

SOAR, [saw(r)], *v.i.* to ascend to a great height in the air, as a bird, to rise high, to mount; (*fig.*) to rise to a high pitch of imagination, thought, or feeling. [OFr. *essorer*].

SOARING, [saw'-ring], *n.* the act of soaring; (*fig.*) intellectual aspiration.

SOARINGLY, [saw'-ring-li], *adv.* in a soaring manner, upwardly.

SOAVE, [sōah'-vā], *adv.* (*mus.*) gently, with sweetness. [It. *soave*].

SOB (**1**), [sob], *n.* the act of sobbing; the sound made by such an act; an involuntary convulsion deep in the throat or chest, a violent catch in the breath due to extreme misery.

SOB (**2**), (**sobbing, sobbed**), [sob], *v.t. and i.* to express by sobs; to utter a sob or a series of sobs; to produce a sound or series of sounds that resemble a sob. [ME. *sobben*].

SOBBING, [sob'-ing], *n.* the act of one who sobs.

SOBER (**1**), [sō'-ber], *adj.* not under the influence of alcohol, not drunk; temperate, of abstemious habits, particularly in relation to alcoholic liquor; having a temperament which does not indulge in extremes of passion or judgment; by nature unable or unwilling to experience abnormal flights of the imagination, not fanciful; having a subdued tone or colour scheme. [L. *sobrius*].

SOBER (**2**), [sō'-ber], *v.t. and i.* to make sober; to become sober.

SOBERIZE, [sō'-ber-īz], *v.t.* to render sober.

SOBERLY, [sō'-ber-li], *adv.* to a sober degree, in a sober manner.

SOBER-MINDED, [sō'-ber-mīnd'-id], *adj.* being by nature cool of judgment, having a disposition which is habitually sober, temperate, and calm.

SOBER-MINDEDNESS, [sō'-ber-mīnd'-id-nes], *n.* the condition of being sober-minded.

SOBERNESS, [sō'-ber-nes], *n.* the state of being sober, sobriety.

SOBERSIDES, [sō'-ber-sīdz], *n.* (*coll.*) a very serious and sedate person.

SOBOLIFEROUS, [sob'-ōl-if'-er-us], *adj.* (*bot.*) bearing suckers. [L. *soboles* sucker and *ferre* to bear].

SOBRANJE, [sob-rahn'-yi], *n.* the national legislative assembly of Bulgaria. [Bulgarian *Sobranje*].

SOBRIETY, [sō-brī'-it-i], *n.* the state of being sober, habitual moderation. [L. *sobrietas*].

SOBRIQUET, SOUBRIQUET, [sōō'-brik-ā], *n.* a nickname; an assumed name. [Fr. *sobriquet*].

SOB-SISTER, [sob'-sist'-er], *n.* (*slang*) a woman journalist who specializes in stories with human appeal on a low, sensational level.

SOB-STUFF, [sob'-stuf], *n.* (*U.S. slang*) highly sentimentalized pathos.

SOC, [sok], *n.* in feudal times, a legal privilege of holding a court in a district; soke; privilege of tenants exempted from certain taxes as part of their tenancy agreement; a miller's privilege to grind all the corn in a district. [OE. *socn*].

SOCAGE, [sok'-ij], *n.* (in feudal society) a tenure of lands permitting exemption from military service in return for certain economic concessions. [LL. *soccagium*].

SOCAGER, [sok'-ij-er], *n.* a tenant by terms of socage.

SO-CALLED, [sō'-kawld'], *adj.* so named, having certain pretensions to being.

SOCCER, [sok'-er], *n.* (*coll.*) a variety of football played under the laws of the Football Association. [Abbreviated from ASSOCIATION].

SOCIABILITY, [sō'-shab-il'-i-ti], *n.* the quality of being sociable, disposition to associate and converse with others; the practice of friendly intercourse.

SOCIABLE (**1**), [sō'-shabl], *n.* (*coll.*) an informal meeting or party with no arrangements for dancing or alcoholic drinks; a four-wheel carriage designed with two opposite seats each for two passengers; a tricycle for two.

SOCIABLE (**2**), [sō'-shabl], *adj.* ready to be friendly, prepared to associate with other people for the sake of their company, willing to strike up an acquaintance, characterized by affability. [L. *sociabilis* easily joined].

SOCIABLENESS, [sō'-shabl-nes], *n.* the quality of being sociable; sociability.

SOCIABLY, [sō'-shab-li], *adv.* in a sociable manner, affably.

SOCIAL (**1**), [sōsh'-al], *n.* a meeting or party for talk and gossip, a sociable.

SOCIAL (**2**), [sōshl], *adj.* relating to, concerned with, man in society; living in a form of society characterized by mutual interdependence; relating to, consisting of, forms of conduct the organization of which has human sanction; disposed to be friendly, fond of convivial intercourse; formed for the purpose of uniting in equal groups seeking diversion or sports; (*biol.*) gregarious; **s. security**, national insurance against unemployment, old-age, sickness, etc. [L. *socialis*].

SOCIALISM, [sō'-shal-izm], *n.* the political theory which advocates public ownership of the means of production, distribution and exchange.

SOCIALIST (**1**), [sōsh'-al-ist], *n.* an advocate of socialism, a member of a socialist party.

SOCIALIST (**2**), [sōsh'-al-ist], *adj.* relating to a socialist or his principles; composed of socialists, under the control of socialists.

SOCIALISTIC, [sōsh'-al-ist'-ik], *adj.* relating to socialism; tending to be influenced by socialism.

SOCIALISTICALLY, [sō'-shal-ist'-ik-al-i], *adv.* by the principles and methods of a socialist.

SOCIALITY, [sōsh'-i-al'-i-ti], *n.* conventional socialness.

SOCIALIZATION, [sō'-shal-īz-ā'-shun], *n.* the act or process of socializing; the state of being socialized.

SOCIALIZE, [sōsh'-al-īz], *v.t.* to render social; to govern according to the principles of socialism.

SOCIALLY, [sōsh'-al-i], *adv.* in a social way, sociably.

SOCIALNESS, [sōsh'-al-nes], *n.* the condition of being social.

SOCIETARY, [sō-sī'-it-er-i], *adj.* relating to society.

SOCIETY (**1**), [sō-sī'-i-ti], *n.* a general form of human association in which men and women live in organized communities accepting a characteristic norm of behaviour which finds its expression in authorized regulations concerned with the ownership of the wealth and the control of the individuals' activities; any people considered collectively from the aspect of their laws and customs; any particular class of human beings the nature of whose work places them in a specific category; the class of society whose privileged position, power, or wealth enables it to indulge in an exclusive refinement of manners and fashion, the upper class; human association, the company of a human being or group; an association of persons for the promotion or protection of some common object or interest. [L. *societas* fellowship].

SOCIETY (2), [sō-sī'-i-ti], *adj.* relating to, consisting of, formed by, members of the privileged upper class of society.

SOCINIAN (1), [sō-sin'-i-an], *n.* a believer in the principles of Socinus, who denied the atonement.

SOCINIAN (2), [sō-sin'-i-an], *adj.* relating to, influenced by, the doctrines of Socinus. [L. *Socinus*, a form of the It. name *Sozzini*, a sixteenth-century theologian].

SOCINIANISM, [sō-sin'-i-an-izm], *n.* the theological principles of Socinus.

SOCIOLOGICAL, [sō'-shi-ō-loj'-ik-al], *adj.* relating to sociology.

SOCIOLOGICALLY, [sō'-shi-ō-loj'-ik-al-i], *adv.* from the point of view of a sociologist.

SOCIOLOGIST, [sō'-shi-ol'-oj-ist], *n.* an expert in sociology.

SOCIOLOGY, [sō'-shi-ol'-o-ji], *n.* the scientific study of the nature of human society and the laws which govern its development. [SOCIAL and Gk. *logos* speech].

SOCK (1), [sok], *n.* a stocking with a short leg covering the foot, ankle, and the lower half of the calf; a detachable sole inserted into a shoe; †shoe worn by the actors in ancient Greek comedy; **to pull up one's socks**, (*coll.*) to prepare oneself for a big effort; **to put a s. in it**, (*coll.*) to subdue the noise one is making. [OE. *socc*].

SOCK (2), [sok], *n.* a ploughshare. [Uncert.].

SOCK (3), [sok], *v.t.* (*slang*) to fling at; to hit, punch.

SOCKDOLOGER, [sok-dol'-oj-er], *n.* (*U.S. slang*) that which settles, a settler, a big one. [Corrupted from DOXOLOGY].

SOCKET, [sok'-it], *n.* a cavity into which something fits, and which permits of movement. [OFr. *soket* small stump].

SOCKET-CHISEL, [sok'-it-chiz'-el], *n.* a strong chisel used in conjunction with a mallet by carpenters for mortising.

SOCKETED, [sok'-it-id], *adj.* set in, having, a socket.

SOCKET-POLE, [sok'-it-pōl], *n.* a pole fitted with an iron socket.

SOCKEYE, [sok'-ī], *n.* a species of *Oncorhynchus*, the so-called blue-back salmon which is tinned on the Pacific coast. [AmerInd. *sukai* fish].

SOCKLESS, [sok'-les], *adj.* not wearing socks, having no socks.

SOCLE, [sokl], *n.* (*arch.*) a plain block or plinth designed to function as a low pedestal; a plain face or projecting plinth at the lower part of a wall. [LL. *socculus*].

SOCRATIC, [sō-krat'-ik], *adj.* relating to Socrates, to his manner of teaching by question and answer, or to his philosophy.

SOCRATICALLY, [sō-krat'-ik-al-i], *adv.* in a Socratic mode.

SOCRATISM, [sō'-krat-izm], *n.* a characteristic or a principle of Socrates.

SOD (1), [sod], *n.* soil covered with grass and compact with its roots; a piece of turf cut in a square or oblong. [~MDu. *sode*].

SOD (2), [sod], *n.* an obscene term of abuse implying sodomitic habits. [Abbreviation of SODOMITE].

SOD† (3), [sod], *pret.* of SEETHE.

SODA, [sō'-da], *n.* a compound of sodium; **washing s.**, carbonate of sodium used for household washing. [It. *soda*, *fem. sing.* of *sodo* hard].

SODA-FOUNTAIN, [sō-da-fownt'-in], *n.* a shop or a counter equipped to sell ice-cream, fruit, and aerated drinks.

SODA-LIME, [sō'-da-līm], *n.* a compound of caustic soda and quicklime.

SODALITE, [sō'-dal-īt], *n.* (*min.*) sodium-aluminium silicate with sodium chloride.

SODALITY, [sō-dal'-i-ti], *n.* fellowship or fraternity, a brotherhood. [L. *sodalis* comrade].

SODA-SALT, [sō'-da-sawlt], *n.* a salt of sodium.

SODA-WATER, [sō'-da-waw-ter], *n.* a weak solution of soda; water charged with carbonic acid gas under pressure, so that it effervesces when the pressure is released.

SODDEN (1), [sod'-en], *adj.* and *p.pt.* of SEETHE; saturated, soaked; heavy and dull with alcohol. [OE. *gesoden*].

SODDEN (2), [sod'-en], *v.t.* and *i.* to make sodden; to become soaked.

SODDY, [sod'-i], *adj.* resembling or consisting of sod; covered with sod.

SODIUM, [sō'-di-um], *n.* a soft metallic element denoted by Na. [SODA].

SODOMITE, [sod'-om-īt], *n.* an inhabitant of Sodom; a person guilty of sodomy. [Gk. *Sodomites* inhabitant of Sodom].

SODOMITIC, SODOMITICAL, [sod'-o-mit'-ik (-al)], *adj.* of, or pertaining to, sodomy or sodomites.

SODOMY, [sod'-om-i], *n.* sexual connexion between males. [*Sodom*, Genesis xix].

SOFA, [sō'-fa], *n.* a kind of long seat or couch, sometimes fitted with back and arms, consisting of a wooden frame containing springs covered with upholstery stuffed with horse-hair. [Arab. *suffah* couch].

SOFA-BED, [sō'-fa-bed'], *n.* a sofa that is designed to be converted into a bed.

SOFFIT, [sof'-it], *n.* (*arch.*) a small ceiling formed into panels; the under part of a cornice presenting a flat surface. [It. *soffitta* ceiling].

SOFT (1), [soft, sawft], *adj.* responding to manipulation, easily pressed, squeezed, compressed, not hard, being of a yielding consistency, easily worked; smooth to the touch; having an even texture, not rough or harsh; having a tender, impressionable nature; expressive of such a nature, merciful, gentle, delicate; not strong, effeminate; disposed to be lenient, humane; free of harsh ingredients; low in tone, not vivid, subdued; having a blurred outline, indistinct; not loud, low of voice, modulated; readily forming a lather; (of drinks) non-alcoholic. [OE. *softe* gentle].

SOFT (2), [soft], *adv.* in a soft manner, gently.

SOFT (3), [soft], *int.* be careful, be still, quiet.

SOFTA, [sof'-ta], *n.* a Moslem engaged in studying theology. [Turk. *softa*].

SOFTEN, [sofn], *v.t.* and *i.* to make soft; to become soft.

SOFTENER, [sof'-ner], *n.* one who, or that which, softens.

SOFTENING, [sof'-ning], *n.* the act of making or becoming softer; the blending of colours harmoniously; (*med.*) a decrease of the consistency of a tissue.

SOFT-GOODS, [soft'-gōōdz], *n.*(*pl.*) drapery, linen.

SOFT-GRASS, [soft'-grahs], *n.* (*bot.*) a grass of the genus *Holcus*.

SOFT-HEARTED, [soft'-haht'-id], *adj.* gentle, tender-hearted, compassionate.

SOFT-HEARTEDNESS, [soft'-haht'-id-nes], *n.* the quality of being soft-hearted.

SOFTISH, [soft'-ish], *adj.* rather soft.

SOFTLY, [soft'-li], *adv.* in a soft fashion.

SOFTNESS, [soft'-nes], *n.* the quality of being soft.

SOFT-SOAP (1), [soft'-sōp], *n.* a viscid soap made from potash lye; (*coll.*) ingratiating flattery.

SOFT-SOAP (2), [soft'-sōp], *v.t.* (*coll.*) to flatter or humour ingratiatingly.

SOFTY, [soft'-i], *n.* (*coll.*) a coward or weakling. [SOFT (1)].

SOG (1), [sog], *n.* marshy ground. [Uncert.].

SOG (2), (**sogging, sogged**), [sog], *v.i.* to become soggy.

SOGGY, [sog'-i], *adj.* wet through; soaked with water; boggy, marshy.

SOHO, [sō-hō'], *int.* a call to attract attention, *esp.* a hunting call.

SOIGNE, soigné, [swun'-yā], *adj.* well groomed. [Fr. *soigner* to look after].

SOIL (1), [soil], *n.* the upper layer of the earth's crust in which plants are nourished, and which may be tilled; country, land. [AFr. *soil*, ~L. *solum* ground].

SOIL (2), [soil], *n.* a stain, a mark that soils; dirt; manure; sewage.

SOIL (3), [soil], *v.t.* and *i.* to make or become dirty; (*fig.*) to stain, tarnish; to manure. [OFr. *soillier*].

SOIL (4), [soil], *v.t.* to purge by feeding on fresh-cut grass; to feed (cattle, etc.) on green provender. [OFr. *saouler* to satiate].

SOILLESS, [soil'-les], *adj.* lacking soil.

SOIL-PIPE, [soil'-pīp], *n.* a pipe for discharging sewage, etc., from a house into the main sewers.

SOIREE, soirée, [swah'-rā], *n.* a social entertainment or party in the evening. [Fr. *soirée*].

SOJOURN (1), [soj'-ern], *n.* a stay, temporary residence.

SOJOURN (2), [soj'-ern], *v.i.* to stay, dwell for a time. [OFr. *sojorner*].

SOJOURNER, [soj'-ern-er], *n.* one who sojourns.

SOJOURNING, [soj'-ern-ing], *n.* a sojourn; the time or period of this.

SOJOURNMENT, [soj'-ern-ment], *n.* a sojourn.

SOKE, [sōk], *n.* (*hist.*, *leg.*) the right or privilege of holding a court in a district; the district subject to this. [OE. *socn*].

SOL (1), [sol], *n.* the sun. [L. *sol*].

SOL (2), [sol], *n.* (*mus.*) the fifth note in the diatonic sol-fa scale. [L. *sol*(*ve*)].

SOLA, [sō'-la], *n.* the East Indian plant, *Æschynomene* *aspera*; the pith of this used for sun helmets. [Hind. *shola*].

SOLACE (1), [sol'-as], *n.* comfort, consolation, relief in grief or disappointment; joy, recreation. [OFr. *solas*].

SOLACE (2), [sol'-as], *v.t. and i.* to offer solace to, comfort, cheer. [OFr. *solacier*].

SOLACEMENT, [sol'-as-ment], *n.* solace.

SOLANACEOUS, [sol'-an-ā'-shus], *adj.* relating to plants of the order which includes the potato, capsicum, and nightshade. [L. *solanum* nightshade].

SOLAN-GOOSE, [sō'-lan-gōōs], *n.* the gannet, *Sula bassana*. [OIcel. *sula* and GOOSE].

SOLAN-GOOSE

SOLANINE, [sol'-an-ēn], *n.* a vegetable poisonous alkaloid from certain species of *Solanum*.

SOLANO, [so-lah'-no], *n.* a hot wind in Spain from the south-east. [Span. *solano*].

SOLANUM, [sō-lā'-num], *n.* a large genus of plants including the nightshades, the potato, etc. [L. *solanum* nightshade].

SOLAR (1), [sōl'-er], *n.* a room built to catch the sun's rays; the living-room of a medieval dwelling. [L. *solarium*].

SOLAR (2), [sōl'-er], *adj.* pertaining to, coming from, due to, by means of, the sun; measured or determined by the sun; **s. plexus**, the epigastric plexus, a network of nerves in the abdomen behind the stomach; **s. system**, the planets and other heavenly bodies which revolve round the sun. [L. *solaris*].

SOLARIZATION, [sōl'-er-īz-ā'-shun], *n.* the act or effect of solarizing; the state of being solarized.

SOLARIZE, [sōl'-er-īz], *v.t. and i.* to over-expose to the sun's rays; (*phot.*) to reverse the negative and positive parts of a film or print.

SOLATIUM, (*pl.* **solatia**), [sō-lā'-shi-um], *n.* compensation for injury, loss, etc., monetary consolation. [L. *solatium*].

SOLD, [sōld], *pret. and p.pt.* of SELL.

SOLDER (1), [sōl'-der, sod'-er, saw'-der], *n.* an easily fusible alloy used for cementing metals together. [OFr. *soudure*].

SOLDER (2), [sōl'-der, sod'-er, saw'-der], *v.t.* to unite or cement with solder.

SOLDERING, [sōl'-der-ing], *n.* the process of uniting by solder; a surface soldered.

SOLDERING-BOLT, [sōl'-der-ing-bōlt'], *n.* a tool used for soldering.

SOLDIER (1), [sōl'-jer], *n.* a man who is a member of an army and undergoing a special training for war; a private soldier as distinct from an officer; a man distinguished for his military achievements; (*slang*) a red herring; (*building*) a wooden block, wedged between the flanges of an iron girder, and used as a foundation for plasterwork. [OFr. *soudiour*, soldier].

SOLDIER (2), [sōl'-jer], *adj.* relating to, resembling, a soldier; **s. crab**, the hermit crab; **s. fish**, the red gurnard; **s. orchis**, an orchid whose flowers are supposed to resemble a soldier, *Orchis militaris*.

SOLDIER (3), [sōl'-jer], *v.i.* to serve as a soldier.

SOLDIER-BIRD, [sōl'-jer-burd'], *n.* the Australian honey-eater, *Myzomela sanguinolenta*, considered to resemble a soldier with its black and red plumage.

SOLDIER-BIRD

SOLDIERING, [sōl'-jer-ing], *n.* the activities or the profession of a soldier.

SOLDIERLIKE, [sōl'-jer-līk'], *adj.* having the style or bearing of a soldier.

SOLDIERLY, [sōl'-jer-li], *adj.* having the appearance of a soldier, straight-backed, brisk and efficient in action; having the mental and emotional characteristics of a soldier, heroic, loyal, brave.

SOLDIERSHIP, [sōl'-jer-ship], *n.* military experience; martial skill, particularly in military strategy.

SOLDIERWOOD, [sōl'-jer-wŏŏd], *n.* the wood of the West Indian tree, *Calliandra purpurea*, which is allied to the mimosa.

SOLDIERY, [sōl'-jer-i], *n.* military men in general, soldiers collectively.

SOLDO, (*pl.* **soldi**), [sol'-dō], *n.* an Italian coin worth a twentieth of a lira. [It. *soldo* from LL. *solidus* coin].

SOLE (1), [sōl], *n.* the underside of the foot between the toes and the arch of the instep; the part of a shoe, boot, etc., on which this rests; the lower or bottom part; a shole. [OFr. *sole*].

SOLE (2), [sōl], *n.* the edible marine flatfish, *Solea vulgaris*. [L. *solea*].

SOLE (3), [sōl], *adj.* only, single, alone, being or acting without another; exclusive; (*leg.*) unmarried. [L. *solus*].

SOLE (4), [sōl], *v.t.* to provide with a new sole.

SOLECISM, [sol'-i-sizm], *n.* a grammatical mistake, incorrect usage in speech; an absurdity, impropriety, a violation of the social conventions. [L. *soloecismus* from Gk. *soloikos* speaking incorrectly, as did the people of Soloi, a city of Cilicia].

SOLECIST, [sol'-i-sist], *n.* one guilty of solecisms.

SOLECISTICAL, [sol'-i-sist'-ik-al], *adj.* of the nature of, constituting, a solecism.

SOLECISTICALLY, [sol'-i-sist'-ik-al-i], *adv.* in solecistical fashion.

SOLECIZE, [sol'-i-sīz], *v.i.* to perpetrate a solecism.

SOLELY, [sōl'-li], *adv.* singly, alone; to the extent of one reason or person.

SOLEMN, [sol'-em], *adj.* characterized by a serious and formal series of acts performed at a slow pace, as at a religious ceremony, worthy of being approached or participated in reverently; grave, important, serious; impressive in dignity of mien; not smiling; affectedly serious. [L. *sollemnis*].

SOLEMNITY, [sol-em'-nit-i], *n.* the condition or quality of being solemn; a ceremonial formality; impressiveness, serious dignity suitable to an important, particularly a religious, occasion. [L. *sollemnitas*].

SOLEMNIZATION, [sol'-em-nīz-ā'-shun], *n.* the act of solemnizing; performance of a religious ceremony.

SOLEMNIZE, [sol'-em-nīz], *v.t.* to celebrate with rites, to perform with due solemnity as proper to ritual ceremonies; to make solemn, to render grave, serious and reverential.

SOLEMNIZER, [sol'-em-nīz-er], *n.* a person who solemnizes; †a person who performs a solemn rite.

SOLEMNLY, [sol'-em-li], *adv.* in a solemn manner, to a solemn degree.

SOLEMNNESS, [sol'-em-nes], *n.* the state of being solemn.

SOLEN, [sō'-len], *n.* (*zool.*) the genus of the razor-shells, *Solen ensis*. [Gk. *solen*].

SOLENOID, [sōl'-en-oid], *n.* (*elect.*) a form of electric wiring consisting of a cylindrical coil. [Gk. *solen* pipe and *oeides* like].

SOL-FA (1), [sol'-fah'], *n.* (*mus.*) a system of spoken syllables designating the notes of the diatonic scale. [SOL and FA].

SOL-FA (2), [sol'-fah], *v.i.* to sing the notes of a scale in terms of the syllabic system, do, re, mi, fa, sol, la, si.

SOLFATARA, [sol'-fa-tah'-ra], *n.* a fissure or hole in the ground acting as a vent for sulphurous and other gases escaping from a dormant volcano. [It. *solfatara* from *solfo* sulphur].

SOLFEGGIO, [sol-fej'-ō], *n.* (*mus.*) a singing exercise using the sol-fa. [It. *solfeggio*].

SOLFERINO, [sol'-fer-ē'-nō], *n.* the crimson colour of rosaniline. [*Solferino*, in Italy, the colour having been discovered in 1859, the year of the battle there].

SOLICIT, [sol-is'-it], *v.t. and i.* to ask, beg for, while fully conscious of the seriousness of the request, to petition earnestly; to make an immoral request, to accost, to importune; to be engaged in solicitation. [L. *sollicitare* to urge].

SOLICITANT, [sol-is'-it-ant], *n.* one who solicits.

SOLICITATION, [sol-is'-it-ā'-shun], *n.* the act of soliciting, earnest request, persistent invitation.

SOLICITOR, [sol-is'-it-or], *n.* a person who solicits; (*leg.*) an attorney, a legal practitioner who, being an expert in the theory and practice of law, conducts suits at law on behalf of others in the lower courts. [OFr. *soliciteur*].

SOLICITOR-GENERAL, [sol-is'-it-or-jen'-er-al], *n.* the second in rank of the law officers of the Crown, junior to the Attorney-General.

SOLICITORSHIP, [sol-is'-it-or-ship], *n.* the office or profession of a solicitor.

SOLICITOUS, [sol-is'-it-us], *adj.* particularly careful, anxious; very concerned; making anxious inquiries. [L. *sollicitus* agitated].

SOLICITOUSLY, [sol-is'-it-us-li], *adv.* in a solicitous manner, anxiously, thoughtfully, displaying concern.

SOLICITOUSNESS, [sol-is′-it-us-nes], *n.* the condition of being solicitous, solicitude.
SOLICITUDE, [sol-is′-i-tewd], *n.* the state of being solicitous, solicitousness, concern, anxiety. [L. *solicitudo*].
SOLID (1), [sol′-id], *n.* that which is solid; (*pl.*) food which is solid (in contrast to slops); (*geom.*) any three-dimensional figure; (*phys.*) a solid body.
SOLID (2), [sol′-id], *adj.* retaining its form under pressure; having a dense consistency, not fluid, compact, firm, hard; substantial; having no empty spaces beneath the surface, completely filled, not hollow; strong, sound, reliable; genuine; characterized by fact, having substantial grounds for argument, valid; grave, profound, deep; unanimous in opinion; (*math.*) existing in, referring to, three dimensions. [L. *solidus* firm].
SOLID (3), [sol′-id], *adv.* without exception, unanimously.
SOLIDARITY, [sol′-id-a′-ri-ti], *n.* unanimity of opinion and resultant action; complete consolidation of communion among members of a community. [Fr. *solidarité*].
SOLID-DRAWN, [sol′-id-drawn], *adj.* drawn out from a solid bar of metal.
SOLIDIFIABLE, [sol-id′-i-fī-abl], *adj.* capable of being solidified.
SOLIDIFICATION, [sol-id′-if-ik-ā′-shun], *n.* the process or the act of solidifying; the state of being solidified.
SOLIDIFY, [sol-id′-i-fī], *v.t. and i.* to make solid; to become solid.
SOLIDITY, [sol-id′-i-ti], *n.* the quality of being solid, firmness, compactness; moral firmness; validity. [L. *soliditas*].
SOLIDLY, [sol′-id-li], *adv.* to a solid degree, in a solid manner.
SOLIDNESS, [sol′-id-nes], *n.* the quality of being solid, solidity; soundness.
SOLIDUNGULATE, [sol′-id-ung′-gyōō-lāt], *n.* (*zool.*) a mammal, such as the horse, the foot of which terminates in a solid, as distinct from a cleft, hoof.
SOLIDUNGULOUS, [sol′-id-ung′-gyōō-lus], *adj.* solidungulate.
SOLIDUS, [sol′-i-dus], *n.* (*archae.*) a Roman gold coin; a slanting stroke used to indicate shillings, as in 2/-. [L. *solidus* (*nummus*) hard (cash)].
SOLIFIDIAN, [sol′-if-id′-i-an], *n.* (*theol.*) one who holds the doctrine that mere faith apart from the moral value of actions is sufficient for salvation. [L. *solus* alone and *fides* faith].
SOLIFIDIANISM, [sol-i-fid′-i-an-izm], *n.* the doctrine of a solifidian.
SOLILOQUIZE, [sol-il′-ōk-wīz], *v.i.* to speak in the form of a soliloquy, to talk to oneself.
SOLILOQUY, [sol-il′-ōk-wi], *n.* talking aloud to oneself; a speech spoken by a character in a play expressing private thoughts out of hearing of other characters; such a speech in its written or printed form; a monologue. [L. *soliloquium*].
SOLIPED, [sol′-i-ped′], *n.* (*zool.*) a solid-hoofed mammal; a solidungulate. [MedL. *solipes*].
SOLIPEDOUS, [sol-ip′-ed-us], *adj.* having a whole hoof, solidungulous.
SOLIPSISM, [sol-ip′-sizm], *n.* (*philos.*) the view that one's self is the basis of knowledge and the universe. [L. *solus* alone and *ipse* oneself].
SOLIPSIST, [sol-ip′-sist], *adj.* of, pertaining to, or based on, solipsism.
SOLITAIRE, [sol′-it-āer′], *n.* a single precious stone, *esp.* a diamond, worn as a piece of jewellery; a game played on the same principle as draughts but using a round board fitted with small pits to hold pegs or marbles; a card game for one, patience; the extinct pigeon of the island of Rodriguez which resembled a dodo; † a recluse. [Fr. *solitaire*].
SOLITARILY, [sol′-it-er-i-li], *adv.* in a solitary manner.
SOLITARINESS, [sol′-it-er-i-nes], *n.* the condition of being solitary.
SOLITARY, [sol′-it-er-i], *adj.* being or living by oneself, living apart from others, not sharing the company of a community, being unaccompanied, alone, lonely; not frequented by people, remote, secluded, not inhabited; desolate, deserted; single, sole. [L. *solitarius*].
SOLITUDE, [sol′-i-tewd], *n.* the state of being solitary; a place barely affected by human activity, a desert. [L. *solitudo*].
SOLLERET, [sol′-er-et′], *n.* a shoe in the form of a series of flexible plates. [OFr. *solleret* little shoe].
SOLMIZATION, [sol′-miz-ā′-shun], *n.* (*mus.*) the act of singing the names of the notes of the sol-fa scale. [Fr. *solmisation*].
SOLO (1), [sō′-lō], *n.* (*mus.*) a tune, air, or strain to be played or sung by a single instrument or voice; a card game based on the principle of whist, particularly a call in such a game made by a player who undertakes to make five tricks. [It. *solo* alone].
SOLO (2), [sō′-lō], *adj.* performed alone.
SOLO (3), [sō′-lō], *adv.* by oneself.
SOLOIST, [sō′-lō-ist], *n.* the performer of a solo.
SOLOMON, [sol′-om-on], *n.* **Solomon's seal**, a six-pointed star formed by interlacing two triangles; (*bot.*) a perennial herb with flowers the shape of bells hanging on curving stems. [*Solomon*, the wise king of Israel].
SOLON, [sō′-lon], *n.* a wise legislator. [*Solon*, an Athenian statesman of the seventh and sixth centuries B.C., famed for his wisdom].
SO-LONG, [sō-long′], *int.* (*coll.*) goodbye, au revoir.
SOLSTICE, [sol′-stis], *n.* the point, north or south, in the ecliptic which marks the sun's extreme limit of distance from the equator. [L. *solstitium* the sun's standing still].
SOLSTITIAL, [sol-stish′-al], *adj.* relating to the solstice; occurring at a solstice.

SOLOMON'S SEAL

SOLUBILITY, [sol′-yōō-bil′-i-ti], *n.* the condition of being soluble, solubleness.
SOLUBLE, [sol′-yōōbl], *adj.* capable of being dissolved in a fluid, capable of solution; **s. glass**, a preparation of silicate of soda with preservative properties. [L. *solubilis*].
SOLUBLENESS, [sol′-yōōbl-nes], *n.* the quality of being soluble, solubility.
SOLUS, [sōl′-us], *adj.* by oneself, alone. [L. *solus*].
SOLUTION, [sol-ōō′-shun], *n.* the act or process of separating out the component parts of any body; the act or process of dissolving a solid in a fluid so that the various elements are absorbed; the act or process of solving a problem, puzzle, or mystery, an explanation, particularly of a difficulty or doubt; a method for discovering an answer to a difficult question or problem. [L. *solutio* a loosening].
SOLUTIONIST, [sol-ōō′-shun-ist], *n.* a person who earns a living by working out possible solutions of newspaper puzzles.
SOLUTRIAN, [sol-ōō′-tri-an], *adj.* (*geol.*) relating to, belonging to, the Palaeolithic period between the Mousterian and Magdalenian. [*Solutré*, Saône-et-Loire, France, where characteristic fossil remains occur].
SOLVABILITY, [sol′-va-bil′-i-ti], *n.* the condition of being solvable, solvableness.
SOLVABLE, [solv′-abl], *adj.* capable of being solved, resolved, or explained; able to be paid.
SOLVABLENESS, [solv′-abl-nes], *n.* the condition of being solvable; solvability.
SOLVE, [solv], *v.t.* to explain by finding the correct relationship of the parts, to provide the right answer to, to clear up, to resolve; to remove the cause of difficulty in. [L. *solvere* to loosen, explain].
SOLVENCY, [solv′-en-si], *n.* the condition of being solvent; ability to pay all debts.
SOLVENT (1), [sol′-vent], *n.* a substance which has the power of dissolving specific substances; an explanation or modification; (*med.*) a menstruum.
SOLVENT (2), [sol′-vent], *adj.* having the power of dissolving; having enough money or wealth to pay all debts.
SOLVER, [solv′-er], *n.* one who, or that which, solves.
SOMA (1), [sō′-ma], *n.* the intoxicating juice of a plant offered in Hindu ritual to a god in order to invigorate him for his fight against evil spirits. [Skr. *soma*].
SOMA (2), [sō′-ma], *n.* the tissue of the body as distinct from the germ cells. [Gk. *soma* body].
SOMATIC, [sō-mat′-ik], *adj.* (*biol.*) relating to, forming, the body as distinct from the reproductive cells. [Gk. *somatikos*].
SOMATOLOGY, [sō′-mat-ol′-o-ji], *n.* the doctrine of material substance or of matter, materialism. [SOMATIC and Gk. *logos* speech].
SOMBRE, [som′-ber], *adj.* presenting a dark and dismal scene, overcast, gloomy in appearance; covered with shadow; having a low tone of colour, subdued; expressing melancholy or depression of

spirits, being in a pessimistic frame of mind, sad, gloomy. [Span. *sombra* shade].

SOMBRELY, [som'-ber-li], *adv.* in a sombre manner; to a subdued extent.

SOMBRENESS, [som'-ber-nes], *n.* the quality of being sombre.

SOMBRERITE, [som-brāer'-īt], *n.* (*min.*) a massive variety of apatite found in the West Indies. [*Sombrero*, a West Indies isle].

SOMBRERO, [som-brāer'-ō], *n.* a type of broad-brimmed soft felt-hat. [Span. *sombrero*].

SOMBROUSLY, [som'-brus-li], *adv.* in a sombrous fashion.

SOMBROUSNESS, [som'-brus-nes], *n.* the condition of being sombre.

SOME (1), [sum], *adj.* a quantity, number, person or thing which is not given a specific definition; approximately, more or less; one or other; (*slang*) fine, great. [OE. *sum*].

SOME (2), [sum], *pron.* an unspecified number of people or objects.

SOMEBODY, [sum'-bod'-i], *n.* a person unknown or uncertain; a person not identified; a person of importance or influence.

SOMEHOW, [sum'-how], *adv.* in some way, in one way or other not yet known; by some means left unspecified.

SOMEONE, [sum'-wun], *pron.* some person.

SOMERSAULT (1), SUMMERSAULT, [sum'-er-sawlt], *n.* a leap in which a person turns heels over head in the air before landing on his feet again; (*fig.*) a volte face. [OFr. *sombre sault*].

SOMERSAULT (2), SUMMERSAULT, [sum'-er-sawlt], *v.i.* to turn a somersault.

SOMERSET, [sum'-er-set'], *n.* a form of saddle padded before the knee and behind the thigh for a man who has lost a leg. [Lord *Somerset*, its inventor].

SOMERVILLITE, [sum'-er-vil-īt], *n.* (*min.*) a yellow Vesuvian mineral. [Dr. *Somerville*].

SOMETHING (1), [sum'-thing], *n.* that which is indicated but left undefined as to characteristics; anything unspecified or indefinite; that which is important; **s. of**, characterized by the possession of (certain features or qualities) but undefined as to degree.

SOMETHING (2), [sum'-thing], *adv.* to some extent or degree; in some degree; **s. like**, having a vague resemblance; approximately, nearly; fine, excellent.

SOMETIME, [sum'-tīm], *adv.* at some time left unspecified; at one time or other hereafter; †formerly.

SOMETIMES, [sum'-tīmz], *adv.* at times; at intervals; at one time; occasionally, now and then.

SOMEWHAT, [sum'-wot], *adv.* in some degree or quantity, rather, to some extent, slightly.

SOMEWHERE, [sum'-wāer], *adv.* in some place unknown or not specified; in one place or another.

SOMITE, [sō'-mīt], *n.* (*biol.*) a distinct body segment of an invertebrate animal. [Gk. *soma* body].

SOMITIC, [sō-mit'-ik], *adj.* (*biol.*) relating to a somite.

SOMNAMBULANT, [som-nam'-byōōl-ant], *adj.* characterized by a tendency to walk while asleep. [L. *somnus* sleep and *ambulans* walking].

SOMNAMBULATE, [som-nam'-byōōl-āt], *v.i.* to walk in one's sleep.

SOMNAMBULATION, [som-nam'-byōōl-ā'-shun], *n.* the act of walking in one's sleep, somnambulism.

SOMNAMBULATOR, [som-nam'-byōōl-ā-tor], *n.* a sleep-walker, a somnambulist.

SOMNAMBULISM, [som-nam'-byōōl-izm], *n.* the practice of walking and performing actions of various kinds in sleep as though in a trance, sleep-walking.

SOMNAMBULIST, [som-nam'-byōōl-ist], *n.* a person who walks in sleep; a person who is subject to somnambulism.

SOMNAMBULISTIC, [som-nam'-byōōl-ist'-ik], *adj.* relating to somnambulism.

SOMNI-, *pref.* inducing, inclined to, affected by, sleep. [L. *somnus* sleep].

SOMNIFEROUS, [som-nif'-er-us], *adj.* causing or inducing sleep, soporific. [L. *somnifer*].

SOMNIFIC, [som-nif'-ik], *adj.* inclined to induce sleep. [SOMNI and L. *facere* to make].

SOMNILOQUISM, [som-nil'-ō-kwizm], *n.* the act or practice of talking in sleep.

SOMNILOQUIST, [som-nil'-ō-kwist], *n.* one who talks in sleep.

SOMNILOQUOUS, [som-nil'-ō-kwus], *adj.* inclined to talk in sleep.

SOMNILOQUY, [som-nil'-ok-wi], *n.* a talk during sleep. [SOMNI and L. *loqui* to speak.]

SOMNOLENCE, [som'-nōl-ents], *n.* a physical and mental condition characterized by drowsiness and a tendency to fall asleep, a condition of being half awake and half asleep. [L. *somnolentia*].

SOMNOLENCY, [som'-nō-len-si], *n.* somnolence.

SOMNOLENT, [som'-nōl-ent], *adj.* tending to fall asleep, sleepy, drowsy; inclined to induce sleep. [L. *somnolentus*].

SOMNOLENTLY, [som'-nō-lent-li], *adv.* in a somnolent manner; to a sleepy degree.

SON, [sun], *n.* a male child in relation to his parent or parents; a form of address used by an old man to a young; a term of affection; a male member of a country; a male member of any group or activity which commands an emotional loyalty, such as a church, a school, etc.; a male person adopted into a family, or regarded by an elder with real paternal affection. [OE. *sunu*].

SONANCY, [sō'-nan-si], *n.* the quality of being sonant.

SONANT (1), [sō'-nant], *n.* (*phon.*) a voiced speech sound.

SONANT (2), [sō'-nant], *adj.* articulated by means of a sound; (*phon.*) voiced. [L. *sonans*, *pres.pt.* of *sonare* to sound].

SONATA, [son-ah'-ta], *n.* a form of musical composition for one or more instruments written in three, or sometimes four, movements; **s. form**, the form typical of the first movement of a classical sonata. [It. *sonata*].

SONATINA, [son'-a-tē'-na], *n.* a short and simplified form of sonata. [It. *sonatina*].

SONG, [song], *n.* a series of modulated sounds produced by a human being or bird by means of the vocal chords in the throat; a musical composition, composed as a setting to a lyric, whose chief characteristic is a well-defined melodic line; a singing of such a composition; such a composition in manuscript form; a short poem emphasizing certain elements of speech best appreciated when sung; poetry in general; the notes of birds; (*slang*) a mere trifle, practically nothing; **to make a s. about**, to make a fuss about. [OE. *sang*].

SONG-BIRD, [song'-burd], *n.* a bird possessing a natural power of song.

SONG-BOOK, [song'-bŏŏk], *n.* a book containing a collection of songs.

SONG-HIT, [song'-hit'], *n.* a popular dance-tune.

SONGLESS, [song'-les], *adj.* not able to sing; not disposed towards singing.

SONG-SPARROW, [song'-spa'-rō], *n.* the hedge-sparrow.

SONGSTER, [song'-ster], *n.* a person who is continually singing; a bird that sings. [OE. *songestere*].

SONGSTRESS, [song'-stres], *n.* a female singer.

SONG-THRUSH, [song'-thrush], *n.* the mavis, *Turdus musicus*.

SONIFEROUS, [son-if'-er-us], *adj.* producing or conveying sound. [L. *sonus* sound and *ferre* to bear].

SON-IN-LAW, [sun'-in-law], *n.* a man married to a parent's daughter, a daughter's husband.

SONLESS, [sun'-les], *adj.* having no son; having lost a son.

SONNET, [son'-it], *n.* a decasyllabic or dodecasyllabic poem of fourteen lines, with one subject. [It. *sonetto*].

SONNETEER, [son'-et-ēer'], *n.* a composer of sonnets. [It. *sonettiere*].

SONNITES, see SUNNITES.

SONNY, [sun'-i], *n.* a young son; a term of endearment; a term reflecting the speaker's sense of superiority in rank or age.

SONOMETER, [son-om'-it-er], *n.* an instrument for measuring the characteristics of sound or for testing its effects. [L. *sonus* sound and METER].

SONOMETER

SONORESCENCE, [son'-o-res'-ents], *n.* (*phys.*) the quality of being sonorescent.

SONORESCENT, [son'-o-res'-ent], *adj.* (*phys.*) capable of emitting sound when affected by heat or light. [L. *sonor* a sound].

SONORITY, [son-o'-rit-i], *n.* the quality of being sonorous, sonorousness. [L. *sonoritas*].

SONOROUS, [son-aw'-rus], *adj.* resonant in quality of sound; emitting a deep, loud sound when struck; yielding sound; high-sounding; rhetorical. [L. *sonorus* resounding].

SONOROUSLY, [son-aw'-rus-li], *adv.* to a sonorous degree, in a sonorous manner.

SONOROUSNESS, [son-aw'-rus-nes], *n.* the quality of being sonorous; magnificence of voice.

SONSY, [son'-zi], *adj.* (*Scots*) buxom, handsome. [Gael. *sonas* good fortune].
SOON, [sōōn], *adv.* in a short time; before the anticipated time, early; without delay, readily, willingly; **as s. as,** at the exact moment that, directly, immediately. [OE. *sona*].
SOOSOO, [sōō'-sōō], *n.* the Gangetic dolphin, *Platanista gangetica*, the blind dolphin.
SOOT (1), [sŏŏt], *n.* a black substance, mostly carbon, deposited in chimneys by fuel during imperfect combustion. [OE. *sot*].
SOOT (2), [sŏŏt], *v.t.* to cover or stain with soot.
SOOTH†, [sōōth], *n.* a true fact, truth, reality. [OE. *soth*].
SOOTHE, [sōōTH], *v.t.* to cause to become less disturbed emotionally, to pacify, calm, placate, to restore to a calm frame of mind by means of kind and sympathetic words; to lessen, mitigate, allay. [OE. *gesothian* to prove].
SOOTHER, [sōō'-THer], *n.* a flatterer; one who, or that which, soothes.
SOOTHING, [sōōTH'-ing], *adj.* having the power to soothe.
SOOTHINGLY, [sōōTH'-ing-li], *adv.* in a soothing manner.
SOOTHSAY, [sōōth'-sā], *v.i.* to predict the future, to foretell.
SOOTHSAYER, [sōōth'-sā-er], *n.* a person who predicts the future, a prognosticator, a prophet, a fortune-teller. [ME. *sothsiggere*].
SOOTHSAYING, [sōōth'-sā-ing], *n.* the art or practice of foretelling.
SOOTINESS, [sŏŏt'-i-nes], *n.* the condition of being sooty.
SOOTING, [sŏŏt-ing], *n.* the deposit of carbon on a motor-car plug.
SOOTISH, [sŏŏt'-ish], *adj.* being slightly affected by, or like, soot.
SOOTY, [sŏŏt'-i], *adj.* consisting of, affected by, soot; relating to, resembling, soot; covered, stained, foul, with soot; **s. tern,** the American bird of the sea, *Sterna fuliginosa*.
SOP (1), [sop], *n.* food such as bread, etc., soaked in liquid such as milk or soup; anything soaked through with liquid, particularly rainwater; (*fig.*) a small concession. [OE. *sopp*.]
SOP (2), (sopping, sopped), [sop], *v.t.* to soak in an edible thick liquid such as soup; to soak, drench; **to s. up,** to remove (water, etc.) by means of an absorbent substance, to mop up.
SOPH, [sof], *n.* (*U.S. slang*) a sophomore. [SOPHOMORE].
SOPHERIM, [sof'-er-im], *n.(pl.)* the Jewish scribes. [Heb. *sopher* scribe].
SOPHISM, [sof'-izm], *n.* an ingenious but fallacious argument, a specious line of reasoning; a fallacy. [Gk. *sophisma*].
SOPHIST, [sof'-ist], *n.* a person expert in putting forward plausible but essentially fallacious arguments, a specious arguer, an unscrupulous publicist or propagandist; formerly, a member of a class of professional lecturers in ancient Greece. [Gk. *sophistes* a clever person].
SOPHISTER, [sof'-ist-er], *n.* a university undergraduate of two years' standing. [OFr. *sophistre*].
SOPHISTICAL, [sō-fist'-ik-al], *adj.* relating to a sophist or his type of argument; containing sophistry, plausible but specious. [Gk. *sophistikos*].
SOPHISTICALLY, [sō-fist'-ik-al-i], *adv.* in a sophistical manner.
SOPHISTICALNESS, [sō-fist'-ik-al-nes], *n.* the quality of being sophistical.
SOPHISTICATE (1), [sō-fist'-ik-āt], *adj.* impure, corrupted, adulterated; not genuine.
SOPHISTICATE (2), [sō-fist'-ik-āt], *v.t. and i.* to translate into terms of sophistry, to make sophistical; to make impure, adulterate, to corrupt; to cause to become artificial or affected in conduct; to be sophistical. [LL. *sophisticare*].
SOPHISTICATED, [sō-fist'-ik-ā-tid], *adj.* affected, artificial, in behaviour; possessing a smartness of social attitude based on an essentially superficial mental capacity; worldly-wise.
SOPHISTICATION, [sō-fist'-ik-ā'-shun], *n.* the state of being sophisticated; an act of one who is sophisticated; the process of making impure or corrupt sophistically.
SOPHISTICATOR, [sō-fist'-ik-ā-tor], *n.* one who sophisticates.
SOPHISTRY, [sŏf'-ist-ri], *n.* the art or method of a sophist; specious reasoning; reasoning which is plausible, notwithstanding its basic fallaciousness. [OFr. *sophistrie*].
SOPHOMORE, [sŏf'-ō-maw(r)], *n.* (*U.S.*) a university or college student in his second year. [Gk. *sophos* wise and *moros* foolish].
SOPHOMORIC, [sŏf'-ō-mo'-rik], *adj.* relating to, characteristic of, a sophomore; bombastic.
SOPHY†, [sŏf'-i], *n.* the title of the Shah of Persia. [Pers. *çafi*].
SOPORIFEROUS, [sop'-or-if'-er-us], *adj.* tending to induce sleep, soporific. [L. *sopor* sleep and *ferre* to bear].
SOPORIFIC (1), [sop'-or-if'-ik], *n.* a medicine or drug which induces sleep.
SOPORIFIC (2), [sop'-or-if'-ik], *adj.* causing or tending to induce sleep. [L. *sopor* sleep and *facere* to make].
SOPPING, [sop'-ing], *adj.* (*coll.*) very wet; **s. wet,** soaked with water. [SOP (2)].
SOPPY, [sop'-i], *adj.* resembling a sop; saturated, soaked, very wet; (*coll.*) having no mental or physical energy; **to be s. on,** to be infatuated with.
SOPRANO (1), [sō-prah'-nō], *n.* music for one with a singing range which reaches the higher notes accessible to a human being or for the treble voice of a boy; a person possessed of such a singing range; the part in a composition written for treble voices. [It. *soprano* supreme].
SOPRANO (2), [sō-prah'-nō], *adj.* with the musical range of a soprano; written for a soprano.
SORB, [sawb], *n.* the service-tree or its fruit, *Pyrus torminalis*. [L. *sorbus*].
SORBATE, [sawb'-āt], *n.* (*chem.*) a salt of sorbic acid formed with a base.
SORBEFACIENT (1), [saw'-bi-fā'-shi-ent], *n.* a medicine or drug which induces absorption.
SORBEFACIENT (2), [saw'-bi-fā'-shi-ent], *adj.* (*med.*) inducing, promoting, absorption. [L. *sorbere* to suck and *faciens* making].
SORBET, [saw'-bet, saw'-bā], *n.* a flavoured water-ice. [Fr. *sorbet* sherbet].
SORBIC, [saw'-bik], *adj.* (*chem.*) derived from, relating to, the service-tree.
SORBINE, [saw'-bin], *n.* (*chem.*) a saccharine substance obtained from the berries of the mountain ash.
SORBONICAL, [saw-bon'-ik-al], *adj.* connected with, belonging to, the Sorbonne. [*Next*].
SORBONIST, [saw'-bon-ist], *n.* a graduate or pupil of the Académie Universitaire de Paris, modern successor to the ancient college of the Sorbonne.
SORCERER, [saw'-ser-er], *n.* one who practises sorcery, a magician, a wizard. [LL. *sortiarius* fortune-teller].
SORCERESS, [saw'-ser-es], *n.* a female sorcerer.
SORCEROUS, [saw'-ser-us], *adj.* relating to sorcery.
SORCERY, [saw'-ser-i], *n.* the art of magic, control of reality or divination by the assistance of evil spirits, or the power of commanding them, witchcraft. [OFr. *sorcerie*].
SORDAVALITE, [saw'-dav-al'-īt], *n.* (*min.*) a black silicate of iron and magnesia. [*Sordavala*, in Finland, where found].
SORDES, [saw'-dēz], *n.* (*med.*) crusted pus forming on a feverish patient's lips and teeth; dregs, filthy refuse. [L. *sordes* dirt].
SORDID, [saw'-did], *adj.* naturally associated with filth, dirty, squalid; given an existence by ignoble methods or motives, contemptible, low in character; base-minded, motivated by a deliberate encouragement of the lowest qualities in mankind, mean, low; **s. dragonet,** a fish characterized by a spotted dorsal fin, *Callionymus maculatus*. [L. *sordidus* squalid).
SORDIDLY, [saw'-did-li], *adv.* in a sordid manner.
SORDIDNESS, [saw'-did-nes], *n.* the condition of being sordid, filthiness; meanness.
SORDINE, SOURDINE, [saw'-dēn'], *n.* a contrivance for muffling sound; a mute for a trumpet. [OFr. *sourdine* from L. *surdus* deaf].
SORE (1), [saw(r)], *n.* a morbid condition of the skin caused by injury or disease, an ulcer, a boil; a painful or irritating memory. [OE. *sar* pain].
SORE (2), [saw(r)], *n.* a hawk in its first year wearing its red plumage; a buck in its fourth year. [AFr. *sore*].
SORE (3), [saw(r)], *adj.* painful when touched or rubbed, as a raw or inflamed part of the body; susceptible of pain, tender, affected with inflammation; hurt, affronted, upset emotionally through an experience of grief, insult, resentment, or anger; †severe, intense, extreme. [OE. *sar*].
SORE (4), [saw(r)], *adv.* †severely, grievously. [OE. *sare*].
SOREHON, [sawr'-hon], *n.* a form of Irish tenancy

which bound a tenant to maintain a chief and his retinue on his estate whenever it was required. [Ir. *sorehon*].

SOREL†, [so'-rel], *n.* a buck in its third year. [OFr. *sorel* reddish-brown].

SORELY, [saw(r)'-li], *adv.* to a sore extent, in a sore manner; severely, greatly.

SORENESS, [saw(r)'-nes], *n.* the quality of being sore; painfulness, tenderness; resentment, rancour.

SORGHUM, [saw'-gum], *n.* (*bot.*) the genus of tall, cereal grasses, allied to the sugar-cane, and including the Indian millet. [It. *sorgo*].

SORICINE, [saw'-ris-in], *adj.* relating to shrews; like a mouse. [L. *soricinus*].

SORIFEROUS, [saw-rif'-er-us], *adj.* (*bot.*) producing, bearing, sori. [Gk. *soros* heap and L. *ferre* to bear].

SORITES, [sō-rī'-tēz], *n.* a form of logical argument based on a series of syllogisms. [Gk. *soreites* heaped up].

SORN, [sawn], *v.i.* to extract unreasonably board and lodging from friends, to sponge upon. [Ir. *coinneamh* free quarters].

SOROPTIMIST, [so-rop'-tim-ist], *n.* a member of a women's Rotary Club. [L. *soror* sister and OPTIMIST].

SORORICIDE, [so-raw'-ris-id], *n.* the murder of one's sister; the murderer of a sister. [L. *sororicida*].

SORORITY, [so-ro'-ri-ti], *n.* a women's club for undergraduates in American universities. [L. *soror* sister].

SOROSIS, [so-rō'-sis], *n.* (*bot.*) a fruit composed of adhering clumps of pulpy flesh like that of the pineapple or the mulberry. [~Gk. *soros* heap].

SORREL (1), [so'-rel], *n.* (*bot.*) **wood s.**, a plant with small pinkish-white flowers, so named from the acid taste of its trefoil leaves. [OFr. *sorel*].

SORREL (2), [so'-rel], *n.* a horse red-brown in colour. [OFr. *sorel*].

SORREL (3), [so'-rel], *adj.* of a reddish-brown colour.

SORREL-TREE, [so'-rel-trē'], *n.* a tree of the heath family, *Oxydendron arboreum*, a native of North America, the elk-tree.

WOOD SORREL

SORRILY, [so'-ri-li], *adv.* in a sorry manner; pitiably, miserably, in a wretched manner.

SORRINESS, [so'-ri-nes], *n.* the quality of being sorry; meanness, despicableness; poverty of quality.

SORROW (1), [so'-rō], *n.* a state of mind and emotion governed by prolonged misery and grief due to a sense of one's own or another's loss, misfortune, affliction, deep unhappiness, sadness; regret for error or sin committed, contrition. [OE. *sorh*].

SORROW (2), [so'-rō], *v.i.* to feel or express sorrow, to grieve; to mourn. [OE. *sorgian*].

SORROWER, [so'-rō-er], *n.* one who sorrows or grieves.

SORROWFUL, [so'-rō-fŏŏl], *adj.* full of sorrow, miserable, sad, unhappy; producing sorrow; grievous; accompanied with sorrow.

SORROWFULLY, [so'-rō-fŏŏl-i], *adv.* in a sorrowful way.

SORROWFULNESS, [so'-rō-fŏŏl-nes], *n.* the quality of being sorrowful, grief.

SORROWLESS, [so'-rō-les], *adj.* unaccompanied by, free from, sorrow.

SORRY, [so'-ri], *adj.* feeling grief, sorrow, regretting, contrite; a term of apology; inferior in quality, worthless; mean, vile; ridiculous. [OE. *sarig*].

SORT (1), [sawt], *n.* a group composed of individual members, objects, persons, etc., having certain qualities in common, a class, species, kind, category; a class of dubious character; degree, quality, condition, manner; (*typ.*) the units of a particular fount; **a good s.**, a generous, likeable person; **out of sorts**, unwell, but not seriously ill; **of sorts**, of a kind. [L. *sors sortis* lot].

SORT (2), [sawt], *v.t.* and *i.* to separate into sorts, classes, or categories, to classify, put into order, arrange in groups; to arrange postal matter for delivery; †to consort; to agree. [L. *sortiri* to divide into lots].

SORTABLE, [sawt'-abl], *adj.* able to be sorted; †suitable, befitting.

SORTATION, [sawt-ā'-shun], *n.* the act of sorting; (*typ.*) the employment of a letter-sorter.

SORTER, [sawt'-er], *n.* one who separates and sorts; a person who earns a living by such employment.

SORTIE, [sawt'-ē], *n.* a sudden raid made by a body of troops from a besieged place on the enemy, a sally; an expedition. [Fr. *sortie*].

SORUS, (*pl.* **sori**), [saw'-rus], *n.* (*bot.*) a cluster of capsules or spore-cases on the under-side of the fronds of ferns. [Gk. *soros* heap].

S.O.S., [es'-ō-es'], *n.* the letters in the Morse code used in an appeal for rescue at sea; a broadcast appeal for a relative or friend of a patient dangerously ill; an urgent appeal.

SO-SO, [sō'-sō'], *adj.* (*coll.*) of mediocre quality; not characterized by excellence; indifferent.

SOSTENUTO, [sos'-ten-ŏŏ'-tō], *adv.* (*mus.*) with a slightly sustained touch; in a prolonged style. [It. *sostenuto*].

SOT (1), [sot], *n.* a dull, drunken, and befuddled fool; a habitual drunkard with his brain sodden by drink. [ME. *sot* foolish].

SOT (2), (**sotting, sotted**), [sot], *v.t.* and *i.* to make stupid by filling with drink; to drink till fuddled in the brain.

SOTERIOLOGY, [sōt-ēer'-i-ol'-o-ji], *n.* the study or science of health; (*theol.*) the doctrine of salvation. [Gk. *soteria* salvation and *logos* speech].

SOTHIC, [sō'-thik], *adj.* relating to the dog-star, by whose heliacal rising the Egyptians calculated their year of 365¼ days. [Gk. *Sothis* Sirius, the dog-star].

SOTNIA, [sot'-ni-a], *n.* a troop of Cossack cavalry. [Russ. *sotnya* hundred].

SOTTISH, [sot'-ish], *adj.* being in the state of a sot, like a sot; given to drinking; fuddled with drink, stupid, weak in the brain.

SOTTISHLY, [sot'-ish-li], *adv.* in a sottish manner.

SOTTISHNESS, [sot'-ish-nes], *n.* the quality of being sottish.

SOTTO-VOCE, [sot'-ō-vō'-chi], *adv.* by means of a whisper, in an undertone. [It. *sotto voce* under the voice].

SOU, [sŏŏ], *n.* a French copper coin, worth five centimes or one-twentieth of a franc. [Fr. *sou*].

SOUARI, [sŏŏ-ah'-ri], *n.* the butternut, a lofty tropical American tree of the genus *Caryocar*, yielding a hard, durable wood. [Native].

SOUBADAR, see SUBADAR.

SOUBISE, [sŏŏ-bēz'], *n.* a French variety of onion sauce. [M. *Soubise*, an eighteenth-century French courtier].

SOUBRETTE, [sŏŏ-bret'], *n.* a waiting-maid; an actress playing the part of a coquettish, pert character in comedy. [OFr. *soubret* cunning].

SOUBRIQUET, see SOBRIQUET.

SOUCAR, SOWKAR, [sow'-kah(r)], *n.* a banker or moneylender of Indian birth. [Hind. *sahukar* magnate].

SOUCHET, [sŏŏ'-shā], *n.* a dish of fish served in the water it is boiled in. [Fr. *souchet*].

SOUCHONG, [sŏŏ'-chong], *n.* a kind of black tea from China with a tarry flavour, notable for its fine quality. [Chin. *hsiao chung* small kind].

SOUFFLE, soufflé (1), [sŏŏf'-lā], *n.* a dish of sweet or savoury, made light by being mixed with the beaten whites of eggs and then baked. [Fr. *soufflé*].

SOUFFLE, soufflé (2), [sŏŏ'-flā], *adj.* consisting of soufflé.

SOUFFLE, [sŏŏfl], *n.* (*med.*) a soft, blowing sound made by the lungs. [Fr. *souffle*].

SOUGH (1), [suf, sow], *n.* a sound of low moaning, or of continuous sighing, such as the wind makes as it blows through the branches and leaves of trees.

SOUGH (2), [suf, sow], *v.i.* to make a sound like the wind sighing. [OE. *swogan*].

SOUGHT, [sawt], *pret.* and *p.pt.* of SEEK; searched for. [OE. *sohte*].

SOUL, [sōl], *n.* the capacity for emotional or spiritual experience conditioning the functioning of conscience, feeling, and rationality which is considered the core or centre of a person's individuality, and credited by religious thought with the potentiality of eternal existence; the vital principle and power which maintains a person in the realm of life; the side of man's nature sustained by the higher, more noble emotions and motives; a person when considered as animated and governed by one of the nobler virtues; a person who provides life and enthusiasm; a spirit believed to have left the body of its owner, and departed elsewhere; a single person, one human being. [OE. *sawol*].

SOUL-BELL, [sōl'-bel'], *n.* the passing-bell tolled at a death or funeral.

SOULFUL, [sōl'-fŏŏl], *adj.* full of a power to stir the nobler emotions, emotional; yearningly sentimental.

SOULFULLY, [sōl'-fŏŏl-i], *adv.* in a soulful way.
SOULFULNESS, [sōl'-fŏŏl-nes], *n.* the condition of being soulful.
SOULLESS, [sōl'-les], *adj.* having no soul; without greatness or nobleness of mind; destitute of human virtues; cruel, merciless; selfish, mean.
SOULLESSLY, [sōl'-les-li], *adv.* in a soulless manner, mercilessly.
SOUL-SICK, [sōl'-sik'], *adj.* suffering from depression or spiritual deficiency, morally diseased.
SOUND (1), [sownd], *n.* a narrow passage of water as between a mainland and an island; a shallow sea or strait forming the means of communication between two seas; the air-bladder of a fish. [OE. *sund*].
SOUND (2), [sownd], *n.* that which is heard, a vibratory disturbance in the air which affects the ear-drum, and stimulates the sense of hearing, an impression received by means of the hearing known to be characteristic of a certain cause; a sound made by the power of speech; noise, report. [OFr. *soun* from L. *sonus*].
SOUND (3), [sownd], *n.* an anatomical instrument used by a surgeon for probing. [Fr. *sonde*].
SOUND (4), [sownd], *adj.* in a properly co-ordinated condition, entire, whole, unbroken; in sound physical condition, undecayed, perfect, healthy; hearty; solid; valid, right, correct in sequence or consequence, logical, sagacious; complete, thorough; designed to produce an orthodox result, efficient, effective; strongly equipped with specific qualities; stout, lusty; unimpaired, reliable, not deranged. [OE. *sund*].
SOUND (5), [sownd], *adv.* in a sound manner; to a whole degree; healthily.
SOUND (6), [sownd], *v.t. and i.* to cause a sound, to cause to make a noise; to express by the voice, to say aloud; to signal by means of a particular sound; to celebrate, honour, announce by sounds; to make a sound or noise; to make an impression of a particular quality on the ear; to make a sound characteristic of a certain condition or event; to seem, appear. [OFr. *souner* from L. *sonare*].
SOUND (7), [sownd], *v.t. and i.* to measure the depth of (water); to attempt to ascertain (opinion or feeling which has not been concretely expressed); (*fig.*) to learn by experience; (*med.*) to test, examine, by means of a sound; (*meteor.*) to examine scientifically by sending up balloons.
SOUND-BOARDING, [sownd'-bawd'-ing], *n.* (*building*) reinforcement of a floor by boards so as to deaden sound.
SOUND-BOW, [sownd'-bō], *n.* the thickest part of a bell where the clapper strikes.
SOUND-BOX, [sownd'-boks'], *n.* the box containing the stylus and diaphragm of a gramophone.
SOUNDER (1), [sownd'-er], *n.* a telegraphic instrument consisting of an electro-magnet, armature and lever, used for signalling by means of sound.
SOUNDER (2), [sownd'-er], *n.* a herd of wild swine; a young boar. [OE. *sunor*].
SOUND-FILM, [sownd'-film], *n.* (*cinema*) a cinematograph film with synchronized sound effects, speech, etc.
SOUND-GATE, [sownd'-gāt'], *n.* the grid through which sound-film is passed in order to reproduce the sound.
SOUND-HEAD, [sownd'-hed'], *n.* that part of a cinematograph employed to reproduce sound.
SOUNDING (1), [sownd'-ing], *n.* the act or process of measuring a depth of water; the measurement obtained by such a process; a place submitted to such a process.
SOUNDING (2), [sownd'-ing], *adj.* full of sound, sonorous; making a noise; providing more noise than meaning or significance.
SOUNDING-BOARD, [sownd'-ing-bawd'], *n.* a board or contrivance suspended over a pulpit to amplify the sound of the preacher's voice; any appliance which helps to increase the resonance of a sound.
SOUNDING-LINE, [sownd'-ing-līn'], *n.* a line for taking soundings with.
SOUNDING-POST, [sownd'-ing-pōst'], *n.* a small peg under the bridge of a violin or violoncello, for transmitting the sound to the body of the instrument.
SOUNDING-ROD, [sownd'-ing-rod'], *n.* (*naut.*) a graduated rod or piece of iron used to measure the depth of water in a ship's hold.
SOUNDING-WIRE, [sownd'-ing-wīer'], *n.* a wire for taking deep-sea soundings with.
SOUNDLESS (1), [sownd'-les], *adj.* characterized by the absence of sound, silent; (*fig.*) still, ghostly.
SOUNDLESS (2), [sownd'-les], *adj.* fathomless.
SOUNDLESSLY, [sownd'-les-li], *adv.* in a soundless manner.
SOUNDLESSNESS, [sownd'-les-nes], *n.* the quality of being soundless.
SOUNDLY, [sownd'-li], *adv.* in a sound manner.
SOUNDNESS, [sownd'-nes], *n.* the quality of being sound.
SOUND-PROOF, [sownd'-prōōf], *adj.* having the structure or properties to shut out sound.
SOUND-SCREEN, [sownd'-skrēn], *n.* a cinema screen specially adapted for sound projection.
SOUND-TRACK, [sownd'-trak'], *n.* (*cinema*) the narrow margin on a celluloid film on which synchronized sound is recorded.
SOUND-TRUCK, [sownd'-truk'], *n.* (*cinema*) a mobile apparatus for recording sounds on the set.
SOUND-WAVE, [sownd'-wāv'], *n.* one of a regular series of disturbances in the air which affects the auditory nerves.
SOUP, [sōōp], *n.* food in the form of water or gravy impregnated with meat or vegetables which have been boiled up in it and strained off, the dish usually being seasoned and served hot; **in the s.**, (*slang*) in trouble. [Fr. *soupe*].
SOUPCON, soupçon, [sōōp'-saw(ng)], *n.* a suggestion, a trace, a taste. [Fr. *soupçon* suspicion].
SOUP-KITCHEN, [sōōp'-kich'-en], *n.* a public establishment with the charitable aim of supplying soup gratuitously to the poor.
SOUP-PLATE, [sōōp'-plāt'], *n.* a plate with a deeper bowl than usual in which soup is served.
SOUP-TICKET, [sōōp'-tik'-it], *n.* a ticket entitling the bearer to obtain free soup from a public kitchen.
SOUPY, [sōōp'-i], *adj.* resembling soup.
SOUR (1), [sowr], *n.* that which is sour.
SOUR (2), [sowr], *adj.* having a quality which is recognizable by tasting as sharp or bitter, acidulous in flavour, astringent; turned, curdled, rancid, as milk; having a peevish nature, disagreeable, acrimonious; impoverished, not rich, as soil. [OE. *sur*].
SOUR (3), [sowr], *v.t. and i.* to turn sour, to cause to become rancid; to make miserable and bitter in feelings, to make cross or peevish; to become acidulous.
SOURCE, [saws], *n.* the place of a spring or fountain from which a stream of water flows; first cause, original, the starting-point of anything; original work providing material for successors. [Fr. *source*].
SOURCE-BOOK, [saws'-bŏŏk], *n.* a collection of original documents recording historical material.
SOURDELINE, [sōōerd'-el-ēn], *n.* a small variety of bagpipes. [Fr. *sourdeline*].
SOURDINE, see SORDINE.
SOURDOUGH, [sowr'-dō], *n.* (*U.S.*) an old-timer.
SOUR-GOURD, [sowr'-gōōerd'], *n.* the Australian tree, *Adansonia digitata*.
SOURING, [sowr'-ing], *n.* that which turns to acid.
SOURISH, [sowr'-ish], *adj.* tasting slightly sour; moderately acid.
SOURLY, [sowr'-li], *adv.* in a sour manner; to a sour degree; with acidity; discontentedly, peevishly.
SOURNESS, [sowr'-nes], *n.* the quality of being sour, acidity, tartness, asperity.
SOURSOP, [sowr'-sop'], *n.* the large green fruit of the small tropical American evergreen tree, *Anona muricata*; the tree itself.

SOUR-GOURD

SOUSE (1), [sows], *n.* something kept steeped in pickle; the ears and feet of pigs, pickled; a downpour of water or rainwater; a ducking in water. [OFr. *sause*].
SOUSE (2), [sows], *v.t.* to pickle, to keep saturated in pickle; to soak with water, to drench; to duck in water.
SOUSE (3), [sows], *v.i.* to move with a violent downward or upward movement, to fall suddenly. [OFr. *sorse* swoop].
SOUSE (4), [sows], *adv.* with a plunge, with a swoop.
SOUSED, [sowst], *adj.* (*coll.*) drunk, inebriated, tipsy.
SOUSLIK, [sōōs'-lik], *n.* the speckled field mouse or ground squirrel found in Europe and Asia. [Russ. *suslik*].
SOUTANE, [sōō-tahn'], *n.* a black robe worn by Roman Catholic priests, a cassock; a wearer of such a robe. [Fr. from LL. *subtana* under-garment].

SOUTENEUR, [sōō'-ten-ur'], *n.* a man who lives on a prostitute's earnings. [Fr. *souteneur* protector].
SOUTH (1), [sowth], *n.* the cardinal point of the compass opposite to the north; that imaginary point facing an observer standing north of the equator and looking towards the sun at noon; the southern hemisphere; a territory, area, or district spoken of collectively as lying south of a certain point or line. [OE. *suth*].
SOUTH (2), [sowth], *adj.* situated in a territory or district in the south, southern; facing the south; coming from, obtained from, grown in, found in, the south.
SOUTH (3), [sowth], *v.i.* to move in a southerly direction.
SOUTH (4), [sowth], *adv.* towards the south.
SOUTHDOWN (1), [south'-down'], *n.* a sheep bred on the South Downs in Sussex or Hampshire.
SOUTHDOWN (2), [sowth'-down'], *adj.* pertaining to a Southdown.
SOUTH-EAST (1), [sowth'-ēst'], *n.* a point of the compass midway between the south and east; a region or district in this direction.
SOUTH-EAST (2), [sowth'-ēst'], *adj.* situated in, facing, moving towards, the south-east; coming from the south-east.
SOUTH-EAST (3), [sowth'-ēst'], *adv.* towards the south-east.
SOUTH-EASTER, [sowth'-ēst'-er], *n.* a south-easterly wind or gale.
SOUTH-EASTERLY (1), [sowth'-ēst'-er-li], *adj.* situated in, directed towards, the south-east, coming from the south-east.
SOUTH-EASTERLY (2), [sowth'-ēst'-er-li], *adv.* in the direction of the south-east.
SOUTH-EASTERN, [sowth'-ēst'-ern], *adj.* belonging to, situated in, the south-east.
SOUTHERLINESS, [suTH'-er-li-nes], *n.* the state of being southerly.
SOUTHERLY (1), [suTH'-er-li], *adj.* towards the south; lying in the south, coming from the south.
SOUTHERLY (2), [suTH'-er-li], *adv.* towards the south.
SOUTHERN, [suTH'-ern], *adj.* situated in, belonging to, the south; lying towards the south; coming from, characteristic of, the south; operating in the south. [OE. *sutherne*].
SOUTHERNER, [suTH'-ern-er], *n.* an inhabitant of the south.
SOUTHERNLY, [suTH'-ern-li], *adv.* in the direction of the south.
SOUTHERNMOST, [suTH'-ern-mōst], *adj.* most southern, farthest south.
SOUTHERNWOOD, [suTH'-ern-wŏŏd], *n.* (*bot.*) an aromatic plant, allied to wormwood, *Artemisia Abrotanum*, native to South Europe.
SOUTHING, [sowTH'-ing], *n.* tendency or motion to the south; course or distance south by drifting from a given course.
SOUTHMOST, [sowth'-mōst], *adj.* farthest towards the south, southernmost.
SOUTHNESS, [sowth'-nes], *n.* the state of being situated in the south; tendency to point towards the south magnetic pole.
SOUTHRON, [suTH'-ron], *n.* an inhabitant of a southern district. [~SOUTHERN].
SOUTHWARD (1), [sowth'-werd], *adj.* directed towards the south.
SOUTHWARD (2), [sowth'-werd], *adv.* in a southerly direction.
SOUTH-WEST (1), [sowth'-west'], *n.* the point of the compass between the south and west; a region or district situated in this direction.
SOUTH-WEST (2), [sowth'-west'], *adj.* situated in, facing, or coming from, the south-west.
SOUTH-WEST (3), [sowth'-west'], *adv.* in the direction of the south-west.
SOUTH-WESTER, [sowth'-west'-er], *n.* a south-westerly wind or gale.
SOUTH-WESTERLY (1), [sowth-west'-er-li], *adj.* towards or coming from the south-west.
SOUTH-WESTERLY (2), [sowth-west'-er-li], *adv.* in the direction of the south-west.
SOUTH-WESTERN, [sowth-west'-ern], *adj.* belonging to, situated in, operating in, the south-west.
SOUVENIR, [sōō'-ven-ēer'], *n.* a small object kept as a reminder, a keepsake. [Fr. *souvenir* memory].
SOU'WESTER, [sow-west'-er], *n.* a strong wind blowing from the south-west; a sailor's waterproof hat enveloping the head and with a flap protecting the back of the neck. [SOUTH and WESTER.]
SOVEREIGN (1), [sov'-rin], *n.* a person acknowledged as possessing a status entitling him to supreme rule, a monarch, king, emperor; a British gold coin worth originally twenty shillings.
SOVEREIGN (2), [sov'-rin], *adj.* possessing the status of supreme dominion, paramount, supreme; powerfully efficient or effective; excellent. [*Prec.*].
SOVEREIGNTY, [sov'-rin-ti], *n.* the state or status of supreme power; supreme dominion; a person or state holding such power. [OFr. *soveraineté*].
SOVIET (1), [sov'-i-et], *n.* the functioning unit of national or local administration in Russia. [Russ. *soviet* council].
SOVIET (2), [sov'-i-et'], *adj.* governed by soviets.
SOW (1), [sow], *n.* an adult female pig; a large mould into which molten metal is run, a bar of iron, etc., cast in such a mould; (*milit.*) †a movable shelter used in attacking walls. [OE. *sugu*].
SOW (2), [sō], *v.t. and i.* to cast seed on the ground, to plant with seed; (*fig.*) to disseminate, inculcate, to scatter the seeds of (some feeling or behaviour); to perform the act of sowing. [OE. *sawan*].
SOWANS, [sō'-enz], *n.* sowens.
SOWAR, [sō'-ah(r)], *n.* an Indian mounted trooper. [Pers. *sawar* rider].
SOW-BREAD, [sow'-bred'], *n.* (*bot.*) a tuberous-rooted plant of the genus *Cyclamen*.
SOWENS, [sō'-enz], *n.* fermented husks of oats, boiled for eating. [Ir. *subhan* sap].
SOWER, [sō'-er], *n.* one who sows.
SOWING-MACHINE, [sō'-ing-ma-shēn'], *n.* a machine for sowing seed in rows.
SOWKAR, see SOUCAR.
SOW-THISTLE, [sow'-thisl], *n.* a thistle of the genus *Sonchus*.
SOY, [soi], *n.* a Japanese fish-sauce made from fermented soya beans, *Glycine Soja*; the bean itself. [Jap. *shoyu*].
SOYA BEAN, [soi'-a-bēn], *n.* the edible bean of *Glycine Soja*. [Du. *soya* from Jap. *shoyu*].
SOZZLE, [sozl], *v.t.* to make drunkenly confused and muddle-headed; to splash, to slop. [Uncert.].
SPA, [spah], *n.* a health-resort with a mineral spring. [*Spa*, in Belgium].
SPACE (1), [spās], *n.* extension between objects, area, the extension supposed to contain the universe, the distance separating objects, a period of time; (*typ.*) a blank interval between words, the available room for matter in a journal; (*mus.*) interval between the lines of a score; **to work on s.,** (*journalism*) to be paid according to the amount of work printed. [L. *spatium*].
SPACE (2), [spās], *v.t.* to arrange (objects) in regard to the spaces between them; **to s. out,** to place at intervals, to place (objects) so that they are separated by a considerable space. [*Prec.*].
SPACIAL, [spā'-shal], *adj.* spatial.
SPACIOUS, [spā'-shus], *adj.* affording ample space, extensive; (*fig.*) broad and unrestricted. [L. *spatiosus*].
SPACIOUSLY, [spā'-shus-li], *adv.* in spacious fashion.
SPACIOUSNESS, [spā'-shus-nes], *n.* the state of being spacious.
SPADASSIN, [spa-das'-in], *n.* a skilled swordsman, a bravo, a bully. [Fr. from It. *spadacchino*].
SPADDLE, [spadl], *n.* a little spade. [~SPADE].
SPADE (1), [spād], *n.* a digging implement, any flat-bladed instrument resembling this; the black suit of playing-cards resembling this; **to call a s. a s.,** to speak plainly and bluntly. [OE. *spadu*].
SPADE (2), [spād], *n.* a gelded animal. [Gk. *spadon* eunuch].
SPADE-BONE, [spād'-bōn], *n.* the shoulder-blade.
SPADEFUL, [spād'-fŏŏl], *n.* as much as a spade will hold.
SPADE-WORK, [spād'-wurk], *n.* the laborious routine work of a project.
SPADGER, [spaj'-er], *n.* (*coll.*) a sparrow. [SPARROW].
SPADICEOUS, [spad-ish'-us], *adj.* relating to a spadix.
SPADILLE, [spad'-il], *n.* the ace of spades at ombre and quadrille. [Span. *espadilla*].
SPADIX, [spā'-diks], *n.* (*bot.*) the spike of flowers surrounded by a spathe. [Gk. *spadix* broken palm-branch].
SPADO, [spā'-dō], *n.* a eunuch, a sterile person. [Gk. *spadon* eunuch].
SPADROON, [spad-rōōn'], *n.* a sword designed both to cut and to thrust. [~L. *spatha* spade].
SPAGHETTI, [spa-get'-i], *n.* an Italian preparation of wheat like small macaroni. [It. *spaghetto* little cord].

SPAHI, [spah'-hē], *n.* formerly a Turkish, now an Algerian, cavalryman. [Pers. *sipahi* soldier].
SPAKE, [spāk], *pret.* of SPEAK. [ME. *spac*].
SPALL, [spawl], *v.t. and i.* to break, chip with a hammer, to dress roughly; to splinter. [ME. *spalden*].
SPALPEEN, [spawl'-pēn'], *n.* a ne'er-do-well, a rascal. [Ir. *spailpin*].
SPALT (1), [spawlt], *n.* a whitish scaly mineral, used in the fusion of metals. [~Germ. *spalten* to split].
SPALT (2), [spawlt], *adj.* brittle, liable to splinter.
SPAN (1), [span], *n.* the distance between the tips of the thumb and little finger when the hand is fully extended, nine inches; a short distance or period, the full period, duration, of anything; the measurement of an aeroplane across the wing-tips; the space between the abutments or supports of an arch; a team of oxen or draught horses. [OE. *spann*].
SPAN (2), [span], *v.t.* to measure by stretching thumb and fingers; to stretch across, or from side to side; to cross over, to extend over a period, to cover, carry over; (*naut.*) to secure with ropes. [OE. *spannan* to clasp].
SPANCEL, [span'-sel], *v.t.* to hobble the hind legs (of a cow). [MDu. *spansel*].
SPANDREL, [span'-drel], *n.* the triangular space between the shoulder and frame of an arch. [~EXPAND].

SPANDREL

SPANDRIL, [span'-dril], *n.* a spandrel.
SPANG, [spang], *n.* a spangle.
SPANGLE (1), [spang'-gl], *n.* a tiny disk of bright metal attached to dress, etc., as an ornament. [ME. *spangel* from OE. *spang* buckle].
SPANGLE (2), [spang'-gl], *v.t.* to set (as) with spangles. [*Prec.*].
SPANIARD, [span'-yerd], *n.* a native of Spain. [OFr. *espaignard*].
SPANIEL, [span'-yel], *n.* a breed of dogs notable for their silky hair and drooping ears; a fawning and subservient flatterer. [ME. *spaignel*].
SPANISH, [span'-ish], *adj. and n.* relating to, coming from, Spain; the language of Spain; (*coll.*) liquorice. [ME. *Spainisch*].
SPANISH-BAYONET, [span'-ish-bā'-on-et], *n.* (*bot.*) a species of yucca, with rigid, sharp-pointed leaves.
SPANISH-BLACK, [span'-ish-blak'], *n.* a soft black from burnt cork.
SPANISH-BROOM, [span'-ish-brōōm], *n.* (*bot.*) a leguminous shrub of the genus *Spartium*.
SPANISH-BROWN, [span'-ish-brown'], *n.* a species of reddish-brown earth used in paints.
SPANISH-CHALK, [span'-ish-chawk'], *n.* a species of steatite obtained from Aragon, in Spain.
SPANISH-CHESTNUT, [span'-ish-ches'-nut], *n.* the edible chestnut, *Castanea vesca*.
SPANISH-FLY, [span'-ish-flī'], *n.* the beetle, *Cantharis vesicatoria*, used for raising blisters.
SPANISH-GRASS, [span'-ish-grahs'], *n.* esparto grass.
SPANISH-JUICE, [span'-ish-jōōs], *n.* liquorice juice.
SPANISH-NUT, [span'-ish-nut], *n.* the fruit of *Corylus Avellana* var. *barceloniensis*.
SPANISH-RED, [span'-ish-red'], *n.* a red ochre.
SPANISH-WHITE, [span'-ish-wit], *n.* a white pigment obtained from chalk.
SPANK (1), [spangk], *n.* a blow (usually on the buttocks) with the flat of the hand.
SPANK (2), [spangk], *v.t. and i.* to strike on or near the buttocks with the open hand or some flat object; to perform the action of spanking; **to s. along,** to move at a brisk pace. [~Dan. *spanke* to strut].
SPANKER, [spangk'-er], *n.* that which, one who, spanks; a horse having a spirited action; (*naut.*) the aftermast sail of a ship; (*coll.*) a good stroke, a remarkable and excellent action or object.
SPANKING (1), [spangk'-ing], *n.* a beating with a flat object.
SPANKING (2), [spangk'-ing], *adj.* brisk; striking.
SPANNER, [span'-er], *n.* a tool for turning nuts, a wrench.

SPANNER

SPAN-NEW, [span'-new], *adj.* quite new. [OScand. *spann-nyr*].
SPAN-ROOF, [span'-rōōf], *n.* a roof sloping on both sides from a common ridge.
SPAN-WORM, [span'-wurm], *n.* a canker-worm; the larva of the "stick caterpillar" or geometer moth.

SPAR (1), [spah(r)], *n.* a pole supporting sails or tackle, a long piece of timber. [ME. *sparre* beam].
SPAR (2), [spah(r)], *n.* a crystalline mineral having various varieties. [OE. *spær(stan)* gypsum].
SPAR (3), [spah(r)], *n.* the act of sparring, a sparring-match.
SPAR (4), [spah(r)], *v.i.* to box, *esp.* to practise boxing without endeavouring to injure one's opponent, to make the motions of striking without actually doing so; (of cocks) to fight. [OFr. *esparer* (of cocks) to strike with the spurs].
SPAR (5), [spah(r)], *v.t.* (*naut.*) to take (a ship) through shallows by spar and tackle.
SPARABLE, [spa'-rabl], *n.* a nail driven into shoe soles. [~SPARROW and BILL].
SPAR-DECK, [spah'-dek'], *n.* the upper deck.
SPARE (1), [spāer], *n.* a spare part, an extra available as replacement.
SPARE (2), [spāer], *adj.* meagre, lean, scanty; left over, not necessary, available as desired, extra, additional, ready for use as a replacement; (of time) not occupied by any necessity, available for leisure or other than essential business. [OE. *spær* frugal].
SPARE (3), [spāer], *v.t. and i.* to be meagre, to refrain from using or performing, to withhold, dispense with, hence, to remit from use, to show mercy to, allow continued existence to, to abstain voluntarily from imposing one's power against a person or thing, to protect, save from injury or punishment, abstain from injuring or destroying. [OE. *sparian* to show mercy].
SPARELY, [spāer'-li], *adv.* in spare degree.
SPARENESS, [spāer'-nes], *n.* the state of being spare.
SPARER, [spāer'-er], *n.* one who spares.
SPARERIB, [spāer'-rib'], *n.* part of the ribs of a bacon pig. [MLGerm. *ribbesper*].
SPARING, [spāer'-ing], *adj.* frugal.
SPARINGLY, [spāer'-ing-li], *adv.* in sparing fashion.
SPARINGNESS, [spāer'-ing-nes], *n.* the quality of being sparing.
SPARK (1), [spahk], *n.* a minute incandescent particle thrown off by a body in a state of combustion, a tiny flash of fire or light; (*fig.*) the germ of animation, the smallest trace of life or intelligence; the flash accompanying electric discharge, the ignition of an internal-combustion engine. [OE. *spearca*].
SPARK (2), [spahk], *n.* a lively, dashing young fellow. [OScand. *sparkr* lively].
SPARK (3), [spahk], *v.i.* to give out sparks. [OE. *spearcian*].
SPARK (4), [spahk], *v.i.* to play the gallant.
SPARKFUL, [spahk'-fōōl], *adj.* lively.
SPARKING PLUG, [spah'-king-plug'], *n.* a device in internal combustion engines, through which the electric current ignites the explosive gas in the cylinder.
SPARKISH, [spahk'-ish], *adj.* like a spark, gay and gallant.
SPARKLE (1), [spahkl], *n.* a scintillation, a rapid glitter, vivacity, witty brilliance, bright conversation. [ME. *sparcle*].
SPARKLE (2), [spahkl], *v.i.* to give out sparks of light, to glitter, to coruscate, to effervesce; to show gaiety and brilliance. [ME. *sparclen*].
SPARKLER, [spahk'-ler], *n.* that which sparkles; (*slang*) a diamond.
SPARKLINESS, [spahk'-li-nes], *n.* the state of being sparkly.
SPARKLING, [spahk'-ling], *adj.* giving off sparkles, flashing, scintillating, brilliantly witty, gay and polished.

SPARKING PLUG

SPARKLINGLY, [spahk'-ling-li], *adv.* in sparkling fashion.
SPARKLINGNESS, [spahk'-ling-nes], *n.* the quality of being sparkling.
SPARKLY, [spahk'-li], *adj.* (*coll.*) sparkling.
SPARLING, [spah'-ling], *n.* the spurling.
SPARRING, [spah'-ring], *n.* practice boxing in which the opponents are not supposed to strike serious blows, the motions of striking without actually hitting, movement of the fists in preparation for a blow; **s. partner,** a person with whom a boxer practises during training. [SPAR (4)].
SPARROW, [spa'-rō], *n.* a small bird of the genus *Passer*, allied to the finches. [OE. *spearwa*].
SPARROW-BILL, [spa'-rō-bil'], *n.* a sparable.
SPARROW-GRASS, [spa'-rō-grahs], *n.* (*slang*) asparagus. [Slang for ASPARAGUS].

SPARROW-HAWK, [spa'-rō-hawk'], *n.* a small species of short-winged hawk, *Accipiter nisus.*
SPARRY, [spah'-ri], *adj.* containing spar.
SPARSE, [spahs], *adj.* growing thinly, not abundant, scarce. [L. *sparsus, p.pt.* of *spargere* to scatter].
SPARSELY, [spahs'-li], *adv.* in sparse fashion.
SPARSENESS, [spahs'-nes], *n.* the state or quality of being sparse.
SPARTALITE, [spaht'-a-lit], *n.* a red oxide of zinc. [*Sparta*, U.S.A., where found, and Gk. *lithos* stone].
SPARTAN, [spaht'-an], *n. and adj.* a native of Sparta, in ancient Greece; courageous and enduring, austerely hardy.
SPARTERIE, [spaht'-er-i], *n.* fabric made from esparto grass. [Span. *esparteria*].
SPASM, [spazm], *n.* a brief, violent, involuntary muscular contraction, a sudden violent physical or mental reaction; a sudden, strong, but brief burst of energy. [Gk. *spasmos* convulsion].
SPASMODIC, [spaz-mod'-ik], *adj.* occurring in, relating to, spasms; violent but infrequent, intermittent. [Gk. *spasmodes*].
SPASMODICALLY, [spaz-mod'-ik-al-i], *adv.* in spasmodic fashion.
SPASMOLOGY, [spaz-mol'-oj-i], *n.* the study of convulsions. [SPASM and Gk. *logos* speech].
SPASTIC, [spas'-tik], *adj.* (*med.*) spasmodic, afflicted with spasms. [Gk. *spastikos*].
SPASTICITY, [spas-tis'-it-i], *n.* the state of being spastic.
SPAT (1), [spat], *n.* the spawn of an oyster. [~SPIT].
SPAT (2), [spat], *n.* a short gaiter for the upper part of the shoe. [~SPATTER].
SPAT (3), [spat], *pret. and p.pt.* of SPIT.
SPATANGUS, [spa-tang'-gus], *n.* a genus of heart-shaped echinoderms. [Gk. *spatanges*].
SPATCHCOCK, [spach'-kok'], *n.* a bird cooked immediately after killing. [Uncert.].
SPATE, [spāt], *n.* a sudden flood, *esp.* of a river after rain. [ME. *spate*].
SPATHACEOUS, [spa-thā'-shus], *adj.* having a spathe.
SPATHE, [spāᴛʜ], *n.* (*bot.*) a sheath protecting an inflorescence. [Gk. *spathe* a broad, flat instrument].
SPATHIC, [spath'-ik], *adj.* resembling, relating to, spar. [Germ. *spath* spar].

SPATANGUS

SPATHIFORM, [spath'-i-fawm], *adj.* having the form or composition of spar.
SPATHOSE (1), [spā'-thōs], *adj.* like a spathe.
SPATHOSE (2), [spath'-ōs], *adj.* spathic.
SPATIAL, [spā'-shal], *adj.* relating to space. [L. *spatium* space].
SPATIALLY, [spā'-shal-i], *adv.* in relation to space.
SPATTEE, [spat'-ē'], *n.* a kind of spat reaching up the leg. [SPAT and (PUTT)EE].
SPATTER (1), [spat'-er], *n.* a light splash.
SPATTER (2), [spat'-er], *v.t. and i.* to sprinkle with drops of liquid, to splash, to befoul; to smirch; to splash, fall in drops. [~Frisian *spatterje* to sprinkle].
SPATTERDASHES, [spat'-er-dash'-iz], *n.(pl.)* leggings worn as protection against mud and splashing. [SPATTER and DASH].
SPATULA, [spat'-yōō-la], *n.* a broad-bladed implement used for spreading paint or plaster; (*med.*) an instrument used for holding down the tongue; a small flattened rod for handling small quantities of chemicals; (*zool.*) the roseate spoonbill. [L. *spatula*].
SPATULATE, [spat'-yōō-lāt], *adj.* (*bot.*) shaped like a spatula; elliptical.
SPATULE, [spat'-yōōl], *n.* (*zool.*) a spatulate formation.
SPAVIN, [spav'-in], *n.* a morbid swelling in the hock-joint of a horse. [OFr. *espavain*].
SPAVINED, [spav'-ind], *adj.* affected with spavin; (*fig.*) lame, crippled.
SPAWL (1), [spawl], *n.* dribble from the mouth.
SPAWL (2), [spawl], *v.t. and i.* to spit gobs of saliva, to spit foully. [Uncert.].
SPAWN (1), [spawn], *n.* the eggs of fish, frogs, etc.; the mycelium of mushrooms; (*slang*) children, offspring.
SPAWN (2), [spawn], *v.t. and i.* (of fish, etc.) to deposit eggs; to produce spawn, to give birth to; to supply with mushroom spawn; (*slang*) to generate copiously. [ME. *spaunen* from OFr. *espandre* expand].
SPAWNER, [spawn'-er], *n.* a female fish.

SPAY, [spā], *v.t.* to sterilize female animals by removin the ovary. [OFr. *espéer* to cut with a sword].
SPEAK, [spēk], *v.t. and i.* to utter words, to utte words without musical modulation, to utter a dis course, to address an audience, to declare, to mak sounds, to convey a meaning (without necessaril putting it in words), to say, express in words, to mak oneself understood in; (*of an organ-pipe*) to soun (a note); **to s. for,** to urge, address on behalf of; **t s. of,** to talk about; **to s. out,** to speak clearly an unrestrainedly; **to s. up,** to speak distinctly. [OE *specan*].
SPEAKABLE, [spēk'-abl], *adj.* able to be spoken o be spoken of.
SPEAKEASY, [spēk'-ēz'-i], *n.* (*U.S.*) a bar where illicit liquor is sold. [SPEAK and U.S. *easy* softly].
SPEAKER, [spēk'-er], *n.* one who speaks, one wh addresses a meeting, the officer presiding in certai parliamentary assemblies, notably the House o Commons; a loud-speaker.
SPEAKERSHIP, [spēk'-er-ship], *n.* the office o parliamentary Speaker.
SPEAKING, [spēk'-ing], *adj.* articulate; **on s. terms** on good enough terms to exchange passing greet ings.
SPEAKING-TRUMPET, [spēk'-ing-trum'-pet], *n.* a megaphone, an instrument for increasing the carryin power of the voice.
SPEAKING-TUBE, [spēk'-ing-tewb], *n.* a tube fo speaking, carried through partitions, etc.
SPEAL-BONE, [spēl'-bōn], *n.* the shoulder-blade [Uncert.].
SPEAR (1), [spēer], *n.* a throwing or thrusting weapon having a sharp-pointed head set on a shaft, anything resembling this; a man armed with a spear. [OE *spere*].
SPEAR (2), [spēer], *v.t.* to pierce with a spear, impal with a spike.
SPEAR-FOOT, [spēer'-fŏŏt], *n.* the off-foot.
SPEAR-GRASS, [spēer'-grahs], *n.* long stiff grass.
SPEARHAND, [spēer'-hand'], *n.* the right hand.
SPEARHEAD, [spēr'-hed'], *n.* the metal head of a spear; (*fig.*) the forces in the van of an attack.
SPEARMAN, [spēer'-man], *n.* a soldier armed with a spear.
SPEARMINT, [spēer'-mint], *n.* the aromatic garden mint, *Mentha viridis.*
SPEAR-THISTLE, [spēer'-thisl], *n.* the spiny thistle, *Carduus lanceolatus.*
SPEARWORT, [spēer'-wurt], *n.* a narrow-leaved species of *Ranunculus.*
SPECIAL (1), [spesh'-al], *n.* anything prepared or designed for a special purpose; a special edition of a newspaper; a voluntary constable enrolled for special emergency.
SPECIAL (2), [spesh'-al], *adj.* of a particular sort, intended for a particular circumstance, distinguished by a peculiar characteristic; detailed, related to specific detail, not general; individual, for one person or purpose in particular; (*coll.*) especially good, out-of-the-ordinary, for a particular occasion; **s. pleading,** (*leg.*) new evidence brought up in court to meet hostile evidence; (*coll.*) a specious argument, an unfair attempt to bias a verdict. [OF. *especial* from L. *specialis*].

SPEARWORT

SPECIALIST, [spesh'-al-ist], *n.* one who specializes in or has special knowledge of a certain subject, *esp.* a branch of medicine.
SPECIALITY, [spesh'-i-al'-it-i], *n.* study, knowledge, occupation in which a person is especially skilled, or to which he gives his main attention; something in the supply of which a trader specializes. [L. *specialitas* peculiarity].
SPECIALIZATION, [spesh'-al-iz-ā'-shun], *n.* the act or process of specializing, the state of being a specialist.
SPECIALIZE, [spesh'-al-iz], *v.t. and i.* to be a specialist, to devote one's abilities and inquiry to a special subject or to some specific branch of accomplishment; (*biol.*) to develop special functions or characteristics; to qualify, make specific.
SPECIALLY, [spesh'-al-i], *adv.* in special, for a particular purpose, particularly.
SPECIALTY, [spesh'-al-ti], *n.* a speciality; (*leg.*) a contract under seal. [OFr. *specialite*].
SPECIE, [spē'shē], *n.* coin, as distinct from paper money. [L. *specie, ablative* of *species* kind, form].

SPECIES, [spē'-shiz], *n.* (*biol.*) a classified set of living organisms, referable to one type, and distinguishable from any other members of its genus by constant, well-marked, inherited characteristics; kind, sort; (*theol.*) the sensory appearance of the consecrated elements. [L. *species* appearance].

SPECIFIC (1), [spes-if'-ik], *n.* a medicine for a specific purpose.

SPECIFIC (2), [spes-if'-ik], *adj.* of a distinct kind, of a certain definite sort; explicit, precise, definite and therefore limited in meaning; relating to a species. [MedL. *specificus*].

SPECIFICALLY, [spes-if'-ik-al-i], *adv.* in a specific manner.

SPECIFICATION, [spes'-if-ik-ā'-shun], *n.* the act of specifying, a detailed description, *esp.* of a projected work; a detailed enumeration. [MedL. *specificatio*].

SPECIFICNESS, [spes-if'-ik-nes], *n.* the state or quality of being specific.

SPECIFY, [spes'-i-fī], *v.t.* to particularize, state specifically, enumerate in detail, indicate precisely. [MedL. *specificare*].

SPECIMEN, [spes'-i-men], *n.* a representative example of a class or division, a typical instance of a whole, a sample, *esp.* when labelled, classified, and preserved for study, a characteristic example; (*coll.*) an eccentric or peculiar individual. [L. *specimen* indication].

SPECIOSITY, [spēsh'-i-os'-it-i], *n.* speciousness. [L. *speciositas* beauty].

SPECIOUS, [spē'-shus], *adj.* outwardly pleasing but deceptive; superficially good or plausible. [L. *speciosus* beautiful].

SPECIOUSLY, [spē'-shus-li], *adv.* in specious fashion.

SPECIOUSNESS, [spē'-shus-nes], *n.* the state of being specious.

SPECK (1), [spek], *n.* bacon; whale-blubber. [Du. *speck*].

SPECK (2), [spek], *n.* a small spot or mark, a minute object, a mark that is only just visible. [OE. *specca*].

SPECK (3), [spek], *v.t.* and *i.* to mark with specks; to become so marked.

SPECKLE (1), [spekl], *n.* a small mark of different colour on a surface, a pattern of such markings.

SPECKLE (2), [spekl], *v.t. and i.* to mark with, become marked with, speckles.

SPECKLEDNESS, [spekld'-nes], *n.* the state of being speckled.

SPECKLESS, [spek'-les], *adj.* spotless.

SPECKTIONEER, [spek'-shon-ēer'], *n.* the chief harpooner in a whaler. [Du. *speksnijer*].

SPECS, [speks], *n.*(*pl.*) (*coll.*) spectacles.

SPECTACLE, [spek'-takl], *n.* something looked at, something displayed for inspection; something remarkable, something arousing pity or contempt; (*pl.*) lenses, supported by a frame, worn to strengthen or correct faults in the vision, eyeglasses. [L. *spectaculum* show].

SPECTACLED, [spek'-takld], *adj.* wearing spectacles.

SPECTACULAR, [spek-tak'-yōō-ler], *adj.* relating to a spectacle, flamboyant, showy; amazing.

SPECTACULARLY, [spek-tak'-yōō-ler-li], *adv.* in spectacular fashion.

SPECTANT, [spek'-tant], *adj.* (*her.*) looking forward. [L. *spectans*].

SPECTATOR, [spek-tāt'-or], *n.* one who watches, an observer, one who witnesses a spectacle. [L. *spectator*].

SPECTATORIAL, [spek'-ta-taw'-ri-al], *adj.* of a looker-on or an eye-witness.

SPECTRAL, [spek'-tral], *adj.* of or relating to a spectre or the spectrum.

SPECTRALITY, [spek-tral'-it-i], *n.* the state of being spectral.

SPECTRALLY, [spek'-tra-li], *adv.* in a spectral manner.

SPECTRE, [spek'-ter], *n.* a ghost, an apparition, a spirit appearing in visible form; (*fig.*) a terrifying but insubstantial danger. [L. *spectrum* appearance].

SPECTRE-BAT, [spek'-ter-bat'], *n.* the American leaf-nosed bat.

SPECTRO-, *pref.* relating to the spectrum. [L. *spectrum* appearance].

SPECTROGRAPH, [spek'-trō-graf], *n.* an instrument for reproducing a spectrum. [SPECTRO and GRAPH].

SPECTRO-HELIOGRAPH, [spek'-trō-hēl'-i-ō-graf], *n.* an instrument for photographing the spectrum of the sun.

SPECTROLOGICAL, [spek'-trō-loj'-ik-al], *adj.* pertaining to, or by means of, spectrology.

SPECTROLOGY, [spek-trol'-oj-i], *n.* the science of analysing the spectrum. [SPECTRO and Gk. *logos* speech].

SPECTROMETER, [spek-trom'-it-er], *n.* an instrument for measuring the deviation of a ray reflected through a prism. [SPECTRO and METER].

SPECTROSCOPE, [spek'-trō'-skōp], *n.* an instrument for analysing a spectrum by a prism which refracts the various elements of light into different positions in the eyepiece. [SPECTRO and SCOPE].

SPECTROSCOPE

SPECTROSCOPIC, [spek'-trō-skop'-ik], *adj.* of, pertaining to, by means of, the spectroscope.

SPECTROSCOPICALLY, [spek'-trō-skop'-ik-al-i], *adv.* by means of the spectroscope.

SPECTROSCOPIST, [spek-tros'-kop-ist], *n.* a student of spectroscopy.

SPECTROSCOPY, [spek-tros'-kop-i], *n.* the study of the spectrum.

SPECTRUM, (*pl.* **spectra**), [spek'-trum], *n.* the image of light split by a prism into bands of different colours, representing the constituents of the incident light; the image retained by the retina after the removal of the stimulus that produces it. [L. *spectrum* image].

SPECULAR, [spek'-yōō-ler], *adj.* relating to the speculum, reflecting. [L. *specularis*].

SPECULATE, [spek'-yōō-lāt], *v.i.* to form theories, wonder about, cogitate; to gamble, to risk a smallish loss for the sake of great gain, *esp.* to gamble in stocks and shares. [L. *speculari* to observe].

SPECULATION, [spek'-yōō-lā'-shun], *n.* the act of speculating, a theory formed by speculating, unconfirmed conjecture; a gamble, an investment without security, gambling on the stock-market. [L. *speculatio* observation].

SPECULATIST, [spek'-yōō-lat-ist], *n.* a theorizer.

SPECULATIVE, [spek'-yōō-lat-iv], *adj.* based on, given to, speculation; risky, of the nature of a gamble.

SPECULATIVELY, [spek'-yōō-lat-iv-li], *adv.* in speculative fashion.

SPECULATIVENESS, [spek'-yōō-lat-iv-nes], *n.* the state of being speculative.

SPECULATOR, [spek'-yōō-lā-ter], *n.* one who speculates, a stock-market gambler. [L. *speculator*].

SPECULATORY, [spek'-yōō-lat-er-i], *adj.* relating to speculation.

SPECULUM, [spek'-yōō-lum], *n.* a mirror, *esp.* of a telescope; (*med.*) an instrument for dilating a cavity; (*ornith.*) a patch of distinct and different colour on a bird's wing. [L. *speculum* mirror].

SPED, [sped], *pret. and p.pt.* of SPEED.

SPEECH, [spēch], *n.* the faculty of expressing meaning orally, a language, a particular form, tone, or manner of speaking, a public address. [OE. *spræc*].

SPEECH-DAY, [spēch'-dā], *n.* an annual celebration at a school, when prizes are awarded, and a visitor delivers an address.

SPEECHIFIER, [spēch'-i-fīer], *n.* one who speechifies.

SPEECHIFY, [spēch'-i-fī], *v.i.* to make a long, silly speech, to make speeches too frequently.

SPEECHLESS, [spēch'-les], *adj.* dumb, silent, unable to be expressed in speech, temporarily prevented from speaking by some strong emotion.

SPEECHLESSNESS, [spēch'-les-nes], *n.* the state of being speechless; muteness.

SPEECH-MAKER, [spēch'-māk'-er], *n.* one who makes public speeches.

SPEECH-READER, [spēch'-rēd-er], *n.* one (usually a deaf person) who can understand speech by observing the lip-movements.

SPEED (1), [spēd], *n.* rapid movement, swiftness; velocity, rate of movement, whether rapid or not. [OE. *sped*].

SPEED (2), [spēd], *v.t. and i.* to move rapidly, to hasten, to make progress, to perform; to help, wish success to, to cause to move rapidly. [OE. *spedan* to succeed].

SPEEDBOAT, [spēd'-bōt'], *n.* a very fast motor-boat.

SPEED-COP, [spēd'-kop'], *n.* (*U.S.*) a policeman whose duty it is to enforce the laws concerning vehicular traffic.

SPEEDER, [spēd'-er], *n.* one who, that which, speeds; a device for regulating speed; a roving machine.

SPEEDILY, [spēd′-i-li], *adv.* with speed, promptly.
SPEEDINESS, [spēd′-i-nes], *n.* the quality of being speedy; dispatch.
SPEEDOMETER, [spēd-om′-it-er], *n.* a device for measuring and indicating the speed of a vehicle.
SPEEDWAY, [spēd′-wā], *n.* a motor-cycle racing track.
SPEEDWELL, [spēd′-wel], *n.* (*bot.*) a herbaceous plant or shrub of the genus, *Veronica.*
SPEEDY, [spēd′-i], *adj.* swift, rapid of movement; prompt, quick. [OE. *spedig* prosperous].
SPEISS, [spīs], *n.* an arsenical compound produced in smelting certain ores. [Germ. dial. *speis*].
SPELD, [speld], *n.* a splinter. [OE. *speld*].
SPELDING, [spel′-ding], *n.* a dried haddock. [Uncert.].
SPELEAN, [spē-lē′-an], *adj.* relating to, inhabiting, caves. [Gk. *spelaion* cave].
SPELK, [spelk], *n.* a splinter of wood. [OE. *spelc*].

SPEEDWELL

SPELL (1), [spel], *n.* a magical charm, a compelling incantation; (*fig.*) a very powerful attraction or influence. [OE. *spell* saying].
SPELL (2), [spel], *n.* a short period, *esp.* one coming or recurring in rotation, a brief space of time; a short turn of activity. [~OE. *gespelia* substitute].
SPELL (3), (spelt), [spel], *v.t. and i.* to write or recite in succession the letters constituting a word; (of the letters) to make a sensible word; (*fig.*) to result in, mean as inevitable consequence; *v.i.* to be able to put the letters of a word in the right order; **to s. out,** to utter a word letter by letter; to decipher with difficulty. [OE. *spellian* to narrate].
SPELLABLE, [spel′-abl], *adj.* able to be spelled.
SPELLBINDER, [spel′-bind′-er], *n.* an orator who can hold his audience spellbound; (ironically) a facile and plausible orator.
SPELLBOUND, [spel′-bownd], *adj.* fascinated, entranced as if by a spell.
SPELLER, [spel′-er], *n.* one who spells, *esp.* correctly.
SPELLICAN, [spel′-i-kan], *n.* a spillikin.
SPELLING, [spel′-ing], *n.* orthography.
SPELLING-BEE, [spel′-ing-bē′], *n.* a spelling game.
SPELLING-BOOK, [spel′-ing-book], *n.* a book for teaching spelling.
SPELT (1), [spelt], *n.* German wheat. [OE. *spelt*].
SPELT (2), [spelt], *pret. and p.pt.* of SPELL.
SPELTER, [spel′-ter], *n.* zinc; a soldering alloy. [LGerm. *spialter* pewter].
SPENCER (1), [spen′-ser], *n.* (*naut.*) a trysail. [Unkn.].
SPENCER (2), [spen′-ser], *n.* a short woollen jacket. [Earl *Spencer*, *c.* 1830].
SPENCERIAN, [spen-sēer′-i-an], *adj.* of or pertaining to the philosopher Herbert Spencer.
SPEND, (spent), [spend], *v.t. and i.* to give, part with, in payment, to exchange money for goods, services, etc.; to expend, to use up strength, resources, to consume; to pay out money. [OE. *spendan*].
SPENDER, [spen′-der], *n.* one who spends freely.
SPENDING-MONEY, [spend′-ing-mun′-i], *n.* money for spending on trifles and small luxuries.
SPENDTHRIFT, [spend′-thrift], *n.* a wasteful, thriftless, extravagant person.
SPENSERIAN, [spen′-sēer′-i-an], *adj.* of or resembling Spenser or his poetry; **S. stanza,** the form of stanza employed by Spenser in *The Faerie Queene.* [Edmund *Spenser*, d. 1599].
SPENT, [spent], *adj., pret. and p.pt.* of SPEND; exhausted, wholly consumed.
SPERM (1), [spurm], *n.* (*also pl.*) the fertilizing germs in the male animal. [Gk. *sperma* seed].
SPERM (2), [spurm], *n.* the sperm-whale; spermaceti. [Abbreviated from SPERMACETI].
SPERMACETI, [spurm′-a-set′-i], *n* a wax-like substance obtained from the head of the sperm-whale, and used for making candles and preparing certain ointments. [Gk. *sperma* sperm and *ketos* whale].
SPERMATIC, [spurm-at′-ik], *adj.* of, relating to, or secreting, sperm. [Gk. *spermatikos*].
SPERMATISM, [spurm′-at-izm], *n.* the discharge of seminal fluid.
SPERMATO-, *pref.* relating to sperm. [Gk. *sperma spermatos*].
SPERMATOBLAST, [spurm′-at′-ō-blast], *n.* (*biol.*) the nucleus of a spermatozoon. [SPERMATO- and Gk. *blastos* sprout].
SPERMATOGENOUS, [spurm′-at-oj′-en-us], *adj.* producing spermatozoa or sperm.
SPERMATOID, [spurm′-at-oid], *adj.* sperm-like.
SPERMATOLOGY, [spurm′-at-ol′-oj-i], *n.* the biological study of the sperm. [SPERMATO and Gk. *logos* speech].
SPERMATOPHORE, [spurm′-at-ō-faw(r)], *n.* the container of spermatozoa in certain invertebrates. [SPERMATO and Gk. *phoros* bearing].
SPERMATORRHOEA, [spurm′-at-ō-rē′-a], *n.* persistent, morbid, involuntary emission of semen. [SPERMATO and Gk. *rheo* I flow].
SPERMATOZOA, [spurm′-at-ō-zō′-a], *pl.* of SPERMATOZOON.
SPERMATOZOIDS, [spurm′-at-ō-zō′-idz], *n.(pl.)* the male germ-cells of ferns, etc.
SPERMATOZOON, (*pl.* **spermatozoa**), [spurm′-at′-ōzo′-on], *n.* the germ-cells in the semen of male animals. [SPERMATO- and Gk. *zoa* living creatures].
SPERMODERM, [spurm′-ō-durm], *n.* (*bot.*) the integument of a seed. [SPERM (1) and Gk. *derma* skin].
SPERM-OIL, [spurm′-oil′], *n.* oil obtained from the sperm-whale.
SPERMOLOGIST, [spurm-ol′-oj-ist], *n.* a student of spermology.
SPERMOLOGY, [spurm-ol′-oj-i], *n.* the scientific study of sperms. [SPERM (1) and Gk. *logos* speech].
SPERM-WHALE, [spurm′-wāl], *n.* the whale from which spermaceti is obtained.
SPERRYLITE, [spe′-ri-līt], *n.* arsenide of platinum. [*Sperry*, the mineralogist, and Gk. *lithos* a stone].
SPEW, SPUE, [spew], *v.t. and i.* to vomit. [OE. *spiwan*].
SPHACELATE, [sfas′-i-lāt], *v.i.* to rot, mortify, become gangrened. [Gk. *sphakelos* gangrene].
SPHACELATION, [sfas′-i-lā′-shun], *n.* the state of being, process of becoming, sphacelate.
SPHACELUS, [sfas′-i-lus], *n.* gangrene; caries. [Gk. *sphakelos*].
SPHAERULITE, [sfēer′-yōō-līt], *n.* a brittle mineral chiefly composed of silica and alumina. [Gk. *sphaira* sphere and *lithos* stone].
SPHAGNOLOGY, [sfag-nol′-oj-i], *n.* the study of the bogmosses. [Gk. *sphagnos* moss and *logos* speech].
SPHAGNOUS, [sfag′-nus], *adj.* of, or pertaining to, bogmoss.
SPHAGNUM, [sfag′-num], *n.* peat-moss, bogmoss. [Gk. *sphagnos* moss].
SPHENE, [sfēn], *n.* (*min.*) titanite; a mineral of foliated texture composed of titanate and silicate of lime. [Gk. *sphen* wedge].
SPHENOGRAM, [sfēn′-ō-gram], *n.* a cuneiform character.
SPHENOGRAPHER, [sfēn-og′-raf-er], *n.* one skilled in sphenography.
SPHENOGRAPHICAL, [sfēn′-ō-graf′-ik-al], *adj.* pertaining to sphenography.
SPHENOGRAPHY, [sfēn-og′-raf-i], *n.* the study of cuneiform writing. [Gk. *sphen* wedge and *graphia* writing].
SPHENOID, [sfēn′-oid], *adj.* wedge-shaped; **s. bone,** (*anat.*) a large bone at the base of the skull. [Gk. *sphen* wedge and *oeides* like].
SPHENOIDAL, [sfēn-oid′-al], *adj.* sphenoid.
SPHERAL, [sfēer′-al], *adj.* like a sphere.
SPHERE, [sfēer], *n.* a solid figure, every point on whose surface is equidistant from the centre, a globe, ball; one of the spherical, hollow bodies in which the stars, planets, etc., were formerly held to subsist; (*fig.*) the scope, area, extent, region of a thing, the circle in which a person moves. [Gk. *sphaira*].
SPHERIC, [sfe′-rik], *adj.* spherical. [Gk. *sphairikos*].
SPHERICAL, [sfe′-rik-al], *adj.* of, relating to, resembling, a sphere.
SPHERICALLY, [sfe′-rik-al-i], *adv.* in the form of a sphere.
SPHERICALNESS, [sfe′-rik-al-nes], *n.* the quality of being spherical.
SPHERICITY, [sfe-ris′-it-i], *n.* sphericalness.
SPHERICLE, [sfe′-rikl], *n.* a small sphere.
SPHERICS, [sfe′-riks], *n.(pl.)* spherical geometry.
SPHEROGRAPH, [sfēer′-ō-graf], *n.* a device for measuring spherical triangles.
SPHEROID, [sfēer′-oid], *n.* a slightly flattened sphere, *esp.* when produced by the revolution of an ellipse. [Gk. *sphairoeides*].
SPHEROIDAL, [sfēer-oid′-al], *adj.* in the form of a spheroid.
SPHEROIDICITY, [sfēer-oid-is′-it-i], *n.* the quality of being spheroidal.
SPHEROMETER, [sfēer-om′-it-er], *n.* an instrument for measuring curvature.
SPHEROSIDERITE, [sfēer′-ō-sid′-er-īt], *n.* (*min.*) carbonate of iron, brownspar. [Gk. *sphaira* a ball and *sideros* iron].

SPHEROSTILBITE, [sfēer'-ō-stil'-bīt], *n.* (*min.*) a variety of stilbite occurring in very small crystals.
SPHERULE, [sfe'-ryōōl], *n.* a little sphere or globe. [L. *sphaerula*].
SPHERULITE, [sfe'-rew-līt], *n.* (*min.*) spherical crystals found in siliceous rock.
SPHERULITIC, [sfe'-rew-lit'-ik], *adj.* containing spherulite.
SPHERY, [sfēer'-i], *adj.* celestial, relating to the spheres.
SPHINCTER, [sfingk'-ter], *n.* a muscular ring closing a bodily orifice. [Gk. *sphigkter* band].
SPHINX, [sfingks], *n.* a fabulous monster having human features and a lion's body, noted for its habit of asking insoluble riddles; (*fig.*) an inscrutable person; the colossal sphinx of Gizeh. [Gk. *sphigx*].

SPHINX

SPHRAGISTICS, [sfraj-ist'-iks], *n.*(*pl.*) the study of seals. [Gk. *sphragistikos*].
SPHYGMIC, [sfig'-mik], *adj.* pertaining to the pulse. [Gk. *sphugmos* pulse].
SPHYGMOGRAPH, [sfig'-mō-graf], *n.* an instrument for measuring the pulse. [Gk. *sphugmos* pulse and GRAPH].
SPHYGMOMANOMETER, [sfig'-mō-man-om'-it-er], *n.* an instrument for measuring blood pressure. [Gk. *sphugmos* pulse and MANOMETER].
SPICATE, [spīk'-āt], *adj.* (*bot.*) in the form of a spike. [L. *spica*].
SPICCATO, [spik-ah'-tō], *adv.* (*mus.*) a term indicating that every note is to have its distinct sound.
SPICE (1), [spīs], *n.* an aromatic tropical product used in flavouring, *esp.* the more pungent of such preparations; (*fig.*) that which flavours, gives taste to a thing. [OFr. *espice* from L. *species* kind].
SPICE (2), [spīs], *v.t.* to flavour with spice.
SPICER, [spīs'-er], *n.* a trader in spices.
SPICERY, [spīs'-er-i], *n.* spices.
SPICE-WOOD, [spīs'-wŏŏd], *n.* any of various woods with a spicy odour, *esp.* when burnt.
SPICIFORM, [spīs'-i-fawm], *adj.* in the form of a spike.
SPICILY, [spīs'-i-li], *adv.* in a spicy manner.
SPICINESS, [spīs'-i-nes], *n.* the quality of being spicy.
SPICK-AND-SPAN, [spik'-an-span'], *adj.* smart, spruce, *esp.* of clothing. [Uncert.].
SPICKNEL, [spik'-nel], *n.* spignel.
SPICOSITY, [spik-os'-it-i], *n.* the state of having or being full of ears, like corn. [L. *spica* ear of corn].
SPICULAR, [spik'-yŏŏ-ler], *adj.* covered with spicules.
SPICULATE, [spik'-yŏŏ-lāt], *adj.* spicular.
SPICULE, [spik'-yōōl], *n.* (*bot.*) a small spike; (*zool.*) a granulation; a component part of a sponge skeleton; a small, sharply pointed object. [L. *spiculum*].
SPICULIFORM, [spik'-yōōl-i-fawm], *adj.* having the form of a spicule.
SPICULIGENOUS, [spik'-yŏŏ-lij'-en-us], *adj.* producing or containing spicules. [SPICULE and Gk. *genes* producing].
SPICY, [spīs'-i], *adj.* flavoured with spice; (*coll.*) piquantly indecent.
SPIDER, [spī'-der], *n.* a member of the order *Arachnida*, distinguished by having eight legs and a capacity for spinning webs to catch prey. [OE. *spithra*].
SPIDERCATCHER, [spī'-der-kach'-er], *n.* an East Indian bird.
SPIDER-CRAB, [spī'-der-krab'], *n.* a crab of the genus *Maia* with long thin legs.
SPIDERDOM, [spī'-der-dom], *n.* the spider world.
SPIDER-FLY, [spī'-der-flī], *n.* a parasitic dipterous insect.
SPIDER-LIKE, [spī'-der-līk], *adj.* like a spider.
SPIDER-LINE, [spī'-der-līn], *n.* a thread of spider-web, *esp.* as used to form the reticle of a telescope.
SPIDER-MONKEY, [spī'-der-mung'-ki], *n.* a small American monkey of the genus *Ateles*, with long slender limbs and sensitive prehensile tail.
SPIDER-ORCHIS, [spī'-der-aw'-kis], *n.* either of two orchids with a yellow-streaked brown lip, *Ophrys aranifera* or *O. fuciflora*.
SPIDERWORT, [spī'-der-wurt], *n.* (*bot.*) one of several species of *Tradescantia*.
SPIDERY, [spī'-der-i], *adj.* like a spider; having long, thin sprawling limbs; (of writing) thin and sprawling.

SPIEGELEISEN, [shpē'-gel-īz-en], *n.* white manganese-iron, used in making Bessemer steel. [Germ. *spiegel* mirror and *eisen* iron].
SPIFFING, [spif'-ing], *adj.* (*coll.*) excellent, splendid. [Uncert.].
SPIFFLICATE, [spif'-lik-āt], *v.t.* (*slang*) to squash utterly, to disconcert, to crush. [Unkn.].
SPIGNEL, [spig'-nel], *n.* (*bot.*) baldmoney, the umbelliferous plant, *Meum athamanticum*. [Unkn.].
SPIGOT, [spig'-ot], *n.* the vent-peg of a cask; (*eng.*) a projecting flange or pin which enables one machined surface to be accurately located on another which has corresponding holes. [ME. *spigot*].
SPIKE (1), [spīk], *n.* a sharp-pointed, tapering rod or projection, *esp.* of metal and intended as a protection; (*bot.*) small sessile flowers about an axis, an ear of corn. [OScand. *spik* nail and L. *spica* ear of corn].
SPIKE (2), [spīk], *v.t.* to pierce with a spike, provide with spikes; to put a cannon out of action by driving a spike into the match hole; (*fig.*) to thwart (a plan).
SPIKELET, [spīk'-let], *n.* a small spike, *esp.* in the inflorescence of grasses.
SPIKE-NAIL, [spīk'-nāl], *n.* a strong nail used for fixing railway lines.
SPIKENARD, [spīk'-nahd], *n.* (*bot.*) an aromatic herb related to valerian, an ointment prepared from this plant; **ploughman's s.**, the composite plant. *Inula Conyza*. [L. *spica nardi* spike of nard].
SPIKY, [spīk'-i], *adj.* covered with spikes; (*coll.*) high-church.
SPILE, [spīl], *n.* a pile driven into the ground to make a foundation; a spigot. [OScand. *spila* narrow piece of wood].
SPILL (1), [spil], *n.* a splinter of wood or twist of paper used for lighting fires or tobacco. [OE. *speld* splinter].
SPILL (2), [spil], *n.* a fall, an upset, a tumble.
SPILL (3), (**spilt**), [spil], *v.t. and i.* to fall, tip out of something, *esp.* of liquid from a vessel; to upset, splash out, allow to fall out and waste; **to s. the beans**, (*coll.*) to divulge a secret, *esp.* unintentionally. [OE. *spillan* destroy].
SPILLER, [spil'-er], *n.* a small net used to remove fish from a larger seine. [Uncert.].
SPILLIKIN, [spil'-i-kin], *n.* a splinter of wood or ivory used in spillikins; (*pl.*) a game in which the players have to extract a spillikin without moving or disturbing the others. [ME. *spellekin*].
SPILLING-LINES, [spil'-ing-līnz], *n.*(*pl.*) (*naut.*) ropes for furling the square-sails.
SPILLWAY, [spil'-wā], *n.* an overflow channel from a mill pond.
SPILT, [spilt], *p.pt.* of SPILL.
SPILTH, [spilth], *n.* overflow, that which is spilt.
SPIN (1), [spin], *n.* the act of spinning; rotation; a short but rapid journey in a vehicle, or by bicycle, taken purely for pleasure; (*aeron.*) a spinning dive.
SPIN (2), (**span, spun**), [spin], *v.t. and i.* to draw and twist yarn, etc., into thread; to make rotate rapidly, to whirl round; (*fig.*) to devise subtly; to perform the act or practice of spinning yarn; to rotate, be whirled round, revolve. [OE. *spinnan*].
SPINACEOUS, [spin-ā'-shus], *adj.* pertaining to spinach.
SPINACH, [spin'-ij], *n.* the edible plant, *Spinacea oleracea*; **s. beet**, a beet whose leaves are cooked and eaten like spinach. [Arab. *aspanakh*].

SPINACH

SPINAL, [spīn'-al], *adj.* of, or pertaining to, the spine; **s. column**, the vertebral column or backbone; **s. cord**, an elongated part of the cerebro-spinal axis contained within the spinal column. [LL. *spinalis*].
SPINATE, [spī'-nāt], *adj.* having spines.
SPINDLE, [spindl], *n.* a thin rod on which is wound the thread from the distaff; the shaft on which something rotates. [OE. *spinel*].
SPINDLE-LEGS, [spindl'-legz'], *n.* spindleshanks.
SPINDLESHANKED, [spindl'-shangkt'], *adj.* having spindleshanks.
SPINDLESHANKS, [spindl'-shangks'], *n.* a person having long, thin legs.
SPINDLE-SHAPED, [spindl'-shāpt], *adj.* having the shape of a spindle, thin, slender, attenuated.

SPINDLE-SIDE, [spindl'-sīd], *n.* the mother's side.

SPINDLE-TREE, [spindl'-trē], *n.* a shrub of the genus *Euonymus*, the wood of which is good for making spindles.

SPINDLE-TREE

SPINDLY, [spind'-li], *adj.* excessively slender.

SPINDRIFT, [spin'-drift], *n.* windblown foam and spray. [~SPOONDRIFT].

SPINE, [spīn], *n.* (*anat.*) the bony column running from head to pelvis in vertebrates, the backbone; any stiff, pointed structure, a quill, spike, a thorn; the part of the back of a book which protects the sewing of the sheets. [L. *spina* thorn].

SPINEL, [spin'-el], *n.* a vitreous crystalline mineral; **s. ruby,** a scarlet gem resembling the true ruby. [OFr. *espinelle*].

SPINELESS, [spīn'-les], *adj.* without a spine; (*fig.*) lacking in courage and determination.

SPINESCENT, [spīn-es'-ent], *adj.* covered with spines.

SPINET, [spin'-et], *n.* a small keyboard musical instrument from which developed the harpsichord. [It. *spinetta*, *dim.* of *spina* quill].

SPINIFEROUS, [spīn-if'-er-us], *adj.* having spines.

SPINIFORM, [spīn'-i-fawm], *adj.* shaped like a spine.

SPINIGEROUS, [spin-ij'-er-us], *adj.* having spines or thorns.

SPINNAKER, [spin'-ak-er], *n.* (*naut.*) a triangular sail carried opposite the mainsail when running before the wind. [Uncert.].

SPINNER, [spin'-er], *n.* one who, or that which, spins.

SPINNERET, [spin'-er-et], *n.* the silk-producing organ of a spider.

SPINNERY, [spin'-er-i], *n.* a spinning-mill.

SPINNEY, SPINNY, [spin'-i], *n.* a small copse. [OF. *espinaie* thicket].

SPINNING, [spin'-ing], *n.* the business, practice, or technique of spinning into thread.

SPINNING-JENNY, [spin'-ing-jen'-i], *n.* a machine for spinning many threads simultaneously.

SPINNING-MILL, [spin'-ing-mil'], *n.* a factory for spinning.

SPINNING-WHEEL, [spin'-ing-wēl], *n.* a primitive spinning machine, usually worked by a treadle.

SPINNY, see SPINNEY.

SPINOSE, [spīn'-ōs], *adj.* spiny [L. *spinosus*].

SPINOSITY, [spin-os'-it-i], *n.* the state of being thorny or crabbed. [L. *spinositas*].

SPINOUS, [spīn'-us], *adj.* spiny, thorny.

SPINOZISM, [spin-ōt'-sizm], *n.* the pantheistic philosophy of Spinoza. [B. de *Spinoza*, the 17th-century philosopher].

SPINOZIST, [spin-ōt'-sist], *n.* a follower of Spinoza the philosopher.

SPINSTER, [spin'-ster], *n.* an unmarried woman, *esp.* if elderly. [ME. *spinnester* female spinner].

SPINSTRY, [spin'-stri], *n.* the business of spinning.

SPINTHARISCOPE, [spinth-a'-ri-skōp], *n.* a device for showing the effects of the disintegration of radium. [Gk. *spintharis* spark and *skopos* watcher].

SPINULE, [spīn'-yōōl], *n.* a minute spine. [L. *spinula*].

SPINULOSE, [spīn'-yōōl-ōs], *adj.* (*bot.*) covered with small spines.

SPINY, [spīn'-i], *adj.*, covered with, full of, spines.

SPIRACLE, [spīer'-rakl], *n.* a respiratory orifice; the blow-hole of a whale. [L. *spiraculum*].

SPIRACULAR, [spi-rak'-yōōl-er], *adj.* of or pertaining to spiracles.

SPIRACULATE, [spi-rak'-yōōl-āt], *adj.* having spiracles.

SPIRAEA, [spī-rē'-a], *n.* a numerous genus of rosaceous plants, including the meadowsweet. [Gk. *spiraia*].

SPIRAL (1), [spīer'-al], *n.* a spiral curve; objects arranged in a spiral.

SPIRAL (2), [spīer'-al], *adj.* in a curve revolving regularly away from a fixed central point; in a curve revolving at a constant distance from a centre, but on a continually shifting plane. [L. *spiralis*].

SPIRAL (3), [spīer'-al], *v.i.* to revolve in, form, a spiral.

SPIRALITY, [spīer-al'-it-i], *n.* the quality of being spiral.

SPIRALLY, [spīer'-al-i], *adv.* in the form of a spiral.

SPIRANT (1), [spīer'-ant], *n.* a consonant made by partial constriction of the air-passage, a fricative consonant. [L. *spirans* breathing].

SPIRANT (2), [spīer'-ant], *adj.* pronounced as a spirant.

SPIRE (1), [spīer], *n.* a tower tapering to a point; anything resembling this. [OE. *spir*].

SPIRE (2), [spīer], *n.* a spiral coil, a twist of a spiral. [Gk. *speira* coil].

SPIRED, [spīerd], *adj.* having a spire.

SPIRILLUM, [spī-ril'-um], *n.* one of a genus of blood parasites like a corkscrew in shape. [L. *spira* coil].

SPIRIT (1), [spi'-rit], *n.* the animating, non-material, divine element in man that gives life and reason, the soul, the intelligent principle; will and intelligence divorced from a body, an immaterial being possessing conation, cognition, or both; a ghost, a spectre; a pervading influence, the feeling that prevails in any particular circumstances; those personal qualities that cannot, apparently, be directly related to the body, *esp.* courage, pride, vivacity of mind; the fundamental principle, true meaning, of a thing; alcohol, a volatile, inflammable liquid; (*pl.*) powerful alcoholic liquor produced by distillation, *esp.* gin, brandy, and whisky; **spirits of salts,** commercial hydrochloric acid. [L. *spiritus*].

SPIRIT (2), [spi'-rit], *v.t.* to inspirit; **to s. away, s. off,** to take away, make to disappear as if by magic.

SPIRITED, [spi'-rit-ed], *adj.* full of spirit, vigour and vitality; full of courage and independence.

SPIRITEDLY, [spi'-rit-ed-li], *adv.* in a spirited manner.

SPIRITEDNESS, [spi'-rit-ed-nes], *n.* the state of being spirited; disposition of mind.

SPIRITFUL, [spi'-rit-fōōl], *adj.* spirited.

SPIRITISM, [spi'-rit-izm], *n.* spiritualism.

SPIRITIST, [spi'-rit-ist], *n.* a spiritualist.

SPIRIT-LAMP, [spi'-rit-lamp'], *n.* a lamp burning methylated spirit.

SPIRITLESS, [spi'-rit-les], *adj.* without spirit, lacking vigour, courage or vitality.

SPIRITLESSLY, [spi'-rit-les-li], *adv.* in a spiritless manner.

SPIRITLESSNESS, [spi'-rit-les-nes], *n.* the state of being spiritless.

SPIRIT-LEVEL, [spi'-rit-lev'-el], *n.* an instrument for ascertaining the true horizontal by means of a bubble of air in a tube of spirit.

SPIRITOSO, [spi'-rit-ōs'-ō], *adv.* (*mus.*) spiritedly. [It. *spiritoso*].

SPIRITOUS, [spi'-rit-us], *adj.* relating to spirit, spirited.

SPIRITOUSNESS, [spi'-rit-us-nes], *n.* the state of being spiritous.

SPIRIT-RAPPER, [spi'-rit-rap'-er], *n.* one who fakes spirit-rapping.

SPIRIT-RAPPING, [spi'-rit-rap'-ing], *n.* a variety of psychic phenomena in which the spirits of the dead are believed to manifest their presence by rapping on material or immaterial objects.

SPIRIT-STIRRING, [spi'-rit-stur'-ing], *adj.* animating the spirit.

SPIRITUAL (1), [spi'-rich-(y)ōō-al], *n.* an American Negro hymn characterized by simple words and sometimes by a syncopated rhythm.

SPIRITUAL (2), [spi'-rich-(y)ōō-al], *adj.* consisting of, relating to, the spirit; relating to the soul, pertaining to religion and its principles, not materialist; inspired by moral or religious motives, not preoccupied with material things. [L. *spiritualis*].

SPIRITUALISM, [spi'-ri-chōō-al-izm], *n.* the belief that the spirits of the dead retain all the interests they possessed in life, and are able and willing to communicate with the living, *esp.* through a medium; the numerous practices based upon this belief.

SPIRITUALIST, [spi'-ri-chōō-al-ist], *n.* a believer in spiritualism.

SPIRITUALISTIC, [spi'-ri-chōō-al-ist'-ik], *adj.* pertaining to spiritualism; due to the presumed agency of spirits.

SPIRITUALITY, [spi'-ri-chōō-al'-i-ti], *n.* the state or quality of being spiritual. [LL. *spiritualitas*].

SPIRITUALIZATION, [spi'-ri-chōō-al-iz-ā'-shun], *n.* the process of spiritualizing, the state of being spiritualized.

SPIRITUALIZE, [spi'-ri-chōō-al-īz], *v.t.* to make spiritual, to refine; to bring into closer relationship with religion.

SPIRITUALIZER, [spi'-ri-chōō-al-īz-er], *n.* one who spiritualizes.

SPIRITUALLY, [spi'-ri-chōō-al-i], *adv.* in spiritual fashion.

SPIRITUALNESS, [spi'-ri-chōō-al-nes], *n.* spirituality.

SPIRITUEL(LE), [spē-rē-tew-el'], *adj.* displaying great refinement and delicacy. [Fr. *spirituel*].

SPIRITUOSITY, [spi'-ri-chōō-os'-it-i], *n.* the state of being spirituous.

SPIRITUOUS, [spi'-ri-chōō-us], *adj.* containing distilled alcohol. [Fr. *spiritueux*].

SPIRITUOUSNESS, [spi'-ri-chōō-us-nes], *n.* the quality of being spirituous.

SPIRITUS, [spi'-rit-us], *n.* (*gram.*) aspiration; **s. asper (lenis)**, the rough (smooth) breathing in Greek. [L. *spiritus* breath].

SPIRKETING, [spurk'-it-ing], *n.* the inside planking of a ship. [Uncert.].

SPIROGRAPH, [spier'-ō-graf], *n.* an instrument for recording the breathing. [L. *spirare* to breathe and GRAPH].

SPIROMETER, [spī-rom'-it-er], *n.* an instrument for measuring the capacity of the lungs. [L. *spirare* to breathe and METER].

SPIRT (1), [spurt], *n.* a sudden, small, vigorous jet of flame, fluid, etc.

SPIRT (2), [spurt], *v.t. and i.* to issue out in a small vigorous jet. [OE. *spryttan* to sprout].

SPIRTLE, [spurtl], *v.i.* to spirt.

SPIRY, [spīer'-i], *adj.* having or resembling a spire.

SPISSITUDE, [spis'-i-tewd], *n.* density. [L. *spissitudo*].

SPIT (1), [spit], *n.* a long, thin, pointed spike or rod, *esp.* such a metal rod impaling meat for roasting; a narrow point of low land running out into the sea. [OE. *spitu*].

SPIT (2), [spit], *n.* the act of spitting, the gob of saliva so ejected from the mouth; a splutter (of rain), a slight fall of liquid.

SPIT (3), [spit], *v.t.* to pierce with a spit.

SPIT (4), (**spat**), [spit], *v.t. and i.* to eject saliva from the mouth; to throw out (liquid) in small drops; to eject anything violently from the mouth. [OE. *spittan*].

SPITCHCOCK, [spich'-kok'], *n.* an eel split and broiled. [Uncert.].

SPITE (1), [spīt], *n.* malevolence, vicious petty hostility; the cause of such a feeling. [~DESPITE].

SPITE (2), [spīt], *v.t.* to injure, annoy through spite, to behave spitefully towards.

SPITEFUL, [spīt'-fōōl], *adj.* malevolent, full of spite towards.

SPITEFULLY, [spīt'-fōōl-i], *adv.* in a spiteful manner.

SPITEFULNESS, [spīt'-fōōl-nes], *n.* the quality of being spiteful.

SPITFIRE, [spit'-fīer], *n.* a hasty, vicious, ill-tempered person, *esp.* a woman of this kind; (*aeron.*) a type of British fighter plane.

SPITTED, [spit'-ed], *adj.* impaled on a spit.

SPITTER, [spit'-er], *n.* one who spits; a young deer.

SPITTLE (1), [spitl], *n.* ejected saliva. [~OE. *spatl*].

SPITTLE (2), [spitl], *n.* a small spade.

SPITTOON, [spit-ōōn'], *n.* a receptacle into which saliva may be ejected.

SPITZ, [shpits], *n.* a Pomeranian dog. [Germ. from *spitz* point].

SPLANCHNIC, [splangk'-nik], *adj.* pertaining to the viscera. [Gk. *splagkhna*].

SPLANCHNOLOGY, [splangk-nol'-oj-i], *n.* the study of the viscera. [Gk. *splagkhna* viscera and *logos* speech].

SPLANCHNOTOMY, [splangk-not'-om-i], *n.* the dissection of the viscera. [Gk. *splagkhna* viscera and *tome* cutting].

SPLASH (1), [splash], *n.* the act of splashing; the noise of splashing; a small quantity of liquid flung on a surface by splashing or squirted from a siphon; a patch of bright colour or light; **to make a s.**, (*coll.*) to cut a dash, indulge in reckless expenditure.

SPLASH (2), [splash], *v.t. and i.* to cause (liquid) to scatter, fly about in drops; to stain, wet, touch a surface by scattering some liquid; to perform with an accompaniment of splashing; (of liquid) to be scattered, to be dashed about, *esp.* as a result of being struck, or violently shaken; (of vessels containing liquids) to permit a liquid to be splashed; to make a bold display of (news, etc.) in a newspaper. [Echoic].

SPLASH-BOARD, [splash'-bawd], *n.* a guard in front of a vehicle to prevent the occupants being splashed with mud; a mudguard.

SPLASHER, [splash'-er], *n.* the mudguard of a locomotive; a board protecting the wall behind a sink, or tap of running water.

SPLASHY, [splash'-i], *adj.* tending to splash.

SPLATTER, [splat'-er], *v.t. and i.* to spatter, to splash lightly.

SPLAY (1), [splā], *adj.* sloping, spreading out at an angle.

SPLAY (2), [splā], *v.t. and i.* to dislocate (a joint), to spread out at an angle; (*arch.*) to slope at an angle. [ME. *splayen*].

SPLAY-FOOT, [splā'-fōōt], *n.* a flat, outward-turned foot.

SPLAY-FOOTED, [splā'-fōōt-ed], *adj.* having splay-feet.

SPLAY-MOUTH, [splā'-mowth], *n.* a wide, gaping mouth.

SPLAY-MOUTHED, [splā'-mowTHd], *adj.* having a splay-mouth.

SPLEEN, [splēn], *n.* a ductless gland situated near the stomach, formerly held to be the seat of ill-humour and melancholy; dejection, ill-tempered despondency. [Gk. *splen*].

SPLEENFUL, [splēn'-fōōl], *adj.* ill-tempered, melancholy.

SPLEENISH, [splēn'-ish], *adj.* tending towards spleen.

SPLEENISHLY, [splēn'-ish-li], *adv.* with spleen.

SPLEENISHNESS, [splēn'-ish-nes], *n.* the state of being spleenish.

SPLEENLESS, [splēn'-les], *adj.* having no spleen; pleasant-tempered.

SPLEENWORT, [splēn'-wurt], *n.* (*bot.*) a fern of the genus *Asplenium*.

SPLEENY, [splēn'-i], *adj.* suffering from spleen.

SPLENDENT, [splend'-ent], *adj.* shining, resplendent. [L. *splendens*].

SPLENDID, [splen'-did], *adj.* gorgeous, magnificent in appearance, dazzling, rich and impressive to the eye; illustrious, pre-eminent, brilliant, glorious; (*coll.*) excellent, admirable. [L. *splendidus*].

SPLENDIDLY, [splen'-did-li], *adv.* in a splendid manner.

SPLENDIDNESS, [splen'-did-nes], *n.* the quality of being splendid.

SPLENDIFEROUS, [splen-dif'-er-us], *adj.* (*slang*) magnificent. [OFr. *splendifere*].

SPLEENWORT

SPLENDOUR, [splen'-der], *n.* gorgeous and radiant brilliance of appearance, magnificence, rich and splendid panoply; pre-eminence, glory, impressive greatness of quality. [L. *splendor*].

SPLENETIC, [splen-et'-ik], *adj.* spleenful; relating to the spleen. [LL. *spleneticus*].

SPLENETICAL, [splen-et'-ik-al], *adj.* splenetic.

SPLENETICALLY, [splen-et'-ik-al-i], *adv.* in a splenetic manner.

SPLENIC, [splēn'-ik], *adj.* belonging to the spleen [Gk. *splenikos*].

SPLENITIS, [splen-ī'-tis], *n.* inflammation of the spleen.

SPLENIUS, [splēn'-i-us], *n.* (*anat.*) a cervical muscle. [Gk. *splenion* bandage].

SPLENIZATION, [splēn'-iz-ā'-shun], *n.* morbid development of an organ in which its tissue comes to resemble that of the spleen.

SPLENOCELE, [splen'-ō-sēl], *n.* hernia of the spleen. [Gk. *splen* spleen and *kele* tumour].

SPLENOLOGY, [splen-ol'-oj-i], *n.* the study of the spleen. [Gk. *splen* spleen and *logos* speech].

SPLENOTOMY, [splen-ot'-om-i], *n.* dissection of the spleen. [Gk. *splen* spleen and *tome* cutting].

SPLENT, [splent], *n.* a splint. [~SPLINT].

SPLENT-COAL, [splent'-kōl], *n.* an inferior kind of cannel-coal from the Scottish collieries.

SPLEUCHAN, [splōō'-khan], *n.* a pouch. [Ir. *spliuchan*].

SPLICE (1), [splīs], *n.* a join in a rope made by intertwining the strands; join of wood by overlapping and binding.

SPLICE (2), [splīs], *v.t.* to join (ropes) by interweaving the strands, to join (timbers) by overlapping or fitting, and binding; (*slang*) to join in marriage; **to s. the main-brace**, to serve out an allowance of spirits in the Navy. [MDu. *splissen*].

SPLINE, [splīn], *n.* a flexible strip used by draughtsmen for drawing curves; the square or fluted end of a wheel shaft fitting into the hub of the wheel, so that shaft and wheel revolve together. [Unkn.].

SPLINE

SPLINT (1), [splint], *n.* a strip of wood tied to a broken limb to keep the ends of bone in position; a strip of split wood used in basket-making; a bony tumour on the splint-bone of a horse. [~Swed. *splint* spike].

SPLINT (2), [splint], *v.t.* to fix with a splint.

SPLINT-BONE, [splint'-bōn], *n.* a bone near the cannon-bone of a horse; (*anat.*) the fibula.

SPLINTER (1), [splint'-er], *n.* a small hard, sharp fragment of anything, roughly broken off from the main body, *esp.* a sliver of wood or a fragment of a projectile or bomb. [MDu. *splinter*].
SPLINTER (2), [splint'-er], *v.t. and i.* to split, smash, shatter into small pointed fragments; to break into sharp, pointed fragments under a blow or heavy pressure.
SPLINTER-BAR, [splint'-er-bah(r)], *n.* a crossbar supporting the springs of a carriage; the rigid bar to which traces are attached.
SPLINTER-BONE, [splint'-er-bōn], *n.* the fibula.
SPLINTER-PROOF, [splint'-er-proof], *adj.* proof against bomb or shell splinters, though not against direct impact.
SPLINTERY, [splint'-er-i], *adj.* tending to splinter.
SPLIT (1), [split], *n.* the process or act of splitting; the result of splitting; a fissure, cleft produced by splitting; (*fig.*) a division, disunion, difference of opinion leading to divergence; an even share, a fifty-fifty division, division according to any proportions; a small portion of spirits; (*basket-making*) a splint; a cake consisting of a scone-like basis filled with jam and whipped cream; (*pl.*) an acrobatic contortion in which the legs are opened to the fullest extent so that they form a straight line at right angles to the trunk.
SPLIT (2), [split], *v.t. and i.* to divide into two or more parts by fissure through the whole body, *esp.* as the result of pressure or impact, to come apart along continuous lines through an entire mass; (*fig.*) to become disunited, to diverge over an issue, to divide up into parties; to cause to divide, to make a fissure in, to separate; to share out with others. [MDu. *splitten*].
SPLIT-PEAS(E), [split'-pēz], *n.(pl.)* husked peas split.
SPLIT-RING, [split'-ring'], *n.* a ring consisting of two turns of a spiral pressed together so as to look as if it were split.
SPLITTER, [split'-er], *n.* one who, or that which, splits.
SPLODGE, [sploj], *n.* a splotch.
SPLOTCH, [sploch], *n.* a smear, a blotch, an irregular patch. [~OE. *splot* spot].
SPLURGE, [splurj], *n.* (*coll.*) pretentious show or talk. [Symbolic].
SPLUTTER (1), [splut'-er], *n.* a noise as of spluttering; the act of spluttering.
SPLUTTER (2), [splut'-er], *v.t. and i.* to spit, sputter out saliva, to speak as if one were so doing. [Echoic].
SPODE, [spōd], *n.* a kind of china ware. [Josiah *Spode*, the potter].
SPODOMANCY, [spod'-ō-man-si], *n.* divination by ashes. [Gk. *spodos* ashes and *manteia* divination].
SPODUMENE, [spod'-yoo-mēn], *n.* (*min.*) a silicate of aluminium and lithium. [Gk. *spodoumenos*].
SPOIL (1), [spoil], *n.* goods captured by violence, booty, the fruits of plunder; (*fig.*) the profits, prizes won by contest. [L. *spolium*].
SPOIL (2), [spoil], *v.t. and i.* to plunder, take spoil from; to injure (a thing), *esp.* to impair its outward appearance; (*fig.*) to detract from the pleasure or merit of; (of persons) to injure the character by excessive indulgence; to become spoiled, to deteriorate, to lose value. [L. *spoliare*].
SPOILAGE, [spoil'-ij], *n.* (*print.*) paper spoiled in printing. [SPOIL (2)].
SPOILER, [spoil'-er], *n.* one who spoils.
SPOIL-SPORT, [spoil'-spawt], *n.* a person who, by untimely self-righteousness, spoils the pleasure of other people.
SPOKE (1), [spōk], *n.* a bar joining the hub and rim of a wheel; a bar used as a drag on the wheel of a vehicle; the rung of a ladder; a handle projecting from the rim of a ship's steering wheel. [OE. *spaca*].
SPOKE (2), [spōk], *pret.* of SPEAK.
SPOKEN, [spōk'-en], *p.pt.* of SPEAK.
SPOKESHAVE, [spōk'-shāv], *n.* a blade set in the middle of a (metal) rod, used in planing the curves of spokes, etc.

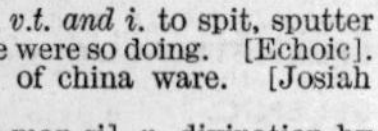

SPOKESHAVE

SPOKESMAN, [spōks'-man], *n.* a person who speaks on behalf of others, *esp.* authoritatively for a government, etc.
SPOLIATE, [spōl'-i-āt], *v.t.* to plunder, despoil. [L. *spoliare*].
SPOLIATION, [spōl-i-ā'-shun], *n.* the act of plundering; (*eccles.*) illegal appropriation of tithes. [L. *spoliatio*].
SPOLIATOR, [spōl'-i-āt-er], *n.* one who commits spoliation, a plunderer. [L. *spoliator*].
SPONDAIC, [spond-ā'-ik], *adj.* consisting of or relating to a spondee or spondees. [Gk. *spondeiakos*].
SPONDEE, [spond'-ē], *n.* (*pros.*) a poetic foot of two long syllables. [Gk. *spondeios*].
SPONDULIC(K)S, [spon-dew'-liks], *n.* (*slang*) money. [Invented].
SPONDYLE, [spond'-il], *n.* one of the vertebrae. [Gk. *spondulos*].
SPONDYLITIS, [spond'-il-it'-is], *n.* inflammation o the vertebrae.
SPONGE (1), [spunj], *n.* a marine creature belonging to the *Porifera*, notable for its fibrous skeleton; the skeleton of this creature used in cleaning because of its absorbent qualities; a sponger; **to throw up the s.**, to admit defeat, give in. [Gk. *spongia*].
SPONGE (2), [spunj], *v.t. and i.* to wipe with a sponge; to dive for sponges; to act the sponger; **to s. on**, to live as the parasite of. [LL. *spongiare*].
SPONGE-CAKE, [spunj'-kāk], *n.* a very light plain sweet cake.
SPONGECLOTH, [spunj'-kloth'], *n.* a fabric having an open texture resembling the surface of a fine sponge.
SPONGELET, [spunj'-let], *n.* a small sponge.
SPONGEOUS, [spunj'-us], *adj.* spongy.
SPONGER, [spunj'-er], *n.* a parasitical hanger-on.
SPONGICOLOUS, [spunj-ik'-ol-us], *adj.* living in sponges.
SPONGIFORM, [spunj'-i-fawm], *adj.* in the form of a sponge.
SPONGINESS, [spunj'-i-nes], *n.* the state of being spongy.
SPONGING-HOUSE, [spunj'-ing-hows], *n.* a bailiff's house in which debtors were formerly kept before being consigned to prison.
SPONGIOLE, [spunj'-i-ōl], *n.* (*bot.*) the absorbent cellular tissue at the extremities of roots.
SPONGIOSE, [spunj'-i-ōs], *adj.* like a sponge.
SPONGY, [spunj'-i], *adj.* like a sponge, yielding, absorbent, boggy and soggy.
SPONSAL, [spon'-sal], *adj.* relating to marriage.
SPONSION, [spon'-shun], *n.* the act of becoming surety for another; (*leg.*) international agreement made by an official not competent to do so. [L. *sponsio* covenant].
SPONSON, [spon'-son], *n.* a platform projecting from the side of a ship; the curved planking on either side of a paddlewheel. [Unkn.].
SPONSOR (1), [spon'-sor], *n.* one who makes an agreement, accepts responsibility for another, one vouching for another. [L. *sponsor* surety].
SPONSOR (2), [spon'-sor], *v.t.* to act as sponsor for; (*U.S.*) to finance (on the radio) an entertainment programme for advertising purposes.
SPONSORIAL, [spon-saw'-ri-al], *adj.* pertaining to a sponsor.
SPONSORSHIP, [spon'-ser-ship], *n.* the state of being a sponsor.
SPONTANEITY, [spont'-an-ē'-it-i], *n.* the state of being spontaneous; spontaneous action.
SPONTANEOUS, [spont-ān'-i-us], *adj.* self-generated, occurring from causes that are purely internal, without the intervention of any outside force; of one's own free will, entirely voluntary; happening without any apparent cause at all. [L. *spontaneus* voluntary].
SPONTANEOUSLY, [spont-ān'-i-us-li], *adv.* in a spontaneous manner.
SPONTANEOUSNESS, [spont-ān'-i-us-nes], *n.* the quality of being spontaneous.
SPONTOON†, [spon-toon'], *n.* a short halberd formerly carried by infantry officers on full-dress parades. [It. *spontone*].
SPOOF (1), [spoof], *n. and adj.* a joking deception, a hoax; bogus, hoaxing. [Invented].
SPOOF (2), [spoof], *v.t.* to deceive, hoax (a person).
SPOOK, [spook], *n.* (*coll.*) a supernatural apparition. [Du. *spook*].
SPOOL (1), [spool], *n.* a bar on which thread is wound; a reel of cotton; the bar on the reel of a fishing-rod; a cylinder on which photographic film is wound. [MDu. *spoele*].
SPOOL (2), [spool], *v.t.* to wind on a spool.
SPOOL-STAND, [spool'-stand'], *n.* a row of upright pegs holding reels of thread.
SPOOM, [spoom], *v.i.* (*naut.*) to drive before the wind. [~SPOON (4)].
SPOON (1), [spoon], *n.* an implement havin

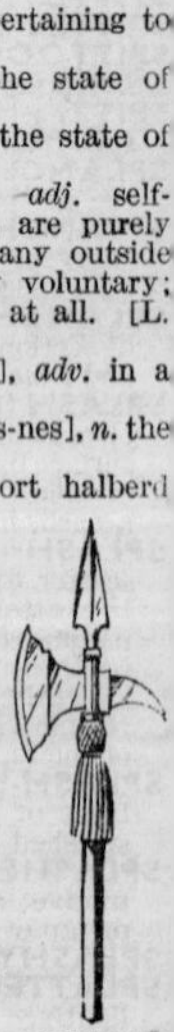

SPONTOON

a long handle supporting a shallow bowl, used for raising, stirring, or drinking liquids; a wooden-headed golf club. [OE. *spon* a shaving].

SPOON (2), [spōōn], *v.t.* to lift, convey, with a spoon; (*golf*) to strike with the spoon; to scoop up or along as if with a spoon.

SPOON (3), [spōōn], *v.i.* (*coll.*) to make sexual advances in a sentimental fashion. [Uncert.].

SPOON† (4), [spōōn], *v.i.* (*naut.*) to move or sail before the wind. [Unkn.].

SPOON-BAIT, [spōōn'-bāt], *n.* a bait in the form of a spoon, used by anglers.

SPOONBILL, [spōōn'-bil], *n.* the wading bird, *Platalea leucorodia*, or a related species.

SPOONDRIFT, [spōōn'-drift], *n.* spindrift. [SPOON (4) and DRIFT].

SPOONERISM, [spōōn'-er-izm], *n.* the involuntary transposition of syllables in adjoining words, *esp.* when the effect is humorous. [Dr. *Spooner*, formerly Warden of New College, Oxford].

SPOONEY, [spōōn'-i], *adj.* spoony.

SPOONFEED, [spōōn'-fēd'], *v.t.* to feed by means of a spoon; to instruct in an elementary way so as to give the recipient no scope for original thought.

SPOONFUL, [spōōn'-fŏŏl], *n.* the amount contained in a spoon.

SPOONILY, [spōōn'-i-li], *adv.* in a spoony manner.

SPOONMEAT, [spōōn'-mēt], *n.* food that is or must be eaten or taken with a spoon.

SPOONY, [spōōn'-i], *adj.* stupidly, gawkishly amorous. [~SPOON (3)].

SPOOR, [spōōer], *n.* the trail of an animal. [Du. *spoor*].

SPORADIC, [spo-rad'-ik], *adj.* occurring at irregular intervals. [Gk. *sporadikos*].

SPORADICALLY, [spo-rad'-ik-al-i], *adv.* in a sporadic manner; separately.

SPORANGIUM, [spo-ranj'-i-um], *n.* (*bot.*) a spore-case. [Gk *spora* spore and *aggeion* little vessel].

SPORE, [spaw(r)], *n.* (*biol.*) one of the minute bodies, formed in flowerless plants after fertilization, from which the new plant develops. [Gk. *spora* seed].

SPORE-CASE, [spaw(r)'-kās], *n.* the container of spores.

SPORIFICATION, [spaw'-rif-ik-ā'-shun], *n.* the production of spores.

SPORODERM, [spawr'-ō-durm], *n.* the covering of a spore.

SPOROGENY, [spo-roj'-en-i], *n.* reproduction by spore. [SPORE and Gk. *genes* producing].

SPORRAN, [spo'-ran], *n.* a Highlander's pouch worn hanging down in front of the kilt and formerly backed with metal as a protection for the genitals. [Gael. *sporan*].

SPORRAN

SPORT (1), [spawt], *n.* activity engaged in as recreation, *esp.* such activity when engaged in by several persons in planned, friendly competition, athletics; fun, pleasure, jest, an amusing occurrence; an object of sport, a plaything; (*biol.*) a spontaneous deviation from normal type; (*pl.*) a meeting for athletic contests; (*coll.*) a good fellow, a sportsman. [~DISPORT].

SPORT (2), [spawt], *v.t. and i.* to disport oneself; to wear for display; **to s. one's oak,** to lock one's outer door.

SPORTER, [spawt'-er], *n.* one who sports.

SPORTFUL, [spawt'-fŏŏl], *adj.* full of frolic.

SPORTFULLY, [spawt'-fŏŏl-i], *adv.* in a sportful manner.

SPORTFULNESS, [spawt'-fŏŏl-nes], *n.* the quality of being sportful.

SPORTING, [spawt'-ing], *adj.* devoted to sports, *esp.* athletics, sportsmanlike; **s. chance,** a possibility having a risk, but with a reasonable likelihood of success.

SPORTIVE, [spawt'-iv], *adj.* playful, frolicsome.

SPORTIVELY, [spawt'-iv-li], *adv.* in a sportive manner.

SPORTIVENESS, [spawt'-iv-nes], *n.* the fact or quality of being sportive.

SPORTLESS, [spawt'-les], *adj.* without sport.

SPORTS JACKET, [spawts'-jak'-et], *n.* a kind of loose jacket, usually made of tweed, suitable for quite informal occasions.

SPORTSMAN, [spawts'-man], *n.* one indulging in athletic activities; a good fellow, a fair, honourable, manly person.

SPORTSMANLIKE, [spawts'-man-līk], *adj.* like or befitting a sportsman, chivalrous, fair-minded.

SPORTSMANSHIP, [spawts'-man-ship], *n.* the qualities of a sportsman.

SPORTSWOMAN, [spawts'-wŏŏm-an], *n.* a woman who indulges in sports.

SPORULE, [spo'-rewl], *n.* a small spore.

SPORULIFEROUS, [spor'-yōōl-if'-er-us], *adj.* bearing sporules.

SPOT (1), [spot], *n.* a small marking, a patch of different colour on a surface, a stain, discoloration, a pimple on the skin; a blemish; a specific place, *esp.* one of very small extent; (*billiards*) the place on the table from which balls are played at the commencement of the game; a black mark on one ball to distinguish it from the other; (*coll.*) a small quantity of drink or food; **s. cash,** payment on delivery; **on the s.,** in a difficult situation, in imminent danger from one's enemies, called to account; **in a s.,** (*U.S.*) in difficulties. [ME. *spot*].

SPOT (2), [spot], *v.t. and i.* to stain, mark with spots; to see, catch sight of, detect; to become marked or spotted.

SPOTLESS, [spot'-les], *adj.* without blemish.

SPOTLESSLY, [spot'-les-li], *adv.* to a spotless degree.

SPOTLESSNESS, [spot'-les-nes], *n.* the state of being spotless.

SPOTLIGHT, [spot'-līt'], *n.* a light that is capable of being directed on a particular spot, *esp.* on a stage; that which draws attention to a particular person or happening.

SPOTTED, [spot'-ed], *pret. and p.pt.* of SPOT.

SPOTTED DOG, [spot'-ed-dog'], *n.* (*coll.*) a Dalmatian dog; a rolled suet pudding containing currants.

SPOTTEDNESS, [spot'-ed-nes], *n.* the quality of being spotted.

SPOTTER, [spot'-er], *n.* one who spots; one who keeps a look-out, *esp.* for impending attack from enemy aircraft.

SPOTTINESS, [spot'-i-nes], *n.* the state of being spotty.

SPOTTY, [spot'-i], *adj.* covered with spots, pimpled.

SPOUSAL, [spowz'-al], *n.* espousal. [~ESPOUSAL].

SPOUSE, [spowz], *n.* a husband or wife. [OFr. *espouse*].

SPOUSELESS, [spowz'-les], *adj.* without a spouse.

SPOUT (1), [spowt], *n.* narrow projection at the orifice of a vessel, serving to direct the flow of its contents, a moulded projection conveying rainwater from a roof, the blow-hole of a whale; a violent gush, jet of water; **down the s.,** lost, ruined irretrievably; **up the s.,** in pawn.

SPOUT (2), [spowt], *v.t. and i.* to gush forth in a strong jet; (*fig.*) to orate copiously; to pour, spurt out in a stream; to declaim copiously. [ME. *spouten*].

SPOUTER, [spowt'-er], *n.* one who, or that which, spouts.

SPOUT-HOLE, [spowt'-hōl], *n.* the spiracle of a whale.

SPOUTLESS, [spowt'-les], *adj.* having no spout.

SPRACK, [sprak], *adj.* brisk, sprightly. [Unkn.].

SPRAG (1), [sprag], *n.* a wooden block used to check a wheel; a mining prop. [Uncert.].

SPRAG (2), [sprag], *n.* a young cod. [Unkn.].

SPRAIN (1), [sprān], *n.* a twist of the muscles or ligaments, leading to painful inflammation.

SPRAIN (2), [sprān], *v.t.* to strain, twist the muscles or ligaments of so as to produce painful and incapacitating inflammation. [OFr. *espreindre*].

SPRAINED, [sprānd], *adj.* affected by a sprain.

SPRAINTS, [sprānts], *n.(pl.)* otter dung. [OFr. *espraintes*].

SPRANG, [sprang], *pret.* of SPRING.

SPRAT, [sprat], *n.* the small sea-fish, *Clupea sprattus*. [OE. *sprott*].

SPRAWL (1), [sprawl], *n.* the act, position, of sprawling.

SPRAWL (2), [sprawl], *v.i.* to sit or recline with the limbs loosely and casually splayed out, to lie or sit in an attitude of ungainly relaxation; (*fig.*) to spread out or over widely and in ugly disorder. [ME. *sprawlen*].

SPRAWLER, [sprawl'-er], *n.* one who sprawls.

SPRAY (1), [sprā], *n.* a flowering branch, a design representing or imitating such a branch. [ME. *sprai*].

SPRAY (2), [sprā], *n.* spume, fine particles of liquid squirted through the air; wind-blown particles of sea-water; a mechanical device for producing a spray, an atomizer. [LGerm. *sprei*].

SPRAY (3), [sprā], *v.t. and i.* to scatter in spray, dampen, disinfect with a spray; to become spray.

SPRAYER, [sprā'-er], *n.* an implement for spraying, a spray.

SPREAD (1), [spred], *n.* the act of spreading, the condition or extent of being spread; the process of diffusion, increasing extension of anything; (*coll.*) a great feast, a table provided with a large amount of food.

SPREAD (2), [spred], *v.t. and i.* to make to cover a larger surface by reducing in height and increasing in length or breadth, *esp.* so to do by pressing out (a substance); to disseminate, scatter widely, cause to be diffused; to circulate, proclaim widely; (*reflex.*) to indulge in self-assertion, be assertively profuse; to extend over a larger surface; to open out (as wings); to be diffused; **to s. out,** to unfold, be unfolded. [OE. *sprædan*].

SPREAD-EAGLE (1), [spred'-ēgl], *n.* (*her.*) an eagle displayed; a bird split open and broiled.

SPREAD-EAGLE (2), [spred'-ēgl], *adj.* (*U.S.*) bombastic.

SPREAD-EAGLE (3), [spred'-ēgl], *v.t.* to tie up with the arms and legs spread out to the fullest extent.

SPREAD-EAGLISM, [spred'-ēgl'-izm], *n.* (*U.S.*) bombastic patriotism.

SPREADER (1), [spred'-er], *n.* that which spreads.

SPREADER (2), [spred'-er], *n.* a crosstree.

SPREADING, [spred'-ing], *adj.* extended, extending, tending to spread.

SPREADOVER, [spred'-ōv-er], *n. and adj.* (relating to) a system by which the weekly quota of working hours may be made up in spells greater (or less) than the average daily amount. [SPREAD (2) and OVER (3)].

SPREE, [sprē], *n.* a bout of drinking and debauchery; a holiday prank, a lark. [Ir. *spre* spark].

SPRIG, [sprig], *n.* a small branching twig, a spray; a headless nail; an off-shoot, a young man. [ME. *sprigge*].

SPRIG-CRYSTAL, [sprig'-kris'-tal], *n.* a cluster of pointed prismatic crystals of quartz.

SPRIGGY, [sprig'-i], *adj.* full of sprigs or small branches.

SPRIGHT, [sprīt], *n.* a sprite. [SPRITE].

SPRIGHTFUL, [sprīt'-ful], *adj.* sprightly.

SPRIGHTLESS, [sprīt'-les], *adj.* dull, spiritless.

SPRIGHTLINESS, [sprīt'-li-nes], *n.* the state of being sprightly; liveliness; briskness; activity.

SPRIGHTLY, [sprīt'-li], *adj.* lively, bright, vivacious, gay and jolly.

SPRING (1), [spring], *n.* the act of springing, the capacity of so doing, the distance sprung, resilience; any body (*esp.* bent metal) tending to return to its original shape or position after distortion by pressure, and so used to store energy; the quality of recoil and bounce possessed by such an object; (*fig.*) mental resilience; that which springs from anything, *esp.* a stream of water rising from the ground; the time of annual vegetable rebirth, the period between winter and summer; the source, origin, or initiating force of anything; (*arch.*) the starting-point of a curve.

SPRING (2), (sprang, sprung), [spring], *v.t. and i.* to leap upwards or forwards by contraction and release of the muscles, or by the release from pressure of an elastic substance; to bound swiftly and suddenly in any direction, *esp.* on to something; to move very rapidly; (*fig.*) to come very rapidly into some position; to gush up (as water) from a source, to arise from, have origin in, to sprout up from the ground, to come into existence, to emerge; (of timber) to become warped, begin leaking; to cause to move, recoil, rapidly; to set off, cause to happen rapidly, to announce unexpectedly; (of wood) to cause to split, warp; to provide with springs. [OE. *springan*].

SPRINGAL†, [spring'-al], *n.* a medieval military engine. [OFr. *espringale*].

SPRINGALD†, [spring'-ald], *n.* a youth. [ME. *springald*].

SPRING-BACK, [spring'-bak'], *n.* a loose-leaf book cover holding the pages by means of a spring.

SPRING-BALANCE, [spring'-bal'-ants], *n.* an instrument measuring weights by means of a spring.

SPRING-BOARD, [spring'-bawd], *n.* a resilient plank used to give impetus for diving.

SPRINGBOK, [spring'-bok], *n.* an African antelope allied to the gazelle, *Antidorcas euchore.* [Du. *springen* to spring and *bok* antelope].

SPRING-BOX, [spring'-boks'], *n.* the barrel containing the mainspring of a watch.

SPRING-CARRIAGE, [spring'-ka'-rij], *n.* a carriage supported on springs.

SPRING-CART, [spring'-kaht], *n.* a cart or carriage, the body of which is supported on springs.

SPRINGE, [sprinj], *n.* a snare for catching birds and small game. [~SPRING (1)].

SPRINGER, [spring'-er], *n.* one who, or that which, springs; a kind of spaniel; (*arch.*) the lowest part of the curve of an arch.

SPRING-GUN, [spring'-gun], *n.* a gun set to go off by the action of trespassers stumbling on to it.

SPRINGHALT, [spring'-hawlt], *n.* the jerk of a horse's leg in walking.

SPRING-HEAD, [spring'-hed'], *n.* a source, origin; spring of water.

SPRINGINESS, [spring'-i-nes], *n.* the state of being springy; elasticity; sponginess.

SPRINGING, [spring'-ing], *n.* the springer of an arch; the sprouting of plants.

SPRINGLESS, [spring'-les], *adj.* devoid of springs.

SPRINGLET, [spring'-let], *n.* a small spring or stream.

SPRINGTAIL, [spring'-tāl], *n.* an insect of the sub-order *Collembola.*

SPRINGTIDE, [spring'-tīd], *n.* the great tide occurring at new and full moon.

SPRINGTIME, [spring'-tīm], *n.* the spring of the year.

SPRING-WHEAT, [spring'-wēt'], *n.* wheat sown in spring.

SPRINGY, [spring'-i], *adj.* resilient, elastic.

SPRINKLE (1), [springkl], *n.* a light scattering of liquid or of solid particles.

SPRINKLE (2), [springkl], *v.t. and i.* to scatter, strew in small drops or particles; to fall in small particles. [ME *sprenkelen*].

SPRINKLER, [springk'-ler], *n.* that which sprinkles, *esp.* a device for fighting fires.

SPRINKLING, [springk'-ling], *n.* a few drops, a few scattered objects.

SPRINT (1), [sprint], *n.* a short dash, a short burst of running at full speed.

SPRINT (2), [sprint], *v.i.* to run at full speed for a short distance. [~OIcel. *spretta*].

SPRINTER, [sprint'-er], *n.* one who sprints.

SPRIT, [sprit], *n.* a spar extending from the mast in an upward diagonal. [ME. *sprete*].

SPRITE, [sprīt], *n.* an elf, a fairy. [*Var.* of SPIRIT].

SPRITSAIL, [sprit'-sal], *n.* (*naut.*) a triangular sail extended by a sprit.

SPROCKET, [sprok'-it], *n.* (*arch.*) a triangular piece of wood used in strengthening wooden frames; (*eng.*) a projection on a gearwheel to engage with a chain; a wheel with such toothed projections on its periphery. [Unkn.].

SPROUT (1), [sprowt], *n.* a young shoot; (*pl.*) the young colewort, brussels-sprouts.

SPROUT (2), [sprowt], *v.t. and i.* to put forth buds, shoots, etc.; to begin to grow; to grow up rapidly; to give forth as by growth. [OE. *sprutan*].

SPRUCE (1), [sproōs], *n.* a coniferous tree related to the pine. [ME. *Spruce* Prussia].

SPRUCE (2), [sproōs], *adj.* neat, spry, dapper. [~*Prec.*].

SPRUCE (3), [sproōs], *v.t.* to make spruce.

SPRUCE-BEER, [sproōs'-bēer], *n.* beer made from the leaves of the spruce.

SPRUCELY, [sproōs'-li], *adv.* in a spruce manner.

SPRUCENESS, [sproōs'-nes], *n.* the quality of being spruce.

SPRUE (1), [sprew], *n.* an aperture for pouring molten metal into a mould; the metal clinging to this aperture. [Unkn.].

SPRUE (2), [sprew], *n.* a tropical disease characterized by enteritis and ulceration of the mouth. [Du. *spruw*].

SPRUIT, [sproit], *n.* a watercourse that is dry except after rain. [Du. *spruit*].

SPRUNG, [sprung], *p.pt.* of SPRING. [OE. *gesprungen*].

SPRY, [sprī], *adj.* brisk, nimble, quick, mentally active, sharp. [Uncert.].

SPUD, [spud], *n.* a small spade; (*slang*) a potato. [ME. *spudde*].

SPUE, see SPEW.

SPUME, [spewm], *n.* foam, froth. [L. *spuma*].

SPUMESCENCE, [spewm-es'-ents], *n.* the state of being spumy.

SPUMESCENT, [spewm-es'-ent], *adj.* foaming. [L. *spumescens*].

SPUMIFEROUS, [spewm-i'-fe-rus], *adj.* producing foam. [L. *spumifer*].

SPUMINESS, [spewm'-i-nes], *n.* the state of being spumy.

SPUMOUS, [spewm'-us], *adj.* spumy. [L. *spumosus*].

SPUMY, [spewm'-i], *adj.* frothy, foamy.

SPUN, [spun], *p.pt.* of SPIN. [OE. *gespunnen*].

SPUN-HAY, [spun'-hā], *n.* strands of hay twisted together.
SPUNK, [spungk], *n.* touchwood; (*coll.*) courage, spirit. [Unkn.].
SPUNKY, [spungk'-i], *adj.* spirited.
SPUN-OUT, [spun'-owt], *adj.* made lengthy.
SPUNYARN, [spun'-yahn'], *n.* rope made of several twisted strands.
SPUR (1), [spur], *n.* a spike or pricking device worn on the heel to goad on a horse; any sharp, pointed projection resembling a spur, *esp.* the horny spike on the leg of a cock; (*fig.*) an incitement, encouragement, goad to endeavour; **to win one's spurs,** to receive knighthood; to attain honour in any profession. [OE. *spora*].
SPUR (2), [spur], *v.t. and i.* to goad, urge on with a spur, to equip with spurs; to use spurs, to ride fast and furiously.
SPUR-DOG, [spur'-dog'], *n.* the shark, *Acanthias vulgaris.*
SPUR-GALL, [spur'-gawl], *n.* a gall or excoriation produced by a spur.
SPURGE, [spurj], *n.* a plant of the genus *Euphorbia.* [OFr. *espurge*].
SPUR-GEARING, [spur'-gēer-ing], *n.* gearing with spur-wheels.
SPURIOUS, [spyōōer'-i-us], *adj.* counterfeit, not genuine; (*biol.*) resembling some organ in appearance but differing from it in function. [L. *spurius*].
SPURIOUSLY, [spyōōer'-i-us-li], *adv.* in a spurious manner.
SPURIOUSNESS, [spyōōer'-i-us-nes], *n.* the quality of being spurious; illegitimacy.
SPURLESS, [spur'-les], *adj.* without spurs.
SPURLING, [spur'-ling], *n.* the smelt, *Osmerus eperlanus*; the sparling. [MLGerm. *spirling*].
SPURLING-LINE, [spur'-ling-līn], *n.* a cord connecting the helm with an indicator. [Unkn.].
SPURN, [spurn], *v.t.* to thrust at, strike, with the foot; to drive away rudely and scornfully, to reject with disdain. [OE. *spurnan* to kick].
SPURNER, [spurn'-er], *n.* one who spurns.
SPURRED, [spurd], *adj.* wearing spurs.
SPURRER, [spur'-er], *n.* one who uses spurs; incitement.
SPURREY, [spu'-ri], *n.* a weed of the genus *Spergula.* [OFr. *spurrie*].
SPURRIER, [spu'-ri-er], *n.* a maker of spurs.
SPUR-ROYAL, [spur'-roi'-al], *n.* a Jacobean gold coin, bearing on its reverse a star resembling a rowel.
SPURT (1), [spurt], *n.* a sudden gush of fluid, flame, etc.; a sudden dash of speed.
SPURT (2), [spurt], *v.t. and i.* to give out a gush of liquid; to gush out in a sudden violent jet; to make a brief but violent increase of speed in running, or of effort in any contest. [OE. *spryttan*].
SPUR-WAY, [spur'-wā], *n.* a bridle-path.
SPUR-WHEEL, [spur'-wēl], *n.* a cogged wheel like a rowel.
SPUR-WINGED, [spur'-wingd], *adj.* (*ornith.*) having a spur on the pinion.
SPUTTER (1), [sput'-er], *n.* the act, noise, of sputtering.
SPUTTER (2), [sput'-er], *v.t. and i.* to make a sound of spitting and spluttering, to speak with such a sound. [Du. *sputteren*].
SPUTTERER, [sput'-er-er], *n.* one who sputters.
SPUTUM, [spewt'-um], *n.* matter that is coughed up. [L. *sputum*].
SPY (1), [spī], *n.* one practising espionage, or keeping another under secret observation, one engaged in discovering what is intended to be secret. [OFr. *espie*].
SPY (2), [spī], *v.t. and i.* to seek to discover secrets, *esp.* of a national or military character on behalf of another country; to espy, observe; **to s. on,** to watch secretly the movements of. [OFr. *espier*].
SPY-BOAT, [spī'-bōt], *n.* a small naval scouting-vessel.
SPY-GLASS, [spī'-glahs], *n.* a small telescope.
SPYHOLE, [spī'-hōl], *n.* an inconspicuous hole for observation.
SPYISM, [spī'-izm], *n.* the act of spying, business of a spy.
SPY-MONEY, [spī'-mun-i], *n.* payment for spying.
SQUAB (1), [skwob], *n.* a nestling pigeon; a sofa; a squab person.
SQUAB (2), [skwob], *adj.* short, squat and plump. [~Swed. *skvabb* loose flesh].
SQUABBISH, [skwob'-ish], *adj.* squabby.
SQUABBLE (1), [skwobl], *n.* a petty, undignified, noisy quarrel. [~Swed. *skvabbel* a quarrel].
SQUABBLE (2), [skwobl], *v.i.* to engage in a squabble.
SQUABBLER, [skwob'-ler], *n.* one who tends to squabble.
SQUABBY, [skwob'-i], *adj.* squab.
SQUAB-PIE, [skwob'-pī], *n.* pigeon-pie; meat-and-apple pie.
SQUACCO, [skwak'-ō], *n.* the squacco heron, *Ardea ralloides.* [It. *squacco*].
SQUAD, [skwod], *n.* a small military detachment, *esp.* a small detachment engaged in drill or physical exercise; (*fig.*) a small, loosely organized group. [It. *squadra* square].
SQUADRON (1), [skwod'-run], *n.* a body of cavalry, usually of about 200 men; a group of warships under the command of a flag-officer; a group of some twelve military aeroplanes; **s. leader,** a rank in the Royal Air Force equivalent to that of major in the Army. [It. *squadrone*].
SQUADRON (2), [skwod'-run], *v.t.* to marshal into a squadron.
SQUAILS, [skwālz], *n.* a game analogous to shove-halfpenny, in which counters are flipped from the edge of the table. [Unkn.].
SQUALID, [skwol'-id], *adj.* dirty, sordid and dingy, mean and poverty-stricken; base, unworthy. [L. *squalidus*].
SQUALIDITY, [skwol-id'-it-i], *n.* squalidness.
SQUALIDLY, [skwol'-id-li], *adv.* in a squalid manner.
SQUALIDNESS, [skwol'-id-nes], *n.* the state of being squalid.
SQUALL (1), [skwawl], *n.* a briefly violent storm of wind; (*fig.*) trouble, discordance, a brief quarrel; a loud, harsh, and unharmonious cry.
SQUALL (2), [skwawl], *v.t. and i.* to utter a squall, to sound loudly and unharmoniously; to utter with a squall. [~OIcel. *skvala* to squeal].
SQUALLER, [skwawl'-er], *n.* one who squalls.
SQUALLY, [skwawl'-i], *adj.* marked by squalls.
SQUALOID, [skwā'-loid], *adj.* resembling a shark. [L. *squalus* shark and Gk. *oeides* like].
SQUALOR, [skwol'-er], *n.* the state of being sordid, dirty and depressing poverty. [L. *squalor* filth].
SQUAMA, [skwā'-ma], *n.* a scale. [L. *squama*].
SQUAMATE, [skwā'-māt], *adj.* scaly. [~L. *squama* a scale].
SQUAMIFORM, [skwā'-mi-fawm], *adj.* having the form of scales.
SQUAMIGEROUS, [skwā-mij'-er-us], *adj.* bearing scales. [L. *squama* scale and *gerere* to bear].
SQUAMOID, [skwā'-moid], *adj.* like a scale. [L. *squama* scale and Gk. *oeides* like].
SQUAMOSAL, [skwā-mōs'-al], *n.* the scaly part of the temporal bone.
SQUAMOSE, [skwā'-mōs], *adj.* squamous. [L. *squamosus*].
SQUAMOUS, [skwā'-mus], *adj.* scaly; covered with scales.
SQUANDER, [skwond'-er], *v.t.* to spend lavishly and wastefully, to dissipate, to expend foolishly. [Uncert.].
SQUANDERER, [skwond'-er-er], *n.* one who squanders.
SQUANDERINGLY, [skwond'-er-ing-li], *adv.* so as to squander.
SQUARE (1), [skwāer], *n.* a plane rectangular figure with four equal sides, anything in the shape of a square; an open space in a town, *esp.* when containing a railed garden in the centre; (*math.*) the product of a quantity multiplied by itself; (*geom.*) an instrument for determining right angles; troops drawn up in a defensive square formation; **on the s.,** honest, on the level. [OFr. *esquare* from L. *quadra*].

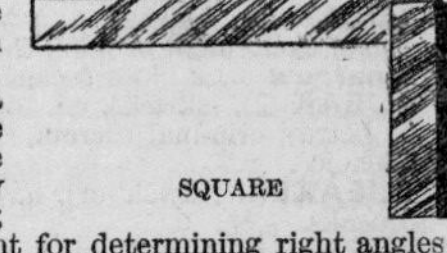
SQUARE

SQUARE (2), [skwāer], *adj.* in the shape or figure of a square, resembling a square, (of persons) short and broad, (of shoulders) straight, not hunched forward; (*math.*) relating to a square; on even terms, with liabilities settled, level; (*coll.*) honest, straightforward; **all s.,** with level scores; **to get s. with,** to be revenged upon, get even with.
SQUARE (3), [skwāer], *adv.* so as to form a right angle; honestly.
SQUARE (4), [skwāer], *v.t. and i.* to make square in shape; (*math.*) to multiply a quantity by itself; (of the shoulders, etc.) to draw back and up, to straighten; to adapt, to reconcile an idea (with a fact); to bribe, to persuade to connive at some illicit action; to be

in agreement (with), harmonize (with); **to s. up,** to adopt a fighting attitude; to settle debts.

SQUAREHEAD, [skwāer′-hed′], *n.* (*U.S.*) a Teuton or Scandinavian.

SQUARELY, [skwāer′-li], *adv.* so as to form a square, at right angles; in square fashion; directly facing.

SQUARE MEASURE, [skwāer′-mezh′-er], *n.* the square of a lineal measure.

SQUARENESS, [skwāer′-nes], *n.* the state of being square; fairness.

SQUARE-RIGGED, [skwāer′-rigd], *adj.* (*naut.*) with horizontal yards, at right angles to the keel.

SQUARE-ROOT, [skwāer′-rōōt], *n.* (*math.*) a number's base or root which, when multiplied by itself, produces that number.

SQUARE-SAIL, [skwāer′-sāl], *n.* a four-cornered sail supported on a yard lying across the mast.

SQUARE-TOED, [skwāer′-tōd], *adj.* with square toes or toe-caps.

SQUARE-TOES, [skwāer′-tōz], *n.* a precise, puritanical person.

SQUARISH, [skwāer′-ish], *adj.* nearly square.

SQUARROSE, [skwo-rōs′], *adj.* rough, scaly. [LL. *squarrosus*].

SQUARSON, [skwah′-sun], *n.* a parson who is also the squire. [SQU(IRE) and (P)ARSON].

SQUASH (1), [skwosh], *n.* a close packing together, a great crowding; the state of being reduced to pulp; drink made from crushed fruits; squash-rackets.

SQUASH (2), [skwosh], *n.* a thick, fleshy fruit eaten as a staple by American Indians. [NAmerInd. *askutasquash*].

SQUASH (3), [skwosh], *v.t. and i.* to pack, squeeze together so as to crush, to press into pulp; (*fig.*) to silence and disconcert; to become crushed, pressed to pulp. [ME. *squacchen*].

SQUASH-BUG, [skwosh′-bug], *n.* the hemipterous insect, *Coreus tristis*, destructive to gourds.

SQUASHER, [skwosh′-er], *n.* one who squashes.

SQUASH-RACKETS, [skwosh′-rak′-its], *n.* a variety of rackets played by two persons with a soft ball.

SQUASHY, [skwosh′-i], *adj.* tending to squash, soft moist and pulpy.

SQUAT (1), [skwot], *adj.* short and thick, stumpy.

SQUAT (2), [skwot], *v.i.* to sit back on the heels, to crouch with the legs drawn up to the body; to settle on land without right or permission; to occupy unenclosed and unclaimed land as a settler. [ME. *squatten*].

SQUATTER, [skwot′-er], *n.* one who squats; one who settles on land without permission; one who settles on government land in the colonies, with a view to eventual ownership.

SQUATTINESS, [skwot′-i-nes], *n.* the state of being squatty.

SQUATTY, [skwot′-i], *adj.* squat.

SQUAW, [skwaw], *n.* an American Indian married woman. [NAmerInd. *squa* woman].

SQUAWK (1), [skwawk], *n.* a short, harsh cry, as of an inharmonious bird, *esp.* a cry of pain or complaint. [Imitative].

SQUAWK (2), [skwawk], *v.i.* to utter a squawk; (*slang*) to betray a criminal undertaking.

SQUAWMAN, [skwaw′-man′], *n.* a white man with an American Indian wife.

SQUEAK (1), [skwēk], *n.* a weak, thin, piercing cry, *esp.* of excitement or pain, the cry made by a mouse; **a narrow s.,** a close escape.

SQUEAK (2), [skwēk], *v.i.* to utter a squeak; (*slang*) to betray criminal secrets, inform on a criminal. [Echoic].

SQUEAKER, [skwēk′-er], *n.* one who, or that which, squeaks.

SQUEAL (1), [skwēl], *n.* a shrill, prolonged, high-pitched cry of pain or excitement.

SQUEAL (2), [skwēl], *v.i.* to utter a squeal; (*slang*) to betray a person or undertaking. [ME. *squelen*].

SQUEALER, [skwēl′-er], *n.* one who squeals.

SQUEAMISH, [skwēm′-ish], *adj.* fastidious, easily nauseated, over-scrupulous. [ME. *squeimous*].

SQUEAMISHLY, [skwēm′-ish-li], *adv.* in a squeamish manner.

SQUEAMISHNESS, [skwēm′-ish-nes], *n.* the condition of being squeamish.

SQUEASINESS, [skwēz′-i-nes], *n.* squeamishness.

SQUEASY, [skwēz′-i], *adj.* squeamish. [*Var.* of QUEASY].

SQUEEGEE, [skwē′-jē′], *n.* a strip of rubber used as a broom on wet surfaces; a similar implement or a rubber roller used for pressing wet photographic prints on to glazing plates; a squeezer. [~SQUEEZE].

SQUEEZABLE, [skwēz′-abl], *adj.* able to be squeezed; amenable to pressure.

SQUEEZE (1), [skwēz], *n.* the act of squeezing, state of being squeezed, a crowding together; an impression, taken by pressure, on a soft surface.

SQUEEZE (2), [skwēz], *v.t. and i.* to press, compress slowly but firmly; to extract moisture by pressure; (*fig.*) to bring moral pressure upon, to constrain by persuasion or threat; to pack, press in tightly; (*bridge*) to play a suit in which one's opponent is short, so as to force the discard of a valuable card, to take an impression on a plastic surface; to get through or into by squeezing. [OE. *cwesan*].

SQUEEZER, [skwēz′-er], *n.* one who, or that which, squeezes.

SQUEEZING, [skwēz′-ing], *n.* the act of compression; that which is extracted by pressure.

SQUELCH (1), [skwelch], *n.* the sound of squelching.

SQUELCH (2), [skwelch], *v.i.* to make a splashing, smacking sound as of watery suction; to walk through mud and produce this sound. [Imitative].

SQUIB, [skwib], *n.* a small exploding firework; an ephemeral lampoon. [Uncert.].

SQUID, [skwid], *n.* a long-tentacled cuttle-fish; an artificial bait in imitation of a squid. [Uncert.].

SQUID

SQUIFFY, [skwif′-i], *adj.* (*coll.*) slightly intoxicated. [Unkn.].

SQUIGGLE (1), [skwigl], *n.* (*coll.*) a wriggly line or flourish. [SQU(IRM) and (WR)IGGLE].

SQUIGGLE (2), [skwigl], *v.i.* to swill out the mouth. [Uncert.].

SQUILL, [skwil], *n.* a genus of plants related to the lily, used in medicine. [OFr. *squille*].

SQUILLITIC, [skwil-it′-ik], *adj.* pertaining to a squill.

SQUINANCYWORT, [skwin′-an-si-wurt], *n.* (*bot.*) the quinsy wort, *Asperula cynanchica.* [MedL. *squinancia* quinsy and WORT].

SQUINCH, [skwinch], *n.* (*arch.*) an arch crossing an interior right angle. [~SCONCE].

SQUINT (1), [skwint], *n.* a condition of the eyes in which both cannot look in the same direction at the same time; an oblique look; a narrow observation hole through a wall. [ME. *a-squint*].

SQUINT (2), [skwint], *v.i.* to look, gaze in a squinting fashion; to peer obliquely.

SQUINT-EYED, [skwint′-īd], *adj.* squinting.

SQUINTING, [skwint′-ing], *adj.* tending to squint.

SQUINTINGLY, [skwint′-ing-li], *adv.* in a squinting fashion.

SQUIRE, [skwīer′], *n.* the body-servant of a medieval knight; a country landowner; a gallant. [~ESQUIRE].

SQUIREARCHY, [skwīer′-ahk-i], *n.* (*coll.*) country gentlemen as a body, *esp.* as a ruling class.

SQUIREEN, [skwīer-ēn′], *n.* a petty squire.

SQUIREHOOD, [skwīer′-hōōd], *n.* the state and rank of a squire.

SQUIRESHIP, [skwīer′-ship], *n.* squirehood.

SQUIRM, [skwurm], *v.t. and i.* to wriggle, writhe the body; to feel humiliated. [Uncert.].

SQUIRREL, [skwi′-rel], *n.* a rodent of the genus *Sciurus.* [OFr. *escurel*].

SQUIRREL-MONKEY, [skwi′-rel-mung′-ki], *n.* a South American monkey of the genus *Chrysothrix.*

SQUIRT (1), [skwurt], *n.* a spurt of liquid; an instrument for producing such a spurt; an insignificant fellow.

SQUIRT (2), [skwurt], *v.t. and i.* to emit, spray with, a jet of liquid. [~LGerm. *swirtjen*].

SQUIRREL

SQUIRTER, [skwurt′-er], *n.* one who, or that which, squirts.

SQUIRTING-CUCUMBER, [skwurt′-ing-kew′-kum-ber], *n.* (*bot.*) a cucumber which bursts its capsules on falling when ripe, *Ecballium elaterium.*

SQUISH, [skwish], *n.* (*coll.*) marmalade. [Echoic].

SRADDHA, [srad′-a], *n.* Hindu funeral oblations. [Skr. *sraddha*].

SRUTI [srōō′-ti], *n.* the sacred tradition of the Hindus. [Skr. *sruti*].

ST., contraction for SAINT.

STAB (1), [stab], *n.* a sudden, fierce thrust with a sharp instrument; (*coll.*) a sudden, treacherous attack; **a s. at,** (*coll.*) an attempt to. [~Swed. *stäbbe* stump].

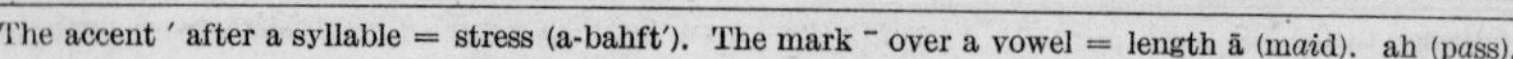

STAB (2), [stab], *v.t. and i.* to pierce, wound with a stab to jab at with a sharp instrument. [*Prec.*].
STABBER, [stab'-er], *n.* one who stabs.
STABILIMENT, [stab-il'-i-ment], *n.* the act of stabilizing.
STABILITY, [stab-il'-it-i], *n.* the state of being stable. [L. *stabilitas*].
STABILIZATION, [stab'-il-īz-ā'-shun], *n.* the process of making or becoming stable.
STABILIZE, [stā'-bil-īz], *v.t.* to make stable, to steady, to confirm. [~L. *stabilis* firm].
STABILIZER, [stā'-bil-īz-er], *n.* one who, or that which, stabilizes.
STABLE (1), [stābl], *n.* a building for keeping horses; a group of racehorses under one ownership. [L. *stabulum*].
STABLE (2), [stābl], *adj.* steady, in equilibrium, firm, well-founded, consistent; (*chem.*) resisting decomposition. [L. *stabilis*].
STABLE (3), [stābl], *v.t.* to put in a stable.
STABLEBOY, [stābl'-boi], *n.* a boy who works in a stable.
STABLEMAN, [stābl'-man], *n.* a man looking after horses in a stable.
STABLENESS, [stābl'-nes], *n.* the condition of being stable.
STABLING, [stāb'-ling], *n.* accommodation for horses in stables.
STABLISH†, [stab'-lish], *v.t.* to establish.
STABLY, [stāb'-li], *adv.* in stability.
STACCATO, [stak-aht'-o], *adv.* (*mus.*) with notes played abruptly and distinctly. [It. *staccato*].
STACK (1), [stak], *n.* a regular pile of hay; an orderly heap; the funnel of a ship or engine; a cluster of chimneys; a tall chimney; **s.-stand,** a stage on which to pile a stack. [OIcel. *stakkr*].
STACK (2), [stak], *v.t.* to arrange in a stack.
STACKYARD, [stak'-yahd], *n.* a yard or enclosure for stacks of hay or corn.
STADDA, [stad'-a], *n.* a saw with a double blade. [Uncert.].
STADDLE, [stadl], *n.* a crutch; a stack-stand. [OE. *stathol*].
STADDLE-ROOF, [stadl'-rōōf], *n.* a covering for a stack forming a canopy over a staddle.
STADIUM, [stăd'-i-um], *n.* a Greek unit of length; a track for athletics; a sports arena. [Gk. *stadion*].
STADTHOLDER, [staht'-hōld'-er], *n.* (*hist.*) the head of the former Dutch Republic. [Germ. *stadthalter*].
STADTHOLDERATE, [staht'-hōld'-er-āt], *n.* the office of stadtholder.
STADTHOLDERSHIP, [staht'-hōld'-er-ship], *n.* the office and rank of a stadtholder.
STAFF, (*pl.* **staffs** or **staves**), [stahf], *n.* a long, slender rod, a pole, a wand of authority, a support; a group of persons working under a single direction to perform some organizational function, military or civil; the five parallel lines on which music is written; **s. notation,** musical notation on staves. [OE. *stæf*].
STAFF-OFFICER, [stahf'-of'-is-er], *n.* an officer attached to a military general staff.
STAG, [stag], *n.* the male red deer; a bachelor; **s. party,** an all-male gathering. [~OIcel. *steggr* male bird].
STAG-BEETLE, [stag'-bētl], *n.* the beetle, *Lucanus cervus,* which has projecting antler-like mandibles in the male.
STAGE (1), [stāj], *n.* a platform, a raised scaffolding; that part of a theatre on which the play is performed; acting as a profession; the theatre, the drama; the scene of an action; a halting place; a period of development. [OFr. *estage*].
STAGE (2), [stāj], *v.t.* to present on the stage; to arrange for dramatic effect.

STAG-BEETLE

STAGE-COACH, [stāj'-kōch], *n.* a horse-drawn coach, with regular route and stopping places.
STAGECRAFT, [stāj'-krahft], *n.* skill in theatrical production, writing, or presentation.
STAGE DOOR, [stāj'-daw(r)'], *n.* the door by which stage performers enter the theatre.
STAGE-DRIVER, [stāj'-drīv'-er], *n.* the driver of a stage-coach.
STAGE FRIGHT, [stāj'-frīt'], *n.* nervous disability and fear when appearing before audiences.
STAGE-MANAGE, [stāj'-man'-ij], *v.t.* to arrange so as to produce an intended effect.
STAGE-MANAGER, [stāj'-man'-ij-er], *n.* the person responsible for the general arrangements for a stage performance.
STAGE-PLAY, [stāj'-plā], *n.* a drama presentable on the stage.
STAGER, [stāg'-er], *n.* one who stages; **old s.,** an experienced person.
STAGERY, [stāj'-er-i], *n.* an exhibition on a stage; stage technique.
STAGE-STRUCK, [stāj'-struk], *adj.* keenly desirous of entering the theatrical profession.
STAG-EVIL, [stag'-ēv'-il], *n.* paralysis of the jaw in horses.
STAGE-WHISPER, [stāj'-wis'-per], *n.* a loud whisper meant to be heard by other people, as by the audience in a theatre.
STAGGARD, [stag'-erd], *n.* a four-year-old stag.
STAGGER (1), [stag'-er], *n.* a staggering movement.
STAGGER (2), [stag'-er], *v.t. and i.* to walk unsteadily; to cause to be unsteady, to disconcert; to set (trenches, etc.) inclined at alternate angles; (of holidays, working hours, etc.) to arrange so as not to meet or coincide. [MDu. *staggeren*].
STAGGERING, [stag'-er-ing], *adj.* tending or causing to stagger.
STAGGERINGLY, [stag'-er-ing-li], *adv.* in staggering fashion.
STAGGERS, [stag'-erz], *n.* a horse and cattle disease of which staggering and reeling are symptoms.
STAGHORN, [stag'-hawn], *n.* (*bot.*) a large fern, *Platycerium*; a club-moss or lycopodium.
STAGHOUND, [stag'-hownd], *n.* a hound trained for hunting stags.
STAGINESS, [stāj'-i-nes], *n.* the quality of being stagy.
STAGING, [stāj'-ing], *n.* theatrical setting; a stage.
STAGIRITE, [stag-ī'-rīt], *n. and adj.* (one) belonging to Stagira; **the S.,** Aristotle. [Gk. *Stageira*, Aristotle's birthplace].
STAGNANCY, [stag'-nan-si], *n.* the condition of being stagnant.
STAGNANT, [stag'-nant], *adj.* (of water) not flowing, undisturbed, foul through remaining undisturbed; inactive. [L. *stagnum* pool].
STAGNANTLY, [stag'-nant-li], *adv.* in a stagnant fashion.
STAGNATE, [stag-nāt'], *v.i.* to be or become stagnant. [L. *stagnare*].
STAGNATION, [stag-nā'-shun], *n.* the state of being stagnant.
STAGY, [stāj'-i], *adj.* crudely theatrical.
STAID, [stād], *adj.* sedate, sober. [~STAY (3)].
STAIDLY, [stād'-li], *adv.* in a staid way.
STAIDNESS, [stād'-nes], *n.* the condition of being staid.
STAIN (1), [stān], *n.* a mark, a blot, a discoloration; a dark colouring matter; a moral blemish.
STAIN (2), [stān], *v.t. and i.* to discolour, to blemish, to impart a dark colour to, to blot, to mar; to become blemished; to tend to become discoloured. [OFr. *disteindre* to colour].
STAINED, [stānd], *adj.* coloured with pigments; besmirched, tarnished, sullied.
STAINER, [stān'-er], *n.* one who, or that which, stains.
STAINLESS, [stān'-les], *adj.* without stain; unblemished; that will not become stained.
STAIR, [stāer], *n.* one of a series of steps; the steps for ascending a building. [ME. *steire*].
STAIR-CARPET, [stāer'-kah'-pet], *n.* a long, narrow carpet for stairs.
STAIRCASE, [stāer'-kās], *n.* a flight of stairs.
STAIR-HEAD, [stāer'-hed], *n.* the top of a staircase.
STAIR-ROD, [stāer'-rod], *n.* a rod for securing in place a stair-carpet.
STAIRWAY, [stāer'-wā], *n.* a staircase.
STAITHE, [stāTH], *n.* a landing-stage or wharf. [OE. *stæth*].
STAKE (1), [stāk], *n.* a pointed wooden pole, such a pole to which people were tied to be burnt to death; that which is risked in a wager. [OE. *staca*].
STAKE (2), [stāk], *v.t.* to mark with a stake; to wager.
STAKE-BOAT, [stāk'-bōt], *n.* a boat used as a mark.
STAKEHOLDER, [stāk'-hold-er], *n.* one holding the stakes in a wager or other transaction.
STAKE-NET, [stāk'-net], *n.* a net stretched on stakes.
STAKHANOVITE, [stak-ahn'-ō-vīt], *n.* a worker who increases his output to an outstanding degree. [*Stakhanov* a Russian miner].
STALACTIC, [stal-ak'-tik], *adj.* like, relating to, a stalactite. [Gk. *stalaktikos*].
STALACTIFORM, [stal-ak'-ti-fawm], *adj.* like a stalactite in shape, appearance or formation.

STALACTITE, [stal'-ak-tīt], *n.* a tapering, calcareous formation, caused by the dripping of limy water, hanging from the roofs of caverns. [Gk. *stalaktikos* dripping].

STALACTITIC, [stal'-ak-tit'-ik], *adj.* of, resembling, or relating to, a stalactite.

STALAGMITE, [stal'-ag-mīt], *n.* a tapering, calcareous formation rising from the floor of a cavern, and caused by the dripping of limy water. [Gk. *stalagmos* dropping].

STALAGMITIC, [stal'-ag-mit'-ik], *adj.* of, resembling, or relating to a stalagmite.

STALAGMITICALLY, [stal'-ag-mit'-ik-al-i], *adv.* in stalagmitic fashion.

STALDER, [stawld'-er], *n.* a frame supporting casks. [Unkn.].

STALE (1), [stāl], *n.* urine of cattle and horses. [Du. *stalle*].

STALE (2), [stāl], *adj.* not fresh, having lost, through the passage of time, some original quality, *esp.* (of food) dry, beginning to decay, having lost its flavour and nutritional value, vitiated, having lost vigour or interest, tedious. [ME. *stale*].

STALELY, [stāl'-li], *adv.* in a stale manner.

STALEMATE (1), [stāl'-māt], *n.* a position in chess in which a player cannot move without bringing his king into check, a draw; (*fig.*) a deadlock.

STALEMATE (2), [stāl'-māt'], *v.t.* to bring to a stalemate.

STALENESS, [stāl'-nes], *n.* the state of being stale; vapidness; triteness.

STALINISM, [stahl'-in-izm], *n.* the theory and practice of Stalin's interpretation of Marxism. [Josef *Stalin* Russian leader].

STALK (1), [stawk], *n.* the stem of a plant, anything resembling a stem, a long, slender support, a thin shaft. [ME. *stalke*].

STALK (2), [stawk], *n.* a stalking gait; the act of stalking game.

STALK (3), [stawk], *v.t. and i.* to walk with a long, stiff angular stride, to walk with lofty dignity; (*fig.*) to progress with silent and terrible irresistibility, to practise the stalking of game; to walk after (game), pursue (enemies) silently and remorselessly, to pursue without being observed. [ME. *stalken*].

STALKED, [stawkt], *adj.* having a stalk.

STALKER, [stawk'-er], *n.* one who stalks.

STALKING, [stawk'-ing], *n.* the practice of hunting or pursuing, game, *esp.* silently, stealthily.

STALKING-HORSE, [stawk'-ing-haws], *n.* a horse used as cover in stalking game; (*fig.*) a pretence, feigned motive.

STALKLESS, [stawk'-les], *adj.* having no stalk.

STALKY, [stawk'-i], *adj.* like a stalk.

STALL (1), [stawl], *n.* a compartment of a stable or cattle-house; a recessed seat in the choir of a church; a small booth, covered stand for selling goods in public open places, markets, etc.; the seats nearest the stage on the ground floor of a theatre; (*fig.*) the best and most comfortable situation for viewing anything; a sheath for protecting an injured finger or toe. [OE. *steall* stable].

STALL (2), [stawl], *v.t. and i.* to place in a stall; (of engines) to stop working, be interrupted; (of aeroplanes) to go out of control through cessation of engine power; to play for time, deliberately delay, avoid a direct issue; **to s. off,** to put off, keep from coming to definite settlement. [*Prec.*].

STALLAGE, [stawl'-ij], *n.* rent paid to set up a stall in a market.

STALLION, [stal'-yon], *n.* an uncastrated male horse. [OFr. *estalon*].

STALWART (1), [stawl'-wert], *n.* an unshakable supporter of a cause.

STALWART (2), [stawl'-wert], *adj.* physically strong, big and muscular; (*fig.*) strong in support of a cause. [OE. *stælwierthe* serviceable].

STALWARTLY, [stawl'-wert-li], *adv.* in a stalwart manner.

STALWARTNESS, [stawl'-wert-nes], *n.* the state of being stalwart.

STAMEN, [stā'-men], *n.* (*bot.*) the pollen-bearing organ of a flower. [L. *stamen* a warp].

STAMEN

STAMENED, [stā'-mend], *adj.* furnished with stamens.

STAMIN, [sta'-min], *n.* a coarse worsted cloth. [OFr. *stamin* from L. *stamina* warp threads].

STAMINA, [stam'-in-a], *n.* capacity for physical endurance, constitutional vigour; (*fig.*) mental toughness and stability. [L. *stamina*, *pl.* of *stamen* warp].

STAMINAL, [stam'-in-al], *adj.* relating to stamens; pertaining to, imparting, stamina.

STAMINATE, [stam'-in-āt], *adj.* having a stamen.

STAMINEAL, [stam-in'-i-al], *adj.* relating to the stamen.

STAMINEOUS, [stam-in'-i-us], *adj.* stamineal. [L. *stamineus*].

STAMINIFEROUS, [stam'-in-if'-er-us], *adj.* having a stamen. [STAMEN and L. *ferre* to bear].

STAMINODE, [stam'-in-ōd], *n.* a sterile stamen.

STAMMEL, [stam'-el], *n.* a rough woollen fabric dyed red. [Fr. *estamel*].

STAMMER (1), [stam'-er], *n.* the act of stammering, a hesitation in speech.

STAMMER (2), [stam'-er], *v.t. and i.* to speak with a stammer, to suffer from a defect of speech marked by involuntary repetitions of a syllable or sound; to utter with a stammer. [OE. *stamerian*].

STAMMERER, [stam'-er-er], *n.* one who stammers.

STAMMERING, [stam'-er-ing], *adj.* with a stammer.

STAMMERINGLY, [stam'-er-ing-li], *adv.* in stammering fashion.

STAMP (1), [stamp], *n.* the act of striking downwards with the foot; an instrument for making impressions by a heavy, usually downward, blow on a softer substance; the impression so made, *esp.* the imprint made by an engraved block; an imprint certifying the validity of a document, the quality of goods, etc., *esp.* a label affixed to postal packages as evidence of the charge required for delivery having been paid, an embossed mark stamped on a document as a receipt of legal payment; (*fig.*) an evident mark of a quality. [OFr. *estampe*].

STAMP (2), [stamp], *v.t. and i.* to strike downwards with the foot, to walk heavily; to mark by striking with an engraved block, to affix a stamp to, to make a lasting impression on; **to s. out,** to extirpate utterly, to suppress completely. [ME. *stampen*].

STAMP-COLLECTOR, [stamp'-kol-ek'-ter], *n.* a philatelist.

STAMP-DISTRIBUTOR, [stamp'-dis-trib'-yŏŏt-er], *n.* an official seller of stamps.

STAMP-DUTY, [stamp'-dewt-i], *n.* a tax on certain legal transactions, so called because documents are stamped as evidence of payment.

STAMPEDE (1), [stam-pēd'], *n.* a sudden, tumultuous rush, usually inspired by panic, *esp.* such a rush by a herd of cattle. [Span. *estampida* crash].

STAMPEDE (2), [stam-pēd'], *v.t. and i.* to cause to stampede; to run in stampede.

STAMPER, [stamp'-er], *n.* one who, or that which, stamps.

STAMPING-MILL, [stamp'-ing-mil], *n.* a machine for crushing ore.

STANCE, [stants], *n.* the attitude in which one stands, the position previous to striking the ball in golf or cricket. [Fr. *stance*].

STANCH, see STAUNCH.

STANCHER, see STAUNCHER.

STANCHION, [stanch'-on], *n.* an upright bar serving as a support. [OFr. *estanchon*].

STANCHLESS, see STAUNCHLESS.

STANCHNESS, see STAUNCHNESS.

STAND (1), [stand], *n.* the act of standing, of stopping, of taking up a position; a position taken up, a place, position, beyond which one will not retreat; a firm opposition to attack, a prolonged resistance at a particular point; (*cricket*) a prolonged period without the loss of a wicket; a place where one may stand, a raised platform for spectators, a station where cabs or public vehicles may wait; a place on which something may be put, a small wooden structure for supporting ornaments, etc.; (*coll.*) a theatrical performance; the witness-box in a court of justice. [OE. *stand*].

STAND (2), [stand], *v.t. and i.* to be at rest in an unsupported upright position; to hold one's ground, to endure; to buy something (usually an alcoholic drink) for (a person); to make to be in an upright unsupported position; to act in the capacity of; **to s. back,** to move away from, stay in the rear; **to s. by,** to support, stay with; **to s. for,** (*coll.*) to tolerate; **to s. in,** to be concerned in; **to s. to,** (*milit.*) to assemble ready and equipped to execute orders; **to s. up,** to stand on one's feet; **to s. up to,** to oppose, refuse to submit to; **to s. with,** to support; **to s. off,** to be distant; to dismiss (an employee) temporarily; **to s. up for,** to defend. [OE. *standan*].

STANDARD (1), [stand'-erd], *n.* a military ensign, a device, elevated on a pole, and used as a symbol or rallying point; a quantity taken as an absolute, with which other quantities may be compared, a certain amount, level, of quantity, quality, or behaviour used as a measuring rod for others of the same kind, a criterion, a general means of judgment; the average degree of a thing to which the rest of the kind are expected to conform. [MedL. *standardum*].
STANDARD (2), [stand'-ard], *adj.* of, or according to, a given standard; accepted; usual.
STANDARD-BEARER, [stand'-erd-bāer'-er], *n.* one who carries a military standard.
STANDARDIZE, [stand'-erd-īz], *v.t.* to make conformable to a standard, to level out irregularities in and bring into uniform pattern.
STANDARD-LAMP, [stand'-erd-lamp'], *n.* a lamp on a tall movable stand.
STANDEL, [stand'-el], *n.* a young tree intended for timber. [Uncert.].
STANDER, [stand'-er], *n.* one who stands.
STANDER-BY, [stand'-er-bī], *n.* a bystander.
STANDING (1), [stand'-ing], *n.* status.
STANDING (2), [stand'-ing], *adj.* established, on a permanent footing; (of armies) permanently in being and under arms; that is always in effect, regular; standing up.
STANDING-STONES, [stand'-ing-stōnz], *n.* (*coll.*) Druidical monoliths.
STANDISH, [stand'-ish], *n.* an inkstand. [ME. *standische*].
STAND-OFFISH, [stand'-off'-ish], *adj.* uncompanionable from a consciousness of superiority.
STAND-PIPE, [stand'-pīp'], *n.* a vertical pipe, *esp.* one connected to a water main, provided with a tap. [STAND (2) and PIPE (1)].
STANDPOINT, [stand'-point], *n.* viewpoint, moral or intellectual position.
STANDSTILL, [stand'-stil], *n.* a complete stoppage.
STAND-UP, [stand'-up], *adj.* (*coll.*) (of conflicts) violently and unashamedly contested.
STANG, [stang], *n.* a wooden beam. [OScand. *stang*].
STANHOPE, [stan'-up], *n.* a light, two-wheeled open carriage. [The Hon. Fitzroy *Stanhope*].
STANK, [stangk], *pret.* of STINK.
STANNARY, [stan'-er-i], *n.* a tin-mine; tin-ware. [~L. *stannum* tin].
STANNATE, [stan'-āt], *n.* a salt of stannic acid.
STANNEL, [stan'-el], *n.* the kestrel. [OE. *stangella*].
STANNIC, [stan'-ik], *adj.* derived from, or pertaining to, tin in its higher valency. [~L. *stannum* tin].
STANNIFEROUS, [stan-if'-er-us], *adj.* containing tin. [*Prec.* and L. *ferre* to bear].
STANNINE, [stan'-in], *n.* (*met.*) an alloy of tin, copper and iron.
STANNOUS, [stan'-us], *adj.* derived from or containing tin in its lower valency.
STANNUM, [stan'-um], *n.* the metallic chemical element denoted by Sn; tin. [L. *stannum*].
STANZA, [stan'-za], *n.* (*pros.*) a number of lines of verse forming a composite unit, and often linked together by various arrangements of rhyme and metre; (*arch.*) a section of a building. [It. *stanza*].
STANZAIC, [stan-zā'-ik], *adj.* containing or pertaining to stanzas.
STAPEDIAL, [sta-pēd'-i-al], *adj.* pertaining to or resembling stirrups. [L. *stapes* stirrup].
STAPES, [stā'-pēz], *n.* (*anat.*) the innermost stirrup-shaped bone of the ear. [~*Prec.*].
STAPHYLE, [staf'-i-li], *n.* (*anat.*) the uvula. [Gk. *staphule* bunch of grapes].
STAPHYLINE, [staf'-i-līn], *adj.* (*anat.*) pertaining to the staphyle.
STAPHYLOMA, [staf'-i-lō'-ma], *n.* (*med.*) a protrusion on the eyeball. [~*Prec.*].
STAPHYLORRAPHY, [staf'-i-lo'-ra-fi], *n.* (*surg.*) a suture of the palate. [Gk. *staphule* inflamed uvula and *raphe* suture].
STAPLE (1), [stāpl], *n.* a place fixed for a market, a market; the chief product of a place; essential raw materials; the pile in wool, etc.; a U-shaped pointed metal rod driven into wood, etc., to form a receptacle for hooks, locks, etc.; (*fig.*) high quality. [OE. *stapol*].
STAPLE (2), [stāpl], *adj.* fixed by agreement or tradition, established; chief (of products and raw materials), principal, basic.
STAPLE (3), (**stapling, stapled**), [stāpl], *v.t.* to sort out different qualities of (wool, thread, flax, etc.).
STAPLER, [stāp'-ler], *n.* one who grades wool, etc.
STAR (1), [stah(r)], *n.* a luminous fixed heavenly body; (*fig.*, *astrol.*) such a body as supposed to control a person's life; a regular pointed figure resembling a heavenly body radiating flashes of light; (*print.*) an asterisk; a white patch on a horse's forehead; a leading actor or actress, *esp.* on the films; **S. of Bethlehem,** (*bot.*) a plant of the genus *Ornithogalum*; **S. of Jerusalem,** (*bot.*) salsify, *Tragopogon porrifolius*; **S. of the Sea,** (*bot.*) the plant, *Aster Tripolium*; **Stars and Stripes,** the national flag of the United States. [OE. *steorra*].
STAR (2), [stah(r)], *v.t.* and *i.* to adorn with stars, to mark with an asterisk to call special attention to; to shine like a star; to take a leading rôle in a dramatic representation.
STAR-ANISE, [stahr'-an'-is], *n.* (*bot.*) the plant, *Illicium anisatum*.
STAR-APPLE, [stahr'-apl'], *n.* (*bot.*) the West Indian fruit of *Chrysophyllum Cainito*.
STAR-BLIND, [stah'-blīnd], *adj.* partially blind.
STARBOARD (1), [stah'-bawd, stah'-berd], *n.* the right side of a ship when looking forward. [STEER and BOARD (1)].
STARBOARD (2), [stah'-bawd, stah'-berd], *adj.* pertaining to, or lying on, the starboard.
STARCH (1), [stahch], *n.* a granular carbohydrate found in plant cells and much used in laundering stiff white linen, etc. [OE. *stearc* stiff].
STARCH (2), [stahch], *adj.* stiff with starch, starchy; rigid.
STARCH (3), [stahch], *v.t.* to stiffen with starch.
STAR-CHAMBER, [stah'-chām'-ber], *n.* an infamously unjust court of criminal justice of Tudor and early Stuart times, so called from the stars decorating the ceiling of the court chamber.
STARCHED, [stahcht], *adj.* stiffened with starch, rigid.
STARCHEDNESS, [stahcht'-nes], *n.* the condition of being starched; (*fig.*) stiffness in manner and bearing.
STARCHER, [stahch'-er], *n.* one who uses starch.
STARCH-HYACINTH, [stahch'-hī-a-sinth], *n.* (*bot.*) the grape hyacinth, *Muscari racemosum*.
STARCHINESS, [stahch'-i-nes], *n.* the condition of being starchy.
STARCHLY, [stahch'-li], *adv.* in a stiff or starchy manner.
STARCHNESS, [stahch'-nes], *n.* (*fig.*) stiffness of manner and bearing.
STARCHY, [stahch'-i], *adj.* pertaining to, or containing, starch; (*fig.*) stiff in manner and bearing.
STARE (1), [stāer], *n.* a starling. [OE. *stær*].
STARE (2), [stāer], *n.* a fixed look with wide-open eyes.
STARE (3), [stāer], *v.t.* and *i.* to look fixedly with wide-open eyes, to affect someone with such a look; **to s. one in the face,** to be obvious to one. [OE. *starian*].
STARER, [stāer'-er], *n.* one who stares.
STARFINCH, [stah'-finch], *n.* the redstart. [OE. *steort* rump and FINCH].
STARFISH, [stah'-fish], *n.* a flat star-shaped echinoderm.
STAR-FORT, [stah'-fawt], *n.* (*fort.*) a fort with angular projections in its outer plan.
STAR-GAZER, [stah'-gāz'-er], *n.* an astrologer.
STAR-GAZING, [stah'-gāz'-ing], *n.* astrology; (*fig.*) absent-mindedness.

STARFISH

STARING (1), [stāer'-ing], *n.* the action of one who stares.
STARING (2), [stāer'-ing], *adj.* looking with a stare; unpleasantly obtrusive.
STARINGLY, [stāer'-ing-li], *adv.* in a staring fashion, with a fixed look.
STAR-JELLY, [stah'-jel'-i], *n.* (*bot.*) a gelatinous lichen, *Nostoc commune*.
STARK (1), [stahk], *adj.* stiff, rigid; bold, strong; absolute, complete. [OE. *stearc*].
STARK (2), [stahk], *adj.* naked, bare. [Short for STARK-NAKED].
STARK (3), [stahk], *adv.* absolutely, completely. [~STARK (1)].
STARK-NAKED, [stahk'-nā'-kid], *adj.* completely naked and bare. [OE. *steort* rump and NAKED].
STARKNESS, [stahk'-nes], *n.* the condition of being stark; implacability, relentlessness.

STARLESS, [stah'-les], *adj.* without the stars being visible.
STARLIGHT (1), [stah'-līt], *n.* light emitted by the stars at night.
STARLIGHT (2), [stah'-līt], *adj.* lit or illuminated by the stars; having the stars visible.
STARLIKE, [stah'-līk], *adj.* resembling a star; bright; shining; stellate.
STARLING (1), [stah'-ling], *n.* a passerine bird of the genus *Sturnus* with black glossy plumage. [OE. *stærling*].
STARLING (2), [stah'-ling], *n.* a ring of piles driven in round the piers of a bridge. [OE. *statholung* foundation].
STARLIT, [stah'-lit], *adj.* lighted by stars.
STAR-NOSE, [stah'-nōz], *n.* a North American insectivore of the genus *Condylura*, related to the mole, with cartilaginous rays on the nose disposed like a star.
STARRED, [stahd], *adj.* studded with stars; influenced in fortune by the stars; playing the part of the star or chief actor or actress.
STARRINESS, [stah'-ri-nes], *n.* the state of being starry.
STARRY, [stah'-ri], *adj.* abounding or adorned with stars; made up of stars; shining like stars; resembling stars.
STAR-SHELL, [stah'-shel'], *n.* a shell which bursts in flight and sheds a bright light around.
STAR-SPANGLED, [stah'-span-gld], *adj.* adorned or spangled with stars; **the s. banner**, the U.S. national flag; the national hymn of the U.S.A. which refers to this.
STARSTONE, [stah'-stōn], *n.* a kind of sapphire or other gem which looks like a six-rayed star.
START (1), [staht], *n.* a sudden movement or twitch from alarm; a little shock; a spring; a sally; a quick spring; a darting; the act of setting out or beginning; **by fits and starts**, spasmodically.
START (2), [staht], *v.t.* to alarm; to startle; to rouse suddenly from concealment; to move suddenly from its place; to raise; to invent; to dislocate; **to s. in**, to begin; **to s. out**, to set forth, intend; **to s. up**, to spring up; to put (an engine) into motion; *v.i.* to move suddenly and spasmodically; to make a sudden involuntary motion of the body; to shrink, wince; to move suddenly aside; to move out of place; to set out, begin, commence. [OE. *steortian*].
STARTER, [staht'-er], *n.* one who, or that which, starts; a dog that rouses game; **self-s.**, the electrical motor for starting the engine of a motor-car.
STAR-THISTLE, [stah'-thisl], *n.* a plant of the genus *Centaurea*, with radiating spines surrounding the flower-heads.
STARTING-POINT, [staht'-ing-point], *n.* the point of departure.
STARTING-POST, [staht'-ing-pōst], *n.* a barrier or line from which competitors begin a race.
STARTLE, [stahtl], *v.t.* and *i.* to start; to feel sudden alarm; to alarm. [OE. *steartlian* to stumble].
STARTLING, [staht'-ling], *adj.* suddenly impressing with fear or surprise; (of dress) vivid, arresting.
STARTLINGLY, [staht'-ling-li], *adv.* in a startling fashion.
STAR TURN, [stah'-turn'], *n.* a leading turn in a variety performance; the best turn at which a performer excels; an amusing or entertaining person.
STARVATION, [stahv-ā'-shun], *n.* the act of starving, or state of being starved; (*fig.*) the condition of having too little nourishment for the mind.
STARVE, [stahv], *v.i.* to perish of hunger; to suffer extreme hunger or want; *v.t.* to deprive of food and nourishment. [OE. *steorfan* to die].
STARVELING (1), [stahv'-ling], *n.* an animal or plant thin and weak from want of food.
STARVELING (2), [stahv'-ling], *adj.* hungry; ill-fed; pining.
STARWORT, [stah'-wurt], *n.* a plant of the genus *Stellaria*; a plant also of the genus *Aster*; **water s.**, a plant of the genus *Callitriche*.
STASIS, [stās'-is], *n.* (*med.*) stagnation of the blood or of other fluid; constipation. [Gk. *stasis* a standing still].
STATABLE, [stāt'-abl], *adj.* able to be stated.
STATANT, [stāt'-ant], *adj.* (*her.*) drawn in profile standing still with all the feet on the ground. [OFr. *statant*].
STATE (1), [stāt], *n.* condition; rank; quality; pomp; dignity; grandeur; a body politic; the whole body of people united under one ruler or government; legislative body. [OFr. *estat* from L. *status*].
STATE (2), [stāt], *adj.* of or pertaining to the state; ceremonial.
STATE (3), [stāt], *v.t.* to give a reasoned statement of; to express the particulars of; to set down; to say, narrate, tell.
STATE-CARRIAGE, [stāt'-ka'-rij], *n.* an official carriage for ceremonial occasions.
STATECRAFT, [stāt'-krahft], *n.* statesmanship; the art of politics or government.
STATE-CRIMINAL, [stāt'-krim'-in-al], *n.* one who offends against the state.
STATED, [stāt-ed], *adj.* settled; established; regular; related, told as a fact.
STATEDLY, [stāt'-ed-li], *adv.* at certain stated times, regularly; allegedly.
STATE-HOUSE, [stāt'-hows], *n.* the house of legislature of a state; a town hall.
STATELESS, [stāt'-les], *adj.* without a state; without ceremonial.
STATELINESS, [stāt'-li-nes], *n.* loftiness of mien or manner; majestic appearance; dignity; haughty formality.
STATELY, [stāt'-li], *adj.* characterized by dignity and loftiness; magnificent; elevated in sentiment; imposing.
STATEMENT, [stāt'-ment], *n.* the act of stating; that which is stated; an account, announcement, or recital; an opinion, judgment; (*comm.*) a setting out of the financial affairs of some business or institution; an account in detail.
STATE-MONGER, [stāt'-mung'-ger], *n.* a person versed in politics, or one who dabbles in state affairs.
STATE-PAPER, [stāt'-pāp'-er], *n.* a document concerned with the political interests or government of a state.
STATE-PRISON, [stāt'-priz'-on], *n.* a public prison; a prison for criminals who have offended against the state.
STATE-PRISONER, [stāt'-priz'-on-er], *n.* a prisoner held for a political crime.
STATER, [stāt'-er], *n.* an ancient Greek and Roman coin of gold or silver of various values. [Gk. *stater* a weight].
STATE-ROOM, [stāt'-rōōm], *n.* a magnificent room in a palace or great house; a private cabin on board ship; an apartment in a railway sleeping-car.
STATES-GENERAL, [stāts'-jen'-er-al], *n.* (in France before the Revolution) the assembly of the three legislative orders of the kingdom, the clergy, nobles and commons. [Fr. *états généraux*].
STATESMAN, [stāts'-man], *n.* a man engaged in affairs of government; an able legislator with foresight and exceptional abilities; (*dial.*) a small land-owner.
STATESMANLIKE, [stāts'-man-līk], *adj.* having the qualities of a good statesman.
STATESMANSHIP, [stāts'-man-ship], *n.* the skill in affairs, the business of a statesman; statecraft.
STATE-TRIAL, [stāt'-trī'-al], *n.* the trial of a person accused of a political crime.
STATIC (1), [stat'-ik], *n.* (*elect.*) atmospheric discharges of electricity, *esp.* as audible on a wireless receiver. [STATIC (2)].
STATIC (2), [stat'-ik], *adj.* stationary; standing still; immovable; pertaining to bodies at rest or in equilibrium; **s. pressure**, pressure exerted by weight without movement. [Gk. *statikos* causing to stand].
STATICAL, [stat'-ik-al], *adj.* static.
STATICALLY, [stat'-ik-al-i], *adv.* in a static way.
STATICS, [stat'-iks], *n.(pl.)* that branch of mechanics which deals with the forces which keep bodies at rest or in equilibrium.
STATION (1), [stā'-shun], *n.* the spot or place where a person or thing stands; post assigned; office; situation; position; place assigned for the rendezvous of troops; employment; occupation; rank; condition of life; a railway depot; a district police office; an Australian stock farm; (*R.C.*) **Stations of the Cross**, the fourteen pictures of scenes from the Passion painted on the walls of churches. [L. *statio* position].
STATION (2), [stā'-shun], *v.t.* to place; to appoint to the occupation of a place, post, or office; (*milit.*) to assign to a certain station.
STATIONAL, [stā'-shun-al], *adj.* pertaining to a station.
STATIONARINESS, [stā'-shun-er-i-nes], *n.* the condition of being stationary.
STATIONARY, [stā'-shun-er-i], *adj.* motionless; fixed; not moving, progressively or regressively; not

appearing to move; not advancing; not improving; operating in one fixed position. [L. *stationarius*].

STATION-BILL, [stā'-shun-bil'], *n.* (*naut.*) a list containing the appointed posts of a ship's company for purposes of navigation.

STATIONER, [stā'-shun-er], *n.* a tradesman who sells all kinds of writing materials. [MedL. *stacionarius* bookseller].

STATIONERY, [stā'-shun-er-i], *n.* writing materials. [~*Prec.*].

STATIONMASTER, [stā'-shun-mahst'-er], *n.* an official in charge of a railway station.

STATISM, [stāt'-izm], *n.* the art of government; statecraft.

STATIST, [stat'-ist], *n.* a statistician.

STATISTIC, STATISTICAL, [stat-ist'-ik(-al)], *adj.* of, or pertaining to, statistics.

STATISTICALLY, [stat-ist'-ik-al-i], *adv.* in a statistical manner; by means of statistics.

STATISTICIAN, [stat'-ist-ish'-an], *n.* one versed in statistics; a statistical expert.

STATISTICS, [stat-ist'-iks], *n.*(*pl.*) the branch of political science dealing with the collection and arrangement of the numerical facts respecting the state of a people, their economy, health, wealth, etc.; the science which treats of these subjects; systematic collection and examination of numerical facts.

STATIVE, [stāt'-iv], *adj.* fixed, *esp.* of a fixed camp of ancient Roman times. [L. *stativus*].

STATOR, [stāt'-er], *n.* (*elect.*) the stationary inductance coil in a dynamo, variometer, etc. [L. *stator* one who stands].

STATUARY, [stach'-ŏŏ-e-ri], *n.* a sculptor; the art of carving statues; statues and sculptured work collectively. [L. *statuarius* sculptor; L. *statuaria* sculpture].

STATUE, [stach'-ŏŏ], *n.* a representation, usually of a human or animal figure, in some solid material as stone, marble, bronze, wood; a sculptured cast or moulded figure in the round. [OFr. *statue* from L. *statua*].

STATUED, [stach'-ŏŏd], *adj.* furnished with statues; represented in the form of a statue.

STATUESQUE, [stach'-ŏŏ-esk'], *adj.* in the style or manner of a statue; having the repose and dignity of a statue.

STATUETTE, [stach'-ŏŏ-et'], *n.* a miniature statue. [Fr. *statuette*].

STATURE, [stach'-er], *n.* the natural height of the body; mental proportions. [Fr. *stature*].

STATURED, [stach'-erd], *adj.* having a certain stature.

STATUS, [stāt'-us], *n.* standing; condition; relative position in society; (*leg.*) legal position; **s. quo,** the existing condition, state, previous position. [L. *status*].

STATUTABLE, [stach'-ōōt-abl], *adj.* made or introduced by statute; statutory.

STATUTABLY, [stach'-ōōt-ab-li], *adv.* according to statute.

STATUTE, [stach'-ōōt], *n.* an enactment by the legislative body of a state; written law; an act of Parliament; the act of a corporation or of its founder, intended as a permanent rule or law. [OFr. *statut*].

STATUTORY, [stach'-ōōt-er-i], *adj.* pertaining to, enacted by a statute; depending on statute for its authority.

STAUNCH (1), STANCH, [stawnch], *adj.* trustworthy, loyal, firm. [OFr. *estanche* seaworthy].

STAUNCH (2), STANCH, [stawnch], *v.t.* to stop or stop partially a flow of blood. [OFr. *estanchier* from L. *stagnare* to cause to become stagnant].

STAUNCHER, STANCHER, [stawnch'-er], *n.* one who staunches.

STAUNCHLESS, STANCHLESS, [stawnch'-les], *adj.* unable to be staunched.

STAUNCHNESS, STANCHNESS, [stawnch'-nes], *n.* the condition of being staunch.

STAUROLITE, [staw'-rō-līt], *n.* (*min.*) a mineral made up of silicate of aluminium, magnesium, and iron, crystallized in prisms, often in the shape of a cross. [Fr. *staurolite*].

STAVE (1), [stāv], *n.* the side timbers of a cask; the rung of a ladder; a staff; stanza, verse of a song; (*mus.*) a set of lines and spaces on which music is written. [OE. *stæf*].

STAVE (2), [stāv], *v.t.* to break a hole in; to burst; to push as with a staff; **to s. off,** to delay, defer, ward off.

STAVESACRE, [stāvz'-āk-er], *n.* the plant *Delphinium Staphisagria*, the seeds from which are used to kill vermin. [Gk. *staphisagria* wild parsley].

STAY (1), [stā], *n.* the time of remaining in one place; period of residence; a halt; (*fig.*) a restraint, curb.

STAY (2), [stā], *n.* (*naut.*) the fore-and-aft rope supports of masts and spars; (*fig.*) support, moral support, comfort. [OE. *stæg* rope].

STAY (3), [stā], *v.t.* to hold back; to stop, delay, obstruct progress of; to endure; *v.i.* to remain, put off one's departure; to reside temporarily. [OFr. *estayer*].

STAY (4), [stā], *v.t.* to hold up, prop, by means of a stay; to satisfy.

STAYER, [stā'-er], *n.* one who stays; one able to stay the course.

STAY-IN, [stā'-in], *adj.* referring to a strike in which the workers remain at their posts but do not work.

STAY-LACE, [stā'-lās], *n.* a thin cord for lacing corsets.

STAYMAKER, [stā'-māk'-er], *n.* one who makes stays.

STAYS, [stāz], *n.*(*pl.*) a corset.

STAYSAIL, [stā'-sāl], *n.* (*naut.*) a triangular sail stretched out on a stay.

STAYTACKLE, [stā'-takl'], *n.* (*naut.*) a large tackle attached to the mainstay by a pendant, and used for hoisting heavy objects as boats and butts of water.

STEAD, [sted], *n.* place, position; **to stand in good s.,** to render useful service to. [OE. *stede*].

STEADFAST, [sted'-fahst], *adj.* firm, constant, unwavering. [OE. *stedefæst*].

STEADFASTLY, [sted'-fahst-li], *adv.* in a steadfast way.

STEADFASTNESS, [sted'-fahst-nes], *n.* the condition of being steadfast; firmness of mind or purpose; firmness of purpose; constancy.

STEADILY, [sted'-i-li], *adv.* in a steady way.

STEADINESS, [sted'-i-nes], *n.* the condition of being steady; firmness of purpose; constancy.

STEADY (1), [sted'-i], *adj.* firm in standing or position; fixed; constant in mind, purpose, or pursuit; not fickle or changeable; unwavering; constant; uniform. [ME. *stedi*].

STEADY (2), [sted'-i], *v.t.* to make or hold steady; *v.i.* to become steady.

STEAK, [stāk], *n.* a thick slice of meat or fish; a thick piece of beef from the rump or fillet. [OIcel. *steik*].

STEAL, [stēl], *v.t.* to take or carry away feloniously the personal goods of another; to withdraw or convey clandestinely; to gain or win by address or by gradual imperceptible means; **to s. a march on,** to gain an advantage over by surprise. [OE. *stelan*].

STEALER, [stēl'-er], *n.* one who steals.

STEALINGLY, [stēl'-ing-li], *adv.* slily, privately.

STEALTH, [stelth], *n.* clandestine or underhand procedure; secret actions. [~STEAL].

STEALTHILY, [stelth'-i-li], *adv.* in a stealthy way.

STEALTHINESS, [stelth-i-nes], *n.* the condition or quality of being stealthy.

STEALTHY, [stelth'-i], *adj.* of stealth; secret; furtive; clandestine.

STEAM (1), [stēm], *n.* the vapour obtained by heating water to the boiling point; the mist formed by vapour when condensing; any exhalation; (*fig.*) **to get up s.,** to get ready for serious business. [OE. *steam*].

STEAM (2), [stēm], *v.t.* to expose to steam; to clean, cook by steam; *v.i.* to rise or pass off in steam; to send off a visible vapour; to move by steam; to open (a sealed letter) by holding it over steam. [OE. *steman* to give out a smell].

STEAMBOAT, [stēm'-bōt], *n.* a boat propelled through the water by power supplied from steam.

STEAM-BOILER, [stēm'-boil'-er], *n.* a boiler where water is converted into steam by applied heat.

STEAM-CARRIAGE†, [stēm'-ka'-rij], *n.* a road carriage driven by steam.

STEAM-CHEST, [stēm'-chest'], *n.* the chamber in a steam-engine through which steam passes into the cylinder.

STEAM-CRANE, [stēm'-krān'], *n.* a crane driven by steam.

STEAM-ENGINE, [stēm'-en'-jin], *n.* an engine driven by the expansion of steam.

STEAMER, [stēm'-er], *n.* a ship propelled by steam-power; a cooking-vessel in which edibles are steamed; a fire-engine worked by steam; **s. lane,** the route used by steamers in crossing the North Atlantic.

STEAM-GAUGE, [stēm'-gāj], *n.* a measuring apparatus attached to a boiler to indicate the pressure of the steam.

STEAM-HAMMER, [stēm'-ham'-er], *n.* a large, powerful forge hammer worked by steam-power.

STEAMINESS, [stēm′-i-nes], *n.* the condition of being steamy.

STEAM-LAUNCH, [stēm′-lawnch], *n.* a launch propelled by steam-power.

STEAM-LAUNCH

STEAM-NAVVY, [stēm′-na′-vi], *n.* an excavator driven by steam.

STEAMPIPE, [stēm′-pīp], *n.* the pipe communicating with the top part of a boiler, through which the steam passes on its way to the cylinder.

STEAM-PLOUGH, [stēm′-plow], *n.* a ploughing machine worked by steam.

STEAM-POWER, [stēm′-pow′-er], *n.* the power of steam when applied to machinery.

STEAM-ROLLER, [stēm′-rōl-er], *n.* a steam-engine provided with a heavy roller, employed to level road surfaces; (*fig.*) an irresistible power.

STEAMSHIP, [stēm′-ship], *n.* a large vessel propelled by steam-power.

STEAM-TRAP, [stēm′-trap′], *n.* a contrivance for allowing the passage of water and stopping the escape of steam.

STEAM-TUG, [stēm′-tug], *n.* a tug driven by steam-power.

STEAM-VESSEL, [stēm′-ves′-el], *n.* a vessel driven by steam-power.

STEAM-WHISTLE, [stēm′-wisl], *n.* a pipe attached to the boiler of a steam-engine, through which steam is discharged, causing a loud, shrill whistle.

STEAMY, [stēm′-i], *adj.* vaporous; covered with, giving off steam; hot and misty.

STEAM-YACHT, [stēm′-yot′], *n.* a yacht driven by steam.

STEANING, see STEENING.

STEARATE, [stēer′-āt], *n.* a salt of stearic acid.

STEARIC, [stēer′-ik], *adj.* derived from stearin.

STEARIN, [stēer′-in], *n.* the chief constituent of solid fats; stearic acid. [Gk. *stear* fat].

STEAROPTENE, [stēer-op′-tēn], *n.* a crystalline substance obtained from certain essential oils, including camphor.

STEAT(O)-, *pref.* fat, fatty. [Gk. *steatos* fatty].

STEATITE, [stē′-a-tīt], *n.* soapstone, amorphous talc, a compound of magnesium and silica of an extremely soapy feel.

STEATITIC, [stē-at-it′-ik], *adj.* from, resembling, steatite.

STEATO-, see STEAT(O)-.

STEATOCELE, [stē-at′-ō-sēl], *n.* a fatty tumour of the scrotum. [STEATO and Gk. *kele* tumour].

STEATOMA, [stē′-a-tōm′-a], *n.* a wen or encysted tumour which contains matter like suet.

STEATOMOUS, [stē′-a-tōm′-us], *adj.* of, like, or pertaining to, a steatoma.

STEATOPYGOUS, [stē′-a-top′-ig-us], *adj.* having an abnormal accumulation of fat on the buttocks. [STEATO and Gk. *puge* buttocks].

STEATOSIS, [stē′-a-tōs′-is], *n.* fatty degeneration. [STEATO and Gk. *osis* condition].

STEED, [stēd], *n.* (*poet.*) horse. [OE. *steda* horse].

STEEL (1), [stēl], *n.* iron combined with carbon; any instrument of steel; a weapon of war; a spike of steel used for sharpening knives; a metal support in a garment; (*fig.*) extreme hardness; obduracy. [OE. *stele*].

STEEL (2), [stēl], *adj.* made of steel; having the qualities of steel; hard and bright; **s. engraving,** engraving on steel plates.

STEEL (3), [stēl], *v.t.* to cover with steel; to sharpen on a steel; to harden; (*fig.*) to render obdurate, hard.

STEEL-CLAD, [stēl′-klad′], *adj.* clad in or armed with steel, wearing armour.

STEELINESS, [stēl′-i-nes], *n.* the condition of being steely.

STEEL-PLATED, [stēl-plāt′-ed], *adj.* plated with steel, armoured.

STEEL-TRAP, [stēl′-trap′], *n.* a trap fitted with a steel spring.

STEELY, [stēl′-i], *adj.* having the qualities of steel; hard and bright; (*fig.*) hard, relentless.

STEELYARD, [stēl′-yahd], *n.* a lever balance with arms of unequal length, used for ascertaining weights, the weight being suspended from the long, and the thing to be weighed from the short, arm. [Uncert.].

STEEN, [stēn], *v.t.* to face or line a well or shaft with bricks, stones or similar material. [OE. *stænan*].

STEENING, STEANING, [stēn′-ing], *n.* the lining of a well or shaft with bricks and stones; the stones or brick so used.

STEEP (1), [stēp], *n.* the action of steeping; the liquor used in steeping.

STEEP (2), [stēp], *adj.* ascending or descending at a high gradient; precipitous; having an abrupt slope; (*coll.*) almost unbelievable; too expensive. [OE. *steap* lofty].

STEEP (3), [stēp], *v.t.* to soak in a liquid; (*fig.*) to imbue, dye deeply. [OIcel. *steypa* to pour].

STEEPEN, [stēp′-en], *v.t.* to render steep; *v.i.* to become steep.

STEEPER, [stēp′-er], *n.* a vessel or vat where things are steeped.

STEEPLE, [stēpl], *n.* a high tapering structure surmounting a building, and often ending in a spire; a church spire. [ME. *stepel*].

STEEPLECHASE, [stēpl′-chās], *n.* a cross-country horserace originally towards a church steeple as a landmark.

STEEPLED, [stēpld], *adj.* having a steeple or steeples.

STEEPLEJACK, [stēpl′-jak′], *n.* a man who builds or repairs steeples and tall chimneys.

STEEPLY, [stēp′-li], *adv.* in a steep fashion.

STEEPNESS, [stēp′-nes], *n.* the condition of being steep; precipitous declivity.

STEEPY, [stēp′-i], *adj.* (*poet.*) steep.

STEER (1), [stēer], *n.* a young ox or bullock up to four years old. [OE. *steor*].

STEER (2), [stēer], *v.t.* to direct the course of a ship, vehicle, or anything moving along; to direct; to guide; *v.i.* to direct and govern a ship in its course; to sail; to be governed; to conduct oneself; to take or pursue a course or way; **to s. clear of,** to keep out of the way of. [OE. *steoran*].

STEERABLE, [stēer′-abl], *adj.* able to be steered.

STEERAGE, [stēer′-ij], *n.* the act of steering; the effect of a rudder on a ship; that part of a ship from which she is steered; the quarters on a ship of the passengers travelling at the cheapest fares; regulation; management.

STEERAGE-WAY [stēer′-ij-wā′], *n.* (*naut.*) movement at a sufficient speed for effective steering.

STEERER, [stēer′-er], *n.* one who steers.

STEERING, [stēer′-ing], *n.* the action of one who steers; the apparatus for steering.

STEERING-GEAR, [stēer′-ing-gēer′], *n.* the apparatus used in steering.

STEERLING, [stēer′-ling], *n.* a young steer; a bullock.

STEERSMAN, [stēerz′-man], *n.* one who steers; the helmsman.

STEERSMANSHIP, [stēerz′-man-ship], *n.* the art of steering.

STEERSMATE, [stēerz′-māt′], *n.* a man who steers; a pilot.

STEEVE (1), [stēv], *n.* the outward slope of an outboard spar used in stowing cargo.

STEEVE (2), [stēv], *v.t.* to slope (a spar) upwards; to pack closely; to stow (cargo). [~STIFF].

STEEVING, [stēv′-ing], *n.* (*naut.*) the angle of elevation that a ship's bowsprit makes with the horizon.

STEGANOPODS, [steg-an′-ō-podz], *n.*(*pl.*) a family of birds with four toes webbed. [Gk. *steganos* covered and *pous podos* foot].

STEGNOSIS, [steg-nō′-sis], *n.* (*med.*) constipation. [Gk. *stegnosis* constriction].

STEGNOTIC, [steg-not′-ik], *n.* (*med.*) an astringent medicine. [Gk. *stegnotikos*].

STEGOGNATHOUS, [steg-og′-na-thus], *adj.* having a jaw of imbricated plates. [Gk. *stego* I cover and *gnathos* jaw].

STEINBOK, [stīn-bok′], *n.* an antelope of the genus *Nanotragus* indigenous to South Africa; the Alpine ibex. [Germ. *stein* stone and *bock* buck].

STEGANO-POD

STELE, [stēl′-ē], *n.* an ancient Greek upright stone slab or column, lacking base or capital, and bearing an inscription or bas-relief. [Gk. *stele*].

STELENE, [stēl′-ēn], *adj.* columnar.

STELL, [stel], *n.* a sheep or cattle fold. [~STALL (1)].

STELLAR, [stel′-er], *adj.* pertaining to stars; astral; starry; of or full of stars; set with stars. [LL. *stellaris*].

STELLARY, [stel′-er-i], *adj.* connected with the stars; stellar.

STELLATE, [stel′-āt], *adj.* like a star; radiated.

STELLATED, [stel′-āt-id], *adj.* stellate.

STELLIFEROUS, [stel-if′-er-us], *adj.* having many

stars; set with stars. [L. *stella* star and L. *ferre* to bear].

STELLIFORM, [stel'-i-fawm], *adj.* star-shaped; radiated. [L. *stella* star and FORM].

STELLITE, [stel'-īt], *n.* a zeolitic mineral found in radiated acicular crystals.

STELLULAR, [stel'-yŏŏl-er], *adj.* resembling little stars; set with little stars. [L. *stellula* little star].

STELLULATE, [stel'-yŏŏl-āt], *adj.* stellular.

STELOGRAPHY, [stel-og'-raf-i], *n.* the art of inscribing characters on steles. [STELE and Gk. *graphia* writing].

STEM (1), [stem], *n.* the ascending axis of a plant; the peduncle of a flower; the stalk; the stock of a family; a branch of a family; a stem-like structure as on a wine-glass; (*naut.*) the prow of a ship; the post to which the two sides of a ship are united at the fore end. [OE. *stemn*].

STEM (2), [stem], *v.t.* to obstruct, stop, hold back. [ME. *stemmen* to stop].

STEM-LEAF, [stem'-lēf], *n.* a leaf which grows from the stem.

STEMLESS, [stem'-les], *adj.* without a stem.

STEMMA, (*pl.* **stemmata**), [stem'-a], *n.* a diagrammatic pedigree. [Gk. *stemma* wreath].

STEMPLE, [stempl], *n.* a crossbar of wood forming steps in a mine-shaft. [Germ. *stempel*].

STENCH, [stench], *n.* an offensive smell; a stink. [OE. *stenc* odour].

STENCHY, [stench'-i], *adj.* smelly; having an offensive odour.

STENCIL (1), [sten'-sil], *n.* a piece of thin metal or other substance perforated with holes that form a design through which colour or ink may be applied to a surface beneath; the design made on the surface beneath by using the stencil; such a device used to reproduce typescript. [~OFr. *estenceler* to spangle].

STENCIL (2), [sten'-sil], *v.t.* to make a copy of by use of a stencil.

STENCILLER, [sten'-sil-er], *n.* one who stencils.

STENCILLING, [sten'-sil-ing], *n.* the art of using a stencil.

STEN GUN, [sten'-gun'], *n.* a form of simple automatic gun. [*S T* the designers' initials and *En*field].

STENO-, *pref.* narrow, constricted. [Gk. *stenos* narrow].

STENOCARDIA, [sten'-ō-kahd'-i-a], *n.* (*path.*) constriction of the heart. [STENO- and Gk. *kardia* heart].

STENOCHROMY, [sten-ok'-rom-i], *n.* the art of printing in several colours at the same time, by the use of several pigment blocks. [STENO- and Gk. *khrome* colour].

STENOGRAPH, [sten'-ō-graf], *n.* one of the characters used in writing in shorthand; shorthand writing. [STENO- and GRAPH].

STENOGRAPHER, [sten-og'-ra-fer], *n.* a shorthand writer.

STENOGRAPHIC, [sten'-ō-graf'-ik], *adj.* of, or pertaining to, stenography.

STENOGRAPHIST, [sten-og'-raf-ist], *n.* a stenographer.

STENOGRAPHY, [sten-og'-raf-i], *n.* the art of writing rapidly by using abbreviations. [STENO- and Gk. *graphia* writing].

STENOSIS, [sten-ōs'-is], *n.* stricture of an aperture. [STENO- and Gk. *osis* condition].

STENOTYPE, [sten'-ō-tīp], *n.* a symbol in shorthand representing a letter, syllable, word, or phrase. [STENO- and TYPE].

STENTOR, [stent'-or], *n.* a man with a powerful voice. [Gk. *Stentor*, the herald in the Trojan War].

STENTORIAN, [stent-aw'-ri-an], *adj.* (of the voice) loud, powerful. [*Prec.*].

STEP (1), [step], *n.* a footfall; a pace; the space between the feet in walking or running; the tread of a stair; a small space; gradation; degree, stage in progression; footstep; gait; proceeding; action; the round of a ladder; a foot-piece; (*naut.*) that on which the foot of a mast rests. [OE. *stæpe* a step].

STEP (2), (stepping, stepped), [step], *v.t.* to set (the foot); (*naut.*) to put (a mast) in place; **to s. aside,** (*fig.*) to give place; **to s. out,** to increase the pace, walk quickly; (*fig.*) to adventure; **to s. on it,** (*coll.*) to go very quickly, hurry; **to s. up,** to increase the rate of; (*elect.*) to increase (the voltage); to arrange as in steps; *v.i.* to advance or recede by a movement of the foot; to go; to walk. [OE. *stæppan*].

STEP-, *pref.* related by the second marriage of one parent. [OE. *steope*].

STEPBROTHER, [step'-bruTH'-er], *n.* a brother who is the son of one's stepfather or stepmother.

STEPDAUGHTER, [step'-dawt'-er], *n.* a daughter of a husband or wife by a former wife or husband.

STEPFATHER, [step'-fahTH'-er], *n.* a mother's second or subsequent husband.

STEPHANITE, [stef'-an-īt], *n.* (*min.*) sulph-antimonite of silver. [Germ. *stephanit* from the Archduke *Stephan* of Austria].

STEPHANOTIS, [stef-an-ōt'-is], *n.* (*bot.*) a tropical genus of plants cultivated on account of their scented flowers. [Gk. *stephanos* wreath].

STEP-INS, [step'-inz], *n.*(*pl.*) underwear, shoes, etc., that can be put on without the use of buttons or fasteners.

STEP-LADDER, [step'-lad'-er], *n.* a ladder with flat treads and a hinged support, opening at an angle for use.

STEPMOTHER, [step'-muTH'-er], *n.* a father's wife by a later marriage.

STEPNEY†, [step'-ni], *n.* a spare wheel for a motor-car. [*Stepney*, the inventor].

STEPPE, [step], *n.* an expanse of uncultivated, arid, treeless plains in the south-east of Europe and the south-west of Asia. [Russ. *stepp*].

STEPPER, [step'-er], *n.* one who steps; a horse with a high-stepping action.

STEPPING-STONE, [step'-ing-stōn'], *n.* a stone to keep the feet above the water or dirt in walking; a means of progress, aid in one's advancement.

STEP-SISTER, [step'-sist'-er], *n.* a stepmother's or stepfather's daughter by a previous marriage.

STEP-SON, [step'-sun'], *n.* a stepmother's or stepfather's son by a previous marriage.

STERCORACEOUS, [stur'-kor-ā'-shus], *adj.* connected with, of, dung. [~L. *stercus* dung].

STERCORAL, [stur'-kor-al], *adj.* pertaining to excrement. [~*Prec.*].

STEREO, [ste'-ri-ō], *n.* a stereotype.

STEREO-, *pref.* firm. [Gk. *stereos* firm, solid].

STEREOCHEMISTRY, [ste'-ri-ō-kem'-ist-ri], *n.* that branch of physical chemistry which deals with the geometrical structure of molecules in relation to their optical or chemical properties. [STEREO- and CHEMISTRY].

STEREOCHROMY, [ste'-ri-ō-krōm'-i], *n.* a method of painting walls by which the colours are preserved with fluoric acid. [STEREO- and CHROME].

STEREOGRAPH, [ste'-ri-ō-graf'], *n.* a stereographic picture or diagram. [STEREO- and GRAPH].

STEREOGRAPHIC, [ste'-ri-ō-graf'-ik], *adj.* made or done in accordance with the rules of stereography; delineated on a plane.

STEREOGRAPHICALLY, [ste'-ri-ō-graf'-ik-al-i], *adv.* in a stereographic fashion.

STEREOGRAPHY, [ste'-ri-og'-raf-i], *n.* the art of delineating solid bodies on a plane. [STEREO- and Gk. *graphia* writing].

STEREOMETER, [ste'-ri-om'-it-er], *n.* an instrument for determining the specific gravity of bodies, also one employed in stereometry. [STEREO- and METER].

STEREOMETRICAL, [ste'-ri-ō-met'-rik-al], *adj.* pertaining to or performed by stereometry.

STEREOMETRY, [ste'-ri-om'-et-ri], *n.* the art of measuring solid bodies, and ascertaining their solid contents; the art of determining the specific gravity of bodies.

STEREOSCOPE, [ste'-ri-ō-skōp], *n.* an optical instrument through which two pictures of the same object appear as one, and cause it to stand out in solid form as though real. [STEREO- and SCOPE].

STEREOSCOPIC, [ste'-ri-ō-skop'-ik], *adj.* of, or pertaining to, the stereoscope or its effect.

STEREOSCOPIST, [ste'-ri-o'-skop-ist], *n.* one skilled in stereoscopy.

STEREOSCOPY, [ste'-ri-o'-skop-i], *n.* the art of using a stereoscope.

STEREOTOMICAL, [ste'-ri-ōt-om'-ik-al], *adj.* pertaining to, or performed by, stereotomy.

STEREOTOMY, [ste'-ri-ot'-om-i], *n.* the art of cutting sections of solid objects. [STEREO- and Gk. *tome* a cutting].

STEREOTYPE (1), [ste'-ri-ō-tīp], *n.* (*print.*) a metallic plate cast from a mould taken from a page of movable type. [STEREO- and TYPE].

STEREOTYPE (2), [ste'-ri-ō-tīp], *v.t.* to cast, print in stereotype; (*fig.*) to fix in one style irrevocably.

STEREOTYPER, [ste'-ri-ō-tīp'-er], *n.* a stereotypist.

STEREOTYPIST, [ste'-ri-ō-tīp'-ist], *n.* one who makes stereotypes.
STEREOTYPOGRAPHER, [ste'-ri-ō-tīp-og'-raf-er], *n.* a stereotype printer.
STEREOTYPOGRAPHY, [ste'-ri-ō-tīp-og'-raf-i], *n.* the art or practice of printing from stereotype.
STERILE, [ste'-rīl], *adj.* barren; unfruitful; producing little or no crop; producing no young; barren of ideas or sentiment; free from septic germs; free from living bacteria, microbes. [L. *sterilis* unfruitful].
STERILITY, [ste-ril'-it-i], *n.* barrenness; unfruitfulness; barrenness of ideas or sentiments; lack of fertility.
STERILIZABLE, [ste'-ril-īz-abl], *adj.* capable of being sterilized.
STERILIZATION, [ste'-ril-īz-ā'-shun], *n.* the act or process of sterilizing; the state of being sterilized.
STERILIZE, [ste'-ril-īz], *v.t.* to render barren; to exhaust of fertility; to destroy bacteria in; to spray or wash with an antiseptic.
STERILIZER, [ste'-ril-īz-er], *n.* one who, or that which, sterilizes, [*esp.* an apparatus for killing bacteria.
STERLET, [stur'-let], *n.* a species of sturgeon, *Acipenser ruthenus*, native to the Caspian Sea and to Russian rivers, from whose roe the finest caviare is made. [Fr. *sterlet* from Russ. *sterlyadi*].
STERLING, [stur'-ling], *adj.* of standard worth; genuine; pure; of excellent quality; (*fig.*) having fine dependable moral qualities. [ME. *sterling* a coin with a star on it].
STERN (1), [sturn, starn], *n.* the rear part of a ship or aircraft; the hinder part. [OIcel. *stjorn*].
STERN (2), [sturn], *adj.* severe in expression; austere; severe in manner and morals; harsh; rigidly steadfast; immovable; unrelenting. [OE. *steorne*].
STERNAL, [sturn'-al], *adj.* of, or pertaining to, the sternum.
STERNALGIA, [sturn-al'-ji-a], *n.* a pain near the breast-bone. [Gk. *sternon* and *algos* pain].
STERNBERGITE, [sturn'-berg-it], *n.* (*min.*) a foliated ore of silver. [Count *Sternberg*].
STERNBOARD, [sturn'-bawd], *n.* (*naut.*) the backward motion of a vessel; the loss of way when making a tack.
STERN-FAST, [sturn'-fahst], *n.* a rope for mooring the stern of a ship.
STERN-FRAME, [sturn'-frām], *n.* the several pieces of timber, etc., forming the stern of a ship.
STERNLY, [sturn'-li], *adv.* in a stern fashion.
STERNMOST, [sturn'-mōst], *adj.* nearest to the stern.
STERNNESS, [sturn'-nes], *n.* the quality of being stern.
STERNOCOSTAL, [sturn'-ō-kost'-al], *adj.* connected with both the sternum and the ribs. [STERNUM and COSTAL].
STERN-PORT, [sturn'-pawt], *n.* a port or door in the stern of a ship.
STERNPOST, [sturn'-pōst], *n.* the timber or casting on which the rudder hangs.
STERN-SHEETS, [sturn'-shēts], *n.*(*pl.*) that part of a boat between the stern and the aftmost seat of the rowers.
STERNUM, [sturn'-um], *n.* the breast-bone, the bone which forms the front of the human chest from the neck to the stomach and to which the upper ribs are joined. [Gk. *sternon* chest].
STERNUTATION, [sturn'-yōō-tā'-shun], *n.* the action of sneezing. [L. *sternutatio*].
STERNUTATIVE, [ster-newt'-at-iv], *adj.* provocative of sneezing.
STERNUTATORY (1), [ster-newt'-at-er-i], *n.* a substance provocative of sneezing.
STERNUTATORY (2), [ster-newt'-at-er-i], *adj.* that causes sneezing.
STERNWAY, [sturn'-wā], *n.* the motion of a ship backward or stern foremost.
STERN-WHEELER, [sturn'-wēl-er], *n.* a steamer propelled by a paddlewheel at the stern.
STERTOROUS, [sturt'-er-us], *adj.* snoring; emitting a sound like snoring. [~L. *stertere* to snore].
STERTOROUSLY, [sturt'-er-us-li], *adv.* in stertorous fashion.
STET, [stet], *v.t.* to let stand; (*print.*) an instruction written on the margin of a proof to intimate to the printer that something which has been deleted is to stand; *v.i.* it may stand. [L. *stet* let it stand].
STETHOMETER, [steth-om'-it-er], *n.* a device for measuring the movement of the walls of the chest during breathing. [Gk. *stethos* breast and METER].
STETHOSCOPE, [steth'-ō-skōp], *n.* an instrument for distinguishing sounds within the body, particularly those connected with the heart and lungs. [Gk. *stethos* breast and SCOPE].

STETHOSCOPE

STETHOSCOPIC, [steth'-ō-skop'-ik], *adj.* of, or pertaining to, the stethoscope.
STETHOSCOPIST, [steth'-o'-skop-ist], *n.* one versed in stethoscopy.
STETHOSCOPY, [steth-o'-skop-i], *n.* the art of using a stethoscope.
STETSON, [stet'-son], *n.* a broad-brimmed felt hat. [*Stetson*, the original maker].
STEVEDORE, [stēv'-i-daw(r)], *n.* a man whose occupation is to stow goods in a ship's hold; a loader or unloader of vessels. [Sp. *estivador*].
STEW (1), [stew], *n.* a fishpond, *esp.* one serving as a store for fish shortly to be used; a brothel. [OFr. *estui*].
STEW (2), [stew], *n.* a dish of stewed meat and vegetables; (*slang*) a state of agitation; **Irish s.,** a stew of mutton and vegetables. [OFr. *estuve* stove].
STEW (3), [stew], *v.t.* to cook (meat or fruit) slowly in a small quantity of liquid; *v.i.* to be boiled in a slow, gentle manner; **to s. in one's own juice,** to cope with one's own difficulties. [OFr. *estuver*].
STEWARD, [stew'-erd], *n.* a man who manages the concerns of a large estate or a great family, superintending the servants, collecting the rents, and keeping the accounts; an officer of state; an officer in a college who provides food for the students, and superintends the concerns of the kitchen; the head of that department in a ship which supplies food or refreshment; a waiter on board ship. [OE. *stigweard*].
STEWARDESS, [stew'-erd-es], *n.* a woman steward.
STEWARDLY, [stew'-erd-li], *adv.* in the manner of a good steward.
STEWARDSHIP, [stew'-erd-ship], *n.* the office, work of a steward; management.
STEWARTRY, [stew'-ert-ri], *n.* stewardship; a territorial district in Scotland under the jurisdiction of a steward, nominated by the king, and having the powers of a sheriff; the county of Kirkcudbright.
STEW-PAN, [stew'-pan], *n.* a pan for stewing food.
STEW-POT, [stew'-pot'], *n.* a pot or saucepan in which food may be stewed.
STHENIC, [sthen'-ik], *adj.* active; vigorous; (*med.*) characterized by excess of organic action. [Gk. *sthenos* strength].
STIACCIATO, [stē'-ach-aht'-ō], *n.* very low relief. [It. *stiacciato*].
STIBIAL, [stib'-i-al], *adj.* containing, or resembling, antimony. [L. *stibium*].
STIBIATED, [stib'-i-āt-ed], *adj.* impregnated with antimony.
STIBIC, [stib'-ik], *adj.* antimonic.
STIBINE, [stib'-ēn], *n.* (*chem.*) hydride of antimony. [STIB(IUM) and (AM)INE].
STIBIUM, [stib'-i-um], *n.* (*chem.*) the metallic element denoted by Sb, antimony. [L. *stibium*].
STIBNITE, [stib'-nīt], *n.* (*chem.*) antimonite, a compound of sulphur and antimony.
STICA, see STYCA.
STICCADO, [stik-ah'-do], *n.* a musical instrument consisting of bars of varying length played with a small mallet. [It. *sticcado*].
STICH, [stik], *n.* a line of verse, of whatever measure or number of feet; a row of trees. [Gk. *stikhos* line of verse].
STICHIC, [stik'-ik], *adj.* pertaining to, or consisting of, lines and stanzas.
STICHOMANCY, [stik'-ō-man-si], *n.* divination by lines or passages in a book, chosen at random. [Gk. *stikhos* line of verse and *manteia* divination].
STICHOMETRY, [stik-om'-it-ri], *n.* a list of books of Scripture with the number of verses each contains; the division of a writing into lines in accordance with the sense or metre. [Gk. *stikhos* stick and *metria* measuring].
STICHOMYTH, STICHOMYTHIA, [stik'-ō-mith, stik'-ō-mith'-i-a], *n.* verse dialogue where two characters speak alternately one line each. [Gk. *stikhomuthia*].
STICK (1), [stik], *n.* a small shoot or branch cut off a tree; a long slender piece of wood or other material; a slender piece; a staff; a printer's tool for composing

type with; a thrust with a pointed instrument that penetrates the body; a stab; a group of bombs released at one time from an aeroplane; (*coll.*) a stiff uninteresting person; **in a cleft s.,** on the horns of a dilemma; **to get hold of the wrong end of the s.,** to misunderstand. [OE. *sticca* stick].

STICK (2), [stik], *v.t.* to pierce; to thrust a pointed instrument into; to stab; to kill by piercing; to thrust; to fasten; to set; to fix in; to set with something pointed; to fix on something pointed; (*coll.*) to endure, put up with; *v.i.* to remain with the point thrust in; to adhere; to cling fast to; to stop; to be impeded; to hesitate; to be embarrassed; **to s. out,** to project; **to s. in one's throat,** (*fig.*) to be very distasteful; hard to accept; **to s. out for,** to insist upon having; **to s. up for,** to defend, champion; **to s. to one's guns,** to defend one's own position or opinions. [ME. *steken* to fix and ME. *stikien* to stab, prick].

STICK (3), [stik], *v.t.* to fasten to a stick or provide with sticks as a support.

STICKER, [stik'-er], *n.* one who, or that which, sticks; (*coll.*) one who sees a thing through, displays great perseverance; an adhesive label.

STICKINESS, [stik'-i-nes], *n.* the quality of being sticky; adhesiveness; viscousness; glutinousness.

STICK-INSECT, [stik'-in'-sekt], *n.* an insect of the *Phasmidæ*, which simulate twigs.

STICK-JAW, [stik'-jaw], *n.* food, toffee, etc., which is sticky and difficult to chew.

STICKLE, [stikl], *v.i.* to take part with one side or other; to insist on the observance of every trifle; to contend obstinately. [ME. *stihtlen* to rule, dispose].

STICKLEBACK, [stikl'-bak'], *n.* a little nest-building fish of the genus *Gasterosteus*, with a spiny back. [OE. *sticel* sting and BACK].

STICKLEBACK

STICKLER, [stik'-ler], *n.* a sidesman to fencers; a second to a duellist; one who stands to judge a combat; an obstinate contender about trivialities; **a s. for,** one who is punctilious about. [~STICKLE].

STICKY, [stik'-i], *adj.* having a tendency to stick to surfaces; glutinous; having adhesive properties; (*coll.*) having many scruples, difficult, over punctilious; **s. end,** an unpleasant, violent death.

STIDDY, [stid'-i], *n.* an anvil; a blacksmith's shop.

STIFF (1), [stif], *n.* (*slang*) a corpse; **big s.,** (*slang*) a blockhead. [*Next*].

STIFF (2), [stif], *adj.* not easily bent; rigid; firm, not fluid; inspissated; strong; violent; stubborn; obstinate; constrained; formal; (*coll.*) exorbitant, excessive, disagreeable; **stiff 'un,** (*slang*) a corpse. [OE. *stif*].

STIFF-BIT, [stif'-bit], *n.* a horse's bit having no joint or branches.

STIFFEN, [stif'-en], *v.t.* to render stiff, rigid; to make less pliable, malleable; (*fig.*) to make more determined, resolute; *v.i.* to become stiff, thicker, less yielding; (*fig.*) to assume a cold and formal manner; to become less amenable and friendly. [~STIFF].

STIFFENER, [stif'-en-er], *n.* something which makes stiff, or causes stiffening; (*slang*) a drink as a stimulant, *esp.* in an emergency.

STIFFENING, [stif'-en-ing], *n.* something which makes stiff.

STIFFISH, [stif'-ish], *adj.* (*coll.*) moderately stiff.

STIFFLY, [stif'-li], *adv.* in a stiff fashion.

STIFF-NECK, [stif'-nek'], *n.* a rheumatic affection of the muscles of the neck in which a lateral movement of the head causes pain.

STIFF-NECKED, [stif'-nekt'], *adj.* (*fig.*) stubborn; standing too much on one's dignity; extremely punctilious.

STIFF-NECKEDNESS, [stif'-nekt'-nes], *n.* the state or quality of being stiff-necked.

STIFFNESS, [stif'-nes], *n.* the state of being stiff.

STIFLE (1), [stīfl], *n.* the joint in a horse's hind leg; a disease affecting this joint. [~STIFF].

STIFLE (2), [stīfl], *v.t. and i.* to suffocate; to choke; to stop the breath temporarily; to extinguish; to deaden; to put down; to smother; to suppress. [OIcel. *stifla* to choke].

STIFLING, [stif'-ling], *adj.* that stifles.

STIFLINGLY, [stif'-ling-li], *adv.* so as to stifle.

STIGMA, (*pl.* **stigmata**), [stig'-ma], *n.* a mark made with a burning iron; a brand; any mark of infamy; moral spot on or imputation attaching to character; (*bot.*) the receptive organ for the pollen grains, placed at the top of a pistil; (*pl.*) (*eccles.*) marks as of five wounds corresponding to those of Christ, sometimes alleged to appear miraculously on the bodies of saints and martyrs. [Gk. *stigma* brand].

STIGMATA, [stig'-ma-ta], *n. pl.* of STIGMA.

STIGMATIC, STIGMATICAL, [stig-mat'-ik(-al)], *adj.* pertaining to a stigma.

STIGMATICALLY, [stig-mat'-ik-al-i], *adv.* in a stigmatical fashion.

STIGMATIFEROUS, [stig'-mat-if'-er-us], *adj.* (*bot.*) having stigmas. [STIGMA and L. *ferre* to bear].

STIGMATIZATION, [stig'-mat-īz-ā'-shun], *n.* the act of stigmatizing; the condition of being stigmatized.

STIGMATIZE, [stig'-mat-īz], *v.t.* to cause to bear a stigma; to brand; to hold up to disgrace; to discredit irrevocably.

STIGMATOSIS, [stig'-mat-ōs'-is], *n.* (*path.*) inflammation of the skin accompanied by spots. [STIGMA and Gk. *osis* condition].

STILAR, [stīl'-er], *adj.* pertaining to the stile of a dial.

STILBITE, [stil'-bīt], *n.* (*min.*) a mineral of the zeolite group, made up of silica, alumina, lime, and water. [~Gk. *stilbo* I glitter].

STILE (1), [stīl], *n.* the gnomon of a sundial. [Gk. *stulos*].

STILE (2), [stīl], *n.* a step or a set of steps or any similar device for ascending and descending over a fence or wall; (*arch.*) an upright piece in framing or panelling. [OE. *stigel*].

STILETTO (1), [stil-et'-ō], *n.* a small dagger having a round blade; a pointed instrument for making eyelet holes. [It. *stiletto*].

STILETTO (2), [stil-et'-ō], *v.t.* to stab with a stiletto.

STILL (1), [stil], *n.* an apparatus used in distilling. [~L. *stillare* to distil].

STILL (2), [stil], *n.* a still (as opposed to a moving) picture.

STILL (3), [stil], *adj.* without movement; motionless; quiet; silent; tranquil; without a sparkle. [OE. *stille*].

STILL (4), [stil], *adv.* to this time, even now; nevertheless, notwithstanding; even more, yet. [OE. *stille* quietly].

STILL (5), [stil], *v.t.* to make still; to quieten, soothe; to render (pain) less acute.

STILLATORY, [stil'-at-er-i], *n.* an alembic; a chemical laboratory. [STILL (1)].

STILL-BORN, [stil'-bawn], *adj.* born dead; abortive.

STILL-BURN, [stil'-burn], *v.t.* to burn during the process of distillation.

STILLER, [stil'-er], *n.* one who stills or quiets.

STILL-HUNTING, [stil'-hunt'-ing], *n.* deer-stalking.

STILLIFORM, [stil'-i-fawm], *adj.* drop-shaped. [L. *stilla* a drop and FORM].

STILLING, [stil'-ing], *n.* a stand for barrels. [LGerm. *stelling*].

STILLION, [stil'-i-on], *n.* stilling. [*Var.* of STILLING].

STILL-LIFE, [stil'-līf'], *n.* (*paint.*) a picture portraying inanimate objects.

STILLNESS, [stil'-nes], *n.* the state of being still.

STILL-ROOM, [stil'-rōōm], *n.* room where distilling is done; a household store-room for jams, pickles, etc.; the room in a hotel, etc., where alcoholic drinks are handled.

STILLY (1), [stil'-i], *adj.* (*poet.*) quiet, tranquil.

STILLY (2), [stil'-i], *adv.* in a still fashion; silently, quietly.

STILT (1), [stilt], *n.* a support of wood with a rest for the foot in walking over rough ground; a long-legged plover of the genus *Himantopus*. [~MDu. *stelte*].

STILT

STILT (2), [stilt], *v.t.* to raise on stilts; to elevate unnaturally.

STILTED, [stilt'-ed], *adj.* affected, bombastic, unnatural; **s. arch,** (*arch.*) an arch springing not directly from the impost but from the horizontal courses of stone above it.

STILTEDLY, [stilt'-ed-li], *adv.* in stilted fashion.

STILTON, [stilt'-on], *n.* a kind of rich soft cheese. [*Stilton* in Huntingdonshire, where first sold].

STIMULANT (1), [stim'-yōōl-ant], *n.* a drink that stimulates; an alcoholic drink; (*fig.*) anything that stimulates to thought or action.

STIMULANT (2), [stim'-yōōl-ant], *adj.* having the power to stimulate.

STIMULATE, [stim'-yōōl-āt], *v.t.* to excite to action or more vigorous exertion; to produce a sudden increase of vital energy in; to stir to thought. [L. *stimulare*].

STIMULATION, [stim'-yo͞ol-ā'-shun], *n.* the act of goading or exciting; a sudden increase of vital energy; mental inspiration.

STIMULATIVE, [stim'-yo͞ol-a-tiv], *adj.* having the power of stimulating.

STIMULATOR, [stim'-yo͞ol-āt-or], *n.* a person or thing that stimulates.

STIMULUS, [stim'-yo͞ol-us], *n.* something which stimulates; a stimulant; a goad; an exciter to thought or action. [L. *stimulus* a goad].

STING (1), [sting], *n.* a sharp, poisonous organ with which certain creatures and plants are armed for their defence; the thrust of a sting into the flesh; anything that gives acute pain; the point of an epigram; that wherein lies the principal pain or which constitutes the chief terror. [OE. *sting*].

STING (2), (**stinging, stung**), [sting], *v.t.* (of insects, etc.) to pierce with a sting; to pain acutely; (*slang*) to get money out of; (*fig.*) to occasion sharp mental pain to; *v.i.* to inflict a sting; to feel a sting or stinging sensation. [OE. *stingan*].

STINGAREE, [sting'-a-rē], *n.* the sting-ray.

STINGER, [sting'-er], *n.* a person or thing that stings.

STING-FISH, [sting'-fish], *n.* the weever fish, a species of the genus *Trachinus*; the father-lasher, *Cottus scorpius*.

STINGILY, [stin'-ji-li], *adv.* in a stingy manner.

STINGINESS, [stin'-ji-nes], *n.* the quality of being stingy.

STINGLESS, [sting'-les], *adj.* having no sting; harmless.

STINGO, [sting'-gō], *n.* a powerful malt liquor. [~STING (1)].

STING-RAY, [sting'-rā], *n.* the sea-fish, *Trygon pastinaca*, having a long tail which is armed with spines.

STINGY, [stin'-ji], *adj.* mean, niggardly; close-fisted; parsimonious. [OE. *stingig* stinging].

STINK (1), [stingk], *n.* an extremely unpleasant and strong odour; a stench; (*slang*) a scandal, a commotion. [*Next*].

STINK (2), [stingk], *v.i.* to emit a strong unpleasant odour; (*fig.*) to be offensive to good taste. [OE. *stincan*].

STINKARD, [stingk'-erd], *n.* a mean, stinking, paltry fellow; the teledu, or stinking badger, *Mydaus meliceps*, found in Java and Sumatra, which gives out a foetid odour when irritated.

STINK-BOMB, [stingk'-bom'], *n.* a bomb emitting an offensive odour when it is let off.

STINKER, [stingk'-er], *n.* one who, or that which, stinks; (*slang*) an unpleasant person or thing.

STINKING, [stingk'-ing], *adj.* giving off an offensive smell, *esp.* of animals and plants when caused by natural secretions.

STINKINGLY, [stingk'-ing-li], *adv.* in a stinking fashion.

STINKPOT, [stingk'-pot'], *n.* an earthen jar filled with powder, grenades, and other materials with an offensive and suffocating smell.

STINKSTONE, [stingk'-stōn], *n.* a variety of carbonate of lime emitting a foetid odour on being struck.

STINKTRAP, [stingk'-trap'], *n.* a contrivance which prevents effluvia returning from a drain.

STINT (1), [stint], *n.* limit; restraint; a small bird of the sandpiper group, a species of *Tringa*; **without s.**, ungrudgingly, without limit.

STINT (2), [stint], *v.t.* to restrict unduly the amount of; to be stingy with, grudging of. [OE. *styntan* to stupefy].

STINTED, [stint'-ed], *adj.* limited to a certain insufficient quantity.

STINTEDNESS, [stint'-ed-nes], *n.* the condition of being stinted.

STINTER, [stint'-er], *n.* one who, or that which, stints.

STIPE, [stīp], *n.* (*bot.*) the base of a frond; the stem of a fungus. [Fr. *stipe* from L. *stipes* stem].

STIPEND, [stīp'-end], *n.* an annual payment for services rendered; a salary, particularly of a clergyman. [L. *stipendium*].

STIPENDIARY, [stīp-end'-i-er-i], *adj.* involving salary in return for services; **s. magistrate**, a paid magistrate in the service of the state. [L. *stipendiarius*].

STIPITATE, [stip'-i-tāt], *adj.* (*bot.*) supported on a stipe; elevated on a stipe. [~L. *stipes* stem].

STIPPLE, [stipl], *v.t.* to paint or engrave by means of dots in place of lines. [Du. *stippelen* to dot].

STIPPLING, [stip'-ling], *n.* drawing, painting, or engraving by means of minute dots instead of lines.

STIPTIC, see STYPTIC.

STIPULA, [stip'-yo͞ol-a], *n.* (*bot.*) a stalk-like appendage at the base of petioles. [L. *stipula* stalk].

STIPULACEOUS, [stip'-yo͞ol-ā'-shus], *adj.* stipular.

STIPULAR, [stip'-yo͞ol-er], *adj.* resembling or made up of stipules; growing on stipules.

STIPULATE (1), [stip'-yo͞ol-āt], *adj.* (*bot.*) having stipules.

STIPULATE (2), [stip'-yo͞ol-āt], *v.t.* to insist upon, demand as a condition; *v.i.* to make an agreement; to contract; to settle terms. [~L. *stipulari*].

STIPULATED, [stip'-yo͞ol-āt'-ed], *adj.* agreed on.

STIPULATION, [stip'-yo͞ol-ā'-shun], *n.* the action of stipulating; contract or bargain; (*bot.*) the situation and structure of the stipules.

STIPULATOR, [stīp'-yo͞ol-āt'-er], *n.* one who stipulates.

STIPULE, [stip'-yo͞ol], *n.* a stipula; a basal appendage to the leaf-stalk or similar structure. [L. *stipula* stem].

STIPULED, [stip'-yo͞old], *adj.* having stipules.

STIR (1), [stur], *n.* disturbance; movement; agitation; agitation of mind; (*slang*) prison, gaol.

STIR (2), [stur], *v.t.* to put in motion, *esp.* to move in a circular direction; to rouse, agitate, excite; *v.i.* to move oneself; to be in a state of movement; to move from one position to another; **to s. up**, to mix; (*fig.*) to agitate, arouse. [OE. *styrian*].

STIRABOUT, [stur'-a-bowt'], *n.* a kind of porridge of oatmeal and water, boiled and stirred about for a few minutes; a bustle; a bustler.

STIRK, [sturk], *n.* (*Scots*) a year-old bullock or heifer; (*coll.*) a dolt. [OE. *stirc*].

STIRLESS, [stur'-les], *adj.* without stir; motionless.

STIRPS, [sturps], *n.* a progenitor; the man who founds a family. [L. *stirps*].

STIRRER, [stur'-er], *n.* a person or thing that stirs.

STIRRING, [stur'-ing], *adj.* active; animating; rousing; thrilling; moving.

STIRRUP, [sti'-rup], *n.* a hoop or ring for the foot, suspended from a strap, to enable a rider to mount or sit steadily on horseback. [OE. *stigrap*].

STIRRUP-CUP, [sti'-rup-kup'], *n.* a parting drink taken on horseback immediately before departure.

STIRRUP-LEATHER, [sti'-rup-leTH'-er], *n.* a stirrup-strap.

STIRRUP-PUMP, [sti'-rup-pump'], *n.* a type of pump used for spraying water, and held in position by inserting the foot in its support. [STIRRUP and PUMP].

STIRRUP-STRAP, [sti'-rup-strap'], *n.* a strap of leather for supporting a stirrup.

STITCH (1), [stich], *n.* the complete action of a needle and thread when sewing; a single turn of the thread round the needle in knitting or crochet; method of doing a stitch; a sharp stabbing pain in the side. [OE. *stice* stab].

STITCH (2), [stich], *v.t.* to sew; to unite with stitches; to embroider; *v.i.* to practise needlework.

STITCHER, [stich'-er], *n.* one who stitches; a sewer.

STITCHERY, [stich'-er-i], *n.* the art of stitching; needlework.

STITCHING, [stich'-ing], *n.* the act of stitching; work done by sewing; the forming of land into ridges.

STITCHWORT, [stich'-wurt], *n.* any of the eighty species of *Stellaria*, the genus which includes the chickweeds. [OE. *sticwyrt*].

STITHY†, [stiTH'-i], *n.* a forge. [~OScand. *stethi*].

STIVE, [stīv], *v.t.* to stew; *v.i.* to be stewed. [OF. *estuver*].

STIVER, [stīv'-er], *n.* a small Dutch coin; a mere nothing. [Du. *stuiver*].

STOA, [stō'-a], *n.* a porch; a colonnade walled at the back; the Stoic philosophy. [Gk. *stoa* colonnade].

STOAT, [stōt], *n.* the ermine, *Mustela erminea*, related to the weasel. [ME. *stote*].

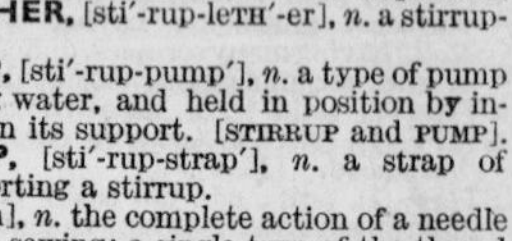

STOAT

STOCCADO, [stok-ahd'-ō], *n.* a stab; a thrust of a rapier. [It. *stoccado*].

STOCK (1), [stok], *n.* the stem of a tree or other plant; a post; a dull, stupid, senseless person; the frame of a rifle; a neckcloth; original progenitor; lineage; a family; a fund; capital; merchandise unsold; share of the public debt; goods on hand; the domestic animals or beasts belonging to a farm; (*bot.*) a plant of the genus *Matthiola*; (*pl.*) a frame in which the legs of criminals were confined; the frame on which a ship rests while building; the public funds; **stocks and stones,** inanimate things; **to take s.,** to make an inventory of stock or goods in hand; (*fig.*) to estimate resources, to appraise. [OE. *stocc* stump].

STOCK (2), [stok], *adj.* kept in stock; (*fig.*) conventional, stereotyped, average.

STOCK (3), [stok], *v.t.* to store for sale or use; to supply; to fill; to lay up in store; to pack; to equip with domestic animals; to plant land.

STOCKADE (1), [stok-ād'], *n.* a palisaded defence; a line of posts or stakes set up as a fence or barrier; an enclosure for cattle. [Fr. *estacade*].

STOCKADE (2), [stok-ād'], *v.t.* to fortify by means of a stockade.

STOCK-BOOK, [stok'-bŏŏk], *n.* a ledger in which stock is entered.

STOCK-BREEDER, [stok'-brēd'-er], *n.* one who breeds animals.

STOCKBROKER, [stok'-brōk-er], *n.* a broker engaged in the purchase and sale of stocks or shares on behalf of his clients.

STOCK-DOVE, [stok'-duv], *n.* the wild pigeon, *Columba œnas.*

STOCK EXCHANGE, [stok'-eks-chānj'], *n.* the corporate body of stockbrokers forming and controlling an official market for stocks and shares; the building where their business is carried out.

STOCK-FARM, [stōk'-fahm], *n.* a farm where the breeding of livestock goes on.

STOCK-FISH, [stok'-fish], *n.* fish, such as cod or ling, dried in the sun without salt.

STOCK-HOLDER, [stok'-hōld'-er], *n.* one who holds stock in the public funds or a public company.

STOCKINESS, [stok'-i-nes], *n.* the condition of being stocky.

STOCKINETTE, [stok'-i-net'], *n.* a knitted fabric of silk, wool, or cotton material used for clothing. [~STOCKING].

STOCKING, [stok'-ing], *n.* a close-fitting knitted or woven covering for the leg and foot made of wool, cotton, or silk. [~STOCK (1)].

STOCKINGED, [stok'-ingd], *adj.* clothed in, wearing, stockings.

STOCKING-FRAME, [stok'-ing-frām], *n.* a machine used for weaving stockings or other hosiery.

STOCKINGLESS, [stok'-ing-les], *adj.* having no stockings.

STOCK-IN-TRADE, [stok'-in-trād'], *n.* stock for carrying on one's business; assets, material or mental, to facilitate the carrying on of one's business.

STOCKISH, [stok'-ish], *adj.* wooden; short and stumpy. [STOCK (1)].

STOCKIST, [stok'-ist], *n.* one who keeps certain goods in stock.

STOCK-JOBBER, [stok'-job'-er], *n.* a member of the Stock Exchange who buys and sells shares for a broker.

STOCK-JOBBERY, [stok'-job'-er-i], *n.* the practices of the stock-jobber.

STOCK-JOBBING, [stok'-job'-ing], *n.* the buying and selling of stocks or shares for brokers.

STOCKLESS, [stok'-les], *adj.* without stock or stocks.

STOCK-LOCK, [stok'-lok'], *n.* a lock fastened in a wooden case or frame.

STOCK-MAN, [stok'-man], *n.* (*Australian*) a man in charge of farm-stock; a herdsman.

STOCK-MARKET, [stok'-mahk'-it], *n.* the Stock Exchange; the market in stocks and shares.

STOCKPOT, [stok'-pot'], *n.* a vessel in which bones, meat, etc., which are to be the basis of soup are stewed and kept.

STOCK-RIDER, [stok'-rīd'-er], *n.* a mounted stockman.

STOCK-STILL, [stok'-stil'], *adv.* as still as a post; motionless.

STOCK-TAKER, [stok'-tāk'-er], *n.* one who takes stock of business goods or properties in hand.

STOCK-TAKING, [stok'-tāk'-ing], *n.* the periodical taking stock of business goods or properties in hand.

STOCKWHIP, [stok'-wip], *n.* a short-handled whip with a thong of great length employed in herding cattle.

STOCKY, [stok'-i], *adj.* small and thickset; of a stumpy build.

STOCKYARD, [stok'-yahd], *n.* a yard or enclosure where cattle are herded.

STODGE, [stoj], *n.* stodgy food; literary material, etc., resembling this.

STODGINESS, [stoj'-i-nes], *n.* the condition of being stodgy.

STODGY, [stoj'-i], *adj.* dull and heavy; (*fig.*) tedious and heavy, lacking inspiration. [Uncert.].

STOEP, STOOP, [stŏŏp], *n.* the verandah of a Dutch South African house. [Afrik. *stoep*].

STOIC, [stō'-ik], *n.* a disciple of the philosopher Zeno, who taught that men should subdue all passion, conform to reason, and accept the inevitable; one who keeps within strict control all emotions; a person with calm fortitude. [Gk. *stoikos* from *stoa* porch].

STOICAL, [stō'-ik-al], *adj.* pertaining to the Stoics or their doctrines; not affected by passion; unfeeling; manifesting indifference to pleasure and pain; displaying a silent fortitude in adversity.

STOICALLY, [stō'-ik-al-i], *adv.* in stoical fashion.

STOICALNESS, [stō'-ik-al-nes], *n.* the condition of being stoical; indifference to pleasure or pain.

STOICHIOLOGY, [stoi'-ki-ol'-oj-i], *n.* the science or doctrine of chemical elements. [Gk. *stoikheion* element and *logos* speech].

STOICHIOMETRY, [stoi'-ki-om'-it-ri], *n.* the science or doctrine of chemical equivalents. [Gk. *stoikheion* element and *metria* measuring].

STOICISM, [stō'-i-sizm], *n.* the opinions and maxims of the Stoics; indifference to pleasure or pain, real or pretended; calm fortitude.

STOKE, [stōk], *v.t. and i.* to shovel (fuel) into a furnace; **to s. up,** (*slang*) to fortify (oneself) with a good meal. [~STOKER].

STOKEHOLD, [stōk'-hōld'], *n.* that part of a ship's hold containing the boilers.

STOKEHOLE, [stōk'-hōl], *n.* the hole through which the furnace is stoked.

STOKER, [stōk'-er], *n.* a man employed to stoke a furnace. [Du. *stoker*].

STOLA, [stōl'-a], *n.* a long garment worn by Roman women of the upper classes. [L. *stola*].

STOLE (1), [stōl], *pret.* of STEAL.

STOLE (2), [stōl], *n.* a stola; a band of silk reaching from the neck to below the waist, worn over both shoulders by priests and bishops and over the left shoulder only by deacons; a long narrow fur necklet. [L. *stola*].

STOLE (3), see STOLON.

STOLEN, [stōl'-en], *p.pt.* of STEAL.

STOLID, [stol'-id], *adj.* impassive, slow, heavy, without animation or vivacity. [L. *stolidus* slow].

STOLIDITY, [stol-id'-it-i], *n.* the quality of being stolid.

STOLIDLY, [stol'-id-li], *adv.* in stolid fashion.

STOLIDNESS, [stol'-id-nes], *n.* stolidity.

STOLON, STOLE, [stō'-lon], *n.* (*bot.*) a trailing stalk or stem which roots at intervals. [L. *stolo* sucker].

STOLONIFEROUS, [stō'-lon-if'-er-us], *adj.* having stolons or suckers. [STOLON and L. *ferre* to bear].

STOLZITE, [stolts'-īt], *n.* (*min.*) a tungstate of lead. [*Stolz*, the discoverer].

STOMA, (*pl.* **stomata**), [stōm'-a], *n.* a breathing pore or orifice as in the epidermis of a leaf. [Gk. *stoma* mouth].

STOMACH (1), [stum'-ak], *n.* a membranous receptacle below the liver and diaphragm, the principal organ of digestion, in which the food is digested for the nourishment of the body; the desire of food; appetite; inclination; liking; anger; sullenness; resentment; pride. [OFr. *estomac* from Gk. *stomakhos*].

STOMACH (2), [stum'-ak], *v.t.* to retain in the stomach; to endure, tolerate. [*Prec.*].

STOMACH-ACHE, [stum'-ak-āk], *n.* pain in the stomach or intestines. [STOMACH (1) and ACHE (1)].

STOMACHER, [stum'-ak-er, stum'-ach-er], *n.* a covering for the breast, often embroidered, part of women's dress in the sixteenth century.

STOMACHIC, [stum-ak'-ik], *adj.* pertaining to the stomach; strengthening to the stomach; stimulating the action of the stomach.

STOMACHLESS, [stum'-ak-les], *adj.* without a stomach; without appetite.

STOMACH-PUMP, [stum'-ak-pump'], *n.* a small medical pump or syringe, with a flexible tube, for drawing liquids from the stomach, or for injecting them.

STOMATA, [stōm'-at-a], *n. pl.* of STOMA.

STOMATIC, [stōm-at'-ik], *adj.* of, relating to, or like a stoma.

STOMATITIS, [stōm'-at-īt'-is], *n.* (*med.*) inflammation of the mouth.

STOMATO-, *pref.* pertaining to the mouth. [~Gk. *stoma* mouth].

STOMATO-GASTRIC, [stōm'-a-tō-gast'-rik], *adj.* (*med.*) pertaining to the mouth and stomach.

STOMATO-PLASTIC, [stōm'-a-tō-plast'-ik], *adj.* (*surg.*) relating to plastic surgery of the mouth.

STOMATOSCOPE, [stŏm-at′-ō-skōp], *n.* an instrument used in examining the mouth.

STONE (1), [stōn], *n.* a small fragment of rock; a gem or precious jewel; anything made of stone; a calculous concretion in the kidneys or bladder; †a testicle; the nut of a drupe or stone-fruit; the weight of fourteen pounds; a weight varying in different trades; a monument; torpidness and insensibility; hard-heartedness. [OE. *stan*].

STONE (2), [stōn], *adj.* made of stone; (*fig.*) hard, unyielding; unfeeling.

STONE (3), [stōn], *v t.* to throw stones at; to injure or kill by throwing stones at; to line or pave with stone; to take out the stones from (fruit).

STONEBACK, [stōn-bak′], *n.* the loach, a fish of the genus *Nemachilus*.

STONEBITER, [stōn′-bīt′-er], *n.* the cat-fish.

STONE-BLIND, [stōn′-blīnd′], *adj.* absolutely blind.

STONE-BOW, [stōn′-bō], *n.* a crossbow from which stones were shot. [OE. *stanboga*].

STONEBRASH, [stōn′-brash′], *n.* (*min.*) a finely crushed rock; a group of oolitic beds. [STONE and BRASH (2)].

STONEBREAKER, [stōn′-brāk′-er], *n.* a man who, or a machine which, breaks up stones for road-making.

STONE-BUTTER, [stōn′-but′-er], *n.* a species of alum.

STONECHAT, [stōn′-chat′], *n.* the small European bird, *Saxicola rubicola*. [STONE (1) and CHAT].

STONE-COAL†, [stōn′-kōl], *n.* coal as opposed to charcoal; anthracite.

STONE-CRAY, [stōn′-krā], *n.* a form of distemper in hawks.

STONECROP, [stōn′-krop′], *n.* a succulent native plant of the genus *Sedum*.

STONECHAT

STONE-CURLEW, [stōn′-kur′-lew], *n.* a species of plover, the thick-kneed *Œdicnemus scolopax*.

STONECUTTER, [stōn′-kut′-er], *n.* a man whose occupation is to cut or hew stones.

STONECUTTING, [stōn′-kut′-ing], *n.* the work of cutting or hewing stones.

STONE-DEAD, [stōn′-ded′], *adj.* absolutely dead.

STONE-DEAF, [stōn′-def′], *adj.* completely deaf.

STONE-DRESSER, [stōn′-dres′-er], *n.* a man who smooths and shapes stones for building purposes.

STONE-EATER, [stōn′-ēt′-er], *n.* a mollusc which bores into stone.

STONE-FALCON, [stōn′-fawlk′-on], *n.* the stone-hawk.

STONE-FLY, [stōn′-flī], *n.* a neuropterous insect of the genus *Perla*, used for bait by trout fishers.

STONE-FRUIT, [stōn′-froot], *n.* fruit whose seeds are covered with a hard shell embedded in pulp, as in the genus *Prunus*.

STONE-HAMMER, [stōn′-ham′-er], *n.* a hammer used in breaking stones; a hammer with a stone head.

STONEHATCH, [stōn′-hach′], *n.* the ringed plover.

STONE-HAWK, [stōn′-hawk], *n.* the merlin, *Falco æsalon*.

STONE-HEARTED, [stōn′-haht′-ed], *adj.* having a heart of stone; hard-hearted, flinty.

STONELESS, [stōn′-les], *adj.* having no stone or stones, *esp.* of fruit.

STONE-LILY, [stōn′-lil′-i], *n.* (*geol.*) a fossil encrinite.

STONE-MASON, [stōn′-mās′-on], *n.* a man who works in building-stone.

STONE-OCHRE, [stōn′-ōk′-er], *n.* an oxide of iron, employed in painting.

STONE-OIL, [stōn′-oil], *n.* a form of petroleum.

STONE PARSLEY, [stōn′-pahs′-li], *n.* the umbelliferous hedge-plant, *Sison Amomum*.

STONE-PINE, [stōn′-pīn′], *n.* an umbrella-shaped coniferous tree, *Pinus Pinea*, of the Mediterranean coastal region.

STONE-PIT, [stōn′-pit], *n.* a pit or quarry where stones are quarried.

STONE-PITCH, [stōn′-pich], *n.* hard inspissated pitch.

STONE-PLOVER, [stōn′-pluv′-er], *n.* the common ringed plover, *Ægialitis hiaticula*; the stone curlew, *Œdicnemus scolopax*.

STONER, [stōn′-er], *n.* one who beats or kills with stones; a man who builds walls with stones.

STONE'S-CAST, [stōnz′-kahst], *n.* the distance which a stone may be thrown; a stone's-throw.

STONE'S-MICKLE, [stōnz′-mikl], *n.* the stonechat, *Saxicola rubicola*.

STONE-SNIPE, [stōn′-snīp], *n.* the North American long-legged tattler, *Totanus melanoleucus*.

STONE-SQUARER, [stōn′-skwāer′-er], *n.* a man who forms stones into squares; a stonecutter.

STONE'S-THROW, [stōnz′-thrō′], *n.* the distance a stone may be thrown; **within a s.,** within a very short distance.

STONESTILL, [stōn′-stil′], *adj.* as still as a stone; absolutely still; motionless.

STONEWALLING, [stōn′-wawl′-ing], *n.* defence by obstructing; (*cricket*) blocking without making runs.

STONEWARE, [stōn′-wāer], *n.* potters' ware of a coarse kind.

STONEWORK, [stōn′-wurk], *n.* masonry.

STONILY, [stōn′-i-li], *adv.* in a stony fashion.

STONINESS, [stōn′-i-nes], *n.* the condition of being stony; hardness of heart.

STONY, [stōn′-i], *adj.* made of, resembling, stone; abounding in stones; petrifying; hard; (*fig.*) obdurate, unrelenting; (*slang*) penniless.

STONY-BROKE, [stōn′-i-brōk′], *adj.* (*coll.*) penniless. [STONY and BREAK (2)].

STONY-HEARTED, [stōn′-i-haht′-ed], *adj.* hard-hearted; cold and relentless.

STOOD, [stŏŏd], *pret. and p.pt.* of STAND.

STOOGE (1), [stōōj], *n.* (*U.S. slang*), a dupe, one who performs humble but necessary tasks to assist another.

STOOGE (2), [stōōj], *v.i.* (*slang*) to act as a stooge; to wander aimlessly. [*Prec.*].

STOOK (1), [stŏŏk], *n.* a group of sheaves of grain piled against each other. [ME. *stouke*].

STOOK (2), [stŏŏk], *v.t.* to build up in stooks for drying and gathering.

STOOL (1), [stōōl], *n.* a seat without a back; a little form with three or four legs as a seat for one person; a seat used in evacuating the bowels; an evacuation; a sucker; **s. of repentance,** (in Scotland) an elevated seat in the church, on which persons formerly sat, during service, as a punishment for their sins; **s.-pigeon,** an apparatus with a wooden pigeon attached, used as a decoy in pigeon-shooting; (*fig.*) a decoy, an informer. [OE. *stol*].

STOOL (2), [stōōl], *v.i.* to ramify; to produce suckers.

STOOL-BALL, [stōōl′-bawl], *n.* an early form of cricket in which the wicket was a stool and the bat held in one hand.

STOOM, [stōōm], *v.t.* to renew fermentation in (wine) by putting bags of herbs or other ingredients into it; to stum. [~STUMP].

STOOP (1), [stōōp], *n.* the action or posture of stooping; a round-shouldered position.

STOOP (2), [stōōp], *v.t.* to bow down; to cause to incline down; *v.i.* to bend down or incline the body; to hold oneself in a round-shouldered position; to condescend; to lower one's dignity by an unworthy act [OE. *stupian*].

STOOP (3), see STOEP.

STOOPER, [stōōp′-er], *n.* one who stoops.

STOOPINGLY, [stōōp′-ing-li], *adv.* in a stooping fashion.

STOP (1), [stop], *n.* a cessation of progressive motion; obstruction; repression; interruption; obstacle; a point or mark in writing for regulating the necessary pauses; (*mus.*) the apparatus by which the sounds of musical instruments are regulated; a diaphragm in a camera; the act of applying the stops; an instruction to stop.

STOP (2), [stop], *v.t.* to close by filling or obstructing; to obstruct; to cause to come to a standstill; to check or withhold; to impede; to repress; to restrain; to intercept; to regulate sounds; to punctuate; *v.i.* to halt; to cease to go forward; to discontinue; to fill (a tooth); to forbid transmission of (a message); (*coll.*) to rest, remain for a while; **to s. up,** to obstruct, clog. [OE. *forstoppian* to stop up].

STOP-COCK, [stop′-kok′], *n.* a tap or valve for regulating flow.

STOPE, [stōp], *n.* (*min.*) one of a number of ledges in which ore is excavated. [Uncert.].

STOP-GAP, [stop′-gap′], *n.* a substitute in an emergency; a temporary expedient.

STOPING, [stōp′-ing], *n.* a series of stopes in a mine.

STOPPAGE, [stop′-ij], *n.* the act of arresting progress or motion; the condition of being stopped; deduction from pay; **s. in transitu,** a right to stop goods in transit when the consignee has become bankrupt.

STOPPER (1), [stop'-er], *n.* one who, or a thing which, stops; that which closes or fills an opening in a vessel, *esp.* a bottle; (*naut.*) a short piece of rope used for making fast.
STOPPER (2), [stop'-er], *v.t.* to shut or secure with a stopper.
STOPPING, [stop'-ing], *n.* something that stops or fills; the filling of a tooth; (*mus.*) the act of using a stop or pressing a string.
STOPPLE (1), [stopl], *n.* that which stops or closes the mouth of a vessel; a cork; a plug; a stopper. [~STOP].
STOPPLE (2), [stopl], *v.t.* to secure with a stopple.
STOP-PRESS, [stop'-pres'], *n.* late news printed in a special space in a newspaper.
STOP-WATCH, [stop'-woch'], *n.* a chronograph; a watch that can be started or stopped at any moment so as to measure the exact time taken by any action.
STORAGE, [staw'-rij], *n.* a placing in store; the safe keeping of goods in a warehouse; the price for keeping goods in a store; the system of storing electricity in cells of grids of lead superficially coated with oxide, which are immersed in dilute sulphuric acid, and polarized by the passage of the current; **cold s.,** keeping food or furs in refrigerating chambers.
STORAX, [staw'-raks], *n.* an odoriferous resin taken from *Styrax officinalis*; a preparation from *Liquidambar orientalis*. [L. *storax* from Gk. *sturax* resin].
STORE (1), [staw(r)], *n.* a stock laid up for supply; abundance; plenty; quantity accumulated; a warehouse, storage place; a shop; (*pl.*) arms, ammunition, provisions and clothing.
STORE (2), [staw(r)], *v.t.* to fill; to supply; to hoard; to reserve; to stow away for safe keeping; to warehouse; to afford storage space for. [OFr. *estorer*].
STOREHOUSE, [staw(r)-hows], *n.* a room or building in which goods are stored; a repository, warehouse; (*fig.*) of the mind, a place stored well with knowledge.
STOREKEEPER, [staw(r)-kēp'-er], *n.* a person who has the care of stores; a shopkeeper.
STORER, [staw'-rer], *n.* a person who lays by a store.
STOREROOM, [staw(r)'-rŏŏm], *n.* a room where articles not in use are stored.
STORES, [staw(r)z], *n.* a large modern shop with many departments; a department store.
STORESHIP, [staw(r)'-ship], *n.* a vessel used for carrying military or naval stores.
STOREY, STORY, [staw'-ri], *n.* one floor of a building; a set of rooms on one floor. [OFr. *estorée*].
STOREYED, STORIED, [staw'-rid], *adj.* having or comprising storeys or floors.
STOREY-POST, [staw'-ri-pōst], *n.* a vertical post employed to support a floor.
STORIATED, [staw'-ri-āt-ed], *adj.* storied. [STORIED (2)].
STORIED (1), [staw'-rid], *adj.* painted with pictures which tell a story; bearing inscriptions full of meaning. [STORY].
STORIED (2), see STOREYED.
STORIOLOGIST, [staw'-ri-ol'-o-jist], *n.* a student of folk-tales.
STORK, [stawk], *n.* a large long-beaked, long-legged wading bird of the genus *Ciconia*. [OE. *storc*].
STORKSBILL, [stawks'-bil], *n.* a plant of the genus *Erodium*, the beak of the fruit of which resembles a stork's bill.

STORKSBILL

STORM (1), [stawm], *n.* (*meteor.*) a violent commotion in the atmosphere, generally widespread and destructive; a tempest; assault on a fortified place; violent civil commotion; insurrection; clamour; tumult; distress; violence; tumultuous force; emotional upheaval; **to take by s.,** to take by a sudden assault; (*fig.*) to get possession of instantaneously. [OE. *storm*].
STORM (2), [stawm], *v.t.* to assault, take by storm; *v.i.* to raise a tempest; to blow with violence; to rage; to give way to violent emotion.
STORMBIRD, [stawm'-burd], *n.* the stormy petrel which supposedly heralds the coming of a storm.
STORMCOCK, [stawm'-kok'], *n.* the fieldfare or missel thrush.
STORM-CONE, [stawm'-kōn], *n.* a large canvas cone, part of a storm-signal.
STORM-DRUM, [stawm'-drum], *n.* a large canvas-covered drum, forming part of a storm-signal.
STORMER, [stawm'-er], *n.* a person who storms.
STORMGLASS, [stawm'-glahs'], *n.* a form of weather-glass.
STORMILY, [stawm'-i-li], *adv.* in stormy fashion.
STORMINESS, [stawm'-i-nes], *n.* the state of being stormy; tempestuousness; the state of being agitated by violent winds.
STORMING-PARTY, [stawm'-ing-pah'-ti], *n.* a party of men chosen to attack a fortified place.
STORMSAIL, [stawm'-sāl], *n.* (*naut.*) a small sail of very strong canvas used in a storm.
STORM-SIGNAL, [stawm'-sig'-nal], *n.* a signal, being an arrangement of a hollow drum of canvas and a hollow cone of canvas, to indicate the approach of a storm, its expected direction, and its intensity.
STORM-TOSSED, [stawm'-tost'], *adj.* suffering from violent storms; (*fig.*) agitated by passion.
STORM-TROOPER, [stawm'-trōōp'-er], *n.* a member of the National Socialist brown-shirt organization. [Trans. of Germ. *sturm abteilung* storm division].
STORM-WIND, [stawm'-wind], *n.* a wind bringing with it a storm; a gale; a hurricane.
STORMY, [stawm'-i], *adj.* tempestuous; accompanied or agitated with furious winds; boisterous; violent; agitated with passion; **s. petrel,** the small sea-bird Mother Carey's chicken, *Procellaria pelagica*.
STORTHING, [staw'-ting'], *n.* the Norwegian parliament. [OScand. *storr* great and *thing* meeting].
STORY (1), [staw'-ri], *n.* an oral narration or written narrative of a series of facts or events; history; a petty tale; a trifling tale; a fiction; a falsehood; an anecdote. [AFr. *storie* from L. *historia*].
STORY (2), see STOREY.
STORYBOOK, [staw'-ri-bŏŏk], *n.* a book of stories or short tales; a romance.
STORYTELLER, [staw'-ri-tel'-er], *n.* a person who tells stories; a historian; a novelist; (*coll.*) a liar.
STORYTELLING, [staw'-ri-tel'-ing], *n.* the practice of telling stories; (*coll.*) lying.
STOUP, [stōōp], *n.* a stoep, a flagon; a basin for holy water; a measure for liquids. [~OIcel. *staup*].
STOUT (1), [stowt], *n.* a dark strong drink resembling porter. [STOUT (2)].
STOUT (2), [stowt], *adj.* strong, lusty, thickset; bold, intrepid, resolute, brave; fat, corpulent. [OFr. *estout*].
STOUT-HEARTED, [stowt'-haht'-ed], *adj.* endowed with a brave heart; courageous, intrepid.
STOUTLY, [stowt'-li], *adv.* in a stout fashion.
STOUTNESS, [stowt'-nes], *n.* the quality or condition of being stout; boldness; fortitude; stubbornness.
STOVAINE, [stōv'-ān], *n.* a local anaesthetic discovered by Fourneau. [Fr. from STOVE (*fourneau*) and (COC)AINE].
STOVE (1), [stōv], *n.* an apparatus enclosing a fire for heating or cooking. [OE. *stofa* heated room].
STOVE (2), [stōv], *v.t.* to keep warm or heat by means of a stove; to fumigate.
STOVEPIPE, [stōv'-pīp], *n.* an iron pipe to carry off the smoke of a stove.
STOVE-PLANT, [stōv'-plahnt], *n.* a plant reared in a hot-house.
STOVE-PLATE, [stōv'-plāt], *n.* a movable plate for filling an aperture on the top of a stove.
STOW, [stō], *v.t.* to place; to put in a suitable place or position; to lay up; to pack; **s. it,** (*slang*) be quiet. [OE. *stowian*].
STOWAGE, [stō'-ij], *n.* the act of stowing; the state of being stowed; room for stowing goods; money paid for stowing things.
STOWAWAY, [stō'-a-wā'], *n.* one who hides in a ship in order to secure a free passage.
STOWER, [stō'-er], *n.* one who stows.
STRABISMUS, [strab-iz'-mus], *n.* a non-coincidence of the optic axes of the eyes upon an object; squinting; a cast in the eye. [~Gk. *strabos* squinting].
STRABOTOMY, [strab-ot'-om-i], *n.* the removal of strabismus by dividing the muscle or muscles causing the obliquity. [Gk. *strabos* squinting and *tome* cutting].
STRAD, [strad], *n.* a Stradivarius.
STRADDLE (1), [stradl], *n.* the act of straddling; distance between legs astraddle.
STRADDLE (2), [stradl], *v.t.* to bestride; *v.i.* to stand or walk with the legs far apart; (*fig.*) to adopt a hesitant attitude, to vacillate. [Uncert.].
STRADIVARIUS, [strad'-i-vāer'-i-us], *n.* a violin or similar stringed instrument made by Antonio Stradivari. [*Stradivarius*, Latin form of *Stradivari*].

STRAFE (1), [strahf], *n.* a concentrated artillery or aerial bombardment. [*Next*].
STRAFE (2), [strahf], *v.t.* to put up a heavy concentration of fire against. [Germ. *strafen* to punish].
STRAGGLE, [stragl], *v.i.* to wander from the direct course or way; to rove; to wander at large without any definite direction or object; to ramble; to shoot too far in growth; to be dispersed; to fall behind the main body. [Uncert.].
STRAGGLER, [strag'-ler], *n.* a person or thing that straggles.
STRAGGLING, [strag'-ling], *adj.* wandering; rambling; scattered; separated from the main place or group; (of hair) in untidy wisps; (of handwriting) unformed and feeble.
STRAGGLINGLY, [strag'-ling-li], *adv.* in a straggling fashion.
STRAGGLY, [strag'-li], *adj.* that straggles.
STRAIGHT (1), [strāt], *adj.* direct; not deviating or crooked; upright; honest, reliable; fair and truthful; frank; undiluted. [OE. *streht*].
STRAIGHT (2), [strāt], *adv.* in a straight line; in a forthright manner; directly; without ambiguity; without diluting.
STRAIGHTAWAY, [strāt'-a-wā'], *adv.* at once, straightway.
STRAIGHT-EDGE, [strāt'-ej'], *n.* a small board or piece of metal having one edge perfectly straight for testing the straightness or levels of objects.
STRAIGHTEN, [strāt'-en], *v.t. and i.* to make straight; to change from a crooked to a straight form.
STRAIGHTENER, [strāt'-ner], *n.* a person or thing that straightens.
STRAIGHTFORTH, [strāt'-fawth], *adv.* henceforth.
STRAIGHTFORWARD, [strāt-faw'-werd], *adj.* proceeding in a straight course; upright; open; frank; simple.
STRAIGHTFORWARDLY, [strāt'-faw'-werd-li], *adv.* in a straightforward fashion.
STRAIGHTFORWARDNESS, [strāt'-faw'-werd-nes], *n.* the condition of being straightforward.
STRAIGHTLY, [strāt'-li], *adv.* in a straight manner.
STRAIGHTNESS, [strāt'-nes], *n.* the condition of being straight.
STRAIGHT-OF-BREADTH, [strāt'-of-bredth'], *n.* (*naut.*) the part of a ship's hull in which the cross-sections are vertical at the sides.
STRAIGHTWAY, [strāt'-wā], *adv.* immediately, straightaway.
STRAIN (1), [strān], *n.* racial descent, breed, lineage; descendants, race; innate quality, inherited tendency; a class or group of people, animals or things linked by common characteristics. [OE. *streon*].
STRAIN (2), [strān], *n.* the action or result of straining or stretching; reach, stretch, muscular effort; a passage of music or poetry or its characteristic style and content. [STRAIN (3)].
STRAIN (3), [strān], *v.t.* to stretch violently; to draw with force; to injure by stretching; to tax to the utmost strength; to filter; to make tighter; to force; to constrain; *v.i.* to make a great effort; to be filtered. [OFr. *estreindre* from L. *stringere* to make tight].
STRAINER, [strān'-er], *n.* an instrument for filtration; a sieve.
STRAINING, [strān'-ing], *n.* the act of straining, stretching; the act of filtering; filtration.
STRAIT (1), [strāt], *n.* a narrow pass or passage in the sea between two portions of land; distress, difficulty; strained means. [STRAIT (2)].
STRAIT (2), [strāt], *adj.* narrow, strict, rigorous, difficult. [AFr. *estreit*].
STRAITEN, [strāt'-en], *v.t.* to make narrow; to contract; to confine; to make tense or tight; to distress; to perplex; to press with poverty or other necessity; to embarrass by want of sufficient room.
STRAIT-JACKET, [strāt'-jak'-it], *n.* a strait-waistcoat.
STRAIT-LACED, [strāt'-lāst'], *adj.* tightly laced in stays; constrained; strict in manners or morals.
STRAITLY, [strāt'-li], *adv.* narrowly, strictly.
STRAIT-WAISTCOAT, [strāt'-wes'-kut, strāt'-wāst'-kōt], *n.* a garment to restrain the arms of a dangerous lunatic.
STRAKE, [strāk], *n.* a curved iron plate connecting the rim segments of a wheel; a single breadth of wood or plating along a ship's side. [ME. *strake*].
STRAMINEOUS, [stram-in'-i-us], *adj.* strawy; consisting of straw; chaffy; like straw; light; straw-coloured. [L. *stramineus*].
STRAND (1), [strand], *n.* the beach, shore. [OE. *strand*].
STRAND (2), [strand], *n.* one twisted thread in yarn or rope; a tress of hair; a feather barb. [OFr. *estran*].
STRAND (3), [strand], *v.t.* to cause to be driven ashore; to leave helpless; *v.i.* to drift or be driven ashore; to run aground.
STRAND (4), [strand], *v.t.* to twist strands together to make rope, etc.
STRANDED, [strand'-ed], *adj.* abandoned, left helpless or without resources.
STRANGE, [strānj], *adj.* foreign; belonging to others; not before known, heard, or seen; wonderful; odd; unusual; reserved; unfamiliar; inexperienced. [OFr. *estrange* from L. *extraneus* outer].
STRANGELY, [strānj'-li], *adv.* in a strange fashion.
STRANGENESS, [strānj'-nes], *n.* the condition of being strange.
STRANGER, [strānj'-er], *n.* a person who belongs to another town or country; one unknown; one unacquainted; a guest; a visitor; (*leg.*) one not party or privy to any act. [OFr. *estrangier* alien].
STRANGLE, [strang'-gl], *v.t* to destroy the life of by stopping respiration; to hinder from birth or appearance; to suppress, stifle. [OFr. *estrangler*].
STRANGLER, [strang'-gler], *n.* a person or thing that strangles.
STRANGLES, [strang'-glz], *n.* an infectious disorder peculiar to young horses, in which a tumour is formed under the jaw. [STRANGLE].
STRANGLEWEED, [strang'-gl-wēd], *n.* the dodder, any of the various species of *Cuscuta*.
STRANGULATE, [strang'-gyōō-lāt], *v.t.* to stop the circulation of by compression; to strangle. [L. *strangulare*].
STRANGULATION, [strang'-gyōō-lā'-shun], *n.* the action of strangling; hysterical constriction of the throat; compression of the intestines in hernia.
STRANGURIOUS, [strang-gyōō(e)r'-i-us], *adj.* (*med.*) labouring under strangury; pertaining to strangury.
STRANGURY, [strang'-gyōō-ri], *n.* (*med.*) a frequent irrepressible desire to pass water, with a difficulty in discharging it, accompanied by pain. [L. *stranguria*].
STRAP (1), [strap], *n.* a long narrow strip of cloth or leather; a strop; an iron plate for connecting two or more timbers; (*naut.*) a piece of rope formed into a circle, used to keep a block in its position; a military strip worn upon the shoulder; (*coll.*) corporal punishment. [OE. *stropp* thong].
STRAP (2), [strap], *v.t.* to fasten, tie up, bind with a strap; to rub on a strap for sharpening; to beat with a strap as a punishment.
STRAPHANGER, [strap'-hang'-er], *n.* a standing passenger steadying himself by holding on to a strap affixed to the side or roof of a vehicle.
STRAPPADO, [strap-ah'-dō], *n.* an old form of torture or military punishment by drawing up a person to a height by a rope and letting him fall with a jerk to the length of the rope. [It. *strappata*].
STRAPPING (1), [strap'-ing], *n.* the material used for straps; diachylon plaster.
STRAPPING (2), [strap'-ing], *adj.* tall, handsome, lusty.
STRAP-SHAPED, [strap'-shāpt], *adj.* resembling a strap in shape; (*bot.*) ligulate.
STRAPWORT, [strap'-wurt], *n.* a plant that grows on the seashore, *Corrigiola littoralis*.
STRASS, [stras], *n.* a variety of flint glass employed in the manufacture of artificial gems. [*Strass(er)* the inventor].
STRATAGEM, [strat'-a-jem], *n.* an artifice, particularly in war; a plan, scheme, or trick for deceiving an enemy or obtaining any advantage. [OFr. *stratageme* from Gk. *strategos* general].
STRATEGIC, [strat-ēj'-ik], *adj.* based on, of, or resembling, strategy.
STRATEGICAL, [strat-ēj'-ik-al], *adj.* strategic.
STRATEGICALLY, [strat-ēj'-ik-a-li], *adv.* in a strategic fashion.
STRATEGIST, [strat'-ej-ist], *n.* one who practises or is versed in strategy.
STRATEGY, [strat'-ej-i], *n.* generalship; the science or art of combining and employing military resources, or of manoeuvring an army; direction of the operations of war; (*fig.*) clever manoeuvring. [Gk. *strategia* office of a general].
STRATH, [strath], *n.* a wide open valley through which a river runs. [Gael. *srath*].
STRATHSPEY, [strath-spā'], *n.* a lively Scottish dance; music for this dance. [*Strathspey*, in Scotland].
STRATICULATE, [strat-ik'-yōōl-āt], *adj.* deposited in a series of thin layers. [L. *straticulum* thin layer].

STRATIFICATION, [strat'-if-ik-ā'-shun], *n.* the process or act of stratifying; the condition of being stratified; the arrangement of strata.
STRATIFIED, [strat'-i-fīd], *adj.* arranged in strata or layers.
STRATIFORM, [strat'-i-fawm], *adj.* in the form of strata. [STRATUM and FORM].
STRATIFY, [strat-i-fī], *v.t. and i.* to form into a layer or layers, as rocks in the earth; to deposit in strata.
STRATIGRAPHICAL, [strat'-i-graf'-ik-al], *adj.* pertaining to stratigraphy.
STRATIGRAPHICALLY, [strat'-i-graf'-ik-al-i], *adv.* in a stratigraphical fashion.
STRATIGRAPHY, [strat-i'-graf-i]. *n.* the science of the geological characteristics of strata. [STRATUM and Gk. *graphia* writing].
STRATOCRACY, [strat-ok'-ras-i], *n.* a military government; government by military leaders and an army. [Gk. *stratos* an army and *kratia* rule].
STRATOGRAPHICAL, [strat'-ō-graf'-ik-al], *adj.* pertaining to stratography.
STRATOGRAPHICALLY, [strat'-ō-graf'-ik-al-i], *adv.* in a stratographical fashion.
STRATOGRAPHY, [strat-og'-raf-i], *n.* the description of armies, or what pertains to an army. [Gk. *stratos* an army and *graphia* writing].
STRATONIC, [strat-on'-ik], *adj.* pertaining to armies; military.
STRATOSPHERE, [strat'-ōs-fēer'], *n.* the upper part of the atmosphere where the temperature no longer falls with an increase in height. [STRATUM and SPHERE].
STRATUM, (*pl.* **strata**), [strāt'-um], *n.* a bed or layer of rock occurring in a series in the crust of the earth; a bed or layer artificially made; (*fig.*) a social level or class. [L. *stratum*].
STRATUS, (*pl.* **strati**), [strāt'-us], *n.* a cloud form, so called from its being spread over the dome of the sky in horizontal layers. [L. *stratus*].
STRAUGHT†, [strawt], *p.pt.* of STRETCH.
STRAW, [straw], *n.* the stalk of certain species of grass, grain, etc.; a mass of such stalks from grain, etc., cut and thrashed; anything proverbially worthless, unreliable. [OE. *streaw*].
STRAWBERRY, [straw'-be-ri], *n.* one of the eight species of the genus *Fragaria*; its fruit; **crushed s.,** a soft pinky colour resembling that of strawberries when crushed. [OE. *streawberige*].
STRAWBERRY-LEAF, [straw'-be-ri-lēf'], *n.* the trifoliate leaf of the strawberry plant; this forming the decoration of the coronet of a duke; a symbol of ducal rank.
STRAWBERRY-TREE, [straw'-be-ri-trē'], *n.* an evergreen tree of the genus *Arbutus*, with fruit somewhat resembling the strawberry.
STRAWBOARD, [straw'-bawd], *n.* a thick paper made of straw; straw pulp.
STRAWBUILT, [straw'-bilt], *adj.* constructed of straw.
STRAW-COLOURED, [straw'-kul'-erd], *adj.* of a pale yellow colour like dry straw.
STRAWCUTTER, [straw'-kut'-er], *n.* a machine for cutting straw for fodder.
STRAW-PLAIT, [straw'-plat'], *n.* plaited straw.
STRAW-ROPE, [straw'-rōp], *n.* a rope made of twisted straw.
STRAWY, [straw'-i], *adj.* made of, resembling, straw.
STRAY (1), [strā], *n.* any domestic animal that has left an enclosure, and wanders at large or is lost; a lost or forlorn child; a waif; (*fig.*) one who wanders from the path of duty or rectitude.
STRAY (2), [strā], *adj.* having strayed; scattered, found here and there irregularly; of a bullet, casual.
STRAY (3), [strā], *v.i.* to wander, move away or aside (from); to deviate; to roam; (*fig.*) to deviate from the course of strict virtue; of one's thoughts, to wander in a desultory fashion. [OFr. *estraier*].
STRAYER, [strā'-er], *n.* a person or animal that strays.
STREAK (1), [strēk], *n.* a line or stripe of a different colour from the ground; a stripe; (*min.*) a mark made by a mineral when drawn across unglazed porcelain; a flash of lightning; (*fig.*) a strain, small endowment; **s. of luck,** a run of luck. [OE. *strica*].
STREAK (2), [strēk], *v.t.* to form streaks in; to stripe; to variegate with streaks; *v.i.* (*coll.*) to flash swiftly. [*Prec.*].
STREAKED, [strēkt], *adj.* marked or variegated with stripes of a different colour, shade, substance or texture; (of lightning) swiftly flashing, forked.
STREAKINESS, [strēk'-i-nes], *n.* the quality of being streaky.
STREAKY, [strēk'-i], *adj.* having streaks, *esp.* of fat and lean meat.
STREAM (1), [strēm], *n.* a current of water or other fluid; a river, brook, or rivulet; a current of air or of light; current; drift; the act of streaming; (*fig.*) a continuously moving crowd or series of objects; the general flow of events or opinions. [OE. *stream*].
STREAM (2), [strēm], *v.t.* to cause to pour out in a stream; *v.i.* to flow; to move or run in a continuous current; to issue in a stream; to move continuously; to run with liquid; to float out.
STREAMER, [strēm'-er], *n.* a long narrow banner; a pennant; a beam or ray of light shooting up from the horizon.
STREAMLESS, [strēm'-les], *adj.* without a stream or streams.
STREAMLET, [strēm'-let], *n.* a little stream.
STREAM-LINE (1), [strēm'-līn], *n.* a gracefully curved shape which presents no projecting portions to act as resistance to air or water.
STREAM-LINE (2), [strēm'-līn], *v.t.* to shape so as to offer the minimum of resistance to air or water.
STREAM-TIN, [strēm'-tin], *n.* tin ore found in beds of streams or the nearby alluvial ground.
STREAM-WORKS, [strēm'-wurks], *n.*(*pl.*) alluvial deposits of tin ore, worked in the open air in Cornwall.
STREAMY, [strēm'-i], *adj.* abounding in running water; flowing in a stream or streak.
STREET, [strēt], *n.* a paved road in a city or town, lined with and including houses; a Roman road; **not in the same s. with,** (*coll.*) greatly inferior to; **on the streets,** being a prostitute; **streets ahead of,** far ahead of. [OE. *stræt* from L. *strata via* paved way].
STREET-ORDERLY, [strēt'-awd'-er-li], *n.* a scavenger; a receptacle for street sweepings.
STREET-SWEEPER, [strēt'-swēp'-er], *n.* a scavenger.
STREET-WALKER, [strēt'-wawk-er], *n.* one who walks the streets; a prostitute.
STRENGTH, [strengkth], *n.* the quality of being strong; active muscular power of an animal body; firmness; solidity, toughness; power or vigour of any kind; power of resisting attacks; support; mental activity and power, intellectual force; robustness; intensity; spirit; force of writing, nervous diction; vividness; physical virtue; legal force; natural force; force; amount of force, military or naval; vehemence; **on the s. of,** because of, relying on. [OE. *strengthu*].
STRENGTHEN, [strengkth'-en], *v.t.* to make strong; to add strength to; to confirm, animate; to cause to increase in power or security; *v.i.* to grow strong or stronger.
STRENGTHENER, [strengkth'-en-er], *n.* one who, or that which, increases the strength.
STRENGTHENING, [strengkth'-en-ing], *adj.* adding to the strength of; nourishing.
STRENGTHLESS, [strengkth'-les], *adj.* without strength or power, weak.
STRENUOUS, [stren'-yŏŏ-us], *adj.* eagerly pressing or urgent; zealous; ardent; bold and vigorous; needing effort; persistent, energetic. [L. *strenuus*].
STRENUOUSLY, [stren'-yŏŏ-us-li], *adv.* in a strenuous fashion.
STRENUOUSNESS, [stren'-yŏŏ-us-nes], *n.* the state of being strenuous; eagerness; active zeal.
STREPENT, [strep'-ent], *adj.* loud, noisy, clamorous. [L. *strepens*].
STREPITANT, [strep'-it-ant], *adj.* loud, noisy.
STREPITOSO, [strep'-it-ō'-so], *adv.* (*mus.*) in a boisterous, impetuous manner. [It. *strepitoso*].
STREPTOCOCCUS, [strept'-ō-kok'-us], *n.* (*path.*) a type of bacillus which occurs arranged in chains. [Gk. *streptos* twisted and *kokkos* berry].
STRESS (1), [stres], *n.* force; urgency; intense pressure; importance; that which bears most weight; violence; strain; emphasis; accent.
STRESS (2), [stres], *v.t.* to subject to a strain; to lay stress on; to emphasize; to draw particular attention to. [OFr. *estrecier*].
STRETCH (1), [strech], *n.* extension in length or breadth; reach; effort; strain; straining; utmost extent of meaning; utmost reach of power; distance travelled on one tack; course; direction; a period of time.
STRETCH (2), [strech], *v.t.* to draw out to greater length or breadth; to spread; to expand; to reach; to

strain towards; to exaggerate; *v.i.* to be drawn out in length or breadth; to be extended; to free one's limbs from the stiffness of sleep; **to s. one's legs,** to go for a brisk walk. [OE. *streccean*].

STRETCHER, [strech'-er], *n.* a person or thing that stretches; a brick or stone laid lengthwise in the surface of a wall; a piece of timber in building; a narrow piece of plank placed across a boat for the rower to set his feet against; a frame or litter for carrying sick or wounded; one of the rods of an umbrella; an expanding device.

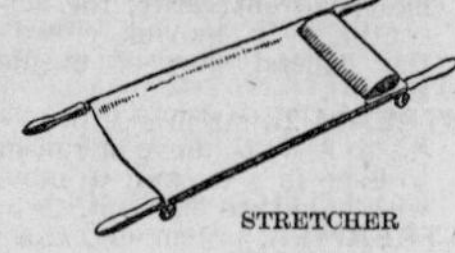

STRETCHER

STRETCHING-COURSE, [strech'-ing-kaws], *n.* (*arch.*) a course or row of stretchers along the side of a wall.

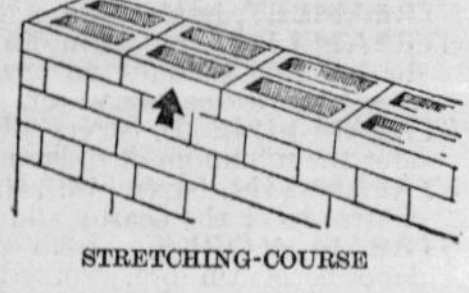

STRETCHING-COURSE

STRETCHY, [strech'-i], *adj.* liable to stretch.

STRETTO (1), [stret'-ō], *n.* a passage (to be) played stretto. [*Next*].

STRETTO (2), [stret'-ō], *adv.* (*mus.*) more quickly. [It. *stretto*].

STREW, [strōō], *v.t.* to scatter; to spread here and there; to sprinkle loosely; to cover by being scattered. [OE. *streawian*].

STREWING, [strōō'-ing], *n.* the action of scattering or spreading over; anything strewed or fit to be strewed.

STREWTH, see STRUTH.

STRIAE, [strī'-ē], *n.(pl.)* small channels, grooves, or thread-like lines; the fillets between the flutes of columns. [L. *stria* a furrow].

STRIATE, STRIATED, [strī'-āt, strī-āt'-ed], *adj.* marked with narrow lines or grooves; channelled; streaked. [L. *striatus* furrowed].

STRIATION, [strī-ā'-shun], *n.* the state of being striated.

STRICK, [strik], *n.* a handful of flax ready to be slivered. [~STRIKE].

STRICKEN, [strik'-en], *adj.* struck down; wearied, afflicted.

STRICKLE, [strikl], *n.* a rod used to strike grain to a level with the measure; a hone for whetting scythes. [OE. *stricel*].

STRICT, [strikt], *adj.* precise, exact, accurate, definite, restricted, severe. [L. *strictus* drawn together].

STRICTLY, [strikt'-li], *adv.* in a strict manner.

STRICTNESS, [strikt'-nes], *n.* the quality of being strict; rigour; severity; inflexibleness.

STRICTURE, [strik'-cher], *n.* severe criticism; censure; animadversion; (*med.*) a morbid contraction of any passage of the body. [L. *strictura* contraction].

STRIDE (1), [strīd], *n.* a long step; a wide stretch of the legs; **to take in one's s.,** to accomplish without extra effort in the ordinary pursuit of one's affairs.

STRIDE (2), [strīd], *v.t.* to cross over with one long step; to bestride; *v.i.* to walk with long steps; to straddle. [OE. *stridan*].

STRIDENCY, [strīd'-en-si], *n.* the fact or quality of being strident.

STRIDENT, [strīd'-ent], *adj.* harsh; loud and raucous. [L. *stridens*].

STRIDENTLY, [strīd'-ent-li], *adv.* in a strident way.

STRIDULANT, [strid'-yōōl-ant], *adj.* strident; chirping in a shrill manner. [L. *stridulus* creaking].

STRIDULATE, [strid'-yōōl-āt], *v.i.* to make a harsh grating noise like a cricket by rubbing parts of the hard integument together.

STRIDULATION, [strid'-yōōl-ā'-shun], *n.* the action of stridulating.

STRIDULATORY, [strid'-yōōl-ā'-ter-i], *adj.* stridulous.

STRIDULOUS, [strid'-yōōl-us], *adj.* characterized by stridulation; making a harsh creaking sound.

STRIFE, [strīf], *n.* contention for superiority; contest or emulation; struggle for victory; dissension, discord. [OFr. *estrif*].

STRIG, [strig], *n.* footstalk. [Unkn.].

STRIGA, (*pl.* **strigae**), [strīg'-a], *n.* (*bot.*) little stiff hairs swollen at their roots. [L. *striga* furrow].

STRIGIL, [strij'-il], *n.* a skin-scraper; an instrument for scraping the skin when bathing. [L. *strigilis*].

STRIGOSE, [strīg'-ōs], *adj.* (*bot.*) with stiff, lanceolate bristles. [~STRIGA].

STRIKE (1), [strīk], *n.* the act of workmen combining in a refusal to work till the employer considers their demands favourably; an attack by aircraft launched from a carrier; (*geol.*) the direction of the outcrop of a stratum; **lucky s.,** a lucky find.

STRIKE (2), [strīk], *v.t.* to hit, deal a blow to; to dash against; to stab with a blow; to reach, arrive at; to sound by percussion; to make by means of stamping; to fill with; to form; to impinge on the mind; to occur to the mind; to cease work and enter upon a strike; *v.i.* to deliver blows; to collide with; to cause to light; to take down one's flag; **to s. at,** to aim at; **to s. in,** to break in; **to s. off,** to cancel; to cut off; **to s. out,** to hit out; to make a bold stroke in swimming or in an enterprise; to cancel; **to s. up,** to begin; **to s. a blow for,** to do something to help; **to s. camp,** to break up an encampment; **to s. while the iron is hot,** to act expeditiously; **to s. oil,** to discover a deposit of mineral oil; (*fig.*) to encounter good fortune. [OE. *strican* to rub, move].

STRIKE (3), [strīk], *v.i.* to take part in a strike.

STRIKE-BLOCK, [strīk'-blok'], *n.* a joiner's plane used in shooting a short joint.

STRIKER, [strīk'-er], *n.* a person or thing that strikes.

STRIKING, [strīk'-ing], *adj.* affecting with strong emotions; surprising; forcible; impressive; effective, smart; that strikes the hours, etc.

STRIKINGLY, [strīk'-ing-li], *adv.* in a striking fashion.

STRIKINGNESS, [strīk'-ing-nes], *n.* the quality of being striking.

STRING (1), [string], *n.* a small rope, line, or cord used for fastening or tying anything; a ribbon; a thread on which a thing is filed; a line of things; the gut or wire cord of a musical instrument, as of a harp; any wire; a fibre; a nerve or tendon; the line or cord of a bow; a series of things; among miners, a small filamentous ramification of a metallic vein; **to have two strings to one's bow,** to have two alternative means of attaining one's object; **to have on a s.,** to have at one's mercy, to gull. [OE. *streng*].

STRING (2), [string], *v.t.* to furnish with strings; to put in tune a stringed instrument; to thread on a string; to render taut; **to s. out,** to extend singly over some distance.

STRING-BAND, [string'-band'], *n.* a band made up of players of stringed instruments.

STRING-BEANS, [string'-bēnz], *n.(pl.)* French beans, so called from the stringy substance found on the back of the pods.

STRING-BOARD, [string'-bawd], *n.* a board with its face next to the well-hole in a wooden staircase.

STRING-COURSE, [string'-kaws], *n.* a projecting horizontal band or line of mouldings on a building.

STRINGED, [stringd], *adj.* furnished with strings.

STRINGENCY, [strinj'-en-si], *n.* the condition of being stringent; strictness.

STRINGENDO, [strinj-end'-ō], *adv.* (*mus.*) in accelerated time. [It. *stringendo*].

STRINGENT, [strinj'-ent], *adj.* strictly enforceable; strict; severe; rigid. [L. *stringens*].

STRINGENTLY, [strinj'-ent-li], *adv.* in a stringent fashion.

STRINGENTNESS, [strinj'-ent-nes], *n.* the condition of being stringent.

STRINGER, [string'-er], *n.* a maker of strings; a horizontal timber or bar serving as a support.

STRINGHALT, [string'-hawlt], *n.* a sudden twitching of the hinder leg of a horse, or an involuntary or convulsive movement of the muscles that extend or bend the hock.

STRINGINESS, [string'-i-nes], *n.* the condition of being stringy.

STRINGLESS, [string'-les], *adj.* without strings.

STRINGY, [string'-i], *adj.* consisting of strings or small threads; filamentous; ropy, viscid; fibrous.

STRINGY-BARK, [stringi'-bahk], *n.* a species of *Eucalyptus*, the bark of which was used by the Australian aborigines for making cordage.

STRIP (1), [strip], *n.* a long narrow piece or band; an edge or border; a shred.

STRIP (2), [strip], *v.t. and i.* to pull or tear off; to take away the covering of; to skin, to deprive; to divest; to pillage; to remove the long loose hair of (a dog); to take off all one's clothes; (*naut.*) to unrig. [OE. *strypan*].

STRIPE (1), [strīp], *n.* a line or a strip of material

of a different colour or texture from the ground; a chevron; a strip attached to something of a different colour; a wale or mark of a lash; a stroke made with a lash or stick. [MDu. *strijpe*].
STRIPE (2), [strīp], *v.t.* to make stripes on; to mark with a stripe or stripes.
STRIPED, [stript], *adj.* having stripes of different colours.
STRIPLING, [strip'-ling], *n.* a youth just passing from boyhood to manhood; a tall growing lad [~STRIP (1)].
STRIPPER, [strip'-er], *n.* one who or that which strips.
STRIP-POKER, [strip'-pōk'-er], *n.* a form of poker in which the loser of each hand must remove a garment.
STRIP-TEASE, [strip'-tēz'], *n.* (*U.S.*) a form of music-hall entertainment in which the performer removes her garments one at a time. [STRIP (2) and TEASE (2)].
STRIPY, [strīp'-i], *adj.* resembling a stripe; striped.
STRIVE, (**strives, striving, strove, striven**), [strīv], *v.i.* to make efforts; to endeavour with earnestness; to labour hard; to struggle; to vie; to fight, contend. [OFr. *estriver*].
STRIVER, [strīv'-er], *n.* one who strives.
STRIVINGLY, [strīv'-ing-li], *adv.* in a striving fashion.
STROB, [strob], *n.* the angular velocity of a radian per second. [Gk. *strobos* a whirling].
STROBILA, [strōb'-il-a], *n.* a tape-worm.
STROBILE, [strōb'-īl], *n.* a hardened catkin, with scale-like carpels as in the pines. [Gk. *strobilos*].
STROBILIFORM, [strōb-il'-i-fawm], *adj.* like a strobile in shape.
STROBILINE, [strōb'-il-īn], *n.* strobiliform.
STROBOSCOPE, [strob'-ō-skōp], *n.* an instrument for determining the frequency of rotation by means of the intermittent lighting of the rotating object. [Gk. *strobos* a whirling and SCOPE].
STROKE (1), [strōk], *v.t.* to rub gently with the hand to show friendliness; to soothe; to rub gently in one direction; to make smooth; to pull stroke-oar and so set the rate of rowing. [OE. *stracian*].
STROKE (2), [strōk], *n.* a blow; the striking of one body against another; a hostile blow or attack; a sudden attack of disease or affliction; calamity; the sound of a clock; the touch of a pencil; a touch; a masterly effort; an effort suddenly or unexpectedly produced; a series of operations; a dash in writing or printing; a line; the working length of a rod; the travel or throw of a valve; the oarsman nearest the stern of the boat and the one who sets the rowing pace; the sweep of an oar. [OE. *strac*].

STROKE

STROKE-OAR, [strōk'-aw(r)], *n.* the oar nearest the stern.
STROKER, [strōk'-er], *n.* one who strokes.
STROLL (1), [strōl], *n.* a saunter; a leisurely walk; a quiet, unhurried walk.
STROLL (2), [strōl], *v.i.* to ramble idly or leisurely; to saunter. [Unkn.].
STROLLER, [strōl'-er], *n.* one who strolls; a strolling player, itinerant actor.
STROLLING, [strōl'-ing], *adj.* moving leisurely from place to place; itinerant.
STROMA, [strōm'-a], *n.* (*anat.*) the groundwork of a tissue, organ, or cell. [Gk. *stroma* covering].
STROMATIC, [strōm-at'-ik], *adj.* miscellaneous; made up of different kinds. [~*Prec.*].
STROMEYERITE, [strō'-mier-īt], *n.* a steel-grey ore of silver, consisting of sulphur, silver, and copper. [*Stromeyer*, the mineralogist].
STRONG, [strong], *adj.* well; having physical power; vigorous; firm; having ability to bear or endure; fortified; powerful; resourceful; violent; forcible; hale; sound; cogent; zealous; of great strength; evil-smelling; affecting a sense forcibly; bright; full of spirit; intoxicating; having great force; having great force of character, intellect, or mind. [OE. *strong*].
STRONG-BOX, [strong'-boks], *n.* a metal box, fitted with strong locks, used for storing valuables.
STRONGHOLD, [strong'-hōld], *n.* a strongly fortified place; a fortress; a place of security; (*fig.*) a strong centre of some opinion or movement.
STRONGLY, [strong'-li], *adv.* in a strong fashion.
STRONG-MINDED, [strong'-mīnd'-ed], *adj.* resolute, determined; free from ordinary human weaknesses.
STRONG-ROOM, [strong'-rōōm], *n.* a strong fire-proof room in which valuables are stored.
STRONG-SET, [strong'-set'], *adj.* strongly made; compact.
STRONG-WATER, [strong'-wawt'-er], *n.* alcoholic drink, spirits.
STRONGYLE, [stron'-jīl], *n.* (*med.*) a round nematoid intestinal worm. [Gk. *strongulos* round].
STRONTIA, [stron'-sha], *n.* (*chem.*) oxide of strontium.
STRONTIAN, [stron'-shan], *adj.* pertaining to, or containing, strontium.
STRONTIANITE, [stron'-shan-īt], *n.* carbonate of strontium.
STRONTITIC, [stron-tit'-ik], *adj.* pertaining to strontium.
STRONTIUM, [strŏn'-shum], *n.* (*chem.*) the ductile metallic element denoted by Sr. [*Strontian* in Argyllshire, where first found].
STROP (1), [strop], *n.* a strip of leather used for sharpening a razor; (*naut.*) a band of leather or rope used for suspending a block. [OE. *stropp*].
STROP (2), [strop], *v.t.* to sharpen on a strop; (*naut.*) to provide with a strop.
STROPHE, [strōf'-i], *n.* in classical Greek drama, the part sung by the chorus when moving to the left; in Greek poetry, the first member of a poem; a stanza. [Gk. *strophe* a turning].
STROPHIC, [stro-fik], *adj.* pertaining to, written in, strophes.
STROPHULUS, [strof'-yōōl-us], *adj.* (*med.*) teeth-rash, a papular skin disease peculiar to babies and young children. [~Gk. *strophos* twisted cord].
STROUDING, [strowd'-ing], *n.* a coarse sort of cloth. [*Stroud* in Gloucestershire].
STROVE, [strōv], *pret.* of STRIVE.
STRUCK, [struk], *pret. and p.pt.* of STRIKE.
STRUCTURAL, [struk'-cher-al], *adj.* of, or pertaining to, structure.
STRUCTURE, [struk'-cher], *n.* manner of building; form; make; construction; a building of any kind, but chiefly one of a certain size or magnificence; an edifice; the arrangement of the elements or parts of anything; texture; manner of organization. [L. *structura*].
STRUCTURED, [struk'-cherd], *adj.* having organic structure; carefully designed and built.
STRUCTURELESS, [struk'-cher-les], *adj.* formless; without structure.
STRUGGLE (1), [strugl], *n.* a strenuous effort to obtain an object or to avoid an evil; contest; contention; agony; contortions of extreme distress.
STRUGGLE (2), [strugl], *v.i.* to use great bodily or mental efforts to attain an end; to strive; to contend; to fight. [ME. *strugelen*].
STRUGGLER, [strug'-ler], *n.* one who struggles.
STRUM, [strum], *v.t.* to strum on; *v.i.* to play badly and noisily on a stringed instrument. [Echoic].
STRUMA, (*pl.* **strumæ**), [strōōm-a], *n.* (*path.*) goitre; (*bot.*) a swelling occurring at the base of a leaf; a dilatation below the base of a moss capsule. [L. *struma*].
STRUMITIS, [strōōm-īt'-is], *n.* (*path.*) acute inflammation of the thyroid gland.
STRUMOSE, [strōōm'-ōs], *adj.* strumous. [L. *strumosus*].
STRUMOSIS, [strōōm-ōs'-is], *n.* dilatation. [L. *struma* swelling and Gk. *osis* denoting condition].
STRUMOUS, [strōōm'-us], *adj.* scrofulous; with a struma or strumae.
STRUMOUSNESS, [strōōm'-us-nes], *n.* the condition of being strumous.
STRUMPET, [strump'-it], *n.* a prostitute. [Uncert.].
STRUNG, [strung], *pret. and p.pt.* of STRING.
STRUT (1), [strut], *n.* a lofty proud step or walk with the head erect; a stiff and unnatural affectation of dignity in walking; a piece of timber obliquely placed to support a rafter; a support; (*carp.*) a prop and brace. [~Dan. *strutte*].
STRUT (2), [strut], *v.i.* to walk in a stiff, haughty, self-important manner; to walk with affected dignity or pomposity. [OE. *strutian* to stand stiffly].
STRUTH, STREWTH, [strōōth], *int.* expressing amazement. [Abbrev. of *God's truth*].
STRUTHIO, [strōōth'-i-ō], *n.* the genus of the ostrich. [Gk. *struthion*].
STRUTHIOUS, [strōōth'-i-us], *adj.* pertaining to or like the ostrich.
STRUTTER, [strut'-er], *n.* a person or creature that struts.
STRUTTINGLY, [strut'-ing-li], *adv.* in a strutting manner; conceitedly, pompously, showing off.

STRYCHNIA, [strik'-ni-a], *n.* strychnine. [Gk. *strukhnos* nightshade].

STRYCHNIC, [strik'-nik], *adj.* of, or pertaining to, strychnine.

STRYCHNINE, [strik'-nēn], *n.* a poisonous alkaloid, in minute quantities valuable as a medicine, usually obtained from the seeds of *Strychnos Nux-vomica.* [~Gk. *strukhnos* nightshade].

STUB (1), [stub], *n.* the stump of a tree after the tree has been cut down; a stub-nail; the short end of a pencil or cigarette when the main part has been used or consumed. [OE. *stybb* tree stump].

STUB (2), [stub], *v.t.* to grub up by the roots; to extirpate; to rid of roots; to strike (the toe) violently against an object.

STUBBED, [stubd], *adj.* short and thick; blunt; obtuse; hardy; not nice or delicate.

STUBBEDNESS, [stub'-id-nes], *n.* the condition of being or resembling a stub.

STUBBINESS, [stub'-i-nes], *n.* the condition of being stubby.

STUBBLE, [stubl], *n.* the short hard stalks of the corn left standing in the ground when the crop has been cut; a growth of beard resembling this. [OFr. *stuble*].

STUBBLED, [stubld], *adj.* covered with or bearing stubble.

STUBBLE-FED, [stubl'-fed'], *adj.* fed on the grass growing among the stubble.

STUBBLE-GOOSE, [stubl'-gōōs], *n.* a goose fed on the grass and grain of a stubble field; the greylag, *Anser cinereus.*

STUBBLE-RAKE, [stubl'-rāk], *n.* a rake having long teeth for raking over stubble.

STUBBLY, [stub'-li], *adj.* pertaining to, resembling, stubble; hard, short, and bristling.

STUBBORN, [stub'-ern], *adj.* obstinate; self-willed; difficult to move either mentally or physically; fixed in opinion; unreasonable; obstinately resisting force of any kind. [ME. *stoburn*].

STUBBORNLY, [stub'-ern-li], *adv.* in a stubborn fashion.

STUBBORNNESS, [stub'-ern-nes], *n.* the condition of being stubborn.

STUBBY, [stub'-i], *adj.* of the nature of a stub; short and stocky; short and thick.

STUB-NAIL, [stub'-nāl], *n.* a nail broken off; a short thick stubby nail.

STUCCO (1), [stuk'-ō], *n.* a fine plaster of any kind used as a coating for walls or for interior decorations; work made of stucco. [It. *stucco*].

STUCCO (2), [stuk'-ō], *v.t.* to plaster; to overlay with fine plaster.

STUCCOED, [stuk'-ōd], *adj.* covered with stucco.

STUCK, [stuk], *pret. and p.pt.* of STICK.

STUCK-UP, [stuk'-up'], *adj.* conceited; affecting an air of consequence.

STUD (1), [stud], *n.* an ornamental knob; a double-headed shirt-button; a small piece of timber or joist for supporting the main timbers; an intermediate post in a partition; a large flat-topped metal nail, one of several used to mark out pedestrian crossings in the streets. [OE. *studu*].

STUD (2), [stud], *n.* a number of pedigree horses, cattle, dogs, or other animals kept for breeding or any special purpose. [OE. *stod*].

STUD (3), [stud], *v.t.* to adorn with studs; to set with detached objects or ornaments; to adorn, to set thickly with small shining objects attractive to the eye.

STUDBOLT, [stud'-bōlt], *n.* a bolt with a thread at both ends.

STUD-BOOK, [stud'-bōōk], *n.* a book in which the pedigree and history of thoroughbred animals are recorded.

STUDDING-SAIL, [stud'-ing-sāl'], *n.* (*naut.*) a sail put alongside the leech of a squaresail; a scudding-sail. [Unkn.].

STUDDLE, [studl], *n.* a trestle. [OE. *stodl*].

STUDENT, [stēwd'-ent], *n.* a person engaged in study; a pupil at a technical school or college; a man devoted to books; one who studies or examines anything in an intensive way; a fellow of Christ Church, Oxford. [L. *studens, pres.pt.* of *studere* to study].

STUDENTSHIP, [stewd'-ent-ship], *n.* the state of being a student; a scholarship.

STUD-FARM, [stud'-fahm], *n.* a farm for breeding horses. [STUD (2) and FARM (1)].

STUD-GROOM, [stud'-grōōm], *n.* a groom at a stud-farm, *esp.* a head groom. [STUD (2) and GROOM (1)].

STUD-HORSE, [stud'-haws'], *n.* a horse kept for the purpose of breeding.

STUDIED, [stud'-id], *adj.* carefully considered; deliberate; elaborate; mannered.

STUDIEDLY, [stud'-id-li], *adv.* in a studied fashion.

STUDIER, [stud'-i-er], *n.* a person who studies; a student.

STUDIO, [stewd'-i-ō], *n.* a room designed for an artist's work-room or for a photographer to take portraits in; a room used for broadcasting or making films or gramophone records. [It. *studio* from L. *studium* study].

STUDIOUS, [stewd'-i-us], *adj.* devoted to the acquisition of knowledge from books; contemplative; diligent or eager to find or effect something; attentive; zealous; favourable to study. [L. *studiosus*].

STUDIOUSLY, [stewd'-i-us-li], *adv.* in a studious fashion; deliberately.

STUDIOUSNESS, [stewd'-i-us-nes], *n.* the state of being studious; the practice or habit of study.

STUDWORK, [stud'-wurk], *n.* brickwork filling up the spaces between the posts of a partition.

STUDY (1), [stud'-i], *n.* application of mind to books or to any subject for the purpose of acquiring knowledge or skill; thoughtful attention; meditation; any branch of learning that is studied; a subject of attention; an apartment devoted to study or literary employment; a work undertaken for improvement in an art; an artist's or musician's preliminary sketch for aid in the composition of a larger work, or as an exercise in technique. [L. *studium*].

STUDY (2), [stud'-i], *v.t.* to apply the mind to; to consider attentively; to con; *v.i.* to fix the mind intently upon a subject; to apply the mind to books; to learn systematically; to endeavour diligently. [OFr. *estudier*].

STUFA, [stōōf'-a], *n.* a jet of steam that issues from the earth. [It. *stufa*].

STUFF (1), [stuf], *n.* a mass of matter or collection of substances; the matter of which anything is formed; furniture; that which fills anything; elemental part; textile material; worthless matter; (*coll.*) **to do one's s.,** to perform one's part in the entertainment or demonstration; **s. and nonsense!** an expression of incredulity. [OFr. *estoffe*].

STUFF (2), [stuf], *v.t. and i.* to fill with stuffing; (*coll.*) to eat to excess; **to s. up,** to choke with stuff, to gull.

STUFFER, [stuf'-er], *n.* a person or thing that stuffs.

STUFFINESS, [stuf'-i-nes], *n.* the state of being stuffy.

STUFFING, [stuf'-ing], *n.* the material used for filling anything; a filling of savoury herbs used in cooking; taxidermy; (*slang*) spirit, courage.

STUFFING-BOX, [stuf'-ing-boks'], *n.* (*eng.*) a box or compartment that contains a packing through which the piston works in the top of a cylinder without losing steam; a contrivance for preventing leakage through the action of a moving part.

STUFFING-BOX

STUFFY, [stuf'-i], *adj.* hot, airless, badly ventilated; (*coll.*) fussy, narrow-minded.

STULM, [stulm], *n.* a shaft for drawing water out of a mine. [Uncert.].

STULTIFICATION, [stult'-if-ik-ā'-shun], *n.* the action of stultifying.

STULTIFY, [stult'-i-fī], *v.t.* to render worthless, make of no avail; to cause to seem foolish or inconsistent. [LL. *stultificare*].

STULTILOQUY, [stul-til'-o-kwi], *n.* foolish talk; vain babbling. [L. *stultus* foolish and *loqui* to speak].

STUM (1), [stum], *n.* must; grape juice unfermented; wine revived by a second fermentation. [Du. *stom* silent, still].

STUM (2), [stum], *v.t.* to renew (wine) by means of mixing must with it and causing a second fermentation. [Du. *stomen*].

STUMBLE (1), [stumbl], *n.* the action of stumbling; a slip, trip, partial fall, moral lapse.

STUMBLE (2), [stumbl], *v.t.* to cause to trip or stop; *v.i.* to trip up, take a false step in walking, to fall over some obstruction; to fall into crime or error; take offence; **to s. at,** to hesitate over, boggle at; **to s. (up)on,** to come across by chance. [ME. *stomblen*].

STUMBLER, [stumb'-ler], *n.* one who stumbles or has a tendency to stumble or blunder.
STUMBLING-BLOCK, [stumb'-ling-blok'], *n.* a cause of stumbling; a difficulty; an impediment, obstacle.
STUMBLINGLY, [stumb'-ling-li], *adv.* in a stumbling fashion.
STUMER, [stewm'-er], *n.* a counterfeit coin or note. [Unkn.].
STUMMEL, [stum'-el], *n.* the bowl and stem of a tobacco pipe. [Germ. *stummel*].
STUMP (1), [stump], *n.* the part of a tree remaining in the earth after the trunk is cut down; the part of a limb or other body remaining after the rest is amputated or destroyed; a remnant; (*cricket*) one of the upright sticks of a wicket; (*slang*) leg. [OIcel. *stumpr*].
STUMP (2), [stump], *v.t.* to lop; to travel round making speeches; (*cricket*) to dismiss (a batsman) for being out of his ground, by dislodging a bail with the ball or hand containing the ball; (*coll.*) to puzzle, defeat; *v.i.* to walk heavily; **to s. up,** (*coll.*) to pay up, fork out.
STUMPER, [stump'-er], *n.* a wicket-keeper in cricket.
STUMP-ORATOR, [stump'-o'-ra-ter], *n.* one who harangues a mob from any tree-stump or other out-of-door place of vantage that offers; one who goes about appealing to the passions of the mob.
STUMP-ORATORY, [stump'-o'-ra-tri], *n.* the practice of the stump-orator; windy talk.
STUMP-SPEECH, [stump'-spēch], *n.* speech as from a stump; an electioneering speech; a windy, incoherent harangue.
STUMPY, [stump'-i], *adj.* pertaining to, resembling, a stump; short and thick.
STUN, [stun], *v.t.* to make senseless by a blow; to blunt or stupefy the hearing of; to confound or make dizzy by loud and mingled sound; to amaze; (*slang*) to captivate, enslave. [OE. *stunian*].
STUNG, [stung], *pret. and p.pt.* of STING.
STUNK, [stungk], *pret. and p.pt.* of STINK.
STUNNER, [stun'-er], *n.* a person or thing that stuns; (*slang*) a fine sight, handsome person or thing.
STUNNING, [stun'-ing], *adj.* producing a stunned condition; (*slang*) splendid, delightful.
STUNSAIL, [stun'-sāl], *n.* (*naut.*) a studding-sail. [~STUDDING-SAIL].
STUNT (1), [stunt], *n.* a feat of skill; a performance; a newspaper sensation or agitation; any trick or course of action for gaining notoriety. [U.S. slang from Germ. *stunde* lesson].
STUNT (2), [stunt], *v.i.* to perform a stunt.
STUNT (3), [stunt], *v.t.* to hinder the growth of; to dwarf. [OE. *stunt* dull, foolish].
STUNTED, [stunt'-id], *adj.* undersized; dwarfed; retarded in development of body or mind.
STUNTEDNESS, [stunt'-id-nes], *n.* the state of being stunted.
STUPA (1), [stew'-pa], *n.* filamentous matter. [L. *stupa* tow].
STUPA (2), [stōō'-pah], *n.* a Buddhist monument or shrine in the form of a domed mound; a dagoba. [Skr. *stupa* a mound].
STUPE, [stewp], *n.* flannel or some other soft material dipped in hot water or medicaments and applied as a fomentation to a wound or sore. [L. *stupa*].
STUPEFACIENT, [stew'-pi-fā'-shi-ent], *adj.* having a stupefying power. [L. *stupefaciens*].
STUPEFACTION, [stew'-pi-fak'-shun], *n.* the action of rendering stupid; a stupefied state; dullness; stupidity.
STUPEFACTIVE, [stew'-pi-fakt'-iv], *adj.* able to stupefy; stupefacient.
STUPEFIER, [stew'-pi-fī-er], *n.* that which stupefies.
STUPEFY, [stew'-pi-fī], *v.t.* to make stupid; to deprive of sensibility; to amaze; to deaden, render incapable of intelligent action. [L. *stupefacere*].
STUPENDOUS, [stew-pend'-us], *adj.* amazing, wonderful, extraordinary. [L. *stupendus* amazing].
STUPENDOUSLY, [stew-pen'-dus-li], *adv.* in a stupendous fashion.
STUPENDOUSNESS, [stew-pen'-dus-nes], *n.* the quality of being stupendous.
STUPEOUS, [stewp'-i-us], *adj.* (*entom.*) having long loose scales or hairs. [L. *stupeus* made of tow].
STUPID (1), [stew'-pid], *n.* (*coll.*) a stupid person.
STUPID (2), [stew'-pid], *adj.* having one's faculties dulled; dull-witted, unintelligent, foolish. [L. *stupidus*].
STUPIDITY, [stew-pid'-i-ti], *n.* the condition or quality of being stupid. [L. *stupiditas*].
STUPIDLY, [stew'-pid-li], *adv.* in a stupid fashion.
STUPIDNESS, [stew'-pid-nes], *n.* stupidity, dulness of wit.
STUPOR, [stew'-por], *n.* a state of torpor or coma when the senses and faculties are numbed; slowness of wit caused by amazement. [L. *stupor*].
STUPOROUS, [stew'-por-us], *adj.* overcome with stupor, pertaining to stupor.
STUPOSE, [stew'-pōs], *adj.* tufted with hair. [MedL. *stuposus* made of tow].
STURDILY, [sturd'-i-li], *adv.* in a sturdy fashion.
STURDINESS, [sturd'-i-nes], *n.* the quality of being sturdy.
STURDY (1), [sturd'-i], *n.* a disease common in sheep, characterized by giddiness. [OFr. *estourdi* stunned, thoughtless].
STURDY (2), [sturd'-i], *adj.* strong, hardy, robust and vigorous; unshakable, well-founded. [*Prec.*].
STURGEON, [stur'-jon], *n.* a large fish of the genus *Acipenser*, found about the coasts and in the rivers of countries bordering on the north Atlantic, valued as the source of caviare and isinglass. [OFr. *esturgeon*].

STURGEON

STURIONIAN, [stew'-ri-ō'-ni-an], *n.* any fish of the family to which the sturgeon belongs. [L. *sturio* sturgeon].
STURNOID, [sturn'-oid], *adj.* of, pertaining to, or resembling a starling. [L. *sturnus* starling and Gk. *oeides* like].
STUTTER (1), [stut'-er], *n.* the defective mode of speech of one who stutters.
STUTTER (2), [stut'-er], *v.t. and i.* to speak with involuntary hesitations, to stammer; to utter with involuntary hesitations. [~ME. *stutten*].
STUTTERER, [stut'-er-er], *n.* one who stutters; a stammerer.
STUTTERING (1), [stut'-er-ing], *n.* involuntary hesitation in speaking.
STUTTERING (2), [stut'-er-ing], *adj.* spoken with, characterized by, a stutter.
STUTTERINGLY, [stut'-er-ing-li], *adv.* in a stuttering fashion.
STY (1), [stī], *n.* a pen where pigs are kept. [OE. *stig*].
STY (2), [stī], *n.* a small sore on the eyelid. [~OE. *stigend*].
STY (3), [stī], *v.t.* to keep or put in a sty.
STYCA, STICA, [stī'-ka], *n.* a small copper coin current in Northumbria from the seventh to the ninth centuries. [OE. *stycas* coins].
STYGIAN, [stij'-i-an], *adj.* (*class. myth.*) pertaining to, or typical of, the infernal river, Styx. [L. *stygius* from Gk. *stugios*].
STYLAGALMATIC, [stī'-la-gal-mat'-ik], *adj.* (*arch.*) pertaining to figures serving as columns. [Gk. *stulos* column and *agalma* image].
STYLAR, [stī'-ler], *adj.* of, or pertaining to, a style of writing.
STYLE (1), [stīl], *n.* (*class. antiq.*) a small instrument for writing on wax, etc., pointed at one end for making the marks, and blunted at the other for erasing them; any similar modern device, as for writing on wax paper; the gnomon of a sundial; (*bot.*) a narrow extension of the ovary, occurring in some plants, that supports the stigma; (*zool., entom.*) a small, pointed, bristle-like process; a mode of expression in writing; the characteristic features of syntax and diction in a piece of writing or composition; the characteristic manner of expression of a writer or group of writers or which was commonly used at one period; fine writing, the characteristics of fine writing; general formal characteristics in any fine art; mode of conduct and behaviour, *esp.* good polite behaviour practised by cultured persons; fashion, *esp.* in dress; deportment; distinction of conduct and bearing, etc.; the mode of living or taste of a person; sort, kind; correct mode of address, full title; a mode of reckoning, *esp.* of date; **in s.,** grandly, expensively. [OFr. *stile* from L. *stilus*].
STYLE (2), [stīl], *v.t.* to address with full titles, to give a title to.
STYLET, [stī'-let], *n.* a small pointed weapon or implement. [OFr. *stilet*].
STYLIFORM, [stīl'-i-fawm], *adj.* shaped like a style.
STYLISH, [stīl'-ish], *adj.* fashionable, smart, showy.
STYLISHLY, [stīl'-ish-li], *adv.* in a stylish fashion.
STYLISHNESS, [stīl'-ish-nes], *n.* the condition of being stylish.
STYLIST, [stīl'-ist], *n.* a writer who exercises great care in matters of style; a writer noted for his style.

STYLISTIC, [stīl-ist'-ik], *adj.* of, or pertaining to, literary style.
STYLISTICALLY, [stīl-ist'-ik-al-i], *adv.* from the point of view of style or a stylist.
STYLITE, [stīl'-īt], *n.* a religious ascetic who dwelt on the top of a pillar. [Gk. *stulites*].
STYLIZE, [stīl'-īz], *v.t.* to bring into line with one style, to conventionalize.
STYLO, [stīl'-ō], *n.* short form of STYLOGRAPH.
STYLOBATE, [stī'-lō-bāt], *n.* (*arch.*) a foundation supporting more than one column, *esp.* supporting columns in a row. [Gk. *stulobates*].
STYLOBATION, [stil'-ō-bā'-shun], *n.* (*arch.*) the pedestal for a column.
STYLOGRAPH, [stīl'-ō-graf], *n.* a variety of fountain pen with a pointed and undivided nib. [STYLE (1) and Gk. *graphia* writing].
STYLOGRAPHIC, [stīl'-ō-graf'-ik], *adj.* like, or pertaining to, a stylograph.
STYLOGRAPHICALLY, [stīl'-ō-graf'-ik-al-i], *adv.* with a stylograph.
STYLOGRAPHY, [stīl-og'-ra-fi], *n.* the use of a style or stylograph. [STYLE (1) and Gk. *graphia* writing].
STYLOID (1), [stīl'-oid], *n.* (*anat.*) the styloid process.
STYLOID (2), [stīl'-oid], *adj.* (*anat.*) **s. process,** a bristle-like projection at the base of the temporal bone. [STYLE (1) and Gk. *oeides* like].
STYLOLITE, [stīl'-ō līt], *n.* (*min.*) a cylindrical formation standing at right angles to the stratification, found in certain limestones. [STYLE (1) and Gk. *lithos* stone].
STYLUS, [stīl'-us], *n.* a style; the bar linking the needle and its holder with the diaphragm in a gramophone sound-box. [L. *stylus*].
STYMIE (1), [stī'-mi], *n.* (*golf*) a situation in which the striker finds that his opponent's ball lies between his own and the hole. [Unkn.].
STYMIE (2), [stī'-mi], *v.t.* (*golf*) to embarrass (one's opponent) by leaving one's own ball directly between his and the hole; (of the ball) to lie between the hole and the striker's ball; also (*fig.*). [Unkn.].
STYPTIC (1), STIPTIC, [stip'-tik], *n.* (*med.*) a substance that checks bleeding.
STYPTIC (2), STIPTIC, [stip'-tik], *adj.* (*med.*) able in check bleeding. [Gk. *stuptikos*].
STYPTICITY, [stip-tis'-i-ti], *n.* the condition of being styptic.
STYRACIN, [stīer'-as-in], *n.* (*chem.*) a crystalline substance obtainable from storax. [Fr. *styracine*].
STYRAX, [stīer'-aks], *n.* a genus of trees and shrubs from all of which resin may be extracted; resin extracted from these plants. [Gk. *sturax*].
STYTHE, [stīTH], *n.* (*dial.*) foul air in a coal-mine, choke-damp; a foul smell. [Unkn.].
STYX, [stiks], *n.* (*class. myth.*) a river of the underworld over which Charon ferried the souls of the dead; **to cross the S.,** to die. [Gk. *stux*].
SUABILITY, [sew'-ab-il'-i-ti], *n.* (*leg.*) the condition of being suable.
SUABLE, [sew'-abl], *adj.* able to be sued.

STYRAX

SUASIBLE, [swā'-zibl], *adj.* able to be persuaded.
SUASION, [swā'-zhun], *n.* persuasion. [L. *suasio*].
SUASIVE, [swā'-ziv], *adj.* having or exercising the power to persuade.
SUASIVELY, [swā'-ziv-li], *adv.* persuasively, in a suasive way.
SUASORY, [swā'-zer-i], *adj.* persuasive.
SUAVE, [swāv], *adj.* bland, urbane, courteous, smooth-mannered; (of wine) smooth to the palate. [L. *suavis*].
SUAVELY, [swāv'-li], *adv.* in a suave way.
SUAVITY, [swa'-vi-ti], *n.* the quality of being suave. [L. *suavitas*].
SUB (1), [sub], *n.* (*coll.*) a subaltern; a sub-editor; a subscription.
SUB (2), [sub], *prep.* **s. judice,** still under consideration; **s. rosa,** in secret. [L. *sub* under].
SUB-, *pref.* below, under; almost, towards, about. [L. *sub* under].
SUBACID (1), [sub-as'-id], *n.* a substance that is subacid.
SUBACID (2), [sub-as'-id], *adj.* somewhat acid or sour. [L. *subacidus*].
SUBACIDITY, [sub'-as-id'-i-ti], *n.* the quality of being subacid.
SUBACRID, [sub-ak'-rid], *adj.* somewhat sharp or acrid; moderately acrid. [SUB- and ACRID].
SUBACUTE, [sub'-ak-ewt'], *adj.* moderately acute.
SUBADAR, SOUBADAR, SUBAHDAR, [sōō'-bad-ah(r)], *n.* a native officer in command of a company in an Indian regiment. [Hind. *subadar*].
SUBAERIAL, [sub-āer'-i-al], *adj.* living or being on the earth's surface.
SUBAERIALIST, [sub-āer'-i-al-ist], *n.* one who believes that geological formations are due to subaerial changes.
SUBAERIALLY, [sub-āer'-i-al-i], *adv.* on the earth's surface.
SUBAGENCY, [sub-ā'-jen-si], *n.* the organization, office, or function of a sub-agent.
SUB-AGENT, [sub-ā'-jent], *n.* an agent employed by another.
SUBAH, [sōō'-bah], *n.* a province in the Mogul Empire. [Urdu *subah*].
SUBAHDAR, see SUBADAR.
SUBALPINE, [sub-alp'-īn], *adj.* (*bot., zool.*) of, pertaining to, inhabiting, regions immediately below the alpine.
SUBALTERN (1), [sub'-al-tern], *n.* (*milit.*) any commissioned officer beneath the rank of captain. [Fr. *subalterne*].
SUBALTERN (2), [sub'-al-tern], *adj.* inferior, subordinate; (*logic*) of a proposition, specific.
SUBALTERNATE (1), [sub'-awl-turn'-at], *n.* (*logic*) a specific proposition.
SUBALTERNATE (2), [sub'-awl-turn'-at], *adj.* (*bot.*) almost opposite but actually alternate. [L. *subalternatus* inferior].
SUBALTERNATION, [sub-awl'-ter-nā'-shun], *n.* (*logic*) the inter-relationship of a universal and a particular; †inferiority. [L. *subalternatio*].
SUBANDEAN, [sub'-an-dē'-an], *adj.* of, or pertaining to, the lower slopes of the Andes.
SUBANGULAR, [sub-ang'-gyōō-ler], *adj.* somewhat angular.
SUBAPENNINE, [sub-ap'-en-īn], *adj.* of, or pertaining to, the lower slopes of the Apennines.
SUBAPOSTOLIC, [sub'-ap-os-tol'-ik], *adj.* pertaining to the period following that of the Apostles.
SUBAQUATIC, [sub'-ak-wat'-ik], *adj.* partly aquatic.
SUBAQUEOUS, [sub-ak'-wi-us], *adj.* being, formed, under water; intended for use under water.
SUBARCTIC, [sub-ahk'-tik], *adj.* pertaining to the region next to the Arctic.
SUBARRATION, SUBARRHATION, [sub'-a-rā'-shun], *n.* an ancient form of betrothal in which the man presented the woman with gifts as a token. [MedL. *subarrhatio*].
SUBASTRAL, [sub-as'-tral], *adj.* being beneath the stars, terrestrial.
SUBASTRINGENT, [sub'-as-trin'-jent], *adj.* weakly astringent.
SUBAUDITION, [sub'-aw-dish'-un], *n.* the mental act of supplying necessary or implied words not verbally expressed.
SUBAURAL, [sub-aw'-ral], *adj.* placed beneath the ear.
SUBAXILLARY, [sub'-ak-zil'-er-i] *adj.* situated under the armpit; (*bot.*) situated beneath the axil.
SUBBASE, [sub'-bās'], *n.* (*arch.*) the lowest section of a base horizontally divided.
SUBBEADLE, [sub'-bēdl'], *n.* an under-beadle.
SUBCALCAREOUS, [sub'-kal-kāer'-i-us], *adj.* somewhat calcareous.
SUBCAUDAL, [sub-kawd'-al], *adj.* being beneath the tail.
SUBCELESTIAL, [sub'-sil-es'-ti-al], *adj.* lying beneath the heavens.
SUBCENTRAL, [sub-sen'-tral], *adj.* situated near or under the centre.
SUBCEREBRAL, [sub-se'-rib-ral], *adj.* (*anat.*) pertaining to that part of the nervous system beneath the brain.
SUBCHANTER, [sub-chahn'-ter], *n.* a deputy precentor.
SUBCLASS, [sub'-klahs'], *n.* a subsection of a class.
SUBCLAVIAN, [sub-klā'-vi-an], *adj.* (*anat.*) situated under the clavicle.
SUBCLAVICULAR, [sub'-klav-ik'-yōō-ler], *adj.* (*anat.*) subclavian.
SUBCOMMITTEE, [sub'-kom-it'-i], *n.* a section of a committee appointed by the main body to deal with some specified minor or subsidiary matter.
SUBCONCAVE, [sub-kon'-kāv], *adj.* somewhat concave.
SUBCONICAL, [sub-kon'-ik-al], *adj.* somewhat conical; slightly tapering. [SUB- and CONICAL].

SUBCONSCIOUS (1) [sub-kon'-shus], *n.* the subconscious mind.
SUBCONSCIOUS (2), [sub-kon'-shus], *adj.* being within the range of consciousness but outside the range of clear mental perception.
SUBCONSCIOUSLY, [sub-kon'-shus-li], *adv.* in a subconscious fashion.
SUBCONSCIOUSNESS, [sub-kon'-shus-nes], *n.* that mental field beyond attention and clear perception; the subconscious mind.
SUBCONTIGUOUS, [sub'-kon-tig'-yōō-us], *adj.* almost touching.
SUBCONTINENT, [sub-kon'-tin-ent], *n.* a mass of land large enough to be reasonably thought of as a continent but not actually classed as one of the five great continents.
SUBCONTINUOUS, [sub'-kon-tin'-yōō-us], *adj.* almost continuous.
SUBCONTRACT (1), [sub'-kon'-trakt], *n.* a contract which is subordinate or subsidiary to another or performed by one contractor for another.
SUBCONTRACT (2), [sub'-kon-trakt'], *v.i.* to enter or make a subcontract.
SUBCONTRACTOR, [sub'-kon-trak'-ter], *n.* a party to a subcontract.
SUBCONTRARY (1), [sub-kon'-trer-i], *n.* (*logic*) a subcontrary proposition.
SUBCONTRARY (2), [sub-kon'-trer-i], *adj.* (*geom.*, *logic*) to some extent contrary.
SUBCONVEX, [sub-kon'-veks], *adj.* somewhat convex.
SUBCORDATE, [sub-kaw'-dāt], *adj.* shaped somewhat like a heart.
SUBCORNEOUS, [sub-kawn'-i-us], *adj.* rather horny; (*anat.*) situated under a nail or other horny growth. [SUB- and L. *corneus* horny].
SUBCOSTAL, [sub-kost'-al], *adj.* (*anat.*) lying below or beneath the ribs.
SUBCRANIAL, [sub-krā'-ni-al], *adj.* (*anat.*) situated below the cranium.
SUBCRYSTALLINE, [sub-kris'-tal-īn], *adj.* partially crystalline.
SUBCULTURE, [sub-kul'-cher], *n.* (of bacteria, etc.) a culture from an earlier culture.
SUBCUTANEOUS, [sub'-kew-tā'-ni-us], *adj.* situated beneath the skin.
SUBCUTANEOUSLY, [sub'-kew-tā'-ni-us-li], *adv.* under the skin.
SUBCUTICULAR, [sub'-kew-tik'-yōō-ler], *adj.* situated under the cuticle.
SUBCYLINDRICAL, [sub'-sil-in'-drik-al], *adj.* almost cylindrical.
SUBDEACON, [sub'-dē'-kon], *n.* a minister immediately lower than a deacon in rank.
SUBDEACONSHIP, [sub-dē'-kon-ship], *n.* the office and rank of a subdeacon.
SUBDEAN, [sub'-dēn'], *n.* the deputy of a dean.
SUBDEANERY, [sub-dē'-ner-i], *n.* (*eccles.*) the rank and function of subdean.
SUBDECANAL, [sub-dek'-an-al], *adj.* (*eccles.*) pertaining to a subdean.
SUBDECUPLE, [sub-dek'-yōōpl], *adj.* being in the proportion of one to ten.
SUBDELIRIUM, [sub'-di-li'-ri-um], *n.* (*med.*) a state verging on delirium.
SUBDENTATE, [sub-den'-tāt], *adj.* (*anat.*) having teeth not clearly distinct.
SUBDEPOSIT, [sub'-di-poz'-it], *n.* a deposit lying under another.
SUBDERIVATIVE, [sub'-di-riv'-at-iv], *adj.* derived from something which is itself not original but derived.
SUBDERMAL, [sub-dur'-mal], *adj.* lying beneath the skin.
SUBDIACONATE, [sub'-dī-ak'-on-āt], *n.* (*eccles.*) the office and function of subdeacon.
SUBDILATED, [sub-di-lā'-tid], *adj.* partly dilated.
SUBDIVERSIFY, [sub'-dī-vurs'-i-fī], *v.t.* to perform a second process of diversification.
SUBDIVIDE, [sub'-di-vīd'], *v.t.* and *i.* to divide up parts; to become a part of a part.
SUBDIVISIBLE, [sub'-di-viz'-ibl], *adj.* able to be subdivided.
SUBDIVISION, [sub'-di-vizh'-un], *n.* the act of subdividing; the condition of being subdivided; a part or section produced by subdivision.
SUBDOMINAL, [sub-dom'-in-al], *adj.* situated below the abdomen. [SUB- and (AB)DOMINAL].
SUBDOMINANT, [sub-dom'-in-ant], *n.* (*mus.*) the fourth note of the diatonic scale, the note below the dominant, the tonic fa. [SUB and DOMINANT (1)].
SUBDORSAL, [sub-daws'-al], *adj.* situated near the back.
SUBDOUBLE, [sub-dubl'], *adj.* being in the proportion of one to two.
SUBDUABLE, [sub-dew'-abl], *adj.* able to be subdued.
SUBDUAL, [sub-dew'-al], *n.* the act of subduing, the condition of being subdued.
SUBDUCE, [sub-dews'], *v.t.* to subduct. [L. *subducere*].
SUBDUCT, [sub-dukt'], *v.t.* to remove, take away. [~L. *subductum*, *p.pt.* of *subducere* to remove].
SUBDUCTION, [sub-duk'-shun], *n.* the act of subducting.
SUBDUE, [sub-dew'], *v.t.* to overcome, conquer, *esp.* by force; to lessen in force or intensity. [OFr. *suduire* from L. *subducere* to lead away].
SUBDUED, [sub-dewd'], *adj.* overcome, repressed, diminished in force or intensity.
SUBDUEDNESS, [sub-dewd'-nes], *n.* the condition of being subdued.
SUBDUER, [sub-dew'-er], *n.* one who subdues.
SUBDUING, [sub-dew'-ing], *adj.* softening, tending to subdue.
SUBDUPLE, [sub-dewpl'], *adj.* (*math.*) being half of a total; subdouble. [LL. *subduplus*].
SUBDUPLICATE, [sub-dew'-plik-at], *adj.* (*math.*) (of a ratio) in the square roots of the two terms.
SUB-EDIT, [sub-ed'-it], *v.t.* to act as assistant editor of.
SUB-EDITOR, [sub-ed'-it-or], *n.* an assistant editor.
SUBELONGATE, [sub-ē'-long-gāt], *adj.* somewhat elongate.
SUBEPIDERMAL, [sub-ep'-i-durm'-al], *adj.* situated under the epidermis.
SUBEQUAL, [sub-ē'-kwal], *adj.* almost equal.
SUBEQUILATERAL, [sub'-ē-kwi-lat'-er-al], *adj.* almost equilateral.
SUBERATE, [sew'-ber-āt], *n.* (*chem.*) a salt of suberic acid. [Fr. *subérate*].
SUBERIC, [sew'-ber-ik], *adj.* pertaining to cork; **s. acid**, (*chem.*) a crystalline acid produced by the action of nitric acid on cork. [Fr. *subérique*].
SUBERIN, [sew'-ber-in], *n.* (*chem.*) a white substance left after the action of solvents on cork. [Fr. *subérine*].
SUBEROSE, [sew'-ber-ōs], *adj.* (*bot.*) corky in texture, resembling cork.
SUBFAMILY, [sub'-fam'-i-li], *n.* a division of a family.
SUBFEBRILE, [sub-fe'-bril], *adj.* somewhat febrile.
SUBFLAVOUR, [sub-flā'-ver], *n.* a secondary flavour.
SUBFLUVIAL, [sub-flōō'-vi-al] *adj.* situated or existing under a river.
SUBFOSSIL, [sub-fos'-il], *adj.* partly fossilized.
SUBFUSC (1), [sub'-fusk'], *n.* subfusc colour; clothing of this colour.
SUBFUSC (2), [sub'-fusk'], *adj.* of a dark or sober hue. [L. *subfuscus*].
SUBFUSCOUS, [sub-fusk'-us], *adj.* subfusc.
SUBGELATINOUS, [sub'-jel-at'-in-us], *adj.* somewhat gelatinous.
SUBGENERIC, [sub'-jen-er'-ik], *adj.* pertaining to a subgenus.
SUBGENUS, [sub-jē'-nus], *n.* a division of a genus.
SUBGLACIAL, [sub-glā'-shal], *adj.* living under a glacier; (of climate) almost glacial in character.
SUBGLOBULAR, [sub-glob'-yōōl-er], *adj.* almost globular.
SUBGLUMACEOUS, [sub'-glōō-mā'-shus], *adj.* rather glumaceous.
SUBGRANULAR, [sub-gran'-yōō-ler], *adj.* partly granular.
SUBGROUP, [sub'-grōōp'], *n.* a subordinate group.
SUBHASTATION, [sub'-has-tā'-shun], *n.* a sale by public auction. [L. *subhastatio*].
SUBHEADING, [sub'-hed'-ing], *n.* the heading or title of a subsection of an essay, article, treatise, etc.
SUBHEPATIC, [sub'-hi-pat'-ik], *adj.* situated under the liver. [SUB- and HEPATIC].
SUB-HUMAN, [sub-hew'-man], *adj.* not quite human.
SUBHYOID, [sub-hī'-oid], *adj.* (*anat.*) situated beneath the hyoid bone.
SUBIMAGO, [sub'-im-ā'-gō], *n.* (*zool.*) a stage of development in the life of some insects between the pupa and imago stages.
SUBINFEUDATION, [sub'-in-few-dā'-shun], *n.* a grant of land made by one who is himself a vassal.
SUBINTESTINAL, [sub'-in-tes'-ti-nal], *adj.* (*anat.*) lying near or under the intestines.
SUBINTRANT, [sub-in'-trant], *adj.* (*med.*) (of fevers)

almost continuous. [L. *subintrans, pres.pt.* of *subintrare* to steal into].

SUBIRRIGATION, [sub′-i-ri-gā′-shun], *n.* irrigation under the surface.

SUBITANEOUS, [sub′-it-ā′-ni-us], *adj.* (*rare*) unexpected, sudden, hasty. [L. *subitaneus*].

SUBITO, [sŏŏb′-it-ō], *adv.* (*mus.*) quickly, suddenly. [It. *subito*].

SUBJACENT, [sub-jā′-sent], *adj.* lying beneath; lying directly underneath. [L. *subjacens*].

SUBJECT (1), [sub′-jekt], *n.* a person under the authority of a king or ruler; a person or thing undergoing a given process or action, one suffering from a stated malady or disease, a person who is the object of medical, pathological, or psychological investigation; the topic, theme, or matter of a literary composition; the object or material subjected to scientific, critical consideration; the theme or matter of learned or studious investigation or dissertation; (*mus.*) a principal musical phrase upon which a composition or part of a composition is founded, a theme; (*gram.*) the nominative phrase or word of a sentence, that part of a sentence about which something is predicated; (*logic*) that about which something is stated; (*philos.*) the actuality of anything contrasted with whatever is attributive to it; the thinking mind or self. [L. *subjectus* a dependant].

SUBJECT (2), [sub′-jekt], *adj.* being under authority; **s. to,** dependent on; liable, tending to. [L. *subjectus, p.pt.* of *subjicere* to throw beneath].

SUBJECT (3), [sub′-jekt], *adv.* **s. to,** provided, conditionally upon.

SUBJECT (4), [sub-jekt′], *v.t.* to place under authority, subdue; **to s. to,** to cause to suffer, undergo; to expose, lay open to (a process, experience, experiment); to proffer or present.

SUBJECTION, [sub-jek′-shun], *n.* the condition of being subject, the act of subjecting. [L. *subjectio*].

SUBJECTIVE (1), [sub-jek′-tiv], *n.* (*gram.*) the case of the subject, the nominative case.

SUBJECTIVE (2), [sub-jek′-tiv], *adj.* (*gram.*) pertaining to the subject of a sentence; (*philos.*) arising from the mind without the aid or influence of anything external to the mind; personal. [LL. *subjectivus*].

SUBJECTIVELY, [sub-jek′-tiv-li], *adv.* in a subjective way.

SUBJECTIVENESS, [sub-jek′-tiv-nes], *n.* the condition of being subjective.

SUBJECTIVISM, [sub-jek′-tiv-izm], *n.* (*philos.*) the doctrine that all knowledge arises from subjective experience only.

SUBJECTIVIST, [sub-jek′-tiv-ist], *n.* one who accepts the doctrine of subjectivism.

SUBJECTIVITY, [sub′-jek-tiv′-i-ti], *n.* subjectiveness, the condition of being subjective; the doctrine that religious belief should be based upon subjective experience.

SUBJECTLESS, [sub′-jekt-les], *adj.* without subjects, having no subject.

SUBJECT-MATTER, [sub′-jekt-mat′-er], *n.* the theme, topic or substance of a literary product.

SUBJOIN, [sub-join′], *v.t.* to make (an addition) to what has been already stated. [OFr. *subjoindre* from L. *subjungere* to append].

SUBJOINT, [sub′-joint′], *n.* (*anat.*) a limb or joint of lesser importance.

SUBJUGABLE, [sub′-jŏŏg-abl], *adj.* able to be subjugated.

SUBJUGATE, [sub′-jŏŏ-gāt], *v.t.* to subdue, place under control or authority. [L. *subjugare*].

SUBJUGATION, [sub′-jŏŏ-gā′-shun], *n.* the act of subjugating, the condition of being subjugated.

SUBJUGATOR, [sub′-jŏŏ-gā-tor], *n.* a conqueror, a person who subjugates. [LL. *subjugator*].

SUBJUNCTIVE (1), [sub-jungk′-tiv], *n.* (*gram.*) the subjunctive mood.

SUBJUNCTIVE (2), [sub-jungk′-tiv], *adj.* (*gram.*) subjoined; **s. mood,** a mood of the verb expressing a wish, command, condition, contingency, possibility, etc. [L. *subjunctivus*].

SUB-KINGDOM, [sub′-king′-dom], *n.* (*bot., zool., etc.*) a subsection of a kingdom.

SUBLANCEOLATE, [sub-lanh′-si-ō-lāt], *adj.* (*bot.*) rather lanceolate.

SUBLAPSARIAN (1), [sub′-lap-sāer′-i-an], *n.* one who accepts sublapsarian, infralapsarian, doctrine.

SUBLAPSARIAN (2), [sub′-lap-sāer′-i-an], *adj.* pertaining to the Calvinist theory that the Fall was permitted but not preordained.

SUBLAPSARIANISM, [sub′-lap-sāer′-i-an-izm], *n.* the belief, teaching, etc., of sublapsarians.

SUBLATE, [sub-lāt′], *v.t.* (*logic*) to deny, reject, assert as a negative. [L. *sublatus, p.pt.* of *tollere* to raise].

SUBLATION, [sub-lā′-shun], *n.* (*logic*) the act of sublating. [L. *sublatio*].

SUBLEASE (1), [sub′-lēs′], *n.* a lease granted by one who is himself a tenant of the property leased.

SUBLEASE (2), [sub-lēs′], *v.t.* to grant a sublease for.

SUBLESSEE, [sub′-les-ē′], *n.* one holding a sublease.

SUBLESSOR, [sub-les′-or], *n.* one granting a sublease.

SUBLET, [sub-let′], *v.t.* to underlet, to let (that which one holds oneself as a tenant).

SUB-LIBRARIAN, [sub′-lī-brāer′-i-an], *n.* an assistant librarian.

SUB-LIEUTENANCY, [sub′-lef-ten′-an-si], *n.* the rank of a sub-lieutenant.

SUB-LIEUTENANT, [sub′-lef-ten′-ant], *n.* a naval officer immediately lower in rank than a lieutenant.

SUBLIGATION, [sub′-lig-ā′-shun], *n.* the act of binding underneath.

SUBLIMABLE, [sub-līm′-abl], *adj.* able to be sublimated.

SUBLIMABLENESS, [sub-līm′-abl-nes], *n.* the quality of being sublimable.

SUBLIMATE (1), [sub′-lim-āt], *n.* (*chem.*) a substance that has been sublimated.

SUBLIMATE (2), [sub′-lim-āt], *adj.* (*chem.*) sublimated, refined by the process of sublimating.

SUBLIMATE (3), [sub′-lim-āt], *v.t.* (*chem.*) to purify by vaporizing and solidifying again; (*fig.*) to refine; (*psychol.*) to transform, apply to other (usually more exalted) ends. [L. *sublimare* to lift up].

SUBLIMATION, [sub′-lim-ā′-shun], *n.* the act of sublimating, the condition of being sublimated; that which is sublimated.

SUBLIME (1), [sub-līm′], *n.* the quality of being sublime; anything evincing the qualities of sublimity.

SUBLIME (2), [sub-līm′], *adj.* lofty, noble, grand, grandiose, impressive; (*fig.*) haughty, conceited, unbending; (*coll.*) extreme; (*anat.*) lying just beneath the surface. [L. *sublimis* lofty].

SUBLIME (3), [sub-līm′], *v.t.* to sublimate, refine. [L. *sublimare* to raise aloft].

SUBLIMELY, [sub-līm′-li], *adv.* in a sublime way.

SUBLIMENESS, [sub-līm′-nes], *n.* sublimity.

SUBLIMINAL, [sub-lim′-in-al], *adj.* (*psych.*) within the range of consciousness but beyond that of perception or attention.

SUBLIMITY, [sub-lim′-i-ti], *n.* the quality of being sublime. [L. *sublimitas*].

SUBLINEATION, [sub′-lin-i-ā′-shun], *n.* the underlining of a word or words in a sentence.

SUBLINGUAL, [sub-ling′-gwal], *adj.* situated underneath the tongue.

SUBLITTORAL, [sub-lit′-er-al], *adj.* living near or on the seashore.

SUBLOBULAR, [sub-lob′-yŏŏl-er], *adj.* situated under a lobe.

SUBLUNAR, [sub-lōōn′-er], *adj.* lying beneath the moon, earthly.

SUBLUNARY, [sub-lōōn′-er-i], *adj.* terrestrial; sublunar.

SUBLUXATION, [sub′-luks-ā′-shun], *n.* (*med.*) a partial dislocation.

SUB-MACHINE-GUN, [sub′-ma-shēn′-gun], *n.* a type of simple machine-gun. [SUB- and MACHINE-GUN].

SUBMAMMARY, [sub-mam′-er-i], *adj.* situated under the mammae.

SUB-MAN, [sub′-man′], *n.* a man of poor physique or low intellect.

SUBMARINE (1), [sub′-ma-rēn′], *n.* a vessel that can travel beneath the surface of the water.

SUBMARINE

SUBMARINE (2), [sub′-ma-rēn′], *adj.* living or capable of travelling beneath the surface of the sea.

SUBMAXILLARY, [sub′-maks-il′-er-i], *adj.* situated beneath the lower jaw.

SUBMEDIAL, [sub-mē′-di-al], *adj.* lying under the middle.

SUBMEDIAN, [sub-mē′-di-an], *adj.* submedial.

SUBMEDIANT, [sub-mē′-di-ant], *n.* (*mus.*) the sixth note of the scale.

SUBMEMBRANOUS, SUBMEMBRANEOUS, [sub-mem′-bra-nus], *adj.* rather membranous.

SUBMENTAL, [sub-men′-tal], *adj.* situated beneath the chin.

SUBMERGE, [sub-murj′], *v.t. and i.* to cause to go

beneath the surface of water, to cover with a liquid; to go below the surface of the water. [L. *submergere* to sink].

SUBMERGENCE, [sub-mur'-jents], *n.* the act of submerging, the condition of being submerged.

SUBMERGIBLE, [sub-murj'-ibl], *adj.* able to be submerged.

SUBMERSE, [sub-murs'], *v.t.* to make to sink under water. [L. *submersus, p.pt.* of *submergere* to sink].

SUBMERSED, [sub-murst'], *adj.* (*bot.*) growing under water. [*Prec.*].

SUBMERSIBLE, [sub-murs'-ibl], *adj.* able to be submersed.

SUBMERSION, [sub-mur'-shun], *n.* the act of submersing; the condition of being submersed. [L. *submersio*].

SUBMETALLIC, [sub'-met-al'-ik], *adj.* rather metallic.

SUBMISSION, [sub-mish'-un], *n.* the act of submitting; the condition of being submitted; the spirit of humble acquiescence, surrender; that which is submitted. [L. *submissio*].

SUBMISSIVE, [sub-mis'-iv], *adj.* characterized by submission, ready to submit, humble, resigned, acquiescing.

SUBMISSIVELY, [sub-mis'-iv-li], *adv.* in a submissive way.

SUBMISSIVENESS, [sub-mis'-iv-nes], *n.* the condition of being submissive.

SUBMIT, [sub-mit'], *v.t. and i.* to yield, surrender; to proffer for consideration and criticism, to urge or put forward; **to s. to,** to acknowledge as superior, yield to, admit the authority of. [L. *submittere* to place beneath].

SUBMITTER, [sub-mit'-er], *n.* one who submits.

SUBMONTANE, [sub-mon'-tān], *adj.* situated on the lower parts of a mountain or mountains.

SUBMUCOUS [sub-mew'-kus], *adj.* somewhat resembling mucus.

SUBMUNDANE, [sub-mun'-dān], *adj.* situated beneath the earth's surface.

SUBMUSCULAR, [sub-musk'-yŏŏl-er], *adj.* situated under a muscle.

SUBNARCOTIC, [sub'-nah-kot'-ic], *adj.* somewhat narcotic.

SUBNASAL, [sub-nāz'-al], *adj.* situated under the nose.

SUBNASCENT, [sub-nā'-sent], *adj.* growing from underneath. [L. *subnascens*].

SUBNATURAL, [sub-nach'-er-al], *adj.* less than is natural.

SUBNEURAL, [sub-newr'-al], *adj.* situated under a nerve. [SUB- and NEURAL].

SUBNORMAL, [sub-naw'-mal], *adj.* under normal.

SUBNUDE, [sub-newd'], *adj.* (*bot.*) having very few leaves.

SUBOCCIPITAL, [sub'-ok-sip'-it-al], *adj.* situated under the occiput.

SUBOCEANIC, [sub'-ō-shi-an'-ik], *adj.* situated under the ocean's surface.

SUBOCELLATE, [sub-ŏs'-el-āt], *adj.* rather ocellate.

SUBOCTAVE, [sub-ok'-tiv], *n.* (*mus.*) the octave below a note. [SUB- and OCTAVE].

SUBOCTUPLE, [sub-okt'-ewpl], *adj.* having the ratio of one to eight.

SUBOCULAR, [sub-ok'-yŏŏl-er], *adj.* situated under the eye.

SUBORBICULAR, [sub'-awb-ik'-yŏŏl-er], *adj.* nearly orbicular.

SUBORBITAL, [sub-aw'-bit-al], *adj.* placed under the orbit of the eye.

SUBORDER, [sub-aw'-der], *n.* a subsection of an order.

SUBORDINACY, [sub-aw'-din-a-si], *n.* the condition of being subordinate.

SUBORDINAL, [sub-aw'-din-al], *adj.* ranking as, or relating to, a suborder.

SUBORDINARY, [sub-aw'-din-er-i], *n.* (*her.*) a charge that is inferior in honour to an ordinary.

SUBORDINATE (1), [sub-aw'-din-at], *n.* one who is subordinate, an inferior.

SUBORDINATE (2), [sub-aw'-din-at], *adj.* inferior in rank, importance, etc.; dependent, subsidiary; **s. clause,** (*gram.*) a clause which qualifies and modifies the principal clause in a sentence, and which is introduced by a relative pronoun (expressed or implied) or an adverbial conjunction, and contains a finite verb. [SUB- and L. *ordinatus, p.pt.* of *ordinare* to appoint].

SUBORDINATE (3), [sub-aw'-din-āt], *v.t.* to give an inferior position to; to make dependent or subordinate.

SUBORDINATELY, [sub-aw'-din-at-li], *adv.* in a subordinate way.

SUBORDINATENESS, [sub-aw'-din-at-nes], *n.* the condition of being subordinate.

SUBORDINATION, [sub-aw'-din-ā'-shun], *n.* the condition of being subordinate, the act of subordinating.

SUBORDINATIONISM, [sub-aw'-din-ā'-shun-izm], *n.* the doctrine that the second and third persons of the Trinity are subordinate to the first.

SUBORDINATIVE, [sub-aw'-din-at-iv], *adj.* tending to subordination; **s. conjunction,** (*gram.*) a conjunction that introduces a subordinate clause.

SUBORN, [sub-awn'], *v.t.* to entice (a person) to commit a crime by bribery or other illegal means. [L. *subornare*].

SUBORNATION, [sub'-aw-nā'-shun], *n.* the act of suborning; the condition of being suborned.

SUBORNER, [sub-aw'-ner], *n.* one who suborns another.

SUBOVAL, [sub-ō'-val], *adj.* subovate.

SUBOVATE, [sub-ō'-vāt], *adj.* almost ovate.

SUBPARIETAL, [sub'-pa-rī'-it-al], *adj.* lying under the parietal bones.

SUBPERITONEAL, [sub'-pe-ri-tō-nē'-al], *adj.* situated under the peritoneum.

SUBPHRENIC, [sub-frĕn'-ik], *adj.* situated under the diaphragm.

SUBPILOSE, [sub-pī'-lōs], *adj.* rather hairy.

SUBPLEURAL, [sub-plōōer'-al], *adj.* situated below the pleura.

SUBPLINTH, [sub'-plinth'], *n.* (*arch.*) a secondary and lower plinth.

SUBPOENA (1), [sub-pē'-na], *n.* (*leg.*) a writ by which a person is summoned to court under threat of penalty for non-appearance. [L. *sub poena* under penalty].

SUBPOENA (2), [sub-pē-na], *v.t.* to issue a subpoena to.

SUBPOLAR, [sub-pōl'-er], *adj.* (*astron.*) beneath the celestial pole; verging on polar.

SUBPREFECT, [sub-prē'-fekt], *n.* an assistant prefect.

SUBPRIOR, [sub-prī'-or], *n.* an official in a religious house who is next to the prior in rank.

SUBPROVINCE, [sub-prov'-ints], *n.* a subdivision of a province.

SUBPYRAMIDAL, [sub'-pi-ra-mid'-al], *adj.* almost pyramidal.

SUBQUADRATE, [sub-kwod'-rāt], *adj.* almost rectangular.

SUBQUADRUPLE, [sub-kwod'-rōōpl], *adj.* being in the ratio of one to four.

SUBQUINTUPLE, [sub-quin'-tewpl], *adj.* being in the ratio of one to five.

SUBRECTOR, [sub-rek'-tor], *n.* a deputy or assistant rector.

SUBREGION, [sub-rē'-jon], *n.* a subsection of a region.

SUBRENT, [sub-rent'], *v.t.* to pay rent for (property) to one who himself is only a tenant.

SUBREPTION, [sub-rep'-shun], *n.* (*leg.*) the illegal acquiring of property by fraud or misrepresentation, etc. [L. *subreptio* theft].

SUBREPTIVE, [sub-rep'-tiv], *adj.* surreptitious.

SUBRETINAL, [sub-ret'-in-al], *adj.* lying below the retina.

SUBRHOMBOIDAL, [sub'-romb-oid'-al], *adj.* almost rhomboidal.

SUBRIGID, [sub-rij'-id], *adj.* somewhat rigid.

SUBROGATION, [sub'-rōg-ā'-shun], *n.* (*leg.*) the substitution of one person or party for another as creditor. [L. *subrogatio*].

SUBROTUND, [sub'-rō-tund'], *adj.* almost rotund.

SUBSACRAL, [sub-sak'-ral], *adj.* situated under the sacrum. [SUB- and SACRAL].

SUBSALINE, [sub-sā'-līn], *adj.* moderately saline.

SUBSALT, [sub-sawlt'], *n.* (*chem.*) a basic salt.

SUBSCAPULAR, [sub-skap'-yōō-ler], *adj.* situated under the scapula.

SUBSCRIBABLE, [sub-skrib'-abl], *adj.* able or requiring to be subscribed to.

SUBSCRIBE, [sub-skrib'], *v.t. and i.* to sign one's name to; (*fig.*) to give one's assent or approval; to give one's allegiance; to contribute, *esp.* at regular intervals; **to s. to,** to buy regularly (a service, newspaper, etc.); to agree with (opinions, etc.). [L. *subscribere*].

SUBSCRIBER, [sub-skrib'-er], *n.* one who subscribes.

SUBSCRIPT, [sub'-skript], *n.* the small iota written

under certain Greek vowels. [L. *subscriptus*, *p.pt.* of *subscribere* to write below].
SUBSCRIPTION, [sub-skrip'-shun], *n.* the act of subscribing, the condition of being subscribed; that which is subscribed. [L. *subscriptio*].
SUBSECTION, [sub'-sek'-shun], *n.* a section of something that is itself only a section.
SUBSELLIUM, [sub-sel'-i-um], *n.* a misericord. [L. *subsellium* bench].
SUBSEPTUPLE, [sub-sept'-ewpl], *adj.* being in the ratio of one to seven.
SUBSEQUENCE, [sub'-si-kwents], *n.* the condition of being subsequent.
SUBSEQUENT, [sub'-si-kwent], *adj.* occurring at a later point of time, following; consequent, resulting. [L. *subsequens*].
SUBSEQUENTLY, [sub'-si-kwent-li], *adv.* at a later time.
SUBSEROUS, [sub-ser'-us], *adj.* somewhat serous.
SUBSERVE, [sub-surv'], *v.t.* to aid, serve, fulfil. [L. *subservire* to be subject to].
SUBSERVIENCE, [sub-surv'-i-ents], *n.* the condition of being subservient.
SUBSERVIENCY, [sub-surv'-i-en-si], *n.* subservience, the state of being subservient.
SUBSERVIENT, [sub-surv'-i-ent], *adj.* serving, promoting, *esp.* in a subordinate capacity; obsequious. [L. *subserviens*].
SUBSERVIENTLY, [sub-surv'-i-ent-li], *adv.* in a subservient way.
SUBSESSILE, [sub-ses'-īl], *adj.* (*bot.*) almost sessile.
SUBSEXTUPLE, [sub-seks'-tewpl], *adj.* being in the ratio of one to six.
SUBSIDE, [sub-sīd'], *v.i.* to collapse (*esp.* of the ground), fall in, sink down; to slacken, diminish, weaken. [L. *subsidere*].
SUBSIDENCE, [sub-sī'-dents], *n.* the fact or process of subsiding. [L. *subsidentia* sediment].
SUBSIDENCY, [sub-sī'-den-si], *n.* the process of subsiding.
SUBSIDIARILY, [sub-sid'-i-er-i-li], *adv.* in a subsidiary fashion.
SUBSIDIARY (1), [sub-sid'-i-er-i], *n.* a person or thing acting in an ancillary capacity.
SUBSIDIARY (2), [sub-sid'-i-er-i], *adj.* aiding or promoting in a secondary capacity, auxiliary, ancillary; having the nature of, or pertaining to, a subsidy; **s. company**, a company of which most of the shares are held by a larger firm. [L. *subsidiarius*].
SUBSIDIZE, [sub'-sid-īz'], *v.t.* to pay a subsidy to.
SUBSIDY, [sub'-sid-i], *n.* a grant made from public funds in support of private enterprise; (*hist.*) a grant made by parliament to the king. [L. *subsidium*].
SUBSIST, [sub-sist'], *v.t. and i.* to exist in reality; to continue in existence; (*rare*) to provide with necessaries for existence. [L. *subsistere* to stand still].
SUBSISTENCE, [sub-sist'-ents], *n.* the act of subsisting; things necessary to maintain life, that on which one subsists, livelihood; **s. money**, an allowance for maintenance. [LL. *subsistentia*].
SUBSISTENCY, [sub-sist'-en-si], *n.* subsistence, continued existence.
SUBSISTENT, [sub-sist'-ent], *adj.* existing, subsisting. [L. *subsistens*].
SUBSOIL, [sub'-soil], *n.* the layer of soil which lies immediately beneath the top layer.
SUBSOLAR, [sub-sōl'-er], *adj.* existing under the sun.
SUBSPECIES, [sub'-spē-shēz], *n.* an intermediate between a species and a variety.
SUBSPECIFIC, [sub'-spis-if'-ik], *adj.* of, or pertaining to, a subspecies.
SUBSPHERICAL, [sub-sfe'-rik-al], *adj.* almost spherical.
SUBSPINOUS, [sub-spī'-nus], *adj.* rather spinous.
SUBSPIRAL, [sub-spīer'-al], *adj.* somewhat or imperfectly spiral.
SUBSTAGE, [sub'-stāj], *n.* an attachment underneath the stage of a microscope.
SUBSTANCE, [sub'-stants], *n.* the essence of a thing, the essential nature, quality or reality of a thing; that of which something is composed or consists; matter; solid matter, body; the meaning or purport of a book, essay, speech, argument, etc.; the essential part or character of a thing; wealth, possessions, resources. [L. *substantia*].
SUBSTANTIAL, [sub-stan'-shal], *adj.* pertaining to substance; having the character of substance, solid, real, firm; (of a meal, etc.) satisfying; concerning substance or purport; important, remarkable, considerable; wealthy. [L. *substantialis*].
SUBSTANTIALISM, [sub-stan'-shal-izm], *n.* the doctrine that there is a permanent reality underlying all phenomena.
SUBSTANTIALIST, [sub-stan'-shal-ist], *n.* one who accepts the doctrine of substantialism.
SUBSTANTIALITY, [sub-stan'-shi-al'-i-ti], *n.* the condition of being substantial.
SUBSTANTIALIZE, [sub-stan'-shal-īz], *v.t.* to make substantial.
SUBSTANTIALLY, [sub-stan'-shal-i], *adv.* to a substantial degree.
SUBSTANTIALNESS, [sub-stan'-shal-nes], *n.* the condition of being substantial.
SUBSTANTIATE, [sub-stan'-shi-āt], *v.t.* to make real, give substance to; to prove to be true, establish [L. *substantiare*].
SUBSTANTIATION, [sub-stan'-shi-ā'-shun], *n.* the act of substantiating, the condition of being substantiated.
SUBSTANTIVAL, [sub'-stan-tīv'-al], *adj.* pertaining to, or serving as, a substantive.
SUBSTANTIVALLY, [sub'-stan-tīv'-al-i], *adv.* in the manner of a substantive.
SUBSTANTIVE (1), [sub'-stan-tiv], *n.* a noun substantive.
SUBSTANTIVE (2), [sub'-stan-tiv], *adj.* having a distinct and real being; (*gram.*) expressing existence; **noun s.**, (*gram.*) a word denoting a specific thing, idea, etc.; **s. rank**, (*milit.*) one's actual paid rank. [L. *substantivus*].
SUBSTANTIVELY, [sub'-stan-tiv-li], *adv.* as a substantive.
SUBSTATION, [sub-stā'-shun], *n.* a subsidiary station.
SUBSTERNAL, [sub-sturn'-al], *adj.* situated under the sternum.
SUBSTITUTE (1), [sub'-sti-tewt], *n.* a person or thing used in place of, or acting instead of, another.
SUBSTITUTE (2), [sub'-sti-tewt], *v.t. and i.* to put or employ instead of another; to act as a substitute. [L. *substituere* to put in place of].
SUBSTITUTION, [sub'-sti-tew'-shun], *n.* the act of substituting; the condition of being substituted. [L. *substitutio*].
SUBSTITUTIONAL, [sub'-sti-tew'-shun-al], *adj.* pertaining to substitution; acting as a substitute.
SUBSTITUTIONALLY, [sub'-sti-tew'-shun-al-i], *adv.* in the manner of a substitute; by substitution.
SUBSTITUTIONARY, [sub'-sti-tew'-shun-er-i], *adj.* pertaining to substitution.
SUBSTITUTIVE, [sub'-sti-tew-tiv], *adj.* able to be substituted.
SUBSTRATOSPHERE, [sub'-straht'-ō-sfēer], *n.* (*meteor.*) the layer of atmosphere lying immediately below the stratosphere.
SUBSTRATUM, (*pl.* **substrata**), [sub-strā'-tum], *n.* an underlying stratum.
SUBSTRUCTURAL, [sub-struk'-cher-al], *adj.* pertaining to a substructure.
SUBSTRUCTURE, [sub-struk'-cher], *n.* (*arch.*) an understructure; that structure upon which a building rests.
SUBSTYLE, [sub'-stīl], *n.* the line on which the gnomon of a dial is set.
SUBSULTORY, [sub-sul'-ter-i], *adj.* moving by sudden leaps or bounds.
SUBSULTUS, [sub-sul'-tus], *n.* (*path.*) a twitching or convulsive movement or motion. [L. *subsultus*].
SUBSUME, [sub-sewm'], *v.t.* to put into a definite stated category; to subordinate. [SUB- and L. *sumere* to take up.
SUBSUMPTION, [sub-sump'-shun], *n.* the act of subsuming; the condition of being subsumed; anything subsumed.
SUBSUMPTIVE, [sub-sump'-tiv], *adj.* pertaining to a subsumption.
SUBSURFACE, [sub'-surf-is], *adj.* situated below the surface.
SUBTANGENT, [sub-tan'-jent], *n.* (*math.*) that part of the axis of a curve lying between the tangent and the ordinate.
SUBTEMPERATE, [sub-tem'-per-at], *adj.* almost or rather less than temperate.
SUBTENANT, [sub-ten'-ant], *n.* a tenant holding property from one who himself holds it only as a tenant.
SUBTEND, [sub-tend'], *v.t.* (*geom.*) to extend under, to be opposite to. [L. *subtendere*].
SUBTENSE, [sub-tents'], *n.* (*geom.*) a line subtending an angle. [~L. *subtensus*, *p.pt.* of *subtendere*].

SUBTEPID, [sub-tep'-id], *adj.* barely warm, cooler than tepid.
SUBTER-, *pref.* beneath; somewhat. [L. *subter* beneath].
SUBTERETE, [sub'-te-rēt'], *adj.* somewhat tapering.
SUBTERFLUENT, [sub-tur'-flōō-ent], *adj.* running under or beneath. [L. *subter* beneath and *fluens* flowing].
SUBTERFUGE, [sub'-ter-fewj], *n.* an artifice, subtle concealment of real conduct or motive, a means of evading discovery. [L. *subterfugium*].
SUBTERNATURAL, [sub'-ter-nach'-er-al], *adj.* less than natural, subnormal.
SUBTERPOSITION, [sub'-ter-pōz-ish'-un], *n.* the state, position, of being beneath.
SUBTERRANE, [sub'-ter-ān], *n.* an underground cave.
SUBTERRANEAN, [sub'-ter-ān'-i-an], *adj.* underground. [L. *subterraneus*].
SUBTERRANEOUS, [sub'-ter-ān'-i-us], *adj.* subterranean.
SUBTERRENE, [sub'-ter-ēn'], *adj.* subterraneous.
SUBTHORACIC, [sub'-thaw-ras'-ik], *adj.* below the thorax.
SUBTILE, [sub'-til, sutl'], *adj.* subtle.
SUBTILELY, [sut'-il-i], *adv.* subtly.
SUBTILIZATION, [sut'-il-īz-ā'-shun], *n.* the act of subtilizing, the state of being subtilized.
SUBTILIZE, [sut'-il-īz], *v.t.* and *i.* to refine, to make subtle; to make subtle distinctions, argue subtly.
SUBTILTY, [sut'-il-ti], *n.* subtlety.
SUB-TITLE, [sub'-tītl'], *n.* the secondary, explanatory title of a book; a caption in a film.
SUBTLE, [sutl], *adj.* intellectually penetrating, with a delicate and accomplished critical sense; artful and cunning of mind, able to devise complex schemes and perceive delicate distinctions; almost indefinable, highly refined, delicate. [L. *subtilis*].
SUBTLENESS, [sutl'-nes], *n.* the quality of being subtle; subtlety.
SUBTLETY, [sutl'-ti], *n.* the quality of being subtle; that which is subtle, a subtle device or argument. [L. *subtilitas* fineness].
SUBTLY, [sut'-li], *adv.* in subtle fashion.
SUBTONIC, [sub-ton'-ik], *n.* (*mus.*) the seventh note of the diatonic scale, the tonic te.
SUBTORRID, [sub-to'-rid], *adj.* less than torrid.
SUBTRACT, [sub-trakt'], *v.t.* to take away (a part) from a quantity; (*math.*) to find the difference between two numbers. [L. *subtractus*, *p.pt.* of *subtrahere* to take away].
SUBTRACTER, [sub-trakt'-er], *n.* one who subtracts.
SUBTRACTION, [sub-trak'-shun], *n.* the act or process of subtracting.
SUBTRACTIVE, [sub-trakt'-iv], *adj.* relating to subtraction, tending to subtract.
SUBTRAHEND, [sub'-tra-hend'], *n.* that which is to be subtracted. [L. *subtrahendus*, *ger.* of *subtrahere* to take away].
SUBTRIPLE, [sub-tripl'], *adj.* in the ratio of one to three.
SUBTRIPLICATE, [sub-trip'-lik-āt], *adj.* in the ratio of the cube roots.
SUBTROPICAL, [sub-trop'-ik-al], *adj.* slightly less than tropical.
SUB-TUTOR, [sub'-tewt'-er], *n.* an under-tutor.
SUBTYPE, [sub'-tīp], *n.* the subdivision of a type.
SUBULATE, [sub'-yōō-lāt], *adj.* (*bot.*, *zool.*) slender and pointed. [~L. *subula* awl].
SUBULICORN, [sub'-yōōl-i-kawn], *adj.* having awl-shaped antennae. [*Prec.* and L. *cornu* horn].
SUBUMBONAL, [sub'-um-bōn'-al], *adj.* beneath the umbo.
SUBUNGUAL, [sub-ung'-gew-al], *adj.* under the nail.
SUBUNGULATE, [sub-ung'-gyōō-lāt], *adj.* (*zool.*) having digited hooves.
SUBURB, [sub'-urb], *n.* a part of a town lying beyond its walls; a residential area lying on the outskirts of a city. [L. *suburbium*].
SUBURBAN, [sub-urb'-an], *adj.* relating to, dwelling in, a suburb; (*fig.*) pettily conventional, narrow-minded. [L. *suburbanus*].
SUBURBIA, [sub-urb'-i-a], *n.* the areas occupied by the suburbs of a large city; the body of opinion and prejudices typical of the inhabitants of these areas. [SUBURB].
SUBURSINE, [sub-ur'-sīn], *adj.* rather ursine.
SUBVARIETY, [sub'-va-rī-it-i], *n.* a subdivision of a variety; a minor variety. [SUB- and VARIETY].
SUBVENTION, [sub-ven'-shun], *n.* the act of supporting; a subsidy. [L. *subventio* assistance].
SUBVERSION, [sub-vur'-shun], *n.* the act of subverting, the state of being subverted. [L. *subversio* overthrow].
SUBVERSIONARY, [sub-vur'-shun-er-i], *adj.* relating to subversion.
SUBVERSIVE, [sub-vurs'-iv], *adj.* tending to subvert.
SUBVERT, [sub-vurt'], *v.t.* to overthrow, *esp.* by means of subtle propaganda; to undermine the loyalty of, *esp.* of the armed forces of a government. [L. *subvertere* to overthrow].
SUBVERTANT, [sub-vurt'-ant], *adj.* (*her.*) upside down.
SUBVERTEBRAL, [sub-vurt'-i-bral], *adj.* beneath the vertebrae.
SUBVERTER, [sub-vurt'-er], *n.* one who subverts.
SUBVERTIBLE, [sub-vurt'-ibl], *adj.* liable to subversion.
SUBVERTICAL, [sub-vurt'-ik-al], *adj.* almost vertical.
SUBVITREOUS, [sub-vit'-ri-us], *adj.* nearly vitreous.
SUBWAY, [sub'-wā], *n.* an underground pathway, *esp.* a passage beneath busy crossings or railway lines; (*U.S.*) a tube railway.
SUBWORKER, [sub'-wurk'-er], *n.* a subordinate worker.
SUCCADE, [suk-ād'], *n.* a crystallized fruit. [Fr. *succade* from L. *succus* juice].
SUCCEDANEOUS, [suk'-si-dān'-i-us], *adj.* serving as substitute. [L. *succedaneus*].
SUCCEDANEUM, [suk'-si-dān'-i-um], *n.* a substitute. [L. *succedaneum*].
SUCCEED, [suk-sēd'], *v.t.* to follow in order immediately after; to replace, to come immediately after; *v.i.* to follow immediately after, to fill an office in place of a deceased person; to achieve an object; to bring to a satisfactory end what is attempted; to be prosperous. [Fr. *succéder*].
SUCCEEDANT, [suk-sēd'-ant], *adj.* (*her.*) following after one another.
SUCCEEDER, [suk-sēd'-er], *n.* successor.
SUCCENTOR, [suk-sent'-er], *n.* the leading bass voice in a choir. [LL. *succentor*].
SUCCESS, [suk-ses'], *n.* the achievement of a desired aim, the prosperous conclusion of what is attempted. [L. *successus*].
SUCCESSFUL, [suk-ses'-fōōl], *adj.* characterized by success, prosperous, brought to a satisfactory conclusion.
SUCCESSFULLY, [suk-ses'-fōōl-i], *adv.* in a successful manner.
SUCCESSFULNESS, [suk-ses'-fōōl-nes], *n.* the condition of being successful.
SUCCESSION, [suk-sesh'-un], *n.* that which succeeds; a series of things or events following upon one another in time or place; the act of succeeding; lineage; (*mus.*) the successive notes in a melody; **Apostolic S.**, the spiritual power transmitted from St. Peter and the Apostles through successive generations of bishops. [L. *successio*].
SUCCESSIONAL, [suk-sesh'-un-al], *adj.* following in a regular order.
SUCCESSIONALLY, [suk-sesh'-un-al-i], *adv.* in order of succession.
SUCCESSIVE, [suk-ses'-iv], *adj.* following or coming by succession or in order, consecutive.
SUCCESSIVELY, [suk-ses'-iv-li], *adv.* in successive manner or order.
SUCCESSIVENESS, [suk-ses'-iv-nes], *n.* the condition of being successive.
SUCCESSLESS, [suk-ses'-les], *adj.* having no success or prosperity.
SUCCESSLESSLY, [suk-ses'-les-li], *adv.* without success.
SUCCESSLESSNESS, [suk-ses'-les-nes], *n.* the state of being without success.
SUCCESSOR, [suk-ses'-er], *n.* one who succeeds; one who takes over the office or rank before held by another. [L. *successor*].
SUCCIDUOUS, [suk-sid'-yōō-us], *adj.* ready to fall. [~L. *succidere*].
SUCCIFEROUS, [suk-sif'-er-us], *adj.* bearing sap. [L. *succus* juice and *ferre* to bear].
SUCCIN, [suk'-sin], *n.* amber. [L. *succinum*].
SUCCINATE, [suk'-sin-āt], *n.* (*chem.*) a salt of succinic acid.
SUCCINATED, [suk'-sin-āt-ed], *adj.* (*chem.*) combined or treated with succinic acid.
SUCCINCT, [suk-singkt'], *adj.* compressed into small space; concise, short. [L. *succinctus* girt in].

SUCCINCTLY, [suk-singkt'-li], *adv.* briefly, shortly.
SUCCINCTNESS, [suk-singkt'-nes], *n.* brevity of style.
SUCCINIC, [suk-sin'-ik], *adj.* (*chem.*) pertaining to, or derived from, amber. [~L. *succinum* amber].
SUCCINITE, [suk'-sin-īt], *n.* an insoluble amber resin.
SUCCINOUS, [suk'-sin-us], *adj.* like, or pertaining to, amber.
SUCCIVOROUS, [suk-si'-ver-us], *adj.* feeding on sap. [L. *succus* juice and *vorare* to devour].
SUCCORY, [suk'-er-i], *n.* chicory. [~CHICORY].
SUCCOSE, [suk'-ōs], *adj.* sappy.
SUCCOTASH, [suk'-ō-tash'], *n.* green maize and beans boiled together. [AmerInd. *sukotash*].
SUCCOUR (1), [suk'-er], *n.* help, relief from trouble or distress; one who, or that which, brings such help. [OFr. *socours*].
SUCCOUR (2), [suk'-er], *v.t. and i.* to give or bring succour to; to relieve distress and want. [L. *succurrere*].
SUCCOURER, [suk'-er-er], *n.* one who succours.
SUCCOURLESS, [suk'-er-les], *adj.* having no succour.
SUCCUBOUS, [suk'-yōō-bus], *adj.* (*bot.*) of the leaves of certain liverworts, having the lower edge of each leaf overlapping the upper edge of the leaf below it away from the apex of the stem. [MdL. *succubus* from L. *sub* under and ~*cumbere* to lie].
SUCCUBUS, [suk'-yōō-bus], *n.* a devil in female form appearing to men in their sleep for sexual intercourse. [~L. *succuba* harlot].
SUCCULA, [suk'-yōō-la], *n.* a kind of capstan. [L. *sucula*].
SUCCULENCE, [suk'-yōōl-ents], *n.* juiciness.
SUCCULENT, [suk'-yōōl-ent], *adj.* juicy (*esp.* of food). [L. *succulentus*].
SUCCULENTLY, [suk'-yōōl-ent-li], *adv.* in a succulent manner.
SUCCUMB, [suk-um'], *v.i.* to submit, fall, yield; to die. [L. *succumbere* to lie down].

SUCCULA

SUCCURSAL, [suk-urs'-al], *adj.* annexed, subsidiary. [Fr. *succursal*].
SUCCUSSATION, [suk'-us-ā'-shun], *n.* a trot; a shaking.
SUCCUSSION, [suk-ush'-un], *n.* the action of shaking, a shake; nervous shaking induced by stimulants. [L. *succussio*].
SUCCUSSIVE, [suk-us'-iv], *adj.* shaking.
SUCH (1), [such], *adj.* of that kind, similar, same, like. [OE. *swylc*].
SUCH (2), [such], *pron.* such a person or thing; the same; it, them. [*Prec.*].
SUCH-AND-SUCH, [such'-and-such'], *adj. and pron.* certain, particular but unspecified.
SUCHLIKE, [such'-lik], *adj.* (*coll.*) like, similar.
SUCK (1), [suk], *n.* the act of drawing in through the mouth by the muscular action of the lips and the inspiration of the lungs; what is drawn in in this manner; milk drawn from the breast, pap.
SUCK (2), [suk], *v.t. and i.* to draw in by means of a suck or series of sucks; to take milk from the breast; to imbibe, draw into the mouth; to absorb; to draw or hold to by exhausting the air; **to s. in**, (*coll.*) to cheat or deceive. [OE. *sucan*].
SUCKATHUMB, [suk'-a-thum'], *n.* a child that sucks its thumb. [SUCK (2) and THUMB (1)].
SUCKER, [suk'-er], *n.* one who, or that which, sucks or draws or holds by a suck; the piston or plunger of a pump; (*bot.*) a shoot from the roots or lower part of the stem of a plant; a fish of the genus *Lepidogaster*; (*U.S.*) a gullible person.
SUCKET, [suk'-it], *n.* a sweetmeat which is meant to be sucked or dissolved in the mouth.
SUCKING, [suk'-ing], *adj.* at the breast, fed by the mother's milk; (*fig.*) very young.
SUCKLE, [sukl], *v.t.* to feed at the breast.
SUCKLER, [suk'-ler], *n.* a suckling.
SUCKLING, [suk'-ling], *n.* a child or animal being still fed at the breast.
SUCROSE, [sewk'-rōs], *n.* cane-sugar. [~Fr. *sucre*].
SUCTION, [suk'-shun], *n.* the action of sucking; the process of drawing a liquid or gas into a vessel in which a partial vacuum is created by withdrawing the air; a similar process by which one thing is made to adhere to another by withdrawing the air between them. [~L. *suctus*, *p.pt.* of *sugere* to suck].
SUCTION-PIPE, [suk'-shun-pip'], *n.* the inlet pipe at the lower end of a pump.
SUCTION-PUMP, [suk'-shun-pump'], *n.* a pump for lifting water and other liquids to a higher level by raising a piston in a cylinder in order to create a vacuum into which the liquid is forced by atmospheric pressure.
SUCTORIAL, [suk-taw'-ri-al], *adj.* having the power to suck or adhere by suction.
SUCTORIAN, [suk-taw'-ri-an], *n.* (*zool.*) an animal with a mouth adapted for sucking or suction.
SUDAMINA, [sew-dam'-in-a], *n.(pl.)* (*med.*) a vesicular eruption with sweating. [~ L. *sudor* sweat].
SUDARIUM, [sew-dāer'-i-um], *n.* the cloth on which Christ wiped his face, and which miraculously preserved an imprint of his features; a vernicle. [L. *sudarium* a cloth for wiping away sweat].

SUCTION-PUMP

SUDATION, [sew-dā'-shun], *n.* sweating. [L. *sudatio*].
SUDATORIUM, [sew'-da-taw'-ri-um], *n.* (*archae.*) a room heated to induce sweating. [L. *sudatorium*].
SUDATORY (1), [sew'-da-ter-i], *n.* a sweating bath; a hothouse. [*Prec.*].
SUDATORY (2), [sew'-da-ter-i], *adj.* causing sweat.
SUDD, [sud], *n.* a mass of floating vegetable remains (*esp.* on the Nile). [Arab. *sudd* obstruction].
SUDDEN (1), [sud'-en], *n.* **of a s., on a s.,** unexpectedly.
SUDDEN (2), [sud'-en], *adj.* occurring without warning or notice; happening unexpectedly; unexpected. [OFr. *soudain*].
SUDDENLY, [sud'-en-li], *adv.* in a sudden fashion.
SUDDENNESS, [sud'-en-nes], *n.* the condition of being sudden.
SUDORIFEROUS, [sew'-der-if'-er-us], *adj.* causing sweating. [L. *sudor* sweat and *ferre* to bear].
SUDORIFIC (1), [sew'-der-if-ik], *n.* a medicine to induce sweating.
SUDORIFIC (2), [sew'-der-if-ik], *adj.* producing sweating.
SUDORIPAROUS, [sew'-der-ip'-er-us], *adj.* secreting sweat. [L. *sudor* sweat and *parere* to produce].
SUDRA, [sōōd'-ra], *n.* the lowest of the four great Hindu castes. [Skr. *sudra*].
SUDS, [sudz], *n.(pl.)* a frothy, bubbly formation on the surface of water in which soap has been dissolved and agitated. [OE. *sud*].
SUE, (**sues, suing, sued**), [sew], *v.t. and i.* (*leg.*) to take proceedings in a court of law to obtain justice; to prosecute; to beg, petition. [AFr. *suer*].
SUEDE, suède, [swād], *n.* soft, pliable, unglazed leather. [Fr. *Suède* Sweden].
SUET, [sōō'-it], *n.* hard animal fat taken from the loins, etc. [OFr. *seu*].
SUET-PUDDING, [sōō'-it-pōōd'-ing], *n.* a (boiled) pudding in which one of the chief ingredients is suet.
SUETY, [sōō'-it-i], *adj.* made of, or similar to, suet.
SUFFER, [suf'-er], *v.t. and i.* to feel and endure physical or mental anguish and distress; to endure, undergo; to lose; to allow (often, unwillingly). [OFr. *soffrir*].
SUFFERABLE, [suf'-er-abl], *adj.* able to be suffered, endured, tolerated, or permitted.
SUFFERABLENESS, [suf'-er-abl-nes], *n.* the condition of being sufferable.
SUFFERABLY, [suf'-er-ab-li], *adv.* tolerably.
SUFFERANCE, [suf'-er-ants], *n.* the bearing of pain and distress; patience, moderation; consent implied by the absence of directions to the contrary; **on s.,** tolerated but unwelcome. [L. *sufferentia*].
SUFFERER, [suf'-er-er], *n.* one who suffers.
SUFFERING (1), [suf'-er-ing], *n.* the bearing of pain and distress; pain and anguish; loss.
SUFFERING (2), [suf'-er-ing], *adj.* bearing pain and distress.
SUFFERINGLY, [suf'-er-ing-li], *adv.* with suffering.
SUFFICE, [su-fis'], *v.t. and i.* to be enough; to be satisfied; to satisfy. [OFr. *suffire*].
SUFFICIENCY, [su-fish'-en-si], *n.* the state of being sufficient or adequate; competence, self-confidence; adequate resources.
SUFFICIENT, [su-fish'-ent], *adj.* enough, adequate, satisfying the needs adequately; competent. [L. *sufficiens*].
SUFFICIENTLY, [su-fish'-ent-li], *adv.* enough, adequately satisfying all needs, competently.

SUFFIX (1), [suf'-iks], *n.* a particle or element added to the end of a word, *esp.* to form a new grammatical or sense development of the original word. [L. *suffixus*].
SUFFIX (2), [suf'-iks], *v.t.* to form or add as a suffix to.
SUFFIXION, [su-fik'-shun], *n.* the process of adding a suffix.
SUFFLATE, [su-flāt'], *v.t.* to inflate. [~L. *sufflatus* blown].
SUFFOCATE, [suf'-ō-kāt], *v.t. and i.* to take away or lose life by stopping respiration. [~L. *suffocare*].
SUFFOCATINGLY, [suf'-ō-kāt-ing-li], *adv.* so as to suffocate.
SUFFOCATION, [suf'-ō-kā'-shun], *n.* the act of suffocating, the state of being suffocated; **to s.,** so as to suffocate.
SUFFOCATIVE, [suf'-ō-kāt-iv], *adj.* tending to suffocate.
SUFFOSION, [su-fō'-zhun], *n.* an undermining. [~L. *sub* under and *fodire* to dig].
SUFFRAGAN, [suf'-rag-an], *n.* (*eccles.*) an assistant to a diocesan bishop or to an archbishop. [MedL. *suffraganeus*].
SUFFRAGANSHIP, [suf'-rag-an-ship], *n.* the rank and duties of a suffragan.
SUFFRAGE, [suf'-rij], *n.* a vote; the right to vote. [L. *suffragium* voting tablet].
SUFFRAGETTE, [suf'-ra-jet'], *n.* a woman who agitated for female suffrage.
SUFFRAGINOUS, [suf'-raj'-in-us], *adj.* pertaining to a beast's knee-joint. [L. *suffrago* pastern].
SUFFRAGIST, [suf'-ra-jist], *n.* one who supports suffrage for women.
SUFFRUTESCENT, [suf'-rōō-tes'-ent], *adj.* woody at the base. [L. *sub* under and *frutex* bush].
SUFFRUTICOSE, [suf-rōōt'-ik-ōs], *adj.* moderately shrubby.
SUFFUSE, [su-fewz'], *v.t.* to flood over, cover. [~L. *suffusus, p.pt.* of *suffundere*].
SUFFUSION, [su-few'-zhun], *n.* that which suffuses; the state of being suffused. [L. *suffusio*].
SUFI, [sōōf'-i], *n.* a Mohammedan mystic. [Arab. *sufi* man of wool].
SUFISM, [sōōf'-izm], *n.* Moslem mysticism. [~Arab. *suf* wool].
SUGAR, [shŏŏg'-er], *n.* a sweet substance, usually crystalline, extracted from various plants, and used extensively in cooking; (*fig.*) gross flattery; (*coll.*) an attractive young female. [OFr. *sucre* from Arab. *sukkar*].
SUGAR-APPLE, [shŏŏg'-er-apl'], *n.* (*bot.*) the sweet-sop, *Anona squamosa*.
SUGAR-BAKER, [shŏŏg'-er-bāk'-er], *n.* a refiner of sugar.
SUGAR-BASIN, [shŏŏg'-er-bās'-in], *n.* a bowl for holding sugar at table.
SUGAR-BEET, [shŏŏg'-er-bēt], *n.* a plant from whose root sugar is extracted, *Beta vulgaris*.
SUGAR-CANDY, [shŏŏg'-er-kan'-di], *n.* a sweet-meat of clear crystallized sugar.
SUGAR-CANE, [shŏŏg'-er-kān], *n.* a grass, *Saccharum officinarum*, from whose stem sugar is extracted.
SUGAR-DADDY, [shŏŏg'-er-dad'-i], *n.* (*coll.*) an old man who provides meals and entertainments for personable young women.
SUGAR-FARMER, [shŏŏg'-er-fahm'-er], *n.* one who grows sugar-beet.
SUGAR-HOUSE, [shŏŏg'-er-hows], *n.* a refinery for sugar.
SUGARINESS, [shŏŏg'-er-i-nes], *n.* sweetness, *esp.* when due to sugar.
SUGAR-KETTLE, [shŏŏg'-er-ketl'], *n.* a receptacle used for boiling sugar in its refining.
SUGARLESS, [shŏŏg'-er-les], *adj.* without sugar.

SUGAR-CANE

SUGAR-LOAF, [shŏŏg'-er-lōf], *n.* a large cone-shaped mass of refined sugar.
SUGAR-MAPLE, [shŏŏg'-er-māpl], *n.* a species of maple whose sap produces sugar.
SUGAR-MILL, [shŏŏg'-er-mil], *n.* a press for extracting sap from sugar-cane.
SUGAR-MITE, [shŏŏg'-er-mīt], *n.* a mite occurring in raw sugar.
SUGAR-PINE, [shŏŏg'-er-pīn], *n.* a coniferous tree, *Pinus lambertiana*.
SUGAR-PLANTER, [shŏŏg'-er-plahnt'-er], *n.* one who cultivates, owns a plantation of, sugar-cane.
SUGAR-PLUM, [shŏŏg'-er-plum'], *n.* a sweetmeat made of sugar.
SUGAR-REFINER, [shŏŏg'-er-ri-fīn'-er], *n.* one who refines sugar.
SUGAR-TONGS, [shŏŏg'-er-tongz'], *n.(pl.)* nippers for transporting small lumps of sugar from a basin at table.
SUGARY, [shŏŏg'-er-i], *adj.* sweet; sickly-sweet.
SUGESCENT, [su-jes'-ent], *adj.* relating to sucking. [~L. *sugere* to suck].
SUGGEST, [su-jest'], *v.t.* to call up (an idea), *esp.* by association; to propose (a plan), to propound (a theory); to imply. [L. *suggerere* to lay beneath].
SUGGESTER, [su-jest'-er], *n.* one who suggests.
SUGGESTIBILITY, [su-jest'-ib-il'-it-i], *n.* the capacity for receiving suggestion.
SUGGESTIBLE, [su-jest'-ibl], *adj.* capable of being influenced by suggestion.
SUGGESTION, [su-jes'-chun], *n.* that which is suggested; the act of suggesting; an implication; an indecent proposal. [L. *suggestio*].
SUGGESTIVE, [su-jest'-iv], *adj.* tending to suggest; having an indecent implication.
SUGGESTIVELY, [su-jest'-iv-li], *adv.* in a suggestive way.
SUGGESTIVENESS, [su-jest'-iv-nes], *n.* the quality of being suggestive.
SUGGESTOR, [su-jest'-er], *n.* one who suggests.
SUGGILATION, [su'-jil-ā'-shun], *n.* a bruise; a suffusion with blood. [L. *suggilatio*].
SUICIDAL, [sew'-i-sīd'-al], *adj.* tending to, relating to, suicide.
SUICIDALLY, [sew'-i-sīd'-al-i], *adv.* in a suicidal way.
SUICIDE, [sew'-i-sīd], *n.* the act of self-destruction, physical or metaphorical; one who destroys himself. [~L. *suus* of himself and *caedere* to kill].
SUILLINE, [sōō'-il-īn], *adj.* relating to swine. [L. *suillus* swine].
SUIT (1), [sewt], *n.* the act of suing, judicial action, request; a set of clothes made of the same stuff; one of the four sets of playing cards. [OFr. *suite*].
SUIT (2), [sewt], *v.t. and i.* to be satisfactory to, harmonious with, appropriate for; to agree with; to match; to be agreeable.
SUITABILITY, [sewt'-a-bil'-it-i], *n.* suitableness.
SUITABLE, [sewt'-abl], *adj.* tending to suit, appropriate, proper, fitting.
SUITABLENESS, [sewt'-abl-nes], *n.* the state of being suitable.
SUITABLY, [sewt'-ab-li], *adv.* in a suitable way.
SUITE, [swēt'], *n.* a retinue; a set of apartments; furniture for one room; (*mus.*) a series of dances or loosely related pieces; the attendants, followers, etc., of a person of importance. [OFr. *suite* following].
SUITING, [sewt'-ing], *n.* a suit of clothes; material for making clothes.
SUITOR, [sewt'-er], *n.* one who makes a suit, *esp.* for a woman's hand in marriage.
SUITRESS, [sewt'-res], *n.* a female suitor.
SULCATE, [sul'-kāt], *adj.* sulcated.
SULCATED, [sul'-kāt-ed], *adj.* grooved, fluted. [~L. *sulcus* furrow].
SULK (1), [sulk], *n.* a sulky mood.
SULK (2), [sulk], *v.i.* to be silently sullen. [Uncert.].
SULKILY, [sulk'-i-li], *adv.* in sulky fashion.
SULKINESS, [sulk'-i-nes], *n.* the state of being sulky.
SULKS, [sulks], *n.(pl.)* sulkiness, the condition of being in a sulky mood.
SULKY (1), [sulk'-i], *n.* a light carriage holding one person only.
SULKY (2), [sulk'-i], *adj.* showing silent ill-temper, sullen, obstinately morose. [~OE. *aseolcan* to be slothful].
SULLAGE, [sul'-ij], *n.* scum on molten metal. [~SULLY].
SULLEN, [sul'-en], *adj.* sombrely sulky, obstinately silent and ill-tempered, lowering. [OFr. *solein* lonely from L. *solus*].
SULLENLY, [sul'-en-li], *adv.* in a sullen manner.
SULLENNESS, [sul'-en-nes], *n.* the quality of being sullen.
SULLENS, [sul'-enz], *n.(pl.)* a fit of sullenness.
SULLY, [sul'-i], *v.t.* to stain, soil, make dirty, tarnish. [OE. *sylian* to soil].
SULPH(O)-, *pref.* relating to, containing, sulphur. [~L. *sulphur*].
SULPHANILAMIDE, [sulf'-an-il'-am-īd], *n.* (*chem.*) one of the group of sulphonamides employed to combat certain diseases caused by *coccus* bacteria. [SULPH(UR), ANIL(INE), and AMIDE].

SULPHATE, [sul′-fāt], *n.* a salt of sulphuric acid containing four atoms of oxygen.
SULPHATIC, [sul-fat′-ik], *adj.* relating to, containing, a sulphate or sulphates.
SULPHIDE, [sul′-fīd], *n.* a compound of sulphur with some other element.
SULPHITE, [sul′-fīt], *n.* a salt of sulphurous acid, containing three atoms of oxygen.
SULPHOCYANIC, [sul′-fō-si-an′-ik], *adj.* relating to sulphocyanogen.
SULPHOCYANOGEN, [sul′-fō-sī-an′-ō-jen], *n.* a compound of sulphur and cyanogen.
SULPHONAMIDE, [sulf-on′-am-īd], *n.* (*chem.*) the amide of a sulphonic acid.
SULPHONIC, [sulf-ōn′-ic], *adj.* (*chem.*) containing the group $SO_2.OH$.
SULPHO-SALT, [sul′-fō-sawlt′], *n.* a salt containing sulphur.
SULPHUR, [sul′-fer], *n.* the chemical element denoted by S, light yellow in colour, inflammable, brittle, insoluble in water. [L. *sulphur*].
SULPHURATE, [sul′-fer-āt], *v.t.* to combine with sulphur, bleach with sulphurous smoke.
SULPHURATION, [sul′-fer-ā′-shun], *n.* the act of sulphurating, the condition of being sulphurated.
SULPHUREOUS, [sul-fewr′-i-us], *adj.* like, relating to, sulphur. [L. *sulphureus*].
SULPHUREOUSLY, [sul-fewr′-i-us-li], *adv.* in a sulphureous manner.
SULPHUREOUSNESS, [sul-fewr′-i-us-nes], *n.* the state of being sulphureous.
SULPHURET†, [sul′-few-ret], *n.* a sulphide.
SULPHURETTED, [sul′-fer-et′-ed], *adj.* in combination with sulphur.
SULPHURIC, [sul-fyōōer′-ik], *adj.* relating to, derived from, containing, sulphur; **s. acid,** oil of vitriol, the corrosive acid, H_2SO_4.
SULPHURING, [sul′-fer-ing], *n.* sulphuration.
SULPHURIZE, [sul′-fer-īz], *v.t.* to cause to combine with sulphur.
SULPHUROUS, [sul-fyōōer′-us, sul′-fer-us], *adj.* containing, resembling, sulphur, *esp.* in its lower valency; (*fig.*) devilish, connected with hell, dangerously passionate.
SULPHUR-ROOT, [sul′-fer-rōōt], *n.* sulphurweed.
SULPHURWEED, [sul′-fer-wēd], *n.* the plant, *Peucedanum officinale*, hog's fennel.
SULPHURWORT, [sul′-fer-wurt], *n.* the umbelliferous herb, *Œnanthe silaifolia.*
SULPHURY, [sul′-fer-i], *adj.* of, or containing, sulphur, like sulphur.
SULTAN, [sul′-tan], *n.* the former emperor of the Ottomans, a Moslem ruling prince; (*bot.*) a plant of the genus *Centaurea.* [Arab. *sultan* victorious].
SULTANA, [sul-tahn′-a], *n.* the chief consort of a sultan; a variety of seedless raisin. [Ital. *sultana*].
SULTANIC, [sul-tan′-ik], *adj.* pertaining to a sultan.
SULTANRY, [sul′-tan-ri], *n.* the kingdom ruled by a sultan.
SULTANSHIP, [sul′-tan-ship] *n.* the office or state of a sultan.
SULTRINESS, [sul′-tri-nes], *n.* the state of being sultry.
SULTRY, [sul′-tri], *adj.* oppressively warm and damp, thundery; (*fig.*) angry, lurid, threatening. [~SWELTER].
SUM (1), [sum], *n.* the total quantity of a thing, the product of numerical addition, the totality of related things or ideas, a quantity of money, a mathematical problem dealing with addition, subtraction, multiplication, or division. [L. *summa*].
SUM (2) [sum], (usually **sum up**), *v.t.* to add up, to total; to review arguments on either side in order to facilitate judgment.
SUMACH, [shew′-mak], *n.* a shrub of the genus *Rheus*, the leaves of which are used medicinally and in dyeing. [Arab. *summaq*].
SUMERIAN (1), [sew-mēer′-i-an], *n.* an inhabitant of Sumeria; the language of Sumeria.
SUMERIAN (2), [sew-mēer′-i-an], *adj.* of, relating to, the people and culture of *Sumer*, an ancient city on the Euphrates.
SUMLESS, [sum′-les], *adj.* immeasurable.
SUMMARILY, [sum′-er-i-li], *adv.* in summary fashion.
SUMMARIST, [sum′-er-ist], *n.* one who summarizes.
SUMMARIZE, [sum′-er-īz], *v.t.* to make a summary of, to abstract and state concisely the principal features of.
SUMMARY (1), [sum′-er-i], *n.* an epitome, a brief, concise abstract of a statement, etc., giving the principal points or heads of argument, a précis.
SUMMARY (2), [sum′-er-i], *adj.* concise, brief and to the point, with the minimum of formality. [L. *summarium* abstract].
SUMMATION, [sum-ā′-shun], *n.* the act of summing up, or forming a grand total. [Fr. *sommation*].
SUMMER (1), [sum′-er], *n.* the annual season of greatest heat, the months between spring and autumn; (*fig.*) a flourishing period, a year of age. [OE. *summor*].
SUMMER (2), [sum′-er], *n.* (*arch.*) a stone supporting an arch, a crosspiece, supported on two uprights, and upholding a structure above it. [Fr. *sommier*].
SUMMER (3), [sum′-er], *adj.* of, in, relating to, the summer months.
SUMMER (4), [sum′-er], *v.i.* to spend the summer.
SUMMER-COLTS, [sum′-er-kōlts], *n.* the shimmering in the air noticeable in extreme heat.
SUMMER-CYPRESS, [sum′-er-sī′-pres], *n.* an annual plant of the genus *Kochia.*

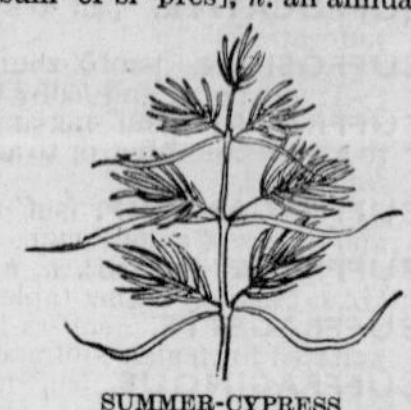
SUMMER-CYPRESS

SUMMER-DUCK, [sum′-er-duk′] *n.* the wood-duck, *Aix sponsa.*
SUMMER-FALLOW, [sum′-er-fal′-ō], *n.* land lying fallow during the summer.
SUMMER-HOUSE, [sum′-er-hows], *n.* an ornamental, open-sided garden shelter for sitting in.
SUMMERING, [sum′-er-ing], *n.* the stone bedding of a vault.
SUMMERSAULT, see SOMERSAULT.
SUMMER-SNIPE, [sum′-er-snīp], *n.* the dunlin.
SUMMER-TEAL, [sum′-er-tēl], *n.* the garganey, *Querquedula circia.*
SUMMER TIME, [sum′-er-tīm], *n.* the summer; a system by which clocks are put on one hour in the summer months; **double s.,** the advancing of clocks by two hours in the summer.
SUMMER-WHEAT, [sum′-er-wēt], *n.* spring wheat.
SUMMERY, [sum′-er-i], *adj.* resembling or suitable for summer.
SUMMING-UP, [sum′-ing-up], *n.* the judge's summary and criticism of the evidence leading to his direction to the jury.
SUMMIT, [sum′-it], *n.* the topmost point of a thing, *esp.* of a hill or material height. [Fr. *sommet*].
SUMMITLESS, [sum′-it-les], *adj.* topless.
SUMMIT-LEVEL, [sum′-it-lev′-el], *n.* the highest level reached by a railway or road.
SUMMON, [sum′-on], *v.t.* to command to be present, imperatively call to a place or to perform a duty; (*leg.*) to serve with a court summons. [OFr. *somoner* from L. *summonere* to remind].
SUMMONER, [sum′-on-er], *n.* one who summons.
SUMMONS (1), [sum′-onz], *n.* a command to attend, *esp.* a legal notice to appear in court. [OFr. *somonse*].
SUMMONS (2), [sum′-onz], *v.t.* (*leg.*) to call to a court of law as witness or defendant.
SUMP, [sump], *n.* a pool of water at the bottom of an excavation; a pit for receiving freshly fused metal; the oil-container of an automobile. [~SWAMP].
SUMPH, [sumf], *n.* a cretin. [Unkn.].
SUMPIT, [sum′-pit], *n.* a Borneo blowpipe. [Malay *sumpitan*].
SUMPTER, [sump′-ter], *n.* a packhorse. [OFr. *sommetier*].
SUMPTUARY, [sump′-chōō-er-i], *adj.* relating to expenditure. [L. *sumptuarius*].
SUMPTUOSITY, [sump′-chōō-os′-it-i], *n.* extravagance. [L. *sumptuositas*].
SUMPTUOUS, [sump′-chōō-us], *adj.* lavish, costly, luxurious, expensively magnificent. [L. *sumptuosus*].
SUMPTUOUSLY, [sump′-chōō-us-li], *adv.* in a sumptuous manner.
SUMPTUOUSNESS, [sump′-chōō-us-nes], *n.* the state of being sumptuous.
SUN (1), [sun], *n.* the heavenly body around which the planetary system revolves, the rays of this heavenly body; any similar star having revolving planets; (*fig.*) a centre of attraction, a magnificent patron. [OE. *sunne*].
SUN (2), [sun], *v.t.* to expose to the sun's rays; (*refl.*) to bask in the sun.
SUN-BATH, [sun′-bahth], *n.* exposure of the body to the sun.
SUNBATHE, [sun′-bāTH], *v.i.* to take a sun-bath.
SUNBEAM, [sun′-bēm], *n.* a ray of the sun.

SUNBIRD, [sun′-burd], *n.* a tropical, long-beaked bird of the *Nectariniidæ*.
SUN-BITTERN, [sun′-bit′-ern], *n.* the striped crane of tropical America, *Europyga helias*.
SUN-BLIND, [sun′-blīnd′], *n.* a blind suitable for keeping out the sun.
SUNBONNET, [sun′-bon′-it], *n.* a bonnet protecting the face from the sun.

SUN-BITTERN

SUNBOW, [sun′-bō], *n.* the rainbow visible in a spray of water caught by the sun.
SUNBURN, [sun′-burn], *n.* darkening or peeling of the skin from exposure to the sun.
SUNBURNT, [sun′-burnt], *adj.* suffering from, enjoying, sunburn.
SUNBURST, [sun′-burst], *n.* a burst of sunshine; a gem arranged in the form of the sun with its rays.
SUNCLAD, [sun′-klad′], *adj.* shining in the sun's rays.
SUNDAE, [sun′-dā], *n.* an ice-cream served with fruits in syrup. [SUNDAY].
SUNDAY, [sun′-di], *n.* the first day of the week. **S.-school,** a school for religious instruction, held on Sunday. [OE. *sunnan dæg*].
SUNDER, [sun′-der], *v.t.* *and* *i.* to sever; to come apart. [OE. *syndrian*].
SUNDEW, [sun′-dew], *n.* a plant of the genus *Drosera*.
SUNDIAL, [sun′-dī′-al], *n.* a device for indicating the hour of the day by means of a shadow thrown by the sun upon a marked plate.
SUNDOG, [sun′-dog′], *n.* an imaginary spot apparently seen a short distance from the sun, a parhelion.
SUNDOWN, [sun′-down], *n.* sunset.
SUNDOWNER, [sun′-down-er], *n.* a tramp, *esp.* one who arrives at sundown to obtain shelter for the night; (*coll.*) an alcoholic drink taken in the evening.
SUNDRIES, [sun′-driz], *n.*(*pl.*) miscellaneous articles or items not listed separately.
SUNDRY, [sun′-dri], *adj.* various, unspecified. [OE. *syndrig* separate].
SUNFISH, [sun′-fish], *n.* a species of the genus *Orthagoriscus*; the opah, *Lampris luna*; the basking shark, *Selache maxima*.
SUNFLOWER, [sun′-flow′-er], *n.* tall yellow-flowered plant of the genus *Helianthus*.
SUN-GLASSES, [sun′-glahs′-iz], *n.* (*pl.*) glasses worn to protect the eyes from the glare of the sun.
SUN-GOD, [sun′-god′], *n.* the sun regarded as a deity.
SUN-HAT, [sun′-hat′], *n.* a hat to protect the head from the sun.
SUN-HELMET, [sun′-hel′-met], *n.* a broad-brimmed helmet worn as a protection from the tropical sun, a topee.
SUNKEN, [sungk′-en], *adj.* having been sunk, lying at the bottom of water; fallen in, hollow, cavernous.
SUNLESS, [sun′-les], *adj.* without sunlight.

SUNFLOWER

SUNLESSNESS, [sun′-les-nes], *n.* the state of being sunless.
SUNLIGHT, [sun′-līt], *n.* the light of the sun; **s. lamp,** an ultra-violet lamp providing a substitute for sunlight.
SUNLIT, [sun′-lit], *adj.* lighted by the sun.
SUN-LOUNGE, [sun′-lownj], *n.* a lounge designed to admit the maximum of sunshine.
SUNN, [sun], *n.* hemp obtained from the bark of a plant. [Hind. *san*].
SUNNA, [soon′-a], *n.* the corpus of Moslem law and doctrine based upon tradition, and not on the direct statement of the Koran. [Arab. *sunna* tradition].
SUNNILY, [sun′-i-li], *adv.* in sunny fashion.
SUNNITES, SONNITES, [soon′-its], *n.*(*pl.*) the orthodox Moslems who accept the Sunna as binding.
SUNNY, [sun′-i], *adj.* exposed to, warmed by, the sun; shining, unclouded; (*fig.*) cheerful, bright.
SUN-PARLOUR, [sun′-pah(r)′-ler], *n.* a sun-lounge.
SUNPROOF, [sun′-proof], *adj.* impervious or resistant to sunshine.
SUNRISE, [sun′-rīz], *n.* dawn, the time when the sun rises above the horizon; the phenomenon of the first appearance of the sun above the horizon daily.
SUNRISING, [sun′-rīz-ing], *n.* sunrise.
SUNSET, [sun′-set′], *n.* the time, process, of the sun's descent below the horizon. [SUN (1) and SET (3)].
SUNSHADE, [sun′-shād], *n.* a light umbrella for protection against the sun, a parasol; a shield for the eyes against sunlight; **s. roof,** a car roof that can be slid back.
SUNSHINE, [sun′-shīn], *n.* the direct light of the sun, as warming and brightening the earth; (*fig.*) radiant happiness.
SUNSHINY, [sun′-shīn′-i], *adj.* marked by sunshine.
SUNSPOT, [sun′-spot′], *n.* a dark, fluctuating spot on the sun, believed to indicate an intense volcanic disturbance.
SUN-SPURGE, [sun′-spurj], *n.* the plant, *Euphorbia Helioscopia*.
SUNSTROKE, [sun′-strōk], *n.* feverish collapse caused by exposure to intense, burning sunlight.
SUN-TRAP, [sun′-trap], *n.* a locality or site which appears to attract the sun's rays.
SUN-UP, [sun′-up], *n.* (*U.S.*) sunrise.
SUNWISE, [sun′-wīz], *adj.* in the direction of the sun's motion.
SUN-WORSHIP, [sun′-wur′-ship], *n.* worship of the sun as a deity.
SUN-WORSHIPPER, [sun′-wur′-ship-er], *n.* one who practises sun-worship.
SUP (1), [sup], *n.* a small mouthful of liquid.
SUP (2), [sup], *v.t.* *and* *i.* to eat supper; to sip; to take liquid in small mouthfuls. [OE. *supan*].
SUPER (1), [soo′-per], *n.* a supernumerary; a film extra.
SUPER (2), [soop′-er], *n.* a super-hive.
SUPER (3), [soop′-er], *adj.* (*coll.*) requiring superlatives to describe.
SUPER-, [soo′-per], *pref.* above in position, superior to, exceeding the normal. [L. *super* above].
SUPERABLE, [soop′-er-abl], *adj.* able to be surmounted.
SUPERABOUND, [soop′-er-a-bownd′], *v.i.* to be very abundant.
SUPERABUNDANCE, [soop′-er-a-bund′-ants], *n.* extraordinary abundance.
SUPERABUNDANT, [soop′-er-a-bund′-ant], *adj.* excessively abounding.
SUPERABUNDANTLY, [soop′-er-a-bund′-ant-li], *adv.* to a superabundant degree.
SUPERACIDULATED, [soop′-er-a-sid′-yoo-lāt-ed], *adj.* highly acidulated.
SUPERADD, [soop′-er-ad′], *v.t.* to add in addition.
SUPERADDITION, [soop′-er-ad-ish′-un], *n.* the act of superadding; that which is superadded.
SUPERADVENIENT, [soop′-er-ad-vēn′-i-ent], *adj.* coming as an unnecessary assistance.
SUPERALTAR, [soop′-er-awlt-er], *n.* a portable consecrated slab used as an altar.
SUPERANGELIC, [soop′-er-an-jel′-ik], *adj.* more than angelic.
SUPERANNUATE, [soop′-er-an′-yoo-āt], *v.t.* to retire on grounds of excessive age. [~SUPER- and L. *annus* year].
SUPERANNUATION, [soop′er-an′-yoo-ā′-shun], *n.* the act of superannuating; the state of being superannuated; a pension or payment enjoyed as of right on being superannuated.
SUPERB, [soo-purb′], *adj.* supremely excellent, splendid, magnificent. [L. *superbus* haughty].
SUPERBLY, [soo-purb′-li], *adv.* in a superb manner.
SUPERBNESS, [soo-purb′-nes], *n.* the quality of being superb.
SUPERCARGO, [soop′-er-kah′-gō], *n.* a person travelling on a ship to take charge of the cargo.
SUPERCELESTIAL, [soop′-er-sil-est′-i-al], *adj.* situated above the firmament.
SUPERCHARGE, [soop′-er-chahj′], *v.t.* to surcharge; (*her.*) to place one bearing over another; to provide with a supercharger.
SUPERCHARGER, [soop′-er-chahj′-er], *n.* (*eng.*) a mechanically driven fan used to increase the pressure of the petrol mixture in an induction system.
SUPERCILIARY, [soop′-er-sil′-i-er-i], *adj.* situated or being above the eyebrow. [L. *supercilium* eyebrow].
SUPERCILIOUS, [soop′-er-sil′-i-us], *adj.* disdainful, contemptuous, nonchalantly haughty. [L. *superciliosus*].
SUPERCILIOUSLY, [soop′-er-sil′-i-us-li], *adv.* in a supercilious manner.
SUPERCILIOUSNESS, [soop′-er-sil′-i-us-nes], *n.* the quality of being supercilious; affected superiority.

SUPERCILIUM, [sōōp′-er-sil′-i-um], *n.* (*anat.*) the eyebrow. [L. *supercilium*].

SUPERCONCEPTION, [sōōp′-er-kon-sep′-shun], *n.* conception when already pregnant.

SUPERCOOL, [sōōp′-er-kōōl], *v.t.* to cool below freezing point without solidifying.

SUPERCRESCENCE, [sōōp′-er-kres′-ents], *n.* a growth upon something already growing. [SUPER- and L. *crescens* growing].

SUPERCRESCENT, [sōōp′-er-kres′-ent], *adj.* in a condition of supercrescence.

SUPERCRETACEOUS, [sōōp′-er-krit-ā′-shus], *adj.* (*geol.*) lying above the chalk.

SUPERDOMINANT, [sōōp′-er-dom′-in-ant], *n.* the note above the dominant.

SUPEREMINENCE, [sōōp′-er-em′-in-ents], *n.* particular eminence.

SUPEREMINENT, [sōōp′-er-em′-in-ent], *adj.* surpassingly eminent.

SUPEREMINENTLY, [sōōp′-er-em′-in-ent-li], *adv.* in a supereminent degree.

SUPEREROGANT, [sōōp′-er-e′-rōg-ant], *adj.* supererogatory.

SUPEREROGATE, [sōōp′-er-e′-rōg-āt], *v.i.* to perform works of supererogation. [L. *supererogare* to spend in addition].

SUPEREROGATION, [sōōp′-er-e′-rōg-ā′-shun], *n.* performance of more than duty requires; **works of s.**, (*R.C.*) those good deeds supposed to have been performed by saints, over and above what is required for their own salvation, the merit of which is held to be transferable to others in need of indulgence. [MedL. *supererogatio*].

SUPEREROGATORY, [sōōp′-er-e-rog′-at-er-i], *adj.* done in supererogation.

SUPERESSENTIAL, [sōōp′-er-is-en′-shal], *adj.* especially essential; (*philos.*) above or apart from the essence of a thing.

SUPEREXALT, [sōōp′-er-egz-awlt′], *v.t.* to exalt especially.

SUPEREXALTATION, [sōōp′-er-egz′-awlt-ā′-shun], *n.* especial exaltation.

SUPEREXCELLENCE, [sōōp′-er-eks′-el-ents], *n.* especial excellence.

SUPEREXCELLENT, [sōōp′-er-eks′-el-ent], *adj.* especially excellent.

SUPEREXCRESCENCE, [sōōp′-er-eks-kres′-ents], *n.* an excrescence upon an excrescence.

SUPER-FATTED, [sōōp-er-fat′-ed], *adj.* of soap, made with a larger proportion of fat than usual.

SUPERFECUNDITY, [sōōp′-er-fik-und′-it-i], *n.* especial fecundity.

SUPERFICIAL, [sōōp′-er-fish′-al], *adj.* relating only to the surface of a thing; not profound. [L. *superficialis*].

SUPERFICIALIST, [sōōp′-er-fish′-al-ist], *n.* one whose knowledge is superficial.

SUPERFICIALITY, [sōōp′-er-fish-i-al′-it-i], *n.* the state of being superficial.

SUPERFICIALLY, [sōōp′-er-fish′-al-i], *adv.* in a superficial manner.

SUPERFICIALNESS, [sōōp′-er-fish′-al-nes], *n.* the quality of being superficial.

SUPERFICIES, [sōōp′-er-fish′-i-ēz], *n.* the outer surface of a thing. [L. *superficies*].

SUPERFINE, [sōōp′-er-fīn], *adj.* especially fine.

SUPERFINENESS, [sōōp′-er-fīn′-nes], *n.* the quality of being superfine.

SUPERFLUENCE, [sōōp′-er-flōō′-ents], *n.* superfluity.

SUPERFLUITY, [sōōp-er-flōō′-it-i], *n.* a quantity that is superfluous; the state of being superfluous. [MedL. *superfluitas*].

SUPERFLUOUS, [sōōp-ur′-flōō-us], *adj.* having, or that is, more than is required; unwanted, useless. [L. *superfluus*].

SUPERFLUOUSLY, [sōōp-ur′-flōō-us-li], *adv.* to a superfluous degree.

SUPERFLUOUSNESS, [sōōp-ur′-flōō-us-nes], *n.* the quality of being superfluous.

SUPERFLUX, [sōōp′-er-fluks], *n.* a superfluity.

SUPERFOETATE, [sōōp′-er-fēt′-āt], *v.i.* to conceive again during pregnancy. [L. *superfetare*].

SUPERFOETATION, [sōōp′-er-fēt-ā′-shun], *n.* superconception.

SUPERFRONTAL, [sōōp′-er-frunt′-al], *n.* an altar cover that hangs down all round.

SUPERHEAT, [sōōp′-er-hēt′], *v.t.* to heat (vapour) above the boiling point of water.

SUPERHEATER, [sōōp′-er-hēt′-er], *n.* an apparatus for superheating steam. [SUPER- and HEATER].

SUPER-HETERODYNE, [sōōp′-er-het′-er-ō-dīn], *n.* a supersonic heterodyne.

SUPER-HIVE, [sōōp′-er-hīv′], *n.* an extra chamber laid over the brood-chamber of a beehive during the summer.

SUPERHUMAN, [sōōp′-er-hew′-man], *adj.* having more than human attributes.

SUPERHUMERAL, [sōōp′-er-hewm′-er-al], *adj.* borne on the shoulders. [SUPER- and L. *humerus* shoulder].

SUPERIMPOSE, [sōōp′-er-im-pōz′], *v.t.* to place above something.

SUPERIMPOSITION, [sōōp′-er-im′-pōz-ish′-un], *n.* the act of superimposing; the state of being superimposed; that which is superimposed.

SUPERINCUMBENT, [sōōp′-er-in-kumb′-ent], *adj.* lying or resting on something else.

SUPERINDUCE, [sōōp′-er-in-dews′], *v.t.* to bring about in addition.

SUPERINDUCTION, [sōōp′-er-in-duk′-shun], *n.* the act of superinducing.

SUPERINFUSE, [sōōp′-er-in-fewz′], *v.t.* to infuse in addition.

SUPERINJECTION, [sōōp′-er-in-jek′-shun], *n.* an injection succeeding another.

SUPERINSPECT, [sōōp′-er-in-spekt′], *v.t.* to superintend.

SUPERINSTITUTION, [sōōp′-er-in-sti-tew′-shun], *n.* the institution of a priest into an already occupied benefice.

SUPERINTELLECTUAL, [sōōp′-er-int-el-ek′-chōō-al], *adj.* of exaggerated intellectuality.

SUPERINTEND, [sōōp′-er-in-tend′], *v.t.* to oversee, to control and direct. [SUPER- and L. *intendere* to attend to].

SUPERINTENDENCE, [sōōp′-er-in-tend′-ents], *n.* the act of superintending; supervision; management.

SUPERINTENDENCY, [sōōp′-er-in-tend′-ens-i], *n.* superintendence.

SUPERINTENDENT, [sōōp′-er-in-tend′-ent], *n.* one who superintends, *esp.* one specially appointed for this purpose; the police rank next above inspector.

SUPERINTENDER, [sōōp′-er-in-tend′-er], *n.* a superintendent.

SUPERIOR (1), [sōōp-ēer′-i-er], *n.* one who is above another in any respect; the ruler of a religious house.

SUPERIOR (2), [sōōp-ēer′-i-er], *adj.* above or higher, in a physical, moral, social, intellectual, or qualitative sense; in greater number; of good quality or attainment, without any direct comparison; above in position. [L. *superior* higher].

SUPERIORESS, [sōōp-ēer′-i-or-es′], *n.* the head of a nunnery or convent.

SUPERIORITY, [sōōp-ēer-i-o′-rit-i], *n.* the state or fact of being superior.

SUPERJACENT, [sōōp′-er-jās′-ent], *adj.* lying upon. [SUPER- and L. *jacens* lying].

SUPERLATIVE (1), [sōōp-ur′-lat-iv], *n.* (*gram.*) the superlative degree; a superlative adjective.

SUPERLATIVE (2), [sōōp-ur′-lat-iv], *adj.* of extreme excellence; (*gram.*) of the highest degree. [L. *superlativus* exaggerated].

SUPERLATIVELY, [sōōp-ur′-lat-iv-li], *adv.* to a superlative degree.

SUPERLATIVENESS, [sōōp-ur′-lat-iv-nes], *n.* the state of being superlative.

SUPERLUNAR, [sōōp′-er-lōōn′-er], *adj.* being above the moon; not sublunary or of this world.

SUPERLUNARY, [sōōp′-er-lōōn′-er-i], *adj.* superlunar.

SUPERMAN, [sōōp′-er-man′], *n.* a man of extra-ordinary attributes.

SUPERMEDIAL, [sōōp′-er-mēd′-i-al], *adj.* lying or being above the middle.

SUPERMOLECULE, [sōōp′-er-mol′-i-kewl], *n.* a combination of single molecules of different kinds.

SUPERMUNDANE, [sōōp′-er-mun′-dān], *adj.* above the earthly.

SUPERNACULAR, [sōōp′-er-nak′-yōō-ler], *adj.* (of wines) excellent.

SUPERNACULUM, [sōōp′-er-nak′-yōō-lum], *n.* excellent wine. [~SUPER- and Germ. *nagel* nail, from the former custom of tipping up the empty wine-glass; if there was left only enough to wet the fingernail it showed the excellence of the wine].

SUPERNAL, [sōōp-ur′-nal], *adj.* celestial. [L. *supernus*].

SUPERNATANT, [sōōp′-er-nāt′-ant], *adj.* floating on the surface. [*Next*].

SUPERNATATION, [sōōp′-er-nat-ā′-shun], *n.* the act of floating entirely on the surface of a fluid, skimming. [SUPER- and L. *natare* to swim].

SUPERNATIONAL, [sōōp'-er-nash'-un-al], *adj.* above nationality.
SUPERNATURAL, [sōōp'-er-nach'-er-al], *adj.* above obedience to natural laws, unbounded by matter.
SUPERNATURALISM, [sōōp'-er-nach'-er-al-izm], *n.* (belief in) the activity of supernatural forces.
SUPERNATURALIST, [sōōp'-er-nach'-er-al-ist], *n.* one who believes in supernaturalism.
SUPERNATURALISTIC, [sōōp'-er-nach'-er-al-ist'-ik], *adj.* relating to supernaturalism.
SUPERNATURALITY, [sōōp-er-nach'-er-al'-it-i], *n.* supernaturalness.
SUPERNATURALIZE, [sōōp'-er-nach'-er-al-īz], *v.t.* to imagine as supernatural.
SUPERNATURALLY, [sōōp'-er-nach'-er-al-i], *adv.* in a supernatural manner.
SUPERNATURALNESS, [sōōp'-er-nach'-er-al-nes], *n.* the quality of being supernatural.
SUPERNUMERARY (1), [sōōp'-er-new'-mer-er-i], *n.* a person in excess of the normal or proper complement of a group.
SUPERNUMERARY (2), [sōōp'-er-new'-mer-er-i], *adj.* exceeding the normal or necessary number.
SUPERNUTRITION, [sōōp'-er-new-trish'-un], *n.* the highest level of nutrition.
SUPERORDINARY, [sōōp'-er-awd'-in-er-i], *adj.* above the ordinary.
SUPERORGANIC, [sōōp'-er-aw-gan'-ik], *adj.* more than material.
SUPERPARASITIC, [sōōp'-er-pa'-ra-sit'-ik], *adj.* living on a parasite.
SUPERPHOSPHATE, [sōōp'-er-fos'-fāt], *n.* an acid phosphate.
SUPERPHYSICAL, [sōōp'-er-fiz'-ik-al], *adj.* psychic.
SUPERPOSE, [sōōp'-er-pōz'], *v.t.* to place above.
SUPERPOSITION, [sōōp'-er-pōz-ish'-un], *n.* the act of being, the state of placing, above or on top.
SUPERPROPORTION, [sōōp'-er-prō-paw'-shun], *n.* an excessive proportion.
SUPERPURGATION, [sōōp'-er-per-gā'-shun], *n.* more purgation than is necessary.
SUPERREFLECTION, [sōōp'-er-ri-flek'-shun], *n.* the reflection of a reflection.
SUPER-REWARD, [sōōp'-er-ri-wawd'], *n.* an extraordinary reward.
SUPER-ROYAL, [sōōp'-er-roi'-al], *adj.* (of paper) larger than royal; 27 in. by 19 in. for writing and drawing paper, and 27½ in. by 20½ in. for printing paper.
SUPERSALIENT, [sōōp'-er-sā'-li-ent], *adj.* leaping above. [SUPER and L. *saliens*].
SUPERSATURATE, [sōōp'-er-sach'-er-āt], *v.t.* to saturate beyond the normal maximum.
SUPERSATURATION, [sōōp'-er-sach'-er-ā'-shun], *n.* the operation of supersaturating; the state of being supersaturated.
SUPERSCRIBE, [sōōp'-er-skrīb'], *v.t.* to write above or on the upper side of. [L. *superscribere*].
SUPERSCRIPT, [sōōp'-er-skript], *adj.* written above a line or letter. [L. *superscriptus* written above].
SUPERSCRIPTION, [sōōp'-er-skrip'-shun], *n.* an inscription above or on a thing; the act of superscribing. [L. *superscriptio*].
SUPERSECULAR, [sōōp'-er-sek'-yōō-ler], *adj.* above secular things.
SUPERSEDE, [sōōp'-er-sēd'], *v.t.* to take the place of. [L. *supersedere* to refrain].
SUPERSEDEAS, [sōōp'-er-sēd'-i-as], *n.* (*leg.*) a writ to stay proceedings. [L. *supersedeas* pray refrain].
SUPERSEDURE, [sōōp'-er-sē'-jer], *n.* the act of superseding.
SUPERSENSIBLE, [sōōp'-er-sens'-ibl], *adj.* beyond the reach of the senses.
SUPERSENSITIVE, [sōōp'-er-sens'-it-iv], *adj.* excessively sensitive.
SUPERSENSITIVENESS, [sōōp'-er-sens'-it-iv-nes], *n.* excessive sensitiveness.
SUPERSENSUAL, [sōōp'-er-sens'-syōō-al], *adj.* supersensible.
SUPERSESSION, [sōōp'-er-sesh'-un], *n.* supersedure.
SUPERSONIC, [sōōp'-er-son'-ik], *adj.* (*phys.*) of, or pertaining to, frequencies or oscillations higher than those of sound; **s.-heterodyne,** a wireless circuit in which a heterodyne of the incoming signals is set up by a local oscillator on an adjacent frequency and further amplification carried out at the resulting supersonic frequency of the beat note. [SUPER- and L. *sonus* sound].
SUPERSTITION, [sōōp'-er-sti'-shun], *n.* that which is believed in face of reason and common sense, *esp.* an irrational belief in the supernatural; the condition of mind that holds superstitions. [L. *superstitio*].
SUPERSTITIOUS, [sōōp'-er-sti'-shus], *adj.* relating to, believing in, superstitions. [L. *superstitiosus*].
SUPERSTITIOUSLY, [sōōp'-er-sti'-shus-li], *adv.* in a superstitious manner.
SUPERSTITIOUSNESS, [sōōp'-er-sti'-shus-nes], *n.* the quality of being superstitious.
SUPERSTRATUM, [sōōp'-er-strāt'-um], *n.* a stratum or layer above another.
SUPERSTRUCTION, [sōōp'-er-struk'-shun], *n.* superstructure. [~L. *superstructum*, *p.pt.* of *superstruere*].
SUPERSTRUCTIVE, [sōōp'-er-struk'-tiv], *adj.* relating to a superstructure.
SUPERSTRUCTURE, [sōōp'-er-struk'-cher], *n.* a structure built above or on top of another.
SUPERSUBSTANTIAL, [sōōp'-er-sub-stan'-shal], *adj.* transcending substance.
SUPERSUBTLE, [sōōp'-er-sutl'], *adj.* over-subtle.
SUPERTAX, [sōōp'-er-taks'], *n.* an additional income tax for large incomes.
SUPERTERRENE, [sōōp'-er-te-rēn'], *adj.* superterrestrial. [L. *superterrenus*].
SUPERTERRESTRIAL, [sōōp'-er-ter-est'-ri-al], *adj.* more than terrestrial.
SUPERTONIC, [sōōp'-er-ton'-ik], *n.* (*mus.*) the note next above the keynote.
SUPERTRAGICAL, [sōōp'-er-traj'-ik-al], *adj.* tragical to excess.
SUPERVENE, [sōōp'-er-vēn'], *v.i.* to come in addition; to come in consequence of, while being in nature different from, the cause. [L. *supervenire* to follow].
SUPERVENIENT, [sōōp'-er-vēn'-i-ent], *adj.* coming in addition. [L. *superveniens*].
SUPERVENTION, [sōōp'-er-ven'-shun], *n.* the act of supervening.
SUPERVISAL, [sōōp'-er-vīz'-al], *n.* supervision.
SUPERVISE, [sōōp'-er-vīz'], *v.t.* and *i.* to oversee; to superintend; to act as supervisor. [~L. *supervisus*, *p.pt.* of *supervidere*].
SUPERVISION, [sōōp'-er-vizh'-un], *n.* the act of supervising; superintendence. [MedL. *supervisio*].
SUPERVISOR, [sōōp'-er-vīz'-er], *n.* one who supervises.
SUPERVISORY, [sōōp'-er-vīz'-er-i], *adj.* pertaining to, or having, supervision.
SUPINATION, [sōōp'-in-ā'-shun], *n.* the act of turning the palm of the hand upwards and outwards; the position when so turned. [L. *supinatio*].
SUPINATOR, [sōōp'-in-āt'-er], *n.* the muscle controlling supination.
SUPINE (1), [sōō'-pīn], *n.* a Latin verbal noun formed upon the past participle stem.
SUPINE (2), [sōō'-pīn], *adj.* lying face upward; (*fig.*) wholly inactive. [L. *supinus*].
SUPINELY, [sōō-pīn'-li], *adv.* in a supine manner.
SUPINENESS, [sōō-pīn'-nes], *n.* the state of being supine.
SUPPEDANEUM, [su'-pid-ān'-i-um], *n.* the footrest on a crucifix. [L. *suppedaneum*].
SUPPER, [sup'-er], *n.* the last meal of the day. [OFr. *soper*].
SUPPERLESS, [sup'-er-les], *adj.* without supper.
SUPPLANT, [su-plahnt'], *v.t.* to displace and take the place of, to usurp the place of. [L. *supplantare* to trip up].
SUPPLANTATION, [su'-plahnt-ā'-shun], *n.* the act of supplanting. [L. *supplantatio*].
SUPPLANTER, [su-plahnt'-er], *n.* one who supplants.
SUPPLE, [supl], *adj.* smoothly pliant, flexible; docile, subtly compliant, adaptable. [L. *supplex* a submissive].
SUPPLEJACK, [supl'-jak'], *n.* a walking-stick made of the twining stem of a species of *Paullinia*.
SUPPLEMENT (1), [su'-pli-ment], *n.* that which is in addition, *esp.* an additional part of a publication giving more detailed treatment to some specific subject; (*geom.*) the amount which an angle requires to become a right angle; an additional charge. [L. *supplementum* that which supplies].
SUPPLEMENT (2), [su'-pli-ment'], *v.t.* to bring in addition to, to supply with additional help.
SUPPLEMENTAL, [su'-pli-ment'-al], *adj.* supplementary.
SUPPLEMENTARY, [su'-pli-ment'-er-i], *adj.* serving as supplement, additional.
SUPPLENESS, [supl'-nes], *n.* the quality of being supple.
SUPPLETORY, [su'-plit-er-i], *adj.* supplementary. [L. *suppletorius*].
SUPPLIAL, [su-plī'-al], *n.* the act of supplying.

SUPPLIANCE, [su'-pli-ants], *n.* the act of a suppliant.

SUPPLIANT (1), [su'-pli-ant], *n.* one who supplicates.

SUPPLIANT (2), [su'-pli-ant], *adj.* supplicating, beseeching humbly. [Fr. *suppliant*].

SUPPLIANTLY, [su'-pli-ant-li], *adv.* in a suppliant manner.

SUPPLICANCY, [su'-plik-an-si], *n.* supplication.

SUPPLICANT, [su'-plik-ant], *n.* one who supplicates. [L. *supplicans*].

SUPPLICATE, [su'-plik-āt], *v.t. and i.* to beg humbly and beseechingly, earnestly to request a favour; to make a humble request to. [L. *supplicare* to kneel down].

SUPPLICATINGLY, [su'-plik-āt-ing-li], *adv.* with supplication.

SUPPLICATION, [su'-plik-ā'-shun], *n.* the act of supplicating, the thing supplicated. [L. *supplicatio*].

SUPPLICATORY, [su'-plik-āt'-er-i], *adj.* by, relating to, supplication. [MedL. *supplicatorius*].

SUPPLIER, [su-plī'-er], *n.* one who supplies.

SUPPLY (1), [su-plī'], *n.* that which is supplied; the whole stock of necessary goods in hand at any time; the total available quantity of a commodity.

SUPPLY (2), [sup'-li], *adv.* in supple fashion.

SUPPLY (3), [sup-lī'], *v.t.* to provide with that which will satisfy a need, *esp.* to provide regularly with necessaries. [L. *supplere* to make good].

SUPPORT (1), [su-pawt'], *n.* that which supports, a prop, a stay; moral encouragement; one who maintains dependents.

SUPPORT (2), [su-pawt'], *v.t.* to bear up, prevent from falling, to sustain; (*fig.*) to provide sustenance for, be responsible for the maintenance of; to endure; to help, back up, be of assistance to. [L. *supportare* to convey].

SUPPORTABLE, [su-pawt'-abl], *adj.* able to be supported.

SUPPORTABLENESS, [su-pawt'-abl-nes], *n.* the state of being supportable or tolerable.

SUPPORTABLY, [su-pawt'-ab-li], *adv.* to a supportable degree.

SUPPORTER, [su-pawt'-er], *n.* one who supports, *esp.* one who supports a cause; (*her.*) one of two figures standing at the side of a coat of arms.

SUPPORTLESS, [su-pawt'-les], *adj.* having no support.

SUPPORTMENT, [su-pawt'-ment], *n.* support.

SUPPOSABLE, [su-pōz'-abl], *adj.* able to be supposed or imagined to exist.

SUPPOSAL, [su-pōz'-al], *n.* supposition.

SUPPOSE, [su-pōz'], *v.t.* to imagine, assume on grounds of probability, but without absolute conviction; to require as a general, but not invariable, concomitant; to expect. [Fr. *supposer*].

SUPPOSEDLY, [su-pōz'-ed-li], *adv.* as one supposes, or is given to suppose.

SUPPOSITION, [su'-pōz-ish'-un], *n.* that which is supposed, an assumption, an opinion held without definite evidence; the act of supposing.

SUPPOSITIONAL, [su'-pōz-ish'-un-al], *adj.* relating to, based on, supposition.

SUPPOSITITIOUS, [su-poz'-it-ish'-us], *adj.* fraudulently substituted, spurious. [L. *suppositicius*].

SUPPOSITITIOUSLY, [su-poz'-it-ish'-us-li], *adv.* in a supposititious manner.

SUPPOSITITIOUSNESS, [su-poz'-it-ish'-us-nes], *n.* the quality of being supposititious.

SUPPOSITIVE, [su-poz'-it-iv], *adj.* suppositional.

SUPPOSITIVELY, [su-poz'-it-iv-li], *adv.* by supposition.

SUPPOSITORY, [su-poz'-it-er-i], *n.* a body introduced into the rectum or vagina for medical purposes. [L. *suppositorius* that which is placed beneath].

SUPPRESS, [su-pres'], *v.t.* to press down, crush; to prevent from expression, to forbid or stifle publication of; to subdue by force, to repress; to ban. [~L. *suppressum*, *p.pt.* of *supprimere* to restrain].

SUPPRESSER, [su-pres'-er], *n.* one who suppresses; (*wirel.*) a device for suppressing extraneous interference.

SUPPRESSIBLE, [su-pres'-ibl], *adj.* able to be suppressed.

SUPPRESSION, [su-presh'-un], *n.* the act of suppressing; the state of being suppressed. [L. *suppressio*].

SUPPRESSIONIST, [su-presh'-un-ist], *n.* an advocate of suppression.

SUPPRESSIVE, [su-pres'-iv], *adj.* tending to suppress; subduing; concealing.

SUPPURATE, [sup'-yŏŏ-rāt], *v.i.* to generate, discharge, pus; to come to a head. [L. *suppurare*].

SUPPURATION, [sup'-yŏŏ-rā'-shun], *n.* the generation of pus. [L. *suppuratio*].

SUPPURATIVE, [sup'-yŏŏ-rat-iv], *adj.* relating to suppuration; producing suppuration.

SUPPUTATION, [sup'-yŏŏ-tā'-shun], *n.* computation; a method of computing. [L. *supputatio*].

SUPRA-, *pref.* above; transcending; before. [L. *supra*].

SUPRA-AXILLARY, [sōō'-pra-ak-zil'-er-i], *adj.* (*bot.*) above the axil.

SUPRACILIARY, [sōō'-pra-sil'-yer-i], *adj.* situated above the eyebrow. [SUPRA- and L. *cilium*].

SUPRACLAVICULAR, [sōō'-pra-klav-ik'-yŏŏ-ler], *adj.* above the collarbone.

SUPRACOSTAL, [sōō'-pra-kost'-al], *adj.* on or above the ribs.

SUPRACRETACEOUS, [sōō'-pra-krit-ā'-shus], *adj.* (*geol.*) above the cretaceous formation.

SUPRAFOLIACEOUS, [sōō'-pra-fō'-li-ā'-shus], *adj.* (*bot.*) inserted into the stem above the leaf or petiole.

SUPRALAPSARIAN, [sōō'-pra-laps-āer'-i-an], *n.* an extreme Calvinist, believing that man was predestined before the Creation. [SUPRA- and L. *lapsus* fall].

SUPRALAPSARIANISM, [sōō'-pra-laps-āer'-i-an-izm], *n.* the doctrine of the supralapsarians.

SUPRALATERAL, [sōō'-pra-lat'-er-al], *adj.* at the top of the side.

SUPRAMAXILLARY, [sōō'-pra-maks-il'-er-i], *adj.* of, or relating to, the upper jaw.

SUPRAMUNDANE, [sōō'-pra-mund'-ān], *adj.* transcending the mundane.

SUPRANATURALISM, [sōō'-pra-nach'-er-al-izm], *n.* supernaturalism.

SUPRA-ORBITAL, [sōō'-pra-aw'-bit-al], *adj.* above the orbit of the eye.

SUPRAPROTEST, [sōō'-pra-prō'-test], *n.* (*comm.*) acceptance of a bill by someone who is not a party to it after it has been protested.

SUPRARENAL, [sōō'-pra-rēn'-al], *adj.* placed above the kidneys.

SUPRASCAPULARY, [sōō'-pra-skap'-yŏŏl-er-i], *adj.* placed above the scapula.

SUPREMACY, [sōō-prem'-as-i], *n.* the state or power of being supreme. [OFr. *suprematie*].

SUPREME, [sōō-prēm'], *adj.* holding absolute power; greater, in any respect, than all others. [L. *supremus* highest].

SUPREMELY, [sōō-prēm'-li], *adv.* in a supreme way.

SUR-, *pref.* beyond; above; in addition. [OFr. *sur* from L. *super*].

SURA, [sōō'-ra], *n.* a chapter, *esp.* of the Koran. [Arab. *sura* step].

SURAH, [sōō'-rah], *n.* an Indian silk. [*Surat* in India, where made].

SURAL, [syŏŏer'-al], *adj.* relating to the calf of the leg. [~L. *sura* calf].

SURBASE, [sur'-bās], *n.* the moulding above the base of a column.

SURBASED, [sur'-bāst], *adj.* having a surbase.

SURBASEMENT, [sur-bās'-ment], *n.* the condition of having a surbase.

SURBATE, [sur-bāt'], *v.t. and i.* to make foot-sore; to become foot-sore. [OFr. *surbatre* to beat hard].

SURBED, [sur-bed'], *v.t.* to set (a stone) edgeways.

SURBASE

SURCEASE (1), [sur-sēs'], *n.* (*arch.*) cessation. [*Next*].

SURCEASE (2), [sur-sēs'], *v.t.* to cease, leave off. [OFr. *surseoir*].

SURCHARGE (1), [sur'-chahj], *n.* a charge over and above another, or more than is usual; an imprint on the face of a postage stamp giving it a postal value other than that at which it was issued; an excessive charge.

SURCHARGE (2), [sur-chahj'], *v.t.* to charge to excess, to charge in addition; to overprint with a different value.

SURCHARGER, [sur'-chahj-er], *n.* one who surcharges.

SURCINGLE, [sur'-sing'-gl], *n.* a belt fastening a load on the back of a horse; the girdle of a cassock. [OFr. *surcengle*].

SURCLE, [surkl], *n.* a twig, a small shoot. [L. *surculus*].

SURCOAT, [sur'-kōt], *n.* a coat worn over armour; a loose outer coat, an overcoat. [SUR- and COAT (1)].

SURCULOSE, [surk'-yōō-lōs], *adj.* (*bot.*) producing suckers. [L. *surculosus*].
SURD, [surd], *n.* (*math.*) a quantity not exactly expressible in figures, an irrational number. [L. *surdus* dull].
SURDIMUTE, [surd'-i-mewt], *n.* one who is deaf and dumb.
SURE (1), [shōōer], *adj.* dependable, certainly reliable, certain, secure, wholly confident. [OFr. *sur* from L. *securus* undisturbed].
SURE (2), [shōōer] *int.* (*U.S.*) certainly, yes. [*Prec.*].
SUREFOOTED, [shōōer'-fōōt'-ed], *adj.* unlikely to stumble.
SURELY, [shōōer'-li], *adv.* safely, securely, certainly, almost certainly.
SURENESS, [shōōer'-nes], *n.* the state of being sure; certainty.
SURETY, [shōōer'-i-ti], *n.* the person responsible for the behaviour of another, a person standing monetary security for a defendant's appearance in court, the sum guaranteed in default of appearance; sureness. [L. *securitas* safety].
SURETYSHIP, [shōōer'-i-ti-ship], *n.* the state of being surety; the obligation of a person to answer for another.
SURF, [surf], *n.* the foamy water of breaking waves, *esp.* waves broken by rocks offshore. [Uncert.].
SURFACE (1), [sur'-fis], *n.* the outer area of a thing; a two-dimensional limit; the outside, superficial appearance of anything; the top of a mass of liquid; the surface works of a mine. [OFr. *surface*].
SURFACE (2), [sur'-fis], *adj.* of, pertaining to, the surface or outside part.
SURFACE (3), [sur'-fis], *v.t.* to treat, polish a surface; to skim on, or come to, the surface of water.
SURFACE-GAUGE, [sur'-fis-gāj], *n.* an apparatus for testing the flatness of a plane surface.
SURFACEMAN, [sur'-fis-man], *n.* a worker maintaining the condition of a railway track.
SURF-BATHING, [surf'-bāᴛʜ'-ing], *n.* bathing in surf.
SURFBOAT, [surf'-bōt], *n.* a boat for use in surf.
SURF-DUCK, [surf'-duk], *n.* a sea-duck, *Œdemia nigra.*
SURFEIT (1), [sur'-fit], *n.* an over-indulgence, excessive quantity of anything, *esp.* of food. [OFr. *sorfait*].
SURFEIT (2), [sur'-fit], *v.t.* to satiate by excess.
SURFEITER, [sur'-fit-er], *n.* a glutton.
SURFEITING, [sur'-fit-ing], *n.* excessive indulgence.

SURFACE-GAUGE

SURFEIT-WATER, [sur'-fit-waw'-ter], *n.* water for the cure of surfeits.
SURFMAN, [surf'-man], *n.* a man who manages a surfboat.
SURF-RIDING, [surf'-rīd'-ing], *n.* the sport of riding on the surf on a specially designed board.
SURF-SCOTER, [surf'-skōt'-er], *n.* the surf-duck.
SURFY, [surf'-i], *adj.* covered with surf.
SURGE (1), [surj], *n.* a billowing heave, a vast heaving movement of a whole surface; the sea; the noise of the sea; a sudden oscillation in an electric current.
SURGE (2), [surj], *v.i.* to billow powerfully over a whole surface, to move tumultuously like the waves of the sea; to move with a surge. [L. *surgere* to rise].

SURF-SCOTER

SURGELESS, [surj'-les], *adj.* unsurging, calm.
SURGEON, [surj'-un], *n.* one practising surgery. [ME. *surgion*, ~CHIRURGEON].
SURGEONCY, [surj'-un-si], *n.* the office or post of surgeon in the Navy, Army, or Air Force.
SURGEON-DENTIST, [surj'-un-dent'-ist], *n.* a dentist holding the diploma of the Royal College of Surgeons.
SURGERY, [surj'-er-i], *n.* medical treatment by manual operation; the dispensary of a doctor. [ME. *surgerie*].
SURGICAL, [surj'-ik-al], *adj.* pertaining to surgeons or surgery; done by means of, or employed in surgery.
SURGY, [surj'-i], *adj.* surging.
SURICATE, [sew'-rik-āt], *n.* the meerkat, a South African mongoose, *Suricata tetradactyla.* [Native].
SURLILY, [sur'-li-li], *adv.* in a surly manner.
SURLINESS, [sur'-li-nes], *n.* the state of being surly.
SURLOIN, [sur'-loin], *n.* the sirloin. [OF. *surloigne*].
SURLY, [sur'-li], *adj.* sullenly ill-tempered and morose. [Uncert.].
SURMASTER, [sur'-mahst-er], *n.* a second master.
SURMISAL, [sur-mīz'-al], *n.* a surmise.
SURMISE (1), [sur'-mīz, ser-mīz'], *n.* a reasonable guess, a conjecture backed by some evidence. [OFr. *surmise*].
SURMISE (2), [sur'-mīz, ser-mīz'], *v.t.* to conjecture, make a surmise.
SURMISER, [ser-mīz'-er], *n.* one who surmises.
SURMOUNT, [ser-mownt'], *v.t.* to overcome; to get on top of. [OFr. *surmonter*].
SURMOUNTABLE, [ser-mownt'-abl], *adj.* that may be surmounted; superable.
SURMOUNTABLENESS, [ser-mownt'-abl-nes], *n.* the state of being surmountable.
SURMOUNTED, [ser-mownt'-ed], *adj.* (*her.*) placed over another charge; (*arch.*) (of an arch) higher than half its span.
SURMOUNTER, [ser-mownt'-er], *n.* one who surmounts.
SURMULLET, [ser-mul'-it], *n.* a sea-fish, the striped mullet, *Multus surmulletus.*
SURMULOT, [sur'-mul-ot], *n.* the brown or Norway rat. [Fr. *surmulot*].
SURNAME, [sur'-nām], *n.* a family name; originally, a nickname. [~Fr. *surnom*].

SURMULLET

SURNOMINAL, [ser-nom'-in-al], *adj.* pertaining to surnames.
SURPASS, [ser-pahs'], *v.t. and i.* to exceed or excel in quality or achievement. [OFr. *surpasser*].
SURPASSABLE, [ser-pahs'-abl], *adj.* able to be surpassed or exceeded.
SURPASSING, [ser-pahs'-ing], *adj.* excelling.
SURPASSINGLY, [ser-pahs'-ing-li], *adv.* so as to surpass.
SURPASSINGNESS, [ser-pahs'-ing-nes], *n.* surpassing excellence.
SURPLICE, [sur'-plis], *n.* the white vestment worn *esp.* by officiating clergy. [OFr. *surplis*].
SURPLUS (1), [sur'-plus], *n.* a quantity above what is necessary; the amount by which receipts exceed expenditure. [MedL. *superplus* excess].
SURPLUS (2), [sur'-plus], *adj.* exceeding what is necessary; **s. value,** the amount by which price exceeds cost of production, and so provides profit.
SURPLUSAGE, [sur'-plus-ij], *n.* surplus.
SURPRISAL, [ser-prīz'-al], *n.* the act of surprising.
SURPRISE (1), [ser-prīz'], *n.* the occurrence of the unexpected; the emotional shock produced by such occurrence; a taking advantage over someone by unexpected action, *esp.* in military sense; (*coll.*) an unexpected pleasure. [OFr. *surprise*].
SURPRISE (2), [ser-prīz'], *v.t.* to shock emotionally by the unexpected, to astonish; to attack, overcome by an unanticipated assault.
SURPRISING, [ser-prīz'-ing], *adj.* causing surprise.
SURPRISINGLY, [ser-prīz'-ing-li], *adv.* in surprising fashion.
SURPRISINGNESS, [ser-prīz'-ing-nes], *n.* the state of being surprising.
SURREALISM, [sōō-rē'-al-izm], *n.* a form of art which claims to express the unconscious mind. [Fr. *surréalisme*].
SURREALIST (1), [sur-rē'-al-ist], *n.* an exponent or admirer of surrealism. [Fr. *surréaliste*].
SURREALIST (2), [sur-rē'-al-ist], *adj.* of, resembling, or pertaining to, surrealism or surrealists. [*Prec.*].
SURREBUT, [sur'-ri-but'], *v.t.* (*leg.*) to reply to (a defendant's rebuttal).
SURREBUTTER, [sur'-ri-but'-er], *n.* the plaintiff's rebuttal of the defendant's rebuttal.
SURREJOIN, [sur'-ri-join'], *v.i.* (*leg.*) to reply as a plaintiff to a defendant's rebutter.
SURREJOINDER, [sur'-ri-join'-der], *n.* the answer of a plaintiff to a defendant's rejoinder.
SURRENDER (1), [su-rend'-er], *n.* the act of surrendering.
SURRENDER (2), [su-rend'-er], *v.t. and i.* to submit to an opponent after defeat, to give way to compulsion; to relinquish under pressure, to yield; to give up (an insurance policy) upon repayment of part of the premiums. [OFr. *surrendre*].
SURRENDEREE, [su-rend'-er-ē'], *n.* the person to whom a thing is surrendered, or a point conceded.

SURRENDEROR, [su-rend'-er-er], *n.* one who surrenders an estate to the holder of the reversion.

SURRENDRY, [su-rend'-ri], *n.* a surrender.

SURREPTION, [su-rep'-shun], *n.* the act of obtaining surreptitiously. [L. *surreptio*].

SURREPTITIOUS, [su'-rep-tish'-us], *adj.* performed or obtained secretly, *esp.* in dishonest fashion. [L. *surrepticius* secret].

SURREPTITIOUSLY, [su'-rep-tish'-us-li], *adv.* in a surreptitious manner.

SURROGATE, [su'-rōg-āt], *n.* a substitute; the deputy of a bishop. [L. *surrogatus*].

SURROUND (1), [su-rownd'], *n.* that which surrounds, *esp.* the bare floor or linoleum around a carpet.

SURROUND (2), [su-rownd'], *v.t.* to encircle, to encompass; (*milit.*) to occupy all lines of a force's advance or retreat; to be present on every side of. [OFr. *surrunder*].

SURROUNDING, [su-rownd'-ing], *adj.* encompassing, everywhere adjacent.

SURSOLID, [ser-sol'-id], *n.* the fifth power of a number.

SURTAX, [sur'-taks'], *n.* an additional tax on incomes exceeding a certain figure.

SURTOUT, [sur-tōō'], *n.* a kind of frock-coat. [Fr. *surtout*].

SURTURBRAND, [sur'-ter-brand'], *n.* fibrous brown coal, lignite. [Icel. *surturbrand*].

SURVEILLANCE, [ser-vāl'-ants], *n.* close observation over a person's activities. [Fr. *surveillance*].

SURVEY (1), [sur'-vā], *n.* a broad, general consideration of a whole situation or field of circumstances; the act, process, methods, or result of inspecting and recording the physical, geological, and geographical characteristics of a tract of land.

SURVEY (2), [ser-vā'], *v.t.* to take a general view of an area or situation; to conduct a geographical and geometrical examination of a tract of country. [OFr. *surveeir* to look over].

SURVEYAL, [ser-vā'-al], *n.* the act of surveying.

SURVEYING, [ser-vā'-ing], *n.* the business of a surveyor.

SURVEYOR, [ser-vā'-er], *n.* one skilled in surveying and measuring land; one who surveys.

SURVEYORSHIP, [ser-vā'-er-ship], *n.* the office of surveyor.

SURVIVAL, [ser-viv'-al], *n.* the state of surviving; anything that survives the rest of its kind.

SURVIVE, [ser-viv'], *v.t. and i.* to outlive, to endure longer than another; to live beyond a certain period; to remain alive after what should have been a fatal disaster; to continue to exist. [L. *supervivere* to outline].

SURVIVENCY, [ser-viv'-en-si], *n.* the state of surviving.

SURVIVING, [ser-viv'-ing], *adj.* remaining alive; that is a survivor.

SURVIVOR, [ser-viv'-er], *n.* one who survives.

SURVIVORSHIP, [ser-viv'-er-ship], *n.* the state of being a survivor; (*leg.*) the rights of the surviving holder of a joint property.

SUSANNITE, [sōō-zan'-it], *n.* a mineral found in Scotland, a compound of sulphate and carbonate of lead. [The *Susanna* mine, where found].

SUSCEPTIBILITY, [su-sept'-i-bil'-it-i], *n.* the state of being susceptible. [MedL. *susceptibilitas*].

SUSCEPTIBLE, [su-sept'-ibl], *adj.* emotionally sensitive, easily influenced by the feelings, readily overcome by sexual attraction. [MedL. *susceptibilis*].

SUSCEPTIBLENESS, [su-sept'-ibl-nes], *n.* the quality of being susceptible.

SUSCEPTIBLY, [su-sept'-ib-li], *adv.* in a susceptible manner.

SUSCEPTIVE, [su-sept'-iv], *adj.* susceptible; receptive of emotional stimuli. [MedL. *susceptivus*].

SUSCEPTIVITY, [su-sept-iv'-it-i], *n.* the state of being susceptive.

SUSCEPTOR, [su-sept'-er], *n.* a godparent. [L. *susceptor*].

SUSCIPIENCY, [su-sip'-i-en-si], *n.* the condition of being suscipient.

SUSCIPIENT, [su-sip'-i-ent], *adj.* recipient. [L. *suscipiens*].

SUSCITATE, [sus'-i-tāt], *v.t.* to stir up, to arouse to activity. [~L. *suscitare*].

SUSLIK, [sōōs'-lik], *n.* a species of gopher, a rodent of the genus *Spermophilus*. [Russ. *suslik*].

SUSPECT (1), [su'-spekt], *n.* a suspected person.

SUSPECT (2), [su'-spekt], *adj.* under suspicion, suspected.

SUSPECT (3), [su-spekt'], *v.t.* to be inclined to believe in the existence of (a thing) without having definite proof; to distrust, disbelieve in (a thing) without adequate evidence for so doing; to consider the probability of a person's guilt without possessing certain knowledge; to mistrust. [L. *suspectare* to mistrust].

SUSPECTABLE, [su-spekt'-abl], *adj.* liable to be suspected.

SUSPECTED, [su-spekt'-ed], *adj.* under suspicion; imagined without proof.

SUSPECTEDLY, [su-spekt'-ed-li], *adv.* so as to be suspected.

SUSPECTEDNESS, [su-spekt'-ed-nes], *n.* the state of being suspected.

SUSPECTER, [su-spekt'-er], *n.* one who suspects.

SUSPECTFUL, [su-spekt'-fōōl], *adj.* ready to suspect.

SUSPECTLESS, [su-spekt'-les], *adj.* unsuspected; unsuspicious.

SUSPEND, [sus-pend'], *v.t.* to hang from above; to hold up, cause to remain in suspense; to cause (an activity) temporarily to cease, to deprive from office for a period or pending a final decision. [L. *suspendere* to hang up].

SUSPENDER, [sus-pend'-er], *n.* one who, or that which, suspends; a device for holding up stockings or socks on the leg.

SUSPENDER-BELT, [sus-pend'-er-belt'], *n.* a belt worn by women round the waist to support suspenders.

SUSPENSE, [sus-pents'], *n.* the state of being suspended; the state of anxiety whilst awaiting news or an important decision.

SUSPENSIBILITY, [sus-pen'-si-bil'-it-i], *n.* the state of being suspensible.

SUSPENSIBLE, [sus-pen'-sibl], *adj.* able to be suspended.

SUSPENSION, [sus-pen'-shun], *n.* the act of suspending; the condition of being suspended; **s. bridge**, a bridge in which the roadway is suspended by chains or cables from piers or towers. [L. *suspensio*].

SUSPENSIVE, [sus-pen'-siv], *adj.* able to suspend; liable to be suspended; in suspense. [MedL. *suspensivus*].

SUSPENSOR, [sus-pen'-ser], *n.* something which suspends.

SUSPENSORY, [sus-pen'-ser-i], *adj.* supporting, relating to suspension.

SUSPICION, [sus-pish'-un], *n.* the act or state of suspecting; a feeling of unprovable mistrust; the smallest possible trace of a thing, a faint indication of something without definite proof of its presence. [L. *suspicio*].

SUSPICIONLESS, [sus-pish'-un-les], *adj.* evoking or having no suspicion.

SUSPICIOUS, [sus-pish'-us], *adj.* feeling suspicion; giving rise to, inviting, suspicion. [L. *suspiciosus*].

SUSPICIOUSLY, [sus-pish'-us-li], *adv.* in a suspicious way.

SUSPICIOUSNESS, [sus-pish'-us-nes], *n.* the state of being suspicious.

SUSPIRATION, [sus'-pi-rā'-shun], *n.* the act of sighing or drawing a long, deep breath, a sigh. [L. *suspiratio*].

SUSPIRE, [sus-pier'], *v.i.* to sigh. [L. *suspirare*].

SUSTAIN, [sus-tān'], *v.t.* to hold up, to take the weight of, to keep from falling, to support; to approve, uphold as correct, to support as just; to suffer, endure; to keep at a certain strength, prolong, maintain; to keep alive, to nourish. [L. *sustinere* to hold up].

SUSTAINABLE, [sus-tān'-abl], *adj.* able to be sustained.

SUSTAINED, [sus-tānd'], *adj.* kept up, maintained.

SUSTAINER, [sus-tān'-er], *n.* one who, or that which, sustains.

SUSTAINMENT, [sus-tān'-ment], *n.* the state of being sustained; support; the act of sustaining.

SUSTENANCE, [sust'-in-ants], *n.* that which supports life; nourishment, food; †maintenance of strength. [LL. *sustinentia* endurance].

SUSTENTACULAR, [sus'-ten-tak'-yōōl-er], *adj.* (*anat., zool.*) serving as a support for an organ or part of it. [*Prec.*].

SUSTENTACULUM, [sus'-ten-tak'-yōō-lum], *n.* (*biol.*) a spine-like projection from the tarsus of the posterior legs of certain spiders. [L. *sustentaculum* support].

SUSTENTATION, [sus'-tent-ā'-shun], *n.* the act or process of sustaining, support, maintenance; the process of maintaining an institution. [L. *sustentatio*].

SUSURRANT, [sew-su'-rant], *adj.* whispering, murmuring in undertone. [L. *susurrans*].

SUSURRATION, [sew'-su-rā'-shun], *n.* a whispering, a murmurous rustling, a hissing sound. [*Prec.*].

SUSURROUS, [sew-su'-rus], *adj.* producing murmurs, susurrant. [L. *susurrus*].

SUTLER, [sut'-ler], *n.* a person who followed an army to sell provisions and liquors. [Du. *zoetelaar* camp worker].

SUTLING, [sut'-ling], *adj.* relating to sutlers; engaged in the pursuits of a sutler.

SUTRA, [sōō'-tra], *n.* a series of aphorisms or precepts in oriental literature. [Skr. *sutra* thread].

SUTTEE, SATI, [sut-ē'], *n.* a Hindu widow who sacrifices herself on the funeral pyre of her husband; the ritual of self-immolation. [Skr. *sati* faithful wife].

SUTTEEISM, [sut-ē'-izm], *n.* the practice of self-immolation among Hindu widows.

SUTURAL, [sōō'-cher-al], *adj.* (*bot.*) relating to a suture or seam; occurring near a suture.

SUTURALLY, [sōōch'-er-al-i], *adv.* in a sutural manner.

SUTURATION, [sōōch'-er-ā'-shun], *n.* the process of forming a suture.

SUTURE, [sōō'-cher], *n.* (*anat.*) the joining of bones or parts of a skull by means of an interlocking serrated seam; (*bot.*) the line or seam formed by a joining; (*surg.*) the act or process of stitching a wound; the line or seam so formed; the stitching material used in such an operation. [L. *sutura* a seam].

SUTURED, [sōō'-cherd], *adj.* having sutures; sewn together.

SUZERAIN, [sōō'-zer-ān], *n.* a supreme authority in feudal times, a lord or superior, a paramount ruler. [OFr. *suzerain*].

SUZERAINTY, [sōō'-zer-ān-ti], *n.* the dominion or authority of a suzerain. [Fr. *suzeraineté*].

SVASTIKA, see SWASTIKA.

SVELTE, [svelt], *adj.* slender, lithesome, supple of figure, graceful. [Fr. *svelte* slim].

SWAB (1), [swob], *n.* a mop for cleaning up spilt liquid, *esp.* on decks; (*naut.*) the epaulet of an officer; (*slang*) a dirty fellow; (*surg.*) an absorbent pad. [~Norw. *svabb* mop].

SWAB (2), (swabbing, swabbed), [swob], *v.t.* to clean up, wash, wipe, sweep, by means of a swab.

SWABBER, [swob'-er], *n.* one who uses a swab to clean a floor or deck; (*slang*) a dirty fellow. [Du. *zwabber*].

SWAD, [swod], *n.* a pod, a husk; (*slang*) a short fat person. [Uncert.].

SWADDLE, [swodl], *v.t.* to wrap up warmly in several layers of garments, pieces of cloth, or bandage, to swathe. [~OE. *swæthel* bandage].

SWADDLING, [swod'-ling], *adj.* made for swathing; binding in tight clothes.

SWADDLING-CLOTHES†, [swod'-ling-klōᴛʜz], *n.(pl.)* bands or clothes wrapped closely round a baby.

SWADESHI, [swad-ā'-shi], *n.* a boycott of British goods as a means of political action taken by Indians. [Bengali *swadeshi* home-made goods].

SWAG (1), [swag], *n.* (*arch.*) an ornamental hanging wreath. [Unkn.].

SWAG (2), [swag], *n.* (*slang*) booty, plunder, stolen goods.

SWAG-BELLIED, [swag'-bel'-id], *adj.* having a prominent stomach.

SWAGE (1), [swāj], *n.* a type of tool used in wrought-iron work. [OFr. *souage*].

SWAGE† (2), [swāj], *v.t.* to ease, to soften; appease, to mitigate. [AFr. *swagier*].

SWAGE (3), [swāj], *v.t.* to manipulate, bend, shape, by means of a swage.

SWAGGER (1), [swag'-er], *n.* the act of swaggering; boastfulness of manner, exaggerated self-conceit manifested in a jaunty gait, dashing talk, or unconventional behaviour.

SWAGGER (2), [swag'-er], *adj.* swaggering, smart, extremely fashionable, swell.

SWAGGER (3), [swag'-er], *v.i.* to show one's sense of superiority by defiantly strutting about the place, insolent in manner, boastful in speech. [Uncert.].

SWAGGER-CANE, [swag'-er-kān], *n.* a soldier's short walking-stick.

SWAGGER-COAT, [swag'-er-kōt], *n.* a loose-fitting, three-quarter length coat or jacket of a smart cut, *esp.* as worn by women.

SWAGGERER, [swag'-er-er], *n.* one who swaggers, a blusterer, a bully.

SWAGGERINGLY, [swag'-er-ing-li], *adv.* in a swaggering manner.

SWAGGY, [swag'-i], *adj.* hanging weightily.

SWAIN, [swān], *n.* a young man, a rustic; (*archaic*) an agricultural labourer; a lover in pastoral poetry, an admiring youth. [OScand. *sveinn* youth].

SWAINISH†, [swān'-ish], *adj.* characteristic of a swain, rustic.

SWAINMOTE, [swān'-mōt], *n.* (*hist.*) a feudal assembly concerned with forestry; a court of administrative duties. [OE. *swangemot*].

SWALE (1), [swāl], *n.* a place in the shade; a vale, a tract of low land characterized by coldness. [Uncert.].

SWALE (2), [swāl], *v.i.* to swag. [Unkn.].

SWALING FIRE, [swāl'-ing-fīer'], *n.* (*dial.*) a fire lit to destroy heather, gorse, etc. [~SWEAL].

SWALLET, [swol'-it], *n.* a hole in a river bed in which the water disappears underground; an underground stream struck in a mine. [Unkn.].

SWALLOW (1), [swol'-ō], *n.* a passerine bird of any species of *Hirundo*, *Chelidon*, or *Cotile*, characterized by a forked tail. [OE. *swalwe*].

SWALLOW (2), [swol'-ō], *n.* the act of swallowing; the throat, the gullet; the amount swallowed in one mouthful; the capacity for eating or drinking, voracity.

SWALLOW (3), [swol'-ō], *v.t. and i.* to pass (food, etc.) from the mouth through the passage of the throat into the stomach, to eat or drink; to cause the muscles of the throat to act as when something is being swallowed; (*fig.*) to feign indifference to, tolerate; to receive implicitly, to accept as true; **to s. up,** to absorb, exhaust, use up; to consume, waste; to engulf; to envelop, shroud; **to s. (one's) words,** to recant. [OE. *swelgan*].

SWALLOWABLE, [swol'-ō-abl], *adj.* able to be swallowed.

SWALLOWER, [swol'-ō-er], *n.* one who swallows; a glutton.

SWALLOW-FISH, [swol'-ō-fish], *n.* the sapphirine gurnard, *Trigla hirundo*, with large pectoral fins resembling wings.

SWALLOW-SHRIKE, [swol'-ō-shrīk], *n.* an Australian bird with a long forked tail like a swallow.

SWALLOW'S-TAIL, [swol'-ōz-tāl], *n.* anything forked like a swallow's tail, a dovetail; (*fort.*) a type of outwork.

SWALLOW-TAIL, [swol'-ō-tāl], *n.* a dress coat; a butterfly of the *Papilionidæ*.

SWALLOW-TAILED, [swol'-ō-tāld], *adj.* having a forked tail, having a form with two points formed either by a split at one end or by a piece cut out of one end in the shape of a V, forked, dove-tailed; **s.-t. kite,** the bird of prey, *Elanoides furcatus*.

SWALLOW-WORT, [swol'-ō-wurt], *n.* (*bot.*) the greater celandine, *Chelidonium majus*.

SWAM, [swam], *pret.* of SWIM. [OE. *swam*].

SWAMI, [swah'-mi], *n.* a form of address to a Brahmin; a teacher of Hindu religious principles; **s. work,** ornamental work in metal representing Hindu gods. [Hind. *swami* prince].

SWAMP (1), [swomp], *n.* a tract of low-lying ground softened and saturated by water to a considerable depth; bog, marsh, morass. [~Du. *zwamp*].

SWAMP (2), [swomp], *v.t.* to overwhelm with water, to cover, saturate, with water, to inundate.

SWAMP-ORE, [swomp'-aw(r)], *n.* (*min.*) an ore of iron found in swamps.

SWAMPY, [swomp'-i], *adj.* consisting of swamp; resembling a swamp; low, wet, and spongy, boggy, marshy.

SWAN, [swon], *n.* a large bird of the genus *Cygneus*, characterized by webbed feet, a long graceful neck, a red bill and black legs, the plumage in the northern hemisphere usually being white; **the S. of Avon,** Shakespeare. [OE. *swan*].

SWAN-FLOWER, [swon'-flow'-er], *n.* a variety of orchid found in tropical America.

SWANG (1), [swang], *n.* a piece of low land open to floods. [Uncert.].

SWANG† (2), [swang], *pret.* of SWING.

SWANHERD, [swon'-hurd], *n.* a person in charge of swans.

SWANK (1), [swangk], *n.* the behaviour of a person who swanks; brag, swagger.

SWANK (2), [swangk], *adj.* (*U.S.*) swanky.

SWANK (3), [swangk], *v.i.* (*slang*) to show off, to act in an ostentatious manner so as to demonstrate one's superiority, to put on side, to swagger. [Unkn.].

SWANKILY, [swangk'-i-li], *adv.* in a swanky manner.

SWANKY, [swangk'-i], *adj.* (*slang*) conceited.

SWAN-LIKE, [swon'-līk], *adj.* having characteristics similar to those of a swan, graceful, *esp.* in the carriage of the neck.

SWAN-NECK, [swon'-nek'], *n. and adj.* (having) a curve resembling a swan's neck.

SWANNEE-WHISTLE, [swon'-i-wisl'], *n.* a musical

instrument of a very simple design consisting of a single hollow tube fitted with a sliding valve.

SWANNERY, [swon'-er-i], *n.* a place where swans congregate to nest.

SWANPAN, SHWANPAN, [swon'-pan'], *n.* a Chinese type of abacus. [Chin. *swanpan* counting board].

SWAN'S-DOWN, [swonz'-down], *n.* the soft underplumage of a swan.

SWAN-SKIN, [swon'-skin], *n.* a thick kind of flannel of a soft, fine texture.

SWAN-SONG, [swon'-song'] *n.* the death rattle in the throat of a swan, transformed by popular imagination into a song; (*fig.*) the last work produced by an artist before death.

SWAN-UPPING, [swon'-up'-ing], *n.* the annual marking of swans on their beaks for identification purposes.

SWAP (1), SWOP, [swop], *n.* the act of swapping; any object which is swapped.

SWAP (2), (swapping, swapped), [swop], *v.t. and i.* to exchange after a bargain, to barter. [~OE. *swap* a blow].

SWAPE, [swāp], *n.* a pole supported by a fulcrum, used for raising water from a well, a pump-handle. [~OIcel. *sveipa* to sweep].

SWARAJ, [swah'-rahj], *n.* Indian home-rule; the movement supporting this. [Hind. from Sanskrit *swa* self and *raj* rule].

SWARD, [swawd], *n.* a stretch of ground covered with short green grass, turf. [OE. *sweard* skin].

SWARDED, [swawd'-id], *adj.* covered with sward.

SWARDY, [swawd'-i], *adj.* slightly resembling sward, swarded.

SWARE†, [swāer], *pret.* of SWEAR (2).

SWARM (1), [swawm], *n.* a large number of bees gathered in an active, compact cluster, *esp.* when they quit a parent hive escorting a queen to build a fresh home; a multitude of people on the move seen as a collective whole, a throng; a large number. [OE. *swearm*].

SWARM (2), [swawm], *v.t. and i.* to cover with a swarm; to gather in great number in the form of a swarm, to congregate, throng, to collect in one place as a moving crowd. [*Prec.*].

SWARM (3), [swawm], *v.t. and i.* to climb (up) anything that is steep or almost perpendicular, clinging very close. [Unkn.].

SWARMING, [swawm'-ing], *adj.* assembling, going in swarms, as bees.

SWART, [swawt], *adj.* dark in colour or complexion, swarthy. [OE. *sweart*].

SWARTH (1), [swawth], *n.* an apparition of a dying person, a wraith, ghost. [*Var.* of WRAITH].

SWARTH (2), [swawth], *adj.* dusky, being of a dark hue; tawny. [*Var.* of SWART].

SWARTHILY, [swawTH'-i-li], *adv.* in a swarthy manner, with a tawny hue.

SWARTHINESS, SWARTHNESS, [swawTH'-i-nes, swawth'-nes], *n.* the state of being swarthy.

SWARTHY, [swawTH'-i], *adj.* having a dark complexion, being of a dark hue, sunburnt.

SWARTISH, [swawt'-ish], *adj.* somewhat swart.

SWASH (1), [swosh], *n.* the sound of splashing water.

SWASH (2), [swosh], *adj.* (*dial.*) soft, like fruit too ripe, squashy.

SWASH (3), [swosh], *adj.* having a swash or swashes.

SWASH (4), [swosh], *v.t. and i.* to dash, splash against; to move about, clashing, like swirling water. [Imitative].

SWASHBUCKLER, [swosh'-buk'-ler], *n.* a swaggering belligerent adventurer, a bully or braggart. [~SWASHING].

SWASHER, [swosh'-er], *n.* an aggressive ruffian, a man who makes a blustering show of bravery.

SWASHING, [swosh'-ing], *adj.* overwhelmingly violent. [Uncert.].

SWASHY, [swosh'-i], *adj.* sloppy, squashy, swash.

SWASH-PLATE, [swosh'-plāt], *n.* a circular plate set obliquely on a rotating shaft so as to give vertical up and down motion to a rod resting on it.

SWASHWORK, [swosh'-wurk], *n.* lathework with the tooling set obliquely to the axis of rotation.

SWASTIKA

SWASTIKA, SVASTIKA, [swost'-i-ka], *n.* the fylfot, gammadion, running cross; a right-angled cross with four equal arms, each having an extension at right angles; a primitive sun-symbol; the badge of the Nazi party of the Third German Reich. [Skr. *swastika* fortunate].

SWAT (1), [swot], *n.* an implement for swatting; a blow with a swat.

SWAT (2), (swatting, swatted), [swot] *v.t.* to strike sharply with the flat of the hand; to hit with a swat.

SWATH, [swawth, swoth], *n.* the amount of grass cut by a scythe at a single sweep; the space cleared by a scythe with one sweep. [OE. *swæth* track].

SWATHE (1), [swāTH], *n.* a bandage, a swath, a wrapping. [O.E. *swathu*].

SWATHE (2), [swāTH], *v.t.* to wrap, to bind with a bandage. [OE. *swathian*].

SWATHING, [swāTH'-ing], *adj.* made for, used for, binding or wrapping.

SWAY (1), [swā], *n.* the act of swaying, the movement of that which sways; the weight or power which causes anything to sway; governing influence, authority of government, dominion, rule, jurisdiction.

SWAY (2), [swā], *v.t. and i.* to cause to move slowly from side to side, to make incline; to control the movement or action of a person, group, or body by reason of authority; to persuade, to cause to swing into line; to swing slowly to the side, to incline, lean; to rule, govern. [OScand. *sveigja* to bend].

SWAYING, [swā'-ing], *adj.* causing to sway; exercising influence.

SWEAL, [swēl], *v.t.* (*dial.*) to singe, to scorch, to burn up. [OE. *swælan* to burn].

SWEAR (1), [swāer], *n.* the act of swearing, an oath; a hearty series of oaths.

SWEAR (2), (swore, sworn), [swāer], *v.t. and i.* to utter as a solemn promise, to declare on oath; to cause to take an oath; to utter a solemn promise; to speak profane oaths, to curse, blaspheme; **to s. by,** to invoke as a solemn witness; to express confidence in; **to s. in,** to administer an oath of office to, to install under oath; **to s. off,** to promise to renounce. [OE. *swerian*].

SWEARER, [swāer'-er], *n.* one who swears.

SWEARING, [swāer'-ing], *n.* the act of affirming on oath; the habit or practice of blaspheming, profanity.

SWEAR-WORD, [swāer'-wurd], *n.* a word used in cursing, swearing profanely or blasphemously.

SWEAT (1), [swet], *n.* moisture exuded through the pores of the skin, perspiration; moisture condensed on the surface of any substance; an emotional or physical state of excitation which causes sweat to be exuded; the process of sweating; (*coll.*) laborious work, drudgery, heavy manual labour; **cold s.,** a state of fear, funk; **old s.,** an old soldier. [~OE. *swat*].

SWEAT (2), [swet], *v.t. and i.* to exude in the manner of sweat; to cause to sweat; to wear down by friction; to force to work hard for long hours at starvation wages; to exude sweat, to perspire; to exude moisture in the manner of sweat; to work hard, to drudge; (*slang*) to suffer; to weld; **to s. out,** to get rid of by means of sweating. [OE. *swætan*].

SWEAT-BAND, [swet'-band'], *n.* the lining round the inside edge of a man's hat, usually made of leather.

SWEAT-DUCT, [swet'-dukt'], *n.* (*anat.*) a small channel conveying the secretion of a sweat gland to the surface of the skin.

SWEATED, [swet'-ed], *adj.* produced by sweating.

SWEATER, [swet'-er], *n.* one who, or that which, causes to sweat; an employer at starvation wages; a thick jersey worn as a protection against cold after exercise.

SWEATILY, [swet'-i-li], *adv.* in a sweaty manner; so as to be moist with sweat.

SWEATINESS, [swet'-i-nes], *n.* the condition of being sweaty.

SWEATING-BATH, [swet'-ing-bahth], *n.* a bath for stimulating perspiration as an aid to physical fitness.

SWEATING-HOUSE, [swet'-ing-hows], *n.* a house for sweating persons in sickness as a cure.

SWEATING-IRON, [swet'-ing-iern], *n.* an implement in the form of a knife to scrape off sweat from horses, a strigil.

SWEATING-ROOM, [swet'-ing-rōōm], *n.* a room heated so as to enable invalids to sweat out sickness; a room for sweating cheese, and carrying off the superfluous juices; a room filled with hot steam in a Turkish bath.

SWEATING-SICKNESS, [swet'-ing-sik'-nes], *n.* an epidemic fever characterized by extreme perspiration as the prelude to death, which swept Europe in the fifteenth century.

SWEATING-SYSTEM, [swet'-ing-sist'-em], *n.* an oppressive system of collective production which employers and firms in the wool and garment trades operated in the eighteenth and nineteenth centuries

SWEAT-SHOP, [swet'-shop'], *n.* (*coll.*) a factory or workroom with a reputation among workers for low wages and long hours.
SWEATY, [swet'-i], *adj.* covered with or moist with sweat; consisting of sweat; smelling of stale sweat; laborious.
SWEDE, [swēd], *n.* a native of Sweden; the Swedish turnip, *Brassica Rutabaga*, whose vegetable root is edible. [MLGerm. *Swede*].
SWEDENBORGIAN (1), [swē'-den-bawg'-i-an], *n.* a follower of Swedenborg and his principles. [E. *Swedenborg*, an eighteenth-century Swedish philosopher].
SWEDENBORGIAN (2), [swē'-den-bawg'-i-an], *adj.* relating to the philosophy of Swedenborg.
SWEDISH (1), [swēd'-ish], *n.* the language of the Swedes.
SWEDISH (2), [swēd'-ish], *adj.* relating to, coming from, made by, the Swedes or Sweden.
SWEEP (1), [swēp], *n.* the act of sweeping; the scope, range, of a movement or stroke, usually of a semicircular nature; a gesture which covers a wide area; a forward movement with a steady power covering a wide area; a comprehensive range or grasp of a subject; a person whose business it is to sweep chimneys; a crossing-sweeper; a dirty person or child; a scamp, blackguard; a curved carriage drive; a long oar; the sail of a windmill; a piece of timber functioning on a fulcrum, a long, gradual curve; a beam-compass; (*coll.*) a sweepstake; an incursion by fighter planes across a considerable area; **to make a clean s. of,** to get rid of, abolish.
SWEEP (2), (swept), [swēp], *v.t.* to remove (dirt or dust) by means of a broom, to clean by brushing, to remove by vigorous action, to carry, brush, drive away; to cause to disappear, abolish, obliterate with a comprehensive, wide-flung movement; to carry off with an energetic swinging movement; to clear with a swift, decisive movement; *v.i.* to pass over a broad surface swiftly and comprehensively, particularly so as to make a clearance, to rush over, to cross with a vigorous driving movement; to move with a stately bearing, to walk with pomp; to stretch, extend in a wide curve; to move with a long reach; to engage in a cleaning with a broom; to pass the fingers over (the strings of a musical instrument). [OScand. *svipa*].
SWEEPER, [swēp'-er], *n.* one who, or that which, sweeps.
SWEEPING, [swēp'-ing], *adj.* having a wide range; comprehending a great deal or a great many; having small regard for details or facts.
SWEEPINGS, [swēp'-ingz], *n.(pl.)* things, rubbish, collected by sweeping, refuse.
SWEEPINGLY, [swēp'-ing-li], *adv.* in a sweeping manner.
SWEEPINGNESS, [swēp'-ing-nes], *n.* the quality of being sweeping.
SWEEP-NET, [swēp'-net'], *n.* a large fishing net for drawing over an extensive area.
SWEEPSTAKE, SWEEPSTAKES, [swēp'-stāk(s)'] *n.* a form of gambling in which each participant pays a specified sum for a ticket entitling him to a chance to draw a competitor in a (horse-)race, the prize money for the successful ticket or tickets being paid out of the common fund provided by the losers. [SWEEP and STAKE].
SWEEP-WASHER, [swēp'-wosh'-er], *n.* the person who extracts from the shop-sweepings of gold and silver the minute grains of the metal left behind.
SWEEPY, [swēp'-i], *adj.* marked by sweeping action; strutting; wavy.
SWEET (1), [swēt], *n.* any substance that tastes sweet; a single piece of confectionery, a sweetmeat made of various forms of sugar and ingredients in various mixtures; a course, eaten at a meal after the meat or main dish, which is of a sweetened nature; a term of affection.
SWEET (2), [swēt], *adj.* having the flavour of honey or sugar, stimulating the palate to experience one of the primary sensations of taste, not bitter, not sour, not salt; seasoned with sugar; agreeable, pleasing to any of the senses, stimulating a feeling of affection and pleasure, delightful; pleasant to the body, restful; fragrant; melodious; soft; having a nature free from viciousness, tender, gentle, mild, kind; (*coll.*) pretty, likeable, nice, charming; **to be s. on,** to be in love with. [OE. *swete*].
SWEET-BAY, [swēt'-bā], *n.* the true bay laurel, *Laurus nobilis*.
SWEETBREAD, [swēt'-bred'], *n.* the pancreas, or thymus gland, of an animal prepared as food.
SWEETBRIER, SWEETBRIAR, [swēt'-bri'-er], *n.* a species of rose, the shrubby plant, *Rosa rubiginosa*, with pink flowers having a delicate fragrance.
SWEET-CALABASH, [swēt-kal'-ab-ash], *n.* (*bot.*) the West Indian passion-flower, *Passiflora maliformis*.
SWEET-CHESTNUT, [swēt'-chest'-nut], *n.* the common Spanish chestnut, *Castanea vesca*, with an edible nut (as distinct from the horse-chestnut).

SWEET-CHESTNUT

SWEET-CICELY, [swēt-sis'-i-li], *n.* (*bot.*) a plant of the genus *Myrrhis*.
SWEET-CORN, [swēt'-kawn], *n.* a variety of maize having a sweet taste, and used, particularly in the U.S., as a vegetable.
SWEETEN, [swēt'-en], *v.t.* and *i.* to make sweet, to season with sugar or honey; to make more agreeable or enjoyable, to make less painful, to soften; to become sweet.
SWEETENER, [swēt'-en-er], *n.* one who, or that which, sweetens.
SWEETENING, [swēt'-ning], *n.* the act of making sweet; a substance or ingredient which sweetens.
SWEET-FLAG, SWEET-RUSH, [swēt'-flag', swēt'-rush'], *n.* (*bot.*) the plant, *Acorus Calamus*, having a thick aromatic rootstock and the form of a rush.
SWEET-GUM, [swēt'-gum], *n.* a tree of the genus *Liquidambar*.
SWEETHEART, [swēt'-haht], *n.* a lover, darling, beloved.
SWEETING, [swēt'-ing], *n.* a sweet apple; †sweetheart.
SWEETISH, [swēt'-ish], *adj.* somewhat sweet.
SWEETISHNESS, [swēt'-ish-nes], *n.* the quality of being sweetish.
SWEETLY, [swēt'-li], *adv.* in a sweet manner; easily, freely.
SWEET-MARJORAM, [swēt-mah'-jer-am], *n.* (*bot.*) a very fragrant perennial plant, *Origanum Majorana*. 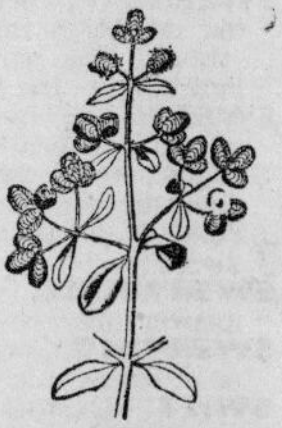
SWEET-MAUDLIN, [swēt-mawd'-lin], *n.* a species of *Achillea*.
SWEETMEAT, [swēt'-mēt], *n.* a confection of sugar, a sweet; fruit preserved with sugar.
SWEETNESS, [swēt'-nes], *n.* the quality of being sweet.
SWEET-OIL, [swēt'-oil], *n.* salad oil, olive oil.
SWEET-PEA, [swēt'-pē'], *n.* (*bot.*) the annual leguminous plant, *Lathyrus odoratus*, with flowers that have a very sweet fragrance.

SWEET-MARJORAM

SWEET POTATO, [swēt'-pōt-ā'-tō], *n.* (*bot.*) the creeper plant, *Ipomœa Batatas*, having an edible root sweet in flavour. 
SWEET-ROOT, [swēt'-rōōt], *n.* liquorice.
SWEET-RUSH, see SWEET-FLAG.
SWEET-SCENTED, [swēt'-sent'-id], *adj.* having a sweet fragrance.
SWEET-SOP, [swēt'-sop'], *n.* the evergreen shrub, *Anona squamosa*; its fruit, which is pulpy and sweet.

SWEET POTATO

SWEETSTUFF, [swēt'-stuf], *n.(pl.)* sugar confectionery, sweets, sweetmeats.
SWEET WILLIAM, [swēt-wil'-yum], *n.* (*bot.*) the plant, *Dianthus barbatus*, having small pink and white flowers forming in a cluster.
SWEETY, [swēt'-i], *n.* (*coll.*) a sweetheart, a lover, *esp.* a woman; (*coll.*) a piece of confectionery.
SWELL (1), [swel], *n.* the act or process of swelling; increase in volume, magnitude, or bulk; a single, gradual undulation of land; the continual undulating motion of the sea, due to powerful deep-sea currents or steady wind, which does not break up the surface into waves; (*coll.*) a rich person, notable for smart

clothes; an important person; (*mus.*) a crescendo; a device in an organ to produce a crescendo.

SWELL (2), [swel], *adj.* (*coll.*) smart, fashionable; first-rate, high-class.

SWELL (3), (swollen), [swel], *v.t.* to cause to swell; to increase in size, bulk, dimension, or volume; to add to the numbers of, increase, augment; to make bigger in arrogance, to puff out with pride; *v.i.* to grow larger, to expand as by dilation or inflation, to increase in size by internal pressure; to be inflated, puffed up, to be blown out, to be bloated; to be puffy or abnormally extended by inflammation; to protrude, to bulge out, to be extended in a curve; to experience a sensation of strength or power due to accumulating emotion; to increase in arrogance, to grow more violent with pride; to rise in a curved protuberance. [OE. *swellan*].

SWELLDOM, [swel'-dom], *n.* (*slang*) high society.

SWELLET, [swel'-it], *n.* (*mining*) an underground stream breaking in upon the works. [Uncert.].

SWELL-FISH, [swel'-fish], *n.* a fish with a defensive physical apparatus by which it can puff itself up.

SWELLING (1), [swel'-ing], *n.* that which swells or is swollen; a natural prominence, an undulation of the earth; a swollen part of the body, a carbuncle, boil, tumour.

SWELLING (2), [swel'-ing], *adj.* marked by a swelling; having a bulging shape, protruding.

SWELLISH, [swel'-ish], *adj.* (*coll.*) characteristic of a swell; rather important; fairly smart.

SWELL-MOB, [swel'-mob'], *n.* (*slang*) a class of well-dressed thieves or pickpockets.

SWELL-MOBSMAN, [swel'-mobz'-man], *n.* (*slang*) a well-dressed pickpocket.

SWELTER (1), [swel'-ter], *n.* the condition of sweltering.

SWELTER (2), [swel'-ter], *v.i.* to be overcome and faint with heat, to be affected by extreme heat, to perspire freely. [OE. *sweltan* to die].

SWELTRY, [swel'-tri], *adj.* characterized by a suffocating heat; oppressive with heat; sultry.

SWEPT, [swept], *pret. and p.pt.* of SWEEP.

SWERVE (1), [swurv], *n.* the act of swerving, a curving deviation from a course, a divergence from a straight line, particularly one followed by a cricket ball in mid-air.

SWERVE (2), [swurv], *v.t. and i.* to cause to deviate; to deviate in a curving line of progress from a set course, to diverge from a straight line, to move suddenly to one side of a line of progression; to suffer a lapse in moral conduct or duty. [OE. *sweorfan* to file].

SWERVELESS, [swurv'-les], *adj.* not liable to swerve, unswerving.

SWERVING, [swurv'-ing], *n.* deviation from any line of progress, rule or standard.

SWIFT (1), [swift], *n.* a soot-black bird of the genus *Cypselus*, resembling a swallow, having long, pointed wings to carry a very light body; a moth of the genus *Hepialus*; a reel on which cotton or yarn is wound.

SWIFT (2), [swift], *adj.* having the power to move at a fast pace, capable of rapid propulsion, moving with speed, rapid, quick, fleet; acting promptly, following quickly in succession. [OE. *swift*].

SWIFT (3), [swift], *adv.* swiftly.

SWIFTER (1), [swift'-er], *n.* (*naut.*) a rope hung below the gunwale to protect the hull from bumps. [~OScand. *svifta* to seep].

SWIFTER (2), [swift'-er], *v.t.* (*naut.*) to extend or stretch.

SWIFT-FOOTED, [swift'-fŏŏt'-id], *adj.* able to run, or running swiftly.

SWIFTLET, [swift'-let], *n.* a small species of swift whose nests the Chinese make into soup.

SWIFTLY, [swift'-li], *adv.* in a swift manner, rapidly.

SWIFTNESS, [swift'-nes], *n.* the quality of being swift, speed, rapid motion, quickness.

SWIG (1), [swig], *n.* a draught of liquor, *esp.* of an alcoholic drink, a gulp; a drink lasting as long as the breath can be held; (*naut.*) a pulley with ropes not set parallel.

SWIG (2), (swigging, swigged), [swig], *v.t. and i.* to drink in large draughts; to take in big gulps; to drink. [Unkn.].

SWILL (1), [swil], *n.* a shallow basket. [Unkn.].

SWILL (2), [swil], *n.* the act of swilling; a copious draught of liquor; food refuse soaked in water for pigs and poultry, hogwash.

SWILL (3), [swil], *v.t. and i.* to wash out and clean with a generous amount of water, to rinse; to drink in great gulps, in large quantities. [OE. *swilian*].

SWILLER, [swil'-er], *n.* one who drinks excessively.

SWILLINGS, [swil'-ingz], *n.*(*pl.*) refuse for pigs, pigs' wash.

SWIM (1), [swim], *n.* the act of swimming; the time spent in swimming; a part of the river usually frequented by fish, a fisherman's pitch; **in the s.,** in the know, fashionable.

SWIM (2), (swimming, swam, swum), [swim], *v.t. and i.* to make swim; to cross by swimming; to compete against as a swimmer; to move through water by using the extremities and limbs or fins as a means of propulsion, to float on or in water; to glide smoothly; to be flooded, overflow; to be giddy, to reel. [OE. *swimman*].

SWIMMER, [swim'-er], *n.* a person who swims; an animal or bird that naturally indulges in swimming.

SWIMMERET, [swim'-er-et], *n.* one of the abdominal limbs of a crustacean which facilitate its swimming.

SWIMMING, [swim'-ing], *n.* the act or the art of moving in water by means of the limbs; dizziness, giddiness.

SWIMMING-BATH, [swim'-ing-bahth], *n.* a large bath equipped for swimming purposes.

SWIMMING-BELL, [swim'-ing-bel'], *n.* the bell-shaped organ of a jellyfish, by means of which it is propelled.

SWIMMING-BELT, [swim'-ing-belt'], *n.* an apparatus consisting of a rubber belt, which may or may not be pneumatic, used to support on the water a person learning to swim.

SWIMMINGLY, [swim'-ing-li], *adv.* easily, smoothly; without obstruction; prosperously.

SWIMMY, [swim'-i], *adj.* giddy. [SWIM (2)].

SWINDLE (1), [swindl], *n.* the act of swindling; deliberate deception for gain under the guise of honesty; an illegal transaction carried on under a legal guise, deliberately framed to defraud; an object which is actually worthless in relation to the high claims made for it. [Germ. *schwindel*].

SWINDLE (2), [swindl], *v.t.* to cheat and defraud grossly; to carry on transactions for gain by means of gross misrepresentations which have a deceptive appearance of honesty and legality. [Germ. *schwindeln*].

SWINDLER, [swind'-ler], *n.* a person who swindles, a cheat, an impostor.

SWINDLERY, [swind'-ler-i], *n.* the wiles of the swindler.

SWINDLING, [swind'-ling], *n.* the act of a swindler, defrauding or cheating by artifice.

SWINDLINGLY, [swind'-ling-li], *adv.* in a swindling manner.

SWINE, [swīn], *n.* a pig; pigs; a term of abuse condemning the person named as disgusting in habits, morals or ethics. [OE. *swin*].

SWINEBREAD, [swīn'-bred'], *n.* a truffle, a fungus of the genus *Tuber*.

SWINECOTE, [swīn'-kōt], *n.* a pen for swine, a pigsty.

SWINE-FEVER, [swīn'-fē'-ver], *n.* a disease affecting pigs, hog-cholera.

SWINE-GRASS, [swīn'-grahs], *n.* (*bot.*) the plant, *Polygonum aviculare*.

SWINEHERD, [swīn'-hurd], *n.* a man who attends to swine, a keeper of pigs.

SWINE-OAT, [swīn'-ōt], *n.* (*bot.*) a kind of oats cultivated particularly in Cornwall for the use of pigs, *Avena nuda*.

SWINEPIPE, [swīn'-pīp], *n.* the redwing thrush.

SWINE-PLAGUE, [swīn'-plāg], *n.* swine-fever.

SWINEPOX, [swīn'-poks'], *n.* a form of chicken-pox with acuminated vesicles containing a watery fluid.

SWINERY, [swīn'-er-i], *n.* a piggery; a pig farm; a pigsty.

SWINE'S-CRESS, [swīnz'-kres'], *n.* (*bot.*) a species of cress of the genus *Coronopus*.

SWINE'S-FEATHER, [swīnz'-feTH'-er], *n.* (*hist.*) the short spear fitting into the muzzle of a fire-arm.

SWINESTONE, [swīn'-stōn], *n.* a variety of limestone called stinkstone, anthraconite. [SWINE and STONE].

SWINE-STY, [swīn'-sti], *n.* a pen for swine, a pigsty.

SWING (1), [swing], *n.* the act of swinging, a movement from side to side, a motion to and fro; the distance traversed by such a motion, the range of that which swings; mode of a person's walk, a free gait with a slight roll of the body from the hips from side to side; unhindered movement, freedom in a specific action; beat, rhythm, extempore jazz music; an apparatus to swing on, *esp.* a loop of rope with a seat attached, which is fastened to a height, on which one sits and is swung backwards and forwards; **in full s.**, at full pressure, with all units functioning; **to make up on the swings what is lost on the roundabouts**, to compensate losses by profits from other sources.

SWING (2), (swung), [swing], *v.t.* to cause to swing, to make move backwards and forwards or from side to side; to hold suspended so that a free movement from side to side is permitted, to dangle; to wave, to brandish; to push or rock on a swing; to cause to move on a pivot; to cause to move rapidly in a semicircular motion; *v.i.* to go or move unobstructedly from side to side like anything weighty suspended in space; to move backwards and forwards, to sway; to vibrate, oscillate; to move in relation to a pivot, actual or imaginary; to move backwards and forwards on a swing; to walk or run with a rhythmic rolling gait; **to s. for,** (*slang*) to be hanged for; **to s. the lead,** to tell lies as an excuse to escape work; **to s. it,** to play (music) with a swing. [OE. *swingan*].

SWING-BOAT, [swing'-bōt], *n.* a boat-shaped seat providing a pleasure swing in a fair ground.

SWING-BRIDGE, [swing'-brij], *n.* a bridge that may be moved by swinging on a pivot.

SWINGE, [swinj], *v.t.* (*archaic*) to hit hard, to beat soundly; to chastise. [OE. *swengan*].

SWINGEL, [swing'-gl], *n.* the flat part of a flail which falls on the grain in threshing. [*Var.* of SWINGLE].

SWINGER, [swing'-er], *n.* one who, or that which, swings; in cricket, a ball bowled so as to swing in the air.

SWINGING, [swing'-ing], *adj.* having the characteristic movement of a swing; rhythmic; very large.

SWINGINGLY, [swing'-ing-li], *adv.* in a swinging manner, with a swing.

SWINGING-POST, [swing'-ing-pōst], *n.* the post or pivot on which a door or gate is hung.

SWINGLE (1), [swing'-gl], *n.* the operation of swingling; the wooden instrument for beating out the fibre from flax, a swingel. [OE. *swingel*].

SWINGLE (2), [swing'-gl], *v.t.* to thrash flax so as to free the fibre from the wood pulp.

SWINGLE† (3), [swing'-gl], *v.i.* to swing, to dangle; to wave hanging, flourish.

SWINGLE-TREE, [swing'-gl-trē], *n.* the pivoted crossbar to which a horse's traces are attached.

SWINGLING-KNIFE, [swing'-gling-nif], *n.* a thin, flat, wooden instrument for cleaning and stripping flax.

SWINGLING-TOW, [swing'-gling-tō], *n.* the coarse part of flax stripped away by swingling.

SWINGLE

SWING-PLOUGH, [swing'-plow], *n.* a crude type of plough without a forewheel under the beam.

SWING-TREE, [swing'-trē], *n.* a swingle-tree.

SWING-WHEEL, [swing'-wēl], *n.* in a clock, the escape-wheel that drives the pendulum.

SWINISH, [swin'-ish], *adj.* having the character of, befitting, or like, swine; gross, hoggish, greedy, coarse.

SWINISHLY, [swin'-ish-li], *adv.* in a swinish way.

SWINISHNESS, [swin'-ish-nes], *n.* the condition of being swinish.

SWINK, [swink], *v.i.* (*coll.*) to labour toilsomely. [OE. *swincan*].

SWIPE (1), [swip], *n.* a strong blow or hit made without taking accurate aim, given with the arm swinging, or with a bat.

SWIPE (2), [swip], *v.t. and i.* to hit hard in a somewhat uncontrolled manner; to aim a strong, but rather wild, blow, *esp.* in cricket; (*slang*) to steal, *esp.* by snatching. [OE. *swipian* to beat].

SWIPES, [swips], *n.(pl.)* weak, washy beer.

SWIRE, [swier], *n.* a hollow between two hills; a depression in the ground on the upper slope of a hill. [OE. *swira* neck].

SWIRL (1), [swurl], *n.* the eddying motion of water, movement of water in a circular, convoluted manner; a twist or curl.

SWIRL (2), [swurl], *v.t. and i.* to cause to swirl, to whirl; to move in a circular, convoluted form, to move in revolving currents of water, to eddy. [OIcel. *svirla* to whirl].

SWISH (1), [swish], *n.* a rapid movement with something flexible which makes a whistling, hissing noise as it cuts through the air; the sound made by such a movement; a short-handled broom. [Echoic].

SWISH (2), [swish], *adj.* (*coll.*) smart, fashionable, fine, posh. [*Prec.*].

SWISH (3), [swish], *v.t.* to move through the air so as to make a hissing or whistling sound; to whip, flog, thrash; to pass through the air with a swift cutting movement. [Echoic].

SWISS (1), [swis], *n.* a native of Switzerland.

SWISS (2), [swis], *adj.* relating to, made in, coming from, Switzerland. [MHGerm. *swiz*].

SWITCH (1), [swich], *n.* a slender, flexible branch, twig, or shoot; a device consisting of a short section of railway line moving on a pivot axis for diverting railway traffic from one line to another; the apparatus for making or breaking an electric circuit. [MDu. *swick* whip].

SWITCH (2), [swich], *v.t. and i.* to lash or thrash with a switch; to move with a quiet swing, to swish; to transfer, divert, shunt by means of a railway switch; to make or break an electric circuit by operating a switch; to be transferred, diverted, shunted to another railway line; to transfer.

SWITCHBACK, [swich'-bak'], *n.* an elevated railway for recreation purposes on an undulating track which imparts an impetus to the carriages.

SWITCHBOARD, [swich'-bawd], *n.* a board or plate fitted with electric switches which are connected to a number of circuits, *esp.* for telephonic purposes.

SWITCHMAN, [swich'-man], *n.* a man who works railway switches by hand, a pointsman.

SWIVEL (1), [swiv'-el], *n.* a link which turns on a pivot; anything which turns on a pivot.

SWIVEL (2), (swivelling, swivelled), [swiv'-el], *v.t. and i.* to cause to move on a swivel; to move round in a socket or staple. [~OE. *swifan* to turn].

SWIVEL-EYE, [swiv'-el-ī'], *n.* (*coll.*) an eye that rolls in its socket, a squint eye.

SWIVEL-HOOK, [swiv'-el-hŏŏk], *n.* a hook that turns in a swivel.

SWIZZLE, [swizl], *v.i.* (*coll. and dial.*) to tipple.

SWIZZLE-STICK, [swizl'-stik], *n.* a stick or whisk for stirring drinks.

SWOLLEN, [swōl'-en], *p.pt.* of SWELL; dilated.

SWOLN†, [swōln], *p.pt.* of SWELL; swollen.

SWOON (1), [swōōn], *n.* the act of swooning; a fainting fit, syncope.

SWOON (2), [swōōn], *v.i.* to experience loss of consciousness and physical control preceded by a reeling giddiness, to faint. [OE. *swogan* to sigh].

SWOONING, [swōōn'-ing], *n.* the act of fainting; (*med.*) syncope.

SWOOP (1), [swōōp], *n.* the act of swooping, a sudden approach with a sweeping movement as though from above, like a bird of prey.

SWOOP (2), [swōōp], *v.t. and i.* to approach rapidly with a swoop and seize; to descend with a sudden sweeping movement which surprises by its rapidity in order to seize, to pounce, as a bird of prey. [OE. *swapan*].

SWOP (1), [swop], *n.* the act of swopping, an exchange, a swap.

SWOP (2), (swopping, swopped), [swop], *v.t.* to swap. [~OE. *swap* blow].

SWORD, [sawd], *n.* a weapon consisting of a sharp-edged blade tapering into a point at one end, and furnished with a hilt at the other; (*fig.*) military power, war, warfare; **at the point of the s.,** under a threat of death; **to cross swords,** to engage in hostilities. [OE. *sword*].

SWORD-ARM, [sawd'-ahm], *n.* the right arm which wields a sword.

SWORD-BAYONET, [sawd'-bā'-on-et], *n.* a bayonet like a short sword.

SWORD-BEARER, [sawd'-bāer'-er], *n.* an attendant official who carries the sword in ceremonies as an emblem of power.

SWORDBELT, [sawd'-belt'], *n.* a belt by which a sword in its sheath is suspended by the side.

SWORDBILL, [sawd'-bil], *n.* the humming-bird, *Docimastes ensiferus*, with a long, sharp beak, found in South America.

SWORD-BLADE, [sawd'-blād], *n.* the blade or cutting edge of a sword.

SWORD-CANE, [sawd'-kān], *n.* a walking-stick concealing a sword inside.

SWORD-CUT, [sawd'-kut], *n.* a cut made by a sword.

SWORD-DANCE, [sawd'-dahnts], *n.* a Highland dance over two swords, laid crosswise, performed with intricate steps without touching them.

SWORD-DOLLAR, [sawd'-dol'-er], *n.* a Scottish silver coin of the 16th century.

SWORDED, [sawd'-id], *adj.* armed with a sword.

SWORD-FIGHT, [sawd'-fīt], *n.* a combat or trial of skill with swords, a bout of fencing.

SWORDFISH, [sawd'-fish], *n.* a large sea-fish of the genus *Xiphias*, or the genus *Histiophorus*, characterized by a prolongation of the upper jaw, which is serrated and sharp like a sword.

SWORDFISH

SWORD-GUARD, [sawd'-gahd], *n.* the part of the hilt affording protection to the swordsman's hand.

SWORD-HILT, [sawd'-hilt], *n.* the handle of a sword.

SWORDKNOT, [sawd'-not'], *n.* a strong ribbon or thong tied to the hilt of a sword, acting as a safety-device round the wrist in case the weapon is knocked out of the wielder's grasp.

SWORD-LAW, [sawd'-law], *n.* power politics, government by force, *esp.* by military reactionaries.

SWORDLESS, [sawd'-les], *adj.* deprived of a sword, defenceless; without recourse to the sword.

SWORD-LIKE, [sawd'-līk], *adj.* having the characteristics of a sword.

SWORD-LILY, [sawd'-lil-i], *n.* (*bot.*) any species of *Gladiolus*.

SWORD-PLAYER, [sawd'-plā'-er], *n.* a professional fencer; a gladiator.

SWORD-SHAPED, [sawd'-shāpt], *adj.* having the form of a sword; ensiform.

SWORDSMAN, [sawdz'-man], *n.* an expert fencer; a soldier, a fighting man.

SWORDSMANSHIP, [sawdz'-man-ship], *n.* skill in the use of the sword.

SWORDSTICK, [sawd'-stik], *n.* a walking-stick which acts also as a sheath for a thin sword.

SWORE, [swaw(r)], *pret.* of SWEAR. [OE. *swor*].

SWORN, [swawn], *adj. and p.pt.* of SWEAR; bound by an oath; **s. enemies**, bitter enemies; **s. friends**, close or intimate friends. [OE. *sworen*].

SWOT (1), [swot], *n.* (*slang*) a person who swots; brain work, *esp.* the concentrated memorizing of facts in preparation for an examination; a term of contempt used by adolescent athletes for scholars.

SWOT (2), (**swotting, swotted**), [swot], *v.i.* (*slang*) to apply oneself assiduously to study, to work hard at memorizing facts for examinations. [*Var.* of SWEAT].

SWOUND†, [swownd], *v.i.* to faint, swoon.

SWUM, [swum], *p.pt.* of SWIM. [OE. *geswummen*].

SWUNG, [swung], *pret. and p.pt.* of SWING. [OE. *geswungen*].

SYBARITE (1), [sib'-er-īt], *n.* a person with wealth enough to indulge continually a liking for luxury, a voluptuary. [Gk. *Subarites* an inhabitant of Sybaris formerly noted for luxurious conditions of life].

SYBARITE (2), [sib'-er-īt], *adj.* luxurious.

SYBARITIC, [sib'-er-it'-ik], *adj.* suited to a sybarite, luxurious, wanton.

SYBARITICALLY, [sib'-er-it'-ik-al-i], *adv.* in the manner of a sybarite.

SYBARITISM, [sib'-er-īt-izm], *n.* the mode of life of sybarites, the practice of effeminacy and luxuriousness.

SYCAMINE, [sik'-a-min], *n.* the black mulberry tree, *Morus nigra*. [Gk. *sukaminos*].

SYCAMORE, SYCOMORE, [sik'-a-maw(r)], *n.* a species of large ornamental maple, *Acer Pseudoplatanus*; a species of fig-tree common in Egypt, *Ficus Sycomorus*. [Gk. *sukomoros* mulberry tree].

SYCAMORE-MOTH, [sik'-a-maw(r)-moth'], *n.* a large moth, *Acronycta aceris*, whose larvae feed on the leaves of the sycamore.

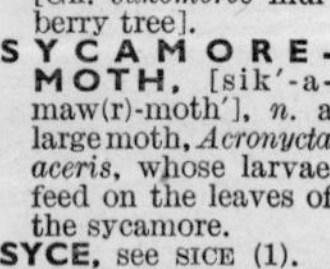

SYCAMORE

SYCE, see SICE (1).

SYCEE, [sī-sē'], *n.* silver in small stamped ingots the shape of a Chinese native shoe used as currency. [Chin. *si sze* fine silk].

SYCHNOCARPOUS, [sik'-nō-kah'-pus], *adj.* (*bot.*) bearing fruit many times without perishing, perennial. [Gk. *sukhnos* many and *karpos* fruit].

SYCOMA, [sīk-ō'-ma], *n.* (*path.*) a tumour with the shape and texture of a fig. [~Gk. *sukon* fig].

SYCOMORE, see SYCAMORE.

SYCONIUM, [sīk-ō'-ni-um], *n.* (*bot.*) a multiple fruit in the form of a fleshy receptacle like that of the fig. [~Gk. *sukon* a fig].

SYCOPHANCY, SYCOPHANTRY†, [sīk'-ō-fan-si], *n.* the practice of a sycophant.

SYCOPHANT, [sīk'-ō-fant'], *n.* a person whose social relationships are based on a deliberate appeal to the pride of his associates, a person who gains the support or friendship of another by means of servile flattery, a parasite, a yes-man, a toady. [Gk. *sukophantes* informer].

SYCOPHANTIC, [sīk'-ō-fant'-ik], *adj.* relating to, characteristic of, like, a sycophant.

SYCOPHANTISH, [sik'-ō-fant'-ish], *adj.* slightly affected by sycophancy.

SYCOPHANTRY†, see SYCOPHANCY.

SYCOSIS, [sī-kō'-sis, sik-ō'-sis], *n.* (*path.*) a pimply fungoid eruption upon the scalp or bearded part of the face, the barber's itch. [Gk. *sukon* fig and *osis* expressing condition].

SYENITE, [sī'-en-īt], *n.* (*min.*) a rock of a granite type in which quartz is present in small proportion to hornblende. [L. *Syenites* (*lapis*, stone) from *Syene*, in Egypt].

SYENITIC, [sī'-en-it'-ik], *adj.* consisting of, like, or containing, syenite.

SYLLABARY, [sil'-ab-er-i], *n.* a list of symbols representing syllables in certain languages. [L. *syllaba* syllable].

SYLLABIC, [sil-ab'-ik], *adj.* relating to a syllable or syllables; consisting of, or based on, a syllable or syllables. [L. *syllaba* syllable].

SYLLABICALLY, [sil-ab'-ik-al-i], *adv.* in a syllabic manner; in separate syllables.

SYLLABICATE, [sil-ab'-ik-āt], *v.t.* to form into syllables; to pronounce in separate syllables.

SYLLABICATION, [sil-ab'-ik-ā-shun], *n.* the act of syllabicating or forming into syllables.

SYLLABIFY, [sil-ab'-i-fī], *v.t.* to form into syllables, to pronounce in separate syllables. [L. *syllaba* syllable and *facere* to make].

SYLLABLE, [sil'-abl], *n.* a speech sound or group of speech sounds consisting of a single vowel, with or without a consonant or consonants, forming a word or a part of a word, and pronounced as a complete unit; the group of symbols or letters giving graphic representation to such a sound; an utterance. [Gk. *sullabe* that which is brought together].

SYLLABUB, see SILLABUB.

SYLLABUS, [sil'-a-bus], *n.* a summary of a subject or outline of a course of studies consisting of heads denoting the main aspects to be covered; (*eccles.*) in the Roman Catholic Church, a list of erroneous beliefs condemned by the Church. [~Gk. *sittuba* tab, book-label].

SYLLEPSIS, [sil-ep'-sis], *n.* (*gram.*) a figure of speech in which one word in a sentence is made to govern two others, one of them in a different or transferred sense. [Gk. *sullepsis* comprehension].

SYLLEPTICAL, [sil-ep'-tik-al], *adj.* of the nature of, relating to, or implying, syllepsis.

SYLLEPTICALLY, [sil-ept'-ik-al-i], *adv.* in the manner of a syllepsis.

SYLLOGISM, [sil'-ō-jizm], *n.* (*log.*) a form of rational argument consisting of three elements, the major and minor premises and the conclusion which follows from the first two, e.g. all men are mortal, John is a man, therefore he is mortal. [Gk. *sullogismos* conclusion].

SYLLOGISTIC, [sil'-ōj-ist'-ik], *adj.* relating to, or consisting of, a syllogism, or in the form of syllogisms. [Gk. *sullogizomai* I infer].

SYLLOGISTICALLY, [sil'-ō-jist'-ik-al-i], *adv.* in a syllogistic manner or form.

SYLLOGIZATION, [sil'-ō-jīz-ā'-shun], *n.* the act or process of reasoning by syllogisms.

SYLLOGIZE, [sil'-ō-jiz], *v.i.* to reason by syllogisms.

SYLLOGIZER, [sil'-ō-jī-zer], *n.* one who syllogizes.

SYLPH, [silf], *n.* a benevolent imaginary spirit like a woman, believed to consist of, and live in, the element of air, and to be light, quick in movement; a slim woman, a woman, *esp.* a young girl, with a graceful figure. [Gk. *silphe* insect].

SYLPHID, [silf'-id], *n.* a small sylph.

SYLPH-LIKE, [silf'-līk], *adj.* resembling a sylph, slender.

SYLVA, [sil'-va], *n.* a descriptive catalogue of trees; a book on forest trees; the trees of a particular region or period considered collectively; †a collection of pastoral poems. [L. *silva* wood].

SYLVAN, see SILVAN.

SYLVANITE, [sil'-van-īt], *n.* (*min.*) a telluride of silver and gold found in crystals.

SYLVICULTURE, [sil'-vi-kul'-cher], *n.* the cultivation of trees, forestry. [L. *silva* wood and CULTURE].

SYLVINE, [sil'-vēn], *n.* (*min.*) crude mineral potassium chloride. [Fr. *sylvine*].

SYM-, *pref.* together. [Gk. *sum* from *sun* with].

SYMBIOSIS, [sim'-bī-ō'-sis], *n.* (*biol.*) the union of two differently constituted organisms dependent for existence on each other. [Gk. *sumbiosis* living together].

SYMBIOTIC, [sim'-bī-ot'-ik], *adj.* relating to, living in, symbiosis.

SYMBIOTICALLY, [sim'-bī-ot'-ik-al-i], *adv.* in the manner of a symbiosis.

SYMBOL, [simb'-ol], *n.* the concrete or graphic representation of one element or aspect of reality; an image or emblem standing for something else as a substitute able to evoke the emotional stimulus of the original by resemblance or suggestion of its qualities and properties; a graphic sign, a letter, a figure signifying a sound or mathematical quality. [Gk. *sumbolon* token].

SYMBOLIC, SYMBOLICAL, [sim-bol'-ik(-al)], *adj.* relating to, serving as, a symbol, representative.

SYMBOLICALLY, [sim-bol'-ik-al-i], *adv.* in a symbolic manner, by symbols or signs.

SYMBOLICALNESS, [sim-bol'-ik-al-nes], *n.* the quality of being symbolical.

SYMBOLICS, [sim-bol'-iks], *n.*(*pl.*) the science or the study of symbols.

SYMBOLISM, [sim'-bol-izm], *n.* the process or practice of taking a fact, object, or incident as a symbol of a larger or deeper source of experience; representation by means of symbols; a system of symbols accepted as representing certain events and ideas; the science of symbols; (*art*) the use of revealed symbols in a poem or painting for the emotive, mystic power they are believed to embody.

SYMBOLIST, [sim'-bol-ist], *n.* one who uses symbols; an artist or poet of the nineteenth-century school of symbolism in France.

SYMBOLISTIC, [sim'-bol-ist'-ik], *adj.* characterized by symbolism, employing symbols.

SYMBOLIZATION, [sim'-bol-īz-ā'-shun], *n.* the process or act of symbolizing; representation of properties. [Fr. *symbolisation*].

SYMBOLIZE, [sim'-bol-īz], *v.t.* to represent as a symbol, to typify.

SYMBOLOGY, [sim-bol'-o-ji], *n.* the study of symbols; the art of expressing by symbols. [SYMBOL and Gk. *logos* speech].

SYMMETRIC, SYMMETRICAL, [sim-et'-rik(al)], *adj.* governed by symmetry; having one half in an exact relationship of size, measurement, shape, and proportion to the other half; having balanced proportions, harmonious in design, having proportionate dimensions.

SYMMETRICALLY, [sim-et'-rik-al-i], *adv.* in a symmetrical form.

SYMMETRICALNESS, [sim-et'-rik-al-nes], *n.* the quality of being symmetrical.

SYMMETRIST, [sim'-et-rist], *n.* a person who likes or demands proportion or symmetry of parts.

SYMMETRIZE, [sim'-et-rīz], *v.t.* to make symmetrical, to render proportional in its parts; to reduce to symmetry.

SYMMETRY, [sim'-et-ri], *n.* the precise correspondence of opposite sides in terms of shape, proportions, and dimensions; regularity of form, the balanced relation of proportionate parts, harmony of structural parts. [Gk. *summetria*].

SYMPATHETIC, [sim'-path-et'-ik], *adj.* relating to, expressing, feeling, sympathy; reacting with mutual emotions; affected by the feelings of others, compassionate, produced by sympathy; inducing sympathy, congenial; acting in unison as the effect of a cause; **s. ink,** ink which is invisible on the paper till subjected to heat. [Gk. *sumpathetikos*].

SYMPATHETICALLY, [sim'-path-et'-ik-al-i], *adv.* in a sympathetic way; by means of sympathy.

SYMPATHIZE, [sim'-path-īz], *v.i.* to feel or express sympathy; to share an emotional experience with another without being subjected to the same causes, to have an affinity.

SYMPATHIZER, [sim'-path-īz-er], *n.* one who sympathizes.

SYMPATHY, [sim'-path-i], *n.* a capacity of experience susceptible to the feelings of others; compassion; correspondence of feelings experienced by two persons in relation to a third realm of experience, sensitive interaction of complementary temperaments; the capacity to share the emotions of another without being subjected to the direct causes of the emotions; (*phys.*) tendency to react or unite, accordance of state or motion; (*med.*) tendency of an organ to react as a result of a condition in another organ or part. [Gk. *sumpatheia* fellow-feeling].

SYMPETALOUS, [sim-pet'-al-us], *adj.* (*bot.*) having united petals. [SYM- and PETALOUS].

SYMPHONIC, [sim-fon'-ik], *adj.* relating to, in the form of, or resembling, a symphony, symphonious; **s. poem,** (*mus.*) a long composition for full orchestra, loosely resembling a symphony, but lacking divisions, and usually of an impressionistic character.

SYMPHONIOUS, [sim-fō'-ni-us], *adj.* characterized by harmony of sound, harmonious; symphonic.

SYMPHONIST, [sim'-fon-ist], *n.* a composer of symphonies.

SYMPHONIZE, [sim'-fon-īz], *v.i.* to sing or play in unison.

SYMPHONY, [sim'-fon-i], *n.* (*mus.*) a composition, usually in three or four movements, the first in sonata form, designed for an orchestra; an overture or prelude; a harmony of sound or colour. [Gk. *sumphonia* harmony].

SYMPHYLLOUS, [sim'-fil-us], *adj.* (*bot.*) bearing leaves joined together. [SYM- and Gk. *phullon* leaf].

SYMPHYSEAL, [sim-fis'-i-al], *adj.* (*anat.*) relating to symphysis.

SYMPHYSIS, [sim'-fis-is], *n.* (*anat.*) the junction of bones affected by means of a cartilage; (*bot.*) abnormal growing together of separate parts of a plant. [Gk. *sumphusis* a growing together].

SYMPIESOMETER, [sim'-pi-ez-om'-it-er], *n.* an instrument for testing atmospheric pressure by means of confined air instead of a vacuum as in the ordinary barometer. [Gk. *sumpiezo* I compress and METER].

SYMPLOCE, [sim'-plos-i], *n.* (*gram.*) a figure of speech consisting of repeating the first and last word of the first phrase in succeeding phrases allotting both words the same position as in the first phrase. [SYM- and Gk. *ploke* knitting].

SYMPODIA, [sim-pō'-di-a], *n.* (*anat.*) a malformation in which the lower limbs are united. [SYM- and Gk. *pous* foot].

SYMPODIUM, [sim-pō'-di-um], *n.* (*bot.*) an apparently primary shoot consisting of a series of forked branches. [SYM- and Gk. *podion* small foot].

SYMPOSIAC (1), [sim-pō'-zi-ak], *n.* a philosophical discussion at a dinner or feast. [Gk. *sumposiakos*].

SYMPOSIAC (2), [sim-pō'-zi-ak], *adj.* relating to, of the nature of, a symposiac.

SYMPOSIARCH, [sim-pō'-zi-ahk], *n.* the president of the feast; a toastmaster. [Gk. *sumposiarkhos*].

SYMPOSIAST, [sim-pō'-zi-ast], *n.* a participator in a symposium; one of a drinking party. [Gk. *sumposiazo* I drink with].

SYMPOSIUM, [sim-pō'-zi-um], *n.* a feast abundantly supplied with drink, and usually accompanied by music, indulged in by the ancient Greeks; a gathering of philosophers; a collection of opinions, often in the form of essays, of different thinkers on a specific subject. [Gk. *sumposion* drinking party].

SYMPTOM, [simp'-tom], *n.* an abnormal change of condition indicating the existence of a hidden causative change, a sign, evidence of organic alteration; (*path.*) a change in physical or mental condition, recognized as abnormal, and accepted as evidence of the existence of disease. [Gk. *sumptoma* chance].

SYMPTOMATIC, [simp'-tom-at'-ik], *adj.* relating to, having the nature of, a symptom, indicative, evident. [Gk. *sumptomatikos*].

SYMPTOMATICALLY, [simp'-tom-at'-ik-al-i], *adv.* according to, by means of, symptoms; in the nature of symptoms.

SYMPTOMATOLOGY, [simp'-tom-at-ol'-o-ji], *n.* the science of the symptoms indicating diseases. [Gk. *sumptoma* chance and *logos* speech].

SYN-, *pref.* with, together.

SYNACMY, [sin-ak'-mi], *n.* (*bot.*) the simultaneous maturity of pistils and stamens. [SYN- and Gk. *akme* a point].

SYNAERESIS, [sin-ēer'-es-is], *n.* (*gram.*) the fusion of two vowels into one. [Gk. *sunairesis* a drawing together].

SYNAGOGAL, [sin-a-gog'-al], *adj.* synagogical.

SYNAGOGICAL, [sin'-a-gog'-ik-al], *adj.* of, or relating to, a synagogue.

SYNAGOGUE, [sin'-a-gog], *n.* a congregation of

Jews for religious purposes; the place set aside for such a meeting, a Jewish place of worship. [Gk. *sunagoge*].

SYNALLAGMATIC, [sin'-al-ag-mat'-ik], *adj.* mutually or reciprocally obligatory. [SYN- and Gk. *allagma* object of barter].

SYNALOEPHA, [sin'-al-ē'-fa] *n.* (*gram.*) the elision of a vowel at the end of a word before another word beginning with a vowel. [Gk. *sunaloiphe*].

SYNANTHOUS, [sin-anth'-us], *adj.* (*bot.*) characterized by bearing leaves and flowers during the same season. [SYN- and Gk. *anthos* flower].

SYNARCHY, [sin'-ah-ki] *n.* jòint rule or sovereignty, *esp.* of the rulers and people. [Gk. *sunarkhia*].

SYNARTHROSIS, [sin'-ahth-rō'-sis], *n.* (*anat.*) union of bones preventing movement; close union, as in sutures. [Gk. *sunarthrosis*].

SYNAXIS, [sin-ak'-sis], *n.* (*eccles.*) a congregation met to celebrate the Eucharist. [Gk. *sunaxis* a gathering].

SYNCARPOUS, [sin-kah'-pus], *adj.* (*bot.*) characterized by having the carpels completely united in a compound fruit. [SYN- and Gk. *karpos* fruit].

SYNCATEGOREMATIC, [sin-kat'-i-go-rim-at'-ik], *adj.* (*log.*) able to be combined with another word, but not constituting a term alone. [Gk. *sugkategorematikos*].

SYNCHONDROSIS, [sin'-kon-drō'-sis], *n.* (*anat.*) the junction of bones by means of cartilage. [Gk. *sugkhondrosis*].

SYNCHORESIS, [sin'-ko-rē'-sis], *n.* (*rhet.*) admission for the purpose of argument. [SYN- and Gk. *khoresis* admission].

SYNCHRONAL, [sin'-kron-al], *adj.* happening at the same time, simultaneous, synchronous.

SYNCHRONISM, [sin'-kron-izm], *n.* the state of being synchronous; arrangement of events in a relation of simultaneity; concurrence of timing relating one set of events to another which runs parallel to it.

SYNCHRONISTIC, [sin'-kron-ist'-ik], *adj.* marked by synchronism, synchronous.

SYNCHRONIZATION, [sin'-kron-īz-ā'-shun], *n.* the fact or process of being synchronized; concurrence of events in time.

SYNCHRONIZE, [sin'-kron-īz], *v.t. and i.* to cause to occur at the same time, to make coincide; to regulate so as to keep time together; to occur or exist simultaneously; to effect a relationship in timing between two parallel sets of events; (*cinema*) to fit a silent film with sound effects; to cause sound effects selected as relevant to a film or part of a film to coincide with the film's action. [Gk. *sugkhronos*].

SYNCHRONOUS, [sin'-kron-us], *adj.* occurring at the same time, simultaneous; (*cinema*) fitted with sound. [Gk. *sugkhronos*].

SYNCHRONOUSLY, [sin'-kron-us-li], *adv.* in a synchronous manner, at the same time.

SYNCHYSIS, [sin'-kis-is], *n.* (*gram.*) an ambiguous order of words in a sentence; (*path.*) abnormal fluidity of humours of the eye. [Gk. *sugkhusis* confusion].

SYNCLASTIC, [sin-klast'-ik], *adj.* (*geom.*) curved on all sides like a ball. [SYN- and Gk. *klastos* bent].

SYNCLINAL, [sin-klī'-nal], *adj.* (*geol.*) sloping downwards towards a line or fold from opposite directions.

SYNCLINE, [sin'-klīn], *n.* (*geol.*) a formation in which the strata are folded to form a trough or basin. [SYN- and Gk. *klino* I bend].

SYNCOPAL, [sin'-kōp-al], *adj.* affected by, relating to, syncope.

SYNCOPATE, [sin'-kōp-āt], *v.t. and i.* to compose or play (a piece of music) so that the beats of the anticipated regular rhythm are for the most part omitted and the accents placed on the off-beat or half-beat, to give a jazzy lilt to; to compose or play with syncopation; (*gram.*) to shorten by leaving out a syllable. [L. *syncopare* to faint away].

SYNCOPATION, [sin'-kōp-ā'-shun], *n.* the act of syncopating.

SYNCOPATOR, [sin'-kōp-ā-tor], *n.* a person expert in syncopation.

SYNCOPE, [sin'-kōp-i], *n.* a fainting fit, a swoon; (*gram.*) the shortening of a word by omission of a medial syllable. [Gk. *sugkope* a cutting short].

SYNCOPIC, [sin-kop'-ik], *adj.* relating to a syncope.

SYNCOPIST, [sin'-kop-ist], *n.* one who contracts words.

SYNCOTYLEDONOUS, [sin'-kot-il-ē'-dun-us], *adj.* (*bot.*) bearing cotyledons joined together.

SYNCRETIC, [sin-krē'-tik], *adj.* characterized by syncretism.

SYNCRETISM, [sin'-kret-izm], *n.* an attempted reconciliation of different philosophical or religious systems into one. [Gk. *sugkretizo* I become an ally].

SYNCRETIST, [sin'-kret-ist], *n.* one who attempts to form a synthesis of opposing systems of thought or belief.

SYNCRETISTIC, [sin'-kret-ist'-ik], *adj.* relating to, characteristic of, the syncretists or syncretism.

SYNCRO-MESH, [sin'-krō-mesh'], *n.* a type of gear affording a smooth change from one ratio to another. [SYNCHRO(NIZE) and MESH].

SYNDACTYLIC, [sin'-dak-til'-ik], *adj.* having webbed digits. [SYN- and Gk. *daktulos* finger].

SYNDESMO-, [sin-dez'-mō], *pref.* binding together. [Gk. *sundesmos* a ligament].

SYNDESMOGRAPHY, [sin'-dez-mog'-ra-fi], *n.* (*anat.*) a description of the ligaments. [SYNDESMO- and Gk. *graphia* writing].

SYNDESMOLOGY, [sin'-dez-mol'-o-ji], *n.* (*anat.*) the branch of anatomy treating of the ligaments. [SYNDESMO- and Gk. *logos* speech].

SYNDESMOSIS, [sin'-dez-mō'-sis], *n.* (*anat.*) the union of two bones by ligaments. [SYNDESMO- and Gk. *osis* expressing condition].

SYNDESMOTOMY, [sin'-dez-mot'-om-i], *n.* (*surg.*) the dissection of the ligaments. [SYNDESMO- and Gk. *tome* cutting].

SYNDIC, [sin'-dik], *n.* an administrative official, *esp.* one having the powers of a magistrate, in various European countries; (in Cambridge University) a member of a special committee of the Senate. [Gk. *sundikos* advocate].

SYNDICALISM, [sin'-dik-al-izm], *n.* a theory which advocates the control of political and economic power by organizations of producers.

SYNDICALIST (1), [sin'-dik-al-ist], *n.* an exponent of syndicalism. [Fr. *syndicaliste*].

SYNDICALIST (2), [sin'-dik-al-ist], *adj.* of, pertaining to, or resembling, syndicalism or syndicalists. [Fr. *syndicaliste*].

SYNDICATE (1), [sin'-dik-at], *n.* a group of business men each of whom puts a certain sum of money into a commercial project, *esp.* in the initial stages of the formation of a limited liability company; a body of syndics, a senate, a council.

SYNDICATE (2), [sin'-dik-āt], *v.t.* to form into a syndicate; (*U.S.*) to publish simultaneously in a number of papers.

SYNDROME, [sin'-drōm-i], *n.* (*med.*) the combination of several symptoms in disease. [Gk. *sundrome*].

SYNECDOCHE, [sin-ek'-do-ki], *n.* (*rhet.*) a figure of speech by which a whole stands for a part or a part for the whole. [Gk. *sunekdokhe*].

SYNECDOCHICAL, [sin'-ek-dok'-ik-al], *adj.* (*rhet.*) expressed by synecdoche.

SYNECHIA, [sin-ē'-ki-a], *n.* (*path.*) a disease of the eye, in which the iris adheres to the cornea or to the crystalline lens. [Gk. *sunekheia* continuity].

SYNECPHONESIS, [sin-ek'-fon-ē'-sis], *n.* (*gram.*) a shortening of two syllables into one. [SYN- and Gk. *ek* out and *phone* sound].

SYNEPY, [sin'-ep-i], *n.* (*rhet.*) the slurring of words while speaking. [SYN- and Gk. *epos* a word].

SYNERGETIC, [sin'-er-jet'-ik], *adj.* working together, co-operating. [Gk. *sunergetikos*].

SYNERGISM, [sin'-erj-izm], *n.* (*theol.*) the principles of the Synergists.

SYNERGIST, [sin'-erj-ist], *n.* (*theol.*) in the Lutheran Church a person who believed divine grace required a correspondent action of the will to make it effectual.

SYNERGY, [sin'-er-ji], *n.* (*med.*) co-operation or correlation of action or function. [Gk. *sunergon*].

SYNGENESIOUS, [sin'-jen-ē'-shus], *adj.* (*bot.*) characterized by being united in a ring, as the anthers of the composite plants.

SYNGENESIS, [sin-jen'-is-is], *n.* (*biol.*) impregnation of an embryo by elements contributed by both male and female parents.

SYNGRAPH, [sin'-graf], *n.* (*leg.*) a contract or deed signed by all the parties concerned.

SYNIZESIS, [sin'-iz-ē'-sis], *n.* elision of two vowels to form one syllable. [Gk. *sunizesis*].

SYNOCHUS, [sin'-ok-us], *n.* continued fever. [Gk. *sunokhos*].

SYNOD, [sin'-od], *n.* (*eccles.*) a council of the clergy, *esp.* of Presbyterians who are delegates from their presbyteries; a council, assembly, convention. [Gk. *sunodos* a meeting].

SYNODAL, [sin'-od-al], *adj.* relating to a synod.

SYNODIC, SYNODICAL, [sin-od'-ik(-al)], *adj.* relating to, sanctioned by, a synod; (*astron.*) relating to the conjunction of two heavenly bodies.

SYNODICALLY, [sin-od'-ik-al-i], *adv.* by means of a synod.

SYNOECIOUS, [sin-ē'-shus], *adj.* (*bot.*) having male and female flowers in one head. [SYN- and Gk. *oikos* house].

SYNOMOSY, [sin-om'-o-si], *n.* a sworn brotherhood of political confederates in ancient Greece. [Gk. *sunomosia*].

SYNONYM, SYNONYME, [sin'-ŏn-im], *n.* a word having the same meaning as another; a word having the same general sense as another but possessing particular implications. [~Gk. *sunonumos*].

SYNONYMIC, [sin'-ŏn-im'-ik], *adj.* relating to a synonym, of similar meaning.

SYNONYMIST, [sin-on'-im-ist], *n.* an expert who studies synonymous words.

SYNONYMITY, [sin'-ŏn-im'-i-ti], *n.* the state, or fact, of being synonymous.

SYNONYMIZE, [sin-on'-im-īz], *v.t. and i.* to express the meaning of in different words; to use synonyms.

SYNONYMOUS, [sin-on'-im-us], *adj.* having the nature of a synonym, having the same general sense, identical in meaning.

SYNONYMOUSLY, [sin-on'-im-us-li], *adv.* by means of a synonym, in a synonymous manner.

SYNONYMY, [sin-on'-im-i], *n.* the condition or the quality of expressing the same meaning by different words. [Gk. *sunonumia*].

SYNOPSIS, [sin-op'-sis], *n.* a statement in summary form giving a brief and characteristic account of a whole by means of a selection from the main parts or heads, an outline. [Gk. *sunopsis* general view].

SYNOPTIC, [sin-op'-tik], *n.* one of the writers of the synoptic gospels. [Gk. *sunoptikos* presenting a general view].

SYNOPTIC(AL), [sin-op'-tik(-al)], *adj.* having the characteristics of a synopsis, relating to a synopsis; **the s. gospels**, (*N.T.*) the gospels of Matthew, Mark, and Luke, which give a conspectus or general view of the life of Christ.

SYNOPTICALLY, [sin-op'-tik-al-i], *adv.* in a synoptical manner, by means of an outline.

SYNOPTIST, [sin-op'-tist], *n.* a writer of a synoptic gospel, a synoptic.

SYNOVIA, [sin-ō'-vi-a], *n.* (*anat.*) a fluid resembling the white of egg, secreted into the cavities of joints as a natural lubricant. [SYN- and L. *ovum* egg].

SYNOVIAL, [sin-ō'-vi-al], *adj.* relating to, affected by, synovia.

SYNOVITIS, [sīn'-ō-vī'-tis], *n.* (*path.*) inflammation of the synovial membrane. [SYNOVIA and Gk. *itis* denoting inflammation].

SYNTACTICAL, [sin-tak'-tik-al], *adj.* relating to syntax; according to the rules of syntax. [Gk. *suntaktikos*].

SYNTACTICALLY, [sin-tak'-tik-al-i], *adv.* in a syntactical form, in conformity to syntax.

SYNTAX, [sin'-taks], *n.* (*gram.*) the arrangement and mutual relationship of words in a sentence; the rules dealing with the order of words in a sentence established by accepted usage. [Gk. *suntaxis* arrangement].

SYNTENOSIS, [sin'-ten-ō'-sis], *n.* (*anat.*) the joining of bones by tendons.

SYNTHERMAL, [sin-thurm'-al], *adj.* having the same temperature.

SYNTHESIS, [sin'-thes-is], *n.* (*chem.*) the process of building up substances into compounds; (*philos.*) the process of testing and working with simple propositions until out of a complex series a final conclusion is deduced; the final stage in a thought-process which follows the thesis and antithesis and embodies the best elements of these two; the opposite of analysis; (*surg.*) the reunion of dissected parts. [Gk. *sunthesis* a putting together].

SYNTHESIST, [sin'-thes-ist] *n.* a person who composes a synthesis.

SYNTHESIZE, [sin'-thes-īz], *v.t.* to make a synthesis of, to introduce as part of a synthesis, to unite in a synthesis, to combine into a whole; to make artificially.

SYNTHETIC(AL), [sin-thet'-ik(-al)], *adj.* pertaining or relating to synthesis; consisting in synthesis or composition; (*chem.*) artificially manufactured as a compound; (*coll.*) bogus. [Gk. *sunthetikos* compounded].

SYNTHETICALLY, [sin-thet'-ik-al-i], *adv.* by means of a synthesis, in a synthetic manner.

SYNTONIC (1), [sin-ton'-ik], *adj.* (*mus.*) sharp, intense. [Gk. *suntonos*].

SYNTONIC (2), [sin-ton'-ik], *adj.* (*wirel.*) tuned to the same wavelength. [SYN- and Gk. *tonos* tone].

SYNTONIN, [sin'-ton-in], *n.* (*chem.*) the basic albuminous substance found in muscular tissue.

SYNTONIZE, [sin'-ton-īz], *v.t.* (*wirel.*) to tune (a wireless set).

SYNTONY, [sin'-ton-i], *n.* (*wirel.*) the correspondence of frequencies of a wireless receiving-set and transmitter. [Gk. *suntonia* agreement].

SYNTROPIC, [sin-trop'-ik], *adj.* (*anat.*) pointing in the same direction. [SYN- and Gk. *tropos* turning].

SYPE, SIPE, [sīp], *n.* water, etc., which has oozed or percolated; a small spring or pool of water. [OE. *sype*].

SYPHER, [sī'-fer], *v.t.* to join up flush with overlapping edges, as two planks. [Unkn.].

SYPHILIS, [sif'-il-is], *n.* a venereal disease, acquired or congenital, caused by a parasite, *Treponema pallidum*, and characterized by skin affections and, finally, paralysis. [From the title of a poem written by G. Fracastoro].

SYPHILITIC, [sif'-il-it'-ik], *adj.* relating to, caused by, or infected with, syphilis.

SYPHILIZATION, [sif'-il-iz-ā'-shun], *n.* the state of being infected by syphilis; the process of inoculating against syphilis.

SYPHILOGRAPHY, [sif-il-og'-raf-i], *n.* the scientific description of syphilis. [SYPHILIS and Gk. *graphia* writing].

SYPHILOID, [sif'-il-oid], *adj.* resembling syphilis. [SYPHILIS and Gk. *oeides* resembling].

SYPHILOLOGIST, [sif'-il-ol'-o-jist], *n.* a student of, or expert in, syphilology.

SYPHILOLOGY, [sif'-il-ol'-o-ji], *n.* the scientific study of syphilis. [SYPHILIS and Gk. *logos* speech].

SYPHON, see SIPHON.

SYREN, see SIREN.

SYRIAC (1), [si'-ri-ak'], *n.* the language of Syria, *esp.* the ancient dialect of Aramaic.

SYRIAC (2), [si'-ri-ak'], *adj.* relating to, written in, coming from, Syria or Syriac. [Gk. *Suriakos*].

SYRIAN (1), [si'-ri-an], *n.* a native of Syria.

SYRIAN (2), [si'-ri-an], *adj.* of, relating to, coming from, made in, Syria.

SYRINGA, [si-ring'-ga], *n.* (*bot.*) a genus of plants comprising the lilacs; (*pop.*) the mock-orange, *Philadelphus coronarius*, with scented white flowers. [Gk. *surigx* pipe].

SYRINGA

SYRINGE (1), [si'-rinj], *n.* an instrument in the form of a cylinder fitted with a piston or rubber bulb by means of which liquid is drawn in by suction and ejected by pressure through a nozzle; **hypodermic s.**, a syringe fitted with a sharp needle for forcing injections under the skin. [*Prec.*].

SYRINGE (2), [si'-rinj], *v.t.* to spray with water or liquid by means of a syringe.

SYRINGEAL, [si-rin'-ji-al, *adj.* relating to the syrinx.

SYRINGOTOMY, [si'-ring-got'-om-i], *n.* (*surg.*) the operation of cutting a fistula. [SYRINGE and Gk. *tome* cutting].

SYRINX, [si'-ringks], *n.* a wind instrument consisting of a set of tuned hollow tubes, Pan's pipes; (*med.*) a fistula. [Gk. *surigx* pipe].

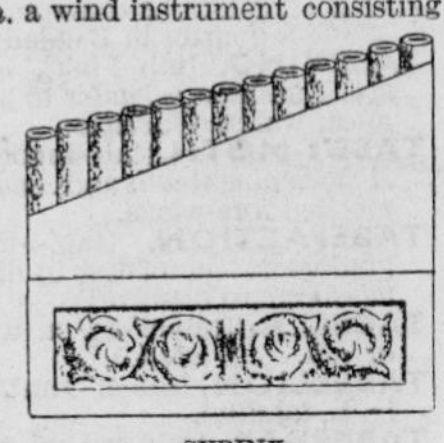

SYRINX

SYRUP, SIRUP, [si'-rup], *n.* a solution of water and sugar; a liquid extracted from the sugar-cane. [OFr. *sirop* from Arab. *sharab* drink].

SYRUPY, [si'-rup-i], *adj.* resembling syrup, treacly, sticky.

SYSTALTIC, [sis-tal'-tik], *adj.* contracting, as in the case of the muscular contraction of the heart. [Gk. *sustaltikos* drawing together].

SYSTEM, [sis'-tem], *n.* a group of units, objects, ideas, or phenomena, functioning in association as a whole; a body of related principles, a classificatory scheme, a plan of categories listed in a possible working relationship; a method of procedure worked out in accordance with an accepted set of principles; the human body as a functioning whole, the constitution. [Gk. *sustema* organized whole].

SYSTEMATIC(AL), [sis'-tem-at'-ik(-al)], *adj.* relating to, consisting of, based on, a system, functioning according to plan. [Gk. *sustematikos*].

SYSTEMATICALLY, [sis'-tem-at'-ik-al-i], *adv.* in a systematic manner, by means of a system.

SYSTEMATISM, [sist'-em-at-izm], *n.* a belief in the fundamental necessity for systems.

SYSTEMATIST, [sis'-tem-at-ist], *n.* one who works according to system.

SYSTEMATIZATION, [sis'-tem-at-īz-ā'-shun], *n.* the act or process of systematizing.

SYSTEMATIZE, [sis'-tem-at-iz], *v.t.* to reduce to system or regular method, to build up into a system.

SYSTEMATIZER, [sis'-tem-at-ī-zer], *n.* a person who systematizes, a systematist.

SYSTEMIC, [sis-tem'-ik], *adj.* of, relating to, the human system or the circulation as a whole as distinct from specialized parts.

SYSTEMLESS, [sis'-tem-les], *adj.* without system.

SYSTEM-MAKER, [sis'-tem-mā'-ker], *n.* a person who forms a system.

SYSTEM-MONGER, [sis'-tem-mung'-ger], *n.* a person who composes and sells systems as a business.

SYSTOLE, [sis'-tol-i], *n.* (*anat., physiol.*) the regular muscular contraction of the heart and arteries (alternating with diastole which pumps the blood outward into circulation). [Gk. *sustole* contraction].

SYSTOLIC, [sis-tol'-ik], *adj.* (*anat., physiol.*) relating to systole or contraction.

SYSTYLE, [sis'-tīl], *n.* (*arch.*) the placing of columns the distance of two diameters apart from each other; a building having columns so spaced.. [Gk. *sustulos*]

SYSTYLOUS, [sis'-til-us], *adj.* (*bot.*) possessing united styles. [~SYN- and Gk. *stulos* column].

SYZYGY, [siz'-ij-i], *n.* (*astron.*) that point of their orbits where two heavenly bodies are in conjunction or opposition; the period during which the sun, moon and earth are in alignment. [Gk. *suzugia* yoke].

T

T, [tē], the twentieth letter of the alphabet; **to a T,** exactly; **to cross one's t's,** to be precise in attention to details.

TA, [tah], *int.* (*coll.*) thank you! [Imitative].

TAAL, [tahl], *n.* the Dutch dialect spoken in South Africa, Afrikaans. [Du. *taal* language].

TAB (1), [tab], *n.* the tongue of a shoe; the end of a boot or shoe lace; a tag, a flap, a strip of material sewn on as a distinctive mark; (*slang*) a check, record; **to keep a t. on,** to keep a check on. [Unkn.].

TAB (2), (tabbing, tabbed), [tab], *v.t.* to provide with a tab.

TABARD, [tab'-ahd], *n.* a military tunic or mantle reaching below the loins, sleeveless, but open at the sides, and worn over armour by knights of the feudal era; the coat of a herald. [OFr. *tabard*].

TABARD

TABARET, [tab'-er-et'], *n.* a strong fabric of satin-striped silk, used for furniture upholstery. [Uncert.].

TABASHEER, [tab'-ash-ēer'], *n.* a siliceous substance found in bamboo canes. [Hind. *tabashir* bamboo sugar].

TABBINET, TABINET, [tab'-in-et'], *n.* a fabric made out of silk and wool, resembling fine damask, and used in interior decoration. [Fr. *tabbinet*].

TABBY, [tab'-i], *n.* a kind of watered silk with a coarse texture; a cat which has a coat mainly light brown or grey in colour but marked with darker patches or stripes, a brindled cat, *esp.* a female cat; a woman who gossips spitefully; a mixture of lime and gravel which hardens as concrete. [Span. *tabi* from Arab. *Attabi* a quarter in Bagdad].

TABBYING, [tab'-i-ing], *n.* the process of rolling stuffs under a calender to give them a wavy appearance; watered fabrics.

TABBY-MOTH, [tab'-i-moth'], *n.* either of two moths, *Aglossa pinguinalis* and *Aglossa cuprealis*, both having mottled fore-wings.

TABEFACTION, [tab'-i-fak'-shun], *n.* (*path.*) a gradual wasting of flesh by disease, emaciation. [~L. *tabefacere* to dissolve].

TABELLA, [tab-el'-a], *n.* a small medicinal lozenge or pill. [L. *tabella*].

TABELLION, [tab-el'-yun], *n.* a notary, a scrivener. [~L. *tabellio*].

TABERDAR, [tab'-erd-ar], *n.* a person who wears a tabard; a foundation scholar of Queen's College, Oxford.

TABERNACLE (1), [tab'-er-nakl'], *n.* a temporary shelter, *esp.* one used by the nomad Israelites in which to worship; a place or house of worship; a niche for a saint's statue; (*eccles.*) a figured chest kept on the altar of a Roman Catholic church to contain the consecrated elements of the Eucharist; (*fig.*) the human body as a temporary receptacle for the spirit; (*naut.*) a socket on deck in which a mast is stepped. [L. *tabernaculum* tent].

TABERNACLE (2), [tab'-er-nakl'], *v.t.* to provide with a tabernacle.

TABERNACLE-WORK, [tab'-er-nakl'-wurk'], *n.* (*arch.*) decorative carvings in the form of canopies.

TABERNACULAR, [tab'-er-nak'-yōō-ler], *adj.* relating to a tabernacle; (*arch.*) formed with delicate tracery; latticed.

TABES, [tā'-bēz], *n.* (*path.*) a wasting away of the body, emaciation. [~L. *tabere* to melt].

TABESCENCE, [tab-es'-ents], *n.* the state of being tabescent.

TABESCENT, [tab-es'-ent], *adj.* having a tendency to waste away, emaciated. [L. *tabescens*].

TABETIC (1), [tab-et'-ik], *n.* a person suffering from tabes.

TABETIC (2), [tab-et'-ik], *adj.* (*path.*) suffering from tabes.

TABID, [ta'-bid], *adj.* (*path.*) wasted by disease, emaciated, consumptive. [L. *tabidus* wasting].

TABIDNESS, [tab'-id-nes], *n.* (*path.*) the condition of being wasted by disease.

TABINET, see TABBINET.

TABLATURE, [tab'-lach-er], *n.* a painting executed on a ceiling or wall; (*mus.*) the notation for a lute. [~L. *tabula* table].

TABLE (1), [tābl], *n.* a piece of furniture consisting of a flat surface of wood on three, or generally four, supports or legs at the corners to a height convenient to a person sitting on a chair to eat or work on; any flat surface; a group of people sitting at a table; the food prepared for one meal; a flat slab of wood, stone, or metal, *esp.* one bearing an inscription, a tablet; the inscription on such a tablet; a list of facts, a synopsis, an index; (*anat.*) either of two flat bony divisions of the skull; (*arch.*) a rectangular, ornamental unit; (*math.*) a system of numbers learnt by heart to facilitate calculations; **at t.,** at meals; **the Round T.,** an order of knights instituted by King Arthur; **to turn the tables on,** to reverse the advantage of. [L. *tabula* a board].

TABLE (2), [tābl], *v.t.* to form into, or place upon, a table; to write a list of, or add to a table; to submit for discussion.

TABLEAU, [tab'-lō], *n.* a representation, a picture; a picture or composition represented by a group of posed persons. [Fr. *tableau*].

TABLE-BEER, [tābl'-bēer], *n.* beer for the table, small beer.

TABLE-BELL, [tābl'-bel'], *n.* a small bell placed on the table, and used for calling servants.

TABLE-BOOK, [tābl'-bōōk], *n.* a small book containing the mathematical tables of multiplication and weights and measures.

TABLE-CLAMP, [tābl'-klamp'], *n.* an adaptable clamp which is fitted to the edge of a table.

TABLECLOTH, [tābl'-kloth'], *n.* a cloth for covering a table.

TABLECOVER, [tābl'-kuv'-er], *n.* a cloth for covering a table.

TABLE-CUT, [tābl'-kut'], *adj.* of a diamond, etc., cut

with a broad rectangular flat surface. [TABLE (1) and CUT (2)].
TABLE D'HOTE, table d'hôte, [tahbl-dōt'], *n.* a meal for which a fixed price is charged, composed of a number of courses chosen by the management. [Fr. *table-d'hôte*].
TABLE-FLAP, [tābl'-flap], *n.* the hinged leaf of a table.
TABLE-KNIFE, [tābl'-nīf], *n.* a knife used at meal-times.
TABLE-LAMP, [tābl'-lamp'], *n.* a small lamp consisting of a lampstand and shade with a light provided by oil, gas or electricity.
TABLELAND, [tābl'-land'], *n.* a stretch of elevated flat land, a plateau.
TABLE-LINEN, [tābl'-lin'-in], *n.* linen for the table.
TABLE-MONEY, [tābl'-mun-i], *n.* an allowance granted to general and flag officers in the Army and Navy for dining expenses, *esp.* when acting as host on official occasions.
TABLE-NEST, [tābl-nest'], *n.* a set of small tables which fit one into the other to save space when not in use.
TABLER, [tāb'-ler], *n.* a person who boards a lodger.
TABLES, [tāblz], *n.(pl.)* backgammon.
TABLE-SHORE, [tābl'-shaw(r)], *n.* a stretch of low, level shore.
TABLESPOON, [tābl'-spōōn], *n.* a large spoon for the table, a soup spoon.
TABLESPOONFUL, [tābl'-spōōn-fŏŏl], *n.* the amount a tablespoon can hold; half a fluid ounce.
TABLET, [tab'-let], *n.* a monument in the form of a flat slab of wood, metal or stone bearing an inscription fixed to a wall; something flat on which to write, a note-pad; a medicine or sweetmeat in a flat round form. [MedL. *tabulata*].
TABLE-TALK, [tābl'-tawk], *n.* conversation of the trivial, gossipy kind spoken at table or meals.
TABLE-TENNIS, [tābl'-ten'-is], *n.* a form of indoor tennis played on a table with small celluloid balls and a wooden racket.
TABLETTE, [tab'-let], *n. (arch.)* a flat projecting coping-stone laid along the top of a wall. [Fr. *tablette*].
TABLE-TURNING, [tābl'-turn-ing], *n.* the act or process of causing a table to move, professedly by spiritualistic agency.
TABLING, [tāb'-ling], *n.* materials such as boards and trestling which form a table; the act of forming into a table; *(carp.)* a form of joining consisting of alternate projections designed to fit into a complementary set.
TABLOID, [tab'-loid], *n. (prot.)* a small round medicinal lozenge, a tablet; a newspaper which provides news in a simple, concentrated, and usually sensational form. [TABLE and Gk. *oeides* like].
TABOO (1), [tab-ōō'], *n.* a prohibition of using or touching an object or person based on religion or magic; a ban or prohibition sanctioned by social convention. [Polynesian *tapu*].
TABOO (2), [tab-ōō'], *adj.* governed by taboo, banned, prohibited by convention, forbidden by the custom of society.
TABOO (3), [tab-ōō'], *v.t.* to prohibit, ban, forbid.
TABOR (1), [ta'-bor], *n.* a camp formed by a ring of wagons. [Turk. *tabor* camp].
TABOR (2), [tā'-bor], *n.* a small drum used to provide a rhythmic accompaniment to a pipe. [OFr. *tabour* from Arab. *tambur* drum].
TABORER, [tā'-bor-er], *n.* one who plays the tabor.
TABORET, [tab'-or-et'], *n.* a taborine. [OFr. *tabouret* stool].
TABORINE, [tab'-or-ēn], *n.* a small tabor, deeper in the drum than the tabor. [L. *taborinus*].
TABOURET, [tab'-ōō-ret'], *n.* a small four-legged seat without arms or back, a low stool. [OFr. *tabouret* stool].
TABULA, [tab'-yōō-la], *n. (zool.)* a plate of hard, brittle tissue forming on the cranium. [L. *tabula* table].
TABULAR, [tab'-yōō-ler], *adj.* arranged in the form of a table; included in a list; having a flat surface; *(zool.)* consisting of thin, flat plates or laminae; **t. spar,** *(min.)* a mineral composed of silicate of lime. [~L. *tabula* board].
TABULARIZE, [tab'-yōō-ler-īz], *v.t.* to tabulate.
TABULARLY, [tab'-yōō-ler-li], *adv.* in a tabular form.
TABULATE (1), [tab'-yōō-lāt], *adj.* having a flat surface; *(zool.)* having laminae.
TABULATE (2), [tab'-yōō-lāt], *v.t.* to arrange in tables or synopses; to provide with a flat surface; to operate a tabulating machine. [L. *tabulatus*].
TABULATION, [tab'-yōō-lā'-shun], *n.* the process of tabulating; the state of being tabulated.
TABULATOR, [tab'-yōō-lā-tor], *n.* a person who tabulates; a device for tabulating.
TACAHOUT, [tak'-a-hōōt], *n.* a gall found on the leaves of *Tamarix indica.* [Native].
TACAMAHAC, [tak'-a-ma-hak'], *n.* a yellowish resin yielded by the tropical American tree, *Calophyllum Tacamahaka*, and used in ointments. [SpanAmer. *tacamahaca*].
TACCA, [tak'-a], *n. (bot.)* a genus of tropical plants which yield a tuber used as food. [Malay *tacca*].
TACE, [tās'-i], *int. (mus.)* be silent. [L. *tace, imper.* of *tacere*].
TACET, [tas'-et, tā'-set], *v.i.* a term used directing a vocal or instrumental part to be silent during a whole movement. [L. *tacet* he is silent].
TACHE, [tach], *n.* a fastening, a catch, a loop; a button. [OFr. *tache* large nail].
TACHOMETER, [tak-om'-it-er], *n.* an instrument for measuring velocity. [Gk. *takhos* speed and METER].
TACHOMETRY, [tak-om'-it-ri], *n.* the science of recording rates of progress. [Gk. *takhos* speed and *metria* measuring].
TACHYCARDIA, [tak'-i-kah'-di-a], *n. (med.)* an affection of the heart characterized by rapid pulsation. [Gk. *takhus* swift and *kardia* heart].
TACHYDRITE, [tak-hī'-drīt], *n.* a deliquescent salt composed of the chlorides of magnesium and lime. [Germ. *tachhydrit*].
TACHYGRAPHIC, [tak'-i-graf'-ik], *adj.* relating to, written in, shorthand.
TACHYGRAPHY, [tak-ig'-raf-i], *n.* the system of notation known as shorthand, stenography. [Gk. *takhus* swift and *graphia* writing].
TACHYLITE, [tak'-i-līt], *n.* any easily fused basalt glass; a kind of impure opal. [Gk. *takhus* swift and *lithos* stone].
TACHYLITIC, [tak'-i-lit'-ik], *adj.* relating to, resembling, tachylite.
TACHYMETER, [tak-im'-it-er], *n.* an instrument used in surveying work for relative location. [Gk. *takhus* swift and METER].
TACHYMETRY, [tak-im'-it-ri], *n. (surveying)* the science of plotting points by means of a tachymeter. [Gk. *takhus* swift and *metria* measuring].
TACIT, [tas'-it], *adj.* implied, not expressed directly, by silence, understood even though left unspoken; silent. [L. *tacitus, p.pt.* of *tacere* to be silent].
TACITLY, [tas'-it-li], *adv.* in a tacit manner, by implication.
TACITURN, [tas'-i-turn], *adj.* naturally inclined to speak little or to remain silent, not talkative, given by temperament to few words. [L. *taciturnus* quiet].
TACITURNITY, [tas'-it-urn'-i-ti], *n.* the quality of being taciturn, habitual silence or reserve in speech. [L. *taciturnitas*].
TACITURNLY, [tas'-i-turn-li], *adv.* in a taciturn manner.
TACK (1), [tak], *n.* a short nail with a broad head; a long loose stitch in needlework making a temporary fastening; *(fig.)* a course of action; *(naut.)* the course of a ship running in an oblique direction to the wind; the side of a ship receiving the wind; a rope for fastening the fore corner at the bottom of a sail; the corner of the sail fastened by such a rope; a shift of direction due to a swing over of the sails calculated to obtain the full benefit of the wind; *(slang)* food in a semi-liquid state; a contemptuous term for food of any kind. [AFr. *taque* nail].
TACK (2), [tak], *v.t. and i.* to fasten or attach by means of a tack or tacks; to stitch together with long loose stitches in a temporary way; to attach, to append; *(naut.)* to cause a sailing vessel to shift its direction by putting the sails in a position to obtain the full benefit of the wind; to chop and change a line of action.
TACKER, [tak'-er], *n.* one who tacks or makes an addition.
TACKET, [tak'-it], *n. (dial.)* a small nail with a large thick head used for studding boots, a hob-nail.
TACKING, [tak'-ing], *n.* the act or process of changing a ship's course; temporary loose stitching; **t. cotton,** cotton used for such stitching.
TACKLE (1), [takl], *n.* a simple mechanism for moving heavy weights, *esp.* a system of ropes and pulleys; any manipulative apparatus or set of instruments, gear, equipment; *(football)* an attempt to rob an opponent of the ball. [ME. *takel*].
TACKLE (2), [takl], *v.t.* to manipulate by means of tackle; *(fig.)* to grapple with, to deal with, to

undertake, to attempt to solve; (*football*) to attempt to rob (an opponent) of the ball.
TACKLING, [tak'-ling], *n.* (*naut.*) rigging of the masts and yards of a ship, such as cordage and sails; a set of implements; harness.
TACKSMAN, [taks'-man], *n.* a lessee. [TACK and MAN].
TACKY, [tak'-i], *adj.* slightly adhesive, sticky.
TACT, [takt], *n.* ability to respond to a person or situation so that the least offence is given, faculty to foresee awkward effects of speech or action and thus lessen social friction, ability to do or say what is most acceptable, discretion, ingenuity which provides extempore forms of expression calculated to lessen the shock of truth. [L. *tactus* sense of touch].
TACTFUL, [takt'-fōōl], *adj.* possessing tact.
TACTFULLY, [takt'-fōōl-i], *adv.* in a tactful way.
TACTIC, [tak'-tik], *n.* mode of operation; an instance of tactics. [Gk. *taktike*].
TACTICAL, [tak'-tik-al], *adj.* of or relating to tactics.
TACTICALLY, [takt'-ik-al-i], *adv.* by means of tactics.
TACTICIAN, [tak-tish'-an], *n.* one expert in tactics.
TACTICS, [tak'-tiks], *n.*(*pl.*) the art or science of manoeuvring forces in battle according to established principles; the art of handling a situation adroitly. [Gk. *taktika*].
TACTILE, [takt'-īl], *adj.* affecting, relating to, the sense of touch; tangible. [L. *tactilis* tangible].
TACTILITY, [takt-il'-i-ti], *n.* the condition of being tactile; tangibleness; perceptibility to touch.
TACTION, [tak'-shun], *n.* the act of touching; contact. [L. *tactio*].
TACTLESS, [takt'-les], *adj.* characterized by absence of tact, destitute of tact.
TACTLESSLY, [takt'-les-li], *adv.* in a tactless manner.
TACTLESSNESS, [takt'-les-nes], *n.* the quality of being tactless.
TACTUAL, [tak'-chōō-al], *adj.* relating to touch; consisting in, or derived from, touch. [~L. *tactus* touching].
TACTUALLY, [tak'-chōō-al-i], *adv.* in a tactual way.
TADPOLE, [tad'-pōl], *n.* a frog, toad, etc., in its first state with a long tail and external gills after leaving the egg. [ME. *tadpolle* toad head].

TADPOLE

TADPOLE-FISH, [tad'-pōl-fish], *n.* the lesser forkbeard fish, *Raniceps raminus*, having a broad head.
TAEL, [tāl], *n.* the Chinese dollar of pure silver worth half a crown, its value varying with the price of silver; a weight of 1⅓ oz. [Malay *tahil* weight].
TA'EN, [tān], *p.pt.* contracted poetical form of *taken*.
TAENIA, [tē'-ni-a], *n.* the tapeworm; (*arch.*) the band over the architrave on a Doric column. [Gk. *tainia* fillet].
TAENIOID, [tēn'-i-oid], *adj.* of or resembling tapeworms.
TAFFETA, [taf'-it-a], *n.* a fabric of fine silk, sometimes mixed with wool or cotton, having a lustrous texture. [Pers. *taftah*].
TAFFRAIL, [taf'-ril], *n.* a handrail placed round a ship's stern. [Du. *tafereel*].

TAFFRAIL

TAFFY, [taf'-i], *n.* (*coll.*) a Welshman. [Wel. *Taffy* David].
TAFIA, [taf'-i-a], *n.* a crude variety of W. Indian rum, distilled from sugar refuse. [Native].
TAG (1), [tag], *n.* that which is tacked on; a supplementary piece attached to the end or edge of something; a loop at the back of a boot; a metal clip fastened round the tip of a piece of string or bootlace; a piece of torn material hanging loose; a year-old sheep; a matted piece of sheep's wool; an actor's catchword, cue; the short refrain of a poem or song; a cliché quotation; a game of pursuit played by children, "he." [~Swed. *tagg*].
TAG (2), (tagging, tagged), [tag], *v.t.* to provide with a tag; to tack on, append, attach; to join, fasten; to touch.
TAGGER, [tag'-er], *n.* one who tags; (*pl.*) lead- or tin-coated plates of iron; very thin plates of these.
TAGILITE, [taj'-i-līt], *n.* (*min.*) a hydrous phosphate of copper. [*Tagilek* in the Ural Mountains].
TAGLIA, [tal'-ya], *n.* a complex combination of pulley for hoisting. [It. *taglia* pulley].
TAGLIACOTIAN, [tal'-ya-kō'-shi-an], *adj.* (*surg* pertaining to an operation for restoring the nose [*Tagliacozzi*, an anatomist].
TAG-RAG, [tag'-rag'], *n.* the lowest class of people riff-raff.
TAG-SORE, [tag'-saw(r)], *n.* a disease affecting th place under the tail of a sheep.
TAG-TAIL, [tag'-tāl], *n.* a worm which has a yellow tail; (*fig.*) a sycophant.
TAGUAN, [tahg'-wan], *n.* a large species of Malaya flying squirrel, *Pteromys petaurista*. [Native].
TAHR, [tāe(r)], *n.* the Himalayan wild goat, *Hemi tragus jemlaicus*. [Native].
TAHSIL, [tah-sēl'], *n.* an area in India as a unit fror which revenue is collected. [Hind. *tahsil* collection
TAI, THAI, [tī], *n.*(*pl.*) a race of people inhabiting th Indo-Chinese peninsula; the Siamese. [Chin. *tai*].
TAIC (1), [tah'-ik], *n.* the language of the Tai.
TAIC (2), [tah'-ik], *adj.* relating to, resembling, mad by, the Tai.
TAIGA, [tī'-ga], *n.* huge stretch of forest-land i Siberia. [Siberian *taiga*].
TAIGLE, [tāgl], *v.t.* to entangle; to retard, impede delay. [ME. *tagil*].
TAIL (1), [tāl], *n.* the part of the backbone in verte brates which extends beyond the trunk and whic is usually long and flexible; any object which ha the characteristics of an animal's tail, any trailin length, an appendage; the lowest or hindermost par of anything; **to have the t. between the legs,** t be disheartened; **to turn t.,** to retreat in flight; (*pl* the side of a coin on the reverse of the head; **tail up,** cheerful. [OE. *tægl*].
TAIL (2), [tāl], *n.* limitation; **estate in t.,** (*leg.*) an estat limited to a particular line of descendants. [OFr *taille* notch].
TAIL (3), [tāl], *v.t.* and *i.* to provide with a tail; to depriv of a tail, *esp.* to cut off a stem or stalk; to track closely trail; **to t. away,** to fade away; to straggle; **to t. off** to fall behind.
TAILBOARD, [tāl'-bawd], *n.* the movable board a the back of a cart.
TAILED, [tāld], *adj.* possessing a tail.
TAIL-END, [tāl'-end'], *n.* the extreme end, fag end.
TAIL-FLOAT, [tāl'-flōt], *n.* (*aeron.*) the landing floa at the rear of a seaplane.
TAILFLOWER, [tāl'-flow(r)], *n.* (*bot.*) the flaming plant, *Anthurium*, of the West Indies.
TAIL-FEATHER, [tāl'-feᴛʜ'-er], *n.* the largest feathe in a bird's tail.
TAILING, [tāl'-ing], *n.* (*arch.*) the part of a projectin stone, timber, or brick inserted and fixed in a wall
TAILINGS, [tāl'-ingz], *n.*(*pl.*) winnowed refuse; or deprived of the metal; faulty calico.
TAILLESS, [tāl'-les], *adj.* possessing no tail.
TAIL-LIGHT, [tāl'-līt'], *n.* a red light attached to the rear of a vehicle as a warning to following traffic.
TAILOR, [tā'-ler], *n.* a person who is expert in makin outer clothes for wear by cutting, sewing and fittin the cloth; a retailer who sells men's suits. [OFr *tailleur*].
TAILOR-BIRD, [tā'-ler-burd], *n.* an Asiatic bird *Orthotomus sutorius*, so called from its habit of sewing together leaves with silk and fibres by means of its bill in order to fashion a nest for itself.
TAILORED, [tāl'-erd], *adj.* tailor-made.
TAILORESS, [tā'-ler-es'], *n.* a woman who makes garments.

TAILOR-BIRD

TAILORING, [tā'-ler-ing], *n.* the occupation of a tailor.
TAILOR-MADE, [tā'-ler-mād'], *adj.* made by a tailor who gives personal attention to the fittings, *esp.* o women's costumes cut in a man's style.
TAILPIECE, [tāl'-pēs], *n.* (*mus.*) a piece of ebony designed to take the strings of an instrument; (*print.*) an ornamental design placed at the end of a chapte or of a book; a closing remark or quotation.
TAILRACE, [tāl'-rās], *n.* the stream of water whic runs below the mill-wheel.
TAILROPE, [tāl'-rōp], *n.* (*mining*) a rope which works a skip.
TAILSKID, [tāl'-skid], *n.* (*aeron.*) a sturdy meta

support at the rear of a plane which acts as a stabilizer when taxi-ing.

TAIL-SPIN, [tāl'-spin], *n.* (*aeron.*) a kind of spinning dive; also (*fig.*).

TAILZIE, [tāl'-zi], *n.* (*Scots leg.*) a deed establishing an entailed estate. [~OFr. *taille* notch].

TAIN, [tān], *n.* a thin sheet of tinfoil for looking-glasses; thin tinplate. [OIcel. *teinn* twig].

TAINT (1), [tānt], *n.* that which taints, tincture or trace of decay, infection, corruption; pollution, contamination; a moral blemish, a stain on a reputation. [Fr. *teinte* tinge].

TAINT (2), [tānt], *v.t. and i.* to impregnate with something which corrupts or pollutes, to infect with decay, to render noxious, to make putrid; to become putrid, to be affected by decaying matter.

TAINTLESS, [tānt'-les], *adj.* characterized by absence of taint or infection.

TAINTLESSLY, [tānt'-les-li], *adv.* in a taintless manner, without taint.

TAJ, [tahj], *n.* the conical cap of a Mohammedan dervish. [Pers. *taj* crown].

TAJACU, [tah-hah-sōō'], *n.* the collared peccary, *Dicotyles tajacu*, which resembles a hog, and is found ranging from Arkansas to Patagonia. [Braz. (Tupi) *tajasu*].

TAKE (1), [tāk], *n.* an amount taken, received, or caught; (*cinema*) the photographing of a single scene; (*print.*) a compositor's share of text to be set up; a section of a press message.

TAKE (2), (took, taken), [tāk], *v.t.* to carry away in the hands, to gain possession of, to get hold of and remove bodily, to seize; to receive into one's possession, to transfer into one's keeping; to catch, seize, trap, ensnare, to make prisoner; to capture; to earn, win in cash; to grasp mentally, to understand; to gain possession of and use, to employ, to adopt as one's own, to undertake, to engage in as an occupation; to swallow, inhale; to choose, select; to endure, withstand; to experience, to stimulate emotionally, to assume in the mind; to do, perform, carry out (an action); to discover, test, ascertain, estimate; to record, to write down; to photograph, to snap; to rent, engage, hire; *v.i.* to be effective, to work according to plan, follow the necessary course; to please, to be popular, to have a good reception; to photograph; **to t. after,** to have a facial or other resemblance to; **to t. away,** to remove, deduct; to deprive of; **to t. back,** to retract; withdraw; **to t. care,** to be cautious, beware; **to t. care of,** to be in charge of; **to t. down,** to remove by lifting down, to transfer to a lower level; to pull down, allow to fall down; to write down; **to t. for,** to judge, consider; **to t. for a ride,** to fool; (*U.S.*) to kidnap and kill; **to t. for granted,** to assume; **to t. hold,** to grasp; to gain influence over; **to t. in,** to enclose, encompass; to comprise; to cheat, impose upon, deceive; to give a place to, to admit, to request to enter, to give comfort or welcome to; to grasp intellectually; **to t. in vain,** to blaspheme; **to t. off,** to doff; to copy; mimic, imitate, parody; to subtract; (of an aircraft) to become airborne; **to t. on,** to undertake; to employ, hire; to challenge; to exhibit distress; **to t. (oneself) off,** to depart, withdraw; **to t. out,** to extract; to obtain (a licence, policy, shares, etc.); to accompany out of doors, cultivate the company of, escort, entertain; **to t. over,** to assume control of; **to t. place,** to happen, occur; **to t. to,** to feel an attraction, to have an affinity for; **to t. to heart,** to feel, *esp.* sorrow, deeply; **to t. up,** to raise, lift; to underwrite; to engross, absorb; to occupy, fill; to engage in; to adopt; to pick up; to resume; to arrest, place in custody; **to t. up with,** to become associated with; **to t. upon oneself,** to assume responsibility for; **t. it from me,** believe me; **to t. th chair,** to act as chairman; **to t. it out of,** to get one's own back on; to exhaust. [OScand. *taka*].

TAKE-IN, [tāk'-in], *n.* (*coll.*) a swindle.

TAKEN, [tāk'-en], *p.pt.* of TAKE.

TAKE-OFF, [tāk'-of], *n.* the act of taking off; the rising of an aircraft from the ground or sea into the air; the manner in which the feet are disposed in the act of jumping; a parody.

TAKER, [tāk'-er], *n.* one who takes or receives; one who catches; one who accepts the odds laid in betting.

TAKING (1), [tāk'-ing], *n.* the act of one who takes, the process of gaining a required effect; seizure, capture; (*pl.*) earnings, cash receipts; (*coll.*) mental distress.

TAKING (2), [tāk'-ing], *adj.* attractive, fetching.

TAKINGLY, [tāk'-ing-li], *adv.* in a taking way.

TAKINGNESS, [tāk'-ing-nes], *n.* the state of being attractive; the quality of pleasing.

TALAPOIN, [tal'-ap-oin], *n.* a mendicant priest of Siam; a species of small African monkey, *Cercopithecus talapoin*. [Taic *tala poi* my lord].

TALARIA, [tal-āer'-i-a], *n.*(*pl.*) the wings or winged sandals attached to the ankles of Mercury, Eros, etc., in classical art. [L. *talaria*].

TALBOT, [tawl'-bot], *n.* a breed of hound, noted for its quick scent when pursuing. [Uncert.].

TALBOTYPE†, [tawl'-bōt-īp], *n.* a process of reproducing a photographic image on the surface of paper specially prepared with chemicals. [Fox *Talbot*, the inventor, and TYPE].

TALC, [talk], *n.* (*min.*) a hydrated silicate of magnesium, used as a particularly fine dusting powder; laminated steatite; mica. [Arab. *talq*].

TALCITE, [talk'-īt], *n.* a variety of talc, nacrite.

TALCOSE, [talk'-ōs], *adj.* relating to, containing, or composed of, talc.

TALCOUS, [talk'-us], *adj.* talcose.

TALCUM, [talk'-um], *n.* french-chalk, powdered talc.

TALCY, [talk'-i], *adj.* containing talc; spattered with, covered with, talc.

TALE (1), [tāl], *n.* a narrative of a series of events, real or imaginary, a story; an account of an incident; a legend; a report, rumour; an anecdote; **to tell tales,** to inform. [OE. *talu* story].

TALE† (2), [tāl], *n.* an amount, reckoning, tally. [OE. *tæl* number].

TALE-BEARER, [tāl'-bāer-er], *n.* a person who tells tales with malicious intent.

TALE-BEARING, [tāl'-bāer-ing], *n.* the act or the practice of telling tales with mischievous intent.

TALENT, [tal'-ent], *n.* natural aptitude for a specific form of activity, a congenital faculty of a creative nature, a particular ability, skill; formerly, a standard weight or money unit, its value differing in various historical periods. [Gk. *talanton* a balance].

TALENTED, [tal'-ent-id], *adj.* possessing talents; having natural ability, skill, or talents.

TALENTLESS, [tal'-ent-les], *adj.* possessing no natural aptitude, without talent.

TALES, [tāl'-ēz], *n.* (*leg.*) the summoning of jurors for a special jury in place of original members who have failed to appear. [L. *tales*, *pl.* of *talis* such].

TALESMAN, [tāl'-ēz'-man], *n.* a person summoned by a tales to act as a juror. [TALES and MAN].

TALETELLER, [tāl'-tel'-er], *n.* one who tells tales or stories.

TALION, [tal'-i-on], *n.* the law of retaliation in kind as a form of punishment for injury. [L. *talio*].

TALIPES, [tal'-i-pēz], *n.* club-foot. [L. *talus* ankle and *pes* foot].

TALIPOT, [tal'-i-pot'], *n.* the great palm, *Corypha umbraculifera*, which has leaves in the shape of a fan. [Skr. *tala* palm and *patra* leaf].

TALISMAN, [tal'-iz-man], *n.* a small object superstitiously considered to possess a protective or lucky influence over the owner, an amulet, a charm. [Gk. *telesma* payment].

TALISMANIC, [tal'-iz-man'-ik], *adj.* relating to, having the properties of, a talisman, magical.

TALK (1), [tawk], *n.* the act of talking, social intercourse by means of speech, mutual discussion, conversation, a chat; the subject of a discussion; a short informal lecture; rumour, gossip; **small-t.,** trivial conversation.

TALK (2), [tawk], *v.t. and i.* to express in words, to speak; to engage in social intercourse by means of speech; to disclose information; **to t. at,** to address obliquely, harangue; **to t. big,** to boast; **to t. down,** to silence by loud or continual talking; **to t. down to,** to address in excessively simple language; **to t. of,** to discuss; relate, tell; **to t. over,** to discuss; to persuade; **to t. round,** to evade the real issue of; to argue into agreement; **to t. to,** to scold. [ME *talken*].

TALKATIVE, [tawk'-at-iv], *adj.* fond of talking, given to much talking, loquacious.

TALKATIVENESS, [tawk'-at-iv-nes], *n.* the quality of being talkative, loquacity.

TALKER, [tawk'-er], *n.* one who talks; a loquacious person; a boaster; one who talks rather than acts.

TALKIES, [tawk'-iz], *n.*(*pl.*) (*coll.*) cinematograph pictures synchronized with sound.

TALKING, [tawk'-ing], *adj.* having the power of speech, able to talk; given to talking, loquacious; expressive.

TALKING-POINT, [tawk'-ing-point'], *n.* a topic on which one can enlarge in order to sell goods or to persuade a waverer to come to a definite decision.

TALKING-TO, [tawk'-ing-tōō], *n.* a scolding.

TALKY-TALKY, [tawk'-i-tawk-i], *n.* (*coll.*) trivial or worthless talk. [TALK (1)].

TALL (1), [tawl], *adj.* above the average in height, relatively high in stature; having an extended height; big; almost incredible, extravagant. [Uncert.].

TALL (2), [tawl], *adv.* (*slang*) boastfully.

TALLAGE, [tal'-ij], *n.* a form of feudal taxation imposed on towns and demesne lands under the Crown. [OFr. *taillage* a cutting].

TALLBOY, [tawl'-boi], *n.* a high chest of drawers. [TALL and BOY (1)].

TALLIER, [tal'-i-er], *n.* one who keeps a tally.

TALLISH, [tawl'-ish], *adj.* tending to be tall, rather tall.

TALLITH, [tal'-ith], *n.* a mantle or scarf with which Jews cover the shoulders while at prayer. [Heb. *tallith* covering].

TALLNESS, [tawl'-nes], *n.* the quality of being tall.

TALLOW (1), [tal'-ō], *n.* animal fat melted down, used for candles or lubrication; **t. tree,** the tree, *Stillingia sebifera*, found in China. [~Icel. *tolg*].

TALLOW (2), [tal'-ō], *adj.* made of tallow.

TALLOW (3), [tal'-ō], *v.t.* to grease with tallow.

TALLOW-CHANDLER, [tal'-ō-chahnd'-ler], *n.* a person who manufactures and sells tallow candles.

TALLOW-FACED, [tal'-ō-fāst], *adj.* having a pale, bloodless complexion.

TALLOWING, [tal'-ō-ing], *n.* the process in animals of forming tallow internally.

TALLOWISH, [tal'-ō-ish], *adj.* somewhat tallowy, having the properties of tallow, greasy.

TALLOWY, [tal'-ō-i], *adj.* containing, resembling, tallow; tallowish.

TALLY (1), [tal'-i], *n.* a piece of wood bearing notches corresponding to those on a similar piece of wood, thus forming a check or account of an amount, number or reckoning; a duplicated account, ticket, label, tag, etc. [OFr. *taille* notch].

TALLY (2), [tal'-i], *v.t. and i.* to record by means of a tally, to reckon, to mark with equal notches; to agree, correspond, *esp.* in number.

TALLY-HO (1), [tal'-i-hō'], *n.* the huntsman's call on sighting the fox. [Fr. *taïaut*].

TALLY-HO (2), [tal'-i-hō'], *v.i.* to utter a tally-ho.

TALLY-MAN, [tal'-i-man'], *n.* a person who keeps or sells goods for a tally-shop.

TALLY-SHEET, [tal'-i-shēt], *n.* a piece of paper on which a tally is written.

TALLY-SHOP, [tal'-i-shop'], *n.* a shop where accounts are kept by means of a tally, payments being made on an instalment system.

TALMA, [tal'-ma], *n.* a long cape or cloak. [François *Talma*, a French actor, d. 1826].

TALMUD, [tal'-mood], *n.* the fundamental code of the Jewish civil and canonical law, consisting of the Mishna, or text, and the Gemara, or commentary. [Heb. *talmud* instruction].

TALMUDIC, [tal-mood'-ik], *adj.* relating to, or contained in, the Talmud.

TALMUDIST, [tal'-mood-ist], *n.* a student of the Talmud.

TALMUDISTIC, [tal'-mood-ist'-ik], *adj.* relating to or resembling the Talmud.

TALON, [tal'-on], *n.* the claw of a bird of prey; (*arch.*) a form of moulding concave at the bottom and convex at the top, an ogee. [Fr. *talon*].

TALONED, [tal'-ond], *adj.* having talons.

TALUK, [tal-ōōk'], *n.* in India, a district paying specified revenue, inferior to a zemindary. [Urdu *taluq*].

TALUKDAR, [tal-ōōk'-dah(r)], *n.* the holder of a taluk, or the head of a revenue department in Southern India. [*Prec.*].

TALUS, [tā'-lus], *n.* (*anat.*) the bone of the foot articulated with the leg bones, the ankle; (*arch.*) a slope; (*fort.*) the sloping side of an earthwork; (*geol.*) the sloping mass of rubble lying at the base of a cliff. [L. *talus* ankle].

TAMABILITY, [tām'-a-bil'-i-ti], *n.* tamableness.

TAMABLE, [tām'-abl], *adj.* capable of being tamed or subdued.

TAMABLENESS, [tām'-abl-nes], *n.* the quality of being tamable.

TAMANDUA, [tam-an'-dew-a], *n.* the caguari or four-toed ant-eater, *Tamandua tetradactyla*, having a prehensile tail with which it clings to the branches of trees. [Braz. *tamandua*].

TAMARACK, [tam'-a-rak'], *n.* the American black larch, *Larix americana*. [Native].

TAMARIN, [tam'-a-rin], *n.* a small South American marmoset of the genus *Midas* with fine silky hair and a tail like a squirrel. [Native].

TAMARIND, [tam'-a-rind], *n.* the tropical leguminous tree, *Tamarindus indica*, which bears yellow flowers. [Arab. *tamr* date and *Hind* India].

TAMARINDS, [tam'-a-rindz], *n.*(*pl.*) the seed-pods of the tamarind tree which contain acid pulp.

TAMARISK, [tam'-a-risk], *n.* the ornamental evergreen tree or shrub, *Tamarix gallica*, with slender branches, minute leaves and spiky flowers; any of the sixty-four species of *Tamarix*. [L. *tamaricus*].

TAMASHA, [tam-ah'-sha], n. (*India*) a public function or display; a fuss. [Arab. *tamasha* promenade].

TAMBOUR, [tam'-bōōer], *n.* a small drum with tiny bells or cymbals attached, a tambourine; a bass drum; a frame, resembling a drum, on which embroidery is done; a species of embroidery worked with gold and silver threads; (*arch.*) a round stone like a drum forming part of a column; (*fort.*) a circular palisade as a defence work for a gate. [Arab. *tambur* drum].

TAMBOURINE, [tam'-bor-ēn'], *n.* a light, shallow drum with a single head and tinkling disks of metal attached to the sides, used for beating out a rhythm as an accompaniment for a dance. [Fr. *tambourin*].

TAMBOURINE

TAME (1), [tām], *adj.* made or disciplined to be responsive to authority, *esp.* to human control; having a nature freed of savagery; subdued, submissive; domesticated; passive; insipid, dull. [OE. *tam*].

TAME (2), [tām], *v.t.* to make tame, to accustom to human command and influence, to domesticate, discipline to human habitation, to make obedient by eliminating any tendencies to wildness and savagery; to make submissive, subdue, curb. [ME *tamien* to tame].

TAMELESS, [tām'-les], *adj.* savage, wild, untamable.

TAMELY, [tām'-li], *adv.* in a tame manner.

TAMENESS, [tām'-nes], *n.* the state of being tame, unresisting submission; lack of vitality.

TAMER, [tām'-er], *n.* one who tames or subdues.

TAMIL (1), [tam'-il], *n.* a Dravidian language spoken in Southern India and Northern Ceylon; one whose native tongue is Tamil. [Native].

TAMIL (2), [tam'-il], *adj.* of, or pertaining to, Tamil or the Tamils.

TAMIS, [tam'-i], *n.* a worsted cloth used for straining sauces; a strainer made of tammy; tammy. [Fr. *tamis* sieve].

TAMISE, [tam-ēz'], *n.* tammy.

TAMKIN, [tam'-kin], *n.* a plug for a barrel, a cannon stopper, a tampion. [*Var.* of TAMPION].

TAMMANY, [tam'-an-i], *n.* originally a society in New York with charitable aims, now a powerful political organization with its headquarters in Tammany Hall.

TAMMY (1), [tam'-i], *n.* a thin worsted cloth used for straining sauces, a strainer; this cloth highly glazed and used for curtains. [Uncert.].

TAMMY (2), [tam'-i], *n.* (*coll.*) a tam-o'-shanter. [TAM O' SHANTER].

TAM-O'-SHANTER, [tam'-ō-shant'-er], *n.* a broad flat cap or bonnet of knitted wool. [*Tam o' Shanter* in the poem by Robert Burns].

TAMP, [tamp], *v.t.* to stop up a hole bored in a rock for blasting with a plug of clay; to obstruct explosion by way of this hole. [Uncert.].

TAMPAN, [tam'-pan'], *n.* a South African tick with a poisonous bite. [Native].

TAMPER, [tamp'-er], *v.i.* **to t. with,** to interfere, meddle with. [*Var.* of TEMPER].

TAMPERER, [tamp'-er-er], *n.* a schemer, meddler.

TAMPICIN, [tamp'-is-in], *n.* a resin obtained from the root of *Ipomæa simulans*. [*Tampico* a town in Mexico].

TAMPING, [tamp'-ing], *n.* the act of filling up of a hole in a rock for the purpose of blasting it; the plug used in such a process.

TAMPION, see TOMPION.

TAMPOE, [tam'-pō], *n.* an Indian fruit resembling an apple. [Native].

TAMPON, [tam'-pon], *n.* (*surg.*) a plug for stopping bleeding. [OFr. *tampon* bung].

TAMPONADE, [tam'-pon-ād], *n.* (*med.*) a method of stopping bleeding by means of a tampon.

TAMPONAGE, [tam'-pon-ij], *n.* (*med.*) the application of, the principle of employing, tampons.

TAMTAM, [tam'-tam'], *n.* a tomtom. [~TOMTOM].

TAN (1), [tan], *n.* a tone of brown imparted to the skin by the sun; the colour of tan, a golden or nut brown; bark bruised and used in the process of tanning; discarded bark from which tannic acid has been extracted. [Fr. *tan*].

TAN (2), [tan], *adj.* having the colour of tan; golden brown, tanny.

TAN (3), (tanning, tanned), [tan], *v.t. and i.* to convert (leather) by steeping in tannic acid; to make brown; (*slang*) to beat, thrash, flog; to become brown in the complexion from exposure to the sun's rays.

TANA, [tah'-na], *n.* an Indian police-station. [Hind. *thana*].

TANAGER, [tan'-a-jer], *n.* an American bird of brilliantly coloured plumage, allied to the finches. [Braz. *tangara*].

TANAGRINE, [tan'-ag-rīn], *adj.* like, or relating to, the tanager.

TANAGROID, [tan'-ag-roid], *adj.* similar to a tanager. [TANAGER and Gk. *oeides* like].

TAN-BED, [tan'-bed'], *n.* a bed made of spent tan; (*hort.*) a bark-bed.

TANDEM (1), [tan'-dem], *n.* a bicycle made for two, with the seats one behind the other, the front rider being in control of the handle-bars; a carriage with two horses harnessed one behind the other. [L. *tandem* at length].

TANDEM (2), [tan'-dem], *adj.* made for two people who sit one behind the other; placed or accommodating one behind or after another.

TANG (1), [tang], *n.* a strong flavour usually of an astringent nature; a penetrating smell; a prolongation of a blade which fits into the hilt or handle. [OIcel. *tange* dagger].

TANG (2), [tang], *n.* a harsh, clanging sound.

TANG (3), [tang], *n.* a kind of seaweed; a tangle. [Dan. *tang* seaweed].

TANG (4), [tang], *v.t.* to provide with a spike, to fit into a handle or shaft.

TANG (5), [tang], *v.t. and i.* to clash together; to clang; to cause to ring loudly; to ring loudly with a metallic sound. [Imitative].

TANGENCY, [tan'-jen-si], *n.* the state of being tangent; a contact or touching.

TANGENT (1), [tan'-jent], *n.* a junction at a point without intersection; (*geom.*) a straight line which touches a curve without cutting it.

TANGENT (2), [tan'-jent], *adj.* meeting at a point without intersecting. [L. *tangens* touching].

TANGENTIAL, [tan-jen'-shal], *adj.* relating to, or in the direction of, a tangent.

TANGENTIALLY, [tan-jen'-shal-i], *adv.* in a tangential manner, in the direction of a tangent.

TANGERINE, [tan'-jer-ēn'], *n.* a native of Tangier; a species of small, scented orange, flattened at opposite ends.

TANGHIN, [tang'-gin], *n.* a Madagascar evergreen tree, the kernel of the fruit yielding a deadly poison. [Native].

TANGIBILITY, [tan'-ji-bil'-i-ti], *n.* tangibleness.

TANGIBLE, [tanj'-ibl], *adj.* capable of being touched, experienced through the sense of touch, tactile, material, concrete; (*fig.*) definite, clear in outline, not vague in form; not visionary, practical. [LL. *tangibilis*].

TANGIBLENESS, [tan'-jibl-nes], *n.* the quality of being tangible.

TANGIBLY, [tan'-jib-li], *adv.* in a tangible manner.

TANGLE (1), [tang'-gl], *n.* a disorderly knot of threads, a mass of interwoven strands hard to disengage; a state of confusion; a kind of seaweed; a dredger consisting of a series of fibre mops. [~Dan. *tang* seaweed].

TANGLE (2), [tang'-gl], *v.t. and i.* to form into a tangle; to become tangled.

TANGLE-PICKER, [tang'-gl-pik'-er], *n.* a shore bird, the turnstone, *Strepsilas interpres*.

TANGLINGLY, [tang'-gling-li], *adv.* in a tangled manner.

TANGLY, [tang'-gli], *adj.* full of tangles, muddled, mixed; covered with tangle.

TANGO (1), [tang'-gō], *n.* an Argentine dance; the French version of this dance. [SpanAmer. *tango*].

TANGO (2), [tang'-gō], *v.i.* to dance the tango.

TANGY, [tang'-i], *adj.* possessing a tang.

TAN-HOUSE, [tan'-hows], *n.* a building in which tanner's bark is stored.

TANIST, [tan'-ist], *n.* in Ireland, the lord or proprietor of a tract of land; the elected heir of a living Irish chief. [Ir. *tanaiste* prince's heir].

TANISTRY, [tan'-ist-ri], *n.* in Ireland, a system by which the chief of a clan held a tenure of lands only for life, the successor being appointed by family election.

TANK (1), [tangk], *n.* a large receptacle, usually rectangular and made of metal, for storing water, oil, or gas, a cistern, basin, reservoir; a chamber in a locomotive for storing water; (*milit.*) a heavily armoured tracked vehicle mounted with guns, and used in attack. [Portug. *tanque*].

TANK (2), [tangk], *v.i.* **to t. up,** to fill the tank of a car or engine with fuel.

TANKAGE, [tangk'-ij], *n.* (space for) storage of water of fuel in tanks; the cost of this.

TANKARD, [tangk'-erd], *n.* a vessel for containing drink, usually made of metal and with a capacity of half a pint or a pint, some designs including a hinged lid. [OFr. *tancquard*].

TANK-ENGINE, [tangk'-en'-jin], *n.* a small type of locomotive requiring no fuel tender.

TANKER, [tangk'-er], *n.* a ship built for transporting petroleum in bulk.

TANNABLE, [tan'-abl], *adj.* capable of being tanned.

TANNAGE, [tan'-ij], *n.* the process of tanning; the materials used in tanning.

TANNATE, [tan'-āt], *n.* (*chem.*) a salt of tannic acid.

TANNER (1), [tan'-er], *n.* one whose craft is to tan hides.

TANNER (2), [tan'-er], *n.* (*slang*) a sixpence. [Uncert.].

TANNERY, [tan'-er-i], *n.* a workshop used for tanning; the process of tanning.

TANNIC, [tan'-ik], *adj.* relating to, or derived from, tannin.

TANNIN, [tan'-in], *n.* tannic acid, an astringent obtained from the bark of oak trees, and used in the manufacture of ink, leather, etc.

TANNING, [tan'-ing], *n.* the process or the craft of converting raw hides into leather.

TANPIT, [tan'-pit], *n.* a vat containing tan in which raw hides are laid.

TANREC, TENREC, [tan'-rek], *n.* a small insectivorous mammal, *Centetes ecaudatus*, allied to the hedgehog. [Malagasy *tandraka*].

TANSPUD, [tan'-spud], *n.* a tool designed for peeling the bark from oak and other trees. [TAN (1) and SPUD].

TAN-STOVE, [tan-stōv], *n.* a hothouse enclosing a bark-bed.

TANSY, [tan'-zi], *n.* (*bot.*) a bitter aromatic plant of the genus *Tanacetum*, bearing clusters of rayless yellow flowers. [OFr. *tanasie*].

TANSY

TANTALIC, [tan-tal'-ik], *adj.* of, containing, tantalum in its higher valency.

TANTALITE, [tant'-a-līt], *n.* (*min.*) a mineral forming in black crystals of tantalic acid, tin, iron, and a little magnesium. [Swed. *tantalit*].

TANTALIZATION, [tant'-al-iz'-ā'-shun], *n.* the act of tantalizing; the state of being tantalized.

TANTALIZE, [tant'-al-īz], *v.t.* to raise to a pitch of frustrated expectation by exhibiting that which fulfils a desire but keeping it out of reach, to torment deliberately by continually retracting a proffered promise.

TANTALIZER, [tant'-al-īz-er], *n.* one who tantalizes.

TANTALIZING, [tant'-al-īz-ing], *adj.* characterized by teasing or tormenting.

TANTALIZINGLY, [tant'-al-īz'-ing-li], *adv.* in a tantalizing manner, so as to tantalize.

TANTALUM, [tant'-al-um], *n.* the metallic element denoted by Ta, very durable, and used in making lamp filaments. [TANTALUS].

TANTALUS, [tant'-al-us], *n.* a decanter stand with a special locking device; a genus of storks, the wood-ibis. [Gk. *Tantalos*, a King of Phrygia, son of Zeus, who revealed the secrets of the gods and was condemned to stand in water up to the chin which he could never drink, while above his head delicious fruits were suspended which receded when he tried to reach for them].

TANTAMOUNT, [tant'-amownt], *adj.* equal, equivalent, in value or signification, having a similar effect. [AFr. *tant amunter* to amount to so much].

TANTIVY (1), [tan'-tiv-i], *n.* a hunting cry; a flourish on a hunting horn. [Imitative].

TANTIVY (2), [tan-tiv'-i], *adj.* swift, pelting.

TANTIVY (3), [tan-tiv'-i], *adv.* with great speed.

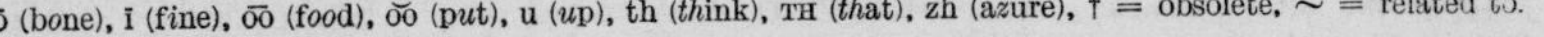

TANTONY, [tan'-ton-i], *n.* the smallest pig in a litter. [(SAIN)T and ANTHONY].
TANTRA, [tan'-tra], *n.* a branch of Hindu literature dealing with the mystical and magical. [Skr. *tantra* loom].
TANTRISM, [tan'-trizm], *n.* the principles embodied in the tantra.
TANTRIST, [tan'-trist], *n.* a student of the tantra.
TANTRUM, [tan'-trum], *n.* an outburst of ill-temper. [Unkn.].
TAN-VAT, [tan'-vat'], *n.* a vat containing tan in which hides are steeped.
TANYARD, [tan'-yahd], *n.* a yard or establishment where the tanning of leather is carried on.
TAOISM, [tow'-izm], *n.* the religion of China founded on principles traditionally established by Lao-tze. [Chin. *tao* way].
TAP (1), [tap], *n.* a light blow, contact with a small area for the shortest possible time; the sound made by such an impact; (*milit.*) lights-out signal.
TAP (2), [tap], *n.* a safety device consisting of a short piece of piping fitted with a control screw which stops up or releases the flow of a liquid held in storage; a tool for cutting the thread of an internal screw; a tap-room; special beer or liquor stored in a vat or cask; **on t.,** stored in a cask ready to hand; **on t.,** (*slang*) always available. [OE. *tæppa*].

TAP

TAP (3), (tapping, tapped), [tap], *v.t. and i.* to hit by means of a tap, to strike lightly and quickly, to touch, making a brief impact; to insert a tapping in; to knock lightly, to give a series of taps, to rap. [OFr. *taper*].
TAP (4), (tapping, tapped), [tap], *v.t.* to fit with a tap; to draw (liquor) from a cask fitted with a tap, to broach; to penetrate in order to make use of available resources; (*slang*) to extract money from; to draw accumulated fluid from (the body); **to t. a line,** to listen in secretly to another's conversation over a telephone. [OE. *tæppan*].
TAPA, [tah'-pa], *n.* a thin fabric of Polynesian cloth made from the inner bark of a species of *Broussonetia*. [Polynesian *tapa*].
TAPBOLT, [tap'-bōlt], *n.* a headed screw designed for use without a nut.
TAPCINDER, [tap'-sind'-er], *n.* the slag produced during the process of puddling iron.
TAP-DANCE (1), [tap'-dahnts], *n.* a dance accompanied by syncopated music to which heel and toe are tapped in rhythm.
TAP-DANCE (2), [tap'-dahnts], *v.i.* to perform a tap-dance.
TAP-DANCER, [tap'-dahns-er], *n.* a person who tap-dances.
TAP-DANCING, [tap'-dahns-ing], *n.* a kind of dancing based on the tapping of heel and toe in rhythmic accompaniment to light music.
TAPE (1), [tāp], *n.* a narrow strip of material, usually of cotton fabric or silk, used for fastening purposes; a roll or strip of paper on which are recorded messages transmitted by an electrical telegraphic system; **red t.,** dilatoriness and enslavement to routine arising from traditional usage and bureaucratic outlook. [OE. *tæppe*].
TAPE (2), [tāp], *v.t.* to fasten by means of tape; to measure; **to have (someone) taped,** (*slang*) to possess a shrewd estimate of (someone's) character.
TAPE-LINE, [tāp'-lin], *n.* a tape measure.
TAPE-MACHINE, [tāp'-ma-shēn'], *n.* the instrument which receives and records on a paper tape messages transmitted by an electrical telegraphic system.
TAPE-MEASURE, [tāp'-mezh'-er], *n.* a tape marked by lines indicating distance, used in dressmaking.
TAPER (1), [tāp'-er], *n.* a thin wax candle; a small light. [OE. *tapur*].
TAPER (2), [tāp'-er], *adj.* having a long shape gradually narrowing to a point at one end.
TAPER (3), [tāp'-er], *v.t. and i.* to cause to taper; to have a form which gradually narrows to a point at one end.
TAPERING, [tāp'-er-ing], *adj.* becoming gradually smaller at one end, narrowing in one direction down to a point.
TAPERINGLY, [tāp'-er-ing-li], *adv.* in a tapering way.
TAPESTRIED, [tap'-est-rid], *adj.* hung with tapestry.
TAPESTRY, [tap'-est-ri], *n.* a hand-woven fabric of linen, wool, silk, etc., into which are worked designs, patterns, pictures, by means of coloured thread, the whole piece being used in interior decoration for adorning walls; a piece of textile in imitation of this, but manufactured by machinery in mass production. [OFr. *tapisserie*].
TAPETI, [tap'-et-i], *n.* the Brazilian rabbit, *Lepus brasiliensis*. [Native].
TAPEWORM, [tāp'-wurm], *n.* a ribbon-shaped worm parasitic in the intestines.
TAPIOCA, [tap'-i-ō'-ka], *n.* grains from the root of the cassava, a species of *Manihot*; **t. pudding,** a pudding made from tapioca baked in milk. [Braz. *tipioca* juice of the cassava].
TAPIR, [tā'-per, ta'-pēer], *n.* one of a genus of ungulates allied to the rhinoceros, of which one species, *Tapirus indicus*, is Malayan, and the four others are South American. [Braz. *tapira*].

TAPIR

TAPIROID, [tāp'-er-oid], *adj.* resembling or characteristic of the tapirs. [TAPIR and Gk. *oeides* like].
TAPIS, [tap'-ē], *n.* the cover of a council table; **(up)on the t.,** under consideration. [Fr. *tapis* carpet].
TAPOTEMENT, [tap-ōt'-ment], *n.* (*med.*) light massage. [Fr. *tapotement* a tapping].
TAPPET, [tap'-it], *n.* a projecting arm or lever of a machine transmitting movement to another part.
TAPPET-LOOM, [tap'-it-lōōm], *n.* a type of loom functioning by means of tappets.
TAPPING, [tap'-ing], *n.* (*surg.*) the operation of draining accumulated fluid from the body; (*elect.*) a connection made in an intermediate part of a coil, etc.
TAPPIT, [tap'-it], *adj.* tufted, crested. [~TOP (4)].
TAP-ROOM, [tap'-rōōm], *n.* a bar in a public-house in which casks of beer are stored and where cheaper drinks are served.
TAP-ROOT, [tap'-rōōt], *n.* a straight enlarged root tapering towards the base.
TAPSTER, [tap'-ster], *n.* a man employed to draw ale or other liquor, a barman. [OE. *tæppestre*].
TAR (1), [tah(r)], *n.* a thick, black, sticky liquid with a resinous smell, obtained by the destructive distillation of wood or coal, used in the preparation of road surfaces, antiseptics, and preservatives; **a touch of the t. brush,** a physical attribute denoting Negro antecedents. [OE. *teoru*].
TAR (2), [tah(r)], *n.* (*coll.*) a sailor. [Abbreviation of TARPAULIN].
TAR (3), (tarring, tarred), [tah(r)], *v.t.* to coat or smear with tar; **to t. with the same brush,** to give the same characteristics to.
TARADIDDLE, TARRADIDDLE, [ta'-ra-didl'], *n.* (*coll.*) a lie. [Invented].
TARANTELLA, [ta'-rant-el'-a], *n.* a vigorous Neapolitan dance; the music in 6-8 time adapted to it. [It. *tarantella*].
TARANTISM, [ta'-rant-izm], *n.* a nervous affliction manifested as a dancing mania, formerly supposed to be caused by the bite of the tarantula. [*Taranto* a town in south Italy].
TARANTULA, [ta-rant'-yōō-la], *n.* a large venomous spider of the genus *Lycosa*. [It. *tarantola*].
TARAXACIN, [ta-raks'-as-in], *n.* (*chem.*) a bitter substance extracted from the dandelion.
TARAXACUM, [ta-raks'-ak-um], *n.* (*bot.*) a genus of twenty-five species of plants including the dandelion, *Taraxacum officinale*, with composite yellow flowers.
TARBOOSH, [tah'-bōōsh], *n.* a brimless cap of felt, a fez; the basic support of the turban. [Arab. *tarbush*].
TARDAMENTE, [tahd'-a-ment'-i], *adv.* (*mus.*) slowly. [It. *tardamente*].
TARDIGRADE (1), [tahd'-i-grād], *n.* a tardigrade animal.
TARDIGRADE (2), [tahd'-i-grād], *adj.* (*zool.*) belonging to the sloths, moving or stepping slowly, sluggish. [L. *tardigradus* stepping slowly].
TARDILY, [tahd'-i-li], *adv.* in a tardy way.
TARDINESS, [tahd'-i-nes], *n.* the quality of being tardy, slowness; lateness.
TARDO, [tahd'-ō], *adv.* (*mus.*) slowly. [It. *tardo*].
TARDY, [tahd'-i], *adj.* slow to act, dilatory, sluggish; given to delaying, late in performance, action, or arrival, behind time. [L. *tardus* slow].
TARE (1), [tāer], *n.* a weed that grows in cornfields, a vetch; the plant, *Vicia hirsuta*. [ME. *tare*].

TARE (2), [tāer], *n.* (*comm.*) allowance or rebate on dutiable goods for weight of packing; the weight of the container. [Arab. *tarhah* a reject].
TARE (3), [tāer], *v.t.* to calculate in respect of tare.
TARGE, [tahj], *n.* a small shield; a target. [OFr. *targe* shield].
TARGET, [tah'-get], *n.* a shield or buckler of a small kind; a mark to aim at, *esp.* a board bearing a series of concentric circles with the smallest one in the centre known as a bull; the objective of an air-raid; **t. area,** the area in which a target stands. [OFr. *targuete*].
TARGETED, [tah'-get-id], *adj.* provided or armed with a target.
TARGETEER, [tah'-get-ēer'], *n.* an infantry soldier armed with a target.
TARGUM, [tah'-gum], *n.* an Aramaic version or paraphrase of the Old Testament. [Chaldean *targum* interpretation].
TARGUMIC, [tah-gōō'-mik], *adj.* relating to, found in, resembling, the Targums.
TARGUMIST, [tah'-gōōm-ist], *n.* the writer of a Targum; a student of the Targums.
TARGUMISTIC, [tah'-gōō-mist'-ik], *adj.* Targumic.
TARIFF (1), [ta'-rif], *n.* a list of goods or articles chargeable for duty on import or export; the amount of a list of items or services with their respective cost, *esp.* the price list of a hotel. [Arab. *tacrif* knowledge].
TARIFF (2), [ta'-rif], *v.t.* to draw up, list, in the form of a tariff.
TARIFF-WALL, [ta'-rif-wawl'], *n.* a means of checking imports by setting high duties payable on foreign goods.
TARLATAN, [tah'-lat-an], *n.* a kind of muslin with an open-work texture. [Fr. *tarlatane*].
TARMAC, [tah'-mak'], *n.* (*prot.*) a road material of tar and macadam. [TAR (1) and MAC(ADAM)].
TARN, [tahn], *n.* a small lake on a mountain side or moor. [~OIcel. *tjörn*].
TARNATION, [tahn-ā'-shun], *n.* (*coll.*) an expletive, a form of damnation.
TARNISH (1), [tahn'-ish], *n.* a film of colour forming on a metallic surface when exposed to the action of heat or damp; (*fig.*) a dulling or tainting of qualities, a blemish.
TARNISH (2), [tahn'-ish], *v.t. and i.* to cause to become dull of surface by exposure to heat, air, or damp, to spoil by affecting the lustre of, to sully; to become tarnished; (*fig.*) to detract from the purity of. [Fr. *ternir*].
TARNOWITZITE, [tahn'-ō-vits'-īt], *n.* (*min.*) a variety of aragonite containing carbonate of lead. [Germ. *tarnowitzit*].
TARO, [tah'-rō], *n.* (*bot.*) the tropical plant, *Colocasia antiquorum*, cultivated for its edible rhizomes. [Polynesian *taro*].
TAROC, [tah'-rok], *n.* tarot. [~*Next*].
TAROT, [ta'-rō], *n.* a pack of seventy-eight playing cards, used *esp.* in fortune-telling; the game played with these. [It. *tarocchi*].
TARPAN, [tah'-pan], *n.* the small wild horse inhabiting the steppes of Central Asia. [Tartar *tarpan*].
TARPAULIN, [tah-pawl'-in], *n.* canvas treated with a coating of tar to render it waterproof; a sailor, a tar. [TAR (1) and PALLING].
TARPAULING, [tah-pawl'-ing], *n.* tarpaulin.
TARPON, [tah'-pon'], *n.* the large jew-fish, *Megalops atlanticus*, of the herring family. [Uncert.].

TARPON

TARRACE, [ta'-ras], *n.* a volcanic pumice rock resembling puzzuolana used as cement; the cement made of this. [Germ. *tarrase*].
TARRADIDDLE, [ta'-ra-didl'], see TARADIDDLE.
TARRAGON, [ta'-ra-gon], *n.* (*bot.*) an aromatic herb, *Artemisia Dracunculus*; **t. vinegar,** vinegar flavoured with tarragon. [MedL. *taragonia* from Gk. *drakon* dragon].
TARRAGONA, [ta'-ra-gōn'-a], *n.* a kind of Spanish red wine. [*Tarragona* in Spain].

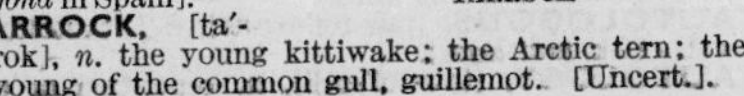
TARROCK

TARROCK, [ta'-rok], *n.* the young kittiwake; the Arctic tern; the young of the common gull, guillemot. [Uncert.].
TARRY (1), [tah'-ri], *adj.* resembling tar, having some of the characteristics of tar; covered with tar.
TARRY (2), [ta'-ri], *v.t. and i.* †to wait for; to be slow in coming, to linger; to remain in a place. [OE. *tergan* to vex].
TARSAL, [tah'-sal], *adj.* relating to the tarsus.
TARSALGIA, [tah-sal'-ji-a], *n.* pain affecting the tarsus. [Gk. *tarsos* foot and *algos* pain].
TARSIA, [tah'-si-a], *n.* a kind of mosaic of coloured woods popular in Italy in the 15th century. [It. *tarsia*].
TARSIER, [tah'-si-er], *n.* an arboreal species of the lemur, *Tarsius spectrum*, found in the East Indies. [Fr. *tarsier*].
TARSUS, [tah'-sus], *n.* the part of the foot to which the leg is articulated, consisting of the ankle, heel, and instep; a joint of the foot in insects. [Gk. *tarsos* the flat of the foot].
TART (1), [taht], *n.* an edible dish consisting of a layer of pastry covered with fruit or jam, which may be of sandwich form by the addition of a top layer of pastry, often decorated with twists of pastry, the whole being baked in an oven and eaten hot or cold as a sweet; a small variety of this eaten as a cake. [OFr. *tarte*].
TART (2), [taht], *n.* (*slang*) a young girl with sex appeal, *esp.* one of easy virtue. [Abbreviated from SWEETHEART].
TART (3), [taht], *adj.* sharp to the taste, acid, sour, sharp; (*fig.*) having an ungenerous, caustic nature, severe. [OE. *teart* acid].
TARTAN (1), [taht'-an], *n.* a woollen fabric with a pattern of stripes crossing each other at right angles, the various patterns being distinctive of particular Highland clans. [Unkn.].
TARTAN (2), [taht'-an], *n.* a small vessel used on the Mediterranean coast, and fitted with one mast and a lateen sail. [Arab. *taridah* small ship].
TARTAN (3), [taht'-an], *adj.* made of tartan.
TARTAR (1), [tah'-ter], *n.* a hard crust of tartrate of potassium forming on the sides of a cask in which fermentation of wine has taken place; a deposit of calcium phosphate accreting on the teeth; **t. emetic,** a compound consisting of tartaric acid combined with oxide of antimony and potassium; **cream of t.,** a substance obtained by boiling and filtering tartar, added to baking-powder, and used medicinally, etc.
TARTAR (2), [tah'-ter], *n.* a native of Tartary in Central Asia; an adult with an ungovernable temper; a mischievous, undisciplined child. [Pers. *tatar*].
TARTAR (3), [tah'-ter], *adj.* of, relating to, the Tartars.
TARTAREAN, [tah-tāer'-i-an], *adj.* relating to Tartarus, characteristic of hell. [L. *Tartareus*].
TARTAREOUS†, [tah-tāer'-i-us], *adj.* (*chem.*) consisting of, or characteristic of, tartar.
TARTARIAN, [tah-tāer'-i-an], *adj.* relating to Tartary; **T. lamb,** (*bot.*) a species of *Dicksonia*.
TARTARIC, [tah-ta'-rik], *adj.* relating to, containing, obtained from, tartar.
TARTARIZATION, [tah'-ter-iz-ā'-shun], *n.* (*chem*). the process of forming tartar.
TARTARIZE, [tah'-ter-iz], *v.t.* (*chem.*) to impregnate with tartar; to treat with the salt of tartar.
TARTAROUS, [tah'-ter-us], *adj.* consisting of tartar; having some of the qualities of tartar.
TARTARUM, [tah'-ter-um], *n.* tartar.
TARTARUS, [tah'-ter-us], *n.* (*myth.*) the deepest, darkest wastes below the surface of the earth; the infernal regions, hell, where the wicked were believed to be punished. [Gk. *Tartaros*].
TARTISH, [tah'-tish], *adj.* inclined to be tart.
TARTLET, [taht'-let], *n.* a small tart.
TARTLY, [taht'-li], *adv.* in a tart manner; severely.
TARTNESS, [taht'-nes], *n.* the quality of being tart; (*fig.*) acerbity of language or manner.
TARTRATE, [taht'-rāt], *n.* (*chem.*) a salt of tartaric acid.
TARTUFFE, [tah-tewf'], *n.* a religious hypocrite. [*Tartuffe*, a character in Molière's play].
TARTUFFISH, [tah-tewf'-ish], *adj.* somewhat affected by pretentious religiosity.
TAR-WATER, [tah'-wawt'-er], *n.* an old-fashioned medicine consisting of water impregnated with tar.
TASEOMETER, [ta'-si-om'-it-er], *n.* an instrument for measuring strains in buildings. [Gk. *tasis* stretching and METER].
TASIMETER, [tas-im'-it-er], *n.* an instrument for recording changes in atmospheric pressure. [Gk. *tasis* stretching and METER].
TASK (1), [tahsk], *n.* a specific piece of work, study, or labour imposed by another, *esp.* such as is likely to

prove troublesome; any job of work which involves laborious effort.

TASK (2), [tahsk], *v.t.* to impose a task on; to provide a severe test of, to tax. [L. *taxare* to value].

TASKER, [tahsk'-er], *n.* one who imposes a task.

TASK-FORCE, [tahsk'-faws], *n.* (*U.S.*) a force dispatched to carry out a specific military or naval undertaking; a commando. [TASK (1) and FORCE (1)].

TASKMASTER, [tahsk'-mahst-er], *n.* a person authorized to impose a task; an authority which demands unremitting effort.

TASKWORK, [tahsk'-wurk], *n.* piece-work.

TASLET†, [tas'-let], *n.* a small tasse. [OFr. *tasselet*].

TASMANIAN (1), [taz-mā'-ni-an], *n.* a native of Tasmania. [A. *Tasman*, the explorer].

TASMANIAN (2), [taz-mā'-ni-an], *adj.* relating to, coming from, made in, Tasmania; **T. devil,** a small flesh-eating marsupial, *Sarcophilus ursinus*; **T. wolf,** a carnivorous marsupial of nocturnal habits.

TASS, [tas], *n.* a small drinking-cup; a drink contained by this. [OFr. *tasse* cup].

TASSE†, [tas], *n.* (*hist.*) a small plate of armour for protecting the thighs, a number of them attached to the corslet forming a kilt. [OFr. *tasse* purse].

TASSEL (1), [tas'-el], *n.* a knot of threads or cords with a bunched fringe hanging from it, the whole forming a decorative pendant for dress or furniture; a book marker in the form of a ribbon sewn to the top of the binding; **t. grass,** (*bot.*) tassel pondweed. [MedL. *tassellus*].

TASSEL (2), (tasselling, tasselled), [tas'-el], *v.t.* to decorate with tassels.

TASTABLE, [tāst'-abl], *adj.* able to be tasted; savoury.

TASTE (1), [tāst], *n.* the act of tasting; the sense by which flavours are distinguished by means of the tongue and palate; a sensation experienced by this sense; the distinctive flavour of anything; that which is tasted; natural or trained appreciation of material providing aesthetic or intellectual experience, a critical discernment of the artistic; a liking, a preference; an example, a sample; a small portion.

TASTE (2), [tāst], *v.t.* and *i.* to experience, perceive, sense by means of the tongue and palate, to test for characteristic flavour; to try by eating a small portion or by sipping, to sample; to participate in, experience; to enjoy; to exercise the sense of taste; to possess a characteristic flavour. [OFr. *taster*].

TASTEFUL, [tāst'-fool], *adj.* characterized by a pleasant flavour, savoury; possessed of, showing, good taste.

TASTEFULLY, [tāst'-fool-i], *adv.* in a tasteful way.

TASTEFULNESS, [tāst'-fool-nes], *n.* the quality of being tasteful.

TASTELESS, [tāst'-les], *adj.* characterized by absence of taste, insipid; showing no good taste.

TASTELESSLY, [tāst'-les-li], *adv.* in a tasteless way.

TASTELESSNESS, [tāst'-les-nes], *n.* the quality of being tasteless.

TASTER, [tāst'-er], *n.* a person employed to taste food or liquor; a sample, specimen; that which contains a sample; a publisher's reader.

TASTILY, [tāst'-i-li], *adv.* in a tasty manner.

TASTY, [tāst'-i], *adj.* characterized by an agreeable flavour, pleasant to the taste, *esp.* savoury.

TAT (1), [tat], *n.* a native Indian pony. [Abbreviated from TATTOO].

TAT (2), (tatting, tatted), [tat], *v.i.* to make a coarse lace with thickish threads. [Unkn.].

TA-TA, [ta-tah'], *int.* (*coll.*) good-bye.

TATLER (1), [tat'-ler], *n.* a tattler.

TATLER (2), [tat'-ler], *n.* the sandpiper, *Totanus hypoleucus*.

TATOUAY, TATOUA, [tat'-ōō-a], *n.* the Peba armadillo, *Tatusia novemcincta*, having an unprotected tail. [Braz. (Tupi) *tatu* armadillo, and *aiba* wounded].

TATTER (1), [tat'-er], *n.* that which is torn or torn off, a shred, a rag. [OIcel. *töturr*].

TATTER (2), [tat'-er], *v.t.* to tear into rags.

TATTERDEMALION, [tat'-er-dem-ā'-li-on], *n.* a person dressed habitually in rags. [Uncert.].

TATTERED, [tat'-erd], *adj.* dressed in rags; torn up into strips.

TATTERY, [tat'-er-i], *adj.* ragged, tatty.

TATTING, [tat'-ing], *n.* lace woven out of coarse, strong threads by a small hand-shuttle; the process of weaving it. [Unkn.].

TATTLE (1), [tatl], *n.* superficial conversation, chatter, gossip, small-talk. [~LGerm. *tateln* to gabble].

TATTLE (2), [tatl], *v.t.* and *i.* to talk superficially about; to gossip. [~LGerm. *tateln* to gabble].

TATTLER, [tat'-ler], *n.* a person who tattles.

TATTLERY, [tat'-ler-i], *n.* futile talk or chit-chat.

TATTLING, [tat'-ling], *adj.* given to chatting.

TATTLINGLY, [tat'-ling-li], *adv.* in a tattling manner.

TATTOO (1), [tat-ōō'], *n.* a military pageant of spectacular scenes presented usually at night; a signal by drum or bugle calling soldiers into barracks for the night; a continuous rapping like a drum roll. [Du. *taptoe*].

TATTOO (2), [tat-ōō'], *n.* an indelible pictorial design on the body made by punctures into which coloured pigments are inserted.

TATTOO (3), [tat-ōō], *v.i.* to beat or sound a tattoo.

TATTOO (4), [tat-ōō'], *v.t.* to decorate by puncturing the skin with a series of small holes into which coloured pigments are inserted so as to form a pictorial design. [Tahiti *tatau*].

TATTY (1), [tat'-i], *n.* a hanging mat or screen of the sweet-smelling cuscus grass which is kept moistened to cool the air, used in the East. [Hind. *tatti* wicker frame].

TATTY (2), [tat'-i], *adj.* tangled, matted; scrappy.

TAU, [taw], *n.* the Greek letter T; a moth, beetle, or fly marked with the shape of this letter. [Gk. *tau* ~Heb. *taw*].

TAUGHT, [tawt], *pret.* and *p.pt.* of TEACH.

TAUNT (1), [tawnt], *n.* a remark calculated to wound another's pride, a penetrating sarcasm, a sneer, a gibe. [TAUNT (4)].

TAUNT (2), [tawnt], *adj.* (*naut.*) tall, towering. [Uncert.].

TAUNT (3), [tawnt], *adv.* (*naut.*) fully rigged. [Uncert.].

TAUNT (4), [tawnt], *v.t.* to wound the pride of, with sneering gibes, to reproach with remarks expressing contempt, to revile. [OFr. *tanter* to provoke].

TAUNTER, [tawnt'-er], *n.* one who taunts.

TAUNTING, [tawnt'-ing], *adj.* having the characteristics of a taunt.

TAUNTINGLY, [tawnt'-ing-li], *adv.* in a taunting manner, sarcastically.

TAUPIE, [taw'-pi], *n.* (*Scots*) a stupid girl. [~Norw. *taape* simpleton].

TAURIAN (1), [taw'-ri-an], *n.* (*astrol.*) a type of person with physical and temperamental characteristics believed to be determined by the ruling of the constellation Taurus.

TAURIAN (2), [taw'-ri-an], *adj.* relating to a bull. [L. *taurus* bull].

TAURIFORM, [taw'-ri-fawm], *adj.* having the form of a bull. [L. *taurus* bull and FORM].

TAURINE (1), [taw'-rin], *n.* (*chem.*) a substance obtained from the bile of the ox.

TAURINE (2), [taw'-rīn], *adj.* having the appearance of, relating to, a bull or bull-fighting. [L. *taurinus*].

TAUROMACHY, [taw-rom'-a-ki], *n.* the practice of bull-fighting; a bull-fight. [Gk. *tauros* bull and *makhe* battle].

TAURUS, [taw'-rus], *n.* the bull, the second sign of the zodiac, which the sun enters about April 20th; (*astrol.*) a constellation which includes the Pleiades. [Gk. *tauros* bull].

TAUT, [tawt], *adj.* stretched tight; secure, firmly connected. [~OE. *togian* to pull].

TAUTEN, [tawt'-en], *v.t.* and *i.* to pull tight, to make taut; to grow taut.

TAUTNESS, [tawt'-nes], *n.* the quality of being taut.

TAUTO-, *pref.* the same. [Gk. *tauto*].

TAUTOCHRONE, [tawt'-ō-krōn], *n.* (*math.*) a curve on which a body, starting from any point on the curve, will reach the lowest point under a given pressure or force of gravity in the same specified time. [TAUTO- and Gk. *khronos* time].

TAUTOCHRONOUS, [taw-tok'-ron-us], *adj.* of or relating to a tautochrone.

TAUTOG, [taw-tog'], *n.* the edible black fish, *Tautoga onitis*, found off the coasts of North America. [NAmerInd. *tautauog*].

TAUTOLOGICAL, [tawt'-ō-loj'-ik-al], *adj.* relating to, having the characteristics of, tautology.

TAUTOLOGICALLY, [tawt'-ō-loj'-ik-al-i], *adv.* in a tautological way.

TAUTOLOGIST, [taw-tol'-oj-ist], *n.* one who uses tautology.

TAUTOLOGIZE, [taw-tol'-oj-īz], *v.i.* to repeat the same idea in different words.

TAUTOLOGOUS, [taw-tol'-og-us], *adj.* tautological. [Gk. *tautologos*].

TAUTOLOGY, [taw-tol'-o-ji], *n.* repetition of an

idea, previously expressed, in different words, redundancy. [Gk. *tautologia*].

AUTOPHONICAL, [tawt'-ō-fon'-ik-al], *adj.* characterized by tautophony.

AUTOPHONY, [taw-tof'-on-i], *n.* a repetition of the same sound, *esp.* vocal. [Gk. *tautophonia*].

AVERN, [tav'-ern], *n.* a house licensed to carry on a retail trade in alcoholic drinks, an inn, a public-house, hotel. [Fr. *taverne* from L. *taberna* shop].

AVERNER, [tav'-ern-er], *n.* one who keeps a tavern, an innkeeper; a person who frequents public-houses.

AW (1), TEW, [taw], *n.* a special variegated marble; a game at marbles; the line toed by marble players. [Unkn.].

AW (2), [taw], *v.i.* to shoot the taw marble.

AW (3), [taw], *v.t.* to convert (skins) into leather by treating them with salts, etc. [OE. *tawian*].

AWDRILY, [tawd'-ri-li], *adv.* in a tawdry fashion.

AWDRINESS, [tawd'-ri-nes], *n.* the state of being tawdry.

AWDRY, [tawd'-ri], *adj.* cheap, gaudy, flashy in substance and appearance, decorated with cheap jewellery or ornaments, *esp.* when these are old and tarnished. [*St. Audrey* on whose day a fair was held annually].

AWER, [taw'-er], *n.* a person who taws hides.

AWERY, [taw'-er-i], *n.* a place where skins are prepared.

AWNINESS, [tawn'-i-nes], *n.* the state of being tawny.

AWNY, [taw'-ni], *adj.* that is golden or bronzed in colour, coloured with a rich yellow-brown, tanned, sunburnt. [ME. *tauni* from OFr. *tanner* to tan].

AWSE, [tawz], *n.* (*Scots*) a thick leather strap, used for beating schoolboys. [Uncert.].

AWTOG, [taw-tog'], *n.* a tautog.

AX (1), [taks], *n.* a means of levying money from the public for national purposes by assessing marketable goods, property, or income; a heavy burden, an exorbitant demand.

AX (2), [taks], *v.t.* to subject to a system of assessment, to compel to pay a specific sum of money as a contribution to national expenditure; to burden, to subject to exacting demands; **to t. with,** to bring an accusation against. [L. *taxare* to value, estimate].

AXABILITY, [taks'-a-bil'-i-ti], *n.* the state of being taxable.

AXABLE, [taks'-abl], *adj.* able to be taxed; legally subject to a tax claim.

AXABLENESS, [taks'-abl-nes], *n.* the state of being taxable, taxability.

AXABLY, [taks'-ab-li], *adv.* so as to be taxable.

AXATION, [taks-ā'-shun], *n.* the act of taxing; the system of taxes; the total sum of money raised either from an individual or from the whole nation.

AX-COLLECTOR, [taks'-kol-ekt'-or], *n.* an official appointed to collect taxes.

AXEL, [taks'-el], *n.* a North American badger. [Native].

AXER, [taks'-er], *n.* one who taxes.

AX-FREE, [taks'-frē'], *adj.* exempt from deductions for tax payments.

AX-GATHERER†, [taks'-gaTH'-er-er], *n.* a tax-collector.

AXI (1), [taks'-i], *n.* a light, low-horse-powered motor-car hired by passengers, the mileage being measured by a taximeter; any motor-car for passenger hire. [Abbreviated from TAXIMETER].

AXI (2), [taks'-i], *v.i.* to go by taxi; (*aeron.*) to glide along a surface with the impetus remaining after the engine is shut off, to free-wheel.

AXICAB, [taks'-i-kab'], *n.* a taxi.

AXIDERMAL, [tak'-si-durm'-al], *adj.* of, or relating to, taxidermy.

AXIDERMIC, [taks'-i-durm'-ik], *adj.* relating to the craft of preserving skins and stuffing animals.

AXIDERMIST, [taks'-i-durm'-ist], *n.* an expert in taxidermy.

AXIDERMY, [taks'-i-durm'-i], *n.* the craft of preserving and stuffing the skins of dead animals and birds so as to present them in a lifelike form. [Gk. *taxis* arrangement and *derma* skin].

AXI-DRIVER, [taks'-i-drīv'-er], *n.* the person employed in driving a taxi.

AXIMETER, [taks'-im-ēt-er], *n.* an instrument which registers automatically on a dial the mileage of a taxi and the fare charged to the passenger. [Fr. *taximètre* from *taxe* charge and *mètre* METER].

AXIN, [taks'-in], *n.* a poisonous substance extracted from the leaves of the yew. [~L. *taxus* yew].

TAXI-RANK, [taks'-i-rangk'], *n.* an official park where taxis wait for fares.

TAXIS, [taks-is], *n.* (*surg.*) an operation by which dislocated parts may be reset by manipulation; (*zool.*) arrangement in categories. [Gk. *taxis* arrangement].

TAXONOMICAL, [taks'-ō-nom'-i'-kal], *adj.* relating to taxonomy.

TAXONOMIST, [taks-on'-om-ist], *n.* an expert in taxonomy.

TAXONOMY, [taks-on'-om-i], *n.* the branch of a science dealing with the classification of its subjects. [Gk. *taxis* arrangement and *nomos* law].

TAXPAYER, [taks'-pā-er], *n.* a person subject to taxes.

TAZZA, [tat'-sa], *n.* a saucer-shaped vessel or vase mounted on a pedestal. [It. *tazza* cup].

TE, [tē], *n.* the seventh note in the tonic-solfa scale, si. [Invented].

TEA (1), [tē], *n.* the dried leaves of the tea-plant, *Thea*; the drink made by infusing these in boiling water; a meal taken in the afternoon or early evening; **Paraguay t.,** maté, *Ilex paraguaiensis*; **t.-plant,** (*bot.*) an evergreen shrub, *Lycium chinense*. [Chin. *chai*].

TEA (2), [tē], *n.* a tea-rose.

TEA (3), [tē], *v.i.* to take tea.

TEA-BOARD, [tē'-bawd], *n.* a tea-tray made of wood.

TEA-CADDY, [tē'-kad'-i], *n.* a box or container for holding tea.

TEA-CAKE, [tē'-kāk], *n.* a large round scone, usually toasted, buttered, and eaten at tea.

TEA-CANISTER, [tē'-kan'-ist-er], *n.* a tea-caddy.

TEACH (1), [tēch], *n.* the last boiler in a sugar-refining works. [Unkn.].

TEACH (2), (taught), [tēch], *v.t. and i.* to lay facts, details, examples, methods, before, with the aim of impressing the memory, to transfer knowledge to, *esp.* by means of a systematic series of studies, to instruct, to develop the intelligence or abilities of; counsel, advise. [OE. *tæcan*].

TEACHABILITY, [tēch'-a-bil'-i-ti], *n.* the state of being teachable.

TEACHABLE, [tēch'-abl], *adj.* able to be taught; apt to learn.

TEACHABLENESS, [tēch'-abl-nes], *n.* the state of being teachable.

TEACHER, [tēch'-er], *n.* one who teaches or instructs; a schoolmaster or schoolmistress.

TEACHERSHIP, [tēch'-er-ship], *n.* the official status and duties of a teacher.

TEA-CHEST, [tē'-chest'], *n.* a large box lined with metal foil, suitable for the transport of tea.

TEACHING, [tēch'-ing], *n.* the act or profession of instructing the young or ignorant; instruction.

TEA-CLIPPER†, [tē'-klip'-er], *n.* a fast sailing ship transporting a cargo of tea.

TEA-CLOTH, [tē'-kloth'], *n.* small tablecloth used at tea-time; a small cloth for drying washed crockery.

TEA-COSY, [tē'-kō'-zi], *n.* a thick cover for keeping a teapot warm.

TEACUP, [tē'-kup], *n.* a small cup for drinking tea out of.

TEACUPFUL, [tē'-kup-fōōl], *n.* the amount a teacup will hold.

TEA-DEALER, [tē'-dēl-er], *n.* a merchant who deals in tea in bulk.

TEA-DRINKER, [tē'-dringk'-er], *n.* one who drinks tea, *esp.* to the exclusion of other types of drink.

TEA-FIGHT, [tē'-fit], *n.* (*coll.*) a tea-party.

TEA-GARDEN, [tē'-gahd-en], *n.* a garden or estate where tea is cultivated; a garden where afternoon tea is served to the public.

TEAK, [tēk], *n.* a tree of the genus *Tectona*, notable for the hardness of its wood. [Malay *tekka*].

TEA-KETTLE, [tē'-ketl'], *n.* a comparatively small kettle in which water is boiled for making tea.

TEAL, [tēl], *n.* the small wild duck, *Anas crecca*. [ME. *tele*].

TEA-LEAF, [tē'-lēf], *n.* a leaf of the tea-plant; one of the fragments of the dried leaf used for making tea.

TEAM (1), [tēm], *n.* a pair, or more, of domesticated animals in draught harness; a group of which each member takes a part in a particular form of work or play, a number of players constituting a side. [OE. *team* team of oxen].

TEAM (2), [tēm], *v.t.* to harness or work together as a team.

TEAMSTER, [tēm'-ster], *n.* one who drives a team.

TEAMWISE, [tēm'-wiz], *adv.* in the manner of a team.

TEAM-WORK, [tēm'-wurk], *n.* work done by a team;

ō (bone), ī (fine), ōō (food), ŏŏ (put), u (up), th (*th*ink), TH (*th*at), zh (a*z*ure), † = obsolete, ~ = related to.

work attempted or achieved by co-operative effort.
TEA-PARTY, [tē'-pah-ti], *n.* a party held in the afternoon at which tea is served.
TEAPOT, [tē'-pot'], *n.* a vessel of china or metal designed with a handle, lid, and spout, in which tea is made.
TEAPOY, [tē'-poi], *n.* a low stand for supporting a tea-tray. [Hind. *tipai*].
TEAR (1), [tēer], *n.* a small drop of translucent moisture secreted by the lachrymal gland in the eye, stimulated by emotion, *esp.* sorrow, and by physical aggravation; a small drop of anything, *esp.* pear-shaped, resembling a tear; **crocodile tears,** grief which is not genuine. [OE. *tear*].
TEAR (2), [tāer], *n.* a split or rent in a piece of a material.
TEAR (3), (tore, torn), [tāer], *v.t. and i.* to make a crude long division in by a violent pull, to divide violently into separate parts, to split into two pieces each being left with jagged edges, to rend; to lacerate; to shatter, destroy; to remove, pull, or drag away by violence so as to leave rough and ragged edges at the breaking points; to put into a state of hostility, to disturb violently; to experience tearing; to move, run, hastily and excitedly, to rush; **to t. away,** to rush off; **to t. down,** to hurry impetuously along; **to t. from,** to deprive by force; **to t. oneself away,** to leave with reluctance; **torn between,** reacting equally to two claims on one's allegiance. [OE. *teran*].
TEAR-DROP, [tēer'-drop'], *n.* a single tear dropping from the eye.
TEAR-DUCT, [tēer'-dukt], *n.* (*anat.*) a passage leading from the lachrymal gland to the nasal orifice.
TEARER, [tāer'-er], *n.* one who tears.
TEARFUL, [tēer'-fōōl], *adj.* full of tears, weeping.
TEARFULLY, [tēer'-fōōl-i], *adv.* in a tearful manner.
TEARFULNESS, [tēer'-fōōl-nes], *n.* the state of being tearful.
TEAR-GAS, [tēer'-gas'], *n.* a type of poison gas which affects the lachrymal glands, and induces a flow of tears.
TEARING, [tāer'-ing], *adj.* (*coll.*) tremendous, violent.
TEARLESS, [tēer'-les], *adj.* not accompanied by tears.
TEA-ROOM, [tē'-rōōm], *n.* a room in a restaurant or hotel where teas are served.
TEA-ROSE, [tē'-rōz], *n.* (*bot.*) a variety of rose, light yellow in colour.
TEARPIT, [tēer'-pit], *n.* a small hollow below the eye in the skull of horses and other ungulates.
TEASE (1), [tēz], *n.* a person who likes teasing others.
TEASE (2), [tēz], *v.t.* to comb out (a matted surface or mass), *esp.* by brushing with a teasel; to annoy, irritate, by persistent impertinence or mockery, to pester, worry. [OE. *tǣsan* to pull apart].
TEASEL (1), [tēz'-el], *n.* (*bot.*) a plant of the genus *Dipsacus*, with a head of hooked prickles set firmly together; the head of this plant adapted as a brush for raising the nap of cloth. [OE. *tǣsel*].
TEASEL (2), (teaselling, teaselled), [tēz'-el], *v.t.* to brush with a teasel.
TEASELER, [tēz'-el-er], *n.* one who uses the teasel.
TEASER (1), [tēz'-er], *n.* a bird of any of several species of *Megalestris*; a skua.
TEASER (2), [tēz'-er], *n.* one who teases; a difficult problem.
TEA-SERVICE, [tē'-surv'-is], *n.* a set of crockery for use at tea-time.
TEA-SET, [tē'-set'], *n.* a tea-service.
TEA-SHOP, [tē'-shop'], *n.* a shop where teas are sold.
TEASINGLY, [tēz'-ing-li], *adv.* in a teasing manner.
TEASPOON, [tē'-spōōn], *n.* a small spoon for stirring tea or coffee in a teacup.
TEASPOONFUL, [tē'-spōōn-fōōl], *n.* the amount contained by a teaspoon; the eighth of a fluid ounce.
TEAT, [tēt], *n.* the small projecting part of the breast, the nipple; the rubber nipple of a child's feeding bottle. [OFr. *tete*].
TEA-TABLE, [tē'-tābl], *n.* a small table on which tea-things are laid.
TEA-THINGS, [tē'-thingz], *n.(pl.)* the crockery and utensils used at tea; a tea-service; a tea-set.
TEA-TIME, [tē'-tīm], *n.* the time of day when tea is taken. [TEA (1) and TIME (1)].
TEA-TRAY, [tē'-trā], *n.* a small tray from which tea may be served.
TEA-TREE, [tē'-trē], *n.* (*bot.*) the plant the leaves of which are dried to produce tea, *Thea sinensis*.
TEA-URN, [tē'-urn'], *n.* a large container, usually of metal, in which water is boiled for tea.
TEA-WAGGON, [tē'-wag'-on], *n.* a small trolley for wheeling tea-things round a drawing-room.
TEBETH, [tē'-beth], *n.* the tenth month of the Jewish ecclesiastical year, corresponding to the moon December to January. [Heb. *tebeth*].
TEC, [tek], *n.* (*slang*) a detective. [(DE)TEC(TIVE)].
TECHILY†, see TETCHILY.
TECHINESS†, see TETCHINESS.
TECHNIC, [tek'-nik], *n.* technique; (*pl.*) the technic side of any subject, *esp.* of the arts. [Gk. *tekhnik* made by art].
TECHNICAL, [tek'-nik-al], *adj.* relating to, ma according to, technique; accurately descriptiv from the aspect of technique.
TECHNICALITY, [tek'-ni-kal'-i-ti], *n.* technica ness; a particular item peculiar to a special bran of knowledge; a detail of formal procedure.
TECHNICALLY, [tek'-nik-al-i], *adv.* in a technic way; by means of technique.
TECHNICALNESS, [tek'-nik-al-nes], *n.* the sta of being technical.
TECHNICIAN, [tek-nish'-an], *n.* a technical exper
TECHNIQUE, [tek-nēk'], *n.* knowledge of establishe theory and practice connected with any activity; sk based on systematic application of accepted principle method in execution. [Fr. from Gk. *tekhnikos* of art
TECHNOCRACY, [tek-nok'-ra-si], *n.* scienti organization and control of industry by skill technicians.
TECHNOCRAT, [tek'-nō-krat'], *n.* an advocate o or technical expert in, technocracy.
TECHNOLOGICAL, [tek'-nō-loj'-ik-al], *adj.* rela ing to technology.
TECHNOLOGIST, [tek-nol'-oj-ist], *n.* an expe in technology.
TECHNOLOGY, [tek-nol'-oj-i], *n.* the science the mechanical and industrial arts. [Gk. *tekhne* a and *logos* speech].
TECHY†, see TETCHY.
TECTIBRANCHIATE, [tek'-ti-brang'-ki-āt], *a* (*zool.*) having gills covered by a mantle, as a gastrop mollusc. [L. *tectus* covered and Gk. *bragkhion* gil
TECTONIC, [tek-ton'-ik], *adj.* relating to the a of building. [Gk. *tektonikos* skilful in building].
TECTONICS, [tek-ton'-iks], *n.(pl.)* the art of buildin
TECTRICES, [tek'-tris-ēz], *n.(pl.)* (*ornith.*) the sma feathers which cover the quill feathers in the wing or tail of a bird. [L. *tectrix* covering].

TECTRICES

TED, (tedding, tedded), [ted], *v.t.* to spread (new-mown grass) for drying. [OIcel. *tethja* to spread].
TEDDART†, [ted'-er], *n.* tether.
TEDDER, [ted'-er], *n.* one who teds; an agricultur machine for tedding grass.
TEDDY BEAR, [ted'-i-bāer'], *n.* a children's toy be made of yellowish-brown plush; **t. b. overcoat,** a kin of loose overcoat made of material resembling th used for teddy bears. [~*Teddy* (Theodore) Roosevel U.S. president 1901-9, and big-game hunter].
TE DEUM, [tē'-dē'-um], *n.* a hymn sung on thank giving occasions. [L. *Te Deum* "Thee, O God," t first words of the hymn].
TEDIOUS, [tē'-di-us], *adj.* producing boredom, e hausting and boring by reason of length, monoto ously dull. [L. *taediosus*].
TEDIOUSLY, [tē'-di-us-li], *adv.* in a tedious manne
TEDIOUSNESS, [tē'-di-us-nes], *n.* the quality being tedious.
TEDIUM, [tē'-di-um], *n.* the state of being tediou wearisomeness. [L. *taedium*].
TEE (1), [tē], *n.* the letter T; that which has this form.
TEE (2), [tē], *n.* an ornament in the shape of an umbrell usually hung with bells, erected on the top of Burmese pagoda. [Burmese *h'ti* umbrella].
TEE (3), [tē], *n.* a small pile of sand or support of rubbe wood, etc., on which a golf ball is placed for the driv the teeing-ground where it is permissible to u such a support; a mark at quoits. [Unkn.].
TEE (4), [tē], *adj.* having the shape of the letter T.
TEE (5), [tē], *v.t.* to place on a tee; **to t. up,** to lay on slightly elevated piece of ground.
TEEING-GROUND, [tē'-ing-grownd] *n.* the flat pie of ground which marks the beginning of a hole on golf-course.
TEE-BOX, [tē'-boks], *n.* the box containing sand o the teeing-ground.
TEEM (1), [tēm], *v.t. and i.* to pour out, to rain heavil to gush, discharge. [OIcel. *tæma*].

EEM (2), [tēm], *v.t. and i.* to produce; to produce in abundance; to contain in great numbers; to be prolific. [OE. *teman*].
EEMER, [tēm'-er], *n.* one who, or that which, teems.
EEMFUL, [tēm'-fŏol], *adj.* characterized by teeming; prolific, brimful.
EEMING, [tēm'-ing], *adj.* producing young; fertile, fruitful.
EEMLESS, [tēm'-les], *adj.* barren.
EENS, [tēnz], *n.(pl.)* the period of adolescence between thirteen and nineteen years of age.
EENY, [tē'-ni], *adj.* very small, tiny. [*Var.* of TINY].
EEPEE, see TEPEE.
EETH, [tēth], *n.(pl.)* of TOOTH.
EETHE, [tēTH], *v.i.* to have the teeth erupting through the gums. [ME. *teth(en)*].
EETHING, [tēTH'-ing], *n.* the process by which the teeth of a baby gradually pierce the gums.
EETOTAL, [tē-tō'-tal], *adj.* relating to, adhering to, teetotalism; non-alcoholic. [Reduplication on the initial *t* of TOTAL].
EETOTALISM, [tē-tō'-tal-izm], *n.* the theory and practice of total abstinence from intoxicating drinks.
EETOTALLER, [tē-tō'-tal-er], *n.* a person who practises total abstinence from all intoxicating drinks.
EETOTUM, [tē-tō'-tum], *n.* a type of top with numbers marked on the sides, one side being marked with a T standing for *totum*, "all" (of the stake).
EG, [teg], *n.* a young sheep that has never been shorn.
EGMEN, (*pl.* **tegmina**), [teg'-men], *n.* (*anat., bot.*) inner coat; integument. [L. *tegmen* covering].
EGULAR, [teg'-yŏo-ler], *adj.* relating to, resembling, a tile; composed of tiles. [~L. *tegula* tile].
EGULARLY, [teg'-yŏo-ler-li], *adv.* so as to be tegular.
EGULATED, [teg'-yŏo-lāt-id], *adj.* (*zool.*) overlapping in form.
EGUMENT, [teg'-yŏo-ment], *n.* a natural covering of an organism; the skin, integument. [L. *tegumentum* covering].
EGUMENTARY, [teg-yŏo-ment'-er-i], *adj.* relating to, or consisting of, teguments.
E-HEE, [tē-hē'], *n.* a high, silly sound made in laughing. [Echoic].
EIL, [tēl], *n.* the lime-tree. [L. *tilia*].
EINDS, [tēndz], *n.(pl.)* (*Scots leg.*) tithes. [OIcel. *tiundi*].
EINOSCOPE, [tī'-nō-skōp], *n.* (*opt.*) an instrument which alters the proportions of an object seen through its specially arranged prisms. [Gk. *teino* I extend and SCOPE].
EKNONYMY, [tek-non'-im-i], *n.* a tribal practice of naming the parent from the child. [Gk. *teknon* child and *onoma* name].
ELAMONES, [tel'-am-ō'-nēz], *n.(pl.)* (*arch.*) representations in stone of men supporting entablatures. [Gk. *telamon*].
ELARY, [tel'-er-i], *adj.* relating to, forming, a web. [L. *tela* web].
ELAUTOGRAPH, [tel-awt'-ō-graf], *n.* an instrument transmitting writing by electricity. [TELE- and AUTO- and GRAPH (1)].
ELE-, *pref.* afar, at a distance. [Gk. *tele* far off].
ELE-ARCHICS, [tel'-i-ahk'-iks], *n.(pl.)* remote control (of aircraft) by wireless. [TELE- and Gk. *arkhikos* relating to rule].
ELEDU, [tel'-ed-ōō'], *n.* the Malayan badger, *Mydaus meliceps*. [Native].
ELEFERIC (1), [tel'-i-fe'-rik], *n.* a teleferic railway.
ELEFERIC (2), [tel'-i-fe'-rik], *adj.* of, pertaining or relating to, transport by means of a telpher. [Fr. *téléphérique*].
ELEGONY, [tel-eg'-on-i], *n.* influence on the offspring of a mother through her previous mating with a different sire. [TELE- and Gk. *gonos* seed].
ELEGRAM, [tel'-i-gram'], *n.* a telegraphic message. [TELE- and Gk. *gramma* that which is written].
ELEGRAMMIC, [tel'-i-gram'-ik], *adj.* relating to telegrams; concise.
ELEGRAPH (1), [tel'-i-graf], *n.* an apparatus consisting of two instruments, a transmitter and receiver, between which an electric circuit is made and broken in a form of code conveying a message over a distance; any device by which a message is signalled. [TELE- and GRAPH (1)].
ELEGRAPH (2), [tel'-i-graf], *v.t. and i.* to send by telegraph; to transmit by telegraph; to signal.
ELEGRAPHIC, [tel'-i-graf'-ik], *adj.* relating to the telegraph; communicated by telegraph; concise in form of verbal expression.
ELEGRAPHICALLY, [tel'-i-graf'-ik-al-i], *adv.* in a telegraphic manner or form, by means of signals.
TELEGRAPHIST, [tel-eg'-raf-ist], *n.* a telegraph operator.
TELEGRAPHY, [tel-eg'-raf-i], *n.* the system of telegraphic communication. [TELE- and Gk. *graphia* writing].
TELEMARK, [tel'-i-mahk], *n.* a kind of turn in skiing. [*Telemark*, a district in Norway].
TELEOLOGICAL, [tel'-i-ō-loj'-ik-al], *adj.* of, or relating to, teleology.
TELEOLOGICALLY, [tel'-i-ō-loj'-ik-al-i], *adv.* in a teleological way.
TELEOLOGIST, [tel'-i-ol'-oj-ist], *n.* one who accepts the principles of teleology.
TELEOLOGY, [tel'-i-ol'-oj-i], *n.* the doctrine that each of the parts of nature is designed to fulfil a particular end, *esp.* as being so designed by God. [Gk. *telos* end and *logos* speech].
TELEPATHIC, [tel'-i-path'-ik], *adj.* of, pertaining to, or resembling, telepathy.
TELEPATHICALLY, [tel'-i-path'-ik-al-i], *adv.* by telepathy.
TELEPATHIST, [tel-ep'-ath-ist], *n.* a believer in or practitioner of telepathy.
TELEPATHY, [tel-ep'-ath-i], *n.* the transmitting of thoughts from one person to another without any apparent means, thought transference. [TELE- and Gk. *pathos* suffering].
TELEPHONE (1), [tel'-i-fōn], *n.* an electrical instrument for transmitting conversation over a distance, *esp.* a single unit consisting of a mouthpiece, earpiece, and stand. [TELE- and PHONE (2)].
TELEPHONE (2), [tel'-i-fōn], *v.t. and i.* to transmit by means of telephone; to use the telephone.
TELEPHONIC, [tel'-if-on'-ik], *adj.* transmitted by, relating to, the telephone.
TELEPHONICALLY, [tel'-if-on'-ik-al-i], *adv.* by means of the telephone.
TELEPHONIST, [tel-ef'-on-ist], *n.* a person employed to operate a telephone or telephone switchboard; †an expert in telephony.
TELEPHONOGRAPH, [tel'-i-fōn'-ō-graf], *n.* an instrument which makes a phonographic record of a telephone message. [TELE- and PHONOGRAPH].
TELEPHONY, [tel-ef'-on-i], *n.* the process and system of sending messages by telephone.
TELEPHOTE, [tel'-i-fōt], *n.* an instrument for transmitting pictures by electricity. [TELE- and Gk. *phos photos* light].
TELEPHOTO, (tel'-i-fōt'-ō], *n. and adj.* (*coll.*) a telephotograph, telephotographic. [TELEPHOTO(GRAPHIC)].
TELEPHOTOGRAPH, [tel'-i-fōt'-ō-graf], *n.* a photograph received and recorded by means of the telephote. [TELE- and PHOTOGRAPH].
TELEPHOTOGRAPHIC, [tel'-i-fōt'-ō-graf'-ik], *adj.* of, pertaining to, or based on a system of lenses, invented by Dallmeyer, by which the distance between the emulsion and the objective is less than the focal length of the system. [TELE(SCOPE) and PHOTOGRAPHIC].
TELEPHOTOGRAPHY, [tel'-i-fō-tog'-ra-fi], *n.* photography using a telephote.
TELEPRINTER, [tel'-i-print'-er], *n.* a form of typewriter operated electrically from a distance. [TELE- and PRINTER].
TELESCOPE (1), [tel'-i-skōp], *n.* an optical instrument, made in different designs of varying complexity, the basis of which is a long tube fitted inside with an arrangement of lenses which makes the viewed object appear nearer. [TELE- and SCOPE].
TELESCOPE (2), [tel'-i-skōp], *v.t. and i.* to cause to pack, *esp.* by force, into a small space by fitting the parts one inside another, as the sections of a collapsible telescope; to fit one into another by pressure.

TELESCOPE

TELESCOPIC, [tel'-i-skop'-ik], *adj.* relating to a telescope; seen only by means of a telescope; having sections which fit one in another.
TELESCOPICALLY, [tel'-i-skop'-ik-al-i], *adv.* by means of the telescope.
TELESCOPIST, [tel-esk'-op-ist], *n.* an expert in the use of the telescope.
TELESEME, [tel'-i-sēm], *n.* an electric apparatus for obtaining service in hotels, etc., by registering signals on an indicator. [TELE- and Gk. *sema* sign].
TELESTICH, [tel'-i-stik], *n.* a poem in which the last

letters of each line when read successively make up a word. [Gk. *telos* end and *stikhos* a line].

TELETYPE, [tel'-i-tīp], *n.* an electric telegraph, which prints automatically. [TELE- and TYPE (1)].

TELEVISE, [tel'-i-vīz], *v.t.* to transmit by television.

TELEVISION, [tel'-i-vizh'-un], *n.* the process and system by which images of moving objects are transmitted, and reproduced as a picture by a receiving set operated by electricity. [TELE- and VISION].

TELEVISOR, [tel'-i-vīz-er], *n.* an apparatus for transmitting or reproducing images by television. [~TELEVISION].

TELIC, [tel'-ik], *adj.* involving an end or purpose. [Gk. *telikos* final].

TELL, (**told**), [tel], *v.t. and i.* to communicate orally, to express in words; to narrate; to inform by word of mouth, to divulge, disclose; to report, admit, explain; to command; to distinguish, disclose; to indicate, teach; †to count, produce as a reckoning; to reveal a secret; to have a distinct effect; **to t. on,** to inform against; to weary, exhaust. [OE. *tellan* to reckon, say].

TELLER, [tel'-er], *n.* one who tells; a narrator; a bank clerk who pays out money; one who counts votes.

TELLERSHIP, [tel'-er-ship], *n.* the office or duties of a teller.

TELLING, [tel'-ing], *adj.* having a great effect.

TELLINGLY, [tel'-ing-li], *adv.* in a telling manner, effectively.

TELLTALE (**1**), [tel'-tāl], *n.* a person who does not keep to himself the confidences given by another, a sneak, a gossip; an indicator; an index. [TELL and TALE].

TELLTALE (**2**), [tel'-tāl], *adj.* tending to reveal what is secret, blabbing.

TELLURAL, [tel-yōōer'-al], *adj.* relating to the earth. [~L. *tellus* earth].

TELLURATE, [tel'-yōō-rāt], *n.* a salt of telluric acid.

TELLURETTED, [tel'-yōō-ret-id], *adj.* combined with tellurium.

TELLURIC, [tel-yōōer'-rik], *adj.* relating to the earth; containing tellurium in its higher valency.

TELLURIDE, [tel'-yōō-rīd], *n.* a compound of tellurium and a metal.

TELLURION, [tel-yōōer'-i-on], *n.* an apparatus for illustrating the movements of the earth. [~L. *tellus* the earth].

TELLURITE, [tel'-yōō-rīt], *n.* telluric ochre, a native oxide of tellurium.

TELLURIUM, [tel-yōōer'-i-um], *n.* (*chem.*) a rare metalloid element, denoted by Te.

TELLUROUS, [tel'-yōō-rus], *adj.* pertaining to tellurium in its lower valency.

TELPHER (**1**), [tel'-fer], *n.* a truck travelling along a cable.

TELPHER (**2**), [tel'-fer], *adj.* pertaining to telpherage. [TELE- and Gk. *phero* I bear].

TELPHERAGE, [tel'-fer-ij], *n.* transport by means of a telpher line.

TELPHER LINE, [tel'-fer-līn'], *n.* an electric overhead cable for trucks.

TELSON, [tel'-son], *n.* (*biol.*) the last section of certain crustaceans. [Gk. *telson* limit].

TELUGU, [tel'-ōō-gōō], *n.* a language of Southern India.

TEMENOS, [tem'-in-os], *n.* the sacred precincts round a temple. [Gk. *temenos*].

TEMERARIOUS, [tem'-er-āer'-i-us], *adj.* rash, headstrong, reckless. [L. *temerarius*].

TEMERARIOUSLY, [tem'-er-āer'-i-us-li], *adv.* in a temerarious way.

TEMERARIOUSNESS, [tem'-er-āer'-i-us-nes], *n.* the quality of being temerarious, temerity.

TEMERITY, [tim-e'-rit-i], *n.* extreme boldness, rashness, audacity. [L. *temeritas*].

TEMEROUS, [tem'-er-us], *adj.* rash, unduly bold.

TEMEROUSLY, [tem'-er-us-li], *adv.* in a temerous fashion.

TEMPEAN, [tem-pē'-an], *adj.* pertaining to the vale of *Tempe* in Thessaly, resembling it in idyllic beauty.

TEMPER (**1**), [tem'-per], *n.* balance, calmness or composure of the emotions and feelings; the quality or state of mind; a passing mood; anger, annoyance, irritation; the condition of a material (a combination of elasticity and hardness) produced by tempering.

TEMPER (**2**), [tem'-per], *v.t. and i.* to moderate the properties of (something) by admixture of something else of neutral or opposite qualities; to produce a desired consistency in (clay) by kneading with water; to make (a metal) hard and elastic by suddenly cooling it from a great temperature and then reheating it to possess or be capable of attaini[ng] a desired consistency or quality. [OE. *tempria[n]*].

TEMPERA, [tem'-per-a], *n.* a painting medium in whi[ch] no oil is used; distemper, such as is used in fresco[es]. [It. *tempera*].

TEMPERAMENT, [tem'-per-a-ment], *n.* ment[al,] moral, and emotional constitution, natural dispo[si]tion; a violent passionate nature; (*mus.*) the slightly i[n]accurate adjustment of the intervals on a keyboa[rd] instrument which makes it possible to play it ha[r]moniously in all keys. [L. *temperamentum*].

TEMPERAMENTAL, [tem'-per-a-ment'-al], *adj.* pe[r]taining to temperament; having a violent, passiona[te] unstable disposition.

TEMPERAMENTALLY, [tem'-per-a-ment'-al-i], *ad[v.]* in a temperamental manner, because of temperamen[t].

TEMPERANCE, [tem'-per-ants], *n.* the condition [or] quality of being temperate; moderation; self-contr[ol]; *esp.* moderation in the use of or total abstinen[ce] from alcoholic or intoxicant drinks; **t. hotel,** a hot[el] where alcoholic liquor cannot be bought. [OF. *temperaunce* from L. *temperantia*].

TEMPERATE, [tem'-per-at], *adj.* equable, moderat[e,] not given to excess, self-controlled; (of climate) sho[w]ing neither extreme cold nor extreme heat.

TEMPERATELY, [tem'-per-at-li], *adv.* in a tempera[te] way.

TEMPERATENESS, [tem'-per-at-nes], *n.* the cond[i]tion of being temperate.

TEMPERATIVE, [tem'-per-at-iv], *adj.* having t[he] quality of tempering.

TEMPERATURE, [tem'-per-ach-er], *n.* the conditi[on] or degree of heat or cold; the warmth or lack of it in living organism; excessive heat of the blood, feveris[h]ness; **to take someone's t.,** to measure the te[m]perature of the blood by a clinical thermometer; **t[o] have a t.,** to be feverish. [L. *temperatura*].

TEMPERED, [tem'-perd], *adj.* moderate; moderate[ly] adjusted in constitution by tempering or admixtur[e].

TEMPERER, [tem'-per-er], *n.* someone or somethi[ng] that tempers.

TEMPEST (**1**), [tem'-pest], *n.* rough violent weather, storm; (*fig.*) anything resembling this, a violen[t] noisy upheaval of some sort. [L. *tempestas*].

TEMPEST (**2**), [tem'-pest], *v.t. and i.* (of persons) to a[ct] like a tempest; to raise into a tempest.

TEMPEST-BEATEN, [tem'-pest-bēt'-en], *adj.* beate[n] and battered with storms.

TEMPEST-TOST, [tem'-pest-tost'], *adj.* tossed an[d] beaten by tempests, weather-beaten.

TEMPESTUOUS, [tem-pest'-yōō-us], *adj.* ve[ry] stormy, turbulent, resembling a tempest; (*fi[g.]*) agitated, excited.

TEMPESTUOUSLY, [tem-pest'-yōō-us-li], *ad[v.]* with great commotion, in a tempestuous manner.

TEMPESTUOUSNESS, [tem-pest'-yōō-us-nes], [*n.*] storminess, the quality of being tempestuous.

TEMPLAR, [temp'-ler], *n.* a member of a religio[us] military order founded at the end of the twelf[th] century to protect the Holy Sepulchre; a studen[t] of law, *esp.* one occupying chambers in the Templ[e,] London, once held by the Knights Templar[s;] one of an order of Freemasons; a member of th[e] temperance society called *Good Templars.* [L. *templarius*].

TEMPLATE, see TEMPLET.

TEMPLE (**1**), [templ], *n.* a building used to worship in; a sacred religious building, a shrine or fane, a church; **the T.,** the sacred building at Jerusalem which wa[s] the centre of Hebrew worship of Jehovah; th[e] two Inns of Court (the *Inner* and *Middle Temple*) in London, standing on a site formerly held by th[e] Knights Templars. [OE. *tempel* from L. *templum*].

TEMPLE (**2**), [templ], *n.* one of the flattened parts [of] the head on each side of the forehead. [OFr. *templ[e]* ~L. *tempora* the fatal spot].

TEMPLE (**3**), [templ], *n.* device on a loom for keepi[ng] the cloth taut. [Unkn.].

TEMPLED, [templd], *adj.* having many temples.

TEMPLET, TEMPLATE, [tem'-plet], *n.* (*building*) [a] flat horizontal piece of wood laid under the end of [a] girder, beam, etc., to distribute the weight; a thi[n] wooden or metal plate used as a guide by stone-, metal[-] or wood-workers. [Unkn.].

TEMPO, [tem'-pō], *n.* (*mus.*) time or speed of mov[e]ment. [It. *tempo*].

TEMPORAL (**1**), [tem'-por-al], *n.* (*anat.*) a tempor[al] bone.

TEMPORAL (**2**), [tem'-por-al], *adj.* of, pertaining [or] adjacent to, the temples.

TEMPORAL (**3**), [tem'-por-al], *adj.* existing und[er] the condition of, controlled or limited by, pertaining to, time; of or pertaining to time as the essential and limiting condition of human life, terrestrial, pertaining to life in this world, earthly, gross and material, transient, worldly; pertaining to worldly and civil affairs as contrasted with things spiritual and ecclesiastical; (*gram.*) pertaining to tense. [L. *temporalis*].

TEMPORALITY, [tem'-por-al'-it-i], *n.* worldly possessions; (*pl.*) the material possessions of the Church. [LL. *temporalitas*].

TEMPORALLY, [tem'-por-al-i], *adv.* with regard to temporal things.

TEMPORALNESS, [tem'-por-al-nes], *n.* (*rare*) worldliness, the quality of being temporal.

TEMPORALTY, [tem'-por-al-ti], *n.* a secular possession, temporality.

TEMPORARILY, [tem'-per-er-i-li], *adv.* for a limited time only.

TEMPORARINESS, [tem'-per-er-i-nes], *n.* the condition of being temporary.

TEMPORARY, [tem'-per-er-i], *adj.* lasting for a limited time only, transient, not permanent.

TEMPORIZATION, [tem'-por-ī-zā'-shun], *n.* the action of temporizing.

TEMPORIZE, [tem'-por-īz], *v.i.* to avoid or delay by hesitation and evasion the taking of a definite or irrevocable decision, in order to gain time; to serve or appear to serve only immediate necessity, bending one's principles to the needs of the moment to compromise.

TEMPORIZER, [tem'-por-ī-zer], *n.* one who temporizes.

TEMPORIZING (1), [tem'-por-ī-zing], *n.* temporization.

TEMPORIZING (2), [tem'-por-ī-zing], *adj.* time-serving; evasive and hesitant.

TEMPORIZINGLY, [tem'-por-ī-zing-li], *adv.* in a temporizing way.

TEMPT, [tempt], *v.t.* to incite, entice; urge, solicit, persuade (to do wrong); to persuade; to allure, attract; (*poet.*) to try, attempt; to test. [OFr. *tempter* from L. *temptare* to touch].

TEMPTABLE, [temp'-tabl], *adj.* able or liable to be tempted.

TEMPTATION, [temp-tā'-shun], *n.* the action of tempting; the condition of being tempted; something that tempts.

TEMPTER, [temp'-ter], *n.* one who tempts or entices to evil; **the T.,** the Devil.

TEMPTING, [temp'-ting], *adj.* attractive, enticing, alluring.

TEMPTINGLY, [temp'-ting-li], *adv.* so as to entice, in a tempting fashion.

TEMPTINGNESS, [temp'-ting-nes], *n.* the condition of being tempting.

TEMPTRESS, [temp'-tres], *n.* a female tempter.

TEMSE, [tems], *n.* (*dial.*) a sieve or strainer. [ME. *temys*].

TEMSE-BREAD, [tems'-bred'], *n.* bread made of well sifted flour.

TEMSE

TEMULENCE, [tem'-yōō-lents], *n.* drunkenness.

TEMULENCY, [tem'-yōō-len-si], *n.* temulence. [LL. *temulentia*].

TEMULENT, [tem'-yōō-lent], *adj.* drunken; given to or connected with drunkenness.

TEN (1), [ten], *n.* the numeral one less than eleven; the symbol for this; a group of persons, things, etc., of this number. [OE. *tene*].

TEN (2), [ten], *adj.* twice five, one less than eleven; **t. times as,** (*coll.*) much more, much better, etc.

TENABILITY, [ten'-ab-il'-it-i], *n.* the condition of being tenable.

TENABLE, [ten'-abl], *adj.* able to be held; sensible, logical; able to be defended. [Fr. *tenable*].

TENABLENESS, [ten'-abl-nes], *n.* the quality of being tenable.

TENACE, [ten'-ās], *n.* (in whist) the name given to the position when the first and third best cards in a suit are held by the same player, his opponent having the intermediate card. [Span. *tenaza* tongs].

TENACIOUS, [ten-ā'-shus], *adj.* holding fast, retentive; tough; (of the mind) retentive; obstinate, determined. [~L. *tenax*].

TENACIOUSLY, [ten-ā'-shus-li], *adv.* in a tenacious fashion.

TENACIOUSNESS, [ten-ā'-shus-nes], *n.* tenacity.

TENACITY, [ten-as'-it-i], *n.* obstinacy, resolution; retentiveness; the quality of being tenacious. [L. *tenacitas*].

TENACULUM, [ten-ak'-yōō-lum], *n.* (*surg.*) a sharp hook used in surgical operations. [L. *tenaculum* a holder].

TENAILLE, [ten-āl'], *n.* (*fort.*) an outwork defending an angle between two bastions. [Fr. *tenaille*].

TENAILLON, [ten-āl'-on], *n.* (*fort.*) an outwork erected on each side of a ravelin. [Fr. *tenaillon*].

TENANCY, [ten'-an-si], *n.* a holding or tenure of property in the position of tenant; property held by a tenant.

TENANT (1), [ten'-ant], *n.* (*leg.*) a person holding real estate for a terminable period; a person holding property by payment of rent; (*poet.*) an inhabitant, dweller. [Fr. *tenant*].

TENANT (2), [ten'-ant], *v.t.* to hold or inhabit as a tenant.

TENANTABLE, [ten'-ant-abl], *adj.* able to be held by, fit for, a tenant.

TENANTED, [ten'-ant-id], *adj.* held by a tenant or tenants ; inhabited.

TENANTLESS, [ten'-ant-les], *adj.* empty, having no tenant, unoccupied.

TENANTRY, [ten'-ant-ri], *n.* tenants regarded collectively.

TENCH, [tench], *n.* a freshwater fish, *Tinca vulgaris*. [OFr. *tenche*].

TEND (1), [tend], *v.t.* to look after, protect, provide with necessaries, etc.; (*naut.*) to stand near to ready to manipulate or control (something). [~ATTEND].

TEND (2), [tend], *v.i.* to move or be moved in a certain direction; to be biased or inclined in a certain way; **to t. to,** to result in, be prone to. [Fr. *tendre* from L. *tendere* to stretch].

TENDANCE, [tend'-ants], *n.* the act of tending or caring for. [~ATTENDANCE].

TENDENCY, [tend'-en-si], *n.* bias, partiality, bent, inclination; the action of tending.

TENDENTIOUS, TENDENCIOUS, [ten-den'-shus], *adj.* biased, written or spoken with a special motive. [Germ. *tendenziös*].

TENDER (1), [tend'-er], *n.* one who tends or looks after, an attendant; a ship operating under orders from the captain of another; a railway truck which immediately follows the locomotive, and carries coal and water supplies.

TENDER (2), [tend'-er], *n.* an offer to carry out a specified piece of work at a stated price; money offered to wipe out a debt; **legal t.,** currency legally recognized as fit and acceptable for the payment of debt.

TENDER (3), [tend'-er], *adj.* soft, delicate, fragile, not strong or firm; (of food) succulent, soft; not robust, delicate, weak in health or constitution, not able to stand exposure, easily hurt or injured; immature, having the delicacy of youth; gentle, not strong or vivid, soft; loving, affectionate; kind, considerate; easily pained, morally scrupulous and susceptible; (of a horse) lame, having an inflamed or sprained pastern. [OFr. *tendre* from L. *tener*].

TENDER (4), [tend'-er], *v.t. and i.* to offer to pay (an amount due) or make (a payment) in satisfaction of a claim; to offer, to present (thanks, apologies, etc.); **to t. for,** to make an offer to contract for (a specified piece of work) at a stated price.

TENDERFOOT, [tend'-er-fōōt'], *n.* a new arrival in a colonial settlement; a novice; a new boy scout.

TENDER-HEARTED, [tend'-er-haht'-id], *adj.* gentle, compassionate.

TENDER-HEARTEDLY, [tend'-er-haht'-id-li], *adv.* in a tender-hearted way.

TENDER-HEARTEDNESS, [tend'-er-haht'-id-nes], *n.* the quality of being tender-hearted.

TENDERLING, [tend'-er-ling], *n.* a young, delicate or effeminate person.

TENDERLOIN, [tend'-er-loin], *n.* (*U.S.*) a part of any city largely devoted to amusements; undercut of sirloin. [TENDER (3) and LOIN].

TENDERLY, [tend'-er-li], *adv.* in a tender way.

TENDERNESS, [tend'-er-nes], *n.* the quality of being tender; softness; fragility; compassion, sensitiveness; love; affection, kindness.

TENDING, [tend'-ing], *n.* the act of looking after or attending.

TENDINOUS, [ten'-din-us], *adj.* pertaining to or like a tendon; sinewy.

TENDON, [ten'-don], *n.* (*anat.*) strong tissue which connects a muscle to a bone or some other part. [OFr. *tendon*].

TENDRIL, [ten'-dril], *n.* a small, string-like organ in climbing plants which projects from the stem and winds itself round anything it touches so as to hold the plant up. [Fr. *tendrille*].

TENDRILLAR, [ten'-dril-er], *adj.* pertaining to or resembling a tendril.

TENEBRAE, [ten'-i-brē], *n.(pl.)* (*R.C.*) the offices of Matins and Lauds for the Thursday, Friday, and Saturday of Holy Week, recited in each case on the preceding day, during which services the candles are gradually extinguished. [L. *tenebræ* darkness].

TENEBRIFIC, [ten'-ib-rif'-ik], *adj.* producing darkness. [L. *tenebrae* darkness and *facere* to make].

TENEBROSE, [ten'-ib-rōs], *adj.* dark and gloomy. [L. *tenebrosus*].

TENEBROSITY, [ten'-ib-ros'-it-i], *n.* darkness, gloom, obscurity.

TENEBROUS, [ten'-ib-rus], *adj.* tenebrose, dark, shadowed, gloomy. [L. *tenebrosus*].

TENEBROUSNESS, [ten'-ib-rus-nes], *n.* the condition of being tenebrous.

TENEMENT, [ten'-i-ment], *n.* (*leg.*) property held by a tenant, anything held by tenure; a dwelling; one set of rooms in a large building where each set is occupied by a different family; (*poet.*) a dwelling-place. [L. *tenementum*].

TENEMENTAL, [ten'-i-ment'-al], *adj.* pertaining to a tenement.

TENEMENTARY, [ten'-i-ment'-er-i], *adj.* tenemental.

TENESMUS, [ten-ez'-mus], *n.* (*path.*) an inclination and effort to clear the bowels without result. [Gk. *tenesmos*].

TENET, [ten'-et, tēn'-et], *n.* any strongly held opinion, principle, dogma, or doctrine. [L. *tenet* he holds].

TENFOLD, [ten'-fōld], *adj. and adv.* ten times more, ten times as many. [TEN and OE. *feald*].

TENNANTITE, [ten'-ant-īt], *n.* (*min.*) a sulpharsenide of copper. [Smithson *Tennant*, a chemist].

TENNER, [ten'-er], *n.* (*coll.*) a ten-pound note.

TENNIS, [ten'-is], *n.* a ball game played in a prepared court divided by a net across which the players (two or four in number) hit the ball to and fro either with their hands or with rackets; lawn tennis. [ME. *teneis*].

TENNIS BALL, [ten'-is-bawl'], *n.* a ball used when playing tennis.

TENNIS COURT, [ten'-is-kawt'], *n.* a prepared court or grass patch where tennis is played.

TENNIS ELBOW, [ten'-is-el'-bō], *n.* inflammation of the elbow due to strain at lawn tennis.

TENON (1), [ten'-on], *n.* (*carp.*) a projection from a piece of wood shaped to fit into a mortise or slot in another piece of wood so as to join the two pieces together. [OFr. *tenoun*].

TENON (2), [ten'-on], *v.t.* (*carp.*) to cut a tenon in.

TENON-SAW, [ten'-on-saw'] *n.* (*carp.*) a small saw used to cut tenons.

TENON-SAW

TENOR (1), [ten'-or], *n.* the import, general meaning of, a writing or utterance; career, course. [L. *tenor* a holding on].

TENOR (2), [ten'-or], *n.* a high pitch of adult male voice, above bass but below alto; the line of notes to be sung by this voice in any composition; a person who sings with such a voice; a violin with a similar pitch, a viola. [Fr. *ténor* from It. *tenore*].

TENOR (3), [ten'-or], *adj.* pertaining to the voice of a tenor.

TENORINO, [ten'-or-ē'-nō], *n.* a high falsetto that can be produced in some male adult voices. [It. *tenorino*].

TENOTOMY, [ten-ot'-om-i], *n.* the operation of severing a tendon. [Gk. *tenon* tendon and *tome* cutting].

TENREC, see TANREC.

TENSE (1), [tents], *n.* (*gram.*) any of the parts of a verb implying the time (past, present, future, etc.) or the nature (i.e. whether continuous or not) of the action expressed by the verb; the quality imparted to a verb by such inflection or root vowel variation. [OFr. *tens* from L. *tempus* time].

TENSE (2), [tents], *adj.* stretched tight, strained, taut; over-wrought but held in restraint, expectant, keyed up; **t. vowel**, (*phon.*) a vowel uttered with the tongue held in a firm, taut position. [L. *tensus*, *p.pt.* of *tendere* to stretch].

TENSE (3), [tents], *v.t.* to make tense, brace up; (*phon.*) to utter (a vowel) tensely.

TENSELY, [tens'-li], *adv.* in a tense fashion.

TENSENESS, [tens'-nes], *n.* the state of being tense.

TENSIBILITY, [ten'-sib-il'-i-ti], *n.* the condition of being tensible; the capability of being stretched.

TENSIBLE, [ten'-sibl], *adj.* tensile, able to be stretched.

TENSILE, [ten'-sīl], *adj.* able to be stretched, ductile.

TENSION, [ten'-shun], *n.* the act of stretching; the state of being stretched; emotional stress. [L. *tensio*].

TENSIONAL, [ten'-shun-al], *adj.* pertaining to tension.

TENSITY, [ten'-sit-i], *n.* the condition of being tense.

TENSIVE, [ten'-siv], *adj.* producing tension, straining, pulling, stretching. [Fr. *tensif*].

TENSON, TENZON, [ten'-son, tenz'-on], *n.* a competition between troubadours in making verses. [OFr. *tenson*].

TENSOR, [ten'-sor], *n.* (*anat.*) a muscle that stretches a part of the body or makes it taut.

TENT (1), [tent], *n.* a portable shelter made of canvas stretched over a pole or poles, and held taut and firm by ropes pegged into the ground. [L. *tenta*].

TENT (2), [tent], *n.* a sweet red wine from Spain, often used at the Eucharist. [Span. *tinto*].

TENT (3), [tent], *n.* (*med.*) a roll of some spongy material used to clean a wound or to keep a wound, sore, or natural orifice open. [Fr. *tente*].

TENT (4), [tent], *v.t. and i.* to camp in a tent; to cover with tents.

TENT (5), [tent], *v.t.* to keep a wound, sore, or natural orifice open or dilated by inserting a tent; †to probe. [Fr. *tenter*].

TENTACLE, [ten'-takl], *n.* a slender, flexible limb that some lower forms of animal life possess, used for gripping or grasping or as a means of moving along. [L. *tentaculum*].

TENTACLED, [ten'-takld], *adj.* having tentacles.

TENTACULA, [ten-tak'-yoo-la], *n.(pl.)* tentacles.

TENTACULAR, [ten-tak'-yoo-ler], *adj.* pertaining to, or resembling, tentacles.

TENTACULATE, [ten-tak'-yoo-lāt], *adj.* tentacled.

TENTACULATED, [ten-tak'-yoo-lā-tid], *adj.* possessing tentacles.

TENTACULIFEROUS, [ten-tak'-yoo-lif'-er-us], *adj.* having tentacles; tentaculated.

TENTATIVE, [ten'-tat-iv], *adj.* provisional, experimental, offered merely as a suggestion or experiment. [MedL. *tentativus*].

TENT-BED, [tent'-bed'], *n.* a bed with a canopy over it; a small collapsible bed for use in a tent.

TENTED, [tent'-id], *adj.* covered with tents.

TENTER (1), [tent'-er], *n.* a man in charge of machinery an attendant or supervisor. [~ATTEND].

TENTER (2), [tent'-er], *n.* a frame over which cloth is stretched so as to prevent it shrinking while drying [OFr. *tenture* tapestry].

TENTER-GROUND, [tent'-er-grownd'], *n.* ground on which tenters are set up.

TENTERHOOK, [tent'-er-hook'], *n.* a hook on a tenter; **on tenterhooks**, keyed up, expectant anxious, nervous.

TENTH (1), [tenth], *n.* the one before the eleventh; one of ten parts of a whole.

TENTH (2), [tenth], *adj.* being between the ninth and the eleventh; pertaining or referring to one of ten parts or fractions of a whole.

TENTHLY, [ten'-thli], *adv.* in the tenth place.

TENTORIUM, [tent-aw'-ri-um], *n.* (*anat.*) a membranous division between the cerebellum and cerebrum; †an awning. [L. *tentorium* tent].

TENT-PEG, [tent'-peg'], *n.* a wooden or metal peg to which the guys of a tent are fastened.

TENT-PEGGING, [tent'-peg'-ing], *n.* a cavalry exercise in which when the horse is at the gallop the rider picks up a peg, fixed firmly in the ground, on the end of a lance.

TENUIFOLIOUS, [ten'-yoo-i-fōl'-i-us], *adj.* (*bot.*) having thin or slender leaves.

TENUIROSTER, [ten'-yoo-i-ros'-ter], *n.* a bird of the *Tenuirostres*; a bird with a slender bill.

TENUIROSTRAL, [ten'-yoo-i-ros'-tral], *adj.* slender-billed, of or pertaining to the *Tenuirostres*.

TENUIS, (*pl.* **tenues**), [ten'-yoo-is], *n.* (*phon.*) a voiceless stop consonant. [L. *tenuis* thin].

TENUITY, [ten-yoo'-it-i], *n.* the condition of being tenuous; slenderness; thinness. [L. *tenuitas*].

TENUOUS, [ten'-yoo-us], *adj.* slender, thin, fine, rare; subtle.

TENUOUSNESS, [ten'-yoo-us-nes], *n.* the quality of being tenuous.

TENURE, [ten'-yer], *n.* the act of holding property; the right to possess property; the action or fact of holding an office; the conditions on which property or office is held. [OFr. *teneure*].

TENURIAL, [ten-yooer'-i-al], *adj.* pertaining to tenure.

TENUTO, [ten-yoo'-tō], *adj.* (*mus.*) of a note, given

or to be given its full time value; sustained. [It. *tenuto*].

TENZON, see TENSON.

TEOCALLI, [tē'-ō-kal'-i], *n.* a heathen temple of the Aztecs. [Mexican *teocalli*].

TEPEE, TEEPEE, [tē'-pē], *n.* an American Indian tent or wigwam, usually conical in shape. [Red Indian *tipi* house].

TEPEFACTION, [tep'-i-fak'-shun], *n.* the act of making tepid.

TEPEFY, [tep'-i-fī], *v.t.* and *i.* to make moderately warm; to become tepid. [L. *tepidus* tepid and *facere* to make].

TEPHIGRAM, [tef'-i-gram], *n.* (*meteor.*) a diagram constructed with reference to entropy and temperature. [TE(MPERATURE), Gk. *phi* the symbol of entropy, and *gramma* written symbol].

TEPHRITE, [tef'-rīt], *n.* a variety of andesite, a volcanic rock which has an ashen colour. [~Gk. *tephra* ashes].

TEPHROITE, [teph'-rō-īt], *n.* (*min.*) an ashen-coloured, crystalline silicate of manganese.

TEPHROMANCY, [tef'-rō-man-si], *n.* divination from the charred remains of burnt offerings. [Gk. *tephra* ashes and *manteia* divination].

TEPID, [tep'-id], *adj.* lukewarm, somewhat warm, warmish. [L. *tepidus*].

TEPIDARIUM, [tep'-id-āer'-i-um], *n.* the moderately warm room in a Roman bath. [L. *tepidarium*].

TEPIDITY, [tep-id'-it-i], *n.* tepidness, the condition of being tepid.

TEPIDNESS, [tep'-id-nes], *n.* moderate warmth.

TER, [tur], *adv.* (*mus.*) three times (used to indicate that the passage so marked is to be repeated twice). [L. *ter* three times].

TERAI, [te'-rī], *n.* a wide-brimmed felt hat worn by whites in tropical or sub-tropical countries. [The *Terai*, a region of marsh and jungle at the foot of the Himalayan Mountains].

TERAPHIM, [te'-ra-fim], *n.*(*pl.*) household gods of the ancient Jews. [Heb. *t'raphim*].

TERATO-, *pref.* pertaining to a monster, resembling or concerning monstrosities. [Gk. *teras teratos* monster].

TERATOGENY, [te'-rat-oj'-en-i], *n.* the birth or production of monsters or freaks. [TERATO- and Gk. *genes* born].

TERATOID, [te'-rat-oid], *adj.* resembling or having the nature of a monster, abnormal, freakish. [TERATO- and Gk. *oeides* like].

TERATOLITE, [te'-rat-ō-līt], *n.* (*min.*) a hydrous silicate of aluminium. [TERATO- and Gk. *lithos* a stone].

TERATOLOGICAL, [te'-rat-ō-loj'-ik-al], *adj.* pertaining to teratology.

TERATOLOGIST, [te'-rat-ol'-oj-ist], *n.* one who studies teratology.

TERATOLOGY, [te'-rat-ol'-oj-i], *n.* the organized and scientific study of freaks and monstrosities in animals and vegetables. [TERATO- and Gk. *logos* speech].

TERBIUM, [tur'-bi-um], *n.* the rare metallic element denoted by Tb. [*Ytterby* in Sweden].

TERCE (1), see TIERCE.

TERCE (2), [turs], *n.* (*Scots leg.*) the right of a widow to one third of her husband's estate provided that the marriage lasted at least a year and a day and produced one living child, and that no other provision is made for her. [*Var.* of TIERCE].

TERCEL, TIERCEL, [tur'-sel], *n.* a male falcon. [Fr. *tercel*].

TERCE-MAJOR, [turs'-māj'-or], *n.* (*card games*) a sequence of the three highest cards.

TERCENTENARY (1), [tur'-sen-tē'-ner-i], *n.* the three hundredth anniversary of an event, the celebrations connected therewith.

TERCENTENARY (2), [tur'-sen-tē'-ner-i], *adj.* pertaining to a tercentenary or a period of three hundred years.

TERCET, TIERCET, [tur'-set], *n.* (*pros.*) a triplet; (*mus.*) a triplet; a third. [Fr. *tercet*].

TERCEL

TEREBENE, [te'-ri-bēn], *n.* oil of turpentine treated with sulphuric acid to make a disinfectant.

TEREBINTH, [te'-rib-inth], *n.* the Chian turpentine tree, *Pistacia Terebinthus*, growing in Mediterranean climates. [Gk. *terebinthos*].

TEREBINTHINE, [te'-rib-inth'-īn], *adj.* pertaining to or like turpentine.

TEREBRA, [te-rē'-bra], *n.* (*zool.*) the organ with which certain insects make a hole in a substance, and bury eggs there. [L. *terebra*].

TEREBRATE, [te'-rib-rāt], *v.t.* to bore into, pierce. [~L. *terebrare* to bore].

TEREBRATION, [te'-rib-rā'-shun], *n.* the act of boring. [L. *terebratio*].

TEREDO, [te-rē'-dō], *n.* a mollusc which bores into the submerged wood of ships, the shipworm. [Gk. *teredon* a wood-worm].

TEREDO

TERETE, [te-rēt'], *adj.* long, smooth, and round like a cylinder. [L. *teres*].

TERGAL, [tur'-gal], *adj.* dorsal, pertaining to the back. [~L. *tergum* back].

TERGIVERSATE, [tur'-ji-ver-sāt'], *v.i.* to act in an evasive manner, to shift about in one's point of view. [~L. *tergiversari*].

TERGIVERSATION, [tur'-ji-ver-sā'-shun], *n.* subterfuge, evasive conduct, the practice of tergiversating.

TERGUM, [tur'-gum], *n.* the back or upper surface of the abdomen in insects and animals. [L. *tergum* back].

TERM (1), [turm], *n.* a limit to a period of time, *esp.* a day fixed by which rent must be paid; a limited period of time, *esp.* a limited period during which an agreement, contract, right, etc., is valid; a fixed number of consecutive weeks in which instruction is given at universities and schools, and the law courts are open for the hearing of cases; one of a set of special and precise names used in the study or science of anything, in an art, profession, etc.; (*Rom. antiq.*) a boundary post; (*log.*) one of the parts of a proposition; (*geom.*) a point, line, or surface which forms a limit or boundary; (*pl.*) the menses; (*pl.*) the stated provisos of an agreement, contract, etc.; (*pl.*) money demanded as payment; (*pl.*) conditions of friendship, personal relations, friendship; (*pl.*) style, phraseology, mode of expression; **terms of reference,** a statement or set of terms defining the scope of an investigation by a person or group of persons. [OFr. *terme* from L. *termen* a boundary].

TERM (2), [turm], *v.t.* to name, give a term to, call, designate.

TERMAGANCY, [tur'-mag-an-si], *n.* tumultuousness, the quality of being a termagant.

TERMAGANT (1), [tur'-mag-ant], *n.* a boisterous, brawling, turbulent woman, so called from a supposed Mohammedan deity represented in morality plays as a boisterous person. [OFr. *tervagant*].

TERMAGANT (2), [tur'-mag-ant], *adj.* boisterous.

TERMAGANTLY, [tur'-mag-ant-li], *adv.* in the manner of a termagant.

TERMER, [tur'-mer], *n.* a person who is serving a term of imprisonment.

TERMES, (*pl.* **termites**), [tur'-mēz, tur'-mīt-ēz], *n.* a group of insects including the white ant. [LL. *termes* wood-worm].

TERM-FEE, [turm'-fē], *n.* (*leg.*) a fee chargeable for each term a cause is in court.

TERMINABILITY, [turm'-in-ab-il'-it-i], *n.* the condition of being terminable.

TERMINABLE, [turm'-in-abl], *adj.* limitable, able to be terminated.

TERMINABLENESS, [turm'-in-abl-nes], *n.* the condition of being terminable.

TERMINAL (1), [turm'-in-al], *n.* (*elect.*) a metal screw, etc., for connecting the ends of some part of a circuit; examinations occurring every term at a school or college; a terminus on a railway.

TERMINAL (2), [turm'-in-al], *adj.* pertaining to a limit or end, situated at an end or limit; concluding, final; lasting for the duration of a term; occurring every term; pertaining to a university or school term. [L. *terminalis*].

TERMINALLY, [turm'-in-al-i], *adv.* at the end; once a term; at regular fixed intervals.

TERMINATE, [turm'-in-āt], *v.t.* and *i.* to limit or bound; to bring to an end; to finish or cause to finish; to be at the end of; to come to an end. [L. *terminare*].

TERMINATION, [turm'-in-ā'-shun], *n.* the act of terminating; the condition of being terminated; an end or conclusion (in time or space); that which is at the end, extremity; (*gram.*) the final part of a word, a suffix or inflexion. [L. *terminatio*].

TERMINATIONAL, [turm'-in-ā'-shun-al], *adj.* (*gram.*) of, or pertaining to, a termination.

TERMINATIVE, [turm'-in-at-iv], *adj.* serving to terminate or determine.

TERMINATIVELY, [turm'-in-at-iv-li], *adv.* absolutely; in a terminative way; bringing to a conclusion.

TERMINATOR, [turm'-in-ā-tor], *n.* someone or something that terminates; (*astron.*) the separating line between the illuminated and unilluminated parts of a planet. [LL. *terminator*].
TERMINATORY, [turm'-in-at-er-i], *adj.* serving to terminate.
TERMINER, [turm'-in-er], *n.* **oyer and t.,** (*leg.*) a Royal Commission granted to judges to hear cases on circuit. [Fr. *terminer* to determine].
TERMINISM, [turm'-in-izm], *n.* the doctrine of a terminist.
TERMINIST, [turm'-in-ist], *n.* one who holds that the period in which Divine Grace is available to an individual is limited.
TERMINOLOGICAL, [turm'-in-ō-loj'-ik-al], *adj.* pertaining to terminology; **t. inexactitude,** a lie.
TERMINOLOGICALLY, [turm'-in-ō-loj'-ik-al-i], *adv.* in a terminological way.
TERMINOLOGY, [turm'-in-ol'-oj-i], *n.* technical terms; a system of technical terms pertaining to any particular art, trade, profession, etc. [L. *terminus* a limit and Gk. *logos* speech].
TERMINTHUS, [tur-min'-thus], *n.* (*med.*) a variety of carbuncle.
TERMINUS, [turm'-in-us], *n.* limit, end, extremity, goal; the end of a railway line, a tram-route, bus-route, etc., a station or depôt at such a place; **t. ad quem,** a point beyond which an argument cannot or is not intended to go; **t. a quo,** the starting point of an argument.
TERMITARY, [turm'-it-er-i], *n.* (*zool.*) a nest of white ants or termites.
TERMITE, [turm'-it], *n.* one of a group of insects commonly called white ants, having the communal habits of ants. [TERMES].
TERMLESS, [turm'-les], *adj.* without limit, boundless.
TERMLY (1), [turm-li], *adj.* occurring term by term.
TERMLY (2), [turm-li], *adv.* term by term.
TERMOR, [turm'-er], *n.* (*leg.*) a person holding an estate for a definite period.
TERN (1), [turn], *n.* one of a group of small gull-like birds; **the common t.,** *Sterna hirundo.* [~OIcel. *therna*].

TERN

TERN (2), [turn], *n.* a group of three. [L. *terni* three each].
TERN (3), [turn], *adj.* arranged in threes. [*Prec.*].
TERNAL, [turn'-al], *adj.* triple, threefold, ternary.
TERNARY (1), [turn'-er-i], *n.* a group of three; the number three.
TERNARY (2), [turn'-er-i], *adj.* arranged in groups of three, triple, threefold; pertaining to such arrangement.
TERNATE, [turn'-āt], *adj.* (*bot.*) arranged in groups of three. [MdL. *ternare* to treble].
TERNION, [turn'-i-on], *n.* a group of three. [L. *ternio*].
TERPSICHOREAN, [turp'-sik-or-ē'-an], *adj.* pertaining to dancing. [Gk. *Terpsichore,* the muse of dancing].
TERRA, [te'-ra], *n.* **t. firma,** dry land as contrasted with the sea; **t. incognita,** unknown, unexplored country. [L. *terra*].
TERRA-ALBA, [te'-ra-al'-ba], *n.* white clay, pipeclay. [L. *terra alba*].
TERRACE (1), [te'-ras], *n.* a raised bank or mound, usually longer than broad, often employed as an ornament in landscape gardening; a row of houses or villas along a street. [OFr. *terrace*].
TERRACE (2), [te'-ras], *v.t.* to make into a terrace, to ornament with or add a terrace to.
TERRACED ROOF, [te'-rast-rōōf'], *n.* the flat roof of an oriental dwelling.
TERRACOTTA, [te'-ra-kot'-a], *n.* a brownish-red pottery. [It. *terra cotta* baked earth].
TERRACULTURE, [te'-ra-kul'-cher], *n.* cultivation of the soil.
TERRAIN, [te-rān'], *n.* a tract of land, a region. [Fr. *terrain*].
TERRAMARA, [te'-ra-mah'-ra], *n.* a fertilizing earth found in the Po valley in Italy; (*pl.*) settlements where this is found. [It. *terramara*].
TERRANEAN, [te-rā'-ni-an], *adj.* pertaining to the surface of land.
TERRANEOUS, [te-rā'-ni-us], *adj.* growing on the earth.
TERRAPIN, [te'-rap-in], *n.* any one of a number of edible turtles found about the Atlantic coasts and estuaries of North America. [AmerInd. *torope*].

TERRAQUEOUS, [ter-āk'-wi-us], *adj.* consisting of land and water. [L. *terra* land and *aqua* water].
TERRA-SIENNA, [te'-ra-si-en'-a], *n.* the earth pigment sienna. [It. *terra di Siena*].
TERRAZZO-PAVING, [te-rat'-sō-pāv'-ing], *n.* (*prot.*) concrete used for building and paving. [It. *terrazzo* terrace].
TERRENE, [te-rēn'], *adj.* pertaining to the earth, mundane, terrestrial. [L. *terrenus*].
TERREPLEIN, [tāer'-plān'], *n.* (*milit.*) the flat platform on a rampart where guns are mounted.
TERRESTRIAL (1), [te-res'-tri-al], *n.* an inhabitant of the earth.
TERRESTRIAL (2), [te-res'-tri-al], *adj.* pertaining to the earth, mundane, earthly; resembling the earth in its ball-like shape; living on land. [OFr. *terrestriel*].
TERRESTRIALLY, [te-res'-tri-al-i], *adv.* in an earthly manner.
TERRESTRIALNESS, [te-res'-tri-al-nes], *n.* the quality of being terrestrial.
TERRET, [te'-ret], *n.* one of the rings in the harness of a carthorse or coachhorse through which the reins pass to the driver's hands. [OFr. *teret*].
TERRE-TENANT, [tāer'-ten'-ant], *n.* a person in actual possession of a landed estate. [AFr. *terre tenaunt*].
TERRIBLE, [te'-ribl], *adj.* evoking horror, fear, awe, monstrous, horrible; (*coll.*) extreme, excessive; very bad, ill-done, disappointing. [L. *terribilis*].
TERRIBLENESS, [te'-ribl-nes], *n.* the quality of being terrible.
TERRIBLY, [te'-rib-li], *adv.* in a terrible way, dreadfully; (*coll.*) extremely; very badly.
TERRICOLOUS, [te-rik'-ol-us], *adj.* inhabiting the soil or earth. [L. *terra* earth and *colere* to inhabit].
TERRIER (1), [te'-ri-er], *n.* a dog of one of several breeds of small dogs very commonly kept as pets, and used in hunting burrowing animals because of their habit of pursuing the animal right into its burrow. [Fr. *terrier* from *terre* earth].
TERRIER (2), [te'-ri-er], *n.* (*coll.*) a territorial soldier. [Shortened from TERRITORIAL].
TERRIER (3), [te'-ri-er], *n.* a document giving legal and other information concerning landed property. [Fr. *terrier* from L. (*liber*) *terrarius* a book about land].
TERRIFIC, [te-rif'-ik], *adj.* dreadful, huge, vast, violent, evoking terror by hugeness or violence. [L. *terrificus*].
TERRIFICALLY, [te-rif'-ik-al-i], *adv.* in a terrific degree, tremendously, violently; (*coll.*) very.
TERRIFY, [te'-ri-fī], *v.t.* to frighten, alarm, overwhelm with terror. [L. *terrificare*].
TERRIGENOUS, [te-rij'-en-us], *adj.* produced by the earth or soil, earth-born. [L. *terra* earth and Gk. *genes* born of].
TERRINE, [te'-rēn], *n.* an earthenware vessel in which a special delicacy is kept. [Fr. *terrine*].
TERRITORIAL (1), [te'-ri-taw'-ri-al], *n.* a soldier in the Territorial Army.
TERRITORIAL (2), [te'-ri-taw'-ri-al], *adj.* pertaining to territory, to a special territory or region; (*milit.*) pertaining to a voluntary force grouped according to certain divisions of the country.
TERRITORIALLY, [te'-ri-taw'-ri-al-i], *adv.* with regard to territory.
TERRITORIED, [te'-ri-ter-id], *adj.* possessing lands.
TERRITORY, [te'-rit-er-i], *n.* a large region or tract of land; a single governmental division of a country; a dependent state, not entirely self-governing; the area traversed by a commercial traveller. [L. *territorium* land round a town].
TERROR, [te'-ror], *n.* a state of extreme fear; extreme, abject fear; a person or thing evoking such fear; a troublesome person, *esp.* a mischievous child. [L. *terror*].
TERRORISM, [te'-ror-izm], *n.* a policy of terror and intimidation, a government or administration founded upon such a policy.
TERRORIST, [te'-ror-ist], *n.* a political fanatic or one of a party of such persons carrying out or proposing to carry out a policy based on terror and intimidation.
TERRORIZATION, [te'-ror-īz-ā'-shun], *n.* the act or result of terrorizing.
TERRORIZE, [te'-ror-īz], *v.t.* to fill with terror, to coerce or intimidate; to rule by intimidation.
TERRORLESS, [te'-ror-les], *adj.* not feeling or not inspiring terror.
TERROR-SMITTEN, [te'-ror-smit'-en], *adj.* stricken with terror.
TERRY (1), [te'-ri], *n.* the uncut loop of a pile fabric. [Unkn.].
TERRY (2), [te'-ri], *adj.* having a pile of uncut loops.

TERSE, [turs], *adj.* brief, concise; (of persons) abrupt almost to rudeness. [L. *tersus, p.pt.* of *tergere* to rub].
TERSELY, [turs'-li], *adv.* in a terse way.
TERSENESS, [turs'-nes], *n.* the condition of being terse.
TERTIAL (1), [tur'-shi-al], *n.* a flight feather in the third row of a bird's wing.
TERTIAL (2), [tur'-shi-al], *adj.* pertaining to a tertial. [~L. *tertius* third].
TERTIAN (1), [tur'-shan], *n.* (*med.*) a tertian malady.
TERTIAN (2), [tur'-shan], *adj.* (*med.*) recurring every other day. [L. *tertianus*].
TERTIARY, [tur'-sher-i], *adj.* third in order of time, importance, etc.; (*geol.*) pertaining to that geological era which followed the Mesozoic. [~L. *tertius* third].
TERTIUM QUID, [tur'-shi-um-kwid'], *n.* something which is intermediate, a compromising alternative, a third suggestion, possibility, etc. [L. *tertium quid* something third].
TERTIUS, [tur'-shus], *adj.* third. [L. *tertius* third].
TERZA RIMA, [täert'-sa-rē'-ma], *n.* a verse form in which the lines are grouped in threes and the rhymes occur thus: aba, bcb, cdc, ded, etc. [It. *terza rima*].
TERZETTO, [täert-set'-ō], *n.* (*mus.*) a song for three voices. [It. *terzetto*].
TESLA COIL, [tez'-la-koil], *n.* (*elect.*) an induction coil which provides a high-frequency alternating current. [*Tesla* an American scientist].
TESLA-CURRENT, [tez'-la-ku'-rent], *n.* (*elect.*) the current produced by a tesla coil.
TESLA-TRANSFORMER, [tez'-la-tranz-fawm'-er], *n.* (*elect.*) a tesla coil.
TESSELLAR, [tes'-el-er], *adj.* consisting of tessera. [L. *tessella* a small cube].
TESSELLATE, [tes'-el-āt], *v.t.* to cover or pave with small stones as in mosaic work. [L. *tessellatus* consisting of small stones].
TESSELLATED, [tes'-el-ā-tid], *adj.* paved with or made of mosaic work.
TESSELLATION, [tes'-el-ā'-shun], *n.* mosaic work, a paving of small stones as in mosaics.
TESSELLITE, [tes'-el-it], *n.* a cubic form of apophylite. [L. *tessella* small cube and Gk. *lithos* a stone].
TESSERA, (*pl.* **tesserae**), [tes'-er-a], *n.* one of a number of small cubes of glass, stone or marble used in mosaic. [Gk. *tessera* four].
TESSERAIC, [tes'-er-ā'-ik], *adj.* tesseral.
TESSERAL, [tes'-er-al], *adj.* pertaining to, or made of, tesserae.
TESSITURA, [tes'-i-tōōer'-a], *n.* (*mus.*) the typical range or notes of a soprano, tenor, etc. [It. *tessitura* texture].
TESSULAR, [tes'-yŏŏ-ler], *adj.* made of, or relating to, tesserae; (of crystals) having equal axes as in the cube.
TEST (1), [test], *n.* the container in a furnace used for refining precious metals, a cupel; a means or method of proving the quality of anything, an examination, a critical survey; (*chem.*) an analysis of a substance; a short written examination less important than and usually in preparation for a vital or authoritative examination; a special fact or circumstance that serves to bring out the true character or work of any person or thing by trying their qualities to the utmost; (*cricket*) a test match; (*hist.*) the oath taken under the Test Act (passed 1672, repealed 1828) which required persons to take the oaths of allegiance and supremacy, declare disbelief in transubstantiation, and receive Holy Communion according to the Anglican rite. [OFr. *test* from L. *testa* pot].
TEST (2), [test], *n.* (*zool.*) the hard shell of molluscs and other invertebrates. [L. *testa* shell].
TEST (3), [test], *v.t.* to try, prove, put to the test, to submit (a person or thing) to trial with a view to ascertaining the nature and strength of his, her, or its qualities; (*chem.*) to analyse.
TESTA, [test'-a], *n.* (*bot.*) the hard covering of a seed. [TEST (2)].
TESTABLE (1), [test'-abl], *adj.* able to be tested.
TESTABLE (2), [test'-abl], *adj.* (*leg.*) able to be disposed of by will.
TESTACEA, [test-ā'-si-a], *n.(pl.)* (*zool.*) creatures with a hard outer shell. [L. *testaceus* covered with a shell].
TESTACEAN (1), [test-ā'-si-an], *n.* (*zool.*) one of the testacea.
TESTACEAN (2), [test-ā'-si-an], *adj.* (*zool.*) having a shell, pertaining to testacea.
TESTACEL, [test'-as-el'], *n.* (*zool.*) a genus of land-slugs, having a small scutate shell, found in Southern Europe and feeding on earthworms. [~TESTACEA].
TESTACEOUS, [test-ā'-shus], *adj.* pertaining to shells; shelly; of the colour of unglazed pottery; (*zool.*) having a shell.
TESTACY, [test'-as-i], *n.* (*leg.*) the condition of being testate.
TESTAMENT, [test'-a-ment], *n.* a declaration; either of the two major sections of the Bible, regarded as covenants of God with Man, called the *Old* and *New Testaments*; (*coll.*) the New Testament; **last will and t.,** a person's will, the document in which he expresses his wishes as to the disposal of his property after death. [L. *testamentum* a statement of one's will].
TESTAMENTAL, [test'-a-ment'-al], *adj.* testamentary.
TESTAMENTARY, [test'-a-ment'-er-i], *adj.* pertaining to a will or wills; bequeathed by or appointed in a will.
TESTAMENTATION†, [test'-a-ment-ā'-shun], *n.* the act of giving by will, or of making a will.
TESTAMUR, [test-ā'-mer], *n.* a university certificate stating that a person has passed an examination; a certificate. [L. *testamur* we testify].
TESTATE (1), [test'-āt], *n.* (*leg.*) a person who dies leaving a valid will.
TESTATE (2), [test'-āt], *adj.* (*leg.*) leaving a valid will at death. [L. *testatus*].
TESTATION, [test-ā'-shun], *n.* the bequeathing of property by will. [L. *testatio*].
TESTATOR, [test-ā'-tor], *n.* (*leg.*) one who makes a will or dies testate; a man so doing or so dying. [L. *testator*].
TESTATRIX, [test-ā'-triks], *n.* a woman who makes a will or dies testate.
TEST CASE, [test'-kās'], *n.* (*leg.*) a suit at law the ruling in which fixes a precedent; a set of circumstances which are likely to provide proof or disproof of something.
TESTER (1), [test'-er], *n.* a person or thing that tests.
TESTER (2), [test'-er], *n.* a canopy over a four-poster bed. [ME. *testere* helmet].
TESTER (3), [test'-er], *n.* (*hist.*) a shilling of Henry VIII; a testoon; a sixpence. [OFr. *testiere* head-piece].
TESTES, see TESTIS.
TESTICLE, [test'-ikl], *n.* one of the male sperm-secreting glands in mammals. [L. *testiculus, dim.* of *testis* testicle].
TESTICULATE, [test-ik'-yŏŏ-lāt], *adj.* (*zool.*) shaped like a testicle; having testicles, or similar organs.
TESTIFICATION, [test'-if-ik-ā'-shun], *n.* the act of testifying or giving evidence; evidence so given. [L. *testificatio*].
TESTIFICATOR, [test'-if-ik-ā'-tor], *n.* one who testifies or gives evidence.
TESTIFIER, [test'-i-fī'-er], *n.* one who gives evidence or bears testimony.
TESTIFY, [test'-i-fī], *v.t. and i.* to give evidence; (*leg.*) to give sworn evidence or testimony; to show signs of, manifest, provide or be evidence of. [L. *testificare* to bear witness].
TESTILY, [test'-i-li], *adv.* in a testy fashion, peevishly.
TESTIMONIAL (1), [test'-i-mōn'-i-al], *n.* a written statement by some responsible person as to the character and abilities of another person; a gift or presentation of some kind made in token of gratitude, admiration, esteem, etc.
TESTIMONIAL† (2), [test'-i-mōn'-i-al], *adj.* pertaining to testimony.
TESTIMONY, [test'-i-mon-i], *n.* evidence given, either written or spoken; that which serves to prove or give evidence of; (*pl.*) the scriptures. [L. *testimonium*].
TESTINESS, [test'-i-nes], *n.* the condition of being testy; peevishness.
TESTING, [test'-ing], *n.* a trial.
TESTIS, (*pl.* **testes**), [test'-is, test'-ēz], *n.* (*anat.*) a testicle. [L. *testis*].
TESTOON, TESTON, [test-ōōn', test'-on], *n.* a shilling of Henry VIII, a tester. [Fr. *teston*].
TEST-TUBE, [test'-tewb], *n.* (*chem.*) a cylindrical phial or vessel of glass, open at the top, rounded and closed at the bottom, used in chemical experiments.
TESTUDINAL, [test-yŏŏ'-din-al], *adj.* pertaining to, resembling, tortoises.
TESTUDINARIOUS, [test'-yŏŏ-din-āer'-i-us], *adj.* mottled like tortoiseshell.
TESTUDINATE(D), [test-yŏŏ'-din-āt(-id)], *adj.* arched like the back of a tortoise.
TESTUDINEOUS, [test'-yŏŏ-din'-ē-us], *adj.* resembling the shell, pace, of a tortoise. [L. *testudinus*].

TESTUDO, [test-yōō'-dō], *n.* (*Rom. antiq.*) a great shield-like engine under cover of which attackers could advance close to the walls of a besieged city or fortress; (*Rom. arch.*) an arched or vaulted roof; (*zool.*) a land-tortoise, one of the *Testudinæ*. [L. *testudo* tortoise].

TESTY, [test'-i], *adj.* peevish, easily annoyed, irritable. [AFr. *testif* headstrong].

TETANIC (1), [tet-an'-ik], *n.* (*med.*) a substance which, when taken, affects the nerves and produces spasms and convulsions like those experienced under tetanus.

TETANIC (2), [tet-an'-ik], *adj.* (*med.*) of, or pertaining to, tetanus. [Gk. *tetanikos*].

TETANUS, [tet'-an-us], *n.* (*path.*) a disease of which the principal symptom is contraction and spasms of the muscles; the similar effect produced by a tetanic. [Gk. *tetanos* cramp].

TETCHILY, TECHILY†, [tech'-i-li], *adv.* in a tetchy way.

TETCHINESS, TECHINESS†, [tech'-i-nes], *n.* the condition of being tetchy.

TETCHY, TECHY†, [tech'-i], *adj.* testy, peevish, touchy.

TETE-A-TETE, tête-à-tête (1), [tāt'-ah-tāt], *n.* a private confidential chat. [Fr. *tête-à-tête*].

TETE-A-TETE, tête-á-tête (2), [tāt'-ah-tāt], *adj.* *and adv.* confidentially, privately, between two people, with one other person.

TETHER (1), [teTH'-er], *n.* a rope which is used to tie an animal to a post or stake, and yet allow a moderate amount of freedom and movement; **to be at the end of one's t.,** to be at the end of one's resources. [OScand. *tiothr*].

TETHER (2), [teTH'-er], *v.t.* to fasten (an animal) with a tether; (*fig.*) to fix, fasten, deprive of freedom.

TETRA-, *pref.* fourfold, containing four parts, consisting of four. [Gk. *tetra*].

TETRABRANCHIATE, [tet'-ra-brang'-ki-āt], *adj.* (*zool.*) pertaining to the *Tetrabranchiata*, a group of cephalopods with four gills.

TETRACHORD, [tet'-ra-kawd], *n.* (*mus.*) a series of four successive tones.

TETRACHOTOMOUS, [tet'-ra-kot'-om-us], *adj.* (*bot.*) separating into four divisions or branches. [Gk. *tetrakha* in four parts and *tome* a cutting].

TETRACOLON, (*pl.* **tetracola**), [tet'-ra-kō'-lon], *n.* (*pros.*) a metrical period containing four parts.

TETRACT, [tet'-rakt], *adj.* (*zool.*) having four rays, *esp.* of sponge spicules.

TETRACYCLIC, [tet'-ra-sī'-klik], *adj.* (*bot.*) possessing four whorls.

TETRAD, [tet'-rad'], *n.* a set or group of four; (*mus.*) a chord made up of four notes; (*biol.*) a group of four cells. [Gk. *tetras* a group of four].

TETRADACTYLOUS, [tet'-ra-dak'-til-us], *adj.* possessing four fingers or toes.

TETRADECAPOD, [tet'-ra-dek'-a-pod], *adj.* (*zool.*) possessing fourteen feet.

TETRADIAPASON†, [tet'-ra-dī'-a-pā'-son], *n.* (*mus.*) an interval of four octaves.

TETRADRACHM, [tet'-ra-dram'], *n.* (*Gk. antiq.*) an ancient Greek coin worth four drachms.

TETRADYMITE, [tet-rad'-i-mīt], *n.* (*min.*) telluride of bismuth.

TETRAGON, [tet'-ra-gon], *n.* (*geom.*) a closed geometrical figure with four sides. [Gk. *tetragonon*].

TETRAGONAL, [tet-rag'-on-al], *adj.* relating to a tetragon; having four angles; (*zool., bot.*) used to describe anything that is quadrangular in section.

TETRAHEDRAL, [tet'-ra-hē'-dral], *adj.* possessing four sides, quadrilateral; (of a three-dimensional figure) enclosed in four plane surfaces.

TETRAHEDRITE, [tet'-ra-hē'-drīt], *n.* (*min.*) a grey copper ore, sulphide of antimony and copper.

TETRAHEDRON, [tet'-ra-hē'-dron], *n.* (*geom.*) a three-dimensional figure contained in four sides.

TETRAHEXAHEDRAL, [tet-ra-heks'-a-hē'-dral], *adj.* having the form of a tetrahexahedron.

TETRAHEXAHEDRON, [tet'-ra-heks'-a-hē'-dron], *n.* (*geom.*) a three-dimensional figure contained in twenty-four sides.

TETRALOGY, [tet-ral'-oj-i], *n.* a related series of four dramas on the same theme or developments of it.

TETRAMETER, [tet-ram'-it-er], *n.* (*pros.*) a line of verse containing four metrical sections.

TETRAPETALOUS, [tet'-ra-pet'-al-us], *adj.* (*bot.*) having four distinct petals.

TETRAPHARMACON, [tet'-ra-fah'-mak-on], *n.* an ointment or medicine containing four ingredients. [TETRA- and Gk. *pharmakon* a drug].

TETRAPHYLLOUS, [tet-raf'-il-us], *adj.* (*bot.*) having four leaves. [TETRA- and Gk. *phullon* leaf].

TETRAPLA, [tet'-rap-la], *n.* a text constructed of four parallel versions; the Old Testament so arranged by Origen. [Gk. *tetrapla*, *neut. pl.* of *tetraplous* fourfold].

TETRAPOD (1), [tet'-ra-pod'], *n.* (*zool., entom.*) a four-footed creature.

TETRAPOD (2), [tet'-ra-pod'], *adj.* having four feet. [Gk. *tetrapous*].

TETRAPTERAN (1), [tet-rap'-ter-an], *n.* an insect that has four wings.

TETRAPTERAN (2), [tet-rap'-ter-an], *adj.* possessing four wings. [TETRA- and Gk. *pteron* a wing].

TETRAPTEROUS, [tet-rap'-ter-us], *adj.* having four wings, tetrapteran.

TETRARCH, [tet'-rahk], *n.* (*Rom. hist.*) the governor of a fourth part of a province; any governor over a small territory. [Gk. *tetrarkhes*].

TETRARCHATE, [tet'-rahk-āt], *n.* (*Rom. hist.*) a province or part of a province under a tetrarch; the office or rank of a tetrarch.

TETRARCHIC, [tet-rahk'-ik], *adj.* (*Rom. hist.*) tetrarchical.

TETRARCHICAL, [tet-rahk'-ik-al], *adj.* (*Rom. hist.*) of or pertaining to a tetrarch or a tetrarchy.

TETRARCHY, [tet'-rahk-i], *n.* (*Rom. hist.*) territory administered by a tetrarch, a tetrarchate.

TETRASPASTON, [tet'-ra-spas'-ton], *n.* a machine having four co-ordinated pulleys. [TETRA- and Gk. *spastos* drawn].

TETRASPERMOUS, [tet'-ra-spur'-mus], *adj.* (*bot.*) having four seeds or seeds in groups of four. [TETRA- and Gk. *sperma* seed].

TETRASTICH, [tet'-ra-stich], *n.* (*pros.*) a stanza containing four lines. [Gk. *tetrastikhos*].

TETRASTYLE (1), [tet'-ra-stīl], *n.* (*arch.*) a building or part of a building having four pillars. [Gk. *tetrastulos*].

TETRASTYLE (2), [tet'-ra-stīl], *adj.* having four pillars.

TETRASYLLABIC, [tet'-ra-sil-ab'-ik], *adj.* containing four syllables.

TETRASYLLABLE, [tet'-ra-sil'-abl], *n.* a word containing four syllables.

TETRODE, [tet'-rōd], *n.* (*elect.*) a thermionic valve that has four electrodes. [TETR(A) and (ELECTR)ODE].

TETTER, [tet'-er], *n.* a skin disease, such as eczema, etc. [OE. *teter* ringworm].

TETTERWORT, [tet'-er-wurt], *n.* the plant *Chelidonium majus*, the greater celandine.

TEUCRIAN, [tew'-kri-an], *adj.* pertaining to Teucer, the first king of Troy, or to Troy or the Trojans. [~Gk. *Teukros*].

TEUTON, [tew'-ton], *n.* a member of one of the Germanic races; (*coll.*) a German. [~L. *Teutones*].

TEUTONIC (1), [tew-ton'-ik], *n.* the primitive Germanic language.

TEUTONIC (2), [tew-ton'-ik], *adj.* pertaining to the Germanic race or to Germanic languages, *esp.* to primitive Germanic.

TEUTONISM, [tew'-ton-izm], *n.* a Teutonic turn of phrase, a German idiom.

TEW, see TAW.

TEWEL, [tew'-el], *n.* (*dial.*) the anus; †a chimney. [OFr. *tuiel* a pipe].

TEXT, [tekst], *n.* the wording of written or printed matter; the written or printed words of which a literary work is composed; the words and phrases originally used by an author as distinct from a later paraphrase, a translation, or amended version; the main body of a literary or academic work as distinct from notes and prefaces and other supplementary matter; a quotation, phrase, or sentence from the Bible, *esp.* one used as the basis or starting point for a sermon or lecture, such a phrase or sentence quoted as authority for an assertion, argument, point of view, etc.; any phrase, proverb, quotation, etc., used to give authority to a writer's or speaker's remarks; the theme or subject of a discourse, discussion, literary work, etc. [L. *textus*].

TEXT-BOOK, [tekst'-bŏŏk], *n.* an informative book on a given subject for use by students, etc., a treatise or compendious summary of knowledge on a given subject.

TEXTILE (1), [teks'-tīl], *n.* a woven stuff or material, a fabric. [L. *textilis*].

TEXTILE (2), [teks'-tīl], *adj.* pertaining to weaving; woven.

TEXTMAN, [tekst'-man], *n.* one who is ready in the quotation of apposite texts from the Bible.

TEXTORIAL, [tekst-aw'-ri-al], *adj.* pertaining to weaving.
TEXTUAL, [teks'-cho͝o-al], *adj.* connected with, pertaining to, a text or texts; (of a translation) word for word.
TEXTUALISM, [teks'-cho͝o-al-izm], *n.* the critical point of view which insists upon a close and exact reference to the author's text.
TEXTUALIST, [teks'-cho͝o-al-ist], *n.* a critic or student primarily interested in problems of text; an editor or critic who insists upon a close and exact reference to the author's text.
TEXTUALLY, [teks'-cho͝o-al-i], *adv.* in accordance with a text; from considerations of the text or textual problems; verbatim.
TEXTUARIST, [teks'-cho͝o-er-ist], *n.* a textualist.
TEXTUARY, [teks'-cho͝o-er-i], *adj.* textual.
TEXTUIST, [teks'-cho͝o-ist], *n.* a person who shows great facility in the quotation of texts.
TEXTURAL, [teks'-cher-al], *adj.* pertaining to texture.
TEXTURE, [teks'-cher], *n.* anything made by weaving; the manner of weaving or character of a woven fabric; the constitution, character, or structure of anything considered with special regard to its real or supposed constituents. [L. *textura* fabric].
THAI, see TAI.
THALAMIUM, [thal-ā'-mi-um], *n.* (*bot.*) the part of a flower on which the carpels are lodged. [~THALAMUS].
THALAMUS, [thal'-am-us], *n.* (*anat.*) a part of the brain in which a nerve is rooted, that part from which the optic nerve comes; (*bot.*) thalamium. [Gk. *thalamos* chamber].
THALASSIC, [thal-as'-ik], *adj.* pertaining to the sea. [Gk. *thalassa* sea].
THALASSOGRAPHY, [thal'-as-og'-ra-fi], *n.* oceanography. [Gk. *thalassa* sea and *graphia* writing].
THALASSOMETER, [thal'-as-om'-it-er], *n.* a tide-gauge, a device for registering the state of the tide. [Gk. *thalassa* sea and METER].
THALER, [tah'-ler], *n.* an obsolete German coin roughly equivalent to a shilling. [Germ. *thaler*].
THALIA, [thal-ī'-a], *n.* (*class. myth.*) the muse of pastoral and comic poetry. [Gk. *Thaleia*].
THALIAN, [thal-ī'-an], *adj.* relating to Thalia; comic.
THALLIC, [thal'-ik], *adj.* (*chem.*) pertaining to, or containing, thallium in its higher valency.
THALLIUM, [thal'-i-um], *n.* (*chem.*) the rare metallic element denoted by Tl. [Gk. *thallos* green shoot (from the green line of its spectrum)].
THALLOGEN, [thal'-ō-jen], *n.* (*bot.*) a thallophyte. [Gk. *thallos* a young shoot and *genes* producing].
THALLOPHYTE, [thal'-ō-fit], *n.* (*bot.*) a plant of the order *Thallophyta*, which is the lowest order of plants, containing those in which stem and leaf are not distinct, and which have no true root, such as algae, fungi, and lichens. [Gk. *thallos* green shoot and *phuton* plant].
THALLOUS, [thal'-us], *adj.* of, or pertaining to, thallium in its lower valency.
THALLUS, [thal'-us], *n.* (*bot.*) a plant structure which has no true root, and in which the stem and leaf are not distinct, as in a lichen, etc. [Gk. *thallos* green shoot].

THALLUS

THALWEG, [tahl'-veg], *n.* (*geog.*) the line at the bottom of a valley which marks the natural watercourse and at which the sides of the valley meet. [Germ. *thalweg* valley way].
THAMMUZ, [tham'-uz], *n.* the name of a Syrian god; the tenth month of the Jewish civil calendar and the fourth of the sacred year. [Heb. *thammuz*].
THAN, [THan], *conj. and prep.* a particle used to express inequality after a comparative.
THANAGE, [thān'-ij], *n.* the rank of a thane; land held by a thane.
THANATO-, *pref.* pertaining to death and mortality. [Gk. *thanatos* death].
THANATOGNOMONIC, [than'-at-ō-nōm-on'-ik], *adj.* indicative of death. [THANATO- and Gk. *gnomonikos* pertaining to sundials].
THANATOID, [than'-at-oid], *adj.* resembling death, as if dead; deadly. [THANATO- and Gk. *oeides* like].
THANATOLOGY, [than-at-ol'-o-ji], *n.* the study or science of death. [THANATO- and Gk. *logos* speech].
THANATOSIS, [than'-at-ō'-sis], *n.* mortification, gangrene. [THANATO- and Gk. *osis* denoting condition].
THANE, THEGN, [thān], *n.* a member of the Anglo-Saxon nobility. [OE. *thegn*].
THANEDOM, [thān'-dum], *n.* the jurisdiction or rank of a thane.
THANE-LANDS, [thān'-landz], *n.*(*pl.*) lands held by thanes.
THANESHIP, [thān-ship], *n.* thanedom.
THANK, [thangk], *v.t.* to express one's gratitude to (someone) in speech or writing; (*fig.*) to be indebted to. [OE. *thancian*].
THANKFUL, [thangk'-fo͝ol], *adj.* grateful; having a proper sense of kindness received or service rendered; expressing or uttering thanks.
THANKFULLY, [thangk'-fo͝ol-i], *adv.* with gratitude.
THANKFULNESS, [thangk'-fo͝ol-nes], *n.* the condition of being thankful, gratitude.
THANKLESS, [thangk'-les], *adj.* (of a person) unthankful; ungrateful; (of an action, etc.) not arousing or unlikely to arouse gratitude in others.
THANKLESSLY, [thangk'-les-li], *adv.* in a thankless fashion.
THANKLESSNESS, [thangk'-les-nes], *n.* the condition of being thankless.
THANKOFFERING, [thangk'-of'-er-ing], *n.* an offering made to express gratitude.
THANKSGIVER, [thangks'-giv'-er], *n.* a person who gives thanks or acknowledges a kindness.
THANKSGIVING, [thangks'-giv'-ing], *n.* the act of rendering thanks or expressing gratitude; a liturgical formula expressing thanks; a special church service to return thanks to God.
THANKSGIVING DAY, [thangks'-giv'-ing-dā'], *n.* (*U.S.*) a day on which thanks are given to God for the harvest and other blessings, usually the last Thursday in November.
THANKWORTHINESS, [thangk'-wurTH-i-nes], *n.* the condition of being thankworthy.
THANKWORTHY, [thangk'-wurTH-i], *adj.* meriting thanks.
THARANDITE, [tha'-ran-dīt], *n.* (*min.*) a yellow crystalline variety of dolomite. [Germ. *tharandit*].
THARM, [thahm], *n.* (*dial.*) catgut, or similar substances prepared from animals' intestines; (*pl.*) the intestines. [OE. *tharm* an intestine].
THAT (1), [THat], *demonstrative pron.* expressing a person or thing pointed out, a person, thing, idea just referred to, a statement, command, or wish just expressed, a phrase just used, etc.; **after t.,** when those things had happened; **by t.,** by that time; **with t.,** thereupon; **t. is,** in other words; **like t.,** thus, after that fashion; **take t.,** receive this blow; **and all t.,** and so on and so forth. [OE. *thæt*].
THAT (2), [THat], *demonstrative adj.* used to emphasize or indicate the person or thing referred to; used before the name of a person or thing to express disapproval; **t. once,** on the indicated occasion only.
THAT (3), [THat], *demonstrative adv.* (*coll.*) to such a degree, to that extent; very, greatly.
THAT (4), [THat], *relative pron.* the person, persons, thing, or things which; (*adverbially*) on which, at which, in which.
THAT (5), [THat], *conj.* used to introduce a subordinate noun clause; used to introduce an exclamatory clause; used to introduce a clause expressing purpose, desire, result; used to introduce a subordinate clause expressing a fact from which the fact expressed in the principal clause might be deduced or upon which it is or might be consequent.
THATCH (1), [thach], *n.* a roof for a house or cottage or covering for the top of a rick, made of reed and straw pegged tightly down; (*fig.*) a thick shaggy head of hair. [OE. *thæc*].
THATCH (2), [thach], *v.t.* to cover with a thatch.
THATCHER, [thach'-er], *n.* one whose trade is to thatch houses.
THATCHING, [thach'-ing], *n.* the act of covering with thatch; the materials used to make a thatch.
THAUMATO-, [thaw'-ma-tō], *pref.* pertaining to a wonder, marvel, miracle, magical trick, etc. [Gk. *thauma* juggling trick].
THAUMATROPE, [thaw'-ma-trōp], *n.* an optical toy consisting of two disks each marked with a different picture which when the disks are rapidly revolved appear to combine into one picture. [THAUMATO- and Gk. *tropos* a turning].
THAUMATURGE, [thaw'-ma-turj], *n.* a magician, a miracle-worker, a wonder-worker; (*fig.*) a conjurer. [Gk. *thaumatourgos* wonder-working].

THAUMATURGIC, [thaw′-ma-tur′-jik], *adj.* pertaining to thaumaturgy.
THAUMATURGICAL, [thaw′-ma-tur′-jik-al], *adj.* thaumaturgic.
THAUMATURGICS, [thaw′-ma-turj′-iks], *n.(pl.)* feats of magic; the science and practice of thaumaturgy.
THAUMATURGIST, [thaw′-ma-turj′-ist], *n.* one who deals in thaumaturgy.
THAUMATURGUS, [thaw′-ma-turg′-us], *n.* a miracle-worker, a title given by the R.C. Church to certain saints.
THAUMATURGY, [thaw′-ma-turj-i], *n.* the act of performing a miracle or miracles, magic, conjuring. [Gk. *thaumatourgia* magic].
THAW (1), [thaw], *n.* the process by which ice, snow, frost, etc., liquefy when the temperature rises; an instance of this; **silver t.,** a frost coming immediately after a thaw.
THAW (2), [thaw], *v.t. and i.* to cause (something that is frozen solid) to melt and become liquid by the application of heat; (of snow, ice) to melt under the influence of heat. [OE. *thawian*].
THAWY, [thaw-i], *adj.* tending to thaw.
THE (1), [THē (stressed), THE, THI (before vowels)], *def. art.* used before a noun to denote that a particular one of a series, group, variety, etc., is referred to; used before nouns denoting things of which only one exists or is known or when one particular example is of special importance and commonly referred to (natural phenomena, geographical phenomena, famous events, movements, etc.); used before names indicating a group or before the name of one specimen of a group taken as typical of the whole; used before titles; used before adjectives used as nouns; used in phrases of measurement to express proportion; used emphatically before a noun to denote that the thing referred to is unique or outstanding. [ME. *the*].
THE (2), [THe], *adv.* by so much (usually followed by a *comp. adj.*).
THEANDRIC, [thē-an′-drik], *adj.* relating to co-operation or combination of the divine and the human. [THEO- and Gk. *aner andros* man].
THEANTHROPIC, [thē′-an-throp′-ik], *adj.* being at once divine and human. [THEO- and Gk. *anthropos* man].
THEANTHROPICAL, [thē′-an-throp′-ik-al], *adj.* theanthropic.
THEANTHROPISM, [thē-an′-throp-izm], *n.* the condition of being God and man; the belief that God appeared in human form.
THEANTHROPIST, [thē-an′-throp-ist], *n.* one who accepts theanthropism.
THEARCHIC, [thē-ah′-kik], *adj.* pertaining to thearchy. [Gk. *thearkhikos*].
THEARCHY, [thē′-ah-ki], *n.* the rule of a deity; the rule of a human person or body of persons claiming that their authority is from God and that their government expresses His will. [Gk. *thearkhia*].
THEATINES, [thē′-at-īnz], *n.(pl.)* (*R.C.*) the members of a religious order founded by St. Cajetan and the Archbishop of Chieti in 1524. [*Theate*, the old name of Chieti in Italy].
THEATRE, [thē′-at-er], *n.* a building consisting of a large hall with seats for spectators facing a stage or platform where dramatic performances are given; a hall or room similarly arranged where lectures are delivered; the place where a connected series of events occur; a body of dramatic writers; the theatrical art and profession generally; dramatic effect; **operating t.,** the room in a hospital where operations are performed. [Gk. *theatron*].
THEATRIC, [thē-at′-rik], *adj.* theatrical, showy.
THEATRICAL, [thē-at′-rik-al], *adj.* pertaining to a theatre or representation; showy, unreal, artificial, merely impressive.
THEATRICALITY, [thē-at′-rik-al′-it-i], *n.* the quality of being showy and theatrical.
THEATRICALLY, [thē-at′-rik-al-i], *adv.* in a theatrical, showy manner.
THEATRICALS, [thē-at′-rik-alz], *n.(pl.)* the hobby of amateur dramatics.
THEAVE, [thēv], *n.* a ewe of the first or second year. [Unkn.].
THEBAINE, [thē′-bā-ēn], *n.* (*chem.*) a very poisonous alkaloid obtained from opium. [*Thebes*, the name of an ancient city on the Nile].
THEBAN (1), [thēb′-an], *n.* an inhabitant of Thebes.
THEBAN (2), [thēb′-an], *adj.* of, or relating to, Thebes.
THECA, [thē′-ka], *n.* (*bot., zool., anat.*) a part of a plant or animal body forming a sheath or case. [Gk. *theke* a case].
THECODONT (1), [thēk′-ō-dont], *n.* (*zool.*) one of the *Thecodontes.*
THECODONT (2), [thēk′-ō-dont], *adj.* (*zool.*) pertaining to an extinct family of saurians whose teeth fixed into sockets in the jawbone, the *Thecodontes.* [Gk. *theke* case and *odous odontos* tooth].
THECOPHORE, [thēk′-ō-faw(r)], *n.* (*bot.*) any part of a plant bearing a theca.
THE DANSANT, thé dansant, [tā′-dah(ng)-sah(ng)′], *n.* afternoon tea accompanied with dancing. [Fr. *thé dansant*].
THEE, [THē], *pers.pron. 2nd pers. sing. objective case of* THOU.˙ [OE. *the*].
THEETSEE, THITSI, [thēt′-sē], *n.* the black varnish obtained from the Malayan tree *Melanorrhœa usitata.* [Native].
THEFT, [theft], *n.* the act of stealing; †anything stolen. [OE. *thiefthe*].
THEGN, see THANE.
THEIC, [thē′-ik], *n.* a constant tea-drinker.
THEIFORM, [thē′-i-fawm], *adj.* having the form of the tea-plant.
THEINE, [thē′-ēn], *n.* (*chem.*) an alkaloid contained in tea, and identical with caffeine.
THEIR, [THāer], *pron. and adj.* possessive case of THEY; of them. [OScand. *theira*].
THEIRS, [THāerz], *pron.* absolute form of THEIR.
THEISM, [thē′-izm], *n.* belief in the existence of God as a deity who makes Himself known by divine revelation. [~Gk. *theos* god].
THEIST, [thē′-ist], *n.* a believer in theism.
THEISTIC, [thē-is′-tik], *adj.* theistical.
THEISTICAL, [thē-is′-tik-al], *adj.* pertaining to theism or to theists.
THEM, [THem], *pron.* objective case of THEY. [OScand. *theim*].
THEMATIC, [thēm-at′-ik], *adj.* (*mus.*) pertaining to themes; (*gram.*) pertaining to the stem of a word. [Gk. *thematikos*].
THEME, [thēm], *n.* a subject of writing, thought, conversation, argument, etc.; (*mus.*) the melodic subject or main melody or figure of any composition; (*gram.*) the section of a word to which suffixes and inflexions are added. [Gk. *thema* a proposition].
THEME SONG, [thēm′-song′], *n.* a song which recurs several times in the course of a musical play, film, or revue.
THEMSELVES, [THem-selvz′], (*pron. pl.*) emphatic or reflexive form of THEM.
THEN (1), [THen], *adj.* existing at that time.
THEN (2), [THen], *adv.* at some specified time either in the past or future; immediately after, next; at a later date; **now t.,** (*coll.*) phrase introducing a warning or threat, or initiating another stage in a conversation. [OE. *thænne*].
THEN (3), [THen], *conj.* in that case; moreover, also.
THENADAYS, [THen′-a-dāz], *adv.* in those times.
THENAL, [thēn′-al], *adj.* (*anat.*) of, or pertaining to, the thenar.
THENAR, [thēn′-er], *n.* (*anat.*) the palm of the hand or the sole of the foot; **t. prominence,** the ball-shaped flesh at the base of the thumb. [Gk. *thenar*].
THENARDITE, [then′-ah-dīt], *n.* (*chem.*) crystalline anhydrous sodium sulphate. [L. J. *Thénard*, a French chemist].
THENCE, [THents], *adv.* from that place or time; from that cause; from that point in the argument, etc., therefore. [ME. *thennes*].
THENCEFORTH, [THents′-fawth], *adv.* from that time onwards.
THENCEFORWARD, [THents′-faw′-werd], *adv.* from that time forward.
THEO-, *pref.* pertaining to God or to gods. [Gk. *theos* God].
THEOBROMA, [thē′-ō-brō′-ma],) *n.* (*bot.*) a group of tropical American trees including the *Theobroma Cacao* from which cacao is obtained for making cocoa and chocolate. [THEO- and Gk. *broma* food].
THEOBROMINE, [thē′-o-brōm′-ēn], *n.* (*chem.*) the volatile alkaloid found in the seeds of the cacao tree.
THEOCENTRIC, [thē′-ō-sen′-trik], *adj.* regarding God as the centre and soul of the universe; centred in God. [THEO- and CENTRIC].
THEOCRACY, [thē-ok′-ras-i], *n.* a government by priests claiming authority from God. [THEO- and Gk. *kratia* rule].
THEOCRASY, [thē-ok′-ras-i], *n.* the mingling or union of the soul with God in mystical exaltation or contemplation. [THEO- and Gk. *krasis* a mingling].

THEOCRAT, [thē'-ō-krat'], *n.* one who takes part in a theocratic government.
THEOCRATIC, [thē-ō-krat'-ik], *adj.* pertaining to a theocracy.
THEOCRITEAN, [thē-ok'-rit-ē'-an], *adj.* written in the style of Theocritus; pastoral. [Gk. *Theokritos*].
THEODICY, [thē-od'-i-si], *n.* a vindication of the justice of God in allowing evil and pain to exist on earth. [THEO- and Gk. *dike* justice].
THEODOLITE, [thē-od'-ō-līt], *n.* the instrument by which a surveyor measures angles. [Unkn.].
THEODOLITIC, [thē-od'-ō-lit'-ik], *adj.* pertaining to a theodolite.
THEOGONIC, [thē'-ō-gon'-ik], *adj.* relating to theogony.
THEOGONIST, [thē-og'-on-ist], *n.* one who is learned in theogony.
THEOGONY, [thē-og'-on-i], *n.* mythology dealing with the birth or origin of the pagan gods. [Gk. *theogonia* birth of the gods].

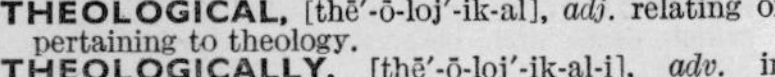
THEODOLITE

THEOLOGIAN, [thē'-ō-lō'-ji-an], *n.* one learned in theology.
THEOLOGICAL, [thē'-ō-loj'-ik-al], *adj.* relating or pertaining to theology.
THEOLOGICALLY, [thē'-ō-loj'-ik-al-i], *adv.* in accordance with the principles of theology.
THEOLOGIST, [thē-ol'-oj-ist], *n.* a student of or authority on theology.
THEOLOGIZE, [thē-ol'-oj-īz], *v.t.* and *i.* to render theological; to speculate in, or discourse on, theology.
THEOLOGIZER, [thē-ol'-oj-īz-er], *n.* a person who theologizes.
THEOLOGY, [thē-ol'-o-ji], *n.* the systematic study of the nature of God; a specific theological theory or system. [Gk. *theologia*].
THEOMACHIST, [thē-om'-ak-ist], *n.* one who strives with God.
THEOMACHY, [thē-ōm'-ak-i], *n.* strife with God; the act of opposing human will to His will; (*myth.*) strife among the gods. [Gk. *theomakhia*].
THEOMANCY, [thē'-ō-man-si], *n.* divination by a divine oracle. [THEO- and Gk. *manteia* divination].
THEOMORPHIC, [thē'-ō-maw'-fik], *adj.* resembling a god. [Gk. *theomorphos* having divine form].
THEOPATHETIC, [thē'-ō-path-et'-ik], *adj.* pertaining to theopathy.
THEOPATHY, [thē-op'-ath-i], *n.* the sense of being surrounded by divine influence; responsiveness to divine influence. [THEO- and Gk. *pathos* suffering].
THEOPHANIC, [thē'-ō-fan'-ik], *adj.* of or relating to theophany.
THEOPHANY, [thē-of'-an-i], *n.* a manifestation of God or any deity to mankind. [Gk. *theophaneia*].
THEOPHILANTHROPISM, [thē'-ō-fil-an'-throp-izm], *n.* a theological system propounded in France at the end of the eighteenth century, and depending on belief in God and the immortality of the human soul. [THEO- and PHILANTHROPIST].
THEOPHILANTHROPIST, [thē'-ō-fil-an'-throp-ist], *n.* a believer in theophilanthropy.
THEOPHILANTHROPY, [thē'-ō-fil-an'-throp-i], *n.* theophilanthropism.
THEOPNEUST, [thē'-ō-pnewst], *adj.* theopneustic. [Gk. *theopneustos*].
THEOPNEUSTIA, THEOPNEUSTY, [thē'-ō-pnew'-sti(-a)], *n.* inspiration from God or from any deity.
THEOPNEUSTIC, [thē'-ō-pnew'-stik], *adj.* given by divine inspiration.
THEORBO, [thē-aw'-bō], *n.* a large double-necked lute very popular in the seventeenth century. [Fr. *téorbe*].
THEOREM, [thēer'-em], *n.* (*math.*) a general statement or proposition which requires proof. [Gk. *theorema* theory].
THEOREMATIC, [thēer'-em-at'-ik], *adj.* pertaining to a theorem or theorems. [Gk. *theorematikos*].
THEORETIC (1), [thēer-et'-ik], *n.* a person devoted to contemplation and speculation.
THEORETIC (2), [thēer-et'-ik], *adj.* theoretical. [Gk. *theoretikos* contemplative].
THEORETICAL, [thēer-et'-ik-al], *adj.* pertaining to theory; in accordance with theory as contrasted with practical experience or knowledge, speculative.
THEORETICALLY, [thēer-et'-ik-al-i], *adv.* according to theory, in a theoretical way.
THEORIST, [thēer'-ist], *n.* one who speculates or forms theories; a person who upholds a certain theory; one learned in the theory of a certain subject.
THEORIZE, [thēer'-īz], *v.t.* and *i.* to form a theory or theories; to speculate concerning; to base one's arguments upon unpractical or speculative grounds.
THEORIZER, [thēer'-īz-er], *n.* a theorist, one who theorizes.
THEORY, [thēer'-i], *n.* a speculative system based upon and offering an explanation of observed facts or phenomena; the underlying laws and principles of a science, art, craft, etc., as contrasted with practical or technical knowledge of it; a systematized statement of these laws or principles; speculation, mental view or imagination; (*coll.*) a notion, fad or fancy; **in t.,** in accordance with theoretical knowledge, though not necessarily with practical experience as well. [Gk. *theoria*].
THEOSOPHIC, [thē'-ō-sof'-ik], *adj.* pertaining to theosophy.
THEOSOPHICAL, [thē'-ō-sof'-ik-al], *adj.* theosophic.
THEOSOPHICALLY, [thē'-ō-sof'-ik-al-i], *n.* in a theosophical way.
THEOSOPHISM, [thē-os'-of-izm], *n.* theosophy.
THEOSOPHIST, [thē-os'-of-ist], *n.* one who believes in theosophy.
THEOSOPHIZE, [thē-os'-of-īz], *v.i.* to practise or discourse upon theosophy.
THEOSOPHY, [thē-os'-o-fi], *n.* a recent mystical and speculative religious system which claims to attain a more profound knowledge and insight by establishing a close and direct relationship between the individual soul and the deity; any speculative system of religious thought claiming a deeper knowledge of nature through a mystical contemplation and knowledge of the deity. [Late Gk. *theosophia*].
THEOTOKOS, [thē-ot'-ok-os], *n.* a title of the Blessed Virgin as the mother of God. [Gk. *theotokos* bearing a god].
THERAPEUTAE, [the'-rap-ew'-tē], *n.*(*pl.*) members of a Jewish sect of the first century A.D., who led a semi-monastic life. [Gk. *therapeutai* healers].
THERAPEUTIC, [the'-rap-ew'-tik], *adj.* relating to the art of healing and the treatment of disease. [Gk. *therapeutike* the art of healing].
THERAPEUTICAL, [the'-rap-ew'-tik-al], *adj.* therapeutic.
THERAPEUTICS, [the'-rap-ew'-tiks], *n.*(*pl.*) the art of healing and curing diseases; that branch of medical science concerned with this.
THERAPEUTIST, [the'-rap-ew'-tist], *n.* one skilled in therapeutics.
THERAPY, [the'-rap-i], *n.* (*med.*) treatment intended to cure.
THERE (1), [THāer], *adv.* in that place or towards that place (always referring to a locality other than that in which the speaker is); (*fig.*) at that point in an argument, discussion, speculation, story, etc.; used as an impersonal pronoun as the subject of a verb (usually the verb *to be*) and at the beginning of a sentence; **to be all t.,** to be very sharp witted; **to get t.,** to attain one's ambition; **t. you are,** I told you so; **t. you go,** you are doing it again. [OE. *thær*].
THERE (2), [THāer], *int.* **there, there,** (when soothing a child) hush, don't cry, dear; **t. now,** I told you it would happen; that's better, isn't it?
THEREABOUT, [THāer'-a-bowt'], *adv.* thereabouts, in that vicinity.
THEREABOUTS, [THāer'-a-bowts'], *adv.* near that place; (*fig.*) approximately that number, degree, or quantity.
THEREAFTER, [THāer-ahf'-ter], *adv.* after that, on subsequent occasions; in accordance with that.
THEREANENT, [THāer'-a-nent'], *adv.* in connection with that.
THEREAT, [THāer-at'], *adv.* at that place or time; in consequence of that, immediately after that.
THEREAWAY, [THāer'-a-wā'], *adv.* in that direction; in those parts or regions.
THEREBY, [THāer'-bī'], *adv.* near that place; by that means.
THEREFOR, [THāer-faw(r)'], *adv.* for that.
THEREFORE, [THāer'-faw(r)], *adv.* on that account, for that reason; consequently. [ME. *therfore*].
THEREFROM, [THāer-from'], *adv.* from that, away from that place.
THEREIN, [THāer-in'], *adv.* in that place; in or within that.
THEREINAFTER, [THāer'-in-ahf'-ter], *adv.* in all which follows (in another document).
THEREINTO, [THāer-in'-tōō], *adv.* into that place.
THEREOF†, [THāer-ov'], *adv.* of that, of those.

THEREON, [THāer-on'], *adv.* on that, on this; after that, as a result of that.

THEREOUT†, [THāer-owt'], *adv.* out of that, outside.

THERETHROUGH†, [THāer-thrōō'], *adv.* through that; by that means.

THERETO, [THāer'-tōō'], *adv.* to that; moreover, in addition.

THERETOFORE†, [THāer'-tōō-faw(r)'], *adv.* previously, up to that time.

THEREUNDER, [THāer-un'-der], *adv.* under that.

THEREUNTO†, [THāer-un'-tōō'], *adv.* to that place.

THEREUPON, [THāer'-up-on'], *adv.* upon that; on account of that; straightway, immediately.

THEREWITH, [THāer-WITH'], *adv.* together with that; immediately following that, straightway.

THEREWITHAL, [THāer'-WITH-awl'], *adv.* over and above that.

THERIANTHROPIC, [thēer'-i-an-throp'-ik], *adj.* having a form partly human and partly animal. [Gk. *ther* animal and *anthropos* man].

THERIANTHROPISM, [thēer'-i-an'-throp-izm], *n.* the worship of therianthropic images and gods.

THERIOMORPHIC, [thēer'-i-ō-maw'-fik], *adj.* like an animal. [Gk. *ther* animal and *morphe* shape].

THERIOMORPHOUS, [thēer'-i-ō-maw'-fus], *adj.* theriomorphic.

THERIOTOMY, [thēer-i-ot'-om-i], *n.* the dissection of animals. [Gk. *ther* animal and *tome* a cutting].

THERM, [thurm], *n.* the amount of heat required to raise one pound of water at its maximum density by one degree Fahrenheit; a unit of heating value used in measuring coal-gas and equal to 100,000 British thermal units. [Gk. *therme* heat].

THERMAE, [thur'-mē], *n.(pl.)* hot springs or baths. [L. *thermae*].

THERMAESTHESIA, [thur-mes-thē'-zi-a], *n.* sense of heat or cold; sensitiveness to heat. [THERMO- and Gk. *aisthesis* perception].

THERMAL, [thurm'-al], *adj.* pertaining to heat; hot, warm.

THERMANTIDOTE, [thurm-an'-tid-ōt], *n.* a device used in hot climates to cool the air. [THERMO- and ANTIDOTE].

THERMATOLOGY, [thurm'-at-ol'-o-ji], *n.* medical treatment by hot mineral springs. [THERMO- and Gk. *logos* speech].

THERMIC, [thurm'-ik], *adj.* thermal, pertaining to heat, hot.

THERMIDOR, [thurm'-id-aw(r)], *n.* the eleventh month in the calendar of the French Revolutionaries, extending from July 19 to August 17. [Fr. *thermidor*].

THERMIDORIAN, [thurm'-id-aw'-ri-an], *n.* a member of the party that overthrew Robespierre on Thermidor 9 (July 27), 1794.

THERMION, [thur'-mi-on], *n.* (*elect.*) an electron emitted by a heated body. [Gk. *thermos* hot].

THERMIONIC, [thurm'-i-on'-ik], *adj.* (*elect.*) relating to thermions; **t. valve,** a vacuum tube used in wireless engineering, containing at least two cathodes, one of which is a heated filament; **t. emission,** the stream of electrons emitted by the heated filament in a thermionic valve.

THERMIONICS, [thur-mi-on'-iks], *n.(pl.)* (*elect.*) the science which deals with the emission of electrons from a heated body.

THERMIT, THERMITE, [thur'-mit, thur'-mīt], *n.* a mixture of very finely granulated aluminium with the oxide of some other metal (usually iron), which, when ignited, burns at a very high temperature. [Germ. *thermit*].

THERMO-, *pref.* pertaining to heat. [Gk. *thermos* hot].

THERMOBAROMETER, [thur'-mō-ba-rom'-it-er], *n.* an instrument which measures the altitude of a given locality by registering the boiling point of water in that locality. [THERMO- and BAROMETER].

THERMOCHEMISTRY, [thur'-mō-kem'-is-tri], *n.* a branch of chemistry which deals with the development of heat by chemical action.

THERMO-COUPLE, [thur'-mō-kupl'], *n.* a device consisting of two different metals joined in two different places, one of these joins being heated more than the other so that an electromotive force is produced, a thermopile. [THERMO- and COUPLE (1)].

THERMO-CURRENT, [thur'-mō-ku'-rent], *n.* an electric current developed by heat, as in a thermocouple.

THERMODYNAMICS, [thur'-mō-dī-nam'-iks], *n.(pl.)* the science which deals with the relationship between thermal energy (heat) and mechanical energy, and the conversion of one into the other.

THERMO-ELECTRIC, [thur'-mō-il-ek'-trik], *adj.* relating to thermo-electricity.

THERMO-ELECTRICAL, [thur'-mō-il-ek'-trik-al], *adj.* thermo-electric.

THERMO-ELECTRICITY, [thur'-mō-il-ek-tris'-i-ti], *n.* electricity developed by the action of heat at the junction of two different metals.

THERMO-ELECTROMETER, [thur'-mō-il-ek-trom'-it-er], *n.* an instrument which, by measuring the heat produced by any given electric current, registers the power of that current.

THERMOGENESIS, [thur'-mō-jen'-is-is], *n.* the generation of heat in an animal body.

THERMOGENETIC, [thur'-mō-jen-et'-ik], *adj.* relating to thermogenesis.

THERMOGENOUS, [thur-moj'-en-us], *adj.* generating or producing heat. [THERMO- and Gk. *genes* producing].

THERMOGRAM, [thur'-mō-gram'], *n.* the diagram produced by a thermograph. [THERMO- and Gk. *gramma* writing].

THERMOGRAPH, [thur'-mō-graf], *n.* a thermometer which makes a record automatically. [THERMO- and Gk. *graphia* writing].

THERMOLOGY, [thur-mol'-o-ji], *n.* the science which deals with heat. [THERMO- and Gk. *logos* speech].

THERMOMETER, [thur-mom'-it-er], *n.* an instrument by which temperature is measured. [THERMO- and METER].

THERMOMETRIC, [thur'-mō-met'-rik], *adj.* thermometrical.

THERMOMETRICAL, [thur'-mō-met'-rik-al], *adj.* pertaining to or measured by means of a thermometer.

THERMOMETRICALLY, [thur'-mō-met'-rik-al-i], *adv.* with or by means of a thermometer.

THERMOMETRY, [thur-mom'-it-ri], *n.* the science and technique of measuring heat. [THERMO- and Gk. *metria* measurement].

THERMOMOTIVE, [thur'-mō-mō'-tiv], *adj.* pertaining to a thermomotor or to motion produced by heat.

THERMOMOTOR, [thur'-mō-mōt'-or], *n.* a motor or engine driven by hot air.

THERMOPHILIC, [thur'-mō-fil'-ik], *adj.* (*biol.*) (of bacteria) flourishing best in warmth. [THERMO- and Gk. *philos* loving].

THERMOPHORE, [thur'-mō-faw(r)], *n.* an apparatus for heating purposes. [THERMO- and Gk. *phoros* bearing].

THERMOPHYLLITE, [thur'-mō-fil'-īt], *n.* a mineral which resembles chlorite.

THERMOPILE, [thur'-mō-pīl], *n.* a thermo-couple.

THERMOPLEGIA, [thur'-mō-plē'-ja], *n.* (*med.*) an apoplectic fit due to exposure to heat, a heat stroke. [THERMO- and Gk. *plege* a blow].

THERMOSCOPE, [thur'-mō-skōp], *n.* an instrument for measuring changes of temperature. [THERMO- and SCOPE].

THERMOSCOPIC, [thur'-mō-skop'-ik], *adj.* pertaining to a thermoscope.

THERMOSCOPICAL, [thur'-mō-skop'-ik-al], *adj.* thermoscopic.

THERMOS FLASK, [thur'-mos-flahsk'], *n.* (*prot.*) a flask of which the sides are a double wall enclosing a vacuum, and which is used to keep liquids at a constant temperature. [~THERMO- and FLASK].

THERMOSTAT, [thur'-mō-stat'], *n.* an instrument which regulates temperature automatically. [THERMO- and Gk. *statikos* causing to stand].

THERMOSTATIC, [thur'-mō-stat'-ik], *adj.* relating to a thermostat.

THERMOSTATICS, [thur'-mō-stat'-iks], *n.(pl.)* the science and theory dealing with the equilibrium of heat.

THERMO-SYPHON, [thur'-mō-sī'-fon], *n.* the movement of water through the cooling system in the engine of a motor-car. [THERMO- and SYPHON].

THERMOTAXIC, [thur'-mō-taks'-ik], *adj.* pertaining to thermotaxis.

THERMOTAXIS, [thur'-mō-taks'-is], *n.* the regulation of bodily heat. [THERMO- and Gk. *taxis* arrangement].

THERMOTHERAPY, [thur'-mō-the'-ra-pi], *n.* the cure of disease by heat.

THERMOTIC, [thur-mot'-ik], *adj.* pertaining to heat or to thermotics. [Gk. *thermotikos* warming].

THERMOTICS, [thur-mot'-iks], *n.(pl.)* the science dealing with heat.

THEROID, [thēer'-oid], *adj.* like an animal in form, habits, etc. [Gk. *ther* wild animal and *oeides* like].

THESAURUS, [thi-saw'-rus], *n.* a collection of any sort, an anthology, lexicon, etc. [Gk. *thesauros* treasury].
THESE, [THēz], *dem. pron. and adj.* (*pl.*) of THIS.
THESIS, [thē'-sis], *n.* (*pros.*) that part of a metrical foot which carries the stress, as contrasted with the unaccented part or arsis; a theory or proposition stated or presented for proof or as a subject for discussion; an academic dissertation on a fixed theme presented by a candidate for a university degree, and usually expected to embody the results of original research. [Gk. *thesis* an arranging or setting forth].
THESMOTHETE, [thez'-mō-thēt], *n.* a judge and lawgiver in ancient Athens; a legislator. [Gk. *thesmothetes*].
THESPIAN (1), [thes'-pi-an], *n.* an actor.
THESPIAN (2), [thes'-pi-an], *adj.* pertaining to acting and the drama. [Gk. *Thespis*, the traditional founder of the drama].
THETA, [thē'-ta], *n.* the letter θ in the Greek alphabet corresponding to *th.* [Gk. *theta*].
THEURGIC, [thē-ur'-jik], *adj.* pertaining to theurgy, magical. [Gk. *theourgikos* magical].
THEURGICAL, [thē-ur'-jik-al], *adj.* theurgic.
THEURGIST, [thē-ur'-jist], *n.* one who practises theurgy or magic.
THEURGY, [thē'-ur-ji], *n.* magic, miracle-working, witchcraft. [Gk. *theourgia* sorcery].
THEW, [thew], *n.* muscle, sinew, bodily strength, moral or mental strength. [OE. *theaw* custom].
THEWED, [thewd], *adj.* having thews, displaying robustness.
THEWLESS, [thew'-les], *adj.* lacking strength either mental or moral.
THEWY, [thew'-i], *adj.* robust, muscular.
THEY, [THā], *pron. 3rd pers. pl., common gender, nom.* those (people or things), those already referred to; (*coll.*) *indefinite pron.* people. [OScand. *theirr*].
THIASUS, [thī'-as-us], *n.* (*Gk. antiq.*) a religious brotherhood formed to do honour to a god; a religious ceremony attended by such a brotherhood. [Gk. *thiasos*].
THIBLE, THIVEL, [thibl, thivl], *n.* a pot-stick, a stick for stirring porridge or any stew which is being cooked. [Unkn.].
THICK (1), [thik], *n.* the thickest place in anything; **to be in the t. of it**, to be in the press of battle surrounded with difficulties, or in the midst of difficult and exacting work.
THICK (2), [thik], *adj.* of considerable size between opposite surfaces; (of fluids) having considerable density, muddy, sluggish; (of a group of objects) placed closely together, crowded; very frequently repeated; (of the voice) harsh and confused, not clear; (of the intellect) dull-witted; (*coll.*) very intimate; **a bit t.**, (*coll.*) scarcely tolerable; **to give a t. ear to**, to give a blow on the ear. [ME. *thikke*].
THICKBACK, [thik'-bak'], *n.* (*U.S.*) the fish, *Solea variegata*. [THICK (2) and BACK (1)].
THICKEN, [thik'-en], *v.t. and i.* to make thick or become thick.
THICKENING, [thik'-ning], *n.* the process of making or becoming thick; that part of an object which grows thicker than the rest; that which serves to make a liquid more dense.
THICKET, [thik'-it], *n.* a small wood, *esp.* one with dense undergrowth. [OE. *thiccet*].
THICKHEAD, [thik'-hed'], *n.* (*coll.*) a dull-witted person; an aching head through over-indulgence in strong drink.
THICK-HEADED, [thik'-hed'-id], *adj.* dull-witted, stupid.
THICKISH, [thik'-ish], *adj.* rather thick.
THICKKNEE, [thik'-nē'], *n.* the stone curlew or great plover, *Œdicnemus scolopax*.
THICKLY, [thik'-li], *adv.* in a thick way, densely, closely, in quick succession.
THICKNESS, [thik-'nes], *n.* the quality of being thick; that dimension of an object obtained by measuring between two opposite surfaces.
THICKSET, [thik'-set'], *adj.* arranged densely and closely together; (of persons, etc.) short and broad, of solid build, sturdy.
THICK-SKIN, [thik'-skin'], *n.* a coarse, insensitive person.
THICK-SKINNED, [thik'-skind'], *adj.* having a thick skin; (*fig.*) (of persons) insensitive, not easily touched by common emotions, *esp.* insensitive to taunts and abuse.
THICK-SKULLED, [thik'-skuld'], *adj.* dull-witted.
THIEF, (*pl.* **thieves**), [thēf], *n.* one who commits robbery; a fault in the wick of a candle. [OE. *theof*].
THIEFCATCHER, [thēf'-kach'-er], *n.* a person employed in apprehending thieves.
THIEVE, [thēv], *v.t. and i.* to commit theft; to steal. [OE. *theofian*].
THIEVERY, [thēv'-er-i], *n.* the practice of stealing, theft, robbery.
THIEVISH, [thēv'-ish], *adj.* of, or addicted to, stealing; resembling a thief.
THIEVISHLY, [thēv'-ish-li], *adv.* in a thievish way.
THIEVISHNESS, [thēv'-ish-nes], *n.* the condition of being a thief; the custom or habit of stealing.
THIGH, [thī], *n.* that part of the human leg between the knee and the trunk; the corresponding part of the leg in apes and birds; the corresponding part of the hind legs of quadrupeds; the thighbone; that part of the clothing which covers the thigh. [OE. *theoh*].
THIGHBONE, [thī'-bōn], *n.* the bone of the thigh, the femur.
THIGHED, [thīd], *adj.* having a thigh or thighs.
THILK, [THilk], *pron.* (*dial., archaic*) the same. [ME. *the ilk*].
THILL, [thil], *n.* the shaft of a cart to which a horse or other animal is attached. [ME. *thille*].
THILLER, [thil'-er], *n.* a thill.
THIMBLE, [thimbl], *n.* a small cap fitted over the middle finger of the right hand (the finger which thrusts the needle) when sewing; any similar article used in mechanical instruments. [OE. *thymel* thumbstall].
THIMBLEFUL, [thimbl'-fo͝ol], *n.* as much as a thimble will hold; a very little (usually applied to liquids).
THIMBLERIG (1), [thimbl'-rig'], *n.* a cheating game in which the operator rapidly shifts a pea or other small object from under one of three inverted thimbles or cups.
THIMBLERIG (2), [thimbl'-rig'], *v.t. and i.* to swindle at thimblerig; to cheat or swindle.
THIMBLERIGGER, [thimbl'-rig'-er], *n.* one who swindles at thimblerig.
THIMBLERIGGING, [thimbl'-rig'-ing], *n.* the act of playing at thimblerig; (*fig.*) dishonest and cheating practice.
THIN (1), [thin], *adj.* not thick, used of an object having a small distance between opposite surfaces; of a person or animal not fat or plump, bony, emaciated; sparsely arranged; of liquids, having a low density; of soup and other liquid foods, not sluggish or heavy; of an argument, etc., being of no great account, easily refuted or improved upon, lacking in thoughtfulness. [OE. *thynne*].
THIN (2), [thin], *v.t. and i.* to make thin or become thin or thinner; **to t. out**, to make or become more sparse.
THINE, [THīn], *poss. pron. and adj. 2nd pers. sg.* (*archaic*) of thee. [OE. *thin*].
THING, [thing], *n.* (*hist.*) an old English or old Scandinavian legal or parliamentary gathering; an animate or inanimate object, made of a material stuff or substance, and forming an entity in itself; any conception of the mind, an idea, a fact, a thought, a subject of conversation, etc.; applied familiarly or colloquially to persons; a circumstance or fact; (*coll.*) that which is suitable, fitting, desirable, etc.; (*pl.*) circumstances, the state of affairs generally, trade, business, the matter in hand; personal belongings, baggage, parcels, clothes, etc.; **to make a good t. of**, to render very profitable; **for one t.**, in the first place; **it's just the t.!** (*coll.*) it's exactly what we want!; **not to feel quite the t.**, (*coll.*) to feel rather unwell; **no such t.!** (*coll.*) certainly not, by no means!; **to know a t. or two**, (*coll.*) to be well informed; **quite the t.**, (*coll.*) (sarcastically) to the manner born. [OE. *thing*].
THINGAMY, see THINGUMMY.
THINGUMABOB, see THINGUMMYBOB.
THINGUMAJIG, [thing'-um-a-jig'], *n.* a thingummy.
THINGUMMY, THINGAMY, [thing'-um-i], *n.* a word used to refer to something the name of which is forgotten for the moment.
THINGUMMYBOB, THINGUMABOB, [thing'-um-i-bob'], *n.* a thingummy.
THINK, [thingk], *v.t. and i.* to exercise the reasoning or contemplative faculties; to reason within the mind, to meditate or reflect; to be of an opinion, to believe without certainly knowing; to hold in the mind, to consider to be (such and such); to anticipate, expect, surmise; to bring oneself into a certain state by too much thought, or by anticipating in the mind the circumstances of that state; **to t. of**, to call to mind, to hit upon in the mind; to remember, reflect upon, turn over in the mind; to be of an opinion

about; **to t. about,** to occupy one's thoughts with, reflect upon, consider, remember, reason about in the mind, contemplate mentally; **to t. better of,** to change one's intention concerning; **not to t. of** (doing something), to have no intention of (doing something); **not to t. much of** (someone or something), to have a low opinion of; **to t. out,** to work out mentally; **to t. up,** (*coll.*) to concoct, invent; **to t. over,** to consider carefully; to reconsider; **I don't t.!** (*coll.*) an emphatic negative used to cancel a statement ironically put in the affirmative; **to t. nothing of,** to hold in low esteem. [OE. *thencan*].

THINKABLE, [thingk'-abl], *adj.* able to be thought of or conceived.

THINKER, [thingk'-er], *n.* one who thinks; a philosopher, a man of intellect.

THINKING (1), [thingk'-ing], *n.* the act of exercising the reasoning and contemplative faculties.

THINKING (2), [thingk'-ing], *adj.* given to thought, thoughtful, capable of thought and reason.

THINKINGLY, [thingk'-ing-li], *adv.* with thoughtfulness.

THINLY, [thin'-li], *adv.* in a thin fashion; sparsely, sparingly.

THINNESS, [thin'-nes], *n.* the quality of being thin.

THINNISH, [thin'-ish], *adj.* somewhat thin.

THIN-SKINNED, [thin'-skind'], *adj.* having a thin skin; unduly sensitive, easily offended.

THIRD (1), [thurd], *n.* that thing or person, etc., in a series coming next after the second; one of three equal parts; (*mus.*) an interval of three consecutive degrees of the scale; (*motoring*) the third gear of a motor engine.

THIRD (2), [thurd], *adj.* the ordinal numeral of the cardinal THREE; coming next after the second; being one of three equal parts or divisions. [OE. *thridda*].

THIRD-BOROUGH†, [thurd'-bu'-rō], *n.* a petty constable or watchman.

THIRD DEGREE, [thurd'-di-grē'], *n.* (*U.S.*) rough handling by the police of a suspected person to obtain information or a confession.

THIRDINGS, [thurd'-ingz], *n.(pl.)* the third of all kinds of produce paid to a landlord by a tenant who occupies his holding upon such condition.

THIRD INTERNATIONAL, [thurd'-in-ter-nash'-un-al], *n.* the international, world-wide communist party organization aiming at world revolution on communistic lines.

THIRDLY, [thurd'-li], *adv.* in the third place.

THIRD MAN, [thurd'-man'], *n.* (*cricket*) a fielder on the offside between slip and point.

THIRD PARTY, [thurd'-pah'-ti], *n.* (*leg.*) a party, other than the two principals, involved in a case; **t. p. risks,** the liability of the holder of an insurance policy with regard to persons or parties not specifically referred to in the policy.

THIRD-RATE, [thurd'-rāt'], *adj.* (*coll.*) of poor quality.

THIRDS†, [thurdz], *n.(pl.)* (*leg.*) the third part of the personalty of her husband to which a widow is entitled.

THIRL (1), THURL, [thurl], *n.* (*dial.*) a bore, perforation, opening or aperture. [OE. *thyrel*].

THIRL (2)†, THURL†, [thurl], *v.t.* to perforate or bore through, *esp.* in mining. [OE. *thyrlian*].

THIRL (3)†, [thurl], *v.t. and i.* to send spinning into the air; to spin or revolve. [Uncert.].

THIRL (4), [thurl], *v.t. and i.* (*Scots*) to bind or be bound to.

THIRLAGE, THRILLAGE, [thur'-lij], *n.* (*Scots leg.*) a form of bondage by which a landlord could compel his tenants to have the corn ground at his mill or at a mill of his choosing. [~THRALL].

THIRST (1), [thurst], *n.* the desire to drink, the painful sensation caused by lack of drink; (*fig.*) any powerful craving, as for knowledge, adventure, etc.; extreme dryness of the soil. [OE. *thyrst*].

THIRST (2), [thurst], *v.i.* to experience thirst, to feel thirsty, to lack drink; **to t. for (or after),** to have a great desire or craving for.

THIRSTILY, [thurst'-i-li], *adv.* in a thirsty way.

THIRSTINESS, [thurst'-i-nes], *n.* the state of being thirsty.

THIRSTY, [thurst'-i], *adj.* suffering from thirst, desiring drink; parched, lacking moisture; causing thirstiness. [OE. *thyrstig*].

THIRTEEN (1), [thur'-tēn'], *n.* one more than twelve.

THIRTEEN (2), [thur'-tēn], *adj.* amounting to one more than twelve. [OE. *threotene*].

THIRTEENTH (1), [thur'-tēnth'], *n.* the next after the twelfth; one of thirteen equal parts or divisions.

THIRTEENTH (2), [thur-tēnth'], *adj.* following next after the twelfth.

THIRTIETH (1), [thur'-ti-eth], *n.* the person or thing in a series which follows next after the twenty-ninth; one of thirty equal parts or divisions.

THIRTIETH (2), [thur'-ti-eth], *adj.* following next after the twenty-ninth.

THIRTY (1), [thurt'-i], *n.* the cardinal number, three times ten; the symbol for this; (*pl.*) the third decade of any century; the third decade of a person's life.

THIRTY (2), [thurt'-i], *adj.* amounting to three times ten. [OE. *thrittig*].

THIRTYFOLD (1), [thur'-ti-fōld], *adj.* multiplied thirty times.

THIRTYFOLD (2), [thur'-ti-fōld'], *adv.* thirty times. [THIRTY and FOLD (1)].

THIS (1), [THis], *dem. pron.* used to refer to a person or thing actually near or that which was last referred to, spoken or thought, or that which will be next referred to or spoken; **all t.,** these things considered collectively; **like t.,** in this manner; **for all t.,** despite these considerations. [OE. *this*].

THIS (2), [THis], *dem. adj.* referring to the one nearest to hand, last referred to, etc.; used with expressions referring to periods of time, e.g. year, morning, week, etc., and meaning, the current one; frequently used in contrast with THAT. [OE. *this*].

THIS (3), [THis], *adv.* **t. much,** so much and no more.

THISNESS, [THis'-nes], *n.* the state or quality of being 'this'; the sense of present and actual existence.

THISTLE, [thisl], *n.* (*bot.*) one of various prickly plants of the genus *Carduus*, *esp.* with yellow or purple flowers; the national emblem of Scotland; **Order of the T.,** a Scottish order of knights (K.T., Knight of the Thistle). [OE. *thistel*].

THISTLE-DOWN, [thisl'-down'], *n.* the long hairs on the seed of thistles, by means of which the seeds are carried along in the air, and so scattered from the parent plant.

THISTLY, [this'-li], *adj.* overgrown with thistles; prickly like a thistle.

THITHER (1), [THiTH'-er], *adj.* lying on the other side, away from the speaker, beyond.

THITHER (2), [THiTH'-er], *adv.* to that place; towards that place, in that direction. [OE. *thider*].

THITHERWARD, [THiTH'-er-werd], *adv.* towards that place, thither, in that direction. [OE. *thiderweard*].

THITSI, see THEETSEE.

THIVEL, see THIBLE.

THLIPSIS, [thlip'-sis], *n.* (*med.*) compression of a blood-vessel by pressure from without. [Gk. *thlipsis* pressure].

THO' [THō], *adv.* (*poet.*) though.

THOLE (1), THOWL, [thōl], *n.* the peg in the gunwale of a rowing boat against which the oar is pulled, the rowlock. [OE. *thol* rowlock].

THOLE (2), [thōl], *v.t.* (*Scots*) to endure, suffer, tolerate. [OE. *tholian*].

THOLE-PIN, [thōl'-pin], *n.* a thole.

THOLOBATE, [thō-lob-āt], *n.* (*arch.*) the structure immediately beneath a dome which bears the weight of the dome. [Gk. *tholos* dome and *bates* one who goes].

THOMAEAN (1), [tō-mē'-an], *n.* a member of the Thomaean Church.

THOMAEAN (2), [tō-mē'-an], *adj.* relating to the Church among the people of the Malabar coast which has existed from early Christian times, and is traditionally supposed to have been founded by St. Thomas the Apostle. [St. *Thomas*].

THOMISM, [tōm'-izm], *n.* the philosophical and theological teaching of St. Thomas Aquinas.

THOMIST (1), [tō'-mist], *n.* a follower of St. Thomas Aquinas.

THOMIST (2), [tōm'-ist], *adj.* pertaining to Thomism.

THOMISTIC, [tō-mis'-tik], *adj.* pertaining to Thomism.

THOMISTICAL, [tō-mis'-tik-al], *adj.* Thomistic.

THOMSONITE, [tom'-son-īt], *n.* (*min.*) a white or brown hydrous silicate of aluminium, sodium, and calcium. [Dr. Thomas *Thomson*, 1773-1852].

THONG, [thong], *n.* a strip of leather used as a strap or lash. [OE. *thwang*].

THORACIC, [thaw-ras'-ik], *adj.* (*anat.*) pertaining to the thorax. [Gk. *thorakikos*].

THORACICS, [thaw-ras'-iks], *n.(pl.)* (*zool.*) fish that have ventral fins situated immediately beneath their pectoral fins.

THORAX, [thaw'-raks], *n.* (*anat., zool.*) in a mammal, that part of the body between the neck and abdomen, including ribs, breasts, and lungs, etc.; the similar part in the lower vertebrates, fish, birds, etc.;

in insects, the middle segment of the body. [Gk. *thorax* chest].

HORITE, [thaw'-rit], *n.* (*min.*) a black or brown silicate of thorium found in Norway. [Swed. *thorit*].

HORIUM, [thaw'-ri-um], *n.* (*chem.*) the rare metallic element denoted by the symbol Th, and found in thorite.

HORN, [thawn], *n.* a spike, spine, or prickle on the twigs and branches of some trees and bushes; a plant bearing these, *esp.* the hawthorn; one of the Old English symbols for the sounds now represented by *th*; (*fig.*) any nuisance, worry, or irritating disability; **a t. in one's side**, a nuisance or annoyance; **a t. in the flesh**, a secret worry, trouble, ailment, or disability. [OE. *thorn*].

HORNAPPLE, [thawn'-apl'], *n.* a weed of cultivated ground with prickly fruits, *Datura stramonium*.

HORNBACK, [thawn'-bak'], *n.* the common ray or skate, *Raia clavata*, so called because it has several rows of short spines or thorns on its back.

THORNBACK

HORNBROOM, [thawn'-brōōm], *n.* (*bot.*) the common furze or gorse, *Ulex europæus*.

HORN-BUSH, [thawn'-bŏŏsh], *n.* any shrub that produces thorns.

HORN-HEDGE, [thawn'-hej'], *n.* a hedge composed of thorn-bearing shrubs.

HORNLESS, [thawn'-les], *adj.* lacking thorns.

HORNSET, [thawn'-set'], *adj.* bristling with thorns.

HORNY, [thawn'-i], *adj.* full of thorns; (*fig.*) presenting many difficulties, by no means easy.

HOROUGH† **(1)**, [thu'-ru], *prep.* through. [OE. *thurh*].

HOROUGH (2), [thu'-ru], *adj.* complete, perfect, entire, out-and-out, downright.

HOROUGH-BASS, [thu'-ru-bās'], *n.* (*mus.*) a notation in which the chords intended for the bass part are indicated by figures; the theory and practice of harmony.

HOROUGHBRACE, [thu'-ru-brās'], *n.* (*U.S.*) one of two strong leather straps which form part of the supports of a coach.

HOROUGHBRED (1), [thu'-ru-bred'], *n.* a thoroughbred creature or plant, *esp.* a horse.

HOROUGHBRED (2), [thu'-ru-bred'], *adj.* (of animals) being of pure breed; (*esp.* of horses) having ancestors which for a considerable number of generations back are recorded in the stud-book; (of human beings) being of aristocratic birth and showing the characteristics of such birth.

HOROUGHFARE, [thu'-ru-fāer'], *n.* a way through, an open road.

HOROUGHGOING, [thu'-ru-gō'-ing], *adj.* going all and any length, uncompromising.

HOROUGH-LIGHTED†, [thu'-ru-lī'-tid], *adj.* having thorough-lights.

HOROUGH-LIGHTS†, [thu'-ru-līts'], *n.*(*pl.*) windows arranged on opposite sides of a room.

HOROUGHLY, [thu'-ru-li], *adv.* completely, entirely, in a thorough fashion.

HOROUGHNESS, [thu'-ru-nes], *n.* the quality of being thorough, of having been thoroughly performed.

HOROUGHPACED, [thu'-ru-pāst'], *adj.* complete, downright, thorough.

HOROUGHPIN, [thu'-ru-pin'], *n.* a disease in horses, which causes the hock to swell.

HOROUGHWAX, [thu'-ru-waks'], *n.* (*bot.*) the plant, *Bupleuram rotundifolium*, with perfoliate leaves.

HOROUGHWORT, [thu'-ru-wawt'], *n.* the plant, *Eupatorium perfoliatum*, found in North America.

HORP, THORPE†, [thawp], *n.* a small village, a hamlet (usually in place-names). [ODan. *thorp*].

HOSE, [THōz], *dem. pron. and adj. pl.* of THAT. [OE. *thas*].

HOU, [THOW], *pron. 2nd pers. sg. nom.* of the personal pronoun now employed chiefly in *dial.*, *poet.* and liturgical language. [OE. *thu*].

HOUGH, [thō], *conj.* despite that, notwithstanding that; nevertheless; **as t.**, as if; **even t.**, even if. [OScand. **thoh*].

HOUGHT (1), [thawt], *n.* the act of thinking, the process of thinking; the capacity to think; the result of thinking, *esp.* a short and sometimes epigrammatical statement of an idea or conception; intellectual outlook, a body of ideas and opinions; reasoned and logical ideas; reflection, consideration, care; opinion, point of view; (*coll.*) a small amount or degree; **to have thoughts of**, to intend; **to take t. for**, to consider, take into account. [OE. *thoht*].

THOUGHT (2), [thawt], *pret. and p.pt.* of THINK. [OE. *thoht(e)*].

THOUGHTFUL, [thawt'-fŏŏl], *adj.* full of thought; pensive, much given to thinking; kind, considerate.

THOUGHTFULLY, [thawt'-fŏŏl-i], *adv.* with thought, in a thoughtful way.

THOUGHTFULNESS, [thawt-fŏŏl-nes], *n.* the quality of being thoughtful.

THOUGHTLESS, [thawt'-les], *adj.* careless, stupid, inconsiderate.

THOUGHTLESSLY, [thawt'-les-li], *adv.* in a thoughtless fashion.

THOUGHTLESSNESS, [thawt'-les-nes], *n.* the quality of being thoughtless, want of consideration, heedlessness.

THOUGHT-PROCESS, [thawt'-prō'-ses], *n.* a sequence of thoughts.

THOUGHT-READER, [thawt'-rēd'-er], *n.* a person who practises thought-reading.

THOUGHT-READING, [thawt'-rēd'-ing], *n.* the power of knowing other people's thoughts by telepathy.

THOUGHT-SICK, [thawt'-sik], *adj.* ill at ease and troubled with too much thought.

THOUGHT-TRANSFERENCE, [thawt'-trans'-ferents], *n.* telepathy.

THOUGHT-WAVE, [thawt'-wāv], *n.* a hypothetical wave of thought travelling between two minds.

THOUSAND (1), [thow'-zand], *n.* the number obtained when 100 is multiplied by 10; (*coll.*) (*pl.*) an immense, uncountable number; **one in a t.**, very good, without equal or rival. [OE. *thusend*].

THOUSAND (2), [thow'-zand], *adj.* ten times one hundred; (*coll.*) very many, indefinite in number.

THOUSANDFOLD, [thow'-zand-fōld], *adj.* multiplied a thousand times. [OE. *thusendfeald*].

THOUSANDTH (1), [thow'-zantth], *n.* one of a thousand equal parts or divisions.

THOUSANDTH (2), [thow'-zantth], *adj.* following the nine hundred and ninety-ninth in a set or series; the thousandth part.

THOWL, see THOLE (1).

THOWLESS, [thow'-les], *adj.* lazy, listless, inefficient. [~THEW].

THRALDOM, [thrawl'-dom], *n.* slavery; bondage, the condition of a thrall.

THRALL, [thrawl], *n.* a slave or serf; slavery, bondage. [OScand. *thræll*].

THRANITE, [thran'-īt], *n.* (*Gk. antiq.*) an oarsman in an ancient trireme, it is supposed one who belonged to the top tier, and so had the hardest work in wielding the longest oars. [Gk. *thranites*].

THRAPPLE, see THROPPLE.

THRASH, [thrash], *v.t. and i.* to beat severely, flog; to separate the grain of (cereal) from the husks and straw by beating; to beat at a game; **to t. out**, to discuss (a problem) very thoroughly; **to t. about**, (as of a swimmer) to move the limbs as if flogging something. [OE. *therscan* to beat].

THRASHER, [thrash'-er], *n.* a person or thing which thrashes; an implement for thrashing corn; the fox-shark, *Alopecias vulpes*.

THRASHER

THRASHING, [thrash'-ing], *n.* a beating; a threshing.

THRASHING-FLOOR, see THRESHING-FLOOR.

THRASHING-MACHINE, see THRESHING-MACHINE.

THRASONICAL, [thras-on'-ik-al], *adj.* boastful, bragging. [*Thraso*, the name of a bragging Greek soldier in Terence's *Eunuchus*].

THRASONICALLY, [thras-on'-ik-al-i], *adv.* in a thrasonical manner.

THRAVE, [thrāv], *n.* two shocks of grain each of which contains twelve sheaves. [~Icel. *threfi*].

THREAD (1), [thred], *n.* a slender cord made of fibres (e.g. of silk, wool, cotton, etc.) and used in sewing; a slender, cylindrical filament; the spiral groove of a screw or of a bolt; the connection in a series of thoughts, ideas, events in a narrative, etc.; **to hang by a t.**, to be in a precarious situation. [OE. *thræd*].

THREAD (2), THRID, [thred], *v.t.* to put (a thread) into the eye of (a needle); to place on a thread, string up; **to t. one's way**, to make one's way with care and caution.

THREADBARE, [thred'-bāer], *adj.* (of a fabric) having

the nap so worn down that the thread is visible; (of persons) shabbily dressed in old, worn clothes; (*fig.*) hackneyed, familiar.

THREADBARENESS, [thred'-bäer-nes], *n.* the condition of being threadbare.

THREADER, [thred'-er], *n.* a person or thing that threads; a machine that cuts the thread on a screw.

THREADINESS, [thred'-i-nes], *n.* the quality of being thready.

THREADLIKE, [thred'-līk], *adj.* fine and slender like a thread.

THREADWORM, [thred'-wurm], *n.* a tiny parasitic worm infesting the human intestines.

THREADY, [thred'-i], *adj.* made of thread; like a thread.

THREAT, [thret], *n.* a menacing statement of intention to hurt, punish or damage; circumstance or circumstances which indicate the probability of an undesirable occurrence. [OE. *threat* a troop, oppression].

THREATEN, [thret'-en], *v.t. and i.* to utter a threat or threats to; to utter threats; to offer an appearance suggesting that some undesirable event will occur; to seem likely to happen. [OE. *threatnian*].

THREATENER, [thret'-en-er], *n.* a person who threatens.

THREATENING, [thret'-en-ing], *adj.* foreboding, menacing, portentous.

THREATENINGLY, [thret'-en-ing-li], *adv.* in a threatening fashion.

THREATFUL, [thret'-fool], *adj.* expressing threats.

THREE (1), [thrē], *n.* the number which is one more than two; the symbol representing this. [OE. *threo*].

THREE (2), [thrē], *adj.* two more than one. [OE. *threo*].

THREE-CORNERED, [thrē'-kawn'-erd], *adj.* shaped with three corners, triangular.

THREE-DECKER, [thrē'-dek'-er], *n.* an old-fashioned sailing ship with three decks; an old-fashioned pulpit with three tiers; a novel in three volumes.

THREEFOLD (1), [thrē'-fōld], *adj.* triple, multiplied by three. [OE. *thrifeald*].

THREEFOLD (2), [thrē'-fōld], *adv.* in a threefold manner, triply.

THREE-HALFPENCE, [thrē-hā'-pents], *n.* the sum of a penny and a halfpenny.

THREE-HANDED, [thrē'-hand'-ed], *adj.* having three hands; suitable for three hands or three players.

THREE-LEGGED RACE, [thrē'-leg'-id-rās'], *n.* a race for pairs of competitors in which the right leg of one competitor in a pair is tied to the left leg of the other.

THREE-MASTER, [thrē'-mah'-ster], *n.* a sailing vessel with three masts.

THREEPENCE, [threp'-ents, thrip'-ents], *n.* the sum of three pennies.

THREEPENNY, [threp'-ni, thrip'-ni], *adj.* costing threepence.

THREEPENNY-BIT, [threp'-ni-bit, thrip'-ni-bit] *n.* a small coin worth three pennies.

THREE-PER-CENTS, [thrē'-per-sents'], *n.(pl.)* British Government bonds which yield interest at 3 per cent.

THREE-PLY (1), [thrē'-plī'], *n.* three-ply wood.

THREE-PLY (2), [thrē'-plī'], *adj.* (of a thread) with three strands; (of wood) consisting of three layers.

THREE-QUARTER (1), [thrē'-kwawt'-er], *n.* (*Rugby football*) one whose playing position is between the half-backs and the full-back; (*pl.*) the sum of three out of four equal parts; the greater part of something.

THREE-QUARTER (2), [thrē'-kwawt'-er], *adj.* being equivalent to or consisting of three of four equal parts of a whole.

THREESCORE, [thrē'-skaw(r)'], *n.* thrice twenty, sixty.

THREESOME, [thrē'-sum], *n.* (*golf*) a game for three persons.

THREE-SPEED, [thrē'-spēd'], *adj.* (*cycling*) (of gearing) having three alternative ratios.

THREE-WHEELED, [thrē'-wēld'], *adj.* having only three wheels.

THREE-WHEELER, [thrē'-wēl'-er], *n.* a motor-car that runs on three wheels.

THREMMATOLOGY, [threm'-at-ol'-o-ji], *n.* the science of breeding domestic animals. [Gk. *thremma* nursling and *logos* speech].

THRENETIC, [thren-et'-ik], *adj.* mournful.

THRENETICAL, [thren-et'-ik-al], *adj.* threnetic.

THRENODE, [thrēn'-ōd], *n.* a threnody. [Gk. *threnoidia*].

THRENODIAL, [thrēn-ō'-di-al], *adj.* of, relating to, a threnody.

THRENODIC, [thrēn-od'-ik], *adj.* threnodial.

THRENODIST, [thrēn'-od-ist], *n.* a writer or singer of a threnody.

THRENODY, [thrēn'-ōd-i], *n.* a dirge or lament, a funeral chant. [Gk. *threnoidia*].

THRESH, [thresh], *v.t.* to beat (corn) so as to separate the grain from the chaff. [*Var.* of THRASH].

THRESHEL, [thresh'-el], *n.* a flail for threshing. [OE. *therscel*].

THRESHER, [thresh'-er], *n.* a person or machine that threshes.

THRESHING-FLOOR, THRASHING-FLOOR, [thresh-ing-flaw(r)], *n.* an area where corn is threshed.

THRESHING-MACHINE, THRASHING-MACHINE, [thresh'-ing-ma-shēn'], *n.* a machine for threshing corn.

THRESHOLD, [thresh-hōld], *n.* the wooden beam or stone lying immediately under a door; the entrance to a room, building, etc.; (*fig.*) a beginning or commencement; **t. of consciousness**, (*psych.*) the border line of consciousness. [OE. *therscold*].

THREW, [throō], *pret.* of THROW (2).

THRICE, [thrīs], *adv.* three times; in a threefold measure. [ME. *thries*].

THRICE-BLESSED, [thrīs'-blest'], *adj.* very greatly blessed.

THRID, see THREAD (2).

THRIFT, [thrift], *n.* frugality and economical management; (*bot.*) the sea-pink, *Armeria maritima*. [OScand. *thrift*].

THRIFTILY, [thrift'-i-li], *adv.* in a thrifty way.

THRIFTINESS, [thrift'-i-nes], *n.* the quality of being thrifty, frugality.

THRIFTLESS, [thrift'-les], *adj.* extravagant and wasteful.

THRIFTLESSLY, [thrift'-les-li], *adv.* in a thriftless fashion.

THRIFTLESSNESS, [thrift'-les-nes], *n.* the condition or quality of being thriftless.

THRIFTY, [thrift-i], *adj.* frugal, thriving by frugality, given to steady saving.

THRILL (1), [thril], *n.* the feeling one has when one's emotions are deeply stirred or great enthusiasm is aroused; the glow of enthusiasm or excitement; (*coll.*) an exciting event or circumstance, *esp.* in a story.

THRILL (2), [thril], *v.t. and i.* to provoke to deep emotional excitement, to stir, rouse the emotions of; to feel great enthusiasm, to be deeply stirred in the emotions; to vibrate. [OE. *thyrelian* to pierce].

THRILLAGE, see THIRLAGE.

THRILLER, [thril'-er], *n.* that which provokes thrills; a sensational tale or novel.

THRILLING, [thril'-ing], *adj.* stirring, rousing, exciting, provoking thrills; (of a voice) clear, ringing.

THRILLINGLY, [thril'-ing-li], *adv.* in a thrilling fashion.

THRILLINGNESS, [thril'-ing-nes], *n.* the quality of providing thrills.

THRIPS, [thrips], *n.* a group of various, very small winged insects that live on the vital juices of plants. [Gk. *thrips* wood-worm].

THRIVE, (**throve, thriven**), [thrīv], *v.i.* (of persons) to prosper, to become steadily better off, to get on in one's profession or calling; (of plants, animals, etc.) to increase and flourish; (of ideas, ideologies, etc.) to spread, gain more and more adherents. [OScand. *thrifa*].

THRIVER, [thrīv'-er], *n.* a person who prospers.

THRIVING, [thrīv'-ing], *adj.* steadily increasing in prosperity; increasing or multiplying in numbers; progressing and developing notably in any way.

THRIVINGLY, [thrīv'-ing-li], *adv.* in a thriving, prosperous fashion.

THRIVINGNESS, [thrīv'-ing-nes], *n.* the condition of being prosperous.

THRO', [throō], *adv.* through. [Short form of THROUGH (2)].

THROAT (1), [thrōt], *n.* (*anat.*) the passage in the neck connecting the mouth and nose with the stomach and lungs, the gullet, the windpipe; the front of the neck; (*fig.*) any similar narrow passage; **to thrust (or ram) (something) down (a person's) t.**, to preach to a person about, or force him to accept (something), even against his will. [OE. *throte*].

THROAT (2), [thrōt], *v.t.* to put a groove or throat on to.

THROATBAND, [thrōt'-band'], *n.* a band that goes round the throat.

THROATINESS, [thrōt'-i-nes], *n.* the condition of being throaty.

THROAT-LATCH, [thrōt'-lach'], *n.* the strap on a bridle which passes under a horse's throat.

THROATPIPE, [thrōt'-pīp], *n.* the windpipe, trachea.
THROATY, [thrōt'-i], *adj.* (of the voice) harsh and guttural.
THROB (1), [throb], *n.* one of a succession of vibrations, a pulsation or beat, a pulse.
THROB (2), [throb], *v.i.* to beat, pulsate, or palpitate, to do this rapidly. [ME. *throbben*].
THROE, [thrō], *n.* a burst of violent pain, a great momentary anguish or agony; (*pl.*) a series of such experiences; **to be in the throes of,** to be busily battling with the difficulties and problems of. [OScand. *thra*].
THROMBIN, [throm'-bin], *n.* (*physiol.*) a substance which causes clotting in the blood. [Gk. *thrombos* a clot].
THROMBOLITE, [throm'-bōl-īt], *n.* a mineral containing copper oxide and oxide of antimony. [Germ. *thrombolit*].
THROMBOSE, [throm'-bōs], *v.t.* to produce thrombosis in.
THROMBOSIS, [throm-bō'-sis], *n.* (*med.*) a stoppage in the blood-stream by the formation of a clot. [Gk. *thrombosis*].
THROMBUS, [throm'-bus], *n.* (*med.*) a clot in the blood-stream.
THRONE (1), [thrōn], *n.* a chair of state, *esp.* of a king, bishop, or archbishop; (*theol.*) an order of angels; (*fig.*) the power and authority of a king; the monarchy; the sovereign himself. [Gk. *thronos* a seat].
THRONE (2), [thrōn], *v.t.* to place on a throne, enthrone; to pay great respect and veneration to.
THRONELESS, [thrōn'-les], *adj.* having no throne, deposed.
THRONG (1), [throng], *n.* a great close-packed crowd of people, a multitude. [OE. *gethrang*].
THRONG (2), [throng], *v.t. and i.* to crowd round, press upon in a crowd; to gather together into a crowd; to fill with multitudes of people; to come in great numbers.
THROPPLE, THRAPPLE, [thropl, thrapl], *n.* the windpipe, *esp.* of a horse or other animal. [OE. *throtbolla*].
THROSTLE, [throsl], *n.* the common thrush or mavis; a certain sort of spinning machine for spinning wool and cotton, etc. [OE. *throstle*].
THROTTLE (1), [throtl], *n.* a throat or neck; anything resembling this, *esp.* the valve in an engine regulating the supply of gas, steam, etc. [ME. *throtel, dim.* of THROAT].
THROTTLE (2), [throtl], *v.t.* to choke by squeezing the throat or windpipe; to kill by this method; (*fig.*) to check, crush, suppress; **to t. down,** to reduce the power (and so the speed) of an engine by closing the throttle.
THROTTLE-VALVE, [throtl'-valv'], *n.* the throttle in an engine.

THROTTLE

THROUGH (1), [thrōō], *adj.* going, stretching, from end to end, unobstructed; (of a train or other vehicle) travelling the entire journey, so that the passengers do not have to change; doing the whole journey without a break.
THROUGH (2), [thrōō], *adv.* from end to end of, from start to finish, right to the very end, completely; **t. and t.,** entirely, completely; **to be t. with,** to refuse to have any further dealings with.
THROUGH (3), [thrōō], *prep.* from end to end of; in the midst of; across; during; by means of. [OE. *thurh*].
THROUGHOUT (1), [thrōō-owt'], *adv.* through each and every part, section, detail, or particular of.
THROUGHOUT (2), [thrōō-owt'], *prep.* through each and every part of; (of time) lasting from the beginning to the end of a given period. [OE. *thurhut*].
THROVE, [thrōv], *pret.* of THRIVE.
THROW (1), [thrō], *n.* the act of throwing; the motions, immediate effects, of anything thrown; distance or degree of displacement; (*geol.*) the direction of displacement of strata in a fault; (*dice, skittles, darts, etc.*) a score.
THROW (2), (threw, thrown), [thrō], *v.t. and i.* to propel through the air, to fling, cast, hurl; to cause to fly from the hand by a jerk of the arm; to shoot, project, to give forth, give away, utter, etc.; to cause to fall, to prostrate; to put or place hurriedly in position, *esp.* of obstacles, impediments opposing troops, etc.; (*U.S.*) to lose deliberately (a game, etc.); **to t. about,** to toss in several or various directions, to scatter; **to t. back,** to revert to a hereditary type; **to t. in,** to give with other things as an extra unspecified and not bargained for; (*cricket*) (of a fielder) to return the ball from the field to the wicket-keeper or bowler; **to t. off,** to get rid of (illness, etc.); (of clothes) to take off hurriedly; to dispense with, discard; to disconcert, put off; to utter, give forth; **to t. (oneself) on (or upon),** to trust oneself to; **to t. open,** to cause to open suddenly (a door, window, etc.); to permit general access to; **to t. out,** to emit, cast forth; to reject; to utter, say; **to t. over (or overboard),** to reject, refuse, discountenance; **to t. up,** to cast upwards; to give up, cease to do or be interested in; **to t. oneself into,** to engage in with all one's strength and enthusiasm; **to t. a fit of temper,** (*coll.*) to be suddenly angry; **to t. a party,** (*slang*) to give a party. [OE. *thrawan* to twist].
THROWAWAY, [thrō'-a-wā], *n.* (*coll.*) a small advertisement, circular, handbill.
THROWBACK, [thrō'-bak'], *n.* a member of a family reverting in some way to an ancestral type.
THROWER, [thrō'-er], *n.* a person or thing that throws; one who twists silk.
THROWING-STICK, [thrō'-ing-stik'], *n.* a short, wooden stick by means of which natives in Australia impart added velocity to spears, etc.
THROWN, [thrōn], *p.pt.* of THROW (2).
THROWN-SILK, [thrōn'-silk'], *n.* silk which has been twisted to make thread.
THROW-OFF, [thrō'-of'], *n.* the beginning of a hunt.
THROW-OUT, [thrō'-owt], *n.* (*coll.*) a person or thing that has been rejected.
THROWSTER, [thrō'-ster], *n.* a person who twists silk, a thrower.
THROWSTICK, [thrō'-stik], *n.* a sort of boomerang; a throwing-stick.
THRUM (1), [thrum], *n.* any one of the ends of the warp remaining on the loom after the web is cut off; the fringe formed thus; any tassel or fringe or loose end of thread. [OE. *thrum* thread].
THRUM (2), [thrum], *v.t.* to give a fringe to.
THRUM (3), [thrum], *v.t. and i.* to strum; to play a musical instrument carelessly or noisily, to strum upon. [~Icel. *thrumma* to rattle].
THRUSH (1), [thrush], *n.* any one of several varieties of song birds of the genus *Turdus*. [OE. *thyrsce*].
THRUSH (2), [thrush], *n.* a disease which most commonly affects the throats and mouths of children, which become inflamed and marked with white spots. [Uncert.].
THRUST (1), [thrust], *n.* the action of thrusting, stabbing, pushing violently; a steady pushing or pressure; (*arch., etc.*) stress; (*geol.*) a displacement of strata by lateral pressure; **cut and t.,** the exchange of blows in a duel or fight; (*fig.*) a rapid exchange of witty remarks.
THRUST (2), [thrust], *v.t.* to push vigorously with a sharp jerk, to make a stab with, to jerk or push forward; to make a series of stabs; **to t. oneself forward,** to cause oneself deliberately to be noticed, to make oneself conspicuous. [OScand. *thrysta*].
THRUSTER, [thrust'-er], *n.* one who thrusts; a person who rides too close to the hounds in a hunt; (*coll.*) one (in business, etc.) who is not over-scrupulous in his determination to succeed.
THRUSTFUL, [thrust'-fŏŏl], *adj.* forceful, energetic, self-assertive.
THRUSTFULLY, [thrust'-fŏŏl-i], *adv.* forcefully.
THRUSTFULNESS, [thrust'-fŏŏl-nes], *n.* the quality of being thrustful.
THRUSTING (1), [thrust'-ing], *n.* the act of pushing suddenly and violently, of stabbing or making a thrust.
THRUSTING (2), [thrust'-ing], *adj.* thrustful, self-assertive, *esp.* used of a member of a hunt who rides too close to the hounds.
THRUSTING-SCREW, [thrust'-ing-skrōō'], *n.* a cheese-press which squeezes the whey out of milk curds.
THUD (1), [thud], *n.* a dull, heavy sound produced by a blow, collision or fall.
THUD (2), [thud], *v.i.* to fall on to, collide with, or strike something with a dull heavy sound. [OE. *thyddan*].
THUG, [thug], *n.* one of a gang of robbers and assassins in northern India who were suppressed at the beginning of the 19th century; a murderer, ruffianly thief, an American gangster. [Hind. *thag* a robber].
THUGGEE, [thug-ē'], *n.* assassination by strangling as committed by Indian thugs. [Hind. *thagi*].
THUGGERY, [thug'-er-i], *n.* ruffianism.

THUGGISM, [thug'-izm], *n.* murder and robbery as practised by Indian thugs.

THULE, [thew'-li], *n.* the northernmost territory known to the ancients; **ultima T.,** (*fig.*) the extreme limits of anything, lying almost beyond the borders of knowledge or experience. [L. *Thule* from Gk. *Thoule*].

THULITE, [thewl'-it], *n.* (*min.*) a reddish-coloured silicate of aluminium and lime found in Norway. [*Prec.*].

THULIUM, [thyōōl'-i-um], *n.* a rare metallic element found in association with yttrium and erbium. [*Thule* a fabulous land in the north of Europe].

THUMB (1), [thum], *n.* the short innermost digit of the human hand which is opposable to the other fingers; the corresponding digit on the hands or feet of animals; that compartment in a glove which covers this digit; **to be under somebody's t.,** to be dominated by someone; **rule of t.,** an empirical method or process. [OE. *thuma*].

THUMB (2), [thum], *v.t.* to touch with the thumb, to make thumb-marks upon; (referring to a book) to use very much and soil with thumb-marks.

THUMBED, [thumd], *adj.* possessing thumbs; soiled with thumb-marks.

THUMB-INDEX, [thum'-in'-deks], *n.* a system of reference consisting of a series of labelled indentations in the side of a book marking where each section commences.

THUMBKINS, [thum'-kinz], *n.(pl.)* thumb-screws.

THUMB-MARK (1), [thum'-mahk], *n.* the mark or stain made by a thumb.

THUMB-MARK (2), [thum'-mahk], *v.t.* to soil or mark with the thumb.

THUMB-NAIL (1), [thum'-nāl], *n.* the nail on the human thumb; (*fig.*) a brief word-picture.

THUMB-NAIL (2), [thum'-nāl], *adj.* (of a drawing) small; (*fig.*) concise, brief.

THUMBPOT, [thum'-pot'], *n.* a very small flower-pot.

THUMB-RING, [thum'-ring], *n.* a ring worn on the thumb; a ring for the thumb on the guard of a sword.

THUMB-SCREW, [thum'-skrōō], *n.* an instrument of torture by means of which a person's thumbs were slowly crushed; a screw with winged tap that can be turned by the finger and thumb.

THUMB-SCREW

THUMBSTALL, [thum'-stawl], *n.* a sheath or covering for the thumb. [THUMB (1) and STALL (1)].

THUMMIM, [thum'-im], *n.* certain ornaments on the breastplate of the Jewish high priest. [Heb. *tummim*].

THUMP (1), [thump], *n.* a dull sound produced by an impact or blow; a blow producing such a sound. [Echoic].

THUMP (2), [thump], *v.t.* and *i.* to strike with a blow producing a dull heavy sound; to give a heavy blow to, to pound, to strike with a series of heavy blows; to fall with a dull, heavy sound; to make such a sound.

THUMPER, [thump'-er], *n.* a person or thing that thumps; (*coll.*) anything excessive or remarkable, *esp.* an exaggerated lie.

THUMPING, [thump'-ing], *adj.* (*coll.*) excessive, very big.

THUNDER (1), [thun'-der], *n.* the sound which follows a flash of lightning; any similar sound; (*fig.*) anger, wrath; **to steal a person's t.,** to anticipate and do what he intended and so rob him of applause or the advantage of novelty. [OE. *thunor*].

THUNDER (2), [thun'-der], *v.i.,* to roar with thunder; to utter a loud thunder-like noise; to speak with great wrath; to move very noisily or with a noise like thunder.

THUNDERBOLT, [thun'-der-bōlt'], *n.* the solid body which is supposed to fall from the heavens in a flash of lightning; (*coll.*) a great surprise.

THUNDERCLAP, [thun'-der-klap'], *n.* one peal of thunder.

THUNDERCLOUD, [thun'-der-klowd'], *n.* a cloud bringing a storm of thunder and lightning, a storm cloud.

THUNDERER, [thun'-der-er], *n.* one who thunders; **The T.,** *The Times* newspaper.

THUNDERING, [thun'-der-ing], *adj.* roaring with thunder; speaking in loud angry tones.

THUNDEROUS, [thun'-der-us], *adj.* thundery, as loud as, resembling thunder; also *fig.*

THUNDERSHOWER, [thun'-der-show'-er], *n.* shower of rain with thunder.

THUNDERSTORM, [thun'-der-stawm'], *n.* a storm of thunder and lightning, usually accompanied by heavy rain.

THUNDERSTRUCK, [thun'-der-struk'], *adj.* (*fig.*) amazed, astonished beyond measure.

THUNDERY, [thun'-der-i], *adj.* accompanied by thunder; hot and heavy with thunder rumbling in the distance as if a storm is blowing up.

THURIBLE, [thew'-ribl], *n.* a censer. [L. *thuribulum*].

THURIFER, [thew'-ri-fer], *n.* (*eccles.*) an incense-bearer.

THURIFEROUS, [thew-rif'-er-us], *adj.* bearing incense.

THURIFICATION, [thew'-ri-fik-ā'-shun], *n.* the act of burning incense.

THURINGITE, [thew'-ring-it], *n.* (*min.*) a hydrous silicate of iron and aluminium. [Germ. *thüringit*].

THURL, see THIRL.

THURSDAY, [thurz'-di], *n.* the fifth day in the week; **Maundy T.,** the fifth day of Holy Week, the day before Good Friday. [OE. *Thunres dæg* the day of Thor].

THUS, [thus], *adv.* in this manner; in the following fashion or way; to this specified degree; **t. far,** only so far. [OE. *thus*].

THWACK (1), [thwak], *n.* a sharp, vigorous blow, *esp.* such as may be given with a staff or stick.

THWACK (2), [thwak], *v.t.* to beat sharply, to give a sharp blow or series of blows to. [Echoic].

THWAITE, [thwāt], *n.* (*dial.*) a piece of ground, *esp.* a clearing in a forest. [OScand. *thveit*].

THWART (1), [thwawt], *n.* a seat in a rowing boat.

THWART (2)†, [thwawt], *adv.* athwart. [OScand. *thvert*].

THWART (3), [thwawt], *v.t.* to oppose, cross, hinder, baulk, impede, to take successful action in opposition to.

THWARTER, [thwawt'-er], *n.* a person who balks or opposes another.

THWARTING, [thwawt'-ing], *adj.* adverse, opposing, balking.

THWARTINGLY, [thwawt'-ing-li], *adv.* in such a way as to thwart.

THWART-SHIPS, [thwawt'-ships], *adv.* (*naut.*) from one side to the other of a boat or ship.

THY, [thī], *poss. adj.* of, pertaining to, or belonging to thee. [OE. *thin*].

THYME, [tīm], *n.* (*bot.*) any of various plants of the genus *Thymus*, *esp.* the garden thyme, *Thymus vulgaris*. [L. *thymum*].

THYMOL, [tīm'-ol], *n.* a preparation from oil of thyme used medicinally, *esp.* as an antiseptic.

THYMUS, (*pl.* **thymi**), [thī'-mus], *n.* (*anat.*) a ductless gland, the purpose of which is unknown, occurring in the lower part of the neck in vertebrates, and which in human beings disperses before or during puberty. [Gk. *thumos*].

THYMY, [tīm'-i], *adj.* covered with thyme.

THYROID (1), [thīer'-oid], *n.* (*anat.*) the thyroid cartilage or the thyroid gland.

THYROID (2), [thīer'-oid], *adj.* (*anat.*) pertaining to the thyroid cartilage or gland; **t. gland,** a ductless gland in the neck of vertebrates; **t. cartilage,** the large cartilage in the throat commonly called the Adam's apple. [~Gk. *thureoeides* shield-shaped].

THYRSE, [thurs], *n.* thyrsus. [Gk. *thursos*].

THYRSOID, [thur'-soid], *adj.* shaped like a thyrsus [THYRSUS and Gk. *oeides* like].

THYRSUS, [thur'-sus], *n.* (*class. antiq.*) a rod on the top of which is a pine cone, a symbol of Dionysos; (*bot.*) a contracted panicle. [L. *thyrsus* from Gk. *thursos* stalk of a plant].

THYSELF, [THī-self'], *pron.* emphatic and reflexive form of THY.

TIARA, [ti-ah'-ra], *n.* a jewelled coronet or head-dress very high at the front and very low at the back now usually worn only by women; any similar head-dress; the Papal crown. [Gk. *tiara*].

TIARAED, [ti-ah'-rad], *adj.* having a tiara on.

TIBIA, [tib'-i-a], *n.* (*anat.*) the shin-bone, that is, the bone in the front of the leg reaching from the knee to the ankle; (*Rom. antiq.*) a flute. [L. *tibia*].

TIBIAL, [tib'-i-al], *adj.* (*anat.*) pertaining to the tibia; (*Rom. antiq.*) of, or pertaining to, a flute. [L. *tibialis*].

TIARA

TIC, [tik], *n.* a nervous facial twitching. [Fr. *tic*].

TICAL, [tik'-al], *n.* a small silver coin of Siam. [Portug. *tical*].
TICCA, [tik'-a], *adj.* hired or for hire. [Hind. *thika* hire].
TIC-DOULOUREUX, [tik'-dōō-lōō-ru(r)], *n.* a twitching of the face accompanied with a neuralgic pain. [Fr. *tic-douloureux*].
TICE, [tīs], *v.t.* to lure, seduce. [Short form of ENTICE].
TICHORRHINE, [tīk'-aw-rīn], *adj.* having subdivided nostrils. [Gk. *teikhos* wall and *rhis rhinos* nose].
TICK (1), [tik], *n.* any one of several small blood-sucking creatures parasitic on men and animals. [ME. *tike*].
TICK (2), [tik], *n.* (*slang*) credit. [Short form of TICKET (1)].
TICK (3), [tik], *n.* the linen cover of a pillow, mattress. [ME. *teke*].
TICK (4), [tik], *n.* a light tapping sound such as is made by a watch or clock; a symbol resembling a V with an elongated upwards stroke, used to indicate approval or correctness. [TICK (5)].
TICK (5), [tik], *v.t. and i.* to make a sound like a tick; to mark with a tick; **to t. off,** (*slang*) to rebuke sharply; **to t. over,** (of a motor) to run gently with the gears not engaged.
TICKBEAN, [tik'-bēn], *n.* a small bean on which farm animals are fed.
TICKER, [tik'-er], *n.* (*slang*) a clock or watch; a telegraphic printing machine.
TICKET (1), [tik'-it], *n.* a receipt made of paper or light cardboard which is proof that the holder has paid for or is otherwise entitled to enjoy a certain privilege, such as to attend a specified entertainment, be carried on a specified public vehicle to a specified place, etc.; any similar small document, printed card or label; **the t.,** the done thing, just what is wanted; **t. of leave,** a document giving a prisoner a certain restricted or conditional liberty before the expiry of his full sentence. [Fr. *étiquette*].
TICKET (2), [tik'-it], *v.t.* to put a ticket on to.
TICKET-DAY, [tik'-it-dā'], *n.* the day before settlement day on the Stock Exchange.
TICKET-PORTER, [tik'-it-paw'-ter], *n.* one of a body of porters at one time controlled by the Corporation of the City of London.
TICKEY, TICKY, TIKKI, [tik'-i], *n.* a threepenny-bit. [Unkn.].
TICKING, [tik'-ing], *n.* cloth for making mattresses.
TICKLE (1), [tikl], *n.* the act or sensation of tickling.
TICKLE (2), [tik], *v.t. and i.* to caress lightly a part of the body till the nerves become irritated, causing spasms or laughter; (of a part of the body) to itch or otherwise feel that this is being done; (*fig.*) to give pleasure to. [Uncert.].
TICKLER, [tik'-ler], *n.* one who tickles; a stick with a bunch of feathers or strips of paper at the end, used at fairs, etc.; (*fig.*) a puzzle or difficulty.
TICKLING, [tik'-ling], *n.* titillation.
TICKLISH, [tik'-lish], *adj.* very sensitive to tickling; (of persons or tasks) difficult to handle.
TICKLISHLY, [tik'-lish-li], *adv.* in a ticklish fashion.
TICKLISHNESS, [tik'-lish-nes], *n.* the condition of being ticklish.
TICKLY, [tik'-li], *adj.* ticklish, easily tickled.
TICK-SEED, [tik'-sēd], *n.* (*bot.*) one of several plants the seeds of which look like the animal called a tick.
TICK-TACK, TICK-TOCK, [tik'-tak', tik'-tok'], *n.* (childish speech) a watch or clock; (racing jargon) a system of signs and gestures used among bookmakers to signal changes in betting prices; **t. man,** a bookmaker's assistant who signals such information.
TICKY, see TICKEY.
TIDAL, [tīd'-al], *adj.* pertaining to or affected by tides.
TIDBIT, see TIT-BIT.
TIDDLER, [tid'-ler], *n.* a stickleback. [Unkn.].
TIDDLEY (1), [tid'-li], *n.* (*slang*) a drink, *esp.* alcoholic. [Unkn.].
TIDDLEY (2), [tid'-li], *adj.* (*slang*) slightly intoxicated. [Unkn.].
TIDDLEYWINKS, [tid'-li-wingks'], *n.* a children's game in which small counters are nipped at the edge with larger ones and so made to spring up in the air, the object being for each player to get by this means as many counters as possible into a wooden bowl. [Uncert.].
TIDE (1), [tīd], *n.* the ebb and flow of the sea; (*fig.*) movement, tendency; †season, *esp.* in the phrase **time and t.** and in certain compounds, e.g. Eastertide. [OE. *tid* time].
TIDE (2), [tīd], *v.t. and i.* **to t. over,** to struggle through, manage to get through; to help to deal with and overcome; (*naut.*) to drift with the tide.
TIDEGATE, [tīd'-gāt], *n.* gates separating a basin from a tidal harbour.
TIDEGAUGE, [tīd'-gāj], *n.* a device that registers the state of the tide.
TIDELESS, [tīd'-les], *adj.* having no tides.
TIDE-LOCK, [tīd'-lok'], *n.* a lock controlling a dock on a tidal river or estuary.
TIDEMARK, [tīd'-mahk], *n.* the mark left by the tide at its highest point.
TIDEMILL, [tīd'-mil], *n.* a mill worked by the action of the tide.
TIDERIP, [tīd'-rip], *n.* a tidal wave or bore; rough water caused by conflicting currents.
TIDESMAN†, [tīdz'-man], *n.* a customs officer.
TIDE-TABLE, [tīd'-tābl], *n.* a table of the times and height of tides.
TIDE-WAITER, [tīd'-wāt-er], *n.* a tidesman.
TIDE-WATER, [tīd'-waw-ter], *n.* (*U.S.*) water moved by tides; tidal water.
TIDEWAY, [tīd'-wā], *n.* a channel in which tidal waters flow; the tidal currents in such a channel.
TIDILY, [tīd'-i-li], *adv.* in a tidy way.
TIDINESS, [tīd'-i-nes], *n.* neat simplicity; neatness; the condition of being tidy.
TIDINGLESS, [tīd'-ing-les], *adj.* bringing no news.
TIDINGS, [tīd'-ingz], *n.(pl.)* news, information. [OE. *tidung*].
TIDY (1), [tīd'-i], *n.* a box, bag, or other receptacle for odds and ends; an antimacassar.
TIDY (2), [tīd'-i], *adj.* arranged in good order, neat; fond of keeping things in good order; (*coll.*) moderately large. [~TIDE (1)].
TIDY (3), [tīd'-i], *v.t.* to make tidy; **to t. up,** to make tidy; to put things in order.
TIE (1), [tī], *n.* a strip of cloth worn round the collar and knotted in front; an emotional or moral bond or obligation; anything which curbs one's freedom; that result in a sporting event in which two competitors or opposing teams obtain equal scores, reach the winning post at the same moment, etc.; an eliminating competition between several competitors or teams; (*mus.*) a small curve printed between notes of identical pitch, the second of which is not intended to be played though the first is to be sustained for the value of both; (*arch., carp., etc.*) a support, link, etc., to make firmer the essential pieces of a structure. [OE. *teah*].
TIE (2), [tī], *v.t. and i.* to fasten or connect with rope or string; to make a knot in; to hamper, bind, rob of liberty; (*carp., arch., etc.*) to provide with a tie or support; to do equally well with a rival in a game, competition, examination, etc.; **to t. down,** to fix firmly down with cord; to hamper, limit the scope of; **to t. up,** to bind into a firm parcel or bundle, etc.; to restrict, corner, limit the freedom, the free use of; to bind or enwrap. [OE. *tigan*].
TIE-BEAM, [tī'-bēm'], *n.* (*arch.*) the beam which connects two principal rafters at the bottom.
TIED HOUSE, [tīd'-hows], *n.* a public-house owned by or under contract to a brewer whose liquors alone may be sold there.
TIER, [tēer], *n.* one of a series of horizontal rows arranged one over the other. [OFr. *tiere*].
TIERCE, TERCE, [tēers], *n.* (*eccles.*) the third canonical hour or the service said then; a position in fencing; a cask that will hold forty-two gallons of wine. [Fr. *tiers* third].
TIERCEL, see TERCEL.
TIERCET, see TERCET.
TIERS ETAT, tiers état, [tyāerz'-ā-tah'], *n.* that one of the three sections of the old French legislative body which represented the commons; the common people generally. [Fr. *tiers état* third estate].
TIFF (1), [tif], *n.* a trifling quarrel; a small draught of liquor. [Uncert.].
TIFF (2), [tif], *v.i.* to be in a peevish mood.
TIFFANY, [tif'-an-i], *n.* a sort of gauze or thin silk. [OFr. *tiffanie* from LL. *theophania* manifestation of God].
TIFFIN, [tif'-in], *n.* lunch among English people in the East. [Uncert.].
TIG, [tig], *n.* a children's game similar to touch. [ME. *tig* to tap].
TIGE, [tēzh], *n.* (*bot.*) a stalk; (*arch.*) the shaft of a pillar. [Fr. *tige* stalk].
TIGELLE, [tēzh-el'], *n.* (*bot.*) a radicle. [Fr. *tigelle*].
TIGER, [tī'-ger], *n.* a fierce carnivorous feline of Asia, *Felis tigris*, whose fur is yellow and marked with black stripes; a very cruel person; a male servant, *esp.* a pageboy; a vigorous and skilful opponent, *esp.*

at tennis or golf; (*coll.*) an extra cheer after the usual three. [L. *tigris*].

TIGER-BEETLE, [tī'-ger-bētl'], *n.* any beetle of the *Cicindelidæ*, of a bright and variegated colour.

TIGER-BITTERN, [tī'-ger-bit'-ern], *n.* a bird of the genus *Tigrisoma* found in South America.

TIGER-CAT, [tī'-ger-kat'], *n.* the South American margay, *Felis tigrina*, or any other wild cat like a tiger in colouring.

TIGER-FLOWER, [tī'-ger-flow(r)], *n.* a plant of the iris family, *Tigridia pavonia*, found in tropical America.

TIGERISH, TIGRISH, [tī'-ger-ish], *adj.* fierce like a tiger.

TIGER-LILY, [tī'-ger-lil'-i], *n.* the tall, bright orange lily, *Lilium tigrinum*.

TIGER-MOTH, [tī'-ger-moth'], *n.* any of several varieties of large spotted English moths.

TIGER'S-EYE, [tī'-gerz-ī'], *n.* a yellow stone used to make ornaments.

TIGER-SHARK, [tī'-ger-shahk'], *n.* a name given to several fierce sharks, *esp.* the zebra shark, *Stegostoma tigrinum*.

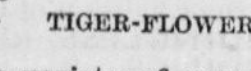

TIGER-FLOWER

TIGER-SHELL, [tī'-ger-shel'], *n.* a variety of cowry.

TIGER-WOOD, [tī'-ger-wŏŏd'], *n.* a wood which is streaked with black and brown, much used in cabinet making, and obtained from a tree which grows in British Guiana.

TIGHT (1), [tīt], *adj.* tied fast, firmly secured and bound taut; cramped, closely packed, compact; close fitting; (of a flask, cask, vessel) not admitting liquids; (of money) hard to come by, scarce; (of persons) ungenerous, given to driving hard bargains; (of a situation or circumstance) presenting grave difficulties, dangerous; (*slang*) drunk. [ME. *tyght*].

TIGHT (2), [tīt], *adv.* tightly, securely; **to sit t.,** to be unshakable in the opinion or position one has taken up; to sit firmly.

TIGHTEN, [tīt'-en], *v.t.* and *i.* to make or become tight or tighter; **to t. up**, to make stricter.

TIGHTLY, [tīt'-li], *adv.* in a tight fashion.

TIGHTNESS, [tīt'-nes], *n.* the condition of being tight; tension.

TIGHT-ROPE, [tīt'-rōp], *n.* a stretched rope for acrobatic performances.

TIGHTS, [tīts], *n.(pl.)* close-fitting breeches; hose reaching to the waist, worn by stage performers, etc.

TIGLIC, [tig'-lik], *adj.* (*chem.*) produced from or connected with croton oil. [Md.L. *tiglium* croton].

TIGRESS, [tī'-gres], *n.* a female tiger.

TIGRINE, [tī'-grīn], *adj.* pertaining to or like a tiger.

TIGRISH, see TIGERISH.

TIKE, TYKE, [tīk], *n.* a mongrel cur; a rustic boor; a Yorkshireman. [OScand. *tik* a bitch].

TIKKI, see TICKEY.

TILBURY, [til'-bur-i], *n.* a light two-wheeled horse carriage of the early nineteenth century. [*Tilbury* the inventor].

TILDE, [til'-di], *n.* (*typ.*) a curved mark or slur over a letter (~). [Span. *tilde*].

TILE (1), [tīl], *n.* a thin, flat clay brick glazed or unglazed; (*coll.*) a hat, *esp.* a top hat. [OE. *tigele*].

TILE (2), [tīl], *v.t.* to roof or line with tiles.

TILE-DRAIN, [tīl'-drān], *n.* a drain made with tiles.

TILE-KILN, [tīl'-kiln], *n.* a kiln for baking tiles.

TILE-ORE, [tīl'-aw(r)], *n.* a red earthy copper ore.

TILER, TYLER, [tīl'-er], *n.* a man who makes roofs of tiles; a doorkeeper at a masonic ceremony.

TILERY, [tīl'-er-i], *n.* a tile kiln.

TILESTONE, [tīl'-stōn], *n.* any flat stone suitable for roofing.

TILIACEOUS, [til'-i-ā'-shus], *adj.* (*bot.*) relating to the *Tiliaceæ*, a family of trees including the linden. [L. *tilia* linden].

TILING, [tīl'-ing], *n.* tiles, *esp.* tiles set in position.

TILKA, [til'-ka], *n.* the caste mark on the forehead of a Hindu. [Hind. *tilak*].

TILL (1), [til], *n.* a cash-box with a drawer, used in a shop. [Uncert.].

TILL (2), [til], *n.* a special hard clay, *esp.* (*geol.*) boulder clay.

TILL (3), [til], *v.t.* to plough and sow. [OE. *tilian*].

TILL (4), [til], *prep.* up to the time of. [OE. and OScand. *til* to].

TILL (5), [til], *conj.* up to the time when.

TILLABLE, [til'-abl], *adj.* able to be tilled.

TILLAGE, [til'-ij], *n.* the practice of tilling; agriculture.

TILLER (1), [til'-er], *n.* a person who tills. [TILL (3)].

TILLER (2), [til'-er], *n.* (*naut.*) the helm, a large handle for working the rudder. [~Du. *tillen* to lift].

TILLER (3), [til'-er], *n.* a young shoot from the root of a plant. [OE. *telgor* twig].

TILLER (4), [til'-er], *v.i.* (of a plant) to send up suckers.

TILLING, [til'-ing], *n.* tillage.

TILLER

TILT (1), [tilt], *n.* the action of tilting; **full t.,** at top speed.

TILT (2), [tilt] *n.* the condition or degree of being tilted.

TILT (3), [tilt], *n.* a canvas hood on a wagon, market stall, etc. [ME. *telt* tent].

TILT (4), [tilt], *v.i.* to charge on horseback with a lance; **to t. at,** to charge with a lance; (*fig.*) to make an attack on, *esp.* in a speech. [ME. *tylten*].

TILT (5), [tilt], *v.t.* and *i.* to move or cause to move into a sloping position. [ME. *tilten* to totter].

TILT-BOAT, [tilt'-bōt], *n.* a boat with a canvas hood.

TILTER, [til'-ter], *n.* one who jousts.

TILTH, [tilth], *n.* the cultivation of the land; the soil so cultivated.

TILT-HAMMER, [tilt'-ham'-er], *n.* a hammer in a forge which is caused to rise and fall by an eccentric wheel.

TILTING, [tilt'-ing], *n.* the act of one who tilts; the state of being tilted.

TILT-YARD, [tilt'-yahd], *n.* a place for tilting or jousting.

TIMBAL, TYMBAL, [tim'-bal], *n.* a kettledrum. [Span. *timbal*].

TIMBALE, [tam-bahl'], *n.* (*cookery*) a small pie of minced fish, fowl, or meat, with a crust. [Fr. *timbale*].

TIMBER (1), [tim'-ber], *n.* wood, *esp.* wood cut from a tree and ready for use; **t. hitch**, a special kind of knot used for tying a rope to a plank. [OE. *timber*].

TIMBER (2), [tim'-ber], *v.t.* to provide timber for, to equip with wooden supports. [OE. *timbrian* to build].

TIMBERED, [tim'-berd], *adj.* made wholly or partly of timber; wooded.

TIMBER-HEAD, [tim'-ber-hed'], *n.* (*naut.*) the end of a beam rising above the deck.

TIMBERLINE, [tim'-ber-līn'], *n.* that altitude above which trees will not grow.

TIMBERLODE, [tim'-ber-lōd'], *n.* (*hist.*) a feudal obligation by which serfs had to transport felled wood for their lord from the forest to his mansion. [TIMBER (1) and OE. *lad* path].

TIMBERMAN, [tim'-ber-man'], *n.* a man who fells trees for timber.

TIMBER-MERCHANT, [tim'-ber-mur'-chant], *n.* a man who sells timber.

TIMBERTOES, [tim'-ber-tōz'], *n.* (*coll.*) a wooden-legged man.

TIMBER-WOLF, [tim'-ber-wŏŏlf'], *n.* the American grey wolf. [TIMBER (1) and WOLF (1)].

TIMBER-YARD, [tim'-ber-yahd'], *n.* a yard where timber is sold or stored.

TIMBRE (1), [tambr], *n.* (*mus.*) the individual quality in the sound of a voice or instrument. [Fr. *timbre*].

TIMBRE (2), [tim'-ber], *n.* a crest on a helmet or over a coat of arms. [Fr. *timbre*].

TIMBREL, [tim'-brel], *n.* a tambourine. [~TIMBRE (1)].

TIME (1), [tīm], *n.* the idea of past, present, and future; the limited duration of the material world contrasted with the eternity of spiritual things; a particular portion of this, a period; a particular point in this, a moment; a system of measuring this; an occasion, the moment at which an event occurs or is repeated, the period in which an event occurs; (*mus.*) ratio of regularly unstressed beats to regularly stressed beats in a composition; (*pl.*) period, era, age; **in t., on t., to t.,** punctually, not late; **in good t.,** punctually and with time to spare; **at times,** sometimes, occasionally; **in no t.,** very quickly; **at all times,** always, constantly; **t. and again,** repeatedly; **from t. to t.,** every now and then; **at the same t.,** nevertheless, all the same, moreover; **for the t. being,** meanwhile, for a little while to come; **what t.,** (*poet.*) meanwhile, at that moment; **to take one's t.,** to be unhurried; **to have a good t.,** to enjoy oneself; **to work against t.,** to have almost more to do than there is time to do it in; **to pass the t. of day with,** to salute with formal greetings; **to do t.,** to suffer imprisonment; **to keep**

good t., (of a clock, watch, etc.) to register the time steadily and accurately; **to beat t.,** to conduct an instrumental or choral performance by waving a wand; **to mark t.,** to raise the feet alternately as if marching, but without moving backward or forward; (*fig.*) to put off or delay. [OE. *tima*].

TIME (2), [tīm], *v.t.* to do or say in season or opportunely; to measure the duration of; to record the instant of; to adjust the happening of.

TIME-BALL, [tīm'-bawl], *n.* a device for marking time, consisting of a ball which falls at a given hour each day.

TIME-BARGAIN, [tīm'-bah'-gin], *n.* an agreement to do something by a fixed date.

TIME-BILL, [tīm'-bil], *n.* a time-table.

TIME-BOOK, [tīm'-bo͝ok], *n.* a book in which a record is kept of how long an employee has worked.

TIME-CARD, [tīm'-kahd], *n.* a card on which is recorded the time of an employee's arrival at and departure from work.

TIMEFUL, [tīm'-fo͞ol], *adj.* timely.

TIME-HONOURED, [tīm'-on'-erd], *adj.* respected for many years, ancient.

TIMEKEEPER, [tīm'-kēp'-er], *n.* one who keeps a record of how long employees spend at their work; a clock.

TIMELESS, [tīm'-les], *n.* eternal, not measured by time.

TIMELESSLY, [tīm'-les-li], *adv.* eternally.

TIMELESSNESS, [tīm'-les-nes], *n.* the condition of being timeless.

TIMELINESS, [tīm'-li-nes], *n.* the condition of being timely.

TIMELY (1), [tīm'-li], *adj.* seasonable, opportune.

TIMELY (2), [tīm'-li], *adv.* opportunely.

TIMEOUS, TIMOUS, [tīm'-us], *adj.* timely.

TIMEOUSLY, [tīm'-us-li], *adv.* opportunely.

TIMEPIECE, [tīm'-pēs], *n.* a clock.

TIMEPLEASER, [tīm'-plēz'-er], *n.* a timeserver.

TIMESERVER, [tīm'-surv'-er], *n.* a person who always does and says the most expedient thing without regard to dignity or principles.

TIMESERVING, [tīm'-surv'-ing], *adj.* obsequious, always careful to do what is expedient.

TIME-SHEET, [tīm'-shēt], *n.* a time-card.

TIME-TABLE, [tīm'-tābl'], *n.* a book, sheet, or pamphlet containing a list of times at which certain events are due to happen (*esp.* the arrival and departure of trains, etc.) or at which certain tasks have to be done; a schedule.

TIMEWORK, [tīm'-wurk], *n.* work paid for by the hour and not by the piece.

TIMEWORN, [tīm'-wawn], *adj.* worn by time; decayed.

TIMID, [tim'-id], *adj.* fearful, shy, nervous, faint-hearted. [L. *timidus*].

TIMIDITY, [tim-id'-it-i], *n.* the state of being timid; fearfulness; want of courage or boldness to face danger; timorousness; habitual cowardice. [L. *timiditas*].

TIMIDLY, [tim'-id-li], *adv.* in a timid fashion.

TIMIDNESS, [tim'-id-nes], *n.* the state of being timid.

TIMIST, [tīm'-ist], *n.* a musician considered as to the manner of his keeping time.

TIMOCRACY, [tīm-ok'-ras-i], *n.* a constitution where government is in the hands of men according to their wealth or glory. [Gk. *timokratia*].

TIMOCRATIC, [tīm'-ō-krat'-ik], *adj.* pertaining to a timocracy.

TIMOROSO, [tim-o-rō'-sō], *adv.* (*mus.*) in a style which expresses awe or fear. [It. *timoroso*].

TIMOROUS, [tim'-or-us], *adj.* full of fear; timid, apprehensive. [~L. *timor* fear].

TIMOROUSLY, [tim'-er-us-li], *adv.* in a timorous fashion.

TIMOROUSNESS, [tim'-er-us-nes], *n.* the state of being timorous; timidity.

TIMOTHY, [tim'-o-thi], *n.* the cat's-tail grass, *Phleum pratense*.

TIMOUS, see TIMEOUS.

TIMPANUM, (*pl.* **timpani**), [tim'-pan-um], *n.* a kettledrum. [Gk. *tumpanon*].

TIN (1), [tin], *n.* the metallic element denoted by Sn; a silvery-white metal, with a slight tinge of yellowish-blue, and very malleable; a thin plate of iron covered with tin; a canister; a box made of sheets of tin; (*slang*) money. [OE. *tin*].

TIN (2), [tin], *v.t.* to cover with tin; to preserve in an air-tight tin can or box.

TINAMOU, [tin'-ā-mo͞o], *n.* any species of a group of Central and South American birds resembling the game-birds and the ostriches. [Native].

TINCAL, [ting'-kal], *n.* crude borax, as imported from the East, *esp.* Malaya. [Malay *tincal*].

TINCHEL, [tin'-chel], *n.* a circle of sportsmen, who, by surrounding a certain stretch of ground and gradually closing in, bring a number of deer within a narrow compass. [Gael. *timchioll* circuit].

TINCT, [tingkt], *n.* a colour, tint, hue. [L. *tinctus*].

TINCTORIAL, [tink-taw'-ri-al], *adj.* connected with colour; used for dyeing.

TINCTURE (1), [tingk'-cher], *n.* a tinge or hue; a slight superadded taste or quality; the finer and more volatile parts of a substance, separated by a solvent; a solution in alcohol; a term applied to metals, colours, and tints used for the field of an emblazoned shield. [L. *tinctura* dyeing].

TINCTURE (2), [tingk'-cher], *v.t.* to tinge, impregnate; to imbue to a slight degree.

TINDAL, [tind'-al], *n.* a Lascar petty officer equivalent to a boatswain's mate. [Malay *tandal*].

TINDER, [tind'-er], *n.* anything inflammable used for catching fire from a spark, *esp.* prepared linen impregnated with saltpetre; (*fig.*) inflammable material or ideas. [OE. *tynder*].

TINDER BOX†, [tind'-er-boks'], *n.* a box where tinder and the materials for striking a light are kept.

TINDER BOX

TINDER-LIKE, [tind'-er-līk], *adj.* like tinder; very inflammable.

TINDERY, [tind'-er-i], *adj.* very dry and inflammable; like tinder.

TINE, [tīn], *n.* the tooth or spike of a fork; a prong; the spike of a harrow; a branch of an antler. [OE. *tind* prong].

TINEA, [tin'-i-a], *n.* (*path.*) a contagious skin disease of several varieties, including ringworm, caused by the presence of minute parasitic fungi; a genus of clothes moths. [L. *tinea* worm].

TINED, [tīnd], *adj.* having tines or prongs.

TINFOIL, [tin'-foil], *n.* an alloy of lead and tin reduced to a thin leaf, much used for wrapping.

TING (1), [ting], *n.* a single, short, sharp ringing made on a metallic object. [Echoic].

TING (2), [ting], *v.t.* and *i.* to ring; to sound a bell. [Echoic].

TINGE (1), [tinj], *n.* a slight degree of some colour, taste, or quality; tincture; hue.

TINGE (2), [tinj], *v.t.* to tint, to colour, stain; to impregnate with something foreign; to alter slightly the colour, taste, or character by something added; (*fig.*) to colour slightly the mind, opinions. [L. *tingere* to dye].

TINGI, [ting'-i], *n.* a Brazilian tree, of the genus *Magonia*, from the seeds of which a kind of soap is made. [Native].

TINGLE (1), [ting'-gl], *n.* the sensation of tingling.

TINGLE (2), [ting'-gl], *v.t.* to cause to feel a sharp thrilling sensation; *v.i.* to feel a sharp stinging sensation; to feel a sharp thrilling pain; to smart; to vibrate. [~TING (1)].

TINGLING, [ting'-gling], *n.* a thrilling sensation; a vibrating.

TIN HAT, [tin'-hat'], *n.* a steel helmet worn by soldiers, etc.; **to put the t. on,** (*slang*) to put an end to, to spoil completely.

TINK, [tingk], *n.* a ringing sound made by striking metal or glass lightly with a hard object. [Echoic].

TINKER (1), [tingk'-er], *n.* one who repairs pots and pans and other household utensils; (*fig.*) an unskilful repairer; a botcher; a bungler; **not to care a tinker's cuss, damn, etc.,** not to care at all. [ME. *tinkere*].

TINKER (2), [tingk'-er], *v.t.* to mend like a tinker; *v.i.* to work at tinkering; **to t. with,** to play about with and try to improve, to construct, repair amateurishly.

TINKERLY, [tingk'-er-li], *adv.* in the way of a tinker.

TINKERSHIRE, [tingk'-er-sher], *n.* (*coll.*) the guillemot. [Unkn.].

TINKLE (1), [tingkl], *n.* the action or sound of tinkling.

TINKLE (2), [tingkl], *v.t.* to cause to clink or make sharp, light metallic sounds; *v.i.* to make a series of sharp, light metallic sounds. [ME. *tynclen*].

TINKLING, [tingk'-ling], *n.* a tinkle.

TINMAN, [tin'-man], *n.* a man who makes tinplate vessels; a dealer in tinware.

TINNED, [tind], *adj.* coated with tin; preserved in tinned cans or boxes; (of music, etc.) recorded.

TINNER, [tin'-er], *n.* a tin miner or tin dredger.

TINNING, [tin'-ing], *n.* the craft of covering or lining anything with melted tin or with tinfoil; the art of preserving food and packing it in canisters.
TINNITUS, [tin-īt'-us], *n.* a sensation as of a ringing in the ears. [L. *tinnitus*].
TINNOCK, [tin'-ok], *n.* the blue tit. [Uncert.].
TINNY, [tin'-i], *adj.* rich in tin; similar to tin; (of a sound) thin and metallic.
TINPLATE, [tin'-plāt], *n.* thin sheet iron coated with tin.
TINSEL (1), [tin'-sel], *n.* something very, but merely, shining and gaudy; thin, shiny metal for theatrical use; (*fig.*) anything showy but worthless. [Fr. *étincelle* spark].
TINSEL (2), [tin'-sel], *adj.* made of tinsel; gaudy, (*fig.*) showy but of no real value, meretricious.
TINSEL (3), [tin'-sel], *v.t.* to cover, decorate with tinsel.
TINSELLY, [tin'-sel-i], *adj.* like tinsel; (*fig.*) meretricious.
TINSMITH, [tin'-smith], *n.* a worker in tin or a maker of tinplate.
TINSTONE, [tin'-stōn], *n.* (*min.*) a common tin ore, native oxide of tin; cassiterite.
TINSTUFF, [tin'-stuf], *n.* ore of tin.
TINT (1), [tint], *n.* hue; shade; colour; surface hue as distinct from groundwork; tinge. [~TINCT].
TINT (2), [tint], *v.t.* to tinge; to give a faint colouring to; to stain the surface of.
TINTAGE, [tint'-ij], *n.* colouring or shading; hue.
TINTER, [tint'-er], *n.* a person who tints; a map-colourer.
TINTINNABULARY, [tin'-tin-ab'-yōōl-er-i], *adj.* pertaining to bells; making the sound of a bell.
TINTINNABULATION, [tin'-tin-ab-yōōl-ā'-shun], *n.* a tinkling of bells; a sound resembling this. [~L. *tintinnabulum* bell].
TINWARE, [tin'-wāer], *n.* goods made of tinplate.
TINY, [tin'-i], *adj.* very small; little; puny; minute. [Unkn.].
TIP (1), [tip], *n.* the small pointed extremity of anything; a gentle hit; a suggestion; a piece of inside information; a small present given as a recognition of services to a servant or an inferior. [ME. *tip*].
TIP (2), [tip], *v.t.* to form a point to; to cover the top or end of; to lower one end of; to cant; to hit gently; to hint; to tell; to give a gratuity to; to empty out; to shoot out of a vehicle; *v.i.* to tilt; **to t. (someone) the wink,** to give information; **to t. a winner,** to give an indication of the horse likely to win a race; **to t. up,** to fall backwards, give up one's money; **to t. over,** to overturn; **to t. out,** to upset, throw out; **to t. off,** (*coll.*) to give a warning to, inform privately. [Prec.].
TIP-AND-A-RUN, [tip'-and-a-run'], *n.* a form of cricket where a run must be attempted for every hit.
TIP-AND-RUN, [tip'-and-run'], *adj.* pertaining to a form of attack in which the hitting of the objective is less important than a safe getaway.
TIP-CART, [tip'-kaht], *n.* a cart in which the body can be tilted up from the frame so as to empty out a load from the back.
TIPCAT, [tip'-kat'], *n.* a game in which a spindle-shaped piece of wood is hit into the air and then knocked forward with a stick.
TIPPET, [tip'-it], *n.* a long narrow kind of cape for the shoulders, fastened round the neck, a small cape of cloth, silk, or fur. [ME. *tipet*].

TIPPET

TIPPING, [tip'-ing], *n.* (*mus.*) a distinct articulation imparted to the flute by striking the tongue against the roof of the mouth.
TIPPLE (1), [tipl], *n.* (*coll.*) liquor.
TIPPLE (2), [tipl], *v.i.* to drink spirituous liquors frequently. [~Norw. *tipla* to dribble].
TIPPLER, [tip'-ler], *n.* a person who tipples; one too fond of strong drink.
TIPPLING-HOUSE, [tip'-ling-hows], *n.* a house where intoxicating liquors are sold; a public-house.
TIPSILY, [tip'-si-li], *adv.* in a tipsy fashion.
TIPSINESS, [tip'-si-nes], *n.* the condition of being tipsy.
TIPSTAFF, [tip'-stahf], *n.* a staff tipped with metal; †an officer of the law who took into custody any person committed to prison by the High Court.
TIPSTER, [tip'-ster], *n.* one who gives tips and inside information in racing and other sports.
TIPSY, [tip'-si], *adj.* almost drunk. [~TIP (2)].
TIPSY-CAKE, [tip'-si-kāk], *n.* a pudding consisting of a sponge cake soaked in sherry, with custard, cream, and blanched almonds. [TIPSY and CAKE (1
TIPTOE (1), [tip'-tō'], *v.t.* to walk on the tips of the toe (*fig.*) to walk carefully, warily.
TIPTOE (2), [tip'-tō'], *adv.* on the tips of the toes; **on t** carefully, warily; with eagerness, excitedly.
TIP-TOP, [tip'-top'], *adj.* first rate; the best imagi able; superlative.
TIPULA, [tip'-yōōl-a], *n.* the genus including th crane-flies; the daddy-longlegs. [L. *tippula* waterbug
TIPULARY, [tip'-yōōl-er-i], *adj.* of, or pertaining t insects of the genus *Tipula*.
TIRADE, [tī-rād'], *n.* an outburst of words; a declama tory speech of invective or abuse; (*mus.*) the fillin of an interval by the intermediate diatonic note [Fr. *tirade*].
TIRAILLEUR, [ti-rī-yur'], *n.* a French rifleman *esp.* of a Colonial regiment. [Fr. *tirailleur* shar shooter].
TIRE (1), TYRE, [tīer], *n.* †apparel, trappings; a ban or hoop usually of iron to bind the felloes of woode wheels; a solid or pneumatic tire, the casing of pneumatic tire; **solid t.,** the solid band of rubbe which encircles the rims of wheels; **pneumatic t.,** rubber tube to be inflated with air, and its rubbe casing, for encircling the rim of a wheel; **inner t** the tube of a pneumatic tire. [~ATTIRE (1)].
TIRE (2), [tīer], *n.* †a head-dress, tiara. [~TIARA]
TIRE (3), [tīer], *v.t.* to exhaust the strength of by to or labour; to weary or fatigue; to bore; *v.i.* t grow weary; to be fatigued; to be bored by. [ME *tiren*].
TIRE (4)†, [tīer], *v.t.* to attire, dress.
TIREDNESS, [tīerd'-nes], *n.* the condition of bein tired.
TIRELESS, [tīer'-les], *adj.* that cannot be tired o wearied.
TIRESOME, [tīer'-sum], *adj.* exhausting the strength wearisome; fatiguing; exhausting the patience tedious; boring.
TIRESOMELY, [tīer'-sum-li], *adv.* in tiresome fashion
TIRESOMENESS, [tīer'-sum-nes], *n.* the state o being tiresome.
TIREWOMAN†, [tīer'-wōō'-man], *n.* a female head-dresser or dresser in general.
TIRING-ROOM, [tīer'-ing-rōōm], *n.* the room in which players dress for the stage.
TIRL (1), [turl], *n.* a twirl, a taste; (*mech.*) a rotating apparatus like a turnstile.
TIRL (2), [turl], *v.t.* to revolve, turn, twist. [~TRILL].
TIRO, TYRO, [tīer'-ō], *n.* a novice, amateur. [L. *tiro* raw recruit].
T-IRON, [tē'-īern], *n.* an iron bar having a cross section in the form of a T.
TIRONIAN, [ti-rōn'-i-an], *adj.* pertaining to the ancient Roman shorthand. [*Tiro*, Cicero's amanuensis].
TISANE, [tiz'-ahn'], *n.* a herbal tea. [Fr. *tisane*].
TISRI, [tiz'-ri], *n.* the first Hebrew month of the civil year and the seventh of the ecclesiastical, corresponding to parts of September and October. [Heb. *tisri*].
TISSUE (1), [tish'-ōō], *n.* a structure formed of cells and cell products; a fabric interwoven with gold or silver or with figured colours; a connected series; a web. [Fr. *tissu* woven fabric].
TISSUE (2), [tish'-ōō], *v.t.* to make into a tissue.
TISSUE-PAPER, [tish'-ōō-pāp'-er], *n.* very thin gauze-like paper used for wrapping.
TIT (1), [tit], *n.* †a small horse; (*coll.*) a woman; a titmouse, a small bird of the genus *Parus*. [OScand. *tittr*].
TIT (2), [tit], *n.* **t. for tat,** a return for something received; an injury for an injury. [Unkn.].
TIT (3), [tit], *n.* (*coll.*) a teat. [~TEAT].
TITAN, [tīt'-an], *n.* one of a race of gigantic beings, representing the primitive powers of nature, with seeming reluctance submissive to the world-order which established itself in the hands of Zeus; a strong nature vainly battling with fate; a person of magnificent powers; anything very powerful. [Gk. *Titan*].
TITANESQUE, [tīt'-an-esk'], *adj.* resembling a Titan; large and powerful.
TITANIC, [tīt-an'-ik], *adj.* huge; pertaining to the Titans; gigantic; (*chem.*) pertaining to or containing titanium.
TITANIFEROUS, [tīt'-an-if'-er-us], *adj.* containing titanium.
TITANITE, [tīt'-an-īt], *n.* the mineral sphene, a compound of titanium.
TITANIUM, [tīt-ān'-i-um], *n.* a metallic element resembling silicon, denoted by Ti. [~TITAN].

TIT-BIT, TIDBIT, [tit'-bit], *n.* a small dainty piece; an appetizing morsel; a piquant item of gossip.
TITHABLE, [tīTH-abl], *adj.* liable to pay tithes.
TITHE (1), [tīTH], *n.* the tenth part of anything; the tenth part of the increase annually arising from the profits of land and stock, allotted to the clergy; a very small part. [OE. *teotha* tenth part].
TITHE (2), [tīTH], *v.t.* to put a tithe upon.
TITHE-BARN, [tīTH'-bahn], *n.* a barn where the grain for the tithe was stored.
TITHING, [tīTH'-ing], *n.* a tithe; †an old Saxon territorial unit which consisted of ten householders, who were sureties or free pledges to each other; a township. [OE. *teothung*].
TITHING-MAN†, [tīTH'-ing-man], *n.* the chief man of a tithing; a collector of tithes.
TITIAN, [tish'-an], *adj.* resembling the works of Titian, *esp.* in colouring; of a rich auburn. [*Titian*, the Italian painter].
TITILLATE, [tit'-il-āt], *v.t.* to tickle; to tempt the palate; to stimulate pleasantly the appetite or the mind. [~L. *titillare* to tickle].
TITILLATION, [tit'-il-ā'-shun], *n.* the action or process of titillating.
TITIVATE, [tit'-iv-āt], *v.t.* to dress up; to bedeck; *v.i.* to make oneself look smart. [Unkn.].
TITIVATION, [tit'-iv-ā'-shun], *n.* the act of titivating.
TITLARK, [tit'-lahk], *n.* a bird, the meadow pipit, *Anthus pratensis*.
TITLE, [tītl], *n.* the inscription put over anything, *esp.* that one in the beginning of a book, denoting the subject of the work; an appellation of dignity, distinction, or pre-eminence; a name; an appellation; right; that which constitutes a just right to exclusive possession; the instrument which is evidence of a right; a title-deed; (*eccles. law*) agreement by which a beneficiary holds a benefice. [OFr. *title* from L. *titulus*].
TITLED, [tītld], *adj.* having a title, *esp.* one denoting nobility.
TITLE-DEED, [tītl'-dēd], *n.* a document in evidence of ownership of real property.
TITLE-PAGE, [tītl'-pāj], *n.* the page at the front of a book giving the subject and the author's name.
TITLER, [tit'-ler], *n.* (*coll.*) a stickleback.
TITLE-ROLE, [tītl'-rōl], *n.* the character in a book or play from which its title is taken.
TITLING (1), [tītl-ing], *n.* the giving of a title; the printing of the title and other preliminary pages of a book; (*typ.*) type faces suitable for title-pages, etc.
TITLING (2), [tit'-ling], *n.* a small tit; the hedge-sparrow.
TITMOUSE, (*pl.* **titmice**), [tit'-mows], *n.* a tit, any one of the small active perching birds of the genus *Parus*.
TITRATE, [tit-rāt'], *v.t.* (*chem.*) to subject to volumetric analysis. [Fr. *titrer*].
TITRATION, [ti-trā'-shun], *n.* (*chem.*) volumetric analysis.
TI-TREE, [tē'-trē], *n.* the cabbage-tree of New Zealand. [Native].
TITTER (1), [tit'-er], *n.* a snigger; a subdued laugh; a giggle.
TITTER (2), [tit'-er], *v.i.* to utter a subdued laugh; to snigger, giggle. [Echoic].
TITTEREL, [tit'-er-el], *n.* the whimbrel, *Numenius phæopus*. [Echoic].
TITTLE, [titl], *n.* a small particle; a jot; an iota. [ME. *titel*].
TITTLE-BAT, [titl'-bat'], *n.* stickleback.
TITTLE-TATTLE (1), [titl'-tatl'], *n.* small talk; gossip.
TITTLE-TATTLE (2), [titl'-tatl'], *v.i.* to gossip; to indulge in idle chatter. [TATTLE].
TITTUP, [tit'-up], *v.i.* to behave in a gay light-hearted way; to step gaily, to prance about, *esp.* of a horse. [TITUBATE].
TITTUPY, [tit'-up-i], *adj.* gay, prancing; unstable.
TITUBATE, [tit'-yōōb-āt], *v.i.* to stagger; to stammer. [L. *titubare*].
TITUBATION, [tit'-yōōb-ā'-shun], *n.* the action of stumbling; a restless fidgety state due to nervous disorder. [L. *titubatio*].
TITULAR (1), [tit'-yōōl-er], *n.* a person invested with the title of an office without performing the duties attached to it.
TITULAR (2), [tit'-yōōl-er], *adj.* of, or pertaining to, a title; holding the title; having the title only, nominal. [~L. *titulus*].
TITULARITY, [tit'-yōōl-a'-ri-ti], *n.* the condition of being titular.
TITULARLY, [tit'-yōōl-er-li], *adv.* nominally; by virtue of title only; in titular style.
TITULARY, [tit'-yōōl-er-i], *adj.* titular.
TIVER, [tiv'-er], *n.* (*dial.*) a sort of ochre used in marking sheep. [OE. *teafor*].
TIVY, [tiv'-i], *adj. and adv.* tantivy.
TIZZY, [tiz'-i], *n.* (*slang*) a sixpence. [Unkn.].
TMESIS, [tmēs'-is], *n.* (*rhet.*) a figure by which a compound word is separated by the interposition of one or more words. [Gk. *tmesis*].
TO (1), [te, tōō, tōō], *prep.* denoting motion towards a place, purpose, object, or thing; denoting extent, degree, or end; in comparison with; denoting addition, junction, or union; denoting opposition or contrast; denoting the indirect object, that is the person or thing indirectly affected by the action or state described in a verb; preceding the simple verb as sign of the infinitive. [OE. *to*].
TO (2), [te, tōō, tōō], *adv.* forward, on; denoting motion towards a junction, union, closing; **t. and fro,** backwards and forwards.
TOAD, [tōd], *n.* an amphibian of the genus *Bufo*, somewhat resembling the frog in form, but thicker and clumsier, and with a warty skin; **sea t.,** a fish, the father lasher, *Cottus scorpius*. [OE. *tadde*].
TOADEATER, [tōd'-ēt'-er], *n.* one who swallowed toads for a mountebank in order to demonstrate the latter's skill in curing a poisoned person; (*fig.*) a fawning obsequious parasite; a mean sycophant.
TOADEATING, [tōd'-ēt'-ing], *n.* sycophancy; parasitism.
TOADFISH, [tōd'-fish], *n.* a North American fish of the genus *Batrachus*, commonly called the puffer.
TOADFLAX, [tōd'-flaks'], *n.* a common European plant of the genus *Linaria*; butter-and-eggs.
TOAD-IN-THE-HOLE, [tōd'-in-the-hōl'], *n.* a savoury dish consisting of sausage or other meat cooked in batter.
TOAD-STONE, [tōd'-stōn], *n.* a variety of dolerite; several forms of stone formerly thought to be found in the body of a toad and to possess magical properties.
TOADSTOOL, [tōd'-stōōl], *n.* an inedible fungus somewhat like a mushroom.
TOADY (1), [tōd'-i], *n.* a toadeater; a sycophant.
TOADY (2), [tōd'-i], *v.i.* to behave like a toady; **to t. to,** to fawn upon and seek for personal motives to obtain the favour of.
TOADYISH, [tōd'-i-ish], *adj.* pertaining to or like a toady.
TOADYISM, [tōd'-i-izm], *n.* mean sycophancy.
TOAST (1), [tōst], *n.* bread browned before the fire; a woman whose health is drunk in honour or respect; he who or that which is named in honour in drinking; the act of proposing a toast. [OFr. *tostée* toasted bread].
TOAST (2), [tōst], *v.t.* to make crisp and brown by exposure to heat; to warm to a comfortable heat; *v.i.* to become so warmed. [OFr. *toster*].
TOAST (3), [tōst], *v.t.* to propose or honour a toast to; *v.i.* to drink a toast.
TOASTER, [tōst'-er], *n.* a person who toasts; apparatus for toasting bread.
TOASTING-FORK, [tōst'-ing-fawk], *n.* a fork for holding the bread when toasting.
TOASTMASTER, [tōst'-mahst'-er], *n.* the announcer of the toasts at a dinner or other formal occasion.
TOAST-RACK, [tōst'-rak'], *n.* a small metal or china rack for serving toast at table.
TOBACCO, [to-bak'-ō], *n.* any of the forty species of the genus *Nicotiana*, the leaves of which when dried are used for smoking and chewing, and in snuff. [Sp. *tobaco*].
TOBACCONIST, [to-bak'-on-ist], *n.* a retailer of tobacco.
TOBACCO-PIPE, [to-bak'-ō-pīp], *n.* a pipe used in smoking tobacco.
TOBACCO-POUCH, [to-bak'-ō-powch'], *n.* a small bag or pouch for carrying tobacco in the pocket.
TOBACCO-STOPPER, [to-bak'-ō-stop'-er], *n.* a plug for pressing down the tobacco in a pipe while smoking.
TOBAS, [tō'-bas], *n.(pl.)* a South American race inhabiting parts of Paraguay and Argentina.
TOBINE†, [tō'-bin], *n.* a stout lustrous twilled silk, used for dresses. [~It. *tabino*].
TOBOGGAN (1), [to-bog'-an], *n.* a light sledge for sliding down a snow-clad slope. [AmerInd. *tobakan*].
TOBOGGAN (2), [to-bog'-an], *v.i.* to ride, coast down a hill, on a toboggan.
TOBY (1), [tōb'-i], *n.* a mug in the shape of a stout man wearing a three-cornered hat; the name of the dog in a punch-and-judy show. [Personal name].

TOBY (2), [tōb'-i], *n.* a highway. [Shelta *tobar*].

TOCCATA, [tok-ah'-ta], *n.* (*mus.*) a prelude designed to display the executant's touch and technique. [It. *toccata*].

TOCHARIAN (1), [to-kāer'-i-an], *n.* a dead language of the Indo-European group preserved in records surviving in Turkestan. [Gk. *Tocharoi* a nomadic Chinese tribe].

TOCHARIAN (2), [to-kāer'-i-an], *adj.* in, of, or pertaining to, Tocharian.

TOCHER, [tokh'-er], *n.* (*Scots*) a portion brought by a wife at her marriage; a dowry. [Gael. *tochar*].

TOCOLOGY, TOKOLOGY, [tok-ol'-oj-i], *n.* obstetrics; midwifery. [Gk. *tokos* childbirth and *logos* speech].

TOCSIN, [tok'-sin], *n.* an alarm-bell or the ringing of it to give the alarm. [Fr. *tocsin*].

TOD†, [tod], *n.* a quantity of wool of about 28 lb.; a bush or thick shrub; a fox. [ON. *toddi* mass, tuft].

TO-DAY (1), [tōō-dā'], *n.* the present day; this very day.

TO-DAY (2), [tōō-dā'], *adv.* on this day; at the present time; now. [OE. *to dæge*].

TODDLE (1), [todl], *n.* the act of toddling.

TODDLE (2), [todl], *v.i.* to walk with little, tottering, uncertain, childish steps; (*coll.*) to walk easily along; to depart, walk away. [~TOTTER].

TODDLER, [tod'-ler], *n.* a person who toddles; a toddling child.

TODDY, [tod'-i], *n.* a juice drawn from a palm tree; a mixture of whisky with hot water and sugar; punch. [~Hind. *tari* juice of the palm tree].

TODDY-BIRD, [tod'-i-burd], *n.* a wood-swallow of the genus *Artamus*, the toddy-shrike; an East Indian bird that feeds on the sap of the palm tree. [*Prec.* and BIRD].

TODDY-SHRIKE, [tod'-i-shrīk'], *n.* the toddy-bird. [TODDY and SHRIKE].

TO-DO, [tōō-dōō'], *n.* ado; disturbance; stir.

TODY, [tōd'-i], *n.* a small, bright-coloured West Indian picarian bird of the genus *Todus*. [Fr. *todier*].

TODY

TOE (1), [tō], *n.* a digit of the foot, corresponding to a finger of the hand; the fore-part of the hoof of a horse or of any other hoofed animal; any prolongation of the foot like a toe; the fore-part of a boot, shoe, or stocking that covers the toe; a projecting portion of an object resembling the human toe; **to tread on a person's toes**, (*fig.*) to hurt a person's feelings. [OE. *ta*].

TOE (2), [tō], *v.t.* to fit with a toe; to place the toe of the foot on (a given point); **to t. the line**, (*fig.*) to obey orders.

TOECAP, [tō'-kap'], *n.* an extra piece over the toe of a boot or shoe.

TOENAIL, [tō'-nāl'], *n.* the nail growing on a toe.

TOFF, [toff], *n.* (*slang*) a well-dressed man; a swell; a gentleman. [Unkn.].

TOFFEE, [tof'-i], *n.* a sweetmeat made of syrup, butter, sugar, etc., boiled together and flavoured; **not for t.**, not at all. [Uncert.].

TOFT, [toft], *n.* a grove of trees; a green knoll; a homestead; (*leg.*) a messuage with right of common; a place where a messuage once stood. [OScand. *topt*].

TOFTMAN, [toft'-man], *n.* the owner of a toft.

TOG, [tog], *v.t.* and *i.* (*slang*) **to t. up**, to dress up. [TOGS].

TOGA, [tōg'-a], *n.* the outer garment of a Roman citizen in peace, long, broad, and flowing, and consisting of a single piece of stuff; **t. praetexta**, a toga with a broad purple border, worn by children, certain magistrates, and priests; **t. virilis**, the manly gown first worn by boys at sixteen. [L. *toga*].

TOGAED, [tōg'-ad], *adj.* wearing a toga.

TOGETHER, [to-geth'-er], *adv.* in company; in or into union; in or into contest; in the same place or time, uninterruptedly; in concert, simultaneously; **t. with**, in union with, accompanied by. [OE. *togædere*].

TOGGERY, [tog'-er-i], *n.* (*slang*) clothes; official garments, outfit. [~TOGS].

TOGGLE, [togl], *n.* (*naut.*) a small wooden pin which tapers at both ends. [Uncert.].

TOGA

TOGGLE-IRON, [togl'-iern], *n.* (*naut.*) a whaler's harpoon with a blade instead of flukes.

TOGGLE-JOINT, [togl'-joint'], *n.* an elbow or knee-joint consisting of two bars that can be brought into a straight line.

TOGGLE-SWITCH, [togl'-swich'], *n.* a switch having a crosspiece to actuate the mechanism.

TOGS, [togz], *n.*(*pl.*) (*slang*) clothes. [Uncert.].

TOIL (1), [toil], *n.* labour with oppressive pain and fatigue; drudgery; strenuous effort over a long period.

TOIL (2), see TOILS.

TOIL (3), [toil], *v.i.* to exert the utmost strength of body or mind in labour; to labour; to work; to walk painfully and with the utmost effort. [OFr. *toillier* to drag about].

TOILER, [toil'-er], *n.* a person who toils.

TOILET, [toil'-et], *n.* the operation of dressing; the costume, the finished effect of performing the toilet; a lavatory. [Fr. *toilette* cloth].

TOILET-COVER, [toil'-et-kuv'-er], *n.* a cover for a dressing-table.

TOILET-GLASS, [toil'-et-glahs'], *n.* a mirror on a dressing-table.

TOILET-PAPER, [toil'-et-pāp'-er], *n.* paper for wiping the anus after defecation.

TOILET-POWDER, [toil'-et-powd'-er], *n.* talcum powder used after shaving, etc.

TOILET-TABLE, [toil'-et-tābl'], *n.* a dressing-table.

TOILETTE, [twah-let'], *n.* toilet; a particular costume usually of an elaborate kind. [Fr. *toilette*].

TOILS, [toilz], *n.*(*pl.*) of TOIL (2); a net, snare, web; **in the toils**, entrapped; fascinated; in the clutches of someone. [Fr. *toile* cloth].

TOILSOME, [toil'-sum], *adj.* necessitating toil; laborious; wearisome.

TOILSOMELY, [toil'-sum-li], *adv.* in a toilsome fashion.

TOILSOMENESS, [toil'-sum-nes], *n.* the condition of being toilsome.

TOILWORN, [toil'-wawn'], *adj.* weary or worn out with toil.

TOISON, [twaz'-aw(ng)], *n.* a fleece; **t. d'or**, a Spanish order of knighthood, the Golden Fleece. [Fr. *toison* fleece].

TOKAY, [tō-kā'], *n.* a rich, aromatic wine made at *Tokay* in Hungary; **essence of T.**, a much esteemed liqueur prepared from Tokay.

TOKEN, [tōk-en], *n.* something intended to represent another thing or event; a sign; a mark; a memorial of friendship; a piece of money not coined by authority but current by sufferance; ten and a half quires of paper; **t. payment**, a small payment made for form's sake. [OE. *tacn*].

TOKENLESS, [tōk'-en-les], *adj.* without a token.

TOKOLOGY, see TOCOLOGY.

TOL†, see TOLL.

TOLA, [tōl'-a], *n.* an Indian weight for gold and silver equal to 180 grains troy. [Hind. *tola*.]

TOLBOOTH, see TOLL-BOOTH.

TOLD, [tōld], *pret.* and *p.pt.* of TELL.

TOLEDO, [tol-ēd'-ō], *n.* a sword-blade of the finest temper, made at *Toledo* in Spain.

TOLERABLE, [tol'-er-abl], *adj.* able to be endured; supportable either physically or mentally; fairly good. [L. *tolerabilis*].

TOLERABLENESS, [tol'-er-abl-nes], *n.* the state of being tolerable.

TOLERABLY, [tol'-er-ab-li], *adv.* in a manner that may be tolerated; moderately.

TOLERANCE, [tol'-er-ants], *n.* the power or the act of tolerating; a disposition to tolerate; forbearance; permissible variation. [L. *tolerantia*].

TOLERANT, [tol'-er-ant], *adj.* disposed to tolerate; permitting, favouring toleration; broad-minded; forbearing.

TOLERANTLY, [tol'-er-ant-li], *adv.* with toleration; in a tolerant fashion.

TOLERATE, [tol'-er-āt], *v.t.* to suffer to be or be done without prohibition or hindrance; to allow or permit negatively by not preventing; to exercise forbearance towards; to endure. [~L. *tolerare*].

TOLERATION, [tol-er-ā'-shun], *n.* the action or state of tolerating; forbearance.

TOLERATIONIST, [tol'-er-ā'-shun-ist], *n.* a person in favour of toleration, particularly in matters of religion.

TOLL (1), TOL†, [tōl], *n.* a tax; a sum to be paid for the right to pass along a certain road or bridge; the portion of wheat kept back by a miller as a fee for grinding; the telephone call for places within a moderate distance of the metropolitan area which are worked from what are called toll exchanges; **to take t. of**, to exact losses from. [OE. *toll*].

TOLL (2), [tōl], *n.* the deep sound of the tolling of a bell.

TOLL (3), [tōl], *v.t.* to cause a bell to sound with notes slowly repeated in regular time; a mournful ringing; *v.i.* to sound as a bell.

TOLL (4), [tōl], *v.t.* (*leg.*) to take away, debar; to vacate. [AFr. *toller*].

TOLL-BAR, [tōl'-bah(r)], *n.* a bar, beam, or gate to stop boats on a canal, or passengers on a road, till toll is paid.

TOLL-BOOTH, TOLBOOTH, [tōl'-bōōth], *n.* a place where goods were weighed to ascertain the duties of toll; (*Scots*) a town prison.

TOLL-BRIDGE, [tōl'-brij'], *n.* a bridge where toll must be paid for passing over it.

TOLL-COLLECTOR, [tōl'-kol-ekt'-or], *n.* a person who collects toll.

TOLL-DISH, [tōl'-dish], *n.* a dish for measuring the toll of grain in mills.

TOLLER, [tōl'-er], *n.* a toll-gatherer; a person who tolls a bell.

TOLL-GATE, [tōl'-gāt], *n.* a gate at which toll is taken.

TOLL-GATHERER, [tōl'-gaTH'-er-er], *n.* a toll-collector.

TOLL-HOUSE, [tōl'-hows], *n.* a house or office at a toll-gate where the collector lives.

TOLLY, [tol'-i], *n.* (*slang*) a candle. [~TALLOW].

TOLSEY, [tōl'-si], *n.* a toll-booth; a kind of market exchange. [ME. *tolseld*].

TOLTEC, [tol'-tek], *n.* a Mexican race that preceded the Aztecs.

TOLU, [tol-yōō'], *n.* a balsam obtained from the bark of the South American tolu tree. [Santiago de *Tolu*, in Colombia].

TOLUENE, [tol'-yōō-ēn], *n.* methyl benzene, obtained first by distillation of tolu balsam. [TOLU].

TOM, [tom], *n.* a male cat. [Hypocoristic form of *Thomas*].

TOMAHAWK (1), [tom'-a-hawk], *n.* a light Indian war and hunting hatchet; a type of U.S. fighter-bomber. [Amer.Indian *tamahak*].

TOMAHAWK

TOMAHAWK (2), [tom'-a-hawk], *v.t.* to cut or slay with a tomahawk.

TOMALLY, [to-mal'-i], *n.* the part of lobster flesh that turns green with boiling. [~TOURMALINE].

TOMATO, [tō-maht'-ō], *n.* a South American plant, *Lycopersicum esculentum*, the reddish yellowy pulpy fruit of which is popularly used in salads. [Span. *tomate* from Mexican *tomatl*].

TOMAUN, [to-mawn'], *n.* a Persian gold coin about fifteen shillings in value. [Pers. *toman*].

TOMB, [tōōm], *n.* a grave; a sepulchre; a monument erected over a grave in memory of the dead; (*fig.*) death. [OFr. *tombe*].

TOMBAC, [tom'-bak'], *n.* an alloy of copper and zinc used for gongs and cheap jewellery. [Port. *tambaca*].

TOMBED, [tōōmd], *adj.* buried in a tomb.

TOMBLESS, [tōōm'-les], *adj.* without a tomb.

TOMBOLA, [tom'-bol-a], *n.* a form of lottery. [It. *tombola*].

TOMBOY, [tom'-boi], *n.* a strong and romping girl. [*Tom* from Thomas].

TOMBSTONE, [tōōm'-stōn], *n.* a stone set over a grave and usually inscribed with the name and particulars of the dead person; a monument.

TOM-CAT, [tom'-kat'], *n.* a male cat.

TOM-COD, [tom'-kod'], *n.* a small North American fish, *Gadus tomcodus*; the young of the cod-fish.

TOME, [tōm], *n.* a book; a large volume; one of several volumes of a large work. [Fr. *tome*].

TOMENTOSE, [tō'-men-tōs], *adj.* (*bot.*) downy; covered with long woolly hairs.

TOMENTUM, [tō-ment'-um], *n.* (*anat.*) the mass of minute vessels on the surface of the brain; (*bot.*) a species of woolly pubescence. [L. *tomentum* stuffing of wool].

TOMFOOL, [tom'-fōōl], *n.* a great fool; a silly trifler.

TOMFOOLERY, [tom'-fōōl'-er-i], *n.* foolish trifling; nonsense; silly behaviour.

TOMIN, [tō'-min], *n.* a Spanish jeweller's weight equal to 12 grains. [Sp. *tomin*].

TOMMY, [tom'-i], *n.* (*coll.*) a private soldier in the British Army, so called from *Thomas* Atkins, the name given as an example in filling up of papers on enlistment; (*slang*) bread, provisions.

TOMMY-GUN, [tom'-i-gun'], *n.* a sub-machine gun with a short barrel. [*Thompson* the maker and GUN (1)].

TOMMY-ROT, [tom'-i-rot'], *n.* (*slang*) nonsense.

TOMNODDY, [tom'-nod'-i], *n.* (*slang*) a dolt, foolish fellow; **Lord T.,** a self-important person.

TOMORROW (1), [tōō-mo'-rō], *n.* the day which comes after to-day.

TOMORROW (2), [tōō-mo'-rō], *adv.* on the day after to-day.

TOMPION, [tom'-pi-on], *n.* the stopper inserted in the mouth of a gun; the iron bottom to which grape-shot were fixed; the inking pad used in lithography. [~TAMPON].

TOMPOT, [tom'-pot'], *n.* the small fish *Blennius gattorugine*, caught in lobster pots. [TOM and POT (1)].

TOMTIT, [tom'-tit'], *n.* the blue titmouse, *Parus cæruleus*.

TOMTOM, [tom'-tom'], *n.* a primitive drum used by the Hindus; the drum of the African races. [Hind. *tamtam*].

TON (1), [tun], *n.* a weight of 20 cwt. or 2,240 lb.; **metric t.,** 2,204·6 lb.; **short t.,** 2,000 lb.; (*fig.*) a very heavy weight; (*pl.*) a great quantity. [~TUN].

TON (2), [taw(ng)], *n.* the fashion; the stylish wear. [Fr. *ton*].

TONAL, [tōn'-al], *adj.* of, or pertaining to, tone.

TONALITY, [tōn-al'-it-i], *n.* tones collectively; (*mus.*) the general quality of the pitch or tone; the relation of notes in conformity with a musical scale.

TONE (1), [tōn], *n.* sound or a modification of sound; accent, or rather a particular inflexion of the voice adapted to express emotion or passion; a whine, a mournful strain of voice; prevailing atmosphere, spirit; a shade, colour, tinge; (*mus.*) an interval of sound; the usual sound of an instrument with regard to softness, etc.; (*med.*) that state of a body in which the animal functions are healthy; (*paint.*) the harmonious relation of the colours of a picture in light and shade; (*mus.*) **t. poem,** a short descriptive piece in music. [Gk. *tonos*].

TONE (2), [tōn], *v.t.* to give tone to; (*phot.*) to modify the colour of by immersion in a bath; *v.i.* to blend agreeably as to colour; **to t. down,** to make the sound or colour of less strong; (*fig.*) to modify, pacify, subdue; **to t. up,** to make the sound, colour stronger; (*fig.*) to strengthen, give more vitality to.

TONE-ARM, [tōn'-ahm'], *n.* the tube which supports the sound-box of a gramophone, and acts as a connexion between the diaphragm and the horn. [TONE (1) and ARM (1)].

TONE-DEAF, [tōn'-def'], *adj.* incapable of distinguishing between sounds of different pitch.

TONED, [tōnd], *adj.* with a tone.

TONELESS, [tōn'-les], *adj.* without tone; unmusical.

TONE-SYLLABLE, [tōn'-sil-abl], *n.* an accented syllable.

TONG (1), [tong], *n.* the sound of a bell being rung sharply. [Echoic].

TONG (2), [tong], *n.* a secret club or society in China. [Chin. *t'ang* hall].

TONGS, [tongz], *n.*(*pl.*) an implement consisting of two bars joined by a pivot or united by a spring, used for handling and lifting, particularly burning fuel and hot metals. [OE. *tang*].

TONGUE (1), [tung], *n.* the organ of taste in animals, and more especially of speech in man; speech; power of utterance; fluency of speech; mode of speaking a language; word or words; the language of a race or nation; a point, as of a buckle; a projecting point of land; a projection along an edge to fit into a groove; the taper part of anything; a thin strip of leather that fits underneath the lace-holes in boots and shoes; **to give t.,** to utter loudly, bark; **to hold the t.,** to be silent. [OE. *tunge*].

TONGUE (2), [tung], *v.t.* to scold; to modify with the tongue the sound of when playing a flute, etc.; *v.i.* to use the tongue in modifying sound.

TONGUED, [tungd], *adj.* with a tongue.

TONGUE-GRAFTING, [tung'-grahft-ing], *n.* (*hort.*) inserting the end of a scion in a special manner.

TONGUELESS, [tung'-les], *adj.* having no tongue; speechless.

TONGUE-TIED, [tung'-tīd], *adj.* having an impediment in the speech; unable to speak freely; awkwardly silent.

TONIC (1), [ton'-ik], *n.* something that stimulates the mind or body; (*med.*) a medicine that gives tone and vigour of nerve and muscle; (*mus.*) the keynote; (*mus.*) the sound produced by a vocal string in a given degree of tension.

TONIC (2), [ton'-ik], *adj.* increasing the strength, tone, *esp.* of the animal system; obviating the effects of debility, and restoring healthy functions; stimulating;

inspiriting; **t. sol-fa**, a style of notation in music, which, dispensing with the staff, its lines, and spaces, indicates the notes by letters, and time and accent by dashes and colons; **t. spasm**, (*med.*) a continuous spasmodic contraction. [Gk. *tonikos*].

TONICITY, [ton-is'-i-ti], *n.* elasticity or contractility of the muscular fibres; (*mus.*) musical tone.

TONIGHT (1), [tŏŏ-nīt'], *n.* this night; the night after the present day.

TONIGHT (2), [tŏŏ-nīt'], *adv.* on this night; on the night of today.

TONITE, [ton'-īt], *n.* an explosive made of gun-cotton and barium nitrate, used for blasting. [~L. *tonare* to thunder].

TONKA-BEAN, [tongk'-a-bēn], *n.* the fruit of the tropical American plant, *Dipteryx odorata*, called also Tonquin bean, noted for its fragrance. [Native].

TONNAGE, [tun'-ij], *n.* the nominal capacity of a ship; the cubical content or burden which a ship can carry in tons; a duty or impost on ships, estimated formerly per ton, now according to bulk. [OFr. *tonnage*].

TONQUIN BEAN, [ton'-kin-bēn'], *n.* the Tonka bean. [~TONKA BEAN and *Tonquin* in Further India].

TONSIL, [ton'-sil], *n.* (*anat.*) one of two glandular bodies in the throat or fauces; lymphoid glands. [L. *tonsillae*].

TONSILLITIC, [ton'-sil-it'-ik], *adj.* pertaining to the tonsils.

TONSILLITIS, [ton'-sil-īt'-is], *n.* inflammation of the tonsils.[~TONSIL and Gk. *itis* denoting inflammation].

TONSORIAL, [ton-saw'-ri-al], *adj.* of, or pertaining to, a barber or to shaving. [L. *tonsorius*].

TONSURE, [ton'-sher], *n.* the action of clipping the hair or of shaving the head; the state of being shorn, as a sign of dedication to the ministry or initiation into holy orders; a shaven bald part on the head of a priest or monk. [L. *tonsura*].

TONSURED, [ton'-sherd], *adj.* having a tonsure; shaven about the head.

TONTINE, [ton'-tīn], *n.* a loan on which annuities are paid instead of interest, each annuity increasing as the number of the subscribers diminishes by death, until the last to survive receives as much as all of them had at first shared amongst them. [It. *tontina*].

TOO, [tŏŏ], *adv.* excessively; over; more than enough; very; in addition; moreover. [OE. *to*].

TOOK, [tŏŏk], *pret.* of TAKE.

TOOL (1), [tŏŏl], *n.* an implement, instrument, apparatus used for performing some operation either by hand or by machinery; the implement used in bookbinding; (*fig.*) equipment for study; a person used as a mere instrument by another. [OE. *tol*].

TOOL (2), [tŏŏl], *v.t.* to shape, mark with a tool; *v.i.* (*coll.*) to drive oneself along in a smooth, brisk way.

TOOL-BAG, [tŏŏl'-bag], *n.* a bag, usually of leather, designed to hold a set of tools. [TOOL (1) and BAG (1)].

TOOLING, [tŏŏl'-ing], *n.* workmanship performed with a tool; marks made on a bookbinding with the tool.

TOONWOOD, [tŏŏn'-wŏŏd], *n.* a wood of a reddish-brown colour, obtained from *Cedrela Toona*, a large East Indian tree. [Hind. *tun*].

TOOT (1), [tŏŏt], *n.* the sounding of a horn.

TOOT (2), [tŏŏt], *v.t. and i.* to sound a horn, *esp.* a motor-car horn; to hoot; to make a noise like the sounding of a horn. [Echoic].

TOOTER, [tŏŏt'-er], *n.* one who toots; a horn.

TOOTH (1), (*pl.* **teeth**), [tŏŏth], *n.* one of the hard, ivory-like instruments growing in the jaws of human beings and animals, used to masticate food; one of a series of wood or metal objects resembling teeth; the prong of a comb; **to cast in the teeth**, to reproach with, blame; **in the teeth of**, in the face of, in spite of; **to be armed to the teeth**, to be thoroughly armed; **to show the teeth**, to grow dangerous, threatening; **to set the teeth on edge**, to irritate greatly, anger; **by the skin of the teeth**, narrowly, only just; **a sweet t.**, a liking for sweet things. [OE. *toth*].

TOOTH (2), [tŏŏth], *v.t.* to provide with teeth, indent; *v.i.* to interlock.

TOOTHACHE, [tŏŏth'-āk], *n.* an ache in the nerves of the teeth or in the gums.

TOOTHACHE-TREE, [tŏŏth'-āk-trē], *n.* the prickly ash, *Xanthoxylum fraxineum*.

TOOTH-BRUSH, [tŏŏth'-brush], *n.* a brush for cleaning the teeth.

TOOTHDRAWER, [tŏŏth'-draw'-er], *n.* one who draws, an instrument for drawing, teeth; a dentist.

TOOTHDRAWING, [tŏŏth'-draw'-ing], *n.* the action of extracting a tooth.

TOOTHED, [tŏŏtht], *adj.* (*bot.*) furnished with teeth or jags; dentate.

TOOTH-EDGE, [tŏŏth'-ej'], *n.* a sensation excited by grating sounds and by the feel of certain substances.

TOOTHFUL, [tŏŏth'-fŏŏl], *n.* a very small quantity.

TOOTH-KEY, [tŏŏth'-kē], *n.* an instrument used in drawing teeth.

TOOTHLESS, [tŏŏth'-les], *adj.* without teeth.

TOOTHLET, [tŏŏth'-let], *n.* a small tooth.

TOOTH-ORNAMENT, [tŏŏth'-awn'-a-ment], *n.* (*arch.*) a decoration peculiar to early English architecture, consisting of a close succession of small four-leaved flowers projecting forward to a central point.

TOOTH-PASTE, [tŏŏth'-pāst], *n.* a dental paste.

TOOTHPICK, [tŏŏth'-pik], *n.* an instrument for cleaning the teeth of food lodged between them.

TOOTH-POWDER, [tŏŏth'-powd'-er], *n.* a powder used for cleaning the teeth.

TOOTHSOME, [tŏŏth-sum], *adj.* appetising, palatable.

TOOTHSOMENESS, [tŏŏth'-sum-nes], *n.* the condition of being toothsome.

TOOTHWORT, [tŏŏth'-wurt], *n.* one of several plants, *esp.* a species of *Lathræa* and a species of *Dentaria*.

TOOTHY, [tŏŏth'-i], *adj.* toothed, displaying teeth.

TOOTLE (1), [tŏŏtl], *n.* the sound made in tootling.

TOOTLE (2), [tŏŏtl], *v.t. and i.* to toot gently; to play the flute or flageolet gently. [~TOOT].

TOP (1), [top], *n.* the highest part of anything; summit; surface; upper side; the highest place or person or degree or rank; the hair on the crown of the head; the head of a plant or the part above the ground; the uppermost division of a fishing-rod; (*naut.*) a sort of platform surrounding the head of the lower mast, and projecting on all sides, serving to extend the shrouds. [OE. *top*].

TOP (2), [top], *n.* a wooden or metal toy in the shape of an inverted pear which children play with by spinning it on its point; (*slang*) **old t.**, old fellow, old girl. [OE. *top*].

TOP (3), [top], *adj.* relating to the top; nearest to, at the top; principal; first, primary; best; **t. gear**, the highest gear in motoring, etc., giving the greatest road speed.

TOP (4), [top], *v.t.* to cover on the top; to cap; to raise above; to excel, surpass; to crop the surface of; *v.i.* to rise aloft; to predominate, be eminent, excel.

TOP-, see TOPO-.

TOPARCH, [top'-ahk], *n.* the ruler or principal man of a small district.

TOPARCHY, [top'-ahk-i], *n.* a small country governed by a toparch; a little state consisting of a few towns. [Gk. *toparkhia*].

TOPAZ, [tō'-paz], *n.* one of the gems, generally yellowish, occurring in rhombic prisms, really a silicate of aluminium with fluorine. [Gk. *topazos*].

TOPAZOLITE, [tōp-az'-ō-līt], *n.* a kind of precious garnet of a topaz-yellow colour. [TOPAZ and Gk *lithos* stone].

TOP-BOOT, [top'-bŏŏt], *n.* one of a pair of riding boots extending nearly to the knee with a broad top of light-coloured leather representing the lining which used to be shown when the upper part of the boot was turned down.

TOP-COAT, [top'-kōt], *n.* an overcoat.

TOP-DRAINING, [top'-drān-ing], *n.* drainage of the surface of land.

TOP-DRESSING, [top'-dres'-ing], *n.* a dressing of manure laid on the surface of land; the final coat of paint or other material in decorating.

TOPE (1), [tōp], *n.* the small species of shark, *Galeus vulgaris*, otherwise known as the dogfish. [Unkn.].

TOPE (2), [tōp], *n.* in India, a grove or clump of trees, usually fruit trees. [Tamil *toppu*].

TOPE (3), [tōp], *n.* a mound or cupola-shaped Buddhist shrine, originally surmounted by a roof in the shape of an extended parasol. [Hind. *top*].

TOPE (4), [tōp], *v.i.* to drink strong or spirituous liquors frequently and to excess. [Fr. *toper*].

TOPEE, TOPI, [tō-pē'], *n.* a pith helmet worn as a protection against the sun. [Hind. *topi* hat].

TOPER, [tōp'-er], *n.* a person who drinks to excess; a drunkard.

TOPFUL, [top'-fŏŏl'], *adj.* full to the brim.

TOPGALLANT, [t-gal'-ant, top'-gal'-ant], *adj.* (*naut.*) above the top or second mast and below the royal; highest; elevated; splendid. [TOP (2) and GALLANT (2)].

TOPGALLANTMAST, [top'-gal'-ant-mahst'], *n.* (*naut.*) the mast above the topmast.
TOPGALLANTSAIL, [top'-gal'-ant-sāl'], *n.* (*naut.*) the sail above the topmast.
TOPHACEOUS, [tōf-ā'-shus], *adj.* gritty; sandy; resembling tophus. [L. *tofaceus*].
TOP HAT, [top'-hat'], *n.* a high cylindrical hat worn by men with formal morning-dress or with certain uniforms.
TOP-HEAVY, [top'-hev'-i], *adj.* having the top or upper part too heavy for the lower; unstable.
TOPHET, [tōf'-et'], *n.* hell or the place of torment; originally, a place south-east of Jerusalem which, in consequence of having been the site of the revolting Moloch worship, had been allowed to be used as a place for burning the city's refuse, so that smoke was constantly rising from it. [Heb. *topheth*].
TOP-HOLE, [top'-hōl'], *adj.* (*slang*) splendid, fine.
TOPHUS, (*pl.* **tophi**), [tōf'-us], *n.* a calcareous concretion forming on the surface of the joints in gout. [L. *tofus* a soft stone].
TOPI, see TOPEE.
TOPIARY, [tōp'-i-er-i], *n.* the art of cutting trees and shrubs into shapes, *esp.* in order to represent birds and animals; a garden of trees thus cut. [L. *topiarius* landscape gardener].
TOPIC, [top'-ik], *n.* a general statement useful in developing an argument; a general truth; the subject of conversation or writing; any subject that is discussed or spoken of at the moment. [Gk. *topikos* belonging to a place].
TOPICAL, [top'-ik-al], *adj.* pertaining to a subject of current interest; (*med.*) pertaining to a local affection of the body.
TOPICALLY, [top'-ik-al-i], *adv.* in a topical manner; (*med.*) locally, with application to a particular part.
TOP-KNOT, [top'-not'], *n.* a knot or bow worn on top of the head; a tuft of hair on top of the head; a kind of flat-fish or flounder of the genus *Zeugoplerus*.
TOPLESS, [top'-les], *adj.* without top; immensely lofty.
TOPLOFTY, [top'-loft-i], *adj.* (*coll.*) haughty; pompous; condescending.
TOPMAN, [top'-man], *n.* one who stands above in sawing; (*naut.*) a man stationed in the top.
TOPMAST, [top'-mahst], *n.* (*naut.*) the mast next above that which rises from the deck, and below the topgallant.
TOPMASTHEAD, [top'-mahst-hed'], *n.* (*naut.*) that part of the topmast above the crosstrees, or, in fore-and-aft vessels, the part above the topsail-halliard block.
TOPMOST, [top'-mōst], *adj.* highest; uppermost.
TOPO-, TOP-, *pref.* place. [Gk. *topos* place].
TOPOGRAPHER, [top-og'-ra-fer], *n.* one versed in topography.
TOPOGRAPHIC, TOPOGRAPHICAL, [top'-ō-graf'-ik(-al)], *adj.* pertaining to topography.
TOPOGRAPHICALLY, [top'-ō-graf'-ik-al-i], *adv.* in a topographical fashion.
TOPOGRAPHY, [top-og'-raf-i], *n.* the art of giving a detailed accurate account of a particular place; such an account when given. [TOPO- and Gk. *graphia* writing].
TOPOLOGY, [top-ol'-ō-ji], *n.* the association of things with places as a help to memory. [TOPO- and Gk. *logos* speech].
TOPONOMY, TOPONYMY, [top-on'-om-i], *n.* the study of names, *esp.* place-names. [TOPO- and Gk. *onoma* name].
TOPPER, [top'-er], *n.* (*slang*) a man's tall silk hat; a good sort, a thoroughly likeable person.
TOPPING (1), [top'-ing], *n.* a top; the cutting off of the top; the top cut off; (*naut.*) the act of pulling one extremity of a yard higher than the other.
TOPPING (2), [top'-ing], *adj.* very high; over-topping, overhanging; (*slang*) first rate, splendid, fine.
TOPPLE, [topl], *v.t.* to throw down; *v.i.* to fall from being top-heavy; to fall forward; to pitch or tumble down; (*fig.*) to fall from a great but unstable eminence. [~TOP (3)].
TOPSAIL, [top'-sel], *n.* (*naut.*) a sail carried on the topmast which, in square-rigged vessels, is usually divided into the upper and lower topsails.
TOP-SAWYER, [top'-saw'-yer], *n.* the man who works the upper handle of the saw in a saw-pit; (*fig.*) a person in a high position, an important man.
TOP-SHELL, [top'-shel'], *n.* a gasteropod mollusc belonging to the genus *Trochus*.
TOPSIDE, [top'-sīd], *n.* the upper portion; that part of a vessel's hull above the waterline; a joint of beef cut from between the leg and the aitchbone.
TOPSMAN, [tops'-man], *n.* a head drover; (*slang*) the public executioner.
TOP-SOILING, [top'-soil'-ing], *n.* the act of taking off the top soil of land before a cutting is begun.
TOP-STONE, [top'-stōn], *n.* a stone forming the top; a coping stone; (*fig.*) the last important item.
TOPSY-TURVY, [top'-si-turv'-i], *adj.* upside down; muddled. [Uncert.].
TOPSY-TURVYDOM, [top'-si-turv'-i-dom], *n.* a topsy-turvy condition.
TOQUE, [tōk], *n.* a small close-fitting, brimless hat worn by women. [Fr. *toque*].
TOR, [taw(r)], *n.* a high pointed hill, rock, or mountain. [OE. *torr*].
TORAH, [taw'-ra], *n.* the Mosaic law; the five books of the Pentateuch. [Heb. *torah* direction].
TORAN, [taw'-ran], *n.* the gateway of a Buddhist temple constructed, like a cromlech, of two pillars and a lintel. [Hind. *toran*].
TORBANITE, [taw'-ban-īt], *n.* a dark-coloured shale yielding petroleum gas. [*Torbane* Hill, near Edinburgh, where first found].
TORCH, [tawch], *n.* a lighted stick carried in the hand; a flambeau; an electric battery and bulb fitted into a case for carrying in the hand; (*fig.*) something that lights up a mental darkness. [OFr. *torche*].
TORCHBEARER, [tawch'-bāer-er], *n.* a person whose office is to bear a torch.
TORCH-DANCE, [tawch'-dahnts], *n.* a dance in which each dancer carries a torch aloft.
TORCHLIGHT (1), [tawch'-līt], *n.* the light of torches.
TORCHLIGHT (2), [tawch'-līt], *adj.* illuminated by torches.
TORCH-LILY, [tawch'-lil'-i], *n.* a garden plant, the red-hot poker, whose flowers resemble a glowing torch. [TORCH and LILY].
TORCHON, [taw'-shon], *n.* bobbin lace of geometrical pattern; strong rough paper used for water colours. [Fr. *torchon* a crumpled rag].
TORCH-THISTLE, [tawch'-thisl], *n.* the cactus, *Cereus strigosus*, used by the North American Indians for torches.
TORE (1), [taw(r)], *n.* long coarse grass. [Unkn.].
TORE (2), [taw(r)], *pret.* of TEAR.
TOREADOR, [to'-ri-a-daw(r)'], *n.* a bull-fighter fighting on horseback. [Sp. *toreador*].
TORERO, [to-rāer'-ō], *n.* a bull-fighter fighting on foot. [Sp. *torero*].
TOREUMATOGRAPHY, [to'-ryōō-mat-og'-raf-i], *n.* the science or description of ancient sculptures and basso-relievos. [Gk. *toreuma* work in relief and *graphia* writing].
TOREUMATOLOGY, [to'-ryōō-mat-ol'-oj-i], *n.* the description of toreutic art. [Gk. *toreuma* work in relief and *logos* word].
TOREUTIC, [to-ryōōt'-ik], *adj.* pertaining to formative art, *esp.* to metal work, cast, chased, or embossed. [Gk. *toreutikos* worked in relief].
TORGOCH, [tawg'-okh], *n.* a species of char, *Salmo perisii*, with a red belly. [Wel. *torgoch*].
TORMENT (1), [taw'-ment], *n.* extreme pain or anguish, bodily or mental; that which causes pain or misery. [L. *tormentum*].
TORMENT (2), [taw-ment'], *v.t.* to put to extreme pain or anguish, bodily or mental; to distress; to harass; to tease, irritate.
TORMENTIL, [taw'-ment-il], *n.* (*bot.*) a plant of the genus *Potentilla*, whose root is used as an astringent in medicine and tanning. [Fr. *tormentille*].
TORMENTING, [taw-ment'-ing], *adj.* occasioning torment or annoyance; harassing.
TORMENTINGLY, [taw-ment'-ing-li], *adv.* in a tormenting fashion.
TORMENTOR, [taw-ment'-or], *n.* a person who torments; (*agr.*) a form of harrow.
TORMINA, [taw'-min-a], *n.* (*med.*) a severe griping pain in the bowels; gripes. [L. *tormina* gripes].
TORMINOUS, [taw'-min-us], *adj.* (*med.*) griping.
TORMODONT, [taw'-mō-dont], *adj.* having teeth, each in its individual socket. [Gk. *tormos* hole and *odous odontos* tooth].
TORN, [tawn], *p.pt.* of TEAR.
TORNADO, [tawn-ā'-dō], *n.* a local tropical thunderstorm; a hurricane; a whirling tempest. [~Span. *tronado* thunderstorm].
TOROSE, TOROUS, [to-rōs', taw'-rus], *adj.* covered with knobs or protuberances; showing muscle-like protuberances. [L. *torosus*].
TOR-OUZEL, [tawr'-ōōz'-el], *n.* the ring-ouzel.
TORPEDO (1), (*pl.* **torpedoes**), [taw-pēd'-ō], *n.* a self-driven cigar-shaped submarine weapon charged

with an explosive, designed for blowing up shipping; **t. boat,** a small swift boat armed with torpedoes; **t. boat destroyer,** a small warship of high speed designed for catching torpedo boats, and other naval purposes; **t. net,** a net hung round a ship as a protection against torpedoes; **t. tube,** the steel tube through which torpedoes are fired; **t. fish,** the electric ray. [L. *torpedo* numbness].

TORPEDO (2), [taw-pēd'-ō], *v.t.* to hit with a torpedo, to destroy by a torpedo.

TORPEDOIST, [taw-pēd'-ō-ist], *n.* a man skilled in the science and management of torpedoes.

TORPENT, [tawp'-ent], *adj.* torpid; sluggish; (*med.*) reducing irritative action. [L. *torpens*].

TORPID (1), [tawp'-id], *n.* a clinker-built eight-oared boat used in the Lent term races at Oxford; (*pl.*) the Lent races at Oxford.

TORPID (2), [tawp'-id], *adj.* having lost the power of exertion; benumbed; destitute of sensibility; inactive; dull; sluggish. [L. *torpidus* benumbed].

TORPIDITY, [tawp-id'-it-i], *n.* the state of being torpid; torpidness; insensibility; inactivity or stupidity.

TORPIDLY, [tawp-id'-li], *adv.* in a torpid fashion.

TORPIDNESS, [tawp'-id-nes], *n.* torpidity.

TORPIFY, [tawp'-i-fī], *v.t.* to render torpid. [L. *torpefacere*].

TORPOR, [tawp'-or], *n.* numbness; inactivity; loss of motion; dulness; laziness; mental sluggishness. [L. *torpor*].

TORPORIFIC, [tawp'-or-if'-ik], *adj.* liable to produce torpor. [L. *torporificus*].

TORQUATED, [tawk-wāt'-ed], *adj.* having a collar or ring round the neck; formed as a torque. [L. *torquatus*].

TORQUE, [tawk], *n.* a collar of twisted wires or of chain worn by the Gauls and Ancient Britons; a collar; (*eng.*) the moment of a rotating or twisting force. [L. *torques*].

TORQUED, [tawkt], *adj.* (*her.*) wreathed.

TORREFACTION, [to'-ri-fak'-shun], *n.* (*met.*) the act, or operation of torrefying.

TORREFY, [to'-ri-fī], *v.t.* to dry by exposure to fire; to roast or scorch (metals); to dry or parch, as drugs. [L. *torrefacere*].

TORRENT, [to'-rent], *n.* a violent rushing stream; a stream suddenly rising and running rapidly downwards; a strong current; (*fig.*) a flow, a gush of words. [Fr. *torrent*].

TORRENTIAL, [to-rensh'-al], *adj.* in the manner of a torrent; caused by, causing a torrent.

TORRICELLIAN, [to'-ri-chel'-i-an], *adj.* of, pertaining to, Torricelli, who discovered the principle of the barometer; **t. vacuum,** the vacuum produced by filling a tube with mercury and allowing it to descend till it is counter-balanced by the atmosphere.

TORRID, [to'-rid], *adj.* parched; dried with the heat of the sun; violently hot; burning or parching; **t. zone,** the zone between the tropics, in which the heat is very great. [L. *torridus*].

TORRIDNESS, [to'-rid-nes], *n.* the condition of being torrid.

TORSE, [taws], *n.* (*her.*) a wreath. [Fr. *torse*].

TORSION, [taw'-shun], *n.* the action of twisting; (*mech.*) the force with which a wire or rod when twisted tends to return to its original state; (*surg.*) the stopping of a haemorrhage by twisting the ends of the blood-vessels; **t. balance,** an apparatus for estimating very minute forces by the action of a twisted thread or wire.

TORSIONAL, [tawsh'-on-al], *adj.* of, or pertaining to, torsion.

TORSIVE, [taws'-iv], *adj.* (*bot.*) spirally twisted. [L. *torsus*].

TORSK, [tawsk], *n.* the tusk, a fish of the cod family, *Brosmius brosme,* valuable for food. [Swed. *torsk*].

TORSO, [taw'-sō], *n.* the trunk of the body; the trunk of a statue deprived of head and limbs. [It. *torso*].

TORT, [tawt], *n.* (*leg.*) a wrong or injury to person or property remediable by a civil action for damages. [Fr. *tort* wrong].

TORTEAU, [tawt'-ō], *n.* (*her.*) a red roundel representing a cake of bread. [Fr. *tourteau*].

TORTFEASOR, [tawt'-fēz-or], *n.* (*leg.*) a person guilty of a tort. [OFr. *tort-fesor*].

TORTICOLLIS, [tawt'-i-kol'-is], *n.* (*med.*) wryneck. [L. *tortus* crooked and *collum* neck].

TORTILE, [tawt'-il], *adj.* twisted; wreathed; coiled; winding. [L. *tortilis*].

TORTILLA, [tawt-il'-a], *n.* a thin flat cake made of soaked maize, baked on an iron plate. [Span. *tortilla*].

TORTIOUS, [taw'-shus], *adj.* (*leg.*) of the nature of, pertaining to, a tort; wrongful. [AFr. *torcious*].

TORTIVE, [tawt'-iv], *adj.* twisted, wreathed. [L. *tortivus*].

TORTOISE, [tawt'-us], *n.* a land or freshwater chelonian reptile from the shell of which protrude the head and tail and the twisted legs (whence its name); †(*milit.*) a defence formed by bucklers held over the heads of soldiers. [~Fr. *tortue*].

TORTOISESHELL, [tawt'-us-shel], *n.* the shell or horny plates of the tortoise; a butterfly of the genus *Vanessa.*

TORTUOSITY, [tawt'-yōō-os'-it-i], *n.* the state of being tortuous.

TORTUOUS, [tawt'-yōō-us], *adj.* twisted, wreathed; winding; crooked; not straightforward; disingenuous. [AFr. *tortuous*].

TORTUOUSLY, [tawt'-yōō-us-li], *adv.* in a tortuous fashion.

TORTUOUSNESS, [tawt'-yōō-us-nes], *n.* the condition of being tortuous.

TORTURE (1), [taw'-cher], *n.* extreme pain; anguish of body or mind; torment; acute pain inflicted judicially, often for the sake of extorting confession. [Fr. *torture*].

TORTURE (2), [taw'-cher], *v.t.* to inflict mental or physical torture upon; to torment; to punish in a painful and cruel manner; to distort, drag out of natural shape. [*Prec.*].

TORTURER, [taw'-cher-er], *n.* a person who tortures.

TORTURINGLY, [taw'-cher-ing-li], *adv.* by, or with, torture.

TORTUROUS, [taw'-cher-us], *adj.* causing torture; of, pertaining to, torture.

TORULA, [to'-ryōō-la], *n.* a small torus; the so-called yeast plant; a chain of fungi. [L. *torulus* little mound].

TORULIFORM, [to'-ryōōl'-i-fawm], *adj.* like a torula in form.

TORULOID, [to'-ryōōl-oid], *adj.* like a torula. [TORULA and Gk. *oeides* like].

TORULOSE, TORULOUS, [to'-ryōōl-ōs], *adj.* (*bot.*) cylindrical, having slight contractions at intervals.

TORUS, [taw'-rus], *n.* (*arch.*) a large moulding employed in the bases of columns; (*bot.*) the floral receptacle, the thalamus, the growing point of the pistil. [L. *torus* swelling].

TORY, [taw'-ri], *n.* a right-wing Conservative in English politics; **the T. Party,** the Conservative Party. [Uncert.].

TORYISM, [taw'-ri-izm], *n.* the practice of the Tories; a policy which upholds established institutions.

TOSH, [tosh], *n.* (*slang*) nonsense; bosh; (*cricket*) feeble bowling. [Unkn.].

TOSS (1), [tos], *n.* a throwing upward or with a jerk; the act of tossing; a throwing up of the head; a particular manner of raising the head with a jerk; the act of spinning a coin; **to take a t.,** to fall, to have a disappointment. [Uncert.].

TOSS (2), [tos], *v.t.* to throw with the hand; to fling upwards; to throw up with a quick, sharp movement; to cause to rise up and down violently; to agitate; (*fig.*) to agitate violently, disturb the mind; *v.i.* to fling; to be in violent commotion; to be agitated; to be tossed about; to spin a coin to decide a course of action. [Uncert.].

TOSSER, [tos'-er], *n.* a person who tosses.

TOSSILY, [tos'-i-li], *adv.* pertly.

TOSSING, [tos'-ing], *n.* the action of throwing upward; a rolling and tumbling.

TOSS-POT, [tos'-pot'], *n.* (*slang*) a habitual drinker, a toper. [TOSS (1) and POT (1)].

TOSS-UP, [tos'-up], *n.* a resort to the spin of a coin; an uncertain issue.

TOSSY, [tos'-i], *adj.* pert.

TOST, [tost], *p.pt.* of TOSS.

TOT (1), [tot], *n.* a very little child; a small quantity of anything; a dram. [Uncert.].

TOT (2), [tot], *n.* the total in addition. [Abbreviated from TOTAL].

TOT (3), [tot], *v.t.* to add (up). [*Prec.*].

TOTAL (1), [tōt'-al], *n.* the whole; the full amount; the result of an addition.

TOTAL (2), [tōt'-al], *adj.* entire, whole, complete; **t. war,** war involving civilians equally with combatants. [L. *totalis*].

TOTAL (3), [tōt'-al], *v.t. and i.* to add up the whole; to arrive at the total; to add up to; to constitute, take together.

TOTALISATOR, [tōt'-al-īz-āt'-or], *n.* an automatic betting machine, where the winnings equal all the money staked less a percentage for expenses.

TOTALITARIAN, [tō-tal′-i-tāer′-i-an], *adj.* of a state or polity, having only one political party, and subject to the domination of a single individual who claims to represent the general will. [~TOTAL (2)].
TOTALITARIANISM, [tō-tal′-i-tāer′-i-an-izm], *n.* totalitarian ideology.
TOTALITY, [tō-tal′-i-ti], *n.* the whole sum or amount; everything; the whole; total eclipse.
TOTALLY, [tōt′-al-i], *adv.* wholly; completely.
TOTALNESS, [tōt′-al-nes], *n.* totality.
TOTE (1), [tōt], *n.* (*coll.*) a totalisator.
TOTE (2), [tōt], *v.t.* (*U.S.*) to carry, lift. [Uncert.].
TOTEM, [tōt′-em], *n.* an animal, plant, or other natural object between which and himself a member of an uncivilized race believes some occult relationship to exist so that he takes it as his hereditary emblem; the representation of this object as a badge, mark, or emblem; **t.-pole,** a column, usually of wood, bearing a representation of a totem. [Uncert.].

TOTEM-POLE

TOTEMIC, [tōt-em′-ik], *adj.* of, or pertaining to, totems.
TOTEMISM, [tōt′-em-izm], *n.* the beliefs and observances regarding totems.
TOTEMISTIC, [tōt′-em-ist′-ik], *adj.* like or pertaining to totemism.
TOTIPALMATE, [tōt′-i-pal′-māt], *adj.* with all four toes connected with webs. [L. *totus* whole and PALMATE].
TOTTER (1), [tot′-er], *n.* the action of tottering; an uncertain hesitating walk.
TOTTER (2), [tot′-er], *v.i.* to walk along with hesitating shaky steps; to shake so as to be in danger of falling; to stagger; (*fig.*) to be on the verge of ruin; to be in process of decay. [ME. *toteren*].
TOTTERINGLY, [tot′-er-ing-li], *adv.* in a tottering fashion.
TOTTERY, [tot′-er-i], *adj.* unsteady, shaky, unstable.
TOUCAN, [tōō-kahn′], *n.* one of a family of picarian birds of tropical America, remarkable for the size of their bright-coloured bills. [Portug. *toucana*].
TOUCH (1), [tuch], *n.* contact; the junction of two bodies at the surface so that there is no space between them; the sense of feeling; the act of touching; test; tried qualities; characteristic manner; the single act of a pencil or brush; feature; act of the hand on a musical instrument; an affection; a stroke; a slight amount; a mild attack; (*football, hockey*) the ground beyond the side lines lying between the extended goal lines; **t. typist,** a person who can type without seeing the keyboard of the typewriter.

TOUCAN

TOUCH (2), [tuch], *v.t.* to come in contact with; to perceive by the sense of feeling; to come to; to reach; to try; to concern; to handle slightly; to meddle with; to affect; to impress; to move; to soften; to delineate slightly; to strike; *v.i.* to be in contact; to be in a state of junction; **to t. at,** to call at (a port); **to t. down,** (in *rugby football*) to touch the ball on the ground within a specified area behind the goal-posts; **to t. on,** to treat of slightly in discourse; **to t. up,** to repair; to put finishing touches to, as a painting; to enhance the colour of (the complexion); to wound a person's feelings by sarcasm; **to t. for,** to (attempt to) borrow from. [OFr. *toucher*].
TOUCHABLE, [tuch′-abl], *adj.* able to be touched; tangible.
TOUCHABLENESS, [tuch′-abl-nes], *n.* the condition of being touchable.
TOUCH-AND-GO, [tuch′-and-gō′], *adj.* risky, capable of eventuating one way or the other.
TOUCHED, [tucht], *adj.* (*slang*) not quite sane; unbalanced.
TOUCHER, [tuch′-er], *n.* one who, or that which, touches.
TOUCH-HOLE†, [tuch′-hōl], *n.* the vent of a cannon, etc., through which the powder was ignited.
TOUCHILY, [tuch′-i-li], *adv.* in a touchy fashion.
TOUCHINESS, [tuch′-i-nes], *n.* the state of being touchy; irritability; extreme sensibility.
TOUCHING (1), [tuch′-ing], *adj.* affecting, pathetic.
TOUCHING (2), [tuch′-ing], *prep.* concerning, as regards.
TOUCHINGLY, [tuch′-ing-li], *adv.* in a touching, affecting manner.
TOUCH-ME-NOT, [tuch′-mē-not′], *n.* a plant of the genus *Impatiens*, the pods of which explode when touched.
TOUCH-NEEDLES, [tuch′-nēdlz], *n.(pl.)* small bars of gold and silver, prepared for trying gold and silver by the touchstone, by comparing the mark which they leave upon it.
TOUCH-PAN†, [tuch′-pan′], *n.* the pan of a gun that holds the priming.
TOUCH-PAPER, [tuch′-pāp′-er], *n.* paper impregnated with saltpetre which causes it to burn slowly.
TOUCHSTONE, [tuch′-stōn], *n.* Lydian stone, a black variety of flinty slate used for ascertaining the purity of gold and silver by the streak traced on it; (*fig.*) something taken as a test or criterion.
TOUCHWOOD, [tuch′-wōōd], *n.* wood tinder; decayed wood used as a match for catching up fire from a spark.
TOUCHY, [tuch′-i], *adj.* peevish, irritable; over-sensitive; apt to fire up.
TOUGH (1), [tuf], *n.* (*slang*) a tough person, a reprobate, criminal.
TOUGH (2), [tuf], *adj.* flexible without being brittle; strong and flexible; firm; not easily broken; able to endure hardship; vigorous; powerful and hardy; difficult, involving much labour; sinewy and hard to clean; (*slang*) difficult to manage, violent. [OE. *toh*].
TOUGHEN, [tuf′-en], *v.t.* to render tough; *v.i.* to grow tough.
TOUGHISH, [tuf′-ish], *adj.* rather tough.
TOUGHLY, [tuf′-li], *adv.* in a tough fashion.
TOUGHNESS, [tuf′-nes], *n.* the state of being tough.
TOUPET, [tōō′-pā], *n.* a little tuft; a front of false hair; a false curl. [Fr. *toupet*].
TOUR (1), [tōōer], *n.* a journey in a circuit; a spell of duty; a journey from place to place for pleasure or business; a ramble; **the grand t.,** an educational tour of France, Italy, Germany, and other European countries. [Fr. *tour*].
TOUR (2), [tōōer], *v.t.* to visit while touring; *v.i.* to make a tour; to travel.
TOURACO, see TURACO.
TOURBILLON, [tōōer-bē′-yaw(ng)], *n.* a firework which rises in a spiral column of fire. [Fr. *tourbillon* whirlwind].
TOURELLE, [tōō-rel′], *n.* a little tower, a turret. [Fr. *tourelle*].
TOURER, [tōōer′-er], *n.* an open car for touring.
TOURIST, [tōōer′-ist], *n.* one who goes on a tour, travelling from place to place for pleasure.
TOURMALINE, [tōōer′-mal-ēn], *n.* a mineral occurring in prisms, varying in chemical composition, used in polarizing light, the finer kinds being much valued by jewellers. [Fr. *tourmaline*].
TOURNAMENT, [tōōer′-na-ment], *n.* in medieval times, a contest between mounted knights armed with lances; a joust; a competition for a sports championship, *esp.* in tennis and croquet; a competitive series of games of chess, etc. [OFr. *tornoiement*].
TOURNEY, [tōōer′-ni], *n.* a medieval tournament; a joust. [OFr. *tornoi*].
TOURNIQUET, [tōōer′-ni-kā′], *n.* a surgical apparatus or bandage, which is straitened or relaxed by twisting, used to check hemorrhages. [Fr. *tourniquet*].
TOURNURE, [tōōr-new(r)′], *n.* apt address; graceful language; a shape; a bustle on a lady's dress. [Fr. *tournure*].
TOUSE, [towz], *v.t.* to tear; worry, tousle. [ME. *tusen*].
TOUSLE, [towzl], *v.t.* to put into disorder, make untidy; to rumple, make dishevelled. [~TUSSLE (2)].
TOUS-LES-MOIS, [tōō′-lā-mwah′], *n.* a starch made of the root of a species of *Canna*, used as a substitute for arrowroot. [Fr. *tous les mois* every month].
TOUSY, [towz′-i], *adj.* tousled, shaggy. [~TOUSE].
TOUT (1), [towt], *n.* one who endeavours by canvassing to obtain custom; a racing tipster. [~TOOT (2)].
TOUT (2), [towt], *v.i.* to try to get custom by canvassing, usually in an importunate manner; to go canvassing for custom; to go about trying to pick up and sell rumours and bits of information about the chances of horses in races.
TOUTER, [towt′-er], *n.* a tout.
TOW (1), [tō], *n.* the coarser fibres of flax and hemp used for ropemaking. [OE. *tow*].
TOW (2), [tō], *n.* the action of towing; **in t.,** being towed; (*coll.*) hanging on; following in attendance.
TOW (3), [tō], *v.t.* to pull along by means of a rope (*esp.* of a boat or broken-down vehicle). [OE. *togian* pull].

TOWAGE, [tō'-ij], *n.* the act of towing, the price paid for this.
TOWARD (1), [tawd], *adj.* ready to do or learn, apt; about to happen, impending. [OE. *toweard*].
TOWARD (2), TOWARDS, [tawd, tawdz], *prep.* in the direction of; in relation to; with respect to; round about; near. [OE. *toweard*].
TOWARDLINESS, [tawd'-li-nes], *n.* towardness.
TOWARDNESS, [tawd'-nes], *n.* the state of being toward.
TOWARDS, see TOWARD (2).
TOW-BOAT, [tō'-bōt], *n.* a boat that tows or is towed.
TOWEL (1), [tow'-el], *n.* a cloth of absorbent material for wiping the person after washing. [OFr. *touaille*].
TOWEL (2), [tow'-el], *v.t.* to dry or rub down with a towel.
TOWEL-HORSE, [tow'-el-haws], *n.* a stand with bars for hanging towels on.
TOWELLING, [tow'-el-ing], *n.* an absorbent cotton or linen material from which towels are made.
TOWER (1), [tow'-er], *n.* a building, either square or circular, of considerable elevation, and generally flat on the top; a citadel; a fortress; a high head-dress; high flight; elevation; (*fig.*) **t. of strength,** someone to be relied on absolutely. [OFr. *tur*].
TOWER (2), [tow'-er], *v.i.* to rise up like a tower; to rear itself; **to t. over,** to exceed in stature or mental power.
TOWERED, [tow'-erd], *adj.* having towers.
TOWERING, [tow'-er-ing], *adj.* very high; lofty; (*fig.*) violent.
TOWER-MUSTARD, [tow'-er-must'-erd], *n.* the plant, *Arabis perfoliata,* which grows on high banks and cliffs.
TOWERY, [tow'-er-i], *adj.* built with towers; defended by towers.
TOWHEE, [tō-hē'], *n.* the American ground robin, a bunting of the genus *Pipilo.* [Echoic].
TOWING-PATH, [tō'-ing-pahth], *n.* a path used by men or horses when towing boats.
TOW-LINE, [tō'-līn], *n.* a tow-rope.
TOWN, [town], *n.* a collection, of indefinite extent, of houses, larger than a village, *esp.* one with a regular market and inferior to a city; a city; the inhabitants collectively of a town or city; the metropolis or its inhabitants; the West End of London. [OE. *tun*].
TOWN CLERK, [town'-klahk'], *n.* an official who keeps the records of, and helps in the administration of, a municipal borough.
TOWN COUNCIL, [town'-kown'-sil], *n.* the elected governing body of a town.
TOWN COUNCILLOR, [town'-kown'-sil-er], *n.* one who is an elected member of the town council.
TOWN CRIER, [town'-krī'-er], *n.* a town functionary whose duty it is to proclaim official and other notices by shouting them in the streets.
TOWNEE, [town'-ē], *n.* an inhabitant of a university town (as distinct from the undergraduates). [TOWN].
TOWN HALL, [town'-hawl'], *n.* a public building used for council meetings and other business of a town.
TOWN HOUSE, [town'-hows'], *n.* a house in town, as distinct from a country house; municipal headquarters.
TOWNISH, [town'-ish], *adj.* pertaining to townsfolk; characteristic of towns.
TOWNLAND, [town'-land'], *n.* a township; the land enclosed within a town.
TOWNLESS, [town'-les], *adj.* devoid of a town.
TOWNSFOLK, [townz'-fōk], *n.(pl.)* the folk of a town.
TOWNSHIP, [town'-ship], *n.* a district having municipal privileges.
TOWNSMAN, [townz'-man], *n.* an inhabitant of a town; an inhabitant of the same town with another.
TOWNSPEOPLE, [townz'-pēpl], *n.* the inhabitants of a town.
TOWNSWOMAN, [townz'-wŏŏm'-an], *n.* a woman who lives in a town.
TOWN-TALK, [town'-tawk], *n.* the subject of common talk.
TOWPATH, [tō'-pahth], *n.* the path along the canal or riverside along which the barge horses walk.
TOW-ROPE, [tō'-rōp], *n.* a rope used during towing operations.
TOWSER, [towz'-er], *n.* a familiar name for a dog. [ME. *tousen* to pull to pieces].
TOWY, [tō'-i], *adj.* resembling tow.
TOXAEMIA, [toks-ēm'-i-a], *n.* blood-poisoning. [TOXIC and Gk. *haima* blood].
TOXIC, [toks'-ik], *adj.* poisonous; caused by poison.
TOXICAL, [toks'-ik-al], *adj.* of a toxic condition.
TOXICO-, TOXIC-, *pref.* pertaining to poison. [Gk. *toxicon* poison in which arrows were dipped].
TOXICOLOGICAL, [toks'-ik-ō-loj'-ik-al], *adj.* pertaining to toxicology.
TOXICOLOGICALLY, [toks'-ik-ō-loj'-ik-al-i], *adv.* in a toxicological fashion.
TOXICOLOGIST, [toks'-ik-ol'-o-jist], *n.* a person versed in toxicology.
TOXICOLOGY, [toks'-i-kol'-o-ji], *n.* the study of poisons, their nature, action, and antidotes. [TOXICO- and Gk. *logos* speech].
TOXIN, [toks'-in], *n.* an organic poisonous substance. [~TOXIC].
TOXODON, [toks'-ō-don], *n.* an extinct ungulate about the size of a large rhinoceros which had long curved crowns to its molar teeth. [Gk. *toxon* a bow and *odous odontos* tooth].
TOXOPHILITE, [toks-of'-il-īt], *n.* an expert in archery. [Gk. *toxon* bow and *philos* loving].
TOY (1), [toi], *n.* a child's plaything; an amusing trifle; anything used as or considered suitable for a plaything. [~Du. *tuig* tool, stuff].
TOY (2), [toi], *v.i.* to trifle; to play; to dally amorously.
TOY-DOG, [toi'-dog'], *n.* a lapdog.
TOYER, [toi'-er], *n.* a person who toys; one who is full of trifling tricks.
TOYFUL, [toi'-fŏŏl], *adj.* full of trifling; playful.
TOYISH, [toi'-ish], *adj.* trifling; wanton.
TOYISHLY, [toi'-ish-li], *adv.* in a toyish fashion.
TOYISHNESS, [toi'-ish-nes], *n.* tendency to dalliance; playfulness.
TOYMAN, [toi'-man], *n.* a man who sells toys.
TOYSHOP, [toi'-shop'], *n.* a shop where toys are sold.
TOYSOME, [toi'-sum], *adj.* inclined to be playful.
TRABEA, [trā'-bi-a], *n.* a toga striped with purple, worn on state occasions. [L. *trabea*].
TRABEATED, [trā'-bi-āt-ed], *adj.* (*arch.*) constructed with horizontal beams, having an entablature. [~L. *trabs* beam].
TRABEATION, [trā'-bi-ā'-shun], *n.* (*arch.*) an entablature.
TRABECULA, [tra-bek'-yŏŏl-a], *n.* a small beam; a strand of tissue; the name of certain different processes of a small size in certain plants and animals, such as one of the fleshy columns in the ventricle of the heart. [L. *trabecula*].
TRABECULAR, [tra-bek'-yŏŏl-er], *adj.* pertaining to a trabecula.
TRABECULATE, [tra-bek'-yŏŏl-āt], *adj.* trabecular.
TRACE (1), [trās], *n.* a strap or chain fastened at one end to the collar of a horse's harness and at the other to the vehicle to be drawn. [OFr. *traits*].
TRACE (2), [trās], *n.* a mark left by anything passing; a footprint; a track; a vestige; remains; a small quantity. [Fr. *trace*].
TRACE (3), [trās], *v.t.* to draw or delineate with marks; to copy through transparent paper or film; to follow by footsteps or tracks; to follow with exactness; to walk over; to traverse; to find; to discover as a result of a process of thought. [OFr. *tracier*].
TRACEABLE, [trās'-abl], *adj.* capable of being traced.
TRACEABLENESS, [trās'-abl-nes], *n.* the condition of being traceable.
TRACEABLY, [trās'-ab-li], *adv.* in a traceable fashion.
TRACE-HORSE, [trās'-haws], *n.* a draught-horse pulling in front of another between the shafts.
TRACER, [trās'-er], *n.* a person who traces; a tracer-bullet.
TRACER-BULLET, [trās'-er-bŏŏl'-it], *n.* a flaming bullet that leaves a trail of smoke behind it.
TRACERY, [trās'-er-i], *n.* a delicate pattern of lines; (*arch.*) the ornamental stonework in the upper part of a Gothic window.
TRACHEA, (*pl.* **tracheae**), [trā'-ki-a', tra-kē'-a], *n.* (*anat.*) the windpipe; (*bot.*) one of the spiral vessels in leaves; (*zool.*) the breathing tube of an insect. [Gk. *trakheid* (*arteria*) rough (*artery*)].
TRACHEAL, [trāk'-i-al], *adj.* pertaining to the trachea or windpipe.
TRACHEAN, [trāk'-i-an], *adj.* furnished with tracheae.
TRACHEARY, [trāk'-i-er-i], *adj.* breathing by tracheae; pertaining to the trachea.
TRACHELIPOD, [trak-el'-i-pod], *n.* a univalve mollusc having a spiral shell. [Gk. *trakhelos* neck and *pous podos* foot].
TRACHEO-, *pref.* neck, throat. [TRACHEA].
TRACHEOBRONCHIAL, [trak'-i-ō-brong'-ki-al], *adj.* pertaining to the trachea and the bronchia.
TRACHEOCELE, [trak'-i-ō-sēl], *n.* a swelling of the thyroid gland. [TRACHEO- and Gk. *kele* tumour].

TRACHEOSCOPY, [trak'-i-os'-ko-pi], *n.* visual inspection of the trachea. [TRACHEO- and Gk. *skopeo* I view].
TRACHEOTOMIST, [trak'-i-ot'-ō-mist], *n.* a specialist in tracheotomy.
TRACHEOTOMY, [trak'-i-ot'-om-i], *n.* the operation of making an incision in the windpipe. [TRACHEO- and Gk. *tome* cutting].
TRACHITIS, [trak-īt'-is], *n.* inflammation of the windpipe. [TRACHEA and Gk. *itis* denoting inflammation].
TRACHOMA, [trak-ō'-ma], *n.* a disease manifested by a granular condition of the mucous lining of the eyelids. [Gk. *trakhoma* roughness].
TRACHYTE, [trak'-īt], *n.* a light-coloured, rough, nearly compact volcanic rock. [Gk. *trakhus* rough].
TRACHYTIC, [trak-it'-ik], *adj.* resembling or pertaining to trachyte.
TRACING, [trās'-ing], *n.* a course; regular track or path; the process of tracing a copy of some drawing through a transparency; the copy thus made.
TRACING-PAPER, [trās'-ing-pāp'-er], *n.* a thin transparent paper used for tracing drawings and engravings.
TRACK (1), [trak], *n.* a mark left by something that has passed along; a mark or impression left by the foot; a road; a beaten path; a running course; (*mech.*) the distance that separates the wheels of a vehicle transversely; a treaded metal belt enclosing the wheels (of a tank, etc.) instead of tyres; **on the t. of,** following, in hot pursuit of; **off the t.,** off the scent, following the wrong course of action; **the beaten t.,** the conventional way; **to conceal one's tracks,** to hide one's projects or affairs; **to make tracks for,** (*coll.*) to make towards. [OFr. *trac*].
TRACK (2), [trak], *v.t.* to follow when guided by a trace or footsteps; to trail; (*mech.*) **to t. up,** to measure and adjust to the right width the transverse distance between a vehicle's wheels; *v.i.* to move in a track.
TRACKAGE, [trak'-ij], *n.* the towing of a boat by a rope operating from the bank.
TRACKBOAT, [trak'-bōt], *n.* a boat towed by a line from the bank.
TRACKER, [trak'-er], *n.* a person or thing that tracks.
TRACKLESS, [trak'-les], *adj.* without a track; marked by no footstep; untrodden.
TRACKLESSLY, [trak'-les-li], *adv.* in a trackless fashion.
TRACKLESSNESS, [trak'-les-nes], *n.* the condition of being trackless.
TRACKMAN, [trak'-man], *n.* (*U.S.*) a man having charge of a section of railroad.
TRACKRAIL, [trak'-rāl], *n.* a flangeless rail laid to take the tread of a flanged wheel.
TRACKROAD, [trak'-rōd], *n.* a towing-path by the river.
TRACKWAY, [trak'-wā], *n.* an open road across a down or common.
TRACT (1), [trakt], *n.* a wide expanse of land, water, or sky; a wide area; an extent; (*anat.*) a system in the body (as all the digestive organs). [L. *tractus*].
TRACT (2), [trakt], *n.* a tractate; a short treatise usually of a political or religious character. [~TRACTATE].
TRACTABILITY, [trakt'-ab-il'-i-ti], *n.* tractableness.
TRACTABLE, [trakt'-abl], *adj.* able to be led, taught, or managed without difficulty; docile; manageable. [L. *tractabilis*].
TRACTABLENESS, [trakt'-abl-nes], *n.* the state of being tractable.
TRACTABLY, [trakt'-ab-li], *adv.* in a tractable fashion.
TRACTARIAN, [trakt-āer'-i-an], *n.* a founder of, or believer in, Tractarianism.
TRACTARIANISM, [trakt-āer'-i-an-izm], *n.* the system of principles advocated in *Tracts for the Times*, published at Oxford between 1833 and 1841, the chief doctrine of which was that the Church, through its sacraments in the hands of a regularly ordained clergy, is the sole divinely appointed channel of the grace of Christ; the Oxford Movement; ritualism.
TRACTATE, [trakt'-āt], *n.* a treatise; a tract. [L. *tractatus*].
TRACTATRIX, [trak-tā'-triks], *n.* (*geom.*) a tractrix.
TRACTILE, [trakt'-il], *adj.* that may be drawn out in length; ductile; that may be withdrawn. [L. *tractilis*].
TRACTILITY, [trakt-il'-i-ti], *n.* the state of being tractile; ductility.
TRACTION, [trak'-shun], *n.* the action of drawing or state of being drawn, *esp.* along a plane against friction; attraction; **t. engine,** a locomotive for drawing anything heavy along the highway.
TRACTIVE, [trakt'-iv], *adj.* having the power necessary to drag anything along a surface; pulling; tending to drag.
TRACTOR, [trakt'-or], *n.* that which draws, or is employed for traction; a vehicle with an internal combustion engine for drawing ploughs, etc.
TRACTORY, [trakt'-er-i], *n.* (*geom.*) a tractrix.
TRACTRIX, [trakt'-riks], *n.* (*geom.*) a curve in which the intercept on its tangent between the point of contact and a fixed straight line is a constant; a parallel curve or line. [MdL. *tractrix* fem. of *tractor*].
TRADE (1), [trād], *n.* the act or business of exchanging commodities; buying and selling; commerce; traffic; the business which a person has learned; occupation, particularly manual or mercantile employment; men engaged in the same occupation; custom; standing practice; **the trades,** the trade-winds. [OFr. *trade*].
TRADE (2), [trād], *adj.* connected with trade or a trade.
TRADE (3), [trād], *adv.* at trade prices.
TRADE (4), [trād], *v.t.* to sell or exchange in commerce; *v.i.* to buy and sell; to traffic; to carry on commerce as a business; **to t. upon,** to take advantage of.
TRADE-BOARD, [trād'-bawd'], *n.* a committee of employers, employees, and experts appointed by the Board of Trade to fix wages and conditions of work in specific industries.
TRADE-MARK, [trād'-mahk], *n.* an exclusive device adopted by a manufacturer, and affixed to his goods as a sign that they are made by him.
TRADE-NAME, [trād'-nām], *n.* a name used in trading.
TRADE-PRICE, [trād'-prīs], *n.* the wholesale price.
TRADER, [trād'-er], *n.* one engaged in trade or commerce; a vessel employed in trading; a merchant vessel.
TRADE-SALE, [trād'-sāl], *n.* an auction of goods by and for a special trade.
TRADESFOLK, [trādz'-fōk], *n.*(*pl.*) tradespeople.
TRADESMAN, [trādz'-man], *n.* a man engaged in trade; a shopkeeper.
TRADESWOMAN, [trādz'-wŏom'-an], *n.* a woman engaged in trade; a woman shopkeeper.
TRADE UNION, [trād'-yōōn'-i-un], *n.* a combination of the workmen in a particular trade or group of trades for mutual support and the defence of their interests as workmen.
TRADE-UNIONISM, [trād'-yōōn'-i-un-izm], *n.* the system employed by the trade unions; the principle of organized association for obtaining and safeguarding equitable working conditions.
TRADE-UNIONIST, [trād'-yōōn'-i-un-ist], *n.* a member of a trade union; an advocate of the principles of trade-unionism.
TRADE-WIND, [trād'-wind], *n.* a wind blowing continuously from the N.E. between 7° and 29° north of the equator, or from the S.E. between 3° and 20° south of the equator.
TRADING, [trād'-ing], *adj.* concerned with carrying on commerce.
TRADITION, [trad-ish'-on], *n.* the handing down of opinions, doctrines or customs from ancestors to posterity, from the past to the present, by oral communication; an opinion, doctrine or custom thus handed down; principles or accumulated experiences of earlier generations handed on to others. [L. *traditio*].
TRADITIONAL, [trad-ish'-on-al], *adj.* according to tradition.
TRADITIONALISM, [trad'-ish'-on-al-izm], *n.* excessive deference to the authority of tradition.
TRADITIONALLY, [trad-ish'-on-al-i], *adv.* according to tradition.
TRADITIONARILY, [trad-ish'-on-er-i-li], *adv.* traditionally.
TRADITIONARY, [trad-ish'-on-er-i], *adj.* delivered orally from father to son; transmitted from age to age; customary.
TRADITIONIST, [trad-ish'-on-ist], *n.* a person who adheres to tradition.
TRADITIVE, [trad'-it-iv], *adj.* transmitted by tradition; traditional. [Fr. *traditif*].
TRADITOR, [trad'-it-or], *n.* a deliverer; a traitor; (*pl.*) a name of infamy given to Christians who, to save their lives, gave up the Scriptures or the goods of their Church to their persecutors. [L. *traditor*].
TRADUCE, [trad-ews'], *v.t.* to misrepresent wilfully and abuse; to calumniate; to defame; to vilify. [L. *traducere* to lead across].
TRADUCER, [trad-ews'-er], *n.* a person who traduces.

TRADUCIANISM, [trad-ews′-i-an-izm], *n.* the belief that soul and body alike are transmitted from posterity and with them sin.
TRADUCIBLE, [trad-ews′-ibl], *adj.* capable of being traduced.
TRADUCINGLY, [trad-ews′-ing-li], *adv.* calumniously.
TRADUCTION, [trad-uk′-shun], *n.* the act of transferring; (*log.*) the art of transferring; the legitimate transference to the same object of a conclusion derived from the premises respecting such object. [Fr. *traduction*].
TRADUCTIVE, [tra-dukt′-iv], *adj.* derivable.
TRAFFIC (1), [traf′-ik], *n.* a moving, transferring to and fro; commerce; trade; amount of traffic; intercourse; vehicles in motion. [Fr. *trafic*].
TRAFFIC (2), [traf′-ik], *v.t.* to exchange in traffic; *v.i.* to trade; to buy and sell wares; to have dealings *esp.* of an illicit nature. [Fr. *trafiquer*].
TRAFFICATOR, [traf′-ik-āt-or], *n.* a direction indicator affixed to motor-vehicles. [TRAFFIC and (INDIC)ATOR].
TRAFFICKER, [traf′-ik-er], *n.* one who carries on traffic; a trader; an illegal dealer.
TRAFFICLESS, [traf′-ik-les], *adj.* devoid of traffic.
TRAFFIC-LIGHTS, [traf′-ik-līts], *n.* (*pl.*) the automatic electric lights serving as traffic signals at crossroads.
TRAGACANTH, DRACANTH, [trag′-a-kanth], *n.* a kind of adhesive gum, obtained from various species of *Astragalus*; gum tragacanth. [Gk. *tragos* goat and *akantha* thorn].
TRAGACANTHIN, [trag′-a-kanth′-in], *n.* the essential element of tragacanth and similar gums.
TRAGEDIAN, [traj-ēd′-i-an], *n.* a dramatist who writes tragedy; a tragic actor.
TRAGEDIENNE, [traj-ēd′-i-en′], *n.* an actress who plays tragic rôles. [Fr. *tragédienne*].
TRAGEDY, [traj′-ed-i], *n.* a play or story dealing with the sufferings of human beings, and ending in disaster; a calamity in real life, a sorrowful and disastrous event or series of events. [OFr. *tragedie* from Gk. *tragoidia*].
TRAGIC, TRAGICAL, [traj′-ik, traj′-ik-al], *adj.* of the nature or character of tragedy; calamitous; expressive of tragedy or sorrow; disastrous.
TRAGICALLY, [traj′-ik-al-i], *adv.* in a tragic fashion.
TRAGICALNESS, [traj′-ik-al-nes], *n.* the state of being tragic.
TRAGICOMEDY, [traj′-i-kom′-ed-i], *n.* a drama in which both tragic and comic scenes occur.
TRAGICOMIC, [traj′-i-kom′-ik], *adj.* having both tragic and comic scenes or aspects.
TRAGICOMICALLY, [traj′-i-kom′-ik-al-i], *adv.* in a tragicomic fashion.
TRAGOPAN, [trag′-ō-pan′], *n.* the horned pheasant, a beautiful Asiatic game-bird of the genus *Ceriornis*. [Gk. *tragopan* a fabulous bird of Ethiopia].
TRAGULINE, [trag′-yōōl-in], *adj.* goat-like.
TRAGUS, [trā′-gus], *n.* (*anat.*) the prominence at the entrance of the external ear, in men and some animals often bearing a tuft of hairs. [Gk. *tragos* he-goat].
TRAIL (1), [trāl], *n.* a mark or track left by anything that has passed; the track followed by a hunter; the scent or spoor left by the animal pursued; anything drawn to length; a trawl; the entrails of a bird; (*milit.*) the end of an artillery carriage, upon which the carriage slides when unlimbered.
TRAIL (2), [trāl], *v.t.* to hunt by the track; to draw along the ground; to carry, as arms, in a horizontal position, muzzles foremost; to tread down grass by walking through it; to lay flat; *v.i.* to be drawn out in length; to run along or climb; to straggle, to be extended along; (*coll.*) to walk slowly and wearily along. [OFr. *traillier* to tow].
TRAILER, [trāl′-er], *n.* a person or thing that trails; a vehicle towed behind another; an advance selection from a film.
TRAIL-NET, [trāl′-net′], *n.* a drag-net; a trawl.
TRAIN (1), [trān], *n.* artifice; stratagem or enticement; something drawn along behind; a trailing extension of a dress; the tail of a bird; a retinue; a series of actions or objects; a procession; a line of gunpowder to lead fire to a charge; a line of vehicles on a railroad; all the apparatus and implements of war; **t. of artillery,** any number of guns accompanying an army; **in t.,** in order, ready.
TRAIN (2), [trān], *v.t.* to educate; to rear and instruct; to teach and form by practice; to drill, exercise; to discipline; to break, reduce to docility; to teach to perform certain tricks; to subject to proper diet and exercise for the performance of some act of physical skill or endurance; (*hort.*) to form to a desired shape by twisting or pruning; *v.i.* to practise; to subject oneself to rigorous diet and exercise so as to arrive at fine physical condition for some athletic contest or other feat. [OFr. *trahiner*].
TRAIN (3), [trān], *v.i.* to travel by railway.
TRAINABLE, [trān′-abl], *adj.* capable of being trained.
TRAINBAND, [trān′-band′], *n.* a band or company of the nature of a militia, instituted in the fourteenth century, and developing later into the militia.
TRAIN-BEARER, [trān′-bāer-er], *n.* an attendant who holds up the train of the gown or robe of a lady or high official personage on occasions of ceremony.
TRAINED, [trānd], *adj.* having a training.
TRAINEE, [trān-ē′], *n.* one who is being trained; one qualified to a limited degree by special short training instead of apprenticeship. [TRAIN (2)].
TRAINER, [trān′-er], *n.* a professional who trains men and women for athletics or horses for racing.
TRAIN-FERRY, [trān′-fe′-ri], *n.* a ferry steamer that carries a whole railway train from shore to shore.
TRAINING, [trān′-ing], *n.* the act of acquiring the necessary qualifications for the performance of some career, occupation, or feat of physical skill or endurance; the condition of being so trained.
TRAINING-COLLEGE, [trān′-ing-kol′-ij], *n.* an educational institution where people are trained in the art of pedagogy.
TRAINING-SHIP, [trān′-ing-ship′], *n.* a ship in which boys are trained to be sailors.
TRAIN-MILE, [trān′-mīl], *n.* a mile run by a train, the basic unit of railway calculations.
TRAIN-OIL, [trān′-oil], *n.* the oil obtained from the blubber or fat of whales by boiling. [MDu. *traen* tear and OIL].
TRAIN-ROAD, [trān-′rōd], *n.* in mines, a light railway for small wagons.
TRAIN-TACKLE, [trān′-takl′], *n.* tackle hooked to the train of a gun to hold it to its place.
TRAIPSE, TRAPES, [trāps], *v.i.* to gad about. [~OFr. *trapesser*].
TRAIT, [trā], *n.* a touch; a distinguishing feature, characteristic.
TRAITOR, [trāt′-or], *n.* one guilty of treason; one who, in breach of trust, delivers his country to its enemy; one who betrays his trust. [OFr. *traiteur*].
TRAITORISM, [trāt′-or-izm], *n.* the practice of a traitor.
TRAITOROUS, [trāt′-er-us], *adj.* like a traitor, guilty of treason; treacherous; perfidious; partaking of treason.
TRAITOROUSLY, [trāt′-er-us-li], *adv.* in a traitorous fashion.
TRAITOROUSNESS, [trāt′-er-us-nes], *n.* the state of being traitorous.
TRAITRESS, [trāt′-res], *n.* a woman who is a traitor.
TRAJECT (1), [tra′-jekt], *n.* a place where boats cross a river; a ferry. [L. *trajectus*].
TRAJECT (2), [tra-jekt′], *v.t.* to carry across; to transmit. [~L. *trajicere*].
TRAJECTION, [tra-jek′-shun], *n.* a crossing; a throwing or darting through; transposition.
TRAJECTORY, [tra′-jekt-er-i], *n.* the curve of a projectile fired through the air.
TRAM (1), [tram], *n.* a large public vehicle propelled by electricity, steam, or horse-power, along lines laid in the streets; a truck used underground for conveyance of coal; a mineral railway. [Uncert.].
TRAM (2), [tram], *v.i.* to travel by tram.
TRAMBLING, [tramb′-ling], *n.* the process of washing tin ore clean with a shovel by moving it about in water.
TRAMCAR, [tram′-kah(r)], *n.* a tram.
TRAMMEL (1), [tram′-el], *n.* a long net for catching birds or fishes; shackles for a horse; that which trammels; a hindrance, impediment; an iron hook to hang vessels over a fire; a carpenter's instrument for drawing ellipses; a beam-compass. [Fr. *tramail* net].
TRAMMEL (2), [tram′-el], *v.t.* to catch; to encumber with trammels; to restrict, shackle.
TRAMMEL-NET, [tram′-el-net′], *n.* a net, supported by corks, and anchored close to the ground by weights.
TRAMONTANA, [tra′-mon-tahn′-a], *n.* a cold, dry, northerly wind from the Adriatic that blows in the Mediterranean.
TRAMONTANE (1), [tra-mon′-tān], *n.* one dwelling beyond the mountains; a stranger.
TRAMONTANE (2), [tra-mon′-tān], *adj.* lying beyond the mountains; transalpine; foreign; barbarous. [It. *tramontano* across the mountains].
TRAMP (1), [tramp], *n.* a vagabond who tramps the roads; a long walk; the sound of heavy feet walking or marching; a cargo boat; the shoulder of a spade.

TRAMP (2), [tramp], *v.t. and i.* to walk heavily along; to plod; to go for a long walk. [ME. *trampen*].
TRAMPER, [tramp'-er], *n.* one who tramps; a vagabond; a hiker.
TRAMPLE (1), [trampl], *n.* the action of trampling; treading under foot.
TRAMPLE (2), [trampl], *v.t.* to tread under foot; to crush; to knock down and crush by treading on; (*fig.*) to bully, oppress; *v.i.* to commit the action of trampling. [ME. *trampelen*].
TRAMPLER, [tramp'-ler], *n.* a person who tramples or treads down.
TRAMPOT, [tram'-pot'], *n.* a socket to hold an upright spindle.
TRAM-ROAD, [tram'-rōd], *n.* a tramway.
TRAMWAY, [tram'-wā], *n.* a system of rails for trams; the whole system of trams and rails.
TRANCE, [trahnts], *n.* (*med.*) a morbid bodily condition resembling sleep wherein all conscious functions are suspended; catalepsy; a mystic rapture during which the soul is felt to be in direct communion with the divine; ecstasy. [OFr. *transe* swoon].
TRANCED, [trahnst], *adj.* in a state of trance.
TRANCEDLY, [trahns'-ed-li], *adv.* as though in a trance.
TRANK, [trangk], *n.* a piece of skin from which a glove is made; the cut-out glove before sewing up. [~Fr. *tranche* a cutting].
TRANQUIL, [trang'-kwil], *adj.* quiet; reposeful; restful; calm, peaceful. [L. *tranquillus*].
TRANQUILLITY, [trang-kwil'-it-i], *n.* the condition of being tranquil.
TRANQUILLIZATION, [trang'-kwil-īz-ā'-shun], *n.* the action of tranquillizing; state of being tranquillized.
TRANQUILLIZE, [trang'-kwil-īz], *v.t.* to calm; to quieten; *v.i.* to become tranquil; to sink into quietness.
TRANQUILLIZER, [trang'-kwil-īz-er], *n.* a person or thing that tranquillizes.
TRANQUILLIZINGLY, [trang'-kwil-īz-ing-li], *adv.* in a manner that tranquillizes.
TRANQUILLY, [trang'-kwil-i], *adv.* in a tranquil way; quietly, calmly.
TRANQUILNESS, [trang'-kwil-nes], *n.* the condition of being tranquil.
TRANS-, *pref.* over, across, beyond; through. [L. *trans*].
TRANSACT, [tran-sakt'], *v.t.* to do; to perform; to manage; *v.i.* to arrange matters; to negotiate. [L. *transactus, p.pt.* of *transigere*].
TRANSACTION, [tran-sak'-shun], *n.* the doing or performing of any business; management of an affair; that which is performed; an affair; (*leg.*) an adjustment of a dispute; (*pl.*) reports of the proceedings of a learned society.
TRANSACTOR, [tran-sakt'-or], *n.* a person who transacts any business.
TRANSALPINE, [tran-zalp'-īn], *adj.* living beyond the Alps from Rome.
TRANSANDINE, [tran-zand'-īn], *adj.* beyond the Andes mountains.
TRANSATLANTIC, [tranz'-at-lant'-ik], *adj.* living, existing, beyond the Atlantic; crossing the Atlantic.
TRANSCALENT, [tranz-kāl'-ent], *adj.* allowing heat to pass. [TRANS- and L. *calens* hot].
TRANSCEND, [tran-send'], *v.t.* to rise higher; to be greater; to exceed; to surpass. [L. *transcendere* step over].
TRANSCENDENCE, [tran-send'-ents], *n.* the condition of being transcendent.
TRANSCENDENCY, [tran-send'-en-si], *n.* transcendence.
TRANSCENDENT, [tran-send'-ent], *adj.* surpassing all others; supreme; (*theol.*) beyond human limitations; divine.
TRANSCENDENTAL, [tran'-send-ent'-al], *adj.* (*philos.*) transcending; (*Kant's philos.*) regulative and constitutive, or treating of what is regulative and constitutive, of what is given in experience, under categories which are of purely *a priori* derivation, and precede, *i.e.*, transcend, experience; transcending the ordinary range of perception or conception; (*math.*) applied to any quantity which cannot be represented by an algebraic expression of a finite number of terms.
TRANSCENDENTALISM, [tran'-send-ent'-al-izm], *n.* a system of philosophy which seeks the fundamental form of thought and perception not empirically but intuitively.
TRANSCENDENTALIST, [tran'-send-ent'-al-ist], *n.* one who believes in transcendentalism.
TRANSCENDENTALLY, [tran'-send-ent'-al-i], *adv.* in a transcendental fashion, surpassingly.
TRANSCENDENTLY, [tran-send'-ent-li], *adv.* in a transcendent fashion.
TRANSCENDENTNESS, [tran-send'-ent-nes], *n.* the state of being transcendent.
TRANSCONTINENTAL, [tranz'-kon'-tin-ent'-al], *adj.* traversing a continent; crossing Europe or America.
TRANSCRIBE, [tran-skrīb'], *v.t.* to copy; to write down; to write over again; to reproduce from hieroglyphics or another alphabet; to arrange (for the piano, etc.). [L. *transcribere* copy].
TRANSCRIBER, [tran-skrīb'-er], *n.* a person or thing that transcribes.
TRANSCRIPT, [tran'-skript], *n.* that which is transcribed; a copy of a document.
TRANSCRIPTION, [tran-skrip'-shun], *n.* the action of transcribing; the thing transcribed.
TRANSCRIPTIONAL, [tran-skrip'-shun-al], *adj.* pertaining to transcription.
TRANSCRIPTIVELY, [tran-skript'-iv-li], *adv.* in the manner of a transcription.
TRANSEPT, [tran'-sept'], *n.* the traverse portion, crossing at right angles before the apse, of a cruciform church. [TRANS- and L. *septum* an enclosure].
TRANSFER (1), [tranz'-fer], *n.* that which is transferred; the removal or conveyance of one person or thing from one place or person to another; a picture, design, or pattern which is so drawn that it can be transferred to another surface usually by some form of pressure or the application of heat; the conveyance of a right or title; (*milit.*) a soldier moved from one company to another.
TRANSFER (2), [tranz-fur'], *v.t.* to convey or remove from one place or person to another; to make over; to convey, as a right; to produce by impression; to print a design, picture, from one surface to another; *v.i.* to change from one place to another. [L. *transferre* to carry over].
TRANSFERABLE, [tranz-fur'-abl], *adj.* capable of being conveyed from one place or person to another; negotiable.
TRANSFEREE, [tranz-fer-ē'], *n.* the person to whom a legal transfer is made.
TRANSFERENCE, [tranz'-fer-ents], *n.* the action of transferring.
TRANSFER-PAPER, [tran'-sfer-pāp'-er], *n.* a specially prepared paper for transferring drawings or printed matter to a printing surface.
TRANSFERRER, [tran-sfur'-er], *n.* a person who transfers, in the legal sense.
TRANSFIGURATION, [tranz'-fig'-yōō-rā'-shun], *n.* change of form; the supernatural change in the personal appearance of Christ on the Mount; a feast on the 6th August in commemoration of this. [L. *transfiguratio*].
TRANSFIGURE, [tranz-fig'-er], *v.t.* to change the outward form or appearance so as to glorify it; to transform. [Fr. *transfigurer*].
TRANSFIX, [tranz-fiks'], *v.t.* to pierce through, as with a pointed weapon; (*fig.*) to amaze, petrify. [L. *transfixus, p.pt.* of *transfigere*].
TRANSFIXION, [tranz'-fik'-shun], *n.* a perforating, boring through. [*Prec.*].
TRANSFORM, [trants-fawm'], *v.t.* to change the form, shape, or appearance of; to change substantially and make seem entirely different; to change the nature of spiritually; (*alg.*) to change (an equation) into another of a different form but of equal value; *v.i.* to be changed in form. [L. *transformare*].
TRANSFORMABILITY, [tranz-fawm'-ab-il'-i-ti], *n.* the capacity for being transformed.
TRANSFORMABLE, [tranz-fawm'-abl], *adj.* capable of transformation.
TRANSFORMATION, [tranz'-fawm-ā'-shun], *n.* the action or operation of transforming; metamorphosis; transmutation; a change of heart in a man; an arrangement of false hair; a partial wig; **t. scene,** an elaborate set of scenery on the stage in which changes take place in view of the audience.
TRANSFORMATIVE, [tranz-fawm'-at-iv], *adj.* able or having a tendency to transform. [Fr. *transformatif*].
TRANSFORMER, [tranz-fawm'-er], *n.* a person or thing that transforms; (*elect.*) an instrument which changes the voltage of a current, transfers oscillations from one circuit to another, or converts direct current into alternating current.
TRANSFORMING, [tranz-fawm'-ing], *adj.* effecting, or capable of effecting, a change of form.
TRANSFUSE, [tranz-fewz'], *v.t.* to put out of one vessel into another; to transfer, as blood, from one animal to another; to cause to be instilled; to imbue.

TRANSFUSER, [tranz-fewz'-er], *n.* a person or thing that transfuses.
TRANSFUSIBLE, [tranz-fewz'-ibl], *adj.* able to be transfused.
TRANSFUSION, [tranz-few'-zhun], *n.* the action or process of transfusing; the act of transferring the blood of one animal into another; transmission, transference. [L. *transfusio*].
TRANSFUSIVE, [tranz-fews'-iv], *adj.* pertaining to transfusion.
TRANSGRESS, [tranz-gres'], *v.t.* to pass beyond any limit; to overstep the bounds of; to offend against; to break or violate in law; *v.i.* to offend by violating a law or ignoring a convention. [Fr. *transgresser*].
TRANSGRESSION, [tranz-gresh'-un], *n.* the action of transgressing; the violation of a law; offence; crime.
TRANSGRESSIONAL, [tranz-gresh'-un-al], *adj.* pertaining to transgression; that violates a law.
TRANSGRESSIVE, [tranz-gres'-iv], *adj.* liable to transgress.
TRANSGRESSIVELY, [tranz-gres'-iv-li], *adv.* in a transgressive fashion.
TRANSGRESSOR, [tranz-gres'-or], *n.* a person who breaks a law or violates a command; a sinner.
TRANSHIP, TRANS-SHIP, [tranz-ship'], *v.t. and i.* to transfer passengers or cargo from one ship or mode of conveyance to another; to betake oneself from one ship to another for a continuation of the journey.
TRANSHIPMENT, TRANS-SHIPMENT, [tranz-ship'-ment], *n.* the act of transhipping.
TRANSIENCE, [trans'-i-ents], *n.* transientness.
TRANSIENT (1), [tran'-si-ent], *n.* one who is passing through; (*phys.*) a surge of sound or electrical energy which rises or falls with sudden intensity.
TRANSIENT (2), [tran'-si-ent], *adj.* passing quickly away; ephemeral; fleeting. [L. *transiens*].
TRANSIENTLY, [tran'-si-ent-li], *adv.* in a transient fashion; fleetingly.
TRANSIENTNESS, [tran'-si-ent-nes], *n.* the condition of being transient.
TRANSIRE, [tran'-sïer'-ē], *n.* (*leg.*) a custom-house warrant for allowing goods to pass. [~L. *transire* to pass over].
TRANSISTHMIAN, [tranz-isth'-mi-an], *adj.* across or crossing an isthmus. [TRANS- and ISTHMUS].
TRANSIT, [tran'-sit], *n.* a passing over or through; conveyance; (*astron.*) the passing of an inferior planet across the sun's disk; the passing of a heavenly body across the meridian of a place. [L. *transitus*].
TRANSIT-INSTRUMENT, [tran'-sit-in'-stroom-ent], *n.* (*astron.*) a mounted telescope employed in observing transits.
TRANSITION, [tran-sizh'-un], *n.* a gradual passage from one place or state to another; change; a passing from one subject to another; the passing from Norman to Early English architecture. [L. *transitio*].
TRANSITIONAL, [tran-sizh'-un-al], *adj.* of, or pertaining to, transition.
TRANSITIVE, [tran'-sit-iv], *adj.* capable of passing from one person or thing to another; (*gram.*) expressive of an action passing from a subject to a direct object. [LL. *transitivus*].
TRANSITIVELY, [tranz'-it-iv-li], *adv.* in a transitive way; by means of a transitive verb.
TRANSITIVENESS, [tranz'-it-iv-nes], *n.* the condition of being transitive.
TRANSITORILY, [tranz'-it-er-i-li], *adv.* in a transitory fashion.
TRANSITORINESS, [tranz'-it-er-i-nes], *n.* the condition of being transitory.
TRANSITORY, [tranz'-it-er-i], *adj.* fleeting; ephemeral. [L. *transitorius*].
TRANSLATABLE, [trans-lāt'-abl], *adj.* able to be translated or rendered into another language.
TRANSLATE, [tranz-lāt'], *v.t.* to remove from one place to another; to convey to Heaven without death; to turn written or spoken words from one language into another; to change, transform from thought into action; *v.i.* to be translatable. [LL. *translatare*].
TRANSLATION, [tranz-lā'-shun], *n.* the action of translating; the act of translating into another language; interpretation; version; motion free from rotation. [L. *translatio*].
TRANSLATOR, [tranz-lāt'-or], *n.* a person who translates.
TRANSLATORY, [tranz-lāt'-er-i], *adj.* pertaining to translation into Heaven; transferring; serving to translate.
TRANSLATRESS, [tranz-lāt'-res], *n.* a woman who translates.
TRANSLITERATE, [tranz-lit'-er-āt], *v.t.* to write (the words of one language) in the corresponding characters of another. [TRANS- and L. *litera* a letter].
TRANSLITERATION, [tranz'-lit-er-ā'-shun], *n.* the action of transliterating; that which is transliterated.
TRANSLOCATION, [tranz'-lōk-ā'-shun], *n.* the moving of things from one place to another; substitution of one thing for another.
TRANSLUCENCE, [tranz-lōōs'-ents], *n.* the condition of transmitting rays of light; transparency.
TRANSLUCENCY, [tranz-lōōs'-en-si], *n.* translucence.
TRANSLUCENT, [tranz-lōōs'-ent], *adj.* transmitting rays of light, but not completely transparent.
TRANSLUCID, [tranz-lōōs'-id], *adj.* translucent.
TRANSLUNAR, TRANSLUNARY, [tranz-lōōn'-er(-i)], *adj.* beyond the moon; far distant; beyond human sight.
TRANSMARINE, [tranz'-ma-rēn'], *adj.* beyond, on the other side of, the sea.
TRANSMIGRANT, [tranz-mī'-grant], *adj.* that migrates from one place to another.
TRANSMIGRATE, [tranz'-mī-grāt'], *v.i.* to remove or migrate; to pass from one country into another; (of the soul) to transfer at death from one body to another about to be born.
TRANSMIGRATION, [tranz'-mī-grā'-shun], *n.* the action of transmigrating; the passing of a thing into another state or condition; the passing of the soul after death into another body.
TRANSMIGRATOR, [tranz'-mī-grāt'-or], *n.* a person who migrates.
TRANSMIGRATORY, [tranz'-mī-grāt'-er-i], *adj.* of, or pertaining to, transmigration; passing from one place, body, or state to another.
TRANSMISSIBILITY, [tranz'-mis-ib-il'-it-i], *n.* the quality of being transmissible; the power to be transmitted.
TRANSMISSIBLE, [tranz-mis'-ibl], *adj.* able to be transmitted.
TRANSMISSION, [tranz-mish'-un], *n.* the act of transmitting; the passing of a substance through any body as light through glass; the state of being transmitted; that which is transmitted. [L. *transmissio*].
TRANSMISSIVE, [tranz-mis'-iv], *adj.* transmitted; transmitting; passed from one to another.
TRANSMIT, [tranz-mit'], *v.t.* to send from one person or place to another; to suffer to pass through; to hand down from one generation to another; to communicate, pass on; to send by wireless. [L. *transmittere*].
TRANSMITTABLE, [tranz-mit'-abl], *adj.* able to be transmitted.
TRANSMITTAL, [tranz-mit'-al], *n.* transmission.
TRANSMITTER, [tranz-mit'-er], *n.* a person or thing that transmits; (*teleg.*) the apparatus for sending out the message over the wires; (*wirel.*) the apparatus that transmits the wireless waves through the air.
TRANSMOGRIFICATION, [tranz-mog'-rif-ik-ā'-shun], *n.* change; transformation.
TRANSMOGRIFY, [tranz-mog'-ri-fī], *v.t.* (*coll.*) to transform; to bring about an absolute change in the nature or look of. [Uncert.].
TRANSMONTANE, [tranz-mont'-ān], *adj.* across the mountains; **t. star**, the North Pole star. [L. *transmontanus*].
TRANSMORPHISM, [tranz-mawf'-izm], *n.* a change in form. [TRANS- and Gk. *morphe* form].
TRANSMUTABILITY, [tranz-mewt'-ab-il'-i-ti], *n.* the quality of being transmutable.
TRANSMUTABLE, [tranz-mewt'-abl], *adj.* able to be changed into a different substance or something of a different nature. [LL. *transmutabilis*].
TRANSMUTABLENESS, [tranz-mewt'-abl-nes], *n.* transmutability.
TRANSMUTABLY, [tranz-mewt'-ab-li], *adv.* able to be transmuted.
TRANSMUTATION, [tranz'-mewt-ā'-shun], *n.* the act of transmuting, or the condition of being transmuted, as the baser metals into gold, according to the alchemists; (*geom.*) the change or reduction of one figure or body into another of the same area or solidity, but of a different form.
TRANSMUTATIONIST, [tranz'-mewt-ā'-shun-ist], *n.* one who believes in the theory of the transmutation of metals or of the transmutation of organic nature.
TRANSMUTE, [tranz-mewt'], *v.t.* to change from one nature, substance, or form into another; (*alchemy*) to change a base metal into gold or silver; to transform. [L. *transmutare*].
TRANSMUTER, [tranz-mewt'-er], *n.* a person who, an instrument which, transmutes; an alchemist.

TRANSOCEANIC, [tranz-ō'-shi-an'-ik], *adj.* across, on the other side of, the ocean; crossing the ocean. [TRANS- and OCEANIC].

TRANSOM, [tran'-sum], *n.* a beam of timber extended across the sternpost of a ship to strengthen the after part and give it proper form; a crossbar; a horizontal mullion or crossbar in a window, or a lintel over a door; the vane of a cross-staff; (*pl.*) pieces of wood which join together the cheeks of gun-carriages. [L. *transtrum* cross-timber].

TRANSOM-WINDOW, [tran'-sum-wind'-ō], *n.* a window divided into two by a transom; a window over a transom.

TRANSPACIFIC, [tranz'-pas-if'-ik], *adj.* across or crossing the Pacific.

TRANSPADANE, [tranz-pad'-ān], *adj.* beyond, north of the River Po. [TRANS- and L. *Padus* the River Po].

TRANSPARENCY, [tranz-pāer'-en-si, tranz-pa'-ren-si], *n.* the state of being transparent; a picture on semi-transparent material seen by light passing through it from behind.

TRANSPARENT, [tranz-pāer'-ent, tranz-pa'-rent], *adj.* having the property of transmitting rays of light so as not to hide the view of objects behind; pervious to light; clear; (*fig.*) obvious; ingenuous, without duplicity.

TRANSPARENTLY, [tranz-pāer'-ent-li], *adv.* in a transparent fashion.

TRANSPARENTNESS, [tranz-pāer'-ent-nes], *n.* the state of being transparent.

TRANSPICUOUS, [tran-spik'-yōō-us], *adj.* transparent.

TRANSPIERCE, [tranz-pēers'], *v.t.* to pierce through.

TRANSPIRABLE, [tranz-pier'-abl], *adj.* emitting or that may be emitted through pores as vapour.

TRANSPIRATION, [tranz'-pi-rā'-shun], *n.* the action or process of transpiring.

TRANSPIRE, [tranz-pier'], *v.t.* to emit through the excretories of the skin; to send off in vapour; *v.i.* to be emitted through the excretories of the skin; to exhale; to become public; to happen, to turn out. [L. *transpirare* to exhale].

TRANSPIRY, [tranz-pier'-i], *n.* the fact of transpiring, coming to light.

TRANSPLANT, [tranz-plahnt'], *v.t.* to take up and plant in another place; to remove; to move away from one district and set up a home in another.

TRANSPLANTATION, [tranz'-plant-ā'-shun], *n.* the act of transplanting.

TRANSPLANTER, [tranz-plahnt'-er], *n.* a person who transplants.

TRANSPLENDENCY, [tran-splend'-en-si], *n.* great splendour; magnificence.

TRANSPLENDENT, [tran-splend'-ent], *adj.* highly resplendent.

TRANSPLENDENTLY, [tran-splend'-ent-li], *adv.* in a transplendent fashion.

TRANSPONTINE, [tranz-pont'-īn], *adj.* across the bridge; on the south side of the Thames. [TRANS- and L. *pons pontis* bridge].

TRANSPORT (1), [tran'-spawt], *n.* transportation; conveyance; a ship used for transporting troops and munitions of war; the conveyances required by an army; rapture; ecstasy.

TRANSPORT (2), [tranz-pawt'], *v.t.* to carry or convey from one place to another; to banish as a criminal; to carry away by violence of passion; to ravish with pleasure. [L. *transportare* to carry across].

TRANSPORTABLE, [tranz-pawt'-abl], *adj.* able to be transported.

TRANSPORTATION, [tranz'-pawt-ā'-shun], *n.* the act of transporting or of being transported.

TRANSPORTEDLY, [tranz-pawt'-ed-li], *adv.* in a state of transport; ecstatically.

TRANSPORTEDNESS, [tranz-pawt'-ed-nes], *n.* a state of transport.

TRANSPORTER, [tranz-pawt'-er], *n.* one who, or that which, transports; a travelling crane for moving goods from one place to another.

TRANSPORTING, [tranz-pawt'-ing], *adj.* used to transport; occasioning transport, rapture.

TRANSPORTINGLY, [tranz-pawt'-ing-li], *adv.* in a manner to occasion transport.

TRANSPOSAL, [tranz-pōz'-al], *n.* the act of transposing; transposition.

TRANSPOSE, [tranz-pōz'], *v.t. and i.* to transfer; to interchange; (*alg.*) to add to or subtract from each of the expressions of an equation one or more of the terms of one expression; (*gram.*) the key of; to be capable of transposition. [Fr. *transposer*].

TRANSPOSITION, [tranz'-pōz-ish'-un], *n.* the action of transferring; transference.

TRANSPOSITIONAL, [tranz'-pōz-ish'-un-al], *adj.* pertaining to, involving transposition.

TRANSPOSITIVE, [tranz-pos'-it-iv], *adj.* made by transposing; characterized by transposition.

TRANS-SHIP, see TRANSHIP.

TRANS-SHIPMENT, see TRANSHIPMENT.

TRANSUBSTANTIATE, [tran'-sub-stan'-shi-āt], *v.t.* to transform into another substance.

TRANSUBSTANTIATION, [tran'-sub-stan'-shi-ā'-shun], *n.* change of substance; (*theol.*) the doctrine of the conversion of substance, *esp.* the conversion of the bread and wine in the Eucharist into the body and blood of Christ.

TRANSUBSTANTIATOR, [tran-sub-stan'-shi-āt-or], *n.* one who believes in the doctrine of transubstantiation.

TRANSUDATION, [tran'-sōōd-ā'-shun], *n.* the act of transuding; that which transudes.

TRANSUDATORY, [tran-sōōd'-at-er-i], *adj.* pertaining to transudation; passing by transudation.

TRANSUDE, [tran-sewd'], *v.i.* to pass through the pores or interstices of texture, as perspiration or other fluid. [TRANS- and L. *sudare* to sweat].

TRANSUMPT, [tran-sumpt'], *n.* (*leg.*) a copy or exemplification of a record; a deed. [L. *transumere*].

TRANSVECTION, [tranz-vek'-shun], *n.* †the act of conveying or carrying over; (*math.*) a method of dealing with variants and co-variants. [TRANS- and L. *vectio* carrying].

TRANSVERSAL (1), [tranz-vurs'-al], *n.* (*geom.*) a straight or curved line which traverses or intersects a system of other lines.

TRANSVERSAL (2), [tranz-vurs'-al], *adj.* transverse; running, lying transverse.

TRANSVERSALLY, [tranz-vurs'-al-i], *adv.* in a transverse direction.

TRANSVERSE (1), [tranz'-vurs], *n.* something lying in a transverse position; (*geom.*) the long axis of an ellipse.

TRANSVERSE (2), [tranz-vurs'], *adj.* lying across; lying in a crosswise direction. [L. *transversus*].

TRANSVERSELY, [tranz-vurs'-li], *adv.* in a transverse direction.

TRANTER, [trant'-er], *n.* a pedlar; a carrier. [ME. *traventer*].

TRAP (1), [trap], *n.* a contrivance that shuts suddenly or with a spring, used for snaring animals; an ambush; a stratagem; a device used in knurr-and-spell, otherwise trap-and-ball; a contrivance to stop foul air escaping from a drain; a light carriage with two wheels, drawn by one horse. [OE. *træppe*].

TRAP

TRAP (2), [trap], *n.* (*geol.*) one of various dark-coloured metamorphic rocks often found in an arrangement of ledges rising one above another like great stairs. [Swed. *trappa* stair].

TRAP (3), [trap], *v.t.* to catch in a trap; to ensnare; to take, capture, by means of a trick; to make a trap for a drain; *v.i.* to set a trap for game or fur-bearing animals; (*fig.*) to lay a trap.

TRAPAN, see TREPAN (3).

TRAP-AND-BALL, [trap'-and-bawl'], *n.* a game in which a ball is jerked up on a trap, and then hit.

TRAP-DOOR, [trap'-daw(r)'], *n.* a hinged door in a floor or roof opening and shutting like a valve.

TRAPES, see TRAIPSE.

TRAPEZE, [trap-ēz'], *n.* a trapezium; a swinging horizontal bar for the exhibition of feats in gymnastics and acrobatic performances. [Fr. *trapèze* from Gk. *trapezion* little table].

TRAPEZIFORM, [trap-ēz'-i-fawm], *adj.* in the form of a trapezium.

TRAPEZIUM, (*pl.* **trapezia**), [trap-ēz'-i-um], *n.* (*geom.*) a plane figure contained within four straight lines, none, or only two of which are parallel; (*anat.*) a bone of the carpus. [Gk. *trapezion* little table].

TRAPEZOHEDRON, [trap-ēz'-ō-hēd'-ron], *n.* a solid, bounded by twenty-four identical trapezia. [TRAPEZIUM and Gk. *hedra* side].

TRAPEZOID, [trap'-ēz-oid], *n.* a plane figure of four unequal sides none of which is parallel to another. [Late Gk. *trapezoeides*].

TRAPEZOIDAL, [trap'-ēz-oid'-al], *adj.* having the form of a trapezoid, or of a trapezium. [*Prec.*].

TRAP-FLOWER, [trap'-flow(r)], *n.* a flower inside which insects are entrapped.
TRAPPEAN, [trap-ē'-an], *adj.* pertaining to or denoting trap rock. [TRAP (2)].
TRAPPER, [trap'-er], *n.* a man whose occupation it is to entrap wild animals, usually for furs.
TRAPPINGS, [trap'-ingz], *n.(pl.)* a horse's harness, *esp.* such as is used on important occasions; (*fig.*) ceremonial dress or uniform. [~TRAPS].
TRAPPIST, [trap'-ist], *n.* a monk of the Cistercian religious order as reformed in the 17th century by the Abbé de Rancé at the monastery of La Trappe.
TRAPPISTINE, [trap'-ist-ēn], *n.* a nun of the religious order of La Trappe; a liqueur made at the Trappist monasteries. [~TRAPPIST].
TRAPPOUS, [trap'-us], *adj.* (*geol.*) resembling the igneous rock, trap. [~TRAP (2)].
TRAPPY, [trap'-i], *adj.* resembling a trap; treacherous; tricky.
TRAPS, [traps], *n.(pl.)* (*coll.*) clothes; personal possessions. [~ME. *trappen* to clothe].
TRAP-SHOOTING, [trap'-shōōt-ing], *n.* shooting at pigeons released from boxes or at clay disks, imitation birds, thrown from a catapult.
TRAPSTICK, [trap'-stik], *n.* a tripstick, a stick used in the game of knurr-and-spell.
TRAP-TUFA, [trap'-tewf'-a], *n.* (*geol.*) a sort of porous rock resembling sandstone found in trap. [TRAP (2) and TUFA].
TRASH, [trash], *n.* rubbish; any waste or worthless matter; a worthless person; cheap, shoddy goods; poor rubbishy literature; **white t.**, the destitute whites of the southern states of America. [Uncert.].
TRASHERY, [trash-er-i], *n.* trash; trashy things.
TRASHILY, [trash'-i-li], *adv.* in a trashy way.
TRASHINESS, [trash'-i-nes], *n.* the condition of being trashy.
TRASHY, [trash'-i], *adj.* like trash; worthless; shoddy.
TRASLING, [tras'-ling], *n.* a freshwater fish, the perch, *Perca fluviatilis.* [Uncert.].
TRASS, [tras], *n.* (*min.*) a pumiceous conglomerate, a volcanic kind of earth, used as a cement. [Du. *tras*].
TRAUMA, [trawm'-a], *n.* (*med.*) a bodily injury occasioned by violence; a psychological injury. [Gk. *trauma* a wound].
TRAUMATIC, [trawm-at'-ik], *adj.* of or pertaining to a trauma; able to cure wounds. [~*Prec.*].
TRAVAIL (1), [trav'-āl], *n.* pains, labour of childbirth. [OF. *travail*].
TRAVAIL (2), [trav'-āl], *v.i.* to labour with pain; to toil; to suffer the pangs of childbirth. [Fr. *travailler*].
TRAVE, [trāv], *n.* a wooden frame to confine a horse while the smith is shoeing it; a beam. [OFr. *trave* beam].
TRAVEL (1), [trav'-el], *n.* a passing on foot; a journey; motion, movement; (*pl.*) journey, tour; a book describing this.
TRAVEL (2), [trav'-el], *v.t.* to traverse, journey over; *v.i.* to go; to move along or from place to place; to make a tour, to visit places; (*mech.*) to make a certain movement; (*comm.*) to go from place to place in search of business orders, to follow the occupation of a commercial traveller. [OFr. *travailler*].
TRAVEL-BUREAU, [trav'-el-bew'-rō], *n.* an office at which the traveller may obtain information, and make all his arrangements for travel.
TRAVELLED, [trav'-eld], *adj.* having travelled extensively.
TRAVELLER, [trav'-el-er], *n.* a person who travels, *esp.* one who travels to secure orders for goods.
TRAVELLER'S CHEQUE, [trav'-el-erz-chek'], *n.* a cheque payable at any branch or by any agent of the bank that issues it, and convenient for tourists.
TRAVELLER'S-JOY, [trav'-el-erz-joi'], *n.* (*bot.*) the old man's beard or virgin's bower, *Clematis vitalba*, a climbing plant with starry white flowers.
TRAVELLER'S-TREE, [trav'-el-erz-trē], *n.* the tree holding water in its leaf-bases, *Ravenala madagascariensis.*
TRAVELLING, [trav'-el-ing], *n.* pertaining to, adapted for, or incurred by travel.
TRAVELOGUE, [trav'-el-og], *n.* (*coll.*) an article or talking film on travel and touring. [TRAVEL and Gk. *logos* speech].
TRAVERSABLE, [tra-vurs'-abl], *adj.* able to be traversed; passable.
TRAVERSE (1), [trav'-ers], *n.* anything laid or built across; something that thwarts, crosses, or obstructs; a turning; a trick; a parapet made across the covert-way to prevent its being enfiladed; a gallery or loft of communication in any large building; (*leg.*) a denial of what the opposite party has advanced in any stage of the pleadings; (*naut.*) a tack when beating to windward; **t. sailing**, the mode of computing the place of a ship by reducing several short courses to one larger course.
TRAVERSE (2), [trav'-ers], *adj.* lying across.
TRAVERSE (3), [tra-vurs'], *adv.* crosswise.
TRAVERSE (4), [trav-urs', trav'-ers], *v.t.* to lay in a cross direction; to thwart, to obstruct; to survey carefully; to turn and point in any direction; to plane across the grain; (*leg.*) to deny what the opposite party has alleged; *v.i.* to turn, as on a pivot; to move round; to swivel; to cut the tread crosswise, as a horse that throws his croup to one side and his head to the other; in fencing, to use the posture or motions of opposition. [Fr. *traverser*].
TRAVERSER, [tra-vurs'-er], *n.* a person or thing that traverses.
TRAVERSE-TABLE, [tra'-vers-tābl], *n.* an apparatus in the form of a travelling platform for shifting railway vehicles from one set of rails to another alongside it; (*naut.*) a table of difference of latitude and departure.
TRAVERTINE, [trav'-er-tin], *n.* (*min.*) a calc-sinter, formed, *esp.* in Italy, as a deposit in limy springs. [It. *travertino*].
TRAVESTY (1), [trav'-est-i], *n.* the representation of a serious work in a burlesque style; a parody; a complete caricature; a perversion.
TRAVESTY (2), [trav'-est-i], *v.t.* to parody; to burlesque; to make a mock of; to render ridiculous. [Fr. *travestir*].
TRAVIS, [trav'-is], *n.* a horse's stall; the wooden partition dividing the stalls in a stable. [~OFr. *travers*].
TRAWL (1), [trawl], *n.* a drag-net held open by a frame near the bottom of the sea; a long buoyed fishing-line from which short lines hang.
TRAWL (2), [trawl], *v.t.* to draw (a net) along after a vessel; *v.i.* to fish by dragging a net along the bottom of the sea. [OFr. *troller* to move about].
TRAWLER, [trawl'-er], *n.* one who trawls; a type of vessel employed for trawling.
TRAWLING, [trawl'-ing], *n.* the act of using a trawl.
TRAY, [trā], *n.* a flat object with a rim, made of wood, metal, or china, used for carrying table appointments, food, or letters; a waiter, salver; an object resembling the domestic tray, and used for other purposes. [OFr. *treie*].
TRAY-TRIP, [trā'-trip], *n.* a kind of draughts.
TREACHEROUS, [trech'-er-us], *adj.* violating allegiance or plighted faith; traitorous to king and country; untrustworthy; deceptive; unreliable; dangerous. [OFr. *trecheros*].
TREACHEROUSLY, [trech'-er-us-li], *adv.* in a treacherous fashion.
TREACHEROUSNESS, [trech'-er-us-nes], *n.* the condition of being treacherous.
TREACHERY, [trech'-er-i], *n.* breaking of faith or allegiance; perfidy; deceitful behaviour; treason. [OFr. *trecherie*].
TREACLE, [trēkl], *n.* molasses; a viscid sugar syrup; a saccharine fluid consisting of the inspissated juices of certain vegetables; (*coll.*) flattery; insincere amiability. [OFr. *triacle* from Gk. *theriake* antidote].
TREACLE-MUSTARD, [trēkl'-must'-erd], *n.* a cruciferous plant of the genus *Erysimum.*
TREACLY, [trēk'-li], *adj.* like treacle; thick and sticky; (*fig.*) over-sweet, nauseatingly amiable.
TREAD (1), [tred], *n.* a step; a manner of walking, a gait; a footstep; that on which one steps or is intended to step, e.g., on a stair; that which presses the ground when one steps, the sole of a shoe; that part of a tyre which presses upon the ground.
TREAD (2), (**trod, trodden**), [tred], *v.t.* to step, walk on; to press under the feet; to trample under the feet; to crush; to oppress; to traverse; to measure out by walking; to work a treadle; *v.i.* to walk, step, go. [OE. *tredan*].
TREADER, [tred'-er], *n.* a person or thing that treads.
TREADLE, TREDDLE, [tredl], *n.* that part of a machine for turning a crank, and worked by the foot; a pedal. [OE. *tredel*].
TREADMILL, [tred'-mil], *n.* a mill turned by persons treading on steps upon the periphery of a wheel, formerly worked by convicts as a part of their punishment; (*fig.*) any trying occupation characterized by sameness and monotony.
TREADWHEEL, [tred'-wēl], *n.* a vertical wheel turned by men or animals walking within its periphery.
TREASON, [trēz'-on], *n.* betrayal of trust; treachery; the offence of trying to betray the state or to subvert

the government of the state to which the offender belongs; **high t.,** treason that immediately affects the monarch; **petty t.,** treason which involves a breach of fidelity to an individual, as the murder of a master by a servant; **t. felony,** high treason treated as a felony instead of as a capital crime. [AFr. *treysoun*].

TREASONABLE, [trēz'-on-abl], *adj.* pertaining to, involving, treason.

TREASONABLENESS, [trēz'-on-abl-nes], *n.* the condition of being treasonable.

TREASONABLY, [trēz'-on-ab-li], *adv.* in a treasonable fashion.

TREASURE (1), [trezh'-er], *n.* money or valuables accumulated and stored; something much valued; money; great abundance; (*coll.*) an invaluable person. [OFr. *tresor*].

TREASURE (2), [trezh'-er], *v.t.* to hoard as treasure; to value highly; to retain in the mind.

TREASURE-HOUSE, [trezh'-er-hows], *n.* a house or place where treasures and stores are kept.

TREASURER, [trezh'-er-er], *n.* one who has the care of funds or a treasury; an officer who receives and takes charge of the money of the public or of private companies, corporations, or societies. [OFr. *tresorier*].

TREASURERSHIP, [trezh'-er-er-ship], *n.* the office of treasurer.

TREASURESS, [trezh'-er-es], *n.* a woman who has charge of funds. [OFr. *tresoresse*].

TREASURE-TROVE, [trezh'-er-trōv'], *n.* any valuables, bullion and the like, found hidden, the owner of which is not known. [AFr. *tresor trové* treasure found].

TREASURY, [trezh'-er-i], *n.* that department of government which has charge of the finances; a repository; a small encyclopedia; **t. bench,** the first row of seats on the Speaker's right in the House of Commons, occupied by cabinet ministers.

TREAT (1), [trēt], *n.* an exceptional entertainment or pleasure which affords great satisfaction; such an entertainment planned for pleasure; (*slang*) a funny person or amusing incident.

TREAT (2), [trēt], *v.t.* to behave or act towards; to handle, deal with in a particular way; to negotiate; to manage, to combat by the use of remedies; to discourse on in speech or writing; to entertain; to bear the expenses for; *v.i.* to discourse; to discuss terms; to deal. [OFr. *traitir*].

TREATABLE, [trēt'-abl], *adj.* easily handled; easily persuaded; manageable; moderate.

TREATER, [trēt'-er], *n.* one who discourses on a subject; a negotiator; one who gives a treat.

TREATISE, [trēt'-iz], *n.* a written discourse in which a particular subject is fully or scientifically treated; a monograph. [AFr. *tretiz*].

TREATMENT, [trēt'-ment], *n.* the act or way of treating; management; manipulation; good or bad behaviour toward; manner of applying remedies; (*med.*) the mode of dealing with a disease.

TREATY, [trēt'-i], *n.* the act of treating; a discussion of differences; an agreement; a formal agreement, league, or contract between states.

TREBLE (1), [trebl], *n.* the highest of the parts in singing or playing; one who sings in the treble or plays a treble instrument.

TREBLE (2), [trebl], *adj.* threefold; of, pertaining to, the third part in music, the boys' voices; hence, the highest part; shrill, sharp, acute, (of a voice) unbroken. [OFr. *treble*].

TREBLE (3), [trebl], *v.t.* to make threefold; *v.i.* to become threefold.

TREBLENESS, [trebl'-nes], *n.* the condition of being treble.

TREBLY, [treb'-li], *adv.* in a threefold fashion.

TREBUCHET, [treb'-yōō-shet], *n.* a small sensitive balance; a trap for small birds; †a military machine for slinging large stones. [OFr. *trebuchet* trap].

TRECENTO, [trā-chent'-ō], *n.* the fourteenth century, *esp.* as a period in Italian art and literature. [It. (*mil*)*trecento* (a thousand and) three hundred].

TREDDLE, see TREADLE.

TREE (1), [trē], *n.* a plant larger than a shrub, and having a single trunk; anything like a tree, consisting of a stem and branches; a piece of wood; the Cross; **genealogical t.,** a family pedigree, a diagram showing lines of descent; **up a t.,** (*coll.*) in difficulties. [OE. *treo*].

TREE (2), [trē], *v.t.* to drive to, or into, a tree; *v.i.* to take to a tree for a refuge.

TREE-CRAB, [trē'-krab'], *n.* a land crab of the genus *Birgus*, living on coconuts.

TREE-CREEPER, [trē'-krēp'-er], *n.* the small bird, *Certhia familiaris*, preying on insects found on trees.

TREE-FERN, [trē'-furn], *n.* a large tropical fern with a bole like a tree.

TREE-FROG, [trē'-frog'], *n.* one of the fourteen genera of frogs that live in trees.

TREELESS, [trē'-les], *adj.* having no trees.

TREE-MALLOW, [trē'-mal'-ō], *n.* the shrubby plant, *Lavatera arborea*.

TREE-NAIL, TRENAIL, [trē'-nāl, tren'-el], *n.* a wooden block used to pin the planks of a wooden ship to the timbers and railway chairs to the sleepers.

TREE-PIPIT, [trē'-pip'-it], *n.* the small pipit, *Anthus trivialis*.

TREE-SPARROW, [trē'-spa'-rō], *n.* a bird of the sparrow genus, *Passer montanus*.

TREFLE, [trefl], *n.* (*fort.*) a mine having three chambers. [Fr. *trèfle* trefoil].

TREFOIL, [tre'-foil], *n.* a plant of the genus *Trifolium*, having leaves of three leaflets, such as clover; (*arch.*) an ornament resembling three-leaved clover. [OFr. *trefueil* from L. *trifolium*].

TREILLAGE, [trel'-ij], *n.* (*hort.*) a kind of railwork, consisting of light posts and rails for supporting espaliers and sometimes wall-trees. [Fr. *treillage*]

TREK (1), [trek], *n.* a journey by ox-wagon; a migration; a journey. [Afrik. *trek*].

TREK (2), [trek], *v.i.* to travel by ox-wagon; to migrate; to journey. [Afrik. *trekken*].

TRELLIS (1), [trel'-is], *n.* a structure of lattice-work for supporting plants. [OFr. *treliz*].

TRELLIS (2), [trel'-is], *v.t.* to fit with a trellis.

TRELLISED, [trel'-ist], *adj.* fitted with a trellis.

TRELLIS-WORK, [trel'-is-wurk'], *n.* small bars nailed across each other, as used for verandas and summer-houses.

TREMANDO, [tre-mand'-ō], *adv.* (*mus.*) to be executed with a general shake of the whole chord. [It. *tremando* trembling].

TREMATODE, [trem'-at-ōd], *n.* (*zool.*) a parasitic worm of the order *Trematoda*; a fluke-worm. [Gk. *trematodes* porous].

TREMATOID, [trem'-a-toid], *adj.* like a trematode.

TREMBLE (1), [trembl], *n.* the act of trembling, a shudder; (*mus.*) a shake.

TREMBLE (2), [trembl], *v.i.* to shake involuntarily as with fear, cold, or weakness; to shake; to quiver; to flutter; (*fig.*) to feel intense anxiety, to be agitated. [Fr. *trembler*].

TREMBLER, [tremb-ler], *n.* a person who trembles; an electric device which trembles as it makes and breaks a circuit.

TREMBLING, [tremb'-ling], *n.* the condition of a person or thing that trembles.

TREMBLINGLY, [tremb'-ling-li], *adv.* in a trembling manner; fearfully.

TREMELLA, [trem-el'-a], *n.* (*bot.*) a genus of jelly-like fungi growing on decayed wood. [~L. *tremulus* shaking].

TREMENDOUS, [trim-end'-us], *adj.* formidable; gigantic; overpowering; (*coll.*) very great, astonishing. [L. *tremendus* causing fear].

TREMENDOUSLY, [trim-end'-us-li], *adv.* in a manner to cause awe or astonishment; (*coll.*) very, extremely.

TREMENDOUSNESS, [trim-end'-us-nes], *n.* the condition of being tremendous.

TREMOLITE, [trem'-ō-līt], *n.* (*min.*) a variety of white or grey hornblende. [*Tremola*, in Switzerland, where found].

TREMOLO, [trem'-ōl-ō], *n.* a shake or trembling of the voice; tremulous delivery. [It. *tremolo*].

TREMOR, [trem'-or], *n.* a sudden access of trembling, shivering, or quivering. [OFr. *tremor* fear].

TREMULANT (1), [trem'-yōō-lant], *n.* a tremulant stop on an organ.

TREMULANT (2), [trem'-yŏŏl-ant], *adj.* tremulous, quivering.

TREMULOUS, [trem'-yŏŏl-us], *adj.* affected with tremors, trembling, uneven; fearful, nervous. [L. *tremulus* shaking, quivering].

TREMULOUSLY, [trem'-yŏŏl-us-li], *adv.* in a tremulous fashion.

TREMULOUSNESS, [trem'-yŏŏl-us-nes], *n.* the condition of being tremulous.

TRENAIL, see TREE-NAIL.

TRENCH (1), [trench], *n.* a long narrow ditch cut or dug in the earth; (*fort.*) such a ditch cut deep into the ground as cover for soldiers; (*pl.*) a military front so fortified; fighting in general. [OFr. *trenche*].

TRENCH (2), [trench], *v.t.* to cut or dig a channel in for water; to furrow; to dig; *v.i.* to encroach; to make a trench in warfare. [OFr. *trenchier* to cut].

TRENCHANCY, [trench'-an-si], *n.* the quality of being trenchant; sharpness of speech.
TRENCHANT, [trench'-ant], *adj.* cutting, sharp; severe, brief and telling in speech, caustic. [OFr. *trenchant* cutting].
TRENCH-COAT, [trench'-kōt], *n.* a belted waterproof coat of the kind worn by soldiers in trenches.
TRENCHER, [trench'-er], *n.* a wooden plate on which to cut meat at table; a bread-platter; food; pleasures of the table; a trencher-cap. [OFr. *trencheoir*].
TRENCHER-CAP, [trench'-er-kap'], *n.* a college cap.
TRENCHER-FLY†, [trench'-er-flī], *n.* a person who haunts the tables of others; a parasite.
TRENCHER-FRIEND, [trench'-er-frend'], *n.* a person who frequents the tables of others; a sponger.
TRENCHERMAN, [trench'-er-man], *n.* one who eats from a trencher; **a good t.**, one with a hearty appetite.
TRENCHER-MATE, [trench'-er-māt], *n.* a companion at table.
TRENCH-FEVER, [trench'-fēv'-er], *n.* a form of fever carried by lice in the trenches during the First World War.
TRENCHING, [trench'-ing], *n.* the digging of a trench or trenches; a thorough form of digging over a garden.
TRENCH-MORTAR, [trench'-mawt'-er], *n.* a short-range mortar for work in trenches.
TRENCH-PLOUGH, [trench'-plow], *n.* a kind of plough for deep ploughing.
TREND (1), [trend], *n.* inclination or tendency; the general course of a speech, etc.
TREND (2), [trend], *v.i.* to move or incline in a particular direction; to take a course; to drift. [~OE. *trendlian* to make round].
TRENDLE, [trendl], *n.* anything round employed in turning or rolling; a little wheel. [OE. *trendel* wheel].
TRENTAL, [trent'-al], *n.* masses offered for thirty days successively after a death. [LL. *trentale*].
TREPAN (1), [trip-an'], *n.* a circular saw for removing a piece of bone from the skull. [Gk. *trupanon* a borer].
TREPAN (2), [trip-an'], *v.t.* (*surg.*) to operate on with a trepan.
TREPAN (3), **TRAPAN**, [trip-an'], *v.t.* to ensnare, entrap, lure. [Unkn.].
TREPANG, [trep-ang'], *n.* the sea-slug. [Malay *trepang*].
TREPANNER, [trip-an'-er], *n.* a surgeon who uses a trepan.
TREPANNING, [trip-an'-ing], *n.* the process of making an opening in the skull.
TREPHINE, [tref-ēn'], *n.* (*surg.*) an improved trepan with a centre-pin, by which it is adjusted and set to work. [Fr. *tréfine*].
TREPID, [trep'-id], *adj.* trembling; nervous. [L. *trepidus* trembling].
TREPIDATION, [trep'-id-ā'-shun], *n.* a state of alarm and anxiety; nervousness; quaking or shivering of the limbs. [L. *trepidatio*].
TRESPASS (1), [tres'-pas], *n.* the act of trespassing; harm caused thereby; transgression; sin. [OFr. *trespas*].
TRESPASS (2), [tres'-pas], *v.i.* to enter unlawfully on the land of another; to intrude, encroach (upon); to sin, transgress, offend; **to t. on a person's time**, to take up a person's time. [OFr. *trespasser*].
TRESPASSER, [tres'-pas-er], *n.* one who enters unlawfully on the land of another; a sinner.
TRESS, [tres], *n.* a long strand or curl of hair; (*pl.*) **tresses**, the hair of the head. [OFr. *tresse* lock of hair].
TRESSED, [trest], *adj.* having tresses; coiled up.
TRESSURE, [tresh'-er], *n.* (*her.*) a border running parallel with the sides of a shield. [Fr. *tressure*].
TRESTLE, [tresl], *n.* two braced legs and a horizontal bar forming a movable frame for a temporary table; a similar framework for supporting anything. [OFr. *trestel*].
TRESTLE-TABLE, [tresl'-tābl], *n.* a table supported on trestles.
TRESTLETREE, [tresl'-trē], *n.* the bar supporting a crosstree.
TRET, [tret], *n.* (*comm.*) an allowance made to purchasers for waste or refuse matter, *esp.* as occasioned by transport. [Fr. *traite* transport].
TREVET, see TRIVET.
TREWS, [trōōz], *n.*(*pl.*) tartan trousers as worn by Highland regiments. [Fr. *trousse* bundle].
TREY, [trā], *n.* the three at cards or dice. [OFr. *treis*].
TRI-, *pref.* three, threefold. [Gk. *tri-* three].
TRIABLE, [trī'-abl], *adj.* able to be tried or tested; liable to trial; requiring to be tried.
TRIABLENESS, [trī'-abl-nes], *n.* the quality of being triable.
TRIACONTAHEDRAL, [trī'-a-kont'-a-hēd'-ral], *adj.* contained by thirty sides, *esp.* thirty rhombs. [Gk. *triakonta* thirty and *hedra* side].
TRIAD, [trī-ad'], *n.* the number three; a union of three elements; (*chem.*) an element, each atom of which, in combining, is equal to three atoms of hydrogen; (*mus.*) a chord consisting of a note sounded along with its third and fifth; a poem with a triple structure. [Gk. *trias* group of three].
TRIADELPHOUS, [trī'-ad-el'-fus], *adj.* (*bot.*) having the stamens in three bundles. [TRI- and Gk. *adelphos* brother].
TRIAL, [trī'-al], *n.* an attempt; examination by test; experience; suffering; temptation; annoyance, irritation; (*leg.*) a judicial examination in a court of law subsequent to a charge; **on t.**, on approbation; **t. run**, a short run in a vehicle for purposes of testing its efficiency; **t. marriage**, a temporary union for the purpose of seeing whether the two parties are compatible; **t. match**, a rehearsal or practice match before the real contest; **method of t. and error**, way of arriving at the best method by testing several. [AFr. *trial* from *trier* to try].
TRIALISM, [trī'-al-izm], *n.* the doctrine of the existence in man of body, soul, and spirit. [TRI- and (DU)ALISM].
TRIALOGUE, [trī'-a-log'], *n.* a conversation in which three persons are engaged. [TRI- and (DI)ALOGUE].
TRIANDROUS, [trī-and'-rus], *adj.* (*bot.*) with three stamens. [TRI- and Gk. *aner andros* man].
TRIANGLE, [trī'-ang'-gl], *n.* a figure bounded by three lines, and containing three angles; a steel percussion instrument in music, bent into the form of an open triangle; †three halberts or poles stuck in the ground and joined at the top, to which soldiers were bound when flogged; (*fig.*) a dramatic situation in which the mutual relations of one woman and two men, or one man and two women, are involved. [L. *triangulus*].
TRIANGLED†, [trī'-ang'-gld], *adj.* divided into triangles; arranged in triangles.
TRIANGULAR, [trī-ang'-gyōōl-er], *adj.* having a triangular form; involving three sides, persons, or groups.
TRIANGULARLY, [trī-ang'-gyōōl-er-li], *adv.* in the form of a triangle.
TRIANGULATE, [trī-ang'-gyōōl-āt], *v.t.* to measure by triangulation.
TRIANGULATION, [trī-ang'-gyōōl-ā'-shun], *n.* employment of a series of triangles in a trigonometrical survey.
TRIANGULOID, [trī-ang'-gyōōl-oid], *adj.* resembling a triangle in shape. [TRIANGLE and Gk. *oeides* like].
TRIAPSIDAL, [trī-ap'-sid-al], *adj.* (*arch.*) with three apses.
TRIARCHY, [trī'-ahk-i], *n.* government by three persons. [TRI and Gk. *arkhia* rule].
TRIAS, [trī'-as], *n.* (*geol.*) the lowest group of Secondary rocks, the series of beds intermediate between the Jurassic and the Permian; New Red Sandstone. [Gk. *trias* three].
TRIASSIC, [trī-as'-ik], *adj.* (*geol.*) pertaining to the Trias.
TRIATIC, [trī-at'-ik], *adj.* (*naut.*) the rope from the foremasthead to the mainmasthead in schooner rig; the jumper stay. [Uncert.].
TRIATOMIC, [trī'-at-om'-ik], *adj.* made up of three atoms.
TRIAXIAL, [trī-aks'-i-al], *adj.* having three axes.
TRIBADISM, [trib'-ad-izm], *n.* homosexuality between women. [Gk. *tribas* female homosexual].
TRIBAL, [trīb'-al], *adj.* of, or pertaining to, a tribe.
TRIBALISM, [trīb'-al-izm], *n.* government by tribes; the characteristics of a tribe.
TRIBASIC, [trī'-bās'-ik], *adj.* having three bases; (*chem.*) containing or combining with three molecules of the base to one of acid.
TRIBE, [trīb], *n.* a social grouping of individuals descending usually from the same progenitor, and kept distinct; a division or distinct class of a people; a number of plants or animals having common qualities; a division; a nation of savages; a number of persons of any character or profession, in contempt. [L. *tribus*].
TRIBELET, [trīb'-let], *n.* a little tribe.
TRIBESMAN, [trībz'-man], *n.* a member of a tribe.
TRIBLET, **TRIBOLET**, [trib'(-ō)-let], *n.* a goldsmith's mandril used in making rings, a cylinder for making tubes; †a caltrop. [Fr. *triboulet*].

RIBOMETER, [trib-om'-it-er], *n.* an instrument for measuring friction. [Gk. *tribo* I rub and METER].
RIBRACH, [trī'-brak'], *n.* a metrical foot of three short syllables. [TRI- and Gk. *brakhus* short].
RIBRACTEATE, [trī-brak'-ti-āt], *adj.* (*bot.*) having three bracts at the base.
RIBULATION, [trib'-yŏŏl-ā'-shun], *n.* great distress; affliction. [L. *tribulatio*].
RIBUNAL, [trī-bewn'-al], *n.* a court of justice; the bench on which the judges sit; any similar body. [L. *tribunal*].
RIBUNARY, [trib'-yōōn-e-ri], *adj.* pertaining to a tribune.
RIBUNATE, [trib'-yōōn-āt], *n.* tribuneship.
RIBUNE (1), [trib'-yōōn], *n.* an ancient Roman military or civil official chosen by the people to defend their privileges; a popular leader. [L. *tribunus*].
RIBUNE (2), [trib'-yōōn], *n.* a platform for a magistrate's official chair; a bishop's throne in a Roman Catholic basilican church; an elevated place from which speeches are delivered. [Fr. *tribune*].
RIBUNESHIP, [trib'-yōōn-ship], *n.* the office of a tribune.
RIBUNITIAL, TRIBUNICIAN, [trib'-yōōn-ish'-al, trib'-yōōn-ish'-an], *adj.* pertaining to a tribune.
RIBUTARILY, [trib'-yŏŏt-er-i-li], *adv.* by way of tribute.
RIBUTARINESS, [trib'-yŏŏt-er-i-nes], *n.* the condition of being tributary.
RIBUTARY (1), [trib'-yŏŏt-er-i], *n.* one paying a tribute; a secondary river running into the main stream.
RIBUTARY (2), [trib'-yŏŏt-er-i], *adj.* paying tribute; paid in tribute; contributing supplies; subsidiary; subordinate.
RIBUTE, [trib'-yōōt], *n.* a sum of money paid by one nation or group to another as a result of conquest or for defence services; a periodical sum paid by a subject to the government or king; (*fig.*) admiration, grateful sentiments expressed by one person for another. [L. *tributum* tax].
RIBUTER, [trib'-yŏŏt-er], *n.* a miner who works his own digging, and pays tribute money to the owner of the ground.
RICAPSULAR, [trī-kap'-syŏŏl-er], *adj.* (*bot.*) having three capsules in the ovary.
RICAR, [trī'-kah(r)], *n.* a three-wheeled motor-car.
RICARPELLARY, [trī'-kahp-el'-er-i], *adj.* (*bot.*) having three carpels.
RICE (1), [trīs], *n.* a moment of time; an instant. [Unkn.].
RICE (2), [trīs], *v.t.* to hoist up (a sail) and make secure by means of a small rope. [MDu. *trisen*].
RICEPHALOUS, [trī-sef'-a-lus], *adj.* having three heads. [TRI- and Gk. *kephale* head].
RICEPS, [trī'-seps'], *n.* the three-headed extensor muscle of the forearm. [L. *triceps* three-headed].
RICHIASIS, [trik-ī'-a-sis], *n.* (*path.*) introversion of the eyelashes; an affection of the kidneys where hair-like formations occur. [Gk. *trikhiasis*].
RICHINA, (*pl.* **trichinae**), [trik-īn'-a], *n.* a minute nematoid parasitic worm infesting the flesh of diseased pigs, and passed on to man in pork. [Gk. *trikhinos* hairy].
RICHINOSIS, TRICHINIASIS, [trik-in-ōs'-is, trik'-in-ī'-as-is], *n.* (*path.*) a disease in either man or animal due to the presence of trichinae in the body.
RICHO-, (*pref.*) hair, of the hair. [Gk. *trikhos*].
RICHOCEPHALUS, [trik'-ō-sef'-a-lus], *n.* a worm which infests the human intestinal canal, and causes a diseased condition there. [TRICHO- and Gk. *kephale* the head].
RICHOGENOUS, [trik-oj'-en-us], *adj.* inducing the growth of hair. [TRICHO- and Gk. *genes* producing].
RICHOLOGIST, [trik-ol'-oj-ist], *n.* a medical specialist in the diseases of the hair.
RICHOLOGY, [trik-ol'-oj-i], *n.* the study of the hair and its diseases; a treatise on hair. [TRICHO- and Gk. *logos* speech].
RICHOME, [trik'-ōm], *n.* (*bot.*) outgrowth from the epidermis in the form of hair, scales, etc. [Gk. *trikhoma*].
RICHOPTERA, [tri-kop'-ter-a], *n.(pl.)* the sub-order of insects including the caddis-flies. [TRICHO- and Gk. *pteron* wing].
RICHORD, [trī'-kawd'], *n.* a three-stringed lyre; a pianoforte having three strings to the key.
RICHOTOMOUS, [trīk-ot'-om-us], *adj.* forking into three branches.
RICHOTOMY, [trīk-ot'-om-i], *n.* division into three parts. [Gk. *trikha* thrice and *tome* a cutting].
TRICHROISM, [trī'-krō-izm], *n.* the property of being able to present three different colours [TRI- and Gk. *khros* tint].
TRICHROMATIC, [trī'-krōm-at'-ik], *adj.* pertaining to three different colours.
TRICK (1), [trik], *n.* an arrangement or device for the purpose of deception; a fraudulent contrivance; a deception; an illusion; a dexterous artifice; legerdemain; a vicious practice; a sly prank; a peculiarity of manner, idiosyncrasy, a curious habit; a round of cards; (*naut.*) a steersman's spell of duty; (*coll.*) **to do the t.**, to achieve the desired end; **a dirty t.**, a mean or treacherous action. [ONFr. *trique*].
TRICK (2), [trik], *v.t.* to cheat, deceive; (*her.*) to delineate (a coat of arms); *v.i.* to practise fraud and treachery; **to t. out**, to bedeck, dress up.
TRICKER, see TRICKSTER.
TRICKERY, [trik'-er-i], *n.* cheating; artifice; roguery. [OFr. *triquerie*].
TRICKILY, [trik'-i-li], *adv.* in a tricky fashion.
TRICKINESS, [trik'-i-nes], *n.* the condition of being tricky.
TRICKING, [trik'-ing], *n.* the act of playing a trick or tricks upon; deceiving.
TRICKISH, [trik'-ish], *adj.* full of tricks; artful; deceptive.
TRICKISHLY, [trik'-ish-li], *adv.* in a trickish fashion.
TRICKISHNESS, [trik'-ish-nes], *n.* the condition of being tricky or characterized by tricks.
TRICKLE (1), [trikl], *n.* a thin stream; a small flow; **t. charger**, a device which charges storage batteries slowly.
TRICKLE (2), [trikl], *v.t.* to make to trickle; *v.i.* to flow in a small gentle stream. [Uncert.].
TRICKLY, [trik'-li], *adj.* trickling.
TRICKSOME, [trik'-sum], *adj.* full of tricks; sportive.
TRICKSTER, TRICKER, [trik'-ster, trik'-er], *n.* one who practises trickery; a rogue; a cheat.
TRICKSY, [trik'-si], *adj.* given to tricks; playful; pretty, fine.
TRICK-TRACK, TRIC-TRAC, [trik'-trak'], *n.* an early variety of backgammon. [Fr. *tric-trac*].
TRICKY, [trik'-i], *adj.* full of tricks; not very straightforward, rather difficult.
TRICLINATE, [trī'-klin-āt], *adj.* (of crystals) having the three axes unequal and obliquely inclined to one another.
TRICLINIARY, [trī-klin'-er-i], *adj.* of, or pertaining to, a triclinium.
TRICLINIC, [trī-klin'-ik], *adj.* (of crystals) triclinate; scalene.
TRICLINIUM, [trī-klin'-i-um], *n.* a couch running round three sides of a table for reclining on during meals, each division usually for three persons; a Roman dining-hall. [Gk. *triklinion*].
TRICOCCOUS, [trī-kok'-us], *adj.* (*bot.*) possessed of a three-grained capsule swelling out in three protuberances. [TRI- and Gk. *kokkos* berry].
TRICOLINE, [trik'-ō-lin], *n.* (*prot.*) a kind of cotton fabric used for frocks and underwear.
TRICOLOUR, [trī'-kul-er], *n.* a national flag of three colours, *esp.* that of France after the 1789 Revolution. [Fr. (*drapeau*) *tricolore* flag of three colours].
TRICOLOURED, [trī'-kul-erd], *adj.* of a flag, having three colours.
TRICORN, [trī'-kawn], *adj.* having three horns, points, or corners. [L. *tricornis*].
TRICORPORAL, [trī-kawp'-er-al], *adj.* with three bodies; three-bodied. [TRI- and L. *corpus corporis* body].
TRICORPORATE, [trī-kawp'-er-at] *adj.* tricorporal.
TRICOSTATE, [trī-kost'-āt], *adj.* with three ribs. [TRI and L. *costa* rib].
TRICOT, [trik'-ō], *n.* knitting; a special style of coarse knitting; a jersey or other garment made of this kind of knitted. [Fr. *tricot* knitted work].
TRICROTIC, [trī-krot'-ik], *adj.* (*physiol.*) showing three undulations of the pulse for every beat of the heart. [TRI- and Gk. *krotos* sound].
TRIC-TRAC, see TRICK-TRACK.
TRICUSPID, [trī-kus'-pid], *adj.* with three points or cusps. [TRI- and L. *cuspis* a point].
TRICUSPIDATE, [trī-kusp'-id-āt], *adj.* tricuspid.
TRICYCLE, [trī'-sikl], *n.* a three-wheeled cycle.
TRIDACNA, [trī-dak'-na], *n.* a genus of bivalve molluscs, having a beautiful shell which, in one species, *Tridacna gigas*, is so large as to be used for fountains and holy-water basins. [Gk. *tridaknos* eaten at three bites].
TRIDACTYL(OUS), [trī-dak'-til(-us)], *adj.* with three toes or fingers. [TRI- and Gk. *daktulos* finger].

TRIDENT, [trī′-dent], *n.* a form of sceptre or spear with three prongs, represented in the hands of Neptune, as god of the sea, and used as a symbol of maritime power. [L. *tridens* three-toothed].
TRIDENTATE, [trī-dent′-āt], *adj.* with three teeth. [TRI-and L. *dentatus* toothed].
TRIDENTINE, [trī-dent′-īn], *adj.* pertaining to the Council of Trent. [L. *Tridentum* Trent].
TRIDIAPASON, [trī-dī-a-pā′-son], *n.* (*mus.*) a triple octave range.
TRIDIGITATE, [trī-dij′-it-āt], *adj.* possessing three fingers or toes.
TRIDIMENSIONAL, [trī′-di-men′-shun-al], *adj.* possessing three dimensions.
TRIDODECAHEDRAL, [trī′-dō-dek-a-hēd′-ral], *adj.* of crystals presenting three ranges of faces, one above another, each containing twelve faces.
TRIDUAN, [trid′-yōō-an], *adj.* lasting three days; taking place every third day. [~L. *triduum*].
TRIDUUM, [trid′-yōō-um], *n.* a period of three days; a religious service lasting three days. [L. *triduum*].
TRIDYMITE, [trid′-im-īt], *n.* a form of silica which crystallizes in the anorthic system. [Gk. *tridumos* threefold].
TRIENNIAL, [trī-en′-i-al], *adj.* of three years' duration; occurring every three years. [L. *triennium* space of three years].
TRIENNIALLY, [trī-en′-i-al-i], *adv.* every three years.
TRIENNIUM, [trī-en′-i-um], *n.* a period of three years; something recurring every third year. [L. *triennium*].
TRIER, [trī′-er], *n.* a person or thing that tries; a tester or test.
TRIERARCH, [trī′-er-ahk], *n.* in classical times, a citizen responsible for the fitting out of a trireme. [Gk. *trierarkhos*].
TRIERARCHY, [trī′-er-ahk-i], *n.* the office of trierarch; the Athenian system of forcing wealthy citizens to contribute triremes to the fleet. [Gk. *trierarkhia*].
TRIFACIAL, [trī-fāsh′-al], *n.* (*anat.*) a branch of the cranial nerve, the trigeminal nerve in the face.
TRIFARIOUS, [trī-fāer′-i-us], *adj.* branching three ways. [L. *trifarius*].
TRIFID, [trī′-fid], *adj.* (*bot.*) split into three parts; threefold. [L. *trifidus*].
TRIFLE (1), [trīfl], *n.* a thing of very little value or importance; sponge cake soaked in custard, and covered with whipped cream. [OFr. *trufle*].
TRIFLE (2), [trīfl], *v.i.* to act or talk with levity; to indulge in light amusements; to play (with); to hurt the feelings of another with thoughtless levity.
TRIFLER, [trīf′-ler], *n.* a person who trifles.
TRIFLING, [trīf′-ling], *adj.* of small value or importance; insignificant.
TRIFLINGLY, [trīf′-ling-li], *adv.* in a trifling fashion.
TRIFLINGNESS, [trīf′-ling-nes], *n.* the condition of being trifling.
TRIFLOROUS, [trī-flaw′-rus], *adj.* having three flowers.
TRIFOLIATE, [trī-fōl′-i-āt], *adj.* bearing three leaves; ternate. [TRI- and L. *foliatus* leaved].
TRIFOLIOLATE, [trī-fōl′-i-ō-lāt], *adj.* bearing three folioles or leaflets. [TRI- and L. *foliolum* a leaflet].
TRIFOLIUM, [trī-fōl′-i-um], *n.* trefoil; clover. [TRI- and L. *folium* a leaf].
TRIFORIUM, [trī-faw′-ri-um], *n.* an arcaded gallery built below a clerestory over the arches of the nave or transept. [TRI- and L. *foris* a door].
TRIFORM, [trī′-fawm], *adj.* with a triple form; having three parts.
TRIFURCATED, [trī′-furk-āt-ed], *adj.* bearing three branches or forks. [~L. *trifurcus* three-forked].
TRIG (1), [trig], *n.* a sprag for a wheel. [Uncert.].
TRIG (2), [trig], *adj.* (*dial.*) trim, neat, smart. [OScand. *tryggr*].
TRIGAMIST, [tri-gam-ist], *n.* one who has three wives or husbands at the same time.
TRIGAMOUS, [tri′-gam-us], *adj.* of or pertaining to trigamy; (*bot.*) having three sorts of flowers in the same head.
TRIGAMY, [tri′-gam-i], *n.* the condition of having three husbands or wives at the same time. [Gk. *trigamia*].
TRIGEMINAL, [trī-jem′-in-al], *adj.* triple.
TRIGGER, [trig′-er], *n.* a catch to hold the wheel of a carriage on a declivity; the catch of a firearm, which if pulled, looses the lock; **t. fish**, *Balistes maculatus*, a fish so called from the longest spine of the three which form its first dorsal fin; **t. circuit, action, etc.**, a circuit, etc., by which a small initial change produces a large resultant change. [~Du. *trekker*].
TRIGINTALS, [tri-jint′-alz], *n.*(*pl.*) trentals. [~ *triginta* thirty].
TRIGLOT, [trī′-glot′], *adj.* written in three languag [TRI- and Gk. *glotta* language].
TRIGLYPH, [trī′-glif′], *n.* the three-grooved orn mental tablet in the Doric frieze, repeated at equ intervals. [Gk. *trigluphos*].
TRIGLYPHIC, [trī-glif′-ik], *adj.* of or pertaining triglyphs.
TRIGON, [trī′-gon], *n.* a triangle; (*astrol.*) a divisi of the zodiac into groups with three signs in eac a trine; (*mus.*) an ancient triangular lyre or har [Gk. *trigonon*].
TRIGONAL, [trī′-gon-al], *adj.* triangular.
TRIGONEUTIC, [trī′-gon-ewt′-ik], *adj.* having thr broods in a year. [TRI- and Gk. *goneuo* I generat
TRIGONIC, [trī-gon′-ik], *adj.* pertaining to a trigo
TRIGONOMETRIC, TRIGONOMETRICA [trig′-on-ō-met′-rik(-al)], *adj.* pertaining to trigon metry.
TRIGONOMETRICALLY, [trig′-on-ō-met′-rik-al-i] *adv.* by or in accordance with trigonometry.
TRIGONOMETRY, [trig′-on-om′-et-ri], *n.* (*math.*) t science of measuring the sides and angles of triangl and their functions. [TRIGON and Gk. *metria* a measu ing].
TRIGONOUS, [trig′-on-us], *adj.* having three angle
TRIGRAM, [trī′-gram], *n.* a figure or letter compose of three lines or strokes.
TRIGRAMMATIC, TRIGRAMMIC, [trī′-gram-at ik, trī-gram′-ik], *adj.* of three letters.
TRIGRAPH, [trī′-graf], *n.* one sound represented b a combination of three letters.
TRIGYNIAN, [trī-jin′-i-an], *adj.* (*bot.*) (of plant having three pistils. [TRI- and Gk. *gune* woman].
TRIHEDRAL, [trī-hēd′-ral], *adj.* of, or resembling, trihedron.
TRIHEDRON, [trī-hēd′-ron], *n.* (*geom.*) a solid th is triangular in section. [TRI- and Gk. *hedra* a side
TRIJUGOUS, TRIJUGATE, [trī′-jōōg-us, trī′-jōō āt], *adj.* (*bot.*) with three pairs of leaflets. [TRI- and *jugum* yoke].
TRILABIATE, [trī-lāb′-i-āt], *adj.* with three lips.
TRILATERAL, [trī-lat′-er-al], *adj.* with three side
TRILATERALLY, [trī-lat′-er-al-i], *adv.* in the mann of a trilateral figure.
TRILBY, [tril′-bi], *n.* a certain shape of soft felt ha [*Trilby* by Gerald du Maurier].
TRILEMMA, [trī-lem′-a], *n.* a choice between thr alternative courses of action. [TRI- and Gk. *lemm* something received].
TRILINEAR, [trī-lin′-i-ar], *adj.* having, or enclose by, three lines.
TRILINGUAL, [trī-ling′-gwal], *adj.* written in, speal ing, three languages.
TRILITERAL, [trī-lit′-er-al], *adj.* consisting of thr letters.
TRILITH, TRILITHON, [trī′-lith(-on)], *n.* a pr historic monument of three large stones placed lil door-posts and a lintel. [TRI- and Gk. *lithos* a stone
TRILL (1), [tril], *n.* a quaver; a shake on two adjace notes in singing or playing; the vibratory notes in bird's song; a warble; (*phon.*) a sound produced b the vibration of the tongue. [Fr. *trille*].
TRILL (2), [tril], *v.t. and i.* to utter with a trill; to si or play with a quavering or tremulous quality; t quaver. [~Fr. *triller*].
TRILLANDO, [tril-and′-ō], *adv.* (*mus.*) in a vibrato manner; with trills. [It. *trillando*].
TRILLION, [tril′-yon], *n.* the product of a millio involved to the third power, and expressed by a un with eighteen zeros; in America, a million times million, that is, a unit of twelve zeros. [TRI- an MILLION].
TRILOBATE, [trī-lō-bāt], *adj.* (*biol.*) bearing three lobe
TRILOBED, [trī′-lōbd′], *adj.* trilobate.
TRILOBITE, [trī′-lō-bīt], *n.* a trilobate sea arachni
TRILOCULAR, [trī-lok′-yōō-ler], *adj.* (*bot.*) thre celled.
TRILOGY, [tri′-loj-i], *n.* a group of three related litera or dramatic compositions. [Gk. *trilogia*].
TRILUMINAR, [trī-lōō′-min-er], *adj.* having thre lights. [TRI-and L. *lumen* light].
TRILUMINOUS, [trī-lōō′-min-us], *adj.* trilumina
TRIM (1), [trim], *n.* good or neat condition; order.
TRIM (2), [trim], *adj.* neat; in good order.
TRIM (3), [trim], *v.t.* to put in order, make neat; t adjust the burning of (a lamp); to adjust the sails (a boat); to ornament the edge of (a garment, etc. to adjust the relationship of (two or more wirele circuits). [OE. *trymman* to fortify].

RIMENSUAL, [trī-men'-sew-al], *adj.* every three months; quarterly.
RIMEROUS, [trī'-mer-us], *adj.* having three segments. [Gk. *trimeres*].
RIMESTER, [tri-mest'-er], *n.* a term or period of three months. [L. *trimestris*].
RIMESTRIAL, [tri-mes'-tri-al], *adj.* trimensual.
RIMETER, [tri'-mit-er], *n.* a verse of three feet. [Gk. *trimetros*].
RIMETRIC, [tri-met'-rik], *adj.* in, relating to, a trimeter.
RIMETRICAL, [tri-met'-rik-al], *adj.* trimetric.
RIMLY, [trim'-li], *adv.* in trim fashion.
RIMMER, [trim'-er], *n.* one who trims; a device for trimming a wireless circuit; (*fig.*) an unprincipled opportunist; a fishing float.
RIMMING, [trim'-ing], *n.* the trimmed edge of a fabric; unessential ornaments.
RIMNESS, [trim'-nes], *n.* the state of being trim.
RIMORPHIC, [trī-mawf'-ik], *adj.* existing in three forms.
RIMORPHISM, [trī-mawf'-izm], *n.* the property of crystallizing or of existing in three distinct forms.
RIMURTI, [tri-mur'-ti], *n.* the Hindu trinity: Brahma, Vishnu, Siva. [Hind. *trimurti*].
RINACRITE, [tri-nak'-rīt], *n.* the brown micaceous mineral found in Sicily. [Gk. *Trinakria* Sicily].
RINAL, [trī'-nal], *adj.* threefold. [L. *trinalis*].
RINARY, [trī'-ner-i], *adj.* ternary. [L. *trinarius*].
RINCOMALEE, [trin-kom'-al-ē'], *n.* the wood of *Berrya ammonilla*. [*Trincomalee*, in Ceylon].
RINDLE, [trindl], *v.t. and i.* to trundle. [ME. *trindelen*].
RINE, [trīn], *n.* the aspect of heavenly bodies 120 degrees apart. [L. *trinus*].
RINERVATE, [trī-nurv'-āt], *adj.* (*bot.*) having three unbranched nerves extending from the base to the apex of a leaf. [TRI- and L. *nervus* nerve].
RINERVED, [trī'-nurvd], *adj.* trinervate.
RINGLE, [tring'-gl], *n.* a curtain-rod; (*arch.*) a narrow rectangular moulding. [Fr. *tringle*].
RINITARIAN, [tri-nit-āer'-i-an], *n.* a believer in Trinitarianism.
RINITARIANISM, [tri'-nit-āer'-i-an-izm], *n.* the doctrine of the Trinity.
RINITROTOLUOL, [trī'-nī-trō-tol'-yōō-ol], *n.* the high explosive T.N.T. obtained by the action of nitric acid on toluene.
RINITY, [trin'-it-i], *n.* a unity consisting of three parts; a group of three things or persons closely connected; (*theol.*) the indivisible unity of Father, Son, and Holy Ghost. [L. *trinitas*].
RINKET, [tringk'-it], *n.* a small ornament, a worthless little jewel. [ME. *trenket* small knife].
RINKETER, [tringk'-it-er], *n.* one who is fond of worthless trinkets; †a Papist.
RINKETRY, [tringk'-it-ri], *n.* trinkets; love of trinkets.
RINOCTIAL, [tri-nok'-shal], *adj.* lasting three nights.
RINODAL, [trī-nōd'-al], *adj.* having three nodes.
RINOMIAL, [trī-nōm'-i-al], *adj.* having three nomes; having three algebraic terms.
RIO, [trē'-ō], *n.* a musical composition for three performers; a group of three persons, *esp.* musical performers. [It. *trio*].
RIOCTAHEDRAL, [trī-ok'-ta-hē'-dral], *adj.* (of crystals) presenting three ranges of faces, one above another, each range containing eight faces.
RIOCTILE, [trī-ok'-tīl], *n.* an aspect of planets distant 135 degrees. [TRI- and L. *octo* eight].
RIODE, [trī'-ōd], *n.* (*wirel.*) a three-electrode valve. [TRI- and Gk. *hodos* path].
RIOLET, [trī'-ō-let], *n.* a stanza of eight lines, the first, third, fourth, fifth and seventh lines having a common rhyme, the second, sixth, and eighth lines rhyming together, the fourth and seventh lines identical with the first, and the eighth identical with the second. [Fr. *triolet*].
RIOR, [trī'-er], *n.* (*leg.*) one judging the validity of a challenge to jurors.
RIP (1), [trip], *n.* a short journey or excursion, a pleasure-voyage; the act of tripping or stumbling; the deliberate tripping of another by interposing one's foot.
RIP (2), [trip], *v.t. and i.* to make to fall by sudden interference with the feet; to catch out in a falsehood or error; to loose (an anchor) by means of a cable; to move with short, light, rapid steps; to stumble through catching one's foot against a thing; (*fig.*) to commit an error, betray oneself. [OFr. *tripper*].

TRIPARTIENT, [trī-pah'-shi-ent], *adj.* dividing into three parts.
TRIPARTITE, [trī-paht'-īt], *adj.* divided into three parts; having three corresponding parts; pertaining to three parties. [L. *tripartitus*].
TRIPARTITION, [trī'-pah-ti'-shun], *n.* a division by three or into three.
TRIPE, [trīp], *n.* the stomach of the ox used as food; literary rubbish. [Fr. *tripe*].
TRIPEDAL, [trī-ped'-al], *adj.* having three feet. [L. *tripedalis*].
TRIPE-DE-ROCHE, [trēp'-de-rosh], *n.* an Arctic lichen, *Gyrophora cylindrica*, used as food.
TRIPERSONAL, [trī-pur'-son-al], *adj.* consisting of three persons in one.
TRIPERSONALITY, [trī'-pur'-son-al'-it-i], *n.* the state of being tripersonal.
TRIPETALOUS, [trī-pet'-al-us], *adj.* (*bot.*) having three petals.
TRIP-HAMMER, [trip'-ham'-er], *n.* a tilt-hammer.
TRIPHANE, [trī'-fān], *n.* the mineral spodumene. [Gk. *triphanes*].
TRIPHIBIOUS, [trī'-fib'-i-us], *adj.* concerning, inhabiting, land, sea, and air; **t. warfare,** actions carried out in all three elements simultaneously, combined operations. [TRI- and (AM)PHIBIOUS].
TRIPHTHONG, [trif'-thong], *n.* a group of three vowels in one compound sound. [TRI- and (DI)PHTHONG].
TRIPHTHONGAL, [trif-thong'-gl], *adj.* pertaining to or consisting of a triphthong.
TRIPHYLINE, [trif'-il-ēn], *n.* a mineral composed of the phosphates of lithium, manganese, and iron.
TRIPHYLLOUS, [trif'-il-us], *adj.* (*bot.*) three-leaved. [Gk. *triphullos*].
TRIPINNATE, [trī-pin'-āt], *adj.* having pinnate leaflets on tertiary petioles.
TRIPLANE, [trī'-plān], *n.* an aeroplane with three planes.
TRIPLE (1), [tripl], *adj.* threefold. [L. *triplus*].
TRIPLE (2), [tripl], *v.t. and i.* to multiply threefold.
TRIPLE-CROWNED, [tripl'-krownd'], *adj.* having three crowns.
TRIPLE-HEADED, [tripl'-hed'-ed], *adj.* having three heads.
TRIPLET, [trip'-let], *n.* one of three children born of a single gestation; a group of three successive rhyming lines.
TRIPLEX, [trip'-lex], *adj.* threefold; (*mus.*) in triple (time); **T. Glass,** (*prot.*) a three-ply amalgam of glass and micaceous substance. [L. *triplus*].
TRIPLICATE (1), [trip'-li-kat], *n.* one of three copies; **in t.,** so as to provide three copies.
TRIPLICATE (2), [tri'-plik-at], *adj.* threefold; in three copies. [L. *triplicatus*].
TRIPLICATE (3), [tri'-plik-āt], *v.t.* to treble.
TRIPLICATION, [tri'-plik-ā'-shun], *n.* the state of being triplicate; the act of triplicating. [L. *triplicatio*].
TRIPLICITY, [tri-plis'-it-i], *n.* the state of being threefold. [L. *triplicitas*].
TRIPLITE, [tri'-plīt], *n.* a crystalline phosphate of the oxides of manganese and iron, cleavable in three directions perpendicular to each other.
TRIPOD, [trī'-pod], *n.* a stool, vessel, supported on three legs; a support with three legs. [Gk. *tripous*].
TRIPOLI, [tri'-pol-i], *n.* an infusorial earth. [*Tripoli*, in North Africa].
TRIPOS, [trī'-pos'], *n.* an honours examination at Cambridge. [Gk. *tripous*, the stool on which the bachelor sat at the degree-giving].
TRIPPANT, [trip'-ant], *adj.* (*her.*) walking or trotting. [OFr. *trippant*].
TRIPPER, [trip'-er], *n.* one who trips; (*coll.*) a holiday excursionist, a tourist.
TRIPPING, [trip'-ing], *adj.* walking nimbly; (of words) coming nimbly off the tongue.
TRIPPINGLY, [trip'-ing-li], *adv.* in a tripping manner.
TRIPSTICK, [trip'-stik], *n.* a trapstick.
TRIPTOTE, [trip'-tōt], *n.* (*gram.*) a noun having three cases only. [Gk. *triptotos*].
TRIPTYCH, [trip'-tik], *n.* a picture or design on three panels, those at the side hinging on that in the centre. [Gk. *triptukhos* having three layers].
TRIPTYQUE, [tript'-ēk], *n.* a customs permit for the temporary importation of a motor-car into a particular country. [Fr. *triptyque*].
TRIPUDIARY, [tri-pew'-di-er-i], *adj.* of, pertaining to, performed by, dancing. [L. *tripudium*].
TRIPUDIATION, [tri-pew'-di-ā'-shun], *n.* a leaping, dancing, in triumph or contempt. [L. *tripudiatio*].

TRIQUETROUS, [trī'-kwet-rus], *adj.* with three edges. [L. *triquetrus*].
TRIRADIATED, [trī-rād'-i-āt-ed], *adj.* having three rays.
TRIREME, [trī'-rēm], *n.* a warship of the classical period, having its oars arranged in banks of three. [L. *triremis*].
TRIRHOMBOIDAL, [trī'-rom-boid'-al], *adj.* having three rhombic faces or sides.
TRISACRAMENTARIAN, [trī-sak'-ra-ment-āer'-i-an], *n.* one who admits of three sacraments, and no more.
TRISAGION, [trī-sāj'-i-on], *n.* a Greek hymn commencing with a threefold invocation to God. [Gk. *trisagion*].
TRISECT, [trī-sekt'], *v.t.* to divide into three equal parts. [TRI- and L. *secare* to cut].
TRISECTION, [trī-sek'-shun], *n.* division into three equal parts.
TRISEPALOUS, [trī-sep'-al-us], *adj.* having three sepals.
TRISKELE, [tris'-kēl], *n.* a device of three radiating spokes, *esp.* the three-legged device of the Isle of Man. [Gk. *triskeles* three-legged].
TRISMEGISTUS, [tris'-mej-is'-tus], *n.* an attributory name of the god Hermes. [Gk. *trismegistos* thrice-greatest].
TRISMUS, [tris'-mus], *n.* tetanus of the jaw. [Gk. *trismos*].
TRISOCTAHEDRON, [tris-ok'-ta-hē'-dron], *n.* a solid bounded by twenty-four equal faces.
TRISPERMOUS, [trī-spur'-mus], *adj.* (*bot.*) three-seeded.
TRISPLANCHNIC, [trī-splangk'-nik], *adj.* pertaining to the three splanchnic nerves.
TRISTE, [trēst], *adj.* melancholy; (*coll.*) unfortunate. [Fr. *triste* sad].
TRISTESSE, [trēs'-tes'], *n.* sadness. [Fr. *tristesse*].
TRISTFUL, [trist'-fōōl], *adj.* sorrowful.
TRISTFULLY, [trist'-fōōl-i], *adv.* in tristful fashion.
TRISTICHOUS, [tri'-stik-us], *adj.* in three ranks. [Gk. *tristikhos*].
TRISULCATE, [trī-sul'-kāt], *adj.* having three furrows. [L. *trisulcus*].
TRISYLLABIC, [tri'-sil-ab'-ik], *adj.* having three syllables.
TRISYLLABLE, [tri-sil'-abl], *n.* a word of three syllables.
TRITE, [trīt], *adj.* commonplace, pettily platitudinous, stale with use, hackneyed. [L. *tritus* rubbed, worn].
TRITELY, [trīt'-li], *adv.* in a trite manner.
TRITENESS, [trīt'-nes], *n.* the quality of being trite.
TRITERNATE, [trī-turn'-āt], *adj.* thrice ternate.
TRITHEISM, [trī'-thi-izm], *n.* the heresy teaching that the Trinity consists of three separate persons.
TRITHEIST, [trī'-thi-ist], *n.* an adherent of tritheism.
TRITHEISTIC, [trī'-thi-ist'-ik], *adj.* of, or pertaining to, tritheism.
TRITOMA, [trī-tōm'-a], *n.* (*bot.*) the torch lily or red-hot poker, *Kniphofia uvaria*. [Gk. *tritomos*].
TRITON, [trī'-ton], *n.* the son of Poseidon and Amphitrite; a sea demi-god. [Gk. *Triton*].
TRITONE, [trī'-tōn], *n.* an interval of three tones. [Gk. *tritonos*].
TRITUBERCULAR, [trī'-tew-burk'-yōō-ler], *adj.* having three tubercles.
TRITURABLE, [trit'-yōō-rabl], *adj.* able to be triturated.
TRITURATE, [trit'-yōō-rāt], *v.t.* to grind to powder, to pulverize. [L. *triturare* to thresh].
TRITURATION, [trit'-yōō-rā'-shun], *n.* the act of triturating; the state of being triturated. [L. *trituratio*].
TRIUMPH (1), [trī'-umf], *n.* the state of triumphing; a great, complete, and glorious victory, a great success; the feeling of exaltation of a victory; (*Rom. hist.*) a processional entry into Rome at the head of his army, granted to a general in honour of an important victory. [L. *triumphus*].
TRIUMPH (2), [trī'-umf], *v.i.* to be gloriously victorious or successful; to exult in victory; **to t. over**, to overcome; to exult over. [L. *triumphare*].
TRIUMPHAL, [trī-um'-fal], *adj.* relating to a triumph; **t. ornaments**, the insignia worn by a triumphing general, *esp.* when awarded as substitute for a full triumph. [L. *triumphalis*].
TRIUMPHANT, [trī-um'-fant], *adj.* triumphing; victorious; exultant. [L. *triumphans*].
TRIUMPHANTLY, [trī-um'-fant-li], *adv.* in triumphant fashion.
TRIUMPHER, [trī'-um-fer], *n.* one who triumphs.
TRIUMVIR, [trī'-um-vur'], *n.* one of three co-rulers (*Rom. hist.*) a member of one of the triple coalition that ruled Rome in the last days of the Republic. [L. *triumviri*].
TRIUMVIRAL, [trī-um'-vi-ral], *adj.* pertaining to a triumvir or triumvirate. [L. *triumviralis*].
TRIUMVIRATE, [trī-um'-vi-rat], *n.* government by three men in coalition. [L. *triumviratus*].
TRIUNE, [trī'-yōōn], *adj.* three in one. [TRI- and L. *unus* one].
TRIUNITY, [trī-yōōn'-it-i], *n.* trinity.
TRIVALENCY, [trī'-vāl'-en-si], *n.* the state of being trivalent.
TRIVALENT, [trī-vāl'-ent], *adj.* combining with three univalent atoms. [TRI- and L. *valere* to be worth].
TRIVALVULAR, [trī-valv'-yōō-ler], *adj.* three valved.
TRIVERBIAL, [trī-vurb'-i-al], *adj.* (*Rom. hist.*) relating to days on which juridical proceedings might be heard. [TRI- and L. *verbum* word].
TRIVET, TREVET, [triv'-it], *n.* a tripod stand for vessel placed over a fire. [Uncert.].
TRIVIAL, [triv'-i-al], *adj.* of little importance, slight [L. *trivialis*].
TRIVIALISM, [triv'-i-al-izm], *n.* a triviality.
TRIVIALITY, [triv'-i-al'-it-i], *n.* a trivial matter [L. *trivialis*].
TRIVIALIZE, [triv'-i-al-īz], *v.t.* to render trivial.
TRIVIALLY, [triv'-i-al-i], *adv.* in trivial fashion.
TRIVIALNESS, [triv'-i-al-nes], *n.* the state of being trivial.
TRIVIUM, [triv'-i-um], *n.* grammar, rhetoric, and logic, the lower division of the seven arts. [L. *trivium* the junction of three roads].
TRI-WEEKLY, [trī-wēk'-li], *adj.* thrice a week; every three weeks.
TROAT, [trōt], *v.i.* to cry, as a buck in rutting time [Echoic].
TROCAR, [trō'-kah(r)], *n.* (*med.*) a surgical instrument for removing fluid from the body. [Fr. *troquart*].
TROCHAIC, [trō-kā'-ik], *adj.* consisting of trochees [Gk. *trokhaikos*].
TROCHANTER, [trō-kant'-er], *n.* (*anat.*) one of the processes at the upper end of the thigh-bone. [~Gk. *trokhos* running].
TROCHE, [trōsh], *n.* a round, flat lozenge. [OF. *trochisque*].
TROCHEE, [trō'-ki], *n.* a foot consisting of a long and a short syllable or a stressed followed by an unstressed syllable. [Gk. *trokhaios*].
TROCHILIC, [trō-kil'-ik], *adj.* able to turn (as a wheel). [Gk. *trokhilos*].
TROCHILICS, [trō-kil'-iks], *n.(pl.)* the science of rotary motion.
TROCHILUS, [trok'-il-us], *n.* a genus of humming birds; (*arch.*) a hollow ring round the base of a column [L. *trochilus*].
TROCHLEA, [trok'-li-a], *n.* a pulley-like arrangement of bones or cartilage. [Gk. *trokhilia* sheaf of a pulley].
TROCHLEAR, [trok'-li-er], *adj.* pulley-shaped.
TROCHLEARY, [trok'-li-er-i], *adj.* pertaining to the trochlea.
TROCHOID, [trō'-koid], *n.* the curve traced by a point on a rolling disk. [Gk. *trokhoeides* wheel-like].
TROCO, [trō'-kō], *n.* an old English variant of billiards in which wooden balls had to be rolled into a series of holes. [It. *trucco* a billiard-board].
TROD, [trod], *pret.* of TREAD.
TRODDEN, [trod'-en], *p.pt.* of TREAD.
TROGLODYTE, [trog'-lōd-īt], *n.* a cave-dweller, *esp.* in contempt. [Gk. *troglodutes*].
TROGLODYTISM, [trog'-lōd-īt-izm], *n.* the state of being a troglodyte.
TROGON, [trō'-gon], *n.* a genus of brilliantly coloured Central American birds. [~Gk. *trogo* I gnaw].
TROJAN (1), [trō'-jan], *n.* an inhabitant of ancient Troy; (*fig.*) a highly energetic, vigorous, and enduring worker. [L. *trojanus*].
TROJAN (2), [trō'-jan], *adj.* of, or relating to Troy.
TROLL (1), [trōl], *n.* (*myth.*) an amphibious giant; dwarf troglodyte. [OScand. *troll*].
TROLL (2), [trōl], *v.t.* and *i.* to sing carelessly and cheerfully; to fish with trailed bait. [OFr. *troller*].
TROLLEY, [trol'-i], *n.* a four-wheeled truck running on rails; a light, two-wheeled push-cart; the overhead arm of an electric tramcar or bus. [Uncert.].
TROLLEY-BUS, [trol'-i-bus'], *n.* a bus propelled by electricity supplied from a trolley.
TROLL-FLOWER, [trōl'-flow'-er], *n.* the plant *Trollius europæus*, the common European globeflower.

TROLLOP, [trol′-op], *n.* a blowsy and disreputable female. [~TROLL].
TROLLOPY, [trol′-op-i], *adj.* trollop-like.
TROLLY, [trol′-i], *n.* a trolley, *esp.* a railway-porter's truck.
TROMBONE, [trom′-bōn′], *n.* a trumpet-like brass wind instrument, whose notes are controlled by a sliding tube or valves. [It. *trombone*].
TROMBONIST, [trom-bōn′-ist], *n.* a player of the trombone.
TROMMEL, [trom′-el], *n.* a mechanical sieve used in mining. [Germ. *trommel* a drum].
TROMP, [tromp], *n.* a device for producing a blast by means of water pressure. [Fr. *trompe*].
TROMPIL, [trom′-pil], *n.* an aperture in a tromp.
TRONA, [trō′-na], *n.* a native mixed carbonate of sodium. [Arab. *tron*].
TROOP (1), [trōōp], *n.* a band, a group; a small body of cavalry; (*pl.*) soldiery, military forces. [LL. *troppus* flock].
TROOP (2), [trōōp], *v.t.* and *i.* to move in large groups; **to t. the colour,** to parade the regimental standard ceremonially.
TROOP-CARRIER, [trōōp′-ka′-ri-er], *n.* an aeroplane designed for the transport of troops.
TROOPER, [trōōp′-er], *n.* a cavalryman; **to swear like a t.,** to swear profusely and hard.
TROOPSHIP, [trōōp′-ship], *n.* a military transport vessel.
TROPAEOLUM, [trō-pē′-ō-lum], *n.* a genus of thirty-five species of American plants, including those popularly known as nasturtiums. [Gk. *tropaion* trophy].
TROPE, [trōp], *n.* an expression used metaphorically or figuratively. [Gk. *tropos* a turn].
TROPHI, [trō′-fī], *n.*(*pl.*) the organs employed in feeding. [Gk. *trophos* feeder].
TROPHIC, [tro′-fik], *adj.* pertaining to nutrition. [Gk. *trophikos*].
TROPHOSPERM, [trof′-ō-spurm], *n.* (*bot.*) that part of the ovary from which the ovules arise. [~Gk. *trophe* food and SPERM].
TROPHY, [trō′-fi], *n.* the spoil taken from a conquered enemy as symbol of victory, *esp.* the pile of enemy arms set up on a battlefield by the victorious party; a prize awarded for a sporting contest. [Gk. *tropaion*].
TROPHY-MONEY, [trō′-fi-mun′-i], *n.* a duty formerly paid by householders toward providing military accoutrements for the militia.
TROPIC (1), [trop′-ik], *n.* the latitude at which the sun is directly overhead at noon at the winter solstice (**t. of Capricorn**) or at the summer solstice (**t. of Cancer**); (*pl.*) the torrid zone between these two latitudes. [Gk. *tropikos* pertaining to a turn].
TROPIC (2), [trop′-ik], *adj.* tropical.
TROPICAL (1), [trōp′-ik-al], *adj.* relating to a trope.
TROPICAL (2), [trōp′-ik-al], *adj.* of, or relating to, the tropics; excessively hot.
TROPICALLY, [trōp′-ik-al-i], *adv.* in tropical fashion.
TROPIC-BIRD, [trop′-ik-burd′], *n.* a long-tailed oceanic bird of the genus *Phaethon* allied to the gannet; the boatswain-bird.
TROPIST, [trō′-pist], *n.* one delighting in tropes.
TROPOLOGICAL, [trōp′-ō-loj′-ik-al], *adj.* relating to the use of tropes.
TROPOLOGY, [trōp-ol′-oj-i], *n.* the use of tropes; the figurative interpretation of the Scriptures. [Gk. *tropologia*].
TROPOSPHERE, [trop′-ō-sfēer], *n.* (*meteor.*) the (lower) layer of the earth's atmosphere, in which increasing altitude is correlated with a fall in temperature. [Gk. *tropos* turn and SPHERE].
TROT (1), [trot], *n.* the act, pace, of trotting; (*coll.*) a silly old person.
TROT (2), [trot], *v.t.* and *i.* (of a horse, etc.) to move at a pace between walking and galloping; (of a person) to run with brief, brisk steps; to make a horse trot; **to t. out,** to bring out (as if of interest) commonplace old sentiments, etc. [ME. *trotten*].
TROTH, [trōth], *n.* fidelity; sworn word. [OE. *treowth*].
TROTHPLIGHT, [trōth′-plīt], *n.* the act of betrothing or plighting faith.
TROTHPLIGHTED, [trōth′-plīt′-ed], *adj.* pledged, betrothed.
TROTSKYITE, [trot′-ski-īt], *n.* a believer in immediate world revolution and the policy of uncompromising hostility to class enemies. [Leon *Trotsky*].
TROTTER, [trot′-er], *n.* one who trots; a pig's foot; (*coll.*) a foot.
TROUBADOUR, [trōō′-ba-dŏŏer′], *n.* a medieval (chiefly Provençal) wandering singer and amorous poet. [Provenc. *trobador*].
TROUBLE (1), [trubl], *n.* inconvenience, laborious difficulty; state of disturbance or affliction; a disease, a persistent ailment; the state of being mentally disturbed, worry. [Fr. *trouble*].
TROUBLE (2), [trubl], *v.t.* and *i.* to stir, disturb, set into movement; to agitate, worry, annoy; to cause inconvenience to, to pester, to bother; to be anxious, to feel agitated; to take care, pay attention. [~L. *turbula* from *turba* a crowd].
TROUBLER, [trub′-ler], *n.* one who troubles or agitates.
TROUBLESOME, [trubl′-sum], *adj.* causing trouble or inconvenience, unruly.
TROUBLESOMELY, [trubl′-sum-li], *adv.* in a troublesome manner.
TROUBLESOMENESS, [trubl′-sum-nes], *n.* the quality of being troublesome.
TROUBLOUS, [trub′-lus], *adj.* troubled, disturbed, agitated.
TROUGH, [trof, truf], *n.* a long, open vessel holding the water and food of domestic animals; the depression between two waves. [OE. *trog*].
TROUNCE, [trownts], *v.t.* to beat severely, thoroughly defeat. [~Fr. *tronce* piece of wood].
TROUNCING, [trown′-sing], *n.* a severe beating.
TROUPE, [trōōp], *n.* a company of players or performers. [Fr. *troupe*].
TROUSERED, [trow′-zerd], *adj.* wearing trousers.
TROUSERING, [trow′-zer-ing], *n.* cloth for trousers.
TROUSERS, TROWSERS†, [trow′-zerz], *n.*(*pl.*) a garment for the lower part of the body, consisting of two tubular coverings for the legs, joining at the groin; long drawers. [Fr. *trousse* bundle].
TROUSSE, [trōōs], *n.* a set of surgical or other instruments in a small case. [Fr. *trousse* bundle].
TROUSSEAU, [trōō′-sō], *n.* the clothes and personal necessaries with which a bride is provided at her marriage. [Fr. *trousseau*].
TROUT, [trowt], *n.* any fish of the genus *Salmo*; a small spotted freshwater fish of this genus; (*slang*) a pigheaded fool. [ME. *trute*].
TROUTING, [trowt′-ing], *n.* fishing for trout.
TROUT-STREAM, [trowt′-strēm], *n.* a stream in which trout breed.
TROUVERE, trouvère, [trōō-vāer′], *n.* one of the French medieval poets who composed the *chansons de geste*, a minstrel. [Fr. *trouvère*].
TROVER, [trō′-ver], *n.* the acquisition of goods by finding or similar means; legal action to recover property wrongfully detained. [OFr. *trover* to find].
TROW, [trō, trow], *v.i.* to believe, assume. [OE. *truwian* to trust].
TROWEL, [trowl], *n.* a small, hollow-bladed implement used for scooping earth in gardening; a flat, diamond-shaped implement used for spreading mortar. [~L. *trulla* ladle].

TROWEL

TROWELLED, [trow′-eld], *adj.* smoothed with a trowel.
TROWSERS†, see TROUSERS.
TROY WEIGHT, [troi′-wāt′], *n.* a weight of 5,760 grains to the ounce by which gold, silver, and precious stones are weighed. [*Troyes*, in France].
TRUANCY, [trōō′-an-si], *n.* the act of playing truant.
TRUANT (1), [trōō′-ant], *n.* a person who remains away from his duty for a personal whim, *esp.* a child who absents himself from school. [OFr. *truant* vagrant].
TRUANT (2), [trōō′-ant], *adj.* being, relating to, a truant.
TRUANTLY, [trōō′-ant-li], *adv.* like a truant.
TRUANTSHIP, [trōō′-ant-ship], *n.* truancy.
TRUCE, [trōōs], *n.* an agreement between combatants to suspend hostilities temporarily without settling the cause at issue. [ME. *trewes*].
TRUCEBREAKER, [trōōs′-brāk′-er], *n.* one who breaks a truce.
TRUCIAL, [trōōsh′-al], *adj.* of, pertaining to, bound or regulated by, a truce. [TRUCE].
TRUCIDATION, [trōō-sid-ā′-shun], *n.* a savage slaughter. [~L. *trucidare*].
TRUCK (1), [truk], *n.* a light wagon for carrying goods; an open railway wagon; (*U.S.*) a lorry. [L. *trochus*].
TRUCK (2), [truk], *n.* trade; commerce; payment in kind; (*coll.*) dealings (with). [Fr. *troque*].

TRUCK (3), [truk], *v.t. and i.* to exchange, to barter; to bargain, have dealings with. [Fr. *troquer*].
TRUCKAGE (1), [truk'-ij], *n.* transport by truck.
TRUCKAGE (2), [truk'-ij], *n.* barter; commercial dealings.
TRUCKER, [truk'-er], *n.* one who traffics by exchange of goods.
TRUCKLE (1), [trukl], *n.* a small wheel or castor; a truckle-bed. [Gk. *trokhilia* sheaf of a pulley].
TRUCKLE (2), [trukl], *v.i.* to submit, to yield obsequiously; *v.t.* to trundle. [*Prec.*].
TRUCKLE-BED, [trukl'-bed'], *n.* a bed that runs on wheels, and may be pushed under another; a trundle-bed.
TRUCKLING, [truk'-ling], *n.* obsequious subservience.
TRUCULENCE, [truk'-yōō-lents], *n.* the quality of being truculent. [L. *truculentia*].
TRUCULENT, [truk'-yōō-lent], *adj.* ferociously insolent, bullyingly violent. [L. *truculentus*].
TRUCULENTLY, [truk'-yōō-lent-li], *adv.* in a truculent manner.
TRUDGE, [truj], *v.i.* to walk with laborious determination, to tramp along wearily. [Uncert.].
TRUDGEN, [truj'-en], *n.* a style of hand-over-hand swimming. [*Trudgen*, who popularized the stroke in the 1860s].
TRUE, [trōō], *adj.* conforming to fact and reality, not false or fictitious; faithful, loyal, honest; rightful, proper; accurate, without variation. [OE. *treow*].
TRUE-BLUE, [trōō'-blōō'], *adj.* of inflexible honesty and steadfastness.
TRUE-BORN, [trōō'-bawn], *adj.* legitimate; true to type.
TRUE-BRED, [trōō'-bred'], *adj.* thoroughbred.
TRUE-HEARTED, [trōō'-haht'-ed], *adj.* loyal, honest, sincere.
TRUE LOVE, [trōō'-luv'], *n.* faithful and exclusive love; the object so loved; the plant, *Paris quadrifolia*.
TRUEPENNY†, [trōō'-pen'-i], *n.* an honest fellow.
TRUFFLE, [trufl], *n.* a fleshy underground fungus, much esteemed in cookery. [Fr. *truffle*].
TRUG, [trug], *n.* a hod for mortar; an old measure of wheat; a shallow gardening basket made of wood. [Uncert.].
TRUISM, [trōō'-izm], *n.* a platitude.
TRULL, [trul], *n.* a trollop. [Germ. *trulle*].
TRULY, [trōō'-li], *adv.* in truth; in true fashion; **yours t.**, a common formal subscription to a business communication.
TRUMP (1), [trump], *n.* a trumpet. [ME. *trump*].
TRUMP (2), [trump], *n.* (*card games*) a card of the suit that, for the time being, ranks above the other three suits. [~TRIUMPH].
TRUMP (3), [trump], *v.t.* to play a trump on (a card of another suit); to play a trump on the card of.
TRUMP (4), [trump], *v.t.* **to t. up**, to fabricate, invent, falsely allege an accusation or excuse. [Uncert.].
TRUMPERY, [trump'-er-i], *adj.* worthless, tawdry, trashy, silly and useless. [Fr. *tromperie*].
TRUMPET (1), [trump'-it], *n.* a brass wind instrument, straight or slightly curved, giving a high, powerful note; the sound of a trumpet; something that proclaims loudly. [Fr. *trompette*].
TRUMPET (2), [trump'-it], *v.t. and i.* to sound on a trumpet, to proclaim; to make a sound like that of a trumpet.
TRUMPETER, [trump'-it-er], *n.* one who sounds a trumpet; the swan, *Cygnus buccinator*.
TRUMPETER-FISH, [trump'-it-er-fish], *n.* a sea-fish so named from its tubular muzzle, *Centriscus scolopax*.
TRUMPET-FISH, [trump'-it-fish], *n.* the Australasian fish, *Latris hecateia*.
TRUMPET-FLOWER, [trump'-it-flow(r)], *n.* a flower so called from its shape, *Tecoma radicans*.
TRUMPET-MAJOR, [trum'-pit-māj'-er], *n.* the leading trumpeter in a cavalry regiment.
TRUMPET-SHELL, [trump'-it-shel'], *n.* a shell of the genus *Triton*.
TRUMPET-TONGUED, [trump'-it-tungd'], *adj.* loud-voiced; loudly proclaiming.
TRUMPET-TREE, [trump'-it-trē], *n.* the tropical American tree, *Cecropia peltata*.
TRUNCAL, [trungk'-al], *adj.* relating to the trunk.
TRUNCATE (1), [trungk'-āt], *adj.* truncated.
TRUNCATE (2), [trungk-āt'], *v.t.* to slice off a projecting angle or edge of so as to leave a plain face; to cut down, cut short. [L. *truncare*].
TRUNCATED, [trungk-āt'-ed], *adj.* truncate; cut off short.
TRUNCATION, [trungk-ā'-shun], *n.* the act of truncating; the state of being truncated. [L. *truncatio*].
TRUNCHEON (1), [trunch'-un], *n.* a short rounded club, used as a wand of office or as a weapon. [OFr. *truncheon*].
TRUNCHEON (2), [trunch'-un], *v.t.* to beat with a truncheon.
TRUNCHEONEER, [trunch'-un-ēer'], *n.* a person armed with a truncheon.
TRUNDLE (1), [trundl], *n.* a castor, a small wheel; a low truck. [~OE. *trendel* ring].
TRUNDLE (2), [trundl], *v.t. and i.* to roll, wheel along heavily; to move along on, or as if on, wheels. [OFr. *trondeler*].
TRUNDLE-BED, [trundl'-bed'], *n.* a truckle-bed.
TRUNDLE-HEAD, [trundl'-hed'], *n.* the wheel that turns a millstone.
TRUNDLE-TAIL, [trundl'-tāl], *n.* a curled tail; a dog, so called from his tail.
TRUNK, [trungk], *n.* the main body of a tree; the torso; a large case or box; a long flexible proboscis; **t.-call**, a long-distance telephone call; **t. road**, a main long-distance road providing communication between important centres. [L. *truncus*].
TRUNK-HOSE, [trungk'-hōz], *n.(pl.)* short, wide breeches, formerly worn, that were gathered in above or just below the knee.
TRUNNION, [trun'-yon], *n.* one of the two supporting pivots of a cannon, etc. [Fr. *trognon* core of a fruit].
TRUNNION-RING, [trun'-yon-ring'], *n.* a ring on a gun next before the trunnions.
TRUSS (1), [trus], *n.* a bundle of hay or straw tied at the ends; a rupture support; a framework of girders used to support a roof, etc. [OFr. *trousse*].
TRUSS (2), [trus], *v.t.* to bind up into, or as if into, a truss.
TRUSSED, [trust], *adj.* bound in a truss.
TRUSSING, [trus'-ing], *n.* the timbers of girders forming a truss.
TRUST (1), [trust], *n.* belief in, reliance on, anything, unquestioning faith in the reliability of a person; something with which a person is entrusted; (*leg.*) a holding of property for the benefit of another, the legal form and framework of such nominal ownership; a business ring to pursue a common interest. [ME. *trust*].
TRUST (2), [trust], *v.t.* to have implicit faith in the reliability of (a person or thing); to hope almost to belief; to entrust. [ME. *trusten*].
TRUSTEE, [trust'-ē'], *n.* one holding property in trust.
TRUSTEESHIP, [trust-ē'-ship], *n.* the office of trustee.
TRUSTER, [trust'-er], *n.* one who trusts or gives credit.
TRUSTFUL, [trust'-fōōl], *adj.* trusting.
TRUSTFULLY, [trust'-fōō-li], *adv.* in a trustful manner.
TRUSTFULNESS, [trust'-fōōl-nes], *n.* the quality of being trustful.
TRUSTILY, [trust'-i-li], *adv.* in a trusty manner.
TRUSTINESS, [trust'-i-nes], *n.* the quality of being trusty.
TRUSTINGLY, [trust'-ing-li], *adv.* with trust.
TRUSTLESS, [trust'-les], *adj.* not worthy of trust; unfaithful.
TRUSTLESSNESS, [trust'-les-nes], *n.* unworthiness of trust.
TRUSTWORTHINESS, [trust'-wur'-THi-nes], *n.* the quality of being trustworthy.
TRUSTWORTHY, [trust'-wur'-THi], *adj.* worthy of trust or confidence.
TRUSTY, [trust'-i], *adj.* that may be safely trusted; faithful.
TRUTH, [trōōth], *n.* that which is true, *esp.* as contrasted with something false, that which is real. [OE. *trewth* fidelity].
TRUTHFUL, [trōōth'-fōōl], *adj.* speaking the truth, in accordance with truth.
TRUTHFULLY, [trōōth'-fōōl-i], *adv.* in a truthful manner.
TRUTHFULNESS, [trōōth'-fōōl-nes], *n.* the state of being truthful.
TRUTHLESS, [trōōth'-les], *adj.* untrue; unfaithful.
TRUTHLESSNESS, [trōōth'-les-nes], *n.* the state of being truthless.
TRUTH-TELLER, [trōōth'-tel'-er], *n.* one who tells the truth.
TRUTTACEOUS, [trut-ā'-shus], *adj.* pertaining to or belonging to trout. [~L. *trutta* trout].
TRY (1), [trī], *n.* an attempt, an endeavour; (in *rugby football*) the scoring of three points when the ball is touched down by a player behind his opponents' goal-posts; the three points thus scored.

RY (2), [trī], *v.t. and i.* to put to trial, to test, to judge (a person) in a court of law; to put a severe strain on; to irritate; to experiment with; to attempt, to make an endeavour. [ME. *trien* to select].
RYING, [trī'-ing], *adj.* irritating; putting a strain on.
RY-ON, [trī'-on'], *n.* a venture or act performed to test the reactions of other persons or parties.
RY-OUT, [trī'-owt'], *n.* a preliminary test, trial, or performance.
RYPANOSOME, [trip'-an-ō-sōm], *n.* a parasitic protozoan that causes sleeping-sickness, etc. [~Gk. *trupanon* piercer].
RYPANOSOMIASIS, [trip'-an-ō-sō-mī'-as-is], *n.* infection by trypanosomes. [TRYPANOSOME and Gk. *asis* morbid state].
RYPSIN, [trip'-sin], *n.* a digestive ferment secreted in the pancreas. [~Gk. *trupsis* friction].
RYPTIC, [trip'-tik], *adj.* pertaining to trypsin.
RYPTONE, [trip'-tōn], *n.* a substance formed by trypsin.
RYSAIL, [trī'-sal], *n.* a fore-and-aft sail without a boom.
RYST (1), [trist], *n.* an assignation, a romantic rendezvous. [ME. *triste*].
RYST (2), [trist], *v.t.* to engage to meet; to set as a rendezvous. [*Prec.*].
RYSTING (1), [trist'-ing], *adj.* concerned with a tryst.
RYSTING (2), [trist'-ing], *n.* a recurring tryst.
SAR, see CZAR.
SAREVITCH, see CZAREVITCH.
SAREVNA, see CZAREVNA.
SARINA, see CZARINA.
SETSE, TZETZE, [tset'-si], *n.* the African fly, *Glossina morsitans*, a carrier of various diseases to human beings and animals. [Native].
SQUARE, [tē'-skwāer], *n.* a drawing instrument shaped like a T.
UATARA, [tew'-a-tah'-ra], *n.* the New Zealand lizard, *Sphenodon punctatas.* [Maori].
UB (1), [tub], *n.* a round wooden vessel, usually for containing water; a clumsy boot; (*coll.*) a bath. [OFr. *tubbe*].
UB (2), [tub], *v.t. and i.* to give a bath to; to take a bath.
UBA, [tew'-ba], *n.* a valved brass wind instrument of very low pitch. [L. *tuba* trumpet].
UBBY, [tub'-i], *adj.* round, short and fat.
UBE, [tewb], *n.* a hollow cylinder, a pipe; an underground railway running through metal tubes. [L. *tubus* pipe].
UBER, [tewb'-er], *n.* (*bot.*) the enlarged underground stem of a plant, containing buds. [L. *tuber* swelling].
UBERCLE, [tewb'-erkl], *n.* a small protuberance; a small morbid growth on a bodily organ; tuberculosis. [L. *tuberculum*].
UBERCLED, [tewb'-erkld], *adj.* having tubercles.
UBERCULAR, [tewb-ur'-kyōō-ler], *adj.* suffering from tuberculosis.
UBERCULATE, [tewb-ur'-kyōō-lāt], *adj.* tubercular; having small knobs or tubercles.
UBERCULIN, [tewb-ur'-kyōō-lin], *n.* a solution of a culture of the tubercle bacillus.
UBERCULOSE, [tewb-ur'-kyōō-lōs], *adj.* tuberculous.
UBERCULOSIS, [tewb-ur'-kyōō-lōs'-is], *n.* an infectious disease marked by the growth of tubercles in the tissues; consumption.
UBERCULOUS, [tewb-ur'-kyōō-lus], *adj.* having tubercles; tubercular.
UBERIFEROUS, [tewb'-er-if'-er-us], *adj.* producing or bearing tubers.
UBEROSE, [tewb'-er-ōz], *n.* the perfumed white garden-plant, *Polianthes tuberosa.*
UBEROSITY, [tewb'-er-os'-it-i], *n.* the state of being tuberous.
UBEROUS, [tewb'-er-us], *adj.* covered with tubers.
UB-FISH, [tub'-fish], *n.* the sapphirine gurnard, *Trigla hirundo.*
UBIFORM, [tewb'-i-fawm], *adj.* in the shape of a tube.
UBINARIAL, [tewb'-i-nāer'-i-al], *adj.* pertaining to the petrels. [L. *tubus* and *naris* nostril].
UBING, [tewb'-ing], *n.* a length of tube; a system of tubes.
UBIPORE, [tewb'-i-paw(r)], *n.* one of a genus of corals; organ-pipe coral, *Tubipora musica.* [L. *tubus* pipe and *porus* a pore].
UB-THUMPER, [tub'-thump'-er], *n.* (*coll.*) a noisy and extravagant preacher or public speaker.

TUBULAR, [tewb'-yōō-ler], *adj.* in the form of a tube.
TUBULATED, [tewb'-yōō-lāt-ed], *adj.* tubular.
TUBULE, [tewb'-yōōl], *n.* a little tube. [L. *tubulus*].
TUBULIFORM, [tewb'-yōōl-i-fawm], *adj.* having the form of a tube.
TUBULOUS, [tewb'-yōō-lus], *adj.* in the form of a tube.
TUB-WHEEL, [tub'-wēl], *n.* a horizontal water-wheel with a series of spiral floats.
TUCK (1), [tuk], *n.* a rapier. [OFr. *estoc*].
TUCK (2), [tuk], *n.* a roll of a drum. [ONFr. *toquer* to strike].
TUCK (3), [tuk], *n.* a fold sewn into cloth; food, delicacies.
TUCK (4), [tuk], *v.t. and i.* to make compact by stuffing or thrusting in; to shorten by sewing up into a fold; **to t. up or in,** to secure the bedclothes of by thrusting the edges beneath the mattress; **to t. in,** to eat largely and rapidly. [ME. *tucken* to pull].
TUCKAHOE, [tuk'-a-hō], *n.* the so-called Indian bread, an edible fungus, *Pachyma Cocos*, growing at the roots of North American trees. [NAmerInd. *tockawhoughe*].
TUCK-BOX, [tuk'-boks'], *n.* a wooden box used by schoolboys for their tuck. [TUCK (3) and BOX].
TUCKER, [tuk'-er], *n.* a band of cloth formerly worn by women across the breasts; **one's best bib and t.,** one's smartest clothes.
TUCKET, [tuk'-it], *n.* a flourish of trumpets. [It. *toccata*].
TUCK-SHOP, [tuk'-shop], *n.* a sweetstuff and pastry shop at a school.
TUCOTUCO, [tōō'-kō-tōō'-kō], *n.* a small South American burrowing rodent of the genus *Ctenomys.* [Native].
TUCUM, [tōō'-kum], *n.* the South American palm *Astrocaryum vulgare.* [Native].
TUDOR, [tew'-der], *adj.* relating to, in the style of, sixteenth-century England. [The *Tudor* Dynasty (1485-1603)].
TUDORESQUE, [tewd'-er-esk'], *adj.* resembling, aping, Tudor fashions or styles.
TUESDAY, [tews'-di], *n.* the third day of the week. [OE. *tiwesdæg*].
TUESITE, [tōō'-i-sīt], *n.* a white variety of lithomarge used for slate pencils. [L. *Tuesa*, the River Spey].
TUFA, [tewf'-a], *n.* a light porous rock of volcanic ashes cemented together; any similar rock. [~L. *tophus*].
TUFACEOUS, [tewf-ā'-shus], *adj.* pertaining to, consisting of, or resembling, tufa.
TUFF, [tuf], *n.* tufa.
TUFT, [tuft], *n.* a loose clump of stalks, hairs, etc., joined at the base, a cluster of grasses. [ME. *tuft*].
TUFTED, [tuft'-ed], *adj.* having a tuft or tufts, *esp.* of hair or feathers on the head.
TUFTER, [tuft'-er], *n.* a hound used for driving a stag out of cover.
TUFTHUNTER, [tuft'-hunt'-er], *n.* one who seeks the company of the rich and important.
TUFTY, [tuft'-i], *adj.* tufted; having tufts.
TUG (1), [tug], *n.* a sudden violent jerk or heave; a vessel used for towing.
TUG (2), [tug], *v.t. and i.* to pull strongly and spasmodically, to jerk violently at; to heave violently. [ME. *tuggen*].
TUGGER, [tug'-er], *n.* one who tugs.
TUGGINGLY, [tug'-ing-li], *adv.* by tugging.
TUG-OF-WAR, [tug'-ov-waw(r)'], *n.* an athletic contest in which two teams tug at opposite ends of a rope, until one party is dragged across a central mark.
TUI, [tōō'-i], *n.* the New Zealand parson-bird, *Prosthemadera novæ-zealandiæ.* [Native].
TUITION, [tew-i'-shun], *n.* the act of teaching; that which is taught. [L. *tuitio*].
TUITIONARY, [tew-i'-shun-er-i], *adj.* pertaining to tuition.
TULA-METAL, [tōō'-la-met'-al], *n.* an alloy of silver with copper and lead. [*Tula*, in Russia].
TULCHAN, [tul'-khan], *n.* a calf's skin stuffed to induce the cow to give milk. [Gael. *tulchan* heap].
TULIP, [tew'-lip], *n.* a brightly coloured liliaceous plant of the genus *Tulipa.* [~Turk. *tulbend* turban].
TULIPOMANIA, [tew'-lip-ō-mān'-i-a], *n.* an excessive passion for tulips.
TULIP-TREE, [tew'-lip-trē], *n.* the North American flowering tree, *Liriodendron tulipiferum.*

TULLE, [tewl], *n.* a kind of fine silk net or muslin. [*Tulle*, in France].
TULWAR, [tōōl'-wah(r)], *n.* an Indian curved sword. [Hind. *tulwar*].
TUMBLE (1), [tumbl], *n.* the act of tumbling.
TUMBLE (2), [tumbl], *v.t. and i.* to stumble and fall, to fall over headlong, to collapse utterly; to turn somersaults; to throw over, to rumple, to copulate with in sudden and informal circumstances. [~OE. *tumbian* to dance].
TUMBLEDOWN, [tumbl'-down'], *adj.* dilapidated.
TUMBLE-HOME, [tumbl'-hōm], *n.* the inward curve from the waterline upwards shown in ships having a rounded midship section.
TUMBLER, [tumb'-ler], *n.* one who tumbles; a clown; a kind of pigeon; a cylindrical drinking glass; the catch of a lock.
TUMBLERFUL, [tumb'-ler-fōōl], *adj.* as much as a tumbler contains (usually half a pint).
TUMBLING, [tumb'-ling], *n.* acrobatic clowning.
TUMBLY, [tumb'-li], *adj.* likely to tumble; tumbled; rumpled.
TUMBREL, TUMBRIL, [tum'-bril], *n.* a dung-cart; the wagon in which the condemned were taken to the guillotine during the French Revolution. [Fr. *tombrel*].
TUMEFACTION, [tew'-mi-fak'-shun], *n.* a tumour; the act of swelling.
TUMEFY, [tewm'-i-fī], *v.t. and i.* to make swell; to become swollen. [Fr. *tumefier*].
TUMESCENCE, [tum-es'-ents], *n.* tumefaction.
TUMESCENT, [tum-es'-ent], *adj.* swelling. [L. *tumescens*].
TUMID, [tew'-mid], *adj.* swollen; congested; pompous. [L. *tumidus*].
TUMIDITY, [tew-mid'-it-i], *n.* tumidness.
TUMIDLY, [tew'-mid-li], *adv.* in a tumid manner.
TUMIDNESS, [tew'-mid-nes], *n.* the state of being tumid.
TUMMY, [tum'-i], *n.* (*coll.*) the belly; the stomach. [~STOMACH].
TUMOROUS, [tew'-mer-us], *adj.* tumid; having a tumour.
TUMOUR, [tew'-mer], *n.* a bodily swelling due to abnormal cell-growth; abnormal protuberance. [L. *tumor*].
TUMOURED, [tew'-merd], *adj.* swollen; having a tumour.
TUMP, [tump], *n.* a hillock; a barrow. [Uncert.].
TUMP-LINE, [tump'-līn], *n.* a strap across the forehead or breast for carrying burdens. [Uncert.].
TUMPY, [tump'-i], *adj.* uneven. [Uncert.].
TUM-TUM, [tum'-tum], *n.* a West Indian dish of boiled plantains. [Uncert.].
TUMULAR, [tewm'-yōō-ler], *adj.* relating to a tumulus.
TUMULOSE, [tewm'-yōō-lōs], *adj.* tumular; full of tumuli.
TUMULOUS, [tewm'-yōō-lus], *adj.* tumulose.
TUMULT, [tew'-mult], *n.* a violent, confused uproar; a public commotion. [L. *tumultus*].
TUMULTUOUS, [tew-mult'-yōō-us], *adj.* in a tumult; furiously disordered.
TUMULTUOUSLY, [tew-mult'-yōō-us-li], *adv.* in a tumultuous manner.
TUMULTUOUSNESS, [tew-mult'-yōō-us-nes], *n.* the state of being tumultuous.
TUMULUS, (*pl.* **tumuli**), [tewm'-yōō-lus], *n.* a barrow; a prehistoric burial-mound. [L. *tumulus*].
TUN, [tun], *n.* a great vat for storing liquor. [OE. *tunne*].
TUNA, [tōōn'-a], *n.* the tunny of the Pacific coast of North America. [Span. *tuna* tunny].
TUNABLE, [tewn'-abl], *adj.* able to be tuned.
TUNABLENESS, [tewn'-abl-nes], *n.* the state of being tunable.
TUNABLY, [tewn'-ab-li], *adv.* in a tunable manner.
TUN-BELLIED, [tun'-bel'-id], *adj.* pot-bellied.
TUN-DISH, [tun'-dish], *n.* a funnel.
TUNDRA, [tun'-dra], *n.* a barren, lichenous, semi-arctic desert, *esp.* in North Russia. [Russ. *tundra*].
TUNDUN, [tun'-dun], *n.* a bull-roarer. [Australian].
TUNE (1), [tewn], *n.* a melody; a series of musical notes arranged harmoniously; **in t.,** in agreement, in harmony, in accordance. [OFr. *tune*].
TUNE (2), [tewn], *v.t.* to put in tune, to adjust musical instruments so that their notes are true; **to t. in,** to adjust (a wireless set) to receive a certain station; **to t. up,** (of an orchestra) to test and adjust the instruments before a musical performance. [*Prec.*].
TUNEFUL, [tewn'-fōōl], *adj.* harmonious; melodious.
TUNEFULLY, [tewn'-fōōl-i], *adv.* in a tuneful manne
TUNELESS, [tewn'-les], *adj.* unmelodious.
TUNER, [tewn'-er], *n.* one who tunes musical instr ments; (*wirel.*) an arrangement of oscillatory circui which may be adjusted for the reception of desire signals.
TUNGSTATE, [tung'-stāt], *n.* a salt of tungst acid.
TUNGSTEN, [tung'-sten], *n.* the metallic eleme denoted by W, used for electric filaments; wolfran **t. steel,** an alloy of steel and tungsten. [Swed. *tu* heavy and *sten* stone].
TUNGSTENIC, [tung-sten'-ik], *adj.* relating tungsten.
TUNGSTIC, [tung'-stik], *adj.* obtained from tungste
TUNIC, [tewn'-ik], *n.* a loose garment covering t trunk; the short, close-fitting coat of a soldier' policeman's, etc., uniform. [L. *tunica*].
TUNICARY, [tewn'-i-ker-i], *n.* an ascidian or se squirt.
TUNICATE, [tewn'-i-kāt], *adj.* tunicated.
TUNICATED, [tewn'-i-kāt-ed], *adj.* covered with tunic or membrane.
TUNICLE, [tewn'-ikl], *n.* a membrane; a vestme worn by the subdeacon at the Eucharist.
TUNING, [tewn'-ing], *n.* the act of putting an instr ment into tune; the adjustment of a wireless set to given wave-length.
TUNING-FORK, [tewn'-ing-fawk], *n.* a fork-lil instrument for setting the note in tuning.
TUNING-HAMMER, [tewn'-ing-ham'-er], *n.* a instrument for tuning pianos.
TUNNEL (1), [tun'-el], *n.* an underground passag *esp.* if cylindrical and artificial. [OFr. *tonnel*].
TUNNEL (2), [tun'-el], *v.i.* to make a tunnel.
TUNNEL-NET, [tun'-el-net'], *n.* a net with a wi mouth at one end and narrow at the other.
TUNNEL-PIT, [tun'-el-pit'], *n.* a shaft sunk from t top of the ground to the level of an intended tunn for drawing up the earth and stones.
TUNNERY, [tun'-er-i], *n.* the area of water enclos between the nets and the shore into which tunni are driven to be caught.
TUNNY, [tun'-i], *n.* a fish of the mackerel famil sometimes of very great size. [Gk. *thunnos*].
TUP, [tup], *n.* a ram. [ME. *tuppe*].
TURACO, TOURACO, [tōō-rah'-kō], *n.* a speci of *Tyracus* or its allied genera, an African bird of t plantain-eater family. [Native].
TURANIAN, [tew-rān'-i-an], *adj.* Ural-Altaic. [Pe *Turan* the country beyond the Oxus].
TURBAN, [tur'-ban], *n.* an Eastern head-dress consis ing of a long strip of fabric wound about a small ca or the head itself. [~Turk. *tulbend*].
TURBANED, [tur'-band], *adj.* wearing a turban.
TURBAN-TOP, [tur'-ban-top'], *n.* a kind of mus room.
TURBARY, [turb'-er-i], *n.* a peat-bed; (*leg.*) the rig to dig turf on another's land. [L. *turba* turf].
TURBID, [tur'-bid], *adj.* thickly confused, disturbe opaque with sediment. [L. *turbidus*].
TURBIDLY, [tur'-bid-li], *adv.* in a turbid manner.
TURBIDNESS, [tur'-bid-nes], *n.* the state of bei turbid.
TURBILLION, [tur-bil'-yon], *n.* a whirling confusio a whirlwind. [OFr. *torbillon*].
TURBINATE, [tur'-bin-āt], *adj.* shaped like a to [L. *turbinatus*].
TURBINATED, [tur'-bin-āt'-ed], *adj.* turbinate.
TURBINATION, [tur'-bin-ā'-shun], *n.* the state whirling like a top. [L. *turbinatio*].
TURBINE, [tur'-bīn], *n.* a rotating wheel driven l water or steam, and used as a prime mover. [~ *turbo* a whirlwind].
TURBINOID, [tur'-bin-oid], *adj.* (*anat.*) turbinat [TURBIN(ATE) and Gk. *oeides* like].
TURBIT, [tur'-bit], *n.* a ruffled and crested pigeo [Uncert.].
TURBOT, [tur'-but], *n.* the large, flat, edible fis *Rhombus maximus*. [Fr. *turbot*].
TURBULENCE, [tur'-byōō-lents], *n.* the state being turbulent; unruliness, lawless disturbance. [*turbulentia*].
TURBULENCY, [tur'-byōō-len-si], *n.* turbulence.
TURBULENT, [tur'-byōō-lent], *adj.* unruly, tumu tuous, violently agitated. [L. *turbulentus*].
TURBULENTLY, [tur'-byōō-lent-li], *adv.* in a turb lent manner.
TURCISM, [turk'-izm], *n.* the religion and customs the Turks.
TURCO, [turk'-ō], *n.* an Algerian soldier. [Fr. *Turc*

TURCOPHILE, [turk'-ō-fil], *n.* an admirer of the Turks.
TURCOPHOBE, [turk'-ō-fōb], *n.* one with fear and hatred of the Turks.
TUREEN, [tyōō'-rēn'], *n.* a deep, oval vessel for serving soup and vegetables. [Fr. *terrine*].
TURF (1), [turf], *n.* the conglomeration of earth and vegetable mould forming the surface layer of the ground; grass-sward; peat; **the t.,** horse-racing. [OE. *turf*].
TURF (2), [turf], *v.t.* to overlay, cover, with turf; **to t. out,** to expel roughly.
TURF-CLAD, [turf'-klad'], *adj.* covered with turf.
TURF-DRAIN, [turf'-drān], *n.* a drain made with bent sods.
TURF-HOUSE, [turf'-hows], *n.* a house, shelter made of dried turf.
TURFINESS, [turf'-i-nes], *n.* the quality of being turfy.
TURFING, [turf'-ing], *n.* the act of covering with turf.
TURFING-IRON, [turf'-ing-ī'-ern], *n.* an implement for paring off turf.
TURFING-SPADE, [turf'-ing-spād], *n.* a tool for undercutting turf when marked out by the plough.
TURFITE, [turf'-it], *n.* a race-goer.
TURF-MOSS, [turf'-mos'], *n.* sphagnum moss found in boggy ground.
TURF-SPADE, [turf'-spād], *n.* a narrow spade for digging out turf.
TURFY, [turf'-i], *adj.* abounding in, resembling, connected with, turf.
TURGENT, [turj'-ent], *adj.* tumid, turgid. [L. *turgens* swelling].
TURGESCENCE, [turj-es'-ents], *n.* the state of being swollen, the act of swelling; bombast, pomposity.
TURGESCENCY, [turj-es'-en-si], *n.* turgescence.
TURGESCENT, [turj-es'-ent], *adj.* swelling, in a state of turgescence.
TURGID, [turj'-id], *adj.* swollen, distended, tumid, inflated, tortuously bombastic. [L. *turgidus*].
TURGIDITY, [turj-id'-it-i], *n.* the state or quality of being turgid.
TURGIDLY, [turj'-id-li], *adv.* in a turgid manner.
TURGIDNESS, [turj'-id-nes], *n.* turgidity.
TURGITE, [tur'-gīt], *n.* a hydrous sesquioxide of iron, similar to haematite. [*Turginsk*, in the Urals].
TURION, [tew'-ri-on], *n.* (*bot.*) an underground shoot growing into a new stem. [L. *turio*].
TURIONIFEROUS, [tew'-ri-on-if'-er-us], *adj.* producing turions.
TURK, [turk], *n.* a member of the Turkish race, an Ottoman; (*coll.*) a young rascal. [It. *turco*].
TURKEY, [turk'-i], *n.* a large bird of the genus *Meleagris*, traditionally eaten on Christmas Day; **to talk t.,** to get down to business, to talk business. [*Turkey*, where supposed to have originated].
TURKEY-BUZZARD, [turk'-i-buz'-erd], *n.* the South American vulture, *Cathartes aura*.
TURKEY CARPET, [turk'-i-kah'-pet], *n.* a kind of brightly coloured woollen carpet of the type exported from Turkey.
TURKEY-OAK, [turk'-i-ōk], *n.* the cerris oak, *Quercus Cerris*.
TURKEY-RED, [turk'-i-red'], *n.* a fine, fast red dye.
TURKEYSTONE, [turk'-i-stōn], *n.* an oil-stone from Turkey.
TURKEY-WHEAT, [turk'-i-wēt], *n.* Indian corn.
TURKISH (1), [turk'-ish], *n.* the native language of Turkey.
TURKISH (2), [turk'-ish], *adj.* of, relating to, Turkey, its inhabitants, or language.
TURKISH-BATH, [turk'-ish-bahth], *n.* originally, a steam bath; now, a steam bath followed by cold douches, massage, etc.
TURKISH-DELIGHT, [turk'-ish-di-līt'], *n.* a sweetmeat made of gelatine and sugar, originally Turkish.
TURKOMAN, [turk'-ō-man], *n.* a member of that branch of the Turkish race inhabiting Turkestan. [Pers. *Turkuman* one resembling a Turk].
TURLOUGH, [tur'-lokh], *n.* a shallow pool that dries up in summer. [Ir. *turloch*].
TURLUPINS, [tur'-lōōp-inz], *n.*(*pl.*) late medieval heretics, who maintained that what was natural was therefore right. [MedL. *turlupinus*].
TURMERIC, [tur'-mer-ik], *n.* the aromatic plant, *Curcuma longa*. [Fr. *terre-méri*].
TURMOIL, [tur'-moil], *n.* tumultuous confusion, noisy agitation. [Unkn.].
TURN (1), [turn], *n.* the act of turning, the motion made in turning, the condition of having turned; a change, alteration, in the condition of a thing; a deflection of ninety degrees; a regularly recurring chance or compulsion to perform some task; a rightful opportunity; a short spell of exercise; a short dramatic performance included amongst others; a sudden shock; a peculiar ability. [OFr. *torn*].
TURN (2), [turn], *v.t. and i.* to cause to change direction, to divert from an intended course; to reverse, to make to face in an opposite direction; to cause to revolve, to spin round; to shape on a lathe; (*fig.*) to present in polished fashion; to transform, to cause to assume some specified form; to sicken, to shock; to direct; (*milit.*) to get behind (an enemy's line of battle); to take a new direction, *esp.* at right angles to the previous one; to face about to a reverse direction; to spin round, to revolve; to become, to be transformed; (of food) to go bad, become sour; to direct the attention (towards), incline (towards); **to t. away,** to rebuff; **to t. back,** to make to return; to return; to give way; **to t. down,** to reject, refuse; **to t. in,** to hand in, to go to bed; **to t. out,** to eject; to fit out; to become; (*milit.*) to summon to parade, to come to parade; to eventuate; **to t. over,** to hand over; **to t. up,** to appear, to arrive, (*U.S. slang*) to reveal; to discover espionage; **to t. upon,** to attack (an associate) unexpectedly. [OE. *turnian*].
TURNCAP, [turn'-kap'], *n.* a chimney-top which turns round with the wind.
TURNCOAT, [turn'-kōt], *n.* a traitor, one who changes his principles to suit his convenience.
TURNCOCK, [turn'-kok'], *n.* one who turns water on and off from the main.
TURNDOWN, [turn'-down'], *adj.* folded down.
TURNER, [turn'-er], *n.* one working on a lathe.
TURNERY, [turn'-er-i], *n.* the craft of working with a lathe; things worked with a lathe; a place where turning is done. [Fr. *tournerie*].
TURNING, [turn'-ing], *n.* a road leading off another; the place at which a road branches off; the practice of working wood, etc., on a lathe.
TURNING-POINT, [turn'-ing-point], *n.* the crux of a matter; the decisive instant at which the course of events changes.
TURNIP, [tur'-nip], *n.* the edible (root of the) plant, *Brassica campestris, var. Rapa*. [~OE. *næp*].
TURNIP-FLY, [tur'-nip-flī], *n.* a fly destructive to turnips.
TURNKEY, [turn'-kē], *n.* a warder in a prison.
TURN-OUT, [turn'-owt'], *n.* the act of turning out, the state of being turned out; (*milit.*) the state of a soldier's uniform and equipment; an equipage.
TURNOVER, [turn'-ō'-ver], *n.* a pastry cake; the money, as distinct from the profits, taken by a business; that which is turned over.
TURNPIKE, [turn'-pīk], *n.* a toll-gate, *esp.* when worked by a pivot.
TURNPIKE-ROAD, [turn'-pīk-rōd'], *n.* a road on which turnpikes or toll-gates were established by law.
TURN-PIN, [turn'-pin], *n.* a cone-shaped implement for widening or stopping up the end of a lead pipe.

TURN-PIN

TURN-SERVING, [turn'-surv'-ing], *n.* a following of interest rather than principle; that which serves one's turn.
TURN-SICK, [turn'-sik], *n.* the gid; a vertigo afflicting sheep.
TURNSOLE, [turn'-sōl], *n.* one of several plants so called because its flowers are said to turn towards the sun. [Fr. *tournesol*].
TURNSPIT, [turn'-spit], *n.* a person who turned a spit; a breed of dog, so called from having been employed to turn the spit.
TURNSTILE, [turn'-stīl], *n.* a small turnpike stopping the passage of cattle and vehicles but allowing pedestrians to pass; a revolving gate for checking the admission of spectators.
TURNSTONE, [turn'-stōn], *n.* a bird of the genus *Strepsilas*, allied to the lapwing.
TURNTABLE, [turn'-tābl], *n.* a large revolving platform for turning locomotives in a different direction; the revolving disk on a gramophone.
TURPENTINE, [tur'-pen-tīn], *n.* an oily secretion of pine trees. [~Gk. *terebinthos*].
TURPENTINE-TREE, [tur'-pin-tīn-trē], *n.* the terebinth.
TURPETH, [tur'-peth], *n.* the root of the Asiatic plant *Ipomœa turpethum*, used as a cathartic. [~Pers. *turbith* a purgative].
TURPITUDE, [turp'-i-tewd], *n.* moral baseness. [L. *turpitudo*].
TURPS, [turps], *n.* (*coll.*) turpentine.

ō (bone), ī (fine), ōō (food), ŏŏ (put), u (up), th (think), TH (that), zh (azure), † = obsolete, ~ = related to.

TURQUOISE (1), [turk'-oiz, turk'-woiz], *n.* a greenish-blue semi-precious stone. [Fr. *turquoise*].

TURQUOISE (2), [turk'-oiz, turk'-woiz], *adj.* of the colour of a turquoise.

TURR, [tur], *n.* a Burmese violin with three strings. [Native].

TURRET, [tu'-ret], *n.* a small tower, usually one of a series comprising fortifications; an armoured rotating gun-emplacement on a warship; a similar fitment on a tank or aeroplane. [Fr. *tourette*].

TURRETED, [tu'-ret-ed], *adj.* having turrets.

TURRET-SHIP, [tu'-ret-ship'], *n.* an armoured warship carrying batteries in the turret.

TURRICULATE, [tu-rik'-yŏŏ-lāt], *adj.* like a turret.

TURTLE, [turtl], *n.* a marine tortoise; any species of the *Chelonidæ*, *esp. Chelone mydas*, the green turtle largely used for soup at banquets. [Uncert.].

TURTLE-DOVE, [turtl'-duv], *n.* the pigeon *Turtur communis*; (*coll.*) an ostentatiously affectionate lover. [L. *turtur* dove and DOVE].

TURTLESHELL, [turtl'-shel'], *n.* tortoiseshell.

TURVES, [turvz], *n. pl.* of TURF.

TUSCAN, [tus'-kan], *adj.* pertaining to Tuscany; **T. order,** the simplest of the five classic orders of architecture.

TUSH, [tush], *int.* nonsense!

TUSK (1), [tusk], *n.* a long tooth projecting from the closed mouth, as in the elephant, walrus, etc.; (*coll.*) a tooth. [OE. *tusc*].

TUSK (2), [tusk], *n.* the torsk, *Brosmius brosme.*

TUSKED, [tuskt], *adj.* furnished with tusks.

TUSKER, [tusk'-er], *n.* an elephant having tusks.

TUSKY, [tusk'-i], *adj.* tusked.

TUSSER, [tus'-er], *n.* a coarse silk from the cocoons of the wild Bengal silkworm. [Hind. *tasar*].

TUSSICULAR, [tus-ik'-yŏŏ-ler], *adj.* pertaining to a cough. [~L. *tussicula* a mild cough].

TUSSIS, [tus'-is], *n.* a cough. [L. *tussis*].

TUSSLE (1), [tusl], *n.* a vigorous, rough, clumsy struggle, a wrestle. [Uncert.].

TUSSLE (2), [tusl], *v.i.* to wrestle, to struggle; to take part in a tussle. [Uncert.].

TUSSOCK, [tus'-ok], *n.* a thick clump of grass. [Uncert.].

TUSSOCK-MOTH, [tus'-ok-moth'], *n.* the moth of the tufted caterpillar, *Dasychira pudibunda.*

TUSSOCKY, [tus'-ok-i], *adj.* abounding in tussocks.

TUSSORE, [tus'-aw(r)], *n.* tusser.

TUT, [tut], *int.* an exclamation of irritation or reproval.

TUTELAGE, [tewt'-il-ij], *n.* the state of being guided and instructed; guardianship. [~L. *tutela*].

TUTELAR, [tewt'-il-er], *adj.* tutelary.

TUTELARY, [tewt'-il-er-i], *adj.* protecting; instructing.

TUTENAG, [tewt'-en-ag], *n.* Chinese alloy of copper, zinc, and nickel. [Skr. *tuttha* blue-vitriol, and *naga* tin].

TUTOR (1), [tewt'-er], *n.* one who instructs; a private teacher; (in universities) a college teacher who arranges and supervises the work of his students. [L. *tutor* protector].

TUTOR (2), [tewt'-er], *v.t.* to teach, be a tutor to.

TUTORAGE, [tewt'-or-ij], *n.* the charge and instruction of a pupil.

TUTORESS, [tewt'-or-es], *n.* a female tutor.

TUTORIAL (1), [tewt-aw'-ri-al], *n.* a session with a tutor.

TUTORIAL (2), [tewt-aw'-ri-al], *adj.* pertaining to a tutor.

TUTORING, [tewt'-er-ing], *n.* the work of a tutor; the act of teaching.

TUTORSHIP, [tewt'-er-ship], *n.* the office of tutor.

TUTRIX, [tew'-triks], *n.* a female guardian. [L. *tutrix*].

TUTSAN, [tut'-san], *n.* the plant, *Hypericum androsæmum.* [Fr. *toute-saine*].

TUTTI, [tŏŏt'-i], *n.* (*mus.*) a direction that all the performers play in concert. [It. *tutti*].

TUTTI-FRUTTI, [tŏŏt'-i-frŏŏt'-i], *n.* fruit-salad; a compote of preserved fruits. [It. *tutti-frutti* all fruits].

TUXEDO, [tuk-sēd'-ō], *n.* (*U.S.*) a dinner-jacket. [*Tuxedo* Park near New York].

TUYERE, tuyère, TWYER, TWEER, [twē-yāer', twī'-er, twēer], *n.* the blast tube of a smelting furnace. [Fr. *tuyère*].

TWADDLE, [twodl], *n.* silly and ridiculous talk. [Uncert.].

TWADDLER, [twod'-ler], *n.* one who talks twaddle.

TWAIN (1), [twān], *n.(pl.)* (*poet.*) two. [OE. *twegen*].

TWAIN (2), [twān], *adj.* in two parts. [OE. *twegen*].

TWAIT, [twāt], *n.* the shad, *Alosa finta.* [Unkn.].

TWAITE, [twāt], *n.* a species of shad. [*Prec.*].

TWANG (1), [twang], *n.* a sharp, ringing sound produced by the rapid vibration of a taut string; a nasal tone of speech. [Echoic].

TWANG (2), [twang], *v.t. and i.* to cause to produce a twang; to utter a twanging sound.

TWANGING, [twang'-ing], *adj.* making a twang.

TWANGLE, [twangl], *v.i.* to twang.

TWANK, [twangk], *n.* a twang.

TWANKAY, [twangk'-ā], *n.* a sort of green tea. [Chin. *tong-ké*].

TWATTLE, [twotl], *n.* silly empty talk. [~TATTLE].

TWAY-BLADE, [twā'-blād], *n.* the green orchis, *Listera ovata*, with two prominent oval leaves at the base of the stem. [OE. *twegen* two and BLADE].

TWEAK (1), [twēk], *n.* a sudden sharp nip or pinch.

TWEAK (2), [twēk], *v.t.* to give a tweak to. [ME. *twikken*].

TWEED, [twēd], *n.* a woollen cloth woven from different coloured yarns. [River *Tweed*, in Scotland, in the district where it is manufactured].

TWEEDLE, [twēdl], *v.t. and i.* to trill, to utter light musical sounds; to wheedle. [Uncert.].

TWEEN, [twēn], *prep.* between.

TWEENY, [twēn'-i], *n.* a between-maid. [(BE)TWEEN].

TWEER, see TUYERE.

TWEEZERS, [twēz'-erz], *n.(pl.)* small pincers for taking hold of small or delicate objects.

TWELFTH (1), [twelfth], *n.* a twelfth part; the twelfth day, etc., *esp.* the 12th August when grouse-shooting begins.

TWELFTH (2), [twelfth], *adj.* the ordinal of twelve. [OE. *twelfta*].

TWELFTH-CAKE, [twelfth'-kāk], *n.* a cake eaten on Twelfth-night.

TWELFTH-DAY, [twelfth'-dā], *n.* Epiphany, which is twelve days after Christmas.

TWELFTH-NIGHT, [twelfth'-nīt], *n.* Epiphany-eve.

TWELFTH-TIDE, [twelfth'-tīd], *n.* Epiphany.

TWELVE, [twelv], *n.* one more than eleven; a dozen. [OE. *twelf*].

TWELVEMONTH, [twelv'-munth], *n.* a year.

TWENTIETH (1), [twent'-i-eth], *n.* a twentieth part; the twentieth day, etc.

TWENTIETH (2), [twent'-i-eth], *adj.* the ordinal of twenty. [OE. *twentigotha*].

TWENTY (1), [twent'-i], *n.* twice ten, a score. [OE. *twentig*].

TWENTY (2), [twent'-i], *adj.* consisting of, containing, twenty.

TWERP, [twurp], *n.* (*slang*) a contemptible, undersized man or youth; a form of contemptuous allusion to any person.

TWIBILL, [twī'-bil], *n.* a two-edged, broad-headed sword; a double-bladed axe; a mattock. [OE. *twibil*].

TWICE, [twīs], *adv.* two times. [ME. *twies*].

TWICER, [twīs'-er], *n.* a printer who is also a compositor.

TWIDDLE, [twidl], *v.t.* to spin round in the fingers; to twist and play idly with. [OScand. *twidla* to stir].

TWIG (1), [twig], *n.* a shoot from the branch of a tree. [OE. *twig*].

TWIG (2), [twig], *v.t.* to grasp mentally, to comprehend. [Ir. *tuigaim* I understand].

TWIGGEN, [twig'-en], *adj.* made from twigs.

TWIGGY, [twig'-i], *adj.* abounding in twigs.

TWILIGHT, [twī'-līt], *n.* the half-light immediately after sunset; (*fig.*) uncertain view, obscurity of understanding. [ME. *twylyght*].

TWILL, [twil], *n.* fabric woven into parallel ribs, by passing the weft irregularly under and over the warp. [OE. *twilic* woven double].

TWIN (1), [twin], *n.* one of a pair of persons or animals born at the same birth; one of an exactly identical pair. [OE. *getwinnas* twins].

TWIN (2), [twin], *adj.* being a twin; being one of an identical pair. [~OIcel. *tvinnr* double].

TWIN-BORN, [twin'-bawn], *adj.* born at the same birth.

TWINE (1), [twīn], *n.* a strong cord made of twisted strands, *esp.* of hemp-strands. [OE. *twin* linen].

TWINE (2), [twīn], *v.t. and i.* to twist, to wind, round about.

TWINER, [twīn'-er], *n.* a twining plant.

TWINGE (1), [twinj], *n.* a sudden spasm of pain; a sudden sharp pinch; a mental qualm. [*Next*].

TWINGE (2), [twinj], *v.t. and i.* to give a twinge to; to feel a twinge. [OE. *twengan* to pinch].
TWINING, [twin'-ing], *adj.* that twines.
TWINKLE (1), [twingkl], *n.* an intermittent, winking light; a sudden gleam; a momentary flash of laughter in the eyes; the shortest possible space of time.
TWINKLE (2), [twingkl], *v.i.* to emit a twinkle; to give out an intermittent winking light; to laugh with the eyes; to move rapidly to and fro. [OE. *twinclian*].
TWINKLING, [twingk'-ling], *n.* the briefest of moments.
TWIN-LIKENESS, [twin'-līk'-nes], *n.* close resemblance.
TWINLING, [twin'-ling], *n.* a twin lamb.
TWINNED, [twind], *adj.* having a twin.
TWIRL (1), [twurl], *n.* that which twirls or is twirled; the act of twirling.
TWIRL (2), [twurl], *v.t. and i.* to make a thing whirl on its own axis; to whirl round. [~OE. *thweran* to stir].
TWIST (1), [twist], *n.* something twined together, a mass of plaited threads; a lump of coarse tobacco; the act of twisting; a tortuous deviation; (*fig.*) a streak of abnormality. [OE. *twist*].
TWIST (2), [twist], *v.t. and i.* to twine, to plait together, to turn, bend, divert out of normal position, to distort by turning; to deviate from the normal, to turn deviously, to writhe; (*fig.*) to behave dishonestly; (*slang*) to swindle. [ME. *twisten*].
TWISTABLE, [twist'-abl], *adj.* able to be twisted.
TWIST-DRILL, [twist'-dril], *n.* a drill having a spiral twist, used in metal working.

TWIST-DRILL

TWISTER, [twist'-er], *n.* that which twists; (*slang*) an untrustworthy person; a swindler.
TWIT (1), [twit], *n.* a silly, low, insignificant person.
TWIT (2), [twit], *v.t.* to reproach in half-humorous, half-nagging fashion; to taunt. [OE. *ætwitan* to reproach].
TWITCH (1), [twich], *n.* a sudden, brief, uncontrollable muscular movement, *esp.* of the facial muscles.
TWITCH (2), [twich], *v.t. and i.* to jerk with a sudden, nervous movement; to give or display a muscular twitch. [ME. *twicchen*].
TWITCHER, [twich'-er], *n.* one who, or that which, twitches; a trowel with raised sides.

TWITCHER

TWITCH-GRASS, [twich'-grahs], *n.* couch-grass.
TWITCHING, [twich'-ing], *n.* the act of one who twitches.
TWITE, [twit], *n.* the mountain linnet, *Linota flavirostris*. [Imitative].
TWITTEN, [twit'-en], *n.* a narrow lane connecting two roads. [Uncert.].
TWITTER (1), [twit'-er], *n.* the rapid, shrill chattering of birds; **all of a t., in a t.,** in a condition of nervous, fluttering excitement.
TWITTER (2), [twit'-er], *v.i.* to utter high, rapid chattering sounds, as birds; to be in a state of feeble excitement. [ME. *twiteren*].
TWITTER-BONE, [twit'-er-bōn], *n.* an excrescence on a horse's hoof.
TWITTERING, [twit'-er-ing], *n.* the act of uttering twitters.
TWITTINGLY, [twit'-ing-li], *adv.* so as to twit.
TWITTLE-TWATTLE, [twitl'-twotl'], *n.* tittle-tattle.
'TWIXT, [twikst], *prep.* betwixt.
TWO, [tōō], *n.* the number between one and three. [OE. *twa*].
TWO-EDGED, [tōō'-ejd'], *adj.* having both edges sharp; ambiguous, having two opposite effects.
TWO-FACED, [tōō'-fāst], *adj.* having two faces; double-dealing.
TWOFOLD (1), [tōō'-fōld], *adj.* double.
TWO-FOLD (2), [tōō'-fōld], *adv.* doubly.
TWO-HANDED, [tōō'-hand'-ed], *adj.* with two hands; meant to be wielded by two hands.
TWO-MASTED, [tōō'-mahst-ed], *adj.* having two masts.
TWONESS, [tōō'-nes], *n.* doubleness.
TWOPENCE, [tup'-ents], *n.* two pennies.
TWOPENNY, [tup'-en-i], *adj.* worth twopence; (*coll.*) worthless.
TWOPENNY-HALFPENNY, [tup'-en-i-hāp'-ni], *adj.* quite worthless.
TWO-PLY, [tōō'-plī], *adj.* of double thickness.
TWOSOME, [tōō'-sum], *n.* a game (usually golf) played by two players. [TWO and OE. *sum* one of].
TWO-STEP, [tōō'-step'], *n.* the original fox-trot.
TWO-TONGUED, [tōō'-tungd], *adj.* deceitful; hypocritical.
TWYER, see TUYERE.
TYCOON, [tī-kōōn'], *n.* the shogun; (*coll.*) a high authority. [Jap. *taikun* great ruler].
TYE, [tī], *n.* a trough used in washing ore. [Uncert.].
TYKE, see TIKE.
TYLER, see TILER.
TYMBAL, see TIMBAL.
TYMP, [timp], *n.* the mouth of a blast furnace. [L. *tympanum*].
TYMPAN, [tim'-pan], *n.* (*print.*) a sheet, formerly of parchment, placed between the platen and the paper during printing. [L. *tympanum* drum].
TYMPANIC, [tim-pan'-ik], *adj.* like a drum; pertaining to the tympanum.
TYMPANITIC, [tim'-pan-it'-ik], *adj.* relating to, suffering from tympanitis.
TYMPANITIS, [tim'-pan-īt'-is], *n.* inflammation of the tympanum.
TYMPANUM, [tim'-pan-um], *n.* the membrane of the ear; the face of a pediment. [Gk. *tumpanon* drum].
TYMPANY, [tim'-pan-i], *n.* a flatulent distension of the abdomen.
TYNWALD, [tin'-wawld], *n.* the parliament of the Isle of Man. [OScand. *thingvöllr*].
TYPE (1), [tīp], *n.* the image, symbol, representation, of a thing; the model of a thing; the kind, variety, general class, of a thing; a representative member of a class or kind, or the representative possessor of a quality; pieces of wood or metal with carved or moulded impressions of letters or characters used in printing. [Gk. *tupos* stamp of a seal].
TYPE (2), [tīp], *v.t. and i.* to typify; to write with a typewriter; to be, or become, typical; to be able to use a typewriter.
TYPEFOUNDER, [tīp'-fownd'-er], *n.* one who casts printing types.
TYPEFOUNDRY, [tīp'-fownd'-ri], *n.* the place where types are cast.
TYPEMETAL, [tīp'-met'-al], *n.* a lead alloy used for printing types.
TYPESCRIPT, [tīp'-skript], *n.* a typewritten document.
TYPESETTER, [tīp'-set'-er], *n.* a person or machine setting type for printing.
TYPEWRITER, [tīp'-rīt'-er], *n.* a small machine for writing with printed characters, by striking lettered keys so that the corresponding symbols are impressed on the paper.
TYPEWRITTEN, [tīp'-ritn], *adj.* written with a typewriter.
TYPHLITIS, [ti-flīt'-is], *n.* inflammation of the caecum and vermiform appendix. [Gk. *tuphlos* closed].
TYPHOID (1), [tī'-foid], *n.* typhoid fever.
TYPHOID (2), [tī'-foid], *adj.* resembling, related to, typhus; **t. fever,** an infectious disease resembling typhus. [TYPHUS and Gk. *oeides* like].
TYPHOMANIA, [tī'-fō-mān'-i-a], *n.* delirium due to typhus.
TYPHON, [tī'-fon], *n.* a Greek mythological monster; the Ancient Egyptian spirit of evil. [Gk. *tuphon*].
TYPHONIC, [tī-fon'-ik], *adj.* pertaining to a typhoon.
TYPHOON, [tī-fōōn'], *n.* a cyclone in the China Sea; a hurricane. [Uncert.].
TYPHOUS, [tī'-fus], *adj.* of, or relating to, typhus.
TYPHUS, [tī'-fus], *n.* contagious spotted fever, usually carried by parasites. [Gk. *tuphos* smoke].
TYPIC, [tip'-ik], *adj.* typical.
TYPICAL, [tip'-ik-al], *adj.* true to type; wholly representative of its kind.
TYPICALLY, [tip'-ik-al-i], *adv.* in typical fashion.
TYPICALNESS, [tip'-ik-al-nes], *n.* the fact of being typical.
TYPIFY, [tip'-i-fī], *v.t.* to exemplify.
TYPIST, [tī'-pist], *n.* one who types for a living.
TYPOGRAPHER, [tī-po'-graf-er], *n.* a printer.
TYPOGRAPHIC, [tī'-pō-graf'-ik], *adj.* typographical.
TYPOGRAPHICAL, [tī'-pō-graf'-ik-al], *adj.* pertaining to printing; emblematic.
TYPOGRAPHICALLY, [tī'-pō-graf'-ik-al-i], *adv.* in respect of typography.
TYPOGRAPHY, [tī-po'-graf-i], *n.* the art of printing.
TYPOLOGY, [tī-pol'-oj-i], *n.* the theory that the Old Testament foretells and prefigures the New.
TYPTOLOGY, [tip-tol'-oj-i], *n.* the study of spirit-rapping. [Gk. *tupto* I beat and *logos* speech].

TYR, [tir], *n.* (*myth.*) a Norse war god. [OScand. *Tyr*].
TYRANNICAL, [tī-ran'-ik-al], *adj.* befitting, characterizing, relating to a tyrant or to his tyrannies. [Gk. *turannikos*].
TYRANNICALLY, [tī-ran'-ik-al-i], *adv.* in tyrannical fashion.
TYRANNICALNESS, [tī-ran'-ik-al-nes], *n.* the quality of being tyrannical.
TYRANNICIDE, [ti-ran'-i-sīd], *n.* the assassination of a tyrant; the slayer of a tyrant. [L. *tyrannicidium*].
TYRANNIZE, [ti'-ran-īz], *v.i.* to play the tyrant. [Gk. *turannizo*].
TYRANNOUS, [ti'-ran-us], *adj.* tyrannical.
TYRANNY, [ti'-ran-i], *n.* the rule, conduct, of a tyrant; a state governed by a tyrant.
TYRANT, [tīer'-ant], *n.* (*hist.*) an absolute ruler seizing and maintaining power by violence or the threat of it; a cruel despot; a non-hereditary absolute ruler; a harsh, oppressive, despotic person. [Gk. *turannos*].
TYRE (1), [tīer], *n.* curdled milk, cream. [Tamil *tayir*].
TYRE (2), see TIRE (1).
TYRIAN, [ti'-ri-an], *adj.* relating to Tyre; of a rich purple colour.
TYRITE, [ti'-rīt], *n.* a mineral allied to fergusonite. [TYR].
TYRO, see TIRO.
TYROLITE, [ti'-rōl-īt], *n.* a greenish or bluish translucent mineral containing arsenic, copper and lime, so called from its being found in the *Tyrol.*
TYRRHENE, [ti-rēn'], *n.* an Etruscan. [*Next*].
TYRRHENIAN, [ti-rēn'-i-an], *adj.* Etruscan. [L. *Tyrrhenia* Etruria].
TYRTAEAN, [tur-tē'-an], *adj.* (of verse) martial. [*Tyrtaeus*, a Spartan poet].
TYSTIE, [tist'-i], *n.* the black guillemot, *Uria grylle.* [Uncert.].
TZETZE, see TSETSE.
TZIGANE, [tsi-gahn'], *n.* a Hungarian gipsy. [Magyar *cigany*].
TZIGANY, [tsi-gahn'-ē], *adj.* of the tziganes. [*Prec.*].

U

U, [yōō], the twenty-first letter of the English alphabet.
UBEROUS, [yōō'-ber-us], *adj.* abundant, fertile.
UBERTY, [yōō'-ber-ti], *n.* abundance, fertility. [~L. *uber* fruitful].
UBICATION, [yōō'-bik-ā'-shun], *n.* the state of being in a particular place. [~L. *ubi* where].
UBIETY, [yōōb-ī'-it-i], *n.* (*philos.*) the state of occupying a relative position.
UBIQUITARIAN, [yōō-bik'-wit-āer'-i-an], *n.* (*theol.*) one who believes that the body of Christ is present in all places at all times.
UBIQUITARIANISM, [yōō-bik'-wit-āer'-i-an-izm], *n.* the belief of a ubiquitarian.
UBIQUITARY, [yōōb-ik'-wit-er-i], *adj.* existing everywhere.
UBIQUITOUS, [yōōb-ik'-wit-us], *adj.* existing everywhere at the same time. [~L. *ubique* everywhere].
UBIQUITOUSLY, [yōōb-ik'-wit-us-li], *adv.* in a ubiquitous fashion.
UBIQUITOUSNESS, [yōōb-ik'-wit-us-nes], *n.* ubiquity.
UBIQUITY, [yōōb-ik'-wit-i], *n.* the condition of being ubiquitous; omnipresence.
U-BOAT, [yōō'-bōt], *n.* a submarine in the German Navy. [Germ. *U*(ntersee)-*boot*].
UDDER, [ud'-er], *n.* an external glandular organ in certain female animals, secreting milk. [OE. *uder*].
UDDERED, [ud'-erd], *adj.* having udders.
UDDERLESS, [ud'-er-les], *adj.* (of a young animal) deprived of its mother's milk.
UGH, *int.* a sound resembling a suppressed cough, expressing great disgust.
UGLIFY, [ug'-li-fī], *v.t.* to make ugly.
UGLILY, [ug'-li-li], *adv.* in ugly fashion.
UGLINESS, [ug'-li-nes], *n.* the condition or quality of being ugly.
UGLY (1), [ug'-li], *n.* any ugly person or thing; † a shade on the front of a lady's bonnet worn in the 19th century.
UGLY (2), [ug'-li], *adj.* utterly lacking in beauty, hideous to behold, repulsive; (*fig.*) morally loathsome or vile; menacing, dreadful, suggesting unpleasant things to come; **an u. customer,** a dangerous opponent. [OIcel. *uggligr* horrible].
UGRIAN (1), [yōō'-gri-an], *n.* a member of a Ugrian race; a language spoken by one of these races.
UGRIAN (2), [yōō'-gri-an], *adj.* of, or pertaining to, certain non-Slavonic races in Russia and to the Magyars and Hungarians. [*Ugra*, the name of territory on either side of the Urals].
UGRIC, [yōō-grik], *adj.* Ugrian.
UGSOME, [ug'-sum], *adj.* ugly, loathsome.
UGSOMENESS, [ug'-sum-nes], *n.* the condition of being ugsome, hideousness.
UHLAN, [yōō'-lan], *n.* a cavalryman in the armies of some central European countries. [Polish *ulan* lancer].
UITLANDER, [oit'-land-er], *n.* (*South Africa*) a foreigner. [Du. *uit* out and *land* land].
UKASE, [yōō-kās'], *n.* a command or decree. [Russ. *ukaz*].
UKULELE, [yōō'-ku-lā'-li], *n.* (*mus.*) a small, soft-toned, four-stringed instrument originating in Hawaii, and employed in dance bands.
ULCER, [ul'-ser], *n.* an open sore which discharges pus; (*fig.*) a source of moral corruption. [L. *ulcer*].
ULCERATE, [ul'-ser-āt], *v.t. and i.* to cause to break out in ulcers; to break out in ulcers; (*fig.*) to cause moral corruption in. [~L. *ulcerare*].
ULCERATION, [ul'-ser-ā'-shun], *n.* the state of being or process of becoming ulcerated. [L. *ulceratio*].
ULCERATIVE, [ul'-ser-ā-tiv], *adj.* causing ulcers; affected with ulcers.

UKULELE

ULCERED, [ul'-serd], *adj.* having an ulcer or ulcers.
ULCEROUS, [ul'-ser-us], *adj.* like an ulcer; ulcerated; morally corrupting.
ULCEROUSLY, [ul'-ser-us-li], *adv.* in an ulcerous fashion.
ULCEROUSNESS, [ul'-ser-us-nes], *n.* the condition of being ulcerous.
ULCUSCLE, [ul'-kuskl], *n.* a little ulcer. [L. *ulcusculum*].
ULEMA, [ōō'-lem-a], *n.*(*pl.*) men skilled in Mohammedan law and doctrine. [Arab. *ulema* wise men].
ULEX, [yōō'-leks], *n.* (*bot.*) a genus of spiny shrubs including gorse and furze. [L. *ulex*].
ULIGINOSE, ULIGINOUS, [yōō-lij'-in-ōs], *adj.* slimy, muddy; (*bot.*) growing in marshy soil. [L. *uliginosus* marshy].
ULLAGE, [ul'-ij], *n.* the difference between the amount of liquor actually in a container and its full capacity. [OFr. *eullage*].
ULLMANNITE, [ul'-man-īt], *n.* (*min.*) a sulphide of nickel containing antimony and arsenic. [Prof. J. C. *Ullmann* the discoverer].
ULMACEOUS, [ul-mā'-shus], *adj.* (*bot.*) pertaining to the *Ulmaceæ*, a family of trees of which the elm is one.
ULMIC, [ul'-mik], *adj.* (*chem.*) pertaining to ulmin.
ULMIN, [ul'-min], *n.* (*chem.*) a sticky substance which exudes from elms and other trees, and occurs in decaying vegetable matter. [~L. *ulmus* elm].
ULNA, (*pl.* **ulnae**), [ul'-na], *n.* (*anat.*) the inner bone of the arm between the wrist and elbow; the corresponding bone in animals. [L. *ulna*].
ULNAR, [ul'-ner], *adj.* (*anat.*) pertaining to the ulna.
ULOTRICHAN, [yōōl-ot'-rik-an], *n.* a member of a woolly-haired race.
ULOTRICHI, [yōōl-ot'-rik-ī], *n.*(*pl.*) the woolly-haired peoples.
ULOTRICHOUS, [yōōl-ot'-rik-us], *adj.* having crisp, woolly hair; pertaining, or belonging, to races having such hair. [Gk. *oulothrix woolly-haired].

ULSTER, [ul'-ster], *n.* a long, loose, heavy overcoat. [*Ulster* in Ireland].
ULT, [ult], *adj.* short for ultimo.
ULTERIOR, [ul-tēer'-i-er], *adj.* remote; **u. motive**, (*coll.*) an unavowed and discreditable reason or purpose. [L. *ulterior* beyond].
ULTERIORLY, [ul-tēer'-i-er-li], *adv.* in an ulterior fashion.
ULTIMA, [ul'-tim-a], *adj.* last, ultimate, final. [L. *ultima*, *fem.* of *ultimus*].
ULTIMATE, [ul'-tim-at], *adj.* last, final; furthest, most remote; fundamental, basic.
ULTIMATELY, [ul'-tim-at-li], *adv.* in the end, finally.
ULTIMATENESS, [ul'-tim-at-nes], *n.* the condition of being ultimate.
ULTIMATUM, (*pl.* **ultimata** *or* **ultimatums**), [ul'-tim-ā'-tum], *n.* a final statement of views and intentions, *esp.* a statement by one of two parties in a negotiation expressing their final terms, and usually accompanied by a threat that, if these are not accepted by a specified time, peaceful negotiations will be at an end. [L. *ultimatum*].
ULTIMITY, [ul-tim'-i-ti], *n.* the final stage (of an action, etc.). [MedL. *ultimitas*].
ULTIMO, [ul'-tim-ō], *adv.* (*comm.*) in the month immediately before this. [L. *ultimo* (*mense*)].
ULTIMO-GENITURE, [ul'-tim-ō-jen'-i-cher], *n.* that social order in which the youngest son is considered heir, not the eldest.
ULTRA (1), [ul'-tra], *n.* a person of extreme opinions.
ULTRA (2), [ul'-tra], *adj.* extreme, *esp.* professing extreme opinions.
ULTRA-, [ul'-tra], *pref.* extreme, or lying beyond. [L. *ultra* beyond].
ULTRAISM, [ul'-tra-izm], *n.* the advocacy of extreme measures or principles.
ULTRAIST, [ul'-tra-ist], *n.* one who advocates extreme measures or principles.
ULTRAMARINE (1), [ul'-tra-ma-rēn'], *n.* ultramarine blue.
ULTRAMARINE (2), [ul'-tra-ma-rēn'], *adj.* lying overseas.
ULTRAMARINE (3), [ul'-tra-ma-rēn'], *adj.* being of a brilliant blue colour.
ULTRA-MICROSCOPE, [ul'-tra-mīk'-rō-skōp], *n.* a microscope permitting observation of objects too small for examination by visible light, but resolvable by ultra-violet rays. [ULTRA-(VIOLET) and MICROSCOPE].
ULTRA-MICROSCOPIC, [ul'-tra-mī'-krō-skop'-ik], *adj.* too minute to be seen even with a microscope.
ULTRAMONTANE (1), [ul'-tra-mon'-tān], *n.* one who lives on the other side of the Alps; (*fig.*) a supporter of extreme Papal claims.
ULTRAMONTANE (2), [ul'-tra-mon'-tān], *adj.* living on the other side of a mountain range, *esp.* on the other side of the Alps (from either point of view); (*fig.*) upholding the most extreme claims of Papal authority.
ULTRAMONTANISM, [ul'-tra-mon'-tān-izm], *n.* the principles advocated by an ultramontane.
ULTRAMONTANIST, [ul'-tra-mon'-tān-ist], *n.* an advocate of ultramontanism.
ULTRAMUNDANE, [ul'-tra-mun'-dān], *adj.* lying beyond this world or the solar system.
ULTRA-SHORT, [ul'-tra-shawt'], *adj.* of wireless waves, having a wave-length of approximately one to fifteen metres.
ULTRA-VIOLET, [ul'-tra-vī'-ōl-et], *adj.* (*phys.*) pertaining to those rays which lie between the X-rays and the violet rays of the visible spectrum.
ULTRA VIRES (1), [ul'-tra-vīer'-ēz], *adj.* (*leg.*) lying beyond the scope of authority. [L. *ultra vires* beyond the powers].
ULTRA VIRES (2), [ul'-tra-vīer'-ēz], *adv.* (*leg.*) beyond the scope of authority.
ULTRONEOUS, [ul-trō'-ni-us], *adj.* spontaneous. [L. *ultroneus*].
ULTRONEOUSLY, [ul-trō'-ni-us-li], *adv.* in an ultroneous way.
ULTRONEOUSNESS, [ul-trō'-ni-us-nes], *n.* spontaneity, the quality of being ultroneous.
ULULANT, [yōōl'-yōō-lant], *adj.* uttering a hoot or howl. [L. *ululans*].
ULULATE, [yōōl'-yōō-lāt], *v.i.* to hoot or howl; to lament. [~L. *ululare* to wail].
ULULATION, [yōōl'-yōō-lā'-shun], *n.* the act of ululating.
UMBEL, [um'-bel'], *n.* (*bot.*) a head of blossom all the stalks of which rise from a single point, and form a more or less flat head. [L. *umbella* sunshade].
UMBELLAL, [um'-bel-al], *adj.* (*bot.*) umbellar.
UMBELLAR, [um'-bel-er], *adj.* (*bot.*) having the shape of an umbel.
UMBELLATE, [um'-bel-āt], *adj.* bearing umbels; umbellal.
UMBELLET, [um'-bel-et], *n.* (*bot.*) a lesser umbel.
UMBELLIFEROUS, [um'-bel-if'-er-us], *adj.* (*bot.*) having umbels.
UMBELLIFORM, [um-bel'-i-form], *adj.* (*bot.*) umbellar.
UMBELLULE, [um'-bel-yōōl], *n.* (*bot.*) an umbellet.
UMBER (1), UMBRE, [um'-ber], *n.* a brownish-yellow pigment which assumes a reddish quality if burnt; the grayling; the umber-bird. [OFr. *ombre* from L. *umbra* shadow].
UMBER (2), [um'-ber], *adj.* having a dark brown colour.
UMBER (3), [um'-ber], *v.t.* to paint with an umber colour.
UMBER-BIRD, [um'-ber-burd'], *n.* (*zool.*) a brown heron-like bird, the *Scopus umbretta*, found in Africa.
UMBERED, [um'-berd], *adj.* coloured with umber.
UMBERY, [um'-ber-i], *adj.* tinted with umber.
UMBILICAL, [um-bil'-ik-al], *adj.* (*anat.*) pertaining to the navel; resembling the navel. [MedL. *umbilicalis*].
UMBILICATE, [um-bil'-ik-āt], *adj.* possessing a navel; resembling a navel. [L. *umbilicatus*].
UMBILICATION, [um-bil'-ik-ā'-shun], *n.* a slight hollow like a navel.
UMBILICULAR, [um'-bil-ik'-yōō-ler], *adj.* pertaining to the navel.
UMBILICUS, [um-bil-īk'-us], *n.* (*anat.*) the navel; anything resembling this; (*class. antiq.*) the boss or handle at either end of a rod carrying a rolled manuscript; (*geom.*) a point on a surface through which every line of curvature passes; †a focus. [L. *umbilicus*].
UMBLE-PIE, see HUMBLE-PIE.
UMBLES†, [umblz], *n.*(*pl.*) entrails of deer. [~HUMBLE].
UMBO, [um'-bō], *n.* the central boss on a shield; any similar projection as a result of which there is a corresponding depression on the reverse; (*bot.*) a similar protuberance on certain fungi; (*zool.*) a protuberance (in a mollusc) which later becomes a valve. [L. *umbo* boss].
UMBONAL, [um'-bō-nal], *adj.* pertaining to an umbo.
UMBONATE, [um'-bō-nāt], *adj.* (*bot.*) resembling an umbo.
UMBONATED, [um'-bō-nāt-ed], *adj.* (*bot.*) umbonate.
UMBRA, [um'-bra], *n.* (*astron.*) the complete darkness or shadow in an eclipse. [L. *umbra* shadow].
UMBRAGE, [um'-brij], *n.* resentment, annoyance; (*poet.*) a shade, shadow; **to take u.**, to be annoyed. [Fr. *ombrage*].
UMBRAGEOUS, [um-brā'-jus], *adj.* shady or shaded; disposed to suspicion or resentment. [Fr. *ombrageux*].
UMBRAGEOUSLY, [um-brā'-jus-li], *adv.* in an umbrageous fashion.
UMBRAGEOUSNESS, [um-brā'-jus-nes], *n.* the quality of being umbrageous.
UMBRAL, [um'-bral], *adj.* (*astron.*) pertaining to an umbra.
UMBRATIC, [um-brat'-ik], *adj.* shadowy; remote, secluded. [L. *umbraticus*].
UMBRATILE, [um'-brat-il], *adj.* remote, secluded; shadowy, unreal. [L. *umbratilis*].
UMBRE, see UMBER (1).
UMBRELLA, [um-brel'-a], *n.* a portable shelter from rain, etc., consisting of a shallow ribbed dome of silk or other cloth, supported on a central stick, folded neatly about it when not in use; a parasol; a large canopy used in oriental ceremonies; (*zool.*) the disk-shaped part of a jellyfish resembling an ordinary umbrella. [It. *ombrella*].
UMBRELLA-BIRD, [um-brel'-a-burd'], *n.* the tropical American perching bird, *Cephalopterus ornatus*.
UMBRELLA-FIR, [um-brel'-a-fur'], *n.* the parasol pine, *Sciadopitys verticillata*.
UMBRETTE, [um-bret'], *n.* the African heron-like wading bird, *Scopus umbretta*.
UMBRIAN, [um'-bri-an], *adj.* of, or pertaining to, Umbria, a district of Central Italy.
UMBRIFEROUS, [um-brif'-er-us], *adj.* casting or offering a shade.

UMBRELLA-BIRD

UMBRIL, [um'-bril], *n.* a visor. [OFr. *ombrel* shade].
UMBROSE, [um'-brōs], *adj.* shady. [L. *umbrosus*].

UMBROSITY, [um-bros'-i-ti], *n.* shadiness.
UMIAK, [ōō'-mi-ak], *n.* an Eskimo boat used by women. [Eskimo *umiak*].
UMLAUT, [ōōm'-lowt], *n.* a sound change in most Germanic languages by which a following vowel (*esp.* i) modifies the vowel in the syllable that precedes. [Germ. *umlaut*].
UMPIRAGE, [um'-pier-rij], *n.* the office and function of an umpire.
UMPIRE, [um'-pier], *n.* an arbitrator; (*cricket*) one appointed to judge the fairness of the play, and give necessary decisions; (*leg.*) a third party who gives a decision when arbitrators cannot come to agreement.
UMPIRESHIP, [um'-pier-ship], *n.* the position of umpire.
UMPTEEN, [ump'-tēn], *n.* (*slang*) an indefinite large number. [*Umpty* representation of Morse signals].
UN- (1), *pref.* used before adjectives, adverbs, and nouns to express negation. [OE. *un*].
UN- (2), *pref.* used before verbs to express negation, separation, or reversal. [OE. *on, un*].
UNA, [yōō'-na], *n.* a special sort of single-masted boat, a cat-boat. [*Una* the name of the first boat of this sort seen in English waters and brought from America].
UNABASED, [un'-a-bāst'], *adj.* not abased or humbled.
UNABASHED, [un-a-basht'], *adj.* not abashed; not put out or confused.
UNABATED, [un-a-bā'-tid], *adj.* not in any way checked or repressed, in full force.
UNABATING, [un-a-bā'-ting], *adj.* not diminishing.
UNABBREVIATED, [un'-a-brē'-vi-ā-tid], *adj.* in full, not shortened.
UNABETTED, [un-a-bet'-id], *adj.* not supported or abetted.
UNABIDING, [un-a-bī'-ding], *adj.* transitory, not permanent or abiding.
UNABLE, [un-ābl'], *adj.* not able.
UNABOLISHABLE, [un-a-bol'-ish-abl], *adj.* incapable of being abolished.
UNABOLISHED, [un-a-bol'-isht], *adj.* valid, current, not abolished.
UNABRADED, [un-a-brā'-did], *adj.* not worn away by friction.
UNABRIDGED, [un-a-brijd'], *adj.* not abridged, in full.
UNABROGATED, [un-ab'-rōg-ā-tid], *adj.* not annulled, not abrogated.
UNABSOLVED, [un-ab-zolvd'], *adj.* not forgiven, not having received absolution.
UNABSORBABLE, [un-ab-sawb'-abl], *adj.* that cannot be absorbed.
UNABSORBED, [un-ab-sawbd'], *adj.* not taken in.
UNABSORBENT, [un-ab-sawb'-ent], *adj.* not absorbing.
UNACCELERATED, [un-ak-sel'-er-ā-tid], *adj.* not quickened.
UNACCENTED, [un-ak-sen'-tid], *adj.* having no stress.
UNACCENTUATED, [un-ak-sent'-yōō-ā-tid], *adj.* lacking emphasis, not accentuated.
UNACCEPTABILITY, [un'-ak-sept'-ab-il'-i-ti], *n.* the quality of being unacceptable.
UNACCEPTABLE, [un-ak-sep'-tabl], *adj.* not welcome or acceptable.
UNACCEPTABLY, [un-ak-sept'-ab-li], *adv.* in an unacceptable way.
UNACCLIMATIZED, [un-a-klīm'-at-īzd], *adj.* not accustomed to the climate.
UNACCOMMODATED, [un-a-kom'-ōd-ā-tid], *adj.* not fitted or suited; not provided with accommodation or lodging.
UNACCOMMODATING, [un-a-kom'-ōd-ā-ting], *adj.* not ready to oblige, not accommodating.
UNACCOMPANIED, [un-a-kum'-pan-id], *adj.* having no companions; (*mus.*) (of a song, etc.) not rendered with an instrumental accompaniment.
UNACCOMPLISHED, [un-a-komp'-lisht], *adj.* not finished or completed; having no accomplishments.
UNACCORDANT, [un-a-kawd'-ant], *adj.* not being in accord.
UNACCOUNTABILITY, [un'-a-kownt'-a-bil'-i-ti], *n.* the condition of being unaccountable.
UNACCOUNTABLE, [un-a-kownt'-abl], *adj.* that cannot be explained or accounted for.
UNACCOUNTABLENESS, [un-a-kownt'-abl-nes], *n.* the quality of being unaccountable.
UNACCOUNTABLY, [un-a-kownt'-ab-li], *adv.* in an unaccountable way.
UNACCREDITED, [un-a-kred'-it-id], *adj.* not authorized or accredited; not generally accepted.
UNACCUSED, [un-ak-yōōzd'], *adj.* not blamed or accused.
UNACCUSTOMED, [un-a-kust'-umd], *adj.* not accustomed, unused; unusual.
UNACHIEVABLE, [un-a-chēv'-abl], *adj.* that cannot be achieved.
UNACHIEVED, [un-a-chēvd'], *adj.* not done; not obtained.
UNACKNOWLEDGED, [un-ak-nol'-ijd], *adj.* not recognized; not owned; not confessed.
UNACQUAINTANCE, [un-a-kwānt'-ants], *n.* lack of acquaintance or knowledge.
UNACQUAINTED, [un-a-kwānt'-id], *adj.* lacking acquaintance.
UNACQUAINTEDNESS, [un-a-kwānt'-id-nes], *n.* the quality of being unacquainted.
UNACQUIRABLE, [un-a-kwier'-abl], *adj.* that cannot be acquired.
UNACQUIRED, [un-a-kwierd'], *adj.* not obtained.
UNACQUITTED, [un-a-kwit'-id], *adj.* not proclaimed innocent.
UNACTABLE, [un-akt'-abl], *adj.* not suitable to act.
UNACTED, [un-akt'-id], *adj.* not performed on the stage.
UNACTUATED, [un-ak'-chōō-āt-id], *adj.* not moved or driven.
UNADAPTABLE, [un-a-dapt'-abl], *adj.* impossible to adapt.
UNADAPTED, [un-a-dapt'-id], *adj.* not suited, unfitting.
UNADDICTED, [un-a-dik'-tid], *adj.* not obsessed (by) or addicted (to).
UNADDRESSED, [un-a-drest'], *adj.* having no address, *esp.* of a letter.
UNADJUDGED, [un-a-jujd'], *adj.* not decided or adjudged.
UNADJUSTED, [un-a-just'-id], *adj.* not adjusted, still requiring adjustment.
UNADMINISTERED, [un-ad-min'-ist-erd], *adj.* not administered.
UNADMIRED, [un-ad-mierd'], *adj.* not held in admiration.
UNADMITTED, [un-ad-mit'-id], *adj.* not allowed to enter; not permitted; not acknowledged or confessed.
UNADMONISHED, [un-ad-mon'-isht], *adj.* not cautioned or admonished.
UNADOPTABLE, [un-a-dopt'-abl], *adj.* that cannot be adopted.
UNADOPTED, [un-a-dopt'-id], *adj.* not adopted.
UNADORED, [un-ad-aw(r)d'], *adj.* not loved or worshipped.
UNADORNED, [un-ad-awnd'], *adj.* plain, without adornment.
UNADULTERATED, [un-ad-ul'-ter-ā-tid], *adj.* genuine, pure, not adulterated.
UNADVENTUROUS, [un-ad-ven'-cher-us], *adj.* not bold; uneventful.
UNADVISED, [un-ad-vīzd'], *adj.* rash; not counselled.
UNADVISEDLY, [un-ad-vīz'-id-li], *adv.* imprudently.
UNADVISEDNESS, [un-ad-vīz'-id-nes], *n.* the quality of being unadvised.
UNAFFABLE, [un-af'-abl], *adj.* not affable; reserved.
UNAFFECTED, [un-af-ek'-tid], *adj.* not affected; plain, natural, without affectation, sincere.
UNAFFECTEDLY, [un-af-ek'-tid-li], *adv.* in an unaffected way.
UNAFFECTEDNESS, [un-af-ek'-tid-nes], *n.* the state or quality of being unaffected.
UNAFFECTIONATE, [un-af-ek'-shun-at], *adj.* lacking in affection.
UNAFFILIATED, [un-af-il'-i-ā-tid], *adj.* not affiliated.
UNAFFLICTED, [un-af-lik'-tid], *adj.* free from trouble, not afflicted.
UNAFFRIGHTED, [un-a-frit'-id], *adj.* not frightened or dismayed.
UNAFRAID, [un-a-frād'], *adj.* bold, daring, undismayed.
UNAGGRESSIVE, [un-a-gres'-iv], *adj.* mild and not aggressive.
UNAGITATED, [un-aj'-it-ā-tid], *adj.* calm, unmoved.
UNAGREEABLE, [un-a-grē'-abl], *adj.* not pleasant or agreeable, distasteful.
UNAIDED, [un-ād'-id], *adj.* unassisted.
UNAIRED, [un-āerd'], *adj.* not aired or ventilated.
UNALARMED, [un-a-lahmd'], *adj.* not disturbed with fear, not frightened.
UNALARMING, [un-a-lahm'-ing], *adj.* not causing alarm.
UNALIENATED, [un-ā'-li-en-ā-tid], *adj.* not alienated or transferred; not diverted (from a purpose).

UNALIST, [yōō'-nal-ist], *n.* a cleric occupying only one benefice. [L. *unus* one and (PLUR)ALIST].
UNALLAYED, [un-a-lād'], *adj.* not pacified.
UNALLEVIATED, [un-a-lēv'-i-āt-id], *adj.* not mitigated or relieved.
UNALLIABLE, [un-al-ī'-abl], *adj.* incompatible.
UNALLIED, [un-al-īd'], *adj.* not connected or allied.
UNALLOTTED, [un-a-lot'-id], *adj.* not reserved, promised, or engaged.
UNALLOWABLE, [un-a-low'-abl], *adj.* that cannot be permitted.
UNALLOWED, [un-a-lowd'], *adj.* forbidden, not permitted.
UNALLOYED, [un-al-oid'], *adj.* pure, unmixed; (of happy emotions) unspoilt.
UNALLURING, [un-a-lyōōer'-ing], *adj.* not tempting, not seductive.
UNALTERABILITY, [un-awl'-ter-ab-il'-i-ti], *n.* the quality of being unalterable.
UNALTERABLE, [un-awl'-ter-abl], *adj.* unchangeable, fixed.
UNALTERABLENESS, [un-awl'-ter-abl-nes], *n.* the quality of being unalterable.
UNALTERABLY, [un-awl'-ter-ab-li], *adv.* in an unalterable fashion.
UNALTERED, [un-awl'-terd], *adj.* unchanged.
UNALTERING, [un-awl'-ter-ing], *adj.* not altering.
UNAMAZED, [un-a-māzd'], *adj.* free from amazement.
UNAMBIGUOUS, [un-am-big'-yōō-us], *adj.* not ambiguous.
UNAMBIGUOUSLY, [un-am-big'-yōō-us-li], *adv.* in an unambiguous fashion.
UNAMBIGUOUSNESS, [un-am-big'-yōō-us-nes], *n.* the quality of being unambiguous.
UNAMBITIOUS, [un-am-bish'-us], *adj.* lacking ambition.
UNAMBITIOUSLY, [un-am-bish'-us-li], *adv.* in an unambitious fashion.
UNAMBITIOUSNESS, [un-am-bish'-us-nes], *n.* the quality of being unambitious.
UNAMENABLE, [un-a-mēn'-abl], *adj.* not amenable or tractable.
UNAMENDABLE, [un-a-mend'-abl], *adj.* that cannot be amended.
UNAMENDED, [un-a-mend'-id], *adj.* not corrected or improved.
UN-AMERICAN, [un-a-me'-rik-an], *adj.* not American in tone or characteristics.
UNAMIABILITY, [un-ā'-mi-ab-il'-i-ti], *n.* the state or quality of being unamiable.
UNAMIABLE, [un-ā'-mi-abl], *adj.* not conciliating, not amiable.
UNAMIABLENESS, [un-ā'-mi-abl-nes], *n.* unamiability.
UNAMIABLY, [un-ā'-mi-ab-li], *adv.* in an unamiable fashion.
UNAMUSED, [un-a-mewzd'], *adj.* not amused.
UNAMUSING, [un-a-mewz'-ing], *adj.* not entertaining.
UNAMUSIVE, [un-a-mewz'-iv], *adj.* not amusing.
UNANALOGICAL, [un-an'-a-loj'-ik-al], *adj.* not based on analogy.
UNANALOGOUS, [un-an-al'-og-us], *adj.* not similar, not corresponding.
UNANALYSABLE, [un-an'-a-līz'-abl], *adj.* incapable of being analysed.
UNANALYSED, [un-an'-al-īzd], *adj.* not analysed.
UNANCHOR, [un-ang'-ker], *v.t. and i.* to free from anchorage; to weigh anchor.
UNANCHORED, [un-ang'-kerd], *adj.* not fastened by an anchor.
UNANELED, [un-an-ēld'], *adj.* (*arch.*) not having received extreme unction. [OE. *ele* oil].
UNANGULAR, [un-ang'-gyōō-ler], *adj.* not having angles.
UNANIMALIZED, [un-an'-im-al-īzd], *adj.* not made animal.
UNANIMATED, [un-an'-im-ā-tid], *adj.* not animated.
UNANIMATING, [un-an'-im-ā-ting], *adj.* not life-giving; (*fig.*) dull, uninteresting.
UNANIMITER, [yōō'-nan-im'-it-er], *adv.* (*leg.*) unanimously. [L. *unanimiter*].
UNANIMITY, [yōō'-nan-im'-i-ti], *n.* the condition or fact of being unanimous.
UNANIMOUS, [yōō-nan'-im-us], *adj.* (of persons) agreed, undivided in opinion; (of resolution, opinion) held by all, agreed to by every one.
UNANIMOUSLY, [yōō-nan'-im-us-li], *adv.* with unanimity.
UNANIMOUSNESS, [yōō-nan'-im-us-nes], *n.* the condition of being unanimous.
UNANNEALED, [un-an-ēld'], *adj.* not annealed or tempered.
UNANNEXED, [un-an-ekst'], *adj.* not annexed.
UNANNOUNCED, [un-a-nownst'], *adj.* not announced.
UNANNOYED, [un-an-oid'], *adj.* not annoyed or irritated.
UNANOINTED, [un-an-oin'-tid], *adj.* not having been anointed.
UNANSWERABILITY, [un-ahn'-ser-ab-il'-i-ti], *n.* the state of being unanswerable.
UNANSWERABLE, [un-ahn'-ser-abl], *adj.* not answerable, that cannot be refuted.
UNANSWERABLENESS, [un-ahn'-ser-abl-nes], *n.* unanswerability.
UNANSWERABLY, [un-ahn'-ser-ab-li], *adv.* beyond refutation, in an unanswerable way.
UNANSWERED, [un-ahn'-serd], *adj.* not answered; unrequited.
UNANTICIPATED, [un-an-tis'-ip-ā-tid], *adj.* not anticipated, unexpected.
UNANXIOUS, [un-angk'-shus], *adj.* not anxious, unconcerned.
UNAPOCRYPHAL, [un-ap-ok'-rif-al], *adj.* genuine, not apocryphal.
UNAPOSTOLIC, [un'-ap-os-tol'-ik], *adj.* not apostolic, lacking apostolic authority.
UNAPPALLED, [un-ap-awld'], *adj.* not daunted or afraid.
UNAPPARENT, [un-a-pa'-rent, un-a-pāer'-ent], *adj.* not visible or apparent.
UNAPPEALABLE, [un-ap-ēl'-abl], *adj.* (*leg.*) (of a decision or sentence) that cannot be appealed against; (of a case) incapable of being contested in a higher court.
UNAPPEASABLE, [un-ap-ē'-zabl], *adj.* incapable of being appeased.
UNAPPEASED, [un-ap-ēzd'], *adj.* not pacified or satisfied.
UNAPPETIZING, [un-ap'-it-īz-ing], *adj.* not appetizing or attractive.
UNAPPETIZINGLY, [un-ap'-it-īz-ing-li], *adv.* in an unappetizing fashion.
UNAPPLAUDED, [un-a-plawd'-id], *adj.* not received with applause.
UNAPPLIABLE, [un-a-plī'-abl], *adj.* inapplicable.
UNAPPLIED, [un-a-plīd'], *adj.* not applied or used.
UNAPPRECIATED, [un-ap-rē'-shi-ā-tid], *adj.* not properly valued.
UNAPPRECIATIVE, [un-ap-rē'-shi-at-iv], *adj.* not showing or feeling appreciation.
UNAPPREHENDED, [un'-ap'-ri-hend'-id], *adj.* not understood; (of a criminal) not held in custody.
UNAPPREHENSIBLE, [un'-ap'-ri-hen'-sibl], *adj.* incomprehensible.
UNAPPREHENSIVE, [un'-ap'-ri-hen'-siv], *adj.* not afraid or suspecting; not quick to apprehend mentally.
UNAPPREHENSIVENESS, [un'-ap'-ri-hen'-siv-nes], *n.* the quality of being unapprehensive.
UNAPPRISED, [un-a-prīzd'], *adj.* not warned beforehand.
UNAPPROACHABILITY, [un'-a-prōch'-ab-il'-i-ti], *n.* unapproachableness.
UNAPPROACHABLE, [un-a-prōch'-abl], *adj.* that cannot be approached; inaccessible, aloof.
UNAPPROACHABLENESS, [un-a-prōch'-abl-nes], *n.* the quality of being unapproachable.
UNAPPROACHABLY, [un-a-prōch'-ab-li], *adv.* in unapproachable fashion.
UNAPPROACHED, [un-a-prōcht'], *adj.* not approached.
UNAPPROPRIATED, [un-a-prōp'-ri-ā-tid], *adj.* not appropriated; (of money) not ear-marked for any particular purpose.
UNAPPROVED, [un-a-prōōvd'], *adj.* not approved.
UNAPPROVING, [un-a-prōōv'-ing], *adj.* disapproving.
UNAPPROVINGLY, [un-a-prōōv'-ing-li], *adv.* disapprovingly.
UNAPT, [un-apt'], *adj.* not apt, unsuitable; lacking skill and readiness, slow.
UNAPTLY, [un-apt'-li], *adv.* in an unapt fashion, inappropriately.
UNAPTNESS, [un-apt'-nes], *n.* the condition of being unapt.
UNARGUED, [un-ah'-gewd], *adj.* not discussed or argued about.
UNARM, [un-ahm'], *v.t. and i.* to disarm; to put aside one's arms.

UNARMED, [un-ahmd′], *adj.* not having or using arms; (*zool., bot.*) not having scales or prickles.
UNARMOURED, [un-ahm′-erd], *adj.* having no armour.
UNARRAIGNED, [un-a-rānd′], *adj.* not accused or brought to trial.
UNARRANGED, [un-a-rānjd′], *adj.* not in any order or arrangement; not prearranged.
UNARRAYED, [un-a-rād′], *adj.* not arrayed or adorned; not disposed in battle formation.
UNARRESTED, [un-a-rest′-id], *adj.* not placed under arrest; not stopped or checked.
UNARTFUL, [un-aht′-fŏŏl], *adj.* guileless.
UNARTFULLY, [un-aht′-fŏŏl-i], *adv.* in an unartful fashion.
UNARTICULATED, [un-ah-tik′-yŏŏ-lā-tid], *adj.* not articulated or spoken clearly.
UNARTIFICIAL, [un-ah′-tif-ish′-al], *adj.* not artificial, natural.
UNARTIFICIALLY, [un-ah′-tif-ish′-al-i], *adv.* not in an artificial manner.
UNARTISTIC, [un-ah-tis′-tik], *adj.* inartistic.
UNASCERTAINABLE, [un-as′-er-tān′-abl], *adj.* impossible to ascertain.
UNASCERTAINED, [un-as′-er-tānd′], *adj.* not known or found out.
UNASHAMED, [un-a-shāmd′], *adj.* not ashamed, brazen.
UNASKED, [un-ahskt′], *adj.* unsolicited; not sought or asked (for).
UNASPIRATED, [un-as′-pi-rā-tid], *adj.* not uttered with aspiration.
UNASPIRING, [un-a-spīer′-ing], *adj.* not ambitious.
UNASSAILABLE, [un-a-sāl′-abl], *adj.* that cannot be assailed; incontestable.
UNASSAYED, [un-a-sād′], *adj.* not assayed; (of a metal) not tested.
UNASSERTED, [un-as-ur′-tid], *adj.* not asserted; not used to its full force; not declared.
UNASSESSED, [un-a-sest′], *adj.* not assessed.
UNASSIGNABLE, [un-a-sīn′-abl], *adj.* not to be transferred by assignment; that cannot be assigned or attributed.
UNASSIGNED, [un-a-sīnd′], *adj.* not assigned; not attributed.
UNASSIMILABLE, [un-as-im′-il-abl], *adj.* incapable of being assimilated.
UNASSIMILATED, [un-as-im′-il-ā-tid], *adj.* not assimilated.
UNASSIMILATING, [un-as-im′-il-ā-ting], *adj.* not mixing easily, not assimilating.
UNASSISTED, [un-as-ist′-id], *adj.* not aided.
UNASSOCIATED, [un-as-ō′-shi-ā-tid], *adj.* not associated.
UNASSORTED, [un-as-aw′-tid], *adj.* not grouped or sorted, not assorted.
UNASSUAGED, [un-as-wājd′], *adj.* not assuaged.
UNASSUMING, [un-a-sewm′-ing], *adj.* not forward, modest.
UNASSURED, [un-a-shŏŏerd′], *adj.* not assured; not insured.
UNATONABLE, [un-a-tōn′-abl], *adj.* not to be atoned (for).
UNATONED, [un-a-tōnd′], *adj.* not atoned (for).
UNATTACHED, [un-a-tacht′], *adj.* not attached; (*milit.*) not connected with any particular regiment.
UNATTACKABLE, [un-a-tak′-abl], *adj.* incapable of being attacked.
UNATTAINABILITY, [un′-a-tān′-ab-il′-i-ti], *n.* unattainableness, the condition of being unattainable.
UNATTAINABLE, [un-a-tān′-abl], *adj.* that cannot be attained.
UNATTAINABLENESS, [un-a-tān′-abl-nes], *n.* unattainability.
UNATTAINTED, [un-a-tānt′-id], *adj.* unblemished.
UNATTEMPERED, [un-a-temp′-erd], *adj.* uncorrupted.
UNATTEMPTED, [un-a-temp′-tid], *adj.* not tried or attempted.
UNATTENDED, [un-a-tend′-id], *adj.* not accompanied by attendants; not attended to medically.
UNATTENDING, [un-a-tend′-ing], *adj.* not attending, unattentive.
UNATTENTIVE, [un-a-tent′-iv], *adj.* not attentive.
UNATTENUATED, [un-a-ten′-yŏŏ-ā-tid], *adj.* not lessened or attenuated.
UNATTESTED, [un-a-test′-id], *adj.* having no attestation, not witnessed to.
UNATTIRED, [un-a-tīerd′], *adj.* disrobed, unclad.
UNATTRACTIVE, [un-a-trak′-tiv], *adj.* not attractive, repellent; not claiming attention.
UNATTRACTIVELY, [un-a-trak′-tiv-li], *adv.* in an unattractive fashion.
UNATTRACTIVENESS, [un-a-trak′-tiv-nes], *n.* the state of being unattractive.
UNAU, [yōō′-naw], *n.* (*zool.*) the bidigitate sloth, *Cholœpus didactylus*, found in South America. [Native].

UNAU

UNAUDITED, [un-awd′-it-id], *adj.* not audited.
UNAUTHENTIC, [un-aw-thent′-ik], *adj.* not genuine, apocryphal.
UNAUTHENTICATED, [un-aw-thent′-ik-ā-tid], *adj.* not authenticated; not supported by authority.
UNAUTHORITATIVE, [un-aw-tho′-rit-at-iv], *adj.* not supported by authority.
UNAUTHORIZED, [un-aw′-ther-īzd], *adj.* not sanctioned by authority.
UNAVAILABILITY, [un′-a-vāl-a-bil′-i-ti], *n.* the fact or quality of being unavailable.
UNAVAILABLE, [un-a-vāl′-abl], *adj.* not available or obtainable.
UNAVAILING, [un-a-vāl′-ing], *adj.* ineffective, having no result, vain.
UNAVAILINGLY, [un-a-vāl′-ing-li], *adv.* in an unavailing fashion.
UNAVENGED, [un-a-venjd′], *adj.* without vengeance having been exacted, unrequited.
UNAVERTED, [un-a-vurt′-id], *adj.* not turned aside or averted.
UNAVOIDABLE, [un-a-void′-abl], *adj.* incapable of being rendered null or void; inevitable, not avoidable.
UNAVOIDABLENESS, [un-a-void′-abl-nes], *n.* the quality of being unavoidable.
UNAVOIDABLY, [un-a-void′-ab-li], *adv.* in an unavoidable fashion.
UNAVOIDED, [un-a-void′-id], *adj.* unshunned.
UNAVOWED, [un-a-vowd′], *adj.* not confessed, unacknowledged.
UNAWAKENED, [un-a-wāk′-end], *adj.* still sleeping; (*fig.*) latent.
UNAWARE (1), [un-a-wāer′], *adj.* uninformed (of), having no knowledge (of), unsuspicious (of).
UNAWARE (2), [un-a-wāer′], *adv.* unawares.
UNAWARES, [un-a-wāerz′], *adv.* unexpectedly, unknowingly, innocently, without full knowledge.
UNAWED, [un-awd′], *adj.* not awed.
UNBACKED, [un-bakt′], *adj.* (of a horse) not yet ridden upon; (*racing*) unsupported by bets; (*fig.*) having no aid, help or support.
UNBAFFLED, [un-bafld′], *adj.* not defeated or tricked; without baffles.
UNBAG, [un-bag′], *v.t.* to take or let out of a bag.
UNBAGGED, [un-bagd′], *adj.* removed from a bag.
UNBAILABLE, [un-bāl′-abl], *adj.* not bailable.
UNBAKED, [un-bākt′], *adj.* not baked.
UNBALANCE, [un-bal′-ants], *v.t.* to put out of balance.
UNBALANCED, [un-bal′-anst], *adj.* not balanced; unsteady, unreliable, temperamental; insane; (of financial accounts) not showing an equal sum on both debt and credit side, *esp.* showing a deficit.
UNBALED, [un-bāld′], *adj.* not done up in bales; not baled out.
UNBALLAST, [un-bal′-ast], *v.t.* to empty of ballast.
UNBALLASTED, [un-bal′-ast-id], *adj.* having no ballast.
UNBANDAGED, [un-band′-ijd], *adj.* not covered with a bandage.
UNBANKED, [un-bangkt′], *adj.* not having banks or sides; (of money, etc.) not lodged at a bank.
UNBANNERED, [un-ban′-erd], *adj.* lacking banners.
UNBAPTIZED, [un-bap-tīzd′], *adj.* not having received baptism.
UNBAR, [un-bah(r)′], *v.t.* to remove the bar from, unlock, open.
UNBARBERED, [un-bahb′-erd], *adj.* not shaved, unkempt, untidy.
UNBARK, [un-bahk′], *v.t.* to strip bare of bark.
UNBARKED, [un-bahkt′], *adj.* naked of bark.
UNBASHFUL, [un-bash′-fŏŏl], *adj.* not bashful.
UNBATED, [un-bāt′-id], *adj.* not checked, lowered, or repressed.
UNBATHED, [un-bāTHd′], *adj.* not having bathed or been bathed.
UNBATTERED, [un-bat′-erd], *adj.* not battered.
UNBEARABLE, [un-bāer′-abl], *adj.* that cannot be borne, intolerable.
UNBEARABLY, [un-bāer′-ab-li], *adv.* intolerably.
UNBEARDED, [un-bēerd′-id], *adj.* beardless.

UNBEARING, [un-bāer'-ing], *adj.* unproductive, barren.
UNBEATEN, [un-bēt'-en], *adj.* not beaten; unsurpassed, unconquered; untrodden, unexplored.
UNBEAUTIFIED, [un-bewt'-i-fīd], *adj.* not adorned or made beautiful by artifice, not beautified.
UNBEAUTIFUL, [un-bewt'-i-fōōl], *adj.* ugly.
UNBECOMING, [un-bi-kum'-ing], *adj.* not suitable or appropriate; indecent; indecorous.
UNBECOMINGLY, [un-bi-kum'-ing-li], *adv.* in an unbecoming fashion.
UNBECOMINGNESS, [un-bi-kum'-ing-nes], *n.* the quality of being unbecoming.
UNBEFITTING, [un-bi-fit'-ing], *adj.* inappropriate, unbecoming.
UNBEFRIENDED, [un-bi-frend'-id], *adj.* not helped by friends; having no friends.
UNBEGOTTEN, [un-bi-got'-en], *adj.* not begotten.
UNBEGUN, [un-bi-gun'], *adj.* not yet started.
UNBEHELD, [un-bi-held'], *adj.* not seen.
UNBEHOLDEN, [un-bi-hōld'-en], *adj.* not dependent upon or under obligation to.
UNBEKNOWN (1), UNBEKNOWNST, [un-bi-nōn(st)'], *adj.* not known.
UNBEKNOWN (2), UNBEKNOWNST, [un-bi-nōn(st)'], *adv.* without one's knowledge, in secret.
UNBELIEF, [un'-bi-lēf'], *n.* lack of faith, disbelief.
UNBELIEVABILITY, [un'-bi-lēv'-a-bil'-i-ti], *n.* the condition of being unbelievable.
UNBELIEVABLE, [un-bi-lēv'-abl], *adj.* incredible.
UNBELIEVABLY, [un-bi-lēv'-ab-li], *adv.* incredibly.
UNBELIEVED, [un-bi-lēvd'], *adj.* not accepted, not taken as true, not credited.
UNBELIEVER, [un-bi-lēv'-er], *n.* one who will not believe; a pagan; an atheist.
UNBELIEVING, [un-bi-lēv'-ing], *adj.* refusing to believe, sceptical.
UNBELOVED, [un-bi-luvd'], *adj.* not loved.
UNBELT, [un-belt'], *v.t.* to remove the belt from.
UNBEND, (**unbent**), [un-bend'], *v.t.* and *i.* to bend from a curved to a straight position; (*fig.*) to cease to be aloof or arrogant, and become gracious and sociable.
UNBENDING, [un-bend'-ing], *adj.* rigid, not bendable; determined, unrelenting, inflexible.
UNBENDINGLY, [un-bend'-ing-li], *adv.* in an unbending fashion.
UNBENDINGNESS, [un-bend'-ing-nes], *n.* the quality of being unbending.
UNBENEFICED, [un-ben'-i-fist], *adj.* with no benefice.
UNBENEFICIAL, [un-ben'-i-fish'-al], *adj.* not profitable or advantageous.
UNBENEFITED, [un-ben'-i-fit-id], *adj.* receiving no benefit.
UNBENIGN, [un-bi-nīn'], *adj.* harsh, not benign.
UNBENT, [un-bent'], *p.pt.* of UNBEND.
UNBESPOKEN, [un-bi-spōk'-en], *adj.* not engaged or ordered beforehand.
UNBESTOWED, [un-bi-stōd'], *adj.* not bestowed.
UNBETRAYED, [un-bi-trād'], *adj.* not betrayed; (*fig.*) kept secret.
UNBEWAILED, [un-bi-wāld'], *adj.* not bewailed or lamented.
UNBEWITCH, [un-bi-wich'], *v.t.* to free from witchcraft or enchantment.
UNBIASED, [un-bī'-ast], *adj.* free from prejudice, impartial.
UNBIASEDLY, [un-bī'-ast-li], *adv.* in an unbiased fashion.
UNBIASEDNESS, [un-bī'-ast-nes], *n.* the quality of being unbiased, impartiality.
UNBIDDEN, [un-bid'-en], *adj.* not bidden, uninvited.
UNBIGOTED, [un-big'-ot-id], *adj.* free from bigotry.
UNBIND, (**unbound**), [un-bīnd'], *v.t.* to take the binding from, to undo; to release.
UNBISHOP, [un-bish'-op], *v.t.* to deprive of episcopal rank.
UNBITT, [un-bit'], *v.t.* (*naut.*) to uncoil (rope) from a pair of bitts.
UNBITTED, [un-bit'-id], *adj.* not held by a bit.
UNBITTEN, [un-bit'-en], *adj.* not bitten; (*slang*) not filled with enthusiasm.
UNBLAMABLE, [un-blām'-abl], *adj.* not to be blamed.
UNBLAMABLENESS, [un-blām'-abl-nes], *n.* the quality of being unblamable.
UNBLAMABLY, [un-blām'-ab-li], *adv.* in an unblamable fashion.
UNBLAMED, [un-blāmd'], *adj.* not blamed or censured.
UNBLASTED, [un-blahst'-id], *adj.* not blasted.
UNBLEACHED, [un-blēcht'], *adj.* not bleached.
UNBLEMISHABLE, [un-blem'-ish-abl], *adj.* that cannot be stained.
UNBLEMISHED, [un-blem'-isht], *adj.* not blemished; (*fig.*) free from blame or reproach.
UNBLENCHED, [un-blencht'], *adj.* not frightened or dismayed; unstained.
UNBLENCHING, [un-blench'-ing], *adj.* not afraid or flinching; brazen.
UNBLENDED, [un-blend'-id], *adj.* pure, not mixed.
UNBLEST, UNBLESSED, [un-blest'], *adj.* having received no blessing; unlucky.
UNBLIGHTED, [un-blīt'-id], *adj.* not blighted; (*fig.*) not spoiled in any way.
UNBLOCK, [un-blok'], *v.t.* to free from hindrance or obstruction.
UNBLOODED, [un-blud'-id], *adj.* not stained with gore; (of a horse) not a thoroughbred.
UNBLOODY, [un-blud'-i], *adj.* not stained with blood; not cruel or fierce.
UNBLOTTED, [un-blot'-id], *adj.* not stained with blots; not erased.
UNBLOWN, [un-blōn'], *adj.* (of a plant) having its buds still closed; (of a bugle, etc.) not sounded; (of a person) not winded with running or exercise.
UNBLUNTED, [un-blunt'-id], *adj.* not made blunt.
UNBLUSHING, [un-blush'-ing], *adj.* brazen, shameless, impudent.
UNBLUSHINGLY, [un-blush'-ing-li], *adv.* in an unblushing fashion.
UNBLUSHINGNESS, [un-blush'-ing-nes], *n.* the condition of being unblushing.
UNBOASTFUL, [un-bōst'-fōōl], *adj.* modest, not given to boasting.
UNBODIED, [un-bod'-id], *adj.* lacking a material body.
UNBOILED, [un'-boild'], *adj.* not boiled, not heated to boiling point.
UNBOLT, [un-bōlt'], *v.t.* to release the bolt of, to open or unfasten by so doing.
UNBOLTED (1), [un-bōlt'-id], *adj.* not locked with a bolt, open, openable.
UNBOLTED (2), [un-bōlt'-id], *adj.* not sifted.
UNBONNETED†, [un-bon'-it-id], *adj.* having the head uncovered.
UNBOOKISH, [un-bŏŏk'-ish], *adj.* not bookish, not well equipped with book learning.
UNBOOT, [un-bōōt'], *v.t.* and *i.* to remove the boots of; to remove one's own boots.
UNBOOTED, [un-bōōt'-id], *adj.* not wearing boots.
UNBORN, [un-bawn'], *adj.* not yet born.
UNBORROWED, [un-bo'-rōd], *adj.* not obtained by borrowing, original.
UNBOSOM, [un-bŏŏz'-um], *v. refl.* to confess one's trouble or worry.
UNBOTTOMED, [un-bot'-omd], *adj.* bottomless.
UNBOUGHT, [un-bawt'], *adj.* not bought; obtained without money; not purchased.
UNBOUND, [un-bownd'], *adj.* free, not chained or shackled; (of a book) having no binding.
UNBOUNDED, [un-bownd'-id], *adj.* having no limit; boundless, unlimited, infinite.
UNBOUNDEDLY, [un-bownd'-id-li], *adv.* without bounds, in an unbounded fashion.
UNBOUNDEDNESS, [un-bownd'-id-nes], *n.* the condition of being unbounded.
UNBOUNTEOUS, [un-bownt'-i-us], *adj.* not bounteous, ungenerous.
UNBOWED, [un-bowd'], *adj.* not bowed or bent; unsubdued, unconquered.
UNBOYISH, [un-boi'-ish], *adj.* not boyish.
UNBRACE, [un-brās'], *v.t.* and *i.* to loosen, untie; to relax, rest.
UNBRAID, [un-brād'], *v.t.* to unweave, to separate the strands of.
UNBRANCHED, [un-brahncht'], *adj.* not having branches.
UNBRANCHING, [un-brahnch'-ing], *adj.* not separating into branches.
UNBREATHABLE, [un-brēᴛʜ'-abl], *adj.* not fit to be breathed or spoken of.
UNBREATHED (1), [un-brēᴛʜd'], *adj.* undivulged.
UNBREATHED (2), [un-bretht'], *adj.* out of breath.
UNBREATHING, [un-brēᴛʜ'-ing], *adj.* not breathing, lifeless; breathless; (*fig.*) not stopping for even a moment.
UNBRED, [un-bred'], *adj.* not bred or trained.
UNBREECH, [un-brēch'], *v.t.* to take the breeches from; (*milit.*) to unlock the breech of (a cannon).
UNBREECHED, [un-brēcht'], *adj.* not yet wearing trousers; deprived of trousers; with bare legs.

UNBRIBABLE, [un-brīb′-abl], *adj.* not open to bribery.
UNBRIBED, [un-brībd′], *adj.* not bribed or corrupted.
UNBRIDGED, [un-brijd′], *adj.* not spanned by a bridge.
UNBRIDLE, [un-brīdl′], *v.t.* to remove the bridle from (a horse); (*fig.*) to free.
UNBRIDLED, [un-brīdld′], *adj.* not bridled; licentious, violent.
UNBRITISH, [un-brit′-ish], *adj.* uncharacteristic, unworthy, of the British.
UNBROKEN, [un-brōk′-en], *adj.* not broken; whole, unshattered; continuous; (of land) unploughed; (of a horse) unbacked, not broken; (of a record) not bettered.
UNBROTHERLINESS, [un-bruTH′-er-li-nes], *n.* the quality of being unbrotherly.
UNBROTHERLY, [un-bruTH′-er-li], *adj.* not according with what is expected of a brother, unfeeling.
UNBRUISED, [un-brōōzd′], *adj.* not bruised, unhurt.
UNBUCKLE, [un-bukl′], *v.t.* to undo the buckle of.
UNBUILT, [un-bilt′], *adj.* not built; (of land) unbuilt on.
UNBUNDLED, [un-bundld′], *adj.* released or taken from a bundle; not made up into bundles.
UNBURDEN, UNBURTHEN, [un-burd′-en], *v.t.* to relieve of a load or burden; (*fig.*) to relieve (one's mind) by confessing one's worry or trouble.
UNBURDENED, [un-burd′-end], *adj.* not burdened or weighed down.
UNBURDENSOME, [un-burd′-en-som], *adj.* not burdensome or oppressive.
UNBURIABLE, [un-be′-ri-abl], *adj.* unfit to be buried.
UNBURIED, [un-be′-rid], *adj.* not buried; disinterred.
UNBURNED, see UNBURNT.
UNBURNING, [un-burn′-ing], *adj.* not burning.
UNBURNT, UNBURNED, [un-burnt′, un-burnd′], *adj.* not consumed by fire.
UNBURROW, [un-bu′-rō], *v.t.* to cause (an animal) to come out of its burrow.
UNBURTHEN, [un-burTH′-en], see UNBURDEN.
UNBURY, [un-be′-ri], *v.t.* to exhume.
UNBUSIED, [un-biz′-id], *adj.* idle, leisurely.
UNBUSINESSLIKE, [un-biz′-nes-līk], *adj.* inefficient, muddled, not businesslike.
UNBUTTON, [un-but′-on], *v.t. and i.* to undo the buttons of; to relax.
UNCAGE, [un-kāj′], *v.t.* to liberate from a cage; (*fig.*) to free, release.
UNCALCULATED, [un-kal′-kyŏŏ-lā-tid], *adj.* not arrived at by calculation; undetermined, indefinite; (*fig.*) accidental, unintentional.
UNCALLED, [un-kawld′], *adj.* not called; **u.-for**, unnecessary; unprovoked.
UNCAMOUFLAGED, [un-kam′-ŏŏ-flahzhd], *adj.* not camouflaged; not disguised.
UNCANCELLABLE, [un-kan′-sel-abl], *adj.* that cannot be cancelled.
UNCANCELLED, [un-kan′-seld], *adj.* not cancelled, still valid.
UNCANDID, [un-kan′-did], *adj.* lacking in frankness and confidence.
UNCANNILY, [un-kan′-i-li], *adv.* weirdly, in an uncanny fashion.
UNCANNINESS, [un-kan′-i-nes], *n.* the quality of being uncanny.
UNCANNY, [un-kan′-i], *adj.* weird, mysterious.
UNCANONIC, [un-kan-on′-ik], *adj.* uncanonical.
UNCANONICAL, [un-kan-on′-ik-al], *adj.* not canonical; outside the canon of Holy Scripture.
UNCANONICALLY, [un-kan-on′-ik-al-i], *adv.* in an uncanonical fashion.
UNCANONICALNESS, [un-kan-on′-ik-al-nes], *n.* the quality or condition of being uncanonical.
UNCANONIZE, [un-kan′-on-īz], *v.t.* to eject from the calendar of saints.
UNCANONIZED, [un-kan′-on-īzd], *adj.* not yet canonized.
UNCANOPIED, [un-kan′-op-id], *adj.* not protected with a canopy.
UNCANVASSED, [un-kan′-vast], *adj.* not sought for by canvassing.
UNCAP, [un-kap′], *v.t. and i.* to remove the cap from; to remove one's own cap.
UNCARED, [un-kāerd′], *adj.* **u.-for**, not loved or looked after.
UNCARESSED, [un-ka-rest′], *adj.* not caressed.
UNCARPETED, [un-kahp′-it-id], *adj.* with no carpet.
UNCART, [un-kaht′], *v.t.* to unload out of a cart.
UNCASE, [un-kās′], *v.t.* to remove from its case.
UNCATALOGUED, [un-kat′-a-logd], *adj.* not entered in a catalogue.
UNCATE, [ung′-kāt], *adj.* uncinate, hooked.
UNCATECHIZED, [un-kat′-ik-īzd], *adj.* not submitted to catechism; (*fig.*) unquestioned.
UNCAUGHT, [un-kawt′], *adj.* not caught.
UNCAUSED, [un-kawzd′], *adj.* not produced by any cause, self-generated.
UNCEASING, [un-sēs′-ing], *adj.* not ceasing, uninterrupted, incessant.
UNCEASINGLY, [un-sēs′-ing-li], *adv.* without ceasing, incessantly.
UNCELEBRATED, [un-sel′-ib-rā-tid], *adj.* not famous; not solemnized.
UNCELESTIAL, [un-si-les′-ti-al], *adj.* not heavenly or divine.
UNCEMENTED, [un-si-ment′-id], *adj.* not cemented; (*fig.*) not firmly joined.
UNCENSORED, [un-sens′-erd], *adj.* not censored; not having the censor's permit.
UNCENSURABLE, [un-sen′-sher-abl], *adj.* not censurable.
UNCENSURED, [un-sen′-sherd], *adj.* not censured.
UNCEREMONIOUS, [un-se′-ri-mōn′-i-us], *adj.* lacking ceremony, curt, rude, abrupt.
UNCEREMONIOUSLY, [un-se′-ri-mōn′-i-us-li], *adv.* in an unceremonious fashion.
UNCERTAIN, [un-sur′-tan], *adj.* not certain, doubtful, undecided; not reliable, fickle; precarious.
UNCERTAINLY, [un-sur′-tan-li], *adv.* in an uncertain fashion.
UNCERTAINTY, [un-sur′-tan-ti], *n.* the state or quality of being uncertain; dubiousness; want of certainty or precision; vagueness, variableness.
UNCERTIFICATED, [un-ser-tif′-ik-āt-ed], *adj.* not possessing a certificate of competence.
UNCERTIFIED, [un-sur′-ti-fīd], *adj.* not holding a certificate, unqualified; not certified, *esp.* as insane.
UNCHAIN, [un-chān′], *v.t.* to remove chains or fetters from; (*fig.*) to free, release, liberate.
UNCHALLENGEABLE, [un-chal′-enj-abl], *adj.* that cannot be challenged.
UNCHALLENGEABLY, [un-chal′-enj-ab-li], *adv.* in an challengeable fashion.
UNCHALLENGED, [un-chal′-enjd′], *adj.* not challenged; not questioned or objected to.
UNCHANCY, [un-chahn′-sē], *adj.* ill-omened; ill-timed; awkward.
UNCHANGEABILITY, [un′-chānj′-ab-il′-i-ti], *n.* the quality of being unchangeable.
UNCHANGEABLE, [un-chānj′-abl], *adj.* not capable of change, immutable.
UNCHANGEABLENESS, [un-chānj′-abl-nes], *n.* the quality of being unchangeable.
UNCHANGEABLY, [un-chānj′-ab-li], *adv.* without change, in an unchangeable fashion.
UNCHANGED, [un-chānjd′], *adj.* not altered; not dressed.
UNCHANGING, [un-chānj′-ing], *adj.* suffering or liable to suffer no alteration.
UNCHANGINGLY, [un-chānj′-ing-li], *adv.* in an unchanging fashion.
UNCHAPERONED, [un-shap′-er-ōnd], *adj.* not accompanied by a chaperone.
UNCHARACTERISTIC, [un-ka′-rak-ter-ist′-ik], *adj.* not characteristic or typical.
UNCHARGED, [un-chahjd′], *adj.* not debited to; (of a gun) not loaded; (of an electric battery) not charged; (of a person) not accused.
UNCHARITABLE, [un-cha′-rit-abl], *adj.* not generous in giving; not in accordance with Christian charity or goodwill.
UNCHARITABLENESS, [un-cha′-rit-abl-nes], *n.* lack of charity.
UNCHARITABLY, [un-cha′-rit-ab-li], *adv.* in an uncharitable fashion.
UNCHARITY, [un-cha′-ri-tē], *n.* lack of charity.
UNCHARTED, [un-chaht′-id], *adj.* not shown on a chart, unexplored, unknown.
UNCHARTERED, [un-chaht′-erd], *adj.* not chartered, unrestricted, unlicensed.
UNCHARY, [un-chāer′-i], *adj.* rash, extravagant.
UNCHASTE, [un-chāst′], *adj.* not chaste; lewd, incontinent.
UNCHASTELY, [un-chāst′-li], *adv.* in an unchaste manner.
UNCHASTISABLE, [un-chas-tī′-zabl], *adj.* that cannot be chastised.
UNCHASTISED, [un-chas-tīzd′], *adj.* not chastised.
UNCHASTITY, [un-chas′-ti-ti], *n.* the quality of being unchaste, incontinence, lewdness.

JNCHECKED, [un-chekt'], *adj.* not checked or hindered; not tried over or tested.
JNCHEERED, [un-chēerd'], *adj.* not given cause to rejoice, not made happy, not cheered.
UNCHEERFUL, [un-chēer'-fōōl], *adj.* not cheerful.
UNCHEERFULNESS, [un-chēer'-fōōl-nes], *n.* lack of cheerfulness.
UNCHEERY, [un-chēer'-i], *adj.* dull, not cheerful.
UNCHEQUERED, [un-chek'-erd], *adj.* not varied, not eventful.
UNCHEWED, [un-chōōd'], *adj.* not chewed.
UNCHIDED, [un-chīd'-id], *adj.* not scolded or rebuked.
UNCHILLED, [un-child'], *adj.* not chilled; not cooled or refrigerated.
UNCHIVALROUS, [un-shiv'-al-rus], *adj.* not gallant or chivalrous.
UNCHIVALROUSLY, [un-shiv'-al-rus-li], *adv.* in an unchivalrous fashion.
UNCHRISTENED, [un-kris'-end], *adj.* unbaptized.
UNCHRISTIAN, [un-kris'-chan], *adj.* contrary to the spirit of Christianity.
UNCHRISTIANLIKE, [un-kris'-chan-līk], *adj.* not befitting a Christian.
UNCHRISTIANLY, [un-kris'-chan-li], *adv.* in an unchristian fashion.
UNCHRISTIANNESS, [un-kris'-chan-nes], *n.* the state of being unchristian.
UNCHRONICLED, [un-kron'-ikld], *adj.* not recorded.
UNCHRONOLOGICAL, [un'-kron-ō-loj'-ikl], *adj.* not in accordance with chronology.
UNCHURCH, [un-church'], *v.t.* to excommunicate.
UNCIA, [un'-si-a], *n.* the twelfth of an as; an inch; an ounce. [L. *uncia*].
UNCIAL (1), [un'-shal], *n.* an uncial character.
UNCIAL (2), [un'-shal], *adj.* in, of, or having, majuscule letters of the type found in early manuscripts. [MedL. (*litterae*) *unciales*].
UNCIFEROUS, [un-sif'-er-us], *adj.* (*zool.*) having a hook. [L. *uncus* hook and *ferre* to bear].
UNCIFORM, [un'-si-fawm], *adj.* shaped like a hook. [L. *uncus*, hook].
UNCINAL, [un'-sin-al], *adj.* shaped like a hook. [~LL. *uncinus*].
UNCINATE, [un'-sin-āt], *adj.* (*zool., bot.*) unciform.
UNCIRCUMCISED, [un-sur'-kum-sīzd], *adj.* not circumcised; pagan; **the U.,** (*N.T.*) the Gentiles.
UNCIRCUMCISION, [un-sur'-kum-sizh'-un], *n.* the state of being uncircumcised, paganism.
UNCIRCUMSCRIBED, [un-sur'-kum-skrībd], *adj.* not limited or circumscribed.
UNCIRCUMSTANTIAL, [un-sur'-kum-stan'-shal], *adj.* not circumstantial.
UNCIRCUMSPECT, [un-sur'-kum-spekt'], *adj.* not tactful or circumspect.
UNCIRCUMSPECTLY, [un-sur'-kum-spekt'-li], *adv.* in an uncircumspect fashion.
UNCIROSTRATE, [un'-si-ros'-trāt], *adj.* having a hook-shaped beak.
UNCITED, [un-sīt'-ed], *adj.* not cited.
UNCIVIL, [un-siv'-il], *adj.* not polite or civil, rude, ill-mannered; uncivilized.
UNCIVILIZABLE, [un-siv'-il-īz'-abl], *adj.* that cannot, or will not, be civilized.
UNCIVILIZATION, [un-siv'-il-īz-ā'-shun], *n.* the state of being uncivilized.
UNCIVILIZED, [un-siv'-il-īzd], *adj.* barbarous.
UNCIVILLY, [un-siv'-il-li], *adv.* in an uncivil fashion.
UNCLAD, [un-klad'], *adj.* not clothed, undressed.
UNCLAIMED, [un-klāmd'], *adj.* not claimed.
UNCLARIFIED, [un-kla'-ri-fīd], *adj.* not made clear.
UNCLASP, [un-klahsp'], *v.t.* and *i.* to release the clasp of, unfasten; to separate, unclench.
UNCLASSABLE, [un-klahs'-abl], *adj.* incapable of being grouped or classified.
UNCLASSICAL, [un-klas'-ik-al], *adj.* not classical.
UNCLE, [ungkl], *n.* he who is brother to one's mother or father, or is married to a sister of either parent; (*slang*) a pawnbroker. [OFr. *oncle*].
UNCLEAN, [un-klēn'], *adj.* not clean, foul; unchaste; not ceremonially clean.
UNCLEANABLE, [un-klēn'-abl], *adj.* incapable of being cleaned.
UNCLEANLINESS, [un-klen'-li-ness], *n.* uncleanness.
UNCLEANLY (1), [un-klen'-li], *adj.* unclean, *esp.* of a person with dirty habits.
UNCLEANLY (2), [un-klēn'-li], *adv.* in an unclean manner.
UNCLEANNESS, [un-klēn'-nes], *n.* the state of being unclean, unregenerate; moral corruption.
UNCLEANSED, [un-klenzd'], *adj.* not cleansed or purified.
UNCLEAR, [un-klēer'], *adj.* obscure. [Germ. *unklar*].
UNCLEARED, [un-klēerd'], *adj.* not rid of or cleared; not proved to be blameless.
UNCLENCH, UNCLINCH, [un-klench'], *v.t.* to open from a tightly closed state or position.
UNCLERICAL, [un-kle'-rik-al], *adj.* not befitting a cleric.
UNCLEW, [un-klōō'], *v.t.* (*naut.*) to unwind; let down.
UNCLIMBABLE, [un-klīm'-abl], *adj.* that cannot be climbed or scaled.
UNCLINCH, [un-klinch'], see UNCLENCH.
UNCLIPPED, [un-klipt'], *adj.* not clipped, not shortened by clipping.
UNCLOAK, [un-klōk'], *v.t.* and *i.* to take off a cloak from; (*fig.*) to reveal; to remove one's cloak.
UNCLOAKED, [un-klōkt'], *adj.* (*fig.*) not hidden or disguised.
UNCLOG, [un-klog'], *v.t.* to free from obstruction or hindrance.
UNCLOISTER, [un-kloi'-ster], *v.t.* to take out of a cloister.
UNCLOSE, [un-klōz'], *v.t.* to open.
UNCLOSED, [un-klōzd'], *adj.* open, not obscured or confined, incomplete.
UNCLOTHE, [un-klōTH'], *v.t.* and *i.* to strip naked.
UNCLOTHED, [un-klōTHd], *adj.* naked, unclad.
UNCLOUD, [un-klowd'], *v.t.* to free from clouds; (*fig.*) to make clean.
UNCLOUDED, [un-klowd'-id], *adj.* free from clouds; (*fig.*) not spoiled in any way.
UNCLOUDEDNESS, [un-klowd'-id-nes], *n.* the condition of being unclouded.
UNCLUTCH, [un-kluch'], *v.t.* to free (something held in a clutch or grip).
UNCO (1), [ung'-kō], *n.* an unknown person or strange object; unusual happening or event. [Scots *var.* of UNCOUTH].
UNCO (2), [ung'-kō], *adj.* strange, marvellous. [*Prec.*].
UNCO (3), [ung'-ko], *adv.* very, unusually, extremely; **the u. guid,** self-righteous moralists.
UNCOAGULABLE, [un-kō-ag'-yōōl-abl], *adj.* that cannot be caused to coagulate.
UNCOAGULATED, [un-kō-ag'-yōōl-ā-tid], *adj.* not coagulated.
UNCOATED, [un-kōt'-id], *adj.* not wearing a coat; without a coating.
UNCOCK, [un-kok'], *v.t.* to release gently the hammer of (a gun) without firing it.
UNCOCKED, [un-kokt'], *adj.* not cocked.
UNCODIFIED, [un-kōd'-i-fīd], *adj.* not subjected to codification.
UNCOIL, [un-koil'], *v.t.* and *i.* to unwind.
UNCOINED, [un-koi-ind'], *adj.* not made into coins; (*fig.*) genuine, not a coinage.
UNCOLLATED, [un-kol-āt'-ed], *adj.* not collated.
UNCOLLECTED, [un-kol-ek'-tid], *adj.* not collected; disordered.
UNCOLLECTEDNESS, [un-kol-ek'-tid-nes], *n.* the condition of being uncollected.
UNCOLOURED, [un-kul'-erd], *adj.* not coloured; (*fig.*) not heightened in narration.
UNCOMBED, [un-kōmd'], *adj.* unkempt, not combed.
UNCOMBINABLE, [un-kom-bīn'-abl], *adj.* not capable of being combined.
UNCOMBINED, [un-kom-bīnd'], *adj.* not combined or compounded.
UN-COME-AT-ABLE, [un'-kum-at'-abl], *adj.* (*coll.*) inaccessible, remote.
UNCOMELINESS, [un-kum'-li-nes], *n.* the condition of being uncomely.
UNCOMELY, [un-kum'-li], *adj.* wanting in grace or beauty; unseemly.
UNCOMFORTABLE, [un-kum'-fer-tabl], *adj.* affording no comfort; not comfortable or at ease.
UNCOMFORTABLENESS, [un-kum'-fer-tabl-nes], *n.* the condition of being uncomfortable.
UNCOMFORTABLY, [un-kum'-fer-tab-li], *adv.* in an uncomfortable fashion.
UNCOMFORTED, [un-kum'-fer-tid], *adj.* not consoled or comforted.
UNCOMMANDED, [un-kom-ahnd'-id], *adj.* not ordered.
UNCOMMEMORATED, [un-ko-mem'-er-ā-tid], *adj.* not celebrated or commemorated.
UNCOMMENDABLE, [un-kom-end'-abl], *adj.* not meriting commendation.
UNCOMMENDED, [un-kom-end'-id], *adj.* not praised or recommended.
UNCOMMERCIAL, [un-kom-ur'-shal], *adj.* not

commercial; not carrying on commerce; not seeking profit; not conforming to commercial standards.
UNCOMMISERATED, [un-kom-iz'-er-ā-tid], *adj.* not pitied or sympathized with.
UNCOMMISSIONED, [un-kom-ish'-und], *adj.* not holding a commission; unauthorized.
UNCOMMITTED, [un-kom-it'-id], *adj.* not done or committed; not bound by any pledge or promise.
UNCOMMON (1), [un-kom'-on], *adj.* not common, scarce, unusual.
UNCOMMON (2), [un-kom'-on], *adv.* (*dial.*) very.
UNCOMMONLY, [un-kom'-on-li], *adv.* in an uncommon degree; not frequently; (*coll.*) very.
UNCOMMONNESS, [un-kom'-on-nes], *n.* the quality of being uncommon.
UNCOMMUNICABLE, [un-kom-ewn'-ik-abl], *adj.* not communicable.
UNCOMMUNICATED, [un-kom-ewn'-ik-ā-tid], *adj.* not disclosed or imparted.
UNCOMMUNICATIVE, [un'-kom-ewn'-i-kat-iv], *adj.* taciturn, not communicative.
UNCOMMUNICATIVENESS, [un'-kom-ewn'-ik-at-iv-nes], *n.* taciturnity.
UNCOMMUTED, [un-kom-ewt'-ed], *adj.* not commuted.
UNCOMPANIONABLE, [un'-kom-pan'-yon-abl], *adj.* not sociable or companionable.
UNCOMPASSIONATE, [un-kom-pash'-un-at], *adj.* unsympathetic, having no pity.
UNCOMPELLABLE, [un-kom-pel'-abl], *adj.* that cannot be compelled.
UNCOMPELLED, [un-kom-peld'], *adj.* not compelled.
UNCOMPENSATED, [un-kom'-pen-sā-tid], *adj.* unrewarded; not compensated.
UNCOMPETITIVE, [un-kom-pet'-it-iv], *adj.* not involving competition.
UNCOMPLAINING, [un-kom-plān'-ing], *adj.* not disposed to complain, patient.
UNCOMPLETED, [un-kom-plēt'-id], *adj.* not complete, unfinished.
UNCOMPLIANT, [un-kom-plī'-ant], *adj.* not compliant, unyielding.
UNCOMPLICATED, [un-kom'-plik-ā-tid], *adj.* not complicated, simple, not involved.
UNCOMPLIMENTARY, [un-kom'-pli-ment'-er-i], *adj.* not complimentary, uncivil.
UNCOMPLYING, [un-kom-plī'-ing], *adj.* not complying, not yielding to request or command.
UNCOMPOSABLE, [un-kom-pōz'-abl], *adj.* that cannot be composed or settled.
UNCOMPOUNDED, [un-kom-pownd'-id], *adj.* not mixed or compounded.
UNCOMPREHENSIVE, [un-kom'-pri-hen'-siv], *adj.* not comprehensive; unable to understand.
UNCOMPRESSED, [un-kom-prest'], *adj.* not compressed.
UNCOMPROMISED, [un-kom'-prom-īzd], *adj.* not compromised.
UNCOMPROMISING, [un-kom'-prom-ī-zing], *adj.* not admitting of compromise; not yielding to compromise; firm, unyielding.
UNCOMPROMISINGLY, [un-kom'-prom-ī-zing-li], *adv.* in an uncompromising fashion.
UNCONCEALED, [un-kon-sēld'], *adj.* not concealed or secret.
UNCONCEIVED, [un-kon-sēvd'], *adj.* not conceived; (*fig.*) not imagined or thought of.
UNCONCERN, [un-kon-surn'], *n.* lack of concern or anxiety.
UNCONCERNED, [un-kon-surnd'], *adj.* not anxious; having no interest or part (in); indifferent, unmoved.
UNCONCERNEDLY, [un-kon-surn'-id-li], *adv.* in an unconcerned fashion.
UNCONCERNEDNESS, [un-kon-surn'-id-nes], *n.* the quality of being unconcerned.
UNCONCERTED, [un-kon-sur'-tid], *adj.* not done in concert or together.
UNCONCILIATED, [un-kon-sil'-i-ā-tid], *adj.* not reconciled or conciliated.
UNCONCILIATING, [un-kon-sil'-i-ā-ting], *adj.* not conciliating.
UNCONCILIATORY, [un-kon-sil'-i-at-er-i], *adj.* not tending to conciliate, hostile.
UNCONCLUDED, [un-kon-klōō'-did], *adj.* not concluded, incomplete.
UNCONCOCTED, [un-kon-kok'-tid], *adj.* not concocted; (*fig.*) true.
UNCONDEMNED, [un-kon-demd'], *adj.* not condemned; not disapproved of.
UNCONDENSABLE, [un-kon-dens'-abl], *adj.* that cannot be condensed, compressed or abbreviated.
UNCONDENSED, [un-kon-denst'], *adj.* not condensed; (*fig.*) not summarized or shortened.
UNCONDITIONAL, [un-kon-dish'-un-al], *adj.* absolute, not limited by any conditions.
UNCONDITIONALITY, [un-kon-dish'-un-al'-i-ti], *n.* the state of being unconditional.
UNCONDITIONALLY, [un-kon-dish'-un-al-i], *adv.* without conditions, in unconditional fashion.
UNCONDITIONED, [un-kon-dish'-und], *adj.* unconditional; not in a good state or condition; (*psych.*) inherent, instinctive; **the u.,** (*philos.*) that which surpasses finite limitations, the infinite.
UNCONDUCTED, [un-kon-duk'-tid], *adj.* lacking a conductor or guide.
UNCONFESSED, [un-kon-fest'], *adj.* not admitted or confessed to; not having made a confession and received absolution.
UNCONFINABLE, [un-kon-fīn'-abl], *adj.* that cannot be confined or shut in.
UNCONFINED, [un-kon-fīnd'], *adj.* loose, free from constraint or control; unlimited.
UNCONFINEDLY, [un-kon-fīn'-id-li], *adv.* without limitation, in an unconfined fashion.
UNCONFIRMED, [un-kon-furmd'], *adj.* not confirmed, attested, or corroborated; not having received Confirmation.
UNCONFORMABILITY, [un'-kon-fawm-ab-il'-i-ti], *n.* the quality of being unconformable.
UNCONFORMABLE, [un-kon-fawm'-abl], *adj.* not conforming, inconsistent; (*geol.*) not parallel.
UNCONFORMABLY, [un-kon-fawm'-ab-li], *adv.* in an unconformable fashion.
UNCONFORMITY, [un-kon-fawm'-i-ti], *n.* incongruity, inconsistency; (*geol.*) a break in the formation of strata.
UNCONFOUNDED, [un-kon-fownd'-id], *adj.* not cast down, disproved, abashed, or confounded.
UNCONFUSED, [un-kon-fewzd'], *adj.* not embarrassed; not in disorder.
UNCONFUSEDLY, [un-kon-fewz'-id-li], *adv.* without embarrassment, in an unconfused fashion.
UNCONFUTABLE, [un-kon-fewt'-abl], *adj.* undeniable; that cannot be confuted.
UNCONGEALABLE, [un-kon-jēl'-abl], *adj.* impossible to congeal.
UNCONGEALED, [un-kon-jēld'], *adj.* not congealed.
UNCONGENIAL, [un-kon-jēn'-i-al], *adj.* not congenial, not in sympathy; repellent.
UNCONGENIALITY, [un-kon-jēn'-i-al'-i-ti], *n.* the quality of being uncongenial.
UNCONGENIALLY, [un-kon-jēn'-i-al-i], *adv.* in an uncongenial fashion.
UNCONJUGAL, [un-kon'-jōōg-al], *adj.* not befitting a married person or marriage.
UNCONNECTED, [un-kon-ek'-tid], *adj.* not physically linked or united; not related as cause and effect, not in logical relationship; not belonging to the same family.
UNCONNECTEDLY, [un-kon-ek'-tid-li], *adv.* in an unconnected fashion.
UNCONQUERABLE, [un-kong'-ker-abl], *adj.* that cannot be overcome; invincible.
UNCONQUERABLY, [un-kong'-ker-ab-li], *adv.* invincibly.
UNCONQUERED, [un-kong'-kerd], *adj.* not defeated; unsubdued.
UNCONSCIENTIOUS, [un-kon'-shi-en'-shus], *adj.* not conscientious.
UNCONSCIENTIOUSLY, [un-kon'-shi-en'-shus-li], *adv.* in an unconscientious way.
UNCONSCIENTIOUSNESS, [un-kon'-shi-en'-shus-nes], *n.* the quality of being unconscientious.
UNCONSCIONABLE, [un-kon'-shun-abl], *adj.* unscrupulous, excessive, unfair.
UNCONSCIONABLENESS, [un-kon'-shun-abl-nes], *n.* the quality of being unconscionable.
UNCONSCIONABLY, [un-kon'-shun-ab-li], *adv.* in an unconscionable fashion.
UNCONSCIOUS (1), [un-kon'-shus], *n.* (*psych.*) the unconscious mind.
UNCONSCIOUS (2), [un-kon'-shus], *adj.* not conscious; not perceiving, unaware; unintentional, involuntary; (*psych.*) unknown to the person or personality that possesses (it), subconscious.
UNCONSCIOUSLY, [un-kon'-shus-li], *adv.* without being aware, in an unconscious fashion.
UNCONSCIOUSNESS, [un-kon'-shus-nes], *n.* the state or quality of being unconscious.
UNCONSECRATED, [un-kon'-sik-rā-tid], *adj.* not consecrated or set apart for sacred use.

UNCONSECRATEDNESS, [un-kon'-sik-rā-tid-nes], *n.* the condition of being unconsecrated.
UNCONSENTING, [un-kon-sent'-ing], *adj.* refusing to consent, unyielding.
UNCONSIDERED, [un-kon-sid'-erd], *adj.* not heeded or considered.
UNCONSOLED, [un-kon-sōld'], *adj.* not consoled.
UNCONSOLIDATED, [un-kon-sol'-id-ā-tid], *adj.* not made firm, compact, or solid; (*fig.*) insecure.
UNCONSOLING, [un-kon-sōl'-ing], *adj.* tendering no consolation.
UNCONSTITUTIONAL, [un-kon'-sti-tew'-shun-al], *adj.* contrary to the constitution.
UNCONSTITUTIONALITY, [un-kon'-sti-tew'-shun-al'-it-i], *n.* an unconstitutional act or condition.
UNCONSTITUTIONALLY, [un-kon'-sti-tew'-shun-al-i], *adv.* in an unconstitutional fashion.
UNCONSTRAINED, [un-kon-strānd'], *adj.* free from constraint; voluntary; unembarrassed and at ease.
UNCONSTRAINEDLY, [un-kon-strān'-id-li], *adv.* in an unconstrained manner.
UNCONSULTED, [un-kon-sult'-id], *adj.* not appealed to for advice or information.
UNCONSUMED, [un-kon-sewmd'], *adj.* not consumed or wasted.
UNCONSUMMATED, [un-kon'-sum-ā-tid], *adj.* not consummated; unfulfilled.
UNCONTAINABLE, [un-kon-tān'-abl], *adj.* incapable of being repressed or held back.
UNCONTAMINATED, [un-kon-tam'-in-ā-tid], *adj.* pure, not having suffered contamination.
UNCONTEMPLATED, [un-kon'-tem-plāt-id], *adj.* not contemplated, unexpected, unconsidered.
UNCONTENDED, [un-kon-tend'-id], *adj.* not opposed, not fought over.
UNCONTENTED, [un-kon-tent'-id], *adj.* not contented.
UNCONTESTED, [un-kon-test'-id], *adj.* not contested; unquestioned; unopposed; not fought over.
UNCONTRACTED, [un-kon-trak'-tid], *adj.* not contracted.
UNCONTRADICTABLE, [un'-kon-tra-dikt'-abl], *adj.* that cannot be contradicted.
UNCONTRADICTED, [un'-kon-tra-dik'-tid], *adj.* not denied or contradicted.
UNCONTRITE, [un-kon'-trīt], *adj.* not sorry or contrite.
UNCONTRIVED, [un-kon-trīvd'], *adj.* not contrived or prearranged.
UNCONTRIVING, [un-kon-trīv'-ing], *adj.* not scheming or plotting.
UNCONTROLLABILITY, [un'-kon-trōl-ab-il'-it-i], *n.* the quality of being uncontrollable.
UNCONTROLLABLE, [un-kon-trōl'-abl], *adj.* that cannot be controlled.
UNCONTROLLABLY, [un-kon-trōl'-ab-li], *adv.* in an uncontrollable fashion.
UNCONTROLLED, [un-kon-trōld'], *adj.* free from restraint; not subject to government control.
UNCONTROLLEDLY, [un-kon-trōl'-id-li], *adv.* in an uncontrolled fashion.
UNCONTROVERSIAL, [un'-kon-trō-ver'-shal], *adj.* not involving controversy.
UNCONTROVERTED, [un-kon'-trō-vurt-id], *adj.* not made a subject of controversy, not opposed in discussion.
UNCONVENTIONAL, [un-kon-ven'-shun-al], *adj.* not according to the usual customs, free from convention.
UNCONVENTIONALITY, [un-kon-ven'-shun-al'-it-i], *n.* the quality of being unconventional.
UNCONVENTIONALLY, [un-kon-ven'-shun-al-i], *adv.* in an unconventional fashion.
UNCONVERSANT, [un-kon-vurs'-ant], *adj.* not familiar (with).
UNCONVERTED, [un-kon-vurt'-id], *adj.* not converted; unchanged in opinion or faith; not Christianized; (*rugby football*) of a try, not converted into a goal.
UNCONVERTIBLE, [un-kon-vurt'-ibl], *adj.* incapable of being changed or converted.
UNCONVINCED, [un-kon-vinst'], *adj.* not persuaded or convinced.
UNCONVINCING, [un-kon-vin'-sing], *adj.* not convincing, lacking in conviction.
UNCONVINCINGLY, [un-kon-vin'-sing-li], *adv.* in an unconvincing fashion.
UNCOOKED, [un-kŏŏkt'], *adj.* not cooked, raw.
UNCOOP, [un-kōōp'], *v.t.* to release from a coop; (*fig.*) to liberate.
UNCORD, [un-kawd'], *v.t.* to free from string or cord.
UNCORDIAL, [un-kawd'-i-al], *adj.* not friendly or cordial.
UNCORK, [un-kawk'], *v.t.* to remove the cork from; (*fig.*) to release.
UNCORONETED, [un-ko'-ron-et-id], *adj.* not having a coronet, without a peerage.
UNCORRECTED, [un-ko-rek'-tid], *adj.* not corrected or rebuked; not revised or amended.
UNCORROBORATED, [un'-ko-rob'-er-ā-tid], *adj.* not corroborated or confirmed.
UNCORRODED, [un-ko-rōd'-id], *adj.* not corroded.
UNCORRUPT, [un-ko-rupt'], *adj.* pure, honest, honourable, not corrupted.
UNCORRUPTED, [un'-ko-rup'-tid], *adj.* uncorrupt.
UNCORRUPTEDNESS, [un-ko-rup'-tid-nes], *n.* the quality of being uncorrupted.
UNCORRUPTIBLE, [un-ko-rup'-tibl], *adj.* incorruptible.
UNCORRUPTNESS, [un-ko-rupt'-nes], *n.* integrity, uncorruptedness.
UNCOUNSELLABLE, [un-kown'-sel-abl], *adj.* not open to advice.
UNCOUNSELLED, [un-kown'-seld], *adj.* unadvised.
UNCOUNTABLE, [un-kown'-tabl], *adj.* that cannot be counted, innumerable.
UNCOUNTED, [un-kownt'-id], *adj.* not counted, not included; untold.
UNCOUNTENANCED, [un-kownt'-in-anst], *adj.* discountenanced.
UNCOUPLE, [un-kupl'], *v.t.* to disengage, disconnect.
UNCOUPLED, [un-kupld'], *adj.* not coupled (together).
UNCOURTEOUS, [un-kur'-ti-us], *adj.* rude, discourteous.
UNCOURTEOUSLY, [un-kur'-ti-us-li], *adv.* in an uncourteous fashion.
UNCOURTEOUSNESS, [un-kur'-ti-us-nes], *n.* the condition of being uncourteous.
UNCOURTLINESS, [un-kawt'-li-nes], *n.* the quality of being uncourtly.
UNCOURTLY, [un-kawt'-li], *adj.* rough, unceremonious, rude.
UNCOUTH, [un-kōōth'], *adj.* (*archaic*) strange, unknown; awkward, clumsy.
UNCOUTHLY, [un-kōōth'-li], *adv.* in an uncouth way.
UNCOUTHNESS, [un-kōōth'-nes], *n.* the quality of being uncouth, awkwardness.
UNCOVENANTED, [un-kuv'-in-ant-id], *adj.* not promised or agreed to.
UNCOVER, [un-kuv'-er], *v.t. and i.* to remove the cover from, to make bare, to expose; (*archaic*) to take off one's hat.
UNCOVERED, [un-kuv'-erd], *adj.* bare; defenceless; not wearing a hat.
UNCOVETED, [un-kuv'-it-id], *adj.* not desired.
UNCOWL, [un-kowl'], *v.t.* to remove the cowl from.
UNCRAMPED, [un-krampt'], *adj.* unconfined, not cramped.
UNCREASABLE, [un-krēs'-abl], *adj.* that cannot be creased.
UNCREATED, [un-kri-āt'-id], *adj.* not produced by creation, spontaneous, eternal; non-existent, unborn, unmade.
UNCREDITED, [un-kred'-it-id], *adj.* not believed, not credited.
UNCRIPPLED, [un-kripld'], *adj.* not crippled; (*fig.*) uninjured.
UNCRITICAL, [un-krit'-ik-al], *adj.* not critical, not willing or able to criticise; not according to strict standards of criticism; undiscriminating.
UNCRITICALLY, [un-krit'-ik-al-i], *adv.* in an uncritical fashion.
UNCRITICIZED, [un-krit'-is-īzd], *adj.* not criticized; not attacked, opposed, or blamed.
UNCROPPED, [un-kropt'], *adj.* not cropped or cut short; uncultivated.
UNCROSS, [un-kros'], *v.t.* to take out of a crossed position; to remove the crossing from (a cheque).
UNCROSSED, [un-krost'], *adj.* not laid one over the other; (of a cheque) not crossed; (of a person, project, etc.) unopposed.
UNCROWDED, [un-krowd'-id], *adj.* not crowded or tightly packed.
UNCROWN, [un-krown'], *v.t.* to take the crown from.
UNCROWNED, [un'-krownd], *adj.* not crowned; **u. king,** a person whose popularity or power is such as to invest him with unchallengeable authority.
UNCRUSHABLE, [un-krush'-abl], *adj.* that cannot be crushed; incapable of being snubbed or rebuffed.

UNCRUSHED, [un-krusht'], *adj.* not crushed, not downcast or disconsolate; not affected by a rebuff.
UNCRYSTALLINE, [un-kris'-ta-lin], *adj.* not having a crystalline form.
UNCRYSTALLIZABLE, [un-kris'-tal-īz-abl], *adj.* not capable of being formed into crystals.
UNCRYSTALLIZED, [un-kris'-tal-īzd], *adj.* not formed into crystals.
UNCTION, [ungk'-shun], *n.* the act of smearing with oil or grease; the oil or grease so used; (*fig.*) anything that soothes; (*fig.*) great fervour or sincerity of manner, *esp.* religious fervour; the affectation of this; a ceremonial anointing, *esp.* of a king; **Extreme U.,** the sacrament administered to the dying of anointing with holy oil. [L. *unctio*].
UNCTUOSITY, [ungk'-choo-os'-it-i], *n.* the quality of being unctuous.
UNCTUOUS, [ungk'-choo-us], *adj.* greasy; resembling oil or grease; (*fig.*) professing an insincere earnestness, sympathy or enthusiasm.
UNCTUOUSLY, [ungk'-choo-us-li], *adv.* in an unctuous fashion.
UNCTUOUSNESS, [ungk'-choo-us-nes], *n.* the quality of being unctuous.
UNCULLED, [un-kuld'], *adj.* not gathered; not segregated.
UNCULPABLE, [un-kulp'-abl], *adj.* not to be blamed.
UNCULTIVABLE, [un-kult'-iv-abl], *adj.* unfertile.
UNCULTIVATED, [un-kult'-iv-ā-tid], *adj.* (of land) not tilled; (*fig.*) uncivilized, unrefined; not developed or fostered.
UNCULTURED, [un-kul'-cherd], *adj.* lacking culture, ill-educated.
UNCUMBERED, [un-kum'-berd], *adj.* not burdened or encumbered.
UNCURB, [un-kurb'], *v.t.* to free (a horse) from the curb; (*fig.*) to let loose, free.
UNCURBED, [un-kurbd'], *adj.* not restrained or controlled; licentious.
UNCURL, [un-kurl'], *v.t.* and *i.* to straighten out or cause to straighten out.
UNCURRENT, [un-ku'-rent], *adj.* not current, not able to be legally tendered as payment.
UNCURSED, [un-kurst'], *adj.* not under a curse.
UNCURTAILED, [un-ker-tāld'], *adj.* not cut down or shortened.
UNCURTAIN, [un-kur'-tan], *v.t.* to take a curtain away from; (*fig.*) to reveal or display.
UNCURTAINED, [un-ker'-tand], *adj.* without curtains; having curtains drawn aside.
UNCUS, (*pl.* **unci**), [ung'-kus, (*pl.*) un'-sī], *n.* (*bot., zool., etc.*) any hook-shaped appendage; a barb. [L. *uncus*].
UNCUSHIONED, [un-koosh'-und], *adj.* lacking cushions, not padded.
UNCUSTOMABLE, [un-kus'-tom-abl], *adj.* not liable to customs duty.
UNCUSTOMARY, [un-kus'-tom-er-i], *adj.* not usual or customary.
UNCUSTOMED, [un-kus'-tomd], *adj.* not having been paid for at the customs; uncustomable.
UNCUT, [un-kut'], *adj.* (of books) having the margins untrimmed; not having the pages cut open; (of gems) not cut and polished.
UNDAM, [un-dam'], *v.t.* to take a dam from.
UNDAMAGED, [un-dam'-ijd], *adj.* not damaged.
UNDAMMED, [un-damd'], *adj.* not blocked or impeded by a dam.
UNDAMNED, [un-damd'], *adj.* not cursed or condemned.
UNDAMPED, [un-dampt'], *adj.* not made damp; (*fig.*) not cast down, uncrushed.
UNDARKENED, [un-dahk'-end], *adj.* not made dark, not obscured.
UNDATE, [und'-āt], *adj.* undulating. [~L. *unda* a wave].
UNDATED (1), [und'-āt-id], *adj.* wavy, undate.
UNDATED (2), [un-dāt'-id], *adj.* having no date, not marked with a date.
UNDAUNTABLE, [un-dawnt'-abl], *adj.* that cannot be daunted, dismayed, frightened.
UNDAUNTED, [un-dawnt'-id], *adj.* bold, undismayed, unafraid, intrepid.
UNDAUNTEDLY, [un-dawnt'-id-li], *adv.* in undaunted fashion.
UNDAUNTEDNESS, [un-dawnt'-id-nes], *n.* the quality of being undaunted.
UNDAZZLED, [un-dazld'], *adj.* not dazzled; (*fig.*) not amazed, having the judgment unimpaired.

UNDE, undé, UNDEE, UNDY, [un'-di], *adj.* (*her.*) waved. [Fr. *ondé*].

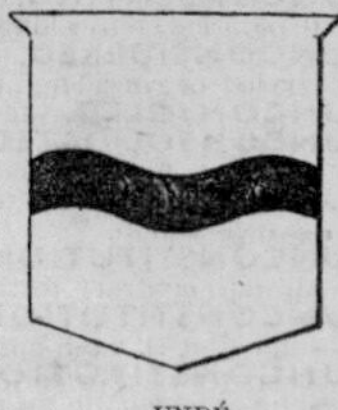
UNDÉ

UNDEBARRED, [un-di-bahd'], *adj.* not forbidden.
UNDEBASED, [un-di-bāst'], *adj.* not debased or lowered in value.
UNDEBATED, [un-di-bāt'-id], *adj.* not argued about.
UNDEBAUCHED, [un-di-bawcht'], *adj.* not having practised debauchery or been debauched.
UNDECAGON, [un-dek'-a-gon], *n.* (*geom.*) a plane figure with eleven sides. [L. *undecim* eleven, and Gk. *gonia* angle].
UNDECAYED, [un-di-kād'], *adj.* not decayed.
UNDECAYING, [un-di-kā'-ing], *adj.* not decaying (*fig.*) undying, immortal.
UNDECEITFUL, [un-di-sēt'-fool], *adj.* honest, not given to trickery.
UNDECEIVABLE, [un-dis-ēv'-abl], *adj.* incapable of being deceived.
UNDECEIVE, [un-dis-ēv'], *v.t.* to explain the deception to, to disillusion.
UNDECEIVED, [un-di-sēvd'], *adj.* not deceived or deluded.
UNDECENARY, [un'-dis-en'-er-i], *adj.* occurring once in eleven years, eleventh. [~L. *undecim* eleven]
UNDECENNIAL, [un'-dis-en'-i-al], *adj.* undecenary
UNDECEPTIVE, [un-dis-ep'-tiv], *adj.* not able or intending to deceive.
UNDECIDABLE, [un-di-sīd'-abl], *adj.* that cannot be decided.
UNDECIDED, [un-di-sīd'-id], *adj.* not decided; not certain in one's own mind; vacillating, irresolute; vague, uncertain.
UNDECIDEDLY, [un'-di-sīd'-id-li], *adv.* in an undecided way.
UNDECIDEDNESS, [un-di-sīd'id-nes], *n.* the quality of being undecided.
UNDECIPHERABLE, [un-di-sīf'-er-abl], *adj.* impossible to decipher.
UNDECIPHERED, [un-di-sīf'-erd], *adj.* not deciphered.
UNDECISIVE, [un-di-sīs'-iv], *adj.* not decisive, inconclusive.
UNDECK, [un-dek'], *v.t.* to remove all adornment from.
UNDECKED (1), [un-dekt'], *adj.* unornamented.
UNDECKED (2), [un-dekt'], *adj.* (of a ship, etc.) not having a deck.
UNDECLARED, [un-di-klāerd'], *adj.* not declared; (of imported goods) not shown to the customs officers.
UNDECLINABLE, [un-di-klīn'-abl], *adj.* that cannot be refused or declined.
UNDECLINED, [un-di-klīnd'], *adj.* not refused or declined; (*gram.*) indeclinable.
UNDECOMPOSABLE, [un'-dē-kom-pōz'-abl], *adj.* incapable of decomposition.
UNDECOMPOSED, [un'-dē-kom-pōzd'], *adj.* not having suffered decomposition.
UNDECORATED, [un-dek'-er-āt-id], *adj.* not decorated or adorned.
UNDECORTICATED, [un'-dē-kaw'-ti-kā-tid], *adj.* without having had the cortex removed.
UNDEDICATED, [un-ded'-ik-ā-tid], *adj.* not dedicated; not consecrated; (of a book) not inscribed to a patron; (of a road) maintained privately.
UNDEE, see UNDÉ.
UNDEEDED, [un-dēd'-id], *adj.* (*leg.*) not transferred by deed.
UNDEFACEABLE, [un-di-fās'-abl], *adj.* not able to be defaced.
UNDEFACED, [un-di-fāst'], *adj.* not disfigured.
UNDEFEASIBLE†, [un-di-fēz'-ibl], *adj.* not defeasible, indefeasible.
UNDEFENDED, [un-di-fend'-id], *adj.* not protected, defenceless; (of a charged person) not having legal advice; (of a suit or action) having no defence or plea offered by the accused party or respondent.
UNDEFIED, [un-di-fīd'], *adj.* not set at defiance.
UNDEFILED, [un-di-fīld'], *adj.* not defiled.
UNDEFINABLE, [un-di-fīn'-abl], *adj.* incapable of being defined.
UNDEFINABLENESS, [un'-di-fīn'-abl-nes], *n.* the quality of being undefinable.
UNDEFINED, [un-di-fīnd'], *adj.* not defined, vague, uncertain; not explained by a definition.

UNDEFORMED, [un-di-fawmd′], *adj.* not marred or deformed.
UNDEFRAUDED, [un-di-frawd′-id], *adj.* not taken in by a fraud, not robbed or defrauded.
UNDEFRAYED, [un-di-frād′], *adj.* not defrayed.
UNDEGRADED, [un-di-grād′-id], *adj.* not lowered in rank or estimation.
UNDELAYED, [un-di-lād′], *adj.* not held up or delayed.
UNDELAYING, [un-di-lā′-ing], *adj.* not delaying or causing delay.
UNDELECTABLE, [un-di-lek′-tabl], *adj.* unpleasant, not delectable.
UNDELEGATED, [un-del′-ig-ā-tid], *adj.* not sent or commissioned to act as a delegate; not entrusted to others to wield or perform.
UNDELIBERATE, [un-di-lib′-er-at], *adj.* hasty, ill-considered, not from design.
UNDELIBERATED, [un-di-lib′-er-āt-id], *adj.* not properly discussed, hasty, ill-considered.
UNDELIGHTED, [un-di-līt′-id], *adj.* not pleased.
UNDELIGHTFUL, [un-di-līt′-fool], *adj.* not giving pleasure.
UNDELIVERABLE, [un-di-liv′-er-abl], *adj.* not capable of being delivered.
UNDELIVERED, [un-di-liv′-erd], *adj.* not delivered or set free; not uttered or spoken; not handed over.
UNDEMOCRATIC, [un-dem′-ō-krat′-ik], *adj.* not democratic, contrary to democratic principles.
UNDEMOLISHED, [un-di-mol′-isht], *adj.* not demolished, still standing.
UNDEMONSTRABLE, [un-dem′-on-strabl], *adj.* that cannot be demonstrated.
UNDEMONSTRATED, [un-dem′-on-strāt′-id], *adj.* not proved or demonstrated.
UNDEMONSTRATIVE, [un-dim-on′-strat-iv], *adj.* not given to a display of feeling, taciturn, reserved.
UNDENIABLE, [un-din-ī′-abl], *adj.* that cannot be denied; indubitable.
UNDENIABLY, [un-din-ī′-ab-li], *adv.* in an undeniable way.
UNDENOMINATIONAL, [un′di-nom-in-ā′-shunal], *adj.* making no distinction between one denomination and another.
UNDENOUNCED, [un-di-nownst′], *adj.* not denounced.
UNDEPENDABLE, [un-di-pend′-abl], *adj.* unreliable.
UNDEPENDING, [un-di-pend′-ing], *adj.* independent.
UNDEPLORED, [un-di-plaw(r)d′], *adj.* not mourned for.
UNDEPOSABLE, [un-di-pōz′-abl], *adj.* that cannot be deposed; firmly established.
UNDEPOSED, [un-di-pōzd′], *adj.* not deposed.
UNDEPRAVED, [un-di-prāvd], *adj.* not ruined by depravity.
UNDEPRECATED, [un-dep′-rik-ā-tid], *adj.* not deplored.
UNDEPRECIATED, [un-di-prē′-shi-ā-tid], *adj.* still at the same value.
UNDEPRESSED, [un-di-prest′], *adj.* not depressed; not melancholy or cast down in spirits.
UNDEPRIVED, [un-di-prīvd′], *adj.* still in possession, office.
UNDER (1), [un′-der], *adj.* inferior, subordinate.
UNDER (2), [un′-der], *adv.* in an inferior or lower position or condition.
UNDER (3), [un′-der], *prep.* below, on a lower level or in a lower position than, beneath the surface of; in the power of, during the reign of; according to; beneath; beneath the cover of; **u. cover,** in a protected position; **u. arms,** equipped with military arms and ready for warfare. [OE. *under*].
UNDER-, (*pref.*) subsidiary; insufficiently; lower.
UNDERACT, [un-der-akt′], *v.t. and i.* to act with insufficient vitality.
UNDERACTION, [un-der-ak′-shun], *n.* a subsidiary element or episode in a story.
UNDER-AGENT, [un′-der-ā′-jent], *n.* a subordinate agent.
UNDERAID, [un′-der-ād′], *v.t.* to help in secret.
UNDERANGED, [un-di-rānjd′], *adj* not deranged, sane.
UNDERARM (1), [un′-der-ahm′], *adj.* (*tennis, cricket, etc.*) with the arm kept below the shoulder.
UNDERARM (2), [un′-der-ahm′], *adv.* in underarm fashion.
UNDERBEARER, [un′-der-bāer′-er], *n.* a man who helps to carry the coffin at a funeral.
UNDER-BELLY, [un′-der-bel-ē], *n.* the part, surface, underneath the middle.
UNDERBID, [un′-der-bid′], *v.t. and i.* to bid less than; (*bridge*) to bid low so as to suggest that one's hand is weaker than actually is the case.
UNDERBIDDER, [un′-der-bid′-er], *n.* one who underbids.
UNDERBITTEN, [un′-der-bit′-en], *adj.* (*etching*) not sufficiently clear on the copper plate through excessive etching of the sides of the lines.
UNDERBOARD, [un′-der-bawd′], *adv.* secretly, dishonestly.
UNDERBRED, [un′-der-bred′], *adj.* ill-bred.
UNDERBRUSH, [un′-der-brush′], *n.* undergrowth.
UNDERCHARGE (1), [un′-der-chahj′], *n.* a low, insufficient price.
UNDERCHARGE (2), [un′-der-chahj′], *v.t.* to charge an insufficient price; to load (a gun) insufficiently.
UNDERCLAY, [un′-der-klā′], *n.* a bed of clay under a stratum of coal.
UNDER-CLERK, [un′-der-klahk′], *n.* a minor clerk.
UNDER-CLERKSHIP, [un′-der-klahk′-ship], *n.* the position of a minor clerk.
UNDERCLIFF, [un′-der-klif′], *n.* a lower cliff beneath a high one.
UNDERCLOTHES, [un′-der-klōTHz′], *n.*(*pl.*) underclothing.
UNDERCLOTHING, [un′-der-klōTH′-ing], *n.* garments worn near or next to the skin and beneath other garments.
UNDERCOAT, [un′-der-kōt′], *n.* a coat that is worn under another, a shorter growth of hair on a furred animal; a first coat of paint.
UNDERCROFT, [un′-der-kroft′], *n.* a crypt; any similar vaulted subterranean chamber.
UNDERCURRENT, [un′-der-ku′-rent], *n.* a current running below the surface of water; an unseen influence or feeling amongst a group of people.
UNDERCUT (1), [un′-der-kut′], *n.* the tender part of sirloin of beef; (*boxing*) an upward blow.
UNDERCUT (2), [un′-der-kut′], *v.t.* to cut beneath or at a lower level; to sell at a cheaper rate than; (*golf*) to strike (the ball) so as to prevent it running very far when it touches the ground again.
UNDERDEVELOP, [un′-der-di-vel′-op], *v.t.* (*phot.*) to fail to develop sufficiently.
UNDERDEVELOPED, [un′-der-di-vel′-opt], *adj.* backward, less developed than normal.
UNDERDITCH, [un′-der-dich′], *v.t.* to drain by digging a deep trench.
UNDERDO, [un′-der-doo′], *v.t.* to do slackly or inadequately; to cook insufficiently.
UNDERDOG, [un′-der-dog′], *n.* a person who is always at the mercy of circumstances or other people.
UNDERDONE, [un′-der-dun′], *adj.* done less than requisite; not cooked enough.
UNDERDOSE (1), [un′-der-dōs′], *n.* a dose less than that required.
UNDERDOSE (2), [un′-der-dōs′], *v.t.* to give an underdose to.
UNDERDRAIN (1), [un′-der-drān′], *n.* a deep trench for drainage.
UNDERDRAIN (2), [un′-der-drān′], *v.t.* to underditch.
UNDERDRAW, [un′-der-draw′], *v.t.* to depict with too little vigour.
UNDERDRESS, [un′-der-dres′], *v.i.* to wear insufficient clothing (for the climate, etc.); to dress meanly or too plainly.
UNDERDRESSED, [un′-der-drest′], *adj.* wearing less than the usual, proper, or suitable, number of garments; (*theatrical*) sketchily clad.
UNDERESTIMATE (1), [un′-der-es′-tim-āt], *n.* an undervaluing, an estimate which is too low.
UNDERESTIMATE (2), [un′-der-es′-tim-āt], *v.t.* to put too low a value on; to value too lightly.
UNDERESTIMATION, [un′-der-es′-tim-ā′-shun], *n.* an undervaluing.
UNDER-EXPOSE, [un′-der-eks-pōz′], *v.t.* (*phot.*) to expose for less than the normal time.
UNDER-EXPOSURE, [un′-der-eks-pōzh′-er], *n.* (*phot.*) the exposing of a sensitized plate, film, or print for less than the normal time; a negative or print thus exposed.
UNDERFACTION, [un′-der-fak′-shun], *n.* a minor party or faction.
UNDERFEED, [un′-der-fēd′], *v.t. and i.* to feed (oneself or someone else) inadequately.
UNDERFLOW, [un′-der-flō′], *n.* a cross-current running deep down in a stream or channel.

UNDERFOOT, [un'-der-fo͝ot'], *adv.* under the feet; (*fig.*) in an inferior position.
UNDERFRAME, [un'-der-frām'], *n.* a frame supporting the main body of anything.
UNDERFUR, [un'-der-fur'], *n.* the shorter hair growing in the coats of some furred animals, an undercoat.
UNDERFURNISH, [un'-der-furn'-ish], *v.t.* to equip or furnish inadequately.
UNDERGARMENT, [un'-der-gahm-ent], *n.* any garment worn near or next to the skin under outdoor clothes.
UNDERGIRD, [un'-der-gurd'], *v.t.* to bind and fasten underneath.
UNDERGLAZE, [un'-der-glāz'], *n.* the process by which a piece of pottery is painted before glazing.
UNDERGO, (**underwent, undergone**), [un'-der-gō'], *v.t.* to suffer, endure.
UNDERGOING, [un'-der-gō'-ing], *n.* the process of suffering or experiencing.
UNDERGRAD, [un-der-grad'], *n.* (*coll.*) an undergraduate.
UNDERGRADUATE, [un'-der-graj'-o͞o-at], *n.* a student at a university who has not yet taken a degree.
UNDERGRADUATESHIP, [un'-der-graj'-o͞o-at-ship], *n.* the rank of an undergraduate.
UNDERGRADUETTE, [un'-der-graj'-o͞o-et'], *n.* (*coll.*) a woman undergraduate.
UNDERGROUND (1), [un'-der-grownd], *n.* an underground railway; an underground association.
UNDERGROUND (2), [un'-der-grownd], *adj.* situated beneath the earth's surface, subterranean; (*fig.*) secret.
UNDERGROUND (3), [un'-der-grownd'], *adv.* beneath the surface of the earth; (*fig.*) in secret.
UNDERGROWN, [un'-der-grown'], *adj.* not fully or normally developed.
UNDERGROWTH, [un'-der-grōth], *n.* shrubs and small trees in a wood.
UNDERHAND, [un'-der-hand'], *adj.* secret, fraudulent, mean.
UNDERHANDED, [un'-der-hand'-id], *adj.* underhand, clandestine; short of employees or assistants.
UNDERHANDEDLY, [un'-der-hand'-id-li], *adv.* in a secret, mean, underhand fashion.
UNDERHOLD, [un'-der-hōld], *n.* (*wrestling*) a grip in which one's arms are below one's opponent's.
UNDERHUNG, [un'-der-hung'], *adj.* (of the lower jaw) projecting further than the upper jaw; having a lower jaw so formed.
UNDERIVED, [un'-di-rīvd'], *adj.* not derived, spontaneous, original; not borrowed; having no known origin.
UNDER-KING, [un'-der-king'], *n.* a vassal monarch.
UNDERLAID, [un'-der-lād'], *adj.* laid beneath; (*print.*) raised.
UNDERLAP, [un'-der-lap'], *v.t.* to project beyond something that is above.
UNDERLAY (1), [un'-der-lā'], *n.* (*print.*) the material used to underlay type; thick felt laid beneath a carpet.
UNDERLAY (2), [un'-der-lā'], *v.t.* to lay beneath; (*print.*) to raise by laying something beneath.
UNDERLEASE, [un'-der-lēs'], *n.* a sublease.
UNDERLET, [un'-der-let'], *v.t.* to sublet.
UNDERLETTER, [un'-der-let'-er], *n.* a tenant who sublets.
UNDERLETTING, [un'-der-let'-ing], *n.* the practice of subletting.
UNDERLIE, [un'-der-lī'], *v.t.* to lie beneath; (*fig.*) to be implicit in, to be the basis of.
UNDERLINE (1), [un'-der-līn], *n.* a mark that underlines.
UNDERLINE (2), [un'-der-līn'], *v.t.* to mark (a word or words) in a book or manuscript with a line underneath; (*fig.*) to emphasize.
UNDERLINEN, [un'-der-lin'-en], *n.* underwear.
UNDERLING, [un'-der-ling], *n.* an inferior person at the beck and call of another.
UNDERLOOKER, [un'-der-lo͝ok-er], *n.* one who inspects the underground parts of a colliery.
UNDERMAN, [un'-der-man'], *v.t.* to provide with insufficient workers or helpers.
UNDERMANNED, [un'-der-mand'], *adj.* (of a ship) having too small a crew.
UNDERMASTED, [un'-der-mahs'-tid], *adj.* (of a ship) having short masts.
UNDERMASTER, [un'-der-mahs'-ter], *n.* a subordinate schoolmaster.
UNDERMENTIONED, [un'-der-men-shund], *adj.* mentioned later on, below; undernoted.
UNDERMINE, [un'-der-mīn'], *v.t.* to excavate the earth from beneath; (*fig.*) to weaken or attack by indirect means.
UNDERMINER, [un'-der-mīn'-er], *n.* a person or thing that undermines.
UNDERMOST, [un'-der-mōst], *adj.* lowest in place, degree, etc.
UNDERNEATH (1), [un'-der-nēth'], *n.* that part or surface of anything which is situated lowest or beneath the rest.
UNDERNEATH (2), [un'-der-nēth'], *adj.* situated beneath or underneath.
UNDERNEATH (3), [un'-der-nēth'], *adv.* under, beneath, below; in a situation directly below. [ME. *undernethe*].
UNDERNEATH (4), [un'-der-nēth'], *prep.* beneath, below.
UNDERNOTE, [un'-der-nōt'], *n.* an undertone.
UNDERNOTED, [un'-der-nōt'-id], *adj.* noted below.
UNDERNOURISHED, [un'-der-nur'-isht], *adj.* insufficiently nourished.
UNDEROGATORY, [un'-di-rog'-at-er-i], *adj.* not adversely or unkindly critical, not derogatory.
UNDERPART, [un'-der-paht'], *n.* a minor part.
UNDERPAY, [un'-der-pā'], *v.t.* to pay inadequate wages to.
UNDERPAYMENT, [un'-der-pā'-ment], *n.* insufficient wages or payment.
UNDERPEOPLED, [un'-der-pēpld'], *adj.* inadequately populated.
UNDERPIN, [un'-der-pin'], *v.t.* to provide a temporary supporting structure for, while existing foundations are repaired or replaced.
UNDERPINNING, [un'-der-pin'-ing], *n.* the act of one who underpins; material used to underpin.
UNDERPLAY, [un'-der-plā'], *v.t.* to underact; (at cards) deliberately to lose a trick when strategically profitable to do so.
UNDERPLOT, [un'-der-plot], *n.* a secondary theme in a story.
UNDER-POPULATED, [un'-der-pop'-yo͞ol-ā-tid], *adj.* insufficiently provided with people.
UNDERPRAISE, [un'-der-prāz'], *v.t.* to praise inadequately.
UNDERPRIZE, [un'-der-prīz'], *v.t.* to value too lightly.
UNDERPRODUCE, [un'-der-prōd-ews'], *v.i.* deliberately to cut production below demand in order to raise prices.
UNDER-PROOF, [un'-der-pro͞of'], *adj.* having less alcohol than proof spirit.
UNDERPROP, [un'-der-prop'], *v.t.* to prop up from beneath.
UNDERPROPPED, [un'-der-propt'], *adj.* supported by props underneath.
UNDERQUOTE, [un'-der-kwōt'], *v.t.* to offer goods at a lower price than.
UNDERRATE (1), [un'-der-rāt], *n.* a price or estimate less than real value.
UNDERRATE (2), [un'-der-rāt'], *v.t.* to estimate or value too low.
UNDER-RECKON, [un'-der-rek'-on], *v.t.* to undervalue, underestimate.
UNDER-RIPE, [un'-der-rīp'], *adj.* not fully ripened or matured.
UNDERRUN, [un'-der-run'], *v.t.* to pass beneath; to examine by passing through the hand.
UNDERSCORE, [un'-der-skaw(r)'], *v.t.* to underline.
UNDER-SECRETARY, [un'-der-sek'-ret-er-i], *n.* an assistant secretary; **Parliamentary U.**, a Member of Parliament assisting a minister who holds a portfolio; **Permanent U.**, a member of the Civil Service who is the head of a state department.
UNDER-SECRETARYSHIP, [un'-der-sek'-ret-er-i-ship'], *n.* the office and position of an under-secretary.
UNDERSELL, [un'-der-sel'], *v.t.* to make lower charges than.
UNDERSELLER, [un'-der-sel'-er], *n.* a trader who undersells.
UNDER-SERVANT, [un'-der-serv'-ant], *n.* a minor, subordinate servant.
UNDERSET (1), [un'-der-set'], *n.* (*naut.*) a current low down in the water running opposite to the main current.
UNDERSET (2), [un'-der-set'], *v.t.* to support from beneath by masonry or other work.
UNDER-SHERIFF, [un'-der-she-rif], *n.* a sheriff's deputy.
UNDERSHIRT, [un'-der-shurt], *n.* a vest or shirt worn next to the skin.
UNDERSHOT, [un'-der-shot'], *adj.* driven by a

stream of water that passes under and not over the wheel.
UNDERSHRUB, [un'-der-shrub], *n.* a small shrub or similar plant.
UNDERSIGN, [un'-der-sīn'], *v.t.* to put one's signature to.
UNDERSIGNED (1), [un'-der-sīnd], *n.* the person who undersigns.
UNDERSIGNED (2), [un'-der-sīnd], *adj.* (of a document) having a signature at the end.
UNDERSIZED, [un'-der-sīzd'], *adj.* smaller than is normal, stunted.
UNDERSKIRT, [un'-der-skurt], *n.* a petticoat, a skirt worn beneath another.
UNDERSLUNG, [un'-der-slung'], *adj.* (of a lorry, etc.) with the spring suspension below axle level.
UNDERSOIL, [un'-der-soil], *n.* the subsoil.
UNDERSONG, [un'-der-song], *n.* the accompanying harmony or part.
UNDERSTAND, (understood), [un'-der-stand'], *v.t. and i.* to perceive in one's mind the meaning (of); to be able to interpret; to perceive what is meant; to possess intelligence; to believe, be informed, have reason to believe; to supply in one's mind something beside what is actually expressed; **to u. each other, one another,** to know and respect each other's views. [OE. *understandan*].
UNDERSTANDABLE, [un'-der-stand'-abl], *adj.* capable of being understood.
UNDERSTANDING (1), [un'-der-stand'-ing], *n.* the faculty of the mind by which it discerns and apprehends; the act of comprehending or apprehending; intelligence, discernment; knowledge; agreement of thought and feeling between two persons; a tacit agreement; **on the u. that,** provided that.
UNDERSTANDING (2), [un'-der-stand'-ing], *adj.* knowing; sympathetic.
UNDERSTANDINGLY, [un'-der-stand'-ing-li], *adv.* in an understanding way.
UNDERSTATE, [un'-der-stāt'], *v.t.* to state with deliberate moderation and with an avoidance of emphasis so as to minimize the importance of what is stated.
UNDERSTATEMENT, [un'-der-stāt'-ment], *n.* a statement that minimizes the gravity or importance of what is discussed.
UNDERSTOCK, [un'-der-stok'], *v.t.* to furnish (a shop, etc.) with less stock than is really necessary.
UNDERSTOOD, [un'-der-stŏŏd'], *pret. and p.pt.* of UNDERSTAND.
UNDERSTRAPPER, [un'-der-strap-er], *n.* an inferior official, an underling.
UNDERSTUDY (1), [un'-der-stud-i], *n.* one who studies an actor's part so as to be able to take his place if required; a substitute.
UNDERSTUDY (2), [un'-der-stud'-i], *v.t.* to learn the part or work of so as to be able to perform it if required.
UNDERTAKE, (undertook, undertaken), [un'-der-tāk'], *v.t. and i.* to take in hand, to set about (to); to promise or contract (to); to take upon one's self (any business, etc.); (*coll.*) to engage in business as an undertaker.
UNDERTAKER, [un'-der-tāk-er], *n.* one whose trade is to manage funerals; one who undertakes a project.
UNDERTAKING, [un'-der-tāk'-ing], *n.* any task or business undertaken; the profession or business of an undertaker.
UNDERTAXED, [un'-der-takst'], *adj.* insufficiently taxed.
UNDER-TENANCY, [un'-der-ten'-an-si], *n.* a tenancy held from one who is himself a tenant of what he is letting.
UNDER-TENANT, [un'-der-ten'-ant], *n.* a tenant of one who is himself a tenant.
UNDERTINT, [un'-der-tint], *n.* a very faint tint.
UNDERTONE, [un'-der-tōn], *n.* a quiet tone, or voice; (*fig.*) an unexpressed feeling; an undertint.
UNDERTOOK, [un'-der-tŏŏk'], *pret.* of UNDERTAKE.
UNDERTOW, [un'-der-tō], *n.* an underset.
UNDERVALUATION, [un'-der-val'-yōō-ā'-shun], *n.* the action of undervaluing, the state of being undervalued.
UNDERVALUE, [un'-der-val'-yōō], *v.t.* to price at too low a rate; not to attach sufficient or proper worth or importance to, to underestimate.
UNDERVEST, [un'-der-vest], *n.* a vest worn under a shirt and next to the skin.
UNDERVIEWER, [un'-der-vew'-er], *n.* a subordinate manager of a mine, an underlooker.
UNDERWEAR, [un'-der-wāer], *n.* undergarments.
UNDERWENT, [un'-der-went'], *pret.* of UNDERGO.
UNDERWING, [un'-der-wing'], *n.* a wing lying under another; (*entom.*) either of the two posterior wings of a four-winged insect; a moth of the genus, *Catocala.*

UNDERWING

UNDERWOOD, [un'-der-wŏŏd], *n.* undergrowth.
UNDERWORK (1), [un'-der-wurk], *n.* work of minor importance.
UNDERWORK (2), [un'-der-wurk'], *v.t. and i.* to fail to obtain sufficient work from; to do less work than one is paid or expected to do; to do work for a lower price than.
UNDERWORLD, [un'-der-wurld], *n.* the world of crime and immorality; (*fig.*) the world of the dead.
UNDERWRITE, [un'-der-rīt'], *v.t. and i.* to write underneath; to insure (*esp.* shipping) against risk; to contract to purchase all shares of an issue not taken up by the public.
UNDERWRITER, [un'-der-rīt-er], *n.* one who insures (*esp.* shipping); one who underwrites an issue of shares.
UNDERWRITING, [un'-der-rīt-ing], *n.* the practice of an underwriter.
UNDESCENDED, [un-di-send'-id], *adj.* that has not descended ; **u. testicle,** a testicle that has failed to descend into the scrotum.
UNDESCRIBABLE, [un-di-skrīb'-abl], *adj.* indescribable.
UNDESCRIBED, [un-di-skrībd'], *adj.* not set forth in description.
UNDESCRIED, [un-di-skrīd'], *adj.* not seen or descried.
UNDESERVED, [un-di-zurvd'], *adj.* not merited, not warranted.
UNDESERVEDLY, [un-di-zurv'-id-li], *adv.* in an undeserved fashion.
UNDESERVEDNESS, [un-di-zurv'-id-nes], *n.* the condition of being undeserved.
UNDESERVING, [un-di-zurv'-ing], *adj.* not deserving, not meriting.
UNDESERVINGLY, [un-di-zurv'-ing-li], *adv.* in an undeserving fashion.
UNDESIGNATED, [un-dez'-ig-nā-tid], *adj.* not designated.
UNDESIGNED, [un-di-zīnd'], *adj.* not planned or designed; (*fig.*) not intended, not deliberate.
UNDESIGNEDLY, [un-di-zīn'-id-li], *adv.* unintentionally, in an undesigned way.
UNDESIGNEDNESS, [un-di-zīn'-id-nes], *n.* the condition of being undesigned.
UNDESIGNING, [un-di-zīn'-ing], *adj.* not scheming, having no guile.
UNDESIRABILITY, [un-di-zīer-ab-il'-it-i], *n.* the quality of being undesirable.
UNDESIRABLE (1), [un-di-zīer'-abl], *n.* an unwanted, troublesome person.
UNDESIRABLE (2), [un-di-zīer'-abl], *adj.* not to be wished for.
UNDESIRABLENESS, [un-di-zīer'-abl-nes], *n.* the state of being undesirable.
UNDESIRABLY, [un-di-zīer'-ab-li], *adv.* in an undesirable fashion.
UNDESIRED, [un-di-zīerd'], *adj.* not desired or sought after.
UNDESIROUS, [un-di-zīer'-us], *adj.* not desirous (of).
UNDESPAIRING, [un-dis-pāer'-ing], *adj.* not yielding to despair, still hopeful.
UNDESPOILED, [un-di-spoild'], *adj.* not ravaged or despoiled.
UNDESTINED, [un-des'-tind], *adj.* not fated.
UNDESTROYABLE, [un-di-stroi'-abl], *adj.* indestructible.
UNDETACHABLE, [un-di-tach-abl'], *adj.* that cannot be detached.
UNDETECTED, [un-di-tek'-tid], *adj.* not detected.
UNDETERMINABLE, [un-di-turm'-in-abl], *adj.* that cannot be determined.
UNDETERMINED, [un-di-turm'-ind], *adj.* not determined or settled, indeterminate; hesitant.
UNDETERRED, [un-di-turd'], *adj.* not constrained by fear to stop or hesitate, resolute; unshaken.
UNDEVELOPED, [un-di-vel'-opt], *adj.* not developed; not worked out fully; not exploited for building purposes, still rural.
UNDEVIATING, [un-dē'-vi-āt-ing], *adj.* not departing from a given way, principle, or purpose; steady.

UNDEVIATINGLY, [un'-dē'-vi-āt-ing-li], *adv.* not in a deviating fashion.
UNDEVOTED, [un-di-vōt'-id], *adj.* showing no devotion.
UNDEVOUT, [un-di-vowt'], *adj.* showing no devoutness.
UNDEXTROUS, [un-deks'-trus], *adj.* not dextrous.
UNDIADEMED, [un-dī'-a-demd], *adj.* not crowned with a diadem.
UNDIAPHANOUS, [un-dī-af'-an-us], *adj.* not diaphanous or filmy.
UNDID, [un-did'], *pret.* of UNDO.
UNDIES, [un'-diz], *n.(pl.)* (*coll.*) women's underwear. [Short for UNDERWEAR].
UNDIFFERENTIATED, [un-dif-er-en'-shi-ā-tid], *adj.* not distinct or distinguished one from another.
UNDIFFUSED, [un-di-fewzd'], *adj.* not scattered or diffused.
UNDIGESTED, [un-di-jest'-id], *adj.* not digested; (*fig.*) not fully grasped and comprehended by the intellect.
UNDIGNIFIED, [un-dig'-ni-fīd], *adj.* not dignified, lacking dignity.
UNDILUTED, [un-dī-lōōt'-id], *adj.* not diluted, pure.
UNDIMINISHABLE, [un-dim-in'-ish-abl], *adj.* not capable of being diminished.
UNDIMINISHED, [un-dim-in'-isht], *adj.* not lessened or decreased.
UNDIMMED, [un-dimd'], *adj.* as bright as ever, not obscured.
UNDINE, [ōōn-dēn'], *n.* a water-nymph. [MdL. *undina*].
UNDINTED, [un-dint'-id], *adj.* not scarred with dents.
UNDIPLOMATIC, [un'-dip-lō-mat'-ik], *adj.* not conforming to diplomatic usages, lacking tact.
UNDIPLOMATICALLY, [un'-dip-lō-mat'-ik-al-i], *adv.* in undiplomatic fashion.
UNDIPPED, [un-dipt'], *adj.* not dipped.
UNDIRECTED, [un-dī-rek'-tid], *adj.* not aimed or directed; unguided, uninstructed.
UNDISBANDED, [un-dis-band'-id], *adj.* not dispersed or broken up.
UNDISCERNED, [un-di-surnd'], *adj.* not seen; (*fig.*) not grasped by the intellect.
UNDISCERNIBLE, [un-di-surn'-ibl], *adj.* incapable of being discerned; imperceptible.
UNDISCERNIBLENESS, [un-di-surn'-ibl-nes], *n.* the quality of being undiscernible.
UNDISCERNIBLY, [un-di-surn'-ib-li], *adv.* in an undiscernible way.
UNDISCERNING, [un-di-surn'-ing], *adj.* lacking in (mental, moral) discernment.
UNDISCHARGED, [un-dis-chahjd'], *adj.* still holding a commission, still on duty; (of an action, duty) not carried out; (of a gun, etc.) not fired; that has not received discharge from bankruptcy.
UNDISCIPLINED, [un-dis'-ip-lind], *adj.* not subject to regular and systematic training and instruction, untrained in military discipline; lacking in self-control; raw; disobedient.
UNDISCLOSED, [un-dis-klōzd'], *adj.* not revealed; still secret.
UNDISCOMFITED, [un-dis-kum'-fi-tid], *adj.* not embarrassed, checked or put off.
UNDISCONCERTED, [un-dis-kon-surt'-id], *adj.* not put out or embarrassed.
UNDISCOURAGED, [un-dis-ku'-rijd], *adj.* not disheartened.
UNDISCOURSED, [un-dis-kawst'], *adj.* not made a subject for discussion.
UNDISCOVERABLE, [un-dis-kuv'-er-abl], *adj.* that cannot be discovered.
UNDISCOVERABLY, [un-dis-kuv'-er-ab-li], *adv.* remotely, beyond discovery.
UNDISCOVERED, [un-dis-kuv'-erd], *adj.* not discovered, not seen, unknown.
UNDISCRIMINATED, [un-dis-krim'-in-āt-id], *adj.* not discriminated.
UNDISCRIMINATING, [un-dis-krim'-in-ā-ting], *adj.* not discriminating, lacking discrimination.
UNDISCRIMINATINGLY, [un-dis-krim'-in-ā-ting-li], *adv.* in an undiscriminating fashion.
UNDISCUSSED, [un-dis-kust'], *adj.* not mentioned, argued about, or debated; not considered.
UNDISFIGURED, [un-dis-fig'-erd], *adj.* not marred or spoilt.
UNDISGRACED, [un-dis-grāst'], *adj.* not in disgrace.
UNDISGUISABLE, [un-dis-gīz'-abl], *adj.* that cannot be disguised, concealed; obtruding on the attention.
UNDISGUISED, [un-dis-gīzd'], *adj.* not disguised; open, candid; deliberately calculated.
UNDISGUISEDLY, [un-dis-gīz'-id-li], *adv.* in an undisguised fashion.
UNDISHEARTENED, [un-dis-haht'-end], *adj.* not disheartened.
UNDISHONOURED, [un-dis-on'-erd], *adj.* with honour unsullied.
UNDISMAYABLE, [un-dis-mā'-abl], *adj.* that cannot be dismayed.
UNDISMAYED, [un-dis-mād'], *adj.* not dismayed or disheartened.
UNDISORDERED, [un-dis-awd'-erd], *adj.* not thrown out of order.
UNDISPARAGED, [un-dis-pa'-rijd], *adj.* not made a subject of disparagement.
UNDISPATCHED, [un-dis-pacht'], *adj.* not sent off.
UNDISPELLED, [un-dis-peld'], *adj.* not scattered or dispelled.
UNDISPENSED, [un-dis-penst'], *adj.* not dispensed.
UNDISPENSING, [un-dis-pen'-sing], *adj.* not dispensing.
UNDISPERSED, [un-dis-purst'], *adj.* not dispersed or scattered.
UNDISPLAYED, [un-dis-plād'], *adj.* not exhibited or displayed.
UNDISPOSED, [un-dis-pōzd'], *adj.* not disposed, bestowed, or allocated; not inclined (to).
UNDISPUTABLE, [un-dis-pewt'-abl], *adj.* indisputable.
UNDISPUTED, [un-dis-pewt'-id], *adj.* not called in doubt; not disputed; sole.
UNDISQUIETED, [un-dis-kwī'-et-id], *adj.* unruffled, calm.
UNDISSECTED, [un-di-sekt'-id], *adj.* not examined by dissection.
UNDISSEMBLED, [un-di-sembld'], *adj.* openly displayed, not hidden or disguised.
UNDISSEMBLING, [un-di-sem'-bling], *adj.* honest, not seeking to deceive.
UNDISSIPATED, [un-dis'-ip-āt-id], *adj.* not scattered or wasted; not having practised dissipation.
UNDISSOLVABLE, [un-di-zolv'-abl], *adj.* indissoluble.
UNDISSOLVED, [un-di-zolvd'], *adj.* not dissolved; (of Parliament, etc.) still in session.
UNDISTEMPERED, [un-dis-temp'-erd], *adj.* not covered with distemper; †not sick or ill; (of the mind) balanced.
UNDISTENDED, [un-dis-tend'-id], *adj.* not stretched or distended.
UNDISTILLED, [un-di-stild'], *adj.* not having been subjected to distillation.
UNDISTINCTIVE, [un-dis-tingk'-tiv], *adj.* lacking distinction and individual quality.
UNDISTINGUISHABLE, [un-dis-ting'-gwish-abl], *adj.* indistinguishable.
UNDISTINGUISHABLY, [un-dis-ting'-gwish-ab-li], *adv.* in an indistinguishable way.
UNDISTINGUISHED, [un-dis-ting'-gwisht], *adj.* not distinguished; not outstanding, ordinary, common; not well-known or famous.
UNDISTINGUISHING, [un-dis-ting'-gwish-ing], *adj.* not discriminating.
UNDISTORTED, [un-dis-tawt'-id], *adj.* not distorted; truthful, honest, not exaggerated.
UNDISTRACTED, [un-dis-trak'-tid], *adj.* not distracted; able to give full and undivided attention to one thing.
UNDISTRACTEDLY, [un-dis-trakt'-id-li], *adv.* in an undistracted manner.
UNDISTRACTEDNESS, [un-dis-trakt'-id-nes], *n.* the quality of being undistracted.
UNDISTRIBUTED, [un-dis-trib'-yōō-tid], *adj.* not distributed, concentrated in one place; **u. middle**, (*log.*) the middle term of a syllogism where the term is not made universally applicable.
UNDISTURBED, [un-dis-turbd'], *adj.* not moved or shifted; calm, unworried.
UNDISTURBEDLY, [un-dis-turb'-id-li], *adv.* calmly, in an undisturbed fashion.
UNDISTURBEDNESS, [un-dis-turb'-id-nes], *n.* the quality of being undisturbed.
UNDISTURBING, [un-dis-turb'-ing], *adj.* not disturbing or causing disturbance.
UNDIVERSIFIED, [un-dī-vurs'-i-fīd], *adj.* uniform, monotonous, not diversified.
UNDIVERTED, [un-dī-vurt'-id], *adj.* not turned aside.
UNDIVIDABLE, [un-di-vīd'-abl], *adj.* incapable of being divided, indivisible; not separable.

UNDIVIDED, [un-di-vīd'-id], *adj.* not separated or divided.
UNDIVIDEDLY, [un'-di-vīd'-id-li], *adv.* in an undivided fashion.
UNDIVINE, [un-di-vīn'], *adj.* not godlike or divine.
UNDIVORCED, [un-di-vawst'], *adj.* not divorced; (*fig.*) not separated.
UNDIVULGED, [un-dī-vuljd'], *adj.* kept secret.
UNDO, (**undoes, undid, undone**), [un-dōō'], *v.t.* to cancel out (what has been done); to untie or unfasten; to ruin; to seduce.
UNDOCK, [un-dok'], *v.t.* to remove from dock.
UNDOER, [un-dōō'-er], *n.* one who undoes, ruins, or seduces.
UNDOING, [un-dōō'-ing], *n.* the act by which something is undone; the cause of a person's ruin.
UNDOMESTIC, [un-dōm-es'-tik], *adj.* undomesticated.
UNDOMESTICATED, [un-dōm-es'-tik-ā'-tid], *adj.* (of animals) not trained to live with or be used by human beings; (of men and women) having little love for home life.
UNDONE, [un-dun'], *adj.* unfastened; not performed; ruined. [*p.pt.* of UNDO].
UNDOUBTED, [un-dowt'-id], *adj.* not doubted, certain, indubitable.
UNDOUBTEDLY, [un-dowt'-id-li], *adv.* beyond doubt, certainly.
UNDOUBTING, [un-dowt'-ing], *adj.* not doubting, trustful, believing.
UNDOUBTINGLY, [un-dowt'-ing-li], *adv.* in an undoubting fashion.
UNDOWERED, [un-dow'-erd], *adj.* lacking a dower.
UNDRAINED, [un-drānd'], *adj.* lacking drainage.
UNDRAMATIC, [un-dra-mat'-ik], *adj.* not dramatic.
UNDRAPED, [un-drāpt'], *adj.* not clad or covered.
UNDRAWN, [un-drawn'], *adj.* not attracted; not drawn.
UNDREADED, [un-dred'-id], *adj.* not dreaded.
UNDREAMED, UNDREAMT, [un-drēmd', un-drempt'], *adj.* not thought of, unimagined.
UNDRESS (1), [un-dres'], *n.* informal attire.
UNDRESS (2), [un-dres'], *v.t.* and *i.* to remove the clothes from; to take one's clothes off.
UNDRESSED, [un-drest'], *adj.* not dressed, not attired, naked; (of game) not paunched or skinned; (of wounds, etc.) not treated and bandaged.
UNDRIED, [un-drīd'], *adj.* not dried, still wet.
UNDRILLED, [un-drild'], *adj.* not drilled or disciplined.
UNDRINKABLE, [un-dringk'-abl], *adj.* not fit to drink.
UNDRIVEN, [un-driv'-en], *adj.* not propelled or driven.
UNDUE (1), [un-dew'], *adj.* not due to be paid.
UNDUE (2), [un'-dew'], *adj.* excessive, unreasonable, unseemly.
UNDULANT, [un'-dyōō-lant], *adj.* undulating.
UNDULATE (1), [un'-dyōō-lāt], *adj.* wavy, undulating. [L. *undulatus*].
UNDULATE (2), [un'-dyōō-lāt], *v.i.* to be shaped in a series of alternate ridges and troughs. [~L. *undulare*].
UNDULATED, [un'-dyōō-lā-tid], *adj.* wavy, made into alternate ridges and troughs.
UNDULATING, [un'-dyōō-lāt-ing], *adj.* rising and falling in alternate troughs and ridges.
UNDULATINGLY, [un'-dyōō-lāt-ing-li], *adv.* in an undulating fashion.
UNDULATION, [un'-dyōō-lā'-shun], *n.* a wave, a rising or falling movement; a vibratory motion.
UNDULATORY, [un'-dyōō-lāt'-er-i], *adj.* wavy, undulating.
UNDULY, [un-dew'-li], *adv.* in an undue fashion.
UNDUTEOUS, [un-dewt'-i-us], *adj.* not dutiful or obedient; not performing duty to parents and superiors.
UNDUTIFUL, [un-dewt'-i-fōōl], *adj.* not dutiful or obedient.
UNDUTIFULLY, [un-dewt'-i-fōōl-i], *adv.* in an undutiful fashion.
UNDUTIFULNESS, [un-dewt'-i-fōōl-nes], *n.* the quality of being undutiful.
UNDY, see UNDÉ.
UNDYING, [un-dī'-ing], *adj.* immortal; having no end or conclusion, unceasing.
UNEARNED, [un'-urnd'], *adj.* not gained by labour; **u. increment,** increase in the value of property which has not been brought about by the owner.
UNEARTH, [un-urth'], *v.t.* to exhume; to drive an animal out of its burrow; (*fig.*) to find in some obscure place.
UNEARTHLINESS, [un-urth'-li-nes], *n.* the condition of being unearthly.
UNEARTHLY, [un-urth'-li], *adj.* not earthly or natural; weird, strange; (*coll.*) unaccustomed.
UNEASILY, [un-ēz'-i-li], *adv.* in an uneasy fashion.
UNEASINESS, [un-ēz'-i-nes], *n.* the quality of being uneasy.
UNEASY, [un-ēz'-i], *adj.* feeling some physical discomfort or pain; restless; disturbed; anxious or worried; not graceful, awkward, embarrassed.
UNEATABLE, [un-ēt'-abl], *adj.* not fit to eat.
UNEATEN, [un-ēt'-en], *adj.* not eaten or consumed.
UNECLIPSED, [un-i-klipst'], *adj.* not eclipsed; (*fig.*) not surpassed.
UNECONOMIC, [un-ēk'-on-om'-ik], *adj.* not according to economic principle; wasteful, lavish.
UNECONOMICAL, [un-ēk'-on-om'-ik-al], *adj.* wasteful.
UNEDIFYING, [un-ed'-i-fī-ing], *adj.* not edifying.
UNEDITED, [un-ed'-it-id], *adj.* not having been edited or published.
UNEDUCATED, [un-ed'-yōō-kāt-id], *adj.* not educated, uncultured.
UNEFFACED, [un-i-fāst'], *adj.* still apparent, not rubbed out or obscured.
UNEFFECTED, [un-if-ek'-tid], *adj.* not done.
UNEFFECTUAL, [un-if-ek'-chōō-al], *adj.* ineffectual.
UNELABORATE, [un-i-lab'-er-at], *adj.* finished with little labour or study; simple.
UNELASTIC, [un-il-as'-tik], *adj.* not elastic; (*fig.*) admitting no variation or variety.
UNELATED, [un-i-lāt'-id], *adj.* not proud or elated.
UNELECTED, [un-il-ek'-tid], *adj.* not elected.
UNELIGIBLE, [un-el'-ij-ibl], *adj.* ineligible.
UNEMANCIPATED, [un-i-man'-si-pāt-id], *adj.* still in bondage.
UNEMBALMED, [un-em-bahmd'], *adj.* not having been embalmed.
UNEMBARRASSED, [un-em-ba'-rast], *adj.* not perplexed or anxious; free from pecuniary difficulties; easy and collected in manner.
UNEMBITTERED, [un-em-bit'-erd], *adj.* not discontented or embittered.
UNEMBODIED, [un-em-bod'-id], *adj.* not incorporated.
UNEMBROIDERED, [un-em-broid'-erd], *adj.* not worked with embroidery; (*fig.*) plain, simple.
UNEMOTIONAL, [un-i-mō'-shun-al], *adj.* lacking emotion; not given to displays of emotion, calm, not easily perturbed.
UNEMPHATIC, [un-em-fat'-ik], *adj.* lacking emphasis.
UNEMPHATICALLY, [un-em-fat'-ik-al-i], *adv.* in an unemphatic fashion.
UNEMPLOYABLE, [un-em-ploi'-abl], *adj.* unfit for employment; not suitable for use.
UNEMPLOYED (1), [un-em-ploid'], *n.* the aggregate of persons out of work at any given time.
UNEMPLOYED (2), [un-em-ploid'], *adj.* not occupied, not busy; not in use; not having a regular job.
UNEMPLOYMENT, [un-em-ploi'-ment], *n.* the condition of having no regular work; the social problem arising when large bodies of workers are unemployed; **u. benefit,** benefit paid to unemployed persons.
UNEMPOWERED, [un-em-pow'-erd], *adj.* not equipped with power or authority.
UNEMPTIABLE, [un-emp'-ti-abl], *adj.* not able to be emptied, inexhaustible.
UNEMULATING, [un-em'-yōō-lāt-ing], *adj.* not ambitious.
UNENCHANTED, [un-en-chahnt'-id], *adj.* under no enchantment; not very pleased or delighted.
UNENCHANTING, [un-en-chahnt'-ing], *adj.* without charm, not attractive.
UNENCLOSED, [un-en-klōzd'], *adj.* not enclosed, hedged in, wrapped up, etc.
UNENCOUNTERED, [un-en-kownt'-erd], *adj.* not met with.
UNENCUMBERED, UNINCUMBERED, [un-in-kumb'-erd], *adj.* not encumbered; free from debt or mortgage.
UNENDEARED, [un-en-dēerd'], *adj.* not endeared.
UNENDEAVOURING, [un-en-dev'-er-ing], *adj.* making little or no effort.
UNENDING, [un-end'-ing], *adj.* not ending, eternal; continual.
UNENDINGLY, [un-end'-ing-li], *adv.* in an unending

fashion, interminably; (*fig.*) to exasperating length.
UNENDOWED, [un-en-dowd'], *adj.* lacking endowment.
UNENDURABLE, [un-en-dyŏŏer'-abl], *adj.* that cannot be endured; intolerable.
UNENDURING, [un-en-dyŏŏer'-ing], *adj.* not lasting or permanent.
UNENERVATED, [un-en'-er-vāt-id], *adj.* not suffering from exhaustion.
UNENFEEBLED, [un-en-fēbld'], *adj.* not made feeble.
UNENFRANCHISED, [un-en-franch'-īzd], *adj.* having no vote.
UNENGAGED, [un-en-gājd'], *adj.* unoccupied, disengaged; free from obligation; not betrothed.
UNENGAGING, [un-en-gāj'-ing], *adj.* not charming or attractive.
UNENGLISH, [un-ing'-glish], *adj.* not according with the customs, preferences, or habits of thought of English people.
UNENJOYED, [un-en-joid'], *adj.* not enjoyed, used, or obtained.
UNENLARGED, [un-en-lahjd'], *adj.* not added to or enlarged.
UNENLIGHTENED, [un-en-līt'-end], *adj.* not enlightened, uninformed, uneducated.
UNENLIVENED, [un-en-līv'-end], *adj.* not enlivened or diversified in any way, dull, monotonous.
UNENSLAVED, [un-en-slāvd'], *adj.* not in slavery or bondage.
UNENTANGLE, [un-en-tang'-gl], *v.t.* to unravel.
UNENTANGLED, [un-en-tang'-gld], *adj.* not in a tangle; (*fig.*) straightforward.
UNENTERPRISING, [un-en'-ter-prīz-ing], *adj.* not adventurous or enterprising.
UNENTERTAINING, [un'-en-ter-tān'-ing], *adj.* not amusing, dull.
UNENTERTAININGNESS, [un'-en-ter-tān'-ing-nes], *n.* the condition of being unentertaining.
UNENTHRALLED, [un-en-thrawld'], *adj.* under no spell or enchantment; (*coll.*) unattracted, disinterested.
UNENTRENCHED, [un-in-trencht'], *adj.* not entrenched.
UNENVIABLE, [un-en'-vi-abl], *adj.* not to be viewed with envy.
UNENVIED, [un-en'-vid], *adj.* not envied.
UNENVIOUS, [un-en'-vi-us], *adj.* not envying.
UNEQUABLE, [un-ek'-wabl], *adj.* irregular and uncertain; intemperate.
UNEQUAL, [un-ē'-kwal], *adj.* not equal; not of the same length, size, etc.; disproportioned; ill-matched; not uniform in quality; **u. to**, not adequate or sufficient for; incapable of performing.
UNEQUALLED, [un-ē'-kwald], *adj.* not equalled; unrivalled.
UNEQUALLY, [un-ē'-kwal-i], *adv.* in an unequal fashion.
UNEQUALNESS, [un-ē'-kwal-nes], *n.* the quality of being unequal.
UNEQUIPPED, [un-ik-wipt'], *adj.* unprepared, ill-adapted, lacking necessary equipment.
UNEQUIVOCAL, [un-ik-wiv'-ok-al], *adj.* not equivocal; not ambiguous; clear.
UNEQUIVOCALLY, [un-ik-wiv'-ok-al-i], *adv.* in an unequivocal fashion, without ambiguity.
UNEQUIVOCALNESS, [un-ik-wiv'-ok-al-nes], *n.* the quality of being unequivocal.
UNERRING, [un-ur'-ing], *adj.* committing no mistake; incapable of error; sure, unfailing.
UNERRINGLY, [un-ur'-ing-li], *adv.* in an unerring way.
UNESCAPABLE, [un-es-kāp'-abl], *adj.* inescapable.
UNESPIED, [un-es-pīd'], *adj.* not seen or noticed.
UNESSAYED, [un-es-ād'], *adj.* not attempted.
UNESSENTIAL, [un-is-en'-shal], *adj.* having no relation to essence; unnecessary; inessential.
UNEVANGELICAL, [un-ē'-van-jel'-ik-al], *adj.* not in accordance with the Gospel; not of the low church school.
UNEVEN, [un-ē'-ven], *adj.* (of a surface) not smooth, rough and broken; not constant in quality, rhythm, etc.; uncertain, not to be counted on; of a number, not exactly divisible by two; odd.
UNEVENLY, [un-ē'-ven-li], *adv.* in uneven fashion.
UNEVENNESS, [un-ē'-ven-nes], *n.* the state or quality of being uneven.
UNEVENTFUL, [un'-i-vent'-fŏŏl], *adj.* not eventful, unmarked by important happenings.
UNEXACT, [un-egz-akt'], *adj.* inexact.
UNEXACTED, [un-egz-akt'-id], *adj.* (of a payment) not exacted; not obtained by demand or compulsion.
UNEXACTING, [un-egz-akt'-ing], *adj.* not requiring precision or meticulous labour.
UNEXAGGERATED, [un-egz-aj'-er-āt'-id], *adj.* not heightened or exaggerated.
UNEXAMINABLE, [un'-egz-am'-in-abl], *adj.* not open to examination.
UNEXAMINED, [un-egz-am'-ind], *adj.* not subjected to examination.
UNEXAMPLED, [un-egz-ahmpld'], *adj.* having no parallel or example; unique.
UNEXCELLED, [un-ek-seld'], *adj.* not surpassed.
UNEXCEPTIONABLE, [un-ek-sep'-shun-abl], *adj.* not liable to any exception or objection, irreproachable.
UNEXCEPTIONABLENESS,[un-ek-sep'-shun-abl-ness], *n.* the condition of being unexceptionable.
UNEXCEPTIONABLY, [un-ek-sep'-shun-ab-li], *adv.* in an unexceptionable fashion.
UNEXCEPTIONAL, [un-ek-sep'-shun-al], *adj.* unexceptionable; not subject to exceptions.
UNEXCISED (1), [un'-ek-sīzd'], *adj.* not subjected to excision.
UNEXCISED (2), [un-ek'-sīzd], *adj.* not taxed by excise duty.
UNEXCITED, [un-ek-sīt'-id], *adj.* not moved or excited.
UNEXCITING, [un-ek-sīt'-ing], *adj.* not exciting.
UNEXCLUDED, [un-eks-klŏŏd'-id], *adj.* not shut out.
UNEXCLUSIVE, [un-eks-klŏŏs'-iv], *adj.* generally available, not exclusive.
UNEXCOMMUNICATED, [un'-eks-ko-mewn'-ik-ā-tid], *adj.* not under excommunication.
UNEXECUTED, [un-eks'-i-kew-tid], *adj.* not performed; (*leg.*) not formally attested and signed.
UNEXEMPLARY, [un-egz-em'-pler-i], *adj.* not fit to be a pattern.
UNEXEMPLIFIED, [un-egz-em'-pli-fīd], *adj.* not displayed in an example.
UNEXEMPT, [un-eg-zempt'], *adj.* not exempt.
UNEXERCISED, [un-eks'-er-sīzd], *adj.* not exercised.
UNEXERTED, [un-egz-urt'-id], *adj.* not used or exerted.
UNEXHAUSTED, [un'-egz-aws'-tid], *adj.* not used up or exhausted.
UNEXORCISED, [un-eks'-aw-sīzd], *adj.* not having been exorcised.
UNEXPANDED, [un-eks-pand'-id], *adj.* not developed, enlarged or expanded.
UNEXPECTANT, [un-eks-pekt'-ant], *adj.* not expectant.
UNEXPECTED, [un-eks-pekt'-id], *adj.* not expected; sudden.
UNEXPECTEDLY, [un-eks-pekt'-id-li], *adv.* in an unexpected fashion.
UNEXPECTEDNESS, [un-eks-pekt'-id-nes], *n.* the quality of being unexpected.
UNEXPENDED, [un-eks-pend'-id], *adj.* not used, paid out, or expended.
UNEXPENSIVE, [un-eks-pen'-siv], *adj.* inexpensive.
UNEXPERIMENTAL, [un'-eks-pe'-ri-ment'-al], *adj.* not having the nature of an experiment.
UNEXPERT, [un-eks'-purt], *adj.* inexpert.
UNEXPIRED, [un-eks-pierd'], *adj.* not having expired, not terminated, still usable.
UNEXPLORED, [un'-eks-plawrd'], *adj.* not explored, unknown.
UNEXPLOSIVE, [un-eks-plōs'-iv], *adj.* not liable or able to explode.
UNEXPORTED, [un'-eks-pawt'-id], *adj.* not sold abroad.
UNEXPOSED, [un-eks-pōzd'], *adj.* sheltered, protected; not denounced.
UNEXPOUNDED, [un-eks-pownd'-id], *adj.* unexplained.
UNEXPRESSED, [un-eks-prest'], *adj.* not expressed.
UNEXPRESSIVE, [un-eks-pres'-iv], *adj.* not expressive; †unutterable.
UNEXPUNGED, [un-eks-punjd'], *adj.* not expunged.
UNEXPURGATED, [un-eks'-pur-gāt-id], *adj.* not expurgated, published or retold in full.
UNEXTENDED, [un-eks-tend'-id], *adj.* not added to, drawn out, or extended.
UNEXTINCT, [un-eks-tingkt'], *adj.* still extant, not extinct; (of a volcano) still liable to erupt.
UNEXTINGUISHABLE, [un-eks-ting'-gwish-abl], *adj.* that cannot be extinguished.
UNEXTINGUISHED, [un-eks-ting'-gwisht], *adj.* not extinguished.
UNEXTIRPATED, [un-eks'-ter-pāt-id], *adj.* not

exterminated, utterly destroyed, or rooted out.
UNEXTORTED, [un-eks-tawt'-id], *adj.* not obtained by extortion.
UNEXTRACTED, [un-eks-trak'-tid], *adj.* not drawn forth or taken out.
UNFABLED, [un-fābld'], *adj.* not described in tales or fables.
UNFACE, [un-fās'], *v.t.* to expose.
UNFADABLE, [un-fād'-abl], *adj.* not fading or liable to fade.
UNFADED, [un-fād'-id], *adj.* not faded.
UNFADING, [un-fād'-ing], *adj.* not fading or liable to fade.
UNFADINGLY, [un-fād'-ing-li], *adv.* in an unfading fashion.
UNFADINGNESS, [un-fād'-ing-nes], *n.* the quality of being unfading.
UNFAILING, [un-fāl'-ing], *adj.* not likely to fail, not failing; sure and certain, trustworthy.
UNFAILINGLY, [un-fāl'-ing-li], *adv.* in an unfailing manner, certainly.
UNFAILINGNESS, [un-fāl'-ing-nes], *n.* the quality of not failing.
UNFAINTING, [un-fānt'-ing], *adj.* unflagging.
UNFAIR, [un-fāer'], *adj.* not according to fair play; unjust.
UNFAIRLY, [un-fāer'-li], *adv.* in an unfair fashion.
UNFAIRNESS, [un-fāer'-nes], *n.* the quality of being unfair.
UNFAITH, [un'-fāth'], *n.* lack of faith.
UNFAITHFUL, [un-fāth'-fŏŏl], *adj.* not observant of promises, allegiance, or duty; treacherous; adulterous; not performing the proper duty; unbelieving; not faithful; not accurate.
UNFAITHFULLY, [un-fāth'-fŏŏl-i], *adv.* in an unfaithful way.
UNFAITHFULNESS, [un-fāth'-fŏŏl-nes], *n.* the state or quality of being unfaithful.
UNFALLEN, [un-fawl'-en], *adj.* not having fallen.
UNFALLOWED, [un-fal'-ōd], *adj.* ploughed.
UNFALTERING, [un-fawl'-ter-ing], *adj.* not faltering.
UNFALTERINGLY, [un-fawl'-ter-ing-li], *adv.* in an unfaltering fashion.
UNFAMILIAR, [un-fam-il'-yer], *adj.* not familiar, not known; not versed in.
UNFAMILIARITY, [un-fam-il'-i-a'-ri-ti], *n.* lack of familiarity.
UNFAMILIARLY, [un-fam-il'-i-er-li], *adv.* in an unfamiliar way.
UNFASHIONABLE, [un-fash'-un-abl], *adj.* not fashionable.
UNFASHIONABLY, [un-fash'-un-ab-li], *adv.* in an unfashionable way; not according to the fashion.
UNFASHIONABLENESS, [un-fash'-un-abl-nes], *n.* the condition of being unfashionable.
UNFASHIONED, [un-fash'-und], *adj.* not shaped, made, or fashioned.
UNFAST, [un-fahst'], *adj.* not securely fastened.
UNFASTEN, [un-fah'-sen], *v.t.* to unfix or loosen.
UNFATHERED, [un-fahTH'-erd], *adj.* having no known or acknowledged father.
UNFATHERLY, [un-fahTH'-er-li], *adj.* not of the nature of a father.
UNFATHOMABLE, [un-faTH'-om-abl], *adj.* incapable of being sounded or fathomed; (*fig.*) obscure or difficult to understand.
UNFATHOMABLENESS, [un-faTH'-om-abl-nes], *n.* the quality of being unfathomable.
UNFATHOMABLY, [un-faTH'-om-ab-li], *adv.* in unfathomable fashion.
UNFATHOMED, [un-faTH'-omd], *adj.* not sounded or fathomed; (*fig.*) not understood.
UNFATIGUED, [un-fa-tēgd'], *adj.* not tired.
UNFAULTY, [un-fawlt'-i], *adj.* having no fault.
UNFAVOURABLE, [un-fāv'-er-abl], *adj.* not favourable or favouring; adverse; unlucky, unpropitious.
UNFAVOURABLENESS, [un-fāv'-er-abl-nes], *n.* the quality of being unfavourable.
UNFAVOURABLY, [un-fāv'-er-ab-li], *adv.* in unfavourable fashion.
UNFAVOURED, [un-fāv'-erd], *adj.* not favoured or helped.
UNFEARED, [un-fēerd'], *adj.* not feared.
UNFEARFUL, [un-fēer'-fŏŏl], *adj.* not terrible or fearful; courageous.
UNFEARING, [un-fēer'-ing], *adj.* not afraid.
UNFEASIBLE, [un-fēz'-ibl], *adj.* not capable of being done.
UNFEATURED, [un-fē'-cherd], *adj.* deformed; not featured; not stressed or singled out.
UNFED, [un-fed'], *adj.* unnourished, not fed.
UNFEED, [un-fēd'], *adj.* not paid by a fee, honorary.
UNFEELING, [un-fēl'-ing], *adj.* lacking feelings, merciless, callous.
UNFEELINGLY, [un-fēl'-ing-li], *adv.* in an unfeeling way.
UNFEELINGNESS, [un-fēl'-ing-nes], *n.* the quality of being unfeeling.
UNFEIGNED, [un-fānd'], *adj.* not feigned or affected, true, genuine.
UNFEIGNEDLY, [un-fān'-id-li], *adv.* in an unfeigned way.
UNFELLOWED, [un-fel'-ōd], *adj.* not matched, having no fellow.
UNFELT, [un-felt'], *adj.* not felt or experienced.
UNFEMININE, [un-fem'-in-in], *adj.* unlike or unfitting for a woman.
UNFENCE, [un-fents'], *v.t.* to remove the fence from.
UNFENCED, [un-fenst'], *adj.* lacking a fence.
UNFERMENTED, [un'-fer-ment'-id], *adj.* not fermented.
UNFERTILE, [un-fur'-til], *adj.* not fertile, unfruitful.
UNFERTILIZED, [un-fur'-til-īzd], *adj.* not treated with a fertilizer; not made fertile, not caused to bear.
UNFETTER, [un-fet'-er], *v.t.* to free from fetters; (*fig.*) to make free.
UNFETTERED, [un-fet'-erd], *adj.* not bound in fetters; (*fig.*) free, uncontrolled, unrestrained.
UNFEUDALIZE, [un-few'-dal-īz], *v.t.* to release from feudalism.
UNFIGURED, [un-fig'-erd], *adj.* not ornamented with figures.
UNFILIAL, [un-fil'-i-al], *adj.* not filial.
UNFILIALLY, [un-fil'-i-al-i], *adv.* in an unfilial way.
UNFILLED, [un-fild'], *adj.* empty, unoccupied, not filled.
UNFILLETED, [un-fil'-it-id], *adj.* not bound by a fillet; not boned.
UNFILMED, [un-filmd'], *adj.* lacking a film; not photographed for the screen.
UNFILTERABLE, [un-fil'-ter-abl], *adj.* that cannot be filtered.
UNFINISHED, [un-fin'-isht], *adj.* not completed or concluded; not exhibiting the highest workmanship, rough, unskilled, clumsy.
UNFIRM, [un'-furm], *adj.* not firm or stable, rickety.
UNFIRMNESS, [un-furm'-nes], *n.* the state of being unfirm.
UNFIT (1), [un-fit'], *adj.* faulty, incapable, not in a fit state (to); not fitted or suited (to).
UNFIT (2), [un-fit'], *v.t.* to make unfit (for), incapable (of).
UNFITLY, [un-fit'-li], *adv.* in an unfit fashion.
UNFITNESS, [un-fit'-nes], *n.* the quality of being unfit.
UNFITTED, [un-fit'-id], *adj.* not supplied with or lacking fittings; not fixed into place; made unfit (for) or incapable (of).
UNFITTING, [un-fit'-ing], *adj.* not suitable; unseemly.
UNFITTINGLY, [un-fit'-ing-li], *adv.* in an unfitting fashion.
UNFIX, [un-fiks'], *v.t.* to release from a fixed state or position.
UNFIXED, [un-fikst'], *adj.* not yet fixed; released from a fixed state or position; (*coll.*) not determined upon.
UNFIXEDNESS, [un-fiks'-id-nes], *n.* the condition of being unfixed.
UNFLAGGING, [un-flag'-ing], *adj.* constant, persevering, unremitting, unwavering.
UNFLAGGINGLY, [un-flag'-ing-li], *adv.* in unflagging fashion.
UNFLATTERED, [un-flat'-erd], *adj.* not having been flattered.
UNFLATTERING, [un-flat'-er-ing], *adj.* not flattering or falsely pleasing.
UNFLATTERINGLY, [un-flat'-er-ing-li], *adv.* in an unflattering fashion.
UNFLAWED, [un-flawd'], *adj.* having no flaw or blemish.
UNFLEDGED, [un-flejd'], *adj.* not yet covered with feathers; (*fig.*) immature.
UNFLESHED, [un-flesht'], *adj.* not yet used to bloodshed; (*fig.*) uninitiated, inexperienced.
UNFLESHLY, [un-flesh'-li], *adj.* not pertaining to the flesh; high-minded, spiritual, other-worldly.
UNFLINCHING, [un-flinch'-ing], *adj.* resolute, not flinching; steadfast amid dangers.
UNFLINCHINGLY, [un-flinch'-ing-li], *adv.* in an unflinching way.
UNFOILED, [un-foild'], *adj.* not foiled or defeated.
UNFOLD, [un-fōld'], *v.t.* and *i.* to open from a folded

state; to expand; (*fig.*) to reveal (something hitherto unknown); to tell (a tale) stage by stage; (of a narrative) to be set forth stage by stage.
UNFOLLOWED, [un-fol'-ōd], *adj.* not followed or pursued.
UNFORBEARING, [un-for-bāer'-ing], *adj.* not forbearing, harsh and unkind.
UNFORBIDDEN, [un-for-bid'-en], *adj.* not prohibited; not warned or ordered not to.
UNFORCEABLE, [un-faws'-abl], *adj.* incapable of being forced.
UNFORCED, [un-fawst'], *adj.* not forced, easy, natural, unconstrained, fluent.
UNFORDABLE, [un-fawd'-abl], *adj.* incapable of being forded.
UNFOREBODING, [un-faw(r)-bōd'-ing], *adj.* not foreboding, not giving ill omen.
UNFOREKNOWN, [un-faw(r)-nōn'], *adj.* not known beforehand.
UNFORESEEN, [un-faw-sēn'], *adj.* not expected or foreseen.
UNFORETOLD, [un-faw-tōld'], *adj.* not described beforehand, not prophesied.
UNFOREWARNED, [un-faw-wawnd'], *adj.* not warned beforehand.
UNFORFEITED, [un-faw'-fit-id], *adj.* not claimed or surrendered as a forfeit.
UNFORGETTABLE, [un-for-get'-abl], *adj.* that cannot be forgotten; striking, memorable.
UNFORGIVABLE, [un-for-giv'-abl], *adj.* that cannot be forgiven.
UNFORGIVEN, [un-for-giv'-en], *adj.* not pardoned.
UNFORGIVING, [un-for-giv'-ing], *adj.* not disposed to forgive, relentless, unmerciful.
UNFORGOTTEN, [un-for-got'-en], *adj.* not forgotten, still remembered.
UNFORMAL, [un-fawm'-al], *adj.* informal.
UNFORMED, [un-fawmd'], *adj.* not yet shaped or given a form, not yet brought into actuality; (of thoughts) vague, nebulous, imperfectly conceived; untrained, undisciplined.
UNFORSAKEN, [un'-for-sāk'-en], *adj.* not forsaken or neglected.
UNFORTIFIED, [un-fawt'-i-fīd], *adj.* defenceless, not fortified.
UNFORTUNATE (1), [un-faw'-chōōn-at], *n.* an unfortunate person.
UNFORTUNATE (2), [un-faw'-chōōn-at], *adj.* not fortunate or lucky; wretched, miserable, dogged with ill-luck; unpropitious; unsuccessful.
UNFORTUNATELY, [un-faw'-chōōn-at-li], *adv.* in an unfortunate fashion, by mischance.
UNFOSSILIZED, [un-fos'-il-īzd], *adj.* not fossilized.
UNFOSTERED, [un-fos'-terd], *adj.* not fostered, cherished, or nourished.
UNFOUGHT, [un-fawt'], *adj.* not fought.
UNFOULED, [un-fowld'], *adj.* not polluted or made foul.
UNFOUNDED, [un-fownd'-id], *adj.* not based on fact, fictitious.
UNFRAMED, [un-frāmd'], *adj.* having no frame.
UNFRATERNAL, [un-frat-urn'-al], *adj.* unbrotherly.
UNFREE, [un-frē'], *adj.* not free, bound, fettered.
UNFREQUENTED, [un-fri-kwent'-id], *adj.* not much visited, solitary.
UNFRETTED, [un-fret'-id], *adj.* not fretted, eroded, or rubbed.
UNFRIABLE, [un-frī'-abl], *adj.* not easily pulverized.
UNFRIENDED, [un-frend'-id], *adj.* having no friends.
UNFRIENDLINESS, [un-frend'-li-nes], *n.* want of kindness; an unkind act.
UNFRIENDLY, [un-frend'-li], *adj.* hostile; unkind; not favourable.
UNFROCK, [un-frok'], *v.t.* to turn out of the priesthood.
UNFROZEN, [un-frōz'-en], *adj.* not frozen.
UNFRUGAL, [un-frōōg'-al], *adj.* not economical, not thrifty.
UNFRUITFUL, [un-frōōt'-fōōl], *adj.* not bearing fruit; barren; unprofitable.
UNFRUITFULLY, [un-frōōt'-fōōl-i], *adv.* in an unfruitful fashion; unsuccessfully.
UNFRUITFULNESS, [un-frōōt'-fōōl-nes], *n.* the quality of being unfruitful; barrenness.
UNFRUSTRABLE, [un-frust'-rabl], *adj.* unable to be frustrated.
UNFULFILLED, [un-fōōl-fild'], *adj.* not fulfilled or accomplished, not achieved.
UNFUNDED, [un-fund'-id], *adj.* lacking funds.
UNFURL, [un-furl'], *v.t. and i.* to unroll (a flag) at the mast; (of a flag) to become opened or spread out.
UNFURNISH, [un-furn'-ish], *v.t.* to remove the furniture from.
UNFURNISHED, [un-furn'-isht], *adj.* containing no furniture; not supplied.
UNFURROWED, [un-fu'-rōd], *adj.* not marked with furrows.
UNFUSED, [un-fewzd'], *adj.* not fused.
UNGAINFUL, [un-gān'-fōōl], *adj.* not profitable.
UNGAINLINESS, [un-gān'-li-nes], *n.* clumsiness, the state of being ungainly.
UNGAINLY, [un-gān'-li], *adj.* clumsy; uncouth.
UNGALLANT, [un-gal'-ant], *adj.* not gallant, discourteous.
UNGALLANTLY, [un-gal'-ant-li], *adv.* in an ungallant fashion.
UNGALLED, [un-gawld'], *adj.* not galled.
UNGARBLED, [un-gahbld'], *adj.* true, not garbled.
UNGARLANDED, [un-gahl'-and-id], *adj.* not garlanded.
UNGARNISHED, [un-gahn'-isht], *adj.* not garnished, unadorned.
UNGARRISONED, [un-ga'-ris-und], *adj.* not garrisoned with troops.
UNGARTERED, [un-gaht'-erd], *adj.* lacking a garter or garters.
UNGATHERED, [un-gaTH'-erd], *adj.* not gathered.
UNGEAR, [un-gēer'], *v.t.* to strip of gear, tackle, clothes, etc.
UNGENERATED, [un-jen'-er-ā-tid], *adj.* not produced or generated.
UNGENERATIVE, [un-jen'-er-a-tiv], *adj.* not producing or generating.
UNGENEROUS, [un-jen'-er-us], *adj.* not generous or liberal; mean, dishonourable.
UNGENEROUSLY, [un-jen'-er-us-li], *adv.* in an ungenerous way.
UNGENIAL, [un-jē'-ni-al], *adj.* not genial or sociable.
UNGENTEEL, [un-jen-tēl'], *adj.* not genteel.
UNGENTEELLY, [un-jen-tēl'-li], *adv.* in an ungenteel fashion.
UNGENTLE, [un-jentl'], *adj.* rough, not tender; low-born.
UNGENTLEMANLIKE, [un-jentl'-man-līk], *adj.* ungentlemanly.
UNGENTLEMANLINESS, [un-jentl'-man-li-nes], *n.* the quality of being ungentlemanlike.
UNGENTLEMANLY, [un-jentl'-man-li], *adj.* vulgar; unfitting, unbecoming a gentleman.
UNGENTLENESS, [un-jentl'-nes], *n.* the quality of being ungentle.
UNGENTLY, [un-jent'-li], *adv.* in ungentle fashion.
UNGEOMETRICAL, [un-jē'-ō-met'-rik-al], *adj.* not geometrical.
UN-GET-AT-ABLE, [un'-get-at'-abl], *adj.* remote, inaccessible.
UNGIFTED, [un-gift'-id], *adj.* not talented.
UNGILD, [un-gild'], *v.t.* to remove the gilt from.
UNGILDED, [un-gild'-id], *adj.* not coloured with gilt.
UNGILT, [un-gilt'], *adj.* ungilded.
UNGIRD, [un-gurd'], *v.t.* to take the girdle from; to take off by undoing one's girdle.
UNGIRT, [un-girt'], *adj.* not girdled; unprepared.
UNGIVEN, [un-giv'-en], *adj.* not bestowed.
UNGIVING, [un-giv'-ing], *adj.* not bestowing.
UNGLADDENED, [un-glad'-end], *adj.* not cheered or gladdened.
UNGLAZE, [un-glāz'], *v.t.* to remove the glass or glaze from.
UNGLAZED, [un-glāzd'], *adj.* not fitted with glass; not glazed.
UNGLORIFIED, [un-glaw'-ri-fīd], *adj.* not praised or worshipped.
UNGLOVE, [un-gluv'], *v.t.* to remove the gloves or glove from.
UNGLOVED, [un'-gluvd'], *adj.* not covered with a glove or gloves.
UNGLUE, [un-glōō'], *v.t.* to separate (something fastened with glue).
UNGOADED, [un-gōd'-id], *adj.* not goaded or pricked on.
UNGODLILY, [un-god'-li-li], *adv.* in an ungodly fashion, to an ungodly degree.
UNGODLINESS, [un-god'-li-nes], *n.* the quality of being ungodly.
UNGODLY, [un-god'-li], *adj.* wicked, impious; having no thought or fear of God; (*coll.*) appalling.
UNGORED, [un-gaw(r)d'], *adj.* not gored.
UNGORGED, [un-gawjd'], *adj.* not replete or sated.

UNGOTTEN, [un-got'-en], *adj.* not born; not gained.
UNGOVERNABLE, [un-guv'-ern-abl], *adj.* incapable of being governed, unruly.
UNGOVERNABLY, [un-guv'-ern-ab-li], *adv.* in an ungovernable way.
UNGOVERNED, [un-guv'-ernd], *adj.* having no rule or governance; unbridled, licentious.
UNGOWN, [un-gown'], *v.t.* to remove the gown from; (of a priest) to unfrock.
UNGOWNED, [un-gownd'], *adj.* not wearing a gown.
UNGRACED, [un-grāst'], *adj.* not graced.
UNGRACEFUL, [un-grās'-fōōl], *adj.* wanting grace or elegance; clumsy.
UNGRACEFULLY, [un-grās'-fōōl-i], *adv.* in an ungraceful way.
UNGRACEFULNESS, [un-grās'-fōōl-nes], *n.* the condition of being ungraceful.
UNGRACIOUS, [un-grā'-shus], *adj.* unkind, discourteous, rude.
UNGRACIOUSLY, [un-grā'-shus-li], *adv.* in an ungracious fashion.
UNGRACIOUSNESS, [un-grā'-shus-nes], *n.* the quality of being ungracious.
UNGRAMMATICAL, [un-gram-at'-ik-al], *adj.* not in accordance with the rules of grammar.
UNGRAMMATICALLY, [un-gram-at'-ik-al-i], *adv.* in ungrammatical fashion.
UNGRANTED, [un-grahnt'-id], *adj.* not allowed or bestowed.
UNGRATE, [un'-grāt'], *n.* an ungrateful person.
UNGRATEFUL, [un-grāt'-fōōl], *adj.* wanting gratitude, unthankful; unprofitable, unpleasant.
UNGRATEFULLY, [un-grāt'-fōōl-i], *adv.* in an ungrateful fashion.
UNGRATEFULNESS, [un-grāt'-fōōl-nes], *n.* ingratitude, the condition of being ungrateful.
UNGRATIFIED, [un-grat'-i-fīd], *adj.* not indulged, not satisfied.
UNGREGARIOUS, [un-grig-āer'-i-us], *adj.* not gregarious, solitary.
UNGROUND, [un-grownd'], *adj.* not crushed or ground.
UNGROUNDED, [un-grownd'-id], *adj.* (of a statement, etc.) having no foundation, without reason or support.
UNGROUNDEDLY, [un-grownd'-id-li], *adv.* in an ungrounded way.
UNGROUNDEDNESS, [un-grownd'-id-nes], *n.* the quality of being ungrounded.
UNGRUDGED, [un-grujd'], *adj.* generously given; not envied.
UNGRUDGING, [un-gruj'-ing], *adj.* giving without stint or envy.
UNGRUDGINGLY, [un-gruj'-ing-li], *adv.* in an ungrudging fashion.
UNGUAL, [ung'-gwal], *adj.* possessing or relating to nails, claws, etc. [~L. *unguis* claw].
UNGUARDED, [un-gahd'-id], *adj.* having no guard or protection, uncircumspect, incautious.
UNGUARDEDLY, [un-gahd'-id-li], *adv.* in an unguarded fashion.
UNGUENT, [ung'-gwent], *n.* an ointment. [L. *unguens*].
UNGUENTARIUM, [un'-gwent-āer'-i-um], *n.* a vessel for holding unguents.
UNGUENTARY, [ung'-gwent-er-i], *adj.* pertaining to unguents.
UNGUENTOUS, [ung-gwen'-tus], *adj.* resembling an unguent.
UNGUESSED, [un-gest'], *adj.* not guessed; carefully calculated.
UNGUICAL, [un'-gwik-al], *adj.* ungual.
UNGUICORN, [un'-gwik-awn], *n.* the horny nail at the tip of a bird's beak.
UNGUICULAR, [ung-gwik'-yōō-ler], *adj.* relating to nails, claws, etc.
UNGUICULATE, [ung-gwik'-yōō-lāt], *adj.* (*bot., zool.*) having nails, claws, or similar appendages.
UNGUICULATED, [ung-gwik'-yōō-lā-tid], *adj.* unguiculate.
UNGUIDED, [un-gīd'-id], *adj.* not guided, conducted or supervised.
UNGUIFEROUS, [un-gwif'-er-us], *adj.* having a nail, claw, etc.
UNGUIFORM, [ung'-gwi-fawm], *adj.* resembling a hoof, claw, or nail in shape.
UNGUILTILY, [un-gilt'-i-li], *adv.* in unguilty manner.
UNGUILTY, [un-gilt'-i], *adj.* not guilty.
UNGUINAL, [un'-gwin-al], *adj.* ungual.
UNGUINOUS, [un'-gwin-us], *adj.* oily, unctuous.
UNGUIROSTRAL, [ung'-gwi-ros'-tral], *adj.* (*ornith.*) having a nail on the beak. [L. *unguis* nail and *rostrum* beak].
UNGULA, [ung'-gyōō-la], *n.* the three dimensional shape which remains when the peak of a cone is cut off along a plane not parallel with the base of the cone. [L. *ungula* hoof].

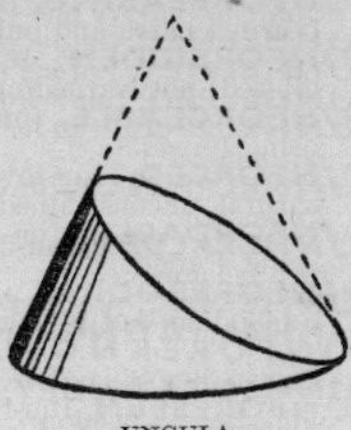
UNGULA

UNGULAR, [un'-gyōō-la], *adj.* ungual.
UNGULATE (1), [ung'-gyōō-lāt], *n.* a mammal that has hoofs.
UNGULATE (2), [ung'-yōō-lāt], *adj.* (*zool.*) having hoofs, belonging to that group of mammals that have hoofs. [~L. *ungula* hoof].
UNGUM, [un-gum'], *v.t.* to unfasten something that is gummed; to remove the gum from.
UNHABITUATED, [un-hab-ich'-ōō-ā-tid], *adj.* not used or accustomed.
UNHACKNEYED, [un-hak'-nid], *adj.* not over-familiar or overquoted, fresh.
UNHALLOW, [un-hal'-ō], *v.t.* to desecrate or profane.
UNHALLOWED, [un-hal'-ōd], *adj.* not consecrated; desecrated; profane, wicked.
UNHAND, [un-hand'], *v.t.* to let go from one's grip.
UNHANDILY, [un-hand'-i-li], *adv.* clumsily.
UNHANDINESS, [un-hand'-i-nes], *n.* the state of being unhandy.
UNHANDLED, [un-handld'], *adj.* not touched with hands.
UNHANDSOME, [un-han'-sum], *adj.* not handsome; ungenerous, uncivil.
UNHANDSOMELY, [un-han'-sum-li], *adv.* in an unhandsome fashion.
UNHANDSOMENESS, [un-han'-sum-nes], *n* the quality of being unhandsome.
UNHANDY, [un-hand'-i], *adj.* not dexterous, clumsy; out of the way.
UNHANG, [un-hang'], *v.t.* to remove the ornaments or hangings from; to release from a hanging position.
UNHANGED, [un-hangd'], *adj.* not hanged.
UNHAPPILY, [un-hap'-i-li], *adv.* unfortunately; wretchedly.
UNHAPPINESS, [un-hap'-i-nes], *n.* the condition or quality of being unhappy, misery.
UNHAPPY, [un-hap'-i], *adj.* not happy, wretched, miserable; unfortunate, ill-timed, tactless.
UNHARASSED, [un-ha'-rast], *adj.* not harassed, not overbusied or worried.
UNHARBOURED, [un-hah'-berd], *adj.* not sheltered or protected; (of opinions, etc.) not cherished or held.
UNHARDENED, [un-hahd'-end], *adj.* not hardened.
UNHARMED, [un-hahmd'], *adj.* free from harm.
UNHARMFUL, [un-hahm'-fōōl], *adj.* harmless.
UNHARMONIOUS, [un-hah-mō'-ni-us], *adj.* not harmonious, discordant.
UNHARNESS, [un-hah'-nes], *v.t.* to remove the trappings or harness from.
UNHASP, [un-hahsp'], *v.t.* to unfasten by loosening the hasp of.
UNHATCHED, [un-hacht'], *adj.* still in the egg; (*fig.*) not matured or revealed.
UNHAZARDED, [un-haz'-erd-id], *adj.* not risked.
UNHAZARDOUS, [un-haz'-erd-us], *adj.* not risky, safe.
UNHEALTHFUL, [un-helth'-fōōl], *adj.* unwholesome, unhealthy.
UNHEALTHFULNESS, [un-helth'-fōōl-nes], *n.* the quality of being unhealthful.
UNHEALTHILY, [un-helth'-i-li], *adv.* in an unhealthy fashion.
UNHEALTHINESS, [un-helth'-i-nes], *n.* the quality of being unhealthy.
UNHEALTHY, [un-helth'-i], *adj.* not healthy, diseased, unwholesome.
UNHEARD, [un-hurd'], *adj.* not heard; **u.- of,** outrageous, unprecedented.
UNHEATED, [un-hēt'-id], *adj.* not heated.
UNHEAVENLY, [un-hev'-en-li], *adj.* not suggestive of heaven.
UNHEDGED, [un-hejd'], *adj.* not bounded by a hedge.
UNHEEDED, [un-hēd'-id], *adj.* not noticed, neglected.
UNHEEDFUL, [un-hēd'-fōōl], *adj.* unheeding.
UNHEEDFULLY, [un-hēd'-fōōl-i], *adv.* in an unheedful way, without care or precaution; rashly.

UNHEEDING, [un-hēd'-ing], *adj.* careless, negligent, inattentive.
UNHEEDINGLY, [un-hēd'-ing-li], *adv.* in an unheeding fashion.
UNHELM, [un-helm'], *v.t. and i.* to remove the helmet from; to remove one's own helmet.
UNHELMED, [un-helmd'], *adj.* not wearing a helmet.
UNHELMET, [un-hel'-mit], *v.t.* to unhelm.
UNHELPED, [un-helpt'], *adj.* not helped.
UNHELPFUL, [un-help'-fo͝ol], *adj.* affording no aid, not helpful.
UNHELPFULLY, [un-help'-fo͝ol-i], *adv.* in an unhelpful fashion.
UNHERALDED, [un-he'-rald-id], *adj.* not announced or proclaimed.
UNHEROIC, [un-hi-rō'-ik], *adj.* not heroic.
UNHESITATING, [un-hez'-it-āt-ing], *adj.* prompt, brisk.
UNHESITATINGLY, [un-hez'-it-āt-ing-li], *adv.* in unhesitating fashion.
UNHEWN, [un-hewn'], *adj.* not hewn.
UNHINDERED, [un-hind'-erd], *adj.* not hindered or delayed.
UNHINGE, [un-hinj'], *v.t.* to remove from the hinges; to make (the mind) unbalanced.
UNHINGEMENT, [un-hinj'-ment], *adj.* the act of unhinging, the state of being unhinged.
UNHIRED, [un-hierd'], *adj.* not taken on hire, not hired.
UNHISTORIC, [un-his-to'-rik], *adj.* not found in history, not momentous.
UNHISTORICAL, [un-his-to'-rik-al], *adj.* unhistoric.
UNHISTORICALLY, [un-his-to'-rik-al-i], *adv.* in an unhistorical way.
UNHITCH, [un-hich'], *v.t.* to undo, unfasten, separate.
UNHIVE, [un-hīv'], *v.t.* to drive from the hive.
UNHOLILY, [un-hō'-li-li], *adv.* in unholy fashion.
UNHOLINESS, [un-hō'-li-nes], *n.* the quality of being unholy.
UNHOLY, [un-hō'-li], *adj.* not holy or hallowed; wicked; (*coll.*) very bad.
UNHONOURED, [un-on'-erd], *adj.* not respected or honoured.
UNHOODED, [un-ho͝od'-id], *adj.* not wearing a hood.
UNHOOK, [un-ho͝ok'], *v.t.* to take off a hook; to undo the hooks of.
UNHOOP, [un-ho͞op'], *v.t.* to take away the hoops of.
UNHOPED, [un-hōpt'], *adj.* not likely, not expected; **u.-for**, not expected.
UNHOPEFUL, [un-hōp'-fo͝ol], *adj.* not hopeful, hopeless.
UNHORNED, [un-hawnd'], *adj.* not possessing horns.
UNHORSE, [un-haws'], *v.t.* to cause to fall from horseback.
UNHOSTILE, [un-host'-il], *adj.* inoffensive, friendly.
UNHOUSE, [un-hows'], *v.t.* to turn out of house.
UNHOUSED, [un-howzd'], *adj.* having no house, homeless.
UNHOUSELED†, [un-howzld'], *adj.* not having partaken of Holy Communion.
UNHUMAN, [un-hew'-man], *adj.* not human.
UNHUMANIZE, [un-hew'-man-iz], *v.t.* to make unhuman, dehumanize.
UNHUMBLED, [un-humbld'], *adj.* not humbled or defeated.
UNHUNG, [un-hung'], *adj.* not hung.
UNHUNTED, [un-hunt'-id], *adj.* not pursued.
UNHURRIED, [un-hu'-rid], *adj.* not hurried; deliberate.
UNHURT, [un-hurt'], *adj.* not hurt, free from injury.
UNHURTFUL, [un-hurt'-fo͝ol], *adj.* not likely to hurt, innocuous.
UNHURTFULLY, [un-hurt'-fo͝ol-i], *adv.* in an unhurtful way.
UNHUSKED, [un-huskt'], *adj.* turned out of the husk.
UNI-, *pref.* single, having only one. [~L. *unus* one].
UNIAT, UNIATE, [yo͞o'-ni-at], *n.* a member of an Eastern church acknowledging the papal authority. [Russ. *uniyata* united].
UNIAXIAL, UNIAXAL, [yo͞o'-ni-aks'-i-al, yo͞o'-ni-aks'-al], *adj.* possessing one axis.
UNIBRANCHIATE, [yo͞o'-ni-brang'-ki-āt], *adj.* (*zool.*) having only one gill.
UNICAMERAL, [yo͞o'-ni-kam'-er-al], *adj.* (of a legislative body) sitting as only one chamber. [UNI- and L. *camera* chamber].
UNICAMERATE, [yo͞o'-ni-kam'-er-āt], *adj.* unicameral.
UNICAPSULAR, [yo͞o'-ni-kap'-syo͞o-ler], *adj.* having only a single capsule in each component.
UNICELLULAR, [yo͞o'-ni-sel'-yo͞o-ler], *adj.* consisting of, comprising, one cell.
UNICORN, [yo͞o'-ni-kawn], *n.* a legendary horse-like creature depicted with a horn in its brow and a lion's or horse's tail. [LL. *unicornis*].

UNICORN

UNICORNOUS, [yo͞o'-ni-kawn'-us], *adj.* having only a single horn.
UNICOSTATE, [yo͞o'-ni-kos'-tāt], *adj.* (*bot.*) (of leaves) having only one rib.
UNICUSPID, [yo͞o-ni-kus'-pid], *adj.* (*anat.*) having one cusp only.
UNICYCLE, [yo͞o'-ni-sīkl'], *n.* a one-wheeled cycle.
UNIDEA'D, UNIDEAED, [un-ī-dē'-ad], *adj.* lacking ideas.
UNIDEAL, [un-ī-dē'-al], *adj.* not ideal.
UNIDENTATE, [yo͞o-ni-dent'-āt], *adj.* having a single tooth.
UNIDENTICULATE, [yo͞o'-ni-dent-ik'-yo͞o-lāt], *adj.* having a single denticle.
UNIDENTIFIED, [un-ī-dent'-i-fīd], *adj.* not identified, recognized or discovered.
UNIDIMENSIONAL, [yo͞o'-ni-dī-men'-shun-al], *adj.* of or having only a single dimension.
UNIDIOMATIC, [un'-id-i-ōm-at'-ik], *adj.* not according to idiom.
UNIFACIAL, [yo͞o-ni-fā'-shal], *adj.* having only one front surface.
UNIFARIOUS, [yo͞o'-ni-fāer'-i-us], *adj.* arranged in a single row.
UNIFIABLE, [yo͞o'-ni-fī'-abl], *adj.* capable of being unified.
UNIFICATION, [yo͞o'-ni-fik-ā'-shun], *n.* the act of unifying, the fact or condition of being unified.
UNIFIER, [yo͞o'-ni-fī'-er], *n.* a person who, or that which, unifies.
UNIFLAGELLATE, [yo͞o'-ni-flaj'-el-āt], *adj.* (*bot.*) having a single flagellum.
UNIFLOROUS, [yo͞o'-ni-flaw'-rus], *adj.* (*bot.*) producing only one flower. [UNI- and L. *flos floris* flower].
UNIFOLIATE, [yo͞o'-ni-fō'-li-āt], *adj.* (*bot.*) possessing a single leaf.
UNIFORM (1), [yo͞o'-ni-fawm], *n.* official or regulation dress.
UNIFORM (2), [yo͞o'-ni-fawm], *adj.* constant, unvarying. [L. *uniformis*].
UNIFORMED, [yo͞o'-ni-fawmd], *adj.* wearing a uniform.
UNIFORMITARIAN, [yo͞o'-ni-fawm'-it-āer'-i-an], *n.* one who believes that all geological processes were, are, and will be due to the same unvarying causes.
UNIFORMITY, [yo͞o'-ni-fawm'-i-ti], *n.* the condition of being uniform.
UNIFORMLY, [yo͞o'-ni-fawm-li], *adv.* in a uniform fashion.
UNIFY, [yo͞o'-ni-fī], *v.t.* to make one of; to make uniform. [MedL. *unificare*].
UNIGENITURE, [yo͞o'-ni-jen'-i-cher], *n.* the condition of being the sole offspring.
UNILABIATE, [yo͞o'-ni-lā'-bi-āt], *adj.* having a single lip.
UNILATERAL, [yo͞o'-ni-lat'-er-al], *adj.* having only one side; pertaining to one party in an agreement.
UNILITERAL, [yo͞o'-ni-lit'-er-al], *adj.* consisting of a single letter.
UNILLUMINATED, [un'-i-lo͞o'-min-ā-tid], *adj.* not illuminated; not enlightened.
UNILLUMINED, [un'-i-lo͞om'-ind], *adj.* not illumined; (*fig.*) not enlightened.
UNILLUSTRATED, [un-il'-us-trā-tid], *adj.* not illustrated; (of a book) without pictures.
UNILLUSTRATIVE, [un-il'-us-tra-tiv], *adj.* not illustrative (of).
UNILOCULAR, [yo͞o'-ni-lok'-yo͞o-ler], *adj.* (*zool.*, *bot.*) having only one cell or loculus.
UNIMAGINABLE, [un-im-aj'-in-abl], *adj.* that cannot be imagined.
UNIMAGINABLY, [un-im-aj'-in-ab-li], *adv.* in an unimaginable fashion.
UNIMAGINATIVE, [un-im-aj'-in-at-iv], *adj.* not imaginative, lacking imagination.
UNIMAGINED, [un-im-aj'-ind], *adj.* not conceived, not thought of, undreamed.
UNIMBUED, [un-im-bewd'], *adj.* not saturated (in), not inspired (with).
UNIMITATED, [un-im'-it-āt-id], *adj.* not imitated.

UNIMPAIRABLE, [un-im-päer'-abl], *adj*. not liable to be or capable of being impaired.

UNIMPAIRED, [un-im-pāerd'], *adj*. not impaired, not damaged or diminished.

UNIMPASSIONATE, [un-im-pash'-un-at], *adj*. dispassionate.

UNIMPASSIONED, [un-im-pash'-und], *adj*. not actuated by passion, dispassionate.

UNIMPEACHABILITY, [un-im-pēch'-ab-il'-i-ti], *n*. the quality of being unimpeachable.

UNIMPEACHABLE, [un-im-pēch'-abl], *adj*. incapable of being impeached; irreproachable, faultless, blameless.

UNIMPEACHABLENESS, [un-im-pēch'-abl-nes], *n*. unimpeachability.

UNIMPEACHABLY, [un-im-pēch'-ab-li], *adv*. in unimpeachable fashion.

UNIMPEACHED, [un-im-pēcht'], *adj*. free from impeachment.

UNIMPEDED, [un'-im-pēd'-id], *adj*. not hindered or impeded; not blocked or obstructed.

UNIMPLICATED, [un-im'-plik-ā'-tid], *adj*. not implicated or involved.

UNIMPLIED, [un-im-plīd'], *adj*. not implied, not intended to be inferred.

UNIMPLORED, [un-im-plaw(r)d'], *adj*. not implored.

UNIMPORTANCE, [un-im-pawt'-ants], *n*. the quality of being unimportant.

UNIMPORTANT, [un-im-pawt'-ant], *adj*. not important, insignificant, immaterial.

UNIMPORTUNED, [un-im'-paw-tewnd], *adj*. not made the object of importunity.

UNIMPOSING, [un-im-pōz'-ing], *adj*. not commanding respect by outward appearance, not imposing.

UNIMPREGNATED, [un-im'-preg-nā-tid], *adj*. not impregnated.

UNIMPRESSED, [un-im-prest'], *adj*. not impressed or attracted.

UNIMPRESSIBLE, [un-im-pres'-ibl], *adj*. incapable of being impressed.

UNIMPRESSIVE, [un-im-pres'-iv], *adj*. not impressive or commanding.

UNIMPRESSIVELY, [un-im-pres'-iv-li], *adv*. in an unimpressive fashion.

UNIMPRISONED, [un-im-priz'-ond], *adj*. not confined or imprisoned.

UNIMPROVABLE, [un-im-proov'-abl], *adj*. not capable of improvement.

UNIMPROVABLENESS, [un-im-proov'-abl-nes], *n*. the state or quality of being unimprovable.

UNIMPROVED, [un-im-proovd'], *adj*. not improved, not made better.

UNIMPROVING, [un-im-proov'-ing], *adj*. not tending to make better, not instructive.

UNIMPUGNABLE, [un-im-pewn'-abl], *adj*. not to be, incapable of being impugned.

UNIMUSCULAR, [yoo'-ni-mus'-kyoo-ler], *adj*. (*zool.*) having only a single muscle.

UNINCENSED, [un'-in-senst'], *adj*. not incensed or enraged.

UNINCLOSED, [un'-in-klōzd'], *adj*. unenclosed.

UNINCORPORATED, [un'-in-kor'-por-āt-id], *adj*. not incorporated.

UNINCUMBERED, see UNENCUMBERED.

UNINDENTED, [un-in-dent'-id], *adj*. not indented.

UNINDIVIDUALIZED, [un'-in-di-vid'-yoo-al-izd], *adj*. not a distinct, complete, individual; (*geol.*) not separated into distinct components.

UNINDORSED, [un-in-dawst'], *adj*. not indorsed; not ratified.

UNINDUCED, [un-in-dewst'], *adj*. not induced.

UNINDUSTRIOUS, [un-in-dus'-tri-us], *adj*. not industrious or diligent.

UNINFECTED, [un-in-fekt'-id], *adj*. not infected or contaminated.

UNINFESTED, [un-in-fest'-id], *adj*. not infested.

UNINFLAMED, [un-in-flāmd'], *adj*. not inflamed; (*fig.*) not angered or impassioned.

UNINFLAMMABLE, [un-in-flam'-abl], *adj*. not inflammable.

UNINFLATED, [un-in-flāt'-id], *adj*. not blown up, deflated.

UNINFLECTED, [un-in-flekt'-id], *adj*. (*gram.*) not having inflections.

UNINFLUENCED, [un-in'-floo-enst], *adj*. not actuated or persuaded by outside influences.

UNINFLUENTIAL, [un'-in-floo-en'-shal], *adj*. lacking any influence.

UNINFORMED, [un-in-fawmd'], *adj*. not having knowledge or information; ignorant.

UNINGENIOUS, [un-in-jē'-ni-us], *adj*. not ingenious.

UNINGENUOUS, [un-in-jen'-yoo-us], *adj*. not frank or ingenuous.

UNINGENUOUSNESS, [un-in-jen'-yoo-us-nes], *n*. the quality of being uningenuous.

UNINHABITABLE, [un-in-hab'-it-abl], *adj*. not capable of being inhabited; unable to support life.

UNINHABITABLENESS, [un-in-hab'-it-abl-nes], *n*. the quality of being uninhabitable.

UNINHABITED, [un-in-hab'-it-id], *adj*. having no inhabitants, deserted.

UNINITIATED, [un-in-ish'-i-ā-tid], *adj*. not initiated.

UNINJURED, [un-in'-jerd], *adj*. not hurt or damaged.

UNINJURIOUS, [un-in-jooer'-i-us], *adj*. not likely to cause hurt or damage.

UNINOMINAL, [yoo'-ni-nom'-in-al], *adj*. consisting of a single word, term; with only one name.

UNINQUIRING, [un-ing-kwier'-ing], *adj*. not curious, not disposed to inquire.

UNINQUISITIVE, [un-ing-kwiz'-it-iv], *adj*. not curious, uninquiring.

UNINSCRIBED, [un-in-skrībd'], *adj*. not having an inscription.

UNINSPIRED, [un-in-spierd'], *adj*. not inspired; lacking inspiration.

UNINSTRUCTED, [un-in-strukt'-id], *adj*. not taught or instructed, not furnished with instructions.

UNINSTRUCTIVE, [un-in-strukt'-iv], *adj*. not likely to instruct.

UNINSTRUCTIVELY, [un-in-strukt'-iv-li], *adv*. in an uninstructive fashion.

UNINSULAR, [un-in'-syoo-la], *adj*. not insular.

UNINSULATED, [un-in'-syoo-lāt'-id], *adj*. (*elect.*) not insulated.

UNINSURED, [un-in-shooerd'], *adj*. not holding, or covered by, an insurance policy.

UNINTEGRATED, [un-in'-tig-rāt-id], *adj*. not integrated.

UNINTELLECTUAL, [un'-in-tel-ek'-choo-al], *adj*. not intellectual, not attracted by intellectual interests or pursuits; without intellectual appeal.

UNINTELLECTUALLY, [un'-in-tel-ek'-choo-al-i], *adv*. in an unintellectual fashion.

UNINTELLIGENT, [un'-in-tel'-ij-ent], *adj*. not gifted with understanding; stupid, foolish, dull.

UNINTELLIGENTLY, [un'-in-tel'-ij-ent-li], *adv*. in an unintelligent way.

UNINTELLIGIBILITY, [un'-in-tel'-ij-ib-il'-i-ti], *n*. the quality of being unintelligible.

UNINTELLIGIBLE, [un'-in-tel'-ij-ibl], *adj*. incapable of being understood; incomprehensible; confused.

UNINTELLIGIBLENESS, [un-in-tel'-ij-ibl-nes], *n*. the quality of not being intelligible.

UNINTELLIGIBLY, [un-in-tel'-ij-ib-li], *adv*. in unintelligible fashion.

UNINTENDED, [un-in-tend'-id], *adj*. not designed, accidental.

UNINTENTIONAL, [un-in-ten'-shun-al], *adj*. unintended.

UNINTENTIONALLY, [un-in-ten'-shun-al-i], *adv*. in unintentional fashion.

UNINTERESTED, [un-in'-ter-est-id], *adj*. not interested, disinterested.

UNINTERESTING, [un-in'-ter-est-ing], *adj*. not exciting interest.

UNINTERESTINGLY, [un-in'-ter-est-ing-li], *adv*. in an uninteresting way.

UNINTERMITTED, [un-in-ter-mit'-id], *adj*. continuous, uninterrupted.

UNINTERMITTING, [un-in-ter-mit'-ing], *adj*. ceaseless, continuous.

UNINTERMITTINGLY, [un-in-ter-mit'-ing-li], *adv*. ceaselessly.

UNINTERMIXED, [un-in-ter-mikst'], *adj*. not mingled or intermixed.

UNINTERPOLATED, [un-in-tur'-pōl-ā-tid], *adj*. not interpolated.

UNINTERPRETABLE, [un-in-tur'-prit-abl], *adj*. incapable of interpretation; transcendent, mystical.

UNINTERPRETED, [un-in-tur'-prit-id], *adj*. not explained or interpreted.

UNINTERRED, [un-in-turd'], *adj*. not interred.

UNINTERRUPTED, [un-in-ter-rup'-tid], *adj*. not interrupted, incessant.

UNINTERRUPTEDLY, [un-in-ter-rup'-tid-li], *adv*. in an uninterrupted way.

UNINTOXICATING, [un-in-toks'-ik-āt-ing], *adj*. not causing intoxication.

UNINTRODUCED, [un-in-trō-dewst'], *adj*. not introduced.

UNINUCLEAR, [yoo'-ni-new'-kli-er], *adj*. having a single nucleus or equivalent structure.

UNINUCLEATE(D), [yōō'-ni-new'-klē-āt(-id)], *adj.* uninuclear.
UNINURED, [un-in-yōōerd'], *adj.* not hardened.
UNINVENTED, [un-in-vent'-id], *adj.* not invented.
UNINVENTIVE, [un-in-vent'-iv], *adj.* not inventive.
UNINVESTED, [un-in-vest'-id], *adj.* not invested.
UNINVESTIGABLE, [un-in-vest'-ig-abl], *adj.* incapable of being investigated; not open to investigation.
UNINVIDIOUS, [un-in-vid'-i-us], *adj.* not invidious, not giving offence.
UNINVITED, [un-in-vīt'-id], *adj.* not invited, not asked for.
UNINVITING, [un'-in-vīt'-ing], *adj.* not attractive or inviting.
UNINVOKED, [un-in-vōkt'], *adj.* not invoked or called upon.
UNINVOLVED, [un-in-volvd'], *adj.* simple, not complex; not concerned (in).
UNION (1), [yōō'-ni-un], *n.* the action of joining together or uniting; the condition of being joined together or united; the unit or unity resulting from a juncture or association of two or more things; a political league or combination; the act of joining two persons in marriage, marriage, the married state; the incorporation of several parishes under a Board of Guardians for the administration of Poor Law relief; the workhouse; the unity of two or more nations in a political entity; an association of non-professional workers, a trade union; a device for connecting together two pipes, etc. [L. *unio*].
UNION (2), ONION, [yōō'-ni-un], *n.* (*archaic*) a large pearl. [L. *unio*].
UNION FLAG, [yōō'-ni-un-flag'], *n.* the flag of the United Kingdom of Great Britain and Northern Ireland.
UNIONISM, [yōō'-ni-un-izm], *n.* (*archaic*) trade unionism; (*hist.*) the policy of centralized imperial government with regard to the British Empire as contrasted with the policy of self-governing dominions; this principle applied in particular to Ireland in the Home Rule controversy.
UNIONIST, [yōō'-ni-un-ist], *n.* (*hist.*) a supporter of the trade union movement; a supporter of imperial unionism, *esp.* one opposing Irish Home Rule; a member of the Conservative Party.
UNION JACK, [yōō'-ni-un-jak'], *n.* the Union flag when flown at a ship's bow; (*coll.*) the Union flag.
UNIPAROUS, [yōō-ni'-pa-rus], *adj.* (*bot.*) having only one axis; (*zool.*) producing only one at a birth.
UNIPARTITE, [yōōn'-i-paht'-īt], *adj.* containing only one part, not subdivided.
UNIPERSONAL, [yōō'-ni-pur'-son-al], *adj.* (*theol.*) contained in or being only one person.
UNIPOLAR, [yōō'-ni-pō'-ler], *adj.* having only a single pole.
UNIQUE, [yōō-nēk'], *adj.* alone in its kind or class, unequalled, resembling nothing else; (*coll.*)marvellous.
UNIQUELY, [yōō-nēk'-li], *adv.* in a unique way.
UNIQUENESS, [yōō-nēk'-nes], *n.* the quality of being unique.
UNIRADIAL, [yōō'-ni-rā'-di-al], *adj.* uniradiate.
UNIRADIATE(D), [yōō'-ni-rā'-di-āt(-id)], *adj.* having a single radius.
UNIRRIGATED, [un-i'-rig-ā-tid], *adj.* not irrigated.
UNIRRITATED, [un-i'-rit-ā-tid], *adj.* not irritated.
UNIRRITATING, [un-i'-rit-ā-ting], *adj.* not irritating.
UNISEXUAL, [yōō-ni-seks'-yōō-al], *adj.* (*bot.*) of one sex only.
UNISOLATED, [un-ī'-sōl-ā-tid], *adj.* not isolated or separate.
UNISON, [yōō'-ni-son], *n.* agreeable concord of sound; (*mus.*) identical pitch; **in u.** (*mus.*) so as to be identical in pitch; (*fig.*) in agreement. [L. *unisonus* having a single sound].
UNISONAL, [yōō-nis-on'-al], *adj.* that is in unison.
UNISONANCE, [yōō-ni'-so-nants], *n.* the condition of being in unison.
UNISONANT, [yōō-ni'-so-nant], *adj.* in unison.
UNISONOUS, [yōō-nis'-on-us], *adj.* in unison.
UNISSUED, [un-ish'-yōōd], *adj.* not issued.
UNIT, [yōō'-nit], *n.* that which is an entity in itself; a convenient subdivision; a standard of measurement; the numeral one; (*fig.*) a single object, person; **abstract u.,** the number one. [Short form of UNITY].
UNITARIAN (1), [yōō-ni-tāer'-i-an], *n.* a member of a religious sect professing itself Christian but denying the Deity of Christ and the doctrine of the Trinity.
UNITARIAN (2), [yōō-nit-āer'-i-an], *adj.* of, or pertaining to, Unitarians or the tenets of Unitarianism.

UNITARIANISM, [yōō-nit-āer'-i-an-izm], *n.* t
religious system of Unitarians.
UNITARY, [yōō'-nit-er-i], *adj.* relating to a unit
units; undivided.
UNITE, [yōō-nīt'], *v.t. and i.* to bring into union,
join together into one body, to form, combine int
one whole; to form or be a connecting link betwee
to join by or in marriage; to become or be capable
being linked, joined together, or combined; to ent
into association, to amalgamate; to agree, or come
agreement; (of a fractured bone) to mend. [~]
unitus, *p.pt.* of *unire* to join].
UNITED, [yōō-nī'-tid], *adj.* joined together, linke
associated, *esp.* in political organization or in affe
tions or principles, etc.; (of an action) undertaken b
various bodies or persons jointly.
UNITEDLY, [yōō-nī'-tid-li], *adv.* in a united manne
in unity, in agreement.
UNITER, [yōō-nī'-ter], *n.* someone or something tha
links or joins.
UNITIVE, [yōō'-nit-iv], *adj.* causing to unite. [L
unitivus].
UNITIZE, [yōō'-nit-īz], *v.t.* to fashion into a unit.
UNITY, [yōō'-nit-i], *n.* the quality or condition
being a unit or being united; the state or quality
agreeing in principles, sentiments, purposes, etc
concord, agreement; the number one; (*leg.*) a join
tenancy; **the three unities,** (*drama*) unity of plo
or story, of place, and of time. [L. *unitas*].
UNIVALVE (1), [yōō'-ni-valv'], *n.* a mollusc that ha
a single valve.
UNIVALVE (2), [yōō'-ni-valv'], *adj.* (of mollusc
having a single valve.
UNIVALVULAR, [yōō'-ni-valv'-yōō-ler], *adj.* un
valve.
UNIVERSAL (1), [yōō'-ni-vurs'-al], *n.* (*log.*) a un
versal proposition; a general idea.
UNIVERSAL (2), [yōō'-ni-vurs'-al], *adj.* pertainir
to the universe; widespread, general; generall
applicable, generally used or usable; **u. joint,**
swivelled pivot or other mechanical device permi
ting movement in every direction. [L. *universalis*
UNIVERSALISM, [yōō'-ni-vurs'-al-izm], *n.* (*theol*
the belief in the ultimate salvation of all humanit
UNIVERSALIST, [yōō'-ni-vurs'-al-ist], *n.* a perso
accepting universalism.
UNIVERSALISTIC, [yōō'-ni-vurs'-al-ist'-ik], *ad*
relating to the doctrine of universalism.
UNIVERSALITY, [yōō'-ni-vurs-al'-i-ti], *n.* the con
dition of being universal.
UNIVERSALIZE, [yōō'-ni-vurs'-al-īz], *v.t.* to rende
universal.
UNIVERSALLY, [yōō'-ni-vurs'-al-i], *adv.* in a un
versal fashion; everywhere and always.
UNIVERSALNESS, [yōō'-ni-vurs'-al-nes], *n.* th
state of being universal.
UNIVERSE, [yōō'-ni-vurs], *n.* the whole of creation
the heavenly bodies and space; space; (*coll.*) th
earth and all it contains. [L. *universum* the world
UNIVERSITY, [yōō'-ni-vurs'-i-ti], *n.* an institutio
consisting of one or more colleges, where students ar
educated in higher branches of learning, wher
research is conducted, and by which degrees ar
awarded; the corporate body of persons employed by
educated at, or connected with, such an institution
any group of persons or team representing such a
institution. [L. *universitas* the whole].
UNIVERSOLOGY, [yōō'-ni-vur-sol'-o-ji], *n.* tha
science which takes the whole universe for its field c
study. [UNIVERSE and Gk. *logos* speech].
UNIVOCAL (1), [yōō-ni'-vō-kal], *n.* a word with
single meaning.
UNIVOCAL (2), [yōō-ni'-vō-kal], *adj.* having a singl
meaning, unambiguous.
UNIVOCALLY, [yōō-ni'-vō-kal-i], *adv.* in a univoca
fashion.
UNIVOCATION, [yōō'-ni-vō-kā'-shun], *n.* con
formity of name and meaning.
UNJAUNDICED, [un-jawn'-dist], *adj.* not jealous
impartial.
UNJEALOUS, [un-jel'-us], *adj.* not jealous.
UNJOIN, [un-join'], *v.t.* to separate, disjoin.
UNJOINED, [un-joind'], *adj.* not joined, separate
UNJOINT, [un-joint'], *v.t.* to unfasten the joints o
UNJOINTED, [un-joint'-id], *adj.* having no joints
UNJOYOUS, [un-joi'-us], *adj.* not joyous.
UNJUDGED, [un-jujd'], *adj.* not judged.
UNJUST, [un-just'], *adj.* contrary to, not actuate
by, justice; unfair, inequitable, prejudiced.
UNJUSTIFIABLE, [un-just'-i-fī-abl], *adj.* that ca
not be justified, *esp.* in the eyes of the law.

NJUSTIFIABLENESS, [un-just'-i-fī-abl-nes], *n.* the quality of being unjustifiable.

NJUSTIFIABLY, [un-just'-i-fī'-ab-li], *adv.* in an unjustifiable manner.

NJUSTIFIED, [un-jus'-ti-fīd], *adj.* not justified.

NJUSTLY, [un-just'-li], *adv.* in an unjust way.

NKEMPT, [un-kempt'], *adj.* uncombed; slovenly, untidy. [OE. *cemban* to comb].

NKENNED, [un-kend'], *adj.* (*Scots*) unknown, unexplored.

NKENNEL, [un-ken'-el], *v.t.* to drive (an animal) from a hole; (*fig.*) to drive from secrecy, to reveal.

NKEPT, [un-kept'], *adj.* not kept or retained.

NKERCHIEFED, [un-kur'-chift], *adj.* not having a kerchief on.

NKIND, [un-kīnd'], *adj.* not kind; inconsiderate, harsh.

NKINDLINESS, [un-kīnd'-li-nes], *n.* the quality of being unkindly; an unkind act.

NKINDLY (1), [un-kīnd'-li], *adj.* unkind, inconsiderate, malignant.

NKINDLY (2), [un-kīnd'-li], *adv.* in an unkind fashion.

NKINDNESS, [un-kīnd'-nes], *n.* unkindliness.

NKINGLIKE, [un-king'-līk], *adj.* unkingly.

NKINGLY, [un-king'-li], *adj.* unworthy of a king.

NKNIGHTLY, [un-nīt'-li], *adj.* not worthy of a knight.

NKNIT, [un-nit'], *v.t.* to separate or undo what is knit or knitted.

NKNOT, [un-not'], *v.t.* to untie the knots in.

NKNOWABLE, [un-nō'-abl], *adj.* incapable of being known; **the u.,** that which cannot be known or comprehended.

NKNOWING, [un-nō'-ing], *adj.* not knowing.

NKNOWINGLY, [un-nō'-ing-li], *adv.* in an unknowing way, unawares.

NKNOWN, [un-nōn'], *adj.* not known, unexplored, inexperienced, lying beyond knowledge.

NLABORIOUS, [un-lab-aw'-ri-us], *adj.* not laborious.

NLABOURED, [un-lāb'-erd], *adj.* easy, unconstrained.

NLACE, [un-lās'], *v.t.* to untie (something that is laced up).

NLACED, [un-lāst'], *adj.* without laces; with laces untied; (of a beverage) lacking a dash of spirits.

NLADE, [un-lād'], *v.t.* to unload.

NLADEN, [un-lād'-en], *adj.* not burdened or loaded.

NLADYLIKE, [un-lā'-di-līk], *adj.* not seemly for a lady.

NLAID, [un'-lād'], *adj.* not set at rest; not arranged or set out; (of paper) not having parallel watermark lines.

NLAMENTED, [un-lam-ent'-id], *adj.* not mourned for, not regretted.

NLAP, [un-lap'], *v.t.* to open or unfold.

NLARDED, [un-lahd'-id], *adj.* not larded.

NLASH, [un-lash'], *v.t.* (of lashings), to undo; to unfasten and remove the lashings from.

NLATCH, [un-lach'], *v.t.* to open by releasing the latch of.

NLAURELLED, [un-lo'-reld], *adj.* not crowned with laurels.

NLAVISH, [un-lav'-ish], *adj.* not lavish.

NLAWFUL, [un-law'-fōōl], *adj.* contrary to the law.

NLAWFULLY, [un-law'-fōōl-i], *adv.* illegally.

NLAWFULNESS, [un-law'-fōōl-nes], *n.* the state of being unlawful.

NLAY, [un-lā'], *v.t.* to unravel (a rope).

NLEARN, [un-lurn'], *v.t.* to forget purposely (what has been learned).

NLEARNED (1), [un-lurn'-id], *adj.* ignorant, illiterate.

NLEARNED (2), UNLEARNT, [un-lurnd', un-lurnt'], *adj.* not learned.

NLEARNEDLY, [un-lurn'-id-li], *adv.* in an unlearned way.

NLEARNEDNESS, [un-lurn'-id-nes], *n.* the quality of being unlearned, ignorance.

NLEARNT, see UNLEARNED (2).

NLEASH, [un-lēsh'], *v.t.* to free from a leash; (*fig.*) to let loose.

NLEASHED, [un-lēsht'], *adj.* let loose from the leash; (*fig.*) unconstrained, unchecked.

NLEAVENED, [un-lev'-end], *adj.* made without yeast.

NLED, [un-led'], *adj.* without guidance; leaderless.

UNLEISURED, [un-lezh'-erd], *adj.* very busy, having no leisure; bereft of leisure.

UNLEISURELY, [un-lezh'-er-li], *adj.* hurried, rushed, very busy.

UNLENT, [un-lent'], *adj.* not parted with as a loan.

UNLESS, [un-les'], *conj.* if . . . not; supposing that . . . not; except, save. [ME. *on lesse*].

UNLEVEL, [un-levl'], *adj.* not level, not smooth.

UNLESSONED, [un-les'-ond], *adj.* not taught.

UNLETTERED, [un-let'-erd], *adj.* unlearned, illiterate.

UNLEVELLED, [un-lev'-eld], *adj.* not made level.

UNLICENSED, [un-lī'-senst], *adj.* not authorized by licence.

UNLICKED, [un-likt'], *adj.* (*coll.*) impudent, ill-mannered, ill-bred; (*slang*) unbeaten.

UNLIGHTED, [un-līt'-id], *adj.* not lighted or illuminated.

UNLIKE (1), [un-līk'], *adj.* dissimilar.

UNLIKE (2), [un-līk'], *prep.* bearing no resemblance to, not according to the character of.

UNLIKELIHOOD, [un-līk'-li-hōōd], *n.* the condition of being unlikely; an event or circumstance unlikely to come about.

UNLIKELINESS, [un-līk'-li-nes], *n.* unlikelihood.

UNLIKELY, [un-līk'-li], *adj.* not likely; not promising success; *adv.* improbably.

UNLIKENESS, [un-līk'-nes], *n.* the state or quality of being unlike.

UNLIMBER (1), [un-lim'-ber], *adj.* not supple.

UNLIMBER (2), [un-lim'-ber], *v.t.* to remove the limber of (a gun).

UNLIMED, [un-līmd'], *adj.* not dressed with lime.

UNLIMITABLE, [un-lim'-it-abl], *adj.* illimitable.

UNLIMITED, [un-lim'-it-id], *adj.* that is without limit or restriction, without constraint or condition; (*coll.*) very great.

UNLIMITEDLY, [un-lim'-it-id-li], *adv.* in an unlimited fashion.

UNLIMITEDNESS, [un-lim'-it-id-nes], *n.* the quality of being unlimited.

UNLINE, [un-līn'], *v.t.* to take the lining out of.

UNLINEAL, [un-lin'-i-al], *adj.* not lineal.

UNLINK, [un-lingk'], *v.t.* to unfasten or disconnect the links of; to separate (things linked together).

UNLIQUEFIED, UNLIQUIFIED, [un-lik'-wi-fīd], *adj.* not turned into a liquid.

UNLIQUIDATED, [un-lik'-wi-dāt-id], *adj.* not liquidated.

UNLIQUIFIED, see UNLIQUEFIED.

UNLISTENING, [un-lisn'-ing], *adj.* not listening.

UNLIT, [un-lit'], *adj.* dark, not illuminated.

UNLIVELINESS, [un-līv'-li-nes], *n.* the quality of being unlively.

UNLIVELY, [un-līv'-li], *adj.* not lively.

UNLOAD, [un-lōd'], *v.t.* to take a load from; to discharge (a load); to remove the charge from (a gun); (of shares, etc.) to sell out.

UNLOCATED, [un-lō-kāt'-id], *adj.* not located; (*U.S.*) not surveyed.

UNLOCK, [un-lok'], *v.t.* to open; (*fig.*) to reveal.

UNLOCKED, [un-lokt'], *adj.* not locked.

UNLOOKED-FOR, [un-lōōkt'-faw(r)], *adj.* unexpected.

UNLOOSE, [un-lōōs'], *v.t.* to make loose, to free.

UNLOOSEN, [un-lōōs'-en], *v.t.* to unloose.

UNLOSABLE, [un-lōōz'-abl], *adj.* that cannot be lost.

UNLOVABLE, [un-luv'-abl], *adj.* not lovable.

UNLOVED, [un-luvd'], *adj.* not loved.

UNLOVELINESS, [un-luv'-li-nes], *adj.* the quality of being unlovely.

UNLOVELY, [un-luv'-li], *adj.* ugly, not lovely.

UNLOVERLIKE, [un-luv'-er-līk], *adj.* not worthy of a lover, not what a lover should do or be.

UNLOVING, [un-luv'-ing], *adj.* not loving, cold.

UNLOVINGLY, [un-luv'-ing-li], *adv.* in an unloving fashion.

UNLUBRICATED, [un-lōō'-brik-ā-tid], *adj.* not oiled.

UNLUCKILY, [un-luk'-i-li], *adv.* in unlucky fashion; unfortunately.

UNLUCKINESS, [un-luk'-i-nes], *n.* the condition of being unlucky.

UNLUCKY, [un-luk'-i], *adj.* experiencing constant bad luck; badly timed, tactless; ill-omened.

UNMADE (1), [un-mād'], *adj.* not made, not fashioned, formed, or shaped.

UNMADE (2), [un-mād'], *pret. and p.pt.* of UNMAKE.

UNMAGNETIC, [un-mag-net'-ik], *adj.* not magnetic; (*fig.*) unattractive.

UNMAIDENLY, [un-mād'-en-li], *adj.* not seemly for a maiden.

UNMAIMED, [un-māmd'], *adj.* not hurt in any limb.

UNMAKABLE, [un-māk'-abl], *adj.* that cannot be made.

UNMAKE, (unmade), [un-māk], *v.t.* to destroy (something made); to cancel, annul.

UNMALLEABILITY, [un-mal'-i-ab-il'-i-ti], *n.* the quality of being unmalleable.

UNMALLEABLE, [un-mal'-i-abl], *adj.* incapable of being hammered into shape.

UNMAN, [un-man'], *v.t.* to take away the courage and manly qualities of; to take the men or crew from.

UNMANACLED, [un-man'-akld], *adj.* not wearing manacles; (*fig.*) free.

UNMANAGEABLE, [un-man'-ij-abl], *adj.* incapable of being managed; not easily governed or directed; out of hand.

UNMANAGED, [un-man'-ijd], *adj.* not managed.

UNMANLIKE, [un-man'-līk], *adj.* not characteristic of a man.

UNMANLINESS, [un-man'-li-nes], *n.* the condition of being unmanly.

UNMANLY, [un-man'-li], *adj.* effeminate, unworthy of a man.

UNMANNED, [un-mand'], *adj.* unnerved; having no crew.

UNMANNERED, [un-man'-erd], *adj.* free from affectation; †ill-bred, impolite.

UNMANNERLINESS, [un-man'-er-li-nes], *n.* the condition of being unmannerly, incivility, rudeness, boorishness.

UNMANNERLY, [un-man'-er-li], *adj.* ill-bred, uncivil.

UNMANTLED, [un-mantld'], *adj.* lacking, not wearing, a mantle.

UNMANUFACTURED, [un'-man-yōō-fak'-cherd], *adj.* not manufactured.

UNMANURED, [un-man-yōōerd'], *adj.* not manured.

UNMARKED, [un-mahkt'], *adj.* having no spots or marks; unsoiled; (of school work) not corrected by the teacher; unnoticed.

UNMARKETABLE, [un-mah'-kit-abl], *adj.* not marketable.

UNMARRED, [un-mahd'], *adj.* not marred.

UNMARRIAGEABLE, [un-ma'-rij-abl], *adj.* too young to be married, unfit for marriage.

UNMARRIAGEABLENESS, [un-ma'-rij-abl-nes], *n.* the quality of being unmarriageable.

UNMARRIED, [un-ma'-rid], *adj.* not married.

UNMARSHALLED, [un-mah'-shald], *adj.* not arranged in order.

UNMASCULINE, [un-mas'-kyōō-lin], *adj.* effeminate.

UNMASK, [un-mahsk'], *v.t. and i.* to strip the mask from; (*fig.*) to reveal or expose; to take off one's own mask; (*fig.*) to appear in one's true character, to stop dissimulating.

UNMASKED, [un-mahskt'], *adj.* no longer wearing a mask; (*fig.*) exposed.

UNMASTERED, [un-mah'-sterd], *adj.* not subdued or conquered; not thoroughly learnt.

UNMATCHABLE, [un-mach'-abl], *adj.* impossible to equal.

UNMATCHED, [un-macht'], *adj.* unequalled.

UNMATED, [un-māt'-id], *adj.* not mated.

UNMATERIAL, [un-mat-ēer'-i-al], *adj.* not made of material, unsubstantial.

UNMATURED, [un-ma-tyōōerd'], *adj.* not yet brought to maturity.

UNMEANING, [un-mēn'-ing], *adj.* having no sense, meaningless.

UNMEANINGLY, [un-mēn'-ing-li], *adv.* in unmeaning fashion.

UNMEANINGNESS, [un-mēn'-ing-nes], *n.* the quality of being unmeaning.

UNMEANT, [un-ment'], *adj.* not intended, accidental.

UNMEASURABLE, [un-mezh'-er-abl], *adj.* incapable of being measured, boundless.

UNMEASURABLY, [un-mezh'-er-ab-li], *adv.* immeasurably.

UNMEASURED, [un-mezh'-erd], *adj.* limitless, unstinted; immoderate, ill-considered.

UNMECHANICAL, [un-mi-kan'-ik-al], *adj.* not mechanical, not depending on mechanics.

UNMECHANICALLY, [un-mi-kan'-ik-al-i], *adv.* in an unmechanical way.

UNMECHANIZED, [un-me'-kan-īzd], *adj.* not mechanized.

UNMEDDLING, [un-med'-ling], *adj.* not meddlesome.

UNMEDITATED, [un-med'-it-ā-tid], *adj.* not thought over; ill-considered; unpremeditated.

UNMEET, [un-mēt'], *adj.* not fitted (for).

UNMEETLY, [un-mēt'-li], *adv.* not fitly, unsuitabl

UNMEETNESS, [un-mēt'-nes], *n.* the quality being unmeet.

UNMELLOWED, [un-mel'-ōd], *adj.* not mellowe or matured.

UNMELODIOUS, [un-mel-ō'-di-us], *adj.* not meloc ous or tuneful.

UNMELODIOUSLY, [un-mel-ō'-di-us-li], *adv.* an unmelodious manner.

UNMELODIOUSNESS, [un-mel-ō'-di-us-nes], the quality of being unmelodious.

UNMELTED, [un-melt'-id], *adj.* not melted; (*fi* unappeased, unsoftened.

UNMENTIONABLE, [un-men'-shun-abl], *adj.* th cannot be spoken of; **unmentionables,** (*col* trousers.

UNMENTIONED, [un-men'-shund], *adj.* not me tioned.

UNMERCANTILE, [un-mur'-kan-tīl], *adj.* not me cantile.

UNMERCENARY, [un-mur'-sen-er-i], *adj.* not co cerned with money.

UNMERCHANTABLE, [un-mur'-chant-abl], *ad* not saleable.

UNMERCIFUL, [un-mur'-si-fōōl], *adj.* cruel, har hearted, showing no mercy.

UNMERCIFULLY, [un-mur'-si-fōōl-i], *adv.* withou mercy, in an unmerciful fashion.

UNMERCIFULNESS, [un-mur'-si-fōōl-nes], *n.* tl quality of being unmerciful.

UNMERITED, [un-me'-rit-id], *adj.* not merited deserved.

UNMETHODICAL, [un-meth-od'-ik-al], *adj.* lacl ing plan or method.

UNMETRICAL, [un-met'-rik-al], *adj.* not written metre; not in accordance with the laws of prosod

UNMETRICALLY, [un-met'-rik-al-i], *adv.* in a unmetrical way.

UNMEWED, [un-mewd'], *adj.* set at liberty.

UNMILITARY, [un-mil'-it-er-i], *adj.* not military.

UNMILKED, [un-milkt'], *adj.* not milked.

UNMILLED, [un-mild'], *adj.* (of a coin) having smooth rim.

UNMINDED, [un-mīnd'-id], *adj.* not intending (to unnoticed; untended.

UNMINDFUL, [un-mīnd'-fōōl], *adj.* not heedfu forgetful.

UNMINDFULLY, [un-mīnd'-fōōl-i], *adv.* in a unmindful fashion.

UNMINDFULNESS, [un-mīnd'-fōōl-nes], *n.* th condition of being unmindful.

UNMINGLED, [un-ming'-gld], *adj.* not mixed mingled.

UNMISSED, [un-mist'], *adj.* not thought to be los unmourned.

UNMISTAKABLE, [un-mis-tāk'-abl], *adj.* that ca not be mistaken or misunderstood.

UNMISTAKABLY, [un-mis-tāk'-ab-li], *adv.* in a unmistakable way.

UNMISTAKEN, [un-mis-tāk'-en], *adj.* not mistake

UNMISTRUSTING, [un-mis-trust'-ing], *adj.* n suspicious.

UNMITIGABLE, [un-mit'-ig-abl], *adj.* not capable being mitigated.

UNMITIGATED, [un-mit'-ig-ā-tid], *adj.* not miti ated; downright; out and out.

UNMIXED, [un-mikst'], *adj.* not mixed; (*fig.*) un qualified.

UNMODERNIZED, [un-mod'-ern-īzd], *adj.* n made modern.

UNMODIFIABLE, [un-mod'-i-fī-abl], *adj.* that ca not be modified.

UNMODIFIED, [un-mod'-i-fīd], *adj.* not altered modified.

UNMODISH, [un-mōd'-ish], *adj.* not in the fashio

UNMODULATED, [un-mo'-jōō-lā-tid], *adj.* n modulated.

UNMOISTENED, [un-mois'-end], *adj.* not mad damp.

UNMOLESTED, [un-mōl-est'-id], *adj.* not disturbe or molested.

UNMOOR, [un-mōōer'], *v.t.* to undo the mooring of (a ship).

UNMORAL, [un-mor'-al], *adj.* not moral; not involv ing moral principles, standards.

UNMORTGAGED, [un-maw'-gijd], *adj.* not mort gaged.

UNMORTIFIED, [un-maw'-ti-fīd], *adj.* not mortified

UNMOTHERLY, [un-muTH-er-li], *adj.* unworthy o unlike, lacking the characteristics of, a mother.

JNMOULD, [un-mōld′], *v.t.* to change or take away the form of.
JNMOULDED, [un-mōld′-id], *adj.* not shaped or moulded.
JNMOUNTED, [un-mownt′-id], *adj.* not mounted; (of a picture, etc.) not displayed on a mount; not riding on horseback.
JNMOURNED, [un-mawnd′], *adj.* not lamented or grieved for.
JNMOVABLE, [un-mo͞ov′-abl], *adj.* immovable; resolute; not capable of being affected by emotion.
JNMOVABLY, [un-mo͞ov′-ab-li], *adv.* in an unmovable fashion.
JNMOVED, [un-mo͞ovd′], *adj.* not moved; not emotionally affected; still resolute, unshaken.
JNMOVING, [un-mo͞ov′-ing], *adj.* motionless, not exciting emotion.
JNMUFFLE, [un-mufl′], *v.t. and i.* to take a muffler from (the face); to take the muffling from (a drum).
JNMURMURING, [un-mur′-mer-ing], *adj.* not murmuring, not complaining, long-suffering.
JNMURMURINGLY, [un-mur′-mer-ing-li], *adv.* in an unmurmuring way.
JNMUSICAL, [un-mewz′-ik-al], *adj.* not musical, harsh-sounding; having no ear for or skill in music.
JNMUSICALLY, [un-mewz′-ik-al-i], *adv.* in an unmusical fashion.
JNMUTILATED, [un-mewt′-il-ā-tid], *adj.* not hurt or maimed.
JNMUZZLE, [un-muzl′], *v.t.* to remove the muzzle from; to allow free speech to.
JNNAMABLE, [un-nām′-abl], *adj.* not to be named; unmentionable.
JNNAMED, [un-nāmd′], *adj.* not having a name; not mentioned; unspecified.
JNNATURAL, [un-nach′-er-al], *adj.* not natural, contrary to the laws of nature, supernatural, monstrous; contrary to human nature, vile or cruel; contrary to the usual course of events, unusual, not to be expected.
JNNATURALIZE, [un-nach′-er-al-īz], *v.t.* to make unnatural.
JNNATURALIZED, [un-nach′-er-al-īzd], *adj.* not naturalized, still alien.
JNNATURALLY, [un-nach′-er-al-i], *adv.* in an unnatural way.
JNNATURALNESS, [un-nach′-er-al-nes], *n.* the quality of being unnatural.
JNNAVIGABLE, [un-nav′-ig-abl], *adj.* not navigable.
JNNAVIGATED, [un-nav′-ig-āt-id], *adj.* not sailed up or through.
JNNECESSARILY, [un-nes′-es-er-i-li], *adv.* in an unnecessary way, needlessly.
JNNECESSARINESS, [un-nes′-es-er-i-nes], *n.* the state of being unnecessary.
JNNECESSARY, [un-nes′-es-er-i], *adj.* not necessary.
JNNECESSITATED, [un-nis-es′-it-āt-id], *adj.* not made necessary.
JNNEEDED, [un-nēd′-id], *adj.* not necessary.
JNNEEDFUL, [un-nēd′-fo͝ol], *adj.* not needful.
JNNEGOTIABLE, [un-neg-ō′-shi-abl], *adj.* (*comm.*) not negotiable.
JNNEIGHBOURLINESS, [un-nā′-ber-li-ness], *n.* the quality of being unneighbourly, an unkind action.
JNNEIGHBOURLY, [un-nā′-ber-li], *adj.* unworthy of a neighbour, not friendly.
JNNERVE, [un-nurv′], *v.t.* to cause to lose courage, to shake the nerve of.
JNNERVED, [un-nurvd′], *adj.* frightened, shaken in courage.
JNNETTED, [un-net′-id], *adj.* not set with, covered with, or protected by, a net or nets.
JNNOBLE, [un-nōbl′], *adj.* not noble.
JNNOTED, [un-nōt′-id], *adj.* not observed or noticed; not distinguished or famous.
JNNOTICED, [un-nōt′-ist], *adj.* not marked or observed, not taken notice of.
JNNOURISHED, [un-nu′-risht], *adj.* not nourished.
JNNUMBERED, [un-numb′-erd], *adj.* innumerable; not distinguished by numbers.
JNNURTURED, [un-nur′-cherd], *adj.* not bred or nurtured.
UNNUTRITIOUS, [un-newt-rish′-us], *adj.* not nutritious.
UNOBJECTED, [un-ob-jek′-tid], *adj.* not raised as an objection.
UNOBJECTIONABLE, [un-ob-jek′-shun-abl], *n.* not to be objected to.
UNOBJECTIONABLY, [un-ob-jek′-shun-ab-li], *adv.* in an unobjectionable manner.
JNOBLIGING, [un-ob-lij′-ing], *adj.* not obliging.
UNOBLITERATED, [un-ob-lit′-er-āt-id], *adj.* not erased, not wiped out.
UNOBSCURED, [un-ob-skyo͞oerd′], *adj.* not darkened or obscured.
UNOBSERVABLE, [un-ob-zurv′-abl], *adj.* not observable.
UNOBSERVANCE, [un-ob-zurv′-ants], *n.* the quality of being unobservant; failure to observe.
UNOBSERVANT, [un-ob-zurv′-ant], *adj.* not taking notice; not naturally observant.
UNOBSERVED, [un-ob-zurvd′], *adj.* not noticed.
UNOBSERVING, [un-ob-zurv′-ing], *adj.* heedless, unobservant.
UNOBSTRUCTED, [un-ob-struk′-tid], *adj.* not hindered, not obstructed.
UNOBSTRUCTIVE, [un-ob-struk′-tiv], *adj.* not causing obstruction.
UNOBTAINABLE, [un-ob-tān′-abl], *adj.* not within reach, not obtainable.
UNOBTAINED, [un-ob-tānd′], *adj.* not obtained.
UNOBTRUSIVE, [un-ob-tro͞os′-iv], *adj.* retiring, diffident.
UNOBTRUSIVELY, [un-ob-tro͞os′-iv-li], *adv.* in an unobtrusive fashion.
UNOBTRUSIVENESS, [un-ob-tro͞os′-iv-nes], *n.* the quality of being unobtrusive or unaggressive.
UNOBVIOUS, [un-ob′-vi-us], *adj.* not obvious.
UNOCCUPIED, [un-ok′-yo͞o-pid], *adj.* (of a person) not busy; (of a house) having no occupant; (of territory) not under military occupation.
UNOFFENDED, [un-ō-fend′-id], *adj.* not offended.
UNOFFENDING, [un-ō-fend′-ing], *adj.* not causing offence, inoffensive, meek.
UNOFFENSIVE, [un-ō-fens′-iv], *adj.* inoffensive.
UNOFFERED, [un-of′-erd], *adj.* not offered.
UNOFFICIAL, [un-ōf-ish′-al], *adj.* not official; (of information) not officially confirmed.
UNOFFICIALLY, [un-ōf-ish′-al-i], *adv.* not officially.
UNOFFICIOUS, [un-ōf-ish′-us], *adj.* not officious.
UNOPENED, [un-ōp′-end], *adj.* not yet opened; (of a book) having the folded sheets not yet cut open.
UNOPERATED, [un-op′-er-āt-id], *adj.* not operated.
UNOPERATIVE, [un-op′-er-at-iv], *adj.* inoperative, not producing any effect.
UNOPERCULATED, [un′-op-ur′-kyo͞o-lā′-tid], *adj.* lacking an operculum.
UNOPPOSED, [un-ōp-ōzd′], *adj.* not opposed.
UNOPPRESSIVE, [un-ōp-res′-iv], *adj.* not oppressive, not tyrannous.
UNORDAINED, [un′-awd-ānd′], *adj.* not ordained or established.
UNORDERED, [un-awd′-erd], *adj.* not ordered; not set in order.
UNORDERLY, [un-awd′-er-li], *adj.* disorderly.
UNORDINARY, [un-awd′-in-eri], *adj.* unusual, strange, uncommon.
UNORGANIZED, [un-aw′-gan-īzd], *adj.* not organized; (*biol.*) not having an organic structure.
UNORIGINAL, [un-o-rij′-in-al], *adj.* not original, merely imitative.
UNORIGINATED, [un′-o-rij′-in-ā-tid], *adj.* having no birth or origin.
UNORNAMENTAL, [un′-awn-a-ment′-al], *adj.* not ornamental.
UNORNAMENTED, [un-awn′-a-ment-id], *adj.* undecorated, not ornamented.
UNORTHODOX, [un-awth′-ō-doks], *adj.* not orthodox.
UNORTHODOXY, [un-awth′-ō-doks-i], *n.* the quality of being unorthodox.
UNOSTENTATIOUS, [un′-os-ten-tā′-shus], *adj.* not ostentatious, modest, not showy.
UNOSTENTATIOUSLY, [un′-os-ten-tā′-shus-li], *adv.* in an unostentatious fashion.
UNOWED, [un-ōd′], *adj.* not owed.
UNOWNED, [un-ōnd′], *adj.* not owned or acknowledged.
UNOXIDIZED, [un-oks′-id-īzd], *adj.* not oxidized.
UNPACIFIC, [un-pas-if′-ik], *adj.* not pacific.
UNPACIFIED, [un-pas′-i-fīd], *adj.* not appeased or pacified.
UNPACK, [un-pak′], *v.t. and i.* to remove from a case, box or package; to empty; to remove clothing and other belongings from cases, etc.
UNPACKED, [un-pakt′], *adj.* not packed.
UNPAID, [un-pād′], *adj.* not paid.
UNPAINED, [un-pānd′], *adj.* not in pain, not pained.
UNPAINFUL, [un-pān′-fo͝ol], *adj.* not painful.
UNPAINTED, [un-pānt′-id], *adj.* not covered with paint.
UNPAIRED, [un-pāerd′], *adj.* not paired, single.

UNPALATABLE, [un-pal'-at-abl], *adj.* not palatable; disagreeable, offensive to the mind.
UNPALATABLY, [un-pal'-at-ab-li], *adv.* in an unpalatable way.
UNPANOPLIED, [un-pan'-ōp-lid], *adj.* not set forth in panoply.
UNPARAGONED, [un-pa'-rag-ond], *adj.* having no equal.
UNPARALLEL, [un-pa'-ra-lel], *adj.* not parallel.
UNPARALLELED, [un-pa'-ra-leld], *adj.* unequalled, unmatched.
UNPARDONABLE, [un-pah'-don-abl], *adj.* not to be pardoned.
UNPARDONABLY, [un-pah'-don-ab-li], *adv.* in an unpardonable fashion.
UNPARDONED, [un-pah'-dond], *adj.* not pardoned.
UNPARDONING, [un-pah'-don-ing], *adj.* unforgiving, not forgiving.
UNPARENTAL, [un-pa-rent'-al], *adj.* not parental.
UNPARENTED, [un-pāer'-en-tid], *adj.* having no parents.
UNPARLIAMENTARINESS, [un-pahl'-i-a-ment'-er-i-nes], *n.* the quality of being unparliamentary.
UNPARLIAMENTARY, [un-pahl'-i-a-ment'-er-i], *adj.* not according to parliamentary usage; rude.
UNPARTED, [un-paht'-id], *adj.* not parted.
UNPASSIONATE, [un-pash'-un-at], *adj.* not passionate.
UNPASSIONED, [un-pash'-und], *adj.* not passioned.
UNPASTORAL, [un-pahst'-er-al], *adj.* not pastoral.
UNPATENTED, [un-pāt'-en-tid], *adj.* not patented.
UNPATHED, [un-pahTHT'], *adj.* having no path.
UNPATHETIC, [un-path-et'-ik], *adj.* not pathetic.
UNPATRIOTIC, [un-pat'-ri-ot'-ik], *adj.* not patriotic.
UNPATRIOTICALLY, [un-pat'-ri-ot'-ik-al-i], *adv.* not patriotically.
UNPATRONIZED, [un-pat'-ron-īzd], *adj.* not patronized, not frequented by customers.
UNPATTERNED, [un-pat'-ernd], *adj.* not patterned.
UNPAVED, [un-pāvd'], *adj.* not paved, without paving.
UNPAWNED, [un-pawnd'], *adj.* not pawned.
UNPEACEABLE, [un-pēs'-abl], *adj.* unpeaceful.
UNPEACEFUL, [un-pēs'-fŏŏl], *adj.* not peaceful.
UNPEDIGREED, [un-ped'-i-grēd], *adj.* having no pedigree.
UNPEELED, [un-pēld'], *adj.* not having been peeled.
UNPEG, [un-peg'], *v.t.* to take down or unfasten (something held by a peg or pegs); to take the pegs out of.
UNPEN, [un-pen'], *v.t.* to let out of a pen.
UNPENETRABLE, [un-pen'-it-rabl], *adj.* impenetrable.
UNPENETRATED, [un-pen'-it-rā-tid], *adj.* not penetrated.
UNPENSIONED, [un-pen'-shund], *adj.* not pensioned.
UNPEOPLE, [un-pēpl'], *v.t.* to depopulate.
UNPEOPLED, [un-pēpld'], *adj.* lacking people.
UNPERCEIVABLE, [un-per-sēv'-abl], *adj.* imperceptible.
UNPERCEIVED, [un-per-sēvd'], *adj.* not perceived.
UNPERFORATED, [un-pur'-fer-āt-id], *adj.* not perforated.
UNPERFORMED, [un-per-fawmd'], *adj.* not performed.
UNPERJURED, [un-pur'-jerd], *adj.* not guilty of perjury.
UNPERMANENT, [un-pur'-man-ent], *adj.* impermanent, temporary.
UNPERMITTED, [un-per-mit'-id], *adj.* not allowed.
UNPERPLEXED, [un'-per-plekst'], *adj.* not puzzled or perplexed.
UNPERSECUTED, [un-pur'-sik-ewt-id], *adj.* not persecuted.
UNPERSUADABLE, [un-per-swād'-abl], *adj.* impossible to persuade.
UNPERSUADED, [un-per-swād'-id], *adj.* not convinced, not influenced by persuasion.
UNPERSUASIVE, [un-per-swās'-iv], *adj.* not persuading.
UNPERTURBED, [un-per-turbd'], *adj.* not perturbed.
UNPERUSED, [un-per-ŏŏzd'], *adj.* not perused.
UNPERVERTED, [un-per-vurt'-id], *adj.* not perverted.
UNPETRIFIED, [un-pet'-ri-fīd], *adj.* not petrified.
UNPHILOSOPHIC, [un'-fil-ō-sof'-ik], *adj.* unphilosophical.
UNPHILOSOPHICAL, [un'-fil-ō-sof'-ik-al], *adj.* not conforming to philosophical principles or method.
UNPHILOSOPHICALLY, [un'-fil-ō-sof'-ik-al-], *adv.* in an unphilosophical way.
UNPHILOSOPHICALNESS, [un'-fil-ō-sof'-ik-(a)l-nes], *n.* the quality of being unphilosophical.
UNPICK, [un-pik'], *v.t.* to undo the stitches of by picking, to unfasten (stitches) by picking.
UNPICKED, [un-pikt'], *adj.* not chosen.
UNPIERCEABLE, [un-pēers'-abl], *adj.* incapable of being pierced.
UNPIERCED, [un-pēerst'], *adj.* not pierced.
UNPILLARED, [un-pil'-erd], *adj.* having no pillar.
UNPILLOWED, [un-pil'-ōd], *adj.* without pillow.
UNPILOTED, [un-pī'-lot-id], *adj.* not piloted.
UNPIN, [un-pin'], *v.t.* to undo (something fastened with a pin or pins).
UNPINIONED, [un-pin'-yond], *adj.* not pinioned.
UNPINKED, [un-pingkt'], *adj.* not pierced or scalloped.
UNPITIED, [un-pit'-id], *adj.* not pitied.
UNPITIFUL, [un-pit'-i-fŏŏl], *adj.* neither feeling nor showing pity, cruel.
UNPITYING, [un-pit'-i-ing], *adj.* not pitying.
UNPITYINGLY, [un-pit'-i-ing-li], *adv.* in an unpitying fashion.
UNPLACED, [un-plāst'], *adj.* not placed; not in the first three.
UNPLAGUED, [un-plāgd'], *adj.* not plagued.
UNPLAIT, [un-plat'], *v.t.* to undo (something plaited).
UNPLANNED, [un-pland'], *adj.* not planned, accidental, haphazard.
UNPLANTED, [un-plahnt'-id], *adj.* not planted.
UNPLAUSIBLE, [un-plaw'-zibl], *adj.* not plausible or credible.
UNPLAUSIBLY, [un-plaw'-zib-li], *adv.* in an unplausible fashion.
UNPLAYABLE, [un-plā'-abl], *adj.* incapable of being struck or played.
UNPLEADABLE, [un-plēd'-abl], *adj.* incapable of being pleaded.
UNPLEADED, [un-plēd'-id], *adj.* not used as a plea.
UNPLEASABLE, [un-plēz'-abl], *adj.* that cannot be suited.
UNPLEASANT, [un-plez'-ant], *adj.* not pleasant.
UNPLEASANTLY, [un-plez'-ant-li], *adv.* in an unpleasant manner.
UNPLEASANTNESS, [un-plez'-ant-nes], *n.* the condition of being unpleasant; bad feeling, a misunderstanding.
UNPLEASED, [un-plēzd'], *adj.* not pleased.
UNPLEASING, [un-plēz'-ing], *adj.* not pleasing, offensive.
UNPLEDGED, [un-plejd'], *adj.* not pawned, not pledged.
UNPLIABLE, [un-plī'-abl], *adj.* not pliant.
UNPLIANT, [un-plī'-ant], *adj.* not pliant.
UNPLOUGHED, [un-plowd'], *adj.* not ploughed; (of a book) untrimmed.
UNPLUG, [un-plug'], *v.t.* to take the plug from; to disconnect by removing a plug.
UNPLUGGED, [un-plugd'], *adj.* not plugged.
UNPLUMBED, [un-plumd'], *adj.* unfathomed.
UNPLUME, [un-plŏŏm'], *v.t.* to strip of feathers.
UNPLUNDERED, [un-plund'-erd], *adj.* not plundered.
UNPOETIC, [un-pō-et'-ik], *adj.* not poetic.
UNPOETICAL, [un-pō-et'-ik-al], *adj.* not poetic.
UNPOETICALLY, [un'-pō-et'-ik-al-i], *adv.* in unpoetical fashion.
UNPOINTED, [un-point'-id], *adj.* not pointed.
UNPOISED, [un-poizd'], *adj.* not poised.
UNPOLARIZED, [un-pō'-ler-īzd], *adj.* not polarized.
UNPOLICIED, [un-pol'-is-id], *adj.* untutored.
UNPOLISHED, [un-pol'-isht], *adj.* not polished.
UNPOLITE, [un-pōl-īt'], *adj.* impolite.
UNPOLITELY, [un-pōl-īt'-li], *adv.* impolitely.
UNPOLITENESS, [un-pōl-īt'-nes], *n.* impoliteness.
UNPOLLED, [un-pōld'], *adj.* not polled.
UNPOLLUTED, [un-pol-ŏŏt'-id], *adj.* not polluted.
UNPOPULAR, [un-pop'-yŏŏ-ler], *adj.* not popular.
UNPOPULARITY, [un-pop'-yŏŏ-la'-ri-ti], *n.* the state or quality of being unpopular.
UNPOPULARLY, [un-pop'-yŏŏ-ler-li], *adv.* in an unpopular fashion.
UNPORTIONED, [un-paw'-shund], *adj.* having no portion.
UNPOSITIVE, [un-poz'-i-tiv], *adj.* doubtful, not assertive.
UNPOSSESSED, [un-pō-zest'], *adj.* not possessed.
UNPOSSESSING, [un-pō-zes'-ing], *adj.* not possessing.
UNPOSTED, [un-pōst'-id], *adj.* not, not yet, posted.

UNPOTABLE, [un-pōt′-abl], *adj.* not fit to drink.
UNPRACTICAL, [un-prak′-tik-al], *adj.* not practical.
UNPRACTICALLY, [un-prak′-tik-al-i], *adv.* in an unpractical fashion.
UNPRACTISED, [un-prak′-tist], *adj.* not skilled; not tried out, not done.
UNPRAISED, [un-prāzd′], *adj.* not praised.
UNPRECARIOUS, [un-prik-āer′-i-us], *adj.* not risky, safe.
UNPRECEDED, [un-pri-sēd′-id], *adj.* not preceded, coming first.
UNPRECEDENTED, [un-pres′-i-dent′-id], *adj.* having no precedent.
UNPRECEDENTEDLY, [un-pres′-i-dent′-id-li], *adv.* in an unprecedented way.
UNPRECISE, [un-pri-sis′], *adj.* not precise.
UNPREDESTINED, [un-pri-dest′-ind], *adj.* not predestined.
UNPREDICTABLE, [un′-pri-dikt′-abl], *adj.* that cannot be predicted.
UNPREDICTED, [un-pri-dik′-tid], *adj.* not prophesied.
UNPREFACED, [un-pref′-ast], *adj.* lacking a preface.
UNPREJUDICED, [un-prej′-ōō-dist], *adj.* not prejudiced or biased.
UNPRELATICAL, [un-pril-at′-ik-al], *adj.* not prelatical.
UNPREMEDITATED, [un-pri-med′-it-ā-tid], *adj.* not previously thought about.
UNPREMEDITATEDLY, [un-pri-med′-it-ā-tid-li], *adv.* in an unpremeditated way.
UNPREPARED, [un-pri-pāerd′], *adj.* not prepared.
UNPREPAREDNESS, [un-pri-pāer′-id-nes], *n.* the quality of being unprepared.
UNPREPOSSESSED, [un-prē′-pō-zest′], *adj.* not prepossessed.
UNPREPOSSESSING, [un-prē′-pō-zes′-ing], *adj.* not prepossessing.
UNPRESENTABLE, [un-pri-zent′-abl], *adj.* not fit to be presented, or exhibited in society.
UNPRESERVABLE, [un-pri-zurv′-abl], *adj.* impossible to be preserved.
UNPRESSED, [un-prest′], *adj.* not pressed.
UNPRESUMING, [un-pri-zewm′-ing], *adj.* modest, not presuming.
UNPRESUMPTUOUS, [un′-pri-zump′-chōō-us], *adj.* unpresuming.
UNPRETENDING, [un-pri-tend′-ing], *adj.* not pretending, modest.
UNPRETENDINGLY, [un-pri-tend′-ing-li], *adv.* in unpretending fashion.
UNPRETENTIOUS, [un-pri-ten′-shus], *adj.* modest, not pretentious.
UNPRETENTIOUSLY, [un-pri-ten′-shus-li], *adv.* in an unpretentious way.
UNPREVAILING, [un-pri-vāl′-ing], *adj.* not prevailing.
UNPREVALENT, [un-prev′-al-ent], *adj.* not prevalent or common.
UNPREVENTABLE, [un-pri-vent′-abl], *adj.* impossible to prevent.
UNPREVENTED, [un-pri-vent′-id], *adj.* not prevented.
UNPRICED, [un-prist′], *adj.* not having been priced.
UNPRIESTLY, [un-prēst′-li], *adj.* not priestly.
UNPRINCELY, [un-prints′-li], *adj.* not befitting a prince.
UNPRINCIPLED, [un-prin′-sipld], *adj.* adhering to no principles, unscrupulous.
UNPRINTABLE, [un-print′-abl], *adj.* not fit for printing.
UNPRINTED, [un-print′-id], *adj.* not printed.
UNPRISONED, [un-priz′-ond], *adj.* not imprisoned.
UNPRIVILEGED, [un-priv′-i-lijd], *adj.* not privileged.
UNPRIZED, [un-prīzd′], *adj.* not prized or valued.
UNPROBED, [un-prōbd′], *adj.* not probed.
UNPROCLAIMED, [un-prō-klāmd′], *adj.* not proclaimed.
UNPROCURABLE, [un-prō-kyōōer′-abl], *adj.* unobtainable.
UNPRODUCTIVE, [un-prō-duk′-tiv], *adj.* not productive.
UNPRODUCTIVELY, [un-prō-duk′-tiv-li], *adv.* in an unproductive way.
UNPRODUCTIVENESS, [un-prō-duk′-tiv-nes], *n.* the quality of being unproductive.
UNPROFANED, [un-prō-fānd′], *adj.* not violated.
UNPROFESSIONAL, [un-prō-fesh′-un-al], *adj.* not conforming to professional usages and standards.
UNPROFESSIONALLY, [un-prō-fesh′-un-al-i], *adv.* in unprofessional fashion; incompetently.
UNPROFICIENCY, [un-prō-fish′-en-si], *n.* lack of proficiency.
UNPROFITABLE, [un-prof′-it-abl], *adj.* not profitable.
UNPROFITABLENESS, [un-prof′-it-abl-nes], *n.* the quality of being unprofitable.
UNPROFITABLY, [un-prof′-it-ab-li], *adv.* in an unprofitable way.
UNPROFITED, [un-prof′-it-id], *adj.* not profited.
UNPROGRESSIVE, [un-prō-gres′-iv], *adj.* not progressive.
UNPROHIBITED, [un-prō-hib′-it-id], *adj.* not prohibited.
UNPROJECTED, [un-prō-jek′-tid], *adj.* not projected.
UNPROLIFIC, [un-prō-lif′-ik], *adj.* not prolific.
UNPROMISING, [un-prom′-is-ing], *adj.* not promising.
UNPROMPTED, [un-promp′-tid], *adj.* not prompted.
UNPRONOUNCEABLE, [un-prō-nownts′-abl], *adj.* impossible to pronounce.
UNPRONOUNCED, [un-prō-nownst′], *adj.* not pronounced.
UNPROP, [un-prop′], *v.t.* to take the props from.
UNPROPHETIC, [un-prōf-et′-ik], *adj.* not prophetic.
UNPROPITIOUS, [un-prō-pish′-us], *adj.* not propitious.
UNPROPITIOUSLY, [un-prō-pish′-us-li], *adv.* in an unpropitious way.
UNPROPITIOUSNESS, [un-prō-pish′-us-nes], *n.* the quality or condition of being unpropitious.
UNPROPORTIONABLE, [un-prō-paw′-shun-abl], *adj.* not proportionable.
UNPROPORTIONAL, [un-prō-paw′-shun-al], *adj.* not proportional.
UNPROPORTIONATE, [un-prō-paw′-shun-at], *adj.* disproportionate.
UNPROPORTIONED, [un-prō-paw′-shund], *adj.* not proportioned.
UNPROPOSED, [un-prō-pōzd′], *adj.* not proposed.
UNPROPPED, [un-propt′], *adj.* not propped.
UNPROSPEROUS, [un-pros′-per-us], *adj.* not prospering.
UNPROSPEROUSLY, [un-pros′-per-us-li], *adv.* in unprosperous fashion.
UNPROSPEROUSNESS, [un-pros′-per-us-nes], *n.* the condition of being unprosperous.
UNPROSTITUTED, [un-pros′-ti-tewt-id], *adj.* not prostituted.
UNPROTECTED, [un-prō-tek′-tid], *adj.* not protected.
UNPROTECTING, [un-prō-tek′-ting], *adj.* not protecting.
UNPROTESTANTIZE, [un-prot′-es-tant-iz], *v.t.* to convert from protestantism.
UNPROTESTED, [un-prō-test′-id], *adj.* not protested.
UNPROTRACTED, [un-prō-trak′-tid], *adj.* not protracted.
UNPROVABLE, [un-prōōv′-abl], *adj.* incapable of being proved.
UNPROVED, [un-prōōvd′], *adj.* lacking proof; untried.
UNPROVIDED, [un-prō-vid′-id], *adj.* not provided.
UNPROVIDENT, [un-pro′-vid-ent], *adj.* improvident.
UNPROVOKED, [un-prō-vōkt′], *adj.* not provoked.
UNPROVOKING, [un-prō-vōk′-ing], *adj.* not provoking.
UNPRUNED, [un-prōōnd′], *adj.* not pruned.
UNPUBLISHED, [un-pub′-lisht], *adj.* not published.
UNPUCKER, [un-puk′-er], *v.t.* to smooth out (something that is puckered).
UNPUCKERED, [un-puk′-erd], *adj.* uncreased.
UNPUNCTUAL, [un-pungk′-chōō-al], *adj.* not punctual.
UNPUNCTUALITY, [un-pungk′-chōō-al′-i-ti], *n.* the condition of being unpunctual.
UNPUNCTUALLY, [un-pungk′-chōō-al-i], *adv.* in an unpunctual fashion.
UNPUNCTUATED, [un-pungk′-chōō-ā-tid], *adj.* not punctuated.
UNPUNISHABLE, [un-pun′-ish-abl], *adj.* not liable or requiring to be punished.
UNPUNISHED, [un-pun′-isht], *adj.* not having been punished.
UNPURCHASABLE, [un-pur′-chas-abl], *adj.* incapable of being bought; not offered for sale.
UNPURCHASED, [un-pur′-chast], *adj.* not purchased.
UNPURGED, [un-purjd′], *adj.* not purged.

UNPURIFIED, [un-pyōōer'-i-fīd], *adj.* not made pure.
UNPURPOSED, [un-pur'-post], *adj.* not purposed.
UNPURSUED, [un-pur-sewd'], *adj.* not pursued.
UNPUTREFIED, [un-pewt'-ri-fīd], *adj.* not putrid.
UNQUAFFED, [un-kwoft'], *adj.* not quaffed.
UNQUAILING, [un-kwāl'-ing], *adj.* not quailing.
UNQUAKING, [un-kwāk'-ing], *adj.* not quaking.
UNQUALIFIED, [un-kwol'-i-fīd], *adj.* not qualified.
UNQUELLABLE, [un-kwel'-abl], *adj.* incapable of being quelled.
UNQUELLED, [un-kweld'], *adj.* not quelled.
UNQUENCHABLE, [un-kwench'-abl], *adj.* that cannot be quenched; inextinguishable.
UNQUENCHABLENESS, [un-kwench'-abl-nes], *n.* the quality of being unquenchable.
UNQUENCHABLY, [un-kwench'-ab-li], *adv.* in unquenchable fashion.
UNQUENCHED, [un-kwencht'], *adj.* not quenched.
UNQUESTIONABLE, [un-kwes'-chun-abl], *adj.* not to be questioned, absolutely certain.
UNQUESTIONABLY, [un-kwes'-chun-ab-li], *adv.* in unquestionable fashion.
UNQUESTIONED, [un-kwes'-chund], *adj.* not questioned.
UNQUESTIONING, [un-kwes'-chun-ing], *adj.* not questioning.
UNQUESTIONINGLY, [un-kwes'-chun-ing-li], *adv.* in unquestioning fashion.
UNQUICKENED, [un-kwik'-end], *adj.* not quickened, not stirring with vitality.
UNQUIET, [un-kwī'-et], *adj.* not quiet, restless, uneasy.
UNQUIETLY, [un-kwī'-et-li], *adv.* in unquiet fashion.
UNQUIETNESS, [un-kwī'-et-nes], *n.* the quality or state of being unquiet.
UNQUIETUDE, [un-kwī'-i-tewd], *n.* unquietness.
UNQUOTABLE, [un-kwōt'-abl], *adj.* unfit for quotation; not to be quoted.
UNQUOTED, [un-kwōt'-id], *adj.* not repeated or quoted.
UNRACKED, [un-rakt'], *adj.* (of wine) not decanted or drawn off from the lees.
UNRAISED, [un-rāzd'], *adj.* not raised.
UNRAKED, [un-rākt'], *adj.* not raked.
UNRANGED, [un-rānjd'], *adj.* not duly ordered.
UNRANSACKED, [un-ran'-sakt'], *adj.* not ransacked.
UNRANSOMED, [un-ran'-somd], *adj.* not liberated by ransom.
UNRATED, [un-rāt'-id], *adj.* not rated.
UNRAVAGED, [un-rav'-ijd], *adj.* not ravaged.
UNRAVEL, [un-rav'-el], *v.t.* to disentangle or extricate; (*fig.*) to work out the solution of (a complex problem).
UNRAVELLED, [un-rav'-eld], *adj.* disentangled, unknitted, frayed.
UNRAVELMENT, [un-rav'-el-ment], *n.* the act of unravelling, the fact of being unravelled.
UNREACHABLE, [un-rēch'-abl], *adj.* unattainable, lying beyond reach.
UNREACHED, [un-rēcht'], *adj.* not reached.
UNREAD, [un-red'], *adj.* not read; illiterate.
UNREADABLE, [un-rēd'-abl], *adj.* not legible; not fit to read; not easy to read.
UNREADILY, [un-red'-i-li], *adv.* in an unready way.
UNREADY, [un-red'-i], *adj.* not prepared; not alert.
UNREAL, [un-rē'-al], *adj.* not real.
UNREALITY, [un'-ri-al'-i-ti], *n.* the quality of being unreal.
UNREALIZABLE, [un-rē'-al-īz-abl], *adj.* not capable of realization.
UNREALIZED, [un-rē'-al-īzd], *adj.* not realized.
UNREALLY, [un-rē'-al-i], *adv.* in an unreal fashion.
UNREAPED, [un-rēpt'], *adj.* not reaped or harvested.
UNREASON, [un-rē'-zon], *n.* want of reason, folly.
UNREASONABLE, [un-rē'-zon-abl], *adj.* not reasonable, irrational.
UNREASONABLENESS, [un-rē'-zon-abl-nes], *n.* the quality or state of being unreasonable.
UNREASONABLY, [un-rē'-zon-ab-li], *adv.* in an unreasonable fashion.
UNREASONED, [un-rē'-zond], *adj.* not reasoned.
UNREASONING, [un-rē'-zon-ing], *adj.* not reasoning, unreasonable.
UNREASONINGLY, [un-rē'-zon-ing-li], *adv.* in an unreasoning way.
UNREBUKABLE, [un-ri-bewk'-abl], *adj.* not open to, or worthy of, rebuke; impervious to rebuke.
UNREBUKED, [un-ri-bewkt'], *adj.* not having been rebuked.
UNRECALLABLE, [un-ri-kawl'-abl], *adj.* incapable of being recalled; irrevocable; that cannot be recollected.
UNRECALLED, [un-ri-kawld'], *adj.* not called back.
UNRECANTED, [un-ri-kant'-id], *adj.* not retracted or recanted.
UNRECEIPTED, [un-ri-sēt'-id], *adj.* not acknowledged by receipt.
UNRECEIVED, [un-ri-sēvd'], *adj.* not received.
UNRECIPROCATED, [un-ri-sip'-rō-kāt-id], *adj.* not returned or reciprocated.
UNRECKONED, [un-rek'-ond], *adj.* not estimated or reckoned.
UNRECLAIMABLE, [un-ri-klām'-abl], *adj.* incapable of being reclaimed.
UNRECLAIMED, [un-ri-klāmd'], *adj.* not reclaimed.
UNRECOGNIZABLE, [un-rek'-og-nīz-abl], *adj.* incapable of being recognized.
UNRECOGNIZED, [un'-rek'-og-nīzd], *adj.* not recognized or acknowledged.
UNRECOMMENDED, [un'-rek-om-en'-did], *adj.* not recommended.
UNRECOMPENSED, [un-rek'-om-penst'], *adj.* not recompensed or rewarded.
UNRECONCILABLE, [un-rek'-on-sīl-abl], *adj.* not reconcilable.
UNRECONCILED, [un-rek'-on-sīld], *adj.* not reconciled.
UNRECONSTRUCTED, [un'-rē-kon-struk'-tid], *adj.* not reconstructed; (*U.S.*) not yet admitted as state of the Union.
UNRECORDED, [un-ri'-kawd'-id], *adj.* not recorded.
UNRECOUNTED, [un-ri-kownt'-id], *adj.* not recounted.
UNRECOVERABLE, [un-ri-kuv'-er-abl], *adj.* irrecoverable.
UNRECOVERED, [un-ri-kuv'-erd], *adj.* not recovered or regained.
UNRECTIFIED, [un-rek'-ti-fīd], *adj.* not rectified; (*chem.*) not distilled again, not refined.
UNRECURRING, [un-ri-kur'-ing], *adj.* not recurrent.
UNREDEEMABLE, [un-ri-dēm'-abl], *adj.* that cannot be redeemed.
UNREDEEMED, [un-ri-dēmd'], *adj.* not redeemed.
UNREDRESSED, [un-ri-drest'], *adj.* not redressed.
UNREDUCED, [un-ri-dewst'], *adj.* not reduced.
UNREDUCIBLE, [un-ri-dews'-ibl], *adj.* irreducible.
UNREEL, [un-rēl'], *v.t.* to wind from a reel.
UNREEVE, (**unrove, unreeved, unroven**), [un-rēv'], *v.t.* (*naut.*) to unfasten something that has been reeved.
UNREFINED, [un-ri-fīnd'], *adj.* not refined, coarse.
UNREFLECTING, [un-ri-flek'-ting], *adj.* not acting as a reflector; not thinking; thoughtless.
UNREFLECTINGLY, [un-ri-flek'-ting-li], *adv.* in an unreflecting way.
UNREFORMABLE, [un-ri-fawm'-abl], *adj.* incapable of being reformed.
UNREFORMED, [un-ri-fawmd'], *adj.* not reformed or amended.
UNREFRACTED, [un-ri-frak'-tid], *adj.* not refracted.
UNREFRESHED, [un-ri-fresht'], *adj.* not refreshed.
UNREFRESHFUL, [un-ri-fresh'-fōōl], *adj.* not refreshing.
UNREFRESHING, [un-ri-fresh'-ing], *adj.* not refreshing.
UNREFUTED, [un-ri-fewt'-id], *adj.* not disproved.
UNREGARDED, [un-ri-gahd'-id], *adj.* neglected.
UNREGARDFUL, [un-ri-gahd'-fōōl], *adj.* lacking in attention or regard.
UNREGENERACY, [un-ri-jen'-er-a-si], *n.* the condition of being unregenerate.
UNREGENERATE, [un-ri-jen'-er-at], *adj.* not regenerate.
UNREGISTERED, [un-rej'-ist-erd], *adj.* not having been registered.
UNREGRETFUL, [un-ri-gret'-fōōl], *adj.* not regretful.
UNREGRETTED, [un-ri-gret'-id], *adj.* not regretted or lamented.
UNREGULATED, [un-reg'-yōō-lāt-id], *adj.* not regulated, disciplined or controlled.
UNREHEARSED, [un-ri-hurst'], *adj.* not rehearsed; not intended to occur.
UNREIN, [un-rān'], *v.t.* to cease holding back with the rein, to loose from the rein.
UNREINED, [un-rānd'], *adj.* not checked by the rein; (*fig.*) uncontrolled.
UNREJOICING, [un-ri-jois'-ing], *adj.* not rejoicing.
UNRELATED, [un-ri-lāt'-id], *adj.* not connected or related.
UNRELAXED, [un-ri-lakst'], *adj.* not slackened.
UNRELAXING, [un-ri-laks'-ing], *adj.* not slackening.

UNRELENTING, [un-ri-lent'-ing], *adj.* not relenting, merciless.
UNRELIABILITY, [un-ri-lī'-a-bil'-i-ti], *n.* the condition of being unreliable.
UNRELIABLE, [un-ri-lī'-abl], *adj.* untrustworthy, not reliable.
UNRELIABLY, [un-ri-lī'-ab-li], *adv.* in an unreliable fashion.
UNRELIEVABLE, [un-ri-lēv'-abl], *adj.* incapable of being relieved.
UNRELIEVED, [un-ri-lēvd'], *adj.* not relieved, not eased or helped, not rescued; not diversified.
UNRELIGIOUS, [un-ri-lij'-us], *adj.* irreligious.
UNREMARKABLE, [un-ri-mahk'-abl], *adj.* not remarkable.
UNREMARKED, [un-ri-mahkt'], *adj.* not noticed.
UNREMEDIABLE, [un-ri-mēd'-i-abl], *adj.* that cannot be cured.
UNREMEDIED, [un-rem'-id-id], *adj.* not remedied.
UNREMEMBERED, [un-ri-memb'-erd], *adj.* not remembered.
UNREMITTED, [un-ri-mit'-id], *adj.* not remitted.
UNREMITTING, [un-ri-mit'-ing], *adj.* not remitting, persistent.
UNREMITTINGLY, [un-ri-mit'-ing-li], *adv.* continuously, in unremitting fashion.
UNREMORSEFUL, [un-ri-maws'-fōōl], *adj.* not remorseful.
UNREMOVABLE, [un-ri-mōōv'-abl], *adj.* irremovable.
UNREMOVABLENESS, [un-ri-mōōv'-abl-nes], *n.* the quality of being irremovable.
UNREMOVED, [un-ri-mōōvd'], *adj.* not removed.
UNREMUNERATIVE, [un-ri-mewn'-er-at-iv], *adj.* not remunerative.
UNRENEWED, [un-ri-newd'], *adj.* not renewed; not replaced by fresh material; not refreshed.
UNRENOUNCED, [un-ri-nownst'], *adj.* not abandoned or renounced.
UNRENOVATED, [un-ren'-ō-vāt-id], *adj.* not reconditioned.
UNRENOWNED, [un-ri-nownd'], *adj.* not famous.
UNREPAID, [un-ri-pād'], *adj.* not paid back.
UNREPAIRED, [un-ri-pāerd'], *adj.* not repaired.
UNREPEALED, [un-ri-pēld'], *adj.* not repealed or countermanded.
UNREPENTANCE, [un-ri-pent'-ants], *n.* the condition of being unrepentant.
UNREPENTANT, [un-ri-pent'-ant], *adj.* not repenting.
UNREPENTANTLY, [un-ri-pent'-ant-li], *adv.* in an unrepentant fashion.
UNREPENTED, [un-ri-pent'-id], *adj.* not repented.
UNREPENTING, [un-ri-pent'-ing], *adj.* not repenting.
UNREPINING, [un-ri-pīn'-ing], *adj.* not complaining or repining.
UNREPININGLY, [un-ri-pīn'-ing-li], *adv.* in an unrepining fashion.
UNREPLENISHED, [un-ri-plen'-isht], *adj.* not replenished.
UNREPORTED, [un-ri-pawt'-id], *adj.* not reported.
UNREPRESENTATIVE, [un-rep'-ri-zent'-at-iv], *adj.* not representative.
UNREPRESENTED, [un-rep'-ri-zent'-id], *adj.* not represented.
UNREPRESSED, [un-ri-prest'], *adj.* not repressed.
UNREPRESSIBLE, [un-ri-pres'-ibl], *adj.* irrepressible.
UNREPRIEVABLE, [un-ri-prēv-abl], *adj.* unable to be reprieved.
UNREPRIEVED, [un-ri-prēvd'], *adj.* not reprieved.
UNREPROACHABLE, [un-ri-prōch'-abl], *adj.* not open to reproach; irreproachable.
UNREPROACHED, [un-ri-prōcht'], *adj.* not reproached.
UNREPROACHFUL, [un-ri-prōch'-fōōl], *adj.* not reproaching.
UNREPROVABLE, [un-ri-prōōv'-abl], *adj.* not open to reproof.
UNREPROVED, [un-ri-prōōvd'], *adj.* not reproved or rebuked.
UNREPUGNANT, [un-ri-pug'-nant], *adj.* not repugnant.
UNREPUTABLE, [un-rep'-yōōt-abl], *adj.* disreputable.
UNREQUESTED, [un-ri-kwest'-id], *adj.* not asked or asked for.
UNREQUIRED, [un-ri-kwīerd'], *adj.* not demanded, not necessary.
UNREQUISITE, [un-rek'-wiz-it], *adj.* not necessary.
UNREQUITABLE, [un-ri-kwīt'-abl], *adj.* not capable of being requited.
UNREQUITED, [un-ri-kwīt'-id], *adj.* not recompensed or reciprocated.
UNRESCINDED, [un-ri-sind'-id], *adj.* not repealed.
UNRESCUED, [un-res'-kewd], *adj.* not rescued.
UNRESENTED, [un-ri-zent'-id], *adj.* not looked upon with anger.
UNRESENTFUL, [un-ri-zent'-fōōl], *adj.* not resentful.
UNRESENTFULLY, [un-ri-zent'-fōōl-i], *adv.* not resentfully.
UNRESENTING, [un-ri-zent'-ing], *adj.* not resenting.
UNRESENTINGLY, [un-ri-zent'-ing-li], *adv.* without resentment.
UNRESERVE, [un-ri-zurv'], *n.* lack of reserve.
UNRESERVED, [un-ri-zurvd'], *adj.* not reserved; very frank of speech; not booked or engaged.
UNRESERVEDLY, [un-ri-zurv -id-li], *adv.* openly, frankly; without reservation.
UNRESERVEDNESS, [un-ri-zurv'-id-nes], *n.* the condition or quality of being unreserved.
UNRESISTED, [un-ri-zist'-id], *adj.* not resisted or opposed.
UNRESISTING, [un-ri-zist'-ing], *adj.* not offering resistance.
UNRESISTINGLY, [un-ri-zist'-ing-li], *adv.* in an unresisting fashion.
UNRESOLVABLE, [un-ri-zolv'-abl], *adj.* incapable of being resolved.
UNRESOLVED, [un-ri-zolvd'], *adj.* hesitant, undecided; not analysed; not solved.
UNRESOLVING, [un-ri-zolv'-ing], *adj.* not resolving.
UNRESPECTED, [un-ri-spek'-tid], *adj.* not held in respect.
UNRESPIRABLE, [un-ri-spīer'-abl], *adj.* not fit to be breathed.
UNRESPITED, [un-res'-pit-id], *adj.* without intermission; unrested.
UNRESPONSIVE, [un-ri-spon'-siv], *adj.* not responsive.
UNRESPONSIVELY, [un-ri-spon'-siv-li], *adv.* in an unresponsive fashion.
UNRESPONSIVENESS, [un-ri-spon'-siv-nes], *n.* the condition of being unresponsive.
UNREST, [un-rest'], *n.* turbulence, agitation; anxiousness, worry.
UNRESTFUL, [un-rest'-fōōl], *adj.* not restful.
UNRESTFULLY, [un-rest'-fōōl-i], *adv.* in an unrestful fashion.
UNRESTFULNESS, [un-rest'-fōōl-nes], *n.* the condition or quality of being unrestful.
UNRESTING, [un-rest'-ing], *adj.* not resting, restless, tireless.
UNRESTINGLY, [un-rest'-ing-li], *adv.* in an unresting way.
UNRESTORED, [un-ri-staw(r)d'], *adj.* not restored.
UNRESTRAINABLE, [un-ri-strān'-abl], *adj.* that cannot be restrained.
UNRESTRAINED, [un-ri-strānd'], *adj.* not restrained.
UNRESTRAINEDLY, [un-ri-strān'-id-li], *adv.* in unrestrained fashion.
UNRESTRICTED, [un-ri-strik'-tid], *adj.* not restricted, unlimited.
UNRETARDED, [un-ri-tahd'-id], *adj.* not retarded.
UNRETENTIVE, [un-ri-tent'-iv], *adj.* not retaining, not retentive.
UNRETRACTED, [un-ri-trak'-tid], *adj.* not retracted.
UNRETURNABLE, [un-ri-turn'-abl], *adj.* not returnable.
UNREVEALED, [un-ri-vēld'], *adj.* not revealed.
UNREVENGED, [un-ri-venjd'], *adj.* not avenged.
UNREVENGEFUL, [un-ri-venj'-fōōl], *adj.* not revengeful.
UNREVERED, [un-ri-vēerd'], *adj.* not respected or revered.
UNREVERSED, [un-ri-vurst'], *adj.* not reversed.
UNREVIEWED, [un-ri-vewd'], *adj.* not reviewed.
UNREVISED, [un-ri-vīzd'], *adj.* not corrected or revised.
UNREVIVED, [un-ri-vīvd'], *adj.* not revived.
UNREVOKED, [un-ri-vōkt'], *adj.* not recalled or revoked.
UNREWARDED, [un-ri-wawd'-id], *adj.* unrecompensed.
UNRHETORICAL, [un-ri-to'-rik-al], *adj.* not rhetorical; plain, straightforward.
UNRHYMED, [un-rīmd'], *adj.* without rhymes.
UNRHYTHMICAL, [un-riTH'-mik-al], *adj.* lacking rhythm; conforming to no rhythmic pattern.

UNRHYTHMICALLY, [un-riTH'-mik-al-i], *adv.* in unrhythmical fashion.
UNRIDDEN, [un-rid'-en], *adj.* not having been ridden on.
UNRIDDLE, [un-ridl'], *v.t.* to solve the puzzle or mystery of.
UNRIFLED, [un'-rifld], *adj.* not plundered.
UNRIG, [un-rig'], *v.t.* to bare (a ship) of rigging.
UNRIGGED, [un-rigd'], *adj.* not carrying rigging.
UNRIGHTEOUS, [un-rī'-chus], *adj.* not godly or righteous; unjust, iniquitous, wicked.
UNRIGHTEOUSLY, [un-rī'-chus-li], *adv.* in unrighteous fashion.
UNRIGHTEOUSNESS, [un-rī'-chus-nes], *n.* wickedness, the state of being unrighteous.
UNRIP, [un-rip'], *v.t.* to tear undone.
UNRIPE, [un-rīp'], *adj.* not ripe or matured.
UNRIPENED, [un-rīp'-end], *adj.* not yet matured.
UNRIPENESS, [un-rīp'-nes], *n.* immaturity, the quality of being unripe.
UNRIVALLED, [un-riv'-ald], *adj.* without a rival, unequalled, incomparable.
UNRIVET, [un-riv'-it], *v.t.* to open, detach (something fastened with rivets); to take the rivets out of.
UNROBE, [un-rōb'], *v.t. and i.* to remove robes or clothing from; to undress.
UNROLL, [un-rōl'], *v.t. and i.* to open (something that has been rolled up); to unfold from a rolled-up position.
UNROMANTIC, [un-rō-mant'-ik], *adj.* not romantic.
UNROMANTICALLY, [un-rō-man'-tik-al-i], *adv.* in an unromantic way.
UNROOF, [un-rōōf'], *v.t.* to remove the roof from.
UNROOFED, [un-rōōft'], *adj.* lacking a roof.
UNROOT, [un-rōōt'], *v.t.* to uproot.
UNROUND, [un-rownd'], *v.t.* (*phon.*) to pronounce without rounding of the lips.
UNROUNDED, [un-rownd'-id], *adj.* not rounded.
UNROUTED, [un-rowt'-id], *adj.* not routed.
UNROYAL, [un-roi'-al], *adj.* unworthy of a king.
UNROYALLY, [un-roi'-al-i], *adv.* not in a royal manner.
UNRUFFLE, [un-rufl'], *v.t.* to smooth the ruffles from.
UNRUFFLED, [un-rufld'], *adj.* not ruffled; calm.
UNRULED, [un-rōōld'], *adj.* ungoverned; (of paper) not having printed lines.
UNRULINESS, [un-rōōl'-i-nes], *n.* the condition of being unruly.
UNRULY, [un-rōōl'-i], *adj.* disobedient, ungovernable.
UNRUMINATED, [un-rōō'-min-ā-tid], *adj.* ill digested; not thought over.
UNRUMPLED, [un-rumpld'], *adj.* not rumpled.
UNSADDLE, [un-sadl'], *v.t.* to take the saddle off (a horse).
UNSAFE, [un-sāf'], *adj.* not safe.
UNSAFELY, [un-sāf'-li], *adv.* in an unsafe way.
UNSAFENESS, [un-sāf'-nes], *n.* the condition of being unsafe.
UNSAFETY, [un-sāf'-ti], *n.* danger.
UNSAID, [un-sed'], *adj.* not said.
UNSAILABLE, [un-sāl'-abl], *adj.* dangerous to sail on.
UNSAINT†, [un-sānt'], *v.t.* to lower from the dignity of a saint.
UNSAINTLY, [un-sānt'-li], *adj.* not befitting a saint.
UNSALABLE, see UNSALEABLE.
UNSALARIED, [un-sal'-er-id], *adj.* not salaried.
UNSALEABLE, UNSALABLE, [un-sāl'-abl], *adj.* not saleable.
UNSALEABLENESS, UNSALABLENESS, [un-sāl'-abl-nes], *n.* the quality of being unsaleable.
UNSALTED, [un-sawlt'-id], *adj.* fresh, not salted.
UNSALUTED, [un-sal-ōōt'-id], *adj.* not saluted.
UNSANCTIFIED, [un-sangk'-ti-fīd], *adj.* not sanctified or consecrated.
UNSANCTIONED, [un-sangk'-shund], *adj.* not allowed, approved, or authorized.
UNSANGUINE, [un-sang'-gwin], *adj.* not sanguine.
UNSANITARY, [un-san'-it-er-i], *adj.* insanitary.
UNSATED, [un-sāt'-id], *adj.* not replete or satisfied.
UNSATISFACTORILY, [un-sat'-is-fak'-ter-i-li], *adv.* in unsatisfactory fashion.
UNSATISFACTORINESS, [un-sat'-is-fak'-ter-i-nes], *n.* the quality of being unsatisfactory.
UNSATISFACTORY, [un-sat'-is-fak'-ter-i], *adj.* not satisfactory.
UNSATISFIABLE, [un-sat'-is-fī-abl], *adj.* incapable of being satisfied.
UNSATISFIED, [un-sat'-is-fīd], *adj.* not satisfied.
UNSATISFIEDNESS, [un-sat'-is-fīd-nes], *n.* the condition of being unsatisfied.
UNSATISFYING, [un-sat'-is-fī-ing], *adj.* not giving satisfaction; not satisfying the appetite.
UNSATURATED, [un-sach'-er-āt-id], *adj.* not saturated.
UNSAVOURILY, [un-sāv'-er-i-li], *adv.* in unsavoury fashion.
UNSAVOURINESS, [un-sāv'-er-i-nes], *n.* the state or quality of being unsavoury.
UNSAVOURY, [un-sāv'-er-i], *adj.* not savoury.
UNSAY, [un-sā'], *v.t.* to cancel or recall (what has been said).
UNSCALABLE, [un-skāl'-abl], *adj.* that cannot be scaled.
UNSCALE, [un-skāl'], *v.t.* to clean the scales off.
UNSCALY, [un-skāl'-i], *adj.* not scaly.
UNSCANNABLE, [un-skan'-abl], *adj.* (*pros.*) that cannot be scanned.
UNSCANNED, [un-skand'], *adj.* not scanned.
UNSCARED, [un-skāerd'], *adj.* not scared or alarmed.
UNSCARRED, [un-skahd'], *adj.* not scarred.
UNSCATHED, [un-skāTHd'], *adj.* undamaged, unharmed.
UNSCATTERED, [un-skat'-erd], *adj.* not scattered.
UNSCENTED, [un-sent'-id], *adj.* not scented.
UNSCEPTRED, [un-sep'-terd], *adj.* having no sceptre.
UNSCHOLARLY, [un-skol'-er-li], *adj.* not befitting a scholar or the work of a scholar.
UNSCHOLASTIC, [un-skol-as'-tik], *adj.* not scholastic.
UNSCHOOLED, [un-skōōld'], *adj.* undisciplined, untrained, lacking experience.
UNSCIENTIFIC, [un'-sī-en-tif'-ik], *adj.* not scientific.
UNSCIENTIFICALLY, [un'-sī-en-tif'-ik-al-i], *adv.* in unscientific fashion.
UNSCORCHED, [un-skawcht'], *adj.* not scorched.
UNSCOURED, [un-skow(er)d'], *adj.* not scoured.
UNSCRATCHED, [un-skracht'], *adj.* not scratched, unhurt, unscathed.
UNSCREENED, [un-skrēnd'], *adj.* not covered with a screen; not sifted.
UNSCREW, [un-skrōō'], *v.t. and i.* to take (a screw, etc.) out by twisting (it); to take the screws out of; to become unscrewed; to be capable of being unscrewed.
UNSCRIPTURAL, [un-skrip'-cher-al], *adj.* not scriptural.
UNSCRIPTURALLY, [un-skrip'-cher-al-i], *adv.* in an unscriptural fashion.
UNSCRUPULOUS, [un-skrōōp'-yōōl-us], *adj.* having no scruples, stopping at nothing.
UNSCRUPULOUSLY, [un-skrōōp'-yōōl-us-li], *adv.* in unscrupulous fashion.
UNSCRUPULOUSNESS, [un-skrōōp'-yōōl-us-nes], *n.* the quality of being unscrupulous.
UNSCULPTURED, [un-skulp'-cherd], *adj.* not sculptured.
UNSCUTCHEONED, [un-skuch'-ond], *adj.* having no scutcheon.
UNSEAL, [un-sēl'], *v.t.* to break, remove the seal of, to open (something sealed).
UNSEALED, [un-sēld'], *adj.* not fastened with a seal.
UNSEAM, [un-sēm'], *v.t.* to undo the seams of.
UNSEARCHABLE, [un-surch'-abl], *adj.* that cannot be found by searching; hidden, inscrutable.
UNSEARCHABLENESS, [un-surch'-abl-nes], *n.* the quality of being unsearchable.
UNSEARCHED, [un-surcht'], *adj.* not searched (for) or explored.
UNSEARCHING, [un-surch'-ing], *adj.* not searching; not diligent or penetrating.
UNSEARED, [un-sēerd'], *adj.* not seared.
UNSEASONABLE, [un-sē'-zon-abl], *adj.* not seasonable; untimely.
UNSEASONABLENESS, [un-sē'-zon-abl-nes], *n.* the quality of being unseasonable.
UNSEASONABLY, [un-sē'-zon-ab-li], *adv.* in an unseasonable fashion.
UNSEASONED, [un-sē'-zond], *adj.* not seasoned.
UNSEAT, [un-sēt'], *v.t.* to remove from or rob of a seat; to throw (a rider) from the saddle; (*parl.*) to deprive (a member) of his right to sit in the House of Commons or other elective body.
UNSEATED, [un-sēt'-id], *adj.* lacking somewhere to sit, standing up; deprived of a seat in Parliament; (of a chair) having the seat missing.
UNSEAWORTHINESS, [un-sē'-wurTH'-i-nes], *n.* the state or quality of being unseaworthy.
UNSEAWORTHY, [un-sē'-wurTH-i], *adj.* not seaworthy.
UNSECONDED, [un-sek'-ond-id], *adj.* having no second or seconder, unsupported.
UNSECRET, [un-sē'-kret], *adj.* not secret.
UNSECTARIAN, [un-sek-tāer'-i-an], *adj.* not sectarian, not conforming to any particular sect.

JNSECTARIANISM, [un-sek-tāer'-i-an-izm], *n.* lack of narrow sectarian prejudice.
JNSECULAR, [un-sek'-yōō-ler], *adj.* not secular.
JNSECULARIZE, [un-sek'-yōō-ler-īz], *v.t.* to make unsecular.
JNSECURED, [un-si-kyōōerd'], *adj.* not financially covered.
JNSEDENTARY, [un-sed'-en-ter-i], *adj.* not sedentary.
JNSEDUCED, [un-si-dewst'], *adj.* not seduced or led astray.
JNSEDUCTIVE, [un-si-duk'-tiv], *adj.* unalluring.
JNSEEDED, [un-sēd'-id], *adj.* (of land) not sown with seed.
UNSEEING, [un-sē'-ing], *adj.* blind, not seeing.
UNSEEMLINESS, [un-sēm'-li-nes], *n.* the quality of being unseemly.
UNSEEMLY, [un-sēm'-li], *adj.* not seemly, indecent.
UNSEEN (1), [un-sēn'], *n.* **the u.,** the divine or spiritual world; the hereafter; **an u.,** a passage (of a text) for translation not previously prepared.
UNSEEN (2), [un-sēn'], *adj.* not seen; spiritual; (of a passage for translation) not previously known or prepared.
UNSEIZABLE, [un-sēz'-abl], *adj.* that cannot be seized.
UNSEIZED, [un-sēzd'], *adj.* not seized.
UNSELECTED, [un-si-lek'-tid], *adj.* not chosen.
UNSELFISH, [un-self'-ish], *adj.* not selfish, charitable, generous, altruistic.
UNSELFISHLY, [un-self'-ish-li], *adv.* in an unselfish fashion.
UNSELFISHNESS, [un-self'-ish-nes], *n.* the condition of being unselfish.
UNSENSATIONAL, [un-sen-sā'-shun-al], *adj.* not sensational.
UNSENSATIONALLY, [un-sen-sā'-shun-al-i], *adv.* in an unsensational way.
UNSENT, [un-sent'], *adj.* not sent, not transmitted or dispatched.
UNSENTENCED, [un-sen'-tenst], *adj.* not sentenced.
UNSENTIMENTAL, [un-sen'-ti-ment'-al], *adj.* not trading on sentiment; not given to sentimental ideas or emotions.
UNSEPARATED, [un-sep'-er-ā-tid], *adj.* not separated.
UNSEPULCHRED, [un-sep'-ōōl-kerd], *adj.* not buried; exhumed.
UNSEQUESTERED, [un-si-kwes'-terd], *adj.* not confiscated; not secluded.
UNSERVED, [un-survd'], *adj.* not served.
UNSERVICEABLE, [un-sur'-vis-abl], *adj.* not fit for use or service.
UNSERVICEABLENESS, [un-sur'-vis-abl-nes], *n.* the quality of being unserviceable.
UNSERVICEABLY, [un-sur'-vis-ab-li], *adv.* in an unserviceable way.
UNSET (1), [un-set'], *adj.* not set.
UNSET (2), [un-set'], *v.t.* to take out of its setting.
UNSETTLE, [un-setl'], *v.t.* to disturb, disarrange, upset.
UNSETTLED, [un-setld'], *adj.* not settled, disturbed, unstable; not paid; not finally determined upon; (*leg.*) not controlled by a settlement.
UNSETTLEMENT, [un-setl'-ment], *n.* the condition of being unsettled.
UNSETTLING, [un-set'-ling], *adj.* disquieting, disturbing.
UNSEVERED, [un-sev'-erd], *adj.* not severed or divided.
UNSEWN, [un-sōn'], *adj.* not sewn.
UNSEX, [un-seks'], *v.t.* to deprive of those qualities characteristic of the sex of.
UNSEXED, [un-sekst'], *adj.* of (chicks, etc.,) not separated according to sex; having become sexually impotent.
UNSHACKLE, [un-shakl'], *v.t.* to unfetter; (*fig.*) to liberate.
UNSHADED, [un-shād'-id], *adj.* not shady; (of a drawing) without shading.
UNSHADOWED, [un-shad'-ōd], *adj.* not dark or shadowed; (*fig.*) not sad or gloomy.
UNSHAKABLE, [un-shāk'-abl], *adj.* not to be shaken, changed, or upset; resolute.
UNSHAKEN, [un-shāk'-en], *adj.* not shaken, resolute, determined.
UNSHAMED, [un-shāmd'], *adj.* not made ashamed.
UNSHAMEFACED, [un-shām'-fāst], *adj.* not shamefaced, impudent.
UNSHAPELINESS, [un-shāp'-li-nes], *n.* the condition of being unshapely.
UNSHAPELY, [un-shāp'-li], *adj.* ill-shapen, ugly.
UNSHAPEN†, [un-shāp'-en], *adj.* not shaped or formed.
UNSHARED, [un-shāerd'], *adj.* not shared.
UNSHAVEN, [un-shāv'-en], *adj.* not shaven; bearded.
UNSHEATHE, [un-shēTH'], *v.t.* to draw out of the sheath.
UNSHED, [un-shed'], *adj.* not poured out or shed.
UNSHEETED, [un-shēt'-id], *adj.* lacking sheets.
UNSHELTERED, [un-shelt'-erd], *adj.* not sheltered, not protected.
UNSHIELDED, [un-shēld'-id], *adj.* not protected.
UNSHIFTING, [un-shift'-ing], *adj.* not shifting; (*fig.*) resolute, firm.
UNSHINGLED, [un-shing'-gld], *adj.* not covered with shingle; (of hair) not cut short in a shingle.
UNSHIP, [un-ship'], *v.t.* to disembark or discharge (from a ship).
UNSHOCKED, [un-shokt'], *adj.* not shocked.
UNSHOD, [un-shod'], *adj.* not wearing shoes.
UNSHOE, [un-shōō'], *v.t.* to take the shoes from.
UNSHORN, [un-shawn'], *adj.* not clipped or shorn.
UNSHOT, [un-shot'], *adj.* not shot or projected; not fired; not hit by a bullet, etc.
UNSHOWERED, [un-show'-erd], *adj.* not watered by showers of rain.
UNSHRINED, [un-shrīnd'], *adj.* not kept in a shrine.
UNSHRINKABLE, [un-shringk'-abl], *adj.* incapable of shrinking or being shrunk.
UNSHRINKING, [un-shringk'-ing], *adj.* not shrinking or hesitating.
UNSHRIVEN, [un-shriv'-en], *adj.* not shriven.
UNSHRUNK, [un-shrungk'], *adj.* not shrunk.
UNSHUNNED, [un-shund'], *adj.* not shunned.
UNSHUT, [un-shut'], *adj.* open, not shut.
UNSHUTTER, [un-shut'-er], *v.t.* to open the shutters of.
UNSIFTED, [un-sift'-id], *adj.* not sifted in a sieve; (*fig.*) not closely examined.
UNSIGHTED, [un-sīt'-id], *adj.* not yet seen or within view; (of a gun) lacking sights.
UNSIGHTLINESS, [un-sīt'-li-nes], *n.* the quality of being unsightly.
UNSIGHTLY, [un-sīt'-li], *adj.* ugly, displeasing to the eye.
UNSIGNALIZED, [un-sig'-nal-īzd], *adj.* not signalized.
UNSIGNED, [un-sīnd'], *adj.* not signed.
UNSILVERED, [un-sil'-verd], *adj.* not covered with silver or silver paint, not coated with a preparation used for silvering mirrors; not of a silvery colour.
UNSINEWED, [un-sin'-yōōd], *adj.* weak and feeble.
UNSINGED, [un-sinjd'], *adj.* not scorched.
UNSINGLED, [un-sing'-gld], *adj.* not separated.
UNSINKABLE, [un-singk'-able], *adj.* designed to keep afloat in all circumstances.
UNSINNING, [un-sin'-ing], *adj.* not sinning or sinful.
UNSISTERLY, [un-sis'-ter-li], *adj.* not befitting a sister.
UNSIZABLE, [un-sīz'-abl], *adj.* not full grown.
UNSIZED, [un-sīzd'], *adj.* not toughened with size.
UNSKILFUL, [un-skil'-fōōl], *adj.* lacking skill, clumsy, not expert.
UNSKILFULLY, [un-skil'-fōōl-i], *adv.* in an unskilful way.
UNSKILFULNESS, [un-skil'-fōōl-nes], *n.* the condition of being unskilful.
UNSKILLED, [un-skild'], *adj.* not skilled.
UNSLACKED, [un-slakt'], *adj.* not made slack.
UNSLACKENED, [un-slak'-end], *adj.* not slackened.
UNSLAKED, [un-slākt'], *adj.* (of lime) not watered; (of thirst) unquenched, not eased.
UNSLEEPING, [un-slēp'-ing], *adj.* not sleeping, having abundant energy, constantly diligent.
UNSLING, (**unslung**), [un-sling'], *v.t.* to take down (something slung up); (*naut.*) to take from the slings.
UNSLUMBERING, [un-slum'-ber-ing], *adj.* not slumbering, wakeful, tireless.
UNSMIRCHED, [un-smurcht'], *adj.* not smirched.
UNSMOKED, [un-smōkt'], *adj.* not smoked or cured.
UNSMOOTH, [un-smōōth'], *adj.* not smooth.
UNSOAPED, [un-sōpt'], *adj.* unwashed; not covered, treated, with soap.
UNSOCIABILITY, [un-sōsh'-a-bil'-i-ti], *n.* unsociableness.
UNSOCIABLE, [un-sōsh'-abl], *adj.* not sociable.
UNSOCIABLENESS, [un-sōsh'-abl-nes], *n.* the quality of being unsociable.
UNSOCIABLY, [un-sōsh'-ab-li], *adv.* in an unsociable fashion.
UNSOCIAL, [un-sō'-shal], *adj.* not social; not suitable for society; lacking community sense.

UNSOCKET, [un-sok'-it], *v.t.* to take out of a socket.
UNSOILED, [un-soild'], *adj.* not soiled.
UNSOLD, [un-sōld'], *adj.* not sold.
UNSOLDER, [un-sōld'-er], *v.t.* to separate (things soldered together).
UNSOLDIERLIKE, [un-sōl'-jer-līk], *adj.* not becoming or befitting a soldier.
UNSOLDIERLY, [un-sōl'-jer-li], *adj.* unworthy of a soldier.
UNSOLICITED, [un-sōl-is'-it-id], *adj.* not solicited.
UNSOLICITOUS, [un-sōl-is'-it-us], *adj.* not solicitous.
UNSOLID, [un-sol'-id], *adj.* not firm and solid.
UNSOLVABLE, [un-solv'-abl], *adj.* inexplicable, incapable of being solved.
UNSOLVED, [un-solvd'], *adj.* not solved or explained.
UNSOPHISTICATED, [un-sōf-is'-tik-ā'-tid], *adj.* not sophisticated.
UNSOPHISTICATEDLY, [un-sōf-is'-tik-ā'-tid-li], *adv.* in an unsophisticated fashion.
UNSOPHISTICATEDNESS, [un-sōf-is'-tik-ā'-tid-nes], *n.* the quality of being unsophisticated.
UNSORROWED, [un-so'-rōd], *adj.* not grieved for.
UNSORTED, [un-sawt'-id], *adj.* not sorted.
UNSOUGHT, [un-sawt'], *adj.* not sought, not asked for.
UNSOULED, [un-sōld'], *adj.* soulless.
UNSOUND, [un-sownd'], *adj.* not sound, rotten, defective; not reasoned, erroneous; not authoritative.
UNSOUNDABLE, [un-sownd'-abl], *adj.* incapable of being sounded.
UNSOUNDED, [unsownd'-id], *adj.* unfathomed.
UNSOUNDLY, [un-sownd'-li], *adv.* in an unsound fashion.
UNSOUNDNESS, [un-sownd'-nes], *n.* the quality of being unsound.
UNSOURED, [un-sow(r)d'], *adj.* not soured.
UNSOWN, [un-sōn'], *adj.* not sown; not seeded.
UNSPARING, [un-späer'-ing], *adj.* not sparing or stinting, liberal; not merciful.
UNSPARINGLY, [un-späer'-ing-li], *adv.* in an unsparing way.
UNSPARINGNESS, [un-späer'-ing-nes], *n.* the quality of being unsparing.
UNSPEAKABLE, [un-spēk'-abl], *adj.* too wonderful to be spoken of or expressed; too bad for description.
UNSPEAKABLENESS, [un-spēk'-abl-nes], *n.* the condition of being unspeakable.
UNSPEAKABLY, [un-spēk'-ab-li], *adv.* in an unspeakable fashion.
UNSPECIALIZED, [un-spesh'-al-īzd], *adj.* not specialized.
UNSPECIFIED, [un-spes'-i-fīd], *adj.* not specified.
UNSPECIOUS, [un-spē'-shus], *adj.* not specious.
UNSPECULATIVE, [un-spek'-yōō-lat-iv], *adj.* not speculative.
UNSPENT, [un-spent'], *adj.* not spent, drained or exhausted.
UNSPHERE†, [un-sfēer'], *v.t.* to take out of its natural sphere.
UNSPIED, [un-spīd'], *adj.* not seen.
UNSPIKE, [un-spīk'], *v.t.* to take the spike or spikes from.
UNSPILT, [un-spilt'], *adj.* not spilt.
UNSPIRITUAL, [un-spi'-ri-chōō-al], *adj.* not spiritual.
UNSPIRITUALITY, [un-spi'-ri-chōō-al'-i-ti], *n.* the quality of being unspiritual.
UNSPIRITUALIZE, [un-spi'-ri-chōō-al-īz], *v.t.* to make unspiritual.
UNSPIRITUALLY, [un-spi'-ri-chōō-al-i], *adv.* in an unspiritual way.
UNSPLIT, [un-split'], *adj.* not split or divided.
UNSPOILED, UNSPOILT, [un-spoild', un-spoilt'], *adj.* not spoiled.
UNSPOKEN, [un-spōk'-en], *adj.* not spoken.
UNSPORTING, [un-spawt'-ing], *adj.* (*coll.*) not fair or sportsmanlike.
UNSPORTSMANLIKE, [un-spawts'-man-līk], *adj.* not like, not worthy of, a sportsman.
UNSPOTTED, [un-spot'-id], *adj.* not spotted, unsoiled; (*fig.*) blameless, untainted.
UNSPOTTEDNESS, [un-spot'-id-nes], *n.* the quality of being unspotted.
UNSPRUNG, [un-sprung'], *adj.* not fitted with springs.
UNSQUARED, [un-skwäerd'], *adj.* not squared.
UNSTABLE, [un-stābl'], *adj.* not stable or steady; (*fig.*) irresolute, inconstant.
UNSTABLENESS, [un-stābl'-nes], *n.* the quality of being unstable.
UNSTAID, [un-stād'], *adj.* not staid; flighty.
UNSTAIDNESS, [un-stād'-nes], *n.* the state or quality of being unstaid; flightiness.
UNSTAINED, [un-stānd'], *adj.* not stained; (*fig.*) not dishonoured.
UNSTAMPED, [un-stampt'], *adj.* not stamped, lacking a stamp.
UNSTANCHED, UNSTAUNCHED, [un-stahncht', un-stawncht'], *adj.* not stanched.
UNSTARCHED, [un-stahcht'], *adj.* not starched or stiff with starch.
UNSTATED, [un-stāt'-id], *adj.* not stated.
UNSTATESMANLIKE, [un-stāts'-man-līk], *adj.* unworthy of a statesman.
UNSTATUTABLE, [un-stat'-yōōt-abl], *adj.* not permitted or enjoined by statute.
UNSTAUNCHED, see UNSTANCHED.
UNSTEADFAST, [un-sted'-fahst], *adj.* not steadfast.
UNSTEADFASTLY, [un-sted'-fahst-li], *adv.* in an unsteadfast fashion.
UNSTEADFASTNESS, [un-sted'-fahst-nes], *n.* the condition of being unsteadfast.
UNSTEADIED, [un-sted'-id], *adj.* not steadied; made unsteady.
UNSTEADILY, [un-sted'-i-li], *adv.* in an unsteady fashion.
UNSTEADINESS, [un-sted'-i-nes], *n.* the condition of being unsteady.
UNSTEADY, [un-sted'-i], *adj.* not firm and steady; unreliable, inconstant, not morally balanced.
UNSTEEPED, [un-stēpt'], *adj.* not steeped.
UNSTEP, [un-step'], *v.t.* (*naut.*) to take (a mast) out of its step.
UNSTICK, [un-stik'], *v.t.* to undo (what is stuck); to separate (things stuck together).
UNSTIMULATED, [un-stim'-yōō-lāt-id], *adj.* not stimulated or invigorated.
UNSTINTED, [un-stint'-id], *adj.* not stinted.
UNSTINTING, [un-stint'-ing], *adj.* ungrudging.
UNSTINTINGLY, [un-stint'-ing-li], *adv.* ungrudgingly.
UNSTIRRED, [un-sturd'], *adj.* not stirred; (*fig.*) not emotionally moved.
UNSTITCH, [un-stich'], *v.t.* to take the stitches out of; to undo (what is stitched up).
UNSTOCKED, [un-stokt'], *adj.* not supplied with stock.
UNSTOCKINGED, [un-stok'-ingd], *adj.* not wearing stockings.
UNSTOOPING, [un-stōōp'-ing], *adj.* not stooping; (*fig.*) unyielding.
UNSTOP, [un-stop'], *v.t.* to clear of obstruction; to remove the stopper from.
UNSTOPPED, [un-stopt'], *adj.* not stopped or blocked up.
UNSTOPPERED, [un-stop'-erd], *adj.* lacking a stopper.
UNSTORED, [un-staw(r)d'], *adj.* not stored.
UNSTORIED, [un-staw'-rid], *adj.* not told in tales or fables.
UNSTRAINED, [un-strānd'], *adj.* not strained, not constrained or forced, natural; not passed through a filter.
UNSTRAITENED, [un-strāt'-end], *adj.* not straitened.
UNSTRAP, [un-strap'], *v.t.* to loosen or remove the strap of.
UNSTRAPPED, [un-strapt'], *adj.* not strapped.
UNSTRATIFIED, [un-strat'-i-fīd], *adj.* (*geol.*) not arranged in strata.
UNSTRENGTHENED, [un-strengk'-thend], *adj.* not strengthened.
UNSTRESSED, [un-strest'], *adj.* not spoken with emphasis, not stressed.
UNSTRING, [un-string'], *v.t.* to loosen or take away the string of; to take (jewels, etc.) off a string.
UNSTRIPED, [un-strīpt'], *adj.* not striped.
UNSTRUCK, [un-struk'], *adj.* not struck.
UNSTRUNG, [un-strung'], *adj.* not strung; (*fig.*) emotionally or nervously unstable.
UNSTUCK, [un-stuk'], *adj.* not stuck together; **to come u.,** to come to grief, fail, break down.
UNSTUDIED, [un-stud'-id], *adj.* not studied; natural.
UNSTUDIOUS, [un-stewd'-i-us], *adj.* not studious.
UNSTUFFED, [un-stuft'], *adj.* not stuffed.
UNSTUNG, [un-stung'], *adj.* not stung.
UNSUBDUABLE, [un-sub-dew'-abl], *adj.* incapable of being subdued.
UNSUBDUED, [un-sub-dewd'], *adj.* not subdued or repressed.
UNSUBMISSIVE, [un-sub-mis'-iv], *adj.* not submissive or obedient; refusing to recognize authority.

UNSUBMISSIVELY, [un-sub-mis'-iv-li], *adv.* in an unsubmissive fashion.
UNSUBMISSIVENESS, [un-sub-mis'-iv-nes], *n.* the quality of being unsubmissive.
UNSUBORDINATED, [un-sub-awd'-in-ā-tid], *adj.* not made subordinate.
UNSUBORNED, [un-sub-awnd'], *adj.* not suborned.
UNSUBSIDIZED, [un-sub'-sid-īzd], *adj.* not subsidized.
UNSUBSTANTIAL, [un-sub-stan'-shal], *adj.* having little or no substance, flimsy; unreal, dreamlike, spiritual.
UNSUBSTANTIALITY, [un-sub-stan'-shi-al'-i-ti], *n.* the condition of being unsubstantial.
UNSUBSTANTIALLY, [un-sub-stan'-shal-i], *adv.* in an unsubstantial way.
UNSUBSTANTIATED, [un-sub-stan'-shi-ā-tid], *adj.* unconfirmed.
UNSUBVERTED, [un-sub-vurt'-id], *adj.* not subverted.
UNSUCCESS, [un-suk-ses'], *n.* lack of success.
UNSUCCESSFUL, [un-suk-ses'-fōōl], *adj.* not successful.
UNSUCCESSFULLY, [un-suk-ses'-fōōl-i], *adv.* in an unsuccessful fashion.
UNSUCCESSFULNESS, [un-suk-ses'-fōōl-nes], *n.* the quality of being unsuccessful.
UNSUCCESSIVE, [un-suk-ses'-iv], *adj.* not successive.
UNSUCKED, [un-sukt'], *adj.* not sucked.
UNSUGARED, [un-shōōg'-erd], *adj.* not sugared.
UNSUITABILITY, [un-sewt'-a-bil'-i-ti], *n.* the quality of being unsuitable.
UNSUITABLE, [un-sewt'-abl], *adj.* not suitable.
UNSUITABLENESS, [un-sewt'-abl-nes], *n.* unsuitability.
UNSUITABLY, [un-sewt'-ab-li], *adv.* in an unsuitable way.
UNSUITED, [un-sewt'-id], *adj.* not suited; having no cards of a particular suit.
UNSUITING, [un-sewt'-ing], *adj.* not suiting or fitting.
UNSULLIED, [un-sul'-id], *adj.* not stained or sullied.
UNSUMMED, [un-sumd'], *adj.* not added up or counted.
UNSUMMONED, [un-sum'-ond], *adj.* not summoned.
UNSUNG, [un-sung'], *adj.* not sung; not lauded in verse.
UNSUNNED, [un-sund'], *adj.* not warmed by, exposed to, sunshine.
UNSUPPLANTED, [un-su-plahnt'-id], *adj.* not supplanted.
UNSUPPLIABLE, [un-su-plī'-abl], *adj.* that cannot be supplied.
UNSUPPLIED, [un-su-plīd'], *adj.* not supplied.
UNSUPPORTED, [un-su-pawt'-id], *adj.* not having, receiving support.
UNSUPPRESSED, [un-su-prest'], *adj.* not suppressed.
UNSURE, [un-shōōer'], *adj.* not sure.
UNSURGICAL, [un-sur'-jik-al], *adj.* not surgical.
UNSURMOUNTABLE, [un-sur-mownt'-abl], *adj.* insuperable, insurmountable.
UNSURMOUNTED, [un-sur-mownt'-id], *adj.* not overcome.
UNSURPASSABLE, [un-sur-pahs'-abl], *adj.* that cannot be surpassed.
UNSURPASSABLY, [un-sur-pahs'-ab-li], *adv.* in unsurpassable fashion.
UNSURPASSED, [un-sur-pahst'], *adj.* not surpassed or exceeded.
UNSURRENDERED, [un-su-rend'-erd], *adj.* not surrendered.
UNSUSCEPTIBLE, [un-su-sept'-ibl], *adj.* not susceptible.
UNSUSPECTED, [un-sus-pek'-tid], *adj.* not suspected.
UNSUSPECTEDLY, [un-sus-pek'-tid-li], *adv.* in an unsuspected fashion.
UNSUSPECTING, [un-sus-pek'-ting], *adj.* not suspicious.
UNSUSPECTINGLY, [un-sus-pek'-ting-li], *adv.* in an unsuspecting fashion.
UNSUSPENDED, [un-sus-pend'-id], *adj.* not suspended.
UNSUSPICIOUS, [un-sus-pish'-us], *adj.* free from suspicion, not causing suspicion.
UNSUSPICIOUSLY, [un-sus-pish'-us-li], *adv.* in an unsuspicious way.
UNSUSPICIOUSNESS, [un-sus-pish'-us-nes], *n.* the condition or quality of being unsuspicious.
UNSUSTAINABLE, [un-sus-tān'-abl], *adj.* that cannot be sustained.
UNSUSTAINED, [un-sus-tānd'], *adj.* not sustained.
UNSUSTAINING, [un-sus-tān'-ing], *adj.* not supporting or sustaining.
UNSWATHE, [un-swāTH'], *v.t.* to free from bandages.
UNSWAYABLE, [un-swā'-abl], *adj.* that cannot be influenced.
UNSWAYED, [un-swād'], *adj.* not influenced or biased.
UNSWEAR, [un-swāer'], *v.t.* to recant by oath what one has already sworn to.
UNSWEETENED, [un-swēt'-end], *adj.* not sweetened.
UNSWEPT, [un-swept'], *adj.* not swept.
UNSWERVING, [un-swurv'-ing], *adj.* not deviating; (*fig.*) resolute, determined.
UNSWERVINGLY, [un-swurv'-ing-li], *adv.* in an unswerving fashion.
UNSWORN, [un-swawn'], *adj.* not sworn.
UNSYMMETRICAL, [un-sim-et'-rik-al], *adj.* not symmetrical.
UNSYMMETRICALLY, [un-sim-et'-rik-al-i], *adv.* in unsymmetrical fashion.
UNSYMPATHETIC, [un-sim'-pa-thet'-ik], *adj.* showing or feeling no sympathy.
UNSYMPATHETICALLY, [un-sim'-pa-thet'-ik-al-i], *adv.* in unsympathetic fashion.
UNSYSTEMATIC, [un-sis'-tem-at'-ik], *adj.* not according to system.
UNSYSTEMATICALLY, [un-sis'-tem-at'-ik-al-i], *adv.* in an unsystematic way.
UNSYSTEMATIZED, [un-sis'-tem-at-īzd], *adj.* not systematized.
UNTACK, [un-tak'], *v.t.* to undo (something lightly sewn together).
UNTACTFUL, [un-takt'-fōōl], *adj.* tactless.
UNTACTFULLY, [un-takt'-fōōl-i], *adv.* in an untactful fashion.
UNTACTFULNESS, [un-takt'-fōōl-nes], *n.* tactlessness.
UNTAINTED, [un-tānt'-id], *adj.* not tainted.
UNTAKEN, [un-tāk'-en], *adj.* not taken.
UNTALENTED, [un-tal'-ent-id], *adj.* not talented.
UNTAMABLE, [un-tām'-abl], *adj.* incapable of being tamed.
UNTAMABLENESS, [un-tām'-abl-nes], *n.* the quality of being untamable.
UNTAMED, [un-tāmd], *adj.* not tamed.
UNTANGLE, [un-tang'-gl], *v.* to unravel, disentangle.
UNTANNED, [un-tand'], *adj.* not tanned.
UNTARNISHED, [un-tahn'-isht], *adj.* not soiled or tarnished.
UNTASKED, [un-tahskt'], *adj.* not burdened with tasks.
UNTASTED, [un-tāst'-id], *adj.* not tasted.
UNTASTEFUL, [un-tāst'-fōōl], *adj.* not tasteful.
UNTAUGHT, [un-tawt'], *adj.* not instructed or taught.
UNTAXED, [un-takst'], *adj.* not taxed.
UNTEACH, [un-tēch'], *v.t.* to teach the reverse of (what has been previously taught).
UNTEACHABLE, [un-tēch'-abl], *adj.* that cannot be taught.
UNTEACHABLENESS, [un-tēch'-abl-nes], *n.* the quality of being unteachable.
UNTEARABLE, [un-tāer'-abl], *adj.* that cannot be torn.
UNTECHNICAL, [un-tek'-nik-al], *adj.* not technical.
UNTEMPER, [un-temp'-er], *v.t.* to take the temper from (previously tempered metal).
UNTEMPERED, [un-temp'-erd], *adj.* not tempered.
UNTEMPTED, [un-tempt'-id], *adj.* not tempted.
UNTEMPTING, [un-tempt'-ing], *adj.* not tempting.
UNTENABLE, [un-ten'-abl], *adj.* not defensible, not tenable.
UNTENABLY, [un-ten'-ab-li], *adv.* in an untenable fashion.
UNTENANTABLE, [un-ten'-ant-abl], *adj.* not tenantable.
UNTENANTED, [un-ten'-ant-id], *adj.* not tenanted.
UNTENDED, [un-ten'-did], *adj.* not tended; neglected.
UNTENDER, [un-ten'-der], *adj.* not tender.
UNTENDERED, [un-ten'-derd], *adj.* not tendered.
UNTENDERLY, [un-ten'-der-li], *adv.* without tenderness.
UNTERMINATED, [un-tur'-min-ā-tid], *adj.* not terminated or concluded.
UNTERRIFIED, [un-te'-ri-fīd], *adj.* not frightened.
UNTESTED, [un-test'-id], *adj.* not tested, proved.

UNTETHER, [un-teᴛʜ'-er], *v.t.* to release from a tether; (*fig.*) to liberate.
UNTHANKED, [un-thangkt'], *adj.* having received no thanks.
UNTHANKFUL, [un-thangk'-fōōl], *adj.* not thankful.
UNTHANKFULLY, [un-thangk'-fōōl-i], *adv.* in an unthankful fashion.
UNTHANKFULNESS, [un-thangk'-fōōl-nes], *n.* the fact or quality of being unthankful.
UNTHAWED, [un-thawd'], *adj.* not thawed.
UNTHINK, [un-thingk'], *v.t.* to think the reverse of (what one has previously thought).
UNTHINKABLE, [un-thingk'-abl], *adj.* unexpected, improbable, outrageous; not to be thought of.
UNTHINKING, [un-thingk'-ing], *adj.* not thinking, inconsiderate.
UNTHINKINGLY, [un-thingk'-ing-li], *adv.* in an unthinking fashion.
UNTHORNY, [un-thawn'-i], *adj.* not thorny.
UNTHOUGHTFUL, [un-thawt'-fōōl], *adj.* not thoughtful.
UNTHOUGHTFULLY, [un-thawt'-fōōl-i], *adv.* not thoughtfully.
UNTHOUGHTFULNESS, [un-thawt'-fōōl-nes], *n.* the quality of being unthoughtful.
UNTHREAD, [un-thred'], *v.t.* to remove the threads from; to disentangle; to take off a thread or string; (*fig.*) to solve (a complicated problem).
UNTHREATENED, [un-thret'-end], *adj.* not threatened.
UNTHRIFTILY, [un-thrift'-i-li], *adv.* in an unthrifty fashion.
UNTHRIFTINESS, [un-thrift'-i-nes], *n.* the condition of being unthrifty.
UNTHRIFTY, [un-thrift'-i], *adj.* not thrifty, prodigal, lavish.
UNTHRIVING, [un-thrīv'-ing], *adj.* not thriving.
UNTHROWN, [un-thrōn'], *adj.* not thrown.
UNTHWARTED, [un-thwawt'-id], *adj.* not frustrated.
UNTIDILY, [un-tī'-di-li], *adv.* in an untidy way.
UNTIDINESS, [un-tī'-di-nes], *n.* the condition of being untidy.
UNTIDY, [un-tī'-di], *adj.* not tidy.
UNTIE, [un-tī'], *v.t.* to unfasten (something tied).
UNTIED, [un-tīd'], *adj.* not tied, undone.
UNTIL (1), [un-til'], *prep.* up to the time of, till. [ME. *untill*].
UNTIL (2), [un-til'], *conj.* up to the time at which, till. [OScand. *und* up to and *till* to].
UNTILE, [un-tīl'], *v.t.* to take the tiles from.
UNTILED, [un-tīld], *adj.* not covered with tiles.
UNTILLED, [un-tild'], *adj.* not tilled.
UNTIMBERED, [un-tim'-berd], *adj.* not made with timbers; not timbered or wooded.
UNTIMELINESS, [un-tīm'-li-nes], *n.* the quality of being untimely.
UNTIMELY (1), [un-tīm'-li], *adj.* premature; inopportune.
UNTIMELY (2), [un-tīm'-li], *adv.* prematurely; at an inopportune moment.
UNTINCTURED, [un-tingk'-cherd], *adj.* not mixed or tinctured.
UNTINGED, [un-tinjd'], *adj.* not tinged.
UNTIRABLE, [un-tīer'-abl], *adj.* indefatigable, unwearying.
UNTIRED, [un-tīerd'], *adj.* not tired.
UNTIRING, [un-tīer'-ing], *adj.* not flagging.
UNTIRINGLY, [un-tīer'-ing-li], *adv.* in untiring fashion.
UNTITHED, [un-tīᴛʜd'], *adj.* not subject to or receiving tithe.
UNTITLED, [un-tītld'], *adj.* not possessing a title.
UNTO, [un'-tōō], *prep.* (*archaic*) to, towards. [ME. *unto*].
UNTOLD, [un-tōld'], *adj.* not told or revealed; not counted; uncountable.
UNTOMB, [un-tōōm'], *v.t.* to remove from a tomb.
UNTORMENTED, [un-taw-ment'-id], *adj.* not tormented.
UNTOUCHABLE (1), [un-tuch'-abl], *n.* a Hindu without caste.
UNTOUCHABLE (2), [un-tuch'-abl], *adj.* not fit to be touched.
UNTOUCHED, [un-tucht'], *adj.* not touched; not affected; not equalled.
UNTOWARD, [un-tō'-erd], *adj.* (*archaic*) perverse, refractory; troublesome, inconvenient.
UNTOWARDLINESS, [un-tō'-erd-li-nes], *n.* the quality of being untowardly; recalcitrance.
UNTOWARDLY, [un-tō'-erd-li], *adv.* untoward
UNTOWARDNESS, [un-tō'-erd-nes], *n.* the condition of being untoward.
UNTRACEABLE, [un-trās'-abl], *adj.* that cannot be traced.
UNTRACED, [un-trāst'], *adj.* not traced.
UNTRACKED, [un-trakt'], *adj.* not tracked.
UNTRACTABLE, [un-trakt'-abl], *adj.* intractable
UNTRAINED, [un-trānd'], *adj.* not trained or disciplined.
UNTRAMMELLED, [un-tram'-eld], *adj.* not shackled or hindered.
UNTRAMPLED, [un-trampld'], *adj.* not trampled (on).
UNTRANSFERABLE, [un-tran-sfur'-abl], *adj.* not transferable.
UNTRANSFERRED, [un-tran-sfurd'], *adj.* not transferred.
UNTRANSLATABLE, [un-tranz-lāt'-abl], *adj.* incapable of being translated.
UNTRANSLATED, [un-tranz-lāt'-id], *adj.* not translated.
UNTRANSPARENT, [un-trans-pāer'-ent], *adj.* not transparent.
UNTRAVELLED, [un-trav'-eld], *adj.* not visited by travellers; not experienced in foreign travel.
UNTRAVERSED, [un-trav'-erst], *adj.* not traversed.
UNTREASURED, [un-trezh'-erd], *adj.* not treasured.
UNTREMBLING, [un-tremb'-ling], *adj.* not trembling.
UNTRIED, [un-trīd'], *adj.* not tasted or experienced; not tested; not having been put on trial in a law court.
UNTRIMMED, [un-trimd'], *adj.* not trimmed.
UNTRITURATED, [un-trit'-yōō-rāt-id], *adj.* not powdered.
UNTROD†, [un-trod'], *adj.* not trodden.
UNTRODDEN, [un-trod'-en], *adj.* not trodden; secluded, unfrequented.
UNTROUBLED, [un-trubld'], *adj.* not troubled by care or sorrow; calm.
UNTRUE, [un-trōō'], *adj.* not true; contrary to fact; disloyal.
UNTRULY, [un-trōō'-li], *adv.* in an untrue fashion.
UNTRUSS, [un-trus'], *v.t.* to unfasten.
UNTRUSSED, [un-trust'], *adj.* not fastened or tied up.
UNTRUSTINESS, [un-trust'-i-nes], *n.* the condition of being untrusty.
UNTRUSTWORTHINESS, [un-trust'-wurᴛʜ-i-nes], *n.* the condition of being untrustworthy.
UNTRUSTWORTHY, [un-trust'-wurᴛʜ-i], *adj.* not trustworthy.
UNTRUSTY, [un-trust'-i], *adj.* not trusty.
UNTRUTH, [un-trōōth'], *n.* falsehood, want of veracity, the quality of being untrue; a lie.
UNTRUTHFUL, [un-trōōth'-fōōl], *adj.* not truthful.
UNTRUTHFULLY, [un-trōōth'-fōōl-i], *adv.* in untruthful fashion.
UNTRUTHFULNESS, [un-trōōth'-fōōl-nes], *n.* the quality of being untruthful; the habit of lying.
UNTUCK, [un-tuk'], *v.t.* to loosen what is tucked up; to remove the tucks from.
UNTUCKERED, [un-tuk'-erd], *adj.* not wearing a tucker.
UNTUMBLED, [un-tumbld'], *adj.* not tumbled or ruffled.
UNTUNABLE, [un-tewn'-abl], *adj.* not tunable.
UNTUNABLENESS, [un-tewn'-abl-nes], *n.* the quality of being untunable.
UNTUNE, [un-tewn'], *v.t.* to make untuneful.
UNTUNED, [un-tewnd'], *adj.* not tuned.
UNTURBANED, [un-turb'-and], *adj.* not having a turban on.
UNTURF, [un-turf'], *v.t.* to take turf from.
UNTURNED, [un-turnd'], *adj.* not turned.
UNTUTORED, [un-tewt'-erd], *adj.* uneducated, untaught; uncouth.
UNTWINE, [un-twīn'], *v.t.* and *i.* to untwist (something twined up); to come untwisted.
UNTWIST, [un-twist'], *v.t.* and *i.* to undo (something twisted up); to disentangle; to come untangled or untwisted.
UNURGED, [un-urjd'], *adj.* not pressed or urged.
UNUSED (1), [un-yōōzd'], *adj.* not used, never having been used.
UNUSED (2), [un-yōōst'], *adj.* not accustomed (to).
UNUSEFUL, [un-yōōs'-fōōl], *adj.* not useful.
UNUSUAL, [un-yōō'-zhōō-al], *adj.* not usual; strange, odd, remarkable.
UNUSUALLY, [un-yōō'-zhōō-al-i], *adv.* in an unusual manner; not in the usual way; (*coll.*) very, extremely.

UNUSUALNESS, [un-yōō'-zhōō-al-nes], *n.* the quality of being unusual.
UNUTILIZED, [un-yōō'-til-īzd], *adj.* not utilized.
UNUTTERABLE, [un-ut'-er-abl], *adj.* indescribable; (*coll.*) utter, absolute.
UNUTTERABLY, [un-ut'-er-ab-li], *adv.* in unutterable fashion.
UNUTTERED, [un-ut'-erd], *adj.* not uttered.
UNVACATED, [un-va-kāt'-id], *adj.* not vacated.
UNVACCINATED, [un-vaks'-in-ā-tid], *adj.* not vaccinated.
UNVALUED, [un-val'-yōōd], *adj.* not thought valuable.
UNVANQUISHABLE, [un-vang'-kwish-abl], *adj.* that cannot be conquered.
UNVANQUISHED, [un-vang'-kwisht], *adj.* not vanquished.
UNVARIABLE, [un-vāer'-i-abl], *adj.* invariable.
UNVARIED, [un-vāer'-id], *adj.* not varied.
UNVARIEGATED, [un-vāer'-i-gāt-id], *adj.* not variegated.
UNVARNISHED, [un-vahn'-isht], *adj.* not varnished; unadorned, simple.
UNVARYING, [un-vāer'-i-ing], *adj.* not varying.
UNVARYINGLY, [un-vāer'-i-ing-li], *adv.* in an unvarying way.
UNVEIL, [un-vāl'], *v.t. and i.* to take the veil from, to uncover; (*fig.*) to reveal, make public; to throw off one's disguise; to lift one's veil.
UNVENERABLE, [un-ven'-er-abl], *adj.* not venerable; not commanding respect.
UNVENTILATED, [un-ven'-til-ā-tid], *adj.* not at all or badly ventilated.
UNVERACIOUS, [un-ve-rā'-shus], *adj.* not true.
UNVERACITY, [un-ve-ras'-i-ti], *n.* lack of truthfulness.
UNVERIFIABLE, [un-ve'-ri-fī-abl], *adj.* that cannot be verified.
UNVERIFIED, [un-ve'-ri-fīd], *adj.* not verified.
UNVERSED, [un-vurst'], *adj.* not skilled or versed; without extensive knowledge.
UNVEXED, [un-vekst'], *adj.* not vexed or troubled.
UNVINDICATED, [un-vin'-dik-ā-tid], *adj.* not vindicated.
UNVIOLATED, [un-vī'-ō-lā-tid], *adj.* not violated.
UNVISITED, [un-viz'-it-id], *adj.* not visited.
UNVITIATED, [un-vish'-i-ā-tid], *adj.* pure, not vitiated or spoiled.
UNVITRIFIED, [un-vit'-ri-fīd], *adj.* not made into glass.
UNVOICED, [un-voist'], *adj.* not spoken; (*phon.*) not spoken so as to cause the vocal chords to vibrate.
UNVOLATILIZED, [un-vol-at'-il-īzd], *adj.* not made volatile.
UNVOUCHED, [un-vowcht'], *adj.* not vouched.
UNVOWED, [un-vowd'], *adj.* not vowed.
UNVOYAGEABLE, [un-voi'-ij-abl], *adj.* incapable of being travelled over.
UNWAKED, [un-wākt'], *adj.* not waked.
UNWAKENED, [un-wāk'-end], *adj.* not wakened.
UNWALLED, [un-wawld'], *adj.* not enclosed by a wall.
UNWANTED, [un-wont'-id], *adj.* not wanted, superfluous.
UNWARILY, [un-wāer'-i-li], *adv.* in an unwary fashion.
UNWARINESS, [un-wāer'-i-nes], *n.* lack of vigilance.
UNWARLIKE, [un-waw'-līk], *adj.* not warlike.
UNWARMED, [un-wawmd'], *adj.* not warmed.
UNWARNED, [un-wawnd'], *adj.* having received no warning.
UNWARP, [un-wawp'], *v.t.* to straighten (what is warped); (*naut.*) to undo the warps of.
UNWARPED, [un-wawpt], *adj.* not warped; (*fig.*) unbiased.
UNWARPING, [un-wawp'-ing], *adj.* not bending, not deviating.
UNWARRANTABLE, [un-wo'-rant-abl], *adj.* not defensible or justifiable.
UNWARRANTABLENESS, [un-wo'-rant-abl-nes], *n.* the quality of being unwarrantable.
UNWARRANTABLY, [un-wo'-rant-ab-li], *adv.* in an unwarrantable way.
UNWARRANTED, [un-wo'-rant-id], *adj.* not authorized; not justified or fitting.
UNWARY, [un-wāer'-i], *adj.* not vigilant or wary.
UNWASHED, [un-wosht'], *adj.* not washed; not touched by water; **the great u.,** the mob.
UNWASTED, [un-wāst'-id], *adj.* not wasted.
UNWATCHED, [un-wocht'], *adj.* not watched.
UNWATCHFUL, [un-woch'-fōōl], *adj.* not watchful.
UNWATCHFULNESS, [un-woch'-fōōl-nes], *n.* the condition of being unwatchful.
UNWATERED, [un-wawt'-erd], *adj.* not watered or irrigated.
UNWAVERING, [un-wā'-ver-ing], *adj.* not wavering or hesitant.
UNWEAKENED, [un-wēk'-end], *adj.* not made weak(er).
UNWEANED, [un-wēnd'], *adj.* not weaned.
UNWEAPONED, [un-wep'-ond], *adj.* having no weapon.
UNWEARIABLE, [un-wēer'-i-abl], *adj.* incapable of being wearied, untiring.
UNWEARIED, [un-wēer'-id], *adj.* not wearied.
UNWEARIEDLY, [un-wēer'-id-li], *adv.* in an unwearied way.
UNWEARIEDNESS, [un-wēer'-id-nes], *n.* the condition of being unwearied.
UNWEARY, [un-wēer'-i], *adj.* not weary.
UNWEARYING, [un-wēer'-i-ing], *adj.* untiring, indefatigable.
UNWEAVE, [un-wēv'], *v.t.* to unravel.
UNWED, [un-wed'], *adj.* not married.
UNWEDDED, [un-wed'-id], *adj.* not married.
UNWEEDED, [un-wēd'-id], *adj.* with weeds growing unchecked.
UNWEIGHED, [un-wād'], *adj.* not weighed; (*fig.*) not duly considered.
UNWEIGHING, [un-wā'-ing], *adj.* not weighing.
UNWELCOME, [un-wel'-kum], *adj.* not welcome.
UNWELL, [un-wel'], *adj.* suffering from ill-health, not well.
UNWEPT, [un-wept'], *adj.* not lamented.
UNWHIPPED, [un-wipt'], *adj.* not whipped.
UNWHISPERED, [un-wisp'-erd], *adj.* not whispered, not rumoured.
UNWHOLESOME, [un-hōl'-sum], *adj.* not wholesome.
UNWHOLESOMENESS, [un-hōl'-sum-nes], *n.* the condition of being unwholesome.
UNWIELDILY, [un-wēl'-di-li], *adv.* in an unwieldy way.
UNWIELDINESS, [un-wēl'-di-nes], *n.* the condition of being unwieldy.
UNWIELDY, [un-wēld-i], *adj.* clumsy, unmanageable.
UNWILLING, [un-wil'-ing], *adj.* not willing, reluctant.
UNWILLINGLY, [un-wil'-ing-li], *adv.* in an unwilling fashion.
UNWILLINGNESS, [un-wil'-ing-nes], *n.* the condition of being unwilling.
UNWILY, [un-wī'-li], *adj.* not wily.
UNWIND, (**unwound**), [un-wīnd'], *v.t. and i.* to undo (that which is wound up); to become unwound.
UNWINKING, [un-wingk'-ing], *adj.* not winking; unceasingly vigilant.
UNWISDOM, [un-wiz'-dom], *n.* folly.
UNWISE, [un-wīz'], *adj.* not wise.
UNWISELY, [un-wīz'-li], *adv.* not wisely.
UNWITHDRAWING, [un-wiTH-draw'-ing], *adj.* stubborn, unyielding.
UNWITHERED, [un-wiTH'-erd], *adj.* not withered, still fresh and vigorous.
UNWITHERING, [un-wiTH'-er-ing], *adj.* not liable to become withered.
UNWITHSTOOD, [un-wiTH-stōōd'], *adj.* unopposed.
UNWITNESSED, [un-wit'-nest], *adj.* not seen or attested by a witness.
UNWITTILY, [un-wit'-i-li], *adv.* not wittily.
UNWITTINGLY, [un-wit'-ing-li], *adv.* in ignorance, unconsciously.
UNWITTY, [un-wit'-i], *adj.* lacking wit.
UNWOMANLY, [un-wōōm'-an-li], *adj.* not womanly.
UNWONTED, [un-wōnt'-id], *adj.* unusual.
UNWONTEDLY, [un-wōnt'-id-li], *adv.* in an unwonted fashion.
UNWONTEDNESS, [un-wōnt'-id-nes], *n.* the quality of being unwonted.
UNWOODED, [un-wōōd'-id], *adj.* lacking trees or woods.
UNWOOED, [un-wōōd'], *adj.* not wooed.
UNWORKMANLIKE, [un-wurk'-man-līk], *adj.* not workmanlike.
UNWORLDLINESS, [un-wurld'-li-nes], *n.* the condition or quality of being unworldly.
UNWORLDLY, [un-wurld'-li], *adj.* not mundane or worldly.
UNWORN, [un-wawn'], *adj.* not worn.
UNWORRIED, [un-wu'-rid], *adj.* not worried.

UNWORSHIPPED, [un-wur'-shipt], *adj.* not worshipped.
UNWORTHILY, [un-wurTH'-i-li], *adv.* in an unworthy way.
UNWORTHINESS, [un-wurTH'-i-nes], *n.* the condition or quality of being unworthy.
UNWORTHY, [un-wurTH'-i], *adj.* not worthy, unbecoming, not suitable.
UNWOUND (1), [un-wownd'], *adj.* straightened out, unravelled.
UNWOUND (2), [un-wownd'], *pret. and p.pt.* of UNWIND.
UNWOUNDED, [un-wōōnd'-id], *adj.* not wounded.
UNWOVEN, [un-wōv'-en], *adj.* not made by weaving, not made into fabric.
UNWRAP, [un-rap'], *v.t.* to take the wrappings from.
UNWREATHE, [un-rēTH'], *v.t.* to remove the wrappings or wreaths from.
UNWRECKED, [un-rekt'], *adj.* not wrecked.
UNWRENCHED, [un-rencht'], *adj.* not wrenched.
UNWRINKLED, [un-ringkld'], *adj.* without wrinkles.
UNWRITTEN, [un-rit'-en], *adj.* not written down, not marked with writing; **u. law,** the justification pleaded for murder done to requite one's honour.
UNWROUGHT, [un-rawt'], *adj.* not done, not made.
UNWRUNG, [un-rung'], *adj.* not wrung, not touched by tender feeling.
UNYIELDED, [un-yēld'-id], *adj.* retained, not surrendered.
UNYIELDING, [un-yēld'-ing], *adj.* resolute, obstinate.
UNYOKE, [un-yōk'], *v.t.* to remove the yoke from; (*fig.*) to make free from some bond or bondage.
UNYOKED, [un-yōkt'], *adj.* having no yoke.
UNZONED, [un-zōnd'], *adj.* not divided into zones; having no girdle.
UP (1), [up], *n.* a movement or thrust upwards; **to have an u. and a downer,** (*coll.*) to skirmish; **ups and downs,** rises and falls, changes of fortune.
UP (2), [up], *adj.* moving upwards; (*fig.*) increasing, developing, improving; travelling towards an important city, *esp.* London.
UP (3), [up], *adv.* expressing transition to, or existence upon, a higher level; expressing growth, development, elevation (physical, moral, social, etc.); expressing increase of value, power, importance, speed, etc.; expressing the ideas of being laid aside after use, disuse, inactivity, etc.; expressing motion towards or existence in the north; expressing the idea of being out of bed; **u. with** (*or* **to**), level with, (*fig.*) equal to; **to be u. to (something),** to be doing (something), *esp.* in a secret way; **to be u. against it,** to have serious difficulties; **what's u.?** (*coll.*) what's the matter?; **it's all u.,** (*coll.*) it's finished, nothing more can be done, we are beaten, etc.; **u. and down,** alternately raised and lowered, or rising and descending; to and fro; hither and thither; here and there; all over; **to be on the u. and u.,** to be progressing. [OE. *uppe*].
UP (4), [up], *prep.* expressing movement towards or existence on a higher level; (*fig.*) expressing increasing importance, worth, power, etc.; along the course of, *esp.* against the current.
UP (5), [up], *v.i.* **to u. and,** to begin to.
UP-, *pref.* in an upward direction or position. [UP (3)].
UPANISHAD, [ōō-pan'-ish-ahd], *n.* a commentary on and development of the Vedas. [Skr. *upanishad*].
UPAS, [yōō'-pas], *n.* a poisonous tree supposed to exist in Java; a Javanese tree, *Antiaris toxicaria*; the poisonous sap of this tree; (*fig.*) any source of corruption. [Malay *upas* poison].

UPAS

UPBEAR, (upbore, upborne), [up-bāer'], *v.t.* to raise, support, sustain.
UPBIND, (upbound), [up-bīnd'], *v.t.* to bind up.
UPBORE, [up-baw(r)'], *pret.* of UPBEAR.
UPBORNE, [up-bawn'], *p.pt.* of UPBEAR.
UPBOUND, [up-bownd'], *pret. and p.pt.* of UPBIND.
UPBRAID, [up-brād'], *v.t.* to chide, reproach, reprove. [ME. *upbreiden*].
UPBRAIDING (1), [up-brād'-ing], *n.* a chiding, a reproof.
UPBRAIDING (2), [up-brād'-ing], *adj.* chiding, reproachful.
UPBRAIDINGLY, [up-brād'-ing-li], *adv.* in upbraiding, scolding or railing fashion; reprovingly.
UPBRINGING, [up'-bring'-ing], *n.* the training and education of a child.
UPCAST (1), [up'-kahst], *n.* that which is cast up; a ventilation shaft in a mine.
UPCAST (2), [up'-kahst], *adj.* cast upwards.
UPCOILED, [up'-koild], *adj.* twisted into a coil.
UP-COUNTRY (1), [up'-kun'-tri], *n.* the interior part of any country.
UP-COUNTRY (2), [up'-kun'-tri], *adj.* relating to the interior of a country.
UP-COUNTRY (3), [up'-kun'-tri], *adv.* towards the interior of a country.
UPCURL, [up-kurl'], *v.t.* to twist, curl upwards.
UP-END, [up'-end'], *v.t.* to put or throw up on end.
UP-GRADE, [up'-grād'], *n.* **on the u.,** improving.
UPGROWTH, [up-grōth], *n.* something which grows up; the act or process of growing up.
UPHAND, [up'-hand'], *adj.* raised by hand.
UPHEAVAL, [up-hēv'-al], *n.* the act of upheaving; an earthquake or any similar eruption; a sudden unexpected trouble or disturbance in normal conditions.
UPHEAVE, [up-hēv'], *v.t.* to heave or raise up.
UPHELD, [up-held'], *pret. and p.pt.* of UPHOLD.
UPHILL (1), [up'-hil'], *adj.* ascending, leading upwards; (*fig.*) difficult, laborious.
UPHILL (2), [up'-hil'], *adv.* towards the top of a hill.
UPHOLD, (upheld), [up-hōld'], *v.t.* to sustain or support; to agree with, encourage, give approval to.
UPHOLDER, [up'-hōld'-er], *n.* a supporter; †an upholsterer, a dealer in second-hand articles.
UPHOLSTER, [up-hōl'-ster], *v.t.* to provide (a room) with furniture and ornaments; to stuff or cover (a chair, etc.).
UPHOLSTERER, [up-hōl'-ster-er], *n.* one who upholsters or deals in upholstery.
UPHOLSTERY, [up-hōl'-ster-i], *n.* household furniture; the covers, springs, and stuffing of chairs, etc.; the trade of an upholsterer.
UPKEEP, [up'-kēp], *n.* maintenance; the cost of maintenance.
UPLAND (1), [up'-land], *n.* higher land on the slopes of hills and mountains above the valleys.
UPLAND (2), [up'-land], *adj.* pertaining to the uplands.
UPLANDISH, [up'-land'-ish], *adj.* upland.
UPLIFT (1), [up'-lift], *n.* upheaval; the act of uplifting; (*coll.*) moral edification and profit.
UPLIFT (2), [up-lift'], *v.t.* to hold up or raise; (*fig.*) to cheer or edify.
UPMOST, [up'-mōst], *adj.* highest, uppermost.
UPON, [up-on'], *prep.* expressing the idea of a state of contact with the upper surface of anything; on. [UP (4) and ON].
UPPER (1), [up'-er], *n.* those parts of a shoe or boot other than the heel and sole; **down on one's uppers,** destitute.
UPPER (2), [up'-er], *adj.* lying or placed above; higher in esteem or rank; greater in power or dignity.
UPPER-CUT, [up'-er-kut'], *n.* (*boxing*) a blow delivered with an upward swing.
UPPER HAND, [up'-er-hand'], *n.* ascendancy; the position of power and advantage.
UPPER-LEATHER, [up'-er-leTH'-er], *n.* leather for the uppers of a shoe or boot.
UPPERMOST (1), [up'-er-mōst], *adj.* highest; (*fig.*) dominant.
UPPERMOST (2), [up'-er-mōst], *adv.* in an uppermost position, on top.
UPPER TEN, [up'-er-ten'], *n.* (*coll.*) the wealthy few, the aristocracy. [Short for *upper ten* thousand].
UPPER-WORKS, [up'-er-wurks'], *n.*(*pl.*) (*naut.*) the parts of a ship higher than the water-line.
UPPISH, [up'-ish], *adj.* (*coll.*) arrogant, self-assertive, impudent, snobbish.
UPPISHLY, [up'-ish-li], *adv.* in an uppish fashion.
UPPISHNESS, [up'-ish-nes], *n.* the quality of being uppish.
UPRAISE, [up-rāz'], *v.t.* to raise up.
UPRIGHT (1), [up'-rīt], *n.* a vertical support in any structure; an upright piano.
UPRIGHT (2), [up'-rīt], *adj.* vertical; (*fig.*) honest, honourable, just; **u. piano,** a piano that has vertical and not horizontal strings. [OE. *upriht*].
UPRIGHTLY, [up'-rīt-li], *adv.* in an upright fashion.
UPRIGHTNESS, [up'-rīt-nes], *n.* the condition or quality of being upright.
UPRISE, (uprose, uprisen), [up-rīz'], *v.i.* to ascend; to stand up.
UPRISING, [up-rīz'-ing], *n.* the act of rising up; the act of getting up from bed; an insurrection, revolt.

UPROAR, [up'-raw(r)], *n.* a great tumult and clamour; a noisy disturbance.
UPROARIOUS, [up-raw'-ri-us], *adj.* very noisy and violent; boisterous, rowdy.
UPROARIOUSLY, [up-raw'-ri-us-li], *adv.* in an uproarious fashion.
UPROARIOUSNESS, [up-raw'-ri-us-nes], *n.* the state of being uproarious, noisy merry-making.
UPROOT, [up-rōōt'], *v.t.* to tear up by the roots; (*fig.*) to exterminate.
UPROSE, [up-rōz], *pret.* of UPRISE.
UPRUSH, [up'-rush'], *n.* a sudden rushing upwards or into consciousness.
UPSET (1), [up'-set'], *n.* a capsizing or overturning; any trouble or disturbance; (*coll.*) a quarrel.
UPSET (2), [up-set'], *v.t. and i.* to cause to capsize; to throw down; to dislocate, throw out, disturb; to make ill; to cause mental distress to; to capsize, to be overthrown.
UPSHOT, [up'-shot], *n.* final issue, result, conclusion.
UPSIDE, [up'-sīd], *n.* the upper surface of anything; that line or section of a railway track on which trains run towards an important city, *esp.* London; **u. down**, with the upper side below.
UP-STAGE (1), [up'-stāj'], *adj.* (*slang*) uppish.
UP-STAGE (2), [up'-stāj'], *adv.* at, or towards the back of the stage, i.e., away from the audience.
UPSTAIRS (1), [up-stāerz'], *n.* the upper rooms of a house.
UPSTAIRS (2), UPSTAIR, [up'-stāer(z)], *adj.* of, or pertaining to, storeys above the ground floor.
UPSTAIRS (3), [up-stāerz'], *adv.* in or towards the upper rooms of a house.
UPSTANDING, [up-stand'-ing], *adj.* (of a man, etc.) straight-backed, well-built.
UPSTART (1), [up'-staht], *n.* a parvenu, a person who by sudden access of wealth or success is raised from insignificance to importance or from a low rank of society to a high one.
UPSTART (2), [up'-staht], *adj.* suddenly raised from insignificance to importance or from comparative poverty to wealth.
UPSTAY, [up-stā'], *v.t.* to support from beneath.
UPSTREAM (1), [up'-strēm'], *adj.* travelling towards the source, against the current.
UPSTREAM (2), [up'-strēm'], *adv.* towards the source, against the current.
UPSTROKE, [up'-strōk], *n.* a stroke made with an upward movement as in writing.
UPSURGE, [up'-surj], *n.* an upward surge.
UPTAKE, [up'-tāk], *n.* perception.
UPTURN, [up-turn'], *v.i.* to overturn, turn up, throw into disorder.
UPWARD (1), [up'-werd], *adj.* moving, caused to move, aimed towards, a higher position, ascending, pointing away from the earth.
UPWARD (2), see UPWARDS.
UPWARDLY, [up'-werd-li], *adv.* upwards.
UPWARDS, UPWARD, [up'-werdz, up'-werd], *adv.* into or towards a higher level, away from the earth.
UR-, [ōōer], *pref.* original, primitive, hypothetical. [Germ. *ur-* primitive].
URAEMIA, [yōō-rē'-mi-a], *n.* (*path.*) the unhealthy state arising in the body when the kidneys fail to cleanse the blood of certain impurities. [Gk. *ouron* urine and *haima* blood].
URAEMIC, [yōō-rē'-mik], *adj.* pertaining to uraemia.
URAEUS, [yōō-rē'-us], *n.* a symbol of supreme power, worn by a ruler in Ancient Egypt, and representing a sacred serpent. [Gk. *ouraios* having a tail].
URAL-ALTAIC (1), [yōōer-al-al-tā'-ik], *n.* a Ural-Altaic language.
URAL-ALTAIC (2), [yōōer-al-al-tā'-ik], *adj.* of, or pertaining to, a group of languages spoken by peoples living mainly between the Ural and Altai mountains.
URALITE, [yōōer'-al-īt], *n.* a variety of hornblende found in the Ural mountains. [Germ. *uralit*].
URANIA, [yōō-rā'-ni-a], *n.* (*class. myth.*) the muse of astronomy. [~Gk. *ouranios* celestial].
URANIAN, [yōō-rā'-ni-an], *adj.* pertaining to non-sexual, spiritual, or homosexual love. [URANIA].
URANIC, [yōō-rā'-nik], *adj.* (*chem.*) pertaining to uranium in its higher valency.
URANITE, [yōōer'-an-īt], *n.* (*min.*) an ore of uranium.
URANITIC, [yōōer'-an-it'-ik], *adj.* (*chem.*) pertaining to uranium or uranite.
URANIUM, [yōō-rā'-ni-um], *n.* a metallic element denoted by the symbol U. [The planet, *Uranus*].
URANO-, *prefix* celestial. [Gk. *ouranos* heaven].
URANOGRAPHIC, [yōōer'-an-og-raf'-ik], *adj.* pertaining to uranography. [URANO- and Gk. *graphia* writing].
URANOGRAPHY, [yōōer'-an-og'-ra-fi], *n.* a description of the heavens and the stars and planets. [URANO- and Gk. *graphia* writing].
URANOLOGY, [yōōer'-an-ol'-o-ji], *n.* astronomy. [URANO- and Gk. *logos* speech].
URANOMETRIA, [yōōer'-a-nō-met'-ri-a], *n.* a list of stars and planets. [URANO- and Gk. *metron* measure].
URANOSCOPY, [yōōer'-an-os'-ko-pi], *n.* the study of celestial bodies. [URANO- and Gk. *skopos* view].
URANOUS, [yōōer'-an-us], *adj.* (*chem.*) pertaining to uranium in its lower valency.
URANUS, [yōō-rā'-nus], *n.* (*Gk. myth.*) the father of Cronus; (*astron.*) the major planet between Saturn and Neptune.
URATE, [yōōer'-āt], *n.* (*chem.*) a salt of uric acid.
URBAN, [urb'-an], *adj.* pertaining to a town or city. [L. *urbanus*].
URBANE, [ur-bān'], *adj.* civil, refined. [L. *urbanus*].
URBANELY, [ur-bān'-li], *adv.* in an urbane way.
URBANITY, [ur-ban'-i-ti], *n.* civility or courtesy, refinement of speech and manner. [L. *urbanitas*].
URBANIZATION, [urb'-an-ī-zā'-shun], *n.* the process of urbanizing, the condition of being urbanized.
URBANIZE, [ur'-ban-īz], *v.t.* to impart the qualities and conditions of a town or city to, to make urban.
URCEOLATE, [ur'-si-ō-lāt], *adj.* (*bot.*) resembling an urn in shape. [~L. *urceolus* a small urn].
URCHIN, [ur'-chin], *n.* (*dial.*) the hedgehog; an uncared-for child. [ME. *urchon* from OFr. *herichon*].
URDU (1), [ur-dōō'], *n.* a form of Hindustani. [Hind. *urdu* camp].
URDU (2), [ur-dōō'], *adj.* in, or pertaining to, Urdu.
UREA, [yōō-rē'-a], *n.* (*chem.*) a crystalline compound found in urine. [~URINE].
UREAL, [yōō'-ri-al], *adj.* (*chem.*) pertaining to urea.
UREDO, [yōō-rē'-dō], *n.* (*bot.*) rust fungi when only partly developed. [L. *uredo* blight].
URETER, [yōō-rē'-ter], *n.* (*anat.*) a duct conveying urine to the bladder. [Gk. *oureter*].
URETERITIS, [yōō-rē'-ter-ī'-tis], *n.* (*med.*) an inflammation of the ureter. [URETER and Gk. *itis* denoting inflammation].
URETHRA, [yōō-rēth'-ra], *n.* (*anat.*) the passage by which urine passes out of the bladder. [Gk. *ourethra*].
URETHRAL, [yōō-rēth'-ral], *adj.* relating to the urethra.
URETHRITIS, [yōō'-rē-thrīt'-is], *n.* (*med.*) an inflammation of the urethra. [URETHRA and Gk. *itis* denoting inflammation].
URETHROSCOPE, [yōō-rēth'-rō-skōp], *n.* an instrument by which the interior of the urethra may be examined. [URETHRA and SCOPE].
URGE (1), [urj], *n.* a powerful incentive, impulse.
URGE (2), [urj], *v.t.* to drive, to compel to advance; to exhort, advise vigorously; to call attention to, vigorously and persistently. [L. *urgere*].
URGENCY, [ur'-jen-si], *n.* the quality of being urgent; great stress or necessity; persistent demand, importunity.
URGENT, [ur'-jent], *adj.* insistent, importunate; very important, impossible to be overlooked or delayed.
URGENTLY, [ur'-jent-li], *adv.* in an urgent way.
URGER, [ur'-jer], *n.* one who urges.
URGING, [ur'-jing], *adj.* importunate, pressing.
URIAL, OORIAL, [ōōer'-ī-al], *n.* a wild sheep found in Asia, *Ovis cycloceros*. [Unkn.].
URIC, [yōōer'-ik], *adj.* pertaining to urine; **u. acid**, an acid which forms a small proportion of the urine of a mammal but a large proportion of the urine of reptiles and birds.
URIM, [yōō'-rim], *n.* in the phrase, **u. and thummim**, which is used in the Bible to refer to certain obscure ornaments on the breastplate of the Jewish high-priest. [Heb. *urim*].
URINAL, [yōōer'-in-al, yōō-rī'-nal], *n.* a vessel into which urine is passed; a public convenience for urinating. [L. *urinalis*].
URINARY, [yōōer'-i-ner-i], *adj.* connected with urine.
URINATE, [yōō'-rin-āt], *v.i.* to discharge urine. [~L. *urinare*].
URINE, [yōōer'-ēn], *n.* the liquid excrement secreted by the kidneys into the bladder and discharged from the body by the urethra. [L. *urina*].
URINIFEROUS, [yōō'-rin-if'-er-us], *adj.* (*anat.*) transmitting urine.
URINOMETER, [yōōer'-rin-om'-it-er], *n.* an instrument for ascertaining the specific gravity of urine.
URINOUS, [yōōer'-in-us], *adj.* (*anat., chem.*) resembling, pertaining to, derived from, urine.

URN, [urn], *n.* a large metal or earthenware vessel, circular at the base, usually having a circular lip and a narrow neck, suitable for holding liquids; a large metal container, with a lid and a tap, in which water or other liquids may be heated. [L. *urna*].
UROCHORD, [yōōer'-ō-kawd'], *n.* (*zool.*) the cartilaginous formation in tunicates which corresponds to the spine of vertebrates. [Gk. *oura* tail and CHORD].
UROSCOPY, [yōōer-os'-kop-i], *n.* (*med.*) diagnosis by inspection of urine.
UROTOXIC, [yōōer'-ō-toks'-ik], *adj.* (*med.*) pertaining to poisons in urine. [Gk. *ouron* urine and TOXIC].
URSA, [ur'-sa], *n.* the name of two constellations in the northern hemisphere, the Great Bear (*U. major*) and the Little Bear (*U. minor*). [L. *ursa* she-bear].
URSIFORM, [ur'-si-fawm], *adj.* resembling a bear in form. [L. *ursus* a bear and FORM (1)].
URSINE, [ur'-sīn], *adj.* relating to or resembling bears. [L. *ursinus*].
URSON, [ur'-son], *n.* a kind of porcupine, *Erethizon dorsatus*. [Fr. *ourson*].
URSULINE (**1**), [urs'-yōō-lin], *n.* a member of an order of nuns founded in the sixteenth century. [St. *Ursula*].
URSULINE (**2**), [urs'-yōō-lin], *adj.* of, or relating to the Ursulines.
URTICACEOUS, [ur'-tik-ā'-shus], *adj.* (*bot.*) pertaining to nettles. [L. *urtica* nettle].
URTICARIA, [ur'-tik-āer'-i-a], *n.* nettle-rash.
URTICATE, [ur'-tik-āt], *v.t.* to sting or whip with nettles. [L. *urticare*].
URTICATION, [ur'-tik-ā'-shun], *n.* the sting of nettles; the act of urticating.
URUBU, [ōō'-rōō-bōō'], *n.* a South American vulture, *Catharesta atrata*. [Native].
URUS, [yōōer'-us], *n.* the European wild ox. [L. *urus*].
US, [us], *oblique case* of WE. [OE. *us*].
USABLE, [yōōz'-abl], *adj.* able to be used.
USAGE, [yōōs'-ij], *n.* manner of use, *esp.* of a word; an established custom or habit. [OFr. *usage*].
USANCE, [yōōz'-ants], *n.* habit, usage; the usual period allowed for the payment of foreign exchange bills. [OFr. *usance*].

URUBU

USE (**1**), [yōōs], *n.* the act of using; ability or right to use; a reason for doing or using; the condition or quality of being useful; something usually done, a habit or custom; (*eccles*) a form of ceremony, a liturgy; (*leg.*) profit derived from a trust or tenancy. [L. *usus* custom].
USE (**2**), [yōōz], *v.t. and i.* to employ as an instrument; to manipulate, operate; to utilize, to employ or avail oneself of in a task, operation, or activity; to cause to operate or have effect; to employ so much that none is left, consume, utterly exhaust; to take as an ingredient; to utter (words, phrases, etc.); to treat, handle in a certain way, adopt a specified attitude or conduct towards; to be wont (to); to be accustomed to have or possess; **to u. up**, to exhaust the supply of. [OFr. *user*].
USEFUL, [yōōs'-fōōl], *adj.* handy, profitable, advantageous to use; helpful.
USEFULLY, [yōōs'-fōōl-i], *adv.* in a useful way.
USEFULNESS, [yōōs'-fōōl-nes], *n.* the quality of being useful.
USELESS, [yōōs'-les], *adj.* not useful, unserviceable.
USELESSLY, [yōōs'-les-li], *adv.* in a useless manner.
USELESSNESS, [yōōs'-les-nes], *n.* the quality or condition of being useless.
USER (**1**), [yōōz'-er], *n.* one who uses (something).
USER (**2**), [yōōz'-er], *n.* (*leg.*) the use or tenure of property and the title to it that can be made out in virtue of such use when long continued. [OFr. *user*].
USHER (**1**), [ush'-er], *n.* an officer at any large public gathering who sees to it that only those entitled to enter do so, and guides them to their places; an officer in a ceremony who precedes an important person; formerly, a junior master in a boarding-school. [OFr. *ussier* from L. *ostiarius* door-keeper].
USHER (**2**), [ush'-er], *v.t.* to perform the duties of an usher for, to direct (someone) to his or her place, or announce his arrival; **to u. in**, to come as a prelude to, to be the first intimation of.
USHERETTE, [ush'-er-et'], *n.* a female attendant who shows people to their seats in a cinema, etc [USHER (2)].
USHERSHIP, [ush'-er-ship], *n.* the office and functio of an usher.
USQUEBAUGH†, [usk'-wi-baw], *n.* whiskey. [Ir *uisge beathe*].
USTION, [us'-chun], *n.* the act of burning; the con dition of being burned.
USTULATE, [us'-tyōō-lāt], *adj.* sered or burnt.
USTULATION, [us'-tyōō-lā'-shun], *n.* the act o burning, the condition of being burnt; †the drying o a moist substance before pulverization. [MedL. *ustul atio*].
USUAL, [yōō'-zhōō-al], *adj.* customary; frequentl done, normal, common, commonplace. [L. *usualis*].
USUALLY, [yōō'-zhōō-al-i], *adv.* in accordance wit habit or custom, habitually, normally.
USUALNESS, [yōō'-zhōō-al-nes], *n.* the quality o being usual.
USUCAPTION, USUCAPION, [yōō'-zhōō-kap'-shun, yōō'-zhōō-kāp'-i-on], *n.* (*leg.*) a right to possess derived from long and unquestioned use. [L. *usucap-(t)io* prescription].
USUFRUCT, [yōō'-zhōō-frukt'], *n.* (*leg.*) the right of temporary possession of what is another's on condition that such possession causes no damage to it. [L. *ususfructus*].
USUFRUCTUARY (**1**), [yōō'-zhōō-fruk'-chōō-er-i], *n.* (*leg.*) a person enjoying usufruct.
USUFRUCTUARY (**2**), [yōō'-zhōō-fruk'-chōō-er-i], *adj.* relating to usufruct.
USURER, [yōō'-zher-er], *n.* one who makes his living by lending out money at very high interest. [LL. *usuarius*].
USURIOUS, [yōō-zhōōer'-i-us], *adj.* pertaining to, or making a practice of, usury.
USURIOUSLY, [yōō-zhōōer'-i-us-li], *adv.* in a usurious fashion.
USURIOUSNESS, [yōō-zhōōer'-i-us-nes], *n.* the condition of being usurious.
USURP, [yōō-zurp'], *v.t.* to take wrongful possession of. [L. *usurpare* to obtain].
USURPATION, [yōō'-zer-pā'-shun], *n.* the act of usurping, the fact of having been usurped. [L. *usurpatio*].
USURPATORY, [yōō'-zer-pā'-ter-i], *adj.* pertaining to a usurper or usurpation.
USURPER, [yōō-zurp'-er], *n.* one who usurps, one who has wrongfully seized the crown.
USURPING, [yōō-zurp'-ing], *adj.* wrongfully seizing and holding.
USURPINGLY, [yōō-zurp'-ing-li], *adv.* in a usurping manner.
USURY, [yōō'-zher-i], *n.* the business of making loans at very high rates of interest; interest and profit on this. [L. *usura* use].
UT, [ōōt], *n.* (*mus.*) the first note of Guido's system; the original first note of the tonic solfa scale, doh. [L. *ut* so that].
UTAS, [yōō'-tas], *n.* (*eccles.*) †an octave, the eight days during which a feast is kept up. [OFr. *huiteus* octaves].
UTENSIL, [yōō-ten'-sil], *n.* any vessel or receptacle employed for culinary or domestic purposes. [OFr. *utensile*].
UTERINE, [yōō'-ter-īn], *adj.* having the same mother but not the same father; (*med.*) connected with the uterus. [LL. *uterinus*].
UTEROGESTATION, [yōō'-ter-ō-jes-tā'-shun], *n.* the development of an embryo in the uterus. [UTERUS and GESTATION].
UTERUS, [yōō'-ter-us], *n.* (*med.*) the womb. [L. *uterus*].
UTILITARIAN (**1**), [yōō-til'-it-āer'-i-an], *n.* a believer in utilitarianism.
UTILITARIAN (**2**), [yōō-til'-it-āer'-i-an], *adj.* pertaining to utilitarianism; practical.
UTILITARIANISM, [yōō-til'-it-āer'-i-an-izm], *n.* the doctrine of Jeremy Bentham based on the ideas that to provide the greatest possible happiness for the greatest possible number is the highest ideal, and that utility is the soundest criterion.
UTILITY, [yōō-til'-i-ti], *n.* the quality of being useful; **u. wear, etc.**, clothing, etc., sponsored by the government at officially controlled prices. [L. *utilitas*].
UTILIZABLE, [yōō'-til-īz-abl], *adj.* able to be utilized.
UTILIZATION, [yōō'-til-ī-zā'-shun], *n.* the act of utilizing; the condition or fact of being utilized.
UTILIZE, [yōō'-til-īz], *v.t.* to make useful or profitable. [Fr. *utiliser*].
UTMOST (**1**), [ut'-mōst], *n.* the fullest extent, the

greatest measure, that which implies the most or greatest possible.
UTMOST (2), [ut'-mōst], *adj.* lying farthest away from the centre; (*fig.*) most extreme, greatest, fullest, most. [OE. *utemæst*].
UTOPIA, [yōō-tō'-pi-a], *n.* a fictitious island which Sir Thomas More describes as possessing a perfect political, religious, legal, and economic system; a book describing a similar ideal community; an ideal state. [Coined by Sir Thomas More from Gk. *ou* not, and *topos* place].
UTOPIAN (1), [yōō-tō'-pi-an], *n.* a dweller in Utopia.
UTOPIAN (2), [yōō-tō'-pi-an], *adj.* pertaining to an ideal state or Utopia.
UTOPIANISM, [yōō-tō'-pi-an-izm], *n.* political or social views of an ideal or Utopian nature.
UTRICLE, [yōō'-trikl], *n.* (*anat.*, *bot.*) a bag-like structure, a hollow in the inner ear. [L. *utriculus* little bag].
UTRICULAR, [yōō'-trik'-yōō-ler], *adj.* pertaining to a utricle.
UTRICULATE, [yōō-trik'-yōō-lāt], *adj.* shaped like a utricle.
UTRIFORM, [yōō'-tri-fawm], *adj.* like a leather bottle in shape.
UTTER (1), [ut'-er], *adj.* absolute, without qualification; total; definite, unconditional; †outer. [OE. *utera*].
UTTER (2), [ut'-er], *v.t.* to speak, pronounce, give forth with the voice; to put into circulation. [Uncert.].
UTTERABLE, [ut'-er-abl], *adj.* able to be uttered.
UTTERANCE, [ut'-er-ants], *n.* the act of uttering; speech, pronunciation; a statement, verbal exposition, a speech.
UTTERER, [ut'-er-er], *n.* a person who utters.
UTTERLY, [ut'-er-li], *adv.* fully, completely, totally.
UTTERMOST (1), [ut'-er-mōst], *n.* the greatest extent, highest measure or degree, etc.
UTTERMOST (2), [ut'-er-mōst], *adj.* farthest from the centre; greatest, strongest possible, utmost. [ME. *uttermost*].
UTTERNESS, [ut'-er-nes], *n.* the state of being absolute or extreme.
UVEA, [yōō'-vi-a], *n.* (*anat.*) the inner cover of the iris. [MedL. *uvea*].
UVEAL, [yōō'-vi-al], *adj.* (*anat.*) pertaining to the uvea.
UVULA, (*pl.* **uvulae**), [yōōv'-yōō-la], *n.* (*anat.*) a soft, pendent extension at the back of the palate; a formation resembling this in the bladder or cerebellum. [L. *uvula*].
UVULAR, [yōōv'-yōō-ler], *adj.* relating to the uvula; (*phon.*) spoken with the uvula.
UVULITIS, [yōōv'-yōō-līt'-is], *n.* soreness of the uvula. [UVULA and Gk. *itis* denoting inflammation].
UXORIAL, [uks-aw'-ri-al], *adj.* relating to a wife.
UXORICIDE, [uks-aw'-ri-sīd], *n.* wife-murder; a man who kills his wife.
UXORIOUS, [uks-aw'-ri-us], *adj.* very devoted to one's wife, *esp.* to a foolish degree; wife-ridden. [L. *uxorius*].
UXORIOUSLY, [uks-aw'-ri-us-li], *adv.* in an uxorious way.
UXORIOUSNESS, [uks-aw'-ri-us-nes], *n.* the condition of being uxorious.
UZBEK (1), [ōōz'-bek], *n.* a member of a people inhabiting Russian Central Asia, related to the Turks; the language of these people.
UZBEK (2), [ōōz'-bek], *adj.* of, pertaining or relating to, in the language of, the Uzbeks

V

V, [vē], the twenty-second letter of the alphabet; a symbol of victory; **v. sign**, a sign made by raising two fingers or thumb and forefinger to form a V.
VA, [vah], *v.i.* (*mus.*) go on. [It. *va*].
VACANCY, [vā'-kan-si], *n.* the state of being vacant; the condition of being unoccupied; an unoccupied post, position, or employment. [L. *vacantia*].
VACANT, [vā'-kant], *adj.* empty, unoccupied; (*fig.*) empty-headed; having no tenant. [L. *vacans*].
VACATE, [va-kāt'], *v.t.* *and* *i.* to make vacant, to leave unoccupied; (*leg.*) to annul; to go away (from a place or position). [~L. *vacare*].
VACATION, [va-kā'-shun], *n.* the act of vacating; a formal holiday from a school, university, or court of law. [L. *vacatio*].
VACATIONIST, [va-kā'-shun-ist], *n.* one on a holiday.
VACCIGENOUS, [vak-sij'-en-us], *adj.* producing vaccine virus.
VACCINATE, [vak'-sin-āt], *v.t.* to inoculate with vaccine. [Fr. *vacciner*].
VACCINATION, [vak'-sin-ā'-shun], *n.* inoculation with vaccine.
VACCINATIONIST, [vak'-sin-ā'-shun-ist], *n.* an advocate of (compulsory) vaccination.
VACCINATOR, [vak'-sin-āt-er], *n.* one who vaccinates.
VACCINE, [vak'-sēn], *n.* the virus of cowpox, obtained in lymph, and used for inoculation against smallpox; any similar virus. [L. *vaccinus* relating to cows].
VACCINIA, [vak-sin'-i-a], *n.* cowpox. [MedL. *vaccinia*].
VACHER, [vash'-ā], *n.* a cattle-keeper. [Fr. from *vache* cow].
VACILLANCY, [vas'-il-an-si], *n.* vacillation.
VACILLANT, [vas'-il-ant], *adj.* vacillating.
VACILLATE, [vas'-il-āt], *v.i.* to sway unsteadily; to hesitate, show indecision. [~L. *vacillare*].
VACILLATING, [vas'-il-āt-ing], *adj.* wavering.
VACILLATINGLY, [vas'-il-āt-ing-li], *adv.* in vacillating fashion.
VACILLATION, [vas'-il-ā'-shun], *n.* the act, state of vacillating; mental hesitancy. [L. *vacillatio*].
VACILLATORY, [vas'-il-āt-er-i], *adj.* wavering.
VACUATION, [vak'-yōō-ā'-shun], *n.* evacuation. [MedL. *vacuatio*].
VACUIST, [vak'-yōō-ist], *n.* one believing in the possibility of a natural vacuum.
VACUITY, [vak-ew'-it-i], *n.* emptiness; mental vacancy. [L. *vacuitas*].
VACUOLE, [vak'-yōō-ōl], *n.* a minute cavity in organic tissue. [Fr. *vacuole*]
VACUOUS, [vak'-yōō-us], *adj.* empty; mentally vacant. [L. *vacuus*].
VACUOUSNESS, [vak'-yōō-us-nes], *n.* the state or quality of being vacuous.
VACUUM, [vak'-yōō-um], *n.* a space containing no matter of any kind whatsoever; a space from which the air has been removed. [L. *vacuus* empty].
VACUUM-CLEANER, [vak'-yōō-um-klēn'-er], *n.* a cleaning tool which removes dust, etc., by suction.
VACUUM-FLASK, [vak'-yōō-um-flahsk'], *n.* an evacuated double-walled glass container with silvered interior surface, designed to keep substances at a constant temperature.
VACUUM-TUBE, [vak'-yōō-um-tewb'], *n.* an evacuated electrical discharge-tube with two or more electrodes.
VADE-MECUM, [vā'-di-mē'-kum], *n.* a manual or handbook for ready reference. [L. *vade mecum* go with me].
VAGABOND (1), [vag'-a-bond], *n.* a wandering rogue, a tramp, a person of no fixed residence or means of support.
VAGABOND (2), [vag'-a-bond], *adj.* vagrant, wandering. [L. *vagabundus*].
VAGABONDAGE, [vag'-a-bond'-ij], *n.* the state of being a vagabond.
VAGABONDIZE, [vag'-a-bond'-īz], *v.i.* to wander like a vagabond.
VAGARIOUS, [vag-āer'-i-us], *adj.* having vagaries.
VAGARY, [vag-āer'-i], *n.* an irrational impulse; a whim. [~L. *vagari* to wander].
VAGINA, [va-jīn'-a], *n.* the passage from the uterus to the external orifice in the female mammal; (*bot.*) the sheath in grasses. [L. *vagina* sheath].
VAGINAL, [va-jīn'-al], *adj.* resembling, relating to, of, a sheath or the vagina; in the form of a sheath.

VAGINANT, [vaj-īn'-ant], *adj.* (*bot.*) sheathing.

VAGINATE, [vaj'-in-āt], *adj.* (*bot.*) sheathed.

VAGINATED, [vaj'-in-āt-ed], *adj.* (*bot.*) furnished with a sheath.

VAGINIPENNATE, [va-jīn'-i-pen'-āt], *adj.* (*entom.*) having the wings covered with a hard sheath; sheath-winged. [VAGINA and L. *penna* wing].

VAGINITIS, [vaj'-in-īt'-is], *n.* (*path.*) inflammation of the vagina. [VAGINA and Gk. *itis* denoting inflammation].

VAGRANCY, [vā'-gran-si], *n.* the state of being or living as a vagrant.

VAGRANT (1), [vā'-grant], *n.* a tramp, a person wandering about the countryside without means of support.

VAGRANT (2), [vā'-grant], *adj.* wandering as a tramp; like, relating to, a vagrant. [ME. *vagaraunt*].

VAGUE, [vāg], *adj.* undefined, not distinct, uncertain; mentally unprecise. [Fr. *vague*].

VAGUELY, [vāg'-li], *adv.* in a vague manner.

VAGUENESS, [vāg'-nes], *n.* the state of being vague.

VAIL, [vāl], *v.t.* to remove (a hat); to lower respectfully. [Fr. *avaler* to let fall].

VAILS, [vālz], *n.*(*pl.*) gratuities to servants. [~AVAIL].

VAIN, [vān], *adj.* empty, useless, fruitless; conceited; **in v.,** idly, to no effect. [L. *vanus* empty].

VAINGLORIOUS, [vān-glaw'-ri-us], *adj.* ostentatiously boastful.

VAINGLORIOUSLY, [vān-glaw'-ri-us-li], *adv.* with vainglory.

VAINGLORY, [vān'-glaw'-ri], *n.* ostentatious vanity; empty pride; boastfulness. [ME. *vainglorie*].

VAINLY, [vān'-li], *adv.* in vain; proudly; foolishly; conceitedly.

VAINNESS, [vān'-nes], *n.* the state, condition of being vain.

VAIR, [vāer], *n.* (*her.*) a kind of fur represented by little bell-shaped pieces, alternately of two colours. [OFr. *vair*].

VAISHNAVA, [vīsh-nah'-vah], *n.* one of a sect among the Hindus, who, in their creed and worship, assign the first place to Vishnu. [Skr. *vaishnava* belonging to Vishnu.

VAISYA, [vīz'-ya], *n.* the third Hindu caste, the merchants and farmers; a member of this. [Skr. *vaisya*].

VAKEEL, [va-kēl'], *n.* a native Indian attorney. [Urdu *wakil*].

VALANCE, [val'-ants], *n.* a drapery hanging down from a window-shelf, the framework of a bed, or an open cupboard, etc. [ME. *valaunce*].

VALE (1), [vāl], *n.* a valley. [L. *vallis* valley].

VALE (2), [vāl'-i], *n.* a farewell salutation. [L. *vale* be well].

VALEDICTION, [val-i-dik'-shun], *n.* a farewell; a bidding farewell. [L. *valedictio*].

VALEDICTORY, [val'-i-dik'-ter-i], *adj.* relating to, of the nature of, a valediction.

VALENCE, [vā'-lents], *n.* valency.

VALENCIANITE, [val-ensh'-an-īt], *n.* a variety of adularia named from the *Valencian* mine in which it was found.

VALENCIENNES, [val'-ahn-syen'], *n.* a kind of lace made at *Valenciennes* in France.

VALENCY, [vāl'-en-si], *n.* the combining potentialities of a chemical substance, measured by comparison with those of hydrogen. [L. *valentia*].

VALENTIA, [val-en'-sha], *n.* a stuff of worsted, cotton and silk. [*Valencia* in Spain].

VALENTINE, [val'-en-tīn], *n.* a greeting-card, usually of an amorous nature, sent on St. Valentine's Day.

VALENTINITE, [val-en'-tin-īt], *n.* oxide of antimony.

VALERIAN, [val-ēer'-i-an], *n.* a perennial plant of the genus *Valeriana*, the medicinal root of *Valeriana officinalis*. [MedL. *valeriana*].

VALERIC, [val-e'-rik], *adj.* derived from valerian.

VALET (1), [val'-et, val'-i], *n.* a male personal servant. [OFr. *valet*].

VALET (2), [val'-et], *v.t. and i.* to care for, or repair (clothes) in the manner of a valet; to act as a valet. [*Prec.*].

VALETUDINARIAN, [val'-i-tewd-in-āer'-i-an], *n. and adj.* one who is, relating to one who is, perpetually sickly; preoccupied with one's own diseases. [L. *valetudinarius*].

VALETUDINARIANISM, [val'-i-tewd-in-āer'-i-an-izm], *n.* the state of being valetudinarian.

VALETUDINARY, [val'-i-tewd'-in-er-i], *adj.* valetudinarian. [L. *valetudinarius*].

VALHALLA, [val'-hal'-a], *n.* (*myth.*) Odin's Hall in Asgard, where heroes slain in battle go. [OIcel. *valhel*].

VALIANCE, [val'-yants], *n.* valour, courage. [OFr *vaillance*].

VALIANCY, [val'-yan-si], *n.* valiantness.

VALIANT, [val'-yant], *adj.* brave, showing valour; requiring great courage to perform. [OFr. *vaillant*].

VALIANTLY, [val'-yant-li], *adv.* bravely.

VALIANTNESS, [val'-yant-nes], *n.* valour.

VALID, [val'-id], *adj.* effectively true, based on good reason; (*leg.*) having legal force, maintainable in a court of law. [L. *validus* strong].

VALIDATE, [val'-i-dāt], *v.t.* to make valid; to maintain the validity of. [~MedL. *validare*].

VALIDATION, [val'-i-dā'-shun], *n.* the act of validating; state of being validated.

VALIDITY, [val-id'-it-i], *n.* the quality of being valid; legal force. [MedL. *validitas*].

VALIDLY, [val'-id-li], *adv.* in a valid manner.

VALIDNESS, [val'-id-nes], *n.* the state of being valid.

VALINCH, [va-linch'], *n.* a tube for drawing liquors from a cask by the bunghole. [Span. *venencia*].

VALISE, [va-lēs'], *n.* a rolled travelling-bag carried slung to a horse's saddle; any large travelling bag. [Fr. *valise*].

VALKYREAN, [val-ki'-ri-an], *adj.* pertaining to the Valkyries.

VALKYR(IE), [val'-kēr, val'-ki-ri], *n.* one of the twelve Norse goddesses who chose those to be killed in battle, and carried them to Valhalla. [OIcel. *valkyrja*].

VALLANCY, [val'-an-si], *n.* a heavy seventeenth-century wig. [Uncert.].

VALLAR, [val'-er], *adj.* pertaining to a rampart. [L. *vallaris*].

VALLARY, [val'-er-i], *adj.* vallar.

VALLATION, [val-ā'-shun], *n.* an earthwork fortification. [L. *vallatio*].

VALLECULA, [va-lek'-yōō-la], *n.* a groove or small furrow. [L. *vallecula*].

VALLEY, [val'-i], *n.* a narrow tract of low-lying land between more or less parallel ridges of higher ground; a low-lying river-basin. [L. *vallis* valley].

VALLEYBOARD, [val'-i-bawd], *n.* a board supporting a gutter along the concave angle of two roofs.

VALLUM, [val'-um], *n.* a rampart of earth. [L. *vallum*].

VALONIA, [val-ōn'-i-a], *n.* the acorn of *Quercus Ægilops* from which tannin is extracted. [It. *vallonia*].

VALOROUS, [val'-er-us], *adj.* valiant; calling for valour. [MedL. *valorosus*].

VALLEYBOARD

VALOROUSLY, [val'-er-us-li], *adv.* in a volorous manner.

VALOUR, [val'-er], *n.* extreme, active, rather spectacular courage. [L. *valor* worth].

VALSE, [vals], *n.* a waltz. [Fr. *valse* waltz].

VALUABLE (1), [val'-yōō-abl], *n.* that which is of value; a costly personal possession or trinket.

VALUABLE (2), [val'-yōō-abl], *adj.* having material worth, being of value; highly useful; estimable.

VALUABLENESS, [val'-yōō-abl-nes], *n.* the quality of being valuable.

VALUATION, [val'-yōō-ā'-shun], *n.* the act of valuing; the estimated monetary worth of a thing; estimation.

VALUATOR, [val'-yōō-āt-er], *n.* one who evaluates.

VALUE (1), [val'-yōō], *n.* worth, importance, monetary price; desirability; quality; exact force (of a word or syllable). [OFr. *value*].

VALUE (2), [val'-yōō], *v.t.* to place a value on; to estimate the worth or monetary price of; to prize.

VALUED, [val'-yōōd], *adj.* regarded as valuable.

VALUELESS, [val'-yōō-les], *adj.* of no value; worthless.

VALUER, [val'-yōō-er], *n.* one who makes valuations.

VALVE, [valv], *n.* an aperture and its covering, regarded as a control over entrance and exit, *esp.* when operated automatically; a door, an opening; a leaf of a folding door; (*elect.*) a vacuum tube used to control the direction and strength of electric currents; (*biol.*) a mollusc shell, one of the leaves of a mollusc shell. [L. *valva* folding-door].

VALVED, [valvd], *adj.* having a valve.

VALVELET, [valv'-let], *n.* a little valve; (*bot.*) one of the pieces which form the outer covering of a pericarp.

VALVULAR, [valv'-yōō-ler], *adj.* containing, relating to, a valve, *esp.* of the heart.

VALVULE, [valv'-yōōl], *n.* (*biol.*) a small, simple valve.

VAMBRACE, [vam'-brās], *n.* armour worn on the forearm. [AFr. *vantbras*].

VAMOOSE, [va-mo͞os'], *v.i.* to go away rapidly; (*slang*) to decamp. [Span. *vamos* let us go].

VAMP (1), [vamp], *n.* a woman who indulges in the art of attracting men. [~VAMPIRE].

VAMP (2), [vamp], *n.* the front portion of a shoe; a patch on a shoe; an improvised musical accompaniment. [OFr. *avampié* before the foot].

VAMP (3), [vamp], *v.t.* to set to work on (a man) in order to attract him sexually. [VAMP (1)].

VAMP (4), [vamp], *v.t. and i.* to patch (a shoe); to do up (old material) to look like new; to improvise a musical accompaniment. [VAMP (2)].

VAMPER, [vamp'-er], *n.* one who vamps.

VAMPIRE, [vamp'-īer], *n.* the malignant spirit of a dead person which brings the body out of its grave to suck the blood of the living; (*fig.*) an unscrupulous extortioner; **v. bat,** a blood-sucking bat. [Fr. *vampire*].

VAMPIRISM, [vamp'-īer-izm], *n.* belief in vampires; the conduct of a vampire.

VAMPLATE, [vam'-plāt], *n.* the guard for the hand in a medieval lance. [AFr. *vaunplate*].

VAMPLET, [vamp'-let], *n.* a vamplate.

VAN (1), [van], *n.* a vanguard, *esp.* the front of an army in line of battle. [~VANGUARD].

VAN (2), [van], *n.* a covered cart or truck. [~CARAVAN].

VAN (3), [van], *n.* a winnowing-fan. [L. *vannus*].

VANADIATE, [van-ād'-i-āt], *n.* a salt of vanadic acid. [VANADIUM].

VANADIC, [van-ad'-ik], *adj.* obtained from vanadium.

VANADINITE, [van-ad'-in-īt], *n.* a mineral, vanadiate of lead.

VANADIUM, [van-ād'-i-um], *n.* the metallic element denoted by V; **v. steel,** steel alloyed with vanadium. [OIcel. *Vanadis*, the goddess Freya].

VAN-COURIER, [van'-ko͝o'-ri-er], *n.* a precursor. [VAN (1) and COURIER].

VANDAL, [van'-dal], *n.* one who destroys or spoils natural beauties or works of art, out of carelessness or deliberate spite. [L. *Vandali*, a Germanic race famed for their destructive violence].

VANDALIC, [van-dal'-ik], *adj.* relating to a vandal or the Vandals.

VANDALISM, [van'-dal-izm], *n.* the behaviour, spirit, of the Vandals; the wanton destruction of beautiful things.

VANDYKE, [van-dīk'], *n.* an elaborately bordered lace collar; a picture painted by Van Dyck; **v. beard,** a close-cut, pointed beard; **v. brown,** a rich brown pigment. [*Van Dyck* the Flemish painter].

VANE, [vān], *n.* a weathercock; one of the wings of a windmill or propeller. [OE. *fana* flag].

VAN-FOSS, [van'-fos], *n.* (*fort.*) a ditch on the outside of the counterscarp. [~Fr. *avant-fossé*].

VANG, [vang], *n.* (*naut.*) a guy rope for the peak of a gaff. [~FANG].

VANGUARD, [van'-gahd], *n.* an advance guard. [Fr. *avant-garde*].

VANILLA, [van-il'-a], *n.* a tropical American plant from the pods of one species of which a flavouring substance is extracted; the flavouring itself. [~Span. *vainilla*].

VANISH, [van'-ish], *v.i.* to disappear suddenly and completely. [~OFr. *esvanir*].

VANISHING, [van'-ish-ing], *adj.* disappearing; **v. cream,** a skin-cream that is absorbed soon after application.

VANITY, [van'-it-i], *n.* uselessness, emptiness, worthlessness; conceit, self-pride; **v. bag,** a small handbag for cosmetics, etc. [L. *vanitas* worthlessness].

VANNER (1), [van'-er], *n.* a horse that pulls a van. [VAN (2)].

VANNER (2), [van'-er], *n.* an ore separator. [VAN (3)].

VANNING, [van'-ing], *n.* winnowing, *esp.* the act of separating ore by shaking in a shovel.

VANQUISH, [vang'-kwish], *v.t.* to conquer; to defeat completely. [OFr. *venquir* from L. *vincere*].

VANQUISHABLE, [vang'-kwish-abl], *adj.* that may be vanquished.

VANQUISHER, [vang'-kwish-er], *n.* one who vanquishes.

VANSIRE, [van'-sīer], *n.* a mongoose inhabiting Madagascar and Bourbon. [Fr. *vansire*].

VANTAGE, [vahnt'-ij], *n.* the state of having advantage in combat; a place that overlooks another; (*tennis*) the next point after deuce. [~ADVANTAGE].

VANTAGE-GROUND, [vahnt'-ij-grownd], *n.* a commanding or advantageous position, *esp.* in military operations.

VAPID, [vap'-id], *adj.* flat, lifeless, stupidly insipid, empty-headed. [L. *vapidus*].

VAPIDITY, [vap-id'-it-i], *n.* vapidness.

VAPIDLY, [vap'-id-li], *adv.* in a vapid manner.

VAPIDNESS, [vap'-id-nes], *n.* the state of being vapid.

VAPORABILITY, [vāp'-er-a-bil'-it-i], *n.* the capacity of being converted into vapour.

VAPORABLE, [vāp'-er-abl], *adj.* capable of being converted into vapour.

VAPORIFIC, [vāp'-er-if'-ik], *adj.* tending to vaporize.

VAPORIMETER, [vāp'-er-im'-it-er], *n.* an instrument for measuring the pressure of a vapour.

VAPORIZABLE, [vāp'-er-īz-abl], *adj.* capable of being converted into vapour.

VAPORIZATION, [vāp'-er-īz-ā'-shun], *n.* the process of vaporizing; the artificial formation of vapour.

VAPORIZE, [vāp'-er-īz], *v.t. and i.* to convert into vapour; to become vapour.

VAPORIZER, [vāp'-or-īz-er], *n.* an apparatus for converting substances into vapour or fine spray.

VAPOROUS, [vāp'-er-us], *adj.* like, consisting of, or filled with, vapour. [L. *vaporus*].

VAPOROUSNESS, [vāp'-er-us-nes], *n.* the quality of being vaporous.

VAPOUR (1), [vāp'-er], *n.* moisture suspended visibly in the air; the gas of a substance; (*fig.*) an empty imagining; (*pl.*) hysterical fainting fits. [L. *vapor*].

VAPOUR (2), [vāp'-er], *v.i.* to spout windy nonsense.

VAPOUR-BATH, [vāp'-er-bahth], *n.* the immersion of one's body in hot vapour; the place where this is done.

VAPOURED, [vāp'-erd], *adj.* suffering from the vapours.

VAPOURER, [vāp'-er-er], *n.* the moth, *Orayia antiqua*, the male of which has a distinctive quivering flight; (*coll.*) a windy, pretentious talker.

VAPOURING, [vāp'-er-ing], *n.* windy, pretentious talk.

VAPOURINGLY, [vāp'-er-ing-li], *adv.* in a pretentiously windy fashion.

VAPOURISH, [vāp'-er-ish], *adj.* tending to suffer from the vapours.

VAPOURY, [vāp'-er-i], *adj.* full of vapours; hypochondriac.

VAPULATION, [vap'-yo͞o-lā'-shun], *n.* flogging. [~L. *vapulare* to flog].

VAQUERO, [va-kāer'-ō], *n.* a herdsman. [Span. *vaquero*].

VARANGIAN, [va-ran'-ji-an], *adj.* relating to those Norsemen who penetrated Russia and served the Byzantine Emperors. [OIcel. *væringi* confederate].

VARANUS, [va-rān'-us], *n.* a monitor lizard. [Arab. *varan*].

VARANUS

VARE, [vāer], *n.* a wand or staff of authority. [Span. *vara*].

VAREC, [va'-rek], *n.* kelp. [Fr. *varec*].

VARI, [vah'-ri], *n.* a species of lemur found in Madagascar. [Malagasy *varianda*].

VARIABILITY, [vāer'-i-a-bil'-it-i], *n.* variableness.

VARIABLE (1), [vāer'-i-abl], *n.* an indeterminate number.

VARIABLE (2), [vāer'-i-abl], *adj.* able, liable, to vary; (*math.*) indeterminate. [L. *variabilis*].

VARIABLENESS, [vāer'-i-abl-nes], *n.* the state of being variable.

VARIABLY, [vāer'-i-ab-li], *adv.* in variable fashion.

VARIAMENTO, [vah'-ri-a-ment'-ō], *adv.* (*mus.*) to be played in a free and varied manner. [It. *variamento*].

VARIANCE, [vāer'-i-ants], *n.* difference of opinion; an observed variation between two similar objects; discrepancy; discord between persons. [L. *variantia*].

VARIANT (1), [vāer'-i-ant], *n.* that which is variant.

VARIANT (2), [vāer'-i-ant], *adj.* varying, differing from type. [L. *varians*].

VARIATE, [vāer'-i-āt], *v.t. and i.* to make different; to vary. [L. *variatus*].

VARIATION, [vāer-i-ā'-shun], *n.* the act or process of varying, a partial modification of qualities or form; a state or form or quality consequent upon change, alteration; degree of change; (*astron.*) change in orbit, *esp.* of the moon in relation to the sun; (*biol.*) organic deviation from a norm; (*naut.*) declination of a

ō (bone), ī (fine), o͞o (food), o͝o (put), u (up), th (*th*ink), TH (*th*at), zh (azure), † = obsolete, ~ = related to.

magnetic needle from true North; (*mus.*) development and elaboration of a theme. [OFr. *variation*].

VARIATIONAL, [vāer'-i-ā'-shun-al], *adj.* of, or pertaining to, (biological) variation or variations.

VARICELLA, [va'-ri-sel'-a], *n.* (*med.*) chicken-pox. [~VARIOLA].

VARICOCELE, [va'-ri-kō-sēl'], *n.* (*path.*) abnormal enlargement of the scrotum veins. [VARICOSE and Gk. *kele* tumour].

VARICOSE, [va'-ri-kōs], *adj.* of, or affected by, abnormal swellings of the veins. [L. *varicosus*].

VARICOSITY, [va'-ri-kos'-it-i], *n.* the state of being varicose.

VARIED, [vāer'-id], *adj.* having variety, characterized by changes.

VARIEGATE, [vāer'-i-gāt], *v.t.* to make parti-coloured. [~LL. *variegare*].

VARIEGATED, [vāer'-i-gāt-id], *adj.* having various colours on one surface, parti-coloured.

VARIEGATION, [vāer'-i-gā'-shun], *n.* the process of variegating; the state of being variegated.

VARIETAL, [va-rī'-it-al], *adj.* (*biol.*) relating to a variety as distinct from a species.

VARIETY, [va-rī'-it-i], *n.* the state or quality characterized by many facets, aspects, and diverse units, antonym of *monotony*; a group of diverse elements or objects; something with distinguishing characteristics, one of a kind; an entertainment in the theatre composed of various short turns, vaudeville; (*biol.*, *bot.*) a sub-group distinguished from a species only by various unimportant characteristic features. [L. *varietas*].

VARIFORM, [vāer'-i-fawm], *adj.* having a variety of form.

VARIFORMED, [vāer'-i-fawmd], *adj.* variform.

VARIOLA, [va-rī'-ō-la], *n.* (*med.*) smallpox. [L. *varius*].

VARIOLAR, [va-rī'-ō-ler], *adj.* (*med.*) relating to smallpox.

VARIOLITE, [vāer'-i-ō-līt], *n.* (*min.*) a dark green variety of felspar with a pock-marked appearance due to the incidence of pieces of lighter stone.

VARIOLOID, [vāer'-i-ō-loid], *n.* (*med.*) a mild attack of smallpox after preliminary vaccination.

VARIOLOUS, [va-rī'-ō-lus], *adj.* variolar.

VARIOMETER, [vāer'-i-om'-it-er], *n.* (*wirel.*) a variable inductance for adjusting a receiving set to different wavelengths. [VARIOUS and METER].

VARIORUM, [vāer'-i-aw'-rum], *adj.* annotated by various experts. [L. *variorum*, *gen. pl.*, of *various*].

VARIOUS, [vāer'-i-us], *adj.* characterized by diversity, different, varied; many, numerous, *esp.* unlike, of different kinds; †versatile. [L. *varius*].

VARIOUSLY, [vāer'-i-us-li], *adv.* by various means.

VARISCITE, [va-ris'-īt], *n.* (*min.*) a phosphate of aluminium. [*Variscia*, where discovered].

VARIX, (*pl.* **varices**), [vāer'-iks], *n.* (*med.*) a varicose vein; (*zool.*) a rib on a shell. [L. *varix* swollen vein].

VARLET†, [vah'-let], *n.* a page, a knight's groom; a rascal, a low-class fellow. [OFr. *varlet* groom].

VARLETRY†, [vah'-let-ri], *n.* the rabble.

VARMINT, [vah'-mint], *n.* (*dial.*) a rascal. [~VERMIN].

VARNISH (1), [vah'-nish], *n.* a resinous, oily substance applied to surfaces to impart a protective gloss; (*fig.*) an appearance of worth designed to conceal faults and flaws. [OFr. *vernis*].

VARNISH (2), [vah'-nish], *v.t.* to cover with varnish; (*fig.*) to hide defects by using brilliant externals or superficialities. [OFr. *vernisser*].

VARNISHER, [vah'-nish-er], *n.* one employed to apply varnish.

VARNISHING, [vah'-nish-ing], *n.* the process of applying a varnish.

VARSITY, [vah'-si-ti], *n.* (*coll.*) university.

VARSOVIENNE, [vah-sō'-vi-en'], *n.* a Polish dance to mazurka rhythm; the music for such a dance. [Fr. (*danse*) *varsovienne*].

VARVELS, [vah'-velz], *n.*(*pl.*) identification rings placed on hawk's legs. [Fr. *vervelles*].

VARVICITE, [vah'-vis-īt], *n.* (*min.*) an oxide of manganese. [MdL. *Varvicia* Warwickshire].

VARY, (**varied, varies, varying**), [vāer'-i], *v.t. and i.* to change, to alter, modify, to diversify, variegate; to become different in condition or quality. [L. *variare*].

VASCULAR, [vas'-kyōō-ler], *adj.* (*biol.*, *bot.*) relating to or possessing a circulatory system. [~L. *vasculum*].

VASCULARITY, [vas'-kyōō-la'-rit-i], *n.* the condition of being vascular.

VASCULIFEROUS, [vas'-kyōō-lif'-er-us], *adj.* (*bot.*) bearing cellular seed-vessels. [VASCULAR and L. *ferre* to bear].

VASCULUM, [vas'-kyōō-lum], *n.* (*bot.*) a metal collecting case. [L. *vasculum* vessel].

VASE, [vahz], *n.* a vessel, usually of a cylindrical form with a deep bowl, wider in girth than the rim, used for holding liquid or as an ornament in the house. [L. *vas* vessel].

VASELINE, [vas'-el-ēn'], *n.* (*prot.*) a preparation of petroleum jelly to apply to the skin.

VASSAL, [vas'-al], *n.* a person kept in a state of subjection, a slave; †a tenant who has sworn fealty and homage to a feudal lord in return for a holding of land. [OFr. *vassal*].

VASSALAGE, [vas'-al-ij], *n.* subjection, servitude; †the social status of a vassal. [MedL. *vassalagium*].

VASSALED, [vas'-ald], *adj.* held in subjection.

VASSALRY†, [vas'-al-ri], *n.* total number of vassals.

VAST, [vahst], *adj.* characterized by enormous size, height, breadth, bulk, or by a great number; extremely important. [L. *vastus*].

VASTITUDE, [vahst'-i-tewd], *n.* vastness.

VASTLY, [vahst'-li], *adv.* to a vast extent; extremely.

VASTNESS, [vahst'-nes], *n.* the condition of being vast.

VASTY†, [vahst'-i], *adj.* vast.

VAT, [vat], *n.* a large tub or storing vessel for liquids, *esp.* spirituous liquors. [OE. *fæt*].

VATIC, [vat'-ik], *adj.* prophetic. [~L. *vates* seer].

VATICAN, [vat'-ik-an], *n.* the papal residence and a district in Rome ruled over by the Pope as a temporal sovereign. [L. *Vaticanus* name of a hill in Rome].

VATICANISM, [vat'-ik-an-izm], *n.* the theory of papal infallibility, ultramontanism.

VATICANIST, [vat'-ik-an-ist], *n.* a believer in Vaticanism.

VATICIDE, [vat'-i-sīd], *n.* the murder or murderer of a prophet. [L. *vates* prophet and *caedere* to kill].

VATICINAL, [vat-is'-in-al], *adj.* resembling, originating in, prophecy, prophetic. [~L. *vaticinus* foretelling].

VATICINATE, [vat-is'-in-āt], *v.t. and i.* to prophesy. [~L. *vaticinari*].

VATICINATION, [vat'-is-in-ā'-shun], *n.* prophecy. [L. *vaticinatio*].

VATICINATOR, [vat-is'-in-āt-or], *n.* a prophet.

VAUDEVILLE, [vō'-de-vil'], *n.* mixed entertainment in a theatre, variety; †a couplet form of light verse popular for humorous use in seventeenth-century France. [*Vau de Vire*, in France, where originated].

VAUDOIS (1), (*pl.* **Vaudois**), [vō'-dwah], *n.* an inhabitant of the canton of Vaud in Switzerland. [Fr. *Vaudois*].

VAUDOIS (2), (*pl.* **Vaudois**), [vō'-dwah], *n.* a member of a much persecuted Protestant sect of Piedmont, etc. [Fr. *Vaudois* from Peter *Waldo*, the founder].

VAULT (1), [vawlt], *n.* an arched roof; a chamber formed by the arched foundations of a building; a strongly guarded and protected room used for the storage of money, valuables, and bonds; an underground cave; a repository for the dead. [LL. *volta*].

VAULT

VAULT (2), [vawlt], *n.* the act of vaulting.

VAULT (3), [vawlt], *v.t. and i.* to leap by using one hand and arm as a support. [OFr. *volter* to leap].

VAULT (4), [vawlt], *v.t.* to equip with a vault.

VAULTAGE, [vawlt'-ij], *n.* space in a vault.

VAULTED, [vawlt'-id], *adj.* built in the form of a vault.

VAULTER, [vawlt'-er], *n.* one who vaults.

VAULTY, [vawlt'-i], *adj.* resembling a vault.

VAUNT (1), [vawnt], *n.* a boast, ostentatious display. [OFr. *vaunt*].

VAUNT (2), [vawnt], *v.t. and i.* to boast, flaunt.

VAUNT-COURIER†, [vawnt-kōō'-ri-er], *n.* an advance guard, a harbinger. [Fr. *avant-courier*].

VAUNTER, [vawnt'-er], *n.* boaster.

VAUNTFUL, [vawnt'-fōōl], *adj.* given to vaunting.

VAUNTING, [vawnt'-ing], *adj.* boasting.

VAUNTINGLY, [vawnt'-ing-li], *adv.* in a vaunting manner.

VAUNTMURE, [vawnt'-mew(r)], *n.* (*fort.*) a work

thrown out in front of the main fortification. [Fr. *avant* before and *mur* wall].
VAUQUELINITE, [vōk'-lin-īt], *n.* (*min.*) a chromate of copper and lead. [Fr. *vauquelinite*].
VAVASOUR, [vav'-a-sōōer], *n.* (*hist.*) a subtenant to a feudal vassal. [OFr. *vavassor*].
VAVASORY, [vav'-a-ser-i], *n.* (*hist.*) the rights and obligations of a vavasour.
VEADAR, [vi-ā'-dah(r)], *n.* the additional month of the Jewish ecclesiastical year. [Heb. *veadar*].
VEAL, [vēl], *n.* flesh of a calf prepared for eating. [OFr. *veal*].
V-BOMB, [vē'-bom'], *n.* any one of various robot projectiles, *esp.* a flying bomb or a rocket, employed by the Germans as "retaliation weapons." [Germ. *Vergehtungswaffe*].
VECTION, [vek'-shun], *n.* the action of carrying. [L. *vectio*].
VECTITATION, [vek'-ti-tā'-shun], *n.* vection. [L. *vectitatio*].
VECTOR, [vek'-ter], *n.* (*math.*) a line from a point to the centre of a circle; a quantity having both magnitude and direction; (*med.*) the animal or channel by which an infectious disease is carried from one human being to another. [L. *vector*].
VEDA, [vā'-da], *n.* a collection of writings stating the fundamentals of Brahminism. [Skr. *veda* wisdom].
VEDANGA, [vā-dang'-ga], *n.* one of the six commentaries on the Veda. [Skr. *vedanga* limb].
VEDANTA, [vā-dan'-ta], *n.* a philosophic system of the Hindus. [VEDA and Skr. *anta* end].
VEDDAH, [ved'-ah], *n.* an aboriginal of Ceylon. [Singhalese *veddah* hunter].
VEDETTE, [ve-det'], *n.* (*milit., hist.*) a mounted sentry. [Fr. *vedette*].
VEDIC, [vā'-dik], *adj.* of, or from the Veda.
VEER, [vēer], *v.t. and i.* (*fig.*) to hold different opinions alternately; to cause to deviate from a course or position; (*naut.*) to pay out chain; **to v. away,** to slacken and let run; **to v. over,** to swing over, to tilt over from one angle to another. [Fr. *virer* to turn].
VEERING, [vēer'-ing], *n.* the process of shifting in the wind.
VEERINGLY, [vēer'-ing-li], *adv.* in a veering manner.
VEGA, [vē'-ga], *n.* (*astrol.*) the most noticeable star in Lyra. [MedL. *Vega*].
VEGETABILITY, [vej'-it-a-bil'-it-i], *n.* the quality of being vegetable.
VEGETABLE (1), [vej'-it-abl], *n.* a plant; (any part of) a plant cultivated as food.
VEGETABLE (2), [vej'-it-abl], *adj.* relating to, composed of, derived from, plants or vegetables. [LL. *vegetabilis* invigorating].
VEGETAL, [vej'-it-al], *adj.* relating to, resembling, a vegetable; (*physiol.*) relating to functional development. [L. *vegetus* vigorous].
VEGETALINE, [vej'-it-al-ēn], *n.* vegetable ivory.
VEGETARIAN (1), [vej'-it-āer'-i-an], *n.* a person who lives on a vegetable diet or a diet excluding flesh.
VEGETARIAN (2), [vej'-it-āer'-i-an], *adj.* consisting of vegetables, made for a vegetarian; relating to the principles of a vegetarian.
VEGETARIANISM, [vej'-it-āer'-i-an-ism], *n.* the theory or practice of a vegetarian.
VEGETATE, [vej'-it-āt], *v.i.* to pass a passive existence like a plant. [~L. *vegetare* to invigorate].
VEGETATION, [vej'-it-ā'-shun], *n.* the process of vegetating; vegetable growth. [LL. *vegetatio*].
VEGETATIVE, [vej'-i-tat-iv], *adj.* able to grow; (*fig.*) passive in mode of life. [MedL. *vegetativus*].
VEGETATIVENESS, [vej'-it-at-iv-nes], *n.* the condition of being vegetative.
VEHEMENCE, [vē'-i-ments], *n.* the condition of being vehement or violent; urgency, ardour. [LL. *vehementia*].
VEHEMENCY, [vē'-i-men-si], *n.* vehemence.
VEHEMENT, [vē'-i-ment], *adj.* full of power, functioning forcefully, violent, ardent, urgent, passionate. [L. *vehemens* eager].
VEHEMENTLY, [vē'-i-ment-li], *adv.* to a vehement degree; in vehement fashion.
VEHICLE, [vē'-ikl], *n.* any means of conveyance on wheels designed for the transport of persons or goods; a means or medium of communication; (*painting*) a medium for paint. [L. *vehiculum* carriage].
VEHICULAR, [vē-hik'-yōō-ler], *adj.* of, relating to, or resembling, a vehicle or vehicles.
VEHICULATORY, [vē-hik'-yōō-lat-er-i], *adj.* vehicular.
VEHMGERICHT, FEHMGERICHT, [fām'-ge-rikht], *n.* a court of justice, usually held in secret, in Germany in the Middle Ages. [Germ. *vehmgericht* court of punishment].
VEHMIC, FEHMIC, [fām'-ik], *adj.* relating to, resembling, or originating in, the vehmgericht.
VEIL (1), [vāl], *n.* a piece of open-work or semi-transparent fabric offering partial concealment; a decorative covering for a woman's face; (*fig.*) that which obscures; **to take the v.,** to enter a convent. [OFr. *veile*].
VEIL (2), [vāl], *v.t.* to cover with a veil; to obscure.
VEILING, [vāl'-ing], *n.* material used for veils.
VEILLESS, [vāl'-les], *adj.* without a veil.
VEILLEUSE, [vā'-yurz'], *n.* a dim night-light. [Fr. *veilleuse* that watches at night].
VEIN (1), [vān], *n.* one of the main tubular channels of the circulation system by which blood passes back to the heart and lungs; that which looks like a vein; (*fig.*) a distinctive trait, underlying quality characteristic of a person's temperament; (*geol.*) a seam of a mineral or minerals running through rock; a streak different in quality from surrounding matter. [OFr. *veine* from L. *vena*].
VEIN (2), [vān], *v.t.* to introduce veins into.
VEINAGE, [vān'-ij], *n.* a collection or system of veins.
VEINED, [vānd], *adj.* having veins.
VEINING, [vān'-ing], *n.* a delicate form of needlework on muslin.
VEINLESS, [vān'-les], *adj.* without veins.
VEINLET, [vān'-let], *n.* a small vein.
VEINOUS, [vān'-us], *adj.* relating to veins.
VEINSTONE, [vān'-stōn], *n.* (*geol.*) the rock surrounding a vein.
VEINULE, [vān'-yōōl], *n.* a very small vein.
VEINY, [vān'-i], *adj.* full of veins.
VELAR, [vēl'-ar], *adj.* of, pertaining to, or sounded by means of, the velum or soft palate. [L. *velaris*].
VELARIUM, [vel-āer'-i-um], *n.* a large protective awning, used in ancient Rome. [L. *velarium*].
VELDT, [felt], *n.* a large stretch of wild open country in South Africa. [Du. *veld*].
VELETA, [vel-ēt'-a], *n.* a kind of ballroom dance based on the waltz. [Invented].
VELIFEROUS, [vel-if'-er-us], *adj.* †fitted with sails; (*zool.*) having a velum. [L. *velum* sail and *ferre* to bear].
VELITE, [vē'-līt], *n.* a lightly armed foot-soldier of ancient Roman armies. [L. *veles velitis*].
VELL, [vel], *n.* a rennet bag. [Unkn.].
VELLEITY, [vel-ē'-it-i], *n.* (*philos.*) volition too weak to express itself in action. [MedL. *velleitas*].
VELLICATE, [vel'-i-kāt], *v.t. and i.* to twitch. [~L. *vellicare*].
VELLICATION, [vel'-ik-ā'-shun], *n.* the act of twitching.
VELLICATIVE, [vel'-ik-at-iv], *adj.* able to twitch.
VELLON, [vel'-on], *n.* (*hist.*) money used in Spain for accounting purposes. [Span. *vellon*].
VELLUM, [vel'-um], *n.* skin specially prepared for use as writing material or bookbinding. [OFr. *velin*].
VELLUMY, [vel'-um-i], *adj.* like vellum.
VELOCE, [vel-ō'-chi], *adv.* (*mus.*) with great speed. [It. *veloce*].
VELOCIMAN, [vel-os'-i-man], *n.* a primitive cycle worked by hand.
VELOCIMETER, [vel'-os-im'-it-er], *n.* an instrument for measuring speed. [L. *velox* swift and METER].
VELOCIPEDE, [vel-os'-i-pēd'], *n.* a kind of wheeled vehicle propelled by the feet of the passenger. [L. *velox* swift and *pes pedem* foot].
VELOCIPEDIST, [vel-os'-i-pēd-ist], *n.* one who rides a velocipede.
VELOCITY, [vel-os'-it-i], *n.* rate of motion, speed, swiftness. [L. *velocitas*].

VELOCIPEDE

VELOUR (1), [vel-ōōer'], *n.* a heavy, velvet-like material; a hat of this material. [OFr. *velour*].
VELOUR (2), [vel-ōōer'], *adj.* made of velour.
VELUM, (*pl.* **vela**), [vē'-lum], *n.* a veil; (*anat.*) the soft palate. [L. *velum* sail].
VELUTINOUS, [ve-lewt'-in-us], *adj.* like velvet. [It. *veluto*].
VELVET (1), [vel'-vit], *n.* a heavy textile of silk, with sometimes a mixture of cotton, woven with a fine, soft nap on one side; **to be on v.,** to be in rich circumstances, fortunately situated; **v. glove,** apparent gentleness masking force. [OFr. *velvet*].

VELVETED, [vel'-vit-id], *adj.* made like velvet.
VELVETEEN, [vel'-vi-tēn'], *n.* imitation velvet made with cotton.
VELVETY, [vel'-vit-i], *adj.* having the characteristics of velvet.
VENA, [vē'-na], *n.* (*anat.*) a vein. [L. *vena*].
VENAL (1), [vēn'-al], *adj.* impure of motive; open to bribery, mercenary. [L. *venalis*].
VENAL (2), [vē'-nal], *adj.* of, or relating to, veins.
VENALITY, [vē-nal'-it-i], *n.* the condition of being venal, corruption, prostitution. [LL. *venalitas*].
VENALLY [vēn'-al-i], *adv.* in a mercenary manner.
VENATIC†, **VENATICAL†**, [vē-nat'-ik], *adj.* relating to the hunt. [L. *venaticus*].
VENATION (1), [vē-nā'-shun], *n.* (*bot., zool.*) systematic arrangement of veins.
VENATION† (2), [vē-nā'-shun], *n.* the act of hunting.
VEND, [vend], *v.t.* to sell. [L. *vendere*].
VENDACE, [ven'-dās], *n.* a species of salmon, *Coregonus vendesius*. [OFr. *vendece*].
VENDEE, [ven-dē'], *n.* (*leg.*) the recipient of an article sold.
VENDETTA, [ven-det'-a], *n.* a blood feud, *esp.* between Corsican families; (*fig.*) a feud. [It. *vendetta* vengeance].
VENDIBILITY, [ven'-di-bil'-it-i], *n.* the quality of being vendible.
VENDIBLE, [ven'-dibl], *adj.* capable of being sold, saleable. [L. *vendibilis*].
VENDIBLENESS, [ven'-dibl-nes], *n.* vendibility.
VENDIBLY, [ven'-dib-li], *adv.* to a saleable degree.
VENDITION, [ven-dish'-un], *n.* the act of selling.
VENDOR, [ven'-der], *n.* a person who offers for sale; (*leg.*) a person who sells real estate.
VENDUE, [ven-dew'], *n.* public auction. [Du. from Fr. dial. *vendue*].
VENEER (1), [ven-ēer'], *n.* a thin layer of expensive wood laid over furniture of cheaper material; (*fig.*) a characteristic or form concealing basic inferiority.
VENEER (2), [ven-ēer'], *v.t.* to apply a veneer to; (*fig.*) to make appear superior to actual quality. [~Fr. *fournir* to furnish].
VENEERING, [ven-ēer'-ing], *n.* the process or craft of treating with a veneer; the product of such craft.
VENEFICAL, [ven-ef'-ik-al], *adj.* poisonous. [~L. *venenum* poison].
VENEFICIAL, [ven'-i-fish'-al], *adj.* able to render poisonous.
VENEFICIOUS, [ven'-i-fish'-us], *adj.* veneficial. [L. *veneficius*].
VENERABILITY, [ven'-er-a-bil'-it-i], *n.* venerableness. [MedL. *venerabilitas*].
VENERABLE, [ven'-er-abl], *adj.* worthy of respect, reverence, or honour, *esp.* by virtue of age or religious associations. [L. *venerabilis*].
VENERABLENESS, [ven'-er-abl-nes], *n.* the condition of being venerable.
VENERABLY, [ven'-er-ab-li], *adv.* in a venerable manner.
VENERATE, [ven'-er-āt], *v.t.* to possess deep feelings of respect for, to reverence; to worship. [~L. *venerari* to reverence].
VENERATED, [ven'-er-āt-ed], *adj.* deeply respected.
VENERATION, [ven'-er-ā'-shun], *n.* the act of venerating; profound respect. [L. *veneratio*].
VENERATOR, [ven'-er-āt-er], *n.* one who venerates.
VENEREAL, [ven-ēer'-i-al], *adj.* of, relating to, communicable by, sexual intercourse. [~L. *venereus*].
VENEREAN, [ven-ēer'-i-an], *adj.* venereal.
VENEREOUS, [ven-ēer'-i-us], *adj.* lecherous. [L. *venereus*].
VENERY† (1), [vēn'-er-i], *n.* the pursuit or enjoyment of sexual pleasure.
VENERY† (2), [vēn'-er-i], *n.* hunting. [~L. *venari* to hunt].
VENESECTION, [ven'-i-sek'-shun], *n.* (*med.*) the art of bloodletting. [MedL. *venae sectio* vein cutting].
VENETIAN (1), [ven-ē'-shun], *n.* a native of Venice. [MedL. *Venetianus*].
VENETIAN (2), [ven-ē'-shun], *adj.* made in, coming from or relating to Venice; **v. blind**, a blind made of wooden slats.
VENGEANCE, [ven'-jants], *n.* the act of exacting a painful retribution for having been wronged or harmed; **with a v.**, with excessive thoroughness and energy. [OFr. *vengeance*].
VENGEFUL, [venj'-fōōl], *adj.* governed by desire to revenge.
VENGEFULLY, [venj'-fōōl-i], *adv.* in a vengeful manner.
VENIABLE, [vēn'-i-abl], *adj.* not serious; pardonable.
VENIAL, [vēn'-i-al], *adj.* pardonable; not deserving o[f] punishment. [LL. *venialis* gracious].
VENIALITY, [vēn'-i-al'-it-i], *n.* the condition of bein[g] venial.
VENIALLY, [vēn'-i-al-i], *adv.* in a venial manner.
VENIALNESS, [vēn'-i-al-nes], *n.* veniality.
VENISON, [ven'-i-zon, ven'-zon], *n.* the flesh of dee[r] prepared for eating. [OFr. *veneson*].
VENITE, [vē-nī'-ti], *n.* the ninety-fifth psalm. [L. *venite* come ye].
VENOM, [ven'-om], *n.* the poisonous secretion o[f] snakes and insects transmitted in their sting; an[y] poison; (*fig.*) vindictiveness, harm. [L. *venenu[m]* poison].
VENOMOUS, [ven'-om-us], *adj.* poisonous; (*fig.*) malicious.
VENOMOUSLY, [ven'-om-us-li], *adv.* to a venomou[s] degree.
VENOMOUSNESS, [ven'-om-us-nes], *n.* the quality of being venomous.
VENOSE, [vēn'-ōs], *adj.* (*bot.*) characterized by veins. [L. *venosus*].
VENOSITY, [vēn-os'-it-i], *n.* the quality of bein[g] venose.
VENOUS, [vē'-nus], *adj.* (*bot.*) venose. [L. *venosus*].
VENT† (1), [vent], *n.* opportunity for sale. [Fr. *vente*].
VENT (2), [vent], *n.* a small opening, natural or manufactured, which allows the escape of air, gas or liquid; a hole, passage, outlet; the act or process of an escape through such a means, emission, egress, discharge; the throat of a volcano; a gimlet for broaching casks. [L. *ventus* wind].
VENT (3), [vent], *v.t. and i.* to allow to escape through a vent; to release from a repressed state. [OFr. *venter*].
VENTAGE, [vent'-ij], *n.* vent capacity; an air-hole in a wind instrument.
VENTAIL, [vent'-āl], *n.* (*hist.*) part of a visor adjustable to permit breathing. [OFr. *ventaile*].
VENTER, [vent'-er], *n.* (*anat.*) abdomen; (*leg.*) mother. [L. *venter* womb].
VENTILATE, [vent'-i-lāt], *v.t.* to provide with a fre[e] circulation of fresh air; to fit with a ventilatio[n] system; (*fig.*) to submit to free discussion. [~L. *ventilare* to fan].
VENTILATION, [vent'-i-lā'-shun], *n.* the act or pro[-]cess of ventilating; a system for ventilating. [L. *ventilatio*].
VENTILATOR, [vent'-i-lāt-er], *n.* an apparatus fo[r] providing ventilation. [L. *ventilator* winnower].
VENTOSITY, [vent-os'-it-i], *n.* the condition of bein[g] windy.
VENT-PEG, [vent'-peg'], *n.* a plug; spile.
VENTRAL, [vent'-ral], *adj.* of, relating to, comin[g] from, the belly. [L. *ventralis*].
VENTRALLY, [vent'-ral-i], *adv.* in or towards th[e] ventral side.
VENTRICLE, [vent'-rikl], *n.* (*anat.*) a small cavity, *esp.* one of the two cardiac chambers. [L. *ventriculus*].
VENTRICOSE, [ven'-tri-kōs], *adj.* (*bot.*) like a belly.
VENTRICOUS, [ven'-trik-us], *adj.* (*bot.*) ventricose.
VENTRICULAR, [ven-trik'-yōō-ler], *adj.* relating t[o] the ventricle.
VENTRICULITE, [ven-trik'-yōō-līt], *n.* (*geol.*) a foss[il] sponge of the Cretaceous Age.
VENTRICULOUS, [ven-trik'-yōō-lus], *adj.* ventri[-]cose.
VENTRILOCUTION, [ven'-tri-lōk-ew'-shun], *n.* th[e] act of a ventriloquist. [L. *venter* belly and LOCUTION].
VENTRILOQUIAL, [ven'-tri-lō'-kwi-al], *adj.* relatin[g] to, based on, ventriloquism.
VENTRILOQUISM, [ven-tri'-lōk-wizm], *n.* the ar[t] of disguising the voice so as to create an illusion o[f] separate identity at a distance.
VENTRILOQUIST, [ven-tri'-lōk-wist], *n.* an exper[t] in ventriloquism.
VENTRILOQUIZE, [ven-tri'-lōk-wīz], *v.t. and i.* t[o] utter in ventriloquial form.
VENTRILOQUOUS, [ven-tri'-lok-wus], *adj.* like [a] ventriloquist.
VENTURE (1), [ven'-cher], *n.* an undertaking, expedi[-]tion, or enterprise involving incalculable or definitel[y] risky factors, a speculation in commerce; **at a v.**, a[t] random, haphazardly. [OFr. *aventure*].
VENTURE (2), [ven'-cher], *v.t.* to expose to incalculabl[e] or dangerous elements, to risk; to presume to express; *v.i.* to dare, to run a risk.
VENTURER, [ven'-cher-er], *n.* one who ventures; † speculator in foreign trade.
VENTURESOME, [ven'-cher-sum], *adj.* daring, bol[d,] taking risks; involving risk or hazard.

VENTURESOMELY, [ven'-cher-sum-li], *adv.* in a venturesome manner.
VENTURESOMENESS, [ven'-cher-sum-nes], *n.* the quality of being venturesome.
VENTURINE, [ven'-cho͞o-rin], *n.* powdered gold used in trepanning. [It. *venturina*].
VENTURING, [ven'-cher-ing], *n.* the act of taking risks.
VENTUROUS, [ven'-cher-us], *adj.* venturesome.
VENTUROUSLY, [ven'-cher-us-li], *adv.* in a venturous manner.
VENTUROUSNESS, [ven'-cher-us-nes], *n.* the quality of being venturous.
VENUE (1), [ven'-yo͞o], *n.* a thrust in fencing. [~Fr. *venir* to come].
VENUE (2), [ven'-yo͞o], *n.* meeting-place; (*leg.*) the place to which a jury is summoned. [Fr. *venue* advent].
VENUS, [vē'-nus], *n.* (*astron.*) the evening star, the major planet whose orbit is between the Earth and Mercury; (*myth.*) the goddess of love and beauty; (*coll.*) a beautiful woman; **Venus' comb,** a plant of the parsley family; **Venus' flower-basket,** a sponge of delicate tubular form; **Venus' fly-trap,** the insect-consuming plant *Dionœa Euplectella*; **Venus' slipper,** the plant also called lady's slipper. [L. *venus* sexual love].
VERACIOUS, [ver-ā'-shus], *adj.* given to telling the truth; relying on or reflecting truth. [~L. *verax* truthful].
VERACIOUSLY, [ver-ā'-shus-li], *adv.* in a veracious manner.
VERACITY, [ver-as'-it-i], *n.* habitual observance of truth, truthfulness.
VERANDA(H), [ver-an'-dah], *n.* a covered-in space built alongside the wall of a house to which it gives access; a ground-floor balcony. [Span. *veranda* balcony].
VERATRIC, [ver-a'-trik], *adj.* obtained from veratrum.
VERATRINE, [ve'-ra-trēn], *n.* a vegetable alkaloid extracted from seeds of hellebore. [L. *veratrum* hellebore].
VERATRUM, [ve'-ra-trum], *n.* (*bot.*) a genus of poisonous plants including the hellebore. [L. *veratrum* hellebore].
VERB, [vurb], *n.* (*gram.*) the part of speech which affirms mode of existence, or what a thing is, does, or how it reacts to external stimuli. [L. *verbum* word].
VERBAL, [vurb'-al], *adj.* relating to, consisting of, words; limited to words; literal, word for word; (*pop.*) not written, oral; (*gram.*) relating to, derived from, a verb. [LL. *verbalis*].
VERBALIST, [vurb'-al-ist], *n.* an expert in the use of words; a loquacious person.
VERBALITY, [verb-al'-it-i], *n.* restriction to use of words.
VERBALIZATION, [vurb'-al-īz-ā'-shun], *n.* the act of verbalizing.
VERBALIZE, [vurb'-al-īz], *v.t. and i.* to express in terms of words; to be verbose.
VERBALLY, [vurb'-al-i], *adv.* in a verbal form; (*pop.*) orally.
VERBARIAN, [ver-bāer'-i-an], *n.* a coiner of words.
VERBASCUM, [ver-bas'-kum], *n.* (*bot.*) a genus of plants comprising the mulleins. [L. *verbascum* mullein].
VERBATIM, [ver-bāt'-im], *adj. and adv.* word for word. [L. *verbatim*].
VERBENA, [ver-bēn'-a], *n.* (*bot.*) a genus of plants comprising the vervains. [L. *verbenae* sacred branches].
VERBENATE, [vurb'-en-āt], *v.t.* to strew with vervain.
VERBERATION, [vurb'-er-ā'-shun], *n.* the act of beating so as to cause noise. [L. *verberatio* a scourging].
VERBIAGE, [vurb'-i-ij], *n.* the use of superfluous words, verbosity. [Fr. *verbiage*].
VERBOSE, [ver-bōs'], *adj.* characterized by superfluous words, talkative, loquacious, prolix. [L. *verbosus*].

VERBENA

VERBOSELY, [ver-bōs'-li], *adv.* to a verbose degree.
VERBOSENESS, [ver-bōs'-nes], *n.* the quality of being verbose.
VERBOSITY, [ver-bos'-it-i], *n.* the condition of being verbose.
VERDANCY, [vur'-dan-si], *n.* the quality of being green; (*fig.*) immaturity, innocence.
VERDANT, [vur'-dant], *adj.* green, like new grass; covered with vegetation; (*fig.*) immature; innocent.
VERD-ANTIQUE, [vurd'-an-tēk'], *n.* a green incrustation due to prolonged action of air, *esp.* on bronze; marble mottled with green. [Fr.† *verd antique*].
VERDANTLY, [vur'-dant-li], *adv.* with verdancy.
VERDERER†, [vur'-der-er], *n.* a forester. [AFr. *verder*].
VERDICT, [vur'-dikt], *n.* (*leg.*) the jury's decision in any tried cause; a judgment, decision, opinion. [OFr. *verdit* from L. *vere dictum* truly said].
VERDIGRIS, [vur'-di-grēs], *n.* the green incrustation forming on copper exposed to air; (*chem.*) acetate of copper used in manufacturing pigment or dyes. [MedL. *viride graecum* green of Greece].
VERDITER, [vur'-dit-er], *n.* a pigment of copper carbonate of blue or green. [OFr. *verd de terre* green of earth].
VERDITURE, [vur'-di-cher], *n.* the colour of very pale green.
VERDUN, [ver-dun'], *n.* a rapier. [*Verdun*, in France].
VERDURE, [vurd'-yer], *n.* green vegetation, new grass. [Fr. *verdure*].

VERDUN

VERDUROUS, [vurd'-yer-us], *adj.* covered with verdure.
VERGE (1), [vurj], *n.* margin, edge, brink; small spindle in a watch; (*hist.*) emblem of authority in the form of a rod; (*leg.*) extent of King's Court jurisdiction. [L. *virga* rod].
VERGE (2), [vurj], *v.i.* to move or incline in a specific direction; **to v. on,** (*fig.*) to tend towards, approach the condition of. [L. *vergere* to bend].
VERGEE, [vur'-jē], *n.* a measure of land equal to four-ninths of an acre. [Fr. *vergée*].
VERGER, [vur'-jer], *n.* an ecclesiastical official bearing a mace before higher church functionaries; a church official. [OFr. *verger*].
VERIDICAL, [ver-id'-ik-al], *adj.* truthful. [L. *veridicus*].
VERIFIABILITY, [ve'-ri-fī'-a-bil'-it-i], *n.* the condition of being verifiable.
VERIFIABLE, [ve'-ri-fī-abl], *adj.* capable of being verified.
VERIFICATION, [ve'-rif-i-kā'-shun], *n.* the act of verifying; process of proving authentic.
VERIFIER, [ve'-ri-fī-er], *n.* one who verifies.
VERIFY, [ve'-ri-fī], *v.t.* to prove authentic, show to be true, to confirm. [L. *verificare*].
VERILY, [ve'-ri-li], *adv.* truly, really.
VERISIMILAR†, [ve'-ri-sim'-il-er], *adj.* likely. [L. *verisimilis*].
VERISIMILITUDE, [ve'-ri-sim-il'-i-tewd], *n.* the appearance of truth, probability. [L. *verisimilitudo*].
VERITABLE, [ve'-rit-abl], *adj.* true, actual. [OFr. *veritable*].
VERITABLY, [ve'-rit-ab-li], *adv.* in a veritable manner.
VERITY, [ve'-rit-i], *n.* the quality of being true; an assertion or proposition to be taken as true. [L. *veritas*].
VERJUICE, [vur'-jo͞os], *n.* the sour liquid obtained from unripe grapes or crab-apples. [OFr. *vertjus*].
VERMEIL (1), [vur'-mil], *n.* bright red, as a garnet. [OFr. *vermeil*].
VERMEIL (2), [vur'-mil], *adj.* bright red in colour.
VERMI-, *pref.* worm. [L. *vermis* worm].
VERMICELLI, [vur'-mi-chel'-i], *n.* thin macaroni. [It. *vermicello* little worm].
VERMICEOUS, [ver-mis'-i-us], *adj.* relating to worms.
VERMICIDE, [vurm'-i-sīd], *n.* a preparation for destroying worms; (*med.*) medicine for killing internal worms. [VERMI- and L. *caedere* to kill].
VERMICULAR, [ver-mik'-yo͞o-ler], *adj.* relating to, resembling, a worm. [~L. *vermiculus* little worm].
VERMICULATE, [ver-mik'-yo͞o-lāt], *v.t.* to decorate with convoluted markings like the tracks of a worm. [L. *vermiculari* to be eaten by worms].
VERMICULATED, [ver-mik'-yo͞o-lāt-id], *adj.* worm-eaten; resembling worm-eaten wood.
VERMICULATION, [ver-mik'-yo͞o-lā'-shun], *n.* the condition or process of being vermiculated.
VERMICULE, [vur'-mi-kewl], *n.* a little worm. [L. *vermiculus*].
VERMICULOSE, [ver-mik'-yo͞o-lōs], *adj.* vermiculous.
VERMICULOUS, [ver-mik'-yo͞o-lus], *adj.* full of worms; having a worm-like appearance; resembling worm-holes or castings. [L. *vermiculosus*].

VERMIFORM, [vurm'-i-fawm], *adj.* having the form of a worm or worms.
VERMIFUGAL, [vurm'-i-fewg'-al], *adj.* relating to, composed of, vermifuge.
VERMIFUGE, [vur'-mi-fewj], *n.* (*med.*) a substance for purging the body of worms. [VERMI- and L. *fugus* fleeing from].
VERMILION (1), [ver-mil'-yun], *n.* brilliant red pigment composed chiefly of red sulphide of mercury; the colour of this. [OFr. *vermillon*].
VERMILION (2), [ver-mil'-yun], *adj.* having the colour of or made of vermilion.
VERMILIONED, [ver-mil'-yund], *adj.* treated with vermilion, made red.
VERMIN, [vur'-min], *n.* animals harmful to game or domestically destructive; insects which thrive in dirty conditions; people contemptible for parasitism or filth. [~L. *vermis* worm].
VERMINATION, [vur'-min-ā'-shun], *n.* breeding of or infestation with vermin. [L. *verminatio*].
VERMINOUS, [vur'-min-us], *adj.* infested by, resembling, caused by, vermin; filthy, disgusting. [L. *verminosus* wormy].
VERMIPAROUS, [verm-ip'-er-us], *adj.* producing worms. [VERMI- and L. *parere* to produce].
VERMIVOROUS, [verm-iv'-or-us], *adj.* worm-eating. [VERMI- and L. *vorare* to devour].
VERMOUTH, [vur'-mōōth], *n.* a sharp-flavoured liqueur, made with wormwood. [Fr. *vermouth* from OHGerm. *wermot* wormwood].
VERNACULAR (1), [ver-nak'-yōō-ler], *n.* the language native to a country or part of a country; language of the common people.
VERNACULAR (2), [ver-nak'-yōō-ler], *adj.* spoken by the people native to a locality; written in dialect. [~L. *vernaculus*].
VERNACULARISM, [ver-nak'-yōō-ler-izm], *n.* vernacular idiom.
VERNACULARLY, [ver-nak'-yōō-ler-li], *adv.* in the vernacular manner.
VERNAL, [vur'-nal], *adj.* belonging to, appearing in, resembling, the spring; fresh; **v. equinox,** equinox occurring in March. [L. *vernalis* of the spring].
VERNANT, [vur'-nant], *adj.* flourishing, as in spring. [L. *vernans*].
VERNATION, [ver-nā'-shun], *n.* (*bot.*) the disposition of leaves in the bud. [L. *vernatio* the sloughing of its skin by a snake in spring].
VERNICLE, [vur'-nikl], *n.* a representation of Christ's face which appeared by a miracle on St. Veronica's veil. [MedL. *veronica*].
VERNICOSE, [vur'-nik-ōs], *adj.* as if varnished.
VERNIER, [vur'-ni-er], *n.* a graduated sliding-scale for calculating subdivisions in surveying, etc.; a supplementary device to provide a fine adjustment. [P. *Vernier*, the French inventor].
VERNILITY, [ver-nil'-it-i], *n.* fawning servility. [~L. *verna* slave].
VERONAL, [ve'-ron-al], *n.* (*prot.*) a soporific drug.
VERONESE, [ve'-ron-ēz], *adj.* relating to, coming from, Verona in Italy.
VERONICA (1), [ver-on'-ik-a], *n.* (*bot.*) a numerous genus of plants including the speedwell. [St. *Veronica*].
VERONICA (2), [ver-on'-ik-a], *n.* a vernicle. [St. *Veronica*].
VERRUCA, [ve'-rōō-ka], *n.* a wart. [L. *verruca*].
VERRUCOSE, [ve'-rōō-kōs], *adj.* covered with warts. [L. *verrucosus*].
VERRUCOSITY, [ve'-rōō-kos'-i-ti], *n.* the condition of being verrucose.
VERRUCULOSE, [ver-ōō'-kyōō-lōs], *adj.* finely verrucose. [L. *verruculosus*].
VERSABILITY, [vur'-sa-bil'-it-i], *n.* versableness.
VERSABLE, [vurs'-abl], *adj.* capable of being turned.
VERSABLENESS, [vurs'-abl-nes], *n.* the capacity for being turned about.

VERONICA

VERSANT, [vurs'-ant], *adj.* familiar, conversant. [~CONVERSANT].
VERSATILE, [vurs'-at-il], *adj.* having many gifts or talents with a facility to turn quickly from one to another; (*bot.*) able to turn freely. [L. *versatilis* revolving].
VERSATILELY, [vurs'-at-il-li], *adv.* in a versatile way.
VERSATILENESS, [vurs'-at-il-nes], *n.* versatility.
VERSATILITY, [vurs'-a-til'-it-i], *n.* the quality of being versatile; aptness at many subjects or tasks.

VERSE (1), [vurs], *n.* a line of words whose metrical o numerical accents are arranged according to the rule of prosody; the technical basis for poetry; a numbe of such lines considered as a unit of poetic form, a stanza of a poem, a piece of poetry; **free v.,** verse whos rhythm does not conform to a metrical pattern. [L *versus* a row].
VERSE (2), [vurs], *v.t. and i.* to compose in verse form
VERSED, [vurst], *adj.* having an extensive knowledg of, skilled, trained.
VERSELET, [vurs'-let], *n.* a short verse.
VERSEMONGER, [vurs'-mung'-ger], *n.* a manufac turer of verses.
VERSER, [vurs'-er], *n.* a composer of verses.
VERSET, [vurs'-et], *n.* a short verse; (*pl.*) trivial verses (*mus.*) a brief organ prelude. [Fr. *verset*].
VERSICLE, [vurs'-ikl], *n.* a short verse, *esp.* one intone in church. [L. *versiculus*].
VERSICOLOROUS, [vurs'-i-kul'-or-us], *adj.* varie gated. [L. *versicolor*].
VERSICOLOURED, [vurs'-i-kul'-erd], *adj.* multi coloured; varying in colour. [L. *versus* turned an COLOUR].
VERSICULAR, [vurs-ik'-yōō-ler], *adj.* relating to characterized by, verses.
VERSIFIABLE, [vurs'-i-fī-abl], *adj.* that may b versified.
VERSIFICATION, [vurs'-if-ik-ā'-shun], *n.* the act or art of composing verse. [L. *versificatio*].
VERSIFICATOR, [vurs'-if-ik-āt-er], *n.* a versifier. [L *versificator*].
VERSIFIER, [vurs'-i-fī'-er], *n.* one who versifies.
VERSIFORM, [vurs'-i-fawm], *adj.* diverse in form.
VERSIFY, [vurs'-i-fī], *v.t. and i.* to put into the form of verse; to compose competent but dull poetry. [L *versificare*].
VERSION, [vur'-shun], *n.* a translation from one language into another; a particular arrangement of something expressed in an artistic medium; a definite account, description, or statement of facts. [L *versio*].
VERSIONIST, [vur'-shun-ist], *n.* a translator.
VERS LIBRE, [vāer-lēbr'], *n.* free verse, verse composed in free rhythms not subject to metrical rules [Fr. *vers libre* free verse].
VERSO, [vurs'-ō], *n.* the left-hand page; the revers side of a coin. [L. *verso, abl. sg.* of *versus* turned].
VERST, [vurst], *n.* a Russian measure of length equa to 3,500 feet. [Russ. *versta*].
VERSUS, [vur'-sus], *prep.* against. [L. *versus*].
VERT, [vurt], *n.* forest vegetation, *esp.* as providing cover for deer; (*her.*) green. [OFr. *vert* from L. *viridis* green].
VERTEBRA, (*pl.* **vertebrae**), [vurt'-i-bra], *n.* (*anat.*) a spinal joint; (*pl.*) the backbone. [L. *vertebra*].
VERTEBRAL, [vurt'-i-bral], *adj.* of, relating to, placed by, or coming from, the spine.
VERTEBRATA, [vurt'-i-brāt'-a], *n.*(*pl.*) (*zool.*) animals with a backbone.
VERTEBRATE (1), [vurt'-i-brāt], *n.* an animal with a backbone.
VERTEBRATE (2), [vurt'-i-brāt], *adj.* having a backbone. [L. *vertebratus* jointed].
VERTEBRATED, [vurt'-i-brāt-id], *adj.* having vertebrae.
VERTEX, (*pl.* **vertices**), [vurt'-eks], *n.* the highest point; (*anat.*) the crown of the head; (*astron.*) the zenith; (*geom.*) the angle opposite a given side of a figure; **v. of a curve,** the point where the diameter meets the curve. [L. *vertex*].
VERTICAL, [vurt'-ik-al], *adj.* relating to, placed at, the vertex; pointing to the zenith, placed in a position or moving in a direction at right angles to the surface of the earth; perpendicular, upright. [~*Prec.*].
VERTICALLY, [vurt'-ik-al-i], *adv.* in a vertical direction.
VERTICALNESS, [vurt'-ik-al-nes], *n.* the condition or characteristic of being vertical.
VERTICIL, [vur'-ti-sil], *n.* (*bot.*) a whorl of florets or similar parts round a centre. [L. *verticillus*].
VERTICILLATE, [vert-is'-il-āt], *adj.* having verticils.
VERTICITY, [vert-is'-it-i], *n.* the power of or the state of being in rotation.
VERTIGINOUS, [ver-tij'-in-us], *adj.* whirling; suffering from, inducing, vertigo.
VERTIGINOUSLY, [ver-tij'-in-us-li], *adv.* in vertiginous fashion.
VERTIGINOUSNESS, [ver-tij'-in-us-nes], *n.* the state of being vertiginous.
VERTIGO, [vurt'-i-gō], *n.* giddiness, faintness, *esp.* when due to disturbance of balance, etc. [L. *vertigo*].

VERTU, [ver′-tōō], *n.* rarity; aesthetic merit; the quality appealing to a connoisseur. [It. *virtù* excellence].
VERVAIN, [vur′-vān], *n.* a plant of the genus *Verbena*, *esp. V. officinalis*, formerly prized for its medicinal properties. [~L. *verbena*].
VERVE, [vurv], *n.* imaginative dash, aesthetic gusto, the quality producing a tasteful flourish, liveliness. [Fr. *verve*].
VERVELS, [vur′-velz], *n.(pl.)* the rings by which a hawk's leash is attached. [OFr. *vervel*].
VERVET, [vur′-vet], *n.* a South African monkey, *Cercopithecus lalandi*. [Fr. *vervet*].
VERY (1), [ve′-ri], *adj.* true, veritable; requisite. [OFr. *verai* true].
VERY (2), [ve′-ri], *adv.* in a great degree, to a great extent; absolutely. [OFr. *verai* from L. *verax* true].
VESICAL, [ves′-ik-al], *adj.* (*anat.*) pertaining to the bladder. [~L. *vesica* a bladder].
VESICANT (1), [ves′-ik-ant], *n.* an application for raising blisters. [L. *vesica* a blister].
VESICANT (2), [vēs′-i-kant], *adj.* causing blistering.
VESICATE, [ves′-ik-āt], *v.t. and i.* to blister; to become blistered.
VESICATION, [ves′-ik-ā′-shun], *n.* the process of blistering; the state of being blistered. [L. *vesicatio*].
VESICATORY, [ves′-ik-āt′-er-i], *adj.* that which blisters.
VESICLE, [ves′-ikl], *n.* a little bladder; a blister. [L. *vesicula*].
VESICULAR, [ves-ik′-yōō-ler], *adj.* vesiculous.
VESICULATE, [ves-ik′-yōō-lāt], *adj.* vesiculous.
VESICULOUS, [ves-ik′-yōō-lus], *adj.* having, relating to, vesicles.
VESPER, [ves′-per], *n.* the evening star; (*pl.*) (*eccles.*) evensong. [L. *vesper* evening].
VESPERTILIO, [ves′-per-til′-i-ō], *n.* a genus of bats. [L. *vespertilio* a bat].
VESPERTINE, [ves′-per-tīn], *adj.* pertaining to or occurring in the evening. [L. *vespertinus*].
VESPIARY, [ves′-pi-er-i], *n.* a wasps' nest. [~L. *vespa*].
VESSEL, [vesl], *n.* a hollow utensil, *esp.* for containing liquids; a ship; (*fig.*) a person, *esp.* when regarded as possessing some special quality. [OFr. *veissel* from L. *vascellum*].
VEST (1), [vest], *n.* a garment worn round the torso, *esp.* next to the skin; (*coll.*) a waistcoat. [L. *vestis* garment].
VEST (2), [vest], *v.t.* to clothe with, to invest; to endow. [L. *vestire*].
VESTA, [vest′-a], *n.* the goddess of the household; a kind of match. [L. *Vesta*].
VESTAL, [vest′-al], *adj.* relating, consecrated, to Vesta; holy, chaste, virginal. [L. *vestalis*].
VESTED, [vest′-id], *adj.* invested, clothed (with), endowed; established and hard to displace.
VESTIARY, [vest′-i-er-i], *adj.* relating to clothes.
VESTIBULAR, [vest-ib′-yōō-ler], *adj.* pertaining to a vestibule.
VESTIBULE, [vest′-i-bewl], *n.* the porch, entrance hall, of a building. [L. *vestibulum*].
VESTIGE, [vest′-ij], *n.* a trace, sign, remnant. [L. *vestigium* footprint].
VESTIGIAL, [vest-ij′-i-al], *adj.* of the nature of a vestige.
VESTING, [vest′-ing], *n.* cloth from which vests are made.
VESTMENT, [vest′-ment], *n.* a garment, *esp.* a ceremonial garment. [L. *vestimentum*].
VESTRY, [ves′-tri], *n.* the part of a church where the vestments are kept and donned; the general assembly of the ratepayers of a parish. [L. *vestiarium* wardrobe].
VESTRYDOM, [ves′-tri-dom], *n.* vestries in general; rule by vestries.
VESTRYMAN, [ves′-tri-man], *n.* a member of a vestry.
VESTUARY, [ves′-chōō-er-i], *n.* a wardrobe.
VESTURAL, [ves′-chōō-ral], *adj.* relating to a vestuary.
VESTURE, [ves′-cher], *n.* clothing. [OFr. *vesture*].
VESTURER, [ves′-cher-er], *n.* a person in official charge of vestments.
VESUVIAN, [ve-sōō′-vi-an], *adj.* relating to Vesuvius or to a volcano. [*Vesuvius*, the Italian volcano].
VET (1), [vet], *n.* (*coll.*) a veterinary surgeon.
VET (2), [vet], *v.t.* (*coll.*) to examine medically; (*fig.*) to revise, check critically.
VETCH, FITCH, [vech, fich], *n.* a common leguminous plant, *Vicia sativa*. [OFr. *veche* from L. *vicia*].
VETCHLING, [vech′-ling], *n.* a leguminous plant of the genus *Lathyrus*, allied to the vetch. [~*Prec.*].
VETCHY, [vech′-i], *adj.* pertaining to or overgrown with vetch.
VETERAN (1), [vet′-er-an], *n.* an experienced person; an old soldier.
VETERAN (2), [vet′-er-an], *adj.* experienced in a service. [L. *veteranus*].
VETERINARIAN, [vet′-er-i-nāer′-i-an], *n.* a veterinary surgeon.
VETERINARY, [vet′-rin-er-i], *adj.* relating to the study and treatment of sickness in animals. [L. *veterinus* relating to beasts of burden].
VETO (1), [vēt′-ō], *n.* an absolute prohibition, *esp.* a constitutional right so to prohibit. [L. *veto* I forbid].
VETO (2), [vēt′-ō], *v.t.* to prohibit absolutely.
VETTURA, [ve-tōōer′-a], *n.* a four-wheeled Italian carriage. [It. *vettura*].
VETTURINO, [ve′-tōō-rēn′-ō], *n.* the driver of a vettura. [It. *vetturino*].
VETUST, [ve′-tust], *adj.* old. [L. *vetustus*].
VEX, [veks], *v.t.* to irritate, annoy, stir to mild anger; to harass. [L. *vexare* to agitate].
VEXATION, [veks-ā′-shun], *n.* the act of vexing, the condition of being vexed. [L. *vexatio*].
VEXATIOUS, [veks-ā′-shus], *adj.* vexing, tending to vex; (*leg.*) done or brought in order to vex or harass.
VEXATIOUSLY, [veks-ā′-shus-li], *adv.* in a vexatious manner.
VEXATIOUSNESS, [veks-ā′-shus-nes], *n.* the condition of being vexatious.
VEXED, [vekst], *adj.* bitterly contested; causing much vexation.
VEXILLAR, [veks-il′-er], *adj.* vexillary.
VEXILLARY, [veks-il′-er-i], *adj.* relating to an ensign or flag. [L. *vexillaris*].
VEXILLATION, [veks′-il-ā′-shun], *n.* a troop of soldiers serving under one standard. [L. *vexillatio*].
VEXILLUM, [veks-il′-um], *n.* (*hist.*) a Roman standard; a vexillation; the vane of a feather. [L. *vexillum*].
VEXING, [veks′-ing], *adj.* tending to vex.
VEXINGLY, [veks′-ing-li], *adv.* in a vexing manner.
VIA, [vī′-a], *prep.* by way of. [L. *via* by road].
VIABILITY, [vī′-a-bil′-it-i], *n.* the condition or quality of being viable.
VIABLE, [vī′-abl], *adj.* capable of remaining alive in a particular environment. [Fr. *viable*].
VIADUCT, [vī′-a-dukt], *n.* a bridge in the form of a series of arches, crossing a road or ravine, *esp.* if bearing a railway. [L. *via* road and DUCT].
VIAL, [vī′-al], *n.* a small vessel; a small bottle containing drugs, etc. [OFr. *fiole* from Gk. *phiale* cup].
VIAMETER, [vī-am′-it-er], *n.* an odometer. [L. *via* road and METER].
VIANDS, [vī′-andz], *n.(pl.)* food, cooked meat. [Fr. *viande*].
VIARIAN, [vī-āer′-i-an], *adj.* relating to roads or to travel by road.
VIATIC, [vī-at′-ik], *adj.* pertaining to travel. [L. *viaticus*].
VIATICUM, [vī-at′-i-kum], *n.* provisions for a journey; (*R.C.*) communion administered to one on the point of death. [L. *viaticum*].
VIBICES, [vī′-bi-sēz], *n.* (*med.*) bright patches of discoloration on the skin in certain fevers. [L. *vibex* weal].
VIBRANT, [vī′-brant], *adj.* vibrating, resonant. [L. *vibrans*].
VIBRATE, [vī-brāt′], *v.t. and i.* to quiver rapidly, to oscillate; to swing on an axis; to cause to quiver. [L. *vibrare*].
VIBRATILE, [vī′-brat-il], *adj.* tending to vibrate.
VIBRATILITY, [vī′-brat-il′-it-i], *n.* the condition of being vibratile.
VIBRATION, [vī-brā′-shun], *n.* the state of vibrating, the extent to which a thing vibrates; oscillation. [L. *vibratio*].
VIBRATIVE, [vī′-brat-iv], *adj.* producing vibration.
VIBRATO, [vi-brah′-tō], *n.* (*mus.*) tremulousness. [It. *vibrato*].
VIBRATOR, [vī-brāt′-or], *n.* that which vibrates; an instrument having a vibratory action; a vibrating reed in an organ.
VIBRATORY, [vī-brāt′-er-i], *adj.* vibrating, tending to vibrate, causing vibration, relating to vibration.
VIBRIO, [vī′-bri-ō], *n.* a small nematoid quivering worm.
VICAR, [vik′-er], *n.* a deputy; the incumbent of a parish who is not entitled to great tithes. [Fr. *vicaire* from L. *vicarius* deputy].
VICARAGE, [vik′-er-ij], *n.* the official residence of a vicar.
VICAR-GENERAL, [vik′-er-jen′-er-al], *n.* (*R.C.*) an assistant, usually the chancellor, to a bishop or

archbishop in ecclesiastical trials, etc.; the principal deputy of a bishop.

VICARIAL, [vi-kāer'-i-al], *adj.* relating to a vicar; vicarious.

VICARIATE, [vi-kāer'-i-āt], *n.* the office or tenure of a vicar.

VICARIOUS, [vi-kāer'-i-us], *adj.* relating to a vicar; serving as substitute; performed on behalf of another. [L. *vicarius*].

VICARIOUSLY, [vi-kāer'-i-us-li], *adv.* in a vicarious way.

VICARSHIP, [vik'-er-ship], *n.* the office of vicar.

VICE (1), [vīs], *n.* moral weakness, *esp.* when translated into action, immoral behaviour; defect. [L. *vitium*].

VICE (2), [vīs], *n.* a mechanical device for gripping an object, a tool for holding tightly by pressure on either side; **hand v.,** a small vice fitted with a handle. [OFr. *vice* from L. *vitis* a vine].

VICE

VICE (3), [vīs'-i], *prep.* in the place of. [L. *vice* by interchange].

VICE-, *pref.* in place of, acting on behalf of (another). [L. *vice* by interchange].

VICE-ADMIRAL, [vīs'-ad'-mir-al], *n.* the rank immediately below that of full admiral. [OFr. *visamiral*].

VICE-CHANCELLOR, [vīs'-chahn'-sel-er], *n.* one next in rank below a chancellor; the official in charge of the administration of an English university.

VICE-CONSUL, [vīs'-kon'-sul], *n.* a subordinate consul.

VICEGERENT, [vīs'-je'-rent], *n.* a deputy entrusted with full powers. [VICE- and L. *gerere* to perform].

VICENARY, [vīs'-en-er-i], *adj.* pertaining to twenty. [L. *vicenarius*].

VICENNIAL, [vīs-en'-i-al], *adj.* pertaining to a period of twenty years. [~L. *vicennium*].

VICE-PRESIDENT, [vīs'-prez'-i-dent], *n.* the deputy of a president; a subsidiary president.

VICEREGAL, [vīs'-rēg'-al], *adj.* pertaining to a viceroy.

VICE-REGENCY, [vīs'-rēj'-en-si], *n.* the office, power, or tenure of a vice-regent.

VICE-REGENT, [vīs'-rēj'-ent], *n.* a person deputed to exercise the powers of his superior.

VICEREINE, [vīs'-rān], *n.* the wife or consort of a viceroy. [VICE- and Fr. *reine* queen].

VICEROY, [vīs'-roi], *n.* a deputy ruling a country in the name of his sovereign. [VICE- and Fr. *roi* king].

VICEROYALTY, [vīs-roi'-al-ti], *n.* viceroyship.

VICEROYSHIP, [vīs'-roi-ship], *n.* the office and duty of a viceroy.

VICE VERSA, [vīs'-i-vurs'-a], *adv.* with the roles or relationships interchanged; conversely. [L. *vice versa* the place turned].

VICINAGE, [vis'-in-ij], *n.* neighbourhood, neighbouring district. [~L. *vicinus* neighbouring].

VICINAL, [vis'-in-al], *adj.* neighbouring; **v. way,** a connecting road or by-way. [L. *vicinalis*].

VICINITY, [vis-in'-it-i], *n.* neighbourhood; the state of being near. [L. *vicinitas*].

VICIOSITY, [vish'-i-os'-it-i], *n.* the state or quality of being vicious.

VICIOUS, [vish'-us], *adj.* performing, tending to, or relating to vice; malevolent; (*coll.*) of a dog, etc., dangerous; **v. circle,** an argument which begs the question; reciprocal aggravation. [L. *vitiosus*].

VICIOUSLY, [vish'-us-li], *adv.* in vicious fashion.

VICIOUSNESS, [vish'-us-nes], *n.* the condition or quality of being vicious.

VICISSITUDE, [vī-sis'-i-tewd], *n.* alteration in affairs, *esp.* one of several changes of fortune. [L. *vicissitudo* alternation].

VICISSITUDINARY, [vī-sis'-i-tewd'-in-er-i], *adj.* tending to, relating to, vicissitudes.

VICISSITUDINOUS, [vī-sis'-i-tewd'-in-us], *adj.* vicissitudinary.

VICTIM, [vik'-tim], *n.* a living creature offered as a religious sacrifice; a person or animal sacrificed for the sake of another; a person suffering through the action of another, or through some uncontrollable quality in himself. [L. *victima*].

VICTIMIZE, [vik'-tim-īz], *v.t.* to make into a victim; to cause to suffer for one's own ends.

VICTIMIZER, [vik'-tim-īz-er], *n.* one who victimizes.

VICTOR, [vik'-ter], *n.* a conqueror. [L. *victor*

VICTORIA, [vik-taw'-ri-a], *n.* a light, two-seater horse-drawn carriage, with a driver's box and a hood. [Queen *Victoria*].

VICTORIA

VICTORIAN, [vik-taw'-ri-an], *adj.* relating to Queen Victoria, her reign and the manners, etc., of her period; old-fashioned; prudish. [Queen *Victoria*].

VICTORINE, [vik'-tor-ēn'], *n.* a woman's fur tippet a kind of peach. [*Victoria*].

VICTORIOUS, [vik-taw'-ri-us], *adj.* having gaine the victory; relating to victory. [L. *victoriosus*].

VICTORIOUSLY, [vik-taw'-ri-us-li], *adv.* in victor ous fashion.

VICTORIOUSNESS, [vik-taw'-ri-us-nes], *n.* th condition of being victorious.

VICTORY, [vik'-ter-i], *n.* a conquest gained ove another, *esp.* a conquest made by battle; a succes gained over anything; **v. roll,** (*aeron.*) a roll made i flight by a victorious fighter pilot.. [L. *victoria*].

VICTRESS, [vik'-tres], *n.* a female conqueror.

VICTRIX, [vik'-triks], *n.* a victress. [L. *victrix*].

VICTUAL, [vit'-al], *v.t.* to supply with provisions [L. *victualia*].

VICTUALLER, [vit'-ler], *n.* one who victuals; a innkeeper.

VICTUALS, [vit'-alz], *n.(pl.)* food. [L. *victualia*

VICUNA, VICUGNA, [vi-kōōn'-ya], *n.* the wil llama. [Span. *vicuna*].

VIDE, [vī'-di], *v. imper.* look at, refer to. [L. *vide* see]

VIDELICET, [vīd-ēl'-i-set], *adv.* namely. [L. *vide licet*]

VIDIMUS, [vīd'-i-mus], *n.* (*leg.*) a formal examination [L. *vidimus* we have seen].

VIDUAGE, [vid'-yōō-ij], *n.* widowhood. [~L *vidua* a widow].

VIDUAL, [vid'-yōō-al], *adj.* pertaining to a widow

VIE, [vī], *v.i.* to strive, to compete. [OFr. *envier*].

VIENNESE (1), (*pl.* **Viennese**), [vē'-en-ēz'], *n.* a inhabitant of Vienna.

VIENNESE (2), [vē'-en-ēz'], *adj.* of, pertaining to, o characteristic of Vienna or the Viennese.

VIEW (1), [vew], *n.* the act of seeing; that which i seen; a natural prospect; the extent or amount of thing that can be seen; the clarity with which a thin is seen; an opinion, a considered impression. [OF *veue* the sense of sight].

VIEW (2), [vew], *v.t.* to look at, observe, inspect, ex amine; to consider, regard, contemplate.

VIEWER, [vew'-er], *n.* one who views or examines an apparatus to assist viewing.

VIEWING, [vew'-ing], *n.* the act of one who views

VIEWLESS, [vew'-les], *adj.* without a view; fro which no prospect is visible; invisible.

VIEW-POINT, [vew'-point], *n.* point of view; vantag point for observation.

VIGESIMAL, [vi-jes'-im-al], *adj.* twentieth. [L *vigesimus*].

VIGESIMATION, [vī-jes'-i-mā'-shun], *n.* (*hist.*) th execution of every twentieth man in a regiment. [L *vigesimatio*].

VIGIL, [vij'-il], *n.* the state of being awake, the actio of watching; a night spent in voluntary wakefulnes for religious reasons. [L. *vigilia*].

VIGILANCE, [vij'-il-ants], *n.* the state of being vig lant; **v. committee,** a committee to keep order i unsettled country, or to watch and report on th moral behaviour of a local population.

VIGILANT, [vij'-il-ant], *adj.* keenly watchful; sus piciously on guard; unsleepingly alert. [L. *vigilans*]

VIGILANTE, [vij'-il-ant'-i], *n.* (*U.S.*) a member o a vigilance committee. [Span. *vigilante*].

VIGILANTLY, [vij'-il-ant-li], *adv.* in vigilant fashion

VIGNERON, [vēn'-yer-aw(ng)], *n.* a vine grower. [F *vigneron*].

VIGNETTE (1), [vēn-yet'], *n.* a small ornamenta engraving at the head or foot of a page; an inset boo illustration; a picture whose edges merge into th background. [Fr. *vignette*].

VIGNETTE (2), [vēn-yet'], *v.t.* to convert into a vign ette. [*Prec.*].

VIGONIA, [vig-ōn'-i-a], *n.* a cloth made of the wool o the vicuna.

VIGOROSO, [vig'-o-rō'-sō], *adv.* (*mus.*) energetically [It. *vigoroso*].

VIGOROUS, [vig'-er-us], *adj.* possessing, displayin

vigour; potent; forceful; in full possession of the physical powers. [L. *vigorosus*].

VIGOROUSLY, [vig'-or-us-li], *adv.* in vigorous fashion.

VIGOROUSNESS, [vig'-or-us-nes], *n.* the condition of being vigorous.

VIGOUR, [vig'-er], *n.* physical strength, potency, animal energy, vitality, force. [OFr. *vigour* from L. *vigor*].

VIKING, [vī'-king], *n.* a Norse pirate. [OScand. *vikingr*].

VILAYET, [vil-ah'-yet], *n.* a Turkish province. [Turk. *vilayet*].

VILE, [vil], *adj.* base, depraved, worthless, morally filthy. [L. *vilis* of little worth].

VILELY, [vīl'-li], *adv.* in a vile way.

VILENESS, [vīl'-nes], *n.* the state of being vile.

VILIFICATION, [vil'-i-fik-ā'-shun], *n.* the act of making vile or of defaming.

VILIFIER, [vil'-i-fī'-er], *n.* one who vilifies.

VILIFY, [vil'-i-fī], *v.t.* to slander, to speak ill of, to represent as vile. [L. *vilificare*].

VILLA, [vil'-a], *n.* a large country house in its own estate, *esp.* in Italy; (*coll.*) a small suburban house. [L. *villa*].

VILLADOM, [vil'-a-dom], *n.* suburbia.

VILLAGE, [vil'-ij], *n.* a small community in a rural district; a collection of houses, etc., less than a town. [OFr. *village*].

VILLAGER, [vil'-ij-er], *n.* an inhabitant of a village.

VILLAGERY, [vil'-ij-er-i], *n.* villages in one district.

VILLAIN, [vil'-an], *n.* a wicked person, an actively vicious and depraved person, a thorough scoundrel; †a villein. [OFr. *villain* from LL. **villanus* attached to a villa].

VILLAINOUS, [vil'-an-us], *adj.* wicked, having the qualities of a villain; ill-done, wholly bad.

VILLAINOUSLY, [vil'-an-us-li], *adv.* in a villainous way.

VILLAINOUSNESS, [vil'-an-us-nes], *n.* the state of being villainous.

VILLAINY, [vil'-an-i], *n.* the act, behaviour, of a villain; a wicked piece of work.

VILLANAGE, see VILLENAGE.

VILLANELLE, [vil'-an-el'], *n.* an elaborate form of poem of nineteen lines rhyming on two sounds. [Fr. *villanelle*].

VILLARSIA, [vil-ah'-zi-a], *n.* a genus of aquatic plants, *Limnanthemum.* [D. *Villars* a botanist].

VILLARSITE, [vil-ah'-zīt], *n.* a mineral, hydrated olivine. [~*Prec.*].

VILLATIC, [vil-at'-ik], *adj.* relating to a villa; rustic. [L. *villaticus*].

VILLEGGIATURA, [vil'-ej-yat-ōō'-ra], *n.* a holiday in a country house; a temporary retirement to the country. [It. *villeggiatura*].

VILLEIN, [vil'-ān], *n.* (*hist.*) a medieval serf bound to the soil. [~VILLAIN].

VILLENAGE, VILLANAGE, [vil'-en-ij], *n.* the position or state of being a villein.

VILLI, [vil'-ī], *n.*(*pl.*) the minute hair-like processes in plants and the intestines. [L. *villus* tuft of hair].

VILLARSIA

VILLOSE, [vil'-ōs], *adj.* villous. [L. *villosus*].

VILLOUS, [vil'-us], *adj.* covered with villi; shaggy; hairy. [L. *villosus*].

VIM, [vim], *n.* (*slang*) vigorous energy. [L. *vim*, *acc.* of *vis* force].

VIMINAL, [vim'-in-al], *adj.* relating to shoots, twiggy. [L. *vimen* a twig].

VIMINEOUS, [vim-in'-i-us], *adj.* consisting of, or resembling, twigs.

VINACEOUS, [vī-nā'-shus], *adj.* relating to wine, or the vine.

VINAIGRETTE, [vin'-ā-gret'], *n.* a metal smelling-box, usually containing a sponge soaked in vinegar. [Fr. *vinaigrette*].

VINCENTIAL, [vin-sen'-shal], *adj.* pertaining to St. Vincent.

VINCIBILITY, [vin'-si-bil'-it-i], *n.* the state of being vincible.

VINCIBLE, [vin'-sibl], *adj.* able to be conquered. [L. *vincibilis*].

VINCIBLENESS, [vin'-sibl-nes], *n.* vincibility.

VINCULUM, [vin'-kyōō-lum], *n.* (*math.*) the sign placed above the several parts of a compound quantity. [L. *vinculum* chain].

VINDEMIAL, [vin-dē'-mi-al], *adj.* characteristic of, relating to, the grape harvest. [~L. *vindemia*].

VINDICABILITY, [vin'-dik-a-bil'-it-i], *n.* the state of being vindicable.

VINDICABLE, [vin'-dik-abl], *adj.* capable of being vindicated.

VINDICATE, [vin'-di-kāt], *v.t.* to validate, to justify, to prove just or correct, to defend successfully. [~L. *vindicare*].

VINDICATION, [vin'-di-kā'-shun], *n.* the act of vindicating.

VINDICATIVE, [vin'-di-kat-iv], *adj.* tending to vindicate; having the power, force, effect of vindicating.

VINDICATOR, [vin'-di-kāt-er], *n.* one who vindicates. [L. *vindicator*].

VINDICATORY, [vin'-di-kat-er-i], *adj.* tending to vindicate.

VINDICTIVE, [vin-dik'-tiv], *adj.* revengeful.

VINDICTIVELY, [vin-dik'-tiv-li], *adv.* in vindictive fashion.

VINDICTIVENESS, [vin-dik'-tiv-nes], *n.* the state or quality of being vindictive.

VINE, [vīn], *n.* the climbing plant, *Vitis vinifera*, which bears grapes; any creeping stem resembling this. [L. *vinea*].

VINE-CLAD, [vīn'-klad'], *adj.* overgrown with vines.

VINEDRESSER, [vīn'-dres'-er], *n.* one who dresses and tends vines.

VINE-FRETTER, [vīn'-fret'-er], *n.* a small insect infesting vines.

VINEGAR, [vin'-i-ger], *n.* an acid liquid used as a condiment, made originally from fermented wine. [OFr. *vineigre*].

VINEGARY, [vin'-i-gar-i], *adj.* resembling, or reminiscent of, vinegar.

VINE-GRUB, [vīn'-grub], *n.* the vine-fretter.

VINERY, [vīn'-er-i], *n.* a glasshouse for the cultivation of vines.

VINEYARD, [vin'-yerd], *n.* a plantation of grape-vines.

VINGT-ET-UN, [va(ng)t'-ā-u(ng)'], *n.* a card game in which the object is to get cards whose pips add up to twenty-one, also called pontoon. [Fr. *vingt-et-un* twenty-one].

VINIC, [vīn'-ik], *adj.* alcoholic.

VINICULTURE, [vin'-i-kul'-cher], *n.* the cultivation of vines.

VINICULTURIST, [vin'-i-kul'-cher-ist], *n.* one who grows vines.

VINOMETER, [vīn-om'-it-er], *n.* an apparatus for measuring the alcoholic content of wine.

VIN-ORDINAIRE, [van(g)'-awd-in-āer'], *n.* a cheap draught wine supplied in French restaurants. [Fr. *vin ordinaire*].

VINOSE, [vīn-ōs'], *adj.* vinous. [L. *vinosus*].

VINOSITY, [vin-os'-it-i], *n.* the state of being vinous. [L. *vinositas*].

VINOUS, [vīn'-us], *adj.* like, relating to, wine; drunk with wine. [L. *vinosus*].

VINT, [vint], *n.* a Russian card game. [Russ. *vint*].

VINTAGE (1), [vint'-ij], *n.* grape gathering, the time of grape gathering; the (quality of) wine made from the grapes of a specific year. [OFr. *vindage*].

VINTAGE (2), [vin'-tij], *adj.* (*coll.*) of good quality, of a particular vintage. [*Prec.*].

VINTAGER, [vint'-ij-er], *n.* one who gathers the vintage grapes.

VINTNER, [vint'-ner], *n.* a wine merchant. [OFr. *vinetier*].

VINTRY, [vint'-ri], *n.* a store place for wine; a wine merchant's place. [ME. *vyntrye*].

VINY, [vī'-ni], *adj.* vinous; abounding in grapes.

VIOL†, [vī'-ol], *n.* a stringed musical instrument, a kind of violin. [Fr. *viole*].

VIOLA (1), [vē-ō'-la], *n.* a tenor violin. [It. *viola*].

VIOLA (2), [vī'-ō-la], *n.* (*bot.*) a numerous genus of flowering plants, including the pansy. [L. *viola*].

VIOLABLE, [vī'-ōl-abl], *adj.* capable of being violated.

VIOLACEOUS, [vī'-ō-lā'-shus], *adj.* of, like, or relating to, the violet.

VIOLAN, [vī'-ō-lan], *n.* a blue-violet mineral.

VIOLATE, [vī'-ō-lāt], *v.t.* to treat with violence; to break rudely into a forbidden place, to blaspheme against; to rape. [~L. *violare*].

VIOLATION, [vī'-ō-lā'-shun], *n.* the act of violating; the state of being violated. [L. *violatio*].

VIOLATIVE, [vī'-ō-lat-iv], *adj.* tending to violate.

VIOLATOR, [vī'-ō-lāt-er], *n.* one who violates. [L. *violator*].

VIOLENCE, [vī'-ō-lents], *n.* vigorously forceful action;

vehement energy; brutal force, violation, unlawfully vigorous action; assault. [L. *violentia*].
VIOLENT, [vī'-ō-lent], *adj.* using, displaying violence; with great strength and vigour; impetuously forcible; very rough. [L. *violens*].
VIOLENTLY, [vī'-ō-lent-li], *adv.* in a violent fashion.
VIOLESCENT, [vī'-ō-les'-ent], *adj.* tending to have a violet colour.
VIOLET (1), [vī'-ōl-et], *n.* a mauve or white flower of the genus *Viola*; the bluish-purple colour characteristic of this flower. [Fr. *violette*].
VIOLET (2), [vī'-ōl-et], *adj.* bluish-purple; coloured like the violet.
VIOLIN, [vī'-ōl-in'], *n.* a stringed musical instrument played with a bow; a fiddle. [It. *violino*].
VIOLINE, [vī'-ōl-īn], *n.* the poisonous principle in the sweet violet.
VIOLINIST, [vī'-ōl-in'-ist], *n.* one who plays the violin.
VIOLIST, [vi-ōl'-ist, vī-ol'-ist], *n.* one who plays the viola or viol.
VIOLONCELLIST, [vi'-o-lon-chel'-ist], *n.* one who plays the violoncello.
VIOLONCELLO, [vi-ō-lon-chel'-ō], *n.* a bass instrument similar in shape and principle to the violin. [It. *violoncello*].
VIOLONE, [vi'-o-lōn'-i], *n.* a double-bass, the largest instrument of the violin class. [It. *violone*].
VIPER, [vī'-per], *n.* a poisonous snake, the adder; (*fig.*) a poisonous person. [L. *vipera*].
VIPERINE, [vī'-per-īn], *adj.* like a viper; relating to vipers.
VIPEROUS, [vī'-per-us], *adj.* having the qualities of a viper; evil, poisonous.
VIRAGINIAN, [vi'-ra-jin'-i-an], *adj.* having the qualities of a virago.
VIRAGINITY, [vi'-ra-jin'-it-i], *n.* the state of being a virago.
VIRAGO, [vi-rā'-go], *n.* a violent, fierce, vixenish woman. [L. *virago*].
VIRE†, [vēer], *n.* a crossbow bolt. [Fr. *vire*].
VIRELAY, [vi'-re-lā], *n.* a roundelay. [OFr. *virelai*].
VIRENT, [vīer'-ent], *adj.* verdant; green. [L. *virens*].
VIREO, [vi'-ri-o], *n.* an American bird, the greenlet. [L. *vireo*].
VIRESCENCE, [vī-res'-ents], *n.* the state of being virescent.
VIRESCENT, [vī-res'-ent], *adj.* turning, beginning to be green. [L. *virescens*].
VIRGATE (1), [vur'-gāt], *n.* a quarter of an acre. [LL. *virgata*].
VIRGATE (2), [vur'-gāt], *adj.* shaped like a rod. [L. *virgatus* made of twigs].
VIRGILIAN, [ver-jil'-i-an], *adj.* pertaining to or resembling Virgil and his poetry. [*Virgil* the Latin poet].
VIRGIN (1), [vur'-jin], *n.* a woman without carnal knowledge of a man; a person who has never had sexual experience; **the V.**, the Virgin Mary, Virgo. [OFr. *virgine* from L. *virgo*].
VIRGIN (2), [vur'-jin], *adj.* chaste; untouched; relating to, characteristic of, a virgin.
VIRGINAL (1), [vur'-jin-al], *n.* a small musical instrument played by means of a keyboard.
VIRGINAL (2), [vur'-jin-al], *adj.* virgin; relating to a virgin. [L. *virginalis*].
VIRGINHOOD, [vur'-jin-hŏŏd], *n.* the state of being a virgin.
VIRGINIA, [ver-jin'-i-a], *n.* an American tobacco grown in Virginia; **V. creeper**, (*bot.*) a climbing plant of the genus *Vitis*. [The *Virgin* Queen, Elizabeth].
VIRGINITY, [ver-jin'-it-i], *n.* the physical and moral state of being a virgin; maidenhood, the maidenhead. [L. *virginitas*].
VIRGO, [vur'-gō], *n.* the Virgin; one of the signs of the Zodiac. [L. *virgo*].
VIRGULE, [vurg'-yōōl], *n.* a comma. [Fr. *virgule*].
VIRID, [vi'-rid], *adj.* green. [L. *viridis*].
VIRIDESCENCE, [vier-id-es'-ents], *n.* the state of being viridescent.
VIRIDESCENT, [vier-id-es'-ent], *adj.* green, turning green; young and vital. [L. *viridescens*].
VIRIDITY, [vi-rid'-it-i], *n.* greenness; youthful vitality. [L. *viriditas*].
VIRILE, [vi'-rīl], *adj.* relating to virility, sexually potent; male; strong and vigorous. [L. *virilis*].
VIRILESCENCE, [vi'-ril-es'-ents], *n.* the development of male qualities by an old female.
VIRILITY, [vi-ril'-it-i], *n.* potency; masculinity; male vigour. [L. *virilitas*].
VIROLE, [vi'-rōl], *n.* a ferrule. [Fr. *virole*].
VIROSE, [vī-rōs'], *adj.* foetid. [L. *virosus* poisonous].
VIRTU, [vur'-tōō], *n.* love of the aesthetically exquisite a combination of rarity, antiquity, and artistic merit [It. *virtù* excellence].
VIRTUAL, [vur'-chōō-al], *adj.* for all intents and purposes. [Fr. *virtuel*].
VIRTUALITY, [vur'-chōō-al'-it-i], *n.* the state of being virtual.
VIRTUALLY, [vur'-chōō-al-i], *adv.* in effect, practically.
VIRTUE, [vur'-chōō], *n.* the quality of being morally good and upright; any particular moral excellence; the inward power or merit of a thing; the moral and psychological strength of a person; sexual continence, chastity; the quality of a thing by which it produces effects. [OFr. *vertu* from L. *virtus*].
VIRTUELESS, [vur'-chōō-less], *adj.* without virtue.
VIRTUOSITY, [vur'-chōō-os'-it-i], *n.* great practical skill in a fine art.
VIRTUOSO, [vur'-chōō-ō'-sō], *n.* one highly skilled and knowledgeable in a fine art. [L. *virtuosus*].
VIRTUOUS, [vur'-chōō-us], *adj.* practising moral virtues; chaste. [L. *virtuosus*].
VIRTUOUSLY, [vur'-chōō-us-li], *adv.* in virtuous fashion.
VIRTUOUSNESS, [vur'-chōō-us-nes], *n.* the condition or quality of being virtuous.
VIRULENCE, [vi'-rew-lents], *n.* the quality of being virulent.
VIRULENCY, [vi'-rew-len-si], *n.* the capacity for being virulent.
VIRULENT, [vi'-rew-lent], *adj.* highly poisonous; bitterly malignant. [L. *virulentus*].
VIRULENTLY, [vi'-rew-lent-li], *adv.* in a virulent way.
VIRUS, [vīer'-us], *n.* poison; (*path.*) a noxious substance, capable of passing through a porcelain filter, giving rise to infectious diseases. [L. *virus* slime].
VIS, [vis], *n.* power, vital force. [L. *vis*].
VISA, [vēz'-a], *n.* an endorsement on a passport permitting the holder to enter certain territories. [L. *visa*, *fem.* of *visus* seen].
VISAGE, [viz'-ij], *n.* the human face, the countenance, the expression of a face. [Fr. *visage*].
VISAGED, [viz'-ijd], *adj.* having a visage.
VIS-A-VIS, [vēz'-ah-vē'], *phr.* face to face. [Fr. *vis-a-vis*].
VISCACHA, [vis-kah'-chah], *n.* the South American pampas hare. [Span. *viscacha*].
VISCACHERA, [vis'-kah-chāer'-a], *n.* a colony of viscachas.
VISCERA, [vis'-er-a], *n.*(*pl.*) the intestines. [L. *viscera*].
VISCERAL, [vis'-er-al], *adj.* relating to the viscera.
VISCERATE, [vis'-er-āt], *v.t.* to eviscerate.
VISCID, [vis'-id], *adj.* slimy and sticky. [L. *viscidus*].
VISCIDITY, [vis-id'-it-i], *n.* the state of being viscid.
VISCOSITY, [vis-kos'-it-i], *n.* the state of being viscous.
VISCOUNT, [vī'-kownt], *n.* the rank of nobility next above a baron; the eldest son of an earl. [OFr. *viscomte*].
VISCOUNTCY, [vī'-kownt-si], *n.* the rank, estates, or tenure of a viscount.
VISCOUNTESS, [vī'-kownt-es], *n.* the wife of a viscount.
VISCOUNTSHIP, [vī'-kownt-ship], *n.* the rank of a viscount.
VISCOUNTY, [vī'-kownt-i], *n.* the rank and position of a viscount.
VISCOUS, [vis'-kus], *adj.* slimily glutinous. [L. *viscosus*].
VISCOUSNESS, [vis'-kus-nes], *n.* the state of being viscous.
VISCUS, [vis'-kus], *n.* an entrail. [L. *viscus*].
VISE, **visé**, [vē-zā'], *n.* (*U.S.*) a visa. [Fr. *visé*].
VISHNU, [vish'-nōō], *n.* a member of the Hindu Trinity, the Preserver. [Skr. *Vishnu*].
VISIBILITY, [viz'-i-bil'-it-i], *n.* the state of the atmosphere in relation to the clarity with which objects are visible; the state or quality of being visible.
VISIBLE, [viz'-ibl], *adj.* able to be seen; apparent to the eye. [L. *visibilis*].
VISIBLENESS, [viz'-ibl-nes], *n.* the state of being visible.
VISIBLY, [viz'-ib-li], *adv.* perceptibly to the eye.
VISIGOTHIC, [viz-i-goth'-ik], *adj.* of, pertaining or relating to, the Visigoths.
VISIGOTHS, [viz'-i-goths'], *n.*(*pl.*) (*hist.*) a branch of the Gothic invaders who settled in South Western Europe. [LL. *Visigothi*].
VISION, [vizh'-un], *n.* the quality by which one perceives with the eyes; that which is so perceived; the power of sight; imaginative perception; intuition;

that which is clearly visualized without sensory aid; a supernatural appearance. [L. *visio*].

VISIONAL, [vizh'-un-al], *adj.* pertaining to a vision.

VISIONARINESS, [vizh'-on-er-i-nes], *n.* the condition of being (a) visionary.

VISIONARY (1), [vizh'-on-er-i], *n.* one who experiences visions; an idealistic dreamer.

VISIONARY (2), [vizh'-on-er-i], *adj.* relating to a vision; subsisting only in impracticable imagination; wildly idealistic, immune from the ordinary realities.

VISIONIST, [vizh'-on-ist], *n.* one who has visions.

VISIONLESS, [vizh'-on-les], *adj.* without vision.

VISIT (1), [viz'-it], *n.* the act of visiting; a temporary stay in a place, usually for some purpose; a brief call; an inspection. [Fr. *visite*].

VISIT (2), [viz'-it], *v.t. and i.* to make a call on; to go to see for a special reason; to inspect; to make visits. [L. *visitare*].

VISITABLE, [viz'-it-abl], *adj.* able to be visited; worth going to see.

VISITANT, [viz'-it-ant], *n.* one who visits. [L. *visitans*].

VISITATION, [viz'-it-ā'-shun], *n.* the act of visiting; a special visit of inspection by a superior; a message or messenger of God, *esp.* in the form of a natural catastrophe; a visit that the visited find unpleasant. [L. *visitatio*].

VISITATORIAL, [viz'-it-a-taw'-ri-al], *adj.* visitorial.

VISITING, [viz'-it-ing], *adj.* authorized to inspect.

VISITING CARD, [viz'-it-ing-kahd'], *n.* a small rectangle of pasteboard on which one's name, etc., is printed, left as an indication that one has paid a call.

VISITOR, [viz'-it-er], *n.* one who visits; an official who pays visits of inspection; one who takes up a temporary sojourn in a place. [Fr. *visiteur*].

VISITORIAL, [viz'-it-aw'-ri-al], *adj.* relating to an official visit or visitor.

VISIVE, [viz'-iv], *adj.* tending to have power to see.

VISON, [vē'-son], *n.* the American mink. [Fr. *vison*].

VISOR, VIZOR, [viz'-er], *n.* the movable frontpiece of a helmet covering the face. [AFr. *viser*].

VISOR

VISORED, [viz'-erd], *adj.* wearing or having a visor.

VISTA, [vist'-a], *n.* a prospect down an avenue; a mental prospect surveying a long period of time or a long series of events. [It. *vista* view].

VISTOMENTE, [vist'-ō-ment'-i], *adv.* (*mus.*) very quickly. [It. *vistomente*].

VISUAL, [vizh'-yōō-al], *adj.* relating to the sight; perceived by the eyes. [L. *visualis*].

VISUALIZATION, [vizh'-yōō-al-īz-ā'-shun], *n.* the act or process of visualizing; that which is visualized.

VISUALIZE, [vizh'-yōō-al-īz], *v.t. and i.* to imagine visually; to picture.

VISUALLY, [vizh'-yōō-al-i], *adv.* by visual means.

VITAL, [vit'-al], *adj.* having life, relating to life; actively alive and vigorous; all-important, urgent, essential. [L. *vitalis*].

VITALISM, [vīt'-al-izm], *n.* a theory based upon the belief in a vital principle.

VITALIST, [vīt'-al-ist], *n.* one who believes in vitalism.

VITALITY, [vī-tal'-it-i], *n.* vital force and vigour. [L. *vitalitas*].

VITALIZATION, [vīt'-al-īz-ā'-shun], *n.* the act of vitalizing, the state of being vitalized.

VITALIZE, [vīt'-al-īz], *v.t.* to impart life to; to animate; to make vital and vigorous.

VITALLY, [vīt'-al-i], *adv.* so as to be vital; essentially.

VITALS, [vī'-talz], *n.(pl.)* the essential organs.

VITAMIN, [vit'-a-min], *n.* one of several chemical substances found in certain foods, and essential to life and health. [~L. *vita* life].

VITELLARY, [vit'-el-er-i], *adj.* of, or pertaining to, the vitellus. [L. *vitellus* yolk of an egg].

VITELLICLE, [vit-el'-ikl], *n.* a yolk sac.

VITELLIN, [vit-el'-in], *n.* the protein in the yolk of an egg.

VITELLUS, [vit-el'-us], *n.* the yolk of an egg. [L. *vitellus*].

VITIATE, [vish'-i-āt], *v.t.* to impair, render ineffective; to sully; to weaken or destroy the effect of. [~L. *vitiare*].

VITIATION, [vish'-i-ā'-shun], *n.* the act of vitiating; the state of being vitiated.

VITICIDE, [vit'-i-sīd], *n.* a pest which attacks vines.

VITICULTURE, [vit'-i-kul'-cher,] *n.* the culture of the grape-vine. [L. *vitis* vine and CULTURE].

VITIOSITY, [vish'-i-os'-it-i], *n.* corruption, depravity. [L. *vitiositas*].

VITIS, [vit'-is], *n.* a genus of climbing plants including the vine. [L. *vitis* grape-vine].

VITRAIN, [vit'-rān], *n.* non-laminated glossy hard coal. [L. *vitrum* glass].

VITREOSITY, [vit'-ri-os'-it-i], *n.* the state of being vitreous.

VITREOUS, [vit'-ri-us], *adj.* relating to, resembling, consisting of, glass. [L. *vitreus*].

VITREOUSNESS, [vit'-ri-us-nes], *n.* vitreosity.

VITRESCENCE, [vi-tres'-ents], *n.* the quality of being glassy.

VITRESCIBLE, [vit-res'-ibl], *adj.* able to be vitrified.

VITRICS, [vit'-riks], *n.(pl.)* the science of glass manufacture.

VITRIFACTION, [vit'-ri-fak'-shun], *n.* the act, process, or operation of converting into glass by heat; the state of being vitrified.

VITRIFIABLE, [vit'-ri-fī-abl], *adj.* capable of being vitrified.

VITRIFICATION, [vit'-ri-fik-ā'-shun], *n.* vitrifaction.

VITRIFIED, [vit'-ri-fīd], *adj.* converted into glass.

VITRIFORM, [vit'-ri-fawm], *adj.* having the form of glass. [L. *vitrum* glass and FORM].

VITRIFY, [vit'-ri-fī], *v.t. and i.* to convert into glass by subjecting to heat and fusion; to become glass in form.

VITRIOL, [vit'-ri-ol], *n.* (*chem.*) (a salt of) sulphuric acid; **blue v.,** copper sulphate; **green v.,** ferrous sulphate; **oil of v.,** sulphuric acid. [L. *vitreolus* made of glass].

VITRIOLATE, [vit'-ri-ōl-āt], *v.t.* to convert into vitriol.

VITRIOLATION, [vit'-ri-ōl-ā'-shun], *n.* the act or process of converting into a vitriol.

VITRIOLIC, [vit'-ri-ol'-ik], *adj.* relating to, containing, having the qualities of, vitriol; obtained from vitriol; (*fig.*) violently penetrative, biting.

VITRIOLIZE, [vit'-ri-ōl-īz], *v.t.* to treat with, or change into, vitriol.

VITRIOLIZED, [vit'-ri-ōl-īzd], *adj.* vitriolated.

VITTA, (*pl.* **vittae**), [vit'-a], *n.* (*bot.*) an oily strip in the fruit of umbelliferous plants. [L. *vitta* band].

VITTATE, [vit'-āt], *adj.* having fillets or vittae. [L. *vittatus*].

VITULAR, [vi'-chōō-ler], *adj.* relating to a calf. [~L. *vitulus* calf].

VITULINE, [vi'-chōō-līn], *adj.* like, or pertaining to, a calf or to veal. [L. *vitulinus*].

VITUPERABLE, [vī-tewp'-er-abl], *adj.* blameworthy.

VITUPERATE, [vī-tewp'-er-āt], *v.t.* to blame abusively, to scold violently. [~L. *vituperare*].

VITUPERATION, [vī-tewp'-er-ā'-shun], *n.* the act of vituperating, blame, abuse.

VITUPERATIVE, [vī-tewp'-er-at-iv], *adj.* having a scolding nature, uttering or containing abuse.

VITUPERATIVELY, [vī-tewp'-er-at-iv-li], *adv.* in a vituperative manner.

VITUPERATOR, [vī-tewp'-er-ā-tor], *n.* one who vituperates. [L. *vituperator*].

VIVA (1), [vē'-va], *n.* a cry or greeting or applause. [It. *viva* may he live].

VIVA (2), [vīv'-a], *n.* (*coll.*) a viva voce examination. [VIVA (VOCE)].

VIVACE, [viv-ah'-chi], *adv.* (*mus.*) in a lively manner. [It. *vivace*].

VIVACIOUS, [viv-ā'-shus], *adj.* having animated manners and a natural liveliness in society; having great vitality. [~L. *vivax* vigorous].

VIVACIOUSLY, [viv-ā'-shus-li], *adv.* in a vivacious manner.

VIVACIOUSNESS, [viv-ā'-shus-nes], *n.* the quality of being vivacious.

VIVACISSIMO, [viv'-a-chis'-im-ō], *adv.* (*mus.*) with great vivacity. [It. *vivacissimo*].

VIVACITY, [viv-as'-it-i], *n.* an inherent quality of temperament characterized by an animated and energetic style of expression in speech and carriage, high spirits. [L. *vivacitas*].

VIVANDIERE, vivandière, [vē-vahn'-di-āer'], *n.* (*hist.*) a woman camp follower of a French regiment. [LL. *vivanda* provisions].

VIVARIUM, [vī-vāer'-i-um], *n.* a place for keeping live animals under natural conditions. [L. *vivarium* enclosure].

VIVA VOCE (1), [vīv'-a-vōs'-i], *n.* (*coll.*) an oral examination. [L. *viva voce* with the living voice].

VIVA VOCE (2), [vīv'-a-vōs'-i], *adj.* oral.

VIVA VOCE (3), [vīv'-a-vōs'-i], *adv.* orally.
VIVE, [vēv], *int.* long live! success to! [Fr. *vive*].
VIVERRINE, [vi-ve'-rīn], *adj.* of or relating to the civets. [L. *viverrinus*].
VIVERS, [vī'-verz], *n.(pl.)* eatables. [OFr. *vivres*].
VIVES, [vīvz], *n.* a disease attacking the ears of horses, causing suppuration of the glands. [OFr. *vives*].
VIVIANITE, [viv'-i-an-īt], *n.* (*min.*) a phosphate of iron forming in blue and green crystals. [J. G. *Vivian*, the discoverer].
VIVID, [viv'-id], *adj.* having form, colour, or characteristics brought out strongly, having an intense brilliance; reproducing in brilliant, lifelike images or form; painted in bright colours. [L. *vividus* vigorous].
VIVIDITY, [viv-id'-it-i], *n.* vividness.
VIVIDLY, [viv'-id-li], *adv.* in a vivid manner; (of a narrative), realistically.
VIVIDNESS, [viv'-id-nes], *n.* the quality of being vivid.
VIVIFIC, [viv-if'-ik], *adj.* vivifical. [L. *vivificus*].
VIVIFICAL†, [viv-if'-ik-al], *adj.* giving life, reviving.
VIVIFICATE, [viv'-if-ik-āt], *v.t.* to give life to, vivify.
VIVIFICATION, [viv'-if-ik-ā'-shun], *n.* the act of vivifying, restoration.
VIVIFICATIVE, [viv'-if-ik'-at-iv], *adj.* reviving.
VIVIFIER, [viv'-i-fī-er], *n.* one who or that which vivifies.
VIVIFY, [viv'-i-fī], *v.t.* to endue with life, to revive, to quicken.
VIVIPARISM, [vīv-vip'-er-izm], *n.* viviparous reproduction.
VIVIPARITY, [vī'-vi-pa'-rit-i], *n.* viviparousness.
VIVIPAROUS, [vī-vip'-er-us], *adj.* giving birth to young in a living state, as opposed to *oviparous*. [L. *vivus* living and *parere* to bear].
VIVIPAROUSLY, [vī-vip'-ar-us-li], *adv.* in a viviparous way.
VIVIPAROUSNESS, [vī-vip'-er-us-nes], *n.* the quality of being viviparous.
VIVISECT, [viv'-i-sekt'], *v.t.* and *i.* to practise vivisection on; to perform a vivisection. [L. *vivus* living and *secare* to cut].
VIVISECTION, [viv'-i-sek'-shun], *n.* the technique or act of operating or experimenting on live creatures for scientific purposes.
VIVISECTIONIST, [viv'-i-sek'-shun-ist], *n.* one who practises or advocates vivisection.
VIVISECTOR, [viv'-i-sek-tor], *n.* one who vivisects.
VIVO, [vē'-vō], *adv.* (*mus.*) with animation. [It. *vivo*]
VIXEN, [viks'-en], *n.* a female fox; a maliciously quarrelsome woman, a shrew. [OE. **fyxen* female fox].
VIXENISH, [viks'-en-ish], *adj.* like a vixen.
VIXENISHLY, [viks'-en-ish-li], *adv.* in a vixenish manner.
VIXENLY, [viks'-en-li], *adj.* having the qualities of a vixen.
VIZ., [viz], *adv.* that is; namely. [~VIDELICET].
VIZARD, [viz'-erd], *n.* a mask. [~VISOR].
VIZIER, [viz'-ēer], *n.* an administrative official of high rank in Mohammedan countries, *esp.* Turkey; †**Grand V.**, the Turkish Prime Minister. [~Arab. *wezir*].
VIZIERATE, [viz'-ēer-āt], *n.* the office of vizier.
VIZOR, see VISOR.
VLACH (1), [vlak], *n.* a native of Wallachia. [Serbian *Vlach*].
VLACH (2), [vlak], *adj.* Wallachian.
VLEI, [vlī], *n.* a hollow, dried-up pond. [Du. *vallei* valley].
VOCABLE, [vōk'-abl], *n.* a word, a term. [L. *vocabulum* name].
VOCABULARY, [vōk-ab'-yōō-ler-i], *n.* a glossary of lingual or technical terms, *esp.* as appended to a text; the total number of words at the command of a person, extent of language. [~*Prec.*].
VOCABULIST, [vōk-ab'-yōō-list], *n.* a person who compiles a vocabulary.
VOCAL, [vō'-kal], *adj.* relating to, produced by, expressed by, the voice; resembling the sound of a voice or voices; having found a means of expression; noisy; **v. chords**, the two membranes in the larynx, at the opening of the glottis, which vibrate to produce vocal sounds; **v. music**, music especially written for the voice; accompanied or unaccompanied singing; **v. thrill**, the vibration of the chest wall when it acts as a resonator to the sound of the voice. [L. *vocalis*].
VOCALION, [vō-kāl'-yun], *n.* a reeded wind-instrument producing sounds resembling the human voice.
VOCALISM, [vō'-kal-izm], *n.* the use of the voice; the specific vowel sounds of a word or language.
VOCALIST, [vō'-kal-ist], *n.* a singer, *esp.* a professional.
VOCALITY, [vō-kal'-i-ti], *n.* the quality of being vocal; the state of being a vowel.
VOCALIZATION, [vō'-kal-i-zā'-shun], *n.* the act of vocalizing; the technique of singing with clear articulation.
VOCALIZE, [vō'-kal-īz], *v.t.* and *i.* to adapt into a form suitable for the voice; to make vocal; to sing vowel sounds; to convert into a vowel.
VOCALLY, [vō'-kal-i], *adv.* by means of the voice; in words.
VOCALNESS, [vō'-kal-nes], *n.* the quality of being vocal.
VOCATION, [vō-kā'-shun], *n.* calling; a natural talent for a particular profession; the adopted profession governing one's life; a trade, occupation; (*theol.*) a call, believed to be of divine origin, to a religious mission. [L. *vocatio* summons].
VOCATIONAL, [vō-kā'-shun-al], *adj.* pertaining to, engaged in, suitable for, a vocation.
VOCATIONALLY, [vō-kā'-shun-al-i], *adv.* in a vocational manner; with reference to a vocation.
VOCATIVE (1), [vok'-at-iv], *n.* (*gram.*) the case used to denote address to a person.
VOCATIVE (2), [vok'-at-iv], *adj.* (*gram.*) forming the case of personal address.
VOCE, [vō'-chā], *n.* (*mus.*) the voice. [It. *voce*].
VOCIFERANCE, [vōs-if'-er-ants], *n.* a state of clamour; clamorousness.
VOCIFERANT, [vōs-if'-er-ant], *adj.* clamorous.
VOCIFERATE, [vōs-if'-er-āt], *v.t.* and *i.* to utter loudly, to shout, cry; to yell, bawl. [~L. *vociferari*].
VOCIFERATION, [vōs-if'-er-ā'-shun], *n.* a violent outcry, exclamation, clamour. [L. *vociferatio*].
VOCIFERATOR, [vōs-if'-er-ā-ter], *n.* one who vociferates.
VOCIFEROUS, [vōs-if'-er-us], *adj.* making a vigorous use of the voice, clamorous; turbulent or noisy.
VOCIFEROUSLY, [vōs-if'-er-us-li], *adv.* in a vociferous way.
VOCIFEROUSNESS, [vōs-if'-er-us-nes], *n.* the quality of being vociferous.
VODKA, [vod'-ka], *n.* an intoxicating spirit drunk in Russia, etc., distilled from rye or potatoes. [Russ. *vodka*].
VOE, [vō], *n.* a creek or inlet. [~OIcel. *vagr*].
VOGLE, [vōgl], *n.* a natural cavity in a Cornish mine. [~Cornish *vooga* cavern].
VOGUE, [vōg], *n.* fashion prevailing at any particular time, a temporary craze; popularity. [Fr. *vogue* drift].
VOICE (1), [vois], *n.* sound expressed by means of the mouth and human larynx; any sound given utterance by breath acting upon the vocal chords, *esp.* words or song; the power of speech; any medium of self-expression, a speaker, a vote; a precept, a command; (*gram.*) aspect of a verb indicating the relation between the subject and predicate; the form indicating this; **to give v.**, to give utterance, to bay. [OFr. *vois* from L. *vox* voice].
VOICE (2), [vois], *v.t.* to express; to express by articulation; to act as a medium of expression for.
VOICED, [voist], *adj.* possessing a voice; uttered with the voice; (*phon.*) uttered with vibration of the vocal chords.
VOICELESS, [vois'-les], *adj.* having no voice or vote.
VOICELESSNESS, [vois'-les-nes], *n.* the condition characterized by loss of voice, state of being speechless.
VOICING, [vois'-ing], *n.* the process of imparting to an organ-pipe its proper tonal quality.
VOID (1), [void], *n.* a large, empty space of indeterminate dimensions, a vacuum; the space between the stars; (*fig.*) a spiritual or emotional deficiency.
VOID (2), [void], *adj.* empty of all concrete matter, unoccupied, vacant, untenanted; destitute, devoid of; legally invalidated, nullified. [OFr. *voide* from LL. **vocitum* empty].
VOID (3), [void], *v.t.* to leave, quit; to get rid of, evacuate; (*leg.*) to nullify, to render ineffective.
VOIDABLE, [void'-abl], *adj.* (*leg.*) able to be annulled or made void; able to be discharged.
VOIDANCE, [void'-ants], *n.* the act of emptying; the act of ejecting from a benefice, vacancy.
VOIDED, [void'-id], *adj.* (*her.*) having an ordinary which seems to be cut in the middle.
VOIDER, [void'-er], *n.* (*leg.*) one who voids; a kind of shallow basket used in agricultural work; (*her.*) a type of ordinary resembling the flanch.
VOIDING, [void'-ing], *n.* the act of voiding, emptying; discharged matter; that which is voided, ejected.

VOIDNESS, [void'-nes], *n.* the state of being void.
VOILE, [voil, vwahl], *n.* a light, semi-transparent, cotton material used for women's and children's clothing and light furnishings. [Fr. *voile* a veil].
VOIVODE, [voiv'-ōd], *n.* the title of the former princes of Wallachia. [Russ. *voevoda* general].
VOLANT, [vō'-lant], *adj.* flying; passing through the air; (*her.*) represented as flying; (*zool.*) having a natural power to fly. [L. *volans*].
VOLAPUK, volapük, [vol'-a-pōōk], *n.* an international language devised by J. M. Schleyer in 1879. [~WORLD and SPEAK].
VOLAR, [vō'-ler], *adj.* (*anat.*) situated in, relating to, the palm of the hand. [~L. *vola* palm of the hand].
VOLATILE, [vol'-a-tīl], *adj.* subject to quick evaporation; (*fig.*) responding quickly and with fickleness to different emotional stimuli, full of a gay, capricious life; **v. alkali,** ammonia. [L. *volatilis* flying].
VOLATILENESS, [vol'-at-īl-nes], *n.* the quality of being volatile.
VOLATILITY, [vol'-at-il'-i-ti], *n.* the quality of being quick in emotional response, capriciousness, fickleness.
VOLATILIZABLE, [vol-at'-il-īz-abl], *adj.* able to be volatilized.
VOLATILIZATION, [vol-at'-il-īz-ā'-shun], *n.* the act or process of volatilizing.
VOLATILIZE, [vol-at'-il-īz], *v.t* to render volatile; to cause to evaporate.
VOL-AU-VENT, [vol'-ō-vah(ng)], *n.* a small pasty filled with mince. [Fr. *vol-au-vent*].
VOLBORTHITE, [vol-bawt'-īt], *n.* (*min.*) vanadiate of copper occurring in small yellow crystals. [Von *Volborth*, its discoverer].
VOLCANIC, [vol-kan'-ik], *adj.* relating to, produced by, a volcano or its action; (*fig.*) subject to violent outbursts.
VOLCANICITY, [vol'-kan-is'-it-i], *n.* the quality of being volcanic.
VOLCANIST, [vol'-kan-ist], *n.* an expert in the phenomena of volcanoes.
VOLCANO, [vol-kā'-nō], *n.* a mountain or hill of ashes and lava which have accumulated round a vent in the earth's crust through which they have been discharged in a molten state; **active v.,** a volcano which continues to discharge vapours, ashes and lava from a vent usually situated in a crater at its summit; **dormant v.,** a volcano known to be periodically active but not at the moment active; **extinct v.,** a volcano in which the vent or vents have become permanently closed, or which has ceased to be active. [It. *volcano* from L. *Vulcanus*].
VOLE (1), [vōl], *n.* a hand in which all the tricks are won by one player; a grand slam. [~L. *volare* to fly].
VOLE (2), [vōl], *n.* a rodent of the genus *Microtus*, resembling a rat; **field v.,** a field mouse. [Uncert.].
VOLE (3), [vōl], *v.i.* to make a vole.
VOLET, [vol'-ā], *n.* a side panel of a triptych. [Fr. *volet* shutter].
VOLITANT, [vol'-it-ant], *adj.* (*zool.*) able to flit. [L. *volitare* to flit].
VOLITATION, [vol'-it-ā'-shun], *n.* (*zool.*) the act of flitting.
VOLITION, [vōl-ish'-un], *n.* the act of willing; faculty or power of determining choice or forming a purpose. [MedL. *volitio*].
VOLITIONAL, [vōl-ish'-un-al], *adj.* relating to, derived from, volition.
VOLITIONALLY, [vōl-ish'-un-al-i], *adv.* by means of volition.
VOLITIONARY, [vōl-ish'-un-er-i], *adj.* volitional.
VOLITIONLESS, [vōl-ish'-un-les], *adj.* deprived of volition.
VOLITIVE, [vol'-it-iv], *adj.* expressing volition.
VOLKSLIED, [folks'-lēt], *n.* a folksong. [Germ. *volkslied*].
VOLKSRAAD, [folks'-rawd], *n.* a S. African legislative assembly; the members of this. [Du. *volk* folk and *raad* counsel].
VOLLEY (1), [vol-i], *n.* a discharge of a number of projectiles more or less simultaneously; in games, the hitting of the ball before it touches the ground; (*fig.*) a vigorous series. [Fr. *volée*].
VOLLEY (2), [vol'-i], *v.t. and i.* to let fly or fire in the form of a volley; to discharge a volley; in games, to hit (the ball) before it touches the ground.
VOLPLANE (1), [vol'-plān], *n.* a gliding descent of an aeroplane with engines shut off.
VOLPLANE (2), [vol'-plān], *v.t. and i.* to (cause to) descend without engine power. [Fr. *vol planer*].
VOLT (1), [vōlt], *n.* the unit of electromotive force or pressure. [A. *Volta*, the Italian scientist].
VOLT (2), [vōlt], *n.* the rearing up of a horse on its hind legs; a leaping manoeuvre in fencing. [~VAULT].
VOLTAGE, [vōlt'-ij], *n.* measurement in volts; electrical pressure measured in volts.
VOLTAIC, [volt-ā'-ik], *adj.* relating to Alessandro *Volta*, the discoverer of voltaism; relating to, consisting of, electrical energy; **v. cell,** a simple electro-chemical cell consisting of a copper and a zinc plate immersed in dilute sulphuric acid.

VOLTAIC CELL

VOLTAIREANISM, [vol-tāer'-i-an-izm], *n.* scepticism typical of *Voltaire*.
VOLTAISM, [volt'-ā-izm], *n.* chemical action between metals immersed in liquids; galvanism.
VOLTAMETER, [volt-am'-it-er], *n.* (*elect.*) an instrument for measuring a quantity of current electricity by the decomposition of an electrolyte.
VOLTI, [vol'-ti], *v.t.* (*mus.*) turn over; **v. subito,** turn over quickly. [It. *volti*].
VOLTMETER, [vōlt'-mē-ter], *n.* an instrument for indicating voltage.
VOLTZITE, [volt'-zīt], *n.* (*min.*) an oxy-sulphide of zinc. [*Voltz*, the discoverer].
VOLUBILITY, [vol'-yōō-bil-i-ti], *n.* the power of being voluble, excessive fluency of speech.
VOLUBLE, [vol'-yōōbl], *adj.* having a natural gift for quick and continuous speech; overwhelming in speech. [L. *volubilis*].
VOLUBLENESS, [vol'-yōōbl-nes], *n.* the quality of being voluble.
VOLUBLY, [vol'-yōō-bli], *adv.* in a voluble way.
VOLUME, [vol'-yōōm], *n.* formerly, a roll of parchment containing literary material; a book, complete in itself or one of a number completing a whole work; compass, dimensions, capacity; amount of solid mass, body of material; (*mus.*) loudness. [L. *volumen* a roll].
VOLUME-CONTROL, [vol'-yōōm-kon-trōl'], *n.* (*wirel.*) the variable resistance on a wireless set which diminishes or increases the volume of sound.
VOLUMED, [vol'-yōōmd], *adj.* having the form of a volume.
VOLUMETRIC, [vol'-yōō-met'-rik], *adj.* relating to measurement by means of standard units of volume.
VOLUMINAL, [vol-yōō'-min-al], *adj.* characterized by, relating to, volume.
VOLUMINOSITY, [vol-yōō'-min-os'-i-ti], *n.* capacity for volume. [L. *voluminosus*].
VOLUMINOUS, [vol-yōō'-min-us], *adj.* containing many volumes; of a size sufficient to occupy many volumes, copious, vast, extensive, numerous. [L. *volumen* roll].
VOLUMINOUSLY, [vol-yōō'-min-us-li], *adv.* to a voluminous degree.
VOLUMINOUSNESS, [vol-yōō'-min-us-nes], *n.* the quality of being voluminous.
VOLUNTARILY, [vol'-unt-er-i-li], *adv.* in a voluntary way.
VOLUNTARINESS, [vol'-un-ter-i-nes], *n.* the attribute of being voluntary.
VOLUNTARY (1), [vol'-unt-er-i], *n.* a solo, usually of an extempore nature, played on a church organ; †a volunteer. [*Next*].
VOLUNTARY (2), [vol'-unt-er-i], *adj.* acting out of reasons not immediately governed or influenced by others, acting willingly and freely; done without compulsion, performed deliberately and freely; supported by charity; **v. conveyance,** (*leg.*) a conveyance of property made unconditionally; **v. hospital, etc.,** a hospital, etc., supported by voluntary contributions. [L. *voluntarius*].
VOLUNTARYISM, [vol'-unt-er-i-izm], *n.* the doctrine that the Church should not come under the jurisdiction of the State; belief in private charitable, as opposed to state, support for hospitals.
VOLUNTEER (1), [vol'-unt-ēer'], *n.* a person who voluntarily offers to serve in any capacity, *esp.* military. [L. *voluntarius* free].
VOLUNTEER (2), [vol'-unt-ēer'], *adj.* a plant, *esp.* a potato, springing up casually; composed of volunteers.
VOLUNTEER (3), [vol'-unt-ēer'], *v.t. and i.* to offer out of one's own free will; to offer oneself as a volunteer, *esp.* for military purposes.
VOLUPTUARY, [vol-up'-chōō-er-i], *n.* a person who habitually seeks voluptuous experiences, a sensualist; a debauchee. [LL. *voluptuarius* voluptuous].

VOLUPTUOUS, [vol-up'-choo-us], *adj.* having an abnormal appetite for sensual or sexual experiences, fond of luxury or controlled lechery; inducing sensual pleasure or sexual excitement. [~L. *voluptas* pleasure].

VOLUPTUOUSLY, [vol-up'-choo-us-li], *adv.* in a voluptuous way.

VOLUPTUOUSNESS, [vol-up'-choo-us-nes], *n.* the quality of, the capacity for, being voluptuous.

VOLUTE, [vol-yoot'], *n.* (*arch.*) the spiral scroll characteristic of the Ionic capital; (*zool.*) a mollusc of the genus *Voluta*, having a spiral shell. [L. *voluta*].

VOLUTED, [vol-yoot'-id], *adj.* (*arch.*) having a volute.

VOLUTION, [vol-ew'-shun], *n.* a spiral turn or wreath; a coiling movement; a convolution.

VOLVOX, [vol'-voks], *n.* (*zool.*) a genus of minute organisms living in stagnant water.

VOLVULUS, [volv'-yool-us], *n.* (*path.*) a twist in the intestines. [L. *volvere* to turn].

VOMER, [vom'-er], *n.* (*anat.*) the thin flat bone between the nostrils. [L. *vomer* ploughshare].

VOMIT (1), [vom'-it], *n.* the foulness of food and gastric juices discharged from the stomach into the mouth, sick; the act of being sick; that which induces vomiting, emetic. [L. *vomitus*].

VOMIT (2), [vom'-it], *v.t. and i.* to eject from the stomach into the mouth; to discharge in a mass; to be rid involuntarily of the contents of the stomach, to be sick. [~L. *vomitum*, *p.pt.* of *vomere*].

VOMITING, [vom'-it-ing], *n.* the act of throwing up involuntarily the contents of the stomach.

VOMITION, [vom-ish'-un], *n.* the act of vomiting. [L. *vomitio*].

VOMITIVE, [vom'-it-iv], *adj.* vomitory, emetic.

VOMITO, [vom'-ē-tō], *n.* yellow fever in its worst stages characterized by excessive vomiting. [Span. *vomitos*].

VOMITORY (1), [vom'-it-er-i], *n.* an emetic; †the principal entrance and exit of a public building.

VOMITORY (2), [vom'-it-er-i], *adj.* relating to vomiting, causing the involuntary discharge of matter from the stomach. [L. *vomitorius*].

VOMITURITION, [vom'-it-yoo-rish'-un], *n.* futile effort to vomit.

VOODOO, [voo'-doo'], *n.* a primitive form of religion or witchcraft practised by the negroes of Haiti and elsewhere in the West Indies and America. [Native].

VOODOOISM, [voo'-doo'-izm], *n.* voodoo beliefs and ritual.

VORACIOUS, [vo-rā'-shus], *adj.* having a powerful undiscriminating appetite, greedy from hunger, having a large, apparently insatiable appetite; (*fig.*) all-consuming. [~L. *vorax* hungry].

VORACIOUSLY, [vo-rā'-shus-li], *adv.* in a voracious manner, ravenously.

VORACIOUSNESS, [vo-rā'-shus-nes], *n.* the quality of being voracious.

VORACITY, [vo-ras'-i-ti], *n.* voraciousness. [Fr. *voracité*].

VORANT, [vo'-rant], *adj.* (*her.*) devouring a live animal. [L. *vorans*].

VORTEX, [vaw'-teks], *n.* a violent whirlpool; a whirling movement of the air, a whirlwind; (*fig.*) an overwhelming set of circumstances into which human society is uncontrollably drawn. [L. *vortex*].

VORTICAL, [vaw'-tik-al], *adj.* having the characteristics of a vortex, whirling.

VORTICALLY, [vaw'-tik-al-i], *adv.* in a vortical way.

VORTICELLA, [vaw'-tis-el'-a], *n.* (*zool.*) a group of the *Vorticellidae*, creating a vortex by moving their cilia. [MdL. *vorticella*].

VORTICOSE, [vaw'-tik-ōs'], *adj.* vortical. [L. *vorticosus*].

VORTIGINOUS, [vaw-tij'-in-us], *adj.* vortical. [L. *vortigo*].

VOTARESS, [vō'-ter-es'], *n.* a woman votary.

VOTARIST, [vō'-ter-ist], *n.* a votary.

VOTARY (1), [vō'-ter-i], *n.* a person who has taken vows dedicating his whole life to a god, an institution, or a particular aim; a practical worker for an ideal; a devotee. [~L. *votum* a vow].

VOTARY (2), [vō'-ter-i], *adj.* consecrated, devoted.

VOTE (1), [vōt], *n.* a means of giving expression to one's preference or opinion concerning a resolution, motion, or choice of a representative by one of various methods such as a ballot-paper or show of hands; the opinion of a person passed officially in this way. [L. *votum* vow].

VOTE (2), [vōt], *v.t. and i.* to express by means of a vote; to consider, estimate; propose; to elect by suffrage to establish by vote; to give judgment by means of a vote.

VOTELESS, [vōt'-les], *adj.* having no vote.

VOTER, [vōt'-er], *n.* a person who is legally entitled to vote; one who records a vote.

VOTING, [vōt'-ing], *n.* the act of a person who votes; **v. paper,** a paper on which an elector marks his vote.

VOTIVE, [vō'-tiv], *adj.* offered in accordance with a vow. [L. *votivus* relating to a vow].

VOTIVELY, [vō'-tiv-li], *adv.* in a votive manner.

VOUCH, [vowch], *v.t. and i.* to offer by way of official evidence, to warrant; to offer proof; **to v. for,** to affirm the truth of, to bear witness to, guarantee. [OFr. *voucher* to cite, from L. *vocare* to call].

VOUCHEE, [vowch-ē'], *n.* (*leg.*) the person summoned into court to warrant a title.

VOUCHER, [vowch'-er], *n.* a person who vouches; a ticket which acts as a substitute for money; a statement or document confirming the truth or fact of certain events, etc.

VOUCHSAFE, [vowch'-sāf'], *v.t.* to permit with condescension. [ME. *vouchen safe*, to guarantee safety].

VOUCHSAFEMENT, [vowch-sāf'-ment], *n.* an act of vouchsafing.

VOUSSOIR, [voo'-swah(r)], *n.* (*arch.*) a wedge-like stone built into an arch. [Fr. *voussoir*].

VOUSSOIR

VOW (1), [vow], *n.* a solemn promise, usually made in the name of a god, a pledge. [OFr. *vou* from L. *votum*].

VOW (2), [vow], *v.t. and i.* to assert in the form and spirit of a vow; to consecrate by a vow, devote, dedicate; to declare.

VOWEL (1), [vow'-el], *n.* (*phon.*) a sound produced in speaking by allowing an air-stream to pass uninterruptedly through the vocal chords and mouth; characters or letters indicating this, as *a*, *e*, *i*, *o*, *u*. [L. *vocalis*].

VOWEL (2), [vow'-el], *adj.* of or relating to a vowel.

VOWELLED, [vow'-eld], *adj.* having vowels.

VOWELLESS, [vow'-el-les], *adj.* having no vowel.

VOWER, [vow'-er], *n.* one who makes a vow.

VOYAGE (1), [voi'-ij], *n.* a journey which necessitates travelling by boat over a comparatively long distance, *esp.* between countries. [OFr. *voiage* journey].

VOYAGE (2), [voi'-ij], *v.i.* to undertake a voyage, to travel by boat.

VOYAGER, [voi'-ij-er], *n.* a traveller who journeys by sea or water.

VOYAGEUR, [vwī'-ah-zhur'], *n.* a Canadian timber-worker. [Fr. *voyageur* traveller].

VRAISEMBLANCE, [vrā'-sahm-blah(ng)s], *n.* appearance of truth. [Fr. *vraisemblance*].

VULCAN, [vul'-kan], *n.* (*myth.*) the god of fire, who specialized in the working of metals. [L. *Vulcanus*].

VULCANIAN, [vul-kān'-i-an], *adj.* relating to Vulcan or to work in iron. [L. *Vulcanius*].

VULCANIC, [vul-kan'-ik], *adj.* relating to Vulcan.

VULCANISM, [vul'-kan-izm], *n.* the action of volcanic heat.

VULCANIST, [vul'-kan-ist], *n.* (*geol.*) an advocate of the theory that geological strata owe their origin to volcanic disturbances.

VULCANITE, [vul'-kan-īt], *n.* rubber mixed with a larger proportion of sulphur.

VULCANIZATION, [vul'-kan-īz-ā'-shun], *n.* the process of vulcanizing.

VULCANIZE, [vul'-kan-īz], *v.t.* to subject (rubber) to heat, and add a high percentage of sulphur so as to produce a rigid, durable substance; to join together by means of this process.

VULGAR (1), [vul'-ger], *n.* †the lower-classes; those who are vulgar.

VULGAR (2), [vul'-ger], *adj.* disregarding the accepted conventions of polite society; **the v. tongue,** the vernacular. [L. *vulgaris* of the multitude].

VULGARIAN, [vul-gāer'-i-an], *n.* a vulgar person.

VULGARISM, [vul'-ger-izm], *n.* an example of vulgarity, *esp.* in speech; a crude grammatical error.

VULGARITY, [vul-ga'-rit-i], *n.* the quality of being vulgar; crudity of manners or language; an expression of bad taste and insensitivity.

VULGARIZATION, [vul'-ger-ī-zā'-shun], *n.* the act of vulgarizing; an instance of vulgarizing.

VULGARIZE, [vul'-ger-īz], *v.t.* to render vulgar.
VULGARLY, [vul'-ger-li], *adv.* in a vulgar way.
VULGARNESS, [vul'-ger-nes], *n.* the quality of being vulgar, vulgarity.
VULGATE (1), [vul'-gāt], *n.* a version of the Scriptures in Latin made during the fourth century A.D. [~L. *vulgare* to make general].
VULGATE (2), [vul'-gāt], *adj.* relating to the Vulgate.
VULNERABILITY, [vul'-ner-a-bil'-i-ti], *n.* the capacity for being vulnerable.
VULNERABLE, [vul'-ner-abl], *adj.* able to be wounded; susceptible to, liable to, injury; (*fig.*) open to criticism; (*contract bridge*) having won one game towards winning a rubber. [L. *vulnerabilis*].
VULNERABLENESS, [vul'-ner-abl-nes], *n.* the state of being vulnerable.
VULNERARY (1), [vul'-ner-er-i], *n.* a cure for wounds.
VULNERARY (2), [vul'-ner-er-i], *adj.* having the power to heal wounds.
VULPICIDE, [vulp'-i-sīd], *n.* the killing of a fox; a fox-hunter. [L. *vulpes* fox and *caedere* to kill].
VULPINE, [vulp'-īn], *adj.* relating to, having the characteristics of, foxes; cunning, crafty. [L. *vulpinus*].
VULPINISM, [vulp'-in-izm], *n.* cunning.
VULPINITE, [vulp'-in-īt], *n.* (*min.*) a siliceous variety of anhydrite. [(*Casta-*) *Volpino*, near Bergamo, Italy].
VULSELLA, [vul-sel'-a], *n.* (*surg.*) a forceps designed with clawed points. [L. *vulsella*].
VULTURE, [vul'-cher], *n.* a large bird of prey, with head and neck bare of feathers, and upper mandible hooked at the tip, living chiefly on carrion; (*fig.*) a person who lives by preying on others. [OFr. *vultur*].
VULTURINE, [vul'-cher-īn], *adj.* of or relating to the vulture; having the characteristics of the vulture; rapacious.
VULTURISH, [vul'-cher-ish], *adj.* like a vulture; rapacious.
VULTURISM, [vul'-cher-izm], *n.* rapacity.
VULTUROUS, [vul'-cher-us], *adj.* vulturish.

VULTURE

VULVA, [vul'-va], *n.* (*anat.*) an orifice, *esp.* the opening of the female genitals; the external female genitals. [L. *vulva*].
VULVAR, [vul'-ver], *adj.* (*anat.*) relating to the vulva.
VULVIFORM, [vul'-vi-fawm], *adj.* (*bot.*) like a cleft with inturned rims. [L. *vulva* wrapper and FORM].
VULVITIS, [vul-vī'-tis], *n.* inflamed condition of the vulva. [VULVA and Gk. *itis* denoting inflammation]
VYING (1), [vī'-ing], *n.* the act of competing.
VYING (2), [vī'-ing], *adj.* striving for superiority.

W, [dubl'-yōō], the twenty-third letter of the English alphabet; **W.C.,** (*coll.*) water-closet, lavatory.
WAAC, [wak], *n.* (*coll.*) a member of the *W*oman's *A*rmy *A*uxiliary *C*orps during the war of 1914-18.
WAAF, [waf, wof], *n.* (*coll.*) a member of the *W*omen's *A*uxiliary *A*ir *F*orce.
WABBLE, see WOBBLE.
WABBLY, see WOBBLY.
WACKE, [wak'-e(r)], *n.* (*min.*) a grey or greenish-brown clay formed from volcanic rock. [MHGerm. *wacke* large stone].
WAD (1), [wod], *n.* a small amount of soft, tightly packed fibres or grasses, etc., used to supplement packing, parcelling, or bandages, a pad, a plug; a thick pile of bank-notes; †a plug to be rammed down the barrel of a gun when loading. [Uncert.].
WAD (2), [wod], *n.* (*min.*) an earthy oxide of manganese; black-lead. [Uncert.].
WAD (3), (**wadding, wadded**), [wod], *v.t.* to form into a wad; to apply to as a wad.
WADABLE, [wād'-abl], *adj.* fordable.
WADDED, [wod'-id], *adj.* formed into a wad or mass; packed tightly by means of a wad.
WADDING, [wod'-ing], *n.* a soft material, *esp.* of cotton-wool, used as padding or absorbent; material out of which wads for guns are manufactured.
WADDLE (1), [wodl], *n.* the act of waddling.
WADDLE (2), [wodl], *v.i.* to walk in an ungainly style characterized by short steps and a rolling from side to side; to move with the gait of a duck. [Unkn.].
WADDLER, [wod'-ler], *n.* one who waddles.
WADDLING, [wod'-ling], *adj.* moving by means of a waddle.
WADDLINGLY, [wod'-ling-li], *adv.* in a waddling manner.
WADDY, [wod'-i], *n.* the wooden war-club of the Australian aboriginals. [Uncert.].
WADE (1), [wād], *n.* the act of wading.
WADE (2), [wād], *v.t.* and *i.* to cross by wading; to walk through water which reaches to a level above the ankle; (*fig.*) to work (through an almost impenetrable mass of dull material); **to w. in,** to proceed to enter in, to participate with vigour. [OE. *wadan*].
WADER, [wād'-er], *n.* one who wades; an angler's long waterproof boot; a bird characterized by wading habits.
WAD-HOOK, [wod'-hŏŏk], *n.* a strong iron screw to extract wads or cartridges remaining in guns.
WADI, [wod'-i], *n.* a deep water-course in which water flows only during the rainy season. [Arab. *wadi*].
WADMAL, [wod'-mal], *n.* a thick woollen cloth. [OIcel. *vathmal* cloth].
WAD-PUNCH, [wod'-punch], *n.* a steel punch with a tubular head, used for making wads for guns, etc.

WAD-PUNCH

WADSET†, [wod'-set], *n.* (*leg.*) in Scotland, a pledge of land as surety for a debt or obligation. [OE. *wed settan* to deposit a pledge].
WADSETTER†, [wod'-set'-er], *n.* one who holds by wadset.
WAE (1), [wā], *n.* (*Scots*) woe. [OE. *wa* woe].
WAE (2), [wā], *adj.* (*Scots*) woeful, sad.
WAFD, [wofd], *n.* a political party in Egypt standing for Nationalist interests. [Arab. *wafd*].
WAFDIST (1), [wof'-dist], *n.* a member of, or sympathizer with, the Wafd.
WAFDIST (2), [wof'-dist], *adj.* of, pertaining to, or resembling the Wafd or Wafdists.
WAFER (1), [wā'-fer], *n.* a piece of very thin biscuit, a flaky layer of baked flour; that characterized by extreme thinness; a round piece of very thin bread used for Holy Communion; a red seal in the form of a circular piece of gummed paper. [OFr. *waufre*].
WAFER (2), [wā'-fer], *v.t.* to form into a wafer; to seal with a wafer.
WAFERY, [wā'-fer-i], *adj.* resembling a wafer.
WAFFLE (1), [wofl], *n.* a batter cake baked in an iron mould. [Du. *wafel*].
WAFFLE (2), [wofl], *v.t.* and *i.* (*coll.*) to talk vague nonsense; to utter vaguely and nonsensically. [~OE. *wlaffian* to stammer].
WAFFLE-IRON, [wofl'-iern], *n.* an iron mould in which waffles are baked.
WAFT (1), [woft], *n.* the act of wafting; that which moves by wafting; a flag at half-mast.
WAFT (2), [woft], *v.t.* and *i.* to cause to move in a light buoyant manner, to carry on an eddying, jerky stream of air or water; to drift or float in the air. [Uncert.].
WAFTAGE, [woft'-ij], *n.* buoyant conveyance.
WAFTER, [woft'-er], *n.* one who, or that which, wafts, *esp.* a passage-boat.
WAFTING, [woft'-ing], *n.* the act of bearing or floating in a fluid.
WAFTURE, [wof'-cher], *n.* the act of waving.
WAG (1), [wag], *n.* the act of wagging.
WAG (2), [wag], *n.* a humorist, a person with a characteristic sense of fun, one with a fund of humorous stories and a comic turn of phrase. [Uncert.].

WAG (3), (wagging, wagged), [wag], *v.t. and i.* to move up and down or to and fro with one end fixed; to shake, vibrate. [~OE. *wagian*].

WAGE (1), [wāj], *n.* a rate of payment for work, usually on a weekly basis; (*pl.*) money paid at regular intervals for work done. [ONFr. *wage*].

WAGE (2), [wāj], *v.t.* to undertake, carry on, organize, to bet, wager. [ONFr. *wagier*].

WAGE-EARNER, [wāj'-urn-er], *n.* one who earns wages.

WAGELESS, [wāj'-les], *adj.* receiving no wages.

WAGER (1), [wāj'-er], *n.* an agreement to stake money or its equivalent on the result of a future event or a question to be settled, a bet; (*leg.*) an oath of innocence sworn by a defendant in conjunction with others. [ONFr. *wageoure*].

WAGER (2), [wāj'-er], *v.t. and i.* to gamble, bet; to make a wager.

WAGERER, [wāj'-er-er], *n.* one who wagers.

WAGE-WORK, [wāj'-wurk], *n.* work done for wages.

WAGE-WORKER, [wāj'-wurk'-er], *n.* a person who works for a wage.

WAGGERY, [wag'-er-i], *n.* the humour, jokes, and tricks of a wag, impish humour.

WAGGISH, [wag'-ish], *adj.* resembling the humour of a wag, done from waggery; merry, comic.

WAGGISHLY, [wag'-ish-li], *adv.* in a waggish manner.

WAGGISHNESS, [wag'-ish-nes], *n.* the quality of being waggish.

WAGGLE (1), [wagl], *n.* the act of waggling.

WAGGLE (2), [wagl], *v.t. and i.* (*coll.*) to move from side to side, to shake up and down, *esp.* of the human body. [~WAG (3)].

WAGGLY, [wag'-li], *adj.* (*coll.*) that waggles.

WAGGON, see WAGON.

WAGGONAGE, see WAGONAGE.

WAGGONER, see WAGONER.

WAGGONET, see WAGONETTE.

WAGNERIAN, [vahg'-nēer'-i-an], *adj.* in the style of Wilhelm Richard *Wagner*, the musical composer, or of his music.

WAGNERIST, [vahg'-ner-ist], *n.* an admirer of Wagner.

WAGNERITE (1), [vahg'-ner-īt], *n.* (*min.*) a phosphate and fluoride of magnesium. [F. M. von *Wagner*, a chemist].

WAGNERITE (2), [vahg'-ner-īt], *n.* a devotee of the music or theories of Richard *Wagner*.

WAGON, WAGGON, [wag'-on], *n.* a sturdy flat-bedded vehicle on four wheels used for carrying heavy loads. [Du. *wagen*].

WAGONAGE, WAGGONAGE, [wag'-on-ij], *n.* payment for haulage in a wagon; †a number of wagons.

WAGONER, WAGGONER, [wag'-on-er], *n.* one who drives and loads a wagon.

WAGONETTE, WAGGONET, [wag'-on-et'], *n.* an open four-wheeled passenger carriage with the back seats facing each other in pairs.

WAGON-LIT, [vag'-aw(ng)-lē'], *n.* a sleeping-car attached to a train. [Fr. *wagon lit* coach bed].

WAGTAIL, [wag'-tāl], *n.* a small bird, belonging to the genus *Motacilla*, named from the wagging of its long tail.

WAGTAIL

WAGWANT, [wag'-wont'], *n.* (*bot.*) the quaking grass, *Briza media*. [WAG (3)].

WAHABI, [wah-hah'-bi], *n.* a follower of Abdel *Wahab*, a Mohammedan, whose doctrines are of a puritanically reforming nature.

WAIF, [wāf], *n.* a person without home, money, food, or job, *esp.* a child; (*leg.*) a piece of lost property. [OScand. *veif* tatter].

WAIL (1), [wāl], *n.* the act of wailing; a high, continuous sound which rises and then falls in pitch and intensity, a plaintive cry, usually the expression of a state of sorrow or pain.

WAIL (2), [wāl], *v.t. and i.* to lament; to make a prolonged high cry or sound which rises and then falls in pitch and intensity, expressive of deep sorrow or pain; to mourn, howl, sigh loudly. [~OScand. *væla* to lament].

WAILER, [wāl'-er], *n.* one who wails.

WAILFUL, [wāl'-fŏol], *adj.* expressive of a state of sorrow, mournful.

WAILING, [wāl'-ing], *n.* mournful cries of sorrow expressed by wails.

WAILINGLY, [wāl'-ing-li], *adv.* in a wailing manner.

WAIN, [wān], *n.* a wagon; (*astron.*) the group of stars called the Great Bear. [OE. *wægn*].

WAINHOUSE, [wān'-hows], *n.* a shed for storing wagons.

WAINROPE, [wān'-rōp], *n.* a rope for fastening a load on a wagon.

WAINSCOT (1), [wānz'-kot], *n.* wooden panelling at the base of a wall. [Du. *wagenschot*].

WAINSCOT (2), [wānz'-kot], *v.t.* to furnish with a wainscot.

WAINSCOTING, [wānz'-kot-ing], *n.* material for a wainscot; a skirting of wood round the base of a wall.

WAINWRIGHT, [wān'-rīt], *n.* a wagonmaker.

WAIST (1), [wāst], *n.* the narrowest part of the trunk between the hips and lowest ribs; the part of a garment designed to fit round this; the widest part of a ship. [ME. *wast*].

WAIST (2), [wāst], *v.t.* to fit with a waist, as a dress.

WAISTBAND, [wāst'-band'], *n.* the band or upper part of trousers or of a skirt, which fits to the waist.

WAISTBELT, [wāst'-belt'], *n.* a belt for fitting to the waist.

WAIST-CLOTH, [wāst'-kloth'], *n.* a strip of cloth worn round the waist and crutch.

WAISTCOAT, [wāst'-kōt, wes'-kut], *n.* a short sleeveless garment for men fitting closely round the waist and chest, opening at the front, and worn beneath a jacket.

WAIST-DEEP, [wāst'-dēp'], *adj.* reaching up to the waist.

WAISTER, [wāst'-er], *n.* (*naut.*) an inexperienced seaman stationed in the waist of a ship.

WAIT (1), [wāt], *n.* an act or period of waiting.

WAIT (2), [wāt], *n.* a member of a group singing Christmas carols outside houses and collecting money. [ONFr. *waite* watcher].

WAIT (3), [wāt], *v.t. and i.* to watch for; to remain in expectancy; to pass the time prior to an expected event, to stay, remain until a certain thing happens; **to w. at,** to serve as a waiter at; **to w. for,** to defer taking another course until; **to w. on,** to serve as a waiter to; to keep in close attendance to. [OFr. *waiter*].

WAIT-A-BIT, [wāt'-a-bit], *n.* (*bot.*) the African grapple-plant, *Uncaria procumbens*.

WAITER, [wāt'-er], *n.* one who waits; a male servant in attendance in a public dining-room; a salver; a customs officer.

WAITING (1), [wāt'-ing], *n.* the act of staying, attendance; the work of a waiter; **in w.,** in attendance.

WAITING (2), [wāt'-ing], *adj.* serving.

WAITING-LIST, [wāt'-ing-list], *n.* a list of names of people waiting their turn for a vacancy falling due, etc.

WAITINGLY, [wāt'-ing-li], *adv.* by means of waiting.

WAITING-MAID, [wāt'-ing-mād], *n.* a female servant who attends at table.

WAITING-ROOM, [wāt'-ing-rŏom'], *n.* a room set aside for waiting passengers, patients, etc.

WAITING-WOMAN, [wāt'-ing-wŏom'-an], *n.* a waiting-maid.

WAITRESS, [wāt'-res], *n.* a woman employed to serve customers at table in a hotel, restaurant, or café.

WAIVE† (1), [wāv], *n.* an outlawed woman. [AFr. *waive*].

WAIVE (2), [wāv], *v.t.* to defer temporarily; to relinquish, not to insist on or claim. [~OE. *wafian* to hesitate].

WAIVER, [wāv'-er], *n.* (*leg.*) the act of consenting to waive.

WAKE (1), [wāk], *n.* an annual vigil or commemoration service of a church dedication; the watching over a corpse by mourners during the night before the funeral; the party with food and drink held during this ritual; a festivity and fair held in the north of England annually. [Uncert.].

WAKE (2), [wāk], *n.* the smooth swirling track of water with an apparently oily surface left behind a moving ship; **in the w. of,** behind, after. [OIcel. *vek* hole in the ice].

WAKE (3), (woke), [wāk], *v.t.* to cause to pass from a state of sleep, to rouse from sleep; to stimulate to a state of consciousness, to quicken in the functioning of the mind and senses; to cause to stir, to revive in the functioning of the parts, to make active, stir, excite; *v.i.* to become awake, to be or remain in a conscious state, to have the senses and mind functioning; to stir the mind into activity, to attain a state of quick realization and mental alertness; to excite out of a state of dormancy or lethargy. [OE. *wacian*].

WAKE (4), [wāk], *v.t.* to participate in a wake.

WAKE-AT-NOON, [wāk'-at-nōōn], *n.* (*bot.*) the plant, *Ornithogalum umbellatum*, the Star of Bethlehem.
WAKEFUL, [wāk'-fōōl], *adj.* not sleeping; unable to sleep; watchful, vigilant.
WAKEFULLY, [wāk'-fōōl-i], *adv.* in a wakeful manner.
WAKEFULNESS, [wāk'-fōōl-nes], *n.* the state of being wakeful.
WAKEN, [wak'-en], *v.t. and i.* to stir into conscious activity; to excite to action or motion by breaking a state of sleep; to wake, to break out of a state of sleep or unconsciousness. [OE. *wæcnan*].
WAKENER, [wāk'-en-er], *n.* one who rouses from sleep.
WAKER (1), [wāk'-er], *n.* one who rouses from sleep.
WAKER (2), [wāk'-er], *n.* one who participates in a wake.
WAKE-ROBIN, [wāk'-rob'-in], *n.* (*bot.*) the plant *Arum maculatum*, lords and ladies, the cuckoo-pint.
WAKING, [wāk'-ing], *n.* the period of being awake; **w. hours,** the hours when one is awake.
WALDENSES, [wawld-en'-sēz], *n.* (*pl.*) a Christian sect with Puritan affinities existing in the Piedmont valleys of the Alps. [P. *Waldo*, the founder].
WALE (1), [wāl], *n.* a ridge raised on the flesh by a blow or lash, etc., a weal; a ridge raised in a fabric. [OE. *walu*].

WAKE-ROBIN

WALE (2), [wāl], *v.t.* to raise wales on.
WALED, [wāld], *adj.* marked with ridges.
WALER, [wāl'-er], *n.* a horse raised in New South Wales.
WALHALLA, see VALHALLA.
WALK (1), [wawk], *n.* the act or action of walking; the manner of walking, gait; distance covered during a time spent in walking; a journey, a route, a road; a place specially laid out for walking in, a promenade, a shaded avenue; a course of life, occupation; social sphere or class; speed of progress by walking, *esp.* of a horse.
WALK (2), [wawk], *v.t. and i.* to proceed by placing one foot alternately before the other, there being always one foot in contact with the ground; to make to proceed by walking; to accompany at walking pace; to proceed, go, travel on foot; **to w. away with,** to win easily; **to w. off with,** to steal; **to w. out with,** to court; **to w. over,** to win with ease or by opponent's absence. [OE. *wealcan*].
WALKABLE, [wawk'-abl], *adj.* able to be walked.
WALKER, [wawk'-er], *n.* one who walks; a person who walks or trains young hounds.
WALKING, [wawk'-ing], *n.* the act of moving on the feet by alternate steps at a slow pace.
WALKING-FAN, [wawk'-ing-fan'], *n.* a fan used as a sunshade.
WALKING-STAFF, [wawk'-ing-stahf], *n.* a walking-stick of a size longer than normal.
WALKING-STICK, [wawk'-ing-stik], *n.* a stick or cane with a plain or ornamented handle, usually tipped with a ferrule at the bottom end, used when out walking either as a means of support or for display.
WALK-OUT (1), [wawk'-out], *n.* a strike of workers who quit their factory in protest.
WALK-OUT (2), [wawk'-out], *v.i.* to leave a factory or shop in protest as a form of strike.
WALK-OVER, [wawk'-ōv-er], *n.* a victory easily gained; a contest in which there is only one competitor.
WALKYR, [val'-kēer], *n.* a valkyrie.
WALL (1), [wawl] *n.* a structure of stone, brick, etc., usually more extended in height than thickness, acting as a means of defence, partition, or privacy for private property; one side of a building; anything acting as a partition; anything of an extended apparently solid nature. [OE. *wall*].
WALL (2), [wawl], *v.t.* to enclose with a wall.
WALLABA, [wol'-ab-a], *n.* a leguminous tree of Guiana, cut for its timber, *Eperua falcata*. [Uncert.].
WALLABY, [wol'-a-bi], *n.* an Australian marsupial allied to the kangaroo; (*coll.*) an Australian. [Native].
WALLACHIAN (1), [wol-ā'-ki-an], *n.* a native of *Wallachia*, a Danubian principality; the language spoken in Wallachia. [~VLACH].
WALLACHIAN (2), [wol-ā'-ki-an], *adj.* relating to, coming from, made in, Wallachia.
WALLAH, [wol'-a], *n.* an Indian employee; (*coll.*) a person, fellow, *esp.* one connected with a specialized job a specialist. [Hindi *wala* belonging to].
WALLAROO, [wol-a-rōō'], *n.* a large Australian kangaroo, *Macropus robustus*, with shaggy and sometimes dark hair. [Native].
WALL-BARLEY, [wawl'-bah'-li], *n.* (*bot.*) a species of wild barley, *Hordeum murinum*, the mouse barley.
WALL-CREEPER, [wawl'-krēp-er], *n.* a small bird, *Tichodroma muraria*, which frequents rocks and walls and feeds on insects.
WALL-CRESS, [wawl'-kres'], *n.* (*bot.*) the rock plant, *Arabis*.
WALLED, [wawld], *adj.* enclosed by a wall.
WALLER, [wawl'-er], *n.* one who builds walls.
WALLET, [wol'-it], *n.* a small pocket-book for holding banknotes or correspondence; a brief-case; †a pilgrim's knapsack. [ME. *walet*].
WALL-EYE, [wawl'-ī], *n.* an affliction of the eye in which the iris turns a whitish colour. [~Icel. *vagl* film over the eye].
WALL-EYED, [wawl'-īd], *adj.* afflicted by wall-eye.
WALLFLOWER, [wawl'-flow'-er], *n.* (*bot.*) the cruciferous plant, *Cheiranthus Cheiri*; (*coll.*) a girl who sits beside a dance floor waiting for a partner.
WALLFRUIT, [wawl'-frōōt], *n.* fruit whose trees need the protection of a wall.
WALL-GAME, [wawl'-gām], *n.* a football game peculiar to Eton College.
WALLING, [wawl'-ing], *n.* materials for walls.
WALL-KNOT, [wawl'-not'], *n.* (*naut.*) a knot to prevent fraying at the end of a rope formed by untwisting the strands and interweaving them.
WALL-LESS, [wawl'-les], *adj.* not built with, or surrounded by, a wall.
WALL-MOSS, [wawl'-mos'], *n.* (*bot.*) a species of lichen growing on walls; the stonecrop, *Sedum acre*.
WALLOON (1), [wol-ōōn'], *n.* a descendant of the old Celtic Belgae in Flanders; their language spoken as a French dialect. [OFr. *wallon*].
WALLOON (2), [wol-ōōn'], *adj.* of or relating to the Walloons; of or in Walloon.
WALLOP (1), [wol'-up], *n.* the act of walloping, a blow, punch; (*slang*) beer.
WALLOP (2), [wol'-up], *v.t. and i.* to beat, punch, hit; to boil. [~GALLOP].
WALLOPING, [wol'-up-ing], *adj.* (*slang*) huge.
WALLOW (1), [wol'-ō], *n.* the act of wallowing; a place where animals wallow.
WALLOW (2), [wol'-ō], *v.i.* to roll with sensual pleasure in (filthy) water or mire; (*fig.*) to take pleasure in moral irregularities; **to w. in money, riches,** to be very rich. [OE. *wealwian*].
WALLOWER, [wol'-ō-er], *n.* one who wallows; a wheel that works the trundle head in a mill.
WALLPAPER, [wawl'-pā'-per], *n.* paper, usually of a coloured or patterned character, pasted in strips on the interior walls of a room as a form of decoration.
WALL-PELLITORY, [wawl'-pel'-it-er-i], *n.* (*bot.*) a plant growing on walls, etc., *Parietaria officinalis*.
WALL-PENNYWORT, [wawl'-pen'-i-wurt], *n.* (*bot.*) the plant, *Cotyledon Umbilicus*.
WALL-PEPPER, [wawl'-pep-er], *n.* (*qot.*) stonecrop.
WALL-PLATE, [wawl'-plāt], *n.* a horizontal timber placed on a wall to take the weight of joists, etc.
WALL-RUE, [wawl'-rōō], *n.* (*bot.*) the fern, *Asplenium Ruta-muraria*.
WALLSEND, [wawlz'-end'], *n.* a superior type of coal. [*Wallsend*, on the Tyne].
WALL-SIDED, [wawl'-sīd-id], *adj.* having perpendicular sides.
WALL-SPRING, [wawl'-spring], *n.* an underground spring issuing from exposed stratified rocks.
WALL-TREE, [wawl'-trē], *n.* a tree trained to grow against a protective wall.
WALL-WASHER, [wawl'-wosh'-er], *n.* an iron plate in the form of a circle or S at the end of a tie-rod as a form of shoring.
WALNUT, [wawl'-nut], *n.* a tree, *Juglans regia*, the timber being used for cabinet work; the edible nut of this tree with a crinkly kernel. [OE. *wealhhnutu*].
WALPURGIS, [vahl-pōōerg'-is], *n.* a witches' ritual held on the eve of May 1, *esp.* on the German Brocken. [St. *Walpurga*].
WALRUS, [wawl'-rus], *n.* a large carnivore, allied to the seals, having a tusk on either side of the mouth, living in the Arctic Ocean. [Du. *walrus*].
WALTZ (1), [wawls], *n.* a dance for two partners, based on three-four or three-two time, and characterized by long sweeping steps governing a series of turns; music for accompanying such a dance. [Germ. *walzen* to revolve].
WALTZ (2), [wawls], *v.t. and i.* to hold so as to waltz; to dance a waltz; to move with a waltzing motion.

WALTZER, [wawls'-er], *n.* a person who waltzes, an expert in waltzing.

WALTZING (1), [wawls'-ing], *n.* the act of dancing a waltz.

WALTZING (2), [wawls'-ing], *adj.* that waltzes; **w. mice,** a breed of mice that spin round rapidly at intervals owing to an inherited defect of the organs of balance.

WAMBLE, [wombl], *v.i.* (*coll.*) to be upset by nausea. [~Dan. *vamle* to feel sick or giddy].

WAMBLE-CROPPED, [wombl'-kropt'], *adj.* feeling sick.

WAMPEE, [wom-pē'], *n.* the Chinese tree, *Cookia punctata*; the edible berry of this. [Chin. *hwang* yellow and *pi* skin].

WAMPUM, [wom'-pum], *n.* strings of beads made from coloured shells, used by the American Indians as money. [NAmerInd. *wambambi*].

WAN, [won], *adj.* pale, pallid. [OE. *wann*].

WAND, [wond], *n.* a small stick, usually smooth and slender, a rod; a staff of authority; a rod used by conjurers; a baton used by orchestral conductors. [~OIcel. *vǫndr* rod].

WANDER, [wond'-er], *v.i.* to proceed by a vague route; to travel in a leisurely manner and not keeping to a direct route, to ramble, roam; to fail to keep to the point in discussion; to lose control of the mind, to be delirious in thought. [OE. *wandrian*].

WANDERER, [wond'-er-er], *n.* one who wanders, *esp.* by habit; a person who deviates from duty.

WANDERING (1), [wond'-er-ing], *n.* the act of one who wanders; extensive travelling, peregrination; delirious rambling of the mind.

WANDERING (2), [wond'-er-ing], *adj.* travelling aimlessly, roaming, rambling; **W. Jew,** a Jew in legend condemned to eternal wandering till Christ's return on earth.

WANDERINGLY, [wond'-er-ing-li], *adv.* in a wandering fashion.

WANDERLUST, [wond'-er-lust], *n.* the urge to travel. [Germ. *wanderlust*].

WANDEROO, [wond'-er-ōō'], *n.* a langur monkey found in Ceylon, a species of *Semnopithecus*; the lion-tailed macaque, *Macacus silenus*, found in India. [Singhalese *wanderu* monkey].

WANDER-PLUG, [wond'-er-plug], *n.* (*wirel.*) a plug which can be connected to various points.

WANE (1), [wān], *n.* the act of waning; diminution of lunar illumination; decline.

WANE (2), [wān], *v.i.* to diminish, lessen, decrease, *esp.* of the illuminated section of the moon visible from the earth. [OE. *wanian*].

WANG†, [wang], *n.* the jaw or cheek; the latchet of a shoe. [OE. *wang*].

WANGHEE, WHANGHEE, [wang'-ē'], *n.* a tough, flexible bamboo, *Phyllostachys nigra*, cut into lengths for walking sticks. [Chin. *hwang*].

WANGLE (1), [wang'-gl], *n.* (*slang*) an act or instance of wangling, fraudulent manipulation.

WANGLE (2), [wang'-gl], *v.t.* (*slang*) to arrange by manipulation which is clever to the point of trickery. [Uncert.].

WANLY, [won'-li], *adv.* in a pale fashion.

WANNED, [wond], *adj.* made wan.

WANNESS, [won'-nes], *n.* the quality of being wan; sickliness.

WANNISH, [won'-ish], *adj.* rather wan.

WANT (1), [wont], *n.* (*dial.*) the mole, *Talpa europæa*. [OE. *wand*].

WANT (2), [wont], *n.* the condition of having an inadequate amount, insufficiency, deficiency, *esp.* of the necessary means of life and comfort, need, poverty, penury, frustration of one's wishes and requirements. [OIcel. *vant* lacking].

WANT (3), [wont], *v.t.* and *i.* to need, to require for one's health's sake, to be destitute of necessaries; to be deficient in quality; to wish to possess, to have a use for; to desire; to be deficient, to be lacking; to fail, fall short. [OIcel. *vanta*].

WANTAGE, [wont'-ij], *n.* deficiency.

WANTING, [wont'-ing], *adj.* lacking, absent; deficient, without essentials.

WANTLESS, [wont'-les], *adj.* having no want.

WANTON (1), [wont'-on], *n.* a person who is wanton, *esp.* a woman of dissolute or flirtatious habits, a harlot.

WANTON (2), [wont'-on], *adj.* lacking moral discipline, characterized by licentious conduct; uncontrollable, irresponsible; capricious, sportive; playing in the wind; extravagant; arbitrary. [ME. *wantoun*].

WANTON (3), [wont'-on], *v.i.* to behave in a wanton manner; to act or grow without restraint; to disport oneself, frolic; to play with licentious intentions, to flirt.

WANTONLY, [wont'-on-li], *adv.* in a wanton way.

WANTONNESS, [wont'-on-nes], *n.* the quality of being wanton; lasciviousness; sportiveness.

WAPACUT, [wop'-a-kut], *n.* the snowy owl found in Hudson Bay, *Nyctea nivea*. [AmerInd.].

WAPENSHAW, [wop'-en-shaw], *n.* (*hist.*) a periodical gathering of Scotsmen able to bear arms; a shooting competition between rival teams. [OScand. *vapn* weapon and ~ SHOW].

WAPENTAKE, [wop'-en-tāk], *n.* a former county division or district, as in Yorkshire, answering to the hundred. [OScand. *vapntak*].

WAPITI, [wop'-i-ti], *n.* the American stag, *Cervus canadensis*, the elk. [NAmerInd. *wapatik*].

WAR (1), [waw(r)], *n.* hostilities undertaken on a large scale between tribes, parties, or nations involving the killing of men; the military profession; the science and tactics of warfare; the means of waging war, armaments; the contest of enemies; **civil w.,** open conflict between armies of opposing factions fighting for control of state power in a nation; **in the wars,** suffering from injury; **holy w.,** war undertaken in religious interests, a crusade; **ideological w.,** a war prosecuted for the sake of a political or social idea, principle; **w. to the knife,** bitter and ruthless warfare, *esp.* as between individuals; **sinews of w.,** the money and materials necessary to make war. [OFr. *werre*].

WAR (2), (**warring, warred**), [waw(r)], *v.i.* to carry on a war, to fight till death or defeat.

WARATAH, [wah'-rat-ah], *n.* (*bot.*) an Australian plant, *Telopea speciosissima*, which has scarlet flowers. [Native].

WARATAH

WAR-BABY, [waw'-bā-bi], *n.* a baby born in wartime, *esp.* of a wartime marriage.

WARBLE (1), [wawbl], *n.* the larva of the bot-fly. [WARBLES].

WARBLE (2), [wawbl], *n.* the act or sound of that which warbles.

WARBLE (3), [wawbl], *v.t.* and *i.* to sing with a tremolo in the voice, to give voice to quavering trills, as a bird; to sing. [OFr. *werbler*].

WARBLER, [wawb'-ler], *n.* a person who warbles; a small songbird of a sub-family of the thrushes.

WARBLES, [wawblz], *n.*(*pl.*) an affection of hard tumours appearing on a horse's back; a disease caused by the larva of the bot-fly. [~Swed. *varbulde* boil].

WARBLING (1), [wawb'-ling], *n.* a warble, a trill.

WARBLING (2), [wawb'-ling], *adj.* having the ability to warble, singing in warbles.

WARBLINGLY, [wawb'-ling-li], *adv.* in a warbling way.

WAR-CRY, [waw'-krī], *n.* a formal cry, shout, cheer, or slogan used as a stimulant before battle.

WARD (1), [wawd], *n.* †a method, position, or place of defence; †a stronghold, castle, fortress; the act of guarding, a defence position in fencing; a room for persons held in custody or under protection, *esp.* one in a prison or hospital; the state of being kept under guard, custody, confinement; a child under the protection of a guardian, a minor; an administrative division of a borough; the characteristic part of a particular lock. [OE. *weard* guard].

WARD (2), [wawd], *v.t.* to act in the capacity of a guardian for; to protect, defend.

WAR-DANCE, [waw'-dahnts], *n.* a ritual dance performed by savages before battle.

WARDCORN, [wawd'-kawn], *n.* (*hist.*) in feudal times, payment in corn in lieu of military service. [WARD (1) and CORN].

WARDEN, [wawd'-en], *n.* a status carrying authority of administration over certain areas; a guardian; a guard, warder; the head of certain Oxford colleges; one appointed for general duties among the civil population during air-raids. [ONFr. *wardein* guard].

WARDENSHIP, [wawd'-en-ship], *n.* the office or administrative power and duties of a warden.

WARDER, [wawd'-er], *n.* a guard over a ward, a prison-guard, a turnkey; a truncheon carried by an officer of arms as a symbol of authority.

WARD-HOLDING, [wawd'-hōld'-ing], *n.* a tenure of land in Scotland held under condition of the tenant's being available for military service.

WARDIAN, [waw'-di-an], *adj.* (*bot.*) descriptive of a glass case for plants. [Dr. N. B. *Ward*, the inventor].

WARD-MOTE, [wawd'-mōt], *n.* an assembly held in a city or borough ward. [WARD (1) and MOOT (1)].

WARD-PENNY, [wawd'-pen'-i], *n.* (*hist.*) payment for watch and ward.
WARDRESS, [wawd'-res], *n.* a female warder.
WARDROBE, [wawd'-rōb], *n.* a large cupboard or piece of furniture where clothes are kept; an outfit of clothes; **w. dealer**, a dealer in old clothes. [~OFr. *garderobe*].
WARDROBE-TRUNK, [wawd'-rōb-trungk'], *n.* an elaborately fitted trunk which, when tipped on end, serves as a wardrobe.
WARD-ROOM, [wawd'-rōōm], *n.* the mess-room of the senior officers of a warship.
WARDSHIP, [wawd'-ship], *n.* the status of being a guardian; the state of being under the protection of a guardian.
WARE (1), [wāer], *n.* (*dial.*) seaweed; (in Scotland) the right of collecting this. [OE. *war*].
WARE (2), [wāer], *n.* an article for sale; manufactured articles, *esp.* earthenware; (*pl.*) products for sale, commodities, merchandise. [OE. *waru*].
WARE (3), [wāer], *adj.* wary. [OE. *wær*].
WARE (4), [wāer], *v.t.* (*coll.*) to beware of. [OE. *warian* to guard].
WARE (5), [wāer], *int.* beware! look out!
WAREFUL, [wāer'-fōōl], *adj.* wary; cautious.
WAREFULNESS, [wāer'-fōōl-nes], *n.* the condition of being wareful.
WARE-GOOSE, [wāer'-gōōs], *n.* the brent goose, *Bernicula brenta.* [WARE (1) and GOOSE].
WAREHOUSE (1), [wāer'-hows], *n.* a large building fitted for storing goods in bulk as a distributing centre to retail traders; a storehouse.
WAREHOUSE (2), [wāer'-hows], *v.t.* to place in a warehouse.
WAREHOUSEMAN, [wāer'-hows-man], *n.* a man employed in a warehouse.
WAREHOUSING, [wāer'-howz-ing], *n.* the act or system of storing in a warehouse, *esp.* in bonded warehouses where goods are not subject to excise duty until put into retail circulation.
WARELESS, [wāer'-les], *adj.* characterized by lack of wariness.
WARELY†, [wāer'-li], *adv.* cautiously.
WARE-ROOM, [wāer'-rōōm], *n.* a room in which wares are displayed.
WARFARE, [waw'-fāer], *n.* the waging of war; the condition of being engaged in war; military service.
WARFARING, [waw'-fāer-ing], *adj.* engaged in carrying on war.
WAR-FIELD, [waw'-fēld], *n.* a theatre of war, battlefield.
WAR-GAME, [waw'-gām], *n.* a game of manoeuvring toy military units.
WAR-HORSE, [waw'-haws], *n.* a cavalry horse, a charger; (*fig.*) a war veteran.
WARILY, [wāer'-i-li], *adv.* in a wary fashion.
WARINESS, [wāer'-i-nes], *n.* the quality of being wary.
WAR-INSURANCE, [wawr'-in-shōōer'-ants], *n.* insurance taken out on ships, etc., in time of war.
WARLIKE, [waw'-līk], *adj.* having a natural propensity for war; relating to war; resembling war; characterized by military factors, martial.
WARLIKENESS, [waw'-līk-nes], *n.* the condition of being warlike.
WARLOCK, [waw'-lok], *n.* (*archaic*) a magician, a wizard. [OE. *wærloga* traitor].
WAR-LORD, [waw'-lawd'], *n.* a military leader who glories in warfare.
WARM (1), [wawm], *n.* the act of warming; **British w.**, an overcoat worn by British Army officers.
WARM (2), [wawm], *adj.* emitting a degree of heat sufficient to be appreciated but not so extreme as to burn or scorch, not hot, characterized by a mild degree of heat, not cold; possessing enthusiasm, ardent, zealous, loyal; heated in response, angry, irritable, impassioned; fanciful; affectionate; rich in tone, reddish in colour; **getting w.**, getting nearer, *esp.* to a concealed mark or object in a child's game. [OE. *wearm*].
WARM (3), [wawm], *v.t. and i.* to impart a degree of heat to, to make warm; to excite, to make deeply interested in, arouse enthusiasm of; to become warm by absorbing heat; **to w. up**, to heat again; to grow warm; to become more enthusiastic.
WARM-BLOODED, [warm'-blud'-id], *adj.* having warm blood, as mammals and birds; quick in emotional response.
WARMER, [wawm'-er], *n.* one who, that which, warms.
WARM-HEARTED, [wawm'-haht'-id], *adj.* having or showing quick sensitivity of affection, cordial.
WARM-HEARTEDLY, [wawm'-haht'-id-li], *adv.* in a warm-hearted fashion, in an affectionate manner.
WARM-HEARTEDNESS, [wawm'-haht'-id-nes], *n.* the quality of being warm-hearted.
WARMING, [wawm'-ing], *adj.* making suitably warm.
WARMING PAN, [wawm'-ing-pan'], *n.* an enclosed metal pan with a long handle, filled with ignited coals, for warming beds.
WARMLY, [wawm'-li], *adv.* in a warm manner; to a warm degree; ardently.
WARMNESS, [wawm'-ness], *n.* the quality of being warm, warmth.
WAR-MONGER, [waw'-mung-er], *n.* a war-lord; one who, for personal gain, encourages warfare.
WARMTH, [wawmth], *n.* the quality of heat retained or emitted, a mild degree of heat; a state of excitement or impassioned ardour, zeal; vehemence; glow of colour, usually reddish in tone; (*coll.*) mild anger.
WARN, [wawn], *v.t.* to inform in advance against approaching or possible danger, to advise caution; to advise care against a failure in performing a duty, admonish; to indicate by a sign. [OE. *wearnian*].

WARMING PAN

WARNER, [wawn'-er], *n.* one who warns.
WARNING, [wawn'-ing], *n.* the act of a person who warns, caution against danger; the means of being warned, previous notice; notice to quit.
WARNINGLY, [wawn'-ing-li], *adv.* in a warning manner.
WAR OFFICE, [wawr'-of'-is], *n.* the British department of State concerned with the administration of the Army and with military affairs.
WARP (1), [wawp], *n.* the threads in a fabric which cross the loom lengthwise at right angles to the woof; mud deposited by tides, and regarded as a land fertilizer; (*naut.*) a rope used for towing. [OE. *wearp*].
WARP (2), [wawp], *v.t. and i.* to put out of shape, to change in shape, *esp.* by twisting, turning, or bending; to turn from truth, to change in purity, to pervert; (*naut.*) to tow by a rope attached to a buoy, etc.; to become twisted out of shape by extremes of temperature; (of cows) to have a miscarriage. [OIcel. *varpa* to throw].
WAR-PAINT, [waw'-pānt] *n.* pigment daubed on the face and other parts of the body on going to war.
WARPATH, [waw'-pahth], *n.* the route followed by American Indians on a marauding expedition; **on the w.**, militant.
WARPED, [wawpt], *adj.* twisted or bent by warping; perverted.
WARPER, [wawp'-er], *n.* the weaver arranging the threads in warp.
WARPING, [wawp'-ing], *n.* arrangement of the warp; fertilization of land by allowing floods to deposit mud; (*naut.*) the use of a warp line.
WARPING BANK, [wawp'-ing-bangk'], *n.* a bank round a field which lets in tidal waters for the purpose of fertilizing the land by mud.
WARPING HOOK, [wawp'-ing-hōōk], *n.* a hook used by ropemakers for hanging yarn on.
WARPING POST, [wawp'-ing-pōst], *n.* a strong post used in warping rope-yarn.
WARPROOF, [waw'-prōōf], *adj.* proof against enemies.
WARRAGAL, WARRIGAL, [wo'-ragl], *n.* the Australian wild dog, *Canis dingo*, the dingo. [Native].
WARRANT (1), [wo'-rant], *n.* an official means of authorization, *esp.* in documentary form; a commission transferring authority to the bearer; a writ of arrest; that which is of a status commanding authority, proof, sanction; **dividend w.**, a document entitling payment of dividend. [OFr. *warant* guarantee].
WARRANT (2) [wo'-rant], *v.t.* to support or sanction in an official or semi-official capacity, to guarantee by implying power to provide proof, to authorize; to justify; to stand by (a statement).
WARRANTABLE, [wo'-rant-abl], *adj.* able to be authorized by warrant; justifiable; **w. stag**, a stag when six years old.
WARRANTABLENESS, [wo'-rant-abl-nes], *n.* the quality of being warrantable.
WARRANTABLY, [wo'-rant-ab-li], *adv.* in a warrantable manner.
WARRANTED, [wo'-rant-id], *adj.* authorized; justified; guaranteed.
WARRANTEE, [wo'-rant-ē'], *n.* the person to whom anything is granted by warrant.
WARRANTER, [wo'-rant-er], *n.* a person who

guarantees a contract or engagement; the official who issues a warrant.

WARRANTING, [wo'-rant-ing], *adj.* authorizing.

WARRANT OFFICER, [wo'-rant-of'-is-er], *n.* an officer, next in rank below a commissioned officer, and acting under a warrant; (*Scots*) a sheriff's officer who issues or delivers a warrant.

WARRANTOR, [wo'-rant-or], *n.* (*leg.*) a person who warrants, a warranter.

WARRANTY, [wo'-rant-i], *n.* authorization, guarantee, security; (*leg.*) manufacturer's assurance that goods are up to standard.

WARREN, [wo'-ren], *n.* a breeding ground for rabbits, riddled with burrows; (*leg.*) a piece of land privileged by grant to be set aside for the breeding of rabbits or game. [ME. *warren* from ONFr. *warir* to preserve].

WARRENER, [wo'-ren-er], *n.* a warren-keeper.

WARRIGAL, see WARRAGAL.

WARRIOR, [wo'-ri-or], *n.* a professional soldier; a man engaged in military life; a soldier who has achieved distinction. [ONFr. *werreour*].

WARRIORESS, [wo'-ri-or-es'], *n.* a female soldier.

WAR-SCOT, [waw'-skot'], *n.* (*hist.*) a feudal tax set aside for the supply of armour and war material.

WARSHIP, [waw'-ship], *n.* a man-of-war; a naval vessel fitted with a full quota of armaments.

WAR-SONG, [waw'-song'], *n.* a song inciting to war, *esp.* one accompanying the war-dance before battle.

WART, [wawt], *n.* a tough knot of cells appearing chiefly on the hands; a spongy excrescence on the hinder pasterns of a horse due to chafing; a protuberance on trees. [OE. *wearte*].

WART-CRESS, [wawt'-kres'], *n.* (*bot.*) a plant of the genus *Coronopus.*

WARTED, [wawt'-id], *adj.* afflicted by small, hard excrescences.

WART-HOG, [wawt'-hog'], *n.* an African ungulate of the genus *Phacochoerus,* allied to the swine.

WART-HOG

WARTIME (1), [waw'-tim'], *n.* time of war.

WARTIME (2), [waw'-tim], *adj.* in or relating to a time of war.

WARTLESS, [wawt'-les], *adj.* having no warts.

WART-WORT, [wawt'-wurt], *n.* (*bot.*) the name applied to several species of plants, generally *Euphorbia Helioscopia,* the sun spurge, believed to cure warts.

WARTY, [wawt'-i], *adj.* covered with, full of, of the nature of, warts.

WARWHOOP, [waw'-hoop], *n.* a full-throated yell raised in charging an enemy; a war cry.

WARWICKITE, [wo'-rik-it], *n.* (*min.*) boro-titanate of magnesium and iron occurring in brown crystals, found at *Warwick* in New York State, U.S.A.

WARY, [wäer'-i], *adj.* cautious of danger; alert, on guard against potential enemies; circumspect. [WARE (3)].

WAS, [woz], *1st and 3rd pret. sing. of* BE. [OE. *wæs*].

WASH (1), [wosh], *n.* the act of washing, *esp.* of dirty clothes; the articles of clothing ready to be sent to the laundry; deposits left by the ebb and flow of water, alluvial mud, a marsh; a lotion for cosmetic or hygienic purposes; dirty water, *esp.* in which food has been cooked, thrown away after kitchen use, usually to pigs; fermented wort from which spirit is extracted; the shallows of a river, *esp.* at the mouth; the blade of an oar; the current of water left behind a moving ship or the blades of the oars; the sound of waves as they ebb and flow over shingle or sand; a weak liquid for drinking, *esp.* weak tea; a thin layer of water infused with a little pigment used by a water-colourist; a thin plating of metal.

WASH (2), [wosh], *v.t.* to cleanse by soaking, rubbing, and scrubbing in water, usually with the help of soap; to cover with water that ebbs and flows, to bathe, to dash against, as the sea; to purify of sin; to move by means of currents or drift; to give a thin metal coating to; *v.i.* to clean oneself with soap and water; to come through a process of washing unchanged; to contact by ebbing and flowing; **to w. down,** to cleanse quickly but not too thoroughly by means of a large quantity of water; **to w. off,** to take off by means of water; **to w. out,** to soak in water, rinse, and squeeze so as to clean; (*coll.*) to cancel; **to w. up,** to cleanse crockery in water; **won't w.,** is unconvincing; **to w. one's hands of,** to refuse responsibility for, to break connexions with; **washed out,** exhausted, tired out pale in complexion. [OE. *wascan*].

WASHABLE, [wosh'-abl], *adj.* able to be washed.

WASHAWAY, [wosh'-a-wā], *n.* a breach caused by a flood washing away the soil.

WASH-BALL, [wosh'-bawl], *n.* a ball of soap used in washing.

WASH-BASIN, [wosh'-bā'-sin], *n.* a basin, usually fitted with running water, for washing in.

WASH-BOARD, [wosh'-bawd], *n.* a board with a ribbed or corrugated surface as an aid for scrubbing dirty clothes in a wash-tub.

WASH-BOTTLE, [wosh'-botl'], *n.* a bottle used for cleansing chemical apparatus.

WASH-BOWL, [wosh'-bōl], *n.* a bowl for washing in.

WASHER, [wosh'-er], *n.* one who or that which washes; a round piece of metal or other material perforated in the centre and placed between the head of a bolt, etc., and the surface against which it is tightened, or between working parts to absorb friction.

WASHERMAN, [wosh'-er-man], *n.* a laundryman.

WASHERWOMAN, [wosh'-er-woo'-man], *n.* a woman employed to wash clothes; a laundress.

WASHHAND-BASIN, [wosh'-hand-bās'-in], *n.* the bowl on a wash-stand in which to wash the hands and face.

WASH-HOUSE, [wosh'-hows], *n.* a house or room in which clothes are washed, a laundry.

WASHILY, [wosh-i-li], *adv.* in a washy manner; to a washy degree.

WASHINESS, [wosh'-i-nes], *n.* the quality of being washy or weak.

WASHING, [wosh'-ing], *n.* the act of cleansing with water; the clothes dispatched to the laundry to be washed at one time.

WASHING MACHINE, [wosh'-ing-mash-ēn'], *n.* a machine used in washing clothes.

WASHING SODA, [wosh'-ing-sō'-da], *n.* hydrous sodium carbonate used for cleaning purposes.

WASHINGTONITE, [wosh'-ing-tun-it], *n.* (*min.*) titaniferous iron. [*Washington,* U.S.A.].

WASHING-UP, [wosh'-ing-up'], *n.* the operation of washing dirty crockery after a meal; the crockery so washed.

WASH-LEATHER, [wosh'-leTH'-er], *n.* a piece of chamois leather for cleaning household articles.

WASH-OUT, [wosh'-owt], *n.* damage caused by flood; a washing out; (*coll.*) a failure.

WASH-POT, [wosh'-pot'], *n.* a vessel in which things are washed.

WASH-STAND, [wosh'-stand'], *n.* a small table on which a wash-basin and toilet requisites are kept.

WASH-TUB, [wosh'-tub], *n.* a tub in which clothes are washed; (*coll.*) a bath-tub.

WASHY, [wosh'-i], *adj.* consisting mostly of water, weak; not firm or hardy; vapid; lacking colourfulness.

WASP, [wosp], *n.* a hymenopterous insect of the genus *Vespa,* characterized by a thin petiole at the waist and alternate markings of black and yellow on the body, and with a sting concealed in the abdomen; **w. waist,** an exaggerated, narrow waist. [OE. *wæps*].

WASP-FLOWER, [wosp'-flow'-er], *n.* (*bot.*) a flower fertilized by wasps.

WASP-FLY, [wosp'-flī], *n.* a species of fly resembling a wasp in colouring, but stingless.

WASPISH, [wosp'-ish], *adj.* having a very slender waist, like a wasp; bad tempered; irascible.

WASPISHLY, [wosp'-ish-li], *adv.* in a waspish manner.

WASPISHNESS, [wosp'-ish-nes], *n.* the quality of being waspish, irascibility.

WASSAIL (1), [wosl, was'-āl], *n.* a festive occasion, *esp.* one accompanied by hard drinking; a spiced ale formerly drunk on such an occasion. [ME. *wes hail* be hale].

WASSAIL (2), [wosl, was'-āl], *v.i.* to participate in a carousal. [ME. *wesseilen*].

WASSAIL-BOWL, [wosl'-bōl], *n.* a vessel containing ale during a festival.

WASSAILER, [wos'-el-er], *n.* a participator at a wassail; a reveller, a drunkard.

WAST, [wost], (*poet.*) *2nd pers. pret. sing.* of BE.

WASTAGE, [wāst'-ij], *n.* the amount lost by waste; waste.

WASTE (1), [wāst], *n.* territory untouched by human habitation, a desolate tract of land, a desert, a barren wilderness; an act of wasting, extravagance, prodigality; rejected matter, refuse; (*leg.*) loss, injury, or destruction of property belonging to an heir.

WASTE (2), [wāst], *adj.* made barren, turned into ruin, converted into a barren tract; untouched by human habitation, deserted, desolate, destitute; rejected as worthless, superfluous. [ONFr. *wast*].

WASTE (3), [wāst], *v.t. and i.* to cause to diminish by unnecessary extravagance, to lose by thoughtless prodigality, to squander, to lose by neglect; **to w. away**, to become emaciated, to lose strength by gradual loss, to become thin from consumption; (*leg.*) to lessen in value by neglect. [ONFr. *waster*].

WASTE-BOOK, [wāst'-bo͝ok], *n.* a book in which temporary entries of transactions are made.

WASTEFUL, (wāst'-fo͝ol], *adj.* causing waste, extravagant, prodigal; expending unnecessarily that which is valuable; destructive, ruinous.

WASTEFULLY, [wāst'-fo͝ol-i], *adv.* in a wasteful manner.

WASTEFULNESS, [wāst'-fo͝ol-nes], *n.* the quality of being wasteful.

WASTE-GATE, [wāst'-gāt], *n.* a gate for draining a pond.

WASTELESS, [wāst'-les], *adj.* involving no waste matter.

WASTENESS, [wāst'-nes], *n.* desolate condition.

WASTE-PAPER BASKET, [wāst'-pā-per-bahsk'-it], *n.* a basket for discarded papers.

WASTE-PIPE, [wāst'-pīp], *n.* a pipe for conveying off waste water or sewerage.

WASTER, [wāst'-er], *n.* any one who squanders money or property; an article damaged in process of being manufactured.

WASTE-WEIR, [wāst'-wēer], *n.* a weir for draining off the surplus water of a canal.

WASTING, [wāst'-ing], *adj.* diminishing by consuming of substance or strength.

WASTREL, [wāst'-rel], *n.* a person who wastes his time and money, a ne'er-do-well.

WATCH (1), [woch], *n.* the act of watching; a period in which sleep is abstained from, vigil; maintenance of a strict and systematic scrutiny, observation of a person's movements; a person or body of men whose duty it is to keep guard, a watchman; a period of the night when a specific guard is on duty; a small portable mechanism for registering the time, a timepiece; (*naut.*) the period allotted for one section of a crew to be on deck. [OE. *wæcce*].

WATCH (2), [woch], *v.t.* to maintain a close observation on, *esp.* with intent to protect, to guard; to tend; to remain in expectancy of; to note carefully; to maintain a strict scrutiny over; *v.i.* to keep awake with intent to guard against dangers, to keep on the alert; to act as a sentry, to keep guard; to look with attention, observe, to function as an onlooker; to take care of an invalid, to keep vigil. [OE. *wæccan* to keep awake].

WATCH-BILL, [woch'-bil'], *n.* (*naut.*) the duty list.

WATCH-BOX, [woch'-boks'], *n.* a sentry-box.

WATCH-CASE, [woch'-kās], *n.* the outer case of a watch.

WATCH-COMMITTEE, [woch'-kom-it'-i], *n.* a committee of a local governing body concerned with police services.

WATCH-DOG, [woch'-dog'], *n.* a dog trained to guard premises; (*fig.*) a chaperone.

WATCHER, [woch'-er], *n.* one who watches.

WATCHET†, [woch'-it], *n.* the colour of pale or light blue; a fisherman's fly of this colour. [Uncert.].

WATCH-FIRE, [woch'-fīer], *n.* a fire used by the guard at night.

WATCHFUL, [woch'-fo͝ol], *adj.* on the alert, vigilant, attentive.

WATCHFULLY, [woch'-fo͝ol-i], *adv.* in a watchful manner.

WATCHFULNESS, [woch'-fo͝ol-nes], *n.* the quality or state of being watchful.

WATCH-GLASS, [woch'-glahs], *n.* a piece of glass for covering the face of a watch; (*naut.*) a half-hour sand glass, for measuring the time of a watch on deck.

WATCH-GUARD, [woch'-gahd], *n.* a chain or strap attached to a watch; a metal grid covering the glass of a watch.

WATCH-HOUSE, [woch'-hows], *n.* a house for the convenience of a guard; a lock-up for the night.

WATCHING, [woch'-ing], *n.* wakefulness.

WATCH-KEY, [woch'-kē], *n.* a key for winding up a watch.

WATCH-LIGHT, [woch'-līt], *n.* a light maintained for the guard; a candle burnt during the night, a night-light.

WATCH-MAKER, [woch'-māk-er], *n.* a person whose occupation is to make or repair watches.

WATCHMAN, [woch'-man], *n.* a sentinel; a man who guards offices or buildings at night; a night policeman; **watchman's rattle**, an instrument which makes a loud rattling sound on being whirled round.

WATCH-NIGHT, [woch'-nīt], *n.* a religious service held towards midnight on New Year's Eve.

WATCH-TOWER, [woch'-tow-er], *n.* a tower giving a commanding view over the countryside, and manned by a sentry.

WATCHWORD, [woch'-wurd], *n.* a word or phrase by which friends recognize each other in battle; a password; a slogan.

WATER (1), [waw'-ter], *n.* a liquid compound consisting of two parts hydrogen to one of oxygen; any large body of water accumulated under natural conditions, a lake, a river; any serum or secretion in the body; urine; **in deep w.**, in trouble; **in low w.**, nearing insolvency; **like a fish out of w.**, out of one's element; **in hot w.**, in trouble; **to hold w.**, (*fig.*) to hang together, to be logical; to stand up to investigation; **of the first w.**, first-class. [OE. *wæter*].

WATER (2), [waw'-ter], *v.t.* to apply water to, to sprinkle, irrigate, to supply with water; to dilute by adding water; to render wavy in surface; to issue new stocks or shares without adding to (the capital of a company, etc.); *v.i.* to imbibe water; to secrete water, to shed in the form of moisture; **to make one's mouth w.**, to stimulate one's expectation of pleasure.

WATERAGE, [waw'-ter-ij], *n.* money paid for transport by water.

WATER-AVENS, [waw'-ter-ā'-venz], *n.* (*bot.*) the plant, *Geum rivale*.

WATER-BAILIFF, [waw'-ter-bā'-lif], *n.* a customs officer with authority for searching ships; a river "game-keeper."

WATER-BATH, [waw'-ter-bahth], *n.* an apparatus for heating by water.

WATER-BEARER, [waw'-ter-bāer'-er], *n.* a water-carrier.

WATER-BED, [waw'-ter-bed'], *n.* a rubber mattress containing water.

WATER-BEETLE, [waw'-ter-bētl], *n.* an aquatic beetle including the species of *Gyrinus*, *Dytiscus*, *Hydrophilus*, *Hydrobius* or *Donacia*.

WATER-BELLOWS, [waw'-ter-bel'-ōz], *n.* a machine for blowing air into a furnace by means of pressure exerted by a descending column of water.

WATER-BIRD, [waw'-ter-burd], *n.* an aquatic bird.

WATER-BISCUIT, [waw'-ter-bisk'-it], *n.* an unsweetened type of biscuit made with water and flour, eaten *esp.* with cheese.

WATER-BLOB, [waw'-ter-blob'], *n.* (*bot.*) the marsh marigold, *Caltha palustris*.

WATER-BOATMAN, [waw'-ter-bōt'-man], *n.* an aquatic insect of the genus *Notonecta*, characterized by long legs by which it moves along the surface of water.

WATERBORNE, [waw'-ter-bawn], *adj.* disseminated or borne by water, *esp.* of disease spread by water; (of troops, etc.) carried in ships or other vessels; (*geol.*) sedimentary.

WATER-BOTTLE, [wawt'-er-botl'], *n.* a bottle or similar container for water, *esp.* as carried by troops on the march or in the field.

WATER-BRASH, [waw'-ter-brash'], *n.* indigestion accompanied by bile.

WATER-BUCK, [waw'-ter-buk'], *n.* a South African antelope of the genus *Cobus*.

WATER-BUFFALO, [waw'-ter-buf'-a-lō], *n.* the domesticated Indian buffalo.

WATER-BUG, [waw'-ter-bug], *n.* (*coll.*) an insect living in water.

WATER-BUTT, [waw'-ter-but], *n.* a large cask in which rain-water gathers.

WATER-CALTROPS, [waw'-ter-kal'-trops], *n.* (*bot.*) the plant *Trapa natans*; the fruit of this. [WATER (1) and ME. *calketrappe* thorny plant].

WATER-CAN, [waw'-ter-kan'], *n.* a watering can; (*bot.*) the yellow water-lily, *Nymphæa lutea*.

WATER-CARRIAGE, [waw'-ter-ka'-rij], *n.* conveyance by water.

WATER-CARRIER, [wawt'-er-ka'-ri-er], *n.* one who carries water for sale in hot countries; (*astron.*) the constellation Aquarius, a sign of the zodiac.

WATER-CART, [waw'-ter-kaht], *n.* a cart bearing a tank of water for spraying roads and gutters.

WATER-CEMENT, [waw'-ter-sim-ent'], *n.* hydraulic cement which hardens under water.

WATER-CHESTNUT, [waw'-ter-chest'-nut], *n.* (*bot.*) the water-caltrops.

WATER-CHUTE, [waw'-ter-sho͞ot], *n.* a sloping board along which water flows, *esp.* one used by bathers as a means of sliding into the water.

WATER-CLOCK, [waw′-ter-klok′], *n.* a clock controlled by a discharge of water.
WATER-CLOSET, [waw′-ter-kloz′-et], *n.* a lavatory flushed by a water system.
WATER-COLOUR, [waw′-ter-kul′-er], *n.* pigment mixed with water, a painting painted in this medium.
WATER-COLOURIST, [waw′-ter-kul′-er-ist], *n.* a person who paints in water-colours.
WATER-COOLED, [waw′-ter-ko͞old], *adj.* fitted with a cooling system of circulating water.
WATERCOURSE, [waw′-ter-kaws] *n.* a stream of water; a passage for water.
WATERCRAFT, [waw′-ter-krahft], *n.* a general name for miscellaneous types of small vessels.
WATER-CRANE, [waw′-ter-krān], *n.* an apparatus for supplying water to locomotives.
WATERCRESS, [waw′-ter-kres′], *n.* (*bot.*) a small creeping plant growing in watery places, the *Nasturtium officinale.*
WATER-CROW, [waw′-ter-krō], *n.* the dipper bird, *Cinclus aqualeicus.*
WATER-CROWFOOT, [waw′-ter-krō′-fo͝ot], *n.* (*bot.*) an aquatic buttercup.
WATER-CURE, [waw′-ter-kyo͞oer], *n.* hydropathy.
WATER-DECK†, [waw′-ter-dek′], *n.* (*milit.*) a painted piece of canvas covering the saddle, bridle, and girths of a horse.
WATER-DEER, [waw′-ter-dēer], *n.* the Chinese deer, *Hydropotes inermis.*

WATERCRESS

WATER-DIVINER, [waw′-ter-di-vin′-er], *n.* a person who detects, or professes to detect, the presence of subterranean water by virtue of a special sense, and usually with the assistance of a forked twig, piece of metal, or other form of dowsing rod.
WATER-DOCTOR, [waw′-ter-dok′-tor], *n.* (*coll.*) a hydropathist.
WATER-DOG, [waw′-ter-dog′], *n.* a dog used to the water; (*pl.*) small clouds, indicative of rain.
WATERDROP, [waw′-ter-drop′], *n.* a drop of water.
WATER-DROPWORT, [waw′-ter-drop′-wurt], *n.* (*bot.*) a poisonous plant of the genus *Œnanthe.*
WATERED, [wawt′-erd], *adj.* supplied with water; made wavy and shiny of surface; diluted.
WATER-ENGINE, [waw′-ter-en′-jin], *n.* an engine to raise water.
WATERER, [waw′-ter-er], *n.* a person who waters.
WATERFALL, [waw′-ter-fawl], *n.* a perpendicular descent of river or stream water, a cascade, a cataract; a place where this occurs.
WATER-FERN, [waw′-ter-furn], *n.* (*bot.*) the royal fern, *Osmunda regalis.*
WATER-FLAG, [waw′-ter-flag′], *n.* (*bot.*) the yellow iris, *Iris pseudacorus.*
WATER-FLEA, [waw′-ter-flē], *n.* an aquatic crustacean found in fresh water.
WATER-FLOOD, [waw′-ter-flud], *n.* an inundation.
WATER-FLY, [waw′-ter-flī], *n.* an insect frequenting fresh water.
WATER-FOWL, [waw′-ter-fowl], *n.*(*pl.*) birds which frequent the water.
WATER-FOX, [waw′-ter-foks′], *n.* the carp.
WATER-FURROW, [waw′-ter-fu′-rō], *n.* a deep furrow made for draining water from the ground; an open drain.
WATER-GALL, [waw′-ter-gawl], *n.* dark, fluffy clouds indicative of rain.
WATER-GAS, [waw′-ter-gas′], *n.* an illuminating gas generated by passing steam over burning carbon or coke.
WATER-GATE, [waw′-ter-gāt], *n.* any type of sluice gate.
WATER-GAUGE, [waw′-ter-gāj], *n.* an instrument for registering the quantity of water in a container.
WATER-GILDER, [waw′-ter-gild′-er], *n.* an expert in water-gilding.
WATER-GILDING, [waw′-ter-gild′-ing], *n.* the process of gilding metals.
WATER-GLASS, [waw′-ter-glahs], *n.* a silicate of soda or potash, transparent in appearance, soluble in hot water, and impervious to the air.
WATER-GOD, [waw′-ter-god′], *n.* a deity believed to control the element of water; Neptune or Poseidon.

WATER-GAUGE

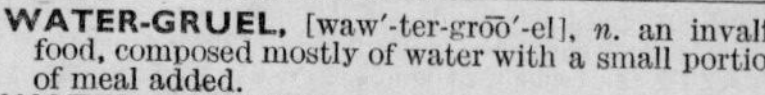

WATER-GRUEL, [waw′-ter-gro͞o′-el], *n.* an invalid food, composed mostly of water with a small portion of meal added.
WATER-HAMMER, [waw′-ter-ham′-er], *n.* the sound which water in a pipe or cylinder makes when its flow is suddenly stopped.
WATER-HEMLOCK, [waw′-ter-hem′-lok], *n.* (*bot.*) the cowbane, *Cicuta virosa.*
WATER-HEN, [waw′-ter-hen′], *n.* the moorhen, *Gallinula chloropus*; the American coot.
WATER-HOLE, [waw′-ter-hōl], *n.* a natural reservoir for water; a waterpool, pond.
WATER-HYACINTH, [waw′-ter-hī′-a-sinth], *n.* (*bot.*) the South American plant, *Eichhornia crassipes.*
WATER-ICE, [waw′-ter-īs], *n.* an ice cream made principally of frozen water and essence of fruits.
WATERINESS, [waw′-ter-i-nes], *n.* the quality or condition of being watery.
WATERING, [waw′-ter-ing], *n.* the act of sprinkling or supplying with water; the process by which a wavy surface is imparted to a fabric.
WATERING-CALL, [waw′-ter-ing-kawl], *n.* (*milit.*) a trumpet call signalling cavalry troopers to water their horses.
WATERING-CAN, [waw′-ter-ing-kan′], *n.* a garden implement for carrying and sprinkling water.
WATERING-CART, [waw′-ter-ing-kaht], *n.* a water-cart.
WATERING-PLACE, [waw′-ter-ing-plās], *n.* a pool or part of a river bank where animals are accustomed to drink; a town by the seaside; a town where medicinal waters are taken.
WATERING-POT, [waw′-ter-ing-pot′], *n.* a watering-can.
WATERING-TROUGH, [waw′-ter-ing-trof′], *n.* a trough containing water for cattle and horses to drink.
WATERISH, [waw′-ter-ish], *adj.* resembling water; somewhat watery.
WATERISHNESS, [waw′-ter-ish-nes], *n.* the quality of being waterish.
WATER-JACKET, [waw′-ter-jak′-it], *n.* a casing containing water for keeping machinery cool.
WATERLAID, [waw′-ter-lād], *adj.* laid under water, as a cable.
WATER-LEMON, [waw′-ter-lem′-on], *n.* (*bot.*) the climbing plant, *Passiflora laurifolia.*
WATERLESS, [waw′-ter-les], *adj.* lacking water.
WATER-LEVEL, [waw′-ter-lev′-el], *n.* the level formed by the surface of still water; an instrument in which water is employed for ascertaining levels.
WATER-LILY, [waw′-ter-lil′-i], *n.* (*bot.*) any one of the aquatic plants of the genera *Nymphæa* and *Nuphar*, with floating leaves and large flowers, growing in ponds.
WATER-LINE, [waw′-ter-līn], *n.* the level of the water on a ship's hull, dock-side, etc.; a mark indicating this; the line corresponding to the maximum permitted draught of a fully laden ship.

WATER-LILY

WATERLOGGED, [waw′-ter-logd′], *adj.* saturated to a point when floating is no longer possible; (*naut.*) lying like a log on the water, the hold being flooded.
WATERLOO, [waw′-ter-lo͞o], *n.* the battle in which Napoleon suffered final defeat; **to meet one's W.,** to suffer defeat after an unbroken run of success. [*Waterloo*, in Belgium].
WATER-MAIN, [waw′-ter-mān], *n.* one of the large pipes carrying a (public) water-supply.
WATERMAN, [waw′-ter-man], *n.* a man employed to look after boats, a boatman; a ferryman.
WATERMANSHIP, [waw′-ter-man-ship], *n.* the art of controlling a rowing-boat; oarsmanship.
WATERMARK, [waw′-ter-mahk], *n.* the mark or limit showing the highest level of a flood; a mark indicating the rise and fall of the tide; a distinguishing mark worked into the texture of paper during manufacture.
WATER-MEADOW, [waw′-ter-med′-ō], *n.* a meadow irrigated by an adjoining stream.
WATER-MEASURE, [waw′-ter-mezh′-er], *n.* a standard of measurement for certain goods brought by sea, as coal, oysters, etc.
WATER-MELON, [waw′-ter-mel′-on], *n.* the plant and edible fruit, *Citrullus vulgaris.*
WATER-METER, [waw′-ter-mē′-ter], *n.* an instrument for ascertaining the volume of water consumed.

WATER-MILFOIL, [waw′-ter-mil′-foil], *n.* (*bot.*) the plant, *Myriophyllum spicatum*, or its allies.
WATER-MILL, [waw′-ter-mil], *n.* a mill turned by water.
WATER-ORDEAL, [waw′-ter-aw-dē′-el], *n.* torture by forced drinking of water.
WATER-OUZEL, [waw′-ter-ōōz-el], *n.* the dipper bird, *Cinclus aquaticus.*
WATER-PARSNIP, [waw′-ter-pahs-nip], *n.* (*bot.*) an umbelliferous aquatic plant belonging to the genus *Sium.*
WATER-PARTING, [waw′-ter-paht-ing], *n.* a watershed.
WATER-PEPPER, [waw′-ter-pep′-er], *n.* (*bot.*) the water-wort, *Elatine hydropiper.*
WATER-PIPIT, [waw′-ter-pip′-it], *n.* the bird, *Anthus spipoletta.*
WATER-PITCHER, [waw′-ter-pich′-er], *n.* a pitcher for water; (*bot.*) a North American marsh plant.
WATER-PLANE†, [waw′-ter-plān], *n.* an aeroplane fitted with floats, a sea-plane.
WATER-PLANT, [waw′-ter-plahnt], *n.* (*bot.*) any plant growing in water.
WATER-PLANTAIN, [waw′-ter-plant′-in], *n.* (*bot.*) a plant belonging to the genus *Alisma.*
WATER-POISE, [waw′-ter-poiz], *n.* an instrument for testing the specific gravity of liquids.
WATER-POLO, [waw′-ter-pō′-lō], *n.* a ball game played in water by two teams of swimmers with rules of play similar to those of football.
WATERPOOL, [waw′-ter-pōōl], *n.* a small pond.
WATER-POT, [waw′-ter-pot′], *n.* a pot for holding water.
WATER-POWER, [waw′-ter-pow′-er], *n.* power derived from the action of water.
WATER-POX, [waw′-ter-poks′], *n.* a form of chicken-pox.
WATERPROOF (1), [waw′-ter-prōōf], *n.* cloth or a coat that has been made proof against water.
WATERPROOF (2), [waw′-ter-prōōf], *adj.* impervious to water.
WATERPROOF (3), [waw′-ter-prōōf], *v.t.* to treat with a preparation so as to render waterproof.
WATER-RAIL, [waw′-ter-rāl], *n.* the wading bird, *Rallus aquaticus.*
WATER-RAM, [waw′-ter-ram′], *n.* a ram operated by hydraulic pressure.
WATER-RAT, [waw′-ter-rat′], *n.* a species of vole which can take to the water.
WATER-RATE, [waw′-ter-rāt], *n.* a charge set by the appropriate authority for the supply of water.
WATER-ROT, [waw′-ter-rot′], *v.t.* to rot in water.
WATERSAIL, [waw′-ter-sāl], *n.* (*naut.*) a small sail set under the lower studding-sail.
WATER-SAPPHIRE, [waw′-ter-sa′-fīer], *n.* iolite, a semi-precious stone of blue colour.
WATERSHED, [waw′-ter-shed′], *n.* a ridge dividing river basins.
WATER-SHREW, [waw′-ter-shrōō], *n.* the insectivore, *Crossopus fodiens.*
WATERSIDE, [waw′-ter-sīd], *n.* land forming the edge of a stretch of water.
WATER-SNAKE, [waw′-ter-snāk], *n.* a snake that inhabits water.
WATER-SOFTENER, [waw′-ter-sof′-ner], *n.* a device fitted to a water supply to remove hardness or chalky elements from the water.
WATER-SOLDIER, [waw′-ter-sōl′-jer], *n.* (*bot.*) the aquatic plant, *Stratiotes aloides*, having long sword-like leaves with serrated edges.
WATER-SPANIEL, [waw′-ter-span′-yel], *n.* a breed of spaniel trained for duck-shooting.
WATER-SPARROW, [waw′-ter-spa′-rō], *n.* the reed warbler, *Acrocephalus scirpaceus*; the reed bunting, *Emberiza schœniclus.*
WATER-SPIDER, [waw′-ter-spīd′-er], *n.* the spider, *Argyoneta aquatica.*
WATERSPOUT, [waw′-ter-spowt], *n.* a whirling column of water spun from a cloud to the sea or lake by a whirlwind.
WATER-SUPPLY, [waw′-ter-sup-lī′] *n.* a system of pipes drawing on a river, lake, or reservoir for supplies of water to be distributed to consumers.

WATER-SOLDIER

WATER-TABLE, [wawt′-er-tābl], *n.* (*arch.*) a string-course moulding or projection in the wall of a building designed to throw rain-water clear of the walls; (*geol.*) the permanent level of subterranean water, *esp.* beneath hills.
WATER-TANK, [waw′-ter-tangk′], *n.* a cistern or small reservoir for holding water.
WATER-THERMOMETER, [waw′-ter-ther-mom′-it-er], *n.* an instrument for registering the degree of cold at which water ceases to be condensed.
WATERTIGHT, [waw′-ter-tīt], *adj.* adapted in such a way as to retain, or not to admit, water, free from leaks.
WATER-TOWER, [waw′-ter-tow′-er], *n.* a tower supporting a tank of water to obtain the necessary pressure for a water-supply.
WATER-TUBE, [waw′-ter-tewb], *adj.* fitted with water tubes passing through the boiler fire.
WATER-VIOLET, [waw′-ter-vī′-ōl-et], *n.* (*bot.*) an aquatic plant belonging to the genus *Hottonia.*
WATER-VOLE, [waw′-ter-vōl], *n.* the water-rat.
WATER-WAGON, [waw′-ter-wag′-on], *n.* a watering-cart; **on the w.,** abstaining from alcoholic drinks.
WATER-WAGTAIL, [waw′-ter-wag′-tāl], *n.* the pied wagtail, *Motacilla lugubris.*
WATER-WAVE, [waw′-ter-wāv], *n.* a wave produced in the hair by setting it with water.
WATER-WAVING, [waw′-ter-wāv-ing], *n.* the process of producing water-waves in hair.
WATERWAY, [waw′-ter-wā], *n.* a navigable river; a canal; (*naut.*) a deck channel for draining water to the scuppers.
WATER-WEED, [waw′-ter-wēd], *n.* (*bot.*) the American water plant, *Elodea canadensis.*
WATER-WHEEL, [waw′-ter-wēl], *n.* a wheel operated by the pressure of running water.
WATER-WINGS, [waw′-ter-wingz], *n.*(*pl.*) walls erected on the banks of rivers, next to bridges, to protect the foundations from erosion; a safety device worn by persons learning to swim, and consisting of a pair of inflatable bladders.
WATER-WITCH, [waw′-ter-wich], *n.* the dipper bird belonging to the genus *Cinclus.*
WATERWORKS, [waw′-ter-works], *n.*(*pl.*) the headquarters of a local water-supply; (*slang*) the organs discharging urine; **to turn on the w.,** to burst into tears.
WATERWORN, [waw′-ter-wawn], *adj.* eroded by the action of water.
WATER-WORT, [waw′-ter-wurt], *n.* (*bot.*) an aquatic plant belonging to the genus *Elatine.*
WATERY, [wawt′-er-i], *adj.* containing an amount of water, *esp.* to a disadvantageous extent, saturated, sodden; resembling water; weak, insipid; misty, rainy.
WATT, [wot], *n.* the unit of electrical power. [James *Watt*, the inventor].
WATTAGE, [wot′-ij], *n.* electrical energy measured in watts; the amount of energy which an electrical circuit, etc., is designed to carry. [WATT].
WATT-HOUR, [wot′-ow(r)′], *n.* the amount of work done by one watt in one hour.
WATTLE (1), [wotl], *n.* a hurdle made by twisting flexible twigs across a frame; the lobe of flesh growing at the neck of poultry or fish; a species of Australian acacia. [OE. *watol*].
WATTLE (2), [wotl], *v.t.* to make with wattles; to bind with twigs; to plait.
WATTLE-BARK, [wotl′-bahk], *n.* the bark stripped from the wattle.
WATTLE-BIRD, [wotl′-burd], *n.* the Australian bird, *Anthochæra caruncculata.*
WATTLED, [wotld], *adj.* bound, plaited, with twigs; (*bot.*) with projections like the wattles of a cock.
WATTMETER, [wot′-mēt-er], *n.* an instrument for measuring wattage. [WATT and METER].
WAUGHT, [wahft], *n.* a deep draught. [Uncert.].
WAUL, WAWL, [wawl], *v.i.* to cry, like a cat. [Echoic].
WAVE (1), [wāv], *n.* the raised ridge of water, sometimes topped with a crest of foam, travelling across the surface of the sea, an ocean swell, a billow, an undulation on the surface of any body of water; a rippling irregularity of any surface or mass, as of silk, hair; (*fig.*) a strong emotional movement stirring a body of people; one of several groups of troops, aircraft, etc., making a series of attacks; (*phys.*) a periodic motion, the transmission of periodic motions through a continuous medium; (*wirel.*) regular disturbances in the ether set up by electrical oscillations radiated by a conductor. [OE. *wæg*, ME. *wawe*].
WAVE (2), [wāv], *v.t. and i.* to cause to undulate, to raise a series of curving ridges in a surface; to manipulate with a series of up and down movements, to

brandish; to raise and flourish the hand as a signal, to beckon; to move in the air from side to side, to sway; to undulate, fluctuate; to grow or be trained in a series of curves, as the hair; to flourish the hand as a signal. [OE. *wafian*].

WAVED, [wāvd], *adj.* possessing or given the form of a series of waves; (*her.*) indented in a sinuous pattern.

WAVELENGTH, [wāv'-length'], *n.* the distance between the peaks of two successive waves; (*wirel.*) the length of electro-magnetic wave (adopted by a transmitting station).

WAVELESS, [wāv'-les], *adj.* free from waves.

WAVELET, [wāv'-let], *n.* a little wave, a ripple.

WAVELIKE, [wāv'-līk], *adj.* having the characteristics of a wave, undulating.

WAVE-LINE, [wāv'-līn], *n.* the shore line left by a receding wave.

WAVELLITE, [wāv'-el-īt], *n.* (*min.*) a hydrated phosphate of aluminium. [Dr. W. *Wavell*, the discoverer, and Gk. *lithos* stone].

WAVEMETER, [wāv'-mē'-ter], *n.* an apparatus for registering or measuring electrical wavelengths.

WAVE-OFFERING, [wāv'-of'-er-ing], *n.* a sacrificial offering waved in the air by the priest in Levitical ritual.

WAVER (1), [wāv'-er], *n.* a sapling left standing by wood-cutters. [Uncert.].

WAVER (2), [wāv'-er], *v.i.* to play or move uncertainly to and fro, to fluctuate; to be unsettled in opinion; to vacillate, to hesitate; to totter. [~OIcel. *vafra*].

WAVERER, [wāv'-er-er], *n.* a person who wavers; an irresolute person.

WAVERING, [wāv'-er-ing], *adj.* fluctuating; trembling, tottering; in doubt.

WAVERINGLY, [wāv'-er-ing-li], *adv.* in a wavering fashion.

WAVERINGNESS, [wāv'-er-ing-nes], *n.* the condition of wavering.

WAVEWORN, [wāv'-wawn], *adj.* worn by the waves.

WAVILY, [wāv'-i-li], *adv.* in a wavy manner.

WAVINESS, [wāv'-i-nes], *n.* the quality of being wavy.

WAVING, [wāv'-ing], *adj.* moving like a wave or waves.

WAVY, [wāv'-i], *adj.* characterized by an undulating surface; full of waves; susceptible to the movement of the breeze; (*bot.*) undulating in form.

WAWL, see WAUL.

WAX (1), [waks], *n.* a firm, plastic substance, yellow in colour, malleable when warm, which bees secrete for the building of cells; a yellow substance secreted by the ear; a substance prepared out of fats and oils, from which candles are made; a secretion of certain plants; beeswax with which cobblers smear their thread; a similar substance extracted from mineral oils. [OE. *weax*].

WAX (2), [waks], *n.* (*schoolboy slang*) a temper, a rage. [Uncert.].

WAX (3), [waks], *v.i.* to increase in size, as the moon; to pass from one state to another, to become. [OE. *weaxan*].

WAX (4), [waks], *v.t.* to smear with wax, to apply wax to.

WAX-BERRY, [waks'-be'-ri], *n.* wax-myrtle.

WAXBILL, [waks'-bil], *n.* a weaver bird of the genus *Estrelda*.

WAX-CANDLE, [waks'-kandl'], *n.* a candle made of wax.

WAX-CHANDLER, [waks'-chahnd'-ler], *n.* a maker or seller of wax and wax-candles.

WAX-CLOTH, [waks'-kloth], *n.* a floor-cloth for polishing.

WAX-DOLL, [waks'-dol'], *n.* a doll with its head modelled out of wax and hardened.

WAXEN, [waks'-en], *adj.* made of wax; having the appearance or properties of wax.

WAX-END, [waks'-end'], *n.* a waxed thread pointed with a bristle, and used by a shoemaker.

WAX-FLOWER, [waks'-flow(r)], *n.* (*bot.*) one of the seventy species of *Hoya*; the orchid *Angræ cum sesquipedale*.

WAXINESS, [waks'-i-nes], *n.* the quality of being waxy.

WAXING, [waks'-ing], *n.* the process of preparing with wax; (*chem.*) the process of stopping out colours in calico-printing.

WAX-INSECT, [waks'-in-sekt], *n.* the insect, *Coccus sinensis*, which secretes a waxy substance.

WAX-LIGHT, [waks'-līt], *n.* a taper made of wax.

WAX-MOTH, [waks'-moth'], *n.* the small moth, *Galleria mellonella*, whose larvae feed on beeswax.

WAX-MYRTLE, [waks'-murtl], *n.* (*bot.*) the candleberry, *Myrica cerifera*, an American shrub from whose berries wax is obtained suitable for candles.

WAX-PALM, [waks'-pahm], *n.* a large South American palm *Ceroxylon andicola*, whose stem is coated with wax; the carnation palm, *Copernica cerifera*.

WAX-PAPER, [waks'-pā'-per], *n.* a type of paper treated with wax.

WAX-PLANT, [waks'-plahnt], *n.* (*bot.*) the honeywort, *Cerinthe major*.

WAX-TREE, [waks'-trē], *n.* any of various trees yielding wax, *esp.* the American gamboge tree, *Vismia guianensis*.

WAXWING, [waks'-wing], *n.* a bird of the genus *Ampelis*, with quills tipped with a substance like red sealing-wax.

WAXWORK, [waks'-wurk], *n.* an effigy in wax; modelling in wax; (*pl.*) a collection of such effigies open to the public.

WAXWORKER, [waks'-wurk-er], *n.* one who models in wax.

WAXY (1), [wak'-si], *adj.* containing, resembling wax; having one or more of the characteristics of wax. [WAX (1)].

WAXY (2), [wak'-si], *adj.* (*slang*) angry. [WAX (2)].

WAY, [wā], *n.* the direction or line of progress from one place to another, a road, street, avenue, path; the route taken, the course of a journey; distance travelled; a direction followed or faced; motion, usually at right-angles to the intended direction; drift; manner, mode, means or method of accomplishing something, the technique of tackling a job of work, a plan of action, a series of practical steps, mode of procedure; a characteristic manner, custom or habit; range, sphere, course of life; characteristic, feature; (*pl.*) the supports taking a ship when launched; **by w. of,** as a means of; **by the w.,** incidentally; **to give w.,** to yield; to retreat; **to go out of one's w.,** to give oneself trouble on behalf of another; **in the family w.,** pregnant; **out of the w.,** inaccessible, not populated; extraordinary; **to pave the w.,** to settle the initial stages; **to put in the w. of,** to provide with an opportunity of; **under w.,** (*naut.*) moving under its own power, travelling; **right of w.,** right of traversing; **ways and means,** method, devices. [OE. *weg*].

WAY-BILL, [wā'-bil], *n.* a record of passengers or goods.

WAYBREAD, [wā'-bred'], *n.* the wayside plant, the plantain. [OE. *wegbræde*].

WAYFARER, [wā'-fāer'-er], *n.* a traveller, *esp.* on foot.

WAYFARING, [wā'-fāer'-ing], *adj.* travelling.

WAYFARING TREE, [wā'-fāer'-ing-trē], *n.* the small hedgerow tree, *Viburnum Lantana*.

WAYGOING, [wā'-gō'-ing], *adj.* taken (as a crop) by a vacating tenant.

WAYGONE, [wā'-gon'], *adj.* weary with travelling.

WAYLAY, [wā-lā'], *v.t.* to assault, seize, or accost by lying in wait for; to ambush.

WAYLAYER, [wā-lā'-er], *n.* one who waylays.

WAYLEAVE, [wā'-lēv], *n.* a right of way.

WAYLESS, [wā'-les], *adj.* having no road or path.

WAYMAKER†, [wā'-māk-er], *n.* one who makes a way, a roadmender.

WAYFARING TREE

WAYMARK, [wā'-mahk], *n.* a sign-post.

WAY-SHAFT, [wā'-shahft], *n.* the shaft in an engine that works the side-valve from the eccentric.

WAYSIDE (1), [wā'-sīd], *n.* the edge of a road; the roadside.

WAYSIDE (2), [wā'-sīd], *adj.* found by, or growing on, the wayside; **w. station,** a small intermediate station, a railway halt.

WAY-THISTLE, [wā'-thisl], *n.* (*bot.*) the thistle, *Carduus arvensis*.

WAY-THORN, [wā'-thawn], *n.* the buckthorn, *Rhamnus catharticus*.

WAY-TRAFFIC, [wā'-traf'-ik], *n.* local traffic.

WAYWARD, [wā'-werd], *adj.* temperamentally inclined to disregard others; perverse; wilful.

WAYWARDEN, [wā'-wawd'-en], *n.* a road surveyor.

WAYWARDLY, [wā'-werd-li], *adv.* in a wayward manner.

WAYWARDNESS, [wā'-werd-nes], *n.* the quality of being wayward, perverseness; irresponsibility.

WAYWISE, [wā'-wiz], *adj.* having a good sense of direction.

WAYWODE, [wā'-wōd], *n.* (*hist.*) a military commander in various Slavonic countries. [~VOIVODE].

WAYWODESHIP, [wā'-wōd-ship], *n.* the office or jurisdiction of a waywode or voivode.

WAYWORN, [wā'-wawn], *adj.* wearied by travelling.

WAYZGOOSE, [wāz'-gōōs], *n.* a printers' annual beanfeast. [Uncert.].

WAZIR, [waz'-ēer'], *n.* a vizier. [Arab. *wazir*].

WE, [wē], *pron. first pers. pl.* of I; also used by royalty, editors, etc., in place of I. [OE. *we*].

WEAK, [wēk], *adj.* lacking in muscular power, deficient in physical strength; puny, feeble; having insufficient power of resistance, support, or strength; unable to withstand pressure or weight; offering little resistance; infirm; defenceless, frail, delicate in constitution; irresolute, indecisive; below standard, lacking strong ingredients; deficient in alcoholic content; insipid, diluted. [ME. *weke*].

WEAKEN, [wēk'-en], *v.t. and i.* to make weaker, to cause to diminish in vigour or powers of endurance; to subtract from the powers of permanence of; to lessen in the capacity to withstand weight or pressure; to make less convincing; to grow weaker, to become weakly; to become less certain.

WEAKENER, [wēk'-en-er], *n.* one who, or that which, weakens.

WEAK-EYED, [wēk'-īd'], *adj.* afflicted with functional weakness of the eyes.

WEAK-HEADED, [wēk'-hed'-id], *adj.* mentally weak.

WEAK-HEARTED, [wēk'-haht'-id], *adj.* having little courage.

WEAK-KNEED, [wēk'-nēd], *adj.* weak in the knees; (*fig.*) having no strength or force of mind.

WEAKLING, [wēk'-ling], *n.* a habitually irresolute person, one with little ability.

WEAKLY (1), [wēk'-li], *adj.* not strong of constitution; delicate in health; infirm.

WEAKLY (2), [wēk'-li], *adv.* in a weak manner.

WEAK-MINDED, [wēk'-mīnd'-id], *adj.* mentally deficient.

WEAKNESS, [wēk'-nes], *n.* the quality of being weak; absence of muscular power; lack of conciseness; irresolution; unhealthiness; defect.

WEAK-SIGHTED, [wēk-sīt'-id], *adj.* having weak eyesight.

WEAK-SPIRITED, [wēk'-spi'-rit-id], *adj.* timid; lacking in moral or emotional drive.

WEAL (1), [wēl], *n.* a healthy or flourishing condition; welfare; happiness, well-being. [OE. *wela* prosperity].

WEAL (2), [wēl], *n.* the mark or long reddish bruise left by a stripe or lash; a wale. [OE. *walu*].

WEALD, [wēld], *n.* an open tract of country stretching through the counties of Surrey, Kent, and Sussex; †forest land. [~OE. *weald*].

WEALDEN, [wēld'-en], *adj.* (*geol.*) relating to, found in, the Weald of Kent and Sussex.

WEALTH, [welth], *n.* the sum total of a nation's or person's resources, money, and property; a state of prosperity accompanied by an amount of material riches above the average, affluence, possession of capital; an abundance, an inordinate amount. [ME. *welthe* pleasure].

WEALTHILY, [welth'-i-li], *adv.* in a wealthy manner, richly.

WEALTHINESS, [welth'-i-nes], *n.* the condition of being wealthy.

WEALTHY, [welth'-i], *adj.* owning wealth, rich, having large possessions; opulent; affluent.

WEAN (1), [wān], *n.* (*Scots*) a child. [Scots *wee ane* little one].

WEAN (2), [wēn], *v.t.* to deprive (a child) gradually of milk from the breast, giving other food as a substitute; (*fig.*) to attract from one interest towards another. [OE. *wenian*].

WEANLING, [wēn'-ling], *n.* an infant or young of a mammal newly weaned.

WEAPON, [wep'-on], *n.* any instrument of offence or defence fitted for the killing or wounding of enemies; (*pl.*) (*bot.*) organic attributes of defence, as thorns, prickles, and stings. [OE. *wæpen*].

WEAPONED, [wep'-ond], *adj.* armed, equipped with weapons or arms.

WEAPONLESS, [wep'-on-les], *adj.* having no weapon.

WEAR (1), [wāer], *n.* the act of wearing; the clothes worn, *esp.* in a collective sense; the act of being used, usage; the process of being impaired in value or quality by persistent use; **w. and tear,** damage to an object, *esp.* a machine, attendant upon regular use.

WEAR (2), (wore, worn), [wāer], *v.t.* to reduce gradually by friction or usage, to cause to diminish bit by bit owing to the action of functioning parts one upon the other, to make inroads into (a solid) by constant rubbing; to waste, exhaust, weary; to carry on the body as clothing or ornament; to possess on one's person; to give expression to, to exhibit, to allow to form; (*Scots*) to be married to; (*coll.*) to tolerate, endure; *v.i.* to endure, last, to withstand severe usage; **to w. away,** to cause to disappear, to consume; to pass out of existence gradually; **to w. down,** to lessen by constant rubbing; to break down; **to w. out,** to cause to become thin by constant usage; to exhaust; to lose substance by attrition; **to w. the breeches,** to rule the roost, to assume command. [OE. *werian*].

WEAR (3), (wore), [wāer], *v.t. and i.* (*naut.*) to turn (a ship's head) away from the wind, to veer. [*Var.* of VEER].

WEARABLE, [wāer'-abl], *adj.* fit or able to be worn.

WEARER, [wāer'-er], *n.* one who wears; that which wastes or diminishes.

WEARIED, [wēer'-id], *adj.* tired, exhausted.

WEARIFUL, [wēer'-i-fōōl], *adj.* wearisome.

WEARILESS, [wēer'-i-les], *adj.* unaffected by exhausting conditions; continual.

WEARILY, [wēer'-i-li], *adv.* in a weary manner.

WEARINESS, [wēer'-i-nes], *n.* the state or quality of being weary.

WEARING, [wāer'-ing], *adj.* denoting what is worn; characterized by power to exhaust.

WEARISH, [wēer'-ish], *adj.* weak; washy.

WEARISOME, [wēer'-i-sum], *adj.* causing weariness; tedious.

WEARISOMELY, [wēer'-i-sum-li], *adv.* in a wearisome manner; tediously.

WEARISOMENESS, [wēer'-i-sum-nes], *n.* the condition of being wearisome; tediousness.

WEARY (1), [wēer'-i], *adj.* sapped of strength by working in exhausting conditions, fatigued, tired; causing fatigue; boring, tedious. [OE. *werig*].

WEARY (2), [wēer'-i], *v.t. and i.* to make weary; to exhaust the interest of a person by persistence; to become weary; (*Scots*) to pine (for).

WEASAND, WEZAND†, [wēz'-and], *n.* the windpipe or trachea. [OE. *wæsand*].

WEASEL, [wēz'-el], *n.* the small carnivore, *Mustela vulgaris*, with a long body and short legs, allied to the stoat. [OE. *wesle*].

WEASEL

WEASEL-FACED, [wēz'-el-fāst], *adj.* having a face like a weasel, sharp featured.

WEASEL-SNOUT, [wēz'-el-snowt], *n.* (*bot.*) the yellow dead-nettle, *Lamium Galeobdolon.*

WEATHER (1), [weᴛʜ'-er], *n.* the atmospheric conditions, depending on the interaction of wind, cloud, and seasonal change, existing at a particular time over a particular area; **under the w.,** not feeling well, depressed. [OE. *weder*].

WEATHER (2), [weᴛʜ'-er], *adj.* (*naut.*) facing towards the wind.

WEATHER (3), [weᴛʜ'-er], *v.t. and i.* to expose to atmospheric conditions; to survive, to bear up against; (*naut.*) to sail to the windward of; to suffer damage from the weather.

WEATHER-ANCHOR, [weᴛʜ'-er-ang'-ker], *n.* the anchor on the windward side of the ship.

WEATHER-BEATEN, [weᴛʜ'-er-bēt'-en], *adj.* affected by the weather, *esp.* in complexion; seasoned.

WEATHER-BOARD, [weᴛʜ'-er-bawd], *n.* the side of a ship facing the wind.

WEATHERBOARDING, [weᴛʜ'-er-bawd'-ing], *n.* lengths of wood so tapered at one longitudinal edge as to permit of their being overlapped when secured.

WEATHER-BOUND, [weᴛʜ'-er-bownd], *adj.* delayed by bad weather.

WEATHER-BOW, [weᴛʜ'-er-bow], *n.* (*naut.*) that side of a ship's bow that is to windward.

WEATHER-BUREAU, [weᴛʜ'-er-bew-rō'], *n.* (*U.S.*) an office dealing with meteorological data.

WEATHERCLOTHS, [weᴛʜ'-er-kloths'], *n.(pl.)* (*naut.*) detachable canvas or tarpaulin screens against rain or spray.

WEATHERCOCK, [weᴛʜ'-er-kok'], *n.* a device usually in the form of a metal plate shaped like a cock, placed on the top of a building, flagpole, etc., to indicate the direction of the wind; (*fig.*) a fickle person.

WEATHER-DRIVEN, [weтн'-er-driv'-en], *adj.* driven by winds.
WEATHERED, [weтн'-erd], *adj.* (*arch.*) designed as a protection against rain; (*geol.*) affected by exposure.
WEATHER-EYE, [weтн'-er-ī], *n.* a watchful eye.
WEATHER-FISH, [weтн'-er-fish], *n.* the largest of European loaches, *Misgurnus fossilis.*
WEATHER-FORECAST, [weтн'-er-faw'-kahst], *n.* a scientific prediction of future weather.
WEATHER-GAGE, [weтн'-er-gāj], *n.* (*naut.*) the situation of a ship when lying to windward of another.
WEATHER-GLASS, [weтн'-er-glahs], *n.* an instrument for recording the state of the atmosphere; a barometer.
WEATHER-HELM, [weтн'-er-helm'], *n.* (*naut.*) the condition of a ship when she is inclined to come too near the wind.
WEATHERING, [weтн'-er-ing], *n.* (*arch.*) weather-boarding to drain off the rain; (*geol.*) disintegration by exposure.
WEATHERLY, [weтн'-er-li], *adj.* (*naut.*) making little leeway.
WEATHERMOST, [weтн'-er-mōst], *adj.* farthest to windward.
WEATHER-MOULDING, [weтн'-er-mōld'-ing], *n.* (*arch.*) moulding over doors and windows to reject rain, a dripstone.
WEATHERPROOF (1), [weтн'-er-prōōf], *n.* a waterproof mackintosh.
WEATHERPROOF (2), [weтн'-er-prōōf], *adj.* adapted to withstand rough weather.
WEATHER-PROPHET, [weтн'-er-prof'-it], *n.* a person who forecasts weather conditions.
WEATHER-ROLL, [weтн'-er-rōl], *n.* (*naut.*) the roll of a ship to windward.
WEATHER-STAINED, [weтн'-er-stānd], *adj.* discoloured, stained, by exposure to the weather.
WEATHER-STRIP, [weтн'-er-strip], *n.* a strip of felt, etc., fitted to the base of a door to exclude draughts.
WEATHER-TIDE, [weтн'-er-tīd], *n.* (*naut.*) the tide meeting the lee-side of a ship, and driving to windward.
WEATHER-VANE, [weтн'-er-vān], *n.* a device indicating the direction of the wind by swivelling in reaction to it, a weathercock.
WEATHER-WISE, [weтн'-er-wīz], *adj.* knowledgeable in weather lore.
WEAVE (1), [wēv], *n.* the basic pattern of a fabric dependent on the method of weaving; a session of weaving.
WEAVE (2), (wove, woven), [wēv], *v.t. and i.* to make into a piece of material by interlacing threads in close texture on a loom, to intertwine, to plait; to arrange in a series of insertions; to practise weaving; in boxing, to make weaving motions with the gloves; (*aeron.*) to fly with a weaving motion; (*fig.*) to put into narrative form; to move drunkenly. [OE. *wefan*].
WEAVER, [wēv'-er], *n.* one who practises weaving.
WEAVER-BIRD, [wēv'-er-burd], *n.* any species of the family *Plocidæ*, which weave material into a nest.
WEAVER-FISH, [wēv'-er-fish], *n.* a species of *Trachinus.*
WEAVING, [wēv'-ing], *n.* the act or craft of one who weaves.
WEAZEN, see WIZEN.
WEAZENED, see WIZENED.
WEB (1), [web], *n.* a piece of woven material, *esp.* one open-worked like a net; the delicate fly-trap of inter-linked threads spun by a spider, a cobweb; a complicated system of organization; the membrane forming between the toes of an aquatic bird; the part of a girder connecting the upper flange to the lower; a large reel of paper from which newspapers are printed; a thin metal plate acting as a partition or means of connexion in machinery; **w. of deceit,** an elaborate tissue of lies. [OE. *webb*].
WEB (2), (webbing, webbed), [web], *v.t.* to form into a web.
WEBBED, [webd], *adj.* (*ornith. and physiol.*) having the digits connected by a web.
WEBBING, [web'-ing], *n.* a strong narrow fabric for supporting upholstery, etc.
WEB-EYE, [web'-ī], *n.* a disease which affects the cornea with a film.
WEB-FINGERED, [web'-fing'-gerd], *adj.* afflicted with webbed fingers.
WEB-FOOT, [web'-fōōt], *n.* a foot with webbed toes.
WEB-FOOTED, [web'-fōōt'-id], *adj.* with webbed feet.
WEBSTERITE, [web'-ster-īt], *n.* (*min.*) aluminite. [T. *Webster*, its discoverer].
WED, (wedding, wedded), [wed], *v.t. and i.* to take a woman for wife or a man for husband, to marry, espouse; to participate in a marriage ceremony with another; (*fig.*) to unite, combine; to be married, to contract matrimony. [OE. *weddian*].
WEDDED, [wed'-id], *adj.* married; closely attached.
WEDDING, [wed'-ing], *n.* the religious or civil ceremony in which a man and woman are joined in marriage.
WEDDING-BREAKFAST, [wed'-ing-brek'-fast], *n.* a party for friends and relations of bride and bridegroom held after the marriage ceremony.
WEDDING-CAKE, [wed'-ing-kāk], *n.* a decorated cake cut following a wedding ceremony and distributed among friends to celebrate the event.
WEDDING-CARD, [wed'-ing-kahd], *n.* a printed card announcing, or inviting to, a wedding.
WEDDING-DAY, [wed'-ing-dā], *n.* the marriage day; its anniversary.
WEDDING-FAVOUR, [wed'-ing-fā'-ver], *n.* a white rosette as a man's buttonhole at a wedding.
WEDDING-FEAST, [wed'-ing-fēst], *n.* a banquet for the guests at a wedding.
WEDDING-RING, [wed'-ing-ring], *n.* a ring given at the marriage ceremony by the bridegroom to the bride as a symbol of the bond.
WEDGE (1), [wej], *n.* a piece of wood or metal shaped down to a thin edge at one end, and designed to be driven into a mass so as to split it, or to act as a support by insertion next to anything that requires a rigid fixture; any mass shaped like a wedge; **the thin end of the w.,** an apparently insignificant incident likely to have undesired consequences. [OE. *wecg*].
WEDGE (2), [wej], *v.t. and i.* to make rigid by means of a wedge; to split by driving a wedge into; to hold fast as if by an inserted wedge.
WEDGE-HEEL, [wej'-hēl], *adj.* denoting a type of shoe in which the heel, in the shape of a wedge, is prolonged under the arch.
WEDGE-SHAPED, [wej'-shāpt], *adj.* having the shape of a wedge; cuneate.
WEDGE-TAILED, [wej'-tāld], *adj.* (*ornith.*) possessing a tail shaped like a wedge.
WEDGEWISE, [wej'-wīz], *adv.* in the manner of a wedge.
WEDGING, [wej'-ing], *n.* the method of fastening by wedges.
WEDGWOOD-WARE, [wej'-wōōd-wāer'], *n.* a valued kind of pottery. [J. *Wedgwood*, a famous potter].
WEDLOCK, [wed'-lok], *n.* the status of a married couple, matrimony. [OE. *wedlac*].
WEDNESDAY, [wenz'-di], *n.* the fourth day of the week. [OE. *Wodnesdæg*].
WEE (1), [wē], *n.* (*Scots*) a little while.
WEE (2), [wē], *adj.* (*Scots*) tiny, very small, minute. [ME. *wei* from OE. *wæge* weight].
WEED (1), [wēd], *n.* any plant whose growth interferes with other cultivated plants, *esp.* one hardy, prolific, and bearing little blossom; (*slang*) a cheap cigar; a weedy fellow; **the w.,** tobacco. [OE. *weod*].
WEED (2), [wēd], *n.* a mourning dress; (*pl.*) sombre clothes and veil worn by a widow. [OE. *gewæde*].
WEED (3), [wēd], *v.t. and i.* to clear of weeds by uprooting them; to purge of obstructive elements; to remove weeds; **to w. out,** to remove by selection. [OE. *weodian*].
WEEDER, [wēd'-er], *n.* one who weeds; a garden tool for uprooting weeds; a chemical weed-killer.
WEED-GROWN, [wēd'-grōn], *adj.* overgrown with weeds.
WEED-HOOK, [wēd'-hōōk], *n.* a gardening tool for lifting out weeds.
WEEDING, [wēd'-ing], *n.* the act of removing weeds.
WEED-KILLER, [wēd'-kil-er], *n.* a substance employed to kill weeds on paths, etc.
WEEDLESS, [wēd'-les], *n.* free from weeds.
WEEDY, [wēd'-i], *adj.* consisting of weeds; invaded by weeds; lanky and underdeveloped.
WEEK, [wēk], *n.* a division of time consisting of seven successive days, *esp.* the period beginning on a Sunday and ending with the following Saturday; (*coll.*) the period from a Monday morning to the following Friday night or Saturday noon, as distinct from the week-end; **Holy W.,** the week before Easter week. [OE. *wicu*].
WEEKDAY, [wēk'-dā], *n.* any day of the week except Sunday.
WEEK-DAY, [wēk'-dā], *adj.* occurring on a weekday.
WEEK-END (1), [wēk-end'], *n.* the period lasting from Friday night to Monday morning, the whole

of Saturday and Sunday, or from Saturday noon till Sunday night; a holiday or visit covering this period.
WEEK-END (2), [wēk'-end'], *adj.* occurring at the week-end.
WEEK-END (3), [wēk'-end'], *v.i.* to pay a visit over a week-end.
WEEKLY (1), [wēk'-li], *n.* a periodical published weekly.
WEEKLY (2), [wēk'-li], *adj.* occurring, published, regularly each week.
WEEKLY (3), [wēk'-li], *adv.* once a week.
WEEL, [wēl], *n.* a kind of wicker trap for snaring eels or fish. [OE. *wile* basket].
WEEM, [wēm], *n.* a primitive underground dwelling. [Gael. *waim* cavern].
WEEN†, [wēn], *v.t.* (*poet.*) to think, opine; imagine; believe, expect. [OE. *wenan* to hope].
WEEP (1), [wēp], *n.* the act or period of weeping.
WEEP (2), (**wept**), [wēp], *v.t. and i.* to shed tears, to drop; lament, bemoan; to fill the eyes to overflowing with tears as an expression of grief or nervous reaction, to cry; to secrete moisture. [OE. *wepan*].
WEEPER, [wēp'-er], *n.* one who weeps; a long crêpe hatband worn by a mourner; a South American monkey of the sapajou group; (*pl.*) (*slang*) side-whiskers; (*pl.*) (*slang*) the eyes.
WEEPING (1), [wēp'-ing], *n.* the action of a person who weeps; lamentation.
WEEPING (2), [wēp'-ing], *adj.* secreting moisture in drops; (of trees) drooping.
WEEPINGLY, [wēp'-ing-li], *adv.* with an accompaniment of weeping; in tears.
WEEPING-ROCK, [wēp'-ing-rok'], *n.* a porous rock exuding water.
WEEPING-SPRING, [wēp'-ing-spring'], *n.* an underground spring that slowly drips water.
WEEPING-TREE, [wēp'-ing-trē], *n.* a tree with drooping branches.
WEEVER, [wē'-ver], *n.* a European fish of the genus *Trachinus* characterized by sharp dorsal fins. [OFr. *wivre*].
WEEVIL, [wēv'-il], *n.* a long-snouted beetle of the family *Curculionidæ*. [OE. *wifol*].
WEEVILLED, [wēv'-ild], *adj.* infested with weevils.
WEEVILY, [wēv'-i-li], *adj.* weevilled.
WEFT (1), [weft], *n.* the threads interwoven with the warp from selvedge to selvedge to form a piece of material or fabric. [OE. *weft*].

WEEVIL

WEFT† (2), [weft], *n.* waif.
WEFTAGE, [weft'-ij], *n.* the order of the threads.
WEIGH (1), [wā], *n.* the act of weighing; the bulk weighed.
WEIGH (2), [wā], *v.t.* to ascertain, record, the weight of, *esp.* by a mechanical balance; to equal the weight of, to test by means of a balance; to subject to a process of consideration, to ponder over, *esp.* with a view to forming a conclusion; to lift, raise, as an anchor; *v.i.* to possess weight, to have the quality of heaviness; to possess significance, to have importance; **to w. down**, to cause to bend, oppress; **to w. in**, to test the specific weight of a jockey before a race; (*fig.*) to plunge in; **to w. out**, to allot measured portions of; to test the specific weight of a jockey after a race; **to w. up**, to form an opinion of; **to w. one's words**, to consider carefully what one has to say. [OE. *wegan* to carry].
WEIGHABLE, [wā'-abl], *adj.* able to be weighed.
WEIGHAGE, [wā'-ij], *n.* tax paid for weighing goods.
WEIGHBRIDGE, [wā'-brij], *n.* an apparatus for weighing laden carts.
WEIGHER, [wā'-er], *n.* one who weighs; a supervisor of official weighing-machines.
WEIGH-HOUSE, WEIGHING-HOUSE, [wā'-hows], *n.* a building where goods are weighed officially.
WEIGHING-CAGE, [wā'-ing-kāj], *n.* a cage in which animals are weighed.
WEIGHING-HOUSE, see WEIGH-HOUSE.
WEIGHING-MACHINE, [wā'-ing-mash-ēn'], *n.* a machine for weighing people or heavy loads.
WEIGHT (1), [wāt], *n.* the amount of heaviness characterizing a mass or object as registered by a pair of scales, the measure of the gravitation of a body towards the centre of the earth; a piece of metal of specific heaviness for ascertaining by balance the heaviness of a body, quantity, or object; a standard system of measuring degrees of heaviness; an object with the function of keeping something held down; a heavy load, a burden; a set of circumstances or facts which by its importance has an oppressive influence; significance, influence, importance. [ME. *weiht*].
WEIGHT (2), [wāt], *v.t.* to equip with weights, to render heavy by adding weights, to load.
WEIGHTILY, [wāt'-i-li], *adv.* in a weighty manner.
WEIGHTINESS, [wāt'-i-nes], *n.* the condition of being heavy; importance.
WEIGHTLESS, [wāt'-les], *adj.* having no weight.
WEIGHTY, [wāt'-i], *adj.* possessing an appreciable weight, distinctly heavy, ponderous; exerting considerable influence in argument, possessing significant or important characteristics, convincing.
WEIR, [wēer], *n.* a dam formed across a river or stream, a trap for fish consisting of stakes placed across a stream. [OE. *wer*].
WEIRD (1), [wēerd], *n.* (*Scots*) fate. [OE. *wyerd*].
WEIRD (2), [wēerd], *adj.* relating to, derived from, fate; strange, queer, uncanny, eerie; (*slang*) eccentric, odd.
WEIRDLY, [wēerd'-li], *adv.* in a weird manner.
WEIRDNESS, [wēerd'-nes], *n.* the condition of being weird.
WEISMANNISM, [vis'-man-izm], *n.* (*biol.*) the theory of heredity that declares acquired characteristics are not passed on from parent to offspring. [A. *Weismann*, biologist].
WEISSITE, [vīs'-īt], *n.* (*min.*) a form of iolite. [C. S. *Weiss*, the crystallographer].
WELCOME (1), [wel'-kum], *n.* the act of making welcome; an occasion of hospitable reception.
WELCOME (2), [wel'-kum], *adj.* given a hospitable reception, received with gladness; accepted as promoting happiness, accepted as supplying a want, gratifying, providing satisfaction; greeted as opportune; offered as gratuitous; **w. to**, at liberty to. [OIcel. *velkominn*, OE. *wilcuma*].
WELCOME (3), [wel'-kum], *v.t.* to offer a welcome to, to greet hospitably; to accept with pleasure.
WELCOMELY, [wel'-kum-li], *adv.* in a welcome manner.
WELCOMENESS, [wel'-kum-nes], *n.* the quality of being welcome.
WELCOMER, [wel'-kum-er], *n.* one who welcomes.
WELD (1), [weld], *n.* (*bot.*) a plant, *Reseda luteola*, used by dyers for the yellow colour it yields, dyer's weed. [ME. *welde*].
WELD (2), [weld], *n.* the act of welding; the join perfected by welding.
WELD (3), [weld], *v.t. and i.* to join (metal) by hammering or pressure when subjected to heat; to unite closely and firmly; to undergo a process of welding. [OE. *wellan* to boil].
WELDABILITY, [weld'-a-bil'-i-ti], *n.* capacity for being welded.
WELDABLE, [weld'-abl], *adj.* able to be welded.
WELDER, [weld'-er], *n.* one employed at welding.
WELDING-HEAT, [weld'-ing-hēt], *n.* the degree of heat needed for the process of welding.
WELFARE, [wel'-fāer], *n.* general level of existence from the point of view of comfort, health, and wealth; prosperity, satisfactory standard of living, *esp.* for a society or community; **w. worker**, a paid person in a factory, local government area, etc., who looks after the health and general circumstances of employees or local inhabitants. [OE. *wel* well and *faran* to go].
WELFARE-CENTRE, [wel'-fāer-sent'-er], *n.* an institution for amelioration of local conditions, *esp.* in connexion with children, expectant mothers, and unemployed.
WELKIN, [wel'-kin], *n.* the sky; **w. eye**, a rolling, blue eye. [~OE. *wolcen*].
WELL (1), [wel], *n.* a place where the water of a subterranean stream is accessible, *esp.* a shaft hollowed out of the earth, with the sides supported by stone or brick, which has access at the bottom to an underground spring; any narrow, deep excavation in the earth; any deep enclosed space; a compartment in a fishing smack or trawler to hold the catch; a central space in a building, *esp.* in a court room; the space provided in a building for a staircase or lift; (*naut.*) space round a ship's pump. [OE. *welle* spring].
WELL (2), [wel], *n.* what is judged good.
WELL (3), [wel], *adj.* possessing good health, physically fit, sound in constitution; advantageous, favourable, suitable; advisable; good.
WELL (4), [wel], *adv.* to a satisfactory degree, in a proper manner; correctly, rightly; not improperly, in a skilful manner, expertly; to an adequate extent, efficiently, thoroughly; to a suitable degree, in a circumspect manner; in a manner worthy of praise, perfectly; to a

convenient extent; **as w.,** as an extra, besides; **as w. as,** together with; **just as w.,** at least as good. [OE. *well*].

WELL (5), [wel], *v.i.* to issue out in a bubbling stream, to gush forth, gain exit. [OE. *wellan* to boil].

WELL (6), [wel], *int.* expressing surprise or resignation, or implying a question. [WELL (3) and (4)].

WELLADAY†, [wel'-a-dā], *int.* alas. [~WELLAWAY].

WELL-ADVISED, [wel'-ad-vizd'], *adj.* supplied with, following, good counsel.

WELL-APPOINTED, [wel'-a-point'-id], *adj.* satisfactorily equipped.

WELL-AUTHENTICATED, [wel'-aw-thent'-ik-āt-id], *adj.* backed by sound authority.

WELLAWAY†, [wel'-a-wā], *int.* an exclamation of grief, welladay. [OE. *wei la wei*].

WELL-BALANCED, [wel'-bal'-anst], *adj.* set in a satisfactory and accurate balance; having good proportions.

WELL-BEHAVED, [wel'-bi-hāvd'], *adj.* possessing exemplary manners, polite.

WELLBEING, [wel'-bē'-ing], *n.* a sound state of health or prosperity.

WELL-BELOVED, [wel'-bi-luvd'], *adj.* well loved.

WELL-BOAT, [wel'-bōt], *n.* a fishing-boat equipped with a well in the hold.

WELLBORING, [wel'-bawr-ing], *n.* the process of sinking wells by means of drills.

WELL-BORN, [wel'-bawn], *adj.* born into an upper-class family.

WELL-BRED, [wel'-bred'], *adj.* possessing hereditary qualities of a high standard; well-mannered.

WELL-CHOSEN, [wel-chōzn'], *adj.* selected with discrimination.

WELL-CONDITIONED, [wel'-kon-dish'-und], *adj.* in a condition suitable for a specific purpose; healthy in body.

WELL-CONDUCTED, [wel'-kon-dukt'-id], *adj.* properly conducted, orderly.

WELL-CONNECTED, [wel'-kon-ekt'-id], *adj.* having relatives of good family or of influence.

WELL-CURB, [wel'-kurb], *n.* the lip of brickwork round the mouth of a well.

WELL-DECK, [wel'-dek'], *n.* a lower deck not covered by upper decks.

WELL-DECKER, [wel'-dek'-er], *n.* a steamship designed with a raised forecastle, bridge-house and quarter-deck.

WELL-DIRECTED, [wel'-di-rekt'-id], *adj.* well aimed.

WELL-DISPOSED, [wel'-dis-pōzd'], *adj.* friendly.

WELLDOING, [wel'-dōō-ing], *n.* moral behaviour.

WELL-DRAIN, [wel'-drān], *n.* a deep channel placed in the centre of wet land for draining purposes.

WELL-DRESSED, [wel'-drest], *adj.* dressed smartly and in the fashion.

WELL-EARNED, [wel'-urnd], *adj.* justly earned.

WELL-EDUCATED, [wel-ed'-yōō-kāt-id], *adj.* that indicates a good education; (of a person) having had a good education, cultured.

WELL-FAVOURED, [wel'-fāv'-erd], *adj.* pleasing to the eye; having handsome features.

WELL-FED, [wel'-fed'], *adj.* having had plenty to eat, or indicating this.

WELL-FOUNDED, [wel'-fownd'-id], *adj.* based on sound reasons, authentic.

WELL-GROUNDED, [wel-grownd'-id], *adj.* amply justified; well instructed in the fundamentals.

WELL-HEAD, [wel'-hed'], *n.* the source of a spring.

WELL-HOLE, [wel'-hōl], *n.* the open space in the middle of a building designed to accommodate a flight of stairs.

WELL-HOUSE, [wel'-hows], *n.* a structure built over a well.

WELL-INFORMED, [wel'-in-fawmd'], *adj.* possessed of an extensive general knowledge; supplied with the appropriate facts.

WELLINGTONIA, [wel'-ing-tō'-ni-a], *n.* a tall coniferous tree of the genus *Sequoia*. [Prec.].

WELLINGTONS, [wel'-ing-tons], *n.(pl.)* long-legged boots (of rubber) made in one piece. [The Duke of *Wellington*].

WELL-INTENTIONED, [wel'-in-ten'-shund], *adj.* meaning well even though failing to achieve the desired end.

WELL-JUDGED, [wel'-jujd'], *adj.* displaying good judgment, well-timed and well-directed.

WELL-KNIT, [wel'-nit'], *adj.* having a compact physique.

WELL-KNOWN, [wel'-nōn], *adj.* widely known.

WELL-MADE, [wel'-mād], *adj.* expertly made.

WELL-MANNERED, [wel'-man'-erd], *adj.* having good manners, polite.

WELL-MARKED, [wel'-mahkt], *adj.* well differentiated, pronounced.

WELL-MEANING, [wel'-mēn'-ing], *adj.* of good intentions.

WELL-MEANT, [wel'-ment'], *adj.* showing kindly intentions.

WELL-MET, [wel'-met'], *int.* welcome.

WELLNIGH, [wel'-nī'], *adv.* almost; nearly.

WELL-NOURISHED, [wel'-nu'-risht], *adj.* well-fed.

WELL-OFF, [wel'-of'], *adj.* having ample means.

WELL-OILED, [wel'-oild'], *adj.* (*slang*) well primed with alcohol, but not drunk.

WELL-ORDERED, [wel'-awd-erd], *adj.* arranged in proper fashion.

WELL-PAID, [wel'-pād], *adj.* highly paid.

WELL-PROPORTIONED, [wel'-prō-paw'-shund], *adj.* having fine proportions, *esp.* in physique.

WELL-READ, [wel'-red'], *adj.* having an extensive and discriminating knowledge of good literature.

WELL-REGULATED, [wel'-reg'-yōō-lāt-id], *adj.* well-ordered.

WELL-ROOM, [wel'-rōōm]; *n.* a space in the hold of a boat where the water is collected; a room supplied by a well, where the waters are drunk.

WELL-SET, [wel'-set'], *adj.* of a compact build, having a firm physique.

WELLSIAN, [wel'-zi-an], *adj.* relating to, characteristic of the style, etc., of, H. G. *Wells* or his Utopian principles and scientific fantasies.

WELL-SINKER, [wel'-singk-er], *n.* one who sinks wells.

WELL-SPOKEN, [wel'-spōk'-en], *adj.* aptly spoken; having an accent and diction free from uncouthness; knowledgeable in conversation.

WELL-SPRING, [wel'-spring], *n.* a natural source of water-supply.

WELL-TEMPERED, [wel'-tem'-perd], *adj.* durable and flexible; (*mus.*) tuned in equal temperament.

WELL-TIMBERED, [wel'-timb'-erd], *adj.* having an ample number of trees.

WELL-TIMED, [wel'-tīmd'], *adj.* opportune.

WELL-TO-DO, [wel'-tōō-dōō'], *adj.* well off, wealthy.

WELL-TRAINED, [wel'-trānd], *adj.* effectively trained.

WELL-TRIED, [wel'-trīd], *adj.* proven.

WELL-TRODDEN [wel'-trod'-en], *adj.* much trodden or frequented; conventional.

WELL-TUNED, [wel'-tewnd], *adj.* correctly tuned; †having a pleasant tune.

WELL-TURNED, [wel'-turnd], *adj.* well expressed.

WELL-WATER, [wel'-waw'-ter], *n.* water that flows into and is drawn from a well.

WELLWISHER, [wel'-wish'-er], *n.* a non-active supporter, a friend.

WELL-WORN, [wel'-wawn], *adj.* threadbare; trite.

WELSH (1), [welsh], *n.* the native Celtic language of Wales; **the W.,** (*pl.*) the native inhabitants of Wales; **W. harp,** a harp with three rows of strings; **W. onion,** (*bot.*) the plant, *Allium fistulosum*, used in salads; **W. poppy,** the yellow-flowered poppy, *Mecanopsis cambrica*; **W. rarebit, rabbit,** toasted cheese. [OE. *welisc* foreign].

WELSH (2) [welsh], *adj.* of, relating to, characteristic of, coming from, made in, Wales; in or of Welsh or the Welsh.

WELSH (3), [welsh], *v.i.* to decamp from a racecourse, as a bookmaker, without paying winnings to backers. [Unkn.].

WELSHER, [welsh'-er], *n.* a bookmaker who welshes.

WELSHMAN, [welsh'-man], *n.* a male inhabitant of Wales; **or I'm a W.!** used to support an assertion.

WELSHWOMAN, [welsh'-wōōm-an], *n.* a female inhabitant of Wales.

WELT (1), [welt], *n.* a form of reinforcement for a hem or border; the thin strip of leather by which the sole of a shoe or boot is attached to the uppers; a mark on the body raised by a lash, a scar, a weal; (*coll.*) a blow, smack. [ME. *welte*].

WELT (2), [welt], *v.t.* to fit with a welt.

WELTANSCHAUUNG, [velt'-an'-show-ōōng], *n.* philosophy treating of the world as a whole. [Germ. *weltanschauung* world-contemplation].

WELTED, [welt'-id], *adj.* fitted with a welt.

WELTER (1), [welt'-er], *n.* a confused mass.

WELTER (2), [welt'-er], *adj.* extra heavy; (in boxing) weighing 147 lb.; (in horse-racing) riding well above average weight. [Uncert.].

WELTER (3), [welt'-er], *v.i.* to slip and roll about uncontrollably in a welter, to wallow. [~OE. *weltan*].

WELTERING, [welt'-er-ing], *adj.* wallowing.
WELTER-WEIGHT, [welt'-er-wāt], *n.* a boxer with a weight between light-weight and middle-weight, about 147 lb.; in racing, any extra heavy weight.
WELTING, [welt'-ing], *n.* the process of equipping with a welt; material for making welts; the welt itself.
WELWITSCHIA, [vel-vitch'-i-a], *n.* (*bot.*) an African plant with long ribbon-shaped leaves. [*Welwitsch*, a botanist].

WELWITSCHIA

WEN, [wen], *n.* a cyst, *esp.* on the head, a wart. [OE. *wenn*].
WENCH (1), [wench], *n.* (*coll.*) a young woman; †a harlot. [ME. *wenche* child].
WENCH (2), [wench], *v.i.* (*slang*) to mix with women for sexual purposes.
WENCHER, [wench'-er], *n.* a man who runs after women, a lecher.
WEND (1), [wend], *n.* a member of a Slavic race that occupied the north-east of Germany. [Germ. *Wende*].
WEND (2), [wend], *v.i.* †to wander; **to w. one's way,** to follow one's road. [OE. *wendan*].
WENDISH (1), [wend'-ish], *n.* the language spoken by the Wends.
WENDISH (2), [wend'-ish], *adj.* relating to, coming from, made by, the Wends.
WENT, [went], *pret.* of WEND and GO.
WENTLETRAP, [wentl'-trap'], *n.* a mollusc of the genus *Scalaria*. [Du. *wenteltrap* spiral staircase].
WEPT, [wept], *pret. and p.pt.* of WEEP.
WERE, [wāer, wur], *pret. pl., pl. and first and third pers. sing. subjunctive* of BE. [OE. *wæron*].
WEREWOLF, [wēer'-wŏolf], *n.* a person fabled to change into a wolf; a person with the voracious nature of a wolf. [OE. *werewulf*].
WERGILD, [wur'-gild], *n.* (*hist.*) the fine paid for committing homicide as compensation to the king and next of kin. [OE. *wer* man and *gild* payment].
WERNERIAN, [vāer-nēer'-i-an], *adj.* (*geol.*) relating to the theories of the German geologist, *Werner*.
WERNERITE, [vāern'-er-īt], *n.* (*min.*) a type of scapolite. [*Werner*, the German geologist].
WERT, [wurt], (*poet.*) *second pers. sing. imperfect subjunctive of* BE.
WERTHERIAN, [vaēr-tēer'-i-an], *adj.* morbidly sweet in sentiment. [*Werther*, a character of Goethe's *Leiden des jungen Werther*].
WESLEYAN (1), [wez'-li-an], *n.* a member of the Methodist sect founded by J. and C. *Wesley*.
WESLEYAN (2), [wez'-li-an], *adj.* relating to John or Charles Wesley or to their tenets, or to the church founded by them.
WESLEYANISM, [wez'-li-an-izm], *n.* the religious doctrines of the Wesleyans.
WEST (1), [west], *n.* the cardinal point of the compass marked by the setting of the sun at the equinox; the area of a country or of the globe situated in this direction in relation to a particular viewpoint.
WEST (2), [west], *adj.* relating to, coming from, opposite to, the west; **W. End,** the fashionable quarter of London.
WEST (3), [west], *adv.* towards the west; **to go w.,** to die; to be lost; to be rendered useless. [OE. *west*].
WEST-END, [west'-end'], *adj.* relating to, proper to, frequenting, the West End; (*coll.*) affected.
WESTERING, [west'-er-ing], *adj.* travelling towards the west. [ME. *westren* to go west].
WESTERLY (1), [west'-er-li], *adj.* relating to, situated in, the west; arriving from the west; moving towards the west.
WESTERLY (2), [west'-er-li], *adv.* in the general direction of the west.
WESTERN (1), [west'-ern], *n.* (*slang*) a cowboy film.
WESTERN (2), [west'-ern], *adj.* relating to, situated in, moving towards, coming from, the west; **W. Church,** the Latin Church.
WESTERNER, [west'-ern-er], *n.* a native of the west; an inhabitant of the west, *esp.* in U.S.A.
WESTERNISM, [west'-ern-izm], *n.* a western idiom.
WESTERNIZE, [west'-ern-īz], *v.t.* to convert to western manners or modes.
WESTERNMOST, [west'-ern-mōst], *adj.* farthest west.
WESTING, [west'-ing], *n.* (*naut.*) the course or drift of a boat westward.
WESTLING, [west'-ling], *adj.* (*Scots*) westward, westerly.
WESTWARD (1), [west'-werd], *n.* a westerly direction or quarter.
WESTWARD (2), [west'-werd], *adj.* western, towards the west.
WESTWARD (3), [west'-werd], *adv.* in a direction towards the west.
WESTWARDLY, [west'-werd-li], *adv.* in the general direction of the west.
WESTWARDS, [west'-werdz], *n., adj. and adv.* westward.
WET (1), [wet], *n.* water, moisture; (*slang*) a characterless person; a drunk.
WET (2), [wet], *adj.* drenched with, covered with, containing, water or other liquid; marked by a downpour of rain, by persistent rainfall; (*coll.*) anti-prohibitionist. [OE. *wæte*].
WET (3), (wetting, wetted), [wet], *v.t.* to make wet, to drench; (*coll.*) to seal (a bargain) with a drink.
WET BLANKET, [wet'-blangk'-et], *n.* a blanket soaked in water in order to put a fire out; (*fig.*) a gloomy or depressing person or event.
WET-BOB, [wet'-bob'], *n.* an athlete trained for water sports.
WET-DOCK, [wet'-dok'], *n.* a dock in which vessels are maintained afloat.
WETHER, [weTH'-er], *n.* a castrated ram. [OE. *wether*].
WETNESS, [wet'-nes], *n.* the quality or state of being wet.
WET-NURSE, [wet'-nurs], *n.* a nurse who suckles another's child.
WET PACK, [wet'-pak'], *n.* an application of wet bandages as a remedial measure.
WETTISH, [wet'-ish], *adj.* rather wet.
WEY, [wā], *n.* a measure of weight varying with different commodities, e.g., 182 lb. of wool, 40 bushels of salt, 48 bushels of oats or barley. [OE. *wæge*].
WEZAND, see WEASAND.
WHACK (1), [wak], *n.* a resounding blow, a thwack; (*slang*) a share. [Echoic].
WHACK (2), [wak], *v.t. and i.* to hit so that the blow resounds; to thwack.
WHACKER, [wak'-er], *n.* (*slang*) a huge one; a particularly audacious lie.
WHACKING (1), [wak'-ing], *n.* a beating.
WHACKING (2), [wak'-ing], *adj.* (*slang*) huge.
WHALE, [wāl], *n.* a large marine mammal of the order *Cetacea*, characterized by its size which is often longer than 60 ft. and by a large caudal fin, and hunted commercially in the Arctic and Antarctic regions; (*slang*) anything big. [OE. *hwæl*].

WHALE

WHALE-BACK, [wāl'-bak'], *n.* a boat, a cargo steamer with upper works designed like the back of a whale.
WHALE-BOAT, [wāl'-bōt], *n.* a long boat designed and equipped for whaling.
WHALEBONE, [wāl'-bōn], *n.* a firm substance growing in the upper jaw of some kinds of whales in place of teeth.
WHALE-FISHERY, [wāl'-fish'-er-i], *n.* an area where whales are caught; the industry of fishing for whales.
WHALE-LOUSE, [wāl'-lows], *n.* a crustacean parasite of the genus *Cyamus*, living on the cetaceans.
WHALEMAN, [wāl'-man], *n.* a man employed in the whaling industry.
WHALE-OIL, [wāl'-oil], *n.* oil extracted from the whale.
WHALER, [wāl'-er], *n.* a ship equipped for whale-fishery; a seaman employed in a whaler.
WHALING (1), [wāl'-ing], *n.* the industry of catching whales.
WHALING (2), [wāl'-ing], *adj.* related to, concerned with, the business of whale-fishery.
WHALING-GUN, [wāl'-ing-gun'], *n.* the apparatus by which the harpoon is fired from a whaler.
WHALING-MASTER, [wāl'-ing-mast'-er], *n.* the officer in charge of a whaler.
WHANG (1), [wang], *n.* a leather strap; the resounding noise that this makes when made to strike something; a large slice.
WHANG (2), [wang], *v.t.* to thrash, *esp.* with a leather strap. [Echoic].
WHANGHEE, see WANGHEE.
WHAP (1), [wop], *n.* a blow. [ME. *wap*].
WHAP (2), (whapping, whapped), [wop], *v.t. and i.* to beat; to flop.
WHARF (1), (wharves), [wawf], *n.* a landing stage where ships are loaded and unloaded. [OE. *hwearf*].

WHARF (2), [wawf], *v.t.* to anchor alongside a wharf.
WHARFAGE, [wawf'-ij], *n.* payment for accommodation at a wharf; the accommodation itself.
WHARFING, [wawf'-ing], *n.* a collection of wharves; materials for building or supporting wharves.
WHARFINGER, [wawf'-in-jer], *n.* an owner or superintendent of a wharf. [~WHARFAGE].
WHAT, [wot], *pron.* who or which (of several alternatives); (*rel.*) that which (of several alternatives); how much; (*interrog.*) which (of several alternatives); how much. [OE. *hwæt*].
WHATE'ER, [wot'-āer'], *pron.* (*poet.*) whatever.
WHATEVER (1), [wot'-ev'-er], *adj.* no matter what.
WHATEVER (2), [wot'-ev'-er], *pron.* regardless of anything, one thing or another, all that, all manner of things.
WHATNOT, [wot'-not'], *n.* a piece of furniture for displaying or storing ornamental odds and ends.
WHATSOE'ER, [wot'-sō-āer'], *pron.* (*poet.*) whatsoever.
WHATSOEVER, [wot'-sō-ev'-er], *pron.* whatever.
WHAUP, [wawp], *n.* (*Scots*) the curlew, *Numenius arquatus*. [Echoic].
WHEAL (1), [wēl], *n.* a pustule; a weal. [ME. *whele*].
WHEAL (2), [wēl], *n.* a mine. [Cornish *hwel*].
WHEAT, [wēt], *n.* a plant of the genus *Triticum* cultivated for its edible seed which is ground into flour. [OE. *hwæte*].
WHEAT-BIRD, [wēt'-burd], *n.* the chaffinch, *Fringilla cœlebs*.
WHEAT-EAR, [wēt'-ēer], *n.* a spike of wheat.
WHEATEAR, [wēt'-ēer], *n.* a small bird, *Saxicola œnanthe*, allied to the stonechat. [OE. *hwit* white and *ears* rump].
WHEATEN, [wēt'-en], *adj.* made of wheat.
WHEAT-FLY, [wēt'-flī], *n.* an insect which infests harvested wheat.
WHEAT-MOTH, [wēt'-moth'], *n.* an insect whose grubs feed on harvested wheat.
WHEATSTONE, [wēt'-stōn], *n.* **w. bridge,** a device for measuring electrical resistance. [*Wheatstone*, an English physicist].
WHEEDLE, [wēdl], *v.t. and i.* to persuade to one's own ends by fawning or flattery, to coax, to cajole; **to w. out of,** to obtain from by flattery. [Uncert.].
WHEEDLER, [wēd'-ler], *n.* one who wheedles.
WHEEDLESOME, [wēdl'-sum], *adj.* characterized by wheedling.
WHEEDLING, [wēd'-ling], *adj.* inducing by fawning and flattery, enticing.
WHEEL (1), [wēl], *n.* a circular piece of any hard material capable of revolving round its centre; such an article of various constructions revolving in a vertical plane on an axle, supporting a vehicle or other load, or transmitting the power of the axle on which it is mounted; any apparatus designed on the principle of this; a single turn of a wheel; any movement which takes in a wide arc; (*naut.*) the steering mechanism; **to break on the w.,** (*hist.*) to bind to the rim of a large wheel and maim by breaking all the bones in the body; also (*fig.*); **to put a spoke in someone's w.,** to obstruct someone's plans or purpose; **to put one's shoulder to the w.,** to give aid in a task; **wheels within wheels,** a complicated series of interdependent agents. [OE. *hweol*].
WHEEL (2), [wēl], *v.t. and i.* to cause to be conveyed by a vehicle fitted with wheels; to cause to move on wheels by pushing, pulling, etc.; to manoeuvre (a body of troops) so that one end keeps its ground, and the other swings round in a wide arc; to revolve on an axis; to change direction so that one end of a line swings round in a wide semicircle; to turn on a pivot so as to face another direction; (of birds, etc.) to fly in a wide arc. [*Prec.*].
WHEEL-ANIMALCULE, [wēl'-an'-i-mal'-kewl], *n.* a species of rotifer.
WHEELBARROW, [wēl'-ba'-rō], *n.* a small sturdy barrow with deep sides set on a more or less triangular frame of which the apex at the front is declined, and fitted with a small single wheel.
WHEEL-BASE, [wēl'-bās], *n.* the area or distance between front and back axles.
WHEEL-BOAT, [wēl'-bōt], *n.* a boat with wheels, a paddle-steamer; a toy boat.
WHEEL-CARRIAGE, [wēl'-ka'-rij], *n.* a large carriage fitted with four wheels.
WHEEL-CHAIR, [wēl'-chāer], *n.* a chair fitted with wheels, *esp.* for use of an invalid.
WHEEL-CUTTING, [wēl'-kut-ing], *n.* a branch of engineering concerned with cutting teeth in wheels; cutting by means of a wheel with a sharpened edge.
WHEELED, [wēld], *adj.* fitted with a wheel or wheel
WHEELER, [wēl'-er], *n.* a maker of wheels; one who or that which, runs on wheels; a cyclist.
WHEEL-HOUSE, [wēl'-hows], *n.* (*naut.*) a structur protecting the wheel of a ship.
WHEELING, [wēl'-ing], *n.* the act of proceeding o wheels; cycling; the action of moving in a wide arc
WHEELLESS, [wēl'-les], *adj.* not provided with wheels
WHEEL-ORE, [wēl'-aw(r)], *n.* (*min.*) a variety o bournonite.
WHEEL-RACE, [wēl'-rās], *n.* the station for a water wheel.
WHEEL-SHAPED, [wēl'-shāpt], *adj.* having the form of a wheel; (*bot.*) monopetalous, rotate.
WHEELTAPPER, [wēl'-tap'-er], *n.* a man who test railway wheels.
WHEEL-WORK, [wēl'-wurk], *n.* a combination o geared or connected wheels functioning as a unit i a machine.
WHEELWRIGHT, [wēl'-rīt], *n.* a craftsman who makes wheels.
WHEETER-WHY, [wē'-ter-wī], *n.* the white-throat a bird of the genus *Sylvia*. [Uncert.].
WHEEZE (1), [wēz], *n.* a breathing accompanied by an involuntary whistling or thin-sounding noise in the chest or at the back of the throat; (*slang*) idea plan, *esp.* for a joke.
WHEEZE (2), [wēz], *v.i.* to breathe hard, making an audible whistling sound in the chest or at the back of the nose. [OE. *hwesan*].
WHEEZILY, [wēz'-i-li], *adv.* in a wheezing manner
WHEEZINESS, [wēz'-i-nes], *n.* the condition o quality of being wheezy.
WHEEZING, [wēz'-ing], *n.* the act of one who wheezes
WHEEZY, [wēz'-i], *adj.* afflicted with wheezing; sounding like one who wheezes.
WHEFT, [weft], *n.* a signaller's flag. [*Var.* of WAFT].
WHELK (1), [welk], *n.* an edible gastropod of the genus *Buccinum* or the genus *Fusus*. [OE. *wiluc*].
WHELK (2), [welk], *n.* a pimple. [OE. *hwylca*].
WHELKY, [welk'-i], *adj.* resembling a whelk in form; tasting like a whelk.
WHELM†, [welm], *v.t.* to engulf, *esp.* in water. [ME. *whelmen* to overturn].

WHELK

WHELP (1), [welp], *n.* the young of a bitch, a puppy; a lion cub; (*coll.*) contemptuous term for a young man. [OE. *hwelp*].
WHELP (2) [welp], *v.t. and i.* to give birth (to offspring) as a bitch.
WHEN (1), [wen], *adv.* which period, at what time, on what date; in what situation; at the time, on the day; at any time, whenever; even though. [OE. *hwænne*].
WHEN (2), [wen], *pron.* on the occasion which; at which time.
WHENCE (1), [wents], *adv.* from where, from what place. [ME. *whennes*].
WHENCE (2), [wents], *conj.* as a result of which.
WHENCE-EVER†, [wents'-ev'-er], *adv.* whencesoever.
WHENCESOEVER, [wents'-sō-ev'-er], *adv.* (*poet.*) from whatever place or source.
WHENEVER, [wen-ev'-er], *adv.* at whatever time or occasion.
WHENSOEVER, [wen'-sō-ev'-er], *adv.* whenever.
WHERE (1), [wāer], *adv.* to what place; at which place; in what particular; at the point at which. [OE. *hwær*].
WHERE (2), [wāer], *pron.* from, to, at, which region, place, etc.; the point at or on which.
WHEREABOUT†, [wāer'-ab-owt'], *adv.* whereabouts.
WHEREABOUTS (1), [wāer'-ab-owts], *n.* the place, situation, area. [WHERE and ABOUT].
WHEREABOUTS (2), [wāer'-ab-owts], *adv.* in which spot, place, area, position, etc. [*Prec.*].
WHEREAS, [wāer-az'], *conj.* but, from an opposite viewpoint, on the other hand, on the contrary, when in fact, since it is established that.
WHEREAT, [wāer-at'], *adv.* at which.
WHEREBY, [wāer-bī'], *adv.* by which; by what.
WHEREFORE (1), [wāer'-faw(r)], *n.* reason.
WHEREFORE (2), [wāer'-faw(r)], *adv.* why, for what reason, on what account; for that reason.
WHEREIN, [wāer-in'], *adv.* into which; in respect of which; where.
WHEREINSOEVER†, [wāer-in'-sō-ev'-er], *adv.* in whatsoever place; in whatsoever connexion.

WHEREINTO†, [wāer-in'-tōō], *adv.* into which.
WHEREOF, [wāer-ov'], *adv.* of which.
WHEREON, [wāer-on'], *adv.* on which.
WHEREOUT†, [wāer-owt'], *adv.* out of which.
WHERESOEVER, [wāer'-sō-ev'-er], *adv.* in whatever place, wherever.
WHERETO, [wāer-tōō'], *adv.* to which; to what; to what end, for what.
WHEREUNTO, [wāer-un'-tōō], *adv.* whereto.
WHEREUPON, [wāer'-up-on'], *adv.* upon which; at which point.
WHEREVER, [wāer-ev'-er], *adv.* at whatever place, in any part, position, etc.
WHEREWITH, [wāer-WITH'], *adv.* with which; with what.
WHEREWITHAL (1), [wāer-WITH-awl'], *n.* the means, the money necessary.
WHEREWITHAL (2), [wāer'-WITH-awl'], *adv.* wherewith.
WHERRY (1), [we'-ri], *n.* a rowing boat with seats for from six to eight passengers; a large sailing barge. [Uncert.].
WHERRY (2), [we'-ri], *n.* a drink made from mashed crab apples. [Uncert.].
WHERRY (3), [we'-ri], *v.t.* to transport by means of a wherry.
WHET (1), [wet], *n.* the act of whetting; an appetizer.
WHET (2), (whetting, whetted), [wet], *v.t.* to rub on the surface of a flat stone so as to put a sharp edge on, to sharpen, to strop; to stimulate. [OE. *hwettan*].
WHETHER† **(1),** [weTH'-er], *pron.* which of two. [OE. *hwæder*].
WHETHER (2), [weTH'-er], *conj.* indicating alternatives of choice, and usually followed by *or*; **w. or no,** no matter if.
WHETHERING, [weTH'-er-ing], *n.* the retention of the afterbirth by a cow.
WHETSTONE, [wet'-stōn], *n.* any hard stone on which tools are sharpened by whetting.
WHETSTONE-SLATE, [wet'-stōn-slāt], *n.* a variety of slate on which steel tools are sharpened.
WHETTER, [wet'-er], *n.* one who or that which whets or sharpens; a stimulant, appetizer.
WHEW (1), [hew], *int.* (expressing surprise) a forcing out of the breath accompanied by half a gasp and half a whistling sound, expressing astonishment, or as a sign of relief or reaction to hot weather. [Echoic].
WHEW (2), [hew], *v.i.* to emit a whew. [*Prec.*].
WHEWELLITE, [hew'-el-īt], *n.* (*min.*) an oxalate of lime. [Dr. *Whewell*, and Gk. *lithos* stone].
WHEY, [wā], *n.* the thin, watery part of milk which remains after removing the curds. [OE. *hwæg*].
WHEYISH, [wā'-ish], *adj.* containing or resembling whey; having the qualities of whey.
WHEY-TUB, [wā'-tub], *n.* a tub for holding whey.
WHICH (1), [wich], *adj.* what, in interrogation; what man, woman, or object; of what sort, type, group. [OE. *hwylc*].
WHICH (2), [wich], *pron.* what one, thing, person, etc., in interrogation; that object or series of objects.
WHICHEVER (1), [wich-ev'-er], *adj.* that, any that.
WHICHEVER (2), [wich-ev'-er], *pron.* either one or the other; which one.
WHICHSOEVER, [wich'-sō-ev'-er], *pron.* whichever.
WHIDAH, see WHYDAH.
WHIFF (1), [wif], *n.* a slight amount of air inhaled by a single sniff; a puff or stream of air slightly tainted with a bad smell; a brief contact with a smell; a sculling boat fitted with outriggers for one rower; (*coll.*) a small, cheap cigar. [Echoic].
WHIFF (2), [wif], *n.* a flatfish resembling the turbot. [Unkn.].
WHIFF (3), [wif], *v.i.* to possess a slight smell, to give off a tainted odour.
WHIFF (4), [wif], *v.i.* to fish for mackerel, etc., by handline.
WHIFFING, [wif'-ing], *n.* the technique of fishing with a handline for mackerel.
WHIFFLE (1), [wifl], *n.* the act of whiffling.
WHIFFLE (2), [wifl], *v.t. and i.* to cause to drift or float away haphazardly by gusts; to blow in intermittent gusts or puffs, to veer; to drift with opinion. [Uncert.].
WHIFFLER, [wif'-ler], *n.* one who vacillates, a trifler; the American golden-eye duck, *Clanguli glaucion.*
WHIFFLETREE, [wifl'-trē], *n.* a whippletree.
WHIFFLING, [wif'-ling], *n.* prevarication; vacillation.
WHIFFY, [wif'-i], *adj.* pervaded with whiffs; (*slang*) slightly smelly.
WHIG (1), [wig], *n.* (*hist.*) a member or supporter of a political party originating with the Scottish Covenanters of the seventeenth century, emerging in the nineteenth century as representative of the middle-class free-traders against the Tory landowners, and later as the Liberal Party. [WHIG(AMORE)].
WHIG (2), [wig], *n.* (*dial.*) curdled milk, whey. [Uncert.].
WHIG (3), [wig], *adj.* relating to the Whigs.
WHIGAMORE, [wig'-a-maw(r)], *n.* (*hist.*) a Scottish Covenanter. [Uncert.].
WHIGGARCHY, [wig'-ahk-i], *n.* government by Whigs. [WHIG (1) and Gk. *arkhia* rule].
WHIGGERY, [wig'-er-i], *n.* the theories and practice, *esp.* malpractices, of the Whigs.
WHIGGISH, [wig'-ish], *adj.* based on, affected by, the principles of Whigs.
WHIGGISHLY, [wig'-ish-li], *adv.* in the manner of a Whig.
WHIGGISHNESS, [wig'-ish-nes], *n.* the theory and practice of the Whigs, *esp.* in a malicious sense.
WHILE (1), [wīl], *n.* time, the trouble or expense spent on something. [OE. *hwil*].
WHILE (2), [wīl], *adv.* as long as, during the same time that; in which case; although.
WHILE (3), [wīl], *v.t.* to cause (time) to pass (away) in pleasant but unimportant occupations.
WHILES, [wīlz], *adv.* (*Scots*) (*coll.*) sometimes.
WHILK, [wilk], *n.* (*dial.*) the scoter, a sea-duck of the genus *Œdemia.* [Uncert.].
WHILOM, [wīl'-um], *adv. and adj.* previously, formerly; once; in ancient times; former. [OE. *hwilum* at times].
WHILST, [wīlst], *conj.* while.
WHIM, [wim], *n.* an idea, a fancy, which has no deep emotional or mental roots, a sudden desire, a capricious wish; a type of windlass functioning at a minehead, usually worked by horses. [~OScand. *hvima* to let the eye stray].
WHIMBERRY, [wim'-be'-ri], *n.* (*bot.*) the fruit of *Vaccinium vitis-idæa*, the bilberry. [*Var.* of WHINBERRY].
WHIMBREL, [wim'-brel], *n.* a small species of curlew, *Numenius phæopus*, with a hooked beak. [Echoic].
WHIMPER (1), [wim'-per], *n.* an act or period of whimpering.
WHIMPER (2), [wim'-per], *v.t. and i.* to cry in the form of low sobs and intermittent whining out of self-commiseration or the after effects of pain; to utter as one who whimpers. [Echoic].
WHIMPERING (1), [wim'-per-ing], *n.* a low, whining sob; a sustained outbreak of these.
WHIMPERING (2), [wim'-per-ing], *adj.* affected by an outburst of whimpers; like a whimper.
WHIMPERINGLY, [wimp'-er-ing-li], *adv.* in a whimpering way.
WHIMPLED, [wimpld], *adj.* covered with little dimples. [*Var.* of WIMPLED].
WHIMSEY†, see WHIMSY.
WHIMSICAL, [wimz'-ik-al], *adj.* full of whimsy, temperamentally inclined to whimsy, expressing a quaint, fanciful capriciousness; freakish, odd, eccentric. [WHIMSY].
WHIMSICALITY, [wimz'-ik-al'-i-ti], *n.* whimsicalness.
WHIMSICALLY, [wimz'-ik-al-i], *adv.* in a whimsical fashion.
WHIMSICALNESS, [wimz'-ik-al-nes], *n.* the quality or state of being whimsical, a fanciful caprice, that which is arch, coy, sentimental, but apt in its way.
WHIMSY, WHIMSEY†, [wim'-zi], *n.* an expression, idea, fanciful to the pitch of fantasy, a caprice, whim. [WHIM].
WHIMWHAM†, [wim'-wam'], *n.* an object or idea characterized by a fanciful playfulness; a toy.
WHIN (1), [win], *n.* gorse; a plant of the genus *Ulex.* [~Norw. *hvine*].
WHIN (2), [win], *n.* whinstone. [Unkn.].
WHINBERRY, [win'-be'-ri], *n.* the whortleberry.
WHINCHAT, [win'-chat'], *n.* the small singing bird, the russet-feathered *Saxicola rubetra*, allied to the stonechat. [WHIN (1) and *chat*, the bird's note].
WHINE (1), [win], *n.* the act of whining, the noise made by a complaining, querulous cry; a weepy, fawning complaint.
WHINE (2), [win], *v.t. and i.* to express with a whine; to give expression to sounds or verbal complaints while weeping and talking through the nose like a hurt child, to complain fretfully like a child asking for pity. [OE. *hwinan*].
WHINER, [win'-er], *n.* one who whines.
WHINING, [win'-ing], *adj.* characteristic of one who whines; wretched.
WHININGLY, [win'-ing-li], *adv.* in a whining manner.

WHINNY (1), [win′-i], *n.* the noise made by a horse when it blows air through its nostrils.
WHINNY (2), [win′-i], *v.i.* to make a noise, as a horse, by blowing air through the nostrils. [Echoic].
WHINSTONE, [win′-stōn], *n.* one of various kinds of sandstone.
WHINYARD, [win′-yahd], *n.* a sword, dirk. [Uncert.].
WHIP (1), [wip], *n.* a flexible thong, lash, or plaited cord, fastened to a handle, and used for beating or thrashing; a lash administered by this instrument; a driver of a carriage; a member of Parliament who organizes the attendance of his party members at divisions; a summons sent out by this member; (*naut.*) a hoisting rope.
WHIP (2), [wip], *n.* the white pennant adorned with the cross of St. George flown by commissioned ships of the British Navy.
WHIP (3), [wip], *v.t.* to strike, hit, lash with a whip, to administer punishment to by means of a whip, to beat, thrash, flog; to beat out, take out, by subjecting to a series of lashes; to conquer, vanquish; to beat into a froth; to sew together (the bases of a fold in a material forming a ridge); *v.i.* to act quickly, to make a movement in a flash; **to w. from,** to snatch away from; **to w. off,** to lift off quickly; to hurry away with a sudden movement; **to w. out,** to draw out quickly; to speak suddenly in a decisive tone of voice; **to w. round,** to pivot suddenly; **to w. up,** to beat into a froth; to pick up suddenly; to stimulate quickly. [ME. *whippen*].
WHIPCORD, [wip′-kawd], *n.* a strong, closely twisted string out of which lashes are made for whips; a strong woollen material woven in a ribbed pattern.
WHIP-CRANE, [wip′-krān], *n.* a light type of crane moving on a pivot.
WHIPGRAFT, [wip′-grahft], *v.i.* to graft by inserting a tongue cut out of the scion into a slit in the stock.
WHIP HAND, [wip′-hand′], *n.* essential control.
WHIP-LASH, [wip′-lash′], *n.* the lash of a whip.
WHIPPER, [wip′-er], *n.* one who whips; (*milit.*) an officer detailed to inflict a legal whipping; (*naut.*) a ship's hand stacking coal in a ship's hold.
WHIPPER-IN, [wip′-er-in′], *n.* an assistant who keeps hounds to the course of a hunt; the competitor to finish last in a race; (*Scots*) (*coll.*) school attendance-officer.
WHIPPER-SNAPPER, [wip′-er-snap′-er], *n.* a small but cheeky boy; an unimportant but presumptuous person. [Uncert.].
WHIPPET, [wip′-it], *n.* a small crossbred greyhound trained for speed; (*milit.*) a small armoured car built for speed. [Uncert.].
WHIPPINESS, [wip′-i-nes], *n.* the quality of being whippy.
WHIPPING, [wip′-ing], *n.* the act of punishing with a whip; the punishment administered by a whip; the state of being whipped; a severe defeat; a close-coiled binding of cord to act as a support.
WHIPPING-BOY, [wip′-ing-boi], *n.* (*hist.*) a boy educated along with an important personage for whose faults he had to take punishment; (*fig.*) one who has to take blame for another's fault.
WHIPPING-POST, [wip′-ing-pōst], *n.* (*hist.*) a post to which offenders were tied when undergoing a whipping by authority.
WHIPPING-TOP, [wip′-ing-top′], *n.* a top spun by being whipped.
WHIPPLETREE, [wipl′-trē], *n.* the bar to which traces are hooked and by which a carriage, a plough, etc., is drawn, a swingle-tree.
WHIPPOORWILL, [wip′-er-wil], *n.* the North American nightjar, *Antrostomus vociferus*. [Echoic].
WHIPPY, [wip′-i], *adj.* thin and pliable, like a whip.
WHIP-RAY, [wip′-rā], *n.* the sea-fish, *Myliobatis aquila*, characterized by a long, pliable tail.
WHIP-ROUND, [wip′-rownd′], *n.* a spontaneously organized collection of voluntary contributions for some charity.
WHIP-SAW, [wip′-saw], *n.* a large type of saw usually set in a frame.
WHIP-SNAKE, [wip′-snāk], *n.* a long, slender snake of the genus *Dryophis*.
WHIP-STITCH (1), [wip′-stich], *n.* a stitch forming a firm ridge of rolled material.
WHIP-STITCH (2), [wip′-stich], *v.t. and i.* to form into whip-stitches; to practise this.
WHIP-STOCK, [wip′-stok′], *n.* the handle to which the lash of a whip is fastened.
WHIP-TAILED, [wip′-tāld], *adj.* possessing a long, thin, tapering tail, resembling the lash of a whip.
WHIP-TOP, [wip′-top′], *n.* a whipping-top.

WHIR (1), WHIRR, WHUR, [wur], *n.* the sound made by anything revolving rapidly.
WHIR (2), WHIRR, WHUR, (whirring, whirred), [wur], *v.t. and i.* to rotate rapidly so as to set up an audible vibration; to make a humming sound by whirling round rapidly. [~Dan. *hvirre* to whirl].
WHIRL (1), [wurl], *n.* the act or condition of whirling, rapid rotation; a hook for twisting strands; **the social w.,** a giddy round of social activities.
WHIRL (2), [wurl], *v.t. and i.* to spin round rapidly as on a pivot, to gyrate; to hurry off. [OIcel. *hvirfla*].
WHIRLABOUT, [wurl′-ab-owt], *n.* the act of whirling about; a whirligig.
WHIRL-BLAST, [wurl′-blahst], *n.* a whirlwind.
WHIRLBONE, [wurl′-bōn], *n.* (*anat.*) the knee-cap.
WHIRLIGIG, [wurl′-i-gig], *n.* a toy turned on a pivot; a roundabout; (*milit.*) punishment by spinning in a wooden cage; **w. beetle,** a beetle of the genus *Gyrinus*, having a gyratory motion. [WHIRL (2) and GIG].
WHIRLING, [wurl′-ing], *adj.* characterized by rapid turning round.
WHIRLING-TABLE, [wurl′-ing-tābl], *n.* a mechanical contrivance for representing several phenomena of centrifugal force.
WHIRLPOOL, [wurl′-pōōl], *n.* a violent current of water eddying round in a circle, a vortex.
WHIRLWIND, [wurl′-wind], *n.* an atmospheric phenomenon consisting of a body of air, revolving violently and made visible by dust drawn into it by suction.
WHIRR, see WHIR.
WHIRRING, [wur′-ing], *n.* the sound produced by that which whirs, *esp.* by a partridge's or pheasant's wings when in flight.
WHISHT, see WHIST (4).
WHISK (1), [wisk], *n.* the act of whisking; a small bunch of straw, stiff hairs, etc., gathered to form a light brush; a small culinary utensil for beating eggs; †a kind of woman's scarf. [OScand. *visk* wisp].
WHISK (2), [wisk], *v.t. and i.* to remove by sweeping smartly away; to swing, flip, toss, fling, twitch; to mix up thoroughly by beating as with a whisk; **to w. out,** to leave rapidly, to move nimbly. [*Prec.*].
WHISKER, [wisk′-er], *n.* one of the prominent hairs growing on the face, *esp.* of a man; a bristle characteristic of the upper lip of the feline species; (*pl.*) a cultivated growth of hair on the cheeks.
WHISKERED, [wisk′-erd], *adj.* formed into whiskers; characterized by a growth of whiskers; **w. tern,** the sea bird, *Hydrochelidon hybrida*.
WHISKEY, [wisk′-i], *n.* whisky distilled in Ireland.
WHISKY, [wisk′-i], *n.* an alcoholic drink distilled in Scotland from malted barley. [Gael. *uisge beatha* water of life].
WHISPER (1), [wisp′-er], *n.* the act of whispering; speech uttered with a low sibilant voice; a subdued hissing sound with no definite articulation; (*fig.*) a suggestion, hint.
WHISPER (2), [wisp′-er], *v.t. and i.* to talk in a low sibilant voice without using the vocal cords; (*fig.*) to intrigue, make mischief by rumour; to give expression to an indistinct hissing or murmuring sound; to give utterance to in a whisper, to communicate secretly by means of a whisper. [OE. *hwisprian*].
WHISPERER, [wisp′-er-er], *n.* one who whispers; a gossip.
WHISPERING (1), [wisp′-er-ing], *n.* the act of one who whispers; that which is whispered.
WHISPERING (2), [wisp′-er-ing], *adj.* characterized by utterance in whispers; **w. campaign,** a campaign of furtive rumour-spreading.
WHISPERINGLY, [wisp′-er-ing-li], *adv.* by means of a whisper.
WHIST (1), [wist], *n.* a game of cards for four players competing in pairs. [*Var.* of WHISK].
WHIST† (2), [wist], *adj.* silent; still.
WHIST (3), [wist], *v.t.* to silence by shushing through the lips.
WHIST (4), WHISHT, [wist], *int.* be silent, hush. [Echoic].
WHISTLE (1), [wisl], *n.* a simple form of musical wind instrument played by finger-stops; the thin, high-pitched sound produced by this, or by forcing air through pursed-up lips with the tip of the tongue resting at the back of the front bottom teeth; any shrill, piercing sound; a small instrument or pipe sometimes containing a dried pea and designed to make such a sound when blown; (*slang*) throat.
WHISTLE (2), [wisl], *v.t. and i.* to give utterance to a high, shrill note or noise by forcing the breath out through pursed-up lips; to make the noise natural

to a bird; to play on a whistle, to blow a whistle; to give vent to a tune by forcing the breath through the teeth and lips; to make the air shriek by forcing a way through it; to produce, *esp.* as music, by whistling; to call by whistling. [OE. *hwistlian*].

WHISTLED, [wisld], *adj.* produced by whistling.

WHISTLE-FISH, [wisl'-fish], *n.* the three-bearded rockling, *Motella tricirrata*.

WHISTLER, [wis'-ler], *n.* one who or that which whistles; (*coll.*) a fast-travelling missile.

WHISTLING, [wis'-ling], *n.* a shrill sound as made by one who whistles.

WHIT (1), [wit], *n.* the minutest fraction, a point, a jot. [OE. *wiht*].

WHIT (2), [wit], *adj.* of, pertaining to, occurring at Whitsun. [WHIT(SUN)].

WHITE (1), [wīt], *n.* colour or paint which is white; that which is white; a person who is white, that is, a man who is of fair complexion as distinct from a negro or oriental; **w. of egg,** the albumen in which the yolk is suspended in the shell; **w. of the eye,** the part of the eyeball around the iris; **W. armies,** the anti-communist armies of Russia defeated by the Communists in the 1917 Revolution; (*pl.*) leucorrhoea.

WHITE (2), [wīt], *adj.* having the colour of driven snow; reflecting the colours of the spectrum as a light characterized by no predominating colour; not dark; pale in colour, of a light tint; deprived of colour, bloodless; pure; free from marks or spots; (*fig.*) good, pure in heart, honest; **w. copper,** an alloy composed of copper, nickel and zinc; **w. feather,** a symbol of cowardice; **w. man,** a member of the white-skinned races of Europe; an honourable and upright man; **the white man's burden,** the responsibility of the white races for civilizing the world; **w. meat,** the flesh of poultry, veal, rabbits, etc.; **w. metal,** an alloy of zinc, etc., used by silversmiths; **w. sheet,** a symbol of doing penance. [OE. *hwit*].

WHITE† (3), [wīt], *v.t.* to make white; to whitewash.

WHITE ANT, [wīt'-ant'], *n.* a destructive tropical social insect resembling an ant, a termite.

WHITEBAIT, [wīt'-bāt], *n.* the small fry of herrings and sprats and other small edible fishes.

WHITEBEAM, [wīt'-bēm], *n.* (*bot.*) the tree, *Pyrus aria*, characterized by a white down on the lower side of the leaves.

WHITEBEARD, [wīt'-bēerd], *n.* an old man.

WHITEBOY, [wīt'-boi], *n.* a member of an association of Irishmen, formed in 1762, who wore white shirts as uniforms.

WHITEBOYISM, [wīt'-boi'-izm], *n.* the principles and practice of the Whiteboys.

WHITE-COLLAR, [wīt'-kol'-er], *adj.* descriptive of the class of workers, mostly clerks, who wear starched white collars.

WHITE-ELEPHANT, [wīt'-el'-i-fant], *n.* the grey elephant held in holy awe by the Siamese, and not trained for work; a failure, a useless possession.

WHITE-FILM, [wīt'-film], *n.* a white film afflicting the eyes of sheep.

WHITE-FISH, [wīt'-fish], *n.* an American fresh-water fish of the genus *Coregonus*; a fish of the genus *Leuciscus* with silver scales; fish with white flesh.

WHITE FRIAR, [wīt'-frī'-er], *n.* a Carmelite monk who wears a white habit.

WHITEHEAD, [wīt'-hed'], *n.* the snow goose, *Anser cærulescens*, characterized by blue wings.

WHITEHEART, [wīt'-haht], *n.* a cherry with white or cream-coloured flesh.

WHITE-HEAT, [wīt'-hēt'], *n.* the degree of heat at which a metal becomes white; (*fig.*) a mental or emotional state in which the faculties function at an unusual intensity.

WHITE HORSE, [wīt'- haws'], *n.* a ridge of foam at the summit of a wave.

WHITE-HOUND, [wīt'-hownd], *n.* a species of small shark, *Galeus vulgaris*.

WHITE-HOUND

WHITE HOUSE, [wīt'-hows'], *n.* the name of the official residence of the President of U.S.A. used (*fig.*) to signify the office itself.

WHITE-IRON, [wīt'-īern], *n.* iron plate treated with tin.

WHITE-LADY, [wīt'-lād'-i], *n.* a cocktail of gin and lemon juice.

WHITE-LIVERED, [wīt'-liv'-erd], *adj.* pale in complexion; cowardly; spiteful.

WHITELY, [wīt'-li], *adv.* to a degree of whiteness.

WHITEN, [wīt'-en], *v.t. and i.* to give a coating of white to, to make white; to bleach; to grow white.

WHITENER, [wīt'-en-er], *n.* one who, or a substance which, bleaches or makes white.

WHITENESS, [wīt'-nes], *n.* the quality of being white; purity, freedom from stain.

WHITENING, [wīt'-ning], *n.* any substance which whitens, whiting.

WHITE-PAPER, [wīt'-pā'-per], *n.* a book or pamphlet issued by the Government on a specific matter of national interest, and bound in white paper.

WHITE-POT, [wīt'-pot'], *n.* a dish made of milk, cream, sugar, and eggs, whipped to a froth and baked in a pot.

WHITE-SALE, [wīt'-sāl], *n.* a sale of white linen.

WHITE-SIDE, [wīt'-sīd], *n.* a species of American duck, the golden-eye, *Clangula glaucion*.

WHITESMITH, [wīt'-smith], *n.* a tinsmith.

WHITE SLAVE, [wīt'-slāv], *n.* a young (white) girl seduced or forced and exported into prostitution.

WHITE-SLAVE, [wīt'-slāv], *adj.* dealing in white slaves.

WHITESTER, [wīt'-ster], *n.* a worker at the craft of bleaching; a whitener.

WHITESTONE, [wīt'-stōn], *n.* a type of granite characterized by a preponderance of white felspar.

WHITE-SWELLING, [wīt'-swel'-ing], *n.* (*path.*) scrofulous inflammation infecting a joint.

WHITE-TAIL, [wīt'-tāl], *n.* the wheatear, *Saxicola œnanthe*.

WHITETHORN, [wīt'-thawn], *n.* (*bot.*) the hawthorn.

WHITE-THROAT, [wīt'-thrōt], *n.* a species of warbler, *Sylvia communis*, characterized by a white-feathered throat.

WHITE-THROAT

WHITEWASH (1), [wīt'-wosh], *n.* a wash containing lime for whitening walls.

WHITEWASH (2), [wīt'-wosh], *v.t.* to paint over with whitewash; (*fig.*) to cause to appear virtuous.

WHITEWASHER, [wīt'-wash'-er], *n.* one who whitewashes.

WHITE-WATER, [wīt'-waw'-ter], *n.* a disease afflicting sheep.

WHITE-WING, [wīt'-wing], *n.* the chaffinch, *Fringilla cœlebs*.

WHITE-WOOD, [wīt'-wŏŏd], *n.* a species of N. American timber tree; the tulip tree of the genus *Liriodendron*.

WHITHER, [wiᴛʜ'-er], *adv.* to what place; in which way; to what point or degree. [OE. *hwider*].

WHITHERSOEVER†, [wiᴛʜ'-er-sō-ev'-er], *adv.* to whatever place.

WHITING, [wīt'-ing], *n.* prepared chalk; Spanish white; the sea-fish, *Gadus merlangus*; **w. pout,** the sea-fish, *Gadus luscus*.

WHITISH, [wīt'-ish], *adj.* light in colour, almost white.

WHITISHNESS, [wīt'-ish-nes], *n.* the quality of being whitish.

WHITLEATHER, [wit'-leᴛʜ'-er], *n.* soft, pliable leather, light in colour, prepared by dressing with alum.

WHITLING, [wit'-ling], *n.* the sea trout, *Salmo trutta*.

WHITLOW, [wit'-lō], *n.* a swollen tumour affecting the tips of the fingers; a disease appearing on the feet of sheep. [ME. *whitlawe*].

WHITLOW-GRASS, [wit'-lō-grahs], *n.* (*bot.*) a cruciferous plant of the genus *Draba*, bearing white flowers believed efficacious for whitlows.

WHITMANESQUE, [wit'-man-esk'], *adj.* characteristic of the style or writings of Walt *Whitman*, American poet.

WHITNEYITE, [wit'-ni-īt], *n.* (*min.*) a mineral containing copper and arsenic. [Prof. J. D. *Whitney*].

WHITSUN (1), [wit'-sun], *n.* a period of the year consisting of the week beginning with Whit Sunday. [ME. *hwit sunnedei* white Sunday].

WHITSUN (2), [wit'-sun], *adj.* relating to, occurring at, Whitsun.

WHIT SUNDAY, [wit'-sun'-di], *n.* the seventh Sunday after Easter, marking a religious festival in commemoration of the descent of the Holy Spirit on the day of Pentecost. [ME. *hwit sunnedei* white Sunday].

WHITSUNTIDE, [wit'-sun-tīd], *n.* the week following Whit Sunday; the Whit Sunday week-end.

WHITTLE (1), [witl], *n.* a pocket knife; a large carving knife. [ME. *thwitel* jack knife].

WHITTLE (2), [witl], *n.* (*dial.*) a double blanket worn as a wrap over the shoulders; a baby's napkin. [OE. *hwitel*].

WHITTLE (3), [witl], *v.t. and i.* to cut down by thin slivers, to slice small strips from with a knife, *esp.* so as to leave white and bare of bark; to make thin by shaving off slices; (*fig.*) to cause to diminish by a process of gradual subtraction.

WHITTLED, [witld], *adj.* cut by whittling with a small knife.

WHITY-BROWN, [wīt'-i-brown], *adj.* coloured with a mixture of white and brown.

WHIZZ (1), [wiz], *n.* the hissing, whirring noise made by passage of a projectile through the air.

WHIZZ (2), [wiz], *v.i.* to make a hissing, whirring sound like an arrow or ball forcing its way through the air. [Echoic].

WHIZZBANG, [wiz'-bang'], *n.* (*milit. slang*) a high velocity shell preceded by a whizzing noise before exploding; (*schoolboy slang*) an exploding firework.

WHIZZING, [wiz'-ing], *adj.* making a whizzing sound.

WHIZZINGLY, [wiz'-ing-li], *adv.* with a whizzing sound.

WHO, [hōō], *pers. rel. and interrog. pron.* that person; which person. [OE. *hwa*].

WHOA, [wō], *int.* stop!

WHOEVER, [hōō-ev'-er], *pers. rel. and interrog. pron.* whatever person, any one.

WHOLE (1), [hōl], *n.* anything in its entirety; the complete entity of a thing in terms of all its parts and qualities, the total number, the complete amount; a regulated system composed of complementary functioning parts or principles.

WHOLE (2), [hōl], *adj.* possessing the parts in a completed aggregate, having an established entity, entire, unbroken, not impaired or defective; †sound in health, cured of sickness. [OE. *hal*].

WHOLE-COLOURED, [hōl'-kul'-erd], *adj.* monochrome.

WHOLE-HEARTED, [hōl'-haht'-id], *adj.* giving of the utmost of one's deepest emotions, loyal, sincere.

WHOLE-HEARTEDLY, [hōl'-haht'-id-li], *adv.* to a whole-hearted degree.

WHOLE-HEARTEDNESS, [hōl'-haht'-id-nes], *n.* the quality or condition of being whole-hearted.

WHOLE-HOGGER, [hōl'-hog'-er], *n.* (*coll.*) one who goes or advocates going the whole hog.

WHOLEMEAL (1), [hōl'-mēl'], *n.* flour which contains the milled husk and kernel of the cereal.

WHOLEMEAL (2), [hōl'-mēl], *adj.* made of wholemeal.

WHOLENESS, [hōl'-nes], *n.* the state of being whole, totality.

WHOLESALE (1), [hōl'-sāl], *n.* the sale of goods in large quantities, carried out *esp.* by the manufacturer or his agent doing business with retailers.

WHOLESALE (2), [hōl'-sāl], *adj.* related to, trading in, goods sold in gross; consisting of commodities sold by wholesale.

WHOLESALE (3), [hōl'-sāl], *adv.* on a wholesale basis; in large amounts; indiscriminately.

WHOLESALER, [hōl'-sāl-er], *n.* one who sells goods wholesale.

WHOLESOME, [hōl'-sum], *adj.* having natural food values, good for maintaining the body in health; having a salutary effect on the mind or morals.

WHOLESOMELY, [hōl'-sum-li], *adv.* in a wholesome fashion.

WHOLESOMENESS, [hōl'-sum-nes], *n.* the quality of being wholesome.

WHOLLY, [hōl'-li], *adv.* entirely, completely; unconditionally.

WHOM, [hōōm], *pers. rel. and interrog. pron.* the objective case of WHO. [OE. *hwam*].

WHOMSOEVER†, [hōōm'-sō-ev'-er], *pers. rel. and interrog. pron.* objective case of WHOSOEVER.

WHOOP (1), [hōōp], *n.* a loud shout uttered in high spirits.

WHOOP (2), [hōōp], *v.i.* to give vent to high spirits by shouting at the top of one's voice, to yell. [Echoic].

WHOOPEE (1), [wōōp'-ē], *n.* a half-yell, half-scream of delight; **to make w.,** (*slang*) to participate in a wild, noisy party; to go on a spree.

WHOOPER, [hōōp'-er], *n.* one of the largest species of British swans, *Cygnus musicus.*

WHOOPING-COUGH, HOOPING-COUGH, [hōōp'-ing-kof'], *n.* an ailment, especially infectious to children, notable for bouts of violent coughing accompanied by a characteristic whooping sound.

WHOP (1), [wop], *n.* a sudden fall, a flop. [WHAP

WHOP (2), [wop], *v.t.* to hit; to defeat, *esp.* in fisticuff

WHOPPER, [wop'-er], *n.* (*slang*) something abnorm ally big, *esp.* a monstrous lie.

WHOPPING, [wop'-ing], *adj.* huge.

WHORE (1), [haw(r)], *n.* a woman who hires her bod to men for sexual use; a woman who breaks th social code of sexual morality, a harlot. [OE. *hore*

WHORE (2), [haw(r)], *v.i.* to associate with a whore

WHOREDOM†, [haw'-dum], *n.* the condition c behaving as a whore; (*O.T.*) idolatry.

WHOREMASTER, [haw'-mah-ster], *n.* a man wh employs whores and lives on their immoral earning

WHOREMONGER, [haw'-mung-ger], *n.* a ma who consorts with whores.

WHORING, [haw'-ring], *n.* fornication; the fre quenting of whores; prostitution.

WHORISH, [haw'-rish], *adj.* acting as a whore, lewe

WHORISHLY, [haw'-rish-li], *adv.* in a whoris manner.

WHORISHNESS, [haw'-rish-nes], *n.* the conditio and conduct of one who is whorish.

WHORL, [wurl], *n.* the form taken by a spiral twist (*bot.*) a ring of leaves or petals round a stem; (*zool.*) coil of a spiral shell. [ME. *whorwhil*].

WHORLED, [wurld], *adj.* characterized by whorl having a spiral form.

WHORT, WHURT, [wurt], *n.* the purple fruit c the whortleberry.

WHORTLEBERRY, HURTLEBERRY, [wurtl'-be ri], *n.* the bilberry, *Vaccinium myrtillus*; the purp fruit of this shrub. [Uncert.].

WHOSE, [hōōz], *pers. rel. and interrog. pron.* th possessive or genitive case of WHO or WHICH.

WHOSESOEVER†, [hōōz'-sō-ev'-er], *pers. rel. an interrog. pron.* possessive case of WHOSOEVER.

WHOSO†, [hōō'-sō], *pers. rel. and interrog. pron* whosoever.

WHOSOEVER†, [hōō'-sō-ev'-er], *pers. rel. an interrog. pron.* any person whatever, whoever.

WHUR, see WHIR.

WHURT, see WHORT.

WHY (1), [wī], *n.* the reason for a thing; **the w('s and wherefore(s),** the precise reason(s) for a cer tain action or thing. [*Next*].

WHY (2), [wī], *adv.* for what cause or reason (in a rela tive or interrogative clause). [OE. *hwi*].

WHYDAH, WHIDAH, [wi'-da], *n.* the Africa widow-bird, a species of *Vidua.* [~WIDOW (1)].

WICK (1), [wik], *n.* a length of twisted or plaited cotto or other fibres set in the middle of a candle or in a vesse containing oil, paraffin or petrol, for the purpose c conducting the fuel to the flame. [OE. *wice*].

WICK (2), [wik], *v.t.* in the game of curling, to caus (the stone) to move off at a tangent. [Unkn.].

WICKED, [wik'-id], *adj.* breaking the laws of God an man which embody the accepted principles of goo thoughts and conduct; by nature or deliberatio following a line of social conduct considered funda mentally vicious, abhorrent, and evil; sinful, immora (*coll.*) malicious, roguish. [ME. *wikked*].

WICKEDLY, [wik'-id-li], *adv.* in a wicked way; (*coll* maliciously.

WICKEDNESS, [wik'-id-nes], *n.* the condition c being wicked; an act of one who is wicked; (*coll.*) mis behaviour, mischief.

WICKER (1), [wik'-er], *n.* an osier; a flexible branc or twig. [MSwed. *viker*].

WICKER (2), [wik'-er], *adj.* made of wickers arrange in a plaited open-work.

WICKERWORK, [wik'-er-wurk], *n.* basket-wor made from plaited wickers.

WICKET, [wik'-it], *n.* a small door built into a large door or gate; (*cricket*) a set of stumps surmounte by a pair of bails, and defended by a batsman; th pitch; a batsman's innings. [AFr. *wiket*].

WICKET-KEEPER, [wik'-it-kēp'-er], *n.* (*cricket*) th fielder protected by pads who stands close up behin the batsman's wicket.

WIDDERSHINS, see WITHERSHINS.

WIDE (1), [wīd], *n.* (*cricket*) a ball bowled out of reason able reach of the batsman; a run counted as a penalty against the side of the bowler of such a ball; **to the w.** to the wide world, utterly.

WIDE (2), [wīd], *adj.* covering a relatively extensive range from side to side, broad; covering a large space extending over a large area, spacious; occurrin some distance from the centre, badly directed; remote distant; all-embracing, general. [OE. *wid*].

WIDE (3), [wīd], *adv.* to a large, or to the fullest, extent at a distance; to an inaccurate degree; **w. of,** far from

WIDEAWAKE (1), [wid'-a-wāk'], *n.* a type of soft, low-crowned, wide-brimmed felt hat.

WIDEAWAKE (2), [wid'-a-wāk'], *adj.* having the eyes wide open and the mind on the alert; being on the lookout for danger.

WIDELY, [wīd'-li], *adv.* with considerable extension; to a great distance; so as to cover a considerable area.

WIDEN, [wīd'-en], *v.t. and i.* to make wide or wider, to extend in breadth; to grow wide or wider; to enlarge, increase in width.

WIDENESS, [wīd'-nes], *n.* the quality of being wide.

WIDESPREAD, [wīd'-spred'], *adj.* covering a great distance or area.

WIDISH, [wīd'-ish], *adj.* somewhat wide.

WIDGEON, [wij'-un], *n.* the migratory duck, *Mareca penelope*; **w. grass**, the plant, *Zostera marina*; **w. leader**, the pintail, *Dafila acuta*.

WIDOW (1), [wid'-ō], *n.* a woman whose husband is deceased and who has not married again; **widow's flower**, (*hort.*) the plant *Scabiosa atro-purpurea*; **grass w.**, a woman whose husband has been obliged to leave her temporarily; **widow's peak**, a triangular growth of hair over the forehead. [OE. *widwe*].

WIDOW (2), [wid'-ō], *v.t.* to make a widow.

WIDOWBENCH, [wid'-ō-bench'], *n.* (*leg.*) a share of her husband's estate allotted to a widow in addition to her jointure.

WIDOW-BIRD, [wid'-ō-burd], *n.* the whydah.

WIDOWER, [wid'-ō-er], *n.* a man whose wife has died.

WIDOWERHOOD, [wid'-ō-er-hŏŏd], *n.* the state of being a widower.

WIDOWHOOD, [wid'-ō-hŏŏd], *n.* the state of being a widow; estate settled on a widow.

WIDTH, [witth], *n.* distance from one side to the other, wideness; also (*fig.*).

WIELD, [wēld], *v.t.* to grasp by the hand and have under control, to manipulate as one in command, to handle. [~OE. *wealdan*].

WIELDABLE, [wēld'-abl], *adj.* able to be wielded.

WIELDER, [wēld'-er], *n.* one who wields.

WIELDLESS, [wēld'-les], *adj.* uncontrollable.

WIELDY, [wēld'-i], *adj.* manageable, easily handled.

WIFE (1), (**wives**), [wīf], *n.* a married woman. [OE. *wif*].

WIFE (2), [wīf], *n.* a woman engaged in the sale of a specific commodity. [*Prec.*].

WIFEHOOD, [wīf'-hŏŏd], *n.* the status or period of being a wife.

WIFELESS, [wīf'-les], *adj.* deprived of a wife, unmarried.

WIFELIKE, [wīf'-līk], *adj.* characteristic of, becoming of or like a wife.

WIFELY, [wīf'-li], *adj.* possessing the virtues of a wife, proper for a wife.

WIFIE, [wīf'-i], *n.* a little wife (used jocularly or as a term of endearment).

WIG, [wig], *n.* a false set of hair as a covering for the head, designed to give the impression of a natural head of hair; a highly artificial head-dress of hair fashionable in the seventeenth and eighteenth centuries; head-covering of a judge, etc.; (*coll.*) a lawyer. [Abbreviation for PERIWIG].

WIGGED, [wigd], *adj.* adorned with a wig.

WIGGERY, [wig'-er-i], *n.* a wig; the sharp practice of lawyers.

WIGGING, [wig'-ing], *n.* (*slang*) a scolding. [Uncert.].

WIGGLE (1), [wigl], *n.* the act of wiggling, a squirm, twist.

WIGGLE (2), [wigl], *v.t. and i.* to make a contorted, twisted movement with the limbs; to waggle, to wriggle. [*Var.* of WAGGLE].

WIGHT† (1), [wīt], *n.* (*coll. and dial.*) a person; poor wretch, fool. [OE. *wiht* creature].

WIGHT (2), [wīt], *adj.* (*dial.*) strong and nimble. [OIcel. *vigt* dexterous].

WIGMAKER, [wig'-māk'-er], *n.* one who makes wigs.

WIGWAM, [wig'-wom'], *n.* a portable tent of the American Indians; an Indian hut. [NAmer. Ind. *wigwaum*].

WIGWAM

WILD (1), [wīld], *n.* territory not occupied by man, an impenetrable area of the earth, wilderness.

WILD (2), [wīld], *adj.* roving at will according to primitive instincts, not tamed by man; seeded by nature; left uninhabited by man, savage, uncivilized, lacking culture; characterized by a state of violent disorder, tempestuous; extremely untidy; loose; emotionally disturbed; mad with anger, furious; irregular in social behaviour, wanton; crazy, frantic, frenzied; ill-considered. [OE. *wilde*].

WILD (3), [wīld], *adv.* to a wild degree.

WILD-BORN, [wīld'-bawn], *adj.* born in a wild state.

WILD-CAT, [wīld'-kat'], *n.* the British wild cat, *Felis sylvestris*, found in Wales and Scotland.

WILDCAT, [wīld'-kat'], *adj.* reckless; hysterical.

WILD-DUCK, [wīld'-duk'], *n.* the mallard, *Anas boscas*.

WILDEBEEST, [wīld'-i-bēst], *n.* the gnu. [Afrik. *wildebeest*].

WILDERNESS, [wild'-er-nes], *n.* a vast tract of country remaining uninhabited and uncultivated because of the impenetrable nature of its geographical features; any enormous area of desolation; any area in which the flora and fauna are allowed to run wild. (*fig.*) a desolate, uninviting place. [ME. *wildern*].

WILDFIRE, [wīld'-fīer], *n.* a highly inflammable substance used by the ancient Greeks in warfare, Greek fire; fire out of control; a disease characterized by quickly spreading inflamed eruptions.

WILDFOWL, [wild-fowl], *n.*(*pl.*) wild birds, game.

WILD-GOOSE, [wīld'-gōōs'], *n.* a wild bird of the goose family.

WILD-GOOSE CHASE, [wīld'-gōōs'-chās], *n.* a vain search, a stupid undertaking.

WILDING, [wīld-ing], *n.* a wild plant, *esp.* one growing from and among cultivated plants.

WILDISH, [wīld'-ish], *adj.* somewhat wild.

WILDLY, [wīld'-li], *adv.* in a wild fashion.

WILDNESS, [wīld'-nes], *n.* the quality or state of being wild.

WILD OAT, [wīld'-ōt], *n.* an uncultivated species of oat, *Avena fatua*.

WILD-WOOD, [wīld'-wŏŏd], *n.* native forest.

WILE (1), [wīl], *n.* a trick, stratagem, or ruse. [OE. *wigel* witchcraft, deception].

WILE (2), [wīl], *v.t.* to trick, beguile, entice.

WILFUL, [wil'-fŏŏl], *adj.* self-willed, perverse, stubborn; done intentionally, premeditated.

WILFULLY, [wil'-fŏŏl-i], *adv.* in a wilful way.

WILFULNESS, [wil'-fŏŏl-nes], *n.* the quality of being wilful.

WILILY, [wīl'-i-li], *adv.* in a wily way.

WILINESS, [wīl'-i-nes], *n.* the quality of being wily.

WILL (1), [wil], *n.* that power of the mind by which we consciously desire and endeavour to carry out our intentions; intention, determining faculty, mental control; purpose, that which is intended; individual choice, determination or volition; a legal testament in which a person declares how he wishes his property to be bestowed or used after his death; (*archaic*) fleshly desire. [OE. *willa*].

WILL (2), [wil], *v.t. and i.* to desire, intend, exercise the will (as to); to control by will power; to be willing or desirous. [OE. *willan*].

WILL (3), (**would**), [wil, wŏŏd], *auxil. v.* expressing future tense; expressing custom or habit; expressing intention as to the future; expressing probability, condition or question; expressing choice in certain circumstances.

WILL (4), [wil], *v.t.* to bequeath by legacy.

WILLEMITE, [wil'-i-mīt], *n.* a crystalline silicate of zinc. [Du. *willemit*].

WILLER, [wil'-er], *n.* one who wills.

WILLET, [wil'-it], *n.* the North American sandpiper, *Symphemia semipalmatus*. [Echoic].

WILLIAMITE†, [wil'-yam-īt], *n.* a follower of King William III.

WILLING, [wil'-ing], *adj.* desiring, wishing (to); eager (to); gladly and voluntarily done.

WILLINGLY, [wil'-ing-li], *adv.* in a willing fashion.

WILLINGNESS, [wil'-ing-nes], *n.* the quality of being willing.

WILLING-HEARTED, [wil'-ing-haht'-id], *adj.* willing, eager.

WILL-LESS, [wil'-les], *adj.* lacking will.

WILLOCK, [wil'-ok], *n.* a bird, the guillemot. [*Will*, personal name].

WILL-O'-THE-WISP, [wil'-o-the-wisp'], *n.* luminous marsh-gas, *Ignis fatuus*; (*fig.*) a person or thing whose whereabouts are always uncertain. [*Prec.* and WISP].

WILLOW (1), [wil'-o], *n.* any tree or plant of the genus *Salix*; (*cricket*) a bat. [OE. *welig*].

WILLOW (2), [wil'-ō], *adj.* like or made of willow.

WILLOW (3), [wil'-ō], *v.t.* to prepare (fibre) in a machine.

WILLOWED, [wil'-ōd], *adj.* having many willows.

WILLOW-HERB, [wil'-ō-hurb'], *n.* any species of the plant genus *Epilobium*.
WILLOW-MOTH, [wil'-ō-moth'], *n.* the moth, *Caradrina quadripuncta*.

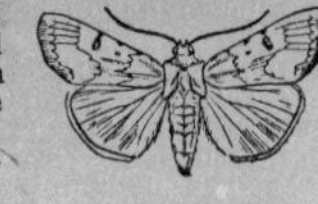

WILLOW-MOTH

WILLOW-PATTERN, [wil'-ō-pat'-ern], *n.* an Oriental pattern in blue, common on English crockery from the eighteenth century onwards.
WILLOW-THORN, [wil'-ō-thawn'], *n.* the plant, *Hippophaë rhamnoides*, the sea-buckthorn.
WILLOW-WREN, [wil'-ō-ren'], *n.* the European bird, *Phylloscopus trochilus*.
WILLOWY, [wil'-ō-i], *adj.* graceful like a willow, drooping.
WILL-POWER, [wil'-pow'-er], *n.* energy of the will, purposefulness, determination.
WILL-WORSHIP, [wil'-wur'-ship], *n.* worship that follows individual whim and fancy.
WILLY, [wil'-i], *n.* a machine for cleaning flax, cotton, or wool by a combing process. [OE. *wilig* a willow basket].
WILLY NILLY, [wil'-i-nil'-i], *adv.* willingly or unwillingly, inevitably. [WILL HE and ME. *nill he*, he does not wish].
WILSOME, [wil'-sum], *adj.* wilful.
WILT (1), [wilt], *v.t.* and *i.* (of plants) to become limp and drooping; to cause to droop. [Uncert.].
WILT (2), [wilt], *2nd pers. sg. pres.* of WILL (3).
WILTON, [wil'-ton], *n.* the name of a town in Wiltshire used to denote a kind of carpet, resembling Brussels but having a pile cut like that of velvet, first made there.
WILY, [wil'-i], *adj.* using wiles to accomplish a purpose, cunning.
WIMBLE (1), [wimbl], *n.* a gimlet, auger, or brace. [ME. *wymble*].
WIMBLE (2), [wimbl], *v.t.* to bore with a wimble.
WIMPLE, [wimpl], *n.* a piece of linen folded across the forehead and down each side of the face, commonly worn by women in the Middle Ages and still by nuns. [OE. *wimpel*].
WIMPLED, [wimpld], *adj.* wearing a wimple.
WIN (1), [win], *n.* the fact of having won, a victory; the act of winning.
WIN (2), **[winning, won]**, [win], *v.t.* and *i.* to achieve or gain in competition with others or despite rivalry or opposition; to obtain, attain or reach by effort; to be victorious or successful in; to be victorious; **to w. over**, to persuade; **to w. through**, to overcome a succession of difficulties; **to w. hands down**, (*coll.*) to obtain a complete victory. [OE. *winnan* to fight].
WINCE (1), [wints], *n.* the act of wincing.
WINCE (2), [wints], *v.i.* to make a nervous involuntary movement in pain or fear; to hesitate through fear, to flinch. [ME. *winchen*].
WINCER, [win'-ser], *n.* one who winces.
WINCEY, [win'-si], *n.* a cloth made of wool and cotton. [Uncert.].
WINCEYETTE, [win'-si-et'], *n.* a stuff made in imitation of real wincey. [WINCEY and (FLANNEL)ETTE].
WINCH, [winch], *n.* a windlass, crank, or pulley.
WINCHESTER (1), [win'-chest-er], *n.* the name of a city in Hampshire, used to denote a series of measures, the standards for which were formerly kept there.
WINCHESTER (2), [win'-chest-er], *n.* a type of breech-loading rifle. [O. F. *Winchester*, the maker].
WIND (1), [wind, wind], *n.* air set in motion by atmospheric conditions; a similar movement of air caused mechanically; the breath and lungs; flatulence; stupid, wordy talk meaning little or nothing; (*mus.*) wind-instruments; (*fig.*) a rumour; **to be in the w.**, to be under consideration and likely to be done; **to get w. of**, to hear a hint or rumour concerning; **to raise the w.**, to raise money when hard pressed for it; **to sail near** (*or* **close to**) **the w.**, to take a matter to the very limits of decency and honesty; **to go like the w.**, to go very fast; **to cast to the winds**, to discard, leave deliberately out of account; **second w.**, the steady breath that comes to a runner in a long race after the first breathlessness. [OE. *wind*].
WIND (2), [wind], *n.* the act of winding; a single revolution, a bend or curve.
WIND (3), [wind], *v.t.* and *i.* to make breathless; to regain a steady breath after breathlessness; (*hunting*) to get the scent of.
WIND (4), [wind], *v.t.* to blow (a bugle, horn, or similar wind instrument); to sound a call on. [WIND (1)].
WIND (5), **(wound)**, [wind], *v.t.* and *i.* to trav[el] or lie along a crooked course, bending this wa[y] and that; to twist like a spiral; to revolve or turn i[n] successive revolutions; to raise by turning a winc[h] or windlass; to form (string, etc.) into a compac[t] lump by twining (it) evenly together; to wrap roun[d] or embrace with; **to w. up**, to twine or coil (strin[g] etc.) into a ball or lump; to twist (a spring or th[e] spring of) into a tight spiral; (*fig.*) to bring t[o] emotional tension; to conclude (proceedings, etc.) to dissolve (a commercial firm); **to w. round (some-thing)**, to twist and twine about it; to **w. one's way** (often *fig.*) to pursue one's course with care; **to w. round one's little finger**, to influence completel[y]. [OE. *windan*].
WINDAGE, [wind'-ij], *n.* the deflection by the win[d] of a projectile from the course it would take if ther[e] were no wind; the amount of this and allowanc[e] made for it; the difference in diameter between th[e] bore of a gun and the shell or bullet, etc., used in it.
WINDBAG, [wind'-bag'], *n.* a wordy talker.
WIND-BAND, [wind'-band'], *n.* an orchestra o[f] wind-instruments.
WIND-BOUND, [wind'-bownd], *adj.* kept in por[t] by a contrary wind.
WIND-BREAK, [wind'-brāk], *n.* a hedge grown, o[r] screen erected, to give shelter from the wind.
WIND-BROKEN, [wind'-brōk'-en], *adj.* (of a horse) suffering from defective breathing.
WIND-CHEST, [wind'-chest'], *n.* the compart-ment in an organ where the air is compressed.
WIND-COLIC, [wind'-kol'-ik], *n.* pain caused by flatulence.
WIND-CUTTER, [wind'-kut'-er], *n.* (in an organ) the inset lip of any pipe.
WIND-DRIVEN, [wind'-driv'-en], *adj.* propelled by the force of the wind.
WIND-EGG, [wind'-eg'], *n.* an egg with a soft shell.
WINDER, [wind'-er], *n.* someone or something tha[t] winds.
WINDFALL, [wind'-fawl], *n.* a fruit blown dow[n] before maturity; (*fig.*) an unexpected piece of goo[d] luck, a legacy.
WINDFALLEN, [wind'-fawl'-en], *adj.* (of fruit) blown down.
WIND-FANNER, [wind'-fan'-er], *n.* a kestrel.
WINDFLOWER, [wind'-flow'-er], *n.* an anemone esp. *Anemone nemorosa*.
WIND-FURNACE, [wind'-fur'-nis], *n.* an artificially blown furnace.
WIND-GALL, [wind'-gawl], *n.* a soft tumour on a horse's fetlock.
WIND-GAUGE, [wind'-gāj], *n.* a device by which the strength of the wind is measured.
WINDHOVER, [wind'-hov'-er], *n.* a wind-fanner.
WINDILY, [wind'-i-li], *adv.* in a windy fashion.
WINDINESS, [wind'-i-nes], *n.* the quality of being windy.
WINDING (1), [wind'-ing], *n.* the course or action of something that winds; a curve, twist, a turn.

WINDFLOWER

WINDING (2), [wind'-ing], *adj.* twisting this way and that, turning in a spiral course.
WINDINGLY, [wind'-ing-li], *adv.* in winding fashion, so as to wind.
WINDING-SHEET, [wind'-ing-shēt'], *n.* a shroud.
WINDING-TACKLE, [wind'-ing-takl'], *n.* an arrange-ment of pulleys consisting of one fixed triple block and a similar movable one.
WIND-INSTRUMENT, [wind'-in'-stroom-ent], *n.* (*mus.*) an instrument sounded by breath or pumped air.
WINDJAMMER, [wind'-jam'-er], *n.* a large sailing vessel; (*coll.*) a type of lumber jacket. [WIND (1) and JAM (3)].
WINDLASS (1), [wind'-las], *n.* a hoisting device con-sisting of a horizontal roller which, when turned, winds the rope about itself. [ME. *windelas*].
WINDLASS (2), [wind'-las], *v.t.* to raise with a wind-lass.
WINDLESS, [wind'-les], *adj.* calm, not windy.
WINDLESTRAW, [windl'-straw'], *n.* a stalk of dry grass. [OE. *windelstreaw*].
WINDMILL, [wind'-mil], *n.* a mill driven by the wind, any similar wind-driven device; **w. plane**, an aero-plane with horizontal revolving vanes.
WINDOW, [win'-dō], *n.* a large gap or space in a wall of a building to admit the light, often glazed so

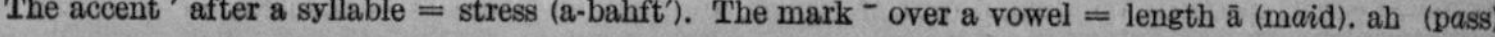

as to be adjustable for ventilation; anything resembling this; **w.-shopping**, the habit of looking much at the goods in shop windows without making purchases. [OIcel. *vindauge* wind eye].
WINDOW-BOX, [win'-dō-boks'], *n.* a box in front of a window for growing plants in.
WINDOW-DRESSING, [win'-dō-dres'-ing], *n.* the displaying of goods in a shop window; (*fig.*) display intended to conceal shortcomings.
WINDOWED, [wind'-ōd], *adj.* furnished with windows.
WINDOW-LEDGE, [win'-dō-lej'], *n.* a ledge or sill at the base of a window.
WINDOWLESS, [win'-dō-les], *adj.* having no windows.
WINDOW-PANE, [win'-dō-pān'], *n.* a sheet of glass for a window.
WINDOW-SEAT, [win'-dō-sēt], *n.* a seat inside a window.
WINDOW-SILL, [win'-dō-sil'], *n.* the sill outside a window.
WINDPIPE, [wind'-pīp], *n.* (*anat.*) the trachea, the passage from lungs to mouth.
WIND-PUMP, [wind'-pump], *n.* a pump driven by the wind.
WIND-ROW, [wind'-rō], *n.* the long heap into which grass is raked to dry after cutting.
WIND-SAIL, [wind'-sāl], *n.* (*naut.*) a tube of canvas for ventilating the lower parts of a ship; one of the sails of a windmill.
WIND-SCREEN, [wind'-skrēn], *n.* a glass or transparent plastic screen in front of the driver's seat in an automobile, etc.
WINDSOR, [win'-zer], *n.* the name of a town and royal castle in Berkshire used to denote certain types of manufactured goods; **w. chair**, a chair with the back formed of upright rods; **w. soap**, a brown or white unperfumed soap.
WIND-SWEPT, [wind'-swept'], *adj.* scoured by the wind.
WIND-TIGHT, [wind'-tīt], *adj.* not admitting the passage of wind.
WIND-UP (1), [wīnd'-up], *n.* the conclusion.
WIND-UP (2), [wīnd'-up'], *n.* (*slang*) panic, alarm; **to get, have, the w.**, to become, be, alarmed. [~ *to have the wind up one's trouser-legs* as a euphemism for *to shake with fright*].
WINDWARD (1), [wind'-(w)erd], *n.* the side or direction from which the wind blows.
WINDWARD (2), [wind'-(w)erd], *adj.* lying on the side exposed to the wind.
WINDY, [wind'-i], *adj.* having the wind constantly blowing; exposed to the wind; (of a speech or speaker) verbose; (*coll.*) scared, nervous; flatulent; (*slang*) angry.
WINE (1), [wīn], *n.* the fermented juice of the grape or other fruits; a rich red colour. [OE. *win*].
WINE (2), [wīn], *v.t.* *and* *i.* to toast; to drink wine.
WINEBAG, [wīn'-bag'], *n.* a skin for holding wine; (*slang*) a person who drinks wine excessively.
WINEBIBBER, [wīn'-bib'-er], *n.* a person who drinks wine excessively.
WINEBIBBING, [wīn'-bib'-ing], *n.* the undue drinking of wine.
WINEBOTTLE, [wīn'-botl'], *n.* a bottle for holding wine.
WINEBOWL, [wīn'-bōl], *n.* a bowl for drinking wine.
WINE-CARRIAGE, [wīn'-ka'-rij], *n.* a small trolley for passing wine round a table.
WINE-CELLAR, [wīn'-sel'-er], *n.* a cellar for wine.
WINE-COOLER, [wīn'-kōōl'-er], *n.* a receptacle for cooling wine with ice.
WINECUP, [wīn'-kup], *n.* a cup for drinking wine.
WINEFAT, [wīn'-fat'], *n.* (*archaic*) a wine-press. [WINE (1) and ~VAT].
WINEGLASS, [wīn'-glahs], *n.* a glass for drinking wine.
WINEGLASSFUL, [wīn'-glahs-fōōl], *n.* the amount of liquid a wineglass will hold.
WINEGROWER, [wīn'-grō-er], *n.* one who grows grapes for wine.
WINELESS, [wīn'-les], *adj.* lacking wine.
WINE-MARC, [wīn'-mahk], *n.* the leavings in a wine-press after the juice has been extracted. [WINE (1) and Fr. *marc* refuse].
WINE-PRESS, [wīn'-pres'], *n.* a place where grapes are crushed in making wine.
WINERY, [wīn'-er-i], *n.* a factory where wine is made.
WINESAP, [wīn-sap'], *n.* a North American variety of dark red apple with a vinous aroma and flavour.
WINESKIN, [wīn'-skin], *n.* a winebottle made of skin.
WINE-STONE, [wīn'-stōn], *n.* the deposit of crude tartar from wine.
WINE-VAULT, [wīn'-vawlt], *n.* a wine-cellar; an (underground) shop where drinks are sold.
WINE-WHEY, [wīn'-wā], *n.* a beverage of whey mixed with wine and sweetened.
WING (1), [wing], *n.* one of the limbs of flight of a bird or other creature; anything resembling this as on an aeroplane, etc.; a lateral extension of a house or other building; the side parts of a stage not visible to the audience; the section of an army in the field protecting the flank of the main body; a group of three Royal Air Force squadrons; (*pl.*) a badge worn by a member of the R.A.F. performing flying duties; (*hockey, football*) a player on either extreme of the forward line; **w.-half**, the left or right half-back in Association football. [OIcel. *vengja*].
WING (2), [wing], *v.t.* *and* *i.* to propel quickly, set in motion or flight; to provide with wings; to wound in the wing; (*fig.*) to injure in the leg or arm; to fly on wings; to soar. [*Prec.*].
WING-BEAT, [wing'-bēt], *n.* one flap of a bird's wing in flight.
WING-CASE, [wing'-kās], *n.* a hard sheath covering the wings of some insects.
WING-COMMANDER, [wing'-kom-ahn'-der], *n.* an officer of the Royal Air Force equivalent in rank to a lieutenant-colonel in the Army.
WINGED, [wingd], *adj.* having wings.
WING-FOOTED, [wing'-fŏŏt'-id], *adj.* having wings on the feet; swift.
WINGLESS, [wing'-les], *adj.* lacking wings.
WINGLET, [wing'-let], *n.* a little wing.
WING-SHEATH, [wing'-shēth], *n.* a wing-case.
WING-SPREAD, [wing'-spred'], *n.* the distance from the tip of one wing to the tip of the other.
WING-STROKE, [wing'-strōk], *n.* one flap of a bird's wing in flight.
WINGY, [wing'-i], *adj.* having wings; swift.
WINK (1), [wingk], *n.* the action of winking; **to tip the w. to**, (*slang*) to give a hint to.
WINK (2), [wingk], *v.t.* *and* *i.* to close and open one or both eyes very quickly; to move (the eyelid) in this way; (of the eyelid) to perform this action; **to w. at**, to make a sign to by winking; to overlook deliberately, connive at. [OE. *wincian*].
WINKER, [wingk'-er], *n.* one who winks.
WINKING, [wingk'-ing], *n.* the action of one who winks; **as easy as w.**, very easy.
WINKINGLY, [wingk'-ing-li], *adv.* with a wink.
WINKLE, [wingkl], *n.* a small shell-fish, a periwinkle. [Short form of PERIWINKLE (2)].
WINNER, [win'-er], *n.* one who wins; (*coll.*) something sure to win or bring victory.
WINNING, [win'-ing], *adj.* victorious; (of a stroke or shot in a game) finally giving victory to one side; charming, winsome.
WINNINGLY, [win'-ing-li], *adv.* in a winning way.
WINNING-POST, [win-ing-pōst], *n.* a post erected to mark the finishing line of a racecourse.
WINNINGS, [win'-ingz], *n.*(*pl.*) profits, *esp.* of gambling.
WINNOW, [win'-ō], *v.t.* to separate (corn) into husks and grain by fanning it or directing an air current upon it in some way; (*fig.*) to discern between what is good and bad in, separating one from the other. [OE. *windwian*].
WINNOWER, [win'-ō-er], *n.* a person who winnows.
WINNOWING, [win'-ō-ing], *n.* the act of one who, or that which, winnows.
WINSOME, [win'-sum], *adj.* charming, attractive. [OE. *wynsum* agreeable].
WINSOMELY, [win'-sum-li], *adv.* in a winsome way.
WINSOMENESS, [win'-sum-nes], *n.* the quality of being winsome.
WINTER (1), [win'-ter], *n.* the cold season between autumn and spring, astronomically considered to begin on December 22, and end on March 20; sometimes used instead of year in reckoning a person's age. [OE. *winter*].
WINTER (2), [win'-ter], *adj.* typical of, coming during, customary in, winter.
WINTER (3), [win'-ter], *v.i.* to spend the winter.
WINTER-APPLE, [win'-ter-apl'], *n.* an apple that ripens in winter.
WINTER-BARLEY, [win'-ter-bah'-li], *n.* a variety of barley usually sown in autumn.
WINTERBERRY, [win'-ter-be'-ri], *n.* the black alder.
WINTER-BLOOM, [win'-ter-blōōm'], *n.* the *Hamamelis virginica*, the American wych-hazel.

ō (bone), ī (fine), ōō (food), ŏŏ (put), u (up), th (*th*ink), TH (*th*at) zh (azure), † = obsolete, ~ = related to.

WINTER-CHERRY, [win'-ter-che'-ri], *n.* a name given to various plants of the family, *Solanaceæ*, and several varieties of *Cardiospermum*.
WINTERCRESS, [win'-ter-kres'], *n.* any plant belonging to the genus, *Barbarea*.
WINTER-CROP, [win'-ter-krop'], *n.* a crop sown late in autumn; a crop whose fruit comes in, or will keep through, the winter.
WINTER-FALLOW, [win'-ter-fal'-ō], *n.* ground left fallow in winter.
WINTER-GARDEN, [win'-ter-gah'-den], *n.* a large hothouse or conservatory with flowers, shrubs, etc.
WINTERGREEN, [win'-ter-grēn'], *n.* an evergreen shrub of the genus, *Gaultheria*, from which an oil is obtained.
WINTER-KILLED, [win'-ter-kild'], *adj.* destroyed by the winter.
WINTERLESS, [win'-ter-les], *adj.* without a winter.
WINTERLY, [win'-ter-li], *adj.* suitable for winter.
WINTER-MOTH, [win'-ter-moth'], *n.* the moth, *Cheimatobia brumata*, the caterpillar of which attacks plum-trees.
WINTER-PEAR, [win'-ter-pāer'], *n.* any pear that will keep well, or ripen, in winter.
WINTER QUARTERS, [win'-ter-kwawt'-erz], *n.(pl.)* a military base used in winter; any habitation occupied in winter.
WINTER SPORTS, [win'-ter-spawts'], *n.(pl.)* games played on snow and ice in winter, *esp.* in Switzerland.
WINTERTIDE, [win'-ter-tīd'], *n.* the winter season.
WINTER-WEIGHT, [win'-ter-wāt'], *adj.* (of under-clothing) sufficiently thick to be worn in winter.
WINTER-WHEAT, [win'-ter-wēt'], *n.* wheat sown just before winter.
WINTRINESS, [win'-tri-nes], *n.* the condition or quality of being wintry.
WINTRY, [win'-tri], *adj.* cold and stormy; (*fig.*) unfriendly, unkind.
WINY, [win'-i], *adj.* having the flavour or other qualities of wine.
WINZE, [winz], *n.* a communicating shaft in a mine. [Uncert.].
WIPE (1), [wīp], *n.* the action of wiping; (*slang*) a handkerchief; a blow.
WIPE (2), [wīp], *v.t.* to rub smoothly and gently with a cloth or other article so as to make dry or clean; **to w. away, w. off, w. up,** to clean away by wiping; **to w. out** to clean by wiping; to clean away by wiping; (*fig.*) to cancel; to exterminate, destroy; **to w. the floor** (*or* **ground**) **with,** to inflict a complete defeat on, to treat with great scorn or aloofness. [OE. *wipian*].
WIPE-OUT, [wīp-owt], *n.* (*wirel.*) the phenomenon by which a louder or near-by transmission blots out reception of a weaker or more distant one on an adjacent wavelength.
WIPER, [wīp'-er], *n.* a person or thing that wipes; that with which one wipes.
WIRE (1), [wier], *n.* a fine thread of metal, sometimes single, sometimes made of woven or twisted filaments like cord; (*coll.*) a telegram; **to pull wires,** to exert a secret influence. [OE. *wir*].
WIRE (2), [wier], *v.t. and i.* to fasten with or provide with wire; to fix wires for (any electrical device); (*fig.*) to send by telegraph; to communicate with by telegraph; **to w. in(to)**, to begin vigorously. [WIRE (1)].
WIRE-CLOTH, [wier'-kloth'], *n.* a cloth of wire.
WIRE-CUTTER, [wier'-kut'-er], *n.* an instrument with which wire is cut.
WIRE-DANCER, [wier'-dahn-ser], *n.* one who performs or dances on a stretched wire.
WIREDRAW, [wier'-draw], *v.t.* to make (metal) into wire; (*fig.*) to handle (an argument) with unnecessary finesse.
WIREDRAWER, [wier'-draw'-er], *n.* one who makes wire.
WIREDRAWING, [wier'-draw'-ing], *n.* the act of drawing out into wire.
WIREDRAWN, [wier'-drawn'], *adj.* drawn out to a great fineness.
WIRE-EDGE, [wier'-ej'], *n.* the easily blunted edge of a knife that has been too finely sharpened.
WIRE-ENTANGLEMENT, [wier'-en-tang'-gl-ment], *n.* (*milit.*) a protective fence of barbed wire twisted to and fro over a line of upright posts.
WIRE-GAUZE, [wier'-gawz'], *n.* gauze made of wire.
WIRE-GRATE, [wier-grāt], *n.* a grating of wire mesh.
WIRE-GUN, [wier'-gun], *n.* a gun the barrel of which is bound with wire.
WIRE-HAIRED, [wier'-hāerd'], *adj.* having stiff, short hair, as in the coats of some terriers.
WIRE-HEEL, [wier'-hēl], *n.* a disease of the foot from which horses suffer.
WIRELESS (1), [wier'-les], *n.* radio; any process or system by which messages can be transmitted by electric waves in the ether without communicating wires; an instrument for receiving such communications; the programmes of entertainment, education, and news provided by a broadcasting station.
WIRELESS (2), [wier'-les], *adj.* having no wires; pertaining to wireless or any system of radio broadcasting.
WIRELESS (3), [wier'-les], *v.t.* to transmit by radio.
WIRELESS-CABIN, [wier'-les-kab'-in], *n.* the room or cabin of a wireless operator.
WIRELESS-OPERATOR, [wier'-les-op'-er-ā-tor], *n.* one responsible for receiving and transmitting wireless messages, *esp.* on board ship.
WIRELESS-STATION, [wier'-les-stā'-shun], *n.* a place where wireless messages may be received or broadcast.
WIREMAN, [wier'-man], *n.* one who fixes wires, *esp.* the wires of an electric system.
WIRE-MICROMETER, [wier'-mī-krom'-it-er], *n.* a micrometer employing fine adjustable parallel wires.
WIRE-NETTING, [wier'-net'-ing], *n.* a wire mesh used in fencing.
WIREPULLER, [wier-pōōl'-er], *n.* one who tries to achieve his ends by using personal or secret influence.
WIREPULLING, [wier'-pōōl'-ing], *n.* the act of employing secret influence to further one's aims.
WIRE-ROPE, [wier'-rōp'], *n.* rope made of wire.
WIREWAY, [wier'-wā], *n.* telpherage; a system of wires connected with transport.
WIREWORKER, [wier'-wurk-er], *n.* one who produces goods made of wire.
WIRE-WORM, [wier'-wurm], *n.* the larva of the click-beetle, so called from its appearance.
WIRE-WOVE, [wier'-wōv'], *adj.* (of paper) of a certain fine quality made in a wire-gauze frame, the form of which can be seen in the watermark.
WIRILY, [wier'-i-li], *adv.* in a wiry fashion.
WIRINESS, [wier'-i-nes], *n.* the state of being wiry.
WIRING, [wier'-ing], *n.* the wires or system of wires in any electrical device.
WIRY, [wier'-i], *adj.* like wire; (of a man) strong and sinewy but not heavily built.
WISDOM, [wiz'-dom], *n.* the condition of being wise; the knowledge and point of view of one who is wise. [OE. *wisdom*].
WISDOM-TOOTH, [wiz'-dom-tōōth'], *n.* the back molar in the human mouth, which does not appear till the late 'teens or early twenties.
WISE (1), [wīz], *n.* manner, way. [OE. *wise*].
WISE (2), [wīz], *adj.* possessing or exhibiting the qualities of clear thinking, careful judgment, tact and understanding; prudent, foreseeing; possessing knowledge; **to be none the wiser,** to be no better informed; **to put (someone) w. to, (on, about)**, (*U.S. slang*) to inform, give hints, of; **to be** (*or* **get**) **w. to,** to be (or become) informed about or aware of. [OE. *wis*].
WISEACRE, [wīz'-āk'-er], *n.* one who pretends to be very wise, usually without cause. [MDu. *wijssegger* wise speaker].
WISECRACK (1), [wīz'-krak'], *n.* (*U.S. slang*) a witticism, joke, smart retort.
WISECRACK (2), [wīz'-krak'], *v.i.* (*U.S. slang*) to utter wisecracks.
WISE GUY, [wīz'-gī], *n.* (*U.S. slang*) a fellow who pretends to know everything.
WISE-HEARTED, [wīz'-haht'-id], *adj.* wise, sympathetic, knowing.
WISELY, [wīz'-li], *adv.* in a wise manner. [WISE (2)].
WISH (1), [wish], *n.* the act of wishing; a longing or desire, a verbal expression of this; the thing longed for.
WISH (2), [wish], *v.t. and i.* to desire, to long for; to desire that; to express a desire in words; to desire (someone else) to have; **to w. for,** to desire to possess, experience, etc. [OE. *wyscan*].
WISHBONE, [wish'-bōn], *n.* a fork-shaped bone in a bird's breast. [WISH (1) and BONE (1)].
WISHER, [wish'-er], *n.* one who wishes.
WISHFUL, [wish'-fōōl], *adj.* anxious, longing, desirous; **w. thinking,** thinking conditioned more by one's wishes than by the actual facts or by reason.
WISHFULLY, [wish'-fōōl-i], *adv.* with longing.
WISHFULNESS, [wish'-fōōl-nes], *n.* a longing or desire; the quality of being wishful.
WISHING-BONE, [wish'-ing-bōn'], *n.* a wishbone.
WISHING-CAP, [wish'-ing-kap'], *n.* a magic cap whose wearer finds his wishes fulfilled.
WISHTONWISH, [wish'-ton-wish'], *n.* the prairie marmot or prairie-dog. [Imitative of its cry].

WISH-WASH, [wish'-wosh'], *n.* (*coll.*) a very weak drink; nonsense.
WISHY-WASHY, [wish'-i-wosh'-i], *adj.* weak and watery; indeterminate, irresolute.
WISKET, [wisk'-it], *n.* (*dial.*) a basket. [Uncert.].
WISP, [wisp], *n.* a thin strand of anything; a small tuft or bunch; a flock of snipe. [ME. *wisp*].
WISPY, [wisp'-i], *adj.* resembling a wisp or wisps.
WIST†, [wist], *v.t.* and *i.* to know. [OE. *wiste*, *pret.* of *witan* to know].
WISTARIA, [wist-āer'-i-a], *n.* a genus of blue-flowered climbing plants. [Prof. Caspar *Wistar*].
WISTFUL, [wist'-fŏŏl], *n.* thoughtful, pensive; longing, yearning, *esp.* in a sad, unhopeful way. [Uncert.].
WISTFULLY, [wist'-fŏŏl-i], *adv.* in a wistful fashion.
WISTFULNESS, [wist'-fŏŏl-nes], *n.* the quality of being wistful.
WISTITI, [wis'-ti-ti], *n.* the marmoset, *Hapale jacchus*. [Fr. *ouistiti*].

WISTARIA

WISTLY†, [wist'-li], *adv.* intently. [Uncert.].
WIT (1), [wit], *n.* the mind, mental vigour and agility; the ability to observe humorous connexions and similarities between one thing and another, and to express them in a neat, memorable way; a person able to do this; (*pl.*) one's faculties. [OE. *witt* mind].
WIT (2), [wit], *v.t.* and *i.* (*hist.*) now only in the phrase, **to w.,** that is, namely. [OE. *witan* to know].
WITAN, [wit'-an], *n.* the Anglo-Saxon deliberative assembly. [OE. *wita*, *witena* wise man].
WITCH (1), [wich], *n.* a woman supposed by the superstitious to have supernatural power and knowledge, a sorceress; any ill-looking, hard-hearted old woman, a hag; a flatfish; (*fig.*) a fascinating woman; **witch's broom,** a broom supposed to be used by witches for locomotion; a witch-knot. [OE. *wicce*].
WITCH (2), [wich], *v.t.* to cast a spell over like a witch.
WITCHCRAFT, [wich'-krahft], *n.* the supernatural power and craft of a witch.
WITCH-DOCTOR, [wich'-dok'-tor], *n.* a tribal medicine-man.
WITCH-ELM, see WYCH-ELM.
WITCHERY, [wich'-er-i], *n.* magic, witchcraft; (*fig.*) fascination.
WITCH-HAZEL, see WYCH-HAZEL.
WITCHING, [wich'-ing], *adj.* enchanting, potent with magic; (*fig.*) fascinating.
WITCHINGLY, [wich'-ing-li], *adv.* enchantingly.
WITCH-KNOT, [wich'-not'], *n.* a cluster of twigs on a tree caused by a disease.
WITENAGEMOT, [wit'-en-a-gē-mōt'], *n.* (*hist.*) the witan or Old English deliberative assembly. [OE. *witena gemot* meeting of counsellors].
WITH (1), [wiTH], *prep.* expressing alliance, agreement, companionship, communication, or physical propinquity; expressing opposition, contrast, proportion, equality, etc.; expressing separation or disagreement; introducing an attribute or possession or the manner, instrument, or cause of an action; expressing similarity of direction or simultaneity. [OE. *with*].
WITH (2), see WITHE.
WITH-, [wiTH], *pref.* expressing opposition and separation. [OE. *with-*].
WITHAL (1), [wiTH-awl'], *adv.* in addition.
WITHAL (2), [wiTH-awl'], *prep.* (used at the end of a phrase or sentence) with.
WITHAMITE, [wiTH'-am-it], *n.* (*min.*) a red-coloured epidote. [H. *Witham*, the discoverer].
WITHDRAW, (**withdrew, withdrawn**), [wiTH-draw'], *v.t.* and *i.* to pull back, remove, or bring back (anything that has been advanced or thrust forward); to retract (what one has said); to come back after having gone forward, to retreat, to go away; to retire; to cancel one's statement, promise.
WITHDRAWAL, [wiTH-draw'-al], *n.* the action of withdrawing.
WITHDRAWER, [wiTH-draw'-er], *n.* a person who withdraws.
WITHDRAWING-ROOM, [wiTH-draw'-ing-rōōm'], *n.* (*archaic*) a lounge or drawing-room.
WITHDRAWMENT, [wiTH-draw'-ment], *n.* a withdrawal.
WITHDRAWN, [wiTH-drawn'], *p.pt.* of WITHDRAW.
WITHDREW, [wiTH-drōō'], *pret.* of WITHDRAW.
WITHE, WITH, [with, wiTH], *n.* a long, slender, tough, flexible twig or shoot. [OE. *withthe*].
WITHED, [wiTHd], *adj.* fastened or bound with withes.
WITHER, [wiTH'-er], *v.t.* and *i.* (of flowers, etc.) to fade, shrivel up, wilt; (*fig.*) to diminish, grow weaker; (*lit.* and *fig.*) to cause to wilt and shrivel; (*fig.*) to confuse, embarrass (a person). [~WEATHER (2)].
WITHERBAND, [wiTH'-er-band'], *n.* a metal band passing under the front of a saddle on a horse. [WITHERS and BAND (1)].
WITHERED, [wiTH'-erd], *adj.* faded and dry; (*fig.*) shrunk, wrinkled, wizened.
WITHEREDNESS, [wiTH'-erd-nes], *n.* the condition of being withered.
WITHERING, [wiTH'-er-ing], *adj.* causing to wither; (*fig.*) embarrassing, scornful, hostile.
WITHERING-FLOOR, [wiTH'-er-ing-flaw(r)'], *n.* a drying floor in a malt factory.
WITHERINGLY, [wiTH'-er-ing-li], *adv.* in a withering way.
WITHERITE, [wiTH'-er-it], *n.* (*min.*) a native carbonate of barium. [W. *Withering*, its first analyser].
WITHERLOCK, [wiTH'-er-lok'], *n.* the part of a horse's mane grasped when mounting. [WITHERS and OE. *locc* hair].
WITHERNAM, [wiTH'-er-nahm], *n.* (*leg.*, *hist.*) a reprisal in an action of replevin; an arrest for debt in the Cinque Ports. [~OIcel. *vithrnam*].
WITHE-ROD, [wiTH'-rod'], *n.* the shrub, *Viburnum nudum*, found in North America.
WITHERS, [wiTH'-erz], *n.* the front of a horse's shoulder next to the neck, against which the collar pulls. [OE. *wither* against].
WITHERSHINS, WIDDERSHINS, [wiTH'-er-shinz'], *adv.* in a direction contrary to that in which the sun seems to move. [MLG. *weddersins*].
WITHER-WRUNG, [wiTH'-er-rung'], *adj.* (of a horse) hurt in the withers.
WITHHELD, [wiTH-held'], *pret.* and *p.pt.* of WITHHOLD.
WITHHOLD, (**withheld, †withholden**), [wiTH-hōld'], *v.t.* to check, keep back, restrain; to keep unused; to retain in one's possession, refuse to grant. [OE. *withhaldan*].
WITHHOLDEN†, [wiTH-hōld'-en], *p.pt.* of WITHHOLD.
WITHHOLDER, [wiTH-hōld'-er], *n.* a person or thing that withholds.
WITHHOLDMENT, [wiTH-hōld'-ment], *n.* the act of withholding, the fact of being withheld.
WITHIN (1), [wiTH-in'], *n.* the inside, interior.
WITHIN (2), [wiTH-in'], *adv.* on the inside, internally; inside a specific space or area; indoors, inside one's house; in the mind or spirit; (*stage*, *archaic*) off stage, in the wings. [OE. *withinnan*].
WITHIN (3), [wiTH-in'], *prep.* in the interior or inside of, inside; not beyond the range or limit of, not beyond the power or resources of; in not more than (a given time); not farther than (a given distance).
WITHINSIDE, [wiTH-in'-sid], *adv.* right inside.
WITHOUT (1), [wiTH-owt'], *n.* the outside.
WITHOUT (2), [wiTH-owt'], *adv.* on the outside, externally; (*archaic*) out of doors, outside the house. [OE. *withutan*].
WITHOUT (3), [wiTH-owt'], *prep.* lacking, not having; not helped by, not using; not accompanied with; (*archaic*) outside, beyond.
WITHSTAND, (**withstood**), [wiTH-stand'], *v.t.* to oppose; to be capable of enduring or keeping out.
WITHSTANDER, [wiTH-stand'-er], *n.* one who withstands.
WITHSTOOD, [wiTH-stŏŏd'], *pret.* and *p.pt.* of WITHSTAND.
WITHY, [wiTH'-i], *n.* a sort of willow. [OE. *widig*].
WITLESS, [wit'-less], *adj.* having no wits, dull, stupid, wanting thought.
WITLESSLY, [wit'-les-li], *adv.* in a witless fashion.
WITLESSNESS, [wit'-les-nes], *n.* want of wit.
WITLING, [wit'-ling], *n.* a person of slight intelligence or understanding.
WITNESS (1), [wit'-nes], *n.* evidence, testimony, manifestation; a person or thing providing evidence; (*leg.*) a person present at the signing of a document, who appends his or her name in testimony of this; one who gives evidence in a court of law. [OE. *witnes*].
WITNESS (2), [wit'-nes], *v.t.* and *i.* to offer proof or testimony (of); to be present at and aware of, to see; to append one's name, seal, or mark to (a document) in declaration that one has seen it legally signed.

WITNESS-BOX, [wit′-nes-boks′], *n.* the place in a court of law where witnesses give evidence.
WIT-STARVED, [wit′-stahvd′], *adj.* lacking wit or understanding.
WITTED, [wit′-id], *adj.* (usually in compounds) having wits.
WITTICHENITE, [wit′-ik-en-īt], *n.* a sulphide of copper and bismuth found at *Wittichen* in Baden, Germany.
WITTICISM, [wit′-i-sizm], *n.* a witty remark, a clever retort. [WITT(Y) and (CRIT)ICISM].
WITTILY, [wit′-i-li], *adv.* in witty fashion.
WITTINESS, [wit′-i-nes], *n.* the condition or quality of being witty.
WITTING, [wit′-ing], *adj.* conscious or intended.
WITTINGLY, [wit′-ing-li], *adv.* intentionally.
WITTOL, [wit′-ol], *n.* a man who complacently submits to his wife's unfaithfulness. [ME. *wetewold*].
WITTY, [wit′-i], *adj.* exhibiting or possessing wit, ingenious. [OE. *witig* knowing].
WITWALL, [wit′-wawl], *n.* the green woodpecker. [ME. *wodewale*].
WIVERN, WYVERN, [wī′-vern], *n.* a legendary winged beast with a dragon's head and two legs. [ONFr. *wivre* viper].
WIVES, [wīvz], *pl.* of WIFE.
WIZARD (1), [wiz′-erd], *n.* a man with magic power; a person who can do things and influence others as if by magic. [ME. *wisard* wise man].
WIZARD (2), [wiz′-ard], *adj.* (*slang*) remarkable, clever.
WIZARDLY, [wiz′-erd-li], *adv.* in the manner of a wizard.
WIZARDRY, [wiz′-erd-ri], *n.* the arts of a wizard; personal charm.
WIZEN, WEAZEN, [wiz′-en, wē′-zen], *adj.* wizened. [~OE. *wisnian* to dry up].
WIZENED, WEAZENED, [wiz′-end, wē′-zend], *adj.* shrivelled.
WOAD, [wōd], *n.* the plant, *Isatis tinctoria*; the blue dye yielded by this. [OE. *wad*].
WOAD-MILL, [wōd′-mil], *n.* a factory where dye is obtained from woad.
WOAD-WAXEN, see WOOD-WAXEN.
WOBBLE, WABBLE (1), [wobl], *n.* the act of wobbling, instability, a swaying to and fro; tremolo.
WOBBLE, WABBLE (2), [wobl], *v.t.* to sway to and fro with instability, to be unstable or shaky; (*fig.*) to be hesitant or vacillating. [~MHGerm. *wabalen*].
WOBBLER, [wob′-ler], *n.* a person or thing that wobbles.
WOBBLY, [wob′-li], *adj.* wobbling, unstable.
WOE (1), [wō], *n.* grief, sorrow, affliction, trouble. [OE. *wa*].

WOAD

WOE (2), [wō], *int.* alas! [WOE (1)].
WOEBEGONE, [wō′-bi-gon′], *adj.* sorrowful, of miserable appearance [WOE and OE. *began* to occupy].
WOEFUL, [wō′-fōōl], *adj.* wretched, sorrowful, mournful.
WOEFULLY, [wō′-fōōl-i], *adv.* in woeful fashion.
WOEFULNESS, [wō′-fōōl-ness], *n.* the condition of being woeful.
WOESOME, [wō′-sum], *adj.* sorrowful.
WOKE, [wōk], *pret.* of WAKE (3). [OE. *woc*].
WOKEN, [wōk′-en], (*coll.*) *p.pt.* of WAKE (3).
WOLD, [wōld], *n.* uncultivated, unwooded land. *esp.* a moor in a limestone district; (*pl.*) downs. [OE. *wald* forest].
WOLF (1), (*pl.* **wolves**), [wōōlf, wōōlvz], *n.* the carnivore, *Canis lupus*; any animal of the same genus; a person who is cruel and greedy like a wolf; a rasping sound in a violin, etc.; **to cry w.**, to give a false alarm. [OE. *wulf*].
WOLF (2), [wōōlf], *v.t.* to eat quickly and greedily.
WOLF-BERRY, [wōōlf′-be′-ri], *n.* the shrub, *Symphoricarpus occidentalis*, found in North America.
WOLF-CUB, [wōōlf′-kub′], *n.* a young wolf; a junior boy scout.
WOLF-DOG, [wōōlf′-dog′], *n.* any large dog kept for hunting, or protection against, wolves; an animal which is a cross between wolf and dog.
WOLF-FISH, [wōōlf′-fish], *n.* the large ocean fish, *Anarrhicas lupus*.
WOLF-HOUND, [wōōlf′-hownd], *n.* a large type of dog first bred to hunt wolves.
WOLFISH, [wōōlf′-ish], *adj.* like a wolf, fierce and greedy; ravenous; voracious. [WOLF (1)].
WOLFISHLY, [wōōlf′-ish-li], *adv.* in a wolfish manner.
WOLFISHNESS, [wōōlf′-ish-nes], *n.* the quality of being wolfish.
WOLF-NET, [wōōlf′-net′], *n.* a sort of fishing net.
WOLFRAM, [wōōlf′-ram], *n.* (*min.*) ore of tungsten, tungsten. [Germ. *wolfram*].
WOLFRAMITE, [wōōlf′-ram-īt], *n.* (*min.*) wolfram.
WOLF'S-BANE, [wōōlfs′-bān], *n.* any of various plants of the genus, *Aconitum*.
WOLF'S-CLAW, [wōōlfs′-klaw], *n.* the plant, *Lycopodium clavatum*, club-moss.
WOLF'S-FIST, [wōōlfs′-fist], *n.* the plant *Lycoperdon bovista*, the puffball.
WOLF'S-FOOT, [wōōlfs′-fōōt], *n.* wolf's-claw.
WOLFSKIN, [wōōlf′-skin], *n.* the skin of a wolf, *esp.* when prepared as a rug, etc.
WOLF-SPIDER, [wōōlf′-spīd′-er], *n.* the tarantula; a spider that leaps on its prey.
WOLLASTONITE, [wōōl′-as-ton-īt], *n.* (*min.*) a native calcium silicate. [W. H. *Wollaston*, 1766-1828].
WOLVERENE, WOLVERINE, [wōōl-ver-ēn′], *n.* a North American carnivore, *Gulo luscus*; this animal's skin. [~WOLF (1)].

WOLF-SPIDER

WOMAN, (*pl.* **women**) [wōō′-man, wim′-in], *n.* an adult person of the female sex; women generally; the essential character of women; a maid, a lady-in-waiting. [OE. *wifman*].
WOMAN-HATER, [wōō′-man-hāt′-er], *n.* a man who has a great dislike of women.
WOMANHOOD, [wōō′-man-hōōd], *n.* the state of being a woman; the essential characteristics of women.
WOMANISH, [wōō′-man-ish], *adj.* effeminate; **old-w.**, fussy about trifles.
WOMANISHLY, [wōō′-man-ish-li], *adv.* in a womanish fashion.
WOMANISHNESS, [wōō′-man-ish-nes], *n.* the condition of being womanish.
WOMANIZE, [wōō′-man-īz], *v.t and i.* to make effeminate; (*coll.*) to have casual sexual intercourse with women.
WOMANKIND, [wōō′-man-kīnd′], *n.*(*pl.*) women in general.
WOMANLESS, [wōō′-man-les], *n.* lacking women.
WOMANLIKE, [wōō′-man-līk], *adj.* like a woman, characteristic of a woman.
WOMANLINESS, [wōō′-man-li-nes], *n.* the quality of being womanly.
WOMANLY, [wōō′-man-li], *adj.* characteristic of the best in women, befitting a woman.
WOMB, [wōōm], *n.* the uterus, the female organ of conception and prenatal development in mammals; any hollow cave or cavity; a matrix. [OE. *wamb*].
WOMBAT, [wom′-bat], *n.* a nocturnal burrowing marsupial of the genus, *Phascolomys*, native to Australia. [Native].
WOMBY, [wōōm′-i], *adj.* hollow like a womb, capacious.
WOMEN, [wim′-in], *n.*(*pl.*) of WOMAN.
WOMENFOLK, [wim′-in-fōk′], *n.*(*pl.*) womankind; one's female relations, etc.
WOMENKIND, [wim′-in-kīnd], *n.*(*pl.*) womankind.
WOMMERA, WOOMERA, [wom′-er-a], *n.* a notched stick used by Australian natives for throwing spears. [Native].
WON (1), [wun], *pret. and p.pt.* of WIN.
WON† (2), [wun], *v.i.* to dwell. [OE. *wunian*].
WONDER (1), [wun′-der], *n.* a person or thing that excites great admiration or astonishment, a prodigy; a marvellous deed, a miracle; strangeness, beauty, prodigious or marvellous quality; an emotion of mingled admiration, awe, and astonishment; (*coll.*) a sensation, a person who does sensational things. [OE. *wundor* glory].
WONDER (2), [wun′-der], *v.i.* to experience an emotion of almost doubting admiration or surprise; to be amazed; to be amazed (at); to desire to be told or get to know. [OE. *wundrian*].
WONDERBERRY, [wun′-der-be′-ri], *n.* a variety of berry resembling a raspberry.
WONDERER, [wun′-der-er], *n.* a person who wonders.

WONDERFUL, [wun'-der-fo͝ol], *adj.* exciting wonder and amazement, marvellous, surpassingly beautiful, miraculous; (*coll.*) very good. [OE. *wundorfull*].
WONDERFULLY, [wun'-der-fo͝ol-i], *adv.* in a wonderful way.
WONDERFULNESS, [wun'-der-fo͝ol-nes], *n.* the condition of being wonderful.
WONDERING, [wun'-der-ing], *adj.* feeling wonder, amazed, almost doubting; expressing wonder.
WONDERINGLY, [wun'-der-ing-li], *adv.* in a wondering fashion.
WONDERLAND, [wun'-der-land], *n.* a land or place of wonders.
WONDERMENT, [wun'-der-ment], *n.* the emotion of wonder; bemused fascination.
WONDERSTRUCK, [wun'-der-struk'], *adj.* overwhelmed with wonder, awestruck.
WONDERWORKER, [wun'-der-wurk'-er], *n.* one who works wonders.
WONDERWORKING, [wun'-der-wurk'-ing], *adj.* performing wonders.
WONDROUS (1), [wun'-drus], *adj.* wonderful.
WONDROUS† (2), [wun'-drus], *adv.* wonderfully, amazingly.
WONDROUSLY, [wun'-drus-li], *adv.* to a wondrous degree; in a wondrous manner.
WONDROUSNESS, [wun'-drus-nes], *n.* the quality of being wondrous.
WONGA-WONGA, [wong'-ga-wong'-ga], *n.* the *Leucosarcia picata*, the Australian pigeon. [Australian aboriginal].
WONKY, [wong'-ki], *adj.* (*slang*) wobbly, unstable; (of a machine, etc.) out of order, working badly; hesitant, doubtful; not very well, in poor health. [~Germ. *wanken* to totter].
WONT (1), [wōnt], *n.* habit.
WONT (2), [wōnt], *adj.* accustomed. [ME. *wuned*].
WON'T, [wōnt], *pres. sing. v.* (*coll.*) will not. [ME. *wol not* will not].
WONTED, [wōnt'-id], *adj.* accustomed, usual.
WONTEDNESS, [wōnt'-id-nes], *n.* the quality of being wonted.
WONTLESS†, [wōnt-les], *adj.* not usual.
WOO, [wo͞o], *v.t.* to court, seek to marry, make love to; to endeavour to get or attain to. [OE. *wogian*].
WOOD, [wo͝od], *n.* a large group of trees, a small forest; the substance of the trunk and branches of a tree; timber; (*sport*) a ball used in bowls; a shot at bowls; (*mus.*) the wood-wind instruments of an orchestra; a wine- or beer-barrel. [OE. *wudu*].
WOOD-AGATE, [wo͝od'-ag'-it], *n.* petrified wood.
WOOD-ANEMONE, [wo͝od'-an-em'-on-i], *n.* an uncultivated anemone growing under trees.
WOOD-ANT, [wo͝od'-ant'], *n.* the red ant.
WOOD-ASH(ES), [wo͝od'-ash'-(iz)], *n.*(*pl.*) ashes left by burnt wood.
WOODBINE, WOOD-BIND, [wo͝od'-bīn, wo͝od'-bīnd], *n.* wild honeysuckle. [OE. *wudubind*].
WOOD-BLOCK, [wo͝od'-blok'], *n.* a block of engraved wood for printing a design; a block of wood used for paving roads.
WOODCARVER, [wo͝od'-kahv'-er], *n.* one who makes woodcarvings.
WOODCARVING, [wo͝od'-kahv'-ing], *n.* a carving done in wood; the art or process of carving in wood.
WOODCHAT, [wo͝od'-chat'], *n.* the bird, *Lanius rutilis*.
WOODCHUCK, [wo͝od'-chuk'], *n.* an American marmot, *Arctomys monax*. [NAmerInd. *wuchak*].
WOOD-COAL, [wo͝od'-kōl], *n.* charcoal made from wood; lignite.
WOODCOCK, [wo͝od'-kok'], *n.* the *Scolopax rusticula*, a migratory bird allied to the sandpiper.
WOOD-CRAFT, [wo͝od'-krahft], *n.* knowledge of how to live in, or travel through, forests.
WOODCUT, [wo͝od'-kut'], *n.* the engraving on, or a print made from, a wood-block.
WOOD-CUTTER, [wo͝od'-kut'-er], *n.* one who engraves wood-blocks; one who fells trees.
WOOD-DOVE, [wo͝od'-duv'], *n.* a wood-pigeon.
WOODED, [wo͝od'-id], *adj.* covered with trees.
WOODEN, [wo͝od'-en], *adj.* made of wood; (*coll.*) clumsy; stiff, dull, stupid.
WOOD-ENGRAVER, [wo͝od'-en-grāv'-er], *n.* (*print.*) one who engraves on wood-blocks.
WOOD-ENGRAVING, [wo͝od-en-grāv'-ing], *n.* the art or process of engraving on wood; an engraving on wood.
WOODENHEAD, [wo͝od'-en-hed'], *n.* a dullard.
WOODEN-HEADED, [wo͝od'-en-hed'-id], *adj.* stupid, slow-witted, incapable of seeing reason.
WOODEN-HEADEDNESS, [wo͝od'-en-hed'-id-nes], *n.* the quality of being wooden-headed.
WOODENLY, [wo͝od'-en-li], *adv.* in a stiff, wooden manner.
WOODENNESS, [wo͝od'-en-nes], *n.* the state or condition of being wooden.
WOODEN-PEAR, [wo͝od'-en-pāer'], *n.* the tree, *Xylomelum pyriforme*, found in Australia.
WOOD-FIBRE, [wo͝od'-fīb'-er], *n.* the fibre contained in wood; fibre made from wood.
WOOD-GAS, [wo͝od'-gas'], *n.* inflammable gas produced from wood by heating.
WOOD-GOD, [wo͝od'-god'], *n.* (*myth.*) a local deity presiding over a wood.
WOOD-GROUSE, [wo͝od'-grows], *n.* a bird of the grouse family, *Tetrao urogallus*.
WOOD-HOUSE, [wo͝od'-hows], *n.* a woodshed.
WOOD-IBIS, [wo͝od'-ī-bis], *n.* any of several sorts of American storks of the subfamily, *Tantalinæ*.
WOODINESS, [wo͝od'-i-nes], *n.* the condition or quality of being woody.
WOODLAND (1), [wo͝od'-land], *n.* a wooded tract of land.
WOODLAND (2), [wo͝od'-land], *adj.* pertaining to woods.
WOODLARK, [wo͝od'-lahk], *n.* a small variety of lark, *Alauda arborea*.
WOODLAYER, [wo͝od'-lā-er], *n.* a young tree planted in a hedge.
WOOD-LEOPARD, [wo͝od'-lep'-erd], *n.* the spotted leopard moth, *Zeuzera pyrina*.
WOODLESS, [wo͝od'-les], *adj.* having no wood or woods.
WOODLESSNESS, [wo͝od'-les-nes], *n.* the condition of being woodless.
WOODLOCK, [wo͝od'-lok], *n.* (*naut.*) a bar of wood fastened under the pintle of a rudder so that the rudder cannot rise in the water.
WOODLOUSE, [wo͝od'-lows], *n.* a small insect of the genus, *Oniscus*.
WOODMAN, [wo͝od'-man], *n.* one who fells, or looks after, trees.
WOODMONGER, [wo͝od'-mung'-ger], *n.* a timber merchant.
WOOD-NOTES, [wo͝od'-nōts], *n.* (*pl.*) a bird's song; (*poet.*) simple, unartificial poetry.
WOOD-NUT, [wo͝od'-nut], *n.* a nut.
WOOD-NYMPH, [wo͝od'-nimpf], *n.* (*myth.*) a nymph living in a forest; a kind of humming-bird; a moth of the genus, *Eudryas*.
WOOD-OFFERING, [wo͝od'-of'-er-ing], *n.* a ritual offering of burning wood.

WOODLOUSE

WOOD-OIL, [wo͝od'-oil], *n.* any oil extracted from a tree.
WOOD-OPAL, [wo͝od'-ōp'-al], *n.* silicified timber.
WOOD-PAPER, [wo͝od'-pāp'-er], *n.* paper manufactured from wood-pulp.
WOODPECKER, [wo͝od'-pek'-er], *n.* any variety of bird of the family, *Picidae*.
WOOD-PIGEON, [wo͝od'-pij'-in], *n.* the ring-dove, *Columba palumbus*, a wild pigeon.
WOOD-PULP, [wo͝od'-pulp'], *n.* pulp made from wood and used to manufacture inferior paper.
WOOD-REEVE, [wo͝od'-rēv], *n.* a chief forest officer.
WOODROCK, [wo͝od'-rok'], *n.* a mineral resembling asbestos; woodstone.
WOODRUFF, WOODROOF, [wo͝od'-ruf], *n.* the herb, *Asperula odorata*. [OE. *wudurofe*].
WOOD-SERE, [wo͝od'-sēer], *n.* that period when a tree has no sap in its upper part.
WOODSHED, [wo͝od'-shed'], *n.* a shed for storing timber.
WOODSKIN, [wo͝od'-skin], *n.* a bark canoe used by natives in Guiana.
WOODSMAN, [wo͝odz'-man], *n.* one who lives in a wood; a forester.
WOOD-SOOT, [wo͝od'-so͝ot], *n.* the soot of burnt wood.
WOOD-SORREL, [wo͝od'-so'-rel], *n.* a small herb of the genus, *Oxalis*, with trifoliate leaves.
WOOD-SPITE, [wo͝od'-spīt], *n.* the green woodpecker.
WOODSTONE, [wo͝od'-stōn], *n.* a siliceous variety of fossil wood.
WOOD-TAR, [wo͝od'-tah(r)], *n.* a tar extracted from wood.
WOOD-TIN, [wo͝od'-tin], *n.* an ore of tin consisting of long fibrous crystals and resembling dead wood.

WOOD-VINE, [wŏŏd'-vīn], *n.* the plant, *Clematis vitalba*.
WOODWALL, [wŏŏd'-wawl], *n.* the green woodpecker. [ME. *wodewale*].
WOOD-WARBLER, [wŏŏd'-wawb'-ler], *n.* an American warbler; the bird, *Phylloscopus sibilatrix*.
WOODWARD, [wŏŏd'-wawd], *n.* a forest officer.
WOOD-WASP, [wŏŏd'-wosp'], *n.* the *Vespa sylvestris*, a wasp found only in woods; a variety of wasp that lays its eggs in rotten wood.
WOOD-WAXEN, WOAD-WAXEN, [wŏŏd'-waks'-en], *n.* the plant, *Genista tinctoria*, dyer's broom. [OE. *wuduweaxe*].
WOOD-WIND (1), [wŏŏd'-wind'], *n.* that section of an orchestra in which wind-instruments generally made of wood are played.
WOOD-WIND (2), [wŏŏd'-wind'], *adj.* pertaining to the wood-wind.
WOODWORK, [wŏŏd'-wurk], *n.* any structure or part of a structure made of wood; carpentry.
WOOD-WREN, [wŏŏd'-ren'], *n.* the bird, *Phylloscopus sibilatrix*, the wood-warbler.
WOODY, [wŏŏd'-i], *adj.* wooded; made of wood; resembling wood.
WOOER, [wōō'-er], *n.* one who woos.
WOOF, [wōōf], *n.* the threads that run at right-angles to the warp; the weft. [OE. *owef*].
WOOFY, [wōōf'-i], *adj.* having a close, fabric-like texture.
WOOING (1), [wōō'-ing], *n.* courtship, the action of a wooer.
WOOING (2), [wōō'-ing], *adj.* intending to persuade or court.
WOOINGLY, [wōō'-ing-li], *adv.* in a wooing manner.
WOOL, [wŏŏl], *n.* the soft hair of a sheep or other similar animal; thread or yarn made from this; a fabric made of such threads; any substance resembling these; (*slang*) hair, *esp.* the curly hair of a negro; **keep your w. on !**, (*slang*) don't get angry; **to lose one's w.**, (*slang*) to grow angry; **to pull the w. over one's eyes**, to trick or deceive one; **dyed in the w.**, wool-dyed; (*fig.*) out and out, absolute. [OE. *wull*].
WOOL-BALL, [wŏŏl'-bawl], *n.* a ball of wool, a matted lump of wool found in a sheep's stomach.
WOOL-CARDER, [wŏŏl'-kahd'-er], *n.* one who cards wool.
WOOL-CARDING, [wŏŏl'-kahd'-ing], *n.* the act of carding wool.
WOOLCOMBER, [wŏŏl'-kōm'-er], *n.* one who prepares wool by combing it.
WOOLCOMBING, [wŏŏl'-kōm'-ing], *n.* the action of combing wool; wool which is so combed.
WOOLD (1), [wŏŏld], *n.* rope used for binding.
WOOLD (2), [wŏŏld], *v.t.* (*naut.*) to wrap round with rope or chain. [MLGerm. *wolen* to compress].
WOOLDED, [wŏŏld'-id], *adj.* (*naut.*) bound with rope.
WOOLDER, [wŏŏld'-er], *n.* (*naut.*) a rope used for woolding.
WOOLDING, [wŏŏld'-ing], *n.* (*naut.*) the action of winding (as a rope round a mast, etc.).
WOOL-DYED, [wŏŏl'-dīd'], *adj.* (of a colour) imparted to the wool before it is spun.
WOOL-FAT, [wŏŏl'-fat'], *n.* lanolin.
WOOL-FELL, [wŏŏl'-fel'], *n.* a sheep's skin with the wool still on. [ME. *wolle felle*].
WOOL-GATHERING (1), [wŏŏl'-gaTH'-er-ing], .. absent-mindedness, dreaminess.
WOOL-GATHERING (2), [wŏŏl'-gaTH'-er-ing], *adj.* dreamy, preoccupied.
WOOL-GROWER, [wŏŏl'-grō'-er], *n.* one who breeds sheep for their wool.
WOOL-HALL, [wŏŏl'-hawl], *n.* a wool market.
WOOLLEN, [wŏŏl'-en], *adj.* made of wool.
WOOLLEN-DRAPER, [wŏŏl'-en-drāp'-er], *n.* one who retails woollen goods.
WOOLLENS, [wŏŏl'-enz], *n.(pl.)* woollen articles.
WOOLLINESS, [wŏŏl'-i-nes], *n.* the condition of being woolly.
WOOLLY (1), [wŏŏl'-i], *n.* a woollen garment, a sweater or jersey.
WOOLLY (2), [wŏŏl'-i], *adj.* made of wool; looking like or feeling like wool; (*fig.*) not precise, vague, muddled; mentally feeble.
WOOLLY-BEAR, [wŏŏl'-i-bāer'], *n.* the large, hairy caterpillar of the Tiger moth.
WOOLMAN, [wŏŏl'-man], *n.* one who deals in wool.
WOOL-MILL, [wŏŏl'-mil'], *n.* a mill where woollen fabric is made.
WOOL-OIL, [wŏŏl'-oil], *n.* lanolin.
WOOLPACK, [wŏŏl'-pak'], *n.* a bag or bale of wool.
WOOLSACK, [wŏŏl'-sak'], *n.* a bale of wool; the large square cushion, supposed to be stuffed with wool but actually with hair, on which the Lord Chancellor sits in the House of Lords; the office and dignity of Lord Chancellor.
WOOLSEY, [wŏŏl'-zi], *adj.* (*rare*) made of wool.
WOOL-SHEARS, [wŏŏl'-shēerz], *n.(pl.)* shears for shearing sheep.
WOOLSORTER, [wŏŏl'-sawt'-er], *n.* one who sorts wool; **woolsorter's disease**, anthrax.
WOOLSTAPLE, [wŏŏl'-stāpl], *n.* a woollen market; the quality of wool.
WOOLSTAPLER, [wŏŏl'-stāp-ler], *n.* one who deals in wool.
WOOLWARD, [wŏŏl'-werd], *adj.* in the phrase **to go w.**, to do penance by wearing wool against the skin.
WOOL-WORK, [wŏŏl'-wurk'], *n.* embroidery done with wool.
WOOMERA, see WOMMERA.
WOORALI, WOURALI, [wōō-rahl'-i], *n.* poison obtained from certain South American trees. [S. AmerInd. *wurali*].
WOORARA, [wōō-rah'-ra], *n.* woorali.
WOOTZ, [wōōts], *n.* an Indian steel. [Canarese *ukku* steel].
WOP, [wop], *n.* (*U.S. slang*) a person from South Europe, *esp.* an Italian. [Unkn.].
WORD (1), [wurd], *n.* a unit of spoken or written language, by itself denoting a thing, idea, action, quality, qualification, or relationship, but not fully significant until associated with other words in a phrase or sentence; the written or printed symbol or symbols representing this; (*theol.*) the Second Person of the Trinity; the Scriptures; the gospel; that which is said, speech, utterance; a short sentence, saying, proverb; a password; a brief conversation; news, information, rumour; a promise; an asseveration not supported by proof but intended to be taken as made in good faith; a plea or recommendation on behalf of a third party; (*pl.*) verses set to music; a speech, remarks; **the last w.**, (*coll.*) the limit; the most modern of its kind; **to have a w. with**, to hold a short conversation with; **to have words (with)**, to quarrel (with); **to say a few words**, to make a short speech; **to be as good as one's w.**, to act up to one's promise; **w. for w.**, literally, exactly; **w. making and w. taking**, a game in which words are spelt out with letters printed on small squares of card. [OE. *word*].
WORD (2), [wurd], *v.t.* to express verbally.
WORDAGE, [wurd'-ij], *n.* the total number of words.
WORD-BOOK, [wurd'-bŏŏk], *n.* a vocabulary, a lexicon.
WORDED, [wurd'-id], *adj.* expressed verbally.
WORD-FORMATION, [wurd'-form-ā'-shun], *n.* the process of constructing one word from another by adding another word or particle.
WORDILY, [wurd'-i-li], *adv.* in a wordy fashion.
WORDINESS, [wurd'-i-nes], *n.* the state of being wordy.
WORDING, [wurd'-ing], *n.* the act of expressing in words; the phrases or style in which anything is expressed.
WORDLESS, [wurd'-les], *adj.* unable to speak, lacking words.
WORD-PAINTER, [wurd'-pānt'-er], *n.* one who excels in verbal description.
WORD-PAINTING, [wurd'-pānt'-ing], *n.* a vivid description in words.
WORD-PLAY, [wurd'-plā], *n.* puns; witty repartee.
WORD-SPLITTING, [wurd'-split'-ing], *n.* unduly precise or subtle use of words.
WORD-SQUARE, [wurd'-skwāer'], *n.* a group of words of equal length so chosen that they may be printed one above the other in the form of a square and read both vertically and horizontally.
WORDY, [wurd'-i], *adj.* verbal, using words; verbose, containing too many words; wont to use too many words.
WORE, [waw(r)], *pret.* of WEAR.
WORK (1), [wurk], *n.* mental or physical action carried out with a serious object in view, labour of mind or body, *esp.* such action regularly performed to earn a living; the results of any given activity or action of any kind; the material instruments necessary for such action, *esp.* needlework; the product of any such activity, *esp.* when of a skilled or artistic nature; a task or duty that must be done; (*phys.*) the energy expended in raising a given weight to a given height, or an equivalent of this; (*pl.*) the moving part or driving mechanism of any instrument or machine;

excavations, buildings, large architectural structures, etc., *esp.* of a military nature or such as are of benefit to the whole community; a factory; (*theol.*) actions done in accordance with one's religious convictions and as an expression of them; **to be out of w.,** to be unemployed, to have no regular means of living; **to set to w.,** to give work to; **to go** (*or* **set**) **to work,** to start work; **to have one's w. cut out,** to be hard pressed; **to make short w. of,** to deal with, overcome, consume, quickly and easily; **to give (one) the works,** (*slang*) to kill by a sub-machine-gun. [OE. *weorc*].

WORK (2), [wurk], *v.t.* to make to do work, to supervise the work of; to cause to act or operate; to shape by pressing or hammering; to perform or achieve, to do; to do work connected with, to make profitable; to dig, till, plough; *v.i.* to do work; to operate or act in the way intended, to be successful; to have effect, to produce results; to progress laboriously (through or over), to penetrate slowly, to spread gradually (through); to come to a certain state (expressed by an *adj.* after the *v.*); to ferment; to be regularly employed; **to w. at,** to devote one's effort and attention to; **to w. in,** to mix in; **to w. in with,** to fit, be capable of adjustment with; **to w. on** (*or* **upon**), to do work in connexion with; to exercise influence upon; **to w. out,** to solve by calculation, to compute; to be able to be solved, to come to a solution; (of an arithmetical problem) to have an answer that has no fractions in it; to be computed or estimated; to carry to a logical conclusion; **to w. up,** to increase or develop; to produce or rouse; to make excited; **to w. it so that,** to arrange matters so that. [OE. *wyrcan*].

WORKABILITY, [wurk'-a-bil'-i-ti], *n.* the state of being workable.

WORKABLE, [wurk'-abl], *adj.* able to be worked; practicable.

WORKABLENESS, [wurk-abl-nes], *n.* workability.

WORKABLY, [wurk'-ab-li], *adv.* in a workable fashion.

WORKADAY, [wurk'-a-dā], *adj.* pertaining to week-days or workdays; ordinary, prosaic. [ON. *verkidagr*].

WORK-BAG, [wurk'-bag'], *n.* a bag for needlework.

WORK-BASKET, [wurk'-bahsk'-it], *n.* a basket for holding needlework.

WORK-BOX, [wurk'-boks'], *n.* a box for needlework and things used in needlework.

WORKDAY, [wurk'-dā], *n.* a day on which most people work.

WORKER, [wurk'-er], *n.* one who works; a neuter bee, ant, etc.

WORK-FELLOW, [wurk'-fel'-ō], *n.* one working in company with another.

WORK-FOLK, [wurk'-fōk], *n.*(*pl.*) people who labour, the working-classes.

WORK-GIRL, [wurk'-gurl], *n.* a girl who does manual labour.

WORKHOUSE, [wurk'-hows], *n.* a public institution maintained under the Poor Law for the support of paupers.

WORKING (1), [wurk'-ing], *n.* the manner or process of work or action, the way something is done or in which a system or instrument operates; (*min.*) the section of the excavation where work is in progress.

WORKING (2), [wurk'-ing], *adj.* engaged in work, moving, operating; used for, connected with, work; necessary for work, business or operations in hand; adapted for immediate needs, makeshift, practical.

WORKING-CLASS (1), [wurk'-ing-klahs'], *n.* the wage-earning section of the community as distinct from salaried and professional workers and those deriving profit from trade, etc.; labourers in general.

WORKING-CLASS (2), [wurk'-ing-klahs'], *adj.* of, pertaining to, characteristic of, the working-class.

WORKING-DAY, [wurk'-ing-dā'], *n.* the number of hours in any day during which one regularly works; a day on which work is done or should be done.

WORKING-MAN, [wurk'-ing-man'], *n.* a man engaged in manual labour, a labourer; a member of the working-class.

WORKING-OUT, [wurk'-ing-owt'], *n.* the development and elaboration of any concept or theme, the series of resulting events from any one cause, etc.

WORKLESS, [wurk'-les], *adj.* unemployed, without work.

WORKMAN, [wurk'-man], *n.* one who does work, a person considered in respect of his work, a manual labourer, a member of the working-class.

WORKMANLIKE, [wurk'-man-līk'], *adj.* done in a skilful way as by a good workman.

WORKMANLY (1), [wurk'-man-li], *adj.* workman-like; having the appearance of a workman.

WORKMANLY (2), [wurk'-man-li], *adv.* in a workmanlike manner.

WORKMANSHIP, [wurk'-man-ship], *n.* the skill of a workman; the skill and craft employed on making anything; something made, *esp.* by manual labour.

WORK-PEOPLE, [wurk'-pēpl'], *n.* members of the working-class, manual workers.

WORK-ROOM, [wurk'-rōōm], *n.* a room for work.

WORKSHOP, [wurk'-shop'], *n.* a place where any work, *esp.* manual work, is done.

WORK-SHY, [wurk'-shī], *adj.* not eager to work, lazy.

WORK-TABLE, [wurk'-tābl], *n.* a table conveniently arranged and fitted for needlework.

WORKWOMAN, [wurk'-wŏŏm-an], *n.* a woman who does (manual) work, *esp.* needlework.

WORLD, [wurld], *n.* the universe, *esp.* the earth and the visible heavens; the earth; a planet resembling, or imagined to resemble, the earth; the earth and all creatures on it; the human race, men and women, society; life, terrestrial existence, this life; a state of existence; a department of terrestrial life and the creatures representing it considered as a unit; a sphere of interest or activity; a number of associated interests and activities and the persons concerned therein, considered as a group; the range of experience and activity of any single person; the ordinary affairs of life; material, temporal, non-spiritual activities and those persons who are more concerned with these than with things spiritual; secular life and its temptations; an era in the history of the human race, a stage in civilization; a great number of anything, a vast amount or extent; **the next w.,** the life after death; **w. without end,** eternally, for ever and ever; **the New W.,** the Americas, the Western Hemisphere; **the Old W.,** the Eastern Hemisphere, including Europe, Asia and Africa; **a man** (*or* **woman**) **of the w.,** one not innocent of the ways and habits of mankind, skilful in business and social adjustments; **for all the w. like** (*or* **as if**), closely resembling, very much as if; **to think the w. of** (*or* **a w. and all of**), to hold in very great affection, esteem. [OE. *weoruld*].

WORLD-HARDENED, [wurld'-hahd'-end], *adj.* hardened by too great fondness for, preoccupation with, worldly things.

WORLD-LANGUAGE, [wurld'-lang'-gwij], *n.* a language used or intended to be used universally, one artificially devised for such use.

WORLDLINESS, [wurld'-li-nes], *n.* the quality of being worldly.

WORLDLING, [wurld'-ling], *n.* one who thinks only of worldly things.

WORLDLY, [wurld'-li], *adj.* pertaining to the world, to this life or the business of human society; mundane, not spiritual, secular; concerned only with earthly pleasure and profit.

WORLDLY-MINDED, [wurld'-li-mīnd'-id], *adj.* devoted to earthly pleasure and profit.

WORLDLY-MINDEDNESS, [wurld'-li-mīnd'-id-nes], *n.* the condition of being worldly-minded.

WORLDLY-WISE [wurld'-li-wīz'], *adj.* possessing that philosphy and knowledge which is directed towards worldly pleasure and profit; knowledgeable in the ways of the world.

WORLD-OLD, [wurld'-ōld], *adj.* of great antiquity.

WORLD-POWER, [wurld'-pow'-er], *n.* a state or nation of major importance having world-wide influence and interests.

WORLD-WEARY, [wurld'-wēer'-i], *adj.* tired of this life.

WORLD-WIDE, [wurld'-wīd'], *adj.* spread into every part of the world.

WORM (1), [wurm], *n.* an invertebrate crawling creature without legs; the earthworm, any similar creature; †a snake, reptile, dragon; (*fig.*) a grovelling, obsequious, mean person; the groove of a screw; (*anat.*) a tendon under the tongue. [OE. *wyrm*].

WORM (2), [wurm], *v.t.* to bore, insinuate; to treat for intestinal worms; **to w. oneself into,** to enter by laborious or cautious means; **to w. one's way through,** to penetrate, pass through with great difficulty and effort; **to w. (information) out of,** to obtain (information) from by laborious and round-about methods. [*Prec.*].

WORM-CAST, [wurm'-cahst], *n.* a little heap of earth left by a worm.

WORM-EATEN, [wurm'-ēt'-en], *adj.* eaten into by worm-like insects; (*fig.*) out of date, so old as to be useless.

WORMED, [wurmd], *adj.* worm-eaten.

WORM-FENCE, [wurm'-fents'], *n.* a fence in which the interlacing palings are set in a zigzag fashion.

WORM-GEAR, [wurm'-gēer], *n.* a mechanical device in which a gear-wheel engages with and is driven by a worm-wheel.
WORM-GRASS, [wurm'-grahs], *n.* an American plant, *Spigelia marilandica.*
WORM-HOLE, [wurm'-hōl], *n.* a hole made by a worm or worm-like larva.
WORMINESS, [wurm'-i-nes], *n.* the state, or quality, of being wormy.
WORMING, [wurm'-ing], *n.* the action of cutting that tendon under a dog's tongue which is called the worm, in order to prevent madness; the process of treatment for intestinal worms.
WORM-LIKE, [wurm'-līk], *adj.* resembling a worm.
WORM-POWDER, [wurm'-pow-der], *n.* a powder for expelling parasitic worms from the intestines.
WORM-SEED, [wurm'-sēd], *n.* any seeds used as a vermifuge.
WORM-WHEEL, [wurm'-wēl'], *n.* a gear wheel cut in the form of a screw.
WORMWOOD, [wurm'-wŏŏd], *n.* the plant, *Artemisia absinthium*, notable for its bitter flavour and property as a vermifuge.
WORMY, [wurm'-i], *adj.* having many worms, worm-eaten; worm-like.
WORN, [wawn], *n.* damaged by continued or protracted use; (of a person's face or hands) marked with heavy toil, tired-looking.
WORN-OUT, [wawn'-owt'], *adj.* rendered useless by continuous service; (*fig.*) tired, exhausted.
WORRICOW, [wu'-ri-kow], *n.* (*Scots*) a hobgoblin; a grotesque person. [WORRY (2) and COW (1)].
WORRIED, [wu'-rid], *adj.* harassed with troubles and worries.
WORRIER, [wu'-ri-er], *n.* one who habitually worries.
WORRILESS, [wu'-ri-les], *adj.* free from worry.
WORRIMENT, [wu'-ri-ment], *n.* worry.
WORRIT (1), [wu'-rit], *n.* (*coll.*) worry.
WORRIT (2), [wu'-rit], *v.t. and i.* (*coll.*) to worry.
WORRY (1), [wu'-ri], *n.* the act of worrying or teasing; the state of being worried; anything that causes one to be worried.
WORRY (2), [wu'-ri], *v.t. and i.* (of a dog) to tease, shake in the teeth; to annoy, irritate, pester, *esp.* with a request or question; to make anxious, to distress, trouble; to feel anxiety, to ponder with vain persistence over some problem or trouble. [OE. *wyrgian*].
WORRYING, [wu'-ri-ing], *adj.* harassing, full of worries.
WORRYINGLY, [wu'-ri-ing-li], *adv.* in a worrying manner.
WORSE (1), [wurs], *n.* that which is worse; a worse state.
WORSE (2), [wurs], *adj.* to a greater extent, or in a greater measure, bad; less good, less satisfactory, less pleasing (than); not so well as before; **to be none the w. for,** to have received no injury on account of. [OE. *wyrsa*].
WORSE (3), [wurs], *adv.* to a worse degree, in a worse fashion. [OE. *wyrs*].
WORSEN, [wurs'-en], *v.t. and i.* to make worse; to grow worse.
WORSENING, [wurs'-en-ing], *n.* the act of growing worse; aggravation.
WORSHIP (1), [wur'-ship], *n.* praise and adoration offered to a deity, *esp.* to God; veneration, admiration, great respect; divine service; a title of a mayor; used in addressing a magistrate. [OE. *weorthscipe*].
WORSHIP (2), [wur'-ship], *v.t. and i.* to offer worship to (a deity); to love almost to excess; to perform an act of worship. [WORSHIP (1)].
WORSHIPABLE, [wur'-ship-abl], *adj.* fit to be worshipped.
WORSHIPFUL, [wor'-ship-fŏŏl], *adj.* deserving to be honoured, *esp.* as a title of mayors, etc.
WORSHIPFULLY, [wur'-ship-fŏŏl-i], *adv.* in a worshipful fashion.
WORSHIPFULNESS, [wur'-ship-fŏŏl-nes], *n.* the quality of being worshipful.
WORSHIPPER, [wur'-ship-er], *n.* one who offers worship; one attending divine service.
WORST (1), [wurst], *n.* that which is worst, most unlucky, or disastrous; the state of being worst.
WORST (2), [wurst], *adj.* in the greatest measure, to the greatest extent, bad. [OE. *wyrsta*].
WORST (3), [wurst], *adv.* in the worst way. [OE. *wyrst*].
WORST (4), [wurst], *v.t.* to overcome, outplay.
WORSTED (1), [wŏŏst'-id], *n.* a high-quality woollen yarn. [*Worstead*, in Norfolk, where first made].
WORSTED (2), [wŏŏst'-id], *adj.* made of worsted.
WORSTED (3), [wurst-id], *pret. and p.pt.* of WORST (4).
WORT (1), [wurt], *n.* a plant. [OE. *wyrt*].
WORT (2), [wurt], *n.* an infusion of malt before it has fermented. [OE. *wyrt*].
WORTH (1), [wurth], *n.* value or price; excellence, good, admirable qualities; the quantity obtainable for a given price. [OE. *wyrth*].
WORTH (2), [wurth], *adj.* possessing a stated value, valued at; having possessions amounting to; profitable; **for all one is w.,** to the utmost of one's powers; **to be w. while,** to be profitable, not useless; **to be w. it,** (*coll.*) to be profitable. [OE. *wyrthe*].
WORTH (3), [wurth], *v.t.* (*archaic, poet.*) in the phrase **woe w.** (with the object following); to happen, fall upon, befall. [OE. *weorthan* to become].
WORTHILY, [wurTH'-i-li], *adv.* in a worthy fashion.
WORTHINESS, [wurTH'-i-nes], *n.* the quality of being worthy.
WORTHLESS, [wurth'-les], *adj.* of no material value; of low principles and character.
WORTHLESSLY, [wurth'-les-li], *adv.* in worthless fashion.
WORTHLESSNESS, [wurth'-les-nes], *n.* the quality of being worthless.
WORTHY (1), [wurTH'-i], *n.* an excellent person, *esp.* one of importance; a notability, *esp.* local.
WORTHY (2), [wurTH'-i], *adj.* of sound principles, honourable, respectable; meritorious; **w. of,** deserving, meriting. [ME. *wurthi*].
WOT†, [wot], *v.i.* to know. [OE. *wat*].
WOULD, [wŏŏd], *pret.* of WILL (3). [OE. *wolde*].
WOULD-BE, [wŏŏd'-bē], *adj.* desiring or pretending to be but not succeeding.
WOULDST†, [wŏŏdst], *second pers. sg.* of WOULD.
WOUND (1), [wŏŏnd], *n.* a hurt to an animal body by which the skin is pierced or ripped; the mark on the skin from such a hurt both before and after healing; any similar hurt and the mark resulting, though not inflicted on an animal body; (*fig.*) pain caused to a person's feelings. [OE. *wund*].
WOUND (2), [wŏŏnd], *v.t.* to hurt as with a wound; (*fig.*) to cause mental or emotional distress to.
WOUND (3), [wownd], *pret. and p.pt.* of WIND (5). [OE. *wand*, *pret.* of *windan* to wind].
WOUNDER, [wŏŏnd'-er], *n.* the person or thing that wounds.
WOUNDING, [wŏŏnd'-ing], *n.* a wound, the act of one who wounds.
WOUNDLESS, [wŏŏnd'-les], *adj.* not wounded.
WOUND-WORT, [wŏŏnd'-wurt], *n.* one of various herbs at one time used in treating wounds.
WOURALI, see WOORALI.
WOU-WOU, see WOW-WOW
WOVE, [wōv], *adj.* **w. paper,** a fine variety of paper, made on a wire-gauze frame. [*Var.* of WOVEN].
WOVEN (1), [wōv'-en], *adj.* manufactured by a process of weaving.
WOVEN (2), [wōv'-en], *p.pt.* of WEAVE.
WOW, [wow], *n.* (*slang*) good fun, a remarkably successful affair.
WOWSER, [wow'-zer], *n.* (in Australia) a fanatical puritan. [Uncert.].
WOW-WOW, WOU-WOU, [wow'-wow], *n.* the silver gibbon found in Java. [Javanese *wawa*].
WRACK, [rak], *n.* a state of ruin; disaster; seaweed, etc., washed ashore. [ME. *wrac*].
WRACKFUL, [rak'-fŏŏl], *adj.* involving ruin, disastrous.
WRACKING, [rak'-ing], *n.* the act of collecting seaweed washed ashore.
WRAITH, [rāth], *n.* a ghost or apparition, *esp* one that appears as an omen of death; (*fig.*) a very thin, ill-looking person. [Unkn.].
WRANGLE (1), [rang'-gl], *n.* a heated argument.
WRANGLE (2), [rang'-gl], *v.i.* to argue or quarrel in a noisy, angry fashion. [ME. *wranglen*].
WRANGLER, [rang'-gler], *n.* one who wrangles; (at Cambridge University) one who is placed in the first class of Part II of the Mathematical Tripos; **senior w.,** a title formerly given to one who was top of the list for first-class honours in mathematics in any one year at Cambridge University.
WRANGLERSHIP, [rang'-gler-ship], *n.* the rank of a wrangler at Cambridge University.
WRANGLESOME, [rang'-gl-sum], *adj.* fond of wrangling.
WRANGLING, [rang'-gling], *n.* a wrangle.
WRAP (1), [rap], *n.* wrapping; a large scarf or other cloth to keep the body warm; **bath-w.,** a large towel.

WRAP (2), [rap], *v.t.* to enclose or enfold (in an outer covering); (*fig.*) to hide or mask; **to w. up,** to enfold in an outer covering; to conceal in verbose language; to put on or wear plenty of warm clothing; **to w. (something) round (something else),** to fold the one about the other. [ME. *wrappen*].

WRAPPAGE, [rap'-ij], *n.* that which is used to wrap something in; packing material.

WRAPPER, [rap'-er], *n.* a person or thing that wraps; something used as an envelope or outer covering; a wrap or scarf.

WRAPPING, [rap'-ing], *n.* that which is used to wrap something else in.

WRAP-RASCAL†, [rap'-rahs'-kal], *n.* a loose outer coat worn in the eighteenth century.

WRASSE, [ras], *n.* a sea-fish notable for its thick lips, found in European waters. [Corn. *wrach*]

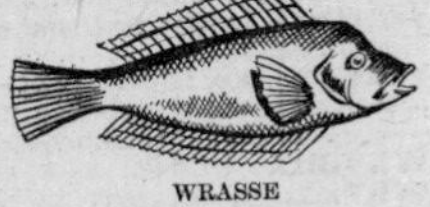
WRASSE

WRATH, [roth], *n.* great and violent anger. [~OE. *wræththu*].

WRATHFUL, [roth'-fōōl], *adj.* very angry.

WRATHFULLY, [roth'-fōōl-i], *adv.* in a wrathful fashion.

WRATHFULNESS, [roth'-fōōl-nes], *n.* the state or quality of being wrathful.

WRATHILY, [roth'-i-li], *adv.* in a wrathful manner.

WRATHLESS, [roth'-les], *adj.* not wrathful.

WRATHY, [roth'-i], *adj.* wrathful.

WRAWL, [rawl], *v.i.* to waul. [Echoic].

WREAK, [rēk], *v.t.* to inflict or execute; †to avenge. [OE. *wrecan* to avenge].

WREAKFUL, [rēk'-fōōl], *adj.* angry, vengeful.

WREAKLESS†, [rēk'-les], *adj.* not avenged.

WREATH, (*pl.* **wreaths**), [rēth, rēTHz], *n.* a circlet of twigs, leaves, and flowers given as a token of remembrance at a funeral, placed on a coffin or grave; a coronet of leaves symbolizing victory; a twisting wisp of vapour, etc.; (of snow) a piled-up drift. [OE. *writha*].

WREATHE, [rēTH], *v.t. and i.* to twist or twine; to wrap or coil round; to encircle with a wreath; to move in a twining, coiling way.

WREATHEN, [rēTH'-en], *adj.* twisted or coiled like a wreath.

WREATHLESS, [rēth'-les], *adj.* having no wreaths.

WREATHY, [rēth'-i], *adj.* twisted like a wreath.

WRECK (1), [rek], *n.* the destruction of, or grave damage done to, a ship by storm, rocks, etc.; an abandoned ship cast upon the shore; a disaster at sea ending in such damage to a vessel; any event of ruin or destruction; ruins left by such an event; (*fig.*) a complete overthrow of plans and ambitions; a person whose state suggests collapse or ruin. [AFr. *wrec*].

WRECK (2), [rek], *v.t. and i.* to bring (*esp.* a ship) to ruin and disaster; to be wrecked or ruined. [WRECK (1)].

WRECKAGE, [rek'-ij], *n.* the condition of being wrecked; the act of wrecking; the remains of a wrecked ship; fragments left over after any great disaster.

WRECKER, [rek'-er], *n.* one who deliberately causes a shipwreck in order to plunder the wreckage; one who deliberately causes ruin or destruction; a person who helps to save cargo from a wrecked ship.

WRECKMASTER, [rek'-mah'-ster], *n.* one responsible for all cargo that can be saved from a wrecked ship.

WREN (1), [ren], *n.* a genus of small passerine birds, the *Troglodites*. [OE. *wrenna*].

WREN (2), [ren], *n.* (*coll.*) a member of the *W*omen's *R*oyal *N*aval *S*ervice.

WRENCH (1), [rench], *n.* a sharp sudden screwing pull; a tool for screwing nuts on or off; a twist or jerk which injures a muscle or tendon; (*fig.*) emotional pain felt at parting with something familiar. [OE. *wrenc*].

WRENCH (2), [rench] *v.t.* to give a wrench to; to interpret in a false or distorting manner. [OE. *wrencan*].

WREST (1), [rest], *n.* a key used in tuning the wires of certain musical instruments.

WREST (2), [rest], *v.t.* to pull out by wrenching or tugging vigorously; to get by toil and effort; (of meanings of words) to twist, misinterpret. [OE. *wræstan*].

WRESTER, [rest'-er], *n.* one who wrests, a false interpreter.

WRESTLE, [resl], *v.t. and i.* to fight with another person by engaging him in a grip and trying to throw him down; to fight in this way; to fight in this way according to certain accepted rules as an athletic exercise; to earn one's living by this sort of fighting; **to w. with,** to struggle with in this way; (*fig.*) to labour in the mind with. [OE. *wræstlian*].

WRESTLER, [res'-ler], *n.* one who wrestles; one who earns a living by wrestling.

WRESTLING, [res'-ling], *n.* the sport in which wrestlers engage, the skill of a trained or professional wrestler.

WREST-PIN, [rest'-pin], *n.* one of the two pins to which either end of a piano string is fastened.

WRETCH, [rech], *n.* one afflicted by poverty or other misery; a person miserably unhappy, a contemptible person, a mean rascal. [OE. *wrecca* exile].

WRETCHED, [rech'-id], *adj.* unfortunate, miserable, unhappy, desperately poor or distressed; having no good qualities, lacking all or any comfort or decency, squalid, utterly undesirable; of very poor quality, contemptible, worthless.

WRETCHEDLY, [rech'-id-li], *adv.* in a wretched fashion or condition, miserably.

WRETCHEDNESS, [rech'-id-nes], *n.* the quality of being wretched.

WRIGGLE, [rigl], *v.t. and i.* to twist about to and fro, to writhe or squirm; (*fig.*) to endeavour to avoid the main issue; to cause to wriggle, to make twist about in a confined space; **to w. out of,** to get out of by wriggling; cleverly to avoid committing oneself on a vital point of discussion. [~LGerm. *wriggeln*].

WRIGGLER, [rig'-ler], *n.* a person or thing that wriggles; one who avoids the main point.

WRIGGLING, [rig'-ling], *n.* the action of one who wriggles.

WRIGHT, [rīt], *n.* (*archaic* and *dial.*) a maker, fashioner (of things, *esp.* ships, wheels, carts, and plays). [OE. *wyrhta*].

WRING (1), [ring], *n.* the act of one who wrings; a similar accomplishment by a machine.

WRING (2), (**wrung**), [ring], *v.t.* to squeeze by twisting very tightly; to grasp and squeeze; (*fig.*) (of an appeal to the feelings) to penetrate, hurt with poignancy; to get (out of) by wringing. [OE. *wringan*].

WRINGER, [ring'-er], *n.* that which wrings; a device for partly drying wet fabrics by squeezing them between rollers.

WRINGING, [ring'-ing], *adj.* in the phrase, **w. wet,** so wet that water could easily be wrung out.

WRINKLE (1), [ring'-kl], *n.* a small crease or furrow, *esp.* on the face. [OE. *wrincle*].

WRINKLE (2), [ring'-kl], *n.* a clever trick, a hint. [~OE. *wrenc*].

WRINKLE (3), [ring'-kl], *v.t. and i.* to make or become wrinkly; **to w. up,** to contract so that the surface becomes puckered; to contract and become wrinkly.

WRINKLY, [ring'-kli], *adj.* having many wrinkles.

WRIST (1), [rist], *n.* the narrow joint between the hand and arm; any similar joint; the lower end of a sleeve; a wrist-pin. [OE. *wrist*].

WRIST (2), [rist], *adj.* (*cricket and other games*) done by suppleness of the wrist.

WRISTBAND, [riz'-band], *n.* the cuff of a shirt.

WRISTLET (1), [rist'-let], *n.* a bracelet or strap for the wrist.

WRISTLET (2), [rist'-let], *adj.* fastened by a wristlet.

WRIST-PIN, [rist'-pin], *n.* a pin that juts out from the flat surface of a wheel, and to which a shaft is attached.

WRIST-PLATE, [rist'-plāt], *n.* a plate or revolving surface which has a wrist-pin attached.

WRIST-WATCH, [rist'-woch], *n.* a watch worn on the wrist, and attached by a strap or bracelet.

WRISTY, [rist'-i], *adj.* (*cricket and other games*) done by suppleness of the wrists.

WRIT (1), [rit], *n.* (*leg.*) a document containing royal instructions or instructions issued, *esp.* under royal authority; †something written; **Holy W.,** the Bible. [OE. *gewrit*].

WRIT† (2), [rit], *pret. and p.pt.* of WRITE.

WRITE, [rīt], *v.t. and i.* to mark paper, etc., with symbols, letters, words, etc.; to produce literary works; to communicate with by letter; to set down on paper, etc.; to give written expression to, to set down and publish in a book; to cover with words, symbols, etc.; to draft, draw up, complete, in writing; **to w. down,** to set down in written characters; to describe with less than the truth; to reduce in value, to simplify to excess; **to w. off,** to liquidate, cancel; **to w. for,** to send for by letter; **to w. up,** to describe in great detail, to give a glowing account of; to bring up to date; **to w. out,** to copy out in a clear, fair hand. [OE. *writan*].

WRITER, [rīt'-er], *n.* one who writes, *esp.* one who writes books, essays, etc.; a clerk; (*Scots*) a solicitor.

WRITER'S CRAMP, [rīt'-erz-kramp'], *n.* a cramp in the hand produced by a long spell of writing.

WRITERSHIP, [rīt'-er-ship], *n.* the position of a clerk or writer.
WRITHE (1), [rīth], *n.* the movement or part of the movement of one who writhes.
WRITHE (2), [rīth], *v.t. and i.* to twist and turn this way and that; to cause to do this. [OE. *writhan*].
WRITING, [rīt'-ing], *n.* the action of a writer, the art of penmanship; the characters and their style in any written document; a document or an inscription; the act of setting down in literary form, authorship.
WRITING-BOOK, [rīt'-ing-bŏŏk], *n.* a book of blank or ruled pages for writing in; a book containing writing exercises.
WRITING-CASE, [rīt'-ing-kās], *n.* a receptacle for pens, ink, paper, etc.
WRITING-DESK, [rīt'-ing-desk'], *n.* a desk or box for writing at, often having a sloping top.
WRITING-INK, [rīt'-ing-ingk'], *n.* ink for use with a pen but not with type.
WRITING-MASTER, [rīt'-ing-mah'-ster], *n.* one who teaches writing.
WRITING-PAPER, [rīt'-ing-pā'-per], *n.* paper that is properly glazed for writing upon.
WRITING-TABLE, [rīt'-ing-tābl'], *n.* a table suitably shaped and fitted for use as a desk.
WRITTEN, [ritn], *adj.* expressed in writing; penned, as opposed to printed or typed.
WRONG (1), [rong], *n.* that which is wrong; an injustice, unkindness, a vicious act (against somebody); evil, wickedness; **to do w.**, to commit sin.
WRONG (2), [rong], *adj.* not right, not just and good, sinful, vicious; false, inaccurate, not true; not well ordered; not as was intended; **the w. end of the stick**, a false impression; **to be on the w. side of**, to have incurred the hostility of; **a w. 'un**, (*coll.*) a person of criminal tendencies. [OE. *wrang*].
WRONG (3), [rong], *adv.* wrongly; **to go w.**, to break down, cease to operate, turn out badly.
WRONG (4), [rong], *v.t.* to do violence or wrong to, to act unjustly or unkindly to; to accuse falsely.
WRONGDOER, [rong'-dōō'-er], *n.* one who does what is wrong, a sinner.
WRONGDOING, [rong'-dōō'-ing], *n.* a wrong action; sin.
WRONGER, [rong'-er], *n.* one who wrongs another person.
WRONGFUL, [rong'-fŏŏl], *adj.* wicked, unfair, mistaken; (*leg.*) adversely affecting another's rights.
WRONGFULLY, [rong'-fŏŏl-i], *adv.* in a wrongful fashion.
WRONGFULNESS, [rong'-fŏŏl-nes], *n.* the quality of being wrongful.
WRONG-HEADED, [rong'-hed'-id], *adj.* obstinately mistaken, stubborn, deliberately perverse.
WRONG-HEADEDNESS, [rong'-hed'-id-ness], *n.* the quality of being wrong-headed.
WRONGLESSLY, [rong'-les-li], *adv.* without doing injury, harmlessly.
WRONGLY, [rong'-li], *adv.* in a wrong way, unfairly, inaccurately.
WRONGNESS, [rong'-nes], *n.* the state or quality of being wrong.
WRONGOUS, [rong'-us], *adj.* (*Scots leg.*) not legal, not just.
WROTE, [rōt], *pret.* of WRITE. [OE. *wrat*].
WROTH†, [rōth, roth], *adj.* very angry. [OE. *wrath*].
WROUGHT (1), [rawt], *adj.* fashioned by beating, and not in a mould. [OE. *geworht*].
WROUGHT (2), [rawt], *pret. and p.pt.* of WORK.
WROUGHT-IRON, [rawt'-iern'], *n.* iron that is shaped by beating, not cast in a mould.
WRUNG, [rung], *pret. and p.pt.* of WRING (2). [OE. *gewrungen*].
WRY, [rī], *adj.* twisted or contorted; **a w. face**, a face for the moment wrinkled up to express disapproval or discomfort. [ME. *wrie*].
WRYBILL, [rī'-bil], *n.* a variety of plover.
WRYLY, [rī'-li], *adv.* in a wry fashion.
WRYNECK, [rī'-nek'], *n.* a bird, the *Iynx torquilla*; a bent neck.
WRY-NECKED, [rī'-nekt'], *adj.* having a deformed or stiff neck.
WRYNESS, [rī'-nes], *n.* the condition of being wry.

WRYBILL

WULFENITE, [wŏŏlf'-en-īt], *n.* (*min.*) a crystalline molybdate of lead. [Germ. *wulfenit*].
WUZZY, [wuz'-i], *adj.* (*coll.*) muzzy. [Symbolic].
WYANDOTTE, [wī'-an-dot], *n.* a breed of U.S. poultry of medium size. [The *Wyandotte* tribe of Red Indians].
WYCH-ELM, WITCH-ELM, [wich'-elm'], *n.* a variety of elm, the *Ulmus montana*. [OE. *wice* a tree with flexible branches and ELM].
WYCH-HAZEL, WITCH-HAZEL, [wich'-hāzl], *n.* a North American shrub, *Hamamelis virginica*, yielding an astringent extract. [~*Prec.* and HAZEL].
WYCLIFFITE (1), [wik'-lif-īt], *n.* a follower of John *Wycliffe*, the English religious reformer.
WYCLIFFITE (2), [wik'-lif-īt], *adj.* of or pertaining to Wycliffe or his doctrines or followers.
WYKEHAMIST, [wik'-am-ist], *n.* a pupil of Winchester College. [William of *Wykeham*, the founder].
WYND, [wīnd], *n.* (*Scots*) a narrow walled alley. [~OE. *gewind*].
WYVERN, see WIVERN.

X

X, [eks], the twenty-fourth letter of the English alphabet; the symbol for ten in Roman figures; an unknown quantity in mathematics; anything unknown.
XANTH-, XANTHO-, [zan'-th(ō)], *pref.* yellow. [Gk. *xanthos* yellow].
XANTHATE, [zan'-thāt], *n.* (*chem.*) a salt produced by xanthic acid.
XANTHEIN, [zan'-thē-in], *n.* a soluble yellow colouring matter found in flowers.
XANTHIAN, [zan'-thi-an], *adj.* relating to *Xanthus* in Asia Minor.
XANTHIC, [zan'-thik], *adj.* yellow; **x. acid**, an organic acid with yellow salts.
XANTHIN, [zan'-thin], *n.* xanthine; the insoluble part of the yellow colouring matter found in flowers.
XANTHINE, [zan'-thēn], *n.* (*physiol.*) a compound found in animal bodies and forming a yellow substance with nitric acid.
XANTHITE, [zan'-thīt], *n.* (*min.*) a yellow crystalline rock.
XANTHOCHROI, [zan-thō'-kroi], *n.*(*pl.*) those races which have a fair complexion and blond hair. [XANTHO- and Gk. *okhros* pale].
XANTHOCHROIC, [zan'-thō-krō'-ik], *adj.* having a fair complexion; pertaining to the xanthochroi.
XANTHOCONITE, [zan'-tho-kon'-īt], *n.* a yellow arsenio-sulphide of silver. [XANTHO- and Gk. *konis* dust].
XANTHOMA, [zan-thō'-ma], *n.* a skin disease symptomized by yellow blotches. [~Gk. *xanthos* yellow].
XANTHOMELANOUS, [zan'-thō-mel'-an-us], *adj.* having a yellowish or brown skin and black hair. [XANTHO- and Gk. *melas* black].
XANTHOPHYLL, [zan'-thō-fil], *n.* the yellow colouring matter in dead leaves. [XANTHO- and Gk. *phullon* leaf].
XANTHOPHYLLITE, [zan-tho'-fil-īt], *n.* (*min.*) a yellow mineral resembling mica.
XANTHORTHITE, [zan-thaw'-thīt], *n.* a yellowish kind of orthite. [XANTH- and ORTHITE].
XANTHOSIDERITE, [zan'-thō-sid'-er-īt], *n.* a yellow or brownish hydrated oxide of iron. [XANTHO- and Gk. *sideros* iron].
XANTHOSIS, [zan-thō'-sis], *n.* a yellow discoloration of the skin associated with cancer. [XANTH- and Gk. *osis* denoting condition].
XANTHOUS, [zan'-thus], *adj.* yellow, belonging to the yellow-skinned races. [Gk. *xanthos*].
XANTIPPE, [zan-tip'-i], *n.* a bad-tempered woman, a scold, shrew. [*Xantippe*, the wife of Socrates].

XEBEC, ZEBEC, ZEBECK, [zē'-bek], *n.* a small Mediterranean sailing vessel. [*Span.* †*xabeque*].
XEMA, [zē-ma], *n.* a genus of birds that includes the fork-tailed gulls. [Invented].

XEMA

XENELASIA, [zen'-i-lāz'-i-a], *n.* the custom by which the Spartans permitted no foreign settlers in their territory. [Gk. *xenelasia*].
XENIAL, [zē'-ni-al], *adj.* relating to the relationship of guest and host. [Gk. *xenia* the status of guest].
XENIUM, (*pl.* **xenia**), [zē'-ni-um], *n.* a gift to a stranger or foreigner. [Gk. *xenion*].
XENO-, [zen'-ō], *pref.* pertaining to things outside, or to hospitality. [Gk. *xenos* stranger].
XENODOCHIUM, (*pl.* **xenodochia**), [zē'-nō-dok'-i-um], *n.* an apartment for guests. [Gk. *xenodokeion*].
XENODOCHY, [ze-nod'-ok-i], *n.* the act of hospitality; a xenodochium.
XENOGAMY, [zen-og'-a-mi], *n.* (*bot.*) fertilization from a different plant of the same species. [XENO- and Gk. *gamos* marriage].
XENOGENESIS, [ze'-nō-jen'-is-is], *n.* the birth of offspring dissimilar from the parents. [XENO- and GENESIS].
XENOGENOUS, [zen-oj'-in-us], *adj.* caused by an outside force.
XENOLITE, [zen'-ō-līt], *n.* a fibrous aluminium silicate. [XENO- and Gk. *lithos* stone].
XENOMANIA, [zen'-ō-mā'-ni-a], *n.* excessive admiration for foreign people, things. [XENO- and MANIA].
XENOMORPHIC, [zen'-ō-mawf'-ik], *adj.* (*geol.*) abnormal in shape on account of pressure from surrounding matter. [XENO- and Gk. *morphe* shape].
XENON, [zen'-on], *n.* (*chem.*) the inert gaseous element denoted by Xe. [Gk. *xenos* strange].
XENOTIME, [zen'-ō-tīm], *n.* (*min.*) a yellow native phosphate of yttrium. [XENO- and Gk. *time* honour].
XERASIA, [zēer-ā'-zi-a], *n.* a dryness of the scalp causing baldness. [Gk. *xerasia*].
XERO-, [zēer'-ō], *pref.* dry. [Gk. *xeros* dry].
XERODERMA, [zē'-rō-dur'-ma], *n.* a diseased dryness of the skin. [XERO- and DERMA].
XERODES, [zē'-rōd-ēz], *n.* a tumour accompanied by dryness.
XEROPHAGY, [zē-rof'-a-ji], *n.* a fast among early Christians at which only dry food was eaten. [Gk. *xerophagia*].
XEROPHILOUS, [zē-rof'-il-us], *adj.* (*bot.*) flourishing in dry ground. [XERO- and Gk. *philos* living].
XEROPHTHALMIA, [zēer'-of-thal'-mi-a], *n.* a dry soreness of the eye, a sort of conjunctivitis. [Gk. *xerophthalmia*].
XEROPHYTE, [zēer'-ō-fīt], *n.* (*bot.*) a plant that grows in very dry ground. [XERO- and Gk. *phuton* plant].
XEROSTOMIA, [zēer'-ō-stō'-mi-a], *n.* great dryness in the mouth. [XERO- and Gk. *stoma* mouth].
XIPHIAS, [zif'-i-as], *n.* the genus of swordfish. [Gk. from *xiphos* a sword].
XIPHIOID, [zif'-i-oid], *adj.* of or like a swordfish. [Gk. *xiphias* swordfish and *oeides* like].
XIPHOID, [zif'-oid], *adj.* shaped like a sword; **x. process,** (*anat.*) an appendage of cartilage from under the sternum. [Gk. *xiphoeides*].
XOANON, [zō'-an-on], *n.* a wooden statue of a god or goddess. [Gk. *xoanon* sculpture in wood].
X-RAYS, [eks'-rāz'], *n.*(*pl.*) rays which are found in the spectrum beyond the ultra-violet and which can penetrate matter opaque to light-rays. [X and RAY].
XYLEM, [zī'-lem], *n.* the harder wood-like part of any plant body. [Germ. *xylem* from Gk. *xulon* wood and (PHLO)EM].
XYLENE, [zī'-lēn], *n.* (*chem.*) xylol.
XYLITE, [zī'-līt], *n.* (*min.*) a fibrous silicate of iron. [XYL(O)- and Gk. *lithos* stone].
XYL(O)-, *pref.* pertaining to wood. [Gk. *xulon* wood].
XYLOBALSAMUM, [zi'-lō-bawl'-sam-um], *n.* the wood of the tree, *Balsamodendron gileadense*, from which balm of Gilead is obtained; balm of Gilead itself. [Gk. *xulobalsamon*].
XYLOCARP, [zī'-lō-kahp'], *n.* a fruit that is hard and woody or a tree that has such fruit. [XYLO- and Gk. *karpos* fruit].
XYLOCHLORE, [zī'-lō-klaw(r)], *n.* a variety of apophyllite found in Iceland. [Germ. *xylokhlor* from Gk. *xulon* wood and *khloros* green].
XYLOGRAPH, [zī'-lō-graf], *n.* a primitive wood-engraving; the graining of wood in paint. [XYLO- and Gk. *graphia* writing].
XYLOGRAPHER, [zī-log'-raf-er], *n.* one skilled in wood-engraving.
XYLOGRAPHIC, [zi'-lō-graf'-ik], *adj.* printed by, or relating to, xylography.
XYLOGRAPHY, [zi-log'-ra-fi], *n.* the craft of engraving; letterpress on wood blocks. [XYLO- and Gk. *graphia* writing].
XYLOID, [zī'-loid], *adj.* resembling wood. [XYLO- and Gk. *oeides* like].
XYLOIDIN, XYLOIDINE, [zī-loi'-din], *n.* a preparation resembling, but less dangerous than, guncotton. [*Prec.*].
XYLOL, [zī'-lol], *n.* (*chem.*) a mixture of isomeric hydrocarbons prepared from wood-spirit.
XYLONITE, [zī'-lon-īt], *n.* celluloid.
XYLOPHAGAN, [zī-lof'-ag-an], *n.* (*zool.*) an insect or larva that feeds on wood by boring into it.
XYLOPHAGOUS, [zī-lof'-ag-us], *adj.* (*zool.*) feeding on wood. [XYLO- and Gk. *phago* I eat].
XYLOPHONE, [zī'-lō-fōn], *n.* a musical instrument consisting of a series of wooden bars, each sounding a different note when struck. [XYLO- and Gk. *phone* sound].
XYLOPYROGRAPHY, [zī'-lō-pier-og'-ra-fi], *n.* the art of making a design on wood by tracing with a red-hot metal implement. [XYLO- and Gk. *pur* fire and *graphia* writing].
XYST, [zist], *n.* (*class. antiq.*) a covered court for athletic exercises; a sheltered path in a garden. [Gk. *xustos*].
XYSTUS, (*pl.* **xysti**), [zist'-us], *n.* a xyst. [Gk. *xustos*].

Y, [wī], the twenty-fifth letter of the English alphabet; anything resembling this in shape.
YACCA-WOOD, [yak'-a-wōōd], *n.* the wood of a small West Indian tree. [Native].
YACHT (1), [yot], *n.* a light sailing vessel; a small pleasure steamer. [Du. *jacht*].
YACHT (2), [yot], *v.i.* to sail a yacht.
YACHT-CLUB, [yot'-klub'], *n.* a club of persons interested in yachting.
YACHTER, [yot'-er], *n.* one who sails a yacht.
YACHTING, [yot'-ing], *n.* the craft of sailing a yacht; the practice of sailing a yacht for pleasure or racing.
YACHTSMAN, [yots'-man], *n.* a yachter.
YACHTSMANSHIP, [yots'-man-ship], *n.* the art of yachting; the skill with which such art is practised.
YAFFLE, YAFFIL, [yafl], *n.* (*prov.*) the green woodpecker. [Echoic].
YAGER, [yā'-ger], *n.* a German rifleman, mounted or on foot; a hunter, sportsman. [Germ. *jager* hunter].
YAHOO, [yah-hōō'], *n.* a member of an imaginary race of creatures, resembling human beings in form, but filthy and animal-like in habits, described in Swift's *Gulliver's Travels*; a human being resembling this. [Coined by Swift].
YAHWEH, [yah'-vā], *n.* the deity of the Jews, Jehovah. [Heb. *Yahaveh*].
YAHWIST, [yah'-vist], *n.* the writer of those portions of the Hexateuch in which the word *Jehovah* is used instead of *Elohim* for *God*.
YAHWISTIC, [yah-vist'-ik], *adj.* of, pertaining or relating to, Yahweh or those parts of the Hexateuch that refer to God as "Yahweh."
YAK, [yak], *n.* a bovine animal, found in Central Asia, and remarkable for its long hair. [Tibetan *gyak*].
YAM, [yam], *n.* any plant of the tropical genus *Dioscorea*; the edible tuber of any such plant. [African].

YAMA, [yah'-ma], *n.* the judge of the dead according to Hinduism. [Skr. *yama*].
YAMUN, YAMEN, [yah'-men], *n.* an administrative office in China, a mandarin's house. [Chin. *yamun*].
YANK (1), [yangk], *n.* (*slang*) a Yankee.
YANK (2), [yangk], *n.* (*slang*) a sharp pull, a tug.
YANK (3), [yangk], *v.t. and i.* (*slang*) to give a yank or tug to, to pull. [Unkn.].
YANKEE, [yangk'-ē], *n.* an American living in New England, *esp.* of the stock of original settlers, or in the northern states generally; an American. [Uncert.].
YANKEE, [yangk'-ē], *adj.* American.
YANKEEFIED, [yang'-ki-fīd], *adj.* made to resemble the corresponding thing in America; having acquired the characteristics of a Yankee.
YANKEEISM, [yang'-ki-izm], *n.* a Yankee habit, Yankee customs in general.
YAOURT, [yah'-awt], *n.* a Turkish beverage of fermented milk. [Turk. *yoghurt*].
YAP (1), [yap], *n.* a quick excited bark from a dog.
YAP (2), [yap], *v.i.* to utter yaps, (*coll., slang*) to chatter. [Echoic].
YAPOCK, [yap'-ok], *n.* a water opossum found in South America. [River *Oyapok* in Brazil].
YAPON, [yawp'-on], *n.* a North American evergreen from the leaves of which a tea can be brewed which acts as a purgative. [Native].
YAPP, [yap], *n.* a manner of bookbinding in limp leather so that the edges of the covers project beyond the leaves. [*Yapp*, a bookseller].
YARBOROUGH, [yah'-bur-er], *n.* a hand of cards containing nothing higher than nine. [The Earl of *Yarborough*, who betted that so poor a hand was impossible].
YARD (1), [yahd], *n.* a length measure of three feet; this length of anything; (in a sailing ship) a subsidiary pole fastened at an angle to the mast and carrying the sails. [OE. *gerd* a rod].
YARD (2), [yahd], *n.* an (often) paved enclosure near a house or farm; any similar enclosed space; a space adjoining industrial buildings or plant, or for assembling and distributing goods trains, etc.; **the Y.,** Scotland Yard, the London Metropolitan Police headquarters. [OE. *geard*].
YARDAGE, [yahd'-ij], *n.* the right to put cattle in a stockyard; the cost of this.
YARD-ARM, [yahd'-ahm], *n.* (*naut.*) either half of a yard as measured from the mast.
YARDMAN, [yahd'-man], *n.* one who works in a (railway) yard.
YARDMASTER, [yahd'-mah'-ster], *n.* an official in charge of a (railway) yard.
YARD-MEASURE, [yahd'-mezh'-er], *n.* a stick a yard long with lesser measurements marked on it.
YARD-STICK, [yahd'-stik], *n.* a yard-measure; a basis of comparison.
YARD-WAND, [yahd'-wond'], *n.* a yard-measure.
YARE†, [yāer], *adj.* active, nimble, ready. [OE. *gearu* ready].
YARELY†, [yāer'-li], *adv.* quickly.
YARN (1), [yahn], *n.* woven fibre for cloth, rope, etc.; (*coll.*) a story, anecdote, *esp.* an exaggerated tale; a comfortable talk or chat. [OE. *gearn*].
YARN (2), [yahn], *v.i.* (*coll.*) to tell a story, to talk in a wordy fashion.
YARROW, [ya'-rō], *n.* the plant, *Achillea millefolium*, otherwise called milfoil. [OE. *gearwe*].
YARWHELP, [yah'-welp], *n.* (*prov.*) a name given to both the bar-tailed godwit and the black-tailed godwit. [Uncert.].
YASHMAK, [yash'-mak], *n.* a veil covering the face from beneath the eyes down, as worn by Mohammedan women. [Arab. *yashmaq*].
YATAGHAN, [yat'-ag-an], *n.* an oriental sword with no hilt and a double-curved blade. [Turk. *yataghan*].
YATE, [yāt], *n.* a name given to two varieties of Australian gum-tree, the *Eucalyptus cornuta* and the *Eucalyptus occidentalis*. [Native].
YAW (1), [yaw], *n.* (*naut.*) the action of yawing. [YAW (2)].
YAW (2), [yaw], *v.i.* (*naut., aeron.*) to follow an uncertain wavering course. [~OIcel. *jaga* to swing on a hinge].
YAWL (1), [yawl], *n.* a small sailing ship equipped with a main mast and a jigger and built like a cutter; a small rowing boat, a ship's boat. [Du. *jol*].
YAWL (2), see YOWL.
YAWN (1), [yawn], *n.* the act of yawning. [*Next*].
YAWN (2), [yawn], *v.i.* to open the mouth wide and breathe in and out as when sleepy; to gape wide open. [~OE. *gesnian*].
YAWNING, [yawn'-ing], *adj.* gaping widely.
YAWNINGLY, [yawn'-ing-li], *adv.* in a yawning fashion, with a yawn.
YAWS, [yawz], *n.* a tropical disease of the skin caused by a protozoan parasite. [Uncert.].
YCLEPT†, **YCLEPED**†, [i-klept', i-klēpt'], *adj.* called, named. [OE. *geclypod*].
YE† **(1),** [yē], *second pers. pl. personal pron.* you. [OE. *ge*].
YE (2), [THē, yē], *def. art.* the. [Initial *y* is a misreading of a similarly shaped letter formerly used for *th*].
YEA, [yā], *int.* (*archaic*) yes. [OE. *gea*].
YEAN, [yēn], *v.t. and i.* to give birth (to a lamb or kid). [OE. *geeanian*].
YEANLING, [yēn'-ling], *n.* a very young kid or lamb.
YEAR, [yēer], *n.* that length of time in which the earth travels once round the sun, reckoned as 365 days, but more accurately 365¼ days; a space of 365 or 366 days; **leap y.,** a year of 366 days occurring as every fourth year; **a y. and a day,** a (legal) formula to make certain that a whole year elapses; **y. by y.,** every year; **y. in and y. out,** year after year successively, with monotonous regularity and seeming endlessness; **full of years,** (*bibl., archaic*) very old. [OE. *gear*].
YEAR-BOOK, [yēer'-book], *n.* a reference book issued in a revised edition each year.
YEARLING (1), [yēer'-ling], *n.* an animal (*esp.* a racehorse) in its second year.
YEARLING (2), [yēer'-ling], *adj.* being one year old.
YEARLONG, [yēer'-long], *adj.* lasting a full year.
YEARLY (1), [yēer'-li], *adj.* annual.
YEARLY (2), [yēer'-li], *adv.* year by year, annually.
YEARN, [yurn], *v.i.* to desire greatly; **to y. for,** to feel a deep love or longing for. [OE. *geornan*].
YEARNFUL, [yurn'-fōōl], *adj.* sad, mournful.
YEARNING (1), [yurn'-ing], *n.* a desire or longing.
YEARNING (2), [yurn'-ing], *adj.* desirous, expressing desire.
YEARNINGLY, [yurn'-ing-li], *adv.* in a yearning manner.
YEAST, YEST†, [yēst, yest], *n.* a pungent yellow fungus organism which, when mingled with sugary fluid, causes fermentation; the same substance when it has been dried for preservation. [OE. *gest*].
YEASTINESS, [yēst'-i-nes], *n.* the quality of being yeasty.
YEASTY, YESTY†, [yēst'-i, yest'-i], *adj.* pertaining to yeast; (*fig.*) frothy, verbose, restless, pointless.
YEGG, [yeg], *n.* (*U.S. slang*) a burglar. [Unkn.].
YELK, see YOLK.
YELL (1), [yel], *n.* the noise made when someone yells.
YELL (2), [yel], *v.t. and i.* to scream, cry, howl very loudly; to laugh very loudly; to say loudly and excitedly. [OE. *gellan*].
YELLING, [yel'-ing], *n.* the act of uttering a yell; a loud outcry.
YELLOW (1), [yel'-ō], *n.* one of the primary colours, which, in combination with blue, makes green, or with red, orange; a pigment giving this colour; (*fig.*) the yolk of an egg. [YELLOW (2)].
YELLOW (2), [yel'-ō], *adj.* having the colour yellow; belonging to a Mongolian race; (*U.S. slang*) timid, cowardly, mean; **y. jack,** yellow fever. [OE. *geolu*].
YELLOWBIRD, [yel'-ō-burd'], *n.* the goldfinch of North America.
YELLOW-BOY, [yel'-ō-boi'], *n.* (*slang*) any gold coin.
YELLOW-EARTH, [yel'-ō-urth'], *n.* a clay pigment producing a yellow colour.
YELLOW-FEVER, [yel'-ō-fē'-ver], *n.* a tropical fever often imparted by a mosquito bite, and marked by jaundice.
YELLOW-HAMMER, [yel'-ō-ham'-er], *n.* the yellow-feathered bird, *Emberiza citrinella*. [YELLOW and OE. *amore, hamere* a kind of bird].

YELLOW-HAMMER

YELLOWISH, [yel'-ō-ish], *adj.* rather yellow.
YELLOWISHNESS, [yel'-ō-ish-nes], *n.* a yellowish quality.
YELLOWNESS, [yel'-ō-nes], *n.* the quality of having a yellow colour.
YELLOW PRESS, [yel'-ō-pres'], *n.* highly sensational news publications, and the organizations behind them.
YELLOWS, [yel'-ōz], *n.* a form of jaundice that attacks cattle.
YELLOW-WORT, [yel'-ō-wurt'], *n.* the yellow-flowered plant, *Chlora perfoliata*.
YELLOWY, [yel'-ō-i], *adj.* somewhat yellow.
YELP (1), [yelp], *n.* a short, high-pitched bark.

YELP (2), [yelp], *v.i.* to give out a yelp. [OE. *gelpan* to boast].
YELPER, [yelp'-er], *n.* one who yelps.
YEN (1), [yen], *n.* a Japanese coin worth, at par, a little more than two shillings. [Jap. *yen*].
YEN (2), [yen], *n.* (*U.S. slang*) an urge or desire. [Unkn.].
YEOMAN, (*pl.* **yeomen**), [yō'-man, yō'-men], *n.* (*hist.*) a superior attendant in a royal or lordly household; a small freeholder or farmer; a member of a mounted force of men of this rank; **the Yeomen of the Guard**, a royal bodyguard now stationed at the Tower of London; **y. service**, invaluable aid. [ME. *yoman*].
YEOMANLIKE, [yō'-man-līk], *adj.* befitting a yeoman.
YEOMANLY, [yō'-man-li], *adj.* yeomanlike.
YEOMANRY, [yō'-man-ri], *n.* (*milit.*) a volunteer cavalry force formerly recruited from the class of small farmers; yeomen and small landholders in general.
YEP, [yep], *int.* (*U.S. coll.*) yes. [~YES].
YERBA, [yur'-ba], *n.* maté. [Span. *yerba* a herb].
YERCUM, [yur'-kum], *n.* a shrub found in the East Indies, the bark of which is used to make a fibre; this fibre. [Tamil].
YERK, [yurk], *v.t.* to jab or stab; to lash or strike. [Unkn.].
YES, [yes], *int.* expressing agreement or affirmation; used interrogatively expressing a desire for further information; [OE. *gese*].
YES-MAN, [yes'-man'], *n.* (*U.S. slang*) a docile, characterless fellow who never dares to disagree.
YEST†, see YEAST.
YESTER-, [yest'-er], *pref.* (*archaic*) relating to yesterday; preceding, last before this. [OE. *geostran*].
YESTERDAY (1), [yes'-ter-di], *n.* the day before this one. [OE. *geostran dæg*].
YESTERDAY (2), [yes'-ter-di], *adv.* on the day before this one.
YESTERNIGHT (1), [yes'-ter-nīt'], *n.* (*archaic*) last night. [OE. *gystran niht*].
YESTERNIGHT (2), [yes'-ter-nīt], *adv.* (*archaic*) last night.
YESTREEN (1), [yes-trēn'], *n.* (*archaic*) last evening.
YESTREEN (2), [yes-trēn'], *adv.* (*archaic*) on the evening of yesterday. [YESTER- and OE. *æfen* evening].
YESTY†, see YEASTY.
YET (1), [yet], *adv.* until and including this moment, still; at this moment and for some time into the future; **. . . nor y.**, not even, not so much as; **as y.**, up to the present, so far. [OE. *get*].
YET (2), [yet], *conj.* moreover, in addition, nevertheless.
YEW (1), [yōō], *n.* the evergreen conifer, *Taxus baccata*; the wood of this tree. [OE. *eow*].
YEW (2), [yōō], *adj.* made of yew wood.
YEWEN, [yōō'-en], *adj.* (*archaic*) made of yew wood.
YEZIDI, [yez'-id-ē], *n.* a member of a religious sect in the eastern parts of Asia Minor and the Euphrates Valley, the peculiarity of whose religion is the deep awe with which they regard the devil. [Uncert.].
Y-GUN, [wī'-gun], *n.* (*nav.*) a gun with two barrels set at an angle.
YID, [yid], *n.* (*slang*) a Jew. [YIDDISH].
YIDDISH (1), [yid-ish], *n.* a Judaized form of German written in Hebrew characters and containing a considerable Slavonic element. [Germ. *jüdisch* Jewish].
YIDDISH (2), [yid'-ish], *adj.* pertaining to or in Yiddish.
YIELD (1), [yēld], *n.* profit, produce, crop.
YIELD (2), [yēld], *v.t. and i.* to produce, give forth, generate (implying profitable production); to surrender, give up willingly; to provide produce or profit; to surrender, admit defeat; to move, withdraw, bend back under physical pressure. [OE. *geldan* to pay].
YIELDER, [yēld'-er], *n.* a person who yields.
YIELDING, [yēld'-ing], *adj.* compliant, submissive, ready to surrender; bendable, pliant, flexible.
YIELDINGLY, [yēld'-ing-li], *adv.* in yielding fashion.
YIELDINGNESS, [yēld'-ing-nes], *n.* the quality of being yielding.
YLANG-YLANG, [il-ang'-il-ang'], *n.* the Malayan tree, *Canangium odoratum*. [Tagalog *alang-ilang*].
Y-MOTH, [wī'-moth], *n.* any moth of the genus *Plusia*, the markings of which are shaped like a Y.
YODEL (1), [yōdl], *n.* any musical phrase sung in alternate natural and falsetto pitch. [YODEL (2)].
YODEL (2), [yōdl], *v.t. and i.* to sing in alternately natural and falsetto pitch in the Tyrolean manner. [Germ. *jodeln*]
YOGA, [yō'-ga], *n.* a meditative Hindu philosophy which aims at uniting the individual soul with the universal spirit. [Hind. *yoga*].
YOGHOURT, [yŏg'-hōōert, yōg-urt], *n.* a European variety of yaourt. [Turk. *yoghurt*].
YOGI, [yō'-gi], *n.* a Hindu who practises yoga. [Hind. *yogi*].
YO-HEAVE-HO, [yō'-hēv-hō'], *int.* (*naut.*) the cry of sailors working a capstan.
YOHIMBE, [yō-him'-bā], *n.* a West African tree of the *Rubiaceæ*. [Native].
YOHIMBIN, [yō-him'-bin], *n.* an alkaloid extracted from yohimbe used as an aphrodisiac.
YOHO, [yō-hō'], *int.* (*naut.*) the shout of sailors working a capstan.
YOICK, [yō'-ik], *v.i.* to utter a yoicks.
YOICKS, [yō'-ikz], *int.* hunting cry. [Unkn.].
YOJAN, [yō'-jan], *n.* a variable Indian measure of distance. [Hind. *yojan*].
YOKE (1), [yōk], *n.* the wooden crosspiece put over the shoulders of cattle used for draught; anything like this; that part of a garment which fits the shoulders; a pair of oxen harnessed together for ploughing; (*fig.*) authority, rule, obligation. [OE. *geoc*].
YOKE (2), [yōk], *v.t.* to harness with a yoke; (*fig.*) to join in the same bond or servitude.
YOKE-FELLOW, [yōk'-fel-ō], *n.* a companion in toil.
YOKEL, [yōkl], *n.* a rustic. [Uncert.].
YOKEMATE, [yōk'-māt], *n.* yoke-fellow.
YOKOHAMA, [yōk'-ō-hahm'-a], *n.* the name of a port in Japan used to denote a breed of ornamental jungle-fowl or a fine kind of crape.
YOLK (1), **YELK**†, [yōk], *n.* the yellow middle part of an egg.
YOLK (2), [yōk], *n.* the oily secretion which keeps the wool of the sheep soft, lanolin. [OF. **eowoca*].
YOLKY (1), [yōk'-i], *adj.* like yolk.
YOLKY (2), [yōk'-i], *adj.* greasy with yolk. [OE. *eowocig*].
YON (1), [yon], *adj.* that over there. [OE. *geon*].
YON (2), [yon], *pron.* (*prov.*) that.
YON (3), [yon], *adv.* over yonder.
YOND† (1), [yond], *adj.* that, further, more distant. [ME. *yeonde*].
YOND (2), [yond], *pron.* (*dial.*) yon.
YONDER (1), [yond'-er], *adj.* situated over there. [ME. *yonder*].
YONDER (2), [yond'-er], *adv.* over there.
YONI, [yō'-ni], *n.* a representation of the female genital organ as a symbol of reproduction. [Skr. *yoni*].
YONKER, see YOUNKER.
YORE, [yaw(r)], *n.* times past; **days of y.**, bygone times. [OE. *geara* formerly].
YORK, [yawk], *n.* the name of the county town of Yorkshire used to designate certain goods produced there, as **Y. ham, Y. paving**, etc. [ON. *Jork*].
YORKER, [yaw'-ker], *n.* (*cricket*) a ball pitching just under the bat and a little inside the crease. [Unkn.].
YORKIST, [yawk'-ist], *n.* (*hist.*) a supporter of the House of York during the Wars of the Roses.
YORKSHIRE, [yawk'-sher], *adj.* belonging to Yorkshire; **Y. pudding**, a light savoury batter pudding; **to come the Y. on**, (*coll.*) to dupe, hoax, deceive.
YOU, [yōō], *second pers. sing. and pl. personal pron., also used indef.* any one. [OE. *eow*].
YOUNG (1), [yung], *n.* young people in general, children, offspring.
YOUNG (2), [yung], *adj.* having lived for a short while, being comparatively recently born; not yet in middle age; of or pertaining to children and adolescents; energetic, youthful; (*fig.*) recent, recently begun; lacking knowledge or experience. [OE. *geong*].
YOUNGISH, [yung'-ish], *adj.* rather young.
YOUNGLING, [yung'-ling], *n.* a young creature, a child.
YOUNGSTER, [yungk'-ster], *n.* a lad, child, boy.
YOUNKER, YONKER, [yung'-ker], *n.* (*coll.*) a young man. [MDu. *jonckher* a young lord].
YOUR, [yōō(e)r], *adj.* belonging to or connected with you; (used indefinitely) such a one as would be commonly imagined. [OE. *eower*].
YOURS (1), [yōō(e)rz], *n. sing. and pl.* friends and relations of you; the letter you wrote.
YOURS (2), [yōō(e)rz], *adj.* belonging to or connected with you.
YOURS (3), [yōō(e)rz], *pron. used abs.*, belonging or pertaining to you.
YOURSELF, (*pl.* **yourselves**), [yōō(e)r-self', yōō(e)r-selvz'], *pron. used emphatically and reflex.* [ME. *youreselfe*].
YOURT, YURT, [yōōert], *n.* a simple dwelling-house of natives of Northern Asia. [Native].

YOUTH, [yōōth], *n.* the condition of being young, the period when a person is young, that is, between childhood and manhood or womanhood; the period of early manhood or womanhood; a young person, *esp.* a young man; strength, activity, vigour; young men and women; **Y. Hostel,** a country hostel for the use of young persons on tour. [OE. *geoguth*].
YOUTHFUL, [yōōth'-fōōl], *adj.* young; having the qualities of youth.
YOUTHFULLY, [yōōth'-fōōl-i], *adv.* in a youthful fashion.
YOUTHFULNESS, [yōōth'-fōōl-nes], *n.* the quality of being youthful.
YOUTHHOOD, [yōōth'-hōōd], *n.* the state or period of youth.
YOUTHLY, [yōōth'-li], *adj.* pertaining to youth, young.
YOWL, YAWL (1), [yowl, yawl], *n.* the cry of an animal that is yowling.
YOWL, YAWL (2), [yowl, yawl], *v.i.* (of various creatures) to utter a wailing cry. [ME. *youlen*].
YO-YO, [yō'-yō'], *n.* a popular toy consisting of a reel spinning up and down a length of string.
YTTERBIC, [it'-er-bik], *adj.* (*chem.*) pertaining to ytterbium.
YTTERBIUM, [it-ur'-bi-um], *n.* (*chem.*) a rare chemical element denoted by Yb. [*Ytterby*, in Sweden, where found].
YTTRIA, [it'-ri-a], *n.* (*chem.*) a white oxide of yttrium.
YTTRIFEROUS, [it-rif'-er-us], *adj.* (*chem.*) containing yttrium.
YTTRIOUS, [it'-ri-us], *adj.* (*chem.*) pertaining to yttrium.
YTTRIUM, [it'-ri-um], *n.* (*chem.*) a rare metallic element denoted by Yt. [*Ytterby*, in Sweden].
YUCCA, [yuk'-a], *n.* a genus of American shrubs which belong to the lily family. [Native].
YUFT, [yuft], *n.* a red leather made in Russia. [Russ. *yuft*].
YUGA, [yōō'-ga], *n.* any of the four great periods into which the duration of the world is divided in Hindu teaching. [Hind. *yuga*].
YUGOSLAV, [yōō'-gō-slahv], *n.* a native of the kingdom of the Southern Slavs which includes Slovenes, Serbs, and Croats. [Serbo-Croat *Yugoslav* southern Slav].
YUGOSLAV, JUGO-SLAV, [yōō'-go-slahv'], *adj.* of, pertaining or relating to, Yugoslavia or the Yugoslavs.
YUKE, [yōōk], *v.i.* (*Scots*) to itch. [~ITCH (2)].
YULAN, [yōō'-lan], *n.* a Chinese magnolia. [Chin. *yulan*].
YULE, [yōōl], *n.* the festival and festivities of Christmas; a pagan Norse festival. [OIcel. *jol*].
YULE-LOG, [yōōl'-log'], *n.* a log of wood burnt at Christmas.
YULETIDE, [yōōl'-tīd], *n.* Christmas time.
YURT, see YOURT.

Z

Z, [zed], the twenty-sixth letter of the English alphabet.
ZABAISM, [sab'-a-izm] *n.* sabaism.
ZAFFER, ZAFFRE, [zaf'-er], *n.* a blue oxide of cobalt used in enamelling. [It. *zaffera*].
ZAMBO, [zam'-bō], *n.* a species of monkey found in America. [Span. *zambo*].
ZAMINDAR, see ZEMINDAR.
ZANY, [zā'-ni], *n.* an idiot, a fool; (*hist.*) a comic actor who appeared with the principal comedian and imitated him. [It. *zani*].
ZANYISM, [zā'-ni-izm], *n.* the state of being a zany, the comic tricks of a zany.
ZANZIBARI (1), [zan'-zi-bah'-ri], *n.* an inhabitant of Zanzibar.
ZANZIBARI (2), [zan'-zi-bah'-ri], *adj.* Zanzibar.
ZAPTIEH, [zap'-ti-ā], *n.* a Turkish policeman. [Turk. *dabtiyeh*].
ZARATHUSTRIAN (1), [za'-ra-thōōs-tri-an], *n.* a Zoroastrian. [*Zarathustra*, the founder of Zoroastrianism].
ZARATHUSTRIAN (2), [za'-ra-thōōs'-tri-an], *adj.* Zoroastrian.
ZAREBA, ZARIBA, ZERIBA, [za-rē'-ba], *n.* a stockade; a camp protected by a stockade. [Arab. *zaribah*].
ZARNICH, [zah'-nik], *n.* a sulphide of arsenic. [Arab. *zarnikh*].
ZAX, [saks], *n.* a slater's hammer or chopper with a point for making holes for the nails.
ZAYAT, [zah'-yat], *n.* a Burmese shelter or meeting-place. [Native].
ZEAL, [zēl], *n.* unflagging and uncompromising enthusiasm, ardour. [Gk. *zelos*].
ZEALFUL, [zēl'-fōōl], *adj.* full of zeal.
ZEALLESS, [zēl'-les], *adj.* lacking zeal.
ZEALOT, [zel'-ot], *n.* a fanatic, an over-enthusiastic supporter. [Gk. *zelotes*].
ZEALOTICAL, [zel-ot'-ik-al], *adj.* having the attributes of a zealot or of zealotry.
ZEALOTISM, [zel'-ot-izm], *n.* zealotry.
ZEALOTRY, [zel'-ot-ri], *n.* the conduct of a zealot.
ZEALOUS, [zel'-us], *adj.* actuated by, expressing, zeal. [MedL. *zelosus*].
ZEALOUSLY, [zel'-us-li], *adv.* in zealous fashion.
ZEALOUSNESS, [zel'-us-nes], *n.* the quality of being zealous.
ZEBEC, ZEBECK, see XEBEC.
ZEBRA, [zē'-bra, zeb'-ra], *n.* a striped South African ungulate quadruped. [Congolese].
ZEBRA-WOOD, [zē'-bra-wōōd], *n.* a wood with a striped grain obtained from a tree in Guiana.
ZEBRINE, [zē'-brīn], *adj.* pertaining to or like zebras.
ZEBU, [zē'-bōō], *n.* a humped ox found in Asia, and domesticated. [Tibetan *mdzopo*].

ZEBU

ZECCHIN, ZECHIN, see SEQUIN.
ZECHSTEIN, [zek'-stīn], *n.* a stratum of limestone in Germany. [Germ. *zechstein*].
ZED, [zed], *n.* the letter Z. [Gk. *zeta*].
ZEDOARY, [zed'-ō-er-i], *n.* an East Indian drug. [Arab. *zēdwar*].
ZEIN, ZEINE, [zē'-in], *n.* a protein extracted from maize. [L. *zea* spelt].
ZELANIAN, [zē-lān'-i-an], *adj.* relating to New Zealand.
ZELOSO, [sel-ō'-sō], *adj.* (*mus.*) with fervour. [It. *zeloso*].
ZEMINDAR, ZAMINDAR, [zem-ēnd'-ah(r)], *n.* in Northern India, a tenant who pays rent for his land direct to the government. [Pers. *zemindar* landholder].
ZENANA, [zen-ah'-na], *n.* a set of rooms for the habitation and isolation of women in India. [Pers. *zenana* pertaining to women].
ZEND, [zend], *n.* an ancient Aryan language, a form of Old Persian. [OPers. *zend* commentary].
ZENITH, [zen'-ith], *n.* that point in the heavens vertically above a person; (*fig.*) the highest point (of achievement, excitement, growth, etc.), peak, apex. [Fr. *zénith* from Arab. *samt* way (overhead)].
ZENITHAL, [zen'-ith-al], *adj.* relating to a zenith.
ZEOLITE, [zē'-ō-līt], *n.* (*min.*) a hydrous silicate found in lava. [Swed. *zeolit*].
ZEOLITIC, [zē'-ō-lit'-ik], *adj.* of, like, or relating to zeolite.
ZEPHYR, [zef'-er], *n.* the west wind; any warm and gentle breeze. [Gk. *zephuros* west wind].
ZEPPELIN, [zep'-el-in], *n.* a large German dirigible balloon. [Count *Zeppelin*, the inventor].
ZERDA, [zur'-da], *n.* the fennec, *Canis zerda*, found in North Africa. [Moorish].
ZERIBA, see ZAREBA.
ZERO, [zēer'-ō], *n.* nought, nothing; the Arabic figure 0; (*arith.*) that amount of which any increase is positive (or plus) and any decrease negative (or minus); that point on a thermometric scale immediately preceding the minimum recognized degree of heat; a

similar point on any other scale; (*fig.*) the lowest point, the state of being nothing; **z. hour,** the time at which an attack is to start. [It. *zero* from Arab. *cifr* cipher].

ZEST, [zest], *n.* an appetizing flavour, piquancy; (*fig.*) eagerness, enthusiasm. [OFr. *zeste* flavouring].

ZETA, [zē'-ta], *n.* the sixth letter of the Greek alphabet. [Gk. *zeta*].

ZETETIC, [zē-tet'-ik], *adj.* conducted by investigation. [Gk. *zetetikos*].

ZEUGMA, [zewg'-ma], *n.* a grammatical figure by which a word is made to agree with, or to apply to, two substantives when strictly it should only agree with, or be applied to, one of them. [Gk. *zeugma* yoke].

ZEUGMATIC, [zewg-mat'-ik], *adj.* relating to or exemplifying zeugma.

ZEUS, [zews], *n.* the supreme deity of Ancient Greek mythology. [Gk. *Zeus*].

ZEUXITE, [zewks'-it], *n.* a brown-coloured variety of tourmaline. [Gk. *zeuxis* joining].

ZHO, ZOBO, [zō, zō'-bō], *n.* a cross between a male yak and a domestic cow. [Tibetan *mdso*].

ZIBELINE (1), [zib'-el-in], *n.* the sable; its fur. [Fr. *zibeline*].

ZIBELINE (2), [zib'-el-īn], *adj.* relating to (the) sable.

ZIGZAG (1), [zig'-zag'], *n.* a crooked line turning from side to side with sharp angles. [Germ. *zickzack*].

ZIGZAG (2), [zig'-zag], *adj.* resembling a zigzag.

ZIGZAG (3), [zig'-zag'], *adv.* in the manner, along the course, of a zigzag.

ZIGZAG (4), (**zigzagging, zigzagged**), [zig'-zag'], *v.i.* to pursue the course of a zigzag.

ZIGZAGGED, [zig'-zagd'], *adj.* shaped like a zigzag; decorated with zigzags.

ZILLAH, [zil'-ah], *n.* (*in British India*) administrative district. [Hind. *dilah*].

ZIMB, [zimb], *n.* an Abyssinian insect pest that attacks cattle. [Native].

ZINC (1), [zingk], *n.* a white metal element denoted by Zn. [Germ. *zink*].

ZINC (2), [zingk], *adj.* made of zinc.

ZINC (3), [zingk], *v.t.* to give a coat of zinc to.

ZINC-BLENDE, [zingk'-blend'], *n.* a native zinc sulphide. [ZINC and BLENDE].

ZINC-BLOOM, [zingk'-bloom], *n.* a hydrous zinc carbonate. [~Germ. *zink-blüthe*].

ZINCIC, [zingk'-ik], *adj.* relating to zinc.

ZINCIFEROUS, [zingk-if'-er-us], *adj.* containing or yielding zinc. [ZINC (1) and L. *ferre* to bear].

ZINCITE, [zingk'-īt], *n.* a native zinc oxide.

ZINCKY, see ZINKY.

ZINCO, [zingk'-ō], *n.* (*print.*) a zincograph. [ZINCO-(GRAPH)].

ZINCO-, *pref.* pertaining to zinc.

ZINCODE, [zingk'-ōd], *n.* (*elect.*) a zinc anode.

ZINCOGRAPH, [zingk'-ō-graf], *n.* a picture made by zincography.

ZINCOGRAPHER, [zingk-og'-raf-er], *n.* one skilled in zincography.

ZINCOGRAPHIC, [zingk'-ō-graf'-ik], *adj.* zincographical.

ZINCOGRAPHICAL, [zingk'-ō-graf'-ik-al], *adj.* relating to zincography.

ZINCOGRAPHY, [zingk-og'-ra-fi], *n.* the technique of printing from zinc plates. [ZINCO- and Gk. *graphia* writing].

ZINCOID, [zingk'-oid], *adj.* resembling zinc. [ZINC (1) and Gk. *oeides* like].

ZINCOTYPE, [zingk'-ō-tīp'], *n.* a zincograph.

ZINCOUS, [zingk'-us], *adj.* relating to zinc.

ZINC-WORKER, [zingk'-wurk'-er], *n.* a craftsman who works in zinc.

ZINGARO, (*pl.* **zingari**), [zing'-ga-rō], *n.* a gipsy. [It. *zingaro*].

ZINGEL, [zing'-gl], *n.* a perch of the genus *Aspro*, *esp.* the *Aspro zingel* which is found in the River Danube. [Germ. *zingel*].

INKENITE, [zingk'-en-īt], *n.* a sulphide of lead and antimony. [Germ. *zinkeneit*].

INKY, ZINCKY, [zingk'-i], *adj.* relating to, resembling, zinc.

INNIA, [zin'-i-a], *n.* (*hort.*) an annual composite garden flower with brightly coloured flowers. [J. G. *Zinn*, a German botanist].

ION, [zī'-on], *n.* a hill in Jerusalem; (*fig.*) the city of Jerusalem; Judaism; Christianity; paradise. [Eccles. L. *Sion* from Heb. *Isiyon*].

IONISM, [zī'-on-izm], *n.* a movement aiming at the establishing of a Jewish National State in Palestine.

IONIST, [zī'-on-ist], *n.* a supporter of Zionism.

IP, [zip], *n.* a ripping or whizzing noise; a zip-fastener; (*coll.*) vigour, energy; liveliness, quickness. [Echoic].

ZIP-FASTENER, [zip'-fahs'-ner], *n.* a joining device consisting of a row of small metal teeth along each of the edges to be joined, which are interlocked by pulling them through a Y-shaped metal rider and unlocked by pulling the rider the other way.

ZIRCON, [zur'-kon], *n.* (*min.*) native crystalline silicate of zirconium. [Pers. *zargun* gold-coloured].

ZIRCONATE, [zur'-kon-āt], *n.* (*chem.*) a salt produced by zirconic acid.

ZIRCONIA, [zur-kō'-ni-a], *n.* zirconium oxide.

ZIRCONIC, [zur-kon'-ik], *adj.* pertaining to, containing, zirconium.

ZIRCONITE, [zur'-kon-īt], *n.* (*min.*) a sort of zircon.

ZIRCONIUM, [zur-kō'-ni-um], *n.* the metallic element Zr, produced from zircon.

ZITHER, [ziTH'-er], *n.* (*mus.*) an instrument of horizontal strings over a sounding board, played by plucking. [Germ. *zither*].

ZITHERIST, [ziTH'-er-ist], *n.* a performer on a zither.

ZIZEL, [zīzl], *n.* the suslik. [Germ. *zeisel*].

ZLOTY, (*pl.* **zloty**), [zwot'-i], *n.* the Polish unit of currency. [Pol. *zloty*].

ZOAEA, see ZOEA.

ZOANTHROPY, [zō-an'-throp-i], *n.* a lunacy in which the sufferer supposes himself an animal. [Gk. *zoon* animal and *anthropos* man].

ZOBO, see ZHO.

ZODIAC, [zō'-di-ak'], *n.* (*astrol.*) a section of the heavens in which the orbits of the chief celestial bodies lie, and which is divided into twelve sections called, and represented by, signs. [Gk. *zodiakos* containing animals].

ZODIAC SIGNS

ZODIACAL, [zō-dī'ak-al], *adj.* relating to the zodiac.

ZOEA, ZOAEA, (*pl.* **zoeae**), [zō-ē'-a], *n.* (*zool.*) a crustacean larva. [Gk. *zoe* life].

ZOETROPE, [zō'-i-trōp], *n.* a toy consisting of a cylinder with vertical slits in it through which a revolving roller, painted with successive and slightly differing representations of a figure in motion, can be seen, so that the figure appears to move. [Gk. *zoe* life and *tropos* turning].

ZOIC, [zō'-ik], *adj.* pertaining to animals, animal; (*geol.*) preserving fossilized animals.

ZOILEAN, [zō-il'-i-an], *adj.* (of a critic) sharp, harsh. [Gk. *Zoilos*, a severe critic of Homer].

ZOILISM, [zō'-il-izm], *n.* nagging, fault-finding criticism. [*Prec.*].

ZOISITE, [zō'-is-īt], *n.* (*min.*) a crystalline silicate of lime and alumina. [Baron von *Zois*, its discoverer].

ZOLAESQUE, [zō'-la-esk'], *adj.* written in the style of Zola.

ZOLAISM, [zō'-la-izm], *n.* the energetic frankness of narrative characteristic of the French novelist Emile *Zola*.

ZOLAIST, [zō-la-ist], *n.* an imitator and admirer of *Zola*.

ZOLAISTIC, [zō-la-ist'-ik], *adj.* Zolaesque.

ZOLLVEREIN, [tsol'-fer-īn], *n.* an economic agreement between a group of nations by which they raise no tariffs against each other and have a uniform rate against other powers. [Germ. *zollverein* customs union].

ZONAL, [zōn'-al], *adj.* relating to zones, divided into zones.

ZONALLY, [zōn'-al-i], *adv.* in a zonal fashion, in zones.

ZONATE, [zōn'-āt], *adj.* divided into zones, marked out in zones.

ZONE, [zōn], *n.* †a girdle; a part of the surface of a sphere in the form of a belt; one of the five climatic divisions of the earth, torrid, north and south temperate, and north and south frigid. [Gk. *zone* girdle].

ZONED, [zōnd], *adj.* divided into, marked with, zones.

ZONELESS, [zōn'-les], *adj.* without zones.

ZONE-TIME, [zōn'-tīm], *n.* the true time at a particular longitude, in contrast with Greenwich time.

ZONING, [zōn'-ing], *n.* the act of dividing (a country, etc.) into zones for purposes of manufacture, building, transport, etc.

ZONULAR, [zōn'-yoo-ler], *adj.* resembling a zonule.

ZONULE, [zōn'-yool], *n.* a little zone or girdle.

ZONURE, [zōn'-yoor], *n.* a South African lizard. [Gk. *zone* girdle and *ouros* tail].

ZOO, [zoo], *n.* a collection of animals in confinement for exhibition and study, *esp.* the one in Regent's Park, London. [Short for *Zoological* Gardens].

ZOO- *pref.* pertaining to animals. [Gk. *zoos* alive].
ZOOBLAST, [zō'-ō-blast], *n.* an animal cell.
ZOO-CHEMICAL, [zō'-ō-kem'-ik-al], *adj.* pertaining to zoo-chemistry.
ZOO-CHEMISTRY, [zō'-ō-kem'-is-tri], *n.* the chemical study of an animal body.
ZOO-GEOGRAPHY, [zō'-ō-ji-og'-ra-fi], *n.* the study of the distribution of animals.
ZOOGRAPHER, [zō-og'-raf-er], *n.* one who paints or describes animals.
ZOOGRAPHIC, [zō'-ō-graf'-ik], *adj.* zoographical.
ZOOGRAPHICAL, [zō'-ō-graf'-ik-al], *adj.* relating to the descriptions or drawings of animals.
ZOOGRAPHY, [zō-og'-ra-fi], *n.* written accounts of animals. [zoo- and Gk. *graphia* writing].
ZOOID, [zō'-oid], *adj.* bearing resemblance to, though not actually classable as, an animal form. [zoo- and Gk. *oeides* like].
ZOOLATROUS, [zō-ol'-at-rus], *adj.* relating to zoolatry.
ZOOLATRY, [zō-ol'-at-ri], *n.* the worship of animals. [zoo- and Gk. *latreia* worship].
ZOOLITE, [zō'-ō-lit], *n.* a fossilized animal. [zoo- and Gk. *lithos* stone].
ZOOLOGICAL, [zō'-ōl-oj'-ik-al], *adj.* relating to zoology.
ZOOLOGICALLY, [zō'-ōl-oj'-ik-al-i], *adv.* in accordance with zoology.
ZOOLOGIST, [zō-ol'-oj-ist], *n.* a student of zoology.
ZOOLOGY, [zō-ol'-o-ji], *n.* the science which is concerned with the form, structure, habits, etc., of animals. [zoo- and Gk. *logos* word].
ZOOM, [zōōm], *v.t. and i.* to cause (an aeroplane) to mount sharply and quickly; to pursue such a course in an aeroplane; to emit a noise like an aeroplane doing this; (*fig.*) to be a great success, to sell quickly and at a high price, etc. [Echoic].
ZOOMETRY, [zō-om'-et-ri], *n.* the science of the measurement of animals. [zoo- and Gk. *metria* measurement].
ZOOMORPHIC, [zō'-ō-mawf'-ik], *adj.* having or representing an animal form. [zoo- and Gk. *morphe* shape].
ZOOMORPHISM, [zō'-ō-mawf'-izm], *n.* representation of deities in animal forms.
ZOONOMY, [zō-on'-o-mi], *n.* the study of animal life and the laws which govern it. [zoo- and Gk. *nomos* law].
ZOOPATHOLOGY, [zō'-ō-path-ol'-o-ji], *n.* the study of the diseases of animals.
ZOOPHAGAN, [zō-of'-ag-an], *adj.* zoophagous.
ZOOPHAGOUS, [zō-of'-ag-us], *adj.* carnivorous. [zoo- and Gk. *phago* I eat].
ZOOPHILIST, [zō-of'-il-ist], *n.* a lover of animals, a supporter of anti-vivisection. [zoo- and Gk. *philos* loving].
ZOOPHILY, [zō-of'-il-i], *n.* affection for animals.
ZOOPHORUS, (*pl.* **zoophori**), [zō-of'-or-us], *n.* (*arch.*) a frieze of carved figures of animals and human beings. [Gk. *zoophoros*].
ZOOPHYSICS, [zō'-ō-fiz'-iks], *n.*(*pl.*) the science of the structure of animal bodies.
ZOOPHYSIOLOGY, [zō'-ō-fiz'-i-ol'-o-ji], *n.* the study of the physiology of animals.
ZOOPHYTE, [zō'-ōf-īt], *n.* an animal that resembles a plant in appearance. [Gk. *zoophuton*].
ZOOPHYTIC, [zō'-ō-fīt'-ik], *adj.* relating to zoophytes.
ZOOPHYTOLOGICAL, [zō'-ō-fīt'-ō-loj'-ik-al], *adj.* relating to zoophytology.
ZOOPHYTOLOGY, [zō'-ō-fīt-ol'-o-ji], *n.* the study of zoophytes. [ZOOPHYTE and Gk. *logos* word].
ZOOPSYCHOLOGY, [zō'-ō-sīk-ol'-o-ji], *n.* the study of the psychology of the lower animals.
ZOOSCOPY, [zō-os'-ko-pi], *n.* a form of nervous disorder in which visions of unknown animals are seen. [zoo- and Gk. *skopos* watcher].
ZOOSPERM, [zō'-ō-spurm'], *n.* a fertilizing cell in the semen of a male animal.
ZOOSPORE, [zō'-ō-spaw(r)'], *n.* a spore that can move about independently.
ZOOTAXY, [zō'-ō-tak-si], *n.* the science of classifying animals. [zoo- and Gk. *taxis* arrangement].
ZOOTECHNY, [zō'-ō-tek'-ni], *n.* the science of breeding animals. [zoo- and Gk. *tekhne* art].
ZOOTOMICAL, [zō'-ōt-om'-ik-al], *adj.* relating to zootomy.
ZOOTOMIST, [zō-ot'-om-ist], *n.* one who practises zootomy.
ZOOTOMY, [zō-ot'-o-mi], *n.* the dissection of animals other than man. [zoo- and Gk. *temno* cut].
ZOOTROPHIC, [zō'-ō-trof'-ik], *adj.* relating to the feeding of animals. [zoo- and Gk. *trophe* nourishment].
ZORIL, [zo'-ril], *n.* the South African polecat, *Ictonyx zorilla*. [Span. *zorillo*].
ZOROASTRIAN (1), [zo'-rō-as'-tri-an], *n.* a follower of *Zoroaster*, founder of the Parsee religion.
ZOROASTRIAN (2), [zo'-rō-as'-tri-an], *adj.* relating to Zoroaster and the religion he founded.
ZOROASTRIANISM, [zo'-rō-as'-tri-an-izm], *n.* the religion of Zoroaster.
ZOSTER, [zos'-ter], *n.* shingles. [Gk. *zoster* girdle].
ZOUAVE, [zōō'-ahv], *n.* a French light infantryman belonging to a regiment at one time recruited in Algeria, and formerly wearing an eastern uniform. [Fr. *zouave*].
ZOUNDS, [zowndz], *int.* (*archaic*) a mild expletive. [Short for *God's wounds*].
ZUCCHETTA, [tsōō-ket'-a], *n.* (*eccles.*) a skull-cap. [It. *zucchetta*].
ZULU, [zōō'-lōō], *n.* a member of certain native South African tribes of Bantu stock; their language; a cone-shaped straw hat for children. [Native].
ZUMBOORUK, [zum'-bōō-ruk], *n.* a small swivel gun tied to a camel's back. [Hind. *zamburak* hornet].
ZWANZIGER, [tsvan'-tsig-er], *n.* an Austrian coin. [Germ. *zwanziger*].
ZWIEBACK, [tsvē'-bak'], *n.* a light rusk. [Germ. *zwie* twice and *backen* to bake].
ZWINGLIAN (1), [tsving'-gli-an], *n.* a follower of Zwingli.
ZWINGLIAN (2), [tsving'-gli-an], *adj.* relating to the doctrine of Ulrich *Zwingli*, a Swiss Protestant of the sixteenth century.
ZYGADITE, [zig'-ad-īt], *n.* (*min.*) a red or yellowish variety of albite. [Germ. *zygadit*].
ZYGAL, [zī'-gal], *adj.* (*anat.*) relating to a zygon.
ZYGO-, [zī'-gō], *pref.* yoke-shaped, going in twos. [Gk. *zugon* yoke].
ZYGODACTYL, [zī'-gō-dak'-til], *n.* a bird with two pairs of toes on each leg, one pair to the front and one to the back. [ZYGO- and DACTYL].
ZYGODACTYLIC, [zī'-gō-dak-til'-ik], *adj.* zygodactylous.
ZYGODACTYLOUS, [zī'-gō-dak'-til-us], *adj.* relating to, characteristic of, a zygodactyl.
ZYGODONT, [zī'-gō-dont'], *adj.* relating to or resembling molar teeth. [ZYGO- and Gk. *odous odontos* tooth].
ZYGOMA, [zī-gō'-ma], *n.* (*anat.*) an arch on each side of the face formed by the junction of the cheek-bone with the temporal bone. [~Gk. *zugon* a yoke].
ZYGOMATIC, [zī'-gō-mat'-ik], *adj.* pertaining to the zygoma, to a process of the temporal bone.
ZYGON, [zī'-gon], *n.* (*anat.*) a bone bridging a fissure in the brain. [Gk. *zugon* yoke].
ZYGOPLEURAL, [zī'-gō-plōōer'-ral], *adj.* balanced and similar on each side. [ZYGO- and Gk. *pleura* side].
ZYGOTE, [zig'-ōt], *n.* (*biol.*) the cell arising when two cells conjugate in reproduction. [Gk. *zugotos* yoked].

ZYGOMA

ZYMOGEN, [zī'-mō-jen], *n.* (*chem.*) a ferment. [Germ. *zymogen*].
ZYMOID, [zī'-moid], *n.* having the characteristics of a ferment. [Gk. *zume* leaven and *oeides* like].
ZYMOLOGICAL, [zī'-mō-loj'-ik-al], *adj.* relating to zymology.
ZYMOLOGIST, [zī-mol'-o-jist], *n.* a student of zymology.
ZYMOLOGY, [zī'-mol'-o-ji], *n.* the study of ferments and fermentation. [Gk. *zume* leaven and *logos* speech].
ZYMOMETER, [zī-mom'-it-er], *n.* an instrument which measures fermentation. [Gk. *zume* leaven and METER].
ZYMOSIS, [zī-mō'-sis], *n.* fermentation; the action of germs or a disease regarded as akin to fermentation. [Gk. *zumosis*].
ZYMOTECHNY, [zī'-mō-tek'-ni], *n.* the technique of fermentation. [Gk. *zume* leaven and *tekhne* art].
ZYMOTIC, [zī-mot'-ik], *adj.* relating to diseases when regarded as similar to fermentation in their development. [Gk. *zumotikos*].
ZYMOTICALLY, [zī-mot'-ik-al-i], *adv.* by zymosis.
ZYMURGY, [zī'-mur-ji], *n.* the chemistry of brewing, distilling, and wine-making, the commercial branch of zymology. [Gk. *zume* leaven and *ergon* work].

APPENDICES

ABBREVIATIONS IN COMMON USE

A(ns)., answer.
a., aged (of racehorse over six years old).
A1, at Lloyds, registered first-class ship; first-class in physical wellbeing.
a.a., account at (valuations).
A.A., Automobile Association; Associate in Arts; Architectural Association; Anti-Aircraft.
A.A.A., Amateur Athletic Association.
A.A.C. (L.), *anno ante Christum*, "in the year before Christ."
A.A.F., Auxiliary Air Force.
A.A.G., Assistant Adjutant-General.
A.A.I., Associate of the Auctioneers' Institute.
A.A.M., Association of Assistant Mistresses.
A. and M., (Hymns) Ancient and Modern.
A.B., Able-bodied seaman; Assistance Board.
A.B.A., Amateur Boxing Association.
abbr., abbrev., abbreviation, abbreviated.
A.B.C., Aerated Bread Company.
A.B.C.A., Army Bureau of Current Affairs.
abd., abdicated.
A.B.E.A., Actors' (British) Equity Association ("Equity").
ab init. (L.), *ab initio*, "from the beginning."
abl., ablative.
Abp., Archbishop.
abt., about.
A.C., Appeal Court; Appeal Cases in this court (in law reports); Alpine Club; Athletic Club; Aircraftman; Air Council; (L) *anno Christi*, "in the year of Christ"; (L.) *ante Christum*, "before Christ"; Anglo-Catholic; alternating current.
A.C.A., Associate of the Institute of Chartered Accountants.
acc(t)., account; accountant; accusative.
A.C.G.B., Arts Council of Great Britain (formerly C.E.M.A.).
A.C.G.I., Associate of the City & Guilds of London Institute.
A.C.I., Army Council Instruction.
A.C.I.S., Associate of the Chartered Institute of Secretaries.
A.C.P., Associate of the College of Preceptors.
A.C.U., Auto-Cycle Union.
A.D. (L.), *anno Domini*, "in the year of our Lord."
ad., advertisement.
a.d., after date.
A.D.C., Aide-de-camp; Amateur Dramatic Club (*esp.* of Cambridge University).
ad eund. (L.), *ad eundem (gradum)*, "admitted to the same degree" (at another University).
ad fin. (L.), *ad finem*, "at, to, the end."
A.D.G.B., Air Defence of Great Britain.
ad inf. (L.), *ad infinitum*, "to infinity."
ad int. (L.), *ad interim*, "meanwhile."
adj., adjective.
Adj(t)., Adjutant.
ad lib. (L.), *ad libitum*, "at pleasure."
ad loc. (L.), *ad locum*, "at the place."
Adm(l)., Admiral.
A.D.O.S., Assistant Director of Ordnance Stores.
Adv., Advent; advocate.
adv., adverb; (L.), *adversus*, "against."
ad val. (L.), *ad valorem*, "according to the value."
advt., advertisement.
A.E.C., Army Educational Corps; Association of Education Committees; Association for Education in Citizenship; Associated Equipment Company; Agricultural Executive Committee (preceded by County name).
A.E.F., Allied Expeditionary Force.
aeg. (L.), *aeger*, "ill."
aegrot. (L.), *aegrotat*, "he is ill."
A.E.L.T.C., All England Lawn Tennis Club.
aeron., aeronautics.
aet., aetat. (L.), *aetatis*, aged (so many years).
A.E.U., Amalgamated Engineering Union.
A.F., Admiral of the Fleet.
A.F.A., Amateur Football Association.
A.F.C., Air Force Cross.
A.F.L., American Federation of Labour.
A.F.M., Air Force Medal.
Afr., African.
A.F.V., Armoured Fighting Vehicle.
A.G., Adjutant-General; Attorney-General; Accountant-General; Agent-General; (Germ.), *Aktiengesellschaft*, "joint-stock company."
agric., agriculture.
A.G.S.M., Associate of the Guildhall School of Music.
Agt., Agent.
Agt.-Gen., Agent-General.
A.H. (L.), *anno Hegirae*, "in the year of the Hegira."
A.H.S. (L.), *anno humanae salutis*, "in the year of human salvation."
A.H.W.C., Associate of the Heriot Watt College
A.I.A., Associate of the Institute of Actuaries.
A.I.C., Associate of the Institute of Chemistry; Army Intelligence Corps.
A.I.C.E., Associate of the Institution of Civil Engineers.
A.I.F., Australian Imperial Force.
A.I.Mech.E., Associate of the Institution of Mechanical Engineers.
A.I.S.A., Associate of the Incorporated Secretaries' Association.
A.L.A., Associate of the Library Association.
Ala., Alabama (U.S.A.).
Alas., Alaska.
A.L.C.M., Associate of the London College of Music.
Ald., Alderman.
A.L.S., Associate of the Linnean Society.
alt., alternate; altitude.
Alta., Alberta (Canada).
A.M. (L.), *Artium Magister*, "Master of Arts" (usually M.A.); Albert Medal.
a.m. (L.), *ante meridiem*, "before noon."
A.M.C., Association of Municipal Corporations.
A.M.D.G. (L.), *ad majorem Dei gloriam*, "to the greater glory of God."
A.M.G., Allied Military Government.
A.M.I.C.E., Associate Member of the Institution of Civil Engineers.
A.M.I.Chem.E., Associate Member of the Institution of Chemical Engineers.
A.M.I.E.E., Associate Member of the Institution of Electrical Engineers.
A.M.I.Mech.E., Associate Member of the Institution of Mechanical Engineers.
A.M.I.P., Associate of the Institute of Patentees.
amp., ampère.
A.M.T.P.I., Associate Member of the Town Planning Institute.
amt., amount.
an., anode (elect.).
Angl., Anglican.
Angl. (L.), *Anglice*, "in English."
anon., anonymous.
antiq., antiquity.
A.N.Z.A.C. (Anzac), Australian and New Zealand Army Corps (in First World War).

A.O., Army Order.
a/o, account of.
A.O.D., Ancient Order of Druids; Army Ordnance Department.
A.O.F., Ancient Order of Foresters.
A.O.H., Ancient Order of Hibernians.
aor., aorist.
ap. (L), *apud*, "according to," "in the works of."
A.P.M., Assistant Provost-Marshal.
Apoc., Apocalypse; Apocrypha.
app., appendix.
appro., approval; approbation.
approx., approximate(ly).
A.P.S., Associate of the Pharmaceutical Society.
A.Q.M.G., Assistant Quartermaster-General.
A.R. (L.), *anno regni*, "in the year of the reign."
A.R.A., Associate of the Royal Academy.
A.R.Ae.S., Associate of the Royal Aeronautical Society.
A.R.A.L., Associate of the Royal Academy of Literature.
A.R.A.M., Associate of the Royal Academy of Music.
A.R.B.A., Associate of the Royal Society of British Artists.
A.R.C., Automobile Racing Club.
A.R.C.A., Associate of the Royal College of Art; Associate of the Royal Cambrian Academy.
A.R.C.I., Associate of the Royal Colonial Institute.
A.R.C.M., Associate of the Royal College of Music.
A.R.C.O., Associate of the Royal College of Organists.
A.R.C.S., Associate of the Royal College of Science.
A.R.E., Associate of the Royal Society of Painter-Etchers and Engravers.
Argyl, Argyllshire.
A.R.H.A., Associate of the Royal Hibernian Academy.
A.R.I.B.A., Associate of the Royal Institute of British Architects.
Ariz., Arizona (U.S.A.).
Ark., Arkansas (U.S.A.).
A.R.M.S., Associate of the Royal Society of Miniature Painters.
A.R.P., Air Raid Precautions.
A.R.P.S., Associate of the Royal Photographic Society.
A.R.R. (L.), *anno regni regis* (*reginae*), "in the year of the king's (queen's) reign."
arr., arrives.
A.R.S.A., Associate of the Royal Scottish Academy; Associate of the Royal Society of Arts.
A.R.S.L., Associate of the Royal Society of Literature.
A.R.S.W., Associate of the Royal Scottish Society of Painters in Water Colours.
A.R.W.A., Associate of the Royal West of England Academy.
A.R.W.S., Associate of the Royal Society of Painters in Water Colours.
A.S., Anglo-Saxon.
A.S.A., Amateur Swimming Association.
A.S.A.A., Associate of the Society of Incorporated Accountants and Auditors.
Asaph, St. Asaph (in signature of Bishop).
A.S.D.I.C., Anti-Submarine Detection and Investigation Committee.
A.S.E., Amalgamated Society of Engineers.
A.S.L.E.&F., Amalgamated Society of Locomotive Engineers and Firemen.
A.S.L.I.B., Association of Special Libraries and Information Bureaux.
Assn., Association.
Assoc., Associate; Association.
Asst., Assistant.
A.S.W., Amalgamated Society of Woodworkers; Association of Scientific Workers.
A.T.A., Air Transport Auxiliary.
A.T.C., Air Training Corps; Air Transport Command.
A.T.C.L., Associate of Trinity College (of Music), London.
A.T.S., Auxiliary Territorial Service.
Att.-Gen., Attorney-General.
A.T.T.I., Association of Teachers in Technical Institutes.
attrib., attributive(ly), attributed to.
at.wt., atomic weight.
A.U., Angström unit (physics).
A.U.C. (L.), *anno urbis conditae*, or *ab urbe condita*, "in the year of the city," or "from the foundation of the city" (Rome).
A.U.T., Association of University Teachers.
auxil., auxiliary.
A.V., Authorized Version (of the Bible).
av., average.
avdp., avoirdupois.

B., Bay; black (of pencil-lead).
b., born; bowled, bye (cricket).
B.A. (L.), *Baccalaureus Artium*, Bachelor of Arts; British Academy; British Association.
B.Agr(ic)., Bachelor of Agriculture.
B.&S., Brown and Sharpe (wire gauge).
B.A.O., Bachelor of Obstetrics.
Bart., Baronet.
Bart's., St. Bartholomew's Hospital.
Bath. & Well., Bath and Wells (in signature of Bishop).
Batt., Battery.
Battn., Battalion.
BB, double black (of pencil-lead).
BBB, treble black (of pencil-lead).
BBC, British Broadcasting Corporation.
B.C., Before Christ; British Columbia (Canada); British Council.
B.C.E., Before Christian Era.
B.Ch. (L.), *Baccalaureus Chirurgiae*, Bachelor of Surgery.
B.Ch.D., Bachelor of Dental Surgery.
B.C.L., Bachelor of Civil Law.
B.Com., Bachelor of Commerce.
B.D., Bachelor of Divinity.
B.D.A., British Dental Association; Bradford Dyers' Association.
Bde., Brigade.
Bde. Maj., Brigade Major.
Bdr., Bombardier.
B.D.S., Bachelor of Dental Surgery (U.S.A.).
B.D.S.T., British Double Summer Time.
B.E., Bachelor of Engineering.
B.E.A., British East Africa; British Engineers' Association.
B.E.C.C., British Empire Cancer Campaign.
B.Ed., Bachelor of Education.
B.E.D.A., British Electrical Development Association.
Beds, Bedfordshire.
B.E.F., British Expeditionary Force.
B.E.I., British East Indies.
Belg., Belgium; Belgian.
B.Eng., Bachelor of Engineering.
Berks, Berkshire.
B.E.S.A., British Engineering Standards Association.
B. ès L. (F.), *Bachelier ès Lettres*, Bachelor of Letters.
B. ès S. (F.), *Bachelier ès Sciences*, Bachelor of Science.
B.E.T.R.O., British Export Trades Research Organization.
B.F.A.S., British Fine Arts Society.
B.F.B.P.W., British Federation of Business and Professional Women.
B.F.B.S., British and Foreign Bible Society.
B.F.U.W., British Federation of University Women.
B.H.A., British Hospitals Association.
B'ham, Birmingham.
B'head, Birkenhead.
b.h.p., brake horse-power.
B.I., British India.
B.I.A.E., British Institute of Adult Education.
Bib., Biblical.
biblio(g)., bibliography; bibliographical.
B.I.F., British Industries Fair.
B.I.P., British Institute in Paris.
biog., biography; biographical.
B.I.S., Bank for International Settlements.
B.I.S.N.C., British India Steam Navigation Company.
bkrpt., bankrupt.
B.L. (L.), *Baccalaureus Legum*, Bachelor of Law.

.l., bill of lading.
., barrel ; bale.
.L.A., British Liberation Army (in Second World War).
.Litt. (L.), *Baccalaureus Literarum,* Bachelor of Letters (Literature).
.I.P.O., British Institute of Public Opinion.
.M., British Museum ; Bench Mark ; (L.), *Baccalaureus Medicinae,* Bachelor of Medicine (more commonly M.B.) ; (L.), *beatae memoriae,* "of blessed memory."
.M.A., British Medical Association.
.M.E., Bachelor of Mining Engineering.
.M.J., British Medical Journal.
.Mus., Bachelor of Music (more commonly Mus.Bac.).
.N.C., Brasenose College, Oxford.
.N.O.C., British National Opera Company.
.o., buyer's option ; branch office.
.O.A., British Olympic Association ; British Optical Association.
.O.A.C., British Overseas Airways Corporation.
.O.A.F.G., British Order of Ancient Free Gardeners.
. of E., Bank of England.
. of T. (or B.O.T.), Board of Trade.
.O.P., Boy's Own Paper.
B.P., British Pharmacopoeia ; the British public (humorous).
b.p., boiling-point ; below proof (of spirits).
B.P.I., Booksellers' Provident Institution.
Bp. Suff., Bishop Suffragan.
B.Q. (L.), *bene quiescat,* "may he (she) rest well."
B.Q.M.S., Battalion Quartermaster Sergeant ; Battery Quartermaster Sergeant.
Br., Brother.
b.r., bills receivable.
B.R.C.S., British Red Cross Society.
b. rec., bills receivable.
Brecon, Brecknockshire.
brev., brevier.
Brig., Brigade ; Brigadier.
Brig.-Gen., Brigadier-General.
Brit., Britain ; British ; Britannia.
Britt. Omn. (L.), *Britanniarum omnium,* "of all the Britains" (on coins).
Bro., Brother.
Bros., Brothers (commercial).
B.S., Bachelor of Surgery; Bachelor of Science (U.S.A.)
b.s., balance-sheet ; bill of sale.
B.S.A., Building Societies Association ; Birmingham Small Arms Company ; British School at Athens.
B.Sc., Bachelor of Science.
B.Sc. (Econ.), Bachelor of Economic Science.
B.Sc. (Eng.), Bachelor of Science (Engineering).
B.S.F., British Standard Fine (of screw threads).
B.S.R., British School at Rome.
B.S.S., British Standard Specification.
B.S.T., British Summer Time.
bt., bought.
B.Th., Bachelor of Theology.
B.T.-H., British Thomson-Houston Company.
B.Th.U., British Thermal Unit.
B.T.U., Board of Trade Unit (elect.).
bu., bushel.
Bucks, Buckinghamshire.
Bulg., Bulgaria ; Bulgarian.
B.U.P., British United Press.
B.V., Bible Version (of the Psalms).
B.V.M. (L.), *Beata Virgo Maria,* "the Blessed Virgin Mary."
B.W.G., Birmingham Wire Gauge.
B.W.I., British West Indies.
B.W.T.A., British Women's Temperance Association.

C., Cape ; Centigrade ; Conservative.
c. (L.), *circa, circum, circiter,* "about"; cent ; centime ; caught (cricket).
C.3., lowest category in physique, efficiency, etc.
C.A., Chartered Accountant ; Clerical Association ; County Alderman ; Court of Appeal ; Church Association ; Church Army.
ca., cathode (elect).
C.A.B., Citizens' Advice Bureau.
Cal., California (U.S.A.).
Cambs, Cambridgeshire.
Can., Canon ; Canto ; Cantoris (of choir).
c. & b., caught and bowled (cricket).
Cant., Canticles (O.T.) ; Canterbury.
Cantab. (L.), *Cantabrigiensis,* of Cambridge.
Cantuar. (L.), *Cantuariensis,* of Canterbury (in signature of Archbishop).
cap. (L.), *caput,* head or chapter ; capital letter ; number of statute in year of reign of sovereign.
Capt., Captain.
Car. (L.), *Carolus,* Charles.
Card., Cardinal.
Cardig, Cardiganshire.
Carliol. (L.), *Carliolensis,* of Carlisle (in signature of Bishop).
Carmaths, Carmarthenshire.
cat., catalogue ; catechism.
cath., cathode (elect.).
Cathol., Catholic.
cav., caveat (law).
C.B., Companion or Commander of the Order of the Bath (civil or military) ; confined to barracks ; Cape Breton (Canada) ; County Borough.
C.B.E., Commander of the Order of the British Empire.
C.B.S., Confraternity of the Blessed Sacrament ; Church Building Society.
C.C., Chamber of Commerce ; Circuit Court; Common Council(man), City of London ; County Council(lor) ; County Court ; Cricket Club ; Cycling Club ; cotton-covered (of electric wire).
c.c., cubic centimetre.
C.C.A., County Councils' Association.
C.C.C., Central Criminal Court.
C.C.F., Co-operative Commonwealth Federation (Canada).
C.C.H.E., Central Council for Health Education.
C.C.M.H., Central Council for Mental Health.
C.C.P., Court of Common Pleas ; Code of Civil Procedure.
C.C.R.P.T., Central Council for Recreative Physical Training.
C.C.S., Ceylon Civil Service ; Casualty Clearing Station.
C.C.S.B., Central Council for School Broadcasting.
C.D., Chancery Division ; Civil Defence ; *Corps Diplomatique* ; Contagious Diseases (Acts).
C.E., Civil Engineer ; Chief Engineer.
C.E.B., Central Electricity Board.
Cels., Celsius (thermometer).
Celt., Celtic.
C.E.M.A., Council for the Encouragement of Music and the Arts (now A.C.G.B.).
C.E.M.S., Church of England Men's Society.
Cent., Centigrade.
cent. (L.), *centum,* 100 ; central ; century.
cert., certificate ; certified.
C.E.S.S.I., Church of England Sunday School Institution.
Cestr. (L.), *Cestrensis,* of Chester (in signature of Bishop).
cet. par. (L.), *ceteris paribus,* other things being equal.
C.E.T.S., Church of England Temperance Society.
C.E.U., Christian Endeavour Union.
C.E.W.M.S., Church of England Working Men's Society.
C.F., Chaplain to the Forces.
cf. (L.), *confer,* compare.
C.G., Captain-General ; Captain of the Guard ; Coastguard ; Coldstream Guards ; Commissary General ; Consul-General.
cg., centigramme.
C.G.H., Cape of Good Hope.
C.G.L.I., City and Guilds of London Institute.
C.G.M., Conspicuous Gallantry Medal.
C.G.S., Chief of the General Staff ; centimetre-gramme-second (system of measurement in science).
C.G.T. (Fr.), *Confédération Générale de Travail,* General Confederation of Labour.
C.H., Companion of Honour.
Ch., Church.
c.h., central heating.
Chap., Chapter ; Chaplain.

Chap.-Gen., Chaplain-General.
Chas., Charles.
Ch.B. (L.), *Chirurgiae Baccalaureus*, Bachelor of Surgery.
Ch. Ch., Christ Church, Oxford University.
Ches, Cheshire.
Ch.M. (L.), *Chirurgiae Magister*, Master of Surgery.
Chmn., Chairman.
chq., cheque.
Chron., Chronicles (O.T.).
chron., chronology ; chronological.
chrs., chambers.
C.I., (Imperial Order of the) Crown of India ; Chief Inspector ; Channel Islands.
Cicester. (L.), *Cicestrensis*, of Chichester (in signature of Bishop).
C.I.D., Criminal Investigation Department (Scotland Yard) ; Committee of Imperial Defence.
C.I.E., Companion of the Order of the Indian Empire.
c.i.f., cost, insurance, freight.
C.I.G.S., Chief of the Imperial General Staff.
C.I.Mech.E., Companion of the Institution of Mechanical Engineers.
C.-in-C., Commander-in-Chief.
C.I.O., Congress of Industrial Organizations (U.S.A.).
circ. (L.), *circa, circiter, circum*, "about."
cit., citation ; cited.
C.J., Chief Justice.
cl., centilitre.
Clar., Clarendon (printing type).
C.L.B., Church Lads' Brigade.
cld., cleared (goods shipping) ; coloured.
C.M. (L.), *Chirurgiae Magister*, Master of Surgery ; Church Missionary ; Certificated Master ; Corresponding Member ; common metre (of hymns).
cm., centimetre.
c.m. (L.), *causa mortis*, "by reason of death."
C.M.A.S., Clergy Mutual Assurance Society.
C.M.B., Central Midwives' Board.
Cmd., Command Paper.
Cmdg., Commanding.
C.M.F., Central Mediterranean Forces.
C.M.G., Companion of the Order of St. Michael and St. George.
C.M.P., Corps of Military Police.
C.M.S., Church Missionary Society.
C.N., Central News (Agency).
C.O., Commanding Officer ; Colonial Office ; Crown Office ; Criminal Office.
Co., Company ; County.
c/o, care of.
c.o., conscientious objector.
C.O.D., Cash on delivery.
C. of E., Church of England.
C. of S., Chief of Staff ; Church of Scotland.
Col., Colonel.
col., column.
Coll., College.
Colo., Colorado (U.S.A.).
Coloss., Colossians (N.T.).
Col.-Sergt., Colour-Sergeant.
Com., Commissioner ; Committee ; Commodore ; Commonwealth ; Communist.
com., common ; commune ; commerce ; communications ; comedy ; commentary ; commission.
Comdr., Commander.
Comdt., Commandant.
Commr., Commissioner.
comp., compositor ; compound.
Com. Serj., Common Serjeant (City of London).
Comy.-Gen., Commissary-General.
Con., Consul.
con. (L.), *contra*, "against"; conics.
conf., conference.
Cong., Congress ; Congregation.
Conn., Connecticut (U.S.A.).
Cons., Conservative ; Consul.
Consols., Consolidated Stock.
constr., construction.
Co-op., Co-operative (Stores).
C.O.P.E.C., Conference on Politics, Economics and Citizenship (Ch. of Eng.).
Copt., Coptic.
Cor., Corinthians (N.T.) ; Coroner.
Corp., Corporation.
C.O.S., Charity Organization Society.
cos., cosine.
cosec., cosecant.
cot., cotangent.
Coy., Company.
C.P., Carriage Paid ; Carter, Paterson & Co. ; Clerk of the Peace ; Common Pleas ; Court of Probate ; Central Provinces (India) ; Cape Province ; Congregation of the Passion (Passionists) ; College of Preceptors ; Co-operative Party.
c.p., candle-power.
C.P.C., Clerk of the Privy Council.
C.P.G.B., Communist Party of Great Britain.
Cpl., Corporal.
C.P.R., Canadian Pacific Railway.
C.P.R.E., Council for the Preservation of Rural England.
C.P.S. (L.), *Custos Privati Sigilli*, Keeper of the Privy Seal.
C.Q.M.S., Company Quartermaster-Sergeant.
C.R., Community of the Resurrection.
Cr., Crown ; credit(or).
cr., created.
C.R.A., Commander, Royal Artillery.
C.R.E., Commander, Royal Engineers.
cresc., crescendo (mus.).
C.S., Chemical Society ; Civil Service ; Clerk to the Signet ; Common Serjeant ; Court of Session ; (L.) *Custos Sigilli*, Keeper of the Seal.
C.S.C., Conspicuous Service Cross.
C.S.C.A., Civil Service Clerical Association.
C.S.I., Companion of the Order of the Star of India.
C.S.M., Company Sergeant-Major.
C.S.M.M.G., Chartered Society of Massage and Medical Gymnastics.
C.S.S.A., Civil Service Supply Association.
C.SS.R., Congregation of the Most Holy Redeemer (Redemptorists).
Ct., Court.
ct., carat (precious metals).
C.T.C., Cyclists' Touring Club.
C.U.A.C., Cambridge University Athletic Club.
C.U.A.F.C., Cambridge University Association Football Club.
cub., cubic.
C.U.A.D.C., Cambridge University Amateur Dramatic Club.
C.U.B.C., Cambridge University Boat Club.
C.U.C.C., Cambridge University Cricket Club.
C.U.G.C., Cambridge University Golf Club.
C.U.H.C., Cambridge University Hockey Club.
cum., cumulative.
Cumb, Cumberland.
cum div., with dividend.
Cum. Pref., Cumulative Preference (shares).
C.U.M.S., Cambridge University Musical Society.
C.U.R.F.C., Cambridge University Rugby Football Club.
C.V.O., Commander of the Royal Victorian Order.
C.W.G., Co-operative Women's Guild.
c.w.o., cash with order.
C.W.S., Co-operative Wholesale Society.
cwt., hundredweight.
cyl., cylinder.

d., date ; daughter ; delete ; (L.) *denarius*, penny, pence ; died.
D.(A.)A.G., Deputy (Assistant) Adjutant General.
Dan., Daniel (O.T.) ; Danish.
D.A.Q.M.G., Deputy Assistant Quartermaster General.
d.b., double-breasted (coat).
D.B.E., Dame Commander of the Order of the British Empire.
D.C., District of Columbia (U.S.A.) ; direct current (elect.).
D.C.C., Double cotton-covered (of electric wire).
D.C.L., Doctor of Civil Law ; Distillers' Company Ltd.
D.C.L.I., Duke of Cornwall's Light Infantry.
D.C.M., Distinguished Conduct Medal.
D.C.S., Deputy Clerk of Session.
D.C.V.O., Dame Commander of the Royal Victorian Order.
D.D., Doctor of Divinity.
d.d. (L.), *dono dedit*, "given as a gift."

D.D.D. (L.), *dat, dicat, dedicat,* "gives, devotes and dedicates."
D.D.S., Doctor of Dental Surgery.
deb., debenture.
Dec., December; Decani (of choir).
dec., deceased.
Def., Deferred (stocks or shares).
def., defendant; definite; definition.
deg., degree.
Del., Delaware (U.S.A.).
del., delegate; delete; (L.) *delineavit*, drawn by (art).
D.E.M.S., Defensively Equipped Merchant Ship.
Dem., Democrat (U.S.A.).
D.Eng., Doctor of Engineering.
denom., denomination.
Dent., dental; dentistry; dentist.
dep., departs (of train, etc.); deputy.
dept., department.
deriv., derivation.
Det. Insp., Detective Inspector.
Deut., Deuteronomy (O.T.).
D.F., Dean of the Faculty; direction finding.
d.f., double-fronted (building).
D.F.C., Distinguished Flying Cross.
D.F.M., Distinguished Flying Medal.
dft., draft.
D.G. (L.), *Dei gratia,* "by the grace of God"; (L.) *Deo gratias,* "thanks to God"; Director-General; Dragoon Guards.
Dg., dekagramme.
dg., decigramme.
D.H.A., Department of Home Affairs (Scottish Office).
diam., diameter.
D.I.C., Diploma of the Imperial College.
dict., dictionary.
diff., difference.
dim., diminutive.
Dioc., Diocese; Diocesan.
Dir., Director.
dis., **disc(t).**, discount.
Dist., District.
dist., distance.
Div., Division (army).
div., dividend; division.
D.L., Deputy Lieutenant.
Dl., dekalitre.
dl., decilitre.
D.L.I., Durham Light Infantry.
D.Lit., Doctor of Literature.
D.Litt., (at Aberdeen) Doctor of Letters.
D.L.P., Divisional Labour Party.
D.M., Doctor of Medicine (Oxford); Deputy Master.
Dm., dekametre.
dm., decimetre.
D.M.I., Director of Military Intelligence.
D.M.R.E., Diploma in Medical Radiology and Electrology.
D.Mus., Doctor of Music (usually Mus.D.).
D.N.B., Dictionary of National Biography.
do., *ditto,* the same.
D.O.M. (L.), *Deo optimo maximo,* "to God the best and greatest."
Dom. (L.), *Dominus,* Lord, Master; Dominion.
D.O.M.S., Diploma in Ophthalmic Medicine and Surgery.
D.O.R.A., Defence of the Realm Act(s).
doz., dozen(s).
D.P., Double pole.
D.P.H., Diploma in Public Health.
D.Ph., **D.Phil.**, Doctor of Philosophy (usually Ph.D.).
D.P.O., Distributing Post Office.
D.P.P., Director of Public Prosecutions.
D.Q.M.G., Deputy Quartermaster-General.
D.R., Dead reckoning.
Dr., Doctor; debtor.
dr., drachm; drawer (banking).
dram. pers. (L.), *dramatis personae,* "characters of the play."
d.s., days after sight (on bills of exchange).
D.S.C., Distinguished Service Cross.
D.Sc., Doctor of Science.
D.S.M., Distinguished Service Medal.
D.S.O., Distinguished Service Order.
d.s.p. (L.), *decessit sine prole,* "died without issue."
D.S.Sc., Diploma in Sanitary Science.
d.t.s, (coll.) delirium tremens.
D.Th., **D.Theol.**, Doctor of Theology.
D.T.M., Diploma in Tropical Medicine.
Du., Dutch.
Dunelm. (L.), *Dunelmensis,* of Durham (*esp.* in signature of Bishop).
D.V. (L.), *Deo volente,* "God willing."
D.V.M., Doctor of Veterinary Medicine.
d.v.p. (L.), *decessit vita patris,* "died during lifetime of father."
D.V.S., Doctor of Veterinary Science (or Surgery).
dwt., pennyweight.

E., earth; east; Eastern (London postal district); second class ship at Lloyd's; Egyptian (in £E).
ea., each.
E. & O.E., errors and omissions excepted.
E.B., Encyclopaedia Britannica.
Ebor. (L.), *Eboracensis,* of York (in signature of Archbishop).
E.C., East Central (London postal district).
Eccles., Ecclesiastes (O.T.).
Ecclus., Ecclesiasticus (Apoc.).
Econ., Economics.
E.C.U., English Church Union.
ed., **edit.**, edited.
Edin., Edinburgh.
edn., edition.
E.D.S., English Dialect Society.
E.E., Envoy Extraordinary; errors excepted (mercantile).
E.E.T.S., Early English Text Society.
e.g. (L.), *exempli gratia,* "for example."
E.G.U., English Golf Union.
Egyptol., Egyptology.
e.h.p., electrical horse-power.
E.I., East Indies; East India.
E.I.C., East India Company.
ejusd. (L.), *ejusdem,* "of the same."
Elien. (L.), *Eliensis,* of Ely (in signature of Bishop).
E.M.B., Empire Marketing Board.
E.M.F., Electromotive force.
E.M.J., Edinburgh Medical Journal.
Emp., Emperor, Empress.
E.M.U., Electromagnetic Units.
encl., enclosure.
Ency., Encyclop(a)edia.
E.N.E., east-north-east.
Eng., England; English.
engr., engraved; engraving.
E.N.S.A., Entertainments National Service Association.
Ent. Sta. Hall., Entered at Stationers' Hall.
Ep., Epistle.
E.P.A., Empire Parliamentary Association.
Eph., Ephesians (N.T.).
Epiph., Epiphany.
episc., episcopal.
E.P.N.S., Electro-Plated Nickel Silver.
E.P.T., Excess Profits Tax.
eq., equal.
equiv., equivalent.
E.R., East Riding (Yorkshire).
E.S.E., east-south-east.
Esq(r)., Esquire.
est., established.
Esth., Esther (O.T.).
E.S.U., Electrostatic units.
et al. (L.), *et alibi,* "and elsewhere"; *et alia,* "and other things"; *et alii,* "and other people."
etc. (L.), *et cetera,* "and (the) other things."
et seq., **et sqq.** (L.), *et sequens, et sequentia,* "and the following."
E.T.U., Electrical Trades Union.
etymol., etymology, etymological.
Ex., Exodus (O.T.).
Exc., Excellency.
exc., except; (L.) *excudit,* engraved by.
ex div., without dividend.
Exod., Exodus (O.T.).
ex off. (L.), *ex officio,* by virtue of office.
Exon. (L.), *Exoniensis,* of Exeter (in signature of Bishop).
ex(o)r., executor
exp., export.
Ez., Ezra (O.T.).
Ezek., Ezekiel (O.T.).

F, firm (of pencil-lead).
F., Fahrenheit ; Father (R.C.).
f., feminine ; farthing ; filly.
F.A., Football Association.
F.A.A., Fleet Air Arm.
f.a.a., free of all average.
F.A.C.S., Fellow of the American College of Surgeons.
fac(s)., facsimile.
Fahr., Fahrenheit.
F.A.I., Fellow of the Auctioneers' and Estate Agents' Institute.
F.A.L.P.A., Fellow of the Incorporated Society of Auctioneers and Landed Property Agents.
F.A.N.Y., First Aid Nursing Yeomanry.
F.A.S., Fellow of the Anthropological Society.
f.a.s., free alongside ship
F.A.S.E., Fellow of the Antiquarian Society, Edinburgh.
F.B.A., Fellow of the British Association.
F.B.I., Federation of British Industries ; Federal Bureau of Investigation (U.S.A.).
F.B.O.A., Fellow of the British Optical Association.
F.B.S., Fellow of the Botanical Society.
F.B.S.E., Fellow of the Botanical Society of Edinburgh.
F.B.U., Fire Brigades Union.
F.C., Football Club ; Free Church.
F.C.A., Fellow of the Institute of Chartered Accountants.
fcap., foolscap.
F.C.F.C., Free Church Federal Council.
F.C.G.I., Fellow of the City and Guilds of London Institute.
F.C.I.I., Fellow of the Chartered Insurance Institute of London.
F.C.I.S., Fellow of the Chartered Institute of Secretaries.
F.C.P., Fellow of the College of Preceptors.
F.C.S., Fellow of the Chemical Society.
F.D. (L.), *Fidei Defensor,* "Defender of the Faith."
Feb(y)., February.
fec. (L.), *fecit,* made by.
fed., federal ; federated.
F.E.I.S., Fellow of the Educational Institute of Scotland.
F.E.S., Fellow of the Entomological Society.
feud., feudal(ism).
ff., folios ; following pages.
F.F.A.S., Fellow of the Faculty of Actuaries in Scotland.
F.F.I., French Forces of the Interior.
F.F.P.S., Fellow of the Faculty of Physicians and Surgeons.
F.F.P.S.G., Fellow of the Faculty of Physicians and Surgeons, Glasgow.
f.g.a., free of general average.
F.G.S., Fellow of the Geological Society of London.
F.H., fire hydrant.
F.I.A., Fellow of the Institute of Actuaries.
F.I.A.A., Fellow Architect Member of the Incorporated Association of Architects and Surveyors.
F.I.A.S., Fellow Surveyor Member of the Incorporated Association of Architects and Surveyors.
F.I.B.D., Fellow of the Institute of British Decorators.
F.I.C., Fellow of the Institute of Chemistry.
F.I.C.S., Fellow of the Institute of Chartered Shipbrokers.
Fid. Def. (L.), *Fidei Defensor,* "Defender of the Faith."
fi. fa. (L.), *fieri facias,* "that you cause to be made" (law).
fig., figure (illustration) ; figurative(ly).
F.I.G.E., Fellow of the Institution of Gas Engineers.
F.I.M.T.A., Fellow of the Institute of Municipal Treasurers and Accountants.
F.I.Inst., Fellow of the Imperial Institute.
F.I.J., Fellow of the Institute of Journalists.
fin., financial ; finis.
F.I.N.A., Fellow of the Institution of Naval Architects.
Finn., Finnish.
Fin. Sec., Financial Secretary.
F.Inst.P., Fellow of the Institute of Physics.
F.I.O., Fellow of the Institute of Ophthalmic Opticians.
F.I.S.A., Fellow of the Incorporated Secretaries Association.
F.I.S.E., Fellow of the Institution of Structural Engineers.
fl. (L.), *floruit,* "he (she) flourished (lived)."
f.l. (L.), *falsa lectio,* "false reading" (of MS., etc.).
F.L.A., Fellow of the Library Association.
Fla., Florida (U.S.A.).
F.L.A.A., Fellow of the London Association of Accountants.
F.L.A.S., Fellow of the Land Agents' Society.
Flem., Flemish.
flor. (L.), *floruit,* "he (she) flourished (lived)."
F.L.S., Fellow of the Linnean Society.
Flt.Lt., Flight-Lieutenant.
F.M., Field-Marshal.
fm., fathom.
F.M.S., Federated Malay States.
F.O., Foreign office.
fo., folio.
f.o.b., free on board.
foll., following.
f.o.r., free on rail.
F.P., fire-plug ; field punishment ; former pupil.
fp., foot-pound ; (It.), *forte-piano,* loud (then) soft (mus.).
f.p.a., free of particular average.
F.Phys.S., Fellow of the Physical Society.
F.P.S., Fellow of the Philosophical Society ; Fellow of the Philharmonic Society.
Fr., French.
fr., franc ; from.
F.R.A.I., Fellow of the Royal Anthropological Institute.
F.R.A.M., Fellow of the Royal Academy of Music.
F.R.Ae.S., Fellow of the Royal Aeronautical Society.
F.R.A.S., Fellow of the Royal Astronomical Society ; Fellow of the Royal Asiatic Society.
F.R.B.S., Fellow of the Royal Botanic Society.
F.R.C.I., Fellow of the Royal Colonial Institute.
F.R.C.M., Fellow of the Royal College of Music.
F.R.C.O., Fellow of the Royal College of Organists.
F.R.C.O.G., Fellow of the Royal College of Obstetricians and Gynaecologists.
F.R.C.P., Fellow of the Royal College of Physicians.
F.R.C.P.E., Fellow of the Royal College of Physicians of Edinburgh.
F.R.C.P.I., Fellow of the Royal College of Physicians of Ireland.
F.R.C.S., Fellow of the Royal College of Surgeons.
F.R.C.S.E., Fellow of the Royal College of Surgeons of Edinburgh.
F.R.C.S.I., Fellow of the Royal College of Surgeons of Ireland.
F.R.C.V.S., Fellow of the Royal College of Veterinary Surgeons.
F.R.Econ.Soc., Fellow of the Royal Economic Society.
freq., frequency.
F.R.F.P.S., Fellow of the Royal Faculty of Physicians and Surgeons (Glasgow).
F.R.G.S., Fellow of the Royal Geographical Society.
F.R.Hist.S., Fellow of the Royal Historical Society.
F.R.Hort.S., Fellow of the Royal Horticultural Society.
Fri., Friday.
F.R.I.B.A., Fellow of the Royal Institute of British Architects.
Frisco, San Francisco (California).
Frl. (Germ.), *Fräulein,* Miss.
F.R.M.S., Fellow of the Royal Microscopical Society.
F.R.Met.S., Fellow of the Royal Meteorological Society.
F.R.N.S.A., Fellow of the Royal Naval School of Architects.
F.R.P.S., Fellow of the Royal Photographic Society.
F.R.P.S.L., Fellow of the Royal Philatelic Society of London.
F.R.S., Fellow of the Royal Society.
F.R.S.A., Fellow of the Royal Society of Arts.
F.R.S.A.I., Fellow of the Royal Society of Antiquaries of Ireland.
F.R.San.I., Fellow of the Royal Sanitary Institute.
F.R.S.E., Fellow of the Royal Society of Edinburgh.

F.R.S.G.S., Fellow of the Royal Scottish Geographical Society.
F.R.S.L., Fellow of the Royal Society of Literature.
F.R.S.S., Fellow of the Royal Statistical Society (formerly F.S.S.).
F.R.S.S.A., Fellow of the Royal Scottish Society of Arts.
F.S., Fleet Surgeon.
F.S.A., Fellow of the Society of Antiquaries; Fellow of the Society of Arts.
F.S.A.A., Fellow of the Society of Incorporated Accountants and Auditors.
F.S.A.(Scot.), Fellow of the Society of Antiquaries of Scotland.
F.S.I., Fellow of the Surveyors' Institute.
F.S.P., Field Security Personnel.
F.S.R., Field Service Regulations.
ft., foot; feet.
F.T.C.D., Fellow of Trinity College, Dublin.
F.T.C.L., Fellow of Trinity College (of Music), London.
fur., furlong.
f.v. (L.), *folio verso*, "on the back of the page."
F.W.A., Factories and Workshops Acts.
F.W.D., Front-wheel drive.
F.Z.S., Fellow of the Zoological Society of London.
F.Z.S. (Scot.), Fellow of the Zoological Society of Scotland.

g., guinea.
G.A., General Assembly.
Ga., Georgia (U.S.A.).
Gael., Gaelic.
Gal., Galatians (N.T.).
gal., gallon(s).
G.B., Great Britain; Gaumont British (Film Company).
G.B. & I., Great Britain and Ireland.
G.B.E., Knight (or Dame) Grand Cross of the Order of the British Empire.
G.B.S., George Bernard Shaw.
G.C., George Cross.
G.C.B., Knight Grand Cross of the Bath.
G.C.I.E., Knight Grand Commander of the Order of the Indian Empire.
G.C.L.H., Knight Grand Cross of the Legion of Honour.
G.C.M., greatest common measure.
G.C.M.G., Knight Grand Cross of the Order of St. Michael and St. George.
G.C.S.I., Knight Grand Commander of the Order of the Star of India.
G.C.V.O., Knight Grand Cross of the Royal Victorian Order.
Gdns., Gardens.
G.E.C., General Electric Company.
gen. (L.), *genus*, kind.
Gen., General; Genesis (O.T.).
G.F.S., Girls' Friendly Society.
G.G., Grenadier Guards; Girls' Guildry.
g.gr., great gross, 144 dozens.
G.H.Q., General Headquarters.
G.I., Government Issue (U.S.A.); (fig.) private soldier (U.S.A.).
Gib. (colloq.), Gibraltar.
G.J.C., Grand Junction Canal.
Gk., Greek.
G.L., Grand Lodge (freemasonry).
Glam, Glamorganshire.
Glos, Gloucestershire.
gloss., glossary.
G.M., George Medal; Grand Master (orders of knighthood and freemasonry); Gold Medallist (Bisley).
gm., gramme.
G.M.B., Great Master of the Bath; good merchantable brand (of metals).
G.M.C., General Medical Council.
G.M.I.E., Grand Master of the Indian Empire.
G.M.M.G., Grand Master of St. Michael and St. George.
G.M.P., Garrison Military Police.
G.M.S.I., Grand Master of the Star of India.
G.M.T., Greenwich Mean Time.
G.O., General Order.
G.O.C., General Officer Commanding.
G.O.C.-in-C., General Officer Commanding-in-Chief.
G.O.M., Grand Old Man.
Goth., Gothic.
Gov., Governor.
Gov.-Gen., Governor-General.
Govt., Government.
G.P., general practitioner (doctor); general paralysis of the insane (also G.P.I.); (L.) *Gloria Patri*, "Glory to the Father."
G.P.D.S.T., Girls' Public Day School Trust.
G.P.M., Grand Past Master (freemasonry).
G.P.O., General Post Office.
G.R. (et I.), (L.), *Georgius Rex* (*et Imperator*), George, King (and Emperor).
gr., grain.
G.R.C.M., Graduate of the Royal College of Music.
Gr. Gds., Grenadier Guards.
G.S., General Staff.
G.S.N.C., General Steam Navigation Company.
G.S.O., General Staff Office(r).
G.T., Good Templar.
Gt. Br., Great Britain.
gtd., guaranteed.
guar., guarantee(d).
G.W.R., Great Western Railway.
gym., gymnasium; gymnastics.

H, hard (of pencil-lead); hydrant.
h., hour.
H.A. Historical Association.
H.A.&M., Hymns Ancient and Modern.
Hab., Habakkuk (O.T.).
hab. (L.), *habitat*, "he lives."
Hab. Corp., Habeas Corpus (writ).
H.A.C., Honourable Artillery Company.
Hag., Haggai (O.T.).
H.A.L. (Germ.), *Hamburg-Amerika Linie*, Hamburg-America Line.
h and c, hot and cold (water supply).
Hants, Hampshire.
HB, hard black (of pencil-lead).
H.B.C., Hudson's Bay Company.
H.B.M., His (Her) Britannic Majesty.
H.C., House of Commons; Heralds' College; Headmasters' Conference.
h.c. (L.), *honoris causa*, honorary.
hcap., handicap.
H.C.F., highest common factor.
hd., hogshead.
hdbk., handbook.
hdqrs., headquarters.
H.E., His Excellency; His Emininence; high explosive.
Heb., Hebrew; Hebrews (N.T.).
H.E.H., His (Her) Exalted Highness (British India).
Herts, Hertfordshire.
HF, hard firm (of pencil-lead).
H.F., High frequency (elect.); Holiday Fellowship.
hf.-bd., half-bound.
H.F.R.A., Honorary Fellow of the Royal Academy.
H.G., Horse Guards; His (Her) Grace; Home Guard.
Hg., hectogramme.
H.H., His (Her) Highness; His Holiness (the Pope).
HH, double hard (of pencil-lead).
hhd., hogshead.
HHH, treble hard (of pencil-lead).
H.I.H., His (Her) Imperial Highness.
H.I.M., His (Her) Imperial Majesty.
hist., history; historical.
H.J.(S). (L.), *hic jacet* (*sepultus*), "here lies (buried)."
H.K., House of Keys (Isle of Man).
H.L., House of Lords.
Hl., hectolitre.
H.L.I., Highland Light Infantry.
H.M., His (Her) Majesty.
Hm., hectometre.
H.M.A.S., His Majesty's Australian Ship.
H.M.C., His Majesty's Customs.
H.M.I.F., His Majesty's Inspector of Factories.
H.M.I.(S.), His Majesty's Inspector (of Schools).
H.M.I.T., His Majesty's Inspector of Taxes.
H.M.O.W., His Majesty's Office of Works.
H.M.P. (L.), *hoc monumentum posuit*, "erected this monument."
H.M.S., His Majesty's Ship; His Majesty's Service.

H.M.S.O., His Majesty's Stationery Office.
H.M.V., His Master's Voice (prot.).
H.O., Home Office.
Hon., Honourable ; Honorary.
Hon. Sec., Honorary Secretary.
hor., horizon.
hort., horticulture ; horticultural.
Hos., Hosea (O.T.).
H.P., House Physician ; Houses of Parliament.
h.p., horse-power ; half-pay ; high pressure ; hire purchase.
h.p.n., horse-power nominal.
H.Q., Headquarters.
hr., hour.
H.R.E., Holy Roman Empire, Emperor.
H.R.H., His (Her) Royal Highness.
H.R.H.A., Honorary Member of the Royal Hibernian Academy.
H.R.S.A., Honorary Member of the Royal Scottish Academy.
H.S., House Surgeon.
H.S.A., Hospital Savings Association.
H.S.E. (L.), *hic situs (sepultus) est*, "here is laid (buried)."
H.S.H., His Serene Highness.
h.t., high tension (elect.).
Hunts, Huntingdonshire.
H.W.(M.), High Water (Mark).
h.w., hit wicket (cricket).
H.W.O.S.T., High Water Ordinary Spring Tides.

I., Idaho (U.S.A.) ; Island.
I.A., Indian Army ; Incorporated Accountant.
Ia., Iowa (U.S.A.).
I.A.A.M., Incorporated Association of Assistant Masters.
I.A.A.S., Incorporated Association of Architects and Surveyors.
I.A.H.M., Incorporated Association of Head Masters.
I.A.R.O., Indian Army Reserve of Officers.
ib(id). (L.), *ibidem*, "in the same place."
i/c., in charge of.
I.C.A., Institute of Chartered Accountants.
I.C.E., Institution of Civil Engineers.
I.C.I., Imperial Chemical Industries.
I.C.S., Indian Civil Service.
I.D., Intelligence Department.
id. (L.), *idem*, "the same."
I.D.N. (L.), *in Dei nomine*, "in the name of God."
i.e. (L.), *id est*, "that is."
I.E.E., Institution of Electrical Engineers.
I.F.T.U., International Federation of Trade Unions.
I.G., Inspector-General.
I.G.E., Institution of Gas Engineers.
ign. (L.), *ignotus*, "unknown" (of painter, etc.).
i.h.p., indicated horse-power.
I.H.S., **J.H.S.** (L.), *Iesus Hominum Salvator*, "Jesus, Saviour of Mankind"; (properly *ΙΗΣ*, in Greek, the first three letters of *ΙΗΣΟΥΣ* Jesus).
I.I.P.A., Institute of Incorporated Practitioners in Advertising.
I.J., Institute of Journalists (now N.A.J.).
Ill., Illinois (U.S.A.).
ill(us)., illustration ; illustrated.
I.L.O., International Labour Office.
I.L.P., Independent Labour Party.
I.M.C.E., Institution of Municipal and County Engineers.
I.Mech.E., Institution of Mechanical Engineers.
I.M.N.S., Imperial Military Nursing Service.
Imp., Imperial ; (L.) *Imperator*, Emperor , *Imperatrix*, Empress.
imp. (L.), *imprimatur*, "let it be printed"; imported.
imperf., imperforated (stamps).
I.M.S., Indian Medical Service.
I.M.T.A., Institute of Municipal Treasurers and Accountants.
in., inch.
I.N.A., Institution of Naval Architects.
I.N.C. (L.), *in nomine Christi*, "in the name of Christ."
Inc., Incorporated (U.S.A.).
incl., including ; inclusive.
incog. (It.), *incognito*, unknown.
Ind., Indiana (U.S.A.) ; India (on coins).
ind., index.
Ind.T(err)., Indian Territory (U.S.A.).
inf. (L.), *infra*, below.
infra dig. (L.), *infra dignitatem*, "beneath one dignity."
I.N.I., **I.N.J.** (L.), *in nomine Iesu*, "in the nam of Jesus."
init. (L.), *initio*, "at (from) the beginning."
in lim. (L.), *in limine*, "on the threshold," "at th outset."
in pr. (L.), *in principio*, "in the beginning."
I.N.R.I. (L.), *Iesus Nazarenus Rex Iudaeorum* "Jesus of Nazareth, King of the Jews."
insc., inscribed (stock).
Insp., Inspector.
Insp.-Gen., Inspector-General.
I.N.S.T. (L.), *in nomine Sanctas Trinitatis*, "in th name of the Holy Trinity."
inst. (Fr.), *instante*, the present month.
Inst.Act., Institute of Actuaries.
Inst.C.E., Institution of Civil Engineers.
Inst.E.E., Institution of Electrical Engineers.
Inst.Mech.E., Institution of Mechanical Engineers
Inst.N.A., Institution of Naval Architects.
int., interest.
int. al. (L.), *inter alia*, "among other things."
inter., intermediate.
inv., invoice.
inv(en). (L.), *invenit*, "he (she) invented, discovered composed (it)."
I.O.F., Independent Order of Foresters.
I.O.H., Independent Order of Hibernians.
I. of M., Isle of Man.
I. of W., Isle of Wight.
I.O.G.T., International Order of Good Templars.
I.O.O., Institute of Ophthalmic Opticians.
I.O.O.F., Independent Order of Odd Fellows.
I.O.P., Institute of Painters in Oil Colours.
I.O.M., Isle of Man.
I.O.U., I owe you (loose form of promissory note).
I.O.W., Isle of Wight.
I.P.A., Institute of Public Administration ; India Pale Ale.
I.P.D. (L.), *in praesentia Dominorum*, "in the presence of the Lords of Session."
ipecac., ipecacuanha.
i.p.i. (L.), *in partibus infidelium*, "in the regions of unbelievers."
I.Q., Intelligence Quotient.
i.q. (L.), *idem quod*, "the same as."
I.R., Inland Revenue.
I.R.A., Irish Republican Army.
I.R.O., Inland Revenue Office.
I.S., Irish Society.
Is., Isaiah (O.T.) ; Island.
I.S.C., Indian Staff Corps.
Isl., Island.
I.S.M., Incorporated Society of Musicians.
I.S.O., (Companion of the) Imperial Service Order.
isth., isthmus.
I.S.U., International Students' Union.
I.T., Indian Territory (U.S.A.); Inner Temple (Inns of Court).
ital., italics.
I.W.E., Institution of Water Engineers.
I.W.T.D., Inland Water Transport Department.
I.W.W., Industrial Workers of the World.
I.Y., Imperial Yeomanry.

J., Judge ; Justice ; joule (elect.).
J.A., Judge Advocate.
J.A.-G., Judge Advocate-General.
Jam., James (N.T.) ; Jamaica.
Jan., January.
Jap., Japanese.
J.C. (L.), *jurisconsultus*, jurisconsult ; Jesus Christ.
J.C.D. (L.), *Juris Civilis Doctor*, Doctor of Civil Law ; (L.) *Juris Canonici Doctor*, Doctor of Canon Law.
J.D. (L.), *Jurum Doctor*, Doctor of Laws.
Jer., Jeremiah (O.T.).
J.H.S., see I.H.S.
J.I.C., Joint Industrial Council.
jn., junction.
Jno., John ; St. John (N.T.).
jnr., junior.
Jo., Joel (O.T.).

Josh., Joshua (O.T.).
J.P., Justice of the Peace.
jr., junior.
J.T.C., Junior Training Corps.
J.U.D. (L.), *Juris utriusque Doctor*, Doctor of both (Civil and Canon) Laws.
Jud., Judith (Apoc.).
Jud(g)., Judges (O.T.).
jun., junior.
junc., junction.
Jun. Opt., Junior Optime (Camb. Univ. Math. Tripos.).
junr., junior.

K., King.
Kal. (L.), *Kalendae*, Calends.
Kan., Kansas (U.S.A.).
K.B., King's Bench.
K.B.D., King's Bench Division.
K.B.E., Knight Bachelor of the Order of the British Empire.
K.C., King's Counsel; King's College.
kc., kilocycle.
K.C.B., Knight Commander of the Bath.
K.C.I.E., Knight Commander of the Order of the Indian Empire.
K.C.M.G., Knight Commander of the Order of St. Michael and St. George.
K.C.S.I., Knight Commander of the Order of the Star of India.
K.C.V.O., Knight Commander of the Royal Victorian Order.
K.G., Knight of the Garter.
Kg., kilogramme.
K.G.C.B., Knight Grand Cross of the Order of the Bath (more usually G.C.B.).
K.G.F., Knight of the Golden Fleece.
K.H.C., Honorary Chaplain to the King.
K.H.P., Honorary Physician to the King.
K.H.S., Honorary Surgeon to the King.
KKK., Ku Klux Klan (U.S.A.).
Kl., kilolitre.
K.L.H., Knight of the Legion of Honour.
K.L.M., Royal Dutch Air Lines.
K.M., Knight of Malta.
Km., kilometre.
K.O.S.B., King's Own Scottish Borderers.
K.O.Y.L.I., King's Own Yorkshire Light Infantry.
K.P., Knight of St. Patrick.
K.R., King's Regulations.
K.R.R.C., King's Royal Rifle Corps.
K.S., King's Scholar.
K.S.G., Knight of St. Gregory.
K.S.I., Knight of the Order of the Star of India.
K.S.L.I., King's Shropshire Light Infantry.
K.T., Knight of the Order of the Thistle; Knight Templar.
Kt., Knight Bachelor.
kw., kilowatt.
Ky., Kentucky (U.S.A.).

L., Lake; Liberal; Latin; left (of stage).
l., left; lira; litre; line.
L.A., Library Association; Legislative Assembly.
La., Louisiana (U.S.A.).
Lab., Labrador; laboratory; Labour.
L.A.C.. London Athletic Club; Leading Aircraftman; Licentiate of the Apothecaries' Company.
L.A.H., Licentiate of Apothecaries' Hall, Dublin.
L.A.M., London Academy of Music.
Lam., Lamentations (O.T.).
Lancs, Lancashire.
Lat., Latin.
lat., latitude.
lav., lavatory.
lb. (L.), *libra*, pound.
l.b., leg-bye (cricket).
l.b.w., leg before wicket (cricket).
L.C., Lord Chancellor; Lord Chamberlain; left centre (of stage).
l.c., (print.) lower case; (L.) *loco citato*, "in the place cited"; letter of credit.
L.C.C., London County Council; Lancashire Cotton Corporation.
L.Ch(ir)., Licentiate in Surgery.
L.C.J., Lord Chief Justice.
L.C.M., lowest common multiple.
L.C.P., Licentiate of the College of Preceptors.
L.-Cpl., Lance-Corporal.
L.C.S., London Co-operative Society.
L.D., Doctor of Letters (U.S.A.); Lady Day; (L.) *laus Deo*, "praise be to God."
L.Div., Licentiate in Divinity.
L.D.S., Licentiate in Dental Surgery; (L.) *laus Deo semper*, "praise be to God for ever."
Leics, Leicestershire.
L. ès L. (Fr.), *Licencié ès Lettres*, Licentiate of Letters.
Lev., Leviticus (O.T.).
L.F., low frequency (elect.).
L.F.B.C., London Federation of Boys' Clubs Incorporated.
L.F.P.S., Licentiate of the Faculty of Physicians and Surgeons.
L.F.P.S.G., Licentiate of the Faculty of Physicians and Surgeons (Glasgow).
L.G., Life Guards.
L.G.U., Ladies' Golf Union.
l.h.d., left-hand drive.
L.I., Long Island (U.S.A.).
Lib., Library; Librarian; Liberal.
Lic.Med., Licentiate in Medicine.
Lieut., Lieutenant.
Lincs, Lincolnshire.
Linn., Linn(a)ean; Linnaeus.
Lit., literally.
Lith., Lithuania; Lithuanian.
litho(g)., lithograph; lithography.
Lit(t). Hum. (L.), *Litterae Humaniores*, Final Classical Honour School, Oxford University, usually known as "Greats."
Litt.D. (L.), *Literarum Doctor*, Doctor of Letters (Literature).
liturg., liturgy; liturgical.
L.J., Lord Justice (of Appeal).
L.J.C., Lord Justice Clerk.
L.L., Lord-Lieutenant.
ll., lines.
L.L.A., Lady Licentiate in Arts.
LL.B. (L.), *Legum Baccalaureus*, Bachelor of Laws.
LL.D. (L.), *Legum Doctor*, Doctor of Laws.
LL.JJ., Lords Justices of Appeal.
LL.M. (L.), *Legum Magister*, Master of Laws.
L.M., Licentiate in Midwifery; Lord Mayor.
L.M.B.C., Lady Margaret Boat Club (St. John's College, Cambridge).
L.M.S., London Missionary Society.
L.M.S.(R.), London, Midland & Scottish (Railway).
L.M.S.S.A., Licentiate in Medicine and Surgery of the Society of Apothecaries.
L.N.E.(R.), London & North Eastern (Railway).
loc. cit. (L.), *loco citato*, "in the place cited."
log., logarithm.
Lond., London.
Londin. (L.), *Londiniensis*, of London (in signature of Bishop).
long., longitude.
loq. (L.), *loquitor*, (he) speaks.
L.P., Labour Party; Lord Provost; letters patent.
l.p., large paper (edition); long primer (type); low pressure.
L.P.O., London Philharmonic Orchestra.
L'pool, Liverpool.
L.P.S., Lord Privy Seal.
L.P.T.B., London Passenger Transport Board.
L.R.A.M., Licentiate of the Royal Academy of Music.
L.R.C., Leander Rowing Club; London Rowing Club.
L.R.C.M., Licentiate of the Royal College of Medicine.
L.R.C.P., Licentiate of the Royal College of Physicians.
L.R.C.P.E., Licentiate of the Royal College of Physicians of Edinburgh.
L.R.C.P.I., Licentiate of the Royal College of Physicians of Ireland.
L.R.C.S., Licentiate of the Royal College of Surgeons.
L.R.C.S.E., Licentiate of the Royal College of Surgeons of Edinburgh.
L.R.C.S.I., Licentiate of the Royal College of Surgeons of Ireland.

L.R.C.V.S., Licentiate of the Royal College of Veterinary Surgeons.
L.R.F.P.S.G., Licentiate of the Royal Faculty of Physicians and Surgeons, Glasgow.
Lrs., Lancers.
L.S. (L.), *loco sigilli*, "the place of the seal" (legal documents); Landing Ship.
L.S.A., Licentiate of the Society of Apothecaries.
L.S.C., London Society of Compositors.
L.S.D., Lightermen, Stevedores and Dockers.
£.s.d. (L.), *librae, solidi, denarii*, pounds, shillings, pence.
L.S.M.A., London Schools' Music Association.
L.S.O., London Symphony Orchestra.
L.S.T., Landing Ship, Tanks.
l.t., low tension (elect.).
L.T.A., Lawn Tennis Association; London Teachers' Association.
L.T.C., Lawn Tennis Club.
L.T.C.L., Licentiate of Trinity College of Music (London).
Lt.-Col., Lieutenant-Colonel.
Lt.-Comm., Lieutenant-Commander (R.N.).
Ltd., Limited.
Lt.-Gen., Lieutenant-General.
Lt.-Gov., Lieutenant-Governor.
L.T.M., Licentiate of Tropical Medicine.
L.V., Licensed Victuallers.
L.W.L., Load Water Line.
L.W.(M.), Low Water (Mark).
L.W.O.S.T., Low Water Ordinary Spring Tides.
LXX., Septuagint.

M. (Fr.), *Monsieur*, Sir.
m., mark (coin); married; metre; mile; minute; maiden (over) (cricket).
M.A., Master of Arts; Mathematical Association.
M.A.B., Metropolitan Asylums Board.
Macc., Maccabees (Apoc.).
M.A.F., Ministry of Agriculture and Fisheries.
mag., magazine; magnetism; magnetic.
M.A.G.B., Mining Association of Great Britain.
M.Agr(ic)., Master of Agriculture (U.S.A.).
Maj., Major.
Maj.-Gen., Major-General.
Mal., Malachi (O.T.).
Mancun. (L.), *Mancuniensis*, of Manchester (in signature of Bishop).
M. and B. 603, May and Baker (sulphonic drug).
Man(it)., Manitoba (Canada).
M.A.P., Ministry of Aircraft Production.
manuf., manufactured; manufacturer.
March., Marchioness.
Marq., Marquess.
Mass., Massachusetts (U.S.A.).
math(s)., mathematics.
matric., matriculation.
Matt., Matthew (N.T.).
M.B. (L.), *Medicinae Baccalaureus*, Bachelor of Medicine.
M.B.E., Member of the Order of the British Empire.
M.C., Military Cross; Master of Ceremonies; Member of Congress; Member of Council.
M.C.C., Marylebone Cricket Club; Middlesex County Council.
M.Ch. (L.), *Magister Chirurgiae*, Master of Surgery.
M.Ch.D., Master of Dental Surgery.
M.Ch.Orth., Master of Orthopaedic Surgery.
M.Com., Master of Commerce (Birmingham).
M.Comm., Master of Commerce and Administration (Manchester).
M.C.P., Member of the College of Preceptors.
M.C.P.S., Member of the College of Physicians and Surgeons.
M.C.S., Malay Civil Service.
M.D. (L.), *Medicinae Doctor*, Doctor of Medicine.
Md., Maryland (U.S.A.).
Mddx, Middlesex.
Mdm., Madam.
M.D.S., Master in Dental Surgery.
Me., Maine (U.S.A.); (Fr.), *Maître*, Master (title applied to barristers, etc.).
M.E.C., Member of Executive Council.
mech., mechanical; mechanics.
Med., Medieval.
med., medical; medicine.
Medit., Mediterranean (Sea).
M.E.F., Middle East Forces.
mem. (L.), *memento*, remember.
memo. (L.), *memorandum*, to be remembered.
M.Eng., Master of Engineering.
Messrs. (Fr.), *Messieurs*, Gentlemen; also as *pl.* of Mr.
MET., Metropolitan (Railway, London).
Met., Metropolitan.
meteor., meteorology.
Method., Methodist.
METRO (Fr.), *Chemin de Fer Métropolitain*, Metropolitan Railway (Paris).
mf. (It.), *mezzo forte*, "moderately loud" (mus.).
mfd., manufactured.
mfg., manufacturing.
M.F.G.B., Miners' Federation of Great Britain.
M.F.H., Master of Fox Hounds.
m.g., machine gun.
mg., milligramme.
M.G.G.S., Major-General, General Staff.
M.G.M., Metro-Goldwyn-Mayer (Films).
Mgr. (Fr.), *Monseigneur*; (It.), *Monsignore* (of Papal dignitaries).
M.H.A., Member of House of Assembly.
M.H.K., Member of the House of Keys (Isle of Man).
mho., unit of conductivity, reciprocal of the ohm (elect.).
M.H.R., Member of the House of Representatives.
Mic., Micah (O.T.).
M.I.C.E., Member of the Institution of Civil Engineers.
Mich., Michaelmas; Michigan (U.S.A.).
M.I.E.E., Member of the Institution of Electrical Engineers.
M.I.J., Member of the Institute of Journalists.
milit., military.
Mil. Att., Military Attaché.
M.I.Mar.E., Member of the Institute of Marine Engineers.
M.I.M.E., Member of the Institution of Mining Engineers.
M.I.Mech.E., Member of the Institution of Mechanical Engineers.
M.I.M.M., Member of the Institution of Mining and Metallurgy.
Min., Minister; Ministry.
min., minute.
M.I.N.A., Member of the Institution of Naval Architects.
Minn., Minnesota (U.S.A.).
Min. Plen., Minister Plenipotentiary.
M.Inst.C.E., Member of the Institution of Civil Engineers.
M.I.P., Member of the Institute of (Incorporated) Patentees.
misc., miscellaneous.
Miss., Mississippi (U.S.A.).
mk., mark (coin).
mkt., market.
ml., millilitre.
M.L.A., Modern Language Association; Member of the Legislative Assembly.
M.L. & N.S., Ministry of Labour & National Service.
M.L.C., Member of the Legislative Council.
Mlle. (Fr.), *Mademoiselle*, Miss.
M.M., Military Medal.
MM., Majesties; (Fr.), *Messieurs*, Gentlemen.
mm., millimetre.
M.M.B., Milk Marketing Board.
Mme. (Fr.), *Madame*, Madam.
M.N.I., Ministry of National Insurance.
M.O., Medical Officer; Money Order.
Mo., Missouri (U.S.A.).
Mod., Modern.
Mods., Moderations (Oxford University).
M. of F., Ministry of Food.
M.O.H., Master of Otter Hounds; Medical Officer of Health; Ministry of Health.
M.O.I., Ministry of Information.
mol.wt., molecular weight.
Mon., Monday; Monmouthshire.
Mont., Montana (U.S.A.).
M.O.O., Money Order Office.
M.O.S., Ministry of Supply.

M.P., Member of Parliament; Ministry of Pensions; Metropolitan Police; Military Police.
m.p., melting-point.
mp. (It.), *mezzo piano*, moderately soft (mus.).
m.p.g., miles per gallon.
M.Ph., Master of Philosophy (U.S.A.).
m.p.h., miles per hour.
M.P.S., Member of the Pharmaceutical Society.
M.R., Master of the Rolls; Municipal Reform (Party, L.C.C.).
Mr., Mister.
M.R.A.S., Member of the Royal Academy of Science; Member of the Royal Asiatic Society.
M.R.C.C., Member of the Royal College of Chemistry.
M.R.C.P., Member of the Royal College of Physicians.
M.R.C.P.E., Member of the Royal College of Physicians of Edinburgh.
M.R.C.P.I., Member of the Royal College of Physicians of Ireland.
M.R.C.S., Member of the Royal College of Surgeons.
M.R.C.S.E., Member of the Royal College of Surgeons of Edinburgh.
M.R.C.S.I., Member of the Royal College of Surgeons of Ireland.
M.R.C.V.S., Member of the Royal College of Veterinary Surgeons.
M.R.G.S., Member of the Royal Geographical Society.
M.R.I., Member of the Royal Institution.
M.R.I.A., Member of the Royal Irish Academy.
Mrs., Mistress.
M.R.S.G.S., Member of the Royal Scottish Geographical Society.
M.R.S.I., Member of the Royal Sanitary Institute.
M.R.S.T., Member of the Royal Society of Teachers.
M.S., Master in Surgery; Military Secretary; (L.), *Memoriae Sacrum*, "Sacred to the Memory."
m.s., month's sight.
MS(S)., manuscript(s).
M.S.A., Member of the Society of Arts.
M.S.C., Madras Staff Corps; Medical Staff Corps.
M.Sc., Master of Science.
M.S.I., Member of the Surveyors' Institution.
M.S.L., mean sea-level.
M.S.M., Meritorious Service Medal.
M.T., Mechanical transport.
Mt., Mount(ain).
M.T.B., Motor Torpedo Boat.
M.T.C.P., Ministry of Town and Country Planning.
mth., month.
Mt. Rev., Most Reverend.
M.U., Motor Union; Musicians' Union.
mus., music; museum.
Mus.B(ac)., Bachelor of Music.
Mus.D(oc)., Doctor of Music.
Mus.M., Master of Music.
M.V., Motor vessel; (It.), *mezza voce*, "subdued voice" (mus.).
M.V.O., Member of the Royal Victorian Order.
M.W., Most Worshipful; Most Worthy.
M.W.B., Metropolitan Water Board; Ministry of Works and Buildings.
M.W.G.M., Most Worshipful (Worthy) Grand Master (freemasonry).

N., north.
N.A., Nautical Almanac; North America(n); numerical aperture.
N.A.A.F.I., Naval, Army, and Air Force Institutes.
N.A.B.C., National Association of Boys' Clubs.
N.A.G.C., National Association of Girls' Clubs.
Nah., Nahum (O.T.).
N.A.H.T., National Association of Head Teachers.
N.A.J., National Association of Journalists.
N.A.L.G.O., National Association of Local Government Officers.
N.A.S., Nursing Auxiliary Service; National Association of Schoolmasters; National Academy of Science (U.S.A.).
Nat., National(ist); Natal.
Nat. Ord., Natural Order.
NAT.S.O.P.A. (Natsopa), National Society of Operative Printers and Assistants.
N.B. (L.), *nota bene*, "note well"; New Brunswick.
n.b., no ball (cricket).
N.B.L., National Book League.
N.C., North Carolina (U.S.A.).
N.C.C.L., National Council for Civil Liberties.
N.C.L., National Council of Labour.
N.C.O., Non-commissioned Officer.
N.C.S.S., National Council of Social Service.
N.C.U., National Cyclists' Union.
N.D.A., National Diploma in Agriculture.
N.Dak., North Dakota (U.S.A.).
N.D.C., National Defence Contribution.
N.D.L. (Germ.), *Norddeutscher Lloyd*, North German Lloyd (steamship company).
N.E., north-east; North-Eastern (London postal district); no effects (banking, on cheque).
Neb(r)., Nebraska (U.S.A.).
N.E.C., National Executive Committee.
N.E.D., New English Dictionary.
N.E.F., New Education Fellowship.
Neh., Nehemiah (O.T.).
N.E.I., Netherlands East Indies.
nem. con. (L.), *nemine contradicente*, "no one contradicting."
nem. dis(s). (L.), *nemine dissentiente*, "nobody dissenting."
N.Eng., New England (U.S.A.).
Neth., Netherlands.
Nev., Nevada (U.S.A.).
N.F., Newfoundland; Norman French; "no funds."
N.F.B.T.O., National Federation of Building Trades Operatives.
N.F.C.C., National Free Church Council.
N.F.C.T., National Federation of Class Teachers.
N.F.F., National Froebel Foundation.
N.F.L., National Film Library.
N.F.S., National Fire Service.
N.F.U., National Farmers' Union.
N.G.C., National Gas Council.
N.H., New Hampshire (U.S.A.).
N.Heb., New Hebrides.
n.h.p., nominal horse-power.
N.H.R.U., National Home Reading Union.
N.H.R(ules), National Hunt Rules.
N.H.T.P.C., National Housing and Town Planning Council.
N.I., Northern Ireland.
N.I.A.B., National Institute of Agricultural Botany.
N.I.I.P., National Institute of Industrial Psychology.
N.I.M.R., National Institution for Medical Research.
ni. pr. (L.), *nisi prius*, "unless previously" (law).
N.J., New Jersey (U.S.A.).
N.L., National Liberal; Navy League.
N.L.C., National Liberal Club.
N.L.F., National Liberal Federation.
N.L.I., National Lifeboat Institution.
N.Mex., New Mexico (U.S.A.).
N.N.E., north-north-east.
N.N.W., north-north-west.
N.O., Natural Order (biol.); New Orleans (U.S.A.).
n.o., not out (cricket).
N.O.D., Naval Ordnance Department.
nol. pros. (L.), *nolle prosequi*, "will not continue" (law).
Non-Coll., Non-Collegiate.
non compos. (L.), *non compos mentis*, "not of sound mind."
Noncon., Nonconformist.
non obst. (L.), *non obstante*, "notwithstanding."
non pros. (L.), *non prosequitur*, "he does not prosecute."
non seq. (L.), *non sequitur*, "it does not follow."
Northants, Northamptonshire.
Northumb, Northumberland.
Norvic. (L.), *Norvicensis*, of Norwich (in signature of Bishop).
No(s). (L.), *numero* (*numeris*), number(s).
Notts, Nottinghamshire.
Nov., November.
N.P., Notary Public.
N.P.A., Newspaper Proprietors' Association.
N.F.Y.F.C., National Federation of Young Farmers' Clubs.
N.P.L., National Physical Laboratory.
N.R., North Riding (Yorkshire).
nr., near.
N.R.A., National Rifle Association; National Recovery Administration (U.S.A.).

N.S., New Style (Gregorian Calendar) ; Nova Scotia ; (L.), *non satis*, "not sufficient."
N.S.H.E.B., North of Scotland Hydro-Electric Board.
N.S.I.C. (L.), *Noster Salvator Iesus Christus*, "Our Saviour, Jesus Christ."
N.S.O., National Symphony Orchestra.
N.S.P.C.C., National Society for the Prevention of Cruelty to Children.
N.S.Trip., Natural Science Tripos (Cambridge University).
N.S.W., New South Wales (Australia).
N.T., New Testament ; Northern Territory (Australia) ; National Trust.
N.U.C.A.W., National Union of Clerks and Administrative Workers.
N.U.D.A.W., National Union of Distributive and Allied Workers.
N.U.G.M.W., National Union of General and Municipal Workers.
N.U.J., National Union of Journalists (now N.A.J.).
N.U.M., National Union of Manufacturers.
Num., Numbers (O.T.).
N.U.P.B.P., National Union of Printing, Bookbinding and Paperworkers.
N.U.R., National Union of Railwaymen.
N.U.S., National Union of Students ; National Union of Seamen.
N.U.S.E.C., National Union of Societies for Equal Citizenship.
N.U.T., National Union of Teachers.
N.U.W.T., National Union of Women Teachers.
N.V.M., Nativity of the Virgin Mary.
N.W., north-west ; North-Western (London postal district).
N.W.F.P., North-West Frontier Province (India).
N.W.T., North-West Territory (Canada).
N.Y., New York (U.S.A.).
N.Y.K. (Jap.), *Nippon Yusen Kaisha*, Japan Mail Steamship Company.
N.Z., New Zealand.

o., over(s) (cricket).
o/a, on account.
ob. (L.), *obiit*, (he) died.
Obad., Obadiah (O.T.).
obb. (It.), *obbligato* (mus.).
O.B.E., Order of the British Empire.
obs., obsolete.
obsol., obsolescent.
O.C., Officer Commanding.
o'c., o'clock.
Oct., October.
oct., octavo (8vo).
O.C.T.U., Officer Cadet Training Unit.
O.D., Ordnance Datum.
O.D.E.L., Odhams Dictionary of the English Language.
O.E.D., Oxford English Dictionary.
offg., officiating.
O.F.M., Order of Friars Minor (Franciscans).
O.F.S., Orange Free State.
O.G.P.U. (Russ.), *Gosudarstvennoe Politicheskoe Upravlenie*, State Political Control.
O.H.B.M.S., On His (Her) Britannic Majesty's Service.
O.H.M.S., On His (Her) Majesty's Service.
O.K., All correct.
Okla., Oklahoma (U.S.A.).
O.L., Officer of the Order of Leopold (Belgium).
Ol., Olympiad.
O.M., Order of Merit.
O.M.I., Oblate of Mary Immaculate.
Ont., Ontario (Canada).
O.P., Old Playgoers (club) ; Old Prices (theatr. hist.) ; opposite prompt (side, in theatre) ; out of print (of books) ; (L.), *Ordo Praedicatorum*, Order of Preachers.
op. (L.), *opus*, work.
o.p., over proof (spirits).
op. cit. (L.), *opere citato*, "in the work cited."
o. pip., observation post.
opp., opposes ; opposite ; opposition.
opt. (L.), *optimus, optime*, best ; optative ; optional.
O.R., Official Receiver ; Official Referee.
Or., Orient(al).
ord., ordained ; order ; ordinary ; ordnance.
Ore., Oregon (U.S.A.).
orig., origin ; original(ly).
O.S., Old Style (Julian Calendar) ; Order of Servites ; Ordinary Seaman ; Ordnance Survey.
O.S.A., Order of St. Augustine.
O.S.B., Order of St. Benedict.
O.S.D., Order of St. Dominic ; Ordnance Survey Datum.
O.S.F., Order of St. Francis.
O.S.M., Order of Servants of Mary (Servites).
O.S.N.C., Orient Steam Navigation Company.
o.s.p. (L.), *obiit sine prole*, "died without issue."
O.T., Old Testament.
O.U.A.C., Oxford University Athletic Club.
O.U.A.F.C., Oxford University Association Football Club.
O.U.A.S., Oxford University Air Squadron.
O.U.B.C., Oxford University Boat Club.
O.U.C.C., Oxford University Cricket Club.
O.U.D.S., Oxford University Dramatic Society
O.U.G.C., Oxford University Golf Club.
O.U.H.C., Oxford University Hockey Club.
O.U.L.T.C., Oxford University Lawn Tennis Club.
O.U.R.F.C., Oxford University Rugby Football Club.
O.U.S., Oxford Union Society.
O.W.I., Office of War Information (U.S.A.).
Oxon. (L.), *Oxoniensis*, of Oxford.
oz., ounce(s).

P., Pawn (chess) ; Progressive (party, L.C.C.) ; President.
p., page ; perch ; pint ; population ; (It.), *piano*, soft (mus.).
P.A., Press Association ; Publishers' Association.
Pa., Pennsylvania (U.S.A.).
p.a. (L.), *per annum*, "by the year."
P.A.C., Public Assistance Committee.
P.A.I.F., Persia and Iraq Force ("Paiforce").
Pal., Palestine.
Pan., Panama.
P. & O., Peninsular and Oriental (steamship line).
par., paragraph ; parallel ; parenthesis ; parish.
P.A.S.I., Professional Associate of the Surveyors' Institution.
P.A.T.A., Proprietary Articles Trade Association.
Pat. Off., Patent Office.
P.A.Y.E., Pay As You Earn (Income Tax).
Paym., Paymaster.
Paym.-Gen., Paymaster-General.
payt., payment.
P.B. (L.), *Pharmacopoeia Britannica*, British Pharmacopoeia ; Plymouth Brother, Brethren ; Prayer Book ; Primitive Baptist.
P.B.I., (slang) Infantry.
P.C., Privy Councillor ; Police Constable.
p.c., post-card ; (L.), *per centum*, "by the hundred."
P.C.R.C., Poor Clergy Relief Corporation.
P.C.S., Principal Clerk of Session.
P.D., Potential difference.
pd., paid.
P.D.A.D., Probate, Divorce, and Admiralty Division.
pdr., pounder (of gun, fish, etc.).
P.E., Protestant Episcopal ; Presiding Elder.
ped., pedal (mus.).
P.E.F., Palestine Exploration Fund.
P.E.I., Prince Edward Island (Canada).
P.E.N., Poets, Essayists, Novelists (club).
pen(in)., peninsula.
Penn., Pennsylvania (U.S.A.).
Pent., Pentateuch.
P.E.P., Political and Economic Planning.
per an. (L.), *per annum*, "by the year, yearly."
per cent. (L.), *per centum*, "by the hundred."
per pro(c). (L.), *per procurationem*, "by proxy" (as agent, etc.).
Pet., Peter (N.T.).
Petriburg. (L.), *Petriburgensis*, of Peterborough (in signature of Bishop).
P.F., Procurator Fiscal.
pf. (It.), *piano-forte*, soft (then) loud (mus.).
pfd., preferred.
P.G.A., Professional Golfers' Association.
P.G.D., Past Grand Deacon (freemasonry).
P.G.M., Past Grand Master (freemasonry).

phar(m)., pharmaceutical; pharmacist; pharmacology; pharmacy.
Ph.B., Bachelor of Philosophy.
Ph.D., Doctor of Philosophy.
Phil., Philippians (N.T.).
pinx. (L.), *pinxit*, "he (she) painted (it)."
pk., peck.
P.K.T.F., Printing and Kindred Trades Federation.
P.L., Primrose League; Poet Laureate; (L.), *Pharmacopoeia Londinensis*, London Pharmacopoeia.
pl., place; plural.
P.L.A., Port of London Authority.
P.L.C., Poor Law Commissioners.
Plen., Plenipotentiary.
P.L.G., Poor Law Guardians.
P.L.M. (Fr.), *Paris-Lyons-Midi* (Railway).
P.L.P., Parliamentary Labour Party.
P.M., Prime Minister; Postmaster; Provost-Marshal; Past Master (freemasonry).
p.m. (L.), *post meridiem*, afternoon.
pm., premium.
P.M.G., Postmaster-General.
P.M.H., production per man-hour.
P.M.O., Principal Medical Officer.
p.n., promissory note.
P.N.E.U., Parents' National Educational Union.
pnxt. (L.), *pinxit*, "he (she) painted (it)."
P.O., Petty Officer (nav.); Postal Order; Post Office; Pilot Officer.
p.o.d., pay on delivery.
pol. econ., political economy.
P.O.P., Printing-out Paper (photog.).
pop., population.
pos., position; positive.
P.O.S.B., Post Office Savings Bank.
P.O.W., prisoner of war.
P.P., Parish Priest (R.C.); (L.), *Pastor Pastorum*, "Shepherd of the Shepherds" (as title of the Pope); Past President; (L.), *Pater patriae*, "father of his country."
pp., pages; (It.), *pianissimo*, "very soft" (mus.).
p.p. (L.), *per procurationem*, "as agent for", "on behalf of."
p.p.c. (Fr.), *pour prendre congé*, "to take leave."
p.p.i., policy proof of interest (insurance).
ppp (It.), *pianississimo*, "as softly as possible" (mus.).
P.P.S., additional postscript; Parliamentary Private Secretary.
P.P.U., Peace Pledge Union.
P.R., Proportional Representation; (L.), *Populus Romanus*, "the Roman people."
Pr., Priest; Primitive; Prince; Provençal.
pr., pair; per; price; printer.
P.R.A., President of the Royal Academy.
P.R.B., Pre-Raphaelite Brotherhood.
P.R.C. (L.), *post Roman conditam*, "after the foundation of Rome."
P.R.C.A., President of the Royal Cambrian Academy.
Preb., Prebendary.
Pref., Preface.
prefd., preferred (stock and shares).
prelim., preliminary (examination).
prem., premium.
prep., preparation; preparatory (school, etc.).
Pres., President; (L.), *Preses*, "presiding."
Presb., Presbyter; Presbyterian.
P.R.H.A., President of the Royal Hibernian Academy.
P.R.H.S., President of the Royal Horticultural Society.
Prim., Primary; Primate; Primitive.
Prin., Principal.
print., printer; printing.
priv., private; privative.
P.R.O., Public Relations Officer.
pro., professional (cricketer, footballer, etc.).
Prob., Probate (Division and Law Reports).
Proc., Proceedings; Proctor.
Prof., Professor.
Prom., promenade (concert).
pron., pronounced; pronunciation.
prop., proprietary; proposition; property (actor's equipment).
Prot., Protestant.
pro tem. (L.), *pro tempore*, "for the time being."
Prov., Proverbs (O.T.); Province; Provost.
Prov.G.M., Provincial Grand Master (freemasonry).
prox. (L.), *proximo*, "in the next month."
prox. acc. (L.), *proxime accessit*, runner-up.
P.R.S., President of the Royal Society; Proportional Representation Society.
prs., pairs.
P.R.S.A., President of the Royal Scottish Academy.
P.R.S.E., President of the Royal Society of Edinburgh.
P.S., Parliamentary Secretary; Permanent Secretary; Police Sergeant; Privy Seal; prompt side (in theatre); (L.), *postscriptum*, postscript.
Ps., Psalms (O.T.).
P.S.A., Pleasant Sunday Afternoons (movement).
p.s.a., Graduate of the Royal Air Force Staff College.
p.s.c., Graduate of the Military (or Naval) Staff College.
P.S.N.C., Pacific Steam Navigation Company.
P.T., Physical Training.
pt., part; payment; pint(s).
Pte., Private (Army).
P.T.O., Please turn over.
pub., publisher; published; public; public house.
P.U.C. (L.), *post urbem conditam*, "after the foundation of the city" (Rome).
P.V., Priest Vicar.
P.W.D., Public Works Department.
P.W.R., Police War Reserve.
pwt. (usually dwt.), pennyweight.
pxt. (L.,) *pinxit*, "he (she) painted (it)."

Q., Queen; question; coulomb (elect.).
q., query; quintal.
Q.A.B., Queen Anne's Bounty.
Q.A.I.M.N.S., Queen Alexandra's Imperial Military Nursing Service.
Q.A.N.T.A.S., Queensland and Northern Territory Air Service.
q.d. (L.), *quasi dicat*, "as if one should say"; (L.), *quasi dictum*, "as if said."
q.e. (L.), *quod est*, "which is."
Q.E.D. (L.), *quod erat demonstrandum*, "which was to be proved."
Q.E.F. (L.), *quod erat faciendum*, "which was to be done."
Q.E.I. (L.), *quod erat inveniendum*, "which was to be found."
Q.F., quick-firing (gun).
Q.I.D.N., Queen's Institute of District Nursing.
Q.M., Quartermaster.
qm. (L.), *quomodo*, "by what means."
Q.M.G., Quartermaster-General.
Q.M.S., Quartermaster-Sergeant.
Qmr., Quartermaster.
qn., question.
qq.v. (L.), *quae vide*, "which (things) see."
qr(s)., quarter(s); quire(s).
Q.S., Quarter Sessions.
q.s. (L.), *quantum sufficit*, "as much as is necessary."
Q.T., (slang) on the quiet.
qt., quart.
qto., quarto (4to).
qu. (L.), *quasi*, "as if"; *quaere*, "query."
quad., quadrangle; quadrant; quadrat; quadruple.
Q.U.B., Queen's University, Belfast.
Que., Quebec (Canada).
quor., quorum.
quot., quotation; quoted.
q.v. (L.), *quod vide*, "which see"; (L.), *quantum vis*, "as much as you like."
qy., query.

r., right; rod; rood; run(s) (cricket).
R, rupee(s).
R.A., Royal Academy; Royal Academician; Rear-Admiral; Royal Arch (freemasonry); Royal Artillery.
R.A.A., Royal Academy of Arts.
R.A.A.F., Royal Australian Air Force.
R.A.C., Royal Armoured Corps; Royal Agricultural College; Royal Automobile Club.
R.A.D., Royal Academy of Dancing.

rad., radical ; (L.), *radix*, root (math.).
R.A.D.A., Royal Academy of Dramatic Art.
R.-Adm., Rear-Admiral.
R.Ae.S., Royal Aeronautical Society.
R.A.F., Royal Air Force.
R.A.F.V.R., Royal Air Force Volunteer Reserve.
R.A.G.C. (R. and A.), Royal and Ancient Golf Club, St. Andrews.
rall. (It.), *rallentando*, gradually more slowly (mus.).
R.A.M., Royal Academy of Music.
R.A.M.C., Royal Army Medical Corps.
R.A.N., Royal Australian Navy.
R.A.O.B., Royal Antedeluvian Order of Buffaloes.
R.A.O.C., Royal Army Ordnance Corps.
R.A.P.C., Royal Army Pay Corps.
R.A.S., Royal Agricultural Society ; Royal Asiatic Society ; Royal Astronomical Society.
R.A.S.C., Royal Army Service Corps.
R.A.V.C., Royal Army Veterinary Corps.
R.B., Rifle Brigade.
R.B.A., Royal Society of British Artists.
R.C., Red Cross ; Roman Catholic ; right centre (of stage).
R.C.A., Royal College of Art ; Railway Clerks' Association.
R.C.A.F., Royal Canadian Air Force.
R.C.I., Royal Colonial Institute (now R.E.S.).
R.C.M., Royal College of Music (London).
R.C.M.P., Royal Canadian Mounted Police.
R.C.O., Royal College of Organists.
R.C.N., Royal Canadian Navy ; Royal College of Nursing.
R.C.P., Royal College of Physicians.
R.C.S., Royal College of Surgeons ; Royal Corps of Signals.
R.C.V.S., Royal College of Veterinary Surgeons.
R.D., Refer to Drawer ; Rural District.
Rd., Road.
R.D.C., Rural District Council.
R.D.S., Royal Drawing Society ; Royal Dublin Society.
R.D.Y., Royal Dockyard.
R.E., Royal Engineers.
Rear-Adm., Rear-Admiral.
Rec., Recorder.
rec., recipe.
recce., reconnaissance.
recd., received.
recit., recitative (mus.).
recogns., recognizances (law).
rect., rectified.
red., reduced.
redupl., reduplicated.
Ref., Referee.
ref., referred ; reference.
Ref. Ch., Reformed Church.
refd., referred.
Reg. (L.), *Regina*, Queen ; (L.), *Registrat*, Register.
reg(d)., registered.
Reg.-Gen., Registrar-General.
Reg. Prof., Regius Professor.
Regt., Regent ; Regiment.
rel., religion ; relative.
Reliq. (L.), *reliquiae*, remains.
R.E.M.E., Royal Electrical and Mechanical Engineers.
Rep., Representative ; Republic ; Report ; Reporter ; (*coll.*) Repertory (Company).
repr., reprinted.
Repub., Republic(an).
R.E.S., Royal Empire Society (formerly R.C.I.).
res., reserve ; resigned ; resident ; residence.
ret(d)., retired ; returned ; retained.
R. (et) I. (L.), *Rex* (*Regina*) (*et*) *Imperator* (*Imperatrix*), "King (Queen) and Emperor (Empress)" (in British Royal signature).
retnr., retainer (law).
Rev., Reverend ; Revelation (N.T.) ; Review.
rev., revolution (mech.) ; reverse(d) ; revised ; revision ; revenue.
R.F. (Fr.), *République française*, French Republic ; Royal Fusiliers ; radio frequency.
R.G.D.(C.), Radio-Gramophone Development (Company).
R.G.G., Royal Grenadier Guards.
R.G.S., Royal Geographical Society.
Rgt., regiment.
R.H., Royal Highlanders ; Royal Highness.
r.h., right hand.
R.H.A., Royal Horse Artillery ; Royal Hibernian Academy.
rhet., rhetoric ; rhetorical.
R.H.G., Royal Horse Guards.
R.Hist.S., Royal Historical Society.
R.H.S., Royal Humane Society ; Royal Horticultural Society.
R.I., Royal Institute of Painters in Water Colours ; Rhode Island (U.S.A.).
R.I.A., Royal Irish Academy.
R.I.B.A., Royal Institute of British Architects.
R.I.I.A., Royal Institute of International Affairs.
R.I.M., Royal Indian Marine.
R.I.P. (L.), *Requiescat in pace*, "may he rest in peace."
rit(ard). (It.), *ritardando*, "gradually more slowly" (mus.).
R.L., Rugby League.
R.L.O., Returned Letter Office.
Rly., Railway.
R.M., Royal Marines.
rm., ream.
R.M.A., Royal Military Academy (Woolwich) ; Royal Marine Artillery ; Royal Military Asylum.
R.M.C., Royal Military College (Sandhurst).
R.Met.S., Royal Meteorological Society.
R.M.S., Royal Mail Steamship ; Royal Microscopical Society ; Royal Society of Miniature Painters.
R.M.S.P., Royal Mail Steam Packet (Company).
R.N., Royal Navy.
R.N.C., Royal Naval College.
R.N.D., Royal Naval Division.
R.N.L.I., Royal National Lifeboat Institution.
R.N.R., Royal Naval Reserve.
R.N.V.R., Royal Naval Volunteer Reserve.
R.N.Z.A.F., Royal New Zealand Air Force.
R.O., Receiving Office(r), Order ; Relieving Officer ; Recruiting Office(r) ; Returning Officer.
Ro. (L.), *recto*, "on the right-hand (page)."
Roffen. (L.), *Roffensis*, of Rochester (in signature of Bishop).
R. of O., Reserve of Officers.
R.O.I., Royal Institute of Oil Painters.
Rom., Romans (N.T.).
rom., roman type.
Roy., Royal.
R.P., Royal Society of Portrait Painters.
R.P.D., Regius Professor of Divinity ; (L.), *Rerum Politicarum Doctor*, Doctor of Political Science.
r.p.m., revolutions per minute.
R.P.S., Royal Photographic Society.
r.p.s., revolutions per second.
rpt., report.
R.Q.M.S., Regimental Quartermaster-Sergeant.
R.R.C., Royal Red Cross (Order).
R.S., Royal Society ; Royal Scots (Regiment).
Rs., Rupees.
R.S.A., Royal Scottish Academy ; Royal Society of Antiquaries ; Royal Society of Arts.
R.S.A.C., Royal Scottish Automobile Club.
R.S.B.S., Royal Society of British Sculptors.
R.S.C., Royal Scottish Corporation.
R.S.D., Royal Society of Dublin.
R.S.E., Royal Society of Edinburgh.
R.S.F., Royal Scots Fusiliers.
R.S.F.S.R., Russian Soviet Federal Socialist Republic.
R.S.G.S., Royal Scottish Geographical Society.
R.S.I., Royal Sanitary Institute.
R.S.L., Royal Society of Literature ; Royal Society of London.
R.S.M., Regimental Sergeant-Major ; Royal School of Mines ; Royal Society of Medicine.
R.S.O., Railway Sorting Office.
R.S.P.A., Royal Society for the Prevention oı Accidents.
R.S.P.C.A., Royal Society for Prevention of Cruelty to Animals.
R.S.S.P.C.C., Royal Scottish Society for the Prevention of Cruelty to Children.
R.S.S., S.R.S. (L.), *Regiae Societatis Socius*, Fellow of the Royal Society.

R.S.V.P. (Fr.), *Répondez s'il vous plaît,* "Please reply."
R.S.W., Royal Scottish Society of Painters in Water Colours.
R/T, radio-telegraphy.
Rt. Hon., Right Honourable.
R.T.O., Railway Transport Officer.
R.T.R., Royal Tank Regiment.
Rt. Rev., Right Reverend.
R.T.S., Religious Tract Society.
R.U., Rugby Union.
R.U.R., Royal Ulster Rifles.
R.U.S.I., Royal United Services Institution.
R.U.S.Mus., Royal United Services Museum.
R.V., Revised Version (of Bible).
R.W.A., Royal West of England Academy.
R.W.A.F.F., Royal West African Frontier Force.
R.W.D.G.M., Right Worshipful Deputy Grand Master (freemasonry).
R.W.G.M., Right Worshipful Grand Master (freemasonry).
R.W.G.S., Right Worthy Grand Secretary (freemasonry).
R.W.G.T., Right Worthy Grand Templar; Right Worthy Grand Treasurer (freemasonry).
R.W.G.W., Right Worthy Grand Warden (freemasonry).
R.W.M., Right Worshipful Master (freemasonry).
R.W.S., Royal Society of Painters in Water Colours.
R.W.S.G.W., Right Worshipful Senior Grand Warden (freemasonry).
Rx., Tens of Rupees.
Ry., Railway.
R.Y.S., Royal Yacht Squadron.

S., south; Saint.
s., second; shilling; singular; son; substantive.
S.A., Salvation Army; South Africa; South Australia; South America.
s.a. (L.), *sine anno,* "without date."
S.A.B.C., Scottish Association of Boys' Clubs.
S.A.E., Society of Automobile Engineers.
Salop, Shropshire.
Sam., Samuel (O.T.).
S. and M., Sodor and Man (in signature of Bishop).
Sarum, Salisbury (*esp.* in signature of Bishop).
S.A.S. (L.), *Societatis Antiquariorum Socius,* Fellow of the Society of Antiquaries.
Sask., Saskatchewan (Canada).
Sat., Saturday.
S.A.T.B., soprano, alto, tenor, bass.
S.B., simultaneous broadcast.
S.B.A., Scottish Bankers' Association.
S. by E., south by east.
S. by W., south by west.
S.C., South Carolina (U.S.A.); Special Constabulary.
sc., scene (play); scruple (weight); (L.), *scilicet,* "namely"; (L.), *sculpsit,* "(he) sculptured (it)."
s.c., small capital letters.
S.C.A., Scottish Clerks' Association.
Scand., Scandinavian.
S.C.A.P.A. (Scapa), Society for Checking the Abuses of Public Advertising.
s.caps., small capital letters (printing).
Sc.B. (L.), *Scientiae Baccalaureus,* Bachelor of Science.
S.C.C., Sea Cadet Corps.
Sc.D. (L.), *Scientiae Doctor,* Doctor of Science.
sch., scholar; school.
sci. fa. (L.), *scire facias,* "do you cause to know" (law).
scil. (L.), *scilicet,* "namely," "being understood."
S.C.M., State Certificated Midwife; Student Christian Movement.
Scot. Nat., Scottish Nationalist.
S.C.P., Society of Correctors of the Press.
scr., scruple (weight).
Scrt., Sanscrit.
sculps., sculpt. (L.), *sculpsit,* "he (she) engraved (it)."
S.C.W.S., Scottish Co-operative Wholesale Society.
S.D., Senior Deacon (freemasonry).
s.d. (L.), *sine die,* "no day (date) being appointed."
S. Dak., South Dakota (U.S.A.).
S.D.N. (Fr.), *Société des Nations,* League of Nations.
S.E., south-east; South-Eastern (London postal district).
S.E.A.C., South East Asia Command.
S.E. by E., south-east by east.
S.E. by S., south-east by south.
Sec., Secretary.
sec., second.
sect., section.
Sem., Seminary.
Sen., Senator; Senate.
Sen. Opt., Senior Optime (Cambridge University).
senr., senior.
Sept., September; Septuagint.
seq., seqq. (L.), *sequens, sequentia,* "the following."
Sergt., Sergeant.
S.F., Sinn Fein.
s.f. (L.), *sub finem,* "towards the end."
sf(z). (It.), *sforzando,* "with sudden emphasis" (mus.).
S.F.A., Scottish Football Association.
S.F.S.U., Scottish Farm Servants' Union.
S.G., Solicitor-General.
s.g., specific gravity.
S.G.W., Senior Grand Warden (freemasonry).
sh., shilling(s).
S.H.A.E.F., Supreme Headquarters (of the) Allied Expeditionary Force.
s.h.p., shaft horse-power.
S.H.R.A., Scottish Home Rule Association.
s.h.v. (L.), *sub hac voce,* or *sub hoc verbo,* "under this word."
S.I.C., specific inductive capacity.
sig(n)., signature.
S.I.M., Sergeant Instructor of Musketry.
sin, sine (trigonometry).
sing., singular; single.
S.J., Society of Jesus (Jesuits).
S.J.C., Supreme Judicial Court (U.S.A.).
S.L., Serjeant-at-law; Solicitor-at-Law.
Slav., Slavonic; Slavic.
s.l.p. (L.), *sine legitima prole,* "without legitimate issue."
S.M., Sergeant-Major; Society of Mary (Marists); short metre (hymns).
Smith. Inst., Smithsonian Institute.
S.M.Lond.Soc. (L.), *Societatis Medicae Londoniensis Socius,* Member of the London Medical Society.
S.M.M. (L.), *Sancta Mater Maria,* "Holy Mother Mary."
S.M.O., Senior Medical Officer.
s.m.p. (L.), *sine mascula prole,* "without male issue."
s.n., (L.), *secundum naturam,* "according to nature."
S.O., Staff Officer; Sub-Office.
s.o., seller's option.
Soc., Society; Socialist.
sol., solicitor; solution.
Sol.-Gen., Solicitor-General.
Som, Somersetshire.
Song of Sol., Song of Solomon (O.T.).
sop., soprano.
S.O.S., signal of distress (Morse Code).
sost(en). (It.), *sostenuto,* "sustained" (mus.).
Soton., Southampton.
sov., sovereign.
S.P., small paper (edition); small pica (typography); starting price (betting).
s.p. (L.), *sine prole,* "without issue."
Span., Spanish.
sp.(nov.) (L.), *species (novum),* species (new).
S.P.C.K. Society for Promoting Christian Knowledge.
S.P.E., Society for Pure English.
spec., special; specification.
specif., specific(ally).
S.P.G., Society for the Propagation of the Gospel.
S.P.G.B., Socialist Party of Great Britain.
sp. gr., specific gravity.
S.P.Q.R. (L.), *Senatus Populusque Romanus,* "The Senate and People of Rome."
S.P.R., Society for Psychical Research.
s.p.s. (L.), *sine prole superstile,* "without surviving issue."
S.P.S.P., St. Peter and St. Paul (papal seal).
sq., square; (L.) *sequens,* "the following."
Sqd. Ldr., Squadron Leader (R.A.F.).
sqn., squadron.
S.R., Southern Railway.

S.R.I. (L.), *Sacrum Romanum Imperium*, "Holy Roman Empire."
S.R.N., State Registered Nurse.
S.R.W.F.S., Scottish Rural Workers' Friendly Society.
SS., Saints; (Collar of) Esses; (L.), *Sanctissimus*, "Most Holy."
S.S., Straits Settlements; Steamship.
S.S.A., Scottish Schoolmasters' Association.
S.S.A.F.A., Soldiers', Sailors' and Airmen's Families Association.
S.S.C., Solicitor before the Supreme Court (Scotland); (L.), *Societas Sanctae Crucis*, "Society of the Holy Cross."
SS.D. (L.), *Sanctissimus Dominus*, "Most Holy Lord" (the Pope).
S.S.E., south-south-east.
S.S.J.E., Society of St. John the Evangelist.
S.S.U., Sunday School Union.
S.S.W., south-south-west.
St., Saint; Street; Strait.
st., stone (weight); stumped (cricket); stanza; stet.
stacc., staccato (mus.).
Staffs, Staffordshire.
stat., statute; static.
S.T.B. (L.), *Sacrae Theologiae Baccalaureus*, Bachelor of Sacred Theology.
S.T.C., Senior Training Corps.
S.T.D. (L.), *Sacrae Theologiae Doctor*, Doctor of Sacred Theology.
Ste. (Fr.), *Sainte*, Saint (feminine).
stereo., stereotype.
stet (L.), "let (it) stand" (printing).
St. Ex., Stock Exchange.
stg., sterling.
Stip., Stipendiary (Magistrate).
S.T.L. (L.), *Sacrae Theologiae Lector*, Reader in Sacred Theology.
stn., station.
S'ton, Southampton.
S.T.P. (L.), *Sacrae Theologiae Magister*, Master of Sacred Theology.
str., stroke (rowing).
S.T.S., Scottish Text Society.
sub., subaltern; submarine boat; subscription; substitute.
succr(s)., successor(s).
Suffr., Suffragan.
Sun., Sunday.
sup., superior; (L.), *supra*, above.
super., supernumerary.
suppt., supplement.
suppy., supplementary.
supt., superintendent.
surg., surgeon; surgery.
Surg.-Gen., Surgeon-General.
Surr., Surrogate.
surv., surveying; surveyor; surviving.
Surv.-Gen., Surveyor-General.
sus. per col. (L.), *suspensis per collum*, "hanging by the neck."
S.V. (L.), *Sancta Virgo*, "Holy Virgin"; (L.), *Sanctitas Vestra*, "Your Holiness."
s.v. (L.), *sub verbo*, "under the heading."
S.W., Senior Warden (freemasonry); south-west; South-Western (London postal district).
S.W. by S., south-west by south.
S.W. by W., south-west by west.
S.W.G., Standard Wire Gauge.
S.Y., steam yacht.
S.Y.H.A., Scottish Youth Hostels Association.
syn., synonym; synonymous.

T., tenor; temperature; territory.
t., ton; (It.), *tempo*, time (mus.); taken (betting); (L.), *tempore*, "in the time of."
T.A., Telegraphic address; Territorial Army; Typographical Association.
T.A.A., Territorial Army Association.
T.A.F., Tactical Air Force.
tal. qual. (L.), *talis qualis*, "just as they come."
tan., tangent (trigonometry).
t. and o., taken and offered (betting).
tar-mac., tar-macadam.
T.B., torpedo boat; tuberculosis.
T.B.D., torpedo boat destroyer.
T.C., Thames Conservancy; Town Councillor.
T.C.D., Trinity College, Dublin.
T.D., Territorial (Officers') Decoration; Telegraph, Telephone Department.
T.D.R., Treasury Deposit Receipts.
t.e.g., top edges gilt.
tel., telegram; telegraph; telephone.
temp., temperature; temporary; (L.), *tempore*, "in the time of."
ten., tenor; (It.), *tenuto*, "held, sustained" (mus.).
Tenn., Tennessee (U.S.A.).
term., termination; terminology.
Ter(r)., Terrace; Territory.
Test., Testament; testamentary; testator.
Tex., Texas (U.S.A.).
text. rec. (L.), *textus receptus*, "the received, accepted text."
t.f., till forbidden.
T.G.W.U., Transport and General Workers' Union.
T.H., Trinity House.
theol., theology.
theos., theosophy.
therap., therapeutics.
Thess., Thessalonians (N.T.).
Thurs., Thursday.
T.H.W.M., Trinity High Water Mark.
T.I.H., Their Imperial Highnesses.
Tim., Timothy (N.T.).
tinct., tincture.
Tit., Titus (N.T.).
T.M., trench mortar.
T.M.O., Telegraph money order (office).
tn., ton.
T.N.T., trinitrotoluene (high explosive).
T.O., Telegraph, Telephone Office; Transport Officer; turn over.
Tob., Tobit (Apoc.).
TocH., Talbot House.
tonn., tonnage.
T.P.I., Town Planning Institute.
tpr., trooper.
Tr., Treasurer; Trustee.
trans., transactions; translation; translated.
transfd., transferred.
T.R.C., Thames Rowing Club.
Treas., Treasurer.
T.R.H., Their Royal Highnesses.
trop., tropic(s); tropical.
Trs., Trustees.
trs., transpose (printing).
Truron., Truro (in signature of Bishop).
T.S., Theosophical Society.
T.S.H., Their Serene Highnesses.
T.S.O., Town Sub-Office.
T.T., total abstainer; Tourist Trophy; torpedo tube.
T.U., Trade Union.
T.U.C., Trades Union Congress.
T.U.C.G.C., Trades Union Congress General Council.
Tues., Tuesday.
Turk., Turkey; Turkish.
T.V.A., Tennessee Valley Authority (U.S.A.).
T.W.G., Townswomen's Guild(s).
T.Y.C., Thames Yacht Club.
typ(og)., typographical; typography.

u.c., upper case (print).
U.C.B.S., United Co-operative Bakery Society.
U.C.C., University Correspondence College.
U.C.L., University College, London.
U.D.(C.), Urban District (Council).
U.F.C., United Free Church (Continuing).
U.G.C., University Grants Committee; Union of Girls' Clubs.
U.G.S.S.S., Union of Girls' Schools for Social Service.
u.i. (L.), *ut infra*, "as below."
U.J.D. (L.), *Utriusque Juris Doctor*, Doctor of both (Civil and Canon) Laws.
U.K., United Kingdom.
U.K.C.T.A., United Commercial Travellers' Association of Great Britain and Ireland.
U.K.A., United Kingdom Alliance.
ult., *ultimo*, in the preceding month.
U.M.F.C., United Methodist Free Churches.
Univ., University; University College, Oxford.

unabr., unabridged.
U.N.C.I.O., United Nations Conference on International Organization.
ung. (L.), *Unguentum*, ointment.
Unit., Unitarian.
unm., unmarried.
U.N.R.R.A., United Nations Relief and Rehabilitation Administration.
u.p., under proof.
up., upper.
U.P.(C.), United Presbyterian (Church).
U.P.W., Union of Post Office Workers.
U.S., United Services ; United States.
u.s. (L.), *ut supra*, "as above."
U.S.A., United States of America.
U.S.M., United States Mail ; United States Marine.
U.S.M.A., United States Military Academy.
U.S.N., United States Navy.
U.S.N.A., United States Naval Academy.
U.S.P., United States Pharmacopoeia.
U.S.S., United States Senate ; United States Ship or Steamer.
U.S.S.C., United States Supreme Court.
U.S.S.R., Union of Soviet Socialist Republics.
Ut., Utah (U.S.A.).
ut dict. (L.), *ut dictum*, "as said."
ut inf. (L.), *ut infra*, "as below."
ut sup. (L.), *ut supra*, "as above."

V., volts (elect.).
v., verse ; (L.), *versus*, "against"; (L.), *vice*, "in the place of"; (L.), *vide*, "see"; (It.), *voce*, "voice."
V1 (Germ.), *Vergeltungswaffe No.* 1, "retaliation weapon No. 1" (the flying bomb).
V2 (Germ.), *Vergeltungswaffe No.* 2, "retaliation weapon No. 2" (the rocket bomb).
V.A., Victoria and Albert (Order) ; Vicar Apostolic ; Vice-Admiral ; Volunteer Artillery.
Va., Virginia (U.S.A.).
v.a. (L.), *vixit annos*, "lived (so many) years."
V.A.D., Voluntary Aid Detachment.
V.-Adm., Vice-Admiral.
val., value.
V. and M., Virgin and Martyr.
var., variant ; variation ; variety.
var. lect. (L.), *varia lectio*, "variant reading" (of MS., etc.).
Vat., Vatican.
vb(l)., verb(al).
V.C., Victoria Cross ; Vice-Chancellor ; Vice-Chairman ; Vice-Consul.
V.D., Volunteer (Officers') Decoration ; venereal disease.
V.D.H., valvular disease of the heart.
Ven., Venerable.
verb. sap. (L.), *verbum sapienti*, "a word to the wise."
vet., veterinary surgeon.
v.f., very fair.
V.G., Vicar-General.
v.g., very good.
Vic., Victoria (Queen).
Vice-Adm., Vice-Admiral.
Vice-Pres., Vice-President.
Vict., Victoria (Australia).
vid. (L.), *vide*, "see."
Vigorn., see WIGORN.
Vis(ct)., Viscount.
viz. (L.), *videlicet*, "namely."
v.l. (L.), *varia lectio*, "variant reading" (of MS., etc.).
Vo. (L.), *verso*, "on the left-hand" (page).
vocab., vocabulary.
Vol., Volume ; volunteer.
V.P., Vice-President ; Vice-Provost.
V.R., Victoria Regina.
V. Rev., Very Reverend.
V.S., Veterinary Surgeon.
v.s. (L.), *vide supra*, "see above"; (It.), *volti subito*, "turn over quickly" (mus.).
vs. (L.), *versus*, "against."
Vt., Vermont (U.S.A.).
Vulg., Vulgate.
vulg., vulgar(ly).
vv., verses.
vv. ll. (L.), *variae lectiones*, "variant readings" (of MS., etc.).

W., west ; Western (London postal district).
w., wicket, wide (cricket) ; with ; wife.
W.A., Western Australia ; West Africa.
W.A.A.C., Women's Army Auxiliary Corps (in First World War).
W.A.A.F., Women's Auxiliary Air Force.
w.a.f., with all faults.
W.Afr.R., West African Regiment.
War, Warwickshire.
Wash., Washington (U.S.A.).
W.A.V.S. (Waves), Women's Auxiliary Voluntary Services (U.S.A.).
W. Aust., Western Australia.
W.B., Water Board ; way bill.
W. by N., west by north.
W. by S., west by south.
W.C., West Central (London postal district) ; water closet.
W.D., War Department.
W.E.A., Workers' Educational Association.
Wed., Wednesday.
w.f., wrong fount (print.).
W.F.L., Women's Freedom League.
W'hampton, Wolverhampton.
whf., wharf.
W.I., West Indies.
Wigorn., **Vigorn.** (L.), *Wigornensis*, of Worcester (in signature of Bishop).
Wilts, Wiltshire.
Winton., Winchester ; (L.), *Wintoniensis*, of Winchester (in signature of Bishop).
W.I.R., West India Regiment.
Wis., Wisconsin (U.S.A.).
Wisd., Wisdom (of Solomon) (Apoc.).
W.J.A.C., Women's Junior Air Corps.
W.J.T.C., Women's Junior Training Corps.
W/L, wave length.
W.L.A., Women's Land Army.
W.M.C., Working Men's College, London.
W.M.S., Wesleyan Missionary Society.
W.N.L.F., Women's National Liberal Federation.
W.N.W., west-north-west.
W.O., War Office ; Warrant Officer.
Wor., Worshipful.
Worcs, Worcestershire.
W.P., weather permitting.
W.P.B., waste-paper basket.
W.R., West Riding (Yorkshire).
W.R.A.F., Women's Royal Air Force (in First World War).
W.R.N.S. (Wrens), Women's Royal Naval Service.
W.S., Writer to the Signet.
W.S.P.U., Women's Social and Political Union.
W.S.W., west-south-west.
W/T., wireless telegraphy, telephony.
wt., weight.
W.T.S., Women's Transport Service.
W.T.U.C., World Trade Union Conference ; Workers' Trade Union Committee.
W.U.S.L., Women's United Service League.
W. Va., West Virginia (U.S.A.).
W.V.S., Women's Voluntary Service.
Wyo., Wyoming (U.S.A.).

x-cp., ex coupon.
xd, x-d(iv)., ex dividend.
x-i., ex interest.
Xmas, Christmas.
x-n., ex new shares.
Xt(ian)., Christ(ian).
XX, XXX, double-X, triple-X (indicating strength of ales, tobacco, etc.).

yd., yard.
yday., yesterday.
Yeo(m)., Yeomanry.
Y.H.A., Youth Hostels Association.
Y.M.C.A., Young Men's Christian Association.
Yorks, Yorkshire.
Y.P.S.C.E., Young People's Society for Christian Endeavour.
yr., year ; your ; younger.
yrs., years ; yours.
Y.W.C.A., Young Women's Christian Association.

Zech., Zechariah (O.T.).
Zeph., Zephaniah (O.T.).
Z.S., Zoological Society.

FAMILIAR WORDS AND PHRASES ADOPTED FROM FOREIGN LANGUAGES

Note on Pronunciation.—The pronunciation given is not necessarily that of the language from which the words or phrases are derived, but the pronunciation *in an English context.* The symbols used are the same as those given in the *Key to Pronunciation* on page ix, except that [a] may have the sound of North Country *a* in *hat*; [ç], which occurs in some German words, has approximately the sound of *h* in *huge*; and the French and German [ü] has the sound betwen [ē] and [o͞o]. An asterisk against a word in an etymology means that the word is in this section.

aberglaube, [ah'-ber-glowb-a], *n.* superstition. [Germ.].

ab extra, [ab'-eks'-tra], *phr.* from outside. [L.].

ab initio, [ab'-i-nish'-i-ō], *phr.* from the beginning. [L.].

ab origine, [ab'-o-ri'-ji-ni], *phr.* from the beginning. [L.].

ab ovo, [ab'-ō'-vō], *phr.* from the earliest stage. [L. from the egg].

absit omen, [ab'-sit-ō'-men], *phr.* let this not be an omen. [L. may the omen be absent].

ab urbe condita, [ab-ur'-bi-kon'-dit-ā], *phr.* from the founding of Rome. [L. from the city founded].

acu rem tangere, [a'-kyo͞o-rem'-tan'-jer-i], *phr.* to hit the nail on the head. [L.].

ad captandum vulgus, [ad'-kap-tand'-um-vul'-gus], *phr.* to catch the popular fancy. [L. in order to catch the common people].

à deux, [ah-dur'], *phr.* for two. [Fr.].

ad hoc, [ad'-hok'], *phr.* for a particular occasion or purpose. [L. to this (end)].

ad infinitum, [ad'-in'-fi-nīt'-um], *phr.* to infinity. [L.].

ad interim, [ad'-in'-ter-im], *phr.* for the time being. [L.].

ad lib., [ad'-lib'], *phr.* ad libitum.

ad libitum, [ad'-lib'-i-tum], *phr.* at will, freely. [L. to what is desired].

ad majorem Dei gloriam, [ad'-mā-jaw'-rem-dē'-ī-glaw'-ri-am], *phr.* to the greater glory of God (motto of the Society of Jesus). [L.].

ad nauseam, [ad'-naw'-zi-am'], *phr.* to the point of disgust. [L. to the point of nausea].

ad rem, [ad'-rem'], *phr.* to the purpose. [L. to the thing].

adscriptus glebae, [ad'-skrip'-tus-glē'-bē], *phr.* in a state of serfdom. [L. attached to the soil].

adsum, [ad'-sum], *phr.* (I am) present. [L.].

ad unguem factus, [ad'-ung'-gwem-fak'-tus], *phr.* finished to the last detail. [L. done up to the finger-nail].

ad valorem, [ad'-val-aw'-rem], *phr.* according to (its) value. [L.].

ad verbum, [ad'-vur'-bum], *phr.* word for word, literally. [L. to the word].

advocatus diaboli, [ad'-vō-kā'-tus-dī-a'-bo-lī], *n.* the Devil's Advocate. [L.].

aet., aetat., abbrev. of *aetatis.*

aetatis, [ē-tāt'-is], *phr.* at the age of. [L.].

à fond, [ah-faw(ng)'], *phr.* thoroughly. [Fr. to the bottom].

a fortiori, [ā'-faw-ti-aw'-rī], *phr.* all the more therefore. [L. so much the more strongly].

aîné, [en'-ā], *adj.* the elder. [Fr.].

Aktiengesellschaft, [akt-syen-gi-zel'-shahft], *n.* a business company. [Germ.].

à l', à la, [ah'-l(ah)'], *phr.* in the . . . manner; **à la française,** [frah(ng)-sez'], in the French manner; **à l'anglaise,** [ah(ng)-glez'], in the English manner; **à l'espagnole,** [es'-pa-nyol'], in the Spanish manner. [Fr. *à la* (*mode*) in the (fashion)].

à la carte, [ah'-lah-kaht'], *phr.* chosen from the menu. [Fr. according to the card].

alea jacta est, [a'-li-a-jak'-ta-est'], *phr.* the die is cast, an irrevocable step has been taken. [L.].

âme damnée, [ahm'-dan'-ā], *n.* a lost soul. [Fr.].

a mensa et thoro, [ā-men'-sā-et'-thaw'-rō], *phr.* from board and bed. [L.].

amicus curiae, [a-mī'-kus-kew'-ri-ē], *n.* a disinterested adviser. [L. friend of the court].

amour propre, [am'-o͞oer-propr'], *n.* pride. [Fr.].

ancien régime, [ah(ng)-sya(ng)-rā-zhēm'], *n.* the old form of government. [Fr. old rule].

animato, [a'-ni-mah'-tō], *adv.* (*mus.*) in lively fashion. [It.].

anno aetatis suae, [a'-nō-ē-tā'-tis-sew'-ē], *phr.* at the age of. [L. in the year of his age].

annus mirabilis, [a'-nus-mi-rā'-bi-lis], *n.* the wonderful year. [L.].

Anschluss, [an'-shlo͞os], *n.* union. [Germ.]

ante meridiem, [an'-ti-me-ri'-di-em'], *phr.* before mid-day. [L.].

aperçu, [a'-pāer-sü'], *n.* a brief presentation. [Fr.].

a posteriori, [a'-po-stēer'-i-aw'-rī], *phr.* (arguing) from effect to cause. [L. from a later thing].

Après moi, le déluge, [a'-prā-mwah-ler-dā'-lüzh], *phr.* disaster will (may) come after my day. [Fr. after me, the deluge].

a priori, [ā'-prī-aw'-rī], *phr.* (of a process of reasoning), from cause to effect. [L. from the prior thing].

à propos, [ah-pro-pō'], *prep.* concerning; **à p. de rien,** [der-rya(ng)'], quite irrelevant(ly); **à p. des bottes,** [dā-bot'], talking of nothing in particular . . . [Fr.].

Arcades ambo, [ah'-ka-dēz-am'-bō], *phr.* blackguards both. [L.].

arcus senilis, [ah'-kus-sen-īl'-is], *n.* (*med.*) a curved yellowish-white band gradually encircling the cornea in old age. [L. senile arc].

argumentum ad hominem, [ah'-gyo͞o-men'-tum-ad'-ho'-mi-nem'], *n.* an argument taking advantage of the character of one's opponent and not based on logic. [L. argument aimed at the man].

arme blanche, [ahm-blah(ng)sh'], *n.* a French cavalry lance or sword. [Fr. white weapon].

arrière pensée, [a'-ryāer-pah(ng)'-sā], *n.* an ulterior motive or mental reservation. [Fr. thought at the back].

ars est celare artem, [ahs'-est-si-lāer'-i-ah'-tem'], *phr.* art lies in concealing art. [L.].

ars longa, vita brevis, [ahs-long'-ga-vī'-ta-bre'-vis], *phr.* art survives, life is short. [L. art long, life short].

auberge, [ō'-bāerzh], *n.* an inn or hostel. [Fr.].

au courant, [ō-ko͞o'-rah(ng)], *phr.* well-informed. [Fr., in the stream].

au fait, [ō-fā'], *phr.* acquainted (with). [Fr.].

Aufklärung, [owf'-klāer-o͝ong], *n.* the spiritual and literary renaissance in Germany in the 18th century; any similar movement. [Germ. enlightenment].

au fond, [ō-faw(ng)'], *phr.* at bottom. [Fr.].

au grand sérieux, [ō-grah(ng)-se-ryur'], *phr.* very seriously. [Fr.].

au pair, [ō-pāer'], *phr.* on a footing of mutual service, without payment. [Fr.].

au pied de la lettre, [ō-pyā'-der-lah-letr'], *phr.* literally. [Fr. at the foot of the letter].

au revoir, [ō'-rer-vwahr], *phr.* good-bye for the present. [Fr. to (our) seeing (each other) again].

Auriga, [aw-rī'-ga], *n.* the northern constellation known as the Wagoner. [L. chariot].

auri sacra fames, [aw'-rī-sa'-kra-fā'-mēz], *n.* the accursed hunger for gold. [L.].

Ausgleich, [ows'-glīç], *n.* a compromise. [Germ.].

aut Caesar aut nullus, [awt-sē'-zar-awt-nul'-us], *phr.* I will have the highest position or none at all. [L. (I will be) either emperor or nobody].

Autobahn, [ow'-tō-bahn], *n.* a specially constructed highway for fast car-traffic. [Germ.]

auto-da-fé, [aw′-tō-dah-fā′], *n.* sentence of the Inquisition or the carrying out of this. [Portug. act of faith].

avant-propos, [a′-vah(ng)-pro′-pō], *n.* a foreword. [Fr.].

baignoire, [ben′-ywahr], *n.* a box level with the stalls. [Fr.].

bain-marie, [ba(ng)′-mah-rē′], *n.* a hot-water bath for heating saucepans. [Fr. bath of Mary].

ballon d'essai, [ba′-law(ng)-des-ā′], *n.* a trial balloon, a preliminary sounding of opinion. [Fr.].

ban, [ban], *n.* the head of an administrative region of Hungary or Croatia. [Pers. lord].

bas bleu, [bah′-blur′], *n.* a blue-stocking. [Fr.].

basso relievo, [bas′-ō-ri-lyā′-vō], *n.* low relief. [It.].

bâton, [ba′-taw(ng)], *n.* a long narrow loaf. [Fr. stick].

béguinage, [beg′-i-nahzh], *n.* a house for beguines. [Fr.].

bel esprit, [bel′-es-prē′], *n.* a clever person. [Fr.].

Benedicite, [ben′-i-dī′-si-ti], *n.* a prayer or hymn invoking a blessing. [L. bless !].

Benedictus, [ben′-i-dik′-tus], *n.* the canticle beginning thus. [L. blessed].

ben trovato, [ben′-trō-vah′-tō], *phr.* aptly invented. [It.].

berceuse, [bāer-surz′], *n.* a lullaby. [Fr.].

Beso las manos, [bā′-sō-lahs-mah′-nos], *phr.* I kiss your hands (a formal greeting). [Span.].

bibelot, [bēb′-lō], *n.* a trinket or collectors' curio. [Fr. plaything].

bis dat qui cito dat, [bis′-dat′-kwi-sit′-ō-dat′], *phr.* he gives twice who gives quickly. [L.].

Blut und Boden, [blŏŏt′-ŏŏnt-bō′-den], *n.* the German doctrine of blood and soil. [Germ.].

Blut und Eisen, [blŏŏt-ŏŏnt-ī′-zen], *n.* the Bismarckian doctrine of blood and iron as the method of rule. [Germ.].

bois de rose, [bwah′-der-rōz], *n.* dull pink. [Fr.].

bon marché, [baw(ng)-mah(r)′-shā], *adv.* cheaply. [Fr.].

bonne, [bon], *n.* a housemaid. [Fr.].

bonne bouche, [bon′-bŏŏsh′], *n.* a tasty morsel. [Fr.].

bonne fortune, [bon′-faw-tün′], *int.* good luck ! [Fr.].

Bon voyage !, [baw(ng)-vwu-yahzh′], *int.* A pleasant (safe) journey ! [Fr.].

borné, [baw′-nā], *adj.* limited (in outlook). [Fr.].

boutonnière, [bŏŏ-ton-yāer′], *n.* a nosegay for the buttonhole. [Fr.].

brutum fulmen, [brŏŏ′-tum-ful′-men], *n.* an empty threat. [L. heavy lightning].

Bundesrat, [bŏŏn′-des-raht′], *n.* the federal council of Switzerland. [Germ. council of the alliance].

bushido, [bŏŏsh′-i-dō], *n.* the code of behaviour of the Samurai. [Jap.].

cacholong, [kach′-o-long], *n.* a kind of opal. [Kalmuck *kashtchilon*].

cacoethes scribendi, [ka′-kō-ē′-thēz-scri-ben′-dī], *n.* an itch to write. [L. (Gk.) *cacoethes* evil disposition, and *scribendi* for writing].

cadit quaestio, [ka′-dit-kwēs′-ti-ō], *phr.* that ends the matter. [L. the question drops].

Cagoulard, [ka′-gŏŏ-lahr], *n.* a member of a French reactionary organization whose members wore a hood. [Fr. from *cagoule* a hood].

Camorra, [ka-maw′-ra], *n.* a secret Neapolitan terrorist organization. [It.].

campo santo, [kam′-pō-san′-tō], *n.* an Italian cemetery. [It. blessed field].

canapé, [ka′-na-pā], *n.* a piece of fried bread having a savoury spread on it. [Fr.].

cantoris, [kan′-taw′-ris], *n.(pl.)* the singers on the north side of the choir in church. [L. of the singer].

caput mortuum, [kap′-ut-maw′-tyŏŏ-um], *n.* the worthless residuum. [L. dead head].

Carbonari, [kah′-bon-ah′-ri], *n.(pl.)* the members of a secret party with republican sympathies, originating in Naples. [It. charcoal-burners].

carte blanche, [kaht′-blah(ng)sh′], *n.* unlimited authority. [Fr. blank card].

cassette, [kas-et′], *n.* (*phot.*) a carrier for holding plates or films in a camera. [Fr.].

casus fœderis, [kā′-sus-fē′-der-is], *n.* the set of circumstances, envisaged by a treaty, in which action is required of one of the parties to it. [L. case of the treaty].

cavaliere servente, [ka′-va-lyāer′-ā-sāer-ven′-ti], *n.* a man who dances attendance on a lady. [It. serving gentleman].

caveat emptor, [ka′-vi-at-emp′-tor], *phr.* at the buyer's risk. [L. let the buyer beware].

c'est le premier pas qui coûte, [sā′-ler-pru′-myā-pah-kē-kŏŏt′], *phr.* it's the first step that counts. [Fr.].

ceterach, [set′-er-ak′], *n.* the fern, *Ceterach officinarum,* closely related to the spleenworts. [MedL.].

cetera desunt, [se′-ter-a-dē′-sunt], *phr.* the rest are missing. [L.].

ceteris paribus, [set′-er-is-pa′-ri-bus], *phr.* other things being equal. [L.].

chacun à son goût, [sha′-ku(ng)-nah-saw(ng)-gŏŏ′], *phr.* every one to his taste. [Fr.].

chanson d'aventure, [shah(ng)-saw(ng)-dav′-ah(ng), tür′], *n.* a poem relating a chance happening. [Fr.].

chanson de geste, [shah(ng)-saw(ng)-der-zhest′], *n.* a poem dealing with the heroic exploits of the Age of Chivalry. [Fr.].

chantage, [shah(ng)′-tahzh], *n.* blackmail. [Fr.].

chaparejos, [cha′-pah-rā′-hōs], *n.(pl.)* chaps. [Mexican-Span.].

chapeau bras, [sha′-pō-brah′], *n.* a flat three-cornered hat, carried under the arm. [Fr. arm hat].

chapelle ardente, [sha-pel′-ah-dah(ng)t′], *n.* a chapel illuminated with candles for the lying in state of a deceased notable. [Fr. glowing chapel].

chassepot, [shas′-pō], *n.* a breech-loading rifle used by the French. [Fr.].

chauffeuse, [shō-furz′], *n.* a female chauffeur. [Fr.]

chef d'orchestre, [shef′-daw-kestr′], *n.* the leader of the orchestra. [Fr. head of the orchestra].

cherchez la femme, [shaēr′-shā-lah-fum′], *phr.* there is a woman in the affair. [Fr. look for the woman].

che sarà sarà, [kā′-sah′-ra-sah′-ra], *phr.* (indicating a resigned outlook) what will be, will be. [It.].

chevalier d'industrie, [sher-va′-lyā-da(ng)′-dü-strē′], *n.* one who lives by his wits. [Fr.].

che va piano va sano, [kā′-vah-pyah′-nō-vah-sah′-nō], *phr.* slow but sure. [It. what goes softly goes healthily].

chevaux de frise, [sher-vō′-der-frēz′], *n.* spikes set up as a rampart ; a formidable obstacle. [Fr. horses of Friesland].

chose jugée, [shōz′-zhü′-zhā], *n.* an issue already decided. [Fr. thing judged].

chota hazri, [chō′-ta-huz′-ri], *n.* a light early breakfast. [Hind. *chhota hazri* little breakfast].

chronique scandaleuse, [kron-ēk′-skah(ng)-dah-lurz′], *n.* a scandalous collection of stories. [Fr.].

cinquecento, [chin′-kwi-chen′-tō], *n.* the 16th century in Italian art and literature. [It. (*mil*) *cinquecento* 1500].

circulus, [sur′-kyŏŏ-lus], *n.* a circle ; **c. in definiendo,** [dē-fī′-ni-en′-dō], the logical fallacy of defining a thing by itself ; **c. in probando,** [prōb-and′-ō], the logical fallacy of arguing in a circle, and begging the question. [L.].

civis romanus sum, [si′-vis-rō-mā′-nus-sum′], *phr.* I am a Roman citizen ; I stand by my rights. [L.].

claro, [klah′-rō], *n.* a light-coloured cigar. [Span. light-coloured].

cocotte, [ko-kot′], *n.* a woman of easy virtue. [Fr.].

cogito ergo sum, [ko′-ji-tō-ur′-gō-sum′], *phr.* I think, therefore I exist. [L.].

comme il faut, [kom′-ēl-fō′], *phr.* as it should be. [Fr.].

compos mentis, [kom′-pos-men′-tis], *phr.* of sound mind ; **non c.m.,** not of sound mind. [L.].

compte-rendu, [kaw(ng)t-rah(ng)-dü′], *n.* a report (of a meeting, lecture, etc.). [Fr.].

con, [kon], *prep.* with. [It.].

con amore, [kon′-a-maw′-rā], *phr.* with enthusiasm. [It.].

concerto grosso, [kon-chāer′-tō-gros′-ō], *n.* a concerted suite for orchestra and soloists. [It. great concerto].

concours d'élégance, [kaw(ng)'-kōōer-del'-ā-gah-(ng)s], *n.* a competition for the smartest turn-out. [Fr. contest in elegance].
confer, [kon-fur'], *int.* compare. [L.].
convenance, [kaw(ng)'-ver-nah(ng)s], *n.* propriety. [Fr.].
coram, [kaw'-ram'], *prep.* in the presence of; **c. me,** in my presence; **c. judice,** before a judge; **c. populo,** publicly. [L.].
cordon sanitaire, [caw'-daw(ng)-sa'-ni-tāer'], *n.* a barrier set up against the dissemination of disease; (*fig.*) a barrier against undesirable political doctrines. [Fr.].
corpus vile, [kaw'-pus-vī'-li], *n.* a vile body; the subject of an experiment. [L.].
corruptio optimi pessima, [ko-rup'-shi-ō-op'-ti-mī-pe'-si-ma], *phr.* the worst of all is the corruption of the best. [L.].
così fan tutte, [co-sē'-fan-tōōt-tā], *phr.* as all (women) do. [It.].
coûte que coûte, [kōōt'-ker-kōōt'], *phr.* cost what it may, at all costs. [Fr.].
credat Judæus Apella, [krē'-dat-jōō-dē'-us-a-pel'-a], *phr.* let the credulous believe that. [L. let the Jew Apella believe (it. I won't)].
credo quia impossibile (est), [krē'-dō-kwī-a-im'-po-si'-bi-li(-est)], *phr.* I believe (it) because it is impossible. [L.].
crême de la crême, [krem'-der-lah-krem'], *n.* the very best. [Fr. cream of the cream].
Crœsus, [krē'-sus], *n.* a fabulously wealthy person. [L. *Crœsus,* King of Lydia].
crosse, [kros], *n.* the long-handled racquet, covered with netting, used to manipulate the ball in lacrosse. [Fr. hook].
croûtons, [krōō'-taw(ng)], *n.(pl.)* cubes of fried bread. [Fr. small crusts].
cucullus non facit monachum, [kyōō-ku'-lus-non-fa'-sit-mo'-na-kum], *phr.* clothing does not make the man; appearances may be deceptive. [L. the cowl does not make the monk].
cui bono ? [kwī'-bō'-nō], *phr.* to whose advantage is it? [L. to whom (is it) an advantage?].
cum, [kum], *prep.* with, including. [L.].
cum grano salis, [kum'-grā-nō-sā'-lis], *phr.* with a grain of salt (of the way an impossible story is to be taken). [L.].
damnosa hereditas, [dam'-no'-sa-hē-red'-i-tas], *n.* a burdensome inheritance. [L.].
danse macabre, [dah(ng)s'-ma-kahbr'], *n.* the dance of death. [Fr. eerie dance].
dartre, [dahtr], *n.* (*path.*) any mild scaly skin-disease. [Fr.].
decani, [dek-ā'-nī], *n.(pl.)* the singers on the south side of the choir in a church. [L. of the deacon].
déclassé, [dā-kla'-sā], *adj.* declassed. [Fr.].
de fide, [dē-fī'-dē], *phr.* requiring to be held as an article of faith. [L. concerning faith].
dégagé, [dā-ga'-zhā], *adj.* at one's ease. [Fr. released].
de gustibus (non est disputandum), [dē-gus'-ti-bus-(non-est-dis'-pyōō-tan'-dum)], *phr.* there is no arguing about personal tastes. [L.].
de haut en bas, [der-ō'-tah(ng)-bah'], *phr.* in condescending fashion. [Fr. below from high up].
Dei gratia, [dē'-ī-grā'-shi-ā], *phr.* by the grace of God. [L.].
déjeuner, [dā'-zher-nā], *n.* lunch; **d. à fourchette,** [ah-fōōer-shet'], a light luncheon. [Fr. lunch (with a fork)].
delineavit, [dē-lin'-i-ā'-vit], *v.* (*paint., etc.*) drew this. [L.].
de minimis non curat lex, [dē-mi'-ni-mis-non-kyōōer'-at-leks'], *phr.* the law is not concerned with trifles. [L.].
de mortuis nil nisi bonum, [dē-maw'-tyōō-is-nil'-nī-sī-bō'-num], *phr.* (speak) nothing but good of the dead. [L.].
de nouveau, [der-nōō-vō'], *phr.* afresh. [Fr.].
de novo, [dē-nō'-vō], *phr.* afresh. [L.].
Deo optimo maximo, [dē'-ō-op'-ti-mō-mak'-si-mō], *phr.* (dedicated) to God the best and greatest. [L.].
Deo volente, [dē'-ō-vo-len'-ti], *phr.* God (being) willing. [L.].
De Profundis, [dē'-prō-fun'-dis], *phr. and n.* out of the depths (of sorrow); an appeal made in great affliction. [L. opening words of Ps. cxxx]
de règle, [der-regl'], *phr.* the rule. [Fr.].
de rigueur, [der-rē-gur'], *phr.* the strict rule. [Fr.]
dernier cri, [dāer'-nyā-krē'], *n.* the latest fashion [Fr. the latest cry].
de trop, [der-trō'], *phr.* surplus, unwanted, in the way. [Fr.].
deus ex machina, [dē'-us-eks'-ma-kī'-nā], *n.* a divine intervention. [L. the god from the stage machinery].
Deus misereatur, [dē'-us-mi-ze'-rē-ā'-tur], *phr.* may God take pity. [L.].
deux temps, [dur'-tah(ng)], *n.* a dance in two-four time. [Fr. two time].
diamanté, [dē'-a-mah(ng)'-tā], *adj.* that sparkles as if covered with diamonds. [Fr.].
Dies Irae, [dī'-ēz-īer'-ē], *n.* the Day of Judgment. [L. day of wrath].
dies non, [dī'-ēz-non'], *n.* a day on which the law-courts do not sit; a day reckoned as not available. [L. *dies non* (*juridicus*) a day not (available for the courts)].
Dieu et mon droit, [dyur'-ā-maw(ng)-drwah'], *phr.* God and my lawful rights. [Fr.].
discobolos, [dis'-ko'-bo-los], *n.* (a statue of) a discus thrower. [Gk.].
diseur, [dē-zur'], *n.* a performer who entertains by a monologue. [Fr. speaker].
disjecta membra, [dis-jek'-ta-mem'-bra], *n.(pl.)* scattered limbs or parts. [L.].
distingué, [dis'-ta(ng)-gā'], *adj.* looking distinguished. [Fr.].
Domine, dirige nos, [do'-mi-ni-di'-ri-ji-nōs'], *phr.* Lord, guide us. [L.].
dolce far niente, [dol'-chi-fah(r)-nyen'-ti], *n.* sweet idleness. [It.].
dono dedit, [dō'-nō-de'-dit], *phr.* he gave it (as a gift). [L.].
Drang nach (dem) Osten, [drang'-nahkh-(dem)-os'-ten], *phr.* the tendency to orientate one's foreign policy, or to expand, towards the east. [Germ. drag towards the east].
dugento, [dōō-jen'-to], *n.* the 13th century in Italian literature, art, etc. [It. (*mil*) *dugento* 1200].
duomo, [dwō'-mō], *n.* an Italian cathedral. [It.].
dura mater, [dyōōer'-a-mā'-ter], *n.* the hard membrane surrounding the brain and the spinal cord. [L. hard mother].
duvet, [dü'-vā], *n.* an eiderdown. [Fr.].
eau de vie, [ō'-der-vē'], *n.* brandy. [Fr. water of life].
éclaircissement, [e'-klāer-sēs'-mah(ng)], *n.* a clarification. [Fr.].
écrasons l'infâme, [ā-krah'-zāw(ng)-la(ng)'-fahm], *phr.* let us crush the iniquity (of superstition). [Fr.].
editio princeps, [i-dish'-i-ō-prin'-seps], *n.* the first edition of a classical author. [L. chief edition].
édition de luxe, [e-dē'-syaw(ng)-der-lüks'], *n.* a sumptuous edition. [Fr.].
eheu fugaces, [ē'-hew-few-gā'-sēz], *int.* alas for the fleeting (years). [L.].
ein Volk, ein Reich, ein Führer, [īn-folk'-īn-rīkh'-īn-für'-er], *phr.* one people, one state, one leader (slogan of the Third German Reich). [Germ.].
ejusdem generis, [ē-jus'-dem-je'-ner-is], *phr.* of the same sort. [L.].
élan vital, [ā'-lah(ng)-vē'-tahl], *n.* a vital urge. [Fr. vital rush].
éloge, [ā-lozh'], *n.* a funeral eulogy. [Fr. eulogy].
embarras de richesse, [ah(ng)-ba-rah'-der-rē-shes'], *phr.* too much of a good thing. [Fr. embarrassment of wealth].
embusqué, [ah(ng)'-büs-kā], *n.* one who has taken a civilian job to avoid military service. [Fr. a soldier not at the front].
émeute, [ā-murt'], *n.* an uproar. [Fr.].
eminence grise, [ā'-mē-nah(ng)s-grēz'], *n.* a powerful adviser behind the scenes. [Fr. "grey eminence" nickname of Fr. Joseph du Tremblay].
employé, [ah(ng)'-plwu-yā'], *n.* an employee. [Fr.].
en bloc, [ah(ng)-blok'], *phr.* wholesale, as one unit. [Fr. in a lump].
en famille, [ah(ng)-fa-mē'], *phr.* together with one's family. [Fr.].
enfant prodigue, [ah(ng)-fah(ng)-pro-dēg'), *n.* a prodigal son. [Fr.].

enfant terrible, [ah(ng)′-fah(ng)-te′-rēbl], *n.* a problem child, a badly behaved child. [Fr. terrible child].
en fête, [ah(ng)-fāt′], *phr.* in a state of public rejoicing. [Fr.].
en masse, [ah(ng)-mas′], *phr.* all together. [Fr. in a mass].
en pension, [ah(ng)-pah(ng)′-syaw(ng)], *phr.* with board and lodging at an inclusive rate. [Fr.].
en rapport, [ah(ng)-ra-pawr′], *phr.* in sympathy, in communication. [Fr.].
en route, [ah(ng)-rōōt′], *phr.* on the way. [Fr.].
entrechat, [ah(ng)′-trer-shah′], *n.* a rapid clicking of the heels during a leap into the air. [Fr. caper].
entre nous, [ah(ng)-trer-nōō′], *phr.* confidentially, between ourselves. [Fr.].
epea pteroenta, [e′-pi-a-pte′-rō-en′-ta], *n.(pl.)* winged words. [Gk.].
eppur si muove, [e′-pōōer-sē-mwō′-vā], *phr.* and yet it (the earth) *does* move. [It.].
espressivo, [es′-pre-sē′-vō], *adv.* expressively. [It.].
esprit d'escalier, [es-prē′-des-ka′-lyā], *n.* a retort or apt remark coming to mind too late to be used. [Fr. staircase wit].
esto perpetua, [es′-to-per-pe′-tyōō-a], *phr.* may it last for ever. [L.].
et hoc genus omne, [et′-hok′-jē-nus-om′-ni], *phr.* and all the rest of this kind. [L.].
et seqq., [et′-sek′], *phr.* and following. [L. *et sequentes*].
evzone, [ev′-zōn], *n.* a lightly armed Greek infantryman. [MdGk. *evzonos*].
Ewigkeit, [ā′-viç-kīt], *n.* eternity. [Germ.].
ewig Weibliche, das, [dus-ā′-viç-vīb′-liç-a], *n.* the eternal feminine principle. [Germ.].
ex animo, [eks′-an′-i-mō], *phr.* cordially, sincerely. [L. from the soul].
ex cathedra, [eks′-ka-thē′-dra], *phr.* authoritative(ly). [L. from the chair].
exceptis excipiendis, [ek-sep′-tis-ek-si′-pi-en′-dis], *phr.* omitting what should be omitted. [L.].
exempli gratia, [ek-zem′-plī-grā′-shi-ā], *phr.* for instance. [L.].
ex gratia, [eks′-grā′-shi-ā], *phr.* as a matter of grace (not of right). [L. out of grace].
ex hypothesi, [eks-hī-po′-thi-sī], *phr.* from the assumption made. [L.].
ex nihilo nihil fit, [eks-nī′-hil-ō-nī′-hil-fit′], *phr.* out of nothing, nothing comes. [L.].
experto crede(re), [eks-pur′-tō-krē′-der-i, -krē′-di], *phr.* (to) believe one who is experienced. [L.].
exposé, [eks-pō-zā], *n.* a summary, an exposition. [Fr.].
ex post facto, [eks′-pōst-fak′-tō], *phr.* by retrospective action. [L. from what is done afterwards].
extra muros, [eks-tra-mewr′-ōs], *phr.* used of studies carried under the aegis of a university by those not in attendance thereat. [L. outside the walls].
ex voto, [eks-vō′-tō], *phr.* in accordance with a vow. [L. from a vow].
facile princeps, [fa′-si-li-prin′-seps], *phr.* easily the chief. [L.].
facilis descensus Averni, [fa′-si-lis-des-sen′-sus-a-vur′-nī], *phr.* the road to hell is an easy one. [L.].
fait accompli, [fet′-ah-kaw(ng)-plē′], *n.* an accomplished action. [Fr.].
falbala, [fal′-ba-lah], *n.* an elaborate trimming. [Fr.].
farceur, [fah-sur′], *n.* a practical joker. [Fr.].
fascismo, [fa-shiz′-mō], *n.* fascism. [It.].
fas est et ab hoste doceri, [fas′-est′-et′-ab-hos′-ti-do-sēer′-ī], *phr.* it is proper to learn even from an enemy. [L.].
fata morgana, *n.* [fah′-ta-maw-gah′-na], *n.* a mirage (as seen in the Straits of Messina). [It. Morgan the fairy].
faute de mieux, [fōt′-der-myu(r)′], *phr.* for lack of better. [Fr.].
faux pas, [fō′-pah′], *n.* a tactless move or remark. [Fr. false step].
femme de chambre, [fum′-der-shah(ng)br′], *n.* a chambermaid. [Fr.].
femme savante, [fum′-sa-vah(ng)t′], *n.* a bluestocking. [Fr. learned woman].
festina lente, [fes-tī′-na-len′-ti], *phr.* make haste gently. [L. hurry slowly].
fête champêtre, [fāt′-shah(ng)-petr′], *n.* a rural festivity or party in the country. [Fr.].
feu de joie, [fur′-der-zhwah′], *n.* a bonfire. [Fr.].
fiat justitia, ruat caelum, [fī′-at-jus-ti′-shi-a-rōō-at-sē′-lum], *phr.* let justice be done though the heavens fall. [L.].
fiat lux, [fī′-at-luks′], *phr.* let there be light. [L. let light be made].
Fidei Defensor, [fi-dē′-ī-dē-fen′-sor], *n.* Defender of the Faith. [L.].
fides punica, [fī′-dēz-pew′-ni-ka], *n.* treachery. [L. Carthaginian faith].
fidus Achates, [fī′-dus-a-kā′-tēz], *n.* a faithful companion. [L. *fidus* faithful, and *Achates* the companion of Aeneas].
fille, [fē], *n.* daughter. [Fr.].
fille de joie, [fē′-der-zhwah′], *n.* a prostitute. [Fr. daughter of joy].
fils, [fēs], *n.* son, junior. [Fr.].
fin de siècle, [fa(ng)′-der-syekl′], *phr.* decadent. [Fr. end of the century].
fine champagne, [fēn′-sham-pahny(e)′], *phr.* liqueur brandy. [Fr. fine (brandy from) Champagne].
finis coronat opus, [fī′-nis-ko′-rō-nat-ō′-pus], *phr.* the end crowns the work. [L.].
flagrante delicto, [fla-gran′-ti-di-lek′-tō], *phr.* in the very act, red-handed. [L.].
flammenwerfer, [flam′-en-vāerf-er], *n.* a flamethrower. [Germ.].
flatus, [flā′-tus], *n.* inspiration. [L.].
fleuron, [flur′-aw(ng)], *n.* a heraldic ornament in the shape of a flower. [Fr.].
fons et origo, [fonz′-et-o-rī′-gō], *phr.* the fount and source. [L.].
fortiter in re suaviter in modo, [for′-tit-er-in-rē-swa′-vi-ter-in-mō′-dō], *phr.* using pressure discreetly. [L. strongly in the affair, gently in the manner].
fortuna favet fortibus, [faw-tew′-na-fa′-vet-faw′-ti-bus], *phr.* fortune favours the bold. [L.].
frate, [frah′-tā], *n.* a friar. [It.].
fuimus Troes, [few′-i-mus-trō′-ēz], *phr.* we have seen better days. [L. we were (once) Trojans].
gallice, [ga′-li-si], *adv.* in French. [L.].
garçon, [gah′-saw(ng)], *n.* boy, waiter. [Fr.].
gaudeamus igitur, [gaw′-di-ā′-mus-i′-ji-tur], *phr.* let us therefore rejoice (students' song). [L.].
geist, [gīst], *n.* spirit. [Germ.].
giallo antico, [ja′-lō-an-tē′-kō], *n.* marble of a rich yellow colour found in Roman ruins. [It. ancient yellow (marble)].
giovine santo, diavolo vecchio, [jo′-vi-nā-san′-tō-dya′-vo-lō-vek′-kyō], *phr.* young, a saint, old, a devil. [It.].
Gleichschaltung, [glīç′-shal-tōōng], *n.* fusion with another organization. [Germ.].
gnothi seauton, [gnō′-thi-sē-au′-ton], *phr.* know thyself. [Gk.].
gorgio, [gaw′-jō], *n.* one who is not a gipsy. [Romany].
Götterdämmerung, [gur′-ter-dā′-mer-ōōng], *n.* the twilight of the gods. [Germ.].
Gott mit uns, [got′-mit-ōōns], *phr.* God (being) with us. [Germ.].
goum, [gōōm], *n.* an Algerian Arab in the French Army. [Arab.].
gourmandise, [gōōer′-mah(ng)-dēz′], *n.* over-indulgence in good living. [Fr.].
Graf, [grahf], *n.* count. [Germ.].
grande passion, [grah(ng)d-pa′-syaw(ng)], *n.* a passionate infatuation. [Fr. great passion].
gup, [gup], *n.* chatter, gossip. [Hind.].
Haggadah, [ha′-gah′-da], *n.* the portion of the Talmud that is legendary. [Heb. legend].
haut goût, [ō′-gōō′], *n.* a "high" taste or flavour. [Fr.].
haute école, [ōt-ā-kol′], *n.* feats of advanced horsemanship. [Fr. high school].
heyduck, [hī′-dōōk], *n.* a liveried Polish servant; a member of the ennobled military class in Hungary. [Pol. *hajduk* brigand].
hic et nunc, [hik′et-nungk′], *phr.* here and now. [L.].
hic jacet, [hik-jā′-set], *phr.* here lies. [L.].

hinc illæ lacrimæ, [hingk′-i-lē-la′-kri-mē], *phr.* hence the trouble. [L. hence those tears].
hird, [hēerd], *n.* the quisling police-force. [Norw.].
hoi polloi, [hoi-po-loi′], *n.* the multitude, the mob. [Gk. the many].
honi soit qui mal y pense, [o′-ni-swah′-kē-mal-ē-pah(ng)s], *phr.* evil to him who evil thinks. [Fr.].
honoris causa, [hon-aw′-ris-kaw′-zā], *phr.* as a mark of esteem. [L. for the sake of honour].
horresco referens, [ho-res′-kō-re′-fer-enz], *phr.* I shudder as I relate it. [L. I shudder relating].
hors concours, [aw(r)-kaw(ng)-ko͞oer′], *phr.* out of the running, not competing. [Fr.].
hortus siccus, [haw′-tus-si′-kus], *n.* a collection of dried plants. [L. dry garden].
hôtel de ville, [ō-tel′-der-vēl′], *n.* a town hall. [Fr.].
hubris, [hew′-bris], *n.* spiritual pride. [Gk.].
humanum est errare, [hew-mā′-num-est-e-rāer-i], *phr.* to err is human. [L.].
ici on parle français, [ē-sē′-aw(ng)-pahrl-frah(ng)′-sā], *phr.* French spoken here. [Fr.].
idée fixe, [ē-dā-fēks′], *n.* an obsession. [Fr. set idea].
id est, [id′-est′], *phr.* that is, namely. [L.].
ignoratio elenchi, [ig′-nor-ā-shō-i-lengk′-ī], *n.* an argument seeking to refute an opponent by disproving what he has not actually asserted. [L. ignoring of the point at issue].
ignotum per ignotius, [ig-nōt′-um-pur-ig-nō-shus], *phr.* (defining) what is unknown by what is even more unknown. [L.].
imperium in imperio, [im-pēer′-i-um-in-im-pēer′-i-ō], *phr.* rule within rule. [L.].
in, [in], *prep.* in; **in absentia,** [in-ab-sen′-shi-ā], in absence; **in articulo mortis,** [in-ah-ti′-kyo͞o-lō-maw′-tis], at the point of death; **in contumaciam,** [in-kon′-tyo͞o-mā-si-am], in contempt (of court); **in esse,** [in-es′-i], in being; **in excelsis,** [in-ek-sel′-sis], to the highest degree; **in extenso,** [in-ek-sten′-so], completely; **in extremis,** [in-ek-strēm′-is], in desperate straits, at the point of death; **in flagrante delicto,** [in-fla-gran′-ti-di-lek′-tō], red-handed, in the act of committing the offence; **in forma pauperis,** [in-faw′-mā-paw′-per-is], as a poor person; **in loco parentis,** [in-lō′-kō-pa-ren′-tis], in the stead of a parent; **in medias res** [in-mē′-di-as-rēz], into the middle of affairs; **in memoriam,** [in′-mi-maw′-ri-am], in, to, the memory of; **in partibus,** [in-pah′-ti-bus], in (heathen) territories; **in posse,** [in-po′-si], as a possibility; **in propria persona,** [in-prō′-pri-ā-per-sō′-nā], personally; **in puris (naturalibus),** [in-pyo͞oer′-is(-nat-yo͞o-rā′-li-bus)], naked; **in re,** [in-rē′], in the matter of, concerning; **in sæcula sæculorum,** [in-sē′-kyo͞o-la-sē-kyo͞o-law′-rum], for ever and ever; **in situ,** [in-si′-tew], in its original situation; **in statu pupillari,** [in-stā′-tew-pew-pi-lāer′-ī], in the position of a minor, *esp.* at a university; **in statu quo ante,** [in-stā′-tew-kwō-an′-ti], in the same position as before (the war); **in terrorem,** [in-te-raw′-rem], as a threat; **in toto,** [in-tō′-tō], totally, as a whole; **in vacuo,** [in-va′-kyo͞o-ō], in a vacuum, in isolation; **in vino veritas,** [in-vī′-nō-ve′-ri-tas], drunk people tell the truth [*lit.* truth in wine].
index expurgatorius, [in′-deks-eks-pur′-ga-taw′-ri-us], *n.* the Roman Catholic Index of prohibited books. [L.].
infra dignitatem, [in′-fra-dig′-ni-tā-tem], *phr.* beneath (one's) dignity. [L.].
initio, [i-nish′-i-ō], *adv.* at the beginning. [L.].
inter alia, [in′-ter-ā′-li-a], *phr.* among other things. [L.].
inter nos, [in′-ter-nōs′], *phr.* between ourselves, confidentially. [L.].
inter vivos, [in′-ter-vī′-vōs], *phr.* between living people. [L.].
invenit, [in-vē′-nit], *v.* designed. [L.].
invita Minerva, [in-vīt′-ā-mi-nur′-va], *phr.* uninspired. [L. Minerva unwilling].
ipsissima verba, [ip-si′-si-ma-vur′-ba], *n.(pl.)* the very words. [L.].
ipso facto, [ip′-sō-fak′-tō], *phr.* by that very fact, automatically. [L.].
jaal, [yahl], *n.* a species of wild goat of Sinai and parts of Egypt. [Heb. *ya'el*].
jacta est alea, see ALEA JACTA EST.
j'adoube, [zha-do͞ob′], *phr.* I adjust (used when a player touches a chessman, but does not intend to move it). [Fr.].
je ne sais quoi, [zher-ner-sā-kwah′], *phr.* I don't know what (of something difficult to define). [Fr.]
jeu d'esprit, [zhur-des-prē′], *n.* a witty trifle. [Fr game of wit].
jeune premier, [zhurn-pru′-myā], *n.* the juvenile lead in a play. [Fr.].
jeunesse dorée, [zhur-nes′-daw′-rā], *n.* gilded youth [Fr.].
joie de vivre, [zhwah-der-vēvr′], *n.* the joy of living, high spirits. [Fr.].
jubilate, [jew-bi-lā′-ti], *n.* an outburst of rejoicing [L. rejoice!].
Judenhetze, [yew′-den-het′-za], *n.* persecution of the Jews. [Germ.].
jure divino, [jo͞oer′-i-di-vī′-nō], *phr.* by Divine Right. [L.].
jus canonicum, [jus′-ka-non′-i-kum], *n.* canon law. [L.].
juste milieu, [zhüst′-mē-lyur′], *n.* the golden mean. [Fr. proper middle].
juvenilia, [jew-ven-il′-i-a], *n.(pl.)* the youthful works of a writer or artist. [L. youthful things].
jupe, [zhüp], *n.* a skirt. [Fr.].
Kapellmeister, [ka-pel′-mī-ster], *n.* the salaried conductor of a choir, orchestra, etc. [Germ.].
kaput, [ka-po͝ot′], *adj.* destroyed, spoilt. [Germ.].
kef, [kef], *n.* the intoxication produced by bhang, hashish, etc. [Arab. well-being].
keffiyeh, [ke-fē′-yā], *n.* a Bedouin head-dress made of a kerchief. [Arab. *kuffiyeh*].
Kinder, Kirche, und Küche, [kin′-der-kēer′-ça-o͞ont-kü′-ça], *phr.* children, church, and the kitchen (as the proper province of women). [Germ.].
kitool, kittool, [ki-to͞ol′], *n.* a species of palm or the black fibre extracted from this. [Sinhalese *kitul*].
kotwal, [kot′-wahl], *n.* a magistrate or chief constable of an Indian town. [Hind.].
kromesky, [krō-mes′-ki], *n.* a kind of rissole, rolled in bacon, and fried. [Russ.].
kshatrya, [kshut′-rē-a], *n.* a member of the second or military Hindu caste. [Hind.].
Kultur, [ko͞ol-to͞oer′], *n.* culture (always *ironically*). [Germ.].
küss' die Hand, [küs′-dē-hant′], *phr.* formal greeting (in Austria). [Germ. I kiss the hand].
laborare est orare, [la′-baw-rāer′-i-est-aw-rāer′-i], *phr.* to work is to pray. [L.].
laisser-aller, laissez-aller, [les′-ā-a′-lā], *phr.* not interfering. [Fr. allow to go].
laisser-faire, laissez-faire, [les′-ā-fāer], *phr.* not interfering, *esp.* of the State in economic matters. [Fr. allow to act].
lamé, [lah′-mā], *n.* material with gold or silver thread in it. [Fr. worked with gold (silver) thread].
langue d'oc, [lah(ng)g-dok′], *n.* the southern dialect of Old French. [Fr. tongue which used "oc" (for "yes")].
langue d'oïl, [lah(ng)g-doi′], *n.* the northerly dialect of Old French. [Fr. tongue which used "oïl" (for "yes")].
lapsus, [lap′-sus], *n.* a lapse or slip; **l. calami,** (ka′-la-mī], a slip of the pen; **l. linguae,** [ling′-gwē], a slip of the tongue. [L.].
lares et penates, [lāer′-ēz-et′-pe-nā′-tēz], *n.(pl.)* the household gods. [L.].
lasciate ogni speranza voi ch' entrate, [la-shyah′-tā-on′-yi-spe-ran′-tsah-voi′-ken-trah′-tā], *phr.* abandon hope all ye that enter. [It.].
lathi, [lah′-ti], *n.* the staff used by the native police of India. [Hind.].
latine, [la-tī′-ni], *adv.* in Latin. [L.].
laudator temporis acti, [law-dā-tor-tem′-por-is-ak′-tī], *n.* one who regrets "the good old days." [L. praiser of time past].
legum, [lē′-gum], *n.(pl.)* of laws. [L.].
l'etat, c'est moi, [le′-tah-sā-mwah′], *phr.* I am the State. [Fr.].
lettre de cachet, [letr′-der-ka′-shā], *n.* (*hist.*) a warrant of imprisonment, formerly granted by the French king. [Fr.].

lev, (*pl.* **leva**), [lev], *n.* the Bulgarian unit of currency. [Bulgarian lion].
levée en masse, [ler-vā′-ah(ng)-mas′], *n.* total conscription. [Fr.].
lever de rideau, [ler′-vā-der-rē′-dō], *n.* the raising of the curtain at the beginning of a play. [Fr.].
lex talionis, [leks′-ta-li-ō′-nis], *n.* the law of retaliation. [L.].
lied, (*pl.* **lieder**), [lēt, lē′-der], *n.* a ballad poem, a song (as cultivated by the great German composers). [Germ. song].
literæ humaniores, [li′-ter-ē-hew-mā′-ni-aw′-rēz], *n.*(*pl.*) the liberal arts; Classical Greats at Oxford. [L. the more humane studies].
lit(t)erarum doctor, [lit′-er-āer′-um-dokt′-or], *n.* doctor of letters (as a university degree). [L.].
litera scripta manet, [li′-ter-ā-skrip′-ta-ma-net′], *phr.* the written word survives. [L.].
loco citato, [lōk′-ō-cit-āt′-ō], *phr.* in the place cited above. [L.].
longue haleine, [law(ng)g′-al-en′], *n.* long perseverance. [Fr. *œuvre de longue haleine* a work requiring lengthy persistence for its completion].
longueur, [law(ng)-gur′], *n.* a boring space of time. [Fr.].
lucus a non lucendo, [lōōk′-us-ā-non-lōōs-en′-dō], *phr.* etymology by contraries. [L. deriving "wood" (*lucus*) from "not shining" (*non lucere*)].
luxe, de [de-lüks′], *adj.* luxury. [Fr.].
Lux Mundi, [luks′-mun′-di], *n.* the Light of the World (as a title of Christ). [L.].
maduro, [ma-dōōer′-ō], *adj.* (of cigars), having a full flavour. [Span.].
magni nominis umbra, [mag′-nī-nō′-mi-nis-um′-bra], *n.* the shadow of a great name. [L.].
maidan, [mī-dahn′], *n.* a parade ground. [Pers.].
maison de santé, [me′-zaw(ng)-der-sah(ng)′-tā], *n.* a lunatic asylum, nursing home, etc. [Fr. house of health].
maître d'hotel, [metr′-dōt-el′], *n.* the manager of a hotel; **m. butter,** butter blended with chopped parsley. [Fr.].
malum in se, [ma′-lum-in-sē], *phr.* evil in itself. [L.].
Mardi gras, [mah′-di-grah′], *phr.* Shrove Tuesday. [Fr.].
mare, [ma′-ri, māer′-i], *n.* sea; **m. clausum,** a sea over which one nation has sovereign rights; **m. liberum,** the high seas; **M. Nostrum,** the Mediterranean viewed by the Italians as their special preserve. [L.].
mariage de convenance, [ma′-ri-ahzh-der-kaw(ng)′-ver-nah(ng)s′], *n.* a marriage arranged on grounds of policy and suitability (as opposed to a love match). [Fr. marriage based upon respect for propriety].
marid, [ma′-rēd], *n.* a jinn of the most powerful class. [Arab. rebel].
marron glacé, [ma′-raw(ng)-glas′-ā], *n.* a sweetmeat made of crystallized chestnuts. [Fr.].
masjid, [muz′-jēd], *n.* a mosque. [Arab.].
matelot, [mat′-lō], *n.* a French sailor. [Fr.].
matzo, [mat′-sō], *n.* a biscuit made of unleavened bread. [Heb.].
maund, [maund], *n.* an Indian measure of weight, usually about 80 lb. [Hind. *man*].
mauvais, [mōv′-ā], *adj.* bad, wicked; **m. sujet,** [süzh′-ā], a "bad lot"; **m. quart d'heure,** [kahr-dur′], a disagreeable quarter of an hour. [Fr.].
mauvaise, [mōv′-ez], *adj.* (*fem.*) bad; **m. honte,** [aw(ng)t], painful social embarrassment. [Fr.].
maya, [mī′-a], illusion. [Skr].
mea culpa, [mē′-a-kul′-pa], *int.* it is my fault. [L.].
media, (*pl.* **mediæ**), [mēd′-i-a], *n.* (*phon.*) a voiced consonant such as *b*, *d*, and *g*. [L. (*littera*) *media* intermediate letter].
medice, cura teipsum, [me′-di-sē-kyōōer′-a-tē-ip′-sum], *phr.* physician, heal thyself. [L.].
medio tutissimus ibis, [mē′-di-ō-tew-ti′-si-mus-ī′-bis], *phr.* the middle course is the safest. [L. you will go safest in the middle].
meistersinger, (*pl.* **meistersinger**), [mīst′-er-zing′-er], *n.* a lyric poet belonging to one of the medieval German guilds of minstrels. [Germ.].
membrum virile, [mem′-brum-vi′-ri-li], *n.* the (human) penis. [L. male organ].
memento mori, [mē-men′-tō-maw′-rī], *int.* remember you must die. [L. remember dying].
ménage à trois, [men′-ahzh-ah-trwah′], *n.* a household of three persons, one cohabiting with the other two. [Fr. household of three].
mens sana, [menz-sān′-a], *n.* a healthy mind. [L. *mens sana* (*in corpore sano*) a healthy mind (in a healthy body)].
meum et tuum, [mē′-um-et-tew′-um], *phr.* yours and mine. [L.].
milady, [mi′-lah-di], *n.* an English lady, *esp.* the wife of a lord. [Fr. from MY LADY].
milord, [mi′-lawr], *n.* an English lord. [Fr. from MY LORD].
mirabile dictu, [mi-rā′-bi-li-dik′-tew], *phr.* marvellous to relate. [L.].
morgue anglaise, [mawg′-ah(ng)-glez′], *n.* cold indifference as a characteristic of the English. [Fr. English haughtiness].
mot juste, [mō-jüst′], *n.* the appropriate word or expression. [Fr. correct word].
motiv, [mō-tēf′], *n.* a musical motif. [Germ.].
moto perpetuo, [mōt′-ō-per-pet′-yōō-ō], *n.* perpetual motion; a musical piece representing this. [It.].
mpret, [mpret], *n.* the title of the ruler of Albania. [Albanian].
mutatis mutandis, [mewt-āt′-is-mewt-and′-is], *phr.* changing what requires to be changed. [L.].
naïf, [nah-ēf′], *adj.* naive. [Fr.].
natura non facit saltum, [na-tewr′-a-non-fa′-sit-sal′-tum], *phr.* Nature does not make a leap. [L.].
nemine contradicente, [nem′-in-i-kon′-tra-dis-ent′-i], *phr.* nobody expressing disagreement. [L.].
nemo me impune lacessit, [nē′-mō-mē-im-pew′-nē-la-se′-sit], *phr.* nobody injures me without being punished. [L.].
ne plus ultra, [nē′-plus-ult′-ra], *n.* the acme, furthest limit, etc. [L. nothing beyond].
nero antico, [nāer′-ō-ant-ēk′-ō], *n.* a species of black marble used by the Romans. [It. (*marmo*) *nero antico* antique black (marble)].
ne sutor ultra crepidam, [nē-sew′-tor-ul′-tra-kre′-pi-dam′], *phr.* let the cobbler stick to his last. [L.].
netsuké, [net-sook′-ā], *n.* a carved ornament in the form of a button, worn by the Japanese. [Jap.].
nihil ad rem, [nī′-hil-ad-rem′], *phr.* not relevant to the question at issue. [L. nothing to the affair].
nil admirari, [nil′-ad′-mi-rāer′-ī], *phr.* be surprised at nothing. [L.].
nil desperandum, [nil′-des-per-an′-dum], *phr.* never despair. [L.].
nisi prius, [nī′-sī-prī′-us], *n.* the hearing of civil lawsuits by a judge of assize. [L. unless (judges come) sooner].
noblesse oblige, [nō-bles′-ō-blēzh′], *phr.* (noble) rank involves obligations. [Fr.].
noisette, [nwuz-et′], *n.* a dish made of small balls of meat. [Fr.].
nolens volens, [nōl′-enz-vōl′-enz], *phr.* willy-nilly. [L. not wishing, wishing].
nolle prosequi, [nol′-i-pros′-ek-wī], *n.* the abandonment of a suit by the prosecutor or plaintiff. [L. not to wish to pursue (a suit)].
nolo episcopari, [nōl′-ō-ep-is′-kō-pāer′-ī], *phr.* I do not wish to be a bishop (used to express refusal to accept a post of responsibility). [L.].
nom de guerre, [naw(ng)-der-gāer′], *n.* a nom de plume. [Fr.].
non, [non], *adv.* not; **n. compos mentis,** [com′-pos-ment′-is], not of sound mind; **n. est,** [est], it does not exist; **n. est inventus,** [est-in-vent′-us], he has not been found; **n. nobis,** [nōb′-is], not to us (but to God are thanks due); **n. placet,** [plās′-et], it does not please; the rejection of a motion in a church or university assembly; **n. possumus,** [pos′-yōō-mus], we cannot; used to denote an unco-operative attitude.
non avenu, [nawn-av′-nü], *phr.* that has not, or is considered as not having, happened. [Fr. not come to pass].
non tali auxilio, [non′-tā-li-awk-zil′-i-ō], *phr.* not with such aid (as this.) [L.].
noscitur a sociis, [no′-sit-ur-ā-sō′-shi-is], *phr.* birds of a feather flock together. [L. he is known from his companions].
nosseigneurs, [nō′-sen-yur′], *n.*(*pl.*) of MONSEIGNEUR.

nota bene, [nōt'-a-bĕn'-i], *phr.* note! [L. note well].
nugæ, [newj'-ē], *n.(pl.)* trifles. [L.].
nulla bona, [nul'-a-bōn'-a], *n.(pl.)* no goods (used by a sheriff when a person has no possessions that can be distrained upon). [L.].
nulli secundus [nu'-lī-sē-kun'-dus], *phr.* second to none. [L.].
nunc dimittis, [nungk'-di-mit'-is], *phr.* now thou dismissest. [L. opening words of the canticle].
obiit, [ob'-i-it], *v.i.* he died (in the year). [L.].
oderint dum metuant, [ō'-der-int-dum'-met'-yōō-ant'], *phr.* let them hate, so long as they fear. [L.].
odium theologicum, [ō'-di-um-thē-ō-lo'-ji-kum], *n.* the hatred of theologians for their rivals. [L.].
omne ignotum, [om'-ni-ig-nō'-tum], *phr.* everything unknown; **o. i. pro magnifico,** [prō-mag-ni'-fi-kō], everything unknown is (taken for) something wonderful. [L.].
opere citato, [o'-per-ĕ-sī-tā'-tō], *phr.* in the work mentioned (above). [L.].
ora pro nobis, [aw'-ra-prō-nō'-bis], *phr.* pray for us. [L.].
orate pro anima, [ō-rā'-tē-prō-a'-ni-mā], *phr.* pray for the soul (of). [L.].
orfe, [awf], *n.* a variety of goldfish. [Fr. and Germ.].
oro è che oro vale, [aw'-rō-ā'-kā-aw'-rō-vah'-lā], *phr.* all is not gold that glitters. [It. gold is what has the value of gold].
o si sic omnia, [ō-sī'-sik-om'-ni-a], *int.* if only all things were like this. [L. oh, if all things thus].
o tempora! o mores! [ō'-tem'-por-a-ō-maw'-rēz], *int.* alas for the times, and the customs! [L.].
otium cum dignitate, [ōsh'-i-um-cum-dig'-ni-tāt'-i], *phr.* leisure with dignity. [L.].
palafitte, [pal'-a-fit], *n.* a prehistoric lake-dwelling. [Fr. from It. *palafitto*].
palikar, [pal'-i-kah(r)], *n.* a member of a band serving under a Greek or Albanian. [MdGk. *palikari*].
palmam qui meruit ferat, [pahl'-mam-kwī-me'-ryōō-it-fe'-rat], *phr.* let him wear the palm of victory who has deserved it. [L.].
panem et circenses [pā'-nem-et-ser-sen'-sēz], *phr.* bread and the Roman circus; food and entertainments at the public expense. [L.].
par excellence, [pahr-eks'-el-ah(ng)s'], *phr.* pre-eminently. [Fr.].
pari passu, [pāer'-i-pas'-ew], *phr.* likewise, to an identical extent. [L. with equal step].
parti, [pah-tē'], *n.* a person considered as a partner to a possible marriage; **p. pris** [prē'], preconception. [Fr.].
parturiunt montes, [pah-tewr'-i-unt-mont'-ēz], *phr.* the mountains are in labour (used as an ironic prelude to a ridiculous happening). [L. *parturiunt montes* (*et nascetur ridiculus mus*) the mountains are in labour (but only a comic mouse is born)].
pavé, [pav'-ā], *n.* a pavement; encrusted jewellery. [Fr.].
pavonazzo, [pav-on-at'-sō], *n. and adj.* (of) a purple or reddish, veined marble. [It. (*marmo*) *pavonazzo* violet (marble)].
pax vobiscum (sit), [paks'-vō-bis'-kum(-sit')], *phr.* peace be with you. [L.].
paysage, [pā'-ē-zahzh], *n.* a painting of a rural landscape. [Fr. landscape].
pêche melba, [pāsh-mel'-ba], *n.* a confection made of peach and ice-cream flavoured with raspberry juice. [Fr. *pêche* peach and Dame Nellie *Melba*, a well-known singer].
peine forte et dure, [pen'-fawt-ā-dür'], *n.* a medieval punishment by which a person who refused to plead was pressed to death. [Fr. heavy and hard punishment].
pendente lite, [pen-dent'-i-līt'-i], *phr.* during a lawsuit. [L.].
per capita, [pur'-ka'-pi-ta], *phr.* counting by heads. [L.].
per caput, [pur'-ka'-put], *phr.* per head. [L.].
per contra, [pur'-kon'-tra], *phr.* on the other hand. [L.].
père, [pāer], *n.* (following a name) senior, the elder. [Fr. father].
perpetuum mobile, [per-pet'-yōō-um-mōb'-i-li], *n.* the principle of perpetual motion. [MedL.].
persona grata, [per-sōn'-a-grāt'-a], *n.* an acceptable person. [L.].
petitio principii, [pet-ish'-i-ō-prin-sip'-i-ī], *n.* (*logic*) a begging of the question. [L.].
phansigar, [fan'-si-gah(r)'], *n.* a thug. [Hind.].
pichiciago, [pich'-i-syāg'-ō], *n.* a small burrowing animal, *Chlamyphorus truncatus*, of Chile. [Span.].
pickelhaube, [pikl'-howb-a], *n.* the spiked helmet worn by certain German regiments. [Germ.].
pied-à-terre, [pyād'-ah-tāer], *n.* accommodation (of a restricted kind) from which to pursue one's activities. [Fr. (one's) foot on the ground].
pindari, [pin-dah'-ri], *n.* (*hist.*) a mounted Indian marauder. [Hind.].
pinxit, [pingks'-it], *v.* painted (this). [L. he painted].
piou-piou, [pyōō'-pyōō'], *n.* a French soldier, a poilu. [Fr.].
pis aller, [pēz-al'-ā], *n.* a course taken or choice made for lack of a better. [Fr.].
plat, [plah], *n.* a course or dish at a meal. [Fr.].
pleno jure, [ple'-no-yōō'-ri], *phr.* with full authority. [L.].
plombé, [plaw(ng)'-bā], *adj.* sealed under official supervision in order to permit transit through the customs. [Fr. leaded].
pococurante, [pōk'-ō-kōō-rant'-ē], *n.* one who is indifferent. [It. caring little].
poissarde, [pwus'-ahd], *n.* a French fish-wife; (*hist.*) one of the market-women who led the riots in the French Revolution of 1789. [Fr.].
poligar, [pol'-i-gah(r)], *n.* (*hist.*) one of the minor feudal chiefs of Southern India; a follower of one of these, *esp.* one given to robbery. [Marathi *palegar*].
pollam, [pol'-am], *n.* (*hist.*) the estate of a poligar. [Teluga *palemu*].
pollice verso, [po'-li-si-vur'-sō], *phr.* with the thumb turned down (as a mark of disapproval). [L.].
pombé, [pom'-bā], *n.* a drink made from fermented African fruit and grain. [Native].
pons asinorum, [ponz'-as-in-aw'-rum], *n.* the nickname of the fifth proposition of Euclid Book I; any problem likely to test the capability of beginners. [L. bridge of asses].
pontificalia, [pon-tif'-ik-āl-i-a], *n.(pl.)* the vestments and appurtenances of a bishop. [L.].
porte cochère, [pawt'-kosh-āer'], *n.* a gateway through a house to admit carriages, etc. [Fr.].
portolano, (*pl.* **portolani**), [pawt'-ō-lahn'-ō], *n.* a portolan. [It.].
post hoc, ergo propter hoc, [pōst'-hok-erg-ō-propt'-er-hok], *phr.* (ironically) after a certain thing, therefore because of it. [L.].
post meridiem, [pōst-me-rid'-i-em], *phr.* after midday (until midnight). [L.].
potlach, [pot'-lach], *n.* the feast given to a tribe by an aspirant to the chieftaincy. [NAmerInd.].
poult de soie, [pōō'-der-swah'], *n.* a fine corded silk stuff, paduasoy. [Fr.].
pour encourager les autres, [pōōr-ah(ng)-kōō-rah'-zhā-lā-zōtr'], *phr.* (ironically, of exemplary punishment) to encourage the others. [Fr.].
pour prendre congé, [pōōr-prah(ng)dr-caw(ng)'-zhā], *phr.* in order to take (one's) leave. [Fr.].
pou sto, [pow'-stō], *n.* a place to stand, a basis for one's operations. [Gk. where can I stand].
predikant, [prā'-di-kahnt'], *n.* a minister of the Dutch Reformed Church. [Du.].
pretzel, [pretsl], *n.* a crisp roll, twisted in the form of a knot, flavoured with salt, and eaten with beer. [Germ.].
preux chevalier, [prur'-cher-val'-yā], *n.* a valiant knight. [Fr.].
prie-dieu, [prē-dyur'], *n.* a desk at which one kneels for prayer. [Fr. from *prier* to pray, and *Dieu* God].
prima buffa, [prīm'-ā-bōōf-a], *n.* the leading comic actress or singer. [It.].
prima facie, [prīm'-a-fāsh'-yē], *phr.* at first sight, judging by first impressions. [L. by first appearance].
primeur, [prēm-ur'], *n.* early fruit out of season; early news of an event. [Fr.].
primo, [prīm'-ō], *adv* in the first place. [L.]

primus inter pares, [prī'-mus-in-ter-pāer'-ēz], *phr.* first among equals. [L.].
privat-dozent, [pri-vaht'-dot-sent'], *n.* a recognized tutor at a German-speaking university not on the salaried staff. [Germ.].
pro bono publico, [prō-bō'-nō-pub'-li-kō], *phr.* for the public good. [L.].
pro forma, [prō-fawm'-ā], *phr.* for the sake of form. [L.].
pro hac vice, [prō-hak-vīs'-ē], *phr.* for this occasion. [L.].
pro re nata, [prō-rē-nāt'-ā], *phr.* for each occasion as it arises. [L.].
pro tanto, [prō-tant'-ō], *phr.* to that extent. [L. for as much].
pro tempore, [prō-temp'-or-i], *phr.* for the time being. [L.].
procès verbal, (*pl.* **procès verbaux**), [pros'-ā-vāer-bahl', vāer-bō'], *n.* a verbatim transcript of proceedings; evidence collected in support of a charge in the French courts. [Fr.].
proneur, [prōn'-ur'], *n.* a flatterer or eulogist. [Fr.].
proveditore, [prov-ed'-i-taw'-ri], *n.* a provedore. [It. †*proveditore*].
pueblo, [pweb'-lō], *n.* a settlement of Indians in Spanish America. [Span. town].
pur sang, [pür-sah(ng)'], *phr.* of pure blood; total. [Fr.].
puy, [püi], *n.* the cone of an extinct volcano in the Auvergne. [Fr. peak].
quamdiu se bene gesserit, [kwam'-di-ōō-sē'-bē'-ni-je'-ser-it], *phr.* (used of the terms of appointment of a judge) so long as he comports himself well. [L.].
quand même, [kah(ng)-mem'], *phr.* all the same, nevertheless. [Fr.].
quantum libet, [kwon'-tum-li'-bet], *phr.* as much as is desired. [L.].
quare impedit, [kwāer'-ē-im'-ped-it], *phr.* used to denote the writ of counter-objection issued when objection has been raised to a presentation to a church benefice. [L. why does he resist?].
quashee, [kwosh'-ē], *n.* a West African negro. [W. Afric. *Kwasi*].
quid pro quo, [kwid'-prō-kwō'], *n.* something in exchange. [L.].
quieta non movere, [kwī-ē'-ta-non-mō-vēer'-i], *phr.* not to disturb things, to let sleeping dogs lie. [L.].
quihai, quihi, [kwī-hī'], *n.* a European resident in India. [Urdu, who's there?].
quis custodiet (ipsos custodes)? [kwis'-kus-tō'-di-et(-ip'-sōs-kus-tō'-dēz)], *phr.* who shall guard the guards themselves? [L.].
qui s'excuse, s'accuse, [kē-sek-sküz'-sa'-küz], *phr.* he who makes excuses (unasked) accuses himself. [Fr.].
qui tam, [kwī-tam'], *n.* an action brought by an informer. [L. who also (sues)].
qui vive, [kē-vēv'], *phr.* **on the q.,** on the alert. [Fr. who lives? (used as a challenge by a sentry)].
quoad hoc, [kwō'-ad-hok'], *phr.* as far as this is concerned. [L.].
quod dixi, dixi, [kwod-dik'-si-dik'-si], *phr,* what I have said, I have said; I stand by what I have said. [L.].
quod erat demonstrandum, [kwod'-e'-rat-de'-mon-stran'-dum], *phr.* which is what was to be proved. [L.].
quod semper, quod ubique, quod ab omnibus, [kwod-sem'-per-kwod-ew-bī'-kwi-kwod'-ab-om'-ni-bus], *phr.* (of Catholicism), eternal, ubiquitous, and (believed) by all. [L.].
quot homines, tot sententiæ, [kwot'-ho'-mi-nēz-tot'-sen-ten'-shi-ē], *phr.* there are as many opinions as there are men. [L.].
quo vadis? [kwō-vā'-dis], *phr.* where art thou going? [L.].
raison d'état, [re'-zaw(ng)-dā-tah'], *n.* reason of state. [Fr.].
Rat(h)skeller, [rahts'-kel-er], *n.* (*U.S.*) a basement bar or saloon. [Germ. cellar of the town hall].
reductio ad absurdum, [rē-duk'-shi-ō-ad'-ab-surd'-um], *phr.* the process of disproving an assertion by drawing from it a logical conclusion which is manifestly absurd; the carrying of a principle to absurd limits. [LL. reduction to the absurd].
reebok, [rā'-bok], *n.* the South African antelope, *Relea capreola.* [Du. roebuck].
reflet, [rer'-flā], *n.* the sheen or lustre on pottery. [Fr. reflection].
répondez s'il vous plaît, [rā-paw(ng)'-dā-sēl-vōō-plā'], *phr.* please reply. [Fr.].
requiescat, [rek'-wi-es'-kat], *n.* a prayer for the repose of the soul of a dead person; **r. in pace,** may he rest in peace. [L. may he (it) rest].
res angusta domi, [rēz'-an-gust'-a-dom-ī'], *phr.* financial embarrassment. [L. affairs at home pinching].
res judicata, [rēz'-jewd-ik-āt'-a], *n.* a matter already settled. [L.].
retenue, [rer'-ter-nü], *n.* reservedness. [Fr.].
revanche, [rer-vah(ng)sh'], *n.* a return match (desired by a defeated contestant). [Fr.].
ritardando, [rit'-ard-and'-ō], *phr.* (*mus.*) a direction to decrease the speed; an instance of this. [It.].
roi le veult, le, [ler-roi'-ler-vurlt'], *phr.* used to signify the royal assent to a Parliamentary bill. [AFr. the king wishes it].
roi s'avisera, le, [ler-roi'-sa-vēz'-er-ah], *phr.* used to signify refusal of royal consent to a Parliamentary bill. [AFr. the king will please himself].
Rollmops, [rol'-mops], *n.* pickled herring. [Germ.].
romaika, [rō-mī'-i-ka], *n.* the Greek national dance. [MdGk. *Rhomaike* Romaic (dance)].
ro(o)inek, [roi'-nek'], *n.* a newcomer to South Africa; †a British soldier in the Boer War. [Du. red neck].
rosarium, [rōz-āer'-i-um], *n.* a rose-garden. [L.].
rusé, [rüz'-ā], *adj.* cunning, full of ruses. [Fr.].
respice finem, [res'-pi-si-fī'-nem], *phr.* keep the end in view. [L.].
resurgam, [rē-sur'-gam], *v.* I shall rise again. [L.].
sabreur, [sab-rur'], *n.* a cavalryman armed with a sabre; **beau s.,** [bō], a handsome, dashing cavalry officer. [Fr.].
sadhu, [sahd'-ōō], *n.* a man of holy life. [Skr. holy].
sakhia, [sahk'-ē-a], *n.* an Arab water-wheel driven by oxen. [Arab. *saqiyah*].
salle à manger, [sal-ah-mah(ng)zh'-ā], *n.* a dining-room. [Fr.].
saltimbanco, [salt'-im-bangk'-ō], *n.* a mountebank. [It.].
sang de bœuf, [sah(ng)-der-buf'], *n.* a deep red colour characteristic of certain Chinese porcelain. [Fr. ox-blood].
sans peur et sans reproche, [sah(ng)-pur'-ā-sah(ng)-rer-prosh'], *phr.* without fear and without reproach. [Fr.].
Sapperment, [sap'-er-ment'], *int.* an oath used by Germans. [~SACRAMENT].
sardelle, [sah-del'], *n.* a Mediterranean fish preserved like sardines. [Germ.].
sartor resartus, [sah'-taw(r)-rē-sah'-tus], *phr.* the tailor retailored. [L.].
satis, [sāt'-is, sat'-is], *adv.* sufficient (used as a pass mark in examinations); **non s.,** [non], not sufficient; **vix s.,** [viks], scarcely sufficient; **s. superque,** [sōō-pur'-kwi], enough and more than enough. [L.].
sauve qui peut, [sōv'-kē-pur'], *n.* a mad scramble for safety. [Fr. escape who can].
savoir faire, [sa'-vwah-fāer], *n.* common sense, nous. [Fr.].
sayyid, seid, [sā'-id], *n.* one who is descended from Mohammed through Fatima and Ali. [Arab. prince].
scaldino, (*pl.* **scaldini**), [skal-dēn'-ō, skal-dēn'-ē], *n.* a brazier made of earthenware. [It.].
scandalum magnatum, [skan'-dal-um-mag'-nā'-tum], *n.* scandalous talk about people in authority. [L. scandal of magnates].
scena, [shā'-na], *n.* a portion or scene of an opera; a vocal and orchestral composition resembling this. [It. scene].
scherzando, [skāert-sand'-ō], *n. and adv.* (*mus.*) (a direction to perform) in the manner of a scherzo. [It. playfully].
sciolto, [shol'-tō], *n. and adv.* (*mus.*) (a direction to perform) as one chooses, or distinctly. [It.].
scire facias, [sīer'-i-fā'-shas], *n.* a writ annulling or enforcing a judgment, etc. [L. let (him) know].

scrinium, (*pl.* **scrinia**), [skrī′-nyum, skrī′-nya], *n.* a box or container for ancient papyrus rolls. [L.].
sebestan, [se-best′-an], *n.* the fruit of the tree, *Cordia Myxa*, etc., used medicinally. [Arab. *sabastan*].
sec, [sek], *adj.* (of wines) dry. [Fr.].
secondo, [si-kon′-dō], *n.* (*mus.*) the second or lower part in a concerted piece. [It. second].
secundo, [sē-kun′-dō], *adv.* secondly. [L.].
secundum, [sē-kun′-dum], *prep.* according to; **s. quid,** [kwid′], to some extent. [L.].
se defendendo, [sē′-dē-fen-den′-dō], *phr.* in self-defence. [L. in defending himself].
sederunt, [sē-dēer′-unt], *n.* a session. [L. they sat].
seid, see *SAYYID.
semper eadem, [sem′-per-ē′-a-dem′], *phr.* always the same. [L.].
semplice, [sem′-pli-chi], *adv.* (*mus.*) simply, without affectation. [It.].
senatus, [se-nā′-tus], *n.* the Roman senate; **s. populusque Romanus,** (pop′-yŏŏ-lus′-kwi-rō-mān′-us], the senate and people of Rome (the official designation of the Roman state); **s. ultimum consultum,** [ul′-ti-mum-con-sul′-tum], a decree of the Roman senate. [L.].
senhor, [sen-yaw(r)′], *n.* Mr. [Portug.].
senhora, [sen-yaw′-ra], *n.* Mrs. [Portug.].
senhorita, [sen-yaw-rē′-ta], *n.* Miss. [Portug.].
se non è vero è ben trovato, [sā-non-ā-vāer′-ō-ā-ben′-tro-vah′-tō], *phr.* if it is not true it is aptly invented. [It.].
sequentes, [si-kwen′-tēz], *n.*(*pl.*) the following (verses, etc.). [L.].
sequentia, [si-kwen′-shi-a], *n.*(*pl.*) the following (words, etc.). [L.].
serein, [ser-ra(ng)′], *n.* fine rain falling like dew from an unclouded sky. [Fr. clear (sky)].
seriema, [se′-ri-ā′-ma], *n.* a Brazilian bird, *Cariama cristata*, that preys on serpents. [Tupi *çariama*].
serioso, [se′-ri-ō′-sō], *n. and adv.* (*mus.*) (a direction to play) solemnly. [It.].
sfumato, [sfŏŏ-mah′-tō], *adj.* painted with blurred outlines. [It. smoked].
shema, [shā′-mah], *n.* the Jewish confession of faith. [Heb. hear (O, Israel)].
sic semper tyrannis, [sik′-sem′-per-tī-ra′-nis], *phr.* so may it always befall tyrants. [L.].
sic transit gloria mundi, [sik′-tran′-sit-glaw′-ri-a-mun′-dī], *phr.* thus worldly glory passes. [L.].
sic volo sic jubeo, [sik′-vol′-ō-sik-jew′-bi-ō], *phr.* thus I wish, thus I command. [L.].
sic vos non vobis, [sik′-vōs′-non-vō′-bis], *phr.* you performed it but the credit is not for you. [L. you (did) thus (but the credit is) not to you].
si jeunesse savait, si vieillesse pouvait! [sē-jur-nes′-sa′-vā-sē-vyā-yes′-pŏŏ-vā], *phr.* if youth knew how, if old age were able. [Fr.].
s'il vous plaît, [sēl′-vŏŏ-plā], *phr.* please. [Fr.].
similia similibus curantur, [si-mil′-i-a-si-mi′-li-bus-kew-ran′-tur], *phr.* like is cured by like. [L.].
sine die, [sī′-ni-dī′-ē], *phr.* indefinitely, without a day assigned. [L. without a day (named)].
sine prole, [sī′-ni-prō-lē], *phr.* without issue. [L.].
sine qua non, [sī′-ni-kwā-non′], *phr.* an essential. [L.].
sirvente, [sēer-vah(ng)t′], *n.* a form of medieval lay of Provençal origin dealing with subjects other than love. [Provenc. *sirventes*].
si vis pacem, para bellum, [sī-vis-pā′-sem-pa′-ra-be′-lum], *phr.* if you desire peace, prepare for war. [L.].
slalom, [slah′-lom], *n.* (*sports*) a ski-race in which artificial obstacles are used to mark out the course. [Norw. *sla-låm*].
soavemente, [sō-ah′-vā-men′-ti], *n. and adv.* (*mus.*) (a direction to perform) gently and smoothly. [It.].
soi-disant, [swu′-dē′-zah(ng)], *adj.* self-styled. [Fr. calling oneself].
soigné(e), [swun′-yā], *adj.* well groomed. [Fr. cared for].
soixante quinze, [swu′-sah(ng)t-ka(ng)z′], *n.* the French 75-mm. gun. [Fr. seventy-five].
soldanella, [sol′-dan-el′-a], *n.* a genus of alpine plants, *esp. Soldanella alpina*, remarkable for their fringed, well-shaped flowers. [It.].
solvitur ambulando, [sol′-vi-tur-am′-byŏŏ-lan′-dō], *phr.* it will be solved as we proceed. [L. it is solved in walking].
sordamente, [saw′-da-men′-ti], *n. and adv.* (*mus.*) in a muffled or muted manner. [It.].
sordino, (*pl.* **sordini**), [saw-dē′-no, saw-dē′-nē], *n.* (*mus.*) a mute; **con sordini,** with mutes. [It.].
sortes virgilianæ, [saw′-tēz-ver-ji-li-ā′-nē], *n.* divination by opening a copy of Virgil at random. [L. from *sors* chance and *Virgilianus* Virgilian].
soutache, [sŏŏ′-tash′], *n.* ornamental braid sewn in patterns on other material [Fr.].
splendide mendax, [splen′-di-di-men′-daks], *phr.* lying in noble fashion. [L.].
spolia opima, [spō′-li-a-o-pī′-ma], *n.*(*pl.*) rich booty or reward. [L.].
sponte sua, [spon′-ti-sew′-ā], *phr.* of his, her, its, own accord. [L.].
stabat mater, [stah′-bat-mah′-ter, stā′-bat-mā′-ter], *n.* a hymn describing the ordeal of the Virgin Mary as she witnessed the Crucifixion; a musical setting of this. [L. the opening words of the hymn].
stat pro ratione voluntas, [stat′-prō-rā′-shi-ō-ni-vo-lun′-tas], *phr.* it is my will, and that serves as the reason. [L. desire stands for the reason].
Sturm und Drang, [shtŏŏerm′-ŏŏnt-drang′], *n.* storm and stress; the period of German culture (1770-1782) characterized by spiritual awakening and emotional unrest. [Germ.].
sua cuique voluptas, [sew′-a-kwī′-kwi-vo-lup′-tas], *phr.* each man has his own pleasures. [L.].
suaviter in modo fortiter in re, [swā′-vi-ter-in-mō′-dō-faw′-ti-ter-in-rē′], *phr.* gently in manner but powerfully in reality. [L.].
subaudi, [sub-aw′-dī], *int.* understand (by implication). [L.].
subauditur, [sub-aw′-di-tur], *n.* an understanding by implication. [L. it is understood].
sub rosa, [sub-rō′-za, rō′-zā], *phr.* confidentially. [L. under the rose].
succès, [sük′-sā], *n.* a success; **s. d'estime,** [des-tēm′], the kind of success accorded to an artistic performance out of personal regard; **s. de scandale,** [der-skah(ng)-dahl′], the success of a play, etc., due to the scandal it creates or to which it gives currency; **s. fou,** (fŏŏ′], success reflected in wild enthusiasm. [Fr.].
suggestio falsi, [su-jest′-i-ō-fawl′-sī], *n.* a suggestion of what is untrue. [L.].
sui generis, [sew′-ī-je′-ner-is], *phr.* unique. [L. of its own kind].
suivez, [swē′-vā], *n. and int.* (*mus.*) (a direction to the accompanist to) accommodate the rhythm to the soloist's performance. [Fr. follow!].
summum bonum, [sum′-um-bō′-num], *n.* the highest good, *esp.* in an ethical system. [L.].
sunt lacrimæ rerum, [sunt-la′-kri-mē-rēer′-um], *phr.* mortal things are suffused with tears. [L.].
suppressio veri, [su-pres′-i-ō-vēer′-ī], *n.* a suppression of what is true. [L.].
supra, [sŏŏ′-pra], *adv.* previously (in this book, etc.). [L. above].
sursum corda! [sur′-sum-kaw′-da], *int.* lift up your hearts! [L.].
sus. per coll., [sus′-per-kol′], *phr.* hanged by the neck. [Abbrev. of L. *suspendatus per collum*].
suum cuique, [sew′-um-kwī′-kwi], *phr.* to each his own. [L.].
tablier, [ta′-bli-ā], *n.* an apron or similar piece of a dress. [Fr.].
tabula rasa, [tab′-yŏŏ-la-rā′-za], *n.* a clean sheet (of paper). [L. a scraped tablet].
tac au tac, [tak′-ō-tak′], *n.* a fencing stroke in which a parry is combined with a riposte; a rapid alternation of attacks and parries. [Fr.].
tædium vitæ, [tē′-di-um-vī′-tē], *n.* weariness with life. [L.].
talis pater, talis filius, [tā′-lis-pā′-ter-ta′-lis-fi′-li-us], *phr.* like father, like son. [L.].
tamanoir, [ta′-ma-nwah(r)′], *n.* the tamandua. [Fr.].
tandstickor, [tand′-sti-ker], *n.* a (Swedish) match. [Swed. *tändstickor* matches].
tempore, [tem′-por-i], *phr.* in the time of, in the reign of. [L.].
tempus fugit, [tem′-pus-few′-jit], *phr.* time flies. [L.].
tenuis, (*pl.* **tenues**), [ten′-yŏŏ-is], *n.* one of the

voiceless stop consonants, *k*, *p*, and *t*. [L. thin].
terra nera, [te'-ra-nāer'-a], *n.* a black pigment used by the artists of the ancients. [It. black earth].
terræ filius, [te'-rē-fī'-li-us], *n.* a son of the soil, the son of a farm-worker. [L.].
tertio, [tur'-shi-ō], *adv.* in the third place. [L.].
tertius gaudens, [tur'-shus-gaw'-denz], *n.* a third party who benefits from the disputes of others. [L. the third rejoicing].
tête-bêche, [tāt'-besh'], *phr.* (of postage stamps) with adjacent impressions mutually inverted. [Fr. head to tail].
til, [tēl], *n.* (*typ.*) the Portuguese tilde (~) used over a vowel to denote nasalization. [Portug. *til* tilde].
timeo Danaos et dona ferentes, [ti'-mi-ō-da'-nā-ōs-et-dō'-na-fe-ren'-tēz], *phr.* I fear the Greeks when they bring presents (used to express suspicion at a gift from a hostile quarter). [L.].
toco, [tō'-kō], n. a thrashing or beating. [Hind. from *tokna* to blame].
totidem verbis, [tot'-i-dem-vur'-bis], *phr.* in those very words. [L.].
toties quoties, [tō'-shi-ēz-kwō'-shi-ēz], *phr.* just as many times as . . . ; so many times . . . [L.].
toto cælo, [tō'-tō-sē'-lō], *phr.* utterly, by a vast amount. [L. by the whole sky].
tour de force, [tooer'-der-faws'], *n.* a piece of virtuosity. [Fr.].
tout court, [too-koor'], *phr.* in a word, briefly, without preface, simply. [Fr. quite brief(ly)].
tout ensemble, [toot'-ah(ng)-sah(ng)mbl'], *phr.* all together; the total appearance. [Fr. altogether].
tracasserie, [trah-ka'-ser-ē'], *n.* a petty vexation. [Fr.].
traduttore traditore, [tra'-doo-taw'-ri-tra'-di-taw'-ri], *phr.* a translator is a traitor. [It.].
trattoria, [tra'-taw-rē'-a], *n.* an eating-house. [It.].
tremolando, [tre-mol-an'-dō], *n. and adv.* (*mus*). (a direction to play) with a tremolo. [It.].
trente et quarante, [trah(ng)t'-ā-ka'-rah(ng)t], *n.* the game of rouge-et-noir. [Fr. thirty and forty].
Triones, [trī-ō'-nēz], *n.*(*pl.*) the stars of the Great Bear or Ursa Major. [L. (*septem*) *triones* (seven) draught oxen].
troika, [trō'-i-ka], *n.* a sledge or carriage drawn by three horses abreast. [Russ.].
trois temps, [trwah'-tah(ng)], *n.* a waltz in 3-4 time. [Fr.].
tromba, (*pl.* **trombe**), [trom'-ba, trom'-bi], *n.* (*mus.*) a trumpet. [It.].
trompe, [trawmp], *n.* (*metal.*) a tromp. [Fr.].
troppo, [tro'-pō], *adv.* (*mus.*) too much; **ma non t.,** (mah-non'], but not too much. [It.].
trouvaille, [troo-vī'], *n.* a discovery. [Fr.].
trumeau, [*pl.* **trumeaux**), [trü'-mō], *n.* (*arch.*) an upright piece of masonry between the two halves of a double door, etc. [Fr.].
tung, [tung], *n.* the Chinese tree, *Aleurites cordata* producing an oil used for varnishing. [Chin. *yu t'ung*].
tu quoque, [tew'-kwō'-kwi], *n.* a retort in kind. [L. you as well].
tutte le strade conducono a Roma, [too' te-lā-strah'-dā-kon-doo'-ko-nō-ah-rō'-ma], *phr.* all roads lead to Rome. [It.].
tuum, [tew'-um], *adj.* thine. [L.].
tyrolienne, [ti'-ro-lyen'], *n.* a dance of the Tyrol. [Fr. (*danse*) *tyrolienne* Tyrol dance].
ubique, [yoo-bī'-kwi], *adv.* everywhere. [L.].
ubi supra, [ew'-bi-soo'-pra], *phr.* in the above-mentioned place (in a book). [L. where above].
ultima ratio, [ul'-ti-ma-rā'-shi-ō], *n.* the last argument, i.e. war. [L.].
ultima Thule, [ul'-ti-ma-thew'-lē], *n.* the remotest boundary, the extreme limit. [L. Thule (which is the) last (land)].
ultra vires, [ul'-tra-vīer'-ēz], *phr.* outside one's legal powers. [L.].
unberufen, [oon'-bi-roofn'], *int.* used to ward off any punishment from the Fates after a boasting remark. [Germ. uncalled upon].
uphroe, [yoo'-frō], *n.* a strip of wood drilled with holes to grip the rope supporting an awning. [Du. *juffrouw* young lady, pulley].
Urbi et Orbi, [ur'-bi-et-or'-bi], *phr.* for Rome and the world (the formula which opens a Papal encyclical). [L. for the city and the world].
ustachi, [oo-stah'-shi], *n.* a member of the forces raised by Pavelitch, the Croat quisling. [Serbo-Croat].
ut supra, [ut-soo'-pra], *phr.* as stated or demonstrated previously (in a book or essay). [L. as above].
uti possidetis, [yoo'-ti-pos'-i-dē'-tis], *phr.* used to denote the principle by which at the conclusion of hostilities, belligerents remain in possession of the territory they have occupied. [L. as you hold (it)].
vade mecum, [vā-di-me-kum], *n.* a manual or handbook for ready reference. [L. go with me].
væ victis, [vē'-vik'-tis], *phr.* woe to the defeated. [L.].
varia lectio, [vāer'-i-a-lek'-shi-ō], *n.* a variant reading in a text. [L. various reading].
vas, (*pl.* **vasa**), *n.* (*physiol.*) a duct; **v. deferens** [dē'-fer-enz], the duct by which the secretion of the testes in mammals is conveyed to the seminal vesicles. [L. vessel].
veilleuse, [vā-yurz'], *n.* a night-light, *esp.* when elaborately decorated. [Fr.].
veloutine, [vel'-oo-tēn'], *n.* a kind of corded fabric; a toilet-powder made of rice-flour and bismuth. [Fr.].
veni, vidi, vici, [vē'-nī-vī'-dī-vī'-sī], *phr.* I came, I saw, I conquered. [L.].
ventre à terre, [vah(ng)tr'-ah-tāer], *phr.* top speed. [Fr. belly to the ground, "flat out"].
verbum sapienti, [vur'-bum-sa'-pi-en'-tī], *phr.* a hint is enough for the wise. [L. *verbum* (*sat*) *sapienti* a word (is enough) for the wise one].
Verein, [fer-īn'], *n.* a union or society. [Germ.].
vers de société, [vāer'-der-so'-sye-tā], *n.* verse of a familiar tone dealing with the elegancies of polite society. [Fr. society verse].
Via Lactea, [vī'-a-lak'-ti-a], *n.* the Milky Way. [L.].
via media, [vī'-a-mē'-di-a], *n.* a middle course (in politics, etc.). [L. middle way].
victor ludorum, (vik'-tor-loo-daw'-rum], *n.* an athletic champion. [L. victor of the games].
vi et armis, [vī'-et-ah'-mis], *phr.* by force of arms. [L. by force and arms].
villanelle, [vi'-la-nel'], *n.* an elaborate verse-form of nineteen lines having only two rhyming sounds. [Fr. from It. *villanella*].
virginibus puerisque, [ver-jin'-i-bus-pewr-is'-kwi], *phr.* to or for girls and boys. [L.].
vixere fortes ante Agamemnona, [vik-sēer'-i-faw'-tēz-an-ti-a'-ga-mem'-no-na], *phr.* there lived great men before Agamemnon. [L.].
vogue la galère, [vōg'-lah-ga-lāer'], *phr.* let things go as they like. [Fr. let the galley drift].
voiturette, [vwu'-tü-ret'], *n.* a light motor-car, a runabout. [Fr.].
volenti non fit injuria, [vō-len'-ti-non-fit-in-jooer'-i-a], *phr.* wrong cannot be inflicted on a consenting party. [L.].
Volksturm, [folk'-shtooerm], *n.* the German equivalent of the Home Guard. [Germ. from *volk* people and *sturm* armed force].
volte-face, [volt'-fahs'], *n.* a rightabout turn; a sudden and unexpected reversal of opinion. [Fr.].
vox, [voks], *n.* voice; **v. angelica,** [an-je'-li-ka], a stop on the organ to give an effect as of celestial music; **v. et præterea nihil,** [et-prē-te'-ri-a-nī'-hil], a voice (or word) and nothing more; **v. humana,** [hyoo-mā'-na], an organ-stop giving a trembling "human" quality to the notes; **v. populi vox Dei,** [po'-pyoo-li-voks-dē'-i], the voice of the people (is) the voice of God. [L.].
Wehrmacht, [vāer'-mahkht], *n.* the German armed forces. [Germ.].
Weltpolitik, [velt'-po'-li-tēk'], *n.* international politics. [Germ. world politics].
Weltschmerz, [velt'-shmāerts], *n.* dissatisfaction with the world and its problems, *esp.* in a vague negative way. [Germ. world grief].
Zeitgeist, [tsīt'-gīst], *n.* the spirit of the age. [Germ. time spirit].
zemstvo, [zemst'-vō], *n.* (*hist.*) an elected body regulating the affairs of a Russian district. [Russ.].
zum Beispiel, [tsoom-bī'-shpēl], *phr.* for instance [Germ.].

STYLES OF ADDRESS FOR PERSONS OF TITLE, RANK, OR OFFICIAL POSITION

AMBASSADOR (BRITISH). "My Lord" *or* "Sir," according to rank. *Envelope:* "His Excellency (*rank or title*) H.M. Ambassador Extraordinary and Plenipotentiary to ——." *Conclusion:* "I have the honour to be, My Lord (*or* Sir), Your Excellency's most humble and obedient servant." *Personal address:* "Your Excellency." The wife of an Ambassador is by courtesy referred to as "Her Excellency."

ARCHBISHOP. "My Lord Archbishop." *Envelope:* "The Most Rev. His Grace the Lord Archbishop of ——." *Conclusion:* "I have the honour to be, My Lord Archbishop, Your Grace's most devoted and obedient servant." *Personal address:* "Your Grace" *or* "My Lord Archbishop." The Archbishop of Armagh is addressed as "His Grace the Lord Primate of Ireland." A Roman Catholic Archbishop is addressed as "The Most Rev. Archbishop of ——." The wife of an Archbishop is simply "Mrs. ——." Retired Archbishop: "Most Rev. Archbishop."

ARCHDEACON. "Venerable Sir." *Envelope:* "The Venerable ——" *or* "The Venerable the Archdeacon of ——." *Personal address:* "Sir."

BARON. "My Lord." *Envelope:* "To the Right Hon. Lord ——," *or* "The Lord ——." *Conclusion:* "I have the honour to be, my Lord, Your Lordship's obedient and humble servant." *Socially:* "Dear Lord ——." *Personal address:* "My Lord" *or* "Your Lordship."

BARONESS. "Madam." *Envelope:* "To the Right Hon. the Baroness ——" *or* "Right Hon. the Lady ——." *Less formally:* "The Lady ——." *Personal address:* "My Lady" *or* "Your Ladyship."

BARONET. "Sir." *Socially:* "Dear Sir (Charles)." *Envelope:* "Sir (Charles) ——, Bart." *Personal address:* "Sir" *or* "Sir (Charles)." *Note:* "Sir" must always be followed by a Christian name or initial, and never by a surname alone, when used of baronets or knights.

BARON'S SON. "Sir." *Envelope:* "Hon. (Charles) ——." *Personal address:* "Sir." The wife is addressed as "The Honourable Mrs. (Charles) ——."

BISHOP. "My Lord." *Envelope:* "The Right Rev. the Lord Bishop of ——." *Formal documents:* "The Right Rev. Father in God by Divine Permission Lord Bishop of ——"; otherwise same as Baron. By virtue of his office the Bishop of London is also a Privy Councillor, and is addressed as "The Rt. Rev. and Rt. Hon. the Lord Bishop of London." A Roman Catholic Bishop is addressed as "The Rt. Rev. the Bishop of ——."

CARDINAL. *Envelope:* "His Eminence Cardinal ——, Bishop (*or* Archbishop) of ——."

CHAIRMAN OF THE LONDON COUNTY COUNCIL. *Envelope:* "The Right Hon. the Chairman of the London County Council."

CLERK IN HOLY ORDERS. "Rev. Sir." *Envelope:* "The Rev. ——." *Conclusion:* "I am, Rev. Sir, Your obedient servant." *Personal address:* "Sir."

COMMANDER, COMPANION OR MEMBER OF ANY ORDER. According to rank, adding after name the initials of the Order, e.g., C.B., C.M.G., D.S.O., etc.

CONSULS. *Envelope:* "—— Esq., H.B.M. Consul-General (*or* Consul *or* Vice-Consul)."

DAMES OF THE ROYAL VICTORIAN AND BRITISH EMPIRE ORDERS. "Madam." *Envelope:* "Dame ——," adding G.C.V.O., D.C.V.O., G.B.E., *or* D.B.E. as the case may be.

DEAN. "Very Rev. Sir." *Envelope:* "The Very Rev. the Dean of ——." *Personal address:* "Sir."

DUKE. "My Lord Duke" *or* "Your Grace." *Envelope:* "His Grace the Duke of ——." *Conclusion:* "I have the honour to be, my Lord Duke, Your Grace's most devoted and most obedient servant." *Personal address:* "Your Grace."

EARL. *Envelope:* "The Right Hon. the Earl (of) ——" *or, less formally,* The Earl of ——." Otherwise, same as Baron.

GOVERNOR OF A CROWN COLONY *or* **HIGH COMMISSIONER OF A PROTECTORATE.** Is styled "His Excellency" before other ranks and titles.

GOVERNOR-GENERAL. *Envelope:* "His Excellency the Governor-General of ——."

"HONOURABLE" IN OVERSEAS DOMINIONS, COLONIES, ETC. Is borne by: (1) All Members of the King's Privy Council for Canada for life, also by members of the Executive Councils of the Commonwealth of Australia and of the States of Victoria and Tasmania. (2) Members of Legislative Councils of other Dominions, Crown Colonies and Protectorates usually during term of office only.

JUDGE. "Sir." *Envelope (official):* "To the Hon. Mr. Justice ——"; *(private):* "Hon. ——." *Personal address:* "Sir"; (*when on the Bench:* "My Lord" *or* "Your Lordship").

JUDGE OF COUNTY COURT. *Envelope:* "To His Honour Judge ——." *Personal address while on the Bench:* "Your Honour."

JUSTICE OF THE PEACE. *Personal address when on the Bench:* "Your Worship." *Envelope:* "——, Esq., J.P."

KNIGHT BACHELOR. *Envelope:* "Sir (Charles) ——." In other respects as Baronet.

LIEUTENANT-GOVERNOR. *Envelope:* "Hon. ——." *Personal address:* "Your Honour."

LORD ADVOCATE. *Envelope:* "The Rt. Hon. the Lord Advocate" *or* "The Rt. Hon. ——."

LORD CHANCELLOR. *Envelope:* "The Rt. Hon. the Lord High Chancellor."

LORD CHIEF JUSTICE. *Envelope:* "The Lord Chief Justice of England" *or* "The Rt. Hon. Baron ——, Lord Chief Justice of England."

LORD MAYOR. *Envelope:* (1) Of London, York and Belfast: "The Right Hon. the Lord Mayor of ——"; (2) of other cities: "The Right Worshipful the Lord Mayor of ——."

LORD OF SESSION. *Envelope:* "Hon. Lord ——." Otherwise, as a Baron.

LORD PROVOST. *Envelope* (1) Of Edinburgh: "The Right Hon. ——, Lord Provost of Edinburgh"; (2) Of Glasgow: "The Right Hon. the Lord Provost of Glasgow."

MARQUESS. "My Lord Marquess." *Envelope:* "The Most Honourable the Marquess of ——" *or, less formally,* "The Marquess of ——." *Personal address:* "My Lord."

NAVAL, MILITARY AND AIR FORCE OFFICERS. Professional rank should precede any social title.

PRINCE. *Envelope:* "His Royal Highness Prince ——." *Begin:* "Sir" *or* "May it please your Royal Highness." *Conclude:* "I remain, Sir, Your Royal Highness's most dutiful and most obedient servant." *Personal address:* "Your Royal Highness."

PRIVY COUNCILLORS. *Envelope:* "The Right Hon." Otherwise in accordance with the rank of the individual followed by "P.C."

RECORDER. The Recorder of London is addressed as "Right Worshipful"; when sitting as a Commissioner in the Central Criminal Court, as "My Lord." Other Recorders are addressed as "The Worshipful" and "Your Worship."

ROYAL DUKE. *Envelope:* "To His Royal Highness the Duke of ——." *Begin:* "Sir." *Conclude:* As for Prince.

SECRETARY OF STATE. *Envelope:* "The Rt. Hon. ——, (or according to rank) His Majesty's Principal Secretary of State for ——" (naming department).

VISCOUNT. *Envelope:* "The Right Hon. the Viscount ——." In other respects as Baron.

PREFIXES AND SUFFIXES
FORMING ELEMENTS OF ENGLISH WORDS

PREFIXES

a- (1), away, on, out, up. [OE. *a-*].
a- (2), on. [OE. *on, an*].
a- (3), of. [OE. *of*].
a- (4), to, towards. [OF. *a-*].
a- (5), from. [L. *a*].
a- (6), from. [AF. *a-*].
a- (7), without. [Gk. *a-*].
ac-, see **ad-**.
ad-, ac-, to, towards. [L. *ad*, etc.].
aero-, aerial. [Gk. *aer* air].
amphi-, both, around. [Gk. *amphi*].
ana-, ano-, afresh, again, back, up. [Gk. *ana-, ano-*].
ano-, see **ana-**.
ant-, see **ant(i)-**.
ante-, before, preceding. [L. *ante*].
ant(i)-, ant-, against. [Gk. *anti*].
apo-, aph-, away, from, off, non- ; detached. [Gk. *apo*, etc.].
arch-, chief, outstanding. [Gk. *arkhos*].
argyr(o)-, containing silver (and). [Gk. *arguron*].
astro-, concerning the stars or astronomy. [Gk. *aster, astros*].
auto-, self-, automatic. [Gk. *autos*].
azo-, containing nitrogen (or its compounds) (and). [Fr. *azo(te)* nitrogen].
be-, about, completely. [OE. *be-*].
bi-, double, doubly, twice. [L. *bi-*].
bio-, life, living. [Gk. *bios* life].
carbo-, containing carbon. [L. *carbo*].
cat(a)-, cath-, according to, away, completely, down. [Gk. *kat(a), kath-*].
caulo-, stem. [Gk. *kaulos*, L. *caulis*].
Celto-, Celtic (and). [L. *Celtus* Kelt].
chole-, bile. [Gk. *khole*].
chondro-, cartilage (and). [Gk. *khondros*].
chori-, separate. [Gk. *khoris*].
Christo-, (of) Christ. [Gk. *Khristos*].
chromo-, containing chromium ; colour. [Gk. *khroma* colour].
chrys(o)-, gold, golden. [Gk. *khrusos* gold].
cine-, motion, the cinematograph. [Gk. *kineo* I move].
cis-, on this side of. [L. *cis*].
citr(o)-, lemon, containing citric acid. [L. *citrus* lemon].
clad(o)-, branch. [Gk. *klados* young shoot].
co-, together. [L. *co-*].
cœl(o)-, hollow. [Gk. *koilos*].
cœno-, in common. [Gk. *koinos* common].
col-, com-, con-, cor-, altogether, completely, with. [L. *col-*, etc.].
concavo-, concave (and). [L. *concavus*].
contra- (1), against. [L. *contra*].
contra- (2), above or below (in pitch). [It. *contra-*].
convexo-, convex (and). [L. *convexus*].
copro-, excrement. [Gk. *kopros*].
cor-, see **col-**.
coralli-, coral. [L. *corallum*].
cosmo-, the cosmos. [Gk. *kosmos*].
cranio-, cranium. [Gk. *kranion* skull].
crio-, ram's horn. [Gk. *krios*].
cryo-, freezing, forming crystals. [Gk. *kruon* frost].
crypto-, secret. [Gk. *kruptos* hidden].
curvi-, curved. [L. *curvus*].
cyano-, dark-blue; containing cyanide. [Gk. *kuanos* dark-blue].
cyclo-, circle, circular. [Gk. *kuklos* wheel].
cyno-, dog. [Gk. *kunos*].
cyst(i)-, cysto-, cyst, bladder. [Gk. *kustos*].
cyto-, cell. [Gk. *kutos*].
de-, reversal, removal ; doubly. [L. and LL. *de-*].
dec(a)-, ten, tenfold. [Gk. *deka* ten].
dec(i)-, in tens, in tenths. [L. *decem* ten].
demi-, half. [Fr. *demi*].
deutero-, second. [Gk. *deuteros*].
di- (1), double, twice. [Gk. *di-*].
di- (2), see **di(s)-**.
di(a)-, entirely, through. [Gk. *dia* through].
dis-, see **di-** (1).
di(s)-, dif-, not, apart, away, out. [L. *dis-, dif-*, etc.].
dodeca-, twelve. [Gk. *dodeka*].
dors(o)-, back (and). [L. *dorsum* back].
dynam(o)-, motive force. [Gk. *dunamis* force].
dys-, bad, difficult, painful. [Gk. *dus-*].
e-, see **e(x)-**.
ec-, off, out. [Gk. *ek-*].
ecto-, external, outside. [Gk. *ektos*].
electro-, electric. [Gk. *elektron* amber].
eleuthero-, free. [Gk. *eleutheros*].
em-, en-, in, into. [L. *em-, en-*].
endo-, internal. [Gk. *endon* within].
ep(h)-, epi-, upon, extra. [Gk. *epi* on].
equi-, equal, equally. [L. *aequus*].
eu-, well, good. [Gk. *eu-*].
e(x)-, from, former, lacking, out. [L. *e(x)* from].
exo-, outer, outside. [Gk. *exo-*].
extra-, outside, additional. [L. *extra* outside].
ferri-, containing iron (in its higher valency). [L. *ferrum* iron].
ferro-, containing iron (in its lower valency). [*Prec.*].
fibro-, containing or concerning fibre. [*fibre*].
fissi-, fisso-, (tending to) split. [L. *fissus* split].
fluo(r)-, containing fluorine. [*fluo(rine)*].
fluor(o)-, fluorescence. [*fluor(escent)*].
fluvio-, river. [L. *fluvius*].
for-, utterly, away. [OE. *for-*].
fore-, before, pre- (usually with native words.) [OE. *fore-*].
form-, formic, formalin. [L. *form(ica)* ant].
Franco-, French (and). [LL. *Francus* Frank].
fronto-, involving the front or forehead. [L. *frons, frontis*].
galacto-, milk. [Gk. *galaktos*].
Gallo-, French, Gaulish (and). [L. *Gallus* Gaul].
gam(o)-, united. [Gk. *gamos* marriage].
gast(e)r(o)-, stomach (and). [Gk. *gaster, gasteros*].
genito-, of the genitals (and). [~L. *genitalis* genital].
geo-, involving the earth or geography. [Gk. *ge* earth].
glycero-, containing glycerin. [*glycerin*].
glyco-, containing glycerin or sugar derivatives. [Gk. *glukus* sweet].
gono-, seminal fluid. [Gk. *gonos* seed].
Gr(a)eco-, Greek (and). [L. *Graecus*].
granulo-, granular (and). [L. *granulum* grain].
grapho-, involving writing. [Gk. *grapho* I write].
Greco-, see **Gr(a)eco-**.
gymno-, naked. [Gk. *gumnos*].
gyn(a)eco-, of women. [Gk. *gune, gunaikos* woman].
gyn(o)-, of women ; of an ovary. [Gk. *gune* woman].
gyro-, of rotation. [Gk. *guros* ring].
hæm(at)o-, blood. [Gk. *haima, haimatos*].
hagio-, sacred, holy. [Gk. *hagios*].
hecto-, hundred. [Gk. *hekaton*].
helio-, involving or employing the sun. [Gk. *helios* sun].
hemi-, half. [Gk. *hemi-*].
hem(at)o-, see **hæm(at)o-**.
hendeca-, eleven. [Gk. *hendeka*].
hepato-, liver. [Gk. *hepar, hepatos*].
hepta-, seven. [Gk. *hepta*].
hetero-, various, abnormal, different. [Gk. *heteros* other].
hexa-, six. [Gk. *hexa-*].
hiero-, sacred, priestly. [Gk. *hieros*].
hippo-, horse, horses. [Gk. *hippos* horse].
hol(o)-, entire(ly). [Gk. *holos* whole].
homo-, same. [Gk. *homos*].
homœo-, like, similar. [Gk. *homoios* like].
hyalo-, transparent. [Gk. *hualos* glass].
hydro-, water, hydrogen, dropsy. [Gk. *hudor, hudros* water].
hyeto-, rainfall. [Gk. *huetos* rain].

hygro-, moisture. [Gk. *hugros* wet].
hylo-, matter, substance. [Gk. *hule*].
hyper-, excessive(ly). [Gk. *huper-*].
hypno-, sleep. [Gk. *hupnos*].
hypo-, insufficient(ly), lower, under. [Gk. *hupo* beneath].
hypso-, altitude. [Gk. *hupsos*].
hystero-, hysteria, the womb. [Gk. *hustera* womb].
ichthyo-, fish. [Gk. *ikhthus*].
icono-, image, portrait, ikon. [Gk. *eikon* image].
ideo-, idea, concept. [Gk. *idea*].
idio-, peculiar, individual. [Gk. *idio-*].
il- (1), see **-in (1)**.
il- (2), see **-in (2)**.
im- (1), see **in- (1)**.
im- (2), see **in- (2)**.
in- (1), il- (1), im- (1), irr- (1), in, into. [L. *in-*, etc.].
in- (2), il- (2), im- (2), irr- (2), not, non-. [L. *in-*, etc.].
Indo-, Indian (and). [L. *Indus*].
infra-, below, on this side of. [L. *infra* below].
inter-, between. [L. *inter*].
intra-, within. [L. *intra*].
irid(o)-, iris, rainbow. [Gk. *iris, iridos* rainbow].
irr- (1), see **in- (1)**.
irr- (2), see **in- (2)**.
iso-, equal. [Gk. *isos*].
Italo-, Italian (and). [L. *Italus* Italian].
juxta-, against, next. [L. *iuxta*].
labio-, lip (and). [L. *labium*].
lachrym(o)-, tears, weeping. [L. *lacrima, lachryma* tear].
lact(o)-, milk. [L. *lac, lactis*].
l(a)evo-, levo-, left, to the left. [L. *laevus* left].
laryng(o)-, larynx. [Gk. *larugx, laruggos*].
lepto-, fine, delicate, small. [Gk. *leptos*].
leuco-, white. [Gk. *leukos* white].
levo-, see **l(a)evo-**.
lingu(o)-, tongue, speech. [L. *lingua* tongue].
lith(o)-, stone. [Gr. *lithos* stone].
longi-, long. [L. *longus*].
lopho-, crest. [Gk. *lophos* crest].
magneto-, magnetic. [*magnet*].
malaco-, soft, soft-shelled. [Gk. *malakos* soft].
male-, ill-, evil. [L. *male-*].
martyr(o)-, martyr, martyrs. [Gk. *martus* and *marturos* martyr].
medic(o)-, medical, medicinal. [L. *medicus* medical].
medi(o)-, middle, intermediate. [L. *medius* middle].
mega-, great, magnifying. [Gk. *megas* great].
megalo-, great, inflated. [Gk. *megale* great].
melo-, music. [Gk. *melos*].
meno-, month, menses. [Gk. *men* month].
mer(o)-, part, partial. [Gk. *meros* part].
mes(o)-, middle, intermediate. [Gk. *mesos* middle].
meta-, after, with, expressing "change." [Gk. *meta* after, with].
mezzo-, middle, intermediate. [It. *mezzo*].
micro-, minute, a millionth. [Gk. *micros* small].
mid-, in the middle (of). [OE. *midd*].
mille-, milli-, thousand, a thousandth. [L. *mille* thousand].
mis-, badly, wrongly. [OE. *mis-*, OF. *mes-*].
mon(o)-, single. [Gk. *monos*].
muc(o)-, mucus. [L. *mucus*].
multi-, many. [L. *multus* much].
myco-, fungus. [~Gk. *mukes* mushroom].
myo-, muscle. [Gk. *muon*].
myria-, ten thousand, great numbers. [Gk. *muria* ten thousand].
mytho-, myth. [Gk. *muthos* myth].
naso-, nose (and). [L. *nasus* nose].
necro-, death, corpse. [Gk. *nekros* corpse].
neo-, new, modern, revised. [Gk. *neos* new].
nephr(o)-, kidney. [Gk. *nephros*].
neur(o)-, nerve(s). [Gk. *neuron* nerve].
nitr(o)-, nitrogen, nitric acid. [Gk. *nitron* nitre].
noct(i)-, night, at night. [L. *nox, noctis* night].
non-, not. [L. *non*].
noto-, back. [Gk. *noton* back].
nuci-, nut(s). [L. *nux, nucis* nut].
ob-, out, forwards, against, completely, inversely. [L. *ob* in the way of].
oct(a)-, octo-, eight. [L. *octo*, Gk. *okto* eight].
odont(o)-, tooth, teeth. [Gk. *odous, odontos*].
oleo-, oil. [L. *oleum* oil].
oligo-, few. [Gk. *oligoi* few].
ombro-, rain. [Gk. *ombros* rain].
omni-, all. [L. *omnis*].
omphal(o)-, navel (and). [Gk. *omphalos*].
on-, on. [OE. *on*].
oneiro-, dream(s). [Gk. *oneiros*].
onto-, being, existence. [Gk. *oun, ontos*].
oo-, egg. [Gk. *oon*].
oppositi-, opposed, opposite. [L. *oppositus*].
ortho-, upright, correct, straight, rectangular. [Gk. *orthos* straight].
osteo-, bone. [Gk. *osteon*].
ostrei-, ostreo-, oyster(s). [L. *ostreum*, Gk. *ostreon*].
out-, out, out of, outwards, so as to surpass, to excess. [OE. *ut-*].
over-, over, above, to excess. [OE. *ofer-*].
ovi- (1), ovo-, egg. [L. *ovum*].
ovi- (2), sheep. [L. *ovis*].
ovo-, see **ovi- (1)**.
oxy- (1), sharp, pointed. [Gk. *oxus* keen].
oxy- (2), oxygen. [*oxy(gen)*].
p(a)ed(o)-, child, boy. [Gk. *pais, paidos*].
pal(a)eo-, ancient, old, prehistoric. [Gk. *palaios* ancient].
pan(to)-, total, all. [Gk. *pas, pantos* all].
para- (1), beside, contrary. [Gk. *para*].
para- (2), protection or guard against. [Fr. from It. *para-*].
pedo, see **p(a)ed(o)-**.
penta-, five. [Gk. *penta*.]
per-, through, completely; *denoting chemical compounds containing the maximum amount of the specified element or acids and their salts in which the radical has more than its normal valency.* [L. *per* through].
peri-, round, around. [Gk. *peri*].
perisso-, odd, uneven. [Gk. *perissos* odd].
petr(o)-, rock, stone. [Gk. *petra* rock].
ph(a)en(o)-, phen(o), light, apparent. [Gk. *phainos* shining, *phainomai* I appear].
phen(o)-, see **ph(a)en(o)-**.
philo-, love, love for. [Gk. *philos* love].
phleb(o)-, vein. [Gk. *phleps, phlebos*].
phon(o)-, sound. [Gk. *phone* voice].
phosph(o)-, phosphorus. [*phospho(rus)*].
phosphor(o)-, phosphorus. [*phosphor(us)*].
photo-, light, photography. [Gk. *phos, photos* light; *photo(graphy)*].
phyll(o)-, leaf. [Gk. *phullon* leaf].
phylo-, race, line of evolution. [Gk. *phulon* tribe].
physic(o)-, physics, physical. [Gk. *phusikos* physical].
physio-, nature. [Gk. *phusis*].
phyto-, plant. [Gk. *phuton*].
piezo-, pressure. [Gk. *piezo* I press].
pinnat(o)-, pinnate. [L. *pinnatus* feathery].
pinni-, webbed, fins. [L. *pinna* fin].
plagio-, crooked, oblique. [Gk. *plagios*].
plano-, plane (and). [L. *planus* level].
plasmo-, plasm, protoplasm. [Gk. *plasma* moulded object].
platin(o)-, platinum (and). [*platinum*].
platy-, flat. [Gk. *platus*].
pleur(o)-, side, pleura. [Gk. *pleura*, side, rib].
pluri-, multi-, of various kinds. [L. *plus, pluris* more].
plut(o)-, wealthy. [Gk. *ploutos*].
pneumato-, air, breath, the Holy Ghost. [Gk. *pneuma, pneumatos* breath].
polari-, polarization. [L. *polaris* polar].
politic(o)-, political (and). [Gk. *politikos* of a citizen].
poly-, many, numerous. [Gk. *polu* much].
porno-, indecency, prostitution. [Gk. *porne* prostitute].
post-, after, subsequent. [L. *post* after].
pre-, before, previous, in front of. [L. *præ* before].
pro- (1), favouring, substitute, deputy. [L. *pro* for].
pro- (2), pre-, before, previous. [Gk. *pro* before].
prot(o)-, primitive, original, earliest. [Gk. *protos* first].
pseud(o)-, false, bogus. [Gk. *pseudos*].
psych(o)-, mind, spirit. [Gk. *psukhe* soul].
ptero-, wing, winged, feather. [Gk. *pteron* wing].
pulmo-, lung(s), respiration. [L. *pulmo* lung].
pycno-, stout, thick, dense. [Gk. *puknos* thick].

py(o)-, pus. [Gk. *puon*].
pyr(o)-, fire. [Gk. *pur*].
quadr(i)-, four. [L. *quadri-*].
quater-, four times, fourfold. [L. *quater* four times].
quinqu(e)-, five. [L. *quinque*].
radio-, radius, radium, wireless. [L. *radius* ray].
re-, again, back. [L. *re-*].
retro-, backwards, behind. [L. *retro*].
rheo-, flow (of current). [Gk. *rheos* flow].
rhin(o)-, nose. [Gk. *rhis, rhinos*].
rhizo-, root. [Gk. *rhiza*].
rhodo-, rose, rose-coloured. [Gk. *rhodon* rose].
Russo-, Russian (and). [Russ. *Rusi* Russians].
sacchar(o)-, sugar, sweet, sweetness. [Gk. *sakkharon* sugar].
sacro-, the sacrum. [L. (*os*) *sacrum*].
sancti-, holy. [L. *sanctus* blessed].
sapro-, decay, decayed. [Gk. *sapros* rotten].
schiz(o)-, split, splitting. [Gk. *skhizo* I split].
scler(o)-, hard, horny. [Gk. *skleros*].
se-, apart, away, without. [L. *se-* apart].
seismo-, earth tremor, earthquake. [Gk. *seismos*].
selen(o)-, moon. [Gk. *selene* moon].
self-, automatic, by, of, or on, oneself, same. [OE. *self* and *selfa*].
semi-, half. [Gk. *semi*].
septem-, septi-, seven. [L. *septem, septi-*].
Serbo-, Serbian (and). [Germ. *Serbo-* from Serbian *Srb* Serbian].
serio-, serious (and). [L. *serius* serious].
sero-, serum (and). [L. *serum* serum].
serrat(o)-, serrate (and). [L. *serratus* serrate].
serri-, serrate, like, or having, a saw-edge. [L. *serra* saw-edge].
sesqui-, one and a half, in the proportion of three to two. [L. *sesqui* one and a half].
sex(i)-, six. [L. *sex*].
silic(i)-, silico-, sand, silicon. [L. *silica* sand].
sinistr(o)-, left, left-handed. [L. *sinister, sinistri* left].
sit(i)o-, food. [Gk. *sitos* and *sition* food].
somat(o)-, the (human) body. [Gk. *soma, somatos*].
somn(i)-, sleep. [L. *somnus*].
spectr(o)-, of a spectre, of the spectrum. [L. *spectrum* image, spectrum].
sperm(at)o-, of sperm, seeds, etc. [Gk. *sperma, spermatos* seed].
sph(a)er(o)-, sphere, spherical. [Gk. *sphaira* ball].
sphen(o)-, wedge. [Gk. *sphen*].
spher(o)-, see **sph(a)er(o)**.
sphygmo-, the pulse. [Gk. *sphugmos*].
spin(i)-, having spines, of the spine. [L. *spina*].
splen(o)-, of the spleen. [Gk. *splen*, spleen].
spor(o)-, of a spore or spores. [Gk. *spora* sowing].
steat(o)-, of fat, plump. [Gk. *stear, steatos* fat].
sten(o)-, narrow, restricted. [Gk. *stenos* narrow].
step-, related only through a second marriage. [OE. *steop* orphaned].
stereo-, solid, involving stereoscopy. [Gk. *stereos* solid].
stern(o)-, sternum (and). [L. *sternum* breastbone].
stomat(o)-, of the mouth or pores. [Gk. *stomatos* mouth].
strato-, stratus. [MdL. *stratus* widespread (cloud)].
sub-, suc-, sup-, sur- (1), under, beneath, somewhat, inversely. [L. *sub-*, etc., under].
subter-, less, secret, inferior. [L. *subter-* under].
suc-, see **sub-**.
sulph(o)-, containing sulphur. [*sulph(ur)*].
sup-, see **sub-**.
super-, over, above, from above, exceeding what is usual, extreme. [L. *super* above].
sur- (1), see **sub-**.
sur- (2), over, superior, additional. [Fr. *sur-*].
syl-, sym-, syn-, with, together, united. [Gk. *sun-*, etc., with].
Syro-, Syrian (and). [L. *Syrus* Syrian].
tach(y)-, fast. [Gk. *takhus*].
taut(o)-, same. [Gk. *tauto* the same].
techn(o)-, craft, industrial work. [Gk. *tekhne* art].
tele-, distant, remote. [Gk. *tele-*].
terato-, monster, monstrous. [Gk. *teras, teratos* monster].
tern-, threefold, in threes. [L. *terni* three each].
tetr(a)-, four. [Gk. *tetra-*].
Teuto(n)-, German, Germanic (and). [L. *Teuto, Teutonis* Teuton].
thanato-, death. [Gk. *thanatos* death].
theo-, God, divinity. [Gk. *theos* god].
therm(o)-, heat. [Gk. *thermos* warm].
top(o)-, place, locality. [Gk. *topos*].
tracheo-, of the trachea. [MedL. *trachea* wind-pipe].
trachy-, hoarse. [Gk. *trakhus*].
trans-, across, through, to a different form or place. [L. *trans* across].
tri-, three, in threes. [Gk., L. *tri-*].
trich(o)-, hair, hairlike. [Gk. *thrix, trikhos* hair].
Turco-, Turkish (and). [LL. *Turcus* Turk].
twi-, double, two. [ME. *twi-*].
typ(o)-, type, printing (type). [Gk. *tupos* model].
ultra-, beyond, extreme(ly). [L. *ultra* beyond].
un- (1), apart, out, loose, dis-. [OE. *un-, on-*].
un- (2), not, negatively, non-. [OE. *un-*].
under-, beneath, subsidiary, insufficiently. [OE. *under-*].
uni-, one, single. [L. *unus* one].
up-, upward(s), up. [OE. *up-*].
urin(o)-, urine. [L. *urina*].
ur(o)- (1), urine. [Gk. *ouron*].
ur(o)- (2), tail. [Gk. *oura*].
ventr(i)-, ventro-, belly. [L. *venter, ventris*].
ver(i)-, true. [L. *verus*].
vermi-, worm. [L. *vermis* worm].
vice-, deputy, subordinate. [L. *vice* in place of].
vin(i)-, wine, vine. [L. *vinum* wine].
viti-, vine. [L. *vitis*].
viv(i)-, alive, living, life. [L. *vivus* alive].
xanth(o)-, yellow, of xanthic acid or related substances. [Gk. *xanthos* yellow].
xen(o)-, stranger, hospitality. [Gk. *xenos* stranger].
xer(o)-, dry. [Gk. *xeros*].
xyl(o)-, wood. [Gk. *xulon*].
yester-, past, previous, last before this. [OE. *geostra(n)*].
zoo-, living, alive, animal. [Gk. *zoos* alive, *zoon* living creature].
zyg(o)-, yoke, linked, paired. [Gk. *zugon* yoke].

SUFFIXES

-a, *fem. sg. of* L. *and* Gk. *nouns*. [L. and Gk. *-a*].
-able, capable of being. [Fr. *-able*].
-ac, *forming adjectives from nouns.* [Gk. *-akos*].
-acal, *forming adjectives from nouns.* [*Prec.* + *-al*].
-acea, *forming the names of orders of animals.* [L. (*animalia*) *-acea*].
-aceæ, *forming the names of families of plants.* [L. (*plantæ*) *-aceæ*].
-aceous, of, resembling. [L. *-aceus*].
-acious, tending to be, full of. [L. *-acius*].
-acity, *forming nouns of quality.* [Fr. *-acité*].
-acy, *forming nouns of state or quality.* [Gk. *-ateia*, L. *-atia, -acia*].
-ad (1), *forming collective numerals.* [Gk. *-as, -ados*].
-ad (2), *forming adverbs and prepositions.* [L. *ad*].
-ade, *forming nouns denoting* an action done or a thing made (*from*). [Fr. *-ade*].
-æ, *forming the pl. of* L. *nouns ending in* -a. [L. *-æ*].
-age, *forming collective nouns, nouns of status, action, amount, cost, or rate.* [Fr. *-age*].
-al, *forming adjectives* (*and nouns*). [L. *-alis*].
-ality, *forming nouns of quality or examples of this quality.* [Fr. *-alité*].
-an, -ane, *forming adjectives denoting* allegiance *or* relationship. [L. *-anus*].
-ana, *forming pl. nouns denoting* anecdotes about, relics of (*a person, etc.*). [L. *-ana* neut. pl.].
-ance, *forming nouns of quality or action.* [Fr. *-ance*].
-ancy, *forming nouns of quality.* [L. *-antia*].
-ane (1), see **-an**.
-ane (2), *forming the names of saturated hydrocarbons.* [*Invented*].
-aneous, *forming adjectives, esp. of time.* [L. *-aneus*].
-ant, *forming adjectives denoting* an act ; *forming nouns denoting* the agent. [L. *-ans, -antis*, Fr. *-ant*].
-ar (1), *forming adjectives* (*and nouns*). [L. *-aris*].

-ar (2), *forming nouns.* [~ *-er* (2)].
-ar (3), *forming nouns of the agent.* [L. *-aris*].
-arch, *forming nouns denoting* a ruler. [Gk. *arkhos*].
-archy, *forming nouns denoting* a form of rule or government. [Gk. *-arkhia*].
-ard, *forming nouns of reproach.* [OFr. *-ard, -art*].
-areous, *forming adjectives.* [L. *-areus*].
-arian, *forming nouns and adjectives denoting* a member of a (religious) sect or pertaining to his opinions; *forming nouns denoting* a person of a certain age (counting by tens or a hundred). [L. *-arianus*].
-arious, *forming adjectives.* [L. *-arius*].
-arium, *forming nouns denoting* a collection, repository, etc. [L. *-arium*].
-ary (1), *forming nouns and adjectives denoting* connexion, purpose, or resemblance. [L. *-arius, -aria, -arium*].
-ary (2), = **-ar (1).** [L. *-aris*].
-asis, *denoting* a state of (*in diseases*). [Gk. *-asis*].
-aster, *forming nouns denoting* contempt, pseudo-. [L. *-aster*].
-ate (1), *forming nouns denoting* rank or office. [L. *-atus*].
-ate (2), *forming nouns denoting* the salts of acids (ending in *-ic*). [L. *-atum*].
-ate (3), *forming adjectives denoting* made of, provided with, or like. [L. *-atus*].
-ate (4), *forming verbs denoting* to make like, to treat with. [L. *-are, -atus*].
-atic, *forming adjectives.* [L. *-aticus*].
-atile, *forming adjectives denoting* tendency. [L. *-atilis*].
-ative, *forming adjectives denoting* tendency. [L. *-ativus*].
-bility, *forming nouns from adjectives in* -ble. [L. *-bilitas*].
-cele, tumour. [Gk. *kele*].
-cide, *forming nouns denoting* the killer of. [L. *-cida*].
-cracy, rule. [Gk. *-kratia* rule].
-crat, ruler, [Gk. *-krates*].
-cule, *forming diminutives of nouns.* [L. *-culus*].
-cy, *forming nouns denoting* state or condition. [Gk. *-kia, -tia,* L. *-cia, -tia,* etc.].
-cyte, *forming nouns denoting* types of cell. [Gk. *kutos*].
-dom, *forming nouns denoting* quality, rank, status, or tenure. [OE. *-dom*].
-drome, arena, track. [Gk. *-dromos* running].
-dyne, force. [Fr. from Gk. *dunamis* force].
-ean, belonging to, resembling. [L. *-eanus*].
-ectomy, excision. [Gk. *ektome*].
-ed (1), *forming the past tense of weak verbs.* [OE. *-de, -ede, -ode*].
-ed (2), *forming the past participle of weak verbs.* [OE. *-d, -ed, -od*].
-ee, *forming nouns denoting* the person to whom the action is done; or the person who is concerned with the specific topic or object. [Fr. *-é*].
-eer, *forming nouns denoting* one concerned with. [Fr. *-ier*].
-en (1), *forming the past participle of strong verbs.* [OE. *-en*].
-en (2), *forming diminutives of nouns.* [OE. *-en*].
-en (3), made of. [OE. *-en*].
-en (4), *forming the plural of weak nouns.* [OE. *-an*].
-en (5), *forming nouns meaning* to make, to become. [OE. *-nian*].
-ence, *forming nouns denoting* action or quality. [Fr.].
-ency, *forming nouns denoting* quality or state. [L. *-entia*].
-ene (1), *forming nouns and adjectives denoting* locality. [L. *-enus*].
-ene (2), *forming names of unsaturated hydro-carbons.* [*Invented*].
-ent, *forming adjectives and nouns denoting* the agent or the action. [L. *-ens, entis*].
-eous, *forming adjectives denoting* of the same nature as. [L. *-eus*].
-er (1), *forming the comparative degree of adjectives, etc.* [OE. *-ra*].
-er (2), *forming nouns denoting* the doer. [OE. *-ere*].
-er (3), *forming nouns denoting* of a certain profession or craft. [AF. *-er*].
-er (4), *forming legal terms denoting* an instance of the action. [OF. *-er*].
-er (5), *forming verbs.* [OE. *-rian*].
-ern, towards. [OE. *-ern*].
-(e)ry, *forming nouns denoting* a place of work, the work itself, a collection, associated ideas. [OF. *-erie*].
-escent, becoming, tending to become. [L. *-escens, -escentis*].
-ese, *forming nouns or adjectives denoting* foreign or outlandish tongues or persons. [OF. *-eis*].
-esque, resembling. [Fr. *-esque*].
-ess, *forming the corresponding female name.* [Fr. *-esse*].
-et, *forming diminutives.* [Fr. *-et*].
-et(e), *forming nouns denoting* the agent. [Gk. *-etes*].
-eth, (*arch.*) *forming the 3rd pers. sg. of present tense of verbs.* [ME. *-eth*].
-ette, *forming diminutives, the corresponding feminine name, the names of substitute materials.* [Fr. *-ette*].
-facient, making or tending to make. [L. *faciens, facientis*].
-faction, *the action or outcome of verbs ending in* **-fy.** [L. *-factio, -factionis*].
-ferous, bearing. [L. *ferre* to bear, and **-ous**].
-fic, -ific, tending to. [L. *-(i)ficus*].
-fication, -ification, *the result or process of verbs ending in* -fy. [L. *-(i)ficatio, -(i)ficationis*].
-fold, repeated or multiplied a specific number of times. [OE. *-fald*].
-form, having a specified shape. [L. *-formis*].
-fuge, that dispels. [L. *-fuga*].
-ful, full of, -ous (usually with native words). [OE. *-ful*].
-fy, to make, bring into a specific state. [Fr. *-fier*].
-gamy, marriage. [Gk. *-gameia*].
-gen, *forming nouns denoting* producer of or growth. [Gk. *-genes* born of].
-geny, *forming nouns denoting* process of development. [Fr. *-génie*].
-gerous, bearing. [L. *-ger* and *-ous*].
-gon, *forming names of many-sided figures.* [Gk. *-gonos* angled].
-grade (1), (degrees on) a scale. [L. *gradus* step].
-grade (2), *forming adjectives denoting* mode of walking. [L. *-gradus* walking].
-gram (1), *forming names of fractions or multiples of a gram.* [Fr. *gramme*].
-gram (2), something written. [Gk. *gramma*].
-graph, *forming nouns denoting* the way a thing is written or a form of record. [Gk. *-graphos* written].
-graphic, *forming adjectives from words ending in* -graph and -graphy. [Gk. *graphikos* of writing].
-graphy, form of writing, research into, or the written literature on, a subject. [Gk. *-graphia*].
-gynous, *forming adjectives denoting* the arrangement of the pistils of flowers. [Gk. *gune* woman].
-head, *forming nouns denoting* state or quality. [OE. **hædu*].
-hood, *forming nouns denoting* state or quality. [OE. *-had*].
-i, *forming plurals of Latin nouns of the second declension ending in* -us, *and Italian nouns ending in* -e *and* -o. [L., It. *-i*].
-ia (1), *forming abstract nouns, esp. of diseases, names of plants, and names of alkaloids.* [L., Gk. *-ia*].
-ia (2), *forming plurals of classes of plants, etc.* [L., Gk. *-ia*].
-ial, *forming adjectives.* [L. *-ialis*].
-ian, *forming adjectives and nouns denoting* resemblance, adherence, location, etc. [L. *-ianus*].
-ible, *forming adjectives denoting* capable of being. [Fr. *-ible* from L. *-ibilis*].
-ic, *forming adjectives from nouns, esp. those denoting a chemical radical in its higher valency.* [Gk. *-ikos,* L. *-icus*].
-ical, *forming adjectives meaning* somewhat. [*-ic* and *-al*].
-ician, *forming nouns denoting* an exponent of. LL. *-icianus*].
-ice, *forming abstract nouns.*
-ics, *forming names of sciences.* [†Fr. *-iques*].
-id (1), *forming names of members of a specific group.* [Gk. *-is, -idos*].
-id (2), resembling. [*Prec.*].
-ide, *forming names of chemical compounds formed directly by an element.* [Fr. *-ide* from *acide* acid].
-ie, see **-y (2).**

-ier, -yer, *forming names denoting* member of a craft or profession. [Fr. *-ière* and ME. *-iere*].
-iety, *forming abstract nouns.* [Fr. *-iété* from L. *-ietas, -ietatis*].
-ific, see **-fic.**
-ification, see **-fication.**
-in, *forming names of neutral organic substances.* [L. *-inus*].
-ina (1), *forming female titles and names of musical instruments.* [L. *-ina*].
-ina (2), *forming plurals of classes of animals, etc.* [L. (*animalia*), *-ina*].
-ine (1), *forming feminine nouns.* [Fr. *-ine*].
-ine (2), *forming abstract nouns from the corresponding verbs.* [Fr. *-ine*].
-ine (3), *forming nouns showing derivation, esp. alkaloids and the paraffin series of hydrocarbons.* [Fr. *-ine*].
-ine (4), *forming adjectives from nouns and denoting* resemblance or relationship. [L. *-inus*, Fr. *-ine*].
-ing (1), *forming patronymics and nouns denoting* having the attributes of. [OE. *-ing*].
-ing (2), *forming verbal nouns.* [~OE. *-ung*].
-ing (3), *forming present participles and participial adjectives.* [ME. *-ing*].
-ion, *forming nouns denoting* state. [Fr. *-ion* from L. *-io, -ionis*].
-iour, *forming nouns denoting* the agent. [Fr. *-eour*].
-ious, see **-ous.**
-ise, see **-ize.**
-ish, *forming adjectives from nouns and adjectives and denoting* belonging to, somewhat (often in a pejorative sense); *denoting, with the hour of the day,* about. [OE. *-isc*].
-ism, *forming nouns denoting a typical or specific attitude or action.* [Gk. *-ismos*].
-ist (1), *forming nouns from verbs ending in* -ize; *forming nouns denoting* an exponent or devotee of, believer in, a movement, creed, or profession; *forming names denoting* performer on. [Gk. *-istes*].
-ist (2), *forming adjectives corresponding in form to nouns in* -ist. [*Prec.*].
-ite, *forming names of persons denoting* connection with; *forming names of minerals, fossils, and salts of acids in* -ous. [Fr. *-ite*, Gk. *-ites*].
-itis, *forming nouns denoting* inflammation of a specific part. [Gk. *-itis*].
-ity, *forming abstract nouns.* [Fr. *-ité* from L. *-itas, -itatis*].
-ium, *forming scientific names of metals and comparable substances.* [MdL. *-ium*].
-ive, *forming adjectives meaning* tending to, of the nature of, *and nouns of the same form as these.* [L. *-ivus, -ivum*].
-ize, -ise, *forming verbs meaning* to act or make like, treat with. [Fr. *-iser*, Gk. *-izo*].
-kin, *forming diminutives.* [~Du. *-ken*].
-later, -olater, worshipper. [Gk. *-(o)latres*].
-latry, -olatry, worship. [Gk. *-(o)latreia*].
-le (1), *forming frequentative or diminutive forms of verbs.* [OE. *-lian*].
-le (2), *forming diminutives of nouns.* [L. *-ellum*].
-le (3), *forming adjectives denoting* tendency or suitability. [ME. *-el*].
-less, lacking, without. [OE. *-leas*].
-let, *forming diminutives of nouns.* [ME. *-let*].
-like, *forming adjectives meaning* resembling. [ME. *-lik*].
-ling, *forming diminutives, forming nouns denoting* connection with, dependence on. [ME. *-ling*].
-lite, *forming the names of minerals.* [Fr. *-lite* from Gk. *lithos* stone].
-lith, *forming the names of stony objects or structures.* [Gk. *lithos* stone].
-lived, having a life of a specified kind. [OE. *lifian*].
-loger, -ologer, an exponent of a science. [Gk. *-(o)logos* and *-er*].
-logic(al), -ological, *forming adjectives from nouns ending in* -logy. [Gk. *-logikos*].
-logist, -ologist, an exponent of a science. [Gk. *-(o)logistes*].
-logue, *forming nouns denoting an account or kind of speech.* [Fr. *-logue* from Gk. *logos* speech].
-logy, -ology, *forming nouns denoting a type of utterance, branch of study, or speech.* [Gk. *-(o)logia* from *logos* speech].
-looking, having a specified appearance. [OE. *locian*].
-ly (1), *forming adjectives from nouns, and denoting* resemblance or frequency of occurrence. [ME. *-ly* from OE. *-lic*].
-ly (2), *forming adverbs from adjectives.* [ME. *-ly* from OE. *-lice*].
-mancer, *forming nouns denoting exponents of specific forms of divination.* [AF. *-mancer*].
-mancy, divination by the corresponding *-mancer.* [OF. *-mancie* from Gk. *manteia* divination].
-mania, craze or mania of a specific kind. [Gk. *mania*].
-maniac, *forming adjectives and nouns from the corresponding noun in* -mania. [*maniac*].
-ment, *forming nouns denoting* means or result. [L. *-mentum*].
-merous, in so many parts. [Gk. *meros* part].
-meter, metrical line (with defining number). [Gk. *metron* measure].
-metry, measurement. [Gk. *-metria*].
-most, *forming the superlative degree of adjectives formed from adverbs and prepositions of place and time.* [OE. *-mest*].
-ness, *forming nouns of quality, state, or condition.* [OE. *-nes, -nis*].
-nosed, having a nose of a specific kind. [*nose* (1)].
-ock, *forming diminutives.* [OE. *-oc*].
-ode, *forming nouns denoting thermionic tubes, esp. with a specified number of electrodes.* [(*electr*)*ode*].
-oid, resembling; that resembles. [Gk. *-oeides* resembling].
-ol (1), *forming names of alcohols.* [(*alcoh*)*ol*].
-ol (2), *forming names of oils and jellies.* [L. *ol*(*eum*) oil].
-olater, see **-later.**
-olatry, see **-latry.**
-ologer, -ologist, -ology, see **-loger, -logist,** etc.
-one, *forming names of a certain series of hydrocarbons.* [*Invented*].
-or (1), *forming nouns of state or condition.* [L. *-or*].
-or (2), *forming nouns denoting* the agent or means, *esp. in legal terms.* [L. *-or*].
-ose (1), *forming names of sugars and other carbohydrates.* [(*gluc*)*ose*].
-ose (2), full of. [L. *-osus*].
-osis, *forming nouns denoting* (diseased) state or condition. [Gk. *-osis*].
-ot, *forming diminutives.* [Fr. *-ot*].
-ot(e), *forming nouns and adjectives denoting* (a native) of the place. [Gk. *-otes*].
-otic, *forming adjectives from nouns ending in* -osis. [Gk. *-otikos*].
-our, *forming nouns of quality, state, or condition.* [AF. *-our*].
-ous, ious, *forming adjectives denoting* full of; *forming names of acids and compounds in a lower state of oxidation.* [OF. *-ous*].
-pathy, feeling, suffering, illness. [Gk. *-patheia*].
-phagous, eating, living on. [Gk. *-phagos*].
-phil(e), that loves, loving, beloved of. [Gk. *-philos* dear to].
-philous, loving. [Gk. *philos* love].
-phobe, that hates, hating. [Gk. *-phobos* hating].
-phobia, fear, hate of. [Gk. *-phobia* hatred of].
-phone, a sound; *forming names of instruments employing sound.* [Gk. *phone* voice].
-phore, that bears. [Fr. *-phore* from Gk. *-phoros* bearing].
-phorous, bearing. [Gk. *-phoros* bearing].
-phyte, plant. [Gk. *phuton*].
-rater, *forming nouns denoting* of a certain rating or standard. [*rate* (1)].
-(r)rhœa, flow, discharge. [Gk. *rhoia* discharge].
-(r)rhynchous, having a beak of a specified kind. [Gk. *rhugkos* beak, snout].
-ry, see **-(e)ry.**
-s (1), *forming adverbs from nouns, etc.* [OE. *-es*].
-s (2), *forming the absolute form of personal pronouns.* [ME. *-es*].
-scope, *forming names of instruments for visual observation.* [Gk. *-skopos* seeing].
-seater, *forming nouns denoting the specific number of seats a conveyance provides.* [*seat* (1)].
-ship, *forming nouns denoting* office, rank, status, quality, or proficiency. [OE. *-scipe*].

-shire, *forming names of counties.* [OE. *scir* shire].
-sighted, having sight of a specific kind. [*sight* (1)].
-skinned, having skin of a specific kind. [*skin* (1)].
-soever, of any kind. [*so* and *ever*].
-som(e), tending to be, suitable for. [OE. *-sum*].
-some, *forming nouns denoting a specific number of persons.* [OE. *sum* one (of)].
-sophy, wisdom, study and knowledge. [Gk. *-sophia* wisdom].
-ster, *forming nouns denoting* occupation; (*coll.*) *forming hypocoristic forms.* [OE. *-ster*].
-storeyed, having a specific number of storeys. [*storey*].
-sy, *forming diminutives (with reduplication).* [Unkn.].
-teen, *forming certain numerals of the second decade.* [OE. *-tene*].
-th (1), *forming ordinals above three.* [OE. *-tha*].
-th (2), *forming abstract nouns of quality.* [OE. *-ath, -oth, -th(o),* and *-th(u)*].
-therapy, curative treatment of a specific kind. [*therapy*].
-tion, *forming nouns denoting* action, quality, or condition. [L. *-tio, -tionis*].
-tome, an instrument for cutting. [Gk. *-tomos* cutting].
-tomy, an incision, cutting. [Gk. *-tomia*].
-tonner, *denoting an object displacing, or having a capacity of, a specific number of tons.* [*ton* (1)].
-trix, *forming nouns denoting feminine agents, esp. in legal terms.* [MedL. (*execu*)*trix* executrix].
-tude, *forming abstract nouns.* [Fr. *-tude* from L. *-tudo*].
-ty (1), *forming abstract nouns.* [Fr. *-té*].
-ty (2), *forming decade names above ten.* [OE. *-tig*].
-ule, *forming diminutives.* [L. *-ulus*].
-ulent, tending to. [L. *-ulens, -ulentis*].
-ure, *forming nouns denoting* action, state, official body, etc. [Fr. *-ure* from L. *-ura*].
-vora, *denoting classes of creatures by their diet.* [L. (*animalia*) *-vora* (animals) eating].
-vore, *forming names of members of a group of* -vora. [*Prec.*].
-vorous, subsisting on. [*-vora*].
-ward(s), toward(s) in a specified direction. [OE. *-w(e)ard,* ME. *-wardes*].
-ways, in a specified direction. [OE. *weges* by way].
-wise, in a specified position, manner, or direction. [OE. *wise* fashion].
-y (1), full of, made of, like. [OE. *-ig*].
-y (2), -ie, *forming diminutives.* [MScots *-y, -ie*].
-y (3), *forming nouns from verbs.* [Fr. *-é, -ée*].
-y (4), *forming adjectives and abstract nouns.* [Fr. *-ie* from L. *-ius, -ia, -ium*].
-yer, see **-ier.**
-yl, *forming names of (organic) chemical radicals.* [Gk. *hule* matter].

THE GREEK ALPHABET

Α	α	alpha [al′-fa]	a
Β	β	beta [bēt′-a]	b
Γ	γ	gamma [gam′-a]	g
Δ	δ	delta [delt′-a]	d
Ε	ε	epsilon [ep-sīl′-on]	e (short)
Ζ	ζ	zeta [zēt′-a]	z
Η	η	eta [ēt′-a]	e (long)
Θ	θ	theta [thēt′-a]	th
Ι	ι	iota [i-ōt′-a]	i
Κ	κ	kappa [kap′-a]	k
Λ	λ	lambda [lam′-da]	l
Μ	μ	mu [mew]	m
Ν	ν	nu [new]	n
Ξ	ξ	xi [ksī]	x
Ο	ο	omicron [o-mīk′-ron]	o (short)
Π	π	pi [pī]	p
Ρ	ρ	rho [rō]	r
Σ (C)	σ (ς)	sigma [sig′-ma]	s
Τ	τ	tau [tau]	t
Υ	υ	upsilon [up-sil′-on]	u
Φ	φ	phi [fī]	ph
Χ	χ	chi [kī]	ch
Ψ	ψ	psi [sī]	ps
Ω	ω	omega [ō′-mig-a]	o (long)

THE RUSSIAN ALPHABET

А	а	a
Б	б	b
В	в	v
Г	г	g
Д	д	d
Е	е	e (short)
Ж	ж	zh
З	з	z
И	и	e or i
Й	й	j
К	к	k
Л	л	l
М	м	m
Н	н	n
О	о	o (long)
П	п	p
Р	р	r
С	с	s
Т	т	t
У	у	u
Ф	ф	f, ph
Х	х	ks, x
Ц	ц	ts
Ч	ч	ch
Ш	ш	sh
Щ	щ	shch
Ы	ы	
Ь	ь	
Э	э	
Ю	ю	yu
Я	я	ya

FAMILIAR WORDS COMMONLY MIS-SPELT

abandon
abandoned
abbey
ability
aboard
abode
abolish
abolished
abominable
abrupt
absence
absolutely
absorbed
absurd
abundance
abundant
abuse
acceptable
acceptance
access
accessible
accessories
accident
accidental
accidentally
accommodate
accommodation
accompanied
accomplish
accordance
accordingly
accountant
accumulate
accuracy
accused
accustomed
ache
achieved
achievement
acknowledge
acquaint
acquaintance
acquire
acres
actor

actually
addition
admission
admits
admitted
advantageous
advertisement
advisable
advisory
aerial
affectionate
affectionately
affiliated
affirmative
affliction
afternoon
aggravate
aggressive
aggrieved
agreeable
agricultural
alarm
alcohol
algebra
alleged
alley
allotment
allotted
all right
aloud
alphabet
already
always
amateur
ammunition
analysis
anchor
angel
ankle
anniversary
annoyance
annually
answer
anxious
apologize

apparatus
appeared
appetite
applause
architect
Arctic
aren't
argument
article
ascend
ascertain
assault
assessment
asset
assistance
association
athletic
atmosphere
attendance
attic
audience
author
automatic
autumn
avenue
average
awful
awfully
awkward
axle

babies
bachelor
badge
baggage
banana
barely
barrel
bazaar
beginning
believe
benefit
benefited
bicycle
biscuit

bitterly
blizzard
blue
bonnet
bosom
brethren
British
Briton
buckle
building
bulletin
bureau
burglar
busiest
busily
business
bus
buses

cabbage
calendar
calves
cancel
canoe
careful
carefully
cargo
carriage
catalogue
ceiling
cellar
census
ceremony
certificate
changeable
channel
chiefly
chilly
chimney
chocolate
choice
choir
choose
chorus
chose

cigarette
circuit
circus
civil
coarse
cocoa
coconut
coffee
collar
college
collision
colonel
column
coming
commission
committed
committee
commonly
comparatively
compass
competition
competitor
compliment
complimentary
conceited
conceive
condemn
condensed
conductor
conferred
confidential
congratulate
connexion
conqueror
conscience
conscientious
conscious
consequently
continually
convenience
conveyance
copying
correspondence
corridor
coupon
courageous
(of) course

crazy
crescent
cruel
crystal
cupboard
curiosity
current
customary
cylinder

debtor
deceased
deceit
deceitful
deceive
deferred
deficiency
deficit
definitely
dense
descended
descent
describe
developing
development
dictionary
dining
disagreeable
disappear
disappeared
disappoint
disastrous
discipline
diseases
disguise
distinguish
divided
dizzy
doctor
does
doesn't
drowned
dutiful

eagle
earache
earnestly

echo
editor
eighth
either
embarrass
embarrassing
endeavour
entirely
envelope
equipment
equipped
errand
especially
essence
evenly
eventful
eventual
exaggerate
excel
excessively
excuse
existence
expense
experience
exquisite
extravagant
extremely

facilities
fairly
faithfully
familiar
families
fascination
fatigue
favourable
feasible
February
feeble
fibre
field
fiery
fifteenth
filing
finally
financial
flannel

foggy
foliage
forbidden
forehead
foreign
foremost
forgetful
formerly
forty
fourth
fuel
fulfil
funeral
furnace

gauge
genuine
glimpse
gorgeous
gossip
government
governor
gradually
grammar
grateful
gravy
grief
grieve
guarantee
guard
guilty
guinea
gymnasium

handful
handkerchief
heroes
heroic
honorary
honourable
hoping
horizon
humorous
hymns

ignorance
imaginary

imitate
immigration
inconvenience
insurance
intelligent
interfere
invisible
island

January
jewellery
journey

kernel
knuckle

label
laboratory
labour
labourer
language
laundry
lawyer
leisure
lettuce
library
(a) licence
licensed
lieutenant
lightening
lightning
linoleum
liquor
locality
locally
lodging
loneliness
loose
lose
luggage
luncheon

machinery
magazine
maintenance
malicious
manly

manufacture
marriage
massacre
meanness
mechanical
melon
mere
merely
mileage
millinery
mirror
miscellaneous
mischief
mischievous
missionary
monotonous
mortgage
muscles

necessary
necessity
negro
negroes
neighbour
neither
nephew
ninety
ninth
nonsense
noticeable
nuisance

occasion
occasionally
occur
occurred
occurrence
offence
offensive
offered
official
omission
omitted
operation
opinion
opportunity
orchestra

originally
orphan

Pacific
palm
pamphlet
parallel
Parliament
parrot
particular
pastime
pavement
perceive
permission
permitted
perpetual
perseverance
persuade
philosophy
photos
physician
piece
pigeon
pillar
pillow
pioneer
pistol
pitiful
plague
plaster
plumber
pneumonia
poisoned
politely
politician
possession
postponed
postscript
potatoes
poultry
preceding
precious
preference
preferred
preliminary
presence
principal (main)

principle
privilege
procedure
professor
programme
prompt
prophecy
prophet
proprietor
psalm
psychology
pulley
pumpkin
puncture
purchaser
purely
purpose

quarantine
quarrel
quarrelling
quarterly
quietly

radiator
radishes
raisin
razor
readiness
receipt
receive
recognize
recommend
refer
reference
referred
reign
religious
remittance
repetition
respectful
restaurant
reverence
rheumatism
rhyme
ridiculous
rogue

rough
route

salary
salmon
salvage
sandals
sandwich
sanitary
satisfactorily
Saturday
sausage
scarcely
schedule
scissors
Scottish
scribbling
scripture
secretary
seize
sentence
separate
separation
sergeant
serviceable
several
severely
sewerage
shepherd
shriek
siege
sincere
sincerely
socialist
socially
societies
solemnly
solitary
souvenir
sovereign
Spanish
special
spectacle
squirrel
stationary (at rest)
stationery(paper)
statistics
stomach
substantial
substitute
subtract
suburb
succeed
success
successful
successor
superficial
surface
surgeon
surplus
survive
suspense
swollen
sympathy

tailor
technical
telegram
telephone
temperature
temporarily
temporary
tendency
theatre
their
theory
thermometer
thieves
thirsty
thirteenth
thirtieth
thistle
thorough
throughout
Thursday
tiresome
tobacco
tomato
tomatoes
tongue
tonnage
tonsil
tonsillitis
totally
tournament
towel
tragedy
traitor
transferred
traveller
treasure
tributary
trifling
triumph
trivial
trousers
truest
truly
tuberculosis
Tuesday
twelfth
twentieth
typed
typical
tyranny

umbrella
unanimous
unconscious
unduly
uneasiness
union
unnecessary
unsatisfactory
unsuccessful
until
unusual
unusually
urging
usable
useful
usually
utility
utterly

vacancies
vacancy
vaccinated
vacuum
vainly
valleys
valve
varieties
vegetable
veil
vein
vengeance
vicinity
view
vigorous
villain
vinegar
violinist
virile
virtually
visible
visitor
vocabulary
volcano
voluntary
volunteer
vomit
vulgar

wagon
warrant
wavy
weather
Wednesday
weigh
welfare
weren't
wharves
whereabouts
whether
whistle
wholly
witnesses
witty
woollen
wrestle
wrinkled

yacht
yearn
yield
yolk

FAMOUS NAMES IN LITERATURE

Examples of the work of an author are printed in italic type

ABERCROMBIE, Lascelles (b. 1881), English poet and critic. *Collected Poems, Theory of Art.*

ADDISON, Joseph (1672–1719), English essayist. *Tatler* and *Spectator Essays.*

AESCHYLUS (525–456 B.C.), Athenian tragic poet. *Agamemnon, Choephori, Eumenides.*

AESOP (c. 570 B.C.), Phrygian manumitted slave whose *Fables* were translated into Greek and Latin.

AINSWORTH, William Harrison (1805–1882), English novelist. *The Tower of London, The Lancashire Witches.*

ANDERSEN, Hans Christian (1805–1875), Danish novelist whose *Fairy Tales* were translated into English in 1846.

ANDERSON, Sherwood (b. 1876), American story writer. *Marching Men, Dark Laughter.*

ARIOSTO, Ludovico (1474–1533), Italian poet. *Orlando Furioso.*

ARISTOPHANES (c. 444–380 B.C.), Athenian comic poet. *The Birds.*

ARISTOTLE (384–322 B.C.), Greek philosopher. *Ethics, Poetics, Politics.*

ARNOLD, Matthew (1822–1888), English essayist and poet. *Essays in Criticism, Sohrab and Rustum, The Scholar Gipsy.*

AUSTEN, Jane (1775–1817), English novelist. *Pride and Prejudice, Emma.*

BACON, Francis (1561–1626), English prose writer. *Essays, The Advancement of Learning, Novum Organum.*

BARBOUR, John (c. 1316–1395), Scottish poet and chronicler. *The Bruce,* a history in rhyme of the life and adventures of Robert the Bruce, King of Scotland.

BARHAM, Richard Harris (1788–1845), English prose writer. *Ingoldsby Legends.*

BARRIE, Sir James (1860–1937), Scottish playwright and story writer. *The Admirable Crichton, What Every Woman Knows, Peter Pan.*

BEAUMONT, Francis (1584–1616), playwright. (See **Fletcher,** John).

BEDDOES, Thomas Lovell (1803–1849), English playwright and poet. *Death's Jest-Book, Dream Pedlary.*

BEERBOHM, Max (b. 1872), English critic, wit and satirist. *A Christmas Garland.*

BELLAMY, Edward (1850–1898), American novelist. *Looking Backward.*

BELLOC, Joseph Hilaire Pierre (b. 1870), English poet and prose writer. *The Path to Rome, The Bad Child's Book of Beasts.*

BENNETT, Arnold (1867–1931), English novelist. *The Old Wives' Tale, Riceyman Steps.*

BENTHAM, Jeremy (1748–1832), English jurist and political philosopher; protagonist of "Utilitarianism"; joint editor of *Westminster Review, Principles of Morals and Legislation.*

BERKELEY, George (1685–1753), Irish philosopher and English prose writer. *Principles of Human Knowledge, Alciphron.*

BINYON, Lawrence (1869–1943), English poet. *London Visions.*

BLACKMORE, Richard Dodridge (1825–1900), English novelist. *Lorna Doone.*

BLAKE, William (1757–1827), English poet. *Songs of Innocence, Songs of Experience.*

BLUNT, Wilfred Scawen (1840–1922), English poet. *The Love Sonnets of Proteus.*

BOCCACCIO, Giovanni (c. 1313–1375), Italian novelist and poet. *Decameron.*

BORROW, George (1803–1881), English prose writer. *The Bible in Spain, Lavengro.*

BOSWELL, James (1740–1795), Scottish biographer. *Life of Samuel Johnson.*

BRIDGES, Robert (1844–1930), English poet. *The Testament of Beauty.*

BRONTË, Charlotte (1816–1855), English novelist. *Jane Eyre.*

BRONTË, Emily (1818–1848), English poet and novelist. *Wuthering Heights.*

BROOKE, Rupert (1887–1915), English poet. *Sonnets* (including *Peace* and *The Soldier*), *Grantchester.*

BROWN, Dr. John (1810–1882), Scottish essayist. *Horæ Subsesivæ* (including *Rab and His Friends*).

BROWNE, Sir Thomas (1605–1682), English prose writer. *Religio Medici.*

BROWNING, Elizabeth Barrett (1806–1861), English poet. *The Cry of the Children, Sonnets from the Portuguese.*

BROWNING, Robert (1812–1889), English poet. *Sordello, The Ring and the Book.*

BUCHAN, John, Lord Tweedsmuir (1875–1940), Scottish novelist. *Greenmantle, The Thirty-Nine Steps.*

BUNYAN, John (1628–1688), English prose writer. *The Pilgrim's Progress.*

BURKE, Edmund (1729–1797), Irish political writer. *Thoughts on the Present Discontents, On American Taxation.*

BURNEY, Frances (Fanny) (1752–1840), English novelist. *Evelina.*

BURNS, Robert (1759–1796) Scottish poet. *The Cottar's Saturday Night, Tam O'Shanter*; also *To a Mouse* and numerous other lyrics, most of which are immortalized with their musical settings in songs such as *My love is like a red, red rose, Mary Morrison,* etc.

BURTON, Sir Richard Francis (1821–1890), English writer; translated into English *Arabian Nights' Entertainments.*

BUTLER, Samuel (1612–1680), English poet. *Hudibras.*

BYRON, George Gordon, Lord (1788–1824), English poet. *Childe Harold's Pilgrimage, The Bride of Abydos, Don Juan.*

CARLYLE, Thomas (1795–1881), Scottish prose writer. *Sartor Resartus, The French Revolution, Heroes and Hero-Worship.*

CATULLUS, Gaius Valerius (c. 87–54 B.C.), Roman poet and epigrammatist.

CELLINI, Benvenuto (1500–1571), Florentine sculptor and author of *Autobiography of B. Cellini* (translated J. A. Symonds).

CERVANTES, Miguel de (1547–1616), Spanish novelist and dramatist. *Don Quixote.*

CHATTERTON, Thomas (1752–1770), English poet. *Rowley Poems.*

CHAUCER, Geoffrey (c. 1340–1400), English poet. *The Canterbury Tales, Troylus and Cryseyde.*

CHEKHOV, Anton Pavlovich (1860–1904), Russian dramatist and novelist. *The Cherry Orchard, Uncle Vanya.*

CHESTERTON, Gilbert Keith (1874-1936), English novelist and poet. *The Flying Inn, The Innocence of Father Brown, The Napoleon of Notting Hill.*

CIBBER, Colley (1671–1757), English actor and dramatist and hero of Pope's *Dunciad. The Careless Husband.*

CICERO, Marcus Tullius (106–43 B.C.), Roman philosophical writer. *De Senectute, Philippics.*

CLEMENS, Samuel Langhorne ("Mark Twain") (1835–1910), American story writer. *Tom Sawyer.*

CLOUGH, Arthur Hugh (1819–1861), English poet. *The Bothie of Tober-na-Vuolich.*

COBBETT, William (1763–1835), English pamphleteer. *Rural Rides.*

COLERIDGE, Samuel Taylor (1772–1834), English poet. *The Rime of the Ancient Mariner, Kubla Khan, Christabel.*

COLLINS, William (1721–1759), English poet. *Ode to Evening, How Sleep the Brave.*

COLLINS, William Wilkie (1824–1889), English novelist. *The Woman in White.*

CONGREVE, William (1670–1729), English playwright. *Love for Love, The Way of the World.*

CONRAD, Joseph (1857–1924), British novelist of Polish birth. *Mirror of the Sea, Almayer's Folly.*

COOPER, James Fenimore (1789–1851), American novelist. *The Last of the Mohicans,* etc. (*The Leather-Stocking Tales*).

CORNEILLE, Pierre (1606–1684), French dramatist. *Le Cid.*

COVERDALE, Miles (1488–1569), English translator of the *Bible,* and of the *Psalms* in the Prayer Book.

COWLEY, Abraham (1618–1667), English poet. *The Mistress.*

COWPER, William (1731–1800), English poet. *John Gilpin, The Task.*

CRABBE, George (1754–1832), English poet. *The Village, The Parish Register.*

CRASHAW, Richard (1613–1649), English poet. *The Flaming Heart.*

CUNNINGHAM, Allan (1784–1842), Scottish poet. *Hame, hame, hame, A wet sheet and a flowing sea.*

DANE, Clemence, English novelist and playwright. *Broome Stages, Wild Decembers.*

DANTE, Alighieri (1265–1321), Italian poet. *Divina Comedia.*

DAUDET, Alphonse (1840–1897), French novelist and short story writer. *Lettres de mon Moulin.*

DAVIDSON, John (1857–1909), Scottish poet. *Romney Marsh, The Runnable Stag.*

DAVIES, William Henry (b. 1871), English poet and prose writer. *The Autobiography of a Super-Tramp.*

DEFOE, Daniel (c. 1660–1731), English novelist. *Adventures of Robinson Crusoe, Moll Flanders, A Journal of the Plague Year.*

DEKKER, Thomas (c. 1570–1632), English playwright. *The Shoemaker's Holiday.*

DE LA MARE, Walter (b. 1873), English poet and novelist. *Peacock Pie, Memoirs of a Midget.*

DE QUINCEY, Thomas (1785–1859), English prose writer. *Confessions of an English Opium Eater.*

DICKENS, Charles (1812–1870), English novelist. *The Pickwick Papers, David Copperfield, A Tale of Two Cities.*

DICKINSON, Emily (1830–1886), American poet. *Complete Poems of E.D.*

DISRAELI, Benjamin, Earl of Beaconsfield (1804–1881), English novelist. *Coningsby, Sybil.*

DODGSON, Charles Lutwidge ("Lewis Carroll") (1832–1898), English writer of children's tales. *Alice's Adventures in Wonderland.*

DONNE, John (1572–1631), English "metaphysical" poet. *Hymn to God the Father, Sonnet to Death.*

DOSTOEVSKY, Feodor Michaelovich (1821–1881), Russian novelist. *Crime and Punishment.*

DOUGHTY, Charles Montagu (1843–1926), English prose writer and poet. *Travels in Arabia Deserta.*

DOYLE, Sir Arthur Conan (1859–1930), English novelist. *The Adventures of Sherlock Holmes, The Hound of the Baskervilles.*

DRAYTON, Michael (1563–1631), English poet. *Polyolbion, Sonnets.*

DREISER, Theodore (b. 1871), American novelist. *An American Tragedy.*

DRINKWATER, John (1882–1937), English poet and dramatist. *Collected Poems, Abraham Lincoln.*

DRUMMOND of HAWTHORNDEN, William (1585–1649), Scottish poet and pamphleteer. *The Cypresse Grove.*

DRYDEN, John (1631–1700), English poet, playwright and critic. *Alexander's Feast, Absolom and Achitophel, All for Love, An Essay on Dramatic Poesy.*

DUMAS, Alexandre (1803–1870), French dramatist and novelist. *The Three Musketeers, The Count of Monte Cristo.*

DUNBAR, William (c. 1465–1530), Scottish poet. *The Thrissill and the Rois, Lament for the Makaris, The Dance of the Sevin Deidly Synnis.*

ELIOT, George (Mary Ann Cross, née Evans) (1819–1880), English novelist. *Adam Bede, The Mill on the Floss, Silas Marner.*

ELIOT, Thomas Stearns (b. 1888), American poet and critic. *The Waste Land.*

EMERSON, Ralph Waldo (1803–1882), American philosopher, poet and essayist. *Essays.*

EURIPIDES (480–406 B.C.), Greek tragedian. *Alcestis, Medea.*

EVELYN, John (1620–1706), English Diarist. *Diary.*

FERGUSON, Robert (1750–1774), Scottish lyrical poet. *Poems.*

FIELD, Eugene (1850–1895), American poet and playwright. *With Trumpet and Drum.*

FIELDING, Henry (1707–1754), English novelist. *Tom Jones, Amelia.*

FITZGERALD, Edward (1809–1883), English poet. Translation of *The Rubáiyát of Omar Khayyám.*

FLAUBERT, Gustave (1821–1880), French novelist. *Madame Bovary.*

FLECKER, James Elroy (1884–1915), English dramatic poet. *Hassan.*

FLETCHER, John (1579–1625), English playwright. (With Francis Beaumont) *Philaster, The Knight of the Burning Pestle.*

FORSTER, Edward Morgan (b. 1879), English novelist and critic. *Howard's End, Aspects of the Novel.*

FRANCE, Anatole (Jacques Anatole Thibault) (1844–1924), French man of letters and short story writer. *Le Crime de Sylvestre Bonnard, Le Livre de mon Ami.*

FRAZER, Sir James (b. 1854), English anthropological author. *The Golden Bough.*

GALSWORTHY, John (1867–1933), English novelist and dramatist. *The Forsyte Saga, The Skin Game.*

GALT, John (1779–1839), Scottish novelist, poet and chronicler. *Annals of the Parish.*

GASKELL, Elizabeth (1810–1865), English novelist and biographer. *Cranford, Life of Charlotte Brontë.*

GAY, John (1685–1732), playwright. *The Beggar's Opera.*

GIBBON, Edward (1737–1794), English historian. *The Decline and Fall of the Roman Empire.*

GISSING, George (1857–1903), English novelist. *The Unclassed, The Private Papers of Henry Ryecroft.*

GOETHE, Johann Wolfgang von (1749–1832), German dramatist and poet. *Faust.*

GOGOL, Nikolai V. (1809–1852), Russian novelist. *Dead Souls.*

GOLDSMITH, Oliver (1728–1774), English poet, novelist and playwright. *The Deserted Village, The Vicar of Wakefield, She Stoops to Conquer.*

GRAHAME, Kenneth (1859–1932), English writer for children. *The Wind in the Willows, The Golden Age.*

GRAY, Thomas (1716–1771), English poet. *Elegy Written in a Country Churchyard, The Bard.*

GRIMM, Jacob Ludwig Carl (1785–1863), German folklorist and writer of fairy tales.

HAGGARD, Sir Henry Rider (1856–1925), English novelist. *King Solomon's Mines, She.*

HAKLUYT, Richard (1553–1616), English prose writer. *The Principal Navigations, Voyages, and Discoveries of the English Nation.*

HARDY, Thomas (1840–1928), English poet and novelist. *The Dynasts, The Return of the Native, Tess of the d'Urbervilles.*

HAWTHORNE, Nathaniel (1804–1864), American novelist. *The Scarlet Letter.*

HAZLITT, William (1778–1830), English essayist and critic. *Table Talk, The Characters of Shakespeare's Plays.*

HENLEY, William Ernest (1849–1903), English poet. *London Voluntaries, Hawthorn and Lavender.*

HENTY, George Alfred (1832–1902), English novelist and writer for boys.

HERBERT, George (1593–1633), English poet. *The Temple.*

HERGESHEIMER, Joseph (b. 1880), American novelist. *Tampico.*

HERRICK, Robert (1591–1674), English poet. *Hesperides.*

HEWLETT, Maurice (1861–1923), English novelist, poet and essayist. *The Forest Lovers.*

HOGG, James, the "Ettrick Shepherd" (1770–1835), Scottish poet. *The Mountain Bard, The Queen's Wake.*

HOLINSHED, Raphael (d. 1580), English historian and chronicler. Holinshed's *Chronicles.*

HOLMES, Oliver Wendell (1809–1894), American essayist. *Autocrat of the Breakfast-Table.*

HOMER (c. 1000 B.C.), Greek epic poet. *Iliad, Odyssey.*

HOOD, Thomas (1799–1845), English poet. *Dream of Eugene Aram, Song of the Shirt.*

HOPKINS, Gerard Manley (1844–1889), English poet. *The Wreck of the Deutschland.*

HORACE (Quintus Horatius Flaccus), (65–8 B.C.), Roman poet. *Odes, Ars Poetica.*
HOUSMAN, Alfred Edward (1859–1936), English poet. *The Shropshire Lad, Last Poems.*
HOUSMAN, Laurence (b. 1865), English author. *Little Plays of St. Francis.*
HOWELLS, William Dean (1837–1920), American novelist. *The Rise of Silas Lapham.*
HUDSON, William Henry (1841–1922), British author and novelist. *A Shepherd's Life, Green Mansions.*
HUGO, Victor-Marie (1802–1885), French poet and novelist. *Ruy Blas, La Lègende des Siècles, Les Misérables.*
HUNT, James Henry Leigh (1784–1859), English poet and essayist. *The Story of Rimini, Table Talk.*
HUXLEY, Aldous (b. 1894), English poet, novelist and essayist. *Point Counter Point.*
IBSEN, Henrik (1828–1906), Norwegian dramatist. *Ghosts, Peer Gynt.*
INGELOW, Jean (1820–1897), English poet. *The High Tide on the Coast of Lincolnshire.*
IRVING, Washington (1783–1859), American essayist and story writer. *Sketch Book.*
JACOBS, William Wymark (1863–1944), English short story writer. *Many Cargoes.*
JAMES, Henry (1843–1916), American novelist and short story writer. *Daisy Miller, The Wings of the Dove, The Turn of the Screw.*
JOHNSON, Samuel (1709–1784), English poet, lexicographer, novelist and critic. *The Vanity of Human Wishes, Rasselas, Prince of Abyssinia, The Lives of the Most Eminent English Poets.*
JONSON, Benjamin (1572–1637), English poet and playwright. *Drink to me only with thine eyes, Hymn to Diana, Every Man in His Humour, Volpone.*
JOYCE, James (b. 1882), Irish novelist. *Ulysses.*
KEATS, John (1795–1821), English poet. *Endymion, Isabella, The Eve of St. Agnes.*
KINGLAKE, Alexander William (1809–1891), English author. *Eothen.*
KINGSLEY, Charles (1819–1875), English novelist. *Alton Locke, Westward Ho!, The Water Babies.*
KIPLING, Rudyard (1865–1936), English poet and story writer. *Barrack-Room Ballads, Stalky and Co., The Jungle Books.*
LAMB, Charles (1775–1834), English essayist. *Essays of Elia,* (with Mary Lamb) *Tales from Shakespeare.*
LANDOR, Walter Savage (1775–1864), English poet and essayist. *To Ianthe, Imaginary Conversations.*
LANG, Andrew (1844–1912), Scottish poet, prose writer and novelist. *Grass of Parnassus, The Mark of Cain.*
LANGLAND, William (c. 1330–1400), English poet. *The Vision Concerning Piers the Plowman.*
LAWRENCE, David Herbert (1885–1930), English novelist. *Sons and Lovers, Lady Chatterley's Lovers.*
LAWRENCE, Thomas Edward (1888–1935), English prose writer. *The Seven Pillars of Wisdom.*
LEWIS, Sinclair (b. 1885), American novelist. *Main Street, Dodsworth.*
LOCKHART, John Gibson (1794–1854), Scottish critic. *Life of Burns, of Scott.*
LONDON, Jack (1876–1916), American novelist. *The Call of the Wild.*
LONGFELLOW, Henry Wadsworth (1807–1882), American poet. *Hiawatha, Evangeline.*
LOVELACE, Richard (1618–1658), English poet. *To Lucasta, To Althea from Prison.*
LUCRETIUS (Titus Lucretius Carus), (c. 99–55 B.C.), Roman poet. *De Rerum Natura.*
LYLY, John (c. 1554–1606), English poet and dramatist. *Euphues, Alexander and Campaspe.*
LYTTON, Edward Bulwer, Lord (1803–1873), English novelist. *Last Days of Pompeii, Eugene Aram.*
MACAULAY, Thomas Babington, Lord (1800–1859), English essayist and poet. *Essays, Lays of Ancient Rome.*
MAETERLINCK, Maurice (b. 1862), Belgian poet and dramatist. *L'Oiseau Bleu.*
MALORY, Sir Thomas (d. 1471), English poet. *Morte d'Arthur.*
MANN, Thomas (b. 1875), German novelist. *Buddenbrooks.*
MANSFIELD, Katherine (Katherine Middleton Murray), (1888–1923), English short story writer. *Bliss, The Garden Party.*
MARLOWE, Christopher (1564–1593), English poet and playwright. *The Passionate Shepherd, Tamburlaine, Dr. Faustus.*
MARRYAT, Frederick (1792–1848), English novelist. *Peter Simple, Mr. Midshipman Easy.*
MARVELL, Andrew (1621–1667), English poet. *The Garden, The Bermudas.*
MARX, Karl (1818–1883), German economist and sociologist. *Das Kapital.*
MASEFIELD, John (b. 1878), English poet. *Salt Water Ballads, The Everlasting Mercy, Reynard the Fox.*
MASSINGER, Philip (1583–1640), English poet and dramatist. *A New Way to Pay Old Debts.*
MAUGHAM, William Somerset (b. 1874), English author and playwright. *Of Human Bondage, The Circle.*
MELVILLE, Herman (1819–1891), American author. *Moby Dick.*
MEREDITH, George (1828–1909), English poet and novelist. *Modern Love, The Ordeal of Richard Feverel, Diana of the Crossways.*
MEYNELL, Alice (1847–1922), English poet and essayist. *The Children, Poems.*
MILTON, John (1608–1674), English poet. *Lycidas, Paradise Lost, Paradise Regained, Comus, Samson Agonistes, Areopagitica.*
MITFORD, Mary Russell (1787–1855), English essayist. *Our Village.*
MOORE, George (1852–1933), English novelist. *Esther Waters.*
MOORE, Thomas (1779–1852), Irish poet. *Irish Melodies.*
MORE, Sir Thomas (1478–1535), English prose writer. *Utopia.*
MORIER, James Justinian (1780–1849), British author. *The Adventures of Hazzi Baba of Izpahan.*
MORRIS, William (1834–1896), English poet and prose writer. *The Life and Death of Jason, The Earthly Paradise.*
NEWBOLT, Sir Henry (1862–1938), English poet. *Songs of the Sea, Songs of the Fleet.*
NOYES, Alfred (b. 1880), English poet. *The Loom of Years.*
OTWAY, Thomas (1652–1685), English dramatist. *Don Carlos.*
OVID (Publius Ovidius Naso), (43 B.C.–A.D. 18), Roman elegiac poet. *Metamorphoses.*
PATER, Walter Horatio (1839–1894), English essayist. *Imaginary Portraits.*
PATMORE, Coventry Kersey Dighton (1823–1896), English poet. *The Angel in the House.*
PEACOCK, Thomas Love (1785–1866), English novelist and poet. *Headlong Hall, Maid Marian.*
PEPYS, Samuel (1633–1703), English diarist. *Diary.*
PERRAULT, Charles (1628–1703), French poet, critic and writer of children's fairy tales. *Histoires et Contes du Temps Passé.*
PHILLPOTTS, Eden (b. 1862), English novelist and playwright. *The Secret Woman, The Farmer's Wife.*
PINDAR (c. 522–442 B.C.), Greek lyric poet. *Epinicia* (triumphal odes).
PINERO, Sir Arthur Wing (1855–1934), English dramatist. *The Second Mrs. Tanqueray.*
PIRANDELLO, Luigi (b. 1867), Italian dramatist. *Six Characters in Search of an Author.*
PLATO (428–347 B.C.), Greek philosopher. *Dialogues* (including the *Republic*).
PLUTARCH (c. A.D. 66), Greek biographer. *Parallel Lives* (of Greeks and Romans).
POE, Edgar Allan (1809–1849), American short story writer. *The Gold Bug.*
POPE, Alexander (1688–1744), English poet, essayist and critic. *The Dunciad, The Rape of the Lock, Essay on Criticism.*
PRÉVOST, The Abbé (1697–1763), French novelist. *L'Histoire de Manon Lescaut.*
PRIESTLEY, John Boynton (b. 1894), English novelist and playwright. *The Good Companions, Laburnum Grove.*
PROUST, Marcel (1871–1922), French Novelist. *A la Recherche du Temps Perdu.*

PUSHKIN, Alexander Sergivich (1799–1837), Russian poet. *Boris Godunov.*

QUILLER-COUCH, Sir Arthur Thomas ("Q") (1863–1943), English critic and novelist. *Adventures in Criticism, Studies in Literature.*

RABELAIS, Francois (1494–1553), French satirist. *Pantagruel.*

RAMSAY, Allan (1686–1758), Scottish pastoral poet who inspired all later vernacular poetry. *The Gentle Shepherd.*

READE, Charles (1814–1884), English novelist. *The Cloister and the Hearth, It's Never Too Late to Mend.*

RICHARDSON, Samuel (1689–1761), English novelist. *Pamela, Clarissa Harlowe.*

ROBINSON, Charles Arlington (1869–1935), American poet. *The Children of the Night.*

ROSSETTI, Christina Georgina (1830–1894), English poet. *Goblin Market.*

ROSSETTI, Dante Gabriel (1828–1882), English poet. *The Blessed Damozel, Ballads and Sonnets.*

ROUSSEAU, Jean-Jacques (1712–1778), French philosophic writer. *Du Contrat Social, Émile.*

RUSKIN, John (1819–1900), English essayist and critic. *Modern Painters, The Seven Lamps of Architecture, Sesame and Lilies.*

RUSSELL, George William ("Æ") (1867–1935), Irish poet. *Deirdre.*

SCOTT, Sir Walter (1771–1832), Scottish poet and novelist. *Marmion, The Lady of the Lake, The "Waverley" Novels.*

SHAKESPEARE, William (1564–1616), English poet and dramatist. *Sonnets, A Midsummer Night's Dream, As You Like It, Twelfth-Night, Hamlet, Macbeth, King Lear, King Richard III, King Henry V.*

SHAW, George Bernard (b. 1856), Irish playwright and writer on social questions. *Man and Superman, The Doctor's Dilemma, Saint Joan, The Intelligent Woman's Guide to Socialism and Capitalism.*

SHELLEY, Percy Bysshe (1792–1822), English poet. *Adonais, The Cenci, Prometheus Unbound.*

SHENSTONE, William (1714–1763), English poet. *The Schoolmistress.*

SHERIDAN, Richard Brinsley (1751–1816), English playwright. *The Rivals, The School for Scandal.*

SIDNEY, Sir Philip (1554–1586), English poet and prose writer. *The Defence of Poesie, Astrophel and Stella.*

SINCLAIR, Upton (b. 1878), American novelist. *The Jungle, Oil.*

SITWELL, Edith (b. 1887), English poet. *Collected Poems.*

SITWELL, Osbert (b. 1892), English poet. *England Reclaimed.*

SITWELL, Sacheverell (b. 1897), English poet and critic. *The Hundred and One Harlequins, The Gothic North.*

SKELTON, John (c. 1460–1529), English poet. *Colyn Cloute.*

SMILES, Samuel (1812–1904), Scottish novelist. *Self-Help.*

SMOLLETT, Tobias (1721–1771), Scottish novelist. *The Adventures of Roderick Random, The Adventures of Peregrine Pickle, The Expedition of Humphry Clinker.*

SOPHOCLES (495–406 B.C.), Greek tragedian. *Oedipus, Antigone.*

SOUTHEY, Robert (1774–1843), English poet and biographer. *My Days among the Dead are Past* and other lyrics, *Life of Nelson.*

SPENSER, Edmund (c. 1552–1599), English poet. *The Shepheard's Calender, The Faerie Queene, Epithalamion.*

STEELE, Sir Richard (1672–1729), English essayist. *Tatler* and *Spectator Essays.*

STENDHAL (Henri Beyle) (1783–1842), French novelist. *Le Rouge et Le Noir.*

STERNE, Laurence (1713–1768), Irish novelist. *Tristram Shandy, A Sentimental Journey.*

STEVENSON, Robert Louis (1850–1894), Scottish novelist and poet. *Treasure Island, Kidnapped, A Child's Garden of Verses.*

STOWE, Mrs. Harriet Elizabeth Beecher (1811–1896), American novelist. *Uncle Tom's Cabin.*

STRACHEY, Giles Lytton (1880–1932), English biographer. *Eminent Victorians, Queen Victoria.*

SWIFT, Jonathan (1667–1745), Irish prose writer and novelist. *A Tale of a Tub, Gulliver's Travels, Journal to Stella.*

SWINBURNE, Algernon Charles (1837–1909), English poet. *Atalanta in Calydon, Mary Stuart.*

SYNGE, John Millington (1871–1909), Irish dramatist. *Riders to the Sea, The Playboy of the Western World.*

TAGORE, Sir Rabindranath (b. 1861), Indian poet. *The Crescent Moon, The King of the Dark Chamber.*

TENNYSON, Alfred, Lord (1809–1892), English poet. *Ulysses, In Memoriam, Morte d'Arthur, Idylls of the King.*

TERENCE (Publius Terentius Afer), (c. 190–159 B.C.), Roman comic poet and dramatist. *Phormio.*

THACKERAY, William Makepeace (1811–1863), English novelist. *Pendennis, Vanity Fair, The Newcomes.*

THOMPSON, Francis (1859–1907), English poet and critic. *The Hound of Heaven, Essay on Shelley.*

THOMSON, James (1700–1748), Scottish poet. *The Seasons, The Castle of Indolence.*

THOMSON, James (1834–1882), English poet. *The City of Dreadful Nights.*

TOLSTOY, Count Leo Nikolaevich (1828–1910), Russian novelist, dramatist and prose writer. *War and Peace, Anna Karenina, What is Art?*

TRELAWNY, Edward John (1792–1881), English author. *Adventures of a Younger Son.*

TROLLOPE, Anthony (1815–1882), English novelist. *The Barchester Novels: The Warden, Barchester Towers, Dr. Thorne,* etc.

TURGENEV, Ivan Sergeivich (1818–1883), Russian novelist. *Fathers and Sons, Smoke.*

TYNDALE, William (1492–1536), English translator of the *Bible.*

UDALL, Nicholas (1505–1556), English dramatist. *Ralph Roister Doister,* the first English comedy.

VEGA, Lope de (1562–1635), Spanish dramatist.

VERGIL (Publius Vergilius Maro), (70–19 B.C.), Roman poet. *The Aeneid.*

VERNE, Jules (1828–1905), French novelist. *Twenty Thousand Leagues Under the Sea.*

VOLTAIRE (Francois Marie Arouet), (1694–1778), French philosophical writer and novelist. *Zadig, Candide.*

WALLER, Edmund (1606–1687), English poet. *On a Girdle, Go, Lovely Rose.*

WALPOLE, Sir Hugh Seymour (1884–1941), English novelist. *The Cathedral, Rogue Herries.*

WALTON, Izaak (1593–1683), English prose writer and biographer. *The Compleat Angler.*

WEBB, Mary (1881–1927), English novelist. *Precious Bane.*

WEBSTER, John (c. 1580–1625), English dramatist. *The Duchess of Malfi.*

WELLS, Herbert George (b. 1866), English novelist. *The Time Machine, Kipps, Tono-Bungay.*

WHARTON, Edith (b. 1862), American novelist. *Hudson River Bracketed.*

WHITE, Gilbert (1720–1793), English prose writer. *Natural History and Antiquities of Selborne.*

WHITMAN, Walt (1819–1892), American poet. *Leaves of Grass.*

WHITTIER, John Greenleaf (1807–1892), American poet. *Snow-Bound.*

WILDE, Oscar Fingal O'Flahertie Wills (1854–1900), English playwright and poet. *The Importance of Being Earnest, Lady Windermere's Fan, The Ballad of Reading Gaol.*

WOOLF, Virginia (1882–1941), English novelist and essayist. *Orlando, A Room of One's Own.*

WORDSWORTH, William (1770–1850), English poet Laureate. *The Prelude, Lyrical Ballads, Intimations of Immortality, The Excursion,* and numerous *Sonnets.*

WYATT, Sir Thomas (1503–1542), English poet. Sonnets, notably *The Lover's Appeal.*

WYCLIFFE, John (c. 1320–1384), English translator of the *Bible.*

YEATS, William Butler (1865–1939), Irish poet and dramatist. *The Wind Among the Reeds, Selected Poems, Lyrical and Narrative, The Countess Cathleen, The Land of Heart's Desire.*

NOTABLE CHARACTERS IN ENGLISH LITERATURE

ABBOT, The (Father Ambrose), *The Abbot,* Sir Walter Scott.
ABOU HASSAN, *The Sleeper Awakened* (*The Arabian Nights' Entertainment*).
ABSOLUTE, Sir Anthony, *The Rivals,* R. B. Sheridan.
ACRES, Bob, *The Rivals,* R. B. Sheridan.
ADAMS, Parson, *Joseph Andrews,* Henry Fielding.
ADMIRABLE CRICHTON, The, *The Admirable Crichton,* Sir James M. Barrie.
ADVERSE, Anthony, *Anthony Adverse,* Hervey Allen.
AEMILIA, *The Comedy of Errors,* W. Shakespeare.
AGNES (Wickfield), *David Copperfield,* Charles Dickens.
AGRAVAIN, Sir, *History of Prince Arthur,* Sir Thomas Malory.
AGUECHEEK, Sir Andrew, *Twelfth-Night,* W. Shakespeare.
AHMED, Prince, *The Arabian Nights' Entertainment.*
ALADDIN, *Aladdin and The Wonderful Lamp* (*The Arabian Nights' Entertainment*).
ALI BABA, *Ali Baba and The Forty Thieves* (*Arabian Nights' Entertainment*).
ALICE, *Alice's Adventures In Wonderland,* Lewis Carroll.
ALISON LEWIS, *The Fountain,* Charles Morgan.
ALLAN-A-DALE, *Ivanhoe,* Sir Walter Scott.
ALLWORTHY, *Tom Jones,* Henry Fielding.
ALMAYER, *Almayer's Folly,* Joseph Conrad.
AMBROSE, Father, *The Abbot,* Sir Walter Scott.
AMELIA, *Amelia,* Henry Fielding; *Vanity Fair,* W. M. Thackeray.
ANCIENT MARINER, *The Ancient Mariner,* S. T. Coleridge.
ANTIPHOLUS, *The Comedy of Errors,* W. Shakespeare.
ANTIQUARY, *The Antiquary,* Sir Walter Scott.
ANTONIO, *The Merchant of Venice; The Tempest; The Two Gentlemen of Verona,* W. Shakespeare.
ARAM, Eugene, *Eugene Aram,* Lord Lytton; *The Dream of Eugene Aram,* Thomas Hood.
ARCHIMAGO, *The Faerie Queene,* Edmund Spenser.
ARDEN, Enoch, *Enoch Arden,* Lord Tennyson.
ARIEL, *The Tempest,* W. Shakespeare; *The Rape of the Lock,* Alexander Pope; *Paradise Lost,* John Milton.
ARTEGAL, *The Faerie Queene,* Edmund Spenser.
ARTFUL DODGER, *Oliver Twist,* Charles Dickens.
ARTHUR, *Morte d'Arthur,* Sir T. Malory; *The Idylls of the King,* Lord Tennyson.
ASHTON, Lucy, *The Bride of Lammermoor,* Sir Walter Scott.
AUDREY, *As You Like It,* W. Shakespeare.
AUTOLYCUS, *The Winter's Tale,* W. Shakespeare.
AYESHA, *She,* Sir H. Rider Haggard.
AYLWIN, *Aylwin,* W. T. Watts-Dunton.
BACKBITE, Sir Benjamin, *The School for Scandal,* R. B. Sheridan.
BAGSTOCK, Major, *Dombey and Son,* Charles Dickens.
BAINES, Constance and Sophia, *The Old Wives' Tale,* Arnold Bennett.
BALDERSTONE, Caleb, *The Bride of Lammermoor,* Sir Walter Scott.
BALFOUR, David, *Kidnapped,* R. L. Stevenson.
BALL, John, *The Dream of John Ball,* William Morris.
BANQUO, *Macbeth,* W. Shakespeare.
BARDELL, Mrs., *The Pickwick Papers,* Charles Dickens.
BARDOLPH, *Henry IV; The Merry Wives of Windsor,* W. Shakespeare.
BARKIS, *David Copperfield,* Charles Dickens.
BARTON, Mary, *Mary Barton* Mrs. Gaskell.
BASSANIO, *The Merchant of Venice,* W. Shakespeare.
BATES, Charley, *Oliver Twist,* Charles Dickens.
BATTLE, Mrs. Sarah, *Essays of Elia,* Charles Lamb.
BEATRICE, *Much Ado About Nothing,* W. Shakespeare.
BEAU TIBBS, *The Citizen of the World,* Oliver Goldsmith.
BECK, Madame, *Villette,* Charlotte Brontë.
BEDE, Adam, *Adam Bede,* George Eliot.
BEDIVERE, Sir, *Morte d'Arthur,* Sir T. Malory; *Idylls of the King,* Lord Tennyson.
BELCH, Sir Toby, *Twelfth-Night,* W. Shakespeare
BELINDA, *The Rape of the Lock,* Alexander Pope; *Belinda,* Miss Edgeworth.
BELMONT, Sir Francis, *Evelina,* Fanny Burney.
BELLONI, Sandra, *Sandra Belloni,* George Meredith.
BELPHOEBE, *The Faerie Queene,* Edmund Spenser.
BENEDICK, *Much Ado About Nothing,* W. Shakespeare.
BENNET, Elizabeth, *Pride and Prejudice,* Jane Austen.
BERNERS, Isopel, *Romany Rye,* George Borrow.
BERTRAM, Harry, *Guy Mannering,* Sir Walter Scott.
BEVERLEY, Constance de, *Marmion,* Sir W. Scott.
BEVIS, *Bevis,* Richard Jefferies.
BICKERSTAFF, Isaac, *The Tatler,* R. Steele.
BIDDLECOMBE, Susan, *Quinneys,* H. A. Vachell.
BLACK DWARF, The, *The Black Dwarf,* Sir Walter Scott.
BLACK MICHAEL, *The Prisoner of Zenda,* Anthony Hope.
BLAIR, Elspeth, *Salute to Adventurers,* John Buchan.
BLAKENEY, Sir Percy, *The Scarlet Pimpernel,* Baroness Orczy.
BLIFIL, *Tom Jones,* Henry Fielding.
BLIMBER, *Dombey and Son,* Charles Dickens.
BOBADIL, Captain, *Every Man in His Humour,* Ben Jonson.
BOIS-GUILBERT, Brian de, *Ivanhoe,* Sir Walter Scott.
BONIFACE, Abbot, *The Monastery,* Sir Walter Scott.
BOOBY, Lady, *Joseph Andrews,* Henry Fielding.
BOOTH, Captain, *Amelia,* Henry Fielding.
BOTTOM, Nick, *A Midsummer Night's Dream,* W. Shakespeare.
BOWLING, Tom, *The Adventures of Roderick Random,* Tobias Smollett.
BOYTHORNE, Laurence, *Bleak House,* Charles Dickens.
BRABANTIO, *Othello,* W. Shakespeare.
BRADWARDINE, Rose, *Waverley,* Sir Walter Scott.
BRAGGADOCHIO, *The Faerie Queene,* Edmund Spenser.
BRAMBLE, Matthew, *Humphry Clinker,* Tobias Smollett.
BRANDT, Margaret, *The Cloister and the Hearth,* Charles Reade.
BRANDON, Archdeacon, *The Cathedral,* Sir Hugh Walpole.
BRASS, Sampson, *The Old Curiosity Shop,* Charles Dickens.
BRECK, Alan, see **Stewart.**
BRIDGENORTH, Alice and Major, *Peveril of the Peak,* Sir Walter Scott.
BRITLING, Hugh, *Mr. Britling Sees It Through,* H. G. Wells.
BRITOMART, *The Faerie Queene,* Edmund Spenser.
BROOKER, *Nicholas Nickleby,* Charles Dickens.
BROWN, Father, *The Innocence of Father Brown; The Incredulity of Father Brown,* etc., G. K. Chesterton.
BROWN, Tom, *Tom Brown's Schooldays,* Thomas Hughes.
BROWNLOW, Mr., *Oliver Twist,* Charles Dickens.
BRUTUS, Marcus, *Julius Caesar,* W. Shakespeare.
BUCKLAW, Laird of, *The Bride of Lammermoor,* Sir Walter Scott.

BUMBLE, Mr., *Oliver Twist,* Charles Dickens.
BUNSBY, Jack, *Dombey and Son,* Charles Dickens.
BURCHELL, Mr., *The Vicar of Wakefield,* Oliver Goldsmith.
BUZFUZ, Mr. Serjeant, *The Pickwick Papers,* Charles Dickens.
CALIBAN, *The Tempest,* W. Shakespeare.
CALIDORE, Sir, *The Faerie Queene,* Edmund Spenser.
CAMPAIGNER, The Old, *The Newcomes,* W. M. Thackeray.
CANDIDA, *Candida,* G. Bernard Shaw.
CANDOUR, Mrs., *The School for Scandal,* R. B. Sheridan.
CARELESS, *The School for Scandal,* R. B. Sheridan.
CARKER, James, *Dombey and Son,* Charles Dickens.
CARTON, Sydney, *A Tale of Two Cities,* Charles Dickens.
CASAUBON, *Middlemarch,* George Eliot.
CASCA, *Julius Caesar,* W. Shakespeare.
CASSIM, *Ali Baba and the Forty Thieves* (*The Arabian Nights' Entertainments*).
CASSIO, *Othello,* W. Shakespeare.
CASSIUS, *Julius Caesar,* W. Shakespeare.
CASTLEWOOD, Beatrix, *Esmond,* W. M. Thackeray.
CATHERICK, Anne, *The Woman in White,* Wilkie Collins.
CATRIONA, *Catriona,* R. L. Stevenson.
CAUDLE, Mrs., *Mrs. Caudle's Curtain Lectures,* Douglas Jerrold.
CEDRIC, *Ivanhoe,* Sir Walter Scott.
CELIA, *As You Like It,* W. Shakespeare.
CHADBAND, Rev. Mr., *Bleak House,* Charles Dickens.
CHAUVELIN, *The Scarlet Pimpernel,* Baroness Orczy.
CHERRYBLE BROS., *Nicholas Nickleby,* Charles Dickens.
CHRISTIAN, *The Pilgrim's Progress,* John Bunyan.
CHUZZLEWIT, Martin, *Martin Chuzzlewit,* Charles Dickens.
CLARE, Angel, *Tess of the D'Urbervilles,* Thomas Hardy.
CLARINDA, *Verses to Clarinda,* Robert Burns.
CLARISSA (Harlowe), see **Harlowe.**
CLAUDIUS, *Hamlet,* W. Shakespeare.
CLAYHANGER, Edwin and Darius, *Clayhanger,* Arnold Bennett.
CLEMENTINE, *Sir Charles Grandison,* S. Richardson.
CLEOPATRA, Queen, *Antony and Cleopatra,* W. Shakespeare; *Caesar and Cleopatra,* G. Bernard Shaw; *All For Love,* John Dryden.
CLINKER, Humphry, *Humphry Clinker,* Tobias Smollett.
CLISSOLD, William, *The World of William Clissold,* H. G. Wells.
CLOTEN, *Cymbeline,* W. Shakespeare.
CODLIN, *The Old Curiosity Shop,* Charles Dickens.
COGIA HOUSSAIN, *Ali Baba and The Forty Thieves* (*Arabian Nights' Entertainment*).
COLLINS, Rev. Mr., *Pride and Prejudice,* Jane Austen.
COMUS, *Comus,* John Milton.
CONINGSBY, *Coningsby,* Benjamin Disraeli.
CONSTANCE, *King John,* W. Shakespeare; *Marmion,* Sir Walter Scott.
COPHETUA, *The Beggar Maid,* Lord Tennyson.
COPPERFIELD, David, *David Copperfield,* Charles Dickens.
CORDELIA, *King Lear,* W. Shakespeare.
CORIOLANUS (Caius Marcius), *Coriolanus,* W. Shakespeare.
COSTARD, *Love's Labour's Lost,* W. Shakespeare.
COVERLEY, Sir Roger de, *The Spectator,* J. Addison.
CRASHAW, Mr., *The Captives,* Sir Hugh Walpole.
CRATCHIT, Bob, *A Christmas Carol,* Charles Dickens.
CRAWLEY, Sir Pitt, *Vanity Fair,* W. M. Thackeray.
CREAKLE, Mr., *David Copperfield,* Charles Dickens.
CRESSIDA, *Troilus and Cressida,* W. Shakespeare.
CRICHTON, The Admirable, see **Admirable Crichton.**
CROSSWAITE, *Alton Locke,* Charles Kingsley.
CRUSOE, Robinson, *Adventures of Robinson Crusoe,* Daniel Defoe.
CRYSEYDE, *Troylus and Cryseyde,* G. Chaucer.
CUTTLE, Captain, *Dombey and Son,* Charles Dickens.
CYMBELINE, *Cymbeline,* W. Shakespeare.
DAGONET, Sir, *Morte d'Arthur,* Sir T. Malory; *Idylls of the King,* Lord Tennyson; *Henry IV,* W. Shakespeare.
DAKERS, Jonathan, *My Brother Jonathan,* F. Brett Young.
DALGETTY, Dugald, *The Legend of Montrose,* Sir Walter Scott.
DANDIE DINMONT, *Guy Mannering,* Sir Walter Scott.
DARKE, Amber, *The House in Dormer Forest,* Mary Webb.
DARLING (Family), *Peter Pan,* Sir James Barrie.
DARNAY, Charles, *A Tale of Two Cities,* Charles Dickens.
DEANS, Jeanie, *The Heart of Midlothian,* Sir Walter Scott.
DEFARGE, Madame, *A Tale of Two Cities,* Charles Dickens.
DERONDA, *Daniel Deronda,* George Eliot.
DESDEMONA, *Othello,* W. Shakespeare.
DESERT, Wilfred, *Flowering Wilderness,* John Galsworthy.
DESPAIR, Giant, *The Pilgrim's Progress,* John Bunyan.
DIANA OF THE CROSSWAYS, see **Merion.**
DICK, Mr., *The Heart of Midlothian; The Fair Maid of Perth,* Sir Walter Scott; *David Copperfield,* Charles Dickens.
DIMMESDALE, Rev. Arthur, *The Scarlet Letter,* Nathaniel Hawthorne.
DINAH, *Uncle Tom's Cabin,* Harriet Beecher Stowe.
DISHART, Gavin, *The Little Minister,* Sir James Barrie.
DIVER, Jenny, *The Beggar's Opera,* John Gay.
DIX, Mr., *Thirteen Travellers,* Sir Hugh Walpole.
DOBBIN, Colonel, *Vanity Fair,* W. M. Thackeray.
DODD, Captain, *Hard Cash,* Charles Reade.
DOGBERRY, *Much Ado About Nothing,* W. Shakespeare.
DOMBEY, Mr., *Dombey and Son,* Charles Dickens.
DON JUAN, *Don Juan,* Lord Byron.
DOOLITTLE, Eliza, *Pygmalion,* G. Bernard Shaw.
DOONE, Lorna, *Lorna Doone,* R. D. Blackmore.
DORA, *David Copperfield,* Charles Dickens.
DROMIO, *The Comedy of Errors,* W. Shakespeare.
DROOD, Edwin, *The Mystery of Edwin Drood,* Charles Dickens.
DURWARD, Quentin, *Quentin Durward,* Sir Walter Scott.
DUVAL, Denis, *Denis Duval,* W. M. Thackeray.
EARLFORWARD, Mr., *Riceyman Steps,* Arnold Bennett.
EARNSHAW, Catherine, *Wuthering Heights,* Emily Brontë.
EDGAR, *King Lear,* W. Shakespeare; *The Bride of Lammermoor,* Sir Walter Scott.
EDITH, *The Lord of the Isles,* Sir Walter Scott.
EGEUS, *A Midsummer Night's Dream,* W. Shakespeare.
EGLANTINE, Madame, *The Canterbury Tales,* G. Chaucer.
ELAINE, *Morte d'Arthur,* Sir T. Malory; *Idylls of the King,* Lord Tennyson.
EMILIA, *The Canterbury Tales,* G. Chaucer; *The Winter's Tale,* W. Shakespeare; *The Adventures of Peregrine Pickle,* Tobias Smollett.
EM'LY, Little, *David Copperfield,* Charles Dickens.
EMMA, see **Woodhouse.**
ENID, *Idylls of the King,* Lord Tennyson.
EPPIE, *Silas Marner,* George Eliot.
ESMOND, Beatrix and Henry, *Esmond,* W. M. Thackeray.
EVELINA (Belmont), see **Belmont.**
EVERDENE, Bathsheba, *Far From the Madding Crowd,* T. Hardy.
EYRE, Jane, *Jane Eyre,* Charlotte Brontë.
FAG, *The Rivals,* R. B. Sheridan.
FAGIN, *Oliver Twist,* Charles Dickens.
FAIRSERVICE, Andrew, *Rob Roy,* Sir Walter Scott.

FAITHFUL, *The Pilgrim's Progress*, John Bunyan.
FAITHFUL, Jacob, *Jacob Faithful*, Captain Marryat.
FALSTAFF, Sir John, *Henry IV*; *Henry V*; *The Merry Wives of Windsor*, W. Shakespeare.
FAT BOY, The, *The Pickwick Papers*, Charles Dickens.
FAUSTUS, Dr., *Dr. Faustus*, Christopher Marlowe.
FENTON, *The Merry Wives of Windsor*, W. Shakespeare.
FERDINAND, *The Tempest*, W. Shakespeare.
FEVEREL, Richard, *The Ordeal of Richard Feverel*, George Meredith.
FINN, Huckleberry, *Huckleberry Finn*, Mark Twain.
FLAMING TINMAN, The, *Lavengro*, George Borrow.
FLANDERS, Moll, *Moll Flanders*, Daniel Defoe.
FLEMING, Marjorie, *Rab and his Friends*, John Brown.
FLIBBERTIGIBBET, *Kenilworth*, Sir Walter Scott.
FLORIMEL, *The Faerie Queene*, Edmund Spenser.
FLORIZEL, *The Winter's Tale*, W. Shakespeare.
FORD, *The Merry Wives of Windsor*, W. Shakespeare.
FORSYTE, Fleur, etc., *The Forsyte Saga*, John Galsworthy.
FOSCO, Count, *The Woman in White*, Wilkie Collins.
FRANKENSTEIN, *Frankenstein*, Mary Shelley.
FRIAR TUCK, *Ivanhoe*, Sir Walter Scott.
FRIDAY, Man, *Adventures of Robinson Crusoe*, Daniel Defoe.
GALAHAD, Sir, *Morte d'Arthur*, Sir T. Malory.
GALATEA, *Pygmalion and Galatea*, Sir W. S. Gilbert; *Philaster, or Love Lies a-bleeding*, Beaumont and Fletcher.
GAMP, Sarah, *Martin Chuzzlewit*, Charles Dickens.
GARETH, Sir, *Idylls of the King*, Lord Tennyson.
GARGERY, Joe, *Great Expectations*, Charles Dickens.
GARVALD, Andrew, *Salute to Adventurers*, John Buchan.
GAWAIN, Sir, *Morte d'Arthur*, Sir T. Malory.
GEIERSTEIN, Anne of, *Anne of Geierstein*, Sir Walter Scott.
GELLATLEY, Davie, *Waverley*, Sir Walter Scott.
GERAINT, Sir, *Idylls of the King*, Lord Tennyson.
GERARD, *The Cloister and the Hearth*, Charles Reade.
GERARD, Brigadier, *The Exploits of Brigadier Gerard*, Sir A. Conan Doyle.
GIAOUR, The, *The Giaour*, Lord Byron.
GILPIN, John, *The Diverting History of John Gilpin*, W. Cowper.
GLORIANA, *The Faerie Queene*, Edmund Spenser.
GLOVER, Catherine, *The Fair Maid of Perth*, Sir Walter Scott.
GLUMDALCLITCH, *Gulliver's Travels*, Jonathan Swift.
GOBBO, Launcelot, *The Merchant of Venice*, W. Shakespeare.
GOLSPIE, Mr., *Angel Pavement*, J. B. Priestley.
GONERIL, *King Lear*, W. Shakespeare.
GORDON, Lord George, *Barnaby Rudge*, C. Dickens.
GRADGRIND, Thomas, *Hard Times*, Charles Dickens.
GRANTLY, Dr., *The Warden* and other Barchester novels, Anthony Trollope.
GRATIANO, *The Merchant of Venice; Othello*, W. Shakespeare.
GRAY, Dorian, *The Picture of Dorian Gray*, Oscar Wilde.
GREATHEART, Mr., *The Pilgrim's Progress*, John Bunyan.
GRESHAM, Mr., *Dr. Thorne*, Anthony Trollope.
GREY, Vivian, *Vivian Grey*, Benjamin Disraeli.
GRIM, Giant, *The Pilgrim's Progress*, John Bunyan.
GRISELDA, *The Canterbury Tales*, G. Chaucer.
GRUNDY, Mrs., *Speed the Plough*, Thomas Morton.
GUEST, Philip, *The Mill on the Floss*, George Eliot.
GUIDO, Franceschini, *The Ring and the Book*, Robert Browning.
GUINEVERE, *Idylls of the King*, Lord Tennyson.
GULLIVER, Lemuel, *Gulliver's Travels*, Jonathan Swift.
GUMMIDGE, Mrs., *David Copperfield*, Charles Dickens.
GUPPY, Mr., *Bleak House*, Charles Dickens.
GURTH, *Ivanhoe*, Sir Walter Scott.
GUYON, Sir, *The Faerie Queene*, Edmund Spenser.
GYNT, Peer, *Peer Gynt*, Henrik Ibsen.
HAIDÉE, *Don Juan*, Lord Byron.
HALCOMBE, Marian, *The Woman in White*, Wilkie Collins.
HAMLET, *Hamlet, Prince of Denmark*, W. Shakespeare.
HANDY ANDY, *Handy Andy*, Samuel Lover.
HARDCASTLE, Kate and Squire, *She Stoops to Conquer*, Oliver Goldsmith.
HARDING, Mr., *The Warden*, Anthony Trollope.
HARLOWE, Clarissa, *Clarissa Harlowe*, Samuel Richardson.
HAROLD, Childe, *Childe Harold's Pilgrimage*, Lord Byron.
HAROUN-AL-RASCHID, *Arabian Nights' Entertainment*.
HARRINGTON, Evan, *Evan Harrington*, George Meredith.
HARRIS, Mrs., *Martin Chuzzlewit*, Charles Dickens.
HARRIS, *Three Men in a Boat*, Jerome K. Jerome.
HARTRIGHT, Walter, *The Woman in White*, Wilkie Collins.
HASSAN, *Hassan*, J. Elroy Flecker.
HATCH, Jack, *Our Village*, Mary Russell Mitford.
HATCHWAY, Lieutenant, *The Adventures of Peregrine Pickle*, Tobias Smollett.
HATTER, The Mad, *Adventures of Alice in Wonderland*, Lewis Carroll.
HATTERAICK, Dirk, *Guy Mannering*, Sir Walter Scott.
HAVISHAM, Miss, *Great Expectations*, Charles Dickens.
HAWK, Sir Mulberry, *Nicholas Nickleby*, Charles Dickens.
HEATHCLIFF, *Wuthering Heights*, Emily Brontë.
HEATHEN CHINEE, The, *The Heathen Chinee*, Bret Harte.
HEDDA GABLER, *Hedda Gabler*, Henrik Ibsen.
HEEP, Uriah, *David Copperfield*, Charles Dickens.
HELENA, *All's Well that Ends Well; A Midsummer Night's Dream*, W. Shakespeare.
HELSTONE, Mr., *Shirley*, Charlotte Brontë.
HEREWARD THE WAKE, *Hereward the Wake*, Charles Kingsley.
HERMIA, *A Midsummer Night's Dream*, W. Shakespeare.
HERMIONE, *The Winter's Tale*, W. Shakespeare.
HERO, *Much Ado About Nothing*, W. Shakespeare.
HERON, Sir George, *The Monastery*, Sir Walter Scott.
HERRIES, Francis, *Rogue Herries*, Sir Hugh Walpole.
HIAWATHA, *Hiawatha*, H. W. Longfellow.
HIERONIMO, *Hieronimo; The Spanish Tragedy*, Thomas Kyd.
HIGGINS, Henry, *Pygmalion*, G. Bernard Shaw.
HIPPOLYTA, *A Midsummer Night's Dream*, W. Shakespeare.
HOBBINOL, *The Shepheard's Calender*, Edmund Spenser.
HODGE, *Gammer Gurton's Needle*, John Still; *The Shoemaker's Holiday*, Thomas Dekker.
HOLMES, Sherlock, *The Adventures of Sherlock Holmes*, etc., Sir A. Conan Doyle.
HOLT, Felix, *Felix Holt, the Radical*, George Eliot.
HONEYCOMB, Will, *The Spectator*, J. Addison.
HONEYMAN, Charles, *The Newcomes*, W. M. Thackeray.
HONEYWOOD, *The Good-Natured Man*, Oliver Goldsmith.
HOOD, Robin, *The Foresters*, Lord Tennyson; *Robin Hood*, Ritson; *Ivanhoe; The Talisman*, Sir Walter Scott.
HOOK, Captain, *Peter Pan*, Sir J. M. Barrie.
HOPEFUL, *The Pilgrim's Progress*, John Bunyan.
HORATIO, *Hamlet, Prince of Denmark*, W. Shakespeare.
HOUYHNHNMS, *Gulliver's Travels*, J. Swift.
HUDIBRAS, *Hudibras*, Samuel Butler.
HUNTER, Mrs. Leo, *The Pickwick Papers*, Charles Dickens.

HYDE, Mr., *The Strange Case of Dr. Jekyll and Mr. Hyde,* R. L. Stevenson.
HYPATIA, *Hypatia,* Charles Kingsley.
IACHIMO, *Cymbeline,* W. Shakespeare.
IAGO, *Othello,* W. Shakespeare.
IDA, *The Princess,* Lord Tennyson.
IMOGEN, *Cymbeline,* W. Shakespeare.
INGOLDSBY, Tom, *The Ingoldsby Legends,* R. H. Barham.
IRAS, *Antony and Cleopatra,* W. Shakespeare; *Cleopatra,* Sir H. Rider Haggard.
ISAAC OF YORK, *Ivanhoe,* Sir Walter Scott.
ISABELLA, *Measure for Measure,* W. Shakespeare.
ISEULT, *Tristram and Iseult,* Matthew Arnold.
ITHURIEL, *Paradise Lost,* John Milton.
IVANHOE, *Ivanhoe,* Sir Walter Scott.
JACQUELINE DE BROYANT, *Flower of the Lily,* Baroness Orczy.
JACQUES, *As You Like It,* W. Shakespeare.
JARLEY, Mrs., *The Old Curiosity Shop,* Charles Dickens.
JARNDYCE, Mr., *Bleak House,* Charles Dickens.
JARVIE, Baillie Nicol, *Rob Roy,* Sir Walter Scott.
JASPER, Old, *The Monastery,* Sir Walter Scott.
JEEVES, *My Man Jeeves,* P. G. Wodehouse.
JEKYLL, Dr., *The Strange Case of Dr. Jekyll and Mr. Hyde,* R. L. Stevenson.
JELLYBY, Mrs., *Bleak House,* Charles Dickens.
JENKINS, Deborah, Matilda and Peter, *Cranford,* Mrs. Gaskell.
JENKINS, Winifred, *Humphry Clinker,* Tobias Smollett.
JENKINSON, Ephraim, *The Vicar of Wakefield,* Oliver Goldsmith.
JENNY (Diver), see **Diver.**
JEREMY, *Jeremy,* Sir Hugh Walpole.
JESSICA, *The Merchant of Venice,* W. Shakespeare.
JINGLE, Alfred, *The Pickwick Papers,* Charles Dickens.
JOAN, Saint, *Saint Joan,* G. Bernard Shaw.
JONES, Tom, *Tom Jones,* H. Fielding.
JORKINS, Mr., *David Copperfield,* Charles Dickens.
JORROCKS, Mr., *Handley Cross,* Robert Surtees.
JUDE, *Jude the Obscure,* Thomas Hardy.
JULIET, *Romeo and Juliet,* W. Shakespeare.
KATHARINA, *The Taming of the Shrew,* W. Shakespeare.
KAY, Sir, *Idylls of the King,* Lord Tennyson.
KETTLE, Captain, in various sea stories by C. J. Cutcliffe Hyne.
KIM, *Kim,* Rudyard Kipling.
KIPPS, Arthur, *Kipps,* H. G. Wells.
KNIGHTLY, Mr., *Emma,* Jane Austen.
KUBLA KHAN, *Kubla Khan,* S. T. Coleridge.
LADY OF SHALOTT, The, *The Lady of Shalott,* Lord Tennyson.
LADY OF THE LAKE, The, *The Lady of the Lake,* Sir Walter Scott.
LAERTES, *Hamlet,* W. Shakespeare.
LANCELOT, *Idylls of the King,* Lord Tennyson.
LANG, Thammas, *Auld Licht Idylls,* Sir J. M. Barrie.
LANGUISH, Lydia, *The Rivals,* R. B. Sheridan.
LAPUTA, *Gulliver's Travels,* J. Swift; *Prester John,* John Buchan.
LATIMER, Darsie, *Redgauntlet,* Sir Walter Scott.
LAURENCE, Friar, *Romeo and Juliet,* W. Shakespeare.
LEAR, King, *King Lear,* W. Shakespeare.
LEATHERSTOCKING, *The Pioneers,* J. Fenimore Cooper.
LEIGH, Amyas, *Westward Ho!,* Charles Kingsley.
LEIGH, Aurora, *Aurora Leigh,* E. Barrett Browning.
LESSWAYS, Hilda, *Hilda Lessways,* Arnold Bennett.
LEWIS, Alison, see **Alison Lewis.**
LEWISHAM, Mr., *Love and Mr. Lewisham,* H. G. Wells.
LIGHTFOOT, Martin, *Hereward the Wake,* Charles Kingsley.
LISMAHAGO, Lieutenant Obadiah, *Humphry Clinker,* Tobias Smollett.
LITTLE BILLEE, *Little Billee,* W. M. Thackeray; *Trilby,* George du Maurier.
LITTLE DORRIT, *Little Dorrit,* Charles Dickens.
LITTLE-ENDIANS, *Gulliver's Travels,* J. Swift.
LITTLE NELL, *The Old Curiosity Shop,* Charles Dickens.
LOB, *Dear Brutus,* Sir J. M. Barrie.
LOCKE, Alton, *Alton Locke,* Charles Kingsley.
LOCHINVAR, *Marmion,* Sir Walter Scott.
LOCKIT, *The Beggar's Opera,* John Gay.
LORD Jim, *Lord Jim,* Joseph Conrad.
LORENZO, *The Merchant of Venice,* W. Shakespeare.
LOTHARIO, *The Fair Penitent,* Nicholas Rowe.
LOVELACE, Robert, *Clarissa Harlowe,* Samuel Richardson.
LUMPKIN, Tony, *She Stoops to Conquer,* Oliver Goldsmith.
LYDIATT, Clare, *Portrait of Clare,* F. Brett Young.
LYSANDER, *A Midsummer Night's Dream,* W. Shakespeare.
MAB, *Queen Mab,* P. B. Shelley.
MACBETH, *Macbeth,* W. Shakespeare.
MACCHOAKUMCHILD, *Hard Times,* Charles Dickens.
MACDUFF, *Macbeth,* W. Shakespeare.
MACGREGOR, Rob Roy, *Rob Roy,* Sir Walter Scott.
MACHEATH, Captain, *The Beggar's Opera,* John Gay.
MAID MARIAN, *The Foresters,* Lord Tennyson; *Polyolbion,* Michael Drayton; *Maid Marian,* T. Love Peacock.
MALAPROP, Mrs., *The Rivals,* R. B. Sheridan.
MALFI, The Duchess of, *The Duchess of Malfi,* John Webster.
MALVOLIO, *Twelfth-Night,* W. Shakespeare.
MAMMON, Sir Epicure, *The Alchemist,* Ben Jonson.
MANETTE, Dr., *A Tale of Two Cities,* Charles Dickens.
MANNERING, Guy, *Guy Mannering,* Sir Walter Scott.
MANTALINI, Alfred, *Nicholas Nickleby,* Charles Dickens.
MARCHIONESS, The, *The Old Curiosity Shop,* Charles Dickens.
MARGARET, *The Cloister and the Hearth,* Charles Reade.
MARIA, *The School for Scandal,* R. B. Sheridan.
MARIANA, *Measure for Measure,* W. Shakespeare; *The Miser,* H. Fielding; *Mariana,* Lord Tennyson.
MARINA, *Pericles,* W. Shakespeare.
MARK ANTONY, *Julius Caesar; Antony and Cleopatra,* W. Shakespeare; *All For Love,* J. Dryden; *Caesar and Cleopatra,* G. Bernard Shaw.
MARLEY, *A Christmas Carol,* Charles Dickens.
MARLOW, *She Stoops to Conquer,* Oliver Goldsmith.
MARMION, *Marmion,* Sir Walter Scott.
MARNER, Silas, *Silas Marner,* George Eliot.
MAZEPPA, *Mazeppa,* Lord Byron.
MEPHISTOPHELES, *Dr. Faustus,* Christopher Marlowe.
MERCUTIO, *Romeo and Juliet,* W. Shakespeare.
MERION, Diana, *Diana of the Crossways,* George Meredith.
MERLIN, *Idylls of The King,* Lord Tennyson.
MERRILEES, Meg, *Guy Mannering,* Sir Walter Scott.
MICAWBER, Wilkins, *David Copperfield,* Charles Dickens.
MIGGS, Miss, *Barnaby Rudge,* Charles Dickens.
MINNEHAHA, *Hiawatha,* H. W. Longfellow.
MIRANDA, *The Tempest,* W. Shakespeare.
MIRIAM, *History of Mr. Polly,* H. G. Wells.
MONIPLIES, Richie, *The Fortunes of Nigel,* Sir Walter Scott.
MONT, Sir Lawrence, *Flowering Wilderness,* John Galsworthy.
MORGANHURST, Miss, *Thirteen Travellers,* Sir Hugh Walpole.
MORGAN LA FÉE, *Morte d'Arthur,* Sir T. Malory; *Earthly Paradise,* W. Morris.
MORGIANA, *Ali Baba and The Forty Thieves* (*Arabian Nights' Entertainment*).
MORLAND, Catherine, *Northanger Abbey,* Jane Austen.
MORRIS, Dinah, *Adam Bede,* George Eliot.
MOWGLI, *The Jungle Books,* Rudyard Kipling.
MOZE, Audrey, *The Lion's Share,* Arnold Bennett.
MURDSTONE, Edward and Jane, *David Copperfield,* Charles Dickens.
NANCY, *Oliver Twist,* Charles Dickens.

NARCISSA, *The Adventures of Roderick Random,* Tobias Smollett.
NEMO, Captain, *Bleak House,* Charles Dickens.
NEWCOME, Colonel Thomas, *The Newcomes,* W. M. Thackeray.
NICKLEBY, Nicholas, *Nicholas Nickleby,* Charles Dickens.
NIGEL, Lord, *The Fortunes of Nigel,* Sir Walter Scott.
NOGGS, Newman, *Nicholas Nickleby,* Charles Dickens.
NYM, Corporal, *Henry V; The Merry Wives of Windsor,* W. Shakespeare.
OAK, Gabriel, *Far From The Madding Crowd,* T. Hardy.
OAKROYD, Jess, *The Good Companions,* J. B. Priestley.
OBERON, *A Midsummer Night's Dream,* W. Shakespeare.
OCHILTREE, Edie, *The Antiquary,* Sir Walter Scott.
O'FERRALL, Trilby, see **Trilby.**
OGILVY, Gavin, *The Little Minister,* Sir J. M. Barrie.
OLDBUCK, *The Antiquary,* Sir Walter Scott.
OLD MORTALITY, see **Paterson.**
OLIVER, *As You Like It,* W. Shakespeare.
OLIVIA, *Twelfth-Night,* W. Shakespeare; *The Vicar of Wakefield,* Oliver Goldsmith.
OMAR KHAYYÁM, *The Rubáiyát of Omar Khayyám,* Edward Fitzgerald (translator).
OPHELIA, *Hamlet,* W. Shakespeare.
ORLANDO, *As You Like It,* W. Shakespeare.
ORVILLE, Lord, *Evelina,* Fanny Burney.
OSBALDISTONE, Frank, *Rob Roy,* Sir Walter Scott.
O'SHANTER, Tam, *Tam O'Shanter,* Robert Burns.
OTHELLO, *Othello,* W. Shakespeare.
OVERREACH, Sir Giles, *A New Way to Pay Old Debts,* Philip Massinger.
PAGE, Ann and Mr., *The Merry Wives of Windsor,* W. Shakespeare.
PALAMON, *The Canterbury Tales,* G. Chaucer.
PAN, Peter, *Peter Pan,* Sir J. M. Barrie.
PANDARUS, *Troylus and Cryseyde,* G. Chaucer; *Troilus and Cressida,* W. Shakespeare.
PANGLOSS, Dr., *The Heir-at-Law,* George Colman.
PARIS, Judith, and Vanessa, *The Fortress; Judith Paris; Vanessa,* Sir Hugh Walpole.
PARSON ADAMS, see **Adams.**
PAUL PRY, *A Comedy,* John Poole.
PATERSON, Robert, *Old Mortality,* Sir Walter Scott.
PATTERNE, Sir Willoughby, *The Egoist,* George Meredith.
PEACHUM, Polly, *The Beggar's Opera,* John Gay.
PECKSNIFF, Mr., *Martin Chuzzlewit,* Charles Dickens.
PEGGOTTY, Daniel, *David Copperfield,* Charles Dickens.
PENDENNIS, *Pendennis,* W. M. Thackeray.
PERDITA, *The Winter's Tale,* W. Shakespeare.
PERRIN, Mr., *Mr. Perrin and Mr. Traill,* Sir Hugh Walpole.
PETRUCHIO, *The Taming of the Shrew,* W. Shakespeare.
PEW, *Treasure Island,* R. L. Stevenson.
PICKWICK, Samuel, *The Pickwick Papers,* Charles Dickens.
PIED PIPER, *The Pied Piper of Hamelin,* R. Browning.
PINCH, Tom, *Martin Chuzzlewit,* Charles Dickens.
PINKERTON, The Misses, *Vanity Fair,* W. M. Thackeray.
PIP, *Great Expectations,* Charles Dickens.
PIPES, Tom, *The Adventures of Peregrine Pickle,* Tobias Smollett.
PIPPA, *Pippa Passes,* R. Browning.
PISTOL, *Henry IV; Henry V; The Merry Wives of Windsor,* W. Shakespeare.
PODSNAP, *Our Mutal Friend,* Charles Dickens.
POLLY, Alfred, *The History of Mr. Polly,* H. G. Wells.
POLONIUS, *Hamlet,* W. Shakespeare.
POMPILIA, *The Ring and the Book,* R. Browning.
PORTIA, *The Merchant of Venice,* W. Shakespeare.
POYSER, Mrs., *Adam Bede,* George Eliot.
PRETTYMAN, Miss, *Mrs. Caudle's Curtain Lectures,* Douglas Jerrold.
PRIG, Betsy, *Martin Chuzzlewit,* Charles Dickens.
PRIMROSE, Dr., *The Vicar of Wakefield,* Oliver Goldsmith.
PRISM, Miss, *The Importance of Being Earnest,* Oscar Wilde.
PROSPER le Gai, *The Forest Lovers,* Maurice Hewlett.
PROSPERO, *The Tempest,* W. Shakespeare.
PROUDIE, Mrs., *Barchester Towers,* A. Trollope.
PRYNNE, Hester, *The Scarlet Letter,* Nathaniel Hawthorne.
PUCK, *A Midsummer Night's Dream,* W. Shakespeare.
PUFF, *The Critic,* R. B. Sheridan.
PUJOL, Aristide, *The Joyous Adventures of Aristide Pujol,* W. J. Locke.
PYGMALION, *The Earthly Paradise,* W. Morris.
QUATERMAIN, Allan, *She,* etc., Sir H. Rider Haggard.
QUICKLY, Mistress, *Henry IV; Henry V; The Merry Wives of Windsor,* W. Shakespeare.
QUILP, Daniel, *The Old Curiosity Shop,* Charles Dickens.
QUIN, Auberon, *The Napoleon of Notting Hill,* G. K. Chesterton.
QUINCE, Peter, *A Midsummer Night's Dream,* W. Shakespeare.
QUINNEY, Joe, *Quinneys,* H. A. Vachell.
QUIRK, Thady, *Castle Rackrent,* Maria Edgworth.
RAINGO, Lord, *Lord Raingo,* Arnold Bennett.
RANDOM, Roderick, *The Adventures of Roderick Random,* Tobias Smollett.
RASSELAS, *Rasselas,* Dr. Johnson.
RASSENDYLL, Rudolf, *The Prisoner of Zenda,* Anthony Hope.
RATTLIN, Jack, *The Adventures of Roderick Random,* Tobias Smollett.
RAVENSWOOD, Edgar of, *The Bride of Lammermoor,* Sir Walter Scott.
REBECCA, *Ivanhoe,* Sir Walter Scott.
RED CROSS KNIGHT, The, *The Faerie Queene,* Edmund Spenser.
REDGAUNTLET, *Redgauntlet,* Sir Walter Scott.
REDLAKE, Jim, *Jim Redlake,* F. Brett Young.
REDLAW, *The Haunted Man,* Charles Dickens.
REGAN, *King Lear,* W. Shakespeare.
RICHMOND, Harry, *The Adventures of Harry Richmond,* George Meredith.
RIDD, John, *Lorna Doone,* R. D. Blackmore.
RIMA, *Green Mansions,* W. H. Hudson.
RIP VAN WINKLE, *The Sketch Book,* Washington Irving.
ROB ROY, see **Macgregor.**
ROBSART, Amy, *Kenilworth,* Sir Walter Scott
ROCHESTER, Mr., *Jane Eyre,* Charlotte Brontë.
RODERICK DHU, *The Lady of the Lake,* Sir Walter Scott.
ROMEO, *Romeo and Juliet,* W. Shakespeare.
ROMOLA, *Romola,* George Eliot.
RONDER, Canon, *The Cathedral,* Sir Hugh Walpole.
ROSALIND, *As You Like It,* W. Shakespeare.
ROSAMOND, *Woodstock,* Sir Walter Scott.
ROSE, Mary, *Mary Rose,* Sir J. M. Barrie.
ROWENA, *Ivanhoe,* Sir Walter Scott.
RUDGE, Barnaby, *Barnaby Rudge,* Charles Dickens.
RUSTUM, *Sohrab and Rustum,* Matthew Arnold.
SADDLETREE, Mr., *The Heart of Midlothian,* Sir Walter Scott.
SALVATION YEO, *Westward Ho!,* Charles Kingsley.
SAMPHIRE, Archibald and Mark, *The Brothers,* H. A. Vachell.
SAMPSON, Dominic, *Guy Mannering,* Sir Walter Scott.
SARN, Prue and Reuben, *Precious Bane,* Mary Webb.
SAWYER, Bob, *The Pickwick Papers,* Charles Dickens.
SAWYER, Tom, *The Adventures of Tom Sawyer; Huckleberry Finn,* Mark Twain.
SCHEHERAZADE, *Arabian Nights' Entertainment.*

SCROOGE, Ebenezer, *A Christmas Carol*, Charles Dickens.
SEBASTIAN, *Twelfth-Night*, W. Shakespeare.
SEYTON, Catherine, *The Abbot*, Sir Walter Scott.
SHADOW, Simon, *Henry IV* (2), W. Shakespeare.
SHALLOW, Mr. Justice, *Henry IV; The Merry Wives of Windsor*, W. Shakespeare.
SHANDY, Tristram, *Tristram Shandy*, Laurence Sterne.
SHARP, Becky, *Vanity Fair*, W. M. Thackeray.
SHE, *She*, Sir H. Rider Haggard.
SHROPSHIRE LAD, The, *The Shropshire Lad*, A. E. Housman.
SHYLOCK, *The Merchant of Venice*, W. Shakespeare.
SIKES, Bill, *Oliver Twist*, Charles Dickens.
SILENCE, *Henry IV*, W. Shakespeare.
SILVER, Long John, *Treasure Island*, R. L. Stevenson.
SINBAD, *Sinbad the Sailor* (*Arabian Nights' Entertainment*).
SKEGGS, Miss, *The Vicar of Wakefield*, Oliver Goldsmith.
SLENDER, *The Merry Wives of Windsor*, W. Shakespeare.
SLIPSLOP, Mrs., *Joseph Andrews*, H. Fielding.
SLOP, Dr., *Tristram Shandy*, L. Sterne.
SLY, Christopher, *The Taming of the Shrew*, W. Shakespeare.
SMIKE, *Nicholas Nickleby*, Charles Dickens.
SNAKE, Mr., *The School for Scandal*, R. B. Sheridan.
SNEERWELL, Lady, *The School for Scandal*, R. B. Sheridan.
SNODGRASS, Augustus, *The Pickwick Papers*, Charles Dickens.
SNOWE, Lucy, *Villette*, Charlotte Brontë.
SNUBBIN, Mr. Serjeant, *The Pickwick Papers*, Charles Dickens.
SORREL, Hetty, *Adam Bede*, George Eliot.
SOUTH, Marty, *The Woodlanders*, Thomas Hardy.
SPENLOW, Mr., *David Copperfield*, Charles Dickens.
SQUEERS, Wackford, *Nicholas Nickleby*, Charles Dickens.
STALKY, *Stalky and Co.*, Rudyard Kipling.
STANDISH, Miles, *The Courtship of Miles Standish*, H. W. Longfellow.
STEENSON, Willie (Wandering Willie), *Redgauntlet*, Sir Walter Scott.
STEERFORTH, James, *David Copperfield*, Charles Dickens.
STELLA, In Sonnets by Sir P. Sidney; *Journal to Stella*, Jonathan Swift.
STEWART, Alan Breck, *Kidnapped; Catriona*, R. L. Stevenson.
STEYNE, Marquis of, *Vanity Fair*, W. M. Thackeray.
STIGGINS, Rev. Mr., *The Pickwick Papers*, Charles Dickens.
STRICKLAND, Charles, *The Moon and Sixpence*, W. Somerset Maugham.
STRULDBRUGS, *Gulliver's Travels*, Jonathan Swift.
SUDDLECHOP, Benjamin and Dame Ursula, *Fortunes of Nigel*, Sir W. Scott.
SUMMERSON, Esther, *Bleak House*, Charles Dickens.
SURFACE, Charles, *The School for Scandal*, R. B. Sheridan.
SWIVELLER, Dick, *The Old Curiosity Shop*, Charles Dickens.
TANQUERAY, Paula, *The Second Mrs. Tanqueray*, Sir A. W. Pinero.
TAPLEY, Mark, *Martin Chuzzlewit*, Charles Dickens.
TAPPERTIT, Simon, *Barnaby Rudge*, Charles Dickens.
TEAZLE, Lady, *The School for Scandal*, R. B. Sheridan.
TESS, *Tess of the D'Urbervilles*, Thomas Hardy.
TEUFELSDRÖCKH, Herr, *Sartor Resartus*, Thomas Carlyle.
THISBE, *A Midsummer Night's Dream*, W. Shakespeare.
THORNE, Dr., *Dr. Thorne*, Anthony Trollope.
THORNHILL, Squire, *The Vicar of Wakefield*, Oliver Goldsmith.
THORPE, Isabella, *Northanger Abbey*, Jane Austen.
TITANIA, *A Midsummer Night's Dream*, W. Shakespeare.
T'KNOWHEAD'S BELL, *Auld Licht Idylls*, Sir James M. Barrie.
TOAD OF TOAD HALL, *The Wind in the Willows*, Kenneth Grahame.
TOBY, *Tristram Shandy*, Laurence Sterne.
TOM, Uncle, *Uncle Tom's Cabin*, Harriet Beecher Stowe.
TOPSY, *Uncle Tom's Cabin*, Harriet Beecher Stowe.
TOUCHSTONE, *As You Like It*, W. Shakespeare.
TRAILL, Mr., *Mr. Perrin and Mr. Traill*, Sir Hugh Walpole.
TRELAWNY, Rose, *Trelawny of the Wells*, Sir A. W. Pinero.
TRILBY (O'Ferrall), *Trilby*, George du Maurier.
TRIM, Corporal, *Tristram Shandy*, Laurence Sterne.
TRISTRAM, *Tristram and Iseult*, Matthew Arnold.
TROILUS, *Troilus and Cressida*, W. Shakespeare.
TROYLUS, *Troylus and Cryseyde*, G. Chaucer.
TRUNNION, Commodore, *The Adventures of Peregrine Pickle*, Tobias Smollett.
TULKINGTON, Mr., *Bleak House*, Charles Dickens.
TULLIVER, Maggie and Tom, *The Mill on the Floss*, George Eliot.
TUPMAN, Mr., *The Pickwick Papers*, Charles Dickens.
TWEEDLEDUM AND TWEEDLEDEE, *Through the Looking Glass*, Lewis Carroll.
TWIST, Oliver, *Oliver Twist*, Charles Dickens.
TYBALT, *Romeo and Juliet*, W. Shakespeare.
UMSLOPOGAAS, Zulu hero of *Allan Quatermain*, Sir H. Rider Haggard.
UNA, *The Faerie Queene*, Edmund Spenser.
VALENTINE, *The Two Gentlemen of Verona; Twelfth-Night*, W. Shakespeare.
VANESSA, see **Paris.**
VARDEN, Dolly, *Barnaby Rudge*, Charles Dickens.
VATHEK, *Vathek*, William Beckford (translator).
VERGES, *Much Ado About Nothing*, W. Shakespeare.
VERNON, Diana, *Rob Roy*, Sir Walter Scott.
VERONICA, Ann, *Ann Veronica*, H. G. Wells.
VIOLA, *Twelfth-Night*, W. Shakespeare.
VIVIEN, *Idylls of the King*, Lord Tennyson.
VYE, Eustacia, *The Return of the Native*, Thomas Hardy.
WADMAN, Widow, *Tristram Shandy*, Laurence Sterne.
WALSINGHAM, Helen, *Kipps*, H. G. Wells.
WARDLE, Mr., *The Pickwick Papers*, Charles Dickens.
WARREN, Mrs., *Mrs. Warren's Profession*, G. Bernard Shaw.
WARRINGTON, George, *Pendennis*, W. M. Thackeray.
WATERS, Esther, *Esther Waters*, George Moore.
WATSON, Dr., *The Adventures of Sherlock Holmes*, Sir A. Conan Doyle.
WEARY WARLD, *The Little Minister*, Sir James Barrie.
WEGG, Silas, *Our Mutual Friend*, Charles Dickens.
WELLER, Sam and Tony, *The Pickwick Papers*, Charles Dickens.
WEMMICK, *Great Expectations*, Charles Dickens.
WENDY (Darling), *Peter Pan*, Sir James Barrie.
WESTERN, Sophia and Squire, *Tom Jones*, Henry Fielding.
WIFE OF BATH, *The Canterbury Tales*, G. Chaucer.
WILDFIRE, Madge, *The Heart of Midlothian*, Sir Walter Scott.
WILLIE, Wandering, *Redgauntlet*, Sir Walter Scott.
WINDERMERE, Lady, *Lady Windermere's Fan*, Oscar Wilde.
WINKLE, Nathaniel, *The Pickwick Papers*, Charles Dickens.
WINTERBOURNE, Giles, *The Woodlanders*, Thomas Hardy.
WOODHOUSE, Emma, *Emma*, Jane Austen.
YAHOOS, *Gulliver's Travels*, J. Swift.
YEOBRIGHT, Clem and Thomasin, *The Return of the Native*, Thomas Hardy.
YORICK, *Hamlet*, W. Shakespeare; *Tristram Shandy*, Laurence Sterne.
ZULEIKA, *The Bride of Abydos*, Lord Byron.

FAMOUS NAMES IN ART

Examples of the work of an artist are printed in italic type

ADAM, Robert (1728–1792) and James (d. 1794), British architects and designers. *Terrace of the Adelphi, London*; *Screen and Gate of the Admiralty, London.*

ADAMS, Wayman (Born 1883), American painter. Portraits of *Booth Tarkington* and *James W. Riley.*

AGASIAS (1st century B.C.), Greek sculptor. *The Borghesi Warrior.*

ALBERTINELLI, Mariotti (1474–1515), Florentine painter. *Christ Appearing to the Magdalen.*

ALTDORFER, Albrecht (1480–1538), German painter. *Suzanna Bathing.*

APELLES (4th century B.C.), Greek painter. Legendary works: *Artemis with a Chorus of Maidens, Aphrodite Rising out of the Sea.*

BAKST, Leon (1866–1924), Russian painter and designer. *Scenery for the Russian Ballets produced by Diaghilev.*

BARRAS, Louis Ernest (1841–1901), French sculptor. *Foundation of Marseilles, Nature Disrobing.*

BARTHOLDI, Frederic A. (1844–1904), French sculptor. *Statue of Liberty,* New York.

BARYE, Antoine Louis (1796–1875), French sculptor. *The Centaur and Lapith, Jaguar Devouring a Hare.*

BEARDSLEY, Aubrey Vincent (1872–1898), English black and white artist. *The Reward of the Dancer*; Frontispiece to *Volpone*; Illustrations to *Morte d'Arthur, The Rape of the Lock, The Yellow Book.*

BEECHEY, Sir William (1753–1839), English painter. *Joseph Nollekens.*

BELLINI, Gentile (1429–1507), Venetian painter. *Procession on the Piazzo San Marco, Preaching of St. Mark at Alexandria.*

BELLINI, Giovanni (1430–1516), Venetian painter. *Doge Lorenzo Loredano*; *Madonna of the Alberetti.*

BENOIST, Guillaume Philippe (1725–1800), French line-engraver. *Sir Isaac Newton, Jupiter and Juno.*

BERNINI, Giovanni Lorenzo (1598–1680), Italian architect and sculptor. *Apollo and Daphne.*

BLAKE, William (1757–1827), English artist. *Nebuchadnezzar, Newton, Oberon and Titania;* Illustrations to *Songs of Innocence, The Book of Job,* etc.

BOLOGNA, Giovanni da (1524–1608), Flemish sculptor. *Mercury, Rape of the Sabines.*

BONINGTON, Richard Parkes (1801–1828), English painter. *Henry IV and the Spanish Ambassador, Francis I and the Duchesse d'Étampes,* Normandy *landscapes.*

BONNART, Robert (1652–1729), French engraver. *The Entrance of the Queen into Arras.*

BOSCH, Jerome (c. 1460–1516), Dutch painter. *The Last Judgment, Adoration of the Magi.*

BOTTICELLI, Sandro (1444–1510), Italian painter. *The Birth of Venus, Primavera.*

BOUCHARDON, Edme (1698–1762), French sculptor. *Hercules.*

BOUCHER, François (1703–1770), French painter. *Venus and Vulcan.*

BOURDELLE, Antoine (1861–1929), French sculptor. Busts in bronze of *Ingres* and others.

BRANGWYN, Sir Frank (Born 1867), English painter and etcher. *Canada's War Record,* in Parliament Building in Winnipeg.

BRAQUE, Georges (Born 1881), French painter. *Still Life, Femmes au Piano.*

BREUGHEL, Peter (the elder) (1525–1569), Flemish painter. *The Village Wedding, The Hunters.*

BROUWER, Adrian (c. 1606–1638), Flemish painter. *The Village Inn.*

BROWN, Ford Madox (1821–1893), English painter. *The Last of England, Work.*

BRUNELESCHI, Filippo (1377–1446), Florentine sculptor and architect. *Dome* of the *Cathedral of Santa Maria del Fiore, Florence.*

BRZESKA, Gaudier (1891–1915), French-Polish sculptor. *Torso,* busts of *Brodzky, Enid Bagnold,* etc.

BUONINSEGNA, Duccio di (1260–1320), Italian painter. *High-altar piece* in the *Cathedral of Siena, Madonna and Child with Saints and Angels.*

BURNE-JONES, Sir Edward (1833–1898), English painter. *King Cophetua and the Beggar Maid.*

CALLCOTT, Sir Augustus Wall (1779–1844), English painter. *Milton Dictating his Poems to his Daughters.*

CALLOT, Jacques (1592–1635), French engraver. *Miseries of War, Temptation of St. Anthony.*

CANALETTO, Antonio (1697–1768), Venetian painter. *View on the Grand Canal, Venice.*

CANO, Alonso (1601–1667), Spanish painter and sculptor. *St. Bruno.*

CANOVA, Antonio (1757–1822), Italian sculptor. Cenotaph of *Clement XIII* in St. Peter's Cathedral, Rome; *Perseus with the Head of Medusa.*

CARPACCIO, Vittorio (c. 1455–c. 1522), Venetian painter. *Dream of St. Ursula.*

CARPEAUX, Jean Baptiste (1827–1875), French sculptor. *Fountain* in the *Jardin du Luxembourg, Paris.*

CARRACCI, Agostino (c. 1557–1602), Bolognese painter. *Last Communion of St. Jerome.*

CARRACCI, Annibale (c. 1560–1609), Bolognese painter. *Christ and the Woman of Samaria.*

CASSATT, Mary (1855–1926), American artist. Studies of mothers and children.

CAZIN, Jean Charles (1841–1901), French painter. *Tobias.*

CELLINI, Benvenuto (1500–1571), Florentine sculptor. *Diana, Perseus.*

CÉZANNE, Paul (1839–1906), French painter. *Portrait of Madame Cézanne, The Bathers, Mount Saint Victoire,* studies in still life.

CHAMPAIGNE, Philippe de (1602–1674), Belgian painter. *The Dead Christ.*

CHARDIN, Jean Baptiste (1699–1779), French painter. *The Housewife, Boy with a Top,* studies in still life.

CHARLET, Nicolas (1792–1845), French painter. *The Grenadier.*

CHAVANNES, Puvis de (1824–1898), French mural painter. *St. Géneviève Watching Paris.*

CHIPPENDALE, Thomas (c. 1718–1779), English furniture designer and cabinet-maker. Furniture in Harewood House and Nostell Priory, Yorkshire.

CHIRICO, Giorgio di, Contemporary Italian painter. *Composition, Deux Chevaux.*

CIMABUE, Cenni (c. 1240–c. 1301), Florentine painter. *The Virgin Enthroned.*

CONSTABLE, John (1776–1837), English painter. *Flatford Mill, Salisbury Cathedral, The Cornfield, The Hay Wain.*

COPLEY, John S. (1738–1815), American painter. *Death of Lord Chatham.*

COQUES, Gonzales (1618–1684), Flemish painter. *The Verhelst Family.*

COROT, Jean Baptiste (1796–1875), French painter. *Une Matinée, The Cathedral of Chartres, The Road to Arras, The Belfry of Douai.*

CORREGGIO, Antonio (1494–1534), Parmese painter. *Mercury and Venus.*

COTMAN, John Sell (1782–1842), English painter and etcher. *Greta Bridge, Yorkshire, Wherries on Breydon.*

COURBET, Gustave (1819–1877), French painter. *Burial at Ornans, The Wave.*

CRANACH, Lucas (1472–1553), German painter. *Rest of the Virgin during the Flight into Egypt, Albert, Elector of Mainz.*

CRANE, Walter (1845–1915), English painter. *The Lady of Shalott, La Belle Dame Sans Merci.*

CROME, John (1769–1821), English painter. *The Porringland Oak.*

CUYP, Albert (1620–1691), Dutch painter. *Riders with the Boy and Herdsman, Piper with Cows.*

DALI, Salvador (Born 1904), Spanish painter. *Suburbs of the Paranoiac-Critical Town.*

DAVID, Gerard (1460–1523), Flemish painter. *Judgment of Cambyses, Adoration of the Magi.*

DAVID, Jacques Louis (1748–1825), French painter. *The Coronation of Napoleon I, Madame Rècamier.*

DAUBIGNY, Charles F. (1817–1878), French painter. *Windmills at Dordrecht.*

DAUMIER, Honoré (1808–1879), French painter and caricaturist. *Third-Class Railway Carriage, Don Quixote and Sancho Panza,* Caricatures in *Le Charivari.*

DEGAS, Edgar (1834–1917), French painter. *Robert le Diable, Dancers, Woman at her Toilet.*

DELACROIX, Eugène (1798–1863), French painter. *Massacre of Chios, Entry of the Crusaders into Constantinople, Liberty Leading the People.*

DELAROCHE, Paul (1797–1856), French painter. *Death of the Duke of Guise.*

DERAIN, André (Born 1880), French painter. *Three Trees, Camillo.*

DE WINT, Peter (1784–1849), English water-colourist. Landscapes.

DIAZ (de la Pena) (1808–1876), French painter. *The Road.*

DOMENICHINO, Zampieri (1581–1641), Italian painter. *The Communion of St. Jerome, Adam and Eve.*

DONATELLO (1386–1466), Florentine sculptor. *David, Judith.*

DUBOIS, Paul (1829–1905), French sculptor and painter. *Narcissus, Eve, The Florentine Singer,* Portrait group of the *Artist's Children.*

DÜRER, Albrecht (1471–1520), German painter and engraver. *Self-portrait, Adoration of the Magi, Melancolia.*

DYCK, Anthony Van (1599–1641), Flemish painter. *King Charles I in Hunting Attire.*

EPSTEIN, Jacob (Born 1880), English sculptor. *Rima* (W. H. Hudson Memorial), *Day and Night,* portrait busts.

ETTY, William (1787–1849), English painter. *Youth at the Prow and Pleasure at the Helm, Cleopatra's Arrival in Cilicia.*

EYCK, Hubert Van (1366–1426), Flemish painter. Part of the *Altarpiece of the Sacred Lamb,* Cathedral of Ghent.

EYCK, Jan Van (1385–1441), Flemish painter. *Madonna of the Chancellor Rollin.*

FABRITIUS, Carel (1624?–1654), Dutch painter. *Goldfinch.*

FANTIN-LATOUR, Ignace H. T. (1836–1904), French artist. *Hommage a Delacroix, Un Coin de Table, Autour du Piano.*

FILDES, Sir Luke (1844–1927), English painter. *The Doctor.*

FLAXMAN, John (1755–1826), English sculptor. *Mercury and Pandora.*

FRA ANGELICO (1387–1455), Florentine painter. *Frescoes* in the *Museo di San Marco,* Florence.

FRA FILIPPO LIPPI (c. 1406–1469), Florentine painter. *Virgin Adoring the Child.*

FRAGONARD, Jean Honoré (1732–1806), French painter. *The Swing.*

FRANCESCA, Piero della (c. 1418–1492), Italian painter. *The Nativity.*

FRY, Roger Elliot (1866–1934), English painter and critic. Landscapes.

GAINSBOROUGH, Thomas (1727–1788), English painter. *Mrs. Siddons, The Blue Boy, The Hay-Waggon, Gainsborough's Daughters.*

GAUGUIN, Paul (1848–1903), French painter. *Jacob and the Angel, Tahitiennes.*

GERARD, François (1770–1837), French painter. *Isabey and His Daughter.*

GÉRICAULT, Jean (1791–1824), French painter. *Officier de Chasseurs à Cheval, Radeau de la Méduse.*

GHIBERTI, Lorenzo (1378–1455), Florentine sculptor. *Doors of the Baptistery,* Florence.

GIBBONS, Grinling (1648–1721), English sculptor. *Charles II,* Carvings in St. Paul's Cathedral.

GILL, Eric Rowland (1882–1940), English sculptor and engraver. *Mother and Child, Christ Driving the Moneylenders out of the Temple.*

GIORGIONE (c. 1478–1510), Italian painter. *Three Philosophers, The Sleeping Venus, Pastoral Symphony.*

GIOTTO, Da Bondone (1267–1337), Italian painter. *Frescoes* at Assisi and Padua of the *Legends of St. Francis.*

GOGH, Vincent Van (1853–1890), Dutch painter. *Sunflowers, L'Arlésienne, View of Arles.*

GOUJON, Jean (c. 1520–c. 1566), French sculptor. Carvings of part of the *Court of the Louvre, Paris.*

GOYA, Francisco (1746–1828), Spanish painter and etcher. *The Family of Charles IV, Maja Desnuda, Disasters of War.*

GOYEN, Jan Van (1596–1656), Dutch painter. *View of the Hague.*

GRANT, Duncan (Born 1885), Scottish painter. Portrait of *Pamela Fry.*

GRECO, El (1542–1614), Spanish painter. *Christ Driving the Money Changers from the Temple, Burial of Count Orgaz* (Toledo).

GREUZE, Jean Baptiste (1725–1805), French painter. *The Broken Pitcher, The Village Bride.*

GRÜNEWALD, Mathias (Active between 1500 and 1530), German painter. *Altarpiece* in the Colmar Museum, *The Crucifixion.*

GUARDI, Francesco (1712–1793), Venetian painter. *Masquerade in the Ridotto, Reception Room in a Convent.*

GUERCINO, Giovanni Francesco Barbieri (1591–1666), Italian painter. *St. Petronilla, The Annunciation.*

HALS, Frans (c. 1581–1666), Dutch painter. *The Laughing Cavalier, The Jester, The Lute Player.*

HARUNOBU, Suzoki (1725–1770), Japanese painter. *The Basin of Red Fish, Horseman on a Bridge Talking to a Woman.*

HELST, Bartholomaeus Van Der (1613–1670), Dutch painter. *The Peace of Münster.*

HILLIARD, Lawrence (d. 1640), English miniature painter. Portraits.

HIROSHIGE, Andro (1797–1858), Japanese painter. *Moonlit Landscape.*

HOBBEMA, Meindert (1638–1709), Dutch painter. *The Avenue at Middelharnois.*

HOGARTH, William (1697–1764), English painter. *The Rake's Progress, Marriage à la Mode, The Shrimp Girl.*

HOKUSAI, K. (1760–1849), Japanese painter. *Travellers, The Wave.*

HOLBEIN, Hans (c. 1497–1543), German painter. *Henry VIII, Erasmus, The Ambassadors.*

HOMER, Winslow (1836–1910), American painter. *Prisoners from the Front, The Voice from the Cliffs.*

HOOCH, Pieter de (1629–c. 1677), Dutch painter. *Courtyard of a Dutch House.*

HOPPNER, John (1758–1810), English painter. *Princess Sophia.*

HOUDON, Jean Antoine (1741–1828), French sculptor. *Diana.*

HUNT, W. Holman (1827–1910), English painter. *The Light of the World, The Scapegoat.*

INGRES, Jean A. D. (1780–1867), French painter. *Odalisque with a Slave, La Source, Apotheosis of Homer.*

ISABEY, Jean B. (1767–1855), French painter. *The First Consul in the Park at Malmaison.*

JOHN, Augustus (Born 1879), British painter. *Smiling Woman, Madame Suggia.*

JONES, Inigo (1573–1651), English architect. *Palace of Whitehall, Designs for Masques.*

JONGKIND, Johann Barthold (1819–1891), Dutch painter and engraver. Landscapes of Paris, Normandy coast, and Dutch canals.

JORDAENS, Jacob (1593–1678), Flemish painter. *The Four Evangelists.*

KAUFFMAN, Angelica (1741–1807), French painter. *Leonardo Expiring in the Arms of Francis I.*

KEENE, Charles (1823–1891), Black and white artist. Drawings for *The Illustrated London News* and *Punch.*

KLEE, Paul (Born 1879), Swiss painter. *Wintergarten.*

KNELLER, Sir Godfrey (1646–1723), Anglo-German painter. Portraits of *Charles II, James II, Queen Anne,* and *William and Mary.*

KORIN, Ogata (c. 1657–1716), Japanese painter.

FAMOUS NAMES IN MUSIC

Examples of the work of a composer are printed in italic type

ALBÉNIZ, Isaac (1860–1909), Spanish composer. *Iberia Suite.*

ALFANO, Franco (b. 1876), Italian operatic composer. *Madonna Imperia.*

ALLEN, Sir Hugh Percy (b. 1869), English conductor.

ALWYN, William (b. 1905), English composer. *Concerto Grossi.*

ANTHEIL, George (b. 1900), Polish-American composer. *Ballet Mécanique.*

ARDITI, Luigi (1822–1903), Italian conductor and composer. *Il Bacio* (*The Kiss*).

ARNE, Michael (1740–1786), English composer. *The Lass With the Delicate Air.*

ARNE, Thomas Augustine (1710–1778), English composer. *Where the Bee Sucks.*

ATKINS, Sir Ivor Algernon (b. 1869), English composer. *Hymn of Faith*: Edition of Bach's *St. Matthew Passion* (with Sir Edward Elgar).

AUBER, Daniel François Esprit (1782–1871), French operatic composer. *Fra Diavolo.*

AUBERT, Louis François Marie (b. 1877), French composer. *Habanera.*

BACH, Johann Sebastian (1685–1750), German composer and organist. *St. Matthew Passion; Chromatic Fantasia and Fugue; Brandenburg Concerto No. 2 in F Major.*

BADARZEWSKA, Thekla (1838–1862), Polish composer. *The Maiden's Prayer.*

BALAKIREF, Mily (1837–1910), Russian composer. *Thamar* (symphonic poem).

BALFE, Michael William (1808–1870), English operatic composer. *The Bohemian Girl.*

BANTOCK, Sir Granville (b. 1868), English composer. *Omar Khayyam; "Hebridean" Symphony.*

BARBIROLLI, John (b. 1899), English conductor.

BARTÓK, Béla (b. 1881), Hungarian composer. *The Wooden Prince* (ballet).

BAX, Sir Arnold Edward Trevor (b. 1883), English composer and Master of the King's Musick. *Tintagel.*

BEECHAM, Sir Thomas (b. 1879), English conductor.

BEETHOVEN, Ludwig van (1770–1827), German composer. *Fidelio; Concerto No. 5 in E Flat ("The Emperor"); Symphony No. 5 in C Minor; "Moonlight" Sonata.*

BENNETT, Sterndale (1816–1875), English composer. *The May Queen* (cantata).

BENOÎT, Peter Léopold Léonard (1834–1901), Belgian composer. *The Children's Oratorio; Rubens Cantata.*

BERKELEY, Lennox (b. 1903), English composer. *Jonah* (oratorio).

BERLIN, Irving (b. 1888), American composer. *Alexander's Rag-time Band.*

BERLIOZ, Louis Hector (1803–1869), French composer. *Symphonie Fantastique; Le Carnival Romain; Hamlet.*

BISHOP, Thomas Brigham (nineteenth century), American composer. *John Brown's Body.*

BIZET, Georges (1838–1875), French composer. *L'Arlésienne; Carmen.*

BLISS, Arthur (b. 1891), English composer. *Colour Symphony; Checkmate* (ballet).

BLOCH, Ernest (b. 1880), Swiss composer. *Macbeth.*

BORODIN, Alexander (1833–1887), Russian composer. *Prince Igor; Symphony No. 2 in B Minor.*

BOUGHTON, Rutland (b. 1878), English composer. *The Immortal Hour.*

BOULT, Sir Adrian (b. 1889), English conductor.

BRAHMS, Johannes (1833–1897), German composer. *Symphony No. 1 in C Minor; Piano Concerto; Hungarian Dances.*

BRITTEN, Edward Benjamin (b. 1913), English composer. *Ballad for Heroes; Peter Grimes.*

BRUCH, Max (1838–1920), German conductor and composer. *Violin Concerto in G Minor.*

BRÜCKNER, Anton (1824–1896), Austrian composer. *Mass in F Minor; Te Deum in C Major.*

BUCK, Sir Percy Carter (b. 1871), English composer and writer of books on music.

BÜLOW, Hans Guido von (1830–1894), German conductor and pianist.

BURLEIGH, Cecil (b. 1885), American composer and violinist. *Violin Concerto.*

BUSH, Alan Dudley (b. 1900), English composer. *Piano Concerto; Dance Overture.*

BUTT, Dame Clara (1873–1936), English contralto.

BYRD, William (1542–1623), English composer of church music.

CARUSO, Enrico (1873–1921), Italian operatic tenor.

CASALS, Pablo (b. 1876), Spanish violoncellist.

CHABRIER, Alexis Emmanuel (1841–1894), French composer. *Le Roi Malgré Lui* (*King Despite Himself*)*; España.*

CHADWICK, George Whitefield (1854–1931), American composer. *Melpomene; Judith.*

CHALIAPIN, Fedor (1873–1938), Russian operatic bass.

CHAMINADE, Cécile (b. 1861), French composer and pianist. *Concerto for Piano and Orchestra.*

CHOPIN, Frédéric François (1810–1849), Polish composer and pianist. *Polonaise; Minute Waltz; Funeral March.*

CIMAROSA, Domenico (1749–1801), Italian operatic composer. *The Secret Marriage.*

COATES, Albert (b. 1882), English conductor and composer. *Samuel Pepys; Pickwick.*

COATES, Eric (b. 1886), English composer. *London Suite.*

COLERIDGE-TAYLOR, Samuel (1875–1912), British composer. *Hiawatha's Wedding Feast; Orchestral Ballad in A Minor.*

CORTOT, Alfred (b. 1877), French pianist.

COWARD, Noel (b. 1899), English composer. *Bitter Sweet; Cavalcade.*

DALE, Benjamin James (b. 1885), English composer. *Piano Sonata in D Minor.*

DARGOMIJSKY, Alexander (1813–1869), Russian composer. *Esmeralda.*

DAVIES, Sir Henry Walford (1869–1941), British composer and Master of the King's Musick. *Everyman* (oratorio).

DEBUSSY, Claude Achille (1862–1918), French composer. *L'Après Midi d'un Faune; Pelléas et Mélisande.*

DELIBES, Clément Leo (1836–1891), French composer. *Coppélia* (ballet) ; *Lakmé* (opera).

DELIUS, Frederick (1862–1934), English composer. *On Hearing the First Cuckoo in Spring; Florida Suite.*

D'INDY, Vincent (1851–1931), French conductor and composer. *Summer Day on the Mountain.*

DOHNÁNYI, Ernst von (b. 1877), Hungarian composer. *Variations on a Nursery Song* (*for Pianoforte and Orchestra*).

DONIZETTI, Gaetano (1797–1848), Italian operatic composer. *Don Pasquale; Lucia di Lammermoor.*

DUKAS, Paul (1865–1935), French composer. *The Sorcerer's Apprentice.*

DUNHILL, Thomas Frederick (b. 1877), English composer. *Tantivy Towers.*

DVOŘÁK, Antonín (1841–1904), Czech composer. *New World Symphony; Slavonic Dances for Pianoforte Duet.*

EDWARDS, Richard (1523–1566), English composer of madrigals.

ELGAR, Sir Edward (1857–1934), English composer and Master of the King's Musick. *Enigma Variations; Dream of Gerontius* (oratorio) ; *Cockaigne* (overture).

FALLA, Manuel de (b. 1876), Spanish composer. *The Three-cornered Hat.*

FAURÉ, Gabriel Urbain (1845–1924), French composer. *Penelope.*

FRANCK, César Auguste (1822–1890), French composer. *Symphonic Variations for Piano and Orchestra.*

GALLI-CURCI, Amelita (b. 1889), Italian operatic soprano.

GERMAN, Sir Edward (1862–1936), English composer. *Merrie England.*

GERSHWIN, George (1898–1937), American composer. *Rhapsody in Blue; Porgy and Bess.*

GIGLI, Beniamino (b. 1890), Italian operatic tenor.

GLINKA, Michael (1804–1857), Russian operatic composer. *Russlan and Ludmilla.*

GLUCK, Christoph Willibald von (1714–1787), German operatic composer. *Orpheus and Eurydice.*

GOOSSENS, Eugène (b. 1893), English conductor and composer. *The Eternal Rhythm.*

GOUNOD, Charles François (1818–1893), French composer. *Faust; Meditation on Bach's Prelude in C; Romeo and Juliet.*

GRAINGER, Percy Aldridge (b. 1882), Australian pianist and composer. *Bridal Song; Molly on the Shore.*

GRANADOS, Enrique (1867–1916), Spanish composer. *Goyescas.*

GRIEG, Edvard Hagerup (1843–1907), Norwegian composer. *Peer Gynt; Piano Concerto in A Minor.*

GRUENBERG, Louis (b. 1883), Russian pianist and composer. *The Emperor Jones.*

HALLE, Adam de la (1230–1287), French poet-composer and song writer. *The Play of Robin and Marion.*

HALLÉ, Sir Charles (1819–1895), German pianist and conductor, settled in England and founded the Hallé Orchestra.

HANDEL, George Frederic (1685–1759), German composer. *Messiah* (oratorio) ; *Dead March* (in *Saul*); *Water Music.*

HARRISON, Julius (b. 1885), English conductor.

HARTY, Sir Herbert Hamilton (1879–1941), English conductor.

HAYDN, Franz Joseph (1732–1809), German composer. *The Creation* (oratorio).

HELY-HUTCHINSON, Christian Victor (b. 1901), British composer and pianist.

HERBERT, Victor (1859–1924), American composer. *Madeleine.*

HESS, Dame Myra (b. 1891), British pianist.

HINDEMITH, Paul (b. 1895), German composer and viola player. *Violin Concerto.*

HOLST, Gustav Theodore (1874–1934), British composer. *The Planets.*

HONEGGER, Arthur (b. 1892), French composer. *King David; Semiramis.*

HUMPERDINCK, Engelbert (1854–1921), German composer. *Hänsel and Gretel.*

IRELAND, John (b. 1879), English composer. *These Things Shall Be; Sea Fever.*

JACOBSON, Maurice (b. 1896), English composer. *David* (ballet).

KREISLER, Fritz (b. 1875), Austrian violinist and composer.

LAMBERT, Constant (b. 1905), English conductor and composer. *Rio Grande.*

LÉHAR, Franz (b. 1870), German composer and violinist. *The Merry Widow; The Count of Luxembourg.*

LEHMANN, Elizabeth Nina Mary Frederika (1862–1918), English singer and composer.

LEONCAVALLO, Ruggiero (1858–1919), Italian composer. *La Bohème; Pagliacci.*

LIND, Jenny (1820–1887), Swedish soprano.

LISZT, Franz (1811–1886), Hungarian pianist and composer. *Hungarian Rhapsody.*

McCORMACK, Count John (b. 1884), Irish-American tenor.

MACDOWELL, Edward Alexander (1861–1908), American composer. *Woodland Sketches; Piano Sonata* ("*Tragica*").

McEWEN, Sir John Blackwood (b. 1868), Scottish composer. *Solway Symphony; Grey Galloway.*

MAHLER, Gustav (1860–1911), German composer and conductor. *The Song of the Earth.*

MASCAGNI, Pietro (1863-1945), Italian operatic composer. *Cavalleria Rusticana.*

MASSENET, Jules Émile Frédéric (1842–1912), French composer. *Salome; Neapolitan Scenes.*

MELBA, Dame Nellie (1861–1931), Australian operatic soprano.

MENDELSSOHN, Felix (1809–1847), German pianist and composer. *Italian Symphony; Elijah* (oratorio) ; *Spring Song; Bee's Wedding; Fingal's Cave Overture.*

MENUHIN, Yehudi (b. 1916), American violinist.

MOISEIWITSCH, Benno (b. 1890), British pianist.

MONTEVERDI, Claudio (1567–1643), Italian composer. *Orpheus* (opera).

MOZART, Wolfgang Amadeus (1756–1791), German composer. *The Magic Flute; Symphony in C* ("*Jupiter*"); *Eine Kleine Nachtmusik.*

MOUSSORGSKY, Modeste (1839–1881), Russian composer. *Boris Godunov; Pictures at an Exhibition; Night on a Bare Mountain.*

NOVELLO, Clara Anastasia (1818–1908), British singer.

NOVELLO, Ivor (b. 1894), British composer. *Keep the Home Fires Burning.*

OFFENBACH, Jacob (1819–1880), German operatic composer. *Tales of Hoffmann; Orpheus in the Underworld.*

PADEREWSKI, Ignacy Jan (1860–1941), Polish pianist and composer. *Minuet in A.*

PAGANINI, Niccolo (1784–1840), Italian violinist.

PARRY, Sir Charles Hubert (1848–1918), English composer. *Jerusalem.*

PATTI, Adelina (1843–1919), Italian soprano.

PERGOLESE, Giovanni (1710–1736), Italian composer. *La Serva Padrona.*

POUISHNOFF, Leff (b. 1891), Russian pianist.

PROKOFIEF, Serge (b. 1891), Russian pianist and composer. *Scythian Suite; Sarcasms.*

PUCCINI, Giacomo (1858–1924), Italian operatic composer. *La Bohème; Madame Butterfly; Turandot.*

PURCELL, Henry (1658–1695), English composer. *Dido and Aeneas; Lilliburlero.*

QUILTER, Roger (b. 1877), English composer. *Children's Overture; To Julia.*

RACHMANINOFF, Sergeï (1873–1943), Russian composer and pianist. *Piano Concerto No. 2 in C Minor; Prelude in C Sharp Minor.*

RAVEL, Maurice (1875–1937), French composer. *Daphnis and Chloë; Bolero.*

RIMSKY-KORSAKOF, Nicholas (1844–1908), Russian composer. *Scheherazade; Le Coq d'Or.*

ROBERTON, Sir Hugh (b. 1874), founder of the Glasgow Orpheus Choir.

ROBESON, Paul (b. 1898), American bass.

ROBINSON, Stanford (b. 1904), British conductor.

RONALD, Sir Landon (1873–1938), English composer and conductor. Incidental music to *The Garden of Allah.*

ROSSINI, Gioacchino Antonio (1792–1868), Italian composer. *The Barber of Seville; William Tell.*

RUBINSTEIN, Anton Gregor (1830–1894), Russian pianist and composer. *Melody in F.*

SAINT-SAËNS, Charles Camille (1835–1921), French composer. *Samson and Delilah; Danse Macabre.*

SARASATE, Pablo (1844–1908), Spanish violinist.

SARGENT, Malcolm (b. 1895), British conductor.

SCARLATTI, Alessandro (1659–1725), Italian composer. *Solo Cantata.*

SCHNABEL, Artur (b. 1882), Austrian pianist.

SCHÖNBERG, Arnold (b. 1874), Austrian composer. *Songs of Gurra; Concerto for Violin and Orchestra.*

SCHUBERT, Franz Peter (1797–1828), Austrian composer. *Unfinished Symphony; Rosamunde; Ave Maria.*

SCHUMANN, Robert Alexander (1810–1856), German composer. *Carnaval; Piano Concerto.*

SCRIABIN, Alexander (1872–1915), Russian composer and pianist. *Prometheus.*

SHARP, Cecil James (1859–1924), English composer. *Folk Songs of England.*

SHOSTAKOVICH, Dmitri (b. 1906), Russian composer. *October Symphony.*

SIBELIUS, Jean (b. 1865), Finnish composer. *The Swan of Tuonela; Finlandia; Symphony No. 1 in E Minor.*

SMETANA, Bedřich (1824–1884), Czech composer. *The Bartered Bride; My Fatherland.*

SMYTHE, Dame Ethel Mary (b. 1858), British composer. *The Wreckers; The Boatswain's Mate.*
SOUSA, John Philip (1856–1932), American composer and bandmaster. *The Stars and Stripes for Ever.*
STOKOWSKI, Leopold (b. 1882), Polish conductor.
STRAUSS, Johann (1825–1899), Viennese composer. *The Blue Danube; Die Fledermaus.*
STRAUSS, Oscar (b. 1870), Viennese composer. *The Chocolate Soldier.*
STRAUSS, Richard (b. 1864), German composer. *Till Eulenspiegel's Merry Pranks; Der Rosenkavalier* (opera).
STRAVINSKY, Igor (b. 1882), Russian composer. *Petroushka* (ballet) ; *Le Baiser de la Fée.*
SUGGIA, Guilhermina (b. 1888), Portuguese violoncellist.
SULLIVAN, Sir Arthur Seymour (1842–1900), British composer. (With W. S. Gilbert as librettist) *The Gondoliers; Iolanthe; The Mikado.*
SUPPÉ, Franz von (1819–1895), Dalmatian composer. *Poet and Peasant* (overture) ; *Boccaccio.*
TALLIS, Thomas (1505–1585), British composer of church music.
TCHAIKOWSKY, Peter (1840–1893), Russian composer. *Pianoforte Concerto in A Flat Minor; Symphony No. 5 in E Minor; Pathétique; The Sleeping Princess* (ballet) ; *Nut-cracker Suite.*
TETRAZZINI, Luisa (1871–1940), Italian operatic soprano.
TOSCANINI, Arturo (b. 1867), Italian conductor.
TOSTI, Sir Francesco Paolo (1846–1916), Italian composer. *Goodbye.*
VAUGHAN WILLIAMS, Ralph (b. 1872), British composer. *A Sea Symphony; Symphony No. 5 in D.*
VERDI, Giuseppe (1813–1901), Italian operatic composer. *La Traviata; Rigoletto; Il Trovatore.*
WAGNER, Richard (1813–1883), German composer. *Tannhauser; Lohengrin; The Mastersingers; The Nibelungs' Ring.*
WALTON, William Turner (b. 1902), British composer. *Façade; Sinfonia Concertante.*
WARLOCK, Peter (Philip Heseltine) (1894–1930), English composer and critic. *The Curlew; Serenade.*
WEBER, Carl Maria von (1786–1826), German composer. *Invitation to the Waltz.*
WEINGARTNER, Paul Felix (1863–1942), Dalmatian conductor.
WILBYE, John (1574–1638), British madrigal composer. *Adieu, Sweet Amaryllis; Sweet Honey-sucking Bees.*
WOOD, Haydn (b. 1882), British violinist and composer. *Roses of Picardy.*
WOOD, Sir Henry (1869–1944), British conductor, composer and arranger, educationist and founder of the Queen's Hall Promenade Concerts.

WELL-KNOWN CHARACTERS IN CLASSICAL MYTHOLOGY

Names printed in italics will be found as separate entries in their alphabetical order

ABSYRTUS, son of King Aeetes of Colchis, accompanied his sister, *Medea,* when she eloped with *Jason.* To delay her father's pursuit Medea killed Absyrtus and scattered his body piecemeal into the sea knowing that Aeetes would stay to gather the pieces.
ACAMAS went with *Diomedes* to Troy to demand *Helen's* return. He was one of the Greeks hidden in the Wooden Horse.
ACASTUS, son of King Pelias, took part in the Argonautic Expedition and in the *Calydonian Hunt.* His wife, *Hippolyte,* was in love with Peleus who scorned her. She thereupon accused him to her husband of dishonourable conduct. Acastus took Peleus's sword while he slept so that he would be defenceless against the *Centaurs.* The Centaur, Chiron, however, saved his life and Peleus, returning later, killed both Acastus and Hippolyte.
ACHILLES (Pelides), son of King Peleus and chief character in Homer's "Iliad." When only six years old he was able to overcome lions. His guardian, Chiron the Centaur, declared that Troy could not be taken without his help and that he would meet his death there. To keep Achilles safe, his mother disguised him as a girl and hid him away. She also dipped him into the *Styx,* from which he emerged immune to wounds except in the heel by which she had held him. *Odysseus* discovered his place of hiding and persuaded him to help the Greeks against Troy. He was killed in battle by an arrow from the bow of *Paris,* which struck his vulnerable heel.
ACIS, a river god, loved by *Galatea* and killed by his rival the Cyclops, *Polyphemus.*
ACTAEON, a famous huntsman who had fifty dogs. One day he intruded upon *Artemis* and her attendants while they bathed and was changed into a stag and killed by his own dogs.
ADMETUS, king of Pherae, made *Apollo* shepherd of his flocks when the god was sent to earth and by his generous treatment won Apollo's friendship. Later, with Apollo's help, he married *Alcestis.*
ADONIS, a handsome, young hunter loved by *Aphrodite,* who persisted, despite the wishes of the goddess, in pursuing his sport until he was killed by a wild boar. Aphrodite found him dead and caused his blood to give rise to the flower anemone.
AENEAS, son of Anchises and *Aphrodite,* and the hero of Vergil's epic the "Aeneid," was a great leader and took *Hector's* place when that hero fell in the Trojan War.
AGAMEMNON, with his brother, *Menelaus,* was driven out of Mycenae by Thyestes, the brother and murderer of their father, Atreus, king of Mycenae. He went to Sparta and there married *Clytemnestra.* Agamemnon later returned to Mycenae and recovered his throne. When *Helen,* wife of Menelaus, eloped with *Paris* to Troy Agamemnon became leader of the Greek expedition against that city. After the fall of Troy, *Cassandra,* daughter of King Priam, was taken captive by Agamemnon, but on his return home with her he was murdered by Clytemnestra and her lover, Aegisthus.
AJAX (i) One of the Greek heroes at the Siege of Troy. He was short in stature but very fleet of foot and possessed of great skill in archery. (ii) Son of Telamon, was bold and handsome and had several combats with *Hector.* He coveted the arms of *Achilles,* and when, after the latter's death, they were awarded to *Ulysses,* Ajax killed himself.
ALCESTIS, daughter of Pelias, was won in marriage by *Admetus,* who, with Apollo's help, was enabled to comply with her father's stipulation that the successful suitor for her hand should arrive in a chariot driven by wild beasts. When the time came for Admetus to die, Alcestis offered her life for his. Ultimately, however, *Heracles* successfully contended with Death for Admetus's life and restored him to Alcestis.
AMAZONS, a race of warlike maidens, who, in their youth, had their right breasts cut off to give them greater freedom to use the bow. Their queen, *Hippolyte,* was killed by *Heracles,* who undertook to carry off her magic girdle. *Theseus* also undertook an expedition against them and carried off their queen, Antiope, sister of Hippolyte. The Amazons invaded Attica but were defeated by Theseus in Athens.
AMOR, see **Eros.**
AMPHITRITE, wife of *Poseidon* and queen of the sea. Triton was the most famous of their children. When, later, Poseidon fell in love with *Scylla*

Amphitrite threw magic herbs into the stream where Scylla bathed and so caused her to be changed into a barking monster.

ANDROMEDA, daughter of Cepheus, king of Aethiopia, and *Cassiopea.* Because her mother claimed to be more beautiful than the Nereids, *Poseidon's* attendant nymphs, the sea god sent a sea monster to ravage their people. Andromeda was chained to a rock by the sea and offered as a sacrifice to the sea monster. *Perseus* killed the monster, turned Phineus, the maiden's betrothed, to stone by means of the *Gorgon's* head, and married Andromeda himself.

ANTAEUS, son of *Poseidon* and *Gaea,* a giant who was invincible only so long as he remained in contact with the earth. *Heracles* discovered this while wrestling with him, lifted him up and strangled him.

ANTIGONE, the daughter of Oedipus, king of Thebes. When her father was banished from his throne and became blind she accompanied him into exile, leading him about and begging in order to supply their needs until he died, when she returned to Thebes. There her two brothers were killed in a quarrel and the usurping king allowed one brother's body to be buried but not the other. Antigone defied this order and buried her brother's body with her own hands. For this disobedience she was condemned to be buried alive, and her lover, Haemon, the king's son, killed himself on her tomb.

APHRODITE (Roman counterpart, *Venus*), said to have been born of sea foam, was the goddess of beauty and love and mother of *Eros* (Cupid). She herself loved the mortals *Adonis* and Anchises and became the wife of *Hephaestus.* It was to her that *Paris* awarded the golden apple in the famous contest of beauty. Aphrodisiac festivals were held in her honour in various parts of Greece.

APOLLO, son of *Zeus.* He is described sometimes as the god of the sun, the god of healing and the god of poetry and music. For myths about him, see **Daphne** and **Hyacinthus.**

ARACHNE, a Lydian maiden who was so proud of her skill in weaving that she counted herself cleverer even than the goddess *Athena.* Athena agreed to a contest and wove a tapestry portraying the majesty of the gods. Arachne wove another in which she showed the unfaithfulness of *Zeus.* Although the maiden's work was more beautiful than that of the goddess, Athena tore it in pieces as a punishment for her irreverence to the gods, changed her into a spider, and left her suspended in the middle of her web.

ARCAS, son of *Zeus* and *Callisto.* His mother was changed into a bear by the jealous *Hera,* and at the request of Zeus the child was cared for by Maia, mother of *Hermes.* When he grew up, Arcas was hunting one day and followed a bear into the temple of Zeus, unaware that the bear was his mother. For going into the temple he could have suffered death, but Zeus placed both mother and son among the stars as the "Great Bear" and the "Little Bear."

ARES (Roman counterpart, *Mars*), an Olympian god and the son of *Zeus* and *Hera.* He was the god of war and was brutal and hard. In battle he had as his attendants, Deimos (Fear), Phobus (Terror), Eris (Strife), Cydoemos (Tumult) and Enyo (Destroyer of Cities).

ARGO, the ship, named after its builder, Argus, in which the *Argonauts* set sail with *Jason.*

ARGONAUTS, the Greek heroes who sailed with *Jason* in quest of the *Golden Fleece.*

ARIADNE, daughter of *Minos,* king of Crete, fell in love with *Theseus* when he came to Crete as one of the seven youths and seven maidens sent annually by Athens as tribute to her father and sacrifice to the *Minotaur* which inhabited the *Labyrinth* of Crete. By giving him a ball of string to unwind as he went into the Labyrinth so that he would be able to find his way back, Ariadne enabled Theseus to kill the Minotaur, and later to escape. Theseus took her with him, promising to marry her, but deserted her on the island of Naxos. *Dionysus* found her weeping there and married her, and *Zeus* gave her immortality.

ARTEMIS (Roman counterpart, Diana), daughter of *Zeus* and twin sister of *Apollo,* was the goddess of the chase and the hunt. She was a maiden divinity, never conquered by love, who demanded strict chastity from those who worshipped her. Artemisia was the festival held in her honour at Delphi.

ATALANTA, a beautiful princess who was nursed by a bear and acquired such great agility that she offered herself as a prize to any suitor who could outstrip her in a race. Hippomenes accepted the challenge and beat her by dropping golden apples one by one along the course, which Atalanta stopped to pick up.

ATHENE or **ATHENA,** also called *Pallas* (Roman counterpart, Minerva), was the daughter of *Zeus* and, as his favourite, shared power over storms. She was the goddess of wisdom, particularly in the art of war, and protected warlike heroes. The legend tells that before her birth Zeus swallowed her mother and that Athene, fully grown and clad in armour, sprang from the head of Zeus with a loud war cry.

ATLAS, one of the *Titans* who fought against the gods under *Zeus* for the overlordship of the world. After the defeat of the Titans, Atlas was placed in the west and condemned to support the heavens on his shoulders.

AUGEAS, a legendary Grecian king who was reputed to have had a stable with 3,000 oxen which had not been cleaned out for more than thirty years and the cleansing of which was one of the twelve labours *Heracles* had to perform for Eurystheus. Augeas was one of the *Argonauts* who sailed with *Jason* in search of the *Golden Fleece.*

BACCHUS, see **Dionysus.**

BAUCIS, see **Philemon.**

BOREAS, the north wind. The Roman name for it was Aquilo.

CALLISTO, see **Arcas.**

CALYDONIAN HUNT, a renowned enterprise in which Meleager led a number of Greek heroes to free his country, Calydonia, from the attacks of a wild boar.

CALYPSO, a nymph, daughter of *Atlas* and queen of the Island of Ogygia where *Odysseus* was shipwrecked. Falling in love with him she offered him immortality if he would remain with her. He refused, but she kept him with her for seven years until *Zeus* insisted that she release him. Calypso died of grief after his departure.

CASSANDRA, daughter of Priam and *Hecuba.* Her loveliness won her the devotion of *Apollo* who promised her the gift of prophecy if she would respond to his suit. She broke her promise and the god punished her by ensuring that no one would trust her, thus making her gift of prophecy useless.

CASSIOPEA, see **Andromeda.**

CENTAURS, a savage race of Thessaly who were addicted to wine, women and war, and in some legends reputed to be half man and half horse.

CEPHALUS, son of *Hermes* and Herse. One day while he was hunting, the goddess Eos, charmed by his beauty, carried him off. But he loved his wife, Procris, and scorned the advances of Eos. Hoping that Procris would not recognize him, Eos changed his appearance and sent him to her with gifts to test her love for him. Procris was about to yield to his suit when he confessed the trick. She fled to Crete where she joined *Artemis.* Later she, in turn, resolved to test the fidelity of Cephalus, and returned to her husband disguised as a boy and won his affection. A reconciliation followed, but she was killed accidentally by her husband.

CERBERUS, the three-headed dog with a mane and tail of serpents that guarded the entrance to *Hades.* *Orpheus* overcame him by the beauty of his music when seeking his wife, *Eurydice.* *Heracles* carried him off to Eurystheus, king of Mycenae, as one of his Twelve Labours.

CERES, see **Demeter.**

CHARON, the ferryman of *Hades* who rowed the dead across the river *Styx.*

CHARYBDIS, daughter of *Poseidon* and *Gaea*, stole some of *Heracles'* cattle and to punish her, *Zeus* transformed her into a monster and hurled her into the sea beneath the rock which thereafter bore her name. There she swallowed a large quantity of water three times a day and spat it forth again causing a dangerous whirlpool and wrecking any ship that sailed too near.

CHIMAERA, a monster whose forepart was lion, the middle goat, and the hind part dragon, and who breathed fire. Bellerophon was sent against her by Iobates, king of Lydia, that he might lose his life, but with the aid of the winged horse, *Pegasus*, he slew the monster.

CHLORIS, a nymph, the personification of Spring. Identified with Flora by the Romans.

CIRCE, a Sorceress whose island kingdom *Odysseus* visited in his wanderings. She changed his men into swine by forcing them to drink a magic potion. *Odysseus* made himself immune by means of a special herb, visited her palace, and forced her to restore his men.

CLYTEMNESTRA, the wife of *Agamemnon*. During the latter's absence in Troy she became the mistress of Aegisthus, who conspired with her to murder Agamemnon on his return home.

COMUS, god of mirth.

CRETAN BULL was captured by *Heracles* as one of his Twelve Labours.

CRONUS (Roman counterpart, Saturn), youngest son of *Uranus* and *Gaea*. He ruled over the Golden Age of the world when the earth, unaided by man, produced everything he required in abundance, and all was peace, happiness and content. To prevent the fulfilment of the prophecy that he would be overthrown by his offspring as he had overthrown his father, Uranus, he swallowed his children. One of them, *Zeus*, escaped this fate, however, and eventually became ruler of the universe.

CYCLOPES, sons of *Uranus* and *Gaea*, were immensely strong, one-eyed giants, the most famous being *Polyphemus*.

CUPID, CUPIDO, see **Eros.**

DANAE, see **Perseus.**

DANAIDES, the name given to the fifty daughters of Danaus, who escaped with their father from Libya to Argos from the fifty sons of Aegyptus, who claimed the land ruled by Danaus. The men followed the maidens and Danaus gave his consent to marriage between them after obtaining from his daughters their promise to kill their husbands on their wedding night. All but Hypermnestra kept this promise. The Danaides, with their father, were afterwards killed by Lynceus, husband of Hypermnestra, and suffered further punishment after death by having perpetually to pour water into a perforated vessel.

DAPHNE, daughter of the river god, Peneus. Attracted by her beauty, *Apollo* pursued her, but just as he was about to capture her, she prayed for power to escape him and was turned into a laurel tree.

DELPHIC ORACLE, the oracle of *Apollo* at Delphi.

DEMETER (Roman counterpart, Ceres), mother of *Persephone*, was one of the twelve chief Grecian deities, the great mother-goddess of agriculture.

DEUCALION married *Pyrrha*, daughter of his uncle, *Epimetheus*. When *Zeus* destroyed the human race by flood, Deucalion built a chest in which he and Pyrrha floated for nine days and nights. They landed on Mount Parnassus and there received a message from Zeus to say that one of their wishes would be granted. Deucalion asked that the human race might be restored. He was told that he and his wife must throw behind them the bones of their mother. They decided that these referred to the stones of mother earth. From those thrown by Deucalion there came men, and from those of Pyrrha, women.

DIANA, see **Artemis.**

DIDO, founder and queen of Carthage, built for herself a funeral pyre which she mounted when her passionate love for *Aeneas* was unrequited.

DIOMEDES, a king of Thrace who fed his horses with the strangers who visited his land. *Heracles,* while performing one of his Twelve Labours, fed Diomedes to the horses and took them to his task-master, Eurystheus.

DIONYSUS, also known as *Bacchus* (Roman counterpart, Liber), the god of wine ; see **Ariadne.**

ECHO, a lovely nymph who, by talking constantly, kept *Hera* away from *Zeus* while he was amusing himself with the nymphs. She fell in love with *Narcissus* but he scorned her love and she pined away until she was only a voice.

ELYSIUM, or the Elysian Fields in the Islands of the Blest, home of the virtuous dead in the nether world, where life was painless and passive.

EPIMETHEUS, whose name indicates afterthought, and to whom *Zeus* sent *Pandora*, whom he accepted at once and without thought as his wife. See **Pandora.**

ERIS (Roman counterpart, Discordia), the goddess of Discord who always caused people to quarrel. Because of this reputation she was the only deity not invited to the marriage of Peleus and Thetis, father and mother of *Achilles*. Angry at being treated thus she threw among the guests the Apple of Discord. On this apple were the words "For the Fairest," and this led to the Judgment of *Paris*, and ultimately to the Trojan War.

EROS (Roman counterpart, Cupid, Amor), the god of love and one of the first beings to arise from Chaos. Afterwards Eros was conceived as the son of *Aphrodite* by either *Ares* or *Hermes*. He was equipped with a bow and arrows and a torch so that he might pierce or inflame the hearts of his victims. Golden wings enabled him to move speedily, and he was blindfolded to represent him as wanton and impartial.

EURYDICE, see **Orpheus.**

EVADNE, the wife of Capaneus who was killed at Thebes. While his body was on the funeral pyre, Evadne threw herself into the flames and was consumed with her husband.

FLORA, Roman goddess of flowers and of spring-time. See **Chloris.**

FORTUNA, Roman goddess of chance.

GAEA (Roman counterpart, Tellus), was the mother of *Uranus*. When Uranus, who hated his children, banished them to *Tartarus*, Gaea called on her sons to rise against their father, but only *Cronus* possessed the courage to do so, and he attacked and killed Uranus. From the blood of Uranus that fell to the ground there sprang the giants, *Gigantes*. Cronus then became ruler.

GALATEA, with whom the *Cyclops*, *Polyphemus*, fell in love. She scorned him, and when the Cyclops came upon her with *Acis*, to whose love she responded, he crushed Acis with a huge stone.

GANYMEDES, the most beautiful of mortals. While tending his father's flocks he was borne away by the eagle of *Zeus* to live among the gods and act as their cupbearer.

GIGANTES, the giants with heads of men and bodies of serpents who sprang from the blood of *Uranus*. See **Gaea.**

GLAUCE, daughter of Creon, king of Corinth. When *Jason* gave up *Medea* to marry Glauce, Medea sent her rival a wedding garment which, on being worn by Glauce, caused her to burn to death.

GOLDEN FLEECE, the prized fleece of a sacred ram in the keeping of Aeetes, king of Colchis, which *Jason* and his *Argonauts* set out to find as the condition of being restored to his father's throne, usurped by Pelias.

GORGONS. The Gorgons were creatures of terrible appearance with writhing serpents in their hair. Of the three, *Medusa* was mortal, and so dreadful was her appearance that whoever looked at her was turned to stone. *Perseus* killed her, and afterwards used her head against his enemies, for it kept its power of turning all who looked at it into stone. See **Perseus.**

HADES, see **Pluto.**

HARPIES, creatures with the body, wings and claws of a bird, the head and breasts of a woman, and the pale mien of ravenous hunger. They personified storms and wasting, destructive powers.

HECTOR, son of Priam and *Hecuba*, and husband

of *Andromeda*, was the leader of the Trojans in the Trojan War and their most successful warrior. Personifying the perfect son, husband, father, and leader. He was killed by *Achilles*.

HECUBA, wife of Priam, king of Troy and mother of *Hector*, *Paris* and *Cassandra*, distinguished as model wife and mother.

HELENA, or Helen, the most lovely of women, was the daughter of *Zeus* and Leda, and the wife of *Menelaus*. While young she was carried off by *Theseus*, rescued by her brothers, and afterwards married Menelaus. *Paris*, son of King Priam of Troy, was entertained by Menelaus and Helen, and persuaded Helen to elope with him to Troy. To avenge the wrong done to Menelaus the Greek chiefs fought the Trojan War, during which Helen's sympathies wavered between the two sides. After the death of Paris, Helen married his brother but betrayed him to the Greeks. Finally, she returned to Menelaus and they lived together for many happy years.

HEPHAESTUS (Roman counterpart, Vulcan), the god of fire, was the son of *Zeus* and *Hera* and married *Aphrodite*. He is supposed to have been born lame, and because of this was thrown from *Olympus* by Hera. The sea goddesses, Thetis and Eurynome, cared for him in a grotto under the sea. He later lived in Lemnos and raised forges to work metals, his workmen being the *Cyclopes* of Sicily.

HERA (Roman counterpart, Juno), daughter of *Cronus* and *Rhea* and sister and wife of *Zeus*. She was the queen of the gods, sharing the throne with Zeus. She is represented as being constantly jealous of her husband, whose amorous adventures peopled and complicated the Olympian drama of the Greek mythology.

HERACLES (Roman counterpart, Hercules), son of *Zeus* and Alcmena, was the most famous hero of Greek mythology. He was brought up at Thebes and before he was eight months old had strangled two snakes sent by the jealous *Hera* to devour him. During his servitude to Eurystheus, who had deprived him of his right to rule over Mycenae, he performed the twelve tasks known as the Twelve Labours of Heracles. These were : (1) to kill the lion of Nemea ; (2) to destroy the Lernaean Hydra ; (3) to capture alive the Arcadian stag celebrated for its swiftness ; (4) to capture a wild boar which ravaged Erymanthus ; (5) to clean in one day, the stables of King *Augeas* where 3,000 oxen had been confined for years ; (6) to kill the birds which ravaged the country near Lake Stymphalus ; (7) to bring into Peloponnesus a wild bull which ravaged Crete ; (8) to capture the mares of *Diomedes* which lived upon human flesh ; (9) to obtain the girdle of *Ares* from the queen of the *Amazons* ; (10) to kill the monster Eurytion and his dog, who guarded the flocks of Geryon which fed upon human beings ; (11) to obtain the golden apples from the garden of the *Hesperides* ; (12) to bring from the lower regions the three-headed dog, *Cerberus*. Later, with the aid of Heracles, Zeus was victorious in the wars against the giants. Heracles introduced the worship of fire and abolished human sacrifice.

HERMAPHRODITUS, the son of *Hermes* and *Aphrodite*, was beloved by the nymph Salmacis, whose love he did not return. He bathed with her, however, and as she embraced him, she prayed to the gods to unite them for ever. Her prayer was answered and they became one body with the characteristics of both sexes.

HERMES (Roman counterpart, Mercury), son of *Zeus*, was the god of wind, of chance and of speech. He was born in a cave on Mount Cyllene and a few hours after birth left his cradle and stole some of *Apollo's* cattle. He invented the lyre by stringing the shell of a tortoise. This he gave to Apollo with whom he became reconciled. He is said also to have invented the Pandean pipes.

HERO, one of *Aphrodite's* priestesses, was loved by *Leander*, who every night swam the Hellespont to visit her in her tower. Finally, he was drowned during a storm and Hero, finding his body, cast herself into the sea.

HESPERIDES, the daughters of *Atlas* and Hesperis, guarded the golden apples presented by *Gaea* to *Hera* as a wedding gift. It was one of *Heracles'* twelve tasks to obtain the golden apples.

HIPPOLYTE, queen of the *Amazons*.

HYACINTHUS, a boy of great beauty, loved by *Apollo*. While playing at quoits, Zephyrus, who also loved Hyacinthus and was jealous of Apollo, diverted from its course a quoit thrown by Apollo so that it struck and killed Hyacinthus. From his blood grew the flower which bears his name.

ICARUS, son of Daedalus, escaped from *Minos* of Crete by means of wings made by his father from feathers and wax. He flew so near the sun that the wax melted and he fell into the sea which was ultimately named after him.

IPHIGENIA, daughter of *Agamemnon* and *Clytemnestra*, whose father was ordered to sacrifice her to appease the goddess, *Artemis*, whom her father had offended by killing a stag, and who, in punishment for this had becalmed the Greek fleet and prevented it from sailing against Troy. When Artemis saw the girl prepared for sacrifice, she took pity on her and put a hind in her place and took her away in a cloud to become a priestess in her temple.

JASON, son of Aeson, king of Iolcus. After his father had been deprived of his throne by Pelias, Jason was cared for by the *Centaur*, Chiron. When he was grown up he set out for Iolcus to demand the return of his father's throne. He helped an old, infirm woman, who was really *Hera* in disguise, to cross a stream in flood, but in doing so lost one of his sandals. When he arrived at the palace in Iolcus and appeared before the king, Pelias noticed that he had only one sandal and remembered a warning he had had concerning a man with only one shoe. He agreed to give up the kingdom if Jason would bring him the *Golden Fleece*. Jason said he would undertake the mission, and led the famous expedition of the *Argonauts* in which many of the greatest of the Greek heroes assisted him. After many adventures he arrived in the land of Aeetes where he was told he could have the Golden Fleece if he could accomplish many terrible tasks. With the assistance of Medea, daughter of Aeetes, he performed these tasks and, taking Medea, whom he later married, with him, he and his men slipped away in the night with the coveted Golden Fleece. On his return, Jason learned that Pelias had killed Aeson and he persuaded Medea to avenge this crime. On pretext of restoring his youth to Pelias Medea had his daughters cut their father to pieces and boil them in a cauldron. For this act Jason and Medea were driven away from Iolcus and lived for some years in Corinth. Later Jason left Medea to marry *Glauce*.

JUNO, see **Hera.**

JUPITER, see **Zeus.**

LABYRINTH, the cavern built for King *Minos* of Crete by Daedalus as a place to keep the *Minotaur*. In it were many passages from which it was difficult to find a way out. See **Ariadne**

LAOCOON, a Trojan priest of *Apollo* who warned the Trojans against receiving into their city the Wooden Horse which the Greeks, in a trick, had left behind them when they pretended to sail away from Troy. He threw a lance into the side of the horse and offended *Athena*. He and his two sons were strangled by a great sea serpent, and the Trojans, thinking this to be a sign that Laocoon's warning was false, admitted the Wooden Horse and thus brought about the fall of Troy.

LAOMEDON, founder and king of Troy, and father of Priam. *Apollo* and *Poseidon* attempted to dethrone him, but *Zeus*, to punish them, forced them to assist Laomedon to build the walls of Troy. When, later, Laomedon refused to pay the agreed price, Apollo sent a plague and Poseidon a sea monster to ravage the country. To appease the monster Laomedon chained his daughter, Hermione to a rock, from which *Heracles* rescued her.

LEANDER, see **Hero.**

MARS, see **Ares.**

MEDUSA, one of the *Gorgons*. She had been turned into a revolting monster by *Athena* for claiming to be as beautiful as the goddess. So hideous was she that all who looked at her were turned to stone.

She was beheaded by *Perseus* who used his shield as a mirror so as not to look at her face.

MENELAUS, brother of *Agamemnon* and husband of *Helen,* who was carried off by *Paris.*

MERCURY, see **Hermes.**

MIDAS, a king of Phrygia who beseeched the god, *Dionysus* to grant him the power to transform all that he touched into gold. When he found that even his food and drink also turned to gold he prayed to be released from his wish. See also **Pan.**

MINERVA, see **Athena.**

MINOS, king of Crete, and the greatest ruler of his time, was the son of *Zeus.* He prayed *Poseidon* to send him a bull for sacrifice, but so fine was the animal that was sent to him that he substituted another. As punishment Poseidon caused Pasiphae, wife of Minos, to fall in love with the bull, and the Minotaur, the son of Pasiphae and the bull, was confined in the *Labyrinth,* built for Minos by *Daedalus.* There *Theseus* later slew the Minotaur, with the help of *Ariadne.*

MINOTAURUS, the Minotaur, half bull and half man, which was kept by *Minos* of Crete in the *Labyrinth.* See **Theseus** and **Ariadne.**

NAIADS, daughters of *Zeus,* who were nymphs presiding over springs, streams and other waters.

NARCISSUS, a beautiful youth who, while wooed by many, refused to respond to any. When the nymph, *Echo,* was scorned by him and pined until she became a mere voice, the other lovers who had been rejected prayed that the gods would punish him. One day, tired and thirsty, he stooped to drink from a pool, and fell in love with his reflection. Unable to satisfy his longing for himself, he pined away, and from the place where he died grew the flower that was named after him.

NEPTUNE, see **Poseidon.**

NIOBE, wife of Amphion, king of Thebes, by whom she had seven sons and seven daughters. Proud of her family, she boasted that she was superior to Leto, mother of *Apollo* and *Artemis,* whom she refused to worship. Leto called upon Apollo and Artemis to punish Niobe, and with their bows and arrows they first killed Niobe's sons as they played in the fields, and then killed her daughters as they mourned their brothers. Amphion killed himself in grief, and Niobe was changed into stone.

NYMPHS were usually lovely maidens who were divinities of lower rank than gods and presided over certain parts of nature.

ODYSSEUS or **ULYSSES** was the husband of *Penelope,* and the most popular of the great Greek heroes and engaged in the war against Troy. After the siege, he began his journey home, which is the subject of the wonderful epic poem, "The Odyssey" by Homer. He travelled far and wide, meeting many adventures as, when on the island of Aeaea, *Circe* changed his men temporarily into swine. Resisting the temptations of the *Sirens,* and surmounting the dangers of *Scylla* and *Charybdis,* after an absence of twenty years, he returned to Ithaca to find his palace occupied and his wealth dissipated by suitors for his wife's hand. With the help of his son, he put the usurpers to death.

OLYMPIA, a place in Greece noted for the sacred grove of *Zeus.* Here Olympic games were celebrated every four years in honour of Zeus.

OLYMPIC GODS, the principal gods of Greek mythology who dwelt on Mount *Olympus.* They included *Zeus, Hera, Athena, Ares, Apollo, Artemis, Aphrodite, Hermes* and *Hephaestus.*

OLYMPUS, a mountain in Thessaly on whose top dwelt the *Olympic gods.* On the highest peak was the palace of *Zeus.*

ORESTES, son of *Agamemnon* and *Clytemnestra,* slew his mother to avenge the murder of his father by Clytemnestra and her lover. His great love for Pylades, who married his sister, Electra, became proverbial.

ORION, a hunter of great beauty and strength. Eos (Aurora), goddess of the dawn, fell in love with him but the gods were jealous of her love and *Artemis* slew him with her arrows. After his death he was placed with his hounds in the heavens as a constellation.

ORPHEUS, son of *Apollo* and the Muse Calliope, was a poet whose skill on the lyre was so great that wild animals were tamed by his music, fish left the water to listen, and the birds flocked around him. He accompanied *Jason* as one of the *Argonauts* and encouraged his companions by his music. He won the nymph, *Eurydice,* for his wife, but soon after their marriage she was stung by a snake and died. Orpheus was heartbroken and descended to the underworld to plead for her return. *Pluto* granted his request on condition that he should precede Eurydice on their way back to the world above, and refrain from looking behind him. Afraid, however, that Eurydice was not following, he disobeyed, and she vanished. In his grief he scorned all women, and the Maenads stoned him to death. All nature mourned for him, and it was said that his lyre continued to sound "Eurydice, Eurydice," long after his death.

PALLAS, see **Athene.**

PAN, son of *Zeus,* and a nymph, was a god of shepherds and hunters. He wandered in woods playing on the pipes which he invented. He challenged *Apollo* to a contest in music, and *Midas,* who was asked to judge, awarded the prize to Pan. To punish Midas for this indignity, *Apollo* caused his ears to be changed into those of an ass.

PANDORA, the first woman on earth, the gift of the gods to man, was endowed with beauty and charm and was carried off by *Hermes* and given to *Epimetheus* in marriage. She had with her a box containing all the vices which she had been forbidden to open ; but one day, overcome with a burning curiosity, she raised the lid to see, and thus liberated the evils to which man has been subject ever since. Then, becoming afraid, she closed the lid quickly, just in time to retain one thing only—Hope.

PARIS, son of Priam and *Hecuba.* For a time he was exposed on Mount Ida, there nursed by a bear, found by a shepherd and brought up by him as his own son. Later, as a result of a contest in which he was successful, he was owned by King Priam as his son. At the marriage between Peleus and Thetis, father and mother of *Achilles,* a dispute arose as to whether *Hera, Athene* or *Aphrodite* was the most beautiful and entitled to the Golden Apple. Paris was chosen to be judge and awarded it to Aphrodite who had promised him the most lovely woman in the world as his wife. Later he visited Sparta where he was entertained by *Menelaus* and *Helena.* He persuaded Helena to elope with him to Troy. This led to the Trojan War and he was killed during the siege of Troy. See **Eris, Helena, Aphrodite.**

PEGASUS, the winged horse, sprang from the body of *Medusa* when she was killed by *Perseus,* flew into the heavens where he was caught and tamed by *Athena* and joined the immortals. With the aid of Pegasus, Bellerophon slew the *Chimaera* and was victorious over the *Amazons.*

PENELOPE, the wife of *Odysseus.* During her husband's long absence she was surrounded by suitors whom she kept at bay by pretending that before she could decide among them she must finish the weaving of a winding sheet for her father-in-law, Laertes. Each night she undid what she had done by day. Odysseus returned in time to protect her and slay the wooers. See **Odysseus.**

PERSEPHONE (Roman equivalent, Prosperpina), was the daughter of *Zeus* and *Demeter,* and the wife of *Hades* or *Pluto.* When Persephone was gathering flowers one day, the earth opened and Pluto carried her off in his chariot to his underworld kingdom where he made her his wife and queen. Demeter wandered over the earth seeking for her daughter and refusing to allow the earth to produce food. At last Zeus sent *Hermes* with orders to Pluto to restore Persephone to her mother. Pluto obeyed but first gave Persephone a part of a pomegranate to eat so that she would have to return to him. Persephone was restored to her mother but, because she had eaten of the pomegranate, she was forced to spend a third of each year with her husband.

PERSEUS, the son of *Zeus* and Danae. Acrisius,

Danae's father, had been told that his daughter would bear a son who would kill him. To prevent this he kept Danae in an underground room, but Zeus visited her there secretly and Perseus was their son. When Acrisius heard of the birth he put Danae and her child in a chest which he threw into the sea. It floated to an island and was found by Dictys, a fisherman, who took the mother and child to his home. There they lived until Perseus was grown up. Polydectes, the king of the island, was in love with Danae and desiring to get rid of Perseus, sent him on a dangerous mission. This was to visit the *Gorgons* and to get the head of *Medusa*. *Athena* and *Hermes* helped Perseus by giving him a shield which shone like a mirror and telling him not to look into Medusa'a eyes, but to watch her image in the mirror and strike off her head. This he accomplished successfully and on his return journey he delivered *Andromeda* from the sea monster and married her. Later his grandfather, Acrisius, was accidentally killed by a discus thrown by Perseus.

PHILEMON and his wife, *Baucis*, were a poor couple who gave welcome and hospitality to *Zeus* and *Hermes* one day, and Zeus rewarded them by transforming their cottage into a temple of the gods and appointing them as priests to be in charge of it. After living to a very old age they were granted their request to die together, and Baucis was transformed into a linden and Philemon into an oak.

PLUTO was the god of the infernal regions. He was the son of *Cronus* and *Rhea*, and a brother of *Zeus*. On the partition of the world he was given the underworld to govern.

POLYPHEMUS, the most famous of the *Cyclopes*. When *Odysseus* and his companions were driven from the shore where Polyphemus lived in a cave, the giant killed four of Odysseus' men. Odysseus plied him with wine until he was drunk, then thrust a burning stake into his one eye and blinded him, thus making it possible for his companions and himself to escape from the cave.

POSEIDON (Roman counterpart, Neptune), son of *Cronus* and *Rhea*, and god of the sea.

PROSERPINA, see **Persephone.**

PSYCHE, the loveliest of three princess sisters, was so beautiful that *Venus* was jealous of her. The goddess sent *Cupid* to cause her to love some person beneath her in rank. Cupid, however, fell in love with her himself, hid her away in a fine palace, but forbade her to look upon him. Lonely in her grandeur, she begged to have her sisters to visit her. They came and persuaded her to break her promise and look upon the god. This she did when he was asleep, but a drop of oil from her lamp fell upon Cupid's shoulder and he vanished. She began to search for him and ultimately approached Venus for help. She was given many hard tasks to perform but, secretly helped by Cupid, she succeeded and at last *Jupiter* interceded with Venus for the lovers, and Psyche was made immortal and married Cupid.

PYGMALION, king of Cyprus, made an ivory statue of a maiden which was so beautiful that he fell in love with it and prayed to *Aphrodite* to give him a wife like the statue. The goddess breathed life into it and she became Pygmalion's wife.

PYRAMUS, a youth who lived in Babylon and was in love with Thisbe, daughter of a neighbouring family. Their parents disapproved of their love and forbade them to meet, so they conversed with each other through a crevice in the wall between their homes. One night they agreed to meet outside the city at the tomb of Ninus. Thisbe arrived first, was surprised by a lioness and fled, dropping her veil as she ran. The lioness, which was eating some animal flesh, seized the veil and soon it was covered with blood. When Pyramus arrived he concluded from the blood-stained condition of the veil that Thisbe was dead, and killed himself. When Thisbe returned she found her lover's body, and in grief killed herself.

PYRRHA, wife of *Deucalion*, was saved, with her husband, when *Zeus* flooded the world to destroy human beings.

REMUS and his twin brother, *Romulus*, were suckled as babes by a she-wolf and later brought up by a shepherd. When they came to decide who was to rule the city which they had agreed to found, a quarrel ensued in which Remus was killed. See **Romulus.**

RHEA, daughter of *Uranus* and *Gaea*, and wife of *Cronus*. Her children were among the most famous in Greek mythology : *Hera, Demeter, Hades, Poseidon* and *Zeus*.

ROMULUS, twin brother of *Remus*, and founder and first ruler of Rome. Through his efforts to increase the population of Rome there occurred the rape of the Sabine women, with the resulting wars in which Rome was victorious. He ruled Rome successfully for many years, and at the end of his life is said to have disappeared in a thunderstorm and become a god.

SATURN, see **Cronus.**

SCYLLA, a dog-like monster, offspring of Typhon, which inhabited a cave in the rock opposite the rock which concealed *Charybdis*, and famed as a legendary menace to shipping.

SIRENS, sea nymphs who, by their singing, enticed to their island those who sailed near and then destroyed them. *Odysseus* took precautions against their power by stuffing the ears of his companions with wax and binding himself to the mast. Thus they all escaped the danger.

SPHINX, a mythical creature who was represented by the Greeks as a monster having the head and bosom of a woman and the body of a lion with wings. She was sent by *Hera* to punish the people of Thebes for the wickedness of their king, and she spared neither rich nor poor. The sphinx proposed a riddle but any one who undertook to solve it and failed was devoured by her. Eventually Oedipus found the correct answer and the sphinx destroyed herself.

STYX, the river of death in the nether world across which *Charon* ferried the souls of the dead.

TARTARUS, the nethermost lower regions to which *Zeus* banished the *Titans*.

TELEMACHUS, son of *Odysseus* and *Penelope*. When his father went to the Trojan War he was left at home. As a young man he went in search of him and later assisted him in his plan to destroy the suitors of Penelope. After his father's death he went to *Circe* who married him and made him immortal.

TELLUS, see **Gaea.**

THESEUS, a mythical king of Athens who, with the help of *Ariadne*, slew the *Minotaur* in the *Labyrinth* at Crete and thus freed Athens from the necessity of sending seven youths and seven maidens as an annual sacrifice to the monster. See **Ariadne.**

TITANES or **TITANS,** sons and daughters of *Uranus* (heaven) and *Gaea* (earth) who ruled the world before the time of *Zeus*. One of them, *Cronus*, aided by his mother, rose against Uranus and deposed him and became king himself. He was in turn overcome by Zeus and the Titans were hurled into Tartarus. See **Cronus.**

URANUS, son of *Gaea* and ruler of the universe. He was the father of the *Titans*, *Cronus*, and many others. Afraid of his children he banished them to Tartarus at birth, but on the suggestion of Gaea, Cronus overthrew him and became king. See **Cronus.**

ULYSSES, see **Odysseus.**

VENUS (Greek counterpart, Aphrodite), a Roman goddess. In Vergil's "Aeneid" she plays an important part. She helped *Aeneas* and his followers on their journey from Troy to Italy. At Carthage, by means of her son, *Cupid*, she caused *Dido*, queen of Carthage, to fall in love with Aeneas.

VULCAN, see **Hephaestus.**

ZEUS (Roman counterpart, Jupiter), warred against *Cronus* and the *Titans* for overlordship of the universe, and eventually became victorious. He was chief of the gods and presided over the Council of the Gods of Olympus. From his numerous amorous adventures sprang many of the characters and much of the fabulous history of the Greek mythology.

TABLES OF STANDARD MEASURES AND EQUIVALENTS

MEASURES OF LENGTH

12 inches	= 1 foot.
3 feet	= 1 yard.
5½ yards	= 1 rod, pole, or perch.
40 poles	= 1 furlong.
8 furlongs	= 1 mile.
1760 yards	= 1 mile.
3 miles	= 1 league.

3 barleycorns	= 1 inch.
3 inches	= 1 palm.
4 inches	= 1 hand.
9 inches	= 1 span.
2½ feet	= 1 pace (military).
5 feet	= 1 pace.
6 feet	= 1 fathom.

7·92 inches	= 1 link.
25 links	= 1 pole.
100 links	= 1 chain.
66 feet	= 1 chain.
10 chains	= 1 furlong.

The hand is used for measuring horses; the fathom for depth measurements of water and mines; the link and chain for land surveying.

The English statute mile	= 1760 yards.
The British nautical mile	= 2026·6 yards.
The international nautical mile (in practice 2,000 yards)	= 2023·23 yards.

The international nautical mile is defined as one-sixtieth part of a degree of longitude at the equator. The geographical mile is one-sixtieth part of the mean degree of latitude = 2025·6 yards.

NAUTICAL MEASURE

6 feet	= 1 fathom.
15 feet	= 1 chain.
100 fathoms	= 1 cable's length.
10 cable's lengths	= 1 (international) nautical mile.
3 nautical miles	= 1 league.
60 nautical miles	= 1 degree.

One knot equals a speed of 1 British nautical mile per hour and is *not* a measure of distance.

SQUARE OR LAND MEASURE

144 square inches	= 1 square foot.
9 square feet	= 1 square yard.
30¼ square yards	= 1 square rod, pole, or perch.
40 square rods, poles, or perches	= 1 rood.
4 roods	= 1 acre.
640 acres	= 1 square mile.
4840 square yards	= 1 acre.

100 square feet	= 1 square of flooring.
272¼ square feet	= 1 rod of brickwork.
30 acres	= 1 yard of land.
100 acres	= 1 hide of land.

62·726 square inches	= 1 square link.
625 square links	= 1 square pole.
16 square poles (10,000 square links)	= 1 square chain.
10 square chains	= 1 acre.
6400 square chains	= 1 square mile.

CUBIC OR SOLID MEASURE

1728 cubic inches	= 1 cubic foot.
27 cubic feet	= 1 cubic yard.

30 cubic feet	= 1 cart load.
40 cubic feet	= 1 ton of shipped merchandise.
42 cubic feet	= 1 ton of shipping.

One cubic foot of water at 62° Fahrenheit at a barometrical pressure of 30 inches = 6·24 gallons and weighs 1000 ounces avoirdupois.

AVOIRDUPOIS WEIGHT

Used for practically all goods sold by weight, other than precious metals and stones.

16 drams	= 1 ounce.
16 ounces	= 1 pound.
14 pounds	= 1 stone.
28 pounds (2 stone)	= 1 quarter.
4 quarters (112 lb.)	= 1 hundredweight.
20 hundredweight	= 1 ton.

100 pounds	= 1 cental.

In the U.S.A., 100 pounds = 1 hundredweight, and the ton of 20 hundredweight = 2000 pounds.

One pound avoirdupois = 14 oz. 11 dwt. 16 grains troy, that is, 7000 troy grains.

TROY WEIGHT

Used for gold, silver, and platinum, etc., and for precious stones.

24 grains	= 1 pennyweight.
20 pennyweights	= 1 ounce.

There is now no troy pound. The former troy pound consisted of 12 troy ounces, and equalled $\frac{14}{17}$ of the pound avoirdupois.

Since 1920 precious stones must be weighed by the troy ounce of 480 grains divided decimally, or by the metric carat ($\frac{1}{5}$ gramme) divided decimally.

The metric carat is equivalent to $\frac{1}{150}$ troy ounce. (The term "carat" as applied to metals means $\frac{1}{24}$th part. Thus, 18-carat gold is $\frac{18}{24}$ths pure gold.)

PEARL AND DIAMOND WEIGHT

3·17 grains	= 1 English carat.
4 pearl grains	= 1 English carat.
151·5 English carats	= 1 ounce (troy).

APOTHECARIES' WEIGHT

Used in mixing medicines.

20 grains	= 1 scruple (℈).
3 scruples	= 1 drachm (ʒ).
8 drachms	= 1 ounce (℥).
12 ounces	= 1 pound (lb.).

The Apothecaries' ounce and grain are the same as the troy ounce and grain.

APOTHECARIES' MEASURE

For fluids—used in mixing medicines.

60 minims (♏)	= 1 fluid drachm (fʒ).
8 fluid drachms	= 1 fluid ounce (f℥).
20 fluid ounces	= 1 pint (O).
8 pints	= 1 gallon (Cong. or C.)
40 fluid ounces	= 1 corbyn.
80 fluid ounces	= 1 Winchester quart.

1 teaspoonful	= 1 drachm.
1 dessertspoonful	= 2 drachms.
1 tablespoonful	= 4 drachms.
1 wineglassful	= 2 fluid ounces.
1 teacupful	= 3 fluid ounces.

MEAT WEIGHT

8 pounds	= 1 stone.
25 stone (beef)	= 1 barrel.
28 stone (pork)	= 1 barrel.

Irish beef:	Irish pork:
8 pounds = 1 piece.	4 pounds = 1 piece.
38 pieces = 1 tierce.	80 pieces = 1 tierce

BREAD AND FLOUR WEIGHTS

1 quartern of flour	= 3 lb. 8 oz. avoirdupois.
1 quartern of bread	= 4 lb. 5 oz. 8½ dr. avoirdupois.
1 peck of flour	= 14 lb. avoirdupois.
1 peck of bread	= 17 lb. 6 oz. 2 dr. avoirdupois.
1 bushel of flour	= 56 lb. (4 pecks).
1 sack of flour	= 280 lb. (5 bushels).

Bread is now generally sold by the 2-lb. or 4-lb. (avoirdupois) loaf.

BUTTER AND CHEESE WEIGHTS

8 pounds = 1 clove.
2 cloves = 1 stone.
16 stone = 1 wey (Suffolk).
21 stone = 1 wey (Essex).
56 pounds (butter) = 1 firkin.
1½ firkins = 1 tub.
4 firkins = 1 barrel.

ALE AND BEER MEASURE

2 pints = 1 quart.
4 quarts = 1 gallon.
9 gallons = 1 firkin.
2 firkins = 1 kilderkin.
2 kilderkins = 1 barrel.
3 kilderkins = 1 hogshead.
2 barrels = 1 puncheon.
2 hogsheads = 1 butt.

---

6 bottles = 1 gallon.
1 leager = 164 gallons.

WINE MEASURE

Used also for spirits, vinegar, oil, cider, honey, etc.

4 gills = 1 pint.
2 pints = 1 quart.
4 quarts = 1 gallon.
10 gallons = 1 anker.
18 gallons = 1 runlet.
31½ gallons = 1 barrel.
42 gallons = 1 tierce.
2 barrels = 1 hogshead.
2 tierce = 1 puncheon.
2 hogsheads = 1 pipe or butt.
2 pipes = 1 tun.

The gill is often known as a quartern. In some parts of England the gill is ½ pint, the ¼ pint measure being called a noggin.

The "bottle" of wine contains about 1⅓ pints, or one-sixth of a gallon.

The "old" wine gallon, by which the anker, barrel, hogshead, etc., are measured, is about five-sixths (·8331) of the Imperial standard gallon. The hogshead contains 52½ Imperial standard gallons.

The old pipe (butt) of Madeira wine is 92 gallons, of sherry 110 gallons, and of port 115 gallons.

One aume of hock equals 31 gallons.

COAL AND COKE WEIGHT

All coal must be sold by avoirdupois weight.

14 pounds = 1 stone.
2 stone = 1 quarter.
4 stone = 1 half-hundredweight.
112 pounds = 1 hundredweight or sack.
2 hundredweight = 1 double sack.
1 keel or barge = 21 tons 4 cwt.
1 shipload = 424 tons.
1 room = 7 tons.
1 chaldron = 25½ cwt.
3 bushels of coke = 1 sack.
12 sacks = 1 chaldron.

GLASS WEIGHT

5 pounds = 1 stone.
24 stone = 1 seam.

TIMBER MEASURE

165 cubic feet = 1 (Leningrad) standard.
100 superficial feet of planking = 1 square.
120 deals = 1 hundred.
108 cubic feet = 1 stack.
120 cubic feet = 1 cord.
50 cubic feet (squared timber) }
40 cubic feet (unhewn timber) } = 1 ton or load.
600 square feet (1-in. planking) }

A *plank* is 10 inches or more in width, and usually 2 inches or more in thickness.

A *deal* is 9 inches wide and from 2 inches to 3 inches thick (the latter thickness is generally understood).

A *board* is 9 inches wide and 1½ inches or less in thickness.

A *floor-board* is usually from 6 to 7 inches wide and from 1 inch to 1¼ inches thick.

WOOL WEIGHT

7 pounds = 1 clove.
2 cloves = 1 stone.
2 stones = 1 tod.
6½ tods = 1 wey.
2 weys = 1 sack.
12 sacks = 1 last.

---

20 pounds = 1 score.
12 score = 1 pack.

CLOTH MEASURE

2¼ inches = 1 nail.
4 nails (9 inches) = 1 quarter.
27 inches = 1 Flemish ell.
4 quarters = 1 yard.
45 inches = 1 English ell.
54 inches = 1 French ell.

YARN MEASURES

Cotton and silk:
1½ yards = 1 thread.
80 threads (120 yards) = 1 skein.
7 skeins (840 yards) = 1 hank.
18 hanks = 1 spindle.

Worsted:
80 yards = 1 wrap.
7 wraps (560 yards) = 1 hank.

Linen:
300 yards = 1 hank.
48 hanks = 1 spindle.
200 hanks = 1 bundle.

FISH MEASURE

2 fish = 1 hand.
37½ imperial gallons = 1 cran.
13,200 fish = 1 last.

PAPER MEASURE

24 sheets = 1 quire.
20 quires = 1 ream.
500 sheets = 1 ream (printing paper).
2 reams = 1 bundle.
5 bundles = 1 bale.

PAPER SIZES
(in inches)

Writing and Drawing Papers

Emperor . .	72×48	Super Royal .	27×19
Antiquarian .	53×31	D'ble Foolscap	26½×16½
D'ble Elephant	40×26¾	Royal . .	24×19
Atlas . .	34×26	Medium . .	22×17½
Colombier .	34½×23½	Large Post .	21×16½
Double Demy .	31×20	Copy or Draft	20×16
Double Post .	30½×19	Demy . .	20×15½
Imperial . .	30×22	Post. .	19×15¼
Elephant . .	28×23	Foolscap . .	16½×13¼
Cartridge . .	26×21	Pott. . .	15×12½

Printing Papers

Quad Demy .	45×35	D'ble Foolscap	27×17
Quad Crown .	40×30	Royal . .	25×20
Double Royal .	40×25	Medium . .	23×18
Double Demy .	35×22½	Demy . .	22½×17½
Imperial . .	30×22	Music Demy .	20×15½
Double Crown .	30×20	Post . .	19¼×15½
Super Royal .	27½×20½	Foolscap . .	17×13½

Brown Papers

Quad Imperial	58×45	Double Four Pound . .	31×21
Double Nicanee	56×45	Imperial Cap .	29×22
Quad Royal .	50×40	Haven Cap .	26×21
Casing . .	46×36	Four Pound Grocers .	26×20
Saddleback .	45×36	Bag Cap .	24×19½
D'ble Imperial	45×29	Kent Cap .	21×18
Elephant . .	34×24	Copy . . .	20×16½
Six Pound Grocers . .	32×22		

HAY AND STRAW MEASURE

36 pounds = 1 truss (straw).
56 pounds = 1 truss (old hay).
60 pounds = 1 truss (new hay).
36 trusses = 1 load (or ton of hay).

1 load weighs (straw) 11 cwt. 64 lb.; (old hay) 18 cwt.; (new hay) 19 cwt. 32 lb.

MEASURES OF CAPACITY

4 gills	= 1 pint.
2 pints	= 1 quart.
4 quarts	= 1 gallon.
2 gallons	= 1 peck.
4 pecks	= 1 bushel.
8 bushels	= 1 quarter.
7¾ gallons (approx.)	= 1 Winchester corn bushel.
2 quarts	= 1 pottle.
2 bushels	= 1 strike.
36 bushels	= 1 chaldron.
5 quarters	= 1 load or wey.
2 loads	= 1 last.

One standard gallon is the capacity of 10 lb. avoirdupois of distilled water at 62° Fahrenheit under a barometrical pressure of 30 inches and equals 277·27 cubic inches.

One standard bushel equals 2218·19 cubic inches. One Winchester corn bushel equals 2150·4 cubic inches and is the standard bushel in U.S.A.

THE METRIC SYSTEM

Measures of Length

10 millimetres	= 1 centimetre.
10 centimetres	= 1 decimetre.
10 decimetres	= 1 metre.
10 metres	= 1 decametre.
10 decametres	= 1 hectometre.
10 hectometres	= 1 kilometre.
10 kilometres	= 1 myriametre.

Measures of Surface

100 square millimetres	= 1 square centimetre.
100 square centimetres	= 1 square decimetre.
100 square decimetres	= 1 square metre.
100 square metres	= 1 square decametre = 1 are.
100 square decametres	= 1 square hectometre.
100 square hectometres	= 1 square kilometre.

10 centiares	= 1 deciare.
10 deciares	= 1 are.
10 ares	= 1 decare.
10 decares	= 1 hectare.

The are and its multiples are used for measuring land; for other purposes the square metre is generally the unit.

Measures of Capacity

10 millilitres	= 1 centilitre.
10 centilitres	= 1 decilitre.
10 decilitres	= 1 litre.
10 litres	= 1 decalitre.
10 decalitres	= 1 hectolitre.
10 hectolitres	= 1 kilolitre.

1 litre = 1 cubic decimetre; 1 kilolitre = 1 cubic metre.

Measures of Weight

10 milligrammes	= 1 centigramme.
10 centigrammes	= 1 decigramme.
10 decigrammes	= 1 gramme.
10 grammes	= 1 decagramme.
10 decagrammes	= 1 hectogramme.
10 hectogrammes	= 1 kilogramme.
10 kilogrammes	= 1 myriagramme.
10 myriagrammes	= 1 quintal.
10 quintals	= 1 millier or tonne.

1 gramme = the weight of 1 cubic centimetre of water at 4° Centigrade (39° Fahrenheit).

1 kilogramme or cubic decimetre of water measures 1 litre.

Cubic Measure

1000 cubic millimetres = 1 cubic centimetre.
1000 cubic centimetres = 1 cubic decimetre.
1000 cubic decimetres = 1 cubic metre.
10 decistères = 1 stère = 1 cubic metre.
10 stères = 1 decastère.
The stère is used for measuring timber.

BRITISH MEASURES AND METRIC EQUIVALENTS

1 millimetre	= 0·0394 inch.
1 centimetre	= 0·3937 inch.
1 metre	= 39·3708 inches.
1 kilometre	= 1093·63 yards
	= 4 furlongs 213 yards 2 feet.

1 inch	= 25·4 millimetres.
1 foot	= 0·3048 metre.
1 yard	= 0·9144 metre.
1 mile	= 1·6093 kilometres.
1 international nautical mile	= 1·852 kilometres.

1 square centimetre	= 0·155 square inch.
1 square metre	= 1·196 square yards.
1 are	= 119·6 square yards.
1 hectare	= 2·471 acres.

1 square inch	= 6·452 square centimetres.
1 square foot	= 9·290 square decimetres.
1 square yard	= 0·836 square metre.
1 acre	= 0·405 hectare.
1 square mile	= 259 hectares.

1 cubic centimetre	= 0·061 cubic inch.
1 cubic metre	= 1·308 cubic yards.

1 cubic inch	= 16·387 cubic centimetres.
1 cubic foot	= 0·028 cubic metre.
1 cubic yard	= 0·765 cubic metre.

1 centilitre	= 0·07 gill.
1 litre	= 1·761 pints.
1 hectolitre	= 2·75 bushels.
1 hectolitre	= 2·83 U.S. bushels.
1 kilolitre	= 3·44 quarters.

1 gill	= 1·42 decilitres.
1 pint	= 0·57 litre.
1 quart	= 1·136 litres.
1 gallon	= 4·546 litres.
1 bushel	= 36·37 litres.
1 U.S. bushel	= 35·23 litres.
1 quarter	= ·29 kilolitre.

1 milligramme	= 0·015 grain.
1 centigramme	= 0·154 grain.
1 gramme	= 15·432 grains.
1 kilogramme	= 2·2046 lb.
1 quintal	= 1·968 cwt.
1 tonne	= 0·984 ton.

1 grain	= 0·0648 gramme.
1 ounce	= 28·350 grammes.
1 pound	= 0·4536 kilogramme.
1 hundredweight	= 50·8 kilogrammes.

1 ton = 1016 kilogrammes = 1·016 tonnes.

COMMERCIAL ABBREVIATIONS

x.c.	without coupon.
x.d.	without dividend.
x.i.	without interest.
%	per cent.
‰	per thousand.
£	pound sterling.
£A	pound Australian.
£E	pound Egyptian.
£NZ	pound New Zealand.
£T	pound Turkish.
$	dollars.
@	at.
⅌	per.
¢	cents.
$	reis.
₱	pesos.
A/A	aerodrome to aerodrome.
a/c	account.
A/c	account of.
A/S	account sales.
a/d	after date.
B/E	bill of exchange.
B/L	bill of lading.
B/S	bill of sale.
c/o	care of.
C/-	coupon.
c.i.f.	cost, insurance, freight.
COD	cash on delivery.
Cr.	credit(or).
d/a	days after acceptance.
d/d	day's date.
Dr.	debit; debtor.
d/s	days' sight.
E. & O.E.	errors and omissions excepted.
f.o.b.	free on board.
J/A	joint account.
L/c	letter of credit.
m/d	month's date.
m/s	month's sight.
n/a	no account.
o/a	on account.
O/D	on demand.
P/N	promissory note.
R/T	radio-telephony.
R/D	refer to drawer.
R(s)	rupee(s).
W/T	wireless telegraphy.

MATHEMATICAL SYMBOLS

+	plus (add), positive.
−	minus (subtract), negative.
±	plus or minus.
×	multiply by.
÷	divide by.
:	is to } signs of proportion.
::	as } signs of proportion.
∵	because.
∴	therefore.
=	equals.
≏	is approximately equal to.
≠	is not equal to.
>	is greater than.
<	is less than.
≦	is equal to or greater than.
≧	is equal to or less than.
≯	is not greater than.
≮	is not less than.
∥	is parallel to.
∦	is not parallel to.
⊥	is perpendicular to.
∠	angle.
∟	right angle.
≚	equiangular.
△	triangle.
□	square.
▭	parallelogram.
⊙	circle.
⌓	semicircle.
◱	quadrant.
⌒	arc.
∼	difference; varies as.
°	degrees.
′	feet, minutes of arc.
″	inches, seconds of arc.
∞	infinity.
√	square root.
∛	cube root.
ρ	radius.
∫	integral.
∟	factorial; also !.
f	function.
△	finite difference.
δ	variation.
d	differential.
Σ	finite sum.
Π	product.
∝	varies as.
⊤	vertical.
π	*pi*, the ratio of circumference to diameter of circle.

ROMAN NUMERALS

I	1	XX	20
II	2	XXX	30
III	3	XL	40
IV*	4	L	50
V	5	LX	60
VI	6	XC	90
VII	7	C	100
VIII	8	CC	200
IX	9	CD	400
X	10	D	500
XI	11	DC	600
XII	12	CM	900
XIV	14	M	1,000
XV	15	MCMXLVI	1946
XIX	19		

When the symbol of a smaller number appears *before* the symbol of a larger, it is subtracted from the latter; thus IX = ten less one = 9; when the symbol of a smaller number *follows* that of a larger, they are added; thus VI = five plus one = 6. Thus, also, XCIV = (one hundred less ten) plus (five less one) = 90 + 4 = 94; CXVI = one hundred plus ten plus five plus one = 116.

A line placed over a letter multiplies it by 1,000; thus $\overline{D}$ = 500,000.

D is sometimes written as IƆ, and M as CIƆ; each Ɔ added to IƆ multiplies it by ten; thus IƆƆƆ = 50,000.

**On clock and watch faces often* IIII